WHO'S WHO

EMPOWERING EXECUTIVES, PROFESSIONALS AND ENTREPRENEURS

HONORS EDITION

2008–2009

For information, contact Cambridge Who's Who Publishing, Inc.
498 RexCorp Plaza
West Tower
Uniondale, NY 11556

ISBN: 978-1-60758-000-3

Manufactured in the United States of America

CAMBRIDGE WHO'S WHO MANAGEMENT AND STAFF

MANAGEMENT TEAM

Chief Executive Officer	Mitchel Robbins
President	Randy Narod
Chief Operating Officer, Chief Technology Officer	Erica Lee
Chief Financial Officer	Brian Wasserman

ADMINISTRATION

Director, Administration	Tina D'Angelo
Administrative Assistants	Roseanne Chillemi
	Kevin Colbert
	Shanay Leonard
	Jessica Nallo
	Aimée Rubinowitz

BOOKKEEPING/ACCOUNTING

Staff Accountants	Barbara Breen
	Stacey Salzano
	Nathalie Strand

EDITORIAL/PROOFREADING/ PRODUCTION DEPARTMENT

Director, Editorial	Meredith Foster
Director, Media Relations	Ellen Campbell
Senior Editor	Dennis Sebayan
Editorial Assistants	Renee Dutcher-Pryer
	Jamie Frevele
	Anna Lacson
	Fatima Naseem
	Michael Viola
Director, Proofreading, Publishing	Sarah Estes
Copy Editors	Danielle Blanchard
	Kristen Giani
	Michael F. Weber
Biographical Assistant	Felicia Henderson
Director, Production	Meredith Foster
Production Assistants	Tracy Gelfand
	Jaclyn Lunetta

HUMAN RESOURCES

Vice President, Human Resources	Deb Morrissey
Human Resource Generalist	Michelle Trabucchi

MARKETING AND ACQUISITION

Directors, Marketing and Acquisition	Janine Alaimo
	Mary Francolini

MEMBERSHIP SERVICES

Vice President, Membership Services	Beth Johnston
Customer Service Associates	Christine DiGiacomo
	Nikki Masih
Membership Services Associates	Moneceya Alston
	Susan Andia
	Tara Crawley
	Donna Fykes
	Stefanie Martinez
	Deb Marmurowski
	Denise Mussillo

NEW MEMBERSHIPS

Directors, New Memberships	Tara Armellino
	Yona Block
	Lorraine Standish
New Membership Associates	Allison Achong
	Patricia Allen
	Richard Alomar
	Arlene Ayabar
	Kareemah Batts
	Christopher Biviano
	Helene Braunstein
	Robin Brunner
	Veronica Cain
	Lucille Cano
	Maria Casal
	Delores Christensen
	Sal Cinglio
	Janice Conway
	Sue Davis
	Krissy DeMonte
	Diane DiGiovani
	Judy Dillon
	Donna Follano
	Denise Forte
	Ray Garcia
	Debra Gettinger
	Jackie Giordano

CAMBRIDGE WHO'S WHO
MANAGEMENT AND STAFF

New Membership Associates (*cont'd*)

Lawrence Glassman
Lilia Golia
Oliver Green Jr.
Rosemarie Grossman
Carla Gwatney
Erica Holmgren
Elaine Huzzar
Jennifer Jacobs
Joyce-Anne Joannou
Tommy Judge
Joan Kay
Lawrence Keller
Leighann Kelly
Elizabeth Kompogiorgias
Ronda Leaderman
Laura Lee
Andrea Lestz
Mary Margarites
Joseph Mortorano
Valerie Mulligan
Beena Nair
Debbie Ombramonti
Elizabeth Peranio
Brian Phelan
Jennifer Prew
Deanna Reid
Joanne Riccardi
Michelle Riordan
Mindy Rosenfield
Tina Ruggiero
Jobanna Sabala
Colette Sam-Boeh
Victoria Schiman
Joan Seiden
Stefani Sguera
Adrian Sobie
Randee Stern
Jon Storey
Elaine Treutle
Kathy Trotta
Susan Tyson
Steven Vagnone
Danica Valentine
Karen Weber
Helen Webster

PREMIER MEMBERSHIP SERVICES

Directors, Premier Member Services	Sandra Anderson
	Laura Oakland
Premier Member Services Associates	Chris Anello
	Shari Brown
	Awilda Cruz
	Stacey Drew
	Mike Fanesi
	Jill Gerdes
	Iris Gettinger
	Mindy Goldschmidt
	Alan Gold
	Lee Goodman
	Darlene Gumas
	Angie Loeffler
	Pamela Marshall
	Dan Metzger
	Glynn Nolan
	Lois Polesky
	Linda Saegert
	Melissa Salib
	Jay Sparber
	Stephanie Standish
	Jackie Tufano
	Heather Villani
	Roger Waldeck

PRODUCT AND CONTENT DEVELOPMENT

Director	Kara Lee
Website and Content Developers	Michelle Lee
	Nikki Masih
Cambridge Travel and Leisure Club Manager	Joanna Defendini

RECRUITMENT/TRAINING

Director of Corporate Recruiting	Stan Pitt
Corporate Recruiter	Caragh Gavin

TECHNOLOGY AND INFORMATION SYSTEMS MANAGEMENT

Network Administrator	Harsh Sethi
Software Developer	Ginny Cui

The Cambridge Who's Who Registry is a compilation of men and women of distinction who are influential within their organization or industry.

The persons described in this volume represent virtually every important field of endeavor. Included are executives and officials in business, healthcare, science, education, philanthropy, religion, government, finance, law, engineering and many other fields.

Although every effort is made to avoid errors in these listings, typographical errors do occur. The publisher requests that such errors be called to our attention so that they may be corrected in future editions.

We are proud of the 2008–2009 Edition and congratulate
all those included.

The Cambridge Who's Who Registry is also available
on the World Wide Web at www.cambridgewhoswho.com.

2008-2009
CAMBRIDGE WHO'S WHO PUBLISHING, INC.
498 RexCorp Plaza
West Tower
Uniondale, NY 11556

EXPLANATION OF REGISTRY LISTING

CODES

BUS:	Type of Business
P/S:	Major Products and Services
MA:	Marketing Area
EXP:	Area of Expertise
D/D/R:	Day to Day Responsibilities
H/I/S:	Hobbies, Interests and Sports
FBP:	Favorite Business Publications
EDU:	Education Degrees
CERTS:	Certifications
A/A/S:	Affiliations, Associations and Societies
A/H:	Awards and Honors
C/VW:	Charities and Volunteer Work
DOB:	Date of Birth
POB:	Place of Birth
SP:	Spouse's Name
CHILD:	Children's Names
W/H:	Work History
C/A:	Career Achievements
A/S:	What do you attribute your success to?
B/I:	How did you become involved in your profession?
H/O:	What was the highlight of your career?
I/F/Y:	Where will you be in five years?

VIP SAMPLE LISTING

MR. JOHN A. SMITH III, ESQ.
Director, Acquisitions and Marketing
AZ Company
123 Main Street
Atlanta, GA 12345
john.smith@azcompany.com, jsmith@aol.com
http://www.azcompany.com, http://www.johnsmith.com

BUS: Manufacturing Company **P/S:** Plastic Products **MA:** Regional **EXP:** Mr. Smith's expertise is in acquisitions and marketing management. **D/D/R:** Overseeing Corporate Management **H/S:** Reading, Traveling **FBP:** Forbes; The Wall Street Journal **EDU:** Bachelor of Arts in Marketing, Harvard University **A/A/S:** Atlanta Businessmen's Association **A/H:** Man of the Year, Atlanta Businessmen's Association **C/VW:** American Heart Association **DOB:** August 14, 1965 **POB:** Atlanta, GA **SP:** Mary **CHILD:** Sam, Peter **W/H:** Supervisor, Plastic Fog Manufacturing Company **C/A:** Citations, Mayor, Atlanta, GA **A/S:** He attributes his career success to his determination and desire to succeed. **B/I:** He became involved in his profession through his interest in the field of mathematics as a child. **H/O:** The highlight of his career was obtaining his current position. **I/F/Y:** In five years, Mr. Smith will have increased his company's earnings by five percent.

In Memoriam

Cambridge Who's Who
dedicates this registry
to the memory of the following
distinguished members:

Anne Marie Behan

Arthur Bowman

Carolyn Bowyer-Brown

Floyd Chambers

Freida Conner

Alan Crowe

Gloria Davis

Jennifer DeNault

Linda Foss

Deborah Gilpin

Debra Hatton

Alice Hubbard

Barbara C. Jett

M. Kelley

Jeanene Laegreid

Celia Livingston

Michael Manore

J. Jason McPhail

William Milbourne Sr.

Greg W. Moeller

Bernice Pressley

Sylvian R. Ray

Elizabeth Robinson

Alvin Rogal

Linda Spencer

Charles Stocker

Marion Voyles

OUTSTANDING PROFESSIONAL OF THE YEAR IN THE MUSIC INDUSTRY

MISSY ELLIOTT

Rapper, Songwriter, Producer, Master of Ceremonies, Clothing Designer, CEO
The Goldmind, Inc.
Aventura, FL United States
mpelove@aol.com
http://www.cambridgewhoswho.com

Type of Business: Entertainment Company

Major Products and Services: Music Recordings

Marketing Area: International

Day to Day Responsibilities: Producing and Composing Music, Writing Songs, Overseeing a Record Label

Hobbies/Interests/Sports: Listening to Music, Interior Designing

Education Degrees: Diploma, Manor High School

Charity/Volunteer Work: Break the Cycle; MAC AIDS Fund

What do you attribute your success to? She attributes her success to her faith in God, determination and her goal-oriented nature.

How did you become involved in your profession? She became involved in her profession because of her interest in singing.

What was the highlight of your career? The most gratifying aspect of her career is being able to bring her ideas to life.

Expanded Bio: Six–time Grammy Award winner Missy Elliott is a songwriter, producer, performer, clothing designer and the chief executive officer of The Goldmind, Inc.

As the music community and her fans wait with great anticipation, Ms. Elliott is currently putting the finishing touches on her seventh studio album, *Block Party*. Elliott has already teased our collective aural palate with *Block Party* album tracks "Best, Best," "Shake Your Pom Pom" and "Ching-A-Ling."

Elliott kicked off 2008 by wowing the world with the first-ever 3D music video for her single "Ching-A-Ling," and has continued to sizzle with a new Pepsi commercial (which premiered during the New York Giants' Superbowl XLII win), a Grammy nomination for Keyshia Cole's "Let It Go," a BET Award win for "Best Female Hip Hop Artist," and notable contributions to 2008's hot chart-topping albums by Janet Jackson, Danity Kane and newcomer Jazmine Sullivan. In addition, Elliott and adidas Originals launched the Respect ME Brand Ambassador campaign which gives girls from around the world the opportunity to join Elliott in future global advertising campaigns and represent Respect ME in their local communities.

Year 2007 was also a good one for Elliott. She enjoyed a wide variety of successes, from writing and producing songs for Fantasia and Keyshia Cole and being feted at VH-1's *Hip Hop Honors* to receiving the "Creative Visionary Award" at the 2nd Annual Black Girls Rock Awards Show at Lincoln Center and remixing country with hip hop for the national television advertising campaign for Doritos Collisions.

Recognized as one of the most influential female artists in contemporary American music, Missy Elliott is the best-selling female hip hop artist of all time with five multi-platinum albums under her belt. She has also gone on to receive innumerable award nominations and wins, including six Grammy Awards and the highly coveted MTV Video Music Award for "Video of the Year." She is one of few women who enjoy an equal amount of success behind the scenes as a prolific songwriter and producer, having garnered a star-studded list of production credits that includes Whitney Houston, Janet Jackson, Christina Aguilera, Justin Timberlake, Aaliyah, Ciara and Destiny's Child, among others. As the head of her own record label, The Goldmind, Inc., Elliott launched the successful career of platinum-selling R&B star Tweet. She created a unique joint venture with adidas for a line of clothing, shoes and accessories under the moniker, Respect ME, which has been met with a tremendous amount of success. In addition to all of this, Elliott has enjoyed phenomenal TV success with her dramality show, UPN's "The Road to Stardom with Missy Elliott" and has a biopic currently in the works. A passionate philanthropist, Elliott is also known for shining a light on the issue of domestic violence and the ways it affects children. In addition, she joined forces with M•A•C cosmetics in 2004 to promote "Viva Glam," which donates 100 percent of its proceeds to the M•A•C AIDS Fund.

For more information about Missy Elliott, contact Anne Kristoff at anne@akpr.net. For the latest news about her projects, including her album *Block Party*, visit http://www.missy-elliott.com.

Executive, Professional and Entrepreneur

Special Section

2008–2009

CAMBRIDGE

WHO'S WHO

PROFESSIONAL OF THE YEAR IN UTILITY SERVICE LAW

MR. RICHARD J. AARON

Partner
Honigman Miller Schwartz and Cohn, LLP
222 N. Washington Square, Suite 400
Lansing, MI 48933 United States
raaron@honigman.com
http://www.honigman.com

Type of Business: Law Firm

Major Products and Services: Legal Services Including Antitrust and Trade Regulation, Bankruptcy, Reorganization and Commercial, Business Immigration, Corporate and Securities, Employee Benefits, Environmental, Insurance, Intellectual Property and Technology, Investment Incentives and Tax Savings, Labor and Employment, Litigation, Real Estate, Regulatory, Tax, Tax Appeals, Tribal Sovereignty and Development Practice, Trusts and Estates

Marketing Area: National

Day to Day Responsibilities: Promoting Landfill-Generated Electricity and Bio-Diesel Bio-Fuels, Litigating Cases on Energy and Renewable Resources Including All Concerns Pertaining to Electricity, Natural Gas, Hydro-Electric Energy and New Frontiers Involving Wind-Generated Electricity

Favorite Business Publications: The Economist

Hobbies/Interests/Sports: Hunting Foxes

Education Degrees: JD, Thomas M. Cooley Law School, Summa Cum Laude (1983)

Affiliations/Associations/Societies: Energy Division, State Bar of Michigan

Spouse: Charlotte

Expanded Biography: Mr. Aaron has presented lectures at the Michigan State University and on various cable television productions regarding energy matters and his published works.

PROFESSIONAL OF THE YEAR IN EDUCATION

TIMOTHY J. ABRAHAM

Professor
Touro College
27-33 W. 23rd Street
New York, NY 10010 United States
timothya@touro.edu
http://www.touro.edu

TOURO ⓣ COLLEGE

Type of Business: Education

Major Products and Services: Curriculum and Teaching

Marketing Area: New York City

Day to Day Responsibilities: Developing Curriculum, Teaching, Coaching Seasoned Teachers on General Equivalency Diploma Subjects

Favorite Business Publications: Educational Leadership

Hobbies/Interests/Sports: Traveling, Theater, Listening to Classical Music

Education Degrees: Doctor of Education, Teachers College, Columbia University (1974); Master of Arts in English, John Carroll University (1962); Bachelor of Arts, John Carroll University (1958)

Affiliations/Associations/Societies: Association for Supervision and Curriculum Development; Association for Teachers of Social Studies; Association of Teacher Educators

Charity/Volunteer Work: Hurricane Katrina Volunteer, American Red Cross; Catholic Charities; Local Church; The Citizens Union

What do you attribute your success to? He attributes his success to the help he has received along the way.

How did you become involved in your profession? He became involved in his profession because he felt that he was privileged to have received such a fine education. He has a genuine interest in helping young people and he feels compelled to give back to the community.

What was the highlight of your career? The most gratifying aspect of his career is whenever a student keeps in contact with him.

PROFESSIONAL OF THE YEAR IN HEALTHCARE LECTURING

DR. AMPAI D. AIMSIRI

Staff Nurse
Perioperative Department
Kaiser Permanente Fontana Medical Center
9961 Sierra Avenue
Fontana, CA 92335 United States
ampaio@earthlink.net
http://www.kaiserpermanente.org

Ampai Aimsiri, DrPH, MS, RN, RD
Nursing & Nutrition Consultant
ampaio@earthlink.net

11667 Pecan Way
Loma Linda, California 92354-3531
(909) 796-4239
Cell (909) 229-5899

Type of Business: Medical Center

Major Products and Services: Healthcare

Marketing Area: Regional

Area of Expertise: Dr. Aimsiri's expertise includes perianesthesia and post-operative care.

Day to Day Responsibilities: Assisting Patients with Pain Management, Specializing in Critical Care Nursing, Promoting Public Health and Nutrition, Lecturing

Favorite Business Publications: Smithsonian; National Geographic; Reader's Digest

Hobbies/Interests/Sports: Traveling, Gardening, Needleworking, Creating Artwork, Making Crafts

Education Degrees: Ph.D. in Public Health Nutrition, Loma Linda University (1995); Master of Science in Biochemistry, Loma Linda University (1978); Bachelor of Science in Chemistry, Philippine Union College (Now Adventist University of the Philippines) (1972); Associate of Science in Nursing, Public Health and Midwifery, Bangkok Sanitarium and Hospital School of Nursing, Bangkok, Thailand (1967); Registered Nurse, State of California; Registered Nurse, Republic of Singapore; Registered Nurse, Bangkok, Thailand

Certifications: Certification in High-Risk Neonate Care, Loma Linda University Medical Center (1994); Registered Dietitian, State of California; Certified Critical Care Registered Nurse, State of California; Certified Doctor of Public Health; Registered Midwife, Bangkok

Awards/Honors: Alumni of the Year Award, Bangkok Adventist Mission Hospital, Thailand (2001)

Charity/Volunteer Work: Volunteer, Mass Cardiopulmonary Resuscitation Instructor, Singapore Cardiology Society (1987); Critical Care Instructor, China Japan Friendship Hospital, Beijing, China (1985, 1987); Nurse, Cambodian Refugee Camp, Thailand (1980)

Place of Birth: Yala

Work History: Staff Nurse, Perioperative Department, Kaiser Permanente Fontana Medical Center (1999-Present); PM Nurse Charge and Preceptor, Perianesthesia Care Unit, Loma Linda University Medical Center (1998-2002); Shift Coordinator and Preceptor, Perianesthesia Care Unit, Loma Linda University Medical Center (1995-1998); Understudy Vice President, Patient Care Services, Florida Hospital Waterman (1994); Understudy Vice President, Patient Care Services, White Memorial Medical Center, CA (1994); Director of Nursing, Youngberg Adventist Hospital, Singapore (1992-1994); Clinical Nurse, Perianesthesia Care Unit, Loma Linda University Medical Center (1990-1992); Senior Research Assistant, Biochemistry Department, Loma Linda University (1980-1984); Team Leader, Clinical Nurse, Multiple Trauma Intensive Care Unite, Loma Linda University Medical Center (1976-1998); Chairman of the Basic Science Department, Nursing Educator, Bangkok Adventist Hospital School of Nursing, Bangkok, Thailand (1973-1976); Associate Dean of Women, Bangkok Adventist Hospital School of Nursing, Bangkok, Thailand; Charge Nurse, Medical-Surgical and intensive Care Units, Bangkok Adventist Hospital, Thailand (1967-1968)

What was the highlight of your career? The most gratifying aspects of her career are helping nurses in other countries and developing her skills and knowledge in pain management and critical care nursing.

Expanded Biography: Dr. Aimsiri has been a guest lecturer and teacher in China, Singapore, Bangkok, Malaysia, the Philippines, Indonesia and Thailand. She is fluent in English, Thai and Chinese.

PROFESSIONAL OF THE YEAR IN QUALITY IMPROVEMENT AND MICROBIOLOGY IN THE CONSUMER PRODUCTS INDUSTRY

DEBRA A. ALBRIGHT, MAED, CQA

Senior Quality Improvement Scientist,
Microbiologist, CQA, MAED
SC Johnson & Son, Inc.
1525 Howe Street
Mail Station 220
Racine, WI 53403 United States
daalbrig@scj.com
http://www.scjohnson.com

Type of Business: Manufacturing and Distribution Company

Major Products and Services: Production and Distribution of Household Storage and Other Consumer Products

Marketing Area: International

Day to Day Responsibilities: Ensuring Quality Improvement, Overseeing Microbiological Functions

Hobbies/Interests/Sports: Coaching Special Olympics, Coaching and Participating in a Variety of Sports, Showing Dobermans

Education Degrees: Master's Degree in Adult Education, University of Phoenix (2006); Bachelor of Science in Biology, Eckerd College (1986)

Affiliations/Associations/Societies: American Society for Quality; ASM

Awards/Honors: Family of the Year, Wisconsin Special Olympics (2007); National Title Holder, Mrs. America's Touch of Class (2005); Coach, Wisconsin Special Olympics (2004); Susan Armacost Medal (2004); Mrs. Wisconsin Americas Touch of Class (2003-2004); Woman of the Year, American Biographical Institute (2003); Coach of the Year, Wisconsin Special Olympics; Herbert F. Johnson Community Service Award

Charity/Volunteer Work: Kiwanis International

Date of Birth: November 27, 1964   **Place of Birth:** Racine, WI, USA

Spouse: Steven   **Children:** Riley, Logan, Cadyn

Work History: SC Johnson, Senior Quality Improvement Scientist and Microbiologist (2000-Present); SC Johnson, Microbiology, Senior Scientist (1997-2000); SC Johnson Wax-Polymer, T-22/T-23 (1995-1997); S.C. Johnson Wax (1995); Chemical Packaging Corp. of America (1994-1995); Racine Industries, Inc. (1991-1994); S.C. Johnson Wax (1987-1991); Milwaukee Area Technical College (1993-2003); University of Wisconsin (1990-1991); Racine County Opportunity Center (1987-1989); Racine Veterinary Hospital (1980-1987)

Career Achievements: SC Johnson Technical Merit Award; SC Johnson Officer Recognition Award

PROFESSIONAL OF THE YEAR IN
FLEET SERVICES, INSPECTION AND REPAIRS

RAYMOND I. ALLOWAY JR.

President
AAF Fleet Service, Inc.
P.O. Box 358
Mc Louth, KS 66054 United States
allowayangus@grapevine.net
http://www.cambridgewhoswho.com

Type of Business: Repairing Company

Major Products and Services: Automotive Repair Services Including Hydraulic, Brake, Drive Train and Clutches

Marketing Area: Kansas, Missouri

Day to Day Responsibilities: Working on Overhead and Underground Power Lines, Repairing Construction Equipment

Favorite Business Publications: Angus Journal

Hobbies/Interests/Sports: Raising Black Angus Cattle, Farming

Certifications: Bucket and Digger Truck Mechanical Training, Altec Industries; Euclid Medium and Heavy Duty Brake Systems Training, Vickers Hydraulic Training School

Date of Birth: January 25, 1956   **Place of Birth:** Bellefontaine, OH

Spouse: Wendy   **Children:** Steven, Amber, Ashley

Expanded Biography: Mr. Alloway works as a mechanic and operator for all types of power plant and power line operations.

EXECUTIVE OF THE YEAR IN
CORRECTIONAL HEALTHCARE ADMINISTRATION

MS. MARGARET E. AMODEI, MSN

Regional Vice President
Correctional Medical Services
830 Bear Tavern Road, Suite 301
Ewing, NJ 08628 United States
m.amodei@cmsstl.com
http://www.cmsstl.com

Type of Business: Healthcare

Major Products and Services: Healthcare Services for Prison Inmates

Marketing Area: National

Area of Expertise: Ms. Amodei's expertise includes clinical corrections management, surgical services, health services administration and strategic decisions.

Favorite Business Publications: The Wall Street Journal; Advanced Nursing; Correct Care; American Journal of Nursing; Spectrum Nursing

Hobbies/Interests/Sports: Golfing, Going to the Beach, Going to the Theater, Bowling, Fishing

Education Degrees: Master of Science in Nursing, Villanova University; Bachelor of Science in Nursing, Gwynedd-Mercy College; Registered Nurse Diploma, Episcopal Hospital School of Nursing

Affiliations/Associations/Societies: National Commission on Correctional Health Care; Advisory Council, Francis J. Curry National Tuberculosis Center

Work History: Sexual Assault Nurse Examiner, Burlington County New Jersey Prosecutors Office; Registered Nurse

What do you attribute your success to? She attributes her success to having excellent mentors.

How did you become involved in your profession? She became involved in the profession because after working in surgery she decided to transition into corrections.

What was the highlight of your career? The highlight of her career was being recognized by colleagues and supervisory staff as a front line leader.

PROFESSIONAL OF THE YEAR IN CHILDBIRTH AND NURSING EDUCATION

CHERYL ANN ANDERSON, RN

Registered Nurse
Melvin E. Sine Elementary School
4932 W. Myrtle Avenue
Glendale, AZ 85301 United States
ospandy@cox.net
http://www.cambridgewhoswho.com

Type of Business: Elementary School

Major Products and Services: Primary Education

Marketing Area: Local

Day to Day Responsibilities: Teaching Childbirth Techniques, School Nursing, Supervising a Clinic for Children without Insurance

Favorite Business Publications: AJN

Hobbies/Interests/Sports: Golfing, Volunteering with Methodist Church

Education Degrees: Associate of Science in Nursing, University of New York

Certifications: Certified Coordinator, Resolve Through Sharing

Affiliations/Associations/Societies: Student Nurses Association of Arizona; National Association of Childbirth Educators

Awards/Honors: Recipient, Star Award (1995, 1998, 2006)

Expanded Biography: Ms. Anderson is instrumental in setting up a nationwide resolve through sharing program, which counsels parents and teaches technicians how to document fetal deaths on obstetric units.

PROFESSIONAL OF THE YEAR IN
NURSING

AURLENE J. ANDREWS

Director of Women and Children Services
San Gabriel Valley Medical Center
438 W. Las Tunas Drive
San Gabriel, CA 91776 United States
aurlene.Andrews@ahmchealth.com
http://www.sangabrielvalleymedctr.org

Type of Business: Not-for-Profit Acute Care Hospital

Major Products and Services: Healthcare Services Including Cardiology, Diagnostic Imaging, Surgical, Gastroenterology, Women's, Emergency, Intensive, Orthopedics, Rehabilitation, Sexual Assault, Acute Care, Pulmonary and Respiratory Care Services

Marketing Area: Regional

Area of Expertise: Ms. Andrews' expertise includes postpartum depression, labor and delivery, quality compliance and maternal and child healthcare.

Day to Day Responsibilities: Overseeing Operations, Budgeting, Coordinating the Staff, Charting Audits for the Perinatal and Intensive Care Unit

Favorite Business Publications: Association of Women's Health, Obstetric and Neonatal Nurses Publications; Joint Commission on Accreditation of Healthcare Organizations Literature; California Health News

Hobbies/Interests/Sports: Cooking, Golfing

Education Degrees: Registered Nurse, St. Francis Medical Center, San Francisco (1958)

Certifications: Certified in Ambulatory Women's Care, Fetal Monitoring and Women's Health (1981)

Affiliations/Associations/Societies: Association of Women's Health, Obstetric and Neonatal Nurses

PROFESSIONAL OF THE YEAR IN OSTEOPATHIC MEDICINE

ARTHUR EUGENE ANGOVE, DO

Doctor of Osteopathy, General Surgeon (Retired)
General Medicine, Surgery, Urgent Care
21501 W. Cleveland Avenue
New Berlin, WI 53146 United States
arthureugene.angove@cwwemail.com
aeangove@wi.rr.com
http://www.cambridgewhoswho.com

Type of Business: Healthcare Center

Major Products and Services: Healthcare

Marketing Area: International

Area of Expertise: Dr. Angove's expertise includes medical and surgical education, basic and advanced disaster life support education and clinical instruction.

Responsibilities: Performing Pastoral Duties

Favorite Business Publications: Journal of the American Medical Association; Journal of American Osteopathic Association

Hobbies/Interests/Sports: Spending Time with his Family, Volunteering Surgical Care for Third World Countries

Education Degrees: Doctor of Osteopathy, College of Osteopathic Medicine, Des Moines University; Bachelor of Science in Pre-Medical, Pre-Theology and Education, Westmar College

Certifications: Licensed Pilot

Affiliations/Associations/Societies: Former President, Wisconsin Association of Osteopathic Physicians & Surgeons; Board of Trustees, Des Moines University; American Osteopathic Association; American Medical Association; American College of Osteopathic Surgeons; Experimental Aircraft Association

Awards/Honors: Aircraft Honors, Aircraft Owners and Pilots Association

Charity/Volunteer Work: Volunteer, Inter-Tribal Medicine; Pastor, United Methodist Church; United Church of Christ; Young Men's Christian Association Heritage Club; Docare International

Spouse: Carmen   **Children:** Julie, Debra, Lori, Steven, Michael, Kristin

Work History: Clinical Instructor, Des Moines University; Clinical Instructor, Midwestern University; Medical Director, Lutheran Mission

What do you attribute your success to? He attributes his success to the support he receives from his wife.

How did you become involved in your profession? He became involved in his profession because of his interest in the medical missionary and was influenced by his uncle who was in the missionary work.

What was the highlight of your career? The highlight of his career was fulfilling all his dreams.

Where will you be in five years? In five years, Dr. Angove hopes to continue his medical education and teaching.

Expanded Biography: Dr. Angove has offered free medical care to people around the world, in nations such as Bolivia, Honduras, Russia and Ecuador.

PROFESSIONAL OF THE YEAR IN
OREGON REAL ESTATE

SALLY A. ARBUS

Real Estate Broker
North Point, Inc.
100 Central Avenue
Coos Bay, OR 97420 United States
sarbus@north-pt.com
http://www.north-pt.com

Type of Business: Real Estate Sales and Services

Major Products and Services: Residential and Commercial Real Estate Services, Land Development, Investment Properties, Mortgage Assistance

Marketing Area: Regional

Day to Day Responsibilities: Representing Clients, Buying and Selling Residential Homes and Apartment Complexes, Helping Clients Find their Perfect Home

Favorite Business Publications: REALTOR; Best Sellers

Hobbies/Interests/Sports: Running, Mountain Climbing, Following the Stock Market, Music, Reading, Weightlifting

Education Degrees: Coursework in Geology, Southwestern Community College

Affiliations/Associations/Societies: PEO Chapter; Oregon Association of Realtors; National Association of Realtors; Coos Bay Yacht Club; SC Wine Grape Growers Association; Rental Owners Association

Charity/Volunteer Work: Warden Episcopal Church; Former Vestry and Junior Warden, Emmanuel Episcopal Church; American Red Cross

Place of Birth: North Bend, OR

Spouse: Bill

Children: Linda, Janet, Mark, Robert

Work History: School Secretary; Welcome Wagon Hostess; UNICEF Director, Coos and Western Douglas Counties; Temporary Hospital Chaplain

Career Achievements: Writer, Four Unpublished Works on 'The American Woman'

PROFESSIONAL OF THE YEAR IN EVANGELISM

ELIZA ARMSTRONG

Pastor
The Last Day Church of God
300 Candler Road S.E.
Atlanta, GA 30317 United States
eliza@bellsouth.net
http://www.cambridgewhoswho.com

Type of Business: Church

Major Products and Services: Non-Denominational Religious Services, Gospel, Ministry, Evangelism

Marketing Area: Local

Area of Expertise: Ms. Armstrong's expertise is in prophecy and evangelism.

Day to Day Responsibilities: Performing Outreach Ministry Services, Conducting Training Classes at the Church, Working for Student Lenders, Teaching Security Identification

Favorite Business Publications: Black Enterprise

Education Degrees: Pursuing Bachelor's Degree in Theology, Minor in Leadership, Beulah Heights University; Associate Degree in Theology, Beulah Heights University (2005)

Certifications: Ordained Pastor (1979)

Children: Angela, Nathaniel (Deceased)

Expanded Biography: Ms. Armstrong is a praying woman who has truly been chosen by God to deliver his message to his people. With the love of God in her heart and belief in lifting as she climbs, she has helped many who were brokenhearted, sick, depressed and downcast. She has a spirit that draws people to her, and if one does not know her, one would not understand her spirit until speaking with her. She is an experienced listener who loves children and the elderly.

PROFESSIONAL OF THE YEAR IN TEACHER EDUCATION

DAVID M. ARNESON, ED.D.

Chairman, Coordinator of Student Teaching
Division of Teacher Education
New York Institute of Technology
Old Westbury, NY 11545 United States
darneson@nyit.edu
http://www.nyit.edu

Type of Business: Nonprofit Educational Institution

Major Products and Services: Higher Education

Marketing Area: International

Area of Expertise: Mr. Arneson's expertise includes teacher, business and marketing education.

Day to Day Responsibilities: Teaching Undergraduate and Graduate Students, Advising Students Majoring in Adolescent Education

Favorite Business Publications: Action; Teacher Education

Hobbies/Interests/Sports: Traveling, Reading, Listening to Country Music

Education Degrees: Doctor of Education, University of Northern Colorado; Master of Arts, University of Northern Colorado; Bachelor of Science, University of Wisconsin

Affiliations/Associations/Societies: The Association of Teacher Educators; Association for Supervision and Curriculum Development; Executive Board Member, New York Association of Colleges for Teacher Education; New York State Association of Teacher Educators; Phi Delta Kappa

Awards/Honors: National Distinguished Award for Education; Distinguished Clinician in Teacher Education Award (1991)

What do you attribute your success to? He attributes his success to his commitment and to the support he receives from his mentors and co-workers.

What was the highlight of your career? The highlight of his career was meeting President Bush in 1990.

SHARON R. ATKIN, MSA, OD

Chief Optometry
Perry Point
VA Maryland Health Care System
Perry Point, MD 21902 United States
aktinod@gmail.com
http://www.cambridgewhoswho.com

Type of Business: Government Organization

Major Products and Services: Healthcare Services for Veterans

Marketing Area: Maryland, Pennsylvania

Area of Expertise: Ms. Atkin's expertise includes vision care, diagnosis and treatment of eye diseases.

Day to Day Responsibilities: Correcting Vision Problems, Educating Optometry Students and Residents, Ensuring Leadership and Administration of the Clinic

Hobbies/Interests/Sports: Reading, Yard Work, Stained Glass

Education Degrees: Doctor of Optometry, Indiana University; Master of Science in Health Administration, Central Michigan University; Bachelor of Science in Physical Therapy, University of Pittsburgh

Affiliations/Associations/Societies: Fellow, American Academy of Optometry; Former Acting Director, Optometry Service, Department of Veterans Affairs; The National Association of Veterans Affairs Optometrists

Charity/Volunteer Work: Planned Parenthood

Spouse: James

What do you attribute your success to? She attributes her success to her hard work, self-motivation, dedication and her commitment to her patients.

How did you become involved in your profession? She became involved in her profession because of the encouragement she received from her friend while attending physical therapy in an optometry school.

Expanded Biography: Ms. Atkin has been featured 15 times in various journals and magazines. She is affliated with nonprofit organizations concerning animal-relatedand environmental causes. She currently holds faculty appointments at four schools and colleges of optometry and has presented numerous professional posters, publications and lectures. She has also participated on the editorial board of optometric journals and served as a referee and guest editor of a journal issue. Ms. Atkin serves as a consultant to a number of corporate healthcare advisory panels and is currently in the process of building a home-based business involving e-commerce, media placement, affiliate marketing and information marketing. She conducts her various business ventures under the name Optopod Enterprises, Inc. She has been appointed to the field advisory group for the director of VA Optometry Service and its executive council.

PROFESSIONAL OF THE YEAR IN ART EDUCATION

LINDA C. BABICH

Art Teacher
Allen Elementary School
2560 Towner Boulevard
Ann Arbor, MI 48104 United States
babich@aaps.k12.mi.us
http://www.cambridgewhoswho.com

Type of Business: School

Major Products and Services: Primary Education

Area of Expertise: Ms. Babich's expertise includes textile and jewelry design, artwork, watercolor painting.

Hobbies/Interests/Sports: Reading, Gardening, Traveling, Visiting the Museums, Attending the Theater

Education Degrees: Master of Arts in Special Education, Concentration in Emotionally Impaired Students, Eastern Michigan University (1990); Bachelor of Fine Arts, Eastern Michigan University (1978); Bachelor of Science in Textiles, Wayne State University (1972)

Certifications: Certificate in Art Education (K-12), Eastern Michigan University

Affiliations/Associations/Societies: Ann Arbor Arts and Crafts; American Academy of Equine Art; National Art Education Association; National Education Association; American Education Association

Charity/Volunteer Work: St. Jude Children's Research Hospital; The Salvation Army

Date of Birth: April 3, 1950   **Place of Birth:** Detroit, MI

What do you attribute your success to? She attributes her success to her hard work and dedication.

How did you become involved in your profession? She became involved in her profession because of her love for children and wanted to share her knowledge.

What was the highlight of your career? The most gratifying aspect of her career is helping children.

Expanded Biography: Ms. Babich does public speaking at St. Mary's University.

PROFESSIONAL OF THE YEAR IN MORTGAGE SERVICES

Ms. Beth Estelle Baker

Senior Loan Representative
Mortgage Loans
Networking Funding Associates, Inc
63 N. First Street
Campbell, CA 95008 United States
info@cambridgewhoswho.com
beth@nfa200.com
http://www.nfa2000.com

Type of Business: Mortgage Brokerage Firm

Major Products and Services: Residential and Commercial Financing

Marketing Area: California

Area of Expertise: Ms. Baker's expertise is in mortgage loans.

Favorite Business Publications: The Wall Street Journal; The San Francisco Chronicle

Hobbies/Interests/Sports: Snorkeling, Painting, Playing Piano

Education Degrees: Coursework in Continuing Education

Date of Birth: December 17, 1953   **Place of Birth:** Tallahassee

Spouse: William   **Children:** Karl, Brian, Bridgette

What do you attribute your success to? She attributes her career success to her pro-active nature, and ability to drive the train and guide the team of players for on time closings of their transactions, even in the face of natural disasters, hurricanes, fires and 9/11.

How did you become involved in your profession? She became involved in her profession after being encouraged in 1976 by a real estate agent to pursue a career in real estate, although she was actually in cosmetology school. Norma Frye said to her, "You don't belong in hair, you belong in Real Estate!"

What was the highlight of your career? The highlights of her career include closing her first tri-state commercial real estate exchange with Norma Frye, working under pressure with brokers and helping the underwriter complete a huge volume.

Expanded Biography: Ms. Baker would like to thank her father, Dr. George Frank, Ph.D. and her mother, Dolly Ann Finkelstein for always being there for her. She would not have been able to get to where she is today without their love and support. She would also like to her wonderful broker, Roger Cummings, and Jennifer Scott, who believed in her during her transition from wholesale to retail. They are both constantly helping her carve out new directions to better serve her clients in an ever-changing market place. She would like to thank her sister Judi Frank for her ongoing support over the last 30 years. Last but not least, Ms. Frank would like to express eternal love and gratitude to her fiancee, Billy, for without him she would not be here, and her three children, who always inspire her to keep going, through the adversities in life that she has personally encountered and endured.

PROFESSIONAL OF THE YEAR IN NONPROFIT INTERNET MARKETING

MELODY BAKER

Owner
Melody's Income Generator
750 S. Petit Avenue, Suite 105
Ventura, CA 93004 United States
mjb2002how@sbcglobal.net
http://www.silentsuccess.org

Type of Business: Nonprofit Organization

Major Products and Services: Marketing, Income Streaming, Sales, Assisting Disabled Individuals in Obtaining a Steady Income

Marketing Area: National

Day to Day Responsibilities: Marketing via the Internet

Favorite Business Publications: BizWebGazzette, The Web Pro Times, Tim's Wholesale Dropshipping

Hobbies/Interests/Sports: Spending Time with Friends

Education Degrees: Associate of Arts, Cuyahoga Community College; Associate of Applied Science, Cuyahoga Community College

Affiliations/Associations/Societies: The Ability Link; Access Watch; Independent Living Resource Center; Ventura City Council

Date of Birth: April 26, 1953   **Place of Birth:** Lowville

What do you attribute your success to? She attributes her success to her perseverance.

Expanded Biography: Ms. Baker is a renowned business owner in Ventura, Florida, who has worked in the industry for two years. She has published content on AC and is an internet marketer for the disabled, helping build them build independence while making an income.

PROFESSIONAL OF THE YEAR IN
SOCIAL WORK IN HIGHER EDUCATION

ANITA P. BARBEE

Professor, Distinguished University Scholar
University of Louisville Kent School of Social Work
Oppenheimer Hall
Louisville, KY 40292 United States
anita.barbee@louisville.edu
http://www.louisville.edu/kent

Type of Business: University School of Social Work that Seeks to Prepare Competently Trained Social Workers who Practice from a Strong Professional Value Base to Serve the Metropolitan Mission of the University

Major Products and Services: Knowledge Development in Social Work, Research and Education

Marketing Area: National

Area of Expertise: Ms. Barbee's expertise includes research on the formation, maintenance and dissolution of relationships, the role of social support, attachment, and emotions in relationship dynamics, evaluation in all areas of child welfare, training program development, execution and evaluation, strategic planning and culture changes.

Hobbies/Interests/Sports: Reading, Going to the Movies, Volunteering

Education Degrees: Master of Science in Social Work, University of Louisville (2001); Ph.D. in Psychology, University of Georgia (1988); Master of Arts in Psychology, University of Georgia (1985); Bachelor of Arts in English and Psychology, Agnes Scott College (1982)

Affiliations/Associations/Societies: American Psychological Association; National Association of Social Workers; International Association of Relationship Researchers; Society for Research in Child Development; National Council on Family Relations; American Public Human Services Association; National Staff Development and Training Association; Society for Social Work and Research; Association for Community Organization and Social Administration; Council on Social Work Education; National Center for Nonprofit Boards

Awards/Honors: Research and Creative Activity Award in Social Sciences, University of Louisville (2003); Recipient, Jeff Frank Teaching Award, Kent School of Social Work (2003); Kentucky Colonel Award, Commonwealth of Kentucky (2003); Recipient, Gerald R. Miller Early Career Award in Personal Relationships, International Network on Personal Relationships (1997); University of Louisville Community Service Award (1996); Junior League Leadership Award (1996); Recipient, President's Outstanding Scholarship

Date of Birth: March 10, 1960   **Place of Birth:** Tallahassee, FL

Children: Robert, Benjamin

Work History: Faculty Member, University of Kentucky, Graduate School (2002-Present); Associate Professor of Research (2002-Present); Assistant Research Scientist, University of Louisville (1990-Present); Faculty Member, University of Louisville, Graduate School (1999-Present); Full Professor, University of Louisville (2005); Tenured Distinguished University Scholar, Kent School of Social Work (1996-2004); Kent Doctoral Faculty (1993-1995); Instructor, Jefferson Community College (1992-1993); Associate, Department of Psychology (1986-1990); Visiting Instructor for Behavioral and Social Sciences, Elmhurst College (1986); Instructor, Department of Psychology, University of Georgia (1984-1985); Instructor, Department of Psychology (1982-1983); Research Assistant for Abe Tesser, Institute for Behavioral Research, English Language Institute (1984); Instructor of English as a Second Language to Japanese of All Ages, Tokyo, Japan

PROFESSIONAL OF THE YEAR IN OCCUPATIONAL THERAPY

MS. DAWN L. BARNIER

Occupational Therapist
Rehabilitation
Phoenix Children's Hospital
1919 E. Thomas Road
Phoenix, AZ 85016 United States
dbarnier@cox.net
http://www.phoenixchildrens.com

Type of Business: Hospital

Major Products and Services: Pediatric Healthcare

Marketing Area: Phoenix, Arizona

Area of Expertise: Ms. Barnier's expertise is in sensory integration.

Favorite Business Publications: Newsweek; BusinessWeek; OT Practice

Hobbies/Interests/Sports: Traveling, Hiking, Horseback Riding, Cooking, Photography

Education Degrees: Bachelor of Science in Occupational Therapy, University of Southern California (1995)

Affiliations/Associations/Societies: American Occupational Therapy Association; Board of Directors, The Children's Center for Neurodevelopmental Studies

Charity/Volunteer Work: Various Healthcare and Prevention Organizations

Expanded Biography: Ms. Barnier has three adult children aged 23, 25 and 28. She was a stay-at-home mom and very active in her children's education and school activities. Three of her service years included serving on the board of directors at the preschool level. In addition, she was very active in the Parent-Teacher Association at the elementary and middle school level and was the president for two years at the high school level. Her career opportunities have included teaching opportunities in Hungary, Vilnius and Lithuania. During these teaching excursions she was fortunate to be able to visit many neighboring eastern European countries and enhance her cultural knowledge, experiences and education.

PROFESSIONAL OF THE YEAR IN
COMMERCIAL AND INDUSTRIAL PROPERTY CONSULTING

CLIFFORD 'BUDDY' BARROWS

Partner, Owner
Meridian Restoration Consultants
30506 Fowler Circle, Suite 1700
Warrenville, IL 60555 United States
buddy@meridian-consultants.net
http://www.meridian-consultants.com

Type of Business: Consulting Services

Major Products and Services: Accountability and Oversight for Restoration for Commercial Property Adjusters

Marketing Area: International

Day to Day Responsibilities: Consulting for Property Loss due to Fire, Water and Other Types of Property Damage, Consulting for Commercial and Industrial Properties

Favorite Business Publications: Business Insurance, Crain's

Hobbies/Interests/Sports: Riding his Harley-Davidson

Education Degrees: Bachelor's Degree in Physical Education and Recreation, Mars Hill College (1978)

Affiliations/Associations/Societies: Property Loss Research Bureau

Charity/Volunteer Work: Willow Creek Church; Heart for Africa; AIDS in Africa

Spouse: Amy

What do you attribute your success to? He attributes his success to his hands-on knowledge, drive and the relationships he has made.

How did you become involved in your profession? He became involved in the profession after seeing the need for consulting while he worked in a company that offered work for large losses.

What was the highlight of your career? The most gratifying aspect of his career is having the opportunity to make a difference in the lives of people who have suffered large losses.

Expanded Biography: Mr. Barrows does speaking presentations for commercial carriers.

PROFESSIONAL OF THE YEAR IN SPECIAL EDUCATION

TERESA A. BARWICK

Special Education Teacher
Hillcrest Middle School
4355 Peach Orchard Road
Dalzell, SC 29040 United States
tnwbarwick@yahoo.com
http://www.cambridgewhoswho.com

Type of Business: Middle School

Major Products and Services: Education

Marketing Area: Local

Area of Expertise: Ms. Barwick's expertise is in academic and life skill services for special needs students.

Favorite Business Publications: 'The Exceptional Child: Inclusion in Early Childhood Education' by K. Eileen Allen and Glynnis Edwards Cowdery

Hobbies/Interests/Sports: Reading, Deer Hunting, Scrapbooking

Education Degrees: Master's Degree in Special Education, University of New Orleans; Bachelor's Degree in Special Education, Concentration in Learning Disabilities, Winthrop University

Affiliations/Associations/Societies: Council for Exceptional Children

Awards/Honors: District Teacher of the Year (1994)

Charity/Volunteer Work: Elder, Local Church; Volunteer, Special Olympics

Date of Birth: September 7, 1961   **Place of Birth:** Sumter

Spouse: Wesley   **Children:** Stephen, Wesley

What do you attribute your success to? She attributes her success to her dedication.

How did you become involved in your profession? She became involved in her profession because her brother has a learning disability and she wanted to make a difference as a teacher.

What was the highlight of your career? The highlight of her career was receiving the District Teacher of the Year award.

Where will you be in five years? In five years, Ms. Barwick hopes to be employed on the district level.

EXECUTIVE OF THE YEAR IN
CUSTOMER EXPERIENCE MANAGEMENT IN HOME BUILDING

MARTHA M. BAUMGARTEN

Vice President, Customer Experience Management
Eliant, Inc.
15631 Alton Parkway, Suite 200
Irvine, CA 92618 United States
marthabaumgarten@hotmail.com
http://www.eliant.com

Type of Business: Consumer Research and Solutions

Major Products and Services: Customer Satisfaction Measurement and Solutions for the New Home and Related Industries

Marketing Area: National

Day to Day Responsibilities: Training in Customer Experience, Facilitation and Design, Improving Organizational Customer Satisfaction Performance

Favorite Business Publications: Harvard Business Review

Education Degrees: Coursework, The Ohio State University

What do you attribute your success to? She attributes her success to continuous learning and her desire to try new things.

How did you become involved in your profession? She became involved in her profession because a mentor encouraged her to try it.

PROFESSIONAL OF THE YEAR IN SOFTWARE DEVELOPMENT

FRANCIS H. BEARDEN

Principal Software Engineer
Philips Medical Systems, Inc.
595 Miner Road
MR4
Highland Heights, OH 44143 United States
frank.bearden@philips.com
http://www.philips.com

Type of Business: Manufacturing Company

Major Products and Services: Diagnostic Equipments Including Medical Research, Magnetic Resonance Imaging, X-Ray and Computed Tomography Imaging Devices, Medical Equipments, Lighting and Silicon System Solutions, Patient Monitoring Systems, Color Televisions and Electric Shavers

Marketing Area: International

Area of Expertise: Mr. Bearden's expertise is in information technology.

Day to Day Responsibilities: Overseeing Software Development and Engineering

Favorite Business Publications: Engineering Times; Software Development

Hobbies/Interests/Sports: Photography, Traveling

Education Degrees: Bachelor of Science in Electrical Engineering, University of Missouri, Columbia (1965)

Affiliations/Associations/Societies: Electronic Engineer, Cincinnati Electronics; Marconi Medical Systems; Picker International

Date of Birth: December 1, 1937   **Place of Birth:** Springfield, MO

Expanded Biography: Mr. Bearden has worked in the magnetic resonance imaging field since 1983. He does public speaking and has published some of his works internationally.

PROFESSIONAL OF THE YEAR IN HIGHER EDUCATION

FRED BEDELLE JR.

Dean of the Carter and Moyers School of Education
Lincoln Memorial University
6965 Cumberland Gap Parkway
Harrogate, TN 37752 United States
bedelle@charter.net
http://www.lmunet.edu

Type of Business: University

Major Products and Services: Higher Education

Marketing Area: International

Day to Day Responsibilities: Overseeing Administrative Works

Favorite Business Publications: Phi Delta Kappa Journal

Hobbies/Interests/Sports: Fishing

Education Degrees: Doctorate Degree in Education, University of Tennessee; Master's Degree in Education, University of Tennessee; Bachelor's Degree in Biology, Lincoln Memorial University

PROFESSIONAL OF THE YEAR IN INDUSTRIAL CONSTRUCTION

CARLOS BEJARANO

Superintendent
Industrial Specialist, LLC
5015 Highway 288 N.
Richwood, TX 77531 United States
cbejarano@indspec.com
http://www.cambridgewhoswho.com

Type of Business: Construction Company

Major Products and Services: Construction Services

Marketing Area: National

Area of Expertise: Mr. Bejarano's expertise is in management and work schedules.

Hobbies/Interests/Sports: Horse Racing, Spending Time with his Family

Education Degrees: Coursework in Management Studies

Charity/Volunteer Work: Local School; Girl Scouts of the USA

Spouse: Edna   **Children:** Karla

What do you attribute your success to? He attributes his success to his flexibility and problem solving skills.

How did you become involved in your profession? He became involved in his profession because of his interest in construction.

What was the highlight of your career? The highlight of his career was attaining his current position.

PROFESSIONAL OF THE YEAR IN DAY CARE SERVICES

MS. LILLIE B. BELLAMY, PH.D.

Director, Owner
Dr. Bellamy's Day Care Center
56 Maple Parkway
Staten Island, NY 10303 United States
bellamy777@aol.com
http://www.cambridgewhoswho.com

Type of Business: Daycare Center

Major Products and Services: Childcare

Marketing Area: Local

Day to Day Responsibilities: Nurturing Children in a Safe and Healthy Environment, Educating Children Between the Ages of 6 Weeks and 12 Years Old, Preaching, Teaching, Counseling, Conducting Seminars

Hobbies/Interests/Sports: Listening to Music, Reading, Teaching the Bible

Education Degrees: Doctor of Philosophical Theology, United Christian College (1991); Doctor of Sacred Theology, United Christian College (1987); Bachelor of Science in the Psychology of Counseling (1987); Master of Religious Education, United Christian College (1986); Associate of Arts in Early Childhood Education

Certifications: Ordained Elder, Board of Presbytery, United Holy Church of America (1996); Certification in Basic Chaplaincy Methodologies and Advanced Methodologies (1996); Licensed Gospel Preacher (1988)

Charity/Volunteer Work: Christian Center; Friends of Crown Heights

Date of Birth: June 7, 1943   **Place of Birth:** Lauringburg, NC

Spouse: Charlie   **Children:** Sheila, Regina

Work History: Associate Pastor, Dean of Bible College, Linden Extension; Ordained Elder, Morning Star Christian Community Center, Linden, NJ (1994); Religious Instructor, United Christian College, Linden, NJ (1989); Religious Instructor, Bishop's School, Staten Island, NY (1987); Missionary, Arthur Kill Correctional Facility, Staten Island, NY (1987); Assistant School Administrator, Full Gospel Tabernacle United Holy Church, Staten Island, NY (1974); Founder, Director, Bellamy Day Care I and II, Staten Island, NY (1970); Evangelist, Superintendent of the Sunday School Department; Treasurer, Church; President, Pastor's Aide Department; Member, Missionary Department

What do you attribute your success to? She attributes her success to God who has led her throughout her life.

How did you become involved in your profession? She became involved in this profession because she has two young children of her own.

What was the highlight of your career? The most gratifying aspects of her career are being able to give children what they do not receive at home and offering them entertainment while encouraging them to do their best.

Expanded Biography: Ms. Bellamy inherited her nurturing spirit from her mother. When she was a young girl, she often cared for her younger brothers and sister for her parents. As a high school student, she often cared for other people's children as a job in addition to occasionally being a companion to senior citizens. She really loves helping children and since she has substantial skills, which far exceed the average childcare provider, she can help change the course of a child's home, community and even the nation. She has prepared herself to be one of the best provider mothers ever. Some of the children she's cared for have become doctors, teachers, policemen, nurses and she is now caring for their children. The anointing that God has placed on her life has allowed her to preach God's word all over the country. She has remained faithful to her home, husband, children and grandchildren. and has changed the lives of many parents and children in her day care. She is an associate pastor at Morning Star Christian Church and has been published in several newspaper publications. Ms. Bellamy is a blessed and highly-favored servant of God.

PROFESSIONAL OF THE YEAR IN HOSPICE CARE

MYRTLE BENJAMIN WEDDERBURN, RN

Registered Nurse, Triage Coordinator, Midwife
Life Path Hospice
3010 W. Azeele Street
Tampa, FL 33609 United States
mbenjamin4@tampabay.rr.com
http://www.lifepath-hospice.org

Type of Business: Not-for-Profit, Community-Based Hospice

Major Products and Services: Pain and Symptom Control, Services Enabling Patients to Carry on Alert, Pain-Free Lives, Programs that Meet the Specialized Needs of the Community, Caregiver Program, Circle of Love Children's Program, Family Camp Program, Nursing Home and Assisted Living Facility Program, Circle of Love Center for Grieving Children and the Outreach Care Program

Marketing Area: Local

Area of Expertise: Ms. Benjamin Wedderburn's expertise is in prostate cancer research.

Day to Day Responsibilities: Offering End-of-Life Care to Patients, Promoting Education for Staff in Nursing Homes and Assisted Living Facilities, Overseeing Quality Assurance Coordination, Ensuring Community Health and Hospice Care

Education Degrees: Registered Nurse, England (1964)

Certifications: Certification in Midwifery (1964)

Affiliations/Associations/Societies: Nursing Division, Caribbean Culture Club

Charity/Volunteer Work: Board of Directors, Safety Harbor Neighborhood Family Center

Expanded Biography: Ms. Benjamin Wedderburn does public speaking on education in end-of-life care.

PROFESSIONAL OF THE YEAR IN
FINANCIAL BUSINESS MANAGEMENT

Ms. Myrna Chérie Bennett

1) President 2) Chief Financial Officer
1) Arbee Inc. 2) Fence Factory 3) C & W Construction Specialties
444 Valley Vista Drive
Camarillo, CA 93010 United States
myrnabennett@roadrunner.com
http://www.cambridgewhoswho.com

Type of Business: 1) Holding Company 2) Fencing Company 3) Manufacturing Company

Major Products and Services: 1) Managing Two Corporations 2) Fencing Services 3) Manufacture and Installation of Guardrail and Commercial Fencing

Marketing Area: 1) California 2) Local 3) Local

Day to Day Responsibilities: Managing Finances for Three Companies

Favorite Business Publications: BusinessWeek

Hobbies/Interests/Sports: Golfing, Traveling, Knitting, Crocheting, Needlework, Reading

Education Degrees: Associate Degree in Business Administration, California State University, Long Beach

Affiliations/Associations/Societies: President, California Federation of Republican Women; Secretary, Treasurer, RASA; Director, 38th District, CRA; President, Beta Sigma Phi

Charity/Volunteer Work: Queen, Red Hat Society; Board Member, Cory Pavin Tournament for Big Brothers Big Sisters; Coalition Against Household Violence; CancerCare; Coalition Against Domestic Violence; American Red Cross; Election Board Member, Ventura County

Children: Cherie, Charlene, Michael, Steven, Laurie, Chuck

What do you attribute your success to? She attributes her success to her caring nature and to the support she receives from her family.

How did you become involved in your profession? She became involved in her profession through a natural progression of opportunities.

What was the highlight of your career? The most gratifying aspect of her career is having four of her six children managing her businesses.

PROFESSIONAL OF THE YEAR IN ENGINEERING CONSULTING

JOHN BERCHTOLD

Partner
Henderson and Bodwell LLP
35 Fairchild Avenue
Plainview, NY 11803 United States
jberchtold@handb.com
http://www.handb.com

Type of Business: Engineering Company

Major Products and Services: Civil Construction, Environmental and Transportation Engineering, Landscaping, Site Plans, Water Resources, Boundary, Topographic and Construction Surveys, Zoning Analysis, Wetlands Mitigation

Marketing Area: National

Area of Expertise: Mr. Berchtold's expertise includes civil and site engineering and infrastructure in residential and commercial sectors.

Day to Day Responsibilities: Designing and Constructing Properties, Managing Business Operations and Finance, Overseeing Housing Development Projects

Favorite Business Publications: Civil Engineering

Hobbies/Interests/Sports: Fishing, Traveling

Education Degrees: Bachelor of Science in Civil Engineering, Merrimack College, North Andover, MA (1994)

Certifications: Licensed Professional Engineer, State of New York

Affiliations/Associations/Societies: American Society of Civil Engineers; American Council of Engineering Companies

PROFESSIONAL OF THE YEAR IN
ELECTRICAL AND COMPUTER ENGINEERING EDUCATION

DR. FREDERICK C. BERRY

Professor
Head of the Electrical and Computer Engineering
Rose-Hulman Institute of Technology
5500 Wabash Avenue
Terre Haute, IN 47803 United States
berry@rose-hulman.edu
http://www.rose-hulman.edu/-berry

Type of Business: Academic Institution

Major Products and Services: Education for Undergraduates in Engineering, Science and Mathematics

Marketing Area: National

Day to Day Responsibilities: Teaching Electrical Engineering, Electronic Power and Controls

Hobbies/Interests/Sports: Collecting Cameras and Beer Steins

Education Degrees: Doctor of Engineering, Louisiana Technical College

Affiliations/Associations/Societies: Senior Member, Institute of Electrical and Electronics Engineers; American Society of Engineering Education; Board Chairman, Global Wireless Education Consortium; ECETA

What do you attribute your success to? He attributes his success to his persistence.

How did you become involved in your profession? He became involved in his profession because his father was an engineer for Boeing and his mother was a teacher, both of whose careers piqued his interest, so he decided to combine them into one career.

PROFESSIONAL OF THE YEAR IN
SEISMIC IMAGING IN THE OIL INDUSTRY

MR. HENRY E. BIGGART

Operations Supervisor
PGS Onshore, Inc.
15150 Memorial Drive
Houston, TX 77079 United States
hbiggart@aol.com
http://www.pgs.com

Type of Business: Geophysical Company

Major Products and Services: Geophysical Services Including 3-D Seismic Images of Plays, Seismic Data Acquisition, Processing, Interpretation and Field Evaluation, 3D-Seismic Data for Oil Industry, Geology, Geophysics, Reservoir and Production

Marketing Area: Statewide

Area of Expertise: Mr. Biggart's expertise is in operations management, product development and positive data acquisition.

PROFESSIONAL OF THE YEAR IN
COSMETIC DENTISTRY

KAREN A. BLAIR, DDS

Dentist
Dentistry By Design
1220 Hobson Road, Suite 132
Naperville, IL 60540 United States
dentistrybydesign1@hotmail.com
http://www.chicagolandcosmeticdentistry.com

Type of Business: Dentistry

Major Products and Services: Cosmetic Dentistry

Marketing Area: Local

Area of Expertise: Ms. Blair's expertise is in cosmetic dentistry.

Favorite Business Publications: American Academy of Cosmetic Dentistry

Hobbies/Interests/Sports: Biking, Boating, Swimming, Reading

Education Degrees: Doctor of Dental Surgery in Cosmetic Dentistry, University of Iowa

Affiliations/Associations/Societies: American Academy of Cosmetic Dentistry; Illinois Dental Association; American Dental Association

What do you attribute your success to? She attributes her success to her love for patient care and dentistry and her commitment to staying current with her educational classes and advances in her profession.

How did you become involved in your profession? She became involved in her profession because she always had a desire to become a dentist and because she enjoys helping people.

What was the highlight of your career? The highlight of her career was receiving the American Top Dentist Award from the Consumer Resource Council of America for 2005, 2006 and 2007.

PROFESSIONAL OF THE YEAR IN PUBLIC SERVICE

MARY JANE BASHAM BLEIER

Machine Processing Equipment Operator, Facilitator,
Secretary, Employee Aid AED Professional
Wage & Investment
Internal Revenue Service Center
6010 Spicewood Avenue
Florence, KY 41042 United States
maryjbleier@hotmail.com
http://www.revenue.ky.gov

Type of Business: Government Organization

Major Products and Services: Tax Collection, Downloadable Income Tax Forms, Instructions, Agency Publications

Marketing Area: National

Day to Day Responsibilities: Facilitating and Instructing Classes, Managing Operations, Training and Mentoring Employees, Overseeing Administrative Duties, Customer Service and Public Service

Favorite Business Publications: Kentucky Revenue; Industry-Related Publications

Hobbies/Interests/Sports: Photography, Biking, Sewing, Participating in Church Activities, Making Crafts, Reading Poetry, Camping, Fishing, Spending Time with her Family

Education Degrees: Coursework in Basic American Sign Language, Northern Kentucky Vocational School (1987); Coursework in Business and Accounting (1983); Diploma, Lloyd Memorial High School (1971)

Certifications: On-the-Job Training Certification, Internal Revenue Service (2007); Certification in Automated External Defibrillator (2005); Certification in CPR (2005); Certification in American Sign Language (1988); Certification in Computer Program Basic I (1981); Certification in Blueprint Reading (1980)

Affiliations/Associations/Societies: The International Executive Guild; Independent Order of Foresters

Awards/Honors: Managerial Award, Internal Revenue Service (2007); Woman of the Year Award, American Biographical Institute (2006); Poetry Award, 'Love is All,' International Library of Poetry Association (2005); Who's Who in Lexington, Kentucky (1999-2000); Employee of the Year Award, Internal Revenue Service (1997); Public Service Award, States of Northern Kentucky, Ohio and Indiana (1997); Service Award, Internal Revenue Service

Charity/Volunteer Work: Volunteers of America; Northern Kentucky Baptist Association; American Red Cross; Clerk, Business Secretary, Youth Director, Children's Church Director, Elsmere Baptist Church; Lost Children Foundation, Fingerprinting Services

Date of Birth: June 1, 1953

Place of Birth: Jefferson County, Louisville

Spouse: Robert

Children: Christine, Chertina, Robert, Crystal, Randall, Catherine

Work History: Control Clerk (1986-2007); Clerk, Assembly, Translator for the Deaf (1985-2007); Equipment Operation (1984-2007); Quality Inspection, Receiving Clerk, Merchandise Handler (1976-2007); Cashier, Clerk (1973-1974)

How did you become involved in your profession? She became involved in her profession through a natural progression of opportunities.

Expanded Biography: Ms. Bleier has worked for VanLuens, Inc., Gap Stores, Inc., Olsten Temporary Services, Adecco Employment Services and Augur Tool & Die company. She owns a photography studio, writes chronicles for churches and does public speaking.

PROFESSIONAL OF THE YEAR IN HEMODIALYSIS

MS. LINDA J. BLOOM SPENCER

Director
Kidney Care Services
635 Maple Avenue
Du Bois, PA 15801 United States
lindaspencercnn@yahoo.com
http://www.cambridgewhoswho.com

Type of Business: Government Outpatient Clinic Offering Dialysis Services in Partnership with Du Bois Regional Medical Center

Major Products and Services: Dialysis Services for People Diagnosed with Chronic Kidney Failure and Disease, Acute Inpatient Dialysis Services

Marketing Area: Local

Area of Expertise: Ms. Bloom Spencer's expertise is in hemodialysis.

Day to Day Responsibilities: Offering a Complete Range of Treatment Options and Support Services for People Living with Chronic Kidney Disease, Performing Administrative Duties

Favorite Business Publications: Dialysis Transplantations, ANNA Journal

Hobbies/Interests/Sports: Reading, Spending Time with Grandchildren

Education Degrees: Pursuing Bachelor's Degree in Nursing, University of Phoenix; Associate of Applied Science in Nursing, Butler Community College (1987)

Certifications: Certified Nephrology Nurse

Affiliations/Associations/Societies: Teacher's Renal Program, American Nephrology Nurses Association; Chamber of Commerce

Expanded Biography: Ms. Spencer is very active in her church.

EXECUTIVE OF THE YEAR IN
WHOLESALE SPORTING GOODS

Mr. Sergio C. Bollazzi

Chief Executive Officer
Tradex
301 N. Conception Street
El Paso, TX 79905 United States
bolazzi@prodigy.net
http://www.sbs-outdoors.com

Type of Business: Sporting Goods Wholesaler

Major Products and Services: Outdoor Products

Marketing Area: Mexico, Central America

Day to Day Responsibilities: Selling Wholesale Products Including Sporting Goods, Fishing Gear and Outdoor Merchandise to Mass Merchants in Mexico, Developing Product Lines, Contacting Vendors and Merchants

Hobbies/Interests/Sports: Fishing, Golfing, Taking Chinese Speaking Lessons

Education Degrees: Bachelor's Degree in Economics, Universidad Nacional Autonoma de Mexico (1987)

Affiliations/Associations/Societies: Saturna Brokerage Services

Spouse: Jose

Expanded Biography: Mr. Bollazzi has been a business owner for 10 years and has 10 years of wholesale experience. He also has three children whom he adores.

PROFESSIONAL OF THE YEAR IN ACCOUNTING

OPAL J. BONTRAGER

1) Accountant II 2) Owner
1) Administrative Services
1) State of Oregon 2) Bontrager Business Enterprises
155 Cottage Street N.E., Unit 90
Salem, OR 97301 United States
Opal.Bontrager@das.state.or.us
http://www.das.state.or.us

Type of Business: 1) Government Organization 2) Online Retail Store

Major Products and Services: 1) Administrative Services for the Public, Internal Services for State Agencies 2) Consulting Services, Internet Marketing and Online Retail Sales

Marketing Area: 1) Local 2) International

Area of Expertise: Ms. Bontrager's expertise includes accounting, tax preparation, consulting and online marketing.

Favorite Business Publications: Journal of Accountancy; The Wall Street Journal

Hobbies/Interests/Sports: Reading, Writing, Bicycling, Walking, Traveling, Visiting Historical Places, Attending Cultural Events, Golfing

Education Degrees: Master of Business Administration in Accounting, University of Phoenix; Bachelor of Arts in Psychology and Social Work, Eastern Mennonite University, Harrisonburg, VA

Certifications: Licensed Tax Consultant, State of Oregon

Affiliations/Associations/Societies: Partner, Professional Golfers Association of America; Deputy Director, International Biographical Center, Cambridge, England; Oregon State Fiscal Association

Work History: Tax Auditor I, Oregon Department of Revenue (1999-2001); Licensed Tax Consultant, Jackson-Hewitt (1999); Licensed Tax Preparer, Jackson-Hewitt (1998); Secretary, Clerical Worker, Kelly Services (1997); Licensed Tax Preparer, Business Helper (1997); Accounting Technician II, Oregon Parks and Recreation Department (1997-1999); Office Temporary, Olsten (1996); Office Specialist I, Accounting Technician, Secretary of State's Office (1994-1996)

PROFESSIONAL OF THE YEAR IN
HOME HEALTHCARE ADMINISTRATION

Ms. Marilyn C. Borromeo-Wesner, RN, BSN

Registered Nurse Manager, Administrator,
Advanced Registered Nurse Practitioner
Home Concept Alternative, Inc.
18707 63rd Avenue N.E.
Kenmore, WA 98028 United States
mbwhca@hotmail.com
http://www.evergreenhealthcare.org/neurosciences/parkinson/default.htm

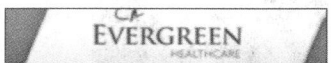

Type of Business: Healthcare Center

Major Products and Services: Healthcare

Marketing Area: Local

Area of Expertise: Ms. Borromeo-Wesner's expertise includes gerontology, dementia and mental health.

Favorite Business Publications: American Journal of Nursing

Hobbies/Interests/Sports: Reading

Education Degrees: Master of Science in Nursing (2006); Bachelor of Science in Nursing, Seattle Pacific University

Certifications: Certified Adult and Gerontological Nurse Practitioner

Affiliations/Associations/Societies: Sigma Theta Tau International; American Holistic Nursing Association; Director of Nursing, ProMed Nursing Agency

Work History: Advanced Registered Nurse Practitioner, Booth Gardner Parkinson's Care Center

What was the highlight of your career? The most gratifying aspect of her career is being dedicated in taking care of the elderly.

Where will you be in five years? In five years, Ms. Borromeo-Wesner hopes to get involved in helping the underserved population.

Expanded Biography: Ms. Borromeo-Wesner is an outreach coordinator for Booth Gardner Parkinson's Care Center and speaks to local community groups. She began her career as a registered nurse more than thirty years ago and established the Home Concept Alternative in 1993.

PROFESSIONAL OF THE YEAR IN SECONDARY EDUCATION

MR. JOHN W. BOWMAN JR.

Mathematics Teacher
Esperanza High School
1830 N. Kellogg Drive
Anaheim, CA 92807 United States
jbowmanjr@pylusd.org
http://www.esperanzahs.com

Type of Business: High School

Major Products and Services: Quality Student Education Services, Athletics, Activities, Special Programs, Teaching, Learning, Academia, Research

Marketing Area: Regional

Day to Day Responsibilities: Teaching Mathematics to High School Students, Coaching Three Olympic Medalist Swimmers, Sixty Five All-American Water Polo Players and Forty All-American Swimmers

Hobbies/Interests/Sports: Golfing, Family Activities, Playing with Twin Children, Swimming, Cooking, Traveling, Reading Mystery Novels

Education Degrees: Master of Business Administration, University of California at Irvine (1982); Bachelor of Science in Mathematics, University of California at Irvine

Certifications: Certificate in Operations Research, University of California at Irvine (1982)

PROFESSIONAL OF THE YEAR IN
SPIRITUAL SERVICES

MICHAEL L. BOYD

Pastor
Grace Apostolic Church
1100 Lischey Avenue
Nashville, TN 37207 United States
elderMLBoyd@comcast.net
http://www.cambridgewhoswho.com

Type of Business: Church

Major Products and Services: Church Services to the Community

Marketing Area: Local

Day to Day Responsibilities: Rebuilding Lives through the Spirit

Hobbies/Interests/Sports: Outdoor Activities, Exercising

Education Degrees: Industry-Related Training and Experience

Charity/Volunteer Work: Union Rescue Mission; Operation Andrew Ministry Group; Citizens Advisory Committee

What do you attribute your success to? He attributes his success to the training he received from his father and the Lord.

How did you become involved in your profession? He became involved in his profession because it was a calling from God and because of his love for humanity.

What was the highlight of your career? The highlight of his career was helping to establish nine new churches in Liberia.

PROFESSIONAL OF THE YEAR IN
RADIATION ONCOLOGY NURSING

CYNTHIA V. BRADLEY

Nurse Manager
University of Miami Sylvester Comprehensive Cancer Center
1475 N.W. 12th Avenue
Miami, FL 33136 United States
cbradley@med.miami.edu
http://www.sylvester.org

Type of Business: University

Major Products and Services: Healthcare Education Including Clinical Trials, Nursing and Medical Services, Radiation Oncology

Marketing Area: Regional

Area of Expertise: Ms. Bradley's expertise is in radiation oncology and nursing.

Favorite Business Publications: Clinical Oncology Nursing

Hobbies/Interests/Sports: Watching Football, Reading

Education Degrees: Bachelor of Science in Nursing, University of Miami (1977)

Certifications: Certified Oncology Nurse (2001); Certified Radiation Oncology Trainer, Oncology Nursing Society

Affiliations/Associations/Societies: President, Miami Dade Chapter, Oncology Nursing Society

PROFESSIONAL OF THE YEAR IN
INTERACTIVE MARKETING

MR. JACK BRECHTEL

Marketing Assistant
Not Rocket Science, Inc.
251 Highway 21, Suite 200
Madisonville, LA 70447 United States
jack@notrs.com
http://www.notrs.com

Type of Business: Customized Software Development Company

Major Products and Services: Application Development, Graphic Design, Handheld Development, Systems Integration, E-Business and Web Development, Web and Database Design, Microsoft Office Integration, Workforce Automation

Marketing Area: Local

Day to Day Responsibilities: Marketing, Performing Administrative Duties, Managing Marketing Principles, Creating and Designing Graphics, Printing Materials, Creating Brochures, Mail-Outs and Updates, Developing and Maintaining the Website, Managing Projects, Consulting on Web Design, Tracking Resumes for Human Resources, Conducting Research, Selling at Trade Shows

Favorite Business Publications: Industry-Related Magazines

Hobbies/Interests/Sports: Exercising, Golfing, Playing Racquetball, Watching Hockey and Football, Reading, Running

Education Degrees: Bachelor's Degree in Electronic Business and Marketing, Texas Christian University (2004)

Affiliations/Associations/Societies: Louisiana Technology Council

PROFESSIONAL OF THE YEAR IN SPECIAL EDUCATION

MRS. PAULA H. BROCK

Teacher
Carver Middle School
Walton County Public School
1095 Good Hope Road N.E.
Monroe, GA 30655 United States
philpaul71@hotmail.com
http://www.walton.k12.ga.us

Type of Business: School District

Major Products and Services: Education

Marketing Area: Regional

Day to Day Responsibilities: Teaching Special Education to Sixth through Eighth-Grade Students

Favorite Business Publications: Educational Leadership; Curriculum Currents

Hobbies/Interests/Sports: Supporting the Georgia Bulldogs, Gardening, Sewing, Making Crafts, Artwork, Decorating, Spending Time with her Family

Education Degrees: Educational Specialist Degree in Administration and Supervision, The University of Georgia (1981); Master of Education, The University of Georgia (1977); Bachelor of Science in Education, The University of Georgia (1969)

Certifications: Certification in Educational Leadership; Certification in Data Collection; Educational Specialist in Adapted Curriculum (Pre-K-12); Educational Specialist in General Curriculum (Pre-K-12); Certification in Special Education, Cognitive Levels in Language Arts, Mathematics, Reading, Science and Social Studies (Pre-K-8)

Affiliations/Associations/Societies: Director, Local Chamber of Commerce; Co-Founder, Greene County Academic Booster Club; Former President, Cartersville Association of Educators; The Professional Association of Georgia Educators; National Science Foundation; Charter Member, Optimist International; Phi Delta Kappa; Former Special Education Chairwoman, Southern Association of Colleges and Schools

Awards/Honors: Teacher of the Year, Carver Middle School Parent-Teacher Association

Charity/Volunteer Work: Director, Miss Greene County Pageant, Greene County Chamber of Commerce; Director, Optimist Club Kiddie Parade; Awana Leader; Sunday School Teacher, Grounds Director, Former Music Director, Woodville Baptist Church; Volunteer, American Cancer Society; Volunteer, Operation Christmas Child

Date of Birth: December 19, 1947   **Place of Birth:** Ironwood, MI

Spouse: Phil   **Children:** Russell, Rosilyn

Work History: Self-Contained MIID Teacher, Carver Middle School (2004-2007); Collaborative Special Education Teacher, Carver Middle School (2001-2004); Consultant in Reading and Writing, Carver Middle School (1999-2001); Teacher, Carver Middle School (1997-1999); Curriculum Director, Greene County Board of Education (1978-1997); Teacher, Greene County High School (1975-1978); Teacher, Union Point Primary School (1974-1975); Teacher, Union Point Elementary School (1973-1974); Teacher, Oglethorpe County Middle and High School (1972-1973); Teacher, Cartersville High School (1971-1972)

What do you attribute your success to? She attributes her success to the support she receives from her family.

How did you become involved in your profession? She became involved in her profession because she was directed and inspired by her father, who was a high school principal.

What was the highlight of your career? The highlights of her career were coaching a female student in a pageant, helping two students raise funds to travel to Europe, and seeing a disabled student she tutored graduate from college.

Where will you be in five years? In five years, Mrs. Brock hopes to continue working with mildly mentally disabled students and help them become functional within their communities.

Expanded Biography: Mrs. Brock consulted for a program called 'Great Expectations in Mathematics and Science,' which is designed to encourage students' interests in mathematics and science. She also participated in 'We Can All Read,' an initiative program designed for children with learning disabilities. She receives much of her satisfaction from seeing her former students excel despite their disabilities.

PROFESSIONAL OF THE YEAR IN GERIATRIC HEALTHCARE

CAROLE BROWN

Licensed Practical Nurse
Washington County Regional Medical Center
894 Warthen Lane
Warthen, GA 31094 United States
carole.brown@cwwemail.com
http://www.cambridgewhoswho.com

Type of Business: Medical Center

Major Products and Services: Healthcare Including Intensive, Obstetrics, Orthopedic, Emergency, Trauma, Pediatric and General Medical-Surgical Care Services

Marketing Area: Regional

Area of Expertise: Ms. Brown's expertise is in geriatric care nursing and patient assistance.

Hobbies/Interests/Sports: Watching Baseball, Spending Time Outdoors

Certifications: Licensed Practical Nurse, Dudley M. Hughes School of Practical Nursing, Macon, GA (1969)

Awards/Honors: Employee of the Month Award; Employee of the Quarter Award

Spouse: Joe

Children: Tess, JoAnna, Sharon

Expanded Biography: Ms. Brown would like to receive more compliments from Dr. Jean R. Sumner.

PROFESSIONAL OF THE YEAR IN SPECIAL EDUCATION

KATHLEEN M. BROWN

Special Education Teacher
Mount Laurel Hartford School
397 Hartford Road
Mount Laurel, NJ 08054 United States
kbrown@mountlaurel.k12.nj.us
http://mtlaurelschools.org

Type of Business: School District

Major Products and Services: The Highest Quality of Educational Services in Eight Schools Serving 4,627 Students in Kindergarten through Eighth Grade, All Subjects and Extracurricular Activities

Marketing Area: Regional

Day to Day Responsibilities: Teaching Special Education to Sixth-Grade Students with Reading Weaknesses, Teaching Writing and Mathematics in a Resource Room, Utilizing the Wilson Reading System as a Means of Instruction

Favorite Business Publications: Wilson Reading System Publications; NJEA Review

Hobbies/Interests/Sports: Family Activities, Bike Riding, Phillies Baseball, Eagles Football

Education Degrees: Master's Degree in Reading, Holy Family University (2003); Bachelor's Degree in Special Education, Marywood University (1976); Bachelor's Degree in Regular Education, Marywood University

Certifications: Certified Wilson Level Reading Instructor (2004)

Affiliations/Associations/Societies: New Jersey Education Association; National Education Association

Date of Birth: March 9, 1954

Spouse: Paul   **Children:** Jeremiah, Zachary, Caitlin

Work History: Special Education Teacher, Mt Laurel, NJ; Special Education Teacher, Pemberton, NJ; Special Education Teacher, Glendo, WY;Special Education Teacher, Pompano Beach, FL; Special Education Teacher, Lake Wales, FL; Special Education Teacher, North Philadelphia, PA

PROFESSIONAL OF THE YEAR IN
FILM INDUSTRY

Mr. Ross Brown

Owner
Brown-West & Associates
7319 Beverly Boulevard, Suite 10
Los Angeles, CA 90036 United States
brownwest@sbcglobal.net
http://www.cambridgewhoswho.com

Type of Business: Entertainment

Major Products and Services: Casting for Theater and Television

Marketing Area: International

Day to Day Responsibilities: Casting Actors and Actresses for More than 600 Movies of the Week, Guiding the Careers of Actors, Producers and Directors, Obtaining Financing for Films

Favorite Business Publications: Hollywood Reporter

Hobbies/Interests/Sports: Sailing, Reading, Watching Tennis

Education Degrees: Doctor of Mathematics, Princeton University (1977); Doctor of Ancient Greek Aramaic, University of Southern California

Affiliations/Associations/Societies: MENSA

PROFESSIONAL OF THE YEAR IN CLINICAL NURSING MANAGEMENT

ALICIA BRUBAKER-KNAB, RN, BSN

Clinical Manager
Institute for Sleep Medicine, Stroke Center
Altoona Regional Health System
620 Howard Avenue
Altoona, PA 16601 United States
aknab@altoonaregional.org
http://www.altoonaregional.org

Type of Business: Nonprofit Healthcare Center

Major Products and Services: Healthcare Including Behavioral Healthcare, Bariatric Surgery, Cancer, Cardiac, Ostomy and Wound Care, Rehabilitation, Surgical and Trauma Services, Sleep and Emergency Medicine and Stroke Treatment

Marketing Area: Local

Day to Day Responsibilities: Performing Administrative Duties, Scheduling, Overseeing Staff and Patients in Pain Management and Outpatient Units, Managing Administrative Duties of Intravenous Therapy

Favorite Business Publications: Clinical Journal of Oncology Nursing; American Journal of Nursing

Hobbies/Interests/Sports: Baking, Cooking

Education Degrees: Bachelor of Science in Nursing, Saint Francis University (1986); Registered Nurse (1986); Associate of Science in Nursing, Mount Aloysius College (1983); Associate Degree in Medical Secretary, Mount Aloysius College (1977)

Affiliations/Associations/Societies: Vice President, Former President, Oncology Nursing Society, South Central Pennsylvania

Charity/Volunteer Work: Girl Scouts of the United States of America

Date of Birth: November 11, 1957   **Place of Birth:** Altoona

Spouse: Mark   **Children:** Mark, Adam, Tyler

Work History: Public Speaker, Integrated Voice and Data Services (2005-2007); Instructor for Patient Care and Pathology, Mercy Hospital School of Radiologic Technology (1993-1995); Medical Secretary, Mercy Hospital, Altoona (Now Altoona Regional Health System)

What do you attribute your success to? She attributes her success to being a girl scout member, believing that women can achieve anything and to her role model Frances Hesselbein, who was a former chief executive officer of Girl Scouts of the United States of America.

How did you become involved in your profession? She became involved in her profession after volunteering at a local home for the elderly.

What was the highlight of your career? The most gratifying aspect of her career is being able to take excellent care of her patients on a daily basis.

Where will you be in five years? In five years, Ms. Brubaker-Knab hopes to retire and would like to do volunteer work for local ministries.

Expanded Biography: Ms. Brubaker-Knab has received various awards for cooking and baking. She was also a religious education teacher.

PROFESSIONAL OF THE YEAR IN ACCOUNTING

DIANE M. BUATTE

President, Owner
Financial Ledger Incorporated
141 N. Meramec Avenue, Suite 107
Saint Louis, MO 63105 United States
dmbuatte@prodigy.net
http://www.cambridgewhoswho.com

Type of Business: Accounting Firm

Major Products and Services: Accounting, Bookkeeping, Financial Services

Marketing Area: International

Day to Day Responsibilities: Making House Calls, Preparing Income Tax Returns and Medicare Claims, Maintaining Financial Records, Paying Clients' Bills, Accounting for Professional Sports Organizations and Individual Players

Favorite Business Publications: The Wall Street Journal; The Journal of the American Medical Association

Hobbies/Interests/Sports: Sports

Education Degrees: Coursework in Interior Design, St. Louis Community College, Meramec; Coursework in Accounting, St. Louis Community College, Meramec

Awards/Honors: The Congressional Medal of Distinction (2007); Recipient, Medal of Distinction, Veteran Advocate (2006); Ronald Reagan Gold Medal Award (2004-2005); Women of the Year Award (2004-2006)

PROFESSIONAL OF THE YEAR IN PATIENT AND PRE-OP EDUCATION

JOANNE M. BUMP

Registered Nurse
Richmond Healthcare Center
Contra Costa Health Services
100 38th Street
Richmond, CA 94805 United States
joannebump@aol.com
http://www.cambridgewhoswho.com

Type of Business: Healthcare Center

Major Products and Services: Healthcare Including Community Health Improvement, Environmental Protection, Alcohol and Drug Prevention Treatments, Health Plans, Outpatient Medical Services, Emergency and Mental Health Services

Marketing Area: Regional

Area of Expertise: Ms. Bump's expertise is in critical care and geriatric nursing.

Day to Day Responsibilities: Educating Patients, Managing the Triage, Answering Calls, Assisting Nursing Students

Favorite Business Publications: RN; Nursing2009; Nursing Made Incredibly Easy

Hobbies/Interests/Sports: Walking, Reading, Traveling

Education Degrees: Bachelor of Science in Nursing, Oregon Health & Science University (1975)

Affiliations/Associations/Societies: California Nurses Association; School of Nursing Alumni Association; Kappa Delta Alumnae Association

Charity/Volunteer Work: Napa Valley Junior Miss Program

Place of Birth: Portland

Spouse: Harold   **Children:** Christine

PROFESSIONAL OF THE YEAR IN DENTAL EDUCATION

Deborah Burch

Dental Assisting Coordinator
Lake Michigan College
2755 East Napier
Benton Harbor, MI 49022 United States
burch@lakemichigancollege.edu
http://www.lakemichigancollege.edu

Type of Business: Two-Year Community College

Major Products and Services: Associate Degrees, Certificates, and a Wide Range of Continuing Education and Business and Industry Training

Marketing Area: Regional

Day to Day Responsibilities: Teaching and Advising Students, Coordinating Three Locations, Supervising Labs and Adjunct Faculty

Favorite Business Publications: Dental Assistant Journal

Hobbies/Interests/Sports: Painting, Crafts

Education Degrees: Master of Science in Career and Technical Education, Ferris State University (1993); Bachelor of Science in Allied Health Education, Ferris State College (1983); Associate Degree in Applied Science, Lake Michigan College (1974)

Certifications: Registered Dental Assistant, Lake Michigan College (2004)

Affiliations/Associations/Societies: MDAA Mara Lee Albrecht Impact Award (2006); Sunstar/Butler/ADAA Pride Award-Educator (2005); Nominee, Who's Who Among America's Teachers (2002, 2005)

Awards/Honors: Lake Michigan College Outstanding Adjunct Faculty of the Year Award (1990); Certificate of Appreciation, Phi Theta Kappa Honor Society;President, Past President, Legislative Chairman, Delegate, Legislative Committee Member, Task Force, MDAA

PROFESSIONAL OF THE YEAR IN ALTERNATIVE EDUCATION

DR. SUE M. BURKHOLDER

School Principal
Genesis Alternative School
2076 Jefferson Highway
Fishersville, VA 22939 United States
sburkhol@staunton.k12.va.us
http://www.staunton.k12.va.us

Type of Business: Public and Alternative Education

Major Products and Services: Middle, High School and Alternative Instruction and Curriculum

Marketing Area: Regional

Day to Day Responsibilities: Addressing Attachment and Behavioral Disorders in Adolescents, School Psychology, Teaching through Alternative Education, Strong Academics, Developing Positive Traits

Favorite Business Publications: Education Week

Hobbies/Interests/Sports: Golfing, Casino Gambling, Landscaping

Education Degrees: Ph.D., University of Virginia (1993); Ph.D. in School Psychology, Child and Family Intervention, University of Virginia; Master of Science in School Psychology, James Madison University; Bachelor of Science in Health and Physical Education, James Madison University

Affiliations/Associations/Societies: National Association of School Psychologists; Virginia Education Association; National Education Association

Awards/Honors: Oxford Round Table (2007)

Career Achievements: Author, 'Alternative Education Models'

PROFESSIONAL OF THE YEAR IN EARLY CHILDHOOD EDUCATION

REV. JACQUELINE JOYCE BURTON

Reverend, Early Childhood Coordinator, Author, Inventor
Stanley Eugene Clark Elementary School
2707 Albemarle Road
Brooklyn, NY 11226 United States
burtonjackiej@aol.com
jburton5@schools.nyc.gov
http://www.ps399.org

Type of Business: School

Major Products and Services: General Education

Marketing Area: Local

Area of Expertise: Rev. Burton's expertise includes early childhood education and a center-based approach to literacy for emergent and fluent readers.

Hobbies/Interests/Sports: Reading, Attending Church

Education Degrees: Master's Degree in Supervision and Administration, Plus 30, CUNY Queens College (1976)

Affiliations/Associations/Societies: Business and Professional Women of Baisley Park; Early Childhood Association; Kappa Delta Pi; Phi Delta Kappa

Charity/Volunteer Work: Board Member, Peninsula Preparatory Academy

What do you attribute your success to? She attributes her success to her faith in the Lord and her personal relationship with God.

How did you become involved in your profession? She became involved in her profession because she decided to become a teacher during her second year of college.

What was the highlight of your career? The highlight of her career was becoming a published author.

Expanded Biography: Rev. Burton believes that the Lord directed her life and she was wise enough to listen, so she gives Him all of the credit. She patented her invention, the Pet Mobile, which is a trolley for pet carriers. She has also published a book entitled 'Because I Don't Want To' and a book on prayer. She consults with other schools and formerly worked as a daycare director and teacher. Rev Burton was ordained as a minister in October of 2006.

PROFESSIONAL OF THE YEAR IN HOSPITAL ADMINISTRATION

CHLETA D. BUTLER, MHA

Department Administrator
Southern California Permanent Medical Group
1011 Baldwin Park Boulevard
Baldwin Park, CA 91706 United States
chleta.d.butler@kp.org
http://www.kaiserpermanente.org

Type of Business: Health System

Major Products and Services: Healthcare

Marketing Area: National

Day to Day Responsibilities: Overseeing Administrative Duties

Favorite Business Publications: The Permanente Journal

Hobbies/Interests/Sports: Reading, Writing Poetry, Swimming, Renovating Home

Education Degrees: Master's Degree in Health Administration, University of Phoenix (2007); Bachelor of Arts in Liberal Studies, The California State University (1994); Associate of Science, Southwestern Christian College, TX

Affiliations/Associations/Societies: President, KPAAA

Awards/Honors: Management Leadership Award (2006); Three-Time Recipient, Top Dog Award; Three-Time Puffball Award

Charity/Volunteer Work: Church Women United, Los Angeles; Habitat for Humanity

Date of Birth: September 13, 1959   **Place of Birth:** Los Angeles, CA

Expanded Biography: Ms. Butler has worked for Kaiser Permanente Medical Group.

PROFESSIONAL OF THE YEAR IN BERMUDIAN FINANCIAL SERVICES

Mrs. Gwynneth Dorothea L. Butterfield, JP

Banking Officer (Retired)
HSBC Bank of Bermuda
6 Front Street
Hamilton, HM11 Bermuda
gdlbutte@logic.bm
http://www.bankofbermuda.com

Bank of Bermuda

Type of Business: Bank

Major Products and Services: Personal and Business Financial Services, Checking and Savings Accounts, Investment Services, Loans, Mortgage Services, International Banking Solutions, Payments and Transfers, Investment Management

Marketing Area: Regional

Day to Day Responsibilities: Overseeing Finances, Assisting Customers, Managing Accounts

Favorite Business Publications: The New York Times

Hobbies/Interests/Sports: Traveling, Exercising, Reading, Playing Card and Board Games Including Bridge and Dominoes.

Education Degrees: Coursework in Foundations of Banking, Bermuda College (1984)

Affiliations/Associations/Societies: Founding Member, Business and Professional Women's Association of Bermuda; American Banking Association

Awards/Honors: Queen Certificate, Badge of Honor (2003)

Charity/Volunteer Work: Bermuda Diabetes Association; Former Treasurer, The Garden Club of Bermuda; President, Senior Learning Center, Bermuda College

Date of Birth: December 8, 1933   **Place of Birth:** KEMH, Paget

Spouse: Ashton Butterfield (Deceased)   **Children:** Michael

Work History: Carpenter

Expanded Biography: Mrs. Butterfield chose her profession as a means of servicing people, which is a task she has carried over into her personal life as well. She is a community volunteer and life member with many charities and organizations. Much of her volunteer work is geared toward helping seniors and the young at heart. Her service career reached a high point in June of 2003 when she was awarded the Queen's Certificate and Badge of Honour in recognition of her extensive community service over the years. During her short life she has been actively involved in 20 charities and community initiatives. The highlight of these efforts was serving the Bermuda Government and general public for 40 years in the capacity of presiding officer and returning officer during general elections. She is equally proud of being elected president of the Seniors Learning Centre at Bermuda College, which consists of more than 800 Members. She became a member of the Garden club of Bermuda in 1991 and served as an honorary deputy treasurer for about four years before becoming their honorary treasurer from 1997 until 1999 as the first and only person of color to hold that position. She has traveled the world and visited 82 countries including England, Dubai, Australia, Hawaii, Mauritius Seychelles and several states in America. Looking back at her much loved career, she would not change it for anything and gives God all the praise and glory. The quote that she lives by is 'Live for self you live in vain; Live for others you will live again.' Her compassion for the employees and customers she encountered over the years separates her from other professionals in the industry; she was never too busy and always managed to lend her time to others. Mrs. Butterfield became the first female of color to hold a supervisory position in any of the local banks when she was promoted to supervisor of the savings department in 1971 and then to banking officer in 1978. These were important milestones for not only her career but for women and other persons of color in Bermuda. She feels one of the greatest achievements in her career occured in 1974 when she was responsible for converting all of the bank's savings accounts from handwritten records into computerised, digital form. This was a massive undertaking and the first and only time such an undertaking had taken place.

PROFESSIONAL OF THE YEAR IN NURSING EDUCATION

LINDA L. BUTZ, RN, CAPA

Registered Nurse
SwedishAmerican Health System
1401 E. State Street
Rockford, IL 61104 United States
lin4550@aol.com
http://www.swedishamerican.org

Type of Business: Hospital

Major Products and Services: Healthcare

Marketing Area: Regional

Area of Expertise: Ms. Butz's expertise includes nursing, nurse management and perianesthesia nursing.

Day to Day Responsibilities: Caring for Patients, Managing Assessments, Dispensing Medication

Favorite Business Publications: RN; Journal of PeriAnesthesia Nursing

Hobbies/Interests/Sports: Spending Time with her Family, Crocheting, Knitting, Walking, Bicycling, Reading

Education Degrees: Registered Nurse, Rockford Memorial Hospital

Certifications: Certified Ambulatory Perianesthesia Nurse, American Society of PeriAnesthesia Nurses

Affiliations/Associations/Societies: American Society of PeriAnesthesia Nurses

Charity/Volunteer Work: CPR Instructor, American Heart Association; Parish Nurse, First Assembly of God; Local Charitable Organizations

Spouse: Thomas   **Children:** Sean, Luke, Ryan, Sara

What do you attribute your success to? She attributes her success to her flexibility.

How did you become involved in your profession? She became involved in her profession because she always wanted to help people.

What was the highlight of your career? The most gratifying aspect of her career is building relationships with her patients and their families and being able to keep them informed and comfortable.

PROFESSIONAL OF THE YEAR IN PUBLIC AFFAIRS, GOVERNMENT RELATIONS AND COMMUNITY SERVICE

MS. JANE A. CAHILL WOLFGRAM

Public Affairs Director
Foley & Lardner LLP
150 East Gilman Street
Madison, WI 53703 United States
info@cambridgewhoswho.com
http://www.foley.com

Type of Business: Law Firm

Major Products and Services: Legal Services

Marketing Area: National

Area of Expertise: Ms. Cahill Wolfgram's expertise includes communications, government and public affairs and environmental regulation practices.

Favorite Business Publications: National Journal

Hobbies/Interests/Sports: Traveling Internationally

Education Degrees: Coursework, University of Wisconsin

Charity/Volunteer Work: Wisconsin Women's Health Foundation; Cameroonian-American Foundation

Expanded Biography: Ms. Cahill Wolfgram has 30 years of experience in public affairs, government relations and community service as a corporate executive, consultant and director of nonprofit programs. She prepares comprehensive public affairs approaches for clients who coordinate government, media, community and employee relations activities. In the government relations area, she develops strategies and plans for designing and implementing policies at the federal, state and local levels, including related political education, and legislative and administrative analysis. Ms. Cahill Wolfgram's lobbying experience includes Congress, the White House, state legislators and government agencies. Her business and nonprofit experience has given her a planning and management focus that facilitates goal-setting, resource allocation and crisis management counseling for her clients. Ms. Cahill Wolfgram joined Foley & Lardner LLP as an executive with PG&E National Energy Group, most recently as the vice president of external affairs. She was responsible for a wide range of regulatory and public policy issues related to taxation, commerce, environmental matters and electric market restructuring, as well as the company's political activities, community outreach, media relations and crisis communications. Her work involved relationship management with business leaders, industry groups, law firms, consultants, and all levels of federal, regional, state and local governmental activity. Before entering the corporate arena, Ms. Cahill Wolfgram founded and was a partner in a full-service government and public affairs consulting firm. The firm assisted companies in the paper, consumer goods and energy industries with regulatory matters, media challenges, policy initiatives and government relationships at the federal, state and local levels. Ms. Cahill Wolfgram's public affairs work began with a decade of directing nonprofit programs involving legal aid, vocational education, and rural development for several state and federal agencies. Ms. Cahill Wolfgram is the chairwoman of the advisory committee of the Wisconsin Women's Health Foundation, an organization that seeks to improve the quality of life for women and their families through information, opportunity and support.

PROFESSIONAL OF THE YEAR IN COSMETIC DENTISTRY

STACIE T. CALIAN

Owner, Dentist
Westchester Smile Design
984 N. Broadway, Suite 410
Yonkers, NY 10701 United States
staciecalian@aol.com
http://www.caliandentistry.com

Type of Business: Dentistry

Major Products and Services: General and Cosmetic Dentistry

Marketing Area: Local

Day to Day Responsibilities: Performing Oral Surgery, Cosmetic, General and Neuromuscular Dentistry, Overseeing Endodontic and Orthodontic Services

Favorite Business Publications: Dental Journals

Education Degrees: Doctor of Dental Surgery, Georgetown University (1988); Master's Degree in Education, Columbia University (1982); Master of Science in Hygiene Education, Columbia University (1981); Master's Degree in Public Health Administration, Columbia University

Certifications: Certification in Invisalign (2006); Lumineers Certified Dentist (2006); Pursuing Certification in Cosmetic Dentistry, American Academy of Cosmetic Dentistry; Pursuing Certification in LBI

What do you attribute your success to? She attributes her success to her hard work, personal drive and being persistent.

How did you become involved in your profession? She became involved in her profession because of her experience and the inspiration she received from her father's friend who was a dentist.

PROFESSIONAL OF THE YEAR IN
STRATEGIC CORPORATE BENEFITS DESIGN

PATRICIA J. CAMPBELL, MAOM

Director of Corporate Benefits
Health Net, Inc.
21650 Oxnard Street
21st Floor
Woodland Hills, CA 91367 United States
pcampbell01@earthlink.net
http://www.healthnet.com

Type of Business: Insurance Company

Major Products and Services: Health and Life Insurance Services

Marketing Area: National

Area of Expertise: Ms. Campbell's expertise is in benefit planning.

Favorite Business Publications: HR Magazine

Hobbies/Interests/Sports: Traveling, Listening to Jazz Music, Sports, Attending Sports Events

Education Degrees: Master of Arts in Organizational Management, University of Phoenix

Certifications: Licensed Life Insurance Agent, State of California

Affiliations/Associations/Societies: Los Angeles Compensation and Benefits Association; Society for Human Resource Management

Charity/Volunteer Work: Southern Poverty Law Center; Feed The Children; Habitat for Humanity

What do you attribute your success to? She attributes her success to her self-motivation, creativity and training.

How did you become involved in your profession? She became involved in her profession because she wanted to instill a good customer service attitude in people.

What was the highlight of your career? The most gratifying aspects of her career are supporting and unifying the interests of her company's management team and employees.

PROFESSIONAL OF THE YEAR IN ONCOLOGY NURSING

CARLA J. CANTOR, RN, MSN, BSN, OCN

Nurse Consultant
Cancer Center
North Broward Hospital District
303 S.E. 17th Street
Fort Lauderdale, FL 33316 United States
nursecantor@aol.com
http://www.browardhealth.org

Type of Business: Cancer Research and Treatment Facility

Major Products and Services: Genetic Counseling and Testing, Screening and Prevention, Treatment of High Risk Women with Pre-Cancer, Treatment of Early Stage and Advanced Breast Cancer

Marketing Area: Local

Area of Expertise: Ms. Cantor's expertise includes oncology, experimental clinical trials, bone marrow transplant coordination and oncology nurse education.

Favorite Business Publications: Cancer Nursing, Oncology Nursing Forum

Hobbies/Interests/Sports: Biking, Reading

Education Degrees: Master of Science in Nursing, Saint Louis University (1998); Bachelor of Science in Nursing, Southern Illinois University (1985)

Certifications: Certified Oncology Nurse; Certified Chemotherapy Nurse

Affiliations/Associations/Societies: Oncology Nursing Society; Sigma Theta Tau International

Awards/Honors: Three-Time Nominee, Top Nurses in Missouri

Charity/Volunteer Work: Relay for Life; Pet Rescue

PROFESSIONAL OF THE YEAR IN
EVENT PLANNING AND PUBLIC RELATIONS

Ms. Gwen L. Carter

President
G. Carter & Associates, LLC
P.O. Box 64
Exton, PA 19341 United States
gwen@consultcarter.com
http://www.consultcarter.com

Type of Business: Event Planning and Public Relations Company

Major Products and Services: Press Releases, Conferences, Event Planning, Special Events

Marketing Area: International

Day to Day Responsibilities: Specializing in Public Relations and Corporate Positioning, Overseeing Media Communications, Managing Employees and Agents in Seven States

Hobbies/Interests/Sports: Watching Professional In-Line Rollerskating

Education Degrees: Bachelor's Degree in Economics and Sociology, Grinnell College (1974)

Affiliations/Associations/Societies: Board and Executive Member, African American Female Entrepreneurs Alliance; Board of Directors, Boys and Girls Club of America; National Adoption Center

Expanded Biography: Ms. Carter also does lecturing, training and makes presentations at conferences and workshops.

PROFESSIONAL OF THE YEAR IN AEROSPACE INSPECTION PLANNING

MS. ROSE M. CASEY

Planning QE
Quality Department
L-3 Communications Crestview Aerospace
5486 Fairchild Road
Crestview, FL 32539 United States
rose.casey@l-3com.com
http://www.l-3com.com

Type of Business: Aerospace Manufacturing Company

Major Products and Services: Communications Equipment and Defense Electronics, Aircraft Modification, Aerostructure Fabrication

Marketing Area: International

Day to Day Responsibilities: Working as the Lead Internal Auditor and Customer Quality Technician, Overseeing the Auditing Processes of All Operations within the Company as Per AS9100, Reviewing, Planning and Creating Inspection Plans for the Quality Department, Approving Plans

Favorite Business Publications: Quality

Hobbies/Interests/Sports: Reading, Organizing Charity Fundraising Events

Certifications: Certified Quality Technician, American Society for Quality; Certification, RABQSA International; Certified AS9100 Lead Auditor

Affiliations/Associations/Societies: American Society for Quality

Awards/Honors: Quality Employee of the Quarter Award (1999); CTE Employee of the Month Award (1992)

Charity/Volunteer Work: Founder, Operation X-Mas Spirit (2000); Boys & Girls Clubs of America; L-3 Crestview Aerospace High Flyers Relay for Life Team; Regional Director, Florida Kids

Date of Birth: May 1, 1950

Children: Carl, Carter

Work History: Stemco Manufacturing Co., Longview, TX (1979)

What do you attribute your success to? She attributes her success to her determination.

How did you become involved in your profession? She became involved in her profession because she always had an interest in investigating.

What was the highlight of your career? The most gratifying aspect of her career is receiving recognition from premier aerospace-industry clients.

PROFESSIONAL OF THE YEAR IN
CHRONIC ILLNESS EDUCATION AND TREATMENT

DR. ISAI CASTILLO

Director
IMAQ SC
416 W. San Ysidro Boulevard
PMB 337
San Ysidro, CA 92173 United States
eldoc@drcastillo.com
http://www.drcastillo.com

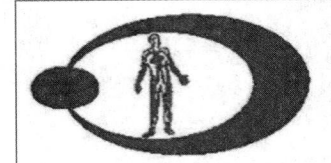

Type of Business: Medical Practice

Major Products and Services: Education and Treatment for Chronic Illness

Marketing Area: International

Day to Day Responsibilities: Improving Patients' Lives by Treating Chronic Illnesses

Hobbies/Interests/Sports: Playing the Guitar and Drums, Collecting Stamps and Coins

Education Degrees: Doctor of Medical Surgeon at Northeast University, Tampico, Tamaulipas, Mexico; Post Graduate Coursework in Geriatrics, Chihuahua, Mexico; Post Graduate Studies in Enzymatic Therapy, Munich, Germany

Affiliations/Associations/Societies: Mexican Society of Medical Doctors

Awards/Honors: Recipient, International Excellence in Improving Quality of Life in Patients Award, Country of Peru (2006)

How did you become involved in your profession? He became involved in his profession because of the opportunities it presented.

What was the highlight of your career? The most gratifying aspects of his career are being able to improve others' lives and live positively.

Expanded Biography: Dr. Castillo was exposed to alternative therapy during his education as a medical doctor, and bases his practice upon the principle that all patients should be educated. He believes in the combination of alternative and traditional medicines and to 'treat patients, not illnesses,' which is advice given to him by his cardiology teacher in 1976. He states, 'I feel truly blessed to have the opportunity to work with both alternative and conventional medicine, creating a complementary medicine.' Dr. Castillo has traveled the United States, Canada and other countries giving seminars about chronic illness and his personal experiences. He feels that it is very important to educate patients so they can become allies in the management of their health.

PROFESSIONAL OF THE YEAR IN
ALTERNATIVE HEALTHCARE THERAPIES

Jennie Charleston-Stokes

Professor Doctor Dame, Doctor of Alternative Medicine,
Founder, Tutor, Lecturer, Author
Medicina Alternativa International
West House Institute of Complementary Healthcare
30 Salem Street
Gosberton, PE11 4NQ United Kingdom
info@CambridgeWhosWho.com
http://www.cambridgewhoswho.com

Medicina Alternativa International (UK)
Presidents { Prof. Dr. Dame Jennie
            { Sir Brian Charleston- Stokes
W.H.I.C.H.
30 Salem Street
Gosberton
Lincolnshire
PE11 4NQ (UK)   Tel/Fax: 01775 840012

Type of Business: Educational Institute of Higher Learning

Major Products and Services: Nonprofit Education, Hands-On Complementary Therapies, Instruction, Services, Research, Communication, Teaching Integration

Marketing Area: International

Day to Day Responsibilities: Integrating Ortho and Fringe Treatments, Teaching the Psychology of Oncology, Researching on Blood Groups and Types Related to Disease and Nutritional Hematology, Serving as a World Authority on Crystalline Acupuncture and Vibrational Healing

Favorite Business Publications: Time; Artist & Illustrators

Hobbies/Interests/Sports: Researching her Family Tree, Studying Gemology and Planetary Meridians

Education Degrees: Master's Degree in Alternative and Complementary Therapies; Bachelor of Science in Literature; Northern Institute of Massage

Certifications: Diploma in Remedial Swedish Massage

Affiliations/Associations/Societies: Medicina Alternativa; International Acupuncture Science Institute; Scandinavian Acupuncture Foundation; International Laser Therapy Association; Fellow, The Homeopathic Foundation; International College of Acupuncture; Chairwoman, International Open University of Complementary Medicine, Sri Lanka; London and Counties Society of Physiologists; Association of Reflexologists; Chinese Medicine Institute

Awards/Honors: Recipient, Dame Knight of Malta for Service to Mankind

Date of Birth: May 16, 1942

Place of Birth: Tamar Bridge between Cornwall and Devon

Spouse: Brian

Children: Kimberly, Karina, Kathryn, John

Expanded Biography: Dr. Charleston-Stokes was raised by herbalist and evangelist parents with a desire to be a medical missionary. She was grounded in traditional medicine, yet trained in orthodox medicine as a doctor. She later changed direction to study alternative medicine on a much deeper level after meeting Dag Hammarskjold and embracing the Alma Ata Declaration of 1962, which culminated in a degree as Doctor of Alternative Medicine under the aegis of the World Health Organization. She is the author of the 'Healers in the Home', a series of self-help books using natural methods to obtain optimum health of body, mind and spirit. She has also lectured on many radio and television stations nationwide, taught students of all ages at the University of the Third Age, and partaken for several years in the Escape programmes organized by the police and social services. She is also qualified in gem identification to jewelers' standards. Having worked for 20 years voluntarily every winter at hospitals and clinics in Sri Lanka, where she holds a chair at the Open International University, she has received many awards and accolades for services to the Third World and humanity, including a knightship in 1997.

PROFESSIONAL OF THE YEAR IN MOTOR TRANSPORT

KEN CHERNIWCHAN

President
KC Transport, Inc.
14510 123 Avenue
Edmonton, AB T5L2Y3 Canada
kctransport@telus.net
http://www.cambridgewhoswho.com

Type of Business: Trucking and Transportation Company

Major Products and Services: Trucking, Warehousing

Marketing Area: Canada

Area of Expertise: Mr. Cherniwchan's expertise is in trucking and transportation.

Favorite Business Publications: Industry Related Journals

Hobbies/Interests/Sports: Golfing

Education Degrees: Coursework, Alberta College

Affiliations/Associations/Societies: Alberta Motor Transportation Association

Charity/Volunteer Work: North American Special Olympics

Date of Birth: November 27, 1948   **Place of Birth:** Vilna

Spouse: Sharon   **Children:** Candice, Angie, Karen

Work History: Owner, KC Show Services (1989-2006); Sales Manager, TNT Alltrans Express, Edmonton, AB (1980-1989); Operations Manager, Territorial Leasing, Edmonton, AB (1978-1980); Terminal Manager, Boychuk Transport, Calgary, AB (1971-1978)

What do you attribute your success to? He attributes his success to his hard work and being service and people-oriented nature.

How did you become involved in your profession? He became involved in his profession because he was inspired by his father who was in the transportation business.

What was the highlight of your career? The highlights of his career were establishing his own company called KC Show Services in 1989 and the great success of the show in which he participated in producing the world's largest petroleum held in Calgary.

Where will you be in five years? In five years, Mr. Cherniwchan hopes to continue his profession and expand the business.

PROFESSIONAL OF THE YEAR IN OCCUPATIONAL THERAPY

DR. STACEY CHILDERS-TEEPLE

Occupational Therapy Department Manager
Occupational Therapy Department
Physical Therapy Specialist Clinic, Inc.
1480 Eighth Street
West Plains, MO 65775 United States
teeplebuffaloranch@hotmail.com
schilders-teeple@ptsconline.com
http://www.cambridgewhoswho.com

Type of Business: Therapy Center

Major Products and Services: Physical Therapy, Occupational Therapy, Speech Therapy, Industrial Rehabilitation, Pediatric and Geriatric Services, Treating Spinal Cord Injuries and Neurological Impairments

Marketing Area: South Central Missouri

Area of Expertise: Ms. Childers-Teeple's expertise is in hand and occupational therapy.

Day to Day Responsibilities: Managing the Occupational Therapy Department, Treating Patients with Sustained Physical, Neurological and Developmental Limitations and Injuries

Favorite Business Publications: Journal of Hand Therapy; American Journal of Occupational Therapy

Hobbies/Interests/Sports: Traveling, Reading, Scrapbooking, Hunting, Rearing Buffalo and Horses, Raising Honey Bees

Education Degrees: Doctorate in Occupational Therapy, Rocky Mountain University of Health Professions, Provo, UT; Bachelor of Health Science in Occupational Therapy, University of Missouri; Associate of Arts, Missouri State University

Affiliations/Associations/Societies: Missouri Occupational Therapy Association; American Society of Hand Therapists; American Occupational Therapy Association; World Federation of Occupational Therapists

Awards/Honors: Tribute Award for Service and Dedication to the Profession of Occupational Therapy (2001)

Charity/Volunteer Work: Relay for Life, American Cancer Society; Paralyzed Veterans of America; Disabled American Veterans

Place of Birth: Farmington, MO

Spouse: Stephen   **Children:** Stephen, James, Melissa

Work History: Inactive United States Navy Engineman, EN3 (1991-1994); Active United States Navy Engineman, EN3 (1987-1990)

What do you attribute your success to? She attributes her success to her self-determination, to the support she receives from her husband and to her faith in God.

How did you become involved in your profession? She became involved in her profession because she was inspired by the occupational therapist who took care of her family when they were in hospital.

What was the highlight of your career? The most gratifying aspect of her career is watching her patients return to their normal health.

Where will you be in five years? In five years, Dr. Childers-Teeple hopes to obtain her certification in hand therapy and intends to work with legislators on healthcare initiatives for veterans and the geriatric population.

Expanded Biography: Dr. Childers-Teeple has developed, designed and built a labor-free mechanical gate for individuals with physical limitations to continue farming without the need of assistance for transfers. She worked as a office manager from 1990 to 1993, laborer in 1994 and as a professional occupational therapist of hand and upper extremities from 2001 to 2003.

PROFESSIONAL OF THE YEAR IN
SPECIAL EDUCATION

MRS. CAMILLA A. CHURCHWELL-SWIFT

Special Education Teacher, Unit Coordinator, Lead Teacher
P226M at P76, Special Education
The New York City Department of Education
220 W. 121st Street, Room 306A
New York, NY 10027 United States
camillaswift@cs.com
cswift2@nycboe.net
http://www.nycboe.net

Type of Business: Department of Education

Major Products and Services: Education Services for Kindergarten through 12th-Grade Students

Marketing Area: Regional

Day to Day Responsibilities: Designing Special Education Plans for Autistic, Mentally Challenged and Emotionally Disturbed Children, Mentoring, Overseeing the Staff

Favorite Business Publications: Ebony; The Network Journal

Hobbies/Interests/Sports: Listening to Music, Reading

Education Degrees: Master of Science, Mercy College, with Distinction (1997); Bachelor's Degree in History and Education, CUNY Queens College (1996); Continuing Education Coursework in Social Skills and Functional Behavior Assessments

Affiliations/Associations/Societies: United Federation of Teachers; ABA

Charity/Volunteer Work: Local Church; The Veteran's Association; United Negro College Fund; Citymeals-on-Wheels; Autism Society of America; Toys for Tots; The Salvation Army

Date of Birth: February 22, 1957 **Place of Birth:** Welch

Spouse: Norton **Children:** Aaron

What do you attribute your success to? She attributes her success to her love for teaching, desire to learn and ability to treat people fairly.

What was the highlight of your career? The most gratifying aspects of her career are being able to motivate others and working with her colleagues, students and their parents.

Expanded Biography: Mrs. Churchwell-Swift does public speaking on social skills.

PROFESSIONAL OF THE YEAR IN BOOK MARKETING

SUE J. CLARK

Owner
SJ Clark Literary Agency
237 L Street
Lincoln, CA 95648 United States
sjclark@psyber.com
http://www.cambridgewhoswho.com

Type of Business: Literary Agency

Major Products and Services: Writing and Publishing Services, Instruction

Marketing Area: National

Day to Day Responsibilities: Editing, Instructing, Writing Poetry, Fiction and Non-Fiction, Conducting Workshops, Public Speaking, Teaching Management Skills

Favorite Business Publications: Writer's Digest

Hobbies/Interests/Sports: Writing Poetry, Reading, Traveling

Education Degrees: Bachelor of Arts in Speech Communication, University of Washington (1952); Associate of Arts, Stephens College (1949); Coursework in Speech Communication, Northwestern University

Affiliations/Associations/Societies: Board of Directors, National Society of Fundraising Executives (1969-1977); Public Relations Society of America (1969-1977); Alpha Delta Pi

Awards/Honors: President's Award (2006); Highest Honor, Military Writers Society of America

Charity/Volunteer Work: President, Lions Clubs International, San Francisco, CA (1991-1993); Easter Seal Society, San Francisco, CA (1974-1977); The Leukemia & Lymphoma Society

Date of Birth: October 17, 1929   **Place of Birth:** Vancouver, Washington

Work History: Instructor, Department of Agriculture (1994-2005); Poetry Instructor, Sierra College; Poetry Instructor of Fiction and Non-Fiction Writing, Adult Education Schools and Community Facilities

Expanded Biography: Ms. Clark previously owned a historic hotel and travel agency. She was also the co-owner of two tourist trade newspapers. She works as an instructor for California Hotel and Motel Management Training. She has also ghost-written a book entitled 'Is Anybody Listening: The True Story About the POW/MIAs in the Vietnam War,' which was published in 2005 and is currently ghost-writing a book about World War II. She is a co-publisher for ShortReads Press.

ENTREPRENEUR OF THE YEAR IN MECHANICAL ENGINEERING

MILES LEE CLYDE, PH.D., PE

Owner
MLC Consulting Services, LLC
7245 W. Emile Zola Avenue
Peoria, AZ 85381 United States
mclyde2@cox.net
http://www.mlc-consulting.com

Type of Business: Consulting Firm

Major Products and Services: Mechanical Engineering Consulting

Marketing Area: International

Area of Expertise: Mr. Clyde's expertise includes failure analysis, fracture mechanics and accident reconstruction.

Favorite Business Publications: National Science Engineering

Hobbies/Interests/Sports: Photography, Landscaping, Web Development, Chaos Services

Education Degrees: Ph.D. in Mechanical Engineering, Oxford University

Certifications: Certified Professional Engineer

Affiliations/Associations/Societies: American Society of Mechanical Engineers; ASM International; National Society of Professional Engineers; Society of Automotive Engineers

Date of Birth: April 8, 1953   **Place of Birth:** Heber City

Children: Lynda, Aaron, Allison, Sara

What do you attribute your success to? He attributes his success to his drive to succeed.

What was the highlight of your career? The highlights of his career were all his areas of study.

PROFESSIONAL OF THE YEAR IN
MODERN EUROPEAN HISTORY EDUCATION

MR. CHARLES ROBERT COLE, PH.D.

Professor
Department of History
Utah State University
Logan, UT 84322 United States
robert.cole@usu.edu
http://www.usu.edu

Type of Business: University

Major Products and Services: Higher Education

Marketing Area: Regional

Area of Expertise: Mr. Cole's expertise is in teaching.

Day to Day Responsibilities: Conducting Research on World War II and British, American and German Propaganda

Favorite Business Publications: Journal of British Studies

Hobbies/Interests/Sports: Exercising, Traveling

Education Degrees: Ph.D., Claremont Graduate University (1971); Master of Arts in History, Kansas State University; Bachelor of Arts, Ottawa University

Affiliations/Associations/Societies: North American Conference on British Studies; Royal Historical Society

Awards/Honors: Grant Recipient, National Endowment for the Humanities; American Philosophical Society; International Studies Association

Date of Birth: August 28, 1939   **Place of Birth:** Harper, KS

Spouse: Llouz   **Children:** Teresa

Career Achievements: Electee, Royal Historical Society; Co-Founder, Western Conference on British Studies

What do you attribute your success to? He attributes his success to his education and to the support he receives from the people around him.

How did you become involved in your profession? He became involved in his profession because of his interest in history.

What was the highlight of your career? The highlight of his career was being invited to lecture in Paris, France.

Where will you be in five years? In five years, Mr. Cole hopes to continue teaching at Utah State University and would also like to continue writing and publish his eight books.

Expanded Biography: Mr. Cole is the author of many books such as 'Britain and the War of Words in Neutral Europe', 'Three-Volume Encyclopedia of Propaganda', 'Propaganda, Censorship and Irish Neutrality in the Second World War', 'Traveler's History of France', 'Traveler's History of Paris' and 'Traveler's History of Germany' and is writing a book entitled 'Propaganda and War'. He previously worked as a part-time lecturer at Pomona College and teaching assistant at Kansas State University.

PROFESSIONAL OF THE YEAR IN COURT REPORTING

JANET A. COLLINS

Manager
J. Collins Reporting, LLC
222 W. Coleman Boulevard
Mount Pleasant, SC 29464 United States
janet@jcollinsreporting.com
http://www.jcollinsreporting.com

Type of Business: Court Reporting Firm

Major Products and Services: Reporting Services Including Real-time Transcriptions, Tutoring Services for Court Reporting Students, Communication Access, Real-Time Translation for the Hearing-Impaired People, Historical and Legal Transcription, Presentations and Demonstrations for Various Legal Groups and Schools

Marketing Area: National

Area of Expertise: Ms. Collins' expertise is in software development.

Day to Day Responsibilities: Reporting in State and Federal Courts, Arranging an Avenue for Individuals, Training Court Reporters, Mediating for a Communication Access Real-Time Translation, Selling and Instructing for Computer-Aided Transcription and Technical Legal Cases, Preparing Court Reporting Instruction

Favorite Business Publications: Journal of Court Reporting

Hobbies/Interests/Sports: Caring for her Dogs, Admiring Nature, Yoga, Listening to Music, Painting

Education Degrees: Associate Degree in Court Reporting, Reporting Academy of Virginia

Certifications: Registered Professional Reporter; Registered Merit Reporter; Certified Real-time Reporter, National Court Reporters Association; Federal Certified Real-time Reporter, United States Court Reporters Association; Certified Court Reporter, State of North Carolina; Caption Master Series Program, The University of Mississippi

Affiliations/Associations/Societies: Secretary, Official Court Reporters Association; Women Work; Secretary, American Business Women's Association; National Court Reporters Association; United States Court Reporters Association

Awards/Honors: Global Register's Who's Who in Executives and Professionals

Date of Birth: April 10, 1969   **Place of Birth:** Suffolk

Spouse: Brock   **Children:** Emma, Eli, Katie, Kassie

Work History: Reporter, United States District Court; Sales Representative, Software Trainer, ProCAT Software

PROFESSIONAL OF THE YEAR IN BILINGUAL EDUCATION

MR. ELIEZER COLON

Bilingual Science Instructor
Streamwood High School
1042 Todd Farm Drive
Apartment 102
Elgin, IL 60123 United States
eliezercolonrivera@sbcglobal.net
http://www.cambridgewhoswho.com

Type of Business: High School

Major Products and Services: Education

Marketing Area: Local

Day to Day Responsibilities: Teaching High School Biology, Chemistry and Environmental Science

Favorite Business Publications: ASCD Journal

Hobbies/Interests/Sports: Wine, Cooking, Listening to Classical Music

Education Degrees: Pursuing Ph.D. in Higher Education; Master of Science in Education, Northern Illinois University; Bachelor of Science in Biology, University of Puerto Rico

Affiliations/Associations/Societies: Association for Supervision and Curriculum Development; Kappa Delta Pi

What do you attribute your success to? He attributes his career success to his patience and dedication.

How did you become involved in your profession? He became involved in education because of his love for science and education.

What was the highlight of your career? The most gratifying aspect of his career is seeing the impact he has made in the lives of his students.

Expanded Biography: Mr. Colón-Rivera is very proud of both of his sons, one who is a staff sergeant in the Air Force and the other who is deployed in Iraq.

PROFESSIONAL OF THE YEAR IN
BLACK THEOLOGY EDUCATION

DR. CECIL W. CONE

1) Professor of Black Theology 2) Theologian, Author, Lecturer, Consultant
1) Spelman College 2) African Methodist Episcopal Church
20 Cross Creek Drive
Lilburn, GA 30047 United States
cecilwconephd@aol.com
http://www.spelman.edu

Type of Business: 1) College 2) Church

Major Products and Services: 1) Higher Education 2) Religious Services, Consulting Services, Lectures, Religious Studies

Marketing Area: International

Area of Expertise: Dr. Cone's expertise includes black theology, systematic theology, philosophy and counseling psychotherapy.

Day to Day Responsibilities: Conducting Research, Identifying Crises in Black Theology, Writing and Lecturing Worldwide

Favorite Business Publications: Journal of the American Academy of Religion; ACA Journals

Hobbies/Interests/Sports: Writing, Exercising

Education Degrees: Master of Arts in Counseling Psychology, University of North Florida (1993); Honorary Doctor of Divinity, Payne Theological Seminary, Wilberforce, OH (1985); Honorary Doctor of Divinity, Philander Smith College, Little Rock, AR (1981); Ph.D. in Systematic Theology, Minor in Philosophy, Atlanta, GA (1974); Honorary Doctor of Divinity, Temple Bible College and Seminary, Cincinnati, OH (1971); Rockefeller Doctoral Fellowship, Emory University (1970-1972); Coursework in Philosophy, Wayne State University (1962-1964); Master of Divinity, Garrett Theological Seminary (Now Garrett-Evangelical Theological Seminary) (1961); Bachelor of Arts, Philander Smith College, Little Rock, AK (1957); Associate of Arts, Shorter College (1955)

Affiliations/Associations/Societies: Lifetime Member, National Association for the Advancement of Colored People; Life Associate Member, National Council of Negro Women; Board Chairman, Co-Founder, Whole Life Health Care; Governor's Commission on Higher Education; Society for the Study of Black Religion; Founding Member, Arkansas Chapter, American Civil Liberties Union; American Academy of Religion; American Counseling Association; National Medical Association; Charter Member, Gamma Beta Boule Chapter, Sigma Pi Phi Fraternity; Alpha Kappa Mu Honor Society; Psi Chi, The National Honor Society in Psychology; Beta Gamma Sigma; Phi Delta Kappa International; Lifetime Member, Alpha Phi Alpha Fraternity, Inc.; Former Member, Commission on Ethics, State of Florida; Former Member, Mayor's Commission on Education; Former Board of Directors Member, The National Association for Equal Opportunity in Higher Education

Awards/Honors: One of the Most Powerful Blacks in Jacksonville, Jacksonville Magazine (1982); 75 Young Leaders in Education, Phi Delta Kappa International (1981)

Charity/Volunteer Work: Chief Consultant, African Hebrew Israelite School of the Prophets Institute of Jerusalem (2005-Present)

Place of Birth: Fordyce

Spouse: Juanita   **Children:** Cecil, Leslie, Charleston

Work History: Professor of Black Theology, Spelman College (2004-Present); Theologian, Lecturer, Consultant, African Methodist Episcopal Church (2002-Present); Theologian, Counselor, Private Practice (1989-1994); President, Edward Waters College (1976-1988); President, Professor of Systematic Theology, Turner Theological Seminary Continuing Education Program (1972-1976); Visiting Professor of Black Theology, Emory University (1970); Professor of Black Theology and Styles of Black Ethics, Candler School of Theology (1970)

Career Achievements: Guest Lecturer, 'The 45-Second Encounter with Yahwah' (2005); Guest Lecturer, 'African Worldview and Conceptual System: Identity Crisis in the Black Religious Experience' (2004); Guest Lecturer, 'Reclaiming our Heritage' (2003); Guest Lecturer, 'A Black Theology of Liberation: An African/Hebraic Interpretation of the Christian Faith' (2002); Guest Lecturer, 'A Black Theology of Absalom Jones: Founder of the African Episcopal Church' (2002); Guest Lecturer, 'Richard Allan and A Black Theology of Liberation' (2001); Guest Lecturer, 'An Introduction to Christian Theology: Telling the Story' (2000); Commencement Speaker, Philander Smith College, Little Rock, AK (1999)

Expanded Biography: Dr. Cone is a theologian, pastor, psychotherapist, lecturer and author. He has served on numerous councils, educational leadership boards and committees for black theology, psychological and religious studies. He is the author of two books, 'The Identity Crisis in Black Theology,' and 'The Identity Crisis in Black Theology: Revised Edition.'

EXECUTIVE OF THE YEAR IN HEALTHCARE ADMINISTRATION

ALICIA R. COOPER

1) Chief Executive Officer 2) Owner
1) Arkansas Specialty Care Centers, PA
2) Dimensions Consulting
600 S. McKinley Street, MS 5410
Little Rock, AR 72205 United States
acooper@arspecialty.com
http://www.arspecialty.com

Type of Business: 1) Comprehensive Neuro-Musculoskeletal Care Organization 2) Consulting Company

Major Products and Services: 1) Orthopedic Treatment for Hands, Upper Extremities and the Spine, Neurosurgery 2) Medical Consultations

Marketing Area: 1) Regional 2) Regional

Area of Expertise: Ms. Cooper's expertise is in healthcare administration and medical group management.

Favorite Business Publications: Harvard Business Review

Hobbies/Interests/Sports: Golfing, Fly Fishing

Education Degrees: Master of Science in Counseling Psychology, University of Central Arkansas (1990)

Affiliations/Associations/Societies: Medical Group Management Association; National Society of Orthopedic Administrators

Awards/Honors: Business Of The Year Award

Spouse: Maryanne

Expanded Biography: Ms. Cooper intends to open her own consulting firm called 'Dimensions' sometime in the near future.

PROFESSIONAL OF THE YEAR IN AESTHETICS

MIHAELA CORCOZ

Owner, Aesthetician
Belladonna Face and Body Clinic
230 S. Robertson Boulevard
Beverly Hills, CA 90211 United States
belladonnaclinic@yahoo.com
http://www.belladonnabeverlyhills.com

Type of Business: European Skin Care Salon

Major Products and Services: Treatments and Services Catering to All Skin Types, Including a Variety of Facials, Waxing, Peels and Lash Tints

Marketing Area: Local

Day to Day Responsibilities: Overseeing Employees and All Clinic Services, Ensuring Client Satisfaction, Training the Staff

Favorite Business Publications: Spa

Hobbies/Interests/Sports: Practicing Yoga, Hiking, Reading, Watching Movies

Certifications: Licensed Aesthetician

What was the highlight of your career? The most gratifying aspect of her career is having so many loyal clients, including celebrities.

Expanded Biography: Ms. Corcoz's business has been featured in Bazaar and Allure magazines. She has participated in many fundraising events for charities including organizations supporting research for AIDS and children with diseases.

EXECUTIVE OF THE YEAR IN INVESTMENT MARKETING

RODOLFO J. CORTINA, PH.D., HDES

Chief Executive Officer
CCC International Services Corporation
11906 Swan Creek Drive
Houston, TX 77065 United States
rjcortina@hotmail.com
http://www.cambridgeswhoswho.com

Type of Business: Investment Marketing Firm

Major Products and Services: Real Estate Investments, Financial Services, Various Export-Import Services, Company and Client Training in Marketing Techniques

Marketing Area: International

Day to Day Responsibilities: Assisting in Real Estate Investing, Helping Establish Companies, Consulting, Determining Companies' Client Base, Strategizing Marketing Ideas, Teaching People How to Obtain Grants for their Business, Protecting Income, Restructuring Debt

Favorite Business Publications: The Economist

Hobbies/Interests/Sports: Reading, Exercising, Cooking

Education Degrees: Ph.D. in Spanish Letters, Case Western Reserve University (1971); Bachelor's Degree in Economics and Spanish Letters, Texas A&M University (1966); Master's Degree in Spanish; Master's Degree in Business

Certifications: Pursuing Securities License; Pursuing Loan Officer License; Licensed in Life, Health, Property and Casualty Insurance, State of Texas

Work History: Professor, University of Houston

Expanded Biography: Dr. Cortina is currently establishing a retirement community in Ecuador and developing conglomerates to help small farmers. He also lectures on entrepreneurship at the University of Houston.

PROFESSIONAL OF THE YEAR IN PHARMACOLOGY

SANDRA J. CRABTREE, RPH, BCOP

Oncology Pharmacist
Western Maryland Health System
900 Seton Drive
Cumberland, MD 21502 United States
scrabtree@wmhs.com
http://www.wmhs.com

Type of Business: Regional Cancer Center

Major Products and Services: Treating Hematology and Oncology Patients, Community Healthcare

Marketing Area: Local

Day to Day Responsibilities: Working as a Medical Oncology Pharmacist, Developing Protocols for Treatments, Preparing Chemotherapy Orders

Favorite Business Publications: American Journal of Oncology Review

Hobbies/Interests/Sports: Doing Yard Work, Reading

Education Degrees: Bachelor of Science in Pharmacy, Duquesne University (1979)

Affiliations/Associations/Societies: American Society of Health System Pharmacists, Board of Pharmaceutical Specialists

PROFESSIONAL OF THE YEAR IN
INDUSTRIAL ENGINEERING AND TECHNOLOGY

DR. J.K. CRAIN, P.E.

Vice President of Engineering,
Research and Development
OptoEngineering, Inc
P.O. Box 52067
Tulsa, OK 74152 United States
jkcrain@optoenginering.com
http://www.optoengineering.com

Type of Business: Commercial Lighting Company Specializing in LED Lighting

Major Products and Services: Design, Fabrication and Installation of Commercial Lighting Fixtures

Marketing Area: National

Area of Expertise: Dr. Crain's expertise is in software systems development and quality assurance .

Favorite Business Publications: Crosstalk, Fortune; How-To publications.

Hobbies/Interests/Sports: Ranching

Education Degrees: Doctorate in Industrial Technology; Master of Science in Computer Science; Master of Science in Industrial Technology; Bachelor of Arts in Mathematics

Affiliations/Associations/Societies: NAIT; SME; IIE

Spouse: Melba

Work History: Faculty Member, Department Head, Industrial Engineering and Technology; Vice President of Engineering and Optoengineering; ISO Auditor, National Aeronautics and Space Administration

What do you attribute your success to? He attributes his success to his ability to capitalize on opportunities that came his way.

Expanded Biography: Dr. Crain presents and lectures at local and national conferences on information pertaining to industrial quality and engineering processes. He published an article in a 2004 edition of Midwestern Business and Economic Review Journal as well as an article in Quality Management Journal. He has edited and performed quality review of textbooks and book chapters.

PROFESSIONAL OF THE YEAR IN
HIGHER EDUCATION ADMINISTRATION

LOIS S. CRONHOLM, PH.D.

Director of Development, Consultant
Educational Housing Service Corporation
240 E. 35th Street
Apartment 9F
New York, NY 10016 United States
lcronholm@studenthousing.org
http://www.studenthousing.org

Type of Business: Educational Housing Center

Major Products and Services: Educational Housing Services

Marketing Area: National

Day to Day Responsibilities: Developing Enhanced Residential Housing Opportunities for Students Attending College in New York and the Tri-State Area Including International Students, Mentoring Young Women Regarding Strategic Planning, Education and Administration

Hobbies/Interests/Sports: Cooking, Gardening, Spending Time with her Granddaughter

Education Degrees: Ph.D. in Microbiology, University of Louisville (1967)

Affiliations/Associations/Societies: Advisory Board Member, School of Public Affairs, The City University New York; Secretary, International Commission, Commission of Arts and Sciences, National Association of State Universities and Land-Grant Colleges

Work History: Former Chairwoman, New York State Educational Department Task Force on Assessment and Institutional Effectiveness (1998-1999); Professor of Biology, Baruch College, The City University of New York; Provost, Baruch College, The City University of New York; Senior Vice President, Interim President, Baruch College, The City University of New York; Former Executive Vice President, Former Chief Executive Officer, Center for Jewish History, City University New York; Former Dean, College of Arts and Sciences, Temple University; Former Dean, College of Arts and Sciences, University of Louisville; Former Chairwoman, Commission of Arts and Sciences, National Association of State Universities and Land-Grant Colleges; Former Board Member, Board of Directors, Journal of the History and Ideas; Former Senior Vice President, Former Chief Executive Officer, College of Arts and Sciences City College of New York

PROFESSIONAL OF THE YEAR IN FIRE FIGHTING

ROBERT D. CROWE

Fire Chief
St. Tammany Fire Protection District No. 11
64279 Highway 3081
P.O. Box 1210
Pearl River, LA 70452 United States
rcrowefirechief@bellsouth.net
http://www.stfpd11.org

Type of Business: Volunteer Fire, Rescue and Emergency Medical Services Company

Major Products and Services: Fire and Rescue Services, and Medical Assistance

Marketing Area: Regional

Day to Day Responsibilities: Managing All Aspects of Fire Rescue, Emergency Medical Services and Fire Duties, Managing the Containment of Hazardous Materials, Assisting with Life and Safety Including Vehicle Extractions

Favorite Business Publications: Fire Chief; Firehouse Magazine

Hobbies/Interests/Sports: Fishing, Hunting

Certifications: Louisiana Emergency Manager Certification (2008); Millages Reassessment, State of Louisiana Office of Legislative Auditor (2008); IS-00100, FEMA Emergency Management Institute (2008); IS-00200, FEMA Emergency Management Institute (2008); Accident Scene Safety Instructor, Scene of The Accident (2006); Pneumatic Heavy Lifting Air Bags Operator, Savatech Corp. (2006); Administrative Process of Adopting Millages, State of Louisiana Office of Legislative Auditor (2006); Waterous Fire Pump Seminar (2006); WMD Emergency Medical Services Training, U.S. Department of Homeland Security (2006); WMD Hands-on Training Course (COBRA), U.S. Department of Homeland Security (2006); WMD Incident Command Course (COBRA), U.S. Department of Homeland Security (2006); WMD Hazardous Materials Technician, U.S. Department of Homeland Security (2005); Disaster Response & Recovery Operations, U.S. Department of Homeland Security (2005); How to Handle People with Tact and Skill, CareerTrack (2005); WMD Hazardous Materials Technician (COBRA), U.S. Department of Homeland Security (2005); WMD Radiological/Nuclear Course, U.S. Department of Homeland Security (2005); Bullard Thermal Imaging, Bullard 2004 Community Safety Education, U.S. Department of Homeland Security (2004); Firefighter Safety, Volunteer Firemen's Insurance Services, Inc. (2004); Fire Service Supervision, National Fire Academy (2004); IS-55 Household Hazardous Materials - A Guide for Citizens, FEMA Emergency Management Institute (2004); Infectious Diseases, Volunteer Firemen's Insurance Services, Inc. (2004); Introduction to National Incident Management System, FEMA Emergency Management Institute (2004); Wildland Urban Interface Fire Operations, U.S. Department of Homeland Security (2004); Critical Incident Stress Management, University of Maryland, Baltimore County (2003); Damage Assessment Training, U.S. Department of Homeland Security (2003); Emergency Vehicle Dynamics, Volunteer Firemen's Insurance Services, Inc. (2003); Emergency Vehicle Driver Training, Volunteer Firemen's Insurance Services, Inc. (2003); Firearm Safety/Use of Lethal Force and Civil Liability, National Rifle Association (2003); Firefighter Safety, Volunteer Firemen's Insurance Services, Inc. (2003); Helicopter Night Landing Course, Acadian Ambulance Service (2003); Incident Command System, Louisiana State University Fire and Emergency Training Institute (2003); NRA Basic Pistol Course, National Rife Association (2003); Urban Search and Rescue Specialist, Louisiana State University Fire and Emergency Training Institute (2003); Certification in Hazardous Materials Awareness, Louisiana State University Fire and Emergency Training Institute (2002); Certification in Command and Control of Incident Operations, National Fire Academy (2002); Certification in Emergency Vehicle Driver Training, Volunteer Firemen's Insurance Services, Inc. (2002); Certification in Emergency Vehicle Response, Volunteer Firemen's Insurance Services, Inc. (2002)

Affiliations/Associations/Societies: St. Tammany Firefighters Association; Louisiana Fire Chiefs Association; Louisiana State Firemen's Association

Awards/Honors: Firefighter of the Year, State of Louisiana (2004); Letter of Recognition, Governor of Louisiana (2002); Recognized by the House of Representatives and the State Senate for his Accomplishments

Charity/Volunteer Work: Volunteer, Educational Program; Local Church Organizations; Volunteer, Local School

Date of Birth: November 23, 1970   **Place of Birth:** Picayune

Spouse: Lisa   **Children:** Natalie, Liana, Robert

Expanded Biography: Mr. Crowe would like to acknowledge all of the fire chiefs and professionals in his industry. He enjoys giving 110 percent to the citizens of his community and ensuring that all fire and rescue equipment is in prime condition. He feels that it makes a big difference in a community to make the best of each situation and for people to give the best of themselves. Mr. Crowe has also been featured in 'Fire Chief' magazine.

PROFESSIONAL OF THE YEAR IN
INFORMATION TECHNOLOGY MANAGEMENT

MR. HARVEY CRUZ

Information Technology Manager
Million Dollar Round Table
325 W. Touhy Avenue
Park Ridge, IL 60068 United States
harveyc@imotion1.com
http://www.cambridgewhoswho.com

Type of Business: Information Technology Management Firm

Major Products and Services: Assisting Worldwide Insurance Companies, Agents, and Financial Advisers to Improve their Business Practices

Marketing Area: International

Day to Day Responsibilities: Managing Projects, Re-Engineering Business Processes, Planning, Developing Engineering Software Applications, Analyzing Cost Benefit Strategies, Consulting with Manufacturing and Utility Industries, Assisting Clients, Monitoring Initiatives Linked to Websphere Portals and iSeries Technology, Overseeing Automatic Content Translation Services, Maintaining Database and Work Flow Processes

Favorite Business Publications: The Economist; CIO; BusinessWeek; Time; PM Magazine

Hobbies/Interests/Sports: Playing Chess, Spending Time with his Family

Education Degrees: Bachelor of Science in Information Technology Management, JEL Institute of Technology

Certifications: Master Certified Professional Project Manager, Villanova University; Master Certification in Information Security Management, Villanova University; Certification in Legacy Systems Integration; iSeries Certification; Certification in DB2; Certification in Web and Portal Implementations, IBM; Certification in Quality Management; Certification in Customer Service; Certification in Quality Software Management; Certification in Software Engineering, AMS; Certification in Software Engineering, McDonnell Douglas

Affiliations/Associations/Societies: Association of Information Technology Professionals, Chicago, IL; Project Management Institute

Work History: iSeries Security Consultant; Y2K Consultant; Chief Information Technology Officer, BJ Services; Chief Information Technology Officer, Baker Performance Chemicals; Chief Information Officer, Hughes Tool Company

PROFESSIONAL OF THE YEAR IN
PERSONAL INJURY LAW

Darla L. D'Amico

Attorney
Law Offices of Frank J. D'Amico, Jr.
240 Fremaux Avenue
Slidell, LA 70458 United States
ddamico1@bellsouth.net
http://www.cambridgewhoswho.com

Type of Business: Private Practice

Major Products and Services: Legal Services, Representation for Personal Injuries, Maritime and Offshore Injuries, Car Accidents, Semi-Tractor-Trailer Accidents, Motorcycle Accidents, Wrongful Death, Medical Malpractice, Birth Injuries, Product Liability, Spine and Brain Injuries

Marketing Area: Regional

Area of Expertise: Ms. D'Amico's expertise is in personal injury litigation and civil law.

Favorite Business Publications: Levy Cites; ABA Journal

Hobbies/Interests/Sports: Water Skiing, Gardening

Education Degrees: JD, Loyola University (1988)

Affiliations/Associations/Societies: The Association of Trial Lawyers of America; American Bar Association; Phi Delta Phi

PROFESSIONAL OF THE YEAR IN SPIRITUAL SERVICES

LAWRENCE A. DALRYMPLE SR.

Pastor
Bethel Worship Center
6060 Kimberly Boulevard
North Lauderdale, FL 33068 United States
admin@bethelworship.us
http://www.bethelworship.us

Type of Business: Church

Major Products and Services: Child Care Center, Preaching

Marketing Area: Local

Day to Day Responsibilities: Offering Ministerial Leadership for Sunday Worship Services

Favorite Business Publications: Fortune 500

Hobbies/Interests/Sports: Reading

Education Degrees: Master's Degree in Social Work and Theology, Adelphi University

Charity/Volunteer Work: Southern Baptist Convention

EXECUTIVE OF THE YEAR IN
JAPANESE AUTOMOTIVE AUTOMATION

MR. RICARDO DAVALOS

President
Buhin Corporation
975 E. Nerge Road, Suite N60
Roselle, IL 60172 United States
davalos@buhincorp.com
http://www.buhincorp.com

Type of Business: Japanese Automotive Automation Distribution

Major Products and Services: Distributing Japanese Factory Automation Products and Electric and Electronic Components to the Automotive Industry

Marketing Area: Nationwide

Area of Expertise: Mr. Davalos' expertise is in business and project management.

Day to Day Responsibilities: Overseeing Daily Operations, Importing and Exporting Goods, Delegating Duties

Favorite Business Publications: Hispanic Business Magazine

Hobbies/Interests/Sports: Watching Movies, Listening to Music, Soccer, Fine Dining

Education Degrees: Bachelor of Science, Illinois Institute of Technology (1994)

Affiliations/Associations/Societies: Chicago Minority Business Development Council

PROFESSIONAL OF THE YEAR IN SUBSTANCE ABUSE COUNSELING

REBECCA C. DAWSON

Substance Abuse Counselor
Home Avenue Clinic
CRC Health Group, Inc.
637 Hampshire Lane
Chula Vista, CA 91911 United States
beckycdawson@cox.net
http://www.crchealth.com

Type of Business: Healthcare Center

Major Products and Services: Medication-Assisted Treatment

Marketing Area: Local

Area of Expertise: Ms. Dawson's expertise is in case management and outside referrals.

Day to Day Responsibilities: Overseeing Outpatient Services, Treating and Offering Medical Assistance to Heroin Addicts, Substance Abuse Counseling, Setting Goals

Favorite Business Publications: Counselor

Hobbies/Interests/Sports: Gardening, Cooking, Walking

Education Degrees: Pursuing Master's Degree in Marriage and Family Therapy; Bachelor of Science in Human Services Management, University of Phoenix (2007); Associate of Arts in Behavioral Science, San Diego City College (2004)

Certifications: Certified Alcohol and Other Drugs of Addiction Counselor-11, California Association of Alcoholism and Drug Abuse Counselors (2006); Certified Addictions Treatment Counselor, California Association for Alcohol/Drug Educators (2000)

Affiliations/Associations/Societies: California Association of Alcoholism and Drug Abuse Counselors; California Association for Alcohol/Drug Educators; California Association of Marriage and Family Therapists; American Association for Marriage and Family Therapy

Where will you be in five years? In five years, Ms. Dawson hopes to become a licensed marriage and family therapist.

Expanded Biography: Ms. Dawson is currently working at the Third Avenue Clinic of CRC Health Group, Inc.

PROFESSIONAL OF THE YEAR IN PERIOPERATIVE NURSING

DONNA JEAN DEAGEL, RN, CNOR

Registered Nurse, Staff Nurse
Reynolds Memorial Hospital
800 Wheeling Avenue
Glen Dale, WV 26038 United States
rndjd@juno.com
http://www.reynoldsmemorial.com

Type of Business: Nonprofit Acute-Care Community Hospital

Major Products and Services: Healthcare Services Including General Medical Surgical Care, Cardiac and Other Intensive Care, Home Health, Obstetrics, Pediatrics, Long-Term Skilled and Personal Care Services

Marketing Area: Local

Area of Expertise: Ms. Deagel's expertise is in operating room and surgical staff nursing.

Hobbies/Interests/Sports: Making Crafts, Traveling

Education Degrees: Associate Degree in Nursing, West Virginia Northern Community College

Certifications: Licensed Practical Nurse, BM Spurr School of Practical Nursing

Affiliations/Associations/Societies: Treasurer, Association of Preoperative Registered Nurses

Awards/Honors: Nurse Excellence Award, Reynolds Memorial Hospital (2007)

Charity/Volunteer Work: Wheeling Health Right; United Way of America; Vice President, Hospital Credit Union; Co-Chairwoman, Nurses Week, Reynolds Memorial Hospital

Date of Birth: March 31, 1948   **Place of Birth:** Wheeling, West Virginia

What do you attribute your success to? She attributes her success to her passion for her profession.

How did you become involved in your profession? She became involved in her profession because she always wanted to be a nurse.

What was the highlight of your career? The highlight of her career was becoming a registered nurse.

Expanded Biography: Ms. Deagel has worked on the medical-surgical floor for two years and in the special care unit for 11 years.

PROFESSIONAL OF THE YEAR IN SOCIAL WORK

KATE H. DeCOU, PH.D., LICSW

1) Consultant 2) Faculty Member
2) School of Social Work
1) Institute for Health and Recovery 2) Springfield College
kdecou@aol.com
http://www.cambridgewhoswho.com

Type of Business: 1) Nonprofit Organization 2) College

Major Products and Services: 1) Consulting, Programs on Substance Abuse, Mental Health and Trauma Issues for Families, Women and Children 2) Higher Education

Marketing Area: Regional

Day to Day Responsibilities: Consulting, Overseeing Gender Responsive Correctional Facilities, Addressing Trauma, Domestic Violence, Mental Health and Homeless Women's Issues, Public Speaking, Coordinating Teams and Women's Employment Programs

Favorite Business Publications: Women & Criminal Justice

Hobbies/Interests/Sports: Yoga, Meditation, Traveling, Reading

Education Degrees: Ph.D. in Social Welfare, SUNY Albany; Master of Social Welfare, The University of Chicago

Certifications: Licensed Independent Clinical Social Worker; Certification, Council on Social Work Education

Affiliations/Associations/Societies: National Association of Social Workers; American Corrections Association; Board of Directors, Behavioral Health Network, MA; Council on Social Work Education

What do you attribute your success to? She attributes her success to her persistence and organizational skills.

How did you become involved in your profession? She became involved in her profession because of her interaction with the sheriff while working on a project.

What was the highlight of your career? The highlight of her career was receiving the national recognition for her gender responsive programs and operations.

Where will you be in five years? In five years, Dr. DeCou hopes to become an international consultant and intends to write a book on sexual and domestic violence issues.

Expanded Biography: Dr. DeCou has also served as an assistant superintendent in a correctional institution.

PROFESSIONAL OF THE YEAR IN OPTHALMOLOGY

DR. ARTHUR JOSEPH DELA HOUSSAYE

Medical Doctor
SEECA
249 Corporate Drive
Houma, LA 70360 United States
drd@seeca.com
http://www.seeca.com

Type of Business: Medical Center

Major Products and Services: Healthcare Including Medinformatix, Medical Software, Retinal Exams, First-Time Glasses or Contact Prescriptions, Pediatrics, Color-Blindness Exams for the Military, Cataract Surgery, Cosmetic Procedures, Retinal Exams without Dilation

Marketing Area: National

Area of Expertise: Dr. Houssaye's expertise is in ophthalmology.

Day to Day Responsibilities: Maintaining Electronic Medical Software and Medical Records

Education Degrees: Doctor of Medicine, Louisiana State University, with Honors (1994)

Affiliations/Associations/Societies: American Medical Association; American Society of Cataractive and Refractive Surgery; American Academy of Ophthalmology

Expanded Biography: Dr. Houssaye takes great pride that SEECA helps medical professionals increase efficiency, thus empowering physicians and administrators.

PROFESSIONAL OF THE YEAR IN
HIGH SCHOOL MATHEMATICS INSTRUCTION

MRS. BETTE J. DeMAYO

Teacher, Advisor, Coordinator for Graduation
and Award Night Ceremonies
Mathematics
North Haven High School
221 Elm Street
North Haven, CT 06473 United States
demayo.bette@north-haven.k12.ct.us
http://www.north-haven.k12.ct.us

Type of Business: Public High School

Major Products and Services: Education

Marketing Area: Local

Area of Expertise: Ms. DeMayo's expertise is in algebra and geometry education.

Day to Day Responsibilities: Training Students in Peer Counseling, Organizing Graduation and Awards Night Ceremonies, Creating and Facilitating Certificates of Employability, Producing School Plays, Piloting the Distance Learning Program

Favorite Business Publications: NCTM Mathematics Teacher; NCTM News Bulletin; Journal for Research in Mathematics Education; Time; Consumer Reports; Reader's Digest

Hobbies/Interests/Sports: Traveling, Playing Bridge, Reading, Going to the Movies, Spending Time with Friends and Family, Baseball, Solving Sudoku Puzzles, Music, Playing Cards, Broadway Musicals

Education Degrees: Master's Degree in Mathematics, Central Connecticut State University; Bachelor's Degree in Mathematics; Coursework, University of Connecticut; Coursework, Quinnipiac College

Affiliations/Associations/Societies: Mathematical Association of America; National Council of Teachers of Mathematics; North Haven Education Association; Connecticut Education Association; National Education Association

Awards/Honors: North Haven Teacher of the Year Award (1999); Ulbrich Fellowship Award (1994); Delio Rotondo Teacher of the Year Award (1988); Who's Who Among American Teachers

Charity/Volunteer Work: Literacy Volunteer; Volunteer, Board of Christian Outreach; Board of Christian Education, Local Church

Date of Birth: November 8, 1949   **Place of Birth:** Concord, NH

Spouse: Robert   **Children:** Gary, Robin, Kristen

Work History: Mathematics Teacher; Sunday School Teacher; Camp Counselor

Career Achievements: Founder, Distance Learning Program, North Haven High School

What do you attribute your success to? She attributes her success to never giving up on her students never letting them give up on themselves, the support she receives from her family, maintaining high standards and expecting her students to give 100 percent to whatever they do. She also tries to catch the imagination and sprouting genius of every student in her class.

How did you become involved in your profession? She became involved in her profession because all she ever wanted to do was teach. She was also inspired by her own experiences in school.

What was the highlight of your career? The highlight of her career was having a former student become a teacher because of her influence.

Where will you be in five years? In five years, Ms. DeMayo will be retired from teaching and working in a different service area.

Expanded Biography: Ms. DeMayo feels that any award or honor she has received must be shared by the man who has supported, encouraged, and mentored her throughout the last several decades, her husband, Bob. She was lucky enough to find and marry her soulmate, who just happens to be her best friend. He has allowed her to grow personally and professionally. Bob is a teacher of psychology, the baseball coach at her high school and extremely gifted in both capacities. He holds the record for the most wins in the state of Connecticut, has been named national coach of the year in baseball, and has been inducted into the National High School Coaches Hall of Fame. He has these same honors at the state level and has been inducted into the North Haven Hall of Fame. Ms. DeMayo is a familiar figure on the bleachers in the spring and misses very few games. She is very proud of her husband and thankful to have been a part of his life.

PROFESSIONAL OF THE YEAR IN CONSTRUCTION

JOSEPH G. DERUBEIS

Owner and Founder
Castle Keep Building and Restoration
414 Central Avenue, Suite 2B
Westfield, NJ 07090 United States
joe@castlekeepbuilders.com
http://www.cambridgewhoswho.com

Type of Business: Construction Company

Major Products and Services: General Construction, Contracting Services, Remodeling, Commercial and Residential Building, Custom Building

Marketing Area: Regional

Area of Expertise: Mr. DeRubei's expertise includes high-end residential construction, finished carpentry and stone masonry.

Favorite Business Publications: LIC Journal, Kitchen Design, Builder

Hobbies/Interests/Sports: Spending Quality Time with Family

Education Degrees: College Coursework

Affiliations/Associations/Societies: New Jersey Business and Industry Association; Better Business Bureau; General Contractors Association

Charity/Volunteer Work: FOP Foundation

PROFESSIONAL OF THE YEAR IN
RECRUITING IN HIGHER EDUCATION

ERIN E. DICKERSON

Coordinator of Minority Recruitment
Ursinus College
P.O. Box 1000
Collegeville, PA 19426 United States
edickerson@ursinus.edu
http://www.ursinus.edu

Type of Business: Institution of Higher Education

Major Products and Services: Twenty-Eight Majors and 49 Minors, Interdivisional Studies, Liberal Studies, Pre-Legal Studies, Pre-Medical Studies, Study Abroad Program, Athletics and Recreation, Career Services, Technology Resources

Marketing Area: National

Day to Day Responsibilities: Conducting Admissions Recruiting and Counseling for Various Counties Along the East Coast, Coordinating the Tour Guide Program, Managing 90 Students, Offering Tours to Prospective Students, Interviewing Families, Reviewing Applications

Favorite Business Publications: Time Magazine, Black Enterprise

Hobbies/Interests/Sports: Writing, Running

Education Degrees: Pursuing Master's Degree in Educational Leadership, St. Joseph's University; Bachelor of Arts in English, Ursinus College (2000)

Affiliations/Associations/Societies: Planning Committee, Pennsylvania Association for College Admission Counseling

PROFESSIONAL OF THE YEAR IN
GOURMET DINING

MS. LINDA M. DILLON

Owner
Blue Duck Bistro
216 N. Main Street
P.O. Box 427
Hutchinson, KS 67504 United States
ldillon3873@yahoo.com
http://www.blueduckbistro.com

Type of Business: Restaurant

Major Products and Services: Fine Dining

Marketing Area: Regional

Day to Day Responsibilities: Managing Operations, Entertaining People, Organizing Food Services

Favorite Business Publications: Departures

Hobbies/Interests/Sports: Mountain Climbing, Scuba Diving, Skiing, Spending Time with her Grandmother, Traveling, Gardening

Awards/Honors: Award for Most Romantic Dining, Hutchinson, KS; Award for Best Fine Dining, Hutchinson, KS

Charity/Volunteer Work: Fox Theater; Cooperative for Assistance and Relief Everywhere; The Hutchinson Theater Guild

Date of Birth: June 5, 1953   **Place of Birth:** Denver, CO

Children: Jennie, Chace, Maggie

What do you attribute your success to? She attributes her success to her hard work, professional service and personal attention to patrons.

What was the highlight of your career? The highlight of her career was meeting actor Bill Murray and original Mercury astronauts Wally Schirra and Alan Sheppard at her restaurant.

Expanded Biography: Ms. Dillon has been nominated for restoring a 1931 Art Deco Fox Theater and for restoring and reusing the Wells Fargo Depot. Her accomplishments include opening a fine-dining restaurant and raising wonderful children.

PROFESSIONAL OF THE YEAR IN PLASTIC SURGERY

BORKO DJORDJEVIC, MD

Medical Doctor
Borko Djordjevic, MD
74-075 El Paseo Drive, Suite D2
Palm Desert, CA 92260 United States
borkomd@aol.com
http://www.timelessbeauty.com

Type of Business: Leading Provider in the Medical Industry with a Specialty in Plastic Surgery

Major Products and Services: Cosmetic and Reconstructive Plastic Surgery

Marketing Area: National

Day to Day Responsibilities: Performing General Plastic Surgery, Aesthetic and Reconstructive Surgery Including Facelifts, Rhinoplasty, Blepharoplasty, Chemical Peels, Breast Augmentations and Reductions, Arm, Leg, Hip and Abdominal Reductions and Reshaping, Liposuction, and Genitalia Repair and Reconstruction

Favorite Business Publications: Aesthetic Surgery

Hobbies/Interests/Sports: Music

Education Degrees: Doctor of Medicine, University of Belgrade (1968)

Affiliations/Associations/Societies: American Medical Association; Fellow, International College of Surgeons; Fellow, American Academy of Cosmetic Surgery

Work History: Chief Resident of Plastic and Reconstructive Surgery, Surgery of the Hand and Genitalia, and Cosmetic Surgery, Riverside Methodist Hospital, Columbus, OH; Associate Professor of Plastic and Reconstructive Surgery, University of Belgrade School of Medicine; Contributing Editor, Journal of Medical Research, University of Belgrade School of Medicine; Director, Cosmetic Surgery Fellowship Training Program, University of Belgrade School of Medicine

Expanded Biography: Mr. Djordjevic received a special appointment from former president Jimmy Carter to assist the Carter Center of Atlanta, Georgia in its efforts to furtherpeace in Bosnia and Yugoslavia.

PROFESSIONAL OF THE YEAR IN EDUCATIONAL PEER ASSISTANCE AND REVIEW

CAROLYN D. DONERSON

Peer Assistance and Review Consulting Teacher
Compton Unified School District
501 S. Santa Fe
Compton, CA 90222 United States
anncarol58@sbcglobal.net
http://www.compton.k12.ca.us

Type of Business: School District

Major Products and Services: Regular Core Curriculum including English, Mathematics, Science, Social Studies, Art, Music, History, Peer Assistance and Review Program

Marketing Area: Regional

Day to Day Responsibilities: Assisting Teachers who Have Difficulty in Attaining Standards for the Teaching Profession, Offering Lessons, Discipline, Assessment and Assistance in Professional Development, Consulting in the Peer Assistance and Review Program

Favorite Business Publications: Newsweek; The Week; House & Garden; Ladies Home Journal

Hobbies/Interests/Sports: Tennis, Hiking, Reading, Watching Game Shows

Education Degrees: Master of Arts in Elementary Education, LaVerne College (Now University of La Verne) (1976)

Certifications: Certification in Beginning Teacher Support and Assessment; Certification in Peer Assistance and Review Program

Affiliations/Associations/Societies: California Teachers Association; National Education Association

Date of Birth: January 4, 1942   **Place of Birth:** Jackson, MI

Spouse: Milton

Work History: Compton Unified School District (1968-Present); Third-Grade Teacher (1967-1968); Elementary School Teacher, Jackson, MI (1965-1967)

Career Achievements: Teacher Leader, Mentor Teacher, BTSA Coach, Peer Assistance and Review Teacher, Compton Unified

Expanded Biography: Ms. Donerson is a peer assistance and review teacher and has worked for 10 years as a mentor teacher. As a PAR teacher and coach, she offers personalized assistance to teachers who desire or need additional help. Some of her program benefits include increasing the use of instructional objectives, developing classroom procedures for enhancing quality student-teacher relationships and developing teaching strategies, verbal interactions, and question styles to address different ability levels in classrooms.

PROFESSIONAL OF THE YEAR IN GOVERNMENTAL PROJECT MANAGEMENT

PAMELA A. DOYLE-PENNE

Project Manager (Retired)
Department of Defense, Office of Economic Adjustment
400 Army Navy Drive
Arlington, VA 22202 United States
pamelapenne@cox.net
http://www.cambridgewhoswho.com

Type of Business: United States Government

Major Products and Services: Defense, Base Closures

Marketing Area: National

Area of Expertise: Ms. Doyle-Penne's expertise is in organization, direction, management and the designation of military bases as prison facilities.

Favorite Business Publications: 'How to Talk to a Liberal (if You Must),' Ann Coulter

Hobbies/Interests/Sports: Exercising, Walking, Resistance Handwriting Analysis, Astrology

Education Degrees: Master's Degree in Business Management, Central Michigan University; Bachelor's Degree in Psychology, Holy Family University, Philadelphia

Affiliations/Associations/Societies: President, National Association of Career Women (1980-1983); Arlington Village Condo Association

Awards/Honors: Who's Who of Washington; Who's Who of Women

Charity/Volunteer Work: St. Mary's Catholic Church

PROFESSIONAL OF THE YEAR IN NURSING MANAGEMENT

SUSAN BRAUN DUGGAR

Vice President of Nursing, Chief Nursing Officer
Spartanburg Regional
101 E. Wood Street
Spartanburg, SC 29303 United States
sduggar@srhs.com
http://www.srhs.com

Type of Business: Regional Medical Center

Major Products and Services: Level One Trauma Center, Level Three Neonatal Intensive Care Unit, Cycle Two Accredited Chest Pain Center, Joint Commission on Accreditation of Healthcare Organizations Accredited Stroke Center and Center of Excellence for Bariatric Surgery

Marketing Area: Regional

Day to Day Responsibilities: Overseeing Cardiovascular Critical Care, Cardiology, Nursing Leadership and Management, Employee Relations, a Staff of 1,600 Nurses, Information Technology and Safety Practices of Bedside Nursing, Collaborating with Physicians and the Community

Favorite Business Publications: Modern Healthcare; AACN Journals; Nursing Management; The Journal of Nursing Administration; The Journal of the American Medical Association; The American Journal of Cardiology

Hobbies/Interests/Sports: Spending Time with her Family, Playing Baseball and Football, Practicing Karate

Education Degrees: Master of Science in Nursing, Concentration in Cardiovascular Clinical Nurse Specialty, Vanderbilt University School of Nursing (1991); Bachelor of Science in Nursing, University of Evansville, IN; Registered Nurse

Affiliations/Associations/Societies: Representative, District One, South Carolina Organization of Nurse Leaders; American College of Healthcare Executives; American Organization of Nurse Executives; American Association of Critical-Care Nurses

Charity/Volunteer Work: March of Dimes Foundation; Diabetes Walk; Obesity Walk; American Heart Walk; Susan B. Komen Cancer Walk; American Heart Association

Place of Birth: Cincinnati

Children: Steven, Lauren

What do you attribute your success to? She attributes her success to her relationship with Jesus, her parents, co-workers and her peers.

How did you become involved in your profession? She became involved in her profession because she wanted to be a nurse and took advantage of management opportunities that presented themselves.

What was the highlight of your career? The most gratifying aspects of her career are working in the cardiac recovery room with Dr. Bender and Dr. Frist, caring for pediatric and adult heart surgery and transplant patients.

Where will you be in five years? In five years, Mrs. Duggar intends to continue working at Spartanburg Regional as the VP/CNO. She has a wonderfully supportive nursing staff that strives every day to deliver the highest quality care using compassion and love for patients. She also expects that they will still be recognized for nursing excellence by maintaining their MAGNET designation, continue to be the leading heart center in the region and the hospital of choice for citizens living in the upstate region of South Carolina.

Expanded Biography: Mrs. Duggar has been published in Nursing Management journal. She is affiliated with the M. D. Anderson Cancer Center. She was always very happy at the bedside taking care of her patients and their families, however, management and leadership opportunities presented themselves and she has been successful in those endeavors. Mrs. Duggar was raised on a very firm foundation of trust and accountability and has been able to use those principals throughout her nursing career, while she treats everyone with respect and dignity. She uses her excellent communication and listening skills to handle conflicts in a way that ensures equal treatment of both parties and a positive outcome for all.

PROFESSIONAL OF THE YEAR IN CAREER CENTER MANAGEMENT

MS. JANET E. DUNN

Assistant Center Manager
Workforce Solutions - Capital Area
6505 Airport Boulevard, Suite 101A
Austin, TX 78752 United States
janetedunn@hotmail.com
http://www.cambridgewhoswho.com

Type of Business: Consulting Firm

Major Products and Services: Training Programs and Workshops for Job Seekers and Employers Including Resume Training, Education

Marketing Area: Regional

Area of Expertise: Ms. Dunn's expertise is in case management.

Day to Day Responsibilities: Managing Operations Including the Workforce Center, Maintaining Records

Hobbies/Interests/Sports: Reading, Swimming, Attending Flea Markets

Education Degrees: Associate Degree in Liberal Arts, San Antonio College (1973)

Awards/Honors: Award for Excellence, State of Texas

Charity/Volunteer Work: Local Food Bank; The Salvation Army; Lisa Hope Chest; Project Helping Others Progress Economically

What do you attribute your success to? She attributes her success to her work ethic, honesty and her ability to work well with others.

What was the highlight of your career? The most gratifying aspect of her career is making a difference in others' lives.

PROFESSIONAL OF THE YEAR IN
NURSING EDUCATION

Ms. Mara Florence Dykas

Clinical Instructor
Milwaukee Area Technical College
700 West State Street
Milwaukee, WI 53233 United States
info@CambridgeWhosWho.com
http://www.cambridgewhoswho.com

Type of Business: Two-Year Educational Institution

Major Products and Services: Allied Health Training, Two-Year Educational Nursing Program

Marketing Area: Statewide

Day to Day Responsibilities: Teaching CPN and CNA Clinicals, and Nursing Medical Assistants, Evaluating Nursing Students for Certification, Working with Students in a Clinical Setting to Teach Them to Draw Blood and Control Infection

Favorite Business Publications: American Journal of Nursing; Nursing 2007

Hobbies/Interests/Sports: Fitness, Reading, Painting

Education Degrees: Pursuing Master of Science in Nursing, Cardinal Stritch University; Bachelor of Science in Nursing and Associate Degree in Nursing, Cardinal Stritch University

Certifications: Licensed Practical Nurse, Milwaukee Area Technical College

Affiliations/Associations/Societies: Wisconsin Nurses Association

Charity/Volunteer Work: Local Jewish League

PROFESSIONAL OF THE YEAR IN INFORMATION SYSTEMS

MS. MARGARET A. EBNER, PMP, MS

Project Manager II
Convergys
285 International Parkway
Heathrow, FL 32746 United States
ebnermarge@yahoo.com
http://www.cambridgewhoswho.com

Type of Business: Telecommunication Company

Major Products and Services: Internet, Cable and Broadband Services

Marketing Area: International

Area of Expertise: Ms. Ebner's expertise is in technical project management and information systems.

Favorite Business Publications: Information Week; Forbes

Hobbies/Interests/Sports: Quilting, Golfing

Education Degrees: Master of Science in Computer Information Systems, University of Phoenix; Bachelor's Degree in Secondary Education, Concentration in English, West Chester University of Pennsylvania

Certifications: Project Management Professional

Affiliations/Associations/Societies: Founding Member, Board of Directors (1996-2002); President, Central Florida Chapter, Project Management Institute (1999-2000)

What do you attribute your success to? She attributes her success to her strong communication, technical and problem solving skills.

What was the highlight of your career? The highlight of her career was becoming a project management professional.

EXECUTIVE OF THE YEAR IN
PROFESSIONAL CASE MANAGEMENT IN THE HEALTHCARE INDUSTRY

CARALEE EICHER

Medical and Vocational Case Manager
Creative Solutions
P.O. Box 4658
Roanoke, VA 24015 United States
caraeigh@cox.net
http://cambridgewhoswho.com

Type of Business: Consulting and Rehabilitation Services Provider

Major Products and Services: Medical and Vocational Case Management for Workers' Compensation Claimants

Marketing Area: Regional

Day to Day Responsibilities: Offering Vocational Services, Assisting with Resume Development and Job Seeking, Analyzing Transferable Skills, Assessing Employability for Long-Term Disability Claimants, Acting as a Medical Case Manager upon Request

Hobbies/Interests/Sports: Practicing Yoga and Tai Chi, Meditating, Arts and Culture

Education Degrees: Master's Degree in Counseling, Virginia Polytechnic Institute (1988); Bachelor's Degree in Music, Goshen College (1964)

Certifications: Pursuing Mediation Certification, State of Virginia; Certified Rehabilitation Counselor; Certified Rehabilitation Provider, State of Virginia

Affiliations/Associations/Societies: International Association of Rehabilitation Professionals

Charity/Volunteer Work: Conflict Transformation Program

PROFESSIONAL OF THE YEAR IN NURSING

DONNA JEAN ELLIOTT, BSN, MSN, RN

Registered Nurse
Maternal Child Health
Sharp Grossmont Hospital
5555 Grossmont Center Drive
La Mesa, CA 91942 United States
donna.elliott@sharp.com
ipushwithyou@aol.com
http://www.sharp.com

Type of Business: Hospital

Major Products and Services: Healthcare

Marketing Area: Local

Area of Expertise: Ms. Elliott's expertise is in labor and delivery nursing.

Day to Day Responsibilities: Working in the Post-Anesthesia Care Unit, Caring for Patients Suffering from Postpartum Depression

Hobbies/Interests/Sports: Playing Tennis, Crocheting, Needlepointing, Spending Time with her Children

Education Degrees: Master of Science, University of Phoenix (1999); Bachelor of Science in Nursing, University of Phoenix (1997); Associate Degree in Nursing, Grossmont College (1987)

Date of Birth: October 21, 1960   **Place of Birth:** Orange

Children: Jessica, John

What do you attribute your success to? She attributes her success to her self-motivation and supportive mother.

How did you become involved in your profession? She became involved in her profession because she was influenced by her mother, who was a registered nurse.

What was the highlight of your career? The highlight of her career was working with the U.S. Army Reserve in Germany.

Where will you be in five years? In five years, Ms. Elliott hopes to retire.

Expanded Biography: Ms. Elliott is a major in the U.S. Army Reserve and was deployed in 2004. She is also a nursing instructor at Kaplan College in San Diego, California.

PROFESSIONAL OF THE YEAR IN
HEALTH AND FITNESS

ELLEN ENNIS GONECONTI

Owner
Premier Fitness
430 Nanuet Mall
Nanuet, NY 10954 United States
Ellen@PremierFitnessNY.com
http://www.PremierFitnessNY.com

Type of Business: Fitness

Major Products and Services: Health and Fitness

Marketing Area: Regional

Day to Day Responsibilities: Teaching Health and Fitness, Overseeing All Purchasing and Business Management, Marketing, Public Relations and Human Resource Functions Managing the Staff, Developing a Handbook on Osteoporosis

Favorite Business Publications: Business Publications

Hobbies/Interests/Sports: Traveling, Horseback Riding

Education Degrees: Bachelor of Science in Nursing, Boston University (1976)

Certifications: Certification, Apex Fitness Group

Charity/Volunteer Work: March of Dimes Fitness Sponsor, United Hospice of Rockland County; Contributer, Tom Foley Premier Fitness; Fitness Sponsor, Walk America, Rockland County

Children: Francesca and Gabrielle

Career Achievements: Creator, First Neonatal Transport Team, Pediatric Intensive Care Unit, Women's Intensive Care Unit, Westchester County Medical Center; First Head Nurse; Creator, Educational Outreach Program Sponsored by Tom Foley Memorial Scholarship Fund, Westchester County Medical Center

What do you attribute your success to? She attributes her success to her determination.

How did you become involved in your profession? She became involved in her profession because she felt the need to educate people in health and fitness.

Expanded Biography: Ms. Ennis Goneconti is a member of the New York State Osteoperosis Prevention and Education Program.

PROFESSIONAL OF THE YEAR IN
DIAGNOSTIC AND INTERVENTIONAL RADIOLOGY

GUSTAVO A. ESPINOSA, MD

Chief Radiologist
FHN Memorial Hospital
1045 W. Stephenson
Freeport, IL 61032 United States
gusespinosa@aol.com
http://www.fhn.org

Type of Business: Healthcare

Major Products and Services: Healthcare Provider

Marketing Area: Local

Area of Expertise: Mr. Espinosa's expertise is in diagnostic and interventional radiology.

Hobbies/Interests/Sports: Hunting, Writing, Traveling

Education Degrees: Doctor of Medicine, University of Illinois

Certifications: Board Certified in Diagnostic Radiology; Board Certified in Vascular and Interventional Radiology

Affiliations/Associations/Societies: Fellow, American College of Radiology; Fellow, American Board of Forensic Examiners; Radiological Society of North America, Inc; ACR; ISMS; AMSUS; AIUM; SIR; ISRS; ABFE; CMS

PROFESSIONAL OF THE YEAR IN PUBLISHING

EMMA SAMUEL ETUK, PH.D.

President
EMIDA International Publishers
1923 Berry Lane
District Heights, MD 20747 United States
emida1@yahoo.com
http://www.emida1.com

Type of Business: Publishing Company

Major Products and Services: Book Publishing Services Including Trade Book Authorship

Marketing Area: International

Day to Day Responsibilities: Overseeing the Management, Distribution and Sale of Books, Writing Books, Offering Motivational Speaking

Favorite Business Publications: Time; Newsweek

Hobbies/Interests/Sports: Singing

Education Degrees: Ph.D. in United States History, Howard University, Washington, DC (1991); Master of Arts in Church History, Ashland Theological Seminary, OH (1983); Bachelor of Arts in Business Administration, Malone College (1981); Higher National Diploma in Estate Management, The Polytechnic Calabar, Nigeria (1979)

Awards/Honors: Irwin Award for Best International Campaign (2005); LABBE Award for the Book 'Recipe for Success' (2005); Leadership Award, Akwa Ibom State Association of Nigeria, USA, Inc. (2005)

Charity/Volunteer Work: Public Speaker, Church of the Living God, Hyattsville, MD

Expanded Biography: Dr. Etuk has published a book entitled 'The Indispensable Visionary.' He travels worldwide to give motivational speeches, conduct seminars and workshops on the topics of leadership and success.

ENTREPRENEUR OF THE YEAR IN ESTHETICS

MS. CONNIE FALFAN

Managing Director
San Miguel Spa and Skin Care
435 S. Curson Avenue
Apartment 6B
Los Angeles, CA 90036 United States
conniefalfan@hotmail.com
http://www.sanmiguelspa.net

Type of Business: Medispa and High Tech Salon

Major Products and Services: Esthetic and Medical Services, NeoSatin Skin Care Products

Marketing Area: Local

Area of Expertise: Ms. Falfan's expertise is in laser skin care and esthetics training.

Day to Day Responsibilities: Managing Operations

Favorite Business Publications: Skin Inc.

Hobbies/Interests/Sports: Running, Reading, Writing, Exercising

Education Degrees: Associate Degree in Psychology, Los Angeles City College

Certifications: Certification in Advanced Esthetics Program

Charity/Volunteer Work: Social Services; Domestic Violence; Women's Shelter

What do you attribute your success to? She attributes her success to her love for what she does and constant pursuit of education.

How did you become involved in your profession? She became involved in her profession because of her interest in skin care and desire to develop quality skin care products.

What was the highlight of your career? The highlight of her career was having her business expand to four other locations.

PROFESSIONAL OF THE YEAR IN PHYSICAL CHEMISTRY

MILTON FARBER

President
Space Sciences, Inc.
135 W. Maple Avenue
Monrovia, CA 91016 United States
milton.farber@cwwemail.com
http://www.cambridgewhoswho.com

Type of Business: Research Center

Major Products and Services: Space Research and Development

Marketing Area: International

Area of Expertise: Mr. Farber's expertise is in physical chemistry.

Favorite Business Publications: ACS Journal; APS Journal

Hobbies/Interests/Sports: Skiing, Playing Tennis, Hiking

Education Degrees: Ph.D., University of Western California (1970); Master's Degree in Chemical Engineering and Chemistry, University of Minnesota (1939); Bachelor's Degree in Chemistry, University of California (1938)

Affiliations/Associations/Societies: American Chemical Society; American Physical Society; ICI

Date of Birth: October 6, 1916   **Place of Birth:** Los Angeles, CA

Spouse: Constance   **Children:** Robert, Richard, Kathleen

Work History: Technologist, Aerojet Electronic Systems Division, Hughes Aircraft Company (1956-1957); Technologist, Jet Propulsion Laboratory, California Institute of Technology (1946-1956)

Expanded Biography: Mr. Farber has published more than 150 articles and enjoys public speaking. He works with electric utility companies, helping to reduce air pollution and improve electrical transformer life. He received United States patent 3768232 for inventing a solvent recovery system in 1972 and United States patent 5659126 for inventing gas chromatography in 1977. He is the author of segments in numerous publications including 'Effect of Gravitational Field in the Thermal Diffusion Separation Method'; 'Solution of Thermochemical Propellant Calculations in a High-Speed Digital Computer'; 'The Vaporization of Graphite Filament'; 'Thermodynamic Properties of the Fluorine Atom and Molecule and Hydrogen Fluoride to 5000 Degrees'; 'Theoretical Study of Recombination Kinetics of Atomic Oxygen'; 'The Thermodynamic and Physical Properties of Beryllium Compounds' and 'A Mass Spectrometric Investigation of Additions in Alkali Seeded H2/O2 Flames.'

EXECUTIVE OF THE YEAR IN AUTOMOTIVE INDUSTRY

NANCY L. FEIN

Vice President of Lexus Customer Service
Toyota Motor Sales, USA
19001 S. Western Avenue
Torrance, CA 90501 United States
nancy_fein@lexus.com
http://www.cambridgewhoswho.com

Type of Business: Automotive Company

Major Products and Services: Automobile Products and Services, Sales, Customer Service, Repair

Marketing Area: National

Day to Day Responsibilities: Overseeing the Service and Parts Department, Ensuring Customer Satisfaction, Facilitating Training Activities

Hobbies/Interests/Sports: Scuba Diving, Flying Airplanes, Golfing

Education Degrees: Master's Degree in Management, University of California at Los Angeles (1989); Bachelor's Degree in Mathematics, Rochester Institute of Technology (1976)

Affiliations/Associations/Societies: Board of Trustees, Rochester Institute of Technology; Board of Managers, San Pedro and Peninsula YMCA; Peninsula Education Foundation

Awards/Honors: Automotive All Star Team (2006); Top 100 Women in the Automotive Industry

Date of Birth: November 22, 1953   **Place of Birth:** Rochester, New York

Spouse: Les

Work History: Eastman Kodak Company (1976-1982); Toyota Motor Sales USA: Vice President, Lexus Customer Service, General Manager, Kansas City Region, Assistant General Manager, Los Angeles Region, Management Positions in Sales, Sales Training, Parts and Service

Career Achievements: Feature, Automotive News (2005)

Expanded Biography: Ms. Fein is active in a number of volunteer organizations.

PROFESSIONAL OF THE YEAR IN MEDICAL ONCOLOGY

KAREN M. FERGUSON, PA-C

Medical Oncology Physician Assistant
South Carolina Oncology Associates
166 Stoneridge Drive
Columbia, SC 29210 United States
kferguson@sconcology.net
http://www.sconcology.net

Type of Business: Medical Center

Major Products and Services: Oncology Treatment Services

Marketing Area: Regional

Area of Expertise: Ms. Ferguson's expertise includes hematology and oncology assistance.

Day to Day Responsibilities: Assisting Doctors with Radiation Oncology, Caring for Patients

Favorite Business Publications: Clinical Advisor

Hobbies/Interests/Sports: Traveling, Kayaking, Swimming, Bicycling, Hiking, Camping, Landscaping, Gardening, Making Jewelry, Watching Movies, Attending the Theater, Dancing, Reading, Collecting Rare Glass Items, Playing Musical Instruments

Education Degrees: Post-Graduate Fellowship in Adult Oncology, The University of Texas MD Anderson Cancer Center (2003); Master of Science in Physician Assistant Studies, Central Michigan University (2002); Associate of Applied Science in Dental Hygiene, Delta College, University Center, MI (1984)

Certifications: Registered Dental Hygienist, State of Michigan (2000); Licensed Dental Hygienist, State of Michigan; Certified Dental Hygienist, State of Michigan; Certified Physician Assistant, State of South Carolina; Certification in Basic Cardiac Life Support; Certification, National Committee on Certification of Physician Assistants

Affiliations/Associations/Societies: Fundraiser, Chairwoman, Board Member, Mortar Board National College Senior Honor Society; American Academy of Physician Assistants

Charity/Volunteer Work: Volunteer, Central Michigan University; Saluki Club of America; Mission Trip, Russia; Adult Supervisor, Boy Scouts of America

Date of Birth: May 1, 1958   **Place of Birth:** Bay City

Children: Amanda, Nicholas

Work History: Physician Assistant in Medical Oncology/Hematology, South Carolina Oncology Associates (2003-2008)

What do you attribute your success to? She attributes her success to her hard work, dedication and education.

How did you become involved in your profession? She became involved in her profession because she was always interested in the medical field, and was drawn to the multidisciplinary approach to patient care.

What was the highlight of your career? The highlight of her career was earning her current position.

Where will you be in five years? In five years, Ms. Ferguson intends to continue working in radiation oncology.

Expanded Biography: Ms. Ferguson is a dental hygienist of 20 years with a specialty in periodontal diseases. She is involved with several professional speaking programs and educates her colleagues about products that can improve patients' health and quality of life.

PROFESSIONAL OF THE YEAR IN PULMONARY ARTERIAL HYPERTENSION

CYNTHIA A. FINK

Pulmonary Vascular Care Nurse Consultant
Pulmonary Vascular Care Consulting
pvcconsulting@yahoo.com
http://www.cambridgewhoswho.com

Type of Business: Healthcare Consulting Firm

Major Products and Services: Support for Pulmonary Hypertension Center Business Development, Building Clinical Databases for Overall Practice Analysis and Quality Improvement, Individualized and Comprehensive Patient and Family Education Booklets for each Pulmonary Hypertension Clinic

Marketing Area: National

Area of Expertise: Ms. Fink's expertise is in medical and community education consultancy with regard to pulmonary arterial hypertension.

Day to Day Responsibilities: Supporting Pulmonary Hypertension Programs and Clinics for Outstanding Pulmonary Hypertension Patient Care

Hobbies/Interests/Sports: Making Crafts, Quilting, Gardening, Woodworking, Caring for her Pets

Education Degrees: Bachelor of Science in Nursing, University of Evansville (1984)

Certifications: Certification, Critical Care Nursing; Certification in the Insertion and Maintenance of Peripherally Inserted Central Catheters

Affiliations/Associations/Societies: Pre-Hospital Registered Nurse Education Committee; Speaker, National Pulmonary Hypertension Association Convention

Awards/Honors: Nominee, Vanderbilt Staff Nurse of the Year Award; Norma J. Shepherd Award for Excellence in Critical Care Nursing, University of Tennessee

Expanded Biography: Ms. Fink delivers speeches at local conferences and various state and community colleges.

PROFESSIONAL OF THE YEAR IN
REAL ESTATE

Ms. Muriel E. Fisher

Realtor
Metro Referrals
11351 Random Hills Road
Fairfax, VA 22030 United States
muriel68@verizon.net
http://www.cambridgewhoswho.com

Type of Business: Real Estate Agency

Major Products and Services: Commercial and Residential Real Estate Exchange

Marketing Area: Statewide

Day to Day Responsibilities: Assisting First-Time Home Buyers

Favorite Business Publications: Southern Living

Hobbies/Interests/Sports: Barrel Horse Racing, Spending Time with her Grandchildren and Great-Grandchildren

Certifications: Licensed Real Estate Agent, State of Virginia (1989); Certification, Graduate Realtor Institute

Affiliations/Associations/Societies: Virginia Association of Realtors; Northern Virginia Association of Realtors; National Association of Realtors; Virginia Quarter Horse Association; National Quarter Horse Association

What do you attribute your success to? She attributes her success to her persistence.

How did you become involved in your profession? She became involved in her profession because she frequently moved herself and wanted to learn the business.

What was the highlight of your career? The most gratifying aspect of her career is finding a home for a first-time home buyer.

EXECUTIVE OF THE YEAR IN
NETWORK MARKETING

LAURA J. FLETCHER

Executive National Vice President
Arbonne International
9067 Forrest Drive
Highlands Ranch, CO 80126 United States
laurafletcher@comcast.net
http://www.arbonne.com

Type of Business: Network Marketing of Skin Care and Health Products

Major Products and Services: Skin Care Products, Body Care, Aromatherapy, Color, Weight Loss, Nutrition, Baby Care

Marketing Area: International

Day to Day Responsibilities: Training, Public Speaking, Recruiting

Favorite Business Publications: Network Marketing, Entrepreneur

Hobbies/Interests/Sports: Traveling, Music, Going to the Theater

Education Degrees: Coursework in Secretarial Administration and Business, Multnomah College, OR (1954); Ongoing Arbonne Training

Affiliations/Associations/Societies: Chamber of Commerce

PROFESSIONAL OF THE YEAR IN
RESPIRATORY THERAPY INSTRUCTION

LOUISE FOLEY

Instructor of Respiratory Therapy, Air Force Lieutenant Colonel (Retired)
Pima Medical Institute
3350 E. Grant Road
Tuscon, AZ 85716 United States
Louise@wvcnet.com
http://www.pmi.edu

Type of Business: Medical Career College

Major Products and Services: Medical Education and Training, Certificate and Associate Degree Programs

Marketing Area: Local

Day to Day Responsibilities: Teaching Core Classes in Respiratory Therapeutics, Specializing in Respiratory Therapy

Favorite Business Publications: Industry-Related Magazines

Hobbies/Interests/Sports: Reading, Crocheting, Spending Time with her Two Puppies, Photography

Education Degrees: Associate Degree in Respiratory Therapy, Pima Medical Institute (1995); Master of Education in Guidance and Counseling, Central State University (1981); Bachelor's Degree in Secondary Education, University of South Carolina (1971)

Affiliations/Associations/Societies: American Association for Respiratory Care; Air Force Association; Retired Military Officers Association of America; Kappa Delta Phi; Lambda Beta Honor Society

Work History: Former Executive Officer-Squadron Commander, Commander Assistant (1991); Air Force-Lieutenant Colonel (1971-1992)

PROFESSIONAL OF THE YEAR IN PSYCHIATRY

LORNA M. FORBES, MD

Medical Doctor, Psychiatrist, Forensic Consultant
Lorna M. Forbes, MD
2055 N. Garey Avenue, Suite 6
Pomona, CA 91767 United States
lorna.forbes1@verizon.net
http://www.cambridgewhoswho.com

Type of Business: Private Psychiatry Practice

Major Products and Services: Psychiatry and Forensic Consulting Services

Marketing Area: Statewide

Area of Expertise: Ms. Forbes' expertise includes forensic court consulting and psychiatric services.

Favorite Business Publications: American Journal of Psychiatry

Hobbies/Interests/Sports: Planting Bonsai, Painting, Creating Needlepoint Work

Education Degrees: Residency Training Program in Psychiatry, Pacific State Hospital (1958); Residency Program in Surgery, Boston, MA (1951); Doctor of Medicine in Psychiatry, Women's Medical College (1946); Fellowship in Forensic Psychiatry

Affiliations/Associations/Societies: American Psychiatric Association; Los Angeles County Medical Association; Southern California Psychiatric Society; ALA

Spouse: Robert

Children: Holly, Victor, Bradford

What do you attribute your success to? She attributes her success to her hard work and competence.

How did you become involved in your profession? She became involved in her profession because she always wanted to work in the medical field.

What was the highlight of your career? The most gratifying aspect of her career is working on important cases where the courts defer to her expertise.

Expanded Biography: Ms. Forbes is a clinical professor at the University of Southern California School of Medicine, and a consultant for the state of California.

PROFESSIONAL OF THE YEAR IN HEALTHCARE INDUSTRY

HILARY E. FORD

Staff Nurse
The Ann Storck Center
871 S. Douglas Road
Pembroke Pines, FL 33025 United States
fordgh@hotmail.com
http://www.ascfl.org

Type of Business: Nationally Accredited, Highly Acclaimed Nonprofit Human Service Organization

Major Products and Services: Residential, Preschool, and Adult Day Training Services for Adults and Children, Life-Enriching Opportunities Including the Expressive Arts Program, Arts in Motion Program, Recreational Services, Annual Events and Celebrations, Assisting Those who are Physically and Mentally Challenged to Live as Normal as Possible

Marketing Area: National

Area of Expertise: Ms. Ford's expertise includes nursing and hospice care and orthopedics.

Day to Day Responsibilities: Working with Mentally and Physically Challenged People, Drawing Blood, Performing Staff Nurse Duties

Favorite Business Publications: Nursing2006, Mayo Clinic Newsletter, Nursing Magazine

Hobbies/Interests/Sports: Sewing, Painting, Gardening, Enjoying Contemporary and Christian Music, Piano Playing

Education Degrees: Coursework, BCC College

Certifications: Licensed Practical Nurse Diploma (1990); Certified Basic Life Support Instructor; Certified Phlebotomist

Charity/Volunteer Work: Holy Sacrament Episcopal Church; Broward Outreach Center; Meals on Wheels; Volunteer, Broward County School; Breakthrough Ministries; Local Fire Department; Habitat for Humanity; Church Sewing Ministry; Friends Reaching Friends Ministries

Date of Birth: March 1, 1948   **Place of Birth:** St. Andrews, Jamaica

Spouse: G. Henry

ENTREPRENEUR OF THE YEAR IN AUTHORSHIP AND MUSICAL COMPOSITION

PATTI FORTÉ

Writer, Author, Artist, Entrepreneur
661 Silver Lake Drive
Danville, CA 94526 United States
pcforte@earthlink.net
http://www.pattiforte.com

Type of Business: Sole Proprietorship

Major Products and Services: Poetry and Screenplay Writing, Artwork and Music Composition

Marketing Area: International

Day to Day Responsibilities: Writing Screenplays, Lyrics and Poetry, Composing Music

Favorite Business Publications: Time

Hobbies/Interests/Sports: Skiing, Hiking, Oil Painting

Education Degrees: Bachelor's Degree in Elementary Education, San Jose State University

Affiliations/Associations/Societies: American Business Women's Association; International Poetry Society; Founding Laureate, International Society of Poets

Expanded Biography: Ms. Forté has worked for the Junior Center of Art and Science, Family Service Guild, Cares and eWomenNetwork.

PROFESSIONAL OF THE YEAR IN
HEALTHCARE CASE MANAGEMENT

DONNA FOWLER BRIAN, RN, CCM, BSN, OCN

Registered Nurse, BSN, Case Manager
Louisville VA Medical Center Home
800 Zorn Avenue
Louisville, KY 40206 United States
donna.brian@va.gov
http://www.louisville.va.gov

Type of Business: Healthcare Center

Major Products and Services: Healthcare Services

Marketing Area: Regional

Day to Day Responsibilities: Caring for Oncology and Bone Marrow Transplant Patients, Counseling, Guiding the Staff, Managing Insurance

Favorite Business Publications: Nursing Made Easy

Hobbies/Interests/Sports: Swimming, Reading, Traveling, Sewing, Cooking, Gardening

Education Degrees: Pursuing Master's Degree, McKendree College; Bachelor of Science in Nursing, McKendree College; Associate Degree in Nursing, Jefferson Community College; Registered Nurse

Certifications: Certified Case Manager; Certified Oncology Nurse

Affiliations/Associations/Societies: Oncology Nursing Association

Charity/Volunteer Work: American Cancer Society

What do you attribute your success to? She attributes her success to her learning skills and ability to understand other's emotions.

How did you become involved in your profession? She became involved in her profession because she was inspired by her grandmother.

What was the highlight of your career? The highlight of her career was completing her bachelor's degree in 18 months at the age of 50.

Expanded Biography: Ms. Brian educates on non-smoking methods and public service awareness. She has also volunteered at state fairs and performed free melanoma screenings.

PROFESSIONAL OF THE YEAR IN
IT SERVICES IN HIGHER EDUCATION

Mr. Stephen L. Frazier

Chief Information Officer
Information Technology
California Maritime Academy
200 Maritime Academy Drive
Vallejo, CA 94590 United States
sfrazier@csum.edu
http://www.csum.edu/personal/sfrazier

Type of Business: Higher Education

Major Products and Services: Education

Marketing Area: Local

Area of Expertise: Mr. Frazier's expertise is in academic computing.

Favorite Business Publications: PMI, Academic Computing Magazine

Hobbies/Interests/Sports: Mountain Biking, Fresh and Salt Water Fishing, Trout Fishing, Canoeing, Kayaking, Computers, Spending Time with Family, Amateur Radio Operator

Education Degrees: Master's Degree in School Computer Studies, Northwest Missouri State University (1985), Bachelor of Arts, Biology and Psychology, Central Methodist College (1972)

Affiliations/Associations/Societies: Project Management Institute; Association of Computing Machinery; SIGUCCS; NERCOMP

Charity/Volunteer Work: Church of Jesus Christ of Latter Day Saints

Spouse: Evelyn Elaine   **Children:** Kimberly, Derek

What do you attribute your success to? He attributes his success to his staff and their knowledge and ability to work as a team.

How did you become involved in your profession? He became involved in his profession because of his passion for education and computers.

What was the highlight of your career? The highlight of his career was becoming a Chief Information Officer.

EXECUTIVE OF THE YEAR IN
CURRICULUM COORDINATION IN EDUCATION

MR. JAMES E. FRENCH

Division Chairman of Education
Missouri Baptist University
1 College Park Drive
James French Education Division
Saint Louis, MO 63141 United States
french@mobap.edu
http://www.mobap.edu

Type of Business: University

Major Products and Services: Educational Services

Marketing Area: International

Area of Expertise: Mr. French's expertise is in curriculum coordination for the entire division.

Day to Day Responsibilities: Overseeing 1990 Students, Handling Curriculum Offerings and Recommendations for Full and Part-Time Students and Faculty, Teaching Courses on Portfolio Development, Presenting Graduate and Undergraduate Strategies for the Brain

Favorite Business Publications: Educational Leadership

Hobbies/Interests/Sports: Reading, Traveling

Education Degrees: Master of Science in Education, Arkansas State University, Jonesboro (1964); Bachelor of Science in Education, Arkansas State University, Jonesboro (1964)

Affiliations/Associations/Societies: Association for Supervision and Curriculum Development; Missouri State Teachers Association; MSCD

Expanded Biography: Mr. French takes part in public speaking and workshops for compatible strategies to assist student learning. He has also authored various published works including 'The Arithmetic Teacher.' He has more than 47 years of experience in educational leadership.

PROFESSIONAL OF THE YEAR IN
ANESTHESIOLOGY

Mr. Charles A. Frisch, CRNA

Director of Anesthesia
Box Butte General Hospital
2101 Box Butte Avenue
Alliance, NE 69301 United States
chuckfri@bbc.net
http://www.cambridgewhoswho.com

Type of Business: Hospital

Major Products and Services: Healthcare

Marketing Area: Local

Day to Day Responsibilities: Managing Pain Using Anesthesia

Favorite Business Publications: Anesthesiologist

Hobbies/Interests/Sports: Traveling, Golfing, Camping, Remodeling his Home

Education Degrees: Fellowship in Pain Management; Master's Degree in Healthcare Administration, University of St. Francis; Bachelor's Degree in Anesthesia

Affiliations/Associations/Societies: Director, Nebraska Nurses Association; Association of periOperative Registered Nurses; American Academy of Pain Management; American Society of Regional Anesthesia and Pain Medicine; American Society of Anesthesiologists; American Association of Nurse Anesthetists

Expanded Biography: Mr. Frisch worked as chairman of anesthesia for a rural small hospital. He has 22 years of nursing experience.

PROFESSIONAL OF THE YEAR IN
GRAPHIC DESIGN IN EDUCATION

JUDITH A. FULLER

Graphic Designer
Valley Christian Schools
100 Skyway Drive, Suite 130
San Jose, CA 95111 United States
jfuller@vcs.net
http://www.vcs.net

Type of Business: School District

Major Products and Services: Education

Marketing Area: Regional

Area of Expertise: Ms. Fuller's expertise is in graphic design.

Day to Day Responsibilities: Designing School Advertisements, Teaching Sewing and Quilting

Favorite Business Publications: Journal of Graphic Design

Hobbies/Interests/Sports: Quilting, Knitting, Crocheting

Education Degrees: Bachelor of Arts in Visual Communication, American InterContinental University; Associate of Arts in Business, Concentration in Accounting, West Valley College

Certifications: Certification in Desktop Publishing and Design

Awards/Honors: Woman of the Year Award, American Biological Women's Advisory Board

Charity/Volunteer Work: Hillside Evangelical Free Church

Date of Birth: May 20, 1959   **Place of Birth:** Redwood City

Children: Robert, Joshua, Sarah

Work History: Administrative Assistant, Calvary Church; Teacher, Valley Christian Schools; Seamstress, The Dance Store

What do you attribute your success to? She attributes her success to her perseverance and her desire to learn.

How did you become involved in your profession? She became involved in her profession because she was always interested in graphic design.

EXECUTIVE OF THE YEAR IN RADIOLOGY INDUSTRY

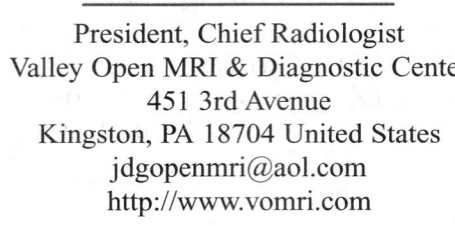

JUAN D. GAIA, MD

President, Chief Radiologist
Valley Open MRI & Diagnostic Center
451 3rd Avenue
Kingston, PA 18704 United States
jdgopenmri@aol.com
http://www.vomri.com

Type of Business: Open MRI and Diagnostic Center

Major Products and Services: All Imaging Modalities, Open MRI Scanner

Marketing Area: Regional

Day to Day Responsibilities: Offering Quality Assurance, Facilitating Efficiency in Daily Operating Procedures, Ensuring Patient Care, Offering Diagnostic Radiology Including Angiology, Mammography, Nuclear Medicine, CTs, Ultrasounds, MRI and Interventional Radiology, Offering CT and Ultrasound Guided Biopsy and Breast Mass Localization Techniques, Performing Peripheral Balloon Angiography Utilizing Inferior Vena Cava Filter Insertion

Favorite Business Publications: The American Journal of Roentgenology Interventional Radiology

Hobbies/Interests/Sports: Fly Fishing, Traveling

Education Degrees: Diagnostic Radiology Residency, Harrisburg Hospital, Harrisburg, Pennsylvania (1973-1975); Rotating Internship, Elyria Memorial Hospital, Elyria, OH (1972-1972); Rotating Internship, Emilio Civit Hospital, Hospital Central de Mendoza and Lagomaggiore Hospital (1970); Doctor of Medicine, Universidad Nacional de Cuyo Facultad de Ciencias Médicas, Mendoza, Argentina (1963-1969); Bachelor of Science, Liceo Agricola y Enológico Domingo Faustino Sarmiento, Mendoza, Argentina (1957-1969)

Certifications: Certified in Vascular and Biliary Wallstent

Affiliations/Associations/Societies: Medical Director, Sonography Program, Lackawanna College; Board Member, Luzerne County Medical Society; American College of Angiology (1984-Present); American College of Radiology (1975-Present); American Medical Association (1976-Present); Pennsylvania Radiological Society (1976-Present); Dauphin County Medical Society (1973-1975); Pennsylvania Medical Society (1972-Present); Radiological Society of North America; Physician Delegate (1998); President, Luzerne County Medical Society (1991-1992); Medical Advisor, Wilkes University Board of Education (1991-1992)

Charity/Volunteer Work: Participant, Denim Day, Breast Cancer Awareness (2003-2004); Sponsor, Pink Ribbon Ball, American Cancer Society (2003); Sponsor, Jingle Bell Run, Arthritis Foundation (2003); Relay for Life, American Cancer Society (2002-2004); Heartwalk Sponsor, American Heart Association (2001); United Way of Wyoming Valley

Date of Birth: July 13, 1944   **Place of Birth:** Mendoza

Work History: Radiologist, Valley Open MRI & Diagnostic Center (Previously Valley Radiology Associates), Kingston, Pennsylvania (July 1979-Present); Professional Consultant, Community Medical Center, Scranton, Pennsylvania (2000-2003); Professional Consultant, Physician's Imaging Center of Wyoming Valley, Wilkes Barre, Pennsylvania (1996-2000); Chairman, Radiology Department, Mercy Hospital, Wilkes Barre, Pennsylvania (1992-1996); Staff Radiologist, Mercy Hospital (1976-1996); Staff Radiologist, Wyoming Valley Imaging Center (MRI), Wilkes Barre, Pennsylvania (19985-1995); Professional Consultant, Veteran's Administration Medical Center, Wilkes Barre, Pennsylvania (1979-1994); Radiology Instructor, United Health & Hospital Services, Inc. Family Practice Residency Program, Kingston, Pennsylvania (1978-1982); Radiology Instructor, Advisor, Hahnemann Medical College and Hospital of Philadelphia-Wilkes University, Wilkes Barre, Pennsylvania (1978-1980); Consultant Radiologist, Hospital Espanol de Mendoza, Mendoza, Argentina (1969-1977); Armed Forces Institute of Pathology, Registry of Radiology Pathology, Washington, DC (May 6, 1974-June 23, 1974); Radiology Instructor, Universidad Nacional de Cuyo, Facultad de Medicina, Mendoza, Argentina (1968-1970)

Expanded Biography: Dr. Gaia has been in practice in the Wyoming Valley more than 30 years. Valley Open MRI represents his commitment to bring the community the most sophisticated imaging resources available anywhere and thus eliminate the need for residents to have to travel to New York or Philadelphia to gain access to such technology. 'The foundation of this technological commitment is an absolute dedication to the physical and emotional comfort of every patient and the clinical needs of their physician. The patient is the center of attention,' says Gaia. The physicians and staff at Valley Open MRI have the skill, experience, expertise and training in the latest techniques required to provide imaging services of the highest quality to the physicians and residents of their community. The physicians and staff are dedicated to offering patients the best quality imaging and evaluation. They strive to provide an environment that affords convenience, privacy and comfort, with a caring staff of professional and specially trained radiologists and technologists. Dr. Gaia is also medical director of the Diagnostic Medical Sonography program at Lackawanna College in Scranton, Pennsylvania.

PROFESSIONAL OF THE YEAR IN
ICU NURSING AND RESPIRATORY CARE

RICHARD ALLEN GANDY, RRT-NPS, RPFT, RN, RCP

Nurse
Intensive Care Unit
Memorial Health System of East Texas
1201 W. Frank Avenue
Lufkin, TX 75904 United States
rgandy@valornet.com
http://www.cambridgewhoswho.com

Type of Business: Healthcare Center

Major Products and Services: Healthcare and Acute Care Services

Marketing Area: Local

Area of Expertise: Mr. Gandy's expertise is in critical and respiratory care nursing.

Day to Day Responsibilities: Assisting the Doctor in Cardiovascular Surgery, Overseeing Intensive Care Unit Operations

Hobbies/Interests/Sports: Scuba Diving, Teaching Aerobics, Participating in Athletics, Traveling, Studying

Education Degrees: Pursuing Bachelor's Degree; Associate Degree in Nursing, Excelsior College; Associate in Applied Arts and Science, California College

Certifications: Certified Personal Trainer; Certified Group Fitness Instructor

Affiliations/Associations/Societies: Pinewoods District TCRC; Texas Nurses Association; Texas Society for Respiratory Care; American Association for Respiratory Care

Charity/Volunteer Work: March of Dimes Foundation; Bowl-A-Thon; Relay for Life, American Cancer Society; Heart Walk, American Heart Association

What do you attribute your success to? He attributes his success to his desire to learn, dedication and to the support he receives from his parents.

How did you become involved in your profession? He became involved in his profession because of his interest in the medical field.

What was the highlight of your career? The most gratifying aspect of his career is helping people every day.

Where will you be in five years? In five years, Mr. Gandy hopes to obtain his bachelor's degree.

EXECUTIVE OF THE YEAR IN HOSPITALITY

Erika L. Garcia

Chief Executive Officer
Cancun Premier Vacations
Sunset Group
444 Brickell Avenue, Suite 51-334
Miami, FL 33131 United States
erikafit@hotmail.com
egarcia@premiercancunvacations.com
http://www.sunsetworld.net

Type of Business: Hotel

Major Products and Services: Hospitality Services, Food and Beverage Services and Entertainment Programs

Marketing Area: International

Day to Day Responsibilities: Working with the Orlando and Miami Communities, Building Relationships, Marketing, Assisting Tourists to Local Destinations and Cancun

Favorite Business Publications: Entrepreneur; Harvard Business Review

Hobbies/Interests/Sports: Playing Soccer, Running

Education Degrees: Bachelor of Arts in Mass Communication, University of California, Irvine; Coursework in Leadership Studies, Mexico City

Affiliations/Associations/Societies: Cancun Hotel Association; American Resort Development Association; CCE; WPSA

Awards/Honors: Bid Award, International Quality Summit, New York

Work History: Sales Director, Sunset Resorts (1996-2000)

EXECUTIVE OF THE YEAR IN MEDICAL RESEARCH

MR. MICHAEL H. GARFIELD

Chief Executive Officer, Chairman
Global Medical Research, LLC
807 W. Morse Boulevard, Suite 202
Winter Park, FL 32789 United States
mgarfield@gmrllc.com
http://www.gmrllc.com

Type of Business: Preeminent Medical Research Company

Major Products and Services: Medical Devices, Research and Development

Marketing Area: International

Day to Day Responsibilities: Offering the Strategic Direction and Leadership, Overseeing Daily Operations, Coordinating Departments, Assessing Product Development

Hobbies/Interests/Sports: Golfing, Softball, Basketball

Education Degrees: Coursework, North Adams State College

Spouse: Daryl   **Children:** Mandi, Jessica, Jason

PROFESSIONAL OF THE YEAR IN FASHION CONSULTING

MS. GLORIA GELFAND

President
Gelfand Marketing Solutions
1410 Broadway
New York, NY 10018 United States
ggelfand@pinsmail.net
http://www.cambridgewhoswho.com

Type of Business: Marketing Firm

Major Products and Services: Merchandising, Consulting Services for Women's Fashion Industry

Marketing Area: Regional

Area of Expertise: Ms. Gelfand's expertise is in merchandising.

Day to Day Responsibilities: Managing the Start-Up Company, Consulting on Structure and Framework, Marketing Niche Products

Favorite Business Publications: Women's Wear Daily; In Style; W; The Week

Hobbies/Interests/Sports: Spending Time with her Five Grandchildren

Education Degrees: Bachelor of Science in Fashion, Fashion Institute of Technology, NY (1947)

Affiliations/Associations/Societies: Board of Directors, Retail Marketing Society; President, Trends; Fashion Group International; Laboratory Institute of Merchandising

What do you attribute your success to? She attributes her success to the support she receives from her mentors.

How did you become involved in your profession? She became involved in her profession after working at several top international design houses including Escada and Louis Féraud.

What was the highlight of your career? The most gratifying aspect of her career is being able to train her protégées.

Expanded Biography: Ms. Gelfand was one among the panel of industry professionals selected for the Gotham Center for New York City History at The CUNY Graduate Center's evening of stores called 'From RAGS to Riches.'

PROFESSIONAL OF THE YEAR IN
CONSTRUCTION PROJECT MANAGEMENT

CYNTHIA A. GIBSON

Project Manager
Barnard & Sons Construction, LLC
3054 Simpson Hwy 13
Mendenhall, MS 39114 United States
cindy@barnardandsons.com
http://www.barnardandsons.com

Type of Business: Commercial Construction

Major Products and Services: Construction

Marketing Area: Regional

Area of Expertise: Ms. Gibson's expertise is in construction project coordination.

Favorite Business Publications: Construction News Magazine

Hobbies/Interests/Sports: Salt Water Fishing, Gardening, Horses

Education Degrees: College Coursework in Drafting, LaSalle University; Coursework in Safety Management

Affiliations/Associations/Societies: Former Vice-President, National Association of Women in Construction, Jackson, MS

Date of Birth: December 26, 1956   **Place of Birth:** Bogalusa

Spouse: Malcolm

Work History: Painting Contractor, Plumbing Contractor, Construction Project Superintendent, Assistant Project Superintendent, Assistant Project Manager, Project Manager

PROFESSIONAL OF THE YEAR IN
LIBRARY MEDIA MANAGEMENT

MRS. KIMBERLY GINGHER

Library Media Specialist
Knox Middle School
Knox Community School Corporation
901 S. Main Street
Knox, IN 46534 United States
kgingher@knox.k12.in.us
http://ms.knox.k12.in.us

Type of Business: School District

Major Products and Services: Education

Marketing Area: Regional

Area of Expertise: Mrs. Gingher's expertise is in bibliographic instruction for children and young adults.

Favorite Business Publications: School Library Journal

Hobbies/Interests/Sports: Reading, Making Crafts

Education Degrees: Master's Degree in Library Science, Indiana University (1990); Master of Education, Indiana University (1983); Bachelor of Liberal Arts, DePauw University

Affiliations/Associations/Societies: Association for Indiana Media Educators; Indiana Library Federation; American Library Association

What was the highlight of your career? The most gratifying aspect of her career is making the children to read.

Expanded Biography: Mrs. Gingher has attended the Educational Technology Endorsement program and the Library Endorsement program.

PROFESSIONAL OF THE YEAR IN JEWELRY DESIGN

KATHY A. GLASS

Owner
Glass Jewelers
3260 Sherwood Way
San Angelo, TX 76901 United States
info@glassjewelers.com
http://www.glassjewelers.com

Type of Business: Jewelry Store

Major Products and Services: Retail Sales, Repairs, Custom Manufactured, Gold, Sterling Silver, One-of-a-Kind Concho Pearl Jewelry

Marketing Area: Local

Day to Day Responsibilities: Offering Goldsmith Services, Designing, Engraving and Casting Custom Pieces

Favorite Business Publications: Instore

Hobbies/Interests/Sports: Hunting, Bowling, Motorcycle Riding

What do you attribute your success to? She attributes her success to support from her family.

How did you become involved in your profession? She became involved in her profession because she comes from five generations of jewelry designers and goldsmiths.

Expanded Biography: Ms. Glass has thirty-two years of experience in the jewelry industry. She has been married for thirty years and has three sons and two grandchildren.

PROFESSIONAL OF THE YEAR IN BUSINESS ADMINISTRATION

LAURA MARINA GOMEZ

Administrative and Accounts Manager
Artex USA-Brenham Texas
6351 Highway 36 S.
Brenham, TX 77833 United States
laura@artex-usa.com
http://www.artex-usa.com

Type of Business: Manufacturing Company

Major Products and Services: Wireline Equipment Including Trucks

Marketing Area: International

Area of Expertise: Ms. Gomez's expertise includes accounting and finance management.

Day to Day Responsibilities: Overseeing the Staff, Reviewing Balance Sheets and Taxes for the Company, Training New Employees

Favorite Business Publications: National Geographic; Discover

Hobbies/Interests/Sports: Flamenco, Jazz and Belly Dancing, Reading

Education Degrees: Bachelor of Science, Double Major in Spanish Literature and Radio-Television-Film, Texas Christian University (2002)

Certifications: Certification in Occupational Safety and Health Administration

Affiliations/Associations/Societies: National Geographic Society

Charity/Volunteer Work: The Leukemia & Lymphoma Society; The American Society for the Prevention of Cruelty to Animals; The National Children's Cancer Society; Greater Good Network

What do you attribute your success to? She attributes her success to her hard work, desire to learn and her ability to utilize the opportunities that came her way.

How did you become involved in your profession? She became involved in her profession because of her desire to work in a challenging field.

What was the highlight of your career? The most gratifying aspects of her career are seeing the growth of her company and her ability to maintain a healthy balance between her work and her family life.

EXECUTIVE OF THE YEAR IN
HEALTHCARE CODING, COMPLIANCE AND STANDARDIZATION

SARAH L. GOODMAN, MBA, CPC-H, CCP, FCS

President, Chief Executive Officer
SLG, Inc.
P.O. Box 37626
Raleigh, NC 27627 United States
slgincconsulting@aol.com
http://www.slgincconsulting.com

Type of Business: Medical Coding Company

Major Products and Services: Coding, Compliance and Standardization Services for Hospitals, Corporate Healthcare Entities and Healthcare Providers

Marketing Area: National

Day to Day Responsibilities: Overseeing Chargemaster Coding, Compliance and Standardization Processes

Favorite Business Publications: Healthcare Financial Management

Hobbies/Interests/Sports: Painting, Drawing, Traveling

Education Degrees: Master of Business Administration, Binghamton University (1991); Bachelor of Arts in Fine Arts, Binghamton University (1984); Associate of Science in Liberal Arts (1981)

Affiliations/Associations/Societies: Region III Governor, Board of Governors, American College of Medical Coding Specialists (2007-Present); Former President, National Advisory Board, American Academy of Professional Coders (2002-2005); Board of Directors, North Carolina Chapter, Healthcare Financial Management Association (2002-2004); Chairwoman, Hospital Services Committee, North Carolina Chapter, Health Care Compliance Association (1999-2001); American Health Information Management Association

Awards/Honors: WakeMed Cary Hospital; Junior League of Raleigh; Wake County Public School System

Work History: Senior Chargemaster Specialist, Tenet HealthSystem Medical, Inc., Nashville, TN (1995-1997); Various Financial Positions, Lourdes Hospital, Binghamton, NY (1982-1995)

Expanded Biography: Ms. Goodman previously worked at Lourdes Hospital in Binghamton, NY for 13 years and has been featured in several healthcare newsletters and publications. SLG, Inc. was incorporated in 1998.

PROFESSIONAL OF THE YEAR IN ONCOLOGY

CRAIG J. GORDON, DO, FACOI

Director of Hematology and Oncology
Clinical Oncology Associates
Botsford Hospital
30160 Orchard Lake Road
Farmington Hills, MI 48334 United States
gordondo@comcast.net
http://www.cambridgewhoswho.com

Type of Business: Hospital

Major Products and Services: Healthcare

Marketing Area: Local

Area of Expertise: Dr. Gordon's expertise includes hematology and oncology.

Favorite Business Publications: American Journal of Clinical Oncology

Hobbies/Interests/Sports: Studying Electronics and Astronomy

Education Degrees: Doctor of Osteopathy, College of Osteopathic Medicine, Des Moines University

Certifications: Board Certification in Medical Oncology and Internal Medicine

Affiliations/Associations/Societies: Oakland County Osteopathic Medical Association; Michigan Osteopathic Association; American Osteopathic Association; Fellow, American College of Osteopathic Internists

Date of Birth: February 10, 1953   **Place of Birth:** Detroit

Spouse: Susan   **Children:** Sari, Scott, Brittany

What do you attribute your success to? He attributes his success to his hard work.

How did you become involved in your profession? He became involved in his profession because of the experiences he had with his parents, who were affected by cancer.

What was the highlight of your career? The highlight of his career was conducting research on breast and pancreatic cancers.

Where will you be in five years? In five years, Dr. Gordon intends to continue in the same profession.

PROFESSIONAL OF THE YEAR IN
PHARMACEUTICAL RESEARCH, DEVELOPMENT AND MANUFACTURING

MR. JACK Z. GOUGOUTAS

Distinguished Research Fellow
Bristol-Myers Squibb
Rt. 206 Province Line Road
Princeton, NJ 08540 United States
gougoutj@bms.com
http://www.bms.com

Type of Business: Pharmaceuticals

Major Products and Services: Research and Development, Manufacture of Pharmaceuticals

Marketing Area: International

Area of Expertise: Mr. Gougoutas' expertise includes solid state chemistry and crystallography.

Education Degrees: Ph.D. in Chemistry, Harvard University (1965)

Affiliations/Associations/Societies: ACA

Expanded Biography: Mr. Gougoutas is the author of hundreds of publications.

EXECUTIVE OF THE YEAR IN EDUCATIONAL LEADERSHIP

MS. BARBARA L. GRAY

President
Shelby County Education Association
6259 Stage Plaza E.
Bartlett, TN 38134 United States
sceapres@bellsouth.net
http://www.shelbycea.org/about_us.html

Type of Business: Educational Association

Major Products and Services: Education

Marketing Area: Local

Area of Expertise: Ms. Gray's expertise is in middle school administration.

Day to Day Responsibilities: Supervising, Teaching Instruction Techniques to Teachers, Mentoring, Developing the Curriculum

Favorite Business Publications: NEA Today; TEACH Magazine

Hobbies/Interests/Sports: Reading, Walking, Participating in Youth Activities

Education Degrees: Master of Education in Curriculum and Instruction, Plus 30, University of Memphis; Bachelor's Degree in Chemistry, The LeMoyne-Owen College

Certifications: Certification in Administration; Certification in Supervision

Affiliations/Associations/Societies: Board Member, Personnel Appeals, City of Millington, TN; National Science Teachers Association; National Council of Teachers of Mathematics; Association for Supervision and Curriculum Development

Awards/Honors: Teacher of the Year Award; National and State Lifetime Membership Award, National Parent Teacher Association

Charity/Volunteer Work: Millington Church of Christ; United Way of America; Susan G. Komen for the Cure

What was the highlight of your career? The most gratifying aspect of her career is seeing her students succeed and become productive citizens.

PROFESSIONAL OF THE YEAR IN OSTEOPATHIC MEDICINE

DR. GINA C. GRECO

Doctor
East Meadow Family Practice
2840 Jerusalem Avenue
Wantagh, NY 11793 United States
davidgmdmmm@aol.com
http://www.cambridgewhoswho.com

Type of Business: Healthcare Facility, Leading Family Practice

Major Products and Services: General and Family Medicine, Internal Medicine, General Pediatrics

Marketing Area: Regional

Day to Day Responsibilities: Diagnosing Illnesses, Prescribing and Administering Treatment for People Suffering from Injury or Disease, Examining Patients, Obtaining Medical Histories, Ordering, Performing and Interpreting Diagnostic Tests, Counseling Patients on Diet, Hygiene, and Preventive Health Care

Favorite Business Publications: American Family Physician

Hobbies/Interests/Sports: Playing and Coaching Soccer, Skiing, Hiking, Gardening, Spending Time with Family

Education Degrees: Doctor of Osteopathic Medicine, New York College of Osteopathic Medicine (1990); Bachelor of Science in Biology, SUNY Stony Brook

Certifications: Board Certified in Family Practice

Affiliations/Associations/Societies: American Osteopathic Association; The Medical Society of Nassau County; The Medical Society of the State of New York; American College of Osteopathic Family Physicians; American Academy of Family Physicians

Work History: Assistant Professor of Family Practice, New York College of Osteopathic Medicine (1994, 1997)

EXECUTIVE OF THE YEAR IN MEDICAL CONSTRUCTION

CHARLES COLEMAN GREGORY JR.

President
The Eden Group, Inc.
229 Retama Place
San Antonio, TX 78209 United States
sunny.gregory@sbcglobal.net
http://www.cambridgewhoswho.com

Type of Business: Construction Company

Major Products and Services: Construction Services for Medical Industry

Marketing Area: Regional

Area of Expertise: Mr. Gregory's expertise is in current trend analysis.

Favorite Business Publications: Fortune

Hobbies/Interests/Sports: Golfing, Attending the Church

Education Degrees: Coursework in Law and Mechanical Engineering; Bachelor's Degree in Economics, St. Mary's University

Charity/Volunteer Work: Local Church; Board of Directors, Boysville; Shriners Club; Precinct Three, South County Constable Office

Children: Gail, Charles

What do you attribute your success to? He attributes his success to his father, who instilled a work ethic in him.

How did you become involved in your profession? He became involved in his profession because he was influenced by his father.

What was the highlight of your career? The highlight of his career was constructing the Pediatric Stem Cell Department for Methodist Hospital.

PROFESSIONAL OF THE YEAR IN
SALES AND FINANCE IN THE MICROBREWERY INDUSTRY

MS. JEANNE E. GROVER

Office Manager
Berkshire Brewing Company Inc.
12 Railroad Street
P.O. Box 141
South Deerfield, MA 01373 United States
mjbbc@comcast.net
http://www.berkshirebrewingcompany.com

Type of Business: Manufacturing Company

Major Products and Services: Beer Including Fine Ales and Lager

Marketing Area: MA, VT, RI and CT

Day to Day Responsibilities: Budgeting, Performing Massage Therapy, Overseeing Administrative Duties, Managing Human Resources, Finance and Sales

Favorite Business Publications: The New York Times; BusinessWeek

Hobbies/Interests/Sports: Practicing Yoga, Golfing, Walking, Gardening, Reading

Education Degrees: Pursuing Master's Degree in Education, Our Lady of the Elms College, Chicopee (Now Elms College); Bachelor of Science in Management, Our Lady of the Elms College, Chicopee (Now Elms College)

Certifications: Licensed Massage Therapist

Affiliations/Associations/Societies: Associated Bodywork & Massage Professionals

Charity/Volunteer Work: Massachusetts Society for the Prevention of Cruelty to Animals; The American Society for the Prevention of Cruelty to Animals

Place of Birth: Greenfield, Ma

Children: Abbigayle

What do you attribute your success to? She attributes her success to the support she receives from others.

How did you become involved in your profession? She became involved in her profession because she was referred by her friend.

What was the highlight of your career? The most gratifying aspect of her career is being successful in her profession.

PROFESSIONAL OF THE YEAR IN GENERAL DENTISTRY

BARBARA A. GUENTHER, DMD

Dentist
Northfield Family Dental Group
1423 Tilton Road, Suite 2
Northfield, NJ 08225 United States
drbarb1025@aol.com
http://www.cambridgewhoswho.com

Type of Business: Dental Clinic

Major Products and Services: Dental Care

Marketing Area: Local

Area of Expertise: Dr. Guenther's expertise is in general dentistry including the installation of Invisalign braces for adults and children.

Favorite Business Publications: Industry-Related Publications

Hobbies/Interests/Sports: Spending Time Outdoors, Traveling, Spending Time at the Church and Beach, Reading

Education Degrees: Doctor of Dental Medicine, University of Medicine and Dentistry of New Jersey

Affiliations/Associations/Societies: International Christian Medical and Dental Association; American Academy of General Dentistry

Charity/Volunteer Work: Trinity Alliance Church

What do you attribute your success to? She attributes her success to her faith in God and her desire to help people.

How did you become involved in your profession? She became involved in her profession because she started her career as a dental assistant and eventually progressed.

What was the highlight of your career? The most gratifying aspect of her career is her success.

Expanded Biography: Dr. Guenther has participated in multiple dental mission trips to Honduras, Haiti, Mali and Mexico.

PROFESSIONAL OF THE YEAR IN
COMPUTER CONSULTING SERVICE AND SUPPORT

PETER GULOTTA

Principal Consultant
Bobcat Consulting, LLC
1120 Dunsinane Hill
Chester Springs, PA 19425 United States
pete@bobcatconsulting.us
http://www.bobcatconsulting.us

Type of Business: Information Technology Consulting

Major Products and Services: HP Systems Administration to Small and Large Businesses, Comprehensive HP-UX and ServiceGuard Consulting Services, HP-UX Installation and Customization for New Servers, HP-UX Patch and System Update Services, HP-UX Performance Analysis and Tuning, ServiceGuard Installation and Configuration, System Recovery Assessment and Backup Planning, High Availability

Marketing Area: National

Day to Day Responsibilities: Managing HP-UX, ServiceGuard, Oracle, Client-Server Systems and Data Centers, Designing, Implementing and Troubleshooting Systems, Managing and Monitoring Performance Levels

Favorite Business Publications: Tech Republic

Hobbies/Interests/Sports: Cooking, Traveling

Education Degrees: Bachelor of Science in Computer Science, Drexel University

Affiliations/Associations/Societies: Computer Measurement Group; Usenix Association; The System Administrators Guild; Independent Computer Consultants Association; Information Technology Service Management Forum

Date of Birth: November 7, 1957

Work History: UNIX Team Leader, AlphaNet Solutions (2000); Systems Architect, North American Performance Group (1998-2000); Senior Consultant, Melillo Consulting

Career Achievements: Speaker, HP World Conference on High Availability Systems

Expanded Biography: Mr. Gulotta established his own consulting firm under the name Bobcat Consulting, LLC where he continues to be dedicated to the delivery of the highest quality consulting service and support. During his 26-year career, Mr. Gulotta has developed specific skills in the areas of UNIX performance management and tuning, high availability design and recovery strategies and overall distributed client-server systems management. He has specific expertise with the OpenView suite of tools in the area of systems and performance management. In addition, he has developed numerous policy and procedure documents currently in use in data centers throughout the United States. Through training, his years of experience and his extensive reading, he has acquired an intimate knowledge of the internals of HP-UX, the performance collection and analysis subsystem of HP-UX, the LVM subsystem of HP-UX, and ServiceGuard, the high availability software package from Hewlett-Packard. He also has a working knowledge of client-server networking protocols, including TCP/IP, and the related network implementation and management issues. Mr. Gulotta has put this knowledge to good use by playing an instrumental role as a technical lead in numerous system implementations, many in a SAP environment. He has also developed a solid understanding of the interrelationships between Oracle's database software and the UNIX operating system, specifically HP-UX. Much of his expertise in systems management has been applied in Oracle environments. He has transmitted much of his knowledge to end-user clients and other consultants through the many classes he has developed and taught, and the white papers he authored.

PROFESSIONAL OF THE YEAR IN INJECTION CLINIC MANAGEMENT

JUDY GUTHRIE, RN

Registered Nurse, Injection Clinic Manager
Kaiser Permanente
3755 Whispering Creek Circle
Stockton, CA 95219 United States
judy.guthrie@kp.org
http://www.kaiserpermanente.org

Type of Business: Healthcare Organization

Major Products and Services: Preventive Healthcare, Prenatal Healthcare, Well-Baby Healthcare, Immunizations, Emergency Well-Baby Healthcare, Diagnostic Screening, Hospital, Medical and Pharmacy Services, Assistance for the Uninsured and Special Needs Populations, Training New Health Professionals, Introduction of New Delivery Methods into the Healthcare Field

Marketing Area: Northern California Central Valley

Day to Day Responsibilities: Consulting Clients Regarding Routine and Travel Immunizations for Vaccine-Preventable Diseases

Favorite Business Publications: Nursing2009; Needle Tips and the Hepatitis B Coalition News; Journal Watch of Infectious Diseases; International Society of Travel Medicine Journal; Travel Med List Serve; GeoSentinel Alerts

Hobbies/Interests/Sports: Gardening, Spending Time with her Grandchildren, Studying Travel Medicine

Education Degrees: Associate Degree in Nursing, San Joaquin Delta College; Coursework in Epidemiology and Prevention of Vaccine-Preventable Diseases

Certifications: Certificate of Knowledge in Travel Health, The International Society of Travel Medicine

Affiliations/Associations/Societies: Alumni Association, San Joaquin Delta College; California Nurses Association; The International Society of Travel Medicine

Charity/Volunteer Work: Epilepsy Foundation of Northern California; Immunization Tracking System, Kaiser Permanente, NC; United Cerebral Palsy Research and Educational Foundation; Volunteer, United Way Annual Neighbors in Health; Immunization Action Coalition; Galt Historical Society; National Wildlife Federation

Date of Birth: January 10, 1944

ENTREPRENEUR OF THE YEAR IN MANUFACTURING

JOHN A. HAHN

Owner
Hahn Tractor Seats
509 E. Main Street
P.O. Box 370
Craigmont, ID 83523 United States
trseats@camasnet.com
http://www.hahn-tractor-seats.com

HAHN TRACTOR SEATS

Type of Business: Manufacturing Company

Major Products and Services: Antique Caterpillar Seats

Marketing Area: International

Day to Day Responsibilities: Managing Operations

Favorite Business Publications: Antique Caterpillar Machinery Owners Club Newsletter

Hobbies/Interests/Sports: Traveling, Attending Tractor Shows, Yard Work

Education Degrees: Associate Degree in Divinity

Affiliations/Associations/Societies: Board Member, The Lewis-Clark Antique Power Club; Antique Caterpillar Machinery Owners Club

Charity/Volunteer Work: Ordained Elder, Local Church

What do you attribute your success to? He attributes his success to his faith in God and to the support he receives from his father.

How did you become involved in your profession? He became involved in his profession because of his love of tractors and heavy machinery.

What was the highlight of your career? The most gratifying aspect of his career is shipping his products internationally.

Expanded Biography: Mr. Hahn ships his products all over the world and to 47 states.

PROFESSIONAL OF THE YEAR IN
TEACHER ADMINISTRATION

MARGARET B. HAMILTON

Principal
St. Peter's School
21 Ridge Street
Haverstraw, NY 10927 United States
mbh0122@yahoo.com
http://www.cambridgewhoswho.com

Type of Business: Private Diocese and Catholic School

Major Products and Services: Education for Students in Grades Pre-Kindergarten to Eighth

Marketing Area: Rockland County, New York

Day to Day Responsibilities: Overseeing Teacher Administration

Favorite Business Publications: Momentum

Hobbies/Interests/Sports: Reading, Traveling

Education Degrees: Master's Degree in Education in Supervision and Administration, Plus 25, College of Saint Rose, Manhattan College and Fordham University; Bachelor's Degree in History and Political Science, Minor in Elementary Education, College of Mount Saint Vincent

Affiliations/Associations/Societies: National Catholic Educators Association; National Association of Elementary School Principals; International Reading Association; National Council for Social Studies; North Rockland Teacher Center Board

Charity/Volunteer Work: St. Peter's Church; Bereavement Counselor, New York Diocese

What do you attribute your success to? She attributes her success to loving what she does, having the support of her husband and family and working with great teachers.

How did you become involved in your profession? She became involved in this profession because both her parents were teachers and she loved working with children.

What was the highlight of your career? The highlight of her career was being promoted to principal.

PROFESSIONAL OF THE YEAR IN
DENTAL HYGIENE

LINDA O. HAMMOND

Dental Hygienist (Retired)
Dr. Kenneth C. West
295 Old Post Road
Mansfield, GA 30055 United States
hootinanny@netscape.com
http://www.cambridgewhoswho.com

Type of Business: Dental Clinic

Major Products and Services: Dentistry Services Including Extractions, Fillings, Root Canals, Cleanings, Preventative Care and X-rays

Marketing Area: Local

Day to Day Responsibilities: Practicing Dental Hygiene, Overseeing X-Rays and Preventative Maintenance Treatments, Educating Patients

Favorite Business Publications: North Georgia News; Newton Citizen; The Covington News

Hobbies/Interests/Sports: Gardening, Crocheting

Education Degrees: Associate of Arts in Dental Hygiene, Clayton State University (1980)

Spouse: Johnny   **Children:** Andrea, Heather

Work History: Women's Army Corps (1965-1968)

What do you attribute your success to? She attributes her success to her love for profession and her learning skills.

How did you become involved in your profession? She became involved in her profession through a natural progression of opportunities.

What was the highlight of your career? The most gratifying aspect of her career is being able to maintain good relationships with her clients.

Expanded Biography: Ms. Hammond served in the Women's Army Corps from 1965 to 1968.

PROFESSIONAL OF THE YEAR IN INFORMATION TECHNOLOGY

MICHAEL HANKEN, BS

General Manager of Information Technology
Multiquip, Inc.
18910 Wilmington Street
Carson, CA 90746 United States
mhanken@multiquip.com
http://www.multiquip.com

Type of Business: Manufacturing Company

Major Products and Services: Construction Equipment

Marketing Area: International

Area of Expertise: Mr. Hanken's expertise includes business management, strategy implementation, information technology planning and execution.

Favorite Business Publications: Fast Company

Hobbies/Interests/Sports: Bicycling, Playing Tennis, Traveling, Spending Time with his Family

Education Degrees: Bachelor's Degree in Computer Science, University of Hagen

Affiliations/Associations/Societies: The Association for Operations Management

Spouse: Anke   **Children:** Felix, Laura, Victoria

What do you attribute your success to? He attributes his success to his creativity.

How did you become involved in your profession? He became involved in his profession because of his interest in manufacturing equipment.

PROFESSIONAL OF THE YEAR IN
AVIATION ENGINEERING

MR. ROBERT B. HARRINGTON

East Coast Aftermarket Sales Manager
FMC Technologies Jetway
8243 Sweetclover Court
Indianapolis, IN 46256 United States
rob.harrington@fmcti.com
http://www.fmctechnologies.com/airportequipmentservices.aspx

Type of Business: Manufacturing Company

Major Products and Services: Aviation Equipment Including Aircraft Air Conditioning, Baggage Handling, Airport Maintenance

Marketing Area: Regional

Day to Day Responsibilities: Meeting Clients and Customers, Inspecting Equipment, Designing and Manufacturing Products Including Passenger Boarding Bridges, Troubleshooting Problems, Ensuring Customer Satisfaction

Favorite Business Publications: GSE Today

Hobbies/Interests/Sports: Playing Soccer, Fishing, Camping

Education Degrees: Bachelor of Science in Aeronautical Sciences, Embry-Riddle Aeronautical University (1986)

Affiliations/Associations/Societies: Aircraft Owners and Pilots Association (1986)

Awards/Honors: The International Who's Who

PROFESSIONAL OF THE YEAR IN
HEALTH ADMINISTRATION AND ADVOCACY

JUDITH A. HARRIS, PH.D.

Owner, Director
Harris Consulting, LTD
6253 Headley Heights Court
Gahanna, OH 43230 United States
judithh@insight.rr.com
http://www.cambridgewhoswho.com

Type of Business: Consulting Company

Major Products and Services: Healthcare Administration Consulting and Advocacy Services

Marketing Area: International

Area of Expertise: Dr. Harris' areas of expertise include administration, public speaking, research and advocacy.

Day to Day Responsibilities: Monitoring and Directing the Program, Speaking on Public Health Issues, Teaching, Reporting on Government Filings

Favorite Business Publications: Industry-Related Publications

Hobbies/Interests/Sports: Reading, Ice-Skating, Golfing

Education Degrees: Ph.D. in Health Administration, The Ohio State University (2004); Ph.D., Concentration in Children with Disabilities, Warren National University (2004); Master's Degree in Human Development, University of Dayton; Master's Degree in Community Counseling, University of Dayton; Bachelor's Degrees in Public Administration, Ohio Dominican University; Bachelor's Degree in Psychology, Ohio Dominican University; Bachelor's Degree in Special Education, Ohio Dominican University; Bachelor's Degree in Legislative Laws, Ohio Dominican University; Bachelor's Degree in Fine Arts and Education, Ohio Dominican University

Certifications: Certified in IOMR/DD, State of Ohio

Affiliations/Associations/Societies: American Association of University Women; American Business Women's Association; National Abortion and Reproductive Rights Action League; Association of University Programs in Health Administration

Charity/Volunteer Work: Children's Health Organizations; Environmental Organizations

Date of Birth: January 20, 1945   **Place of Birth:** Gallipolis

Spouse: James

Work History: Executive Director, Five Nonprofit Health Organizations

What do you attribute your success to? She attributes her success to her personal drive, the support she receives from her husband, and her desire to make the world a better place to live.

How did you become involved in your profession? She became involved in her profession because she wanted to study the effects of environmental issues on childbirth.

What was the highlight of your career? The highlight of her career was being nominated to go to China as an ambassador to discuss children's and women's issues with other professionals.

Expanded Biography: Dr. Harris authored a book entitled 'Consequences of Pollution and Contamination on the Human Body.' She has worked for county, state and federal governments and The Ohio State University, and implemented a program that changed the lives of more than one million people.

MR. DARRYL K. HARRISON

Director
Department of Public Safety
Georgetown University
37th and O Street N.W.
Washington, DC 20057 United States
dh2@georgetown.edu
http://www.georgetown.edu

Type of Business: University

Major Products and Services: Higher Education Including Biomedical and Health Sciences, Business, Economics, International, Regional and Ethnic Studies, History, Classical Studies, Languages and Linguistics, Literature, Cultural Studies, Law, Government, Politics, Multi- and Interdisciplinary Studies, Science, Mathematics, Technology, Social Sciences, Theology, Philosophy, Religious Studies, Visual and Performing Arts, Public Safety, Law Enforcement

Marketing Area: Local

Area of Expertise: Mr. Harrison's expertise is in law enforcement.

Day to Day Responsibilities: Ensuring Public Safety, Overseeing Management

Favorite Business Publications: The Wall Street Journal

Hobbies/Interests/Sports: Traveling, Reading, Fishing

Education Degrees: Bachelor of Arts, American University

Affiliations/Associations/Societies: International Association of Chiefs of Police; International Association of Campus Law Enforcement Administrators; The National Organization of Black Law Enforcement Executives

Spouse: Judith   **Children:** Daria, Brian, Rachel

What do you attribute your success to? He attributes his success to his quiet drive, determination and motivation to do the best job he can.

How did you become involved in your profession? He became involved in his profession after a recruiter encouraged him to be a police officer, he pursued the law enforcement field and found that he enjoyed it and could really make a difference.

Expanded Biography: Mr. Harrison enjoys visiting different parts of the world.

PROFESSIONAL OF THE YEAR IN RESIDENTIAL REMODELING

ALLYN E. HARTH

President, Chief Executive Officer
A.E. Harth, Inc. dba Harth Builders
1 Mill Race
Spring House, PA 19477 United States
allyn.harth@harthbuilders.com
http://www.harthbuilders.com

Type of Business: Construction Company

Major Products and Services: Building, Remodeling

Marketing Area: Local

Day to Day Responsibilities: Managing Sales, Estimating, Overseeing Administrative Duties, Marketing, Selling and Constructing Custom and Panel Package Homes, Visiting Sites

Favorite Business Publications: Remodeling; Qualified Remodeler; Progressive Remodeler

Hobbies/Interests/Sports: Spending Time at his Shore House in Delaware, Traveling

Education Degrees: Bachelor's Degree in Industrial Engineering, North Dakota State University; Coursework in Computer Science, Gwynedd-Mercy College

Certifications: Licensed Realtor; Certification, National Association of the Remodeling Industry

Affiliations/Associations/Societies: North Penn Chamber of Commerce; Remodelers Advantage; National Institute of Fire Restoration; Institute of Inspection, Cleaning and Restoration

Awards/Honors: Chrysalis Award for Residential Kitchens Under $40,000 (2007); Regional CotY Award, Residential Kitchen $30,000 to $60,000, Residential Bath $30,000 to $60,000 (2007); Chrysalis Award for Best Room Addition Over $100,000 (2006); Professional Achievement Award, Residential Kitchens Under $30,000, Residential Interiors Over $100,000, Bucks-Mont National Association of the Remodeling Industry (2005); Award, Residential Additions Under $100,000 (2004); Big50 Award (2004)

Charity/Volunteer Work: The American Legion; Boy Scouts of America

Spouse: Janice   **Children:** Jeffrey, Gregory, Amy

What do you attribute your success to? He attributes his success to his high energy level and people management skills.

How did you become involved in your profession? He became involved in his profession after working as a carpenter and attending engineering school.

What was the highlight of your career? The highlight of his career was being selected by Remodeling Magazine as one of the Top 50 remodeling contractors in 2004 in the United States.

Expanded Biography: Mr. Harth was the first Eagle Scout in his boy scout troop and the president of his high school freshman and senior classes. Both of his sons are also Eagle Scouts. He started his remodeling company and developed it into a multi-million dollar business after retiring in 1996 with over 50 years of experience. He also served in the United States Marine Corps and is a public speaker.

PROFESSIONAL OF THE YEAR IN
CREATIVE WRITING

JON F. HASSLER

Novelist
jhassl@aol.com
http://www.cambridgewhoswho.com

Type of Business: Novelist

Major Products and Services: Writing Novels

Marketing Area: International

Day to Day Responsibilities: Writing Novels, Teaching English and Creative Writing

Hobbies/Interests/Sports: Writing

Education Degrees: Honorary Doctoral Degree, Notre Dame University (2000); Master's Degree in American Literature, University of North Dakota (1980); Bachelor's Degree in English, St. John's University (1955)

What do you attribute your success to? He attributes his success to his knowledge of human nature.

How did you become involved in your profession? He became involved in his profession because he always had a strong desire to write.

What was the highlight of your career? The highlight of his career was received an honorary doctorate from Notre Dame University.

Expanded Biography: Mr. Hassler has published 17 novels, including 'The New Woman', 'Staggerford', 'North of Hope', 'Deans List', 'A Green Journey' and 'Dear James'. He taught English and creative writing for 42 years at various high schools and colleges.

PROFESSIONAL OF THE YEAR IN NURSING

Diane Denny Hayes

Registered Nurse Supervisor
Valley Pediatrics
4896 Main Street
Jasper, TN 37347 United States
diane2729@bellsouth.net
http://www.cambridgewhoswho.com

Type of Business: Healthcare Center

Major Products and Services: Healthcare, Pediatric Care

Marketing Area: Regional

Area of Expertise: Ms. Hayes' expertise is in nursing.

Day to Day Responsibilities: Billing, Supervising the Staff, Overseeing Patient Diagnosis, Assisting Nurse Practitioners for Billing Purposes, Managing Patient Accounts, Updating Charts

Favorite Business Publications: American Journal of Nursing

Education Degrees: Associate Degree in Nursing, Georgia State University

Charity/Volunteer Work: Local Church; American Cancer Society; Special Olympics

Spouse: Gary

ENTREPRENEUR OF THE YEAR IN HORTICULTURE

MR. PETER J. HECKER

Owner, President, Manager
PH Enterprises, LLC
415 S. 30th Street
Manitowoc, WI 54220 United States
info@CambridgeWhosWho.com
http://www.cambridgewhoswho.com

Type of Business: Neighborhood Landscaping Company

Major Products and Services: Spring and Fall Clean-Up Work, Seasonal Preparations Including Snow Removal, Full Range of Lawn and Yard Service and Maintenance at Reasonable Prices

Marketing Area: Regional

Day to Day Responsibilities: Designing Landscapes, Offering Maintenance Services, Performing Woodwork for Flower Beds and Lawn Borders, Acquiring and Retaining Clientele, Thatching, Pruning, Running the Daily Operations of the Company, Training and Overseeing the Staff, Consulting on Gardening

Favorite Business Publications: Organic Gardening Care, Gardening Literature

Hobbies/Interests/Sports: Woodworking

Education Degrees: Degree in Custodial Maintenance with Horticulture Training, Lakeshore Technical College (1980-1981)

Affiliations/Associations/Societies: Manitowoc Marine Band

Date of Birth: April 22, 1961   **Place of Birth:** Manitowoc, Wisconsin

Work History: Sanitation Engineer

ENTREPRENEUR OF THE YEAR IN
REAL ESTATE APPRAISING

Ms. Marilyn L. Hembree

Owner
Ozark Appraisal Service of Joplin
1820 E. 20th Street, Suite 50
Joplin, MO 64804 United States
mhembree@fastfreedom.com
http://www.cambridgewhoswho.com

Type of Business: Realty

Major Products and Services: Appraisal Service

Marketing Area: Regional

Day to Day Responsibilities: Appraising Residential Real Estate

Hobbies/Interests/Sports: Spending Time with Family

Certifications: Certified Appraiser (2003)

Affiliations/Associations/Societies: Joplin Board of Realtors; Better Business Bureau

What do you attribute your success to? She attributes her success to hard work.

How did you become involved in your profession? She made a natural progression into her current career.

What was the highlight of your career? The highlight of her career is seeing her business do well.

PROFESSIONAL OF THE YEAR IN REAL ESTATE

BILL E. HENSON JR.

Founder, Chief Executive Officer
SilverPointe Properties, LLC
501 Corporate Centre Drive, Suite 260
Franklin, TN 37067 United States
bhenson@silverpointe.com
http://www.silverpointe.com

Type of Business: Real Estate Agency

Major Products and Services: Real Estate Exchange Including Relocation, Mortgage Assistance

Marketing Area: National

Area of Expertise: Mr. Henson's expertise is in brand management.

Day to Day Responsibilities: Marketing, Managing Residential and Consumer Product Sales

Hobbies/Interests/Sports: Participating in Politics, Football, Tennis, Jogging, Skiing

Education Degrees: Bachelor's Degree in Business Administration, Major in Marketing, The University of Tennessee (1982)

Certifications: Certified Residential Specialist (2007); Accredited Buyer Representative

Affiliations/Associations/Societies: Advisory Board Member, Southern Land Company; Cool Springs Chamber of Commerce; Council of Residential Specialists; Former Chairman, Legislative Committee, Greater Nashville Association of Realtors; Tennessee Association of Realtors; National Association of Realtors

Awards/Honors: Businessman of the Year Award, NRCC

Charity/Volunteer Work: Board of Directors, Habitat for Humanity of Williamson County; Ordained Deacon, The People's Church, Franklin, TN; Volunteer Speaker, Williamson County School District

Spouse: Wanda

Expanded Biography: Mr. Henson is a multi-million dollar listing agent and has been recognized three times as No. 1 realtor in the nation. He has twenty-one years of experience in consumer product sales, marketing, management and field-based brand management.

MS. MELISSA D. HESHMAT

Chief Financial Officer
Mohawk Innovative Technology, Inc.
1037 Watervliet-Shaker Road
Albany, NY 12205 United States
mheshmat@miti.cc
http://www.miti.cc

Type of Business: Manufacturing Company

Major Products and Services: Machinery Including Gas Turbine Engines, Turbochargers, Compressors, Cryogenic Pumps with Integration of Advanced Foil Bearings, Oil Free Bearings and Foil Seals

Marketing Area: International

Area of Expertise: Ms. Heshmat's expertise is in research for the development of hi-tech companies, startup business financing, cost analysis and government accounting.

Hobbies/Interests/Sports: Reiki Training, Practicing Healing Arts

Education Degrees: Bachelor of Business Administration in Accounting, The Pennsylvania State University (1977)

Affiliations/Associations/Societies: Small Business Innovative Research Initiative; University of Wyoming

PROFESSIONAL OF THE YEAR IN MUSIC CAMP MANAGEMENT

WANDA HIGGINS

Chief Executive Officer
Hummingbird Music Camp
104 Hummingbird Lane
Jemez Springs, NM 87025 United States
wanda.higgins@cwwemail.com
http://www.hummingbirdmusiccamp.org

Type of Business: Music Camp

Major Products and Services: Music Instruction, Band Training, Vocal Training, Hiking, Storytelling, Outdoor Cookouts, Performances, Art Gallery, Programs for Children Ages 8-14

Marketing Area: Regional

Day to Day Responsibilities: Teaching Piano, Choir, Band and Guitar Performance, Overseeing Private Lessons for Children

Hobbies/Interests/Sports: Painting, Playing Bridge, Cooking

Education Degrees: Coursework in Nursing; Coursework in First Aid

Expanded Biography: Ms. Higgins co-founded the camp with her husband in 1959. Her family includes five children, 12 grandchildren and six great-grandchildren. She has been a Girl Scout Leader for more than 20 years and speaks at various church functions and concerts. Ms. Higgins has published articles in the Albuquerque Journal and is the recipient of numerous gubernatorial awards.

EXECUTIVE OF THE YEAR IN
WATER WORKS

BOBBIE T. HINDE

Executive Director
American Water Works Association, Florida Section
500 S. Orange Avenue, Suite 518
Orlando, FL 32801 United States
bobbie.hinde@verizon.net
http://www.fsawwa.org

Type of Business: Scientific and Educational Nonprofit Association of Water Industry Professionals

Major Products and Services: Certification and Training, Continuing Education, Networking, Legislative Advocacy Related to Water Industry Issues

Marketing Area: Florida, Southeastern United States

Area of Expertise: Ms. Hinde's expertise includes association management, public administration, training, certification, economic development, strategic planning, marketing, board governance and staff oversight.

Favorite Business Publications: Florida Trends

Hobbies/Interests/Sports: Photography, Traveling, Writing, Reading

Education Degrees: Bachelor's Degree, University of Washington

Certifications: Certified Public Manager, Florida State University

Affiliations/Associations/Societies: American Society of Association Executives; Association of Boards of Certification; American Society of Association Executives, Florida Chapter

PROFESSIONAL OF THE YEAR IN
BROADCASTING

CYNTHIA C. HITE

Co-Host, News Anchor
Seaview AM 960
12853 Calais Circle
Palm Beach Gardens, FL 33410 United States
cindy@cindyhite.com
http://www.cindyhite.com

Type of Business: Broadcasting, Public Relations and Marketing

Major Products and Services: Public Relations Services, Marketing Strategies, Sales/Marketing, Media Placement, Writing Copy, Creative Concepts/Slogans, Theme Songs/Jingles Narration and Voice Over

Area of Expertise: Ms. Hite's expertise includes organizational management and communications.

Day to Day Responsibilities: Narrating, Offering Voice-Over Artistry and Creative Concepts, Writing

Favorite Business Publications: Fortune, Small Business

Hobbies/Interests/Sports: Women's Fencing Champion, Swimming, Sailing, Poetry, Music, Scrapbooking

Education Degrees: Bachelor of Science in Organizational Management, Palm Beach Atlantic University, West Palm Beach, FL, Magna Cum Laude (2005)

Affiliations/Associations/Societies: Phi Beta Alpha Chapter of the Alpha Sigma Lambda Honor Society; Public Relations Society of America; UDC

Awards/Honors: MacArthur ORM Leadership Award, PBAU (2006); Green Eyeshade Award (1997); Florida Emmy Award (1989)

Place of Birth: Greenwich   **Spouse:** Brian

What do you attribute your success to? She attributes her success to the values that her parents taught her.

How did you become involved in your profession? She became involved in her profession because she has an extensive family history in broadcasting and media.

What was the highlight of your career? The highlights of her career were receiving the Southeastern Regional Fencing Champion and National Competitor Awards in 1971 and 1972.

Expanded Biography: Ms. Hite gained experience in television, broadcasting and related industries with Kinship Productions under Bob Hite, Jr. in Tampa, Florida. She wrote the lyrics and composed the music for a number of songs and jingles, all of which she performed as an accomplished vocalist, guitarist and narrator. A music video called 'Kingdom of the Sea,' written, composed and performed by Ms. Hite and produced by her brother Bob Hite, earned them two Florida Emmy Awards in 1989. Ms. Hite has hosted two TV shows, 'Medical Review' and 'Inside Pro-Baseball,' both produced in Palm Beach County. She has been the on-camera talent and voice talent in numerous TV and radio commercials. In addition, she has narrated full- length documentary films, such as 'Journey into Wilderness' and 'Lady of the Glades.' Some of her major commercial work includes training films for Motorola and AT&T and vocal accompaniments at the Disney World Motorola Pavilion. As an experienced vocalist and guitarist, Ms. Hite has performed in several concerts and theater productions, where she excelled in classic or modern leading roles. As, Viola in 'Twelfth Night,' she set Feste's poems to music, sang and played them on guitar.

EXECUTIVE OF THE YEAR IN
COMMUNITY DEVELOPMENT AND SOCIAL SERVICES

Ms. Kari Hogan

Executive Director
PPEP, Inc.
802 E. 46th Street
Tucson, AZ 85713 United States
khogan@ppep.org
http://www.ppep.org

Portable Practical Education Preparation, Inc

Type of Business: Nonprofit Multi-Service Organization

Major Products and Services: Employment and Training, Education Programs, General Equivalency Diplomas, Emergency Assistance, Workforce Investment Act Programs, Community Service Block Grants, Case Management, Senior Programs, Youth Summer and After School Programs

Marketing Area: Statewide

Day to Day Responsibilities: Managing, Directing and Implementing Programs for Youth and Adults in the Areas of Employment, Training, Case Management and Emergency Services, Working with Communities, Developing Partnerships to Leverage Funding for the Sustainability of Programs, Overseeing Career Development and Economic Development Strategies within High Growth and High-Demand Occupations, Working with Regional and National Coalitions on Legislative Issues Surrounding Employment and Training, Managing Funding in Excess of 4 Million Dollars, Monitoring the Budget for Optimum Output, Overseeing 15 Programs and Grants and 47 Staff Members in Arizona

Hobbies/Interests/Sports: Participating in Outdoor Activities

Education Degrees: Diploma, St. Regis High School, MT (1978)

Certifications: Certificate, The Grantsmanship Center (1996); Certification, Pima Community College

Affiliations/Associations/Societies: Executive Board Member, Association of Farmworker Opportunity Programs; President, Rocky Mountain High Coalition; Board Member, Western Alliance of Farmworker Advocates

Date of Birth: January 2, 1960   **Place of Birth:** Great Falls

Children: Bret, Brad, Victoria, Craig

What do you attribute your success to? She attributes her success to her supervisor of the last 15 years, who has been a mentor and guide. She has given constructive criticism and has always been honest. She has let her fail at times in order to find her path and the right direction in order to find success.

How did you become involved in your profession? She became involved in her profession because a friend encouraged her to apply for a position with the company.

What was the highlight of your career? The most gratifying aspects of her career are being able to give people an opportunity to achieve their dreams, and watching adults and youth walk down the aisle in their caps and gowns to their graduation ceremony, something they thought they would never achieve.

Where will you be in five years? In five years, Ms. Hogan intends to become the newest chief administrative officer of the company.

Expanded Biography: Ms. Hogan began working for PPEP in July of 1987 and has held a number of positions throughout the past 21 years of employment with the agency. She has shown the agency and its management that she has the ability to do what it takes to manage, develop and maintain successful programs and devote the time necessary to achieve those goals. Through her hard work, she has been able to achieve success despite obstacles and disappointments.

PROFESSIONAL OF THE YEAR IN
EDUCATION FOR TRANSITIONAL STUDIES

MRS. ELEANOR HOLMES PELCHER

Assistant Professor
Monroe Community College
717 E. Henrietta Road
Rochester, NY 14623 United States
epelcher@monroecc.edu
http://www.monroecc.edu

Type of Business: Community College

Major Products and Services: Higher Education Including 70 Different Career, Transfer and Certificate Programs, Athletics and Academic Counseling

Marketing Area: Local

Area of Expertise: Mrs. Holmes Pelcher's expertise is in English and mathematics instruction for transitional students and freshman orientation programs.

Hobbies/Interests/Sports: Traveling, Gardening, Sewing, Making Home Improvements

Education Degrees: Master's Degree in Education, Plus 45, Nazareth University (1984)

Certifications: Certification in Special Education; Certification in General Education; Certification in Reading

Affiliations/Associations/Societies: Rochester Museum Women's Council; Mathematics Committee, Monroe Community College; Language Committee, Scholarship Committee, Hospitality Committee, Monroe Community College; Landmark Society; Alpha Sigma Tau; American Association of University Women

Awards/Honors: Lucile Klipp Book Award

Charity/Volunteer Work: Volunteer, American Heart Association

Place of Birth: Philipsburg, PA

Children: Rian, David, Stephan, Timothy, Amanda, Deborah

How did you become involved in your profession? She became involved in her profession after deciding at the age of 7 that she wanted to be a teacher.

Expanded Biography: Mrs. Holmes Pelcher has lectured at national conferences, organized 'trash-to-treasures' sales at McQuaid Jesuit High School, and designed hall murals. While she taught at Rochester City Schools, Mrs. Holmes Pelcher was called a master teacher. She also supervised student teachers from Brockport University. In addition, she was the co-chairwoman of Taste Sensations as well as a contributing member for other fundraisers. She also started a scholarship at Monroe Community College in memory of her best friend. Mrs. Holmes Pelcher was the former recording secretary at the Rochester Museum of Science. One of her favorite quotes is 'Knowledge is Power,' by Francis Bacon.

ENTREPRENEUR OF THE YEAR IN
CHINESE ANTIQUES

MARIE L. HOOD

Owner
Hood Antiques
2834 Adams Avenue
San Diego, CA 92116 United States
marie.hood@cwwemail.com
http://www.cambridgewhoswho.com

Type of Business: Antique Store

Major Products and Services: Antiques

Marketing Area: International

Day to Day Responsibilities: Collecting Ancient Chinese and General Antiques

Favorite Business Publications: Industry-Related Publications

Hobbies/Interests/Sports: Reading

Education Degrees: Master's Degree in History and Government Studies, University of Illinois

Affiliations/Associations/Societies: Phi Beta Kappa; Delta Kappa Gamma

Charity/Volunteer Work: Board of Directors, Adult Protective Services, San Diego

What do you attribute your success to? She attributes her success to her knowledge and honesty.

How did you become involved in your profession? She became involved in her profession because of her interest in collecting antiques.

PROFESSIONAL OF THE YEAR IN ART EDUCATION

LAURIE A. HOOVER-ATWOOD

1) Artist, Creative Design Director
2) Entrepreneur, Charity Builder 3) Teacher
1) Laurie with Love 2) Look2Day
3) Salem-Keizer Schools
1115 Madison Street N.E., PMB 235
Salem, OR 97301 United States
look2day@comcast.net
http://laurieh.myexpose.com • http://www.look2day.com

Type of Business: 1) Art Ministry 2) Online Store 3) School

Major Products and Services: 1) Fundraisers Including Ministry Events and Activities, Charity Support, and the Sale of Art Including Wearable Art and Other Products, Art Services, Logos and Banners, CD Covers, E-cards, a Gallery, Photography and Poetry, Journal Articles, and the Moderation of Online Art and Parent Groups 2) Retail Items 3) Elementary Education

Marketing Area: 1) International 2) International 3) Local

Day to Day Responsibilities: Teaching Art, Leading Workshops and Parenting Classes, Creating Fine Artwork, Selling Art, Raising Funds for Children's Assistance, Illustrating Children's Books, Designing Logos, CD Covers and Cards, Publishing Poetry

Favorite Business Publications: The Writer; Poetry Today; Artist's Magazine; National Geographic Traveler; ARTnews; Instructor; ASCD Today; Teaching K-8; Fast Company; Woman Business Magazine

Hobbies/Interests/Sports: Creating Art, Teaching, Writing Stories, Articles and Poetry, Listening to Music, Playing and Composing Music, Hiking, Photography, Gardening, Researching, Solving Problems, Traveling

Education Degrees: Endorsement, English for Speakers of Other Languages (1992); Master's Degree in Educational Leadership, Portland State University (1991); Bachelor's Degree in Education, Western Oregon University (1989); Coursework in Early Childhood Development (1981)

Affiliations/Associations/Societies: Affiliate Business Woman of America; Oregon Reading Council; Salem Art Association; Friends of the Visual Arts; Association for Supervision and Curriculum Development; Oregon Reading Association; International Reading Association; Salem Education Association; Oregon Education Association; National Education Association; Art Guild, Salem

Awards/Honors: Best International Poet (2006); Visual Arts Award (2004); Most Caring Teacher Award (2004); Elected Honorary Professor of Arts, Duca, Italy (2003); People's Choice Award (2000)

Charity/Volunteer Work: Look2Day.org; PROJECT Hands4Him

Place of Birth: Washington

Spouse: Sheridan

Work History: Pre-K-Sixth Grade Teacher; Newsletter Illustrator, State Farm Insurance; Illustration Artist, Writer's Exchange; Literacy Leader, Reading Is Fundamental Coordinator; Art Vendor; Journalist and Photographer, International Travel Writers Photographers Alliance; Online Business Operator

Career Achievements: Best International Poet (2006); Published Poet and Writer, Best Poems and Poets (2004); Honorary Professor, Department of Arts, Academia Internationale via Duca degli Italy (2003); Visual Artist of the Year (2003)

What do you attribute your success to? She attributes her success to her perseverance, courage and faith in God.

How did you become involved in your profession? She became involved in her profession because she always had a passion for expression and wanted to touch the lives of others through her creative work.

What was the highlight of your career? The highlight of her career was witnessing her first group of students graduate from high school and make a difference in the world.

Where will you be in five years? In five years, Ms. Hoover-Atwood hopes to continue helping children, use her art to offer additional funds and write to bring hope to the lives of children.

Expanded Biography: Ms. Hoover-Atwood pledges to continually work toward healing children and families in a hurting world through the use of the creative arts. She is dedicated to reaching children in orphanages and areas throughout the world where at-risk children live, so that they may have a glimmer of hope and express their feelings through painting, sound and dance.

PROFESSIONAL OF THE YEAR IN ART EDUCATION

JULIA L. HOVANEC, M.ED.

1) Professor of Art Education 2) Art Teacher Supervisor
1) Art 2) Art and Education
1) Kutztown University 2) Moravian College
jhovanec2007@comcast.net
hovanec@kutztown.edu
http://www.kutztown.edu

Type of Business: 1) University 2) College

Major Products and Services: 1) Higher Education 2) Higher Education

Marketing Area: 1) Regional 2) Regional

Area of Expertise: Ms. Hovanec's expertise is in art education.

Day to Day Responsibilities: Supervising Students, Teaching Visual Arts, Special Topics Courses and Workshops for Artists at the Intermediate Level

Favorite Business Publications: Art Education; School Arts Magazine

Hobbies/Interests/Sports: Reading, Spending Time with her Family, Baking, Cooking

Education Degrees: Pursuing Doctoral Degree in Art Education, Concentration in Curriculum and Instruction, Capella University; Master of Education, Kutztown University (1996)

Certifications: Certified Art Teacher for Kindergarten through 12th-Grade

Affiliations/Associations/Societies: Chairwoman, Yearbook Committee, Parent-Teacher Association; National Art Education Association; Association for Supervision and Curriculum Development

Charity/Volunteer Work: Local Church; Local Charitable Organizations; National Multiple Sclerosis Society; American Cancer Society; Girl Scouts of the United States of America

What do you attribute your success to? She attributes her success to her interest in art education and the support she receives from her mother.

How did you become involved in your profession? She became involved in her profession because of her interest in the field of education and her passion for art.

What was the highlight of your career? The most gratifying aspect of her career is teaching at the graduate level.

PROFESSIONAL OF THE YEAR IN SNACK AND BEVERAGE SERVICES

GARY L. HUBLER

Owner, Manager
Gary's Snack Shop
19901 Germantown Road
Germantown, MD 20874 United States
gary.hubler@cwwemail.com
http://www.cambridgewhoswho.com

Type of Business: Retail Store

Major Products and Services: Snacks and Beverages

Marketing Area: Local

Day to Day Responsibilities: Managing Operations, Training

Hobbies/Interests/Sports: Writing

Education Degrees: Bachelor's Degree in Animal Science, University of Maryland

Certifications: License, State of Maryland; Certified Biologist

Awards/Honors: Carrier of the Year Award, Washington Evening Star (1970)

Charity/Volunteer Work: American Cancer Society

Date of Birth: December 17, 1952   **Place of Birth:** Washington, DC

What do you attribute your success to? He attributes his success to his hard work, organizational skills and training as a scientist.

Expanded Biography: Mr. Hubler attended the federal work-study program at the University of Maryland. He has also completed various college level training programs at a rehabilitation center.

PROFESSIONAL OF THE YEAR IN HOSPITALITY OPERATIONS

MS. MINNIE L. HUGHES

Owner
Osage Express Truck Plaza Casino
11 Oakley Drive
Hammond, LA 70401 United States
minniehughes@bellsouth.net
http://www.cambridgewhoswho.com

Type of Business: Casino

Major Products and Services: Entertainment Services Including Food and Beverages

Marketing Area: Regional

Area of Expertise: Ms. Hughes' expertise lies in her strategic leadership and entrepreneurial skills.

Day to Day Responsibilities: Ensuring Customer Satisfaction, Building Relationships, Managing Operations

Favorite Business Publications: Industry-Related Publications

Hobbies/Interests/Sports: Rescuing Animals, Sports

Education Degrees: Ph.D.; High School Diploma

Expanded Biography: Ms. Hughes is the owner of the Hughes Estate and Family Camping Grounds.

PROFESSIONAL OF THE YEAR IN CONTINUING EDUCATION FOR THE CLERGY

REV. DONALD K. HUMMEL, D.MIN.

Director of Ongoing Formation and Continuing Education of Priests
Roman Catholic Archdiocese of Newark
171 Clifton Avenue
P.O. Box 9500
Newark, NJ 07104 United States
hummeldo@rcan.org
http://www.rcan.org

Type of Business: Clergy

Major Products and Services: Continuing Education of Priests

Marketing Area: Statewide

Day to Day Responsibilities: Directing Priests, Collaborating with Law Enforcement Officials, Counseling for Addiction Problems, Enforcing Emergency Response Measures

Favorite Business Publications: America

Hobbies/Interests/Sports: Enjoying Poetry, Attending Theater, Listening to Classical Music, Hiking, Former Football and Baseball Player

Education Degrees: Doctorate of Ministry and Pastoral Ministry, St. Mary's Seminary and University, Baltimore, MD (1991); Certified Counselor; Certified Master Police Chaplain; Certification in Thanatology

Affiliations/Associations/Societies: General Society of the War of 1812; Sons of Union Veterans of the Civil War; National Society Sons of the American Revolution; Fellow, American Psychological Association; American Catholic Association; American Christian Counseling Association

Awards/Honors: Silver Buffalo Award (2004)

Charity/Volunteer Work: Boy Scouts of America; Mothers Against Drunk Driving; United Way of America; Law Enforcement Emergency Management

Expanded Biography: Rev. Hummel is a former football and baseball player. He wrote an article in Catholic Advocate titled, 'Came to Believe, Healing the Wounds of Addiction.' His father's family has been in the United States since 1640.

PROFESSIONAL OF THE YEAR IN EMERGENCY HEALTHCARE

ANDREA W. HUNT

Administrative Director
Ashland Boyd County Catlettsburg Medical Reserve Corporation
info@CambridgeWhosWho.com
http://www.cambridgewhoswho.com

Type of Business: Medical Facility, Emergency Surgical Personnel

Major Products and Services: Medical-Surgical Capacity, WMDs, CBERN, Natural and Man-Made Disasters, Natural and Acquired Disease, Isolation, Treatment, Prevention

Marketing Area: National

Area of Expertise: Ms. Hunt's expertise is in program and exercise design.

Day to Day Responsibilities: Managing WMD and CBERN Problems, Treating Diseases

Favorite Business Publications: Nursing2006, Games, National Geographic

Hobbies/Interests/Sports: Reading, Needlework, Playing Computer Games, Spending Time with her Three Grandchildren

Education Degrees: Coursework, Marshall University (1973-1977)

Certifications: Licensed Practical Nurse, Roanoke Memorial Hospital (1982); Certified Paralegal, SUNY Albany

Awards/Honors: Who's Who of American Women; Who's Who in Health and Medicine; Who's Who in the World; America's Registry of Outstanding Professionals

Spouse: David   **Children:** Kristopher, Laura Ann

Expanded Biography: Ms. Hunt does public speaking locally and nationally.

EXECUTIVE OF THE YEAR IN COLLECTION OPERATIONS

PAUL R. HUNZIKER JR.

Chairman
Capital Management Services, L.P.
726 Exchange Street, Suite 700
Buffalo, NY 14210 United States
phunzikerjr@cms-collect.com
http://www.cms-collect.com

Type of Business: Financial Services Company

Major Products and Services: Collections Services, Delinquent Receivables Management and Resolution, Portfolio Management, Liquidations, Legal and Audit Compliance, Process Management

Marketing Area: International

Day to Day Responsibilities: Managing Collection Operations, Implementing Strategic Financial Planning

Hobbies/Interests/Sports: Exercising

Education Degrees: Bachelor's Degree in Finance, Franklin University

Awards/Honors: Who's Who in Western New York Financial Executives

Charity/Volunteer Work: Finance Committee Member, Our Lady of Pompeii

What do you attribute your success to? He attributes his success to being performance driven, self-disciplined and focused.

How did you become involved in your profession? He became involved in his profession through a natural progression of opportunities, from an entry-level position to an executive level position.

What was the highlight of your career? The highlight of his career has been obtaining his current position as owner and chairman of capital management services.

Expanded Biography: Mr. Hunziker's leadership is the driving force behind Capital Management Services' growth from a staff of 120 to 1200 employees and increased revenues from 6 million to over 100 million dollars. Capital Management has also added operations in Houston, Texas and Greenville, South Carolina and a successful joint venture in New Delhi, India. He is directly involved in the integration of the Houston and Greenville sites, thereby offering a consistent level of excellence for all of Capital Management clients, which include the top credit issuer as well as the largest buyers of consumer debt. He has over 24 years of successful senior executive collection management experience. Prior to joining Capital Management Services, he was responsible for the entire collection operations in Great Lakes Collection Bureau, where he was the senior vice president leading over 1500 employees and 130 clients portfolios, in seven separate sites. Under Mr. Huntziker's leadership, his staff recovered more than $1.2 Billion in delinquencies owed.

PROFESSIONAL OF THE YEAR IN ELEMENTARY EDUCATION

MS. MAXINE M. HYMAN-SPELLS

Educator
Orangeburg Consolidated School District Five
137 Nimmons Road
Orangeburg, SC 29118 United States
Maxinemhyman@hotmail.com
http://www.orangeburg5.k12.sc.us

Type of Business: Public School District

Major Products and Services: Primary Education for Students

Marketing Area: Local

Day to Day Responsibilities: Teaching Language Arts, Science and Reading to Second-Grade Students, Coordinating Parent Involvement Programs

Hobbies/Interests/Sports: Reading, Exercising, Traveling

Education Degrees: Pursuing Doctoral Degree, Nova Southeastern University, North Miami Beach, FL (2004); Master of Science in Elementary Education, South Carolina State University, Orangeburg, SC (1985); Bachelor of Science in Health and Physical Education, Minor in Biology, South Carolina State University, Orangeburg, South Carolina (1978)

Certifications: Master Teacher, National Teacher Training Institute (2004); Certificate of Completion, Five Leadership Academy (2003); Certificate of Completion, Arbitration Program-First Judicial Circuit Solicitor's Office, Orangeburg, SC (1999); Brown Belt in Karate and Ju Jitsu (1976)

Awards/Honors: Teacher of the Year, Rivelon Elementary School (2003-2004); Individual Incentive Reward, Orangeburg School District Three (1998); Nominee, Outstanding Young American Award (1985); Teacher of the Year, North Elementary School (1984-1985); Winner, First Annual Physical Education Majors and Minors Literacy Contest, Health and Physical Education Department, South Carolina State University (1977-1978); Second Place Trophy, Aiken Karate Tournament, Aiken, SC (1976)

Charity/Volunteer Work: Team Leader, Chairwoman, Parent Involvement Program

Spouse: Johnny   **Children:** Kenneth

PROFESSIONAL OF THE YEAR IN HIGHER EDUCATION

SISTER JANICE IVERSON

Business Manager, Healthcare Coordinator
Benedictine Sisters of Mother of God Monastery
110 28th Avenue S.E.
Watertown, SD 57201 United States
janice.iverson@cwwemail.com
sjiverson@hotmail.com
http://www.watertownbenedictines.org

Type of Business: Ministry

Major Products and Services: Religious Services Including Hospitality, Education and Healthcare

Marketing Area: National

Area of Expertise: Sis. Iverson's expertise includes ministry management, property maintenance and healthcare administration.

Day to Day Responsibilities: Overseeing Missionary Work, Maintaining Facilities, Managing Transportation Services, Scheduling, Coordinating Healthcare Programs, Performing CPR Procedures, Teaching Religious Education

Favorite Business Publications: Forbes; Fortune; Business 2.0; Scriptures; Benedictine Leadership

Hobbies/Interests/Sports: Reading, Playing Basketball and Soccer, Biking, Woodworking, Tinkering with Inventions

Education Degrees: Master's Degree in Education and Exercise Physiology, Concentration in Cardiac Rehabilitation and Intervention, Virginia Polytechnic Institute and State University (1981); Master's Degree in Health, Physical Education, Recreation and Dance, South Dakota State University (1972); Bachelor of Arts in Elementary Education, Mount Marty College, Yankton, SD (1968)

Affiliations/Associations/Societies: Benedictine Community of Religious Sisters; Mother of God Monastery; American Association of Cardiac and Pulmonary Rehabilitation; Conference of Religious Treasurers; National Association for Treasurers of Religious Institutes; Leadership Conference for Women Religious

Charity/Volunteer Work: American Diabetes Association

Date of Birth: March 3, 1941   **Place of Birth:** Miranda, SD

Work History: Physical Education Instructor, Watertown Home and School for Girls, Watertown, SD (1999-2001); Sabbatical, Mother of God Monastery, Watertown, SD (1998-1999); Clinical Exercise Physiologist, Mercy Medical Hospital, Nampa, ID (1987-1998); Director of Brookings Hospital, South Dakota State University (1981-1987); Physical Educator, Immaculate Conception School, Watertown, SD (1973-1974); Boys Basketball Coach, St. Bernard's Mission School, Fort Yates, ND; Athletic Director, Physical Educator, Girl's Basketball and Volleyball Coach, Harmony Hill High School, Watertown, SD; Administrative Assistant to Pastor, Athletic Director, Physical Educator, Volleyball Coach, Assistant Girl's Basketball Coach, Sacred Heart School, East Grand Forks, MN (1970-1976); Educator, St. Joseph's School, Pierre, SD; Educator, St. Mary's School, Aberdeen, SD; Educator, Grade High School Physical Education and Girls Basketball Coach, St. Mary's School, Richardton, ND; Women's Volleyball Coach, Assistant Women's Basketball Coach, Mary College; Graduate Assistant in Human Physiology, Tennis Instructor, Virginia Polytechnic and State University; St. Joseph's Health Care Center, Dickinson, ND

Expanded Biography: Sis. Iverson's life has been gifted and blessed with many opportunities to experience the world at its fullest and saddest conditions of despair. She believes that for every beginning there is an end and she entered the race and finished. Sis. Iverson has published research articles on physiology, cardiac rehabilitation education on glucose intolerance and lipid profiles on exercise. She is involved with Camp Chance, a summer program with the police department for first and sixth-grade students.

PROFESSIONAL OF THE YEAR IN EMERGENCY MEDICAL SERVICES

JILL A. JAEHNE

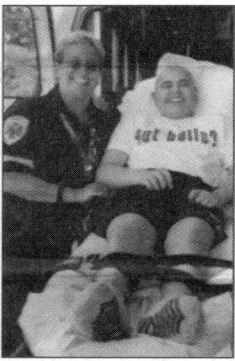

Emergency Medical Technician, Field Training Officer
American Medical Response, Inc.
607 Single Spur Court
Scotts Valley, CA 95066 United States
jaehnej@aol.com
http://www.cambridgewhoswho.com

Type of Business: Healthcare Center

Major Products and Services: Emergency Medical Services

Marketing Area: California

Day to Day Responsibilities: Overseeing Emergency Medical Services and the Medical Strike Team, Conducting Emergency Vehicle Operation Courses

Favorite Business Publications: Journal of Emergency Medical Services

Hobbies/Interests/Sports: Gardening, Reading, Riding Motorcycles, Participating in Motorcycle Races

Education Degrees: Associate of Arts in Liberal Arts; Coursework in Special Operations Team Training, American Medical Response; Coursework in Field Training Officer Program, American Medical Response; Coursework in Anesthesia Training, Nottingham and East Midlands School of Anesthesia

Certifications: Certified Information Security Manager, American Medical Response; Certified Emergency Medical Technician, CA; Certified Emergency Vehicle Operations Instructor, American Medical Response; Certification in CPR, American Heart Association; Certification in Basic Cardiac Life Support, American Heart Association; Automated External Defibrillator Certification, American Heart Association

Affiliations/Associations/Societies: Critical Incident Stress Management Team, American Medical Response (2004-2008); Special Operations Strike Team (2004-2008); Shop Steward, American Medical Response (2004-2008); DAR

Date of Birth: April 26, 1956   **Place of Birth:** Orange, CA

Work History: Emergency Medical Technician, Silicon Valley Ambulance (2004); Emergency Medical Technician, California Medical Transport (2002-2003); Field Training Officer, California Medical Transport (2002-2003); Operations Manager, American Express Financial Advisors (1995-2002); Operations Officer, Utility Clerk, Customer Service Representative, Wells Fargo (1980-1995)

Expanded Biography: Ms. Jaehne excels in bariatric, one-on-one advanced life support, CCT-P and CCT-RN medical procedures.

PROFESSIONAL OF THE YEAR IN SPECIAL EDUCATION

LAURIE K. JEFFRIES

Special Education Teacher
Brownsville Road Optional School
Memphis City Schools
3832 Kenwood Cove
Memphis, TN 38122 United States
lauriejkj@aol.com
jeffrieslk@mcs.k12.net
http://www.cambridgewhoswho.com

Type of Business: School District

Major Products and Services: Education

Marketing Area: Regional

Day to Day Responsibilities: Working with Small Groups, Writing Individual Education Plans, Planning Programs for Individual Child and Inclusion Teachers

Favorite Business Publications: Council for Exceptional Children

Hobbies/Interests/Sports: Swimming, Making Crafts, Needlework

Education Degrees: Master's Degree in Rehabilitation and Special Education, Plus 45, University of Memphis (1978); Bachelor of Science in Special Education, University of Memphis (1973)

Certifications: Certification in Special Education for Gifted and Disabled Children (K-12)

Affiliations/Associations/Societies: Council for Exceptional Children

Awards/Honors: Kipling's Who's Who of Leading Business Professionals

Children: Daniel, Elliot

PROFESSIONAL OF THE YEAR IN GERIATRICS

CAROLYN ADAIR JOHNSON, MD, CMD

Clinical Professor, Medical Director (Retired)
University of Minnesota
carolyn-johnson-md@concast.net
http://www.cambridgewhoswho.com

Type of Business: University

Major Products and Services: Higher Education

Marketing Area: Regional

Area of Expertise: Ms. Johnson's expertise is in geriatrics.

Favorite Business Publications: American Family Physician

Hobbies/Interests/Sports: Traveling, Playing the Piano, Spending Time with her Grandchildren

Education Degrees: Doctor of Medicine, University of Minnesota; Bachelor of Arts, University of Minnesota; Bachelor of Science, University of Minnesota

Certifications: Certified Clinical Professor, University of Minnesota (1994)

Affiliations/Associations/Societies: Board Member, Minnesota Medical Directors Association; President, Ramsey County Senior Physicians; American Medical Directors Association; Board Certified Diplomate, American Board of Family Medicine (1978); Lifetime Member, American Academy of Family Physicians

Expanded Biography: Ms. Johnson enjoys public speaking.

PROFESSIONAL OF THE YEAR IN WELLNESS ACUPUNCTURE

KARIN I. JOHNSON, BSN

Acupuncturist
Acusource Healing, LLC
96 Bowden Road
Cedar Grove, NJ 07009 United States
balance4u@verizon.net
http://www.acusourcehealing.com

Type of Business: Therapy Center and Day Spa

Major Products and Services: Wellness Acupuncture, Infrared, Craniosacral and Microcurrent Colorlight and Massage Therapy Services

Marketing Area: Local

Area of Expertise: Ms. Johnson's expertise is in pain relief therapy.

Day to Day Responsibilities: Practicing Integrative Medicine, Performing Acupuncture, Rejuvenation and Craniosacral Therapies

Favorite Business Publications: Alternative Therapies in Health and Medicine; Industry-Related Publications

Hobbies/Interests/Sports: Swimming, Hiking, Traveling, Practicing Yoga, Eastern Studies

Education Degrees: Bachelor of Science in Nursing, The University of North Carolina at Greensboro

Certifications: Diplomate in Acupuncture, Eastern School of Acupuncture, Montclair, NJ

Affiliations/Associations/Societies: Eastern School Alumni Association; Cedar Grove Historical Society

Charity/Volunteer Work: Morris Land Conservancy; New Jersey Conservation Foundation; March of Dimes Foundation; Habitat for Humanity

Date of Birth: January 1, 1949

Children: Melanie, Liam

What do you attribute your success to? She attributes her success to her dedication to service, self-confidence and customer service skills.

Expanded Biography: Ms. Johnson is a nursing professional of 41 years who found a deep personal satisfaction helping people in their times of need, from maternal care, to wound care, home health care and geriatric care, among others. In her continuing commitment to promote healthier lifestyle information and choices, she studied traditional Chinese medicine and became an accredited practitioner. Her love for humanity extends beyond her profession into her community service efforts, which include preserving cultural heritage, addressing environmental issues and working with the mentally challenged. Ms. Ferguson is proud to be able to offer her expertise in eastern and western modalities and fully embraces the responsibilities that come with her knowledge. She reaffirms daily her commitment to care for and help all people who are interested in becoming and staying well.

PROFESSIONAL OF THE YEAR IN
MANAGEMENT AND ORGANIZATION

ROXIEANN ELLA JOHNSON

Assistant Principal
John H. Finley Campus School
425 W. 130th Street
New York, NY 10027 United States
rjohnso6@schools.nyc.gov
http://www.cambridgewhoswho.com

Type of Business: School

Major Products and Services: Education

Marketing Area: Local

Day to Day Responsibilities: Overseeing After School Programs, Implementing and Developing the Curriculum

Education Degrees: Master's Degree in Educational Administration, The City University of New York (1994)

Expanded Biography: Ms. Johnson has received numerous grants for arts and science.

EXECUTIVE OF THE YEAR IN
MEDICAL EQUIPMENT MARKETING

DENISE D. JONES

Co-Owner
B&D Enterprises of Texas
2610 W. Marshall Drive, Suite 5
Grand Prairie, TX 75051 United States
ddjones@bdenterprises.net
http://www.bdenterprises.net

Type of Business: Chiropractic Equipment, Supplies and Service Company

Major Products and Services: Chiropractic and Medical Equipment and Supplies, Treatment and Adjusting Tables, Decompression and Traction Therapy Equipment, Electrotherapy Products, Ultrasound Products, Low-Level Laser Therapy Products, Exercise and Rehabilitative Products, Veterinary Treatment Supplies, Online Store and Services, Used Equipment, Learning Center, Seminars, Mobile Showroom

Marketing Area: Regional

Day to Day Responsibilities: Selling and Marketing Medical Equipment and Supplies, Managing Finances, Accounting

Hobbies/Interests/Sports: Reading, Cooking

TERESA JONES

Hispanic Marketing Consultant
Fisher Comm - UNIVISION Seattle
140 4th Avenue North
Seattle, WA 98109 United States
tjones@kunstv.com
http://www.kunstv.com

Type of Business: Television Sales

Major Products and Services: Television Station

Marketing Area: Seattle-Tacoma, WA

Area of Expertise: Ms. Jones' expertise is in marketing to Hispanic communities and advertising.

Favorite Business Publications: Hispanic Business; Hispanic Journals

Hobbies/Interests/Sports: Movies, Hiking, Spending Time with Family and Friends, Traveling, Live Theater

Education Degrees: Industry-Related Training and Experience

Affiliations/Associations/Societies: Professional Women of Color Network; Washington State Hispanic Chamber of Commerce; Vila Art Foundation

Work History: Account Executive, UNIVISION Seattle (2006-Present); Account Executive, Hispanic Marketing Consultant, KKMO Radio Sol, Salem Communications, Seattle, WA (2005-2006); Real Estate Sales Associate, Skyline Properties, Seattle, WA (2004-2006); News Editor, Technician, Playback Operator, Tape Coordinator, KCBS, Channel 2, Los Angeles, CA (1997-2004); Series Producer, Host, 'Reflexiones', Magazine Producer and Writer, 'Arizona Illustrated', KUAT-TV, PBS, Tucson, AZ (1980-1996); Founding Member, Teatro Libertad Bilingual Theater Group, Tucson, AZ (1978-1980); Marketing Director, Office Administrator, Grant Writer, Actress

What do you attribute your success to? She attributes her success to her great mentors and to her willingness to listen and keep an open mind.

How did you become involved in your profession? She became involved in her profession due to her passion for working with and promoting the Hispanic community.

What was the highlight of your career? The most gratifying aspect of her career is offering services to underprivileged people on a daily basis.

Expanded Biography: Ms. Jones has 20 years of experience producing, directing and writing.

PROFESSIONAL OF THE YEAR IN ELECTRICAL DESIGN

STEPHEN L. JOSLIN

Senior Test Engineer (Retired)
Gavial Engineering & Manufacturing, Inc.
1752 Little Orchard Street
San Jose, CA 95125 United States
steve.joslin@gavial.com
http://www.gavial.com

Type of Business: Engineering and Manufacturing Company

Major Products and Services: Integrated Fabrication, Aerospace Fabrications, Control Panels, Cable Assemblies, Circuit Cards, Custom Fabrications, Test Equipment, Nuclear Power Equipment, Nuclear Instrumentation Services, Quality Control Engineering Tests, Engineering Consulting, Project Management

Marketing Area: United States

Area of Expertise: Mr. Joslin's expertise includes nuclear instrumentation, power range and start-up systems, process loop controls and test design.

Day to Day Responsibilities: Preparing and Writing Test Procedures Based on System or Instrument Specifications, Developing New Products, Designing Replacement Circuitry for Analog Instruments

Favorite Business Publications: Electrical Design News; PC World; Windows Pro; Smart Computing

Hobbies/Interests/Sports: Crystal Radios, Computers, Hiking

Education Degrees: Associate of Arts in Electronics Technology, American River College, Sacramento, CA

Date of Birth: June 4, 1946   **Place of Birth:** Riverside, CA

Career Achievements: Patent Holder, Voltage Regulation

What was the highlight of your career? The highlights of her career were becoming involved in the design of analog system equipment and conducting test procedures on the equipment.

PROFESSIONAL OF THE YEAR IN
HOME AND BUSINESS REMODELING

MR. JOHN P. KAPICA

Owner
Kapica's Home Renovations
214 Howard Road
Rochester, NY 14606 United States
kappi60@frontiernet.net
http://www.cambridgewhoswho.com

Type of Business: Home Remodeling Business

Major Products and Services: Contracting and Remodeling of Homes and Businesses

Marketing Area: Regional

Day to Day Responsibilities: Remodeling Kitchens, Baths, Walk-In Bathtubs, Windows and Doors, Negotiating and Formulating Contracts, Maintaining Client Relationships, Acquiring Necessary Construction Materials, Ensuring Customer Satisfaction

Favorite Business Publications: Remodeling Magazine

Hobbies/Interests/Sports: Fishing, Woodworking

Education Degrees: High School Diploma

Expanded Biography: Mr. Kapica has 30 years of experience in his field.

PROFESSIONAL OF THE YEAR IN CONCERT PERFORMANCE

DALE M. KASTBERG, PH.D.

Concert Musician
Dale Martin Kastberg, Ph.D.
1523 W. Shore Drive
Delafield, WI 53018 United States
dmk6@juno.com
http://www.cambridgewhoswho.com

Type of Business: Fine Arts and Music Performance

Major Products and Services: Spiritual Music, Choir, Hymns, Sacred Music, Concert Organist

Marketing Area: International

Day to Day Responsibilities: Making International Contributions through Art, Church and Organ Music

Hobbies/Interests/Sports: Gardening, Traveling, Oil Water and Acrylic Painting, Stained Glass

Education Degrees: Ph.D. in Music, Brentwood, England (2000); Master's Degree in Organ Performance, University of Wisconsin, Madison (1972)

Certifications: Ordained Theologian Minister (1976)

Affiliations/Associations/Societies: Wisconsin State Choir; National Cathedral Association

Awards/Honors: Men of Achievement (1977); Who's Who in Music (1975)

Expanded Biography: Dr. Kastberg has been an ordained theologian for 31 years. He visited Belgium as a lecturer of music in 1976 and was the State of Wisconsin's Ambassador of Goodwill in 1970. He speaks about fine arts and music in various forums around the world.

EXECUTIVE OF THE YEAR IN
EVENT PLANNING AND MANAGEMENT

JODI B. KATZMAN

Director, Events Management and Production
JBK Productions
307 E. 44th Street, Suite 410
New York, NY 10017 United States
jbkatzman@mindspring.com
http://www.cambridgewhoswho.com

Type of Business: Events Management and Production

Major Products and Services: Production and Management of High-Profile Events, Business Programs and Television Projects for Leading Organizations

Marketing Area: International

Area of Expertise: Ms. Katzman's expertise includes talent booking and coordination, television and theatrical production, stage management, promotion, logistics and on-site management.

Day to Day Responsibilities: Spearheading Projects from Inception to Execution in Support of Product Launches, Celebrations, Sports Competitions, Promotions, Fundraising Efforts, City-Wide Cultural Events, Conferences, Conventions, TV Programs, Award Shows, Parades, Festivals and Theatrical Productions

Favorite Business Publications: Variety, BizBash, Crain's New York Business, Industry-Related Magazines

Hobbies/Interests/Sports: Collecting Autographs and Memorabilia, Writing Script and Song Parodies, Playing Music, Attending Arts and Entertainment Events in New York City, Participating in Community Theater

Education Degrees: Bachelor of Arts in Mass Communications and Theatre, Hartt School of Music, University of Hartford, Cum Laude

Affiliations/Associations/Societies: Board Member, NY Coalition of Professional Women in the Arts & Media; Arts & Sciences Advisory Board, University of Hartford; Women in Sports & Events; New York Women in Communications; New York Women in Film & Television; Stage Managers' Association; National Academy of Television Arts & Sciences; Society of Industry Leaders

Awards/Honors: President's Award, Avon Products (2001); Executive & Professional of the Year in Event Planning & Management, Cambridge Who's Who (2006 & 2007); Arts & Sciences Advisory Board, University of Hartford (Since 2007); 2 Telly Awards/Verizon FiOS (2007); Esprit Award-Winning Promotion/Mercedes-Benz S-Class Launch (1999); Special Events Magazine Gala Award/Hong Kong USA Festival (1996); Published Articles in Public Relations Journal and PR Week Magazine (Two Feature Stories, Four Product Launch Campaigns)

Charity/Volunteer Work: Board of Directors, Vice President, Village Light Opera; Volunteer, Community Organization

Work History: Corporate Executive, Avon Products

Expanded Biography: Ms. Katzman has been producing award-winning events for leading organizations for more than 20 years. She has orchestrated over 100 high-profile, world-class events, business programs and TV projects. Her knack for bringing the 'wow factor' to every event she manages has contributed to her success, garnering repeat and referral business from world-class organizations in the for-profit and nonprofit sectors. She offers an extensive portfolio of success elevating profitability, visibility and image and manages multiple programs concurrently from concept through execution, on-time, on budget with a strong return on investment. Her experience includes work with Fortune 500 corporations, event companies, production houses, nonprofit organizations and independent projects, with an outstanding roster of annual and once-in-a-lifetime production credits. Selected accomplishments include: the 2008 Beijing Olympics, a Mercedes-Benz Launch, Blockbuster Video Game Championships, a Grammy Awards Celebration, two Presidential Conventions, Billie Jean King's Annual Salute to Women in Sports, World Archery Championships, an Atlanta Olympics Tennis Venue, three Miss America Pageants, four United Cerebral Palsy Telethons, BMW Goldeneye Press Launch, Nickelodeon Studios' Grand Opening, the First Annual Snapple Festival, Columbus 500th, Hong Kong USA Festival, Chase Holiday Festivals and the Desert Storm Parade. In addition, she has offered stage management, production and talent coordination services for shows including the Tony Awards, Grammy Awards, Night of 100 Stars, Irving Berlin 100th, Liberty Weekend Closing, 9/11 Memorial Services and was production manager for four Verizon FiOS corporate videos. Ms. Katzman has earned an equally strong reputation as a savvy and collaborative dealmaker, meticulous project manager and creative cost-cutter, slashing costs by millions of dollars, negotiating unprecedented contract terms and securing appearances by A-list televison, film, recording, business, sports personalities and athletes. Some of her favorite quotes include: 'Shoot for the moon; even if you miss it, you will land among the stars,' by Les Brown; 'Having fun is not a diversion from a successful life; it is the pathway to it,' by Oprah Winfrey; and 'Quality is never an accident. It is always the result of intelligent effort,' by John Ruskin.

EXECUTIVE OF THE YEAR IN LAW

DONEENE KEEMER DAMON, ESQ.

Director
Richards, Layton & Finger, PA
One Rodney Square
920 N. King Street
Wilmington, DE 19801 United States
damon@rlf.com
http://www.rlf.com

Type of Business: Law Firm

Major Products and Services: Legal Services Including Corporate Law, Restructuring, Bankruptcy, Tax Law and Pro Bono Services

Marketing Area: National

Day to Day Responsibilities: Managing Structured Finance, Asset Securitizations, Trust and Agency Services, Overseeing Trust-Preferred Transactions, Commercial Transactions and Banking Services

Favorite Business Publications: Asset Securitization Report

Education Degrees: JD, James E. Beasley School of Law, Temple University, Cum Laude (1992); Bachelor of Science in Accounting, Saint Joseph's University, Cum Laude (1989)

Affiliations/Associations/Societies: Delaware State Bar Association; The District of Columbia Bar; American Securitization Forum; Chairwoman, Committee on Trust Indentures and Indenture Trustees, American Bar Association

Expanded Biography: Ms. Keemer Damon is the co-author of PLI's 'Equipment Leasing.'

EXECUTIVE OF THE YEAR IN PHARMACY SERVICES

Ms. Angela Andes Kelley, RPH

1) Chief Executive Officer 2) Pharmacist
1) Professional Business Services, Inc. 2) Walgreen's
208 Brittany Park
Anderson, SC 29621 United States
tkak123@aol.com
http://www.premiernotesolutions.net

Type of Business: 1) Entrepreneurial Company 2) Pharmacy

Major Products and Services: 1) Products from Multi-Billion Dollar Companies 2) Pharmaceuticals

Marketing Area: 1) International 2) Local

Area of Expertise: Ms. Kelley's expertise is in management.

Day to Day Responsibilities: Gathering Loyal Customers for Multi-Billion Dollar Companies, Introducing the Business to Others, Distributing Pharmaceuticals

Favorite Business Publications: Your Business at Home, Money

Hobbies/Interests/Sports: Playing Tennis, Traveling, Helping Others

Education Degrees: Bachelor of Science in Pharmacy, Medical University of South Carolina

Affiliations/Associations/Societies: South Carolina Pharmacy Association

Spouse: Thomas   **Children:** Bryce, Layne

What do you attribute your success to? She attributes her success to her determination and desire to succeed.

How did you become involved in your profession? She became involved in her profession because she was always interested in real estate.

What was the highlight of your career? The highlights of her career were achieving success in her own business and becoming a pharmacist.

Where will you be in five years? In five years, Ms. Kelley hopes to be retired.

PROFESSIONAL OF THE YEAR IN
REGISTERED NURSE CASE MANAGEMENT

MAUREEN R. KELLY

Registered Nurse, Case Manager
Nursefinders
1541 Alta Drive, Suite 306
Whitehall, PA 18052 United States
Maureen.Kelly@cwwemail.com
http://www.nursefinders.com

Type of Business: Healthcare Center

Major Products and Services: Healthcare Services Including Residential Healthcare, Long-Term, Short-Term and Intermittent Care

Marketing Area: National

Area of Expertise: Ms. Kelly's expertise is in case management.

Day to Day Responsibilities: Overseeing Pediatric and Intermittent Healthcare Services, Dealing with Insurance Claims, Managing Admissions and Discharges

Hobbies/Interests/Sports: Reading, Traveling, Spending Time with her Grandson

Education Degrees: Associate Degree in Nursing, Northampton Community College, Bethlehem, PA (1994); Registered Nurse, Northampton Community College, Bethlehem, PA (1994)

Date of Birth: January 14, 1958   **Place of Birth:** Jersey City, NJ

Spouse: James   **Children:** Kevin, Matthew

Work History: Head Nurse, Zahra Pediatrics (1995-2002); Medical and Surgical Nurse, Sacred Heart Hospital, Allentown, PA (1995)

What do you attribute your success to? She attributes her success to her caring nature and the support she receives from her family and friends.

Expanded Biography: Ms. Kelly pursued her bachelor's degree at the age of 32. She finds deep personal fulfillment in her work, which allows her to observe people in a non-clinical setting and make a difference in their lives. She is constantly inspired by the resilience of the people whose hardships she witnesses.

CHRISTINE A. KENNEDY SCHOOLMAN

Dentist, Pharmacist
Forba, LLC Small Smiles
7104 Ticonderoga Road N.E.
Albuquerque, NM 87109 United States
cksmile@excite.com
http://www.cambridgewhoswho.com

Type of Business: Dental Center

Major Products and Services: Pediatric Dentistry

Marketing Area: Regional

Day to Day Responsibilities: Administering Dental Procedures Including Examinations, Fillings, Extractions, Crowns, Root Canals, Cleanings and X-Rays, Rendering Dental Education, Treating Pediatric Patients

Favorite Business Publications: ADA News, Woman Dentist Journal

Hobbies/Interests/Sports: Reading, Swimming

Education Degrees: Doctor of Dental Surgery, University of Missouri, Kansas City (2004); Doctor of Pharmacy, The University of New Mexico (2000)

Affiliations/Associations/Societies: American Dental Association; American Pediatric Dental Society

Expanded Biography: Dr. Kennedy Schoolman's work has been published in pharmacy journals.

PROFESSIONAL OF THE YEAR IN PHOTOGRAPHY

BRIAN RICHARD KERR

LSWPP, HE, DG, FAOE, FABI
Kerr Photography
P.O. Box 44926
London
England, N9 0WA United Kingdom
brianrichard.kerr@cwwemail.com
http://www.kerrphotography.co.uk

Type of Business: Photo Studio

Major Products and Services: Photography including Press, Commercial, Wedding, Portraiture and Social Functions

Marketing Area: International

Day to Day Responsibilities: Photographing for Press, Wedding, Commercial and Social Portraiture Functions, Writing Wedding Poems

Favorite Business Publications: Forbes Global; Fortune; Telegraph Newspaper; Time

Hobbies/Interests/Sports: Listening to Music, Playing the Drums, Piano and Violin, Writing, Motivational Reading, Spending Time with his Family

Education Degrees: Pursuing Diploma in Information Technology, Scheidegger Training College; Coursework in Photography, New York Institute of Photography; Coursework in Accounting, Business, Personal and Management Training

Affiliations/Associations/Societies: Deputy Governor, Distinguished Research Board of Advisers, ABI; Association of Christian Writers; American Order of Excellence; Order of International Ambassadors, ABI

Awards/Honors: Man of the Year, ABI (2005-2006); Distinction Award, Society of Wedding and Portrait Photograpehrs; International Cultural Diploma of Honor, ABI; International Peace Prize, United Cultural Convention, ABI; American Medal of Honor; Featured Member, Great Minds of the 21st Century; Featured Member, 500 Greatest Geniuses of the 21st Century, ABI; The Key Award, ABI; World Medal of Freedom, ABI

Charity/Volunteer Work: Assemblies of the First Born Church; Edmonton Baptist Church

Place of Birth: Balham

Spouse: Carol   **Children:** Lewis

Expanded Biography: Mr. Kerr's favorite quotes include 'Seize the moment;' 'If I expect things around me to change then I must change things within myself first of all;' and 'Do good to others always and good will follow you.'

PROFESSIONAL OF THE YEAR IN MOTHER AND BABY NURSING

SHAMEEZA KHAN, RN-C, ASN+

Registered Nurse Certified, Staff Nurse
Queens Hospital Center
82-68 164th Street
Jamaica, NY 11432 United States
zamsham@aol.com
http://nyc.gov/html/hhc/qhn/html/qhc.html

Type of Business: Full-Service Medical Center

Major Products and Services: High Quality Healthcare Services

Marketing Area: International

Day to Day Responsibilities: Offering Healthcare Services in the Mother and Baby Unit, Consulting and Educating Mothers, Supporting and Assisting Patients

Favorite Business Publications: American Journal of Nursing; American Nurse; LPN

Hobbies/Interests/Sports: Spending Quality Time with Family and Friends, Traveling

Education Degrees: Bachelor of Science in Nursing, York College; Associate of Science in Nursing, Queensborough Community College

Certifications: Certified Perinatal Nurse; Certification in Breastfeeding

Affiliations/Associations/Societies: Infection Control Representative, New York State Nurses Association; Phi Theta Kappa

Date of Birth: June 16, 1980   **Place of Birth:** Guyana

Spouse: Zameer   **Children:** Fardeen, Ameisha

What do you attribute your success to? She attributes her success to her very supportive parents and family.

How did you become involved in your profession? She became involved in her profession after discovering that this career was right for her.

What was the highlight of your career? The most gratifying aspect of her career is teaching mothers how to care for their newborn babies.

PROFESSIONAL OF THE YEAR IN
COURT ADMINISTRATION

NATHANIEL H.C. KIM

Department Head
Hawaii State Judiciary
1111 Alakea Street
Sixth Floor
Honolulu, HI 96813 United States
kimnatekim@aol.com
http://www.courts.state.hi.us

Type of Business: Government Organization

Major Products and Services: Judicial Administration

Marketing Area: Statewide

Area of Expertise: Mr. Kim's expertise is in court administration.

Favorite Business Publications: Fortune

Hobbies/Interests/Sports: Archery, Reading, Writing

Education Degrees: Master of Social Work, University of Hawaii; Bachelor of Arts in English Literature, University of Hawaii

Charity/Volunteer Work: The Silver Lining Foundation

Expanded Biography: Mr. Kim is the author of the books entitled 'Khwarazm', 'Blue Wolf, Fallow Doe', 'Sara', 'Of Time and Destiny' and 'I, Chinggis Quan.'

EXECUTIVE OF THE YEAR IN RESTAURANT FRANCHISING

KAREN L. KING

President
The King Group, Inc.,
c/o McDonalds of Orange Park
372-1 Blanding Boulevard
Orange Park, FL 32073 United States
jwrklk@bellsouth.net
http://www.cambridgewhoswho.com

Type of Business: Highly Qualified Franchising Company Playing a Major Role in the Success of McDonald's Franchising Around the World

Major Products and Services: Three McDonald's Franchises with a Commitment to Satisfying Customers in the Community with Quality Food and Customer Service

Marketing Area: National

Area of Expertise: Ms. King's expertise is in the administration and management of three McDonald's franchises with a personal commitment to the time and energy needed to run a fast food business.

Favorite Business Publications: Bottom Line Personal; The Kiplinger Letter

Hobbies/Interests/Sports: Reading Business and Self-Help Books, Dancing, Collecting Angels

Education Degrees: Associate Degree in Business Administration and Economics, Okalossa Walton College (1973); Diploma, Willard High School, OH (1959); Coursework in Franchise, Hamburger University

Affiliations/Associations/Societies: Women Business Owners; Women's Operators Network of McDonald's; Clay County Chamber of Commerce

Awards/Honors: Appointee, Planning and Zoning Commission (1999-2007); Clay County Business Person of the Year (1985)

Charity/Volunteer Work: Volunteer Prayer Minister, Christian Healing Ministers, Jacksonville, FL; Board of Directors, Salvation Army of Clay City

Date of Birth: November 6, 1941   **Place of Birth:** Dubois, PA

Spouse: John   **Children:** Eugene

Work History: Franchise Owner, McDonald's

Expanded Biography: Ms. King opened the first McDonald's in Clay County in 1974. She married her husband John in 1993 and has two granddaughters, Kassidy and Victoria. Her son Eugene is a second-generation McDonald's franchise owner.

EXECUTIVE OF THE YEAR IN
PROPERTY AND CASUALTY INSURANCE

STANLEY KLECKNER

President
Polar International Brokerage Corporation
369 Lexington Avenue
New York, NY 10017 United States
stanley.kleckner@cwwemail.com
http://www.rampartinsurance.com

Type of Business: Insurance Company

Major Products and Services: Insurance Services Including Personal, Commercial and Life Insurance, Brokerage Services

Marketing Area: Regional

Day to Day Responsibilities: Interacting with Clients, Representing Clients in Property and Casualty Insurance Coverage and Claims

Hobbies/Interests/Sports: Playing Tennis, Spending Time with his Family, Watching Basketball

Education Degrees: Bachelor's Degree, New York University

Affiliations/Associations/Societies: Associate, Hadassah

Work History: United States Army (1945-1946)

How did you become involved in your profession? He became involved in his profession because of his education.

What was the highlight of your career? The highlight of his career was being the largest provider of Aetna products before they were sold.

Expanded Biography: Mr. Kleckner has won more than 150 tennis tournaments worldwide.

EXECUTIVE OF THE YEAR IN BIOSTATISTICS

CHARLES J. KOCIAN, DDG, LFIBA

Owner
International Pyrotechnics Apparatus, Inc.
Apartment 103
Washington, DC 20006 United States
charles.kocian@cwwemail.com
http://www.cambridgewhoswho.com

Type of Business: Distribution Firm

Major Products and Services: Firefighting Apparatus Including Fire Engines, Ambulances, Pump Trucks and Firefighting Gear

Marketing Area: International

Area of Expertise: Mr. Kocian's expertise is in biostatistics.

Favorite Business Publications: Entrepreneur

Hobbies/Interests/Sports: Volunteering, Philanthropy

Education Degrees: Master's Degree, American University; Master's Degree, Rensselaer Polytechnic Institute; Bachelor of Business Administration, Lycoming College

Affiliations/Associations/Societies: British Embassy; Canadian Embassy; Australian Embassy; United States Department of Health and Human Services, Office of the Surgeon General; American Biographical Institute Research Association; Vice President, World Congress on Communication and Arts; Masonic Organization

Awards/Honors: Leading Intellectuals of the World, American Biographical Institute (2006-2007); International Biographical Center Directory (2005-2006); Leading Intellectuals of the World, International Biographical Center (2005); Man of the Year Award (2000); 2000 Outstanding Intellectuals of the 21st Century, International Biographical Center; Outstanding Intellectual of the 21st Century Award; Great Minds of the 21st Century Award, American Biogeographical Institute; Who's Who of Professionals; American Biographical Institute; Featured Member, The First Five Hundred, International Biographical Center; Living Legends, International Biographical Centre; International Register of Profiles, International Biographical Centre; Lexington Who's Who; Marquis Who's Who; Featured Member, International Directory of Experts and Expertise

Charity/Volunteer Work: Local Charitable Organizations; President, Salvadoran American Humanitarian Foundation

Date of Birth: March 31, 1921   **Place of Birth:** Lansford, PA

Spouse: Jean

Work History: United States Army Civilian, Office of the Surgeon General, United States Department of Health & Human Services (1965-1976); Supervisory Statistician, Rural Electrification Administration, United States Department of Agriculture (1963-1965); United States Army Civilian, Military Sea Transportation Service (1961-1963); United Mine Workers of American Welfare and Retirement Fund Medical Care Program (1950-1961)

Expanded Biography: Mr. Kocian has published two articles entitled 'Medical Statistics in World War II' and 'Neuropsychiatry in World War II' for the United States Army.

PROFESSIONAL OF THE YEAR IN PERIODONTICS

DAVID L. KORCHEK, DMD

Periodontist
Dr. David L. Korchek
414 N. Camden Drive
Beverly Hills, CA 90210 United States
info@CambridgeWhosWho.com
http://www.cambridgewhoswho.com

Type of Business: Dental Practice

Major Products and Services: Periodontal Services

Marketing Area: California

Day to Day Responsibilities: Practicing Periodontics

Hobbies/Interests/Sports: Photography

Education Degrees: Doctor of Dental Medicine, Harvard School of Dental Medicine (1957); Master's Degree, University of Southern California (1953); Bachelor of Arts and Sciences in Zoology and Bacteriology, University of Southern California (1951)

Affiliations/Associations/Societies: California Dental Association; American Dental Association; Beverly Hills Academy of Dentistry; American Academy of Periodontics

Date of Birth: July 19, 1929   **Place of Birth:** Detroit, MI

Children: Jeffrey, Cathie

Work History: Private Periodontal Practice (Present); Instructor of Undergraduate Students and Post-Graduate Students in Periodontics, University of Southern California Dental School (1961-1985); Mexico University (1961-1980); Instructor of Oral Diagnostics, University of Southern California Dental School (1957-1958); Teaching Assistant in Anatomy, University of California, Los Angeles (1951-1953); Teaching Assistant in Histology, University of California, Los Angeles (1950-1951); Teaching Assistant in Chemistry, University of California, Los Angeles (1949-1950)

PROFESSIONAL OF THE YEAR IN
ACADEMIC ACHIEVEMENT ADMINISTRATION

DR. LOIS MAE KOSTER-PETERSON

Administrator, Academic Achievement
Sacramento City Unified School District
5735 47th Avenue, Box 720
Sacramento, CA 95824 United States
petersol@sac-city.k12.ca.us
http://www.scusd.edu

Type of Business: Urban Public Education System

Major Products and Services: General Elementary and Secondary School Curriculum, Arts, Music, Physical Education, Language Arts, Special Education, Learning Resources, Extracurricular Activities, Athletics, Student Clubs and Organizations

Marketing Area: Regional

Area of Expertise: Dr. Koster-Peterson's expertise is in educational leadership.

Favorite Business Publications: Industry-Related Publications

Hobbies/Interests/Sports: Biking, Walking, Traveling, Reading

Education Degrees: Doctorate in Educational Leadership, Northern Arizona University; Education Specialist Degree in Educational Leadership, Point Loma Nazarene University; Master of Arts in Secondary Leadership, Iowa State University; Bachelor of Arts in Business Education, Physical Education and Coaching, Buena Vista University

Affiliations/Associations/Societies: Association for Supervision and Curriculum Development; National Association of Secondary School Principals; Advisory Board Member, The Principals' Center at Harvard University; Phi Delta Kappa; Association of California School Administrators; National School Principals Association; Joan L. Curcio International Women's Leadership Conference, Oxford University (2007); Principals' Center Emeritus Advisory Board Member, Harvard University (2007); Harvard University Principals' Center, 25th Anniversary and Lessons Learned Institute (2006); An Evolving Vision, Harvard University Principals' Center (1999); Lifetime Emeritus Member Parent Teacher Association, Shawnee Mission North High School (1997)

Awards/Honors: Most Supportive Faculty Award, Shawnee Mission North High School (1997); School Administrator of the Year, Shawnee Mission School District (1995 – 1996); Thespian Administrator of the Year, State of Kansas (1995-1996); North Winneshiek Sincere and Devoted Effort Award (1988); Conference and Regional Coach of the Year, Softball and Basketball, Colo Community School (1979 – 1982)

Place of Birth: Carroll, Iowa

Spouse: Kent R. Peterson

Work History: Colo Community Schools, Colo, IA; Dubuque Wahlert High School, Dubuque, IA; North Winneshiek School, Decorah, IA; Dodge City Junior High School, Dodge City, KS; Winterset High School, Winterset, IA; Olive Pierce Middle School, Ramma, CA; Shawnee Mission North High School, Shawnee Mission, KS; Albert Einstein Middle School, Sacramento, CA; Sacramento City Unified School District, Sacramento, CA; Former Adjunct Faculty Member, California State University at Sacramento; Former Adjunct Faculty Member, MidAmerica Nazarene University, Olathe, KS; Part-Time Faculty, Sacramento State University, Sacramento, CA

Career Achievements: National Blue Ribbon Nominee, No Child Left Behind (2006); California Distinguished School (2005); California Title One Academic Award (2005-2006); National Advisory Board Member, Principals' Center, Harvard Graduate School of Education

What do you attribute your success to? She attributes her success to her desire to support education.

How did you become involved in your profession? She became involved in her profession because she always wanted to be a teacher and had a desire to help others.

What was the highlight of your career? The highlight of her career was attaining her current position.

PROFESSIONAL OF THE YEAR IN HUMAN RESOURCES

Ms. Beverly E. Kramer, PHR

Human Resources Manager
Quaker Tropicana Gatorade (QTG) Division
PepsiCo
750 Oakhill Road
Mountain Top, PA 18707 United States
beverly_kramer@quakeroats.com
http://www.cambridgewhoswho.com

Type of Business: Manufacturing Company

Major Products and Services: Food and Beverage Products Including Ready-to-Eat Food Products and Cereals, Fruit Juices, Soft Drinks, Soda, Gatorade, Tropicana, Flavored Water and Quaker Products

Marketing Area: International

Day to Day Responsibilities: Offering Human Resource Leadership and Support for 240 Salaried and Hourly Associates, Negotiating Contracts, Overseeing Communications, Safety and Community Relations and Benefits and Employee Labor Relations, Focusing on Systems Improvement, Utilizing Total Productive Maintenance Programs, Recruiting, Managing Talent, Ensuring Manager Quality, Building Empowered Cultures

Favorite Business Publications: The Wall Street Journal; SHRM Journal

Hobbies/Interests/Sports: Camping and Hiking in Pennsylvania State Parks, Reading, Scrapbooking, Spending Time with her Family

Education Degrees: Pursuing Master of Science in Organization and Management, Misericordia University; Bachelor's Degree in English, Kutztown University, PA (1985); Associate Degree in Business Administration, Pennsylvania State University (1982)

Certifications: Professional in Human Resources Certification, Human Resource Certification Institute, Society for Human Resource Management (2007); Certification in Employment Law, Institute for Applied Management and Law (2004); Certified Trainer, DDI Training Institute (2002); Certified Targeted Selection Administrator (2002); Certified Secondary Education Teacher, Albright College (1990)

Affiliations/Associations/Societies: Society for Human Resource Management; Northeastern Pennsylvania Society for Human Resource Management

Charity/Volunteer Work: Band Parent, Crestwood High School; Girl Scouts of the United States of America; Susan G. Komen Race for the Cure; Relay for Life, American Cancer Society; Board Member, Wyoming Valley Chapter, American Red Cross; Board Member, Pennsylvania Chapter, American Red Cross

Date of Birth: November 17, 1962   **Place of Birth:** Pottsville, PA

Spouse: Brian Sr.   **Children:** Brian Jr., Victoria

Work History: Human Resources Manager, Kraft Foods (2002-2005); Human Resources Administrator, Sony Electronics (1998-2000); Communications Manager, Alcoa Engineered Products (1998-2000); Human Resources Representative, Premier Beverage Packers (1997-1998); Human Resources Representative, Interstate Intercom (1995-1997); Adjunct Faculty Member, Schuylkill Institute of Business and Technology; Adjunct Faculty Member, Reading Area Community College

Expanded Biography: Ms. Kramer was a teacher from 1990 to 1995. She resides in Mountaintop, PA, with her husband Brian and their children Brian Jr. and Victoria. Brian Jr. is in the United States Navy and is currently serving his tour of duty in the Mediterranean region.

EXECUTIVE OF THE YEAR IN TECHNOLOGY-BASED SERVICES FOR THE FINANCIAL ADVISORY INDUSTRY

DR. HELGA ELIZABETH KROEGER

President and CEO
DRSdigital, LLC
230 Park Avenue, 10th Floor
New York, NY 10169 United States
liza.kroeger@drs-digital.com
http://www.drs-digital-usa.com

Type of Business: Technology-Based Services for the Financial Advisory Industry

Major Products and Services: Financial Advising, DRSdigital, The Virtual Data Room Platform, DRSq+a Tool, The Online Q&A Management PlatformDRSDocMaster, The Administration Tool for DRSdigital Virtual Data Rooms

Marketing Area: International

Area of Expertise: Dr. Kroeger's expertise includes international investments, mergers and acquisitions, corporate governance, strategic decisions and operations.

Favorite Business Publications: The New York Times

Hobbies/Interests/Sports: Traveling, Attending the Theater and Ballet, Visiting Museums

Education Degrees: JD, Earned in Frankfurt, Germany; Ph.D. in Law, Earned in Frankfurt, Germany; Master of Laws, University of California at Berkeley

Affiliations/Associations/Societies: California Bar Association; Frankfurt Bar Association; American Bar Association; Advisory Board Member, Frankfurt International School

Spouse: Frank   **Children:** Alexandra

What do you attribute your success to? She attributes her success to working hard, thriving on knowledge and taking risks.

How did you become involved in your profession? She became involved in her profession because she came from a rural town and decided she liked working across borders.

What was the highlight of your career? The highlight of her career was gaining partner status in a competitive firm on Wall Street.

Expanded Biography: Dr. Kroeger speaks English, German and French. She established DRSdigital, LLC in 2005.

PROFESSIONAL OF THE YEAR IN CONSTRUCTION LAW

KRISTINE A. KUBES, JD

Attorney
Meagher & Geer, PLLP
33 S. Sixth Street, Suite 4400
Minneapolis, MN 55402 United States
kkubes@meagher.com
http://www.meagher.com

Type of Business: Law Firm

Major Products and Services: Legal Services Including Construction Law, Contract Negotiation, Proactive Project Management, Counseling, Professional Liability Defense and Business Services, Mediation Services for Business and Construction Disputes

Marketing Area: National

Area of Expertise: Ms. Kubes' expertise includes construction law and the mediation of construction and business disputes.

Day to Day Responsibilities: Representing Design Professionals, Architects, Engineers and Contractors

Hobbies/Interests/Sports: Cooking, Entertaining, Singing, Reading, Watching College Football

Education Degrees: JD, University of Minnesota Law School; Bachelor of Arts in English and Political Science, The College of St. Catherine, St. Paul, MN

Affiliations/Associations/Societies: Hennepin County Bar Association; Construction Law Section, Minnesota State Bar Association; Division 3 Steering Committee, Forum on the Construction Industry Program, American Bar Association; Minnesota Women Lawyers; Associate Member, American Institute of Architects Minnesota; Vice Chair, Minnesota State Board of Architecture

Place of Birth: Minneapolis, MN

Work History: Meagher & Geer, PLLP (2002-Present); Associate Attorney, Thomas R. Olson & Associates (1998-2002); Law Clerk to Judge Robert Schumacher (1998); Law Clerk to Judge Fred Norton (1993-1998); Law Clerk to Judge Doris Ohlsen Huspeni, Minnesota Court of Appeals (1990-1992)

Expanded Biography: Ms. Kubes was featured in the American Bar Association's forum on the construction industry in 2006. Since 2005, she has been teaching an annual course on construction documents and services for the American Institute of Architects Minnesota.

PROFESSIONAL OF THE YEAR IN PODIATRY

DR. DARLINE M. KULHAN

President, Doctor of Podiatric Medicine and Surgery
Scarsdale Foot Specialists, PC
32 Harney Road
Scarsdale, NY 10583 United States
duchessdarline@aol.com
http://www.real4reel.com

Type of Business: Podiatry Clinic

Major Products and Services: Aesthetic Foot and Podiatric Surgery

Marketing Area: Regional

Area of Expertise: Dr. Kulhan's expertise includes surgical foot reconstruction and podiatric surgical practice management.

Day to Day Responsibilities: Lecturing Nationwide on Foot Aesthetics, Performing Botox and Sculptra Injections in Foot and Aesthetic Foot Makeovers

Favorite Business Publications: The Journal of Foot & Ankle Surgery

Hobbies/Interests/Sports: Skiing, Skating

Education Degrees: Doctor of Podiatric Medicine, New York College of Podiatric Medicine (1978); Residency in Podiatric Surgery, Washington Memorial Hospital, NJ

Certifications: Board Certified in Podiatric Surgery (1995)

Affiliations/Associations/Societies: Physicians Advisory Board, National Republican Congressional Committee (2005-2007); Board of Directors, International Aesthetic Foot Society (2005-2007); Diplomate, American Board of Podiatric Surgery (1995); Fellow, American College of Foot and Ankle Surgeons (1995); Fellow, American College of Foot and Ankle Surgeons (1995); Pi Delta (1978); Diplomate, American Board of Podiatric Examiners (1978); American Podiatric Medical Society; Life Member, President's Task Force, Republican Party

Awards/Honors: New York Physician of the Year Award, National Republican Congressional Committee (2006)

Children: Harry, Annette

Expanded Biography: Dr. Kulhan is currently writing the memoirs of her father John Kulhan, who won numerous awards and accolades for his charitable work in Russia. She and her family have been instrumental in helping to build a church dedicated to Divine Mercy in Praznovce, Slovakia. They were also involved in the canonization of the first saint of the new millennium, which earned them an apostolic blessing from Pope John Paul II in 2000.

PROFESSIONAL OF THE YEAR IN
GENETIC RESEARCH AND DEVELOPMENT

THOMAS K. KUPKA

1) Owner 2) Researcher
1) Serendipity Labs 2) Parkway Electric
2009 Portland Avenue
Minneapolis, MN 55404 United States
thomas.kupka@cwwemail.com
http://www.cambridgewhoswho.com

Type of Business: 1) Laboratory 2) Electrical Contracting Company

Major Products and Services: 1) Genetic Research and Development Services 2) Electrical Contracting Services Including Design, Maintenance and Installation of Electrical, Voice and Data Systems and Laser Knives

Marketing Area: Regional

Day to Day Responsibilities: Conducting Research on Genetics, Utilizing Existing Research Facilities, Creating New Ideas

Favorite Business Publications: Science; Nature

Education Degrees: Ph.D. in Plant Genetics, Ludwig-Maximilians-University, Munich, Germany (1970)

Affiliations/Associations/Societies: New York Academy of Sciences; American Chemical Society

Expanded Biography: Dr. Kupka received the Fulbright traveling scholarship and holds 131 patents.

PROFESSIONAL OF THE YEAR IN
PERIOPERATIVE NURSING

BOJAN M. KUURE, RN

Director of Surgical Services
Island Hospital
1211 24th Street
Anacortes, WA 98221 United States
bkuure@islandhospital.org
http://www.islandhospital.org

Type of Business: Hospital

Major Products and Services: Healthcare

Marketing Area: Regional

Area of Expertise: Ms. Kuure's expertise includes operating room and anesthesia nursing, and operating room management.

Day to Day Responsibilities: Overseeing the Operating Room, Administering Anesthesia, Performing Central Service Including Endoscopy, Managing Procedure Flow in Operating Rooms, Ensuring Doctors' and Operating Room Staff's Welfare, Ordering Specific Items, Supplies and Implants

Hobbies/Interests/Sports: Diving, Skiing, Gardening

Education Degrees: Registered Nurse, University of Finland (1964)

Affiliations/Associations/Societies: Association of periOperative Registered Nurses

Charity/Volunteer Work: HTC WWA; Oregon Chapter, HTC; Midlantic Chapter, HTC; Northeast Chapter, HTC; Interplast; Operation Smile

Date of Birth: November 14, 1942

Expanded Biography: Ms. Kuure completed research on open-heart procedures, including bypass surgeries, in her native Finland. She has also trained surgical nurses.

PROFESSIONAL OF THE YEAR IN OFFICE ADMINISTRATION

Ms. Pauline M. Lagace

Office Clerk
Sigma Systems, Inc.
201 Boston Post Road
Marlborough, MA 01752 United States
plgc8074@msn.com
http://www.cambridgewhoswho.com

Type of Business: IT, Employment Recruiter, Executive Searches

Major Products and Services: Recruiting Employees for Clients

Marketing Area: Local

Area of Expertise: Ms. Lagace's expertise is in office administration.

Hobbies/Interests/Sports: Spending Time with her Children

Education Degrees: Coursework in Business, Mount Wachusett College

Awards/Honors: Shining Star Award for Volunteer Work, Arc Community Service

Charity/Volunteer Work: Arc Community Service; Veterans Groups; Korean War Veterans

Work History: Nursing Assistant, Doctor's Office

Expanded Biography: Ms. Lagace has five grandchildren, Aaron, Corey, Brad, Justin and Curtis.

PROFESSIONAL OF THE YEAR IN ASSISTED LIVING SUPPORT

MS. D. JANE LAMBERT

Windows Support Coordinator
Country Meadows Retirement Community
451 Sand Hill Road
Hershey, PA 17033 United States
JLambert@countrymeadows.com
http://www.countrymeadows.com

Type of Business: Assisted Living Retirement Community

Major Products and Services: Family-Owned and Operated Retirement Community with 24-Hour Care and Four Levels of Care

Marketing Area: Statewide

Day to Day Responsibilities: Working with Residents Showing Signs of Dementia, Assisting Residents with Staying Alert and Mentally Stimulated, Coaching Residents Using Posit Science Audible Computer Programs to Increase Cognitive Abilities

Favorite Business Publications: Newsweek

Hobbies/Interests/Sports: Creating Gift Baskets and Wreaths, Sports, Watching Football, Hockey and Soccer

Education Degrees: Pursuing Certification in Speaking with Individuals in a Vegetative State, The Validation Training Institute; Associate Degree in Hotel Management; Associate Degree in Allied Health, Harrisburg Area Community College; Coursework in Gerontology, Harrisburg Area Community College

Date of Birth: June 8, 1943   **Place of Birth:** Pennsylvania

Spouse: Len   **Children:** Leon, Drew

Work History: Controller, Hershey Entertainment, Inc.; Office Manager, Christmas Wholesaler; Country Meadows Retirement Community

Career Achievements: Board of Directors, Children's Playroom, Harrisburg, PA; Board of Directors, Lower Dauphin High School Alumni Association

Expanded Biography: Ms. Lambert wanted to work with seniors since her childhood. After a career in hotel accounting and raising her two children, she decided to pursue her dream of working with the senior population. She enjoys assisting residents in all levels of care and independent, assisted living. At the age of 60 she continued her education in allied health. The most rewarding aspects of her profession are listening to patients and touching their lives with just a smile or hug. Her passion for her profession can best be described by a quote from publisher Katharine Graham which states, 'To love what you do, and feel that it matters. How could anything else be more fun?'

PROFESSIONAL OF THE YEAR IN DAIRY FARMING

CAROLYN E. LANDIS

Co-Owner
Misty-Octoraro Farm
439 Creek Road
Christiana, PA 17509 United States
canonelan@earthlink.net
http://www.cambridgewhoswho.com

Type of Business: Dairy Farm

Major Products and Services: Dairy Products

Marketing Area: Regional

Area of Expertise: Ms. Landis' expertise is in operations management.

Favorite Business Publications: Farm Journal

Hobbies/Interests/Sports: Watercolor Painting, Photography, Playing the Piano, Decorating

Education Degrees: Coursework in Computer Science; Coursework in Christian Counseling

Affiliations/Associations/Societies: Pennsylvania Farm Bureau; Women of Faith Association; American Association of Christian Counselors

Charity/Volunteer Work: Local Church

Spouse: J. Kenneth   **Children:** Jeffrey, Lisa

What do you attribute your success to? She attributes her success to hard work and dedication.

How did you become involved in your profession? She became involved in her profession because it was her family business.

What was the highlight of your career? The most gratifying aspect of her career is offering her spiritual presence to others through her business.

Expanded Biography: Ms. Landis is a Sunday school teacher.

PROFESSIONAL OF THE YEAR IN SOCIAL SERVICES AND FAMILY SCIENCE

CLARA LANE-BROWN

Owner, Licensed Social Worker
Special Gifts for Social Workers
6616 Red Bud Road
Fort Worth, TX 76135 United States
swclara@aol.com
http://www.cambridgewhoswho.com

Type of Business: Retail Store

Major Products and Services: Handmade Items Created with Social Work Jargon

Marketing Area: National

Area of Expertise: Ms. Lane-Brown's expertise is in social services including mental health and gerontology.

Day to Day Responsibilities: Coordinating Outreach Programs for Elderly Guardianship and At-Risk Children

Favorite Business Publications: NASW Newsletter; Fort Worth Star Telegram; Azle News; Play Therapy

Hobbies/Interests/Sports: Making Crafts, Interior Designs, Traveling, Swimming, Clog Dancing

Education Degrees: Master's Degree in Child Development, Texas Woman's University (2000); Bachelor of Arts in Social Work, with a Concentration in Psychology and Sociology, University of Oklahoma (1966)

Certifications: Licensed Social Worker

Affiliations/Associations/Societies: Graduate Honor Society; Honorary Member, National Association of Social Workers

Awards/Honors: Who's Who Among Professionals

Date of Birth: February 7, 1943   **Place of Birth:** Okemah, OK

Spouse: Lesley   **Children:** Toby

Work History: Social Worker, Buckner Children's Home; Social Worker, Denton State School; Master Teacher, Child Care Associates, Fort Worth, TX; Part-Time Administrative Social Worker, Guardianship Services, Fort Worth

What was the highlight of your career? The highlights of her career were obtaining her master's degree at the age of 57 and starting her own business.

Expanded Biography: Ms. Lane-Brown came to Dallas in 1966 and began her career with Buckner Children's Home. She worked as a social work consultant for two nursing homes, and has administered several outreach programs and procedural policies.

EXECUTIVE OF THE YEAR IN
BEVERAGE MANUFACTURING AND LOGISTICS

DAVID E. LAPP

Vice President Worldwide Manufacturing
The Pepsi Bottling Group, Inc.
44 Charter Ridge Drive
Sandy Hook, CT 06482 United States
david.lapp@pepsi.com
http://www.pbg.com

Type of Business: Manufacturing Company

Major Products and Services: Pepsi-Cola Products

Marketing Area: International

Day to Day Responsibilities: Overseeing Staff Members and Logistics Operations, Manufacturing Strategies

Favorite Business Publications: Industry-Related Publications

Hobbies/Interests/Sports: Snow and Water Skiing, Running, Restoring Homes, Traveling

Education Degrees: Bachelor's Degree in Economics, University of California, Davis (1988)

Affiliations/Associations/Societies: Council of Logistics Management

Charity/Volunteer Work: Juvenile Diabetes; American Cancer Society Relay for Life; Race for the Cure

What do you attribute your success to? He attributes his success to leadership and vision.

How did you become involved in your profession? He became involved in his profession through a natural progression of opportunities.

PROFESSIONAL OF THE YEAR IN PEDIATRIC HOME CARE

BECKY LATHROP

Licensed Practical Nurse
rblathrop@sbcglobal.net
http://www.cambridgewhoswho.com

Type of Business: Foster Care Center

Major Products and Services: Foster Care and Healthcare Services

Marketing Area: Local

Day to Day Responsibilities: Caring for Disabled Foster Children, Offering in-Home Care for Families with Special Needs Children who are Dependent on Technology, Giving Emotional Support to Families

Favorite Business Publications: Mind & Body Magazine

Hobbies/Interests/Sports: Reading, Quilting, Gardening, Sports

Certifications: Licensed Practical Nurse, Dodge City Community College (1976)

Affiliations/Associations/Societies: Kansas Foster and Adoptive Parent Association; Families Together, Inc.

Awards/Honors: Award, Court Appointed Special Advocates

Charity/Volunteer Work: Local Hospice; Pratt Friends Church

Date of Birth: August 30, 1955   **Place of Birth:** Los Angeles

Spouse: Robert   **Children:** Lindsey, Katie, Matthew

Work History: Meade District Hospital; Dr. R.H. Hill Pratt Regional Medical Center; Southwind Hospice, Inc.; Care 2000 Home HealthCare Services Inc.

What do you attribute your success to? She attributes her success to the support she receives from her family and having good friends in the nursing community.

How did you become involved in your profession? She became involved in her profession because she loves children and caring for their specific needs.

What was the highlight of your career? The most gratifying aspect of her career is seeing children loved, happy and cared for.

Expanded Biography: Ms. Lathrop is a foster parent of special children who are dependent on ventilators.

EXECUTIVE OF THE YEAR IN INVESTMENTS

YUK CHUN LAU

Chief Executive Officer
God the Creator Heritage
P.O. Box 7148
Alhambra, CA 91802 United States
infoalh@aol.com
http://www.cambridgewhoswho.com

Type of Business: Educational Institution

Major Products and Services: Higher Education

Marketing Area: International

Area of Expertise: Ms. Lau's expertise is in Hong Kong media approvals.

Day to Day Responsibilities: Working on Technology Including Energy Tree, Translating with a Digital Library, Dictionary and Language, Organizing Mother and Infant Care Outreach Programs, Teaching Mathematics and Nuclear Mathematics, Rendering Healthcare Services Including Home, Mental Health, Day, Child and Elderly Care Services

Hobbies/Interests/Sports: Traveling, Reading, Swimming, Participating in Track and Field Events

Education Degrees: Bachelor of Science, California State University, Los Angeles

Certifications: Certification, Graduate Realtor Institute

Affiliations/Associations/Societies: California Association of Realtors; Founder, The University of Hong Kong; The Chinese University of Hong Kong; The Hong Kong University of Science and Technology; The Hong Kong Polytechnic University; The Hong Kong Institute of Education

Awards/Honors: Dean's List, California State University, Los Angeles

Charity/Volunteer Work: Founder, Hong Kong Mental Health; Founder, Prince of Wales Hospital, Hong Kong

Date of Birth: January 1, 1957   **Place of Birth:** Hong Kong

Children: Kenneth, Adelaide, Angela, Barney

What do you attribute your success to? She attributes her success to her hard work and faith in God. **How did you become involved in your profession?** She became involved in her profession because of her interest in finance and her desire to help people.

What was the highlight of your career? The highlight of her career will be exploring outer space.

Expanded Biography: Ms. Lau has also taught mathematics, English as a second language, integrated science, special education, fashion design, psychology and nuclear mathematics.

PROFESSIONAL OF THE YEAR IN GLOBAL FINANCE

RACHEL S. LAWRENCE MINARD

Contract Negotiator
Corbin Capital Partners
870 Market Street, Suite 1201
San Francisco, CA 94102 United States
rachelminard@hotmail.com
rminard@corbincapital.com
http://www.corbincapital.com

Type of Business: Finance Company

Major Products and Services: Marketing, Finance and Investment Services

Marketing Area: International

Area of Expertise: Ms. Lawrence Minard's expertise includes product and client management, and leadership.

Day to Day Responsibilities: Investing and Managing Globally, Marketing, Global Branding, Raising Assets, Developing Global Partnerships and Distribution Channels, Hiring and Training Staff

Favorite Business Publications: Pensions and Investments; InvestHedge; The Wall Street Journal; Financial Times

Hobbies/Interests/Sports: Skydiving, Motorcycling, Running, Traveling, Trekking

Education Degrees: Bachelor's Degree in Journalism, Northeastern University; Coursework, Wharton Investment Institute

Awards/Honors: Profit Maintainer of the Year, FEMM (2004); Global Public Speaker; Rising Star

Expanded Biography: Ms. Minard recently accepted a position in contract negotiation with a new firm.

PROFESSIONAL OF THE YEAR IN INSURANCE INVESTIGATIONS

LARRY D. LEE

Unit Manager, Special Investigation Unit
Westfield Group Insurance Company
10300 Alliance Road, Suite 260
Cincinnati, OH 45242 United States
larrylee@westfieldgrp.com
http://www.westfieldgrp.com

Type of Business: Insurance Company Specializing in Property and Casualty Insurance

Major Products and Services: Structured Settlements, Flood Program and Specialty Brokerage Services

Marketing Area: National

Day to Day Responsibilities: Conducting Claim Investigations

Favorite Business Publications: SIU Awareness

Hobbies/Interests/Sports: Fishing, Hunting, Sports

Education Degrees: Pursuing Bachelor's Degree in Criminal Justice and Business, University of Phoenix; Pursuing Certification in Fraud Examination; Certified Field Examiner; Graduate, Northwestern University 200-Hour Course on Managing Criminal Investigators; Certified Fraud Investigator; Senior Claims Law Associate; Fraud Claims Law Associate; Casualty Claims Law Associate; Fraud Claims Law Specialist; Property Claim Law Associate; Certified Insurance Fraud Investigator; Legal Principal Law Specialist

Affiliations/Associations/Societies: Ohio Chapter, International Association of Arson Investigators; Ohio Chapter, International Association of Auto Theft Investigators; Ohio Chapter, International Association of Special Investigation Units; Association of Certified Fraud Examiners; Former Member, County Arson Task Force

Awards/Honors: Achievement Award for the Successful Completion of the Traffic Institute's 200 Hour Series on Management of Criminal Investigation, Northwestern University Traffic Institute (1995); Dual-Recipient, Outstanding Young Police Officer of the Year; Recognition for Specific Criminal Investigation, Internal Revenue Service

Date of Birth: July 26, 1956

Spouse: Pamela   **Children:** Amy B. Cash, Amy R. Settle, David Sheppard, Susan Lancaster

Work History: City Police Department; Chief Operator of Communications, West Virginia State Police; Manager, Special Investigation Unit

Career Achievements: Officer in Charge of Investigations, Local Police Department; Member, Special Investigation Unit, Local Insurance Company; Manager, Investigating Casualty and Property Claims and Major Case Investigations

Expanded Biography: Mr. Lee's experience in law enforcement and insurance investigation has allowed him exposure to the criminal and civil sides of investigations. He is fortunate to have completed continued education and training in the field of civil and criminal investigations, and to have worked alongside some of the industry's best investigators.

ROSEMARY CARRASCO LEÓN, MD

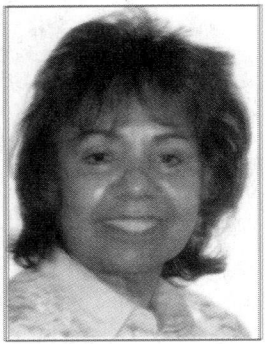

Physician
Rosemary C. León, MD
32665 Ray Court
Visalia, CA 93292 United States
rosecleon@sbcglobal.net
http://www.cambridgewhoswho.com

Type of Business: Medical Clinic

Major Products and Services: Healthcare Including Gynecology Services, Women's Healthcare and Minor Surgical Procedures

Marketing Area: Regional

Area of Expertise: Dr. Leon's expertise includes obstetrics and gynecology, high-risk pregnancy, infertility, women's health issues and the treatment of patients with diabetes and lupus.

Favorite Business Publications: Contemporary OB/GYN

Hobbies/Interests/Sports: Reading, Knitting, Sewing, Crocheting, Participating in Water Sports

Education Degrees: Fellow, American College of Obstetricians and Gynecologists; Doctor of Medicine, School of Medicine, University of California, Los Angeles (1980); Coursework in Pre-Pharmaceutical Studies, University of California, Los Angeles; Coursework, San Francisco School of Pharmacy (1975)

Certifications: Certified Obstetrician and Gynecologist

Affiliations/Associations/Societies: California Medical Association; American Medical Association

Date of Birth: January 24, 1951   **Place of Birth:** Hanford

Children: Liliana, Carlo

Work History: Gynecologist, Dr. Rene Charles Practice (2006); Obstetrician and Gynecologist, Tule River Indian Health Center (2004-2005); Obstetrics and Gynecology Private Practice (1988-2001); Obstetrician and Gynecologist, Portervine Health Center (1985-1988)

Career Achievements: Outstanding Physician, Kaweah Delta Hospital (1991)

Expanded Biography: Dr. Leon performs depression and anxiety consultations for non-pregnant women, men and children, and gives presentations at schools about the importance of higher education. She also works with low-income patients and as an independent contractor with a doctor.

PROFESSIONAL OF THE YEAR IN MENTAL HEALTH COUNSELING

Ms. Diane Karen Lessner

1) Owner, Rehabilitation Mental Health Specialist 2) Vocational Rehabilitation Counselor
1) Consult Rehab 2) Department of Veterans Affairs (VA Greater Healthcare System)
1924 Prosser Avenue
Los Angeles, CA 90025 United States
fouru2b4u@earthlink.net
http://www.cambridgewhoswho.com

Type of Business: 1) Healthcare, Mental Health and Vocational Counseling Service 2) Healthcare System

Major Products and Services: 1) Rehabilitation and Mental Health Counseling 2) Healthcare

Marketing Area: 1) National 2) National

Area of Expertise: Ms. Lessner's expertise includes vocational rehabilitation and job placement.

Day to Day Responsibilities: Working with Returning Soldiers from Iraq and Afghanistan with Polytrauma Issues and Helping Them Find Employment in the Private Sector

Favorite Business Publications: Psychology Today; Discover Magazine; U.S. News & World Report

Hobbies/Interests/Sports: Ballet Dancing, Swimming, Movies, Writing Poetry

Education Degrees: Master's Degree in Vocational Rehabilitation, University of Hawaii (1992); Master's Degree in Physiological Psychology, Stony Brook University (1978); Coursework in Physiological Psychology, University of Washington

Certifications: Licensed Mental Health Practitioner (2005); Certified Rehabilitation Counselor (1992); Licensed Neurolinguistic Programmer (1982)

Affiliations/Associations/Societies: American Counseling Association; International Association of Rehabilitation Professionals; People to People Ambassador Program to South Africa; American Board of Disability Analysts

Work History: Heritage Counseling Services; Crawford Rehab

Expanded Biography: Ms. Lessner is currently working on a book.

ENTREPRENEUR OF THE YEAR IN PEDIATRIC CONSULTING

MRS. KAREN S. LEWIS, MSN, RN, ARNP

Nurse Practitioner and Owner
Carolina Heartland Healthcare
214 Buck Run Drive
Goldsboro, NC 27530 United States
smokey53@earthlink.net
http://www.cambridgewhoswho.com

Type of Business: Independent Contractor

Major Products and Services: Healthcare

Marketing Area: Local

Day to Day Responsibilities: Specializing in Pediatric Endocrinology, Pediatric Psychopharmacology, Working with Special Needs Children, and Patients with Type I and II Diabetes, Autistic Spectrum Disorders, ADHD and Behavioral Problems, Parenting, Consulting, Serving as an Expert Witness

Favorite Business Publications: American Journal of Pediatrics; Pediatric Consultant; Advance

Hobbies/Interests/Sports: Oil Painting, Writing Poetry, Backpacking

Education Degrees: Master of Science in Nursing, Medical College of Virginia (1990); Bachelor of Science in Nursing, Arizona State University (1979)

Affiliations/Associations/Societies: American Academy of Nurse Practitioners; Sigma Theta Tau International Honor Society of Nursing; North Carolina Pediatric Society; Phi Kappa Phi; Retired Chairman, Southeast North Carolina Nurse Practitioner Association; American College of Nurse Practitioners

Charity/Volunteer Work: American Cancer Society Relay for Life; Community Work

Spouse: Robert   **Children:** Carrie

Expanded Biography: Mrs. Lewis is a breast cancer survivor.

PROFESSIONAL OF THE YEAR IN PHARMACY SERVICES

Ronald E. Lim

1) Pharmacist 2) President
1) Susanville Family Pharmacy, Inc. 2) Lim's Family Pharmacy, Inc.
1035 Placer Street, Suite 110
Redding, CA 96001 United States
rlim@charter.net
http://www.cambridgewhoswho.com

Type of Business: 1) Clinical Pharmacy 2) Clinical Pharmacy

Major Products and Services: 1) Prescription Drugs, Over-the-Counter Medications, Beauty Products, Men's Products, Women's Products 2) Prescription Drugs, Over-the-Counter Medications, Beauty Products, Men's Products, Women's Products

Marketing Area: 1) Regional 2) Regional

Day to Day Responsibilities: Filling Prescriptions, Overseeing the Day-to-Day Operations of Two Pharmacies

Hobbies/Interests/Sports: Flying, Boat Racing

Education Degrees: Pharm.D., University of the Pacific (1972)

Affiliations/Associations/Societies: California Pharmacist Association; American Pharmaceutical Association

EXECUTIVE OF THE YEAR IN HUMAN SERVICES

DEBORAH A. LINDRUD

Senior Vice President
Department of Talent Management and Development
United Way of Central Maryland
100 S. Charles Street
Fifth Floor
Baltimore, MD 21201 United States
deborah.lindrud@uwcm.org
http://www.uwcm.org

Type of Business: Nonprofit Organization

Major Products and Services: Community Services Including Global Outreach and Human Development, Information Resources

Marketing Area: Regional

Area of Expertise: Ms. Lindrud's expertise includes talent management and development.

Day to Day Responsibilities: Overseeing and Training Three Staff Members

Favorite Business Publications: Forbes; Harvard Business Review; SHRM Newsletter

Hobbies/Interests/Sports: Walking, Exercising, Gardening, Enjoying Fine Dining and Spirits

Education Degrees: Coursework in Organizational Development, ASIU (1982); Master of Arts in Educational Leadership, Southern Illinois University (1978)

Certifications: Certified Four Lenses Temperament Discovery Facilitator of Emotional Intelligence Competencies and Character Development (2005); Certification in Leadership Training, American Management Association (1979)

Affiliations/Associations/Societies: Society for Human Resource Management; Human Capital Task Force; American Society for Training and Development

Charity/Volunteer Work: Human Resources Committee, Young Men's Christian Association

Expanded Biography: Ms. Lindrud is the system chairwoman and a presenter at The National Staff Leaders Conference.

PROFESSIONAL OF THE YEAR IN
INFORMATION TECHNOLOGY SUPPORT

RANDA J. LISBURG

Information Systems Specialist
AgCountry Farm Credit Services
1900 44th Street S.
Fargo, ND 58103 United States
randa.lisburg@agcountry.com
http://www.agcountry.com

Type of Business: Agricultural Lending Company

Major Products and Services: Credit and Integrated Financial Management Services for Farmers and Ranchers, Facility and Real Estate Loans and Leases, Farm Cash Management, Appraisal Services, Record-Keeping and Enterprise Analysis, Tax Planning and Preparation, Life and Disability Insurance, Agribusiness

Marketing Area: Regional

Area of Expertise: Ms. Lisburg's expertise includes data quality assurance and integrity.

Day to Day Responsibilities: Offering Technological Support, Maintaining Phone Systems, Maintaining Expertise in the Field of Technology and Supporting Association Staff by Being Responsive to their Needs, Serving as the Association Data Security Officer, Establishing and Maintaining All Data Security Policies for the Association

Favorite Business Publications: Company Newsletters

Hobbies/Interests/Sports: Arts and Crafts, Spending Time with Family and Pets

Education Degrees: Certificate of Completion in Computer Operations, North Dakota State College of Science (1974); Training of IBM System/36 (1986), IBM AS/400 (1992), Banyan Vines Networking; Novel Networking with a Certificate of Completion in Network Administration (1995); Folio (1995); Crystal (1997); Windows and ZEN (1997-2001); Microsoft Office Applications Including Word, Excel, Access, PowerPoint, Project (1995-2001); Avaya Phone System (2003); PDA's (2003); Certificate of Completion, Microsoft Active Directory Training (2004); Managing Interpersonal Relations-Social Style Analysis Sessions (2004); Beyond Culture Program (2005); Internal Customer Service Program (2006)

Awards/Honors: Certificate of Appreciation for More than 25 Years of Dedicated Service to AgCountry Farm Credit Services (2003)

PROFESSIONAL OF THE YEAR IN
OFFICE FURNITURE MANUFACTURING

DONNA LONG

Dealer, President
GOVSOLUTIONS, Inc.
2424 Litchfield Way
Virginia Beach, VA 23453 United States
donna@govsoultionsinc.com
http://www.govsolutionsinc.com

Type of Business: Distribution Firm

Major Products and Services: Office Furniture for Federal Government Agencies, Design Services, Installation Services, Flooring, Minor Interior Construction, Electrical Services, Plumbing Services, Heating, Ventilation and Air Conditioning, Data and Telecommunications Services

Marketing Area: National

Area of Expertise: Ms. Long's expertise includes sales and administration.

Day to Day Responsibilities: Selling to the Government through General Services Administration Contracts and Government Agencies

Favorite Business Publications: Interior Source; BusinessWeek

Hobbies/Interests/Sports: Mountain Biking, Swimming

Education Degrees: College Coursework

Affiliations/Associations/Societies: National Contract Management Association; Treasurer, Litchfield Manor Homeowners Association; Hampton Roads Association for Commercial Real Estate; Hampton Roads Chamber of Commerce; Tidewater Association for Service Contractors

Work History: Government Specialist, Office Pavilion, Herman Miller Office Furniture Dealership, San Diego, California (2000-2005); Procurement Specialist, Navy Exchange, Exmouth, Australia (1990-2001); Communications Specialist, The United States, Puerto Rico and Bermuda (1993-2000); Owner, Operator and Liaison CCC, Watchstanders, Exmouth, Australia (1988-1990); Navy in Adak, Alaska (1987-1988); National Capitol Region Manager, UNICOR Federal Prison Industries; Dealer Principal, GOVSOLUTIONS, Inc.

PROFESSIONAL OF THE YEAR IN
BAIL BONDING

MR. DAVEY A. LOONEY

President
Looney Bonding, LLC
dba Free Bird Bonding Company
3617 Old Route 100 Road
Pulaski, VA 24301 United States
topbonds@hotmail.com
http://www.cambridgewhoswho.com

Type of Business: Bail Bond Company

Major Products and Services: Bail Bonding Services

Marketing Area: National

Day to Day Responsibilities: Troubleshooting, Collaborating with Other Bondsmen and Licensed Bail Enforcement Agents, Managing a Professional Agency with a Focus on Improving the Image of the Industry

Favorite Business Publications: Virginia Sheriff Magazine; Virginia State Trooper Magazine; Cigar International Publications; Newsweek; BusinessWeek

Hobbies/Interests/Sports: Golfing, Fishing, Hunting, Playing Chess, Playing Tennis, Swimming

Education Degrees: College Coursework

Certifications: Licensed Bail Bondsman, United States Department of Criminal Justice; State Board Certified Bail Enforcement Agent

Affiliations/Associations/Societies: Better Business Bureau; Professional Bail Agents of the United States; Chairman, Congressional Party, VA

Charity/Volunteer Work: Volunteer, Community Services

Date of Birth: September 7, 1968   **Place of Birth:** Buchanan County

Expanded Biography: Mr. Looney appeared on television news in a documentary on West Virginia. He has published newspaper articles in the 'Roanoke Times' and 'Southwest Times.' He has also participated in the Virginia Law Enforcement Torch Run, supports girls' softball of Hillsville, VA, and sponsors the Dublin Cubs, tee ball, men's softball and the Volvo truck team.

PROFESSIONAL OF THE YEAR IN
NURSING, NEUROLOGY, AND NEUROSURGERY

ANGELEA M. LORETTA

Registered Nurse
Interim Healthcare
1111 Van Voorhis Road
Morgantown, WV 26505 United States
ruralrn2002@excite.com
http://www.health.wvu.edu/hospitals

Type of Business: Healthcare Center

Major Products and Services: Home Healthcare, Education and Supervision Services

Marketing Area: Regional

Area of Expertise: Ms. Loretta's expertise is in the supervision of home healthcare.

Day to Day Responsibilities: Practicing Neurology and Neurosurgery, Precepting New Staff Members and Students, Working in the Epilepsy Management Unit, Assessing and Treating Patients in the Pain Management Unit Including those with Fibromyalgia and Multiple Sclerosis, Researching, Acting as a Staff Nurse and Charge Nurse, Overseeing Orientation for New Home Health Nurses and Aides, Overseeing Fragile Children in their Homes who have Undergone Tracheotomies, Dialysis, Ventilators, Intravenous Therapy Infusion, Intravenous Therapy Antibiotics, Supervising Home Care Nurses, Acting as an Advocate for Patients, Writing for Much Needed Funding, Advising and Monitoring Nutrition, Monitoring Heart, Weight and Glucose Via Telemonitor Systems so that Adjustments can be Made Spontaneously, Managing a Staff of over 300 Nurses and Aides

Favorite Business Publications: Journal of Diabetes Science and Technology; AJN

Hobbies/Interests/Sports: Painting, Exercising

Education Degrees: Pursuing Master of Science in Nursing, West Virginia University; Bachelor of Science in Nursing, West Virginia University (2002); Bachelor's Degree in Psychology and Chemistry, St. Andrews Presbyterian College (1999)

Certifications: Certified Emergency Medical Technician-Basic

Affiliations/Associations/Societies: Utilization Team, West Virginia University Hospital; American Association of Neuroscience Nurses; American Association of Diabetes Educators; Phi Kappa Phi; Pi Gamma Mu; Sigma Theta Tau International Honor Society of Nursing

Expanded Biography: Ms. Loretta has published an article on music therapy for the hospital research utilization team. She also taught pharmacology, anatomy and physiology as an adjunct faculty member at West Virginia Junior College.

PROFESSIONAL OF THE YEAR IN
SAFETY IN THE CONSTRUCTION INDUSTRY

MR. JOHN LOTT, CSM

Safety Director
Satterfield and Pontikes Construction, Inc.
11000 Equity Drive, Suite 100
Houston, TX 77041 United States
jlott@satpon.com
http://www.satpon.com

Type of Business: Commercial Construction

Major Products and Services: Commercial Construction, High Rises and Retail Stores

Marketing Area: Local

Day to Day Responsibilities: Managing a Crew of Four Safety Managers who Travel to Sites, Handling Workers' Compensation Cases and Attending Hearings, Creating Policies and Procedures, Performing Job Audits

Favorite Business Publications: ENR Business

Hobbies/Interests/Sports: Fishing

Education Degrees: Associate of Applied Science; Licensed in 17 States

Affiliations/Associations/Societies: American General Contractors Association; American Builders Association; World Safety Organization

Awards/Honors: National Safety Award, American General Contractors Association; Runner-up, National Safety Award, American Builders Association

Spouse: Linda   **Children:** Misty, Krystal

Work History: Scaffolding Work, Statue of Liberty

What do you attribute your success to? He attributes his personal and professional success to his dedication to getting to know colleagues on a one-to-one basis.

How did you become involved in your profession? While working in the construction business for more than 20 years, he consistently saw co-workers getting injured and, subsequently, not being treated properly. He then decided he wanted to make a difference and help other construction workers.

What was the highlight of your career? The highlight of his career was receiving the National Safety Award and being able to offer help to construction workers in need.

Expanded Biography: Mr. Lott observed that most companies have similar issues and concerns, and has since served on a peer group of seven companies to share ideas and views. He is also a speaker for the American General Contractors Association.

PROFESSIONAL OF THE YEAR IN
COMPUTER GRAPHICS AND VISUAL AIDS

ALFRED ROBERT LUBIENSKI

1) President 2) Owner
1) Renaissance Technology 2) Internet Retail Business
1717 Allard Avenue
Grosse Pointe Woods, MI 48236 United States
rentech@comcast.net
http://www.cambridgewhoswho.com

Type of Business: 1) Graphic Design Company 2) Retail Store

Major Products and Services: 1) Computer Graphics for the Automotive Industry 2) Miniature Vintage Cars, Lighthouses, Toy Soldiers and Holiday Specialty Items

Marketing Area: 1) International 2) International

Area of Expertise: Mr. Lubienski's expertise is in visual aids.

Day to Day Responsibilities: Overseeing Hallways and Conference Room Visuals, Developing Self-Taught Computer Graphics for Manufacturing Purposes, Working to Create Visual Aids for the Handicapped, Managing Internet Sales of Specialty Collectible Items, Working as a Movie Historian with Manuals and Biographies for More than 2,000 Movies, Preparing Panels for Automotive Industries, Producing Line, Developing Brochures

Education Degrees: Bachelor of Arts in Business, Wayne State University (1956)

Affiliations/Associations/Societies: Republican Party

Charity/Volunteer Work: Various Police Organizations

Work History: Speaker and Lecturer, American Hospital, San Francisco, CA

Expanded Biography: Mr. Lubienski previously owned Votrex, a voice synthesis company that created and synthesized the phone voice used by most companies today. He has been featured in newspapers for Votrex and previously served in the U.S. Navy from 1956 to 1960. He has worked on various projects all over the world, including constructing or developing buildings, office quarters, restaurants, schools and libraries.

PROFESSIONAL OF THE YEAR IN GAMING INDUSTRY

DENISE A. LUNDBY

Cage Manager
Flamingo, O'Shea's, Harrah's
3555 Las Vegas Boulevard S.
Las Vegas, NV 89109 United States
lundbyd@harrahslasvegas.com
http://www.cambridgewhoswho.com

Type of Business: Gaming

Major Products and Services: Casino, Restaurants, Shopping, and Hospitality and Spa Services

Marketing Area: Regional

Day to Day Responsibilities: Interacting with People, Training Others

Hobbies/Interests/Sports: Cooking, Creating Crafts, Making Baskets

Education Degrees: Diploma, Valley High School, Las Vegas

Affiliations/Associations/Societies: Co-Chairwoman, Heroes; Co-Chairwoman, Harrah's Community Service; United Way of America

Spouse: Michael   **Children:** Taylor Humphry, Jamison Humphry, Lydia Lundby, Tyler Lundby

What do you attribute your success to? She attributes her success to her love of making people happy and making a difference in their lives.

How did you become involved in your profession? She became involved in her profession because of her love for the gaming industry and her desire to meet new people.

What was the highlight of your career? The most gratifying aspect of her career is having great customer service and making people happy.

Expanded Biography: Ms. Lundby has two Yorkshire Terriers named Luigi and Sophia Loren.

PROFESSIONAL OF THE YEAR IN COMPUTER SERVICES

BARBARA L. LYMAN

Senior Computer Consultant
3440 Parkwood Court
Hermitage, TN 37076 United States
bllyman@worldnet.att.net
http://www.cambridgewhoswho.com

Type of Business: Consulting Company

Major Products and Services: Consulting Services

Marketing Area: National

Area of Expertise: Ms. Lyman's expertise is in consulting, with an emphasis on PeopleSoft.

Day to Day Responsibilities: Working for a Client in Columbus, OH, Creating Enhancements to Streamline Processing, Programming Mainframes, Installing Software, Troubleshooting, Designing Systems

Favorite Business Publications: PC Magazine

Hobbies/Interests/Sports: Playing Baseball, Square Dancing, Cross Stitching, Solving Puzzles

Education Degrees: Pursuing Master's Degree; Bachelor's Degree in Business Administration and Data Processing, Nazareth College (1985)

Certifications: PRO Certification in PeopleSoft

Affiliations/Associations/Societies: Association for Computing Machinery

Awards/Honors: Piece of the Puzzle Award

Charity/Volunteer Work: Lutheran World Relief; Give the Kids the World; Dream Makers

Date of Birth: August 2, 1945   **Place of Birth:** Saco

Spouse: Lynn   **Children:** Angela

Work History: Fisher-James Co.; New England Division of Maramont Corp.; Woodland Mutual Insurance; National Lumberman's Bank; Borgess Medical Hospital; SCB Computer Technology; Nashville Electric Co.; Anderson-Tully Co.; Indianapolis Water Co.; Ingram Industries Corporate Office; Jitney Jungle; Cardinal Point; Publicis; Xpedia Solutions; Knoxville Utility Board; Surrex Solutions; LimitedBrands; PeopleSoft Consulting

What do you attribute your success to? She attributes her success to her persistence and her ability to update her knowledge with current trends.

How did you become involved in your profession? She became involved in her profession because she started out as a keypuncher and eventually progressed.

What was the highlight of your career? The most gratifying aspect of her career is the gratitude she receives from her clients.

Expanded Biography: Ms. Lyman has worked for various state governments including those of Indiana, Tennessee and Arkansas.

PROFESSIONAL OF THE YEAR IN HUMANITIES EDUCATION

DR. MARIANNE MACNICHOL

Professor of Humanities
Orange Park Campus
St. Johns River Community College
283 College Drive
Orange Park, FL 32065 United States
trousdale@comcast.com
http://www.sjrcc.cc.fl.us
http://www.stjohnsriverscommunitycollege.edu

Type of Business: Community College

Major Products and Services: Higher Education, Research, Associate of Arts Degrees, Associate of Science Degrees, Technical and Vocational Certificates

Marketing Area: National

Day to Day Responsibilities: Teaching Humanities and Communications, Lecturing on Music, Paintings, Architecture, Sculptures, Literature and Dance, Teaching English Courses

Favorite Business Publications: Forbes; Money

Hobbies/Interests/Sports: Traveling, Ballet, Theater, Photography, Reading Art and Sociology Books, Visiting her Beach Condominium

Education Degrees: Ph.D. in Interdisciplinary Humanities and Literature, Florida State University (1982); Master of English (1973); Master's Degree in Interdisciplinary Humanities (1971); Bachelor of Arts in History, Minor in English, Texas Christian University (1963); Bachelor of Fine Arts, Minor in Theatre, Texas Christian University (1963)

Awards/Honors: Who's Who Among American Teachers (1996, 1998, 2000, 2005); Cambridge Blue Book Award (2005); Great Minds of the 21st Century (2004); 2000 Notable American Women (2003); Woman of the Year (2003); 2000 Outstanding Intellectuals in the 21st Century (2003); Nisod Award (2002); International Executive Club (2001)

Place of Birth: Jacksonville

Work History: Full-Time Faculty, St. Johns River Community College (1978-2002); Adjunct Faculty, Florida Community College at Jacksonville (1974-2001); Duval County School System (1963-1970, 1971-1972, 1974-1978)

Career Achievements: Faculty, St. Johns River Community College; Award Recipeint, National Institute for Staff and Organizational Development (2002); International Professional of the Year (2005)

Expanded Biography: Dr. MacNichol teaches architectural reflection of culture, which offers a chronological look at architecture as a reflection of major cultural concerns in the western world from prehistoric times to the twentieth century. Each major period is thematically approached and studied with visual aids and discussions. The course focuses on the psychological and sociological impact of the ethos upon man's architectural monuments as an extension of his personal needs and basic instinct for physical survival and mental well-being. This course is loosely based on Joseph Campbell's idea that buildings are the product of the needs and dominant ideas or major concerns of any historical period. Dr. MacNichol also taught architectural courses at St. Johns River Community College.

PROFESSIONAL OF THE YEAR IN PAROCHIAL SCHOOL EDUCATION

AGNES E. MALEAKAS

Principal
St. Thomas of Canterbury School
336 Hudson Street
Cornwall on Hudson, NY 12520 United States
agnes122@optonline.net
http://www.cambridgewhoswho.com

Type of Business: Catholic School

Major Products and Services: Catholic Education for Kindergarten through Eighth-Grade Students

Marketing Area: Local

Area of Expertise: Ms. Maleakas' expertise is in leadership development.

Day to Day Responsibilities: Mentoring, Overseeing Administrative Duties

Favorite Business Publications: Principal

Hobbies/Interests/Sports: Traveling, Spending Time at the Beach, Casino, Shopping

Education Degrees: Master's Degree in Counseling, The University of Scranton

Certifications: Certification in Supervision and Administration

Affiliations/Associations/Societies: Catholic School Administrators Association of New York State; National Association of Elementary School Principals; National Association of Supervision and Curriculum Development; National Catholic Educational Association

Charity/Volunteer Work: Dutchess County Society for the Prevention of Cruelty to Animals; American Heart Association

What do you attribute your success to? She attributes her success to her love for working with children and being a part of their formation.

How did you become involved in your profession? She became involved in her profession because she was inspired by her family members who were in the education field.

What was the highlight of your career? The most gratifying aspect of her career is the gratitude she receives from her former students.

EXECUTIVE OF THE YEAR IN CONSTRUCTION

MR. WILLIAM MANFREDONIA

President, Chief Executive Officer
Cost Calculations, Inc.
23 Lincoln Street
Ramsey, NJ 07446 United States
manfredonia@msn.com
http://www.cambridgewhoswho.com

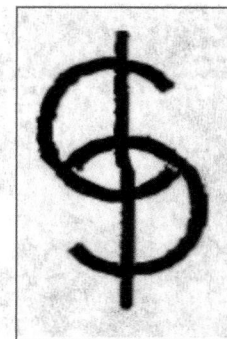

Type of Business: Construction

Major Products and Services: Cost Construction, Hard Bid Claims, Insurance Claims, Damage Assessments

Marketing Area: National

Area of Expertise: Mr. Manfredonia's expertise includes architecture, general contracts and sub-contracts.

Day to Day Responsibilities: Making Cost Estimates, Contracting with Real Estate Firms, Handling All Trades, Consulting, Accurately Forecasting the Cost of Future Projects

Hobbies/Interests/Sports: Fishing

Education Degrees: Bachelor of Science in Construction Management, Pratt Institute (1970); Coursework in Construction Claims, Worcester Polytechnic Institute

Certifications: Certified Professional Estimator

Affiliations/Associations/Societies: American Society of Professional Estimators; The Construction Specifications Institute; American Association of Cost Engineers; Garden State Chapter, American Society of Professional Estimators

Awards/Honors: Several Recognition Awards from Various Organizations (2002-Present); Gold Medal Recipient, Republican Congressional Committee (2002-2003); Leadership Award, Businessman Advisory Council

Date of Birth: January 21, 1943

Spouse: Stephanie   **Children:** Joseph, Andrea, Anthony

Work History: Founder and President, Cost Calculations, Inc.; Principal, M2 Inc.=M Squared Inc.; Diesel Construction Company; Morris Park Contracting; Jeffery Brown, Inc.; A.J. Contracting; York Hunter; Gazetten Contracting Inc.; Aark Construction Co. Inc.; Construction Inspector, United States Treasury Department; Cost Consultant, New York State Department of Economic Development; Arbitrator in Construction and Insurance Cases; Estimating Teacher, Pratt Institute; Estimating Teacher, Rutgers, The State University of New Jersey; Estimating Teacher, New Jersey Institute of Technology

Expanded Biography: Mr. Manfredonia believes that in order to be successful in any business, a person needs to be a good teacher as well as a good student. When mastering one's trade, one must be patient and learn as much as he can. With these attributes, he can achieve his goals and become successful in anything he wants to do.

PROFESSIONAL OF THE YEAR IN THE
HEALTHCARE AND FOOD SERVICE INDUSTRIES

JUDITH E. MANN, RN

President
Celiac Solution, LLC
South Yarmouth, MA United States
judith@celiacsolution.com
http://www.celiacsolution.com

Type of Business: 1) Healthcare 2) Food Service

Major Products and Services: 1) Gluten-Free Lifestyle Management 2) Gluten-Free Baked Goods

Marketing Area: Regional

Area of Expertise: Ms. Mann's expertise includes consulting, nursing and gluten-free baking.

Favorite Business Publications: Cooks Illustrated; Cape Cod; Boston Globe Times

Hobbies/Interests/Sports: Cooking, Windsurfing, Spending Time with her Husband and her Dog

Education Degrees: Associate Degree in Nursing, County College of Morris

Affiliations/Associations/Societies: American Dietetic Association; Celiac Sprue Association; Gluten Intolerance Group of North America; Society for Nutritional Education; Association of Pediatric Gastroenterology and Nutrition Nurses; National Foundation for Celiac Awareness; Healthy Villi Massachusetts Division CSA; Celiac Center For Research, Columbia University, NY; National Foundation for Celiac Awareness

Spouse: Phillip

What do you attribute your success to? She attributes her success to her illness, which encouraged her to move forward with her business.

How did you become involved in your profession? She became involved in her profession after being diagnosed with Celiac Disease, which opened her eyes to the need for a business that dealt in gluten-free goods.

What was the highlight of your career? The highlight of her career was moving forward with a large project that will open many doors for her business.

Expanded Biography: Ms. Mann has been married for 10 years. In her spare time, she enjoys playing with her dog Abby.

ENTREPRENEUR OF THE YEAR IN NATIONAL REAL ESTATE INVESTING

Ms. Tanya M. Marchiol, MBA

Broker, President
Team Investments, Inc.
3145 E. Chandler Boulevard, Suite 110410
Phoenix, AZ 85048 United States
tanya@teaminvestmentsinc.com
http://www.teaminvestmentsinc.com
http://www.tidaily.com

Type of Business: Client-Focused, Full-Service Independent Real Estate Firm

Major Products and Services: Real Estate Services Including Divisions of Single-Family Homes, Multi-Family Homes, Property Management, Land, Foreclosures, Fix and Flip, Personal Family Homes, and Bulk Real Estate Owned and Broker Priced Opinion Divisions

Marketing Area: National

Day to Day Responsibilities: Writing a Column for 'Moves' Magazine, Teaching Athletes and Professionals how to Create Wealth through Real Estate, Overseeing all Aspects of the Show 'The Real Deal' on iBusiness.

Hobbies/Interests/Sports: Traveling, Skydiving

Education Degrees: Bachelor of Arts, Indiana University (1996)

Affiliations/Associations/Societies: Steadman Hawkins Research Foundation

Awards/Honors: Businesswoman of the Year Award, President George W. Bush (2006)

Charity/Volunteer Work: Arizona Cardinals Charity Events

Date of Birth: April 18, 1974

Expanded Biography: Ms. Marchiol is an author, entrepreneur, real estate guru and financial adviser. She was recently selected to host 'The Real Deal,' a new business-oriented talk show on iBusinessChannel.com. On the show, she interviews prominent entrepreneurs from the sports, entertainment, fashion and real estate industries. By having her guests discuss how they got their start and some of the challenges they've had to overcome, she educates her viewers on what to expect as they embark on their own business ventures. In addition, as guests describe their successes, they offer positive examples and reinforce good business principles. For example, during an interview with venture capitalist and founder of Byrd Alliance Group, LLC, Al Byrd, they learned how important it is to have a solid business plan and to make sure their business has a strong, experienced management team. They also learn how a venture capital firm may be able to help their company grow. A casual and accessible approach makes the show entertaining and enjoyable to watch, and it breaks complicated business concepts down to laymen's terms so the audience is able to easily retain the information. Also, 'The Real Deal' is not only an educational tool for aspiring entrepreneurs, but also a promotional vehicle for those already successful in their fields. Ms. Marchiol offers seminars on building wealth cycles and real estate. She has been interviewed on '20/20' and CNBC, and is writing a book entitled 'Prosperity Principles.' Ms. Marchiol also played professional volleyball in Italy for two years.

EXECUTIVE OF THE YEAR IN
MOTOR CARRIER TRANSPORTATION

DEBRA D. MARKELONIS

Vice President
Visionary Solutions, LLC
111-B Union Valley Road
Oak Ridge, TN 37830 United States
dmarkelonis@vs-llc.com
http://www.vs-llc.com

Type of Business: Private Waste Transportation and Management Company

Major Products and Services: Safe Transportation of Radioactive and Other Hazardous Materials, Waste and Classified Materials for Government and Commercial Customers in Industries Including Steel, Chemical, Machinery, Explosives and Building Materials

Marketing Area: International

Day to Day Responsibilities: Overseeing Finances, Transportation and Motor Carriers, Chemical Engineering, Negotiating Ventures

Hobbies/Interests/Sports: Knitting, Reading, Researching Genealogy

Education Degrees: Bachelor's Degree in Chemical Engineering, Tennessee Technical University (1986)

Affiliations/Associations/Societies: United Way of Andersen; Chamber of Commerce; Three Time Honoree, Inc. 500

What do you attribute your success to? She attributes her success to keeping her faith in God and to respecting other people's relationships.

What was the highlight of your career? The highlight of her career was competing against much larger firms on a full and open competition and winning the $27 million contract. Her company was able to complete 1,882 shipments over eight months, successfully and in full compliance of regulations.

Expanded Biography: Ms. Markelonis is beginning negotiations on a joint venture with an Alaska Native Company.

EXECUTIVE OF THE YEAR IN EXECUTIVE COACHING

MS. SUSAN A. MARSHALL

President
Executive Advisor, LLC
1109 Emerson Drive
Oconomowoc, WI 53066 United States
execadvise@mac.com
http://www.executiveadvisorllc.com

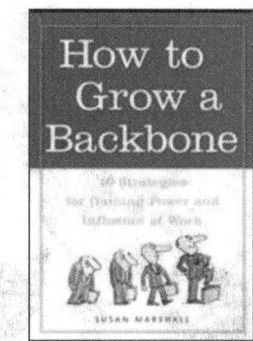

Type of Business: Consulting Company

Major Products and Services: Executive Development and Speaking Services

Marketing Area: National

Day to Day Responsibilities: Executive Coaching, Speaking, Writing, Presenting, Offering Client Services

Favorite Business Publications: Harvard Business Review; The Wall Street Journal

Hobbies/Interests/Sports: Reading, Writing, Watching Football, Running with her Dog

Education Degrees: Master of Business Administration, Cardinal Stritch University (1996); Bachelor of Science in Management, Cardinal Stritch University (1987)

Certifications: Certification in Leadership Effectiveness Analysis 360

Affiliations/Associations/Societies: Mount Mary College; Stephen M. Ross School of Business at the University of Michigan; Global Business Partnership

Charity/Volunteer Work: Healthy Families; United Way of America

Date of Birth: April 7, 1955   **Place of Birth:** Milwaukee

Children: Jennifer, Kelly

What do you attribute your success to? She attributes her success to her perseverance, positive outlook, dedication to service and ability to build good working relationships with others.

How did you become involved in your profession? She became involved in her profession because she developed an early interest in the field and accumulated experience across a variety of disciplines.

What was the highlight of your career? The most gratifying aspects of her career are watching people realize their capabilities and step up to challenges.

Where will you be in five years? In five years, Ms. Marshall intends to lead the formation of The Backbone Institute.

Expanded Biography: Ms. Marshall is the president of Executive Advisor, LLC, an independent consulting firm founded in 1997 that specializes in executive leadership development. She has served as an adjunct faculty member for Prof. Noel Tichy's Cycle of Leadership executive program since 2000. She is the author of 'How to Grow a Backbone: 10 Strategies for Gaining Power and Influence at Work,' published in 2000, which has been translated into multiple languages and is particularly popular in Asia. She is a regular columnist for 'Today's Wisconsin Woman' and 'Small Business Times.' She has worked with General Motors Corporation, BestBuy, Subaru of America, Inc., Harley-Davidson, Apple Inc., GE Healthcare, Boys & Girls Clubs of America, and many other organizations. She led a successful turnaround of a privately held marketing firm in the mid-1990s. Ms. Marshall teaches a leadership course for a new master of business administration program at Mount Mary College in Milwaukee, WI. She has been welcomed as a guest-lecturer at several University of Wisconsin campuses, and at Marquette University, Alverno College, the Stephen M. Ross School of Business at the University of Michigan and The University of Chicago Graduate School of Business. She has two daughters, two sons-in-law and three granddaughters.

EXECUTIVE OF THE YEAR IN
MEDICAL AND PUBLIC HEALTH EDUCATION

PHILLIP J. MARTY, PH.D.

Associate Vice President
Health Department
University of South Florida
12901 Bruce B. Downs Boulevard
Tampa, FL 33612 United States
pmarty@hsc.usf.edu
http://www.cambridgewhoswho.com

Type of Business: University

Major Products and Services: Higher Education, Healthcare

Marketing Area: National

Area of Expertise: Dr. Marty's expertise includes preventive medicine, social and behavioral science.

Favorite Business Publications: The New England Journal of Medicine; Journal of Public Health

Hobbies/Interests/Sports: Fishing, Camping

Education Degrees: Ph.D. in Curriculum, Instruction and Preventative Medicine, University of Wisconsin-Madison; Master's Degree in Curriculum, University of Wisconsin-Madison; Bachelor of Science in Biology and Bio Sciences, Wisconsin State University, Whitewater

Affiliations/Associations/Societies: Society for Public Health Education; University Research Administration; Association of American Medical Colleges; National Council of University Research Administrators

Charity/Volunteer Work: Local Church; American Cancer Society; American Heart Association

Spouse: Marianne   **Children:** Adam, Melissa, Megan

What do you attribute your success to? He attributes his success to his work ethic and personal drive.

How did you become involved in your profession? He became involved in his profession because he was always interested in healthcare.

What was the highlight of your career? The highlight of his career was working as a dean for the college of public health where he was able to establish a new program and curriculum.

BRENDA K. MATTSON

Artist
Artist Brenda Mattson
6931 Windwater Court
Muskegon, MI 49444 United States
brendamattson@msn.com
http://www.brendamattson.com

Type of Business: Art Gallery

Major Products and Services: Artwork, Pastels and Oil Paint, Sensitive Portraits, Landscapes Including Teaching Art Education

Marketing Area: International

Day to Day Responsibilities: Painting Portraits, Landscapes and Animals, Utilizing Mixed Media Techniques Including Pastels and Paint, Exhibiting Art Work in Galleries, Teaching Art

Favorite Business Publications: Artist International

Hobbies/Interests/Sports: Golfing, Hiking, Photography

Education Degrees: Coursework in Art Studies

Affiliations/Associations/Societies: Devon Equestrian Life Art Exhibition, PA (2006-2007); The Gallery Up Town, Grand Haven, MI (2006); Jack Richeson Gallery, Kimberly, WI (2005-2007); Alliance Group Show Detroit, MI (2006); Alliance Group Show, Crooked Tree Gallery, Petoskey, MI (2006); International Association of Pastel Societies (2004-2005); Alliance Group Show, The Gallery Up Town, Grand Haven, MI (2004); One Trick Pony Gallery, Grand Rapids, MI (2002); Ella Sharp Museum GLPS Juried Exhibition, MI (2001); American Artist Juried Exhibition Show, Pasadena, California (2000); Lansing Art Gallery Botanical Exhibition (2000); Exhibition Chairwoman, International Association of Pastel Societies; Signature Member, Pastel Society of America; Historian, Great Lakes Pastel Society; Portrait Society of America; Vice President, Artist Alliance Member, Lakeland Artists; National Portrait Convention, Washington, DC; International Pastel Convention, Albuquerque, NM; International Association of Pastel Society

Awards/Honors: Award, West Michigan Regional Competition (2006)

Work History: Art Instructor, Grand Rapids Art Museum (1999-2006); Art Instructor, International Association of Pastel Societies (2003-2005)

Expanded Biography: Ms. Mattson's artwork has been featured in 'Bio in Pastel Journal,' 'International Pastel,' 'Tole Art Magazine,' 'American Artist,' 'The Artist Magazine' and 'Art News.'

PROFESSIONAL OF THE YEAR IN
PERFORMANCE IMPROVEMENT IN THE HEALTHCARE INDUSTRY

DIANE K. MAXWELL

Performance Improvement Coordinator
Memorial Hermann Healthcare System
9250 Pinecroft Drive
Shenandoah, TX 77380 United States
diane.maxwell@memorialhermann.org
http://www.memorialhermann.org

Type of Business: Nonprofit Healthcare System

Major Products and Services: Healthcare Including Surgery, In-Patient and Out-Patient Care and Specialty Services

Marketing Area: Houston, Texas

Area of Expertise: Ms. Maxwell's expertise is in healthcare.

Day to Day Responsibilities: Ensuring that Appropriate Care is Practiced Among Physicians and Staff Members and Evidence-Based Medicine is Implemented, Working with Doctors, Reporting Data Nationally, Collaborating with TMF Health Quality Institute, Following CMS Regulations

Hobbies/Interests/Sports: Traveling, Gardening, Hiking

Education Degrees: Bachelor of Science in Nursing, Regents College, University of the State of New York (1990)

Certifications: Certified Nurse, Worthington Community College, MN (1982); Certified Emergency Medical Technician, Southwest Technical Institute, Jackson, MN (1979)

Affiliations/Associations/Societies: Texas Association for Healthcare Quality; National Association for Healthcare Quality

Awards/Honors: Diamond Homer Award (1995)

Children: Scott, Stephanie, Sandra

Where will you be in five years? In five years, Ms. Maxwell would like to use her experience and skills to benefit organizations that support quality in healthcare.

Expanded Biography: Ms. Maxwell has written many policies and procedures, and directed several initiatives for process changes. She has experience in negotiating, politics, contract and proposal writing, budgeting, personnel and world travel. She also participates in the medical peer review process to facilitate medical peer-to-peer interaction on complex hospital cases.

PROFESSIONAL OF THE YEAR IN
HUMAN RESOURCES LEADERSHIP DEVELOPMENT

MICHELLE M. MAY

Human Resource Program Manager
The Clorox Company
2121 Broadway
Oakland, CA 94612 United States
mmay_ccr@yahoo.com
http://www.thecloroxcompany.com

Type of Business: Consumer Products and Goods Manufacturing Company

Major Products and Services: Household Products, Home Care Products, Laundry Additives, Water Filtration Products, Automobile Care Products, Dressings, Sauces and Seasonings, Bags, Wraps, Containers, Charcoal, Cat Litter, Leadership Development Programs

Marketing Area: International

Area of Expertise: Ms. Mayworm's expertise is in human resource leadership development.

Favorite Business Publications: ASTD Publications

Hobbies/Interests/Sports: Mountain Biking, Cycling, Hiking

Education Degrees: Master of Arts in Human Resource Management, Golden Gate University (1993)

Affiliations/Associations/Societies: American Society for Training and Development

What do you attribute your success to? She attributes her success to her education and the relationships she has built along the way.

How did you become involved in your profession? She became involved in this profession because she always had an interest in leadership development.

What was the highlight of your career? The most gratifying aspects of her career are her daily achievements.

PROFESSIONAL OF THE YEAR IN
LEGAL NURSE CONSULTING

JANET K. MCCABE, RN, BSN, MN, CLNC

RN, BSN, MN
Lakeland Legal Nurse Consultants
127 E. Creek Road
Greenwood, SC 29646 United States
jkmccabe@earthlink.net
http://www.cambridgewhoswho.com

Type of Business: Major Referral and Medical Center

Major Products and Services: Advanced Health Care Services to a Population of More than a Quarter of a Million People in the Lakelands Region of Upstate South Carolina

Marketing Area: National

Day to Day Responsibilities: Working in Level III Neonatal Intensive Care, Dealing with Pediatrics, Serving as the Regional Director for Neonatal Resuscitation Program for the American Academy of Pediatrics

Favorite Business Publications: Neonatal Network

Hobbies/Interests/Sports: Reading, Going to the Beach

Education Degrees: Master's Degree in Nursing, University of South Carolina (1988); Bachelor of Science in Nursing, Clemson University, South Carolina (1976)

Certifications: Legal Nurse Consultant Certification

Affiliations/Associations/Societies: Sigma Theta Tau International Honor Society of Nursing; South Carolina Neonatal Association; National Alliance of Certified Legal Nurse Consultants

PROFESSIONAL OF THE YEAR IN PHARMACY SERVICES

MS. ANNE FREYER MCCLUSKEY, MS

Director of Health Systems
Cardinal Health
7000 Cardinal Place
Dublin, OH 43017 United States
anne.mccluskey@cardinal.com
http://www.cardinal.com

Type of Business: Healthcare

Major Products and Services: Pharmaceutical Supply Chain, Integrated Solutions for Healthcare

Marketing Area: International

Day to Day Responsibilities: Working with the Pharmacy Supply Division, Identifying and Implementing Solutions to Meet Clients' Needs

Favorite Business Publications: American Journal of Health-Systems Pharmacy

Hobbies/Interests/Sports: Golfing, Reading

Education Degrees: Master's Degree in Pharmacy Administration, College of Pharmacy, The University of Arizona

Affiliations/Associations/Societies: American Society of Health-System Pharmacists; ACHCE; Advisory Board Member, College of Pharmacy University of Arizona; Advisory Board Member, Pharmacy Technician Program

Charity/Volunteer Work: The Neighborhood Christian Clinic; Fresh Start

What do you attribute your success to? She attributes her success to her expertise, vision, natural inclination, practicality and problem-solving skills.

How did you become involved in your profession? She became involved in her profession because she enjoyed science and medical topics.

What was the highlight of your career? The highlight of her career was attaining her current position.

PROFESSIONAL OF THE YEAR IN
ELECTRICAL CONTRACTING

DON L. MCCORD

Owner
McCord Lighting Contractors
13800 County Road 29
Centre, AL 35960 United States
dmccord@powernet.org
http://www.cambridgewhoswho.com

Type of Business: Electrical Contracting Company

Major Products and Services: Residential and Commercial Electrical Services

Marketing Area: Regional

Day to Day Responsibilities: Overseeing Electrical Contracting, Offering Residential and Commercial Utility Line Work

Hobbies/Interests/Sports: Caring for his Ten Horses, Vacationing in the Mountains

Education Degrees: Industry-Related Training

PROFESSIONAL OF THE YEAR IN
REAL ESTATE

REBA B. MCFADDEN

Realtor, Educator (Retired)
Coldwell Banker Mackey Co.
2783 Water Pointe Circle
Mount Pleasant, SC 29466 United States
rbmac1@aol.com
http://www.coldwellbanker.com

Type of Business: Full Service Real Estate Company

Major Products and Services: Personalized Services for Home Buyers and Sellers, Multiple Listing Service, Instant Market Analysis, Mortgage Advice and Assistance, Land Sales, Single Family Homes

Marketing Area: National

Day to Day Responsibilities: Listing and Selling Residential Homes, Moderately-Priced Homes and Multi-Family Homes

Favorite Business Publications: Realtor Specialist

Hobbies/Interests/Sports: Family Time, Cooking, Gardening

Education Degrees: Bachelor's Degree in Business Education, Winthrop University (1954)

Affiliations/Associations/Societies: National Association of Realtors; Louisiana Realtors Association; GBRAR

PROFESSIONAL OF THE YEAR IN ENGINEERING

Mr. Harry J. McIntyre

Consultant for Engineering Staff
Control Electronics Department
Xerox Corporation
701 S. Aviation Boulevard
El Segundo, CA 90245 United States
hjmcintyre@ca.rr.com
http://www.xerox.com

Type of Business: Document Management Company

Major Products and Services: Office Products and Equipment, Electronics Design, Document Services, Consulting, Outsourcing Services

Marketing Area: International

Area of Expertise: Mr. McIntyre's expertise includes analytic and driver design.

Favorite Business Publications: Design News; Electric Engineering Times

Hobbies/Interests/Sports: Golfing, Tennis, Photography

Education Degrees: Bachelor of Science in Engineering, University of California, Los Angeles (1982)

Affiliations/Associations/Societies: Institute of Electrical and Electronics Engineers, Inc.

EXECUTIVE OF THE YEAR IN
MENTAL HEALTH SERVICES

DR. CAILLEAN MCMAHON-TRONETTI

Medical Director
Chautauqua County Mental Health Services
319 Central Avenue
Dunkirk, NY 14048 United States
caileenmc@yahoo.com
http://www.co.chautauqua.ny.us/mhealth/clinics.htm

Type of Business: Healthcare Center

Major Products and Services: Mental Healthcare Services, Confidential and Discreet Assessment and Evaluation, Individualized Treatment Planning, Individual Therapy, Group Therapy Specifically Designed to Assist the Individual with an Understanding of Self and Skill Development, Case Management Services, Psychiatric Services, Referral Services, Management of Gay, Lesbian and Transsexual Treatment Services

Marketing Area: Regional

Area of Expertise: Dr. McMahon-Tronetti's expertise is in forensic psychiatry.

Favorite Business Publications: Archives of General Psychiatry

Hobbies/Interests/Sports: Horseback Riding, Hiking, Playing Rugby

Education Degrees: Coursework, Duke University (1990); Coursework, Temple University (1989); Postdoctoral Fellowship in Medicine and Forensic Psychiatry, Temple University (1988); Postdoctoral Fellowship in Electro-Seizure Therapy

Awards/Honors: Exemplary Psychiatrist Award, National Alliance for the Mentally Ill (1993)

Expanded Biography: Dr. McMahon-Tronetti published research articles in 1996.

PROFESSIONAL OF THE YEAR IN CHILD PSYCHOLOGY

DR. MICHELE MEAUX

School Psychologist (Retired)
Specialized Services
Chicago Public Schools
1451 E. 55th Street
Apartment 1020N
Chicago, IL 60615 United States
cebmmb1@yahoo.com
http://www.cps.k12.il.us

Type of Business: School District

Major Products and Services: Education, Psychological Evaluations and Counseling

Marketing Area: Chicago, Illinois

Area of Expertise: Dr. Meaux's expertise includes early childhood preparation and education.

Day to Day Responsibilities: Observing Crises in Chicago Schools, Interacting with Students, Teaching, Conducting Psychological Tests for Adults and Children

Favorite Business Publications: Psychology Today; U.S. News & World Report

Hobbies/Interests/Sports: Listening to Music, Traveling to Different Countries, Reading

Education Degrees: Ph.D. in Educational Psychology, Loyola University Chicago; Master's Degree in Educational Counseling, Governors State University; Bachelor of Science in Psychology, Loyola University Chicago

Affiliations/Associations/Societies: Illinois School Psychologists Association; National Association for Female Executives

Charity/Volunteer Work: World Vision; American Cancer Society; United Negro College Fund; Mercy Home for Boys and Girls; Salesian Missions

Date of Birth: June 22, 1947   **Place of Birth:** Chicago

Spouse: Curtis   **Children:** Darius

Work History: Teacher; Psychologist

What do you attribute your success to? She attributes her success to her mother, who was dedicated to her and her eight brothers and sisters.

How did you become involved in your profession? She became involved in her profession after enrolling in an introductory psychology course.

Expanded Biography: Dr. Meaux worked as a classroom teacher for 15 years and then became a reading specialist in order to serve children better. After four years as a reading specialist, she became a school psychologist. Her personal philosophy is 'If at first you don't succeed, try, try again!' The eldest of nine children, she was expected to help her brothers and sisters, who always looked up to her. Dr. Meaux credits all the success that she and her siblings enjoyed to their mother, who was dedicated to each of her children and motivated them to do their best.

EXECUTIVE OF THE YEAR IN CORPORATE RETIREMENT PLANNING

MR. DANFORD R. MEISCHEN, CIMA, ARPC, AIF, CFP

First Vice President
Merrill Lynch
1221 McKinney, Suite 3900
Houston, TX 77010 United States
danford_meischen@ml.com
http://fa.ml.com/BOM_Team

Type of Business: Financial Services

Major Products and Services: Executive and Employee Retirement and Retention Plans for both for-profit and nonprofit organizations

Marketing Area: Mostly Texas and surrounding states; however, client companies are located from South Carolina to Alaska.

Area of Expertise: Mr. Meischen's expertise includes qualified and non-qualified retirement plans, and stock award programs.

Day to Day Responsibilities: Assisting in the Development of 401(k) Platforms for Corporations and Services for Participants, Helping Thousands of Employees to have a More Enjoyable Retirement

Favorite Business Publications: Plan Adviser; Plan Sponsor: Defined Contribution News; Pensions and Investments; IOMA

Hobbies/Interests/Sports: Fishing, Riding his Harley-Davidson Motorcycle, Hunting, Skiing, Reading, Working on his Ranch

Education Degrees: Bachelor of Science in Engineering, United States Military Academy at West Point

Certifications: Certified Investment Analyst; Accredited Retirement Plan Consultant; Certified Investment Planner; Accredited Investment Fiduciary

Awards/Honors: One of the Nation's Top 25 Retirement Plan Financial Advisors, Plan Sponsor Magazine; Recognized Consistently for Excellence in Individual and Corporate Retirement Plans, Merrill Lynch; Corporate Retirement Planning Executive of the Year

Charity/Volunteer Work: Texas Children's Hospital; Ronald McDonald House; West Point Society

Date of Birth: March 13, 1947   **Place of Birth:** Corpus Christi

Spouse: Susie   **Children:** Molly, Matthew, Ryan

Work History: Merrill Lynch (1974-Present); Various Command Positions, U.S. Army (1969-1974)

What do you attribute your success to? He attributes his success the support and understanding of his wife Susie, as he puts in long hours and works weekends to service clients.

How did you become involved in your profession? He became involved in his profession through a natural progression of opportunities.

What was the highlight of your career? The highlight of his career was being selected as one of the Top 25 Retirement Plan Financial Advisors by Plan Sponsor Magazine and being nominated as The Top Retirement Plan Financial Advisor.

Where will you be in five years? In five years, Mr. Meischen intends to work with existing and new corporate clients.

Expanded Biography: Mr. Meischen was one of the first at Merrill Lynch to become a Certified Financial Planner, and one of only nine financial advisors to be selected for the Business Financial Services Council.

PROFESSIONAL OF THE YEAR IN CLINICAL PSYCHOLOGY

DR. SUSAN JOY MENDELSOHN

Clinical Psychologist, Author
Dr. Susan J. Mendelsohn, P.A.
9420 Towne Square Avenue, Suite 18
Cincinnati, OH 45242 United States
drsusie@transformempowersoar.com
http://www.transformempowersoar.com

Type of Business: Private Mental Healthcare Practice

Major Products and Services: Individual and Group Psychotherapy, Relationship and Couples Counseling

Marketing Area: National

Area of Expertise: Dr. Mendelsohn's expertise includes the treatment of eating and body dysmorphia disorders, body image distortion and related illnesses.

Day to Day Responsibilities: Practicing Psychotherapy with Eating Disorders, Mood, Anxiety, Adjustment and Addictive Disorders, Counseling Victims of Sexual, Verbal, Emotional and Physical Abuse, Relationship Counseling, Consulting with a Multi-Disciplinary Treatment Team of Physicians and Dieticians, Improving her Clinical Skills through Continuing Education and Conferences, Keeping Up-to-Date with the Latest Research

Favorite Business Publications: American Psychologist; Psychotherapy Networker; Psychology Today; The National Psychologist

Hobbies/Interests/Sports: Reading, Traveling, Kickboxing, Playing Tennis, Jogging, Writing, Exercising

Education Degrees: Doctor of Clinical Psychology, CCAS (1999); Master of Psychology, CCAS (1994); Master of Professional Studies in Counseling, New York Institute of Technology (1991); Bachelor of Science in Education, University of Miami (1985)

Certifications: Licensed Clinical Psychologist

Affiliations/Associations/Societies: Ohio Psychological Association; American Psychological Association; National Eating Disorders Association

Awards/Honors: VIP Member, Presidential Who's Who among Business and Professional Achievers (2008-2009); Alumni of the Year, CCAS (2007); Businesswoman of the Year, NRCC (2004)

Charity/Volunteer Work: Survivors Network of those Abused by Priests; Fundraiser, National Eating Disorders Awareness Week

Date of Birth: August 25, 1963   **Place of Birth:** Milwaukee

Work History: International Psychological Consultant, eDiets.com

Career Achievements: Author, 'It's Not About Weight, Attacking Eating Disorders from the Inside Out;' Chapter Author, '101 Interventions in Group Therapy'

What do you attribute your success to? She attributes her success to her genuine concern for the welfare of her clients, non-judgmental attitude, unconditional acceptance of her clients and her passion and belief of the need for the profession of psychology.

How did you become involved in your profession? She became involved in her profession because she believes that she is able to empathize with people in a way that others are not capable of and felt it was her calling from God.

What was the highlight of your career? The most gratifying aspect of her career is being able to help her clients to regain their lives and recover from their illnesses.

Where will you be in five years? In five years, Dr. Mendelsohn hopes to continue with her private practice, publish another book and work on the lecture circuit for educating doctors, dieticians and other clinicians about the diagnosis and treatment of eating disorders.

Expanded Biography: Dr. Mendelsohn has worked as a professor of psychiatry for 12 years and has been in private practice for 14 years. She encourages and empowers others to achieve success, and is a firm believer that one cannot change yesterday, but has the chance to start the next day anew. She draws from experiences of negativity in her own life, having triumphed over obstacles despite being told that she would never achieve anything great and that being overweight and single would be detrimental to her success.

PROFESSIONAL OF THE YEAR IN
NATIVE AMERICAN HEALTHCARE EDUCATION

DR. SHARON ELIZABETH METCALFE,
ED.D., RN, MSN

Assistant Professor of Nursing
Western Carolina University
Cullowhee, NC 28723 United States
metcalfe@email.wcu.edu
http://www.wcu.edu

Type of Business: University

Major Products and Services: Higher Education

Marketing Area: Statewide

Day to Day Responsibilities: Collaborative and Distance Learning, Working in Clinical Nursing Administration, Managing Seven Counties, Advising Online

Favorite Business Publications: Journal of Nursing Education; Sigma Theta Tau Publications

Hobbies/Interests/Sports: Listening to Music, Attending Concerts, Exercising

Education Degrees: Doctor of Education, North Carolina State University; Master of Science in Nursing, University of Colorado; Bachelor of Science in Nursing, University of Colorado

Affiliations/Associations/Societies: The 100 Great, NC (2005-2006)

What do you attribute your success to? She attributes her success to the support she receives from her parents.

How did you become involved in your profession? She became involved in her profession after her sister passed away as the result of premature birth.

Expanded Biography: Dr. Metcalfe is collaborating with a Native American tribe to open up a nursing program for Cherokee people. She is also working as a teacher and conducting 12-week classes on high-risk parenting skills.

EXECUTIVE OF THE YEAR IN
AUDIT AND FINANCIAL SERVICES

CYNTHIA J. MICHAUD, MD, CIA, CFE

President, Chief Executive Officer
CJM Associates, LLC
P.O. Box 125
Simsbury, CT 06070 United States
cjm_associates@comcast.net
http://www.cambridgewhoswho.com

Type of Business: Accounting and Finance Company

Major Products and Services: Auditing, Implementation of Internal Controls, Fraud Prevention and Detection, Safeguarding of Assets across All Industries, Investigations for Privacy and Reputation Protection, Strategic Planning and Cost Benefit Analysis across All Industries, Healthcare Restructuring Services to Improve Efficiency without Hindering Patient Care

Marketing Area: International

Day to Day Responsibilities: Overseeing Internal and External Audits in the Healthcare, Insurance and Finance Industries, Practicing Forensics, Ensuring Medical Compliance and Risk Management, Offering Key Initiatives to Ensure that Clients' Needs for Preventative Control are Met in the Workplace Regarding Healthcare Fraud, Banking and Insurance

Education Degrees: MD, University of Connecticut Health Center (2005); Bachelor of Science in Pre-Medical Studies and Accounting, Long Island University (1987); Coursework in Medical Studies, Yale-New Haven Hospital, CT

Certifications: Post-Baccalaureate Certification in Medical Studies, University of Connecticut Health Center (2001)

Affiliations/Associations/Societies: Cystic Fibrosis Foundation; Resident Affairs Liaison, Yale-New Haven Hospital; Bridge to Peace; Who's Who Among American Women

Awards/Honors: Woman of the Year Award, Farmington Valley, CT

Charity/Volunteer Work: American Cancer Society

Children: Arianna, Albert III

Expanded Biography: Dr. Michaud is a single mother. Given all the responsibilities she had at the time she became pregnant, this was certainly not an easy task. However, for all the challenges she endured, the benefits have definitely outweighed the negative. She has become an even more driven, focused and independent person, a stronger leader and an even more compassionate mother. Although it was difficult finding herself alone wearing so many hats, she grew both independently and spiritually. Basically, she had two choices: one was to continue to ask the 'what if' questions and not proceed with her ambitions. The other was to do what she had always done in the past when life took an unexpected turn of events: take control of her own crisis and deal with it in the best way she knew. She has always said that if she is okay, then her family, co-workers and friends will be as well. Today, she has more control over her life and future. She can multi-task in even more areas than she thought possible, while ensuring that she gives her absolute best to each area. Even though she is pulled in many directions, she firmly believes that one needs to step out of one's comfort area to be successful. She believes that people need the courage to raise their hands when in need of help, and reach out to the people they know and trust to receive the best guidance possible. Her advice is: 'Let people help you when asked! Regardless of your profession, you can't be perfect at everything and a successful professional admits what they don't know, and defers to others. You must ask yourself daily if you did the best at whatever endeavor you were accomplishing. If the answer is no, then you're not serious enough to achieve what you are pursuing.' She counsels people continuously by asking the fundamental question: What happens if you try your absolute best at something and fail? Although there are many answers to this question, since it is based on the situation, she usually responds by saying try again, and ask for advice. That's how she became successful. Although the experience can be humbling, it was the best advice she received from seasoned professionals in order to be effective and successful in her professions. She still relies on those mentors and will never forget the support and guidance they have given her. Dr. Michaud was fortunate to learn some of her life's lessons at an early age. It took a crisis for her to learn, 'Change is imminent. It is how you deal with the change and how you rise from that situation that describes the type of person, or leader, you are or will be.' After founding CJM Associates, she wore many hats: Doctor, Chief Executive Officer, mom, dad and head of the household. Here are some of her favorite quotes: 'A woman is like a tea bag, you don't know how strong she is until you put her in hot water,' Nancy Regan; 'When will our consciences grow so tender that we will act to prevent human misery rather than avenge it?,' Eleanor Roosevelt; 'Lasting change is a series of compromises. And compromise is all right, as long your values don't change,' Jane Goodall; 'The mind should be at peace but the heart debauches it perpetually,' Marie de Sevigne; 'I trust you I just need to verify,' Ronald Regan; 'A man does what he must in spite of personal consequences, in spite of obstacles and dangers and pressures, and that is the basis of all human morality,' John F. Kennedy; 'It is not living that matters, but living rightly,' Socrates; 'Blessed is he who has found his work; let him ask no other blessedness,' Thomas Carlyle; 'No one on their death bed ever said that they wish they had spent more time at work,' Anonymous.

PROFESSIONAL OF THE YEAR IN
COLLEGE PREPARATORY EDUCATION

DOROTHY E. MILEVSKIY

English as a Second Language Teacher, College Counselor
The Winchendon School
172 Ash Street
Winchendon, MA 01475 United States
dmilevskiy@yahoo.com.au
http://www.winchendon.org

Type of Business: School

Major Products and Services: Education Including French, Spanish, American Culture, Psychology, Graphic Arts, Computer Programming, Word Processing and Typing

Marketing Area: Regional

Day to Day Responsibilities: Volunteering, Participating in Community Activities, Offering Divorce Counseling and Employee Assistance, Fundraising

Hobbies/Interests/Sports: Sewing, Making Crafts, Cooking, Listening to Music, Archery

Certifications: Diploma in Teaching, James Cook University, Australia (1978)

Affiliations/Associations/Societies: Queensland College of Teachers

Awards/Honors: Who's Who Among America's Teachers (2006-2007); Connecting Teachers to the Future Award (1997); Advanced Skills Teacher Award (1994); Curriculum Leadership Award, Technology (1992)

Work History: Student Teacher Supervisor, James Cook University, Australia

Expanded Biography: Ms. Milevskiy worked in two Australian schools as a computer science teacher and system administrator for 20 years.

ENTREPRENEUR OF THE YEAR IN DANCE CHOREOGRAPHY

HEATHER M. MIRTO

Owner, Director
Miss Heather's School of Dance
2478 S. Dupont Highway
Middletown, DE 19709 United States
missheather@mhdance.com
http://www.mhdance.com

Type of Business: Dance Studio

Major Products and Services: Dance Instruction

Marketing Area: Local

Area of Expertise: Ms. Mirto's expertise includes tap, jazz, ballet, lyrical, cheerleading, tumbling, hip hop and pointe.

Favorite Business Publications: Middletown Transcript

Hobbies/Interests/Sports: Spending Time with her Two Children

Certifications: Certified, Dance Masters of America

Affiliations/Associations/Societies: Everette Theatre; Better Business Bureau

Charity/Volunteer Work: Middletown High School; Red Lion Christian Academy; Christina Cultural Arts Center; Rotary Club of Southern New Castle County; St. Anne's Episcopal School; MOT Charter School; Appoquinimink

Spouse: Anthony   **Children:** Anthony, Angelina

What do you attribute your success to? She attributes her success to support from her family.

How did you become involved in your profession? She became involved in this profession because she has been dancing since she was two years old and wanted to share her passion.

What was the highlight of your career? The most gratifying aspect of her career is being able to work with children and being a positive influence on their lives.

EXECUTIVE OF THE YEAR IN
BUSINESS DEVELOPMENT

MR. RANDALL L. MOAKE

Business Development Executive
Business Development
Triple Canopy, Inc.
2250 Corporate Park Drive, Suite 300
Herndon, VA 20171 United States
randy.moake@triplecanopy.com
http://www.triplecanopy.com

Type of Business: Communications, Logistical, Medical and Life Support Services Firm

Major Products and Services: Assessments, Training, Crisis Management, and Protective Services

Marketing Area: International

Day to Day Responsibilities: Consulting, Managing Security Operations, Analysis and Planning, Developing Business, Giving Presentations, Writing Proposals

Favorite Business Publications: Security Management

Hobbies/Interests/Sports: Camping, Rock Climbing, Fishing

Education Degrees: Master of Arts in Business and Organizational Security Management, Webster University (2004); USAF Police Administration Course (1987); Advanced Leadership and Management Education (1978-1998); Master of Science in Administration, Central Michigan University (1998); FBI National Academy (1997); Bachelor of Science in Criminal Justice Administration, Park University (1988); Associate of Applied Science in Industrial Security, Community College of the Air Force (1987); Associate of Applied Science in Criminal Justice, Community College of the Air Force (1985)

Certifications: Certificate, Criminal Justice Education (1997); Aerospace Management Certificate (1992)

Affiliations/Associations/Societies: Lifetime Member, Air Force Association; American Society for Industrial Security

Awards/Honors: Five Meritorious Service Medals; Air Force Commendation Medal; Two Air Force Achievement Medals; Two Southwest Asia Service Medals; Air Force Recognition Ribbon; National Defense Service Medal; Humanitarian Service Medal; Small Arms Expert Marksmanship Ribbon; Six Air Force Outstanding Unit Awards; Two Air Force Organizational Excellence Awards; Five Air Force Good Conduct Medals

Date of Birth: January 3, 1957   **Place of Birth:** Fort Wayne

Work History: Account Manager, Security Analysis and Planning-Triple Canopy, Inc. (2004-Present); Manager, Systems Security Planning and Validation-Protection Technology Los Alamos (1998-2004); Chief, Security Force Inspections, Air Force Material Command, U.S. Air Force (1995-1998); Headquarters Staff Office, Air Force Security Police Agency, E1-S. Air Force (1994-1995); Chief and Deputy Chief of Security Police-Limit Air Station, Turkey, U.S. Air Force (1992-1994); Superintendent, Missile Security Nuclear Policy & Doctrine-Strategic Air Command, U.S. Air Force (1990-1992)

Career Achievements: General Managers Award, PTLA (1999); Decorated Security Forces, Non-Commissioned Officer; Outstanding Leadership, Air Force Sergeants Association (1994); Outstanding Senior Non-Commissioned Officer of the Year, U.S. Air Force (1993); FBI National Academy (1997); Honor Graduate and Zero Track Award, Mutual of Omaha, Insurance Company (1977); Strategic Missile Wing Outstanding NCO of the Year (1987); Excellence in Competition Bronze Pistol Shot Badge (1990); US Air Force Outstanding Security Police Senior NCO of the Year (1993); Air Force Chief Master Sergeant Award for Outstanding Leadership (1994)

Expanded Biography: Mr. Moake has experience in DOE and DOD security management in anti-terrorism and force protection, nuclear security operations, training, canine operations, security operations planning, performance-based evaluation programs, vulnerability assessments, bargaining unit management, and business acumen in dynamic security environments. Mr. Moake's leadership in DOE protective force operations led to significant improvement in tactical response capabilities and upgrades in protection strategy, equipment, weapons, ammunition and armored vehicles against the postulated threat. He also has experience with the U.S. Air Force in positions of increasing responsibility guiding highly-successful nuclear and aerospace security operations around the world. Mr. Moake is a decorated security forces officer and nuclear security specialist. He served in several capacities gaining experience in positions of increasing responsibility and leadership, including operational units, headquarters command staffs, chief and deputy chief of security police, and chief of the air force material command inspector general security force inspector staff. Mr. Moake has three sons and two daughters. He has authored several USAF security policy documents and an article in 'Law Enforcement Online' and given presentations on Asymmetric Threats and Government Security Regulations to corporate and private security clients.

PROFESSIONAL OF THE YEAR IN
MENTAL HEALTH

DR. MARGIE MOLINET-MOLINA, PSY.D., NCSP

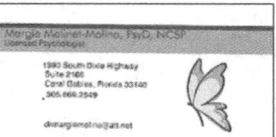

1) Psychologist 2) School Psychologist
1) Private Practice 2) Miami-Dade County Public Schools
1390 S. Dixie Highway, Suite 2106
Coral Gables, FL 33146 United States
drmargiemolina@bellsouth.net
http://www.cambridgewhoswho.com

Type of Business: 1) Private Practice 2) School District

Major Products and Services: 1) Healthcare Including Child and Adolescent Psychology 2) Education

Marketing Area: 1) Local 2) Local

Area of Expertise: Dr. Molinet-Molina's expertise includes child and adolescent psychology, regression therapy and the treatment of adult chronic illness.

Day to Day Responsibilities: Offering Psychotherapy and Psychological Assessments to Patients, Supervising Students and Patients

Favorite Business Publications: Monitor; Psychology Today; Industry-Related Publications

Hobbies/Interests/Sports: Traveling, Gardening, Spending Time with her Family, Attending the Theater

Education Degrees: Post-Doctoral Fellowship, University of Miami School of Medicine at Jackson Memorial Hospital; Doctor of Clinical Psychology, with Distinction, Carlos Albizu University; Pre-Doctoral Internship, University of Miami School of Medicine at Jackson Memorial Hospital; Master's Degree in Clinical Psychology, with Distinction, Carlos Albizu University; Master's Degree in School Psychology, Florida International University; Bachelor's Degree in Psychology, InterAmerican University

Certifications: Licensed Psychologist, State of Florida; Licensed School Psychologist, State of Florida; National Certified School Psychologist; Certified Cognitive Behavioral Therapist; Certified Kindergarten through 12th-Grade Teacher, State of Florida

Affiliations/Associations/Societies: Psi Chi, The National Honor Society in Psychology; National Association of School Psychologists; National Academy of Neuropsychology; American Psychological Association; American Psychotherapy Association

Charity/Volunteer Work: The Children's Initiative

Date of Birth: June 10, 1954   **Place of Birth:** Havana

Spouse: David   **Children:** Manny, Stephanie

Work History: School Psychologist (1986-2007); Research Associate, University of Miami (1983-1986)

What do you attribute your success to? She attributes her success to her dedication, perseverance and commitment.

How did you become involved in your profession? She became involved in her profession because of her education and through a natural progression of opportunities.

What was the highlight of your career? The highlight of her career was opening her own practice and working independently toward developing a holistic approach to mental health.

Where will you be in five years? In five years, Dr. Molinet-Molina intends to expand her business to include other practitioners with similar approaches to mental health.

Expanded Biography: Dr. Molinet-Molina conducts presentations and lectures at the University of Miami. She has published a number of papers, including 'Bilingual Receptive Vocabulary in Hispanic Preschool Children' in 1992 and 'Using a Neuro-psychoeducational Evaluation Approach to Identify Fine Motor Deficits in Preschool Children with Developmental Verbal Dyspraxia' in 2002.

PROFESSIONAL OF THE YEAR IN
TISSUE DONATION AND TRANSPLANT SERVICES

MONICA MARIA MONTENERO, MD, PH.D.

Director of International Tissue Services
Musculoskeletal Transplant Foundation
125 May Street
Edison, NJ 08837 United States
monica_montenero@mtf.org
http://www.mtf.org

Type of Business: Nonprofit Service Organization

Major Products and Services: Musculoskeletal Tissue Donation, Processing and Transplant Services

Marketing Area: International

Area of Expertise: Dr. Montenero's expertise is in international donor services.

Favorite Business Publications: AATB Publications

Hobbies/Interests/Sports: Practicing Yoga, Swimming, Skiing, Listening to Philharmonic and Opera Music

Education Degrees: MD, Università degli Studi di Roma 'La Sapienza,' Italy; Ph.D., Joslin Clinic

Certifications: Board Certified Pathologist, Earned in Europe and the United States

Affiliations/Associations/Societies: International Chairman, Food Allergy Initiative; American Association of Tissue Banks; European Association of Tissue Banks; American Medical Association

Charity/Volunteer Work: American Diabetes Association; European Association for the Study of Diabetes; FAI

Date of Birth: December 18, 1953   **Place of Birth:** Rome

Children: Raffaele, Annie

What do you attribute your success to? She attributes her success to her dedication to her profession.

How did you become involved in your profession? She became involved in her profession because she had an interest in the field, and followed the footsteps of her father and grandfather into the profession.

What was the highlight of your career? The highlights of her career were the accomplishments that her foundation made in the United States, Europe and South America.

EXECUTIVE OF THE YEAR IN
INTEGRATED WORKPLACE MANAGEMENT SYSTEMS

MR. NICK A. MOORE

President
Cougar Software, Inc.
208 W. 30th Street, Suite 802
New York, NY 10001 United States
nick.moore@cougarsoftware.com
http://www.cougarsoftware.com

Type of Business: The World's Premier Privately-Owned Company Specializing in the Development, Implementation and Support of Forward-Looking Real Estate Financial Analysis Software

Major Products and Services: Investment, Corporate Real Estate, Comprehensive Business Solution for All Sizes of Real Estate Owner, Investor, Corporate User, Government or Service Provider

Marketing Area: International

Area of Expertise: Mr. Moore's expertise includes software applications for real estate management and real estate investments.

Favorite Business Publications: Forbes; Fortune; Time

Hobbies/Interests/Sports: Golfing, Water Sports, Sport Shooting

Education Degrees: Bachelor of Commerce in Finance and Accounting, University of New South Wales, Australia (1990)

Certifications: Certified Public Accountant

Affiliations/Associations/Societies: National Association of Real Estate Investment Trusts; CPA Australia

Place of Birth: Sydney

PROFESSIONAL OF THE YEAR REPRESENTING HIV/AIDS HEALTHCARE CONSULTING

GRACIELA MORALES-SCOTT, PH.D.

Educational Consultant
Scott Consulting Services
14255 Sunset Street
Hesperia, CA 92345 United States
drgphd740@msn.com
http://www.cambridgewhoswho.com

Type of Business: Bilingual Consulting Company

Major Products and Services: Nonprofit Management and Consulting Services for New, Small and Mid-Sized Nonprofit and Faith-Based Organizations in the Areas of HIV/AIDS, Primary Healthcare, Adult Day Care, Domestic Violence, Homelessness, High-Risk Youth, and Drug and Alcohol Treatment

Marketing Area: National

Day to Day Responsibilities: Offering Bilingual, Nonprofit Consulting Services Including Training, Grant Writing, Board, Staff and Program Development, Strategic Planning and Evaluation, Evaluating Curriculums and Programs, Mentoring

Favorite Business Publications: AAGP Journal

Hobbies/Interests/Sports: Gardening, Dancing, Sewing, Traveling, Reading, Exercising, Playing the Piano

Education Degrees: Ph.D. in Education, University of California, Los Angeles; Master's Degree in Educational Counseling; Bachelor's Degree in Psychology, California State University, San Bernardino; Professional Degree in Theology, Latin American Bible Institute, La Puente, CA

Certifications: Pursuing Certification in Grant Writing; Certified Anger Management Trainer; Certified Mediator; Certified HIV/AIDS Trainer and Counselor; Certified Psychology Instructor; Certified Teacher in English as a Second Language and Spanish

Affiliations/Associations/Societies: American Association of Grant Professionals; American Indian Professional Association; California State University Alumni Association; Hispanic Scholarship Fund; Southern California Association for Healthcare Development; National Family Caregivers Association; National Association for Female Executives; California Community College Alumni Association; National Parenting Association; Psi Chi, The National Honor Society in Psychology; Pi Lambda Theta

Awards/Honors: Outstanding Student Alumnus Award for Outstanding Contributions to Persons with HIV/AIDS, California State University (1996); Award for Development and Administration of the First Program for Services for HIV Positive Women, T.H.E. Clinic for Women, Inc. (1994); First Human Rights Award, California Association for Counseling and Development (1992); First Native American and Latina Inductee, Victor Valley Community College Annual Hall of Fame (1991); First Latina to be Featured in the HBO Award-Winning Presentation on Women and HIV; Four-Time Recipient, Professional Commendations in Domestic Violence Training; Six-Time Recipient, Professional Recognitions for Community Service; Six-Time Recipient, Professional Recognitions for HIV Outreach and Education

Charity/Volunteer Work: Disabled American Veterans

Date of Birth: July 20, 1940   **Children:** Deborah, Michael, Rene

Work History: California Dance Center, Los Angeles, CA (2004-Present); President, Chief Executive Officer, Scott Consulting Services, Hesperia, CA (1995-Present); Understanding Principles for Better Living Church, Los Angeles, CA (2004-2006); New Beginnings Fellowship Center, Fountain Valley, CA (2004-2005); Spanish Pacific Latin American District, La Puente, CA (2004-2005); National Adult Day Care Foundation, Culver City, CA (2003-2005); Each One Teach One, Los Angeles, CA (2002-2005); Chief Executive Officer, National Healthcare Foundation, Inc., Culver City, CA (2003-2004); La Oportunidad Inc., Los Angeles, CA (2002-2004); Grayson's Outreach, Inc., Los Angeles, CA (2002-2004); Peacemakers, Inc., Los Angeles, CA (1999-2003); Women's Haven of Tarrant County, Fort Worth, TX (2000-2001); Family Counselor, Homeless Health Care Los Angeles (1999–2000)

Expanded Biography: Dr. Morales-Scott is a bilingual consultant for Centers for Disease Control and Prevention in Atlanta, GA and has worked on many committees addressing HIV/AIDS to develop a national organization. She has been serving as an HIV/AIDS consultant for 25 years, and has been focusing her expertise on grant writing and nonprofit management services since 1997. She has written various articles on HIV/AIDS for 'La Opinion' and 'The Los Angeles Times,' in addition to co-authoring 'Psychodynamic Theory and AIDS Counseling,' published in 'Beyond the Faces of AIDS,' a University of California, San Francisco publication. She was featured in two educational videos, 'Women and AIDS,' produced in Los Angeles, and 'Women and AIDS,' a national HBO production. Dr. Scott has also appeared on ABC, NBC and Univision as an HIV/AIDS expert.

PROFESSIONAL OF THE YEAR IN NAVAL JOURNALISM

MR. SAMUEL LORING MORISON

Journalist, Naval Historian, Author
1482 Carlyle Court
Crofton, MD 21114 United States
s.morison@verizon.net
http://www.cambridgewhoswho.com

Type of Business: Journalism

Major Products and Services: Books, Articles, United States Navy Research

Marketing Area: International

Day to Day Responsibilities: Writing More than 200 Published Articles for Military and Naval Newspapers Including 'Navy Times,' 'Naval History Magazine' and 'United States Naval Institute Proceedings,' Writing Book Reviews

Favorite Business Publications: Warships of the World; U.S. Naval Institute Proceedings; Navy Times; Warships International Fleet Review

Education Degrees: Bachelor of Arts in History, Minor in Naval Science, University of Louisville (1967)

Affiliations/Associations/Societies: Navy League of the United States; American Legion; International Naval Research Organization; United States Naval Institute; National LSM/LSMR Association; PT Boats, Inc.; United States Navy

Work History: Junior Grade Lieutenant, United States Navy (1967-1969)

Expanded Biography: Mr. Morison has written eight books on the military and is currently working on his ninth. He is widely credited for possessing the best files and records on naval matters outside of the Pentagon.

EXECUTIVE OF THE YEAR IN
HEALTH FOUNDATION CONSULTING

MRS. J. MORROW

President
J. Morrow, Inc.
P.O. Box 660038
Birmingham, AL 35266 United States
jmorrow@mrrbusa.com
http://www.cambridgewhoswho.com

Type of Business: Women and Children's Health Foundation

Major Products and Services: Foundation for Women and Children's Health

Marketing Area: International

Day to Day Responsibilities: Women and Children's Health Consulting

Hobbies/Interests/Sports: Traveling, Working with Computers

Education Degrees: Ph.D. in Health Services, The Walden Institute, University of Minnesota

Affiliations/Associations/Societies: Alabama Department of Public Health; Arthritis and Osteoporosis Unit; Cancer Registry; General Federation of Women's Clubs; Foundation for Women's Health; Sight Savers of Alabama; Secretary, Treasurer, Morrow Railroad Builders

Spouse: James

What do you attribute your success to? She attributes her success to meeting people who recognized her abilities and believed in her.

How did you become involved in your profession? She became involved in her profession after initially majoring in premedical studies and working with junior memberships at a women's club.

What was the highlight of your career? The highlight of her career was being on the Health Services Advisory Board and contributing to the development of the Brookwood Women's Medical Center.

PROFESSIONAL OF THE YEAR IN EXECUTIVE COACHING

ANNE B. MOSES, MA, MBA, CPC

Executive Coach, Consultant
1837 Harris Avenue
San Jose, CA 95124 United States
anne.moses@evistaconsulting.com
http://www.evistaconsulting.com/coaching.asp

Type of Business: Consulting

Major Products and Services: Working with Groups or Individuals to Achieve Growth for Desired Goals

Marketing Area: Regional

Day to Day Responsibilities: Offering Management Consulting in Healthcare and Social Services, Managing Leadership Development and Emergency Disaster Preparedness

Favorite Business Publications: Harvard Business Review; The Wall Street Journal

Hobbies/Interests/Sports: Fly-Fishing, Photography, Writing

Education Degrees: Master of Business Administration, University of Chicago (1977); Master of Social Work, University of Chicago (1977)

Certifications: Professional Coach Certification, Hudson Institute of Santa Barbara

Affiliations/Associations/Societies: California Writers Club; National Association of Social Workers; International Coaches Federation; Planned Parenthood; American Red Cross; American Lung Association

Awards/Honors: Short Story Award, California Writers Group (2005); Woman of Achievement Award (1980)

Expanded Biography: Ms. Moses self-published, 'Take 2 and Hit to Write' and 'Hello, Hello, There's a Story or 2 I'd Like to Tell You.'

EXECUTIVE OF THE YEAR IN FOOD SCIENCE

FRANCINE M. MOUDRY

Director of Operations
Bell Brands USA
602 W. Main Street
Leitchfield, KY 42754 United States
fmoudry@belbrandsusa.com
http://www.cambridgewhoswho.com

Type of Business: Manufacturing Company

Major Products and Services: Cheese Products

Marketing Area: International

Area of Expertise: Ms. Moudry's expertise includes food science, plant and production management, research development and quality assurance.

Day to Day Responsibilities: Managing Employees, Accounting

Favorite Business Publications: Cheese Market News; Dairy Foods; Quality; Control

Hobbies/Interests/Sports: Playing the Violin and the Piano, Reading, Traveling, Discovering New Places and People

Education Degrees: Ph.D. in Food Science, Ensaia Institute, France

Affiliations/Associations/Societies: Kentucky Milk Safety Board; International Dairy Foods Association

Date of Birth: October 4, 1962

What do you attribute your success to? She attributes her success to her hard work and tenacity.

How did you become involved in your profession? She became involved in her profession because of her interest in food science.

What was the highlight of your career? The highlight of her career was rallying 300 people for one project.

Expanded Biography: Ms. Moudry feels that her largest professional accomplishment to date was getting the plant ready for the future. It moved from manual to automated operations in a very tight frame while continuing to produce and maintain the familial identity. Ms. Moudry was born in France and completed her education there. She has been working with her current company for 20 years and has held various position within it, steadily progressing throughout her career to become the leader of the plant in Leichtfield, KY.

PROFESSIONAL OF THE YEAR IN RELIGIOUS SERVICES

MONTY W. MULKEY

Senior Pastor
International Association of Deliverance Churches
2060 E. Avenida de los Arboles, Suite D
Thousand Oaks, CA 91362 United States
iadc2000@aol.com
http://www.wccd.com

Type of Business: Church

Major Products and Services: Religious Services, Education, Spiritual Guidance and Counseling

Marketing Area: International

Day to Day Responsibilities: Preaching to Large Congregations, Ministering on Personal Relationships, Coordinating the Growth and Financial Programs of the Congregation, Establishing Churches, Ministering in Areas Needed to Promote Education, Counseling

Hobbies/Interests/Sports: Listening to Music, Fishing

Education Degrees: Doctor of Divinity, World Christianship Ministries, with Honors

Certifications: Certification in Ordination

Affiliations/Associations/Societies: International Who's Who of Entrepreneurs

PROFESSIONAL OF THE YEAR IN
LEGAL ADMINISTRATIVE SUPPORT

LINDA A. MURA

Executive Legal Secretary
1828 L Street N.W., Suite 1111
Washington, DC 20036 United States
lamura@vssp.com
http://www.cambridgewhoswho.com

Type of Business: Law Firm

Major Products and Services: Legal Services

Marketing Area: Washington Metropolitan Area

Day to Day Responsibilities: Assisting High-Profile Executives, Scheduling Events and Board Meetings, Making Travel Arrangements, Overseeing Client Billing and Interactions

Favorite Business Publications: Leader to Leader Journal

Hobbies/Interests/Sports: Traveling, Swimming, Bowling, Reading, Gardening

Education Degrees: High School Education

Affiliations/Associations/Societies: National Association of Legal Secretaries (Now Association for Legal Professionals)

Charity/Volunteer Work: Local Fire Department; Local Police Department; St. Jude Children's Research Hospital

Place of Birth: Fredericksburg   **Children:** Zakk, Danielle, Niki, Brooke

What do you attribute your success to? She attributes her success to her self-motivation, work ethic, determination and networking skills.

What was the highlight of your career? The most gratifying aspect of her career is working with respected professionals in Washington.

PROFESSIONAL OF THE YEAR IN EARLY CHILDHOOD EDUCATION

LORETTO HALEY MURPHY

Classroom Teacher
C.A. Moore Elementary School
21 Seagull Place
Vero Beach, FL 32960 United States
blmurphy@comcast.net
http://plato.stlucie.k12.fl.us/html

Type of Business: Elementary School

Major Products and Services: Primary Education

Marketing Area: Regional

Area of Expertise: Ms. Murphy's expertise is in early childhood education.

Day to Day Responsibilities: Teaching All Subjects to Kindergarten through Third-Grade Students, Acting as a Liaison to Teachers

Favorite Business Publications: Phi Delta Kappan Publications; Chi Omega Booklet

Hobbies/Interests/Sports: Studying Genealogy, Watching University of Miami Hurricane Club Football

Education Degrees: Education Specialist Degree in Educational Computers, Barry University (1989); Master's Degree in Early Childhood Education, Florida International University, Miami (1979); Bachelor of Science in Elementary Education, Florida International University

Affiliations/Associations/Societies: Florida Education Association; Chi Omega National Fraternity; International Honorary Member, Phi Delta Kappa; Former President, Association of Childhood Education International; President, Ladies Ancient Order of Hibernians

Awards/Honors: Recipient, Outstanding Student Award, School of Education, Florida International University

What do you attribute your success to? She attributes her success to her tenacity.

How did you become involved in your profession? She became involved in her profession because of her love for children.

What was the highlight of your career? The most gratifying aspect of her career is seeing her students succeed.

Expanded Biography: Ms. Murphy was a clinical teacher for the University of Miami. She has also published newsletters.

PROFESSIONAL OF THE YEAR IN
STATE LAW ENFORCEMENT

LINDA A. MYS

Sergeant
Michigan State Police Newaygo Post
360 Adams Street
Newaygo, MI 49337 United States
mysla318@live.com
http://www.michigan.gov/msp

Type of Business: Police Department

Major Products and Services: Law Enforcement

Marketing Area: Michigan

Day to Day Responsibilities: Multi-Tasking, Ensuring Troopers are Knowledgeable, Teaching Guidelines, Sharing Knowledge of All Laws

Hobbies/Interests/Sports: Watching NASCAR Racing, Golfing, Riding All Terrain Vehicles, Swimming, Hiking

Education Degrees: Industry-Related Training

Affiliations/Associations/Societies: Michigan Concerns of Police Survivors; Former Member, Fraternal Order of Police; Marshall Memorial Park Committee; National Law Enforcement Officers Memorial Fund

Charity/Volunteer Work: Former Senior Coordinating Committee Member, The Humane Society of the United States; World Wildlife Federation

Work History: Military Police Officer, United States Army

What do you attribute your success to? She attributes her success to her motivation and determination, and to the support she receives from her colleagues.

How did you become involved in your profession? She became involved in her profession because she always wanted to be a police officer.

What was the highlight of your career? The most gratifying aspect of her career is being able to help victims' families find justice.

Expanded Biography: Ms. Mys was the first woman assigned to serve in the Reed City Post.

EXECUTIVE OF THE YEAR IN LAND DEVELOPMENT

LESCEILLEA M. NAPUE

President, Owner
Pine Stone Estates, LLC
23810 96th Street
Elk River, MN 55330 United States
lesceillea.napue@cwwemail.com
http://www.cambridgewhoswho.com

Type of Business: Construction Company

Major Products and Services: Construction Services, Developing Land for Single-Family Homes

Marketing Area: Local

Day to Day Responsibilities: Constructing Single-Family Homes, and Lakefront Properties, Woods and Wetlands

Favorite Business Publications: Business Monthly

Hobbies/Interests/Sports: Reading, Cleaning, Traveling

Education Degrees: Master's Degree in Educational Psychology and Guidance, University of Minnesota; Bachelor of Science in Elementary Education, University of Nebraska

Affiliations/Associations/Societies: Delta Kappa Gamma

Charity/Volunteer Work: Glendale Seventh-Day Adventist Church

PROFESSIONAL OF THE YEAR IN NEONATAL NURSING

Sharon L. Neely, RN

Registered Nurse
Lee Memorial Health Systems
9981 S. Healthpark Drive
Fort Myers, FL 33901 United States
info@CambridgeWhosWho.com
http://www.cambridgewhoswho.com

Type of Business: Healthcare

Major Products and Services: Full-Service Hospital

Marketing Area: Local

Area of Expertise: Ms. Neely's expertise is in neonatal intensive care.

Favorite Business Publications: Neonatal Network

Hobbies/Interests/Sports: Attending the Florida State Fair, Reading, Traveling, Gardening, Crafts, Needlepoint

Education Degrees: Registered Nurse Diploma, Parkview Methodist Hospital

Affiliations/Associations/Societies: National Neonatal Association

Charity/Volunteer Work: March of Dimes Foundation

What do you attribute your success to? She attributes her success to staying current with industry advancements.

What was the highlight of your career? The highlight of her career was receiving a plaque for her work at the nursery in 1981.

PROFESSIONAL OF THE YEAR IN PRIMARY EDUCATION

GWENDALYN V. NEWMAN-JONES, MA

Professional Educator
Ninety-Second Street Elementary School
Los Angeles Unified School District
9211 Grape Street
Los Angeles, CA 90002 United States
newmanjones13@hotmail.com
http://www.cambridgewhoswho.com

Type of Business: School District

Major Products and Services: Education

Marketing Area: Local

Day to Day Responsibilities: Teaching Professional Education for New Teachers, Mentoring First-Grade Students, Conducting Workshops

Favorite Business Publications: UTLA Journal

Hobbies/Interests/Sports: Traveling, Photography

Education Degrees: Master of Arts in Curriculum and Instruction, University of San Francisco (1983); Bachelor's Degree in Child Development, California State University, Los Angeles (1975)

Certifications: Certified English as a Second Language Teacher (1990); Certified Administrator (1984); Certification in Adult Education (1980); Certification in Early Childhood Education (1979)

Affiliations/Associations/Societies: Board Member, Women in Educational Leadership; Children's Nature Institute; Board Member, Freemont High School Alumni Association; Board Member, National Association for the Education of Young Children; Alpha Kappa Alpha; Phi Delta Kappa

Awards/Honors: Leadership Award, National Geographic Board

PROFESSIONAL OF THE YEAR IN PHARMACEUTICAL DISTRIBUTION

MRS. AMELIA NIEVES

President, Owner
Wholesale Drug Distributor
312 32nd Villa Nevarez, Americo Miranda Avenue
San Juan, PR 00927 United States
bnieves@wddpr.com
http://www.wddpr.com

Type of Business: Pharmaceutical Distributor

Major Products and Services: Pharmaceuticals

Marketing Area: International

Day to Day Responsibilities: Distributing Pharmaceutical Drugs

Hobbies/Interests/Sports: Walking, Swimming

Education Degrees: Bachelor of Science

Certifications: Registered Pharmacist

Affiliations/Associations/Societies: Pharmaceutical Industry Association of Puerto Rico

Charity/Volunteer Work: St. Jude Children's Research Hospital

What do you attribute your success to? She attributes her success to her dedication and determination.

How did you become involved in your profession? She became involved in her career because she always knew she wanted to be a pharmacist.

What was the highlight of your career? The highlight of her career was being able to open her own business.

EXECUTIVE OF THE YEAR IN ADVERTISING AND PUBLIC RELATIONS

MR. JOHN A. NORTH JR.

President (Retired)
Baker & North, Inc. (Dissolved)
info@cambridgewhoswho.com
http://www.cambridgewhoswho.com

Type of Business: Advertising and Public Relations Company

Major Products and Services: Promotions, Advertising, Production of 'What in the World' TV Quiz Show

Marketing Area: Regional

Day to Day Responsibilities: Advertising and Public Relations Producing Creative Work, Working with Nonprofit Organizations

Favorite Business Publications: Smithsonian; Architectural Digest; Advertising Age

Hobbies/Interests/Sports: Golfing, Fishing, Gardening, Landscaping, Working with Nonprofit Organizations

Education Degrees: Bachelor of Arts in English, Trinity College

Affiliations/Associations/Societies: Board Member, Chairman, Zoning Board of Appeals and Tax Review; Former Director, Visiting Nurse Association of Greater Hartford; Former Director, Long Rivers Council of Boy Scouts; Former Director, Better Business Bureau of Greater Hartford; Former Director, Connecticut Foundation of Independent Schools; Charter Member, Vice President, Farmington Valley Junior Chamber of Commerce; Member and Chairman, Simsbury Zoning Board of Appeals; Trustee, Former President, Ames Hill-Marlboro Community Center; Chairman of Trustees, Marlboro Meeting House; Vice President, Director, Camp Waubanong; Chairman of the Board, Southern Vermont Natural History Museum; Member, Alden Kindred of America

Awards/Honors: Hometown Hero Award (1994); Recipient, Outstanding Young Man of the Year Award (1963); Former Chairman, Easter Seals of Connecticut; Former President, Easter Seal's Greater Hartford Rehabilitation Center; Former President, Greater Hartford Advertising Club; Former Trustee, Connecticut River Watershed Council; Trinity College Alumni Association; Trustee, Marlboro Meeting House

Date of Birth: April 30, 1931   **Place of Birth:** Hartford

Spouse: Jean (Deceased)   **Children:** John III, Sterling, Susan

What do you attribute your success to? He attributes his success to getting along with people and being very creative in advertising development.

How did you become involved in your profession? He became involved in his profession after starting in the field while still in school.

What was the highlight of your career? The highlight of his career was being asked to serve on the board of several nonprofit organizations.

Expanded Biography: Mr. North produced the 'What in the World' television program.

DONALD M. NULL JR., MD

Medical Director, Neonatal ICU
Primary Children's Medical Center
100 N. Medical Drive
Salt Lake City, UT 84113 United States
donald.null@intermountainmail.org
http://www.pcmc.org

Type of Business: 232-Bed Pediatric Medical Center, Part of a Nonprofit Healthcare System

Major Products and Services: Adolescent Medicine, Allergy, Anesthesiology, Asthma, Birth Defects, Bone Marrow Transplant, Brace Shop and Orthotics Lab, Cancer Treatment, Cerebral Palsy, Child Abuse and Neglect, Child Life, Diabetes, Down Syndrome, Emergency Service, Endocrinology, Epilepsy, Family Centered Care, High-Risk Infant Follow-Up, Newborn Critical Care, Nutrition, Ophthalmology, Orthodontics, Pediatric and Adolescent Gynecology, Pediatric Surgery, Spina Bifida

Marketing Area: Regional

Area of Expertise: Dr. Null's expertise is in neonatology.

Day to Day Responsibilities: Working on a Research Project Regarding Ideology and the Prevention of Lung Injury in Premature and Term Newborns

Favorite Business Publications: Pediatrics

Hobbies/Interests/Sports: Snow Skiing, Collecting Antiques

Education Degrees: MD, West Virginia University (1969)

Affiliations/Associations/Societies: American Pediatric Society; American Academy of Pediatrics; Society of Critical Care Medicine

Spouse: Kathy   **Children:** Mildred, Julie

Expanded Biography: Dr. Null is a local, national and international public speaker. He organizes an annual High Frequency Ventilation Conference and has published articles and chapters in several books.

PROFESSIONAL OF THE YEAR IN FAMILY MEDICINE

THOMAS G. O'BRIEN II, MS, DO

Family Physician
Thomas G. O'Brien II, MS, DO, PC
244 Madison Avenue
Apartment 3G
New York, NY 10016 United States
baccracr@aol.com
http://www.communityhealtheducation.com

Type of Business: Private Practice

Major Products and Services: Healthcare Including Community Outreach Programs, Health Education and Services

Marketing Area: Regional

Day to Day Responsibilities: Educating Healthcare Providers and Patients through Television and Radio, Enriching Under-Served Communities in New York City through Community Outreach Programs, Treating Patients, Administering Surgical Services for Members of the Police Department

Favorite Business Publications: Medical Economics

Hobbies/Interests/Sports: Weight Training, Roller-Skating

Education Degrees: Bachelor's Degree in Biology, New York Institute of Technology (1997); Associate Degree in Biology, Nassau Community College (1996); Doctor of Osteopathy, College of Osteopathic Medicine, Des Moines University, IA (1995); Master's Degree in Clinical Nutrition, New York Institute of Technology (1990)

Certifications: Certified in Emergency Management and Family Medicine, Federal Emergency Management Association

Affiliations/Associations/Societies: Commanding Officer, New York Guard; 1102 Forward Medical Support Detachment, 88th Brigade, New York Guard; American Osteopathic Board of Family Physicians; American Medical Association; Team Physician, United States of America Amateur Boxing Federation

Awards/Honors: Dual Recipient, New York Guard Operations Support Medal; Humanitarian Award for Healthcare Excellence; BETA Award for Best Health Education Show

Charity/Volunteer Work: Community Outreach Programs; Clothing and Food Drives; Health Screening Events

Date of Birth: June 6, 1964

Expanded Biography: Dr. O'Brien holds the rank of captain in the New York Guard and, in July 2007, was promoted to commander of the 1102 Forward Medical Support Detachment. He hosts his own cable television show called, 'Ask Dr. Tommy O,' a health education show in New York. He and his colleagues established a triage center on September 11, 2001 for 9-11 survivors at Stuyvesant High School in Manhattan, NY. He is also a ringside boxing physician. Dr. O'Brien has published several health-related articles and currently holds a United States patent for a medical instrument that he developed.

PROFESSIONAL OF THE YEAR IN LACTATION CONSULTANCY

FLORENCE I. OBANYA

Registered Nurse, Independent Business Consultant
Business Connections International,
Dynamic and Futuristic Concepts
Dallas, TX United States
fobanya@yahoo.com
email@obanyainternational.info
http://www.obanyainternational.info

Type of Business: E-commerce

Major Products and Services: Health and Nutritional Products, Personalized Health Care for Heart and General Nutrition, Genetics Testing, e-Spring Water Purification, Beauty Products, Weight-Loss Products, Energy Drinks, Health and Wellness Consulting

Marketing Area: International

Day to Day Responsibilities: Educating People on Health-Related Products, Consulting on Health, Wellness and Breastfeeding, Managing Customer Relations

Favorite Business Publications: Time; Books Business

Hobbies/Interests/Sports: Exercising, Walking, Reading, Spending Time with her Family and Friends, Writing

Education Degrees: Bachelor of Science in Nursing, Earned in Canada

Certifications: Registered Nurse, Earned in United States and Canada; Certified Midwife, Earned in United Kingdom; Registered Sick Children's Nurse, Earned in United Kingdom; MSI-Skin Analyzer Magnifier Machine Certification for Facial Type Analysis; International Board Certified Lactation Consultant

Affiliations/Associations/Societies: Canadian Nurses Association; American Nurses Association; People to People International

Date of Birth: October 9, 1943   **Place of Birth:** Asaba

Children: Irene, Winifred, Richard, Dorothy

Work History: Registered Nurse, Children's Emergency Clinic (1966)

Expanded Biography: Ms. Obanya was among a group of lactation consultants from the United States, Canada and Australia chosen to visit South Africa in 2004. She worked as an obstetrics and lactation nurse in Canada for 20 years, and is currently working as an RN and lactation nurse in Texas and with the University of Texas Southwestern Medical Center at Dallas.

PROFESSIONAL OF THE YEAR IN
INTERNATIONAL AND DIPLOMATIC GOVERNMENT RELATIONS

FRANCIS G. OKELO

Ambassador, Former United Nations Special Envoy
United Nations Organization
17 Barnard Road
New Rochelle, NY 10801 United States
fgokelo@hotmail.com
fgocii@yahoo.com
http://www.un.org

Type of Business: Nonprofit Organization

Major Products and Services: Development of International Diplomatic Relations Including Solving Issues Related to National, Regional and International Conflict Resolution, Real Estate Development and Investments, Humanitarian Measures

Marketing Area: International

Day to Day Responsibilities: Communicating, Building Relationships

Favorite Business Publications: BusinessWeek; Money; Forbes; Investor's Business Daily; The Economist

Hobbies/Interests/Sports: Golfing

Education Degrees: Master's Degree in Finance and Management; Coursework in History, Philosophy and Economics, Makerere University, Uganda, with Honors (1969)

Affiliations/Associations/Societies: Deputy Special Representative, Secretary to Palestinian Liberation Organization and Palestinian Authority (2000-2004); Deputy Special Coordinator, Mideast Peace Process (1999); Director of Office Special Representative (1991-1997); United Nations Peacekeeper

Awards/Honors: Highest Civilian Award 'Ordre De Mono' for the Significant Role Played in the Peaceful Resolution of the Nine-Year Civil War in Sierra Leone, Economic Community of West African States (1999)

Work History: Acting United Nations Special Coordinator (2005); Deputy Special Coordinator, Middle East Peace Process, Special Representative, United Nations Secretary, General, Palestinian Liberation Organization and Palestinian Authority (2000-2004); United Nations Special Envoy, Sierra Leone (1997-1999); Deputy Special Envoy to Afghanistan, United Assistance Mission to Afghanistan (1995-1997); Uganda Ambassador, European Economic Communities, Belgium, Luxembourg and Kenya (1979-1986)

Expanded Biography: Mr. Okelo served in several positions with the United Nations in New York, Namibia, Haiti, Afghanistan, Brazil and Guatemala.

PROFESSIONAL OF THE YEAR IN ELEMENTARY EDUCATION

JUNE M. OMEL

Third-Grade Teacher
Kiona-Benton City Elementary School
1107 Grace
Benton City, WA 99320 United States
lovecake@netzero.net
http://www.kibesd.org

Type of Business: Elementary School

Major Products and Services: Elementary Education Including Arts, Music, Physical Education, Special Programs, Learning Resources, Student Support Services, Athletics, Extracurricular Activities

Marketing Area: Local

Day to Day Responsibilities: Teaching Second through Fourth-Grade Students, Planning and Developing Lessons for Knowledge Amidst Fun and Creativity within the Classes

Favorite Business Publications: Industry-Related Publications

Hobbies/Interests/Sports: Reading, Writing for School's Town Newspaper, Arts, Listening to Music, Gardening

Education Degrees: Bachelor's Degree in Elementary Education, Minor in Speech Communications, Luther College; Coursework, Antioch University; Coursework, Fresno Pacific University; Coursework, Portland State University

Affiliations/Associations/Societies: Washington Teachers Association; National Education Association; Association for Supervision and Curriculum Development

Awards/Honors: Nominee, Who's Who of America's Teachers (2002, 2005)

Date of Birth: June 4, 1945   **Place of Birth:** Spring Grove

Spouse: Alexander (Deceased)   **Children:** Andrei, Peter

Work History: Teacher, Turkey Hill Elementary, Orange, CT (1967-1969)

Career Achievements: Nominee, Who's Who of America's Teachers (2002, 2005); Nominee, Who's Who of American Women (2007)

What do you attribute your success to? She attributes her success to her hard work, creative thinking and love for her profession.

How did you become involved in your profession? She became involved in her profession because she had always wanted to be a teacher.

What was the highlight of your career? The most gratifying aspect of her career is seeing her students succeed.

PROFESSIONAL OF THE YEAR IN
INTERNAL MEDICINE AND RHEUMATOLOGY

DR. MOHAMMAD E. OREIZI-ESFAHANI

Faculty, Rheumatologist
Medicine
Good Samaritan Hospital
5601 Loch Raven Boulevard
Smyth Building, Suite 200
Baltimore, MD 21239 United States
moreiz1e41@aol.com
http://www.goodsam.org

Type of Business: Hospital

Major Products and Services: Medical Care in Over 30 Specialties Covering Education, Prevention, Treatment of Illness, Injury and Other Sickness

Marketing Area: Regional

Day to Day Responsibilities: Teaching Residents, Practicing Internal Medicine and Rheumatology

Favorite Business Publications: The New England Journal of Medicine; Annals of Internal Medicine; Arthritis and Rheumatism

Hobbies/Interests/Sports: Gardening, Hiking, Listening to Classical Music, Reading, Bike Riding

Education Degrees: Post-Doctoral Fellow, Division of Rheumatology and Clinical Immunology, School of Medicine, University of Maryland (1996); Chief Residency in Medicine, Maryland General Hospital, Baltimore (1994); Residency in Medicine, Maryland General Hospital, Baltimore (1993); Chief Residency in Medicine, American University of Beirut, Lebanon (1992); Residency in Medicine, American University of Beirut, Lebanon (1991); Internship in Medicine, American University of Beirut, Lebanon; Doctor of Medicine, St. Joseph University School of Medicine, Lebanon (1989); Coursework, Notre Dame College of Jamhour, Lebanon (1982); Coursework in Internal Medicine, American University of Beirut, Lebanon

Certifications: Licensed Federal Examiner; Recertification in Internal Medicine and Rheumatology

Affiliations/Associations/Societies: Fellow, American College of Rheumatology; American College of Physicians; American Board of Rheumatology; American Board of Internal Medicine; Educational Committee Member, Foreign Medical Graduates

Awards/Honors: Golden Apple Award, Department of Medicine, Maryland General Hospital (2005); Physician of the Year Award, Maryland General Hospital, Baltimore (2005); Golden Apple Award, Department of Medicine, Maryland General Hospital (2003); Physician of the Year Award, Maryland General Hospital, Baltimore (2002); Customer Service Award, Maryland General Hospital, Baltimore; Finalist, Health Care Hero, City of Baltimore, Maryland; Mayor's Citation, City of Baltimore, Maryland

Charity/Volunteer Work: Local Charitable Organizations

PROFESSIONAL OF THE YEAR IN
HEALTHCARE CONSULTING

MR. RONALD A. ORTH

President, Founder
Clinical Reimbursement Solutions, LLC
215 W. Maple Street
Apartment 107
Milwaukee, WI 53204 United States
ron.orth@clinicalreimbursement.com
http://www.clinicalreimbursement.com

Type of Business: Consulting Firm

Major Products and Services: Healthcare Consulting and Educational Services for Long-Term Care Medicare Regulations, Billing and Compliance, Clinical Reimbursement Systems and Solutions

Marketing Area: National

Day to Day Responsibilities: Consulting for Medicare Regulations and Compliance, Managing Billing and Long-Term Care Facilities

Favorite Business Publications: PPS Alert for Long-Term Care; MDS Alert; ECPN; Milwaukee Journal Sentinel

Hobbies/Interests/Sports: Traveling, Reading, Appreciating Unique Artwork, Caring for his Pets

Education Degrees: Bachelor's Degree in Healthcare Administration, Concordia University Wisconsin (1996); Associate Degree in Nursing (1995)

Certifications: Licensed Nursing Home Administrator, State of Arizona

Affiliations/Associations/Societies: Advisory Board Member, PPS Alert for Long-Term Care; Advisory Board Member, MDS Alert; Association of Registered Health Care Professionals; Leading Instructor, Medicare Boot Camp, HCPro; American Association of Nurse Assessment Coordinators; American Academy of Professional Coders

Charity/Volunteer Work: The Humane Society of the United States; World Wildlife Fund; American Forest Preserve

Place of Birth: Racine

What do you attribute your success to? He attributes his success to his dedication, and interest in the rules and regulations that govern the long-term industry.

How did you become involved in your profession? He became involved in his profession after his family encouraged him to attend nursing school and he developed an interest in the rules and regulations that governed his field.

Where will you be in five years? In five years, Mr. Orth would like to expand his business to offer a greater array of services, making it a 'one-stop shop.'

PROFESSIONAL OF THE YEAR IN CARDIAC SURGERY

DR. JAMES H. OURY

Cardiovascular Surgeon
James H. Oury Medical Corporation
2805 Fifth Street, Suite 100
Rapid City, SD 57701 United States
jourymd@rushmore.com
http://www.cambridgewhoswho.com

Type of Business: Healthcare Center

Major Products and Services: Healthcare Including Cardiac Surgery

Marketing Area: Regional

Day to Day Responsibilities: Performing the Ross Procedure, General and Cardiothoracic Surgery Including Valve Repair and Natural Tissue Valves, Lecturing on Cardiac Surgery

Favorite Business Publications: The Journal of Thoracic and Cardiovascular Surgery

Hobbies/Interests/Sports: Triathlons, Running Marathons, Participating in Long-Distance Horse Races

Education Degrees: MD; Bachelor of Science

Affiliations/Associations/Societies: European Association for Cardio-Thoracic Surgery; Community Medical Center, Missoula, MT; Rush Medical College, Chicago, IL; San Francisco General Hospital; Fellow, American College of Surgeons; American Association for Thoracic Surgery; U.S. Naval Hospital

Expanded Biography: Dr. Oury has lectured at an international-level conference on cardiac surgery. He also lectured at the Society for Cardiovascular Anesthesiologists on surgical considerations in aortic valve disease during their 'Fourth Annual Comprehensive Review and TEE Update' on clinical decision-making in the cardiac surgery patient in 2001. He has served as an expert medical witness and has authored several articles regarding the Ross procedure.

PROFESSIONAL OF THE YEAR IN ONCOLOGY

PAOLO A. PACIUCCI, MD

Physician
The Mount Sinai Hospital
114 E. 72nd Street
New York, NY 10021 United States
paciucci@neoplastic-diseases.com
http://www.mountsinai.org

Type of Business: One of the Country's Oldest and Largest Voluntary Teaching Hospitals

Major Products and Services: Minimally Invasive Surgery, Adolescent Health, Neurology, Alzheimer's Disease, Treatment Neurosurgery, Anesthesiology, Obstetrics and Gynecology, Brain Surgery, Occupational Health, Breast Health, Oncology, Ophthalmology, Oral Surgery, Cardiothoracic Surgery, Organ Transplants, Cardiovascular Diseases, Orthopaedics and Child Psychiatry

Marketing Area: Regional

Day to Day Responsibilities: Diagnosing and Treating Cancer, Specializing in the Clinical and Preclinical Development of New Drugs and Treatments for Patients with Cancer

Hobbies/Interests/Sports: Soccer

Education Degrees: MD, University La Sapienza, Rome, Italy, Summa Cum Laude

Affiliations/Associations/Societies: New York Academy of Sciences; American Association for Society of Clinical Oncology; American Cancer Research

Expanded Biography: Dr. Paciucci has been published in the 'Journal of Clinical Oncology' and in 'Annals of Internal Medicine.' An associate professor in practice, he also does public speaking locally and at national conferences.

EXECUTIVE OF THE YEAR IN GLOBAL EDUCATION

MR. FRANK S. PALATNICK

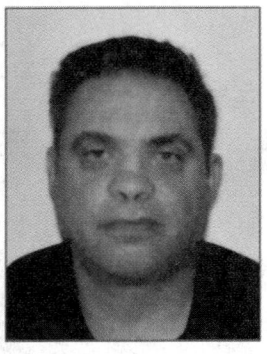

Educational Advisor
United Nations
23338 38th Drive
Little Neck
Douglaston, NY 11363 United States
fpalatnick@nyc.rr.com
http://www.cambridgewhoswho.com

Type of Business: International Association of Governments

Major Products and Services: International Law, Security, Economic Development, Social Progress and Human Rights, Achieving World Peace

Marketing Area: International

Day to Day Responsibilities: Facilitating Educational Administration Standards, Overseeing Educational Testing Services

Favorite Business Publications: Educational Leadership

Hobbies/Interests/Sports: Reading, Attending Seminars

Education Degrees: Bachelor's Degree in Education, Ashworth University

Affiliations/Associations/Societies: Nassau County Bar Association; Suffolk County Bar Association; American Bar Association; Alumnus, National Society for Experiential Education; Center for Education Policy; Research and Development Corporation; Council for Adult and Experiential Learning; Association for Supervision and Curriculum Development; National Civil Rights Organization, Montgomery, AL; National Career Development Association; Department of Homeland Security, United Nations; Vice President, World Congress of Arts, Sciences and Communication

Awards/Honors: Nominee, Nobel Peace Prize (2008); American Medal of Honor; International Medal of Honor; Lifetime Achievement Award; Great Minds of the 21st Century Award; International Order of Merit; Life Fellowship, International Biographical Association; Award, Cambridge University; Proclamation, The White House; Letter of Acknowledgment for Expertise in Career Development, Cornell University; Listed on Wall of Tolerance

What do you attribute your success to? He attributes his success to the support he receives from his mother.

How did you become involved in your profession? He became involved in his profession because of his interest in the field of education and desire to improve it.

What was the highlight of your career? The highlight of his career was having dinner with the Premier of China.

Expanded Biography: Mr. Palatnick delivered a keynote speech at Oxford University in April 2008.

EXECUTIVE OF THE YEAR IN
CONSULTING IN THE QUALITY ASSURANCE INDUSTRY

MS. DOROTHY J. PAPIN, CEO

President, Chief Executive Officer
Gryphon's Lair Productions
701 W. Graham Avenue, Suite C
Lake Elsinore, CA 92530 United States
dpapin9421@aol.com
http://www.glair.biz

Type of Business: Consultation and Self-Help Program

Major Products and Services: Technical Writing, Consultations, Quality Assurance, Nonprofit Services

Marketing Area: International

Area of Expertise: Mrs. Papin's expertise includes quality assurance, safety coordination and executive duties.

Day to Day Responsibilities: Managing Stress, Coordinating Company Safety with Occupational Safety & Health Administration Requirements, Overseeing Technical and Grant Writing

Favorite Business Publications: Reiki Magazine

Hobbies/Interests/Sports: Writing Fantasy Adventure Novels

Education Degrees: Ph.D. in Ancient Religion, Universal Life Church

Certifications: Certification, Occupational Safety & Health Administration

Affiliations/Associations/Societies: Executive Board Member, Cops for Kids; Elsinore Valley Arts Network; Rotary International; American Society for Quality

Date of Birth: December 3, 1946

Spouse: William

What do you attribute your success to? She attributes her success to her perseverance, self-confidence and focus on her goals.

What was the highlight of your career? The highlight of her career was establishing her own business, which showed her that she can achieve anything that she sets her mind to.

Expanded Biography: Mrs. Papin has extensive experience in the manufacturing industry among large and small corporations.

PROFESSIONAL OF THE YEAR IN MEDICAL TECHNOLOGY

VIRGINIA PARSEGHIAN

Medical Technologist
USB Cancer Center, Nyack Hospital
111 N. Highland Avenue
Nyack, NY 10960 United States
thecoronakid@verizon.net
http://www.rocklandhemonc.com

Type of Business: Hospital

Major Products and Services: Healthcare Including Research, Diagnosis and Treatment of Diseases of the Blood, Evaluation and Treatment of Anemia, Thrombocytopenia, Enlarged Lymph Nodes or Spleen, Bleeding and Clotting Disorders and other Abnormalities of the Blood, Cancer Treatment, Chemotherapy, Immunotherapy

Marketing Area: Regional

Day to Day Responsibilities: Supervising the Laboratory, Patient Care and the Staff

Favorite Business Publications: ONS; Men's Health Magazine; AMT Journal

Hobbies/Interests/Sports: Reading, Caring for her Pets

Education Degrees: Bachelor of Science in Bioscience, Empire State College (1981)

Certifications: Licensed in Medical Technology, New York State

Affiliations/Associations/Societies: American Association of Bioanalysts; American Society for Clinical Laboratory Science

Charity/Volunteer Work: Dogswalk Against Cancer

PROFESSIONAL OF THE YEAR IN
CARDIAC SURGERY INTENSIVE CARE

Evelyn R. Paul, BSN, CCRN

Staff Nurse IV
Cardiac Surgery Intensive Care Unit
Pitt County Memorial Hospital
2100 Stantonsburg Road
Greenville, NC 27834 United States
epaul57778@aol.com
epaul@pcmh.com
http://www.uhseast.com

Type of Business: Hospital

Major Products and Services: Healthcare

Marketing Area: Regional

Day to Day Responsibilities: Charge Nursing for an Eight-Bed Cardiac Surgery Intensive Care Unit, Managing Patient Flow, Transferring Patients from the Operating Room to the Intermediate Care Unit, Staffing, Reviewing Patient Care Assignments Based on Patient Acuity and the Staff's Level of Competence or Experience, Intensive Care Nursing for Cardiac Surgery Patients, Overseeing the Open-Heart Surgery Recovery Unit

Favorite Business Publications: Nursing2009; American Journal of Nursing

Hobbies/Interests/Sports: Photography, Reading, Attending Church

Education Degrees: Bachelor's Degree in Nursing, The University of North Carolina at Chapel Hill

Certifications: Critical Care Registered Nurse; Certification in Basic Life Support; Certification in Advanced Cardiac Life Support

Affiliations/Associations/Societies: East Carolina Chapter, American Association of Critical-Care Nurses (1983-2008); Board of Directors, School of Nursing Alumni Association, The University of North Carolina at Chapel Hill (2003-2007); Chairwoman, Alumni Awards Committee (2005-2006); Council on Cardiovascular Nursing; Board Member, School of Nursing, The University of North Carolina at Chapel Hill

Awards/Honors: Divisional Nurse of the Year Award, Cardiovascular Division, Pitt County Memorial Hospital (1996)

Charity/Volunteer Work: Civil War Preservation Trust; American Cancer Society; American Heart Association; National Trust for Historic Preservation

Date of Birth: May 10, 1953   **Place of Birth:** New Bern

Work History: Staff Nurse, Surgical Intensive Care Unit, Medical University of South Carolina, Charleston, SC (1979-1985); Charge Nurse, Surgical Intensive Care Unit, Medical University of South Carolina, Charleston, SC (1979-1985); Chief Nurse, Surgical Intensive Care Unit, Medical University of South Carolina, Charleston, SC (1979-1985); Staff Nurse, Intensive Care Unit, Beaufort County Hospital, Washington, NC (1975-1979); Charge Nurse, Intensive Care Unit, Beaufort County Hospital, Washington, NC (1975-1979)

What do you attribute your success to? She attributes her success to her dedication, concern for her patients and ability to work with a team.

How did you become involved in your profession? She became involved in her profession after her father's interest in healthcare inspired her to volunteer with local rescue squads.

What was the highlight of your career? The highlight of her career was serving on the board of directors of the School of Nursing Alumni Association at The University of North Carolina at Chapel Hill.

Expanded Biography: Ms. Paul is a deacon and Sunday school teacher at Silver Hill Christian Church. She also works in the East Carolina Heart Institute. Ms. Paul was recognized in the Greenville, NC newspaper, 'The Daily Reflector,' as part of its salute to nurses during 'Nurse's Week' in 2008.

PROFESSIONAL OF THE YEAR IN MIDDLE SCHOOL COUNSELING

MR. VICTOR G. PEARSON

Middle School Counselor
Robin Mickle Middle School
Lincoln Public Schools
5901 O Street
Lincoln, NE 68510 United States
vgpearson@hotmail.com
http://www.cambridgewhoswho.com

Type of Business: School District

Major Products and Services: Education

Marketing Area: Local

Day to Day Responsibilities: Assisting Students in their Transition from Fifth to Sixth-Grade and Eighth to Ninth-Grade, Consulting, Managing Professional Educational Services, Performing Vocal and Instrumental Music, Working with Structured Groups, Utilizing a Combination of Music Therapy Including Art and Counseling Techniques to Enhance Students' Personal, Social and Emotional Development

Favorite Business Publications: National Counseling Journal

Hobbies/Interests/Sports: Singing, Traveling, Gardening, Spending Time with his Grandchildren, Performing in Musicals

Education Degrees: Master's Degree in Guidance and Counseling, Northwest Missouri State University (1986); Bachelor's Degree in Music Education, James Madison University (1969)

Affiliations/Associations/Societies: Nebraska State Education Association; National Education Association; The American Counseling Association; Life Member, Phi Mu Alpha

Charity/Volunteer Work: Calvary Community Church, Lincoln, NE

What was the highlight of your career? The highlight of his career was implementing an anti-bullying program called 'Mickel Allies Advocates' for Robin Mickel Middle School.

Expanded Biography: Mr. Pearson served as a vocal and band adjudicator for the state of Iowa for 20 years, and retired from the Iowa School System at the age of 55.

PROFESSIONAL OF THE YEAR IN
PREACHING AND COUNSELING GOD'S WORD

DINO J. PEDRO, D.MIN.

Senior Pastor, President
New Testament Baptist Church
13900 Griffin Road
Southwest Ranches, FL 33330 United States
dpedrone@newtestbaptist.org
http://www.thegatheringplacefl.org

Type of Business: Church and Christian School

Major Products and Services: Adult Bible Study Classes, S.O.S. Six, AWANA Kids Club, College and Career Visions Classes, Children's Sunday Bible Study, Worship Ministry, Youth Ministry, Evangelism, Women's Ministry, Men's Ministry

Marketing Area: Regional

Day to Day Responsibilities: Overseeing Ministry Services in Two Counties, Training 2,600 Church Members, 1,700 Christian School Students and 300 Employees, Sharing, Preaching, Counseling, Enhancing the Growth of Membership

Education Degrees: Doctor of Ministry, Luther Rice College & Seminary, Lithonia, GA (1992)

Affiliations/Associations/Societies: President, Florida Association of Christian Colleges & Schools; Southwide Baptist Fellowship

Expanded Biography: Dr. Pedro has been featured in many books, journals and articles.

ENTREPRENEUR OF THE YEAR IN
MEDICAL REFERENCE PUBLISHING

DESI J. PENINGTON, MD

President
MedInfo, Inc. dba MD Pocket
10650 Irma Drive, Suite 17C
Denver, CO 80233 United States
penington@mdpocket.com
http://www.mdpocket.com

Type of Business: Publishing Company

Major Products and Services: Medical Reference Guides and Medical Information Materials for Students and Residents

Marketing Area: National

Area of Expertise: Dr. Penington's expertise is in internal medicine.

Favorite Business Publications: New England Journal of Medicine

Hobbies/Interests/Sports: Skiing, Biking, Hiking

Education Degrees: MD, University of Colorado; Master of Science, Purdue University; Bachelor of Arts, Metropolitan State College of Denver; Bachelor of Science, Metropolitan State College of Denver

Affiliations/Associations/Societies: American College of Physicians; American Medical Association

Charity/Volunteer Work: Local Clinics

What do you attribute your success to? She attributes her success to her perseverance and her marketing skills.

How did you become involved in your profession? She became involved in her profession because of her educational background and her interest in the medical field.

What was the highlight of your career? The most gratifying aspect of her career is watching the growth of her business.

PROFESSIONAL OF THE YEAR IN HEALTH SERVICES ADMINISTRATION

Ms. Maryanne E. Percuoco, RNC, BA

Health Services Administrator
UMass Correctional Health Program
University of Massachusetts Medical School
30 Administration Road
Bridgewater, MA 02324 United States
mpercuoco@doc.state.ma.us
maryanneper@msn.com
http://www.umasscorrectionalhealth.org

Type of Business: Medium Treatment Facility for Sex Offenders

Major Products and Services: Mental Healthcare, Medical Correctional Healthcare, Healthcare for Incarcerated Males

Marketing Area: Regional

Day to Day Responsibilities: Managing Operations at the Massachusetts Treatment Center, Overseeing Physicians, Psychologists and Staff

Favorite Business Publications: The Wall Street Journal; Forbes; RN

Hobbies/Interests/Sports: Reading, Knitting, Traveling, Skiing, Spending Time with her Family and Friends

Education Degrees: Bachelor of Science in Human Services, Stonehill College

Certifications: Registered Nurse, Cambridge, MA; Certified Psychiatric Nurse; Certified Correctional Health Professional

Affiliations/Associations/Societies: Former Member, South Shore Visiting Nurse Association; National Commission on Correctional Health Care, American Correctional Association; American Psychiatric Nurses Association

Awards/Honors: Certificate of Recognition, Department of Corrections

Charity/Volunteer Work: MSPCA Animal Shelters

Place of Birth: Boston   **Children:** Marc

How did you become involved in your profession? She became involved in her profession because she always wanted to become a nurse.

ENTREPRENEUR OF THE YEAR IN COSMETOLOGY

LOUISE PERRY

Owner
Holliswood Beauty Center
14434 184th Street
Rosedale, NY 11413 United States
louise.perry@cwwemail.com
http://www.cambridgewhoswho.com

Type of Business: Salon

Major Products and Services: Cosmetology and Other Industry-Related Services

Marketing Area: Local

Day to Day Responsibilities: Overseeing Operations, Applying Makeup, Performing Manicures, Pedicures and Facials, Styling Hair

Hobbies/Interests/Sports: Bowling, Making Hats, Cooking, Spending Time with her Children, Grandchildren and Great Grandchildren

Education Degrees: Diploma, DeFran's Beauty School, Jamaica, NY; Diploma, Bettis Junior College High School; Coursework, Edgefield Academy

Certifications: Certification in Cosmetology, State of New York

Affiliations/Associations/Societies: New York State Beauty Association; Examiner, New York State Certifying Board for Cosmetology; Officer, Jamaica Unit 105; Officer, New York State Beauty Culturist Association

Charity/Volunteer Work: Choir, Morning Star Missionary Baptist Church, Jamaica, NY; President, Get Together Group, Morning Star Missionary Baptist Church, Jamaica, NY

Place of Birth: Edgefield   **Children:** Louis, Vivian

Expanded Biography: Ms. Perry opened Holliswood Beauty Center in Jamaica, NY in 1979.

PROFESSIONAL OF THE YEAR IN BLOOD BANK MANAGEMENT

LJILJANA PETKOVIC

Certified Blood Bank Manager, Reimbursement Specialist
Northwest Community Hospital
800 W. Central Road
Arlington Heights, IL 60005 United States
lpetkovic@nch.org
http://www.nch.org

Type of Business: Hospital

Major Products and Services: Healthcare

Marketing Area: Regional

Day to Day Responsibilities: Managing All Three Laboratory Areas, Serving as the Laboratory Reimbursement Specialist Liaison for the Hospital, Handling Compliance Issues Regarding Laboratory Testing, Working in the Blood Bank, Immunology and Laboratory Send-Out Departments

Favorite Business Publications: The New York Times; Archives of Pathology & Laboratory Medicine

Hobbies/Interests/Sports: Gardening, Traveling, Bicycling, Reading

Education Degrees: Leadership Academy (2007-2008); Bachelor's Degree in Medical Technology, Northwestern University, Feinberg School of Medicine (1977)

Certifications: Assessor, American Association of Blood Banks (1984); Medical Technologist, American Society for Clinical Pathology; Technologist in Blood Banking, American Society for Clinical Pathology; Specialist in Blood Banking Technology, American Society for Clinical Pathology; Certification in Project Management

Affiliations/Associations/Societies: American Society for Clinical Pathology; Illinois Association of Blood Banks; American Association of Blood Banks; Blood Drive Coordinator, Northwest Community Hospital

What do you attribute your success to? She attributes her success to having great mentors at Northwest University and Northwest Community Hospital.

How did you become involved in your profession? She became involved in her profession because she was interested in pathology and guidance counseling.

What was the highlight of your career? The most gratifying aspect of her career is playing dual roles that enable her to be a well-rounded individual, and give her a better understanding of the goals of the hospital and her department.

Expanded Biography: Ms. Petkovic gets great fulfillment from having multiple responsibilities within a quality healthcare environment.

PROFESSIONAL OF THE YEAR IN EDUCATION CONSULTING

C. SUE PHELPS, PH.D.

President, Owner
Phelps and Associates
2706 Clearview Drive S.W.
Rocky Face, GA 30740 United States
phas@alltel.net
http://www.cambridgewhoswho.com

Type of Business: Educational Consultancy

Major Products and Services: Education, Curriculum and Instruction Design, Industry Task Analysis, Staff Training

Marketing Area: National

Day to Day Responsibilities: Developing Curriculum, Teaching Mathematics, Instruction Design and General Education

Favorite Business Publications: ASCD Journal

Hobbies/Interests/Sports: Reading, Attending Art Shows

Education Degrees: Ph.D. in Mathematics and Education, Georgia State University; Master's Degree in Mathematics, Ohio State University; Bachelor's Degree in Mathematics, University of Kentucky

Affiliations/Associations/Societies: Chamber of Commerce; National Council for Accreditation of Teacher Education; National Education Association; Association for Supervision and Curriculum Development

What do you attribute your success to? She attributes her success to her basic value system and her desire to make a difference.

How did you become involved in your profession? She became involved in her profession after starting her career as a teacher in a one-room school, gradually progressing to the high school level and deciding to establish her own business.

Expanded Biography: Dr. Phelps published an article in a medical journal.

PROFESSIONAL OF THE YEAR IN PERSONAL TAXES

CARL MAXEY PHILLIPS

Owner, Founder
Carl Maxey Phillips, EA
P.O. Box 2689
Cookeville, TN 38502 United States
frznrth@juno.com
http://www.frznrth.com

Type of Business: Tax Consulting Firm

Major Products and Services: Tax Consulting, Tax Planning, Tax Preparation, Tax Representation

Marketing Area: Regional

Area of Expertise: Mr. Phillips' expertise includes personal tax consulting, tax planning, tax preparation and tax representation.

Favorite Business Publications: The Wall Street Journal

Hobbies/Interests/Sports: Watching Movies, Reading Science Fiction

Education Degrees: Associate of Applied Science in Management and Supervision, Bevill State Community College (1978); Master of Arts in Journalism, University of Alabama (1975); Master of Science in Instructional Media, Jacksonville State University (1975); Bachelor of Arts in German, Jacksonville State University

Certifications: Accredited Investment Fiduciary Advisor; Accredited Tax Advisor; Accredited Tax Preparer

Affiliations/Associations/Societies: Chapter President, American MENSA, Montgomery, AL (1982-1985); Chapter President, Alabama State Employees Association, Montgomery, AL (1983-1985); Presidents Council, Montgomery, AL (1983-1985); American Flag Dedication, Republican Presidential Task Force (1982); Founders Club, National Republican Senatorial Committee (1989); Sunday School Secretary, Dexter Avenue United Methodist Church, Montgomery, AL (1982-1985); President, Men's Club, Dexter Avenue United Methodist Church, Montgomery, AL (1983-1985); Life Member, American Legion; Life Member, American MENSA; American Numismatic Association; Benefactor, Life Member, National Rifle Association; Life Member, Tennessee Numismatic Society; American Society of Tax Problem Solvers; Associate Member, Association of Certified Fraud Examiners; Affiliate Member, Association of Fundraising Professionals; Cookeville Area-Putnam County Chamber of Commerce; Financial Planning Association; Institute of Certified Professional Compilers of Canada; Associate Member, National Association of Certified Valuation Analysts; National Association of Enrolled Agents; National Association of Tax Professionals; National Federation of Independent Business; National Society of Accountants; National Society of Tax Professionals; National Tax Association; Associate Member, Society for Human Resource Management; Turnaround Management Association

Awards/Honors: Outstanding Membership Growth Award, Montgomery-Wiregrass MENSA Chapter, American MENSA (1986); Golden Apple Award, Dexter Avenue United Methodist Church (1985); Academic Excellence Award, UAB Junior College Academic Bowl (1978); Dean's List (1977-1978); Fort Campbell Zebra Wives' Club Scholarship (1969); Jacksonville State University Letter of Appreciation (1974); Jacksonville State University Student Government Association Outstanding Service Award (1974-1976); Sons of the American Revolution Medal (1972); WLJS-FM Certificate of Appreciation (1975); Golden Key Society; Alexis de Tocqueville Society of Northwest Georgia; Certificate of Appreciation, Revenue Chapter, Alabama State Employees Association (1985); Presidential Order of Merit, National Republican Senatorial Committee (1991); Certificate of Appreciation, Alabama Republican Party (1987); Certificate of Appreciation, Bush-Quayle Reelection Committee (1992); Certificate of Appreciation, National Republican Congressional Committee (1990); Certificate of Recognition, National Republican Congressional Committee (1982-1984); Certificate of Recognition, National Republican Committee (1990-1992); Century Society, St. Labre Indian School Educational Association (1998); Certificate of Recognition, American MENSA (1989, 2004); Certificate of Recognition, National Association of Tax Professionals (2002); Certificate of Salutation, Saint Joseph's Indian School (1990); Eminent Fellow of the American Biographical Institute (2001); Nominee, Bishop N. Barron State Employee of the Year (1984); Honorary Diploma, St. Labre Indian School (2002); James and Sis Brown Fellow (1999); Century Society, St. Labre Indian School Educational Association (1998); Letter of Appreciation, State of Alabama Emergency Management Agency (1985); World Science Fiction Convention, Voter-Hugo Awards (1979-1991)

Work History: Research Department Head, H & R Block, Pelham, AL (1993); Out of State Specialist, H & R Block, Pelham, AL (1993); Income Tax Consultant, H & R Block, Montevallo, AL (1989-1992); Revenue Examiner, Special Audit/Federal Audit Section, Income Tax Division, Alabama Department of Revenue, Montgomery, AL (1982-1988); Statistician, Research Section, Research and Statistics Division, Alabama Department of Industrial Relations, Montgomery, AL (1981-1982); Statistician, Reports Section, Research and Statistics Division, Alabama Department of Industrial Relations, Montgomery, AL (1979-1981); Career-Related Instructor, 'Forgiveness of Debt and Net Operating Loss,' Level II, H & R Block, Pelham, AL (1991)

PROFESSIONAL OF THE YEAR IN PSYCHOTHERAPY

MR. DUANE H. PIEL

Licensed Clinical Social Worker
Duane H. Piel, LCSW
1377 Sanden Ferry Drive
Decatur, GA 30033 United States
dhpiel@bellsouth.net
http://www.cambridgewhoswho.com

Type of Business: Proven Leader in the Healthcare Industry, Mental Health, Private Practice

Major Products and Services: Psychotherapy for Clients, Individuals, Couples, Families and Groups, Specializing in Grief and Death, Offering Motivation Consultation, Nutritional Consultation, Psychotherapy Instructor at Gupton-Jones College of Funeral Services

Marketing Area: Local

Day to Day Responsibilities: Offering Grief, Death and Dying Therapy

Favorite Business Publications: NASW Journal; Mortician Journal

Hobbies/Interests/Sports: Reading, Traveling, Enjoying his Pet Rabbit Bugs and his 1950 Black Buick, Cooking and Baking

Education Degrees: Associate of Science in Funeral Service, Gupton-Jones (2004); Master's Degree in Social Work, University of Georgia School of Social Work (1988); Bachelor of Arts in Psychology, Emory University (1985)

Affiliations/Associations/Societies: National Association of Social Workers

PROFESSIONAL OF THE YEAR IN
LIBRARY SCIENCE

SHERRILL M. PINCKNEY, MLIS

Interim Head Librarian
University of South Carolina, Salkehatchie Campus
767 James Brandt Boulevard
Allendale, SC 29810 United States
pinckney@gwm.sc.edu
http://uscsalkehatchie.sc.edu

Type of Business: Small Rural University, Part of the University of South Carolina

Major Products and Services: Social Sciences, Arts and Languages, Mathematics and Science, Professional Studies

Marketing Area: Local

Day to Day Responsibilities: Ordering New Books, Cataloging, Technical Processing, Offering Services for Books Sent from the Cataloging Department, Managing Inter-Library Loans, Circulation, Training and Bibliographic Instruction

Hobbies/Interests/Sports: Studying Genealogy, Watching Movies, Going to the Theater, Participating in Church Activities, Maintaining the Church Library, Reading Romance Novels

Education Degrees: Master's Degree in Library Science, University of South Carolina (1990); Bachelor of Science in History, Minor in Library Science, Georgia Southern University (1971)

Affiliations/Associations/Societies: South Carolina Library Association

PROFESSIONAL OF THE YEAR IN
HIGHER EDUCATION FINANCIAL AID

HELENE ELIZABETH PLANK

Assistant Director of Financial Aid
Mercer County Community College
Financial Aid Office
1200 Old Trenton Road
West Windsor, NJ 08550 United States
plankh@mccc.edu
http://www.mccc.edu

Type of Business: Community College

Major Products and Services: Associate Degree Programs, Credit and Noncredit Certificate Programs, Continuing Education, Customized Training for Businesses, Career Training, Youth Programs and Summer Camps for Children, Financial Aid Programs

Marketing Area: Regional

Day to Day Responsibilities: Managing All Financial Aid-Related Issues, Liaising between the College and the State of New Jersey, Overseeing All Grants and Scholarships, Answering Student Questions on the Grants Process, Evaluating at-Risk Students Academically for Financial Aid and Appeals

Favorite Business Publications: Money

Hobbies/Interests/Sports: Crafting

Education Degrees: Master's Degree, Rider University, NJ (1992); Bachelor's Degree, Trenton State College, NJ, Summa Cum Laude (1979); Associate Degree, Mercer County Community College, NJ, Summa Cum Laude (1977)

Affiliations/Associations/Societies: Phi Kappa Phi; Advisorship, Phi Theta Kappa Honor Society

Awards/Honors: Advisor of the Year (2005)

Spouse: William

Expanded Biography: Ms. Plank's academic history has long been one of an honor student. While attending college at Mercer County Community College, the trend continued. At that time, there was no honor society at Mercer, yet she had graduated with a 4.0 cumulative average. As she continued her education at Trenton State College (now the College of New Jersey), she maintained that 4.0 average. Trenton State inducted her into the Phi Kappa Phi National Honor Society. She was very happy to again be honored for her academic achievements. Once she started her career and had the opportunity to work at Mercer, her alma mater, she discovered that Mercer had established a chapter of Phi Theta Kappa, the International Honor Society for Two-Year Colleges (PTK). She was excited to hear the news, but discovered the honor society would not offer membership to previous graduates. Although she was disappointed, she understood the task that would accompany such an offer. But she always wished for the chance to be part of PTK. In October 2002, she was asked to become an advisor for the PTK chapter, and she was ecstatic about the opportunity. When she spoke with her first-year slate of chapter officers, she explained to them her unfulfilled dream to be a PTK member. By the fall semester of 2003, the officers surprised her by inducting her into the chapter as an honorary member. That single event has been one of the highest points of her career at Mercer. She has been a PTK advisor for the past five years, and it has been one of the most rewarding experiences in her 22 years at Mercer. Since she has retired from her full-time position at the college, she continues to work there part-time in the alumni area. This academic year, she hopes to combine her love for both the honor society and alumni development by chartering a PTK chapter alumni society. This will be a milestone in her work at Mercer, but she plans to continue to expand alumni and PTK even further in the years to come. Retirement has become a new beginning for her at Mercer County Community College.

PROFESSIONAL OF THE YEAR IN
PROJECT MANAGEMENT

ANGELICA PODIAS

Project Manager, JCPenney Direct Inventory Teams
JCPenney
6501 Legacy Drive
Plano, TX 75024 United States
apodias@jcpenney.com
http://www.jcpenney.com

Type of Business: Distribution Firm

Major Products and Services: Apparel for Women, Men and Children, Shoes, Jewelry, Bed and Bath Products, Window Treatments, Home Furnishings, Housewares

Marketing Area: International

Day to Day Responsibilities: Planning, Allocating, Forecasting, Training on Testing, Implementing the Roll-Out of New Systems

Favorite Business Publications: BusinessWeek

Hobbies/Interests/Sports: Gardening, Watching Sports, Volunteering

Education Degrees: Bachelor's Degree in Business Economics and Social Sciences, Minor in Business, Fordham University (1978)

Affiliations/Associations/Societies: Project Management Institute; Philoptochos Women's Philanthropic Society

Awards/Honors: Award, Girl Scouts of the USA; Outstanding Leader Award; Outstanding Volunteer Award

Charity/Volunteer Work: Green Angel; Heart of Gold

PROFESSIONAL OF THE YEAR IN CARTOGRAPHY

THOMAS J. POLLOCK

Principal Planner and Cartographer
Middlesex County Planning Department
21 Kingsley Way
Freehold, NJ 07728 United States
tp.prs@comcast.net
http://www.cambridgewhoswho.com

Type of Business: Government Organization

Major Products and Services: Planning and Cartography Services

Marketing Area: Regional

Day to Day Responsibilities: Overseeing Administrative Duties, Planning, Addressing Computer Issues, Managing Data, Reviewing and Correcting Information from the Census to Create Maps, Preparing Presentations, Coordinating the Placement of Houses, Developing Reports on Various Maps, Industrial Areas, Roadways, Sewage Systems and Bus Routes

Favorite Business Publications: Digital Photography

Hobbies/Interests/Sports: Hiking, Camping, Caving, Traveling, Writing, Photography

Education Degrees: Bachelor's Degree, Rutgers, The State University of New Jersey (1973)

Affiliations/Associations/Societies: North American Nature Photography Association; Fellow, Lifetime Member, The National Speleological Society

Awards/Honors: PRS Consulting Firm Award

Expanded Biography: Mr. Pollock has served for three years in the United States military. His speech at the National Speleological Society Convention on Preservation was published in 'Caving' magazine.

PROFESSIONAL OF THE YEAR IN VETERINARY ORTHOPEDIC PATHOLOGY

DR. ROY R. POOL

Professor of Pathology
Department of Veterinary Pathobiology
College of Veterinary Medicine
Texas A&M University
College Station, TX 77843 United States
rpool@cvm.tamu.edu
http://www.cvm.tamu.edu

Type of Business: University

Major Products and Services: Veterinary Education, Medical Research

Marketing Area: International

Area of Expertise: Dr. Pool's expertise includes veterinary orthopedic pathology, spontaneous diseases of bones, joints, tendons and ligaments of dogs and athletic horses as well as healing of these structures facilitated by embryonic stem cells, and dissecting and examining the joints of race horses to study the pathogenesis of repetitive microtrauma in the development of common joint lesions and osteochondrosis.

Favorite Business Publications: Journal of the American Veterinary Medical Association; Compendium for the Veterinarian; Journal of Equine Veterinary Science

Hobbies/Interests/Sports: Golfing, Caring for Animals, Photography

Education Degrees: Ph.D. in Veterinary Pathology, University of California, Davis (1967); Doctor of Veterinary Medicine, Oklahoma State University (1964); Bachelor of Science, Duke University (1957)

Affiliations/Associations/Societies: Veterinary Cancer Society; Pathology of Tendon and Ligament Disease of Horses and Dogs; Pathogenesis of Equine Navicular Disease and Athletic Injuries; American Veterinary Medical Association; International Academy of Pathology

Awards/Honors: Pegasus Equine Research Award (1991); Norden Distinguishing Teaching Award; International Pegasus Equine Research Award, National Council on Radiation Protection and Measurements

Place of Birth: Raleigh

Spouse: Bettye   **Children:** Marlen, Kathryn

Work History: Professor of Pathology, Michigan State University, College Of Veterinary Medicine (2000-2002); Senior Lecturer and Hospital Pathologist, Cornell University (1999-2000); Orthopedic Path Consultant, IDEXX Laboratories (1995-1998); Emeritus Professor of Pathology, University of California, Davis (1969-1994); Clinical Professor of Pathology, Texas A&M University

Expanded Biography: Dr. Pool has directed a bone pathology research program on the effects of internal radioactive emitters on the bone and bone marrow of 1,500 beagle dogs. His research on spontaneous bone and joint tumors involving more than 5,000 dogs allowed him to develop a bone tumor classification system that formed the basis for the WHO classification of bone tumors. He has received several awards for his studies on the pathogenesis of bone and joint injuries in racehorses, and continues to contribute to the understanding of navicular disease and the pathogenesis of osteochondosis and sesmoid fractures of the horse. He has received and examined musculoskeletal specimens and histopathology slides and radiographs from animal patients mostly in the United States of America but also from European clients. He is a co-author of 'WHO Classification of Bone and Joint Tumors of Animals.' He is the chief of the surgical pathology service that primarily supports staff clinicians in Texas A&M University College of Veterinary Medicine and chief of service for the osteopathology specialty service of the department of veterinary pathobiology. He also lectures veterinary students, faculty, pathologists and practitioners in the USA, Australia, South America and Europe.

PROFESSIONAL OF THE YEAR IN NURSING

FRANCES M. POWELL, RN

Registered Nurse
Kaiser Permanente
9400 E. Rosecrans Avenue
Bellflower, CA 90706 United States
stampin.rn@verizon.net
http://www.kaiserpermanente.org

Type of Business: Healthcare

Major Products and Services: Quality Care for Members and Their Families

Marketing Area: Southern California

Area of Expertise: Ms. Powell's expertise includes obstetrics and gynecology, and patient safety.

Day to Day Responsibilities: Treating Patients with Dysplasia

Favorite Business Publications: Nurses World Magazine

Hobbies/Interests/Sports: Collecting Rubber Stamps, Reading

Education Degrees: Associate Degree in Nursing, Cerritos College

Affiliations/Associations/Societies: American Legion Auxiliary; Officer Bellflower Registered Nurses Association; Kaiser Permanente Workplace Safety Committee

What do you attribute your success to? She attributes her success to her hard work and determination.

How did you become involved in your profession? She became involved in her profession because of her life-long desire to be a nurse.

What was the highlight of your career? The highlight of her career was decreasing the number of work-related injuries at the company by 50 percent.

PROFESSIONAL OF THE YEAR IN LEGAL NURSE CONSULTING

MISSY JO PRIEST, RN, CEN, CCRN, CLNC

1) Registered Nurse 2) Forensic Specialist
1) Nursing Education Unlimited
2) East Texas Medical-Legal Nurse Consultants
1131 VZ County Road 2513
Canton, TX 75103 United States
missyjo.priest@cwwemail.com
missy2043@aol.com
http://www.cambridgewhoswho.com

Type of Business: 1) Educational Center 2) Consulting Firm

Major Products and Services: 1) Nursing Education 2) Consulting Services Including Assistance to Attorneys in Medical Legal Matters, Forensic Services

Marketing Area: 1) National 2) National

Area of Expertise: Ms. Priest's expertise includes critical care education and forensic consultation.

Day to Day Responsibilities: Evaluating Legal Work, Performing Forensic Tasks, Reading Medical Charts, Assisting Attorneys

Favorite Business Publications: American Journal of Nursing; Critical Care Nurse

Hobbies/Interests/Sports: Fishing, Horseback Riding, Caring for her Pets, Playing the Piano, Raising Horses, Cooking, Spending Time with her Family, Working on Computers, Volunteering, Writing

Education Degrees: Bachelor of Science in Forensic Science; Associate of Science in Nursing, Tyler Junior College

Certifications: Registered Nurse, Tyler Junior College; Certified Forensics Analyst

Affiliations/Associations/Societies: Texas Nurses Association

Charity/Volunteer Work: St. Jude Children's Research Hospital; Feed the Children; Katrina Relief; American Red Cross

Date of Birth: December 14, 1959   **Place of Birth:** Downey

Spouse: Dusty   **Children:** Diana, Anthony, Cody

What do you attribute your success to? She attributes her success to the support she receives from her family.

How did you become involved in your profession? She became involved in her profession because she was inspired by the nurses who cared for her when she suffered from rheumatic fever as a child. She later ventured into forensic science and became involved in the legal profession because she wanted to help people who are given low-quality medical care.

What was the highlight of your career? The most gratifying aspect of her career is developing her knowledge on bedside nursing techniques and critical care nursing.

Expanded Biography: Ms. Priest has taken her work on the national level, lecturing in several states. She has also embarked on speaking engagements in the United Kingdom.

PROFESSIONAL OF THE YEAR IN BARIATRIC SURGERY

LYUDMILA S. PUPKOVA

Doctor, Independent Contractor
Absolute Bariatric Surgery, LLC
8 Jennifer Drive
East Hanover, NJ 07936 United States
lpupkova@optonline.net
http://www.absolutebariatric.com

Type of Business: Medical Center

Major Products and Services: Comprehensive Program for Obese Patients

Marketing Area: Local

Area of Expertise: Dr. Pupkova's expertise includes general and bariatric surgery.

Hobbies/Interests/Sports: Reading, Traveling, Attending the Opera, Ballet and Broadway Shows

Education Degrees: Ph.D. in Urology and Biochemistry, Saint Petersburg Medical Academy of Postgraduate Studies, Saint Petersburg, Russia; MD, Pavlov State Medical University of Saint Petersburg, Russia; Fellowship in Laparoscopic Bariatric Surgery, SUNY Stony Brook

Affiliations/Associations/Societies: American College of Surgeons; American Society for Bariatric Surgery; International Federation for the Surgery of Obesity; Association of Women Surgeons; Medical Society of New Jersey; Fellow, American College of Surgeons

What do you attribute your success to? She attributes her success to her persistence and perseverance in pursuing a career with a steep learning curve.

How did you become involved in your profession? She became involved in her profession because she always wanted to be surgeon.

PROFESSIONAL OF THE YEAR IN EDUCATIONAL CONSULTING AND TUTORING

Mrs. Karen L. Rabe, M.Ed.

1) Educator 2) Educator
1) Highland Elementary School
2) Academic Associates Learning Center
11095 36th Street N.E.
Lake Stevens, WA 98258 United States
dkrabe@iglide.net
http://www.academic-associates.com

Type of Business: 1) Elementary School 2) Learning Center

Major Products and Services: 1) General Elementary Curriculum Including Arts, Music, Physical Education, Learning Resources, Student Support Services, Athletics and Extracurricular Activities 2) Tutoring Services in Reading and Mathematics

Marketing Area: 1) Local 2) International

Day to Day Responsibilities: Teaching, Offering Science Consulting Services, Tutoring Reading and Mathematics

Favorite Business Publications: Ranger Rick

Hobbies/Interests/Sports: Hiking, Traveling, Kayaking

Education Degrees: Master of Education in Remedial Reading, Pacific University; Master's Degree in Curriculum Development Using Technology, Lesley University

Affiliations/Associations/Societies: Who's Who Among America's Teachers (2005, 2006, 2007); Washington Education Association; National Education Association

Charity/Volunteer Work: Local Church, Everett Gospel Mission

Date of Birth: April 18, 1949 **Place of Birth:** Alberta

Spouse: Dennis **Children:** D.J., Heather, Russ, Desirae, Grant, Ryan

Work History: Elementary Education Teacher, Vancouver, WA; Preschool Owner and Home School Consultant, Lynnwood, WA; Elementary Education Teacher, Los Angeles, CA; Elementary Education Teacher, Lake Stevens, WA

What do you attribute your success to? She attributes her success in education to her dedication and hard work, and to the support she receives from her family and friends.

How did you become involved in your profession? She became involved in education because of her desire to help others improve their quality of life through learning skills.

What was the highlight of your career? The most gratifying aspect of her career is knowing that no matter how much knowledge she amasses, the most important thing to her students is that she truly cares for them and their futures.

Expanded Biography: Mrs. Rabe is a lifelong learner who strives to pass on her love of learning to her students. She studies with national experts in their fields, including archeologists, environmentalists, zoologists and marine biologists, and brings these exciting curricula to her classes. In addition to teaching elementary school, Ms. Rabe joined her husband in establishing a tutoring center in reading and mathematics, training under an English language expert who founded the Academic Associates Learning Centers. She and her husband also tutor students internationally. She also established a preschool and wrote a children's book.

PROFESSIONAL OF THE YEAR IN SPECIAL EDUCATION

CINDA L. RACHOW, MS

Learning Supports Coordinator
Loess Hills Area Education Agency 13
Council Bluffs, IA United States
crachow@aea13.org
http://www.aea13.org

Type of Business: Education Institution

Major Products and Services: Special Education Services for Students with Disabilities

Marketing Area: Regional

Day to Day Responsibilities: Overseeing the Strategic Planning Committee for the School District, Organizing Donations for Books to New Mothers, Overseeing Learning Support Systems and Social Emotional Learning, Coordinating Services for 31 School Districts

Favorite Business Publications: Educational Leadership

Hobbies/Interests/Sports: Gardening, Playing the Piano, Spending Time with her Family

Education Degrees: Master of Science in Special Education, Plus 30, University of Nebraska; Bachelor of Science in Behavioral Psychology, University of Nebraska

Certifications: Certified Teacher, Buena Vista University

Affiliations/Associations/Societies: Association for Supervision and Curriculum Development; Phi Delta Kappa

Charity/Volunteer Work: Local Charitable Organizations; Closing the Gap

Spouse: Roger

What do you attribute your success to? She attributes her success to her helping nature, passion for her profession and the support she receives from her husband.

How did you become involved in your profession? She became involved in her profession because she saw that children with emotional and learning disabilities need special training and supervision.

What was the highlight of your career? The highlight of her career was seeing the rollout of school-wide discipline and the positive effect it had on children in school.

EXECUTIVE OF THE YEAR IN INTERIOR DESIGN

ALBERTO RAMOS

Interior Designer, Project Manager, Chief Executive Officer
M.A. Esteves, Inc.
48th Street S.E.
La Riviera 1272
San Juan, PR 00921 United States
aramos@maesteves.com
http://www.maesteves.com

Type of Business: Manufacturing and Supply Company

Major Products and Services: Custom-Designed Office Furniture, Space Planning Services, Binders and Binding Supplies, Calendars, Planners, Briefcases, Accounting Supplies, Computer Hardware, Computer Supplies, Data Storage and Supplies, Files and Filing Supplies, Forms, Record Keeping and Reference Forms, Furniture and Accessories, Janitorial and Maintenance Supplies, Labels, Label Makers, Tags and Stamps, Mailroom and Packing Materials, General Office Supplies, Paper, Envelopes, Mailers, Pens and Pencils, Presentation and Meeting Supplies, Printer Supplies and Accessories

Marketing Area: International

Area of Expertise: Mr. Ramos' expertise includes interior design, space planning, project management and consulting.

Hobbies/Interests/Sports: Sports, Listening to Music, Spending Time with his Children, Reading

Education Degrees: Bachelor's Degree in Advertising and Public Relations, Universidad del Sagrado Corazón, Puerto Rico

Affiliations/Associations/Societies: American Society of Interior Designers; CODE; Manager, Women's National Selection Soccer Team; International Interior Design Association

What do you attribute your success to? He attributes his success to his passion for his profession, hard work and education.

What was the highlight of your career? The most gratifying aspect of his career is being able to share his knowledge and love with others.

PROFESSIONAL OF THE YEAR IN
HIGHER EDUCATION MATHEMATICS

AGNES M. RASH

Professor, Mathematics and Computer Science
Department of Mathematics and Computer Science
Saint Joseph's University
5600 City Avenue
Philadelphia, PA 19131 United States
arash@sju.edu
http://www.sju.edu/arash

Type of Business: University

Major Products and Services: Higher Education

Marketing Area: Regional

Day to Day Responsibilities: Teaching Mathematics and Computer Science, Developing Curriculum, Mentoring, Conducting Research

Favorite Business Publications: The American Mathematical Monthly; Mathematics Teacher; Journal for Research in Mathematics Education; Philadelphia Inquirer

Hobbies/Interests/Sports: Golfing, Fly-Fishing, Traveling

Education Degrees: Ph.D. in Mathematics Education, University of Pennsylvania (1974); Master of Science in Mathematics, University of Notre Dame (1966); Bachelor of Arts, Holy Family University (1963)

Certifications: Certified Teacher, States of Pennsylvania and New Jersey

Affiliations/Associations/Societies: National Council of Teachers of Mathematics; Mathematical Association of America; Pi Mu Epsilon; Sigma Xi; Phi Beta Kappa

Awards/Honors: Teaching Award; Research Award; Service Award

Date of Birth: February 11, 1942

Work History: Mathematics Instructor, California Polytechnic State University (1973-1974); Mathematics Instructor, Temple University (1966-1968)

Career Achievements: Several National Science Foundation Grants; Who's Who in American Education

What was the highlight of your career? The most gratifying aspects of her career are assisting students with their research projects and mentoring young women.

Expanded Biography: Dr. Rash has published four textbooks and more than 30 articles on mathematics education research and curriculum development. She has been elected as the chairwoman of the mathematics and computer science department six times. She has also led more than 100 presentations.

PROFESSIONAL OF THE YEAR IN PHYSICAL EDUCATION

ELIZABETH M. REDNER

Teacher of Physical Education, Teacher of the Handicapped
Ringwood Board of Education
121 Carletondale Road
Ringwood, NJ 07456 United States
rednerlish@yahoo.com
http://www.ringwoodschools.org

Type of Business: Board of Education

Major Products and Services: Education

Marketing Area: Regional

Area of Expertise: Ms. Redner's expertise is in physical education.

Day to Day Responsibilities: Teaching Handicapped Students

Favorite Business Publications: The Journal of Physical Education, Recreation & Dance

Hobbies/Interests/Sports: Traveling

Education Degrees: Master's Degree in Education, Plus 45, Marygrove College; Bachelor of Arts in Teaching the Handicapped Education, William Patterson University

Affiliations/Associations/Societies: Association for Supervision and Curriculum Development; American Alliance for Health; National Education Association

Awards/Honors: Nominee, Teacher of the Year Award (Twice); New Jersey Governor's Teacher Recognition Student Choice Teacher of the Year Award

Charity/Volunteer Work: Special Olympics

Spouse: Lester   **Children:** Christine

What do you attribute your success to? She attributes her success to her love for children and teaching.

How did you become involved in your profession? She became involved in her profession because she was influenced by her family members who were teachers.

What was the highlight of your career? The most gratifying aspect of her career is watching her students succeed.

PROFESSIONAL OF THE YEAR IN CHILD PSYCHIATRIC NURSING

MS. KATHLEEN M. REGAN, RN, MHA, CNA, BC

Nurse Manager
Child Assessment Unit
Cambridge Health Alliance
1493 Cambridge Street
Cambridge, MA 02139 United States
kregan@challiance.org
http://www.challiance.org

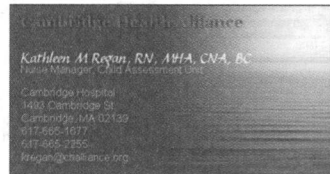

Type of Business: Healthcare Center

Major Products and Services: Healthcare Including Psychiatric Care

Marketing Area: Regional

Area of Expertise: Ms. Regan's expertise includes nursing administration and psychiatric care.

Hobbies/Interests/Sports: Reading, Writing

Education Degrees: Leadership Education in Neurodevelopmental Disabilities Program, University of Massachusetts Medical School, Suffolk University, The Shriver Center (2004); Master's Degree in Health Administration, Suffolk University; Bachelor of Science in Nursing, Boston College; Bachelor of Arts in Sociology, Stonehill College

Certifications: Board Certified Nurse Administrator, American Nurses Credentialing Center

Affiliations/Associations/Societies: Steering Committee Member, Position Paper and Revision of Standards for Restraint and Seclusion (2007); Board of Directors, Adoptive Families Together (1998-2004); Former President, Adoptive Families Together; President, BOD of AFT (2004); Founding Member, Board of Directors, Massachusetts Coalition for Adoption (1997-1998); Advisory Board Member, Foundation for Children with Behavioral Challenges; Advisory Board Member, Step Up for Kids; American Psychiatric Nursing Association; American Medical Writers Association; American Psychiatric Association; International Society of Psychiatric-Mental Health Nurses

Work History: Program Director, Crisis Services, South Shore Mental Health (1993-2001); Assistant Clinical Director, CIT, South Shore Mental Health (1991-1993); Staff Nurse, CIT, South Shore Mental Health (1986-1991), Psychiatric Staff Nurse, The Arbour Hospital (1981-1986); Associate Director, Day Treatment Center, South Shore Mental Health (1976-1981), Staff Registered Nurse, McLean Hospital (1976-1976); Social Worker, Division of Child Guardianship (1968-1972)

Career Achievements: Staff Trainer, Camp XCite and Step Up for Kids; Crisis Planning Presentation, Foundation for Children with Behavioral Challenges (2006); 'Letting Go of the Level System' Panel Presenter, Annual Massachusetts Department of Mental Health Round Table for Restraint/Seclusion Reduction Initiative (2006); 'Paradigm Shifts in Inpatient Psychiatric Care of Children,' Second International Institute of Family Centered Care, San Francisco (2005); 'Humane Strategies for Parenting Children with Challenging Behaviors,' BAMSI, Parent Information Network, Spring Workshop Series (2005); 'Reducing and Eliminating Restraints on a Child Inpatient Psychiatric Unit,' Cambridge Health Alliance Psychiatry Grand Rounds (2004); Gold Award for Service Excellence and Innovation for Psychiatric Services, American Psychiatric Association, Boston, MA (2003); 'Reducing and Eliminating Restraint and Seclusion on a Child Inpatient Psychiatric Unit':American Academy of Child and Adolescent Psychiatry, Miami, FL (2003); 'Changing the Culture and Model of Care on a Child Inpatient Unit to Eliminate Restraints.' DMH Annual Restraint Reduction Conference for Child and Adolescent Inpatient Units (2002); 'Eliminating Restraints on a Child Inpatient Unit,' Massachusetts General Hospital Conference on Violent Youth, The Treatment Challenge (2002); 'Changing the Culture and Model of Care on a Child Inpatient Unit to Reduce Restraints,' Boston Medical Center, Department of Psychiatry (2002); 'Need for Post-Adoption Services for Families,' Legislative Breakfast, Nurses Hall, State House Boston (1997); Presenter, DMH State-Wide Training for Providers and Vendors (1998); 'Working in Collaboration with Families,' Three State-Wide Training Seminars, The Massachusetts Behavioral Health Partnership to Improve Customer Service (2000); 'Opening Our Arms: Helping Troubled Kids Do Well' (2006); 'Journal of Child and Adolescent Psychiatric Nursing' (2006); 'Paradigm Shifts in Inpatient Psychiatric Care of Children: Approaching Child-Centered and Family Centered Care'; 'Advance for Nurses, When Daddy Hits Mommy' (2003); 'Nursing Spectrum, Loosening Restraints' (2003); Educational Pamphlet Series, 'Restraint and Seclusion: What Parents Need to Know (2003); 'Advance for Nurses, More Than Lip Service, Putting the 'Child' Back in 'Child-Centered Care' (2003); AFT, Inc. Educational Pamphlet Series, 'When the Going Gets Touch' Handling a Psychiatric Crisis or Emergency; What To Do When You Have a Crisis on Your Hands (1999)

What was the highlight of your career? She considers the work she and her staff have accomplished to improve the psychiatric care of children to be her greatest professional accomplishment.

Expanded Biography: Ms. Regan wrote a book entitled 'Opening our Arms...Helping Troubled Kids do Well,' published by Bull Publishing Company in 2006.

PROFESSIONAL OF THE YEAR IN WELLNESS

MS. LuAnn Reitmeier-Budiselic

1) Executive Regional Vice President 2) Owner
1) Arbonne International 2) Big Horn Developers LLC
1106 Rosemary Circle
Corona, CA 92879 United States
LuAnn@myarbonne.com
http://www.luann.myarbonne.com

Type of Business: 1) Health and Wellness 2) Home Building

Major Products and Services: 1) Anti-Aging Skin Care Products, Aromatherapy, Weight Loss Vitamins 2) Custom Built Homes and Log Cabins

Marketing Area: 1) International 2) Regional

Area of Expertise: Ms. Reitmeier-Budiselic's expertise includes marketing, sales, advertising and finance.

Favorite Business Publications: Networking Times

Hobbies/Interests/Sports: Traveling, Exercising, Weight Training, Golfing, Water Skiing, Swimming, Reading

Education Degrees: Diploma in Travel, Kinman Business University

Certifications: Makeup Artist

Affiliations/Associations/Societies: Corona Chamber of Commerce

Charity/Volunteer Work: Sojourner Center

PROFESSIONAL OF THE YEAR IN GOVERNMENT COMMUNICATIONS

FRANK REYSEN JR., MS

Communications Manager
New Jersey Planning Officials
31 Mountain Boulevard
Warren, NJ 07059 United States
frank.reysen@cwwemail.com
http://www.njpo.org

Type of Business: Government Agency

Major Products and Services: Municipal Plans, Education, Seminars, Publications, Legislation

Marketing Area: Regional

Day to Day Responsibilities: Editing, Writing, Reporting on Land Use Issues, Maintaining Websites, Managing Public Relations, Representing the Organization at State Conferences

Favorite Business Publications: Playthings

Hobbies/Interests/Sports: Reading, Collecting Autographs, Attending and Participating in Literary Events

Education Degrees: Candidate, Doctoral Degree in Journalism, Southern Illinois University; Master of Science in Journalism, West Virginia University (1965); Bachelor of Arts in Classical Languages, Fordham University (1963)

Affiliations/Associations/Societies: Alumni Association, Fordham Preparatory School; Kappa Tau Alpha

Awards/Honors: Neal Award, American Business Press; Public Service Award, Community Action Network; Three Bronze Stars and One Army Commendation Medal, Vietnam, Unites States Army

Date of Birth: April 13, 1942   **Place of Birth:** Bronx

Work History: Adjunct Professor, C.W. Post Campus, Long Island University; Director, Department of Defense High School News Service; Combat Information Officer, United States Army; Sports Editor, Media-Scope Magazine; Editor, Licensing Trends Newsletter; Editor, Playthings Magazine; Executive Editor, Incentive Marketing; News Editor, 'Daily Republican'

Career Achievements: Bronze Star, Army Commendation Medal, Vietnam, Unites States Army (Three Times); Neal Award, American Business Press; Public Service Award, Community Action Network

What do you attribute your success to? He attributes his success to his hard work and being goal-oriented.

How did you become involved in your profession? He became involved in his profession because of his interest in journalism.

What was the highlight of your career? The highlights of his career were receiving three bronze stars, an Army Commendation Medal, a Neal Award and a Public Service Award.

Expanded Biography: Mr. Reysen's published works include: 'A Comparative Survey of Sports Information Programs at American Colleges and Universities' (1965). He is also a public speaker and presented 'A Career in Business Press' at C.W. Post Campus, Long Island University and West Virginia University.

PROFESSIONAL OF THE YEAR IN BROADCASTING

MR. STEVEN E. RICHARDS

Operations Technician
Sinclair Broadcast Group
110 Technology Drive
Asheville, NC 28803 United States
tvmco13@netzero.com
http://www.sbgi.net

Type of Business: Broadcasting Company

Major Products and Services: Entertainment Including Television Shows and News

Marketing Area: National

Day to Day Responsibilities: Maintaining on-Air Programs for Television Stations, Rendering Technical Assistance to the News Department, Managing Engineering Duties, Satellite Feeds for News and Various Programs

Hobbies/Interests/Sports: Bowling, Reading, Exercising, Watching Movies

Education Degrees: Ph.D. in Educational Psychology, University of Pennsylvania (2002); Master of Education in Educational Psychology, Pennsylvania State University (1987); Master's Degree in Science and History, Temple University (1985); Bachelor of Arts in Music, Arkansas State University (1982); Bachelor of Science in History, Arkansas State University (1982)

Charity/Volunteer Work: American Red Cross; North Shore Animal League America

Date of Birth: July 16, 1961   **Place of Birth:** Washington

Work History: Radio Talk Show Host, Producer, WCGC, Charlotte, NC; Studio Engineer, Carolina Panthers Radio Network

Expanded Biography: Mr. Richards is a master control operator for 'Tuning in on Live Shots.' He has also worked as a DJ in commercial production and voice work.

PROFESSIONAL OF THE YEAR IN
ADVANCED NURSING

MS. KAY M. RICKEY, RN, MS, CNS, CWOCN

Director of Advanced Nursing Practice and Magnet
Upper Valley Medical Center
3130 N. Dixie Highway
Troy, OH 45373 United States
krickey@uvmc.com
http://www.uvmc.com

Type of Business: Nonprofit Community Magnet Designated Hospital

Major Products and Services: Medical-Surgical-Telemetry Care, Emergency Services, Intensive Care, Progressive Care, Women's Service, Level One Nursery, Cancer Care Center, Adult Rehab Unit, Cardio-Pulmonary Rehabilitation, Behavioral Health (Adult, Youth, Clinic), Home Health Care, Acute and Chronic Dialysis, Surgical Services, Outpatient Surgery, Occupational Health, Wound/Ostomy Patient Care Services, Education, Sports Medicine, Sleep Disorder Center and Wellness Programs

Marketing Area: Local

Day to Day Responsibilities: Medical-Surgical, Intensive Care, Emergency Room, Certified Wound Ostomy and Continence Nursing, Working as a Magnet Writer for Magnet Designation Journey, Mentoring and Supporting Advanced Practice Nurses, Preparing Documents for Magnet Redesignation, Working as a Research Facilitator for UVMC

Hobbies/Interests/Sports: Reading, Attending Church Activities, Nursing Home Ministry, Walk to Emmaus, Camping, Traveling

Education Degrees: Master of Science in Nursing, Wright State University; Registered Nurse

Certifications: Certified Wound, Ostomy and Continence Nurse

Affiliations/Associations/Societies: Sigma Theta Tau International Honor Society of Nursing; Wound, Ostomy and Continence Nurses Society; National Association of Clinical Nurse Specialists; Ohio Organization of Nurse Executives, Greater Dayton Area Nursing Research Symposium; Miami Valley Hospital School of Nursing Alumni Association

Awards/Honors: Cameos of Caring Nurse (2004); Upper Valley Nursing Excellence Award (2004)

What do you attribute your success to? She attributes her success to the support of her co-workers and the organization.

How did you become involved in your profession? She became involved in her profession because she was influenced by her mother, who was a nurse. Through her mother she noticed her own talents in caring for people and joined the medical field.

What was the highlight of your career? The highlight of her career was assisting in the successful Magnet Designation pursuit, earned in October 2004.

PROFESSIONAL OF THE YEAR IN MEDICAL-SURGICAL NURSING

KATHERINE M. RILEY-UPSHAW

Licensed Practical Nurse
Surgery
Presbyterian Medical Group
201 Cedar Street S.E., Suite 306
Albuquerque, NM 87106 United States
krileyups@phs.org
http://www.phs.org

Type of Business: Healthcare System

Major Products and Services: Healthcare Including Adult Neurology, Pediatrics, Surgery and X-rays

Marketing Area: New Mexico

Day to Day Responsibilities: Practicing Medical-Surgical Nursing

Hobbies/Interests/Sports: Hiking, Traveling

Certifications: Licensed Practical Nurse

Affiliations/Associations/Societies: Center for Development and Disability, University of New Mexico

PROFESSIONAL OF THE YEAR IN FIRE SAFETY

JACK J. RISO

1) Chief of Fire and Emergency Services
2) Fire Chief
1) Presidio of Monterey Fire Department
2) U.S. Department of Defense
4400 General Jim Moore Boulevard
Seaside, CA 93955 United States
jack.riso@us.army.mil
http://www.cambridgewhoswho.com

Type of Business: 1) Fire Department 2) Government Organization

Major Products and Services: 1) Fire and Emergency Rescue Services 2) Defense Services

Marketing Area: 1) Regional 2) National

Day to Day Responsibilities: Firefighting, Overseeing Emergency Services

Favorite Business Publications: Firehouse; IAFC Journal

Hobbies/Interests/Sports: Exercising, Walking, Caring for his Dog, Spending Time with his Family

Education Degrees: Associate Degree in Fire Science, Monterey Peninsula College

Certifications: Certification, Intumescent Fire Seals Association; Certification, International Fire Service Training Council

Affiliations/Associations/Societies: Monterey County Fire Chiefs Association; Monterey Fire Safe Council; Monterey County Fire Training Officers Association; The International Association of Fire Chiefs

Charity/Volunteer Work: California State Sheriffs' Association; California Police Activities League; Disabled American Veterans; Combined Federal Campaign

What do you attribute your success to? He attributes his success to his dedication.

How did you become involved in your profession? He became involved in his profession because of his interest in emergency rescue services.

What was the highlight of your career? The most gratifying aspect of his career is being able to work with great people.

PROFESSIONAL OF THE YEAR IN WASHINGTON REAL ESTATE

MS. KRIS ROBBS

Associate Broker
Coldwell Banker
2649 78th Street S.E.
Mercer Island, WA 98040 United States
krisrobbs@cbbain.com
http://www.krisrobbs.com

Type of Business: Real Estate Agency

Major Products and Services: Real Estate Services

Marketing Area: Local

Day to Day Responsibilities: Selling Waterfront and Upper-End Real Estate Property

Hobbies/Interests/Sports: Boating, Skiing, Traveling

Certifications: Certified Residential Specialist; Associate Broker; e-PRO Designation; Diploma, Graduate Realtor Institute

Affiliations/Associations/Societies: National Association of Realtors; Forum XXII

Awards/Honors: Number One Agent, Coldwell Banker Bain Mercer Island International (2006); Number Two Agent, Coldwell Banker Bain Mercer Island Office (2000-2005); Number One Agent, Coldwell Banker Bain Mercer Island Office (1999); Number Three Agent, Coldwell Banker Bain Puget Sound Offices (1999)

Charity/Volunteer Work: Hospital Board, Swedish Medical Center Foundation; Fundraising, Local Community Organizations

What do you attribute your success to? She attributes her career success to her hard work.

How did you become involved in your profession? She became involved in her profession because of the encouragement of her mother, who was in real estate.

What was the highlight of your career? The highlight of her career is being able to take care of her clients.

Expanded Biography: Ms. Robbs has ranked consistently among the top 10 agents in the community and in the top 1 percent of real estate professionals in the company.

EXECUTIVE OF THE YEAR IN
FINANCIAL SERVICES IN THE BEVERAGE INDUSTRY

THOMAS D. ROBERTS

Senior Vice President and Treasurer
Constellation Brands, Inc.
370 Woodcliff Drive, Suite 300
Fairport, NY 14450 United States
tom.roberts@cbrands.com
http://www.cbrands.com

Type of Business: Importer, Marketer and Manufacturer

Major Products and Services: Importation, Market and Manufacture of Wines and Spirits, Beer Importation

Marketing Area: International

Area of Expertise: Mr. Roberts' expertise includes finance and insurance.

Favorite Business Publications: The Wall Street Journal

Hobbies/Interests/Sports: Reading, Golfing

Education Degrees: Master's Degree in Business; Roosevelt University

Affiliations/Associations/Societies: Treasury Leadership Council; Risk Management Insurance Association

PROFESSIONAL OF THE YEAR IN CORRECTIONAL SERVICES

JUNE L. ROBINSON

Facility Director
Claremont Custody Center
185 W. Gale Avenue
Coalinga, CA 93210 United States
bandit4860@att.net
http://www.coalinga.com/ccc

Type of Business: Correctional Facility

Major Products and Services: Correctional Services Including Inmate Care, Education, Employment Assignments, an Animal Shelter and Adoption Program, a Vehicle Service Center and a Recycling Plant

Marketing Area: Local

Area of Expertise: Ms. Robinson's expertise includes cognitive behavior, anger management and parenting.

Day to Day Responsibilities: Overseeing Operations, Managing the Staff, Ensuring Proper Inmate Behavior, Designing Programs, Offering Educational and Vocational Training

Favorite Business Publications: Forbes; Industry-Related Publications

Hobbies/Interests/Sports: Reading, Gardening

Education Degrees: Bachelor of Science in Criminology, University of Phoenix (2005)

Certifications: Certification in Narcotic Symptomology Background Investigations, Internal Affair Investigations and Classroom Presentations

Affiliations/Associations/Societies: California Gang Task Force

Awards/Honors: President's Citation; Employee of the Year Award, West Hills College Coalinga; Highest Net Profit, Circle K Stores, Inc.; Award for Program Excellence, International City/County Management Association

Charity/Volunteer Work: Local Charitable Organizations

Date of Birth: October 19, 1956

What do you attribute your success to? She attributes her success to her hard work and the support she receives from her colleagues.

How did you become involved in your profession? She became involved in her profession because she wanted to make a positive impact on her community.

What was the highlight of your career? The highlight of her career was creating the infrastructure for five operations in the city including an animal shelter, a recycling facility and an auto service center.

Where will you be in five years? In five years, Ms. Robinson hopes to expand the facility and convert it to a re-entry facility.

Expanded Biography: Ms. Robinson creates innovative programs for inmates and has served on the safety committee for Assemblywoman Nicole Parra.

PROFESSIONAL OF THE YEAR IN
FINE ART

JENNIFER L. ROE, LMT

1) Owner 2) Owner 3) Owner 4) Owner
1) Energi Essentials 2) JLROE Fine Art Print Making
3) JT Productions 4) Behzat, Inc.
3413 Doe Run
Austin, TX 78748 United States
jlroelmt@yahoo.com
jlroe@behzat.com
http://www.energiessentials.com

Type of Business: 1) Therapy Center 2) Fine Art Company 3) Consulting Firm 4) Trading Company

Major Products and Services: 1) Therapy Services 2) Fine Arts 3) Consulting Services 4) Handcrafted Art Jewelry

Marketing Area: 1) International 2) International 3) International 4) International

Area of Expertise: Ms. Roe's expertise includes fine arts, and print-making using linoleum, woodcuts and metals.

Day to Day Responsibilities: Intermediating between the Community and Pharmaceutical Companies

Favorite Business Publications: Art in America

Hobbies/Interests/Sports: Artwork, Traveling, Hiking, Architecture, Reading Fiction and Non-Fiction Books

Education Degrees: Pursuing Bachelor's Degree in Fine Arts, University of Northern Texas

Certifications: Certification in CEU; Licensed Massage Therapist; Certification in Craniosacral Therapy

Affiliations/Associations/Societies: Austin Visual Arts Association; Women Print Makers of Austin

Charity/Volunteer Work: Local Charitable Organizations; Run for the Rovers

What do you attribute your success to? She attributes her success to her personal drive and creativity.

How did you become involved in your profession? She became involved in her profession because she always wanted to work in an industry where she can utilize her creativity.

What was the highlight of your career? The highlight of her career was earning her current position.

Where will you be in five years? In five years, Ms. Roe hopes to open a massage therapy center.

Expanded Biography: Ms. Roe coordinates community education and opens venues for members of the community to voice their opinions, informing them when a new drug for AIDS is in development. She is currently taking classes on Myofascial Release.

PROFESSIONAL OF THE YEAR IN NONPROFIT MANAGEMENT

WILLIAM D. ROLLINS JR.

Director of Field Services
Paralyzed Veterans of America
801 18th Street N.W.
Washington, DC 20006 United States
bor@pva.org
http://www.pva.org

Type of Business: Nonprofit Organization

Major Products and Services: Healthcare Services for Veterans

Marketing Area: National

Area of Expertise: Mr. Rollins' expertise includes operations management.

Day to Day Responsibilities: Managing Operations Including Projects and Human Resources, Directing Services for Paralyzed Veterans, Training, Reviewing Bills, Implementing Plans, Overseeing Field Operations and Public Speaking on Education, Hiring, Training and Caring for Paralyzed Veterans

Hobbies/Interests/Sports: Golfing, Shooting

Education Degrees: Bachelor's Degree in Psychology, National University

Charity/Volunteer Work: Fisher House

Spouse: Trish   **Children:** Monica, Liam

What do you attribute your success to? He attributes his success to his passion for his profession.

How did you become involved in your profession? Mr. Rollins was motivated by PVA service officer Charlie Rowe, who was a quadriplegic. When Mr. Rollins first went to him seeking assistance, he learned quickly that Mr. Rowe overcame more every day just to go to and perform at work, than he would ever face. Mr. Rowe's strength and desire to help others, even those more fortunate than himself, was an inspiration.

What was the highlight of your career? The highlight of his career was earning his current position.

PROFESSIONAL OF THE YEAR IN GENERAL FAMILY DENTISTRY

PATRICIA E. ROMANO, DDS

Doctor of Dental Surgery, Registered Nurse
Romano's Family Dentistry, PLLC
5962 State Route 31
Cicero, NY 13039 United States
peromanodds@aol.com
http://www.romanofamilydentistry.com

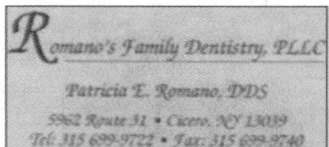

Type of Business: General Family Dentistry Office, Solo Practice

Major Products and Services: Family Dental Care, Patient Services, General and Cosmetic Dental Services, Quality Oral Care

Marketing Area: Regional

Day to Day Responsibilities: Specializing in General Family Dentistry, Orthodontics, Cosmetic Dentistry, Patient Education on Oral Care, Collaborative Research with Veterinarians on the Correlation between Oral Hygiene and Physical Well-Being in Humans and Pets

Favorite Business Publications: The Journal of the American Dental Association; Journal of Orthodontics; New York State Dental Association Journal; Journal of Prosthodontics; The Wall Street Journal; The New York Times

Hobbies/Interests/Sports: Painting, Sculpture, Hockey, Football, Caring for her Eight Shih-Tzus

Education Degrees: Doctor of Dental Surgery, Georgetown University (1985); Bachelor of Science, Le Moyne College (1981); Associate Degree in Nursing, Maria Regina College (1979)

Affiliations/Associations/Societies: Fifth District, New York State Dental Association; American Dental Association; American Veterinary Dental Association; Board Member, Society for the Prevention of Cruelty to Animals

Charity/Volunteer Work: Rosamond Gifford Zoo; Ginger and Tiger Pharmacy Fund; Sponsor, Several Children's Sports, Dance and Marching Band Programs; Sponsor, Society for the Prevention of Cruelty to Animals Pet Walk

Place of Birth: Syracuse

Work History: Public Health Service, States of Pennsylvania and New York

DR. RONALD L. ROSSMILLER

Owner
Storm Water Consultants
7933 Van Buren Road
Everson, WA 98247 United States
ronaldrnr@aol.com
http://www.cambridgewhoswho.com

Type of Business: Consulting Firm

Major Products and Services: Studies, Designs, Calculations, Reports, Short-Course Teaching

Marketing Area: National

Day to Day Responsibilities: Designing Overall Drainage Systems, Writing Books, Rendering Consultations Regarding Stormwater Drainage Facilities in Terms of Quality and Quantity Stormwater Runoffs

Hobbies/Interests/Sports: Spending Time with his Grandchildren, Reading, Gardening

Education Degrees: Ph.D. in Water Resources, Iowa State University (1975); Master of Science in Civil Engineering, Iowa State University (1971); Bachelor of Science in Civil Engineering, Purdue University (1955)

Affiliations/Associations/Societies: American Society of Civil Engineers (1981); Urban Water Resources Research Council; National Urban Water Resources Research Institute; American Public Works Association; American Water Works Association; American Society of Civil Engineers; Chi Epsilon; Tau Beta Pi; Phi Kappa Phi; Sigma Xi

Awards/Honors: Engineer of the Year, University of Wisconsin (1999); Professional Engineer, State of Washington; Distinguished Service Citation (1999); Distinguished Service Citation, University of Wisconsin (1999); Iowa State University Charles Schafer Faculty Award for Excellence in Teaching Civil Engineering (1986); Listed in Who's Who in the Midwest (1984); Outstanding Member of the Class, American Society of Civil Engineers, Purdue University (1955)

Date of Birth: January 3, 1932   **Place of Birth:** Milwaukee

Spouse: Susan

Work History: Principal Engineer, Designer, Marketer, Wright Water Engineers, Inc., Denver, CO (1986-1990); Instructor, Full Professor, Department of Civil Engineering, Iowa State University, Ames, IO (1972-1986); Highway Engineer II, Preliminary Bridge Section, IA State Highway Commission, Ames, IO (1967-1972); Realtor, Gilbert Realty Company, Walnut, CA (1965-1967); Associate Civil Engineer, Los Angeles County Flood Control District, CA (1955-1965)

What do you attribute your success to? He attributes his success to his knowledge, and to his friendly and accessible personality.

How did you become involved in your profession? He became involved in his profession because he wanted to be a civil engineer since junior high school.

Expanded Biography: Dr. Rossmiller served as the national program director for storm water management for more than 40 United States offices, and served as a designer and mentor for several projects over the past 52 years. He also worked in Henningson, Durham, & Richardson Engineering from 1990 to 1998. He authored two chapters in the American Public Works Association Special Report No. 49, Urban Storm Water Management, Chapter 6: 'Storm water Collection Systems Design' and Chapter 9: 'Engineering Design of On-site Detention Facilities.' He also was the vice-chairman for preparing two chapters and was a contributing author to the second and third chapter for the American Society of Civil Engineers Manual of Practice No. 77, Design and Construction of Urban Storm Water Management Systems. He is currently writing a book entitled 'Design of Culverts.' He has also authored numerous papers and has published proceedings. Dr. Rossmiller teaches short courses at the University of Wisconsin on storm sewer design, culvert design, water surface profiles and detention basins.

PROFESSIONAL OF THE YEAR IN
HIGH SCHOOL DIPLOMA PROGRAM COORDINATION

JANE BARNETT ROYAL, MA

International Baccalaureate Diploma Program Coordinator
North Mecklenburg High School
11021 Old Statesville Road
Huntersville, NC 28078 United States
jbroyal722@hotmail.com
http://www.cms.k12.nc.us/allschools/north/index.html

Type of Business: Public High School

Major Products and Services: General Secondary Curriculum, Language Arts, Fine Arts, Music, Physical Education, Learning Resources, Student Support Services, Athletics, Extracurricular Activities, Student Clubs and Organizations

Marketing Area: Local

Day to Day Responsibilities: Coordinating Diploma Programs

Favorite Business Publications: Newsweek; Time

Hobbies/Interests/Sports: Spending Time with her Family, Knitting, Walking, Reading, Traveling, Watching Old Movies and CNN News, Gardening, Cooking, Entertaining her Friends, Spending Time with her Students

Education Degrees: Master's Degree in History, Concentration in International Relations, Virginia Polytechnic Institute and State University; Bachelor's Degree in Secondary Education, Concentrations in English, History and Political Science, Minors in Theater Arts and Psychology, University of Cincinnati

Affiliations/Associations/Societies: National Education Association; American Historical Association; Susan G. Komen for the Cure, Race for the Cure; Knitting Donations, Bag Program, Project Comfort; Project Linus; Habitat for Humanity International; Katrina Relief Community Outreach Program

What do you attribute your success to? She attributes her success to respecting her students and establishing a rapport with them in her classroom.

How did you become involved in your profession? Her involvement in education was inspired by her high school history teacher, Betsy Bolander, a demanding but excellent teacher. Her family's interest in history and politics also played an important role in her career path. Her students have also been a great inspiration to her.

What was the highlight of your career? The highlight of her career was when the students of one of her U.S. History classes decided to petition the government for a special visa. The purpose of the visa was to allow the brother of a classmate, who was from Poland, to attend the graduation of his sibling. Their success in this achievement was an inspiring and moving moment in her career.

Expanded Biography: Ms. Royal is very proud of her three boys, who have grown into well-rounded individuals. One son is a teacher, another a musician and the third is a graduate student.

PROFESSIONAL OF THE YEAR IN
MENTAL HEALTH

DR. ALICE RUSCALLEDA

Chief Executive Officer, Psychologist
Clinical Support Group
1432 Calle Barracuda
Bahia Vistamar
Carolina, PR 00983 United States
druscalleda@aol.com
http://www.cambridgewhoswho.com

Type of Business: Healthcare Center

Major Products and Services: Mental Healthcare, Geriatrics, Internal Medicine, Social Work, Occupational Therapy and Physical Therapy

Marketing Area: Regional

Area of Expertise: Dr. Ruscalleda's expertise includes clinical psychology and human resource management.

Day to Day Responsibilities: Managing Operations, Hiring Nurses, Social Workers and Clinicians, Meeting Owners of Homes for the Elderly, Supervising Clinicians from the University of Puerto Rico, Processing Payroll, Overseeing Administration Including Long-Term Care, Office Practice, Home Health Facilities and Nursing Homes

Favorite Business Publications: APA Journals

Hobbies/Interests/Sports: Sailing, Snorkeling

Education Degrees: Ph.D. in Clinical Psychology, University of Bern (1998); Ph.D. in Human Resource Management, La Salle University (1996); Master's Degree in Human Resource Management, La Salle University (1996); Bachelor of Science in Pre-Medicine, University of Puerto Rico, Rio Piedras (1977)

Affiliations/Associations/Societies: Council of University Directors of Clinical Psychology; American Aging Association; American Psychological Association

Charity/Volunteer Work: Volunteer, Home Healthcare Facility

Place of Birth: New York

Spouse: Hector   **Children:** Steven, Sophia, Alice, Hector

What was the highlight of your career? The most gratifying aspect of her career is helping the elderly.

Expanded Biography: Dr. Ruscalleda does regional, national and international speaking for American Airlines and American Eagle. She also writes a column for a local newspaper and has published a book entitled 'Dementia and Depression in the Elderly.'

PROFESSIONAL OF THE YEAR IN CARDIOLOGY

DR. RICHARD O. RUSSELL JR.

Cardiologist, Clinical Professor (Retired)
Cardiovascular Associates, Inc.
4408 Kennesaw Drive
Birmingham, AL 35213 United States
rorussell@charter.net
http://www.cambridgewhoswho.com

Type of Business: Healthcare Center

Major Products and Services: Healthcare Including Cardiology

Marketing Area: Regional

Day to Day Responsibilities: Caring for Patients with Cardiovascular Disease Including Coronary Artery and Hypertension Disease, Assisting Medical Students, Interns, Residents and Cardiology Fellows

Favorite Business Publications: The Journal of the American Medical Association

Hobbies/Interests/Sports: Spending Time with his Family

Education Degrees: Fellowship in Cardiology, University of Alabama at Birmingham (1963); Residency, Peter Bent Brigham Hospital, Harvard Medical School (1960); Internship, Peter Bent Brigham Hospital, Harvard Medical School (1956); MD, Vanderbilt University (1956); Bachelor of Arts, Vanderbilt University (1953)

Certifications: Board Certification in Internal Medicine and Cardiology

Affiliations/Associations/Societies: Fellow, Chairman, Annual Scientific Session, American College of Cardiology (1994); American College of Chest Physicians; American Heart Association; American Medical Association

Awards/Honors: Silver Antelope Award, Boy Scouts of America; Silver Beaver Award, Boy Scouts of America; Distinguished Eagle Scout Award, Boy Scouts of America; Commendation Medal, U.S. Army

Charity/Volunteer Work: Volunteer, Boy Scouts of America; Kiwanis Club of Birmingham

Date of Birth: July 9, 1932   **Place of Birth:** Birmingham

Spouse: Phyllis   **Children:** Scott, Katherine, Meredith, Stephen

Work History: Professor of Medicine in Cardiology, University of Alabama at Birmingham

What do you attribute your success to? He attributes his success to having an interest in people and their problems, an intellectual curiosity for cardiology and medicine, and concern for his patients.

How did you become involved in your profession? He became involved in his profession because he had an interest in the human heart and was inspired by his father, who was an internist.

Expanded Biography: Dr. Russell published a book on the management of coronary artery disease with Charles E. Rackley in 1976.

PROFESSIONAL OF THE YEAR IN SOCIAL WORK

JOAN R. RYCRAFT, PH.D.

Chief Academic Officer
School of Social Work
The University of Texas at Arlington
211 S. Cooper Street
P.O. Box 19129
Arlington, TX 76010 United States
rycraft@uta.edu
http://www.uta.edu/gradcatalog/social_work

Type of Business: University

Major Products and Services: Higher Education

Marketing Area: Local

Area of Expertise: Dr. Rycraft's expertise is in social work.

Day to Day Responsibilities: Developing Curriculum, Scheduling Classes, Overseeing Student Activities

Favorite Business Publications: NASW Journal

Hobbies/Interests/Sports: Traveling, Reading

Education Degrees: Ph.D. in Social Work, University of Denver

Affiliations/Associations/Societies: National Association of Social Workers; Council on Social Work Education; Society for Social Work and Research

Awards/Honors: Child Welfare Scholar Award (2003)

Charity/Volunteer Work: International Society for Prevention of Child Abuse and Neglect

PROFESSIONAL OF THE YEAR IN PHARMACEUTICAL FACILITIES SERVICES

ALISON M. SAFKER

Associate Manager of Building Services
Bristol-Myers Squibb Company
1 Squibb Drive
New Brunswick, NJ 08901 United States
alijos@optonline.net
http://www.bms.com

Type of Business: Pharmaceutical Company

Major Products and Services: Pharmaceuticals Including Ostomy Care, Wound Therapeutics and Nutritional Products

Marketing Area: International

Area of Expertise: Ms. Safker's expertise includes customer satisfaction, building management and special event coordination.

Day to Day Responsibilities: Overseeing Housekeeping, Landscaping and Recycling Services Including the Removal of Non-Hazardous Materials

Favorite Business Publications: Dining Out; People

Hobbies/Interests/Sports: Golfing, Water Sports, Watching NASCAR, Spending Time at the Beach

Education Degrees: Coursework in Customer Service; Coursework in Fall Protection Safety

Certifications: Dale Carnegie Training; Training in Hazardous Materials Safety

Affiliations/Associations/Societies: American Society of Safety Engineers

Awards/Honors: Star Award, Consolidation of Departments, Bristol-Myers Squibb Company (2003); Whatever It Takes Award, Bristol-Myers Squibb Company (2003); Dale Carnegie Highest Achievement Award

Charity/Volunteer Work: Children's Hospital of New Jersey; Make-A-Wish Foundation; Order Sons of Italy in America

Spouse: Joseph

What do you attribute your success to? She attributes her success to her hard work and prudence.

How did you become involved in your profession? She became involved in her profession because of her experience in customer service.

What was the highlight of your career? The highlight of her career was receiving several awards.

Expanded Biography: Ms. Safker owned a racing car collectibles store for six years.

PROFESSIONAL OF THE YEAR IN
ENERGY SOLUTIONS

SHANA SANTONI

Manager of Sponsorships
Direct Energy
909 Lake Carolyn Parkway, Suite 1100
Irving, TX 75039 United States
shana.santoni@directenergy.com
http://www.directenergy.com

Type of Business: Energy and Energy Solutions Company

Major Products and Services: Energy Management, Engineering Services and Energy Information Systems

Marketing Area: International

Day to Day Responsibilities: Overseeing Major Sponsorships in the United States, Working with the Dallas Cowboys, Houston Rockets and Cleveland Indians to Execute and Activate Sponsorships, Trade Show Marketing, Overseeing All Major Sponsorships in Texas

Favorite Business Publications: DMNews; Advertising Age

Hobbies/Interests/Sports: Volunteering at a Local Children's Hospital; Serving on a Nonprofit Board of Directors

Education Degrees: Pursuing Bachelor's Degree in Business, University of Phoenix

Charity/Volunteer Work: Board Member, Greater Dallas Restaurant Association; Auxiliary Council Member, Texas Scottish Rite Hospital for Children; Terence Newman's Rising Stars Foundation

Date of Birth: January 4, 1971   **Place of Birth:** Casper

What was the highlight of your career? The highlight of his career was working with the Dallas Cowboys.

Expanded Biography: Ms. Santoni has helped developed a multi-faceted program.

PROFESSIONAL OF THE YEAR IN
UROLOGY

DR. NEIL J. SAYEGH

Urologist
Yonkers Urology, PC
944 N. Broadway, Suite G6
Yonkers, NY 10701 United States
yonkersurology@optonline.net
http://www.cambridgewhoswho.com

Type of Business: Urology Practice

Major Products and Services: Diagnosis and Treatment of Various Urological Conditions

Marketing Area: Regional

Area of Expertise: Dr. Sayegh's expertise includes urology and the treatment of sexual dysfunction.

Day to Day Responsibilities: Treating and Caring for Patients

Education Degrees: Post-Graduate Surgical Residency; MD, New York Medical College

Certifications: Board Certified Surgeon

Affiliations/Associations/Societies: Fellow, American College of Surgeons; New York Urological Association; American Urological Association

Date of Birth: November 11, 1950   **Spouse:** Sana

Children: Najwa, Michael, Briggette, Matthew, Mark, Danielle

Work History: Director of Surgery and Chief of Urology, St. Joseph's Hospital

What do you attribute your success to? He attributes his success to his persistence, hard work and compassion.

What was the highlight of your career? The highlights of his career were becoming a fellow of the American College of Surgeons and an assistant professor of surgery at New York Medical College.

Where will you be in five years? In five years, Dr. Sayegh would like to continue working in the same profession.

Expanded Biography: Dr. Sayegh performs free yearly prostate screenings at his practice and does local public speaking. He has published 10 articles.

PROFESSIONAL OF THE YEAR IN COMMERCIAL RETAIL REAL ESTATE

SUSAN SCHAEFF

General Manager
Madison Marquette Realty
1585 W. Lane Avenue
Upper Arlington, OH 43221 United States
sschaeff@mmrs.com
http://www.theshopsonlaneavenue.com

Type of Business: Commercial Real Estate Agency

Major Products and Services: Implementation of Creative Solutions for Retail Opportunities, Delivering Outstanding Investment Returns for Clients

Marketing Area: National

Day to Day Responsibilities: Managing Operations, Marketing

Favorite Business Publications: Shopping Today Magazine

Hobbies/Interests/Sports: Riding Roller Coasters, Sky Diving

Affiliations/Associations/Societies: Chamber of Commerce; MDA, Special Olympics; Pilot Dog

Awards/Honors: Upper Arlington Businesswoman of the Year (2004); Winner, Florida Businesswoman of the Year (Two Times)

Expanded Biography: Ms. Schaeff worked as a general mall manager for five years, and was responsible for overseeing several retail shops and ensuring the smooth running of daily operations.

PROFESSIONAL OF THE YEAR IN MUSIC PRODUCTION

M. Star Schatten

1) Owner 2) Owner 3) Owner
1) Schatten Properties Management
2) Lionsway Farm 3) Star Clement Productions
1420 Moran Road
Franklin, TN 37069 United States
lionsway@mac.com
http://www.cambridgewhoswho.com

Type of Business: 1) Real Estate Agency 2) Breeding Farm 3) Music Studio

Major Products and Services: 1) Real Estate Services 2) Horse Breeding 3) Music Production

Marketing Area: 1) International 2) International 3) International

Area of Expertise: Ms. Schatten's expertise includes operations management, leadership and property management, music production and equine breeding.

Favorite Business Publications: The Wall Street Journal

Hobbies/Interests/Sports: Horseback Riding, Listening to Music, Artwork, Playing String Instruments

Education Degrees: Coursework in Real Estate, Coastal Carolina Community College, University of Southern California; Coursework, Aquinas University, David Lipscomb University, Nashville State Technical Institute, Belmont University

Affiliations/Associations/Societies: United States Equestrian Federation; United States Tennis Association

Awards/Honors: Children's and Adult Jumper Championship Award, Middle Tennessee Hunter Jumper Association (2006)

Charity/Volunteer Work: Volunteer, Cheekwood Society; Smithsonian Legacy Society; Vanderbilt-Ingram Cancer Center

Place of Birth: Nashville   **Children:** Stephanie

Expanded Biography: Ms. Schatten has been quoted in M. Scott Peck's book, 'The Road Less Traveled.' She also worked as a realtor and a luthier.

PROFESSIONAL OF THE YEAR IN
LABOR AND EMPLOYMENT LAW

MR. KARL A. SCHMIDT, ESQ.

Shareholder, Department Chair
Parker, Milliken, Clark, O'Hara & Samuelian
555 S. Flower Street
30th Floor
Los Angeles, CA 90071 United States
kschmidt@pmcos.com
http://www.pmcos.com

Type of Business: Law Firm

Major Products and Services: Representation of Governmental Entities and a Diverse Clientele of Smaller, Privately-Held Businesses, Entrepreneurs and Individuals, Five Key Practice Areas: Business Transactional Law, Environmental Law, Estate Planning, Labor and Employment Law, and Litigation

Marketing Area: Regional

Day to Day Responsibilities: Practicing Labor and Employment Law, Union Negotiations, Concessionary Bargaining, Benefits Bargaining and Bankruptcy Reorganization, Managing

Favorite Business Publications: The Economist

Hobbies/Interests/Sports: Tennis, Hiking, Cooking, Basketball

Education Degrees: JD, University of California at Berkeley (1974); Bachelor of Science in Accounting and Finance, University of California at Berkeley (1969)

Certifications: Martindale-Hubble AV Rating

Affiliations/Associations/Societies: Los Angeles County Bar Association; American Bar Association; California Bar Association; Los Angeles Rotary; Board of Directors, Goodwill Industries of Southern California

Awards/Honors: Super Lawyer in the Top Five Percent, 'Los Angeles Magazine' (2004, 2006)

Expanded Biography: Mr. Schmidt was published in the area of executive termination in 'Major Tax Planning' in 2003. He was recently inducted into 'The Best Lawyers in America' reference book.

PROFESSIONAL OF THE YEAR IN
INFORMATION TECHNOLOGY AND ASSURANCE

MR. JAMES A. SCHOLZ

President, Owner, Founder
Computer Security Consulting, Inc.
509 Tracy Lane, Suite 1B
Warrensburg, MO 64093 United States
j.scholz@csc-inc1.com
http://www.csc-inc1.com

Type of Business: Information Assurance and Technology Consulting Company for All Levels of Government Including Local, State and Federal

Major Products and Services: Technological Support Services for Several Federal, State and Local Government Agencies, Contracts with Private Businesses in the Areas of Certification and Accreditation, Security Architecture, Network Security, Full Security Integrated Life Cycle Software Development, Database Design and Management, Information System Security Program Development, Business Continuity Planning, Disaster Recovery Planning, Data Center Consolidation, Enterprise Storage Management, Independent Verification and Validation, Counter Terrorism and Courthouse Security, In-Class and Computer-Based Training

Marketing Area: National

Day to Day Responsibilities: Offering Security Services to the Federal Government, Working with Banks, Schools, Hospitals and Other Organizations as a Subcontractor, Inventing Ways to Streamline Processes and Offer Total Cost of Ownership for Employees

Favorite Business Publications: Magazine Storage; Information Systems Control Journal

Education Degrees: Bachelor's Degree in Information Technology, University of Phoenix (2000)

Certifications: Pursuing Six Sigma Certification; Pursuing Certification in Capability Maturity Model Software

Affiliations/Associations/Societies: Information Systems Audit and Control Association; Microsoft and Cisco Partners

Spouse: Susan

Expanded Biography: Mr. Scholz does national public speaking. He's the prime reseller for 'NGSSQuirreL' software. His company was established in 1998. CSCI is an emerging, certified Native American, service disabled, veteran-owned small business with an extensive and successful past performance history working with federal and state government agencies. With his staff of 10 employees, Mr. Scholz offers training for any business, improving management processes and data center designs.

PROFESSIONAL OF THE YEAR IN OCCUPATIONAL THERAPY

EMILY K. SCHULZ, PH.D., OTR/L, CFLE

Research Consultant
University of Alabama at Birmingham
1717 11th Avenue S.
Birmingham, AL 35205 United States
schulze@uab.edu
http://main.uab.edu

Type of Business: World-Renowned Research University and Health Care Center

Major Products and Services: Research, Education, Health Care and Community Service

Marketing Area: Regional

Day to Day Responsibilities: Practicing Occupational Therapy and Family Studies, Spirituality, Religiosity and Faith as Relating to Health and Well-Being, Planning Methodology, Preparation and Presentations Nationally and Internationally, Teaching Online Courses on Complimentary Care for Occupational Therapy, Running Support Groups for Persons with HIV/AIDS Living in Poverty, Instituting Community-Based Practice and Research

Favorite Business Publications: Journal of Marriage and the Family; Journal of Occupational Therapy

Hobbies/Interests/Sports: Gardening, Listening to Music

Education Degrees: Ph.D. in Family Studies, Texas Woman's University (2003); Ph.D. in Occupational Therapy, Texas Woman's University (2002); Master of Science in Occupational Therapy, Tufts University (1988)

Affiliations/Associations/Societies: Phi Kappa Phi; American Public Health Association; National Council on Family Relations, Occupational Therapy Association; Society for the Study of Occupation

PROFESSIONAL OF THE YEAR IN NURSE ANESTHESIA

WINIFRED S. SCHWEIGER

Nurse Anesthetist (Retired)
University of Michigan Health System
1500 E. Medical Center Drive
Ann Arbor, MI 48109 United States
winifred@umich.edu
http://www.med.umich.edu

Type of Business: Nonprofit Hospital

Major Products and Services: Home Education, Patient Care, Research, Children's Hospital, Cancer Center, Cardiovascular Center, Depression Center, Information

Marketing Area: National

Day to Day Responsibilities: Administering Anesthesia to Patients, Scheduling, Staffing, Recruiting, Supervising More than 100 Employees, Conducting Interviews, Negotiating Union Contracts, Managing Equipment Issues, Developing Improved Planning for the New Cardiovascular Center, Overseeing Daily Operations and Duties as Chief Nurse

Favorite Business Publications: American Journal of Nursing; U.S. News & World Report

Hobbies/Interests/Sports: Golfing, Knitting, Volunteering to Teach Children, Reading, Music, Growing Flowers and Vegetables

Education Degrees: Master's Degree in Adult Education, University of Detroit Mercy; Industry-Related Training, United States Navy; Coursework, The George Washington University

Certifications: Certified Anesthetist

Affiliations/Associations/Societies: American Association of Nurse Anesthetists; Michigan Association of Nurse Anesthetists; Adjunct Instructor, University of Michigan School of Nursing; United States Golf Association; Former President, HVWOG; Ann Arbor Women's City Club; Knitting Girls of America; Volunteer Counselor, Family Life Services

What do you attribute your success to? She attributes her success to her expert knowledge, excellent work ethic and ability to think outside of the box.

What was the highlight of your career? The highlight of her career has been the tremendous growth that the company has experienced over the past ten years. She is very proud to have played a crucial role in that growth.

PROFESSIONAL OF THE YEAR IN
REHABILITATION CLINIC MANAGEMENT

DR. SONYA MARIE SCONIERS

Operating Manager
Sonam Group, LLC
800 Niagara Avenue, Suite 203
Niagara Falls, NY 14305 United States
ssconiers1@yahoo.com
http://www.cambridgewhoswho.com

Type of Business: Consulting Firm

Major Products and Services: Service Coordination, Clinic Management, Customer Care and Financial Management

Marketing Area: Statewide

Day to Day Responsibilities: Facilitating Cultural Competence, Assisting Injured Workers, Managing Long-Term Care for Patients, Consulting on Healthcare, Practicing Clinical Management and Program Development

Favorite Business Publications: Advance for Physical Therapists and Physical Therapy Assistants; Money; Smithsonian Associates

Hobbies/Interests/Sports: Singing, Ballroom and Modern Dancing, Practicing Ballet, Attending the Theater

Education Degrees: Doctor of Health Administration, University of Phoenix; Master's Degree in Physical Therapy, Texas Woman's University; Bachelor's Degree in Occupational Therapy, SUNY Buffalo

Certifications: Certified Disability Analyst

Affiliations/Associations/Societies: Washington Performing Arts Society; Alumni Association Network; American Board of Disability Analysts; American College of Healthcare Executives; National Association for Female Executives; Board of Advisers, American Biographical Institute; Who's Who of Women Worldwide; Who's Who Among American High School Students; Alpha Kappa Alpha; Buffalo Chapter, The Alpha Eta

Awards/Honors: Two Thousand Notable American Women; Silver's Who's Who (1977-1990): Dean's Award, School of Occupational Therapy; Travel Grant to Guatemala for Academic Achievement; Recognition by State Assemblyman for Academic Achievement; American Cyanamid Fellowship; Recognition for Contribution to the Student Occupational Therapy Association, SUNY Buffalo

What do you attribute your success to? She attributes her success to her hard work, dedication, positive attitude, and passion for her profession, and to the support she receives from her family and mentors.

How did you become involved in your profession? She became involved in her profession because of her passion for helping ill or injured people live a better quality of life.

What was the highlight of your career? The highlights of her career were receiving the dean's award from the school of occupational therapy and completing her doctorate.

Where will you be in five years? In five years, Dr. Sconiers intends to transition to the academic environment, travel to other parts of the world in assisting with healthcare initiatives and occasionally enjoy island retreats.

Expanded Biography: Dr. Sconiers received a scholarship for academic excellence and professional potential from the American Physical Therapy Association.

EXECUTIVE OF THE YEAR IN BUSINESS OPERATIONS

SAMUEL J. SEASE

Vice President
Central Virginia Area Service
Colonial Webb Contractors
2820 Ackley Avenue
Richmond, VA 23228 United States
sam.sease@colonialwebb.com
http://www.colonialwebb.com

Type of Business: Contracting Company

Major Products and Services: Contracting Services Including Heating, Ventilation, Air Conditioning, Plumbing, Electrical, Process Piping, Refrigeration, Water Treatment

Marketing Area: National

Area of Expertise: Mr. Sease's expertise is in career development.

Day to Day Responsibilities: Managing Business Operations, Overseeing Staff, Sales, Marketing, Administration, Recruiting Employees

Hobbies/Interests/Sports: Golfing, Spending Time with her Family

Education Degrees: Bachelor of Science in Mechanical Engineering, University of South Carolina (1983)

Affiliations/Associations/Societies: International Facility Management Association; American Society of Heating, Refrigerating and Air-Conditioning Engineers

Charity/Volunteer Work: The Federal Club

Spouse: Susan   **Children:** Sierra, Cassidy, Brie

Expanded Biography: Mr. Sease is a coach for the co-ed Rockville soccer team. He also does international public speaking.

PROFESSIONAL OF THE YEAR IN
LAW ENFORCEMENT FOR THE U.S. FOREST SERVICE

VICKIE SELL

Law Enforcement Officer (Retired)
United States Department of Agriculture, Forest Service
3941 Highway 76
Chatsworth, GA 30705 United States
morganza@alltel.net
http://www.cambridgewhoswho.com

Type of Business: Government Agency

Major Products and Services: Management of Public Lands in National Forests and Grasslands

Marketing Area: National

Day to Day Responsibilities: Maintaining and Protecting the Public and Forest Resources

Hobbies/Interests/Sports: Training her Dog, Spending Time with her Nephews and Nieces, Friends and Family

Education Degrees: Associate Degree in Forestry, Dekalb Community College (1980)

Affiliations/Associations/Societies: Georgia Sheriff's Association; Federal Law Enforcement Officers Association; International Association of Women Police

Awards/Honors: First Barriers to Bridges Award for First Female Law Enforcement Officer for the Forest Service in the Southeastern Region, National Forests in South Carolina (1996); Certificate of Commendation for Participation in the Western Fire Season, Governor of Alabama (1989); Certificate of Recognition, Female Forest Service Officer; Service to the Community; Outstanding Young Women of Accomplishments Award (1987); Certificate of Recognition for Work During the 'Siege of 87' Wildfires in the West (1987); Certifications of Merit for Work as a Law Enforcement Officer with the Forest Service; First Woman Patrol Officer on Marijuana Details for the Forest Service in Southeast Kentucky

Expanded Biography: Ms. Sell was honored with numerous awards during her time in law enforcement.

EXECUTIVE OF THE YEAR IN CLINICAL HEALTHCARE

MARTHA J. SHADEL, DO

Medical Director
Bridgeview Family Medicine and Urgent Care
39833 Bridgeview Street
Harrison Township, MI 48045 United States
mshadel@mcrmc.org
http://www.bridgeviewmedicalclinic.org

Type of Business: Medical Center

Major Products and Services: Urgent Care, Family Practice and Occupational Medicine for Routine and Urgent Medical Issues

Marketing Area: Regional

Day to Day Responsibilities: Treating Occupational and Emergency Medicine Injuries along with Practicing Family Medicine and Evaluating Drug Screens

Favorite Business Publications: The Wall Street Journal

Hobbies/Interests/Sports: Painting, Rollerblading, Exercising

Education Degrees: Doctor of Osteopathy, The College of Osteopathic Medicine of the Pacific (Now Western University of Health Sciences) (1988); Bachelor of Science as a Physician Assistant, Western Michigan University (1976); Bachelor of Arts in Sociology, Indiana University (1972)

Certifications: Medical Review Officer Certification, American Association of Medical Review Officers (2005); Board Certified Emergency Medicine Physician; Certificate of Added Qualifications in Occupational Medicine (2006)

Affiliations/Associations/Societies: Michigan Osteopathic Association; American Osteopathic Association; American Osteopathic College of Occupational and Preventive Medicine; American College of Osteopathic Emergency Medicine; Sigma Sigma Phi

What was the highlight of your career? The most gratifying aspect of her career was opening her clinic.

Expanded Biography: Dr. Shadel practiced emergency medicine at St. John Macomb Hospital prior to founding her clinic, and continues to do so.

PROFESSIONAL OF THE YEAR IN LEGAL COMPLIANCE

ROBERT A. SHAPIRO

Director of Corporate Legal Affairs
Casio, Inc.
128 Robinhood Road
Clifton, NJ 07013 United States
bshapiro@casio.com
http://www.casio.com

Type of Business: Manufacturing Company

Major Products and Services: Consumer Electronics

Marketing Area: International

Day to Day Responsibilities: Managing Legal Affairs and Compliance

Favorite Business Publications: Fast Company; Wired; Technology; Business 2.0; Inc.com

Hobbies/Interests/Sports: Photography, Skiing

Education Degrees: Master's Degree in Business and Information Systems, Goddard College (1980); Bachelor of Arts in Biology and Chemistry, Montclair State University, Summa Cum Laude (1972)

Affiliations/Associations/Societies: New Jersey State Policemen's Benevolent Association; National Contract Management Association; Electronic Industries Alliance; Homeland Security Industries Association

Expanded Biography: In his spare time, Mr. Shapiro embarks on public speaking engagements.

PROFESSIONAL OF THE YEAR IN DENTURE FABRICATION

MS. DIANA S. SHELBY, DPD

Owner, Denturist
Dentures 4 U, PLLC
5219 W. Clearwater Avenue, Suite 3
Kennewick, WA 99336 United States
dentures4u@gmail.com
http://www.cambridgewhoswho.com

Type of Business: Dental Clinic

Major Products and Services: Dentures, Partials and Examinations

Marketing Area: Local

Day to Day Responsibilities: Administering Dental Examinations and Evaluations, Producing Dentures and Partials

Favorite Business Publications: Industry-Related Publications

Hobbies/Interests/Sports: Embroidery, Quilting, Participating in Church Activities

Education Degrees: Associate Degree in Dental Technology, Northwest College; Associate Degree in Denturism, Bates Technical College

Affiliations/Associations/Societies: Better Business Bureau; National Denturist Association; National Federation of Independent Businesses

What do you attribute your success to? She attributes her success to her supportive family and excellent mentors.

How did you become involved in your profession? She became involved in her profession because of her interest in dentistry.

What was the highlight of your career? The highlight of her career was establishing her own business.

PROFESSIONAL OF THE YEAR IN HIGHER EDUCATION

DR. CLAIRE V. SIBOLD

Professor, School of Education
Biola University
13800 Biola Avenue
La Mirada, CA 90639 United States
claire.sibold@biola.edu
http://www.biola.edu

Type of Business: Private Christian University

Major Products and Services: Academic Programs, Doctoral Degrees to Bachelors Degrees, In-service and Workshops in Literacy and Children's Literature

Marketing Area: National

Area of Expertise: Dr. Sibold's expertise includes literacy and teacher preparation, elementary and secondary reading methodology, children's literature and comprehensive examination preparation.

Day to Day Responsibilities: Writing Credential Documents for California, Teaching 12 Units

Favorite Business Publications: Journal of Adolescent & Adult Literacy

Hobbies/Interests/Sports: Reading, Swimming, Hiking, Researching

Education Degrees: Ph.D. in Secondary Curriculum with Corollaries in Research and Reading Education, Arizona State University (1984); Master of Arts in Education, with Emphases in Curriculum Development and Literacy, University of Washington (1978); Bachelor of Arts in English, University of Washington (1971)

Affiliations/Associations/Societies: Distinguished Volunteer Service Award from Local School (2000); Orange County Reading Professors' Network (1999); California Reading Initiative (1999); Chairwoman of Two Committees, Biola University; Phi Delta Kappa (1983); International Reading Association (1972); California Reading Association; Who's Who in Education

Charity/Volunteer Work: Volunteer, Animal Rescue Organization

Date of Birth: April 25, 1950   **Place of Birth:** Seattle

Spouse: Jon Cohn   **Children:** Genoa, Bryn

Work History: Professor, Department of Education, Biola University, La Mirada, CA (1987-Present); Editor/Project Director, New Product Development CTB/McGraw-Hill, Monterey, CA (1987-1988); Visiting Assistant Professor, Department of Reading Education, Arizona State University, Tempe, AZ (1986-1987); Adjunct Professor, Department of Secondary Education, Arizona State University, Tempe, AZ (1984-1986); Instructor/Graduate Assistant, Center for Reading Education, Arizona State University, Tempe, AZ (1980-1984); Secondary Teacher, Judson Private School, Scottsdale, AZ (1984-1985); Secondary Teacher and Reading Consultant, Shoreline High School, Seattle, WA (1979-80; 1980-1981); Substitute Teacher, Seattle Public Schools, Seattle, WA (1976-1977); Secondary Teacher, North Kitsap High School, Poulsbo, WA (1971-1972; 1973-1976); Secondary Teacher, South Kitsap High School, Port Orchard, WA (1972-1973); Student Teaching, Nathan Eckstein Junior High School, Seattle, WA (1971)

Expanded Biography: Dr. Sibold does public speaking and is a manuscript reviewer for Houghton Mifflin. She has made presentations at the Oxford Round Table and Pruitt Symposium at Baylor University. She has also presented at international, national and state conferences, and is the author of articles published in professional and Christian journals and books. Dr. Sibold recently published a book on context clues for 'Creative Teaching Press.'

EXECUTIVE OF THE YEAR IN PHILANTHROPY

BRYAN DAVID SISSON, MS, MPH

President
The Antioch Foundation
1133 Kelly Lane
Lewisville, TX 75077 United States
info@CambridgeWhosWho.com
http://www.antiochfoundation.org

Type of Business: Philanthropy

Major Products and Services: Gifts to Support Mission Work, Nonprofit, Anthropology

Marketing Area: International

Area of Expertise: Mr. Sisson's expertise is in communication studies.

Favorite Business Publications: Anthropology Today

Hobbies/Interests/Sports: Singing, Playing a 1918 Wurlitzer Starke Model Harp

Education Degrees: Master of Science in Allied Anthropology, Toulouse School of Graduate Studies; Bachelor of Applied Arts and Sciences, Applied Anthropology and Sociology, University of North Texas

Affiliations/Associations/Societies: American Anthropological Association; Society for Applied Anthropology; General Anthropology; National Association of Student Anthropologists; Division of American Anthropological Association

What do you attribute your success to? He attributes his personal success to his faith.

What was the highlight of your career? He feels his recent travels to Jordan on an expedition, where he found a jar handle in Square E1, which held an inscription from the 11th century B.C., was the highlight of his career. The handle is currently displayed in the Department of Antiquities of Jordan with his name.

Expanded Biography: Mr. Sisson is currently studying cross-cultural communication at the Dallas Christian College.

PROFESSIONAL OF THE YEAR IN DENTISTRY

KAREN E. SKORUPPA-KEY

Dentist
Karen Key, DDS Family Dentistry
1900 Avenue G N.W., Suite A
Childress, TX 79201 United States
drkarenkey@sbcglobal.net
http://www.cambridgewhoswho.com

Type of Business: Private Dental Practice

Major Products and Services: Dental Healthcare Services, Cleanings, General Check-Ups and Compassionate Patient Care

Marketing Area: Local

Area of Expertise: Ms. Skoruppa-Key's expertise includes family dental care and oral hygiene.

Day to Day Responsibilities: Conducting Research for the U.S. Department of Agriculture

Favorite Business Publications: The Journal of the American Dental Association

Hobbies/Interests/Sports: Hiking, Camping, Gardening

Education Degrees: Doctor of Dental Surgery, The University of Texas Health Science Center at San Antonio (2005)

Affiliations/Associations/Societies: Texas Dental Association; American Dental Association

PROFESSIONAL OF THE YEAR IN MUSIC EDUCATION

MARILYNN J. SMILEY

Distinguished Teaching Professor
State University of New York at Oswego
Tyler Hall Music Dept
Route 104
Oswego, NY 13126 United States
smiley@oswego.edu
http://www.oswego.edu

Type of Business: Comprehensive College, One of 13 University Colleges in the 64-Campus SUNY System

Major Products and Services: More than 110 Undergraduate Majors, Minors, Cooperative and Graduate Programs

Marketing Area: Local

Area of Expertise: Ms. Smiley's expertise is in musicology.

Day to Day Responsibilities: Researching Music History, Teaching Courses on Music History, Women in Music and All Periods of Music

Favorite Business Publications: All Journals from the Societies

Hobbies/Interests/Sports: Traveling, Collecting Flutes, Photography

Education Degrees: Ph.D., University of Illinois at Urbana-Champaign; Master's Degree in Music, Northwestern University; Bachelor of Science in Music, Ball State University; Studied Music with Nadia Boulanger

Affiliations/Associations/Societies: Society for American Music; American Musicological Society; American Association of University Women

Expanded Biography: Ms. Smiley has conducted research and published works in Renaissance and American Music. She is currently a historian for New York state.

EXECUTIVE OF THE YEAR IN
PETROLEUM EXPLORATION AND EVALUATION

CONLEY P. SMITH

President
Conley P. Smith Operating Company
1512 Larimer Street, Suite 1000
Denver, CO 80202 United States
cmcnabbsmith@comcast.net
http://www.cambridgewhoswho.com

Type of Business: Energy Firm

Major Products and Services: Oil and Gas Exploration, Development, Acquisitions, Unconventional Projects

Marketing Area: National

Area of Expertise: Mr. Smith's expertise includes oil and gas exploration, property evaluations, oil and gas evaluations, new ventures and explorations.

Favorite Business Publications: American Oil & Gas Reporter; Oil & Gas Investor Journal; Journal of Petroleum Technology; ENP Global Exploration Production

Hobbies/Interests/Sports: Skiing, Reading, Walking

Education Degrees: Master's Degree in Petroleum Engineering, The University of Oklahoma; Bachelor of Science in Petroleum Engineering, Louisiana Technical University

Affiliations/Associations/Societies: Independent Petroleum Association of Mountain States; Independent Petroleum Association of America

Awards/Honors: Wildcatter of the Year Award (1988); Graves Award, The Golden Gate Seminary; Denver Petroleum Man of the Year Award (1989); Rocky Mountain Hall of Fame

Charity/Volunteer Work: International East and West Ministries; The Golden Gate Seminary

What do you attribute your success to? He attributes his success to his hard work and exposure to the lobbying industry.

How did you become involved in your profession? He became involved in his profession after switching from chemical engineering to oil engineering while in college. He felt that working with oil was more fascinating and offered more creative possibilities.

What was the highlight of your career? The most gratifying aspect of his career is being successful in the field.

Expanded Biography: Mr. Smith is affiliated with Stonebridge Energy.

PROFESSIONAL OF THE YEAR IN
NEW ZEALAND PARLIAMENTARY SERVICES

MS. JOAN R. SMITH

Strategic Advisor
Parliamentary Services
Wellington, New Zealand
joansmith@xtra.co.nz
http://www.govt.nz

Type of Business: Administrative and Support Services for the Running of Parliament

Major Products and Services: Offers Members of Parliament Offices, Secretarial and Personal Assistance, Travel Arrangements, Research and Information Services

Marketing Area: Statewide

Day to Day Responsibilities: Assisting the Chief Executive, Offering Advice on Organizational Development, Offering Solutions to Address Functional Gaps and Risk Areas for the Purpose of Ensuring that Objectives and Strategies are Feasible, Managing Business Operations and Development, Offering Care and Support to People of All Ages

Favorite Business Publications: Fortune; Time

Hobbies/Interests/Sports: Jazz, Watching French Movies, Dining with Friends, Attending Orchestras

Education Degrees: Post-Graduate Diploma in Economics, Lincoln University (1970); Bachelor of Science, University of Otago

Affiliations/Associations/Societies: New Zealand Institute of Directors; Former President, Current Treasurer, Institute of Public Administration New Zealand; Fellow of the New Zealand Institute of Management; Trustee, Dowse Foundation

Expanded Biography: Ms. Smith is a public speaker at universities. She has also published a book entitled, 'The Hidden Viruses Within You.'

PROFESSIONAL OF THE YEAR IN EDUCATIONAL LEADERSHIP

VALORIE SMITH WATKINS, M.ED., BA

Principal
Swainsboro Primary School
308 Tiger Trail
Swainsboro, GA 30401 United States
sow12vs@yahoo.com
http://www.emanuel.k12.ga.us/SwainsboroPrimary.cfm?subpage=73829

Type of Business: Education

Major Products and Services: Primary School, Kindergarten through Second Grade

Area of Expertise: Ms. Smith Watkins' expertise is in educational leadership.

Day to Day Responsibilities: Teaching Language Arts and Social Studies to Seventh-Grade Students, Offering Special Education, Working with Mildly and Moderately Intellectually Disabled Students in Grades Six through Eight, Teaching in a Self-Contained Setting, Supervising, Scheduling, Meeting with Parents, Setting Learning Goals

Favorite Business Publications: Educational Leadership Publications

Education Degrees: Master's Degree in Educational Leadership, Georgia College, State University of Georgia (2000); Bachelor's Degree, Pane College, Georgia (1993)

Affiliations/Associations/Societies: Association for Supervision and Curriculum Development; Georgia Educator Association; National Education Association; Delta Sigma Theta

Awards/Honors: Teacher of the Year (1999)

PROFESSIONAL OF THE YEAR IN
FAMILY MEDICINE

JAN SONANDER

Physician
Jan Sonander, MD
11 Doctors Park Drive
Santa Rosa, CA 95405 United States
josmd@sonic.net
http://www.cambridgewhoswho.com

Type of Business: Private Practice

Major Products and Services: Healthcare

Marketing Area: Regional

Area of Expertise: Mr. Sonander's expertise is in family medicine.

Favorite Business Publications: The Economist; Sonoma County Business Publications

Hobbies/Interests/Sports: Sailing, Skiing

Education Degrees: Doctor of Medicine, University of California, Davis; Master of Science, University of California, Davis; Bachelor of Science, University of California, Davis

Certifications: Board Certified Physician, American Board of Family Medicine

Affiliations/Associations/Societies: Former President, Sonoma County Medical Association; California Medical Association; Former Chief of Staff, Chairman of Credentials, Santa Rosa Memorial Hospital; American Academy of Family Physicians

PROFESSIONAL OF THE YEAR IN MICROBIOLOGY

Ms. Coleen Gae Spalsbury, MS, SM (AAM), MT (ASCP)

Clinical Micro Biologist
Long Beach Memorial Medical Center
2801 Atlantic Avenue
Long Beach, CA 90801 United States
info@cambridgewhoswho.com
http://www.memorialcare.org/long_beach

Type of Business: Hospital

Major Products and Services: Diagnostic Clinical Microbiology

Marketing Area: Local

Area of Expertise: Ms. Spalsbury's expertise is in bacteriology mycology.

Hobbies/Interests/Sports: Skiing, Bicycling

Education Degrees: Master of Science in Microbiology, California State University, Long Beach (1972); Medical Technology Trainee, Memorial Medical Center, Long Beach (1962); Bachelor of Science in Microbiology, California State University, Long Beach (1961)

Certifications: Biological Sciences Instructor Credential, California Community Colleges; American Society of Clinical Pathologists Credential; National Registry of Microbiology Credential; Clinical Laboratory Scientist Credential, California Stage Department of Public Health; Credential, National Certification Agency for Medical Laboratory Personnel

Affiliations/Associations/Societies: American Society of Microbiology; Phi Kappa Phi; American Society of Clinical Laboratory Science; American Society of Clinical Chemistry

Date of Birth: April 7, 1938   **Place of Birth:** Powers Lake

What do you attribute your success to? She attributes her success to her natural curiosity.

What was the highlight of your career? The highlight of her career was making a positive change in her work environment.

PROFESSIONAL OF THE YEAR IN PSYCHOLOGICAL ASSESSMENT

CHARLES D. SPIELBERGER, PH.D.

Distinguished Research Professor
and Professor Emeritus
University of South Florida
11313 Carrollwood Drive
Tampa, FL 33618 United States
spielber@cas.usf.edu
http://www.usf.edu

Type of Business: University

Major Products and Services: Higher Education

Marketing Area: International

Area of Expertise: Dr. Spielberger's expertise includes clinical and health psychology, and psychological assessment.

Education Degrees: Research Fellow, The Netherlands Institute for Advanced Study (1979-1980, 1985-1986); Ph.D., The University of Iowa (1954); Master of Arts in Psychology, The University of Iowa (1953); Bachelor of Arts in Psychology, The University of Iowa (1951); Bachelor of Science in Chemistry, Georgia Institute of Technology (1949)

Certifications: Diplomate in Clinical Psychology, American Board of Professional Psychology

Affiliations/Associations/Societies: Council Representative, American Psychological Association (2000-2006); President, International Association for Applied Psychology (1998-2002); Chairman, International Psychology Committee, National Academy of Sciences (1996-2000); Chairman, National Council of Scientific Society Presidents (1996-1997); President, American Psychological Association (1991-1992); National Treasurer, American Psychological Association (1987-1990); Distinguished Practitioner, National Academies of Practice; Fellow, Sigma Xi, The Scientific Research Society; Former President, Society for Personal Assessment; Former President, Society for Test Anxiety Research; Former President, International Council of Psychologists; Former President, Southeastern Psychological Association; Former President, Psi Chi, The National Honor Society in Psychology; Academy of Behavioral Medicine Research; Psychonomic Society; Society for Psychophysiological Research; The New York Academy of Sciences

Awards/Honors: Lifetime Achievement Award, International Stress and Anxiety Research Society (1998); American Psychological Association Award (1993); Society for Personality Assessment Award (1990); Divisions of Clinical, Community and International Psychology Award, Florida Psychological Association (1977, 1988)

Spouse: Carol

What was the highlight of your career? The highlight of his career was being appointed as the president of the American Psychological Association.

Expanded Biography: Dr. Spielberger's research regarding anxiety and anger measures have been translated, adapted and published in many different languages around the world. His State-Trait Anxiety Inventory and State-Trait Anger Expression Inventory have become the standard international measures used in research on those fundamental concepts. His current research focuses on anxiety, curiosity, depression and the experience, expression and control of anger, job stress and stress management, and the effects of stress, emotions and lifestyle factors on the etiology and progression of hypertension, cardiovascular disorders and cancer. His books include 'Anxiety and Behavior,' 'Contributions to General Psychology,' 'Anxiety and Educational Achievement,' 'Anxiety: Current Trends in Theory and Research,' 'Cognitive and Affective Learning Strategies,' 'Police Selection and Evaluation,' 'Understanding Stress and Anxiety,' 'Anxiety in Sports,' 'Cross-Cultural Anxiety,' 'Personality Assessment in America,' 'Test Anxiety: Theory, Assessment and Treatment' and the continuing 17-volume research series on 'Stress and Emotion' with I. Sarason. Dr. Spielberger founded the 'American Journal of Community Psychology' in 1971, serving as its editor for seven years, and currently serving as associate editor of the 'Journal of Occupational Health Psychology' and the 'International Journal of Stress Management.' He was also editor of the LEA series, 'Advances in Personality Assessment,' and two continuing book series, 'Clinical and Community Psychology,' and 'Health Psychology and Behavioral Medicine.'

EXECUTIVE OF THE YEAR IN EMPLOYMENT SERVICES

MR. RAYMOND H. STALLKAMP III

Chief Executive Officer
Careers, Inc.
1946 N. 13th Street
Toledo, OH 43624 United States
careersinc@bex.net
http://www.careersinc.us

Type of Business: Employment Services Company

Major Products and Services: Vocational Rehabilitation

Marketing Area: Regional

Day to Day Responsibilities: Offering Services to Individuals with Employment Barriers

Hobbies/Interests/Sports: Traveling, Flying, Power Boating

Education Degrees: Master's Degree in Organizational Management, Spring Harbor University (2002); Bachelor of Science in Business Administration and Psychology, Lourdes College (1996); Associate Degree in Law Enforcement, Advocacy in Counseling, Police Administration from Terra Community College (1986)

Affiliations/Associations/Societies: Chamber of Commerce; Better Business Bureau, Commission on Accreditation of Rehabilitation Facilities

Charity/Volunteer Work: Lucas County Commissioners Committee for Veterans

Work History: Professor, Terra Community College

Expanded Biography: Mr. Stallkamp served in the U.S. Navy and the Ohio National Guard during the Vietnam War.

PROFESSIONAL OF THE YEAR IN
MILITARY SERVICE IN THE NATIONAL GUARD

Barbara J. Stephens

Chief Warrant Officer (Retired)
United States Army
405 Citrus Circle
Orangewood Estates 63
San Juan, TX 78589 United States
bjscds@prodigy.net
http://www.cambridgewhoswho.com

Type of Business: Government Organization

Major Products and Services: Defense Services

Marketing Area: National

Area of Expertise: Ms. Stephens' expertise is in military finance.

Day to Day Responsibilities: Overseeing Operations, Preparing Written Instruction Manuals, Co-Teaching Classes

Hobbies/Interests/Sports: Cross-Stitching, Golfing

Education Degrees: Associate of Arts in Business, Richland College (1975)

Affiliations/Associations/Societies: United States Warrant Officers Association; Disabled American Veterans; National Guard Association of the United States; The American Legion

Awards/Honors: Meritorious Service Medal; Dual Recipient, Army Commendation Medal; Armed Forces Reserve Medal; Federal Woman of the Year Award, Federal Women's Program

Date of Birth: March 31, 1942   **Place of Birth:** Fort Sam Houston

Spouse: Charles   **Children:** Russell, Dana

Work History: Chief Warrant Officer (1982-1998); Warrant Officer (1982); Sergeant in Personnel Records (1980); Arkansas Army National Guard (1976-1980); Corps of Engineers Regional Officer (1976-1997); Federal Civil Service Agent, Kelly Air Force Base, San Antonio, TX (1965-1976)

What do you attribute your success to? She attributes her success to her faith in God and the values she learned from her parents.

How did you become involved in your profession? She became involved in her profession by joining the Arkansas National Guard.

What was the highlight of your career? The most gratifying aspect of her career is assisting soldiers and their families.

Expanded Biography: Ms. Stephens' full-time job was with the Arkansas Army National Guard in finance. Her military position was in personnel, ensuring that records were correct and up-to-date at all times. Ms. Stephens retired in 1998.

PROFESSIONAL OF THE YEAR IN SPECIAL EDUCATION

Ms. Loretta Marie Stevens, M.Ed.

Supervisor for Special Education
Warren County Public Schools
210 N. Commerce Avenue
Front Royal, VA 22630 United States
LStevens@shentel.net
http://www.wcps.k12.va.us

Type of Business: Education

Major Products and Services: Special Education

Marketing Area: Local

Day to Day Responsibilities: Testing and Diagnosing Students in Special Education Programs

Favorite Business Publications: Learning Disabilities Research

Hobbies/Interests/Sports: Horseback Riding, Breeding and Training Horses, Hiking, Traveling

Education Degrees: Master's Degree in Educational Administration, Shenandoah University; Special Education Degree, James Madison University; Bachelor's Degree in Elementary Education and Psychology, Shenandoah University

Affiliations/Associations/Societies: American Society for Clinical Pathology; Learning Disabilities Association; Council for Exceptional Children; Association for Supervision and Curriculum Development; Virginia Association of Special Education Administrators

Charity/Volunteer Work: Special Olympics, Therapeutic Riding Association

PROFESSIONAL OF THE YEAR IN INFORMATION TECHNOLOGY

MR. MARC L. STIEHR

Senior Director of Network Technology
YMCA of Metropolitan Chicago
801 N. Dearborn Street
Chicago, IL 60610 United States
mstiehr@ymcachgo.org
http://www.ymcachgo.org

Type of Business: Nonprofit Organization

Major Products and Services: Fitness and Wellness Programs, Child Care, Housing and Counseling Services, Job Preparation Training, Recreational Activities, Value-Based Programming

Marketing Area: Regional

Area of Expertise: Mr. Stiehr's expertise includes needs assessment, project planning, hardware and software acquisition, the regulation of departmental policies and procedures, and the evaluation of emerging technologies.

Day to Day Responsibilities: Overseeing Corporate Technology, Establishing Strategies and Ensuring Network Operations, Managing the Technical Help Desk, Voice Communications, Technology Licensing, Systems Security and Wireless Mobile Technologies

Favorite Business Publications: CIO; CIO Insight

Hobbies/Interests/Sports: Singing

Education Degrees: Bachelor of Science in Economics and Urban Planning, The University of Wisconsin Oshkosh

Affiliations/Associations/Societies: Association of Information Technology Professionals

Awards/Honors: Computerworld Smithsonian Award

Spouse: Bari   **Children:** Matthew, Kristin

How did you become involved in your profession? He became involved in his profession because he started his career in the city programming and planning field.

Expanded Biography: Mr. Stiehr has been a vocalist for 16 years for the Spirit of Life Christian singing group and he conducts 16 concerts a year. He has enhanced and implemented wide area network operations by standardizing 700 PCs in 40 locations onto the same platform, standardized the telephone system platform and then implemented a voice-over-IP platform that connects thirty-three locations, and implemented a point-of-sale environment. He has also developed a business continuity plan that includes a disaster recovery data center with real-time backup of transactional data, allowing the main data center to be shut down on weekends.

PROFESSIONAL OF THE YEAR IN
ELEMENTARY EDUCATION

CLARA V. STONE

Fourth-Grade Teacher
Cahokia School District 187
1700 Jerome Lane
Cahokia, IL 62206 United States
clarastone@charter.net
http://www.cahokia.stclair.k12.il.us

Type of Business: Elementary School

Major Products and Services: Education Including Curriculum Development, Reading Program, Arts, Music, Physical Education, Learning Resources, Student Support Services, Athletics, Extracurricular Activities

Marketing Area: Regional

Day to Day Responsibilities: Teaching Reading, Accelerated Reading, Mathematics, Social Studies, English, Spelling and Science

Favorite Business Publications: The Teacher's Guide

Hobbies/Interests/Sports: Fishing, Cooking, Watching Baseball and Football

Education Degrees: Bachelor of Arts in Education, Southern Illinois University Edwardsville, Plus 16 (1978); Associate Degree, Belleville Area College

Affiliations/Associations/Societies: Who's Who Among American Teachers; Former Member, Alpha Delta Kappa

Date of Birth: February 13, 1945   **Place of Birth:** Belleville

Spouse: Michael   **Children:** Michael Jr., Kenneth

Expanded Biography: Ms. Stone previously taught in private schools for 22 years, and worked in a nursing home and a grocery store throughout college.

PROFESSIONAL OF THE YEAR IN
ARCHITECTURE AND INTERIOR DESIGN

NINA STRACHIMIROVA

Principal
Nina Strachi, Architect
31-62 29th Street, Suite 2M
Long Island City, NY 11106 United States
boninaarch@aol.com
http://www.cambridgewhoswho.com

Type of Business: Architecture and Interior Design Company

Major Products and Services: High-Quality Architectural Services

Marketing Area: Regional

Area of Expertise: Ms. Strachimirova's expertise includes architecture and design.

Favorite Business Publications: Architectural and Design Magazines and Books

Hobbies/Interests/Sports: Tennis, Gymnastics, Music, Theater

Education Degrees: Two Master's Degrees in Architecture, Bulgaria and Germany

Affiliations/Associations/Societies: Institute of Classical Architecture and Classical American;
International Union of Architects; International Academy of Architecture

What do you attribute your success to? She attributes her success to her work ethic.

How did you become involved in your profession? She became involved in profession because of her
love for drawing.

PROFESSIONAL OF THE YEAR IN
SPECIAL EDUCATION IN INDIANA

SHERRY A. STROUGH

Learning Disabilities Teacher, Instructor for
Mildly Mentally Handicapped
Indianapolis Public Schools
120 E. Walnut Street
Indianapolis, IN 46204 United States
sstrough@sbcglobal.net
http://www.cambridgewhoswho.com

Type of Business: School District

Major Products and Services: Education for Learning Disabled and Mentally Handicapped Students

Marketing Area: Local

Day to Day Responsibilities: Supervising and Directing Classes, Preparing Lesson Plans, Coordinating Special Education Programs, Teaching Learning Disabled and Mildly Mentally Handicapped Students

Favorite Business Publications: Industry-Related Publications

Hobbies/Interests/Sports: Traveling, Scrapbooking

Education Degrees: Master's Degree in Special Education, Indiana University; Bachelor's Degree in Elementary Education, University of Indianapolis

Affiliations/Associations/Societies: Learning Disabilities Association of America

Awards/Honors: ABCD Award for Outstanding Performance, Indianapolis Public Schools; Who's Who Among America's Teachers (2004-2006)

Expanded Biography: Ms. Strough has been featured twice in 'American Teacher,' a newspaper offering coverage on a wide range of activities of educators.

PROFESSIONAL OF THE YEAR IN GUIDANCE COUNSELING

MR. WILLIAM T. SUMEREL, M.ED., GCDF

School Counselor
Riverside High School, Guidance Department
Greenville County School District
794 Hammett Bridge Road
Greer, SC 29650 United States
wsumerel@greenville.k12.sc.us
wsumerel@charter.net
http://www.greenville.k12.sc.us/rsidehs/index.htm

Type of Business: School District

Major Products and Services: General Secondary Curriculum including Arts, Music, Physical Education, Language Arts, Special Programs, Learning Resources, Support Services, Athletics, Extracurricular Activities, Student Clubs and Organizations

Marketing Area: Regional

Area of Expertise: Mr. Sumerel's expertise includes student support services, career development and counseling.

Day to Day Responsibilities: Instructing, Inspiring and Preparing Students

Favorite Business Publications: School Counselor; Industry-Related Publications

Hobbies/Interests/Sports: Spending Time with his Two Children and Wife, Spending Time at the Beach, Reading

Education Degrees: Master's Degree in Guidance and Counseling, Clemson University (2007); Bachelor's Degree in Business Administration, University of South Carolina (1992)

Certifications: National Certification in Global Career Development

Affiliations/Associations/Societies: Southeastern Employment and Training Association, Inc.; South Carolina School Counselor Association; American School Counselor Association; American Counseling Association

Awards/Honors: High Performer Program Award; Outstanding Specialist Award; Awards, Jobs for South Carolina Graduates; Award, Jobs for America's Graduates

Charity/Volunteer Work: Knights of Columbus

Date of Birth: July 30, 1969   **Place of Birth:** Lawton

Spouse: Jennifer   **Children:** Elizabeth, Donald

Work History: Job Specialist, Chesnee High School, Spartanburg District; Customer Service Manager, Retention Specialist, Senior Workforce Specialist, Upstate Workforce Development Board, Spartanburg County Government; Job Coordinator, ACHIEVE Program, University of South Carolina Upstate; School-To-Work Coordinator, Boiling Springs High School, Spartanburg District

What do you attribute your success to? He attributes his success to his education, business contacts and the support he receives from his family and friends.

How did you become involved in your profession? He became involved in his profession after working as a school-to-work coordinator at a local high school but realized that his calling was to assist young people with career and personal decisions, academics and overall life success.

What was the highlight of your career? The most gratifying aspects of his career are seeing the progress made by young people in their academic and career choices and assisting his students with their decisions and offering them the most up-to-date information that is available.

Where will you be in five years? In five years, Mr. Sumerel hopes to continue to work as a school counselor, assisting students with the best services possible to enable them to be successful in the future.

Expanded Biography: Mr. Sumerel works as a job specialist, counseling 'at-risk' students in a high school setting in the South Carolina graduate program for all four years of high school. He assisted with the implementation of this program. He utilizes a classroom setting, teaching employability, workplace and life skills. In addition, he works with students individually, covering academic, personal and social problems as they come about in their lives. He also offers academic assistance tools for students and parents to use while working with teachers for academic success inside and outside the classroom. He also assists other members of the counseling staff with testing, classroom guidance, student registration, promoting the academic success of the school and offering administrative assistance in the overall operation of the school. He assists and prepares them for a bright and rewarding career and life.

EXECUTIVE OF THE YEAR IN
QUALITY ASSURANCE IN MANUFACTURING

SUSAN SUTHERLAND

Vice President of Quality Assurance
OSI Optoelectronics
12525 Chadron Avenue
Hawthorne, CA 90250 United States
ssutherland@osioptoelectronics.com
http://www.udt.com

Type of Business: Engineering and Manufacturing Company

Major Products and Services: Silicon Photodiodes, Standard and Custom Photodiodes, Opto-Assembly, X-ray Products, Medical Products, Telecommunications and Datacommunications Applications, Military and Aerospace Specialties, Tool and Die Injection Molding, Book Mold and Prototyping, Production Tooling and Machining, Plastic and Metal Components, Precision Laser Trimming, Heat Staking and Ultrasonic Welding, Custom Tooling, Computer Peripherals and Medical Electronics

Marketing Area: International

Day to Day Responsibilities: Ensuring Quality

Favorite Business Publications: More

Hobbies/Interests/Sports: Exercising, Practicing Yoga

Education Degrees: Coursework in Quality Management, University of Phoenix (1991); Associate Degree in Urban Planning, University of Southampton (1965)

Affiliations/Associations/Societies: American Society for Quality

What do you attribute your success to? She attributes her success to using common sense.

How did you become involved in your profession? She became involved in her profession through a natural progression of opportunities.

What was the highlight of your career? The highlight of her career was being included in the American Biographical Institute.

PROFESSIONAL OF THE YEAR IN
DANCE COMPETITION WEAR

MELISSA SWEITZER

CEO
Best Ballroom Shoes
6 Mendonshire Drive
Honeoye Falls, NY 14472 United States
info@bestballroomshoes.com
http://www.bestballroomshoes.com

Type of Business: Retailer of High-Quality Ballroom Dance Shoes with Custom Shoe Service which Allows the Customer to Design their Dream Shoe, Popular with Bridal Parties

Major Products and Services: High-Quality and Affordable Ballroom Dance Shoes for Men, Women and Children, Custom Shoe Service Allows the Customer to Pick Style, Color, Heel and Size from Hundreds of Styles, Over 100 Materials and 11 Heels, Custom Line is Very Attractive for Theatrical Groups, Brides, Bridal Parties, Proms and Other Special Occasions

Marketing Area: International

Area of Expertise: Ms. Sweitzer's expertise includes ballroom dancing and the engineering of dance footwear.

Day to Day Responsibilities: Consulting with Dancers Regarding Specific Needs Based on Foot Issues, Dancing Style and Experience Level

Favorite Business Publications: Mechanical Design Journal

Hobbies/Interests/Sports: Ballroom and Latin Dancing, Skiing, Rollerblading, Biking, Gardening, Gourmet Cooking

Education Degrees: Master of Science in Engineering Management, National Technological University (1984); Master of Science in Mechanical Engineering, Syracuse University (1985); Bachelor of Science in Mechanical Engineering, Clarkson College (1983)

Certifications: Licensed Professional Engineer (1990)

Affiliations/Associations/Societies: Sigma Xi Honorary Society for Scientific Researchers (1984); American Society of Mechanical Engineers; U.S. American Amateur; U.S. Dance

Awards/Honors: Best Solo Routine Award, Arthur Murray Competition, Buffalo, NY (2001)

Expanded Biography: Ms. Sweitzer is involved with engineering the Chandra X-Ray Observatory Project for NASA through Eastman Kodak.

PROFESSIONAL OF THE YEAR IN FAMILY MEDICINE

PHIL H. SYNAR, MD

Medical Doctor
2260 Lower Waterfall Road
Grove, OK 74344 United States
phil.synar@cwwemail.com
http://www.cambridgewhoswho.com

Type of Business: Healthcare Center

Major Products and Services: Healthcare

Marketing Area: Regional

Day to Day Responsibilities: Practicing Family and Emergency Medicine in the Emergency Room, Contracting

Education Degrees: Doctor of Medicine, Tulane University, New Orleans (1976)

Affiliations/Associations/Societies: Fellow, American Academy of Family Physicians

Work History: Adjunct Faculty, Oklahoma University

Where will you be in five years? In five years, Dr. Synar hopes to teach and train medical students and residents.

PROFESSIONAL OF THE YEAR IN HOSPICE NURSING

SUSAN C. TALLEY

Patient Care Manager
Vista Care Hospice
st1951@grandecom.net
http://www.cambridgewhoswho.com

Type of Business: Hospice Center

Major Products and Services: Hospice Care

Marketing Area: National

Area of Expertise: Ms. Talley's expertise includes obstetric nursing, end of life care and hospice services.

Favorite Business Publications: National Hospice Journal

Hobbies/Interests/Sports: Reading, Crocheting, Making Jewelry, Riding her Motorcycle

Education Degrees: Pursuing Master of Science in Nursing; Associate Degree in Nursing, McLennan Community College

Certifications: Pursuing Registered Nurse

Affiliations/Associations/Societies: Texas New Mexico Hospice Association; National Hospice Association

Charity/Volunteer Work: Toys for Tots Foundation; American Heart Association; American Cancer Society

Spouse: Richard   **Children:** Angela, Jessica, Jennifer, Christopher

What do you attribute your success to? She attributes her success to her flexibility and desire to help others.

How did you become involved in your profession? She became involved in her profession because she wanted to help families get through difficult times with their loved ones.

What was the highlight of your career? The highlight of her career was earning her current position.

PROFESSIONAL OF THE YEAR IN
VISITOR SERVICES

MS. WENDY L. TATAROUNS

Assistant Manager of Visitor Services
Museum of Science
1 Science Park
Boston, MA 02114 United States
wtatarouns@hotmail.com
http://www.mos.org

Type of Business: Science Museum

Major Products and Services: Exhibits, Shows, Events and Activities Including Earth and Space Science, Science and Technology, Life Sciences and the Natural World

Marketing Area: Regional

Day to Day Responsibilities: Ensuring Visitor Satisfaction by Offering the Best Experience and Service Possible, Responding to Written Complaints, Maintaining Strong Customer Service, Managing Six Supervisors and a Staff of 100 Employees

Hobbies/Interests/Sports: Playing Ice Hockey and Softball, Jet-Skiing, Traveling

Education Degrees: Bachelor of Science in Sociology, The University of New Hampshire (1995)

Awards/Honors: Merit Award, International Society of Photographers

Date of Birth: November 20, 1972   **Place of Birth:** Woburn

Work History: House Manager, AMC Loews Boston Common 19, Loews Cineplex Entertainment Corporation

PROFESSIONAL OF THE YEAR IN
WELFARE AND HEALTH BENEFITS ADMINISTRATION

MR. PATRICK F. TEDALDI

Administrative Manager
Office of Labor Relations
City of New York
40 Rector Street, Third Floor
New York, NY 10006 United States
ptedaldi@olr.nyc.gov
http://www.cambridgewhoswho.com

Type of Business: City Government Agency

Major Products and Services: Welfare and Health Benefits

Marketing Area: Local

Day to Day Responsibilities: Utilizing his Extensive Government Background, Addressing Complaints, Performing Emergency Work, Managing Health and Welfare Fund Benefits

Favorite Business Publications: Journal of Accountancy

Hobbies/Interests/Sports: Bowling, Watching Sports

Education Degrees: Master of Science in Industrial Relations, Pace University (1982); Master of Science in Taxation, Iona College (1978); Master of Business Administration, Iona College (1976); Bachelor of Science in Business Administration, Manhattan College (1973); Diploma, Cardinal Spellman High School (1963)

Affiliations/Associations/Societies: President, New York City Catholic Alumni Club (2005-2007); Cardinal Spellman High School Alumni Association (2005)

Date of Birth: October 10, 1944   **Place of Birth:** New York

Spouse: Reisha

Work History: Office of Labor Relations, City of New York (1971-Present); H&R Block (1982-1983); New York Police Department (1969-1971); First National City Bank (1963-1969)

Expanded Biography: Mr. Tedaldi began his career at First National City Bank on July 22, 1963. He worked for their tax department at 399 Park Avenue in New York City for several years. This was interrupted by military services from 1965-1967. Upon returning from military service, he was assigned to 55 Wall Street and worked in bond services for about two years. There, he dealt with government municipal securities. After taking the Civil Service Exam for a police administration aide, he was selected in October 1969 to work as a civilian in the New York Police Department. In December 1971, he left the police department to work in the department of labor relations. He deals with health and welfare fund benefits.

PROFESSIONAL OF THE YEAR IN PEDIATRIC ENDOCRINOLOGY

SVETLANA TEN, MD

Pediatrician
Infants and Children's Hospital of Brooklyn at Maimonides Hospital
977 48th Street
Brooklyn, NY 11219 United States
tenlanna@aol.com
http://www.maimonidesmed.org

Type of Business: Nonprofit Hospital

Major Products and Services: Pediatric Endocrinology, Anesthesiology, Blood Donation Center, Cancer/Oncology, Critical Care, Dental, Dermatology, Ear, Nose and Throat Treatment, Otolaryngology, Emergency Medicine, Endocrinology and Metabolism, Gastroenterology, Geriatrics, Intensive Care Services, International Patient Services, Mature Woman's Program, Medical Genetics, Geriatrics

Marketing Area: Regional

Day to Day Responsibilities: Treating Patients with Diabetes, Thyroid and Endocrine Disorders, Managing Academic Activities, Overseeing Direct Supervision of Medical Residents, Developing Academic Programs for the College Hospital

Hobbies/Interests/Sports: Swimming, Biking, Listening to Music, Reading Russian Novels

Education Degrees: Fellowship in Pediatric Endocrinology, Cornell University (2002); Fellowship in Pediatric Endocrinology, Akita, Japan (1992-1993); Fellowship in Pediatric Endocrinology, Moscow State University (1989); Doctor of Medicine, Belarus-Minsk Medical University (1984)

Affiliations/Associations/Societies: Fellow, American Academy of Pediatrics; Lawson Wilkins Pediatric Endocrine Society; American Association of Clinical Endocrinologists; American Medical Association; Richmond County Medical Society; Fellowship Program Director, SUNY Downstate Medical Center

Expanded Biography: Dr. Ten speaks at Grand Rounds and makes presentations for pediatricians nationally and internationally. Her research and expert knowledge has been featured in more than 20 articles and publications.

PROFESSIONAL OF THE YEAR IN EDUCATIONAL LEADERSHIP

MARILUPE MIER Y TERÀN

Principal
Saint John of the Cross School
8175 Lemon Grove Way
Lemon Grove, CA 91945 United States
smarilup@stjohncross.org
http://www.stjohncross.org

Type of Business: School

Major Products and Services: Education

Marketing Area: Regional

Area of Expertise: Ms. Teràn's expertise includes administration, curriculum development and operations management.

Hobbies/Interests/Sports: Swimming, Reading

Education Degrees: Master's Degree in Theology, Corpus Christi State University; Master's Degree in Education, La Salle University, Mexico

Affiliations/Associations/Societies: Council of Christian Scholarly Societies; Association for Supervision and Curriculum Development; National Catholic Educational Association

PROFESSIONAL OF THE YEAR IN MUSICAL PERFORMANCE

WANDA G. THERIAC

Manager
The Chesterfield Quartet
51 Orange Hills Drive
Chesterfield, MO 63017 United States
wtmus@sbcglobal.net
http://www.chesterfieldquartet.com

Type of Business: Entertainment Firm

Major Products and Services: String Music

Marketing Area: Regional

Day to Day Responsibilities: Consulting with Clients in Order to Meet their Expectations, Overseeing Administrative Duties, Performing with a String Quartet with a Repertoire of More than 775 Tunes, Managing Private String Instruments

Favorite Business Publications: Chamber Music

Hobbies/Interests/Sports: Listening to Music, Spending Time with her Grandchildren, Playing Musical Instruments

Education Degrees: Master's Degree, Eastman School of Music (1948); Bachelor's Degree in Music Performance, Central Methodist University (1947)

Affiliations/Associations/Societies: American String Teachers Association

How did you become involved in your profession? She became involved in her profession because it was her family business.

What was the highlight of your career? The most gratifying aspect of her career is working in an industry that she was always interested in.

Expanded Biography: Ms. Theriac was a public school orchestra director for 28 years and is a former public school music teacher. She started attending violin classes at the age of four.

PROFESSIONAL OF THE YEAR IN MISSOURI REAL ESTATE

JANICE N. THOMAS

Realtor
Realty Executives West County
1795 Clarkson Road, Suite 150
Chesterfield, MO 63017 United States
connectwithjan@charter.net
http://www.janthomas.net

Type of Business: Real Estate

Major Products and Services: Executive-Level Real Estate Services

Marketing Area: International

Day to Day Responsibilities: Working with Buyers and Sellers

Favorite Business Publications: St. Louis Business Journal

Hobbies/Interests/Sports: Book Club, Singing, Traveling, Writing

Education Degrees: Bachelor of Science in Education, Mississippi College, Clinton, MS

Affiliations/Associations/Societies: Local Chapter President, Women's Council of Realtors (2006); Local Chapter Secretary, Women's Council of Realtors (2005); St. Louis Association of Realtors; Missouri Association of Realtors; National Association of Realtors; Business Network International; Marketing Coordinator, West Chapter Business Connection; St. Louis Metro Singers; St. Louis Food Bank; Professional Women's Advisory Board Member, American Biographical Institute

Awards/Honors: Excel Award, Metropolitan St. Louis Chapter, Women's Council of Realtors (2006)

Charity/Volunteer Work: Susan G. Komen Breast Cancer Foundation; American Red Cross; Habitat for Humanity International

PROFESSIONAL OF THE YEAR IN JUVENILE CORRECTIONS

MR. BEAUFORD THOMPSON

Consultant
Jeffrey C. Wardle Academy
1100 Slater Road
Wheatland, WY 82201 United States
beauf@wyomail.com
http://www.fcs-inc.net

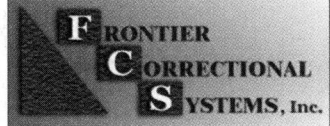

Type of Business: Juvenile Correctional Facility

Major Products and Services: Secured Facility Serving the State and the Community, Education, Treatment Programs, Rehabilitation, Alternative Supervision Programs, Security

Marketing Area: Regional

Day to Day Responsibilities: Directing All Educational Programs, Overseeing the Day Treatment Program

Favorite Business Publications: Education Leadership; ASCD Journal; Phi Delta Kappan

Hobbies/Interests/Sports: Studying Technology, Using Computers

Education Degrees: Master of Education in Administration of Education, University of Wyoming (1972); Bachelor's Degree in Instruction, University of Wyoming (1964)

Affiliations/Associations/Societies: Phi Delta Kappa International; Council for Exceptional Children; Association for Supervision and Curriculum Development; Cheyenne Teachers Education Association; Wyoming Education Association, Regional Board of Directors; Instructor, Educational Courses, Business Courses, Preston University; Adjunct Instructor, University of Wyoming; Wyoming Grape Growers Association; Minnesota Grape Growers Association

Awards/Honors: Teacher of the Year; Scholarship, University of Wyoming (1960)

Charity/Volunteer Work: Local Charities and Community Efforts

Place of Birth: Branson

Spouse: Starley   **Children:** Danae, Richard

Work History: Education Consultant (2003-2007); Director of Education, Jeffrey C. Wardle Academy (2002-2007); Classroom Teacher, Cheyenne, WY (1967-2002); Classroom Teacher, Lusk, WY (1964-1967); Technology Staff Trainer, Laramie County School District 1

What do you attribute your success to? He attributes his success to his devotion to the improvement of society through education of youth, and the improvement of interaction and teaching processes.

What was the highlight of your career? The highlight of his career was being honored by his colleagues as Teacher of the Year in 1995-1996.

Expanded Biography: Mr. Thompson's research and expert knowledge has been published in several articles, and he has received numerous awards and honors. He is retired and living on a ranch in rural Wyoming, where he is experimenting with wine grapes. Mr. Thompson is affiliated with Swan Hill Vineyards. He is testing which grape varieties can withstand harsher climates. He serves on community boards and organizations that offer services, and focuses on the heritage of the community. He was instrumental in changing science education for middle and elementary schools in Wyoming, and assisted in the development of technology programs for classroom use. He also published the 'Sounding Board,' a newsletter for institution schools in Wyoming.

PROFESSIONAL OF THE YEAR IN
PHYSICAL THERAPY AND REHABILITATION FOR THE ELDERLY

MS. JULIE A. THOMPSON, PT

Physical Therapist, Director of Rehabilitation
Hallmark Rehabilitation, Inc., Autumn Winds Retirement Lodge
2453 Grove Park
Schertz, TX 78154 United States
jthompson930@satx.rr.com
http://www.cambridgewhoswho.com

Type of Business: Physical Rehabilitation Clinic

Major Products and Services: Occupational, Physical and Speech Therapy Services for the Elderly

Marketing Area: Regional

Area of Expertise: Ms. Thompson's expertise is in physical therapy.

Day to Day Responsibilities: Overseeing Program Development, Managing a Multidisciplinary Staff, Finances and Equipment, Coordinating with Facility Staff, Evaluating and Treating Patients, Administering Neurological and Orthopedic Therapy, Managing Wound Care Issues, Educating Patients and Staff

Favorite Business Publications: PTmagazine

Hobbies/Interests/Sports: Photography, Scrapbooking, Exercising, Swimming, Reading

Education Degrees: Pursuing Doctoral Degree, Hardin-Simmons University; Bachelor of Science in Physical Therapy, University of Puget Sound (1981); Industry-Related Training, Neuro-Developmental Treatment Association

Affiliations/Associations/Societies: Texas Physical Therapy Association; American Physical Therapy Association; Physical Therapy Association of Washington; Texas Physical Therapy Education and Research Foundation; United States Army, European Command; International Weightlifting Association; Neuro-Developmental Treatment Association

Awards/Honors: On-the-Spot Cash Special Act Award Recipient; Hallmark Award for Excellence in Customer Relations

PROFESSIONAL OF THE YEAR IN
HIGHER EDUCATION ADMINISTRATION

JOSEFINA VILLAMIL TINAJERO, ED.D.

Dean
College of Education
The University of Texas at El Paso
500 W. University Avenue
El Paso, TX 79902 United States
tinajero@utep.edu
http://www.utep.edu

THE UNIVERSITY OF TEXAS AT EL PASO

Type of Business: University

Major Products and Services: Education

Marketing Area: Local

Area of Expertise: Dr. Tinajero's expertise is in college administration.

Day to Day Responsibilities: Overseeing the Management of the College, Budgeting, Planning Curriculum, Participating in Teacher Education, Lecturing

Favorite Business Publications: Research; Industry-Related Publications

Hobbies/Interests/Sports: Decorating, Gardening

Education Degrees: Doctor of Education, Texas A&M University (1980); Master's Degree in Education, Supervision and Administration, The University of Texas at El Paso (1976); Bachelor's Degree in Education and Reading, The University of Texas at El Paso (1973)

Affiliations/Associations/Societies: Board of Directors, American Association of Colleges for Teacher Education; Board of Directors, National Association for Bilingual Education; Governing Board Member, National Network for Educational Renewal

Awards/Honors: 80 Most Influential Hispanics in the United States, Hispanic Business Magazine (2005); Texas Professor of the Year, Carnegie Foundation for the Advancement of Teaching and the Council for the Advancement and Support of Education (2002); Outstanding United States Bilingual Educator, Education Ministry of Spain (2002); Chancellor's Council Award for Teaching Excellence, UT System/UTEP; REACH Award; Maestro TESOL Award; Diamond Jubilee Gem Award for Outstanding Service, UTEP; Orgullo Hispano for Outstanding Service as Role Model to Hispanics; Outstanding Educator Award, LULAC Council 335; Outstanding Service to the Community, Hispanic and Business Alliance for Education; Inductee, El Paso Women's Hall of Fame; Star Award, Mother-Daughter Program, Texas Higher Education; Multicultural Educator Award, National Association for Multicultural Education

Expanded Biography: Dr. Tinajero has published seven books and 50 articles.

PROFESSIONAL OF THE YEAR IN PHYSICAL THERAPY

Ms. Mary Darlene Tom, BS, PT

Owner, Manager
Island Wide Physical Therapy, LLC
1001 Dillingham Boulevard
Room 203
Honolulu, HI 96817 United States
dtom@hawaii.rr.com
http://www.cambridgewhoswho.com

Type of Business: Physical and Massage Therapy Center

Major Products and Services: Physical Therapy for Treatment of Personal and Work-Related Injuries

Marketing Area: International

Area of Expertise: Ms. Tom's expertise includes deep tissue massage, myofascial release and sports therapy reflexology.

Day to Day Responsibilities: Performing Manual Mobilization, Hydrotherapy and Manipulation Massage Therapy

Hobbies/Interests/Sports: Traveling, Ballroom Dancing, Watching Movies, Fine Dining, Playing the Guitar, Singing

Education Degrees: Bachelor's Degree in Physical Therapy, University of Perpetual Help, Philippines

Certifications: Board Certified in Physical Therapy; Board Certified in Massage Therapy

Affiliations/Associations/Societies: Hawaii State Sheriff Association; Batch 82 Group Foundation, Philippines

Charity/Volunteer Work: Aloha Medical Mission to the Philippines

Spouse: Raymond   **Children:** Alexis

Work History: Physical Therapy Clinic (1993-Present)

What do you attribute your success to? She attributes her success to her dedication to quality service.

How did you become involved in your profession? She became involved in her profession because she enjoys making others feel better.

What was the highlight of your career? The most gratifying aspect of her career was building her entire business on referrals from clients.

Where will you be in five years? In five years, Ms. Tom plans to retire.

PROFESSIONAL OF THE YEAR IN
PROJECT MANAGEMENT IN THE HOSPITALITY INDUSTRY

MR. BYRON G. TRAFTON

Project Manager, PMP
Marriott International
10400 Fernwood Road
Dept. 51/954.61
Bethesda, MD 20817 United States
byron.trafton@marriott.com
http://www.marriott.com

Type of Business: Leading Worldwide Hospitality Company with Nearly 2,800 Lodging Properties Located in the United States, and 66 other Countries and Territories

Major Products and Services: Accommodations, Vacation Packages, Timeshares, Corporate Incentives, Meeting and Conference Spaces, Wedding Receptions and Events, Rewards Program

Marketing Area: International

Day to Day Responsibilities: Directing and Implementing All New Software, Hardware and Rollouts, Global Field Services to Properties, Implementing Project Rollout for All Departments, Individualizing Reservations, Human Resources, Accounting, Purchasing, Training Staff, Lecturing, Training and Educating Using New Properties

Hobbies/Interests/Sports: Videography, Local Bird Expert

Education Degrees: Bachelor's Degree in Hotel Administration, Washington State University (1976)

Certifications: Nationally Certified Project Management Professional (2003)

Work History: Senior Assistant Manager, Westin Hotels; Front Office Manager, Mauna Kea Beach Hotel

PROFESSIONAL OF THE YEAR IN EDUCATIONAL ADMINISTRATION

KAREN A. TRIMBOLI, CAGS, M.ED.

Principal
Ludlow Elementary School, PreK-6
45 Main Street
Ludlow, VT 05149 United States
trimboli@ludlowelementary.org
http://www.ludlowelementary.org

Ludlow Elementary School

Type of Business: Education

Major Products and Services: Elementary Education

Marketing Area: Local

Area of Expertise: Ms. Trimboli's expertise includes leadership, assessment, and curriculum development.

Favorite Business Publications: ASCD Journal

Hobbies/Interests/Sports: Golfing, Playing the Guitar, Kayaking, Cross Country Skiing, Snow Shoeing, Spending Time with her Family and Friends, Traveling, History

Education Degrees: CAGS, Administration, Castleton State College; Master of Education Degree in Special Education, College of St. Joseph; Bachelor of Science in Elementary Education, College of St. Joseph

Affiliations/Associations/Societies: Vermont Principals Association; National Elementary School Principals Association; Association for Supervision and Curriculum Development; Regional Standards Board for Administration

Charity/Volunteer Work: United Way of America; Volunteer, Various Local Community Organizations

Work History: Adjunct Professor, Castleton State College

What do you attribute your success to? She attributes her success to her communication skills, and senses of humor and fairness.

How did you become involved in your profession? She became involved in her career because she had worked as a substitute teacher while her children were in school and decided it was something she wanted to further pursue.

What was the highlight of your career? The highlight of her career was helping a difficult class to succeed.

ENTREPRENEUR OF THE YEAR IN TRUCKING TRANSPORT SERVICES

Mr. James A. Troyer

Owner
J.T. Trucking
1025 Seldenright Road
Sugarcreek, OH 44681 United States
troyerjimbo@cs.com
http://www.cambridgewhoswho.com

Type of Business: Transportation Service Company

Major Products and Services: Trucking Services, Dump Trucks, Flatbed Trucks

Marketing Area: Ohio

Day to Day Responsibilities: Overseeing the Business Operations of the Entire Transportation Company

Favorite Business Publications: INK.Com

Affiliations/Associations/Societies: Better Business Bureau

Date of Birth: October 20, 1972

Place of Birth: Dover

PROFESSIONAL OF THE YEAR IN
NURSING MIDWIFERY

Eileen Twidt, RN, CNM, SRN, CNM

Nurse Midwife
Department of Obstetrics and Gynecology
Kaiser Permanente
43112 15th Street W.
Lancaster, CA 93534 United States
etwidt@msn.com
http://www.kp.org

Type of Business: Nonprofit Healthcare Organization

Major Products and Services: Healthcare, Preventive Medicine, Prenatal Care and Immunizations, Emergency Medicine, Screening and Diagnostic Tests, Pharmacy Care Services

Marketing Area: Regional

Area of Expertise: Ms. Twidt's expertise is in nursing.

Day to Day Responsibilities: Educating Patients, Assisting with Labor and Deliveries, Overseeing Clinical Operations, Conducting Breast Examinations

Hobbies/Interests/Sports: Golfing, Reading

Education Degrees: Nursing Degree in Midwifery, Newcastle University, United Kingdom (1977)

Certifications: Registered Nurse, Northumberland School of Nursing, United Kingdom (1975)

Date of Birth: June 17, 1948   **Place of Birth:** Wallsend

What was the highlight of your career? The highlights of her career were opening a hospital in Saudi Arabia and delivering over 16,000 babies around the world.

Expanded Biography: Ms. Twidt has practiced midwifery around the world including the United Kingdom, United States, Saudi Arabia and Abu Dhabi. She has taught many young doctors the art of midwifery, helping to close the gap between midwives and doctors.

PROFESSIONAL OF THE YEAR IN NURSING

EVALENA T. UNFRIED, RN

Staff Nurse, Registered Nurse
Mt. Vernon Countryside Manor
606 E. IL Highway 15
Mount Vernon, IL 62864 United States
evalena.unfried@cwwemail.com
http://www.mtvernoncountrysidemanor.com

Type of Business: Healthcare Center

Major Products and Services: Healthcare from Gestation through Geriatrics Care

Marketing Area: Local

Area of Expertise: Ms. Unfried's expertise is in nursing.

Favorite Business Publications: RN; Nursing2009; The Ladies' Home Journal

Hobbies/Interests/Sports: Spending Time with her Family, Reading, Listening to Music, Playing Basketball, Bicycling, Walking

Education Degrees: Associate Degree in Nursing, Rend Lake College (1982)

Certifications: Licensed Practical Nurse, Rend Lake College; Registered Nurse

Charity/Volunteer Work: St. Clements Catholic Church

Date of Birth: October 11, 1943   **Children:** Teresa, Rikki, Coty, Desireé, Hunter, Chance

Work History: Registered Nurse (1982-2008); Licensed Practical Nurse (1975-1982); Nurse's Aide (1972-1975); Dental Assistant (1968-1971); Teacher, First to 12th-Grade Students, McLeansboro School

Expanded Biography: Ms. Unfried has worked in the medical field for about 40 years as a dental assistant, licensed practical nurse and registered nurse. She has also served in the U.S. Army as a veteran.

Patricia L. Vachon, MS, BA

Production Planning Manager
Raytheon Company
350 Lowell Street
Andover, MA 01810 United States
patricia_l_vachon@raytheon.com
http://www.raytheon.com

Type of Business: Manufacturing Company

Major Products and Services: State of the Art Electronic Devices Including Missile Systems, Radars, and Satellite Communications Systems as well as a Broad Range of Mission Support Services

Marketing Area: International

Day to Day Responsibilities: Managing Logistics, Inventory and JMRP Planning

Favorite Business Publications: Purchasing

Hobbies/Interests/Sports: Reading, Sewing

Education Degrees: Master's Degree in Supply Chain Management, University of San Diego (2004); Bachelor's Degree in Business Administration, Emmanuel College, Boston (2000)

Certifications: Certification, American Production and Inventory Control Society; Certified Supplied Chain Manager

Charity/Volunteer Work: Volunteer, House of Hope; McNeill Pediatric Aids Foundation

Expanded Biography: Ms. Vachon was featured in the 'Society of Manufacturing Engineers' publication in 2004.

PROFESSIONAL OF THE YEAR IN
MEDICAL RESEARCH AND EDUCATION

RICHARD D. VEENSTRA, PH.D.

Professor
Department of Pharmacology
SUNY Upstate Medical University
750 E. Adams Street
Syracuse, NY 13210 United States
veenstrr@upstate.edu
http://www.upstate.edu

Type of Business: University

Major Products and Services: Higher Education

Marketing Area: International

Day to Day Responsibilities: Researching on Cardiovascular Electrophysiology, Ion Channels and Gap Junctions

Favorite Business Publications: Biophysical Journal; The Journal of Physiology; Circulation Research; American Journal of Physiology; Cardiovascular Research

Hobbies/Interests/Sports: Running, Riding his Bicycle, Cross Country Skiing, Sports, Attending the Theater, Watching Movies

Education Degrees: Ph.D. in Physiology and Biophysics, The University of Iowa (1983); Bachelor's Degree in Zoology, Iowa State University (1977)

Affiliations/Associations/Societies: Hamilton White Society; Biophysical Society; Society of General Physiologists; Iroquois Chapter, Sierra Club Earth Day Cleanup; The American Physiological Society; League of American Bicyclists; The American Society for Cell Biology

Awards/Honors: Finalist, Louis N. Katz Basic Science Research Prize for Young Investigators, American Heart Association (1986)

Charity/Volunteer Work: Executive Board, Onondaga Cycling Club; Nature Conservancy; American Heart Association; League of American Bicyclists; United Way of America; World Wildlife Fund

Date of Birth: June 2, 1955   **Place of Birth:** Des Moines

Work History: Associate Professor, Department of Pharmacology, SUNY Upstate Medical University (1992-2006); Assistant Professor, SUNY Upstate Medical University (1986-1992); Research Associate, Department of Anatomy and Cell Biology, Emory University School of Medicine (1986); National Institutes of Health Postdoctoral Fellow, Emory University (1984-1986)

What do you attribute your success to? He attributes his success to his desire to learn, self-motivation and his ability to utilize the opportunities that came his way.

What was the highlight of your career? The highlight of his career was being featured in the journal 'Science' which vaulted him to his first and only faculty appointment.

Expanded Biography: Mr. Veenstra has published more than 12 book chapters and 39 peer-reviewed scientific articles. He has also participated and done public speaking at the National Scientific Conferences and Biannual International Gap Junction Conference. He has sought the opportunity to apply a new methodology to pairs of embryonic chick cardiac myocytes as an NIH postdoctoral research fellow at Emory University.

PROFESSIONAL OF THE YEAR IN
PEDIATRIC HEMATOLOGY AND ONCOLOGY EDUCATION

TERESA J. VIETTI, MD

Professor Emeritus of Pediatrics
Washington University School of Medicine
in St. Louis
1 Childrens Place
Saint Louis, MO 63110 United States
vietti@kidswustl.edu
http://medschool.wustl.edu

Type of Business: University Medical School

Major Products and Services: Graduate Programs in Biology and Biomedical Sciences, Medical Scientist Training Program, Health Administration, Occupational Therapy, Physical Therapy, Continuing Medical Education, Graduate Medical Education, Clinical Research Education, Genetic Epidemiology, Psychiatric Epidemiology, Hematology and Oncology Research and Treatment

Marketing Area: Local

Day to Day Responsibilities: Training Students, Interns, Residents and Fellows in the Care of Children with Cancer and Blood Diseases, Training Pediatric Hematology and Oncology Fellows about the Basic Pathophysiology of these Diseases, and How to Design and Activate Clinical Research Studies in Collaboration with Other Investigators of All Disciplines at their Institution and Others

Hobbies/Interests/Sports: Medical Knowledge, History

Education Degrees: Doctor of Medicine, Baylor University (1953); Bachelor of Arts, Rice University (1949)

Affiliations/Associations/Societies: Midwest Pediatric Research Society, St. Louis Pediatric Society; American Society of Hematology; International Society of Hematology; American Society of Clinical Oncology; The American Pediatric Society; American Society for Cancer Education; American Association for Cancer Research; American Academy of Pediatrics; CEMPROC; Cell Kinetic Society; Missouri State Medical Association; American Society of Pediatric Hematology/Oncology; International Society of Paediatric Oncology; Alpha Omega Alpha

Awards/Honors: UNICO Award; Distinguished Alumnus, Rice University; Tomorrow's Children's Institute Award; John Krey III Memorial Award/American Cancer Society; Aphrodite Jannopoulo Hofsommer Award from Washington University School of Medicine; Distinguished Career Award, The American Society of Pediatric Hematology/Oncology; Cover Dedication, Cancer Research, September 15, 1996, Vol. 56, Issue 18; The Return of the Child Award, Leukemia Society of America; Spirit of Health, American Cancer Society Award

Date of Birth: November 5, 1927   **Place of Birth:** Fort Worth

Work History: Professor, Emeritus of Radiology, Washington University School of Medicine, St. Louis, Missouri (1998-Present); Professor, Emeritus of Pediatrics, Washington University School of Medicine, St. Louis, Missouri (1998-Present); Professor of Pediatrics in Radiology, Washington University School of Medicine, St. Louis, Missouri (1980-1998); Professor of Pediatrics, Washington University School of Medicine, St. Louis, Missouri (1972-1998); Associate Professor of Pediatrics, Washington University School of Medicine, St. Louis, Missouri (1965-1972); Assistant Professor of Pediatrics, Washington University School of Medicine, St. Louis, Missouri (1961-1965); Rockefeller Visiting Professor, Hachettepe's Children's Hospital, Ankara Turkey (1960-1961); Instructor in Pediatrics, University of Texas Southwestern Medical School, Dallas, Texas (1958-1960); Instructor in Pediatrics, Wayne State University, Detroit, Michigan (1958)

ENTREPRENEUR OF THE YEAR IN FINANCIAL SERVICES

MERCEDES C. VILLALPANDO

Notary Public, Paralegal, Certified Public Accountant, Owner
MJF Tax General Service
2600 Wilkinson Avenue
Fort Worth, TX 76103 United States
mecheypaco580866@aol.com
http://www.cambridgewhoswho.com

Type of Business: Finance Company

Major Products and Services: Financial Services Including Accounting, Tax Preparation, Paralegal and Notary Public

Marketing Area: National

Day to Day Responsibilities: Preparing Income Taxes and General Taxes, Bookkeeping, Generating Quarterly Reports, Managing Notary and Paralegal Services

Favorite Business Publications: Finance-Related Publications

Hobbies/Interests/Sports: Traveling, Spending Time with her Children

Education Degrees: Coursework in Economics and Finance, Rio Hondo Community College

Certifications: Licensed Public Accountant, State of Mexico (1990); Certified Foster Parent Instructor (2005); Certified Paralegal (1991); Certified Nurse Practitioner (1985); Certified Public Accountant

Affiliations/Associations/Societies: National Notary Association

Children: Jose, Louis, Mercedes

EXECUTIVE OF THE YEAR IN
HOME HEALTHCARE NURSING

KAREN JEAN VOLOSIN

President, Administrator
Innovative Nursing, Inc.
499 E. Central Parkway, Suite 100
Altamonte Springs, FL 32701 United States
karen@innovativenursing.org
http://www.innovativenursing.org

Type of Business: Healthcare Center

Major Products and Services: Healthcare Including Intermittent, Rehabilitative Services, Chronic Care Services

Marketing Area: Regional

Day to Day Responsibilities: Managing Operations, Infusion Nursing, Ensuring Safety Practices, Overseeing Pharmacy and Intravenous Therapy Operations

Favorite Business Publications: Journal of Infusion Nursing

Hobbies/Interests/Sports: Scuba Diving, Playing the Guitar

Education Degrees: Master of Science in Nursing Education and Administration, University of Phoenix (1999); Bachelor of Science in Nursing, Saint Peter's College (1992)

Affiliations/Associations/Societies: National Home Infusion Association; Infusion Nurse's Society; Oncology Nursing Society; Sigma Theta Tau International Society of Nursing

PROFESSIONAL OF THE YEAR IN CORPORATE WELLNESS MANAGEMENT

Ms. Tonya P. Vyhlidal

Wellness Manager
Lincoln Plating
600 W. East Street
Lincoln, NE 68522 United States
tonyav@lincolnplating.com
http://www.lincolnplating.com

Type of Business: Manufacturing Company

Major Products and Services: Metal Finishing Products

Marketing Area: International

Area of Expertise: Ms. Vyhlidal's expertise includes health and wellness management, safety and productivity management.

Day to Day Responsibilities: Personal Training, Instructing Yoga, Fitness and College Internship, Overseeing Workers' Compensation, Occupational Health, Health Benefits and Healthcare Administration

Favorite Business Publications: American Journal of Health Promotion

Hobbies/Interests/Sports: Exercising, Practicing Yoga, Reading, Traveling, Spending Time with her Family

Education Degrees: Master's Degree in Education, University of Nebraska-Lincoln (1996); Bachelor of Science in Physical Education and Health, University of Nebraska

Affiliations/Associations/Societies: Society for Human Resource Management; American College of Sports Medicine; National Strength and Conditioning Association; Aerobics and Fitness Association of America; Yoga Fit; Advisor Council, WEICOA; Board Member, Work Well

PROFESSIONAL OF THE YEAR IN AMBULATORY CARE

EILEEN W. WAGNER

President
South Windsor Ambulatory Care Center, Inc.
2800 Tomarack Avenue, Suite 105
South Windsor, CT 06074 United States
ewilsonwagner@yahoo.com
http://www.swacci.com

Type of Business: Medical Center

Major Products and Services: Healthcare

Marketing Area: Local

Day to Day Responsibilities: Overseeing the Physical Examination Process and Workers' Compensation, Medical Treatment of Patients, Screening for Drugs, Managing Operations, Breath Alcohol Testing

Favorite Business Publications: Journal of the American Medical Association; Fortune; Forbes

Hobbies/Interests/Sports: Writing, Painting, Reading

Affiliations/Associations/Societies: South Windsor Chamber of Commerce; Board Member, St. Phillips Church

Charity/Volunteer Work: American Cancer Society; The Leukemia & Lymphoma Society; National Kidney Foundation

Spouse: Donald   **Children:** Jared

What do you attribute your success to? She attributes her success to her dedication and her ability to communicate well with patients.

How did you become involved in your profession? She became involved in her profession because of her experience in healthcare service and decided to open her own facility.

What was the highlight of your career? The most gratifying aspect of her career is managing her business successfully.

PROFESSIONAL OF THE YEAR IN AVIATION

DEBRA L. WALKER

Aircraft Maintenance, Operations,
Auto Fuel Supplemental Type Certificate Coordinator
Experimental Aircraft Association
1145 W. 20th Avenue
Oshkosh, WI 54902 United States
dwalker@eaa.org
http://www.cambridgewhoswho.com

Type of Business: Membership Organization

Major Products and Services: Aviation Museum, Pilot Services, Aviation Education, Youth Programs, Online Products

Marketing Area: Local

Area of Expertise: Ms. Walker's expertise is in aircraft maintenance.

Favorite Business Publications: Administrative Professional

Hobbies/Interests/Sports: Advocating for Veterans

Education Degrees: Associate Degree in Personnel, Community College of the Air Force (1990); Associate Degree in Business, Community College of the Air Force (1988)

Affiliations/Associations/Societies: Former Member, National Association for Female Executives; State Commander, Veterans of Foreign Wars; Chartered Member and Treasurer, Oshkosh Chapter, Women in Aviation, International

Awards/Honors: Dual Recipient, Meritorious Service Medal; Air Force Achievement Medal; Four-Time Recipient, Outstanding Unit Award; Four-Time Recipient, Longevity Service Award; Dual Recipient, Air Force Reserve Medal; Kuwaiti Service Medal; Bronze Star Medal; Professional Military Award; Basic Training Ribbon

Expanded Biography: Ms. Walker was a technical sergeant in the United States Army. She is a Gulf War veteran and retired in 1995.

PROFESSIONAL OF THE YEAR IN
EDUCATION AND CURRICULUM DEVELOPMENT

DR. KATHRYN L. WALSH

Principal
Preston Veterans Memorial School
304 Parish Hill Road
Chaplin, CT 06235 United States
kwalsh@parishhill.org
http://www.parishhill.org

Type of Business: Elementary School

Major Products and Services: Primary Education

Marketing Area: Regional

Area of Expertise: Dr. Walsh's expertise includes science and curriculum development.

Favorite Business Publications: National Association of Secondary School Principals Publications

Hobbies/Interests/Sports: Reading, Gardening, Boating, Collecting Antique Cars

Education Degrees: Doctor of Education in Educational Leadership, Management and Policy, Seton Hall University; Master of Science in Curriculum and Instruction, Western Connecticut State University; Bachelor's Degree in Horticulture Education, University of Maryland

Affiliations/Associations/Societies: Connecticut Association of Schools; National Association of Secondary School Principals; Association for Supervision and Curriculum Development; American Association of School Administrators; Operation Respect; Phi Delta Kappa; Kappa Delta Pi

Charity/Volunteer Work: Various Charitable Organizations; Covenant Food Mission; Volunteer, Domestic Violence Program

What do you attribute your success to? She attributes her success to her ability to face challenges, the opportunities that came her way and passion for her profession.

How did you become involved in your profession? She became involved in her profession because of her desire to help children succeed and desire to make a difference in their lives.

What was the highlight of your career? The highlight of her career was attaining her current position.

EXECUTIVE OF THE YEAR IN RISK ANALYSIS

REBECCA WALZAK

President, Chief Executive Officer
Walzak Risk Analysis
5550 Glades Road, Suite 303
Boca Raton, FL 33431 United States
rwalzak@walzakrisk.com
http://www.walzakrisk.com

Type of Business: Risk Management Company

Major Products and Services: Risk Management Services Including Strategic Consulting Services and Risk Evaluation

Marketing Area: National

Day to Day Responsibilities: Overseeing Operational and Enterprise Risk Management

Favorite Business Publications: Mortgage Banking; Harvard Business Review

Hobbies/Interests/Sports: Traveling, Writing, Boating

Education Degrees: Master of Business Administration, University of Maryland University College (1994)

Certifications: Certification in Quality Management, George Washington University

Affiliations/Associations/Societies: Mortgage Bankers Association of America; Risk Management Association; American Society for Quality; Founder, Florida Quality Council; Women of Tomorrow

What do you attribute your success to? She attributes her success to her ability to take concepts from other industries and use them successfully.

What was the highlight of your career? The most gratifying aspect of her career is owning a successful company.

Expanded Biography: Ms. Walzak is a leader in innovative operational risk management programs. She has experience in consulting for mortgage banking and other types of consumer lending. She has been recognized by Fannie Mae and Freddie Mac as an industry expert in risk management. She has written numerous articles for industry trade publications, and enjoys speaking at national and regional forums.

PROFESSIONAL OF THE YEAR IN EDUCATIONAL CONSULTING

MARGARET ANNE WARNER, ACP, DIP. SMS, MA, F. COLL.T

International Education Consultant,
Teacher Trainer, HLTA Assessor
MAW Education, 27 Old Gloucester Street
Camden, London, WC1N 3XX United Kingdom
maweducation@easynet.co.uk
http://www.maweducation.co.uk
http://www.discover-multiple-intelligences.com

Type of Business: Educational Consulting and Life Coaching Company

Major Products and Services: Educational Consulting, Teacher Training Workshops, Internet Website and Life Coaching Services

Marketing Area: International

Area of Expertise: Ms. Warner's expertise includes teacher and educator training through workshops, and the promotion of educational leadership, middle management and school consultancy.

Day to Day Responsibilities: Developing School Performance Management Systems, Conducting School Needs Analysis and Observational Research, Overseeing One-on-One Life Coaching

Favorite Business Publications: ASCD Publications; The TES; Harvard Education Letter; Harvard Educational Review; The Economist

Hobbies/Interests/Sports: Gardening, Listening to Music, Traveling

Education Degrees: Master's Degree in Educational Studies, Roehampton University, London (1990): Diploma in School Management Studies, College of Preceptors (1979)

Certifications: New Insights Certified Life Coach with High Distinction (2007); Certification in English as a Second Language, Associate of the College of Preceptors (1976); Teacher's Certification in Mathematics, Froebel Educational Institute (1964); Accredited Mentor

Affiliations/Associations/Societies: Fellow, College of Teachers, UK (2008); Biographical Recorder, Marquis Who's Who (2006-2008); Madison Who's Who (2005-2007); Empire Who's Who (2003-2007); Deputy Governor, Research Board of Advisers, Fellow, American Biographical Institute (2006); Treasurer, Institute of Registered Inspectors of Schools (2002-2005); National Foundation for Educational Research; Consultant, Department for Education and Skills Trained Performance Management; Chairman, London Diocesan Head Teachers' Council; Primary Heads' Representative, Inner London Education Authority Head Teachers' Consultative Committee; Secretary, Programs, Projects and Communications Committee, Council for Education in the Commonwealth

Awards/Honors: Professional of the Year Representing Education in Consultancy and Training, Cambridge Who's Who (2008-2009); Distinguished Service Order, American Biographical Institute (2008); Woman of the Year, American Biographical Institute (2008); Nominee, Dictionary of International Biography, Cambridge, England (2005-2007); World Lifetime Achievement Award, American Biographical Institute (2006); Legion of Honor, United Cultural Convention (2006); International Peace Prize, United Cultural Convention (2005); Woman of the Year, American Biographical Institute (2005-2006)

Charity/Volunteer Work: Local Charitable Organizations

Date of Birth: September 4, 1943   **Place of Birth:** Epsom

Expanded Biography: Ms. Warner published an e-book entitled 'An Introduction to Multiple Intelligences.' She has also published 78 full-length Ofsted inspection reports and three short Ofsted inspection reports. She has worked as a primary class teacher where no child left her class unable to read, and made contributions both in school and the community. She has also carried out action research on spelling, handwriting and word processing skills, Internet research and multiple intelligences. She was head teacher of a primary school for ten years during the social regeneration of Isle of Dogs in London. She was also the head of the department in three secondary and secondary special schools. As a registered inspector for eight years, she led teams across England, and was recognized by head teachers of the schools she inspected as being fair and supportive. Ms. Warner is also a teacher trainer. She has supervised students on teaching practice in the United Kingdom and, employed by CfBT Education Trust, she has trained teachers in Qatar. She has written and led workshops on multiple intelligences across India including Amritsar, Assam, Bangalore, New Delhi and Mumbai, working in partnership with The Achievers' Programme. In 2008, she contributed to the fourth year course for student teachers at Sétif University in Algeria. Ms. Warner has also supervised teachers in training in London schools and has been one of the tutors on an induction course for European teachers run by the Roehampton Institute and ILEA. She has taught in Australia and made educational visits in Brussels, Malaysia, New Guinea, Malta and South Africa. In 2007, she was invited to take part in educational research by The National Foundation for Educational Research. She also qualified as a New Insights Life Coach, to help others achieve their own goals in life. Since 2006, she has been an assessor of higher level teaching assistants in the United Kingdom, alternating with her international consultancy commitments.

PROFESSIONAL OF THE YEAR IN TAX PREPARATION

TERRA M. WASHINGTON

Chief Executive Officer
Tax One
2210 Wynnton Road, Suite 100
Columbus, GA 31906 United States
taxone1@yahoo.com
http://www.taxone.com

Type of Business: Tax Preparation Firm

Major Products and Services: Personal Income and Comprehensive Tax and Financial Statements Preparation Services

Marketing Area: Local

Day to Day Responsibilities: Managing Income Funds, Processing Payroll, Generating Financial Reports, Teaching Tax Preparation Courses

Favorite Business Publications: Forbes

Hobbies/Interests/Sports: Running, Football

Education Degrees: Associate Degree in Banking and Finance, Chattahoochee Valley College (1999)

Certifications: Certified Tax Preparation Instructor; Certified Notary Public

Affiliations/Associations/Societies: Order of the Eastern Star; National Republican Congressional Committee (2006)

PROFESSIONAL OF THE YEAR IN
MILITARY AEROSPACE INSTRUCTION

WALTER L. WATSON JR.

Senior Aerospace Science Instructor
Air Force Junior ROTC Unit
C.A. Johnson Preparatory Academy
2219 Barhamville Road
Columbia, SC 29204 United States
cajafjrotc@aol.com
http://www.cambridgewhoswho.com

Type of Business: Training Academy

Major Products and Services: Citizenship Training, Aerospace Education, Leadership Development, Cadet Corp Activities

Marketing Area: Regional

Day to Day Responsibilities: Teaching Aviation

Favorite Business Publications: Aerospace Today; Air & Space

Hobbies/Interests/Sports: Traveling

Education Degrees: Master of Arts in Human Resources, Chapman University College (1983); Bachelor of Science in Mechanical Engineering, Howard University (1971)

Affiliations/Associations/Societies: Air Force Association; Blackbird Association

Awards/Honors: Brigadier General Noel Parrish Award (2003); Tuskegee Airmen Award

Charity/Volunteer Work: Alma Mater; School District; Various Charitable Organizations

Spouse: Joyce   **Children:** Alexandria, Walter

Work History: United States Air Force (1971-1996)

What do you attribute your success to? He attributes his success to his hard work.

How did you become involved in your profession? He became involved in his profession because of his interest in the air force.

What was the highlight of your career? The highlight of his career was receiving 'The Brigadier General Noel Parrish Award.'

EXECUTIVE OF THE YEAR IN HUMAN SERVICES

MR. STEVEN J. WEINDORF

Executive Director
Community Residence Corporation
1851 Washtenaw Road
Ypsilanti, MI 48197 United States
steven@communityresidence.org
http://www.communityresidence.org

Type of Business: Nonprofit Human Services Organization

Major Products and Services: Residential and Supportive Services for People with Disabilities

Marketing Area: Local

Day to Day Responsibilities: Overseeing the Administrative Staff and Administration of a $5 Million Annual Budget, Managing Budgets, Negotiating Contracts, Building Relationships with Funding Agencies

Favorite Business Publications: The New York Times

Hobbies/Interests/Sports: Reading, Traveling, Rose Gardening, Landscaping, Hiking, Biking

Education Degrees: Bachelor of Arts in Political Science, Michigan State University

Affiliations/Associations/Societies: Ypsilanti Area Chamber of Commerce; Michigan Assisted Living Association; Michigan Nonprofit Association

Date of Birth: October 15, 1960   **Place of Birth:** Ann Arbor

Spouse: Marielle   **Children:** Edsell, Elizabeth

Work History: Cavass Director, Development Director, Board Member, Michigan Committee, SANE Nuclear Policy (1985-1990); Agriculture Instructor, U.S. Peace Corps, Sierra Leone West Africa (1982-1984)

Expanded Biography: Mr. Weindorf has worked as a personnel manager, director of operations and associate director with his company, and taught 65 farmers to develop inland swamp land for paddy rice cultivation which helped to more than triple SANE's membership in the state of Michigan and successfully stopped funding for the MX Missile Program. He has worked to eliminate a $300,000 deficit in 2001 to a positive fund-balance of $231,677 in 2007.

PROFESSIONAL OF THE YEAR IN RESPIRATORY CARE

STEPHANIE D. WELLS

Respiratory Care Practitioner
Marietta Memorial Hospital
401 Matthew Street
Marietta, OH 45750 United States
travisstephw@aol.com
http://www.mmhospital.org

Type of Business: Hospital

Major Products and Services: Healthcare

Marketing Area: Local

Day to Day Responsibilities: Practicing Respiratory Care

Favorite Business Publications: Advance for Respiratory Care Practitioners

Hobbies/Interests/Sports: Spending Time with her Family

Education Degrees: Coursework in Respiratory Protection

Certifications: Certified Respiratory Care Practitioner, Marietta College; Certified Tobacco Treatment Counselor; Certified Basic Life Support Instructor

Affiliations/Associations/Societies: American Association for Respiratory Care

EXECUTIVE OF THE YEAR IN FINANCIAL MANAGEMENT

RAYMOND B. WHITE

Chief Executive Officer
The Watson Institute
301 Campmeeting Road
Sewickley, PA 15143 United States
raywh@thewatsoninstitute.org
http://www.thewatsoninstitute.org

Type of Business: Educational Institution

Major Products and Services: Educational Programs for Special Need Students, Special Education for Children Aged Three to 21 Years Old Who Have been Diagnosed with Cerebral Palsy, Autism, Spectrum Disorders, Brain Injuries, Neurological Impairments and Emotional Challenges

Marketing Area: Regional

Area of Expertise: Mr. White's expertise includes financial management, strategic planning, marketing, program development and community outreach services.

Favorite Business Publications: BusinessWeek; Forbes; Fortune; The Wall Street Journal

Hobbies/Interests/Sports: Golfing, Traveling, Spending Time with his Family

Education Degrees: Coursework in Marketing Management, Columbia University Graduate School of Business (1992); Bachelor of Science in Business Administration, West Virginia University (1965)

Certifications: Certification, The College of Insurance, Insurance Society of New York (1971)

Affiliations/Associations/Societies: President, Pittsburgh Philharmonic; Board President, Pittsburgh Chapter, West Virginia University Alumni Association; Board Member, Boys' Club of Pittsburgh; Chairman, Dean's Visiting Committee, West Virginia University College of Business and Economics; Board Member, Pittsburgh Symphony; Board Member, Ursuline Center; Board Member, Boyd Community Center and Library; Board President, Allegheny Country Club; Duquesne Club; Rolling Rock Club; Who's Who in Finance and Industry; Board President, Craig House dba Craig Academy; Former President, Board of Trustees, Margaret H. W. Watson Foundation

Date of Birth: January 22, 1943   **Place of Birth:** Clarksburg

Spouse: Cherry   **Children:** Drew, Chris, Holly, Fraser

Work History: Principal, Senior Vice President, Johnson & Higgins

PROFESSIONAL OF THE YEAR IN BOOKKEEPING AND TAX SERVICES

MS. DORIS L. WHITWORTH

Owner, Tax Accountant, Master Bookkeeper
Doris L. Whitworth
6000 Apache Trail
Knoxville, TN 37920 United States
dotax4you@aol.com
http://www.cambridgewhoswho.com

Type of Business: Accounting Firm

Major Products and Services: Bookkeeping, Offering Income Tax Services

Marketing Area: Regional

Day to Day Responsibilities: Managing Quarterly and Monthly Bookkeeping for the Local Community, Overseeing Operations of the Business and Income Tax

Favorite Business Publications: Tax Hotline; General Ledger

Education Degrees: Associate Degree in Accounting, University of Tennessee (1975)

Affiliations/Associations/Societies: American Institute of Professional Bookkeepers

Children: Danny, Amy

What was the highlight of your career? The highlight of her career was establishing her own business.

EXECUTIVE OF THE YEAR IN NON-PROFIT ADMINISTRATION

LAURA S. WIJKOWSKI

Chief Executive Officer
Sooner Council, Inc
Girl Scouts of the United States of America
laurasw@live.com
http://www.cambridgewhoswho.com

Type of Business: Nonprofit Organization

Major Products and Services: Community Services for Young Girls

Marketing Area: Oklahoma

Area of Expertise: Ms. Wijkowski's expertise is in operations management.

Day to Day Responsibilities: Managing the Staff, Overseeing Nonprofit Management, Human Resources, Marketing, Operations, Policies and Procedures, Strategic Planning and Fundraiser Development

Favorite Business Publications: Fast Company; The Chronicle of Philanthropy

Hobbies/Interests/Sports: Knitting, Crocheting, Spinning Wool, Making Jewelry, Caring for her Pets, Golfing

Education Degrees: Bachelor's Degree in Human Relations and Agency Management, Missouri Valley College; Coursework, Graduate Management Program, Simmons College

Certifications: Certified in Nonprofit Management, Case Western Reserve University; Certified in Asset Management, Harvard University

Affiliations/Associations/Societies: Main Street Board, Chickasha Chamber of Commerce; Human Relations Commissioner, City of Chickasha

Charity/Volunteer Work: Festival of Lights; Chamber of Commerce; Gold Coast President, Sertoma International

Place of Birth: Chicago

Spouse: Stanley   **Children:** Andrea, Dawn

What do you attribute your success to? She attributes her success to her commitment, extensive education and experience.

How did you become involved in your profession? She became involved in her profession because she was a Girl Scout as a child and wanted to improve the lives of young girls.

What was the highlight of your career? The most gratifying aspect of her career has been helping to facilitate change in her organization.

Where will you be in five years? In five years, Ms. Wijkowski would like to work for another nonprofit organization.

Expanded Biography: Ms. Wijkowski supports local fundraisers.

EXECUTIVE OF THE YEAR IN BIOMEDICS

MICHAEL J. WILCOX, PH.D.

Chief Executive Officer
Hyperacuity Systems
6555 Delmonico Drive
Apartment 212
Colorado Springs, CO 80919 United States
mike.wilcox@aqueousbio.com
http://www.aqueousbio.com

Type of Business: Biomedical Device Company

Major Products and Services: Innovative Products in Cardiovascular Stents and Cancer Treatment

Marketing Area: International

Area of Expertise: Mr. Wilcox's expertise includes biological composites and the vision information processing system.

Day to Day Responsibilities: Overseeing Daily Operations, Conducting Scientific Research in the Laboratory, Manufacturing, Conducting Verification Tests on Final Devices and Products

Favorite Business Publications: EETimes; Neuroscience Magazine; Science

Hobbies/Interests/Sports: Motorcycling, Weightlifting, Precision Modeling, Camping, Hiking, Computer Simulation, Cooking

Education Degrees: Post-Doctoral Degree, CNRS, Marseille, France; Ph.D. in Biophysics, Purdue University; Master of Science in Biology; Bachelor of Science in Psychology

Certifications: Electro-Visual Diagnostics Training, Doheny Eye Institute, Keck School of Medicine, University of Southern California

Affiliations/Associations/Societies: Institute of Electrical and Electronics Engineers, Inc.; International Society for Optical Engineering; American Association for the Advancement of Science; Sigma Xi; Sigma Pi Sigma; Beta Beta Beta; Association for the Advancement of Medical Instrumentation

Awards/Honors: Celebrate Technology Award (2005); Patent Award for Glaucoma Shunt (2005); Frank J. Seiler Award for Research Excellence (2000); Science and Engineering Award, United States Air Force (1999); John C. Johnson Award for Research Excellence (1998)

Charity/Volunteer Work: Board of Directors, FalconWorks

Date of Birth: March 20, 1948   **Place of Birth:** Detroit

Children: Christopher, Marc

Work History: Aqueous Shunts LLC, Aqueous Biomedical, Inc.; Purdue University; Centre Nationale de la Recherche Scientifique, University of Puerto Rico; Keck School of Medicine, University of Southern California; Doheny Eye Institute, University of New Mexico School of Medicine; United States Air Force Academy

Expanded Biography: Mr. Wilcox has published his works and delivered local, national and international public speeches. He also mentors cadets of the United States Air Force Academy. He has received the 'Biomedical Company of the Year' award for Aqueous Biomedical, Inc. in 2006. He designed, tested and implemented the first glaucoma shunt device that operates without forming a blister on the eye surface, designed a drug delivery device that performs without complications caused by fibrosis, experimented with a drug and dye delivery system that controls penetration at a cellular level and is available to treat nerve cells non-invasively, developed a control system for the repair of soft tissue injuries without scar tissue formation, developed the first visual system with sub-pixel resolution in real-time, and designed a wavefront sensor to allow earth-based telescopes to make unprecedented high resolution images. This 'fly-eye' technology is patented.

PROFESSIONAL OF THE YEAR IN
MOLECULAR BIOLOGY AND BIOTECHNOLOGY EDUCATION

ARTHUR L. WILLIAMS, PH.D.

Professor, Chairman
Morgan State University
1700 E. Cold Spring Lane
Baltimore, MD 21251 United States
awillia5@morgan.edu
http://www.jewel.morgan.edu/-biology

Type of Business: State University

Major Products and Services: Comprehensive Range of Academic Programs in Business, Engineering, Education, Architecture, Social Work, Hospitality Management, Arts and Sciences

Marketing Area: Regional

Day to Day Responsibilities: Teaching Molecular Biology and Biotechnology Courses, Teaching Gene Regulation and Gene Structure, Managing Administration of Department, Assessing Graduate and Undergraduate Curriculum, Liaising between University, Grant Agencies and State Agencies, Overseeing Faculty Recruitment, Hiring and Firing Staff

Favorite Business Publications: Science

Hobbies/Interests/Sports: Bowling, Hiking

Education Degrees: Ph.D. in Molecular Biology, Purdue University (1975); Master of Science in Biology, Atlanta University (1971)

Affiliations/Associations/Societies: American Society for Microbiology; American Society for Bioengineering; Governor's Board for Biosciences, State of Maryland

Expanded Biography: Dr. Williams has 45 completed publications and 116 abstracts. He presents at conferences both nationally and internationally.

PROFESSIONAL OF THE YEAR IN
FAMILY AND CHILD DEVELOPMENT IN EDUCATION

SUE W. WILLIAMS, ED.D.

Professor of Family and Consumer Sciences Education
Texas State University-San Marcos
601 University Drive
San Marcos, TX 78666 United States
sw10@txstate.edu
http://www.txstate.edu

Type of Business: University

Major Products and Services: Higher Education

Marketing Area: National

Area of Expertise: Ms. Williams' expertise includes family and consumer sciences education.

Day to Day Responsibilities: Overseeing the Child Development Center and Laboratory School with 20 Staff Members, Implementing the International Exchange Programs in the Stockholm Institute of Education, Conducting Research on Program Administration, Comparative Child Studies and Child Guidance

Favorite Business Publications: The New York Times; Time

Hobbies/Interests/Sports: Reading, Gardening

Education Degrees: Master of Education, Oklahoma State University (1980)

Affiliations/Associations/Societies: Director, Child Development Center; Advisor, The Foundation for Child Development; Society for Research in Child Development; Texas State Employees Union; National Association for the Education of Young Children; Advisor, Phi Beta Chi; Kappa Omicron Nu; Phi Kappa Phi; SRHD

PROFESSIONAL OF THE YEAR IN SPECIAL EDUCATION

CAROLYN H. WILSON, ED.D.

Associate Professor
Virginia State University
1 Hayden Drive
P.O. Box 9077
Petersburg, VA 23806 United States
cwilson@vsu.edu
http://www.vsu.edu

Type of Business: University

Major Products and Services: Higher Education

Marketing Area: International

Day to Day Responsibilities: Teaching Individuals with Disabilities, Conducting Workshops in Public Schools, Writing Grant Proposals for Special Education Teachers

Favorite Business Publications: The Journal of Special Education; CEC Journal

Education Degrees: Doctor of Education, The George Washington University (1998); Coursework in Administration, Old Dominion University (1987); Master of Science, Old Dominion University (1983)

Affiliations/Associations/Societies: Phi Delta Kappa; Delta Sigma Theta

Awards/Honors: Teacher of the Year Award (1994-1995); Special Olympics Coordinator of the Year Award (1992)

Date of Birth: January 31, 1949   **Place of Birth:** Clinton

What do you attribute your success to? She attributes her success to the support she receives from her students.

Expanded Biography: Ms. Wilson has published an article entitled 'The Negative Impact of High Stakes Testing: A Literature Review' in the 'International Journal of Arts & Sciences.'

PROFESSIONAL OF THE YEAR IN LITERATURE

MAUREEN E. WILSON

Author
Mommy's Moments
355 Hale Street
Prides Crossing, MA 01965 United States
texaswilsons@juno.com
http://www.cambridgewhoswho.com

Type of Business: Sole Proprietorship

Major Products and Services: Books, Poetry and Short Stories

Marketing Area: International

Day to Day Responsibilities: Teaching, Composing Music, Writing Poetry on Right-to-Life, Nature and Family Issues

Hobbies/Interests/Sports: Photography, Writing Poetry, Recording Song Lyrics on Tapes and Compact Discs, Singing in the Church Choir

Education Degrees: Bachelor's Degree in Business Administration, Johnson & Wales University, Rhode Island, Cum Laude (1976)

Affiliations/Associations/Societies: Vice President, Manchester Singers; American Women's Association

Awards/Honors: Best Photos of Multiple Year Awards, Who's Who in Poetry

Charity/Volunteer Work: Local Charitable Organizations, Cambodia

What do you attribute your success to? She attributes her success to her creativity and her faith in God.

Expanded Biography: Ms. Wilson's work has been featured in United Kingdom, Asia and United States publications.

PROFESSIONAL OF THE YEAR IN
RESPIRATORY CARE ADMINISTRATION

MRS. SUSAN L. WILSON

Physician Extender, Vice President
Respiratory Critical Care Associates
2325 18th Street, Suite 210
Columbus, IN 47201 United States
wilsonwine@comcast.net
http://www.cambridgewhoswho.com

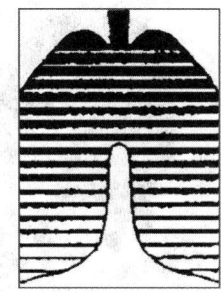

Type of Business: Medical Group

Major Products and Services: Healthcare Services for Patients with Lung Disease, Critical Care Medicine, Clinical Instruction, Education

Marketing Area: Regional

Day to Day Responsibilities: Coordinating Patient Care, Assisting the Pulmonologist, Offering Clinical Instruction and Respiratory Therapy, Utilizing Pulmonary Function Technology

Favorite Business Publications: AARC Times; American Journal of Respiratory and Critical Care Medicine; Advance for Managers of Respiratory Care; Respiratory Care Journal

Hobbies/Interests/Sports: Traveling, Reading, Skiing, Parasailing, Boating, Exercising Including Running, Biking, Step Aerobics and Weight Training, Practicing Yoga

Education Degrees: Master of Business Administration, Indiana Wesleyan University (2000); Bachelor of Science in Health Arts, University of St. Francis (1996); Coursework, Indiana Vocational Technical College (1977)

Certifications: Certified Respiratory Therapist; Registered Respiratory Therapist; Certified Pulmonary Function Technologist; Registered Pulmonary Function Technologist; Certified Aerobics Instructor, Aerobics and Fitness Association of America; Licensed Respiratory Care Practitioner, Indiana Health Professions Bureau

Affiliations/Associations/Societies: Indiana Society for Respiratory Care; American Association for Respiratory Care

Awards/Honors: Richard Alan Literary Award for an Article Regarding F102s (1978)

Date of Birth: February 4, 1954 **Place of Birth:** Fort Wayne

Spouse: David **Children:** Tony, Moss, Amy, Andrew, Abigail Wilson

Work History: Critical Care Medicine (1995-Present); Conducted Workshops for Nine Instructors, Taught Fundraising Volunteer Classes for Heart Disease and Cancer (1988-2000); Clinical Instructor for Respiratory Care Students from Indiana Vocational Technical College and for Students from California College for Health Sciences (1974-1995); Home Care Services (1988-1991); Clinical Technician, Columbus Occupational Health Association; Various Outpatient Procedures and Tests for Patient Physicals (1978-1980); Physician Extender, Respiratory Critical Care Associates; Assistant, Columbus Regional Hospital; RCCA Office Duties; Patient Care Coordinator of Outpatient Care, Policies and Procedures; Direct Patient Care for Patients with Lung Diseases; Registered Respiratory Therapist, Columbus Regional Hospital-Respiratory Care Department; Registered Respiratory Therapist; Respiratory Care Services (RCS); AFAR Certified Aerobics Instructor; Owner, Operator, Energy Plus! Aerobic Dance; Teacher, Exercise Classes, Gold's Gym and Ladies Only Clubs

Expanded Biography: Mrs. Wilson has been published in 'The Journal of Ventilation.' She co-authored a piece regarding F102s during mechanical ventilation while she was a student in 1976 and wrote 'EKG Interpretation for the Respiratory Therapist,' which was published in the 'Indiana Society for Respiratory Care Newsletter' in 1978.

PROFESSIONAL OF THE YEAR IN
NEURORADIOLOGY AND INTERVENTIONAL RADIOLOGY

JOAN C. WOJAK, MD

Director
Neuroradiology and Interventional Radiology
Our Lady of Lourdes Regional Medical Center
611 St. Landry Street
Lafayette, LA 70506 United States
wojakj@lourdesrmc.com
http://www.lourdes.net

Type of Business: Healthcare, Hospital-Based Group

Major Products and Services: Healthcare

Marketing Area: National

Area of Expertise: Dr. Wojak's expertise is in diagnostic radiology.

Day to Day Responsibilities: Consulting on Complicated Cases Including TIA, Strokes, Aneurysms and Complicated Spines to Assist in Deciding what Treatment the Patient Needs, Performing Interventional Procedures, Treating Aneurysms, Preventing and Treating Strokes, Installing Stents and Balloons, Performing Minimally-Invasive Spine Procedures

Hobbies/Interests/Sports: Showing her own Hunter, Jumper and Pleasure Horses at U.S. Equestrian Federation, Palomino Horse Breeders Association and American Quarter Horse Association Shows, Breeding Thoroughbred Horses

Education Degrees: Radiology Residency and Neuroradiology Fellowship, Louisiana State University School of Medicine, New Orleans, LA (1990-1996); Doctor of Medicine, New York University (1983); Neurosurgery Residency, Bellevue Hospital Center, New York, NY (1983-1990)

Affiliations/Associations/Societies: Society of NeuroInterventional Surgery; American Society of Neuroradiology; Society of Interventional Radiology; American Stroke Association; American Society of Neurosurgery Association; Speakers Bureau, GE, Pharmaceutical Industry

Charity/Volunteer Work: Volunteers and Serves on the Board of Acadiana Therapeutic Riding Organization

Date of Birth: September 12, 1958   **Place of Birth:** Bethpage

What do you attribute your success to? She attributes her success to her commitment to the advancement of the field and treatment of patients and her unwillingness to compromise on these points.

How did you become involved in your profession? She became involved in her profession because she switched from neurosurgery after spending time with one of the pioneers in the field during her neurosurgery residency.

What was the highlight of your career? The highlight of her career was co-authoring the most widely read textbook in interventional neuroradiology.

Where will you be in five years? In five years, Dr. Wojak intends to continue offering the most technologically advanced care in a new hospital.

Expanded Biography: Dr. Wojak is an acclaimed researcher and groundbreaker in the field of neuroradiology. Here is an excerpt from an article published by Acadiana Profile entitled, 'The Battle Against Strokes,' by Wes Milligan: 'The most common form of treatment for an ischemic stroke is to intravenously administer the blood-thinning agent t-PA, or tissue plasminogen activator. But this drug must be given within three hours of the onset of the stroke, because after three hours the risk of giving the drug significantly increases the chance of brain bleed. Due to the limited time period, most patients do not make it to the hospital in time to receive this treatment, leaving doctors with only the option of controlling certain factors, such as the patient's blood pressure. In order to increase the time window for treating ischemic strokes, an increasing number of doctors are beginning to believe in interventional stroke therapy, in which doctors can thread a catheter through the body directly to the blood clot to administer t-PA, rather than pumping a larger dose of the drug throughout the whole body intravenously. Devices that mechanically retrieve the clot are also used. According to Dr. Joan Wojak, medical director of the Neurosciences Department at Our Lady of Lourdes Regional Medical Center in Lafayette, this type of therapy can increase the time window to six hours. This treatment requires a smaller dosage of t-PA, thus decreasing the chance of brain bleed into the extended time window, she observes. Dr. Wojak is a pioneer in the field of interventional neuroradiology, which uses innovative methods to treat patients with conditions affecting the brain and spine. She says these aggressive approaches are proving to be successful and are drawing more interest to the field.' Dr. Wojak co-authored the 1999 book, 'Interventional Neuro-radiology: Strategies and Practical Techniques,' and she has sat on several national committees for neuroscience training and treatment. She runs a monthly neuroscience roundtable involving presentations on topics of interest and a review of interesting cases brought by the physician audience. She also does public speaking at professional association meetings in her field.

PROFESSIONAL OF THE YEAR IN PUBLISHING

DR. AZI U. WOLFENSON

Board President
Montecristo Editores
3781 N.E. 208th Terrace
Aventura, FL 33180 United States
aziwolfenson@aol.com
http://www.larazon.com.pe

Type of Business: Publishing Company

Major Products and Services: 250,000 Local and Regional Daily Newspapers in Peru

Marketing Area: International

Area of Expertise: Dr. Wolfenson's expertise is in project development.

Day to Day Responsibilities: Overseeing Business Operations

Favorite Business Publications: The Economist

Hobbies/Interests/Sports: Soccer, Reading

Education Degrees: Ph.D. in Engineering, The World University Roundtable, with Honors (1987); Ph.D. in Engineering Management, Century University (1985); Ph.D. in Engineering Management, Pacific Western University (1983); Master of Science in Industrial Engineering, University of Michigan (1966); Bachelor of Science in Professional, Mechanical and Electrical Engineering, University of Peru (1955)

Affiliations/Associations/Societies: Aventura Turnberry Jewish Center Beth Jacob; Executive Committee, Greater Miami Jewish Federation; Fellow, Institute of Production Engineers; Institute of Administrative Management; Institution of Manufacturing Engineers; Institution of Electrical Engineers; American Society of Mechanical Engineers; Senior Member, American Institute of Industrial Engineers; American Society for Engineering Education; American Management Association; Life Patron, Deputy Governor, Research Board of Advisors, American Biographical Institute; British Institute of Management; The Association of Energy Engineers; Founder, The World University Roundtable; Executive Member, World Association of Newspapers

Awards/Honors: International Man of the Year; One in a Million Award, International Biographical Center; Man of the Year Award (1990); Bronze Medal of the Congress (1989); Biography of the Year Award (1987); Grand Ambassador of the Year, American Biographical Institute; International Cultural Diploma of Honor, American Biographical Institute; Diploma of Recognition, Ministry of Defense, Government of Israel (1967)

Date of Birth: August 1, 1933   **Place of Birth:** Riskani

Spouse: Rebeca

Children: Michael, Ida (Deceased), Jeannette, Ruth, Moises, Alex

Work History: General Manager, Director, La Republica (1981); Private Consultant in Peru and Latin America (1959-1981); Executive President, Electroperu (1976-1980); President, Despro (1973-1977); Chairman, PROA Project Promotion AG; Chairman, Institute for the Development of the Americas; Board President, Editora Sport S.A.; Board President; Editores Montecristo; Founder, Director, La Razón

Expanded Biography: Dr. Wolfenson is the author of 'Work Communications,' 'Programmed Learning,' 'Production, Planning and Control,' 'Transfer of Technology,' 'National Electrical Development,' 'Energy and Development' and 'El Gran Desafio.' He is also the co-author of 'Hacia Una Politica Alternativa.' He is a professional mechanical, electrical and industrial engineer, and serves as a chairman for the PROA Project Promotion AG in Luzern, Switzerland and as a chairman of the Institute for the Development of the Americas. He is president of the board of Editora Sport S.A. and Editores Montecristo. He created the program of mini-hydroelectric plants to attend the rural demands of 1500 different towns in the Peruvian mountains. He was the co-founder of many Peruvian newspapers including 'La Republica' in 1981, 'El Popular' in 1983, 'El Nacional' in 1985, 'Todo Sport' in 1993, 'El Chino' in 1995, 'La Reforma' in 1997, 'El Men' in 1999, 'La Razón' in 2001 and 'Rocoto' in 2003.

PROFESSIONAL OF THE YEAR IN LABOR EMPLOYMENT AND LAW

PATRICIA A. WOOD, ESQ.

Assistant General Counsel
State of Maryland Commission on Human Relations
6 Saint Paul Street, Ninth Floor
Baltimore, MD 21202 United States
pwood@mail.mchr.state.md.us
http://www.mchr.state.md.us

Type of Business: State Government Agency

Major Products and Services: Case Processing, Mediation, Community Outreach, Education, Litigation, Publications, Governance

Marketing Area: Regional

Area of Expertise: Ms. Wood's expertise includes civil rights, labor, employment law and litigation management.

Day to Day Responsibilities: Handling Employment and Housing Discrimination Cases, Overseeing Jury Trials and Case Appeals

Hobbies/Interests/Sports: Watching Movies, Playing Tennis, Roller-blading, Sewing

Education Degrees: JD, University of Baltimore School of Law; Master's Degree in Criminal Justice, University of Baltimore

Certifications: Certification in Mediation

Affiliations/Associations/Societies: Maryland State Bar Association; Maryland Volunteer Lawyers Service

What do you attribute your success to? She attributes her success to her hard work and tenacity.

How did you become involved in your profession? She became involved in her profession because of her caring nature and desire to help the hearing impaired settle their legal issues.

What was the highlight of your career? The highlight of her career was winning a case in front of the Appellate Court of Appeals, the highest court in the state of Maryland.

PROFESSIONAL OF THE YEAR IN
PARAMEDICS AND FIRE FIGHTING

LORI A. WORTMAN

Paramedic, Firefighter
Washington Township Fire Department
2310 Adamsville Road
Zanesville, OH 43701 United States
lwortman@columbus.rr.com
http://www.cambridgewhoswho.com

Type of Business: Government Organization

Major Products and Services: Fire and Emergency Rescue Services

Marketing Area: Regional

Day to Day Responsibilities: Overseeing Paramedic Emergency Care, Firefighting

Favorite Business Publications: JEMS

Education Degrees: Associate Degree in Mental Health, Muskingum Area Technical College (1990)

Certifications: Certified Paramedic; Certified Firefighter

Affiliations/Associations/Societies: President, Mental Health Club (1990)

Charity/Volunteer Work: Local Church

PROFESSIONAL OF THE YEAR IN FREELANCE WRITING

MARY F. WUELLENWEBER

Children's Storybook Writer and Illustrator
The Rebbe's Workshop
48 Dunbarton Center Road
Bow, NH 03304 United States
mary48@comcast.net
http://www.cambridgewhoswho.com

Type of Business: Freelance Writing and Illustrating

Major Products and Services: Children's Storybooks

Marketing Area: International

Day to Day Responsibilities: Writing and Illustrating Children's Storybooks

Favorite Business Publications: Children's Writers & Illustrators Journal; Harvard Review

Hobbies/Interests/Sports: Writing, Gardening, Reading History, Designing and Sewing Period Costumes

Education Degrees: Montessori Training; Industry-Related Training and Experience

Affiliations/Associations/Societies: The Society for Children's Book Writers and Illustrators

Charity/Volunteer Work: American Cancer Society; Shriners Children's Hospital; March of Dimes Foundation; Disabled American Veterans

What do you attribute your success to? She attributes her success to the inspiration she received from her creative parents, and encouragement from her friends and teachers.

How did you become involved in your profession? She became involved in this profession because she was inspired by a trip she took to Jerusalem, during which she became enamored with Israel, and decided to positively mentor children to help improve society.

What was the highlight of your career? The highlight of her career was receiving a patent for her work.

PROFESSIONAL OF THE YEAR IN NURSING

RACHEL G. YANDELL, RN, BS, M.ED.

Diabetes Educator
Presbyterian Healthcare
200 Hawthorne Lane
Charlotte, NC 28204 United States
rachel.yandell@cwwemail.com
http://www.cambridgewhoswho.com

Type of Business: Hospital

Major Products and Services: Healthcare

Marketing Area: Regional

Area of Expertise: Ms. Yandell's expertise includes diabetes and nursing education.

Favorite Business Publications: NCNA Journal

Hobbies/Interests/Sports: Reading, Attending the Church

Education Degrees: Master of Education, The University of North Carolina

Affiliations/Associations/Societies: Chairwoman, Residential Health Committee; Planning Committee, Metrolina Association of Diabetes Educators; The National Diabetes Foundation

Charity/Volunteer Work: Treasurer, Women's Department, Local Church; Habitat for Humanity International

What do you attribute your success to? She attributes her success to the support she receives from her family.

How did you become involved in your profession? She became involved in her profession because of her desire to help people.

What was the highlight of your career? The highlight of her career was receiving the best nurse award.

PROFESSIONAL OF THE YEAR IN LAW ENFORCEMENT

ANN ELIZABETH YOUNG

Captain
Detective Support and Vice Division
Los Angeles Police Department
Central Traffic Division
251 E. Sixth Street
Los Angeles, CA 90014 United States
younga@lapd.lacity.org
http://www.lapdonline.org

Type of Business: Police Department

Major Products and Services: Law Enforcement Services

Marketing Area: Regional

Area of Expertise: Captain Young's expertise is in law enforcement.

Day to Day Responsibilities: Overseeing Administrative Duties and Court Services, Managing Operations and Detective Funds, Investigating Hate Crimes, Threat Management, Working with Mentally Ill People and Finding Missing People

Favorite Business Publications: Mystery Novels by James Patterson

Hobbies/Interests/Sports: Gardening, Reading Mystery Novels by James Patterson, Traveling

Education Degrees: Master's Degree in Education, University of Nevada, Las Vegas; Bachelor's Degree in Kinesiology, University of California, Los Angeles

Affiliations/Associations/Societies: Women in Business; Former President, Los Angeles Women Police Officers Association; Oscar Joel Bryant Foundation; Black Law Enforcement Association; National Organization of Black Law Enforcement Executives; FBI National Academy Associates

Expanded Biography: Captain Young was promoted to the rank of detective in July 1988. She also worked in the 77th area, the juvenile division, the robbery homicide division and the department of internal affairs. She was promoted to the rank of sergeant in 1991 and was transferred to the south traffic division. She was promoted to the rank of sergeant II in 1994. She was assigned to the tactical planning division and was promoted to the rank of lieutenant in July 1995. She was promoted to the rank of lieutenant II in March of 1999 and was assigned to the Van Nuys Operations Support Division. She was the first African-American to be promoted to the rank of captain I within the Los Angeles Police Department, which took place in April of 2000. She received a diploma from the FBI National Academy Associates in Quantico, VA in 1998. She is also a graduate of the West Point Leadership Program at the Supervisory Leadership Institute.

EXECUTIVE OF THE YEAR IN MINING

FRAN YUNGWIRTH

Chief Executive Officer
Moneta Porcupine Mines, Inc.
65 Third Avenue
Timmins, ON P4N 1C2 Canada
franyung@vianet.ca
http://www.monetaporcupine.com

Type of Business: Mining Company

Major Products and Services: Strategic Planning, Project Development and Management, Gold Mining

Marketing Area: National

Day to Day Responsibilities: Evaluating Resources, Financing, Managing Projects, Structure Consulting

Favorite Business Publications: Mining Engineering; CIM Magazine

Hobbies/Interests/Sports: Construction, Carpentry, Collecting Coins, Public Speaking

Education Degrees: Bachelor of Laws, University of Saskatchewan (1976); Bachelor of Science in Mining and Engineering, University of Saskatchewan (1973)

Affiliations/Associations/Societies: Association of Professional Engineers and Geoscientists of the Province of Manitoba; Association of Professional Engineers of Ontario; The Law Society of Upper Canada; The Law Society of Manitoba; The Canadian Bar Association; Rotary Club of Timmins-Porcupine; Prospectors & Developers Association of Canada; Canadian Institute of Mining, Metallurgy and Petroleum

Awards/Honors: Appreciation Award, Canadian Institute of Mining, Metallurgy and Petroleum (2001); Rotary International Recognition Award (1995)

Date of Birth: June 29, 1951

Spouse: Claudette   **Children:** Grace, Francis, Dale, Claudette

Expanded Biography: Ms. Yungwirth is a lecturer and published an article about the trout lake mine operation in 1989.

PROFESSIONAL OF THE YEAR IN HEALTH EDUCATION

Ms. Fern R. Zahlen

Owner
Zahlen Professional Seminars
6082 Eaglecrest Drive
Huntington Beach, CA 92648 United States
fzahlen@aol.com
http://www.cambridgewhoswho.com

Type of Business: Consulting Firm

Major Products and Services: Education Consulting for Teachers and Administrators, Health, Accident and Life Insurance Agents

Marketing Area: Regional

Area of Expertise: Ms. Zahlen's expertise is in health education.

Day to Day Responsibilities: Supervising Students and Teachers, Managing Medical Subsidy, Overseeing Sales of Aflac Insurance

Hobbies/Interests/Sports: Traveling, Dancing

Education Degrees: Master's Degree in School Administration and Management, Pepperdine University; Master's Degree in Public Health, University of Minnesota

Certifications: Registered Nurse, University of Minnesota; Licensed Insurance Agent

Affiliations/Associations/Societies: California Association of Supervisors of Child Welfare and Attendance; Association of California School Administrators; The American Nurses Association; United States Department of Education

Awards/Honors: Academic Excellence Award, Teacher Training

Charity/Volunteer Work: Hoag Hospital, Newport Beach; American Cancer Society

Spouse: George

What do you attribute your success to? She attributes her success to her honesty and creativity.

What was the highlight of your career? The highlight of her career was participating in the Academic Excellence Bilingual Education program.

PROFESSIONAL OF THE YEAR IN POLKA MUSIC INDUSTRY

MS. TERESA ZAPOLSKA

President, Floral Designer
Polka Towne Florist & Gifts
1998 Ladenburg Drive
Westbury, NY 11590 United States
polkatowne@verizon.net
http://www.polkatowneflorist.net

Type of Business: Retail Store

Major Products and Services: Floral Arrangements, Custom Designs, Silk and Dried Flowers, Gift Items and Novelties, Gift Baskets for All Occasions, Wedding and Party Consultations, Polka Records, Tapes and Compact Discs

Marketing Area: Regional

Area of Expertise: Ms. Zapolska's expertise is in business management.

Day to Day Responsibilities: Overseeing Operations

Hobbies/Interests/Sports: Caring for and Playing with her Dogs, Reviewing New Polka Releases, Contacting Radio Fans

Certifications: Certification in Floral Design

Awards/Honors: Two Entertainment Awards (2006); Best Female Vocalist Award, International Polka Association; Most Talented Store Owner, Westbury, NY; Inducted into the Polka Hall of Fame (2008)

Work History: Vice President, Gateway Industries and Recording Studios, Pittsburgh, PA; Consultant and Advisor, Premier Albums; Radio Industry Executive, WBAB-WGR; Program Licensed Engineer and Producer, WUSB-FM; Founder, Polka Towne Record Distributors; Recording Artist, RCA Victor, Polo, Musico, Rex, Dana, Silverbell, Dyno, Rim, Eurotone and Polka Towne; Featured Band Vocalist; Medical Secretary

Expanded Biography: Ms. Zapolska had many responsibilities during her time in the record industry. While at Gateway Industries and Recording Studios, her responsibilities included overseeing artists and repertoire for the record labels Dyno and Rim. During her time at Premier Albums, her responsibilities included visiting distributors, stores and radio shows nationwide for the Jay Jay polka label. Ms. Zapolska also performs as a featured singer with 20 orchestras in New York, New Jersey, Connecticut and Massachusetts. She is a member of Frank Wojnarowski's band and has written songs, helped run the band, planned tours, written band orchestration, designed costumes and recorded songs. She appeared on two television music series during the 1970s including eight additional shows for television release. She has also written songs and published for Broadcast Music, Inc. since 1963. She has had her own band for 29 years.

EXECUTIVE OF THE YEAR IN PHARMACEUTICALS MANUFACTURING

THOMAS R. ZIMMERMAN JR., MD

Vice President of Research and Development
Asubio Pharmaceuticals, Inc.
395 West Passaic Street
Rochelle Park, NJ 07662 United States
tzimmerman@asubio.com
http://www.asubio.com

Type of Business: Pharmaceuticals Manufacturer and Research Company

Major Products and Services: Medical and Pharmaceutical Research for the Treatment of Cardiovascular Diseases, Ailments of the Central Nervous System, Immunologic Conditions and Hormonal Irregularities

Marketing Area: International

Day to Day Responsibilities: Developing Drugs, Budgeting, Overseeing Clinical Development Plans, and Workplace Safety for 30 Employees and 50 Vendors

Hobbies/Interests/Sports: Music

Education Degrees: Doctor of Medicine, University of Medicine and Dentistry of New Jersey (1986)

Affiliations/Associations/Societies: AAN; AMA; AGS; Drug Information Association

VIP

SPECIAL SECTION

2008–2009

CAMBRIDGE WHO'S WHO

Mr. Arthur J. Abbate
President
Grout Rescue, Inc.
23 Center Court
Center Moriches, NY 11934 United States
aabbate@groutrescue.com
http://www.groutrescue.com

BUS: Contracting Company Dedicated to Providing Quality Home Improvement Services **P/S:** Restoration, Construction, Contracting, Kitchens and Bathrooms **MA:** Regional **EXP:** Mr. Abbate's areas of expertise are in restoration and construction. **H/I/S:** Golfing **FBP:** Fortune Magazine **EDU:** Master of Business Administration, Saint Joseph College (2005); Master of Science in Organizational Management, Saint Joseph College (2002) **A/A/S:** Center for Social Entrepreneurship

Suellen G. Abbott
Reading and Music Teacher
Hemphill Independent School District
PO Box 1950
Hemphill, TX 75948 United States
suellena@mail.hemphill.esc7.net
http://www.hemphill.esc7.net

BUS: School District **P/S:** Education **MA:** Local **D/D/R:** Teaching the 'Voyager,' an Intervention Reading Program, to Kindergarten and First-Grade Students, Teaching Music to Prekindergarten through Fourth-Grade Students, Mentoring Students, Creating Special Musical Programs for All Grade Levels **H/I/S:** Writing, Collecting Fenton Art Glass and Antiques, Art, Playing the Piano, Spending Time with her Family **FBP:** Industry-Related Publications **EDU:** Bachelor of Science in Education, Stephen F. Austin State University **A/A/S:** Texas State Teachers Association; Secretary, Local Chapter, Phi Delta Kappa; Poetry Society of America; Order of the Eastern Star; Lion's Club International; National Garden Clubs; Hemphill Chamber of Commerce; Former Worthy Matron of Texas; Former Deputy, State of Texas; Founder, Community Music Program **A/H:** Golden Apple Award for Outstanding Teachers of East Texas in Education; Miss Hemphill, Hemphill High School (1959); Certificates of Appreciation, Thomas Johnson High School **C/VW:** First Baptist Church **DOB:** December 6, 1941 **POB:** Port Arthur, TX **SP:** Bill **CHILD:** Julee, Jason **A/S:** She attributes her success to her perseverance, dignity, respect, patience and the support she receives from her family. **B/I:** She became involved in her profession because she always enjoyed music and wanted to help and inspire others. **H/O:** The most gratifying aspect of her career is to watch a child grow academically.

GEORGE T. ABERMATHY, MD

Cardiologist
Heart Institute of Venice
1370 East Venice Avenue Suite 102
Venice, FL 34285 United States
askthedr@heartinstituteofvenice.com
http://www.heartinstituteofvenice.com

BUS: Healthcare Healthcare-Doctor **P/S:** Cardiology Practice, Providing Excellent Pre-Op and Post-Op Services and Consulting Services to Cardiologists **MA:** Regional **D/D/R:** Non Invasive Cardiology **H/I/S:** Boating, Fishing, Swimming, Breeding Quarter Horses for Competitive Cutting **FBP:** Journal of American Cardiology **EDU:** MD, Emory University School of Medicine; Bachelor's Degree, Emory University School of Medicine **CERTS:** Board Certified- Intern of Medicine and Cardiology **A/A/S:** Fellow, American College of Cardiology; Fellow, American Heart Association; Fellow, American College of Chest Physicians; ASEC

MS. RACHEL M. ABRAHAMS

Program Officer
The Avi Chai Foundation
1015 Park Avenue
New York, NY 10028 United States
http://www.avichai.org

BUS: Philanthropy **P/S:** Programs to Assist in Furthering Jewish Education and Heritage **MA:** National **EXP:** Ms. Abrahams' expertise is in philanthropy in Jewish education. **EDU:** JD, Cardoza Law School; Master's Degree, Law, Bernard Revel School, Yeshiva University **CERTS:** Certified in Bible Studies **A/A/S:** Council on Philanthropy; Jewish Founders Network **C/VW:** Jewish Women's Organizations **A/S:** She attributes her success to her personal values and devotion to Jewish education. **B/I:** She became involved in this profession because she has always been involved with her synagogue and was looking for a new job other than the law field. **H/O:** The highlight of her career is being able to develop very exciting programs such as helping women to study at home and teaching Hebrew, history and culture.

CAROL ABSHIRE
Science Laboratory Manager
Lamar State College-Orange
410 W. Front Street
Orange, TX 77630 United States
carol.abshire@lsco.edu
http://www.orange.lamar.edu

BUS: College **P/S:** Education **MA:** Regional **D/D/R:** Teaching Medical Lab Technology Programs, Conducting Courses in Phlebotomy and Urinalysis, Co-teaching an On-line Introduction to Clinical Laboratory Science Course, Managing the Laboratory, Overseeing Behind-the-scenes Set Up, Mixing Chemical Solutions and Ordering Supplies, Equipment and Materials for Laboratories. **H/I/S:** Photography **FBP:** Phlebotomy Today **EDU:** Bachelor's Degree in General Studies, Lamar State-Beaumont (2006) **A/A/S:** American Society for Clinical Pathology **C/VW:** Relay for Life; College for Kids

SANDRA L. ACKERMAN, RN
RN
Valley Health-Winchester Medical Center
1840 Amherst Street
Winchester, VA 22604 United States
ackerman3@adelphia.net
http://www.Valleyhealthlink.com

BUS: Medical Center **P/S:** Healthcare **MA:** Regional **D/D/R:** Working as a Registered Nurse, Assisting with Cardiovascular Surgery and Intensive Care Unit **H/I/S:** Reading **EDU:** Bachelor of Science in Nursing, The Pennsylvania State University; Associate Degree in Nursing, Allegheny Community College **A/A/S:** American Association of Critical-Care Nurses **A/S:** She attributes her success to family support and encouragement from her husband to continue her education. **B/I:** She was prompted to enter her profession because her mother was a nurse. **H/O:** The highlight of her career was receiving her Bachelors Degree.

CECILIA L. ADAM
Senior Laboratory Technician
Mastertaste, Inc.
546 U.S. Highway 46
Teterboro, NJ 07608 United States
skisaphir@aol.com
http://www.mastertaste.com

BUS: Manufacturing Company **P/S:** Fragrance Oils and Flavors **MA:** International **EXP:** Ms. Adam's expertise is in chemistry. **D/D/R:** Making Candles, Testing Fragrances **H/I/S:** Gardening, Snow Skiing **FBP:** Inside the Vatican **EDU:** Bachelor's Degree in Chemistry, St. Joseph's College (1981) **A/A/S:** American Chemical Society **C/VW:** Saint Matthias Church

ALANA KAY ADAMS, RN, BSHS
Patient Care Manager
VistaCare Hospice
14232 N. 23rd Street
Phoenix, AZ 85022 United States
alanakay.adams@cwwemail.com
http://www.vistacare.com

BUS: Hospital **P/S:** Healthcare **MA:** Regional **D/D/R:** Overseeing All Patients, Nurses, Managers and Social Workers, Managing Patient Care and Visits from Chaplains, Reviewing Medicare Documents and All Clinical Record Information, Budgeting, Complying with the Centers for Medicare and Medicaid Services **H/I/S:** Hiking, Spending Time with her Grandchildren, Traveling, Gardening **FBP:** RN; The American Journal of Managed Care **EDU:** Bachelor of Science in Health Service Administration, Northern Arizona University (1989); Associate of Science in Nursing (1977) **A/A/S:** Phi Kappa Phi; Arizona Hospice and Palliative Care Organization **A/H:** Magna Cum Laude

MR. MICHAEL B. ADAMS
Vice President
Turner Lightning Protection Co., Inc.
2845 Wilson Avenue
Cincinnati, OH 45251 United States
mikeadams@lightningpro.com
http://www.lightningpro.com

BUS: Full System Supplier of Lightning Protection and Power Quality Consulting **P/S:** Government and Commercial Lightning Protection, Surge Suppressors, Lightning Rods, Design, Engineering and Installation **MA:** OH, PA, KY, MI, IN **D/D/R:** Client Relations, Problem Solving, Lightning Protection Specialists **H/I/S:** Spending Time with Family, Camping, Swimming, Traveling **EDU:** Bachelor's Degree in Communication Sciences, Ohio University (1989) **A/A/S:** Better Business Bureau; Lightning Protection Institute; Honorary Chairman, National Republican Congressional Committee; Underwriter's Laboratories **A/H:** Kentucky Colonel Recipient, Governor Paul Patton (2003)

TAWANA B. ADAMS
Teacher
Parker Elementary
640 S. Highway 22A
Panama City, FL 32404 United States
adamsangelfish@yahoo.com
http://www.bayschools.com/pkesportal

BUS: Proven Leader in Public Education **P/S:** Elementary Education of Children in Grades K-6, General Studies, Arts, Science, Physical Education, Special Education Programs **MA:** Regional **D/D/R:** Helping to Develop Young Minds and Preparing them for Secondary Schooling, **H/I/S:** Spending Time with her Children, Piano, Singing, Crocheting, Reading, Sewing, Baton Twirling, Basketball, Writing Poetry, Story Telling, Acting **FBP:** NEA Publications; Children's Literature; Weekly Reader; Scholastic; Mailbox **EDU:** Master's Degree in Educational Leadership, Florida State University (1995); Bachelor of Arts, Old Dominion University **A/A/S:** ABCE; National Education Association; Bay County Reading Association; American Federation of Teachers; American Cancer Association; Storytellers Group; Boys Book Club **A/H:** Who's Who American Teachers (2003-2005)

MAUREEN ADAMS-HEGWOOD
Handicapped Learner Specialist
Jefferson County Public Schools
445 S.E. Buff Street
Madras, OR 97741 United States
mo1949@telePort.com
http://www.jcsd.com

BUS: Public School **P/S:** Special Education, Basic Reading, Writing, Mathematics and Social Skills **MA:** Local **D/D/R:** Offering Special Needs Education for Handicapped Children since 1974 **H/I/S:** Camping, Boy Scouts, Sewing, Crafts, Hunting and Fishing along with her Husband. **FBP:** Boys' Life **EDU:** Bachelor's Degree in Elementary Education, University of Hawaii; Coursework in Special Education **A/A/S:** National Education Association; Boy Scouts of America **A/H:** Wood Badge Course Director Vigil Honor, Boy Scouts of America; Silver Beaver, Boy Scouts of America **C/VW:** Special Olympics; Shriners' Hospital for Children, Arthritis Foundation, Concerned Women for America **A/S:** She attributes her success to her ability to do her best in working together with child and family. **B/I:** She became involved in her profession by accident. The school had a shortage in her profession and she enjoyed it so much she stayed in it. **H/O:** The highlight of her career is seeing the progress made by the students she works with.

REBECCA ELIZABETH ADDO-NARTEY, PT, DPT
Pediatric Physical Therapist
Children's Specialized Hospital
10 Oak Drive
Edison, NJ 08837 United States
rebeccadan1@verizon.net
http://www.childrens-specialized.org

BUS: Hospital **P/S:** Healthcare, Early Intervention, Family-Based Pediatric Services and Physical Therapy **MA:** Central New Jersey **D/D/R:** Performing Physical Therapy for Children, Working with Special Orthotic Equipment and Caring for Children with Neurological Disorders. **H/I/S:** Spending Time with her Family **FBP:** Exceptional Parent Magazine; Journal of Developmental Medicine and Child Neurology **EDU:** Doctor of Physical Therapy, Simmons College (2006); Master of Theology, Princeton Theological Seminary (1995); Bachelor of Science in Biology, Simmons College (1985) **A/H:** Performance Award **C/VW:** Teacher, Sunday School, Local Church; Community Outreach Program; Mission in Sierra Leone and Liberia; Ghana Congregation **A/S:** She attributes her success to the support she receives from her mentors, educators and supervisors. **B/I:** She became involved in her profession through a natural progression of opportunities. **H/O:** The most gratifying aspect of her career is having the opportunity to serve people at Sikoma, West Africa, Puerto Rico, Mexico, Egypt, Pakistan and Ghana.

BONNIE C. ADKINS
Licensed Affiliated Broker
Sellers Realty Co.
119 Charles Sievers Boulevard
Clinton, TN 37716 United States
sellreal@bellsouth.net
http://www.cambridgewhoswho.com

BUS: Real Estate Brokerage Firm **P/S:** Residential and Commercial Real Estate Services, Mortgage Assistance, Luxury Homes, Property Search **MA:** Regional **D/D/R:** Handling Real Estate Services for Lake Properties and Horse Farms **H/I/S:** Motorcycles, Horses **EDU:** College Coursework **CERTS:** Realtors License (1995); GRI Certified **A/A/S:** Anderson Association of Realtors; Knoxville Area Association of Realtors; Tennessee Association of Realtors; National Association of Realtors; **DOB:** August 23, 1947 **CHILD:** Two Sons, Three Grandchildren

MS. BARBARA J. AFFONCE
Nursing Information Systems Specialist
Professional Development Department
Southcoast Hospitals Group
101 Page Street
New Bedford, MA 02740 United States
affonceb@southcoast.org
http://www.southcoast.org

BUS: Healthcare Systems **P/S:** Healthcare Including Brain, Spine and Weight Loss Surgery, Cardiac Care, Diabetes, Maternity, Neurosurgery, Radiology and Rehabilitation Services **MA:** Regional **EXP:** Ms. Affonce's expertise is in nursing information technology on the Meditech healthcare software application. **D/D/R:** Monitoring Quality Assurance of the Healthcare System, Working for Professional Development Department, Teaching Trainers, Maintaining Dictionaries for Order Entry, e-Mail Systems and Order Entry System **EDU:** Associate's Degree in Computer Technology, Fisher College (2005) **CERTS:** Certified Health Unit Coordinator (1988) **A/A/S:** Nursing Documentation Committee **A/H:** National Educator of the Year Award, National Association of Health Unit Coordinator (1995)

DR. KERRI-RAE AGIN
Dentist, Owner
Herbie Dental
1413 Diamond Hill Road
Woonsocket, RI 02895 United States
herbiedental@juno.com
http://www.ridentist.com

BUS: Dental Practice Dedicated to Providing the Very Best 'Gentle' Dental Care **P/S:** General Dentistry Services, Examinations, Cleanings, Oral Hygiene Instruction, Fillings, Crowns, Dentures, Newest In Cerec Technology (CAD-CAM), Laser Technology **MA:** Regional **D/D/R:** Utilizing New Equipment, Laser Technologies, Digital X-Ray, Pediatrics and Adult Dentistry, Cosmetic Dentistry, Family Practice, Cerec Technology **H/I/S:** Participating in Outdoor Sports, Traveling, Running Marathons **FBP:** Woman Dentist Journal; Adult Dentistry **EDU:** Doctor of Medical Dentistry, Tufts University (1992) **CERTS:** Certification in Laser Surgery (2006); CAD-CAM Certification (2004); Orthodontic Certification (1999) **A/A/S:** American Dental Association; Pierre Fauchard Academy; New England Dental Society; Rhode Island Dental Society; United States Air Force **A/H:** The Sackler Award for Dental Research (1992); Company Grade Officer of the Year (1995)

NORMA A. AGUAYO, MS
Educator
Peralta Elementary School, Estrella CC
7125 W. Encanto Boulevard
Phoenix, AZ 85035 United States
norma.aguayo@nau.edu
http://www.cambridgewhoswho.com

BUS: Education **P/S:** Provide Education for Grades K-5 **MA:** Local **EXP:** Educator. **H/I/S:** Walking, Jogging, Family Activities **EDU:** Pursuing Master's Degree in Bilingual Multicultural Education; Master's Degree in Educational Leadership, North Arizona University; Master's Degree in Elementary Education, North Arizona University **A/A/S:** Phi Kappa Phi **C/VW:** Donates and Teaches in Maricopa County, AZ **A/S:** She attributes her personal and professional success to her drive, motivation and experiences. **B/I:** She has always had an interest in the field and was motivated by one of her high school teachers.

JUAN M. AGUILÓ-GARLAND
Architect
JMA Architecture Interior Design
268 Ponce de Leon
Suite 503
Hato Rey, PR 00918 United States
jaguilo@jmarq.com
http://www.jmarq.com

BUS: Architectural Company **P/S:** Leaders in Providing Architectural and Interior Design Services **MA:** National **D/D/R:** Residential High End Design, Start to Finish Interior Decorating and Design, Overseeing the Company **EDU:** Master's Degree in Architecture, University of Puerto Rico (1985); Bachelor of Science in Architecture, Ohio State University (1985) **CERTS:** Licensed in Architecture, Florida and Puerto Rico **A/A/S:** Colegio de Arquitectos y Arquitectos Paisajistas; American Institute of Architects

MR. KEVIN W. AHEARN
Superintendent
Carteret School District
599 Roosevelt Avenue
Carteret, NJ 07008 United States
kahearn@carteretschools.org
http://www.cambridgewhoswho.com

BUS: School District **P/S:** Education **MA:** Regional **D/D/R:** Overseeing Five Schools, Managing Different Programs and Curriculums for the District, Ensuring a Safe and Nurturing Environment that Affirms the Worth and Diversity of All Students **H/I/S:** Golfing **EDU:** Master's Degree in English Literature and Educational Administration, Manhattan College; Master's Degree in Special Education, Staten Island University Hospital; Master's Degree in Theatre, New York University; Bachelor of Arts in English Literature, Iona College **A/A/S:** Council for Exceptional Children; New Jersey Principals and Supervisors Association; New Jersey Staffing Alliance **A/H:** Nominee, Central New Jersey Superintendent of the Year

CYNTHIA AIELLO
Head Nurse, Administrator
Hearts Together
188 Miller Avenue
Elmwood Park, NJ 07407 United States
Cynthia.Aiello@cwwemail.com
http://www.cambridgewhoswho.com

BUS: Nonprofit Organization **P/S:** Mental Health Services, Physical Therapy for Babies and Children Addicted to Drugs **MA:** Local **D/D/R:** Overseeing Nursing Staff Performance, Monitoring and Assessing Children's Progress, Caring for Children with Mental and Physical Impairments Resulting From Drug-addicted Parents, Speaking to the People who Seek to Adopt Children. **H/I/S:** Spending Time with her Family, Caring for her Pets **FBP:** RN Magazine **EDU:** Bachelor of Science in Nursing, William Paterson University (1986); Associate Degree in Nursing (1984)

ERICA AITKEN
President
Rods and Cones, Inc.
501 Mission Street
Suite 3
Santa Cruz, CA 95060 United States
erica@rodsandcones.com
http://www.rodsandcones.com

BUS: Consulting for Work Flow Solutions **P/S:** Workflow Systems and Technical Services for Advertising and Graphic Agencies, Photo Studios, Prepress Services Agencies, Print Providers and In-House Creative Groups **MA:** National **EXP:** Ms. Aitken's areas of expertise are in business development and sales. **H/I/S:** Running, Reading, Spending Time with her Family **FBP:** The New Yorker **EDU:** Bachelor of Fine Arts, Ecole de Recherches Graphiques, Brussels, Belgium **A/A/S:** Printing Industries of Northern California; GATS

WANDA K. AKI III
Librarian III
Public Safety
Kauai Community Correctional Center
35351 Kuhio Highway
Lihue, HI 96766 United States
exploradadora@yahoo.com
http://www.cambridgewhoswho.com

BUS: Correctional Center **P/S:** Correctional and Rehabilitation Services **MA:** Local **D/D/R:** Researching with Touch Sonic Technology, Teaching Inmates to Research on Case Laws **H/I/S:** Dancing **FBP:** Industry-Related Publications **EDU:** Master's Degree in Library Science, University of Hawaii **A/A/S:** Library Science Alumni Association; Hale O Na Alii **A/H:** National Award for Success for Non-Traditional Schooling for a Native Hawaiian **A/S:** She attributes her success to her hard work, determination and confidence. **B/I:** She became involved in her profession because of her personal experiences. **H/O:** The highlight of her career was being a part of a pilot research program.

CLAUDETTE P. ALAIMO
Realtor
Century 21 Alaimo & Corrado
25 Palomba Drive
Enfield, CT 06082 United States
claudettealaimo@ctmove.com
http://www.claudettealaimo.com

BUS: Sales, Real Estate **P/S:** Real Estate Property **MA:** Local **D/D/R:** Selling Residential, Condo and Multi-Family Investments **H/I/S:** Snow Skiing, Kayaking, Hiking, Biking **CERTS:** Certified Residential Specialist **A/A/S:** Executive Realtor, Connecticut Association Board of Realtors Region 3VP; Greater Hartford Board of Realtors **C/VW:** School Activities, Parent Teacher Associations, Boost Club, Cancer Research Fundraising **A/S:** She attributes her personal and professional success to her ability to meet the needs of customers. **B/I:** She was influenced by her father-in-law to enter the field and truly enjoys her work. **H/O:** The highlight of her career is having satisfied customers and receiving awards along the way.

BARBARA M. ALBERTS
Claims Service Representative
Brown and Brown, Empire State
500 Plum Street
Syracuse, NY 13206 United States
balberts@bbempirestate.com
http://www.cambridgewhoswho.com

BUS: Insurance Agency **P/S:** Commercial Insurance **MA:** National **EXP:** Ms. Albert's expertise is in claims management. **H/I/S:** Reading, Knitting, Gardening **EDU:** Bachelor of Arts in Mathematics and Science; Bachelor of Arts in Sociology, SUNY Cortland **A/A/S:** IANI; AIC; ARM; ACFR **A/S:** She attributes her success to her love of knowledge. **B/I:** She became involved in this profession because she started as an insurance coder and continually got promoted. **H/O:** The highlight of her career was becoming a claims manager.

TAMARA ALDREDGE
Director, Owner
Rainbow Child Care Too
5599 Hilliard Rome Office Park
Hilliard, OH 43026 United States
rainbowchildcaretoo@yahoo.com
http://www.rainbowchildcare-too.com

BUS: Child Day Care Facility **P/S:** Quality Affordable Care for Children From Ages 6 Weeks to 12 Years Where Children Learn, Play and Grow in a Safe and Secure Environment, Stimulating and Growing Experience through Emotional, Social and Intellectual Supportive Activities **MA:** Regional **EXP:** Ms. Aldredge's areas of expertise are in child care, leadership and management. **D/D/R:** Ensuring Quality Care for Children **EDU:** Bachelor of Science in Education, Otterbein College **A/A/S:** National Advisory Committee on Immunization

CHERYL ALDRIDGE, MN, RN, CPNP

Nurse Practitioner Manager
Parkland Health and Hospital System
5201 Harry Hines Boulevard
Dallas, TX 75235 United States
caldri@parknet.pmh.org
http://www.cambridgewhoswho.com

BUS: County Hospital **P/S:** Healthcare, Research and Education **MA:** Local **EXP:** Ms. Aldridge's expertise is in pediatric care. **H/I/S:** Cross Stitching, Reading **EDU:** Master's Degree in Nursing, University of Kansas **A/A/S:** Texas Nurse Practitioners; American Academy of Nurse Practitioners; The Greater Texas Chapter of Pediatric Nurse Practitioners; National Association of Pediatric Nurse Practitioners **C/VW:** Child Advocacy Center for Denton County; AIDS Services of North Texas **A/S:** She attributes her success to always wanting to learn more and her family's support. **B/I:** She became involved in this profession because she always wanted to help others and she had an interest in medicine. **H/O:** The highlight of her career was being recognized as Practitioner of the Year by the state.

STEPHANIE A. ALEX

Assistant Director of Special Education
Imagine Schools
18052 North Black Canyon Highway
Phoenix, AZ 85053 United States
salex@imagineschools.com
http://www.cambridgewhoswho.com

BUS: Special Education **P/S:** Special Education **MA:** National **D/D/R:** Serving as Assistant Director **H/I/S:** Reading, Painting, Photography **FBP:** Educational Leadership; Special Educators Association Publication **EDU:** Master of Arts in Education, Curriculum and Instruction, University of Phoenix; Bachelor of Arts, University of California, Irvine **CERTS:** Special Education Certification, University of California. Riverside **A/A/S:** Association of Curriculum Instructors; Learning Disabilities Association of America; Special Educators Administrators Association **A/H:** National Teacher of the Year, Imagine Schools **C/VW:** Women's Ministries, Christ Church Lutheran, Phoenix, Arizona **A/S:** She attributes her success to her hardworking parents and the values they instilled in her. **B/I:** She became involved in the profession after working for the Walt Disney Company until 1991 and realizing her desire to teach. **H/O:** The highlight of her career was returning to school.

Dr. Carolyn J. Alexander
Reproductive Endocrinologist, Infertility Specialist, Associate
Residency Program Director, Obstetrics and Gynecology
Cedars-Sinai Medical Center
8700 Beverly Boulevard
Los Angeles, CA 90048 United States
cjoya77@yahoo.com
http://www.csmc.edu, http://www.csmc.edu/12928.html

BUS: Medical Center **P/S:** Healthcare Services **EXP:** Dr. Alexander's expertise is in reproductive endocrinology. **D/D/R:** Treating Infertility Patients, Performing Surgery, Conducting Research, Administering Ultrasounds **H/I/S:** Spending Time Outdoors, Swimming, Reading, Volunteering **FBP:** Fertility and Sterility; The Johns Hopkins Manual of Gynecology and Obstetrics **EDU:** MD, University of California, Los Angeles (2000) **CERTS:** Board Certified in Obstetrics and Gynecology **A/A/S:** Society for Endocrinology; American Society of Reproductive Medicine; American Medical Association; American College of Obstetricians and Gynecologists **A/H:** Teaching Award, Council on Resident Education in Obstetrics and Gynecology (2008) **C/VW:** March of Dimes; Fertile Hope **POB:** Los Angeles

Patricia L. Alexander
Elementary Teacher
Irvington Elementary School
611 S. First Street
Irvington, KY 40146 United States
patti.alexander@break.ky.schools.us
http://www.cambridgewhoswho.com

BUS: Education **P/S:** Education **MA:** Local **EXP:** Ms. Alexander's expertise is in elementary education. **H/I/S:** Spending Time with her Family, Traveling, Reading, Enjoying Outdoor Activities **EDU:** Master's Degree, Eastern Kentucky University; Bachelor's Degree, Eastern Kentucky University **C/VW:** St. Jude Children's Research Hospital, American Red Cross, Church **A/S:** She attributes her success to her supportive family. **B/I:** She chose the profession because she comes from a family of educators. **H/O:** The highlight of her career is her educational success.

VICTORIA FORD ALEXANDER
Elementary Teacher (Retired)
Oakland Unified School District
1025 Second Avenue
Oakland, CA 94606 United States
brookstex@aol.com
http://www.cambridgewhoswho.com

BUS: School District **P/S:** Education **MA:** Local **D/D/R:** Teaching Elementary Education, Drama and Music **H/I/S:** Traveling, Gardening, Cooking, Attending Music Events **FBP:** Gardening and Cooking Magazines **EDU:** Bachelor's Degree in Counseling, University of Phoenix **A/A/S:** Soloist, San Francisco Russian Choir; Oakland Education Association; National Education Association **C/VW:** Local Church; Veterans of Foreign Wars **A/S:** She attributes her success to caring for children. **B/I:** She became involved in her profession because she was inspired by her father and because she always enjoyed working with children. **H/O:** The most gratifying aspect of her career is seeing her students succeed.

WARENE D. ALFORD
Contractor Industrial Relations Specialist (Retired)
U.S. Department of Army, Corps of Engineers
819 Taylor Street
Room 2A-19
Fort Worth, TX 76102 United States
Warene.D.Alford@swf02.usace.army.mil
http://www.usace.army.mil

BUS: Government Agency Providing Quality, Responsive Engineering Services to the Nation, Made up of Approximately 34,600 Civilian and 650 Military Men and Women **P/S:** Planning, Designing, Building and Operating Water Resources and Other Civil Works Projects such as Navigation, Flood Control, Environmental Protection and Disaster Response, Designing and Managing the Construction of Military Facilities for the Army and Air Force, Offering Design and Construction Management Services to Defense and Other Federal Agencies **MA:** International **D/D/R:** Labor and Civil Works Projects, Monitoring Government Contracts on Contractors for The Davis Bacon and Related Acts for Compliance **H/I/S:** Traveling, Sports **FBP:** People; Better Homes & Gardens; Ebony; Jet **EDU:** Coursework, El Centro College; Diploma, Dunbar High School, Oakwood, TX **A/A/S:** Ft. Hood Modularity Development Project **A/H:** Project Delivery Team of the Month (2004); Certificate of Appreciation, US Army Medical Department Facility, Fort Polk, LA (1999); Performance Award (1991-1993); Official Commendation, Department of the Army (1983-1988); Superior Sustained Performance Award, Department of Agriculture (1974) **C/VW:** Greater El Bethel Baptist Church, Dallas, TX

CAROL L. ALISESKY
Special Education Teacher (Retired)
Intermediate Unit #1
One Intermediate Unit Drive
Coal Center, PA 15423 United States
carol.alisesky@verizon.net
http://www.cambridgewhoswho.com

BUS: School **P/S:** Special Education for 3-5 Year Olds **MA:** Regional **D/D/R:** Teaching Special Education, Early Childhood Development **H/I/S:** Swimming, Vacationing, Walking, Reading **EDU:** Bachelor's Degree in Special Education, California University of Pennsylvania (1985) **A/A/S:** NCRR **C/VW:** United Cerebral Palsy **A/S:** She attributes her success to her education, determination and achievements. **B/I:** She became involved in the profession because her daughter has special needs. **H/O:** The most gratifying aspect of her career is watching children achieve.

AUDREY W. ALLEN
Director of Nursing
Highland Park Care Center
2714 Morrison Street
Houston, TX 77009 United States
audrey.allen@sbcglobal.net
http://www.cambridgewhoswho.com

BUS: Residential Care Center **P/S:** Healthcare **MA:** Regional **EXP:** Ms. Allen's expertise is in nursing. **D/D/R:** Overseeing Dietary Issues and Procedures, Ensuring All Systems Functions **H/I/S:** Gardening, Horseback Riding, Caring for Animals **FBP:** Journal of Gerontological Nursing **EDU:** Associate of Arts, North Harris Montgomery Community College (1984) **A/A/S:** BNA; ACNA **SP:** Napolean **CHILD:** Andrea, Natasha

JACQUELINE L. ALLEN
Real Estate Associate Broker
Century 21 J. L. Allen
299 Shell Road
Carneys Point, NJ 08069 United States
info@jlallen.info
http://www.cambridgewhoswho.com

BUS: Real Estate Agency **P/S:** Commercial and Residential Real Estate Exchange **MA:** Local **D/D/R:** Selling Residential Properties. **H/I/S:** Traveling, Attending the Game Show Tapings **CERTS:** Industry-Related Training **A/A/S:** New Jersey Association of Realtors; National Association of Realtors **C/VW:** Carneys Point Historic Society **A/S:** She attributes her success to her love for her profession. **B/I:** She became involved in her profession because she wanted to be in the real estate industry since childhood. **H/O:** The most gratifying aspect of her career is owning her real estate business.

KATHIE ALLEN, DDS
Private Practice
Kathie Allen, DDS, PA
836 Sunset Lake Boulevard
Suite 204
Venice, FL 34292 United States
drkathie@verizon.net
http://www.drkathie.net

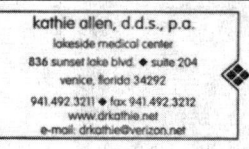

kathie allen, d.d.s., p.a.
lakeside medical center
836 sunset lake blvd. ◆ suite 204
venice, florida 34292
941.492.3211 ◆ fax 941.492.3212
www.drkathie.net
e-mail: drkathie@verizon.net

BUS: Dental Office Dedicated to Providing High Quality Comprehensive Dental Treatment in a Comfortable and Caring Atmosphere **P/S:** Bonding, Cosmetic Contouring, Crowns and Bridges, Specialty Dentures, Cosmetic Fillings, Implants, Restorations, Veneers, Whitening, Sealants, Root Canal Therapy, Extractions Scaling and Root Planing, Dentures, Fillings **MA:** Regional **EXP:** Dr. Allen's areas of expertise are in cosmetic and restorative dentistry. **H/I/S:** Horseback Riding, Theatre, Art, Working Out **EDU:** Doctor of Dental Surgery, University of Detroit Mercy (1990) **CERTS:** Certified Dental Hygienist, Ferris State University (1981) **A/A/S:** Advisory Board, Manatee Community College Dental Hygiene (2000-Present); State Board Examiner for State of Florida, Dentistry and Dental Hygienists (1999-Present); Academy of General Dentistry; West Coast Dental Association; Sarasota County Dental Association; Florida Dental Association; American Dental Association; Sharks Tooth: Venice Chapter, Seattle Study Club; Sarasota Study Group; Female Study Group; Venice-Sarasota Study Group; Sarasota Implant Study Group; Florida Emergency Mass Disaster Team Forensics; Alpha Omega Dental Fraternity; Pi Delta Alpha; Phi Eta Sigma

LYNNE W. ALLEN, MBA, BS
Business Manager
Stargate School
3954 Cottonwood Lakes Boulevard
Thornton, CO 80241 United States
lynne.allen@adams12.org
http://www.stargateschool.org

BUS: Chartered Educational K-8 Facility **P/S:** High Quality Educational Services for Intellectually Gifted and Talented Students **MA:** Local **EXP:** Ms. Allen's areas of expertise are in accounting and business management. **H/I/S:** Skiing, Traveling **EDU:** Master of Business Administration, Clarkson University; Bachelor of Science in Political Science and Economics, St. Lawrence University (1983)

SUSAN E. ALLEN
President
Allen Insurance Agency and Associates, Inc.
1809 Main Street
Valrico, FL 33594 United States
aia96@aol.com
http://www.cambridgewhoswho.com

BUS: Insurance Company **P/S:** Property and Casualty Insurance Services **MA:** Regional **D/D/R:** Offering Personal and Commercial Insurance for Homes, Automobiles and Life Insurance and Ensuring Customer Satisfaction. **H/I/S:** Golfing, Spending Time with her Family **EDU:** Bachelor of Science in Marketing, University of Tampa (1991)

THERESE M. ALLIN
Mathematics Educator
Centralia High School
813 Eshom Road
Centralia, WA 98531 United States
allint@comcast.net
http://www.cambridgewhoswho.com

BUS: School **P/S:** Education **MA:** Local **EXP:** Ms. Allin's expertise is in mathematics. **EDU:** Master's Degree in Educational Leadership, University of Portland **A/A/S:** Washington Education Association; National Education Association; National Council of Teachers of Mathematics **B/I:** She became involved in her profession because she had the ability to explain mathematics to others.

MARJORIE N. ALMEDA, DO
Doctor of Osteopathy
Visiting Physicians Association
3840 Packard Road
Suite 170
Ann Arbor, MI 48108 United States
teamalameda@voyager.net
http://www.visitingphysicians.com

BUS: Healthcare **P/S:** House Calls, Primary Care **MA:** Local **EXP:** Dr. Almeda's areas of expertise are in internal medicine, geriatrics, Alzheimer's, hospice and end of life care. **H/I/S:** Mothering her Three Boys, Traveling **FBP:** Clinical Geriatrics; Industry-Related Journals **EDU:** Doctor of Osteopathic Medicine, Michigan State University (1998) **A/A/S:** Diplomat, American College of Osteopathic Internists; American College of Osteopathic Internists; American Osteopathic Association; The American Geriatrics Society **SP:** Lawrence **CHILD:** Joseph, James, John

DARELENE M. ALOOT
Vice President
Quantitative Management Consultants, LLC
1818 Sixth Avenue
Apartment 216
San Diego, CA 92101 United States
darelene.aloot@theqmcgroup.com
http://www.theqmcgroup.com

BUS: Consulting Firm **P/S:** Consulting Services Including Information Technology, Quantitative Statistical Analysis and Financial Consulting **MA:** National **D/D/R:** Her expertise is in Marketing, Communicating, Contracting, Consulting on Government Relations, Procurements and Proposals. **H/I/S:** Traveling, Photography, Art, Painting **EDU:** Post Graduate Coursework in Marketing and Business Analysis; Bachelor's Degree in Business Administration, Eastern Michigan University (1979) **A/A/S:** Alpha Kappa Psi **A/H:** Who's Who of Executive Leaders **C/VW:** Academy of Friends; United Way; San Francisco Society for the Prevention of Cruelty to Animals

STAN ALTMAN
Senior Financial Advisor
Delta Equity
2787 E. Oakland Park Boulevard
Fort Lauderdale, FL 33306 United States
saltman@deltaequity.com
http://www.cambridgewhoswho.com

BUS: Investment Firm **P/S:** Financial Planning Including Annuities, Mutual Funds, Stocks and Bonds **MA:** National **D/D/R:** Financial and Retirement Planning **H/I/S:** Acting, Fishing, Boating, Artwork **EDU:** Coursework in Business Administration **CERTS:** License in Life, Fixed, Variable Annuity and Health Insurance; Registered Investment Advisor; Series 63 Financial Certification, Florida Department of Financial Services Registered Agency; Licensed Notary Public; Notary Signing Agent **A/A/S:** National Association of Securities Dealers **C/VW:** Volunteer, Hurricane Disaster Relief; Various Cancer Organizations **A/S:** He attributes his success to his personal drive and his knowledge in the business. **B/I:** He became involved in his profession because of his interest in the field of stock brokerage.

CRISTINA ALVAREZ
Mechanical Designer, CAD Manager
M-E Engineers, Inc.
10113 Jefferson Boulevard
Culver City, CA 90232 United States
calvarez@me-engineers-la.com
http://www.me-engineers.com

BUS: Mechanical and Electrical Engineering **P/S:** Mechanical and Electrical Consultants, Heating, Ventilation, Air Conditioning **MA:** National **EXP:** Ms. Alvarez's areas of expertise are in AutoDesk, AutoCAD and project design. **H/I/S:** Sports **EDU:** Bachelor of Science in Computer Visualization Technology, IGT Technical Institute **A/S:** She attributes her success to her dedication and desire to keep moving. **B/I:** She became involved in this profession because her drawing has always been an interest. **H/O:** The highlight of her career is being able to grasp the knowledge from her colleagues.

Ms. MELISSA J. ALVES, RN, BSN
Registered Nurse
The Hospital of Central Connecticut-New Britain General Campus
100 Grand Street
New Britain, CT 06050 United States
mimiadpi@yahoo.com
http://www.nbgh.org

BUS: Hospital **P/S:** High-Quality, Accessible and Cost-Effective Pediatric and Gynecological Nursing and Healthcare Services **MA:** Central Connecticut **D/D/R:** Performing Post-Operative Women's Health Services, Treating Children with Asthma, Distributing Medications, Following Up with Patient Healthcare, Checking Patient Vital Signs, Assisting with Ambulatory Services, Performing Transfusions and Cardiac Catheterization **H/I/S:** Reading, Going to the Gym, Spending Time with her Friends **FBP:** Advance for Nurses; American Journal of Nursing; Nursing Spectrum **EDU:** Bachelor of Science in Nursing, Western Connecticut State University (2001) **A/A/S:** Alpha Delta Pi

JANET ALVORD RYAN, BSN, MPH, RN
Public Health Nurse Consultant (Retired)
2431 N.W. 41st Street
Apartment 5406
Gainesville, FL 32606 United States
http://www.cambridgewhoswho.com

BUS: Proven Leader in the Healthcare Industry **P/S:** Nursing, Public Health, Gerontology and Healthcare Services for the State of Florida **MA:** Local **D/D/R:** Surveying Healthcare Facilities for Adherence to License Regulations and Medicare and Medicaid Regulations, Visiting Patients **H/I/S:** Spending Time with her Family, Playing Budge **FBP:** RN; Nursing2009; American Journal of Nursing **EDU:** Master of Public Health, University of Michigan (1967); Bachelor's Degree in Nursing, University of the Incarnate Word (1953) **A/A/S:** Florida Nurses Association; American Heart Association; Daughters of the American Revolution **A/H:** Recipient, Scholarship for Master of Public Health Degree, Florida State Board of Health (1966); **DOB:** January 4, 1932 **W/H:** Diploma Program, University of the Incarnate Word, San Antonio

A. LOREN AMACHER, MD
Neurosurgeon
Evangelical Medical Services Foundation
3 Hospital Drive
Suite 318
Lewisburg, PA 17837 United States
aljamach@ptd.net
http://www.evanhospital.com

BUS: Hospital **P/S:** Healthcare Including Family Medicine, Internal Medicine, Pediatrics, Pathology, Neurology, Rehabilitation, Emergency Care and Surgical Services **MA:** North Central Region **EXP:** Mr. Amacher's expertise is in neurosurgery. **H/I/S:** Reading, Writing Essays, Novels and Poetry, Spending Time with his Family **FBP:** Economist **EDU:** Fellowship, Royal College of Physicians and Surgeons of Canada (1969); MD, University of Western Ontario (1962) **CERTS:** Certification, Royal College of Physicians and Surgeons of Canada (1969) **A/A/S:** President, Pennsylvania Neurosurgical Society (1997); Trustee, Pennsylvania Medical Society; New York Academy of Sciences; American Association of Neurological Surgeons; American Association for the Advancement of Science; Academy of American Poets; Canadian Congress of Neurological Sciences **A/H:** Harriman Award, Bucknell University; Back Court Award, Bucknell University **DOB:** October 22, 1938 **SP:** Jane **CHILD:** Jon, Marc **W/H:** Department Director, Geisinger Medical Center (1987-2003); Professor of Neurology, University of Connecticut, Hartford Hospital (1983-1987); Associate Professor, University of Western Ontario (1970-1983) **C/A:** Honored Guest, Neurosurgical Society of Alabama (2002); Honored Guest, Spanish Neurosurgical Society (1982)

DEBRA J. AMBROFF, RN, BSN, CCM
Western Clinical Supervisor, Regional Manager
Sedgwick Claims Management Services, Inc
701 S. Parker Street
Suite 5000
Orange, CA 92868 United States
dambroff@sedgwickcms.com
http://www.cambridgewhoswho.com

BUS: Claims Management Company **P/S:** Worker's Compensation and Case Management Services **MA:** National **EXP:** Ms. Ambroff's expertise is in human resources management. **D/D/R:** Recruitment, Hiring, Staffing and Training New Staff Members, Managing Overall Clinical Operations for Assigned Teams and Offices, Developing and Implementing Clinical Objectives and Initiatives **H/I/S:** Reading, Walking, Visiting New Places **FBP:** The Case Manager **EDU:** Bachelor of Science in Nursing, University of Phoenix **CERTS:** Certified Case Manager, Case Management Society of America; Certified Public Health Nurse **DOB:** January 12, 1954 **CHILD:** Brett, Tami **W/H:** Regional Manager; Case Manager; Labor and Delivery Nurse; Operating Room Nurse; Registered Nurse **A/S:** She attributes her success to her passion for nursing and education. **B/I:** She became involved in the profession because she feels that nurses should be passionate about her work and tries to mentor nurses with that same feeling.

WILLIAM MATTHEW AMES
Chief Executive Officer, Engineer
WTG, Inc.
PO Box 1235
Folsom, CA 95763 United States
williamames@comcast.net

BUS: Invention Consulting Agency **P/S:** Invention Consulting Services, Wire Snigger, Quick Ream **MA:** International **EXP:** Mr. Ames' areas of expertise are in design, engineering and invention consulting. **D/D/R:** Managing and Executing Tasks and Timelines for Multiple Clients **H/I/S:** Swimming, Martial Arts, Archery, Watching Movies, Traveling **FBP:** Electrical Contractor; CNN **EDU:** Industry-Related Training and Experience **A/A/S:** International Brotherhood of Electrical Workers **A/H:** United States Patent Holder **C/VW:** Leukemia & Lymphoma Society; National Multiple Sclerosis Society; UTT Consulting **DOB:** February 1, 1967 **A/S:** He attributes his success to being inspired by Benjamin Franklin and his realization that everyone wants to think 'outside the box' so he teaches them that there is no box. **B/I:** He became involved in the profession after working in electrical contracting, where he invented the wire snagger. **H/O:** The highlight of his career was receiving a U.S. patent. The most gratifying aspect of his career is being able to help others achieve their dreams on a daily basis.

ROSE E. AMOAH, RN, BSN

Acting Assistant Director of Programs
Metro Day Treatment Center
Washington, DC 20011 United States
rosyosei@aol.com
http://www.cambridgewhoswho.com

BUS: School for the Mentally Challenged and Physically Handicapped **P/S:** Education **MA:** Local **D/D/R:** Nursing **H/I/S:** Traveling, Physical Fitness, Reading **FBP:** Nursing Spectrum; Prevention; Good Housekeeping **EDU:** Bachelor of Science in Nursing, Howard University **A/A/S:** American Nurses Association **A/S:** She attributes her success to her love of helping people and the satisfaction she gets from doing her job well. **B/I:** She wanted to help people and decided this was the career she wanted to pursue. **H/O:** The highlight of her career is bring able to help people who can not help themselves.

LOIS A. ANAPLE, RN

Registered Nurse
Mercy Health Partners Mount Airy Campus
2446 Kipling Road
Cincinnati, OH 45239 United States
lanaple@fuse.net
http://www.cambridgewhoswho.com

BUS: Healthcare **P/S:** Healthcare **MA:** Local **D/D/R:** Specializing in Nursing, Same Day Surgery, Preadmission Testing **H/I/S:** Choir and Community Activities, Golfing, Traveling, Reading, Crocheting, Gardening **FBP:** American Journal of Nursing **EDU:** Registered Nurse, Allegheny General Hospital School of Nursing, Pittsburgh, PA **CERTS:** Certified in Advanced Cardiac Life Support **C/VW:** Open Door Pantry; Hamilton Symphonic Chorale; Hamilton Presbyterian Church Regular and Contemporary Choirs; Voices of the Ascension Choir; Village Voices; Stephen Ministry; Parish Health Ministry; Healing Touch **A/S:** She attributes her success to her desire to help others in their time of need and her commitment to provide her patients with quality care. **B/I:** She became involved in this profession due to her long-time desire to be a nurse and to help people. **H/O:** The highlight of her career was helping to make her patients feel comfortable and secure and to help them get well.

ARNOLD B. ANDERSON
President
Educational EmPorium
1004 E. 211th Street
Bronx, NY 10469 United States
aande1004@aol.com
http://www.cambridgewhoswho.com

BUS: Multimedia Company **P/S:** Multimedia Classroom Tools **MA:** New York **D/D/R:** Teaching, Advising, Managing Business Operations and Real Estate Sales, Preparing Tax Returns **H/I/S:** Studying Economics **FBP:** Reader's Digest; Ebony; The New York Times **EDU:** Bachelor of Arts in Economics, Major in Accounting, Lehman College (1986); Bachelor of Arts in Mathematics (1968); Bachelor of Arts in History (1968); Bachelor of Arts in Latin, University of London (1964) **C/VW:** Episcopal Church **A/S:** He attributes his success to his interest in enhancing the knowledge of the people. **B/I:** He became involved in his profession because he found the business to be a profitable one. **H/O:** The most gratifying aspect of his career is being able to interact with people.

CHERIE L. ANDERSON
Budget Manager
Alaska Aerospace Development Corporation
4300 B Street
Suite 101
Anchorage, AK 99503 United States
cherie.anderson@akaerospace.com
http://www.akaerospace.com

BUS: Commercial and Military Aerospace Industry **P/S:** Space Launch Services Dedicated to Fostering New Pace-Related Industries in the State and to Stimulate Interest in Space Careers and Technology Among Alaska's Young People **MA:** National **D/D/R:** Overseeing the Accounting, Offering Management and Budget Management Services, Running the Accounts Receivable Department **H/I/S:** Practicing Aromatherapy, Working with Essential Oils, Studying her Native American Heritage, Practicing Spirituality **FBP:** Alaska Journal of Commerce **EDU:** Bachelor's Degree in Natural Science, Alaska Methodist University (Now Alaska Pacific University) (1970) **A/A/S:** Challenger Learning Center

DONALD T. ANDERSON II
President, Chief Executive Officer
Anderson's Lion Den Corporation
6368 Coventry Way, Suite 125
Clinton, MD 20735 United States
dtaii@juno.com
donaldanderson@globalfinancial.net
http://www.lionsdenservices.com/

BUS: Consulting Firm **P/S:** Consulting Services, Mortgage Banking, Financial Management **MA:** National **EXP:** Mr. Anderson's expertise is in credit restoration. **D/D/R:** Overseeing Mortgage Operations, Counseling, Assisting People, Handling Field Reviews **H/I/S:** Golfing, Fishing, Bowling, Reading, Traveling, Listening to Jazz, Blues, Rhythm and Blues, and Gospel Music **FBP:** Inc 500; Black Enterprise; The Wall Street Journal; National Mortgage Broker; Consumer Reports; BusinessWeekly; Money; Fortune; Mortgage Banking **EDU:** Coursework, Salisbury University **A/A/S:** Homebuilders Association of Maryland; Charles County Chamber of Commerce; Coalition of Nonprofit Housing and Economic Development; Waldorf Visionaries Referral Exchange Group; Potomac MEWS Association; Unity Economic Development Corporation **A/H:** Top businessman of the Year Award (2007)

JOYCE EULALIE ANDERSON
Senior Minister
New York Center of Truth for Better Living, Inc.
600 Linden Boulevard
Brooklyn, NY 11203 United States
joyful615a@aol.com
http://www.nycot.org

BUS: New Thought Christian Ministry **P/S:** Weekly Religious Services, Weddings, Classes on Metaphysics **MA:** Regional **EXP:** Ms. Anderson's expertise is in early childhood education. **D/D/R:** Coordinating Activities, Teaching, Expanding the Ministry **H/I/S:** Traveling, Reading, Watching Movies, Dancing, Writing Poetry **FBP:** Unity; New Thought; Science of Mind; Ode; Black Enterprise; Consumer Guide **EDU:** Master of Science in Early Childhood Education, Brooklyn College; Bachelor's Degree in Education, Brooklyn College **CERTS:** Advanced Certification in School Administration and Supervision, Brooklyn College; Certified Minister, Universal Foundation for Better Living **A/A/S:** Advanced Toastmaster, Toastmasters International; National Teachers Association; International Society of Poets; Universal Foundation for Better Living; University of Metaphysics **A/H:** Bronze Teacher of the Year, New York City Public Schools (1991); ATM Silver Toastmasters Award **C/VW:** American Red Cross; Save Abandoned Babies Foundation; Disabled American Veterans **SP:** Robert **CHILD:** Andrea **W/H:** New York City Board of Education; Brownsville Head Start **A/S:** She attributes her success to her creativity, hard work and desire to help and inspire others. **B/I:** She became involved in her profession because she loves people, especially children. **H/O:** The highlight of her career was publishing three poetry books. **I/F/Y:** In five years, Ms. Anderson plans to enjoy her retirement by publishing more books and traveling around the world as an inspirational speaker.

LORI B. ANDERSON, RN, BSN
Operating Room Manager
Bon Secours Mary Immaculate Hospital
2 Bernardine Drive
Newport News, VA 23602 United States
lori_anderson@bshsi.com
http://www.cambridgewhoswho.com

BUS: Full-Service Hospital Featuring a New Surgical Pavilion **P/S:** Healthcare **MA:** National **D/D/R:** Minimally Invasive Surgery Nursing **H/I/S:** Spending Time with Family **FBP:** American Journal of Registered Nurses; OR Orthopedics **EDU:** Bachelor of Science in Nursing; Registered Nurse, Virginia **C/VW:** American Heart Association; Volunteer Reader; Volunteer, Senior Citizen's Hospital **A/S:** She attributes her success to high energy. **B/I:** She became involved in her profession because of her experiences as a child. **H/O:** The highlight of her career has been building the surgical pavilion.

LYNROSE R. ANDERSON
New York State Licensed Funeral Director
John Jay College of Criminal Justice
899 10th Avenue
New York, NY 10019 United States
mortich1@aol.com
http://www.cambridgewhoswho.com

BUS: College **P/S:** Education **MA:** Regional **EXP:** Ms. Anderson's areas of expertise are in hematology and mortuary science. **H/I/S:** Traveling, Playing the Piano, Visiting Aquariums, Playing Computer Games, Listening to Music, Spending Time with her Friends and Family, Exploring Life **FBP:** American Funeral Director; Journal of the American Medical Association; Industry-Related Publications **EDU:** Pursuing Coursework in Forensic Science, John Jay College of Criminal Justice; Degree in Mortuary Science, American Academy McAllister Institute of Funeral Service; Bachelor of Science in Medical Technology, The Manhattan Institute **CERTS:** Licensed Funeral Director, State of New York; Licensed Notary Public **A/H:** Mu Sigma Alpha; Nancy Flynn Scholarship **C/VW:** Local Charitable Organizations **A/S:** She attributes her success to being goal-oriented, her determination and the support she receives from her family. **B/I:** She became involved in her profession because she has always been interested in the medical field and she wanted to help people. **H/O:** The most gratifying aspect of her career is being a source of comfort for families in their time of need. **I/F/Y:** In five years, Ms. Anderson hopes to have influenced many lives by providing comfort, strength and closure to those in need by working diligently to provide answers to forensic questions.

ROBERT A. ANDERSON
ComPonent Engineer
Detector Electronics
6901 W. 110th Street
Bloomington, MN 55438 United States
bob.anderson@detronics.com
http://www.detronics.com

BUS: Fire and Gas Detection Company **P/S:** Ultraviolet and Infrared Sensors for Flame Detectors, Catalytic Gas Sensors Used in Combustible Gas Detectors and Electronic Personal Computer Board, Detector and Controller Assemblies **MA:** International **D/D/R:** Specifying Parts for Electronics, Analyzing and Logging Data **H/I/S:** Studying for School **EDU:** Pursuing Degree in Organizational Administration, Metropolitan State University; Associate Degree in Business Analysis, Hennepine Technology College (2007)

VENA V. ANDERSON
Rehabilitation Teacher
State of Tennessee Department of Human Services
Div. Rehabilitation Services
88 Hermitage Avenue
Nashville, TN 37210 United States
http://www.cambridgewhoswho.com

BUS: State Government **P/S:** Helping People with Vision Loss to be More Independent in Daily Living **MA:** Regional **D/D/R:** Rehabilitation, Teaching Daily Living Skills to Blind and Visually Impaired Individuals, Enabling them to Increase their Independence **H/I/S:** Swimming, Reading, Spending Quality Time with her Family, Seeing Movies **EDU:** Master's Degree in Community Health Education, West Virginia University; Graduate Certification in Gerontology, West Virginia University; Bachelor of Arts in Pre-Med, Minor in Psychology, West Virginia University **A/A/S:** Health Education Organization; CHES **C/VW:** Good Will, Salvation Army **A/S:** She attributes her success to her education and experiences. **B/I:** She became involved in her profession after working in social work. **H/O:** The highlight of her career has been helping people and giving them hope after doing social work.

DEBORAH ANDRES
Director of International Relations
National Funeral Directors Association
13625 Bishops Drive
Brookfield, WI 53005 United States
dandres@nfda.org
http://www.nfda.org

BUS: Funeral Service Organization **P/S:** Education, Legislation and Expo Organization **MA:** International **EXP:** Ms. Andres' areas of expertise are in logistics and international relations. **D/D/R:** Managing Sales, Organizing Large Trade Shows for Funeral Services, Working with International Vendors and Funeral Directors on Repatriation **H/I/S:** Swimming, Fishing, Horseback Riding **FBP:** Director; NFDA Publications **EDU:** Bachelor's Degree in Police Sciences, Vanier College, Montreal (1982) **CERTS:** Certified Junior Leader (1977) **A/A/S:** IFTA; ASAE International Circle; Council, International Association of Exhibitions and Events; National Parent Teacher Association

DR. GENEVIEVE ANDREWS SHEPHERD
School Principal
Tom Bradley Elementary School
Los Angeles Unified School District
3875 Dublin Avenue
Los Angeles, CA 90008 United States
shep4hugday@yahoo.com
http://www.lausd.com

BUS: School District **P/S:** Primary Education **MA:** Regional **EXP:** Dr. Andrews Shepherd's expertise is in multicultural education. **D/D/R:** Incorporating Innovative Strategies for Teaching Children and Staff Development, Ensuring Quality Services and Safe Environments, Promoting a Fine Learning Experience, Conducting Workshops and Presentations on Teaching Strategies, Training New Principals and Those Who Aspire to Become Principals **H/I/S:** Writing Poems, Volunteering in Community Outreach Programs **FBP:** NEA Literature; Educational Journal **EDU:** Ph.D. in Education, Golden State University (1985); Master of Education in Administration and Leadership, Pepperdine University (1978); Bachelor of Science in Education, California State University (1958) **A/A/S:** President, Black History Club of Los Angeles; Instructor, Aenon Bible College, West Coast; Council of Administrators; Adventure Activities Licensing Authority, California School of Educators; National Alliance of Black School Educators; Phi Delta Kappa **C/VW:** Secretary, Bethlehem Temple Church; Board of Managers, Young Men's Christian Association **SP:** Edell **CHILD:** Gene, Deborah, Jaime **H/O:** The most gratifying aspect of her career is seeing her students succeed.

JONATHAN L. ANENSON, BS, MS
Lutheran Church of Hope
925 Jordan Creek Parkway
West Des Moines, IA 50266 United States
jon.anenson@hopewdm.org
http://www.hopecitybranch.org

BUS: Evangelical Lutheran Church **P/S:** Religious Services **MA:** Regional **EXP:** Mr. Anenson's expertise is in the development of satellite congregation churches. **H/I/S:** Spending Time Outdoors, Golfing, Watching Movies, Spending Time with her Friends, Sports **FBP:** The Journal of Student Ministries; Relevant **EDU:** Pursuing Master's Degree in Theology, Bethel Seminary; Bachelor's Degree in Communications, Waldorf College **C/VW:** Local Church; Local Charitable Organizations; Compassion International **A/S:** He attributes his success to God's strength and vision for him. **B/I:** He became involved in his profession because it was a vision that God planted in his heart. **H/O:** The highlights of his career are the relationships that he has developed in his ministry.

VERONICA ANOKUTE, BSN, RNC, MPA
Administrative Nursing Supervisor
East Orange General Hospital
300 Central Avenue
East Orange, NJ 07018 United States
vanokute@yahoo.com
http://www.evh.org

BUS: Independent, Fully Accredited, Acute Care Hospital **P/S:** Finest Health Care Services Coupled with the Best in Personal Care and Concern, Quality, Safe, Cost Effective Care to Patients through the Support and Actions of Administration, Medical Staff and Personnel **MA:** Regional **D/D/R:** Managing the Nursing Staff, Perinatal Nursing, Conducting Clinical Research at the University of Medicine and Dentistry of New Jersey **H/I/S:** Reading, Praying, Physical Fitness **FBP:** Longevity **EDU:** Master's Degree in Public Administration, Farleigh Dickinson University (1991); Bachelor's Degree in Nursing, Southern Nazarene University at Bethany, Oklahoma (1982) **CERTS:** Certified Prenatal Nurse **A/A/S:** New Jersey Nurses Association; American Nurses Association

432 • CAMBRIDGE WHO'S WHO 2008–2009

VIP MEMBERS

GENA N. ANSLEY
Medical Assistant
Willow Creek Family Medicine
3235 Sparks Road
Cheyenne, WY 82001 United States
genanoelle@hotmail.com
http://www.cambridgewhoswho.com

BUS: Family Healthcare Practice **P/S:** General Healthcare **MA:** Local **EXP:** Ms. Ansley's expertise is in customer service. **D/D/R:** Checking In Patients, Drawing Blood, Giving Immunizations, Coordinating Immunizations with the State **H/I/S:** Helping Out on a Cattle Ranch **CERTS:** Registered Medical Assistant, Institute of Business and Medical Careers, Fort Collins, Colorado **C/VW:** The Humane Society of the United States, Salvation Army **A/S:** She attributes her success to her ability to interact well with the patients and her desire to help them. **B/I:** She became involved in her profession because she has always enjoyed taking care of people. **H/O:** The most gratifying aspect of her career is the gratitude her patients show.

CARLA MARIE ANTOINE
Director
New Life Youth and Senior Center
96 Longwood Court
Marrero, LA 70072 United States
raneya@aol.com
http://www.myspace.com/ladycarlaantoine
http://www.christianmanual.com

BUS: Family Life Center **P/S:** Religious, Public and Social Services **MA:** Statewide **EXP:** Ms. Antoine's expertise is in computer operations management, media design and curriculum development. **D/D/R:** Overseeing Administrative Duties and Ministerial Services for the Youth, Working with Ministry and Nonprofit Organizations, Fundraising, Teaching, Creating Original Logos and Programs, Writing Grants **H/I/S:** Reading, Traveling, Designing **FBP:** Gospel Today; Christianity Today **EDU:** Bachelor of Science in Christian Counseling, Liberty Theological Seminary & Graduate School; Diploma, McDonogh #35 Senior High School **CERTS:** Certified Curriculum Developer **A/A/S:** Perspective Custom Builders; Home Builders Association of Greater New Orleans; Louisiana Home Builders Association; National Association of Home Builders; Better Business Bureau **A/H:** MMAC Community Service Award, Mayor Marc Morial; Achievement Medal, U.S. Navy; Southwest Asia Service Medal; Letter of Commendation, President Bill Clinton **C/VW:** Community Service Volunteer, Mount Airy Baptist Church **POB:** New Orleans **SP:** Raney **CHILD:** Raney, Jr., Kayla, Y'vonne **W/H:** Director of Administration and Media Relations, New Life Family Center; Operation Desert Shield, Persian Gulf, Saudi Arabia, U.S. Navy; Operation Desert Storm, Persian Gulf, Saudi Arabia, U.S. Navy **A/S:** She attributes her success to her faith, ability to design and passion for ministerial services. **B/I:** She became involved in her profession because of her personal experiences. **H/O:** The highlight of her career was pioneering the New Life Family Center. **I/F/Y:** In five years, Ms. Antoine hopes to expand the center and inter-build stronger families locally and statewide.

STEPHANIE APOSTOLOU
Marketing Specialist
Utilities Employees Credit Union
2850 Windmill Road
Sinking Spring, PA 19608 United States
saPostolou@uecu.org
http://www.uecu.org

BUS: Finance **P/S:** Deposit Options, Advantages Checking, IRAs, Credit Cards, Loan Options, Insurance, Mutual Funds and Investing, Current Rates, Fee Schedule and UECU Reach Program **MA:** National **D/D/R:** Offering Members Financial Information through Newsletters, Writing and Proofreading Text for Six Different Newsletters **H/I/S:** Riding her Harley, Collecting Native American Artifacts and Memorabilia **EDU:** Diploma, Reading High School **A/A/S:** Various Community Organizations

MARY H. SALINAS ARANDA
Special Education Teacher
Corpus Christi Independent School District
801 Leopard Street
Corpus Christi, TX 78403 United States
http://www.cambridgewhoswho.com

BUS: School District **P/S:** Special Need Education First through Fifth Grade **MA:** Regional **EXP:** Ms. Arand's expertise is in special education. **D/D/R:** Mentoring **H/I/S:** Shopping, Reading Novels, Completing Word Puzzles, Traveling, Spending Time with her Parents **FBP:** American Federation of Teachers Union **EDU:** Master of Science in General Counseling, Texas A&M University; Bachelor of Science in Education, Texas A&M University; Associate Degree, Del Mar Junior College **C/VW:** United Way of America; March of Dimes; Goodwill Industries International **A/S:** She attributes her success to the fact that she is creative, resourceful and people oriented. **B/I:** She became involved in this profession because she's always had an affinity for teaching and helping people.

MR. MICHAEL J. ARCANA SR.
President, Chief Consultant
Arcana Technologies Solutions
1205 Crossover Road
Fayetteville, AR 72701 United States
arcanam@arkansas.net
http://www.cambridgewhoswho.com

BUS: Proven Leader in the Field of Technology Solutions **P/S:** Quality Consulting Services on All Aspects of Technology, Information Technology **MA:** Local **D/D/R:** Specializing in Information Security, Technology Solutions, Hardware and Software and Operating Systems **H/I/S:** Golfing, Fishing, Spending Quality Time with his Family **FBP:** CIO; CESP Computer Security Magazine **EDU:** Bachelor of Science in Business Information Systems, John Brown University (2000) **A/A/S:** Computer Security Institute; International Computer Security Association **C/VW:** Boy Scouts; Fund Raising; Security Analyst, Tyson Food **SP:** Shannon **CHILD:** Kara, David, Christina, Christopher; Grandchildren: Faith, Troy, Yvonne

MR. KEVIN L. ARCHER
Executive Vice President
VMT Long Term Care Management
4201 Connecticut Avenue
Suite 208
Washington, DC 20008 United States
karcher@vmtltc.com
http://www.vmtltc.com

BUS: Healthcare **P/S:** Nursing Home, Home Healthcare, Nursing School, Pharmacy Tech Programs **MA:** Local **EXP:** Mr. Archer's expertise is in business management. **H/I/S:** Watching Football and Basketball **EDU:** Master of Business Administration, George Washington University **A/A/S:** President, Community Advisory Board **C/VW:** Christian Children's Fund **A/S:** He attributes his success to his personal drive, strong family foundation and the motivation to succeed at helping people in his community. **B/I:** He became involved in his profession because he was given an opportunity and made a natural progression from there. **H/O:** The highlight of his career was being recognized by his staff for all of the work he has done to improve their work environment.

STEPHANIE L. ARDEN, BS, RRT, RCP, LRTR
Registered Respiratory Therapist, Respiratory Care Practitioner
Braxton County Memorial Hospital
100 Hoylman Drive
Gassaway, WV 26624 United States
stephanie.arden@braxtonmemorial.org
http://www.cambridgewhoswho.com

BUS: Hospital **P/S:** High Quality Healthcare Services for Patients in a Rural Areas **MA:** West Virginia **D/D/R:** Working with Acute Care, Trauma Care, Setting Up and Managing Ventilators and High-Frequency Ventilators, Administering Electrocardiograms and Pulmonary Function Tests, Educating Patients about Chronic Obstructive Pulmonary Diseases, Cardiac Stress Testing, Specializing in Arterial Blood Gases **H/I/S:** Horseback Riding, Camping, Hiking, Flower Gardening, Antiquing, Walking, Listening to Music, Rescuing Animals **FBP:** AARC Times; Journal for Respiratory Care; Advance **EDU:** Bachelor of Science in Respiratory Care, University of Charleston **CERTS:** Registered Respiratory Therapist; Registered Level II Practitioner; Registered Respiratory Care Practitioner **A/A/S:** West Virginia Society for Respiratory Care; American Association for Respiratory Care **C/VW:** Volunteer, The Humane Society of the United States; Little Kanawha Trail Riders Club; The American Society for the Prevention of Cruelty to Animals **W/H:** Charleston Area Medical Center, Memorial Division, Charleston, WV; Braxton County Memorial Hospital, Gassaway, WV; United Hospital Center, Clarksburg, WV

DAYANA ARGOTI
Graduate Research Assistant
The Barnett Institute
Northeastern University
360 Huntington Avenue
Boston, MA 02115 United States
argoti.s@neu.edu
http://www.barnett.neu.edu

BUS: University **P/S:** Higher Education **MA:** Regional **EXP:** Ms. Argoti's areas of expertise are in analytical chemistry and mass spectrometry. **D/D/R:** Conducting Research on Drug Metabolism and Biomolecules **H/I/S:** Traveling, Playing Soccer **FBP:** Journals of Mass Spectrometry **EDU:** Pursuing Ph.D. in Bioanalytical Chemistry, Northeastern University; Bachelor's Degree in Chemistry, Clarkson University (2002) **A/H:** Dean's List Undergraduate Award; The Gates Millennium Scholarship **C/VW:** Big Brothers Big Sisters of America

MARY K. ARMOUR
President (Retired)
HRI, Inc.
1410 W. Northfield Boulevard
Murfreesboro, TN 37129 United States
marykatherine513@aol.com
http://www.cambridgewhoswho.com

BUS: Recruiting Firm **P/S:** Staffing Services **MA:** Regional **EXP:** Ms. Armour's areas of expertise are in evaluation, recruitment and employment security. **H/I/S:** Golfing, Traveling **FBP:** Business Weekly **EDU:** Master's Degree in Marketing, Minor in Personnel, The University of Tennessee

TAMMY ARNALL, RN, CPSN, CPAN, RAC-CT
Nurse Consultant
Myers and Stauffer
11440 Tomahawk Creek Parkway
Leawood, KS 66211 United States
tarnall@mslc.com
http://www.mslc.com

BUS: Proven Leader in the Field of Healthcare **P/S:** Consulting on Reimbursement Systems Design Issues, Defending Reimbursement Rates and Audit Findings from Healthcare Provider Administrative and Judicial Challenges and Performing Data Management and Analysis Services to Assist Clients in Better Managing Government-Sponsored Healthcare Programs **MA:** National **D/D/R:** Reviewing Medical Records for Support of Billed Claims to Medicare and Medicaid Agencies, whose Findings are Presented to the Various State Medicare and Medicaid Congressional Committees, Liaison with Various States, Utilizing her Passion for Taking Care of the Individual and Seeing the Whole Picture, Working as a Plastic Surgery Nurse with Breast Reconstruction for Women, Taking Care of Cancer Patients **H/I/S:** Boating, Swimming, Marching Band Parent, Reading, Playing the Piano and Drums with her Children **FBP:** Coastal Living; Travel Magazine; Nursing2009; Long Term Care Provider; RN **EDU:** Bachelor of Science in Nursing, UMKC School of Nursing (1985); Registered Nurse Diploma, Research Medical Center School of Nursing (1981) **CERTS:** Certified Post-Anesthesia Nurse; Certified Plastic Surgical Nurse; Certified Resident Assessment Coordinator **A/A/S:** Midwest Regional Coordinator, American Society of Plastic Surgeons; American Association of Nurse Assessment Coordinators **C/VW:** Volunteer, Blue Springs South High School; Guest Editor, Southern Living Magazine **SP:** Bruce **CHILD:** Travis, Brittney

ANNETTE ARNOLD, BA, LBSW, MA, LLPC
Recipient Rights Representative
Office of Recipient Rights
Detroit Wayne County Community Mental Health Agency
640 Temple
Detroit, MI 48205 United States
nucie50@hotmail.com
http://www.waynecounty.com/mhealth

BUS: Mental Health Agency **P/S:** Mental Health and Substance Abuse Services and Programs **MA:** Local **EXP:** Ms. Arnold's expertise is in mental health advocacy. **D/D/R:** Serving as an Advocate for Mental Healthcare Recipients, Managing a Caseload of more than 100 Recipients, Visiting Adult and Children Foster Homes to Investigate Alleged Abuse and Neglect of Mentally Disabled Adults and Children **H/I/S:** Gardening, Traveling, Reading Mystery Novels and Self-Help Books **FBP:** Midwest Living Magazine; Counselor; Travel **EDU:** Master of Arts in Community Counseling, University of Detroit Mercy (2007); Bachelor's Degree in Interdisciplinary Studies, Wayne State University (2000); Bachelor's Degree in Social Work, Wayne State University (2000) **CERTS:** Licensed Professional Counselor, University of Detroit Mercy (2007); Licensed Social Worker **A/A/S:** Michigan Counseling Association; Michigan Marriage and Family Counseling Association; Michigan Association of Multi-Cultural Counseling and Development; Michigan College Counseling Association; Michigan Career Development Association; Recipient Rights Officers Association of Michigan **H/O:** The most gratifying aspect of her career is helping others.

KAREN MICHELE ARNOLD
Library Media Specialist (Retired)
King Open School
Cambridge Public Schools
850 Cambridge Street
Cambridge, MA 02141 United States
speicalkma@comcast.net
http://www.cambridgewhoswho.com

CAMBRIDGE PUBLIC SCHOOLS
159 THORNDIKE STREET CAMBRIDGE, MASSACHUSETTS 02141

BUS: Professional Development and Social Justice School **P/S:** Family Partnerships Education, Teacher Training, Multi-Grade Classrooms, Integrated Curriculum Including Reading, Writing, Social Studies and Language Studies, Library **MA:** Regional **D/D/R:** Working in the Library, Researching, Utilizing Various Media, Acting as a Reading Advisor, Overseeing the Collection Development, Encouraging the Use of Instructional Technology **H/I/S:** Reading, Foodie **FBP:** School Library Journal; American Libraries; Knowledge Quest; Book Links **EDU:** Master's Degree in Library Studies, Salem State College; Bachelor of Science in Elementary Education, Boston University **CERTS:** Certification in Elementary Education; Certified Library Media Specialist; Certified Educational Technology Specialist **A/A/S:** American Library Association; American Association of School Librarians; National Education Association; Cambridge Teachers Association; Massachusetts Teachers Association **DOB:** August 19, 1951 **SP:** Richard **CHILD:** Sarah **W/H:** Library Media Specialist, Wilmington, MA (1988-1991); Digital Equipment Corp Foxboro Company ATEX Inc.; Library Media Specialist, Lincoln, MA; Library Power, Cambridge, MA; Library Media Specialist, Cambridge, MA

SHARON R. AROS, MS
Licensed Educational Psychologist
Educational Psychology
1320 Melville Drive
Riverside, CA 92506 United States
sharonschpsy@yahoo.com
http://www.cambridgewhoswho.com

BUS: Consulting Firm **P/S:** Consulting Services, Psycho-Educational and School Neuropsychological Evaluations **MA:** Local **D/D/R:** Assessing Learning Disabled Students, Evaluating Gifted Students with Attention Deficit Disorders and Reading Disabilities, Evaluating and Accommodating Learning and Disabled Undergraduate and Graduate College Students **H/I/S:** Making Crafts, Woodworking, Gardening **FBP:** Journal of School Psychology **EDU:** Master's Degree in Counseling, University of La Verne, CA (1984); Bachelor's Degree in Secondary Education, University of Hawaii, Manoa (1982) **CERTS:** Certified Clinical Neuropsychologist; Certification in School Psychology, School Counseling and Secondary Education, CA; Certification in Community College Counseling; Licensed Educational Psychologist; License in Exam Development **A/A/S:** California Association of School Psychologists; Subject Matter Expert, Board of Behavioral Sciences; Diplomate, American Board of School Neuropsychology; National Academy of Neuropsychology; National Association of School Psychologists

TERESA L. ARROWOOD, RN
Registered Nurse
Holzer Medical Center-Jackson
Burlington Road
Jackson, Oh 45640
arrowood4@verizon.net
http://www.cambridgewhoswho.com

BUS: Healthcare **P/S:** Healthcare **MA:** Local **EXP:** Ms. Arrowood's expertise is in coronary care. **H/I/S:** Photography, Scrapbooking **FBP:** RN **EDU:** Associate of Applied Science in Nursing, University of Rio Grande **C/VW:** Relay for Life **A/S:** She attributes her success to parental support. **B/I:** She chose the profession because she has always wanted to be a nurse.

WILLIAM E. ARTHUR
Owner
Golden Gate Dairy Queen
4895 Golden Gate Parkway
Naples, FL 34116 United States
wmenaples@aol.com

BUS: Fast Food Restaurant Dedicated to Providing Quality Products and Food Services **P/S:** Ice Cream Sundaes, Cones, Milkshakes, Sandwiches **MA:** Local **D/D/R:** Overseeing a Staff of 10 **H/I/S:** Watching NASCAR **FBP:** Restaurant News **A/A/S:** President, Florida Lion's Eye Bank (1969); Lion's Club

JENNIFER R. ARWAS, OBE
Head of School
British School of Washington
4715 16th Street N.W.
Washington, DC 20011 United States
jarwas@britishschool.org
http://www.britishschool.org

BUS: School **P/S:** High Quality Education in a Structured, Positive and Caring Environment **MA:** Washington, DC, Virginia, Maryland **EXP:** Ms. Arwas' areas of expertise are in school leadership and management. **H/I/S:** Spending Time with her New Grandson, Reading, Attending the Cinema and Theater, Spending Time with her Husband **CERTS:** Certificate of Education, England **A/A/S:** Council of International Schools; European Council of International Schools; IAPC; English Speaking Union; Association for Supervision and Curriculum Development; British Schools of America; National Association of Secondary School Principals

ERICA R. ASFAHL
Project Engineer
Mechanical
Marshalltown Company
2200 Industrial Drive
Fayetteville, AR 72701 United States
erica@marshalltown.com
http://www.marshalltown.com

BUS: Manufacturing **P/S:** Manufacturer of Concrete Construction Hand Tools **MA:** International **EXP:** Ms. Asfal's areas of expertise are in product development and tooling, communication, and field testing. **H/I/S:** Cycling, Mountain Biking, Sailing, Backpacking **FBP:** Design; Manufacturing Engineering; Concrete Construction **EDU:** Bachelor's Degree in Mechanical Engineering, Minor in Architecture, University of Arkansas **CERTS:** EIT 6378 Certification **A/A/S:** ASME; Women in Engineering **C/VW:** Search and Rescue **B/I:** She became involved in this profession because she really enjoyed working with her hands and moving parts.

JANET ASHCRAFT
Massage Therapist
Massage by Janet
520 Oak Hill
Benton, AR 72015 United States
angelwanab_1@yahoo.com
http://www.cambridgewhoswho.com

BUS: Healthcare Service Company **P/S:** Relaxation Massage in Clients' Homes **MA:** Arkansas **D/D/R:** Specializing in Relaxation Massage and Physical Therapy **H/I/S:** Riding Motorcycles, Attending Live Sporting Events Especially Football, Supporting her Favorite Teams **FBP:** Advance for Physical Therapists **EDU:** Associate of Applied Science, Ozarka College, Melbourne, AK **A/A/S:** National Association of the Self-Employed; Arkansas Physical Therapy Association **C/VW:** United Way **A/S:** She attributes her success to her hard work, genuine desire to help people and being blessed with healing hands. **B/I:** She became involved in her profession because she knew from an early age that she was blessed with healing hands. **H/O:** The most gratifying aspect of her career is witnessing healing miracles.

JENNIFER ANNE ASHER, RN
Registered Nurse
Western Baptist Hospital
2501 Kentucky Avenue
Paducah, KY 42003 United States
jennifer.asher@bshi.com
http://www.cambridgewhoswho.com

BUS: Hospital **P/S:** Healthcare **MA:** Regional **D/D/R:** Neonatal Nursing. **H/I/S:** Reading, Spending Time with her Family **CERTS:** Registered Nurse, West Kentucky Community & Technical College **A/H:** Award, Nursing School **A/S:** She attributes her success to her faith in God. **B/I:** She became involved in the profession because she always wanted to be a nurse and help others. **H/O:** The most gratifying aspect of her career is helping others.

VALERIE L. WESCO ASHWORTH
Owner
A & A Ink
105 E. Main Street
Troy, OH 45373 United States
dannysays4@hotmail.com

BUS: Tattoo and Body Piercing Studio **P/S:** Tattoos, Body Piercings, Retail Items **MA:** Local **D/D/R:** Running the Store, Performing Body Piercings, Ordering Supplies, Creating Tattoo Art **A/A/S:** National Tattoo Association **C/VW:** American Cancer Society, American Disabled Veterans Associations **A/S:** She attributes her success to her desire to make people happy and her love of the profession. **B/I:** She became involved in the field through her husband, a tattoo artist. **H/O:** The highlight of her career is being a successful female business owner.

KATHLEEN M. ASLANIAN
Biology Teacher
North Brookfield Junior-Senior High School
10 New School Drive
North Brookfield, MA 01535 United States
turtlz@verizon.net
kaslanian@nbschools.org
http://www.cambridgewhoswho.com

BUS: Junior-Senior High School Facility **P/S:** Secondary Education **MA:** Regional **D/D/R:** Teaching Advanced Placement Biology, College Prep Biology, Ecology, Anatomy, Physiology **EDU:** Pursuing Master's Degree; Bachelor of Science in Biology, Worcester College (1997) **A/A/S:** Founder, North Brookfield Parent-Teacher Association

BRIDGET IRENE ATKINS, LCSW
Clinical Therapist, Licensed Clinical Social Worker
Youth Home, Inc.
20400 Colonel Glenn Road
Little Rock, AR 72210 United States
bridget.atkins@youthhome.org
http://www.youthhome.org

BUS: Residential Treatment Facility **P/S:** Mental Health Services, Individual, Group, Family and Adolescent Therapy, Case Management, Discharge and Treatment Services, Court Appearances, Education for Staff, Patients and Families, Field Instruction for Graduate Students **MA:** Regional **D/D/R:** Working with Adolescents with Depression and Sexual Abuse Victims, Offering Family Therapy, Performing Adoption Home Studies for Private Attorneys **H/I/S:** Traveling, Cooking, Quilting, Crafts **EDU:** Master of Social Work, University of Arkansas at Little Rock; Bachelor of Psychology, University of Arkansas at Little Rock **A/H:** Elbert H. Leigh Award for Clinical Excellence (2005); Dual Recipient, Employee of the Month, Youth Home, Inc. (2002, 2005) **DOB:** April 10, 1970 **SP:** Allen **CHILD:** Laura **W/H:** Field Instructor, Graduate Social Work Interns, University of Arkansas, Little Rock (2001-Present); Clinical Therapist, Licensed Clinical Social Worker, Youth Home, Inc. (2000-Present); Licensed Clinical Social Worker, New Day (1999-2000); Licensed Clinical Social Worker, Department of Health and Human Services, Division of Children and Family Services (1996-1999); Licensed Clinical Social Worker, Little Rock School District (1996) **A/S:** She attributes her success to her hard work and effort. **B/I:** She became involved in her profession because she was raised to help others. **H/O:** The most gratifying aspect of her career is the peaceful feeling she gets when her patients recover.

ANNETTE G. ATWELL, RN, ADN, CPAN
Peri Anesthesia Staff Nurse
The Medical Center of Bowling Green
250 Park Street
Bowling Green, KY 42101 United States
atwellag@chc.net
http://www.cambridgewhoswho.com

BUS: Hospital **P/S:** Healthcare **MA:** Local **EXP:** Ms. Atwell's areas of expertise are in medical and surgical nursing, peri anesthesia and risk management. **H/I/S:** Gardening, Reading, Sewing **FBP:** Nursing Management **EDU:** Associate Degree in Nursing, Western Kentucky University **CERTS:** Certified Peri Anesthesia Nurse **A/A/S:** American Society of PeriAnesthesia Nurses; American Association of Critical Care Nurses; American Society for Healthcare Risk Management **C/VW:** The Commonwealth Health Free Clinic; Relay For Life, American Cancer Society; American Breast Cancer Society

VIRGINIA AUKAMP, RN, PH.D.
St. Paul's Lutheran Church
352 W. Wood Street
Decatur, IL 62522 United States
lvaparish@aol.com
http://www.stpaulsdecatur.org

BUS: Church **P/S:** Spiritual Services **MA:** Local **D/D/R:** Caring for Children, Staffing, Evaluating, Maintaining Clean and Sterile Facilities **H/I/S:** Reading, Solving Crossword Puzzles, Spending Time with her Grandchildren, Volunteering **FBP:** American Journal of Nursing **EDU:** Ph.D. in Nursing, Administration and Research, University of Texas at Austin; Master's Degree in Maternal Child Health, Texas Woman's University; Bachelor of Science in Nursing, Sangamon State University; Bachelor of Science in Education and Psychology, Millikin University **A/A/S:** American Nursing Association **C/VW:** American Red Cross **H/O:** The most gratifying aspect of her career is interacting with the people at the church.

FELICIA P. AUSTIN

Correctional Officer
Danville Correctional Center
3820 E. Main Street
Danville, IL 61834 United States
fgrgtwn@aol.com
http://www.cambridgewhoswho.com

BUS: Correctional Facility **P/S:** Corrections **MA:** Regional **D/D/R:** Working in an All Male, Level III Corrections Facility **H/I/S:** Spending Time Outdoors, Playing Softball, Spending Time with her Family **EDU:** Bachelor's Degree in Behavioral Science, Concentration In Corrections, Morehead State University **A/A/S:** Illinois Corrections Association; American Corrections Association; National Association of Blacks in Criminal Justice; Illinois Association of Minorities in Government **C/VW:** Boys and Girls Club of America **A/S:** She attributes her success to determination, consistency and the enjoyment she gets from talking to people. **B/I:** She became involved in the profession so she could help people and because she was curious as to why people think the way they do. **H/O:** The highlight of her career is making a difference and doing her job to the best of her ability. She has also won 'Officer of the Year' for Illinois State and Danville Correctional Center.

LAURA AVAKIANS, MS

Teacher, Staff Developer
Public School 214, New Yorker City Board of Education
2944 Pitkin Avenue
Brooklyn, NY 11208 United States
iavakians@nycboe.net
http://www.nycboe.net

BUS: Education **P/S:** Public Education **MA:** Local **EXP:** Ms. Avakians' areas of expertise are in staff development and education. **H/I/S:** Gardening **EDU:** Master of Science in Special Education, Touro College; Master of Science in School Supervision and Administration; Touro College; Bachelor of Arts in Psychology, Queens College **A/A/S:** National Association of Elementary School Principals; Association of Supervision and Curriculum Development **C/VW:** New York Cares **A/S:** She attributes her success to her work ethic. **B/I:** She chose the profession because English is not her native language and when learning she realized how difficult it is to learn, so she wanted to help others with their struggle. **H/O:** The highlight of her career was obtaining her second masters degree.

NICOLE AVERY
Office Manager
Rusty's Truck Repair, Inc.
512 State Fair Boulevard
Syracuse, NY 13204 United States
niki_a_22@msn.com
http://www.cambridgewhoswho.com

BUS: Automotive **P/S:** Repairing 18-Wheelers **MA:** National **D/D/R:** Overseeing Accounts Payable and Receivable, Payroll, Bank Deposits, QuickBooks, Customer Service and Sales **FBP:** Tow Time; American Tow Man **EDU:** Community Health and Science Coursework, SUNY Onondaga Community College **A/A/S:** Alumni, International Scholar Laureate Program Delegation on Nursing

DAWN AXAM
Director, Owner, Artist
Axam Dance Theatre Experience
722 Flamingo Drive
Atlanta, GA 30311 United States
dawnaxam@comcast.net
axam_dte@yahoo.com
http://www.cambridgewhoswho.com

BUS: Proven Leader in the Arts Industry **P/S:** Wide Variety of High Quality Dance and Theatre Services **MA:** National **D/D/R:** Dancing, Instructing and Acting, Choreographing for The Wiz, Dreamgirls, Pippin, Jesus Christ Superstar, Little Shop of Horrors and Bricktop at Metro Stage **EDU:** BSA, New York University Tisch School of Arts **A/A/S:** International Dance Association **A/H:** Star Teacher Award (2006)

MR. HUGO AZZOLINI
President
Different Perspective Productions, Inc.
5728 Major Boulevard
Suite 250
Orlando, FL 32819 United States
hugo@dppad.com
http://www.dppad.com

BUS: Full Service Advertising, Marketing, Design and Production Agency **P/S:** Services Ranging from Print to Web to Video, Commercial Spots, Brochure Design, Small Informational Websites to Full e-Commerce **MA:** National **D/D/R:** Specializing in Marketing, Increasing Awareness of Businesses through Advertising, Branding Realtors and Creating Identities **H/I/S:** Basketball, Volleyball, Soccer, Orlando Magic Fan **FBP:** Videomaker **EDU:** Bachelor of Arts, UGF, Brazil (2000); Associate of Arts in Marketing, ESPM, Brazil (1999) **A/A/S:** Board of Directors, Different Perspective Productions, Inc.

DEBRA JANE BACCHI
Myopathic Mascular Therapist
Muscle Manipulators
1416 Sugar Maple Avenue
Gardenerville, NV 89410 United States

BUS: Healthcare Medical Services **P/S:** Myopathy, Massage, Reflexology **MA:** Local **D/D/R:** Offering Three-Day Muscular Therapy for Accidents and Injured Patients **H/I/S:** Fine Dining, Boating, Swimming **EDU:** Certification, Massage Integrative School **A/A/S:** National Republican Congressional Committee; Nevada Republican Women; Myopathic Muscular Therapy Association

JOHN THOMAS R. BACON
Rector
Nativity of the Virgin Mary Orthodox Church
110 Washington Avenue
Chelsea, MA 02150 United States
burbank302@aol.com
http://www.orthodoxchelsea.org

BUS: Church **P/S:** Religious Services and Education, Counseling **MA:** Local **EXP:** Rev. Bacon's areas of expertise include eastern Orthodox canon law and public speaking. **H/I/S:** Watching Old Movies, Working with the Boy Scouts **FBP:** The Orthodox Church; Psychology Today **EDU:** Master of Theological Studies, Holy Cross Greek Orthodox School of Theology; Master of Education, Cambridge College, MA **CERTS:** Certified Boy Scout Camp Chaplain **A/A/S:** Orthodox Theological Society in America; Society for the Law of the Eastern Churches **A/H:** Silver Beaver Award **C/VW:** Chaplain, National Camping School, Northeast Region Boy Scouts of America; Lions Clubs International **DOB:** July 26, 1948 **POB:** Barnstable **SP:** Pamela **CHILD:** Daniel, Juliana **A/S:** He attributes his success to his efforts and ability to connect with people. **B/I:** He became involved in his profession because he felt a calling from God to serve His people. **H/O:** The most gratifying aspect of his career is maintaining his parish in a difficult inner city. **I/F/Y:** In five years, Rev. Bacon hopes to retire from active ministry.

SHARON A. BADGLEY
Tutor, Owner (Retired)
L and S Tutoring
801 South Road
Lisle, IL 60532 United States
silverswan@earthlink.net
http://www.cambridgewhoswho.com

BUS: Educational Institution **P/S:** Education **MA:** Local **D/D/R:** Teaching Mathematics, Managing the Church Library **H/I/S:** Reading, Quilting, Gardening, Listening to Classical Music, Crocheting, Knitting **FBP:** Mathematics Teacher; Educational Leadership **EDU:** Bachelor's Degree in Mathematic Education, Chicago State College (1964) **CERTS:** Certified Teacher, State of Illinois (1965) **A/A/S:** Mathematics Academic Association; Former Member, Association for Supervision and Curriculum Development; National Council of Teachers of Mathematics **C/VW:** Local Police and Fire Department; Mission Aviation Fellowship; National Council of Teachers of Mathematics; Heifer International; Hope International

ELBA BAEZ
Administrator
Banco Popular - North America
120 Broadway
16th Floor
New York, NY 10271 United States
ebaez@bPop.com
http://www.bancoPopular.com

BUS: Largest Hispanic Bank in the United States **P/S:** Personal Banking Services, a Wide Array of Personal Banking, Investment and Financial Planning Services, Providing a Diverse Selection of Innovative Checking and Savings Products to Fit Clients' Unique Banking Needs **MA:** International **D/D/R:** Serving the Community, Financing, Budgeting, Managing Accounts Payable **H/I/S:** Music, Reading **EDU:** Degree, Earned in Puerto Rico (1968) **A/A/S:** Mothers Against Drunk Driving

JON BAHL
Sales Director
ADP, Inc.
5680 New Northside Drive
Atlanta, GA 30328 United States
jonathan_bahl@adp.com
http://www.adp.com

BUS: Business Solution Company **P/S:** Broad Range of Employer Services and Business Solutions that Effects the Employee Life-Cycle from Recruitment to Retirement **MA:** National **D/D/R:** Overseeing 35 District Managers who work with 50 to 999 Employees, Offering Consultations on the Best Practices for Workforce Management, Making Sales, Assisting Employers, Handling Human Resources and Benefit Administration **H/I/S:** Golfing, Traveling **FBP:** Harvard Business Review **EDU:** Bachelor's Degree in Business Administration, The University of Texas **A/A/S:** American Payroll Association; Society for Human Resource Management **SP:** Amber **A/S:** He attributes his success to his work ethic and motivation. **B/I:** He became involved in his profession because he was confident that his company can help any business prosper. **I/F/Y:** In five years, Mr. Bahl plans to continue working at ADP.

Thomas 'Ted' Baildon
Tax Accountant
Weston Solutions, Inc.
1400 Weston Way
West Chester, PA 19380 United States
ted.baildon@westonsolutions.com
http://www.westonsolutions.com

BUS: Leading Employee-Owned Environmental and Redevelopment Firm, Delivering Comprehensive Solutions to Complex Problems for Industry and Government **P/S:** Restoring Efficiency to Essential Resources such as Air, Land, Water, People and Facilities, Developing Solutions that Maximize Resource Value and Turn Environmental Responsibility into Economic Growth, Restoring Assets to Full Use, Making Operations More Productive, Enhancing Competitive Advantage **MA:** International **D/D/R:** Fixed Asset and Tax Accounting **H/I/S:** Bowling, Making Home Improvements **FBP:** IRS GuideWire **EDU:** Bachelor's Degree, The Pennsylvania State University (1997) **A/A/S:** National Fire Protection Agency; Eagle Scout; Mainliners Barbershop Chorus **SP:** Tracy **CHILD:** Mackenzie, William **W/H:** SEI Investments

Mr. George R. Bailey
Business Owner (Retired)
424 Park Avenue North
Tifton, GA 31794 United States
http://www.cambridgewhoswho.com

BUS: Retail **P/S:** Retail **MA:** Regional **D/D/R:** Running a Laminating Studio from his Home **EDU:** Coursework in Electronics, University of Minnesota (1946); Diploma, Tifton High School (1942) **A/A/S:** Chairman, Fund Drive, Red Cross Blood Program; First President, Optimist Club; Charter Member, Jaycees; Charter Member, Civitan's Club; Charter Member, Kiwanis International **W/H:** State Executive Committee, OH (1972-1975); Vice Mayor City of Tifton (1971); Chairman, Fund Drive, American Red Cross (1970); Owner, Bailey Tifton Tire Company (1965); Manager, Retail Auto Parts Store (1961); Instructor, Dale Carnegie Leadership Course (1955-1961); Traveling Sales Representative (1945)

SHELIA W. BAILEY, RN, BSN
Registered Nurse, Case Manager, Appeals Coordinator
Case Management Department
Methodist Healthcare South
1300 Wesley Drive, Memphis, TN 38116 United States
baileys@methodisthealth.org
sheilabailey@aol.com
http://www.cambridgewhoswho.com

BUS: Healthcare Center **P/S:** Healthcare Including Acute Care Services **MA:** Local **EXP:** Ms. Bailey's areas of expertise are in obstetrics, gynecology, pediatrics, medical-surgery and urology. **D/D/R:** Staff Nursing, Instructing Nurses, Case Management Nursing, Overseeing the Labor and Delivery Unit, Directing and Coordinating the Case Management Department **H/I/S:** Reading, Writing, Baking **FBP:** Case Management Journal **EDU:** Bachelor of Science in Nursing, Union University **CERTS:** Certified Legal Nurse Consultant; Certified Case Manager, Case Management Society of America **A/A/S:** Case Management Society of America **C/VW:** Local Church; Health Fairs **DOB:** December 23, 1954 **POB:** Memphis, TN **SP:** Clyde **CHILD:** Nicole **W/H:** Director, Case Management, Interim; Appeals Coordinator, Methodist Healthcare **A/S:** She attributes her success to her faith in God. **B/I:** She became involved in her profession because of her interest in nursing since childhood when she started volunteering as a candy striper. **H/O:** The most gratifying aspects of her career are working as a bedside nurse and a teacher. **I/F/Y:** In five years, Ms. Bailey hopes to obtain her master of business administration and start her own business.

SHERA LYNNE THACKERY BAKE, MA, MBA, CISA, CISM, CISSP-ISSMP
Lead Senior Auditor
Information Technology Audits
Florida Auditor General
111 W. Madison Street, Tallahassee, FL 32399 United States
sherabake@aud.state.fl.us
http://www.state.fl.us/audgen

BUS: Government Agency **P/S:** Independent, Unbiased, Timely and Relevant Information on Florida Legislation and Entity Management which can be Used to Improve the Operations and Accountability of Public Entities **MA:** Florida **EXP:** Ms. Bake's areas of expertise are in information security and assurance related to government auditing of information technology services supporting the state and local government. **D/D/R:** Auditing and Advising State Agencies on Issues Related to Information Technology, Especially Security Related Issues, Offering Services to Citizens, Specializing in Fiscal Management, Meeting Regulatory Requirements **H/I/S:** Reading, Ballroom Dancing **FBP:** CSO; Information Security **EDU:** Master of Business Administration, Florida State University; Master of Arts in Mathematics, Samford University; Bachelor of Science in Mathematics, Birmingham-Southern College **CERTS:** Certified Information Systems Security Professional, The International Information Systems Security Certification Consortium; Certified Information System Security Management Professional, The International Information Systems Security Certification Consortium; Certified Information Systems Auditor, Information Systems Audit and Control Association; Certified Information Security Manager, Information Systems Audit and Control Association **A/A/S:** Information Systems Audit and Control Association; Information Systems Security Association; Board of Directors, Treasurer, InfraGard Tallahassee Members Alliance; International Information Systems Security Certification Consortium; Computer Security Institute; Institute of Electrical and Electronics Engineers, Inc. **W/H:** Florida Auditor General (1974-Present); Lead Senior Auditor, Compu-Time (1970-1974); Systems Analyst, Boeing Company (1967-1969); Associate Research Engineer **A/S:** She attributes her success to her education and supportive family. **B/I:** She became involved in her profession because she loves mathematics and wanted to work with computers. **H/O:** The highlight of her career was working on the Saturn-Apollo program. **I/F/Y:** In five years, Ms. Bake plans to retire.

DEBRA J. BAKER
Realtor
RE/MAX Integrity Realtors
20241 W. 67th Avenue
Suite A
Glendale, AZ 85308 United States
debbiebaker3@msn.com
http://www.remax.com

BUS: Real Estate Agency **P/S:** Residential and Commercial Real Estate Exchange Including Luxury Homes, Property Search, Moving Assistance, Mortgage Assistance **MA:** Local **D/D/R:** Working on New Sales and Re-Sales, Assisting First-Time Buyers, Public Speaking, Mentoring, Selling Residential Real Estate Properties **H/I/S:** Horseback Riding, Practicing Yoga, Caring for her Horses **FBP:** Broker/Agent; CRS Publication; AAR Online **EDU:** College Coursework **CERTS:** Licensed Realtor (1987); Certified Residential Specialist; Graduate, Realtor Institute; Certified Yoga Instructor **A/A/S:** National Association of Realtors **A/S:** She attributes her success to her leadership skills.

KIMBERLY A. J. BAKER
Co-Owner
Yee-haw Sisterhood, LLC
9892 S. Hoyt Court
Littleton, CO 80127 United States
kim@yee-hawsisterhood.com
http://www.yee-hawsisterhood.com

BUS: Retail **P/S:** Retail Sales of Horse-Related Jewelry, Clothing and Gifts **MA:** National **EXP:** Ms. Baker's areas of expertise are in website development, usability and functionality, program management, natural and holistic horsemanship. **H/I/S:** Riding Horses, Hiking, Camping, Traveling **FBP:** Equine Wellness; Natural Horse; Trail Blazer **EDU:** Master of Science in Integrated Sciences, University of Colorado; Bachelor of Ecology and Evolutionary Biology, University of Arizona **A/A/S:** Arabian Horse Association; Return to Freedom; Colorado Arabian Horse Club **A/H:** Who's Who Among University Students **C/VW:** Make-A-Wish Foundation of Colorado, Horse Protection League of Colorado, Front Range Equine Rescue, American Society for the Prevention of Cruelty to Animals **A/S:** She attributes her success to hard work, dedication and passion. **H/O:** The highlight of her career is building relationships with people.

MS. TRISHA J. BAKER, M.ED.
Special Education Teacher, Data Manager
Special Services
Evanston-Skokie School District 65
1500 McDaniel Avenue
Evanston, IL 60201 United States
bakersquare1@yahoo.com
http://www.cambridgewhoswho.com

BUS: School District **P/S:** Education **MA:** Regional **D/D/R:** Teaching Special Education **H/I/S:** Watching and Coaching Basketball, Watching Movies, Traveling, Shopping, Playing Tennis and Softball **FBP:** Educational Leadership **EDU:** Master of Education, National-Louis University; Bachelor of Arts in Special Education, Alcorn State University **A/A/S:** Association for Supervision and Curriculum Development; International Reading Association **W/H:** Special Education Teacher, Duval County Florida Public School System; Vocational Coordinator, Chicago, IL; Resource and Self-Contained Special Education Teacher, Local Middle School; Technology Support Teacher, Department of Special Services **A/S:** She attributes her success to the inspiration she received from her mother. **B/I:** She became involved in her profession because she felt it was a spiritual calling to become a teacher. **H/O:** The most gratifying aspect of her career is watching her students succeed. **I/F/Y:** In five years, Ms. Baker hopes to obtain her Doctoral Degree and become a school superintendent.

MIRIAM BALAGUER
Vice President
Banco Santander Central Hispano
45 E. 53rd Street
New York, NY 10022 United States
mbalaguer@schny.com
http://www.cambridgewhoswho.com

BUS: Finance Company **P/S:** Financial Services Including Investment and Banking Services **MA:** International **D/D/R:** Money Marketing, Handling Fixed Income and Derivative Products, Working in an Administrative Position, Conducting Foreign Exchange Operations **H/I/S:** Woodworking **EDU:** Bachelor's Degree in Accounting, SUNY New Paltz (1985) **A/A/S:** National Association for Female Executives; National Notary Association

Nan M. Baldwin
Career Counselor (Retired)
Rutgers, The State University of New Jersey School of Law
123 Washington Street
Newark, NJ 07102 United States
nanb22om@aol.com
http://www.rutgers.edu

BUS: Law School **P/S:** Education **MA:** Local **EXP:** Ms. Baldwin's areas of expertise are in career counseling, spiritual education and feng shui. **D/D/R:** Counseling, Facilitating Seminars, Conducting Myers Briggs Workshops, Overseeing the Work Study Program **H/I/S:** Traveling, Reading, Writing, Feng Shui **EDU:** Master of Public Administration, Rutgers, The State University of New Jersey **CERTS:** Licensed Unity Teacher, Unity Center of New York City; Unity Prayer Chaplain **A/A/S:** World Seido Karate Organization **C/VW:** Unity Center, Silent Unity **POB:** Cattawba Spring **A/S:** She attributes her success to her spirituality and belief in the inner presence of God. **B/I:** She became involved in her profession because she enjoys helping others. **H/O:** The highlight of her career was studying in China, England and Africa as well as having the opportunity for extensive national and international travel. **I/F/Y:** In five years, Ms. Baldwin hopes to be traveling and attending book signing receptions for her best-selling book.

Diana K. Ball
Realtor
Century 21 Heartland
130 Sangamon Avenue
Rantoul, IL 61866 United States
rdball908@yahoo.com
http://www.soldonrantoul.com

BUS: Real Estate Agency **P/S:** Seller and Buyer of Quality Commercial and Residential Properties **MA:** Regional **D/D/R:** Listing and Selling of Residential and Commercial Properties **H/I/S:** College Football, Softball, T-Ball, Spending Time with her Six Grandchildren **FBP:** Realtor **EDU:** Coursework, Parkland College **CERTS:** Real Estate License (1993) **A/A/S:** Chamber of Commerce; Champaign County Association of Realtors

KATRINA R. BALLENGER
Second Grade Teacher
Pine Ridge Elementary School
PO Box 129
Ellerslie, GA 31807 United States
ballenger-k@harris.k12.ga.us
http://www.cambridgewhoswho.com

BUS: Elementary School **P/S:** Primary Education **MA:** Local **D/D/R:** Teaching Second Grade **H/I/S:** Baking, Shopping **FBP:** The Mailbox **EDU:** Master of Arts in Elementary Education, Troy University, Phenix City, AL (2006) **A/A/S:** National Education Association; Georgia Association of Educators **C/VW:** Junior Firefighter Program; Disabled American Veterans **A/S:** She attributes her success to her ability to communicate with her students. **B/I:** She became involved in her profession because she was inspired by her fifth-grade teacher. **H/O:** The most gratifying aspect of her career is seeing her students succeed.

DR. JOHN T. BALSAMO
Doctor of Chiropractic
Life is Beautiful Family Chiropractic
430 West Main Street
Babylon, NY 11702 United States
drjbalsamo@optonline.net
dr.john@balsamochiropractic.com

BUS: Family Chiropractic Practice **P/S:** Pediatrics, Family Care **MA:** NY, NJ, CT **EXP:** Dr. Balsamo's areas of expertise are in chiropractic pediatrics and family care. **D/D/R:** Specializing in Upper Cervical Alignment **H/I/S:** Spending Time with his Labradors, Fishing, Surfing, Practicing Martial Arts, Gun Enthusiast, Pyrotechnics **FBP:** Money Magazine **EDU:** Doctor of Chiropractic, Life University (1999); Bachelor of Arts in Biology and English, SUNY Stony Brook (1994); Coursework in Physiotherapy, New York Chiropractic College **A/A/S:** Foundation for the Advancement of Chiropractic Education; World Trade Center Site Chiropractor; Pyrotechnics Guild International; Order of the Sons of Italian Americans **C/VW:** Chiropractors Restoring Energy Worldwide, Third World Missions, Long Island Breast Cancer Walk, Babylon Junior Senior High School Health and Wellness Forum, Big Brother Big Sister at SUNY Stony Brook **A/S:** He attributes his success to his parents and belief in the philosophy of chiropractic medicine. **B/I:** He became involved in his profession because he wanted to become involved in proactive care for a healthy life and help others. **H/O:** The most gratifying aspect of his career is being involved in various rewarding mission trips.

CONNIE MELINDA BANCROFT
Classroom Teacher
Prospect School
2450 Prospect School Road
Cleveland, TN 37312 United States
cbancroft@bradleyschools.org
http://www.cambridgewhoswho.com

BUS: School **P/S:** Education **MA:** Bradley County **D/D/R:** Teaching Third-Grade Students **EDU:** Master's Degree in Administration and Supervision, Plus 45, Trevecca Nazarene University; Bachelor's Degree in Elementary Education, Lee University; Associate Degree in Education, Cleveland State Community College **A/A/S:** Local Chapter, Red Clay Council; Local Education Association; International Reading Association; Delta Kappa Gamma; Board Member, Parent-Teacher Organization **A/H:** Who's Who Among American Teachers; **C/VW:** The Children's Church **A/S:** She attributes her success to her desire to help children learn. **B/I:** She became involved in her profession because she wanted to care for children. **H/O:** The most gratifying aspect of her career is working with children.

GAIL Y. BANKS
1) President, Board of Directors 2) Active Volunteer
1) Westminster Manor 2) Presbyterian of Cayuga-Syracuse
105 Whedon Road
Apartment 20
Syracuse, NY 13219 United States
banksgy@yahoo.com
http://www.cambridgewhoswho.com

BUS: 1) Nonprofit Adult Home Facility 2) Judicatory Level Presbyterian Church **P/S:** 1) Healthcare Including Excellent Care for the Elderly 2) Religious and Spiritual Services **MA:** 1) Local 2) Local **D/D/R:** Volunteering, Serving the Elderly, Overseeing Administrative Duties, Ensuring the Facility to Run the Program Efficiently, Caring for the Residents with Comfort, Ensuring Care for Residents, Attending Monthly Board Meetings, Working with the Executives to Oversight the Facility **H/I/S:** Camping, Traveling, Studying Lighthouse History, Making Crafts **EDU:** College Coursework **CERTS:** Certification, Administrative Personnel Association; Level I and Level II Certification, Presbyterian Women of the Presbyterian Church **A/A/S:** Presbyterian Women of the Presbytery; Camillus Canal Society, Camillus Erie Canal Park; Presbyterian Women in the Synod of the Northeast; Administrative Personnel Association **A/H:** Honorary Life Member, Presbyterian Women of the Presbyterian Church **C/VW:** Volunteer, Amber Cemetery Association **POB:** Syracuse, NY **SP:** Frederic **W/H:** Business Administrator, Presbyterian Church **H/O:** The most gratifying aspect of her career is to interact with the residents and get to know them personally to ensure that the quality care is maintained. **I/F/Y:** In five years, Ms. Banks hopes to ensure the availability of the needs of the elderly in the community.

DANIELLE BARBARO
Manager of Global No Sugar Cola Product Development
Pepsi
100 Stevens Avenue
Valhalla, NY 10595 United States
danielle.barbaro@pepsi.com
http://www.cambridgewhoswho.com

BUS: Beverage **P/S:** No Sugar Cola **MA:** International **EXP:** Ms. Barbaro's areas of expertise are in product development and new innovation. **H/I/S:** Dancing, Skiing **EDU:** Master's Degree in Food Science, Rutgers, The State University of New Jersey; Bachelor's Degree in Food Science and Nutrition, University of Delaware **A/A/S:** Institute of Food Technology **A/S:** She attributes her personal and professional success to her hard work, drive, diligence and interpersonal relationships. **B/I:** After being exposed to the food industry, she developed an interest in nutrition. **H/O:** The highlight of her career is having other people value her input.

JOHN D. BARBER
President
Kinetic Holdings, Inc.
1093 Beach Boulevard
Suite 225
Jacksonville, FL 32250 United States
jbarberkinetic@aol.com
http://www.kineticholdingsgiftshop.com

BUS: Aviation Company **P/S:** Charter Flights **MA:** International **EXP:** Mr. Barber's expertise is in aeronautics. **D/D/R:** Selling Real Estate Properties **H/I/S:** Spending Time with his Family, Scuba Diving, Skiing **FBP:** Journal of Emergency Medical Services; U.S. Business News **EDU:** Bachelor of Science in Aeronautics, Embry-Riddle Aeronautical University **A/A/S:** Aircraft Owners and Pilots Association; Northeast Mycological Federation; Clan MacLeod Society USA **C/VW:** Various Charitable Organizations **POB:** Madison **SP:** Jasna **CHILD:** Justin, Shaun, Ivan, Kyra **A/S:** He attributes his success to his hard work and perseverance. **B/I:** He became involved in his profession because of his interest in aircraft and aviation. **H/O:** The highlight of his career was flying in the Bosnian War and saving two Danish soldiers from a mine field.

MELONIE A. BARBOUR, RMC, CPC

Office Manager
Goldsboro Medical Clinic, PA
2400 Wayne Memorial Drive
Suite J
Goldsboro, NC 27534 United States
meloniebarbour@yahoo.com
http://www.cambridgewhoswho.com

BUS: Internal Medicine Practice **P/S:** Healthcare **MA:** Local **EXP:** Ms. Barbour's areas of expertise are in coding and billing management. **D/D/R:** Overseeing Insurance and Billing Services **H/I/S:** Spending Time with her Family, Shopping, Exercising **FBP:** Coding Edge **EDU:** High School Diploma **CERTS:** Certification in Coding, Billing and Insurance, Johnston Community College **A/A/S:** Association of Registered Health Care Professionals; American Academy of Professional Coders **DOB:** February 3, 1969 **SP:** Randy **CHILD:** Charisma, Jordan **A/S:** She attributes her success to her husband.

LORI A. BARGAR, MHA, PT

Physical Therapist
Greenwich Hospital Hospice
5 Perryridge Road
Greenwich, CT 06830 United States
labpt@aol.com
http://www.cambridgewhoswho.com

BUS: Hospice Care **P/S:** Healthcare and Rehabilitation, Business Consulting and Mentoring **MA:** Local **D/D/R:** Caring for Patients, In Home Physical Therapy, Marketing Orthopedic Products, Business Management Consulting **H/I/S:** Playing Racquetball, Playing Softball, Scrapbooking **EDU:** Master's Degree, University of North Florida **A/A/S:** American Physical Therapy Association **C/VW:** Former President and Treasurer, Parent Teacher Association; Leader, Treasurer, Council for Troop 44, Girl Scouts of America; Softball Coach, Silent Auction Volunteer, Elementary School **A/S:** She attributes her success to her communication skills and taking into consideration all aspects of patient healthcare and their lifestyles. **B/I:** Her long time desire to work in the medical field motivated her to pursue her current career. **H/O:** The highlight of her career was being director in San Diego and overseeing eight departments.

BERNADINE LIVESAY BARKER
Owner, Consultant Dietitian
Barkers Dietary Consultant Business
Keosauqua, IA 52565 United States
bernieb38@netins.net
http://www.cambridgewhoswho.com

BUS: Consulting Company **P/S:** Consulting Care, Nutrition Planning **MA:** Local **EXP:** Ms. Barker's expertise is in dietary nutrition. **D/D/R:** Assessing Patients Quarterly and Annually, Making Menu Recommendations, Approving Menus, Observing Clients, Conducting Dietary Consultations **H/I/S:** Collecting Antiques, Spending Time with her Children and Grandchildren, Dancing, Reading, Studying History **FBP:** American Dietetic Association Journal **EDU:** Master of Public Health in Nutrition, University of Minnesota; Bachelor's Degree in Home Economics and Chemistry Education, Iowa State University **A/A/S:** American Dietetic Association; Consultants of Dietitians for Health Care **C/VW:** Senior Housing Board Member, Good Samaritans Long-Term Care Centers **A/S:** She attributes her success to her perseverance and her drive to succeed and become skilled in the field. **B/I:** She became involved in her profession because she was interested in the field at a young age and later took college courses to learn about the field. **H/O:** The highlight of her career was helping get the senior center build in her town in the 1970s.

SUSAN BARKER
Family Nurse Practitioner, Women's Health Coordinator
VA Medical Center
325 Montgomery Cross Road
Savannah, GA 31406 United States
susan.barker@med.va.gov
http://www1.va.gov/health

BUS: Out-Patient Clinic Dedicated to the Health and Well Being of Veteran Residents **P/S:** Excellence in Patient Care **MA:** Regional **D/D/R:** Offering Women's Health and Primary Care, Overseeing 900 Female Patients and 900 Primary Care Patients **H/I/S:** Boating, Reading, Spending Time with Family **FBP:** Nurse Practitioner; Women's Health **EDU:** Post-Graduate Degree in Nurse Practitioner Studies (1995); Master's Degree in Nursing, Georgia Southern University (1993) **A/A/S:** Nurse Practitioner Council of Coastal Georgia; National Women's Health Nurse Practitioner; Georgia Nursing Association

BONNIE-JO BARNABY
Associate Broker
Coldwell Banker Legacy
4000 Southern Boulevard
Rio Rancho, NM 87124 United States
bbarnaby@albuquerquenmproperties.com
http://www.albuquerquenmproperties.com

BUS: Real Estate **P/S:** Real Estate **MA:** Local **EXP:** Ms. Barnaby's expertise is in new home construction. **D/D/R:** Buying and Selling Homes **EDU:** College Coursework **C/VW:** Habitat for Humanity; Food Pantry **A/S:** She attributes her personal and professional success to her determination and consistency. **H/O:** The highlight of her career is making her customers happy.

ALAINA B. BARNES
Military Police and Linguist
United States Army
900 Adams Avenue
A CO, 55 BDE BTB
Scranton, PA 18510 United States
alaina.barnes@us.army.mil
http://www.army.mil

BUS: Military **P/S:** Surveillance, Weapons Handling, Information and Contact Collection **MA:** National **EXP:** Ms. Barnes' areas of expertise are in leadership, linguistics, interpersonal skills, weapons and meticulous planning. **H/I/S:** Reading, Playing Volleyball, Skiing, Snowboarding, Ice Hockey, Weightlifting, Practicing the Trumpet and Guitar, Listening to Music, Cooking **FBP:** The New York Times; International Social Science Review **EDU:** Pursuing Master's Degree in Security and Intelligence Studies; Bachelor's Degree in Political Science; Associate Degree in Intelligence Operations **A/A/S:** Pi Sigma Alpha; Pi Gamma Mu **A/H:** Reserve Achievement Medal; National Defense Service Medal; Armed Forces Expeditionary Medal; Global War on Terrorism Medal; Armed Forces Reserve Medal; Noncommissioned Officer Professional Development Medal; General White Award; General Stewart Award; Army Service Ribbon

Patricia A. Barnes, MD

MD
Nighthawk Radiology Services
250 Northwest Boulevard
Suite 202
Coeur D'Alene, ID 83814 United States
xray478@aol.com
http://www.cambridgewhoswho.com

BUS: Radiology Center **P/S:** Teleradiology and Diagnostic Radiology Services **MA:** International **EXP:** Ms. Barnes' areas of expertise are in general radiology, imaging, mammography, neuro CAQ radiology and teleradiology. **H/I/S:** Cooking, Listening to Music, Traveling **FBP:** Radiology Publications **EDU:** Fellowship in CT Scan and Ultrasound, University of Texas MD Anderson Hospital; Residency, University of Texas, Houston; MD, Anderson Medical School, University of Texas Medical School, Houston (1976) **CERTS:** Board Certified Radiologist **A/A/S:** Lafayette Parish Medical Society; Louisiana Parish Medical Society; Radiology Society of Louisiana; American Roentgen Ray Society; American College of Radiology; Radiology Society of North America **A/H:** Top Doctor of Radiology (2006)

Dana M. Barnett, LPN

Licensed Practical Nurse, Case Coordinator, Clinical Director Assistant
Kindred Care Hospice
2153 Riverchase Office Road
Birmingham, AL 35244 United States
dmbsew@bellsouth.net
http://www.cambridgewhoswho.com

BUS: End of Life Care **P/S:** Healthcare **MA:** Local **EXP:** Ms. Barnett's expertise is in patient care. **H/I/S:** Sewing **FBP:** American Journal of Nursing **EDU:** Pursuing Bachelor of Science in Nursing **CERTS:** Licensed Practical Nurse, Itwamba Community College **C/VW:** Various Child-Oriented Charities **A/S:** She attributes her success to enjoying what she does and the people she works with. **B/I:** She became involved in her profession because it is a family profession. **H/O:** The highlight of her career has been working towards becoming a nurse practitioner.

Sarah A. Barnett
Controller
Washington College
300 Washington Avenue
Chestertown, MD 21620 United States
sbarnett2@washcoll.edu
http://www.washcoll.edu

BUS: First College Established in the United States, Founded in 1782 **P/S:** Quality Higher Education Services, Graduate and Undergraduate Degree Programs in Various Areas of Study **MA:** National **D/D/R:** Directing All Business Office Operations, Administrating All Payroll and Accounts Payable Functions, Overseeing College Assets, Endowments and Annuities **H/I/S:** Crafts, Jewelry Making **FBP:** CFO **EDU:** Master of Business Administration, Webster University (2006); Bachelor's Degree in Business Administration, Southern Illinois University (1977) **CERTS:** Certified Public Accountant (1981) **A/A/S:** American Institute of Banking **A/H:** Award, Financial Executives Institute (1977); President's Award, American Institute of Banking (1975)

Natalio Barquet, Jr.
President
N. Barquet Jewelers
201 Calle Fortaleza, Bo Palmas
Catano, PR 00962 United States
nbarquet@spiderlink.net
http://www.cambridgewhoswho.com

BUS: Designer Jewelry **P/S:** Sales, Italian Designers **MA:** Local **EXP:** Mr. Barquet's areas of expertise are in diamonds and fine retail jewelry. **FBP:** Industry-Related Publications **EDU:** Bachelor's Degree in Economics, University of Puerto Rico **A/S:** He attributes his success to his wife, Helen R. and daughters, Natalio R., Daniela M., Elena M. **B/I:** He became involved in this profession because of his father and grandfather and he started as a clerk.

TRILLA ANNE REEVES BARR
Social Worker
Lee Memorial Health Systems
696 Del Prado Boulevard S.
Cape Coral, FL 33990 United States
trillab@msn.com
http://www.cambridgewhoswho.com

BUS: Nonprofit Healthcare Organization **P/S:** Healthcare Including Palliative Care **MA:** Regional **EXP:** Ms. Barr's expertise is in palliative care. **H/I/S:** Traveling, Cooking, Reading, Exercising **EDU:** Master of Social Work, San Diego State University **CERTS:** Board Certified Diplomat in Clinical Social Work; Licensed Clinical Social Worker, State of California **A/A/S:** Matlacha Hookers **A/S:** She attributes her success to her hard work, passion for her profession and to the support she received from her mentors. **B/I:** She became involved in her profession because she was always interested in social work. **H/O:** The most gratifying aspect of her career is working with bone marrow transplant patients.

ILDEFONSO BARRIENTOS JR.
Fourth Grade Bilingual Teacher
Goose Creek Consolidated Independent School District, Lamar
Elementary School
816 N. Pruett Street
Baytown, TX 77520 United States
abarrientos@gccisd.net
http://www.cambridgewhoswho.com

BUS: Public School District **P/S:** Elementary Education **MA:** Local **D/D/R:** Specializing in Bilingual Education **H/I/S:** Reading, Fishing **FBP:** Hispanic **EDU:** Master's Degree in Administration, University of Houston; Bachelor's Degree in Elementary Education, University of Texas Pan American **A/A/S:** Science Teacher's Association **C/VW:** Junior Baseball Little League for Baytown North **A/S:** He attributes his personal and professional success to his supportive and encouraging father. **B/I:** He has always had an interest in the field and a love for working with children. **H/O:** The highlight of his career was winning the Teacher of the Year Award in 2004.

LISA B. BARRON
Editor, Reporter
Kobliner Communications
1350 N. Lake Shore Drive
Apartment 602
Chicago, IL 60610 United States
lisabarron600@yahoo.com
http://www.cambridgewhoswho.com

BUS: Publishing Company **P/S:** Publishing and Printing Service **MA:** Local **D/D/R:** Writing about International Politics, Domestic Crime and Financial Journalism **H/I/S:** Reading, Watching Movies, Scuba Diving, Running **FBP:** Economist; Fortune; People **EDU:** Master of Philosophy, London School of Economics **A/A/S:** National Strategy Forum; American Women in Radio and Television **A/S:** She attributes her success to her determination. **B/I:** She became involved in her profession because of being inspired by her mother who was also a writer. **H/O:** The highlight of her career was working for CBS radio.

MARGARET M. BARTH
Owner
Ecocessories
13 E. Upsal Street
Philadelphia, PA 19119 United States
Mbarth@ecocessories.com
http://www.cambridgewhoswho.com/

BUS: Manufacturing, Fashion Art To-Wear **P/S:** Fashion and Art To-Wear including Upscale Accessories, Outerwear for Children and Adults **MA:** National **EXP:** Ms. Barth's areas of expertise are in art design and the innovative translation of design. **D/D/R:** Marketing, Focusing on Environmentally Green Products **H/I/S:** Hiking, Kayaking, Cooking and Baking, Skydiving and Adventuring **FBP:** Craft Report; Cookie; Children's Magazines **EDU:** Apprenticeship, Theater Costume Design, Metropolitan Opera Company, New York, NY **C/VW:** American Cancer Society, Sisters of St. Joseph **A/S:** Margaret attributes her success to being an innovator with incredible drive and creativity. **B/I:** She became involved because of a desire to create a product that would leave behind a legacy, showing the beauty that can come from recycled items. **H/O:** The rapid growth of the business within the first year and the tough business decisions learned as a result of the growth are some of the career highlights of Margaret's career.

Elizabeth M. Barton, MBA, LCSW, Ph.D.
Psychotherapist
1221 Pearl St. #8
Boulder, CO 80302 United States
elizabeth1150@comcast.net

BUS: Healthcare, Private Practice **P/S:** Child, Adolescent, Adult and Family Therapy and Clinical Supervision **MA:** Colorado **D/D/R:** Offering Individual and Family Therapy for Clients of All Ages Suffering from Emotional and Behavioral Problems Including ADHD, Trauma, Grief and Loss, Interpersonal and Family Conflict, Adoption Issues Including Interracial Adoption, Parenting and Step-Parenting Issues, Offering Developmentally Appropriate Strengths-Based Treatment Including Dialectical Behavior Therapy, EMDR, Play Therapy, Jungian-Based Sandtray Therapy, Client-Centered Supportive Therapy, Solution-Focused Therapy and Cognitive-Behavior Therapy **H/I/S:** Fossil Hunting, Armchair Mountaineering, Midnight Gardening, Multi-genre Reading, Travel, Yoga, Jewelry Design, Mountain Hiking, Neighborhood Walking, Interior Design **FBP:** New Yorker; New York Times; New England Journal of Medicine **EDU:** Master of Social Work, University of Denver (2001); Master of Business Administration, The Pennsylvania State University (1981); Ph.D., Individual and Family Studies, The Pennsylvania State University (1978) **A/A/S:** Boulder Psychotherapist Guild, Inc.; National Association of Social Workers; People To People Ambassador Program; International Dark Sky Association; Democratic Congressional Campaign Committee; AARP **C/VW:** Planned Parenthood, ACLU **DOB:** January 30, 1950 **POB:** Columbia, Missouri **SP:** legion **CHILD:** Sarah Barton Studer, Zachary Barton Studer, Gordon Studer, Gretchen Studer **A/S:** He attributes his success to his compassion, skill and curiosity. **B/I:** He became involved in his profession after teaching, researching and deciding to do professional clinical work.

Mrs. Ruth F. Bascom
Mayor, Councilor (Retired)
The City of Eugene
65 W. 30th Avenue
Suite 3512
Eugene, OR 97405 United States
jbascomr@pacinfo.com
http://www.eugene-or.gov

BUS: Government Organization **P/S:** Public Services **MA:** Regional **D/D/R:** Overseeing the Groundwork for New Library and Improved Passenger, Rail System Route from Eugene, Oregon to British Columbia, Developing Parkland Seven Mile Riverbank Trail **H/I/S:** Bicycling, Tree Farming, Singing in the Church Choir **EDU:** Master's Degree in Social Psychology, Cornell University (1949) **A/A/S:** Board Member, 1000 Friends of Oregon (1999-2005); Chairwoman, Passenger Rail (1993-2005) **C/VW:** Local Church **DOB:** February 4, 1926 **POB:** Ames **SP:** John **CHILD:** Lucinda, Rebecca, Ellen, Thomas, Paul, Mary **A/S:** She attributes her success to her hard work, determination and to the support she receives from her family. **B/I:** She became involved in her profession because of her interest in community services. **H/O:** The most gratifying aspect of her career is receiving support from her family member.

LONA G. BASS
Licensed Practical Nurse
Forcht Wade Corrections
7990 Caddo Drive
Keithville, LA 71047 United States
jbass2@sport.rr.com
http://www.cambridgewhoswho.com

BUS: Healthcare, Law Enforcement **P/S:** Inmate Corrections **MA:** Louisiana **D/D/R:** Nursing **H/I/S:** Fishing, Arts and Crafts, Playing Croquet, Exercising, Spending Time with her Children **FBP:** LPN **EDU:** Pursuing Degree in Registered Nursing, State of Ohio **CERTS:** Licensed Practical Nurse, Arkansas Technical University **A/A/S:** American Nurses Association; NMCA **C/VW:** American Police Association, Local Department, United Way, American Red Cross **A/S:** She attributes her success to loving her job and her ability to take care of people. **B/I:** She became involved in her profession through her parents, who were involved in nursing. **H/O:** The highlight of her career has been participating in nursing conventions throughout the United States.

SARA BATEN
Owner
Abbate-Baten, LLC dba Abbate Florist
326 Silas Deane Highway
Wethersfield, CT 06109 United States
batensara@yahoo.com
http://www.cambridgewhoswho.com

BUS: Retail Store **P/S:** Floral Products, Crafts, Gifts and Gourmet Food Baskets **MA:** International **EXP:** Ms. Baten's expertise is in operations management. **D/D/R:** Overseeing the Sale of Floral and Gift Products, Gourmet Crafts, Arranging for All Occasions Including Weddings and Funerals **H/I/S:** Making Crafts **FBP:** SAF Publications **EDU:** High School Diploma **A/A/S:** The Business Advisory Council, National Republican Congressional Committee (2007); Glastonbury Chamber of Commerce; The Society of American Florists; Teleflora **A/H:** National Leadership Award (2007) **C/VW:** Local Community Organizations

JUAN CARLOS BATLLE
President, Chief Executive Officer
Santander Asset Management Corporation
Calle B-7 Tabonuco
Suite 1800
Guaynabo, PR 00968 United States
jcbatlle@sampr.com
http://www.santandersecurities.com

BUS: Proven Leader in the Financial Industry **P/S:** High Quality Services and Customer Care in the Field of Asset Management **MA:** Regional **D/D/R:** Investment Advisor, Asset Management, Working with Different Companies to Help with Asset Management **H/I/S:** Golfing, Fishing **EDU:** Bachelor's Degree in Economics, University of Michigan (1996) **A/H:** 40 Under 40 Award, Caribbean Business

CAROL J. BAUER
Owner, Secretary, Treasurer
Stasney Mechanical, Inc.
1574 Third Avenue S.W.
Suite 2
New Prague, MN 56071 United States
stasmech@bevcomm.net
http://www.cambridgewhoswho.com

BUS: Plumbing and Heating Company **P/S:** Plumbing, Heating, Ventilation, Air Conditioning, Refrigeration **MA:** Local **D/D/R:** Performing Administrative Duties Including Hiring, Answering Service Calls, Ordering Supplies, Overseeing Accounts Receivable, Managing 10 Employees and 6 Trucks **H/I/S:** Traveling, Spending Time with her Husband, Five Children and Three Grandchildren **FBP:** The News; Industry-Related Publications **EDU:** Diploma, New Prague High School **A/A/S:** Veterans of Foreign Wars Ladies Auxiliary; American Legion Auxiliary **A/H:** First Runner-Up, Township Leader of the Year (2005)

LINDA BAUNE
Speech-Language Pathologist, Co-Owner
SPoT Rehabilitation
2835 W. Germain Street
Suite 300
St. Cloud, MN 56301 United States
lindyslp@aol.com
http://www.sPot-rehab.com

BUS: Speech, Physical and Occupational Therapy Center **P/S:** Occupational, Physical and Speech Therapy for Children and Adults Including Assistive Technology, Industrial and Ergonomic Services, Body Weight Supported Gait Training, Programs for Seniors, Contract Therapy, Sensory Integration, Driver Review Program, Serial Casting and Splinting, Feeding and Oral Motor Program, Specialized Equipment Assessment, Home Health Care, Vital Stimulation and Aquatic Therapy **MA:** Local **D/D/R:** Offering Augmentative Services, Speech Therapy to Children and Adults with Various Disabilities, New Vital Stimulation for Patients with Stroke and Swallowing Difficulties **H/I/S:** Reading, Horseback Riding, Counted Cross-Stitching **EDU:** Master of Science, St. Cloud State University **A/A/S:** Minnesota Speech-Language-Hearing Association; American Speech-Language-Hearing Association **A/H:** Judd Jacobson Memorial Award (2006); Spirit Award, United Cerebral Palsy of Central Minnesota (2005); Jay and Rose Phillips Award (2001)

MR. ROGER D. BAUSMAN, RN, BSN, CLNC
Registered and Travel Nurse,
Certified Legal Nurse Consultant, BSN (Retired)
PRN Health Services, Inc.
4321 W. College Avenue, Suite 200
Appleton, WI 54914 United States
rbaus@earthlink.net
http://www.prnhealthservices.com

BUS: Staffing Company **P/S:** Recruiting Qualified Healthcare Professionals in the Industry, Temporary and Contract Placement of Nurses in Acute Care and Inpatient Facilities such as Hospitals, Rehabilitation Centers, Subacute and Long Term Care Facilities **MA:** Local **EXP:** Mr. Bausman's expertise is in cardiac, medical-surgical, telemetry and palliative nursing. **H/I/S:** Camping **FBP:** American Journal of Nursing; Nursing2009; American Journal of Preventive Medicine; Advance in Skin and Wound Care **EDU:** Bachelor's Degree in Nursing, Saint Francis Medical Center School of Nursing (1999)

JENNIFER L. BAXTER

Nurse Charge Auditor
Mercy Health Center
4300 W. Memorial Road
Oklahoma City, OK 73103 United States
jbaxter@ok.mercy.net
http://www.mercyok.net

BUS: Hospital **P/S:** Healthcare **MA:** International **EXP:** Ms. Baxter's expertise is in revenue management, auditing and oncology and respiratory nursing. **H/I/S:** Tennis, Traveling, Reading, Collecting Fine Artworks Including Porcelain Pieces and Crystals **FBP:** American Journal of Nursing **EDU:** Bachelor of Arts, University of Arkansas; Associate Degree, Westark Sate College **CERTS:** Registered Nurse, Carl Albert State College; Certified Oncology Nurse **A/A/S:** Former Member, Oncology Nurses Society; Former Member, Neurological Nurses Society; Oklahoma Healthcare Compliance Group; Oklahoma Hospital Association; American Nurses Association **C/VW:** Medical Society Alliance; Junior League; Make-A-Wish Foundation; Children's Emergency Center **A/S:** She attributes her success to her dedication, hard work, personal drive and her desire to learn about medicine. **B/I:** She became involved in her profession because she was encouraged by her family friend. **H/O:** The most gratifying aspects of her career are researching on neurophysiology and practicing oncology nursing.

PENNY BAYKO

Director, Business Process Improvement-People Services
NOVA Chemicals
1550 Coraopolis Heights Road
Moon Township, PA 15108 United States
baykop@novachem.com
http://www.novachem.com

BUS: Commodity Chemicals Company, Chemical Manufacturing **P/S:** Business to Business Manufacturer of Raw Materials, Olefins, Polyolefins and Styrenics Polymers, Produces Commodity Plastics and Chemicals that are Essential to Everyday Life, Develops and Manufactures Materials for Customers Worldwide Who Produce Consumer, Industrial and Packaging Products **MA:** International **D/D/R:** Consulting on In-House Human Resources Issues, Improving Business Processes, Managing Talent **H/I/S:** Reading, Golfing **FBP:** HR; Harvard Business Review **EDU:** Coursework, Southern Alberta Institute of Technology, Canada **A/A/S:** Society of Human Resource Management

PHYLLIS BAYNES-SUPERVILLE
Broker, Accountant
PBS Homes Realty, Inc.
144-19 107th Avenue
Jamaica, NY 11435 United States
psupervill@aol.com
http://www.pbsintl.com

BUS: Professional Real Estate Agency and Accounting Firm **P/S:** Excellent Accounting and Financial Services as well as Providing Quality Residential Real Estate **MA:** Regional **D/D/R:** Bookkeeping, Preparing Taxes, Advising on Financial Issues, Overseeing Home Sales and Rentals of Residential Properties **H/I/S:** Sewing, Dress Designing, Tennis **FBP:** Business Week **EDU:** Bachelor's Degree in Accounting, Baruch College, The City University of New York (2006) **A/A/S:** New York Association of Realtors; National Association of Realtors; National Society of Tax Preparers

MARY S. BEAL-THORP
Senior Branch Office Administrator
Edward Jones
1412 N.E. 134th Street, Suite 240
Vancouver, WA 98685 United States
mary.beal-thorp@edwardjones.com
http://www.edwardjones.com

BUS: Investments **P/S:** Investment Services **MA:** Local **EXP:** Ms. Beal-Thorp's areas of expertise are in customer service and administration. **H/I/S:** Reading, Gardening, Spending Time with Family, Sports **FBP:** The Wall Street Journal **C/VW:** Local Church; Order of the Eastern Star; National Guard; Armed Services; Shriners Hospitals for Children **A/S:** She attributes her success to her family and to her faith. **B/I:** She became involved in this profession because she always loved crunching numbers and customer service. **H/O:** The highlight of her career is her current position.

ANITA BEASLEY
Reading Specialist
Daughtry Elementary School
Butts County Public Schools
150 Shiloh Road
Jackson, GA 30233 United States
acbeasley@charter.net
http://www.cambridgewhoswho.com

BUS: Elementary School **P/S:** Education **MA:** Local **D/D/R:** Helping Students with Reading, Testing, Overseeing a Federal Grant, Teaching Reading, Mentoring Teachers, Testing Students **H/I/S:** Traveling, Reading, Scrapbooking **FBP:** Reading Teacher; Reading Today **EDU:** Ed.S in Leadership, Lincoln Memorial University; Master of Arts in Reading and Early Childhood Education, The University of West Georgia; Bachelor of Science in Early Elementary, Georgia State University **CERTS:** National Board Certified Teacher in Early Childhood Education; Certified General Reading Specialist; Certified Teacher Support Specialist **A/A/S:** Professional Association of Georgia Educators; Georgia Reading Association; International Reading Association; Henry Heritage Reading Council; McIntosh Reading Council; Concern for Effect in Reading Education; Parent-Teacher Organization; The Delta Kappa Gamma Society International; Association for Supervision and Curriculum Development **A/H:** Georgia Reading Leadership Award, Georgia Reading Association (2008); Lucille Cornetet Professional Development Award, The Delta Kappa Gamma Society International (2007); Who's Who Among America's Teachers (2005-2006); Who's Who in American Education (2005-2008); Teacher of the Year, Anderson Elementary School, Clayton County (1999) **C/VW:** Ferst Foundation for Childhood Literacy **DOB:** August 4, 1956 **POB:** Atlanta **SP:** Wayne **CHILD:** Chad, Kirk, Eric **A/S:** The attributes her success to her supportive parents, who raised her to respect everyone in the education field and instilled in her a love of reading. **B/I:** She became involved in her profession because she wanted to be a teacher since childhood. **H/O:** The highlight of her career was receiving her national board certification. **I/F/Y:** In five years, Ms. Beasley would like to be become either the director or coordinator of reading education.

LILLIAN J. BEATO
Pastor, Founder
New Hope and Deliverance
10772 Rhode Island Avenue
Beltsville, MD 20705 United States
aPostlebeato@aol.com
http://www.cambridgewhoswho.com

BUS: Church **P/S:** Religious Services **MA:** Regional **D/D/R:** Mentoring, Teaching, Conducting Services, Counseling for Marriage, Drug and Alcohol, Unwed Mothers and Abused Women **H/I/S:** Home Decorating **FBP:** Charisma Magazine **EDU:** International Ministries Fellowship, Jameson University (1988); Coursework, Bible School **CERTS:** Certification, Appointed Church of God in Christ **A/A/S:** West Virginia Jurisdiction Department of Women

MR. JOHN BEAUMONT
Director, Manager
John C. Beaumont Earthmoving
2673 Cunningham Highway
Willowbank, 4306 Australia
jcbeau@gil.com.au
http://www.cambridgewhoswho.com

BUS: Proven Leader in the Contracting Industry **P/S:** Quality Services, Earthmoving Contracting, Construction, Mining **MA:** Citywide **D/D/R:** Overseeing All Aspects of Civil Construction and Mining **H/I/S:** Playing Golf and Fishing **FBP:** Business Review Weekly; The Economist **DOB:** October 29, 1963 **SP:** Kay

CAROLYN M. BEBOUT, RN
Registered Nurse, Staff Nurse
Knox Community Hospital
1330 Coshocton Road
Mount Vernon, OH 43050 United States
beboutfarms@voyager.net
http://www.cambridgewhoswho.com

BUS: Hospital **P/S:** Patient Care **MA:** Local **EXP:** Ms. Bebout's expertise is in critical-care nursing, diagnostic imaging, invasive procedure assistance care, cat scans and radiology critical care. **H/I/S:** Gardening, NeedlePoint, Spending Time with Family **FBP:** Nursing2009; Critical-Care Nurse **EDU:** Diploma in Nursing, Good Samaritan Hospital School of Nursing **CERTS:** Certified in Advanced Cardiac Life Support; Certified in Pediatric Advanced Life Support; Certified Breast Health Navigator **A/A/S:** American Association of Critical-Care Nurses; Oncology Nursing Society **C/VW:** Church, The Salvation Army **DOB:** December 25, 1960 **POB:** Highland Park **SP:** Charles **CHILD:** Paul **W/H:** Nurse **A/S:** She attributes her success to loving her job, keeping a positive outlook and wanting to help people. **B/I:** She chose the profession because she always wanted to be a nurse. **H/O:** The most gratifying aspect of her career is being the best nurse she can be. **I/F/Y:** In five years, Ms. Bebout hopes to still be working in the same capacity and to have earned her oncology nursing certification.

PROF. DONNA MARIE BECK, CSJ
Chairwoman, Music Therapy Department
Duquesne University, Mary Pappert School of Music
600 Forbes Avenue, Room 104
Pittsburgh, PA 15282 United States
beckd@duq.edu
http://www.music.duq.edu

BUS: Higher Education University Committed to Providing Quality Music Therapy Education Services **P/S:** Higher Education Services, Undergraduate and Graduate Degree Programs in Music Education, Music Technology, Music Performance, Music Therapy Specialization in Bonny's Method of Guided Imagery and Music (FAMI) **MA:** International **EXP:** Prof. Beck's areas of expertise are in music and spirituality, music therapy and education. **H/I/S:** Listening to Music, Reading, Cooking, Art **FBP:** Spirituality and Health; Psychology Today; Spiritual Direction **EDU:** Ph.D. in Formative Spirituality and Music, Duquesne University Institute of Formation Science; Master of Arts Degree; Master of Music Education; Bachelor of Music Education **CERTS:** First-Level Training in Mandala Assessment **A/A/S:** American Music Therapy Association; Fellow, Association of Music and Imagery; West Virginia Institute of Formative Spirituality **A/H:** Lifetime Achievement Award, American Music Therapy Association (2003) **DOB:** April 30, 1932 **W/H:** Music Therapist, Polk State Center (1976-1979); Professor of Music Therapy, Duquesne University, Pittsburgh; Marywood University, Scranton, PA **C/A:** Co-Founder, Music Therapy Undergraduate Program, Marywood University, Scranton, PA; Published in Association of Music and Imagery Journal, AMI Journal (2006, 2007)

ANN W. BECKER
Director
Women's Health Research
6036 N. 19 Avenue
Suite 400A and 401
Phoenix, AZ 85015 United States
beckerconsulting@cox.net
http://www.whraz.com

BUS: Arizona Clinical Research Organization **P/S:** Coronary Health, Vascular Health, Menstrual Disorders, Endometriosis, Contraception, Post-Partum Anemia, Hysterectomy, Urinary Incontinence, Osteoporosis, Obesity, HPV, Genital Herpes, Vaginitis and Yeast Infections, Devices, Menopause, Hot Flashes and Sterilization **MA:** International **D/D/R:** Directing the Clinical Research Site, Negotiating Contracts and Budgets, Advertising, Recruiting, Assessing Quality Data, Working on New Business Development, Overseeing Recruitment Activities for Clinical Trials, Creation of Promotional and Marketing Plans, Including Strategic Development Planning **H/I/S:** Reading, Photography **FBP:** DIA; Focus **EDU:** Bachelor of Business Administration in Healthcare Management, American Intercontinental University (2005) **A/A/S:** Regulatory Affairs Professional Society

SUSANNE BECKER-PETERSON
Business Segment Partner Care Delivery
Kaiser Permanente
4480 Hacienda Dr
Pleasanton, CA 94566 United States
sue.becker@kp.org
http://www.kaiserpermanente.org

BUS: HMO Healthcare Provider **P/S:** Healthcare Information Technology **MA:** National **D/D/R:** Developing Information Technology Systems for Healthcare **H/I/S:** Attending Plays, Enjoying Art, Investing in Homes **EDU:** Master's Degree in Computer Science, Stanford University; Bachelor of Science in Pre-Medicine, Fairleigh Dickinson University **A/A/S:** American Society for Clinical Pathology **C/VW:** Women's Shelters, San Jose

SAMUEL W. BECKWITH
Training/Safety Senior Manager
ARAMARK
2875 Michelli Drive
Baton Rouge, LA 70805 United States
beckwith-samuel@aramark.com
http://www.aramark.com

BUS: Facilities Support Services Service Organization **P/S:** Product Distribution to Corporations **MA:** International **D/D/R:** Conducting Training and Safety Programs **H/I/S:** Powerlifting **FBP:** Forbes **EDU:** Bachelor's Degree, Georgia Southern University **A/A/S:** Safety Champion, ARAMARK

MRS. LINDA K. BEERBOWER
Manager
Beerbower's P.A. Accounting and Tax Service
103 S. West Street
Edgerton, OH 43517 United States
nbeerbower@yahoo.com
http://www.cambridgewhoswho.com

BUS: Accounting Company **P/S:** Tax Preparation, Payroll and Bookkeeping Services Including Setting Up Businesses **MA:** Regional **D/D/R:** Managing Operations Including Customer Service, Administration and Communications, Working with Small Businesses on Taxes, W-2s, Preparing Personal Income Tax Returns and Audits, Reviewing for Senior Citizens **H/I/S:** NASCAR, Fishing, Camping **EDU:** High School Education **A/A/S:** Edgerton Chamber of Commerce; Fraternal Order of the Eagles

REBECCA L. BEGAZO
Special Education Coordinator
beckybegazo@netscape.net
http://www.cambridgewhoswho.com

P/S: Bilingual Inclusion Program, Coordinating Tutorial Program **MA:** Local **D/D/R:** Supervising the Inclusion Program **H/I/S:** Reading, Traveling **EDU:** Master's Degree, Howard University **A/S:** She attributes her success to her dedication and perseverance.

ELIZABETH A. BEIRO, LMT, CT
Massage Therapist/Colon Hydrotherapy
Harris Health Center
1221 Cleveland Street
Clearwater, FL 34681 United States
http://www.cambridgewhoswho.com

BUS: Healthcare **P/S:** Chiropractic Services and Massage Therapy **MA:** Local **EXP:** Ms. Biero's areas of expertise are in massage therapy and colon hydrotherapy. **H/I/S:** Ballroom and Belly Dancing **EDU:** Industry-Related Training and Experience **A/A/S:** Florida Massage Therapy Association **C/VW:** Free Life, Go Ji Kids Charity **A/S:** She attributes her personal and professional success to her determination, people skills and good reputation with her clients. **B/I:** She has always had an interest in the field and enjoys helping others.

CAPT. ANDREW J. BELCHER, NREMT-P, FF1
Captain, Vice President
Union Dale Volunteer Fire Company
PO Box 191
Union Dale, PA 18470 United States
bubbabelcher@gmail.com
http://www.uniondalefire.com

BUS: Emergency Service Center **P/S:** Fire Prevention and Control, Emergency Medical Services **MA:** Regional **D/D/R:** Overseeing Emergency Medical Services, Quick Response Services and Advanced and Basic Life Support Services, Working as a Paramedic, Supervisor and Ski Patroller for Elk Mountain and as a Line Officer for the Volunteer Department **H/I/S:** Skiing, Hunting, Playing Softball, Traveling, Quad Riding, Camping **FBP:** Journal of Emergency Medical Services; Firehouse; Ski; Skiing; Powder **EDU:** Coursework in Paramedic Studies, Luzerne County Community College (2004); Diploma, Mountain View School (2000) **CERTS:** Pursuing Critical Care Paramedic Certification, Harrisburg Area Community College; Certified Advanced Life Support Paramedic (2006); Nationally Registered Emergency Medical Technician and Paramedic; Certified Firefighter I; Certified Emergency Medical Technician and Paramedic, State of Pennsylvania; Certification, Pennsylvania State Fire Academy; Certification in Basic Trauma Life Support; Certification in Neonatal Advanced Life Support; Certification in Advance Cardiac Life Support; Certification in Pediatric Advanced Life Support; Certified HAZMAT Technician **A/A/S:** National Rifle Association; National Elk Foundation **C/VW:** Chairman, Knights of Columbus (2007); Emergency Medical Service Coordinator, Distance Run, Rails to Trails **DOB:** February 9, 1982 **POB:** Scranton **W/H:** Cottage Hose Ambulance Rescue Company (2005); Senior Patroller, National Ski Patrol (2001); Elk Mountain Ski Patrol (2000); Uniondale Fire Department (1999); Pleasant Mount Emergency Services, Belmont Corners Fire Company (1998); Clifford Township Volunteer Fire Company (1996); 911 Dispatcher; Emergency Medical Services Technician; Fireman; Line Officer; Administration Officer; Instructor, Academy of Hospital Administration **A/S:** He attributes his success to his willpower and desire to succeed. **B/I:** He became involved in his profession through a natural progression of opportunities. **H/O:** The most gratifying aspect of his career is the gratitude he receives from people for his volunteer work. **I/F/Y:** In five years, Mr. Belcher hopes to continue his education and grow professionally.

CANDACE 'CANDY' J. BELL, ABR
Associate Broker
Rio Rico Home and Land
1060 2A Yavapai Drive
Rio Rico, AZ 85648 United States
candy@candybell.com
http://www.candybell.com

BUS: Real Estate Company **P/S:** Sales of Homes and Land **MA:** Local **D/D/R:** Specializing in Residential Sales and Relocation **H/I/S:** Traveling **FBP:** Arizona Realtors Digest **EDU:** Accredited Buyers Representative; Certified Associate Broker **A/A/S:** Real Estate Buyers Agent Council Inc. **C/VW:** Humane Society; Alzheimer's Association

GAYLE M. BELL
Lecturer/School Psychologist
University of Idaho
gayleid4@aol.com
http://www.cambridgewhoswho.com

BUS: Education **P/S:** Neuropsychological Evaluations, Treatment Recommendations **MA:** Regional **D/D/R:** Neuropsychology, Differential Diagnosis Testing and Evaluation of Effects of Neurological Disorders on Cognition and Behavioral Function **FBP:** CNS Spectrums; NEI **CERTS:** Educational Development Specialist, University of Northern Colorado **A/A/S:** Society of Pediatric Psychology; Society for Behavioral and Neuropsychology **C/VW:** ICARE; Kootenai County Search and Rescue; Kootenani County Sheriff Posse, The Humane Society **A/S:** She attributes her personal and professional success to her desire to make a difference. **B/I:** She has always had an interest in the field and a passion for neuropsychology. **H/O:** The highlight of her career is having successful cases with children.

MAY S. BELL
Chartered Property Casualty Underwriter, Owner
A&B Insurance Solutions, LLC
2002 Richard Jones Road
Suite 304C
Nashville, TN 37215 United States
mayb@abinsurance.com
http://www.abcinsurance.com

BUS: Insurance Brokerage **P/S:** Wholesale Brokerage, Commercial Insurance **MA:** United States **D/D/R:** Overseeing Primary and Excess Casualty **H/I/S:** Golfing **FBP:** Fortune; Small Business **EDU:** College Coursework **A/A/S:** Insurance Association of Tennessee; National Association of Professional Surplus Lines Offices

VIRGINIA E. BELL
Director
Department of Health Information Management
Franklin Square Hospital Center
9000 Franklin Square Drive
Rosedale, MD 21237 United States
virginia.bell@medstar.net
http://www.franklinsquare.org

BUS: Hospital **P/S:** Healthcare **MA:** Local **D/D/R:** Coaching, Mentoring and Directing the Operations of the Hospital Information Management System, Overseeing Employees Dealing with Coding, Medical Records and Discharge Analysis **H/I/S:** Reading, Traveling **EDU:** Bachelor of Science in Health Records Administration, CUNY York College (1987) **A/A/S:** President, Alumni Association, CUNY York College; Fellow, Advisory Board of the Healthcare Administration; American College of Healthcare Executives **A/H:** Distinguished Member Award, Maryland Health Information Management Association **C/VW:** Goodwill; Maryland State Fraternal Order of Police; United Way

LINDA J. BELLEVUE
Broker
Congdon and Coleman Real Estate
57 Main Street
Nantucket, MA 02554 United States
lindab@congdonandcoleman.com
http://www.congdonandcoleman.com

BUS: Full-Service Nantucket Real Estate Brokerage Company Specializing in the Marketing, Sales and Rental of Residential and Commercial Properties **P/S:** Quality Real Estate Services, Residential and Commercial Sales, Rentals, Property Listings, Marketing **MA:** International **D/D/R:** Selling High-End Residential, Vacation and Second Homes **H/I/S:** Gardening, Traveling **FBP:** DuPont Registry; Estate Magazine; Traditional Home **CERTS:** GRI Certified; Certified Buyer Representative **A/A/S:** Cape Cod and Islands Association of Realtors; Massachusetts Association of Realtors

SHERRI BELLUOMINI
Real Estate Consultant
First Marin Realty
145 Lomita Drive
Mill Valley, CA 94941 United States
sherri@firstmarin.com
http://www.firstmarin.net

BUS: Real Estate Agency **P/S:** Residential and Commercial Real Estate Exchange **MA:** Regional **EXP:** Ms. Belluomini's expertise is in property management. **D/D/R:** Consulting, Overseeing Sales, Negotiating Contracts **H/I/S:** Golfing **CERTS:** Licensed Realtor **A/A/S:** Marin Association of Realtors; California Association of Realtors; National Association of Realtors; President, GVHCA

Ms. Sarah A. Belsha, LOTR
Occupational Therapist
sarahlotr@yahoo.com
http://www.cambridgewhoswho.com

BUS: Private Practice **P/S:** Occupational Therapy **MA:** Local **EXP:** Ms. Belsha's expertise is in pediatrics. **D/D/R:** Treating Neurological Deficits **H/I/S:** Tap Dancing, Spending Time with her Family **FBP:** OTPractice **EDU:** Bachelor of Science in Occupational Therapy, Northeast Louisiana University **A/A/S:** Louisiana Occupational Therapy Association; American Occupational Therapy Association; Phi Mu **C/VW:** St. Jude Children's Research Hospital **A/S:** She attributes her success to her determination to help people and make a difference in their lives. **B/I:** She became involved in her profession because of her interest in science and anatomy. **H/O:** The highlight of her career was speaking at the Vernon Parish Pilot Club on stroke rehabilitation.

Janie Benckert, RN, CDE
Certified Diabetic Registered Nurse
Newberry County Memorial Hospital, Wellness Center
2605 Kinard
Suite 100
Newberry, SC 29108 United States
junglejanern@yahoo.com
http://www.cambridgewhoswho.com

BUS: Hospital **P/S:** Diabetes Education and Training **MA:** National **D/D/R:** Nursing **H/I/S:** Reading, Missionary Work, Exercising **FBP:** Nursing2009 **EDU:** Registered Nurse **A/A/S:** American Association of Diabetes Educators; BCNF **C/VW:** Peru South American Missionary, Local Community Charities **A/S:** She attributes her success to her hard work, bilingual education and caring for others. **B/I:** She became involved in the profession because her mother was a nurse and she was surrounded by the industry. **H/O:** The most gratifying aspect of her career is seeing people get better.

SHAUN V. BENFORD-CRUMP

Shaun V. Benford-Crump
230 Bradberry Street S.W.
Atlanta, GA 30313 United States
svbis123@hotmail.com
http://www.cambridgewhoswho.com

BUS: Foster Care Agency **P/S:** Foster Care Including Homes for Children with AIDS, Autism, Cerebral Palsy, Fetal Alcohol Syndrome, Prenatal Drug Exposure and the Lasting Effects of Severe Physical Abuse, Trainings for Foster Parents, Youth Groups and Enrichment Experiences for the Children **MA:** Regional **D/D/R:** Consulting on Foster Care, Managing Business Operations Including Finances, Overseeing Information Technology, Facilities and Human Resources **H/I/S:** Cooking, Traveling, Horseback Riding **FBP:** BusinessWeek **EDU:** Master's Degree in Business Administration, Keller Graduate School (2007); Bachelor's Degree in Communications, Columbia College of Chicago (1984) **CERTS:** Pursuing Certification in Senior Professional in Human Resources; Licensed Funeral Director and Embalmer **A/A/S:** Atlanta Union Mission; Society for Human Resource Management **C/VW:** Local Charitable Organizations; Christian Children's Fund; American Cancer Society

MYRTLE BENJAMIN WEDDERBURN, RN

Registered Nurse, Triage Coordinator, Midwife
Life Path Hospice
3010 W. Azeele Street
Tampa, FL 33609 United States
mbenjamin4@tampabay.rr.com
http://www.lifepath-hospice.org

BUS: Nonprofit, Community-Based Hospice **P/S:** Pain and Symptom Control, Services Enabling Patients to Carry on Alert, Pain-Free Lives, Programs that Meet the Specialized Needs of the Community, Caregiver Program, Circle of Love Children's Program, Family Camp Program, Nursing Home and Assisted Living Facility Program, Circle of Love Center for Grieving Children and the Outreach Care Program **MA:** Local **D/D/R:** Offering End-of-Life Care for Patients, Promoting Education for Staff in Nursing Homes and Assisted Living Facilities, Overseeing Quality Assurance Coordination, Ensuring Community Health and Hospice Care **EDU:** Registered Nurse Degree, England (1964) **CERTS:** Certification in Midwifery (1964) **A/A/S:** Nursing Division, Caribbean Culture Club; Board of Directors, Safety Harbor Neighborhood Family Center

CORRINNE BENNETT
Teacher, Educator
Moffet Elementary School
127 W. Oxford Street
Philadelphia, PA 19122 United States
cbennet@phila.k12.pa.us
http://www.phila.k12.pa.us

BUS: Proven Leader in the Field of Primary Education **P/S:** Quality Student Education Services, Teaching, Learning, Special Programs, Activities **MA:** Local **D/D/R:** Teaching First Grade **H/I/S:** Bowling, Reading, Sewing **FBP:** Teachers Magazine; PFT; AFT Magazine **EDU:** Master's Degree, Antioch University (1975) **CERTS:** CSAP Certified Coordinator **A/A/S:** Leadership Committee, National Education Association **A/H:** Moffet School Teacher of the Year (1995); Semi-Finalist, Philadelphia School District Teacher of the Year (1995) **C/VW:** Superintendent of Sunday School; Director of Vacation Bible School

JEANNE BENNETT
Coordinator of Professional Development and Curriculum,
Mathematics Teacher
Spring Lake Park Schools
711 91st Avenue N.E.
Blaine, MN 55434 United States
ebenne@district16.org
http://www.cambridgewhoswho.com

BUS: School **P/S:** Education **MA:** Local **EXP:** Ms. Bennett's areas of expertise are in professional development and mathematics. **H/I/S:** Golf, Travel, Reading, Gardening, NeedlePoint **EDU:** Master of Arts Plus 60 in Mathematics Education, University of Minnesota (1993); Bachelor of Arts in Mathematics Education, University of Minnesota (1983) **A/A/S:** Association for Supervision and Curriculum Development; National Staff Development Council; National Council of Teachers of Mathematics; Minnesota Council of Teachers of Mathematics, Phi Kappa Phi **A/S:** She attributes her success to her curiosity. **B/I:** She became involved in her profession because she has always been good at mathematics and enjoys dealing with education standards and curriculum.

MARY G. BENNETT
Executive Director
Project GRAD Newark
24 Commerce Street
13th Floor
Newark, NJ 07102 United States
mary.bennett@cwwemail.com
http://www.cambridgewhoswho.com

BUS: Nonprofit Organization **P/S:** Educational Support **MA:** Local **EXP:** Ms. Bennett's expertise is in education assessment, facilitation and team building. **D/D/R:** Directing the Organization, Supporting and Arranging Scholarships **H/I/S:** Traveling, Reading, Journaling, Spending Time with her Grandchildren **FBP:** Educational Leadership **EDU:** Master of Education in Curriculum Development, Rutgers, The State University of New Jersey **A/A/S:** Phi Delta Kappa; Middle School Principals Association; Association for Supervision and Curriculum Development; National Association of Secondary School Principals; National Association of Elementary School Principals **C/VW:** Celebrity Reading Program; Metropolitan Baptist Church; United Way of America **A/S:** She attributes her success to being passionate in her belief that education is essential for people to contribute to their family and the society. **B/I:** She became involved in her profession because she was the first person in her family who did not grow up on a farm and pursued school full time. **H/O:** The highlight of her career was serving as a high school principal where she created a safe and caring environment for children. **I/F/Y:** In five years, Ms. Bennett hopes to retire.

KRISTIN G. BENSEN-HAUSE
Adjunct Instructor
Broome Community College
901 Upper Front Street
Binghamton, NY 13902 United States
bensenhause@sunybroome.edu
http://www.sunybroome.edu

BUS: Education **P/S:** Critical Thinking and Writing, English Composition **MA:** Local **D/D/R:** Testing Theories of Intelligence and Multiple Learning Styles, Promoting Self-Awareness and Personal Growth in Students **H/I/S:** Drumming, Writing Poetry, Singing **FBP:** Calyx; Hunger Mountain **EDU:** Master of Arts Degree, American Literature, Vermont College; Bachelor of Arts Degree, Cultural Studies, Empire State College; Pursuing Ph.D., Walden University **A/A/S:** National Council of Teachers of English **C/VW:** Volunteer, Reader, Elderly Nursing Home **A/S:** She attributes her success to her excitement and passion for the subject matter. **B/I:** She became involved in her profession because of an opportunity that was presented to her. **H/O:** The highlight of her career was the opportunity to convert a student to a major after they took her class.

MYRTLE BENSON CALBERT
Executive Manager
Earth's Outlet
PO Box 201272
Austin, TX 78720 United States
myrtle@earthsoutlet.com
http://www.earthsoutlet.com

BUS: Distribution Company **P/S:** Distributing Organic Materials and Natural Products **MA:** International **D/D/R:** Marketing, Managing, Nursing **H/I/S:** Writing, Arts, Watching Classical Ballet, Cooking Gourmet Dishes **FBP:** The Wall Street Journal; Forbes **EDU:** Registered Nurse; Master of Science, Triple Major in Education, Counseling and Business, Nova Southeastern University; Bachelor of Science in Nursing, Florida State University **A/A/S:** National Rehabilitation Association **C/VW:** Rape Crisis Hotline **DOB:** January 18, 1941 **POB:** Palm Beach, FL **W/H:** Administrative Director, Mt. Sinai, Miami, FL.; Professor of Nursing, Broward Community College, Fort Lauderdale, FL.; National Consultant, St. Louis, MO,; Catastrophic Medical Case Manager **C/A:** President's Committee on People with Disabilities **A/S:** She attributes her success to her hard work and dedication. **B/I:** She became involved in her profession through her friend who gave her the opportunity. **H/O:** The highlight of her career was earning her current position.

SHIRLEE E. BENVIE
Registered Nurse
Brockton Hospital
680 Centre Street
Brockton, MA 02302 United States
shirleebenvie@hotmail.com
http://www.cambridgewhoswho.com

BUS: Hospital **P/S:** Healthcare **MA:** Local **D/D/R:** Working in the Special Care Nursery **H/I/S:** Gardening, Traveling **FBP:** RN **EDU:** Bachelor's Degree in Nursing, Salve Regina University **A/A/S:** Massachusetts Nurses Association **C/VW:** Relay for Life, American Cancer Society **A/S:** She attributes her success to her desire to work in the medical field. **B/I:** She became involved in her profession because she worked as a candy striper when she was younger and found that she enjoyed working with patients. **H/O:** The highlight of her career was receiving her bachelor's degree.

KIMBERLY BERG
Artist
Isis Rising
489 East Road
Cadyville, NY 12918 United States
kdegas@artlover.com
http://www.isisrising.net

BUS: Sole Proprietorship **P/S:** Goddess Paintings, Poetry and Artwork **MA:** National **EXP:** Ms. Berg's expertise is in the creation of artwork. **FBP:** Art in America; American Artist **EDU:** Coursework in History, Minor in Chemistry and Literature, University of Wisconsin (1964) **A/A/S:** Leader, Life Drawing Group; Poets & Writers; Society for Art of Imagination; Women's Caucus for Art; North County Council of the Arts; American Association of University Women

MELODY A. BERGEVIN
Senior Mortgage Consultant
First New England Mortgage Company
157 Main Dunstable Road
Nashua, NH 03060 United States
mbergevin@fnem.com
http://www.fnem.com

BUS: Mortgage Firm **P/S:** Financial Services Including Home Mortgages, Challenged Credit Loans, Second Mortgage Loans, High Debt Ratio Loans, Construction Loans, Investor Loans **MA:** New England **D/D/R:** Assisting Clients with Residential, Reverse and Renovation Mortgages **H/I/S:** Woodworking, Cabinetry, Interior Designing, Spending Time with her Children and Grandchildren **FBP:** Connections **EDU:** Coursework in Liberal Arts, Mars Hill College **A/A/S:** Treasurer, Secretary, Nashua Chapter, Women's Council of Realtors; New Hampshire Chapter, Women's Council of Realtors; Greater Manchester Nashua Board of Realtors; National Association of Realtors **C/VW:** American Heart Association; Big Brothers Big Sisters of America; Locks of Love; Salvation Army **A/S:** She attributes her success to her consistency, love for people, reliability and her ability to maintain relationships with her clients. **B/I:** She became involved in her profession because of her work experience. **H/O:** The most gratifying aspect of her career is being in the top 10 to 15 percent in the state for her profession.

Patricia M. Bergin, RN, LMSW
Registered Nurse
Inpatient Psychiatry
Kings County Hospital
541 Clarkson Avenue
Brooklyn, NY 11203 United States
patbrg3@verizon.net
http://www.cambridgewhoswho.com

BUS: Hospital **P/S:** Healthcare **MA:** Local **D/D/R:** Specializing in Inpatient Psychiatry **H/I/S:** Outdoor Activities **EDU:** Master of Social Work, CUNY Hunter College; Bachelor of Arts in Psychology and Sociology, Hunter College; Associate Degree in Nursing, New York City College of Technology; Registered Nurse **A/A/S:** The Phi Beta Kappa Society **C/VW:** Local Charities; Volunteer, Soup Kitchen **A/S:** She attributes her personal and professional success to her social work experience. **B/I:** She became involved in the profession because she always enjoyed helping others. **H/O:** The most gratifying aspect of her career is her success with her patients.

Elynor Berkowitz
Case Manager
American Imaging Management
4931 Birchwood Avenue
Skokie, IL 60077 United States
ellweb21@aol.com
http://www.americanimaging.net

BUS: Imaging Center **P/S:** Diagnostic Imaging Management Services Including Home Healthcare, Rehabilitation and Outpatient Therapy **MA:** Local **EXP:** Ms. Berkowitz's expertise is in case management and radiological services. **H/I/S:** Crocheting **FBP:** Professional Case Management **EDU:** Master's Degree in Human Resource Management, National-Louis University (1986); Bachelor of Science in Nursing, Northern Illinois University **CERTS:** Certification in Case Management

LILY J. BERNABE
Chief Executive Officer, Designer
LJB Interior Design, Inc.
1950 E. Chapman Avenue
Suite 6
Fullerton, CA 92831 United States
ljbdesigngroup@earthlink.net
http://www.ljbhoteldesign.net

BUS: Interior Design Firm **P/S:** Trend-Setting Interior Designs, Helping Clients Develop their Vision and Design Requirements **MA:** National **D/D/R:** Managing Hotel Design Services, Interior and Exterior Design, Design Purchases and Floral Arrangements **H/I/S:** Collecting Antiques, Traveling, Creating Floral Designs **FBP:** Interior Design Magazine **EDU:** Bachelor's Degree in Interior Design, University of Santo Thomas, Philippines (1978) **CERTS:** Certified in Interior Design, California Council for Interior Design Certification

MRS. MELANIE ANN BERNBECK
Treasurer of Church Board, Deaconess, Librarian
First Christian Church
123 N. Garfield Street
Utica, KS 67584 United States
scooter3@gbta.net
http://www.cambridgewhoswho.com

BUS: Church **P/S:** Religious Services, Volunteering, Helping Others in Need **MA:** Local **D/D/R:** Helping Others, Editing the Church Letter **H/I/S:** Reading, Making Crafts **FBP:** NAR Publications **EDU:** Bachelor's Degree in Elementary Education, Minor in Early Childhood Education, Fort Hayes State University; Associate Degree in Arts, Minor in Childhood Education, Fort Hayes State University **A/A/S:** National Rifle Association; Phi Theta Kappa **C/VW:** Secretary and Treasurer, May Day Parade and Works; Relay for Life, American Cancer Society; Local Church

SALLY L. BERO
Registered Nurse
Cross Country TravCorp
9246 County
Route 125
Chaumont, NY 13622 United States
sallybero@aol.com
http://www.cambridgewhoswho.com

BUS: Private Staff Nursing Organization **P/S:** Healthcare, Nursing Services **MA:** Regional **D/D/R:** Assisting Cancer, Cardiac Care, Renal Transplant, Geriatrics, Orthopedic and Stroke Care Patients, Overseeing Medical-Surgical, Emergency Room and Psychiatric Nursing, Instructing Team Members **H/I/S:** Reading, Cooking, Traveling, Golfing **FBP:** American Journal of Medicine **CERTS:** Registered Nurse, Manhattan State School of Nursing **A/A/S:** Florida Nurses Association

CYNTHIA A. BERRIOS REYES, PH.D.
Psychologist
Centro de Desarrollo Psico—Organizacional y Psicoartístico
1474 Avenue San Ignacio, Urb Altamesa
San Juan, PR 00921 United States
cabreyes@hotmail.com
cberriosreyes@gmail.com
http://www.cambridgewhoswho.com

BUS: Private Practice **P/S:** Mental Healthcare, Psychological Services **MA:** Regional **H/I/S:** Reading, Listening to Music, Swimming, Traveling **FBP:** The Journal of General Psychology; APA Journal **EDU:** Ph.D. in Psychology, University of Puerto Rico, Rio Piedras Campus; Bachelor of Arts in Psychology, University of Puerto Rico, Rio Piedras Campus **CERTS:** First Degree in Reiki Usui Shiki Ryoho, Institute of Natural Healing, Carolina, Puerto Rico (2005) **A/A/S:** Former Member, Alumni Association, University of Puerto Rico; American Psychological Association **A/H:** Recognition, Center of Academic Excellence (2000); Distinguished Professor, Rio Piedras Campus **C/VW:** Conference Speaker, 'Pet Assisted Therapy,' Recreational Therapist Week (2008); Landscaping and Ornamentation Volunteer, Juan B. Huyke Elementary School (2007-2008); Integrated Services and Recovering Center, ASSMCA **POB:** Rio Piedras **I/F/Y:** In five years, Dr. Berrios Reyes hopes to improve her clinical practice.

LISA B. BERRY, MS, APN, BC

Nurse Practitioner
Eastern Illinois Physician Group
1400 W. Park Street
Urbana, IL 61862 United States
lisabee@net66.com
http://www.cambridgewhoswho.com

BUS: Healthcare Center **P/S:** Healthcare Including Emergency Medical Services **MA:** National **EXP:** Ms. Berry's expertise is in emergency medical services. **D/D/R:** Treating, Diagnosing and Referring Patients **H/I/S:** Spinning, Knitting, Gardening, Cooking **FBP:** Clinician Journal **EDU:** Master's Degree in Nursing Science, University of Illinois (1997); Bachelor's Degree in Graphic Design, Southern Connecticut State University (1979) **A/A/S:** Illinois Society for Advanced Nurse Practitioners; American College of Nurse Practitioners

JULIE A. BERTHELOTE

Executive Assistant
Cadigan Venture Group of Companies - Ross Display Fixture Company
& Contemporary Countertops
3419-3421 First Avenue S.
Seattle, WA 98134 United States
j.berthelote@yahoo.com
http://www.rossdisplay.com

BUS: Investments **P/S:** Manufacturing **MA:** International **D/D/R:** Offering Executive and Administrative Support **H/I/S:** Athletics, Cooking, Education, Equestrian Sports, Linguism, Playing the Piano, Reading. **FBP:** Forbes; Fortune; Fortune Small Business (FSB) **EDU:** Pursuing Bachelor's Degree in International Business, Minor in Criminal Justice Administration **C/VW:** American Diabetes Association, Arthritis Foundation, Feed the Children, Seattle Union Gospel Mission, Younglife, YWAM **A/S:** She attributes her success to hard work. **B/I:** She chose the profession because likes working long hours.

YVONNE N. BESHANY
Shareholder
Beshany Law Group, LLC
1117 22nd Street S.
Suite 203
Birmingham, AL 35205 United States
yvonne@beshanylaw.com
http://www.beshanylaw.com

BUS: Outstanding Law Firm **P/S:** Legal Services **MA:** Alabama, Texas, Nevada **EXP:** Ms. Beshany's expertise is in civil litigation, insurance disputes and commercial suits. **H/I/S:** Reading, Raising her Two Sons **FBP:** The Wall Street Journal; ABA Journal **EDU:** JD, University of Alabama School of Law, Cum Laude (1997); Bachelor of Science in Business Administration, Minor in English, Magna Cum Laude, Samford University (1991) **A/A/S:** Nevada Trial Lawyers Association; Texas State Bar Association; Alabama State Bar Association; Nevada State Bar Association; American Bar Association

SALLY BEST-BARTHEL
Certified Rehabilitation Registered Nurse
St. Luke's Medical Center
6508 E. Sandra Terrace
Scottsdale, AZ 85254 United States
sallybe23@aol.com
http://www.cambridgewhoswho.com

BUS: Proven Leaders in Healthcare Services **P/S:** Inpatient and Outpatient Medical Care **MA:** Regional **D/D/R:** Nursing, Specializing in Acute Rehabilitation, Caring for Patients with Hip, Knee, Head and Traumatic Brain Injuries Including Stroke Patients **EDU:** Associate Degree in Nursing, Maui Community College (1986); Coursework, Barrow Neurological Institute **A/H:** Gateway Community College Enthusiasm Award (2006); Honorable Mention, Phoenix Needlepoint Show (1993)

JENNY BETTS, RN
Registered Nurse and Unit Manager
Franklin United Methodist Community
1070 W. Jefferson Street
Franklin, IN 46131 United States
jburton@fumeth.com
http://www.cambridgewhoswho.com

BUS: Retirement Community Center **P/S:** Housing Services **MA:** Regional **D/D/R:** Overseeing 45 Residents and 10 Employees **H/I/S:** Selling Beauty Products, Reading **FBP:** American Journal of Nursing; RN **EDU:** Associate Degree in Nursing, Indiana University **CERTS:** Certification in Geriatric Care **A/A/S:** Mary Kay Cosmetics **C/VW:** Alzheimer's Association **A/S:** She attributes her success to her problem solving skills and passion for her profession. **B/I:** She became involved in her profession because of her personal experience. **H/O:** The highlight of her career was earning her current position.

GAYLE S. BEYER, MCSP
Real Estate Broker
Welcome Center Realty
3585 S.W. Corporate Parkway
Palm City, FL 34990 United States
gb@fla777.com
http://www.fla777.com

BUS: Real Estate **P/S:** Residential and Commercial Realty; Buyers Agent **MA:** Regional **D/D/R:** Selling Residential and Commercial Real Estate **H/I/S:** Traveling **FBP:** IDEAS; New Homes and Designs **EDU:** Bachelor's Degree in Public Relations and Journalism, Georgia State University; Graduate Coursework **A/A/S:** Women's Council of Realtors; Saint Lucie County Association of Realtors; Sales and Marketing Team, National Association of Home Builders **A/H:** Salesperson of the Year, Treasure Coast Builders Association **A/S:** She attributes her success to having excellent mentors, being determined, driven and thinking positive. **B/I:** She became involved in her profession after working as a recruiter. She feels she has the ability to help others in either capacity. **H/O:** The highlight of her career was being named Salesperson of the Year for the Central Coast Builders Association.

LORI BIALA-SMITH, RN, BSN, MBA
Director of Nursing
Norwood Crossing
6016-20 N. Nina Avenue
Chicago, IL 60631 United States
lbialasmith@norwoodcrossing.org
http://www.norwoodcrossing.org

BUS: Proven Leader in the Healthcare Industry, Senior Care Center with 200 Beds **P/S:** Quality Geriatric Services, Enhancing the Independence and Well-Being of Older Adults, Programs and Services to Address Physical, Emotional and Spiritual Needs **MA:** Local **EXP:** Ms. Biala-Smith's areas of expertise are in nursing administration, medical-surgical nursing, critical and long-term care and quality resource management. **H/I/S:** Spending Quality Time with Family, Crafts, Sewing, Dancing **FBP:** Nurse Leader; American Journal of Critical Care **EDU:** Master of Business Administration, Dominican University (1996); Bachelor of Science in Nursing, Loyola University (1974) **A/A/S:** American Organization of Nurse Executives; National Healthcare Cost and Quality Association; Board of Directors, Learning House Foundation; Advisory Board, Triton College; Advisory Board, Nursing and Certified Nursing Assistant Programs

LINDA L. BICKOS
Chief Executive Officer, Publisher and Designer
Country Computers and Publishing
1004 State Highway 7, Suite C
Unadilla, NY 13849 United States
ccandp@frontiernet.net
mabickos@yahoo.com
http://www.ccandp.net

BUS: Computer Sales and Service, Custom-Designed Stationery **P/S:** Publishing and Desktop Design, Custom Invitations, Business Stationary, Booklets, Brochures and Other Printed Materials, Custom-Built Computer Systems, Refurbished Computers and Laptops, Computer Repair and Consultation Services, Photo Restoration, Media Reproduction Services **MA:** Statewide **EXP:** Ms. Bickos' expertise is in custom-designed stationery, invitations and other printed materials. **D/D/R:** Overseeing Operations, Interacting with Customers, Vendors and Business Associates, Bookkeeping, Ordering, Billing, Handling Payroll **H/I/S:** Singing, Photography, Needlework, Restoring Furniture **EDU:** Industry-Related Training and Experience **A/A/S:** Recording Secretary, Unadilla Chamber of Commerce; Vision 21 Foundation; Business and Professional Women; Former District Director, New York State Federation of Women's Clubs; President, Former Recording Secretary, Unadilla Women's Club; Director, Unadilla Foundation; Unadilla Historical Society; Mayor, Village of Unadilla; New York Conference of Mayors; Catskill Choral Society **A/H:** Community Pride Award, Unadilla, NY (2008); Honor Roll, New York Federation of Women's Clubs (2008); Business of the Year Award (2005) **C/VW:** American Red Cross; Food Pantry; Head Start; Local Church Groups; Unadilla Carnival of Sales; CROP Walk; Relay for Life **DOB:** October 3, 1955 **POB:** Binghamton **SP:** James **CHILD:** Michael, Brian, Jessica, Stephen **A/S:** She attributes her success to her faith in the Lord and the support she receives from her family, friends and associates. **B/I:** She became involved in her profession because she has always had an interest in art and design and a desire to work for herself. **H/O:** The most gratifying aspect of her career is meeting and working with a diverse group of people and making them happy.

RHONDA BIENEK, RN
Registered Nurse
Needville High School
16319 Highway 36
Needville, TX 77461 United States
bienekr@needville.isd.esc4.net
http://classroom.needvilleisd.com/webs/nhs

BUS: Educational Facility **P/S:** Superb Teaching Services **MA:** Regional **D/D/R:** Keeping Medical Records and Updating Immunizations, Handling Injuries on School Grounds, Speaking on Health Programs and Promoting Good Health throughout the School **H/I/S:** Gardening, Outdoor Activities, Spending Time with Family **FBP:** RN **EDU:** Bachelor of Science, Texas Women's University, Houston (1978); Registered Nurse, State of Texas (1978) **C/VW:** TSNA; Aim for Success; Volunteer, District Blood Drive; The Leukemia Society; Sponsor, Bluejays Against Alcohol and Drugs

NICOLE E. BIGELOW
Product Manager
Giddy Up, LLC
3630 Plaza Drive, Suite 6
Ann Arbor, MI 48108 United States
nicole@giddyup.com
http://www.giddyup.com

BUS: Children's Toys **P/S:** Children's Activities **MA:** International **D/D/R:** Developing and Licensing Production **H/I/S:** Sailing, Horseback Riding, Attending the Theater **FBP:** Bottom Line **EDU:** Bachelor's Degree in Psychology, University of Michigan **C/VW:** Making Strides Against Breast Cancer, Soup Kitchens **A/S:** She attributes her success to the ability to take on more Responsibilities. **B/I:** She became involved in the profession because it is a career that is always changing and that appealed to her. **H/O:** The highlight of her career is being recognized by other people.

CATHERINE M. BILL, MBA
Clinical Affairs Manager
Kozy Korner
74 Harmony Station
Phillipsburg, NJ 08865 United States
robbiebill@myway.com
http://www.cambridgewhoswho.com

BUS: Pharmaceutical Drug and Device Research **P/S:** Healthcare **MA:** Regional **EXP:** Ms. Bill's expertise is in project, oncology clinical trial and clinical site management. **H/I/S:** Antiquing, Buying and Selling Real Estate for Vacation Properties **FBP:** Pharmaceutical Executive; Working Woman **EDU:** Master of Business Administration in Healthcare Systems Management, DeSales University of Allentown **A/A/S:** Association of Cancer Society Oncologists; American Urological Association; American Academy of Allergy, Asthma and Immunology **C/VW:** Catholic Charities, Battered Wives, Knights of Columbus, Breast Cancer Walk, Susan G. Komen Breast Cancer Foundation, DeSales University Alumni, Sentary College Alumni **A/S:** She attributes her success to her passion, to her training and to her ability to network. **B/I:** She became involved in this profession because she feels that the healthcare profession is her calling. **H/O:** The most gratifying aspect of her career is working as a public speaker at meetings.

MARVIN A. BILLSZAR
Safety and Loss Prevention Director
Ikea
20700 S. Avalon Boulevard
Carson, CA 90746 United States
MNBR@memo.ikea.com
http://www.ikea.com

BUS: Retail **P/S:** Home Furnishing Company **MA:** Worldwide **D/D/R:** Conducting Internal and External Investigations, Ensuring the Safety of Customers and Employees, Preventing Loss **H/I/S:** Watching Football, Exercise, Spending Time with Family **FBP:** Loss Prevention Magazine **EDU:** Bachelor's Degree in Business Management, San Jose State University **A/A/S:** American Society for Industrial Security **C/VW:** Family Foothill Church **A/S:** He attributes his success to good communication skills, treating others well, empowering others and a great staff. **B/I:** He became involved in his profession through a natural progression of opportunities. **H/O:** The highlight of his career was contributing to his former employees' promotions.

TIMOTHY L. BINGHAM
Office Manager
First US Mortgage & Associates
13075 New Halls Ferry Road
Florescent, MO 63033
tim2tim92002@yahoo.com
http://www.cambridgewhoswho.com

BUS: Real Estate **P/S:** Residential and Commercial Mortgage Lending **MA:** KS, MO, TN **D/D/R:** Managing Human Resources, Mortgage Loans and Marketing **H/I/S:** Coaching Football and Wrestling **FBP:** The Wall Street Journal **C/VW:** Glad Tidings, Big Brothers **A/S:** He attributes his success to internal motivation and never giving up. **B/I:** He chose the profession because he wanted the challenge of making his own money. **H/O:** The highlight of his career was making $10,000 in one month.

LILI BINNS
Field Case Manager, Registered Nurse, Certified Case Manager, CIRS
Hope Integrated Services
841 Smallwood Street
Colton, CA 92324 United States
merbilil@cs.com
http://www.cambridgewhoswho.com

BUS: Private Healthcare Company **P/S:** Disability Insurance, Medical Coordination, Case Management, Rehabilitation of Injured Workers **MA:** California **D/D/R:** Supervising Nurses in Hospitals, Teaching Nursing, Vocational Rehabilitation and Medical Terminology, Handling Orthopedics and Catastrophic Injuries **H/I/S:** Oil Painting **FBP:** American Journal of Nursing **EDU:** Registered Nurse, University of Costa Rica School of Nursing; Bachelor's Degree in Orthopedic Gerontology, University of Florida **A/A/S:** Former Secretary, President, Costa Rica Nurses Association

JENNIFER R. BIRDSONG
Chief Information Officer
Rural Health Group
2064 Highway 125
Roanoke Rapids, NC 27870 United States
jennifer.birdsong@rhgnc.org
http://www.rhgnc.org

BUS: Healthcare **P/S:** Pediatric Care, Family Planning, Contraception, Adolescent Medicine, Women's Health, Men's Health, Geriatrics, Limited Pharmacy Assistance, Preventative Medicine, Dental Care, Chronic Disease Management, Information Technology **MA:** Regional **EXP:** Ms. Birdsong's expertise is in information technology, computers and network engineering. **FBP:** IT Security **EDU:** Master's Degree in Science and Technical Systems, East Carolina University (2006)

EUNICE BIROTTE, LMSW
Social Worker II
Parkland Health and Hospital Systems
141 Meadowcrest Drive
DeSoto, TX 75115 United States
ebirot@parknet.pmh.org
http://www.parklandhospital.com

BUS: County Teaching Hospital with Community Primary Care Clinics **P/S:** Inpatient and Outpatient Healthcare Services **MA:** Local **D/D/R:** Performing Pediatric Healthcare, Interviewing Patients and Families, Assessing Problems, Acting as a Shared Medical Appointment Facilitator, Organizing Educational Classes, Case Management, Teaching Field Placement to Social Work Students **H/I/S:** Going on Cruises, Reading, Spending Time with her Long-Haired Dachshund, Playing Word Games, Putting Together Puzzles with her Grandchildren **EDU:** Master's Degree in Social Work, University of Houston **CERTS:** Licensed Master Social Worker **C/VW:** St. Labre Indian School; Health Ministries, St. Elizabeth of Hungary Catholic Church; Volunteer, Disproportionally Program, Dallas, TX; Volunteer, Navy Relief Society; Volunteer, American Red Cross; Volunteer, USMC and USN Bases **DOB:** December 22, 1939 **POB:** Galveston **W/H:** Pediatric Social Worker, Parkland Health and Hospital Systems, Dallas, TX; Foster Care Social Worker Supervisor, Maternity Program, Catholic Charities, Houston, TX; Social Worker, Financial Counselor, Family Service Center, Parris Island United States Marine Corps Base, United States Marine Corps Air Base, Beaufort, SC; Counselor, Volunteer Coordinator, Citizens Opposed to Domestic Violence Shelter, Beaufort, SC **A/S:** She attributes her career success to her children, family, education, efforts to live life in a positive manner and the population she serves. **B/I:** She became involved in her profession after volunteering with military families. **H/O:** The most gratifying aspect of her career is being able to work with children.

JANE E. BISHOP, LPN
Licensed Practical Nurse, Unit Secretary
Wayne Memorial Hospital
500 Osborn Boulevard
Sault Sainte Marie, MI 49783 United States
sweetgrass91@yahoo.com
http://www.wmh.org

BUS: Hospital **P/S:** Healthcare Including Assisted Living and Audiology Services, Auxiliary and Behavioral Healthcare, Cardiology and Child Birth Care, Bone Density Testing, Childbirth Education **MA:** Local **EXP:** Ms. Bishop's expertise is in nursing. **D/D/R:** Overseeing Residential Healthcare, Primary and Hospice Care, Performing Medical Surgery and Physical Therapy, Assigning Overseers in Patient Care, Assisting Doctors, Executing Doctors' Orders, Acting as Liaison between Nurses and Doctors **H/I/S:** Scrapbooking, Sewing **FBP:** LPN2009; Nursing2009 **CERTS:** Licensed Practical Nurse, Grand Rapids Community College **A/A/S:** Board Member, Agricultural Fair; Michigan Farm Bureau Family of Companies; Michigan Licensed Practical Nurses Association; Leader, 4-H

JOANNE MARIE BISIGNANI
Educator
Mountain View School District
2825 Walnut Avenue
Ontario, CA 91761 United States
madoli@mac.com
http://www.cambridgewhoswho.com

BUS: Public School **P/S:** Education **MA:** Local **D/D/R:** Teaching Kindergarten through Fifth-Grade Students **H/I/S:** Photography, Traveling **FBP:** Phi Delta Kappa News **EDU:** Master's Degree in School Administration and Management, Pepperdine University (1980) **A/A/S:** National Teachers Association (2007); Phi Delta Kappa; National Education Association; California Education Association **C/VW:** Choir Member, St. Andrews **A/S:** She attributes her success to staying up to date in her field and enjoying her work. **B/I:** She became involved in her profession because she likes working with children. **H/O:** The highlight of her career was being contacted by a former student who wanted to thank her.

SHERRIE BJURSTROM
Special Education Teacher, Gifted Teacher
Lockland City Schools
249 W. Forrer Street
Cincinnati, OH 45215 United States
sbjurstrom2003@yahoo.com
http://www.cambridgewhoswho.com

BUS: Public School **P/S:** Education **MA:** Local **H/I/S:** Pottery, Quilting, Gardening, Photography, Cooking **FBP:** Architectural Digest; Cucina Italiana **EDU:** Master of Education Plus 50 in Education, Specialization in Emotionally Disturbed Children, Xavier University **C/VW:** Various Charitable Donations **A/S:** She attributes her success to enjoying kids, the curriculum she is teaching and helping special education students. **B/I:** She became involved in this profession after finishing her teaching certification. When she did her student teaching she knew she was in the right place. **H/O:** The highlight of her career was helping a second grade class achieve the highest standardizes scores in the district.

JONI BLACK
Manager of Human Resources
Human Resources
BCS Insurance Group
2 Mid America Plaza, Suite 200
Oakbrook Terrace, IL 60181 United States
jblack@bcsigroup.com
http://www.bcsigroup.com

BUS: Insurance Agency **P/S:** Health, Life, Property and Casualty Insurance **MA:** National **D/D/R:** Offering Human Resources and Generalist Knowledge **H/I/S:** Running, Reading, Walking her Dog, Watching Movies **FBP:** BusinessWeek **EDU:** Bachelor's Degree in Human Resource Management, De Paul University **A/A/S:** Society for Human Resource Management; Human Resources Management Association of Chicago **C/VW:** Park Community Church; Volunteer, Local Homeless Shelter; Little Brothers; Friends of the Elderly

MELISSA BLACKBURN
Nurse Practitioner, Owner
Monson Pediatrics PC
218 Cedar Swamp Road
Monson, MA 01057 United States
monsonped@aol.com
http://www.cambridgewhoswho.com

BUS: Primary Healthcare **MA:** Local **EXP:** Pediatrics. **H/I/S:** Spending Time with her Children **FBP:** New England Journal of Medicine **EDU:** Master of Science Degree, University of Massachusetts **A/S:** She attributes her success to great family support. **B/I:** She chose the profession because she had an interest in helping children. **H/O:** The highlight of her career is owning her business.

TRACEY R. BLACKSHEAR
Owner, Hair Replacement Technician
Elite Hair Replacement, LLC
5114 E. Southern Avenue
Suite 167
Mesa, AZ 85206 United States
tblackshear3@cox.net
http://www.elitehair-replacement.com

BUS: Upscale Beauty Salon **P/S:** Hair Replacement for a Fuller, More Natural Appearance **MA:** National **EXP:** Ms. Blackshear's expertise is in non-surgical hair replacement. **H/I/S:** Traveling, Roller Skating, Singing, Cooking **FBP:** The Wall Street Journal **EDU:** Industry-Related Training and Experience **A/H:** Business Woman of the Year, National Republican Congressional Committee (2006) **C/VW:** Honorary Chairman, National Republican Congressional Committee; Business Advisory Committee **A/S:** She attributes her success to applying her knowledge of the hair industry to meet customers' needs and restore or elevate their self-esteem. **B/I:** She became involved in her profession after a personal experience watching a loved one deal with the emotional effects of Alopecia. **H/O:** The highlight of her career is witnessing on a daily basis the tears of joy shed by a grateful client.

REBECCA ELIZABETH BLAIS
School Psychologist
Schodack Central School District
80 Scott Avenue
Castleton, NY
beccablais@yahoo.com
http://www.cambridgewhoswho.com

BUS: School, Education **P/S:** Education **MA:** Local **EXP:** Ms. Blais' expertise is in school psychology. **H/I/S:** Running, Reading **FBP:** National Association of School Psychologists **EDU:** Master of Science in Education, Counseling and School Psychology, College of Saint Rose; Bachelor of Arts in English, State University of New York at Plattsburgh **CERTS:** Certified in School Psychology, New York State **A/A/S:** New York Association of School Psychologists; National Association of School Psychologists; Secondary Teachers Association **C/VW:** Teaching Sunday School at Church **A/S:** She attributes her success to her focus and hard work. **B/I:** She became involved in her profession because she enjoyed working with children. **H/O:** The highlight of her career was when a student at her old job with autism was able to successfully deal with school and a daily schedule because of her help.

JOY E. BLAKER
Licensed Practical Nurse, Patient Care Coordinator
Medi Home Health
211 S. Market Street
Ligonier, PA 15658 United States
http://www.cambridgewhoswho.com

BUS: Home Healthcare **P/S:** Home Healthcare **MA:** Local **H/I/S:** Hiking **CERTS:** Licensed Practical Nurse, West Moreland County Community College **C/VW:** Local Church, Life-Way Pregnancy Care Organization **A/S:** She attributes her success to being conscientious, hard working and going beyond just fulfilling duties. **B/I:** She became involved in the profession due to her compassion and love for people. She wanted to touch peoples lives in a positive way. **H/O:** The highlight of her career was obtaining her current position.

TERESA M. BLANCHETTE, MS, CCC-SLP
Speech Language Pathologist
Ann Arundel County Public Schools
2544 Riva Road
Annapolis, MD 21401 United States
tblanchette@aacps.org
http://www.cambridgewhoswho.com

BUS: Education **P/S:** Education **MA:** Local **EXP:** Ms. Blanchette's expertise is in speech and language education. **H/I/S:** Taking Acting Classes, Doing Charity Work **FBP:** ASHA Leader **EDU:** Master of Science in Speech Language Pathology, Towson University **A/A/S:** Maryland Speech and Hearing Association; American Speech-Language-Hearing Association **C/VW:** Great Stride Walk of Annapolis, Cystic Fibrosis Foundation, Susan G. Komen Breast Cancer Foundation, American Heart Association **A/S:** She attributes her success to hard work and her desire and ability to keep herself educated on topics related to the profession. **B/I:** Her interest in healthcare motivated her to pursue her current career. **H/O:** The highlight of her career was having some students make extreme progress.

JOHN M. BLANKENSHIP, CCEMT-P, F-PC
Manager
Children's Hospital of the King's Daughters
601 Children's Lane
Norfolk, VA 23507 United States
ccemtp@cox.net
http://brotherjohn.net2go.com

BUS: Hospital **P/S:** Healthcare **MA:** Regional **D/D/R:** Overseeing Critical Care of Children and Flight Paramedic Services **H/I/S:** Playing Guitar, Playing Blue Grass Music **FBP:** Air Medical Journal; EMS Magazine **EDU:** Coursework in Emergency Medical Services and Critical Care, Northern Virginia Community College **CERTS:** Certified in Critical Care, Certified Flight Paramedic; Pediatric Advanced Life Support; Advanced Cardiac Life Support; Emergency Medical Service Firefighter **A/A/S:** International Association of Flight Paramedics **C/VW:** Medical Missionaries, Feed the Children **A/S:** He attributes his success to his desire to never stop learning. **B/I:** He became involved in his profession while working part time as a volunteer firefighter. He was persuaded to get more involved with emergency medical technician work and loved it. **H/O:** The most gratifying aspect of his career is working with children.

GARY E. BLAZER
Senior Pastor
Believers Destiny Church
124 Spring Chase Lane
Rocky Point, NC 24857 United States
geblazer@cfaith.com

BUS: Church **P/S:** Non-Denominational Religious Services **MA:** Local **D/D/R:** Bringing Hope to Others, Helping and Healing Our World Preaching and Teaching the Word **H/I/S:** Spending Time Outdoors, Hunting, Fishing, Hiking, Water Skiing, Snow Skiing **FBP:** Charisma Magazine **EDU:** Master's Degree, Beacon University (2008) **C/VW:** Missionary Work, China; American Red Cross; Life Center; State Director, RMAI

MARY JANE BASHAM BLEIER
Machine Processing Equipment Operator, Facilitator,
Secretary, Employee Aid AED Professional
Wage & Investment, Internal Revenue Service Center
6010 Spicewood Avenue
Florence, KY 41042 United States
maryjbleier@hotmail.com
http://www.revenue.ky.gov

BUS: Government Organization **P/S:** Tax Collection, Downloadable Income Tax Forms, Instructions, Agency Publications **MA:** National **D/D/R:** Facilitating and Instructing Classes, Managing Operations, Training and Mentoring Employees, Overseeing Administrative Duties, Customer Service and Public Service **H/I/S:** Photography, Biking, Sewing, Participating in Church Activities, Making Crafts, Reading Poetry, Camping, Fishing, Spending Time with her Family **FBP:** Kentucky Revenue; Industry-Related Publications **EDU:** Coursework in Basic American Sign Language, Northern Kentucky Vocational School (1987); Coursework in Business and Accounting (1983); Diploma, Lloyd Memorial High School (1971) **CERTS:** On-the-Job Training Certification, Internal Revenue Service (2007); Certification in Automated External Defibrillator (2005); Certification in CPR (2005); Certification in American Sign Language (1988); Certification in Computer Program Basic I (1981); Certification in Blueprint Reading (1980); Certification in Computer Programming, Boone County Vocational School (1980); **A/A/S:** The International Executive Guild; Independent Order of Foresters **A/H:** Managerial Award, Internal Revenue Service (2007); Woman of the Year Award, American Biographical Institute (2006); Employee of the Year Award, Internal Revenue Service (1997); Public Service Award, States of Northern Kentucky, Ohio and Indiana (1997); Who's Who in Lexington, Kentucky (1999-2000); Service Award, Internal Revenue Service **C/VW:** Volunteers of America; Northern Kentucky Baptist Association; American Red Cross; Clerk, Business Secretary, Youth Director, Children's Church Director, Elsmere Baptist Church; Lost Children Foundation, Fingerprinting Services; Community Activist **DOB:** June 1, 1953 **POB:** Jefferson County, Louisville **SP:** Robert **CHILD:** Christine, Chertina, Robert, Crystal, Randall, Catherine **W/H:** Control Clerk (1986-2007); Clerk, Assembly, Translator for the Deaf (1985-2007); Equipment Operation (1984-2007); Quality Inspection, Receiving Clerk, Merchandise Handler (1976-2007); Cashier, Clerk (1973-1974) **B/I:** She became involved in her profession through a natural progression of opportunities.

DEBRA M. BLOMME
President
MD/DC Ladies Ministries
8511 Clarkson Drive
Fulton, MD 20759 United States
dmblomme@cavtel.net
http://www.cambridgewhoswho.com

BUS: Life Coaching for Families **P/S:** Empowering Women to be Strong Leaders and Empowering Families to Work Together Toward Success **MA:** Regional **D/D/R:** Creative Venues to Teach Families to Live Better Lives **H/I/S:** Reading, Gardening and Sports **FBP:** Business Week **EDU:** Coursework in Business, Black Hawk College **CERTS:** Licensed Notary Public **C/VW:** PTA, United Pentecostal Church International; New Beginnings, Haven of Hope, Lighthouse Ranch for Boys **A/S:** She attributes her success to her sensitivity, always caring for people's feelings and loving to help people. **B/I:** She chose the profession because she wanted to make a difference in the lives of others and empower women. **H/O:** The highlight of her career was when she organized an event for Ben Carson to speak with parents and children within her organization.

MR. JAMES M. BLOOMFIELD, CPA
Senior Tax Accountant
Porte Brown, LLC
845 Oakton Street
Elkgrove Village, IL 60007 United States
jmb@Portebrown.com
http://www.Portebrown.com

BUS: Tax Services **P/S:** Trust and Estate Tax Services **MA:** Statewide **EXP:** Mr. Bloomfield's expertise is in corporate partnership services. **EDU:** Coursework, DePaul University **A/A/S:** The American Institute of Certified Public Accountants

JUDY MARIE BLYSTONE
Account Executive
American HomePatient
204 Independent Drive
Sanford, NC 27330 United States
j.m.blystone@ahom.com
http://www.cambridgewhoswho.com

BUS: Home Healthcare Provider **P/S:** Home Care Respiratory Products and Therapy **MA:** National **D/D/R:** Educating Referral Sources **H/I/S:** Sewing, Reading, Arts and Crafts, Baking, Traveling **FBP:** Industry-Related Publications **EDU:** Industry-Related Experience **C/VW:** Cub Scouts of America; Relay for Life **A/S:** She attributes her success to always going the extra mile to help others. **B/I:** She became involved in her profession because she enjoys working with people. **H/O:** The highlight of her career was working with Stanley DuBrine in California.

BRUCE S. BOCHNER, MD
Professor of Medicine
Johns Hopkins University School of Medicine,
Division of Allergy and Clinical Immunology,
Johns Hopkins Asthma and Allergy Center
5501 Hopkins Bayview Circle
Baltimore, MD 21224 United States
bbochner@jhmi.edu • http://www.hopkinsmedicine.org/allergy

BUS: Research and Educational Institution **P/S:** Promoting Discovery, Understanding and Treatment of Allergies, Asthma and Other Immunological Disorders **MA:** International **D/D/R:** Training Physicians and other Scientists, Evaluating and Treating Individuals with a Wide Variety of Allergic Disorders Including Asthma, Allergic Rhinitis, Anaphylaxis and Eosinophilic Disorders, Conducting Human-Based Research on the Mechanisms of Allergic Diseases **H/I/S:** Listening to Jazz, Traveling, Wine Tasting, Golfing **FBP:** Journal of Allergy and Clinical Immunology **EDU:** Fellowship at John's Hopkins University School of Medicine, Division of Allergy and Clinical Immunology (1985-1988); Bachelor of Arts in Natural Sciences, with Honors, Johns Hopkins University (1978); Medical Degree, with Honors, University of Illinois at Chicago (1982); Residency in Internal Medicine at University of Illinois at Chicago (1982-1985) **CERTS:** Diplomat of the American Board of Internal Medicine, Diplomat of the American Board of Allergy and Immunology **A/A/S:** Board of Directors, American Association of Allergy Asthma and Immunology; American Association of Immunology; American College of Physicians; Association of American Physicians **C/VW:** Allergy, Asthma & Immunology Education and Research Trust; American Academy of Allergy Asthma and Immunology **DOB:** February 5, 1957 **POB:** Chicago, IL **SP:** Jacqueline **CHILD:** David **A/S:** He attributes his success to being present in a positive environment and to being intellectually challenged. **B/I:** He became involved in his profession through exposure to outstanding mentors. **H/O:** The highlight of his career was earning his current position as a full professor at Johns Hopkins University and giving his first plenary lecture at a conference with his mother there.

504 • CAMBRIDGE WHO'S WHO 2008–2009   VIP MEMBERS

NATHAN BODE
Owner, Executive Chief
Kraemers Catering/ Absolute Beverage
240 N. River Ridge Circle
Burnsville, MN 55337 United States
nathan@kraemerscatering.com
http://www.kraemerscatering.com

BUS: Food Catering **P/S:** Full Service Catering for Both Food and Beverages **MA:** Regional **D/D/R:** Creating Custom Gourmet Menus with Wine Pairings **H/I/S:** Entertaining Friends and Family, Working on His House **FBP:** Food and wine **EDU:** Bachelor's Degree in Applied Science, Le Cordon Bleu **A/A/S:** Canvas and Vines; Burnsville Chamber of Commerce; Betty Business Bureau; Saint Pauls Chamber of Commerce; NACE

DANIEL T. BOEMMELS
Insurance Agent
Boccarossa Insurance
220 Bridgeport Avenue
Milford, CT 06460 United States
boemmed@nationwide.com
http://www.boccarossainsurance.com

BUS: Insurance and Financial Services **P/S:** Commercial Insurance Packages **MA:** Local **D/D/R:** Insuring Large and Small Businesses **H/I/S:** Mountain Biking, Rappelling, Skydiving **FBP:** Various Industry-Related Publications **EDU:** Bachelor of Science in Business Management, Southern Connecticut State University **CERTS:** Licensed Notary Public, State of Connecticut **A/A/S:** Lead Group, Chamber of Commerce **C/VW:** Local Police Department; Donor, Local Blood Drives; Donor, Local Charities **A/S:** He attributes his success to persistence and a strong understanding of the business. **B/I:** He became involved in his profession after attending a life insurance seminar with his father and becoming intrigued with the business.

AIMEE E. BOGAN
Teacher
Discovery House
27 2nd Street
Bangor, ME 04401 United States
Pooltiurf77@aol.com
http://www.cambridgewhoswho.com

BUS: Pre-School **P/S:** Education **MA:** Local **D/D/R:** Teaching Pre-School **H/I/S:** Kayaking, Spending Time with her Husband and Daughter **EDU:** Bachelor of Arts in Human Services, Mental Health and Childhood Development, University of Maine **C/VW:** Bangor Y **A/S:** She attributes her success to her hard work and ability to learn from others. **B/I:** She became involved in the profession because she was interested in educating children. **H/O:** The most gratifying aspect of her career is enjoying every day.

PATRICIA M. BOHMANN
Speech and Language Pathologist (Special Education Teacher)
Lake Villa School District 41
131 N. McKinley Avenue
Lake Villa, IL 60046 United States
pbohman@district41.org
http://www.cambridgewhoswho.com

BUS: Public School District **P/S:** Education **MA:** Local **EXP:** Ms. Bohmann's expertise is in special education. **H/I/S:** Reading, Walking, Crocheting, Photography **FBP:** Teaching; Communication Disorders Quarterly **EDU:** Master's Degree in Speech Pathology, Bradley University **A/A/S:** American Speech-Language-Hearing Association; Council for Exceptional Children **C/VW:** American Diabetes Association; Susan G. Komen Breast Cancer Foundation; St. Jude Children's Research Hospital

CAROLE S. BOIKE-DILLNER
Teacher
Northside Intermediate School
159 Northside Drive
Milton, WI 53563 United States
dillnerc@mail.k12.milton.wi.us
http://www.milton.k12.wi.us/schools/nis/website/

BUS: Public Education **P/S:** Quality Education through Core Academic Classes such as Mathematics, Reading, Science, Social Studies and English **MA:** Regional **D/D/R:** Teaching All Elementary Content Areas with a Concentration in Science and Social Studies **H/I/S:** Gardening, Home Improvement, Decorating **EDU:** Master's Degree in Curriculum and Instruction, Plus 20, University of Wisconsin, Whitewater (1991); Bachelor's Degree in Education, Northern Illinois University (1973) **A/A/S:** Alpha Phi; Phi Kappa Phi **A/H:** Nominee Disney Teacher of the Year; Nominee, NFL Teacher of the Year; Nominee, Golden Apple Award, Local Television Station

GLORIA G. BOKEN
Mathematics Teacher
Sylvan Learning Center
1865 S. Nevada Avenue
Colorado Springs, CO 80906 United States
ggboken@yahoo.com
http://www.cambridgewhoswho.com

BUS: Tutoring Center **P/S:** Extracurricular Education and Instruction **MA:** National **D/D/R:** Teaching Kindergarten through Post-12th Grade Mathematics **H/I/S:** Exercising, Teaching, Playing Golf **EDU:** Master's Degree in Mathematics, Plus 64, Rutgers, The State University of New Jersey; Bachelor of Arts in Mathematics, Boulder University **A/S:** She attributes her career success to to her college professors and high school teachers. **B/I:** She was encouraged to pursue a career in education by her professors. **H/O:** She feels that being able to teach calculus for sixteen years and helping all of her students to pass has been the highlight of her career.

ANNABELLE G. BOLIG, RN
Parish Nurse
Mt. Zion United Methodist Church
4685 Mt. Zion Drive
Enola, PA 17025 United States
rbolig785@comcast.net
http://www.mountzionumc.org

BUS: United Methodist Church **P/S:** Religious Services as well as Quality Healthcare Services, Declares the Gospel of Jesus Christ in Loving and Redemptive Ways, the Caring, Sensitive Fellowship Described in the Scriptures, Reaches out to the Community with Ministries that Meet Social and Spiritual Needs **MA:** Regional **D/D/R:** Teaching in the Certified Nursing Assistant Program, Teaching Long-Term-Care, Writing a Column for the Church Newsletter, Visiting Hospitals and Nursing Homes, Conducting Health and Blood Pressure Screenings, Cardiac, Newborn and Respiratory Nursing **H/I/S:** Crocheting, Basketball, Soccer **FBP:** RN Magazine **EDU:** Associate Degree in Nursing, Harrisburg Area Community College (1984) **A/A/S:** Democratic Women's Club **C/VW:** Sunday School Teacher, Former Choir Director, Mt. Zion United Methodist Church; Former Girl Scout Leader **CHILD:** Eight Grandchildren

NATALIYA A. BOLSHEVA, MD, PH.D.
Spiritual Advisor
Spiritual Unification Institute of AIWP
406 16th Avenue
San Francisco, CA 94118 United States
nbolshevapsy@yahoo.com
http://www.cambridgewhoswho.com

BUS: Spiritual Service Company **P/S:** Spiritual Services for Clients, Spiritual Advisement and Education **MA:** Statewide **D/D/R:** Offering Spiritual Services for Individuals, Couples, Groups and Married Couples **H/I/S:** Traveling, Reading, Listening to Music, Watching Movies **FBP:** Women's Magazines **EDU:** Ph.D. in Clinical Psychology (2006); MD, Earned in Europe; Master's Degree in Divine Studies **C/VW:** St. Jude Children's Research Hospital **DOB:** December 11, 1955 **POB:** Odessa **SP:** Yevgeniy **CHILD:** Alla, Andrew

MARSHA A. BOND, RN
Registered Nurse
St. Bernard's Medical Center
225 E. Jackson Avenue
Jonesboro, AR 72401 United States
nursemarsha2000@yahoo.com
http://www.sbrmc.com

BUS: Hospital Dedicated to Heal All Patients through Education, Treatment and Health Services **P/S:** Experienced, Responsive and Compassionate Patient Health Services, Centers for Cancer Treatment, Heart Care, Senior and Women's Health Care as well as Clinical and Diagnostic Services, Extended Care and Rehab Centers **MA:** Local **D/D/R:** Precepting Intensive Care Nurses **H/I/S:** Playing Volleyball **EDU:** Associate Degree in Nursing, Arkansas State University (1997)

MS. MICHELLE M. BONELLI
District Manager
Department of Human Services
3011 Golden Rock
Christiansted, VI 00820 United States
bonellimiche@hotmail.com
http://www.cambridgewhoswho.com

BUS: Government Organization **P/S:** Public Services Including Education and Training **MA:** Virgin Islands **D/D/R:** Overseeing the Execution of All Operations, Implementing Projects and Administration, Overseeing Staff, Organizing Job Programs, Helping Single Mothers in Education **H/I/S:** Fashion Designing, Participating in Beauty Pageants **FBP:** Black Enterprise; Time **EDU:** Master's Degree in Public Administration, University of the Virgin Islands, St. Thomas (1990); Bachelor's Degree in Sociology, Morgan State University **A/A/S:** Parent-Teacher Association; St. Croix Educational Complex; NOPA **CHILD:** Marcel, Malcolm **A/S:** She attributes her success to the support she receives from her children and her faith in God.

CHERYL E. BONILLA
President, Owner
Arctic Fire Mechanical, LLC
7124 Jefferson Street N.E.
Albuquerque, NM 87109 United States
mikecherylba@msn.com
http://www.cambridgewhoswho.com

BUS: Manufacturing Company **P/S:** Trane, Carrier, York, Bryant, Heating, Cooling, Plumbing **MA:** Regional **D/D/R:** Handling All Vendor Relations and Customer Service Issues, Overseeing Employees, Management, Accounts Payable and Receivable and Payroll, Bidding, Organizing Meetings, Budgeting **H/I/S:** Golfing, Bowling **FBP:** BusinessWeek **EDU:** Pursuing Associate Degree in Business Administration, Eastern New Mexico University **CERTS:** MM98 License **A/A/S:** Better Business Bureau; Dunn and Bradstreet; NFID **C/VW:** Shrine Club; American Cancer Society **A/S:** She attributes her success to her husband's support. **B/I:** She became involved in her profession because she had previously worked with her husband in the same field. **H/O:** The most gratifying aspect of her career is being a successful minority businesswoman.

ANDREA E. BONNY
Medical Doctor
MetroHealth Medical Center
2500 Metro Health Drive
Cleveland, OH 44109 United States
abonny@metrohealth.org
http://www.cambridgewhoswho.com

BUS: Hospital **P/S:** Healthcare **MA:** Local **D/D/R:** Creating Two Divisions of Adolescent Medicine, Conducting Clinical and Educational Research **H/I/S:** Reading, Traveling, Competing in Triathlons, Spending Time with her Three Children **FBP:** Pediatrics Journal **EDU:** MD, Washington University, Saint Louis (1994) **A/A/S:** American Academy of Pediatrics; OVSAM **C/VW:** School Health Council; Health Committee Elementary **A/S:** She attributes her success to being a socially focused person, working hard, being dedicated and obtaining her degree. **B/I:** She became involved in her profession because she wanted to care for others, especially in under-served populations. **H/O:** The highlight of her career was creating a division for Hispanic services.

EVELYN SMITH BOOKER
General Sales Manager
Capital Broadcasting Company, WRAZ-TV Fox50
512 S. Magnum Street
Durham, NC 27701 United States
ebooker@fox50.com
http://www.fox50.com

BUS: Television Station **P/S:** Television Programming **MA:** National **D/D/R:** Supervising Sales Operations, Managing Inventory Control, Establishing Rates, Overseeing Managers and Research Directors **H/I/S:** Tennis, Golfing, Reading **FBP:** Media Week **EDU:** Bachelor's Degree in English, North Carolina Central University **A/A/S:** American Women in Radio and Television; Raleigh-Durham Triangle Apartment Association; Chairwoman, SAC Committee for Fox **A/H:** Five Star Award, Capitol Broadcasting **C/VW:** United Way; American Heart Association; Chairwoman, Deaconess Board

LAUREN C. BOOTH
Commercial Real Estate Appraiser,
South Carolina Real Estate Agent
Jayroe Appraisal Company & Real Estate Consultants
1704 Oak Street
Myrtle Beach, SC 29577 United States
lauren_4realestate@yahoo.com

BUS: Real Estate Agency **P/S:** Commercial Real Estate Appraisals **MA:** Statewide **EXP:** Ms. Booth's expertise is in commercial real estate appraisal. **H/I/S:** Taking Advantage of the Beautiful Beaches Along the South Carolina Coast, Traveling **FBP:** Industry-Related Publications **EDU:** Associate Degree in Business, Horry-Georgetown Technical College **CERTS:** Licensed Real Estate Agent (2005); Licensed Real Estate Appraiser, Fortune Academy (2003) **A/A/S:** Myrtle Beach Chamber of Commerce; Coastal Carolina Association of Realtors; South Carolina Association of Realtors; National Association of Realtors; Former Member, National Association of Home Builders **DOB:** April 6, 1981 **W/H:** Real Estate Agent, State of South Carolina (2005); Commercial Real Estate Appraiser (2003)

FRANCES R. BORDONARO
Owner
Fran's Concession
PO Box 85
South Glastonbury, CT 06073 United States
frances.bordonaro@cwwemail.com
http://www.cambridgewhoswho.com

BUS: Restaurant **P/S:** Food and Beverage Service Including Seasonal Food Concession **MA:** National **D/D/R:** Preparing Italian Sausage, Overseeing Catering Arrangements for Fairs and Festivals **H/I/S:** Making Paper Dolls, Collecting Plates, Reading, Working as a Pastry Chef **FBP:** Money; Investment **CERTS:** Certified Food Handler, National Restaurant Association; Industry-Related Training **W/H:** Welder, Pratt & Whitney **A/S:** She attributes her success to her hard work. **B/I:** She became involved in her profession through a natural progression of opportunities. **H/O:** The highlight of her career was working as a welder at Pratt & Whitney.

MR. MANUEL R. BORRELL, MHA
Corporate Director of Logistics
Novant Health
1578 Roger Dale Carter Road
Kannapolis, NC 28081 United States
mborrell@novanthealth.org
http://www.novanthealth.org

BUS: Nonprofit Healthcare Leader **P/S:** Operation of Eight Hospitals and 200 Physician Practices and Clinics, Distribution of Medical Supplies **MA:** Regional **D/D/R:** Running a Supply Chain, Directing and Operating a Medical Supply Distribution Center, Hiring and Training Staff Members **H/I/S:** Playing Guitar, Golfing, Enjoying All Sports **EDU:** Master's Degree in Healthcare Administration, Central Michigan University (1988); Bachelor of Science in Psychology, University of Puerto Rico **A/A/S:** Association of Healthcare Administrators

LINDA S. BOSTIAN
Teacher of the Deaf and/or Hard of Hearing
Katy Independent School District
PO Box 159
Katy, TX 77492 United States
wbostian@aol.com
http://www.cambridgewhoswho.com

BUS: School **P/S:** Education, Language, Communication and Support **MA:** Katy, Texas **D/D/R:** Communicating with Deaf and/or Hard of Hearing Children From Ages Three to 20 **H/I/S:** Outdoor Activities, Horseback Riding **EDU:** Bachelor of Science in Communications, University of Texas **A/A/S:** Association of Texas Professional Educators **C/VW:** Military Order of the Purple Heart; American Society for the Prevention of Cruelty to Animals; Defender of the Wildlife **A/S:** She attributes her success to her good education, supportive family, self-motivation and passion for helping children and young adults. **B/I:** She became involved in her profession because of her family influence and inner love for teaching those who require special communication skills. **H/O:** The highlight of her career was seeing students years later leading successful, fully functioning lives.

DEBBIE G. BOSWELL
Owner, Sole Proprietor
Crafts by Grace
687 Midwood Street
Brooklyn, NY 11203 United States
craftsbygrace@msn.com
http://www.cambridgewhoswho.com

BUS: Arts and Crafts **P/S:** Soaps and Candles **MA:** Local **D/D/R:** Creating Homemade Soaps and Candles, Selling Products at Fairs and Flea Markets, Creating Tye Dyes, Working on T-Shirts, Preparing Tax Returns **H/I/S:** Reading, Writing, Animals **FBP:** Creative Screenwriting; Script; Writer's Digest **EDU:** Bachelor of Science in Accounting, Marymount Manhattan College **CERTS:** Enrolled Agent, Internal Revenue Service **A/A/S:** American Screenwriters Association

PATRICIA J. BOUCHER
Jingle Writer
Jazzy Jingles Advertising
7311 Parrot Drive
Port Richey, FL 34668 United States
jazzy@jazzyjingles.net
http://www.cambridgewhoswho.com

BUS: Advertising **P/S:** Advertising Jingles, Business Slogans and Tag Lines **MA:** National **D/D/R:** Creating Clever and Creative Ads, Slogans, Tag Lines and Jingles **H/I/S:** Traveling, Reading, Attending Concerts, Riding Recreational Vehicles, Watching NASCAR, Extreme Sports and Movies **FBP:** Advertising Age **EDU:** Bachelor of Arts in Liberal Arts, Hofstra University **A/A/S:** West Pasco Chamber of Commerce **C/VW:** American Humane Society; American Society for the Prevention of Cruelty to Animals **A/S:** She attributes her success to being blessed with a wonderful mind. **B/I:** She became involved in her profession because she began generating great ideas for advertising jingles. **H/O:** The highlight of her career has been being able to be involved in show business and meeting celebrities.

SHIRLEY BOULTER-DAVIS, GRI
Residential Realtor
RE/MAX Premier
15150 Preston Road
Dallas, TX 75248 United States
shirley@shirley-homes.com
http://www.shirley-homes.com

BUS: Real Estate **P/S:** Single Family Housing, Real Estate Services and Sales, Residential Properties **MA:** Local **D/D/R:** Listing and Marketing Residential Real Estate Properties **EDU:** Master's Degree in Music, Eastern Texas State University **A/A/S:** National Association of Realtors; Graduate Realtor Institute **A/S:** She attributes her success to her hard work and determination and great customer service. **B/I:** She became involved in this profession because she enjoys the field and has people skills. **H/O:** The highlight of her career is her success so far.

MR. LAWRENCE N. BOURGET, AIFA
Retirement Plan Consultant
Nationwide Mutual Insurance Companies
3100 Twin Leaf Drive
Raleigh, NC 27613 United States
larsbourget@yahoo.com
http://www.nationwidefinancial.com

BUS: Insurance and Financial Company **P/S:** Innovative Protection, Accumulation and Wealth-Transfer Solutions, Life Insurance and Annuities for Individual Retirement Needs **MA:** National **EXP:** Mr. Bourget's areas of expertise include the design of retirement plans and investment portfolio structures. **D/D/R:** Consulting, Implementing Design Plans **H/I/S:** Traveling Internationally, Spending Time with his Family, Reading, Kitesurfing, Heliskiing, Tennis **FBP:** Harvard Business Review **EDU:** Bachelor's Degree in Accounting, Bentley College **CERTS:** Accredited Investment Fiduciary Auditor, Joseph M. Katz Graduate School of Business, University of Pittsburgh (2003); Plan Sponsor Retirement Plan Professional **A/A/S:** American Society of Pension Actuaries and Administrators; Center for Fiduciary Studies **C/VW:** St. Timothy's Episcopal Church; The Kadampa Center **A/S:** He attributes his success to his hard work, loyalty, dedication and supportive spouse.

MARIA LYNN BOUTON
Special Education Teacher
204 N. Cleveland Avenue
Long Beach, MS 39560 United States
boutonm@lbsd.k12.ms.us
http://www.lbsd.k12.ms.us

BUS: Middle School **P/S:** Secondary Education Including Special Education, Athletics, Safety and Discipline, Clubs and Organizations, Personal and Academic Guidance and Counseling **MA:** Local **D/D/R:** Teaching Reading and Mathematics **H/I/S:** Playing Bridge **EDU:** Master's Degree, Delta State University (1974) **A/A/S:** Kappa Delta Phi; Golden Key International Honour Society; ALTA

PATRICIA G. BOWEN
Assistant Teacher
J.W. Stewart Head Start Center
Henry Street
Gadsden, AL 35901 United States
patricia.bowen@cwwemail.com
http://www.cambridgewhoswho.com

BUS: Educational Institution **P/S:** Education **MA:** Local **EXP:** Ms. Bowen's expertise is in teaching. **H/I/S:** Reading, Volunteering for Underprivileged Children **EDU:** Pursuing Associate Degree in Early Childhood Education **C/VW:** United Givers Fund; Boy Scouts of America; Section Holy Church **B/I:** She became involved in her profession because of her love for children and her desire to see them better themselves.

DEYDRA 'DEDE' D. BOWERS
Assistant Business Office Director
Permian Regional Medical Center
720 Hospital Drive
Andrews, TX 79714 United States
bowersdede@hotmail.com
http://www.permianregional.com

BUS: Medical Center **P/S:** Healthcare Including Emergency Medical Services and Education **MA:** Regional **D/D/R:** Overseeing Data Entry, Insurance, Credit and Collections, Working on Meditech Computer Systems for Financial Modules, Admission Demographics and Reporting, PBX, switchboard, Medicare and Medicaid **H/I/S:** Attending Son's Sports Activities, Sports, Spending Time at the Church, Collecting Photographs, Photography, Scrapbooking **FBP:** Money; Inc. **EDU:** Coursework in Basics and Financial Management, Odessa College **CERTS:** Training in Tax Preparation and Bookkeeping **A/A/S:** Senator, Jaycees, TX; Treasurer, Vice President of Management and Individual Development, Chairwoman, Board of the Andrews, Jaycees **C/VW:** Den Leader, Tiger Coach, Cub Scout, Boy Scouts of America; Mustang Band Boosters

STEPHANIE M. BOWLER, BSN
Registered Nurse
Erie County Medical Center
Grider Street
Buffalo, NY 14125 United States
msbowler@adelphia.net
http://www.cambridgewhoswho.com

BUS: Woman's Health Center, Maternal **MA:** Regional **D/D/R:** Nursing in the Step-Down Trauma Unit and Women's Health **H/I/S:** Giving her Love and Time to her Nieces and Nephews **FBP:** Let's Live American Journal of Nursing Amercian of Nursing **EDU:** Bachelor of Science Degree in Nursing, Niagara University; Coursework in Women's Health, University of Buffalo **CERTS:** Certified in Advanced Cardiac Life Support; **A/A/S:** Sigma Theta Tau International ; Delta Epsilon Sigma; United States Achievement Academy Directory **C/VW:** March of Dimes **A/S:** She attributes her success to her loving family and their support. **B/I:** She chose the profession because she always wanted to help people and assist in their well being.

GRETCHEN C. BOWMAN
Intake Supervisor
Mahoning County Children Services Board
222 W. Federal Street
Youngstown, OH 44503 United States
http://www.mahoningkids.com

BUS: Nonprofit Organization **P/S:** Social Services Including Protecting Children and Preserving Families, Investigating Child Abuse and Neglect Situations, Adoption, Foster Parents **MA:** Local **EXP:** Ms. Bowman's expertise is in child welfare and neglect issues including abuse investigations and assessments. **H/I/S:** Gardening, Spending Time with her Grandchildren and Dogs **FBP:** Various Research Journals and Publications **EDU:** Master of Science in Counseling, Youngstown State University (1995); Bachelor of Science in Social Work, Youngstown State University (1991); Associate of Science in Nursing, Youngstown State University (1970), Registered Nurse **A/A/S:** National Board for Certified Counselors **C/VW:** Disabled American Veterans; Local Rescue Mission; The Humane Society of the United States; Volunteer, Park Systems; Youth Mentor **A/S:** She attributes her success to her good work ethic and honesty. **B/I:** She became involved in her profession because after completing an internship as a nurse with child services she found that she had a passion for the field. **H/O:** The highlight of her career was obtaining her current position.

CAROLYN J. BOWYER-BROWN
Nurse Practitioner
Bon Secours Hospital
53 Krouse Court
Aberdeen, MD 21001 United States
http://www.cambridgewhoswho.com

BUS: Medical Hospital **P/S:** Quality and Compassionate Health Care to Anyone in Need, Experienced and Compassionate Medical Services to Patients in a Safe and Responsive Environment **MA:** Regional **D/D/R:** Caring for Geriatric Patients **H/I/S:** Supporting the Pittsburgh Steelers, Bowling **EDU:** Degree in Nurse Practitioner Studies, University of Maryland (1973) **A/A/S:** American Nurses Association **C/VW:** Volunteering for the Community

M. FRANKLIN BOYD, JD
1) Principal 2) Attorney
1) Boyd Level, LLC 2) M. Franklin Boyd Esq.
18 Harrison Street, 3rd Floor
New York, NY 10013 United States
franklin@boydlevel.com
http://www.boydlevel.com

BUS: 1) Arts 2) Legal Services **P/S:** 1) New Collector Development for Contemporary Art 2) Legal Services **MA:** 1) International 2) New York State **D/D/R:** Remaining Current with Emerging Art Forms, Practicing Intellectual Property and General Commercial Law **H/I/S:** Triathlon, Swimming, Running, Traveling, Scuba Diving **FBP:** Industry-Related Publications **EDU:** JD, New York University; Bachelor of Science in Foreign Services, School of Foreign Services, Georgetown University **A/A/S:** New York Bar Association; New York Arts Organization **C/VW:** Volunteer Lawyer for the Arts, Creative Time, LMCC **A/S:** She attributes her personal and professional success to her supportive family. **H/O:** The highlight of her career is owning her own company.

MRS. CARLEY BOYER, RN
Owner, Registered Nurse (Retired)
Shorty's Apartments
8123 E. Marlin Drive
Globe, AZ 85501 United States
cjvirgo6@hotmail.com
http://www.cambridgewhoswho.com

BUS: Property Management Firm **P/S:** Real Estate Rentals and Leasing Services **MA:** Regional **EXP:** Mrs. Boyer's expertise is in operations management and nursing. **D/D/R:** Managing Properties, Leasing Eight Apartments and Commercial Units, Interviewing Prospective Clients, Accompanying Clients to Property Sites, Facilitating Lease Negotiations, Caring for Patients in Hospice Center and Intensive Care Unit, Assisting in Surgeries **H/I/S:** Glass Design, Exercising, Gardening, Writing **EDU:** Associate Degree in Nursing, GateWay Community College, Phoenix, AZ (1994) **A/H:** Dean's List **SP:** Roland **CHILD:** KaMisha, Mark **B/I:** She became involved in her profession because it was her family business. **I/F/Y:** In five years, Ms. Boyer hopes to sell her investment property and write a book on her family history and her unusual childhood experiences.

PATRICIA E. BOYLE, RN, MSN
Executive Director
New Mexico Center for Nursing Excellence
3200 Carlisle N.E.
Suite 223
Albuquerque, NM 87110 United States
pboyle@nmnursingexcellence.org
http://www.nmnursingexcellence.org

BUS: Nonprofit Organization **P/S:** Promotion of Nursing **MA:** Statewide **D/D/R:** Overseeing Administration and Health Policies **H/I/S:** Gardening, Basket Weaving, Creating Arts and Crafts, Reading Mysteries **EDU:** Master of Science in Nursing, University of New Mexico; Bachelor of Science in Nursing, University of Northern Colorado **A/A/S:** Former President, New Mexico Organization of Nurse Executives; American Organization of Nurse Executives **C/VW:** Vice President, Friends of the Belen Library

MARY FAYE BOZE
Owner
Boze Properties
925 Robinhood Court
Maitland, FL 32751 United States
chamchambo@yahoo.com
http://www.cambridgewhoswho.com

Faye Boze
Property Investments
407-644-1055
407-488-6730

BUS: Real Estate Company **P/S:** Investing, Remodeling and Reselling Services **MA:** Regional **D/D/R:** Buying Houses, Fixing, Reselling and Renting Real Estate, Finding Properties **H/I/S:** Playing and Spending Time with her Dog **FBP:** Local Florida Newspaper; Stock-Market Section **EDU:** High School Diploma; Industry-Related Experience **A/S:** She attributes her success to her hard work and desire to work in the industry. **B/I:** She became involved in her profession because of her willpower and interest in real estate. She started out as a real estate salesperson. **H/O:** The most gratifying aspect of her career is seeing the business she created prosper.

TINA B. BRABANDT, ABR
Broker
RE/MAX Realty Consultants
2150 Country Club Road
Winston Salem, NC 27104 United States
tinabrab@aol.com
http://www.1carolinahomes.com

BUS: Real Estate **P/S:** Sales, Real Estate, Marketing **MA:** Local **EXP:** Ms. Brabandt's expertise is in residential and commercial relocation. **H/I/S:** Traveling **EDU:** Coursework in Sociology, University of North Carolina, Greensboro **CERTS:** Licensed Broker, State of North Carolina; Certified Accredited Buyers Representative; Pursuing Residential Specialist Certification **A/A/S:** North Carolina Association of Realtors; National Association of Realtors **C/VW:** Children's Miracle Network; Brenner Children's Hospital; Habitat for Humanity **A/S:** She attributes her success to hard work, determination and dedication. **B/I:** She became involved in her profession after initially working in real estate investing and then moving into sales. She is now in broker management. **H/O:** The most gratifying aspects of her career are the investments she has made.

LINDA R. BRACKIN
Positive Psychotherapist, Life Coach
Renewal Counseling and Coaching
701 Adams Dam Road
Wilmington, DE 19807 United States
lbrackin@comcast.net
http://www.renewalcounselingcoaching.com

BUS: Coaching and Counseling Company **P/S:** Positive Psychotherapy Life Coaching **MA:** National **EXP:** Ms. Brackin's areas of expertise include positive psychology, relationship enhancement and loss and grief recovery. **D/D/R:** Nurturing Relationships with Families and Friends, Promoting Healthy Self-Evaluation, Counseling Individuals, Coaching on Life and Communication Skills **H/I/S:** Performing Contemporary Dances, Traveling, Reading, Enjoying Nature, Sound Healing, Building Tree Houses **FBP:** Psychology Today **EDU:** Master's Degree in Clinical Specialist Studies, Graduate School of Social Work and Social Research, Bryn Mawr College **A/A/S:** Institute of Noetic Sciences; International Lyme and Associated Diseases Society **C/VW:** Habitat for Humanity, Angel Network; The Nature Conservancy; Heron Dance; Sunray Peace Village; World Trust Federation; Public Research Organizations **DOB:** May 14, 1945 **POB:** Noranda **CHILD:** Ian, Erin **W/H:** Coordinator, Delaware Hospice; Family Service of Philadelphia; Child Study Center of Philadelphia **A/S:** She attributes her success to commitment to others. **B/I:** She became involved in her profession because she is committed to the well-being of others. **H/O:** The highlights of her career were facilitating a weekly sustainable happiness life coaching group and witnessing others embrace their signature character strengths as tools for transformation. **I/F/Y:** In five years, Ms. Brackin intends to continue working actively in her private practice.

MS. DEBORAH ANN BRADLEY, RN, PAHM
Registered Nurse, Professional, Academy for Healthcare Management
D2 Hawkeye
130 Turner Street
Waltham, MA 02453 United States
dbradley@d2hawkeye.com
sbradley2@nycap.rr.com
http://www.d2hawkeye.com

BUS: Healthcare Analytics Company **P/S:** Care Management Strategy Consulting Services Including Analytics, Predictive Modeling, Risk Management and Data Processing **MA:** International **D/D/R:** Defining Solutions for Pre-Claims Risks, Developing Strategies for Care Management Programs, Offering Sales Training, Developing Competitive Analysis, Speaking at Conferences, Coordinating with Product Development and Market Needs for Product Enhancements, Crafting Solution Packages to Address Business Issues, Presenting New Ideas and Improving Practices for Health Plans to Increase Revenue, Decreasing the Cost of Care and Increasing Efficiency while Improving the Health Status and Outcomes of the Organization's Members **H/I/S:** Gardening, Hiking, Kayaking **FBP:** Disease Management News; American Journal of Nursing **EDU:** Registered Nurse, Utica State Hospital (1975) **CERTS:** Certification in Product Management (2007); Certified Professional, The Academy for Healthcare Management; Certification in Pragmatic Marketing **A/A/S:** New York State Nurses Association; American Nurses Association; Case Management Society of America **A/H:** Chairman's Club Award, TriZetto (2005, 2006); Extra Mile Award (1997) **C/VW:** Alzheimer's Association **DOB:** June 22, 1954 **POB:** Troy **SP:** Scott **CHILD:** Timothy, Molly **W/H:** The TriZetto Group, Inc.; St. Luke's Hospital Center, Utica, NY; St. Peters Hospital; Children's Hospital; Dr. Douglas Larson; Voorheesville Elementary School; Travelers Corporation; Preferred Care; Novalis Corporation **A/S:** She attributes her success to her awareness of care management and data trends, remaining active in the industry and innovation. **B/I:** She became involved in her profession because she was inspired by a friend who made positive care management changes by moving from the clinical side of healthcare to the business side. **H/O:** The highlight of her career was being recognized for her contributions to the advancement of care management. **I/F/Y:** In five years, Ms. Bradley sees herself being promoted to a senior leadership position at D2 Hawkeye.

KAREN BRADLEY
Vice President
Bank of America
500 Northlake Drive
Peachtree City, GA 30269 United States
karen.a.bradley@bankofamerica.com
http://www.cambridgewhoswho.com
http://www.mortgage.bankofamerica.com/karenabradley

BUS: Mortgage Company **P/S:** Residential Mortgages **MA:** National **EXP:** Ms. Bradley's expertise is in the oversight of financial services, residential mortgages, one-time close construction loans and government loan programs. **H/I/S:** Reading, Spending Time with her Family, Traveling **FBP:** WCR Publications **CERTS:** Industry-Related Training and Experience **A/A/S:** Treasurer, Women's Council of Realtors; President Elect, LineCreek Civilian Club; National Association of Realtors **A/H:** Spirit Award **C/VW:** Special Olympics; Christian City **POB:** Atlanta **SP:** Russell **A/S:** She attributes her success to her persistence, leadership skills and goal-oriented nature. **H/O:** The highlight of her career was winning the spirit award.

MR. WESLEY C. BRADLEY
President
University Housing Group, Inc.
2758 Electric Road
Suite B
Roanoke, VA 24018 United States
wcs@studenthome.com
http://www.studenthome.com

BUS: Housing Company Dedicated to Providing College Students with a Unique Living Environment of Convenience, Comfort and Privacy at an Affordable Price **P/S:** Building of Quality Student Housing throughout the Nation, Variety of Floor Plans, Exciting Amenity Packages, Excellent Locations **MA:** National **D/D/R:** Researching on and Developing Real Estate, Managing Operations, Selecting Sites **H/I/S:** Snow Skiing, Travel, Hiking **FBP:** The Economist; Real Estate Journals **EDU:** Bachelor's Degree in Business Marketing and Finance, Radford University (1992) **A/A/S:** Homebuilders Association of Virginia; National Multi-Family Housing Council

Anita Nanda Brahme, DDS, MDS
Dentist, Oral Surgeon
Clinikas del Camino Real
200 S. Wells Road
Suite 200
Venticia, CA 93006
nanndab@aol.com
http://www.cambridgewhoswho.com

BUS: Dentistry **P/S:** Dentistry **MA:** Regional **D/D/R:** Performing Oral Surgery **H/I/S:** Traveling, Spending Time with Family, Continuing her Education **FBP:** Journal of Oral and Maxillofacial Surgery **EDU:** Doctor of Dental Surgery, UCLA; Associate Degree in Business Accounting, Marketing and Management **CERTS:** Practicing License, California; Certifications in Management; Certification in Sales **A/A/S:** American Dental Association; ADH; Indian Dental Association; Punjabi Dental Association; American Association of Physicians of Indian Origin **C/VW:** Indian Dental Association; Punjabi Dental Association **A/S:** She attributes her success to the encouragement she receives from her family and colleagues. **B/I:** She became involved in her profession because she wanted to work in the medical field. **H/O:** The highlight of her career was obtaining her current position.

Mr. Arthur Branagan
Regional Supervisor
State of Maine Department of Health and Human Services
176 Hogan Road
Bangor, ME 04401 United States
artbran@hotmail.com
http://www.maine.gov/dhhs

BUS: Government Organization **P/S:** Social Work for Developmental Disabled Individuals **MA:** Local **EXP:** Mr. Branagan's expertise is in psychology and the social sciences. **D/D/R:** Working with Computers **H/I/S:** Riding Motorcycles, Swimming, Going to the Beach, Running a Computer Business for Computer Coaching **FBP:** Popular Science **EDU:** Graduate Coursework in Corporate Management; Bachelor of Arts in Psychology and Social Sciences, University of Maine (1989) **A/A/S:** Elks Club; Supervisor, Maine State Employees Association; Gold Wing Road Riders Association

SANDRA JEAN BRANNON
Realtor, Owner
Brannon Properties
9233 Gloxinia Drive
Garden Ridge, TX 78266 United States
sandy@brannonproperties.com
http://www.brannonproperties.com

BUS: Real Estate Agency Committed to Providing Quality, Comprehensive Services **P/S:** Residential and Commercial Properties, Listings, Marketing, Financial Advise **MA:** Regional **D/D/R:** Selling and Buying Real Estate **H/I/S:** Basketball, Bowling, Riding Horses and Breeding Quarter Horses **FBP:** Real Estate Journal **A/A/S:** American Quarter Horse Association; National Cutting Horse Association; National Association of Realtors

RICHARD J. BRAUN
Licensed Practical Nurse
Central Vermont Medical Center
130 Fisher Road, PO Box 547
Barre, VT 05641 United States
rickbraun65@msn.com
http://www.cambridgewhoswho.com

BUS: Nursing Home **P/S:** Long-Term Care, Rehabilitation **MA:** Local **EXP:** Mr. Braun's expertise is in geriatrics. **H/I/S:** Enjoying Outdoor Activities, Hunting, Fishing, Managing Property **EDU:** Associate Degree in Electrical Engineering Technology, Vermont Technical College; Associate Degree in Computer Technology, Vermont Technical College **CERTS:** Certified Licensed Practical Nurse, Vermont Technical College, with Honors **C/VW:** International Fellowship of Christians and Jews **A/S:** He attributes his personal success to his perseverance self-discipline, consistency in performance and the support of his loving family. **B/I:** He chose to enter the profession of nursing because he found it to be very rewarding, especially in the fact that he is having a positive effect on peoples' lives. **H/O:** The highlight of his career has been the ability to go through a major career change and maintain success, and also the satisfaction he feels knowing that he is helping others in need.

JESSICA M. BRAYDICH
Administrative Assistant
Montgomery County Board of County Commissioners
451 W. 3rd Street
11th Floor
Dayton, OH 45422 United States
Braydichj@hotmail.com
http://www.mcohio.org

BUS: County Government **MA:** Local **C/VW:** Culture Works; United Way of America **A/S:** She attributes her success to her upbringing. **B/I:** She was prompted to enter her profession because she had an interest in the field. **H/O:** The highlight of her career was obtaining her current position.

SARAH JEAN BREEDEN
Associate Broker
William E. Wood and Associates
1321 Baskin Road
Virginia Beach, VA 23451 United States
sarahbreeden@cox.net
http://www.sarahbreeden.com

BUS: Real Estate Agency **P/S:** Residential Real Estate Sales **MA:** Local **D/D/R:** Selling Residential Properties, Overseeing New Construction Sites, Managing Marketing and Advertising, Communicating with Clients and Builders **H/I/S:** Horsesback Riding, Spending Time Outdoors, Exercising, Traveling, Spending Time with her Family and Friends **FBP:** Buyer Representative **EDU:** Coursework in Physical Education, Old Dominion University **CERTS:** Certified New Homes Sales Professional **A/A/S:** National Home Builders Association; National Association of Realtors; Sales and Marketing Council **C/VW:** Board of Directors, Virginia Beach Society for the Prevention of Cruelty to Animals; Society for the Prevention of Cruelty to Animals; Seton House; Local Charitable Organizations **A/S:** She attributes her success to her education, persistence and her dedication. **B/I:** She became involved in the profession because she enjoyed working with people. **H/O:** The highlight of her career was seeing the excitement on the faces of the family at her first closing.

FAITH BRENNER
Assistant Professor
Richland Community College
1 College Park
Decatur, IL 65221 United States
fbrenner@richland.edu
http://www.richland.edu

BUS: Comprehensive Community College of Higher Education **P/S:** Baccalaureate, Technical, Continuing Education and Community Service Programs, Several Degrees in its Baccalaureate and Transfer Program Including an Associate in Arts, Associate in Science, Associate in Fine Arts and Associate in Engineering Science, Customized Training, Life Long Learning Programs **MA:** Regional **D/D/R:** Computer Programming, Web Designing, Advising Students, Developing the Curriculum, Serving On the Quality Improvement Committee, Serving on the Strategic Task Force, Department Faculty Search Committee and Outcome Assessment Team **H/I/S:** Crafting, Reading **FBP:** Certification Magazine; Strategic Task Force Maintenance **EDU:** Master's Degree in Speech Pathology and Audiology, Illinois State University (1984) **CERTS:** Certification in Computer Programming (2000) **A/A/S:** American Speech-Language-Hearing Association; ICE; IBEA; SQIN

JENNY BRESELOW
Founder
Rocket Careers, Inc.
582 Market Street
Suite 1101
San Francisco, CA 94104 United States
jbreselow@rocketcareers.com
http://www.rocketcareers.com

BUS: Executive Search **P/S:** Biotech and Pharmaceutical Recruiting and Staffing Service **MA:** National **EXP:** Ms. Breselow's expertise is in business management. **H/I/S:** Playing Golf and Tennis, Traveling **FBP:** San Francisco Business Times **EDU:** Bachelor's Degree in Medical Technology, University of Wisconsin-Madison **C/VW:** Susan G. Komen Breast Cancer Foundation; Special Olympics; Habitat for Humanity; National Brain Tumor Foundation; Goodwill Industries International; Salvation Army; San Francisco Food Drive **A/S:** She attributes her career success to her integrity and excellent work ethic. **B/I:** She has always enjoyed the recruitment industry and so she decided to begin her own staffing agency. **H/O:** She feels that the recognition her company has earned within the biotech community is the highlight of her career.

SANDRA J. BREW, RN, MSN
Educator, Staff Nurse
McGuire VA Hospital
6555 Belmont Woods Road
Chester, VA 23831 United States
bubbasmom65@hotmail.com
http://www.cambridgewhoswho.com

BUS: Healthcare **P/S:** 486 Bed VA Teaching Hospital **MA:** Regional **D/D/R:** Administering Medical, Surgical and Critical Care **H/I/S:** Raising and Selling of Pure-Bred Cats **FBP:** Nursing Journal of Excellence **EDU:** Master of Science Degree in Nursing, University of Phoenix; Bachelor of Science Degree in Nursing, University of Phoenix; Bachelor of Science Degree in Education, University of North Dakota **A/A/S:** Sigma Theta Tau International; American Association of Critical-Care Nursing **C/VW:** Richmond Kennel Club **A/S:** She attributes her success to her ability to set and achieve goals. **B/I:** She became involved in her profession after her husband was injured on his job, and they both decided to become nurses. **H/O:** She feels that her current position is the highlight of her career.

JUDITH ANNE BREWER
Department Co-Chair, Teacher Consultant, Special Education
Lake Orion Community Schools
495 E. Scripps Road
Lake Orion, MI 48360 United States
jbrewer1@lakeorion.k12.mi.us
http://www.lakeorion.k12.mi.us

BUS: School District **P/S:** Educational Services for Students **MA:** Local **D/D/R:** Offering Academic Support to Students, Parents and Administration, Conducting Assessments for Special Education Students, Mentoring, Teaching, Training at High Schools **H/I/S:** Reading, Knitting, Sewing, Boating, Swimming, Spending Time with Family **FBP:** Council for Exceptional Children Magazine **EDU:** Master of Arts in Teaching in Special Education for Learning Disabled Plus 32, Oakland University; Bachelor of Science in Special Education for Emotionally Impaired, Western Michigan University **CERTS:** Pursuing Supervisor of Special Education Certification **A/A/S:** Association for Supervision and Curriculum Development; Council for Exceptional Children; Former Vice President, Lake Orion Education Association **C/VW:** Christ the Redeemer Catholic Church; Baldwin Shelter

LILLIAN D. BREWINGTON, MLS
Special Collections Librarian
University of North Carolina at Pembroke
1 University Drive
Pembroke, NC 28372 United States
lillian.brewington@uncp.edu
http://www.uncp.edu

BUS: Educational Facility-University **P/S:** Leaders in Providing Higher Education and Teaching Services in Various Degree Programs **MA:** Regional **D/D/R:** Receiving Publications, Handling Processing, Labeling and Cataloging of Publications, Government Documents and Special Collection Services **H/I/S:** Basketball, Reading, Computers **FBP:** Photo Shop Journal **EDU:** Master's Degree in Library Science, North Carolina Central University (1988); Bachelor's Degree in English, University of North Carolina at Pembroke (1986) **A/A/S:** North Carolina Library Association; American Library Association **A/H:** State lifetime Award for 30 years of successful employment within the state of North Carolina **H/O:** The most rewarding aspect of her job is going back and looking at the history of the University and the history of people in the community and providing information to those in need of it whether it is students or anyone from all over the country.

CHERYL R. BREWTON
Executive Assistant
Omega Protein, Inc.
2101 Citywest Boulevard
Building 3, Suite 500
Houston, TX 77042 United States
cbrew1121@aol.com
http://www.omegaproteininc.com

BUS: Distributor **P/S:** Distribution of Fish Oil **MA:** International **D/D/R:** Supporting the Marketing and Sales Department **H/I/S:** Playing for an Adult Soccer Team **FBP:** ASAS **EDU:** Associate Degree in Television Production, Montgomery College; Bachelor's Degree in Communication, University of Maryland **A/S:** She attributes her success to her drive and dedication. **B/I:** She became involved in her profession after being hired temporarily, then promoted to marketing assistant and again to executive assistant. **H/O:** The highlight of her career was being promoted to executive assistant.

MR. BOBBY R. BRIDGES
Patient Advocate, Public Relations Professional
Ambu Star
1248 Boiling Springs Road
Spartanburg, SC 29303 United States
bobby.bridges@ambustar.com
http://www.cambridgewhoswho.com

BUS: Transportation Company **P/S:** Transportation Services for the Healthcare Industry Including Ambulance and Wheelchair Transport Services **MA:** Regional **EXP:** Mr. Bridges' expertise is in non-emergency medical care transportation. **D/D/R:** Caring for Patients **H/I/S:** Spending Time with his Wife at the Mountains and the Beach, Home Renovation, Spending Time with his Family and Friends **EDU:** Coursework in Sales **CERTS:** Certified CPR and First Aid Instructor; Training in Sales and Marketing; Dale Carnegie Training **A/A/S:** South Carolina Association of Residential Care Homes; Union City Community Partnership **A/H:** Shining Star Award (2006); Employee of the Year Award (2005) **C/VW:** Local Church; Local Nursing Homes; Local Ministry; Volunteer, Ombudsman **A/S:** He attributes his success to his hard work, dedication and passion for his profession. **B/I:** He became involved in his profession because of the experience he gained by starting a wheelchair program. **H/O:** The most gratifying aspect of his career is serving patients.

REGINA A. BRIGGS
Co-Owner, Operator, Poet, Minister of the Gospel, Substitute Teacher
Current River Beach Resort
7937 Highway 67 N.
Biggers, AR 72413 United States
crbbeachbabe@yahoo.com
http://www.arkansas.com

BUS: Resort **P/S:** Hospitality Including Swimming, Camping, Fishing and Boating **MA:** National **EXP:** Ms. Briggs' expertise is in operations management and building public relationships. **H/I/S:** Jet Skiing, Swimming, Writing Poetry, Fishing, Singing Karaoke, Reading The Holy Bible **EDU:** Bachelor's Degree in Retail Sales Management, East Central College; Associate Degree in Automotive Office Assistance Studies, East Central College **A/A/S:** Arkansas State Chamber of Commerce **C/VW:** Cohort Program; First Assembly of God; Freedom Crusade Missions; World Missions **A/S:** She attributes her success to her upbringing, dedication and focused nature. **B/I:** She became involved in her profession because it was her husband's business. **H/O:** The most gratifying aspect of her career is making a positive impact on people's lives.

LOUANNE M. BRIGHT, RN
Registered Nurse
Home Solutions, Infusion Therapy
3 Regent Street
Livingston, NJ 07039 United States
mamaskis2004@yahoo.com
http://www.cambridgewhoswho.com

BUS: Healthcare **P/S:** Home Infusion Therapy **MA:** Eastern United States **EXP:** Ms. Bright's expertise is in home infusion therapy. **H/I/S:** Skiing, Singing, Crafts **FBP:** Advance for Nurses **EDU:** Associate of Applied Science, County College of Morris; Registered Nurse, State of New Jersey **A/S:** She attributes her personal and professional success to her willpower and ability to set and achieve goals. **B/I:** She has always had an interest in the field and a desire to help others. **H/O:** The highlight of her career is getting to know her patients on a more personal level.

MS. GISELA BRINKER-GABLER
Professor, Chairwoman of Comparative Literature
Comparative Literature
Binghamton University
Department of Comparative Literature
Binghamton, NY 13902 United States
gbrinker@binghamton.edu
http://www.brinker-gabler.com

BINGHAMTON UNIVERSITY
State University of New York

Gisela Brinker-Gabler, Dr. Phil.
Professor and Chair
Department of Comparative Literature

Binghamton, New York 13902-6000
gbrinker@binghamton.edu
607-777-2890   www.brinker-gabler.com

BUS: University **P/S:** Higher Education, Research Facilities at the Public Universities of the Northeast, Strong Academic Programs, Twenty-Six specialized Research Centers, Distinguished Faculty, Bachelor's, Master's and Doctoral Degrees, Affordable Tuition, Talented Students, Diversity, International Education **MA:** Regional **D/D/R:** Teaching as an Internationally Known Scholar of Comparative Literature, Philosophy, Culture and Women's and Gender Studies **H/I/S:** Traveling, Enjoying Photography, Creating Art **EDU:** Ph.D., University of Cologne (1973) **A/A/S:** Director of Graduate Programs, Graduate Council, Faculty Senate and Various Professional Executive and University Committees, Binghamton University; Modern Language Association; American Comparative Literature Association; Modern Studies Association; American Association of Teachers of German; Women in German; International Comparative Literature Association **A/H:** Who's Who in Germany **CHILD:** Kai **W/H:** Professor, Chairwoman of Comparative Literature, Binghamton University; Co-Director, Doctoral Program in Philosophy, Literature and the Theory of Criticism (2002); Associated Faculty Member, Doctoral Program in Philosophy, Interpretation and Culture (2001); Affiliated Faculty Member, Department of History, Doctoral Program in German History (1997); Affiliated Faculty Member, Program in Women's Studies (1995); Affiliated Faculty Member, Translation Research and Instruction Program (1993); Visiting Associate Professor, Comparative Literature, Binghamton University (1989-1993); Lecturer, Department of German, University of Cologne, Germany (1983-1988); Lecturer, Department of Comparative Literature, University of Essen (1976-1983); Assistant Professor on Tenure Track, Department of German, University of Florida (1974-1975); Editor, 'Die Frau in der Gesellschaft.=Texte und Lebensgeschichte,' Fischer Verlag, Frankfurt A.M., Germany (1978-1986) **C/A:** Founding Listee, 'Leading Educators of the World,' International Biographical Centre, Cambridge, England (2006); Professional Women's Advisory Board, The American Biographical Institute; Appointed Member, Editorial Board, State University of New York Press, Albany, NY (2005);Käthe Leichter Visiting Professor, Gender and Women's Studies Endowed Chair, University of Vienna (2000); Dean, Harpur College, 'Modernity and Identity' Workshop-Series Grant, Binghamton University (1998); Executive Committee, Division for Nineteenth and Early Twentieth Century German Literature, Modern Language Association (1995-1998); Chair, Executive Committee, Division for Nineteenth and Early Twentieth Century German Literature, Modern Language Association (1997); 'Ingeborg Bachmann Symposium' Conference Grant, DAAD German Academic Exchange Service, NY (1996); 'Ingeborg Bachmann Symposium Conference Grant,' Austrian Culture Institute, NY (1996); Honorary Appointment, Research Board of Advisors, American Bibliographical Advisory Board (1993); Invited Guest Speaker, Annual Meeting of the Canadian Association of Teachers of German, Charlottetown, Prince Edward Island, Canada (1992); Distinguished Visiting Scholar, National Endowment for the Humanities, University of Minnesota, Morris (1991); Conference Grant, 'The Question of the Other,' John Kade Foundation, NY (1991); Conference Grant, 'The Question of the Other, DAAD German Academic Exchange Service, NY (1991); Research Fellowship, German Research Society (1986-1988); Research Grant, Ministry of Science and Research of the State of Northrhine Westphalia, Düsseldorf (1985-1986); Research Grant, Ministry of Science and Research of the State of Northrhine Westphalia, Düsseldorf (1983-1985); Invited Guest Speaker, German-Netherland-Society, Amsterdam, Den Haag, Utrecht and Nijmegen (1984)

Dr. Penny C. Britt, EED
Principal
Long Branch Elementary School
Public Schools of Robeson County
506 Rowan Road
Lumberton, NC 28358 United States
brittpc.longbr@robeson.k12.nc.us
http://www.robeson.k12.nc.us

BUS: Public School District **P/S:** Education **MA:** Local **D/D/R:** Teaching Educational Leadership, Early Childhood and Elementary Education, Developing Curriculum, Maintaining Discipline **H/I/S:** Spending Time with her Family, Reading, Spending Time at the Beach **FBP:** Educational Leadership **EDU:** Doctor of Education in Educational Leadership, Fayetteville State University; Master of Education in School Leadership, East Carolina University; Master of Education in Early Childhood Education, University of North Carolina, Pembroke; Bachelor of Science in Early Childhood Education, University of North Carolina, Pembroke **A/A/S:** National Education Association; National Middle School Association; Association for Supervision and Curriculum Development; National Association of Secondary School Principals; Alumni Organization, University of North Carolina, Pembroke; Alumni Organization, Fayetteville State University **C/VW:** Volunteer Tutor, United Way; Little People of America **A/S:** She attributes her success to her determination and to the support she receives from her mother and family. **B/I:** She became involved in her profession because she always wanted to be a teacher. **H/O:** The highlight of her career was obtaining her master's degree.

Eileen Lilley Broas
Gifted Science Teacher, Science Department Head, Science Coach
Miami-Dade Public Schools, Ruben Dario Middle School
350 N.W. 97th Avenue
Miami, FL 33172 United States
eelilley@dsli.com
http://www.cambridgewhoswho.com

BUS: Middle School **P/S:** Education **MA:** Local **D/D/R:** Teaching Gifted Education and Gifted Geology **H/I/S:** Reading, Traveling **EDU:** ABD, Florida International University; Master's Degree in Science Education, Florida International University; Bachelor's Degree in Health and Business Administration, Florida International University **A/A/S:** National Education Association **C/VW:** Girl Scouts of the U.S.A, Boy Scouts of America **A/S:** She attributes her success to her upbringing, dedication and passion for education youth. **B/I:** She became involved in the profession because she always had an interest in the field and a desire to educate others. **H/O:** The most gratifying aspect of her career is making a positive impact on the lives of children.

SHARON L. BROCKMAN
Assistant IT Manager, Systems Administrator
Grand Traverse Resort and Casino
2605 N.W. Bay Shore Drive
Peshawbestown, MI 49682 United States
sharon.brockman@gtbindians.com
http://www.cambridgewhoswho.com

BUS: Gaming **P/S:** Gaming **MA:** Local **EXP:** Ms. Brockman's expertise is in information technology and systems administration. **H/I/S:** Spending Time with her Children **EDU:** Associate Degree in Computer Science, Minnesota West Community and Technical College **C/VW:** Susan G. Komen Breast Cancer Foundation **A/S:** She attributes her success to the support of her wonderful family. **B/I:** She became involved in her profession because at her previous job her employers were impressed by her work with computers and offered to send her to school for computers. **H/O:** The highlight of her career is being able to consistently progress and grow.

RICHARD G. BRODY
Senior Consultant
RGB Consultation Services
10 Bayside Avenue
Port Washington, NY 11050 United States
rgbrody@aol.com
http://www.portwashingtonlongislandhouses.com

BUS: Consulting Firm **P/S:** Consulting for Finance, Real Estate and Computers, Conference Management, Marketing **MA:** International **EXP:** Mr. Brody's expertise is in business management and marketing. **D/D/R:** Consulting for Finance, Design and Operations Management, Making Professional Power Point Presentation **H/I/S:** Boating, Playing Tennis **FBP:** Meetings and Conventions **EDU:** Bachelor of Arts in Psychology, CUNY Queens College (1972) **CERTS:** Certification in Nonprofit Management, C.W. Post Campus, Long Island University (2003); Certified Real Estate Cyberspace Specialist **A/A/S:** Real Estate CyberSpace Society; Long Island Board of Realtors; Manhasset Port Washington Real Estate Board; Association of Fundraising Professionals

WANDA K. BROM
Owner
Bkw Commercial Cleaning
PO Box 35878
Des Moines, IA 50315 United States
wandabrom@hotmail.com
http://www.cambridgewhoswho.com

BUS: Janitorial Company **P/S:** Commercial Cleaning Services Including Floor Stripping and Waxing **MA:** Local **D/D/R:** Overseeing Business Operations, Supervising Employees **H/I/S:** Traveling, Collecting Baskets, Volunteering **EDU:** Bachelor of Arts in Education, University of Northern Iowa; Associate Degree in Secretarial English, Indian Hills Community College, Centerville, IA **C/VW:** Jehovah's Witnesses **A/S:** She attributes her success to her advertising skills. **B/I:** She became involved in her profession because of her desire to start her own business.

KIMBERLY M. BROOKER, RN
Registered Nurse, Nurse Manager
Plaza Surgery Center, HCA
3901 University Boulevard S.
Jacksonville, FL 32216 United States
kimberly.brooker@hcahealthcare.com
http://www.cambridgewhoswho.com

BUS: Outpatient Surgery Center **P/S:** Healthcare Including All Specialties in Surgery, Nursing Management **D/D/R:** Overseeing the Surgery Center and 50 Employees, Working in Operating Rooms, Offering Pre-Operation and Recovery Room Care, Managing Risks, Coordinating Quality Improvement **FBP:** AORN Journal **CERTS:** Registered Nurse, Florida Community College (1987); Licensed Risk Manager, State of Florida **A/A/S:** Association of Operating Room Nurses **C/VW:** Co-Leader, Girl Scouts of the United States of America

APRIL E. BROOKS, LPC
Licensed Professional Counselor
Professional Counseling Group
1324 Trotwood Avenue, Suite 6
Columbia, TN 38401 United States
aebpfg@gmail.com
http://www.cambridgewhoswho.com

BUS: Mental Healthcare Center **P/S:** Aid for Children with Academic Issues, Aid for Adolescents, Women and Men, Social and Parenting Skills Training, Relationship Skills Training, Spiritual Counseling, Anger Management, Treatment for Depression, Post-Traumatic Stress Disorder, Selective Mutism, Asperger's Syndrome, Oppositional Defiant Disorder, Behavioral Issues, Attention Deficit Hyperactivity Disorder, Reactive Attachment Disorder, Addictions and Substance Abuse **MA:** Local **EXP:** Ms. Brooks' expertise is in couples' and relationship counseling. **D/D/R:** Treating Anger Management Issues, Helping Children with Academic Behavioral Issues and Depression, Helping People Suffering from Post-Traumatic Stress Disorder **H/I/S:** Studying Genealogy, Knitting, Crocheting, Listening to Classical Music, Participating in Drum Corps International **FBP:** Psychology Today **EDU:** Pursuing Associate Degree in Religion; Master's Degree in Psychology and Counseling, Liberty University in Lynchburg, VA (1996); Bachelor's Degree in Psychology and Counseling (2003); Associate Degree in Nursing (1988) **A/A/S:** American Counseling Association; American Association of Christian Counselors; Drum Corps International **C/VW:** Pro Bono Counseling

ELEANOR D. BROOKS
Vice President, Owner
Prestige Towing Recovery
947 Old Route 17
Harris, NY 12742 United States
towman@hvc.rr.com
http://www.cambridgewhoswho.com

BUS: Towing Company **P/S:** Twenty-Two Tow Trucks, Four Tractor-Trailer Car Carriers, Heavy Duty Trucks Providing Services for Oversize Vehicles, Rental Car Company Providing Service to Customers that Break Down **MA:** Northeastern United States **D/D/R:** Managing Financing for the Company, Accounts Payable and Receivable, Making Business Decisions **H/I/S:** Weightlifting at the Gym, Spending Time with her Children **FBP:** Tow Times Magazine **EDU:** Coursework, Trade School

RONNIE G. BROOKS
Business Banker
Regions Banking
6200 Popular Avenue
Memphis, TN 38119 United States
ronnie.brooks@regions.com
http://www.regions.com

BUS: Investment Firm **P/S:** Investment Services Including Securities Brokerage, Trust and Asset Management Services **MA:** International **EXP:** Mr. Brooks' expertise is in managing finance, consulting, training, overseeing staff management, prospecting, recognizing and capitalizing on opportunities. **EDU:** Bachelor's Degree in Economics, University of Memphis (2003) **A/A/S:** Inside Downtown; South Main Association; Downtown Neighborhood Association Memphis; RISE Association; Memphis Debt Collaborative; 100 Black Men of Memphis

ROCHELLE ANNETTE BROOME
Corporate Medical Director
Department of Primary Care
CHD Meridian Healthcare
40 Burton Hills Boulevard, Suite 200
Nashville, TN 37215 United States
rochelle.broome@takecarehealth.com
http://www.chdmeridian.com

BUS: Healthcare Center **P/S:** Healthcare, Integrated Disease Management, Corporate Healthcare Programs for Large and Mid-Sized Employers **EXP:** Ms. Broome's expertise is in family medicine. **H/I/S:** Traveling, Wine Tasting, Gourmet Cooking **FBP:** Journal of American College Health **EDU:** MD, Northeastern Ohio Universities College of Medicine and Pharmacy **A/A/S:** Fellow, American Academy of Family Physicians; Accreditation Council for Pharmacy Education; American College of Physician Executives **C/VW:** Board Member, Nashville Cares **A/S:** She attributes her success to her communication skills and being goal-oriented. **B/I:** She became involved in her profession because of her interest in the medical field. **H/O:** The highlight of her career was earning her current position.

JANE M. BROSNAN, CPNP
Certified Pediatric Nurse Practitioner
Mt. Sinai at Elmhurst Hospital-PS7Q School Base Clinic
4820 88th Street
Elmhurst, NY 11373 United States
brosnanj@nychhc.com
http://www.cambridgewhoswho.com

BUS: Proven Leader in the Healthcare Field **P/S:** Pediatric Healthcare Specifically Located on School Grounds to Ensure the Health and Welfare of the Students **MA:** Regional **D/D/R:** Nursing, Working in the School Facility as a Pediatric Nurse, Conducting Medical Assessments and Student Testing, Working with and Educating School Staff and Parents in Relation to Healthcare, Administering Physical Examinations, Writing Prescriptions and Referrals **H/I/S:** Swimming, Tennis, Skiing **FBP:** Journal of the National Association of Pediatric Nurse Associates and Practitioners **CERTS:** Certified Nurse Practitioner, Cornell NYU Hospital (1976) **A/A/S:** National Association of Pediatric Nurse Associates and Practitioners

JANICE K. BROWER
Library Tech III
Jim E. Hamilton Correctional Center
53468 Mineral Springs Road
Hodgen, OK 74939 United States
janice.brower@doc.state.ok.us
http://www.cambridgewhoswho.com

BUS: Department of Corrections **P/S:** Minimum Security Prison **MA:** Statewide **EXP:** Ms. Brower's expertise is in leisure library processes. **H/I/S:** Going to Museums, Visiting Historical Sites, Attending Civil War Reenactments **FBP:** Booklist **EDU:** Bachelor of Science in Library Science, Illinois State University (1975); Associate of Arts, Lincoln College, IL (1973) **CERTS:** Certified-Level IV, Oklahoma Department of Libraries **A/A/S:** Oklahoma Library Association **A/H:** Librarian of the Year, Oklahoma Department of Corrections (1991) **C/VW:** Volunteer, Friends of Peter Conser; Operator in Training, Fort Smith Trolley Museum **DOB:** July 29, 1952 **POB:** Chicago **W/H:** University of Oklahoma (1985-1987); Chicago Public Library (1975-1980, 1981-1983) **A/S:** She attributes her success to her parents, who stressed the Importance of education to her. **B/I:** She became involved in this profession due to her long-time interest in libraries. **H/O:** The highlight of her career was receiving a Librarian of the Year Award from the Department of Corrections in 1991. **I/F/Y:** In five years, Ms. Brower hopes to have continued growth.

ARTHUR L. BROWN
Director of Nursing Services
Public Health Trust
New Horizons Community Mental Health Center, Inc.
1321 N.W. 13th Street, First Floor
Miami, FL 33125 United States
abrown4526@aol.com
http://www.um-jmh.org

BUS: Medical Center **P/S:** Healthcare Including Mental Healthcare and Rehabilitation Services **MA:** Regional **D/D/R:** Overseeing Mental Healthcare and Stabilization Services **H/I/S:** Playing Football **FBP:** RN Journal; Journal of Correctional Healthcare **EDU:** Master of Science, Nova Southeastern University (1981); Bachelor of Science in Nursing (1973); Registered Nurse (1972) **A/A/S:** American Correctional Association; National Commission on Correctional Healthcare

BEVIN L. BROWN, CRNA
Certified Registered Nurse Anesthetist
Troy Regional Medical Center
1330 Highway 231
Troy, AL 36081 United States
bevinb@wmconnect.com
http://www.cambridgewhoswho.com

BUS: Healthcare **P/S:** Full-Service Rural Hospital **MA:** Local **EXP:** Mr. Brown's expertise is in anesthesia. **H/I/S:** Biking, Backpacking, Traveling, Spending Time with his Wife and Children **FBP:** Industry-Related Publications; AANA Journal **EDU:** Associate of Science in Registered Nursing, Adventist University; Diploma in Nursing, Madison Hospital School of Anesthesia, Madison, Tennessee **CERTS:** Certified Registered Nurse Anesthetist, American Association of Nursing Anesthetists **A/A/S:** Alabama Association of Nursing Anesthetists **C/VW:** Troy Seventh-Day Adventist Church, Various Local Charities, Three Angels Broadcasting Network, Goodwill **A/S:** He attributes his success to his concern for others. **B/I:** He became involved in his profession because he was inspired by his father. **H/O:** The most gratifying aspect of his career is being a part of the advancement in anesthesia practices.

Caretha E. Brown
Founder, President
Living Hope International Ministry
909 29th Street
Orlando, FL 32805 United States
carethabrown@bellsouth.net
http://www.livinghopecdc.org

BUS: Social Service Program **P/S:** Residential Education and Training for Battered and Abused Women and Children, Education Life Skill Program for the Incarcerated in the Orange County Jail, Workshops, Seminars, Conferences and Support Groups **MA:** Local **D/D/R:** Offering Oversight of the Organization and of Community Relations, Fundraising, Marketing **H/I/S:** Traveling, Reading **FBP:** Charisma **EDU:** Bachelor of Science in Nursing Education, Florida A&M University **CERTS:** Licensed Bible Teacher, International Bible Institute and Seminary; Licensed Minister, International Bible Institute and Seminary; Ordained Minister, Faith Christian Fellowship International **A/A/S:** Nurses for Christ Association; Christian Chamber of Commerce; Inmate Resource Program; Orlando Evening Rotary Club **C/VW:** Orange County Jail Ministry; Various Local Churches **A/S:** She attributes her success to hard work, sticking to difficult tasks, and community and family support. **B/I:** She became involved in this profession because she has always tried to help people in her community overcome problems. **H/O:** The highlight of her career is seeing individuals overcome their problems and become successful in society.

Christine Ozog Brown
Information Technology Manager
Met Life
651 Brookfield Parkway
Greenville, SC 29607 United States
cozogbrown@metlife.com
http://www.cambridgewhoswho.com

BUS: Insurance Company **P/S:** Group Insurance Technical Support **MA:** Regional **EXP:** Ms. Brown's expertise is in mainframe restoration. **H/I/S:** Restoring Mustangs **EDU:** Bachelor of Science in Computer Science and Business, Furman University **C/VW:** Various Local Charities **DOB:** July 8, 1974 **SP:** Lee **A/S:** She attributes her success to her desire to learn and grow.

MR. DARREN BROWN
President
Arivium, Inc.
354 Glen Arbor Drive N.E.
Rockford, MI 49341 United States
dbrown@arivium.com
http://www.arivium.com

BUS: Consulting Firm **P/S:** Implementation Management, Business Management Consulting, Vendor Management, Program Management, Technology Evaluation, Communication Planning **MA:** Regional **EXP:** Mr. Brown's expertise is in technology consulting, business development, product commercialization, manufacturing and finance management for life science, pharmaceutical and transportation industries. **H/I/S:** Coaching Soccer and Football, Playing Softball and Volleyball **FBP:** Entrepreneur; Fast Company; Bio-IT World **EDU:** Bachelor's Degree in Information Science, Western Michigan University (1988) **A/A/S:** Grand Rapids Chamber of Commerce

DEMORY K. BROWN
Special Education Teacher, Resource Teacher
for Kindergarten through Fifth Grade
Solvang Elementary School
565 Atterdag Road
Solvang, CA 93463 United States
demoryb@hotmail.com
http://www.cambridgewhoswho.com

BUS: Special Education **P/S:** Elementary Education **MA:** Local **D/D/R:** Teaching Special Education **H/I/S:** Exercising, Golfing, Surfing, Gardening, Hiking, Cooking, Spending Time Outdoors **EDU:** Associate of Arts in General Studies; Bachelor's Degree in Liberal Studies, Minor in Child Development, California Polytechnic State University **CERTS:** Teacher Credentials, Antioch University **A/A/S:** California Teachers Association; California Association of Resource Specialists Plus; Student Study Team; School Site Council; Solvang Yearbook Chairwoman **C/VW:** Relay for Life, Multiple Sclerosis Society, Special Olympics **A/S:** She attributes her success to her passion for her career, being professional and having a strong mindset. **B/I:** She became involved in the profession because she was a special education student and admired her educators and wanted to help offer other special education students the same education she received. **H/O:** The most gratifying aspect of her career is when her students understand what they are learning.

GRACE G. BROWN
Real Estate Sales
Corcoran Group
PO Box 2761
Palm Beach, FL 33480 United States
grace.brown@corcoran.com
http://www.corcoran.com

BUS: Leading Residential Real Estate Company in Palm Beach, New York City, the Hamptons and the East End **P/S:** Brokerage Sales and Leases of Upscale Residential Real Estate in Palm Beach, FL, the Hamptons, and New York City, Specifically in Manhattan and Brooklyn's Trendiest and Most Upscale Neighborhoods **MA:** Regional **D/D/R:** Working with Buyers and Sellers, Assisting Clients with Relocations and Second Homes, Specifically from New York **H/I/S:** Gardening, Playing Tennis, Reading, Investing in Real Estate **FBP:** Real Estate; Home and Garden; Architectural Digest; Palm Beach Cottages and Gardens **EDU:** Bachelor of Science Degree in Political Science, University of North Carolina, Chapel Hill (1983) **CERTS:** License in Real Estate (1995) **A/A/S:** Young Friends, Norton Museum of Arts **A/H:** Recipient, Polly Earl Award for Historic Preservation (2006); Outstanding Service Award, Palm Beach Board of Realtors (2002-2003) **C/VW:** First Families of North Carolina; Preservation Foundation of Palm Beach

JULIE F. BROWN
Staff Accountant
Accounting
First Choice America Community Federal Credit Union
3501 Main Street
Weirton, WV 26062 United States
aug_mar_8@hotmail.com
http://www.cambridgewhoswho.com

BUS: Finance Company **P/S:** Financial Services **MA:** Upper Ohio Valley, WV **EXP:** Ms. Brown's areas of expertise include reports, balancing and the general ledger. **H/I/S:** Walking, Reading **FBP:** The Wall Street Journal **EDU:** Bachelor of Science in Accounting, Franciscan University of Steubenville **CERTS:** Credit Union Accounting Certificate (2004) **C/VW:** American Heart Association **A/S:** She attributes her success to thoroughly completing each job and being eager to learn new things. **B/I:** She became involved in her profession while she was in high school. She realized that she loved accounting and decided to pursue a career in it. **H/O:** The most gratifying aspects of her career are knowing that her co-workers are confident in her and feel comfortable delegating tasks to her.

Ms. Karen R. Brown
Gifts Trainer
Discover Your Gifts
1872 114th Avenue N.W.
Minneapolis, MN 55433 United States
nik43br@aol.com
http://www.cambridgewhoswho.com

BUS: Leader in Education **P/S:** Consulting and Counseling **MA:** National **D/D/R:** Counseling, Consulting, Education relating to life, special education, counseling and assisting individuals on their understanding and discovery of their gifts. **H/I/S:** Reading, Writing **FBP:** Sun Magazine **EDU:** Master's Degree in Special Education, Bemidji State University (1993); Bachelor of Science in Education, St. Cloud State University (1968) **A/A/S:** Minnesota Public Radio; Foundation of Faith, Family and Friends; Plymouth Writers Group **C/VW:** Disabled American Veterans; Local Church

Lori L. Brown, BSM-B, RMA, CMOM
Office Manager
ABC Women's Care
300 Medical Arts Building
Suite 300
Kittanning, PA 16201 United States
brownl@acmh.org
http://www.cambridgewhoswho.com

BUS: OB/GYN Office **P/S:** Women's Healthcare **MA:** Local **D/D/R:** Managing Two Offices and One Satellite Office, Scheduling Employees **H/I/S:** Reading Management Books **EDU:** Pursuing Bachelor's Degree in Management, University of Phoenix **CERTS:** Registered Medical Assistant; Certified Child Passenger Safety Instructor **A/A/S:** American Medical Technologies **C/VW:** Safe Kids Worldwide

MARY J. BROWN, RN, MSN
Patient Safety Officer, Assistant Chief, Nursing Practice
Mercy Medical Center, Des Moines
1111 6th Avenue
Des Moines, IA 50314 United States
mbrown@mercydesmoines.org
http://www.cambridgewhoswho.com

BUS: Medical Center **P/S:** Healthcare **MA:** Regional **D/D/R:** Nursing, Patient Care and Safety **H/I/S:** Traveling, Reading **EDU:** Master of Science Degree in Nursing, Drake University; Executive Fellowship in Inpatient Safety Leadership, Health Forum **A/A/S:** American Association of Critical-Care Nurses; National Patient Safety Foundation; Sigma Theta Tau International **C/VW:** Church, School, Easter Seals **A/S:** She attributes her success to being deeply rooted in her passion for good patient care. **B/I:** She became involved in this profession because of her desire to be involved in patient care. **H/O:** The highlight of her career is being recognized as 1 out of 100 great nurses in Iowa.

REBECCA CRAY CRAFT BROWN, ESQ.
Attorney
Bailes, Craig & Yon
401 Tenth Street, Suite 500
Huntington, WV 25701 United States
rcb@bcyon.com
http://www.cambridgewhoswho.com

BUS: Law Firm **P/S:** Legal Services **MA:** Local **D/D/R:** Practicing Healthcare, Medical Defense and Transactional Law **H/I/S:** Cooking, Family **EDU:** JD, Chase College of Law, Northern Kentucky University **A/A/S:** American Bar Association; Registered Nurse Advisory Board, Ashland Community and Technical College; American Registry of Outstanding Professionals **C/VW:** March of Dimes; American Cancer Society; St. Jude Children's Research Hospital **A/S:** She attributes her success to the support of her family. **B/I:** She became involved in her profession because she had been a nurse and decided that she wanted to help nurses in the legal field. **H/O:** The highlight of her career has been being made partner.

SHARON K. BROWN
Owner, President
Brown Electric, Inc.
7367 Bear Ridge Road
North Tonawanda, NY 14120 United States
brownelectric81@yahoo.com
http://www.cambridgewhoswho.com

BUS: Electrical Construction Company **P/S:** Electrical Construction, Repairs, Maintenance **MA:** International **D/D/R:** Meeting with Clients, Business, Companies, Overseeing Nine Employees and Administrative Duties, Consulting, Managing Operations **H/I/S:** Spending Time with her Family, Hunting, Traveling, Cooking, Sewing **CERTS:** Industry-Related Training **A/A/S:** Better Business Bureau **C/VW:** Local Charitable Organizations; National Charitable Organizations **CHILD:** Eileen, Christopher **A/S:** She attributes her success to her determination, passion for her profession and to the support she receives from her colleagues. **B/I:** She became involved in her profession because of her personal and work experience. **H/O:** The highlight of her career was successfully increasing the sales of the business. **I/F/Y:** In five years, Ms. Brown hopes to continue in her profession.

TRACY R. BROWN
Business Manager
St. Francis of Assisi Catholic Church
8000 El Dorado Parkway
Frisco, TX 75034 United States
tbrown@stfoafrisco.org
http://www.stfoafrisco.org

BUS: Church **P/S:** Religious Services **MA:** Regional **D/D/R:** Managing Financial Operations and Accounts Payable, Processing Payroll, Maintaining Personnel Records, Configuring Reports **H/I/S:** Traveling, Scuba Diving **FBP:** Fortune; NACBA Ledger **EDU:** Pursuing Master's Degree in Nonprofit Management and Corporate Finance, University of Dallas; Bachelor of Science in Business Administration, Belhaven College, Mississippi (1999) **A/A/S:** National Association of Church Business Administration

Mr. Walter H. Brown, NCC
Guidance Counselor
Perry Hall Christian School
3919 Schroeder Avenue
Perry Hall, MD 21128 United States
waltcher@comcast.net
http://www.cambridgewhoswho.com

BUS: Counseling, Education **P/S:** Christian Education for Students in Kindergarten through 12th Grade **MA:** Local **D/D/R:** Counseling, Teaching Mathematics, Coaching Wrestling, Baseball and Soccer **H/I/S:** Spending Time with Family, Singing in the Church Choir, Counseling, Teaching **FBP:** James Dobson **EDU:** Master's Degree in Mathematics, Johns Hopkins University; Master's Degree in Administration, Clinical Psychology and Counseling, Loyola University; Bachelor's Degree in Pre-Law, University of Baltimore **A/A/S:** National Board for Certified Counselors; American Association of Christian Counselors **A/S:** He attributes his success to his love of children and counseling and the answers he has found in scripture. **B/I:** He became involved in the profession because he always wanted to teach. He began with the Baltimore Orioles baseball team, worked in an administrative position for the Federal Bureau of Investigation and then at General Motors before he began teaching. **H/O:** The most gratifying aspect of his career is finding his calling as counselor, teacher and coach.

Penny Brownfield
Special Education Teacher
Ponca City Senior High School
927 N. Fifth Street
Ponca City, OK 74601 United States
brownp@poncacity.k12.ok.us
http://www.poncacity.k12.ok.us

BUS: Public High School **P/S:** Education **MA:** Regional **D/D/R:** Teaching Developmentally Delayed, Impaired, Severe, Profound, Challenged, Autistic Kindergarten through Twelfth Grade Students and other Health Impaired Students with Attention Deficit Disorder and Attention Deficit Hyperactivity Disorder, Alternate Assessments, Individualized Education Programs **H/I/S:** Traveling, Boating, Water Skiing, Gardening, Reading **EDU:** Bachelor's Degree in Special Education, Oklahoma State University **A/A/S:** Oklahoma Education Association; Association of Classroom Teachers; Alpha Chi Omega **A/H:** Who's Who Among American High School Teachers **C/VW:** First Presbyterian Church; Chairman, Local High School Committees; Sponsor, Staff Council and Asian Club

CAROL A. BROWNLEE
Teacher
Grove Avenue School
900 S. Grove Avenue
Barrington, IL 60010 United States
carolbrownlee@earthlink.net
http://www.cambridgewhoswho.com

BUS: School **P/S:** Education **MA:** Local **EXP:** Ms. Brownlee's expertise is in primary education. **H/I/S:** Reading, Teaching a Fitness Class **EDU:** Master's Degree in Elementary Education, National-Louis University **C/VW:** PEO, Local YMCA **A/S:** She attributes her personal and professional success to her love for teaching. **B/I:** She became involved in the profession because she was inspired by her first grade teacher. **H/O:** The most gratifying aspect of her career is having children come back to thank her for her positive influence.

PATRICIA S. BRUBAKER
Family Medicine Nursing Supervisor
Luke Air Force Base Clinic
United States Air Force Medical Group 56
16044 W. Washington Street
Goodyear, AZ 85338 United States
patyjoaz@cox.net
http://www.cambridgewhoswho.com

BUS: United States Air Force, Healthcare Center **P/S:** Defense, Healthcare **MA:** Regional **D/D/R:** Training, Managing Human Resources, Overseeing Staff Development **H/I/S:** Reading, Gardening, Spending Time with her Family **FBP:** Journal for Nurses in Staff Development **EDU:** Pursuing Master's Degree in Nursing Education; Master's Degree in Human Resource Management, Webster University (2004); Bachelor of Science in Nursing, Barton College **A/H:** Training Nurse of the Year Award, Air Education and Training Demand (2005); Outstanding Program Award, United States Air Force Reserve Annual Training Program (2005)

MR. CARL A. BRUICE
National Nutrition and Agronomy Manager
Wilbur-Ellis
4703 Nicole Court
Rocklin, CA 95765 United States
cbruice@wilburellis.com
http://www.wilbur-ellis.com

BUS: Privately-Held Agricultural Chemical and Fertilizer Retail Marketing and Distribution **P/S:** Agricultural Product Marketer and Distributor, Agribusiness Division, Seed Treatments, Forestry, Nursery, Greenhouse, Vegetation Management **MA:** National **D/D/R:** Working in Crop Nutrition, Managing National Nutrition and Agronomic Resources within 20 States, Directing the Development of Prescription Crop Fertility Programs **H/I/S:** Golfing, Skiing, Working Out, Gardening **FBP:** Western Farm Press **EDU:** Master's Degree in Integrated Pest Management, University of California (1981); Bachelor of Science in Zoology, Humboldt State University (1979) **CERTS:** Certified Crop Advisor, American Society of Agronomy; Licensed Pest Control Advisor, State of California **A/A/S:** Fluid Fertilizer Foundation; Former Member, California Foundation for Agriculture in the Classroom; Former Member, California Fertilizer Research and Education Program

CAROL L. BRUMLEY
Director
King's Kids Preschool
38325 Cedar Boulevard
Newark, CA 94560 United States
cbrumagape@yahoo.com
http://www.cambridgewhoswho.com

BUS: Christian Preschool **P/S:** Early Childhood Development **MA:** Regional **D/D/R:** Teaching Reading and Literacy to Children as well as Arts and Crafts **H/I/S:** Reading, Watching Movies, Crocheting **EDU:** Bachelor of Arts in Early Childhood Development, Bethany University **A/A/S:** PACE; National Association for the Education of Young Children; Association for Christian Schools International **C/VW:** St. Jude Children's Research Hospital; Trackathon **A/S:** She attributes her success to her love for children. **B/I:** She was prompted to enter her profession because she enjoys working with children. **H/O:** The greatest aspect of her career is feeling accomplished when she sees the children succeed.

BRADLEY W. BRUNER, MD
Orthopedic Surgeon
Orthopedic and Sports Medicine at Cypress
9300 E. 29th Street
Suite 205
Wichita, KS 67226 United States
http://www.cambridgewhoswho.com

BUS: Group Medical Practice **P/S:** Sports Medicine and Arthroscopic Knee Surgery **MA:** Local **D/D/R:** Specializing in Orthopedic Surgery **H/I/S:** Golfing, Spending Quality Time with his Wife of 13 Years and Nine Children **FBP:** American Journal of Sports Medicine **EDU:** MD, University of Kansas School of Medicine (1985); Residency, University of Wisconsin-Madison **A/A/S:** Fellow, American Academy of Orthopedic Surgeons; Mid-America Orthopedic Association

HANNAH E. BRYAN
Distance Learning Instructor
Choctaw Nation of Oklahoma
16th and Locust
Durant, OK 74702 United States
hbryan@choctawnation.com
http://www.choctawnation.com

BUS: Native American Tribal Nation **P/S:** Education **MA:** Local **D/D/R:** Teaching the Choctaw Language **H/I/S:** Reading **EDU:** Master's Degree in Divinity, University of Dubuque Theological Seminary **A/A/S:** Choctaw Nation of Oklahoma **A/S:** She attributes her personal and professional success to her commitment to teaching. **B/I:** She has always had an interest in the field and a desire to teach.

LaToya N. Bryant
Patient Services Representative
Charter Oak Health Center
21 Grand Street
Hartford, CT 06112 United States
bryantangels@yahoo.com
http://www.thecharteroak.org

BUS: Nonprofit Community Healthcare **P/S:** Medical, Optical, Mental and Dental Health Services, Counseling **MA:** Regional **D/D/R:** Ensuring that Clinical Patients Receive Proper Care and Treatment, Maintaining the Patient Database, Translating Spanish and English for the Government Healthcare Center **H/I/S:** Reading Various Massage Therapy Books, Acting, Cooking, Traveling **C/VW:** Ryan White Organization

Mr. Ronald S. Bryant
Quality Assurance Chief Inspector
McEntire Joint National Guard Base
1325 S. Carolina Road
Eastover, SC 29044 United States
ronald.bryant@scmcen.ang.af.mil
http://www.scang.ang.af.mil

BUS: Military National Guard Base **P/S:** Aircraft Inspections and Maintenance **MA:** International **EXP:** Mr. Bryant's expertise is in quality inspection. **D/D/R:** Acting as the Quality Assurance Chief Inspector and First Sergeant **H/I/S:** Yard Work, Fishing, Playing the Guitar and Piano **EDU:** Industry-Related Training and Experience **CERTS:** Registered Barber, State of South Carolina **A/H:** Family of the Year, South Carolina Air National Guard (2005) **C/VW:** Assisted Living Programs; Volunteer Pastor, Singer, Speaker, Generations Home for Assisted Living, Chapin, SC **DOB:** November 22, 1955 **POB:** Columbia **SP:** Diane **CHILD:** Shawn, Christian, Kelli **A/S:** He attributes his success to his faith in God. **B/I:** He became involved in his profession because he decided he belonged in the National Guard and continued to pursue a career there. **H/O:** The highlight of his career was being named the 2005 Family of the Year. **I/F/Y:** In five years, Mr. Bryant hopes to be retired from the National Guard and working full-time in ministry.

CHERYL BRYANT BRUCE, MD
President, Medical Director, Owner
Elite Personal Physician Services, Inc.
9663 Santa Monica Boulevard, Suite 446
Beverly Hills, CA 90210 United States
doctorbb@elitepersonalphysician.com
http://www.elitepersonalphysician.com

BUS: Healthcare Facility, Wellness Management and Personal Improvement Consultant **P/S:** Leading Personal Private Physician Providing Excellent Patient and Healthcare Services Including Anti-Aging, Aesthetics, Personal Improvement and Image Management, Traveling to Clients' Location of Choice for On-Site Services **MA:** Regional **D/D/R:** Managing Wellness, Travelling to Patients' Homes and Offices **H/I/S:** Professional Entertaining, Dancing, Acting **FBP:** American Family Physicians; Journal of the American Medical Association; Journal of Family Practice **EDU:** Fellowship in Family Development, Morehouse School of Medicine (1997); Residency in Family Practice, Morehouse School of Medicine (1994-1996); Internship, Army Hospital, Fort Bragg (1989); MD, Tufts University (1989) **A/A/S:** American Medical Association; American Academy of Family Physicians; American College of Physician Executives; National Association for Female Executives; National Medical Association; American Association of Anti-Aging Medicine; Diplomat, American Board of Family Medicine; Diplomat, American Association of Hyperbaric Medicine **A/H:** Strathmore's Who's Who; National Who's Who; International Who's Who; Outstanding Young Women of America

JOSEPHINE MARY BUCCAFUSCO DEVITO, PH.D., RN
Assistant Professor
Seton Hall University - College of Nursing
400 South Orange Avenue
South Orange, NJ 07748 United States
JosDeVito@aol.com
http://www.shu.edu

BUS: College of Nursing **P/S:** Education **MA:** National **D/D/R:** Offering Maternal Child Nursing Education **H/I/S:** Reading, Playing Guitar **FBP:** Journal of Gerontological Nursing; American Journal of Maternal Child Nursing **EDU:** Ph.D. in Nursing Research, New York University (2005); Master of Science in Nursing, Seton Hall College (1985); Registered Nurse, Seton Hall College of Nursing (1978) **CERTS:** Certified School Nurse, State of New Jersey **A/A/S:** Sigma Theta Tau International; President-Elect, Gamma Nu Chapter; New Jersey Nurses Association; American Nurses Association; Eastern Nursing Research Society

VALERIA M. BUCK
Paramedic
Nashville Fire Department
500 Second Avenue N.
Nashville, TN 37201 United States
valeria.buck@cwwemail.com
http://www.cambridgewhoswho.com

BUS: Fire Department **P/S:** Fire and Emergency Rescue Services **MA:** Regional **D/D/R:** Caring for Patients, Teaching a Advanced Wilderness Life Support Course, Overseeing Emergency Rescue and Paramedic Services **H/I/S:** Backpacking, Camping, Hiking, Horseback Riding, Photography, Sketching, Reading, Spending Time with her Grandchildren **FBP:** Journal of Emergency Medical Services **EDU:** Associate of Science in Emergency Medical Technology, Hocking College **CERTS:** Certification in Advanced Wilderness Life Support (2007) **A/A/S:** International Association of Fire Fighters **C/VW:** National Audubon Society; Wilderness Society; St. Jude Children's Research Hospital; Susan G. Komen for the Cure **A/S:** She attributes her success to her hard work and dedication. **B/I:** She became involved in her profession because of her work experience. **H/O:** The most gratifying aspect of her career is seeing her patients recovery.

LISA LYNN BUCZYNSKI, OTR/L
Occupational Therapist
Meadowcrest Nursing Center
1200 Brawn Road
Bethel Park, PA 15102 United States
heineck464@yahoo.com
http://www.cambridgewhoswho.com

BUS: Healthcare Center **P/S:** Long-Term Care **MA:** Local **D/D/R:** Coordinating Facility Rehabilitation, Performing Occupational Therapy, Offering Long-Term Care **EDU:** Master's Degree in Occupational Therapy, Duquesne University; Bachelor's Degree in Health Sciences **A/A/S:** Pennsylvania Occupational Therapists Association, American Occupational Therapists Association **A/S:** She attributes her personal and professional success to her hard work. **B/I:** She has always had an interest in the field and a desire to help others. **H/O:** The highlight of her career is helping people everyday.

MR. GREGORY L. BUELL
Professor
Chemeketa Community College
500 N. Hill Road
McMinnville, OR 97128 United States
gregory.buell@comcast.net
http://www.cambridgewhoswho.com

BUS: College **P/S:** Higher Education **MA:** Regional **D/D/R:** Teaching Grammar, Composition and Writing, Developing Reading and Spelling Curricula, Offering Education Consulting for Companies **H/I/S:** Practicing Martial Arts, Boxing, Playing Soccer and Softball, Golfing, Bowling **EDU:** Master's Degree in Teaching, Lewis & Clark, Portland, OR (1984) **A/A/S:** Chemeketa Adjunct Professors Association; Oregon Education Association; National Education Association **A/H:** Teacher of the Year Award (1997) **DOB:** September 1, 1948 **CHILD:** Luke, Justine, Kaitlan **W/H:** Chemeketa Community College (1994-2007); Western Oregon University (1992-1994); Linn-Benton Community College (1990-1992); Clark College (1986-1987); Portland Community College (1984-1985); Covington Middle School (1983-1979); Vancouver Public Schools (1976-1979) **I/F/Y:** In five years, Mr. Buell hopes to write another book.

JANINE MICHELLE BUGGLE, RN, BSN
Registered Nurse
Jersey Shore University Medical Center
1945 Carlies Ave
Neptune, NJ 07753 United States
bahbuggs@optonline.net
http://www.mycmsite.com/janinebuggle

BUS: Hospital **P/S:** Healthcare **MA:** Local **EXP:** Ms. Buggle's expertise is in neonatal intensive care. **H/I/S:** Tennis, Hiking, Scrap Booking, Creative Memories Consultant **FBP:** Sigma Theta Tau International Nursing Journal **EDU:** Bachelor of Science in Nursing, University of Rhode Island **A/A/S:** Sigma Theta Tau International **A/S:** She attributes her success to being a strong patient advocate and believing in the importance of the work she does. **B/I:** She became involved in her profession because she had always liked the medical field and children. **H/O:** The highlights of her career were passing the state boards and being recognized for a project on pain scales for neonates that she is working on.

PAMELA K. BUIE-ELL-PROKOP
Owner, President
Affordable Cleaning
8900 S.W. Sweek Drive Unit 517
Tualafin, OR 97062 United States
ellees@comcast.net
http://www.cambridgewhoswho.com

BUS: Cleaning Company **P/S:** Cleaning of Businesses and Homes **MA:** Local **D/D/R:** Cleaning, Assisting Customers **H/I/S:** Boston Terrier Puppies, Gardening **EDU:** Diploma, Canby Union High School **C/VW:** Veterans, Foster Parents **A/S:** She attributes her success to her hard work, determination and dependability. **B/I:** She became involved in her profession because she got divorced and needed a job to support her children. She started cleaning for a construction company and eventually was able to open her own business. **H/O:** The highlight of her career was owning her own business.

APRIL S. BULGER, BA
Owner
Visionary Venture, LLC
New York, NY United States
abulger@visionaryventure.biz
http://www.cambridgewhoswho.com

BUS: Event Management Company **P/S:** Event Planning **MA:** Regional **D/D/R:** Planning Events for Large Scare Corporate, Nonprofit and Social Events **H/I/S:** Traveling, Photography, Fine Dining, Participating in Outdoor Activities **FBP:** Cranes; The Chronicle of Philanthropy; Biz Bash; Forbes **EDU:** Bachelor's Degree in Communications, Virginia Union University (1995) **A/A/S:** Manager in Commissioners Office, National Basketball Association; Alpha Kappa Alpha

JESSICA R. BULLARD
Human Resources Generalist
District 4
King County Public Hospital
9575 Ethan Wade Way S.E.
Snoqualmine, WA 98065 United States
jessicab@snoqualmiehospital.org
http://www.snoqualmiehospital.org

BUS: Hospital **P/S:** 24-Hour Emergency Room, Geropsychiatric Unit, Cardiopulmonary Clinic, Digital X-rays and Computed Tomography Scans, On-Site Laboratory Services, Outpatient Surgery, Specialty Clinics and Services, Bone Density Clinic **MA:** Local **EXP:** Ms. Bullard's areas of expertise are in administration and human resources. **D/D/R:** Hiring and Training Employees, Advertising, Interfacing with Employers and Employees, Handling Benefits, Making Presentations **H/I/S:** Baseball, Basketball, Reading Murder Mysteries **FBP:** HR **EDU:** Master of Business Administration, Keller Graduate School of Management (2007); Bachelor's Degree in Business Administration, Central Washington University (2005) **CERTS:** Certified Human Resources Professional, The Keller Graduate School of Management **A/A/S:** Society for Human Resource Management

JOHN W. BULLIS
Managing Director
Southern Pines Women's Health Center
145 Applecross Road
Southern Pines, NC 28374 United States
wjbullis@spwhc.com
http://www.cambridgewhoswho.com

BUS: Healthcare Center **P/S:** Healthcare Including Obstetrics and Gynecology Surgery and Pelvic Reconstruction Care Services **MA:** Local **D/D/R:** Practicing Obstetrics and Gynecology **H/I/S:** Golfing, Playing Tennis **FBP:** Green Journal **EDU:** MD, Georgetown University, Madigan Army Medical Center **A/A/S:** North Carolina Medical Society; American College of Obstetricians and Gynecologists; American Medical Association; American Urogynecologic Society **C/VW:** United Way

B.H. 'BART' BUNTING
Account Executive (Retired)
Milne and BNC Insurance Service
1750 E. Glendale Avenue
Phoenix, AZ 85020 United States
bbunting@milnebnc.com
http://www.milnebnc.com

BUS: Insurance Brokerage Firm **P/S:** Commercial Insurance, Bonds, Employee Benefits, Personal Insurance, Claims Management, Risk Control **MA:** Local **D/D/R:** Working with Troubled Accounts and Hard-to-Place Express and Surplus Lines **H/I/S:** Dancing, Golfing, Practicing Fitness **FBP:** Golf Digest **EDU:** Diploma, Libbey High School **CERTS:** Certified Insurance Counselor; LUTC **A/A/S:** Independent Insurance Agents Group **C/VW:** First Christian Church **A/S:** He attributes his success to discipline and perseverance. **B/I:** He became involved in his profession because of his interest in insurance. **H/O:** The highlight of his career was earning his current position.

CARMELLA A. BURDI
GIS Analyst
Argonne National Laboratory
9700 S. Cass Avenue
Argonne, IL 60439 United States
cburdi@anl.gov
http://www.cambridgewhoswho.com

BUS: Department of Energy **P/S:** Research **MA:** National **EXP:** Ms. Burdi's expertise is in geographic information systems. **H/I/S:** Reading, Spending Time with Family and Two Chocolate Labs **EDU:** Bachelor's Degree in Geographic and Environmental Planning, Elmhurst College; Pursuing Master's Degree in Geographic Information Systems **A/A/S:** Geospatial Information and Technology Association; ESRI **C/VW:** Planned Parenthood, Make a Wish Foundation **A/S:** She attributes her success to having the opportunity to work with great professionals and mentors throughout her career. **B/I:** She became involved in her profession because she took a course in geography in college and really got interested in it. **H/O:** The highlight of her career is her current position.

LEAH CHAMP BURDICK
Teacher
Henry A. Wolcott School
71 Wolcott Road
West Hartford, CT 06110 United States
lilchamp@hotmail.com
http://www.cambridgewhoswho.com

BUS: Public, Higher Order Thinking- Arts Based School **P/S:** Education **MA:** Local **EXP:** Ms. Burdick's expertise includes communication, Spanish and videography. **H/I/S:** Swimming, Bicycle, Running **EDU:** Master of Education, Concentration in Instructional Technology, American InterContinental University; Bachelor of Arts in Visual Arts, Wheelock College **A/A/S:** Wheelock Alumni Association; National Education Association **A/S:** She attributes her career success to her dedication to finishing what she starts. **B/I:** She became involved in her profession after working in a preschool and deciding to pursue a career in education. **H/O:** The highlight of her career was obtaining her master's degree.

JANIE BUREL
Associate Broker
RE/MAX Greater Atlanta 400/Lanier
1100 Turner Road
Cumming, GA 30041 United States
burel@alltel.net
http://www.mylakelady.com

BUS: Real Estate Company **P/S:** Real Estate Services **MA:** Local **D/D/R:** Buying and Selling Residential and Commercial Properties, Recruiting Agents, Facilitating Relocations **H/I/S:** Flower Gardening, Bicycling, Practicing Pilates, Snow Skiing, Water Sports **FBP:** The Realtor; Mark Leader Literature; Mr. Internet Literature **EDU:** Coursework in Leadership, Brian Buffini and Company (2007); Master's Degree in Real Estate Brokerage (2005); Bachelor's Degree in Elementary Education, Toccoa Falls College (1973) **CERTS:** Senior Real Estate Specialist (2007); e-Pro Certified Realtor (2004); Certified Real Estate Consultant (1993); Certified Residential Broker (1990); Certified Residential Specialist (1990) **A/A/S:** Graduate Realtors Institute (1991); Leader, Women's Council; 400 North Board of Realtors; Georgia State Board of Realtors; National Association of Realtors **A/H:** Phoenix Award **C/VW:** Susan G. Komen for the Cure

MARY ANN BURGESS, LPN
Licensed Practical Nurse
Self-Employed
717 Taylor Street
Chelsea, MI 48118 United States
http://www.cambridgewhoswho.com

BUS: Proven Leader in the Healthcare Industry **P/S:** Healthcare Services **MA:** Local **D/D/R:** Offering Home Care Nursing **H/I/S:** Spending Quality Time with her Grandchildren **CERTS:** Licensed Practical Nurse Degree, Ann Arbor Practical Nurse Center **A/A/S:** Michigan Licensed Practical Nurse Association; Representative, Catholic Council on Aging

RUTH J. BURGUS
Registered Nurse
Banner Mesa Medical Center
1010 N. Country Club Drive
Mesa, AZ 85201 United States
julieburgus@aol.com
http://www.cambridgewhoswho.com

BUS: Hospital **P/S:** Healthcare **MA:** National **EXP:** Ms. Burgus' expertise is in oncology. **FBP:** Nurses Week **EDU:** Nurses Degree, Iowa Methodist, School of Nursing **C/VW:** American Cancer Society; Salvation Army; Susan G. Komen Breast Cancer Foundation **A/S:** She attributes her success to her dedication and a strong work ethic. **B/I:** She became involved in her profession because she likes people and loves to help people. **H/O:** The highlight of her career has been being a preceptor.

SUSAN M. BURK
Staff Assistant
Alltel
1 Allied Drive
Little Rock, AR 72202 United States
whiasian@gmail.com
http://www.cambridgewhoswho.com

BUS: Telecommunications Company **P/S:** corporate Cellular Phones **MA:** National **D/D/R:** Overseeing Customer Service **H/I/S:** Watching Movies, Relaxing, Spending Time with her Four Children, Computers **EDU:** Pursuing Bachelor's Degree in Information Technology, University of Phoenix; Associate Degree in Business Technology, Remington College **A/A/S:** Team Alltel **C/VW:** The Salvation Army **A/S:** She attributes her success to her drive. **B/I:** She became involved in her profession because she started in the wire live side of the business and then developed a broader knowledge of wireless communications. **H/O:** The most gratifying aspect of her career is the knowledge she has gained. She consistently goes above and beyond and enjoys the recognition from her peers and coworkers.

EVELYN F. BURKE
Owner/Videographer
P.H.C. Audio-Video/Comcast
44 Lisa Lane
Mashpee, MA 02649 United States
phcav@juno.com

BUS: Video Service Provider **P/S:** Videos and CDs (Audio), Post Production **MA:** Local **D/D/R:** Editing Post Production **H/I/S:** Gardening and Crafts **EDU:** Pursuing Bachelor of Arts in Visual Communications, American InterContinental University Online **A/A/S:** American Home Builders **C/VW:** Local Church; Good Samaritan; The Salvation Army; Feed the Children

JULI A. BURKS, RN, BSN, CCRC
Registered Nurse
Cardio-Thoracic Surgeons, P.C.
48 Medical Park E. Drive
Suite 151
Birmingham, AL 35235 United States
jburks@cardio-thoracic.com
http://www.cambridgewhoswho.com

BUS: Healthcare Research **P/S:** Research **MA:** International **H/I/S:** Reading, Traveling **FBP:** Association of Clinical Research Professionals **EDU:** Bachelor of Science in Nursing, Rockford College **CERTS:** Certified Clinical Research Coordinator, Association of Clinical Research Professionals **A/A/S:** Association of Clinical Research Professionals **C/VW:** Clear Branch United Methodist Church **A/S:** She attributes her career success to her excellent upbringing, her intrinsic motivation and competitive spirit, to her desire to be a better person, and to her ability to work quickly and accurately. **B/I:** After beginning her career as a licensed practical nurse, she wanted to pursue positions that would offer her better options, so she marketed herself well and moved up through the ranks. **H/O:** She feels that receiving her certification in Critical Care Nursing has been the highlight of her career.

REV. ELIZABETH BURNETT
Pastor
Tree of Life Church
702 E. Harry Street
Wichita, KS 67211 United States
hannahotrod@att.net
http://www.cambridgewhoswho.com

BUS: Church **P/S:** Religious Services **MA:** Regional **D/D/R:** Offering Spiritual Counseling, Pastoring Adults and Unmarried Individuals **EDU:** Master's Degree in Psychology, Northwest Nazarene University (1941); Bachelor of Science in Psychology, Northwest Nazarene University **A/A/S:** Red Hat Society; Business and Professional Women's Club **C/VW:** Organic Gardening Club; Eagle Lodge; Black Captain Society

DEE ANN BURNS
Vice Chairwoman
Travis County Republican Party
deeannburns@sbcglobal.net
http://www.cambridgewhoswho.com

BUS: Political Party **P/S:** Public Services **MA:** Regional **D/D/R:** Managing Political Operations, Handling Public Relations, Electing Candidates to Republican Office **H/I/S:** Spending Time with her Family, Volunteering Community Services, Shopping **FBP:** National Republican Party **EDU:** Bachelor of Arts in Business Administration, University of Houston, TX (1974) **A/A/S:** Chairwoman, Seaton Golf (2007); National Community of Republicans; National Federation of Women; Travis County Republican Committee; Lake Travis Men's Club **C/VW:** Seaton Sisters of Charity; Emmaus Catholic Church **A/S:** She attributes her success to her hard work and people management skills. **B/I:** She became involved in her profession because she has always been motivated politically and has strong Republican values. **H/O:** The highlight of her career was being elected for two terms in a historically male club.

NORMA L. BURNS
Owner, Operator
Many-Stars Collectibles
PO Box 5517
Kalispell, MT 59903 United States
many_stars@centurytel.net
http://www.manystarscollectibles.com

BUS: Retail Store **P/S:** Vintage Dolls, Figurines, Toys, Sports Memorabilia Items, Star Wars Collectibles **MA:** Local **EXP:** Ms. Burns' expertise is in sales and marketing. **H/I/S:** Camping, Hiking, Listening to Music, Playing the Piano, Reading, Gourmet Cooking, Baking **FBP:** Doll Reader; Collector's Digest; Toy Shop; Entrepreneur; Sports Illustrated **EDU:** Coursework in Business Relations, Marketing, Public Speaking and Economics **A/H:** Retail Sales Award, Avon Products (1967-1968) **C/VW:** Toys for Tots; The Salvation Army **W/H:** Sales Representative, Con-Stan Industries (1969-1972) **A/S:** She attributes her success to her customer service skills. **B/I:** She became involved in her profession because she wanted to display all her collectibles.

Dr. Frank R. Burrelli
Corporate Pilot, Evangelist
Frank Burrelli Evangelistic Ministries, Inc.
830 Santa Barbara Boulevard
Cape Coral, FL 33991 United States
drburrelli@inbarq.com
http://www.cambridgewhoswho.com

BUS: Ministry **P/S:** Religious Services **MA:** Local **D/D/R:** Using Illusions as Illustrations while Preaching **H/I/S:** Traveling **EDU:** Doctor of Theology, Gulf Shore Baptist Seminary (1990); Master of Divinity, New Orleans Baptist Theological Seminary **A/A/S:** Southern Baptist Evangelist Association; Southern Baptist Convention; Lieutenant, United States Coast Guard Auxiliary; Chaplain, Former Board Member, Sheriff Department **A/H:** Who's Who Christian Leadership Award (1989)

Sabrina Burrow
Director, Owner
Burrow's Child Development Center, Inc.
110 W. Bank Street
Petersburg, VA 23803 United States
sbu7852921@aol.com
http://www.cambridgewhoswho.com

BUS: Child Care and Learning Center **P/S:** Advancement of Children **D/D/R:** Offering Childcare and Child Development Services for Two to 12-Year-Old Children, Overseeing Programs, Meals and Transportation, Ensuring the Safety of 50 Children **H/I/S:** Computers, Reading **FBP:** Industry-Related Literature **EDU:** Associate Degree in Early Childhood Education, John Tyler Community College **CERTS:** Licensed Childcare Provider, State of Virginia **A/A/S:** Parent-Teacher Association

JENNIFER L. BURTON
Vice President, Geoscientist
Griffis
1001 Fannin Street, Suite 3875
Houston, TX 77002 United States
jburton@rgriffis.com
http://www.anadarko.com

BUS: Exploration, Production **P/S:** Upstream Oil and Gas, Exploration and Production Energy **MA:** Statewide **EXP:** Ms. Burton's expertise is in strategic planning. **H/I/S:** Playing with her Son, Traveling **FBP:** The Wall Street Journal **EDU:** Master's Degree in Geoscience, University of North Carolina; Bachelor of Science in Geology, University of Memphis **A/A/S:** American Association of Petroleum; Houston World Affairs Council; Association of Women Geoscientists **C/VW:** Humane Society; American Cancer Society **A/S:** She attributes her success to her professors who educated her all the way. **B/I:** She became involved in her profession because she was always interested in science. **H/O:** The highlight of her career was earning her current position.

BECKI G. BURTSCHER
Chief Executive Officer
Live Longer at Home Health Care Services, Inc.
313 W. Oak Street
Arcadia, FL 34266 United States
beckyg1@aol.com
http://www.cambridgewhoswho.com

BUS: Home Healthcare Agency **P/S:** Healthcare Including Medical Services for Daily Living Activities, Transportation Services **MA:** Local **D/D/R:** Analyzing Financial Strategies, Managing Employees, Overseeing Business Development Operations, Marketing **EDU:** Master of Business Administration, University of Phoenix (2001) **A/A/S:** Chairwomen, Florida Disaster Management Team for Home Health Care; Kettle Women's Association of Florida; American Association for Health Freedom; Associated Home Health Industries of Florida; American Quarter Horse Association **A/H:** Honorary Chairman Award, Business Advisory Council (2007) **A/S:** She attributes her success to her faith in God and the support she receives from her grandfather and mentor.

NANCY J. BUSH
Fifth Grade Teacher
Fuerte Elementary School
11625 Fuerte Drive
El Cajon, CA 92020 United States
bush@cajonValley.net
http://www.cajonValley.net/Fuerte

BUS: Elementary School **P/S:** Education **MA:** Local **D/D/R:** Teaching Mathematics, Writing, Social Studies and Physical Education, Mentoring and Assisting New Teachers **H/I/S:** Traveling, Cycling, Hiking, Exercising at the Gym, Gardening **FBP:** The Commander **EDU:** Master's Degree in Curriculum and Instruction, San Diego State University; Bachelor's Degree in Liberal Studies, San Diego State University **CERTS:** Certified Gifted and Talented Educator; Certified in English as a Second Language **A/A/S:** National Council of Teachers of Mathematics; Beginning Teacher Support and Assessment, California Department of Education **C/VW:** Local Church

CHLETA D. BUTLER, MHA
Department Administrator
Southern California Permanent Medical Group
1011 Baldwin Park Boulevard
Baldwin Park, CA 91706 United States
chleta.d.butler@kp.org
http://www.kaiserpermanente.org

BUS: Health System **P/S:** Healthcare **MA:** National **D/D/R:** Overseeing Administrative Duties **H/I/S:** Reading, Writing Poetry, Swimming, Renovating her Home **FBP:** The Permanente Journal **EDU:** Master's Degree in Health Administration, University of Phoenix (2007); Bachelor of Arts in Liberal Studies, The California State University (1994); Associate of Science, Southwestern Christian College, TX **A/A/S:** President, Kaiser Permanente Asian Association **A/H:** Three-Time Recipient, Management Leadership Award (2006); Three-Time Recipient, Top Dog Award; Puffball Award **C/VW:** Church Women United, Los Angeles; Habitat for Humanity **DOB:** September 13, 1959 **POB:** Los Angeles, CA

WENDY S. BUTLER, ESQ.
W. Butler Legal Services, LLC
11330 Lakefield Drive
Building 2, Suite 200
Johns Creek, GA 30097 United States
wbutler@wsblegal.com
http://www.cambridgewhoswho.com

BUS: Law Firm **P/S:** Full Range of Legal Services in Real Estate Law, Including the Areas of Real Estate Acquisition, Planning, Development, Financing, Investment **MA:** Regional **D/D/R:** Overseeing Real Property and Environmental Development, Regulatory and Transactional Litigation **H/I/S:** Biking, Yoga **FBP:** Atlanta Business Chronicle **EDU:** JD, Chicago Kent College of Law (1999) **A/A/S:** Executive Board, John's Creek Chamber of Commerce; Atlanta Bar Association; Georgia Bar Association; Greater North Fulton Chamber of Commerce; John's Creek Area Council; Chairwoman, Economic Development Community; John's Creek Rotary

JENNIFER M. BUTTERFIELD
Vice President
Tim Butterfield Drilling, Inc.
395 Reed Street
Somerset, WI 54025 United States
butterfielddrilling@hotmail.com
http://www.cambridgewhoswho.com

BUS: Proven Leader in the Field of Water Well Drilling **P/S:** High Quality Services Including Drilling Water Wells and Pumping Repairs **MA:** Regional **D/D/R:** Overseeing All Paperwork and Financial Aspects of the Water Well Drilling and Pump Repairing Business, Bookkeeping, Offering Customer Contact and Customer Services, Managing Company Marketing and Advertising **H/I/S:** Golfing, Spending Time with her Children **FBP:** Fleet Owner **EDU:** College Coursework **A/A/S:** Former Senior Airman, United States Air Force (1999-2005); Republican National Committee; Republican Senatorial Inner Circle; Business Advisor Council for State of Wisconsin

MR. BOBBY G. BUTZKE
Construction Manager
CB&I
2103 Research Forest Drive
The Woodlands, TX 77380 United States
bbutzke@cbi.com
http://www.cbi.com

BUS: Engineering, Procurement and Construction Company **P/S:** Industrial Refinery Work Including Capital and Maintenance Projects and Turnkey Projects, Specialization in Projects for Customers that Produce, Process, Store and Distribute the World's Natural Resources **MA:** International **D/D/R:** Managing Turnaround Projects, Working with Engineering Procurement Construction, Following Projects from their Inception to Completion, Overseeing a Staff of 50 to 750 Employees **H/I/S:** Competitive Clog Dancing, Woodworking, Creating Stained Glass Work **EDU:** Coursework in Engineering, North Harris Community College **CERTS:** Certified Judge, National Clogging Organization **A/A/S:** Director, Clog Dancing Team **DOB:** April 19, 1971

DENNIS R. BUZZATTO
Owner
Buzzatto Flooring
PO Box 731
Bridgeville, PA 15017 United States
dennis.buzzatto@cwwemail.com
http://www.cambridgewhoswho.com

BUS: Home Improvement Company **P/S:** Installation of Carpets for Residential and Commercial Properties **MA:** Pennsylvania **D/D/R:** Consulting, Carpeting, Managing Operations, Ensuring Customer Satisfaction **EDU:** High School Diploma **CHILD:** Jarrod

DIANE BYNUM, MS, LAC, LADC
Associate Director
Horizon Adolescent Treatment Program
Western Arkansas Guidance and Counseling Center
3113 S. 70th Street
Fort Smith, AR 72903 United States
diane_bynum@wacgc.org
http://www.cambridgewhoswho.com

BUS: Counseling Center **P/S:** Mental Health Substance Abuse Treatment, Family and Adolescent Therapy **MA:** Local **D/D/R:** Treating 13-18 Year-Old Children for Concurrent Disorders, Diagnosing Clients, Overseeing Screening and Assessments, Marketing **H/I/S:** Walking, Boating, Camping with her Family, Enjoying Nature, Tennis **FBP:** Addiction **EDU:** Master's Degree in Community Counseling and Family Therapy; Bachelor of Science in Organizational Management, John Brown University **CERTS:** Licensed in Marriage, Family and Community Counseling, John Brown University (2007); Master's Level Certified Substance Abuse Counselor; Licensed Associate Counselor; Certified Drug Abuse Counselor **A/A/S:** Former President and Vice President, Arkansas Association of Alcohol and Drug Abuse Counselors; Alcoholism and Substance Abuse Providers

PROF. WILLIAM J. BYRNES
Dean
College of Performing and Visual Arts
Southern Utah University
351 W. University Boulevard
Cedar City, UT 84720 United States
byrnes@suu.edu
http://www.suu.edu/pva

BUS: University **P/S:** Higher Education **MA:** Local **D/D/R:** Overseeing Braithwaite Fine Arts Gallery, Conducting Seminars in the Arts Administration Program, Developing the Curriculum, Overseeing the Art, Design, Music, Theater and Dance Departments **H/I/S:** Hiking, Biking **FBP:** BusinessWeek; MIT Sloan Management Journal; Management Review **EDU:** Master's Degree in Fine Arts, University of California, Los Angeles (1972); Bachelor's Degree in English, University of New Mexico (1970) **A/A/S:** Association of Arts Administration Educators; Association for Theater in Higher Education; National Theater Conference; United States Institute for Theater Technology; Board of Governors, Utah Shakespearean Festival; Board Member, Entertainment Services and Technology Association **DOB:** January 1, 1947 **SP:** Christine **CHILD:** Alison, Emily, Matt **C/A:** Fellow and Former President, United States Institute for Theater Technology (2000-2002)

Melissa Cabre Piovanetti, AIA

Principal Architect
MCP Group
1767 Jesus T. Pinero Avenue
San Juan, PR 00920 United States
cabre@mcpgroup.net
http://www.mcpgroup.net
http://www.cambridgewhoswho.com

BUS: Architectural Design and Consulting Firm **P/S:** Residential Design Services for Residential Complexes, Commercial and Mixed-Use Buildings **MA:** Regional **D/D/R:** Designing Commercial and Residential Structures **H/I/S:** Playing Racquetball, Walking, Enjoying Nature and her Dogs **FBP:** Architectural Record; Urban Land Institute Publications; Interior Design **EDU:** Bachelor's Degree in Architecture, Syracuse University (1994); Coursework, One Year Abroad Design Program, Florence, Italy **A/S:** She attributes her success to the strong passion she has for her work.

John M. Cade, Ed.D.

Associate Vice President
Tennessee State University
1239 General George Patton Road
Nashville, TN 37221 United States
cade1239@comcast.net
jcade@tnstate.edu
http://www.tnstate.edu

BUS: Time-Honored Leader in Higher Education **P/S:** Comprehensive, Urban, Coeducational Land-Grant University Offering 45 Bachelor's Degrees and 24 Master Degrees, Doctoral Programs Including Biological Sciences, Psychology, Public Administration, Computer Information Systems Engineering, Administration and Supervision, Curriculum and Instruction **MA:** Regional **D/D/R:** Managing Enrollment **EDU:** Doctorate of Education, Tennessee State University (1998) **A/A/S:** National Association for the Care and Resettlement of Offenders; Scottish Association for the Care and Resettlement of Offenders; TACRO

MS. JAYNE L. CAFARO, MH

1) President 2) President 3) President
1) Authentic Herbs and Vitamins 2) Cafaro Studios
3) Atek-Art Technology
214 Daniel Road N.
North Massapequa, NY 11758 United States
jaynecafaro@gmail.com
http://www.cambridgewhoswho.com

BUS: 1) Nutritional and Herbal Supplement Retail and Consulting Company 2) Movie Production Studio 3) Graphic Design Studio **P/S:** 1) Herb and Vitamin Sales and Consultations 2) Movie, Film and Music Productions, Editing Services 3) Art, Design, Computer Graphics, Illustration, Logo Design, Advertising Services **MA:** 1) National 2) Regional 3) Regional **EXP:** Ms. Cafaro's expertise is in herbology, graphic design, technical illustration and movie production. **H/I/S:** Designing a Custom Classic Racing Car, Caring for her Pets, Studying Herbal Remedies for Dogs and Cats, Food Connoisseur, Cooking Exotic Gourmet Dishes, Victorian-Style Decorating, Organic Herbal and Vegetable Gardening, Taking Nature Walks to Empower Both the Body And Soul, Painting in Oil Acrylics and Watercolors, Creating Ceramics, Making Crafts, Dancing, Singing, Swimming, Bicycling, Sleigh Riding, Playing Badminton and Ping Pong, Conducting Television Interviews for News 12 of Long Island **FBP:** AAIM Journal; The Herb Quarterly; The Artist's Magazine; Professional Photographer; Advanced Photoshop **EDU:** Master's Degree in Herbal Studies, College of Herbal Education (2007); Coursework, Nassau County Citizens Police Academy (1998); Coursework in Computer Graphics, State University of New York, Farmingdale (1993); Associate in Applied Science in Advertising Art and Design, The State University of New York (1974) **CERTS:** Certified Master Herbalist, College of Herbal Education (2008); Certified Nutritional Herbologist, The School of Natural Healing (2006); Certified Family Herbalist, The School of Natural Healing (2005); Certification, Community Emergency Response Team, Nassau County Office of Emergency Management; Certification in Fine Art and Calligraphy, with a Concentration in Copperplate and Gilding with 24 Karat Gold Leaf, Long Island Scribes; Certification, First Aid for Dogs and Cats; Certificate of Training, Nassau County Police Department; Certification in Law and Jurisprudence **A/A/S:** Official Photographer, Nassau County Citizens Police Academy; Television News 12 Long Island; Nassau County Police Academy Alumni Association, Nassau County Police Department; Nassau County Police Commissioner James H. Lawrence; American Association of Integrative Medicine; The Herb Society of America; Integrative Practitioner; National Health and Wellness Organization; Creative Arts Home Association; Oldsmobile Club of America; Long Island Cat Fanciers Club; Charter Member, International Society of Artists **A/H:** Certificate of Recognition, Outstanding Hard Work and Commitment to Making a Difference in the Lives of the People Of Nassau County, Nassau County Legislature; Third Place Trophy, National Trust for Historic Preservation; First and Second Prize Award, Best Recipes, The Cooks Guild; Certificate of Appreciation, American Association of Integrative Medicine **C/VW:** Community Emergency Response Team, Nassau County Office of Emergency Management; Historic Preservation Society; The American Society for the Prevention of Cruelty to Animals **DOB:** November 2, 1954 **POB:** New York, NY **SP:** DVD Producer, 'Memories Before Retirement,' **W/H:** Graphic Design Artist, Illustrator, Volt Information Sciences, Syosset, NY (1994-1998); Creative Computer Designer, Nynex Yellow Pages Clients (1994-1998); Technical Illustrator, Cartographer, Vantage Art, Massapequa (1983-1992); Art Director, Town & Country Kitchens, Farmingdale, NY (1978-1983); Graphic Artist, Illustrator, Valdes Art, Westbury, NY (1974-1983) **I/F/Y:** In five years, Ms. Cafaro hopes to continue to push boundaries, further her horizons and pursue her life-long goal of making society a better place to live.

TRACI LAVERNE CAIN-TIGGS

AP Coordinator, Science Teacher
East High School
474 Bennington Avenue
Youngstown, OH 44505 United States
TraciLTiggs@msn.com
http://www.cambridgewhoswho.com

BUS: High School **P/S:** Education **MA:** Local **D/D/R:** Specializing in Science Curriculum, Instruction and Administration **H/I/S:** Reading, Traveling **FBP:** Journal of Chemical Education **EDU:** Pursuing Master's Degree in Administration, Youngstown University; Master's Degree in Chemistry and Education, Youngstown University; Bachelor's Degree in Chemistry and Education, Youngstown University **A/A/S:** National Science Teachers Association; State and Local National Education Association; American Chemistry Society; Delta Sigma Theta **A/S:** She attributes her success to her spiritual and ethical values. **B/I:** She became involved in this profession because she was always interested in the field and found out she enjoyed it as a peer tutor in college. **H/O:** The highlight of her career is her nomination for the Teacher of the Year Award (2004-2005).

DOLORES C. CALAF
Director-Lawrence Regional Center
Cambridge College
60 Island Street
Lawrence, MA 01840 United States
dolores.calaf@cc.edu
http://www.cambridgewhoswho.com

BUS: Educational Center **P/S:** Education, Degree/Non-Degree Programs, Accelerated Focused Learning **MA:** Regional **D/D/R:** Overseeing the Center and Academic Calendar, Staffing **H/I/S:** Tennis, Dancing, Traveling, Music **FBP:** ATA Chronicle; Hispanic Magazine **EDU:** Master's Degree in Media, Emerson College **A/A/S:** American Translator Association; Board Member, Museum of Science; Chamber of Commerce; Businesses of Greater Boston; Latino Professional Network **C/VW:** Big Brother Big Sisters of America **A/S:** She attributes her success to having a supportive family, positive attitude, her empathy, her respect for others and her belief in herself. **B/I:** She became involved in her profession because she enjoyed media production and community development. **H/O:** The highlights of her career are the relationships she has built within the company.

ROSA C. CALANDRIELLO, CAS
Teacher, Science Department Chairwoman Administrator
Middle School 101
New York City Board of Education
2750 Lafayette Avenue
Bronx, NY 10461 United States
rosacalandriello@aol.com
http://www.cambridgewhoswho.com

BUS: Board of Education **P/S:** Secondary Education **MA:** Regional **D/D/R:** Teaching Science, Conducting Workshops, Private Tutoring and Communicating in Five Languages Including Italian, English, Spanish, French and Arabic **H/I/S:** Fencing, Step Dancing **EDU:** Master's Degree in Education, Pace University; Coursework, University of Massachusetts **CERTS:** Certified Administrative Supervisor, Mercy College **A/A/S:** Pi Lambda Theta; National Science Teachers Association; Association for Supervision and Curriculum Development; Committee Member, National Junior Honor Society; Academic Olympics **A/H:** Continental Who's Who Award (2007-2008) **CHILD:** Amedo, Joseph, Gerado **I/F/Y:** In five years, Ms. Calandriello hopes to start a school for kindergarten through fifth-grade students and intends to write proposals and start a new project with two of her colleagues.

SARAH D. CALDWELL
President
The Caldwell Consulting Group, LLC
245 Eighth Avenue
Suite 388
New York, NY 10011 United States
sarahcaldwell@tcconsultinggroup.net
http://www.cambridgewhoswho.com

BUS: Privately-Owned Company **P/S:** Management Consulting **MA:** National **D/D/R:** Developing the Business in Nonprofit Companies, Overseeing Leadership and Board Development, Coaching, Strategic and Operational Planning, Planning Leadership Transitions, Planning and Implementing Capital Projects **H/I/S:** Sailing **EDU:** Bachelor's Degree in Urban Planning, Hunter College (1993) **A/A/S:** Management Chamber of Commerce; Institute of Management Consulting; Association of Fundraising Professionals; Greenwich Village Chelsea Chamber of Commerce

GEORGE J. CALES JR.
President
Jeff Cales Custom Aviation, LLC
8101 St. Rt. 44/Building A
Ravenna, OH 44266 United States
jcales@customaviation.com
http://www.customaviation.com

BUS: Aviation **P/S:** All Aspects of Aircraft Refinishing **MA:** National **EXP:** Mr. Cales' expertise is in business management, aircraft painting and design. **H/I/S:** Bike Riding **A/A/S:** National Federation of Independent Business Owners

MR. GARY D. CALKINS
Commercial Division Specialist
Panda Realty
4327 W. 13th Street N.
Wichita, KS 67212 United States
garycalkins@hotmail.com
http://www.cambridgewhoswho.com

BUS: Real Estate Firm **P/S:** Commercial and Residential Real Estate Exchange **MA:** National **EXP:** Mr. Calkins' expertise is in architecture and consulting services. **D/D/R:** Assisting Clients, Managing Information Services **H/I/S:** Renovating his Home **FBP:** Wichita Business Journal **EDU:** High School Diploma **A/A/S:** Commercial Real Estate Division; Kansas Association of Realtors; Commercial Source; National Association of Realtors **C/VW:** Habitat for Humanity **A/S:** He attributes his success to his ability to solve problems and to being detail-oriented. **H/O:** The most gratifying aspect of his career is seeing his clients happy during a real estate transaction.

MARY J. CALLAN
Consultant
Self-Employed
11 Half Penny Lane
Old Saybrook, CT 06475 United States
marycallan5@comcast.net
http://www.cambridgewhoswho.com

BUS: Consulting Firm **P/S:** Human Resource Consulting Services **MA:** International **EXP:** Ms. Calla's expertise is in human resource management. **D/D/R:** Consulting on Human Resources, Recruiting, Working with New Hires to Acclimate them to their New Workplace **H/I/S:** Reading, Gardening **FBP:** Forbes **EDU:** Master of Business Administration, University of New Haven (2006); Bachelor's Degree in Business Management, Albertus Magnus College (2004) **A/A/S:** Society for Human Resource Management **C/VW:** Local Church **A/S:** She attributes her success to her integrity and work ethic. **B/I:** She became involved in her profession because of the experience she gained in staffing coordination at Pfizer Pharmaceuticals. **I/F/Y:** In five years, Ms. Callan hopes to teach business management at the college level.

April L. Calton, DDS
Dentist, Owner
About Smiles Dentistry
507 S. Cherry Grove Avenue
Annapolis, MD 21401 United States
aboutsmiles@gmail.com
http://www.aboutsmilesdentistry.com

BUS: Healthcare Facility **P/S:** Latest Dental Technologies for Comfort and Care, Tooth Whitening, Video Dentistry, Full Range of Dental Treatment Including Preventative Measures such as Cleaning, Polishing and Periodontal Care, Restorative Services such as Crowns, Bridges, Implants, Fillings and Dentures, Cosmetic Procedures such as Whitening, Bonding and Veneers **MA:** Local **D/D/R:** Offering General and Cosmetic Dentistry, Applying Fillings and Veneers, Processing Applications **H/I/S:** Traveling, Skiing, Attending Church Activities **FBP:** Journal of the American Dental Association; The Journal of Cosmetic Dentistry; AGD Impact **EDU:** Doctor of Dental Surgery, New York University (2000); Bachelor's Degree, Florida State University (1996) **A/A/S:** Maryland State Dental Association; American Dental Association; American Academy of General Dentistry **C/VW:** Stanton Center

Patricia J. Cameron
Teacher (Retired)
Los Angeles Unified School District
450 N. Grand Avenue
Los Angeles, CA 90012 United States
patricia.cameron@cwwemail.com
http://www.cambridgewhoswho.com

BUS: School District **P/S:** Education **MA:** Local **EXP:** Ms. Cameron's expertise is in language arts and thematic teaching. **D/D/R:** Teaching Social Interaction Skills and Summer Classes for Teachers **H/I/S:** Traveling, Spending Time with her Grandchildren, Caring for her Dog, Reading **EDU:** Master of Education, The California State University; Bachelor of Arts in Psychology, Occidental College **A/A/S:** Federal Bureau of Prisons **A/S:** She attributes her success to the support she received from her mother and grandmother. **B/I:** She became involved in her profession because she always wanted to be a teacher. **H/O:** The highlight of her career was helping a child with attention deficit hyperactivity disorder learn enough to work in his mother's firm.

MICHELE G. CAMET
Registered Nurse
Parish Pain Specialists
4500 Clearview Parkway
Metairie, LA 70006 United States
rmcamet@cox.net
http://www.cambridgewhoswho.com

BUS: Healthcare **P/S:** Interventional Pain Clinic, Treatment of Spine and Nerve Diseases **MA:** Local **EXP:** Ms. Camet's expertise is in pain management. **H/I/S:** Playing Tennis, Hiking **FBP:** American Society for Pain Management Nursing Journal and Newsletter **EDU:** Bachelor of Science in Nursing, Louisiana State University School of Nursing **CERTS:** Certificate in Pain Management, American Nurses Credentialing Center **A/A/S:** Louisiana Society for Pain Management Nursing; American Society for Pain Management Nursing **C/VW:** Vietnam Veterans of America; Secretary, Louisiana Pain Society **A/S:** She attributes her success to the encouragement from her friends and family and the influence of her role model. **B/I:** She became involved in the profession when she worked as a candy striper. **H/O:** The highlight of her career is the ability to learn something new everyday and to help her patients cope with their diseases.

BIRGIT CAMPANA, CMT, NCTMB
President
Dansk Day Spa
212A Commerce Street
Occoquan, VA 22125 United States
info@danskdayspa.com
http://www.danskdayspa.com

BUS: Day Spa **P/S:** Massage Therapy Services **EXP:** Ms. Campana's expertise is in massage therapy. **D/D/R:** Consulting, Lecturing, Marketing, Specializing in Human Resources **H/I/S:** Spending Time with her Children, Reading, Traveling **EDU:** Associate Degree in General Studies, Central Texas College **A/A/S:** Prince William Regional Chamber of Commerce; Associated Bodywork and Massage Professionals; American Civil Liberties Union **A/S:** She attributes her success to her common sense and personal drive. **B/I:** She became involved in her profession because she wanted to start her own business. **H/O:** The most gratifying aspects of her job are helping her clients feel good about themselves and educating them on body awareness. **I/F/Y:** In five years, Ms. Campana hopes to expand her business and start consulting on nutrition.

CHARLES CAMPBELL
Chief Cardiac Surgeon
Mt. Sinai Hospital, Michael Reese Hospital
357 N. Canal Street
Chicago, IL 60606 United States
http://www.cambridgewhoswho.com

BUS: Healthcare-Cardiac and Thoracic Surgery **P/S:** Superb Cardiac Medical Services **MA:** Regional **D/D/R:** Performing Cardiac and Thoracic Surgery Procedures Including Coronary and Heart Bypass Surgery, Offering Lung Surgery and General Skilled Healthcare Services **H/I/S:** Playing Tennis, Motorcycle Riding **FBP:** Journal of Thoracic and Cardiovascular Surgery **EDU:** MD in Cardiovascular Medicine, University of Pittsburgh (1970) **A/A/S:** Society of Thoracic Surgeons; American Association for Thoracic Surgery

MS. LINDA CAMPBELL, MA
Sixth Grade Teacher
Language Arts, Social Studies
Laurel Middle School
725 Washington Avenue
Laurel, MT 59044 United States
lindac@imt.net
http://www.cambridgewhoswho.com

BUS: Middle School **P/S:** Regular Core Curriculum Including Reading, Mathematics, English, Science, Social Studies, Art, Music, History, Languages and Physical Education **MA:** Regional **D/D/R:** Teaching All Language Arts Subjects to an Average of 50 Sixth and Eighth Grade Students, Instructing Driver's Education Courses **H/I/S:** Enjoying the Outdoors, Hiking, Fishing, Camping **FBP:** Educator **EDU:** Master's Degree in Technology and Education, Cambridge-Lesley University (2007); Bachelor's Degree in Elementary Education, Montana State University, Billings **A/A/S:** Montana Education Association; National Education Association **DOB:** February 10, 1952 **SP:** Significant Other, Dave **CHILD:** Kori, Kacie **W/H:** Teacher, Laurel Middle School, MT; Teacher, Australia **A/S:** She attributes her success to the support of her family, the love she has for children, a good sense of humor, a hard work ethic and her determination to make a difference in the lives of her students. **B/I:** She became involved in her profession because she loves children and has a very caring and nurturing personality and knew from a young age that she had the potential to change many young lives. **H/O:** The most gratifying aspects of her career are seeing her former students lead successful lives and earning an online Master's degree in technology from Cambridge University while still enjoying teaching Language Arts and Social Studies to her sixth grade students.

MERLINE M. CAMPBELL, MT (ASCP)
Medical Technologist
Jefferson Comprehensive Health Center
225 Community Drive
Fayette, MS 39069 United States
lcmpb8@aol.com
http://www.cambridgewhoswho.com

BUS: Proven Leader in the Healthcare Industry **P/S:** High Quality Healthcare Services **MA:** Local **D/D/R:** Supervising the Laboratory, Conducting Technical Consultations **H/I/S:** Singing **FBP:** Laboratory Medicine **EDU:** Bachelor of Science in Biology, Tennessee State University **CERTS:** Certified Medical Technologist, Meharry Medical College **A/A/S:** Delta Sigma Theta; American Society of Clinical Pathology **C/VW:** Local Church; St. Jude Children's Research Hospital; Habitat for Humanity

CAROL CAMPBELL-NORRIS
Bereavement Counselor
Hospice of the Comforter
480 W. Central Parkway
Altamonte Springs, FL 32714 United States
ccampbellnorris@yahoo.com
http://www.cambridgewhoswho.com

BUS: Nonprofit Organization **P/S:** Counseling **MA:** Local **D/D/R:** Counseling on Grief, Bereavement, Marriage and Family Issues **H/I/S:** Spending Time with Family **FBP:** Psychotherapy Today **EDU:** Master's Degree in Marriage and Family Counseling, Stetson University **A/A/S:** Florida Association for Marriage and Family Therapy; American Association for Marriage and Family Counseling; CMI **C/VW:** Local Charities **A/S:** She attributes her success to her empathy for others. **B/I:** She became involved in the profession because she wanted to help others. **H/O:** The highlight of her career was earning her master's degree.

KIMBERLY JEANNE CAMPING, BA
Realtor
Independence Realty Professionals, Inc.
4535 S. Lakeshore Drive
Ste. 4
Tempe, AZ 85282 United States
kcamping@cox.net
http://www.cambridgewhoswho.com/

BUS: Real Estate Company **P/S:** Real Estate **MA:** Phoenix Metropolitan Area **D/D/R:** Working with Buyers and Sellers **EDU:** Bachelor's Degree in Business Management, University of Phoenix **A/A/S:** National Association of Realtors; Arizona Association of Realtors; South East Valley Associations of Realtors **C/VW:** Children's Inc. **A/S:** She attributes her success to her customer service and an aggressive marketing plan. **B/I:** She became involved in her profession because both of her parents were involved in real estate and she loves her profession. **H/O:** The highlight of her career are the customer referrals she receives.

SANDRA A. CAMPO
Owner
Bull Dawg Cafe
2600 E. County Line Road
Ardmore, PA 19003 United States
sandic601@aol.com
http://www.cambridgewhoswho.com

BUS: Cafe **P/S:** Breakfast, Lunch, Table Service **MA:** Local **D/D/R:** Running the Cafe, Preparing Food **H/I/S:** Relaxing, Going out with Friends, Attending Movies **EDU:** High School Diploma **A/A/S:** Ardmore Business Association **C/VW:** Hurricane Katrina Bake Sale; Lemonade Stand; Local Fundraisers **A/S:** She attributes her success to hard work and determination. **B/I:** She became involved in her profession because she had an interest in cooking since childhood. **H/O:** The highlight of her career was opening up her own shop.

JULIE M. CANDICE
Vice President of Finance
Pointandship Software, Inc.
2200 Powell Street
Unit 1080
Emeryville, CA 94608 United States
jcandice@pointandship.com
http://www.pointandship.com

BUS: Multi-Million Dollar Privately Held Corporation in the Shipping Expense Management Software Industry **P/S:** Web-Based Shipping Management Software Giving Businesses Greater Control Over their Express, Ground and Supply Chain Distribution Services **MA:** International **D/D/R:** Overseeing Finance, Accounting and Client Services **H/I/S:** Art, Theater, Fund Raising, Charity Events **FBP:** Forbes **EDU:** Bachelor of Arts, Loughborough University, England (1994)

KIMBERLY M. CANGRO, RN, CHPN
Registered Nurse
United Hospice of Rockland
11 Stokum Lane
New City, NY 10956 United States
kcrn3boyz@yahoo.com
http://www.cambridgewhoswho.com

BUS: Facility Committed to Improving End-of-Life Care for Patients and their Families **P/S:** Hospice and Palliative Care Information, Advance Care Planning, Advance Directives, Living Wills, Nursing Care, Pain and Grief Counseling, Financial Planning **MA:** Regional **D/D/R:** Offering Symptom and Pain Management for 12 to 15 Patients a Week, Overseeing Anxiety and Crisis Management for Patients and Their Families, Nursing in Cardiac Care, Working with the Mentally Disabled **H/I/S:** Reading, Horseback Riding, Gardening, Scuba Diving **EDU:** Associate Degree in Nursing, Rockland Community College (1999) **CERTS:** Certified Hospice and Palliative Nurse (2007) **A/A/S:** NHPC **C/VW:** American Red Cross

CHERIE CANNON
Professor of Speech, Writing Communications
Miami Dade College
11010 N.W. 27th Avenue
Miami, FL 33168 United States
cherie.cannon@mdc.edu
http://www.faculty.mdc.edu/ccannon

BUS: Multicampus, State-Supported College, One of the Largest and Best Colleges in America **P/S:** More than 150 Associates Degrees in Accounting, Architecture, Allied Health Technologies, Aviation, Biology, Business and Computers, Child Development, Criminal Justice, Engineering, Entertainment Technologies, Fire Science, Foreign Languages, History, Human Services, Legal Assisting, Mass Communication, Mathematics, Physical Therapy, Psychology, Social Work, Teaching, Arts **MA:** Regional **D/D/R:** Teaching Speech and Writing Communication, Public Speaking, Creative Writing **H/I/S:** Playing Bridge, Gardening, Travel **FBP:** Educator; Harvard Review **EDU:** Pursuing Doctorate in Higher Education Administration and Supervision, Barry University; Master's Degree in Speech Pathology, Minor in Audiology, University of Miami (1977); Bachelor of Arts in Education and Speech Communications **A/A/S:** National Communication Association; Florida Communication Association; American Council on Education; Pembroke Pines City Educational Advisory Board **A/H:** Who's Who of Women in Education

MICHELE LEE CANNON
Realtor
Kappel & Kappel
1919 Peabody Road
Vacaville, CA 95687 United States
mcannonrealtor@msn.com
http://www.mcannonrealtor.com

BUS: Real Estate Agency **P/S:** Commercial Real Estate **MA:** Local **H/I/S:** Boating, Spending time With Family **EDU:** Coursework in General Studies, Sacramento State University; Industry-Related Training and Experience **A/A/S:** California Association of Realtors; National Association of Realtors **C/VW:** American Cancer Association, Leukemia & Lymphoma Foundation **A/S:** She attributes her success to client referrals and the support she receives from her family. **B/I:** She became involved in her profession through a natural progression of opportunities. **H/O:** The most gratifying aspect of her career is being a top producer.

KATHLEEN G. CANTAGALLO
Director of Strategy & Planning
Astra Zeneca
1800 Concord Pike
Wilmington, DE 19850 United States
kathleen.cantagallo@astrazeneca.com
http://www.astrazeneca.com

BUS: One of the World's Leading Pharmaceutical Companies **P/S:** Neuroscientific Therapy Products Including a Broad Product Portfolio Including Many World Leaders and a Range of High Potential Medicines Designed to Meet the Needs of Patients and Healthcare Professionals **MA:** International **D/D/R:** Overseeing Global Market Purchasing and Drug Development in the Area of Neuroscience **FBP:** Fortune; The Wall Street Journal **EDU:** Master's Degree in Industrial Management, Widener University (1985) **A/A/S:** Society of Women Engineers; International Society for Pharmaceutical Engineering; American Association of Pharmaceutical Scientists

CHRISTINE A. CANTRELL
Senior Human Resource Specialist
Pinellas County School Board
301 Fourth S.W.
PO Box 2942
Largo, FL 33770 United States
cantrell@pcsb.org
http://www.cambridgewhoswho.com

BUS: School Board **P/S:** Education **MA:** Local **D/D/R:** Teaching Special Education, Mentoring and Training New Teachers **H/I/S:** Sewing, Boating, Listening to Music **FBP:** Educational Leadership; Just ASK Publications **EDU:** Master's Degree in Educational Leadership, University of South Florida **C/VW:** Volunteer, Local Schools **A/S:** She attributes her success to her tenacity and passion to provide her students with a strong education. **B/I:** She became involved in her profession because she always wanted to be a teacher. **H/O:** The most gratifying aspect of her career is hearing that her former students are successful.

JAMES L. CAPO
Owner, Package Design Engineer, Consultant
JMar Package Consultants
4902 Brookhaven Drive
Middletown, OH 45044 United States
jmarconsultants@cinci.rr.com
http://www.cambridgewhoswho.com

BUS: Packaging Company **P/S:** Consulting and Packaging Services Including Folding Carton Patents, Dual Purpose Carton, Pop-Out Carton, Separable Carton, Dispensing Carton, Reclosable Carton with Tear-Open Spout, Poultry Tray, Food Service Container and Lid, Wrap Around Package and Twirlee Toy **MA:** National **D/D/R:** Designing Physical Structures and Folding Cartons for Packaging, Developing Wrappers, Troubleshooting on Machinery Problems, Consulting **H/I/S:** Photographing **FBP:** Packaging Digest; Package Design **EDU:** Coursework in Engineering, Rockland Community College; Coursework in Packaging and Environment, Sinclair Community College **A/H:** Excellence Award for Mott's Applesauce Package; Excellence Award for Mint Spearmint Package; Excellence Award for Hardee's Biscuits Pop-Up Action Meal Package; Excellence Award for Heinz Mighty High Mini Desserts; Excellence Award for Mrs. Smith's Quiches, Paperboard Packing Council; Silver Key Award, Chef America CS; Best Packaging Award for Rondele' Bagel Cream Cheese Items, Eastern Dairy Deli and Bakery Association; Excellence Award, Kroger Holiday Pack, National Paperboard Package Association (Twice) **SP:** Marlene **CHILD:** Marylynn, Carl, Micheal

THERESA 'TERI' CAPPABIANCA
Licensed Real Estate Agent
Coldwell Banker Real Estate
508 Mamaroneck Avenue
White Plains, NY 10605 United States
teri.cappabianca@cbmoves.com
http://www.cambridgewhoswho.com

BUS: Full Service Real Estate **P/S:** Real Estate Sales **MA:** International **D/D/R:** Buying and Selling Residential and Commercial Properties **H/I/S:** Exercising, Yoga, Spending Time with her Family **FBP:** Forbes; New York Magazine **EDU:** Associate of Science in Marketing, Westchester Community College **A/A/S:** Multiple Listing Service; National Association of Realtors **A/H:** Diamond Award (2005) **C/VW:** Cancer Research Hospice; American Lung Association; American Heart Association **A/S:** She attributes her success to being patient and understanding the needs of her clients. **B/I:** She became involved in this profession because she worked in a small real estate office and was recommended that she get her license. **H/O:** The highlight of her career is when she is recognized for a job well done because that will lead to repeat business and referrals.

JANELLE E. CARDIEL
Sales Director
Shiseido Cosmetics (America) Ltd.
900 Third Avenue
New York, NY 10022 United States
jcardiel@charter.net
janellee.cardiel@sca.shiseido.com
http://www.cambridgewhoswho.com

BUS: Cosmetics Firm **P/S:** Skincare, Cosmetics, Fragrances **MA:** National **D/D/R:** Directing Sales, Mentoring, Maintaining National Specialty Accounts, Driving Retail and Net Sales **H/I/S:** Spending Time with her Son, Traveling, Reading **FBP:** Women's Wear Daily; Smart Money **EDU:** Associate of Arts in Retail Administration, Fashion Institute of Los Angeles **A/A/S:** Shiseido Fifteen-Year Recognition Award; Nordstrom Vendor of the Year (1997) **C/VW:** Local Charities **A/S:** She attributes her success to her professionalism and mentoring skills. **B/I:** She became involved in her profession because she has a passion for retail. **H/O:** The highlight of her career was having seven people under her receive promotions.

KAREN M. CARDILLO, RN, MSN, HSMI
Professor of Health and Physical Education
Monroe Community College
1000 E. Henrietta Road
Rochester, NY 14623 United States
kcardillo@monroecc.edu
http://www.monroecc.edu

BUS: College **P/S:** Higher Education **MA:** Regional **D/D/R:** Teaching Health and Physical Education, Developing the Curriculum, Lecturing on Stress Management, Physical, Mental and Spiritual Wellness **H/I/S:** Kayaking, Riding her Motorcycle, Quilting, Gardening, Reading **EDU:** Master of Science in Nursing, University of Rochester (1979) **CERTS:** Certification in Holistic Stress Management **A/A/S:** National Wellness Institute

V. Jauhara Care, MA
Director of Education
Everest Institute
1000 Blue Gentian Road
Suite 250
Eagan, MN 55121 United States
jcare@cci.edu
http://www.cambridgewhoswho.com

BUS: Higher Education **P/S:** Vocational and Technical Education **MA:** State Wide **H/I/S:** Gardening, Painting, Hiking, Photography and Reading **EDU:** Ph.D. in Philosophy and Religion, California Institute of Integral Studies; Master's Degree in Spirituality, Holy Name University, Magna Cum Laude; Bachelor of Arts in Psychology and Counseling, College of Santa Fe, Cum Laude **A/A/S:** Minnesota Board, American Council on Education **C/VW:** Women to Women International **A/S:** She attributes her success to input from others, having good mentors and co-workers and working as a team to accomplish goals. **B/I:** She became involved in her profession because she started as a teacher and was offered a position at the Bryman Institute. She has enjoyed the setting in a community college and she likes the interaction with students and faculty. **H/O:** The highlight of her career has been being able to help others and impact their lives.

Gina M. Carey
Purchasing Agent
Merrick-Industries Inc.
10 Arthur Drive
Lynn Haven, FL 3244
gina@merrick-inc.com
http://www.merrick-inc.com

BUS: Manufacturing **P/S:** Environmentally Friendly Industrial Weight Scale and Coal Feeders Manufacturer **MA:** International **D/D/R:** Procuring Electronic Components for All the Machines Used by the Company **H/I/S:** Teaching Kick Boxing, Playing Community League Softball **FBP:** Purchasing **EDU:** Bachelor's Degree in History, Florida State University (2003) **C/VW:** Local Rescue Mission, Volunteer Fundraiser, Heart Walks **A/S:** She attributes her success to her sales her background and good interpersonal skills. **B/I:** She became involved in this profession after working as a retail sales manager at another company and deciding to get on the other end of the business. **H/O:** The highlight of her career was working out a deal with a vendor that saved the company $10,000.

SUSAN P. CARLEN
President
Solutions in Practice Management
1326 Viewtop Drive
Clearwater, FL 33764 United States
sipm0303@aol.com
http://www.mybillingsolutions.com

BUS: Healthcare **P/S:** Practice Management, Billing and Administrative Services **MA:** Tampa Bay Area **EXP:** Ms. Carlen's expertise is in administration. **H/I/S:** Spending Time with Family, Listening to Music with Family, Church **A/A/S:** Psychiatric Practice Management Association; Alliance of Behavioral Health Professionals **C/VW:** Church, Military Order of the Purple Heart **A/S:** She attributes her success to her persistence and her ability to find ways to get past road blocks. **B/I:** She became involved in her profession because a friend asked for her assistance with running his business. **H/O:** The highlight of her career has been setting up her own successful business.

JANE M. CARLOCK, EMT
Emergency Medical Technician, Intermediate
Arkansas Valley Ambulance Service
PO Box 210
Cotopaxi, CO 81223 United States
darylcarlock@yahoo.com
http://www.cambridgewhoswho.com

BUS: Ambulance Service **P/S:** Community Patient Care and Transportation Services **MA:** Local **EXP:** Ms. Carlock's expertise is in education and training. **H/I/S:** Hiking, Outdoor Activities and Enjoys Spending Time with Family and her Dogs **FBP:** EMS Journal of Prehospital Emergency Care **CERTS:** Certificate, EMT Intermediate Course, Trinidad State Junior College **C/VW:** Local Camp Counselor, Camp Iona; Board Member, Camp Cherith **A/S:** She attributes her success to God, her family's support and a love for what she does. **B/I:** She became involved in the profession because she always had an interest in medicine. During high school, working as a lifeguard, she went on a ride along with local Emergency Medical Technicians and was intrigued, turning it into a career. **H/O:** The highlight of her career is having the ability to make a difference in her community.

PAMELA L. CARLSON, RN
Registered Nurse
Summa Health System
444 N. Main Street
Akron, OH 44310 United States
lightworker@chasethecrew.com
http://www.cambridgewhoswho.com

BUS: Healthcare Center **P/S:** Healthcare Including Orthopedic and Trauma Care **MA:** Local **EXP:** Ms. Carlson's expertise is in case management and field staff nursing. **D/D/R:** Overseeing Case Management, Acting as a Training Preceptor for the Department, Filling in for the Supervisor, Practicing Field Staff Nursing **H/I/S:** Reading, Needlework, Listening to Music, Traveling **FBP:** RN 2008; Journal of Orthopedic Nursing **EDU:** Bachelor's Degree in Psychology, Baldwin-Wallace College **CERTS:** Registered Nurse, Summa St. Thomas School of Nursing **A/H:** Exceptional Staff Award, Ohio Nurses Association (2000-2006); Summit-Portage County Leadership Award; Certificate of Appreciation for Handling an On-Board Emergency, Continental Airlines **C/VW:** Local Church; Amnesty International; Sierra Club; International Campaign for Tibet **A/S:** She attributes her success to her ability to deal with people. **B/I:** She became involved in her profession because she was always interested in the medical field and wanted to help others. **H/O:** The most gratifying aspect of her career is being in her current position.

DIANE C. CARLYON, BSN, RN, MSHCA
Neighborhood Manager
Providence Extended Care Center
4900 Eagle Street
Anchorage, AK 99503 United States
dcarlyon@provak.org
http://www.cambridgewhoswho.com

BUS: Long-Term Care Center **P/S:** Long-Term Care Including Skilled Care and Rehabilitation Services **MA:** Regional **EXP:** Ms. Carlyon's expertise is in infusion therapy. **H/I/S:** Hiking, Exercising **EDU:** Master's Degree in Health Administration, Bellevue University **A/S:** She attributes her success to her persistence, hard work and determination. **B/I:** She became involved in her profession because she began her career as a nurse. **H/O:** The highlight of her career was becoming an clinical instructor for the college's senior nursing program.

RAYMOND W. CARON
Hospice Registered Nurse
VNA of Manchester and Southern New Hampshire
1870 Elm Street
Manchester, NH 03104 United States
raynman617@aol.com
http://www.cambridgewhoswho.com

BUS: Visiting Nurses Associations **P/S:** Quality Care to All Hospice Patients **MA:** Local **EXP:** Mr. Caron's expertise is in hospice nursing. **H/I/S:** Riding Motorcycles, Going to the Gym, Baseball, Hockey **FBP:** Nursing2009 **EDU:** Associate Degree in Nursing, New Hampshire Community Technical College **C/VW:** Volunteer, Local Nursing Home; United Nations Association **A/S:** He attributes his success to having an incredible support group including friends, family and colleagues. **B/I:** He became involved in his profession after taking nursing courses because he was influenced by his friend, who was a nurse. **H/O:** The highlight of his career was getting a job with VNA Hospice.

ELIZABETH CARPENTER DAVIS
Owner
Davis Movers
2602 E. Voltaire Avenue
Phoenix, AZ 85032 United States
lee@davismovers.com
http://www.davismovers.com

BUS: Moving Service **P/S:** Moving Household Goods **MA:** Statewide **D/D/R:** Managing the Business **H/I/S:** Traveling, RVing **FBP:** Spotlight **EDU:** Coursework in Business, Chaffey College, California **C/VW:** Local Church

Joshua A. Carr, DC
Doctor of Chiropractic
Coral Canyon Chiropractic
1141 W. State Street
Suite 12
Hurricane, UT 84737 United States
dr.carr@ycoralchiro.com
http://www.coralchiro.com

BUS: Chiropractic Healthcare and Wellness Center **P/S:** Manual Therapies for Musculoskeletal Conditions, Cervical and Lumbar Decompression, Electrical Muscle Stimulation, Ultrasound, Therapeutic Exercises, Neuromuscular Reeducation **MA:** Southern Utah **D/D/R:** Caring for Patients, Rehabilitating the Spine, Partnering to Accomplish Business and Administrative Duties, Overseeing the Practice **H/I/S:** Studying Archeology, Mythology, Religion, Belief Systems and Philosophy, Practicing Mixed Martial Arts, Tang Soo Do **FBP:** Spine Biomechanics; Journal of Manual and Physical Therapies; Chiropractic Economics; Journal of Body Work **EDU:** Doctor of Chiropractic Medicine, Palmer College **CERTS:** Certification in Whiplash and Brain Traumatology; Certified Independent Chiropractic Examiner **A/A/S:** American Chiropractic Association; Pi Tau Delta International Chiropractic Honor Society; Local Chamber of Commerce **A/H:** International Physician of the Year (2006) **C/VW:** Church; Boy Scouts of America; Volunteer Fight Doctor, Mixed Martial Arts **DOB:** September 16, 1976 **POB:** Millington **CHILD:** Jacob, Sadie **A/S:** He attributes his success to his hard work and following the example of the great leaders in his life. **B/I:** He became involved in his profession after being involved in a car accident, with a drunk driver, which left him with injuries that required rehabilitation. **H/O:** The highlight of his career was starting his own practice.

Leticia Carrasco
Teacher
City of Lynn
90 O'Callahan Street
Lynn, MA 01902 United States
carrascoleticia@hotmail.com
http://www.ci.lynn.ma.us/Public_Documents/index

BUS: City Government Agency **P/S:** Public Services Including Assessment, Elections, Tax Collections, Community Development, Information Technology, Legal Services, Recreation, Human Resources and Water and Sewer Maintenance **MA:** Local **D/D/R:** Teaching Spanish to Seventh and Eighth-Grade Students **H/I/S:** Working Out, Running, Reading **FBP:** Time **EDU:** Master's Degree in English as a Second Language, Salem State College (2002)

MICHELLE M. CARRIERE
Owner
Health and Body Solutions
12743 Rosedale Highway
Bakersfield, CA 93312 United States
healthandbodysoultions@yahoo.com
http://www.cambridgewhoswho.com

BUS: Healthcare Facility, Herb Specialist **P/S:** Health Products such as Bare Essentials and Natures Sunshine **MA:** Regional **D/D/R:** Assisting Clients in Product Preparation to Enhance Health and Well Being, Healing Using Holistic Alternatives to Spa Treatments **H/I/S:** Scrapbooking **EDU:** Coursework in Herbal Treatment

MARY J. CARRILLO
Program Director, Medical Radiography
Gateway Community College (MCCD)
108 N. 40th Street
Phoenix, AZ 85034 United States
mary.carrillo@gwmail.maricopa.edu
http://www.gatewaycc.edu

BUS: Fully Accredited, Comprehensive Institution Emphasizing Both Academic and Occupational Programs **P/S:** Academic Programs, Occupational Programs, Research, Online Courses **MA:** Statewide **D/D/R:** Performing Diagnostic Medical Imaging, Teaching, Training New Faculty **H/I/S:** Skiing, Dancing, Spending Quality Time with Family **FBP:** National Geographic **EDU:** Master of Business Administration, University of Phoenix **A/A/S:** Association of Collegiate Educators in Radiologic Technology; Arizona State Society of Radiologic Technologists; American Society of Radiologic Technologists; American Registry of Radiologic Technologists; International Society for Clinical Densitometry, Inc.; SIR

JOY J. CARRINGTON, MSW, M.DIV.
Agency Program Coordinator
Arkansas Department of Health-Office of
Minority Health and Health Disparities
4815 W. Markham Street, Slot 22
Little Rock, AR 72205 United States
joy.carrington@arkansas.gov
http://www.healthyarkansas.com

BUS: Government Organization **P/S:** Development, Dissemination and Coordination of Initiatives, Policies, Programs and Activities Focused on the Improvement of Public Health **MA:** Statewide **D/D/R:** Coordinating Programs, Informational Dissemination and Resources, Training, Managing Technical Assistance **H/I/S:** Instructing Liturgical Dance, Bicycling, Swimming **FBP:** American Journal of Public Health; Journal of Cultural Diversity; Journal of National Medical Association **EDU:** Pursuing Doctor of Ministry, Austin Presbyterian Theological Seminary; Master of Divinity, Johnson C. Smith Seminary ITC (1994); Master of Social Work, Atlanta University (1988); Bachelor of Arts in Psychology, Spelman College (1986) **A/A/S:** National Association of Social Workers; National Genealogical Society

SAM J. CARROLL
Vice President, Office Group
Graham and Company, LLC
110 Office Park Drive
Suite 200
Birmingham, AL 35223 United States
samc@grahamcompany.com
http://www.grahamcompany.com

BUS: Real Estate Firm **P/S:** Brokerage Services, Property Management, Investment, Development, Appraisals **MA:** Alabama **D/D/R:** Selling Real Estate **H/I/S:** Golfing, Spending Time with his Family **FBP:** Forbes **EDU:** Bachelor of Arts, University of Alabama **CERTS:** Certified Commercial Investment Member **A/A/S:** Society of Industrial and Office Realtors; National Association of Industrial and Office Properties; Alabama Association of Realtors; National Association of Realtors **C/VW:** Presbyterian Church; Habitat for Humanity

ALMA D. CARTER
Certified Physician Assistant
Saint Marie Clinic PA
305 E. Expressway 83
Mission, TX 78572 United States
almadg_2000@yahoo.com
http://cambridgewhoswho.com

BUS: Healthcare Clinic **P/S:** Healthcare **MA:** Local **D/D/R:** Assessing Patients, Devising Treatment Plans **EDU:** Bachelor's Degree in Physician Assistant, University of Texas-Pan American **A/A/S:** American Academy of Physicians Assistants **C/VW:** American Cancer Society **A/S:** She attributes her success to her dedication and sacrifices. **B/I:** She became involved in her profession because her grandfather was a doctor and inspired her. **H/O:** The highlights of her career are the daily interactions with patients.

MS. GWEN L. CARTER
President
G. Carter & Associates, LLC
PO Box 64
Exton, PA 19341 United States
gwen@consultcarter.com
http://www.consultcarter.com

BUS: Event Planning and Public Relations Company **P/S:** Press Releases, Conferences, Event Planning, Special Events **MA:** International **D/D/R:** Specializing in Public Relations and Corporate Positioning, Overseeing Media Communications, Managing Employees and Agents in Seven States **H/I/S:** Watching Professional In-Line Rollerskating **EDU:** Bachelor's Degree in Economics and Sociology, Grinnell College (1974) **A/A/S:** Board and Executive Member, African American Female Entrepreneurs Alliance **C/VW:** Board of Directors, Boys and Girls Club of America; National Adoption Center

JEFFREY P. CARTER
Industrial Source Reduction and Control Program Manager
United Water Services, Inc.
740 N. Lake Street
Burbank, CA 91502 United States
jeff.carter@unitedwater.com
http://www.cambridgewhoswho.com

BUS: Wastewater Treatment Facility **P/S:** Public Utility, Contract Operations and Management **MA:** National **EXP:** Mr. Carter's expertise is in environmental compliance. **H/I/S:** Restoring MG Midgets, Snorkeling, Scuba Diving **EDU:** Bachelor's Degree in Chemistry, University of Hawaii **CERTS:** Certification in Pre-Treatment Pollution Prevention and Storm Water Community Technician Program **A/A/S:** Past Chairman, Vice President, Colorado River Basin Section, California Water Environment Association; Vice Chairman, Tri-State Seminar on the River **C/VW:** Executive Member, American Youth Soccer Organization **A/S:** He attributes his success to his perseverance. **B/I:** He became involved in his profession because he wanted to utilize his educational background. **H/O:** The highlights of his career were acting as the Chairman of Pre-Treatment Pollution Prevention and Storm Water Committee for the California Water Environment Association and as the Chairman for the Tri-State Seminar on the River.

LINDA A. CARTER
Teacher
Vernon-Verona-Sherrill Central Schools
5275 State Route 31
Verona, NY 13478 United States
lindacarter_@excite.com
http://www.cambridgewhoswho.com

BUS: High School **P/S:** Education **MA:** Local **D/D/R:** Directing the Band, Acting as Co-Teacher in the Music Department **H/I/S:** Golfing, Spending Time With her Children **FBP:** School Music News **EDU:** Master's Degree in Music and Education, Morehead State University, KY; Bachelor's Degree in Music Education and Performance, Syracuse University **A/A/S:** Music Education National Conference; New York State School Music Association; New York State Band Directors Association; Association for Supervision and Curriculum Development; Phi Kappa Phi; Pi Lambda Theta **C/VW:** Susan G. Komen Breast Cancer Foundation **A/S:** She attributes her success to hard work. **B/I:** She became involved in this profession because she always loved kids and taught a summer music program. **H/O:** The highlight of her career was putting together a concert focusing on African music in order to influence the music department to broaden their horizons.

SALLY CARTER LaPLANT
Director
Worcester Masonic Learning Center
1 Ionic Avenue
Worcester, MA 01608 United States
mlc33@verizone.net
http://www.childrenslearningcenters.org

BUS: Proven Leader in the Education Industry **P/S:** Education, One-on-One Tutoring for Dyslexic Students **MA:** Central Massachusetts **D/D/R:** Tutoring Children with Dyslexia After School, Training Adults in the Orton-Dillingham Method for Dyslexia, Working with Grades One through 12 **H/I/S:** Raising American Saddle Breed Horses **EDU:** Bachelor of Science in Education **CERTS:** Certified Orton-Gillingham Tutor and Trainer **A/A/S:** International Dyslexia Association; International Multisensory Structured Language Education Council **C/VW:** Special Olympics

ANDRIEA CARTER-KAHN
Team Leader, Realtor
Keller Williams-Cupertino
20230 Stevens Creek Boulevard
Suite E
Cupertino, CA 95014 United States
alcarter@kw.com
http://www.homesbyandriea.com

BUS: Real Estate Company Committed to Providing Quality Services **P/S:** Home Evaluations, Buying and Selling Homes, Listings, Marketing, School and Community Information, Reports, Mortgage Services **MA:** Local **D/D/R:** Teaching and Mentoring Agents, Selling Real Estate **H/I/S:** Women's Stand-Up Jet Skiing **FBP:** Realtor **EDU:** Bachelor's Degree in Business Management, San Francisco State University (1988) **A/A/S:** California Association of Realtors; National Association of Realtors

ZELIA M. CARVALHO
Sales Representative
Regional Sales in Traffic Control Systems
Western Pacific Signal, LLC
zcats1@sbcglobal.net
http://www.cambridgewhoswho.com

BUS: Distribution Firm **P/S:** Medical Equipment **MA:** National **EXP:** Ms. Carvalho's expertise includes purchase orders and operations and human resource management. **H/I/S:** Biking, Decorating Home Projects, Volunteering **FBP:** Newsweek **EDU:** Associate Degree in Computer Science and Accounting, Heald College **A/H:** Successful in Business Award, Bank of America

MR. ANDRES CASANOVA, PE
Vice President
Administration
Westernbank Puerto Rico
268 Avenida Muñoz Rivera, 11th Floor
San Juan, PR 00918 United States
andres.casanova@wbpr.com
http://www.wbpr.com

BUS: Financial Institution **P/S:** Consultations, Call Center, Workforce Management, Customer Service, Banking Services Include Online Banking, Savings, Checking Accounts and Telephone Banking **MA:** Regional **D/D/R:** Taking Measurements, Improving Processes, Supervising Branch Operations, Developing Metrics, Managing Human Resources, Overseeing the Incentives Program **H/I/S:** Playing the Drums, Piloting Single Engine Planes, Basketball **FBP:** Workforce Management; Chief Learning Officer **EDU:** Bachelor's Degree in Industrial Engineering, University of Puerto Rico (1995) **CERTS:** Licensed in Engineering (2001); Certified Color Code Trainer; Licensed Professional Engineer **A/A/S:** Colegio de Ingenieros y Agrimensores de Puerto Rico **SP:** Neyda **CHILD:** Nicole, Andrea

ANGELA CASELLA
Medical Biller
127 Pine Street
Montclair, NJ 07042 United States
beaglebaby302@aol.com
http://www.cambridgewhoswho.com

MA: Local **D/D/R:** Processing Insurance Claims and Medical Billing **H/I/S:** Spending Time with her Family and Friends, Caring for her Pets, Dining Out **CERTS:** Certified Medical Assistant, Medical Arts School; Datalogics PC Training for Typesetting, Chicago (1984); Impala PC Training in Typesetting, Boston (1977); Diploma in Medical Assistant Studies (1969) **A/H:** Typesetting Composition Award (1989) **C/VW:** St. Jude Children's Research Hospital; Paralyzed Veteran's Association; Make-A-Wish **DOB:** October 24, 1950 **POB:** Newark, NJ **W/H:** Typesetter, Prudential **A/S:** She attributes her success to her knowledge, work experience and perseverance. **B/I:** She became involved in her profession because she was influenced by her friend to pursue a career in the medical field.

DEVIN CASHA
Landscape Supervisor
Pleasant Places, Inc.
449 Long Point Road
Mt. Pleasant, SC 29464 United States
dvc@pleasantplaces.com
http://www.pleasantplaces.com

BUS: Commercial Landscape Installation and Maintenance **P/S:** Landscaping Services **MA:** Regional **EXP:** Mr. Casha's expertise is in management and installation. **H/I/S:** Golfing, Motorsport Racing **FBP:** Time; Entrepreneur **EDU:** Industry-Related Training and Experience **A/A/S:** Charleston Chamber of Commerce **C/VW:** March of Dimes; Habitat for Humanity; Miracle League **A/S:** She attributes her success to knowing the industry and being the best in what she does. **B/I:** She became involved in her profession when she took advantage of an opportunity after moving from California. **H/O:** The highlight of her career was completing the jobs she was hired to do.

MARY CASLIN
Associate Broker
Daniel Gale Sotheby's International
Manhasset, NY 11030 United States
marycaslin@danielgale.com
http://www.danielgale.com

BUS: Real Estate Company **P/S:** Residential Real Estate, Listings, Marketing, Sales, Appraisals, Open Houses **MA:** Regional **D/D/R:** Listing and Selling Homes in All Price Ranges, Working with Buyers and Sellers, First-Time Home Buyers, Money Referrals and Attorneys, Developing Full Knowledge of Homes **H/I/S:** Watching Sports, Traveling Internationally **FBP:** Architectural Digest; Town and Country; Financial Publications **EDU:** Bachelor's Degree in English, St. John's University **A/A/S:** New York State Association of Realtors; National Association of Realtors **C/VW:** Ellis Island Foundation

JULIANNE CASSIN-SHARP, ESQ.
Attorney at Law
Maroko and Landau, P.C.
32255 N.W. Highway, Suite 214
Farmington Hills, MI 48334 United States
julianne.cassinsharp@cwwemail.com
jcassin@m-l-law.com
http://www.marokoandlandau.com

BUS: Law Firm **P/S:** Legal Services **MA:** National **EXP:** Ms. Cassin-Sharp's expertise is in immigration and nationality law. **H/I/S:** Playing the Piano **FBP:** Harvard Law Review **EDU:** JD, University of Detroit Mercy School of Law; Bachelor's Degree in Political Science, Western Michigan University **A/A/S:** Hispanic Bar Association of Michigan; American Bar Association; American Immigration Lawyer Association **C/VW:** Alumni Fund; University of Detroit Mercy School of Law; Western Michigan University; Society of Jesus; American Stroke Association

MARIA CECILIA CASTILLO
Product Developer
Kassatex, Inc.
295 Fifth Avenue
Suite 814
New York, NY 10016 United States
cecilia@kassatex.com
http://www.kassatex.com

BUS: Distribution Firm **P/S:** Home Furnishing Textiles Including a Collection of Towels, Bath Rugs and Terry Cloth Robes **MA:** National **EXP:** Ms. Castillo's expertise is in product development and designs. **D/D/R:** Designing Collections, Diversifying her Products with Category Expansion, Selling Private Labels to Retail Customers, Attending Many Seasonal Shows around the World Including China, Paris and other European Countries, Preparing to Show New Products and Designs to the Market each Year **H/I/S:** Playing Volleyball, Scuba Diving **FBP:** The New York Times; Home Textiles Today **EDU:** Master of Business Administration, Pontificia Universidad Catolica de Chile; Bachelor's Degree in Product Design; Coursework in Textile Design **A/H:** Travel Industry Association Award, Best Tonal Look, Hampton Collection (2008); Travel Industry Association Award, Best Relaxed Living Look (2007); Dual Recipient, TIA Award in Featured Patterns, Home Textiles Magazine **C/VW:** Salvadoran American Humanitarian Foundation; Worldfund **DOB:** October 9, 1970 **POB:** San Salvador, El Salvador **A/S:** She attributes her success to her adaptability. **B/I:** She became involved in her profession because of her work experience in product design. **H/O:** The most gratifying aspects of her career are seeing the company grow into different categories, including adding an embroidery category in addition to her collection of solids. **I/F/Y:** In five years, Ms. Castillo hopes to expand her business.

ANGELA M. CASTRO, RNC
Certified Registered Nurse
Bayfront Medical Center
701 Sixth Street S.
St. Petersburg, FL 33701 United States
castroam@msn.com
http://www.cambridgewhoswho.com

BUS: Healthcare **P/S:** Labor and Delivery **MA:** National **D/D/R:** Assisting in Caesarian Sections, Serving as the Release Charge Nurse, Nursing in the Labor and Delivery Unit, Managing and Caring for Antepartum and Intrapartum Patients **H/I/S:** Kickboxing, Horseback Riding **FBP:** Nursing2009 **EDU:** Industry-Related Training and Experience **A/A/S:** NCC **A/S:** She attributes her success to her upbringing and the influence of her mother. **B/I:** She became involved in her profession because all women in her family were in the nursing profession. **H/O:** The highlight of her career was earning her position and moving up.

KAREN STADLER CATE
Executive Director
Fully Effective Christians/ Malachi Project
101 Surrywood Road
Greenville, SC 29607 United States
http://www.havenplace.com

BUS: Christian Service Organization **P/S:** Training for Christian Service **MA:** Regional **D/D/R:** Training for Service to At-Risk Youths and Young Adults **H/I/S:** Enjoys Cooking Gourmet Foods and Gardening **FBP:** The Wall Street Journal **EDU:** Bachelor's Degree in Church Music, Leigh University; Master's Degree in Church Music, Leigh University **CERTS:** Licensed Minister **C/VW:** Christian Service Organization **A/S:** She attributes her success to the love she has for people which was given to her from God. **B/I:** She chose this profession because she has been involved in Christian Ministry her entire life. After the shooting at Columbine High School, she was motivated to build the organization she now runs. **H/O:** The highlight of her career was having her songs published on two CD's, 'Quiet Places' and 'Still Worthy.' She is also proud of her work as a minister of music for multiple churches in her area.

DR. KATHERINE CAUSEY
Chairwoman of the Business Economic Department
LeMoyne-Owen College
807 Walker Avenue
Memphis, TN 38126 United States
katherine_causey@loc.edu
http://www.loc.edu

BUS: One of the Oldest Institutions of Higher Learning in the Mid-South **P/S:** Higher Education, Research **MA:** Local **EXP:** Dr. Causey's expertise is in international business and management. **H/I/S:** Music **FBP:** Academy of Management Review **EDU:** Ph.D. in Business, Argosy University (2005) **A/A/S:** Academy of Management; Rock and Roll Hall of Fame; United in Group Harmony Association; FAME

DR. RONALD K. CAVANAUGH
Director of Treatment, Department of Corrections
State of Alabama
301 S. Ripley Street
Montgomery, AL 36104 United States
ron.cavanaugh@doc.alabama.gov
http://www.cambridgewhoswho.com

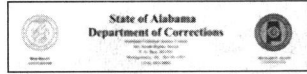

BUS: Government Corrections Office **P/S:** Correctional Services **MA:** Statewide **D/D/R:** Working as a Clinical Psychologist, Specializing in Correctional Health Care Administration and Forensic Psychology **H/I/S:** Listening to Music, Enjoying Art and Entertainment, Traveling **FBP:** APA Journal; Law and Human Behavior **EDU:** Doctorate in Clinical Psychology, Forest Institute of Professional Psychology; Master's Degree in Clinical Psychology, Ball State University; Bachelor's Degree in Psychology, Brigham Young University **A/A/S:** American Psychological Association; American Association for Correctional and Forensic Psychology; National Commission on Correctional Health Care **C/VW:** Alabama Public Radio; Make-A-Wish Foundation; March of Dimes; Disabled American Veterans; American Cancer Society; National Federation for the Blind; Center for Science in the Public Interest **DOB:** February 7, 1951 **POB:** Washington, D.C. **A/S:** He attributes his success to his perseverance. **B/I:** He became involved in the profession because he always wanted to help others. **H/O:** The highlights of his career were implementing a comprehensive system of mental health care standards and treatments within the Alabama Department of Corrections as well as standardizing all drug treatment programs.

DEBORAH L. CAYWOOD
Quality Assurance Team Leader
Bristol Compressors
15185 Industrial Park Road
Bristol, VA 24202 United States
debbiecaywood@bristolcompressors.com
http://www.cambridgewhoswho.com

BUS: Manufacturing **P/S:** Manufacture Compressors for Air Conditioners **MA:** International **EXP:** Ms. Caywoods's expertise is in quality assurance. **H/I/S:** Painting, Drawing, Spending Time with her Grandchildren, Reading Fiction Novels **EDU:** Industry-Related Training and Experience **A/A/S:** American Society for Quality Assurance **A/S:** She attributes her personal and professional success to her hard work and education. **B/I:** She has always had an interest in the field and enjoys working with numbers. **H/O:** The highlight of her career was receiving her mechanical inspection certificate.

MELANIE L. CECH
Flamework Glass Artist, Owner, Founder
The Glass Menagerie, Green Sun Glass Studio
3360 Bluestone Avenue
Spring Hill, FL 34609 United States
melaniesglass@earthlink.net
http://www.cambridgewhoswho.com

BUS: Private Glass Art Company **P/S:** Glass Jewelry, Wedding Cake Tops, Nautical Sculptures, Original Designs and Custom Pieces in Glass Art, Sculptured Glass Figures, Wholesale Gifts for Resale **MA:** Regional **D/D/R:** Creating Custom Glass Pieces, Consulting **H/I/S:** Decorating, Listening to Classical Piano and Other Music **FBP:** The Flow; Glassline **EDU:** High School Diploma (1989) **A/A/S:** National Honor Society **A/H:** Merit Award in Fine Arts, Orlando, FL (2007); Second Place in 3D Sculpture, Sanibel Island, FL (2007); Award of Distinction for Fine Crafts (2002); Second Place, General Merchandise Retailing Supervisory (1989); Sixth Place, Industry-Related National Competition (1989)

MS. DIANE ELIZABETH CELLA JAMISON, M.ED., MS
Speech-Language Pathologist (Retired)
dcella4153@sbcglobal.net
http://www.cambridgewhoswho.com

BUS: Healthcare Center **P/S:** Home Healthcare and Rehabilitation Services **MA:** Local **D/D/R:** Assisting Patients with Motor Speech Disorders, Dysphagia and Dementia, Administering Geriatric Home Healthcare to Stroke Victims and People with Medical Problems that Affect Speech, Swallowing and Memory **H/I/S:** Spending Time with her Grandchildren **FBP:** BusinessWeek **EDU:** Master of Science in Speech-Language Pathology, University of Louisiana at Lafayette; Master of Education in Secondary Education, Minor in Deaf Education, University of Louisiana at Lafayette **CERTS:** Certified Speech-Language Pathologist in Vital Stimulation and Deep Pharyngeal Neuromuscular Stimulation **A/A/S:** American Speech-Language-Hearing Association **A/S:** She attributes her career success to her caring nature, problem solving skills and her ability to empathize with the people she works with. **B/I:** She became involved in her profession because of her interest in communication and desire to help people. **H/O:** The most gratifying aspect of her career is being able to help people achieve and relearn important communication skills.

LISA M. CERCHIARO
Former Senior Vice President
Wachovia Bank
604 S. Washington Square
Apartment 1312
Philadelphia, PA 19106 United States
lcerchiaro@comcast.net
http://www.wachovia.com

BUS: Finance Company **P/S:** Financial Services Including Banking and Brokerage, Asset and Wealth Management, Corporate and Investment Banking **MA:** International **D/D/R:** Budgeting, Auditing, Handling Client Issues, Overseeing Personal Trust Investments and Capital Management, Supervising the Staff, Offering Compliance Reviews and Risk Management **H/I/S:** Playing Tennis, Golfing, Athletics, Traveling **FBP:** The Wall Street Journal; USTA Magazine **EDU:** Master of Business Administration, Rider University **A/A/S:** Financial Analysts of Philadelphia; Philadelphia Securities Association **C/VW:** Alzheimer's Association; Fox Chase Cancer Center **A/S:** She attributes her success to her personal drive, honesty and ambition. **B/I:** She became involved in her profession because of her experience in the brokerage industry. **H/O:** The highlight of her career was earning her current position.

TONY CERULLO
Owner
VA Cerullo Landscaping and General Contracting
717 Pennington Street
Elizabeth, NJ 07202 United States
vsuperone@aol.com
http://www.cambridgewhoswho.com

BUS: Landscape Contracting Company **P/S:** Landscaping and Construction Services **MA:** Regional **D/D/R:** Landscaping, Laying Cement Using Asphalt Concrete, Negotiating Contracts, Overseeing Residential and Corporate Drainage Services, Consulting, Removing Snow **H/I/S:** Playing Soccer and Football, Reading Landscaping and Nursing Magazines **FBP:** Organic Gardening **EDU:** Coursework in Automotive Mechanism, Edison Vocational High School (1968) **A/A/S:** Vallarta Club

MR. MICHAEL J. CESTONE, DMD
Orthodontist
Cestone Orthodontics
829 Second Street Pike
Richboro, PA 18954
cestoneortho@gmail.com
http://www.cambridgewhoswho.com

BUS: Dental Clinic **P/S:** Orthodontic Services Including the Application of Self-Ligating Brackets, Invisible Ceramic Braces and Invisalign **MA:** Statewide **EXP:** Mr. Cestone's expertise is in orthodontics. **H/I/S:** Spending Time with his Family, Playing Soccer and Tennis, Golfing, Playing the Guitar, Hiking, Hockey **FBP:** Industry-Related Publications **EDU:** Doctor of Dental Medicine, University of Pennsylvania **CERTS:** Board Certified Orthodontist; Diplomate, American Board of Orthodontics **A/H:** Middle Atlantic Society of Orthodontics; Pennsylvania Dental Association; American Dental Association; American Association of Orthodontists; Psi Chi; Omicron Kappa Upsilon; Delta Upsilon Sigma **C/VW:** Coach and Trainer, Local Soccer Associations **A/S:** He attributes his success to his hard work, dedication and desire to make people feel better about themselves. **B/I:** He became involved in his profession because of his interest in dentistry. **H/O:** The highlight of his career was seeing the excitement of a 55-year-old patient who had her braces removed. Her self-esteem increased dramatically and the experience changed her life.

APRIL S. CHAFFEE, MS
First Grade Teacher
Morningside Elementary School
10521 Morningside Drive
Garden Grove, CA 92843 United States
aprilabc123@hotmail.com
http://www.cambridgewhoswho.com

BUS: Elementary School **P/S:** Regular Curriculum Including English, Mathematics, Science, Social Studies, Art, Music, History, Reading, Writing and English Language Development **MA:** Regional **D/D/R:** Instructing Kindergarten through Second-Grade Students in All Core Subjects **H/I/S:** Practicing Yoga, Reading **EDU:** Master's Degree in Education Curriculum and Instruction, California State University at Fullerton (1988); Bachelor of Arts in Liberal Studies, California State University at Fullerton (1986) **A/A/S:** California Teachers Association; National Education Association; National Association for the Education of Young Children **A/H:** Who's Who Among American Teachers (2004-2006) **DOB:** April 17, 1964 **W/H:** Teacher, Morningside Elementary School, Garden Grove, CA

CARMEN M. CHALOUX
Administrative Assistant
Department of Corrections
State of Vermont
1229 Portland Street, Suite 101
St. Johnsburg, VT 05819 United States
http://www.doc.state.vt.us

BUS: Government Department **P/S:** Criminal Justice and Incarceration **MA:** Statewide **D/D/R:** Fulfilling Administrative Duties **H/I/S:** Camping, Creating Arts and Crafts, Painting, Spending Time with her Grandson **FBP:** Better Homes and Gardens **EDU:** Industry-Related Training and Experience **A/S:** She attributes her personal and professional success to her hard work and continued interest in the profession. **B/I:** She became involved in her profession because of her desire to succeed as a single parent. **H/O:** The highlight of her career was being promoted to administration services.

SHAWNNA M. CHAMBERLIN
Teacher
Big Spring High School
100 Mount Rock Road
Newville, PA 17241 United States
schamberlin@bigspring.k12.pa.us
http://www.cambridgewhoswho.com

BUS: School **P/S:** Education **MA:** Local **EXP:** Ms. Chamberlin's expertise is special education. **D/D/R:** Managing the Department **H/I/S:** Traveling, Scrapbooking **FBP:** CEC Journals **EDU:** Master's Degree, Shippensburg University **A/A/S:** Local Union **C/VW:** Local Church, The Four Diamonds Fund **A/S:** She attributes her success to making people understand that all children can learn. **B/I:** She became involved in her profession because she started as a drug and alcohol counselor, but decided she needed something less stressful. **H/O:** The highlight of her career is watching her students graduate.

SHELIA A. CHAMBERS, BSN, RN
1) Registered Nurse 2) Mark Kay Consultant
1) Girling Healthcare, Inc. 2) Mary Kay Cosmetics
213 W. Southmore
Pasadena, TX 77502 United States
schambers48@aol.com
http://marykay.com/schambers48

BUS: 1) In-Home Healthcare Facility 2) Beauty Consulting Firm **P/S:** 1) At Home Healthcare 2) Independent Beauty Consulting **MA:** 1) Texas 2) Statewide **D/D/R:** Managing Cases, Specializing as a Field Nurse, Advocating for her Patients **H/I/S:** Football, Cooking, Sewing, Cooking on the Barbecue, Interior Decorating, Caring for Plants **FBP:** Nursing Today; Nurse2007; Journal of Psychiatry; Nursing Made Incredibly Easy **EDU:** Bachelor of Science in Nursing, University of Texas, Galveston **CERTS:** Licensed Vocational Nurse, San Jacinto College; Certified Nursing Assistant, Houston **A/A/S:** American Nurses Credentialing Center **C/VW:** Galveston County Ministerial Alliance; Scholarship Fund for Katrina Victims **SP:** David **CHILD:** Nicole, Joronica **A/S:** She attributes her success to her strong family values, her mother and her family background in health care. **B/I:** She became involved in her profession because she always wanted to become a nurse since the age of ten. **H/O:** The highlight of her career was when her team spent the weekend with Willy Nelson on his ranch as an outing for the oncology team of the Sisters of Charity St. Joseph Hospital.

MS. KATHLEEN A. CHAN, MSW, LCSW
Lead Counselor (Retired)
Department of Counseling
Catholic Charities
abraggdon@netzero.net
http://www.cambridgewhoswho.com

BUS: Social Service Agency **P/S:** Community Counseling, Refugee Resettlement, Immigration and Foster Care Services **MA:** Regional **D/D/R:** Performing Psychodynamic Brief Therapy Including Trauma Treatment **H/I/S:** Creative Writing, Cooking, Listening to Music, Studying History and Theosophy **FBP:** Psychodynamic Diagnostic Manual; National Geographic Magazine **EDU:** Master of Social Work, University of Denver (1989); Master of Arts in Anthropology, San Francisco State University (1978); Bachelor of Arts in Anthropology, University of California (1968) **A/H:** Commendation Award, Colorado Mental Health Institute, Fort Logan **DOB:** May 27, 1943 **SP:** Donald **A/S:** She attributes her success to her dedication and work ethic. **B/I:** She became involved in her profession because of her desire to help others. **H/O:** The highlights of her career were receiving licensure and developing her expertise through mentoring of students.

JOHN A. CHAPMAN
Chief Chemist
Polymer Research Corporation
700 Highway 33 S.
Centreville, MS 39631 United States
cousinjacx3@yahoo.com
http://www.cambridgewhoswho.com

BUS: Chemical Manufacturing Company **P/S:** Polymers for Water Treatment Services **MA:** International **EXP:** Mr. Chapman's expertise lies in environmental compliance. **D/D/R:** Conducting Lab Research for Quality Improvement, Managing and Integrating Projects, Overseeing Plant Safety, Training **H/I/S:** Golfing, Solving Word and Logic Puzzles, Reading **FBP:** Chemical Processing; Aldrichimica Acta **EDU:** Bachelor of Science in Mineral Engineering and Chemistry, Colorado School of Mines (1969) **A/A/S:** American Mensa; Cornish American Heritage Society **A/H:** NASA Silver Snoopy Award (1998) **C/VW:** St. Joseph's Catholic Church **DOB:** November 18, 1946 **POB:** Boulder **SP:** Jacquie **CHILD:** Joshua, Dylan, Kyle

MR. GEORGE R. CHARETTE
Owner, Sole Proprietor
Charette Services
286 Whipple Street
Fall River, MA 02721 United States
charetteservices@aol.com
http://www.cambridgewhoswho.com

BUS: Wastewater and Biotechnical Company **P/S:** Data Acquisition, System Integration **MA:** National **D/D/R:** Controlling Programming and Instrumentation for Water, Wastewater and Biotechnical Industries, Working in Industrial Facilities, Overseeing Six Contracts **H/I/S:** Golfing, Playing Racquetball **EDU:** Associate Degree in Electrical Engineering, Bristol Community College (1996); Associate Degree in Mechanical Engineering, Bristol Community College (1996); Associate Degree in Computer Maintenance, Bristol Community College (1996) **A/A/S:** Instrument Society of America; Waterworks Association

NICOLE D. CHARLES
United Auto Workers Employee Support Services Representative
Automotive Components Holding, LLC
1508 Long Meadow Trail
Ann Arbor, MI 48108 United States
ncharle2@yahoo.com
http://www.cambridgewhoswho.com

BUS: Automotive Manufacturing **P/S:** Employee Support **MA:** National **EXP:** Ms. Charles' expertise is in employee assistance programs. **H/I/S:** Crocheting, Knitting, Making Jewelry **EDU:** Bachelor of Science in Business Administration, Northwood University **C/VW:** Elyse Bryant Educational Grant Foundation **A/S:** She attributes her success to good mentors and having been put in good situations. **B/I:** She became involved in the profession and became the person everyone went to and trusted. Her chairman saw this and promoted her to her current position. **H/O:** The highlight of her career is when people come back to thank her for her assistance.

DIONICIO CHARLES JR.
Senior Directional Supervisor
Diamond Back Quantum
Houston, TX United States
donniecharlesjr@yahoo.com
http://www.quantumdm.com

BUS: Oil to Gas Service Provider **P/S:** Directional Drilling **MA:** International **D/D/R:** Directing Drills **H/I/S:** Cooking, Reading, Hunting **EDU:** College Coursework; High School Education

BARBARA G. CHATMAN, M.Ed.
Guidance Counselor, Administrator
Hamilton County Department of Education
1020 N. Moore Road
Chattanooga, TN 37411 United States
bdchat@bellsouth.net
http://www.cambridgewhoswho.com

BUS: Education **P/S:** Education **MA:** Local **D/D/R:** Teaching, Counseling, Managing Administration **H/I/S:** Traveling, Painting, Watching College Football, Reading, Going to the Movies, Bowling, Playing Tennis, Spending Time with Family and Friends **EDU:** Bachelor of Arts in History and Sociology, Miles College, Birmingham, AL; Master's Degree in School Counseling, Alabama State University at Montgomery **CERTS:** Certified in Administration, University of Alabama at Birmingham **A/A/S:** Tennessee Education Association; Alpha Kappa Alpha Sorority, Inc.; National Association for the Advancement of Colored People; National Dropout Prevention Network **A/H:** ALCA Emerging Leader Award, Alabama Counseling Association **C/VW:** Project Safe Domestic Violence **A/S:** She attributes her success to her perseverance and determination. **B/I:** She became involved in her profession because she wanted to be in education since she was a child. **H/O:** The highlight of her career was obtaining her current position.

NORMA CHAVEZ
Certified Bilingual Teacher (Retired)
Glass Elementary School
701 N. 42nd Street
Waco, TX 76710 United States
hh4432006@yahoo.com
http://www.cambridgewhoswho.com

BUS: Elementary School **P/S:** Primary Education **MA:** Regional **D/D/R:** Teaching Second Grade Students in English and Spanish, Coaching Students in Storytelling, Developing the Curriculum, Translating between English and Spanish **H/I/S:** Cooking, Gardening, Fishing, Crocheting **EDU:** Master's Degree in General Education, Sul Ross State University, Alpine, TX (1995); Bachelor of Arts in Elementary Education, Boise, ID (1980) **CERTS:** Certified Lay Minister **H/O:** The highlight of her career was helping her student named Mansy to receive first prize in competitions.

TeVerra P. Chavous

Chief Executive Officer, Property Manager
CoChav Holdings, LLC
9003 Overlook Boulevard
Brentwood, TN 37027 United States
tivo60@bellsouth.net
http://www.cambridgewhoswho.com

BUS: Property Management and Real Estate Firm **P/S:** Housing Rentals **MA:** National **EXP:** Ms. Chavous' expertise is in psychometry. **D/D/R:** Managing and Coordinating Properties, Counseling, Working as a Vocational Director, Making Vocational Assessments, Career Coaching **H/I/S:** Creative Writing, Gardening, Sports, Interior Design, Attending Bible Study Classes, Dactyology, Lending Moral Support to Others **FBP:** Charles Schwab Investing Publications **EDU:** Bachelor of Arts in Sociology, Minors in French and English, Paine College **A/A/S:** Liaison, Aiken County Board of Disabilities (1998-2000); National Association for the Advancement of Colored People; South Carolina Professional Staff Association **C/VW:** Community Service, Local Church; Neighborhood Crime Watch; Adult Literacy Council **DOB:** April 5, 1943 **POB:** Marion **SP:** Jimmy **CHILD:** Jamie, Corey, Matea **A/S:** She attributes her success to her sense of fairness and personal integrity. **B/I:** She became involved in her profession because her son started the company and appointed her to oversee it. **H/O:** The most gratifying aspect of her career receiving positive feedback fro others.

Vladimir Chelyshkov

Instructor
Georgia State University
750 COE 7th Fl. 30 Pryor Street
Atlanta, GA 30303 United States
matvxc@langate.gsu.edu
http://www.cambridgewhoswho.com

BUS: Higher Education **P/S:** Education **MA:** International **D/D/R:** Applying Mathematics and Mechanics **EDU:** Ph.D. in Computational Fluid Mechanics, Ukraine Academy of Sciences **A/A/S:** American Mathematical Society **A/S:** He attributes his success to consistency, determination and luck. **B/I:** He was prompted to enter his profession because he had a passion for mathematical science. **H/O:** The highlight of his career was being able to combine education and research.

MR. JOHN S. CHENG
Associate
JP Morgan Chase and Company
Four Chase Metrotech Center
Brooklyn, NY 11245 United States
chengjsl@hotmail.com
http://www.chase.com

BUS: Finance Company **P/S:** Financial Services **MA:** International **EXP:** Mr. Cheng's expertise is in systems and network administration. **H/I/S:** Reading, Traveling **FBP:** MIS **EDU:** Bachelor's Degree in Computer Science, New York Institute of Technology (1991)

DIANE O. CHIARELLA, RN, BSN
Clinical Reimbursement Coordinator
Cranbury Center
Genesis Healthcare
292 Apple Garth Road
Monroe Township, NJ 08831 United States
dchia1022@aol.com
http://www.genesishcc.com

BUS: Healthcare Center **P/S:** Subacute and Long-Term Healthcare **MA:** National **D/D/R:** Conducting Assessments for Medicare **H/I/S:** Needlework, Reading, Gardening **FBP:** Nursing Spectrum **EDU:** Bachelor's Degree in Nursing, Rutgers, The State University of New Jersey; Associate of Science in Nursing, University of Medicine and Dentistry of New Jersey **C/VW:** Disabled American Veterans **A/S:** She attributes her personal and professional success to her true dedication to helping others. **B/I:** She has always had an interest in the field and a desire to care for others. **H/O:** The highlight of her career was returning to school at age 50 to acquire her bachelor's degree in nursing.

BECKY SUE CHILDREE, BSN, ACHRN
Hyperbaric Unit Coordinator
South Georgia Medical Center
2501 N. Patterson Street
Valdosta, GA 31602 United States
becky.childree@sgmc.org
http://www.cambridgewhoswho.com

BUS: Hospital **P/S:** Healthcare Including Wound Care, Hyperbaric Oxygen Therapy, Apheresis **MA:** Regional **EXP:** Ms. Childree's expertise is in hyperbaric oxygen therapy, wound care and therapeutic plasma exchanges. **D/D/R:** Educating Patients and Staff, Supervising Hyperbaric Oxygen Treatments, Performing Simple and Complex Wound Care, Minor Debridement and Apheresis Procedures **H/I/S:** Whitewater Rafting, Horseback Riding **FBP:** Undersea and Hyperbaric Medicine Journal; Pressure; Nursing2009 **EDU:** Bachelor of Science in Nursing, Medical College of Georgia; Associate Degree in Nursing, Abraham Baldwin Agricultural College **CERTS:** Advanced Certified Hyperbaric Registered Nurse; Certification in Advanced Cardiac Life Support, Advanced Transcutaneous Oximetry Certification **A/A/S:** Underwater Hyperbaric Medical Society; Baromedical Nurses Association; Baptist Nursing Association **A/H:** Nurse of the Year, Pulmonary Department, South Georgia Medical Center (2006) **C/VW:** First Baptist Church of Doerun, GA; Women on Missions Group, Covenant House; World Vision **DOB:** May 24, 1959 **POB:** Moultrie **W/H:** Tift General Hospital, Tift, GA; Jefferson Hospital, Louisville, GA; St. Mary's Hospital, Athens GA; South Georgia Medical Center, Valdosta, GA **A/S:** She attributes her success to the satisfaction she finds in seeing patients get well. **B/I:** She became involved in her profession because she wanted to help others. **H/O:** The highlight of her career was receiving her Advanced Hyperbaric Registered Nurse certification. **I/F/Y:** In five years, Ms. Childree hopes to have continued growth.

PAUL M. CHIMOCK
Owner, Vice President, Mortgage Specialist
NEPA Home Loans
HIMC, Inc.
201 S. Webster Avenue, Suite A
Scranton, PA 18505 United States
paul@nepahomeloans.com
http://www.nepahomeloans.com

BUS: Mortgage Company **P/S:** Mortgage Services, Home Loans **MA:** Regional **D/D/R:** Overseeing Residential Mortgage Services, Business and Operations Management **H/I/S:** Skiing, Playing Golf and Tennis **FBP:** Scotsman Guide **EDU:** Bachelor of Arts in Communication and Business, Wilkes University (1997) **A/A/S:** Scranton Board of Realtors; Scranton Chamber of Commerce; Pennsylvania Association of Mortgage Brokers; BIA

LESLIE A. CHLADNY, RT(R), CT
CAT SCAN Technologist
Greater Lafayette Health Services
2400 South St.
Lafayette, IN 47904 United States
lesterchat1279@aol.com
http://www.cambridgewhoswho.com

BUS: Nonprofit Hospital **P/S:** Trauma, Emergency and General Care **MA:** National **EXP:** Conducting In- and Outpatient Exams, CAT Scans and Intravenous Therapy, Assisting Radiologists with Cardiac CTA Procedures **H/I/S:** Softball, Exercise, Spending Time with Family and Friends **FBP:** RT Image **EDU:** Associate Degree in Allied Health Career Specialties, Southern Illinois University; Associate Degree in Radiologic Technology, Southern Illinois University **A/A/S:** American Registry of Radiologic Technologists **C/VW:** Relay for Life, American Cancer Society; Local Church **A/S:** She attributes her success to her upbringing, strong work ethic and continuous education. **B/I:** She was prompted to enter her profession because she wanted to help people. **H/O:** The highlight of her career is when her co-workers and patients recognize her hard work and dedication to other patients.

MARGRETHE ROSE CHOROSER
Business Manager, LBN
Chevron Corporation
PO Box 2516
Liverpool, NY 13090 United States
crmr@chevron.com
http://www.chevron.com

BUS: Oil Industry Company **P/S:** Oil, Fuel and Lubricant Sales **MA:** International **EXP:** Ms. Choroser's expertise is in marketing. **H/I/S:** Traveling, Exercising, Volunteering, Spending Time with her Family **EDU:** Bachelor of Arts in Psychology, Le Moyne College, Syracuse; Associate of Arts in Business Administration, Erie Community College, North Campus **A/A/S:** Sales Award (2006); Premium Product Growth Award (2006); Contribution Margin Growth Award (2006); North American Top Performer Award **C/VW:** Volunteer, Hospice Family Care Giver; Confirmation Teacher, St. John's Parish; Booster President, Softball League **A/S:** She attributes her success to her determination and faith. **B/I:** She became involved in this profession because she has always worked in sales for a premium product. She started in the food industry working for Nabisco and then moved into the oil industry. **H/O:** The most gratifying aspect of her career is her success.

PATRICIA A. CHRISMAN
Registered Nurse
UK HealthCare Good Samaritan Hospital
310 S. Limestone Street
Lexington, KY 40508 United States
patricia.chrisman@cwwemail.com
http://www.samaritanhospital.com

BUS: Hospital **P/S:** Healthcare **MA:** Local **D/D/R:** Working in the Pediatric Extended Care Unit **H/I/S:** Traveling, Cross-Stitching, Bicycling **FBP:** Nursing2009 **EDU:** Associate Degree in Nursing, Kentucky State University **A/A/S:** Disabled American Veterans **C/VW:** Volunteer, Three Mission Trips **A/S:** She attributes her success to her ability to work with people. **B/I:** She became involved in her profession because she always wanted to become a nurse. **H/O:** The most gratifying aspect of her career is working in the critical care unit.

DON 'DOC' CHRISTIAN
Caretaker, Manager, Teacher
1) Lincoln Tree Farm 2) Tacoma School District #10
28001 Mountain Highway E.
Spanaway, WA 98387 United States
dondoc.christian@cwwemail.com
http://www.tacoma.k12.wa.us

BUS: 1) Farm 2) Public School **P/S:** 1) Vocational Forestry 2) Education Including Instruction and Curriculum Development **MA:** 1) International 2) Local **EXP:** Mr. Christian's expertise is in forestry. **D/D/R:** Teaching, Maintaining the Acreage, Landscaping, Logging, Inventing **H/I/S:** Fishing, Clam Digging, Golfing, Hunting **FBP:** National Geographic; U.S. News & World Report; Reader's Digest; Technology Review; Discover; Bottom Line **EDU:** Bachelor of Arts in Education, Pacific Lutheran College (1951) **CERTS:** Vocational Certificate, State of Washington (1974); Certification in Standard General Teaching **A/A/S:** North American Hunting Club; President, Village Condo Association (1980) **C/VW:** Lions Club; Veterans of Foreign Wars **SP:** Donna **CHILD:** Linda, Kelly, Steve, Steve

ROBIN A. CHRISTIE
Real Estate Agent
Century 21 Southern Homes, Inc.
205 St. James Avenue
Suite 509
Goose Creek, SC 29445 United States
robinchristie@comcast.net
http://www.cambridgewhoswho.com

BUS: Real Estate Company **P/S:** Real Estate **MA:** Local **D/D/R:** Marketing **H/I/S:** Barrel Racing **EDU:** Bachelor of Science in Computer Science **A/A/S:** Charleston Board of Realtors; National Association of Realtors **C/VW:** Local Hospitals **A/S:** She attributes her personal and professional success to her customer service referrals and continued education. **B/I:** She has always had an interest in the field and enjoys the flexibility of the profession. **H/O:** The highlight of her career is helping first-time buyers.

TRACEY JEAN CHRISTY, RN, BSN
Nursing Administrative Manager
St. John Hospital and Medical Center
22101 Moross Street
Detroit, MI 48236 United States
traceycrn@aol.com
http://www.cambridgewhoswho.com

BUS: Hospital and Medical Center **P/S:** Healthcare **MA:** Regional **EXP:** Ms. Christy's expertise is in emergency medicine, nursing administration and legal nurse consulting. **H/I/S:** Spending Time with Family **FBP:** AACN Journal **EDU:** Bachelor of Science in Nursing, Grand Valley State University **CERTS:** Certified in Advanced Cardiac Life Support; Certified in Pediatric Advanced Life Support; Certified Nursing Assistant, Stevens High School **A/A/S:** Association of Legal Nurse Consultants **C/VW:** The United Way, Habitat for Humanity **A/S:** She attributes her personal and professional success to her continued learning and open mind. **B/I:** She has always had an interest in the field and a desire to make a difference. **H/O:** The highlight of her career is seeing nurses that she mentored become successful staff members.

IRENA M. CHRUSTOWICZ-POSTIFF, MBA, MSEM
Continuous Improvement Engineer
TRW Automotive
4505 W. 25 Mile Road
Washington, MI 48094 United States
irena.postiff@trw.com
http://www.trw.com

BUS: Automotive Company **P/S:** Active and Passive Systems Including Active Control Retractors, Curtain Airbag Systems, Active Suspension Systems, Electronic Stability Control, Chassis Components, Steering Gears, Body Control Systems and Engineered Fasteners and Components **MA:** National **D/D/R:** Scheduling, Tracking, Consulting, Lecturing, Training, Testing Medical Fluid, Steering Gears and Chassis Components, Engines and Transmissions in the Laboratory **H/I/S:** Gardening, Cooking, Hiking **FBP:** Science **EDU:** Pursuing Master of Business Administration, University of Phoenix; Master of Science in Engineering Management, Oakland University (1998); Bachelor's Degree in Mechanical Engineering, Lawrence Technical University, MI (1994); Bachelor's Degree in Medical Technology, Eastern Michigan University (1986) **A/A/S:** Polish Engineering Society; American Society of Clinical Pathologists

JULIE A. CHURCHILL-MICKLEY
Official Court Reporter
Julie A. Churchill-Mickley
c/o US Courthouse
5400 Federal Plaza
Hammond, IN 46320 United States
julie_churchill@innd.uscourts.gov
http://www.cambridgewhoswho.com

BUS: Court Reporting Company **P/S:** Legal Services Including Court Reporting Services, Federal Court, Judiciary, Environmental Protection Agency System and Medical Product Liability Patents **MA:** Local **D/D/R:** Court Reporting on Areas such as Medical and Labor Law, Environmental Protection and U.S. Equal Employment Opportunity Commission **H/I/S:** Participating in Church Activities, Reading 'Seven Habits of Highly Effective People' by Stephen Covey **EDU:** Coursework in Court Reporting Studies, College of Commerce, Chicago (1976); Associate Degree in Business Studies **CERTS:** Illinois Court Reporting License #1608 6155; California Court Reporting License **A/A/S:** National Court Reporters Association; Society for the Technological Advancement of Reporting **C/VW:** President, The Church of Jesus Christ of Latter-day Saints **W/H:** Official Reporter, U.S. District Court, Hammond, IN (1995-Present); Owner, Operator, Custom Service Reporting, Chicago, IL (1993-1994); Official Reporter, Federal Court of Los Angeles (1988-1992); Owner, Operator, Eisenhower Medical Center (1982-1983); Freelance Reporter, U.S. District Court, Chicago, IL (1975-1981)

Nikki Cianni, MBA
Human Resource Administrator
Northern Habilitative Services and Northstar Services, Inc.
227 W. Lake Street
Chisholm, MN 55719 United States
nc@nhs-nss.com
http://www.nhs-nss.com

BUS: Healthcare **P/S:** Care and Support for People with Disabilities **MA:** Local **D/D/R:** Specializing in Human Resources for Healthcare Providers **H/I/S:** Traveling, Spending Time with Family **FBP:** HR **EDU:** Pursuing Ph.D. in Leadership and Human Resource Management, Capella University; Master of Business Administration, Concentration in Human Resource Management, University of Phoenix **A/A/S:** Society for Human Resource Management; Arrowhead Human Resource Management Association **C/VW:** Charities through her Organization **A/S:** She attributes her success to her desire to develop herself, patience and openness, which make her approachable. **B/I:** She became involved in her profession because while she was working in a home healthcare agency she became more attached to the employees and wanted to assist them. **H/O:** The highlight of her career has been the opportunity to work with a healthcare organization and combine healthcare with her human resources experience and education.

Ms. Andrea Cifizzari, NCTMB
Nationally Certified Massage Therapist
Therapeutic Massage and Bodywork
118 Washington Street
Holliston, MA 01746 United States
distarblue@comcast.net
http://www.cambridgewhoswho.com

BUS: Proven Leader Dedicated to Excellence in Healthcare **P/S:** Massage Therapy **MA:** Regional **D/D/R:** Performing Deep Tissue, Thai/Shiatsu Combination and Yoga Massages, Traveling Nationally and Internationally to Meet with Clients **H/I/S:** Playing Music, Yoga, Traveling **FBP:** Massage Therapy Journal **EDU:** Coursework in Bodywork and Massage Therapy, Bancroft School of Massage Therapy (1997) **CERTS:** Nationally Certified Massage Therapist, American Massage Therapy Association **DOB:** September 16, 1961 **W/H:** Professional Musician

LISA CIRACO
Director, Special Education Therapist
For Kids Only Day Care
900 and 904 Morris Park Avenue
Bronx, NY 10462 United States
craklee123@aol.com
http://www.cambridgewhoswho.com

BUS: Day Care Facility Offering Quality Child Care in a Safe Environment **P/S:** Services and Care for Children Aged Two Months to Five Years **MA:** Regional **D/D/R:** Running an Inclusion Day Care for 160 Children, Overseeing Teachers Regarding Curriculum, Working with Children with Special Needs, Checking the Children for Any Special Needs, Encouraging Parent Education, Addressing Behavior Issues, Hiring and Firing, Reviewing Staff Certifications, Receiving Referrals from TheraCare (a Private Agency), Conducting Evaluations and Testing for Two Month to Five-Year-Old Children **H/I/S:** Walking, Jogging, Exercising **FBP:** Autism and Attention Deficit Publications **EDU:** Master's Degree in Special Education, College of New Rochelle (2004); Master's Degree in Early Childhood Education, College of New Rochelle (1992); Bachelor's Degree in Elementary Education, St. John's University (1983) **CHILD:** Donna, Stephen

GLORIA J. CISSNE, MSN, CPNP
Pediatric Nurse Practitioner
Lancaster Pediatric Associates
2106 Harrisburg Pike
Lancaster, PA 17601 United States
gloria.cissne@villanova.edu
http://www.cambridgewhoswho.com

BUS: Private Practice **P/S:** Healthcare **MA:** Local **D/D/R:** Offering Primary Care **H/I/S:** Camping, Hiking, Snow Skiing, Spending Time with her Two Labs **FBP:** Journal of Pediatric Healthcare **EDU:** Master's Degree in Pediatric Nurse Practitioner, Villanova University; Bachelor's Degree in Nursing, LaSalle University **A/A/S:** Sigma Theta Tau International; National Association of Pediatric Nurse Practitioners; Pediatric Nurse Certification Board **A/S:** She attributes her success to her ability to stay current in her field and network with other professionals. **B/I:** She became involved in her profession because she has a rare genetic disorder so she had to spend a lot of time with doctors and enjoyed the field. **H/O:** The highlight of career is being able to reassure parents.

JANICE HOPE MARIA CLACKEN, LPN
Independent Contractor, Licensed Practical Nurse
Family Private Care
PO Box 1169
Hobesound, FL 33475 United States
jan_eyez@yahoo.com
http://www.Cambridgewhoswho.com

BUS: Healthcare **P/S:** Healthcare **MA:** Local **EXP:** Ms. Clacken's expertise is in psychiatric nursing. **H/I/S:** Playing Tennis, Dancing, Going to the Beach and Cooking Island Foods. **CERTS:** Licensed Practical Nurse, Medgar Evers Community College, Brooklyn, NY **C/VW:** Veterans of Foreign Wars; Silent Unity; Treasurer, Samaritan Village **A/S:** She attributes her personal and professional success to her passion for helping . **B/I:** She became involved in the healthcare industry while helping people in Jamaica and trying to make a difference. **H/O:** The highlight of her career is her patients being able to understand and relate to the face behind the voice.

BETTY W. CLARK
Owner, Manager
Mansion House Art and Antiques
120 N. Church Street
Smithfield, VA 23430 United States
mansiongallery@charter.net
http://www.mansiongallery.net

BUS: Art and Antiques Shop **P/S:** Antiques, Oil Paintings, Hair Jewelry, Estate Jewelry, Figurines, Accessories, Furniture, Oil Restoration **MA:** Regional **D/D/R:** Restoring Paintings Appraising and Selling Artwork from 1820-1950, Selling Silver, Porcelain and Estate Jewelry, Matching Flatware, Managing Operations **H/I/S:** Gardening **FBP:** Antiques **EDU:** College Coursework **A/A/S:** Tidewater Area Retail Alliance Association **A/S:** She attributes her success to her honesty and high standards.

DANNY L. CLARK SR., PH.D.
Curriculum Specialist
Miami-Dade County Public Schools
1450 N.E. 2nd Avenue
Miami, FL 39132 United States
dannlclark@aol.com
http://www.cambridgewhoswho.com

BUS: Education **P/S:** Instruction and Curriculum, Public School Education Support **MA:** Regional **EXP:** Dr. Clark's expertise is in curriculum development and mathematics. **D/D/R:** Supporting Schools, Administration, Department Chairs, Teachers and Students, Working with Middle and High School Students to Improve the Quality of Education **H/I/S:** Most College Sports, Baseball, Football, Track, Baseball, Golfing **FBP:** ASCD Magazines **EDU:** Ph.D. in Administrative Educational Leadership, Mathematics, Curriculum and Instruction, Union Institute and University (2005) **A/A/S:** Association for Supervision and Curriculum Development

DIANNE S. CLARK
Teacher
Rosehill Elementary School
9801 Rosehill Road
Lenexa, KS 66215 United States
rhclark@smsd.org
http://www.teacherweb.com/ks/rosehill/dianneclark

BUS: Elementary School **P/S:** Primary Education **MA:** Regional **D/D/R:** Teaching All Subjects to Second through Fourth-Grade Students, Selecting Textbooks, Writing Grants **H/I/S:** Reading, Traveling, Playing Tennis and Volleyball, Scrapbooking, Watching Movies, Sewing, Spending Time with her Grandchildren and Relatives **FBP:** Phi Delta Kappan; Instructor; Mailbox; Teacher's Helper **EDU:** Master's Degree in Curriculum and Instruction, Webster University; Bachelor of Science, The University of Kansas **A/A/S:** Parent-Teacher Association; District Curriculum Council; National Science Teachers Association; National Council of Teachers of Mathematics; National Education Association; Phi Theta Kappa; Gamma Phi Beta; Phi Delta Kappa; International Reading Association **A/H:** Outstanding Junior Award, School of Education, University of Kansas; Who's Who Among America's Teachers; Harvest Moon Queen, Phi Delta Kappa **C/VW:** Local Church; The Madison Project **POB:** Shreveport, LA **CHILD:** Christy, Cara **C/A:** Leader, Cadet Mathematics Program, District 49

JAMES R. CLARK
Pharmacist Supervisor
Parkway Apothecary
89 Genesee Street
Rochester, NY 14611 United States
jclark@unityhealth.org
http://www.unityhealth.org

BUS: Healthcare Center **P/S:** Healthcare Including Medication Preparation, Administration and Drug Interactions **MA:** Local **D/D/R:** Supervising the Pharmacy Staff, Dispensing Medications, Preparing Intravenous Medications, Drug Consulting, Consulting with the Staff, Reviewing Charts for Nursing Homes **H/I/S:** Playing Tennis, Playing the Guitar and Drums, Boating **FBP:** Pharmacist's Letter; Pharmacy Times **EDU:** Bachelor of Science in Pharmacy, University at Buffalo (1999); Associate of Science, Monroe Community College (1996) **A/A/S:** Kappa Psi Pharmaceutical Fraternity; Rho Chi Honor Society

LAURA ANN CLARK
Manager of Radiology
Sublette County Rural Healthcare District
PO Box 548
Big Piney, WY 83113 United States
cindy2b@yahoo.com
http://www.cambridgewhoswho.com

BUS: Healthcare Center **P/S:** Healthcare **MA:** Local **EXP:** Ms. Clark's expertise is in radiography. **D/D/R:** Budgeting, Scheduling the Staff, Training New Employees, Administering Patient Care **H/I/S:** Gardening, Cleaning, Cooking, Surfing the Internet **FBP:** ASRT Journal **EDU:** Associate Degree in Radiologic Technology, Western Wyoming Community College, Rock Springs **A/A/S:** American Society of Radiologic Technologists; American Registry of Radiologic Technologists **C/VW:** Juvenile Diabetes Research Foundation; National Breast Cancer Foundation **A/S:** She attributes her success to her desire to better herself. **B/I:** She became involved in her profession because of the variety and challenges that exist within the profession.

DR. ORVIN R. CLARK

Associate Professor,
Department Chairman of Educational Administration
University of Wisconsin
PO Box 2000, Belknap and Catlin
Superior, WI 54880 United States
oclark@uwsuper.edu
http://www.uwsuper.edu

BUS: University **P/S:** Higher Education **MA:** Regional **EXP:** Dr. Clark's expertise is in the oversight of the educational administration department and the development of individualized plans for students. **D/D/R:** Advising, Strategic Planning, Budgeting **H/I/S:** Cross Country and Downhill Skiing, Snowshoeing, Boating **FBP:** Association of School Business Officials Publications; American School Board Journal **EDU:** Doctor of Education in Educational Administration, Northern Illinois University (1995); Master of Science in Educational Administration, University of Wisconsin-Milwaukee (1971); Bachelor of Science in Business Administration, Wisconsin State University-Superior (1966) **CERTS:** Certified Chief School Business Official, Illinois State Board of Education; Certified School Business Manager, Department of Public Instruction, State of Wisconsin; Registered School Business Administrator, International Association of School Business Officials **A/A/S:** Wisconsin Association of School Business Officials; Illinois Association of School Business Officials; ; International Association of School Business Officials; American Association of School Administrators; American Management Association; American Educational Finance Association; Association for Supervision and Curriculum Development; Association of Educational Data Systems; Association of Educational Negotiators **C/VW:** Foundation Board, University of Wisconsin-Superior; Fundraiser, Hall of Fame, University of Wisconsin-Superior; Executive Director, Class of 1959 Educational Foundation, Superior Central High School

SHAWNA L. CLARK

President
Big Red Fasteners, Inc.
608 N. Walnut Avenue
Broken Arrow, OK 74012 United States
sclark@bigredfasteners.com
http://www.bigredfasteners.com

BUS: Wholesale Fastener Distributor **P/S:** Manufacturing, Construction, Petroleum Industry, Structural Bolts, Anchors, B7 Studs, Screws **MA:** National **D/D/R:** Overseeing Customer Service, Taking Care of Large Accounts, Packaging **CERTS:** Certified Minority Supplier, State of Oklahoma **A/A/S:** National Association of Woman Business Owners **A/H:** Talk of the Year Award, National Association of Woman Business Owners

Ms. Christine A. Clarke
Staff Pharmacist
Cottage Hospital
Swiftwater Road
Woodsville, NH 03785 United States
chris11m4@yahoo.com
http://www.cambridgewhoswho.com

BUS: Hospital **P/S:** Healthcare **MA:** Northern New Hampshire, Vermont **D/D/R:** Monitoring and Dispensing Patient Drugs, Resolving Issues with Insurance Companies **H/I/S:** Sullivan's American Kenpo Karate, First Degree/Brown Belt **EDU:** Pursuing Master's Degree in Forensic Toxicology; Bachelor of Science in Pharmacy, University of Rhode Island College of Pharmacy **CERTS:** Nationally Registered Emergency Medical Technician, New Hampshire Society of Hospital Pharmacists **A/S:** She attributes her success to hard work, and always striving constantly towards improving herself. **B/I:** She chose the profession due to influence from her uncle, who was also a pharmacist. **H/O:** The highlight of her career was being accepted into graduate school.

Marcia D. Clarke
Sales Executive
Manhattan Place Realty
99 Park Ave
Hoboken, NJ 07030 United States
marcia@manhattanplacerealty.com
http://www.manhattanplacerealty.com

BUS: Real Estate Company **P/S:** Full Service Real Estate Sales **MA:** Hudson County **EXP:** Ms. Clarke's expertise is in commercial and residential sales. **H/I/S:** Spending Time with her Family **FBP:** Realty Magazine **EDU:** Bachelor's Degree in Nursing, Thomas Damby University of Leeds, England **CERTS:** Real Estate License (2002) **A/A/S:** New Jersey Board of Realtors; National Association of Realtors; National Association for the Advancement of Colored People **C/VW:** St. Jude Children's Hospital **A/S:** She attributes her success to excellent mentoring from her boss.

KEVIN D. CLAUSIUS
Graphic Artist, Technology Service Co-HEAD
Focus
PO Box 1210
Greeley, CO 80632 United States
kclausius@focusonline.org
http://www.focusonline.org

BUS: Catholic College Ministry Organization Mentoring Catholic Students in Chastity, Sobriety and Excellence; **P/S/:** Campus Ministry **P/S:** Catholic College Ministry Organization Mentoring Catholic Students to Chastity, Sobriety and Excellence **MA:** International **EXP:** Ms. Clausius' expertise is in ministry. **D/D/R:** Enhancing Graphic and Print Layouts through Adobe Software **H/I/S:** Karate, Visual Arts Including Icon Painting and Black and White Photography **EDU:** Bachelor of Fine Arts, Graphic Design and Printmaking, Minor in Public Relations, Culver-Stockton College **A/A/S:** Lambda Chi Alpha **C/VW:** Church **A/S:** He attributes his success to wonderful parents, always offering support and providing inspiration. **B/I:** He became involved in this profession because he started as a resident assistant in college and he discovered a desire to help college students. **H/O:** The highlight of his career is his ability to make a positive impact on the lives of students.

JAMES A. CLEMENT, RWCS
Director, Risk Management and Insurance
Samford University
800 Lakeshore Drive
301 Samford Hall
Birmingham, AL 35229 United States
jaclemen@samford.edu
http://www.samford.edu

BUS: University **P/S:** Higher Education **MA:** International **EXP:** Mr. Clement's expertise is in accounting. **D/D/R:** Overseeing Risk Management, Property and Casualty Insurance, Managing Workers' Compensation and Legal Arbitration **H/I/S:** Collecting Movie Memorabilia and Autographs **EDU:** Bachelor's Degree in Accounting, University of Tennessee (1989); Bachelor's Degree in Marketing, Samford University (1979)

NANCY L. LIVINGSTON CLEMENTS
Art Teacher
Dummerston School
52 School House Road
East Dummerston, VT 05346 United States
clement4@sover.net
http://www.dummerstonschool.org

BUS: School **P/S:** Art Education **MA:** Local **EXP:** Ms. Clements' expertise is in visual arts. **H/I/S:** Painting **FBP:** School Arts; Art Activities **EDU:** Bachelor's Degree in Art Education and Psychology, Central Michigan University **A/A/S:** Vermont Art Education Association **A/H:** Teacher of the Year Award, Wal-Mart Corporation (2006) **C/VW:** Arts Council; Boy Scouts of America **A/S:** She attributes her success to her determination. **B/I:** She became involved in her profession because art was always an interest for her. **H/O:** The highlight of her career was receiving the Wal-Mart Teacher of the Year Award in 2001.

CHRISTINE J. CLEVELAND
Cardiac Rehabilitation Registered Nurse
St. Margaret Mercy Hospital
5454 Hohman Avenue
Hammond, IN 46320 United States
wcannie@xvi.net
http://www.cambridgewhoswho.com

BUS: Hospital **P/S:** Cardiac Care, Rehabilitation and Education **MA:** Local **EXP:** Ms. Cleveland's expertise is in cardiac rehabilitation. **H/I/S:** Reading, Bike Riding, Hiking, Outdoor Activities, Traveling with Family, Cooking, Sewing **FBP:** American Journal of Nursing **EDU:** Bachelor of Science in Nursing, Valparaiso University **CERTS:** Certified in Advanced Cardiac Life Support **A/A/S:** Indiana Society of Cardiovascular and Pulmonary Rehabilitation **C/VW:** Board Member, American Heart Association; Local Community Volunteer **A/S:** She attributes her personal and professional success to her strong educational background and positive attitude. **B/I:** She has always had an interest in the field and a desire to care for others. **H/O:** The highlight of her career is the exciting and challenging nature of the profession.

TERESA A. CLIFFORD
Nurse Manager
Covenant Medical Center
3007 N. Frankford Avenue
Lubbock, TX 79416 United States
trscliffrd@aol.com
http://www.covenanthealth.org

BUS: Healthcare Institution **P/S:** Behavioral Health, Cancer, Cardiac, Diabetes, Trauma, Emergency, Hospice and Neurology Services, Pain Management, All Types of Surgery Services, Primary Care, Rehabilitation and Sports Medicine, Senior, Spiritual and Wound Care **MA:** National **D/D/R:** Managing Staff, Running All Codes, Administrating for After-Hours Calls, Troubleshooting **H/I/S:** Football, Swimming, Four-Wheel Biking **FBP:** Nursing Journals **EDU:** Bachelor of Science in Nursing Health Sciences **A/A/S:** Texas Nurses Association **C/VW:** Volunteer, Ronald McDonald House

REBECCA A. CLOTHEY
Assistant Professor, Director of High Education
Drexel University
3141 Chestnut Street
Philadelphia, PA 19104 United States
rebecca.a.clothey@drexel.edu
http://www.cambridgewhoswho.com

BUS: University **P/S:** Higher Education **MA:** Local **D/D/R:** Teaching International Education, Managing the Online Program as the Higher Education Administer, Overseeing Faculty **H/I/S:** Traveling, Reading, Bicycling **EDU:** Ph.D. in Education, University of Pittsburgh; Master's Degree in International Relations, American University; Bachelor of Arts in English, University of Pittsburgh **A/A/S:** Fulbright Association; Association for the Study of Higher Education; Comparative and International Education Society **A/S:** She attributes her success to her hard work, passion and motivation to accomplish her goals. **B/I:** She became involved in her profession after studying abroad in China. **H/O:** The highlight of her career was visiting Bosnia.

Ms. Linda Coady Richardson
Horticulture Supervisor, Landscape Architect
Oregon Zoo
4001 S.W. Canyon Road
Portland, OR 97221 United States
linda.richardson@oregonzoo.org
http://www.oregonzoo.org

BUS: Public Zoo **P/S:** Housing and Care for 1,029 Specimens Representing 200 Species of Birds, Mammals, Reptiles, Amphibians and Invertebrates, Education on Animals and their Habitats, Botanical Garden with More than 1,000 Species of Exotic Plants, Including Firebird Heliconia, Pelican Flower and Ground Orchid, Exhibits and Tours **MA:** Regional **D/D/R:** Designing, Building and Caring for the Zoological Garden Collection, Supervising the Landscape Architecture and Horticulture Department **H/I/S:** Soccer, Gardening, Overseeing Home Renovation **FBP:** Landscape Architecture Quarterly **EDU:** Master's Degree in Intercultural Studies, Western Seminary (1990); Bachelor of Science in Landscape Architecture, Oregon State University (1977) **CERTS:** Registered Landscape Architect (1990) **A/A/S:** Board Member, Association of Zoological Horticulture; American Society of Landscape Architects; American Public Garden Association; Oregon Association of Nurseries

Regina K. Coats
Registered Nurse, Quality Care Coordinator
Erickson Retirement Communities, Henry Ford Village
5101 Ford Road
Dearborn, MI 48126 United States
http://www.erickson.com

BUS: Retirement Community **P/S:** Independent Living Housing, Assisted Living and Nursing Home Care Center **MA:** Local **D/D/R:** Overseeing a 30-Bed Unit in an Alzheimer's and Dementia Unit, Supervising Two Charge Nurses, Attending Care Conferences and Annual Evaluations **H/I/S:** Reading, Camping, Enjoying Recreational Vehicles with her Family **FBP:** American Journal of Nursing **EDU:** Associate Degree; Registered Nurse **A/H:** Nominee, Best of the Best Leadership Award, Henry Ford Village **C/VW:** Local Church; Schultz Lewis Home for Orphaned Children **A/S:** She attributes her success to her wonderful staff that requires minimal supervision and to the mentorship the director of nursing has shown her, teaching her the importance of organizing and prioritizing and how to prepare her unit for the annual state surveys. **B/I:** She became involved in this profession after working as a nursing assistant for many years and then receiving an offer to return to school as a licensed practical nurse. **H/O:** The highlight of her career was becoming manager of the department after going back to school for her degree and knowing that she was fully qualified for her position.

JANICE A. COBURN
Assistant Principal
Milford Elementary School
100 West Street
Milford, NH 03055 United States
coburnbjka@adelphia.net
http://www.cambridgewhoswho.com

BUS: Education **P/S:** Elementary Education **MA:** Local **EXP:** Ms. Coburn's expertise is in staff and curriculum development. **D/D/R:** Staff Development, Curriculum Development **H/I/S:** Spending time with family, Socializing with friends **EDU:** Master's Degree in Education Administration, Rivier College; Bachelor's Degree in Elementary Education, Concentration in Early Childhood Development, Salem State College **A/A/S:** New Hampshire Association of Elementary School Principals; National Association of Elementary School Principals **C/VW:** Board of Directors, Milford Lion's Club **A/S:** She attributes her personal and professional success to her love for her work. **B/I:** She has always had an interest in the field and a love for working with children. **H/O:** The highlight of her career is networking and meeting people.

MARILYN A. COCHRAN
Administrative Assistant
Proximity Real Estate
1221 Bridgeway
Sausalito, CA 94965 United States
marilyncochran@sbcglobal.net
http://www.cambridgewhoswho.com

BUS: Real Estate Company **P/S:** Real Estate Exchange Services **MA:** National **D/D/R:** Managing the Office **H/I/S:** Spending Time with her Twin Grandsons, Traveling, Reading **FBP:** Ladies' Home Journal; Realtor **EDU:** Coursework and Training in Real Estate **CERTS:** Licensed Real Estate Agent, State of California **A/A/S:** Graduate Realtor Institute **C/VW:** Local Charitable Organizations **A/S:** She attributes her success to her drive, motivation and family. **B/I:** She became involved in her profession because she wanted a career for herself after her divorce. **H/O:** The highlights of her career are all of the goals she has accomplished.

JACK COE
Evangelist
Jack Coe Ministries, Inc.
PO Box 398538
Dallas, TX 75339 United States
jackcoe@jackcoe.org
http://www.jackcoe.com

BUS: Ministry **P/S:** Spiritual Services Including Religious Books, CD's and DVD's **MA:** Local **D/D/R:** Public Speaking, Writing Books **H/I/S:** Riding his Motorcycle **FBP:** Forbes; The Wall Street Journal; Time **EDU:** Coursework, Southwestern Assemblies of God University **A/A/S:** International Convention of Faith Ministries

FAYE COFFELT
Early Childhood Health Services Coordinator
Cumberland County Schools
PO Box 2357
Fayetteville, NC 28302 United States
fayeco@ccs.k12.nc.us
http://www.ccs.k12.nc.us

BUS: School District **P/S:** Educational Services Including Extracurricular Activities and Athletics **MA:** Regional **D/D/R:** Overseeing 20 Nurses and Four Counselors, Promoting Exceptional School Programs, Working with Special Needs and Handicapped Children, Performing Tube Feedings and Accucheck **H/I/S:** Spending Time at Beach **FBP:** School Health Alert **CERTS:** Registered Nurse, Chowan University (1972) **A/A/S:** Local Chapter, School Nurses Association; Program Coordinator, School Nurse Association of North Carolina; School Health Advisory Council; Vice President, Secretary, Exceptional Children's Parent Advisory Council **DOB:** September 29, 1951 **CHILD:** Casey, Crissy **W/H:** Pediatric Office Nurse (1976-1990); Staff Nurse, Newborn and Intensive Care Nursery (1972-1975)

JOSEPH H. COFFIN
Pastor
Upper Deer Creek Church
5019 E. 1400 S.
Galveston, IN 46932 United States
jhcoff@aol.com
http://www.udc@upperdeercreek.com

BUS: Church **P/S:** Religious Services **MA:** Local **D/D/R:** Working as a Pastor **H/I/S:** Woodworking **FBP:** New Christ Bible Institute Publications **A/A/S:** CAM

DIANE E. COHEN, RHIA
Director, Privacy Officer
Health Information Management
Schervier Nursing Care Center
2975 Independence Avenue
Bronx, NY 10463 United States
diane_cohen@bshsi.org
http://www.scherviercares.org

BUS: Nonprofit Healthcare Organization **P/S:** Healthcare Including Alzheimer's, Palliative, Respite, Short-Term and Long-Term Care, Rehabilitation and Skilled Nursing Services **MA:** Regional **D/D/R:** Managing Health Information Systems, Maintaining Medical Records, Overseeing Staff and Privacy Training **H/I/S:** Watching New York Area Hockey and Football Sports Teams, Reading, Traveling, Listening to Music **FBP:** Journal of AHIMA **EDU:** Master's Degree in Nutrition, New York Medical College (1986); Bachelor's Degree in Nutrition, Lehman College (1983) **CERTS:** Post-Baccalaureate Certification in Health Information Management, Health Science Center, SUNY Brooklyn (1999) **A/A/S:** President, Tappan Zee Health Information Management Association; Chairwoman, Award Committee, New York Health Information Management Association; Secretary, Long-Term Care Section Board; American Health Information Management Association **W/H:** Director of Health Information Management, St. Cabrini Nursing Home, Dobbs Ferry

ROBERT E. COHEN, MA.ED, C.A.S, ED.ADM

Executive Director
The American Seminary for Contemporary Judaism
885 E. Seaman Ave
Baldwin, NY 11510 United States
rc7119@aol.com
http://www.theascj.org

BUS: Professional Jewish Education **P/S:** Professional Education for Students in Jewish Education **MA:** NY Metro Area **D/D/R:** Overseeing Administration, Supervision and Curriculum, Programming, Scheduling, Training Cantors, Rabbis and Educators **H/I/S:** Playing Tennis and Soccer, Swimming, Music, Theater, Reading, Old Movies, Collecting Currency from Around the World, Collecting Stamps, Collecting Art **FBP:** Education Weekly; Association of Supervision and Curriculum Development; Principal Leadership; Time; Newsweek; US News and World Report **EDU:** Master's Degree in Elementary Education, Adelphi University; Master's Degree in Special Education, Adelphi University; Master's Degree in Curriculum and Development, Adelphi University **A/A/S:** Association for Supervision and Curriculum Development; National Secondary School Principals; Coalition for Advanced Jewish Education; International Childhood Association **C/VW:** North American Conference of Rabbi's; North American Federation of Synagogues Inc.

EVELYN COLBERT

Registered Nurse
Stratford VNA
2340 North Avenue
Apartment 2C
Bridgeport, CT 06604 United States
rngramec@aol.com
http://www.stratfordvna.org

BUS: Nonprofit Organization **P/S:** Residential Healthcare Including Nursing and Medical Services **MA:** Regional **D/D/R:** Caring for Patients **H/I/S:** Traveling **EDU:** Associate Degree in Nursing, University of Bridgeport (1974)

KAT COLE
Vice President of Training and Development
Hooters of America, Inc.
1815 The Exchange N.E.
Atlanta, GA 30339 United States
kcole@hooters.com
http://www.hooters.com

BUS: Atlanta-Based Operator and Franchiser of over 450 Hooters Locations in 46 States and 26 Countries **P/S:** Quality Food Service **MA:** National **EXP:** Ms. Cole's expertise is in administration. **D/D/R:** Organizing Training and Development Programs, Ensuring Client Satisfaction, Overseeing Responsible Business Practices and Alcohol Services **H/I/S:** Practicing Yoga, Painting **FBP:** Nation's Restaurant News **EDU:** Associate Degree, University of North Florida (1998) **A/A/S:** Georgia Restaurant Association; Multicultural Food Service & Hospitality Alliance; The Council of Hotel & Restaurant Trainers; National Restaurant Association; CHRT; MSHA **H/O:** The most gratifying aspects of her career are attaining her current position and working to improve the company's performance.

RONJA COLE, MSN, APN, CNP
Nurse Practitioner
Hashemi Medical Group
4 Executive Court
Suite 3
South Barrington, IL 60010 United States
ronjacole@sbcglobal.net
http://www.cambridgewhoswho.com

BUS: Healthcare Center **P/S:** Healthcare **MA:** Local **EXP:** Ms. Cole's expertise is in family medicine including diabetes, geriatrics, wound care and preventive medicine. **D/D/R:** Managing Long-Term Care, Consulting for Quality Improvement for Long-Term Care Facilities **H/I/S:** Spending Time with her Family **FBP:** Diabetes Forecast; Advance for Nurse Practitioners **EDU:** Master's Degree in Nurse Practitioner Studies, University of Alabama, Birmingham (2000); Master's Degree in Nursing, The University of Alabama, Huntsville (1999) **CERTS:** Board Certified Family Nurse Practitioner, American Nurses Credentialing Center; Certification in Basic Life Support **A/A/S:** American Academy of Nurse Practitioners; American Association of Diabetes Educators; American Diabetes Association; Association For the Advancement of Wound Care

VICKI A. COLEMAN, RN, NCTM, CIMI
Registered Nurse, National Certified Therapeutic Massage, Certified
Infant Massage Instructor
Centegra Health System
3701 Doty Road
Woodstock, IL 60098 United States
vicki0201@sbcglobal.net
http://www.vcoleman@centegra.com

BUS: Hospital **P/S:** Healthcare **MA:** Local **D/D/R:** Nursing, Delivering Chemotherapy and Massage Therapy **H/I/S:** Gardening, Swimming, Fishing **FBP:** RN Magazine; Massage Therapy **EDU:** Associate Degree in Nursing, Tennessee State University **CERTS:** Nationally Certified in Therapeutic Massage; Certified in Infant Massage Instruction **A/S:** She attributes her success to the encouragement from her patients. **B/I:** She became involved in the profession because she used to work in a physicians office. **H/O:** The highlight of her career is her education.

PEDRO COLLAZO-ORNES, MD
MD
SP Radiology
202 A San Justo Street
Apartment 209
San Juan, PR 00901 Puerto Rico
http://www.cambridgewhoswho.com

BUS: Healthcare **P/S:** Radiology **MA:** International **EXP:** Mr. Collazo-Ornes' expertise is in neuroradiology. **H/I/S:** Traveling, Boating **EDU:** MD, University of Puerto Rico **A/A/S:** American College of Radiology; Neurological Society of North America

ANITRA COLLINS
Program Assistant
James J. Peters Veterans Affairs Medical Center
130 W. Kingsbridge Road
Bronx, NY 10468 United States
anitra.collins@va.gov
http://www.cambridgewhoswho.com

BUS: Healthcare **P/S:** Healthcare **MA:** Regional **D/D/R:** Coordinating Programs **H/I/S:** Reading, Dancing, Surfing the Web **C/VW:** Cancer Research **DOB:** December 18, 1961 **CHILD:** Charmaine **A/S:** She attributes her success to hard work and determination. **B/I:** She became involved in the profession because she was very interested in it. **H/O:** The highlight of her career was having such amazing mentors.

JANET A. COLLINS
Manager
J. Collins Reporting, LLC
222 W. Coleman Boulevard
Mount Pleasant, SC 29464 United States
janet@jcollinsReporting.com
http://www.jcollinsReporting.com

BUS: Court Reporting Firm **P/S:** Reporting Services Including Real-time Transcriptions, Tutoring Services for Court Reporting Students, Communication Access, Real-Time Translation for the Hearing-Impaired People, Historical and Legal Transcription, Presentations and Demonstrations for Various Legal Groups and Schools **MA:** National **EXP:** Ms. Collins' expertise is in software development. **D/D/R:** Reporting in Official State and Federal Courts, Training Court Reporters, Mediating for a Communication Access Real-Time Translation, Selling and Instructing for Computer-Aided Transcription and Technical Legal Cases, Preparing Court Reporting Instruction **H/I/S:** Caring for her Dogs, Admiring Nature, Yoga, Listening to Music, Painting **FBP:** Journal of Court Reporting **EDU:** Associate Degree in Court Reporting, Reporting Academy of Virginia **CERTS:** Registered Professional Reporter; Registered Merit Reporter; Certified Realtime Reporter, National Court Reporters Association; Federal Certified Realtime Reporter, United States Court Reporters Association; Certified Court Reporter, State of North Carolina; Caption Master Series Program, The University of Mississippi **A/A/S:** Secretary, Official Court Reporters Association, NC; Women Work; Secretary, American Business Women's Association; National Court Reporters Association; United States Court Reporters Association **A/H:** Global Register's Who's Who in Executives and Professionals **DOB:** April 10, 1969 **SP:** Brock **CHILD:** Emma, Eli, Katie, Kassie **W/H:** Reporter, United States District Court; Sales Representative, Software Trainer, ProCAT Software

PATRICIA J. COLLINS
Senior Administrator, Financial Advisor
Alliance Data Systems, Inc.
17655 Waterview Parkway
Dallas, TX 75252 United States
patricia.collins@alliancedata.com
http://www.alliancedata.com

BUS: Finance Company **P/S:** Financial Services Including Retail, Utility and Mail Service Transactions **MA:** National **D/D/R:** Maintaining Accounts Payable and Receivable and Spreadsheets, Forming Projections, Evaluating Contracts, Overseeing the Procurement Department and Lease Services, Arranging Travel for the Director and Marketing Coordinator **FBP:** Fortune **EDU:** Associate Degree in Business, University of Texas (1996) **C/VW:** Various Charitable Organizations

STACI M. COLLINS
Realtor, Trade Show Manager
Urban Realty
1411 Sweetbriar Road
Orlando, FL 32806 United States
stacicollins@cfl.rr.com
http://www.agentcollins.com

BUS: Real Estate **P/S:** Investments, Residential and Commercial Real Estate Sales **MA:** Local **EXP:** Ms. Collins' expertise is in commercial real estate and investment properties. **H/I/S:** Spending Time With Family & Friends, Bike Riding **FBP:** Money **EDU:** Associate of Science in Business Management **CERTS:** Real Estate License **A/A/S:** Chamber of Commerce; National Association of Realtors **A/S:** She attributes her success to her drive. **B/I:** She chose the profession she has always been interested in real estate. **H/O:** The highlight of her career is helping build a better community.

NICOLE BIVENS COLLINSON
Vice President, Trade Negotiations and Legislative Affairs
Sandler Travis & Rosenberg, P.A.
1300 Pennsylvania Avenue N.W.
Washington, DC 20004 United States
nbc@strtrade.com
http://www.strtrade.com

BUS: International Trade and Customs Law Firm **P/S:** International Trade and Customs Practice, International Trade and Government Relations, Border Security Program, Labor and Corporate Social Responsibility, International Trade Law, Intellectual Property **MA:** International **D/D/R:** Lobbying for International Trade Policies and United States Trade Agreements, Customs Requirements, Attending Multinational Association and Foreign Government and International Conferences **H/I/S:** Practicing Yoga, Playing Ultimate Frisbee **FBP:** Washingtonian; The Hill **EDU:** Master's Degree in International Relations, The George Washington University (1988) **A/A/S:** President, Women in International Trade; Women in Government Relations; Washington International Trade Association; Board of Trustees, Georgetown College; Board of Directors, Imojeans

ENNIO M. COLÓN, MD
MD
South Florida Pediatric Partners
7800 S.W. 8th Avenue
Suite C-350
Miami, FL 33173 United States
emcolon@pol.net
http://www.cambridgewhoswho.com

BUS: Pediatric Healthcare Group **P/S:** Healthcare Services to Pediatric Patients from their Ten Offices in the Tri-County Area of Miami-Dade, Broward and Palm Beach **MA:** Regional **D/D/R:** Specializing in General Pediatric Care, Dealing with Newborns to 21-Year-Olds, Treating Pediatric Infectious Diseases and Autism in Children, Educating the Public on Autism, Training Residents at Local Hospitals and Universities **H/I/S:** Playing Soccer, Cycling, Swimming **EDU:** Fellowship, Tulane University (1990-1992); MD, University of Puerto Rico Central (1987); Bachelor of Science in Biology and Pre-Med, University of Puerto Rico Central (1983) **A/A/S:** Fellow, American Academy of Pediatrics; Medical Association; National Alliance for Autistic Research; Medico Americano Academy of Inter-American Doctors

LORETTA COLORATO
Realtor
Century 21 McMullen
6400 N.W. Highway
Chicago, IL 60631 United States
lcolorato@sbcglobal.net
http://www.century21mcmullen.com

BUS: Real Estate Agency **P/S:** Commercial and Residential Real Estate Exchange **MA:** Regional **EXP:** Ms. Colorato's expertise is in the sale of condominiums and multi-family properties. **H/I/S:** Traveling, Reading **FBP:** Realtor **A/A/S:** Harwood Heights Chamber of Conference; Multiple Listings Service; Chicago Association of Realtors; National Association of Realtors

MARSHA A. COMBE
Vice President of Call Centers
America First Credit Union
1344 W. 4675 S.
Riverdale, UT 84405 United States
mcombe@americafirst.com
http://www.cambridgwhoswho.com

BUS: Credit Union **P/S:** Financial Services **MA:** Local **D/D/R:** Managing Call Centers, Lending **H/I/S:** Golfing, Snowmobiling **EDU:** High School Education **CERTS:** Certified Credit Union Executive, CUNA Management School **A/A/S:** Ogden-Weber Chamber of Commerce; Spikers Ambassador, Military Affairs **C/VW:** United Way; Chamber of Commerce; In-House Credit Union Donations Committee **H/O:** The highlight of her career was becoming vice president.

KEVIN SCOT COMBS, DO
Internal Medicine Attendant
Family Health Care Associates of Southwest Virginia, P.C.
143 W. Main Street
PO Box 369
Lebanon, VA 24266 United States
kcombs_nch@yahoo.com
http://www.cambridgewhoswho.com

BUS: Private Practice **P/S:** Healthcare **MA:** Local **EXP:** Dr. Combs' expertise is in internal medicine. **D/D/R:** Assessing Patients, Prescribing Medicines, Overseeing Internal Medicine and Geriatric Rotations **H/I/S:** Collecting Coins **EDU:** Doctor of Osteopathic Medicine, Pikeville College School of Osteopathic Medicine **A/A/S:** American Osteopathic Association; American Medical Association; American College of Osteopathic Internists **A/H:** National Dean's List **DOB:** May 1, 1971 **A/S:** He attributes his success to his determination and persistence. **B/I:** He became involved in his profession because of his personal experience with family illnesses. **H/O:** The most gratifying aspect of his career is being able to care for his patients.

GAIL L. CONAWAY, RN, CCRC, CIP
Associate Director
Chesapeake Research Review, Inc.
7063 Columbia Gateway Drive
Columbia, MD 21046 United States
gconaway@irbinfo.com
http://www.chesapeakeirb.com

BUS: Research and Ethics Review Business and Risk Management Partner **P/S:** Research Oversight, Consulting, Training and Education, and the Advancement of Public Understanding of Research **MA:** International **EXP:** Ms. Conaway's expertise includes human research protection and human subject safety review. **H/I/S:** Fishing, Snowmobiling, Camping, Rock Climbing, Gardening **FBP:** Applied Clinical Trials **EDU:** Associate Degree in Nursing, Catonsville Community College (1974); Registered Nurse (1974) **CERTS:** Certified Clinical Research Coordinator; IRB professional **A/A/S:** Board Member, Local Chapter, Association of Clinical Research Professionals **DOB:** May 21, 1952 **SP:** John **CHILD:** John, Brian

BEULAH ANN CONDREY
Instructor, Advisor
Blue Ridge Community College
180 W. Campus Drive
Flat Rock, NC 28731 United States
annc@blueridge.edu
http://www.blueridge.edu

BUS: Comprehensive Community College **P/S:** Degree Programs, Diploma Programs, Certificate Programs **MA:** Regional **EXP:** Ms. Condrey's expertise is in American sign language. **D/D/R:** Interpreting, Advising Students on Course Selection and Job Searches, Developing Courses through Distant Learning Formats Including Television and Online, Conducting Workshops Related to American Sign Language, Deaf Culture, Codas and Establishing Deaf Ministry **H/I/S:** Writing **EDU:** Master's Degree in Advanced Studies in Deaf Education, Gallaudet University, Washington, DC (2002) **A/A/S:** National Association of the Deaf; American Sign Language Teachers Association; Registry of Interpreters for the Deaf **A/H:** Excellence in Teaching Award, State Board of Community Colleges (2001); Outstanding Teacher Award; Excellence Community Service Award; Outstanding Young Woman, Henderson County; Outstanding Individual in the Community, Mayor's Committee; Recognition Pin, North Carolina Governor Jim Martin

FLORENCE G. CONFORTI FELANO
Physical Education and Adapted Education Instructor (Retired),
Sports Coach
Wayne Board of Education
50 Nellis Road
Wayne, NJ 07470 United States
http://www.cambridgewhoswho.com

BUS: School District **P/S:** Education for Grades Kindergarten through 12th **MA:** Local **D/D/R:** Physical Education, Special Education Adapted Physical Education, Coaching Roller Skating, Basketball, Soccer, Ice Skating, Bocci, Track and Field, Bowling and Swimming, Special Olympic Team **H/I/S:** Walking, Reading, Gardening **FBP:** U.S. News & World Report **EDU:** Master of Arts in Special Education, William Paterson University **CERTS:** Certified in Early Childhood Education, William Paterson University; Certified in Supervision, William Paterson University; Certified in Learning Disabled Teacher Consulting, William Paterson University **A/A/S:** New Jersey Association of Physical Education; New Jersey Association of Health, Physical Education, Recreation and Dance; Board Member, Montclair State University Alumni Association **C/VW:** Member, Foster Parent Group; Our Lady of the Valley Church; Old Timers Athletic Association of the Patterson Greater Area

ANNE K. CONLEY-GOLDSTEIN, PH.D., HSPP
Clinical Psychologist
Private Psychology Practice
10585 N. Meridian
Suite 340
Indianapolis, IN 46290 United States
drakcg2005@yahoo.com
http://www.cambridgewhoswho.com

BUS: Therapy and Psychological Assessment **P/S:** Private Psychology Practice **MA:** Indianapolis and Surrounding Areas **EXP:** Ms. Conley-Goldstein's expertise is in adolescent psychological treatment. **H/I/S:** Spending Time With Family, Reading, Cooking **FBP:** APA Journals **EDU:** Ph.D., Pacific Graduate School of Psychology, CA **A/A/S:** American Psychology Association **C/VW:** Planned Parenthood **A/S:** She attributes her personal success to her hard work, perseverance, and mentors. **B/I:** She has always had an interest in the field and was inspired by her mentors. **H/O:** The highlight of her career was completing her pre-doctoral internship.

CLAUDINE L. CONNELL
Home Delivery Manager
Eau Claire Press Company
701 S. Farwell Street
Eau Claire, WI 54701 United States
cconnell@ecol.net
http://www.leadertelegram.com

BUS: Media and Publishing Company **P/S:** Two Newspapers, Commercial Printing, Internet Service Provider **MA:** Regional **D/D/R:** Overseeing Circulation and Home Delivery, Marketing **H/I/S:** Listening to Music, Attending the Theatre, Playing Volleyball **FBP:** Publication Journals **EDU:** Coursework, University of Wisconsin **C/VW:** The United States Junior Chamber; Committee Member, Sawdust City Days and Air Show **A/S:** She attributes her success to her hard work and perseverance. **B/I:** She became involved in her profession after starting as a part-time employee and taking advantage of opportunities for advancement. **H/O:** The most gratifying aspect of her career is being able to relate to her employees because she once worked in their positions.

ALICE L. CONNERS, MS, MBA
Market Researcher
IMV Medical Information Division
1400 E. Touhy Avenue, Suite 250
Des Plaines, IL 60017 United States
alconners1@yahoo.com
http://www.cambridgewhoswho.com

BUS: Medical Imaging **P/S:** Medical Imaging Equipment Research **MA:** National **D/D/R:** Marketing Research Reports **H/I/S:** Reading and Playing with her Cats **FBP:** US News and World Report **EDU:** Bachelor's Degree, Coe College; Master of Science, Iowa State University; Master of Business Administration, University of Chicago **A/A/S:** The Phi Beta Kappa Society; Phi Kappa Phi; Daughters of the American Revolution **C/VW:** Mental Health Organizations **A/S:** She attributes her success to her ability to respond to others in a positive way and applying her knowledge to new endeavors. **B/I:** She became involved in the profession when she took a market research course in college and really enjoyed it. **H/O:** The highlight of her career was launching two products that went international.

CONSTANCE J. CONNOR
Laboratory Section Supervisor
Alaska Native Medical Center
4315 Diplomacy Drive
Anchorage, AK 99508 United States
cconnor@anthc.org
http://www.anmc.org

BUS: Hospital **P/S:** Healthcare Including Primary, Tertiary and Acute Care **MA:** Local **EXP:** Ms. Connor's expertise is in hematology. **D/D/R:** Supervising the Staff, Training and Teaching Students **H/I/S:** Watching ATV Races, Riding Snowmobiles **FBP:** College of American Pathologists Publications; American Society for Clinical Pathology Publications; Transfusion **EDU:** Bachelor of Science in Medical Technology, Northern State University (1972) **A/A/S:** American Society for Clinical Pathology **SP:** Robert **CHILD:** Tamara, Steven

C. R. CONRAD, MS, MA
1) Teacher (Retired) 2) Minister
1) Davis-Townsend School 2) New Jerusalem United Church of Christ
1270 Beck's Nursery Road
Lexington, NC 27292 United States
bconrad652003@yahoo.com
http://www.cambridgewhoswho.com

BUS: 1) School District 2) Church **P/S:** 1) Education 2) Religious Services **MA:** 1) Regional 2) Regional **D/D/R:** Visiting Hospitals, Caring for Sick Patients, Singing Gospel, Teaching Mathematics and History to Fourth-Grade Students, Preaching, Coordinating Events, Conducting Bible Classes, Counseling **H/I/S:** Sports, Reading, Traveling **FBP:** Christianity Today; US News & World Report **EDU:** Master of Arts in Theology, Houston Graduate School of Theology (2006); Master's Degree in School Administration, North Carolina A&T State University (1986); Master's Degree in Intermediate Education, North Carolina A&T State University (1983); Bachelor of Arts in History, High Point University (1969); Associate of Arts in Business Administration, Davidson County Community College (1967) **A/H:** Lion of the Year Award (2008); Teacher of the Year Award (1980) **C/VW:** Crisis Ministry; Former Secretary, Lions Club; Board of Directors, North Carolina Western Association of the United Church of Christ **H/O:** The most gratifying aspect of his career is being able to build relationships with people. **I/F/Y:** In five years, Mr. Conrad hopes to obtain his Doctoral Degree in theology.

EILEEN M. CONROY
Second Vice President, Marketing Director
Principal Financial Group
710 Ninth Street
Des Moines, IA 50309 United States
econroy632@aol.com
http://www.cambridgewhoswho.com

BUS: Finance Company **P/S:** Financial Services **MA:** International **EXP:** Ms. Conroy's expertise is in direct marketing, product branding, new product development and business-to-business marketing. **H/I/S:** Playing Tennis, Watching Movies, Visiting Art Museums **FBP:** Harvard Business Review **EDU:** Master of Business Administration, Harvard Business School; Bachelor of Arts in Economics and Political Science, Wellesley College **C/VW:** Alumni Organizations; Art Museums **A/S:** She attributes her success to her open-mindedness. **H/O:** The highlight of her career was creating a new product and introducing it to the market.

MR. ALLAN G. CONWAY
Managing Director, Founder, Author
Consultant Graphologists
14 Orford Court
Marsh Lane
Stanmore, HA7 4TQ United Kingdom
graphology@allanconway.co.uk
http://www.allanconway.com

BUS: One of Europe's Foremost Graphologists **P/S:** Consultant in the Field of Recruitment Selection, Regular Lecturer at both Oxford and Cambridge Universities, Provides Valuable Insights Based on Handwriting **MA:** International **D/D/R:** Conducting Detailed Handwriting Evaluations, Detecting Fraudulent Signatures, Determining Career Occupations and Marriage Partners through Handwriting Analysis, Consulting, Lecturing, Acting as an Expert Witness in Fraud Investigations **H/I/S:** Keeping an Unbroken Diary for 55 Years, Lecturing, Traveling, Spending Time with his Two Grandchildren **FBP:** Institute of Directors UK **EDU:** Bachelor's Degree in Psychology, Open University (1983) **A/A/S:** Association of Certified Examiners; British Institute of Graphology **SP:** Marion **CHILD:** Jeremy, Debra, Edward

MARGARET M.J COOK-DANCER, PA-C
Physicians Assistant
Stewartsville Medical Clinic, DeKalb Medical Clinic & Cameron
Regional Medical Center
106 S. Fourth Street
Stewartsville, MO 64490 United States
jmdancer2000@yahoo.com
http://www.cameronregional.org

BUS: Nonprofit General Acute Care Hospital **P/S:** Emergency Services, Radiology, Surgical Services, Laboratory Services, Home Health Care, Hospice Care, Inpatient and Outpatient Rehabilitation, Intensive Care, Obstetrics and Gynecology **MA:** Local **EXP:** Ms. Cook-Dancer's expertise is in family medicine and emergency room patient care. **D/D/R:** Dealing with Patients of All Ages, Working Directly with Surgeons, Overseeing the Women's Health Clinic Affiliated with the Hospital, Consulting with Other Hospitals, Assisting with Psychiatric Programs **H/I/S:** Collecting Antiques, Volleyball, Basketball, Swimming **FBP:** Audio Digest; American Family Physicians; CME **EDU:** Bachelor's Degree, Oklahoma State University (1987); Coursework, Physician Assistant Program, United States Army **CERTS:** Licensed Practical Nurse, Southeast Community College (1981) **A/A/S:** Missouri Association of Physician Assistants; National Association of Physician Assistants; National Commission on Certification of Physician Assistants; American Academy of Physician Assistants; NCMS **C/VW:** American Heart Association **H/O:** The most gratifying aspects of her career are enjoying the diagnostic aspect of her job, figuring out what is wrong with her patients and being able to treat them appropriately.

MRS. LAURA MORIN COONEY
French and Spanish Teacher
World Languages Department
Lebanon Junior High School
75 Bank Street
Lebanon, NH 03766 United States
lcooney@sau88.net
http://www.sau88.net

BUS: School District **P/S:** Education **MA:** Local **D/D/R:** Teaching French and Spanish **H/I/S:** Cooking **FBP:** Smithsonian; Time **EDU:** Bachelor of Arts in French, Rivier College (1968) **CERTS:** New Hampshire Mentoring Program, National Education Association (2005) **A/A/S:** New Hampshire Association of World Language Teachers **A/H:** Scholastic Bowl Coach Award, Lebanon Junior High School (1996) **C/VW:** New Hampshire Celebrates Wellness (1996-2008); Lebanon Junior High School Representative; District Wellness Committee; Former Member, Lebanon Community Chorus; Lifetime Member, Cooking Club of America **W/H:** Teacher, Mascoma High School (1969-1973); Teacher, Hollis High School (1968-1969)

CARA COOPER
Teacher, Student Activities Director
Sachse High School
3901 Miles Road
Sachse, TX 75048 United States
cjcooper@garlandisd.net
http://www.garlandisd.net

BUS: High School **P/S:** Education **MA:** Local **D/D/R:** Teaching Social Studies to Freshman Students, Directing Student Activities, Acquiring Sponsors, Approving Fundraisers for the Booster Club, Choir and Band, Making Daily Announcements, Tracking Student and Faculty Identification Badges, Maintaining the Master Calendar **H/I/S:** Reading, Watching Football and Basketball **EDU:** Bachelor's Degree in Liberal Arts, Southern Methodist University (2002) **A/A/S:** Ambassador, Sachse Chamber of Commerce **C/VW:** First Christian Church **DOB:** August 11, 1980 **POB:** Garland **A/S:** She attributes her success to her parents, who taught her the value of hard work and dedication.

KELLI E. COOPER
Sales Representative
Liberty Mutual Insurance Company
1811 Center Point Circle
Naperville, IL 60563 United States
kelli.cooper@libertymutual.com
http://www.libertymutual.com

BUS: Insurance Company **P/S:** Market Home Owners, Automotive and Life Insurance Policies **MA:** Statewide **D/D/R:** Marketing Home, Automobile and Life Insurance, Advising Clientèle on Identity Theft, Winterizing Individual Properties, Overseeing Cellular Phone Safety and Saving Gasoline at the Pump Programs **H/I/S:** Attending her Son's Baseball and Soccer Games, Traveling, Reading **FBP:** People **EDU:** Associate of Arts, Harper College (1989) **A/A/S:** Naperville Country Club; Chamber of Commerce **C/VW:** GSP **CHILD:** Tyler **A/S:** She attributes her career success to her excellent people and listening skills. **B/I:** She became involved in the insurance industry because she wanted to offer a more personal sales approach to her clients. **H/O:** The highlight of her career has been getting to know her clients.

PHYLLIS G. COOPER, RN, MN
President
1) Cooper Consulting 2) A Healthy Life for Everyone
PO Box 5037
Playa del Rey, CA 90296 United States
1) cconsulting@gmail.com 2) 4ahlife@gmail.com
http://www.phyllisgcooper.com

BUS: 1) Healthcare Education Consulting 2) Spiritual Coaching Provider **P/S:** 1) Education, Process Evaluation, Coaching 2) Community Health Nursing and Editor of Nursing Forum **MA:** 1) Local 2) Local **D/D/R:** Developing Educational Programs, Spiritual Coaching, Editing a Nursing Forum Journal, Advocating for Patients **H/I/S:** Water Fitness, Playing Tennis, Reading **FBP:** Fortune; Nursing Forum Journal **EDU:** Master of Science in Nursing, University of California, Los Angeles; Bachelor of Science in Nursing, Boston University **A/A/S:** Sigma Theta Tau International; National Association of Nurses in Business; Organization of Healthcare Educators; National League of Nursing; American Nurses Association **C/VW:** Myotonic Muscular Dystrophy Association and Awareness Support Group; Student Mentor

ROSALIE ANN COOPER
Author
rac962@roadrunner.com
http://www.cambridgewhoswho.com

BUS: Sole Proprietorship **P/S:** Poetry, Books **MA:** International **D/D/R:** Writing Poetry and Books **H/I/S:** Writing, Drawing **EDU:** Bachelor of Science in Electrical Engineering Technology, Buffalo State University; Associate Degree in Electrical Engineering Technology, Niagara County Community College; Associate Degree in Computer Science, Jamestown Community College **A/A/S:** International Society of Poets **A/H:** Best Poet, Poetry.com (2002-2007); Best Poems, Poetry.com (2002-2007); Found Woman Award (2004); Ambassador of Poetry, Poetry.com **C/VW:** Volunteer, Veterans Administration Hospital; County President, Ladies Auxiliary Veterans of Foreign Wars; Lifetime Member, Disabled American Veterans; WAVES National **A/S:** She attributes her success to the professionals she has met and worked with over the years as well as her self-motivation, dedication and persistence. **B/I:** She became involved in her profession because of her passion for writing and desire to express her feelings. **H/O:** The highlight of her career was being featured in The New York Times Book Review. **I/F/Y:** In five years, Ms. Cooper hopes to become a well-known author.

PATRICIA B. COPE
Clinical Research Associate
Novartis Pharmaceuticals
4082 S.W. Bamberg Street
Port St. Lucie, Fl 34953 United States
butchpj@aol.com
http://www.cambridgewhoswho.com

BUS: Pharmaceutical **P/S:** Federal Regulations and Conducting of Research with Human Subjects **MA:** International **D/D/R:** Auditing Clinical Trials **H/I/S:** Spending Time with her Pug Peggy Sue **FBP:** Newsweek **EDU:** Associate of Arts in Business Management, Jacksonville University **A/A/S:** Association of Clinical Research Professionals **C/VW:** American Heart Association; Multiple Sclerosis Society; Association of Intestinal Diseases; Veterans Administration **A/S:** She attributes her success to her drive, hard work and determination. **B/I:** She became involved in her profession because she had a desire to find better and safer drugs for the treatment of disease. **H/O:** The highlight of her career has been being able to mentor others using her knowledge and education.

JANICE E. COPPLE
Teacher, Counselor
Saddleback Valley Unified School District
10 El Potro
Rancho Santa Margarita, CA 92688 United States
bradcopple@cox.net
http://www.svusd.k12.ca.us

BUS: Outstanding Educational System **P/S:** Primary and Secondary Education for Regular and Gifted Students, Adult Education Courses, Special Education, Recreation and Community Services **MA:** National **D/D/R:** Teaching Regular and Gifted Third-Grade Classes, Counseling Students in All Elementary Grades, Counseling Children and Adults through the Community Church **H/I/S:** Reading Healthful Living, Going to the Gym, Enjoying Life with her Family and Children **EDU:** Master's Degree in Counseling and Psychology, Laverne University **A/A/S:** Saddle Back Valley Education Association; National Education Association **C/VW:** Fun Divorce Recovery Workshop; Saddle Back Church

CATHERINE C. CORBETT
Sales Executive
Coldwell Banker Realty Group
9427 S. Highway 1259
McDaniels, KY 40152 United States
cathycorbet@moreland.com
http://www.moreland.com

BUS: Real Estate and Land Development **P/S:** Waterfront Development, Luxury Exclusives **MA:** Local **EXP:** Ms. Corbett's expertise is in management. **H/I/S:** Enjoying Horses, Boating **FBP:** The Wall Street Journal **EDU:** Bachelor of Arts in Management Development, Aurora University **A/A/S:** Greater Louisville Association of Realtors; Kentucky Association of Realtors; National Association of Realtors; Chamber of Commerce **C/VW:** Habitat for Humanity **B/I:** After working for thirty years in the nuclear power industry, she wanted to pursue a career that would require less traveling. **H/O:** She feels that working for fourteen months with nuclear power executives after the fall of the Berlin Wall has been the highlight of her career.

BRAD L. CORBIN
Firefighter, Fire Medic
Anderson Fire Department
44 W. Fifth Street
Anderson, IN 46011 United States
caninekop782@sbcglobal.net
http://www.cambridgewhoswho.com

BUS: City Government **P/S:** Firefighting **EXP:** Mr. Corbin's expertise is in firefighting, emergency medical response, hazardous materials and dive rescues. **H/I/S:** Scuba Diving, Fishing, Playing Basketball and Softball **FBP:** Firehouse **EDU:** Industry-Related Training and Experience **A/A/S:** International Association of Firefighters; NMG **C/VW:** Indiana Mentors Association, Criminal Justice Task Force **A/S:** He attributes his success to her family. **B/I:** He became involved with the fire department because many of his family members work in law enforcement. **H/O:** The highlight of his career was being named EMT of the year.

LILLIAN A. CORDERO
Maternal Child Health Coordinator
Englewood Hospital & Medical Center
661 Martense Avenue
Teaneck, NJ 07666 United States
lillian.cordero@cwwemail.com
http://www.englewoodhospital.com

BUS: Hospital **P/S:** Healthcare **MA:** Local **D/D/R:** Managing Neonatal Pediatrics, the Maternity and Obstetric Departments **H/I/S:** Attending the Opera **FBP:** Pediatric Annuals; CB **EDU:** Bachelor of Science in Nursing, Seton Hall University, South Orange, NJ (1968)

DARRELYNN D. CORESON
Instructor
Linn Benton Community College
6500 Pacific Boulevard S.W.
Albany, OR 97321 United States
dodi.coreson@linnbenton.edu
http://www.linnbenton.edu

BUS: College **P/S:** Higher Education Including Professional and Technical Training, Continuing Education Classes and Education Programs for Students with Disabilities **MA:** Regional **D/D/R:** Teaching Computer Science and Mathematics Including Java, C++ and Oracle Databases **H/I/S:** Dancing **EDU:** Master's Degree in Mathematics, Oregon State University (1974) **A/A/S:** Leadership Team, Association of Judges, OR; Board of Directors, Dance Drill Coaches Association of Oregon **C/VW:** Local Church

PAM R. CORNEJO
Payroll Operations Manager
National Semiconductor Corporation
2900 Semiconductor Drive
Santa Clara, CA 95051 United States
pam.cornejo@nsc.com
http://www.national.com

BUS: The Manufacturing Industry's Premier Analog Company **P/S:** Semiconductor Components, High-Performance Analog Devices and Subsystems **MA:** National **D/D/R:** Managing Accounting and Payroll **H/I/S:** Bowling **FBP:** Payroll Managers Letter **EDU:** Diploma, Piedmont Hills High School (1969) **A/A/S:** American Payroll Association; United States Bowling Congress

MR. ROY CORNETT III, MBA
Owner
Cornett Enterprises
107 Woodlake Drive
Santa Rosa, CA 95405 United States
roycornett@sbcglobal.net
http://www.hmgwebmeeting.com/rc3

BUS: Internet Services **P/S:** Marketing **MA:** International **EXP:** Mr. Cornett's expertise is in leadership and coaching. **H/I/S:** Traveling, Music, Avid Reader **FBP:** The Wall Street Journal; Success **EDU:** Bachelor of Arts, Ball State University (1979); Master of Business Administration, University of San Francisco **C/VW:** United Way of America

MS. BETH CORREA
Chief Executive Officer
Official Payroll Advisor
PO Box 565
Enumclaw, WA 98022 United States
beth@officialpayrolladvisor.com
http://www.officialpayrolladvisor.com

BUS: Consulting Firm **P/S:** Strategic Payroll Implementation Services **MA:** National **EXP:** Ms. Correa's expertise is in operations management. **D/D/R:** Consulting, Overseeing Strategic Payroll Implementation Services **H/I/S:** Horseback Riding, Caring for Alpacas **FBP:** Horse Illustrated **EDU:** Master of Business Administration, Kent State University **A/A/S:** Board Member, Oracle HCM Users Group **C/VW:** The Humane Society of the United States; Thoroughbred Retirement Foundation; American Red Cross; St. Jude Children's Research Hospital **SP:** Zachary **A/S:** She attributes her success to her knowledge and her passion for her profession. **B/I:** She became involved in her profession through a natural progression of opportunities. **H/O:** The highlight of her career was opening her own company.

MARJORIE M. CORREIA
President
Bermuda Bowling Club, Inc.
47 Middle Road
Warwick, INTL WK05 Bermuda
marjorie@logic.bm
http://www.cambridgewhoswho.com

BUS: Membership Club **P/S:** Ten Pin Bowling **MA:** Local **D/D/R:** Performing Business Managerial Duties Including All Aspects of Leadership, Development and Project Management **H/I/S:** Traveling, Gardening, Bowling **EDU:** High School Education **C/VW:** Bermuda Society for the Prevention of Cruelty to Animals

DEBBIE J. CORSON
Managing Partner
Corson Creative Consulting LLC
1604 S.W. Ninth Street
Fort Lauderdale, FL 33312 United States
corsoncreative@bellsouth.net
http://www.outhousead.com

BUS: Full-Service Advertising Industry **P/S:** Quality Advertising Services, Public Relations, Communications, Account Services, Creative Services, Production Services, Media Services, Integrated Marketing Services, Branding, Research **MA:** Regional **D/D/R:** Overseeing Public and Media Relations, Branding, Marketing **H/I/S:** Camping **FBP:** AdvertisingAge **EDU:** Industry-Related Training; Coursework in Journalism and Public Relations, Indiana University of Pennsylvania **A/A/S:** Advertising Federation of Minnesota; Chamber of Commerce

HAROLD R. COSBY
Pastor
Harmony Missionary Baptist Church
292 McAllister Road
Battle Creek, MI 49014 United States
Mrctrans@netscape.com
http://www.cambridgewhoswho.com

BUS: Church **P/S:** Worship Services, Bible Studies, Community Outreach and Counseling Services, Spreading the Word of God **MA:** Regional **D/D/R:** Overseeing the Entire Organization Including Youth Programs, Working in Conjunction with Sister Churches, Servicing the Elderly, Sick and Underserved Populations in the Area **H/I/S:** Collecting Model Cars, Gardening, Reading Historical and Archaeological Books **EDU:** Associate Degree in Bible Studies, English and History, Northeast Mississippi Community College (1954) **CERTS:** Ordained (1952); Master Gardener **A/A/S:** Leila Arboretum Society; Former President, Equifax Users Group

PATRICIA COSIANO, M.ED, S.ED.
Lead Literacy Teacher Grades Three through Five
Memorial Park Elementary School
22800 Fox Avenue
Euclid, OH 44123 United States
pc4729@sbcglobal.net
http://www.euclid.k12.oh.us

BUS: Elementary School **P/S:** Reading, Mathematics, English, Science, Social Studies **MA:** Regional **D/D/R:** Teaching Reading in All Content Area, Science and Social Studies, Helping her Students Succeed, Coaching, Collaborating, Consulting **H/I/S:** Reading, Crafts, Basket Weaving, Sewing, Reading **FBP:** NEA Magazine **EDU:** Specialist Degree in Reading Education, Bowling Green State University (1994); Master's Degree in Reading, Bowling Green State University (1993); Bachelor of Science Degree in Elementary Education, Bowling Green State University (1983) **A/A/S:** North Eastern Ohio Education Association; Ohio Education Association; National Education Association; Euclid Teachers Association; Academic Achievement Team, Ohio Council of Teachers of English and Language Arts; Highly Qualified and Effective Teacher Committee, National Board Certification for Middle Childhood Education (2001)

CHRISTINE A. COSTELLO
Director of Fine Arts
Tantasqua Union-61 Regional School District
320 Brookfield Road
Fiskdale, MA 01518 United States
costelloc@tantasqua.org
http://www.tantasqua.org

BUS: Public School System with Seven Schools in Two Counties **P/S:** Educational Services for Students **MA:** Hampton and Worcester Counties **EXP:** Ms. Costello's expertise is in fine arts administration and curriculum design and education. **D/D/R:** Overseeing 27 Faculty Members in Seven Schools in Five Towns, Running the Visual Arts Program for Students in Kindergarten through Twelfth Grade **H/I/S:** Gourmet Cooking, Spending Time with Family **FBP:** Educational Leadership; Music News **EDU:** Pursuing Master of Education in Educational Leadership, Worcester State College; Master's Degree in Music, University of Connecticut **CERTS:** Master's Certification in Choral Music; Master's Certification in Principalship **A/A/S:** Massachusetts Music Educators Association; National Association for Music Education; American Choral Directors Association; Massachusetts Teachers Association; Association for Supervision and Curriculum Development **A/H:** Who's Who Among American Teachers; Who's Who Among American Women; Who's Who in the World; Who's Who in America **C/VW:** Director of Music and Church Organist, Zion Lutheran Church

NICOLE ANNE COSTELLO, BA, EL.ED
Eighth Grade Teacher
St. Mark School
1024 Radcliffe Street
Bristol, PA 19007 United States
cjsmommy1014@hotmail.com
http://www.cambridgewhoswho.com

BUS: Elementary School **P/S:** Education **MA:** Local **D/D/R:** Teaching Mathematics, Running the Student Council, School Safety Patrol Program, Mathletes and Varsity Cheerleading, Directing the Yearbook Staff **H/I/S:** Spending Time with Children **EDU:** Bachelor of Arts in Elementary Education, Holy Family University **CERTS:** Certification in Middle School Education **C/VW:** Basilica; Susan G. Komen Breast Cancer Foundation **A/S:** She attributes her success to her strong background in mathematics. **B/I:** She became involved in her profession because she wanted to be a teacher since she was in second grade. **H/O:** The most gratifying aspect of her career is having former students return and tell her how much she affected their lives.

TARA COTÉ
Realtor
Prudential California Realty
1400 Newport Center Drive
Suite 200
Newport Beach, CA 92660 United States
taracote@msn.com
http://www.coterealtygroup.com

BUS: Real Estate Agency **P/S:** Investment, Home Buyers and Multi-Unit Services **MA:** Regional **D/D/R:** Representing Clients in Orange County, Investment Properties Services **H/I/S:** Tennis, Walking, Going to the Beach **FBP:** BusinessWeek **EDU:** Bachelor's Degree in Political Science, University of California at Irvine (1999) **A/A/S:** Corona-Norco Association of Realtors; Orange County Association of Realtors; Pacific West Association of Realtors; California Association of Realtors; National Association of Realtors; Kappa Alpha Theta

SUSAN COTTLER, PH.D.
Division Chairwoman of Humanities,
Department Chairwoman of History
Westminster College
1340 Westminster Avenue
Salt Lake City, UT 84105 United States
scottler@westminstercollege.edu
http://www.westminstercollege.edu

BUS: Only Private, Comprehensive Liberal Arts College in Utah Offering a Strong Liberal Education Combined with Cutting-Edge Professional Programs at Both the Undergraduate and Graduate Levels **P/S:** Degree Programs in Business, Fine Arts, Nursing and Health Sciences, Education, Aviation, Environmental Studies, Social Sciences, Anthropology, Music, Communication and English **MA:** International **D/D/R:** Teaching Pop Culture as a Rock and Roll Historian, Studying the Connection to Rhythm and Blues and Soul to Civil Rights, Teaching Nineteenth Century Cultural and Social History of Europe **H/I/S:** Skiing, Traveling, Surfing, Thai Boxing, Shopping, Movies **FBP:** Vanity Fair; ESPN; Esquire; Vogue; Newsweek; Rolling Stone **EDU:** Ph.D. in Latin American History, The University of Utah (1982); Bachelor of Arts, University of Vienna (1970); Master's Degree in Latin American History, University of Utah **A/A/S:** Pop Culture Association; American Culture Association

LISA A. COUGHLIN, MS, CCC-SLP
Speech-Language Pathologist
Heritage Education Program
1 Delaware Road
Kenmore, NY 14217 United States
jc410lc@aol.com
http://www.cambridgewhoswho.com

BUS: Proven Leader in the Education Industry **P/S:** Assessments and Preschool Classes for Children with Developmental Disabilities Ages Three to Five Years, as well as Inclusion Classes in Conjunction with a 'Typical' Day Care Facility Located on Site **MA:** Regional **D/D/R:** Working with Handicapped Individuals from Birth to 21 Years of Age, Serving on a Multi-Disciplinary Evaluation Team of Social Workers, Special Education Professionals, Occupational Therapists and Physical Therapists, Making Home and Classroom Visits as Part of an Early Intervention Program Offering Pull-Out, Push-In and Inclusion Endeavors, Addressing Issues such as Feeding, Articulation, and Language **H/I/S:** Reading, Needlepointing, Admiring Antique Cars **FBP:** ASHA Leader; Advance; Parenting Magazines **EDU:** Master of Science in Speech Pathology, Buffalo State College (2005); Master of Science in Special Education, Canisius College (1998) **A/A/S:** American Speech-Language Hearing Association

ANN D. COUTURE
Special Education Resource Specialist
J.G. Johnson Elementary School
900 E. Jack Rabbit Street
Pahrump, NV 89048 United States
swmystic@pahrump.net
http://jgjohnson.nye.k12.nv.us

BUS: Elementary School **P/S:** Primary Education **MA:** Local **D/D/R:** Assisting Students with Learning Disabilities, Teaching Mathematics, Reading and Writing **H/I/S:** Reading, Volunteering **EDU:** Bachelor's Degree in Special Education, Fitchburg State College **A/A/S:** International Reading Association **A/S:** She attributes her success to her love for her profession. **B/I:** She became involved in her profession because of her interest in special education.

KNUTE COVER
Realtor
Century 21 Real Estate Champions
9021 Oakhurst Road
Suite D
Seminole, FL 33776 United States
kc@kccover.com
http://www.kccover.com

BUS: Real Estate Agency **P/S:** Residential Real Estate Exchange **MA:** National **D/D/R:** Managing Relocations and Investment Properties and Foreclosures **H/I/S:** Spending Time with his Children and Grandchildren, Making Crafts **FBP:** The Wall Street Journal; Real Estate Magazine **CERTS:** Accredited Buyers Representative; Certified Relocation Specialist; Certified MatureMoves Specialist; Certified E-Pro **A/A/S:** Greater Largo Chamber of Commerce; Pinellas County Board of Realtors; Florida Association of Realtors; National Association of Realtors **A/H:** Centrillion Award, 2005 **C/VW:** Easter Seals; Susan G. Komen for the Cure **SP:** Conchita **A/S:** He attributes his success to his honesty and customer service skills. **B/I:** He became involved in his profession because of his interest in real estate.

MR. DARRELL L. COWAN II
Chief Financial Officer, Owner
Independent National Security
1442 E. Lincoln Avenue
Apartment 332
Orange, CA 92865 United States
dcowan@inspatrol.com
http://www.inspatrol.com

BUS: Security Service Agency **P/S:** Protection and Courtesy Patrol Services **MA:** California **EXP:** Mr. Cowan's expertise is in business management and finance. **EDU:** Coursework, Fullerton College Police Academy; Coursework, Orange Country Sheriff Academy; Coursework, Douglas County Reserve Academy; Coursework, Western Nevada Police Academy **A/A/S:** California Association of Licensed Security Agencies, Guards and Associates; Apartment Association Greater Inland Empire; Apartment Association of Orange County; California Association of Community Managers **DOB:** May 29, 1987 **SP:** Brenda **CHILD:** Faith, Julie, Anna **H/O:** The most gratifying aspect of his career is providing a safe and happy work environment for his employees with all the benefits.

Jo Anne Cox, RN, MSN, CRNI, OCN
Clinical Staff Registered Nurse
Virginia Mason Medical Center
1100 Ninth Avenue
Seattle, WA 98111 United States
joacox@seanet.com
http://www.cambridgewhoswho.com

BUS: Specialty Hospital **P/S:** Healthcare, Infusion Therapy **MA:** Local **EXP:** Ms. Cox's expertise is in infusion therapy, chemotherapy and venous access. **H/I/S:** Reading, Crocheting **FBP:** ONS Journal **EDU:** Master of Science in Nursing, Seattle Pacific University **A/A/S:** Oncology Nursing Society; Infusion Nurses Society; American Nurses Association; Sigma Theta Tau International **A/S:** She attributes her success to her desire for growth and professional achievements. **B/I:** She became involved in her profession because she wanted to help other people through difficult times. **H/O:** The highlight of her career was returning to school and having her master's thesis published in a journal.

Mrs. Octavia L. Cox
Owner, Manager
Octavia's Daycare
1508 S. Walter Reed Drive
Arlington, VA 22204 United States
http://www.cambridgewhoswho.com

BUS: Daycare **P/S:** High Quality Professional Care and Education for Children Ages One to Four Years-Old **MA:** Regional **D/D/R:** Caring for and Teaching Children, Preparing Children for a Bright Future by Instilling them with Good Values **H/I/S:** Caring for Children, Dancing, Theater, Fine Dining, Traveling **EDU:** Coursework in Child Development **CERTS:** Licensed Daycare Center **C/VW:** Various Charitable Organizations; J.E. Eubanks Foundation **DOB:** October 24, 1955 **POB:** Alexandria **SP:** Robin **W/H:** Owner, Founder, Manager, Octavia's Daycare; Childcare Provider, Various Private Homes **C/A:** Founder, J.E. Eubanks Foundation **A/S:** She attributes her success to her late parents, brothers, sisters and friends who knew that she watched other people's children and they encouraged her to open her own daycare even though she had no children of her own. **B/I:** She became involved in her profession because she is a caring person who wants to spread her love around and teach children that they are not alone. **H/O:** The most gratifying aspect of her career is knowing that she makes many children happy and seeing that many of them have grown up to be successful adults.

Barbara K. Coy, RS, LPN
Food Industry Specialist
Michigan Department of Agriculture-Food and Dairy Division
525 W. Allegan
Lansing, MI 48909 United States
coyb9@michigan.gov
http://www.cambridgewhoswho.com

BUS: Food Safety Industry **P/S:** Food Service Sanitation, Section of MDA-Local Health Department, Food Service Inspection Programs **MA:** Statewide **EXP:** Ms. Coy's expertise is in the application of food safety through hazard analysis and critical control point programs. **D/D/R:** Application of Food Safety through HACCP **H/I/S:** Painting (Acrylics and Pastels), Singing, Sewing, Outdoor Activities **FBP:** Toastmaster Magazine **EDU:** Bachelor's Degree in Biology, Lake Superior State University **CERTS:** Licensed Practical Nurse, Hindsdale Sanitarian Hospital School of Practical Nursing; Registered Environmental Sanitarian, State of Michigan **A/A/S:** Toastmasters International; Association of Food and Drug Officials; Michigan Environmental Health Association; Past President, Great Lakes Conference on Food Protection **C/VW:** Local Church; Leukemia & Lymphoma Foundation **A/S:** She attributes her success to her commitment to serve, conviction from the Lord and her caring, supportive family.

Ms. Leslie D. Craig-Stubbs
Speech-Language Pathologist
Speech Therapy Services
Clark County School District
2625 E. St. Louis Avenue
Las Vegas, NV 89104 United States
lesliecmc@msn.com
http://www.mycmsite.com/lesliestubbs

BUS: School District **P/S:** Education **MA:** Regional **D/D/R:** Conducting Speech-Language Assessments for Pre-Kindergarten through Fifth-Grade Students, Participating in the Student and School Intervention Process, Participating as a Multidisciplinary Team Member to Determine the Eligibility of Special Education Students, Writing Reports, Collaborating with the School Nurse and Psychiatrist, Working Within Self-Contained Preschool Classes, Facilitating and Empowering Teachers, Focusing on Functional Communication, Developing New Programs **H/I/S:** Scrapbooking, Horseback Riding, Spending Time with her Children **EDU:** Master's Degree in Communication Disorders, Plus 40, Abilene Christian University (1988); Bachelor's Degree in Communication Disorders, Abilene Christian University (1986) **A/A/S:** Nevada Speech-Language-Hearing Association; American Speech-Language-Hearing Association; National Education Association **C/VW:** Sunrise Children's Foundation; Kifaru Jitsu Rhino Squad **DOB:** February 19, 1964 **POB:** Albuquerque **W/H:** Abilene State School, Abilene, TX; Special Children's Clinic, Las Vegas, NV; Clark County School District Speech Therapy Services, Las Vegas, NV **A/S:** She attributes her success to her determination to helping children. **B/I:** She became involved in her profession because of her desire to help children with communication disorders. **H/O:** The most gratifying aspect of her career is making a difference in the life of a child. **I/F/Y:** In five years, Ms. Craig-Stubbs intends to continue working with children.

MARGARET ANN CRAMER, RN
Licensed Practical Nurse
Brookdale Senior Living
2601 W. Northwest Expressway
Oklahoma City, OK 73112 United States
http://www.maximhealth.com

BUS: Full Service Staffing Company **P/S:** Temporary and Permanent Positions at Hospitals and Clinics to Potential Employees **MA:** Regional **D/D/R:** Serving as a Staff Nurse for Long Term Acute Care, Conducting Reassessments, Administering Intravenous Therapy, Distributing Medications, Drawing Blood, Consulting with Doctors and Family Members, Facilitating Family Nurses **H/I/S:** Fishing, Sewing **EDU:** Registered Nurse, Platt College, Oklahoma City (2007); Bachelor's Degree in Education and Science, South Eastern Oklahoma State University; Associate Degree in Nursing, Oklahoma State Community College **C/VW:** Christ Legacy Church

CAROLYN CRAWFORD
Executive Director, Owner
In His Name, Inc.
618 Ingleside Avenue
Athens, TN 37303 United States
inhisnameinc@msn.com
http://www.cambridgewhoswho.com

BUS: Healthcare **P/S:** Medical Supplies, Hospital Supplies, Walkers, Canes, Wheelchairs, Crutches and Braces **MA:** Regional **D/D/R:** Loaning Medical Equipment to Individuals **H/I/S:** Making Jewelry, Knitting, Painting **EDU:** Bachelor of Science in Nursing, Easton College, PA (1960) **A/A/S:** Board of Directors, Good Faith Clinic; Board of Directors, TOWEL Disciples; WOM

ANTOINETTE CRAWFORD-WILLIS
Executive Director
Dance Kentucky
6203 Port Antonio Road
Louisville, KY 40228 United States
antoinetteedctr@bellsouth.net
http://www.cambridgewhoswho.com

BUS: Community Service **P/S:** Dance Festivals **MA:** National **D/D/R:** Advocating for Dance Education, Performing **H/I/S:** Dancing, Children **EDU:** Master's Degree in Dance Education, Ohio State University **A/A/S:** National Registry of Dance Educators **A/S:** She attributes her success to her persistence and the support of her family. **B/I:** She became involved in her profession because she loved dancing since an early age and was recruited as a teacher because of her ability. **H/O:** The highlight of her career was reconstructing 'Helen Tamar's Negro Spirituals' and touring the act throughout Kentucky.

RENEE M. CRETAL
Accounts Payable Specialist
IPS-Sendero
7272 E. Indian School Road
Suite 300
Scottsdale, AZ 85251 United States
rmcretal2004@hotmail.com
http://www.cambridgewhoswho.com

BUS: Information Technology Firm **P/S:** Information Technology Services Including Accounts Receivable, Accounts Payable, Billing, Financial Software **MA:** International **EXP:** Ms. Cretal's expertise is in accounts payable and expenses management and advising companies on accounts. **D/D/R:** Training on How to Submit Expense Reports and Getting Approvals, Training Individuals for All New Hires, Managing Accounts Receivable and Payable, Interacting with Advisories that Travel, Training Advisories on Reports, Preparing Financial Statement Analysis, Overseeing Trends in the Market, Troubleshooting for the Company, Lecturing and Consulting on Financial and Trend Analysis **H/I/S:** Hiking, Rafting, Camping, Spending Time Outdoors **FBP:** The Wall Street Journal **EDU:** Bachelor's Degree in Accounting, University of Phoenix **A/H:** The Apple Award; Above and Beyond Award **C/VW:** Arizona Adopt A Greyhound **A/S:** She attributes her success to her creativity, organizational and problem solving skills, education, experience, hard work and being detail-oriented. **B/I:** She became involved in her profession because of her interest in working with numbers. **H/O:** The highlight of her career was receiving the Apple and Above and Beyond Award. **I/F/Y:** In five years, Ms. Cretal hopes to grow professionally, pursue her master's degree in accounting and earn her public accountant license.

FRANCES A. CRIST, MAE
Fourth Grade Teacher
Westview Elementary School
Berkeley County School District
100 Westview Drive
Goose Creek, SC 29445 United States
cristf@berkeley.k12.sc.us
http://www.berkeley.k12.sc.us

BUS: School District **P/S:** Education **MA:** Regional **D/D/R:** Teaching Mathematics and Science, Conducting Manipulative and Hands-On Activities **EDU:** Master's Degree in Elementary Education and Reading Endorsement, Plus 45, Ball State University (1979); Bachelor of Science in Elementary Education and Mathematics Endorsement, Ball State University (1975); Diploma, Alexandria-Monroe High School (1970) **A/A/S:** South Carolina Science Council; International Reading Association; Beta Sigma Phi **C/VW:** Saint John's Catholic Church

SHARI L. CROCKETT, M.Ed.
1) Adult Education Director (Retired) 2) Director
1) Monroe Randolph Regional Office of Education 2) Monroe
Randolph Transit District
1 Taylor Street
Chester, IL 62233 United States
scrocket@randolph.k12.il.us
http://www.randolph.k12.il.us

BUS: 1) Government Organization 2) Transportation Company **P/S:** 1) Education 2) Transportation Services **MA:** 1) Regional 2) National **D/D/R:** Teaching Adult Education and Core Subjects for Kindergarten, Sixth and Eighth-Grade Students, Writing Grants for Low-Income and General Educational Development Students, Working with State and Federal Agencies on Public Transportation, Overseeing Seven Buses and Eight Employees **H/I/S:** Collecting Antiques, Attending Auctions, Traveling, Reading **EDU:** Master's Degree in Education Administration, Plus 75, Southern Illinois University, Edwardsville (1993) **A/A/S:** Co-Chairwoman, National Conference, Adult Basic Education Committee (2000); Former President, Illinois Administrator and Continuing Educators Association **A/H:** Award, Monroe and Randolph Transit District (2006); Award, Family Literacy Program (2005); President Award, Illinois Administrator and Continuing Educators Association

JANA S. CROSBY
Reading Specialist, Early Childhood Consultant
505 Farmington Court
Nashville, TN 37221 United States
janacrosby@comcast.net
http://www.cambridgewhoswho.com

BUS: Early Learning Initiative Working with Child Care Centers **P/S:** Ensuring Disadvantaged Children are Ready to Start School by Providing Books to Centers, Classroom Materials, Curricula and Professional Development for Teachers and Literacy Coaches, Supporting Family Literacy within the Centers **MA:** Regional **D/D/R:** Training Early Preschool and Elementary Teachers in Literacy, Working with Community-Based Agencies, Training Large Groups, Reading Aloud to Children, Promoting a Love for Reading, Consulting **H/I/S:** Following Nashville Predators Hockey, Reading, Spending Time with Family, Playing with her Dogs, Shopping **FBP:** Education Weekly; The Reading Teacher; Reading Research Quarterly; Reading Today; Young Children **EDU:** Master's Degree in Education, Reading Specialist, Harding University (1992); Bachelor of Arts in K-12 Special Education, Minor in Elementary Education (1-6), Harding University, Cum Laude (1990); Liberal Arts Diploma, Harding Academy of Memphis (1987) **CERTS:** Kindergarten Certification, Harding University (1992); **A/A/S:** Former Treasurer, Vice President, Advisory Board Tennessee Reading Association; International Reading Association; Former President, Former Director of Membership Development, Middle Tennessee Reading Association; Advisory Board, Nashville Area Association for the Education of Young Children; Membership Committee, Tennessee Association for the Education of Young Children; National Association for the Education of Young Children; Southern Early Childhood Association **A/H:** Walter Heims Service Award, Tennessee Reading Association (2006) **C/VW:** Board Member, Book'Em (2003-2005)

RAYMOND L. CROUSER
Fifth Grade Teacher
Whiteriver Unified School District #20
PO Box 190
Whiteriver, AZ 85941 United States
lazyr@wmonline.com
http://www.cambridgewhoswho.com

BUS: School **P/S:** Education **MA:** Local **D/D/R:** Teaching Children **H/I/S:** Gardening, Theater, Reading, Hiking, Camping, Fishing, Traveling, Music **FBP:** Instructor; American Educator **EDU:** Master of Arts in Education Administration, Northern Arizona University; Bachelor's Degree in Elementary Education, Arizona State University **A/S:** He attributes his success to his high school drama teacher, who served as his mentor and the wonderful parents and students he has met. **B/I:** He became involved in high school drama because of his love for children. **H/O:** The highlight of his career was being named one of America's Top 100 Educators.

DOROTHY S. CROWDER, MS, RN, CCE

Associate Professor of Nursing
Bon Secours Memorial School of Nursing
8550 Magellan Parkway
Richmond, VA 23227 United States
dorothy_crowder@bshsi.com
http://www.cambridgewhoswho.com

BUS: Higher Education **P/S:** Caring and Implementing Nursing Interventions to Improve Health for Clients **MA:** International **EXP:** Ms. Crowder's expertise is in maternal, child and women's health. **H/I/S:** Walking, Biking, Reading **EDU:** Master of Science in Nursing, Minor in Education, Medical College of Virginia School of Nursing, Virginia Commonwealth University; Bachelor of Science in Nursing, Medical College of Virginia School of Nursing, Virginia Commonwealth University **CERTS:** Certified Childbirth Educator **A/A/S:** American Nurses Association; Virginia Nurses Association; Sigma Theta Tau International; Association of Women's Health, Obstetric and Neonatal Nursing **C/VW:** Highland United Methodist Church; Donlop Farms Homeowners Association; American Red Cross; March of Dimes Foundation **A/S:** She attributes her success to the grace of God, her parents and support from her husband. **B/I:** She became involved in this profession because she always wanted to be in nursing and after trying other professions she went back to it. **H/O:** The highlight of her career is furthering nursing education for students and guiding them.

TAMERA D. CROWE, MD

Medical Doctor
Richland Community Healthcare Association
120 Clarkson Street
Eastover, SC 29044 United States
tamibodenhamer@msn.com
http://www.cambridgewhoswho.com

BUS: Healthcare Center **P/S:** Healthcare **MA:** Local **D/D/R:** Diagnosing and Treating Patients of All Ages, Overseeing Community Healthcare Services **H/I/S:** Traveling, Reading, Scrapbooking, Spending Time with her Husband, Caring for her Pets **FBP:** Journal of the American Academy of Family Physicians; Journal of the American Medical Association **EDU:** Residency, University of Missouri, Kansas City (2005); MD, University of Missouri, Kansas City (2002) **A/A/S:** American Medical Association **C/VW:** Volunteer, Local Church; Local Medical Missions **DOB:** June 6, 1978 **POB:** Nairobi **SP:** Kenneth **A/S:** She attributes her success to the support she receives from her family and mentors and her faith in God. **H/O:** The most gratifying aspect of her career is helping her patients physically, emotionally and spiritually.

IVY-LYNNE CROWELL
Certified General Contractor, Co-Owner
M & I General Contracting
1197 E. Altamonte Drive
Altamonte Springs, FL 32701 United States
bidbusters@aol.com
http://www.bidbustersconstruction.com

BUS: Construction Company **P/S:** Construction of Residential and Commercial Properties, Painting, Repairing, Remodeling, Renovations, Demolition, Commercial Management and Maintenance of Custom Homes **MA:** Central Florida **D/D/R:** Writing Proposals, Managing Administrative Duties, Ensuring Customer Satisfaction, Overseeing Human Resources and Finance **H/I/S:** Playing Football **FBP:** Orlando Business Journal **EDU:** Associate of Arts in Construction, St. Johns River Community College (1994) **CERTS:** Licensed Real Estate Broker; Licensed Mortgage Broker **A/A/S:** Associated General Contractors of Greater Florida

MICHELLE M. CRULL
Senior Structural Engineer
United States Army Engineering and Support Center
4820 University Square
Huntsville, AL 35816 United States
mcrull@yahoo.com
http://www.cambridgewhoswho.com

BUS: Federal Government Organization **P/S:** Engineering Services **MA:** International **EXP:** Dr. Crull's expertise is in explosion effects, explosives safety and the design of engineering controls to mitigate the effects of explosions. **D/D/R:** Conducting Explosives Safety Studies **H/I/S:** Reading, Cooking, Bicycling, Practicing Tai Chi, Golfing **EDU:** Ph.D. in Structural Engineering, Vanderbilt University (1989); Master of Science in Civil Engineering, University of Mississippi (1984); Bachelor of Science in Civil Engineering, University of Mississippi (1982) **CERTS:** Registered Professional Engineer, State of Alabama **A/A/S:** Society of American Military Engineers **A/H:** Chief of Engineers 'Hero' (2008); Coastal America Partnership Award (2004); Civilian Engineer of the Year Award, Corps of Engineers (2003); Engineer of the Year Award, Huntsville Center (2003) **C/VW:** Habitat for Humanity; Huntsville Downtown Rescue Mission **W/H:** United States Army Engineering and Support Center, Huntsville (1995-2008); University of Alabama in Huntsville (1988-1985); United States Department of Agriculture Sedimentation Lab (1985); University of Mississippi (1983-1985); United States Army Corps of Engineers, Waterways Experiment Station (1984) **A/S:** She attributes her success to her hard work and the support she receives from her family and friends. **H/O:** The highlight of her career was completing a study of barricades for the army. It is estimated that the results will save the army millions of dollars over the next several years.

DONNA M. CRUZ, LPN
Disability Case Specialist
Reed Group
10155 Westmoor Drive
Suite 210
Westminster, CO 80021 United States
Lunars-35107@mypacks.net
http://www.rgl.net

BUS: Medical Management Firm **P/S:** Absence and Medical Disability Case Management Services **MA:** Local **D/D/R:** Overseeing Operations Including Case Management, Clinical Orthopedic and Neurology Units, Long-Term Disability and Utilization Review, Generating Reports **H/I/S:** Camping, Fishing **FBP:** Industry-Related Publications **EDU:** Pursuing Bachelor's Degree in Business Communications, University of Denver **CERTS:** Licensed Practical Nurse, Emily Griffith Opportunity School **A/A/S:** Election Judge, Adams, CO; Golden Key International Honour Society **A/H:** International Who's Who Among Professional Management **A/S:** She attributes her success to her flexibility and her ability to face challenges. **B/I:** She became involved in her profession because of her interest in healthcare industry. **H/O:** The most gratifying aspect of her career is being able to maintain a good relationship with her patients and clients.

MR. GONZALO CARLOS CUBILLOS
Principal Space Planning Designer
24246 E. Bellewood Drive
Aurora, CO 80016 United States
gccubillos@atkinsengineers.com
protraning@earthlink.net
http://www.atkinsengineers.com

BUS: Forensic Engineering Firm **P/S:** Forensics and Conversion Turnovers, Budgeting for Developers, Quality Assurance for Preventive Measures, On-Site Visits **MA:** National **D/D/R:** Working Hand-in-Hand with Contractors During Construction, Ensuring Quality **H/I/S:** Spending Time with his Family, Traveling, Skiing, Playing Soccer, Cycling, Swimming, Running, Practicing Karate **EDU:** Bachelor of Science in Construction Management, School of Engineering, Florida International University **CERTS:** Certified Personal Trainer (1998) **A/A/S:** General Contractors Association; The American Institute of Architects; Alpha Omega **C/VW:** Cycling and Running Events; Local Charitable Organizations; American Heart Association; American Cancer Society; Kids in Distress **DOB:** November 20, 1958 **POB:** Bogotá, Colombia **SP:** Solangel Raquel **CHILD:** Brandonlee, Luzmarialee **A/S:** He attributes his success to his dedication and to the inspiration he received from his parents. **B/I:** He became involved in his profession through a natural progression of opportunities. **H/O:** The most gratifying aspect of his career is being a part of the Miami skyline.

H. JUDITH CUE, MSN, RN
Nursing Instructor
Arkansas Northeastern College
1032 W. Kings Highway
PO Box 458
Paragould, AR 72451 United States
jcue@anc.edu
http://www.anc.edu

BUS: Education **P/S:** Providing Nursing Higher Education for Associate Degree Nursing **MA:** Regional **EXP:** Ms. Cue's expertise is in nursing education. **H/I/S:** Spending Time With Family, Gardening, Genealogy and Writing Prose and Poetry **FBP:** American Journal of Nursing **EDU:** Master's Degree in Adult Health Nursing, Arkansas State University; Bachelor's Degree in Nursing **A/A/S:** National League of Nurses; National League for Nursing Accrediting Commission **C/VW:** Relay for Life, American Cancer Society; American Red Cross **A/S:** She attributes her success to caring tremendously about her profession and providing her students with an outstanding educational foundation. **H/O:** The highlight of her career is having students since each one is a highlight for her. She helps them to improve their lives as well as their patients.

LILLIA CUFFY
President
Bluekap Financial Group
7901B W. McNab Road
Tamarac, FL 33321 United States
lillia.cuffy@bluekap.com
http://www.bluekap.com

BUS: Mortgage and Banking Company **P/S:** Mortgage and Banking Services **MA:** Regional **D/D/R:** Working with Company Finances, Recruiting, Assisting in Account Management **H/I/S:** Gardening, Cooking, Playing Tennis **FBP:** Scottsman Guide; ABA Journal **EDU:** JD, Nova Southeastern University (2001); Bachelor's Degree in Business and Finance, Florida State University **A/A/S:** National Association for the Advancement of Colored People; Florida Association of Mortgage Brokers

DOTTIE CULLOP
Secretary, Bookkeeper
JW Cullop, Inc.
7900-A Cessna Avenue
Gaithersburg, MD 20877 United States
account@jwcullopinc.com
http://www.cambridgewhoswho.com

BUS: Commercial Contractors **P/S:** Heating, Ventilation and Air Conditioning **MA:** Local **D/D/R:** Bookkeeping, Managing the Secretarial Payroll **H/I/S:** Singing, Traveling, Spending Time with her 11 Grandchildren and Two Great-Grandchildren **FBP:** Guidepost **EDU:** Industry-Related Training and Experience **C/VW:** Deacon Ministry, Church of the Brethren **A/S:** She attributes her success to her excellent customer service and concern for quality services provided to customers. **B/I:** She became involved in her profession because she worked her way up in the organization. **H/O:** The highlight of her career was seeing satisfied customers and knowing that her customers refer others for repeat business.

MR. MIKE CUMMINGS
Owner, Artist
Inksomnia Tattoo Studios, Inc.
11890 Douglas Road
Alpharetta, GA 30004 United States
inksomnia@bellsouth.net
http://www.inksomniatattoo.com

BUS: Body Art Studio **P/S:** Custom Tattoos **MA:** Regional **D/D/R:** Managing Operations, Custom Designing, Overseeing the Staff, Ensuring Customer Satisfaction **H/I/S:** Boating **FBP:** Tattoo **EDU:** College Coursework; High School Diploma **A/A/S:** Better Business Bureau

Mr. William F. Cummins Jr.
Director of Radiology
United Medical Center
214 23rd Street
Cheyenne, WY 82001 United States
bcummins@umcwy.com
http://www.umcwy.info

BUS: Nonprofit, County Hospital, One of the Oldest Hospitals in the Western United States, Community-Centered Hospital **P/S:** Acute Rehabilitation Unit, Bariatric Surgery, Behavioral Health Services, Case Management, Emergency Department, Home Care, Hospice, Maternal Child Services, Medical-Oncology, Radiation Therapy, Senior Care, Sleep Lab, Social Services, Trauma Center, Weight Loss Surgery, Women's Imaging Center **MA:** National **EXP:** Mr. Cummins' expertise is in management and diagnostic intervention. **H/I/S:** Camping, Outdoor Activities **FBP:** Diagnostic Imaging; Internet **EDU:** Associate of Science in Radiology (2002) **CERTS:** Certified Radiology Administrator (2003) **A/A/S:** American Healthcare Radiology Administrators; American Registry of Radiologic Technologists; Wyoming Society of Radiology; American Society of Radiology Technicians

Lucy P. Cupp, BS, MS, MA
Retired Associate Pastor, Senior Administrator, Guidance Counselor
(Retired)
Bayview Christian School, Ryan Academy
Norfolk Public Schools
Norfolk, VA United States
funcupp@aol.com
http://www.cambridgewhoswho.com

BUS: Ministry **P/S:** Education **MA:** Local **EXP:** Ms. Cupp's expertise is in administration and staff development. **H/I/S:** Reading **FBP:** Leadership **EDU:** Master of Science in Administration and Development, Old Dominion University; Master of Arts in Counseling, Liberty University **A/A/S:** American Association of Christian Counselors; United Federation of Teachers; Norfolk Education Association; National Education Association **C/VW:** First Baptist Church; Ministry Outreach Worship Program, Assisted Living Facility **A/S:** She attributes her personal and professional success to her encouraging mother. **B/I:** She became involved in the profession because she has always had an interest in education. **H/O:** The most gratifying aspect of her career is seeing the children grow and succeed.

KEVIN C. CURREY
Health, Safety and Environmental Professional
Hercules Offshore
Houston, TX United States
kcurrey722@hotmail.com
http://www.cambridgewhoswho.com

BUS: Oil Company **P/S:** Oil and Gas Drilling **MA:** International **EXP:** Mr. Currey's areas of expertise include health and environmental safety, management and public speaking. **H/I/S:** Golfing, Traveling, Woodworking **FBP:** Professional Safety Manager; Golf Digest; Texas Monthly; Woodsmiths **EDU:** Bachelor's Degree in Safety Management, Central Missouri State University (1992) **A/A/S:** American Society of Safety Engineers; National Safety Management Society **C/VW:** Interface of the Woodlands **A/S:** He attributes his success to his honesty. **B/I:** He became involved in this profession through a natural progression of opportunities. **H/O:** The highlight of his career is being the director of health and safety for a major organization.

CHRISTIANA A. CURRY
Owner
BC Mechanical, LLC
Smithville, MO 64089 United States
cacurry25@aol.com
http://www.cambridgewhoswho.com

BUS: Proven Leader in the Heating and Cooling Industry **P/S:** Skilled Commercial and Residential Heating and Cooling Services **MA:** Regional **D/D/R:** Overseeing Commercial and Residential Heating and Cooling, Managing Accounts Payable and Receivable **H/I/S:** Softball, Volunteering **A/A/S:** Chamber of Commerce; Better Business Bureau **C/VW:** Park Board, City of Smithville; Vice President, Smithville Soccer Club; President, Hills of Shannon Homeowners Association

STEPHEN A. CURRY, CHE
Director of Networking and Imaging
Princeton Community Hospital
PO Box 1369
Princeton, WV 24740 United States
scurry@pchonline.org
http://www.pchonline.org

BUS: Hospital **P/S:** Healthcare Services **MA:** Local **D/D/R:** Overseeing Radiologic Technology and Imaging, Managing Communications in Four Clinics **H/I/S:** Working on Computers **FBP:** Modern Healthcare **EDU:** Master's Degree in Public Administration, Concentration in Healthcare Management, Auburn University **CERTS:** Certification, American College of Healthcare Executives **A/A/S:** Board Member, Bluefield College

HAZEL L. CURTIS
Sales Associate
Realty Executives
5 Victory Lane
Liberty, MO 64068 United States
hazellcurtis@yahoo.com
http://www.hazelcurtis.com

BUS: Leaders in Real Estate Services **P/S:** Real Estate Listings for Residential Homes, Buying, Selling, Relocating and Vacant Land **MA:** Kansas City Area **D/D/R:** Assisting Clients with Residential and Vacant Land Property Sales and Service, Selling Investment Properties **H/I/S:** Reading, Traveling, Athletic Events, Basketball and Football **FBP:** National Geographic **EDU:** Bachelor of Science in Education, Evangel University (1967) **CERTS:** Licensed in Real Estate, State of Missouri (1984) **A/A/S:** Women's Council of Realtors; Missouri Association of Realtors; National Association of Realtors **A/H:** Three-Time Recipient, Five Star Best in Client Satisfaction, Kansas City Magazine

Ms. Laura A. Cuthbert
Senior Mechanical Engineer
Raytheon
350 Lowell Street
Andover, MA 01810 United States
laura_a_cuthbert@raytheon.com
http://www.raytheon.com

BUS: Defense and Government Electronic Engineering **P/S:** Mission Systems Integration, Mission Support and Assurance, Information Technology, Technical Services, Business Aviation, Special Mission Aircraft **MA:** International **D/D/R:** Managing Mechanical Design Work and Materials, Overseeing Engineering Selection, Evaluating Selection in Areas of Corrosion Prevention and Electro-Magnetic Interference Shielding and Radar Systems **H/I/S:** Piloting, Breeding and Showing Boxers, Working with Stained Glass **EDU:** Bachelor of Science in Mechanical Engineering, University of Texas (1983)

Alina G. Czub
Account Executive
Pinnacle Advertising & Marketing
1435 N. Plum Grove, Suite C
Schaumburg, IL 60173 United States
alinaandtig@sbcglobal.com
http://www.pinnacle-advertising.com

BUS: Advertising Agency **P/S:** Advertising and Marketing **MA:** National **EXP:** Ms. Czub's expertise is in automotive and Hispanic marketing. **H/I/S:** Spending Time with her Family **FBP:** Advertising Age **EDU:** Bachelor of Arts in Journalism and TV Production, Columbia College **C/VW:** American Cancer Society; The Leukemia & Lymphoma Society **A/S:** She attributes her success to determination and drive. **B/I:** She has naturally progressed to her current position. **H/O:** The highlight of her career is the recognition she receives in the work place.

LORRAINE A. D'AGOSTINO, M.ED.
Teacher (Retired)
North Syracuse School District
auntrenee@webtv.net
http://www.cambridgewhoswho.com

BUS: School District **P/S:** Education **MA:** Onondaga County **EXP:** Ms. D'Agostino's expertise is in elementary education. **H/I/S:** Playing the Piano, Listening to Music, Sculpting, Cartooning **EDU:** Master of Science in Elementary Education, SUNY Oswego (1982); Bachelor of Science in Elementary Education, SUNY Oswego (1976); Associate of Applied Science, SUNY Onondaga Community College **CERTS:** Certification in Education (N-6), SUNY Oswego (1976); Executive Secretarial Certificate, Powelson Business Institute **A/A/S:** New York State United Teachers; National Teachers Association; North Syracuse Education Association **A/H:** North Syracuse Excellence in Teaching Award (1989); Who's Who Among American Teachers (1998-2006); Professional Best Leadership Commendation (1990) **C/VW:** Vira Health and Hospice **A/S:** She attributes her success to her sense of humor. **B/I:** She became involved in her profession because she loves working with children. **H/O:** The highlight of her career was being inducted into Who's Who Among American Teachers.

STEPHANIE N. D'ANGIO
Elementary School Teacher
Primary
Fresno Unified School District
1780 W. Sierra Avenue
Fresno, CA 93711 United States
princessdancer2@hotmail.com
http://www.fresno.k12.ca.us

BUS: School District **P/S:** Education **MA:** Local **D/D/R:** Teaching Elementary School Children, Implementing Autism Programs, Teaching Second-Grade Art **H/I/S:** Ballroom Dancing, Shopping, Party Planning, Decorating **FBP:** Fresno Magazine **EDU:** Masters Equivalent in Early Childhood Education, Fresno State University; Bachelor of Arts in Anthropology, Fresno State University **CERTS:** Certification in Cross-Cultural, Language and Academic Education **A/A/S:** Fresno Teachers' Association; California Teachers Association; National Teachers Association; Fresno State Alumni Association **A/H:** Honoree, Who's Who Among America's Teachers (2005-2006) **C/VW:** San Joaquin River Parkway and Conservation Trust; National Smooth Dancers; Central California Big Band Dance Society; President, Homeowners Association of Woodward Lake, Subdivision Americana Shores **DOB:** November 1, 1957 **POB:** Fresno, CA **SP:** Fiance, Steven **W/H:** Teacher, Starr Elementary School (1985-Present); Fourth-Sixth Grade Science Teacher (1985); Special Assignment Teacher

JEAN D'ORIO
Registered Nurse, Charge Nurse
Middlesex Hospital
28 Crescent Street
Middlesex, CT 06457 United States
http://www.cambridgewhoswho.com

BUS: Nonprofit Hospital **P/S:** Nonprofit Hospital Healthcare **MA:** Local **D/D/R:** Charge Nursing **H/I/S:** Playing the Organ, Line Dancing, Volunteering at the Hospital, Treasurer for Local Chapter of the AARP **EDU:** Bachelor of Science Degree in Registered Nursing, Yukon University **A/A/S:** Catholic Nurses Association **A/H:** 30 Year Participation Certificate, Harvard Nurses Medical Society **C/VW:** Coordinator, Church Clinic; Volunteer Line Dancer, Local Nursing Home **A/S:** She attributes her success to hard work and determination. **B/I:** She became involved in this profession because she always wanted to help people. **H/O:** The highlight of her career is bringing up a family while working and always having time for her children.

NANCY DABB HALL
Kindergarten Teacher
Honeoye Central School
8528 Main Street
Honeoye, NY 14471 United States
nhall@honeoye.org
http://www.honeoye.org

BUS: School **P/S:** Education **MA:** Regional **EXP:** Ms. Dabb Hall's expertise is in public speaking. **D/D/R:** Teaching Speech and Language to Kindergarten Students, Facilitating Early Intervention Programs, Implementing Motor Activities Involving Music and Movement, Utilizing Computer and Pilot Programs **H/I/S:** Scrapbooking, Participating in Church Activities **FBP:** Newsweek; Learning **EDU:** Master's Degree in Early Childhood Education, Nazareth College, Rochester, NY (1995); Bachelor of Science in Education, Keuka College (1993) **A/A/S:** NAECA **C/VW:** Bristol Springs Free Church **POB:** Buffalo **SP:** David **CHILD:** Jacob, Philip

JANICE D. DADE
Coder
Nicka & Associates, Inc.
5501 Independence Parkway, Suite 316
Plano, TX 75023 United States
jdenised@msn.com
http://www.cambridgewhoswho.com

BUS: Healthcare Company **P/S:** Coding for Emergency Room Physicians **MA:** Local **EXP:** Ms. Dade's expertise is in coding. **H/I/S:** Playing Volleyball, Sewing Clothes, Collecting Shoes, Spending Time with her Family and Friends **EDU:** Bachelor of Arts in Home Economics, Louisiana Tech University (1983); Diploma, Ouachita Parish High School (1976) **A/A/S:** American Academy of Professional Coders **C/VW:** Junior Usher, Greater Northpark Church of God in Christ **POB:** Monroe **A/S:** She attributes her success to her hard work. **B/I:** She became involved in her profession through a natural progression of opportunities. **H/O:** The highlight of her career was becoming a coder.

JO A. DAHLIN, RN, BSN
Private Duty Nurse, Case Manager
Care Quiet Home Healthcare
1530 SSW Loop 323, Suite 125
Tyler, TX 75701 United States
joadahlin6@hotmail.com
http://www.cambridgewhoswho.com

BUS: Proven Leader in the Healthcare Industry **P/S:** Exceptional Care for Exceptional Children **MA:** Regional **EXP:** Ms. Dahlin's expertise is in home healthcare. **H/I/S:** Horseback Riding, Running her Ranch **FBP:** Forbes **EDU:** Bachelor of Science in Nursing, University of Texas at Arlington; Associate Degree in Nursing, Grayson County College; Associate Degree in Applied Science, Paris Junior College **A/A/S:** Texas Nursing Association; The Phi Beta Kappa Society; Sigma Theta Tau International **C/VW:** Troop Leader, Girl Scouts of America; Leader, 4-H

BONNIE MEIER DAHLKE
Certified Registered Nurse, Intensive Care Unit
Arrowhead Hospital, Johns Hopkins School of Nursing
18701 N. 67th Avenue
Glendale, AZ 85310 United States
bdahlkel@cox.net
http://www.cambridgewhoswho.com

BUS: Hospital **P/S:** Healthcare **MA:** Local **D/D/R:** Intensive Care Nursing **H/I/S:** Traveling, Reading **EDU:** Registered Nurse Degree, The Johns Hopkins University Hospital School of Nursing **A/A/S:** American Association of Critical Care Nurses **A/S:** She attributes her success her compassion and caring nature. **B/I:** She became involved in her profession because she had always wanted to be a nurse. **H/O:** The highlight of her career has been the satisfaction she receives from helping others.

MARION J. DALTON
Director
Whakatane Shuttle Bus Ltd.
11 Te Poi Road
ID 3
Mata Mata, INTL 0 New Zealand
marion1@wave.co.nz
http://www.cambridgewhoswho.com

BUS: Transportation Company **P/S:** Transportation, Small Bus and Limousine Services **MA:** National **D/D/R:** Overseeing Administrative Duties and Corporate Operations, Working as the Owner and Operator of Country Tavern **H/I/S:** Spending Time with Family **FBP:** NZTF Publications; HANZ Publications **EDU:** College Coursework **A/A/S:** Secretary, New Zealand Taxi Federation Limited Inc.; Hantz Group

JANE M. DANCOSSE
Chief Executive Officer
1) Janry Kennels 2) Christie's
470 Route 173
Stewartsville, NJ 08886 United States
janry101@msn.com
http://www.janrykennels.com

BUS: 1) Full-Service Grooming Salon and Spa, Doggie Day Care 2) Restaurant **P/S:** 1) Pet Care, Training, Retail 2) Fine Dining, In-House and Off-Premise Catering **MA:** 1) Warren and Hunterdon Counties 2) Eastern Pennsylvania **EXP:** Ms. Dancosse's expertise is in management. **H/I/S:** Traveling, Breeding German Shepherds **A/A/S:** German Shepherd Dog Club of America; Chamber of Commerce **A/S:** She attributes her success to her love for animals, her continuing education and her excellent people skills. **H/O:** The highlight of her career was the facility she built, which is referred to as 'Doggie Disneyland.'

LINDA DANIEL
Realtor
Nancy Chandler Associates
701 W. 21st Street
Norfolk, VA 23517 United States
lindadaniel@nancychandler.com
http://www.lindadaniel.net

BUS: Recognized Industry Leader in Resale and New Construction Property Transactions in the Varied Neighborhoods of Hampton Roads **P/S:** Residential Single Family Home **MA:** Local **D/D/R:** Offering Assistance to Clients Buying a New House, Selling their Home or Relocating, Ensuring a Variety of Professional Real Estate Services in the Hampton Roads Area of Virginia **H/I/S:** Traveling, Fine Dining **EDU:** Coursework, Tidewater Community College **CERTS:** Accredited Buyer Representative; Senior Real Estate Specialist **A/A/S:** Virginia Association of Realtors; National Association of Realtors **A/H:** Award, Tidewater Association of Realtors; Award, Hampton Roads Realtors Association; Circle of Excellence; Gold, Silver and Bronze Levels, Million Dollar Club (1995-Present); **C/VW:** Townpoint Club; Downtown Norfolk Council; Colonial Place Pacific League; Colonial Place Riverview Civic League

SHARON K. DANIELS
Director, Early Childhood Educator
Ironton-Lawrence County CAO Head Start
305 N. Fifth Street
Ironton, OH 45638 United States
sdaniels@headstartworks.org
http://headstartworks.org/

BUS: High Quality Early Educator and Child Care Center **P/S:** Preschool Programs for Children Ages Birth through Five Years Old, Special Services for Pregnant Women, Infants and Toddlers **MA:** Statewide **D/D/R:** Specializing in Elementary and Special Education as well as Early Childhood Development, Running the Day-to-Day Operations of the Center, Overseeing All Services Offered through the Center Including Training and Employment Opportunities, Working as an Adjunct Professor at Ohio University, Training in Early Childhood Education, Writing Grants, Consulting through the Child Development Association and Students Headstart Review Team **FBP:** Ironton Tribune **EDU:** Pursuing Doctor of Education; Master's Degree in Special Education, Ohio University (1990); Bachelor of Arts in Elementary Education, Ohio University (1981) **CERTS:** Licensed Social Worker, State of Ohio; Certified Teacher (B-8), State of Ohio; Certified in Early Childhood Intervention, State of Ohio; Certified in Special Education **A/A/S:** Ohio Head Start Association; National Association for the Education of Young Children; Council for Exceptional Children

EVA A. DANKHA-KELLY
Assistant Civil Engineer
City of Modesto
1010 10th Street
Modesto, CA 95354 United States
edkelly@modestogov.com
http://www.modestogov.com

BUS: Government Organization **P/S:** Public Services, History, Arts and Entertainment, Dining and Nightlife, Education, Points of Interest, Recreation, Shopping **MA:** Local **EXP:** Ms. Dankha-Kelly's expertise is in development services. **D/D/R:** Public Speaking, Reviewing All New Development Projects Coming into the City, Tending to Engineering Plans **H/I/S:** Spending Time with her Family, Playing Tennis, Spending Time at the Beach, Watching her Children's Play Soccer, Attending School Plays, Playing the Piano **FBP:** Journal of American Society of Civil Engineers; Parent & Child **EDU:** Bachelor of Science in Civil Engineering, California State University, Fullerton (1987) **A/A/S:** American Society of Civil Engineers **A/H:** Employee Recognition Award (2003) **C/VW:** Local Modesto Engineers Club

LaDrena D. Dansby
Construction Manager
URS Corporation
915 Wilshire Boulevard
Suite 800
Los Angeles, CA 90017 United States
ladrena_dansby@urscorp.com
http://www.urscorp.com

BUS: Engineering Design Firm **P/S:** Comprehensive Range of Professional Planning, Design, Systems Engineering and Technical Assistance, Program and Construction Management, Operations and Maintenance Services **MA:** Regional **EXP:** Ms. Dansby's expertise is in civil engineering. **D/D/R:** Managing Hospital Buildings and Infrastructures **EDU:** Bachelor's Degree in Civil Engineering, California State University, Northridge (1993)

Evelina Darlington, BSN, MSN
Clinical Nurse Specialist, Nurse Educator (Retired)
Nursing Department
Georgetown University Medical Center
1720 Lake Shore Crest Drive, Apartment 13
Reston, VA 20190 United States
evydarlington@yahoo.com
http://gumc.georgetown.edu

BUS: University, Medical Center **P/S:** Higher Education, Healthcare **MA:** International **EXP:** Ms. Darlington's expertise is in midwifery and medical-surgical psychiatric nursing. **H/I/S:** Walking, Reading, Traveling, Listening to Music, Meditation **EDU:** Master of Science in Nursing, Wayne State University (1963); Bachelor of Science in Nursing, Wayne State University (1962); Diploma in Nursing, Trinidad and Tobago, West Indies (1948) **CERTS:** Certified Clinical Nurse Specialist (1994) **A/A/S:** American Nurses Association; American Association of University Professors; Sigma Theta Tau International **A/H:** International Book of Honor (1985); American Biographical Institute (1986); Colegio de Professionales de Enfemeria de Puerto Rico; Princess Mary Nursing Gold Medal Recipient (1948)

KATHY L. DARREL
Senior Programmer Analyst, Contract Programmer
Silver Legacy Resort Casino
407 N. Virginia Street
Reno, NV 89501 United States
kat.darrel@yahoo.com
http://www.cambridgewhoswho.com

BUS: Computer Programming **P/S:** Computer Programs, Systems and Training **MA:** National **D/D/R:** Programming Computers, Analyzing Systems, Overseeing Financial, Human Resources and Hospitality Industry Applications **H/I/S:** Needlepoint, Reading **EDU:** Industry-Related Training and Experience **C/VW:** Loyal Order of Moose, Moose Heart, Moose Haven, Police Department, Pet Patrol **A/S:** She attributes her success to her ability to stay current and learn on the job and management support. **B/I:** She was prompted to enter her profession because she had an interest in computers and enjoyed training. **H/O:** The highlight of her career is bringing on new programs and successfully training new users.

APRIL M. DARTY, RN, BSN
Registered Nurse
Lifebridge Health
2434 W. Belvedere Avenue
Baltimore, MD 21215 United States
trvlnurse376@yahoo.com
http://www.lifebridgehealth.org

BUS: Health System, Two Hospitals, Two Nursing Homes **P/S:** Healthcare **MA:** National **EXP:** Ms. Darty's expertise is in medical-surgical nursing and geriatrics. **D/D/R:** Teaching Licensed Practical Nurse Students at Sojourner-Douglass College **H/I/S:** Reading **FBP:** Advance for Nurses **EDU:** Bachelor of Science in Nursing, North Carolina Agricultural and Technical State University; Registered Nurse, State of Maryland

Ms. Lena Dashnaw
President
Adirondack Golf & Country Club
88 Golf Road
Peru, NY 12972 United States
lmd@adirondackgolfclub.com
http://www.adirondackgolfclub.com

BUS: Clinton County, New York's Finest Golf and Country Club **P/S:** 18-Hole Championship Golf Course, Practice Range, Putting Green, Lounge and Banquet Facilities, Offers Private Memberships and is Open to the Public, 500 Building Site Lots Available for Developing Homes **MA:** Regional **D/D/R:** Running the Office, Handling the Budget, Overseeing the Pro-Shop, Maintaining the Grounds, Putting Green, Golf Course, Two Banquet Rooms and Restaurants **H/I/S:** Golfing, Sewing, Bowling **FBP:** New York Magazine; Vermont Links **EDU:** Associate Degree in Business Administration, Clinton Community College **A/A/S:** Chamber of Commerce; National Golf Course Owners Association **SP:** Henry

Mr. Michael D. Davenport
President, Chief Executive Officer
Executive Office
INTEGRIS Federal Credit Union
4900 N. Portland Avenue, Suite 101
Oklahoma City, OK 73112 United States
mdd496@yahoo.com
http://www.integrisfcu.org

BUS: Federally Chartered Credit Union **P/S:** Full Service Banking and Financial Services **MA:** Oklahoma Statewide **EXP:** Mr. Davenport's expertise includes executive management, personal budget and business development and financial services. **H/I/S:** Martial Arts (MMA), Football, Firearms **A/A/S:** Oklahoma Credit Union Political Action Committee; Former President, Oklahoma Karate Association; Founder, Former Chairman, Oklahoma Sport Karate Association, Inc; Association of Hostage Negotiators; International Association of Law Enforcement Firearms Instructors **A/H:** Rookie of the Year Award **C/VW:** Red Shoe Gala, Ronald McDonald House Children's Charities; Kiwanis International; Oklahoma Coalition for Crime Victims Right **A/S:** He attributes his success to surrounding himself with quality people and always trying to do the right thing. **H/O:** The highlight of his financial management career was progressing into a full-service credit union.

DORINDA J. DAVIDSON
Associate Broker
Re/Max First
95 Allens Creek Road
Rochester, NY 14618 United States
dorindadavidson@remax.net
ddavidsonsold@frontiernet.net
http://www.dorindadavidson.com

BUS: Real Estate Company **P/S:** Real Estate Services **MA:** Regional **D/D/R:** Informing Applicants of the Home-Buying Process, Assisting First-Time Home Buyers, Selling Lakefront Properties and Residential Real Estate, Working as a Seller's Agent, Selling Existing Properties, Keeping Sellers Up-to-Date on the Market for the Purpose of Adjusting their Prices **H/I/S:** Reading, Golfing, Gardening **FBP:** Realtor **CERTS:** Pursuing Accredited Buyer Representative License; Licensed Broker (2008); Licensed Real Estate Agent (2000) **A/A/S:** Women's Council of Realtors; Board of Directors, Gennesee Valley Board of Realtors; Greater Rochester Association of Realtors; New York State Association of Realtors; National Association of Realtors **A/H:** Pinnacle Award, Greater Rochester Association of Realtors (2003) **C/VW:** Children's Miracle Network; Mercy Flight; Habitat for Humanity

MRS. LUCY DAVIDSON
Owner, Color Specialist
O'Haira Salon
712 Holmes Street
Gaffney, SC 29341 United States
http://www.cambridgewhoswho.com

BUS: Salon **P/S:** Hair Services Including Color Treatments **MA:** Regional **D/D/R:** Treating Hair with Color **FBP:** Chi **EDU:** Coursework in Color Training, Farouk Systems **CERTS:** Licensed Cosmetologist, American Academy of Beauty **A/A/S:** National Cosmetology Association **C/VW:** March of Dimes Foundation; Meals on Wheels; Local Charitable Organizations **A/S:** She attributes her career success to her hard work, the ethics instilled in her by her parents, the knowledge that she can achieve anything she puts her mind to and her determination to never give up. **H/O:** The highlight of her career was being selected by Farouk Systems to attend a conference in the Middle East among 3,500 hairdressers representing 78 different countries.

MR. STEVEN C. DAVIDSON
Attorney
Law Office of S.C. Davidson
2 Ganett Drive
Suite 102
White Plains, NY 10604 United States
sdavidsonesq@aol.com
http://www.scdavidsonlaw.com

Law Office Of S.C. Davidson
Criminal Defense Lawyers

BUS: Law Firm Dedicated to Providing the Best Quality Criminal Representation Reasonably Possible **P/S:** High Quality Criminal Defense Legal Services **MA:** New York, Massachusetts, Washington DC **EXP:** Mr. Davidson's expertise is in criminal defense. **H/I/S:** Traveling, Spending Time with his Two Children **FBP:** American Lawyer; The Champion **EDU:** JD, New York Law School (1990) **A/A/S:** The District of Columbia Bar (2004); Massachusetts Bar Association (1998); The New York State Bar Association (1990); American Bar Association; Grievance Committee, Westchester County Bar Association; National Association of Criminal Defense Lawyers; Association of Trial Lawyers of America; New York State Defenders Association **DOB:** November 10, 1965 **SP:** Shari **CHILD:** Stacey, Phoebe **C/A:** Admission, United States Supreme Court (2003)

CORENE ODETTE DAVIS
Registered Nurse
Saint Louise Regional Hospital
9400 N. Name Uno
Gilroy, CA 95020 United States
corenedavis@sbcglobal.net
http://www.cambridgewhoswho.com

BUS: Hospital **P/S:** Healthcare **MA:** Regional **EXP:** Ms. Davis' expertise is in geriatric care nursing and writing. **H/I/S:** Singing, Playing the Piano, Crocheting, Knitting **FBP:** Advance for Nurses **EDU:** Master's Degree in Elementary Education, University of Oregon; Bachelor of Science in Curriculum and Instruction, University of Oregon; Associate of Science in Nursing **CERTS:** Registered Nurse, Blue Mountain Community College; Certification in Basic Cardiac Life Support; Certification in Advanced Cardiac Life Support **A/A/S:** California Nurses Association **C/VW:** New Life Fellowship, Hollister, CA; Disabled American Veterans; March of Dimes; American Cancer Society; World Financial Group **A/S:** She attributes her success to her persistence, tenacity and being goal oriented. **B/I:** She became involved in her profession through a natural progression of opportunities. **H/O:** The highlight of her career was earning her master's degree.

MR. ERIC C. DAVIS
Maintenance Technician
Department of Technical and Adult Education
Middle Georgia Technical College
80 Cohen Walker Drive
Warner Robins, GA 31088 United States
edavis@middlegatech.edu
http://www.middlegatech.edu

BUS: College **P/S:** Higher Education **MA:** Regional **D/D/R:** Overseeing In-House Electrical Duties for the College, Maintaining Air Conditioning, Plumbing, Electrical and Office Responsibilities **H/I/S:** Listening to the Radio, Reading Books **FBP:** Maintenance Solutions; Building Operating Management; Buildings & Grounds; Buildings; Campus Magazine; College Planning & Management; Housekeeping Solutions; The News **EDU:** Pursuing Coursework in Business Management and Business Technology, Macon State College; Technical Degree in Mechanical Control Systems (2005); Technical Degree in Industrial System (2001); Technical Degree in Air Conditioning Systems (1992) **A/A/S:** President, Middle Georgia Technical College's Alumni Association; Minority Advising Program, Macon State College; Middle Georgia Technical College; National Technical Honor Society **DOB:** February 14, 1958

JACQUELINE Z. DAVIS
Executive Director
The New York Public Library for the Performing Arts
40 Lincoln Center Plaza
New York, NY 10023 United States
jacdavis@nypl.org
http://www.cambridgewhoswho.com

BUS: Library **P/S:** Access to Collections of Public Music, Theater, Galleries, Exhibitions, Recorded Sounds **MA:** Local **EXP:** Ms. Davis' expertise is in arts administration and theater management. **D/D/R:** Overseeing Musical, Dance and Theater Galleries and Exhibitions **H/I/S:** Broadway Shows **FBP:** The New York Times **EDU:** Master's Degree in French Literature, University of Kansas; Bachelor's Degree in French Literature, Dunbarton College **A/A/S:** Association of the Performing Arts; International Society of the Performing Arts; American Theater Wing; Voter, Former Nominator, Tony Awards **C/VW:** Lied Center of Kansas; Next Wave Festival; Brooklyn Academy; The Joyce Theater **A/S:** She attributes her success to her love of the work, tenacity and good role models. **B/I:** She became involved in this profession because of her love of the arts. **H/O:** The highlight of her career is building the Performing Arts Center at University of Kansas.

JOYCE W. DAVIS
Teacher
Lake Arbor Elementary
10205 Lake Arbor Way
Mitchellville, MD 20721 United States
joyce2.davis@pgcps.org
http://www.cambridgewhoswho.com

BUS: Elementary School **P/S:** Elementary Education **MA:** Prince Georgia County **D/D/R:** Teaching Early Childhood Education and Visual Arts **H/I/S:** Traveling, Event Planning, Making Crafts **EDU:** Master's Degree in Education, Trinity College **A/A/S:** Educational Development Association **C/VW:** Red Hat Society; Internationally-Recognized Youth Choir, Local Church; River of Scholarship Committee **A/S:** She attributes her success to her ability to communicate with children and their parents. **B/I:** She became involved in her profession because she was influenced by her family, her love of children and teaching. **H/O:** The most gratifying aspect of her career is knowing that two of her former students became a senator and a doctor.

LORETTA L. DAVIS
Licensed Practical Nurse
Home Sweet Home
812 W. Seventh Street
Winona, MN 55987 United States
loretta_john@yahoo.com
http://www.cambridgewhoswho.com

BUS: Homecare **P/S:** Private Pay Hospice and Homecare Augmentation **MA:** Local **D/D/R:** Specializing in Homecare and Hospice Care **H/I/S:** Gardening, Traveling **FBP:** Home Healthcare Nurse **CERTS:** Licensed Practical Nurse, South East Technical School, Winona, Minnesota (1999) **C/VW:** The Humane Society of the United States **B/I:** She became involved in this profession because her close family members had become very ill and she enjoyed her experience in helping them so she went into the medical field. **H/O:** The highlight of her career is wonderful referrals.

MARION DAVIS
General Partner
TLS Enterprises dba H&R Block
1331 S.W. Barlow Street
Oak Harbor, WA 98277 United States
madavis@hrblock.com
http://www.cambridgewhoswho.com

BUS: Tax Preparation Company **P/S:** Tax Preparation Services for Corporations, Partnerships, Individuals, Estates and Trusts **MA:** Local **EXP:** Ms. Davis' expertise is in operations management and tax preparation. **D/D/R:** Overseeing Business Operations, Hiring Employees, Managing Technology **H/I/S:** Reading, Making Jewelry from Natural Stones **FBP:** The Wall Street Journal **A/A/S:** Oak Harbor Chamber of Commerce **A/S:** She attributes her success to her hard work and dedication. **B/I:** She became involved in her profession because of her interest in tax preparation. **H/O:** The highlight of her career was attaining her current position.

MAXINE M. DAVIS, LPN
Licensed Practical Nurse
Immanuel-Saint Joseph's Hospital
Mayo Health Systems
101 Martin Luther King Jr. Drive
Mankato, MN 56001 United States
maxdavis@hickorytech.net
http://www.cambridgewhoswho.com

BUS: Hospital System **P/S:** Healthcare **MA:** Regional **EXP:** Ms. Davis' expertise is in renal care. **H/I/S:** Collecting Antique Textiles, Linens and Furniture **FBP:** Nursing2009 **CERTS:** Licensed Practical Nurse, South Center College **A/A/S:** Board of Directors, Minnesota Licensed Practical Nurses; United Neonatal Nurses Advisory Board **C/VW:** Labor Management Committee, Immanuel-Saint Joseph's Hospital **A/S:** She attributes her success to her commitment. **B/I:** She became involved in her profession because she always wanted to become a nurse. **H/O:** The highlight of her career was being recognized as a leader in the profession.

SHEILA K. DAVIS
ARI Reading Coach
Birmingham City Schools
3681 Charleston Lane
Birmingham, AL 35216 United States
shkdavis@aol.com
http://www.cambridgewhoswho.com

BUS: Public Education School District **P/S:** Education for Local Students **MA:** Regional **D/D/R:** Teaching Reading in a Group Setting to Second and Third-Grade Students, Helping Teachers Improve Students' Reading Skills through Interactive Activities **H/I/S:** Enjoying Music, Spending Time with her Cats, Completing Jigsaw Puzzles, Walking, Reading **FBP:** Reading Teacher **EDU:** Master's Degree in Religious Education, Southwest Seminar (1976); Bachelor of Science in Elementary Education, Samford University (1974) **A/A/S:** Birmingham Education Association; National Education Association; International Reading Association **A/H:** Teacher of the Year (1993); Technology Teacher of the Year (1992); Distinguished Teacher of the Year (1987)

SYLVIA ANNE DAVIS, RN
Registered Nurse
Oklahoma State University Medical Center
744 W. 9th Street
Tulsa, OK 74127 United States
rondavis2@netzero.net
http://www.healthsciences.okstate.edu

BUS: Osteopathic Hospital Dedicated to the Health and Well Being of Area Residents **P/S:** Highest Quality Medical Care with High Caliber Staff Physicians, Nurses, Technicians and other Healthcare Professionals **MA:** Regional **D/D/R:** Holistic Nursing Involving the Body, Mind and Spirit, Treating Patients Using Nutrition and Herbs and Less Clinical Medications, Reviewing Charts, Precepting **H/I/S:** Reading, Writing, Walking, Nature, Fishing, Traveling with Husband **FBP:** RN; Nursing **EDU:** Bachelor of Arts in Theology, Baptist Theology Seminary (1982); Registered Nurse, Indiana University (1979) **CERTS:** Ordained Minister (1986); Certified in Advanced Cardiac Life Support **A/A/S:** National Nurses Association **C/VW:** Joshua 1:3 Ministry, INC. Oklahoma (1988) **DOB:** July 26, 1946 **POB:** New Castle, IN **SP:** Ronnie Lee **CHILD:** John Allen, Sherry Lynn **W/H:** Registered Nurse (1979-Present); Supervisor; Travel Nurse

TRACY A. DAVIS
Principle Designer
Urban Dwellings, LLC
422 ½ Fore Street
Portland, ME 04101 United States
tdavis@urban-dwell.com
http://www.urban-dwell.com

BUS: Leader in the Field of Interior Design **P/S:** Programming, Space Planning, Schematic Design, Design Development, Documentation, Construction Administration, Custom Millwork Design **MA:** National **D/D/R:** Designing Contemporary Interiors for Residential Properties **H/I/S:** Mountain Biking **FBP:** Maine Home and Design **EDU:** Bachelor of Arts, Bowling Green State University **A/A/S:** Board Member, Portland Symphony Orchestra Showhouse (2007); Allied Member, American Society of Interior Designers; Adjunct Faculty, Boston Architectural College

VICKI L. DAVIS
Realtor
Imani Realty and Associates, Inc.
600 Beverly-Rancocas Road
Willingboro, NJ 08046 United States
vdavis@imanirealtors.com
http://www.imanirealtors.com

BUS: Real Estate **P/S:** Buying and Selling Real Estate **MA:** Local **EXP:** Ms. Davis' expertise is in residential home sales. **H/I/S:** Travel, Reading, Spending Time with her Three Children **FBP:** Realtor **EDU:** Master's Degree in Public Administration, Massachusetts Institute of Technology; Bachelor's Degree in Biology, South Carolina State University **A/A/S:** Delta Sigma Theta **C/VW:** Church, Goodwill, Salvation Army **A/S:** She attributes her career success to her hard work. **B/I:** After she retired, she realized that she was interested in a new career, so she became a realtor. **H/O:** She feels that her retirement as a GM14 in her past career has been the highlight of her career.

KIM DAVIS BAILEY
Bookkeeper
Saluda Trail Middle School
2300 Saluda Road
Rock Hill, SC 29730 United States
kbailey@rock-hill.k12.sc.us
http://www.cambridgewhoswho.com

BUS: Middle School **P/S:** Education for Young Adults **MA:** Local **D/D/R:** Accounting **H/I/S:** Going to Basketball Games; Spending Time with Family and Friends **EDU:** Coursework in Accounting, Business and Banking **A/A/S:** President, Beta Sigma Phi **C/VW:** Children's Attention Home; American Red Cross **A/S:** She attributes her success to hard work and dedication. **B/I:** She became involved in her profession because she was fascinated with the banking industry.

TERESA D. DAVISON
Educator
Title I Early Childhood
Springfield Public Schools R-12
940 N. Jefferson Avenue
Springfield, MO 65802 United States
tdavison@spsmail.org
http://www.springfieldpublicschoolsmo.org

BUS: Proven Leader in the Education Industry **P/S:** High-Quality Educational Services for Students Including Communication Arts, Speech, Journalism, Drama, Science, Social Studies and Mathematics **MA:** Regional **D/D/R:** Working with At-Risk Title I Four and Five-Year-Old Students, Preparing Students for Kindergarten, Instilling a Love for Reading in her Students **H/I/S:** Reading, Working on Arts and Crafts, Scrapbooking **FBP:** The Mailbox **EDU:** Master of Education, Missouri State University (Formerly Southwest Missouri State) (1992) **CERTS:** Certification in Early Childhood Education, Missouri State University (1992) **A/A/S:** Missouri State Teachers Association; Honorary Life Member, Missouri Congress of PTA (1999); Kappa Delta Pi Honor Society **A/H:** Wal-Mart Teacher of the Year (1999)

VIVIENNE E. DAWKINS
Bureau Chief for Community Health Nursing
Illinois Department of Human Services
1112 S. Wabash Avenue
Fourth Floor
Chicago, IL 60605 United States
viviennedawkins@sbcglobal.net
http://www.dhs.state.il.us

BUS: Government Organization **P/S:** Public and Maternal Child Health Services **MA:** Local **EXP:** Ms. Dawkins' expertise is in public health nursing. **D/D/R:** Establishing a Nurse Midwifery Service and Prenatal Education Program for Pregnant Methadone Maintained Narcotic Addicts, Conducting Prenatal Classes for Pregnant Teenagers and a Disease Prevention and Health Promotion Program **H/I/S:** Tennis, Gardening, Traveling **FBP:** Time; National Geographic **EDU:** Master of Science in Maternal Child Health, University of Illinois College of Nursing, Chicago (1975); Coursework, American College of Nurse Midwives, Washington, DC (1975); Bachelor of Science in Nursing, University of Illinois College of Nursing, Chicago (1972) **CERTS:** Certification in Nurse-Midwifery, Central Midwives Board, London, England (1962); Diploma in Nursing, Wembley Hospital School of Nursing, England (1960); License, State of Illinois **A/A/S:** Illinois Public Health Association; Jamaica Association of Healthcare Professionals; American College of Nurse Midwives; Board Member, New Moms; Nutrition Services Advisory Committee, Illinois Department of Health; Board Member, Perinatal Association of Illinois; Board Member, Chicago Care Pregnancy Center **A/H:** Certificate of Appreciation, Alpha Lambda Chapter, Eta Phi Beta; Outstanding Award for Dedicated Service, Abstinence Program, IL (2002); Distinguished Service Award, Department of Nursing, Cook County Hospital, Chicago, IL (1997); Outstanding Nurse Recognition Award for Service, March of Dimes, Birth Defects Foundation (1990); Faculty of the Year Award by Senior Students, College of Nursing, Chicago State University (1979)

CHERYL LOUISE DAY
Administrative Assistant
United Methodist Church
205 N. Mulberry Street
Mount Vernon, OH 43050 United States
collegemom6145@hotmail.com
http://www.cambridgewhoswho.com

BUS: Religious **P/S:** Information Technology **MA:** Local **EXP:** Ms. Day's expertise is in information technology. **H/I/S:** Reading, Camping, Crocheting **FBP:** Fortune **EDU:** Bachelor of Arts in Business Administration, Mount Vernon Nazarene University **C/VW:** Church **A/S:** She attributes her success to determination. **B/I:** She chose the profession because she wanted to help others. **H/O:** The highlight of her career is knowing she is making a positive difference in the live of others.

MARLENE E. DAY, MS.ED.
Fifth Grade Teacher
Loranger Middle School
148 Saco Avenue
Old Orchard Beach, ME 04064 United States
mday@oobschools.org
http://www.cambridgewhoswho.com

BUS: Middle School **P/S:** Education **MA:** Local **D/D/R:** Teaching Fifth Grade Students **EDU:** Master's Degree in Reading and Education, Plus 15, University of Southern Maine; Bachelor's Degree in Elementary Education (K-8), University of Maine, Orono **A/A/S:** National State Teachers Association; Associate for Supervision and Curriculum Development; Phi Delta Kappa; International Reading Association; Kappa Pi; Phi Mu; Maine State Teacher of the Year Award (1983) **C/VW:** World Youth Day at Church; Teaches Religious Instruction; American Diabetes Association; American Cancer Society

PATRICIA A. DAYFIELD
Teacher, National Creating Independence through
Student-Owned Strategies Trainer
Creating Independence through Student-Owned Strategies
40 Second Street E., Suite 249
Kalispell, MT 59901 United States
pattypat44@hotmail.com
http://www.projectcriss.com

BUS: Educational Institution **P/S:** Education Including Professional Development Program **MA:** National **EXP:** Ms. Dayfield's expertise is in classroom management and teaching strategies. **H/I/S:** Spending Time Outdoor, Reading, Traveling **FBP:** Time; Newsweek; Cobblestone **EDU:** Bachelor's Degree in Education, Concord College, WV (1965) **A/H:** Teacher of the Year Award (Four Times)

JOHN A. DE LA GARZA
Sub-Region Safety Manager
Maxim Crane Works
7085 Fannett Road
Beaumont, TX 77705 United States
jdelagarza@maximcrane.com
http://www.maximcrane.com

BUS: World's Largest Crane and Equipment Company **P/S:** Rental and Sales of All Types of Lift Equipment: Hydraulic Truck Cranes, Rough Terrain Cranes, Crawler Cranes, Tower Cranes, Conventional Truck Cranes, Boom Trucks and Carry Decks **MA:** National **D/D/R:** Ensuring Employees and Companies Adhere to Safety Policies when Working on Cranes, Overseeing 85 Employees, Conducting Safety Meetings with Companies **H/I/S:** Golfing, Hunting, Fishing, Skeet Shooting **FBP:** Golf Digest; Occupational Health and Safety Magazine; Success **CERTS:** Training Certificate, Occupational Safety and Health Administration; Training Certificate, Dixon Crane Company **A/A/S:** Golden Triangle Business Round Table; St. Jude Catholic Church

MS. MELINDA DE METRI
Owner
UltraClean
399 Business Park Court
Suite 515
Windsor, CA 95492 United States
blinds@ultracleanexperts.com
http://www.ultracleanexperts.com

BUS: Janitorial Service Company **P/S:** Janitorial Services Including Blind Cleaning, Sales and Repairs, Screen Repair **MA:** Regional **D/D/R:** Cleaning, Repairing, Installing, Selling Blinds and Screens, Working in Residential and Commercial Settings **H/I/S:** Collecting Movies, Reading **FBP:** Today's Home **EDU:** College Coursework; High School Education **A/A/S:** Santa Rosa Chamber of Commerce **A/H:** Honoree, Who's Who Among America's Teachers (2004-2006)

ANDY V. DEAN
Firefighter, Emergency Medical Technician I, Hazardous Technician
Lockheed Martin Aeronautics Company
86 South Cobb Drive
Marietta, GA 30062 United States
andy@trucking-ins.com
http://www.cambridgewhoswho.com

BUS: Fire and Emergency Services **P/S:** Fire Prevention and Medical Response **MA:** Local **EXP:** Mr. Dean's expertise is in firefighting and emergency medical services. **H/I/S:** Racing Motorcycles **EDU:** College Coursework **CERTS:** Certification, Department of Defense **A/A/S:** American Medical Association; National and State Emergency Medical Technician **C/VW:** Church, Local Charities **A/S:** He attributes his personal and professional success to his perseverance and willingness to progress. **B/I:** He has always had an interest in the field and was inspired by a friend to become involved. **H/O:** The highlight of his career was rescuing a woman from a riptide while on vacation.

DONNA M. DEAN
Author
Heartfelt Ministries
8651 S.W. Second Street
Okeechobee, FL 34974 United States
ddean4349@earthlink.net
http://heartfeltministries.webs.com

BUS: Inspirational Books **P/S:** Books **MA:** National **D/D/R:** Writing Inspirational and Religious Books, Helping Others Write Books, Speaking at Functions, Helping Abused and Homeless Women **H/I/S:** Bowling, Listening to Music, Singing, Writing, Sewing, Spending Time with her Family, Swimming, Reading, Creating Crafts, Athletics **FBP:** Women's Magazines; Writer's Magazines **EDU:** Coursework, St. David's Catholic College **CERTS:** Secretarial Certification, Ridley-Lowell, Business and Technical Institute **C/VW:** Local Charities to Help the Poor; Local Ministries and Churches; Local Women's Shelters **DOB:** May 4, 1943 **POB:** Endicott **SP:** Larry **CHILD:** Kay, Paul, Kathy, Karleen **A/S:** She attributes her success to her personal drive and faith in God. **B/I:** She became involved in her profession through a natural progression of opportunities. **H/O:** The most gratifying aspects of her career are giving hope, love and encouragement to people and seeing women's lives changed for the better by God. **I/F/Y:** In five years, Ms. Dean hopes run a shelter and publish more of her books.

MR. MARK ANTHONY DEANGELIS
District Sales Manager
Sodexo
9801 Washingtonian Boulevard
Gaithersburg, MD 20878 United States
mstrpwrlftr@yahoo.com
http://www.sodexo.com

BUS: Facility Management Company **P/S:** Facility Management Services **MA:** International **EXP:** Mr. DeAngelis' areas of expertise lie in supply and sales management, budgeting and forecasting. **D/D/R:** Managing Regional Protein Contracts **H/I/S:** Playing in a Contemporary Christian Band, Woodworking, Golfing, Power Lifting **FBP:** The Wall Street Journal **EDU:** Master's Degree in Theological Studies, John Leland Center for Theological Studies (2006); Bachelor of Arts in Technology Management, University of Maryland (1987) **A/A/S:** The Crosstones Christian Band; Shiloh Baptist Association; Pastor, Church **C/VW:** Forest Grove Baptist Church **DOB:** December 11, 1963 **POB:** Milwaukee **SP:** Jeannine **CHILD:** Nicolina, Dominick **A/S:** He attributes his success to his honesty. **B/I:** He became involved in the profession because he was encouraged by his father to enter the field. **H/O:** The highlight of his career was being named the manufacturer representative of the year in 2003. **I/F/Y:** In five years, Mr. DeAngelis plans to continue working for Sodexo.

KAREN DEBERRY
Executive Director
Project Linden
1410 Cleveland Avenue
Suite 2
Columbus, OH 43211 United States
kdeberry@project-linden.org
http://www.project-linden.org

BUS: Private Nonprofit Outpatient Alcohol and Drug Treatment and Prevention Services Center **P/S:** Outpatient Treatment and Referrals to other Treatment Centers, Prevention Services Targeting Preschool to the Elderly Population with a Special Focus on Women's Issues, Incarcerated Individuals, High Risk Youth, the Homeless Population, Clergy Community, Unemployed Persons and Community Based Services **MA:** Regional **D/D/R:** Overseeing Executive Administration of All Programs and Fiscal Management of the Agency, Organizing Client Charts, Passing All Audits which Show Documentation to Funders, Overseeing a Staff of 40 **H/I/S:** Jet Skiing, Water Sports, Fishing, Swimming **EDU:** Bachelor of Science in Education, California University of Pennsylvania (1977) **CERTS:** Licensed Social Worker, State of Ohio (1992) **A/A/S:** Hero Award for Community Shelter Board (2007); Commissioned Minister, Volunteers of America; Outstanding Achievement for Working with Homeless People

MARY ANN DECARO
Owner, Vice President
Albuquerque Bicycle Center
1570 Juan Tabo Boulevard N.E.
Albuquerque, NM 87112 United States
mary.decaro@cwwemail.com
http://www.albbicyclecenter.com

BUS: Retailer **P/S:** Bicycle Sales and Service **MA:** International **D/D/R:** Servicing Customers, Lecturing about the Importance of Bicycles in Today's Economy, Governing 25 Employees **H/I/S:** Painting, Gardening, Bicycling, Modeling **FBP:** New Mexico Magazine **C/VW:** Spike's Ride; Museum of Natural History; Local Charitable Organizations **A/S:** She attributes her success to her love for working with people. **B/I:** She became involved in her profession because she had prior entrepreneurial exposure and experience. **H/O:** The most gratifying aspect of her career is helping others.

JACQUELYN P. DEEDS, PH.D.
Professor
Mississippi State University
Box 9731
Mississippi, MS 39762 United States
jdeeds@ais.msstate.edu
http://www.ais.msstate.edu

BUS: University **P/S:** Higher Education **MA:** National **EXP:** Ms. Deeds' expertise includes teaching, leadership and youth development. **H/I/S:** Traveling, Reading, Sewing **EDU:** Ph.D., Ohio State University, Columbus; Master's Degree in Education, Oregon State University **A/A/S:** Former President, American Association for Agricultural Educators; CTE; Phi Kappa Phi; Gamma Sigma Delta **C/VW:** The Humane Society of the United States; American Heart Association; Business and Professional Women Foundation

JOANNA M. DEFEO
English Curriculum Director
Swampscott Public Schools
207 Forest Avenue
Swampscott, MA 01907 United States
joanna.defeo@verizon.net
http://www.cambridgewhoswho.com

BUS: High School **P/S:** Education, Curriculum Development **MA:** Local **D/D/R:** Developing the Curriculum **H/I/S:** Spending Time with Family **FBP:** Industry-Related Publications **EDU:** Master's Degree in English, Dartmouth University (1979) **A/S:** She attributes her success to her education and hard work. **B/I:** She became involved in the profession because she always wanted to teach. **H/O:** The most gratifying aspect of her career is seeing children learn.

GEORGE P. DeGEORGE
Curriculum Consultant (Retired)
Connecticut State Department of Education
20 Woodsedge Drive
Apartment 3C
Newington, CT 06111 United States
gdegeorge@snet.net
http://www.cambridgewhoswho.com

BUS: Education Center **P/S:** Educational Programs Including Leadership, Curriculum, Research, Planning, Evaluation, Assessment, Data Analysis and Other Assistance **MA:** International **D/D/R:** Training Bilingual and English Language Educators, Promoting Professional Development **FBP:** The New Yorker; Educational Leadership; Phi Delta Kappan **EDU:** Master of Arts in French, The City College of The City University of New York (1967); Bachelor of Arts in French, St. Francis College (1963) **CERTS:** Certification in Advanced Graduate Study, Boston University (1998) **A/A/S:** Board Member, Friends of the Newington Public Library; Docent, Wadsworth Atheneum Museum of Art (2004) **DOB:** April 23, 2008 **SP:** Denise **CHILD:** Ruth Ellen, Matthew **W/H:** English as a Second Language Teacher (1973-1987); French and Spanish Teacher, High School and College Students (1963-1973); Curriculum Consultant (Retired), Connecticut State Department of Education **A/S:** He attributes his success to hard work, dedication, and the motivation he receives from the students and teachers he has served. **B/I:** He became involved in his profession because of his desire to teach world languages. **H/O:** The highlight of his career was working for the state department of education, where he was able to enhance teacher training and support the improvement and expansion of services for English learners.

CYNTHIA A. deGUZMAN
Real Estate Broker
DeGuzman Realty
961 Sandoval Drive
Virginia Beach, VA 23454 United States
cdeguzman@roseandwomble.com
http://www.cambridgewhoswho.com

BUS: Real Estate Sales Company **P/S:** Residential Property Sales and Management **MA:** Local **EXP:** Ms. deGuzman's expertise is in office management. **H/I/S:** Sports **FBP:** The Wall Street Journal **EDU:** Bachelor's Degree in Computer Science **A/A/S:** National Association of Realtors; Virginia Association of Realtors **C/VW:** United Way of America; Autumn Speaks **A/S:** She attributes her success to her tenacity. **B/I:** She became involved in her profession because it was a natural progression. **H/O:** The most gratifying aspect of her career is owning her business.

DIANA A. DeLaHAYE, LMHC
LMHC
The Woman's Path
9 Loomis Lane
Groton, MA 01450 United States
dianadelww@aol.com
http://www.Delahaye-thwomanspath.com

BUS: Mental Healthcare Center **P/S:** Healthcare **MA:** Local **EXP:** Ms. DeLaHaye's expertise is in women's empowerment and healing therapy. **H/I/S:** Creative Art, Creative Writing **FBP:** Psychotherapy **EDU:** Master's Degree in Mental Health, River College; Bachelor's Degree in Human Services, Lesley College **CERTS:** Licensed Mental Health Clinician **A/A/S:** AMAC **A/S:** She attributes her success to her integrity, self esteem and being good at what she does. **B/I:** She became involved in her profession because she is a people person and wanted to help other women empower themselves. **H/O:** The most gratifying aspect of her career is having the opportunity to help other women.

MILDA DELENA
Realtor Associate
Southeast Coast Realty
4209 N. Federal Highway
Pompano Beach, FL 33064 United States
mildadelena@earthlink.net
http://www.cambridgewhoswho.com

BUS: Real Estate Firm **P/S:** Residential Real Estate Exchanges, Expert Services for Home Sellers and Buyers **MA:** Local **D/D/R:** Specializing in Residential Real Estate Sales **H/I/S:** Traveling, Gardening **FBP:** Realtor **EDU:** Bachelor's Degree in Teaching, The Vilius Teaching Institute **CERTS:** Licensed Real Estate Agent **A/A/S:** Florida Association of Realtors; National Association of Realtors **C/VW:** The Humane Society of Broward County; United Way of America **DOB:** January 30, 1958 **A/S:** She attributes her success to her outstanding customer service for both sellers and buyers. **B/I:** She became involved in her profession because she loves meeting people and helping them find the perfect home.

ADA I. DELGADO
Channel Development Manager
Unilever P.R.
997 San Roberto Street
Professional Office Park, Suite 7
San Juan, PR 00926 United States
ada.delgado@unilever.com
http://www.unilever.com

BUS: Multinational Consumer Products Company **P/S:** Marketing of Consumer Products **MA:** International **D/D/R:** Managing National Accounts, Overseeing the Wal-Mart Team in Puerto Rico, Managing Five Customer Business Managers, Sales Analysts and Ten Field Sales Personnel, Leading the Team in Directions and Strategies for Sales **H/I/S:** Dominoes, Bowling, Water Sports, Skiing **EDU:** Master in Business Administration, Puerto Rico (1992)

MR. LAWRENCE E. DELL
President
Dell Abstract & Title Company
10435 Dell Road
Kingsley, MI 49649 United States
dellabstract@aol.com
http://www.dellabstract.com

BUS: Title and Abstract Company **P/S:** Curative, Due Diligence, Oil and Gas Abstracts, Regular Abstracts of Title, Ownership/Leasehold Reports, Real Estate Title Searches and Related Title Services for All Types of Real Estate Transactions including, but not Limited to, Right of Ways, Pipeline Acquisitions and the Recordation of Small or Large Detailed Legal Real Estate Transactions, Service All 50 United States and Canada, Performance of All Personnel Management Functions, Mapping and Site Research **MA:** National **D/D/R:** Advocating for Oil and Gas Mineral Rights, Overseeing Operations and Purchasing, Training, Research on Titles and Abstracts, Conducting Phase I Site Environmental Studies and Cellular Tower Acquisitions **H/I/S:** Traveling with his Wife in their Motorhome, Spending Time with their Children and Grandchildren **FBP:** Oil and Gas News **EDU:** High School Diploma (1968) **A/A/S:** Fraternal Order of the Eagles

MR. JAMES G. DeLORBE
President
DMW, Ltd.
210 Justice Court N.E.
Washington, DC 20002 United States
jamesdelorbe@yahoo.com
http://www.cambridgewhoswho.com

BUS: Consulting **P/S:** Fundraising Consulting **MA:** National **EXP:** Mr. DeLorbe's expertise is in organizational development. **D/D/R:** Fundraising for the Annual Fund, Capital Campaigns and Nonprofit Initiatives **H/I/S:** Classic Cars, Architecture and Interior Designing **FBP:** The Wall Street Journal **EDU:** Master's Degree in Organizational Development (1990); Bachelor of Arts in Public Relations, George Mason University (1988) **A/A/S:** Association of Fundraising Professionals; Engineer's Club **A/S:** He attributes his career success to his hard work and passion for his work. **B/I:** He became involved in consulting through his interest in public relations and experience in the field. **H/O:** The highlight of his career was earning his current position.

JoAnn M. Demarais
Instructional Aid
Missisquoi Valley Union High School
http://www.cambridgewhoswho.com

BUS: High School **P/S:** Education **MA:** Local **EXP:** Ms. Demarais' expertise is one-on-one teaching. **H/I/S:** Sewing, Researching History **EDU:** Bachelor of Arts in Early Childhood Education, Trinity College; Degree in Special Education, Trinity College **A/A/S:** National Education Association; 4-H Camp; ARC; BPW **C/VW:** 4-H Leader; Animal Group; Sunday School Teacher, Local Church **A/S:** She attributes her success to being driven, motivated and focused. **B/I:** She became involved in her profession because she always wanted to teach. **H/O:** The most gratifying aspect of her career is working with children.

Toni M. Demetri
Pediatric Nurse Practitioner
Jacobi Medical Center, Pediatric Emergency Room
1400 Pelham Parkway
Bronx, NY 10461 United States
tmdemetri@yahoo.com
http://www.cambridgewhoswho.com

BUS: Medical Center **P/S:** Healthcare, Nursing **MA:** Regional **EXP:** Ms. Demetri's expertise is in pediatrics. **H/I/S:** Dancing, Reading, Traveling **FBP:** Pediatrics Review Journal; Newsweek **EDU:** Master of Science in Nursing, New York University **A/A/S:** National Association of Pediatric Nurse Associates and Practitioners **C/VW:** American Society for the Prevention of Cruelty to Animals **A/S:** She attributes her success to family support and a strong education. **B/I:** She chose the profession because she has always been passionate about pediatrics, and the holistic approach. **H/O:** The highlight of her career is doing something she enjoys doing.

CHRISTOPHER R. DEMPSEY, BSc, MSc
Manager, Coal Technology
Burton Coal Pty., Ltd.
PO Box 108 (Postal)
Burton Mine Site
Glenden, 4743 Australia
cdempsey@burtoncoal.com.au
http://www.mining-technology.com/projects/burton

BUS: Leader in the Coal Industry, in Operation since 1996, Dedicated to Providing Mining-Industry Equipment, Products and Service **P/S:** Metallurgy, Coal, Abrasion Resistant Materials, Shaft Equipment, Winding and Winches, Electrical Equipment and Lighting, Drilling and Blasting, Mine and Resource Management Software, Workshop Equipment, Consumables and Lubricants, Loaders and Haulage, Safety Systems and Equipment **MA:** International **EXP:** Ms. Dempsey's expertise is in coal research, technology, marketing and science. **H/I/S:** Squash, Cricket, Bush Walking, Sailing, Music, Fine Wine and Food **FBP:** The Bulletin; Technical Research Papers **EDU:** Master's Degree, University of Wollongong (1992); Bachelor's Degree, University of Adelaide (1980) **A/A/S:** Australasian Institute of Mining and Metallurgy; Chairman, Australia Coal Association Research Program; International Coal and Carbon Club **DOB:** February 17, 1955 **SP:** Carol **CHILD:** Louise, Allison, Jannah

MR. JOHN R. DENBO, PH.D.
Chief Executive Officer
Phelps County Regional Medical Center
1000 W. 10th Street
Rolla, MO 65401 United States
denboj@pcrmc.com
http://www.pcrmc.com

BUS: One of Missouri's Leading Regional Referral Centers, Serving over 150,000 Residents in South Central Missouri **P/S:** Quality Healthcare Services, Patient Care, Treatment, Rehabilitation, Intensive Care, Maternity Services, Medical Imaging, Outsource Laboratory, Psychiatric Services, Radiation **MA:** Regional **EXP:** Mr. Denbo's expertise is in corporate governing and strategic planning. **H/I/S:** Tennis, Bicycling **FBP:** Modern Healthcare **EDU:** Ph.D. in Physiology, Southern Illinois University (1974) **A/A/S:** American College of Healthcare Executives

CAROLYN R. DENNIS
Creative Director
Carolyn Dennis Creative
151 Clark Hill Road
Milford, CT 06460 United States
carolyn.dennis@mac.com
http://www.cambridgewhoswho.com

BUS: Independent Contractor of Graphic Design and Project Management Services **P/S:** Graphic Design **MA:** Regional **EXP:** Ms. Dennis' expertise is in information design and logo manuals. **H/I/S:** Sewing, Golfing, and Gardening **FBP:** How and Fast Company **EDU:** Bachelor of Science in Fine Arts, Southern Connecticut University **C/VW:** St. Gabriel's School and Parish Volunteer; Milford Public Library; Pro Bono Graphic Design Services, Local Community Groups **A/S:** She attributes her success to great service, honesty, strong work ethic, and the ability to easily identify with all levels of people. **B/I:** She chose the profession because she comes from a family of graphic artists, so choosing the career was quite natural as she always had artistic ability.

DEBORAH S. DENSON, RNC
Nurse Manager
Sierra Medical Center
1625 Medical Center Drive
El Paso, TX 79902 United States
ddenson@elp.rr.com
http://www.cambridgewhoswho.com

BUS: Medical Center **P/S:** Healthcare **MA:** Regional **EXP:** Ms. Denson's expertise is in bedside neonatal nursing. **H/I/S:** Reading, Traveling, Participating in the Church Choir, Leadership Programs for Adults and Youth, Spending Time at the Church **FBP:** Advances in Neonatal Care; Neonatal Network **EDU:** Pursuing Master of Business Administration in Healthcare Management; Bachelor of Science in Psychology, University of Texas at El Paso; Bachelor of Science in Nursing, University of Texas at El Paso **A/A/S:** Treasurer, El Paso Area Association of Neonatal Nurses; National Association of Neonatal Nurses **C/VW:** Local Church; Sponsor, Compassion International; World Vision **A/S:** She attributes her success to her perseverance and to the support she receives from her family and co-workers. **B/I:** She became involved in her profession by starting out in the field of psychology and wanting to do more. **H/O:** The most gratifying aspect of her career is seeing the pre-term babies return home healthy.

TARA L. DEONARINESINGH
Regional Director
United Realty Group
1364 Silverado
North Lauderdale, FL 33068 United States
tsingh@uhmcfl.com
http://www.cambridgewhoswho.com

BUS: Real Estate Company **P/S:** Residential Properties **MA:** Local **D/D/R:** Selling Real Estate Including Jewelry Parlors **H/I/S:** Jewelry Parlors **A/A/S:** Florida Association of Mortgage Brokers; Florida Regional Board of Realtors; National Association of Realtors

MRS. ANITA L. DEPREY
Dance Teacher, Owner
Anita Deprey Studio of Dance and Performing Arts Center
1096 Silver Lane
East Hartford, CT 06118 United States
anitadepreysod@comcast.net
http://www.anitadepreystudioofdance.com

BUS: Dance Studio **P/S:** All Types of Dance Instruction for Children through Adults, Musical Theater Workshops **MA:** Regional **D/D/R:** Teaching Tap, Jazz, Ballet, Lyrical, Contemporary, Acro-Gymnastics, Hip-Hop and Musical Theater **H/I/S:** Horseback Riding, Swimming, Caring for her Dogs **FBP:** Dance Teachers; Dance Spirits **EDU:** High School Education **A/A/S:** Chapter President, National Board Member, National Association of Dance and Affiliated Arts **A/H:** Best Dance Studio (2004)

MARYANNE M. DeRosa, RN, ADN, APCUM
Registered Nurse, Assistant Care Unit Manager
Staten Island University Hospital
475 Seaview Avenue
Staten Island, NY 10305 United States
mnikkismom@aol.com
http://www.cambridgewhoswho.com

BUS: Healthcare **P/S:** Direct Patient Care, 600-Bed Community Hospital **MA:** Regional **D/D/R:** Managing the Medical-Surgical Unit, Administering Patient Care **H/I/S:** Spending Quality Time with her Family **FBP:** Nursing Made Easy; Nursing2009; Nursing Spectrum **EDU:** Associate Degree in Nursing, College of Staten Island **A/A/S:** Association of Part-Time Care Unit Managers **C/VW:** St. Mary's Church; Various Animal Societies **A/S:** She attributes her career success to her dedication to her profession and to her passion for nursing. **B/I:** While still in high school, she earned her licensed practical nursing degree. **H/O:** She feels that the satisfaction she earns from helping her patients is the highlight of her career.

DEBORAH ANN DeSANTIS
1) Student and Faculty Services Coordinator 2) Professor
1) Wilmington College, Wilson Graduate Center
2) Delaware Technical Community College
31 Reads Way
New Castle, DE 19720 United States
m4bunny@aol.com
http://www.cambridgewhoswho.com

BUS: 1) College 2) University **P/S:** 1) Associate, Bachelor's, Master's and Doctoral Degrees in Education, Technology, Medicine, Behavioral Science, General Studies and Business Management 2) Associate, Bachelor's, Master's and Doctoral Degrees in Education, Technology, Medicine, Behavioral Science, General Studies and Business Management **MA:** 1) Regional 2) Regional **D/D/R:** Performing Administrative and Technological Duties, Offering Educational Leadership **H/I/S:** Attending Art Exhibits, Assisting with Family-Related Events, Sporting Events, Fashion Shows, and ITAC Division Awards Banquets, Attending Leadership Conventions, Playing Badminton, Participating in Breast Cancer Walks, MS Walks and Diabetes Walks, Singing, Traveling, Working as a Full-Time Nanny **FBP:** BusinessWeek; Consumer Reports **EDU:** Pursuing Master of Education, Wilmington University; Associate Degree in Office Administration and Technology, Delaware Technical Community College; Bachelor of Science in General Studies, Wilmington College **A/A/S:** Delta Epsilon Rho; National Honor Society, Wilmington College; Former Vice President, Alpha Zeta Kappa Chapter, Phi Theta Kappa; Lambda Alpha Epsilon; Business Professionals of America Organization; Former Secretary and Vice President, Student Government Association; Information Technology and Advanced Communication Club, Iota Theta Alpha Kappa Chapter; Diamond Ambassador, Delaware Technical and Community College; Student Ambassador, Wilmington College; Secretary, Human Services Club; National Art Honor Society; President, Future Homemakers of America; Participant, Young American's National Outreach Tour; Wilmington College Alumni Association; Criminal Justice Honor Society **A/H:** Delaware Technical and Community College Presidents Lists; National Dean's List; Who's Who in American Junior Colleges; USA All-State Academic Scholarship—Runner-Up; LEWIS Award; Full Scholarship, Wilmington College; **C/VW:** Holy Rosary Church Choir; Volunteer, Church Carnival; Religious Services for the Elderly; Ronald McDonald House, Salvation Army **A/S:** She attributes her success to the encouragement of her older sister. **B/I:** She became involved in her current career because she likes working in administration. **H/O:** The most gratifying aspect of her career is having earned so many credentials at such a young age.

STEFANIE L. DeSANTIS
Unit Clerk
The Reading Hospital and Medical Center
PO Box 16052
Reading, PA 19612 United States
sldesantis@comcast.net
http://www.cambridgewhoswho.com

BUS: Nonprofit Healthcare Center **P/S:** Healthcare, Acute Care, Post-Acute Rehabilitation, Behavioral and Occupational Healthcare **MA:** Local **EXP:** Ms. DeSantis' expertise is in oncology nursing, reflex, Swedish and pregnancy massage therapy. **H/I/S:** Reading, Caring for Animals **EDU:** Coursework, Berks Technical Institute (1998); Coursework in Massage Therapy (1998) **C/VW:** The Humane Society of the United States; American Society for the Prevention of Cruelty to Animals; Co-Captain, Relay for Life, American Cancer Association **A/S:** She attributes her success to her hard work and perseverance. **B/I:** She became involved in her profession after being recommended for the position by a client. **H/O:** The most gratifying aspect of her career is seeing improvements in her patients.

MR. SURESH DESHMUKH
President
Fire Prevention Company of New York, Inc.
9102 91st Avenue
Woodhaven, NY 11421 United States
ssdeshmukh@aol.com
https://http://www.cambridgewhoswho.com

BUS: Leading Fire Prevention Consulting Service **P/S:** Inspection, Tests and Recommendations of Fire Prevention Measures, Assistance for Commercial Companies Looking to Fulfill Requirements of City and State Fire and Building Codes **MA:** International **D/D/R:** Preventing Fires, Hosting Fire Prevention Courses, Teaching Fire Safety Work, Offering Fire Services and Fire Prevention Systems **H/I/S:** Playing Bridge, Watching Television **FBP:** National Fire Protection Association **EDU:** Associate Degree in Fire Engineering, School of London (1964) **A/A/S:** Fire Safety Director's Association of Greater New York; National Fire Protection Association

ROBIN A. DESROSIERS, NP-C
Certified Nurse Practitioner
Walden Medical, PLLC
142 S. Montgomery Street
Walden, NY 12586 United States
rdesro5566@aol.com
http://www.cambridgewhoswho.com

BUS: Private Practice **P/S:** Healthcare Including Primary Care **MA:** Local **EXP:** Ms. desRosiers' expertise is in medical-surgical nursing and patient care. **H/I/S:** Reading, Traveling, Spending Time with her Family, Attending Sporting Events **FBP:** Nurse Practitioner; Sigma Theta Tau International **EDU:** Master of Science in Nursing, Mount Saint Mary College, Newburgh, NY; Bachelor of Science in Nursing, Mount Saint Mary College **A/A/S:** Nurse Practitioner Association of Hudson Valley; New York State Nurses Association; Sigma Theta Tau International **C/VW:** Memorial Sloan-Kettering Cancer Center; Leukemia & Lymphoma Society; American Diabetes Association **A/S:** She attributes her success to her self-motivation and personal drive. **B/I:** She became involved in her profession because of her interest in helping others and the inspiration she received by taking care of her mother and grandparents who were diabetic patients. **H/O:** The most gratifying aspect of her career is taking care of patients.

NINA A. DEVINCENTIS
Gift Administrator
Boxed Love, Inc.
27 Horseneck Road
Fairfield, NJ 07004 United States
ninadee@boxedlove.org
http://www.boxedlove.org

BUS: Nonprofit Organization **P/S:** Children's Social Services **MA:** Statewide **H/I/S:** Camping, Hiking, Horseback Riding, Playing Tennis, Enjoying the Outdoors **FBP:** Entrepreneur; Forbes **EDU:** Associate Degree in Prenursing **A/A/S:** Women's Executive Network **C/VW:** Bovec Love, Inc. **A/S:** She attributes her success to her longevity and sticking to it. **B/I:** She chose the profession because she wanted to work with children. **H/O:** The most gratifying aspect of her career is knowing that she is making a difference in the lives of her patients.

ZACHARY J. DEVINE
Special Education Teacher
Park High School
8040 80th Street S.
Cottage Grove, MN 55016 United States
zdevine@sowashco.k12.us
http://www.cambridgewhoswho.com

BUS: Educational Facility with Special Educational Services **P/S:** Special Education and Teaching Services for Students **MA:** Regional **EXP:** Mr. Devine's expertise is in special education for mentally retarded and autistic children with emotional or behavioral problems. **D/D/R:** Completing Federal Paperwork **H/I/S:** Golfing **FBP:** Journal of Applied Behavioral Analysis **EDU:** Master's Degree in Special Education, University of South Dakota (2003); Bachelor of Science in Physical and Special Education, University of South Dakota (2001) **A/A/S:** South Dakota Education Association; National Education Association; Association of Applied Behavioral Analysis; Council for Exceptional Children; American Swimming Coaches Association

BARBARA A. DeVOE
Staff Nurse, Licensed Practical Nurse
Indian River Memorial Hospital
315 Perch Lane
Sebastian, FL 32958 United States
dragonbad@aol.com
http://www.cambridgewhoswho.com

BUS: Hospital **P/S:** Healthcare **EXP:** Ms. DeVoe's expertise is in healthcare, critical care admissions and bed control. **D/D/R:** Finding the Appropriate Bed for Admitted, Post-Operative and Unit Transfer Patients, Promoting the Hospital's Community Value by Helping the Case Management Staff Meet or Exceed Patient Needs **H/I/S:** Reading, Knitting, Making Crafts, Walking, Traveling throughout the United States, Spending Time with her Family, Friends and Pets **CERTS:** Licensed Practical Nurse, Ulster County BOCES **A/A/S:** Former Chairwoman, Clinical Practice Council; General Federation of Women's Clubs; Correspondence Secretary, Sebastian Women Juniors Clubs **C/VW:** Metro Ministries; Grace Bible Church; Knits Hats for Cancer Patients; Supply Donator, Community Food Banks and Schools **DOB:** June 6, 1949 **POB:** Newburgh **A/S:** She attributes her success to her ability to learn from her mistakes, love for helping others and sharing knowledge as well as to the smart, dedicated caregivers she works with. **B/I:** She became involved in her profession because she was inspired by her mother, who was a practical nurse. **H/O:** The most gratifying aspect of her career is being able to learn from her patients. **I/F/Y:** In five years, Ms. DeVoe hopes to remain in her current position.

GEORGE DEWEY
ESE Teacher
Miami-Dade County Public Schools,
Thomas Jefferson Middle School
525 N.W. 147th Street
Miami, FL 33168 United States
georgedewey@dadeschools.net
http://www.cambridgewhoswho.com

BUS: Public School **P/S:** Education, Inclusion Classes **MA:** Local **D/D/R:** Educating Students with Profound Handicaps, Sponsoring Federally Funded Programs for the Handicapped **H/I/S:** Cooking **FBP:** Exceptional Children **EDU:** Master's Degree in Special Education, Florida Atlantic University; Bachelor's Degree in Philosophy, Florida Atlantic University; Associate of Arts in Liberal Arts, Miami Dade Junior College (Now Miami Dade College) **C/VW:** Paralyzed Veterans, United Way, Salvation Army **A/S:** He attributes his success to his intuitive nature and being able to focus on the abilities and not the disabilities in others. **B/I:** He became involved in his profession because he was interested in civil rights and working with the mentally handicapped. **H/O:** The highlight of his career was getting programs for autistic children established, which took more than 10 years.

BETTY DeWOODY
RN, Nurse Manager
Alliance Surgery Center
2525 Eye Street
Suite A
Bakersfield, CA 93301 United States
bdewoody@healthsmartcorp.com

BUS: Outpatient Surgery Center, Proven Leader in the Healthcare Industry **P/S:** Surgery, Medical Services, Patient Care and Services **MA:** Regional **D/D/R:** Recruiting Doctors, Staffing, Scheduling Surgery, Purchasing All Safety and Education Packets for the Corporation Overseeing Interviews, Payroll, Risk Management, Infection Control, and State Recording Reporting **H/I/S:** Spending Time with her Grandchildren **FBP:** RN **EDU:** Registered Nurse, Bakersfield Community College (1995) **CERTS:** Registered Nurse Administrative Certification (2001) **A/A/S:** DAORN

AMY CHRISTINE DEYOUNG
Manager of Respiratory Care
Orlando Regional Lucerne Hospital
818 Main Lane
Orlando, FL 32801 United States
http://www.cambridgewhoswho.com

BUS: Healthcare **P/S:** Full-Service Hospital **MA:** Local **D/D/R:** Acting as a Medical Intensive Care and Pulmonary Rehabilitation Respiratory Therapist **H/I/S:** Gardening, Dogs, Biking, Yoga **FBP:** Harvard Business Review **EDU:** Master of Business Administration, Webster University; Bachelor's Degree in Professional Administration, Barry University; Associate Degree in Respiratory Care, Valencia Community College **A/A/S:** Florida Society for Respiratory Care; American Association for Respiratory Care; American Association for Cardiovascular and Pulmonary Rehabilitation; National Board for Respiratory Care **C/VW:** American Lung Association; American Heart Association **A/S:** She attributes her personal and professional success to her good role models. **B/I:** She has always had an interest in the field and was inspired by the respiratory therapist who helped her.

JUDY P. DIAL
1st Grade Teacher
Christ the King Catholic School
5858 Crittenden Avenue
Indianapolis, IN 46220 United States
http://www.cambridgewhoswho.com

BUS: Elementary School **P/S:** Education **MA:** Local **D/D/R:** Teaching in Kindergarten-Eighth Grade Self-Contained Classrooms **H/I/S:** Reading, Spending Time with Grand Son **EDU:** Master of Science in Elementary Education, Ball State University **C/VW:** Christ the King Parish **A/S:** She attributes her success to her love for children and the support of the children and their parents. **B/I:** She became involved in her profession because she has always loved working with children. **H/O:** The highlight of her career has been watching her children make progress as they move into the next grade.

MR. DANIEL E. DIAZ, BS, MS
Writer, Producer of Motion Pictures
Papillon Motion Picture Productions, Inc.
7095 Hollywood Boulevard
Suite 1219
Hollywood, CA 90028 United States
papillonfilms@aol.com
http://papillonproductionsinc.com

BUS: Motion Picture Production Company **P/S:** Television and Motion Picture Production **MA:** International **D/D/R:** Writing and Producing Motion Pictures **H/I/S:** Hang Gliding, Flying Ultralights and Single Engine Aircraft **FBP:** The Hollywood Reporter; Variety Weekly; AOPA Journal **EDU:** Master of Science in Film and Television, Zweite Deutsche Fernsehen (1976); Bachelor of Science in Hotel and Restaurant Management, Liechtenstein, Black Forest, Germany(1971) **A/A/S:** Ministerio Cultura in Caracas; Venezuela also Centro de Cine; Aircraft Owners and Pilots Association **A/H:** James A. Carroll Award for Excellence in Military Club Management; Gold Seal Awards, United States Army **A/S:** He attributes his success to being able to work with the Oscar award winning director Mr. John Clayton of East Canaan, Connecticut and the award winning writer, producer and former president of the Producers Guild of America Mr. Michael J. Musto of Tampa. **B/I:** He became involved in his profession because of his interest in film production. **H/O:** The highlight of his career was working eighteen hours everyday. **I/F/Y:** In five years, Mr. Diaz hopes to update his biography.

SHAWNE D. DIAZ, MA, LCMHC
Licensed Clinical Mental Health Counselor
Elliot Behavioral Health Services
445 Cypress Street
Suite 8
Manchester, NH 03103 United States
sdd56@verizon.net
http://www.cambridgewhoswho.com

BUS: Mental Health Service Company **P/S:** Adult Psychotherapy, Depression and Anxiety Disorders Treatment, Anger Management and Faith Based Counseling, Personal Coaching for Life Transitions Including Life and Career Changes and Retirement **MA:** Local **D/D/R:** Treating Depression, Anxiety and Personality Disorders, Offering Anger Management Counseling, Life, Retirement and Career Coaching **H/I/S:** Participating in Church Functions, Studying the Bible, Drawing, Painting, Attending Sporting Events, The Symphony and Opera **FBP:** American Counseling Association Journal; AMHCA Newsletter **EDU:** Master's Degree in Counseling Psychology, Notre Dame College, Manchester, NH; Bachelor of Fine Arts, Kutztown University **A/A/S:** American Counseling Association; American Mental Health Counselors Association; National Alliance for the Mental Ill **A/H:** Dean's List (2006) **C/VW:** Multiple Sclerosis Society; Special Olympics; Children International **POB:** Allentown, PA **W/H:** Personal Coaching Practice, Elliot Behavioral Health Services (2008); Adult Outpatient Therapist (2004 -Present); Emergency Crisis Team, Riverbend Community Mental Health (2003); Licensed Clinical Mental Health Counselor, Inpatient Crisis Unit, Community Council of Nashua (2002-2003) **C/A:** Dean's List (2006); Service Award, Elliot Health Systems **A/S:** She attributes her success to her faith in God and hard work. **B/I:** She became involved in her profession after working in preservation film, she decided to change her career path in order to follow what she felt was her calling. **H/O:** The most gratifying aspect of her career is knowing that her clients are able to live full lives after she has successfully closed their cases. **I/F/Y:** In five years, Ms. Diaz plans to expand her personal coaching practice.

MISS GERALDINE M. DiCAMILLO
Executive Administrator - New England Division
United States Professional Tennis Association
41 Taber Street
West Kingston, RI 02892
jerridicamillo@cox.net
http://www.uspta.com

BUS: Professional Tennis Organization **P/S:** More than 30 Profession Benefits to Over 14,000 Members Worldwide Including Certifications and Continuing Education **MA:** National **D/D/R:** Coaching, Teaching Tennis, Graphic Designing for Three Newsletters per Year, Creating Convention Brochures, Acting as a Liaison Between the World Headquarters and the New England Division **H/I/S:** Gardening, Cultural Arts Events, Reading **FBP:** Tennis Life; Tennis Week **EDU:** Master's Degree in Physical Education, Ithaca College; Bachelor's Degree in Physical Education, SUNY Cortland **CERTS:** Certified Tennis Teaching Professional, U.S. Professional Tennis Association **A/A/S:** US Professional Tennis Association **A/H:** Cortland College Hall of Fame (2005) **C/VW:** Local Chamber of Commerce, Local Hospice Center **A/S:** She attributes her success to the upbringing she received from her family, the people she has worked with in the field and loving what she does. **H/O:** The highlight of her career is being elected the first woman to the New York State Public High School Athletic Association Executive Committee.

GERALD A. DIEHL
President, Founder
Diehl Appraisal Service, Inc.
6837 E. Monterra Way
Scottsdale, AZ 85262 United States
gerald.diehl@cwwemail.com
http://www.cambridgewhoswho.com

BUS: Real Estate Agency **P/S:** Commercial and Residential Real Estate Exchange Including Appraisal Services **MA:** National **D/D/R:** Managing the Sale of Residential Single Family Homes **H/I/S:** Volunteering **FBP:** Appraisal-Related Publications **EDU:** Associate of Arts, Highland Community College **A/A/S:** Corvette Association, AL; ARBS

CHARLES E. DIETERLE
Owner, Chief Executive Officer, Gear Design Consultant
C-Dot Engineering
14900 Robinwood Drive
Plymouth, MI 48170 United States
c_dieterle@comcast.net
http://www.cambridgewhoswho.com

BUS: Engineering Company **P/S:** Automotive Design Engineering **MA:** National **EXP:** Mr. Dieterle's expertise is in the design of gears and splines. **H/I/S:** Golfing, Bowling **EDU:** Coursework in Mathematics, Michigan State Normal College; Diploma, Ypsilanti High School **A/A/S:** Society of Automotive Engineers; American Gear Manufacturers Association; B-92 Spline Standard Committee, American National Standards Institute **DOB:** March 24, 1928 **SP:** Dorothy **CHILD:** Jill **W/H:** Design Consultant, C-Dot Engineering; Hydramatic Division, General Motors Corporation; Machine Designer, Buhr Machine; Engineer, Garwood Industries **C/A:** Designer, Chain Drive for Front Wheel Drive Cars; Creator, Computer Programs, Gears & Splines **A/S:** He attributes his success to his education and his open-mindedness. **B/I:** He became involved in his profession because of his interest in engineering. **H/O:** The most gratifying aspect of his career is seeing his business succeed.

MR. JOSEPH S. DIGLIO
Officer In Charge
United States Postal Office
494 Broad Street
Newark, NJ 07102 United States
jdiggs51@yahoo.com
joseph.diglio@usps.gov
http://www.cambridgewhoswho.com

BUS: Government Organization **P/S:** Postal Services Including Overnight Mailing, Address Changes, Passports, Package Delivery, Envelopes and Postage **MA:** National **D/D/R:** Overseeing the Operation and Delivery of 1,400 Carryouts, Consulting, Lecturing, Public Speaking at the Postal Events **H/I/S:** Boating, Traveling **FBP:** BusinessWeek **EDU:** Associate Degree in Business Management, Fairleigh Dickinson University **A/A/S:** American Power Boat Association; National Association of Postmasters of the United States **H/O:** The most gratifying aspect of his career is meeting and interacting with new people. **I/F/Y:** In five years, Mr. Diglio hopes to continue working in the same field.

CATHY I. DILLON
Clinical Safety Nurse
Virginia Oncology Associates
5900 Lake Wright Drive
Norfolk, VA 23502 United States
cathy.dillon@usoncology.com
http://www.cambridgewhoswho.com

BUS: Private Oncology Practice **P/S:** Blood Disorders and Cancer Healthcare Services **MA:** Local **D/D/R:** Administering Treatments, Working in the Triage, Caring for Patients, Reviewing All Chemotherapy Regimens **H/I/S:** Traveling, Spending Quality Time with her Family **FBP:** NJN **EDU:** Associate Degree in Nursing, Norfolk State University **CERTS:** Certified in Oncology Nursing **A/A/S:** Oncology Nurses Association **A/S:** She attributes her success to liking what she does. **B/I:** She became involved in her profession because of a family member who had lung cancer. She always had an interest in taking care of people. **H/O:** The most gratifying aspect of her career is being able to help people and make an impact on their lives.

CATHY DiMUZIO
Director of Therapy Development
Gambro
10810 W. Collins Avenue
Lakewood, CO 80215 United States
cathy.dimuzio@us.gambro.com
http://www.gambro.com

BUS: Medical Technology Company **P/S:** Manufacturing and Supplying Medical Products, Therapies and Services for In-Center Care and Self Care Hemodialysis, Peritoneal Dialysis, Renal Intensive Care and Hepatic Care **MA:** International **D/D/R:** Overseeing Marketing, Clinical Works and Strategic Planning **H/I/S:** Reading, Traveling **FBP:** Harvard Business Review; BusinessWeek **EDU:** Master of Business Administration, University of Phoenix (2000); Bachelor of Science in Nursing, California State University, Fullerton

CINDY SUE DiNUNNO

Project Engineer
Rotorcraft Division
Boeing IDs
Route 291 and Stewart Avenue
Ridley Park, PA 19078 United States
cindy.s.dinunno@boeing.com
http://www.boeing.com

BUS: Aerospace **P/S:** Helicopters and V22 Osprey **MA:** International **D/D/R:** Developing Testing, Assuring Helicopters are Operating to Standard, Upgrading as per Customer Request **H/I/S:** Playing Tennis, Traveling, Reading **FBP:** ASQ Publications **EDU:** Master of Quality Systems Management, The National Graduate School; Bachelor's Degree in Mechanical Engineering, The Pennsylvania State University **A/A/S:** Adjunct Faculty Teacher, National Graduate School; The Pennsylvania State University **C/VW:** United Way of America; Cancer Foundation Inc.; Alzheimer's Foundation of America; Mentor for Girls in Engineering, University of Delaware **A/S:** She attributes her success to her hard work, determination and persistence. **B/I:** She became involved in this profession because she had an interest in technical work. **H/O:** The highlight of her career is being the first engineer to fly on the experimental V22 Osprey Aircraft.

W. JANICE DIPLEY, MSN, RN, FNP-C

Director of Health Services
Department of Student Health
Missouri Southern State University
3950 E. Newman Road
Joplin, MO 64801 United States
dipley-j@mssu.edu
http://www.mssu.edu

BUS: University **P/S:** Higher Education **MA:** National **EXP:** Ms. Dipley's expertise is in nursing. **D/D/R:** Teaching Health Science **H/I/S:** Reading, Traveling, Working on Computers, Exercising **FBP:** Clinician Reviews; Industry-Related Publications **EDU:** Master of Science in Nursing, University of Missouri-Kansas City; Bachelor of Science in Nursing, Missouri Southern State University; Associate of Science in Nursing, Missouri Southern State University **A/A/S:** Sigma Theta Tau International

MARCIA DIXON
Business Teacher
C.H. Price Middle School
140 N. CR 315
Interlachen, FL 32148 United States
carrmac@hotmail.com
http://www.cambridgewhoswho.com

BUS: Educational Facility **P/S:** Computer Applications and Learning Services **MA:** Regional **D/D/R:** Specializing in Education and Computer Applications, Tutoring, Working with the School Improvement Team **H/I/S:** Shopping, Singing, Going to Church, Playing in a Bell Choir, Making Gift Baskets **EDU:** Master's Degree in Education, Northern Kentucky University (1981); Bachelor's Degree in Business Education, Western Illinois University (1973) **CERTS:** Certificate Business Teacher, Grades Six through Twelve, State of Florida; Certification in Middle Level Integrated Curriculum; Endorsement, English for Speakers of Other Languages; Certification in Vocational Business Education, Grades Six through Twelve, State of Kentucky **A/A/S:** National Business Education Association **A/H:** Teacher of the Year; Technology Teacher of the Year; ESE Inclusion Teacher of the Year; Hall of Fame, Florida Future Business Leaders of America **C/VW:** Ladies Ensemble Choir **DOB:** November 16, 1951 **POB:** Herrin **SP:** William **A/S:** She attributes her success to her supportive parents and hard work. **H/O:** The most gratifying aspect of her career is being visited by her former students who tell her how much they learned in her class and how it has helped them in life.

ADAM T. DODSON
President
Emergency Medical Services Provider Program
The Maryland Institute for Emergency Medical Services Systems
PO Box 3442, Baltimore, MD 21225 United States
emsdodson@hotmail.com
a.dodson@mdemsp.org
http://www.mdemsp.org

BUS: Medical Services Program **P/S:** Critical Care Development and Implementation, Emergency Medical Services, Education, Fire Prevention, Suppression, Rescue Management and Mass Casualty, Pre-Hospital Care and Critical Care Services **MA:** National **EXP:** Mr. Dodson's expertise includes the creation of critical care transport teams, communication, management, quality assurance and improvement, and equipment. **D/D/R:** Educating, Training and Precepting All New Employees, Critical Care Teams and Emergency Management Undergraduates, Offering Continuing Education for Co-Workers and Staff Members Involved with Patient Care, Creating Critical Care Transport Teams, Staffing **H/I/S:** Reading, Playing Volleyball, Basketball, Football, Teaching, Volunteering in Community Services **FBP:** Annals of Emergency Medicine; JEMS; EMS Update; The Merck Manual of Medical Information **EDU:** Associate of Applied Science, Cecil College (2003); Master of Science, U.S. Army Medical Department Center & School Portal (1996); Diploma, Aberdeen High School, with Honors (1993); Coursework in Medical Laboratory Technology and Psychology, Harford Community College **CERTS:** Advanced International Trauma and Life Safety Instructor (2007); Certified MFRI Level III Instructor, University of Maryland, College Park (2006); RSI Certified (2004); Certified Advanced Cardiac Life Support Instructor (2003); Certified Basic Life Support Instructor (2003); Certified Advanced Life Support Provider (2000); Certified Incident Commander, Trench and Confined Space Rescue Specialist (1994); Certified Emergency Medical Technician (1992); Nationally Certified Firefighter I, II, III, State of Maryland; Nationally Registered Paramedic; Certified Cardiac Rescue Technician, State of Maryland **A/A/S:** National Registry of Emergency Medical Technicians; National Fire Academy; National Safety Council; Level III Instructor, Maryland Fire and Rescue Institute; Board Member, Bylaws Committee **A/H:** President of the United States Award (2008); Empire Who's Who for being a Proven Leader in the Field of Public Service, Fire Rescue, Emergency Medical Services, Pre-Hospital Care and Critical Care Services (2007); Nominee, Hero of the Year Award, University of Maryland (2005); Army Achievement Medal (2000); Call to Service Award; Volunteer Service Award **C/VW:** Volunteer, Maryland Emergency Medical Services Program; National Association of Emergency Medical Technicians **POB:** Havre de Grace **SP:** Carol **CHILD:** Mariah, Noah, Addison **W/H:** Operations Supervisor (2005-2006); Communications Manager, Lifestar Response of Maryland, Johns Hopkins Critical Care Team (2004-2005); DC Operations Manager (2003-2004); Communications Manager (2002-2003); Communications Manager (2002-2003); Chairman, Recruitment and Retention Committee (2001); Communications Supervisor, Field Training Officer, Operations Manager, Rural/Metro Corporation (2001); Absolute-Care Ambulance, Baltimore, MD (1998); Cardiac Laboratory In-Charge, Walter Reed Army Medical Center **A/S:** He attributes his success to his perseverance, motivations and inspirations. **B/I:** He became involved in his profession because he was inspired by his elder brother and friends who were firefighters. **H/O:** The highlight of his career was receiving the Army Achievement Medal in March 2000 for saving lives while stationed at Walter Reed Army Medical Center.

PETRINA J. DOLBY
Partner
SECOR Consulting
390 Bay Street
Suite 2400
Toronto, Ontario MSH2Y2 Canada
pdolby@secor.ca
http://www.secor.biz

BUS: Consulting Company **P/S:** Services for Strategic Consulting, Technology, Outsourcing, Local Professionals, Leadership, Development and Implementation **MA:** International **D/D/R:** Offering Financial Services, Wealth and Change Management **H/I/S:** Golfing, Skiing **FBP:** The Economist; BusinessWeek **EDU:** Master's Degree in Business Administration, Cranfield School of Management, United Kingdom (1990); Bachelor's Degree in European Business, The University of Nottingham, with Honors (1984) **CERTS:** Certified Investment Management Analyst

MARILYN MAY DOLVEN
Associate Professor of Education
Brenau University
500 Washington Street S.E.
Gainesville, GA 30501 United States
mmay@brenau.edu
http://www.brenau.edu

BUS: University **P/S:** Higher Education **MA:** International **EXP:** Ms. Dolven's expertise lies in her leadership skills and methods to improve the quality of education and curriculum development. **D/D/R:** Teaching Media Technology, Art and Social Studies, Supervising Student Teachers, Teaching Undergraduate and Graduate Students **H/I/S:** Traveling, Water Color Landscapes and Scenic Paintings **FBP:** Journal of Social Studies Research **EDU:** Doctoral Degree in Curriculum Design, Kansas State University; Master's Degree in Media Technology Integration; Bachelor's Degree in Education **CERTS:** Certified Teacher (K-12) **A/A/S:** Association for Supervision and Curriculum Development; National Council on Geography Education; National Council of Social Studies Education; Kappa Delta Pi; International Society for Technology in Education **A/H:** Elementary Art Teacher of the Year, Kansas State University

KAREN DOMINGUEZ
Manager
Automatic Payroll Processing
2267 Brunswick Pike
Lawrenceville, NJ 08648 United States
autopayroll@comcast.net
http://www.cambridgewhoswho.com

BUS: Service **P/S:** Business Payroll, Company Insurance **MA:** Local **D/D/R:** Advising on Financial Issues **H/I/S:** Traveling, Studying for Financial Planning Certification **FBP:** Barron's **EDU:** Bachelor of Science in Economics and Spanish, Rutgers, The State University of New Jersey **CERTS:** Pursuing Financial Planning Certification **A/S:** She attributes her success to her perseverance and drive. **B/I:** She became involved in her profession because her father is an accountant. **H/O:** The most gratifying aspect of her career is being independently employed.

MRS. NANCY DONATIELLO
Realtor
Lattimer Realty
397 Route
Suite 46
Fairfield, NJ 07004 United States
nancydonatiello@yahoo.com
http://www.lattimerrealty.com

BUS: Real Estate Firm **P/S:** Real Estate Sales **MA:** Local **D/D/R:** Working with Residential Relocations and Land **H/I/S:** Traveling **A/A/S:** Parent Teacher Association; Board of Realtors **C/VW:** Make-A-Wish Foundation; American Cancer Society; Co-Chair, Board Committees

Emily Elizabeth Donelson, RN, BSN
Clinical Nurse
Yale New Haven Psychiatric Hospital
184 Liberty Street
New Haven, CT 06510 United States
emily.e.donelson@gmail.com
http://www.ynhh.org/ynhph/ynhph.hml

BUS: Psychiatric Hospital **P/S:** Inpatient Mental Healthcare **MA:** Statewide **EXP:** Ms. Donelson's expertise includes psychiatric nursing and pediatric mental health. **H/I/S:** Reading, Traveling **FBP:** Journal of the American Psychiatric Nurses Association; American Journal of Nursing; Industry-Related Publications **EDU:** Pursuing Master of Science in Advanced Practice Psychiatric Nursing, Yale University School of Nursing; Bachelor of Science in Nursing, University of Florida **A/A/S:** Sigma Theta Tau International; Nomination Committee, American Psychiatric Nurses Association **A/S:** She attributes her success to her mentors and co-workers. **B/I:** She became involved in the profession because she loves working in healthcare and making a difference in people's lives.

Ms. Mary Atkins Donnelly, RN, BSN
Staff Registered Nurse, Intensive Care Unit
Indiana Regional Medical Center
835 Hospital Road
Indiana, PA 15701 United States
mtdonnelly04@hotmail.com
http://www.cambridgewhoswho.com

BUS: Healthcare Center **P/S:** Healthcare **MA:** Regional **EXP:** Ms. Donnelly's expertise is in intensive care unit nursing and assessments. **D/D/R:** Caring for Patients, Discharging, Planning, Counseling Families **H/I/S:** Spending Time with her Family, Genealogy, Listening to Music, Gardening, Stain Glass Painting,Traveling **FBP:** Journal of the American Medical Association; American Journal of Nursing; American Journal of Critical Care **EDU:** Bachelor of Science in Nursing, University of Pittsburgh, PA **A/A/S:** Sigma Theta Tau International **C/VW:** Local Church **SP:** Barry **CHILD:** Robert, Michael, Jamie, Brian **W/H:** Nurse, Lee Regional Hospital **A/S:** She attributes her success to self-motivation and her work experience. **B/I:** She became involved in her profession because she was inspired by her mother who was a nurse. **H/O:** The most gratifying aspects of her career are serving as a mentor to others and encouraging her co-workers to pursue their dreams and attain their goals.

NAOMI DONSON, MA
Columnist, Writer
1) Self-Employed 2) Herald-Tribune
12229 Hernando Road
North Port, FL 34287 United States
http://www.cambridgewhoswho.com

BUS: 1) Freelance Writer 2) Newspaper **P/S:** 1) Publications 2) News **MA:** 1) International 2) International **D/D/R:** Reviewing, Writing **H/I/S:** Traveling, Reading, Writing **FBP:** The New York Times **EDU:** Master's Degree in International Relations, University of Southern California **CERTS:** Certified in Scandinavian Literature, University of Copenhagen **A/A/S:** Independent Writers Association; Sigma Delta Chi **A/H:** Muse Award, Art and Culture Alliance (2004) **C/VW:** Private Organizations **B/I:** She became involved in her profession because she has always been surrounded by a well-educated family. Consequently, she became interested in the written word. **H/O:** The highlight of her career was winning the Muse Award.

JEANNE B. DORANCY
1) Educator 2) Educational Consultant
1) PS 77 2) CLC
450 Clarkson Avenue
Brooklyn, NY 11203 United States
http://www.cambridgewhoswho.com

BUS: 1) School 2) Consulting Firm **P/S:** 1) Education 2) Consulting **MA:** 1) Local 2) Local **EXP:** Ms. Dorancy's expertise is in special education. **D/D/R:** Teaching Autistic Children, Educational Consulting **H/I/S:** Church Minister **FBP:** Educational Leadership **EDU:** Ph.D. in Counseling and Religion, University of California; Master's Degree in Special Education, Brooklyn College **A/A/S:** Black Educators Alliance; International Reading Association; Phi Delta Kappa **C/VW:** Church; Paralyzed Veterans Association; Doctors Without Borders **A/S:** She attributes her success to her determination. **B/I:** She became involved in her profession because her child has cerebral palsy and she wanted to be able to help her and others with similar afflictions. **H/O:** The highlight of her career was earning her current position.

SUSAN A. DOTSKI
Internet Technical Support Analyst
TDS Telecom
525 Junction Road
4th Floor N.
Madison, WI 53717 United States
esdotski@centurytel.net
http://www.cambridgewhoswho.com

BUS: Telecommunications Company **P/S:** Service to 6 Million Customers in 36 States with Telephone and Internet Telecommunications **MA:** National **D/D/R:** Offering Internet Technical Support **H/I/S:** Cooking, Crocheting, Reading, Spending Time with her Cat **FBP:** USA Today; Time **EDU:** Technical Diploma, Madison Area Technical College, Madison, WI **C/VW:** Volunteers and Donates, Area Retarded Citizens, Columbia County, WI; Volunteers and Chaperones, Special Olympics; Donates to Humane Society, Columbia County, WI **A/S:** She attributes her personal and professional success to her hard work and willingness to learn. **B/I:** She became involved in the technical support industry through a progression of advancements in her company. **H/O:** The highlight of her career is serving in her current capacity as support analyst.

LINDA R. DOTY
Principal
Oswego City School District, Fitzhugh Park Elementary School
195 E. Bridge Street
Oswego, NY 13126 United States
ldoty@oswgo.org
http://www.oswego.org

BUS: School **P/S:** Education **MA:** Local **EXP:** Ms. Doty's expertise is in administration. **H/I/S:** Spending Time with her Grandchildren **FBP:** Association for Supervision and Curriculum Development Publications **A/A/S:** Association for Supervision and Curriculum Development; Phi Delta Kappa; Association of American Educators; New York State Council of School Superintendents **C/VW:** Care 'N' Share; United Way of America; Susan B. Komen Breast Cancer Foundation; Various Charitable Organizations **A/S:** She attributes her success to her family support. **B/I:** She became involved in the profession because she wanted to work with children.

Ms. Mary K. Dougherty, MSPT

MSPT, Site Manager
Aqua Care
20684 John Jay Williams Highway, Suite 2
Lewis, DE 19958 United States
marydoc1@yahoo.com
http://www.cambridgewhoswho.com

BUS: Rehabilitation and Therapy Center **P/S:** Rehabilitation, Physical Therapy **MA:** Local **EXP:** Ms. Dougherty's expertise is in orthopedic and Sports medicine. **H/I/S:** Participating in Triathlons, Coaching Basketball **FBP:** Journal of the American Physical Therapy Association **EDU:** Master's Degree in Physical Therapy, Thomas Jefferson University **A/A/S:** American Physical Therapy Association **C/VW:** March of Dimes **A/S:** She attributes her success to her caring nature and her love for her profession. **B/I:** She became involved in her profession because she was a high school athlete who needed physical therapy and wanted to work in the healthcare field. **H/O:** The most gratifying aspect of her career is being able to work in different settings. **I/F/Y:** In five years, Ms. Dougherty hopes to start her own practice or own clinic.

Stella Douros, MD

Ophthalmologist, Vitreoretinal Specialist
Stella Douros, MD, PC
7501 Sixth Avenue
Brooklyn, NY 11209 United States
stella.douros@cwwemail.com
sdouros@pol.net
http://www.cambridgewhoswho.com

BUS: Private Medical Practice **P/S:** Ophthalmology Services Including Diagnosis, Medical and Surgical Treatment of Retinal Diseases **MA:** Regional **D/D/R:** Making Retinal Consultations, Performing Medical and Surgical Treatments for Vitreoretinal Diseases, Participating in Clinical Research Projects, Educating Patients, Supervising Employees **H/I/S:** Reading, Traveling **FBP:** Retina; The Journal of Retinal and Vitreous Diseases **EDU:** MD, Albert Einstein College of Medicine (1991) **A/A/S:** Fellow, American College of Surgeons; Fellow, American Academy of Ophthalmology; Brooklyn Ophthalmological Society; New York State Ophthalmological Society; Hellenic Medical Society; Association for Research Vision and Ophthalmology **A/H:** Super Doctors of New York Award (2008); America's Top Ophthalmologists Award (2002-2008); Physician's Recognition Award, American Medical Association (1998-2008) **H/O:** The most gratifying aspect of her career is helping patients.

TERRI ELLEN DOVER
Practice Consultant
Elsevier/CPMRC
600 28th Street
Grand Rapids, MI 49509 United States
trdover@msn.com
http://www.cambridgewhoswho.com

BUS: Healthcare Company **P/S:** Healthcare, Marketing, Training, Medication Management, Research, Best Practice Implementation **MA:** International **EXP:** Ms. Dover's expertise is in healthcare safety, electronic systems, hospital presentations and research. **H/I/S:** Reading, Traveling, Writing, Crocheting **EDU:** Master's Degree in Business Management, Breyer State University **A/A/S:** National Society of Insurance Premium Auditors **C/VW:** National Spinal Cord Injury Board; NAPSAC **A/S:** She attributes her success to her willingness to work hard and fact-finding abilities. **B/I:** She became involved in her profession because she wanted to move into a clinical role that would still impact patient care and safety. **H/O:** The most gratifying aspect of her career is making a difference and seeing positive changes occur because of her work.

JOHN F. DOWN
Contractor
Insap, Inc.
1120 Route 735
Marlton, NJ 08053 United States
jdown@csc.com
http://www.csc.com

BUS: Professional Service Firm **P/S:** Consulting Services for Information Technology, Training, Development Services and Outsourcing Options **MA:** National **EXP:** Mr. Down's expertise is in system engineering, logistic and project management and business analysis. **H/I/S:** Skiing, Golfing, Cycling, Exercising, Gardening, Landscaping, Painting, Astronomy, Stamp and Coin Collecting, Reading Civil War History Books **FBP:** Money; Forbes **EDU:** Master of Business Administration, Monmouth University (1985); Master's Degree in Political Science, Ohio State University (1970) **A/A/S:** Life Loyal Member, Sigma Chi; Reserve Officers Association; Roanoke Civil War Round Table; National Home Gardening Club; Washington Chapter, SPIN; The Highlands Historical Society; Railway & Locomotive Historical Society

REBECCA DOWNS, CCC-SLP

Speech Pathologist
USD 308 Hutchinson Public Schools
Hutchinson, KS 67502 United States
crazyoverspeech@yahoo.com
http://www.cambridgewhoswho.com

BUS: School District **P/S:** Education **MA:** Regional **EXP:** Ms. Downs' expertise is in cognitive and dysphagia rehabilitation. **D/D/R:** Caring for Patients with Traumatic Brain Injuries, Swallowing Disorders and Articulation and Language Deficiencies, Performing Electrical Stimulation Treatments, Teaching Elementary Education **H/I/S:** Spending Time with her Twelve Grandchildren **FBP:** Forbes; ASHA Journals **EDU:** Pursuing Master's Degree in Administration, Southwestern Oklahoma State University; Master's Degree in Speech Pathology, Northeastern State University (1996); Bachelor's Degree in Elementary Education, Southwestern Oklahoma State University (1989)

SHIRLEY M. DOYLE, RRT

Educational Coordinator
Ingham Regional Medical Center
401 W. Greenlawn Avenue
Lansing, MI 48910 United States
shirley.doyle@irmc.org
http://www.cambridgewhoswho.com

BUS: Nonprofit Teaching Hospital **P/S:** Healthcare **MA:** Local **EXP:** Ms. Doyle's expertise is in disease management and treatment. **H/I/S:** Skiing, Swimming, Biking, Camping, Traveling **FBP:** Respiratory Care Magazine **EDU:** Bachelor of Science in Respiratory Therapy, Michigan State University; Associate of Science in Respiratory Therapy, Lansing Community College **A/A/S:** Michigan Society of Respiratory Care; American Association of Respiratory Care **C/VW:** American Diabetes Association; Local Church **A/S:** She attributes her success to being a life-long learner and her love of teaching. **B/I:** She became involved in her profession while in school. She was interested in physical therapy and took a course. **H/O:** The highlight of her career has been speaking at the Michigan Convention for the Society of Respiratory Care.

CHRISTINE A. DRAKE
Board Member, Secretary
West Michigan Veterans Association
349 S. Division
Grand Rapids, MI 49503 United States
christinedrake@sbcglobal.net
http://www.cambridgewhoswho.com

BUS: Nonprofit Charitable Service Provider **P/S:** Social and Human Services for United States Veterans **MA:** Regional **D/D/R:** Volunteering Time to Assist Male and Female Veterans in Need, Helping the Homeless, Assisting with Funding for Healthcare, Food, Housing and Insurance, Working with the Veterans Assistance Program and Disabled Veterans **H/I/S:** Reading, Cross Stitching **EDU:** College Coursework **C/VW:** Air Force Sergeants Association; Disabled Veterans Chapter 2; Veterans of Foreign War

APRIL D. DRAYTON
Business Analyst
Blue Cross and Blue Shield of Alabama
5926 Southwood Parkway
Bessemer, AL 35022 United States
aprildrayton@hotmail.com
http://www.cambridgewhoswho.com

BUS: Insurance Company **P/S:** Healthcare Coverage **MA:** Local **EXP:** Ms. Dayton's expertise is in business strategy analysis. **D/D/R:** Auditing and Promoting Healthcare Insurance, Consulting with Clients **H/I/S:** Relaxing, Watching Movies, Tennis **FBP:** Internal Auditor; Black Enterprise **EDU:** Master of Business Administration, Webster University; Bachelor's Degree in Computer Science **A/A/S:** The Institute of Internal Auditors

MS. DIANNE D. DRESSOR
Interpreter for the Deaf
6905 Cisco Road N.W.
Albuquerque, NM 87120 United States
dddressor@gmail.com
http://www.cambridgewhoswho.com

BUS: Sole Proprietorship **P/S:** Freelance Interpretation for the Deaf **MA:** Regional **EXP:** Ms. Dressor's expertise is in interpretation for the deaf community. **D/D/R:** Attending Physician's Appointments, Arranging Meetings and Conferences with the Clients **H/I/S:** Horseback Riding, Working on Computers, Watching Star Trek, Photography **FBP:** RID Magazine; View **EDU:** Master's Degree in Training and Learning Technology, University of New Mexico (1993); Bachelor's Degree in Special Education, University of Northern Colorado (1973) **A/A/S:** New Mexico Registry of Interpreters of the Deaf; Registry of Interpreters for the Deaf

PEGGY A. DROGEMULLER, RN
Registered Nurse
Verdugo Hills Hospital
1812 Verdugo Boulevard
Glendale, CA 91208 United States
peggyrn@earthlink.net
http://www.verdugohillshospital.org

BUS: Hospital **P/S:** Healthcare **MA:** Local **EXP:** Ms. Drogmuller's expertise is in medical-surgical nursing. **D/D/R:** Precepting New Nurses, Treating Diseases, Assessing Patients **H/I/S:** Gardening **FBP:** Nursing2009 **EDU:** Associate of Science in Nursing, Pacific Union College **CERTS:** Certification in Chemotherapy

MR. HERBERT DRUCKER
Information Technology Manager
SC Department of Mental Health
PO Box 848
Columbia, SC 29202 United States
hed00@scdmh.org
http://www.scdmh.org

BUS: Healthcare **P/S:** Care for Adults, Children, and their Families Affected by Serious Mental Illnesses and Significant Emotional Disorders **MA:** South Carolina **D/D/R:** Overseeing All Information Technology Operations **H/I/S:** Poker **FBP:** Government Technology Magazine **EDU:** Bachelor of Science in Mathematics, DC Teachers College **A/A/S:** College of Information Healthcare Management

NATALIE JOAN DUBANOWITZ
Environmental Engineer
US Powergen
18-01 20th Avenue
Astoria, NY 11105 United States
ndubanowitz@uspowergen.com
http://www.cambridgewhoswho.com

BUS: Environmental Plant **P/S:** Power Generation through Steam Generation **MA:** Regional **EXP:** Ms. Dubanowitz's expertise is in environmental health and safety for steam generation and electrical projects. **H/I/S:** Skiing, Fishing, Golfing, Traveling, Running **FBP:** Harvard Business Journal **EDU:** Bachelor of Science in Environmental Science, Engineering and Biotechnology, James Madison University **A/A/S:** Office of Emergency Management **C/VW:** Children of Chernobyl Relief Fund; St. Jude Children's Research Hospital **A/S:** She attributes her personal and professional success to her hard work and level head. **B/I:** She has always had an interest in the field and enjoys the challenges of the profession. **H/O:** The highlight of her career is her progression within the company.

MARGOT D. DuBois
Distribution Services Operations Assistant
American Public Television
55 Summer Street
Fourth Floor
Boston, MA 02110 United States
margot_dubois@aptonline.org
http://www.aptonline.org

BUS: Entertainment Firm **P/S:** Innovative Programs and Creative Distribution Techniques, Distribution of More than 300 Series and Specials in a Variety of Genres Including Documentary, Cooking and Lifestyle, Travel, Feature Film Packages, Drama, Music and Entertainment **MA:** International **D/D/R:** Receiving Broadcast Tapes and On-Air Promotional Reels, Compiling Information on Satellite Feeds and Refeeds, Maintaining the Media Library, Tracking Station and Airing Programs and their Corresponding Satellite Feeds, Contributing to the Production of APT Teleconferences **H/I/S:** Reading, Playing Baseball, Rollerblading, Listening to Music, Visiting Museums, Studying Architecture, Attending Theater in the Boston Area **FBP:** APT Monthly **EDU:** Bachelor of Fine Arts in Theater, Boston University (2003) **A/A/S:** Actor's Equity Association; Stage Source; The Greater Boston Theater Alliance; The Union for Professional Actors and Stage Managers of the United States

CYNTHIA G. DUCKETT
Army Nurse
U.S. Army Nurse Corps
110 Mallard Cove
Vass, NC 28394 United States
cynthia.duckett@us.army.mil
http://www.cambridgewhoswho.com

BUS: Government Organization **P/S:** Nursing Care for U.S. Army Personnel Including Research, Healthcare Education, Wellness Promotion and Community Healthcare **MA:** International **D/D/R:** Discharging Scrub and Circulating Duties, Overseeing Administrative Duties, Recruiting Nurses, Assisting in Surgeries Including Open-Heart Surgery **H/I/S:** Skydiving, Scuba Diving, Boating **EDU:** Bachelor's Degree in Nursing, Syracuse University (1987) **A/A/S:** Association of Operating Room Nurses; Military Officers Association of America **H/O:** The most gratifying aspect of her career is being able to interact and treat patients.

GENE C. DUFF
Consultant
Gene C. Duff, Consultant
geneduff@comcast.net
http://www.cambridgewhoswho.com

BUS: Consulting Practice **P/S:** Consulting for Textile and Carpet Companies **MA:** Regional **D/D/R:** Investigating Carpet Research and Development, Offering Technical Services for Mohawks, Assisting in the Development of New Products and Machinery **H/I/S:** Traveling, Visiting Museums, Reading **EDU:** Degree in Junior Accounting, National College of Business & Technology (1961); Coursework in Textile Engineering

KRISTINA MARIANNE DUFRESNE
Teacher
Norwalk/LaMirada Unified School District
12820 Pioneer Boulevard
Norwalk, CA 90650 United States
toy02@earthlink.com
http://www.cambridgewhoswho.com

BUS: Education **P/S:** Intermediate Education, Grades 6-8 **MA:** Local **D/D/R:** Specializing in Physical Education and Health **H/I/S:** Kayaking, Travel **FBP:** Prevention; Women's Health; People **EDU:** Pursuing Master's Degree in Administration, Concordia University; Bachelor's Degree in Physical Education and Health, California State University, Chico **A/A/S:** California Association for Health, Physical Education, Recreation and Dance **C/VW:** Salvation Army, American Veterans **A/S:** She feels that her success lies in the fact that she understands where the kids are coming from, and she believes that adults need to take time to get to know the students. **B/I:** She became a teacher because she loves working with young people. She feels that often times they are stifled and unable to express their ideas; she works to let them grow and be creative. **H/O:** She feels that the highlight of her career happens when her students come back to visit her.

JODY A. DUGRENIER, PA-C
Certified Physician Assistant
Wentworth-Douglass Hospital
789 Central Avenue
Dover, NH 03820 United States
jdugrenier@hotmail.com
http://www.cambridgewhoswho.com

BUS: Hospital **P/S:** Patient Care **MA:** Local **EXP:** Ms. Dugrenier's expertise is in internal medicine. **H/I/S:** Going on Healthcare Missions, Trekking, Hiking, Camping, Reading **FBP:** The New England Journal of Medicine **EDU:** Master's Degree in Physician Assistant Studies, Massachusetts College of Pharmacy and Health Sciences; Bachelor of Science in Medical Laboratory Sciences, University of New Hampshire, Minor in Criminal Justice Studies **CERTS:** Certified Physician Assistant **A/A/S:** New Hampshire Society of Physician Assistants; American Academy of Physician Assistants; National Commission on Certification of Physician Assistants **C/VW:** Helping Hands Health Education **A/S:** She attributes her success to her motivation and determination. **B/I:** She became involved in her profession because she always had an interest in the field and wanted to help others. **H/O:** The most gratifying aspect of her career is helping patients.

ANNE DUKEHART
Registered Nurse, BSN
Johnson Memorial Hospital
201 Chestnut Hill
Stafford Springs, CT 06071 United States
dukeheal@aol.com
http://www.cambridgewhoswho.com

BUS: Hospital **P/S:** Healthcare **MA:** Local **D/D/R:** Caring for Patients **H/I/S:** Running, Working Out, Skiing **EDU:** Bachelor of Science in Nursing, University of Connecticut **A/A/S:** ARC; ACS **A/S:** She attributes her personal and professional success to her continued education. **B/I:** She has always had an interest in the field and was greatly influenced by her mother. **H/O:** The highlight of her career is her ability to help new nursing graduates transition from students to professional nurses.

ROGER WAYNE DUNAGAN
Owner, Manager
Triple R Contracting, LLC
103 Fannin Drive
Kerrville, TX 78028 United States
dun1043@ktc.com
http://www.cambridgewhoswho.com

BUS: Construction Company **P/S:** Construction Services **MA:** Regional **EXP:** Mr. Dunagan's expertise is in organizational management . **D/D/R:** Working with a Staff of 15 **H/I/S:** Hunting, Fishing **FBP:** Texas Contractor **EDU:** Bachelor's Degree in Criminal Justice, Evangelical and Christian University **CERTS:** Certified Police Officer **A/A/S:** Future Farmers of America **C/VW:** Church of Christ

ANGELA DE SOTO DUNCAN, PE
Lead Structural Engineer
U.S. Army Corps of Engineers, New Orleans District
7400 Leake Avenue
New Orleans, LA 70118 United States
palmter@bellsouth.net
http://www.cambridgewhoswho.com

BUS: Federal Government Agency **P/S:** Flood Control and Navigation **MA:** National **EXP:** Ms. Duncan's expertise is in concrete design. **H/I/S:** Spending Time with her Family **EDU:** Bachelor of Science in Civil Engineering, Tulane University **A/A/S:** American Society of Civil Engineers; Licensing Executives Society; American Concrete Institute **C/VW:** Local Charitable Organization **A/S:** She attributes her success to her hard work and ability to determine and set goals. **B/I:** She became involved in her profession because she always had an interest in construction.

DOROTHY A. DUNCAN, RN, BSN, CPHQ
Associate Director Healthcare Inspector
Department of Veterans Affairs
City Center Square
1100 Main Street
Kansas City, MO 64105 United States
http://www.cambridgewhoswho.com

BUS: Healthcare Agency **P/S:** Healthcare and Hospitalization Services for United States Veterans at Low to No Cost **MA:** Local **EXP:** Ms. Duncan's expertise is in management, quality assurance and veteran patient care evaluations. **H/I/S:** Playing Piano, Watching College Football, Golfing, Knitting **FBP:** RN 2005; Journal of Healthcare Quality **EDU:** Pursuing Master's Degree in Healthcare Administration; Bachelor's Degree in Nursing, University of Nebraska **A/A/S:** National Association for Healthcare Quality **C/VW:** American Cancer Society; Planned Parenthood **SP:** Michael **CHILD:** Jessica, Katy

ALISON M. DUNCH
Physical Therapist
Round Rock Medical Center
2400 Round Rock Avenue
Round Rock, TX 78681 United States
adunch@austin.rr.com
http://www.cambridgewhoswho.com

BUS: Medical Center, Hospital **P/S:** Healthcare **MA:** Regional **EXP:** Ms. Dunch's expertise is in wound care and acute care physical therapy. **H/I/S:** Scrapbooking, Gardening, Family Time, Boating **FBP:** Advance for Physical Therapists and Physical Therapy Assistants **EDU:** Master's Degree in Physical Therapy, Philadelphia College of Pharmacy and Science; Bachelor's Degree in General Health Sciences, Purdue University **A/A/S:** American Physical Therapy Association **C/VW:** Church; Paralyzed Veterans of America; Texas Chapter, Paralyzed Veterans of America; Cystic Fibrosis Foundation **B/I:** She became involved in her profession because she has always had a calling for helping others. **H/O:** The highlight of her career is her success with many of her acute care patients.

Ms. Janet E. Dunn
Assistant Center Manager
Workforce Solutions - Capital Area
6505 Airport Boulevard, Suite 101A
Austin, TX 78752 United States
janetedunn@hotmail.com
http://www.cambridgewhoswho.com

BUS: Consulting Firm **P/S:** Training Programs and Workshops for Job Seekers and Employers Including Resume Training, Education **MA:** Regional **EXP:** Ms. Dunn's expertise is in case management. **D/D/R:** Managing Operations and the Work Force Center, Maintaining Records **H/I/S:** Reading, Swimming, Attending Flea Markets **EDU:** Associate Degree in Liberal Arts, San Antonio College (1973) **A/H:** Award for Excellence, State of Texas **C/VW:** Local Food Bank; The Salvation Army; Lisa Hope Chest; Helping Others Progress Economically **A/S:** She attributes her success to her work ethic, honesty and her ability to work well with others. **H/O:** The most gratifying aspect of her career is making a difference in the others lives.

Cheryl A. Dupre
Registered Respiratory Therapist
Abbeville General Women & Children's Hospital
PO Box 295
Youngsville, LA 70592 United States
cheryldup@aol.com

BUS: Hospital **P/S:** Healthcare **MA:** Local **EXP:** Ms. Dupre's expertise is in advanced respiratory care. **H/I/S:** Motorcycling **FBP:** Ride Texas; AARC; Advance; Wing World; Road Runners **EDU:** Coursework in Advanced Respiratory Care **C/VW:** Pediatric Brain Tumor Foundation; Ride for Kids; Local Church

M. Joanelle Duran-Wennersten
Owner, Floral Designer
Joanelle's
2025 Hampshire Road
Fort Collins, CO 80526 United States
jnllduran@yahoo.com
http://www.cambridgewhoswho.com

BUS: Floral, Weddings **P/S:** Floral Design **MA:** Statewide **D/D/R:** Designing Wedding Flower Arrangements, Coordinating Weddings **H/I/S:** Reading, Watching Bridezilla's, Extreme Home Makeover and Whose Wedding Is It Anyway on Television **FBP:** The Knot; Bride **EDU:** Coursework in Floral Design and Horticulture, Colorado State University **CERTS:** Certified in Cosmetology and Hair Design in Colorado **A/A/S:** North Colorado Wedding Network Group **C/VW:** Habitat for Humanity **A/S:** She attributes her success to her ability to work with the public. **B/I:** She became involved in her profession because of her creative nature.

Denise B. Durham
Quality Assurance Manager
PepsiCo-Gatorade
409 S. 104th Avenue
Tolleson, AZ 85353 United States
denise_durham@quakeroats.com
http://www.pepsico.com

BUS: Food and Beverage Company **P/S:** Food and Beverages Including Pepsi Products, Frito-Lay, Tropicana, Quaker and Gatorade **MA:** National **EXP:** Ms. Durham's expertise is in quality assurance. **D/D/R:** Approving All Productions, Managing Sanitation **H/I/S:** Hiking, Scuba Diving, Horseback Riding **FBP:** DiversityInc **EDU:** Pursuing Master's Degree in Leadership Management, Capella University **A/A/S:** The National Society of Black Engineers; Society for Food Science and Technology **C/VW:** Soup Kitchen Volunteer, Society of St. Vincent de Paul

SCOTTY DURISEK
Realtor
Jack Gaughen Realtor ERA
5050 Linglestown Road
Harrisburg, PA 17112 United States
scotty.durisek@jgr.com
http://www.jgr.com

BUS: Real Estate Agency **P/S:** Real Estate Services **MA:** Regional **EXP:** Ms. Durisek's expertise is in real estate. **D/D/R:** Listing Properties, Managing the Purchase and Sale of Residential Properties, Assisting First-Time Homebuyers, Making Smooth Transactions **H/I/S:** Reading, Water Skiing, Swimming **EDU:** College Coursework **CERTS:** Licensed Realtor; Certified Residential Specialist; Certified Safety Professional; Leadership Training Graduate; Graduate Realtor Institute **A/A/S:** Pennsylvania Association of Realtors; National Association of Realtors **A/H:** Salesperson of the Year Award **C/VW:** Board of Directors, Cystic Fibrosis Foundation **H/O:** The most gratifying aspect of her career is the gratitude she receives from her clients.

DR. HEATHER M. B. DUSSAULT
Assistant Professor, Electrical Engineering
SUNY Institute of Technology
PO Box 3050
Utica, NY 13504 United States
dussauh@sunyit.edu
http://turing.sunyit.edu/dussauh

BUS: University **P/S:** Higher Education **MA:** National **D/D/R:** Instructing a Graduate Reliability Course, Performing Object-Oriented Programming, Working on Command and Control Systems **H/I/S:** Playing Volleyball, Hiking, Reading, Gardening, Caring for her Pets **FBP:** Scientific American; IEEE Spectrum; Communications of the ACM **EDU:** Ph.D. in Nuclear Engineering and Science, Rensselaer Polytechnic Institute (1995); Master's Degree in Nuclear Engineering and Reliability, Rensselaer Polytechnic Institute **A/A/S:** New York Academy of Science; New York State Engineering Technology Association; Association for Computing Machinery; American Nuclear Society; American Society of Engineering Educators; Society of Women Engineers; Institute of Electrical and Electronics Engineers; Alumni Association, Rensselaer Polytechnic Institute **A/S:** She attributes her success to her hard work and perseverance. **B/I:** She became involved in her profession because she always wanted to make a difference in students' lives. **H/O:** The highlight of her career was working at the Defense Advanced Research Agency.

Ms. Marian June DuVal
Registered Professional Reporter (Retired)
Los Angeles Superior Court
5860 Hazeltine Avenue
Apartment Five
Van Nuys, CA 91401 United States
vannuysmarian@yahoo.com
http://www.cambridgewhoswho.com

BUS: Court Reporting for a Private Industry **P/S:** Non-Machine Verbatim Shorthand Reporting Services Including Depositions, Conferences, and Witness Statements **MA:** Regional **D/D/R:** Specializing in Shorthand as a Court Reporter, Handling Court Records, Recording Witness Testimonies, Overseeing Court Transcripts **H/I/S:** Massage Therapy, Nutrition, Enjoying Ballet and Music **FBP:** Court Reporters Journal: The Wall Street Journal **EDU:** Pursuing Bachelor's Degree in Liberal Arts; Associate Degree in Liberal Arts, Los Angeles Valley College **A/A/S:** National Court Reporters Association; Los Angeles Court Reporters Association **A/H:** Certificate of Proficiency Award **C/VW:** Animal Rights Organizations; Environmental Organizations; Nature Conservatory **A/S:** She attributes her success to her hard work, ambition and determination.

Grace E. Dyjak
Special Education Teacher
Gulliver Schools
7500 S.W. 120th Street
Miami, FL 33156 United States
dyja@gulliverschools.org
http://www.cambridgewhoswho.com

BUS: School District **P/S:** Education **MA:** Local **D/D/R:** Helping Children Reach their Potential, Focusing on Middle School Students, Treating Each Student as an Individual **H/I/S:** Camping, Traveling, Reading **FBP:** National Geographic **EDU:** Bachelor of Arts in Exceptional Student Education **A/S:** She attributes her success to having a desire to learn and work at helping children succeed. **B/I:** She became involved in her profession because she always wanted to work with exceptional children. **H/O:** The most gratifying aspect of her career is working with the children and seeing their daily progress.

MERVEL L. EAGANS SR.
Director
United Drug Information Network, Inc.
412 E. Wilden Avenue
Goshen, IN 46528 United States
mleagans@verizon.net
http://www.cambridgewhoswho.com

BUS: Drug Abuse Intervention Center **P/S:** Drug Intervention Instructions and Services **MA:** Local **EXP:** Mr. Eagans' expertise is in editing. **H/I/S:** Gardening, Fishing **FBP:** Industry-Related Publications **EDU:** Bachelor's Degree, The George Washington University **A/A/S:** Goshen Citizens Police Academy; Basic Ministry for the Imprisoned; Adventists Prison Ministries Association; National Geographic Society **C/VW:** Arbor Day Foundation; Center for Positive Thinking

LEONA M. EANES
Billing Systems Analyst
Quantum Medical Business Services
2800 Keagy Road
Salem, VA 24153 United States
leanes@qmbs.com
http://www.qmbs.com

BUS: Medical Billing Company **P/S:** Medical Billing, Business Services, Quality Control to Ensure Clients are Satisfied **MA:** National **EXP:** Ms. Eanes' expertise includes education, communication and evaluation. **D/D/R:** Training Employees, Offering Continual Training to Employees for HIPAA Compliance, Troubleshooting, Handling HIPAA Regulations Electronically **H/I/S:** Gardening, Reading, Painting, Playing the Piano **EDU:** Industry-Related Training and Experience **C/VW:** National Multiple Sclerosis Society; American Diabetes Association

HILLARY K. EATON
Occupational Therapist
Rehabilitation Hospital of the Cape and Island
22 Barberry Lane
Brewster, MA 02631 United States
hillarykeaton@yahoo.com
http://www.rhci.org

BUS: State-of-the-Art Hospital Dedicated to Rehabilitation Care **P/S:** Cardiac Monitoring (Telemetry), EMG and Nerve Conduction Lab, Hearing Evaluations, Laboratory, On-site Dialysis, Orthotics Clinic, Pharmacy, Prosthetics Clinic, Respiratory Services, Video Fluoroscopic Evaluations, X-Ray Suite **MA:** Regional **D/D/R:** Administering Acute Care and Rehabilitation for Stoke Patients, Teaching Home Management for Patients Including Cooking and Cleaning, Following-Up on Patients **H/I/S:** Gardening, Kayaking, Fencing, Walking **EDU:** Master's Degree in Education, Springfield College (2000); Bachelor of Arts in Art History and Costume Design, Hobart and William Smith College **A/A/S:** American Journal of Occupational Therapy; National Education Alliance for Borderline Personality Disorder; Formerly Board Member New England Personality Disorder Association

MR. PETER N. EBERE, PH.D.
Chief Executive Officer
Total Healthcare
3333 Knollcrest Lane
Mesquite, TX 75181 United States
totalhealth@sbcglobal.com
care@swbell.net
http://www.totalhealthcare.com

BUS: Home Healthcare Agency **P/S:** Services for Seniors, Homebound and Chronically Disabled Individuals from a Personally Selected and Screened Team of Home Healthcare Providers **MA:** Texas **D/D/R:** Overseeing Operations and Business Administration, Complying with Regulations, Handling Finances, Marketing and Community Relations **H/I/S:** Running, Playing Soccer **EDU:** Pursuing Ph.D. in Community Health, Walden University; Master of Science in Operations Management, University of Arkansas (1994); Bachelor of Science in Hospital Administration, Southern Illinois University (1993) **A/A/S:** American College of Health Executives **C/VW:** Seventh Day Adventist Church **W/H:** DT3, United States Navy (1989-1994)

JOHN J. ECKEL JR.
Network Technician (Retired)
Verizon Communications
4075 Highway Nine
Freehold, NJ 07728 United States
johnhafeken@verizon.net
http://www.verizon.com

BUS: Telecommunication Company **P/S:** Telecommunication Services Including Wireless Network, Wireless Telephones and Devices, Wireless Service Plans for Individuals and Businesses, Customer Service, Call Center, Broadcasting, Product Instructions, Yellow Pages Advertising and Conference Services **MA:** International **EXP:** Mr. Eckel's expertise is in inter-office facility management. **H/I/S:** Designing Model Railroads **FBP:** IBW Journal **EDU:** High School Diploma **A/H:** Bronze Star Award **C/VW:** Veterans of Foreign Wars Post 2290; American Legion Post 1000

NEIL SETH EDELMAN
Partner, Chief Executive Officer
Sleepy Hollow Development Co., LLC
2350 Ocean Avenue
Brooklyn, NY 11229 United States
geotwn@aol.com
http://www.cambridgewhoswho.com

BUS: Proven Leader Committed to Excellence in the Building and Developing Industry **P/S:** Building Services for One and Two-Family Homes **MA:** Regional **D/D/R:** Purchasing Raw Property for the Development of Residential Homes, Building High-Rise Homes, Offering Property Management Services **H/I/S:** Golfing **EDU:** Bachelor of Arts in Accounting, Franklin Pierce College, New Hampshire (1976) **A/A/S:** National Association of Home Builders; Building Industry Association of New York City; RSA

DR. MARLOW EDIGER
Professor Emeritus
Truman State University
Kirksville, MO 63501 United States
mediger2@cox.net
http://www.truman.edu

BUS: One of the Nation's Premier Public Liberal Arts and Sciences Institutions **P/S:** Higher Education, Research, Academic Advising, General Education, Associate of Arts Degree, General Honors Program, Graduate Studies, Liberal Studies Program, Major and Degree Worksheets, Undergraduate Research and Scholarship Grants **MA:** International **D/D/R:** Writing, Speaking, Teaching, Lecturing Regionally and Nationally for Teachers and Instructors **H/I/S:** Going Out to Dinner with Wife, Playing Baritone Horn, Visiting with his Three Children and Six Grandchildren **EDU:** Doctoral Degree in Curriculum and Instruction, University of Denver (1963); Master's Degree in School Administration, Emporia State University (1960); Bachelor of Science in Elementary Education, Emporia State University (1958) **A/A/S:** Phi Delta Kappa Honorary Society; National Council of Teachers of English; International Reading Association; National Council for Social Studies; Association for Supervision and Curriculum Development; Life Member, National Education Association; External Examination Committee, Mother Teresa University, St. Xavier University, University of Madras **A/H:** Missouri State Senate Resolution for Outstanding Work in Education (1985); Project Innovations Award of Education (1985)

SHEILA R. EDMONDS-WILLIAMS, CSM
Licensed Funeral Director and Embalmer
AB Coleman Mortuary
5660 Moncrief Road
Jacksonville, FL 32218 United States
sheilarew@netscape.net
http://www.cambridgewhoswho.com

BUS: Funeral Home and Mortuary **P/S:** Mortuary and Funeral Services to Local Community **MA:** Local **D/D/R:** Helping Grieving Families **H/I/S:** Participating in Outdoor Activities, Walking **FBP:** Entrepreneur **EDU:** Master of Business Administration, University of Phoenix (2007); Bachelor of Arts in Business, Columbia College **CERTS:** Licensed Funeral Director **A/A/S:** Florida Funeral Directors Association; National Funeral Directors Association **C/VW:** Volunteer, Assisting the Elderly and Young **B/I:** She was motivated to enter her profession by personal experiences. **H/O:** The highlight of her career was the transition she made from Commander Sergeant Major in the army to civilian life as a funeral director.

Bess M. Edwards
President
The Annie Oakley Foundation
333 N. Troy Street
Suite 906
Royal Oaks, MI 48067 United States
bessedwards@wowway.com
http://www.annieoakleyfoundation.org

BUS: Nonprofit Organization **P/S:** Community Services, Accurate Information on the Life and Legend of Annie Oakley to Disseminate Educational Materials, and Create and Maintain the Annie Oakley Education, Cultural and Sports Activity Center **MA:** Michigan **EXP:** Ms. Edwards' expertise is in the recounting of Annie Oakley's life story. **EDU:** Coursework, Business School

Mr. Earl Ezekiel Edwards, MS, RRT-NPS
Respiratory Therapist
Kings County Hospital Center
Brooklyn, NY 11203 United States
edwardsrrtnps@aol.com
http://www.cambridgewhoswho.com

BUS: Hospital **P/S:** Healthcare **MA:** Local **EXP:** Mr. Edwards' expertise is in respiratory therapy and education, and community health with a specialization in management. **D/D/R:** Managing and Educating Patients with Pulmonary Problems **H/I/S:** Playing Cricket and Volleyball, Reading **FBP:** American Association of Respiratory Care; American Journal of Health System Pharmacy **EDU:** Master of Science in Community Health, Concentration in Management, Long Island University; Bachelor of Arts, College of Liberal Arts and Science, CUNY City College, Cum Laude; Associate of Applied Sciences, Borough of Manhattan Community College **CERTS:** Registered Respiratory Therapist, National Board of Respiratory Care and the State Of New York; Perinatal and Pediatric Certification, National Board of Respiratory Care; Laboratory Technician, Mandl School, The College of Allied Health (1974) **A/A/S:** American Association Of Respiratory Care; American Society of Health-System Pharmacist **A/H:** Certificate of Excellence in Community Health Research, Long Island University (2007); Alpha Kappa Chapter, Phi Theta Kappa (1983) **C/VW:** Catholic Conference for Refugees **DOB:** December 14, 1948 **POB:** Curacao **SP:** Divorced **CHILD:** Michelle, Renee, Tamika, Kurth **A/S:** He attributes his success to his family's support and encouragement and his dedication. **B/I:** He became involved in his profession because he wanted to help his friends as well as those in the community who were suffering from asthma. **H/O:** The most gratifying aspect of his career was when he graduated from CUNY City College. **I/F/Y:** In five years, Mr. Edwards would like to be involved in higher education.

KEITH A. EDWARDS, RN-C
Nurse Manager
Florida Hospital
1210 US Highway 27 N.
Lake Placid, FL 33852 United States
kjdesign1@yahoo.com
http://www.floridahospital.com

BUS: Hospital **P/S:** Healthcare Including Mental Health and Emergency Services, Radiology, Cardiology, Oncology, Pediatric and Renal Care, Obstetrics and Gynecology **MA:** Local **EXP:** Mr. Edwards' expertise is in risk management and behavior and mental health evaluation. **D/D/R:** Overseeing 32 Employees **H/I/S:** Fishing, Boating **FBP:** Nursing Journals **CERTS:** Registered Nurse, South Florida Community College (1990); Certification in Psychiatric Nursing **A/A/S:** Florida Nurses Association; American Psychiatric Nurses Association **A/H:** Anna B. Critz Award for Leadership **C/VW:** Co-Chairman, Restraint/Falls Prevention Committee; Crisis Intervention Team; Risk Management and Safety Committee; Local Nursing Council

MS. SHARON K. EDWARDS, RN
Registered Nurse, Charge Nurse
Call A Nurse For Children Division
Methodist Children's Hospital
7299 Ewing Halsell, Suite 320
San Antonio, TX 78229 United States
shed13911@aol.com
http://www.cambridgewhoswho.com

BUS: Children's Hospital **P/S:** Healthcare Including Pediatric Medical Care Services **MA:** Texas **EXP:** Ms. Edwards' expertise is in pediatric telephone triage nursing. **D/D/R:** Answering Calls from Parents Seeking Advice Concerning Sick or Injured Children Including Home Care, Emergency Room Visits, Primary Care and Physician Follow-Up, Working in a Charge Nurse Position, Training New Staff Members on Assigned Duties and Monitoring their Progress **H/I/S:** Spending Time at the Beach and Coast with her Family, Vacationing, Reading Books **FBP:** Nursing2009; Nursing Spectrum **EDU:** Associate Degree in Nursing, San Antonio College (1995) **CERTS:** Licensed Vocational Nurse (1978); Certified in CPR **A/H:** Team Spirit Award, Fourth Quarter, Patient Satisfaction Committee (1998) **C/VW:** Volunteer, Hurricane Katrina Relief Effort; United Way **DOB:** August 31, 1960 **POB:** Nixon, TX **CHILD:** Cassandra, Tim **W/H:** Registered Nurse, Step Down Unit for Preemies and Sick Newborns (1995-2001); Agency Nurse, Floor Float in Medical-Surgical, Gerontology, NBN, Antepartum Floors (1991-1995); Charge Nurse, Licensed Vocational Nurse, Nursing Home (1979-1981); Registered Nurse, Charge Nurse, Pediatric Call Center, Methodist Children's Hospital **A/S:** She attributes her success to the support she receives from her parents and siblings. **B/I:** She became involved in her profession because she had always wanted to be a nurse. **H/O:** The highlights of her career were attending 100 delivery cases without the presence of doctors and obtaining her associate degree as a registered nurse. **I/F/Y:** In five years, Ms. Edwards intends to continue working in the telephone triage nursing and would like to gain experience to seek other avenues in her nursing career.

KERN H. EGGER
Real Estate Agent
Kelly Williams Realty, Coastal Bend
3820 S. Alameda, Suite 38
Corpus Christi, TX 78411 United States
kern@kernegger.com
http://www.kernegger.com

BUS: Real Estate Company **P/S:** Residential and Commercial Real Estate Services **MA:** Regional **D/D/R:** Marketing Real Estate, Building Townhouses **H/I/S:** Tap and Jazz Dancer **FBP:** Texas Realtor Magazine; The Women's Council of Realtors **EDU:** Associate Degree in Marketing, Nassau Community College **CERTS:** Certification, Graduate Realtor Institute; Accredited Buyer Representative; Certified Residential Specialist **A/A/S:** Former President, Women's Council of Realtors; Local Builders Association **C/VW:** Salvation Army; Goodwill; Board Member, Church **A/S:** She attributes her success to her tenacity, perseverance, determination and remaining detail oriented with excellent follow through. **B/I:** She became involved in her profession because she was in banking for 15 years prior to moving into real estate. **H/O:** The highlight of her career has been striving to be number one in her industry.

MR. THOMAS H. EHRENSBERGER
Chief Executive Officer
Pittsburgh Tower Erectors, LLC
5895 Heckert Road
Suite 106
Bakerstown, PA 15007 United States
tehrensberger@pghte.com
http://www.pghte.com

BUS: Construction Company **P/S:** Engineering and Construction of Telecommunications Towers for Major Companies **MA:** International **D/D/R:** Designing Towers that Blend in with their Surroundings and Follow Proper Safety Conditions, Managing Corporate Budget Review, Determining the Company's Budget, Overseeing 60 Staff Members **H/I/S:** Playing Hockey **FBP:** RCR Wireless News **EDU:** Master of Business Administration, University of Maryland University College (2000); Bachelor of Science, Indiana University of Pennsylvania (1994) **CERTS:** Certified Instructor of Safety, Occupational Safety and Health Administration

MARCELLUS EKWEBELEM UNAEGBU
Doctor, Teacher
1) Prince George's County Public Schools
2) District of Columbia Public Schools
8000 Croom Road
Upper Marlboro, MD 20772 United States
ekwemmarc@yahoo.com
http://www.pgcps.org

PRINCE GEORGE'S COUNTY PUBLIC SCHOOLS
Frederick Douglass High School
"Eagles Expecting Excellence"
8000 Croom Road
Upper Marlboro, Maryland 20772
Telephone 301-952-2400 ~ Fax 301-627-3377
http//www.pgcps.org/~douglass

BUS: 1) School District 2) School District **P/S:** 1) Education 2) Education **MA:** 1) Regional 2) Regional **D/D/R:** Teaching Chemistry, Physics and Biology to High School Students, Counseling 10th through 12th-Grade Students **H/I/S:** Listening to Music, Dancing, Swimming **EDU:** Ph.D. in Nutritional Biochemistry, Howard University (1982); Master's Degree in Environmental Health, Howard University (1978); Bachelor of Science in Zoology, Howard University (1974) **A/A/S:** American Chemistry Council; Prince George's County Educators Association; The Washington Teachers' Union **A/H:** Science Teacher of the Year Award, Prince George's County Public Schools (2005-2006) **W/H:** Associate Professor of Nutritional Sciences, Anambra State University of Science and Technology, Enugu, Nigeria (1984-1987)

CLAUDIA L. ELDRED
General Manager
Jimmy Johns
6402 S. Westnedge Avenue
Portage, MI 49002 United States
claudiaeld@charter.net
http://www.jimmyjohns.com

BUS: Sandwich Franchise **P/S:** Submarine and Gourmet Sandwiches **MA:** National **D/D/R:** Overseeing Food Service Management **H/I/S:** Playing Volleyball, Building Furniture **FBP:** Restaurant **C/VW:** Habitat for Humanity; Local School Events; Local Charities **B/I:** She became involved in this profession because she has been in the food industry service since she was 16 and truly loves working with people. **H/O:** The highlight of her career is being able to interact with people everyday.

DANEEN E. ELLER
President, Board of Directors
Central Nervous System Vasculitis Foundation, Inc.
5170 Nash Drive
Flint, MI 48506 United States
daneen@cnsvfinc.org
http://www.cnsvfinc.org

BUS: Nonprofit Organization Providing Health Education and Awareness for Central Nervous System Vasculitis **P/S:** Information and Support to Patients, Families and the Medical Community, Diagnosis and Treatment in Order to Improve Overall Quality of Life, and Assist in Discovering a Cure through Scientific Research **MA:** National **D/D/R:** Editing Website Content, Researching, Fund Raising, Searching for Doctors and Facilities that Treat Diseases, Educating Frontline Health Care Professionals **H/I/S:** Reading, Freelance Writing **FBP:** Popular Science; Online Publications; NORD **EDU:** Nursing Degree, Lamar University, TX (1993) **C/VW:** Vasculitis Association

KELLY R. ELLIOTT, RN, BSN, MSN, APRN-BC
Family Nurse Practitioner, Owner
C-Worth Family Walk-In Clinic
2976 Highway 76
Suite B
Chatsworth, GA 30705 United States
cworth1@alltel.net
http://www.cambridgewhoswho.com

BUS: Healthcare Center **P/S:** Family Practice, General Medical Care **MA:** Regional **EXP:** Mr. Elliott's expertise is in family medicine. **H/I/S:** Swimming, Decorating **FBP:** Nurse Practitioner **EDU:** Master of Science in Nursing, Southern Adventist University (2005) **A/A/S:** American Nurses Association; American Academy of Nurse Practitioners

Deborah G. Ellis
Founder, Director
Veterans Memorial Day Tribute, Inc.
8125 Hampstead Way
Granite Bay, CA 95746 United States
dgene525@aol.com
http://www.coloradoveteransmonument.org

BUS: Nonprofit Corporation **P/S:** Event Planning and Promotion **MA:** National **EXP:** Ms. Ellis' expertise is in event planning, marketing, computer graphics illustration and sales. **H/I/S:** Spending Time with her Family, Gardening, Writing, Painting, Photography, Computer Graphics, Art **FBP:** Time; Newsweek; Business Journal; Fraternal Publications **EDU:** Bachelor of Fine Arts, University of Nebraska **A/A/S:** United Veterans Committee of Colorado; Award for Fundraising, The National World War II Memorial **C/VW:** American Cancer Society; Eureka Public School District; American Heart Association; Colorado Gerontological Society Website Administration; Administration-Youth Lacrosse Club; Veterans Advocate

Mr. James E. Ellis
President
Ellis Packaging Solutions
1867 N. Tin Strap Trail
Prescott, AZ 86314 United States
jellis@ellispackaging.net
http://www.cambridgewhoswho.com

BUS: Manufacturing and Packaging **P/S:** Global Solutions of Contract Packaging **MA:** International **EXP:** Mr. Ellis's expertise is in sales and product development. **D/D/R:** Manufacturing and Packaging Material **H/I/S:** Horses, Skiing **FBP:** Contract Packaging Magazine **EDU:** Coursework, U.S. Army Administrative School; Coursework, Glendale College **A/A/S:** President, Contract Packaging Association **C/VW:** Toy Foundation; American Diabetes Association

AMY ELLIS SMITH, ESQ.
Attorney, Associate
Barrister Capital Group
P. O. Box 7127
Louisville, KY 40257 United States
amy@barristercapitalgroup.com
http://www.barristercapitalgroup.com

BUS: Attorney Owned and Operated Company **P/S:** Automobile Accidents, Employment Discrimination Cases, Medical Malpractice, Nursing Home Abuses, Personal Injury Cases, Sexual Harassment, Slip and Fall Cases, Commercial Litigation Cases, Structured Settlement, Wrongful Death Cases, Wrongful Termination, Product Liability Cases **MA:** National **D/D/R:** Practicing Juvenile, Personal Injury and Criminal Law **H/I/S:** Snow Skiing, Tennis, Bicycling, Football, Basketball, Lacrosse **FBP:** KBA Journal; Web **EDU:** JD, Brandeis University School of Law (1989); Bachelor of Arts, University of Louisville (1986) **A/A/S:** Lecturer, Kentucky Bar Association; Council Member, Prosecutors Council, KY **C/VW:** Quick Recall Coach, Quix Bowl; Athletic Director, St. Margaret Mary School

MICHAEL B. ELLISON, PH.D.
Associate Professor
Bowling Green State University
Department of Theatre and Film, 338 South Hall
1001 E. Wooster Street
Bowling Green, OH 43403 United States
ellison@bgnet.bgsu.edu
http://www.michaelellison.net

BUS: College **P/S:** Education **MA:** International **D/D/R:** Directing, Choreographing, Teaching Musical Theater and Performance for Entrepreneurs, Acting, Performing Songs and Arias, Directing Theater for Social Change, Performing Transformational Body Energy Work **H/I/S:** Singing, Dancing, Traveling, Reading **EDU:** Ph.D. in Theatre, University of Minnesota; Master of Arts in Acting and Directing, University of Arizona; Bachelor of Arts in Theatre, Trinity University, San Antonio, Texas **A/A/S:** Vice President of Conference, Association for Theatre in Higher Education (2006) **A/H:** Kennedy Center American College Theater Festival, Preliminary Judge, Irene Ryan Competition **A/S:** He attributes his success to his openness and ability to enjoy the journey of life. **B/I:** He became involved in the profession because he wanted to touch lives and open new possibilities. **H/O:** The highlight of his career was spending three months in the Philippines as the acting coach, choreographer and composer for 'The Music of Alain Boublil and Claude-Michel Schonberg in Concert.'

SUE E. ELZEY
Sales Associate
Reeves Williams
868 Goodman Road
South Haven, MS 38671 United States
franklinfarms@reeveswilliams.com
http://www.reeveswilliams.com

BUS: Real Estate **P/S:** Construction Company, Buying and Selling **MA:** Mississippi and Tennessee **EXP:** Ms. Elzey's expertise is in new construction. **H/I/S:** Antiques, Reading **FBP:** Architectural Digest **EDU:** Coursework in Business, Jonesboro Business College **CERTS:** License in Real Estate, State of Tennessee **A/A/S:** Million Dollar Club **C/VW:** Independent Presbyterian Church, Fireman and Police Funds **A/S:** She attributes her success to a good product and hard work. **B/I:** She became involved in this profession because she was in her own business as a general contractor and transitioned into real estate. **H/O:** The most gratifying aspect of her career is the money she makes helping people.

SAMANTHA L. EMBRY
Owner
Samantha's House Cleaning and Pet Sitting Service
10011 S.W. 84th Avenue
Gainesville, FL 32608 United States
samanthaembry@yahoo.com
http://www.cambridgewhoswho.com

BUS: Sole Proprietorship **P/S:** Private Home and Office Cleaning, Pet Sitting at Owner's Home or her Own **MA:** Local **D/D/R:** Cleaning Private Residences and Offices, Caring for Animals **H/I/S:** Fishing, Sightseeing, Spending Time with her Family and Dogs **FBP:** Forbes **EDU:** Degree in Animal Science, Harcourt Online University (2001) **C/VW:** People for the Ethical Treatment of Animals; The Humane Society of the United States **A/S:** She attributes her success to hard work, determination and loving what she does. She has a constant drive to take care of herself. **B/I:** She became involved in her profession by working as a veterinary assistant and taking courses in animal science. She took care of people's animals and eventually started cleaning their homes as well. **H/O:** The highlight of her career is making relationships with her clients.

KANANA M. EMERY
Proprietor
Ms. K's Pralines, LLC
1000 W. Oaks Mall
Suite 445
Houston, TX 77082 United States
kmememem@yahoo.com
http://www.mskspralines.com

BUS: Sweets **P/S:** Handmade Chocolates **MA:** Local **D/D/R:** Making Candy **H/I/S:** Reading **EDU:** Pursuing Bachelor's Degree in Business Administration, University of New Orleans **C/VW:** Local Charities **A/S:** She attributes her success to putting her whole self into the business and being involved. **B/I:** She became involved in this profession because this was a family recipe that had been handed down and she took it to the next level. **H/O:** The highlight of her career is opening the business.

MR. WILLIAM F. EMLICH SR., DO
William F. Emlich Sr., DO
4559 Columbus Road
Centerburg, OH 43011 United States
william.emlich@cwwemail.com
http://www.cambridgewhoswho.com

BUS: Private Practice **P/S:** Healthcare Including Family Medicine **MA:** Regional **EXP:** Mr. Emlich's expertise is in family medicine. **H/I/S:** Collecting Guns, Farming, Reading **FBP:** The New England Journal of Medicine **EDU:** Internship, Doctor's Hospital, Columbus, OH (1959); Doctor of Osteopathic Medicine, Kirksville College of Osteopathic Medicine (1958); Bachelor of Science, Muskingum College (1954) **CERTS:** Certification in Family Medicine (1991) **A/A/S:** Columbus Medical Association; Ohio Osteopathic Association; American Osteopathic Association; Knox County Medical Society (Now Knoxville Academy of Medicine); Board Member, Chief of Staff, Knox Community Hospital **A/H:** Family Physician of the Year Award, State of Ohio (1955); National Recognition Award, State Recognition Award for Service **C/VW:** Director, Hiller Township Emergency Squad **SP:** Norma Thomas **CHILD:** Kerry Ann **W/H:** Clinical Professor, Osteopathic Medical Society, Ohio University

TINA ENCHEVA
Realtor
Realty One Group
1401 N. Green Valley Parkway
Suite 200
Las Vegas, NV 89074 United States
tinaencheva@gmail.com
http://www.calltinaforvegashomes.com

BUS: Real Estate **P/S:** Representing Buyers and Sellers, Helping others Achieve their Goals **MA:** Local **D/D/R:** Specializing in Residential Real Estate **H/I/S:** Reading, Biking, Working Out, Traveling **FBP:** Las Vegas Review Journal; Newsweek **EDU:** Bachelor's Degree in Biotechnology **A/A/S:** Las Vegas Association of Realtors; Nevada Association of Realtors; National Association of Realtors; Bulgarian Society of Nevada

KAREN L. ENGLAND
Owner
Edgehill Herb Farm
2360 Edgehill Road
Vista, CA 92084 United States
circlekengland@msn.com
http://www.edgehillherbfarm.com

BUS: Leading Herb Farmer and Herb Product Manufacturer, Authoress and Popular Speaker **P/S:** All Herb-Related Items Including Cookbooks, Books and Videos, Soaps and Oils, Posy Pins, Vases and Bottles, Calendars, Everything the Customer Could Want to Know about Herbs and their Use Thereof **MA:** International **D/D/R:** Overseeing Product Development, Marketing and Production **H/I/S:** Sewing, Quilting **EDU:** Bachelor of Science in Christian Education, Biola University (1982) **A/A/S:** International Herb Association; Herb Society of America; International Geranium Society; Board Member, Vista Garden Club; San Diego Herb Society

Dr. Alicia M. English

Clinical Director
Center for Elders Independence
510 17th Street
Oakland, CA 94612 United States
alicia.english@gmail.com
http://www.cambridgewhoswho.com

BUS: Long-Term Senior Care Facility **P/S:** Residential Living, Program of All-Inclusive Care for the Elderly **MA:** Local **D/D/R:** Treating Patients Suffering from Personality Disorders, Substance Abuse, Chemical Dependency Issues and Trauma, Administering Psychological Testing **H/I/S:** Traveling, Reading, Hiking, Playing the Hammered Dulcimer **FBP:** Journal of Personality Disorders **EDU:** Ph.D., California Institute of Integral Studies **A/A/S:** San Francisco Society for Lacanian Studies; Society for Personality Assessment; American Psychological Association; International Society for the Study of Personality Disorders **A/S:** She attributes her success to her tenacity, ambition and deep concern for patients with mental health issues. **B/I:** She became involved in her profession after she took a class in high school and found that she loved the industry. **H/O:** The highlight of her career was earning her current position.

Linda K. English, Ed.S.

Assistant High School Principal
West Helena School District- Central High School
103 School Road
West Helena, AR 72390 United States
lkenglish@go.com
http://www.cambridgewhoswho.com

BUS: Public School **P/S:** Handling Federal Programs and Grant Applications and Monitoring **MA:** Local **D/D/R:** Specializing in Curriculum and Instruction **H/I/S:** Reading, Walking, Movies, Writing, Spending time with Daughter **EDU:** Pursuing Doctor of Education, Arkansas State University; Educational Specialist Degree, Arkansas State University; Bachelor's Degree, University of Arkansas, Pine Bluff; Master's Degree, Gifted and Talented Education, Arkansas State University **A/A/S:** Arkansas Association of Education Administrators; Association for Supervision and Curriculum Development **C/VW:** March of Dimes Foundation; United Negro College Fund; St. Jude Children's Research Hospital; Rotary International; American Legion Auxiliary **A/S:** She attributes her personal and professional success to her faith in God, family support, and determination. **B/I:** She has always had an interest in the field and a desire to make a difference in the lives of children. **H/O:** The highlight of her career is seeing the underprivileged children graduate.

JANICE G. ENGQUIST, RN, BSN
Registered Nurse
Huntsville Hospital
13254 Dickens Lane
Madison, AL 35756 United States
janern8@hotmail.com
http://www.huntsvillehospital.org

BUS: Hospital **P/S:** Healthcare Including Cancer Care, Cardiac Care, Neurological Care, Maternity Care, Orthopedic, Outpatient Services, Pediatric Care, Surgical, General Surgery, Advanced Laparoscopy and Geriatric Surgery, Behavioral Health, Diabetes Control, Endoscopy, Home Health, Medical Imaging, Laboratory, Occupational Medicine, Pain Management, Respiratory, Rehabilitation, Treatment for Sleep Disorders, Sports Medicine, Therapy, Wellness, Wound Care and Emergency Medical Services **MA:** Regional **D/D/R:** Nursing on a Progressive Surgical and Trauma Step-down Unit, Specializing in Assisting with Alzheimer's Patients and the Developmentally Disabled **H/I/S:** Gardening, Cross-Stitching, Needlepointing, Cooking, Painting, Swimming **FBP:** American Journal of Nursing **EDU:** Bachelor of Science in Nursing, The University of Alabama in Huntsville (1999); Registered Nurse **CERTS:** Certified Nursing Assistant **DOB:** September 3, 1946 **CHILD:** William **W/H:** Adjunct Professor, West Virginia State University

DEE ENRICO-JANIK, MPA, LSW
Assistant Director, Advocate Specialist
Client Services
Indiana Protection & Advocacy Services
4701 N. Keystone Avenue, Suite 222
Indianapolis, IN 46205 United States
denrico-janik@ipas.in.gov
http://www.in.gov/ipas

BUS: Independent State Agency **P/S:** Advocacy for the Rights of Individuals with Disabilities **MA:** Statewide **EXP:** Ms. Enrico-Janik's expertise is in human services administration and management. **D/D/R:** Overseeing Five People and Three Divisions, Helping People with Mental Illnesses and Developmental Disabilities **H/I/S:** College Basketball, Exercising **FBP:** Behavioral Healthcare **EDU:** Master's Degree in Public Administration, Indiana University (1974); Bachelor's Degree in Sociology, Indiana University **CERTS:** Licensed Social Worker; Certification in Advocacy Professional Development, National Disability Rights Network **A/A/S:** Charter Member, Pi Alpha Alpha; Indiana Consortium for Mental Health Services Research; Chairwoman, Community Education and Self-Advocacy Committees, National Disability Rights Network; American Society for Public Administration **A/H:** International Who's Who of Professionals (1999); Who's Who Among Human Services Professionals (1989); Distinguished Alumnus Award, School of Public and Environmental Affairs, Indiana University; Service Award, Tri-City Community Mental Health Center; Key Consumer Empowerment Award; Collaboration Award, ATTIC Inc. **C/VW:** United Way of Lake County; United Way of Central Indiana; Alumni Council, The School of Public and Environmental Affairs, Indiana University Alumni Association; Mentoring Program, Indiana University Alumni Association **W/H:** Mental Health Association, Marion County; Lake County Employment and Training Programs; Lake County Department of Public Welfare

ANN EPPERSON
Chemistry Supervisor
Centennial Medical Center
2300 Patterson Street
Nashville, TN 37203 United States
nancy.epperson@hcahealthcare.com
http://www.cambridgewhoswho.com

BUS: Hospital **P/S:** Healthcare **MA:** Local **D/D/R:** Maintaining the Chemistry Department and the Hospital Clinical Lab **H/I/S:** Hot Air Ballooning, Reading **EDU:** Bachelor's Degree in Chemistry, Vanderbilt University; Associate Degree in Chemistry and Biology, Columbia State Community College **A/A/S:** American Clinical Chemistry Organization **C/VW:** National Humane Society **A/S:** She attributes her success to her work ethic and ability to manage people in an effective manner. **B/I:** She became involved in her profession because her father was a doctor and her mother was a nurse. **H/O:** The highlight of her career was being asked to participate in a focus group for various committees.

FRANCE-MICHELE R. ERDMAN, RN, BSHA
Supervisor, Assistant Health Administrator
Oasis Home Care
901 Northpoint Parkway
West Palm Beach, FL 33407 United States
ziedel@bellsouth.net
http://www.cambridgewhoswho.com

BUS: Healthcare Center **P/S:** Healthcare **MA:** Local **EXP:** Ms. Erdman's expertise is in home healthcare services and healthcare administration oversight. **D/D/R:** Overseeing Heart and Trauma Nursing **H/I/S:** Reading, Artwork, Sewing, Cooking, Baking **FBP:** The Wall Street Journal; Journal of Advanced Nursing **EDU:** Bachelor of Science in Health Administration, Florida Atlantic University **CERTS:** Registered Nurse, Northampton Community College; Certification in Advanced Cardiac Life Support; Certification in CPR; Emergency Response Team Certification, Palm County; Certification in Intravenous Therapy; Certification in Peripherally Inserted Central Catheter; Certification in Psychology and Alzheimer; Certified Quality Improvement Supervisor; Certified Quality Assurance Supervisor **A/A/S:** The American Israel Public Affairs Committee **A/H:** 30-Year Service Award; Honoree, International Who's Who of Professional Management **C/VW:** Cook, Soup Kitchen; Caridad Center; Boy Scouts of America; Faith Farm Ministry; Board of Directors, Country Fair; Theatrical Group; ACOF **DOB:** November 30, 1947 **POB:** Easton, PA **A/S:** She attributes her success to her compassion and her love for her profession. **B/I:** She became involved in her profession through a natural progression of opportunities. **H/O:** The most gratifying aspect of her career is seeing her patients recover.

DR. TRINE ERICHSEN-VINAGRE

School Adjustment Counselor
E.C. Brooks Elementary School
212 Nemasket Street
New Bedford, MA 02740 United States
tvinagre@newbedford.k12.ma.us
http://www.newbedford.k12.ma.us

BUS: Elementary School Dedicated to Excellence in Education **P/S:** Regular Curriculum Including English, Science, Art, Music, Social Studies, History, Mathematics, Physical Education **MA:** Regional **D/D/R:** Handling All Paperwork and Counseling, Special Education Curriculum and Long and Short-Term Crisis Intervention **H/I/S:** Traveling, Activities with her Children **FBP:** The Psychology Networker **EDU:** Ph.D., LaCrosse University (2004); Master's Degree, Harvard University (1992); Bachelor of Arts in Psychology, Salve Regina University, Rhode Island (1991) **CERTS:** Certified CPI Trainer (2003); **A/A/S:** New Bedford, Harvard-Radcliffe Club; Massachusetts School Counselors Association; Psychological Association of America

DR. BETH M. ERICKSON

Speaker, Personal Coach, Consultant, Spiritual Mentor
Erickson Consulting
5200 Willson Road, Suite 150
Edina, MN 55424 United States
drbetherickson@aol.com
http://www.drbetherickson.com
http://www.mirrorsofthesoul.com

BUS: Proven Leader in Healthcare and Business Development **P/S:** Management **MA:** International **D/D/R:** Facilitating Personal Growth, Inspirational Speaking, Spiritual Mentoring **H/I/S:** Writing, Reading, Beading, Watercolor Painting, Singing **FBP:** Spirituality and Health Publications **EDU:** Post-Doctoral Training in Family and Marital Therapy, Northwestern University (1981); Ph.D., University of Minnesota (1976) **SP:** Paul **W/H:** Chief Therapist, Private Child Welfare Agency; Family and Marital Therapist, Private Practice **C/A:** Author, 'Helping Men Change: The Role of the Female Therapist'; Author, 'Longing for Dad: Father Loss and its Impact'; Author, 'Aging isn't for Sissies: Overcoming the Psychological and Spiritual Challenges Top Vital Aging'

BRENDA L. ERIKSEN, MD
Medical Director
Northwest Indiana Pathology Consultants
901 MacArthur Boulevard
Munster, IN 46321 United States
beriksen@comhs.org
http://www.cambridgewhoswho.com

BUS: Consulting Firm **P/S:** Consulting Services Including High Quality Healthcare and Pathology Services **MA:** Regional **EXP:** Ms. Eriksen's expertise is in cytopathology and molecular testing. **D/D/R:** Purchasing Equipment, Strategic Planning, Overseeing Clinic Lab Operations, Analyzing Quality, Checking Quality for Service Lines and Instrumentation **H/I/S:** Speaking French, Swimming **FBP:** CAP Today **EDU:** MD, Rush Medical College (1986) **A/A/S:** College of American Pathologists; American Society of Clinical Pathology; American Association of Blood Banks; American Association of Clinical Chemistry; Indiana State Medical Association; American Medical Association

CONNIE C. ERRINGTON, LPN
Supervising Floor Nurse, Licensed Practical Nurse
87 Staley Road
Orwell, OH 44076 United States
http://www.cambridgewhoswho.com

BUS: Long Term Care Facility **P/S:** Long Term Health Care **MA:** Local **EXP:** Ms. Errington's expertise is in geriatrics. **H/I/S:** Crocheting, Completing Arts and Crafts, Sewing **CERTS:** Licensed Practical Nurse **C/VW:** Veterans' Associations; The Salvation Army **A/S:** She attributes her career success to her hard work. **B/I:** She has wanted to be a nurse since the first grade. **H/O:** She feels that being able to take care of the elderly while befriending them is the highlight of her career.

HOWARD L. ERWIN
Director of Laboratory Services (Retired)
12521 Palermo Drive
Silver Spring, MD 20904 United States
bigrederwinlu42@verizon.net
http://www.cambridgwhoswho.com

BUS: Laboratory **P/S:** Laboratory Services Including Drug Research and Testing **MA:** International **EXP:** Mr. Erwin's expertise is in laboratory testing of chemotherapy drugs. **H/I/S:** Watching Football, Reading **EDU:** Bachelor of Science in Chemistry, Lincoln University **A/A/S:** American Association for the Advancement of Science

OLIMPIA V. ESCUDERO, MA, RN
Director of Continuing Care, Case Management
Palisades Medical Center
7600 River Road
North Bergen, NJ 07047 United States
oescudero@palisadesmedical.org
http://www.palisadesmedical.org

BUS: Community Hospital **P/S:** Quality Healthcare Services **MA:** Local **EXP:** Ms. Escudero's expertise is in case management. **D/D/R:** Nursing in the Operating Room and Critical-Care Unit, Using Hands-On Healing Techniques, Working on Grant Research and Safety Goals **H/I/S:** Music, Crafts, Making Candy **FBP:** Nursing Journals **EDU:** Master's Degree in Guidance Counseling and Social Work, Montclair State University **CERTS:** Leadership Certificate, New Jersey City University; Certified Massage Therapist **A/A/S:** Association Operating Room Nurses; American Holistic Nurses Society; American Nurses Society **C/VW:** Board of Palisades Medical Auxiliary, St. Jude; Various Church Organizations

KENNETH ESLINGER

Associate Professor of Sociology
John Carroll University
20700 N. Park Boulevard
Administration Building, Department of Sociology
University Heights, OH 44118 United States
KEslinger@jcu.edu
http://www.jcu.edu

BUS: Catholic and Jesuit University Dedicated to Bestowing Women and Men with the Knowledge and Character to Lead and Serve **P/S:** Undergraduate and Graduate Programs that Encourage Academic Excellence and Challenge Students **MA:** International **D/D/R:** Teaching Courses on Urban Sociology, Social Problems, Social Theory and Human Ecology **H/I/S:** Bass Fishing, Spending Time Outdoors **FBP:** American Sociological Review; Sociologic Focus; Newsweek; The New Yorker **EDU:** Ph.D., Ohio State University (1971); Master's Degree in Sociology, Ohio State University (1968); Bachelor's Degree in History, Indiana State University (1965) **A/A/S:** North Central Sociological Association; American Sociological Association

DIANE ESPOSITO

Manager of Documentations and Authorizations
Professional Home Care Services, Inc.
104 Sebethe Drive
Cromwell, CT 06416 United States
dianee@phcsivdme.com
http://www.phcsivdme.com

BUS: Healthcare Center **P/S:** Healthcare Including Respiratory and Pediatric Care, Specialty Infusion Services and Specialty Pharmacy **MA:** Regional **D/D/R:** Ensuring Insurance Qualifications, Training, Interviewing, Hiring, Firing, Scheduling Six Direct Reports, Consulting, Overseeing Medicare Reimbursement, Commercial Insurance and Infusion Therapy, Ensuring Customer Satisfaction **H/I/S:** Reading **EDU:** Bachelor's Degree in Business and Economics, Albertus Magnus College (1991)

CYNTHIA W. ESTEP, RN, PHN, M.ED.
Registered Nurse, School Nurse
Claremont Unified School District
2080 N. Mountain Avenue
Claremont, CA 91711 United States
cindyestep@gmail.com
http://www.cambridgewhoswho.com

BUS: School **P/S:** General Education, Special Education, Arts, Music, Physical Education, Learning Resources, Student Support Services, Extracurricular Activities **MA:** Local **EXP:** Ms. Estep's expertise is in education. **D/D/R:** Teaching Physically Disabled and Medically Fragile Children, Supervising Elementary and Special Education Students from the Ages of Three to 21 **H/I/S:** Reading, Gardening, Traveling to Europe **FBP:** School Nurses Journal **EDU:** Master of Education in School Nursing, Cambridge University, Ontario, CA; Bachelor of Science in Nursing, California State University at Los Angeles; Registered Nurse **A/A/S:** National Association of School Nurses **C/VW:** PKU Research; The Leukemia & Lymphoma Society; St. Jude Children's Research Hospital; Veterans of America

MELISSA DAWN ESTEPP
Microbiology and Chemistry Technical Supervisor
Williamson Memorial Hospital
211 Kara Lane
Delbarton, WV 25670 United States
melissadawn.estepp@cwwemail.com
http://www.cambridgewhoswho.com

BUS: Hospital Facility Dedicated to Excellence in Healthcare **P/S:** Laboratory, Radiology, Cardiac Catheterization, Rehabilitation, Diabetes, Respiratory Health, Emergency Services, Surgical Services, Intensive Care **MA:** Regional **D/D/R:** Offering Consistent Patient Care in an Efficient and Cost-Effective Manner, Supporting Physicians, Contributing to the Community **H/I/S:** Fishing, Flower Gardening **FBP:** Advance for Medical Laboratory Professionals **EDU:** Bachelor of Science; Associate of Applied Science in Medical Laboratory Technology **A/A/S:** American Society of Clinical Pathologists

ENRQIDUE 'HENRY' ESTRADA
Owner, Realtor
Hilltop Realty
881 N. Chappell Road
Hollister, CA 95023 United States
estradasold@yahoo.com
http://www.hilltoprealtyhomes.com

BUS: Real Estate Agency **P/S:** Buying and Selling of Homes, Property, Businesses and Home Loans **MA:** Local **D/D/R:** Selling Real Estate **H/I/S:** Playing Racquetball and Softball **FBP:** Hispanic Business; Forbes **EDU:** Coursework, Heald Business School **A/A/S:** Local Board of Realtors **A/S:** He attributes his success to his honesty, ethics and referrals. **B/I:** He became involved in the profession because he saw a need for more Spanish-speaking realtors. **H/O:** The most gratifying aspect of his career is selling and procuring new homes and loans.

DAVID LOUIS EVANS
Professor of English (Retired)
Brigham Young University
davidLouis.evans@cwwemail.com
http://www.cambridgewhoswho.com

BUS: University **P/S:** Higher Education **MA:** Regional **D/D/R:** Teaching Modern, American and British Literature in Comparative and Renaissance Studies, Assuring Advanced Education in English, Language and Literature Including Comparative Literature in European Languages **H/I/S:** Mountain Climbing, Skiing, Photography, Creating Slides and Negatives, Printing Photographs **EDU:** Ph.D. in English, The University of Utah (1968); Master's Degree in English, The University of Utah (1958); Bachelor of Arts in English, Idaho State University (1948) **A/H:** Maser Award (1989) **B/I:** He became involved in his profession because of his desire to become a teacher.

EARLENE ADAMS EVANS
Owner, Lead Teacher
Storybook Lodge Nursery and Preschool
717 Bakertown Road
Lynchburg, TN 37352 United States
earlene_evans@hotmail.com
http://www.cambridgewhoswho.com

BUS: School **P/S:** Education **MA:** Local **D/D/R:** Teaching and Mentoring Children **H/I/S:** Playing Tennis, Volleyball, Cake Decorating, Photography **FBP:** Early Childhood **EDU:** Coursework, Early Childhood Education; Industry-Related Training and Experience **A/A/S:** President, Moore Coffee Early Learners Association **A/H:** Honoree, Tennessee State University Center of Excellence **C/VW:** St. Jude Children's Research Hospital **A/S:** She attributes her success to a string desire to help students and parents. **B/I:** She chose the profession because she could not find any pre-school providers that she trusted, so she decided to open her own business. **H/O:** The highlight of her career is being the first person in the area to become nationally accredited.

JEFFREY L. EVANS
Broker, Agent
Colliers Dickinson
One Independent Drive, Suite 2401
Jacksonville, FL 32202 United States
jevans@colliersdickinson.com
http://www.colliersdickinson.com

BUS: Real Estate Company **P/S:** Sales, Leasing and Property Management Services **MA:** Regional **D/D/R:** Managing the Office for Industrial Real Estate in Northeast Florida, Overseeing 15 Real Estate Locations **H/I/S:** Running and Weight Training **FBP:** Florida Real Estate Journal; SE Real Estate News **EDU:** Bachelor of Science in Business Administration, University of Florida (1982) **CERTS:** Licensed Realtor; Licensed Broker **A/A/S:** Board of Directors, National Association of Industrial and Office Properties; Government Relations Committee, Building Owners and Managers Association; FCMA; CREW; JCC

NANCY FLEMING EVANS
Psychologist II
Wayne County Public Schools
Po Drawer 1797
Goldsboro, NC 27830 United States
necats@aol.com
http://www.cambridgewhoswho.com

BUS: Education **P/S:** Education, Full Service, Local Facility Serving Grades Pre-K to 12 **MA:** Local **D/D/R:** Treating Traumatic Brain Injuries and Autism **H/I/S:** Gardening, Scrapbooking, Quilting, Traveling and Reading **FBP:** National School Psychologist Journal **EDU:** Master's Degree in Education, Appalachian State; Master's Degree, East Carolina University **CERTS:** Certificate in Advanced Study in School Psychology, East Carolina University **A/A/S:** Regional Director, Delta Kappa Gamma; North Carolina School Psychologists; National Association for School Psychologists **C/VW:** Fundraiser, Church Circle; American Cancer Society; Autism Association; Parkinson's Association, NCSPA; School Psychologist Association **A/S:** She attributes her success to her determination and passion for ensuring children's rights are protected. **B/I:** She became involved in her profession after teaching English and Special Education. **H/O:** The highlight of her career has been the respect she has earned as a Psychologist.

MRS. MARY EVANS SEELEY
President
A Presidential Christmas
16612 Millan de Avila
Tampa, FL 33613 United States
mls42@aol.com
http://www.whitehousechristmas.com

BUS: Proven Leader in the Retail Industry **P/S:** Publishing, 'Season's Greetings from the White House', Variety of Gift Items, Laura Bush Boot, Signed Uncle Sam Nutcracker, Official White House Ornament, Bush Gift Print, The Commemorative White House Ornament, White House Book End, Armed Forces Ornament, Regency Egg, The Great Seal Rug, Capitol Under Glass Ornament **MA:** National **D/D/R:** Writing and Publishing Books **H/I/S:** Collecting Presidential Christmas Memorabilia, Genealogy **EDU:** Master of Arts, University of Nebraska (1970)

DENORIS H. EVERETT
Delivery Engineer
Michigan Department of Transportation
38257 Mound Road
Sterling Heights, MI 48310 United States
everett@voyager.net
http://www.cambridgewhoswho.com

BUS: Government Agency **P/S:** Public Transportation Services **MA:** Regional **EXP:** Ms. Everett's expertise is in project management. **D/D/R:** Overseeing Construction Services, Supervising the Staff **H/I/S:** Playing Basketball and Baseball **EDU:** Master's Degree in Business and Finance, Michigan State University; Coursework in Civil Engineering, University of Detroit

MR. TIMOTHY J. FABRY, MS.ED., BA, AA
School Counselor
Unified School District #446, Lincoln School
701 W. Laurel Street
Independence, KS 67301 United States
tfabry@indyschools.com
http://www.indyschools.com

BUS: Elementary School and School District **P/S:** Excellent and Relevant Education for Students in Pre-Kindergarten through Grade Twelve **MA:** Regional **D/D/R:** Counseling Students One-on-One, Chairing the Student Care Team, Counseling Groups, Teaching Classroom Guidance, Coordinating Testing, Consulting with Staff and Parents, Mentoring Students, Participating in the After-School Tutoring Program **H/I/S:** Golfing, Reading, Volunteering, Participating in Church Activities, Mentoring **FBP:** American School Counseling Journal **EDU:** Master of Science in Education, Southern Illinois University, Edwardsville, IL; Bachelor of Arts in Education, Concordia University, Chicago, IL; Associate of Arts in Education, St. Paul's Junior College, Concordia, MO **A/A/S:** National Education Association; Kansas Counseling Association; Missouri Counseling Association; The American Counseling Association **C/VW:** Volunteer, Big Brothers and Big Sisters; School Crisis Team

MR. MANUEL FACHADO JR., DO
Doctor
Fig Tree Medical Consulting, LLC
PO Box 699
Lyman, SC 29365 United States
ficustreeus@hotmail.com
http://www.cambridgewhoswho.com

BUS: Proven Leader in the Fields of Healthcare, Medical Computing and Information Technology **P/S:** Medical Computing, Documentation Software for Physicians to Assist in Physicians Filing, Medical Reports, Billing, and Investigative Diagnosis Computing **MA:** National **EXP:** Mr. Fachado's expertise is in family practice, emergency medicine, medical computing for physicians, integrity technology in computing systems and diagnosis. **H/I/S:** Landscaping, Fishing **FBP:** JAMA; New England Journal of Medicine **EDU:** Pursuing JD, Northwestern California University School of Law; Degree in Osteopathic Medicine, University of Health Sciences College, Kansas City; Doctor of Osteopathy, University of Medicine and Dentistry of New Jersey; Internship in Surgery, Philadelphia College of Osteopathic Medicine; Residency in Family Practice **CERTS:** Certification in Manipulation under Anesthesia **A/A/S:** American Osteopathic Association; American Medical Association; Undersea and Hyperbaric Medical Association; American College of Osteopathic Family Physicians **C/VW:** American Diabetes Association

DOLLY M. FAIRCLOUGH
Attorney, Chief Executive Officer
Law Officer of D.M. Fairclough
235 Peachtree Street
Suite 400
Atlanta, GA 30303 United States
dmfairclough@bellsouth.net
http://www.cambridgewhoswho.com

BUS: Law Firm **P/S:** Legal Services **MA:** International **D/D/R:** Practicing Immigration, Criminal and International Law **H/I/S:** Traveling, Researching Legal Documents, Networking **FBP:** The Wall Street Journal **EDU:** JD, John Marshall Law School **A/A/S:** American Immigration Lawyers Association; Georgia Association of Criminal Defense Lawyers **A/H:** Business Woman of the Year **C/VW:** Georgia Innocence Project; Local High School; Mock Trial Team **A/S:** She attributes her success to her determination and parents. **B/I:** She became involved in the profession while working in banking and getting court experience. **H/O:** The most gratifying aspect of her career is working with international law.

BRANDON FALKNOR
General Manager, Owner
The Blue Pacific Grill
4150 Levis Commons Boulevard
Perrysburg, OH 43551 United States
brandon.falknor@hotmail.com
http://www.cambridgewhoswho.com

BUS: Restaurant **P/S:** Food and Beverage Services **MA:** Local **D/D/R:** Overseeing Operations Including Inventory, Accounts, Analyzing Profit and Loss, Troubleshooting, Ensuring Customer Satisfaction **H/I/S:** Playing Baseball and Basketball **EDU:** Associate Degree in Business Management, Clark State Community College (2003) **C/VW:** National Business Association

JOHN FALTO
Real Estate and Financial Consultant
Professional Real Estate Services
11251 S. Orange Blossom Trail
Orlando, FL 32837 United States
askjohn@realestateandmortgagehotline.com
http://www.realestateandmortgagehotline.com

BUS: Real Estate and Financial Services Company **P/S:** Residential, Commercial Real Estate and Mortgage Services, Foreclosure Specialist **MA:** Regional **D/D/R:** Selling Residential and Commercial Real Estate, Assisting Buyers with Mortgages, Working with First-Time and Seasonal Clients **H/I/S:** Spending Time with his Family, Playing Outside Laser Tag **FBP:** Kiplinger's Personal Finance **EDU:** Bachelor of Arts in Marketing and Accounting, New York City Technical College **CERTS:** Licensed Mortgage Broker; Licensed Real Estate Agent; Licensed in Insurance Products (1981); Licensed in Financial Products **A/A/S:** National Association for the Self-Employed; National Association of Tax Professionals; Florida Association of Realtors; National Association of Realtors; National Association of Personal Financial Advisors; National Association of Mortgage Brokers **C/VW:** American Red Cross **DOB:** January 25, 1959 **POB:** Manhattan **W/H:** Mortgage Broker and Realtor, Professional Mortgage Services of Central Florida, Inc. (2003-Present); Financial Service Representative, MetLife Financial Services (1999-2003); Sales Associate, Century21-Papp Realty (1997-1999); Sales Associate, Schlaeffer Associates, NJ (1995-1997); Phoenix Data (1988-Present)

MICHELLE M. FARABAUGH
Partner
Lenser
899 Northgate Drive
San Rafael, CA 94930 United States
michelle.farabaugh@lenser.com
http://www.lenser.com

BUS: Multi Channel Retail **P/S:** Retail Store **MA:** National **D/D/R:** Consulting, Strategic Planning with a Focus on Catalog and Internet **H/I/S:** Traveling and Sailing **FBP:** Harvard Review and The Wall Street Journal **EDU:** Master's Degree in Business, Babson College; Bachelor's Degree in Marketing, Bryant University **A/A/S:** Direct Marketing Association **A/S:** She attributes her success to focus and learning. **B/I:** She chose the profession because she loves the retail industry and people. **H/O:** The highlight of her career is her current position.

JEAN ANNE SOLON FARLEY
Orthodontist, Owner
Drs. Farley and Solon Orthodontics
1809 Alexandria Pike
Highland Heights, KY 41076 United States
jeanfarley@fuse.net
http://www.cambridgewhoswho.com

BUS: Orthodontic Dentistry **P/S:** Orthodontic Care **MA:** Local **EXP:** Ms. Farley's expertise is in orthodontics. **H/I/S:** Playing Tennis, Exercising, Walking, Bicycle Riding **FBP:** Orthodontics Journal; JCO Magazine **EDU:** Doctor of Medical Dentistry, University of Louisville (1985); Residency, University of Louisville (1987) **A/A/S:** American Association of Orthodontists **C/VW:** Fort Thomas Educational Fund; Local Charities **A/S:** She attributes her success to having a strong type A personality and always wanting to achieve the best. **H/O:** The highlight of her career is doing what she loves to do.

CYNTHIA JANE FARR, RN

RN, Charge Nurse
Gallup Indian Medical Center
Nizhoni Boulevard
Gallup, NM 87301 United States
cindyfarrrn@yahoo.com
http://www.cambridgewhoswho.com

BUS: Hospital **P/S:** Healthcare **MA:** Regional **D/D/R:** Charge Nursing **H/I/S:** Motor Sports, Camping, Hiking, Fishing **FBP:** Journal of Oncology Nursing; RN; Nursing2009 **EDU:** Associate Degree in Nursing, St. Elizabeth College of Nursing **A/A/S:** Oncology Nursing Society **C/VW:** United Way of America; Feed the Children; The Victory of Junction Gang **A/S:** She attributes her personal and professional success to her positive attitude. **B/I:** She has always had an interest in the field and developed experience in caring for her mother and father after an accident. **H/O:** The highlight of her career was becoming chemotherapy certified.

JILL A. FARROW, RN

Registered Nurse
Hospice of Orange & Sullivan Counties
800 Stony Brook Court
Newburgh, NY 12550 United States
mango1026@aol.com
http://www.hospiceoforange.com

The circle is love
the branch life;
the blossom,
dignity in the darkness

BUS: Specialized Care Program for Terminally Ill Patients, Working in Tandem with Primary Care Physicians to Ensure the Best Care **P/S:** Nursing Care, Pain and Symptom Control, Patient and Family Instructions on Care, Home Health Aide Services, Social Work Services, Spiritual Care, Volunteer Services for Patients and Families, Complimentary Bereavement After Care Program for Hospice Families, Medical Equipment Services **MA:** Local **D/D/R:** Public Speaking, Nursing **H/I/S:** Horseback Riding, Swimming, Reading, Photography **FBP:** Nursing2009; Journal of Advanced Nursing; American Journal of Nursing; RN **EDU:** Bachelor's Degree in Nursing, SUNY New Paltz; Associate Degree in Nursing, Sullivan County Community College; Board Certified **A/A/S:** Phi Theta Kappa; Sigma Theta Tau International **A/H:** Beacon Scholar **CHILD:** Nichole **C/A:** Author, Journal Article

DAVID A. FAUL, CPA
CPA
David A. Faul, CPA
30 Vine Sreet, Suite 2
PO Box 823
Landsdale, PA 19446 United States
cpafaul@mindspring.com
http://www.cambridgewhoswho.com

BUS: Accounting **P/S:** Tax Return Preparation, QuickBooks Pro Advisor **MA:** Local **EXP:** Mr. Faul's expertise is tax return preparation using QuickBooks Pro. **H/I/S:** Bowling, Fishing, Archery **FBP:** The Wall Street Journal **EDU:** Bachelor's Degree in Accounting, Temple University **A/A/S:** Pennsylvania Institute of Certified Public Accountants **C/VW:** Local Fire Department; United Way of America; Various Other Charities **A/S:** He attributes his success to his appetite for work. **B/I:** He became involved in this profession because he grew up in it. **H/O:** The highlight of his career is building his practice.

JOAN FAVOR
Assistant Vice President
Management Systems International, Inc.
600 Water Street S.W.
Washington, DC 20024 United States
jfavor@msi-inc.com
http://www.cambridgewhoswho.com

BUS: Management Consulting **P/S:** Consulting Services **MA:** International **EXP:** Ms. Favor's expertise is in human resources, finance and contracts administration. **H/I/S:** Traveling, Youth and Senior Citizens; Sports **EDU:** Bachelor of Science in Business Administration, Voorhees College, Magna Cum Laude **A/A/S:** Delta Sigma Theta **C/VW:** Church, Local Charities **A/S:** She attributes her success to her mother who taught her to nurture, teach and train to see others prosper. **B/I:** She became involved in this profession because she likes to help people. **H/O:** The highlight of her career is traveling to third world countries and helping employees be financially secure.

EIKO FAZIO
Business Analyst
IMP Consulting, Inc.
1 State Street
Boston, MA 02109 United States
eikofaz@yahoo.com
http://www.cambridgewhoswho.com

BUS: Consulting Firm **P/S:** Financial Services for Financial Institutions and Investment Management Companies **MA:** Regional **D/D/R:** Overseeing System Upgrades and Implementations, Offering Client Training and Support **H/I/S:** Traveling, Skiing, Painting **FBP:** BusinessWeek **EDU:** Bachelor of Science in Management Information Systems and Computer Science, Simmons College, MA **A/H:** Management Information Systems Award (2003); Liberty Mutual Scholarship Academy (2003) **DOB:** December 1, 1967 **W/H:** Associate Analyst, Liberty Mutual Insurance Company (2004-2006) **A/S:** She attributes her success to taking risks, learning and being motivated to excel.

ROSEMARY M. FEDERICO, RN, MS
RN, Manager
St. Joseph's Hospital and Medical Center
350 W. Thomas Road
Phoenix, AZ 85013 United States
rfederi@chw.edu
http://www.stjosephs-phx.org

BUS: Hospital **P/S:** Level One Trauma Center, Teaching Hospital, Nonprofit, 565 Beds **MA:** Regional **D/D/R:** Specializing in Oncology and Telemetry **H/I/S:** Spending Time with her Family **EDU:** Master of Science Nursing Degree, Regis University; Bachelor of Science in Nursing, University of Phoenix **A/A/S:** Phoenix Oncology Nurses Society; Oncology Nurses Society; American Nurses Association **C/VW:** United Way of America; St. Jude Children's Research Hospital; Local Food Drive; Easter Basket Donations **SP:** Arnold Federico **CHILD:** Arnold and Moussa **A/S:** She attributes her success to constantly striving to improve her personal being, as well as working in a very supportive environment. **B/I:** She became involved in her profession because, since childhood, nursing has been the only profession she has wanted to pursue. After taking Certified Nursing Assistant classes in junior in high school, she became a licensed practical nurse as a senior. **H/O:** The most satisfying aspects of her career are feeling that her role as both a nurse and manager have enabled her to help both patients and those who help patients.

JOHN I. FEHN
Director of Property Operations
Double Tree Hotel
1150 Ninth Street
Modesto, CA 95354 United States
john_fehn@hilton.com
http://www.doubletree.com

BUS: Leader in the Hospitality Industry **P/S:** Quality Hospitality Services, Accommodations, Restaurants, Conrad Hotels, Embassy Suites Hotels, Hampton Inn and Hampton Inns and Suites, Hilton Hotels, Hilton Garden Inn, Homewood Suites by Hilton **MA:** International **EXP:** Mr. Fehn's expertise is in carpentry. **D/D/R:** Managing Day-to-Day Operations, Maintaining Hotel Security, Engineering, Air Conditioning, Electrical Services and Remodeling, Managing Safety **H/I/S:** Riding Dirt Bikes, Softball **EDU:** Bachelor's Degree in Carpentry, Los Angeles Trade Technical College (1982)

YVONNE C. FEKKERS
Owner
The Camelot Room
1331 W. Gonzales Road
Oxnard, CA 93036 United States
Fekkers3@aol.com
http://www.cambridgewhoswho.com

BUS: Bar, Social Club **P/S:** Social Gatherings, Beverages, Entertainment **MA:** Local **D/D/R:** Managing All Aspects of the Business **H/I/S:** Traveling **FBP:** The Bartender's Guide **C/VW:** Local Charitable Donations **A/S:** She attributes her success to her hard work and knowledge of the field. **B/I:** She became involved in the profession because her mother owned a bar and she grew up understanding the industry. **H/O:** The most gratifying aspect of her career is having never experienced a violent problem in her bar.

MICHELLE FELKER
Production Assistant
michellefelker@bonitz.com

A/S: She attributes her career success to her positive personality, and to her ability to work in a fast-paced environment. **B/I:** While job searching, she was offered a position as a production assistant, which she accepted. **H/O:** She feels that her current position is the highlight of her career.

DR. J. LOUIS FELTON
Pastor
The Galilee Baptist Church
1216 N. Westnedge Avenue
Kalamazoo, MI 49007 United States
jlf2@sbcglobal.org
http://www.gbckazoo.org

BUS: Proven Leader in the Field of Religious Services **P/S:** Religious Leadership, Prayer and Worship Services, Counseling, Community Outreach **MA:** Regional **D/D/R:** Teaching, Counseling and Mentoring Others through the Word of God **H/I/S:** Traveling, Visiting Museums and Historical Sites **EDU:** Honorary Doctoral Degree, St. Thomas Christian College, Jacksonville, FL (2004); Master's Degree in Theology, McCormick Theological Seminary, Chicago (1989); Bachelor of Arts in History and Political Science, Western Michigan University (1982) **A/A/S:** President, Nationwide Multicultural Alliance of Kalamazoo; National Baptist Convention; National Association for the Advancement of Colored People, Kalamazoo Chapter **C/VW:** Board Member, Kalamazoo Community Foundation

MS. TERRI FENSEL
Freelance Photographer
PO Box 2664
Lafayette, LA 70502 United States
terri@terrifensel.com
http://www.terrifensel.com

BUS: Sole Proprietorship **P/S:** Photography **MA:** International **D/D/R:** Taking Photographs for Magazines, Newspapers, Music Artists and Corporations **H/I/S:** Traveling, Gardening, Golfing, Canoeing **EDU:** Coursework in Photography, The Art Institute of Pittsburgh **A/A/S:** Louisiana Press Association; American Society of Media Photographers **A/H:** Photographer of the Year, OffBeat Magazine (2007) **C/VW:** Jeep Jaunt; American Lung Association **POB:** Cleveland **A/S:** She attributes her success to her dedication and talents. **B/I:** She became involved in her profession because she believed photographing was a creative way to tell a story. **H/O:** The most gratifying aspect of her career is sharing a subject with her viewer through photography. **I/F/Y:** In five years, Ms. Fensel would like continue photographing while working as a photo editor in the magazine industry.

ANITA C. FERBER
Director of Contracts
The Aerospace Corporation
2350 E. El Sequndo Boulevard
El Sequndo, CA 90245 United States
anita.c.ferber@areo.com
http://www.areo.org

BUS: Federally Funded Research and Development Center **P/S:** Knowledge, Information and Innovative Solutions **MA:** National **D/D/R:** Negotiating DOD and Commercial Contracts **H/I/S:** Spending Time with her Family, Gardening, Scuba Diving, Reading **FBP:** BusinessWeek; Cross Link **EDU:** Master's Degree in Technology Management, University of Phoenix **A/A/S:** NCMA **C/VW:** Orange County Children's Hospital; Red Cross; Saint Jude's Hospital **A/S:** She attributes her success to staying focused and on track. **B/I:** She chose the profession because she always enjoyed the field. **H/O:** The highlight of her career is her current position.

CHERIE D. FERGUSON
Administrative Assistant
Gallatin Airport Authority
850 Gallatin Field Road
Suite 6
Belgrade, MT 59714 United States
cherie.ferguson@gallatinfield.com
http://www.gallatinfield.com

BUS: Airport Authority **P/S:** Keeping the Airfield Operating Smoothly, Airport Authority **MA:** Regional **EXP:** Ms. Ferguson's expertise includes bookkeeping, administration, aviation and life coaching. **H/I/S:** Horseback Riding, Walking, Bird Watching, Crafts, Reading **EDU:** College Coursework **C/VW:** Mentor **B/I:** She became involved in this profession because she had joined the Air Force back in 1969 and was doing computer operation and progressed into bookkeeping and software development. **H/O:** The highlight of her career is having more responsibilities.

MS. JONEL FERGUSON KINSER, RN, BSN
Clinical Audit Coordinator
North Carolina Baptist Hospital
Wake Forest University Baptist Medical Center
S. Hawthorne Road, Medical Center Boulevard
Winston Salem, NC 27157 United States
jkinser@wfubmc.edu
http://www1.wfubmc.edu

BUS: Medical and Tertiary Referral Center **P/S:** Level I Trauma Care, Wide Range of Medical Services Including Oncology, Urology, Geriatrics, Ear, Nose and Throat Care, Heart Surgery and Orthopedics **MA:** International **EXP:** Ms. Ferguson Kinser's expertise is in cardiovascular care. **D/D/R:** Handling Third Party Billing Audits and Patient Complaints, Reporting to the Director of Corporate Compliance and the Hospital President **H/I/S:** Quilting, Wheel Pottery, Reading **EDU:** Bachelor's Degree, Winston Salem State University (2008); Associate Degree in Nursing, Asheville-Buncombe Technical Community College (1990) **CERTS:** Certification in Auditing and Coding, American Association of Certified Coders and Auditors **A/A/S:** Professional Practice Advocacy Council, North Carolina Nurses Association (2008); American Nurses Association **SP:** Bryan **A/S:** She attributes her success to her hard work and determination. **B/I:** She became involved in her profession because it was her lifelong dream to become a nurse just like her great aunts.

PEDRO J. FERNANDEZ
Psychiatrist
Dr. Pedro Fernández, CSP
55 Calle De Diego E., Suite 301
Mayaguez, PR 00680 United States
sierraz85@prtc.net
http://www.cambridgewhoswho.com

BUS: Private Practice **P/S:** Healthcare Including Psychiatric Care **MA:** Puerto Rico **EXP:** Mr. Fernandez's expertise is in psychiatric nursing. **D/D/R:** Consulting, Conducting Research on Psychopharmacology, Speaking at Seminars and Conferences **H/I/S:** Collecting Muscle Cars **FBP:** Medical Journal; Muscle Car **EDU:** MD in Psychosomatic Medicine, Bronx-Lebanon Hospital Center **A/A/S:** American Psychiatric Association; American Medical Association; Society for Puerto Rican Psychiatrists **A/S:** He attributes his success to the support he receives from his father. **B/I:** He became involved in his profession because he was recommended by his friend. **H/O:** The most gratifying aspect of his career is helping his patients.

LILLIE FERRELL
Management Consultant
Executive and Technical Services
30 Cattano Avenue
Suite 419
Morristown, NJ 07960 United States
lillieferr@aol.com
http://www.exectechservices.com

BUS: Nonprofit, Community Based Organization **P/S:** Consulting **MA:** National **D/D/R:** Management Consulting, Upgrading Technology Systems, Training, Building Teams, Offering Technical Assistance for Government Agencies **H/I/S:** Traveling, Reading **FBP:** The Wall Street Journal **EDU:** Master of Education, Florida State University (1976); Bachelor's Degree in Political Science, Florida State University (1974) **A/A/S:** National Speakers Bureau; Houston Speakers Bureau

MARY P. FETTE
Nurse Manager
Waseca Medical Center - Mayo Health System
501 N. State Street
Waseca, MN 56093 United States
fettemary@mayo.edu
http://www.mayohealthsystem.org

BUS: Medical Center that Works to Improve the Well Being of the Communities it Serves by Healing and Educating Patients While Teaching Healthcare Professionals **P/S:** Access to Local Healthcare through the Clinic, Hospital, Emergency Room, Urgent Care and many Outpatient Services **MA:** Local **EXP:** Ms. Fette's expertise is in nurse management. **D/D/R:** Overseeing 22 Nurses, Supervising Procedures, Covering the Medical-Surgical Floor **H/I/S:** Scrapbooking **FBP:** Critical Care Nurses **EDU:** Pursuing Bachelor's Degree, University of Phoenix (2007) **A/A/S:** ENA; CCNA

LENA FEYGIN, Ed.D, DIP LC
President
FROG Enterprises
FROG Enterprises, Corp
New York, NY 10280 United States
lenafeygin@frogent.com
http://www.frogent.com

BUS: Consulting Company **P/S:** Individual Life Coaching Services, Coaching Services for Women Juggling a Career and a Family, Family Life Coaching Services, Business Consulting and Coaching Services for Entrepreneurs to Develop Customized Business Models, Corporate Business Consulting Services **MA:** International **EXP:** Ms. Feygin's expertise is in business consulting and life coaching. **H/I/S:** Going to the Theater, Taking Walks in Central Park, Fine Dining **FBP:** Forbes; Forbes for Small Business **EDU:** Doctor of Education, Amstead University; Bachelor of Arts in Psychology, Fordham University **CERTS:** Diploma in Life Coaching, The Life Coach Institute **A/A/S:** International Coaching Federation; New York Women's Agenda **C/VW:** Police Athletic League **POB:** Moscow **A/S:** She attributes her success to her supportive mother. **B/I:** She became involved in her profession because she had a background in educational coaching and wanted to make a difference in the lives of others. **H/O:** The most gratifying aspect of her career is seeing her clients succeed.

ROBERTA K. FIELD
Independent Insurance Agent
RKF Insurance Services
3101 Farnborough court
Silver Spring, MD 20906 United States
bobbes@comcast.net
http://www.cambridgewhoswho.com

BUS: Insurance Brokerage **P/S:** Health Insurance **MA:** National **D/D/R:** Offering BlueCross BlueShield Insurance, Representing StarMark and Uni-Care **H/I/S:** Sculpturing **FBP:** Health Insurance Underwriters **A/S:** She attributes her success to her determination. **B/I:** She became involved in the profession because she was working with hospital supplies and transitioned to medical insurance.

ARLENE G. FIGGINS, RN, BSN, CDE
Registered Nurse, CDE
Diabetes Management Program
Valley Health
333 W. Cork Street, Suite 620
Winchester, VA 22601 United States
afiggins@Valleyhealthlink.com
http://www.Valleyhealthlink.com

BUS: Medical Facility **P/S:** Diabetes Assessment and Education, Medical Nutrition Therapy, Youth Type-One and Adult Type-One and Type-Two Diabetes, Insulin Pump Therapy, Pre-Diabetes, Gestational Diabetes and Follow-Up Care **MA:** Regional **D/D/R:** Offering Diabetes Education, Contracting with Endocrinologists for Study Coordination **H/I/S:** Spending Time with her Children **FBP:** Diabetes Forecast; Diabetes Self Management; Diabetes Educator; American Association of Diabetes Educators Journal **EDU:** Bachelor of Science in Nursing, Alderson-Broaddus College (1983) **CERTS:** Certified Diabetes Educator (2005) **A/A/S:** American Association of Diabetes Educators

COLLEEN M. FINCH
Executive Administrative Assistant
Harcourt Assessment Inc.
19500 Bulerde Road
San Antonio, TX 78259 United States
colleen_finch@harcourt.com
http://www.cambridgewhoswho.com

BUS: Publishing **P/S:** Test Publishers for Clinical and Educational Publications **MA:** International **EXP:** Ms. Finch's expertise lies in her organizational skills. **H/I/S:** Reading **FBP:** Industry-Related **EDU:** Associate Degree in Business, North Harris County **C/VW:** Children's Schools; Reading is Fundamental; Kiwanis International **A/S:** She attributes her success to the support she received from her coworkers, family, friends and students. **B/I:** She became involved in her profession because she had always wanted to do something in business. **H/O:** The highlight of her career was seeing projects from start to finish.

MR. LAWRENCE G. FINK
Fire Chief
Brookhaven Fire Department
2486 Montauk Highway
Brookhaven, NY 11719 United States
esd11@optonline.net
http://www.cambridgewhoswho.com

BUS: Fire Department **P/S:** Fire Protection, Technical and Emergency Rescue Services **MA:** Local **EXP:** Mr. Fink's expertise is in overseeing emergency services. **D/D/R:** Utilizing the Incident Command System, Pre-Planning, Ensuring Public Safety, Overseeing Emergency Services **H/I/S:** Traveling, Scuba Diving, Sailing, Downhill Skiing, Photography **FBP:** Fire Engineering **EDU:** College Coursework **A/A/S:** Brookhaven Town Fire Chiefs Association; South Country Ambulance Company; National Fire Protection Association; The International Association of Fire Chiefs **DOB:** November 8, 1960 **SP:** Tetyana **CHILD:** Alex

SANDRA P. FINKELSTEIN
Mathematics Teacher (Retired)
East Windsor Regional Schools
25A Leshin Lane
Hightstown, NJ 08520 United States
Sandra.Finkelstein@cwwemail.com
http://www.eastwindsorregionalschools.com

BUS: School District **P/S:** Education **MA:** Regional **D/D/R:** Teaching Mathematics, Acting as a Faculty Advisor for the Student Council, Choreographing Musical Productions **H/I/S:** Gardening, Horseback Riding, Choreographing, Playing Number Games, Assisting in Music Productions **FBP:** Mathematics Teacher; NEA Today **EDU:** Master of Science in Education, Brooklyn College; Bachelor's Degree in Education, Brooklyn College **A/A/S:** New Jersey Education Association; Retired Educators Association; National Education Association **A/H:** Who's Who Among American Teachers **C/VW:** Sierra Club; National Wildlife Federation; World Wildlife Fund; Co-Chairwoman, Key Club International **A/S:** She attributes her success to her open mind. **B/I:** She became involved in her profession because she wanted to be a teacher. **H/O:** The highlight of her career was developing a mathematics program.

JEANNE FIORE-ZYDALLIS
Educator, Assistant
South Brunswick Public Library
P. O. Box 69, Amboy Avenue
Fords, NJ 08863 United States
felixjeannegianna@msn.com
http://schools.privateschoolsReport.com/NewJersey/
Fords/OurLadyOfPeaceElemSchool

BUS: Catholic Elementary School **P/S:** Education in Reading, Mathematics, English, Science, Social Studies, Art, Music, History, Languages, Physical Education, Religion **MA:** Regional **D/D/R:** Teaching All First Grade Core Subjects, Tutoring After-School for Students Needing Extra Help, Assisting in the Children's Department of the South Brunswick Public Library **H/I/S:** Reading **FBP:** Young Children **EDU:** Master's Degree in Early Childhood Education, Concentration in Reading, Wheelock College, Boston, MA (1987) **A/A/S:** National Association for Education of Young Children; Former Member, Rhode Island Honor Society **A/H:** Catholic School Teacher of the Year, Our Lady of the Peace

CARI D. FISH
President/Secretary
B Fish Enterprises DBA/Oregon Rain Landscapes Irrigation
4672 Northeast Columbia Boulevard
Portland, OR 97218 United States
fishc@qwest.net

BUS: Landscaping Contractor **P/S:** Commercial and Residential Landscaping **MA:** Local **EXP:** Ms. Fish's expertise is in commercial landscaping. **H/I/S:** Loves Singing, Snow Skiing, Water Skiing, Rock Climbing **FBP:** Landscaping Magazines; Women's Health **EDU:** Coursework, Brigham Young University; Diploma, Oregon High School **C/VW:** Mission Fund, Youth Program, Church of Jesus Christ Latter Day Saints

GAIL D. FISHER
President
Central Iowa Real Estate Services
5161 Maple Drive
Pleasant Hill, IA 50327 United States
gailcirs@aol.com
http://www.help4realtors.net

BUS: Real Estate Services Company **P/S:** Real Estate Exchange Services **MA:** Iowa **EXP:** Ms. Fisher's expertise in real estate management. **D/D/R:** Overseeing All Aspects of the Closing Process, Conducting Training Classes for Local Real Estate Companies **H/I/S:** Farming, Participating in Shooting Sports **EDU:** Industry-Related Training and Experience **CERTS:** Licensed Real Estate Agent (1973) **A/A/S:** Former Treasurer and President, Women's Council of Realtors; Des Moines Association of Realtors; National Association of Realtors **C/VW:** Blank Children's Hospital; American Heart Association; The Leukemia & Lymphoma Society **A/S:** She attributes her success to her ability to get along with people, which results in many referrals and repeat business. **B/I:** She became involved in her profession through a natural progression of opportunities. **H/O:** The highlight of her career was starting her own business.

MS. BERNADETTE J. FISHER-CHARLES, CAC II, RAC, NAFC
Counselor
Department of Health
1905 E. Street S.E.
Washington, DC 20002 United States
BChristylove@msn.com
http://www.cambridgewhoswho.com

BUS: Social Services **P/S:** Social Work **MA:** Local **D/D/R:** Counseling Individuals on Addiction and Reproductive Issues, Instructing on Black Parenting Techniques **H/I/S:** Writing, Listening to Music, Writing Poetry **FBP:** American Counseling Association Nationa Association for Forensic Counselors **EDU:** Bachelor's Degree in Sociology, Minor in Elementary Education, Temple University **CERTS:** Certified Treatment Counselor **A/A/S:** NAADAC - The Association for Addiction Professionals; National Counselors Association; PADACA **C/VW:** Salesian Mission, Jesuit Volunteer Corps, Peace Corps, Purple Hearts **A/S:** She attributes her success to her empathy, understanding her clients and knowing how to help them.

JOANN V. FISKE
Owner
JoAnn's Childcare
107 Indian Avenue
Forest City, IA 50436 United States
joannjones@yahoo.com
http://www.cambridgewhoswho.com

BUS: Home Childcare **P/S:** Childcare **MA:** Local **D/D/R:** Caring for Children from Birth through Adolescence **H/I/S:** Traveling, Reading, Horseback Riding **C/VW:** Local Church; Girl Scouts of the USA; Boy Scouts of America; American Cancer Society **A/S:** She attributes her success to being both honest and fair. **B/I:** She chose the profession because she loves her children. **H/O:** The highlight of her career is being able to watch her children grow.

SHARON A. FITZGERALD, ESQ.
Esquire, Partner
Fitzgerald Law Firm
2108 Warren Avenue
Cheyenne, WY 82001 United States
lawyers@fitzgerald.com
http://www.fitzgeraldlaw.com

BUS: Law Office **P/S:** Legal Services **MA:** National **D/D/R:** Specializing in Catastrophic Injury and Law for Plaintiffs **H/I/S:** Spending Time with Family, Painting **FBP:** Wyoming State Bar Publication **EDU:** JD in Law, University of Wyoming; Bachelor of Arts in English, University of Wyoming **A/A/S:** American Association of Appellate Lawyers; Million Dollar Advocate Forum; Wyoming State Bar **A/H:** Best Lawyers in America (2007) **C/VW:** Fitzgerald Foundation for Children **A/S:** She attributes her success to her hard work, determination and integrity. **B/I:** She became involved in this profession because she always loved the challenge of helping people with their legal issues. **H/O:** The most gratifying aspect of her career is helping people in need.

MARY JANE FIZER
Teacher (Retired)
Leesylvania Elementary
Prince William County Schools
1284 Dawson Court
Woodbridge, VA 22191 United States
mfizer5038@aol.com
http://www.pwcs.edu/leeslvania

BUS: Elementary School **P/S:** Education **MA:** Local **D/D/R:** Teaching All Subjects to First Grade Students **H/I/S:** Reading, Traveling, Solving Crossword Puzzles **FBP:** NEA Journal **EDU:** Master of Education, George Mason University; Bachelor's Degree in Elementary Education, Concord University **A/A/S:** Prince William Education Association; Virginia Education Association; National Education Association **C/VW:** Organist, United Methodist Church; Cancer Society **POB:** Crumpler, WV **SP:** Harry Fizer **CHILD:** Karen, Timothy, Tina **W/H:** First Grade Teacher, Leesylvania Elementary School, Woodbridge, VA (1996-2007); First Grade Teacher, Rippon Elementary School, Woodbridge, VA (1968-1996); First Grade Teacher, Potomac View Elementary School, Woodbridge, VA (1966-1967); Kindergarten Teacher, Cokesbury United Methodist Kindergarten, Woodbridge, VA (1965-1966); First Grade Teacher, Lorton Elementary School, Lorton, VA (1962-1965); Second Grade Teacher, Rose Hill Elementary School, Alexandria, VA (1960-1962); Seventh Grade Teacher, Stonewall Jackson Elementary School, Alexandria, VA (1958-1959); Fifth Grade Teacher, Brushfork Elementary School, Bluefield, WV (1957-1958) **C/A:** Outstanding Elementary Teacher of America (1975); Who's Who Among Elementary Teachers (Four Times); Phi Delta Kappa **A/S:** She attributes her success to her love for children. **B/I:** She became involved in the profession because she always wanted a career in education. **H/O:** The most gratifying aspect of her career is having former students who have reached adulthood return to visit her.

MR. MATTHEW G. FLANIGAN
Chief Executive Officer
Flanigan and Associates
389 Clubhouse Drive, W3
Gulf Shores, AL 36542 United States
flanig40@yahoo.com
http://www.cambridgewhoswho.com

BUS: Leading Consulting Firm **P/S:** Consultant to Presidents, Provosts, and Enrollment Officers for Feasibility and Marketing Studies Focusing on Growth and Quality Improvement for Undergraduate and Graduate Enrollment Goals for Adult Learners and Traditional Students **MA:** National **D/D/R:** Consulting on Admissions and Degree Completion, Building Enrollment in Institutions, Fundraising **H/I/S:** Football **FBP:** Chronicle of Higher Education **EDU:** Master's Degree in History, DePaul University (1972) **CERTS:** Certified in College Counseling, University of California at Los Angeles (1990) **A/A/S:** Former President, National Association for College Admission Counseling **DOB:** June 22, 1940 **SP:** Judie **CHILD:** Sarah, Andrew, Bridget, Siobhan **W/H:** Vice President, St. Norbert College, WI; President, Marian College, WI; Vice President of Development, Jacksonville University, FL; Vice President of New Ventures, Adult Division, Jacksonville University, FL

SUSAN M. FLEEGE, JD, CIPP
Compliance Officer
The Hartford Administrative Services Company
500 Bielenberg Drive
Woodbury, MN 55125 United States
susan.fleege@hartfordlife.com
http://www.cambridgewhoswho.com

BUS: Finance **P/S:** Mutual Funds **MA:** International **EXP:** Ms. Fleege's expertise is in securities, banking and financial compliance from a legal aspect. **H/I/S:** Acting as a Court Appointed Guardian **FBP:** Privacy Advisor **EDU:** JD, William Mitchell College of Law **CERTS:** Certified Information Protection Officer, International Association of Protection Professionals **A/A/S:** Minnesota Bar Association; Money Laundering Committee Member, Investment Company Institute **A/S:** She attributes her success to her focus and her diligence. **B/I:** She made a natural progression into her current profession. **H/O:** The highlight of her career was setting up a bank and setting up a company in India.

MARTHA FLEMING
School Nurse
Waco Independent School District
501 Franklin Avenue
Waco, TX 76708 United States
zignrob@aol.com
http://www.wacoisd.org

BUS: Public School System **P/S:** Special Needs Children in a Public School Setting, Working with All Different Types of Disabilities **MA:** Local **D/D/R:** Working with Severely Sick Children in Public Schools **H/I/S:** Being Heavily Involved with her Children's Activities **EDU:** Bachelor of Science in Nursing, University of Texas; Registered Nurse **A/A/S:** Parent-Teacher Association; School Nurses Association **C/VW:** Center for Women and Children

DONNA J. FLETCHER, PH.D.
Director of Risk Management Research,
Associate Professor of Finance
Bentley College
175 Forest Street
Waltham, MA 02452 United States
dfletcher@bentley.edu
http://www.bentley.edu

BUS: Business College **P/S:** Higher Education for Students, Generates Knowledge by Uniting the Rigor, Relevance, Creativity and Intellectual Dynamics of Business and the Liberal Arts, Bachelor's and Master's Degree Programs, Research, Athletics, Clubs and Organizations, Housing, Spiritual Life, Personal and Academic Counselors, Community Service **MA:** Regional **D/D/R:** Handling Fixed-Income Securities and Currency Swaps, Assessing Risk Management, Overseeing the Faculty **EDU:** Ph.D. in Business and Economics, Lehigh University (1991); Bachelor of Science Degree in Accounting and Economics, Minor in French, Lehigh University (1978) **A/A/S:** Financial Women's Association; American Finance Association; American Institute of Certified Public Accountants; Eastern Finance Association; Financial Management Association International; International Association of Financial Engineers; WCI; Finance Executive Institution; Beta Alpha Psi; Beta Gamma Sigma **A/H:** Arthur E. Humphrey Teaching Assistant Award (1988)

LISA R. FLETCHER-DAVID
Accounts Payable Director
The Catholic University of America
620 Michigan Avenue N.E.
Washington, DC 20064 United States
fletche1@cua.edu
http://www.cua.edu

BUS: University **P/S:** Higher Education Including Special Programs **MA:** Regional **EXP:** Ms. Fletcher-David's expertise is in accounting. **D/D/R:** Working with Staff Members **H/I/S:** Water Aerobics, Shopping, Spending Time with her Family **FBP:** BusinessWeek **EDU:** Pursuing Ph.D. in Business Administration, University of Phoenix; Master of Business Administration in Accounting, University of Phoenix; Associate of Arts in Business Administration, Prince George's Community College; Bachelor of Science in Accounting and Business Management, University of Maryland **DOB:** December 28, 1968 **SP:** John **CHILD:** John

MS. JOETTE L. FLIPPING
Speech Pathologist III
Saint Agnes Medical Center
1303 E. Herndon Avenue
Fresno, CA 93720 United States
joette.flip@gmail.com
http://www.cambridgewhoswho.com

BUS: Leader in Healthcare Services **P/S:** Full Service Community Medical Center for Inpatient and Outpatient Care **MA:** Local **EXP:** Ms. Flipping's area of expertise include speech pathology instruction, pediatrics, rehabilitation therapy, dysphagia management, neurorehabilitation, cognitive and laryngectomy rehabilitation. **D/D/R:** Training, Offering Direct Input for New Hires, Treating Adult and General Population Patients with Brain Injuries, Tumors and Strokes **H/I/S:** Power Walking, Biking, Hiking, Traveling, Practicing Horticulture, Reading **EDU:** Master's Degree in Communication Disorders, Adams State College (1982); Bachelor's Degree in Speech, California University of Pennsylvania (1978) **A/A/S:** California Speech-Language-Hearing Association; American Speech-Language-Hearing Association; National Aphasia Association; International Association of Laryngectomies; Former Member, National Brain Injury Association; Alpha Kappa Alpha

ARLENE FLORES
Teacher, English Language Learner Program Site Coordinator
Colton Middle School
670 Laurel Street
Colton, CA 92324 United States
aflores57@hotmail.com
http://www.cambridgewhoswho.com

BUS: Middle School **P/S:** Education for Primary a Minority Immigrant Population **MA:** Local **D/D/R:** Teaching English to Immigrant Students **H/I/S:** Dancing and Choreography, Drawing, Painting, Portraits **EDU:** Bachelor's Degree in English and Liberal Studies, Minor in Spanish, California State University at San Bernardino **A/A/S:** Phi Kappa Phi **C/VW:** Teacher, Vacation Bible School, Europe **A/S:** She attributes her success to her love for learning and teaching. **B/I:** She became involved in her profession because she always loved teaching. **H/O:** The highlight of her career was seeing her students come back.

MARIA I. FLORES, MA, BA
Foreign Language Supervisor
Prince George's County Public School
9201 E. Hampton Drive
Capital Heights, MD 20743 United States
maria.flores@pgcps.org
http://www.cambridgewhoswho.com

BUS: Public School **P/S:** Secondary Education **MA:** Regional **D/D/R:** Establishing New Foreign Language Programs, Beginning New Initiatives Where People Realize a Second Language is Imperative in the Work Force **H/I/S:** Reading, Shopping, Traveling **FBP:** ASCD Magazine **EDU:** Fellowship, China (2006); Fellowship in Italian Culture and Language (2005); Master of Arts in Latin American Literature, University of Maryland, College Park; Bachelor's Degree in Humanities Education and Spanish, Minor in History, Universidad del Turabo, Puerto Rico **CERTS:** License in ADM2 (2007); Certified Teacher K-12; Certified in Administration **A/A/S:** Association for Supervision and Curriculum Development; Maryland Foreign Language Association; Greater Washington Association of Teachers of Foreign Language; American Council of Foreign Language Teachers; State President, American Association of Teachers of Spanish and Portuguese; National Association of District Supervisors of Foreign Language; National Network of Early Language Learning; The Office of Chinese Language International Council

NANCY A. FLORES, RN, BSN
Registered Nurse (Retired)
Veterans Administration Medical Center
1443 Hepner Street S.E.
Palm Bay, FL 32909 United States
http://www.cambridgewhoswho.com

BUS: VA Medical Center **P/S:** Healthcare **MA:** Local **D/D/R:** Staff Nursing, Managing Cases, Scheduling, Reporting, Skin Nursing, Precepting and Mentoring, Intravenous Consulting, Charge Nursing **EDU:** Bachelor of Science in Nursing, Catholic University of Ponce, Puerto Rico **A/H:** Suggestion Award **CHILD:** Angel, Magda

VIRGINIA K. FLORES
1) Teacher 2) Teacher
1) Oakland Unified School District 2) Berkeley Adult School
1) 2455 Church Street 2) 1701 San Pablo Avenue
Oakland, CA 94702 United States
FloresVK@yahoo.com
http://cambridgewhoswho.com

BUS: 1) Public School District 2) Adult School **P/S:** 1) Education, English as a Second Language 2) Graduate Equivalency Diploma Courses, English as a Second Language Courses for Adults **MA:** 1) Local 2) Local **D/D/R:** Teaching English as a Second Language **H/I/S:** Singing in Sunday School Choir, Playing the Piano **EDU:** Master's Degree in Bilingual and Bicultural Education, University of San Francisco; Bachelor of Arts in Education, University of California at Berkeley **A/A/S:** California Teachers Association; Oakland Education Association; National Education Association **C/VW:** The Chicana and Latina Foundation First Mexican Baptist Church **A/S:** She attributes her success to her patience and productivity. **B/I:** She became involved in her profession after taking an opportunity to teach and naturally progressing into the field. **H/O:** The most gratifying aspect of her career is watching her students succeed.

GLADYS C. FLOYD
Registered Nurse
Florida Hospital
601 E. Rollins Street
Orlando, FL 32803 United States
lollipoprn@aol.com
http://www.cambridgewhoswho.com

BUS: Medical Center **P/S:** Healthcare **MA:** Regional **EXP:** Ms. Floyd's expertise is in emergency critical-care nursing and CPI instruction. **H/I/S:** Listening to Music, Spending Time with Family and Friends, Reading, Singing, Going to the Theater, Staying Fit **FBP:** Nursing2009; Emergency Nursing Journal; CPI Journal **EDU:** Pursuing Master of Science in Nursing, Excelsior College; Associate of Applied Science Degree in Nursing, New York College of Health Professions **CERTS:** Certified Basic Life Support Instructor; Certified Advanced Cardiac Life Support Instructor; Certified Emergency Nurse **A/A/S:** American Heart Association **C/VW:** Nursing Home Ministry; Christian Ministry; Club-Cup of Joy; Children International; Cystic Fibrosis Worldwide; American Heart Association; Orlando Union Rescue Mission; St. Jude Children's Research Hospital **A/S:** She attributes her success to persistence. **B/I:** She chose the profession because she wanted to become a nurse since she was a child.

KAREN R. FLYNN
Mortgage Loan Officer
Coastway Credit Union
25 Lovell Avenue
Cranston, RI 02910 United States
kflynn@coastway.com
http://www.coastway.com

BUS: Commercial and Retail Financial Services **P/S:** Financial **MA:** National **D/D/R:** Accounting, Managing Finances and Projects **H/I/S:** Gardening and Skiing **FBP:** The Wall Street Journal **EDU:** Bachelor of Business Administration in Accounting, Providence College; Master of Business Administration, Bryant University; Certificate of Advanced General Studies **A/A/S:** Junior League of Rhode Island; North Kingston Chamber of Commerce **C/VW:** American Red Cross; Celebrate Rhode Island; American Heart Association; Arthritis Foundation; St. Mary's Home for Children **A/S:** She attributes her success to family support and dedication. **B/I:** She chose the profession because she wanted to assist people obtain their dream. **H/O:** The highlight of her career was becoming senior vice president of Fleet Bank, and mentoring people.

JANET E. H FOGH, MS
Middle School Principal
Vacaville Christian Schools
1117 Davis Street
Vacaville, CA 95687 United States
jfogh@go-vcs.com
http://www.go-vcs.com

BUS: Middle School **P/S:** Educational Services Including English, Mathematics, Reading, Science, Social Studies, Art, Music, History, Languages, Physical Education and Honors Courses **MA:** Regional **D/D/R:** Managing Operations and Administrative Duties, Mentoring, Supervising the Entire Middle School, Chairing the Mathematics Department, Teaching Sunday School, Serving on Accreditation Teams, Hiring, Developing and Orienting Staff Members **H/I/S:** Spending Time with her Family, Traveling, Swimming, Camping, Singing, Bible Study **FBP:** Comment **EDU:** Master of Science in Human Resources, Chapman University (1990); Bachelor of Arts in Computer Science, Baylor University (1986); Doctoral Degree in Business Administration, Argosy University **CERTS:** Certified Professor, State of California (1989); Certification in Administration and Teaching Grades K-12 **A/A/S:** Association of Christian Schools International; Western Association of Schools and Colleges **A/H:** Who's Who Among American Teachers (2005); Teacher of the Year Award, Reporter Campus Star, Vacaville (1998); Air Force Commendation Medal (1990) **C/VW:** Prayer Ministry **W/H:** Personnel Programs Officer, U.S. Air Force

MARTIN A. FOLCH
Realtor
Casa Pueblo Realty
1926 Main Street
Santa Ana, CA 92707 United States
folchmar@sbcglobal.net
http://www.cambridgewhoswho.com

BUS: Real Estate Agency **P/S:** Real Estate **MA:** Local **D/D/R:** Soliciting Clients Using Real Estate Knowledge and Customer Service Skills to Address Clients Needs **H/I/S:** Running with his Two Dogs, Kickboxing, Practicing Martial Arts, Spending Time with Friends **FBP:** Real Estate Publications **EDU:** Pursuing Degree, Santa Ana College **CERTS:** Licensed Realtor, State of California **A/A/S:** Pacific West Realtors **A/S:** He attributes his success to going above and beyond and always doing his best for his clients. **B/I:** He became involved in his profession because he took his real estate exams after moving to California.

JESÚS JUAN FONSECA, MD
MD, Owner
The Medicine Clinic
5419 N. Lovington Hwy., Suite 10
Hobbs, NM 88240 United States
kacike@aol.com
http://www.cambridgewhoswho.com

BUS: Internal Medicine Practice **P/S:** Consistent Excellent and Accessible Healthcare Services to Patients in Need of Care Such as Internal Medicine **MA:** Local **EXP:** Mr. Fonseca's expertise is in internal medicine. **D/D/R:** Seeing 30-40 Patients Per Day, Practicing Internal Medicine, Running All Administrative Responsibilities in Practice **H/I/S:** Running, Playing Tennis, Golfing **FBP:** New England Journal of Medicine **EDU:** MD, University of Central Caribbean (1992) **A/A/S:** FACGF; Board of Geriatric Specialists; Board of Hospital Physicians

LORNA M. FORBES, MD
MD
Lorna M. Forbes, MD
2055 N. Garey Street, Suite 6
Pomona, CA 91767 United States
lorna.forbes1@verizon.net
http://www.cambridgewhoswho.com

BUS: Psychiatry **P/S:** Medicines, Psychiatry, Forensic Consulting for the Courts **MA:** Statewide **D/D/R:** Specializing in Psychiatry **H/I/S:** Bonsai Plants, Needlepoint, Painting **FBP:** American Journal of Psychiatry **EDU:** MD in Psychiatry, Women's Medical College **A/A/S:** Los Angeles County Medical Association; Southern California Psychiatry Society; American Association of Psychiatry; American Psychiatric Association; ALA **SP:** Robert **CHILD:** Holley, Victor, Bradford **A/S:** She attributes her success to her hard work and competence. **B/I:** She became involved in the profession because she always wanted to work in the medical field. **H/O:** The most gratifying aspect of her career is working on important court cases where the courts defer to her expertise.

MARY FRANCES FORD
Compensation and Benefit Manager
KPSS, Inc.
981 Corporate Boulevard
Linthicum Heights, MD 21090 United States
mary.ford@kpss-hair.us
MaryFord28@Verizon.net.
http://www.goldwellusa.com

BUS: Manufacturers and Distributors of Superb Professional Hair Color and the Best Hair Care and Styling Products Available **P/S:** Providing Salons throughout the Country with Superior Product Innovations using State-of-the-Art Technology **MA:** Worldwide **D/D/R:** Performing all Duties Related to Payroll, Benefit, Compensation and Retirement Plans for over 200 Employees, Evaluating Employee Benefits, Ensuring that All Retirement and Compensation Packages are Aligned and Appropriate Following the Company's Merger **H/I/S:** Swimming, Kickboxing, Practicing Calligraphy, Stamp Collecting **FBP:** Economist **EDU:** Bachelor of Science in Environmental Science and Geography, Towson University (1997) **A/A/S:** Society for Human Resource Management

MILTORIA R. FORDHAM
Chief Executive Officer,
Partners for Self-Employment, Inc.
3000 Biscayne Boulevard
Suite 102
Miami, FL 33137 United States
toria@microbusinessusa.org
http://www.microbusinessusa.org

BUS: Nonprofit Organization **P/S:** Business and Financial Education, Microloans, Literacy Training, Managerial Skills **MA:** Local **D/D/R:** Writing Grants, Supporting Entrepreneurs **H/I/S:** Reading, Walking, Listening to Music, Ballet **FBP:** The Wall Street Journal; South Florida Business Journal **EDU:** Bachelor of Science in Health and Human Services, St. Thomas University, FL **A/H:** Future Education of America Award for Outstanding Community Service **C/VW:** Boy Scouts of America; St. Jude Children's Research Hospital; Community Action Agency **A/S:** She attributes her success to her ability to listen to others. **B/I:** She became involved in the profession because she progressed naturally into position after helping foster children in her home. **H/O:** The most gratifying aspect of her career is helping 43 individuals buy homes and six individuals start their own businesses.

GAIL LYNNE FOREMAN
Special Education Teacher
Booker High School, Sarasota
2207 51st Street W.
Bradenton, FL 34209 United States
gforce123@tampabay.rr.com
http://www.cambridgewhoswho.com

BUS: High School **P/S:** Secondary Education **MA:** Local **D/D/R:** Teaching Special Education to Ninth through 12th-Grade Students **H/I/S:** Camping, Traveling, Golfing, Softball, Mountain Biking **EDU:** Master's Degree in Special Education, Youngstown State University (2002) **A/A/S:** Council for Exceptional Children; Association for Supervision and Curriculum Development; Golden Key International Honour Society; Kappa Delta Pi; Pi Kappa Pi **C/VW:** Special Olympics; Big Brothers Big Sisters of America **A/S:** She attributes her success to her consistency. **B/I:** She became involved in her profession because of her desire to help people in need. **H/O:** The most gratifying aspect of her career is seeing her students succeed.

WALTER 'BUD' FORREST
Chief Executive Officer
Shores Sales & Management, Inc.
1200 Orange Avenue
Coronado, CA 92118 United States
bud@ilovecoronado.com
http://www.ilovecoronado.com

BUS: Real Estate Agency **P/S:** Real Estate Sales for Coronado and San Diego **MA:** Regional **D/D/R:** Offering Real Estate Sales and Property Management, Leasing and Renting Property **H/I/S:** Horseback Riding, Open Wheel Car Racing **FBP:** Fortune **EDU:** Bachelor of Arts in Marketing, University of California, Los Angeles **CERTS:** Certification, Graduate Realtor Institute; Accredited Buyer Representative **A/A/S:** Chamber of Commerce; President, Coronado Association of Realtors; National Association of Realtors **A/H:** Realtor of the Year, Coronado Association of Realtors (1997) **C/VW:** Coronado Rotary; March of Dimes Foundation **A/S:** He attributes his success to his perseverance and consistency. **B/I:** He became involved in this profession because of a recommendation from his mentor in San Marino. **H/O:** The most gratifying aspect of his career is the continued success of his company for 23 years.

BRENDA JOYCE FORTES
Adjunct Teacher
Boyertown Area School District
911 Montgomery Avenue
Boyertown, PA 19512 United States
bfortes@aol.com
http://basd.netjunction.com
http://www.mc3.edu

BUS: School District **P/S:** Education **MA:** Regional **D/D/R:** Teaching Literature, Writing, Organizing Drafted Reading Remediation Programs, Instructing Higher Education Writing Courses **H/I/S:** Caring for her Dog, Walking, Tricycling, Bread Baking, Reading **FBP:** NCTE Journal **EDU:** Master of Education, Plus 21, Eastern University (1998); Bachelor's Degree in English Literature, Eastern University (1972) **A/H:** Nominee, Disney's American Teacher Award (2002) **DOB:** August 27, 1949 **CHILD:** Lauren, Elita, Angela **W/H:** High School English Teacher, Boyertown Area School District; Adjunct English Faculty, Montgomery County Community College **A/S:** She attributes her success to her love for her profession and children.

RHEA FORUM, PH.D.
Educational and Family Consultant
Rhea Forum, Ph.D. Education and Family Consultant
5486 Collins Loop
Florence, OR 97439 United States
rforum@aol.com
http://www.cambridgewhoswho.com

Rhea Forum, Ph.D.
Educational & Family Consultant

5486 Collins Loop, Florence, OR 97439
(541) 902-1588   Fax (541) 902-7969
e-mail: rforum@aol.com

BUS: Psychological and Life Counseling Company **P/S:** Learning Styles Identification, Education, Life Coaching, Counseling **MA:** Statewide **D/D/R:** Teaching Talented and Gifted Children, Supporting Parents, Overseeing Placement for Children **H/I/S:** Reading, Teaching Sunday School, Providing Grief Counseling **FBP:** Bulletin of Psychological Type **EDU:** Master of Arts in Family Therapy, Northwest Christian College (1993); Ph.D. in Curriculum and Instruction, University of Oregon (1980); Bachelor of Arts in Education, Arizona State University (1964); Master of Education, University of Oregon **CERTS:** Certified Myers-Briggs Type Indicator; International Board Certified Christian Counselor **A/A/S:** Pi Lambda Theta; Association for Psychological Type International; American Counseling Association; American Association of Christian Counselors **A/H:** Who's Who Among American Teachers (1994, 1992) **C/VW:** Sunday School Teacher; Grief Counselor **DOB:** November 23, 1942 **POB:** Miami, AZ **SP:** Don **A/S:** She attributes her success to her education and experience, and her ability to work with gifted students and their families. **B/I:** She became involved in her profession because she enjoyed working with talented and special students. **H/O:** The most gratifying aspect of her career is having the ability to offer seminars for parents to modify their responses for their children's success.

LAURA 'LOU' A. FOSTER
Certified Practitioner
Herb Fancy
PO Box 872
Dahlgren, VA 22448 United States
herbfancy@yahoo.com
http://herbfancy.myshopify.com

BUS: Retailer **P/S:** Food and Drug Administration Approved Organic and Wildcrafted Herbs and Essential Oils, Herbs, Teas, Room Mists, Crystals, Reiki and Crystal Healing Sessions and Classes, Massages **MA:** International **D/D/R:** Handling Coordination, Organization and Administration, Offering Services as a Reiki Master and Teacher, Herbalist, Crystal Healer, Massage Practitioner and Ordained Minister **H/I/S:** Reading Science Fiction and Holistic Healing Books, Collecting Rocks, Practicing Shamanism **EDU:** Associate Degree in Business Administration **CERTS:** Certified Reiki Master; Certified Master Crystalogist **A/H:** International Who's Who (2001) **DOB:** May 18, 1961 **W/H:** Owner, Operator, Herb Fancy Gifts, LLC (2001-Present); Secretary, Naval Surface Warfare Center, Dahlgren Division (1998-Present) **A/S:** She attributes her success to her strong faith and spirit. **B/I:** She became involved in her profession because she was inspired by her grandmother and read books about herbs at a young age. **I/F/Y:** In five years, Ms. Foster plans to continue healing people using holistic practices.

MARY BETH FOSTER, MSN, APRN, BC
Nurse Practitioner
Gobinder S. Chopra M.D. & Associates
3201 S. Maryland Parkway
Las Vegas, NV 89109 United States
Lvfnp@cox.net
http://www.cambridgewhoswho.com

BUS: Medical Office **P/S:** Neurological Services **MA:** Regional **EXP:** Ms. Foster's expertise is in neurology. **H/I/S:** Traveling, Hiking, Reading and Writing **FBP:** American Nurse Practitioner Journal **EDU:** Master's Degree in Nursing, University of Nevada **A/A/S:** Sigma Theta Tau International; American Nursing Association; American Association of Nurse Practitioners **A/S:** She attributes her success to hard work and determination. **B/I:** She became involved in her profession from a long desire to be in the medical field. She decided to become a nurse rather than a doctor to allow herself more flexibility.

LISA KAY FOUNTAIN
Owner, Founder
At Your Service Limousine
1700 Buckner Street
Longview, TX 75604 United States
LKLimos@aol.com
http://www.cambridgewhoswho.com

BUS: Limousine Company **P/S:** Limousine Services **MA:** National **D/D/R:** Ensuring Customer Satisfaction, Offering Transportation for all Occasions, Managing Business Operations **H/I/S:** Traveling, Reading **EDU:** Coursework in American Sign Language, Kilgore College **C/VW:** Make-A-Wish Foundation **A/S:** She attributes her success to her positive attitude and charisma. **B/I:** She became involved in her profession because she originally worked as a driver for the company and took over the business when the owner sold it. **H/O:** The most gratifying aspects of her career are the facts that she has been able to be independent and run the business on her own.

JANET S. FOWLER
Kindergarten Teacher
Mountain View Elementary School
2600 Judson Bulloch Road
Manchester, GA 31816 United States
fowlerjs@yahoo.com
http://www.cambridgewhoswho.com

BUS: Elementary School **P/S:** Primary Education **MA:** Local **D/D/R:** Instructing in Reading, Computers, Art and Music, Teaching Learning Focus Strategies, Discussing the Reading Program with Teachers, Overseeing the Supply of Lunch, Storytelling, Providing the Georgia Performance Standards to Teach Full-Day Academic Kindergarten **H/I/S:** Spending Time with her Grandchild and Family, Gardening **FBP:** Instructor Magazine **EDU:** Master of Education in Early Childhood Education, Columbus State University; Bachelor of Science in Elementary Education, Columbus State University **A/A/S:** Delta Kappa Gamma **A/H:** Teacher of the Year Award (2005-2006) **A/S:** She attributes her success to her love for working with children. **B/I:** She became involved in her profession because she was always interested in teaching. **H/O:** The most gratifying aspect of her career is having a positive effect on the lives of her students.

MELISSA G. FOWLER
Registered Dental Hygienist
Dr. Perry M. Whites, DMD, Dr. Adam W. Hodges, DMD
702 Highway 82 W.
Suite A
Greenwood, MS 38930 United States
mgm_18_99@yahoo.com
http://www.cambridgewhoswho.com

BUS: General Dentistry **P/S:** General Dentistry **MA:** Local **EXP:** Ms. Fowler's expertise is in prophylaxis. **H/I/S:** Working Out, Watching Movies **FBP:** Dimensions **EDU:** Associate Degree in Liberal Arts, Holmes Community College; Associate Degree in Dental Hygiene, Mississippi Delta Community College **A/A/S:** American Dental Hygienists' Association **A/S:** She attributes her success to improving the lives of her patients. **B/I:** She became involved in the profession because she was always interested in dentistry. **H/O:** The highlight of her career is meeting so many people.

JUDY FOX JACKSON
Educator
Franklin Special School District
510 New Highway 96 W.
Franklin, TN 37064 United States
jfoxj@webtv.net
http://www.fssd.org

BUS: School District **P/S:** Education **MA:** Regional **EXP:** Ms. Jackson's expertise includes teacher mentorship and workshop presentation. **D/D/R:** Developing Curriculum, Evaluating Classroom Assessments, Teaching All Subjects to First-Grade Students **H/I/S:** Traveling, Meeting People, Walking, Reading **FBP:** Delta Kappa Gamma Bulletin; Educational Leadership **EDU:** Master's Degree, Plus 30, Middle Tennessee State University (1999); Master's Degree in Curriculum and Instruction, Middle Tennessee State University (1976); Bachelor's Degree in Elementary Education, Middle Tennessee State University (1971) **A/A/S:** Director, Delegate, Forum Chairman Area VI, Xi State, Delta Kappa Gamma Society International (2007-Present); International Who's Who of Professional Educators (2000); Co-Chairwoman, Annual State Legislature Educational Forum; Franklin Special School District Education Association; National Education Association; **A/H:** Who's Who Among America's Teachers (2000); Teacher of the Year Award, Franklin Special School District **DOB:** August 8, 1949 **SP:** Donald **CHILD:** Eric **W/H:** Workshop Presenter, Demonstration Teacher, Facilitator, Franklin Special School District **A/S:** She attributes her success to the support she receives from her family and colleagues. **B/I:** She became involved in her profession because of her interest in the education field. **H/O:** The most gratifying aspects of her career are having the ability to develop non-readers into fluent readers and teaching first-grade students.

CAROL FRANCES, PH.D.
Professor
Seton Hall University
400 S. Orange Avenue
South Orange, NJ 07079 United States
franceca@shu.edu
http://www.shu.edu

BUS: University **P/S:** Education Including Undergraduate, Master's Degree, Doctoral, Dual Degree Programs **MA:** New Jersey **EXP:** Ms. Frances' expertise is in economics, finance, information technology and class preparation. **H/I/S:** Volleyball, Traveling **EDU:** Ph.D. in Economics and Finance, Duke University; Master of Science in International Relations, Yale University; Bachelor of Arts in International Relations, University of California, Los Angeles **A/A/S:** Former Chief Economist, American Council on Education; Association for the Study of Higher Education; Congress of Political Economists International; The European Higher Education Association; American Association of University Women; International Federation of University Women

VALERIE L. FRANCIS
Senior Training Consultant
Rockhurst University Continuing Education Center, Inc.
6901 W. 63rd Street
Shawnee Mission, KS 66202 United States
vfrancis55061@everestkc.net
http://www.nationalseminarstraining.com

BUS: University, Continuing Education Center **P/S:** Higher Education Including Corporate Training Services, Training Seminars and other Education Services **MA:** National **D/D/R:** Corporate Training, Consulting with Businesses to Improve Quality, Managing Employees **H/I/S:** Reading, Watching Movies, Lively Discussions **FBP:** Training Magazine **EDU:** Bachelor's Degree in Radio, TV and Film, University of Missouri (1988) **A/A/S:** Association and Society for Training Development; Association of Administrative Professionals; International Customer Service Association

DIANA E. FRANCOIS
Director of Logistics Center of Excellence
Whitney, Bradley and Brown, Inc.
1604 Spring Hill Road
Vienna, VA 22182 United States
dfrancois@wbbinc.com
http://www.wbbinc.com

BUS: Defense Organization **P/S:** Defense Consulting **MA:** International **D/D/R:** Hosting Consultations on Logistic Related Matters Regarding Military, Commercial, Federal Government and Industrial Defense **H/I/S:** Traveling **EDU:** Pursuing Master of Business Administration in Supply Chain Management, Strayer University; Bachelor of Engineering Sciences, United States Air Force Academy (1980) **A/A/S:** Logistics Officers Association; Association of Graduate Air Force Academy; National Defense Industrial Association; Women in Defense; Association of The United States Army; National Defense Transportation Association; Air Force Association **C/VW:** Veteran's Activities **A/S:** She attributes her success to her hard work, self discipline and the support she receives from her co-workers and family. **B/I:** She became involved in her profession after spending time in the military working in logistics and aircraft maintenance. After she completed her duties, she was still interested in the field. **H/O:** The highlight if her career was earning her current position. She is among one of six women out of a company of 150 workers.

HEIDI FRANKLIN
Cardiac Registered Nurse
Blanchard Valley Medical Associates
200 W. Pearl Street
Findlay, OH 45840 United States
heidifranklin@sbcglobal.net
http://www.cambridgewhoswho.com

BUS: Healthcare **P/S:** Healthcare **MA:** Local **H/I/S:** Scrapbooking, Reading, Spending Time with her Kids **FBP:** Journal of Medicine **EDU:** Associate of Science in Cardiology, Owens Technical College **CERTS:** Certified in Advanced Cardiac Life Support **A/H:** Biltmore Who's Who **C/VW:** St. Jude Children's Research Hospital **B/I:** She became involved in this profession because she always wanted to be a nurse. **H/O:** The highlight of her career is the respect she has gained from her peers.

RUTH JOHNSTON FRANKS, RN, BS
Registered Nurse Consultant
Indiana Emergency Medical Services
2816 W. Sample Street
South Bend, IN 46619 United States
ruthfranks@comcast.net
http://www.cambridgewhoswho.com

BUS: Healthcare Transportation **P/S:** Ambulance Transportation **MA:** National **EXP:** Ms. Franks' expertise is in nurse consultancy and healthcare coordination. **H/I/S:** Natural Gardening, Reading, Walking, Spending Time with her Grandchildren **EDU:** Bachelor's Degree in Administration, Siena Heights University, Adrian, MI; Associate Degree in Nursing, Siena Heights University **A/A/S:** Michigan Executive Director of Nursing, Indiana Healthcare Association; Healthcare Centennial Case Mix Consultant of the Year Award **C/VW:** Compassion International; Local Church; In Touch; World Vision; Church Student Ministry **A/S:** She attributes her success to her fortitude and her desire to continue to serve the community. **B/I:** After working as a nurse she made a natural progression into her current position. **H/O:** The highlight of her career is when others tell her she has helped them to go onto a career they enjoy.

DR. MICHAEL A. FRASCA
Chiropractic Physician
Integrated Health, Inc
953 Niles-Cortland Road S.E.
Warren, OH 44484 United States

BUS: Integrated Health Practice **P/S:** Healthcare, Chiropractics **MA:** Local **EXP:** Dr. Frasca's expertise is in Sports medicine and chiropractic care. **H/I/S:** Football, Collecting Baseball Memorabilia **EDU:** Coursework, Life Chiropractic Institute, DC **A/A/S:** Ohio State Chiropractic Association; American Chiropractic Association

WENDY FRAZER
Physician Assistant
Vascular Surgery
Beth Israel Deaconess Medical Center
750 Farm Road, Apartment 109
Marlboro, MA 01752 United States
frazerwendy@earthlink.net
http://www.bidmc.harvard.edu

BUS: Medical Center **P/S:** Emergency Care, Oncology, Cardiology, Psychological Care, Reconstructive Surgery, Diagnostic Testing, Healthcare Education **MA:** Regional **D/D/R:** Assisting with Vascular Surgery, Discharging Patients, Offering Clinical Care **H/I/S:** Massage Therapy **EDU:** Associate Degree in Physician Assistant Studies, Cuyahoga Community College, Cleveland, OH (1983)

LEIF FREDIN, PH.D.
President, Chief Executive Officer,
Chief Technology Officer
TLMI Corporation
2111 W. Braker Lane, Suite 500
Austin, TX 78758 United States
lfredin@tlmicorp.com
http://www.tlmicorp.com

TLmi corporation

BUS: World-Class Leader in Wafer Bumping and Flip Chip Interconnect Technology **P/S:** Specialty Services, Interconnects, Semiconductors, Solder and Gold, Copper, Indium and Pad Redistribution, Mask Design, Backgrinding, Dicing, Pick and Place, Custom Services, Chemistry, Physics, Process Engineering **MA:** International **EXP:** Mr. Fredin's expertise is in chemistry and physics. **H/I/S:** Sailing, Photography **FBP:** Investor's Business Daily **EDU:** Ph.D., Lund University, Sweden (1974) **A/A/S:** American Chemical Society; Materials Research Society; Institute of Electrical and Electronics Engineers; Society of Photo-Optical Instrumentation Engineers; IMAPS; Sigma Xi; ASM **DOB:** October 23, 1945 **SP:** Jan **W/H:** TLMI Group (2002-Present); Radiant Photomos (2000-2002); Systems and Process Engineering (1996-2000); SI Diamond (1992-1996) **C/A:** Author, 75 Published Reports; Author, One Book; Patent Holder, Nine United States Patents

ANGELICA A. FREELING, PHR
Recruitment Coordinator
Center for Family Services
584 Benson St.
Camden, NJ 08103 United States
angelica_freeling@hotmail.com
http://www.cambridgewhoswho.com

BUS: Nonprofit **P/S:** Social and Human Service **MA:** Local **EXP:** Ms. Freeling's expertise is in human resources. **H/I/S:** Reading **FBP:** The New York Times **EDU:** Bachelor's Degree, Management and Human Resources, The Pennsylvania State University **CERTS:** Certified Professional in Human Resources, Human Resource Certification Institute **A/A/S:** Society for Human Resource Management; National Organization for Women **C/VW:** Planned Parenthood; American Civil Liberties Union; United Way of America **A/S:** She attributes her success to her drive and motivation to help people. **B/I:** She became involved in this profession because she was drawn to the nonprofit sector and she is business minded. **H/O:** The highlight of her career is running the human resources department at the previous company and also passed professional Human Resource Certificate.

GAIL L. FREEMAN, RN
Registered Nurse
Memorial Hospital
1400 E. Boulder
Colorado Springs, CO 81009 United States
gail132@juno.com
http://www.memorialhealthsystem.com

BUS: World-Class Hospital System **P/S:** Birthing Center, Blood Bank, Cancer Center, Cardiac Care, Classes and Events, Memorial Hospital for Children, Disease Management, Emergency and Trauma, Laboratory, Orthopedics, Pediatric Care, Radiology, Rehabilitation and Surgery **MA:** Regional **D/D/R:** Nursing in the Cardiac Unit, Psychiatric Nursing, Caring for Geriatric Patients, Specializing in the Neonatal Intensive Care Unit Level III, Reviewing Charts, Conducting Peer Review Evaluations, Working with Premature Babies and Sick Infants **H/I/S:** Owning Horses, Goats, Dogs, Cats, Spending Time with Grandchildren, Involved in 4-H Club with Granddaughter **FBP:** Neonatal Network **EDU:** Associate of Science in Registered Nursing, Moraine Valley Community College (1986) **A/A/S:** Academy of Neonatal Nurses; National Association of Neonatal Nurses; Phi Theta Kappa **DOB:** April 17, 1953 **CHILD:** John, Christine **W/H:** Level III Nurse, Memorial Health Systems Children's Hospital, Colorado Springs, CO (2002-Present); Registered Nurse, Colorado Mental Health Institute of Pueblo, Pueblo, CO (2000-2002); Registered Nurse, St. Thomas More Hospital, Canon City, CO (1996-2000); Registered Nurse, St. Joseph Manor (1996-2000); Registered Nurse, Home Health Nursing Home (1996-2000); Registered Nurse, Kremmling Hospital, Kremmling, CO (1993-1996); Level III Nurse, St. Joseph Hospital, Denver, CO (1988-1993); Registered Nurse, Denver Presbyterian Hospital (1986-1988)

PATRICIA A. FREHNER
Professor
1) The Art Institute of Phoenix 2) Ottawa University
3733 N. 75th Avenue
Phoenix, AZ 85033 United States
trifree@earthlink.net
http://www.cambridgewhoswho.com

BUS: 1) Educational Institution 2) University **P/S:** 1) Education on Graphic, Interior and Web design 2) Higher Education **MA:** 1) National 2) National **D/D/R:** Teaching Art History, English and Arts **H/I/S:** Traveling **FBP:** Educational Leadership **EDU:** Ph.D. in Education and Leadership Studies, Capella University **A/A/S:** Association for Supervision and Curriculum Development; National Middle School Association **A/S:** She attributes her success to her desire for learning. **B/I:** She became involved in her profession because she always had an interest in teaching. **H/O:** The most gratifying aspect of her career is watching her students succeed.

JANET M. FRENCH, BS
Teacher
South View Middle School
4100 Elk Road
Hope Mills, NC 28348 United States
janetfrench@ccs.k12.nc.us
http://www.cambridgewhoswho.com

BUS: Public Middle School **P/S:** Education **MA:** Local **D/D/R:** Teaching Mathematics to Middle School Students **H/I/S:** Reading, Playing Piano, Cross-Stitching, Spending Time with Family **EDU:** Bachelor of Science in Elementary Education, Bowling Green State University **CERTS:** Licensed in Elementary Education (K-6); Certified in Mathematics (6-9) **A/A/S:** National Council of Teachers of Mathematics **C/VW:** Local Church **A/S:** She attributes her success to her faith, continued education and her mother. **B/I:** She became involved in the profession because she wanted to teach since she was a child. **H/O:** The most gratifying aspect of her career is being able to have a career and spend time with her children.

MICHAEL M. FRIEDMAN, DDS
Dentist
North Ocean Dental, P.C.
99 N. Ocean Avenue
Patchogue, NY 11772 United States
skip30py@aol.com
http://www.drmichaelfriedman.com

BUS: Dental Clinic **P/S:** Cosmetic and General Dentistry Services, Dental Healthcare **MA:** Local **EXP:** Mr. Friedman's expertise is in cosmetic dentistry, oral healthcare consultancy and oral health maintenance education. **H/I/S:** Practicing Karate, Woodworking **FBP:** Inside Dentistry; Dentistry Today **EDU:** Doctor of Dental Surgery, New York University College of Dentistry (1975) **A/A/S:** Director of Admissions, American Society for Dental Aesthetics; American Board of Family Dentistry; Fellow, American College of Dentists; Fellow, International College of Dentists; Fellow, Academy of General Dentistry

MIRTA ROMERO FRIMTZIS, PSY.D.
Educational Psychologist
Desert Counseling and Assessment Center
41750 Rancho Las Palmas Drive
Suite L16
Rancho Mirage, CA 92270 United States
drmiaf@aol.com
http://www.desertcounseling.org

BUS: Psychologist Assessment, Diagnostic and Counseling Center **P/S:** Psychology Testing, Counseling Academic Testing, Full Range Therapy Services **MA:** Local **EXP:** Ms. Frimtzis' expertise is in biofeedback and neurofeedback. **H/I/S:** Reading, Biking, School Psychology, Photography **FBP:** Journal of Marital and Family Therapy **EDU:** Master's Degree in Counseling; Master's Degree in Educational Psychology; Master's Degree in Marriage and Family Counseling, Chapman University; Bachelor of Arts in Psychology and Interdisciplinary Studies, California State University, Long Beach **A/A/S:** California Association of Marriage and Family Therapists; California Association of School Psychologists; National Association of School Psychologists; American Association for Marriage and Family Therapy **A/S:** She attributes her success to her dedication and compassion. **B/I:** She became involved in her profession because she always wanted to help people. **H/O:** The highlight of her career was opening the counseling center.

MOLLY M. FRITZ
General Manager
Marche
898 Santa Cruz Avenue
Menlo Park, CA 94025 United States
molly@restaurantmarche.com
http://www.restaurantmarche.com

BUS: Restaurant **P/S:** Fine Dining **MA:** Local **EXP:** Ms. Fritz's expertise is in restaurant management and name recollection. **H/I/S:** Reading, Cooking **EDU:** Associate of Arts Degree **C/VW:** American Cancer Society, ASPCA **A/S:** She attributes her career success to her ability to recall names. **B/I:** She became involved in restaurant management because she loves working with food and wine. **H/O:** The highlight of her career was earning the position of general manager.

PATRICIA A. FRYE
English Department Chairwoman,
Foreign Language Department Chairwoman
Plymouth Christian Academy
43065 Joy Road
Canton, MI 48187 United States
fryep@plymouthchristian.org
http://www.cambridgewhoswho.com

BUS: College Preparatory School **P/S:** Education **MA:** Local **D/D/R:** Mentoring New Teachers and Students **H/I/S:** Traveling, Reading **FBP:** BusinessWeek; The Wall Street Journal **EDU:** Bachelor of Arts in English and Speech, Eastern Michigan University; Reading Endorsement, Eastern Michigan University **C/VW:** Community Outreach, Local Church **A/S:** She attributes her success to her genuine compassion and concern. **B/I:** She became involved in her profession because she always wanted to be a teacher. **H/O:** The highlight of her career was guiding several Canadian students, helping them improve their grades and succeed in school.

JUDITH A. FULLER
Graphic Designer
Valley Christian Schools
100 Skyway Drive, Suite 130
San Jose, CA 95111 United States
jfuller@vcs.net
http://www.vcs.net

BUS: School District **P/S:** Education **MA:** Regional **EXP:** Ms. Fuller's expertise is in graphic design, sewing and quilting. **D/D/R:** Designing for School Advertisements **H/I/S:** Quilting, Knitting, Crocheting **FBP:** .Journal of Graphic Design **EDU:** Bachelor of Arts in Visual Communication, American InterContinental University; Associate of Arts in Business, Concentration in Accounting, West Valley College **CERTS:** Certification in Desktop Publishing and Design **A/H:** Woman of the Year Award, American Biological Women's Advisory Board **C/VW:** Hillside Evangelical Free Church **DOB:** May 20, 1959 **POB:** Redwood City **CHILD:** Robert, Joshua, Sarah **W/H:** Administrative Assistant, Calvary Church; Teacher, Valley Christian Schools; Seamstress, The Dance Store **A/S:** She attributes her success to her perseverance and her desire to learn. **B/I:** She became involved in her profession because she was always interested in graphic design.

RAEANN M. FULLER, RN, CCRN
Nurse Manager
Intensive Care Unit
Condell Medical Center
801 S. Milwaukee Avenue
Libertyville, IL 60048 United States
rfuller@condell.org
http://www.condell.org

BUS: Medical Center **P/S:** General, Heart and Brain Surgery, Cancer Care, Childbirth Facilities, Radiology, Women's Health, Magnetic Resonance Imaging and Positron Emission Tomography Scans, Physical Therapy, Chemotherapy **MA:** Local **D/D/R:** Overseeing 25 Bed Intensive Care Units, Offering Critical-Care Including Medical, Surgical and Cardiothoracic Nursing, Managing Stress, Precepting Nurses **H/I/S:** Cross Stitching, Spending Time with her Daughter **CERTS:** Board Certification in Critical Care, American Association of Critical Care Nurses (1981); Registered Nurse, School of Nursing, Michael Reese Medical Center (1977) **A/A/S:** American Association of Critical Care Nurses; American Heart Association **C/VW:** International Critical Incidence Stress Foundation **SP:** James **CHILD:** Courtney Alyse

JOYCE ANN FUNK
Accountant, President
Funktional Bookkeeping & Payroll, Inc.
1409 Potter Drive, Suite 201
Colorado Springs, CO 80909 United States
fbooks@qwest.net
http://www.cambridgewhoswho.vom

BUS: Accounting **P/S:** Accounting and Payroll Services **MA:** Local **D/D/R:** Financial Reporting **H/I/S:** Hunting, Fishing, Hiking, Driving All-Terrain Vehicles, Enjoying Outdoor Activities **FBP:** Various Government Publications **EDU:** Coursework in Accounting, Pikes Peak Community College **C/VW:** Choir, Deacon, Local Church **A/S:** She attributes her success to her attention to detail and honesty. **B/I:** She chose the profession because she enjoys the industry. **H/O:** The highlight of her career is having her own company.

LAURIE A. FURST
Art Teacher
Shelby High School
541 N. State Street
Shelby, MI 49455 United States
lalee@alldial.net
http://hs.shelby.k12.mi.us

BUS: High School **P/S:** Education for Students in Ninth through Twelfth Grade **MA:** Local **D/D/R:** Teaching Painting **H/I/S:** Reading, Traveling, Painting, Creating Art **EDU:** Master's Degree in Reading, Grand Valley State University **A/A/S:** National Art Education Association; Lakeshore Artists Association **C/VW:** National Wildlife Federation; Friend, Local Library

MARY GABBERT-ALLBRIGHT
Chief Executive Officer, Owner
Higher Ground Financial Services, Inc.
1270 N. Wickham Road
Suite 16 PMB 503
Melbourne, FL 32935 United States
highergroundfinsvc@cfl.rr.com
http://www.cambridgewhoswho.com

BUS: Finance Company **P/S:** Financial and Mortgage Services **MA:** National **EXP:** Ms. Gabbert-Allbright's expertise is in commercial mortgages and credit restructuring. **D/D/R:** Conducting Financial Seminars, Developing Leadership and Entrepreneurship Skills, Consulting Nationally, Training on Commercial Brokerage for Residential Brokers **H/I/S:** Sewing, Painting **FBP:** Entrepreneur; Trump World **EDU:** Coursework in Education, Montgomery County Community College **CERTS:** Licensed Mortgage Broker; Microsoft Certified Professional, Fashion Institute of Technology **A/A/S:** eWomenNetwork; Cocoa Beach Area Chamber of Commerce; North American Mission Board; Chief Executive Officer, IBI Global **C/VW:** Volunteer, Local Budgeting Workshops **I/F/Y:** In five years, Ms. Gabbert-allbright hopes to move into the commercial sector.

L. SUE GABRIEL
Assistant Professor
BryanLGH College of Health Sciences, School of Nursing
5035 Everett Street
Lincoln, NE 68506 United States
sue.gabriel@bryanlgh.org
http://www.bryanlgh.org

BUS: Comprehensive Continuum of Patient-Centered Care in Cooperation with Other Healthcare Providers **P/S:** Education to Healthcare Professionals, Promoting Wellness, Quality Healthcare Services for those in Need **MA:** National **D/D/R:** Educating Students as an Assistant Professor of Pediatrics, Family, Community Health and Forensic Nursing, Reviewing Textbooks **FBP:** Forensic Nursing Journal **EDU:** Pursuing Doctoral Degree; Master of Science in Nursing, Nebraska Wesleyan University (2005); Master of Forensic Science, Nebraska Wesleyan University (2003); Bachelor of Science in Nursing, University of Nebraska Medical Center (1971) **CERTS:** Certified Sexual Assault Nurse Examiner (2004); Certification in Forensic Science, Southeast Community College (1999) **A/A/S:** National League of Nursing; Sigma Theta Tau International; American College of Forensic Examiners; International Association of Forensic Nurses; American Academy of Forensic Science

LISA BACH GAGER
President
All Sports Childcare
4213 N. Pine Island Road
Sunrise, FL 33351 United States
allsportskids@aol.com
http://www.cambridgewhoswho.com

BUS: Childcare **P/S:** After School and Summer Camp Competitive Sports and Activities **MA:** Local **EXP:** Ms. Gager's expertise is in gymnastics, cheerleading and dance. **H/I/S:** Cheerleading, Dancing **EDU:** Bachelor of Science in Physical Education, Ithaca College **A/A/S:** Chamber of Commerce **C/VW:** Hunter's Hope; Ronald McDonald House; American Cancer Society **A/S:** She attributes her success to a love for what she does. **B/I:** She became involved in this profession because she has a background in health and fitness and saw a need for kids in her area to increase their physical activity. **H/O:** The highlight of her career is the success she has with the kids and her opportunity to assist them to preserve.

DIANE M. GAHAGEN
Registered Nurse, Owner, Consultant
Rock Mountain Medical Review
2816 W. 115th Circle
Westminster, CO 80234 United States
dmgahagen@comcast.net
http://www.cambridgewhoswho.com

BUS: Hospital Facility Dedicated to Excellence in Healthcare **P/S:** Small Business Auditing to Ensure Accurate Billing, Insurance and Case Reviews **MA:** Regional **D/D/R:** Treating Post-Heart Surgery Patients, Handling Human Resources for Nurses, Ensuring Staff is Up-to-Date with Policies, Assisting Staff with Equipment **H/I/S:** Golfing, Scrapbooking **EDU:** Diploma in Nursing, College of St. Mary's (1976)

JUNE DUCKER GAINES
Special Education Teacher and Inspiration (Retired)
Chester Upland School District
112 Jennifer Way
Marcus Hook, PA 19061 United States
buns53@hotmail.com
http://www.cambridgewhoswho.com

BUS: School District **P/S:** Education and Inspiration **MA:** National **EXP:** Ms. Gaines' expertise is in special education. **D/D/R:** Overseeing Summer Camps, Tutoring, Working and Supplying Materials for Students throughout the School Year, Organizing Parent Meetings **H/I/S:** Listening to Jazz Music, Attending Jazz Events, Traveling, Attending Educational Workshops **EDU:** Master's Degree in Special Education and Elementary Education, Beaver College (Now Arcadia University) (1979); Bachelor of Arts in Education, Benedict College (1974) **A/H:** Teacher Under the Sun, Sun East (2007); Teacher of the Year, Wal-Mart **C/VW:** Sunday School Teacher, Shiloh Baptist Church; Scholarship Committee **DOB:** September 1, 1951 **POB:** Louisville **SP:** Robert **CHILD:** Joel, Jerrold **W/H:** Teacher in Elementary Education; Teacher in Special Education; Director, Pre-School Program, Chester Eastside Ministries; Director, Summer Camp, Chester Eastside Ministries; Director, After-School Program, Chester Eastside Ministries **A/S:** She attributes her success to her desire to help the youth and her faith in God. **B/I:** She became involved in her profession because she was inspired by her mother, who was a teacher and social worker, and her interest in the education field. **H/O:** The highlights of her career were being recognized as the Teacher of the Year by Wal-Mart and receiving the President's Award from the National Association for the Advancement of Colored People in 2006.

FLORDELIZA PIA TORIO GALAPON
Realtor
Prudential Americana Group, Realtors
8337 W. Sunset Road
Suite 150
Las Vegas, NV 89113 United States
pialasvegas@cox.net
http://www.cambridgewhoswho.com

BUS: Real Estate Agency **P/S:** Commercial and Residential Real Estate Exchange **MA:** National **EXP:** Ms. Galapon's expertise is in land, residential, commercial and investment property sales. **D/D/R:** Marketing, Relocating Properties **H/I/S:** Writing, Traveling, Dancing **FBP:** Filipino Newspapers; Industry-Related Publications **EDU:** Bachelor of Science in Psychology, Saint Joseph's University **A/A/S:** Filipino American Society **A/H:** Presidential Service Award; Teacher of the Year Award **C/VW:** Filipino American Charities **A/S:** She attributes her success to her honesty. **B/I:** She became involved in her profession because of her interest to make home buying, a pleasant experience for her clients. **H/O:** The highlights of her career were receiving the teacher of the year award and the presidential service award for her volunteering services.

CARLOS GALINDO
Quality Assurance / Quality Control Program Manager
Environmental Quality Laboratories
1399 Feria Street Stop 20 Santurce
San Juan, PR 00910 United States
cgalindo@eglab.com
http://www.cambridgewhoswho.com

BUS: Environmental Agency **P/S:** Inorganic, Metal and Organic Analysis of Drinking Water, Domestic and Industrial Wastes **MA:** Statewide **D/D/R:** Ensuring and Controlling Quality **H/I/S:** Reading, Going to the Movies **FBP:** Today's Chemists **EDU:** Bachelor of Science in Chemistry, Bayamon Central University **A/A/S:** Colegio de Quimicos de Puerto Rico **C/VW:** Drug Addiction and AIDS-Related Charities; Puerto Rico Chemistry College

MARIA ANGELINA GALLO
Educator
Oceanside Unified School District
2111 E. Mission Avenue
Oceanside, CA 92054 United States
mgallo4@cox.net
http://www.cambridgewhoswho.com

BUS: Educational Facility **P/S:** Education **MA:** Local **D/D/R:** Teaching Computer Education and Languages **H/I/S:** Traveling, Photography, Scrapbooking, Reading, Working on her Computer, Cooking **FBP:** Instructor; National Geographic Traveler; The Week **EDU:** Master's Degree in Computers and Education, National University **A/A/S:** Kappa Delta Pi; National Education Association **C/VW:** Habitat for Humanity **A/S:** She attributes her career success to her hard work, determination and efforts to be the best she can be. **B/I:** She became involved in her profession after being inspired by her third grade teacher and mentor.

ELIZABETH GALLUP, MD, JD, MBA
President
Heart with Hands Elder Care
236 Arapaho Circle E.
Lake Quivira, KS 66217 United States
emgallupmd@aol.com
http://cambridgewhoswho.com

BUS: Medical Group **P/S:** Working in Conjunction with Local Doctors and Church Pastors, to Identify Communities and Areas where Medical Needs are Unmet **MA:** National **D/D/R:** Overseeing the Physicians Group Care in Nursing Facilities, Building Physicians' Organization, Managing a Hospital at a Senior Vice President Level, Directing and Managing Pharmaceutical Research **H/I/S:** Bird Watching, Exercising, Looking at the Lake, Playing Catch with her Three Dogs, Leo, Beamer and Lulu **FBP:** The American Academy of Family Physicians Journal **EDU:** Master of Business Administration, University of South Florida (1998); JD, The University of Toledo College of Law (1986); MD, Ohio State University (1981) **DOB:** October 9, 1956 **SP:** Col. Wilson **W/H:** Medical Director, Transworld Airlines; New Century Health; Liberty Mutual Insurance; Senior Vice President, Shawnee Mission Medical Center; Senior Consultant, William M. Mercer; Assistant General Counsel, American Academy of Family Physicians

ROBERTO H. GALVÁN
Occupational Safety and Health Officer III
Gila River Indian Community
PO Box 147
Sacaton, AZ 85247 United States
robert.galvan@gric.nsn.us
http://www.gric.nsn.us.com

BUS: Nonprofit Organization **P/S:** Resources for many Shared Social Needs, Recreational Activities, Cultural Projects, Services and Protection **MA:** Regional **EXP:** Mr. Galván's expertise is in federal safety inspections. **D/D/R:** Training in Occupational Safety, Instructing on Research and Development, Inspecting Compliance Safety for Businesses on Tribal Land, Consulting for Businesses in the Development of Safety Programs **H/I/S:** Weight Lifting, Traveling, Dancing **EDU:** Bachelor's Degree in Business Administration, West Texas A&M University, Canyon, TX (1984) **CERTS:** Certification in Construction and Industry Compliance, Occupational Safety and Health Administration; Certification in Hazardous Waste Identification and Disposal **A/H:** Recognition Award, City of Phoenix (2004); Excellence in Safety Award, Burlington Northern Santa Fe Railway (1997) **DOB:** July 14, 1960 **W/H:** Data Entry Specialist, ASARCO Copper Refinery; Car Inspector, Burlington Northern Santa Fe Railway; Safety Analyst, City of Phoenix

PATRICIA GAMBINO
Relocation Specialist
Coldwell Banker Residential
1070 Old Country Road
Plainview, NY 11803 United States
patricia.gambino@cbmoves.com
http://www.cambridgewhoswho.com

BUS: Residential Real Estate **P/S:** All Facets of Real Estate Services, Including Relocation, Sales, Investment Properties, Mortgage Assistance **MA:** Nassau and Suffolk Counties **D/D/R:** Real Estate with a Specialty in Relocation, Providing Service Above and Beyond the Expectations of Home Buyers and Sellers with an Emphasis on Enhancing the Entire Real Estate Experience, Market Analysis, Bilingual in Italian and English **H/I/S:** Traveling, Walking, Reading People Magazine, Enjoying her Eight Children **FBP:** Realtor; Reader's Digest **EDU:** Coursework in Real Estate **A/A/S:** President's Circle; National Association of Realtors

EDGAR J. GANNAWAY
Senior Pastor
Temple Baptist Church
PO Box 327
Dermott, AR 71638 United States
http://www.cambridgewhoswho.com

BUS: Church **P/S:** Worship **MA:** Local **EXP:** Mr. Gannaway's expertise is in worship. **H/I/S:** Gardening, Hunting, Fishing **FBP:** The Bible **EDU:** Bachelor of Arts Degree, Ouachita University **A/S:** He attributes his personal and professional success to his obedience and education. **B/I:** She has always had an interest in the field and feels it was her calling to become involved. **H/O:** The highlight of her career is reaching others.

DOUGLAS GANTT
Instructor
Hampton University
253 Town Center Drive
Virginia Beach, VA 23462 United States
dgtoon@hotmail.com
http://www.hamptonu.edu

BUS: University **P/S:** Higher Education **MA:** National **D/D/R:** Teaching Multidisciplinary Science **H/I/S:** Cartooning **FBP:** Wizard Magazine **EDU:** Master's Degree in Biology, Hampton University; Bachelor of Science in Marine Science, Hampton University **A/A/S:** American Society of Limnology and Oceanography **A/S:** He attributes his success to his hard work, determination and persistence. **B/I:** He became involved in his profession because he was inspired by his professors. **H/O:** The highlight of his career was obtaining his master's degree.

FRANK GARBER JR., RN, BSN, CEN
Registered Nurse, Teacher, APRN Student
Lafayette General Medical Center, University of Louisiana
1214 Coolidge Street
Lafayette, LA 70503 United States
frankgarber667@cs.com
http://www.cambridgewhoswho.com

BUS: Medical Center **P/S:** Healthcare, Education **MA:** Regional **D/D/R:** Nursing, Emergency Nursing **H/I/S:** Running, Boating **FBP:** American Journal of Nursing; Journal of Emergency Nursing; The Nurse Practitioner **EDU:** Pursuing Master's Degree in Adult Health Nurse Practitioner, McNeese State University; Bachelor's Degree in Nursing, University of Southwest Louisiana; Bachelor's Degree in Zoology, University of Southwest Louisiana **CERTS:** Certified Emergency Room Nurse **A/A/S:** Emergency Nurses Association; Louisiana Association of Nurse Practitioners **A/S:** He attributes his success to his constant desire to improve. **B/I:** He became involved in his profession because he wanted to help people. **H/O:** The most gratifying aspect of his career is being able to teach other nurses.

Susan Young Garces
Director of Nursing Services
Chaparral House
1309 Allston Way
Berkeley, CA 94702 United States
sygarces@sbcglobal.net
http://www.cambridgewhoswho.com

BUS: Long-Term Care Facility **P/S:** Healthcare **MA:** Local **EXP:** Ms. Garces' expertise is in geriatric nursing. **D/D/R:** Developing the Staff, Caring for the Elderly **H/I/S:** Watching Baseball, Walking, Reading, Cooking, Making Crafts **EDU:** Bachelor of Arts in Liberal Studies, California State University, East Bay; Associate of Science in Nursing, Samuel Merritt College **A/A/S:** Lumetra; Live Oak Institute; Toastmasters International **C/VW:** Shiloh Christian Fellowship **A/S:** She attributes her success to her faith in God. **B/I:** She became involved in her profession because she always wanted to help people in nursing homes. **H/O:** The most gratifying aspect of her career is making the residents of the nursing home feel comfortable.

Jose L. Garcia
Validations
Mentor Technical Group
HC 04 Box 4086
Las Piedras, PR 00771 Puerto Rico
jose.garcia@engineer.com
http://www.cambridgewhoswho.com

BUS: Pharmaceutical Group **P/S:** Consulting Services **MA:** International **D/D/R:** Ensuring Regulatory Compliance **H/I/S:** Reading, Watching Movies **EDU:** Master of Business Administration, University of Turado **A/A/S:** Puerto Rico Engineering Association; American Society of Mechanical Engineers

LENORE GARCIA
Owner
Lenore's La Casita
2338 Planet Avenue
Salina, KS 67401 United States
lenore.garcia@cwwemail.com
http://www.cambridgewhoswho.com

BUS: Restaurant **P/S:** Food and Beverages **MA:** Local **EXP:** Ms. Garcia's expertise is in Mexican cuisine preparation. **D/D/R:** Overseeing Operations **H/I/S:** Traveling, Cooking, Spending Time with her Great Grandchildren **EDU:** Diploma, Roosevelt-Lincoln High School **C/VW:** St. Jude Children's Research Hospital **A/S:** She attributes her success to her experience and to the support she receives from her family.

MILDRED A. GARCIA, MBA
Law Enforcement Assistant
DOI-BIA- Law Enforcement Services
4505 Columbine Avenue N.W.
Albuquerque, NM 87113 United States
haskeetwo@aol.com
http://www.cambridgewhoswho.com

BUS: Law Enforcement **P/S:** Law Enforcement for Indian Country **MA:** Local **EXP:** Ms. Garcia's expertise is in program support. **H/I/S:** Raising Cattle and Horses **FBP:** Fortune **EDU:** Master's Degree in Accounting, University of Phoenix; Bachelor's Degree in Accounting, University of Phoenix **C/VW:** Homeless Shelters **A/S:** She attributes her personal and professional success to her perseverance. **B/I:** She has always had an interest in the field and was offered a position out of college.

CAROLINA GARCIA-MOROS
Business Development Manager
Stampa
7275 N.W. 61st Street
Miami, FL 33166 United States
carogarciamoros@yahoo.com
http://www.stampa.com

BUS: International Purchasing Company Specializing in Industrial Products **P/S:** Equipment, Accessories, Tools and Instruments, Machinery, Spare Parts, Vehicles, Computers, Raw Materials, Communications Services **MA:** International **EXP:** Ms. Garcia-Moros' expertise is in international purchasing. **H/I/S:** Reading History Books, Studying Foreign Languages **EDU:** Coursework in Political Science Administration, Rafael Urdaneta University, Venezuela

ROSALIE M. GARDNER
Curriculum Coordinator
Columbia CUSD No. 4
100 Parkview Drive
Columbia, IL 62236 United States
rosegar2000@yahoo.com
http://www.cambridgewhoswho.com

BUS: Leader in the Education Industry **P/S:** Quality Public Education **MA:** Local **D/D/R:** Mentoring, Coordinating the Curriculum, Ensuring State Compliance, Educating Students **H/I/S:** Reading, Needlework **FBP:** Educational Leadership **EDU:** Master of Science in Education, Plus 32, Western Illinois University (1982) **A/A/S:** Illinois Reading Council; National Council of English Teachers; Phi Delta Kappa; Association for Supervision and Curriculum Development **C/VW:** Former Auditor for Curriculum Management and Systems; First Baptist Church of Waterloo

FRANCES GARNER, ABR, CRS, SRES
Realtor
Bob Parks Realty
2319 Crestmoor Road
Nashville, TN 37215 United States
garnerf@realtracs.com
http://www.homesbyfrances.com

BUS: Real Estate Agency **P/S:** Real Estate Services for Clients **MA:** Middle Tennessee **D/D/R:** Working with Residential Properties **H/I/S:** Traveling, Reading, Knitting, Outdoor Activities **EDU:** Diploma, Mebane High School **CERTS:** Licensed Real Estate Sales Associate, Middle Tennessee Region Multiple Listing Service; Accredited Buyer Representative; Certified Residential Specialist; Certified Senior Real Estate Specialist **A/A/S:** Greater Nashville Association of Realtors; Tennessee Association of Realtors; National Association of Realtors **C/VW:** Make-A-Wish Foundation; Child Reach; Making Strides Against Breast Cancer; Susan G. Komen Breast Cancer Foundation; March of Dimes

CRAIG G. GARRETT
Instructor
Contemporary Goju Karate
555 Santa Rosa Street
Arvin, CA 93203 United States
CraigDGarrett@hotmail.com
http://www.cambridgewhoswho.com

BUS: Karate Instruction and Community Service **P/S:** Martial Arts Classes **MA:** Regional **D/D/R:** Educating Women and Children on Self-Defense **H/I/S:** Art, Studying Martial Arts **FBP:** Industry-Related Publications **EDU:** College Coursework in Art; High School Diploma **A/A/S:** North American Black Belt Association (2002); World Black Belt Association (1996) **C/VW:** Scholarships to High Schools **H/O:** The highlight of his career was going on his first martial arts trip to India to teach. Sensei Garrett has traveled to India 5 more times over the years. The induction into the World Black Belt and North American Hall of Fame were unexpected honors.

JENNIFER O'CONNOR GARRETT
Lead School Nurse
Macon County Public Health Center
1830 Lakeside Drive
Franklin, NC 28734 United States
jgarrett@maconnc.org
http://www.cambridgewhoswho.com

BUS: Healthcare **P/S:** Management of Health Department **MA:** Local **D/D/R:** Practicing Pediatric Nursing **H/I/S:** Crafts **FBP:** Journal of Pediatrics; Journal of School Health **EDU:** Bachelor of Science in Nursing, Western Carolina University **CERTS:** Certified Pediatric Nurse **A/A/S:** National Association of Respiratory Training; North Carolina Nursing Association; Western North Carolina Public Health Association **C/VW:** March of Dimes; American Red Cross; Relay for Life; Coordinator, Special Olympics; Governor Appointed Facilitator, Task Force for Early Childhood **A/S:** She attributes her personal and professional success to her love for her work and great role models. **B/I:** She has always had an interest in the field and was inspired by her mother and father.

SUSAN M. GARRETT, CRNFA
Certified Registered Nurse First Assistant
Sarasota Assisting PA
3325 Bougainvillea Street
Sarasota, FL 34239 United States
susangarrett3325@comcast.net
http://www.cambridgewhoswho.com

BUS: Surgical First Assisting **P/S:** Healthcare **MA:** Local **D/D/R:** Practicing Medical-Surgical Nursing **H/I/S:** Gardening, Making Stained Glass and Fused Glass **FBP:** AORN Journal **EDU:** Pursuing Master of Science in Nursing, University of South Florida; Pursuing Bachelor of Science in Nursing, University of South Florida; Associate of Science in Nursing, Manatee Community College; Registered Nurse Diploma, Manatee Community College **A/A/S:** Association of perioperative Registered Nurses; American Society of Bariatric Surgery **C/VW:** School Volunteer, PALS **A/S:** She attributes her success to perseverance and hard work. **B/I:** She became involved in the profession because her grandmother was a nurse and she volunteered as a young girl. She fell in love with the profession. **H/O:** The highlight of her career is being a member of the ASBS and the Bariatric Program which she is heavily involved in through patient care and support groups.

VIRGINIA J. GARRISON
Staff Nurse
St. Joseph Medical Center
4932 S. State Street
Tacoma, WA 98409 United States
virginiagarrison@fhshealth.org
http://www.fhshealth.org

BUS: Medical Center **P/S:** Healthcare, Healing in a Comfortable and Compassionate Way, Safe Environment for Patients, Families and Visitors **MA:** Regional **EXP:** Ms. Garrison's expertise includes medical, surgical, charge and resource nursing. **D/D/R:** Ensuring Quality **EDU:** Bachelor of Science in Nursing, Saint Joseph's College, ME (1998); Bachelor of Arts in Education, Pacific Lutheran University (1975) **CERTS:** Registered Nurse; Certification in Medical-Surgical Nursing, American Nurses Credentialing Center **C/VW:** Founder, Nursing Team, Trinity Lutheran Church

MARGARET ANN GARY, BSN
Director, Critical Care
Chester River Hospital Center
100 Brown Street
Chestertown, MD 21620 United States
magary@dmv.com
http://www.cambridgewhoswho.com

BUS: Hospital **P/S:** Acute Care **MA:** Local **D/D/R:** Specializing in Critical Care Nursing **H/I/S:** Quilting, Playing the Organ and the Piano **FBP:** Critical Care Nursing Journal **EDU:** Bachelor of Science Degree in Nursing, Wesley College **CERTS:** Certified Critical Care Nurse **A/A/S:** American Association of Critical Care Nurses **C/VW:** American Heart Association; American Cancer Society; Local Church **A/S:** She attributes her success to the support of her family and staff as well as loving what she does. **B/I:** She became involved in her profession because she always had the desire to help care for people and make a difference in their lives. **H/O:** The highlight of her career was when a former patient who had a heart transplant returned years later to thank her and the staff for their care.

MARGARET E. GASCOIGNE
Educator
Overland Avenue School
10650 Ashby Avenue
Los Angeles, CA 90064 United States
mgascoigne@labridge.com
http://www.cambridgewhoswho.com

BUS: Public Elementary School **P/S:** Education **MA:** Local **EXP:** Ms. Gascoigne's expertise is in elementary education. **H/I/S:** Gardening, Yoga, Dance, Arts, Opera, Reading, Classical Music, Ballet **FBP:** Instructor **EDU:** Master's Degree in Special and Gifted Education, California State University at Northridge **CERTS:** National Board Certified Teacher **C/VW:** Environmental Charity; Heifer International; American Society for the Prevention of Cruelty to Animals **A/S:** She attributes her personal and professional success to her creativity. **H/O:** The highlight of her career is being inducted into the National Board of Certified Teachers.

GWENDOLYN BROWN GASTON
Senior Director of Ambulatory Services
Children's Medical Center
1935 Motor Street
Dallas, TX 75235 United States
gwendolyn.gaston@childrens.com
http://www.childrens.com

BUS: Pediatric Hospital **P/S:** All Facets of Pediatric Healthcare **MA:** Statewide **D/D/R:** Performing Pediatric Ambulatory Nursing **H/I/S:** Crocheting, Reading, Traveling **EDU:** Master's Degree in Nursing, University of Phoenix **C/VW:** American Heart Association, American Cancer Society, Society of Pediatric Nursing **A/S:** She attributes her success to drive, determination, and her sensitive nature. **B/I:** She chose the profession because a good opportunity was presented to her, and she took it.

DONALD E. GATEWOOD
Teacher, Coach (Retired)
Denver Public Schools
900 Grant Street
Denver, CO 80203 United States
donaldgatewood@msn.com
http://www.cambridgewhoswho.com

BUS: School District **P/S:** Education **MA:** Local **D/D/R:** Coaching Track and Field, Teaching Physical Education **H/I/S:** Traveling, Watching Track Meets **EDU:** Master of Arts in Education and Administration, Colorado State University **A/A/S:** Board Member, Colorado State Coaches Association; Director, National Federation for High Schools; All American Football League **A/H:** State Championship Award, 100 Yard and 200 Yard Dash **A/S:** He attributes his success to the influence of his brother, his love for sports and his love for children. **B/I:** He became involved in his profession because he was an athlete and was inspired by his brother who was a teacher in addition to being a coach. **H/O:** The highlight of his career was coaching the Manuel High School team to the first state championship in 1974.

MARGARITA GAUTIER RIVERA, RN
Registered Nurse
South Jersey Health System, Regional Medical Center
1505 W. Sherman Avenue
Vineland, NJ 08360 United States
margriv@msn.com
http://www.sjhs.com

BUS: Charitable Nonprofit Health Care Organization **P/S:** Patient Care, Outpatient Services, Cancer Services, Wellness Services, Women's and Children's Healthcare, Orthopedic Services **MA:** Statewide **D/D/R:** Working in the Emergency Room as Staff Nurse, Treating and Directing Patients, Utilizing the Triage System, Rotating from the Fast Track Area, Acting as a Resource Person to New Registered Nurses and Students, Precepting, Mentoring **H/I/S:** Reading, Crafts, Church Activities, Working with Girls at Church, Missionettes **FBP:** Joyce Meyer Magazine **EDU:** Associate Degree in Nursing, Bronx Community College, NY (1970); Coursework in Registered Nurse Studies, Bronx Community College, NY (1970) **CERTS:** Pursuing Emergency Nurse Certification; Certified in Pediatric Advanced Life Support; Certified Basic Life Support; Certified in Trauma Nurse Core Curriculum **A/A/S:** Emergency Nurses Association; ENTC **C/VW:** Cumberland County Traffic Safety Committee

DEE M. GEARHART
Author, Writer
65500 Saint Lucie Boulevard
Fort Pierce, FL 34946 United States
clownsheart@comcast.net
http://www.cambridgewhoswho.com

BUS: Writing **P/S:** True Crime and Mystery Books **MA:** National **D/D/R:** Writing Mystery and Crime Books **H/I/S:** Bowling, Line Dancing, Swimming, Socializing **FBP:** American Society of Authors and Writers **EDU:** Associate Degree in Medical Assistant Studies, Cedar Rapids **A/A/S:** American Association of Medical Assistants **A/H:** Award, American Society of Authors and Writers **C/VW:** Children's Charities, Homeless Animals **A/S:** She attributes her success to setting personal goals. **B/I:** She became involved in her profession because her husband was in a coma for two years, so she stayed at home. **H/O:** The highlight of her career was having her first book published.

JEAN M. GEISSLER
Medical Office Manager
Barry M. Schwartz, MD, PC
23 E. 79th Street
New York, NY 10021 United States
http://www.cambridgewhoswho.com

BUS: Proven Leader in the Field of Healthcare **P/S:** High Quality General Medicine and Compassionate Patient Care, Specializing in Urology **MA:** Regional **D/D/R:** Performing Office Administrative Duties, Bookkeeping **H/I/S:** Reading, Listening to Music, Appreciating Art, Attending the Ballet and Opera, Studying Egyptology **FBP:** American Association of Medical Assistants **EDU:** Coursework, Payne Hall (1949) **CERTS:** Certified Urologist Assistant **A/A/S:** American Association of Medical Assistants; American Urological Association

COLLEEN GEMMILL
Administrator
D. E. Gemmill, Inc.
10174 Chapel Church Road
Red Lion, PA 17356 United States
colleen@degemmill.com
http://www.degemmill.com

BUS: Privately Owned Company Committed to Excellence in the Contracting Industry **P/S:** Traffic Control Line Painting, Sign Manufacturing, Safety Gear Sales **MA:** Regional **D/D/R:** Selling Safety Gear, Reviewing Applicants, Handling Accounting and Book Work **H/I/S:** Volunteering **CERTS:** Certified Basic Firefighter; Certification in Vehicle Rescue; Certification in Hazardous Materials Management; Certified in CPR; Certified First Responder **A/A/S:** Junior Firefighter Association; Committee Member, County Builders Association; Vice President, Red Lion Business Association **C/VW:** Make-A-Wish Foundation; Volunteer Firefighter

MR. JOSEPH M. GENTILE
Special Education Teacher
Cedar Hill Intermediate
2843 Community Lane
High Ridge, MO 63049 United States
jgentile@nwr1.k-12.mo.us
http://www.nwr1.k12.mo.us

BUS: Board of Education **P/S:** Curriculum and Instruction Development **MA:** Regional **D/D/R:** Working in the Classroom Setting, Overseeing After-School Programs, Teaching Special Education, Managing Individualized Education Plans for Students with Special Needs, Training through Positive Intervention Procedures **H/I/S:** Participating in Scouts Activities, Coaching Volleyball and Soccer, Playing Basketball and Baseball **FBP:** CEC Publications **EDU:** Master's Degree in Special Education, Lindenwood University (2002); Bachelor's Degree in Education, Harris-Stowe State University **CERTS:** Certified Administrator **A/A/S:** Council for Exceptional Children; Learning Disabilities Association of America **C/VW:** Leader, Boy Scouts of America

FAITH D. GEORGE, MA
Assistant Principal
U.S. Virgin Islands Department of Education
71-75R Mars Hill
Frederiksted
St. Croix, VI 00840 United States
fgeorge@stx.k12.vi
http://www.cambridgewhoswho.com

BUS: Elementary School **P/S:** Educational Services for Kindergarten through Sixth-Grade Students, Educational Administration **MA:** Regional **D/D/R:** Teaching Elementary Education to Kindergarten through Sixth-Grade Students, Educating Adults Giving Workshop Presentations, Presenting at the University of the Virgin Islands **H/I/S:** Reading, Walking, Relaxing at the Beach **FBP:** Principal **EDU:** Master of Arts in Educational Administration, University of the Virgin Islands; Bachelor of Arts in Elementary Education **A/A/S:** Association for Supervision and Curriculum Development; National Association of Elementary School Principals; National Alliance of Black School Educators **A/H:** Teacher of the Year Award (2003-2004) **C/VW:** Ebenezer Methodist Church; St. Croix Reading Council **DOB:** March 25, 1965 **POB:** St. Croix, US Virgin Islands **W/H:** Multi-age Classroom Teacher, Adult Basic Education Teacher (1988-2004); Elementary School Administrator (2004); Foreign Language Teacher; Remedial Reading Teacher; Primary Classroom Teacher **A/S:** She attributes her success to receiving hugs from children at the end of a rough day and being able recognize understanding in children's faces. **B/I:** She became involved in her profession because she wanted to make a difference in the instructional process. **H/O:** The most gratifying aspects of her career are being able to mentor other teachers who have the potential to be administrators and provide learning opportunities.

MANDY GEORGE
Bookkeeper
Marks Realty, Inc.
445 N. Pennsylvania Street
Suite 810
Indianapolis, IN 46204 United States
mgeorge@markscompanies.com
http://www.cambridgewhoswho.com

BUS: Real Estate **P/S:** Commercial Property Management, Real Estate, Leasing **MA:** Local **D/D/R:** Reconciling Accounts, Preparing Profit and Loss Statements, Performing Administrative Duties **H/I/S:** Attending School **FBP:** Indianapolis Business Journal **EDU:** Pursuing Associate Degree in Accounting, Ivy Tech Community College **A/A/S:** Phi Theta Kappa National Honor Society **A/H:** National Dean's List (2006, 1998) **B/I:** She became involved in her profession because she likes to analyze things. **H/O:** The highlight of her career is her current position.

CAROLE GERHARD-HOSTETTER
Enrichment Facilitator
Cornwall-Lebanon School District - South-Lebanon Elementary School
1825 S. Fifth Avenue
Lebanon, PA 17042 United States
chostetter@clsd.k12.pa.us
http://www.clsd.k12.pa.us

BUS: Elementary School Dedicated to Excellence in Education **P/S:** Enthusiastic, Engaging and Structured Curriculum to Elementary School Students **MA:** Local **D/D/R:** Working with Gifted First through Fifth Grade Students with High IQs and Talents, Utilizing Junior Great Books and Out-of-Grade Level Mathematics **H/I/S:** Cooking, Exercising, Calligraphy, Traveling **FBP:** Gifted Quarterly **EDU:** Master's Degree in Elementary Education, Plus 60, Bloomsburg University (1972); Bachelor of Science in Elementary Education, Bloomsburg University (1967) **A/A/S:** Delta Kappa Gamma Society International; Cornwall-Lebanon Education Association; Pennsylvania Education Association; National Education Association; Lebanon County Education Honor Society **C/VW:** Delegate, Lebanon County Christian Ministry; St. Jude Children's Hospitalhildren's Hospital

MR. DEREK GERSTENSCHLAGER
Auctioneer Broker
The Prudential Real Estate Affiliates, Inc.
3173 S. Church Street
Murfreesboro, TN 37127 United States
gerstend@realtracs.com
http://www.derekgteam.com
http://www.prudentialrowlandauctions.com

BUS: Real Estate Agency **P/S:** Commercial and Residential Real Estate Exchange Including Representation of Buyers and Sellers of Residential Properties and Auction Sales **MA:** National **D/D/R:** Managing Brokerage Services Using Technology for Cost-Effective Service, Selling Houses, Boats, Businesses and Planes, Facilitating Rapid Disposal, Auctioneering for the United States Marshal Service and Department of Justice **H/I/S:** Aviation, Scuba Diving, Traveling **FBP:** Aviation-Related Journals; People **EDU:** Coursework, Graduate Realtor Institute (2005); Bachelor of Science in Business, The University of Tennessee (1982) **CERTS:** Licensed Broker (1982); Certified Auction Manager; Certified in Real Estate Finance; e-PRO Certification; Certified Residential Specialist; Certified Relocation Professional **A/A/S:** Central West Tennessee Association of Realtors; Tennessee Association of Realtors; National Association of Realtors; Graduate Realtor Institute; National Auctioneers Association **A/H:** Valued Investor, Rutherford County (2005-2006); Sales Achievement Award (2004-2006) **C/VW:** Volunteer, American Red Cross; Cystic Fibrosis Foundation; Brain Tumor Society; Habitat for Humanity **CHILD:** Nikolaus, Natasha

REV. KENNETH R. GHASTIN, OFM
Deacon, Reverend
Order of Friars Minor
50 Sommerset Street
Apartment 3
Clearwater Beach, FL 33767 United States
kenneth.ghastin@cwwemail.com
http://www.cambridgewhoswho.com

BUS: Roman Catholic Church **P/S:** Catholic Religious Services **MA:** International **D/D/R:** Preaching, Managing Administrative Duties **H/I/S:** Reading, Writing, Making Arts **EDU:** Coursework, Saint Vincent College (1983-1985); Associate Degree in Scripture, Minor in Church History, Aquinas College (1973); Coursework in the New Testament Scripture, Christology and Modern Catechetic, Georgian Court College; Coursework in Basic Doctrine and Methods, Diocese of Wichita; Coursework in Intermediate Bible and Liturgy, Religious Information Bureau, Knights of Columbus; Coursework in the Kingdom of Jesus; Coursework in Religious Studies; Coursework in Thomas Aquinas College; Coursework, Georgian Court College; Coursework, Saint Vincent Archabbey **CERTS:** Certification in Teaching, St. Anne's Parish (1993); Certified Student Advisor, Duquesne University (1992); Ordained Deacon **A/A/S:** Hungarian Franciscans (1955) **A/H:** Award of Merit, St. Ann's Parish, Marlborough, Massachusetts (1993) **C/VW:** Director of Religious Training, Duquesne University; Director of Religious Training, Bordentown School for Retarded Children

MARY LYNN GIACOBBE
President
JMG Heating and Air Conditioning, Inc.
6587 N. Manlius Road
Kirkville, NY 13082 United States
mgiacob2@twcny.rr.com
http://www.cambridgewhoswho.com

BUS: Heating, Ventilation and Air Conditioning Company **P/S:** Heating, Ventilation and Air Conditioning Installation and Maintenance **MA:** Local **D/D/R:** Working with Commercial, Residential and New Home Construction Properties **H/I/S:** Creating Art, Camping, Playing with her Sled Dogs, Spending Time with her Family **EDU:** Bachelor's Degree in Music Education, SUNY Potsdam **A/A/S:** National Association of Home Builders **C/VW:** Music Director, Youth Groups Church

CLAIRE MARIE GIBBONS
Special Education Teacher
Norwich City School District
1 Midland Drive
Norwich, NY 13815 United States
clairemh1019@mac.com
http://www.cambridgewhoswho.com

BUS: Education **P/S:** Public High School **MA:** Local **EXP:** Ms. Gibbons' expertise is in special education. **H/I/S:** Painting, Reading, and Volunteering **FBP:** Journal for Behavior **EDU:** Master's Degree in Special Education, College of St. Rose; Bachelor's Degree in Psychology Education, Hamilton College **A/A/S:** Council for Exceptional Children; Transition Planning Committee; Norwich Instructs Character Education **A/H:** Teacher of the Year Award (2005) **C/VW:** Local Church; New York State Division of Veterans' Affairs; Order of the Eastern Star **A/S:** She attributes her success to having patience. **B/I:** She chose the profession because she always wanted to teach and be creative. **H/O:** The highlight of her career was going back to school at a later age, and finishing.

MRS. JOYCE M. GIBOUR
Clerk (Retired)
Milwaukee County
jychgb@wi.rr.com
http://www.milwaukeecounty.org

BUS: Government Organization **P/S:** Public and Social Services **MA:** Regional **D/D/R:** Overseeing Administrative Duties **H/I/S:** Sewing, Making Crafts, Quilting, Singing, Square Dancing, Teaching Dance **FBP:** PC Magazine; Investment Management Review; Money; Harvard Business Review **EDU:** High School Diploma **CERTS:** Training, Coalition of Wisconsin Aging Groups (2006) **C/VW:** Local Church

MELVIN K. GIBSON
Senior Health Services Administrator
Central Florida Reception Center
7000 HC Kelley Road
Orlando, FL 32822 United States
http://www.cambridgewhoswho.com

BUS: Healthcare **P/S:** State Prison Facility **MA:** Local **EXP:** Mr. Gibson's expertise is in health services administration. **H/I/S:** Playing Tennis, Fishing, Hunting, Golfing **EDU:** Bachelor of Science in Health and Physical Education and Recreation, Minor in Social Sciences and Religion, University of North Carolina **CERTS:** Certified Tennis Instructor **A/A/S:** Non Commissioned Officers Association; Tennis Association; Masonic Association **C/VW:** American Society for the Prevention of Cruelty to Animals; Mentor, Department of Corrections; Veterans of Foreign Wars; The American Legion **A/S:** He attributes his success to the staff he works with and the strong sense of team work they all share. **B/I:** After retiring from the military he followed in his family's footsteps and got into his current profession. **H/O:** The highlight of his career was being selected to supervise a reception center.

DR. STEPHEN T. GILBERT
Plastic Surgeon
New Zealand Institute of Plastic Cosmetic Surgery
243 Remuera Road
Auckland, New Zealand
stg@plasticsurgeons.co.nz
http://www.plasticsurgeons.co.nz

BUS: New Zealand's Largest Private Plastic and Cosmetic Surgical Practice **P/S:** Ongoing Training and Research, Botox, Breast Augmentation, Tummy Tucks, Liposuction, Rhinoplasty, Skin Care, Brow lift, Facelift **MA:** International **D/D/R:** Performing Cosmetic Surgery, Specializing in Facial Enhancement and Face Lifts, Breast Enhancement and Breast Reconstruction after Mastectomies **A/A/S:** Fellow, Royal College of Surgeons, England; Fellow, Royal Australian College of Surgeons; New Zealand Foundation for Cosmetic Plastic Surgery; International Society of Aesthetic Plastic Surgery; American Society of Plastic Surgeons

STEPHANIE K. GILCHRIST
Kindergarten Teacher
Floresville ECC
1200 Fifth Street
Floresville, TX 78114 United States
smileyag2000@yahoo.com
http://www.cambridgewhoswho.com

BUS: Public School District **P/S:** Public Education **MA:** Local **D/D/R:** Teaching Kindergarten, Overseeing Campus Technology **H/I/S:** Camping **FBP:** Mailbox **EDU:** Bachelor's Degree in Interdisciplinary Studies, Texas A&M University **A/A/S:** Texas Computer Education Association; Former Member, Association for Supervision and Curriculum Development; Association of Texas Professional Educators **A/H:** Teacher of the Year, Floresville Independent School District (2006)

STEPHEN R. GILFUS
Co-Founder
Blackboard, Inc.
1899 L St NW
Washington, DC 20036 United States
gilfus7@yahoo.com
http://www.blackboard.com
www.gilfus.com

BUS: Enterprise Software and Services Provider **P/S:** Enterprise Software Platform Development in the Education Sector **MA:** International **EXP:** Mr. Gilfus' expertise includes strategic business planning and product development. **FBP:** IT Software **EDU:** Bachelor of Science, Cornell University **A/A/S:** NVTC **C/VW:** Cornell Advisory Board

KATHLEEN P. GILL
Intervention Specialist
Boulevard Elementary School
1749 Lee Road
Cleveland Heights, OH 44118 United States
k_gill@staff.chuh.org
http://www.cambridgewhoswho.com

BUS: Elementary School **P/S:** Primary Education **MA:** Local **D/D/R:** Teaching Kindergarten through Eighth-Grade Students, Caring for Inclusion Students, Teaching Language Arts Intervention, Reading and Mathematics **H/I/S:** Gardening, Cooking, Camping, Reading **EDU:** Pursuing Master's Degree in Curriculum and Development, Ashland University; Bachelor's Degree in Special Education, Central Michigan University **A/A/S:** Association for Supervision and Curriculum Development; International Reading Association **A/S:** She attributes her success to her love for working with students and to the support she receives from her family. **H/O:** The highlight of her career was writing nine grants that have been funded for student activities.

MS. BENITA L. GILLIARD
Assistant Director of Program Management
IT Portfolio Management Office
Ohio State University Medical Center
640 Ackerman Street, Room C200P
Columbus, OH 43202 United States
benita.gilliard@osumc.edu
http://www.cambridgewhoswho.com

BUS: University Hospital **P/S:** Healthcare, Education **MA:** Regional **EXP:** Ms. Gilliard's expertise includes project management and strategic planning for information technology. **D/D/R:** Managing Program Teams in Business Technology Portfolios Including Applications, Construction, Renovation, Technology and Information Warehouses **H/I/S:** Mentoring, Walking, Reading **FBP:** Black Enterprise **EDU:** Pursuing Master of Business Administration, Fisher College of Business; Bachelor of Arts in Computer Science, Grambling State University, LA, Magna Cum Laude (1982) **A/A/S:** Project Management Institute; Healthcare Information and Management Systems Society; Black Data Processing Associates **C/VW:** Pastor, Local Church; Local Youth Ministries and Outreach Programs **W/H:** Officer, United States Air Force **A/S:** She attributes her success to her integrity, honesty and Christian values. **B/I:** She became involved in her profession because of her passion and complexity of technology. **H/O:** The most gratifying aspects of her career are mentoring junior managers into seasoned project managers and being able to implement and deliver large-scale programs.

JENNIFER L. GILMOUR, BS
Fifth-Grade Teacher
Horace Mann School
Beverly Hills Unified School District
8701 Charleville Boulevard
Beverly Hills, CA 90211 United States
jenny.gilmour@gmail.com
http://www.bhusd.k12.ca.us

BUS: School District **P/S:** Education, Dynamic Interdisciplinary Curriculum, Exemplary Instructional and Support Team, Student-Centered Active Learning, Respect for Diversity, Strong Parent and Community Involvement, and a Nurturing Environment where Students and Staff Share a Common Purpose and Joy for Learning **MA:** Local **D/D/R:** Teaching All Subjects to Fifth-Grade Students, Developing the Curriculum, Working with the Mathematics Planning Committee, Creating Benchmark Assessments **H/I/S:** Playing Tennis, Softball, Listening to Vocal Music, Volunteering **EDU:** Bachelor of Science in General Studies, Concentration in Music, University of Southern California (2005) **CERTS:** Certified Teacher (K-8), State of California; Certification in Clear Language and Design **A/A/S:** Vice President, Kappa Delta Pi, University of Southern California; California Teachers Association; Registrar, Kappa Kappa Gamma; Mentor, Women and Youth Supporting Each Other; Fundraising Chairman, USC Pepsters; Greeks Administering the Mature Management of Alcohol; Golden Key International Honour Society; Order of Omega; Rho Lambda; Gamma Sigma Alpha **A/H:** Best Director Award, USC Songfest (2003); Dean's List, Magna Cum Laude **C/VW:** Coach, Teacher, Representative, Parent-Teacher Association; Volunteer, High School Youth Group Leader, Bel Air Presbyterian Church **DOB:** March 11, 1983 **POB:** Van Nuys, California

JANE GINN
Managing Director
Sedona Cyber Link
1040 E. Park Ridge Drive
Sedona, AZ 86336 United States
jane@sedonacyberlink.com
http://www.sedonacyberlink.com

BUS: International Trade and Global Business Strategies Planning **P/S:** Global Business Strategies Planning, International Marketing, e-Business Design **MA:** International **D/D/R:** Conducting Business Planning for Global Trade Companies with Resource Management **H/I/S:** Swimming, Hiking, Reading **FBP:** The Economist; International Herald Tribune **EDU:** Master of Regional Planning in Environmental Science and Regional Planning, Washington State University (1998); Bachelor of Arts in Geography, University of Oklahoma (1981) **CERTS:** Certification in Applied Information Technology, Information Technology Institute (2001) **A/A/S:** Environmental Export Council of Washington; Environmental Technology Trade Advisory Committee; Former Fellow, Institute for Resource Management **C/VW:** CARE; March of Dimes Foundation **A/S:** She attributes her success to her entrepreneurial spirit and staying active. **B/I:** She became involved in her profession because of her background in environmental science and concern for pollution control. **H/O:** The highlight of her career was being appointed to the Environmental Trade Advisory Committee five times.

PATRICIA R. GIROUX
Licensed Practical Nurse, Allergy Nurse
Raleigh Ear, Nose and Throat
3010 Anderson Drive
Raleigh, NC 27609 United States
giroux2@webtv.net
http://www.raleighent.net

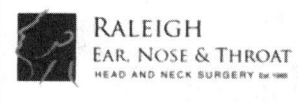

BUS: Medical Practice **P/S:** Ear, Nose and Throat Services, Head and Neck Surgery, Allergy Treatment **MA:** Local **EXP:** Ms. Giroux's expertise includes medical-surgical, trauma, endoscopy and allergy Nursing. **H/I/S:** Singing **CERTS:** Licensed Practical Nurse, Muskegon Community College **A/A/S:** American Academy of Otolaryngic Allergy **C/VW:** Local Church

ELLEN M. GIVEN
Flutist, Founder, Manager
Trio Desjardins
60 Green Hill Road
Sudbury, MA 01776 United States
ellengiven@comcast.net
http://www.cambridgewhoswho.com

BUS: Entertainment Firm **P/S:** Entertainment Including Music Shows **MA:** Regional **EXP:** Ms. Given's expertise is in creative expression. **D/D/R:** Playing the Flute, Performing Music, Writing, Lecturing **H/I/S:** Watching Women's Soccer, Architectural Design, Landscaping **FBP:** Architectural Digest; Poets & Writers; Art & Antiques **EDU:** Bachelor's Degree in Music, Philadelphia Musical Academy, The University of the Arts (1968) **A/A/S:** Local 9, Boston Musicians' Association; National Trust for Historic Preservation; The Academy of American Poets; Institute of Contemporary Art, Boston; American Association of University Women; American Biographical Institute; International Biographical Center **A/H:** International Peace Prize, United Cultural Convention (2006); International Peace Prize, Legion of Honor (2004); Top 100 Musicians of the Year Award, International Biographical Center (2005) **C/VW:** World Forum; Southern Poverty Law Center **POB:** Darby **CHILD:** Jennine, Marnie **A/S:** She attributes her success to her hard work and her ability to utilize the opportunity that came her way. **B/I:** She became involved in her profession because she was inspired by her family members who were musicians. **H/O:** The highlight of her career was attending the World Forum at the University of Oxford.

BETH GLASS
Librarian
South Plains College, Reese Center
819 S. Gilbert Drive
Lubbock, TX 79416 United States
eglass@southplainscollege.edu
http://www2.southplainscollege.edu

BUS: College **P/S:** Higher Education **MA:** Regional **EXP:** Ms. Glass' expertise is in library science. **D/D/R:** Managing the Library and Staff, Overseeing Operations, Budgeting, Planning and Organizing Professional Development Programs, Overseeing the Information Literacy Program for Faculty and Students **H/I/S:** Creative Writing, Bowling **A/A/S:** Texas Library Association; Texas Association of Community Colleges; American Association of University Women; Former Member, Toastmasters International

DELLA A. GLEASON
Firefighter, First Responder
Darlington Fire Department, Inc.
102 S. Franklin Street
Darlington, IN 47940 United States
jelippbrowen@yahoo.com
http://www.cambridgewhoswho.com

BUS: Fire Department **P/S:** Fire and Rescue Services **MA:** Local **D/D/R:** Offering Fire and Medical Services **H/I/S:** Mechanics, Spending Time with her Five Children **FBP:** IVFA Publications **EDU:** College Coursework **C/VW:** Volunteer, Fire Department; Volunteer, Church; Indiana Volunteer Firefighters Association **A/S:** She attributes her success to her family's support and encouragement. **B/I:** She became involved in the profession because her friends encouraged and inspired her to enter the field. **H/O:** The most gratifying aspect of her career is enjoying and trusting her co-workers.

Ms. Pearlie A. Gleghorn

Respiratory Blood Gas Technician
University Medical Center
1800 W. Charleston Boulevard
Las Vegas, NV 89102 United States
pagalnme@cox.net
http://www.cambridgewhoswho.com

BUS: Hospital **P/S:** Healthcare, Medical Services **MA:** Local **D/D/R:** Sampling and Analyzing Arterial Blood **H/I/S:** Attending Church, Listening to Classical Music, Interior Decorating, Reading, Spending Time with her Family, Collecting Stamps and Coins **FBP:** Industry-Related Publications; Eastern Press Periodicals **EDU:** Coursework, Polk Community College, Winter Haven, FL **CERTS:** Certification in Respiratory Therapy **C/VW:** Church of Greater Harvest Ministry; Winter Haven Hospital; American Cancer Society; Paralyzed Veterans of America **DOB:** November 7, 1950 **POB:** Gretna **SP:** Alfred (Deceased) **CHILD:** Dexter, Charis, Ernesta, Eboni **W/H:** Dr. R.D. Prabhu Pulmonology, Las Vegas, NV (1996-2002); Valley Hospital and Medical Center, Las Vegas, NV (1984-1996); Community Hospital, North Las Vegas, NV (1978-1984); Polk General Hospital, Bartow, FL (1976-1977) **A/S:** She attributes her success to her motivation and compassion for others. **B/I:** She became involved in the profession after being presented with an opportunity while working at the hospital. **H/O:** The most gratifying aspect of her career is being able to provide peace to her critically-ill patients.

Deborah L. Glenney, MSW

Behavior Specialist Consultant
Safety Net Counseling, Inc.
7 W. Hillcrest Drive
Bloomsberg, PA 17815 United States
billglenney@evenlink.com
http://www.cambridgewhoswho.com

BUS: Mental Health Practice Committed to Providing Quality, Comprehensive Patient Care in a Professional and Compassionate Environment **P/S:** Behavioral Health Care and Counseling **MA:** Regional **D/D/R:** Offering Therapeutic Services, Treatment Plans and TSS Supervision, Working with Children, Promoting Anger Management and Coping Skills, Treating Attention Deficit Hyperactivity Disorder, Working with Several Children's Agencies, Running a Mobile Therapy Center **H/I/S:** Traveling, Exercising, Enjoying Outdoor Activities, Walking **EDU:** Master's Degree in Social Administration, Temple University (2003) **A/A/S:** Phi Kappa Phi; Phi Alpha Honor Society; Board Member, Victims of Crime

KAREN M. GLOTFELTY
Owner
Enviro-Tech Systems & Services, LLC
N4955 Sunny Hill Road
Weyerhaeuser, WI 54895 United States
glots@brucetel.net
http://www.cambridgewhoswho.com

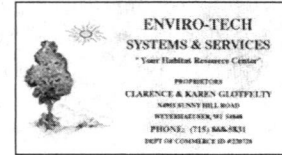

BUS: Installation Company **P/S:** Installation of Residential and Commercial Septic Systems, Plumbing, Perk Tests, Sewer Preparations **MA:** Regional **EXP:** Ms. Glotfelty's expertise is in the design and installation of privately-owned wastewater treatment sites. **D/D/R:** Managing Family-Owned Plumbing and Septic Installation Services, Working with Homeowners, Contractors, Suppliers and Subcontractors, Evaluating Sites **H/I/S:** Hiking, Cross-Country Skiing, Hunting, Golfing **FBP:** Industry-Related Publications **EDU:** Coursework in Landscaping Design **A/A/S:** Rusk County Trail Association **C/VW:** Concerned Women for America

DeLON R. GOBELI, GRI, ABR, CBR, CHMS
Sales Associate
TRAPP GMAC Real Estate
3321 Cedar Heights Drive
Cedar Falls, IA 50613 United States
drgobeli@mchsi.com
http://www.cambridgewhoswho.com

BUS: Real Estate Agency **P/S:** Commercial and Residential Real Estate Exchange **MA:** Regional **D/D/R:** Selling Residential and Commercial Properties, Handling Relocations, Referrals and Investment Properties, Analyzing Market Strategies **H/I/S:** Spending Time with his Friends and Family, Volunteering for Community Services **EDU:** Associate Degree in Accounting, Hawkeye Community College **CERTS:** Licensed Real Estate Agent; Accredited Buyer Representative; Certified Buyer Representative; Certified Home Marketing Specialist **A/A/S:** Waterloo Cedar Falls Board of Realtors; Iowa Association of Realtors; Blackhawk Community Credit Union; Iowa Credit Unions; Waterloo Iowa Exchange Club; Landlords of Black Hawk County; Elk's Club **A/H:** Community Service Award, Board of Directors (2001-2003); Rookie of the Year Award, Waterloo Exchange Club (2001-2003); National Director of the Year Award (1992-1993); Volunteer of the Year Award, National Youth Board; Robert L. Curry Scholarship (1993); Silver Iowa Achievement Award, National Association of Realtors; Three-Time Recipient, Bronze Iowa Achievement Award National Association of Realtors **C/VW:** Board Member, Waterloo Community Playhouse **CHILD:** Mark, Dawn, Heather, Adam **A/S:** He attributes his success to his hard work and determination. **B/I:** He became involved in his profession because of his interest in real estate. **H/O:** The highlight of his career was receiving an award from the National Credit Union in Las Vegas.

HEMWATIE GOBERDHAN, RN, BSN, MSN, SNP
Nurse
Lincoln Medical Center
234 E. 149th Street
Bronx, NY 10451 United States
hemanur@aol.com
http://www.cambridgewhoswho.com

BUS: Hospital Facility Dedicated to Excellence in Health Care **P/S:** Level I Trauma Center, Critical Healthcare, Bariatric Surgery and Obesity Programs, Birth Center, Burn Center, Senior Healthcare, Diabetes and Endocrinology, Cancer Care, Heart Healthcare, Rehabilitation **MA:** Regional **D/D/R:** Working as Staff Nurse, Charge Nurse and Certified Trauma Nurse **H/I/S:** Traveling **FBP:** NP Magazine **EDU:** Master of Science in Nursing, College of St. Vincent's (2007); Bachelor of Science in Nursing, Hunter College (2001) **CERTS:** Certification in Trauma Care; Certification in Advanced Cardiac Life Support; Certification in Basic Cardiac Life Support; Certification in Pediatric Advanced Life Support **A/A/S:** Ethics Committee, Lincoln Medical Center

SHARON M. GOETZ
Owner, Partner
Lowake Steak House
24913 FM 381
P. O. Box 24
Lowake, TX 76855 United States
lowakesteakhouse1@yahoo.com
http://www.lowake-steakhouse.com

BUS: Privately Owned Restaurant **P/S:** Perfectly Prepared Steaks, Over-Sized Steaks, Seating for 200 Persons **MA:** Regional **D/D/R:** Working as the Chief Financial Officer, Overseeing Payroll, Managing a Staff of 22 Employees, Training the Staff, Running the Entire Restaurant **H/I/S:** Refereeing Volleyball **FBP:** Cheers **EDU:** Diploma, Ballinger High School (1972)

YVETTE Y. GOLAN
President, Chief Executive Officer
World Innova Corporation, Two Allen Center
Two Allen Center
1200 Smith Street, Suite 1600
Houston, TX 77002 United States
ygolan@worldinnova.com
http://www.worldinnova.com

BUS: Corporation **P/S:** Manufacturing, Distribution and Licensing of Patent Rights for Consumer Products **MA:** National **EXP:** Ms. Golan's expertise is in law and licensing. **EDU:** JD, Cornell University Law School; Bachelor of Arts, University of Texas at Austin **CERTS:** Licensed Lawyer, States of Illinois and Texas **A/A/S:** Licensing Marketing Association; Ohio Bar Association; American Bar Association **C/VW:** Child Advocates **A/S:** She attributes her success to her hard work and determination to succeed. **B/I:** She became involved in her profession because she has always loved the process of product creation and development. **H/O:** The highlight of her career was opening her own business.

CAROL G. GOLDMAN, CSA, CLTC
Consultant
Carol G. Goldman & Associates
430 Franklin Village Drive
PMB 230
Franklin, MA 02038 United States
http://www.carolggoldman.com

BUS: Consulting Company **P/S:** Motivation and Leadership Training, Seminars, Financial Services Recruitment, Professional Training **MA:** National **EXP:** Ms. Goldman's expertise is in business consulting. **H/I/S:** Playing Badminton and Volleyball, Reading, Public Speaking, Spending Time with her Family and Friends **FBP:** Financial Advisor; 'Raising Financially Fit Kids' by Joline Godfrey; 'Networking: How to Build Relationships that Count' by Colleen S. Clark; 'Little Black Book of Connections' by Jeffrey Gitomers **CERTS:** Licensed in Life, Accident and Health Insurance, Series 6 & 63, States of MA, FL, GA, ME, NH and RI (1963); Certified Senior Advisor; Certified Long-Term Care Designation; Certified Networker **A/A/S:** Former President, BNI; Former President, LeTip International, Inc; Newton Needham Chamber of Commerce; National Association of Insurance and Financial Advisors **A/H:** Dual Recipient, Person of the Year Award; Employer of the Year, Boston University's Center for Psychiatric Rehabilitation; Ambassador of the Year, Toastmasters International **C/VW:** Former Deacon, Community Church of West Medway; Former Stewardship Chair, Former Co-Chair, Single Parenting Group; Women's Initiative **A/S:** She attributes her success to her faith in God, supportive mother and husband and referrals from clients. **B/I:** She became involved in her profession at the encouragement of a friend, who invited her to join the financial services field. **H/O:** The most gratifying aspects of her career are receiving professional recognition from her peers and becoming good friends with her clients. **I/F/Y:** In five years, Ms. Goldman intends to continue keynote speaking, producing seminars and helping clients manage their finances.

MR. BUD R. GOLDSBY
President
Resource Potentials, Inc.
1343 Main Street
Suite 502B
Sarasota, FL 34236 United States
brg@resourcepotentials.com
http://www.resourcepotentials.com

BUS: Environmental Consulting **P/S:** Consulting Solutions for All Types of Properties Including Commercial, Residential and Industrial, on both Private and Public Land Parcels, Giving any Organization the Knowledge and Experience to Improve and Protect their Investments **MA:** Regional **D/D/R:** Acquiring Permits for Land Management, Alteration and Development Purposes of Coastal Resources and Wetlands **H/I/S:** Boating, Fishing, Racquetball, Water-Skiing, Hiking, Scuba Diving **EDU:** Bachelor of Science Degree, School of Forest Resources and Conservation, University of Florida (1998) **CERTS:** Certified Arborist, International Society of Arboriculture; Certification, State of Florida Wetland Delineation **A/A/S:** Elected Chair, UF Student Chapter, Society of American Foresters **A/H:** Most Valuable Member, Society of American Foresters

JOSE J. GOMEZ
President
Jogony Music
100 Park Terrace W.
Apartment 4K
New York, NY 10034 United States
jogo@jogomusic.com
http://www.jogomusic.com

BUS: Premier Music Recording Company **P/S:** Music Programs and CD's **MA:** International **D/D/R:** Writing Lyrics, Performing Shows Including Pop, Rock, Rhythm and Blues, Adult Contemporary and Jazz Music **H/I/S:** Playing Baseball, Skiing, Horseback Riding, Collecting Antique Phonographs **FBP:** Billboard; Keyboard; Recording **EDU:** Bachelor of Arts in Songwriting, Piano and Voice, Berklee College of Music (1979) **A/H:** 18-Time Recipient, Yearly Award, American Society of Authors, Composers, and Publishers

MARIA T. GOMEZ
Teacher
Thomas Edison Middle School
60 Glenmod Road
Brighton, MA 02135 United States
m120268@aol.com
http://www.cambridgewhoswho.com

BUS: Public Middle School for Sixth through Eighth Grade **P/S:** Educational Services **MA:** Regional **D/D/R:** Educating Special Needs Students, Teaching Special Education Science and Social Studies to Seventh and Eighth-Grade Students, Coaching **H/I/S:** Traveling **FBP:** National Geographic; Reader's Digest **EDU:** Bachelor's Degree in Education and Psychology, Cambridge College **A/A/S:** American Federation of Teachers; Representative, Boston Teacher Union; Advertising Specialty Institute **C/VW:** Volunteer, Local School

AMY S. GONZALES
District Manager
Bayview Irrigation District 11
110 S. San Roman Road
Los Fresnos, TX 78566 United States
bayviewirigation@earthlink.net
http://www.cambridgewhoswho.com

BUS: Government Organization **P/S:** Irrigation Water Supply **MA:** Local **D/D/R:** Overseeing Five Employees, Managing Delivery of Water to Farmers, Answering Phone Calls, Selling Irrigation to Farmers **H/I/S:** Web Designing **FBP:** TexasMonthly **EDU:** Associate Degree, South Texas Vocational Technical Institute; Coursework in Bookkeeping, South Texas Vocational Technical Institute **A/A/S:** Secretary, Treasurer, Lower Rio Grande Valley Water District Managers Association; Texas Water Conservation Association **C/VW:** Local Charitable Organizations **A/S:** She attributes her success to her hard work and determination. **B/I:** She became involved in her profession after retiring as a general manager, she was suggested that she would be best for the district manager position. **H/O:** The most gratifying aspect of her career is the gratitude she receives from her colleagues. **I/F/Y:** In five years, Ms. Gonzales hopes to continue improving the district.

BERMARY E. GONZALEZ
Preschool Director
Piece of Heaven Preschool
1283 Liberty Avenue
Hillside, NJ 07205 United States
bgon19@hotmail.com
http://www.cambridgewhoswho.com

BUS: Preschool **P/S:** Early Childhood Education **MA:** Local **D/D/R:** Directing the Preschool **H/I/S:** Traveling, Reading, Shopping **FBP:** Early Childhood Today **EDU:** Master's Degree in Early Childhood Education, New Jersey City University **A/A/S:** Kappa Delta Pi **C/VW:** Big Brothers Big Sisters **A/S:** She attributes her success to her patience. **B/I:** She was prompted to enter her profession because she always had an interest in the field. **H/O:** The highlight of her career is seeing her students learn.

JUAN GONZALEZ
Environmental Service Director
HCR Manor Care
1510 Collingwood Road
Alexandria, VA 22308 United States
jgonzalez0@comcast.net
http://www.hcr-manorcare.com

BUS: Healthcare Facility with 96 Beds **P/S:** Services for the Retirement Community **MA:** Regional **D/D/R:** Overseeing Administration for the Community, Managing Inventory and Maintenance, Procurement and Quality Assurance, Overseeing a Staff of 11, Overseeing Laundry and Housekeeping, Reporting Directly to the Faculty Administrator **H/I/S:** Reading, Outdoors, Family, Bowling, Jazzercise **FBP:** Long-Term Care Journal; Environmental Compliance Alert **EDU:** High School Education, Venezuela (1981); Coursework in Graphic Design, Venezuela (1980)

ROBERT A. GONZALEZ JR.
Physical Therapy Assistant
Corpus Christi Home Care
5350 S. Staples Street
Corpus Christi, TX 78411 United States
robertchanogonz@yahoo.com
http://www.cambridgewhoswho.com

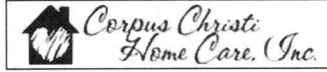

BUS: Home Healthcare Association **P/S:** Physical Therapy Services **MA:** Statewide **D/D/R:** Practicing Physical Therapy **H/I/S:** Spending Time with his Family, Watching Movies, Fishing **FBP:** Business Journals; Physical Therapy Journals **EDU:** Associate Degree in Physical Therapy Assistant Studies, St. Philip's College **CERTS:** Licensed Physical Therapy Assistant

JUAN GONZALEZ-FELICIANO
Chief Executive Officer, Owner
G-Management Corporation
751 Acuario Avenue
San Juan, PR 00926 United States
gmancorp@gmail.com
http://www.cambridgewhoswho.com

BUS: Housing Management and Community Organization **P/S:** Oversight of Local and Government Funds for Low-Income Families **MA:** Puerto Rico, United States, the Caribbean **D/D/R:** Overseeing Operations and Management, Organizing the Community, Counseling, Public Speaking, Managing 300 Employees **H/I/S:** Reading, Spending Time with his Family **EDU:** Pursuing Master's Degree, University of El Turabo; Bachelor's Degree, University of Puerto Rico (1974) **CERTS:** Certified Registry Housing Manager **A/A/S:** Liga de Cooperativas; President, Community Foundation of Puerto Rico **C/VW:** Community **A/S:** He attributes his personal and professional success to his love for helping others. **B/I:** He has always had an interest in the field and a desire to help low-income families. **H/O:** The highlight of his career is helping families reach for their dreams.

REBECCA GOODELL
Realtor, Accredited Buyers Representative, Military Market Specialist
Coldwell Banker West Realty Co.
2500 Military Road, Suite 1
Columbus, MS 39705 United States
rgoodell@westrealtycompany.com
http://www.rebeccagoodell.com

BUS: Real Estate Company **P/S:** Real Estate **MA:** Lowndes County **EXP:** Ms. Goodell's expertise is in relocation. **D/D/R:** Representing Buyers and Military Personnel **H/I/S:** Her Dogs, Shopping **FBP:** National Women Council of Real Estate **EDU:** University of Memphis **A/A/S:** Mississippi Association of Real Estate; Golden Triangle Association of Realtors; National Association of Realtors; National Women's Council of Realtors; Real Estate Buyers Agent Council; Columbus Chamber of Commerce; Base Community Council **C/VW:** Make-A-Wish Foundation; St. Jude Children's Research Hospital; Special Olympics; Habitat for Humanity **A/S:** She attributes her success to her hard work. **B/I:** She became involved in her profession because a broker had suggested it to her. **H/O:** The highlight of her career was being on the cover of the Mississippi Association of Realtors Magazine.

ISABEL HARTLEY FOX GOODMAN
Vision Specialist (Retired)
isablegoodman@aol.com
http://www.cambridgewhoswho.com

MA: Local **D/D/R:** Working with Blind and Visually Impaired Students, Consulting, Transcribing Print Materials in Braille **H/I/S:** Listening to Classical Music, Playing the Piano, Attending Concerts, Reading **EDU:** Doctoral Degree, Columbia University; Master of Arts in Supervision and Administration, New York University; Master's Degree, CUNY Hunter College **A/A/S:** Alumni Association, New York University; Council for Exceptional Children; National Association for Visually Handicapped; National Society for the Prevention of Cruelty to Children **C/VW:** Susan G. Komen for the Cure **A/S:** She attributes her success to her determination, courage and love of her profession and students. **B/I:** She became involved in her profession because she worked with a visually impaired girl when she was younger and decided to help people with the same. **H/O:** The highlight of her career was having some of her students go on to prestigious universities.

DIANE E. GOOLD, BS
Newspaper in Education Director
St. Joseph News-Press
825 Edmond Street
St. Joseph, MO 64501 United States
niediane@npgco.com
http://www.stjoeslive.com

BUS: Educational Journalism **P/S:** Journalism, Newspaper and News Press **MA:** Regional **D/D/R:** Education, Program Development, Teaching Students and Teachers the Benefit of Reading Newspapers **H/I/S:** Music, Singing, Playing the Piano and Organ, Being Outside and Enjoying Nature, Spending Time with her Three Grandchildren **FBP:** Education Week Digest **EDU:** Bachelor of Science in Education, Minor in Music, Northwest Missouri State University, Maryville **A/A/S:** Prairie Lands Writing Project; Saint Joseph's Area Literacy Coalition; Missouri Press Association **C/VW:** United Way of America; Lions Club; Optimist Club; Community of Christ Church **A/S:** She attributes her success to her hard work, perseverance and her passion for her job. **B/I:** She became involved in her profession because she enjoys working with people, students, teachers and sponsors. **H/O:** The highlight of her career has been being published on several occasions locally, nationally and state wide.

DEANETH A. GORDON
Teacher
Morningside Elementary School
6620 N.E. 5th Avenue
Miami, FL 33138 United States
dgordon2@dadeschools.net
http://www.cambridgewhoswho.com

BUS: School **P/S:** Elementary Education **MA:** Local **EXP:** Ms. Gordon's expertise is in elementary education. **D/D/R:** Teaching First-Grade Students, Helping Students Learn to Read **H/I/S:** Singing, Playing the Guitar **FBP:** School Adhesive **EDU:** Master's Degree in Education, Nova Southeastern University; Bachelor of Science in Education, Northwest Carolina University; Diploma in Teaching, Earned in Jamaica **CERTS:** Certified in English for Speakers of Other Languages **A/A/S:** National Reading Association; National Education Association **A/H:** Teacher of the Year (2000) **C/VW:** Church; Local Youth Group **A/S:** She attributes her success to her determination and commitment. **B/I:** She became involved in the education industry through her mother, who was also a teacher, and taught her that students will remember everything they learn if the lessons are made fun and interesting. **H/O:** The most gratifying aspect of her career is watching her students excel and achieve high learning goals in school. **I/F/Y:** In five years, Ms. Gordon hopes to be retired and writing children's literature.

TREVOR L. GORDON
President
TIC Properties, LLC
101 N. Main Street
Suite 1203
Greenville, SC 29615 United States
trevor.gordon@ticproperties.com
http://www.ticproperties.com

BUS: Real Estate Syndications Investment Program Syndicator **P/S:** Tenant-in-Common Investment Programs **MA:** Local **D/D/R:** Acquiring, Syndicating and Managing Institutional Grade Commercial Real Estate Assets Nationwide **H/I/S:** Travel **FBP:** Barrons; Forbes; WSJ Inc; Local Business Journals **EDU:** Master of Business Administration, Kennedy Western University **A/A/S:** Veterans of Foreign Wars; Founding Member, ICA; Board of Directors, Center for Developmental Services **C/VW:** Congregation of the Sisters of Saint Joseph of Peace

HALLIE J. GORE
Material Manager
The Industrial Company
2211 Elk River Road
Steamboat Springs, CO 80487 United States
hallieg@ticus.com
http://www.ticus.com

BUS: Heavy Industrial Contractor **P/S:** Construction of Facilities for Power, Mining and Materials Processing, Renewable Energy, Food and Beverage **MA:** International **EXP:** Ms. Gore's expertise includes material management and warehousing. **H/I/S:** Oil Painting Landscapes, Sculpting **EDU:** High School Education **C/VW:** Local Church

DANUTA M. GOROCH
1) Dentist 2) Race Horse Trainer
1) Indian Rock Dental
25 Indian Rock Road, Suite 27
Windham, NH 03087 United States
dkutt@msn.com
http://www.cambridgewhoswho.com

BUS: 1) Family and Cosmetic Dentistry 2) Racing **P/S:** 1) Dental Care 2) Thoroughbred Horse Racing **MA:** 1) Local 2) National **EXP:** Ms. Goroch's expertise includes general dentistry and horse racing. **H/I/S:** Horse Racing **FBP:** Thoroughbred Times **EDU:** Doctor of Medical Dentistry, Tufts University **A/A/S:** Merrimack Valley Dental Society; American Dental Association **C/VW:** Local Nursing Home **A/S:** She attributes her success to hard work. **B/I:** She became involved in the profession because she became interested in the field in high school. **H/O:** The highlight of her career was having her horse win an allowance race at the Aqueduct Racetrack in New York.

TERESA A. GOSS
Autistic and Profound Disabled Teacher
Liberty High School
319 Summit Drive
Liberty, SC 29657 United States
gossta@picken.k12.sc.us
http://www.pickens.k12.sc.us

BUS: Public Education **P/S:** Public Education, Special Education **MA:** Local **D/D/R:** Educating and Helping to Initiate Students with Autism and Profound Mental Disorders into the Community **H/I/S:** Spending Quality Time with her Family **FBP:** Council for Exceptional Children Publications **EDU:** Pursuing Master's Degree in Special Education, Clemson University; Bachelor of Arts in Special Education, Piedmont College **A/A/S:** Autism Society; Council for Exceptional Children; Team Member, Augmented Committee for Assisted Technology **A/H:** Teacher of the Year, Liberty High School (2000) **C/VW:** Prevent Child Abuse-Pickens County; Muscular Dystrophy Association **A/S:** She attributes her career success to her role as a lifetime learner, her hard work, her ability to form strong relationships with the community and her students. **B/I:** After studying education in college, she knew that she wanted to pursue a career as a teacher. **H/O:** She feels that the positive relationships she has developed with her students' parents are the highlights of her career.

MAUREEN GOSSOO
Mathematics Teacher
Kingswood-Oxford Upper School
170 Kingswood Road
West Hartford, CT 06119 United States
dgossoo@aol.com
http://www.cambridgewhoswho.com

BUS: School **P/S:** Mathematics Education **MA:** Local **D/D/R:** Teaching Algebra, Trigonometry and Pre-Calculus in Regular and Advanced Placement Classes **H/I/S:** Playing the Piano, Knitting, Crocheting, Cross-Stitching, Reading, Attending her Son's Varsity Swimming and Sailing Events **FBP:** National Council of Teachers of Mathematics Publications; Bon Appetit **EDU:** Master of Arts in Counseling, Central Connecticut State University (1972); Bachelor of Arts in Mathematics, SUNY Albany **A/A/S:** Connecticut Association of Mathematics Teachers; National Council of Teachers of Mathematics **A/H:** Mathematics Teacher of the Year, University of Connecticut (2003); Student Council Advisor of the Year (2001); Award for Community Service, Newington Schools **C/VW:** St. John Fisher; National Multiple Sclerosis Society; American Cancer Society **A/S:** She attributes her success to her availability to help students inside and outside of the classroom. **B/I:** She became involved in her profession because she had wanted to be a mathematics teacher since she was very young and always helped out as a student. **H/O:** The highlights of her career were being named outstanding advisor by the student council and mathematics teacher of the year for the entire state of Connecticut.

MS. SUZANNE M. GOULET-BUCKLEY
President, Chief Executive Officer, Owner, Founder
Artistic Inspirations Unlimited
821 Heron Road
Weston, FL 33326 United States
smbuckley821@aol.com
http://www.cambridgewhoswho.com

BUS: Hand, Painted Glassware **P/S:** Hand Painted Glassware, Personalized High End Glass Items **MA:** Florida **D/D/R:** Selling Unique Custom and Personalized Painted Glass Items **H/I/S:** Tennis, Golfing, Reading, Painting **FBP:** Business Journal for Ft. Lauderdale; Western Lifestyle Magazine **EDU:** Bachelor's Degree in Sociology, Florida South College **A/A/S:** Chamber of Commerce of Ft. Lauderdale, Tower Club, NANBU **C/VW:** Women in Distress; Kids in Distress; Autism Speaks; St. Thomas Aquinas; St. Paul's Lutheran **A/S:** She attributes her success to her drive. **B/I:** She became involved in her profession because she has always enjoyed painting. **H/O:** The highlight of her career is painting for private clubs.

MS. KAY A. GOWENS
Registered Nurse, Home Care Nurse
Maxim Health Care Services
406 Garden Wood Place
Valrico, FL 33594 United States
kay.gowens@cwwemail.com
kaygowens@yahoo.com
http://www.cambridgewhoswho.com

BUS: Healthcare Center **P/S:** Healthcare **MA:** Regional **EXP:** Ms. Gowens' expertise is in patient care. **D/D/R:** Offering Nursing Services for the Elderly and Disabled in the Comfort of their Homes **H/I/S:** Spending Time at the Church, Spending Time with her Family, Exploring and Sharing Health Alternatives, Reading, Traveling **FBP:** RN; Spectrum **EDU:** Registered Nurse, Bronson Western Michigan University (1961)

RHONDA GRABOW
Senior Vice President of Strategic Planning
Innoviant, Inc.
11 Scott Street, Suite 150
Wausau, WI 54403 United States
rhonda.grabow@innoviant.com
http://www.innoviant.com

BUS: Pharmacy Benefits Administrator **P/S:** Prescription Benefit Administration Focused on Lowest Net Cost, Trend Management and Service Excellence for Self-Funded Employer Groups, Health Plans, Union and Coalitions **MA:** National **EXP:** Ms. Grabow's expertise includes product development, project management, marketing, communications, employee development and long-range planning. **H/I/S:** Fishing, Swimming, Reading **FBP:** Managed Healthcare Executive; Business Insurance; Harvard Business Review **EDU:** Coursework in Management, Kellogg School of Management, Northwestern University **CERTS:** Certification, Health Insurance Association of America **A/A/S:** National Association for Female Executives; Association of Managed Care Pharmacy; Governor's Panel, State of Wisconsin **A/H:** Business Insurance's Top 40 Executives Under the Age of Forty **C/VW:** Impact Team Member for Family Violence, United Way; Secretary of Board of Directors, The Neighbors' Place **DOB:** April 3, 2008 **POB:** Wausau **SP:** Ken **CHILD:** Cassady, Grant, Heather **C/A:** Creator, Pharmacy Benefits Management, TPA; Founder, Independent Company

CATHERINE C. GRAEFF, R.Ph., MBA
Senior Vice President of Communication and Industry Relations
National Council for Prescription Drug Programs
9240 E. Raintree Drive
Scottsdale, AZ 85260 United States
cgraeff@ncpdp.org
http://www.ncpdp.org

BUS: Nonprofit Healthcare Center **P/S:** Healthcare **MA:** National **D/D/R:** Managing Operations, Prescribing Drug Benefits, Ensuring Healthcare Standards, Educating, Public Speaking **H/I/S:** Cooking, Gardening, Skiing **EDU:** Master of Business Administration, University of Houston; Bachelor of Science, College of Pharmacy, University of Nebraska Medical Center **A/A/S:** Workgroup for Electronic Data Interchange; National Community Pharmacists Association; Medical Group Management Association; America's Health Insurance Plans **C/VW:** The Association of Junior Leagues International Inc; Heard Museum **A/S:** She attributes her success to the support she receives from her family. **B/I:** She became involved in her profession after working as a delivery person at a pharmacy.

JOYCE E. GRAHAM, BSN, RN
Registered Nurse
Kaiser Permanente
2100 Pennsylvania Avenue N.W.
Washington, DC 20037 United States
joyce.graham@kp.org
http://www.cambridgewhoswho.com

BUS: HMO **P/S:** Quality Healthcare for All Patients **MA:** Local **EXP:** Ms. Graham's expertise is in rheumatology. **D/D/R:** Assisting in the Ear, Nose and Throat, Cardiology, Allergy and Neurology Departments **H/I/S:** Movies, Word Games, Reading, Church Activities **FBP:** American Journal of Nursing; Permanente Journal **EDU:** Bachelor of Science in Nursing, University of the District of Columbia **C/VW:** President, Church Health League; Adopted Grandmother; Various Community Outreach Programs **A/S:** She attributes her personal and professional success to her flexibility, sense of humor and passion for her work. **B/I:** She has always had an interest in the field and a desire to serve others. **H/O:** The highlight of her career was earning her BSN.

YVETTE GRAHAM, MBA
System Director
Allstate Insurance Company
3075 Sanders Road, Suite G2F
Northbrook, IL 60062 United States
ygraham@allstate.com
http://www.allstate.com

BUS: Insurance Company **P/S:** Insurance Services Including Property, Casualty, Life and Automobile Insurance **MA:** National **EXP:** Ms. Graham's expertise is in enterprise portfolio management. **H/I/S:** Bowling, Attending Church Activities **EDU:** Master of Business Administration, University of Illinois **CERTS:** Certification in Women's Senior Leadership Program, Center for Executive Women, Kellogg School of Management **A/A/S:** Center for Executive Women, Kellogg School of Management; Mayor's Council of Technology Advisors; Black Data Processing Association **C/VW:** Sunday School Teacher, Metropolitan Community Church; President, Ushers Ministry

MARCIA A. GRANDSTAFF, RN, MSN, CCRN
Clinical Nurse Specialist
Community Health Network
1500 N. Ritter Avenue
Indianapolis, IN 46219 United States
mgrandstaff@ecommunity.com
http://www.ecommunity.com

BUS: Nonprofit Community Health Network **P/S:** Community Health Network for Services on a Nonprofit Basis **MA:** Local **D/D/R:** Rehabilitation Nursing, Overseeing Policies and Procedures, Managing Projects **H/I/S:** Reading, Cooking **EDU:** Master of Science in Nursing, Indiana University School of Nursing; Bachelor of Science in Nursing, Indiana University **A/A/S:** Sigma Theta Tau International; Association of Rehabilitation Nurses **C/VW:** Girl Scouts of America; Mount Comfort United Methodist Church **A/S:** She attributes her success her hard work, determination and setting goals for herself. **B/I:** She became involved in her profession because she always enjoyed helping people. **H/O:** The highlight of her career has been working with other nurses and seeing them improve.

MR. DON W. GRANTHAM
Director, Chief Executive Officer
Evolve Media
175 N. Indian Hill Boulevard, Suite B200
Claremont, CA 91711 United States
don@evolvemedia.com
http://www.evolvemedia.com

BUS: Strategic Interactive Design and Development Firm **P/S:** Web Design, Online Applications, Graphic and Interactive Design, Deep Technology Expertise, Content Management, Interactive Services, Email Marketing, Creative Services, Hosting, Process Services, Financial Tools, Search Engine Optimization and Pay Per Click Campaigns, Virtual Iris, Project Management Services, Technical Services **MA:** International **D/D/R:** Managing Business Operations, Negotiating Deals with Clients, Programming, Designing **H/I/S:** Scuba Diving, Traveling **FBP:** Hell Magazine **EDU:** Bachelor of Arts in Business Management, Minor in Computer Applications, California State University at Fullerton (1989) **A/A/S:** American Institute of Graphic Arts; AIP

GAIL GRAY
Teacher (Retired)
Las Lomas High School
1460 S. Main Street
Walnut Creek, CA 94596 United States
gray1@comcast.net
http://www.cambridgewhoswho.com

BUS: High School **P/S:** Public High School Education **MA:** Local **D/D/R:** Teaching Fine Arts Education in High School **H/I/S:** Kayaking, Art, Going to Museums **FBP:** The Artist's Magazine; Southwest **EDU:** Bachelor of Arts in Fine Arts, University of Montana at Missoula **C/VW:** American Cancer Society **A/S:** She attributes her success to her interest in teaching and watching her students grow and learn. **B/I:** She became involved in her profession because she had a desire to share her knowledge and love of art with her students. **H/O:** The highlight of her career was being able to see her students understand the concepts she was teaching.

NANCY GRAY
Owner
Fourth Street Gallery and FSG Art Consulting
508 E. Fourth Street
Lampasas, TX 76550 United States
nancy@fourthstreetgallery.com
http://www.fourthstreetgallery.com

BUS: Fine Art Dealer and Custom Framing Service **P/S:** Paintings, Sculpture, and Works on Paper by Exceptional European and American Artists **MA:** International **D/D/R:** Working with Clients and Artists in the United States, France and Italy, Collaborating with Interior Designers for Corporate and Private Clients, Finding the Right Piece for the Client's Needs, Managing Projects, Consulting, Maintaining the Database of Itemized Existing Art **H/I/S:** Reading, Painting, Swimming, Sculpting **FBP:** Decor Magazine; PSM Magazine; Art News; Metropolitan; Elements; American Style **EDU:** Bachelor's Degree in Fine Arts, University of Texas (1992); Coursework in Finance, The University of Texas at San Antonio **A/A/S:** National Oil Painters Society (1998); Professional Picture Framers Association; American Society of Interior Design **A/H:** Standing Ovation Award (1999); Confluence Jurors Award, National Exhibit Jury Competition (1998); Nominee, Gold Medal

TINA GRAY-RUSSELL, BSW, LSW
Self-Employed In-Home Provider
Department of Health
1900 Kanawha Boulevard E.
Building E, Building 6
Charleston, WV 25305 United States
samuri872003@yahoo.com
http://www.cambridgewhoswho.com

BUS: In-Home Services **P/S:** Family Crisis Assistance **MA:** Local **D/D/R:** Offering Parenting Instruction, Conducting Home Study Evaluations and Home Studies for Potential Foster Homes, Mentoring, Working with Children with Behavior Problems **H/I/S:** Traveling, Reading, Bicycling, Hiking **EDU:** Bachelor's Degree in Social Work, Concord University **A/A/S:** National Association of Social Workers **C/VW:** St. Jude Children's Research Hospital

DANIELLE ANN GREANEY
Elementary School Teacher
Monroe Woodbury Central School District
278 Route 32
Central Valley, NY 10917 United States
daniellegreaney@hotmail.com
http://www.cambridgewhoswho.com

BUS: School District **P/S:** Education **MA:** Local **EXP:** Ms. Greaney's expertise is in reading development. **D/D/R:** Teaching All Subjects to Third-Grade Inclusion Students **H/I/S:** Traveling **FBP:** Reading Teacher **EDU:** Master's Degree in Literacy, Long Island University; Bachelor's Degree in Special Education and Childhood Education, SUNY Cortland **A/A/S:** Kappa Delta Phi **C/VW:** Volunteer, Local Charitable Organizations

CHARLES L. GREEN
Program Director
Minnequa Community Corrections
2411 Lake Avenue
Pueblo, CO 81004 United States
cgreen@mcc.nexep.com
http://www.cambridgewhoswho.com

BUS: Offender Rehabilitation/Community Corrections **P/S:** Community Corrections, Program, Substance Abuse TMT, Domestic Violence, Urine Screenings, Anger Management, Relapse Prevention, Cognitive Groups **MA:** Local **EXP:** Mr. Green's expertise is in substance abuse and mental health rehabilitation. **EDU:** Master's Degree in Psychology, University of Northern Colorado **CERTS:** Certified Counselor, State of Colorado **C/VW:** National Association for the Advancement of Colored People; USC Veteran's Club **A/S:** He attributes his personal and professional success to his supportive family. **B/I:** He has always had an interest in the field and a desire to help others. **H/O:** The highlight of his career was receiving an advanced degree.

KAREN L. GREEN, DVM
Veterinarian
Banfield, The Pet Hospital
3589 River Rapids Drive
Coon Rapids, MN 55448 United States
moor0378@hotmail.com
http://www.banfields.net

BUS: Pet Hospital **P/S:** Veterinary Medicine **MA:** Local **EXP:** Ms. Green's expertise is in small animal medicine. **H/I/S:** Visiting Zoos **FBP:** Compendium Magazine **EDU:** Doctor of Veterinary Medicine, University of Minnesota **A/A/S:** American Veterinary Medical Association; American Animal Hospital Association **C/VW:** American Society for the Prevention of Cruelty to Animals **B/I:** She became involved in her profession because of her love of animals. **H/O:** The highlight of her career has been being able to treat sick pets and have them get well.

PAMELA S. GREEN
1) Tag Agency of Enid, Inc. 2) Paradise Donuts of Enid, Inc.
122 N. Oakwood Road
Enid, OK 73703 United States
momok_pam@yahoo.com
http://www.okstate.tax

BUS: 1) Independent Branch of Department of Motor Vehicles 2) Donut Shop **P/S:** 1) Financial Administration 2) Baked Goods, Donuts **MA:** 1) Local 2) Local **EXP:** Ms. Green's expertise includes administration and financial operations. **D/D/R:** Managing the Taxes and Fees Associated with the Registration and Tagging of Vehicles, Overseeing Daily Operations of the Two Entities **H/I/S:** Watching her Husband Race Cars **FBP:** Consumer Products **EDU:** Associate of Arts in Elementary Education, Northern Oklahoma College (2003) **A/A/S:** Air Force Association

DR. RUBY GREEN
Pastor, Chief Executive Officer
Victory Bible Church
501 W. Block Street
El Dorado, AR 71730 United States
vbcinc@hotmail.com
http://www.vbc-inc.org

BUS: Church **P/S:** Religious Services, Bible Study, Teaching the Word of God, Deliverance Ministry, Prophetic Ministry **MA:** Regional **D/D/R:** Specializing in Family and Youth Counseling, Evangelism, Conference, Workshop and Motivational Speaking and Prayer, Acting as a Civil Service Commissioner of El Dorado **H/I/S:** Traveling, Reading **FBP:** Charisma; Newsweek **EDU:** Honorary Doctoral Degree, Houston Theological Institute (2005) **A/A/S:** District Prayer Coordinator, Arkansas Concert Of Prayer; United States Strategic Prayer Network **A/H:** Spirit Award (2007); Friend of Education Award

DOTTIE M. GREENAGE
Realtor, Team Leader
Keller Williams Realty Central Delaware, Greenage Group
1671 S. State Street
Dover, DE 19901 United States
dgreenage1@comcast.net
http://www.exceedingexpectations.cc

BUS: Real Estate **P/S:** Real Estate Sales **MA:** Regional **EXP:** Ms. Greenage's expertise is in residential real estate. **H/I/S:** Gardening, Writing Poetry, Writing Articles on Real Estate Topics **EDU:** Coursework in Business Administration, University of Delaware **A/A/S:** Kent County Association of Realtors; Delaware Association of Realtors; National Association of Realtors **C/VW:** Keller Williams Cares Community Outreach; Habitat for Humanity; Local Church; Local Nursing Home **A/S:** She attributes her personal and professional success to her faith in God. **B/I:** After working in the retail industry for many years, she changed her career direction to real estate. **H/O:** The highlight of her career is making the dreams of others come true.

MS. JOANIE T. GREENE, PH.D.
President
Christian Outreach Bible Institute
507 Person Street
Fayetteville, NC 28301 United States
obifnc@aol.com
http://www.cambridgewhoswho.com

BUS: Bible Institute Dedicated to Exceptional Ministry Services **P/S:** Excellence in Religious Education, Bible Study, Outreach Ministry Services, Counseling, Student Services **MA:** National **D/D/R:** Reviewing the Curriculum, Working as an Administrator, Reviewing Criteria for Admission, Overseeing Operations, Helping Bible Institutes, Colleges and Churches Achieve a National Status, Working within the Community, Feeding the Homeless, Working as a Liaison with Other Schools, Mentoring **H/I/S:** Exercising, Bowling, Rollerskating **EDU:** Ph.D. in Religious Education, Lighthouse Christian College, Beebe, Arkansas (1997); Doctorate in Religious Education, United Theological Seminary, Orlando, Florida (1993) **A/A/S:** Accrediting Commission International, Beebe, AK **C/VW:** CLURT International Assemblies with Bishop George G. Bloomer, Durham, North Carolina

PETRA L. GREENE (PATTY)
Realtor
Keller Williams Realty
PO Box 3536
Ventura, CA 93006 United States
patty@venturalovelyhomes.com
http://www.venturalovelyhomes.com

BUS: Independently Owned and Operated Real Estate Company **P/S:** Buying and Selling Residential Properties, Land Sales, Single and Multi-Family Homes, New Construction, Condominiums, Relocations, First Time Home Buyers, Investment Properties **MA:** International **D/D/R:** Handling Investment Properties **H/I/S:** Golfing, Reading, Walking **FBP:** Homes and Land Magazine **EDU:** Registered Nurse, Pasadena City College (1963); Coursework in Computer Science; Coursework in Business Education **CERTS:** Certification in Business **A/A/S:** Ventura County Fire Historic Society; Ventura County Coastal Association of Realtors; National Association for Hispanic Real Estate Professionals; Navy League **C/VW:** Ventura County Speakers Bureau; Elks Club; Assistant League of Ventura County

JOSHUA A. GREENWALD, MD
Plastic Surgeon
Cosmetic Surgery Association of Westchester, PLLC
10 Chester Avenue
White Plains, NY 10601 United States
drgreenwald@gmail.com
http://www.drgreenwald.com
http://www.drjoshuagreenwald.com

BUS: Cosmetic and Reconstructive Practice **P/S:** Cosmetic Treatments, Collagen Injections, Breast Augmentation, Liposuction, Tummy Tuck, Laser Skin Treatments, Vein Injections **MA:** Regional **EXP:** Mr. Greenwald's expertise includes aesthetic breast and facial surgery and body contouring. **H/I/S:** Swimming, Reading, Scuba Diving **FBP:** Journal of Plastic and Reconstructive Surgery **EDU:** MD, New York University School of Medicine (1995); Bachelor of Arts, Columbia University (1991); Coursework in General Surgery, New York University; Research Fellowship, New York University Institute for Reconstructive Plastic Surgery **CERTS:** Board Certified, American Board of Plastic Surgery **A/A/S:** American Society of Plastic Surgeons; Westchester County Medical Society; American Society for Aesthetic Plastic Surgeons **A/H:** Research Award, White Plains Hospital Center; Research Award, Northern Westchester Hospital Center; Research Award, United Hospital Medical Center; Research Award, Putnam Hospital Center **DOB:** July 15, 1970

JANET S. GREER
Instructor Emeritus
University of Southern Indiana
8600 University Boulevard
Evansville, IN 47715 United States
jsgreer@usi.edu
http://www.cambridgewhoswho.com

BUS: Higher Education **P/S:** Education **MA:** National **D/D/R:** Teaching Education Courses **H/I/S:** Spending time with Family, Traveling, Cooperating with Musical Organizations, Attending Musical Events **FBP:** Educational Leadership **EDU:** Master's Degree in Education, Indiana State University; Bachelor of Arts in Education, College of Saint Benedict **A/A/S:** International Reading Association; Association for Supervision and Curriculum Development; National Association for Music Education; MSNC **C/VW:** Local Church; American Heart Association; Special Olympics; Diabetes Association; Arthritis Association **A/S:** She attributes her success to her love for working with students and future teachers. **B/I:** She became involved in the profession because she always wanted to be a teacher. **H/O:** The most gratifying aspect of her career is seeing her students serve on a state and national level.

SANDRA M. GREIWE
Owner, President
Reuse Caboose
14 Willowbrook Place
Saint Charles, MO 63301 United States
sandra.greiwe@cwwemail.com
http://www.cambridgewhoswho.com

BUS: Recycling Firm **P/S:** Recycling Services **MA:** International **EXP:** Ms. Greiwe's expertise is in environmental education. **H/I/S:** Playing Tennis, Art work, Making Crafts, Biking, Fishing, Spending Time Outdoors **FBP:** Smithsonian; National Geographic **EDU:** College Coursework **CERTS:** Registered Nurse **A/H:** Hardy's Hometown Hero Environmental Award (1993); Pam Bran Environmental Achievement Award, Women of Action, Missouri

JUDITH EVADNEY GREY
Kindergarten Teacher
Ludlam Elementary School
6639 S.W. 74th Street
South Miami, FL 33143 United States
239823@dadeschools.net
http://www.cambridgewhoswho.com

BUS: Elementary School **P/S:** Education **MA:** Local **D/D/R:** Teaching Elementary School Students **H/I/S:** Cooking, Reading, Traveling **FBP:** Education Journals **EDU:** Pursuing Doctor of Education in Educational Leadership, Saint Thomas University; Master of Science in Teaching English to Speakers of Other Languages, University of Miami; Bachelor's Degree in Early Childhood Education, Sojourner-Douglass College **CERTS:** National Board Certified Teacher **A/A/S:** National Board for Professional Teaching Standards **C/VW:** Tutor, Love Fellowship Ministries **A/S:** She attributes her success to her determination and desire to set an example for her family. **B/I:** She became involved in her profession because she always wanted to be a teacher and make a difference in the lives of her students. **H/O:** The most gratifying aspect of her career is watching her students grow and succeed in life.

COLLEEN GRIFFIN
Art Director
The Ant Farm
110 S. Fairfax Avenue
Suite 200
Los Angeles, CA 90036 United States
six13@hotmail.com
http://www.cambridgewhoswho.com

BUS: Motion Picture Advertising Company **P/S:** Movie Posters, Trailers, Advertisements **MA:** International **EXP:** Ms. Griffins expertise includes graphic design, art direction and fine arts. **D/D/R:** Working in Adobe Photoshop and Illustrator and Other Programs to Create Movie Posters, Sketching, Scheduling Photo Shoots, Meeting with Clients **H/I/S:** Writing, Dancing, Traveling, Designing Jewelry, Hiking **FBP:** Communication Arts; Dynamic Graphics; Print; STEP; HOW **EDU:** Bachelor's Degree in Fine Arts and Communications, SUNY Geneseo **A/H:** Finalist, Key Art Award (2008); Finalist, Golden Trailer Award (2008); Nominee, Key Art Award (2005); Finalist, Publicity Club of New England Bell Ringer Award (2003); Finalist, Publicity Club of New England Bell Ringer Award (2000); Publicity Club of New England Bell Ringer Award (1999) **C/VW:** Food on Foot **A/S:** She attributes her success to her passion for her profession and developing good relations with her coworkers, employers and clients. **B/I:** She became involved in her profession because she decided to try her luck in entertainment after working as a designer in Boston and New York. **H/O:** The highlight of her career was being nominated for the Key Art Award, the highest honor in her profession.

KATHY J. GRIFFIN, BS
Teacher Third Grade
Hamilton County School
c/o Board Central Hamilton Elementary School
553 Chan Bridge Drive
griffin-k@firn.edu
http://www.cambridgewhoswho.com

BUS: Education **P/S:** Elementary Education **MA:** Local **EXP:** Ms. Griffin's expertise is in reading. **D/D/R:** Reading **H/I/S:** Reading Mysteries, Shopping, and Fitness **FBP:** Industry-Related Material **EDU:** Bachelor's Degree, Elementary Education, Florida A & M University; Pursuing Master of Educational Leadership, Florida A & M University **A/A/S:** Association of Supervision and Curriculum Development; National Education Association, Golden Key International Honour Society **A/H:** Teacher of the Year (2006) **A/S:** She attributes her success to hard work and determination. **B/I:** She became involved in her profession due to the children's interest in learning. **H/O:** The highlight of her career is in seeing her students succeed.

VERNICE M. GRIFFIN, CDT
Owner, CDT
VMB Dental Arts
8911 Greeneway Commons Place
Suite 201
Louisville, KY 40220 United States
vmdentalarts@yahoo.com
http://www.VMB-DENTALARTS.com

BUS: Dental Laboratory **P/S:** Crown and Bridge Prosthesis **MA:** National **EXP:** Ms. Griffin's expertise is in dental technology. **H/I/S:** Reading, Gardening, Playing the Violin, Attending Mixed Martial Arts Matches **FBP:** Journal of Dental Technology; Lab Management Today; Interior Design; Dentistry Today; Cosmetic Dentistry **EDU:** Bachelor of Arts in Psychology, University of Kentucky; Associate in Applied Science, Lexington Community College **CERTS:** Certification in Simplifying Posterior Dental Anatomy (2000); Certification in Accredited Dental Technology, National Board for Certification in Dental Laboratory Technology; Certification, National Board for Certification in Crown and Bridge **A/A/S:** Alumni Association, University of Kentucky; American Cosmetic Dentistry Laboratory Association **C/VW:** Cancer Research Society **A/S:** She attributes her success to her education. **B/I:** She became involved in the profession because she was encouraged by a friend in high school. **H/O:** The most gratifying aspect of her career is helping her patients value themselves.

LINDA R. GRIGGS, RN, BSN, MCP
Registered Nurse, Foster Parent
Sharp Grossmont Hospital
Grossmont Center Drive
La Mesa, CA 91942 United States
osllrg@sbcglobal.net
http://www.sharp.com

BUS: Largest Healthcare Facility in East San Diego County **P/S:** Emergency and Critical Care, Cardiac Care, Orthopedics, Rehabilitation, Behavioral Health, Neurology, Women's and Children's Health and Hospice Care **MA:** Local **D/D/R:** Foster Parenting for Premature and Drug-Affected Babies, Promoting Premature Infant Health and Development **H/I/S:** Camping, Hiking, Singing, Music **FBP:** RN; Neonatal Nursing; Harvard Mental Health Newsletter **EDU:** Certified in Infant and Preschool Mental Health, Alliant International University (2007); Master's Degree in Clinical Counseling and Psychology; Master's Degree in Religious Studies, Southern California Seminary; Bachelor of Science in Nursing, San Diego State University **A/A/S:** Association of Neonatal Nurses; Association of Christian Counselors **C/VW:** Order of St. Luke; Foster Parent Association; Domestic Violence Annual Conference

BARBARA J. GRIMM, ACTIS, MBA
Web Development Lead
Altair Avionics Corp.
63 Nahatan Street
Norwood, MA 02062 United States
bgrimm@altairavionics.aero
http://www.managementquality.com

BUS: Aerospace **P/S:** Aircraft Engine Monitoring, Data Analysis Services **MA:** International **EXP:** Ms. Grimm's expertise is in web development and management. **H/I/S:** Designing Jewelry **EDU:** Master of Business Administration, Northeastern University **C/VW:** Massachusetts Society for the Prevention of Cruelty to Animals **A/S:** She attributes her success to perseverance and keeping up with change in the industry. **B/I:** She was prompted to enter her profession because she had an interest in the field. **H/O:** The highlight of her career was obtaining her current position.

JACQUELINE A. GROGAN
Registered Nurse
Southwestern Vermont Medical Center
100 Hospital Drive
2 West
Bennington, VT 05201 United States
http://www.svhealthcare.org

BUS: Community Hospital with 96 Beds Committed to Excellence in Healthcare **P/S:** Cardiological, Birthing, Diabetes, Emergency, Therapies, Laboratories, Nutrition Counseling, Occupational Health, Rehabilitation, X-Rays, Imaging **MA:** Regional **EXP:** Ms. Grogan's expertise is in medical-surgical nursing. **D/D/R:** Coordinating and Overseeing the Care of Acutely Ill Patients, Directing a Team of Licensed Practical Nurses and Licensed Nursing Assistants **H/I/S:** Bowling, Vacations **EDU:** Associate of Science in Nursing, Vermont Technical College **CERTS:** National Certification in Medical-Surgical Nursing, American Nurses Credentialing Center; Certified Preceptor; Certified in Telemetry and Conscious Sedation **A/A/S:** Phi Theta Kappa; Professional Practice Council **A/H:** Magnet Award for Nursing Excellence

GLORIA GROOMES
Registered Nurse, Mental Health Specialist
Department of Corrections, Lake Correctional Institution
2762 Valiant Drive
Clermont, FL 34711 United States
kvg157@aol.com
http://www.dc.state.fl.us

BUS: State Correctional Facility **P/S:** Custody, Control, Care, Treatment and Rehabilitation of Inmates **MA:** Regional **D/D/R:** Charge Nursing in the Mental Health Department, Working the Floor, Responding to Psychiatric Crises and Chronic Medical Issues, Educating the Staff as Needed **H/I/S:** Fishing **FBP:** American Journal of Nursing **EDU:** Bachelor of Science in Nursing, Florida A&M University (1985) **CERTS:** Certification, American Nurses Credentialing Center (1998-2003) **A/A/S:** Florida Nurses Association; Representative, American Nurses Association

LORI L. GROSSMAN
Administrator, Instructional Coordinator
Houston Independent School District
4400 W. 18th Street
Houston, TX 77092 United States
lgrossma@houstonisd.org
http://www.houstonisd.org

BUS: Public School System **P/S:** Education **MA:** Local **D/D/R:** Developing and Coordinating Training for Mentors of New Teachers and Induction **H/I/S:** Reading, Traveling, Coaching Volleyball and Softball **FBP:** Educational Leadership **EDU:** Master's Degree in Elementary Education, Stephen F. Austin State University; Bachelor of Science in Elementary Education, Stephen F. Austin State University **A/A/S:** National Staff Development Council; Texas State Development Council; Kappa Delta Phi; Alpha Chi National Honor Society; Board Member, Brook School; Association for Supervision and Curriculum Development; National Education Association; International Reading Association **A/H:** Nomination, Who's Who Among American Teachers

Ms. Jeanne E. Grover
Office Manager
Berkshire Brewing Company, Inc.
12 Railroad Street
PO Box 141
South Deerfield, MA 01373 United States
mjbbc@comcast.net
http://www.berkshirebrewingcompany.com

BUS: Manufacturing Company **P/S:** Beer Including Fine Ales and Lager **MA:** MA, VT, RI, CT **D/D/R:** Budgeting, Performing Massage Therapy, Managing Administration, Human Resources, Finance and Sales **H/I/S:** Practicing Yoga, Golfing, Walking, Gardening, Reading **FBP:** The New York Times; BusinessWeek **EDU:** Pursuing Master's Degree in Education, Our Lady of the Elms College, Chicopee; Bachelor of Science in Management, Our Lady of the Elms College, Chicopee **CERTS:** Licensed Massage Therapist **A/A/S:** Associated Bodywork and Massage Professionals **C/VW:** Massachusetts Society for the Prevention of Cruelty to Animals; American Society for the Prevention of Cruelty to Animals **POB:** Greenfield, Ma **CHILD:** Abbigayle **A/S:** She attributes her success to the support she receives from others. **B/I:** She became involved in her profession because she was referred by her friend. **H/O:** The most gratifying aspect of her career is being successful in her profession.

Betty J. Grulke
Receptionist, Administrative Assistant (Retired)
Garst Seed Company
2369 330th Street
Slater, IA 50244 United States
bettygrulke@hotmail.com
http://www.cambridgewhoswho.com

BUS: Seed, Corn and Soybean Company **P/S:** Seed, Corn and Soybean **MA:** International **D/D/R:** Acting as a Receptionist and Administrative Assistant **H/I/S:** Reading, Volunteering Work, Her Grandchildren, Church **EDU:** Coursework in Education, Drake University **A/A/S:** Questers International **A/H:** Volunteer of the Year Award (2005) **C/VW:** Special Olympics **A/S:** She attributes her success to the support she gets and because she finds her work very interesting. **B/I:** She became involved in her profession because she enjoys helping people and is interested in studying antiques. **H/O:** The highlight of her career is serving as an officer in Trivent Financial for Lutherans.

KATE GUERIN
Public Relations Associate
Ruder Finn, Inc
301 E. 57th Street
Third Floor
New York, NY 10022 United States
kate.guerin@gmail.com
http://www.ruderfinn.com

BUS: Public Relations Firm **P/S:** Public Media Relations **MA:** National **EXP:** Ms. Guerin's expertise includes media relations, writing and strategic planning. **EDU:** Bachelor's Degree in English Literature, University of Connecticut

EDGAR JESUS G. GUERRERO
E.I.T., Civil Engineer
AIA, Ltd.
7909 Heid Avenue
El Paso, TX 79915 United States
egguerrero8484@yahoo.com
http://www.cambridgewhoswho.com

BUS: Engineering Company **P/S:** Geotechnical Services, Engineering, Consulting, Apprenticeship **MA:** National **EXP:** Mr. Guerrero's expertise is in structural and geo-technical lab work. **D/D/R:** Analyzing Data, Giving Presentations throughout Corporate America, Promoting Awareness and Sponsorship of the Steel Bridge and Concrete Canoe Competition, Studying Structural Engineering and Bridge Designs **H/I/S:** Watching Football and Basketball, Playing Chess **EDU:** Bachelor of Science in Civil Engineering, The University of Texas, El Paso (2007) **A/A/S:** National Scholars Honor Society; American Society of Civil Engineers **A/H:** National Dean's List **DOB:** August 4, 1984

SHARMIN GUGAT, M.ED.
Educator
Mesa Valley School District # 51 - Broadway Elementary School
2115 Grand Avenue
Grand Junction, CO 81501 United States
sharming@mesa.k12.co.us
http://www.mesa.k12.co.us

BUS: Elementary School Committed to Fostering Achievement of High Academic and Ethical Standards **P/S:** Education, Special Education, Guidance, Counseling, Transportation, Food Services, After-School Programs **MA:** Regional **D/D/R:** Teaching Reading, Mathematics, Social Studies, Science and Spelling to Fourth-Grade Students, Participating in the Teacher Effectiveness Team for Special Education and Gifted Children, Working on the Report Card, Mathematics and Social Studies Committees **H/I/S:** Working Out, Spending Time with her Dogs **FBP:** Teacher's Helper **EDU:** Master of Education in Reading, University of Northern Colorado (2000); Bachelor of Arts in Elementary Education, University of Northern Colorado **A/A/S:** National Education Association; MVEA

MS. SANDRA S. GUINN
Sales Representative
Midwest Fastener Corporation
9031 Shaver Road
Portage, MI 49024 United States
sandyguinn@locl.net
http://www.fastenerconnection.com

BUS: Distribution Company **P/S:** Packaged Fasteners **MA:** Northern Indiana **EXP:** Ms. Guinn's expertise is in fastener sales to regional hardware and lumber yard stores. **H/I/S:** Bowling, Traveling, Gardening **EDU:** Diploma, Garrett High School, IN **A/H:** Woman Bowler of the Year (2007); Top Award (2002); Diamond Ring Recipient, Over One-Half Million Dollars in Sales **C/VW:** Superintendent, Sunday School **DOB:** November 8, 1949 **POB:** Garrett, IN **SP:** Divorced **W/H:** Sales Representative, Midwest Fastener Corporation; Lumber Yard Worker **A/S:** She attributes her success to her product knowledge. **B/I:** She became involved in her profession through a natural progression of opportunities. **H/O:** The highlight of her career was receiving an award for earning over one-half million dollars in sales.

MARTHA J. GUMBS
Owner, Founder
Auntie M's Crafts
14499 Brentwood Court
Dale City, VA 22193 United States
auntiemscrafts@aol.com
http://www.AuntieMsCraft.com

BUS: Crafts Company **P/S:** Lady Shadow Box and Wood Roses **MA:** Regional **D/D/R:** Offering Handmade Crafts and Sign Name Items, Filling Special Orders, Producing Custom Gift Baskets and Silk Florals **H/I/S:** Participating in Craft Shows **FBP:** Crafters **EDU:** Degree in Business, Queensboro College

CAROLYN R. GUNTON-LEWIS
Broker, Owner
Century 21 Lake Region Realty, Inc.
106 N. Shore Drive
Elysian, MN 56028 United States
c21-lake@myclearwave.net
http://www.c21-lake.com

BUS: Real Estate Agency **P/S:** Commercial and Residential Real Estate Exchange **MA:** Regional **D/D/R:** Selling Lakeshore Residential and Commercial Properties, Assisting Clients, Managing Real Estate Exchange and Business Operations **H/I/S:** Traveling **EDU:** Coursework in Business Studies, Laramie County Community College **CERTS:** Licensed Broker, State of Minnesota (1985); Licensed Real Estate Agent (1980) **A/A/S:** Local Chamber of Commerce; Board of Directors, National Association of Realtors **C/VW:** Epiphany Lutheran Church; American Legion Auxiliary **A/S:** She attributes her success to her ability to interact with people. **B/I:** She became involved in her profession because she believed that the real estate would be an interesting venture. **H/O:** The most gratifying aspect of her career is meeting different people.

VAUGHN D. GURSSLIN
Owner, President
V.G. Enterprises
7706 Rochester Road
Gasport, NY 14067 United States
egleflyt@hotmail.com
http://www.mypowercheck.com

BUS: Identity Theft Protection **P/S:** Identity Theft Prevention **MA:** New York **EXP:** Mr. Gursslin's expertise is in computer science and engineering software. **EDU:** College Coursework **C/VW:** American Heart Association **A/S:** He attributes his success to his advertising skills. **B/I:** He became involved in the profession because he had his identity stolen. **H/O:** The most gratifying aspect of his career is helping others.

SALLY A. GUSTAFSON
1) Counseling Supervisor 2) Pastor, Counseling Supervisor
1) Pittsburg Ministry Center 2) Bridgeway Church
3415 Oakley Road
Antioch, CA 94509 United States
sallyagus@yahoo.com
http://www.cambridgewhoswho.com

BUS: 1) Ministry Center 2) Church **P/S:** 1) Counseling 2) Religious Services, Counseling **MA:** 1) Local 2) Local **D/D/R:** Counseling Families **H/I/S:** Spending Time with Family, Oil Painting **EDU:** Bachelor of Arts in Counseling Psychology, Delta Bible College; Licensed Cosmetology Instructor (1970); Licensed Pastor (2005) **A/A/S:** Art and Culture Foundation **A/H:** Recipient, Awards in Cosmetology (1968) **C/VW:** Antioch Pregnancy Center; International Fellowship of Christians and Jews **A/S:** She attributes her success to her faith in God.

JUDY GUTHRIE, RN
Registered Nurse, Injection Clinic Manager
Kaiser Permanente
3755 Whispering Creek Circle
Stockton, CA 95219 United States
judy.guthrie@kp.org
http://www.kaiserpermanente.org

BUS: Healthcare Organization **P/S:** Preventive Healthcare, Prenatal Healthcare, Well-Baby Healthcare, Immunizations, Emergency Well-Baby Healthcare, Diagnostic Screening, Hospital, Medical and Pharmacy Services, Assistance for the Uninsured and Special Needs Populations, Training New Health Professionals, Introduction of New Delivery Methods into the Healthcare Field **MA:** Northern California Central Valley **D/D/R:** Consulting Clients Regarding Routine and Travel Immunizations for Vaccine-Preventable Diseases **H/I/S:** Gardening, Spending Time with her Grandchildren, Studying Travel Medicine **FBP:** Nursing2009; Needle Tips and the Hepatitis B Coalition News; Journal Watch of Infectious Diseases; International Society of Travel Medicine Journal; Travel Med List Serve; GeoSentinel Alerts **EDU:** Associate Degree in Nursing, San Joaquin Delta College; Coursework in Epidemiology and Prevention of Vaccine-Preventable Diseases **CERTS:** Certificate of Knowledge in Travel Health, The International Society of Travel Medicine **A/A/S:** Alumni Association, San Joaquin Delta College; California Nurses Association; The International Society of Travel Medicine **C/VW:** Epilepsy Foundation of Northern California; Immunization Tracking System, Kaiser Permanente, NC; United Cerebral Palsy Research and Educational Foundation; Volunteer, United Way Annual Neighbors in Health; Immunization Action Coalition; Galt Historical Society; National Wildlife Federation **DOB:** January 10, 1944

APRIL D. GUTKNECHT
President, CEO
Patriot Pool, Inc.
290 Lake Park Road, Suite 804
Lewisville, TX 75057 United States
pres@patriotpool.com
http://www.patriotpool.com

BUS: Regional, Dallas, Ft. Worth Metropolitan Area **P/S:** Complete Pool Service **MA:** Organizational Management and Entrepreneurship **EXP:** Ms. Gutknecht's expertise is in swimming pool construction and remodeling. **H/I/S:** Rock Climbing, Reading **FBP:** Wall St. Journal **EDU:** Associate Degree, Brookhaven College **A/A/S:** Better Business Bureau; National Public Radio **A/S:** She attributes her success to her integrity. **H/O:** The highlight of her career was starting the company.

JILL M. HAALA, DC
Chiropractor
In-Line Chiropractic, LLC
512 2nd Street
Morgan, MN 56266 United States
info@inlinechiro.com
http://www.inlinechiro.com

BUS: Healthcare **P/S:** Chiropractic Services from Infants to the Elderly **MA:** Minnesota **D/D/R:** Specializing in Functional Medicine, Nutrition and Rehabilitation **H/I/S:** Traveling, Spending Time with Family and Friends **FBP:** Industry-Related Publications **EDU:** Doctor of Chiropractic, Northwestern Health Sciences University; Bachelor of Science in Human Biology, Minnesota State University; Certified in Functional Medicine (2003); Certified in Graston Technique (2003) **A/A/S:** American Chiropractic Association; Minnesota Chiropractic Association; Institute for Functional Medicine **A/H:** National Deans List (2003) **DOB:** March 21, 1979 **SP:** Steven **CHILD:** Rylee **W/H:** Chiropractor, In-Line Chiropractic, LLC (2004-Present); Sleepy Eye Chiropractic (2004-2006); Intern, Northwestern Health Sciences University (2003); Intern, Eagle Creek Chiropractic (2003)

MR. TOM R. HACKETT, MD
Orthopaedic Surgeon
The Steadman Hawkins Clinic
181 W. Meadow Drive
Vail, CO 81657 United States
tomhackett@hotmail.com
http://www.steadman-hawkins.com

BUS: Private Academic Surgical Practice **P/S:** Sports Medicine, Trauma Surgery, Ligament and Joint Reconstruction, Sports Medicine, Arthroscopic Surgery, General Orthopaedics, Athletic Injuries, Sports Injuries, Knee Surgery, Rotator Cuff Injuries, Anterior Cruciate Ligament Repair, Spinal Disorders and Injuries, Hand Injuries, Liquissentials Line of Products **MA:** National **D/D/R:** Specializing in Sports Medicine, Directing the Mountain Climbers Association, Lecturing and Teaching in Cuba, China **EDU:** Sports Medicine Fellowship, Kerlan-Jobe Clinic, Los Angeles; Residency, Boston's New England Medical Center, Tufts University; MD, Creighton University(1998) **A/A/S:** Irish American Orthopaedic Society; American College of Sports Medicine; American Association of Nurse Anesthetists; American Orthopaedic Society for Sports Medicine; WMS

ELIZABETH JANE HAGAN-DURKIN, RDH

Registered Dental Hygienist
Dr. Scott Kelly, DDS
3700 Parsons Avenue
Columbus, OH 43207 United States
rdhjane86@sbcglobal.net
http://www.cambridgewhoswho.com

BUS: Dentistry **P/S:** Healthcare, Dentistry **MA:** Local **EXP:** Ms. Hagan-Durkin's expertise is in elementary education. **H/I/S:** Traveling, Gardening, Walking **FBP:** RDH Magazine **EDU:** Bachelor of Science in Health Education, Ohio State University **A/A/S:** Ohio State University Alumni Association; The ALS Association **C/VW:** Wish Kids; American Cancer Society; The Humane Society of the United States **A/S:** She attributes her success to her determination, people skills and listening ability. **B/I:** She became involved in her profession because she had friends in the dental profession. **H/O:** The highlight of her career was being able to touch peoples lives and better their dental health.

VIKE HAGHNAZARIAN

Broker Associate
Windermere Real Estates/S.C.A., Inc.
16261 Redmond Way
Redmond, WA 98052 United States
vikeh@windermere.com
http://www.VikeSellsRedmond.com

BUS: Real Estate **P/S:** Single Family Residential Homes **MA:** Regional **D/D/R:** Selling Residential Real Estate and New Construction Properties, Luxury Homes and Condominiums **H/I/S:** Bicycling, Basketball, Traveling, Reading **EDU:** Graduate Realtor Institute; Accredited Buyer's Representative; Accredited Seller's Representative; Accredited Staging Professional; Certified Residential Specialist; Bachelor's Degree in Engineering, Seattle University **A/A/S:** Council of Residential Specialists; Northwest Multiple Listing Service; Washington Association of Realtors; National Association of Realtors **C/VW:** Helping the Homeless; Boys & Girls Clubs of America **A/S:** He attributes his personal and professional success to his perseverance and ability to go above and beyond expectations. **B/I:** He has always had an interest in the field and a desire to help others. **H/O:** The highlight of his career is loving the work he does every single day.

HYEOUK CHRIS HAHM, LCSW, PH.D.
Assistant Professor
Boston University School of Social Work
264 Baystate Road
Boston, MA 02215 United States
hahm@bu.edu
http://www.bu.edu

BUS: Independent, Co-Educational, and Non-Sectarian Institution of Higher Education and Research **P/S:** Arts & Sciences Communication, Continuing Education, Dental Medicine Education, Engineering, Fine Arts, General Studies, Health and Rehabilitation Sciences, Hospitality, Administration, Law Management Medicine, Public Health, Social Work, Theology, University Professors Program, Departments, Libraries, Centers & Institutes Journals Bulletins (Catalogs), Services Medical Campus **MA:** National **D/D/R:** Teaching Clinical Practice and Research for the Masters Program, Conducting Research on Adolescent Health of Asian-Americans, Studying Health and Risk Behaviors, STD, HIV/AIDS, Licensed Clinical Social Worker **H/I/S:** Reading, Singing, Spending Time with her Three Children, Cooking for Guests, Golfing **FBP:** Harvard Business Review **EDU:** Ph.D. in Social work, Columbia University (2002); Public Health Fellowship - University of California at Berkeley **A/A/S:** American Public Health Association; American Psychological Association; Society for Social Work and Research; Society of Research on Child Development

RICHARD A. HAHN
FAA Airframe and Powerplant Mechanic,
Supervisor of Technical Center West
Technical Help Desk Department
Dassault Falcon Jet Corp.
4300 S. Kennedy Street
Boise, ID 83705 United States
rich.hahn@falconjet.com • http://www.dassaultfalcon.com

BUS: Manufacturing Company **P/S:** Business Jet Aircraft **MA:** International **D/D/R:** Assisting Clients, Troubleshooting, Developing Jet Aircraft Design with Computer-Based Cockpits **H/I/S:** Sailing **FBP:** Business & Commercial Aviation **CERTS:** Licensed Airframe and Powerplant Mechanic, Federal Aviation Administration, Teterboro School of Aeronautics (1986) **A/A/S:** Society of Automotive Engineers; Professional Aviation Maintenance Association; Former Aviation Ground Support Equipment Technician, US Navy **DOB:** April 25, 2007 **SP:** Karen **B/I:** He became involved in his profession through a natural progression of opportunities. **H/O:** The highlight of his career was being selected to head up new operations in the Western United States.

WILLIAM R. HAIRSTON
Head Counselor
United States Department of Veterans Affairs
421 N. Main Street
Leeds, MA 01053 United States
williamhairston@med.va.gov
http://www.va.gov

BUS: Government Organization **P/S:** Public Services, Healthcare for Veterans and their Families **MA:** Western Massachusetts **D/D/R:** Treating Addiction Patients, Supervising Counselors, Coordinating Programs, Reaching out to the Community **H/I/S:** Softball, Jogging, Martial Arts **FBP:** Counselor **EDU:** Coursework, University of Massachusetts **A/A/S:** Massachusetts Association for Alcoholic and Drug Abuse Counselors; National Association of Alcoholism and Drug Abuse Counselors **A/H:** Employee of the Year Award (2005) **C/VW:** Deacon, Local College Church; Jesse's House; Men's Group **CHILD:** Timothy, Tracey **A/S:** He attributes his success to his honesty. **H/O:** The highlight of his career was having Hairston House named after him.

WANDA COLLEEN HALE
Cosmetologist, Salon Owner
Wanda's Beauty Salon
1536 17th Street
Mitchell, NE 69357 United States
wanda.hale@cwwemail.com
http://www.cambridgewhoswho.com

BUS: Salon **P/S:** Hair Cutting and Coloring **MA:** Local **D/D/R:** Cutting, Coloring and Perming Hair, Applying Makeup, Giving Manicures **H/I/S:** Dancing, Playing Cards **EDU:** High School Education **CERTS:** Licensed Cosmetologist, State of Nebraska (1960) **A/A/S:** National Cosmetology Association **C/VW:** Federated Church, Mitchell, Nebraska; Member, Church Choir **CHILD:** Sandra, Richard, Jerry, Tommy **A/S:** She attributes her success to her hard work and to implementing her abilities in her profession. **B/I:** She became involved in her profession because her husband passed away when her four children were young and this was a good way for her to be there for her children and take care of them financially. **H/O:** The highlight of her career was opening her business.

CHRISTOPHER MARK HALL
Consultant
Self-Employed
1539 Day Valley Road
Aptos, CA 95003 United States
fyzzyx@att.net
http://www.cambridgewhoswho.com

BUS: Engineering, Integrated Circuits **P/S:** Consulting, Engineering, Integrated Circuits **MA:** California **EXP:** Mr. Hall's expertise includes science, engineering, methodology, research, failure analysis and instruction. **H/I/S:** Sports Cars, Bikes **FBP:** Scientific American **EDU:** Master's Degree in Electrical and Computer Engineering, University of California at Santa Barbara (1981); Bachelor of Arts in Physics, Reed College (1978) **A/A/S:** Eta Kappa Nu Engineering Honor Society

GLORIA ANN HALL
Home Health Field Nurse, Licensed Practical Nurse
WRMC Progressive Home Care
1929 Harrison Street
Batesville, AR 72501 United States
annhall2004@yahoo.com
http://www.cambridgewhoswho.com

BUS: Hospital-Based Home Health Agency **P/S:** Healthcare **MA:** Local **EXP:** Ms. Hall's expertise includes skilled and home-health nursing, wound care and diabetic education. **H/I/S:** Sewing, Quilting **CERTS:** Licensed Practical Nurse Certification, Ozarka Vocational Technical College **A/S:** She attributes her success to her hard work and dedication. **B/I:** She became involved in this profession because she has always had an interest in the field and a desire to help others. **H/O:** The most gratifying aspect of her career is having the ability to aid in the health improvement of others.

LISA F. HALL
Entrepreneur, Business Owner
It's TYME
heylisa@vmdirect.com
http://www.itstyme.com

BUS: Leader in the Marketing Industry Dedicated to Connecting People through a World-Class Communication Platform **P/S:** Marketing and Advertising, Exclusive Web-Based Products Designed to help Manage Digital Content with One Easy to Use Application **MA:** International **D/D/R:** Marketing, Streaming Videos for Worldwide Communications, Creating Jingles, Helping Entrepreneurs Execute their Dreams, Minimizing Costs, Maximizing Exposure **H/I/S:** Gardening, Sailing, Skating, Networking **FBP:** AdvantEdge **EDU:** General Equivalency Diploma **CERTS:** Licensed Notary Public **A/A/S:** Women's Leadership Team; Chamber of Commerce; Better Business Bureau **C/VW:** Volunteer, Battered Women and Victims of Child Abuse; Volunteer, Local Television Station; Local Charitable Organizations **DOB:** February 11, 1966

MARY D. HALL
Registered Nurse
St. John Hospital and Medical Center
Moross Road
Detroit, MI United States
wmmaryh@semol.com
http://www.cambridgewhoswho.com

BUS: Healthcare **P/S:** Acute Care Nursing **MA:** Local **EXP:** Ms. Hall's expertise includes general, transplant and pediatric surgery. **H/I/S:** Gardening **FBP:** Garlik Goodies Cookbook **EDU:** Bachelor of Arts, Cambridge University **A/A/S:** American Association of perioperative Registered Nurses **C/VW:** American Legion, Auxiliary, VFW Auxiliary, AVVA **A/S:** She attributes her success to hard work and dedication. **B/I:** She chose the profession due to her father's encouragement. **H/O:** The highlight of her career is her current position.

BARBARA LYNN HALLACK
Loan Consultant
Washington Mutual
barbara.hallack@wamu.net
http://www.wamuloans.com//barbarahallack

BUS: Bank **P/S:** Mortgage Loans, Equity Lines **MA:** Local **D/D/R:** Offering Financial and Mortgage Planning Services **EDU:** Coursework, Ventura College, Antelope Valley College, Valley College **CERTS:** Certified Mortgage Planning Specialist **A/A/S:** Greater Antelope Valley Association of Realtors **C/VW:** Antelope Valley Children's Center

MRS. ROSALEE C. HALLSTEAD, RN
Staff Registered Nurse
Women's Center
Jersey Community Hospital
Maple Summit Road
Jerseyville, IL 62052 United States
upsrn@frontiernet.net
http://www.jch.org

BUS: Hospital **P/S:** Dialysis Center, Emergency Room, Physical Therapy, Radiology, Obstetrics, Sleep Disorder Center, Ambulatory Care Services, Chemotherapy, Dietary Counseling, Gastrointestinal Diagnostic Testing, Intensive Care Unit, Outpatient Services and Surgery **MA:** Local **D/D/R:** Specializing in Labor and Delivery **H/I/S:** Bowling, Crocheting Blankets and Donating them for Premature Babies in the Hospital **FBP:** Nursing2009 **EDU:** Registered Nurse Diploma, Lewis and Clark College; Certified in Advanced Cardiac Life Support **C/VW:** President, Monday Night Bowling League; Relay for Life; Moose Lodge

KIM L. HALULA
Associate Dean, College of Health Sciences
Marquette University
604 N. 16th Street
Milwaukee, WI 53233 United States
kim.halula@marquette.edu
http://www.marquette.edu

BUS: Education **P/S:** Higher Education **MA:** International **EXP:** Ms. Halula's expertise is in administration and dental hygiene. **H/I/S:** Traveling, Reading **FBP:** Journal of Allied Health **EDU:** Registered Dental Hygienist; Ph.D., Marquette University **A/A/S:** Association of Schools of Allied Health Professions **C/VW:** Alliance Bible Church, Various Charities through her Community **A/S:** She attributes her success to her parents and mentors. **B/I:** She was prompted to enter her profession because she always wanted to be a teacher. **H/O:** The highlight of her career is getting people to work together.

MS. CONNIE HAMBROCK, PH.D., NBCMT, CHI
President, Center Director
Heaven & Earth Environmental Education & Healing
297 Herndon Parkway, Suite 105
Herndon, VA 20170 United States
dr.hambrock@gmail.com
http://www.heavenandearthhealing.com

BUS: Healthcare Center **P/S:** Healthcare Including Complimentary and Alternative Medicine, Craniosacral Therapy, Hypnotherapy and Massage Therapy, Deep Tissue and Energy Work **MA:** Virginia **EXP:** Ms. Hambrock's expertise is in hypnobirth techniques including craniosacral and holistic therapy, clinical instruction and life coaching. **H/I/S:** Making Jewelry **FBP:** Entrepreneur; Town and Country; Mother Earth News; American Holistic Healing Journal; NGH Journals; Massage Therapy Related Publications **EDU:** Ph.D. in Herbology, Shepperton University (2002); Master of Science in Holistic Medicine, Shepperton University (2000); Master of Science in Hypnotherapy, Austin, TX; Bachelor of Arts in Communication, University of West Florida **A/A/S:** Northern Virginia Chapter, National Association of Women Business Owners; American Massage Therapy Association; National Guild of Hypnotists; American Holistic Medical Association; American College of Emergency Physicians **SP:** Paul **CHILD:** Kent, Shannon

EDITH A. HAMELIN
Medical Assistant Program Director
Brigham Young University-Idaho
Rexburg, ID 83460 United States
ehamelin@cableone.net
http://www.byui.edu

BUS: University **P/S:** Higher Education, Healthcare **MA:** Local **D/D/R:** Developing the Curriculum and Clinical Applications, Administering the Programs, Teaching Medical Law **H/I/S:** Reading **EDU:** Bachelor of Science in Nursing, University of Colorado **A/A/S:** The American Association of Medical Assistants **C/VW:** The Church of Jesus Christ of Latter-Day Saints **A/S:** She attributes her success to providing a high level of educational services and seeing the rewards from the effort she has made. **B/I:** She became involved in her profession because she had always wanted to be a nurse and took advantage of the opportunity to teach. **H/O:** The most gratifying aspect of her career is being able to influence a number students.

DEBORAH K. HAMILTON
Owner
Bitterroot Equine Marketing Services, LLC
1914 Middle Bear Creek Road
Victor, MT 59875 United States
debbiekh@bluequestfarm.com
http://www.bluequestfarm.com

BUS: Horse Marketing Agency **P/S:** Horse Marketing for Professional Trainers and Breeders **MA:** International **D/D/R:** Managing the Website, Taking Pictures, Researching Horses **H/I/S:** Riding Horses, Photography, Artwork **FBP:** National Geographic **EDU:** Coursework in Large Animal Rescue; Coursework in Computer Graphic **C/VW:** Volunteer, Animal Rescue; Various Animal Charities **A/S:** She attributes her success to her skills, education, hard work and dedication. **B/I:** She became involved in her profession because she has been involved with horses her whole life. **H/O:** The highlight of her career was making sales in every state.

MARGARET B. HAMILTON
Principal
St. Peter's School
21 Ridge Street
Haverstraw, NY 10927 United States
mbh0122@yahoo.com
http://www.cambridgewhoswho.com

BUS: Private Diocese and Catholic School **P/S:** Education for Students in Grades Pre-Kindergarten to Eighth **MA:** Rockland County, New York **D/D/R:** Overseeing Teacher Administration **H/I/S:** Reading, Traveling **FBP:** Momentum **EDU:** Master's Degree in Education, Plus 25 Credits in Supervision and Administration, College of Saint Rose, Manhattan College and Fordham University; Bachelor's Degree in History and Political Science, Minor in Elementary Education, College of Mount Saint Vincent **A/A/S:** National Catholic Educators Association; National Association of Elementary School Principals; International Reading Association; National Council for Social Studies; North Rockland Teacher Center Board **C/VW:** St. Peter's Church; Bereavement Counselor, New York Diocese **A/S:** She attributes her success to loving what she does, having the support of her husband and family and working with great teachers. **B/I:** She became involved in this profession because both her parents were teachers and she loved working with children. **H/O:** The highlight of her career was being promoted to principal.

TONI M. HAMILTON, BSN, RN-C
Assistant Nurse Manager
St. Vincent's Medical Center
1800 Barrs Street
Jacksonville, FL 32204 United States
hamlt@earthlink.net
http://www.cambridgewhoswho.com

BUS: Medical Center **P/S:** Healthcare **MA:** Local **D/D/R:** Specializing in Medical-Surgical Nursing **H/I/S:** Baking, Walking **FBP:** American Journal of Nursing **EDU:** Bachelor of Science in Nursing, Jacksonville University; Associate of Science in Nursing, Lake City Community College **CERTS:** Certification in Medical-Surgical Nursing **A/A/S:** Sigma Theta Tau International; Lambda Rho **C/VW:** Veterans Association; Police Association **A/S:** She attributes her success to her perseverance and determination to be the best at her job. **B/I:** She became involved in her profession because she was determined to pursue a nursing career once she began college.

JOAN E. HAMMOND
Second Grade Teacher
Vista San Gabriel Elementary School
18020 E. Avenue O
Palmdale, CA 93591 United States
http://www.cambridgewhoswho.com

BUS: Elementary School **P/S:** Education **MA:** Local **D/D/R:** Teaching Second-Grade Students **H/I/S:** Volunteering with Local Marching Band **EDU:** Teachers Credential, State of California Bakersfield **A/A/S:** National Education Association, California Teachers Association **C/VW:** Second Grade Chairwoman, English Language Advancement Committee; Union Treasurer; Local Church

MARILYN HAMOUDA
President
Parent Teacher Association
6006 23rd Avenue
Brooklyn, NY 11204 United States
m1d3l6@netzero.net
http://www.cambridgewhoswho.com

BUS: Nonprofit **P/S:** Funding Programs **MA:** Local **D/D/R:** Fundraising for the School, School Store, and Picture Day **EDU:** Coursework in Business **C/VW:** Leader, Girl Scouts of the United States of America

THELMA G. HAMPTON
Teacher
Critzer Elementary School
Pulaski County School System
345 Vaughan Avenue
Dublin, VA 24084 United States
thampton@pcva.us
http://www.pcva.us

BUS: School District **P/S:** Education **MA:** Regional **D/D/R:** Attending Steering Committee Meetings, Instructing Students, Working with Children who Have Deficit Disorders **H/I/S:** Dancing, Reading, Exercising **EDU:** Bachelor of Science in Elementary Education, Radford University (1978) **CERTS:** Certified Paraprofessional (1974) **A/A/S:** National Teachers Association; Professional Construction Estimators Association; Dublin Educators Association; National Education Association; Delta Kappa Gamma **A/H:** Teacher of the Week Award, Pulaski County (2005); Teacher of the Month Award (2002); Who's Who Among American Teachers (2002); Nominee, Teacher of the Year, Walt Disney (1999) **C/VW:** Community Services Association

KATHY HANCOCK
Special Education Teacher
Belleview-Santos Elementary School - Marion County Schools
9600 S.E. US Highway 441
Belleview, FL 34420 United States
pigsfly@wfeca.net
http://www.marion.k12.fl.us/schools/bse

BUS: Kindergarten through Fifth Grade School Site **P/S:** High Quality Educational Services for Students **MA:** Regional **D/D/R:** Teaching Behavior Modification, Social Skills and Academics to Emotionally Handicapped Students in Kindergarten through Fifth Grade, Specializing in Teaching in a Self-Contained Classroom so Students can be Mainstreamed back to Regular Education Classrooms **H/I/S:** Pottery, Golfing **EDU:** Bachelor's Degree in Art, Edinboro University of Pennsylvania (1974); Bachelor's Degree in Special Education K-12, University of Central Florida **A/A/S:** National Education Association **C/VW:** School Improvement Committee

ROENA M. HANKUS-COSTA, RNC
Staff Nurse
Central Texas VA Medical Center
1901 S. First Street
Temple, TX 76501 United States
http://www.cambridgewhoswho.com

BUS: Veteran Medical Center **P/S:** Healthcare Services **MA:** Local **D/D/R:** Psychiatric Nursing, Offering Substance Abuse, Vocational Rehab and Health Maintenance Programs **H/I/S:** Spending TIme with Family, Gardening, Crafts, Cross Stitching, Crocheting, Knitting **FBP:** RN Journal; American Journal of Nursing; Psychiatry Journal **EDU:** Associate Degree in Registered Nursing, Central Texas College **CERTS:** Certified Psychiatric Nurse; Certified Anger Management Therapist **A/A/S:** American Nurses Association; American Psychiatric Nursing Association

LILLIE 'LOU' T. HANNAH
President, Owner
Creative Destinations, Inc.
10858 Anderson Road
Piedmont, SC 29673 United States
lou@creativedestinationsinc.com
http://www.creativedestinationsinc.com

BUS: Travel Agency **P/S:** Travel Programs for Leisure, Company and Employee Incentives **MA:** International **D/D/R:** Building Relationships with Vendors and Clients, Assisting with Program Setups, Managing Operations, Overseeing the Travel Programs **H/I/S:** Spending Time with her Grandson, Spending Time at the Beach, Attending Youth Baseball, Reading **FBP:** ProSales; Travel Weekly; Recommend **EDU:** Bachelor's Degree in Accelerated Business, East Mississippi Community College (1964) **A/A/S:** Lumbermen's Association of Texas; SBMA **C/VW:** National Breast Cancer Foundation; Palmer Home for Children; Paralyzed Veterans of America **DOB:** November 30, 1944 **POB:** Gholson **SP:** Tom **CHILD:** Morgan, Jonathan **W/H:** President, Owner, Creative Destinations, Inc (2002-Present); Partner, Head of the Incentive Division, Travel Agency (1994-2002); Director, Local Travel Agency (1990-1994); Travel Coordinator, BMA (1980-1990) **A/S:** She attributes her success to her integrity, morals, hands-on attitude and positive disposition. **B/I:** She became involved in her profession after being hired as a travel coordinator for the incentive division of a large corporation. **H/O:** The most gratifying aspect of her career is forming relationships with her clients and vendors. **I/F/Y:** In five years, Ms. Hannah hopes for professional growth.

SYLVIA HANNIBAL-JONES
Professor Emeritus
Kentucky Community and Technical College System
901 S. 43rd Street
Louisville, KY 40211 United States
sjones9968@aol.com
http://www.kctcs.edu

BUS: State's Largest Two-Year, Comprehensive Community and Technical College **P/S:** More Than 300 Options in Academic and Technical Programs Including Automotive Technology, Computer Information Systems, Engineering Technology, Human Services, and Nursing **MA:** Regional **D/D/R:** Teaching Various Classes, Coordinating Student Activities **EDU:** Master's Degree in Social Work, University of Wisconsin (1965); Bachelor of Science in Biology and Sociology, Kentucky State University (1962) **A/A/S:** National Association of Social Workers; Academy of Certified Social Workers

MICHAEL T. HANSEN, FACHE
Chief Executive Officer
Pender Community Hospital District
603 Earl Street, Box 100
Pender, NE 68047 United States
hansemic@mercyhealth.com
http://www.pendercommunityhospital.com

BUS: Hospital **P/S:** Healthcare Including Acute Care, Long Term Care, Assisted Living **MA:** Regional **EXP:** Mr. Hansen's expertise is in healthcare administration. **D/D/R:** Managing Human Resources **H/I/S:** Reading, Playing Racquetball **FBP:** Modern Healthcare **EDU:** Master's Degree in Healthcare Administration, Webster University; Master's Degree in Human Resources Development, Webster University **CERTS:** Certified Healthcare Executive; Certified Senior Professional in Human Resources **A/A/S:** Society for Human Resource Management; Fellow, American College of Healthcare Executives **C/VW:** The Young Men's Christian Association

DAVID J. HANSWIRTH, DMD
Dentist
Hanswirth Dentistry
30 Lake Street
White Plains, NY 10603 United States
drdavehans@aol.com
http://www.hanswirthdentistry.com

BUS: Dentistry **P/S:** Implants, Cosmetics, CAD and CAM Restorations, TMJ Treatment, Neuromuscular Dentistry **MA:** Local **EXP:** Mr. Hanswirth's expertise is in implants and cosmetic dentistry. **H/I/S:** Golfing, Spending Time with Family **EDU:** Doctor of Medical Dentistry, Boston University School of Dental Medicine **A/A/S:** American Dental Association; Academy of General Dentistry; Prosthetic Master and Diplomat, International Congress of Oral Implantologists; Associate Fellow, American Academy of Implant Dentistry; Master, Academy of General Dentistry; Diplomat, American Academy of Pain Management; Associate Fellow, World Clinical Lazor Institute **C/VW:** Susan G. Komen Breast Cancer Foundation; Cerebral Palsy Foundations; March of Dimes; White Plains Hospital **A/S:** He attributes his success to dedication and enjoyment of his profession. **B/I:** He became involved in the profession because his family was involved in dentistry and he developed an interest. **H/O:** The most gratifying aspect of his career is working with his co-workers and seeing results in his patients.

PENNIE A. HARCUS
Principal
Marana Unified School District, Quail Run Elementary School
4600 W. Cortaro Farms Road
Tucson, AZ 85742 United States
P.A.Harcus@maranausd.org
http://www.cambridgewhoswho.com

BUS: Public Elementary School **MA:** Local **EXP:** Mr. Harcus' expertise is in educational leadership. **EDU:** Educational Doctorate in Student Education in Leadership, University of Arizona; Dual Master's Degree in Educational Leadership and Bilingual Multicultural, Northern Arizona University; Bachelor of Science Degree in Elementary Education, University of Arizona **CERTS:** Endorsement in English as a Second Language, Northern Arizona University **A/A/S:** Association for Supervision and Curriculum Development; National Association of Elementary School Principals; School Law Reporter, Kappa Kappa Gamma Sorority, University of Arizona **C/VW:** Local Charitable Organizations **A/S:** She attributes her success to her commitment to education and surrounding herself with good people who all want to make good things happen for children. **B/I:** She chose the profession because she has wanted to be a teacher since she was in the first grade. **H/O:** The highlight of her career is when both parents and students express their gratitude and testify that she has had a positive impact on their lives.

PATRICIA A. HARDINA
Managing Director
Citi
233 S. Wacker Drive
Suite 8500
Chicago, IL 60606 United States
patty.hardina@citigroup.com
http://www.citi.com

BUS: Financial Institution **P/S:** Financial Services, Corporate and Investment Banking **MA:** National **D/D/R:** Specializing in Sales to Institutional Clients **H/I/S:** Golfing, Volunteering Time for Community Service **FBP:** The Wall Street Journal **EDU:** Bachelor of Science in Finance, University of Dayton **A/A/S:** The Executives Club of Chicago **C/VW:** St. Clement Moms Stewardship **A/S:** She attributes her success to her diligence and passion for the business. **B/I:** She became involved in this profession because she used her degree and progressed from different positions through her career into her current position. **H/O:** The highlight of her career was becoming a managing director for Citigroup.

COLLEEN T. HARDY, RN
Quality Assurance Officer, Infection Control Nurse
Dothan Surgery Center
1450 Ross Clark Circle, Suite 4
Dothan, AL 36301 United States
colleen@dothansurgerycenter.com
http://www.cambridgewhoswho.com

BUS: Outpatient Same-Day Surgery Center **P/S:** GI Endoscopy Surgery **MA:** Tri-State Area **D/D/R:** Supervising Quality Assurance **H/I/S:** Watching her Son and Husband Play Golf, Spending Time with her Grandchildren **FBP:** Hospital Infection Control **EDU:** Associate Degree in Nursing, Wallace College **C/VW:** Board of Directors, Mental Health Association **A/S:** She attributes her success to her honesty and hard work. **B/I:** She became involved in her profession because she was once hospitalized for a long period of time and saw the wonderful work of the nurses. **H/O:** The highlight of her career was being promoted to quality assurance officer.

MARCIA R. HARDY
Transplant Information Specialist
The Johns Hopkins Hospital, Comprehensive Transplant Center
720 Rutland Avenue, Turner 36
Baltimore, MD 21205 United States
mrwhardy@msn.com
http://www.johnshopkinsmedicine.org

BUS: Healthcare **P/S:** Comprehensive Transplant Center **MA:** International **D/D/R:** Managing Medical Information of Patients for Kidney and Pancreas Transplantation **H/I/S:** Reading, Dancing, Studying **EDU:** Associate Degree in Health Information Technology, DeVry University **C/VW:** Multiple Sclerosis Society, Maryland Mental Health Association **A/S:** She attributes her success to her hard work, determination and being a team player. **B/I:** She became involved in her profession because she began working in the industry as a nursing technician and moved into administration of patient care. **H/O:** The highlight of her career has been being able to move from bed side care to administrative.

SANDY S. HAREN
Business Manager
Sioux City Allergy & Asthma Associates, PC
4280 Sergeant Road
Suite 230
Sioux City, IA 51106 United States
scallergy@cableone.net
http://www.cambridgewhoswho.com

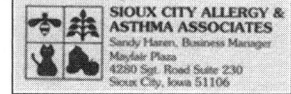

BUS: Medical Center **P/S:** Healthcare Including Allergy, Asthma and Immunology Treatments **MA:** Regional **D/D/R:** Managing Operations, Billing, Overseeing Insurance Plans **H/I/S:** Golfing, Home Decoration **FBP:** Allergy Coding Alert; Medical Office **CERTS:** Licensed Practical Nurse, Hawkeye Community College, Waterloo, IA (1968) **A/A/S:** Iowa Medical Group Management Association **A/S:** She attributes her success to her hard work, determination and to the support she receives from her colleagues. **B/I:** She became involved in her profession because of her interest in nursing.

RENEE S. HARKER
Director of Food and Nutrition Department
Long Beach Medical Center
455 E. Bay Drive
Long Beach, NY 11561 United States
rsharker@aol.com
http://www.cambridgewhoswho.com

BUS: Medical Center **P/S:** Healthcare **MA:** Local **EXP:** Ms. Harker's expertise is in dietary administration and public health management. **H/I/S:** Gardening, Painting, Wallpapering, Reading Mysteries **FBP:** Food Management; Restaurants & Institutions **EDU:** Master's Degree in Nutrition and Public Health, Teachers College, Columbia University **A/A/S:** American Dietetic Association; National Society for Healthcare Foodservice Management; American Society for Healthcare Food Service Administrators **C/VW:** American Red Cross **A/S:** She attributes her success to her commitment, hard work and interest in dietetics. **B/I:** She became involved in her profession through a natural progression of opportunities. **H/O:** The highlights of her career were becoming an administrator of dietetics at Johns Hopkins Hospital, a surveyor for the New York State Department of Health and the public health nutritionist of Baltimore.

TERRI L. HARLAND
Information Technology Analyst
John Deere Parts Distribution Center
1600 1st Avenue E.
Milan, IL 61264 United States
Harlandterril@johndeere.com
http://www.johndeere.com

BUS: Industrial Manufacturing Company **P/S:** Agricultural Equipment, Construction and Forestry Equipment, Commercial and Consumer Equipment, Power Systems, Risk Protection, Agricultural Services **MA:** International **D/D/R:** Analyzing Information Technology, Supporting International Systems for Operations, Overseeing Managerial Reports for Orders, Consulting **H/I/S:** Spending Time with Family **FBP:** Newsweek **EDU:** Bachelor of Arts, St. Ambrose University (1988) **A/A/S:** Board, Figure Skating Club of the Quad Cities; Davenport Chamber of Commerce **C/VW:** United Way; Junior Achievement Organization

REBECCA LEANN HARMON
Executive Marketing, Creative Director
Nancy Larson Publishers, Inc.
27 Talcott Farm Road
Old Lyme, CT 06731 United States
leann.harmon@nancylarsonpublishers.com
http://www.nancylarsonpublishers.com

BUS: Educational Publishing **P/S:** Quality Materials for Education for Teachers and Students **MA:** National **D/D/R:** Creative Marketing, Working on Kindergarten, Fourth and Fifth Levels of the Science Program **H/I/S:** Writing, Skiing, Traveling, College Football **FBP:** Entrepreneur; Pink; Fortune; Kiplinger's **EDU:** Bachelor of Science in Letters and Psychology, University of Oklahoma **A/A/S:** Delta Gamma; University of Oklahoma Theatre Guild **C/VW:** Delta Gamma Foundation; Library for the Blind; Reach Out and Read Organization; Nancy Larson Foundation **A/S:** She attributes her success to being clear on what makes her happy. **B/I:** She became involved in this profession because she always enjoyed writing and is very creative. **H/O:** The highlight of her career was launching a new science program for first through third grades.

OZIE HAROLD, LPN
Licensed Practical Nurse, Crisis Care Nurse
Baptist Hospice Agency
301 Interstate Drive
Montgomery, AL 36109 United States
ozozieh@aol.com
http://www.cambridgewhoswho.com

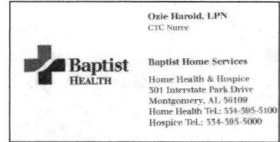

BUS: Hospice Agency **P/S:** Home Healthcare and Hospice Services **MA:** Local **EXP:** Ms. Harold's expertise is in palliative care for terminally ill patients. **D/D/R:** Utilizing Core Components of Nursing Practice to Offer the Highest Level of Care to Patients and their Families, Educating Families to Meet the Needs of their Loved Ones **H/I/S:** Traveling, Crocheting, Fishing, Solving Crossword Puzzles, Reading **FBP:** LPN2009; NURSING made Incredibly Easy; Lippincott Manual; Home Care Nurse; Taste of Home; Readers Digest **EDU:** Coursework, St. Jude School of Nursing (1971) **CERTS:** Licensed Practical Nurse, State of Alabama; Certification in Business Management, Floyd's Commercial School (1967); Certification in Commercial Works **A/A/S:** President, Montgomery Chapter, Licensed Practical Nurses Association **A/H:** Second Runner-Up, Nurse of the Year Award (2008); Nominee, Woman of the Year Award for Medicine and Healthcare (2008); Runner-Up, Nurse of the Year Award (2006); Nominee, Nurse of the Year Award (2004-2006); Employee of the Month Award, Fairview Medical Center; Employee of the Month Award, Baptist Home Health; Life Award, Hospice Peers **C/VW:** Sensation Social; Civic Club; American Heart Association; Relay for Life, American Cancer Society; Church Women United; Easter Seals of America; Arthritis Foundation; American Institute for Cancer Research **POB:** Montgomery **CHILD:** Dover **A/S:** She attributes her success to her flexibility and her ability to face challenges. **B/I:** She became involved in her profession because she always loved helping others. **H/O:** The highlight of her career was being nominated for the nurse of the year award from 2004 to 2008. **I/F/Y:** In five years, Ms. Harold hopes to face challenges and be more creative to move her career in the right direction.

Mr. Johnny M. Harper
Owner
JM Harper Enterprise LLC
583 Sinclair Way
Jonesboro, GA 30238 United States
harperenterprise@bellsouth.net
http://www.cambridgewhoswho.com

BUS: Real Estate Investment Company **P/S:** Market-Driven Housing Rehabilitation Services **MA:** Local **D/D/R:** Managing Construction and Rehabilitation Services of Single-Family Homes, Selling Residential Real Estate **H/I/S:** Watching Horse Races and College Football, Traveling, Spending Time with his Family **FBP:** Ebony **EDU:** Bachelor of Arts in Sociology, California State University, Sacramento **A/A/S:** Co-Chairman, Business Advisory Council **C/VW:** Board Member, Clayton County Grassroots Leadership Institute **A/S:** He attributes his success to his listening skills and desire to learn and grow. **B/I:** He became involved in his profession because of the experience he gained by working in construction while in college. **H/O:** The most gratifying aspect of his career is meeting with influential people in his community.

Donna W. Harr
1) Owner
1) Red Bank Ranch 2) Americana Collection
16100 Red Bank Road
Red Bluff, CA 96080 United States
maeharr@earthlink.net
http://www.cambridgewhoswho.com

BUS: 1) Agriculture Firm 2) Art Gallery **P/S:** 1) Walnut Orchards 2) Art and Antique Collection and Sales **MA:** 1) International 2) National **D/D/R:** Raising Walnuts for Commercial Market, Western and Indian Art, Holding Private Showings of Collections, Auctioning Art **H/I/S:** Participating in Equestrian Activities, Reading **FBP:** Range Magazine; AG Alert **EDU:** Master's Degree in Education, San Francisco State University; Bachelor's Degree in Education, San Francisco State University **A/A/S:** Local Chamber of Commerce; Stewards of the Range; American Farm Bureau; Bits 'n' Spurs Riding Club; League of Women's Voters; Republican Women's Association; Charter Member, American Business Women's Association **A/S:** She attributes her success to her hard work and having a true interest in people and their well being. **B/I:** She became involved in her profession because she and her husband came from farm backgrounds and antique collections. **H/O:** The most gratifying aspect of her career is serving the community with her husband.

WILLIAM R. HARRELL
Professor of Agricultural Mechanization, Retired
Sam Houston State University
221 Westridge Drive
Huntsville, TX 77340 United States
b.harrell@shsu.edu
http://www.shsu.edu

BUS: State University **P/S:** Undergraduate Degree Programs, Masters Degree Programs, Doctoral Degree Programs in Criminal Justice, Educational Leadership, Counselor Education and Clinical Psychology **MA:** International **D/D/R:** Teaching Agricultural Mechanization, Maintaining Agricultural Equipment, Structures and Environmental Controls, Electric Power, Power Machinery and Soil and Water Conservation **H/I/S:** Square Dancing, Traveling, Fishing **FBP:** Resource; Newsweek **EDU:** Ph.D. in Agricultural Education with Research Support in Agricultural Mechanization, University of Missouri, Columbia (1972); Bachelor of Science, Texas A&M University, Commerce (1963); Master of Science, Texas A&M University, Commerce (1967) **A/A/S:** Lifetime Member, Teaching Fellow, North American Colleges and Teachers of Agriculture (2003); Texas Future Farmers of America; National Future Farmers of America; Vocational Agriculture Teachers Association of Texas; Houston Livestock Show and Rodeo Association; Walker County Fair Association; American Society of Agricultural and Biological Engineers; Texas Agricultural Mechanics Committee; National Agricultural Mechanics Committee; Texas Chapter, American Society of Agricultural and Biological Engineers **A/H:** Texas FFA Blue and Gold Award (2004); International Who's Who of Professionals (2003); ; Sam Houston State University Faculty Excellence in Service Award (2002); Hall-of-Honor Houston Livestock Show & Rodeo (1998); Educator Award, Professional Agricultural Workers of Texas (1998); VIP Award, National FFA (1995); Teacher Educator Award, Vocational Agriculture Teachers Association of Texas (1992); NACTA John Deere Agricultural Mechanization Award (1991); Distinguished Service Award, Vocational Agriculture Teachers Association of Texas (1990); Honorary American Farmer, National FFA (1983); President, Texas College Teachers of Agricultural Mechanization (1981); Superintendent, National FFA Agricultural Mechanics Contest (1979-1981); Outstanding Young Vocational Agriculture Teacher; Texas and Southern Region of U.S., U. S. Steel Corporation (1968); Honorary Lone Star Farmer, Texas FFA (1967) **C/A:** Board of Directors, National Association of Schools and Colleges of Agriculture and Natural Resources (1992-1995); Superintendent, Texas FFA Agricultural Mechanics Career Development Event (1998-1999); President, Agricultural Consortium of Texas (1989); Board of Directors, Ag Workers Mutual Auto Insurance Company, Fort Worth; Superintendent, Houston Livestock Show and Rodeo FFA & 4-H Agricultural Mechanics Project Show; Superintendent, Texas FFA Tractor Technician Career Development Event

ELAINE C. HARRINGTON
Professor Emeritus
2712 Gunn Avenue
Tuskegee, AL 36088 United States
harringtonec@bellsouth.net
http://www.cambridgewhoswho.com

BUS: School **P/S:** Education **MA:** Statewide **D/D/R:** Teaching English and Liberal Arts **H/I/S:** Music **FBP:** Black Enterprise **EDU:** Coursework, University of Connecticut **A/A/S:** National Education Association; New Jersey Education Association; American Guidance Association

CYNTHIA J. HARRIS
Art Instructor
Kankakee Junior High School
1850 S. 17000 W. Road
Reddick, IL 60961 United States
tmtlabs@bysys.net
http://www.cambridgewhoswho.com

BUS: High School **P/S:** Secondary Education Including Reading, Mathematics, Art, Music, Science, Social Studies and Physical Education **MA:** Regional **EXP:** Ms. Harris' expertise is in audio-visual work and art. **H/I/S:** Playing Soccer and Baseball, Volunteering with the Boy Scouts of America and the Girl Scouts of the USA, Coaching Softball **FBP:** Scholastic Art **EDU:** Master's Degree in Curriculum and Instruction, Olivet Nazarene University (2005); Bachelor's Degree in Art Education, Illinois State University (1988); Associate Degree, Lincoln University (1986) **CERTS:** Certified Mentor **A/A/S:** Illinois Education Association; National Education Association **C/VW:** Local Hospice **A/S:** She attributes her success to her education and supportive parents. **B/I:** She became involved in her profession because she always wanted to be a teacher. **H/O:** The most gratifying aspect of her career is having a positive impact on her students education.

G. CHANNING HARRIS
Graduate Student
channingonly@gmail.com
http://www.cambridgewhoswho.com

BUS: Graduate School **P/S:** Education **MA:** Local **D/D/R:** Counseling **H/I/S:** Foreign Films, Reading, Music **EDU:** Pursuing Master's Degree in Counseling; Bachelor of Arts in French, Belmont University **A/A/S:** Nashville Psychotherapy Institute; American Psychological Association; American Counseling Association

Ms. Lauren E. Harris
Vocational Counselor
University of Maryland Medical Center
Harbor City Unlimited
1227 W. Pratt Street
Baltimore, MD 21223 United States
lololaurenh@aol.com
http://www.medschool.umaryland.edu/community/psychiatry.asp

BUS: Psychosocial Rehabilitation Center **P/S:** Psychosocial Rehabilitation Services **MA:** Local **D/D/R:** Connecting People with Services in the Community, Helping People in Filling Applications, Working with Adults, Therapists and Psychiatrists, Conducting Classes, Overseeing Leading Discussion Groups and Outpatient Day Program, Assisting in Independent Living and Employment Programs **H/I/S:** Reading, Traveling, Camping, Interior Decoration **FBP:** Monitor; Psychology Today; The Baltimore Sun **EDU:** Pursuing Master's Degree in Counseling, Capella University; Bachelor of Arts in Psychology, Hood College (1998) **A/A/S:** American Psychological Association

Naomi T. Harris
Realtor
Jackson Real Estate & Auction
PO Box 248
Strawberry Plains, TN 37871 United States
charris785@bellsouth.net
http://www.jacksonjackson.com

BUS: Real Estate **P/S:** Real Estate Services, Home Sales, Permanent Homes, Condos, Lake Front, Acreage, Commercial, Vacation Homes, Multi-Family Homes, Mountain Properties, Lots **MA:** National **D/D/R:** Representing Buyers and Sellers for Resales and New Home Construction, Working for Builder and Building Sub-Divisions, Single and Two Story Homes, Redesigning Homes around Buyers **H/I/S:** Reading, Cooking **FBP:** Realtor **EDU:** Bachelor of Science in Biology, Federal City College (1976) **CERTS:** Licensed Realtor, Tennessee (2005); Licensed Realtor, Maryland (1989-1994) **A/A/S:** Knoxville Area Association of Realtors; Lakeway Area Association of Realtors; National Association of Realtors **A/H:** Gold Award (2000-2006)

TRACEY L. HARRIS
Fourth Grade Teacher
Tippecanoe School Corporation, James Cole Elementary
21 Elston Road
Lafayette, IN 47909 United States
tharris@tsc.k12.in.us
http://www.tsc.k12.in.us

BUS: Educational Corporation **P/S:** Fine Arts, Foreign Language, Mathematics, Language Arts, Science, Social Studies and Physical Education Services **MA:** Regional **D/D/R:** Teaching All Fourth-Grade Subjects, Teaching Summer School, Computer Lab and IA Coordination **H/I/S:** Horseback Riding **FBP:** Mailbox **EDU:** Master of Education, Indiana Wesleyan University (1997) **A/A/S:** Delta Kappa Gamma; Indiana State Teachers Association; TEA

JEANETTE YVONNE HARRIS-MCNAIR
Director of Commercial Operations
WPXA/ ION Media TV
200 Cobb Parkway N.
Marietta, GA 30062 United States
ruhamah@bellsouth.net
http://www.cambridgewhoswho.com

BUS: Broadcast Communication **P/S:** Television Programs, Advertising, Programming, Commercials **EXP:** Ms. Harris-McNair's expertise is in project management. **D/D/R:** Coordinating All Commercial and Television Program Schedules, Ensuring the Quality of Programming and Sequence **H/I/S:** Martial Arts, Basketball, Bowling, Dancing **FBP:** Broadcast **EDU:** Ph.D. in Business Administration, Kennedy Western University; Master's Degree, Keller Williams University (2001); Master of Arts in Business Communication, Concentration in Project Management (2001); Bachelor of Arts in Broadcast Communication, The University of Alabama (1981)

EZRA HARRISON
Nurse Manager
Bowie Town Medical Practice
3060 Mitchellville Road
Suite 103
Bowie, MD 20716 United States
eharrison11@hotmail.com
http://www.cambridgewhoswho.com

BUS: Healthcare Center **P/S:** Healthcare Including Cardiological, Neurological and Psychological Care **MA:** Regional **EXP:** Ms. Harrison's expertise is in psychiatric care and nursing. **D/D/R:** Conducting Detoxification Programs, Managing Staff, Counseling Patients with Diabetes, Dealing with Detoxification Problems for Young Adults **H/I/S:** Reading, Relaxing, Spending Time with her Family **FBP:** Nursing2009; ADvantage **EDU:** Bachelor's Degree in Nursing (2000)

MR. DANIEL R. HART
President
Hart Development
288 Newbury Street
Suite 308
Boston, MA 02115 United States
dhart@hartdev.com
http://www.hartdev.com

BUS: Excellency in the Real Estate Industry **P/S:** Superior Real Estate Development, Quality Commercial and Residential Real Estate, Premier Properties **MA:** Regional **D/D/R:** Selling Residential, Commercial and Mixed-Use Properties **H/I/S:** Playing Football, Running **FBP:** Fortune **EDU:** Bachelor of Arts, Bowdoin College (1995) **A/A/S:** Director and Former President, Bowdoin Club of Boston; Rental Housing Association; National Association of Industrial and Commercial Properties

BARBARA S. HARTGROVE-HOLLEY
1) Ohio State Director 2) Director
1) Zeta Phi Beta Sorority, Inc. 2) Midstate Educators Credit Union
1501 Demorest Road
Columbus, OH 43228 United States
bsgghholley@aol.com
http://www.cambridgewhoswho.com

BUS: 1) Sorority 2) Credit Union **P/S:** 1) International Sorority 2) Credit Union **MA:** 1) International 2) National **D/D/R:** Developing and Implementing Policies, Planning Conferences, Budgeting, Leadership, Helping other People Excel through Mental, Physical and Spiritual Excellence, Sitting on Committees, Planning Meetings, Making Policy Evaluations **H/I/S:** Boating, Fishing, Reading, Self-Improvement **FBP:** Seven Habits of Highly Effective People **EDU:** Bachelor of Science in Elementary Education, Central State University (1972) **A/H:** Community Service Award Finalist, Columbus Dispatch (2001); Dual Recipient, Martha Holden Jennings Award (1995-1996); Educator of the Year (1986-1987) **C/VW:** ZHOPE

HELEN 'HERBIE' HARTMAN, CRS
Realtor
Long & Foster Real Estate, Inc.
321 Main Street
Reisterstown, MD 21136 United States
herbie@longandfoster.com
http://www.homesbyherbie.com

BUS: Real Estate Agency **P/S:** Home Sales and Listings **MA:** Regional **D/D/R:** Listing Residential Homes, Mentoring New Agents at the Company, Offering a Variety of Real Estate Products through the Largest Privately Owned Real Estate Company Worldwide **H/I/S:** Traveling, Reading, Spending Time with her Family **FBP:** Realtor Journals; Various Business Publications **CERTS:** Licensed Realtor, State of Maryland; Certified Residential Specialist; Certified Relocation Specialist; Certified Senior Housing Specialist **A/A/S:** Maryland Association of Realtors; National Association of Realtors; Women's Council of Realtors; Founders Club, Long & Foster Real Estate; Co-Chairman, Long and Foster Community Service Committee; President, Homeowners Association; Gold Team Member, Long & Foster Real Estate **A/H:** Outstanding Service Award, Greater Baltimore Board of Realtors (2003) **C/VW:** Charity Basket Bingo, Long & Foster Real Estate; Katrina Relief Fund; At Home with Diversity; Smart Home **B/I:** She became involved in this profession because she was interested in the flexibility of the field and being able to help people find a home that they love. **H/O:** The most gratifying aspect of her career is being able to assist first-time home buyers and help people sell their home and search for a more affordable residence.

SARAH A. HARTZ, BS
Civil Engineer, Facilities Engineer, EIT
California Department of Transportation
13171 Telfair Avenue
Suite 101
Sylmar, CA 91342 United States
sarah_hartz@dot.ca.gov
http://www.dot.ca.gov

BUS: Proven Leader in the Government Transportation Industry **P/S:** Manages more than 45,000 Miles of California's Highway and Freeway Lanes, Inter-City Rail Services, Assists more than 100 Public General Aviation Airports, Works with Local Agencies **MA:** Local **D/D/R:** Overseeing All Aspects of Expansion and Widening Projects of Bridges from Beginning to End, Acting as a Structural Representative **H/I/S:** Traveling, Horseback Riding, Motorcycle Riding **EDU:** Pursuing Master of Science in Structural Analysis, California State University at Northridge; Bachelor of Science in Civil Engineering, California State University at Northridge (2004); Associate of Arts in Liberal Studies, Antelope Valley College (2000) **CERTS:** Licensed Facilities Engineer, State of California **A/A/S:** American Society of Civil Engineers; Society of Women Engineers; American Institute of Steel Construction

PATRICK J. HASKELL
Voice Infrastructure Engineer
Logic Technology Inc.
232 Thimbleberry Road
Ballston Spa, NY 12020 United States
pjhaskell@ltionline.com
patrick.haskell@ge.com
http://www.ltionline.com

BUS: Consulting Firm **P/S:** Information Technology Consulting Services Including Project Management and Telecom Systems Implementation **MA:** International **EXP:** Mr. Haskell's expertise is in telecommunications management. **D/D/R:** Designing, Coordinating, Implementing and Managing Voice Network Equipment and Facilities Installation, Inspecting Project Sites, Procuring, Upgrading Video-Conferencing Systems and Other Conference Room Equipment **H/I/S:** Golfing, Listening to Music, Traveling, Reading **FBP:** Telecommunications **EDU:** Master's Degree in Education, Touro University, Summa Cum Laude (2005); Bachelor of Science, The New School (2003) **CHILD:** Jessica, Hannah, Rebecca, Lauren **W/H:** Master Sergeant, U.S. Air Force (2006)

ALLAN J. HASTINGS
Professor, Director of Product Design Studies
Kansas State University, College of Architecture, Planning and Design
115 Seaton Hall
Manhattan, KS 66506 United States
hasting@ksu.edu
http://www.k-state.edu

BUS: University **P/S:** Higher Education **MA:** National **EXP:** Mr. Hasting's expertise is in product exhibitions and automotive design. **H/I/S:** Golfing, Watercolor Painting, Illustrating **FBP:** Innovation; Scientific American **EDU:** Master's Equivalency in Design; Bachelor's Degree in Professional Arts, Product Transportation and Design, Art Center College of Design, Pasadena, CA; Bachelor's Degree in Architecture, Kansas State University **A/A/S:** Industrial Designers Society of America; Chamber of Commerce **A/S:** He attributes his success to his love for his profession. **B/I:** He became involved in his profession through a natural progression of opportunities. **H/O:** The most gratifying aspect of his career is seeing a new student understand a conceptual design and succeed in it.

KAREN S. HATCH
Realtor
New Horizons Realty
106 E. Church Street
Marshalltown, IA 50158 United States
khtch18karen@aol.com
http://www.cambridgewhoswho.com

BUS: Real Estate **P/S:** Residential and Rental Properties **MA:** Statewide **D/D/R:** Buying and Selling Residential and Rental Properties **H/I/S:** Gardening, Fitness, Reading **FBP:** Real Estate Magazine **A/A/S:** Iowa Association of Realtors; National Association of Realtors **C/VW:** American Cancer Society; Alzheimer's Association; American Veterans Society **A/S:** She attributes her personal and professional success to her grandchildren. **B/I:** She has always had an interest in the field and a love for helping others. **H/O:** The highlight of her career is investing in rental properties.

CARRIE L. HATHAWAY
Administrative Assistant
Swedish Medical Center Ballard
5300 Tallman Avenue N.W.
Seattle, WA 98107 United States
carriehathaway@swedish.org
http://www.swedish.org

BUS: Largest, Most Comprehensive, Nonprofit Health Care Provider in the Pacific Northwest, Committed to Excellence in Medical Care **P/S:** Emergency Services, Oncology, Cardiology, Women's Health Care, Pediatrics, Rehabilitation, Behavioral Health, Primary Care, Surgical Services, Orthopedics, Neuroscience **MA:** Local **D/D/R:** Assisting with Purchasing, Managing 10 to 20 Vendor Contracts, Ordering, Entering Data, Making Travel Arrangements and Bids **H/I/S:** Camping, Country Music, Reading **FBP:** Country Weekly **EDU:** Coursework in Construction and Project Management, Shoreline Community College

DIANE L. HATTENDORF, MA
Principal
Peotone Community School District 207U
9526 W. 255th Street
Frankfort, IL 60423 United States
http://www.cambridgewhoswho.com

BUS: School **P/S:** Providing a Positive, Safe, Nurturing Environment Where We Inspire Students To Achieve Their Full Potential In Collaboration With Family, Community And Staff **MA:** Local **D/D/R:** Communicating with Parents, Public Speaking **H/I/S:** Gardening, Making Crafts, and Baking **FBP:** Educational Leadership Magazine **EDU:** Master's Degree in Education, Governor State University; Master's Degree in Educational Administration, Plus 30, Governor State University **A/A/S:** Illinois Reading Association; Association for Supervision and Curriculum Development **C/VW:** Local Church; American Cancer Society; Katrina Relief Organization **A/S:** She attributes her success to having the ability to listen and make decisions. She takes each day like a new experience and she always puts the children first. **B/I:** She became involved in the profession because at the age of six she knew she wanted to be a teacher. She later went into administration to help mentor up and coming educators. **H/O:** The highlight of her career was having her first classroom after graduating from college.

MARCIA I. HAUSMAN
Secondary Mathematics Teacher
Sunman Dearborn Middle School
8356 Schuman Road
Saint Leon, IN 47012 United States
thausman@hsonline.net
http://sunmandearborn.k12.in.us/sdms

BUS: Safe and Caring Secondary School that Enables and Encourages High Achievement for all Students through the Effective Use of Resources **P/S:** Teaching Gifted and Talented Middle School Students, Programs in Art, Music, Computers, English, Mathematics, Social Studies, Science and Health **MA:** Regional **D/D/R:** Teaching the Gifted and Talented in Secondary Mathematics **H/I/S:** Traveling, Photography **FBP:** NCTM Journal **EDU:** Bachelor of Science in Mathematics, Purdue University (1993); Master of Science in Secondary Education, Indiana University (1978) **CERTS:** Certified Mentor **A/A/S:** National Education Association; Mathematics Advisory Council, Purdue University (1998-2001); SDA; IST

BARBARA SPENCER HAWK
President
Crossbridge Communications, LLC
339 Forrer Boulevard
Dayton, OH 45419 United States
bspencerhawk@cs.com
http://www.crossbridgecommunications.com

BUS: Business, Technical Consulting and Communications Industry **P/S:** Strategies, Applications, Enterprise Networks and Infrastructure Solutions Across Various Industries **MA:** National **D/D/R:** Assisting Companies to Improve the Quality of Written Communications, Offering Training and Analysis of Strategic Approaches to Communications **H/I/S:** Knitting, Gardening **EDU:** Master of Public Administration, University of Dayton (1979); Bachelor's Degree in International Studies, Miami University (1975) **C/VW:** Volunteer, American Friends

PATHENIA L. HAWTHORNE
Medical Library Technician
VA Medical Center
508 Fulton Street
NG 014
Durham, NC 27705 United States
pathenia.hawthorne@med.va.gov
http://www.cambridgewhoswho.com

BUS: Medical Center **P/S:** Health Care Services Including Assessment and Rehabilitation **MA:** National **D/D/R:** Purchasing Books for the Library, Interlibrary Loaning Of Books, Articles and Videos, Requesting Materials from Other Libraries throughout the U.S. And Canada, Maintaining Budgets, Processing Books **H/I/S:** Reading, Listening to Music **FBP:** Business Week **EDU:** Associate of Science in Secretarial Science, Croft Business College (1968)

JEFF HAYENGA
Realtor
Keller Williams Realty
1801 S. Mo-Pac Expressway
Suite 100
Austin, TX 78746 United States
jeffhayenga@austinhomebroker.com
http://www.kw.com

BUS: Real Estate Agency **P/S:** Real Estate Exchange **MA:** Texas **D/D/R:** Assisting First Time Home Buyers and Sellers, Overseeing Residential and Commercial Sales and Market Analysis **H/I/S:** Traveling, Golfing, Riding his Harley-Davidson **CERTS:** Licensed Realtor (2001) **A/A/S:** Keller Williams Realty Luxury Realty **C/VW:** Local Charitable Organization; Keller Williams Cares; Save the Children; Harley Davidson Charity **A/S:** He attributes his success to his ability to interact with people and help them buying their homes. **B/I:** He became involved in his profession because he always wanted to be in the sales field. **H/O:** The highlights of his career were selling a $2.7 million home and working with a single mother for a year to help her buy a home. **I/F/Y:** In five years, Mr. Hayenga hopes to represent his clients ethically and professionally.

JANET L. HAYES
ADON, TCU Manager, PPS/MDS Coordinator, Wound Specialist
Billings Health and Rehabilitation Community
2115 Central Avenue
Billings, MT 59102 United States
jhayes@thegoodmangroup.com
http://www.billingshealth.com/index.htm

BUS: Rehabilitation and Long-Term Care Community **P/S:** Long-Term Care, Skilled Nursing, Rehabilitation, Pharmacy Services, Individual and Group Activities, Family Involvement, Social Services **MA:** Regional **D/D/R:** Managing All Medicare Patients and Cases, Completing Patient Documentation, Assisting in Wound Care and Skin Care Issues **H/I/S:** Making Jewelry **FBP:** Gerontological Nursing **EDU:** Diploma in Nursing, Beaver Falls, PA (1972) **CERTS:** Certified MDS Coordinator, American Association of Nurse Assessment Coordinators **A/A/S:** National Alliance of Wound Care Specialists

KATHRYN E. HAYNES, RN
Registered Nurse
Procedure Center
Queen of the Valley Medical Center
100 Trancas Street
Napa, CA 94558 United States
kgrn62@aim.com
http://www.thequeen.com

BUS: Hospital **P/S:** General Healthcare **MA:** Local **D/D/R:** Offering Outpatient Chemotherapy and Infusion Services, Conscious Sedation for Endoscopy Procedures and Other Small Procedures Including Thoracentesis, Paracentesis, Bronchoscopies, Bone Marrow Biopsies, Lumbar Punctures and Blood Patches **H/I/S:** Traveling, Scrapbooking, Reading, Hiking **FBP:** Journal of Christian Nursing **EDU:** Pursuing Bachelor of Science in Nursing, California State University, Chico; Associate Degree in Nursing, Shasta College, Redding, CA **A/A/S:** Oncology Nursing Society **C/VW:** Griefshare Group; Valley Christian Fellowship **DOB:** April 27, 1962 **POB:** Page **SP:** Aaron **CHILD:** Ricky, Bob, Brett, Taylor **W/H:** Charge Nurse, Inpatient Oncology Floor; Outpatient Chemotherapy Nurse, Oncology Practice; Endoscopy Nurse; Small Procedure Nurse **A/S:** She attributes her success to her natural talent in the medical field. **B/I:** She became involved in her profession because she always wanted to become a nurse. **H/O:** The most gratifying aspect of her career is hearing her cancer patients' success stories. **I/F/Y:** In five years, Ms. Haynes hopes to have earned her bachelor's degree.

ROSE M. HAYNES, M.ED.
Special Education Teacher
Crossett Public School
219 Main Street
Crossett, AR 71635 United States
rhaynes@csd2.k12.ar.us
http://www.cambridgewhoswho.com

BUS: Education **P/S:** Education **MA:** Local **D/D/R:** Special Education, Leadership, Teaching Children and Assisting Senior Citizens in the Community **H/I/S:** Going to Church, Reading, Spending Time with her Grandchildren and Mother **FBP:** Educational Leadership **EDU:** Master of Arts in Special Education, University of Arkansas, Fayetteville; Bachelor's Degree, University of Arkansas at Monticello **CERTS:** Certified in Elementary Education; Certified in Special Education (K-12) **A/A/S:** Arkansas Education Association; National Education Association; CEA; ANEA; Professional Alliance of Women **A/H:** Best Teacher Award, Hastings Elementary School (1997-1998) **C/VW:** New Bethel Missionary Baptist Church; Youth Leader, Youth Department of New Bethel; Young Adult Ushers **A/S:** She attributes her success to the school she works in and to the pastor in her church. **B/I:** She became involved in her profession because of the events of her personal life. **H/O:** The highlight of her career is seeing her students progress and show social skills.

VALERI J. HEALD
Hospice Patient Care Coordinator
Hoosier Uplands Home Health and Hospice
PO Box 9
Mitchell, IN 47446 United States
vheald@hoosieruplands.org
http://www.hoosieruplands.org

BUS: Local Nonprofit Agency that Serves as an Area Agency on Aging, Community Action Agency and Licensed Home Health Care and Hospice Agency **P/S:** Supplying Medications and Equipment Related to Terminal Diagnosis, Holistic Care for the Client and Family Members, Comfort and Symptom Management to Ensure that the Client's Dying Wishes are Met, Home Health Aide Services to Assist with Personal Care, Social Work and Chaplain Services, Volunteer Services **MA:** Regional **D/D/R:** Critical Care Nursing, Emergency Room Nursing, Offering Hospice and Palliative Care **H/I/S:** Spending Quality Time with Family, Attending her Children's School and Sport Activities, Spending Relaxing Evenings at Home with her Husband **FBP:** Journal of Hospice and Palliative Nursing; American Journal of Hospice and Palliative Medicine **EDU:** Pursuing Certification in Hospice and Palliative Care Nursing; Associate Degree in Nursing, Spencerian College (2002) **CERTS:** Licensed Practical Nurse, Ivy Tech State College (1999); Certified in Basic Life Support; Certified in Advanced Cardiac Life Support **A/A/S:** Indiana Association for Home and Hospice Care; Indiana Hospice and Palliative Care Organization; Community Health Accreditation Program; National Hospice and Palliative Care Organization; National Association for Home Care and Hospice **DOB:** January 8, 1972 **SP:** Carlos **CHILD:** Charlie, Audriana, Jenny, Kerry, Kevin **W/H:** Health South Rehabilitation Hospital, Terre Haute, IN; Hospice, Oncology, Emergency Room, Louisville VA Hospital; Emergency Room, University of Louisville Medical Center; Emergency Room, Norton Hospital, Louisville, Kentucky; Hoosier Uplands Home Health and Hospice

NATALIE M. HEARD HACKETT
Principal
Paterson Board of Education
33 Church Street
Paterson, NJ 07505 United States
natalieheard1@aol.com
http://www.cambridgewhoswho.com

BUS: Board of Education **P/S:** Education Including Elementary, Middle School, Art and Physical Education **MA:** Regional **D/D/R:** Working as an Adjunct Professor at the New Jersey City University, Monitoring All Classrooms, Handling Disciplinary Actions, Ensuring Teachers Follow Curriculum Guidelines, Developing Staff for Three Inclusion Classes **FBP:** Education Leadership **A/A/S:** New Jersey Principals and Supervisors Association; Elementary Principals and Supervisors Association; Association for Supervision and Curriculum Development

LINDA SUSAN HEATH
Teacher
Cherry Hill High School East
1750 Kresson Road
Cherry Hill, NJ 08003 United States
mthtchr43@comcast.net
http://east.cherryhill.k12.nj.us

BUS: High School **P/S:** Education Services, Core Curricula in Mathematics, Science, Social Studies, English and World Language, College Preparatory Courses, Scholarships, Field Trips, Guidance **MA:** Local **D/D/R:** Teaching Higher-Level Mathematics, Honors Geometry, Advanced Placement Calculus, Integrated Remedial Mathematics Classes, Making Presentations at Conferences and Workshops, Speaking Publicly **H/I/S:** Coaching Bowling, Singing in Choirs, Participating in Multicultural Activities **FBP:** Mathematics Teacher **EDU:** Bachelor of Arts in Mathematics, Plus 11, Rutgers, The State University of New Jersey (1974) **CERTS:** Certification in K-12 Mathematics; Certification in Advanced Placement **A/A/S:** Association of Mathematics Teachers of New Jersey; National Council of Teachers of Mathematics

SHARYL L. HEAVIN
Head of Test Kitchen
DCS by Fisher & Paykel
5800 Skylab Drive
Huntington Beach, CA 92647 United States
sheavin@dcsappliance.com
http://www.cambridgewhoswho.com

BUS: Manufacturing Company **P/S:** Manufacturing Home Appliances **MA:** International **D/D/R:** Testing New Appliances; Working with Engineers on Designs **H/I/S:** Gardening, Cooking, Hiking **FBP:** Industry-Related Publications **EDU:** Bachelor's Degree in Education, California State University at Los Angeles **A/A/S:** American Association of Family and Consumer Science; Family and Community Home Economists; Investment Club **C/VW:** American Diabetes Association; American Heart Association; Local Charitable Organizations **A/S:** She attributes her success to her hard work and continuous learning. **B/I:** She became involved in the profession because she wanted to work in a field that combined teaching and cooking. **H/O:** The highlight of her career was earning her current position.

M. ANJANETTE HEBERT, CHPA
Director of Security, Safety and Emergency Preparedness
Lafayette General Medical Center
1214 Coolidge Boulevard
Lafayette, LA 70503 United States
ahebert@lgmc.com
http://www.lgmc.com

BUS: Nonprofit Hospital **P/S:** Healthcare **MA:** Regional **D/D/R:** Specializing in Security, Safety and Emergency Management **H/I/S:** Spending Quality Time with her Children **EDU:** Bachelor of Science, University of Louisiana **A/A/S:** International Association for Healthcare Security and Safety; Louisiana Homeland Security and Emergency Preparedness **C/VW:** United Way **A/S:** She attributes her career success to her excellent networking skills. **B/I:** She became involved in security after taking a criminal justice course while in college and finding it fascinating. **H/O:** The most gratifying aspect of her career is being able to mentor professional organizations in security and safety.

NORMA J. HEDGES
Funeral Director
Hedges Funeral Homes, LLC
100 Hedges Drive
Camdenton, MO 65020 United States
hedges1941@sbcglobal.net
http://www.cambridgewhoswho.com

BUS: Funeral Home **P/S:** Three Funeral Homes, Two Crematoriums, Two Cemeteries and a Mausoleum **MA:** Local **D/D/R:** Arranging Furniture, Conducting Visitations, Funerals, Cremations and Burials **H/I/S:** Reading **EDU:** Bachelor's Degree in English, University of Missouri-Columbia **A/A/S:** Literary Society **C/VW:** Local Fundraisers, Local Schools and Hospitals **A/S:** She attributes her career success to public acceptance of death. **B/I:** She entered the business after her husband began his first funeral home. **H/O:** She feels that the highlight of her career is yet to come.

CANDACE MICHELLE HEFNER, LMT
Licensed Massage Therapist
Lucky You Massage Therapy
1880 N. Germantown Parkway
Cordova, TN 38016 United States
candace_hefner@hotmail.com
http://www.cambridgewhoswho.com

BUS: Healthcare **P/S:** Natural Healing Arts in Licensed Massage Therapy for Improved Client Health **MA:** National **EXP:** Ms. Hefner's expertise includes natural healing arts including ancient Chinese and traditional therapies, aromatherapy, deep tissue and Swedish massage. **H/I/S:** Traveling, Fitness, Building International Relationships **FBP:** American Massage Therapy Association Journal **CERTS:** Licensed Massage Therapist, States of Mississippi and Tennessee; Certified in Aromatherapy; Certified in Natural Healing Arts; Certified in CPR **A/A/S:** American Massage Therapy Association **C/VW:** Make-A-Wish Foundation; Elite Therapist, World Series Poker Tour; Ideal Health **A/S:** She attributes her career success to the many client referrals she receives. **B/I:** Although she received a medical scholarship to Emory University for medical studies, she found that she wanted to pursue a career that would allow her more hands-on healing, so she chose massage therapy as her career. **H/O:** The highlight of her career was when she was asked to be the official massage therapist for the National power Tour, corporate clientele.

JULIE ANNE HEIBERGER, NCARB, AIA
Senior Design Architect, Project Architect
Hoffman, LLC
N434 Greenville Center
Appleton, WI 54914 United States
jheiberger@hoffman.net
http://www.hoffman.net

BUS: Proven Leader in the Planning, Architecture and Construction Management Services Industry **P/S:** Fully Integrated Planning, Architecture and Construction Management Services within the Following Primary Markets: Education, Healthcare, Corporate, Professional, Senior Living, Women's Religious Planners, Expertise and Quality Service **MA:** National **D/D/R:** Working with Senior Living Services, Women's Religious Planners, Architects, Engineers and Construction Managers **H/I/S:** Traveling, Reading, Spending Quality Time with her Two Children, Coaching T-Ball **FBP:** Design; Architects; AIA Record **EDU:** Master's Degree in Architecture, University of Wisconsin (1996) **A/A/S:** NACARB; SAGE; AIA

HOPE ROSE HEIDERSCHEIDT
Licensed Representative
Citigroup Global Mortgage
6451 N. Charles Street
Towson, MD 21212 United States
hope.heiderscheidt@citi.com
http://www.cit.com

BUS: Mortgage Company **P/S:** Variety of Living Arrangements, Amenities, Services, Meal Plans, Social Activities and Care **MA:** International **EXP:** Ms. Heiderscheidt's expertise is in assisted living services coordination. **D/D/R:** Managing Operations Including Hiring and Firing Staff, Supervising Care Plans, Scheduling, Ensuring Satisfactory Resident Care, Encouraging Independence, Family Involvement and Social Interaction for Residents **H/I/S:** Horseback Riding, Reading Science Fiction and Fantasy Novels **EDU:** Bachelor's Degree in Mass Communication and Sociology, York College (2001)

GAIL A. HEINTZ
RN Case Manager
Lower Keys Medical Centre
5900 College Road
Key West, FL 33040 United States
gail.heintz@lkmc.hma-corp.com

BUS: Acute Care Hospital **P/S:** Healthcare **MA:** National **EXP:** Ms. Heintz's expertise is in case management. **H/I/S:** Reading **FBP:** Newsweek **EDU:** Bachelor of Science in Nursing, University of Miami (1985); Registered Nurse, Jackson Memorial Hospital (1974) **A/A/S:** Florida Nurses Association **A/S:** She attributes her success to hard work, enjoying what she does and working for a good company. **B/I:** She became involved in this profession after high school. **H/O:** The highlight of her career is the day she received her registered nurse degree.

JANET L. HELMBOLD
School Psychologist, Area Coordinator (Retired)
Delta-Schoolcraft Intermediate School District
2525 Third Avenue S.
Escanaba, MI 49829 United States
janet.helmbold@cwwemail.com
http://www.cambridgewhoswho.com

BUS: School District **P/S:** Education **MA:** Local **D/D/R:** Treating Psychological, Educational and Learning Disorders Including Retardation and Emotional Problems in Students **H/I/S:** Reading, Listening to Music, Philately, Traveling, Spending Time at the Church, Singing **EDU:** Educational Specialist Degree in Psychology and Education, University of Michigan **A/A/S:** Former Member, Council for Exceptional Children; Former Member, Michigan Association of School Psychologists; Former Member, National Association of School Psychologists **A/H:** Outstanding Person in Education Award, Region 17-BC, Michigan Education Association (2005); Distinguished Service Award, Schoolcraft County Mental Health Services Board (1997) **C/VW:** Local Church; Project Hope; ChildReach; Feed the Children; AmeriCares; Habitat for Humanity **DOB:** June 10, 1945 **POB:** West Branch, MI **W/H:** Area Coordinator, Delta-Schoolcraft Intermediate School District (1980-2005); School Psychologist, Delta-Schoolcraft Intermediate School District (1975-2005); School Psychologist, Sanilac Intermediate School District (1970-1975); Director, Summer Head Start Program (1968-1969); Waitress, Wayside Grill (1965); Waitress, Hamilton Stores (1964) **A/S:** She attributes her success to the support she receives from her parents. **B/I:** She became involved in her profession because she was inspired by her mother who was involved in special education. **H/O:** The most gratifying aspect of her career is being successful.

MARY A. HELSELL
Owner, Director, Teacher
Momma Mary's Daycare
613 Highway 33 E.
West Bend, WI 53095 United States
mhelsell@wi.rr.com
htt://http://www.cambridgewhoswho.com

BUS: Day Care Center **P/S:** Child Care **MA:** Local **D/D/R:** Scheduling Activities, Preparing Lesson Plans, Planning Projects, Maintaining Logs For Children Under Two Years ff Age, Taking Care of Children from Six Weeks to 12 Years Old **H/I/S:** Reading Novels, Gardening, Making Educational Crafts, Golfing **EDU:** Associate Degree in Early Childhood Education, Moraine Park Technical College **A/A/S:** Phi Theta Kappa; National Association for the Education of Young Children; OWEKA **A/H:** National Who's Who for Junior Colleges in Early Childhood Education, Moraine Park Technical College (2007) **C/VW:** Children with Special Needs **DOB:** November 3, 1954 **POB:** West Bend, WI **SP:** Alan **CHILD:** Eric, Alan **W/H:** Assistant Day Care Teacher, Supportive Care Giver, Washington County Mental Health Services **A/S:** She attributes her success to the support she receives from her family and mentors. **B/I:** She became involved in her profession through a natural progression of opportunities. **H/O:** The highlight of her career was earning her state license before receiving her degree.

STACEY R. HELVIN, RN, BSN, PHN, CRRN, CLCP
Registered Nurse, Certified Life Care Planner
Quality Life Care Plans, Inc.
19907 Trotter Lane
Yorba Linda, CA 92886 United States
stacey@qlcp.net
http://www.cambridgewhoswho.com

BUS: Healthcare Center **P/S:** Healthcare and Life Care Plans for Individuals with Chronic and Disabling Conditions **MA:** Regional **D/D/R:** Working with Attorneys to Develop Plans for Individuals Suffering with Long-Term Disabilities, Preventing Medical Malpractice, Treating Patients with Personal Injuries Including Brain, Spinal Cord, Burns and Birth Injuries **H/I/S:** Walking, Reading, Cooking, Spending Time with her Children **FBP:** Legal Nurse Consulting Resource **EDU:** Bachelor of Science in Nursing, California State University, Dominguez Hills **CERTS:** Certified Rehabilitation Registered Nurse, Association of Rehabilitation Nurses; Certification in Life Planning, Commission on Healthcare Certification **A/A/S:** Secretary, Association of Rehabilitation Nurses; International Association of Rehabilitation Professionals; National Spinal Cord Injury Association; International Academy of Life Care Planners

MARILYN HEMPHILL SMITH
President, Owner
Metro Christian Family Living Magazine
2 Northpointe Cove
Jackson, MS 39211 United States
http://www.jacksonchristianfamily.com

BUS: Publishing Company **P/S:** Family Publications with a Christian Perspective **MA:** Regional **D/D/R:** Overseeing all Operations, Selling Ads, Writing Articles, Circulating 25,000 Magazines **H/I/S:** Playing the Piano at Church **FBP:** Metro Christian Family Living Magazine **EDU:** Master of Music in Piano Performance, Mississippi College; College Coursework, University of Mississippi **A/A/S:** American Christian Writers; Southern Christian Writers **C/VW:** Mission Mississippi; Board of Directors, Drama Ministry Fishtale

PATRICIA W. HENDERSON, RN
Registered Nurse, Case Manager
Select Specialty Hospital
5903 Ridgewood Road
Jackson, MS 39211 United States
phende5908@bellsouth.net
http://www.cambridgewhoswho.com

BUS: Acute Long-Term Care Facility **P/S:** Healthcare **MA:** Local **D/D/R:** Specializing in Patient Advocacy, Ensuring Patients Needs are Met and Rights are Protected for Safe Discharge from Hospital Care **H/I/S:** Camping, NASCAR **FBP:** RN **EDU:** Associate Degree in Nursing, Hinds Community College **A/A/S:** Phi Theta Kappa **C/VW:** American Lung Association, Salvation Army

SANDRA E. HENDERSON, RNRAC
Registered Nurse Assessment Coordinator
Port Orange Nursing and Rehab
5600 Victoria Gardens Boulevard
Port Orange, FL 32127 United States
sandrahenderson1@aol.com
http://www.cambridgewhoswho.com

BUS: Long-Term Care Skilled Nursing and Short-Term Rehab Facility **P/S:** Healthcare **MA:** Local **D/D/R:** Assessing Patient Needs, Initiating Care Plans **H/I/S:** Spending Time at the Beach, Walking, Gardening, Spending Time with her Husband, Anthony and Son, Charles **EDU:** Associate Degree in Nursing, Daytona Beach Community College; Registered Nurse Diploma, Daytona Beach Community College **A/H:** Department Recognition, AHCA (2006) **C/VW:** Pet Rescue, Best Friends, St. Jude Children's Research Hospital, Shriners Children's Hospital **A/S:** She attributes her success to her love for her work and her organizational skills. **B/I:** She became involved in her profession because her mother was a nurse. **H/O:** The highlight of her career is working in geriatric medicine.

JULIE NICOLE HENDRICKSON, RN
Registered Nurse
Mercy Hospital
2525 S. Michigan Avenue
Chicago, IL 60616 United States
jules0902@yahoo.com
http://www.cambridgewhoswho.com

BUS: Hospital **P/S:** Healthcare **MA:** Local **D/D/R:** Overseeing the Labor Unit and Special Care Nursery **H/I/S:** Running, Swimming, Practicing Yoga, Scrapbooking, Reading **EDU:** Associate Degree in Nursing, College of DuPage (2007); Bachelor's Degree in Business Management, Minor in Psychology, Northern Illinois University (2001); Registered Nurse, College of DuPage **A/H:** Social Services Director of the Year Award, Illinois Healthcare Association (2005) **H/O:** The most gratifying aspect of her career is educating her patients.

MR. ROBERT R. HENKEL
President
3DC Solutions
3676 Gamble Street
Schertz, TX 78154 United States
robert_3dc@satx.rr.com
http://www.3dcsolutions.com

BUS: Construction and Consulting Business **P/S:** Construction Support to Engineers, Environmental Project Management **MA:** International **D/D/R:** Bidding on Contracts, Working with Subcontractors, Consulting in Project Management **H/I/S:** Spending Time with his Children **FBP:** American Military Engineers **EDU:** Master's Degree in Public Administration, Golden Gate University (1987); Bachelor of Civil Engineering, Virginia Military Institute (1978); Coursework in Resource Management **A/A/S:** Society of American Military Engineers **W/H:** U.S. Air Force

TIMOTHY P. HENNESSY
Vice President
Garrison Litigation Management Group
120 East Avenue
Suite 101
Rochester, NY 14604 United States
hennessytim@hotmail.com
http://www.cambridgewhoswho.com

BUS: Litigation Management Group Committed to Providing Quality, Comprehensive Services **P/S:** Litigation Management **MA:** National **EXP:** Mr. Hennessy's expertise includes litigation management, personal injury and asbestos cases. **H/I/S:** Sports, Enthusiast on NFL Teams Pittsburgh Steelers and Pirates **FBP:** Inside Counsel; Counsel to Counsel Magazine **EDU:** JD, University of Pittsburgh (1975) **A/A/S:** New York State Bar Association; American Bar Association

REV. MAYTHIA HENRIQUEZ-ABNEY
Senior Pastor
Warriors for Christ Ministries and Tabernacle Inc
445 Sterling Road at Route 196 North
Tobyhanna, PA 18466 United States
maythia45@aol.com
http://www.warriorsforchristministries.com

BUS: Religion, Religious Organization Religion/Spiritual Services **P/S:** Preaching and Teaching The Word of God Mentor **MA:** International **D/D/R:** Counseling to Youth and Youthful Offenders, Public Speaking, Drug and Alcohol Counseling, Preaching and Teaching the Word of God **H/I/S:** Travel, Reading, Coin Collecting, Hunting & Golf **FBP:** Oprah; Black Enterprise **EDU:** Doctor of Theology, New Greater Bethel Bible Institute; Master of Social Work, New Greater Bethel Bible Institute; Bachelor's Degree in Theology, New Greater Bethel Bible Institute **A/A/S:** Association of Black Social Workers **C/VW:** Pocono Mountain Clergy Association; Police Officers for Christ

TRISHA M. HENRY
Educator, Coach
Pierce City High School
300 N. Myrtle Street
Pierce City, MO 65723 United States
thenry@pcschools.net
http://www.cambridgewhoswho.com

BUS: High School Facility Dedicated to Excellence in Education **P/S:** Regular Core Curriculum including English, Mathematics, Reading, Science, Social Studies, Art, Music, History, Physical Education, Languages, Computers **MA:** Regional **D/D/R:** Teaching English, Coaching Volleyball **H/I/S:** Volleyball, Basketball, Baseball **FBP:** The English Journal **EDU:** Bachelor's Degree, Missouri State University (2000) **A/A/S:** Phi Kappa Phi; American Volleyball Coaches Association; National Council of English Teachers; United States Association of Volleyball Coaches

LORI A. HEPLER
Realtor
RE/MAX Real Estate Services
8141 Kaiser Boulevard, #311
Anaheim Hills, CA 92808 United States
lorihepler@adelphia.net
http://www.lorihepler.com

BUS: Real Estate **P/S:** Real Estate Services and Sales, Property Management, Investments **MA:** Local **D/D/R:** Selling Residential Real Estate **H/I/S:** Boating, Traveling, Reading **FBP:** The Realtors Guide; The Wall Street Journal **EDU:** Bachelor of Science in Political Science and Public Law, University of California at Los Angeles **A/A/S:** Pacifica West Association of Realtors; California Association of Realtors; National Association of Realtors **C/VW:** Children's Health Network; Mater Dei High School **A/S:** She attributes her success to the support she gets from her family and to being people oriented. **B/I:** She became involved in the profession because she wanted to help people make one of the biggest purchases of their lives. **H/O:** The highlight of her career was having her daughter write an essay about her which recognized her as a role model and a successful woman.

LELA HERBERT
President
Hopes Drapery and Manufacturing
815 Jones Street
Berkeley, CA 94710 United States
http://www.cambridgewhoshwho.com

BUS: Manufacturer, Custom Draperies, Restorer of Antique Draperies **P/S:** Draperies, Residential and Commercial, Curtains, Valances, Swags, Bedspreads, Cornices, Pillows, Table Coverings, Fabrics, Lining, Traverse Rods, Furniture, Carpet, Lamps, Mirrors, Installation **MA:** Regional **D/D/R:** Designing and Manufacturing Fancy, Custom-Made Draperies, Restoring Antique Draperies Including Reconstruction and Reweaving of Fabrics, Teaching Custom Drapery Work **H/I/S:** Attending Lectures **EDU:** Associate Degree in Teaching Credentials, Laney College (1972) **A/A/S:** San Francisco Merchandise Mart

WAYNE R. HERMAN
Financial Treasurer (Retired)
Ohio State Local Union
oneuptight@aol.com
http://www.cambridgewhoswho.com

BUS: Labor Union **P/S:** New York State Contracts for Labor Practices **MA:** Local **EXP:** Mr. Herman's expertise is in finance. **H/I/S:** Using the Computer **EDU:** Diploma, Belden High School **C/VW:** Veteran Chairman, Elks Club; Veterans of Foreign War **A/S:** He attributes his success to his hard work and determination. **B/I:** He became involved in the profession because he wanted to make a difference in people's lives. **H/O:** The highlight of his career was being recognized for his achievement.

MR. ANDRES HERNANDEZ
Exceptional Student Education Teacher
Riviera Middle School
10301 S.W. 48th Street
Miami, FL 33165 United States
andres0917@msn.com
http://www.cambridgewhoswho.com

BUS: Middle School **P/S:** Education **MA:** Local **D/D/R:** Teaching Science and Social Studies to Mentally and Physically Handicapped Students **H/I/S:** Reading, Traveling **EDU:** Pursuing Master's Degree in Community Mental Health Counseling and School Counseling, Florida International University **A/A/S:** Phi Sigma Iota; Delta Epsilon Iota **C/VW:** Coach, Special Olympics **A/S:** He attributes his success to his willingness to learn, setting goals and to the support of his family. **B/I:** He became involved in his profession because he enjoyed working with children and wanted to make a difference in their lives. **H/O:** The most gratifying aspect of his career is being able to have a career while pursuing a new degree.

LUIS F. HERNANDEZ
Accountant
Super Carniceria La Chiquita
1000 W. Main Street
Santa Maria, CA 93458 United States
felipe.hernandez@lachiquita.com
http://www.lachiquita.com

BUS: Retail Store **P/S:** Retail Sales of Supermarket Items **MA:** National **EXP:** Mr. Hernandez's expertise is in accounting and finance management. **H/I/S:** Playing Basketball, Biking **FBP:** Hispanic Business **EDU:** Bachelor of Arts in Accounting, University of Sinaloa, Mazatlan, Mexico (1990) **A/A/S:** Treasurer, Latino Business & Community Council

MARIA E. HERNANDEZ VIVIANO
Vice President, General Manager
Cellstar Corp
601 S. Royal Lane
Coppell, TX 75019 United States
maria.viviana@yahoo.com
http://www.cambridgewhoswho.com

BUS: Telecommunications Company **P/S:** Telecommunications Distribution and Logistical Services **MA:** International **EXP:** Ms. Hernandez Viviano's expertise is in business management. **H/I/S:** Listening to Music, Bicycling, Cooking **FBP:** BusinessWeek **EDU:** Bachelor of Science Degree, University of Texas **A/A/S:** DHCFC; GSA **C/VW:** Local Catholic Church

DARLENE R. HERPS, RPSGT
Supervisor of the Sleep Medicine Center
Norton's Kosair Children's Hospital
231 E. Chestnut Street
Louisville, KY 40202 United States
darlene.herps@nortonhealthcare.org
http://www.cambridgwhoswho.com

BUS: Hospital **P/S:** Sleep Medicine for Children **MA:** Healthcare **EXP:** Ms. Herps' expertise is in sleep medicine. **H/I/S:** Camping **FBP:** Journal of Sleep **EDU:** Coursework in Nursing, Eastern Kentucky University **A/A/S:** American Academy of Sleep Medicine; Kentucky Sleep Society; The Board of Registered Polysomnographic Technologists **C/VW:** Divine Savior Lutheran Church, Helping Hands Thrift Shop, Outreach Thrift Shop **C/A:** City Council Member, Pioneer Village (2007) **A/S:** She attributes her success to her patience and always taking the next step. **B/I:** She became involved in this profession because she read a book for sleep disorders and was interested in it. **H/O:** The highlight of her career is doing scientific research.

MISS MARIA LUISA HERRERO
President, Owner
Tecnina Industrial, S.A
Av. San Martin No. 284
Santo Domingo, 10513 Dominican Republic
tisa@codetel.net.do
http://www.tisa.com.do

BUS: Sales and Distribution Company **P/S:** Sales and Distribution Services for Automotive Workshops, Specialty Tools and Equipment **MA:** International **EXP:** Ms. Herrero's expertise is in business operations management. **H/I/S:** Traveling, Reading, Spending Time with her Family **FBP:** The Wall Street Journal; The New York Times **EDU:** Bachelor's Degree in Business and Economics, INTEC Technology Institute of Santo Domingo, Dominican Republic **A/A/S:** OAC **C/VW:** Dominican Cancer Institute **POB:** Cáceres, España **CHILD:** Fernando, Christian **A/S:** She attributes her success to her hard work and determination. **B/I:** She became involved in her profession because it is a family business. **H/O:** The highlight of her career was earning her current position.

RUTH HERRING, RN
Registered Nurse
Bronx Lebanon Hospital Fulton Division
1276 Fulton Avenue
Bronx, NY 10956 United States
harring.03@yahoo.com
http://www.cambridgewhoswho.com

BUS: Healthcare **P/S:** Magnet Status Hospital Addressing the Healthcare Needs of the Community **MA:** Regional **EXP:** Ms. Herring's expertise is in psychiatric nursing. **H/I/S:** Gardening, Traveling **FBP:** American Journal of Nursing; Psychiatric Nursing **EDU:** Associate Degree in Nursing, University of Nicaragua **CERTS:** Certified in Advanced Cardiac Life Support; Certified in Basic Life Support; Certified in Advanced Pediatric Life Support **C/VW:** Volunteering at the Spring Valley Seventh Day Adventist Church **A/S:** She attributes her success to her loyalty, dedication and her caring spirit for the sick. **B/I:** She became involved in this profession because she loves caring for sick people and began teaching health in Nicaragua. When she moved to New York she moved into psychiatric nursing. **H/O:** The highlight of her career is the high level of responsibility and credibility that she has.

ALICE M. HERTZLER
Owner, Life Transition Coach, Licensed Clinical Social Worker, Mentor
A Bridge Beyond Coaching
5311 Highgate Green
Williamsburg, VA 23188 United States
alice@abridgebeyondcoaching.com
http://www.abridgebeyondcoaching.com

BUS: Human Development Company **P/S:** Life Transforming Coaching, Education on How to Relax the Body to Promote Strength, Clearing the Mind and Freeing the Spirit to Create the Ultimate Life **MA:** National **EXP:** Ms. Hertzler's expertise is in clinical social work. **D/D/R:** Coaching Individuals to Help Fulfill their Dreams and Develop their Inner Creative Skills, Training, Empowering Individuals to Live Spontaneously and Take Responsibility for their Lives **H/I/S:** Dancing, Sailing **FBP:** Fast Company; Science and Spirit **EDU:** Master's Degree in Social Work, University of South Carolina (1981); Bachelor's Degree in Psychology, University of South Carolina (1979) **CERTS:** Licensed Clinical Social Worker (1990) **A/A/S:** Toastmasters International; National Association of Social Workers; Peninsula Women's Network

THERESA M. HESEBECK
Realtor
Coldwell Banker Brenizer Realtors
237 South Main Street
Rice Lake, WI 54868 United States
RealEstate@TheresaHesebeck.com
http://www.SoldWithTheresa.com

BUS: Real Estate Agency **P/S:** Real Estate Services for Everyone from the First-Time Buyer to the Experienced Investor, Sales and Purchases of Residential and Commercial Real Estate, Mortgage Assistance **MA:** Regional **D/D/R:** Assisting the Client with all Aspects Including Making an Offer, Negotiating, Financing, Mortgage Rates and Moving **H/I/S:** Golfing, Bowling, Fishing, Snowmobiling **FBP:** Realtor; REBAC Magazine **CERTS:** Licensed Realtor, Wisconsin Technical College (2001); Certified in e-PRO Technology **A/A/S:** Coldwell International Diamond Society; ABR; SRES

MR. DAVID HESSERT
Executive Manager
Nurse Anesthesia of Maine
489 State Street
Bangor, ME 04401 United States
david.hessert@nurseanesthesiaofmaine.com
http://www.nurseanesthesiaofmaine.com

BUS: Medical Company **P/S:** Trauma, Surgical and Regional Anesthesia Services, Clinical Instruction **MA:** Eastern Maine **EXP:** Mr. Hessert's expertise is in anesthesia services. **H/I/S:** Traveling, Golfing, Boating, Swimming, Listening to Music **FBP:** AANA Journal **EDU:** Master's Degree in Anesthesia, University of New England (1993); Bachelor of Science in Nursing, The University of Maine (1979) **A/A/S:** Board of Directors, Maine Association of Nurse Anesthetists; American Association of Nurse Anesthetists **A/H:** Professional Outstanding Achievement Award, Maine Hospital Association (2008) **A/S:** He attributes his success to being open-minded, compassionate and dedicated even at a high executive level. **B/I:** He became involved in his profession because he always enjoyed a challenge, and finds working so closely with patients to be rewarding. **H/O:** The highlight of his career has been witnessing the rapid growth of his company while maintaining a high level of morale with his employees.

PETRA L. HEWITT, MA, BS
Elementary School Teacher
Atlantic City Board of Education
1300 Atlantic Avenue
Sixth Floor
Atlantic City, NJ 08401 United States
encompassingall@comcast.net
http://www.acboe.org

BUS: Education **P/S:** Curriculum and Instruction **MA:** Regional **D/D/R:** Teaching Language Arts and Writing to Sixth Grade Students in a Self-Contained Classroom, Helping Students Improve their Reading and Writing Skills and Abilities **H/I/S:** Writing Poems, Playing Basketball **FBP:** Phi Delta Kappan Publications **EDU:** Pursuing Ph.D., Walden University; Master's Degree in Administration and Supervision, Rowen University (2005); Bachelor of Science in Criminal Justice, Troy State University, Alabama (1987); Diploma, St. Croix Central High School (1979) **CERTS:** Certified Supervisor, State of New Jersey; Principal Eligibility Certification, State of New Jersey; Certified Elementary School Teacher, State of New Jersey **A/A/S:** Executive Board Member, National Association for the Advancement of Colored People; Phi Delta Kappa International; Alpha Lambda Epsilon; Venice Park Civic Association **A/H:** Nominee, Junior National Young Leaders Conference **A/S:** She attributes her success to her sincere love for children. **B/I:** She became involved in her profession because Ms. Nina Chavis and Mr. Steve Murphy encouraged and supported her in becoming a teacher.

MICHAEL J. HIBBS
Head of Employment Law, Service Partner
Shakespeare Putsman, LLP
Somerset House
Temple Street
Birmingham, B2 5DJ United Kingdom
michael.hibbs@shakespeares.co.uk
http://www.shakespeares.co.uk

BUS: Law Firm **P/S:** Legal Services **MA:** International **EXP:** Mr. Hibbs' expertise is in employment law litigation. **H/I/S:** Spending Time with his Family, Gardening **FBP:** Business and Financial Midlands; Personnel Today **EDU:** Bachelor of Law, The University of Nottingham (1980) **A/A/S:** Employment Lawyers Association; The Association of Midlands Mediators; The Society of Legal Scholars **SP:** Helen **CHILD:** Charlotte, James

TOMMIE L. HICKOX
Chef, Owner
Island Cuisine Restaurant and Catering
16691 HWY 520
Freeland, WA 98249 United States
islandcuisine@whidbey.com
http://www.cambridgewhoswho.com

BUS: Restaurant and Catering **P/S:** Seafood, Island Style Specialty Food Service Specializing in Loganberry Products such as Syrups, Jellies and Salad Sauces **MA:** Local **D/D/R:** Producing Quality Food, Serving Customers, Catering **FBP:** Gourmet Magazine **EDU:** High School Diploma **A/H:** Second Place, 'Specialty Salad Sauces' Jefferson County Fair (2003); Second Place, 'Loganberry Pie' Jefferson County Fair (2003); 'Best Clam Chowder', Pacific Rim (2003); Third Place, 'Triple Chocolate Fudge Cheesecake,' Oregon Chocolate Classic Cookoff (1999) **C/VW:** Whidbey Island Charities **DOB:** July 9, 1957 **POB:** Fort Worth Texas **A/S:** His ability to provide fine dining at affordable prices, both in his restaurant and his catering business.

SUSAN M. HIGGINS, MA
Academic Fieldwork Coordinator
New England Institute of Technology
2500 Post Road
Warwick, RI 02886 United States
shiggins@neit.edu
http://www.neit.edu

BUS: Education **P/S:** Occupational Therapy Assistant Technology **MA:** International **EXP:** Ms. Higgins' expertise is in field work and mental health. **H/I/S:** Enjoys Crafts, Sewing and Breeding Pugs **EDU:** Master's Degree in Occupational Therapy, Tufts University **A/A/S:** Rhode Island Occupational Therapy Association; American Occupational Therapy Association; American Board of Disability Analysts; Allen Cognitive Advisors; New England Occupational Therapy Education Council **C/VW:** Organist, Local Church; Local School Events **A/S:** She attributes her success to personal motivation. **B/I:** She became involved in the profession after seeing an occupational therapist take care of her grandfather. She wanted to do the same type of work. **H/O:** The highlight of her career has been doing different types of research for her Masters Degree.

Jan R. Hilburn
Assistant Director, Transportation Training Specialist
Alhambra School District, Transportation Department
4501 N. 39th Avenue
Phoenix, AZ 85019 United States
jhilburn@alhambra.k12.az.us
http://www.alhambra.k12.az.us

BUS: Educational Organization **P/S:** Academic and Social Skills Necessary to be Successful in an Evolving, Diverse Society, Quality Student Education Services, Special Programs **MA:** Local **D/D/R:** Holding General Assemblies in All Schools Regarding Bus Safety, Addressing Child Abuse Issues, Managing Bus Drivers Including Training and Certifications, Scheduling, Ensuring Safety, Working with Principals, Handling Student Problems and Parent Complaints, Maintaining Employee Relationships **H/I/S:** Participating in Church Activities, Spending Time with her Family, Studying the Bible **EDU:** High School Education; Associate Degree **CERTS:** Certification in Training and Testing, Department of Public Safety for Other Drivers; Certified Agility Tester for Drivers **A/A/S:** Arizona Association for Pupil Transportation; National Association for Pupil Transportation; Transportation Administrators Association **SP:** Richard **CHILD:** Adam, David, Dawn, April, Tim

Ms. Allison C. Hill
Firm Administrator
Dudley, Topper and Feuerzeig, LLP
Law House
1000 Frederiksberg Gade
St. Thomas, 802
ahill@dtflaw.com
http://www.dtflaw.com

BUS: Private Practice Law Firm **P/S:** General Civil Legal Services Concentrating in Transactional Law and Litigation **MA:** International **D/D/R:** Supervising Overall Management and Technology Management, Overseeing Legal Administration **H/I/S:** Participating in Water Activities, Reading **FBP:** ALA Legal Management; HR **EDU:** Coursework, Tarrant County Community College, Fort Worth, TX **A/A/S:** Association of Legal Administrators; Society for Human Resources Management

CANDICE R. HILL
Legal Document Preparer Assistant
North Valley Paralegal
319 Sixth Street
Marysville, CA 95901 United States
candyrh@prodigy.net
candy.nvp@comcast.net
http://northValleyparalegal.com

BUS: Paralegal Office **P/S:** Divorce Services, Child Custody, Adoption, Guardianship, Document Preparation Service, Notaries-Public, Paralegal Services and Business Services, Grants and Deeds **MA:** Local **D/D/R:** Preparing Family Law Documents, Overseeing Divorce Services, Child Custody, Adoption and Guardianship Cases, Offering Notarial Services **H/I/S:** Horseback Riding, Participating in Bike Runs for Charities **CERTS:** Certification in Business and Office Administration, California Institute of Technology **C/VW:** Make-A-Wish Bike Runs

KATHY L. HILL, PH.D.
Associate Professor
General Business and Finance
Sam Houston State University
PO Box 2056
Huntsville, TX 77341 United States
KHill@shsu.edu
http://www.shsu.edu

BUS: University **P/S:** Teaching and Research, Five Colleges within the University- Arts and Sciences, Business Administration, Criminal Justice, Education, and Humanities and Social Sciences **MA:** International **D/D/R:** Teaching Business Communication, Research Design and Intercultural Research Classes **EDU:** Ph.D. in Communications, Concentration in Organization, University of Oklahoma (1990); Master's Degree in Business Education, University of Oklahoma (1976); Bachelor's Degree in Business Education, Oklahoma Baptist University (1972) **A/A/S:** Association of Business Communication; Allied Academics; Academy of Business Administration; Academy of Business Discipline; Federation of Business Discipline

Patricia J. Hill
Owner
Edmund Hill Art
53660 Avenida Mendoza
La Quinta, CA 92253 United States
patriciadunlophill@msn.com
http://www.cambridgewhoswho.com

BUS: Art Gallery **P/S:** Artwork Sales **MA:** Regional **EXP:** Ms. Hill's expertise is in sales management of art reproductions and cards of artist Edmund Hill. **H/I/S:** Photography, Swimming, Exercising, Leading Bible Study Groups, Listening to Music **FBP:** Southwest Art **EDU:** Coursework in Christian Education, Moody Bible Institute, Chicago, IL **A/A/S:** Palm Springs Art Museum **C/VW:** La Quinta Art Foundation; Southwest Community Church **A/S:** She attributes her success to her commitment to sell her husband's artwork. **B/I:** She became involved in her profession because she was inspired by her husband. **H/O:** The highlight of her career was selling a large quantity of her husband's artwork.

Kevin Hillman
Consultant Microbiologist
22 Fairway Avenue
Inverurie
Aberdeenshire, AB51 3WY United Kingdom
kh@gutbugs.com
http://www.gutbugs.com

BUS: Sole Proprietorship **P/S:** Consultancy and Research Services in Intestinal Microbiology for Animals and Humans **MA:** International **D/D/R:** Consulting and Training on Intestinal Microbiology, Animal and Human Probiotics, Writing Classical Microbiology Techniques, Editing and Proofreading **H/I/S:** Gardening, Fishing **FBP:** Agricultural Related Publications; New Scientist **EDU:** Ph.D. in Microbiology of Rumen Ciliate Protozoa, University of Wales (1987); Bachelor of Science in Microbiology, University of Wales, with Honors (1981) **DOB:** April 5, 1960 **SP:** Carole **CHILD:** Stuart, Joanna **W/H:** Research and Teaching Microbiologist, Veterinary Sciences Division, Scottish Agricultural College, Aberdeen (1992-2005); Higher Scientific Officer, Rowett Research Institute, Aberdeen (1989-1992); Research Fellow, Department of Microbiology, University of Wales, Cardiff (1988-1989); Research Fellow, Department of Genetics and Microbiology, University of Aberdeen (1985-1988); Research Assistant, Department of Microbiology, University of Wales, Cardiff (1981-1982) **C/A:** Contributor, Journal of Applied Bacteriology (2003)

JANET M. HILSABECK
Medical Technologist
St. Francis Hospital
2016 S. Main Street
Maryville, MO 64468 United States
mmatww@grm.net
http://www.cambridgewhoswho.com

BUS: Hospital **P/S:** Healthcare **MA:** Local **D/D/R:** Supervising Blood Bank **H/I/S:** Sports, Black Angus Cattle Farm **FBP:** Lab Magazine **EDU:** Bachelor's Degree in Medical Technology, Northwest Missouri State University **C/VW:** Local Schools, Scholarship Programs, The Humane Society, The National Arbor Day Foundation **A/S:** She attributes her success to her drive to achieve and the support of her parents. **B/I:** She became involved in the profession because she was interested in working with medicine. **H/O:** The highlight of her career was when she became a blood bank supervisor in 1990.

CHARLEEN M. HIMMELBERG
Reading Specialist for Kindergarten through Sixth Grade
Hastings Public Schools-Hawthorne Elementary
2100 W. Ninth Street
Hastings, NE 68901 United States
chimmelb@esu9.org
http://www1.hastings.esu9.k12.ne.us

BUS: Educational Institution for Kindergarten through Twelfth Grade **P/S:** State and Nationally Approved Educational Instruction **MA:** Local **D/D/R:** Ms. Himmelber's expertise is in the improvement and enhancement of reading instruction. **H/I/S:** Painting, Creating Ceramics, Refurbishing Old Houses **EDU:** Master of Arts in Reading, University of Nebraska at Kearney; Bachelor of Arts in Education, Hastings College **A/A/S:** Alpha Delta Kappa; International Reading Association **C/VW:** PEO Chapter W, Blue Hill United Methodist Church

DR. MARGARET L. HINDLEY
Senior Engineer
Schering Plough Research Institute
556 Morris Avenue
Building S-7
Summit, NJ 07901 United States
margaret.hindley@spcorp.com
http://www.spcorp.com

BUS: Pharmaceutical and Chemical Company **P/S:** Pharmaceutical Products for Allergy and Respiratory Care, Animal Health, Anti-Infectives, Arthritis and Immunology, Cancer Therapies, Cholesterol Control, Cardiovascular Health, Erectile Dysfunction, Foot Care, Hepatitis, Skin Disorders and Sun Care **MA:** National **D/D/R:** Managing Regulated Equipment for the Business Unit, Leading Monthly Presentations for the Business Unit to the Senior Management, Conducting Compliance-Orientated Training Seminars for the Entire Department, Writing, Reviewing and Approving Standard Operating Procedures as well as Laboratory Procedures, Overseeing Staff, Supervising Vendor Activities **H/I/S:** Cooking, Interacting with her Children, Spending Time with her Son **FBP:** Chemical & Engineering News **EDU:** Post-Doctoral Degree in Chemistry, University of Pennsylvania (2000); Ph.D. in Bio-Organic Chemistry, University of Maryland, College Park (1998); Master of Science in Chemistry, Villanova University (1992); Bachelor of Science in Biochemistry and Molecular Biology, Chestnut Hill College, PA (1988) **A/A/S:** Chairman, Departmental Safety Committee; American Chemical Society; Institute of Validation Technology; American Management Association; American Society for Quality **C/VW:** March of Dimes **DOB:** June 1, 1967 **POB:** Philadelphia **SP:** George **CHILD:** Jimmy, Timothy **W/H:** Senior Scientist, Analytical Development, Schering-Plough Research Institute (2000-2004); Postdoctoral Associate, Department of Chemistry, University of Pennsylvania (1998-2000); Team Leader, Task Force for the Departmental Safety Program; Chemical Hygiene Officer, Coordinator, Technology Transfer of 16 Clarinex-D

STANLEY J. HINSHAW
Quality Assurance Coordinator
Community Hospital of Anderson and Madison County
1515 N. Madison Avenue
Anderson, IN 46011 United States
sjhinshaw@aol.com
http://www.cambridgewhoswho.com

BUS: Full-Service 207-Bed Hospital **P/S:** Healthcare **MA:** Local **EXP:** Mr. Hinshaw's expertise is in clinical laboratory quality assurance, clinical laboratory accreditation inspections and standards. **H/I/S:** Landscaping, Spending Time with his Family **FBP:** Laboratory Medicine **EDU:** Bachelor of Science in Pre-Medical Studies and Medical Technology, Ball State University **CERTS:** Certification in Medical Technology & Specialist in Chemistry by the American Society for Clinical Pathology **A/A/S:** American Society for Clinical Pathology; Board of Directors, Community Hospital of Anderson and Madison County **A/H:** Recognition for Continued Focus on Patient Satisfaction **C/VW:** United Way **A/S:** He attributes his success to his hard work and perseverance. **B/I:** He became involved in his profession because of his love for both chemistry and medicine. **H/O:** The highlight of his career was being recognized by the board of directors for his efforts and focus on quality assurance.

PROF. DAVID E. HINTON, PH.D.
Professor
Environment and Earth Sciences
Duke University, Nicholas School
333 Science Drive
Durham, NC 27708 United States
dhinton@duke.edu
http://www.env.duke.edu/people/faculty/hinton.html

BUS: University **P/S:** Higher Education **MA:** International **D/D/R:** Teaching Ecotoxicology and Cell Biology of Fish **H/I/S:** Traveling, Fishing, Caring for his Pets **FBP:** Aquatic Toxicology **EDU:** Ph.D. in Anatomy, The University of Mississippi Medical Center (1968); Master of Science in Anatomy, The University of Mississippi Medical Center (1967); Bachelor of Science in Zoology, Mississippi College (1965) **C/VW:** United Way; Watershed Management Group **SP:** Judith **CHILD:** Daniel, Benjamin, Emily, Susan, Jill **A/S:** He attributes his success to his ability to switch between two fields. **B/I:** He became involved in his profession because of his fascination with small fish, structural sciences and the effect of environmental pollution on sea-dwelling organisms. **H/O:** The highlight of his career was earning his distinguished professorship from Duke University.

TONYA B. HIPPS
Supply Chain Superintendent
Southern Nuclear Operating Company
11028 Hatch Parkway
Baxley, GA 31513 United States
tbhipps@southernco.com
http://www.southernco.com

BUS: One of the Largest Generators of Electricity with a 120,000-Square-Mile Service Territory Spanning Most of Georgia and Alabama, Southeastern Mississippi, and the Panhandle Region of Florida **P/S:** Fortune 500 Company with Services including, Retail Electricity, Electronic Data Interchange, Wireless Telecommunications, Dark Fiber and Wholesale Energy **MA:** National **D/D/R:** Purchasing and Maintaining Equipment for Nuclear Plants **H/I/S:** Football **EDU:** Bachelor of Arts in Business Administration, Faulkner University (1997) **A/A/S:** CGP

MR. JOHN HISCOX
Corporate Director of Safety
Koch Companies, Inc.
424 Harding Street
Minneapolis, MN 55413 United States
john.hiscox@kochcompanies.com
http://www.kochcompanies.com

BUS: Transportation and Distribution Company **P/S:** Commercial Freight Transportation, Logistics, Warehousing Services, Freight Brokerage, Equipment Leasing **MA:** National **EXP:** Mr. Hiscox's expertise is in Transportation safety and compliance. **D/D/R:** Ensuring the Companies are in Compliance with Federal and State Regulations, Developing Accident Reduction Programs, Training, Managing 1,400 Trucks Including Local, Regional and Long Haul Freight Vehicles, Overseeing General Commodities **H/I/S:** Listening to Music, Playing Instruments with Frets and Strings, Riding Motorcycles **FBP:** Transport Topics **EDU:** Coursework, Embry-Riddle Aeronautical University (1996); Bachelor of Arts in Management, Western Illinois University (1981) **CERTS:** Certified Risk Manager (1996); Certified Director of Safety, North American Transportation Management Institute, University of Central Florida; Certified Transportation Security Professional, Center for Integrated Transportation Safety & Security **A/A/S:** President, Safety Council, Minnesota Trucking Association; Truckload Carriers Association; Safety and Security Division, Truckload Carriers Association **A/H:** Safety Professional of the Year Award, Minnesota Trucking Association (2006); National Fleet Safety Award, Truckload Carriers Association (2005, 2006); Herb Ney Memorial Award, Minnesota Trucking Association (2005)

JUDY A. HOBERG
Public Health Nurse and Clinical Care Coordinator
Allegany County Department of Health
7 Court Street
Belmont, NY 14813 United States
hobergj@alleganyco.com
http://www.cambridgewhoswho.com

BUS: Full Service Health Department **P/S:** Traditional Home Care and Long Term Nursing, Immunizations, Occupational Therapy **MA:** Local **D/D/R:** Home Healthcare **H/I/S:** Reading, Scrapbooking, Bowling, Camping, Fishing, Hiking **FBP:** American Journal of Nursing **EDU:** Bachelor's Degree, Alfred University **A/A/S:** New York State Nursing Association; Sigma Theta Tau International; New York State Nurse Registry **C/VW:** American Red Cross, American Cancer Society, U.S. Freedom Corp, Medical Reserve Corp, Camp Day Dreams **A/S:** She attributes her success to her faith. **B/I:** She became involved in her profession because it was her life long dream. **H/O:** The highlight of her career was being able to service and care for Hurricane Katrina.

MARY ANNE HOCHADEL, PHARM.D., BCPS
Vice President, Editor in Chief
Gold Standard, Inc.
302 Knights Run Avenue, Suite 800
Tampa, FL 33602 United States
hochadel.m@goldstandard.com
http://www.goldstandard.com

BUS: Information Technology Company **P/S:** Developing Software for Drug and Medical Content Information **MA:** International **D/D/R:** Overseeing Drug Informatics Including Medical and Clinical Contents **H/I/S:** Oil Painting, Environmental Work, Participating in Church and Mission Activities **FBP:** The Journal of the American Medical Association; Annals of Internal Medicine **EDU:** Doctor of Pharmacy, The University of Arizona (1989); Bachelor of Science in Pharmacy, The University of Arizona (1998) **CERTS:** Board Certified Pharmacotherapy Specialist (1995) **C/VW:** Foundation for International Missions **POB:** Lockbourne Air Force Base **B/I:** She became involved in her profession because of her experience in the field of pharmacy and internal medicine. **H/O:** The most gratifying aspects of her career is developing various products and educating the elderly people about the effects of their medications.

APRIL LYNN HODGES
President
RL Instruments
9 Main Street, Suite 2E
Manchaug, MA 01526 United States
april.h@rlinst.com
http://www.rlinstruments.com

BUS: Laboratory Instrument Distributor **P/S:** Food, Beverage, Chemicals, Waste Water, Plastics, Testing Equipment, Laboratory Instruments **MA:** International **D/D/R:** Overseeing Company Activities **H/I/S:** Cooking, Camping, Reading **FBP:** American Laboratory **EDU:** Associate Degree in Business Administration, St. Lawrence College, St. Laurent **A/A/S:** IFT **C/VW:** Local Churches, City of Hope Cancer Society **A/S:** She attributes her success to her perseverance. **B/I:** She became involved in the profession because it was a family-owned business. **H/O:** The most gratifying aspect of her career is running a business successfully for 15 years.

DOROTHY MARIE HOEHNE, PH.D., RN
Associate Professor (Retired)
D'Youville College
320 Porter Avenue
Buffalo, NY 14201 United States
http://www.cambridgewhoswho.com

BUS: College **P/S:** Education, Graduate Education in Nursing **MA:** Local **D/D/R:** Researching and Evaluating, Directing Instructional Communication, Developing Curriculum **H/I/S:** Sketching and Drawing Cartoons, Reading Professional Publications and Mysteries, Refinishing Furniture, Gardening, Camping, Playing the Keyboard **EDU:** Ph.D. in Instructional Communication, Research and Evaluation, University at Buffalo, with Honors; Master of Education in Maternal Child Health, Nursing and Curriculum Higher Education, Teachers College, Columbia University, with Honors; Bachelor of Science in Nursing, Teachers College, Columbia University **A/A/S:** University at Buffalo Alumni Association; Columbia University Teachers College Nursing Education Alumni Association; New York State Nurses Association **A/H:** New York State Scholarship; Children's Bureau Scholarship **C/VW:** University at Buffalo Foundation; Teachers College, Columbia University; Roswell Park Alliance Foundation; Society for the Prevention of Cruelty to Animals; The Mouth and Foot Painting Artists; Alzheimer's Disease Fund; Guiding Eyes for the Blind; Habitat for Humanity; American Lung Association; National Multiple Sclerosis Society; Muscular Dystrophy Association; Salvation Army; Sierra Club **A/S:** She attributes her success to her determination, perseverance and to the love and support she received from her parents. **B/I:** She became involved in her profession because of her desire to be a nurse and her love of education. **H/O:** The most gratifying aspects of her career are seeing her students succeed and the recognition and appreciation she receives from her students and colleagues.

REV. LORI A. HOFF
1) Global Account Manager 2) Chief Executive Officer
1) AT&T 2) Outreach Ministries, Inc.
228 Cedar Street
South Amboy, NJ 08879 United States
lori@omifocus.org
http://www.omifocus.org

BUS: 1) Telecommunication Company 2) Nonprofit Organization **P/S:** 1) Telecommunication Services 2) Youth Development Services and Religious Services **MA:** 1) International 2) Regional **D/D/R:** Overseeing Ministerial Duties and Operations, Managing New Projects, Mentoring and Counseling At-Risk Youth, Developing Life and Social Skills and Community Outreach for Abused Women, At-Risk Children and their Families, Performing Social Work, Conducting Parenting Seminars and Family Intervention Programs **H/I/S:** Hiking, Spending Time Outdoors, Cooking, Entertaining, Playing Volleyball **FBP:** Forbes **EDU:** Pursuing Master's Degree in Counseling; Bachelor's Degree in Counseling, Calvary Theological Seminary, National Christian Counselors Association **CERTS:** Ordained Minister; Licensed Counselor (2005) **A/A/S:** Former President, AT&T Pioneers; Covenant Ministries International **C/VW:** Local Charitable Organizations **A/S:** She attributes her success to her hard work and persistence. **I/F/Y:** In five years, Rev. Hoff hopes to organize a relationship conference with Dr. Grace and Telecom Pioneers in New York City.

MARIAN R. HOFFMAN
Singer, Teacher
Hoffman Studios
646 Dale Court S.
Shoreview, MN 55126 United States
marianhoffman@comcast.net
http://www.cambridgewhoswho.com

BUS: Home Studio **P/S:** Coaching and Singing Lessons **MA:** Local **EXP:** Ms. Hoffman's expertise is in vocal education. **H/I/S:** Gardening, Traveling **EDU:** Master's Degree in Vocal Performance, University of Minnesota **A/A/S:** National Association of Teachers of Singing; Sigma Alpha Iota **C/VW:** Young People's Center **A/S:** She attributes her success to staying current and up to date in her profession. **B/I:** Growing up in a family with musicians inspired her to pursue her current career. **H/O:** The highlight of her career has been being her church soloist for the past 30 years.

JULIE A. HOGAN
Lecturer
State University of New York at Plattsburgh
Ward Hall Draper Ave
Plattsburgh, NY 12901 United States
Hgooey@aol.com
http://www.beartracksband.com

BUS: Education **P/S:** School Counseling, Mental Health, Student Affairs **MA:** Regional **D/D/R:** Educating, Supervising Counseling **H/I/S:** Playing in a Bluegrass Country Band, Writing Songs, Spending Time with Family **FBP:** New York State School Counseling Association Journal **EDU:** Master of Science in School Counseling and Marriage and Family Therapy, SUNY Plattsburgh; Bachelor of Science in Sociology, SUNY Plattsburgh **CERTS:** Certificate in Advanced Studies in School Counseling; **A/A/S:** New York State School Counseling Association; American School Counseling Association; American Counseling Association **C/VW:** Career Day Speaker, Local Schools; Local Charitable Organizations **A/S:** She attributes her success to her kids, those who have supported her, good friends and family, and always maintaining a positive attitude. **B/I:** She chose the profession because she has always loved kids, and she loves having the ability to comfort them in a safe environment. She believes in the developmental approach to counseling. **H/O:** The highlight of her career to counsel a public school student, and the outcome was positive.

RACHEL K. HOGANCAMP
Managing Partner
Rasa Spa
310 Taughanock Boulevard
Ithaca, NY 14850 United States
rachel@rasaspa.com
http://www.rasaspa.com

BUS: Day Spa **P/S:** A Full Service Day Spa Offering Body Treatment, Facials, and Other Services **MA:** Local **D/D/R:** Handling Operations, Performing Massage Therapy **H/I/S:** Hiking **FBP:** Spa Magazine **EDU:** Bachelor of Science, Ithaca College **W/H:** Teacher, Finger Lakes College

BILLIE S. HOGGARD, M.ED.
Educator
Jonesboro Public Schools - Hillcrest Elementary School
1804 Hillcrest Drive
Jonesboro, AR 72401 United States
billiesuehoggard@yahoo.com
http://www.jps.k12.ar.us/elemen/hill

BUS: Primary Level Public Education **P/S:** Assisting Students to Develop the Skills Necessary for Lifelong Learning Using a Scientifically Based Academically Enriched Curriculum **MA:** Regional **D/D/R:** Teaching Fifth Grade Level Reading, American History and Language Arts, Running for State Legislature **H/I/S:** Reading, Playing Piano, Singing, Traveling **EDU:** Master of Science in Elementary Education, Plus 60, Arkansas State University (1994) **CERTS:** National Board Certified Facilitator; Certified in Principalship **A/A/S:** Jonesboro Teachers Association **C/VW:** JFAST; Nettleton Lions Club; Choir Member, Community Fellowship Church; Women's Auxiliary American Legion

TIA R. HOHLER
Science Teacher
Comstock High School
2107 N. 26th Street
Kalamazoo, MI 49048 United States
hohlert@comstockps.org
http://www.comstockps.org

BUS: Public High School **P/S:** Education **MA:** Kalamazoo **D/D/R:** Teaching Earth Science and Biology, Safety Standards and Innovations **H/I/S:** Cooking, Traveling, Composing Music **FBP:** Industry-Related Journals **EDU:** Pursuing Master's Degree in Education Technology, Western Michigan University; Bachelor of Science, Ferris State University **A/A/S:** Michigan Science Teachers Association; National Association of Biology Teachers; Golden Key National Honor Society **A/H:** Biology Education Student of the Year (2003); Who's Who Among College Students **A/S:** She attributes her success to her desire to always set and achieve higher goals for herself. She has a true love of her profession and wants to work for the good of others. **B/I:** She became involved in her profession by taking an externship in college, which sparked her love of teaching and prompted her to enter the field. **H/O:** The highlight of her career was receiving several grants for the high school, which allowed her to increase her involvement with students.

SISTER CARRIE HOLDER
Author, Gospel Singer
carrie.holder@cwwemail.com
http://www.cambridgewhoswho.com

BUS: Sole Proprietorship **P/S:** Religious Poetry and Music **MA:** International **EXP:** Sister Holder's expertise includes poetry, gospel music and singing. **H/I/S:** Preaching, Writing Songs and Poetry **FBP:** Industry-Related Publications **CERTS:** Industry-Related Training **A/A/S:** World Gospel Musical Association **A/H:** Martin Luther King, Jr. Commemorative Commission, New Jersey Department of State (2008); Proclamation, Governor Jon Corzine, State of New Jersey (2008); Award, New Jersey Municipal Council (2008); Women of the Year Award, Bethel Baptist Church (1995) **C/VW:** Bethel Baptist Church **DOB:** February 12, 1943 **POB:** Greensburg, LA **SP:** Samuel **W/H:** Principal, Payroll Clerk, Typist, Department of Labor, New Jersey Division of Disability Services (1971-2003) **C/A:** President, Poetry Department, World Gospel Musical Association **A/S:** She attributes her success to her faith in God. **B/I:** She became involved in her profession because of her passion for singing. **H/O:** The highlights of her career were having her first book of poetry published in 2000 and her gospel CD released in 2005. **I/F/Y:** In five years, Sister Holder would like to publish her second book and release another gospel CD.

Mr. Nicholas Holian
Global Information Technology Manager
Hewlett Packard
3404 E. Harmony Road
Stop B5
Fort Collins, CO 80528 United States
nholian@comcast.net
http://www.hp.com

BUS: Information Technology Company **P/S:** Computers, Printers, Electronics **MA:** International **EXP:** Mr. Holian's expertise is in program management. **D/D/R:** Managing Automation Systems, Testing Strategies for High-End Servers, Improving Electrical Processes and Engineering Systems, Overseeing Staff **H/I/S:** Cycling, Running **FBP:** Industry-Related Publications **EDU:** Bachelor of Science in Construction Science, Texas A&M University (1997) **CERTS:** Certified Microsoft Systems Engineer (2003); Certified Microsoft Professional (2003); Certified Microsoft Professional (2002); Novell Certified Linux Professional (2000) **A/A/S:** Project Management Institute **C/A:** Patent Holder, United States Patent for Mechanical Engineering; Patent Holder, United States Patent for ASIC; Patent Holder, United States Patent for Hardware Engineering; Patent Holder, Taiwanese Patent for Hardware Engineering

Ms. Virginia 'Ginny' M. Holland, PMP
Global Program Manager
Strategic Pricing and Deal Management Department
AVAYA
211 Mount Airy Road
Basking Ridge, NJ 07920 United States
mvholland@avia.com
http://www.cambridgewhoswho.com

BUS: Telecommunications Company **P/S:** Telecommunications Services Including Software and Hardware **MA:** International **EXP:** Ms. Holland's expertise is in project management. **EDU:** Master of Arts, Seton Hall University; Bachelor of Arts, Merrimack College; Coursework, Carnegie Mellon University **CERTS:** Certified Project Management Professional (1996) **A/A/S:** Project Management Institute **A/H:** Marquis Who's Who in America; Who's Who Among American Women

KELLEE L. HOLLENBACK
National Sales Manager
Department of Sales
Savoy House
625 Braselton Parkway
Braselton, GA 30517 United States
khollenback@savoyhouse.com
http://www.savoyhouse.com

BUS: Retail Store **P/S:** Sales Including Wide Range of Coordinating Styles for an Unsurpassed Sense of Freedom in Home Decorating, Residential Decorative Lighting, Elegant Lighting Designs and Home Accessories **MA:** International **EXP:** Ms. Hollenback's expertise is in selling residential decorative lighting. **D/D/R:** Overseeing Sales Representatives, Encouraging Point of Sale Purchases, Promoting Web Development, Marketing and Visual Merchandising **H/I/S:** Motorcycling, Spending Time with her Family, Reading **FBP:** Fast Company **CERTS:** Certified Lighting Specialist, American Lighting Association (2005) **A/A/S:** Accessories Resource Team; American Lighting Association

CHARLOTTE A. HOLLISTER
Principal
JES Arts Consulting
3321 Old Dominion Boulevard
Alexandria, VA 22305 United States
chollister@jesarts.com
http://www.jesarts.com

BUS: Consulting Firm **P/S:** Consulting Services **MA:** National **EXP:** Ms. Hollister's expertise is in management consulting for performing arts organizations, strategic planning and board development. **FBP:** Harvard Business Review **EDU:** Ph.D. in Chemistry, Yale University (1965); Master of Business Administration, Earned in United Kingdom (2006); Bachelor of Arts in Chemistry, Vassar College **A/A/S:** President, Board of Directors, Jane Franklin Dance (2008); Association for Computing Machinery; Virginians for the Arts; Cultural Alliance of Greater Washington **C/VW:** Pro Bono Consulting; Counterpointe Ballet Company **A/S:** She attributes her success to her ability to take challenges. **B/I:** She became involved in her profession because she saw a need for management expertise in the field of performing arts. **H/O:** The highlight of her career was running a department of 35 software developers and managing all projects.

JOYCE E. HOLLOWELL
Agricultural Research Specialist I
Plant Pathology
North Carolina State University
Box 7903
Raleigh, NC 27695 United States
joyce_hollowell@ncsu.edu
http://www.ncsu.edu

BUS: State University **P/S:** Agriculture and Life Sciences, Design, Education, Engineering, Graduate School, Humanities and Social Sciences, Management, Natural Resources, Physical and Mathematical Sciences, Textiles, Veterinary Medicine **MA:** National **EXP:** Ms. Hollowell's expertise is in plant pathology. **D/D/R:** Researching Peanut Disease, Leaf Spot, Root and Stem Disease, Working on Epidemics, Doing On-Farm Tests, Conducting Greenhouse Experiments, Testing in and Managing the Lab Ordering Supplies for the Lab, Overseeing Graduate Students who Assist Farmers and Faculty, Cooperating with County Extension Agents **H/I/S:** Gardening, Softball, Photography, Traveling **FBP:** The Peanut Farmer **EDU:** Bachelor of Arts in Botany, University of North Carolina at Chapel Hill (1978) **A/A/S:** American Peanut Research and Education Society; American Phytopathological Society; Turfgrass Council of North Carolina, Plant Pathology Society of North Carolina **A/H:** SPA Leadership Award (1996-1997); Outstanding SPA Employee Award (1996) **DOB:** December 5, 1955 **W/H:** Agricultural Research Specialist I, Plant Pathology Department, North Carolina State University (1979-Present)

BEVERLY ALICE HOLMES, RN
Director of Clinical Services
Maxim Healthcare
1845 Business Center Drive
San Bernardino, CA 92408 United States
konagal@sbcglobal.com
http://www.maximhealthcare.com

BUS: Healthcare **P/S:** In-Home Nursing, Healthcare **MA:** Local **EXP:** Ms. Holmes' expertise is in the administration and supervision of clinical services. **H/I/S:** Golfing, Spending Time with Family, Traveling, Church **EDU:** Pursuing Bachelor of Science in Nursing, Concentration in Healthcare Administration, California State University; Associate Degree in Nursing, Riverside Community College **CERTS:** Certified in Public Relations and Aides Instruction **A/A/S:** American Medical International School of Management **A/H:** Outstanding Achievement Award, Interim Healthcare (1992) **C/VW:** March of Dimes, HIV Instructor, Court Appointed Special Advocate **B/I:** She was prompted to enter her profession because she always wanted to be a nurse.

KIMBERLY A. HOLMES
Registered Nurse
Orange Park Medical Center
2001 Kingsley Avenue
Orange Park, FL 32073 United States
foxscout09@yahoo.com
http://www.cambridgewhoswho.com

BUS: Community Hospital **P/S:** Healthcare **MA:** Local **D/D/R:** Managing the Intensive Care Unit **H/I/S:** Scrapbooking, Sewing, Making Crafts, Going to Church, Photography **FBP:** Critical-Care Nurse; American Journal of Critical Care **EDU:** Pursuing ANRP; Bachelor of Science Degree in Human Development, St. Mary's College of Maryland **A/A/S:** American Association of Critical-Care Nurses **C/VW:** Advisor, Crossroad Lutheran Church, American Heart Association, United Way **A/S:** She attributes her success to being independent and a strong leader.

RONNIE R. HOLMES, RN
Assistant Head Nurse
Central Florida Kidney Center
745 W. State Road 734
Suite A
Longwood, FL 32750 United States
gizmousmc89@yahoo.com
http://www.cambridgewhoswho.com

BUS: Healthcare **P/S:** Kidney Dialysis and Treatment **MA:** Local **D/D/R:** Managing, Assisting and Training Nurses **H/I/S:** Pencil Drawings **EDU:** Registered Nurse Diploma, Macon State College **A/A/S:** American Legion **C/VW:** Florida Sheriffs, American Cancer Society **A/S:** He attributes his success to his discipline and drive, desire to succeed and enjoying what he does. **B/I:** He became involved in this profession because he served in the marines for four years. After that his wife and sister-in-law encouraged him to pursue nursing.

JUSTIN M. HOLUB
Graduate Student, Ph.D.
New York University
100 Washington Square E.
New York, NY 10003 United States
jmh456@hotmail.com
http://www.nyu.edu/

BUS: One of the Largest Private Universities in the United States **P/S:** Undergraduate and Graduate Degree Programs, Professional Programs, International and Study Abroad Programs, Innovative Research **MA:** Regional **D/D/R:** Conducting Research and Design, Troubleshooting, Experimenting with Different Techniques, Teaching Classes, Writing **H/I/S:** Tennis, Scuba Diving **FBP:** Science; Nature; Nature Chemical Biology **EDU:** Pursuing Ph.D., New York University; Bachelor of Science in Biochemistry, Rider University (2001); Master of Science in Chemistry **A/A/S:** New York Academy of Sciences; American Association for the Advancement of Science; American Chemical Society **A/H:** Kramer Fellowship Award, New York University (2006)

SUSAN DEBRA HOOD, M.ED., MSW, LCSW, CDVC
1) Psychotherapist 2) Clinician
1) The Professional Counseling Center
2) Massachusetts Society for the Prevention of Cruelty to Children
466 County Street
New Bedford, MA 02740 United States
http://www.mspcc.org

BUS: 1) Outpatient Clinic Dedicated to Protecting and Promoting the Rights and Well-Being of Individuals and Their Families 2) Nonprofit Organization Dedication to the Prevention of Child Abuse, Individual and Family Support Services **P/S:** 1) Self-Employed Psychotherapist in an Outpatient Clinic Setting 2) Fee-for-Service Clinician Providing Individual and Family Counseling, Treatments Available in Schools, Residential Programs and Foster Placements **MA:** 1) Local 2) Statewide **D/D/R:** Preparing Patient Intakes, Devising Treatment Plans and Discharge Summaries, Treating Patients in a Variety of Settings, Networking with Agencies within the Community, Assessing Patients' Diagnosis, Preparing Treatment Plans, Completing CAFAS and TOPS Evaluations, Discharge Planning **H/I/S:** Listening to Music, Watching Movies, Shopping at Thrift Stores, Traveling, Learning New Cultures, Being Near the Ocean, Gardening **FBP:** People; Travel **EDU:** Master's Degree in Social Work, Boston University (2000); Master's Degree in Education, Concentration in Agency Counseling, Bridgewater College (1986) **A/A/S:** National Association of Forensic Counselors; National Association of Social Workers

BUS: High School **P/S:** Business Education **MA:** Statewide **EXP:** Ms. Hooper's expertise is in technology and business principles, basic keyboarding, Microsoft Word, Excel and PowerPoint instruction. **D/D/R:** Advising and Encouraging Students to Become Business Leaders, Accompanying Students to Competitive Events **H/I/S:** Traveling, Attending Plays **FBP:** Ebony Magazine **EDU:** Master of Science in Administration and Supervision, Seton Hall University **A/A/S:** A&T State University Alumni Association

BUS: Publishing Company **P/S:** Formatted International Materials with Images, Stories, Maps and Information Index for Veterans and their Families **MA:** International **EXP:** Ms. Hopkins' expertise is in website development for Vietnam veterans and research. **D/D/R:** Helping Veterans and their Families, Responding to e-Mails **H/I/S:** Photography **FBP:** Vietnam; Vietnam Veterans of America Journal; Bay State Veteran Publications **EDU:** Associate of Arts in Business Administration, Glendale Community College, with Honors (1991); Diploma, North Phoenix High School (1959); Bachelor of Arts in English, University of Ottawa **A/A/S:** Associate Member, Local Chapter 432; Lifetime Alumnus Member, Phi Theta Kappa; Mensa International; Honor Society, Glendale Community College; Honor Society, University of Ottawa; Honor Society, Arizona State University **C/VW:** Vietnam Veterans of America **H/O:** The most gratifying aspect of her career is being able to make a difference in the lives of veterans.

DONNA M. HOPP
Corporate President
Hopp Accounting and Tax Service, PC
804 Walnut Avenue
Elgin, IL 60123 United States
donna@hoppcpa.com
http://www.hoppcpa.com

BUS: Accounting Firm **P/S:** Accounting, Income Tax Preparation and Financial Services **MA:** Regional **EXP:** Ms. Hopp's expertise is in accounting, sales management and income tax preparation. **D/D/R:** Overseeing All Corporate Books and Checks, Preparing Monthly Reports, Managing a Staff of Six Members **H/I/S:** Supporting Chicago Cubs Fan, Crocheting **FBP:** Debits and Credits; IAA Newsletter **EDU:** High School Education **A/A/S:** Independent Accountants Association of Illinois; National Association of Tax Professionals; Board of Directors, Treasurer, Vice President, President, Vocalist, Elgin Choral Union; Audition for Directors; American Bankers Association

MR. J. WILSON HORN
Human Resources and Industrial Relations Manager
Human Resources, Industrial Relations Division
Rust Constructors, Inc., PO Box 151
0039 Grass Mesa Road
Rifle, CO 81650 United States
wilson.horn@shawgrp.com
http://www.shawgrp.com

BUS: Construction Company **P/S:** Construction and Maintenance Services Including Consulting, Plant Services, Total Plant Maintenance, Supplemental Maintenance, Shutdowns, Turnarounds, Small Capital Project Support, Production Support and Technical Support **MA:** International **D/D/R:** Supervising Employees, Managing the Industrial Engineering Procurement Firm, Building Manufacturing Plants, Mills, Power and Energy Plants **H/I/S:** Hunting, Gardening **FBP:** ENR; Construction News **EDU:** Bachelor of Business Administration, Northwestern University (1965) **A/A/S:** Society for Human Resources Management; HRCC; Gulf Coast Workforce Initiative

ELIZABETH J. HORNE
Office Manager, Ministry Assistant
First Baptist Church
106 W. Taylor Street
PO Box 809
Griffin, GA 30224 United States
bethhorne@fbcgriffin.org
http://www.fbcgriffin.org

BUS: Church **P/S:** Managing Staff, Scheduling, Assisting Members **MA:** Regional **D/D/R:** Coordinating and Planning Special Events and Religious Services **H/I/S:** Reading, Spending Time with her Daughter **EDU:** Bachelor of Arts in Recreation, Georgia Southern University **A/A/S:** Georgia Baptist Association of Assistants **C/VW:** American Red Cross, Chamber of Commerce, School, Parent Teachers Organization **A/S:** She attributes her personal and professional success to her passion, hard work and dedication. **B/I:** She became involved in the profession because she always enjoyed helping others and enjoys working on publications.

ERIN C. HORROCKS
Direct Marketing Manager
Babies "R" Us
1 Geoffrey Way
Wayne, NJ 07470 United States
ehorrocks@excite.com
http://www.cambridgewhoswho.com

BUS: Specialty Retailer **P/S:** Baby Gear, Juvenile Products **MA:** National **EXP:** Ms. Horrocks' expertise includes direct and database marketing and print advertising. **H/I/S:** Painting, Crafts, Martial Arts **FBP:** Fast Company; The Week **EDU:** Bachelor's Degree in Marketing, Fairleigh Dickinson University, 1998 **A/A/S:** National Association for Female Executives; Alpha Kappa Psi; National Association of Professional Women **A/S:** She attributes her success to the support she receives from those around her and her belief in the company she works for. **B/I:** She became involved in her profession because she was studying to be a graphic designer and found she was allergic to paint so she switched to advertising.

KATHY Y. HORTON, MA
Special Education Teacher
Green Bay Avenue Elementary School
3872 N. Eighth Street
Milwaukee, WI 53206 United States
horton262@aol.com
http://www.cambridgewhoswho.com

BUS: Education **P/S:** Elementary Education **MA:** Local **EXP:** Ms. Horton's expertise is in special education and leadership counseling. **H/I/S:** Spending Time with her Family **EDU:** Master of Arts in Special Education, Cardinal Stritch University **A/A/S:** National Education Association; Wisconsin Education Association **C/VW:** St. Jude Children's Research Hospital, Children's Cancer Research, Juvenile Diabetes **A/S:** She attributes her success to her love of teaching children. **B/I:** She chose the profession because she has an inner drive to teach and give guidance to children. **H/O:** The highlight of her career is her current position.

MS. ROBERTA V. HOUCEK, CHT, APP
Founder, President
The Houcek Group, LLC
5398 Hallford Drive
Atlanta, GA 30338 United States
rv@houcek.cbeyond.com
http://www.robbiehoucek.com

BUS: Holistic Healing Center **P/S:** Energy Therapy, Clinical Hypnotherapy, Acupressure, Ontological Kinesiology **MA:** National **H/I/S:** Practicing Yoga, Belly Dancing **FBP:** Yoga Journal **EDU:** Bachelor's Degree in Business Administration and Computer Science, The University of New Mexico **CERTS:** Certification, Mind Body Reflexology Institute (2007); Certification in Ontological Kinesiology (2005); Certification in Polarity Therapy (2004); Ordained Interfaith Minister (2004); Certified Clinical Hypnotherapist, American Council of Hypnotist Examiners (1999) **A/A/S:** American Polarity Therapy Association

BONNIE L. HOUSER
Chief of Enlisted Professional Military Education Programs
Headquarter Air Force-Manpower in Personnel
United States Air Force
114 Douglas Street
Langley AFB, VA 23665 United States
bonnie.houser@pentagon.af.mil
http://www.cambridgewhoswho.com

BUS: Government Organization **P/S:** Defense **MA:** International **EXP:** Ms. Houser's expertise is in leadership development, staff instruction, school guidance, budget planning and execution, instructor selection, training and development, manpower resourcing and policy development for instructor selection. **H/I/S:** Reading, Teaching **EDU:** Master's Degree in Education, Troy University (2003); Bachelor's Degree in Management, University of Maryland (1998) **A/A/S:** Lifetime Member, Non-Commissioned Officer's Association; Lifetime Member, Air Force Sergeant's Association

ADRIENNE M. HOWARD RN, MSN, FNP/C
1) Registered Nurse 2) Registered Nurse
1) VA Northern Indiana Healthcare System 2) Ambucare Clinic
1700 E. 38th Street
Marion, IN 46953 United States
amhrnp@indy.rr.com
http://www1.va.gov/directory/guide/facility.asp?ID=755

BUS: 1) Proven Leader in the Healthcare Industry 2) Healthcare Facility **P/S:** 1) Coordinated, Compassionate and Comprehensive Quality Primary Care, Mental Health Services and Extended Care to Veterans in a Timely, Accessible and Cost Effective Manner 2) Healthcare Services **MA:** 1) Local 2) Local **EXP:** Ms. Howard's expertise includes diabetic education and family care. **H/I/S:** Sewing, Traveling **FBP:** Journal of the American Academy of Nurse Practitioners **EDU:** Master of Science in Nursing and Family Nurse Practitioner Studies, Indiana Wesleyan University (2006); Bachelor's Degree in Nursing, Wesleyan University (1994) **A/A/S:** Indiana Wesleyan University Alumni Organization; Parish Nurse, American Association of Diabetic Educators; American Association of Nurse Practitioners; Indiana Coalition for Nurse Practitioners; National Organization of Veterans Advocates; Sigma Theta Tau International **A/H:** Registered Nurse of the Year (2003); Disabled Veterans Service Award **C/VW:** Minority Health Coalition; Parish Nurse Program at Church; Volunteer, Marion General Hospital; Volunteer Family Nurse Practitioner, Local Indigent Clinic

KATHERINE S. HOWARD
Occupational Therapist
The Ohio State University Medical Center
1670 Upham Drive
Columbus, OH 43210 United States
katherine.howard@osumc.edu
http://www.cambridgewhoswho.com

BUS: Healthcare Center **P/S:** Healthcare Including Medical Education **MA:** Statewide **D/D/R:** Performing Inpatient and Outpatient Therapy **H/I/S:** Reading, Studying Archaeological and Biblical History, Gardening, Working with Copper **FBP:** National Geographic; Smithsonian; Scientific American **EDU:** Bachelor of Science in Occupational Therapy, The Ohio State University **A/A/S:** Ohio Occupational Therapy Association; Advisory Board, Occupational Therapy Department, School of Allied Medical Professions, The Ohio State University; Allen Cognitive Network; Public Broadcasting Service; The American Occupational Therapy Association; National Public Radio; Former Member, Children and Adults with Attention Deficit/Hyperactivity Disorder **C/VW:** Local Church; National Alliance on Mental Illness; Youth for Christ, USA **A/S:** She attributes her success to her networking skills, open-mindedness and compassionate nature. **B/I:** She became involved in her profession because she was encouraged by a guidance counselor. **H/O:** The most gratifying aspects of her career were making a positive impact on her patients and receiving appreciation from them.

CHARLIE LYNN HOWE
Confidence Coach
Global Relationship Centers
charliehowe@msn.com
http://www.centertoselfreliance.com

BUS: Training and Development **P/S:** Personal Growth and Inspiration **MA:** National **EXP:** Ms. Howe's expertise includes management, enrollment, personal development, positive thinking and confidence coaching. **H/I/S:** Gardening, Yoga, Collecting Beanie Babies, Jewelry Fashion and Design, Dancing **EDU:** Associate Degree in Business Administration and Fashion Merchandising, North Hampton County Area Community College **A/A/S:** UYO Training, Global Industries **C/VW:** St. Joseph Children's Hospital **W/H:** Whitney Education Group

CINDY K. HOWETH
Senior Mortgage Consultant
1st Priority Home Loans a Division of Universal Lending
6775 E. Evans Avenue
Demuer, CO 80224 United States
choweth@1stpriorityhomeloans.com
http://www.1stpriorityhomeloans.com

BUS: Financial Lending **P/S:** Mortgages **MA:** Local **D/D/R:** Assisting First-Time Home Buyers, Lending Mortgages **H/I/S:** Spending Time with Pets, Reading, Traveling **EDU:** Master of Arts in Applied Communications **A/S:** She attributes her success to always trying to provide the best mortgage for her clients and caring about their needs and how the outcome will affect them. **B/I:** She became involved in this profession because she was in real estate for many years but realized there were not enough lenders to take care of the number of applicants.

JOSEPH L. HUBBARD
Director of Golf Maintenance
Broken Sound Club
2401 Willow Springs Drive
Boca Raton, FL 33496 United States
taterjoe@aol.com
http://www.brokensoundclub.org

BUS: Golf Club **P/S:** Golf Course Including Championship Golf Courses, Addison Mizner Style Clubhouse, Stadium, Tennis Court, State of the Art Fitness Center, Spa and Cuisine **MA:** International **D/D/R:** Designing Golf Courses and Policies for Structure, Developing Five Year Capital Expense Programs, Overseeing Daily Operations, Instructing Golf for College Students, Interacting with Committees and the Executive Board **H/I/S:** Fly Fishing **EDU:** Associate Degree in Turf Management, Northern Virginia Community College (1989); Associate Degree in Journalism, Skagit Valley Community College (1982) **A/A/S:** United States Golf Association; FGCSAA; Former National Director, Toll Brothers Golf Course **C/VW:** GCSSA

VICTORIA I. HUDGINS
Realtor
Patterson-Schwartz Real Estate
140 Greentree Drive
Dover, DE 19904 United States
vhudgins@psre.com
http://www.victoriahudgins.com

BUS: Real Estate Company **P/S:** All Types of Real Estate **MA:** Regional **D/D/R:** Assisting Buyers and Sellers with the Sale and Purchase of Property **H/I/S:** Figure Skating, Swimming, Going to the Beach **FBP:** Realtor **EDU:** Bachelor of Education, Earned in Russia **A/A/S:** Delaware Association of Realtors; National Association of Realtors **C/VW:** Sending Care Packages to Families in Ukraine and Russia **A/S:** She attributes her success to hard work and doing the best for her clients. **B/I:** She became involved in this profession because she wanted a position that offered her flexible hours and independence. **H/O:** The highlights of her career include learning English in one year and being recognized as a leading real estate agent in the United States in 2005.

ALISON C. HUDSON
Manager of Assessment and Remediation
EHS Technology Group, LLC
965 Capstone Circle
Miamisburg, OH 45342 United States
ahudson@ehstech.com
http://www.ehstech.com

BUS: Consulting Company **P/S:** Environmental Consulting and Remediation Services **MA:** National **D/D/R:** Researching on Geoenvironmental Science, Banking, Building Relationships with Commercial Lenders, Visiting Industrial and Commercial Sites and Retail Stores **H/I/S:** Bowling, Golfing, Gardening, Spending Time with her Two Children **FBP:** Dayton Business Journal **EDU:** Bachelor of Science in Geology and Geophysics, Wright State University, with Honors **CERTS:** Certified Asbestos Hazard Evaluation Specialist, State of Ohio; Certified Asbestos Abatement Project Designer, Department of Health **A/A/S:** National Ground Water Association; Southwest Ohio Water Environment Association; Geological Society of America; Big Brothers Big Sisters of America **SP:** Randy **A/S:** She attributes her success to her work ethic and her positive attitude. **B/I:** She became involved in her profession because she had a love for environmental science and geology. **H/O:** The most gratifying aspect of her career is completing her projects.

JANET A. HUDSON
Owner
Hudson Family Daycare
28 Good Rock Road
Levittown, PA 19057 United States
rsecondhome@comcast.net
http://www.cambridgewhoswho.com

BUS: Child Care **P/S:** Child Care **MA:** Local **EXP:** Ms. Hudson's expertise is in child care. **H/I/S:** Taking Care of Family, Traveling **FBP:** Parents; Working Mother **EDU:** Pursuing Bachelor's Degree in Early Childhood Education, Ashworth College **CERTS:** Certificate in Child Development, Buck County Community College **A/A/S:** Monitor, Local Government Food Program **C/VW:** Volunteer, Breastfeeding Association, St. Jude Children's Research Hospital **A/S:** She attributes her success to hard work and having compassion for children. **B/I:** She became involved in the profession after having four children. She wanted to stay home with them and needed to make a living. **H/O:** The highlight of her career is getting back all that she gives to the children.

MARLENE HUDSON
Massage Therapist, Reflexologist, Education
Self-Employed
311 Booker Avenue
Egg Harbor, NJ 08234 United States
essentialeducation@msn.com
http://www.cambridgewhoswho.com

BUS: Continuing Education for Somatic Therapists **P/S:** Reflexology, Aromatherapy, Somatic Modalities **MA:** International **D/D/R:** Connecting Emotional Ramifications to Resulting Physical Conditions for the Purpose of Healing **H/I/S:** Traveling, Walking, Weight Lifting, Reading **FBP:** Scientific American **EDU:** Bachelor's Degree in Nutrition, Clayton College of Natural Health **CERTS:** Registered Medical Assistant; Certified in Reflexology; Certified Massage Therapist; Certified Reiki Master **A/A/S:** Associated Bodywork & Massage Professionals Reflexology Association **C/VW:** Battered Women's Shelters, Homeless Shelters **A/S:** She attributes her success to her diligence, studying, having a passion for what she does and the mentoring she receives. **H/O:** The highlight of her career has been working with one particular doctor.

JUDITH A. HUFF
RN/CHPN (Retired)
Hospice of Cincinnati
Cooper Road
Cincinnati, OH
jarluff3@aol.com
http://www.cambridgewhoswho.com

BUS: Hospice **P/S:** Healthcare **MA:** Local **H/I/S:** Spending Time with Grandchildren and Gardening **FBP:** RN **EDU:** Nursing Diploma, Deconess Hospice School of Nursing **CERTS:** Certified in Hospice and Palliative Care Nursing **C/VW:** American Heart Association **A/S:** She attributes her success to her education, and the great training she has received. **B/I:** She chose the profession because she always wanted to help others. **H/O:** The highlight of her career if the certification she has received.

SUSY HUFFORD
Facilitator, Teacher
Meridian Joint School District No. 2
10762 Blackhawk Drive
Boise, ID 83709 United States
hufford.susy@meridianschools.org
http://www.meridianschools.org

BUS: School District **P/S:** Education **MA:** Local **D/D/R:** Creating an Integrated Curriculum, Coordinating School Fair Programs, Recruiting Mentors **H/I/S:** Traveling, Gardening, Reading, Writing **EDU:** Master of Education in Literacy; Bachelor of Arts in English; Bachelor of Science in Elementary Education **CERTS:** National Board Certified Teacher (2001) **A/A/S:** Adjunct Professor, Northwest Nazarene University; Idaho Education Association; National Science Teachers Association; Association for Supervision and Curriculum Development **A/S:** She attributes her success to her curiosity, creativity and to the support she receives from her family. **B/I:** She became involved in her profession because of her desire to become a teacher since childhood. **H/O:** The most gratifying aspect of her career is the gratitude she receives from her students.

BELINDA L. HUGHES
Executive Assistant
Texas Tech University Health Science Center
3601 4th Street
MS # 6298
Lubbock, TX 79430 United States
bhughes0707@yahoo.com
http://www.arbonne.com

BUS: Leader in Education and Patient Care **P/S:** Higher Education **MA:** International **D/D/R:** Scheduling and Coordinating All Activities for the Vice President of the Health Science Center, Overseeing Traveling, Expenses, Budgets, Accounting and Contracts **H/I/S:** Reading 'The Gift,' by Shad Helmstetter, Arbonne International Products Including Make-Up, Skin Care, Health and Wellness, Traveling, Spending Time with Family **EDU:** Coursework in Business, Law and Accounting, Howard Junior College **A/A/S:** Children's Miracle Network; Susan G. Komen Breast Cancer Foundation

JEWELL A. HUGHES
Owner, Founder
Madison Surgical Appliance Center
4222 Milwaukee Street
Suite 2
Madison, WI 53714 United States
msac@jvl.com
http://www.cambridgewhoswho.com

BUS: Surgical Appliance Center **P/S:** Medical Services Including Ladies Foundation Apparel, Support for Post Mastectomy, Lymphedema, Compression Hosiery, Orthopedic Supports, Twenty-First Century Lingerie **D/D/R:** Fitting People into Durable Medical Lingerie, Selling Durable Medical Equipment **H/I/S:** Bicycling, Cooking, Writing Stories, Listening to Music, Art, Sports **EDU:** High School Diploma **A/A/S:** Chamber of Commerce; Women's Expo

PAMELA PARSONS HUGHES, MA
Realtor
Jenny Pruitt & Associates
5290 Roswell Road
Atlanta, GA 30342 United States
pamhughes@jennypruitt.com
http://www.jennypruitt.com

BUS: Real Estate Agency **P/S:** Real Estate **MA:** Greater Atlanta Area **D/D/R:** Helping Physicians, Educators and Other Professionals Relocate, Selling Residential Homes **H/I/S:** Dining at Fine Restaurants, Playing Tennis, Traveling, Reading, Skiing **FBP:** Atlanta Business Chronicle **EDU:** Master of Arts in South Asian History, University of Virginia (1977); Bachelor of Arts in Political Science and History, University of California, San Jose (1967) **A/A/S:** National Association of Realtors; Secretary, Georgia Tennis Foundation **C/VW:** Out of Hand Theater **A/S:** She attributes her success to impeccable customer service, listening to her clients and tremendous word-of-mouth referrals. **B/I:** She became involved in real estate through the realtor who sold her home to her. **H/O:** The highlight of her career was winning the crystal Phoenix Award in 2006.

CAROL A. HUKARI
Vice President of Customer Service
Customer Service
Arbonne International, LLC
9400 Jeronimo Road
Irvine, CA 92618 United States
chukari@arbonne.com
chukari@sbcglobal.net • http://www.arbonne.com

BUS: Manufacturing Company **P/S:** Skin Care and Personal Care Products for Children, Teens, Men and Women **MA:** United States, Canada, Australia, United Kingdom **EXP:** Ms. Hukari's expertise is in strategic planning, marketing communications, sales management, warehousing, distribution, international business and customer service. **D/D/R:** Redesigning Distribution Systems, Negotiating Contracts for the Indiana Distribution Facility, Handling Remodeling and Facility Acquisition for Corporate Headquarters **H/I/S:** Traveling, Reading Fiction and Non-Fiction Books, Solving Crossword Puzzles and Paoman **FBP:** Direct Selling News; The Wall Street Journal; Harvard Business Review **EDU:** Bachelor of Arts in Social Studies and Education, Indiana University (1974) **A/A/S:** Direct Selling Association; Co-Chairwoman, World Congress; World Federation of Direct Selling Association (1999) **C/VW:** Make-A-Wish Foundation; Second Harvest; American Cancer Society **DOB:** November 15, 1948 **POB:** Cambridge, MA **SP:** David **CHILD:** Lori, Erica **W/H:** Vice President of Sales Operations, Shaklee Corporation; Vice President of Marketing, Shaklee Corporation; Vice President of International Business, Shaklee Corporation; Senior Vice President of Customer Operations, Shaklee Corporation; Chief Operating Officer, Natrol, Inc. **A/S:** She attributes her success to her hard work, fortune and to the support she receives from her mentors including John Tefft and Charles Orr. **B/I:** She became involved in her profession because of her experience in advertising agency, her interest in direct selling and network marketing business and her ability to make a positive impact in others life.

KATHRYN B. HULL
Owner, Teacher, Consultant
Hull Music Studio and for the Arts
PO Box 947
La Quinta, CA 92247 United States
kathyhull@aol.com
http://www.cambridgewhoswho.com

BUS: Music Studio **P/S:** Piano and Music Theory for All Ages **MA:** Regional **D/D/R:** Teaching Music, Consulting for the Arts **H/I/S:** Reading, Traveling, Listening to Music **FBP:** American Music Teacher **EDU:** Bachelor of Arts in Music, Point Loma University **CERTS:** Nationally Certified Teacher of Music, Coachella Valley Arts Alliance **A/A/S:** Coachella Valley Arts Alliance; Steinway Society of Riverside County; Music Teachers National Association; California Association of Professional Music Teachers; Music Teachers of the Desert, ENCORE! Series

CYNTHIA M. HULSEBUS
Principle Systems Engineer
General Dynamics
112 Lakeview Canyon Road
Thousand Oaks, CA 91362 United States
cynthiahulsebus@gd-ais.com
http://www.cambridgewhoswho.com

BUS: Defense Contractor **P/S:** Defense **MA:** International and Nationwide **EXP:** Ms. Hulsebus' expertise is in systems test engineering. **H/I/S:** Reading, Web Design, Swimming, Aerobics Classes, Playing the Piano, Needlepointing **FBP:** Working Woman; Health **EDU:** Bachelor's Degree in Mathematics, Indiana State University **C/VW:** Church, American Humane Society, American Cancer Society **A/S:** She attributes her success to her internal drive. **B/I:** She became involved in this profession because she always enjoyed math. **H/O:** The highlight of her career is working with the navy Department on F-14s.

REV. DONALD K. HUMMEL, D.MIN.
Director of Ongoing Formation and Continuing Education of Priests
Roman Catholic Archdiocese of Newark
171 Clifton Avenue
PO Box 9500
Newark, NJ 07104 United States
hummeldo@rcan.org
http://www.rcan.org

BUS: Clergy **P/S:** Continuing Education of Priests **MA:** Statewide **D/D/R:** Directing Priests, Collaborating with Law Enforcement Officials, Counseling for Addiction Problems, Enforcing Emergency Response Measures **H/I/S:** Enjoying Poetry, Attending Theater, Listening to Classical Music, Hiking, Former Football and Baseball Player **FBP:** America **EDU:** Doctorate of Ministry and Pastoral Ministry, St. Mary's Seminary and University, Baltimore, Maryland (1991) **CERTS:** Certified Counselor; Certified Master Police Chaplain; Certification in Thanatology **A/A/S:** Silver Buffalo Award (2004); General Society of the War of 1812; Sons of Union Veterans of the Civil War; National Society Sons of the American Revolution; Fellow, American Psychological Association; American Catholic Association; American Christian Counseling Association; Boy Scouts of America; Mothers Against Drunk Driving; United Way; Law Enforcement Emergency Management

CRAIG W. HUNT
Vice President
Accounting Data Services, Inc. dba Hunt's Computers
7686 N. State Street
Lowville, NY 13367 United States
craig@huntcomp.com
http://www.huntcomp.com

BUS: Computer Retail Store **P/S:** Computer Sales and Service **MA:** Local **EXP:** Mr. Hunt's expertise includes virus protection, spyware removal and business development. **H/I/S:** Golfing, Racing Snowmobiles **FBP:** VARBusiness **EDU:** Associate Degree in Electrical Engineering Technology, Canton College of Technology (1984) **A/A/S:** Chamber of Commerce; New York Water Cross Association **C/VW:** Breast Cancer Awareness **A/S:** He attributes his success to his patience. **B/I:** He became involved in his profession because it is the family business and he grew up seeing his father work in computer sales as a child. **H/O:** The highlight of his career was maintaining and expanding the business after his father's retirement.

PAMELA HUNT
Director of Continuing Dental Education
and Quality Improvement Coordinator
Wake Forest University School of Medicine-Department of Dentistry
Medical Center Boulevard
Winston-Salem, NC 27157 United States
phunt@wfubmc.edu
http://www1.wfubmc.edu

BUS: Dental Education and Services **P/S:** Provides General Dentistry for Adults and Children, Periodontal Services, Endodontic Services, Specialty Referrals and/or Specialty Care, Oral Maxillofacial Surgery, Orthodontics and Dentofacial Orthopedics **MA:** Regional **D/D/R:** Programming Continuing Education for Dentists, Dental Hygienists, Conducting Re-Certification Workshops for Dentists and Hygienists, Lecturing on General Dentistry **H/I/S:** Waterskiing, Snowskiing **FBP:** The Journal of the American Dental Association **EDU:** Bachelor of Science, University of North Carolina, Chapel Hill (1981) **A/A/S:** ADHA; In Charge of Continuing Dentist Education Component for Northwest ATTEL

RUSS HUNTER
Partner
The Group Inc.
4239 Applegate Court
Fort Collins, CO 80526 United States
rhunter@thegroupinc.com
http://www.thegroupinc.com

BUS: Proven Leader in the Real Estate Industry **P/S:** Variety of High Quality Real Estate Services to Clients Including Selling Residential Properties **MA:** Regional **D/D/R:** Selling Residential Properties **H/I/S:** Golf, Baseball, Football **FBP:** Sports Illustrated **EDU:** High School Education **CERTS:** Licensed Broker, State of Colorado; Licensed Realtor; Certified New Home Sales Professional; **A/A/S:** National Association of Realtors; Northern Colorado Association of Realtors; Fort Collins Board of Realtors; The Ram Booster Club

NANCY HURLEY, RN
RN Supervisor
Hebrew Home and Hospital
1 Abrahms Boulevard
West Hartford, CT 06117 United States
Hurlsfour@msn.com
http://www.cambridgewhoswho.com

BUS: Hospital **P/S:** Long-Term, Rehabilitative, Psychiatric and Acute Medical Care **MA:** Regional **EXP:** Ms. Hurley's expertise is in gerentology management. **D/D/R:** Gerontology /Management **H/I/S:** Traveling, Photography, Skiing **FBP:** Advance for Nurses; RN **EDU:** Bachelor of Arts in Communication and Human Relations, Western Connecticut State University; Bachelor of Science in Nursing, State University of New York **C/VW:** St Jude Children's Research Hospital **A/S:** She attributes her success to the support of her family, perseverance and being flexible. **B/I:** She became involved in her profession because she always wanted to be a nurse. **H/O:** The highlight of her career has been the ability to balance her family life with her career.

SANDRA M. HURST, LBSW
Operations Director
New Light Consultants, Inc.
PO Box 359
Millington, MI 48746 United States
Shurst.nlc@tds.net
http://www.newlightconsultants.net

BUS: Private, Nonprofit Healthcare Organization **P/S:** Mental Health and Substance Abuse Counseling and Treatment **MA:** Local **D/D/R:** Developing Programs and Policies, Writing Grants, Speaking and Teaching in the Community Regarding Children's Issues, Counseling Families **H/I/S:** Camping, Reading, Gardening **FBP:** NASW Journal; Entrepreneur **EDU:** Master of Business Administration in Healthcare Management, University of Phoenix (2005); Bachelor of Social Work in Psychology, Michigan State University (1985) **A/A/S:** National Association of Social Workers; Local Chairwoman, Child Abuse and Neglect Council; Board Member, Blue Water Center for Independent Living **W/H:** Adjunct Human Services Instructor, Baker College

MaryLou Stack Huske

1) Calligrapher (Retired) 2) Landscaper
1) Sole Proprietorship 2) Sole Proprietorship
bhuske@aol.com
http://www.cambridgewhoswho.com

BUS: 1) Script Shop 2) Freelance Landscaping **P/S:** 1) Script Shop, Calligraphy Supplies 2) Freelance Landscape Consultations **MA:** 1) Local 2) Local **D/D/R:** Practicing Calligraphy, Performing Freelance Landscaping for Residential and Commercial Properties **H/I/S:** Reading History, Traveling **FBP:** World **EDU:** Bachelor's Degree in History and English, Salem International University **A/A/S:** Member, Washington Council of Mount Vernon Association; Christian Women's Club; Daughters of the American Revolution; Clan MacNeil Association of America; Cape Fear Assembly **C/VW:** Highland Presbyterian Church; Samaritan's Purse **A/S:** She attributes her success to the Lord. **B/I:** 1) She became involved in her profession because she felt it was her calling. She thought calligraphy illuminated words with an attractive flair and was a form of artistic expression. 2) She became involved in her profession through gardening circles and being raised around plants. Her mother enjoyed gardening as well as gardening clubs and her grandparents owned a large farm. **H/O:** 1) The most gratifying aspect of her career is being able to give friends and strangers something of beauty that they can enjoy. 2) The highlight of her career was when her city won first place in the Sears Annual Competition for Community Beautification.

Jane E. Huston

Dental Hygienist
Freelance
15 Broad Street
Nashua, NH 03064 United States
hstj1@aol.com
http://www.cambridgewhoswho.com

BUS: General Practice **P/S:** General Dentistry Practice **MA:** Local **EXP:** Ms. Houston's expertise is in dental and oral hygiene. **H/I/S:** Hiking, Bird Watching, Sewing, Doing Needlework **FBP:** Audubon Magazine **EDU:** Associate of Science in Dental Hygiene, University of Rhode Island **A/A/S:** American Dental Hygienists' Association; Harris Center for Conservation **C/VW:** Monadnock Congregation Church; National Audubon Society **A/S:** She attributes her personal and professional success to her ability to help others. **B/I:** She became involved in the profession after being encouraged by her dentist. **H/O:** The highlight of her career was being recognized by her patients.

SHEILA M. HUTTON
Owner
The Scarlet Pimpernel Herb Company
2296 E. Dexter Trail
Dansville, MI 48819 United States
http://www.cambridgewhoswho.com

BUS: Agriculture Farm **P/S:** Farming, Poultry, Ducks, Turkeys, Eggs, Vegetables, Herbs **MA:** Local **D/D/R:** Growing Herbs and Vegetables, Making Herbal Medicines, Selling Products at Farmers' Markets, Raising Chickens, Turkeys and Ducks **H/I/S:** Spending Time with her 9 Dogs, Cross Country Skiing **FBP:** Herb Quarterly **EDU:** Bachelor's Degree in Horticulture, Michigan State College (1997); Associate Degree in Marketing, Bakersville College (1995) **A/A/S:** Distributor for Nature Sunshine Products

TAMA L. HYCHE
Staff Registered Nurse
Self-Employed
Jasper, AL 35501 United States
bwhyche@peoplepc.com
http://www.cambridgewhoswho.com

BUS: Healthcare Services **P/S:** Internal Medicine **MA:** Regional **EXP:** Ms. Hyche's expertise includes upper and lower gastrointestinal and pulmonary testing and phlebotomy. **D/D/R:** Caring for Geriatric and Disabled Patients **H/I/S:** Gardening, Reading Mysteries and Christian Books, Spending Time with her Grandchildren (Currently 6) **EDU:** Registered Nurse, Bevill State College (1986); Associate Degree in Science, Bevill State College **CERTS:** Certified in Advanced Cardiac Life Support **A/A/S:** Hunter Chapel; Holy Church of Christ; President of the Fraternal Police Auxiliary and the Alabama Chapter; Walker County Head Start Program (Fundamental Program)-Mentoring

DAWN M.J. HYMAN
Marketing Coordinator
Providence of Brookfield Homes
8500 Executive Park Avenue
Suite 300
Fairfax, VA 22031 United States
dhyman@brookwash.com
http://www.providenceofbrookfieldhomes.com

BUS: Residential Builder and Active Adult Community **P/S:** Real Estate **MA:** Regional **D/D/R:** Marketing **H/I/S:** Reading, Jewelry Design, Listening to Jazz Music **EDU:** Bachelor of Arts in Interior Design, Mary Mount University; Bachelor's Degree in Marketing, Towson State University **C/VW:** Suited for Change **A/S:** She attributes her success to her personality, work ethic, and belief in her product. **B/I:** She chose the profession because she had an interest in interior design . **H/O:** The highlight of her career is her current position.

DEBORAH C. HYSELL, M.Ed.
Teacher and Team Leader
Tropical Elementary School
1500 S.W. 66 Avenue
Plantation, FL 33317 United States
http://www.cambridgewhoswho.com

BUS: Public Elementary School **P/S:** Education **MA:** Local **EXP:** Ms. Hysell's expertise is in technology and professional development. **H/I/S:** Gardening, Reading, and Traveling **EDU:** Master's Degree in Educational Technology, Florida Atlantic University; Bachelor of Science in Elementary Education, Bowling Green University **A/A/S:** Phi Kappa Phi; FACE **A/H:** Who's Who Among American Teachers (2001-2005) **C/VW:** Women's Club of Coconut Creek; Make-A-Wish Foundation; Guiding Eyes for the Blind, American Cancer Society **B/I:** She chose the profession because she has always loved children, and enjoys watching them learn and grow.

ERIC E. IDEHEN
Vice President
Wells Fargo Bank, NA
2840 Ingersoll Avenue
Des Moines, IA 50312 United States
eric.idehen@wellsfargo.com
http://www.wellsfargo.com

BUS: Financial Institution Bank **P/S:** Financial Products and Services **MA:** International **EXP:** Mr. Idehen's expertise is in community development and management. **H/I/S:** Soccer **FBP:** The New York Times **EDU:** Bachelor of Science, Auchi Polytechnic Institute **A/A/S:** Lutheran Church of Hope, Multiple Community Boards

CLAUDIA MIREYA IMA, ESQ.
Attorney
Law Offices of Claudia M. Ima, PA
15175 Eagle Nest Lane, Suite 102
Miami Lakes, FL 33014 United States
ima_lawoffice@yahoo.com
http://www.cambridgewhoswho.com

BUS: Law Firm **P/S:** Legal Services **MA:** National **D/D/R:** Litigating for Immigration Law, Offering Legal Aid for Citizenship, Green Cards, Employment Visas, Family Petitions, Political Asylum and Naturalization **H/I/S:** Dancing, Swimming **FBP:** Fiction **EDU:** JD, Albany Law School, Union University (1999) **A/A/S:** Florida Bar Association; American Immigration Lawyers Association

MELISSA ANN INFERRERA
First Grade Educator
Joseph C. Shaner Elementary School
5801 Third Street
Mays Landing, NJ 08330 United States
maismiles527@aol.com
http://www.hamiltonschools.org/~inferreram

BUS: Elementary School **P/S:** Education **MA:** Local **D/D/R:** Teaching General Studies, Reading, Writing, Mathematics, Social Studies, Science and Technology **H/I/S:** Writing Poetry, Reading, Playing Tennis, Surfing the Internet **FBP:** Rolling Stone **EDU:** Bachelor of Arts in Elementary Education and Psychology, Rowan University **A/H:** Best of the Best, Best Teacher Cumberland County, NJ (2008) **C/VW:** Mentor, Big Brother Big Sister **DOB:** May 27, 1981 **POB:** Vineland **A/S:** She attributes her success to her supportive mother, friends and family. **B/I:** She became involved in her profession because her mother is a teacher and found it very rewarding. **H/O:** The highlight of her career was when her class, for the past two years, received the Manner Banner, which is awarded to the class with the best manners and discipline.

MR. SAM W. INGLE, MBA
Sales and Leasing Advisor
Leading Edge Commercial Real Estate Services
374 Meridian Parke Lane
Greenwood, IN 46142 United States
samwingle@sbcglobal.net
http://www.cambridgewhoswho.com

BUS: Full Service Commercial Real Estate **P/S:** Commercial Real Estate Services for Clients **MA:** Local **EXP:** Mr. Ingle's expertise is in commercial sales and consulting. **H/I/S:** Fitness, Traveling, Spending Time with Family **FBP:** Indianapolis Business Journal **EDU:** Master of Business Administration, Indiana Wesleyan University (1996), Bachelor of Science in Marketing and Business Administration, Indiana University (1986) **A/A/S:** Adjunct Faculty Member, Indiana Wesleyan University; Former Chairman, Leadership Council; Church

URSULA INGOLFSSON-FASSBIND
Director, President
The Leopold Mozart Academy & Franz Fassbind Foundation
7453 Old York Road
Elkins Park, PA 19027 United States
lmozartacademy@aol.com
http://www.leopoldmozartacademy.com

BUS: Music School **P/S:** Music Education Including Pre-College Coursework, Private and Class Instruction in Piano, Cello, Violin, Viola, Flute, Clarinet, Percussion, Chamber Music, Music Theory and Solfeggio, Performance Training Classes, Music History Classes **MA:** International **D/D/R:** Developing the Curriculum, Overseeing Staff, Students' Progression and Concert Services, Teaching General Music to Gifted and Mentally Challenged Children **H/I/S:** Reading, Painting Porcelain, Designing **FBP:** The Educator; The Economist **EDU:** Coursework in Performance and Composition, The University of Arizona; Diploma in Soloist Piano Performance **CERTS:** National Certified Swiss Teacher, Switzerland **A/A/S:** Port Huron Music Teachers Association; GMI; Nebraska Music Teachers Association

TERESA J. INGRAM, LCSW
Director of Recovery Services
Terros, Inc.
3003 N. Central Avenue
Suite 200
Phoenix, AZ 85012 United States
teresai@terros.org
http://www.terros.org

BUS: Nonprofit Organization **P/S:** Social Services Including Treatment for Adults, Behavioral Healthcare, Addiction Treatments **MA:** Local **D/D/R:** Overseeing Social Services Including Treatment for Trauma, Mental Healthcare and Family Services, Managing Five Programs and 17 Facilities, Managing and Planning Policies and Curriculum, Training **H/I/S:** Reading, Making Crafts, Quilting, Swimming, Cooking, Sewing, Scrapbooking, Crocheting, Shopping **EDU:** Master of Social Work, University of South Florida **A/A/S:** Youth Athletic Association; Victim/Witness Services; Arts and Science Honor Society (1991); National Association of Social Workers; Phi Kappa Phi (1991) **A/H:** Social Work Student of the Year, National Association of Social Workers Heartland Unit (1995); Who's Who's Who Among American High School Students (1976, 1977) **C/VW:** Coach, Youth Soccer (1988-1992); PAYC (1981-1984); FACUS (1981-1984); Captain, Crime Watch Block (1982-1983); Blood Donor **DOB:** December 10, 1958 **POB:** Wichita, KS **SP:** Billy **CHILD:** Daniel, Rachel **W/H:** Director of Recovery Services (2005); Director, SMI Services (2004-2005); Associate Director, SMI Services (2004); Associate Director, Residential Services, Community Living Program, Glendale, AZ (2002-2004); Sexual Assault Response Team Advocate and Coordinator, Victim and Witness Services for Coconinoo County, Northern Arizona Center Against Sexual Assault (2001-2002); Program Supervisor, Children's Home Society of Florida, Central Florida Division, Crisis Nursery (2000-2001); Program Director, Children's Home Society of Florida, Brevard Division, Hacienda Girl's Ranch (1999-2000); Clinical Supervisor, Center for Drug Free Living-ATC (1998-1999); Outpatient Therapist, Sexual Abuse Treatment Team, Peace River Center for Personal Development, Inc. (1994-1998); Outreach Therapist, School Consultation and Treatment Peace River Center for Personal Development, Inc.(1993-1995); Outreach Therapist, Intensive Crisis Counseling Program Peace River Center for Personal Development, Inc. (1993); Case Manager, Family Services Planning Team, Peace River Center for Personal Development, Inc. (1992-1993); Counselor, Therapeutic Foster Home Program, Peace River Center for Personal Development, Inc. (1985-1992); Associate Teaching Parent, CARE Center, Peace River Center for Personal Development, Inc. (1984-1985); Parent Resource Consultant, Day Nursery of Lakeland and Tri-County Child Care (1981-1984); Latchkey Director, Parent Coordinator, Day Nursery of Lakeland and Tri-County Child Care (1983); Teacher, Director, Day Nursery of Lakeland and Tri-County Child Care (1981-1983); Mental Health Technician II, Lakeland Manor Hospital and Palmview Hospital (1981); Psychiatric Assistant, Lakeland General Hospital, Lakeland Regional Medical Center (1978-1981); Field Instructor, Department of Social Work, Arizona State University (2003-2008); Field Instructor, Department of Nursing, Arizona State University (2003-2008); Field Instructor, Department of Social Work, Northern Arizona University (2002); Field Instructor, Department of Social Work, USF (1997); Finance Chair, National Association of Social Workers Heartland Unit (1995-1997) **A/S:** She attributes her success to the support she receives from her mentors. **B/I:** She became involved in her profession after serving as a certified nursing assistant in the psychology department. **H/O:** The most gratifying aspects of her career are working with sexually abused children and seeing them recover.

THERESA MARIE IOSA, RN
Registered Nurse
St. Vincent's Medical Center
350 Crossing Boulevard
Orange Park, FL 32073 United States
tia_rn627@yahoo.com
http://www.cambridgewhoswho.com

BUS: Hospital **P/S:** Medical Services Including Highly Ranked Cardiac Facilities **MA:** Regional **EXP:** Ms. Iosa's expertise is in the care of kidney dialysis patients and cardiac telemetry. **D/D/R:** Acting as a Preceptor for New Nurses with Initial Training Reinforcement and Unit Charge Nurses, Working within the Cardiac Unit **FBP:** American Journal of Nursing; RN **EDU:** Associate Degree in Nursing, Naugatuck Valley Community College, CT (1997) **A/A/S:** Nurse Retention Committee **A/H:** Nominee, Top 100 Nurses in Northeastern Florida; Nominee, Nurse Recognition Award (2007); Five Years Service Award, St. Vincent's Medical Center

GLORIA Y. IRIGOYEN
Court Administrator
Sunland Park Municipal Court
1000 McNutt Road, Suite F
Sunland Park, NM 88063 United States
g_irigoyen_2000@yahoo.com
http://www.cambridgewhoswho.com

BUS: Municipal Court **P/S:** Assistance for Misdemeanor Crimes within the City Limits, Driving While Intoxicated, Traffic Tickets and City Ordinance Violations **MA:** Local **D/D/R:** Overseeing Management and Administration, Utilizing Fire Technology, Fine Arts and Advertising, Serving as a Child Passenger Restraint Technician **H/I/S:** Going to the Movies with her Son, Traveling, Gardening **FBP:** Hispanic Business; Newsweek; Workforce Management **EDU:** Master of Business Administration and Human Resources, University of Phoenix (2004); Bachelor of Science in Business Administration (2003) **A/A/S:** Board of Directors President, New Mexico Court Clerks Association; Former President Elect, Secretary, Treasurer, Historian, New Mexico Court Clerks Association **A/H:** International Who's Who in Professional Management; First Paid Female Fire Chief, New Mexico (1990); Court Clerk of the Year, New Mexico Municipal League (2006)

MARY LYNN IRVING
Curator
The Martin and Frances Lehnis Railroad Museum
700 E. Adams Street
Brownwood, TX 76801 United States
mirving@ci.temple.tx.us
http://www.rrhm.org

BUS: Nonprofit History Museum **P/S:** Tourism, Education On Railroads Impacted the Western Expansion of America **MA:** National **EXP:** Ms. Irving's expertise is in historical subject and design research, design exhibition and museum planning. **H/I/S:** Painting, Fiber Art, Design, Reading Science Fiction **FBP:** Aviso **EDU:** Bachelor of Arts in Art History and Studio Art, West Chester University of Pennsylvania (1981) **A/A/S:** Texas Association of Museums; National Railway Historical Society; The Embroiderers' Guild of America (1982); American Association of Museums **A/H:** John L. Nau, III Award of Excellence in Museums (2005); Citation of Honor for Outstanding Contributions for the Preservation of Texas History (1990) **CHILD:** John, Michael, Kathyrn

MR. JIMMY DALE ISBELL
Licensed Real Estate Agent, Associate Broker
RE/MAX Realty Brokers, Inc.
5588 Apple Park Drive
Birmingham, AL 35235 United States
jimdisbell@hotmail.com
http://www.remax.com

BUS: Major Real Estate Network **P/S:** Residential and Commercial Real Estate **MA:** Regional **D/D/R:** Selling Residential, Farm and Vacant Land Real Estate, Assisting Buyers **H/I/S:** Playing Bridge **FBP:** Broker Agent **CERTS:** Licensed Associate Broker (2007) **A/A/S:** Birmingham Multiple Listing Service; Former President, St. Clair County Association of Realtors (1999); National Association of Realtors; Director, Board of Directors, Children's Advocacy Place **A/H:** Realtor of the Year (2000); Top Selling Agent, Saint Clair County (1995-1999); Eagle Award, RE/MAX; Rookie of the Year (1990)

TERESA L. IVERSON, LPN
Staff Nurse
Regency Home Health Staff
teresai1@msn.com
http://www.cambridgewhoswho.com

BUS: Leader in the Healthcare Industry **P/S:** Quality Healthcare Services **MA:** National **D/D/R:** Traveling to Homes, Setting up Medications, Conducting Assessments, Reporting to the Case Manager **H/I/S:** Gardening, Reading **FBP:** Nursing2009 **CERTS:** Licensed Practical Nurse, Minnesota Community College (1979) **A/A/S:** Minnesota Technical Institute

MRS. REX A. IVEY
Real Estate Agents
1st Choice Realty
3276 Goodman Road E.
Southaven, MS 38672 United States
cynthiaivey@1stchoicems.com
realestaterex@yahoo.com

BUS: Real Estate Broker **P/S:** All Aspects of Real Estate **MA:** Local **D/D/R:** Marketing Homes for Sales **H/I/S:** Boating, Bowling, Motorcycling, Swimming, Animals **EDU:** Licensed Real Estate Agent **A/A/S:** Million Dollar Club, NAR, Republican Women's Association, MARPAC, Trinity Baptist Church

Eduardo Mauricio Izquierdo
Registered Nurse
Larkin Community Hospital
7031 S.W. 62nd Avenue
Miami, FL 33143 United States
izquierdoe@bellsouth.net
http://www.cambridgewhoswho.com

BUS: Hospital **P/S:** Healthcare Services **MA:** Local **D/D/R:** Practicing Intensive Care Nursing **H/I/S:** Reading, Swimming, Dining Out **FBP:** Critical Care; Nursing2009 **EDU:** Diploma in Nursing, Miami-Dade Community College **A/A/S:** American Cancer Society; St. Jude Children's Research Hospital **A/S:** He attributes his success to his hard work, determination and keeping himself updated on the latest medical methodologies. **B/I:** He became involved in his profession because he was influenced by a family illness and wanted to help people. **H/O:** The most gratifying aspect of his career is seeing patients making progress everyday.

Billy Ray Jackson
Teacher/Tennis Pro
BRJ Tennis LLC
8-12 Briarcliff Drive
Ossining, NY 10562 United States
tennisbrj@aol.com

BUS: Tennis Service Provider **P/S:** Tennis Instruction Coaching **MA:** Local **D/D/R:** Conducting High-Performance Tennis Coaching **H/I/S:** Fitness Training, Competition **FBP:** TENNIS **EDU:** Master's Degree, Thornhill University

CYNTHIA A. R. JACKSON
Math Specialist
Oak Ridge City Schools
125 Aubodon Road
Oak Ridge, TN 37830 United States
cjackson@ortn.edu
http://www.cambridgewhoswho.com

BUS: Public Elementary School **P/S:** Working with Teachers, Working with Students in Small Groups to Better Mathematics **MA:** Local **D/D/R:** Conducting Personal Mathematics Coaching and Staff Development **H/I/S:** Fishing, Camping, And Spending Time with Family **FBP:** Math Journals and Gardening Journals **EDU:** Education Specialist Degree, Lincoln Memorial University **A/A/S:** National Council of Teachers of Mathematics; Association for Supervision and Curriculum Development; National Education Association; TEA; Delta Kappa Gamma; Phi Delta Kappa **C/VW:** Disabled Veterans Association, March of Dimes, United Way **B/I:** She chose the profession because her mother was a teacher. **H/O:** The highlight of her career was receiving national board certification

EVELYN JACKSON
Chief Operating Officer
2nd Solution, LLC
260 Peachtree Street, Suite 220
Atlanta, GA 30303 United States
evelyn@bass-ent.com
http://www.cambridgewhoswho.com

BUS: Finance Company **P/S:** Financial Services Including Debt Collections **MA:** Regional **D/D/R:** Managing Business Operations, Overseeing Finance and Debt Collections for Major Accounts **H/I/S:** Motorcycling **FBP:** FCDPA

KATHY B. JACKSON
Senior Vice President
Access Health Solutions, LLC
400 Sawgrass Corp Parkway
Sunrise, FL 33325 United States
kathyjackson@accessmpn.com
http://www.accessmpn.com

BUS: Healthcare Network **P/S:** Minority Physician Network, Limited Liability Corporation **MA:** International **EXP:** Ms. Jackson's expertise is in government relations. **H/I/S:** Reading, Patron of Arts Throughout the United States **FBP:** Business Week; New England Journal of Medicine; Alternate Medicine **EDU:** Ph.D. in Health Administration, Kennedy Western University

NELSON E. JACKSON JR.
Registered Representative
Primerica Financial Services
12150 E. Briarwood Avenue, Suite 204
Englewood, CO 80112 United States
hondoj@gmail.com • njackson.sts5602@primerica.com
http://www.primerica.com/njacksonjr1954
http://www.primericafna.com

BUS: Financial Service Company **P/S:** Assistance for Families Looking to Become Debt-Free and Financially Independent through Education, Financial Solutions and Business Opportunities, Business-to-Business Retirement Plans, Employee Education and Financial Solutions **MA:** Colorado **D/D/R:** Analyzing Finances for Families in an Effort to Help them Achieve their Financial Goals and Continue within a Comfortable Budgetary Lifestyle, Overseeing Marketing and Distribution for the Company, Working with Medium-Sized Businesses and Independent Retirement Accounts as a Financial Consultant **H/I/S:** Riding his Motorcycle, Horseback Riding, Sky Diving, Scuba Diving, Flying, Hunting **FBP:** Forbes; Money **EDU:** Master of Science in Systems Management, University of Denver (1991); Bachelor of Arts, University of Wisconsin-Madison (1976) **CERTS:** Licensed in Series 6, 63 and 26 Securities; Licensed in Accident and Health Insurance, States of Colorado, Nebraska, Wisconsin and Oklahoma

SHERRI L. JACKSON, RN, BSN
Registered Nurse, Clinical Compliance Coordinator
Hallmark Nursing Center
3701 W. Radcliff Avenue
Denver, CO 80236 United States
wellinvr@msn.com
http://www.cambridgewhoswho.com

BUS: Long Term Geriatric Care **P/S:** Rehabilitation, Caring for the Elderly **MA:** National **EXP:** Ms. Jackson's expertise is in long-term care. **D/D/R:** Managing All Medicare Insurance of Patients from the Day of Admission until Discharge **H/I/S:** Traveling, ATVing **FBP:** American Journal of Nursing **EDU:** Bachelor of Science in Geriatrics, University of Phoenix **A/A/S:** American Association of Nurse Assessment Coordinators **A/S:** She attributes her success to her compassion and her caring nature toward her patients. **B/I:** She became involved in her profession because she loved taking care of others. **H/O:** The highlight of her career was receiving her bachelor's degree.

MABLE L. JACKSON-ROBINSON, DD
Chief Executive Officer, Founder
1) New Life in Christ Jesus Ministry
2) Layman in Training Institute
73 High Street
Lockport, NY 14094 United States
mablerobinson08@yahoo.com
http://www.newlifeinchristjesusministry.com

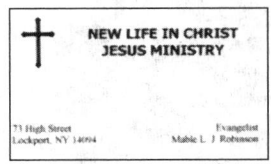

BUS: 1) Ministry 2) Educational Institution **P/S:** 1) Religious Services Including Distribution of Free Gifts, Bibles, Faith Rocks, Christians, Tracts and Cards 2) Education **MA:** 1) Local 2) Local **EXP:** Ms. Jackson-Robinson's expertise includes Christian spiritual guidance and encouragement and English and language arts secondary education. **H/I/S:** Reading, Supervising an After-School Tutoring Program **FBP:** Christian Growth and Educational Materials **EDU:** Doctor of Divinity (2007); Master's Degree in English Education, Niagara University (1992); Bachelor of Arts in English Education, Niagara University (1982) **CERTS:** Certification in Ordination (2007) **A/A/S:** Experience Works (2006); Aspire; New York State United Teachers; The Salvation Army; American Federation of Teachers **DOB:** June 20, 1946 **A/S:** She attributes her success to her passion for teaching and her faith in God. **B/I:** She became involved in her profession due to her own children who inspired her to pursue the academic area and help other children. **H/O:** The most gratifying aspect of her career is seeing her students succeed.

CHRIS ANN JACOBS
Medical Technologist
Reproductive Biology Associates
1150 Lake Hearn Drive
Atlanta, GA 30342 United States
jchrisann@yahoo.com
http://www.cambridgewhoswho.com

BUS: Private Medical Practice **P/S:** Reproductive Medicine, Clinical Laboratory Testing **MA:** Atlanta **EXP:** Ms. Jacob's expertise includes reproductive biology, microbiology and endocrinology. **H/I/S:** Collecting Coins, Conducting Biblical Research **EDU:** Bachelor of Arts in Medical Technology, University of Michigan, with Honors; Bachelor's Degree in Theology **CERTS:** Certification in Medical Technology, American Society for Clinical Pathology **A/A/S:** American Society of Clinical Pathology **C/VW:** Church **A/S:** She attributes her success to her genuine love for the field, hard work and her attention to detail. **B/I:** She became involved in the profession because she had an interest in science and a high aptitude in biological sciences. **H/O:** The most gratifying aspect of her career is being able to teach others.

MRS. SUSAN O. JACOBS
Real Estate Broker, Owner
Jacobs Team Buyers & Sellers Realty
Assist-2-Sell
7515 Presidential Avenue
Manassas, VA 20109 United States
home4sale@mris.com
http://www.virginiabuyersandsellers.com

America's Leading Discount Real Estate Company

BUS: Real Estate Agency **P/S:** Real Estate Services **MA:** Manassas, Bristow, Gainesville, Haymarket and Centreville, Prince William County, Northern Virginia **D/D/R:** Marketing, Overseeing the Sale of Custom-Built, Resale, Veterans Affairs Foreclosure, Housing and Urban Development, Land, Commercial, Auction, Short Sale and Real Estate Owned Properties **H/I/S:** Cooking, Attending and Hosting Parties, Gardening **FBP:** Washington Business Journal; Shape; Living; Cooking; Health and Gardening-Related Publications **EDU:** Coursework, National Institute of Real Estate; Diploma, Garfield High School **CERTS:** Certified Relocation Specialist; Certified Realtor, State of Virginia; Certified Real Estate Consultant; Certified REO Specialist; Senior Housing Specialist; Licensed Broker, State of Virginia; CyberStar; VA Foreclosure Certified Agent; HUD Foreclosure Certified Agent; Certified Buyer Broker; Certification in Appraisal, Financing Level I and II and Tax Laws **A/A/S:** Executive Board of Directors, Chair Elect, Vice President of Programs, Vice President of Membership Service, Vice President of Membership Recruitment, Member Retention, Greater Manassas Chamber of Commerce (1999-2006); Chairwoman, Greater Manassas Chamber of Commerce (2004-2005); Metropolitan Regional Information Services; Prince William Board of Realtors; Northern Virginia Association of Realtors; National Association of Realtors; Business Network International **A/H:** Best Realtor of the Year (2007); Top Team Award, Long & Foster Top Team (1998); National Sales Award, The Realty Alliance (1997); Top Producer, P.W.A.R. (1991-2006); Dual Recipient, Member of the Month Award **C/VW:** Habitat for Humanity; Light the Night Leukemia Walk; SERVE; MDA **DOB:** September 11, 1957 **POB:** Somerset, PA **SP:** Neil **CHILD:** Monica **C/A:** Long & Foster Chairman's Club (1997, 1999-2005); Lifetime Member, Chairman's Club, Long & Foster (1997); REMAX 100 Percent Club (1991-1996); REMAX Presidents Club (1990); P.W.A.R. Million Dollar Club (1988-2006); REMAX Executive Club (1989) **A/S:** She attributes her success to her self-motivation, personality, honesty and helping her clients with correct information. **I/F/Y:** In five years, Mrs. Jacobs hopes to sit on the Lido deck of a cruise ship and assist clients with all their real estate needs.

GARY A. JACOBSON
Technical Specialist
Greenwich Hospital
5 Perryridge Road
Greenwich, CT 06830 United States
garyj@greenhosp.org
http://www.greenhosp.org

BUS: Blood Bank **P/S:** Medical Diagnosis **MA:** Local **D/D/R:** Supervising the Blood Bank, Overseeing Daily Operations, Taking Inventory, Ensuring Patients Receive Correct Infusions **H/I/S:** Running a Ceramic Program at a Local School **FBP:** Transfusion **EDU:** Bachelor of Science in Biochemistry, Pace University **A/A/S:** American Association of Blood Banking; Blood Bank of New York; Connecticut Red Cross **C/VW:** St. Sebastian, Salvation Army **H/O:** The highlight of his career is working for St. Josephs in Paterson, New Jersey as the manager of the blood blank infusions.

CECILIA M. JACQUES
Guest Services Training Manager
Treasure Island Resort Hotel
3300 Las Vegas Boulevard S.
Las Vegas, NV 89109 United States
cejacques@hotmail.com
http://www.treasureisland.com

BUS: Hospitality **P/S:** Hospitality and Service for the Gaming Industry **MA:** Local **D/D/R:** Offering Customer Service, Training Employees, Developing Customer Training **H/I/S:** Golfing, Bicycling, Creating Gift Baskets **EDU:** Continuing Education Coursework in Leadership, University of Washington **A/A/S:** Las Vegas Chamber of Commerce **C/VW:** VOICE Volunteer, Childhaven **A/S:** She attributes her personal and professional success to her drive and passion for the profession. **H/O:** The highlight of her career is the development and successful launch of the Platinum IT Employee Training and Development Plan.

SANDRA M. JAMERSON, M.ED., BA
Music Instructor, Choir Director, Minister of Music, First Baptist
Cordell
Barton Junior High School
400 W. Faulkner
El Dorado, AR 71730 United States
lilpea22002003@yahoo.com
http://www.cambridgewhoswho.com

BUS: Junior High School **P/S:** Education **MA:** Local **EXP:** Ms. Jamerson's expertise is in music education. **H/I/S:** Reading Avidly, Watching Home and Garden Television, Spending Time with her Family, Listening to Music **FBP:** 'The Power of a Praying Woman' by Stormie Omartian **EDU:** Bachelor's Degree in Music Education, Lane College (1983); Master's Degree in Education, Southern Arkansas University **A/H:** Teacher of the Year, African-American Society (2003); Achievement Award, First Baptist Cordell Church (2002); Gospel Music Workshop of America; Vice Chairwoman, Deaconess of First Baptist Cordell; Board Member, South Arkansas Arts Center, **C/VW:** American Diabetes Foundation; St. Jude Children's Hospital **A/S:** She attributes her success to her strong faith and belief in God. **B/I:** She became involved in the profession because she always wanted to be in a position to make a difference in children's lives. **H/O:** The highlight of her career was earning her master's degree.

EDMAN L. JAMES JR.
Director of Transportation
Aillet, Fenner, Jolly & McClelland, Inc.
1055 Louisiana Avenue
Shreveport, LA 71101 United States
sjames@afjmc.com
http://www.afjmc.com

BUS: Highway and Transportation Design Consulting Firm **P/S:** Civil, Environmental and Structural Engineering Services for Federal, State, and Local Governmental Projects, Industrial, Commercial, Institutional and Private Projects, MEP **MA:** Regional **D/D/R:** Overseeing Highway Projects on Interstate and State Roadways, Managing a Staff of 16 Engineers, Implementing and Executing Engineering Plans and Designs **H/I/S:** Playing Football, Hunting **EDU:** College Coursework **A/A/S:** The American Railway Engineering and Maintenance-of-Way Association; American Society of Civil Engineers; Institute of Transportation Engineers; American Council of Engineering Companies of Louisiana; American Council of Engineering Companies

MR. PHILIP F. G. JAMES, RN
Registered Nurse Instructor
Best Care
1784 Flatbush Avenue
Brooklyn, NY 11210 United States
philip.james@cwwemail.com
http://www.cambridgewhoswho.com

BUS: Educational Facility **P/S:** Nursing Education to Train Nurse Aides and Personal Care Aides **MA:** Local **D/D/R:** Conducting Classes, Training Students **H/I/S:** Traveling, Gardening **FBP:** American Journal of Nursing **EDU:** Bachelor of Science in Hospital Administration, St. Joseph's College; Registered Nurse, Queens General Hospital **CERTS:** Diploma in In-Service Nursing Education, St. Joseph's College **A/A/S:** New York Nurses Association; Long Island Nurses Association **C/VW:** Volunteer, Local Church and Community; Brotherhood of St. Andrew; Warden, St. Bartholomew; St. Bartholomew's Church; Long Island Corsilla Movement

HEATHER ANN JANKOVICH
Program Administrator
Gatewood Program for Educating Exceptional Preschoolers
1241 Gatewood Road
Newport News, VA 23601 United States
heather.jankovich@nn.k12.va.us
http://sbo.nn.k12.va.us/schools/peep.shtml

BUS: Education **P/S:** Supervision of Teachers and Special Needs Students **MA:** Local **EXP:** Ms. Jankovich's expertise includes special and early childhood education and administration. **H/I/S:** Reading, Traveling, Swimming, Nutrition, Spending Time with his Family **FBP:** Education Week **EDU:** Master of Arts, Hampton University, VA; Associate of Arts, Shenandoah University, Winchester, VA; Advanced Graduate Coursework in Educational Leadership, Cambridge College **A/A/S:** Association for Supervision and Curriculum Development; Alpha Delta Kappa; Soroptimist International; Christian Foundation for Children and Aging; National Association for the Education of Young Children; National Education Association; Virginia Education Association **C/VW:** CFCA; Relay for Life; United Way **A/S:** She attributes her success to her parents and their belief in a limitless life. **B/I:** She became involved in the profession after making the decision to impact the lives of children with special needs and after starting her own family. **H/O:** The highlight of her career was planning and implementing the first school carnival, the Book Fair, Open House and several volunteer programs.

Teresa L. Janz, LMT, RN
Certified Massage Therapist, Registered Nurse
Spiritual Expression
14001 N. 184th Avenue
Surprise, AZ 85388 United States
circhawk@yahoo.com
http://www.cambridgewhoswho.com

BUS: Massage Therapy **P/S:** Massage Therapy for People and Animals **MA:** Arizona **EXP:** Ms. Janz's expertise is in myofacial release. **EDU:** Master's Degree in Education, Lynchburg College; Bachelor of Science in Nursing, Lynchburg College **C/VW:** Native American Universities, Native American Rights Fund **A/S:** She attributes her success to her passion, love of life and family's support. **B/I:** She became involved in her profession because she loves to help people and make them feel better. **H/O:** The most gratifying aspect of her career is saving lives.

Connie A. Jastrenski, RN, MS, MBA
Chief Nursing Officer, Vice President of Patient Care Services
Bassett Healthcare
1 Atwell Road
Cooperstown, NY 13326 United States
connie.jastrenski@bassett.org
http://www.bassett.org

BUS: Medical Center **P/S:** Healthcare Including Heart Care for Women and Children, Cancer Service, Behavioral Health, Alternative Medicine and Diabetes Program **MA:** Local **EXP:** Ms. Jastrenski's expertise is in nursing. **D/D/R:** Overseeing all Departments Including the Operating Room, Emergency Department and Laboratory, Preoperative Nursing, Bed Management, Admission and Transportation Services, Solving Problems **H/I/S:** Kayaking, Canoing, Golfing **FBP:** Journal of Nursing Administration; Journal of Healthcare Management **EDU:** Master of Business Administration, Syracuse University (1997); Master's Degree in Education, University of Maryland (1982); Bachelor of Science in Nursing, University of Maryland (1980); Diploma in Nursing, University of Pittsburgh (1969) **A/A/S:** New York Organization of Nurse Executives; American Association of Nurse Executives; Society of Critical Care Medicine; American Nurses Association; NTS Nurses Association; Sigma Theta Tau International; American Association of Neuroscience Nurses; Society of Trauma Nurses

LAURETTA J. JAYSURA
Director of Medical Staff Affairs, Manager
Jacobi Medical Center
1400 Pelham Parkway S.
Bronx, NY 10461 United States
lauretta.jaysura@nbhn.net
http://www.nbhn.net

BUS: Hospital **P/S:** Complete Range of Acute, Specialty, General and Psychiatric Services **MA:** Regional **D/D/R:** Offering Leadership in Medical Staff Affairs, Verifying Credentials, Compliance and Regulatory Issues, Enforcing Policies and Procedures for Medical Staff Affairs, Overseeing Healthcare Administration, Offering Leadership in Training Surveys, Analyzing Information, Overseeing a Staff of Seven **H/I/S:** Swimming, Bicycling **EDU:** Associate Degree in Business Administration, Bronx Community College (1995) **CERTS:** Certified Toastmaster (2007) **A/A/S:** National Association of Medical Staff Services; African American Association of the Bronx; Toastmasters International

MS. LYNDA G. JEFFERS-CAIN
Vice President, Branch Manager
First National Bank of New Mexico
919 Martinez Street
Logan, NM 88426 United States
lcain@fnbofnm.com
http://www.fnbofnm.com

BUS: Premier Privately Owned Bank with Branches in Northeastern New Mexico **P/S:** ATM and Debit Card Services, Competitive Rates, TeleBank, Safe Deposit Boxes, Online Banking, Loan Services **MA:** Regional **D/D/R:** Overseeing Consumer and Agricultural Loans, Managing Daily Operations **H/I/S:** Rodeos, Cutting Horses, Four-Wheeling, Spending Time with Grandchildren **EDU:** Bachelor of Science in Agricultural Business and Economics, New Mexico State University (1977) **CERTS:** Commercial Credit Certificate, Western States School of Banking **A/A/S:** National Cutting Horse Association; New Mexico Cattle Grower's Association; Logan Chamber of Commerce **A/H:** Outstanding Senior of Agricultural College, New Mexico State University

Sharen K. Jeffries, MD
Medical Doctor
Premier ENT
399 E. Highland Avenue
503
San Bernardino, CA 92404 United States
skjeffries@verizon.com
http://www.cambridgewhoswho.com

BUS: Medical Spa **P/S:** Head and Neck Surgery, Cosmetic Laser Center, Ear Nose and Throat Care **MA:** Local **EXP:** Ms. Jeffries' expertise includes otolaryngology, facial plastic and reconstruction. **H/I/S:** Traveling, Reading, Farming, Reading Fiction Novels **EDU:** MD, Specialization in Ear Nose and Throat Care, Baylor College of Medicine **A/A/S:** American Medical Association; California Medical Association; Society of Head and Neck Surgery; Board of Directors, Symphony; Parish Nurse Program

Linda K. Jenkins
Registered Nurse, Access Manager, Charge Nurse
DaVita Renal Care
4802 Broadway
Gary, IN 46408 United States
lindakj3333@sbcglobal.net
http://www.davita.com

BUS: Healthcare Center **P/S:** Healthcare Including Hemodialysis, Peritoneal Dialysis, Acute Dialysis, Laboratory Services, Clinical Research, Disease Management and Education **MA:** Regional **EXP:** Ms. Jenkins' expertise is in patient care. **D/D/R:** Overseeing Medications and Staff, Assessing Dialysis Using Fistulas, Grafts and Catheters, Making Referrals to Physicians, Ensuring Efficiency **H/I/S:** Toile Painting, Gardening **FBP:** The Dialysis Transport Magazine **EDU:** Bachelor of Science in Nursing, Indiana University (1995) **CERTS:** Diploma, Trinity Lutheran Hospital, School of Nursing, Kansas City, MO (1965); Certified Nephrology Nurse **A/A/S:** American Nurses Association; American Nephrology Nurses Association

PAULA SUE JENKINS, BS
Educator (Retired)
Orange County School District
Orlando, FL United States
http://www.cambridgewhoswho.com

BUS: Education **P/S:** Elementary Education **MA:** Local **D/D/R:** Teaching Kindergarten **H/I/S:** Crafts, Collecting Cottages **FBP:** Reader's Digest; Children's Magazines **EDU:** Bachelor of Science in Elementary Education, The University of Central Florida at Orlando **A/A/S:** International Poets Society **C/VW:** Easter Seals, American Cancer Society, Feed the Children, United Way, Local Sheriff's Association **A/S:** She attributes her success to never giving up and remaining persistent. **B/I:** She became involved in her profession because she had wanted to teach since she was little.

GWENDOLYN A. JENNINGS
Owner
J&J Construction
4188 Dustin Drive
Acworth, GA 30101 United States
Jerry007@bellsouth.net

BUS: Custom Furniture Construction **P/S:** Framing, Custom Cabinets, Custom Furniture **MA:** Local **H/I/S:** Family, Reading, Gardening, Cooking, Woodworking **EDU:** Master's Degree in Chef Management, Culinary Art Institute of NY; Master of Business Administration, University of Pennsylvania

MRS. SANDRA K. JENSEN
Poet
Sandra Noe Jensen
911 E. Denver Avenue
Turkey, TX 79261 United States
sandra@sandranoejensen.net
http://www.sandranoejensen.net

BUS: Publishing Company **P/S:** Books, Poems **MA:** International **EXP:** Mrs. Jensen's expertise is in writing inspirational poetry. **H/I/S:** Reading Smithsonian and Non-Fiction Books, Sewing, Making Crafts, Painting, Archery, Playing Tennis, Horseback Riding **FBP:** Writer's Digest; The Wilson Quarterly; AARP The Magazine; AARPBulletin; Guideposts; Believer's Voice of Victory; Highways; This Old House **CERTS:** Industry-Related Training **A/A/S:** Noble House Publishers; Sparrow Grass Publications; Prairie Dog Press; Arcadia Poetry Press; World of Poetry Press; The International Who's Who in Poetry; Poetry International **C/VW:** Disabled American Veterans; Kenneth Copeland Ministries **DOB:** June 26, 1943 **POB:** Rockford, IL **SP:** Randolph **CHILD:** John, Shelly, Joshua **A/S:** She attributes her success to her faith in God. **B/I:** She became involved in her profession because of her interest in poetry. **H/O:** The highlight of her career was receiving several awards for her poetry. **I/F/Y:** In five years, Mrs. Jensen hopes to continue writing and publishing.

MR. WILLIAM D. JEROME
1) Owner 2) President 3) Owner
1) Jerome Distributors, Inc. 2) Martin Coffee Company
3) Quick Q Barbeque of Pinellas Park Inc.
4900 Park Boulevard
Pinellas Park, FL 33781 United States
mrsnackman1@yahoo.com
http://www.martincoffee.com

BUS: 1) Distribution Company 2) Manufacturing Company 3) Catering Company **P/S:** 1) Food Products Including Baked Goods, Coffee, Espresso, Cappuccinos and Snack Foods 2) Coffee Services for Offices, Restaurants and Coffee Shops 3) Food Services **MA:** 1) Florida 2) Local 3) Local **D/D/R:** Supplying Prepackaged Baked Goods and a Wide Variety of High Quality Products with a 30-Day Shelf Life, Ensuring Customer Satisfaction, Managing Administrative Duties, Overseeing Business Development for More Than 220 Locations **H/I/S:** Fishing **EDU:** Coursework in Architectural Drafting, Michigan State University (1972) **A/A/S:** Pinellas Park Chamber of Commerce; National Barbecue Association; International Hotel & Restaurant Association

SHERRY W. JESSUP
Elementary School Teacher
Shoals Elementary School
1800 Shoals Road
Pinnacle, NC 27043 United States
jessupsh@surry.k12.nc.us
http://www.cambridgewhoswho.com

BUS: School for Exceptional Children **P/S:** Education **MA:** Local **D/D/R:** Helping Children Reach their Potential **H/I/S:** Reading, Scrapbooking, Painting **EDU:** Bachelor of Arts in Education, Lees McCrae College **B/I:** She became involved in her profession because she was working at another profession and a friend told her about the great satisfaction that comes from teaching so she decided to pursue it. **H/O:** The highlight of her career is seeing her students succeed.

LETICIA L. JIMENEZ
Clinic Assessor
Del Norte Clinics, Inc.
935 B. Market Street
Yuba City, CA 95991 United States
jimenezl@dnci.org
http://www.cambridgewhoswho.com

BUS: Nonprofit Organization **P/S:** Personal Care for Low-Income Individuals **MA:** Regional **D/D/R:** Visiting Clinics, Assessing Clinic Workers and Facilities **H/I/S:** Traveling **EDU:** Pursuing Associate Degree in Business Management, Yuba Community College **C/VW:** Seventh Day Adventist Church; Pathfinders; Homeless Feeding Ministry; Volunteer, Carehome; Volunteer, Prison Writing and Visiting Ministry **A/S:** She attributes her success to her faith in Jesus. **B/I:** She became involved in her profession through a natural progression of opportunities. **H/O:** The most gratifying aspect of her career is serving people.

KARLA R. JOHANNING, PA-C
Physician Assistant
Dakota Clinic
125 E. Frazee Street
Detroit Lakes, MN 56501 United States
kjohanning@dakcl.com
http://www.dakotaclinic.com

BUS: Healthcare Facility **P/S:** Superb Healthcare Services in Multiple Disciplines **MA:** Regional **D/D/R:** Specializing in Women's Health and Diabetes, Attending to Patients of All Ages **H/I/S:** Playing the Piano, Spending Time with her Husband and Two Children **FBP:** JAAPA **EDU:** Master's Degree in Physician Assistant Studies, The University of Iowa (1998) **A/A/S:** American Academy of Physician Assistants

ALLISON T. JOHNSON
Co-President
The Adason Group
1745 Phoenix Boulevard
Suite 240
Atlanta, GA 30349 United States
ajohnson@theadasongroup.com
http://www.theadasongroup.com

BUS: Advertising **P/S:** Unique Opportunities for Clients to Generate Additional Revenue through Advertising and Consulting Services for a Variety of Industries **MA:** National **EXP:** Ms. Johnson's expertise is in strategic communications. **D/D/R:** Strategic Communications **H/I/S:** Golfing, Cooking **FBP:** The Wall Street Journal; The New York Times; BusinessWeek **EDU:** Bachelor's Degree in Journalism, University of Georgia **A/A/S:** Mentor, Public Elementary School District; Ordained Elder; High Museum of Art

CHRISTINE M. JOHNSON, PLS
Principal
Clear Path
2280 Grass Valley Highway
Suite 242
Auburn, CA 95603 United States
christine@clear-path.net
http://www.andregg.com

BUS: Time-Honored Leaders in Engineering and Land Surveying **P/S:** Mapping and Geomatics, Consulting Services, Orthophotography, Geographic Information Systems, Remote Sensing, Topographic and Hydrographic Surveys **MA:** Regional **D/D/R:** Offering Professional Consulting and Project Management as a Principal-in-Charge and Project Manager, Conducting Surveying and Civil Engineering, Overseeing Project Leadership for Land Development Projects Including the Design and Calculation of Subdivisions, Land Divisions, Route Layout, Legal Descriptions for Property, Easements and Utilities and Construction Projects Including Shopping Centers and Apartment Complexes **H/I/S:** Training and Breeding Dogs, Photography, Gardening **FBP:** Sacramento Business Journal; Entrepreneur **EDU:** Bachelor of Science in Education, Mancato State College **A/A/S:** American Congress of Surveying and Mapping; California Land Surveyors Association; Society of Women Engineers; Recipient, Journal Women who Mean Business Award, Sacramento Business (2005)

ELAINE S. JOHNSON
Speech and Language Pathologist
Harris Hill Elementary School
Penfield Central Schools
2590 Atlantic Avenue
Penfield, NY 14625 United States
eljoe@rochester.rr.com

BUS: Elementary School **P/S:** Primary Education **MA:** Local **D/D/R:** Offering Early Childhood Language Development for Disabled Children **H/I/S:** Reading, Traveling, Spending Time with her Family and Friends **FBP:** American Speech-Language-Hearing Association Journals **EDU:** Master's Degree in Speech Pathology, SUNY Geneseo; Master's Degree in Early Childhood Education, Nazareth College **A/A/S:** American Speech-Language-Hearing Association; Geneseo Valley Speech and Language Hearing Association **C/VW:** Volunteer, Public Library; Sponsor, International Children **A/S:** She attributes her success to her wonderful mentors and administrators. **B/I:** She became involved in the profession because she enjoys working with people. **H/O:** The most gratifying aspect of her career is when the children remember what she has done for them and show their appreciation.

GLYNDOL K. JOHNSON
Purchasing Agent
Walton County Board of County Commissioners
176 Montgomery Circle
DeFuniak Springs, FL 32435 United States
johglyndol@co.walton.fl.us
http://www.co.walton.fl.us

BUS: Government Board of County Commissioners **P/S:** Government Administration Services, Community Service, Public Services, Projects, Special Programs **MA:** Regional **D/D/R:** Supervising and Evaluating Staff, Bidding, Purchasing, Advertising, Warehousing **H/I/S:** Water Sports, Shopping, Spending Time with Family **FBP:** NIGP Newsletter **CERTS:** Certified Public Purchasing Buyer (2004) **A/A/S:** National Institute of Governmental Purchasing, Inc., Gulf Coast Chapter **DOB:** April 20, 1958 **SP:** Kenneth **CHILD:** Brent, Lauren, Jeremy, Keith **W/H:** Purchasing Agent (2001-Present); Clerk of Courts (1975-1987); Purchasing Agent, Department of Corrections, State of Florida

JOHN J. JOHNSON
Executive Managing Director
Whiteweld and Company
200 Park Avenue
New York, NY 10166 United States
jjohnson@whiteweld.com
http://www.whiteweld.com

BUS: Investment Firm **P/S:** Real Estate Development **MA:** Local **EXP:** Mr. Johnson's expertise includes real estate, banking and philanthropy. **H/I/S:** Golfing, Tennis, Playing Racquetball, Horseback Riding **FBP:** Fortune **EDU:** Bachelor's Degree in Business Administration, Pace University **A/A/S:** Union League Club; President, The Whiteweld Foundation **A/S:** He attributes his success to his hard work and communication skills. **B/I:** He became involved in his profession through luck and circumstance. **H/O:** The highlight of his career was buying a piece of property from an estate.

KATHARINA JOHNSON
Broker Associate, Owner
Key Real Estate Advisors, Inc.
9230 Daniels Parkway #102
Fort Myers, FL 33912 United States
katharinaj@msn.com
http://www.keyrealestateadivosrs.com

BUS: Real Estate Company **P/S:** Real Estate, Residential Sales and Investment Properties **MA:** Lee County, Florida **D/D/R:** Selling Investment, New Construction, Country Living Properties **H/I/S:** Painting, Enjoying Arts and Crafts, Spending Quality Time with her Children **FBP:** Realtor **EDU:** Master of Business Administration, Germany; Bachelor of Arts in Business Administration, Germany **A/A/S:** National Association of Realtors; Florida Association of Realtors **C/VW:** Make-A-Wish Foundation, Church **A/S:** She attributes her success to being able to deal with all types of people. **B/I:** She became involved in her profession because she liked the flexible ours. **H/O:** The highlight of her career was being able to provide home purchasers and investors what they need.

LAURA A. JOHNSON, BA, MLS
Assistant Principal (Retired)
West Charlotte High School
2219 Senior Drive
Charlotte, NC 28216 United States
laura.johnson@cms.k12.nc.us
http://www.cms.k12.nc.us

BUS: High School **P/S:** Secondary Education **MA:** Local **D/D/R:** Working in the Media Center of an Alternative School, Overseeing Administrative Duties, Utilizing Educational Media Technology, Mentoring Teachers and Young Ladies **H/I/S:** Golfing, Reading, Traveling **FBP:** Educational Leadership **EDU:** Master's Degree in Library Science, University of North Carolina, Greensboro; Coursework in Advanced Educational Media, University of North Carolina, Charlotte **A/A/S:** North Carolina Association of School Administrators; National Association of Black School Educators; Alpha Kappa Alpha; Billy Graham Evangelistic Association **A/H:** Finalist, Harris Educators Award for Teacher of the Year **C/VW:** Seigle Avenue First Church of God; United Way; American Red Cross **DOB:** April 3, 1954 **POB:** Charlotte, NC **SP:** Timothy **W/H:** Coordinator, International Studies, Lincoln Heights Elementary School; Site Administrator, Mayfield Alternative Middle School **A/S:** She attributes her success to her people management and listening skills. **B/I:** She became involved in her profession because of her educational background and the experience she gained in teaching at Sunday school during her childhood. **H/O:** The highlight of her career was being a finalist for the Harris Educators Award for Teacher of the Year on a district level.

LIANNE M. JOHNSON, DH
Registered Dental Hygienist
Disaster Mortuary Operational Response Teams
Florida Emergency Mortuary Response System
599 William Ellery Street
Orange Park, FL 32073 United States
lujohnson7@msn.com
http://www.cambridgewhoswho.com

BUS: Disaster Management Company **P/S:** Identification of Disaster Victims **MA:** National **D/D/R:** Practicing Forensic Ontology and Periodontal Work **H/I/S:** Spending Time with her Family, Socializing with People through the Internet, Swimming, Exercising **FBP:** Modern Hygienist **EDU:** Associate of Science in Dental Hygiene, Pensacola Junior College **CERTS:** Registered Dental Hygienist **A/A/S:** Northeast Florida District Four Medical Examiners Office **C/VW:** United Way; World Vision; Ridge wood Baptist Church; American Cancer Society **A/S:** She attributes her success to her perseverance and desire to help people. **B/I:** She became involved in her profession because of her interest in the field. **H/O:** The highlight of her career was serving in the Ivan and Katrina hurricane disaster relief.

MARDINE JOHNSON
Senior Consultant
McKesson Provider Technologies
5995 Windward Parkway
Alpharetta, GA 30005 United States
Mardi@JohnsonPDX.com
http://www.mckesson.com

BUS: Healthcare Information Technology and Pharmaceutical Distribution Company **P/S:** Pharmaceuticals, Medical Supplies and Technologies that Make Healthcare Safer while Reducing Costs **MA:** International **EXP:** Ms. Johnson's expertise is in software development and implementation. **D/D/R:** Teaching Staff how to Build and Use the Systems and Roll them Out to End Users, Performing In-House Training, Developing Methodology for Implementations, Growing the Software Side of the Business **H/I/S:** Traveling, Hiking, Exercising **FBP:** Laboratory Medicine **EDU:** Master of Business Administration, Oregon State University (1988) **A/A/S:** ASCP

Patricia A. Johnson
Enrolled Agent/Franchisee
H&R Block
112 E. Washington Street
Momence, IL 60954 United States
paljohn@sbcglobal.net
http://www.cambridgewhoswho.com

BUS: Tax Services **P/S:** Tax Preparation **MA:** National **EXP:** Ms. Johnson's expertise is in tax preparation. **H/I/S:** Quilting, Scrapbooking, Traveling **FBP:** Kiplinger's **EDU:** Coursework in Accounting, Kankakee Junior College **A/A/S:** Chamber of Commerce **A/S:** She attributes her success to hard work, persistence, support from her family and ability to work well under pressure. **B/I:** She became involved in this profession because she always enjoyed working with number and the opportunity arose.

Ruby N. Johnson
Realtor
Metro Brokers GMAC Real Estate
3330 Satellite Boulevard
Duluth, GA 30096 United States
ruby.johnson@metrobrokers.com
http://www.metrobrokers.com

BUS: Real Estate Agency **P/S:** Residential and Commercial Real Estate Exchanges, Financial, Title Closing, Insurance and Brokerage Services **MA:** International **D/D/R:** Selling Residential Properties, Dealing with First-Time Home Buyers **H/I/S:** Reading, Traveling, Spending Time with her Grandchildren **EDU:** Education Specialist Degree in Vocational Education, Georgia State University (1985); Master's Degree in Education and Mathematics, Atlanta University (1972); Bachelor of Arts in Elementary Education, Clarke University (1969); Ph.D. **CERTS:** Pursuing Buyer Representative Accreditation; Certified New Home Sales Professional (2007); Certification in Commercial Real Estate (2007); Certification in Elegant Homes (2006); Certification in Premier Service (2006); Quality Service Certified Real Estate Professional (2006); Certification in Educational Leadership and Supervision (1992); Certified Vocational Director (1985); Licensed Real Estate Agent **A/A/S:** Atlanta Board of Realtors; Georgia Association of Realtors; National Association of Realtors; Georgia Retired Educators Association; Alpha Kappa Alpha; **C/VW:** New Birth Missionary Baptist Church; Lecturer, Order of the Eastern Star

MR. SCOTT W. JOHNSON
Vice President of Construction
D.R. Horton Inc.
2300 Clayton Road
Concord, CA 94520 United States
swjohnson@drhorton.com
http://www.drhorton.com

BUS: Construction **P/S:** Development, Construction and Sales of Single-Family Homes, Town Homes and Condominiums **MA:** National **EXP:** Mr. Johnson's expertise is in project management. **D/D/R:** Overseeing Daily Operations of Construction Job Sites in the San Francisco Bay Area, Budgeting, Scheduling, Developing Business Plans for the Construction Department **EDU:** High School Education

TAMMIE L. JOHNSON
Primary Teacher
Sand Gap Elementary
Jackson County Board of Education
PO Box 320
Sand Gap, KY 40481 United States
miller@prtcnet.org
http://www.jackson.k12.ky.us

BUS: Board of Education **P/S:** Education Including Arts and Physical Education **MA:** Regional **D/D/R:** Teaching Kindergarten Students, Managing All Areas of Curriculum Including Reading, Addition, Subtraction and Spelling **H/I/S:** Gardening **EDU:** Master's Degree in Elementary Education, Union College (2001) **A/A/S:** Kentucky Education Association **C/VW:** Mission of Hope

CONNIE M. JOHNSTON
Bookkeeper, Office Manager
Turlock Eye Physician Medical Group
880 Delbon Avenue
Turlock, CA 95382 United States
http://www.cambridgewhoswho.com

BUS: Healthcare Provider **P/S:** Healthcare Services Including Eye Care **MA:** Regional **D/D/R:** Overseeing Payroll, Accounting and Taxes, Ordering Supplies, Performing Human Resources Duties **H/I/S:** Skiing **EDU:** Coursework in Medical Studies, Union College **CERTS:** Certified Office Manager, Reynold and Reynolds General Motors

SARAH A. JOHNSTON
Inventory Analyst
Citgo Petroleum
6100 S. Yale Avenue
Tulsa, OK 74136 United States
sjohnst@aol.com
http://www.cambridgewhoswho.com

BUS: Petroleum Company **P/S:** Producing Oil and Gas Products **MA:** International **D/D/R:** Taking Daily Inventory for Products, Monitoring Traders' Performances and Data from Other Departments **H/I/S:** Reading, Scrapbooking **EDU:** Bachelor of Arts in Accounting, Oklahoma State University **A/A/S:** Phi Kappa Phi, Beta Alpha Phi **C/VW:** Susan G. Komen Breast Cancer Foundation, Race for the Cure **A/S:** She attributes her success to her tenacity to work until the problem is solved. **H/O:** The most gratifying aspect of her career is being able to work on several special government projects for the company.

STEPHANIE A. JONAH, RN
Registered Nurse
EZ Visions
8455 Indigo Harbor Avenue
Las Vegas, NV 89117 United States
ezvisions@hotmail.com
http://www.cambridgewhoswho.com

BUS: Publisher **P/S:** The Book, 'Transitions Along the Way-A Guide to the Dying Process for Children and Young Adults' **MA:** National **EXP:** Ms. Jonah's expertise is in mental, physical, emotional, and spiritual healing and well-being. **H/I/S:** Scuba Diving, Traveling, Watching Movies, Dancing **FBP:** National Geographic **EDU:** Associate of Applied Science in Nursing, Pierce College; Registered Nurse **CERTS:** Certification in Basic Life Support; Certification in Advanced Cardiac Life Support; Certification, Neonatal Resuscitation Program **A/H:** Recipient of Several Service Excellence Awards **C/VW:** Volunteer Educator in Healthcare Standards and Techniques, Romanian Orphanage; Volunteer, Groups of Children Whose Parents had Life Threatening Illnesses **W/H:** Labor and Delivery Nurse, Acute Hospital Facility **A/S:** She attributes her success to her desire to help people. **B/I:** She became involved in her profession because she wanted to help people. **H/O:** The highlight of her career is having the ability to relate with people in whatever process they are going through on their journey through life. **I/F/Y:** In five years, Ms. Jonah hopes to publish several more books.

CARISSA JONES
U.S. Sales, Marketing Director
Mercodia Inc.
150 S. Stratford Road
Suite 515
Winston Salem, NC 27104 United States
carissa.jones@mercodia.com
http://www.mercodia.com

BUS: Developer and Manufacturer of High Quality Diagnostic Kits **P/S:** Immunoassays, ELISA Technology for Clinical and Research Applications within Cardiovascular Disease and Diabetes, Offers Assays Applicable in Human and Mammalian Models **MA:** International **D/D/R:** Mentoring, Overseeing Running Sales, Giving Presentations, Attending Conferences, Interacting with Researchers **H/I/S:** Tennis, Photography, Reading, Running, Scrap Booking, Gardening, Baking **EDU:** Bachelor of Arts in Biology, University of North Carolina at Greensboro (1995) **A/A/S:** Gamma Sigma Sigma

MR. FRANKLIN JONAH JONES
Senior Claims Examiner
Tristar Risk Management
203 N. Golden Circle
Santa Ana, CA 92705 United States
franklin.jones@tristargroup.net
http://www.cambridgewhoswho.com

BUS: Risk Management Company **P/S:** Risk Management Services and Claims Management for Insurance Claims **MA:** CA, TX, AZ, NV **EXP:** Mr. Jones' expertise is in litigation. **D/D/R:** Assisting with Final Settlement Claims and Closures, Evaluating Medical Reports **H/I/S:** Gardening, Caring for Pets, Studying Classical Voice, Playing Chess, Volleyball and Racquetball, Reading, Watching Movies, Swimming **EDU:** College Coursework; High School Diploma **CERTS:** Certification, Insurance Education Association; Certified Worker's Compensation Professional, Insurance Education Association (2001); Certified Self-Insured Employer (1997) **A/H:** SPOT Award for Adoption of Bulk Mailout System, EOS Group, Irvine, CA (1999-2000) **DOB:** April 27, 1958 **W/H:** Amtrak (1979-1989) **A/S:** He attributes his success to his positive attitude and love for his profession. **B/I:** He became involved in his profession after starting his career as a data entry operator. **H/O:** The highlight of his career was obtaining a position at Tristar Risk Management.

GEORGE CHAVIER JONES
Chief Executive Officer, Owner
Nation Mortgages and Investments, LLC
550 Pharr Road, Suite 207
Atlanta, GA 30305 United States
gjones@nationsmi.com
http://www.nationsmi.com

BUS: Finance Company **P/S:** Residential Home Loan Financing **MA:** Regional **D/D/R:** Offering Financial Counsel **H/I/S:** Cars, Basketball **EDU:** Bachelor's Degree in Radiology, Emory University **A/A/S:** 100 Black Men's Club; Mortgage Broker Association; One Ninety- One Club

HELEN J. JONES
President
Sound Tracks Productions
1009 N. Central Avenue
Muncie, IN 47303 United States
ssoundtrackss@yahoo.com
http://www.cambridgewhoswho.com

BUS: Music Production Company **P/S:** Making CDs and Demos **MA:** Local **D/D/R:** Singing Gospel Music **H/I/S:** Fishing **FBP:** Industry-Related Publications **EDU:** Industry-Related Training and Experience **C/VW:** Church, Various Charities **B/I:** She became involved in her profession because she has been singing for her entire life. **H/O:** The most gratifying aspect of her career is having her own business.

MS. JOCELYNNE ELYCE JONES
Second Grade Teacher
M.M. Generali Elementary School
3196 E. Main Street
Waterbury, CT 06705 United States
elycect@sbcglobal.net
http://www.cambridgewhoswho.com

BUS: Elementary School **P/S:** Education **MA:** Local **D/D/R:** Teaching All Subjects, Implementing Individualized Education Plans for Special Education and Autistic Students, Developing the District's Science Curriculum, Serving as the Union Representative, Supervising Paraprofessionals during School Dismissal **H/I/S:** Spending Time with Friends and Family, Writing, Exercising, Reading, Visiting Museums and Exhibits, Traveling, Surfing the Web, Singing Karaoke **FBP:** Time; Newsweek; U.S. News & World Report; O, the Oprah Magazine; People; Shape; Essence; Ebony **EDU:** Master of Arts in History and International Relations, Western Connecticut State University; Bachelor of Science in Elementary Education and American Studies, Western Connecticut State University **A/A/S:** Phi Alpha Theta; Who's Who Among College Students; The National Scholars Honor Society; Connecticut Education Association; National Education Association **C/VW:** Volunteer, After-School Programs; American Cancer Society Relay for Life; Food Drives **DOB:** March 21, 1978 **A/S:** She attributes her success to praying, being positive, staying focused, creating a safe and loving environment for her students, spending time with her family and friends, and working with a dedicated staff. **B/I:** She became involved in her profession because she was influenced by her mother and second-grade teacher. **H/O:** The most gratifying aspects of her career are helping others and teaching young children. It is rewarding to see their eyes sparkle when they learn something. **I/F/Y:** In five years, Ms. Jones intends work in a profession where she can help others.

MARGARET ANN JONES, BS, PO
Police Officer, Peer Support Team Member, Field Training Officer
Warwick Police Department
99 Veterans Memorial Drive
Warwick, RI 02886 United States
MargaretJ143@cs.com
http://www.warwickpd.org

BUS: Police Department **P/S:** Tactical Patrol, Firearms Instructor, SWAT Operator **MA:** Local **D/D/R:** Instructing on Firearms Use, Conducting Field Training, Training Officers to Use Less Lethal Force **H/I/S:** Enjoying Long Distance Cycling and All Outdoor Sports **FBP:** American Police Beat **EDU:** Bachelor of Science in Criminal Justice, Roger Williams University **CERTS:** Certified SWAT Operator; Certified Field Training Officer; Certified Firearms Instructor **A/A/S:** Rhode Island Tactical Officers Association; Former Military Intelligence (Technical) Analyst; Relay for Life; Feinstein Mentoring Program; Special Olympics

NADINE JONES
Human Resources Director (Retired)
Curtis Lumber Co., Inc.
885 Route 67
Ballston Spa, NY 12020 United States
jones@curtislumber.com
http://www.curtislumber.com

BUS: Retail Lumber Company **P/S:** Lumber and Supplies for the Largest Residential Contractor Customer Base in the State, Specialized Wood Imported From Around the World for Custom Design **MA:** Statewide **D/D/R:** Establishing Positive Employee Relations, Recruiting, Maintaining Employee Retention and Benefits, Enforcing Policies and Procedures, Conducting New Hire Orientation and Training **FBP:** HR **EDU:** Bachelor of Business Administration, Davenport Business College **CERTS:** Professional in Human Resources, Davenport Business College **A/A/S:** Judge, Junior Miss New York State Beauty Pageant; Society for Human Resource Management; Capital Regents Association of Human Resources **C/VW:** Participant, Relay for Life, American Cancer Society; American Diabetes Association

Pastor Barbara Lisa Jones

Amherst-Aurora Congregational Church
PO Box 25
Aurora, ME 04428 United States
sonflowergrrl@yahoo.com
http://www.cambridgewhoswho.com

BUS: Religion **P/S:** Ministry **MA:** Local **D/D/R:** Preaching, Leading, Worshipping **H/I/S:** Horseback Riding, Concerts **FBP:** Christian Seminary Magazine **EDU:** Master's Degree, Bangor Theological Seminary **A/A/S:** UCC **C/VW:** Homeless Shelter; Animal Shelter; The Humane Society of the United States **A/S:** She attributes her success to God. **B/I:** She became involved in this profession because it was a calling from God. **H/O:** The highlight of her career is helping people.

Sally Fogg Jones, LRCP, RPSGT

Sleep Disorder Center Manager
St. Clare Hospital
Franciscan Health Systems
11307 Bridgeport Way S.W.
Lakewood, WA 98499 United States
sallyjones@fhshealth.org
http://www.fhshealth.org/location/sch.asp

BUS: Community Hospital **P/S:** Emergency Center, Acute Medical and Surgical Services, Diagnostic Imaging, Laboratory Services, Rehabilitation Services, Sleep Disorders Laboratory, Spiritual Care, Transfusion-Free Medicine and Surgery Program **MA:** Regional **D/D/R:** Managing the Treatment of Sleep Disorders Including Obstructive Sleep Apnea, Supervising 19 Employees in an Eight-Bed Laboratory, Overseeing the AWAKE Group, Assisting in a Laboratory Class for Highline Community College in their Polysomnographic Program **H/I/S:** Gardening, Knitting, Reading **FBP:** APT Journal **EDU:** Associate of Applied Science in Respiratory Care Therapy, Tacoma Community College **CERTS:** Registered Polysomnographic Technologist; Licensed Respiratory Care Practitioner **A/A/S:** American Association for Respiratory Care; Association of Polysomnographic Technologists

THELMA JONES, MD, FACP, FAPA, FMBCCH

Physician
Options for Wellness
397 Grand Boulevard
Scarsdale, NY 10583 United States
docthel@gmail.com
http://www.optionsforwellness.net

BUS: Healthcare Center **P/S:** Healthcare **MA:** Regional **EXP:** Ms. Jones' expertise is in integrative medicine. **H/I/S:** Sports, Swimming, Playing the Piano, Spending Time with her Grandson **EDU:** MD, SUNY Downstate Medical Center; Bachelor's Degree in Pre-Medicine and Psychology, Barnard College, Columbia University, Cum Laude; Diploma, Bronx High School of Science **A/A/S:** Fellow, American College Physicians; American Medical Women's Association; American Medical Association; Fellow, National Board for Certified Clinical Hypnotherapists; Fellow, American Psychotherapy Association **A/S:** She attributes her success to her personality, education and to the motivation she receives from her mother. **B/I:** She became involved in her profession because of her love for working with people and her desire to help them. **H/O:** The most gratifying aspect of her career is seeing her patients recovery.

VICKI L. JONES

Registered Nurse, Intensive Care Specialist
Western Baptist Hospital
2501 Kentucky Avenue
Paducah, KY 42003 United States
vicki_jones_29@excite.com
http://www.westernbaptist.com

BUS: Hospital **P/S:** Healthcare Including Occupational Health and Wellness, Cardiac Services, Children's Services, Diagnostic Imaging Services, Emergency Services, Laboratory Services, Oncology Services, Outpatient Services, Rehabilitation Services, Respiratory Care Services and Surgical Services **MA:** National **D/D/R:** Working with Surgical, Intensive Care Unit, Cardiac Recovery and Open Heart Surgery Patients, Working as an Interpreter of American Sign Language for Deaf Persons and in the Social Services Office, Overseeing and Instructing Critical Care Nursing, Training New Staff Members **H/I/S:** Playing the Piano, Reading, Crocheting, Oil Painting **FBP:** Nursing Management; American Journal of Nursing; Critical Care Nursing **EDU:** Pursuing Master of Science in Nursing; Bachelor of Science in Education, Tennessee Temple University (1976) **CERTS:** Certified Deaf Interpreter (1980) **CHILD:** Michelle, Nicole

W. JACQUE JONES
Administrator of Constituent Services for the Osage Nation
Executive Office and Principal Chiefs
Osage Nation Executive Branch
627 Grandview
Pawhuska, OK 74056 United States
jjones@osagetribe.org
http://www.osagetribe.org

BUS: Government Agency **P/S:** Social Services, WIC, Housing, EPA, Transportation, Education **MA:** Local **D/D/R:** Overseeing All Administrative Duties **H/I/S:** Ceremonial Dancing, Beading Native American Clothing, Creating Osage Ribbon Work **FBP:** Osage News Tribal Newspaper **CERTS:** Certified in Microsoft Office; Certified Business Administrator, Tri County Technical College **A/A/S:** Who's Who Among Business Professionals of America **C/VW:** Osage Language Program; Women and Children in Crisis **POB:** Green Bay **SP:** Shannon **CHILD:** Allison, Jade, Mia, Lily **W/H:** Breastfeeding Coordinator, Osage Nation; Administrative Assistant, Osage Nation Executive Branch; Constituent Services Administrator, Osage Nation **A/S:** She attributes her success to her passion and dedication for serving the Osage people. **B/I:** She became involved in her profession because she always had interest in the field and a desire to help others. **H/O:** The most gratifying aspect of her career is finding and providing available services for all Osage people.

DR. EMMA B. JONES
Bishop, Executive Director
The Church at South Seattle and Koinonia Community Service
3019 S. Angeline Street
Seattle, WA 98108 United States
emma.jones@comcast.net
http://www.koinoniaedu.org

BUS: Church, Community Resource Provider **P/S:** Education **MA:** Local **D/D/R:** Preaching, Teaching, Mentoring **H/I/S:** Writing Music, Writing Books, Making Sound Tracks, Playing for a Choir **FBP:** Computing; Psychology Today **EDU:** Doctor of Theology in Family Counseling, Bishop A.L. Hardy Academy of Theology, Seattle, WA **A/A/S:** National Library of Poetry; American Society of Composers, Authors and Publishers; American Association of Christian Counselors; National Black Achievers Award (1996); Union Gospel Mission

JANE E. JONIETZ, BS
Second Grade Teacher
St. Luke School
1305 Davidson Road
Brookfield, WI 53045 United States
jjonietz@stlukebrookfield.org
http://www.stlukebrookfield.org

BUS: Catholic Elementary School **P/S:** Primary Education **MA:** Regional **D/D/R:** Teaching All Subjects Including Religion, Preparing Students For Their First Holy Communion **H/I/S:** Traveling, Sailing, Counted-Cross Stitching **EDU:** Bachelor of Science in Education, University of Wisconsin-Milwaukee **A/A/S:** Who's Who Among American Teachers; Wisconsin Council for the Social Studies; University of Wisconsin Milwaukee Alumni Association; Milwaukee Archdiocesan Pastoral Council **C/VW:** Volunteer, SHARE **A/S:** She attributes her success to the support she receives from her mentors, her students and their parents. **B/I:** She became involved in her profession because of her interest in school sociology. **H/O:** The most gratifying aspect of her career is seeing her students succeed.

DELPHINE S. JORDAN
Reading and Language Arts Teacher
Westport Traditional Middle School and Fine Arts Academy
8100 Westport Road
Louisville, KY 40222 United States
delphine.jordan@jefferson.kyschools.us
http://www.cambridgewhoswho.com

BUS: School **P/S:** Education **MA:** Local **D/D/R:** Teaching Reading and Remediation, Mentoring Students **H/I/S:** Writing, Western Dancing, Scouting, Camping, Spending Time Outdoors **FBP:** Ebony **EDU:** Master's Degree in Counseling, University of Louisville (2008); Master's Degree in Teaching, Union College, Schenectady, NY (1977) **A/A/S:** Barbados Reading Association; Louisville Credit Union; School Board Council Member; International Reading Association **C/VW:** Associate Chief and Commissioner, Barbados Girl Scout Leader Training; Girl Scouts of the United States of America, Barbados **A/S:** She attributes her success to her love for children and her ability to assist them in achieving their goals. **B/I:** She became involved in her profession because she was inspired by her first-grade teacher and wanted to help people. **H/O:** The most gratifying aspect of her career is working with at-risk children and helping them to stay in school. **I/F/Y:** In five years, Ms. Jordan hopes to get involved in counseling services.

MAUREEN JILL JORDAN, RN-C, BSN
Chief Nurse IV, Assistant Nurse Manager
Cedars-Sinai Medical Center
8700 Beverly Boulevard
West Hollywood, CA 90048 United States
jill.jordan@cshs.org
mjjordan01@sbcglobal.net
http://www.cshs.org

BUS: Nonprofit Acute Care Hospital **P/S:** Healthcare **MA:** Local **D/D/R:** Overseeing the Neonatal Intensive Care Unit **H/I/S:** Practicing Yoga, Golfing, Scrapbooking, Bicycling **FBP:** Neonatal Network Journal **EDU:** Pursuing Master of Science in Nursing, California State University, Los Angeles; Bachelor of Science, California State University **CERTS:** Registered Neonatal Nurse, American College of Obstetricians and Gynecologists; Certified Pediatric Acute Life Support Instructor; Certified Basic Life Support Instructor **A/A/S:** Sigma Theta Tau International **C/VW:** Good Beginnings; Parent Support Network **A/S:** She attributes her success to her ability to care for patients. **B/I:** She became involved in her profession because she found her niche in the healthcare field after working as an intern in the neonatal unit. **H/O:** The highlight of her career was earning her current position.

VANESSA B. JORDAN
Owner, Chief Executive Officer
Jordan Concepts, LLC
5729 Janice Lane
Temple Hills, MD 20748 United States
jordanconcepts@verizon.net
http://www.jordanconceptsllc.com

BUS: Design, Merchandising **P/S:** Graphic Design **MA:** National **EXP:** Ms. Jordan's expertise is in graphic design and leadership. **H/I/S:** Bowling, Painting, Spending Time with Family **A/A/S:** Avon **A/H:** Ranked Number Two in District for Sales (2005)

PAULETTE J. JORGENSON
Registered Nurse, Charge Nurse
Med Center One
300 N. Seventh Street
Bismarck, ND 58501 United States
babyrn@bismidco.net
http://www.cambridgewhoswho.com

BUS: Hospital **P/S:** Healthcare, Patient Care and Services **MA:** Regional **D/D/R:** Nursing, Instructing on Infant Massages, Counseling on Lactation, Serving as a Charge Nurse **H/I/S:** Spending Time with her Two Children, Walking, Camping **FBP:** RN **EDU:** Bachelor's Degree in Nursing, Jamestown College **A/A/S:** Certified Infant Massage Instructor, Certified Lactation Counselor **C/VW:** Seeds of Hope, Church, Local Schools, Parent Teacher Organization **A/S:** She attributes her success to her family's support and to her love of helping others. **B/I:** She became involved in her profession because she is a people person and wanted to help in the medical field since grade school and chose nursing. **H/O:** The highlight of her career was being a preceptor for the new nurses.

GEORGÍNA D. JOYA, RN
Registered Nurse
LAC-USC Medical Center
1200 N. State Street
Los Angeles, CA 90033 United States
http://www.cambridgewhoswho.com

BUS: Healthcare Facility **P/S:** Healthcare **MA:** Local **D/D/R:** Specializing in Critical-Care Nursing, Labor and Delivery **H/I/S:** Traveling, Riding her Motorcycle in the Country **FBP:** Critical-Care Nurse **EDU:** Bachelor of Science in Nursing, California State University, Los Angeles; Bachelor of Science in Microbiology, California State University, Los Angeles **A/A/S:** Recognition Award for 20 Years of Service, American Association of Critical-Care Nurses **A/S:** She attributes her personal and professional success to her determination and dedication. **B/I:** She became involved in her profession after working for a physician as a teenager. **H/O:** The most gratifying aspect of her career is the longevity she has had in her position.

DAVID ROBERT JULIAN, MSW, LSW

School Social Worker
Seaside Heights Elementary
1200 Bay Boulevard
Seaside Heights, NJ 08751 United States
Fireguy3054@aol.com
http://www.cambridgewhoswho.com

BUS: Elementary School **P/S:** Elementary Education **MA:** Local **EXP:** Mr. Julian's expertise is in social work for children and families and special education law. **D/D/R:** Coordinating Special Education Services, Preparing State and Federal Funding Special Education Reports, Assisting with the Completion of the Quality Assurance Annual Report, Acting as the Affirmative Action Officer, Alternative Proficiency Assessment Coordinator, Homeland Security Team Contact and Coordinator of Student Services, Assisting the Principal with Daily Operations Including Attendance, Assemblies, Discipline and Emergency Procedures, Assisting the Assistant Business Administrator with the Special Education Budget **H/I/S:** Playing the Saxophone, Reading, Rooting for the New York Yankees and Dallas Cowboys **FBP:** Education Week; First Responder News **EDU:** Master of Social Work in Policy Planning and Administration, Fordham University **CERTS:** Pursuing Administrative Certification; Certified Firefighter 1; Hazardous Materials Certification; Certification in Operational Multi-Hazard Emergency Planning for Schools, Certification in Weapons of Mass Destruction Awareness; Introduction to Disaster Mental Health and Trauma Counseling Certification; Certified Disaster Response Crisis Counselor **A/A/S:** Future Business Leaders of America; Phi Beta Lambda; New Jersey School Social Workers Association; National Association of School Social Workers **A/H:** Dean's List (1997); Honored Member, Cambridge Who's Who Among Executives and Professionals **C/VW:** Boy Scouts of America; Volunteer, Pleasant Plains Fire Department; Ocean County Fire Police; Jackson Township First Aid Squad; Toms River Office of Emergency Management **DOB:** May 1, 1976 **W/H:** Child Support Enforcement Division, Youth and Family Services Juvenile Justice Commission; Parent Educator, Alternative High School; Consultant; Police, Fire and Emergency Medical Services Dispatcher **A/S:** He attributes his success to his mother's support, instilling in him that he could be anything he aspires to be. **H/O:** The highlight of his career was placing a four-year-old child for the New Jersey Department of Children's Services.

ROBIN L. JUNG

Staff Nurse
West Bay Rehabilitation and Nursing Center
3865 Tampa Road
Oldsmar, FL 34677 United States
http://www.cambridgewhoswho.com

BUS: Healthcare **P/S:** Rehabilitation and Nursing Home Care **MA:** Local **EXP:** Ms. Jung's expertise is in geriatric care. **FBP:** Nursing2009 **CERTS:** Licensed Practical Nurse **C/VW:** Humane Society of the United States, Disabled American Veterans **A/S:** She attributes her success to working one on one with people and being a patient advocate. **H/O:** The highlight of her career is the respect she receives from her superiors.

SHELLY A. JUSKIEWICZ
Pastor to Women
Mariners Church
5001 Newport Coast
Irvine, CA 92603 United States
sjuskiewicz@marinerschurch.org
http://www.marinerschurch.org

BUS: Church **P/S:** Religious Services **MA:** Local **D/D/R:** Helping Women Emotionally and Spiritually, Managing Programs for New Believers, Conducting Meetings, Teaching Weekly Bible Classes **H/I/S:** Traveling, Snowboarding, Reading, Running **FBP:** Harvard Business Review; Leadership **EDU:** Bachelor of Arts in Economics, University of Southern California **A/A/S:** Board of Directors, Miracle Ranch Children's Home **C/VW:** Local Church **A/S:** She attributes her success to the support she received from her family to develop her creativity skills. **B/I:** She became involved in her profession because she found her niche in religious services. **H/O:** The most gratifying aspects of her career are being the first woman on the executive team at her church and being involved in decision-making at the executive level. **I/F/Y:** In five years, Ms. Juskiewicz hopes to publish one or two books and complete her book on curriculum.

REBECCA RUBY KAAMINO
Clinical Chemist Scientist, Manager Immunochemistry
Immunology, Spectra Laboratories
48818 Kato Road
Department of Immunology
Fremont, CA 94538 United States
ruby.kaamino@fmc-na.com
http://www.spectralabs.com

BUS: Leaders in the Clinical Chemistry Industry **P/S:** Specialized Testing Services, Industry-Leading Software and Clinical Research Capabilities that Assist Hospitals, Dialysis Clinics and other Medical Facilities **MA:** National **EXP:** Ms. Kaamino's expertise is in technology and administration. **D/D/R:** Managing 28 Employees Directly, Validating Tests Before In-House, Making Recommendations Based on Study Analysis, Conducting Quality Control for Patient's Tests, Researching Hepatitis, HIV, PTH, Therapeutic Drugs, and Thyroid Functions, Investigating an Efficient Antigen to Use Against Hepatitis C **H/I/S:** Football, Reading **FBP:** Nephrology Magazine; CAP Today **EDU:** Graduate Coursework in Immunochemistry; Bachelor's Degree in Medical Technology, Far Eastern University, Philippines, Manila (1973) **CERTS:** Licensed Clinical Chemist Scientist (1983); Licensed Medical Technologist, State of New York (1974) **A/A/S:** American Association for Clinical Chemistry; CAMCT; American Society for Clinical Laboratory Science

HELEN KAGAN, PH.D., LCSW
Wellness Consultant
New York Healing; Wellness World, Inc.
PO Box 630853
Miami, FL 33163 United States
elkaheal@yahoo.com
http://www.nyhealing.com; http://www.wellnessproworld.com

BUS: Wellness **P/S:** Wellness Services and Products **MA:** National **EXP:** Ms. Kagan's expertise includes psychotherapy counseling, holistic therapy healing, spiritual counseling and substance abuse. **H/I/S:** Dancing, Jogging, Biking, Yoga, Painting, Music, Martial Arts, Cooking, Hiking, Dogs, Travel, the Arts, Wellness **FBP:** Prevention Magazine **EDU:** Master of Science, St. Petersburg University, Russia; Ph.D. in Science, Novosibirsk University, Russia; Master of Arts in Psychology, St. Petersburg State University, Russia; Master of Social Work, Adelphi University, NY **CERTS:** Nationally Certified Polarity Practitioner, American Polarity Therapy Association; Certified and Ordained Spiritual Counselor, IM School of Healing Arts, NY **A/A/S:** NASW; National Polarity Association **B/I:** She became involved in her profession because she felt it was her destiny to help people in betterment of their lives.

CARRIE W. KAHN
Executive Dean of Workforce Development
Erie Community College
4140 Southwestern, Bldg. 7
Orchard Park, NY 14127 United States
kahn@ecc.edu
http://www.ecc.edu

BUS: Community College **P/S:** Higher Education **MA:** Regional **D/D/R:** Managing Four Divisions Including Workforce Investment Services, Community Service, Corporate Training and Driver Transportation **H/I/S:** Traveling, Reading Cook Books, Spending Time with her Family **FBP:** Harvard Business Review; The New York Times; The Wall Street Journal **EDU:** Coursework in Entrepreneurial Leadership, University at Buffalo (2004); Master's Degree in Marketing and Management, University at Buffalo **A/A/S:** Buffalo Niagra Partnership Leadership Education; Continuing Education Association of New York; National Council for Workforce Education; American Association of Community Colleges; Advanced Leadership Institute

ANDRENE KAIWI-LENTING, M.ED.
Assistant Director of Student Life and Leadership
California Polytechnic State University
University Union 217
San Luis Obispo, CA 93407 United States
akaiwile@calpoly.edu
http://www.calpoly.edu

BUS: Nationally Ranked Four-Year Comprehensive Public University **P/S:** Undergraduate Programs, Graduate Programs, Continuing Education, Special Programs and Projects **D/D/R:** Arranging Student Orientation, Setting up New Student Programs, Supervising Other Student Program Coordinators **H/I/S:** Gardening **EDU:** Master's Degree in Education, California Polytechnic State University (2006); Bachelor's Degree in Home Economics, California Polytechnic State University (1991) **A/A/S:** National Orientation Directors Association; American College Personnel Association

GLENDA L. KAMINSKI
Clinical Nurse Specialist
Oncology
Lakeland Regional Medical Center
1324 Lakeland Hills Boulevard
Lakeland, FL 33805 United States
glenda.kaminski@lrmc.com
http://www.lrmc.com

BUS: Medical Center **P/S:** Healthcare Services in All Medical Specialties **MA:** Regional **EXP:** Ms. Kaminski's expertise includes oncology and infusion therapy nursing. **D/D/R:** Assessing and Consulting with Complex Patients from Various Disciplines, Coaching and Mentoring Staff Nurses, Educating the Staff and Community about Cancer-Related Issues **H/I/S:** Spending Quality Time with her Family, Going to the Movies **FBP:** Oncology Nursing Forum **EDU:** Pursuing Ph.D. in Nursing, Barry University; Master of Nursing in Oncology, University of South Florida (1991); Registered Nurse, St. Francis General Hospital, Pittsburgh, PA (1983) **CERTS:** Certified Infusion Registered Nurse; Advanced Oncology Certified Nurse **A/A/S:** Sigma Theta Tau International Honor Society of Nursing; Imperial Polk Florida Chapter, Infusion Nurses Society, Oncology Nursing Society **A/H:** Volunteer Hope Award, American Cancer Society; Nurse of Hope Award, American Cancer Society **C/VW:** Breast Health Educator and Trainer, American Cancer Society; Co-Facilitator, Cancer Dialogue Support Group; Education Consultant, Support Group, The Leukemia & Lymphoma Society **SP:** Stephen **CHILD:** Katie, Holly, Kimberly **W/H:** Lakeland Regional Medical Center, FL (1992-Present); H. Lee Moffitt Cancer Center & Research Institute, Tampa, FL (1986-1992) **A/S:** She attributes her success to the inspiration and learning opportunities she received from various people throughout her life. **B/I:** She became involved in her profession when she was recruited at graduation to the oncology unit at St. Francis Hospital.

CHRISTINA KANG
Founder
Paradigm Art
112 W. 18th Street
Suite 5A
New York, NY 10011 United States
info@paradigmart.com
http://www.paradigmart.com

BUS: Art Consulting Firm **P/S:** Contemporary Art and Art Education **MA:** International **D/D/R:** Finding Talented Artists, Promoting and Contacting Artists **H/I/S:** Traveling, Movies, Yoga **FBP:** The New York Times; Financial Times **EDU:** Master's Degree in Visual Arts Administration, New York University **A/A/S:** Ivy League Club; Harvard Business Club; Manhattan Chamber of Commerce **C/VW:** World Vision **A/S:** She attributes her success to her generosity with various causes. **B/I:** She became involved in art because her parents are art collectors and she has always been surrounded by it. **H/O:** The highlight of her career has been helping women in the industry.

DAWN M. KANOHO
Realtor Associate
Eric M. Watanabe Realty, Inc.
98-030 Hekaha Street
Suite 12
Aiea, HI 96701 United States
dwatanabe@emwrealty.com
http://www.emwrealty.com

BUS: Full Service Real Estate Agency **P/S:** Representing Buyers and Sellers of Residential Properties **MA:** Local **D/D/R:** Focusing on Residential Properties for First-Time Buyers and Investors, Assisting Clients from Marketing to Closing **H/I/S:** Playing Keyboard, Saxophone and Vocals in her Family's Band **FBP:** Money; Fortune **EDU:** Bachelor of Science in Elementary Education, University of Hawai'i

MS. MORGAN KAPNECK
Vice President, Co-Founder
Continental Carpet-Tile-Marble
1964 N.E. Fifth Avenue
Boca Raton, FL 33432 United States
grandmizner@aol.com
http://www.cambridgewhoswho.com

BUS: Retail Floor Coverings **P/S:** Floor Coverings Including Marble, Tile, Wood, Granite, Carpet, Decorating Services **MA:** Regional **EXP:** Ms. Kapneck's expertise is in interior design and customer service. **D/D/R:** Offering High Quality Products and Workmanship Including Custom Flooring, Marble, Granite, Tile, Wood and Carpeting **H/I/S:** Tennis, Boating, Skiing **FBP:** Architectural Digest; W Magazine **EDU:** Bachelor of Science in Rhetoric and Communication, Emerson College; Graduate Coursework in Communications, Kent State University **A/A/S:** Emerson College Alumni Association; Kappa Gamma Chi **CHILD:** Elissa, Dylan

ISMAIL J. KARIM, PH.D.
Chief of Staff, Architecture Supervisor
Bechtel
50 Beale Street
San Francisco, CA 94105 United States
ijkarim@bechtel.com
http://www.bechtel.com

BUS: Architecture Firm **P/S:** Engineering and Construction Management Services **MA:** International **EXP:** Mr. Karim's expertise includes engineering management and the functional review of architecture. **H/I/S:** Walking, Reading, Listening to the News **EDU:** Ph.D. in Architecture, Technical University of Berlin; Master of Engineering, Budapest Technical University, Budapest, Hungary; Bachelor's Degree, The American University of Afghanistan, Kabul **CERTS:** Certification in Royal British Architecture, Hong Kong; Licensed in General Construction **A/A/S:** Oregon Department of Transportation; RBIA; CSI **A/H:** Award of Excellence for Design Coordination, Disney (1987) **A/S:** He attributes his success to his dedication, education and goal-oriented attitude. **B/I:** He became involved in his profession because he was encouraged by a professor who believed he had the potential to be successful in engineering. **I/F/Y:** In five years, Mr. Karim hopes to open his own business.

DR. JOSHUA A. KATZ
Physician, Director
Montgomery Colorectal Surgery, LLC
9715 Medical Center Drive
Suite 233
Rockville, MD 20850 United States
jakatz@mcrsllc.com
http://www.mcrsllc.com

BUS: Clinic **P/S:** Healthcare Including Colorectal Surgery **MA:** Regional **D/D/R:** Treating Patients with Colorectal, Inflammatory Bowel and Anorectal Disease, Incontinence and Constipation, Colon and Rectal Cancer **H/I/S:** Studying History, Spending Time with his Family, Traveling **FBP:** British Journal of Surgery; Diseases of the Colon and Rectum **EDU:** Fellowship in Colorectal Surgery, Cleveland Clinic, FL (2002); Residency, Bellevue Hospital Center, New York University (2000); Fellowship in Surgical Metabolism, Weill Cornell Medical Center (1997); MD, Weill Medical College of Cornell University (1993); Bachelor of Arts, Major in Chemistry and History, Yale University (1989) **C/VW:** Crohn's & Colitis Foundation of America; National Association for Continence **A/S:** He attributes his success to his determination, perseverance, love for his profession and to the support he receives from his family. **B/I:** He became involved in his profession because he was fascinated by colorectal surgery. **H/O:** The highlight of his career was establishing his own medical practice.

JOAN M. KAUP
Vice President, Business Development
Iacono Productions
412 Central Avenue
Cincinnati, OH 45202 United States
joan@iaconoproductions.com
http://www.iaconoproductions.com

BUS: Media Communication Company **P/S:** Creative Audio Visual, Production, Design, Lighting, Writing Scripts, Video Power Point, Project Management **MA:** International **D/D/R:** Overseeing Marketing and Sales, Managing Projects, Creating Solutions and Action Plans **EDU:** Master of Business Administration, Xavier University; Bachelor of Science in Marketing, University of Cincinnati **A/A/S:** International Association CCD; International DT Association; Over the Reign, Chamber of Commerce

SUSAN R. KAY, MS
Administrator
Planned Giving and Endowments
Jewish Federation of Palm Beach County
4601 Community Drive
West Palm Beach, FL 33417 United States
skayinwpb@bellsouth.net
http://www.jewishpalmbeach.org

BUS: Nonprofit Community Service Organization **P/S:** Community Services such as Volunteering, Fundraising, Leadership Development and Education **MA:** Regional **D/D/R:** Working with Computers, Teaching Microsoft Office Programs, Handling Funds, Managing Operations, Processing Checks **H/I/S:** Golfing, Walking, Reading, Knitting, Photography **FBP:** PC World **EDU:** Master's Degree in Information and Communications Sciences, Ball State University; Bachelor of Science in Home Economics, University at Buffalo **CERTS:** Certification in Microsoft Office Programs **C/VW:** American Cancer Society **DOB:** August 23, 1945 **POB:** Brooklyn **A/S:** She attributes her success to her caring nature. **B/I:** She became involved in her profession because she wanted to work with people. **H/O:** The highlight of her career was receiving her master's degree.

MS. MARY E. KEARIN
Client Information Paralegal
Mayer Brown LLP
230 S. La Salle Street
Eighth Floor
Chicago, IL 60604 United States
marykearin@msn.com
http://www.mayerbrownrowe.com

BUS: Global Law Firm **P/S:** Legal Services **MA:** International **D/D/R:** Maintaining Contact with Attorneys for Engagement Letters and Waivers from Clients, Reviewing and Profiling Letters for Conformity with Firm Policies **H/I/S:** International Traveling, Listening to Classical Music, Walking, Fine Arts **EDU:** Master's Degree in Library and Information Science, Dominican University; Ph.D. in Humanities, Concentration in English, Florida State University; Master of Arts in Humanities, Concentration in English, Florida State University; Bachelor of Arts in Humanities, Concentration in English, Florida State University **CERTS:** Generalist Paralegal Certificate, Roosevelt University **W/H:** Paralegal, Illinois Bankers Association; Second Lieutenant, Military Intelligence, United States Army; English Professor, Morris College, SC; Loan Documentation Preparer; Bank Reviewer

SARAH KECK
Vice President
American Nutraceuticals, Inc.
1920 Northgate Boulevard
Suite A5
Sarasota, FL 34234 United States
sarah@888vitality.com
http://www.888vitality.com

BUS: Manufacturing Company **P/S:** Health Food Products Including Vitamins and Supplements **MA:** International **D/D/R:** Overseeing Office Operations, Developing Products, Ensuring Customer Service, Monitoring Patient Protocols, Accounting **H/I/S:** Playing Golf, Photography, Hiking, Spending Time with Friends and Family **FBP:** Natural Solutions Magazine **EDU:** Bachelor's Degree in Biology, Oglethorpe University, Atlanta, GA (1998)

DENISE O. KEELING
1) Special Education Coordinator 2) Owner
1) District of Columbia Public Schools Drew Elementary 2) O-So Nice
1401 Michigan Avenue N.E.
Washington, DC 20017 United States
doknice@rcn.com
http://www.cambridgewhoswho.com

BUS: 1) School District 2) Catering Service Company **P/S:** 1) Education 2) Food Services for all Events **MA:** 1) Local 2) Local **EXP:** Ms. Keeling's expertise is in social work. **D/D/R:** Meeting Counselors, Parents and Students to Determine Eligibility, Counseling, Chairing Meetings, Conducting Training Workshop and Resolution Meetings with Attorneys, Training the School Staff, Assessing the Social Service and special Education Needs of Kindergarten through Sixth-Grade Students **H/I/S:** Traveling, Playing Softball **FBP:** Council for Exceptional Children Publications **EDU:** Educational Specialist Degree, George Washington University (2007); Master of Social Work, Catholic University (1986) **A/A/S:** Council for Exceptional Children; National Council of Negro Women; National Association of Social Workers; Alpha Kappa Alpha

HELEN KEISER-PEDERSEN, RN, BSN, RVT
Registered Nurse
Department of Vascular Surgery
Yale University, School of Medicine
333 Cedar Street, FMB 137
New Haven, CT 06510 United States
helen.pedersen@yale.edu
http://www.yale.edu

BUS: University **P/S:** Higher Education Including Research **MA:** Local **EXP:** Ms. Keiser-Pedersen's expertise is in vascular technology. **H/I/S:** Reading, Traveling **EDU:** Bachelor of Science in Nursing, University of Miami, Coral Gables, FL, Cum Laude (1984) **CERTS:** Certified Vascular Technologist, American Registry for Diagnostic Sonography (1986); Certification in Medical and Surgical Nursing, Ocean County College, Toms River, NJ (1973) **A/A/S:** Society of Vascular Nurses; Society for Vascular Ultrasound **C/VW:** Catholic Relief Services; Food for the Poor; Community Service **A/S:** She attributes her success to her optimism. **B/I:** She became involved in her profession because she felt it was her calling. **H/O:** The most gratifying aspect of her career is helping her patients. **I/F/Y:** In five years, Ms. Keiser-Pedersen hopes to retire and plans to look for opportunities to involve herself in healthcare issues for the poor and disadvantaged.

SUZANNE R. KELLAM, RN
Registered Nurse, Burn Clinician
Sentara Norfolk General Hospital, Burn Clinic
Sentara Health Systems
600 Gresham Drive
Norfolk, VA 23507 United States
srkellam@sentara.com
http://www.sentara.com

BUS: Hospital **P/S:** Healthcare Including Level I Trauma Center, Breast Center, eICU, Emergency and Trauma Care, Genital and Pelvic Reconstruction, Cardiac Care, Hospital for Extended Recovery, Imaging, Minimally Invasive Surgery, Neuroscience, Nightingale Air Ambulance Service, Robotic Surgery, Sleep Disorders Center, Stroke Center, Transplant Center, Vascular and Weight Loss Surgery **MA:** Regional **D/D/R:** Treating Inpatient and Outpatient Burns, Coordinating Care, Evaluating, Working under Trauma Physicians, Teaching Burn Care Education, Wound Care and Nursing Protocols, Lecturing **H/I/S:** Spending Time with her Son, Watching Basketball and Soccer **EDU:** Pursuing Bachelor of Science in Nursing, Jacksonville University **CERTS:** Registered Nurse, Sentara Norfolk General Hospital (1990); Diploma, St. Mary's Academy, Alexandria, VA (1982); Certified Trauma Nurse

CHRISTINA L. KELLER
Human Resources Manager
Sturgill Chrysler Dodge Jeep, Inc.
169 Conowingo Road
Conowingo, MD 21918 United States
ckeller.sturgills@hotmail.com
http://www.sturgillchrysler.com

BUS: Privately Owned Car Dealership Dedicated to Excellence in the Automobile Industry **P/S:** New and Used Cars, Service, Parts **MA:** Regional **D/D/R:** Handling Personnel Management, Medical and Dental Benefits, Payroll, Accounts Payable and Receivable, Working on the Financial Side of the Automotive Business **H/I/S:** Scrapbooking, Outdoor Activities, Hiking, Camping **EDU:** Pursuing Bachelor's Degree in Human Resources, Cecil Community College **DOB:** June 4, 1981

JENNIFER L. KELLEY
Project Leader
Sanofi Aventis
9 Great Valley Parkway
Malvern, PA 19355 United States
jennifer.kelley@sanofi-aventis.com
http://www.sanofi-aventis.com

BUS: Healthcare and Pharmaceutical Company **P/S:** Research and Development to Design and Develop New Effective and Well-Tolerated Medicines for Therapeutic Challenges **MA:** International **EXP:** Ms. Kelley's expertise is in clinical data management. **H/I/S:** Reading, Running, Traveling **FBP:** Clinical Trials **EDU:** Master of Business Administration, University of Phoenix; Bachelor of Science, University of Michigan **A/A/S:** Society for Clinical Data Management; Drug Information Association; DAA **C/VW:** Local Fire Department; Local Police Department; Leukemia & Lymphoma Society; Diamonds for Dogs, Biden Breast Health Initiative; Student Drinking and Driving Education **A/S:** She attributes her success to hard work and commitment. **B/I:** She became involved in her profession because she was interested in the field. **H/O:** The most gratifying aspect of her career is seeing people she has mentored succeed.

Virginia L. Kelley, BSEd.
Childcare Director
Carlisle Family YMCA Child Development Center
311 S.W. Street
Carlisle, PA 17013 United States
http://www.cambridgewhoswho.com

BUS: Child Services **P/S:** Day Care Services to Youth from Six months to Five Years Old **MA:** Local **D/D/R:** Overseeing All Aspects of Program Planning and Development, Programming for Kindergarten Including Swimming and Library Time **H/I/S:** Spending Time With her Husband, Outdoor Activities, Writing, Music **FBP:** Early Child Education **EDU:** Bachelor's Degree in Education, Shippensburg University (1996) **A/A/S:** Newburg United Methodist Church; National Association for the Education of Young Children; Lifetime Member, Girl Scouts; Church Choir **SP:** Norman **W/H:** Camp Counselor; Pre-K Teacher English Teacher; Social Studies Teacher; Daycare Director; Bank Teller

Alyson J. Kelly, RN, CCRN
Assistant Director of Nursing
Eddy Ford Nursing Home
421 Columbia Street
Cohoes, NY 12047 United States
kellya@nehealth.com
http://www.cambridgewhoswho.com

BUS: Nursing Home **P/S:** Long-Term Care and Rehabilitation **MA:** Local **D/D/R:** Geriatric Nursing, Working in Long-Term Care in a 122 Bed Facility **H/I/S:** Walking, Hiking, Watching Movies, Spending Time with her Family **FBP:** Registered Nurse; Advance for Nurses; Long-Term Care **EDU:** Bachelor of Science in Nursing, Villanova University (1986) **A/A/S:** New York State Head Start Association **C/VW:** Schenectady Food Bank; Volunteer, Alzheimer's Association **B/I:** She became involved in the profession because she was always interested in science and wanted to help provide care for others. **H/O:** The most gratifying aspect of her career is making a difference in people's lives and having the ability to work as an advocate for her patients.

JOAN KELLY
Owner
Dancesteps Etc.
24 Buck Street Extension
Epsom, NH 03234 United States
joan108@gmail.com
http://www.dancesteps-etc.com

BUS: Dance Studio **MA:** Teaching Dance **EXP:** Ms. Kelly's expertise is in classical ballet. **EDU:** Bachelor's Degree, University of New Hampshire **A/A/S:** Royal Academy of Dance; Dance Masters of America **C/VW:** Local Theater **A/S:** She attributes her career success to her passion and love of her profession. **B/I:** She was taught dance by her father, who is a dance instructor, and followed in his footsteps by opening her studio. **H/O:** The most gratifying aspect of her career is being able to teach the children of her former students .

SHERRY J. KELLY
Division Chief, Special Security Officer
6002 Waterman Drive
Fredericksburg, VA 22407 United States
jai_64@hotmail.com
http://www.cambridgewhoswho.com

BUS: Government Organization **P/S:** Public Services, Safety Programs **MA:** Local **D/D/R:** Overseeing Security Operations **H/I/S:** Playing Racquetball **FBP:** Education **EDU:** Doctoral Degree, Old Dominion University; Master's Degree in Education, Old Dominion University

HOLLI L. KEMMER
Realtor
Lighthouse Realty
PO Box 431
Ocean Park, WA 98640 United States
hkemmer@lighthouseproperty.com
http://www.lighthouseproperty.com

BUS: Proven Leader in the Real Estate Industry, Co-Operating Brokerage **P/S:** Wide Variety of the Highest Quality of Real Estate Services to Clients Including but not Limited to Home Buying and Selling **MA:** Washington and Oregon **D/D/R:** Listing and Selling Residential, Commercial and Investment Properties, Arranging Profiles for Clients, Handling All Paperwork, Assisting Buyers throughout the Entire Process, Negotiating **H/I/S:** Camping, Recreational Sports, Coaching T-Ball, Volunteering in the Community **FBP:** Realtor **EDU:** Coursework in Education, Clark Community College **CERTS:** Licensed in Real Estate (2006) **A/A/S:** Bluegrass Festival Committee; National Association of Realtors; Washington Association of Realtors; Cowlitz County Association of Realtors; Regional Multiple Listing Service; Northwest Multiple Listing Service; Board Member, Boys and Girls Clubs of America **DOB:** January 27, 1973 **SP:** Chuck **CHILD:** Taylor, Jaymi, Carli

SANDRA R. KEMPER, RDH
Executive Director
Smiles Forever
10914 Rainier Avenue S
Seattle, WA 98178 United States
sandykemper@smileforever.org
http://www.206-smilesforver.org

BUS: Nonprofit Dental Hygiene Vocational Training for Indigenous Women in Cochabamba, Bolivia **P/S:** Vocational Training for Women to Become Dental Hygienists and Leaders in the Community **MA:** International **EXP:** Ms. Kemper's expertise is in dental hygiene and the organization of local facilities. **H/I/S:** Water Skiing, Skiing, Traveling **FBP:** Time **EDU:** Bachelor of Science in Dental Hygiene, University of Iowa **A/A/S:** Eastern University; Washington State Dental Association; Washington State Dental Hygienists' Association; Dental Hygiene Program, Eastern Washington University **C/VW:** Smiles Forever **A/S:** She attributes her success to family and friends continued support. **B/I:** She chose the profession because she wanted to be in the medical industry since she was a child. She enjoys helping others, especially within the community. **H/O:** The highlight of her career was seeing her first class graduate.

NATALIE J. KENDRICK
Owner
Jenna's House of Christian Child Care and Preschool
39 Calla Court
Oakley, CA 94561 United States
natygurl@yahoo.com
http://www.cambridgewhoswho.com

BUS: Day Care Center **P/S:** Child Care, Primary Education **MA:** Regional **D/D/R:** Working with Young Children, Supporting Families, Fundraising, Organizing Community Outreach and Christian-Based Programs **EDU:** Pursuing Bachelor's Degree in Child Psychology and Child Development, Los Medanos College **CERTS:** Certification in CPR; Certification in First Aid Procedures; Certification in Infant Specialty Training; Certification in Business Communication; Certification in Time Management; Certification in Infant Visual Stimulation; Certification in Play Through Learning **A/A/S:** Contra Costa Child Care Council; Lions Club, City of Oakley **C/VW:** Local Charitable Organizations; Volunteer, Sudden Infant Death Syndrome Awareness Program; St. Jude Trike-A-Thon **DOB:** January 9, 1961 **POB:** Sacramento, California **CHILD:** Michael, Shawn, Kenneth, Jenna

JANETTE L. KENNEDY
Third and Fourth Grade Teacher (Retired)
South-Western City Schools
3646 Richard Avenue
Grove City, OH 43123 United States
jkennedy006@columbus.rr.com
http://www.swcs.k12.oh.us

BUS: Local City School District **P/S:** Educational Program Striving to Meet the Educational Needs of a Diverse Population of Learners **MA:** Local **D/D/R:** Teaching Third through Fifth Grades in Multi-Age Classes, Working as a Substitute Teacher, Coordinating the Intervention Assistance Team, Making Recommendations, Writing Reports, Tutoring Children in Reading and Mathematics **H/I/S:** Reading, Making Jewelry, Volunteering at a School Working with Special Needs Children **EDU:** Graduate Coursework in Education, Concentration in Reading, Mathematics and English as a Second Language; Bachelor's Degree in Education, Ohio University, Athens (1971) **A/A/S:** Reading Recovery; Coordinator, Intervention Assistance Team; Collaborator, Reading Program, Ohio State University **A/H:** Various Awards through the School District; Martha Holden Jennings Teacher Award-1993

SHARON KENNEDY-KELLER
President
Keller Construction Group, Inc.
315 Montana Avenue
Nokomis, FL 34275 United States
teamtiebeam@verizon.net
http://www.kellerconstruction.com

BUS: Construction Company Dedicated to Providing Quality Services **P/S:** Masonry, Structural Concrete and New Construction Services, Renovations, Site Evaluations, Design **MA:** Florida **D/D/R:** Overseeign Operations and Management, Handling Insurance, Investments, Construction and Taxes, Dealing with Residential and Commercial Properties, Conducting Occupational Safety and Health Administration Training **H/I/S:** Working Out, Scuba Diving, Fishing **FBP:** Concrete News; Travel **EDU:** Bachelor's Degree in Computer Science, University of Florida (1985) **A/A/S:** Gulf Gate Church; Special Olympics; American Red Cross; The Salvation Army **SP:** Joseph **CHILD:** Joseph

LISA M. KENNIS
Human Resources Generalist
All-Pak, Inc.
1195 Washington Pike
Bridgeville, PA 15017 United States
kennisl@all-pak.com
http://www.all-pak.com

BUS: Packaging Company **P/S:** Glass, Metal and Plastic Packaging **MA:** International **D/D/R:** Overseeing Human Resources Including Recruiting and Payroll **H/I/S:** Golfing **FBP:** HR **EDU:** Bachelor's Degree in Psychology, The Pennsylvania State University **A/A/S:** Society for Human Resource Management, Pittsburgh Human Resource Association **A/S:** She attributes her career success to her thirst for knowledge. **B/I:** She pursued a career in human resources because she enjoys working with and helping other people. **H/O:** She feels that her current education level is the highlight of her career.

NORMA RAMÍREZ KENT
Nutrition Director
Harvard Street Neighborhood Health Center
632 Blue Hill Avenue
Boston, MA 02121 United States
norma.kent@harvardstreet.org
http://www.cambridgewhoswho.com

BUS: Health Center **P/S:** Healthcare **MA:** Local **EXP:** Ms. Kent's expertise includes diabetic nutrition, dialysis, periodontal disease, Hepatitis C and eating disorders. **FBP:** Christian Today **EDU:** Master's Degree in Nutrition **A/A/S:** American Diabetes Association **C/VW:** Diabetes Association, Project Red to Combat Hunger **A/S:** She attributes her success to loving her job. **B/I:** She became involved in her profession through a natural progression of positions. **H/O:** The most gratifying aspect of her career is taking care of others and helping them feel better.

MILLIE G. KEPLER, CRS, GRI
Broker Associate, Realtor
Koenig and Strey GMAC
100 N. Milwaukee Avenue
Libertyville, IL 60048 United States
mkepler@ksgmac.com
http://www.ksgmac.com

BUS: Real Estate Agency **P/S:** Real Estate Sales and Brokerage, Residential, Executive and Hi-End Properties, Condos, Town Homes, Golf Homes, Gated and Horse Properties **MA:** National **D/D/R:** Constructing New Properties, Relocating Clients, Acting as a Buyer Broker, Selling Residential and Executive Homes, Condos, Golf Homes Gated and Horse Properties **H/I/S:** Spending Time with her Children and Grandchildren, Biking and Walking Along the Beach **FBP:** Money **A/A/S:** Illinois Association of Realtors; National Association of Realtors; Hospital Auxiliary **A/H:** Founders Award, President's Club; United Methodist Church

MELISSA L. KERESZTES-FISCHER, RN

Registered Nurse
University of Michigan
E. Medical Center Drive
Ann Arbor, MI 48109 United States
ffischer@mvfi.com
http://www.umich.edu

BUS: Proven Leader in the Education and Healthcare Industry **P/S:** University Research Hospital, Teaching Institute, Cardiovascular and Cancer Center, Children's Hospital **MA:** Ann Arbor **D/D/R:** Offering Cardiovascular Services **H/I/S:** Spending Time with her New Daughter, Downhill Skiing **FBP:** Critical-Care Nurse **EDU:** Bachelor's Degree in Nursing, Madonna University, Livonia, Michigan (2001) **A/A/S:** Sigma Theta Tau International; American Heart Association; Susan G. Komen Breast Cancer Foundation; Avon Breast Cancer Walk

HOPE R. KERKOF

President
Coast Capital Mortgage Group, Inc.
8524 10th Avenue N.W.
Bradenton, FL 34209 United States
hkerkof@tampabay.rr.com
http://www.coastcapitalmortgagegroup.com

BUS: Mortgage Company **P/S:** Mortgages Lending, Refinance and Financial Consulting Services **MA:** Regional **D/D/R:** Assisting Brokers, Putting Together Loans for Clients, Dealing with IRA Non-Recourse Loans **H/I/S:** Caring for her Dog **FBP:** The Wall Street Journal **EDU:** Bachelor's Degree in Organizational Communication, University of Central Florida (1994) **A/A/S:** Florida Association of Mortgage Brokers; Better Business Bureau; National Association of Mortgage Brokers; Who's Who in Business

MR. ROBERT D. KERNS
President
Transplant Technologies, LLC
kernsrobert@bellsouth.net
http://www.cambridgewhoswho.com

BUS: Medical Consulting Firm **P/S:** Medical Consulting Services, Transplant Medicine, Organ Procurement, Staffing and Education for Agencies **MA:** International **EXP:** Mr. Kerns' expertise is in operations management and the use of technology in the transplant clinical environment. **H/I/S:** Teaching Scuba Diving **FBP:** Journal of Transplantation; New England Journal of Medicine **A/A/S:** Professional Association of Diving Instructors; North American Transplant Coordinators Organization; American Heart Association; Lambda Chi Alpha **A/S:** He attributes his success to his integrity and dedication.

TERESA KERRIGAN
Managing Partner
1) Impact Consultancy Group 2) Congrats Books, Inc.
Plantation, FL United States
tkerrigan@impactconsultancygroup.com
http://www.impactconsultancygroup.com

BUS: 1) Consulting Firm 2) Publishing Company **P/S:** 1) Business Development Consulting Services, Leadership Training and Exceptional Telephone Skills Training 2) Books **MA:** 1) National 2) International **EXP:** Ms. Kerrigan's expertise is in performance development and appraisals. **D/D/R:** Managing All Aspects of Corporate Training Including Task and Soft Skills Training, Food and Beverage Services, Implementing and Developing Programs, Overseeing Management Training and Hospitality Services, Mentoring Teachers of English for Speakers of Foreign Languages **H/I/S:** Spending Time with her Family, Traveling **FBP:** Entrepreneur **EDU:** Coursework in Psychology and Sociology, Earned in England; Diploma in Hotel Management, Austria, with Honors; Diploma in Teaching English as a Foreign Language, Earned in Dublin; Diploma in Teaching English to Speakers of other Languages, Earned in London **CERTS:** Certified Train-the-Trainer; Basic Safety and Firefighting Training; Critical Incident Distress Training; Certification in Crisis Management; Certified Crowd Control Officer; Coaching Skills Training **A/A/S:** Teachers of English to Speakers of Other Languages; The National Speakers Association; American Society for Training and Development; National Association of Professional Women **A/H:** Employee Development Award, University of North Florida (2006); Corporate University Best in Class Award (2004-2005); Honorable Mention Award (2004); Employee Excellence Award, University of North Florida; Corporate University Best in Class Award, Best Mature Corporate University; Runner-Up, Most Innovative Industry Resources **C/VW:** Local Charitable Organizations **A/S:** She attributes her success to her focused nature, her personal drive and her passion for her work. **B/I:** She became involved in her profession through a natural progression of opportunities.

ANNE A. KETZER, MAOM, BSN, RNC
Registered Nurse, Legal Nurse Consultant
Anne Ketzer Consulting
7920 Elizabeth Street
Cincinnati, OH 45231 United States
aketzer@aol.com
http://www.cambridgewhoswho.com

BUS: Legal Services, Healthcare **P/S:** Advisory Services, Expert Witness, Acute Care, Risk Management **MA:** National **EXP:** Ms. Ketzer's expertise is in medical-surgical nursing. **H/I/S:** Singing in the Church Choir, Traveling **FBP:** Nursing Management **EDU:** Master's Degree in Organizational Management, University of Phoenix; Bachelor of Science in Nursing, Miami University **A/A/S:** Sigma Theta Tau International **C/VW:** Local Church, NAPM **A/S:** She attributes her success to the support she receives from her family and friends. **B/I:** She became involved in her profession because she has always wanted to be a nurse. **H/O:** The highlight of her career was obtaining her master's degree.

GWEN KEYLON
Account/MT Manager
Cy Med
2807 North Parham
Richmond, VA 23294 United States
gkeylon@cymedinc.com
http://www.cambridgewhoswho.com

BUS: Healthcare **P/S:** Medical Transcription Services to Handle Healthcare Facilities, Offices of Over Flow **MA:** National **D/D/R:** Mentoring, Acting as a Medical Transcriptionist **H/I/S:** Enjoying Country Music Performed by Jeffery Stelle with her Friends **FBP:** Forbes **CERTS:** Certified Medical Transcriptionist; Registered Healthcare Information Technologist **A/A/S:** American Association for Medical Transcription **C/VW:** Former President of the Middle Tennessee Chapter of the AAMT **A/S:** She attributes her success to her ability to build rapport with colleagues and her communication skills. **H/O:** The highlight of her career has been making a difference in people's lives on a daily basis.

KRISTA B. KHONE
Vice President
Bentonville, Bella Vista Chamber of Commerce
202 East Central Avenue
Bentonville, AR 72712 United States
kkhone@bbvchamber.com
http://www.bbvchamber.com

BUS: Chamber of Commerce **P/S:** Services for Community Businesses **MA:** Local **D/D/R:** Supervising Leadership Programs, Coordinating Events, Special and Community Projects **H/I/S:** Spending Time with Family and Friends, Softball and Volleyball, Music **EDU:** Master's Degree in Adult Education, University of Arkansas; Bachelor's Degree in Elementary Education, University of Arkansas **A/A/S:** Association of Chamber of Commerce Executives; Association of Fundraising Professionals; National Association of Community College Trustees; Arkansas Two Year College Association **C/VW:** Local Associations; YMCA; Chairwoman, Benton County Women's Shelter; Board of Trustees, Northwest Arkansas Community College; Students in Free Enterprises; Community Colleges; John Brown University **A/S:** She attributes her success to the support of her parents who encouraged her in every aspect of her life. **B/I:** She became involved in her profession because a position within the community college became available. **H/O:** The highlight of her career has been the success of the Northwest Arkansas Women's Business Conference.

TERESA P. KIDD
North America Supply Chain Manager and Controller
SGL Carbon, LLC
8600 Bill Ficklin Dr.
Charlotte, NC 28269 United States
teresa.kidd@sglcarbon.com
http://www.sglcarbon.com

BUS: Manufacturing Company **P/S:** Graphite **MA:** International **EXP:** Ms. Kidd's expertise is in supply chain management and control. **H/I/S:** Traveling **FBP:** APICS **EDU:** Master of Business Administration, Virginia Polytechnic Institute and State University; Bachelor's Degree in Business Administration, Averett College **CERTS:** Certification, APICS The Association for Operations Management **A/A/S:** APICS **A/S:** She attributes her success to her hard work and dedication to her profession. **B/I:** She became involved in her profession because she felt it was exciting and fast moving. **H/O:** The highlight of her career is her current position.

CARLA A. KILLAM
President, Land Owner, Author
Killam-Evans Transport, Rahonce Drive Court
317 Smith Street
Rock Springs, WY 82901 United States
scooter406@msn.com
http://www.cambridgewhoswho.com

BUS: Transportation Company **P/S:** Transportation of RVs, Campers and Trailers to Factories Across the Country **MA:** National **EXP:** Ms. Killam's expertise is in administration. **D/D/R:** Executing Financial Tasks, Ensuring that RVs, Trailers and Campers Reach their Destinations **H/I/S:** Spending Time with her Family and Pets, Gardening, Yard Work, Reading, Writing **EDU:** Coursework in Criminal Justice, Western Wyoming Community College **C/VW:** The Humane Society of the United States **A/S:** She attributes her success to her generosity and willingness to trust others. **B/I:** She became involved in the profession because her boyfriend believed that the transportation business would be successful and suggested that she join the business. She then financed the business and became a partner. **H/O:** The highlight of her career was becoming a published author.

TAMMY K. KILMER
Territory Manager
Hills Pet Nutrition
400 S.W. 8th Avenue
Topeka, KS 66603 United States
tammy-kilmer@hillspet.com
http://www.cambridgewhoswho.com

BUS: Animal Products **P/S:** Prescription Diet and Science Diet Pet Food **MA:** National **D/D/R:** Managing 150 Offices and Clinics throughout Central and Northern Missouri and Illinois **H/I/S:** Bowling, Spending Time with her Family, Boating, Fishing **EDU:** Bachelor's Degree in Biology, Lincoln University **C/VW:** American Cancer Society, United Way **A/S:** She attributes her success to a great support system, family and friends, a strong work ethic and good morals. **B/I:** She became involved in the profession because she was always interested in animals and worked for a veterinary clinic her junior year of high school; she has progressed within the industry since then.

BETTE L. KINCAID
Chief Executive Officer, Manufacturer
Bette K New People Products, LLC
P. O. Box 60161
Renton, WA 98058 United States
betteknpp@aol.com
http://www.cambridgewhoswho.com

BUS: Natural Products Manufacturer **P/S:** Specially Formulated Moisturizing Creams, Soaps, and Cosmetics Manufacturer **MA:** National **D/D/R:** Manufacturing all Natural Creams, Soaps, and Cosmetics from an Old American-Indian Formula **H/I/S:** Walking, Exercising Daily, Gardening, Decorating **FBP:** O, The Oprah Magazine **EDU:** High School Diploma **A/H:** Certified Woman Minority Award; Several Insurance Agent of the Year Awards; Various Achievement and Outstanding Insurance Agent Awards; Various Cosmetic Awards **C/VW:** Various Community Events **W/H:** Mary Kay Beauty Consultant; Insurance Agent **C/A:** Founder, Product Line **A/S:** She attributes her success to being a hands on Chief Executive Officer who is able to keep abreast of changes in the market place, combined with persistence and meeting the needs of her clients.

DR. ERICA J. KING
Assistant Professor
The University of West Alabama
5319 Colonial Oaks Drive N.
Mobile, AL 36618 United States
blessed40@bellsouth.net
http://www.uwa.edu

BUS: University **P/S:** Higher Education **MA:** Local **D/D/R:** Teaching Special Children, Scheduling, Teaching Undergraduate and Graduate Students Who are Pursuing Degrees in Special Education **H/I/S:** Shopping, Traveling, Reading **FBP:** CEC Journal; Teaching Pre K-8 **EDU:** Doctor of Education, Nova Southeastern University (2006); Master's Degree in Special Education, Alabama State University (2000); Bachelor's Degree, University of South Alabama (1995) **A/A/S:** UWA Lions Club; Mid-South Educational Research Association; Chairwoman, Special Education Scholarship Committee, The University of West Alabama; The Mobile Association for Retarded Citizens **A/H:** The National Dean's List (1997-1998); Academic Excellence Award **C/VW:** Holy Family Catholic Church; Saint Mary's Church; Catholic Youth Organization; Afro-American Club; Black Student Union (1989-1995) **DOB:** December 8, 1970 **POB:** Mobile **SP:** Terry **CHILD:** DeMario, Kelcie **W/H:** Inclusion Teacher, Baker High School; Eligibility Chairwoman; Inclusion Teacher; Special Education Tracking Systems Administrator; IEP Team Leader; Department Chairwoman

JAMES KING
Partner
Couch White LLP
540 Broadway
Albany, NY 12207 United States
jking@couchwhite.com
http://www.couchwhite.com

BUS: New York-Based Law Firm with a National Reputation **P/S:** Energy Law, Construction Law, Commercial Litigation, Commercial Transactions, Environmental Law and Telecommunications **MA:** National **D/D/R:** Practicing Energy and Environmental Law, Representing Large Industrial Consumers in Project Development, Presenting at Conferences and Energy Symposiums **EDU:** JD, Georgetown University (1977) **A/A/S:** Energy Bar Association; New York Bar Association; District of Columbia Bar Association; University of Virginia Alumni Association

LEE R. KING, BSN, RN
Nurse Manager
United Health Services
33-57 Harrison Street
Johnson City, NY 13790 United States
lee_king@uhs.org
http://www.uhs.net

BUS: Level II Hospital Trauma Center **P/S:** Patient Care Consisting of Alcohol and Drug Therapy, Inhalation, Occupational, Physical and Speech Therapy, Psychiatric Services, Coronary Care, Neonatal Care, Obstetrics, All Emergency Services **MA:** Regional **D/D/R:** Administering Respiratory and Critical Care, Managing a 28-Bed Unit, Enforcing Policies and Procedures, Staffing, Maintaining Compliance, Issuing Yearly Evaluations, Overseeing the Pediatric and Gynecological Units **H/I/S:** Woodworking, Camping, Boating **FBP:** RN; This Old House **EDU:** Bachelor of Science in Nursing, Misericordia University (2007); Associate of Nursing, Broome Community College (1992) **A/A/S:** Board of Directors, Credit Union

DOROTHY I. KING-DICKERSON
Writer
Circle DIBKD
620 Horseshoe Drive
Cadiz, KY 42211 United States
dorothy.kingdickerson@cwwemail.com
http://www.cambridgewhoswho.com

BUS: Publishing Company **P/S:** Publishing Books, Writing **MA:** Local **EXP:** Ms. King-Dickerson's expertise is in homespun humor, journalism and poetry. **H/I/S:** Traveling, Walking, Exercising, Attending ISP Meetings, Caring for her Dog **FBP:** Writer's Digest **EDU:** Associate Degree in English, Lansing Community College; Coursework in Nursing **A/A/S:** Health Camp, FL; Quandas; The Widows Group; School Book Club Association **A/H:** Editors' Choice Awards, International Society of Poets **C/VW:** Den Mother, Brownies, Girl Scouts of America; Kiwanis Club; Singer, Church Choir **DOB:** July 1, 1926 **POB:** Fort Wayne, IN **SP:** Nelson, Odis **CHILD:** David, Tonia, Denis, Teresa, Joey, Randy, Timothy **W/H:** Trainer, Breeder, Cocker Spaniel Puppies; Teacher, Sunday School **C/A:** Author, It Takes a Heap of Living **A/S:** She attributes her success to her ability to face challenges. **B/I:** She became involved in her profession after participating in a poetry contest in her childhood.

SUSAN E. KINNIN
Teacher
Grade Six Inclusion Classroom
Wales Elementary School
41 Main Street, Wales, MA 01081 United States
skinnin@hotmail.com
kinnins@tantasqua.org
http://www.tantasqua.org/wales

BUS: Elementary School **P/S:** Prekindergarten through Sixth Grade Public Education **MA:** Local **D/D/R:** Teaching Mathematics in an Inclusion Classroom Setting for Mainstream Special Education Students, At-Risk Students and Students with Emotional, Behavioral and Learning Disabilities **H/I/S:** Spending Time with her Family, Listening to Music, Walking, Going to the Beach, Practicing Yoga, Learning about and Supporting Tibetan Culture and Causes **EDU:** Bachelor of Arts in Liberal Arts, Concentration in Elementary Education, Bay Path College **C/VW:** Co-Founder, Board of Directors, Drong-ba Western Tibet Foundation, Inc.; International Campaign for Tibet; American Heart Association **DOB:** June 17, 1956 **POB:** Brooklyn, NY **A/S:** She attributes her success to hard work, care, respect for everybody and her determination to see her students achieve success. **B/I:** She became involved in this profession because it was a way to connect with many people to help them grow and learn. She wanted to instill a lifelong love of learning and an openness and curiosity about the world in students. **H/O:** The most gratifying aspect of her career is when her students come back to visit her and are successful in their respective careers.

CHASSIE A. KIRBY
Certified Registered Nurse
Northwest Arkansas Surgical Clinic
724 Deaver Street
Springdale, AR 72764 United States
chassie.kirby@cwwemail.com
http://www.cambridgewhoswho.com

BUS: Medical Center **P/S:** Healthcare **MA:** Regional **D/D/R:** Nursing in the Surgery and Cardiology Units, Counseling Inpatients and Outpatients, Making Daily Rounds, Assisting in Surgeries and Cardio Catheterization Laboratory Procedures **H/I/S:** Spending Time with her Family **FBP:** RN; American Journal of Nursing; AORN Journal **EDU:** Master of Science in Nursing, Concentration in Acute Care, University of Arkansas for Medical Sciences; Bachelor of Science in Nursing, University of Arkansas for Medical Sciences **A/A/S:** Association of Operating Room Nurses; American College of Nurse Practitioners; American Association of Critical Care Nurses **C/VW:** American Hospice Foundation; The Salvation Army

CASHARION A. KIRK
Registered Nurse, President, Owner
Consulting Accreditation Resource Educators, LLC
2021 E. Dublin Grandville Road
Suite 260
Columbus, OH 43229 United States
ckirk@carellc.com
http://www.carellc.com

BUS: Healthcare Consulting **P/S:** Training, Management, Education, Regulatory Compliance **MA:** Local **EXP:** Ms. Kirk's expertise includes healthcare management, administrative nursing services and training, employee development, performance and quality improvement management and principles and practices. **H/I/S:** Writing Poetry **FBP:** AJN **EDU:** Associate of Applied Science in Nursing, Hocking College **A/A/S:** Ghana Cyber Group

Yvonne M. Kirk, Ph.D.
Vice President of Nursing Services
Mercy Medical Center
2700 Stewart Parkway
Roseburg, OR 97479 United States
http://www.mercyrose.org

BUS: Community-Based Medical Center **P/S:** Family Birthplace, Surgery, Shaw Heart and Vascular Center, Respiratory Care, Emergency, Home Health, Hospice, Nursing Services, Imaging Services, Laboratory, Behavioral Health, Ambulatory Therapy Clinic, Sleep Lab and Inpatient Rehabilitation Unit **MA:** National **D/D/R:** Directing a Staff of 24, Overseeing All Nursing Issues for the Hospital, Including Policy Developments, Procedures and Patient Issues **H/I/S:** Drawing, Painting **FBP:** Assorted Nursing Journals **EDU:** Doctoral Degree, University of Wisconsin (2005) **A/A/S:** National Association of Female Executives; Northwest Organization of Nurse Executives; United Way; Walk America for Cancer; March of Dimes; ERTN; CCNO

Jane W. Kiser
Owner, BeautiControl Independent Consultant
Regeneration Skin and Spa
2959 Emissary Drive
Roanoke, VA 24019 United States
beautigal@cox.net
http://www.beautipage.com/janekiser

BUS: International Manufacturer and Party-Plan Direct-Sales Company **P/S:** Skincare, Cosmetics, Spa Products, Microdermabrasion, Chemical Peels, Sun Care, Men's Products **MA:** National **D/D/R:** Enhancing the In-Home Spa Experience Using BeautiControl Products, Performing Microdermabrasion, Chemical Peels, Makeovers, Relaxing Foot Baths, Applying Glamour Makeup **H/I/S:** Gourmet Cooking, Biking **FBP:** Achiever **EDU:** Associate Degree in Liberal Arts, Virginia Western Community College, Magna Cum Laude (1992) **A/A/S:** Phi Theta Kappa

KATHLEEN KISZKA
Mathematics Department Chair
Queen of Peace High School
191 Rutherford Place
North Arlington, NJ 07031 United States
kz315@aol.com
http://www.qphs.org

BUS: Religious High School Committed to Excellence in Education **P/S:** Regular Curriculum Including Reading, Music, Art, History, Social Studies, Science, Mathematics and Physical Education **MA:** Regional **D/D/R:** Teaching Applied Mathematics and Geometry to High School Students **H/I/S:** Photography **FBP:** NCTM Publications **EDU:** Bachelor's Degree in Mathematics and Computer Science, Saint Peter's College (1974) **CERTS:** Certified Mathematics Teacher, Seton Hall University (1976); Certification in Mathematics Education (Kindergarten through 12th Grade), State of New Jersey **A/A/S:** National Council of Teachers of Mathematics **A/H:** Catholic High School Educator Award (2008); John Baptist DeLaSalle Educator Award (2006); Teacher of the Year, Archdiocese of Newark (1999) **DOB:** February 22, 1952

LISSA M. KIVISTO
Assistant Art Director
Mary Bell Gallery
311 W. Superior
Chicago, IL 60654 United States
lkivisto@gallerykh.com
http://www.gallerykh.com

BUS: Art Gallery **P/S:** Retail and Resales of Fine Art, Contemporary American Artists Collection in Various Styles and Media, Framing Services **MA:** International **D/D/R:** Consulting on Fine Art, Promoting Artists, Acquiring Items for Showcasing, Conducting All Administrative Duties for the Business **H/I/S:** Traveling, Watching Kansas Basketball and Sporting Events, Photography, Writing, Meditating **FBP:** American Art Collector; Psychology Today **EDU:** Coursework in Art in Business, Styles in Art and Contemporary Art, Sotheby's Institute of Art, London, United Kingdom (2008); Coursework in Women's Studies, University of Kansas (2005) **A/A/S:** Contemporary Art Museum of Chicago **C/VW:** Project Single Parent; Meals on Wheels **DOB:** August 19, 1982 **POB:** Wichita **W/H:** Sem Group, Oklahoma City; Lea Sutton Interiors, OK

Dr. Ana Maria Klein
Professor
SUNY Fredonia
E-242 Thompson
Fredonia, NY 14063 United States
kleina@fredonia.edu
http://www.fredonia.edu

BUS: Higher Education, Part of the State University of New York System **P/S:** Wide Array of Degree Programs, Providing a Choice of 82 Majors and 41 Minors **MA:** Local **D/D/R:** Specializing in Mathematics and Cultural Studies, Researching on Test Anxiety and Standardized Testing **H/I/S:** Swimming, Traveling, Reading **FBP:** Journals in Mathematics and Cultural Issues **EDU:** Doctoral Degree, McGill University at Montreal (2000); Master's Degree, Venezuela (1992); Bachelor's Degree, Venezuela (1981) **A/A/S:** American Education Research Association; Oxford Round Table; Mathematics Association; Bilingual Education Association

Kristen Lynn Kleinberg
Regional Sales Manager
GreyStone Staffing
201 Willowbrook Boulevard
Wayne, NJ 07470 United States
kristenk@greystonestaffing.com
http://www.greystonestaffing.com

BUS: Staffing Agency **P/S:** Hiring and Permanent Placement for Information Technology, Creative Services, Accounting and Finance, Legal and Healthcare Industries **MA:** Regional **EXP:** Ms. Kleinberg's expertise is in temporary and permanent staffing. **H/I/S:** Dancing, Spending Time with her Beagle **FBP:** Human Resource Management Journal **EDU:** Bachelor of Arts in Psychology and Criminal Justice, Montclair State University **A/A/S:** Commerce and Industry Association of New Jersey; Society for Human Resource Management; TriCounty Area Chamber of Commerce; New Jersey Staffing Alliance; Human Resources Association of New York **A/H:** President's Club Award (2003-2004) **C/VW:** The Cancer Institute of New Jersey; The Marty Lyons Foundation

MR. ROBERT A. KLINE
Prison Superintendent (Retired)
Virginia Department of Corrections
PO Box 160
White Post, VA 22663 United States
circ01@hughes.net
http://www.vadoc.state.va.us

BUS: Government Organization **P/S:** Correctional Services **MA:** National **D/D/R:** Overseeing Correctional Services **H/I/S:** Photography, Working on Computers, Spending Time with his Family, Model Railroading **FBP:** Industry-Related Publications **EDU:** Pursuing Bachelor of Arts in History, University of Maryland **A/A/S:** Secretary, National Jail Managers' Association: American Correctional Association; Virginia Correctional Association; Friendship Volunteer Fire Company; Fairfax County Citizens Action Committee; Former President, Parent Teacher Association, Boyce Elementary School; Former Captain, Friendship Fire, Rescue and Salvage Unit **A/H:** Law Enforcement Officer of the Year Award, Winchester-Frederick County Jaycees (1975) **DOB:** November 11, 1946 **SP:** Linda **CHILD:** Roy, Melissa **W/H:** Police Dispatcher, Police Officer, Chief Correctional Officer, Field Operations Sergeant, Corrections Training Officer, Manager, State Court and Legal Services Unit; Assistant Prison Superintendent, Prison Superintendent

SUSAN M. KLINGER
Teacher
Trinity Academy
130 Academy Lane
Ashland, PA 17921 United States
skeng@ptd.net
http://www.cambridgewhoswho.com

BUS: Educational Academy **P/S:** Education **MA:** Local **D/D/R:** Teaching English, Music and Theology **EDU:** Master's Degree in Education, Bloomsburg University; Bachelor of Science in Elementary Education, Bloomsburg University **CERTS:** Certified Reading Specialist, Bloomsburg University **A/A/S:** National Education Association; International Reading Association **C/VW:** ACA; Relay For Life; National Multiple Sclerosis Society **A/S:** She attributes her success to the support she receives from her family and students. **B/I:** She became involved in her profession because of her desire to work with students.

SUZANNE L. KMET, SPHR
Director of Human Resources
Peddicord, Wharton, Spencer, Hook, Barron & Wegman, LLP
405 Sixth Ave
Des Moines, IA 50309 United States
suekmet@msn.com
http://www.cambridgewhoswho.com

BUS: Law Firm **P/S:** Workers' Compensation, Employee Relations Law **MA:** Regional **EXP:** Ms. Kmet's expertise includes human resources, employee training and development. **D/D/R:** Human Resources, Employee Training and Development **H/I/S:** Traveling, Golfing **FBP:** Fast Company **EDU:** Pursuing Master of Science in Human Resource Management and Administration,; Bachelor of Science in Professional Aeronautics, Emery Riddle Aeronautical University, Daytona Beach, FL **CERTS:** Certification in Aerospace and Aviation Safety, Embry-Riddle Aeronautical University; Certified Human Resource Professional, Society of Human Resource Management **A/A/S:** Society of Human Resource Management **C/VW:** American Business Women's Association **A/S:** She attributes her success to her hard work, constant learning, listening skills and compassionate nature. **H/O:** The highlights of her career are the awards she has received.

MR. GREGORY J. KNAPP
Project Manager
Ebara International
350 Salomon Circle
Sparks, NV 89434 United States
GKnapp@ebaraintl.com
http://www.cambridgewhoswho.com

BUS: Pump Manufacturing, Assembly, Production and Shipping Company **P/S:** Cryogenic Submersible Pumps for Liquefying Natural Gas, Petroleum and Mining Industries Inclusive of Federal Operations, Full Performance Testing of Liquefied Gas Pumps Using the Actual Service Fluids **MA:** International **D/D/R:** Working in the Pump Industry, Managing Projects and Relationships, Scheduling, Overseeing Profits, Making Strategic Decisions, Mechanical Engineering, Monitoring Internal Operations **H/I/S:** Snow Skiing, Hiking, Enjoying Outdoor Activities **FBP:** Pump Technology; Project Management Literature **EDU:** Bachelor's Degree in Marine Engineering, United States Merchant Marine Academy **CHILD:** Elizabeth, Allison

EARLENE W. KNIGHT
Physical Education Teacher, Coach (Retired)
Jefferson County High School
50 David Road
Monticello, FL 32344 United States
knight_e@firn.edu
http://www.cambridgewhoswho.com

BUS: High School **P/S:** Secondary Education **MA:** Local **D/D/R:** Teaching Physical Education, Public Speaking, Consulting **H/I/S:** Fishing, Gardening, Spending Time Outdoors, Building Models **EDU:** Bachelor of Arts in Elementary Education **CERTS:** Certified Physical Education Teacher; Certified Music Teacher **A/A/S:** Florida Alliance for Health, Physical Education, Recreation, Dance and Sport **C/VW:** Florida Green Industries **A/S:** She attributes her success to her passion for her profession and her caring nature for children. **B/I:** She became involved in her profession because she always wanted to become a physical education teacher and help children. **H/O:** The most gratifying aspect of her career is the gratitude she receives from her students.

LOUISE A. KNIGHT, MSW, LCSW-C, OSW-C
The Harry J. Duffey Family - Patient and Family Services
The Sidney Kimmel Comprehensive Cancer Center
Johns Hopkins Hospital
401 N. Broadway, Suite 1210
Baltimore, MD 21231 United States
scherlo@jhmi.edu
http://www.hopkinskimmelcancercenter.org

BUS: Healthcare Facility **P/S:** Active Programs in Clinical Research, Laboratory Research, Education, Community Outreach, Prevention, Control and Palliative Medicine **MA:** International **FBP:** Journal of Psychology; Journal of Sociology; Journal of Clinical Oncology

JANICE ETTELT KNIPP, M.A.
Bank Examiner
United States Treasury, Office of the Comptroller of the Currency
Washington, DC United States
rknipp@adelphia.net
http://www.cambridgewhoswho.com

BUS: Federal Regulators, National Banking System **MA:** National **EXP:** Ms. Knipp's expertise is in finance. **H/I/S:** Fine Arts **EDU:** Master of Arts, California State University at Fullerton; Bachelor of Science, University of Illinois **A/A/S:** OCC Professional Women's Network; Kappa Tau Alpha Journalism Honor Society **A/H:** 'Outstanding Graduate Student,' California State University at Fullerton; 'Top Three in Nation' for Masters Thesis **C/VW:** American Lung Association; National Mental Health Association; National Jewish Medical and Research Center; American Diabetes Association **A/S:** She attributes her success to overcoming adversity, perseverance, having strong role models, working hard and strong family support. **B/I:** She became involved in this profession because she was a private banker for 13 years and became a bank examiner and federal regulator for the US Treasury. **H/O:** The highlight of her career is seeing small business flourish and grow and professionals become successful due to her portfolio management.

COURY M. KNOWLES, MS
Specially Designed Physical Education
Teacher and Baseball Coach
Seminole County Public Schools
1722 W. Airport Boulevard
Sanford, FL 32771 United States
coury_knowles@scps.k12.fl.us
http://www.scps.k12.fl.us

BUS: School District **P/S:** Education **MA:** Regional **D/D/R:** Teaching Physical Education, Managing Physical Education Programs for 10 Schools, Motivational Speaking for High School and Universities, Sharing and Dealing with his Own Experiences **H/I/S:** Playing Football, Running, Swimming, Watching Movies **EDU:** Doctoral Degree in Curriculum and Instruction, University of Central Florida (2007) **A/A/S:** Graduate Assistant, Former Equipment Manager, Florida Gators **A/H:** Teacher of the Year Award, Seminole County Chapter, Council for Exceptional Children (2007); Teacher of the Year Award (2004)

JACQUELINE R. KNOX
Licensed Practical Nurse Supervisor
Spring Gate
847 Lynwood Drive
Memphis, TN 38116 United States
jdnknx72036@midsouth.rr.com
http://www.cambridgewhoswho.com

BUS: Healthcare **P/S:** Patient Care, Focus on Mental Disorders **MA:** Local **EXP:** Ms. Knox's expertise is in geriatrics and mental disability. **H/I/S:** Reading, Tennis, Working with Disabled Children **FBP:** American Journal of Nursing **EDU:** Bachelor of Arts in Education, University of Oregon **CERTS:** Licensed Practical Nurse **A/S:** She attributes her personal and professional success to her determination and love for the profession. **B/I:** She has always had an interest in the field and enjoys helping others. **H/O:** The highlight of her career is seeing the condition of her patients improve.

PAT M. KNUTSON
Registered Massage Therapist, Owner
Pat Knutson, RMT
4214 Medical Parkway
Suite 209
Austin, TX 78756 United States
patknutsonrmt@yahoo.com
http://www.cambridgewhoswho.com

BUS: Massage Therapy Practice **P/S:** Therapeutic Body Work, Massage Therapy **MA:** Local **D/D/R:** Administering Deep Tissue and Myofascial Massage Therapy for Chronic, Acute Pain and Injuries, Joint Mobilization and Range of Motion **H/I/S:** Wake Boarding, Mountain Biking, Riding Motorcycles, Custom Woodworking **CERTS:** Registered Massage Therapist, Austin School of Massage Therapy

MS. TERESA KOCHMAR GOODWIN
President
The Christ College of Nursing and Health Sciences
2139 Auburn Avenue
Cincinnati, OH 45219 United States
Terbgoodwin@fuse.net
http://www.thechristcollege.org

BUS: Private, Nonprofit, Non-Denominational, Institution of Higher Learning **P/S:** Quality Healthcare Education at the Associate Degree Level to Qualified Men and Women Primarily from the Tri-State Area **MA:** Regional **EXP:** Ms. Kochmar Goodwin's expertise includes administration, nursing education, consulting and writing. **H/I/S:** Tennis, Crafts, Boating, Writing, Dancing **EDU:** Master's Degree in Education, Xavier University; Bachelor's Degree in Nursing, Carlow University **A/A/S:** National League for Nursing; Ohio League for Nursing; National Association of Female Executives; OCHBSN; Strathmore's Who's Who

ELIZABETH 'BETTY' M. KOEHLER
Public Health Nurse Coordinator
Arkansas State Health Department
3000 N. First Street
Jacksonville, AR 72076 United States
elizabethkoehler@arkansas.gov
http://www.healthyarkansas.com

BUS: Healthcare Center **P/S:** Healthcare Including Public Health Education **MA:** Regional **D/D/R:** Coordinating Nurses, Managing a Health Department Clinic **H/I/S:** Reading, Needlework, Spending Time with her Family and Friends, Acting as a Caregiver **FBP:** American Journal of Nursing **EDU:** Coursework in Nursing, St. Vincent Infirmary **CERTS:** Registered Nurse **A/A/S:** President, Social Chairman, Treasurer, Preceptor Chapter, Beta Sigma Phi; Local State Agencies **C/VW:** First Methodist Church of North Little Rock, Arkansas; Prayer Chain; Sunday School Teacher; Various Nursing Organizations **A/S:** She attributes her success to her good health and her love for her job. **B/I:** She became involved in her profession because of her educational background. **H/O:** The most gratifying aspect of her career is helping others.

LINDA KOENIG-BROWN
Clinical Counselor
Shawnee State University
940 Second Street
Portsmouth, OH 45662 United States
http://www.cambridgewhoswho.com

BUS: Clinical Counseling **P/S:** Counseling Sex Offenders and Substance Abusers **MA:** Regional **EXP:** Ms. Koenig-Brown's expertise is in sex offender treatment. **H/I/S:** Spending Time with Family **EDU:** Master's Degree, Counseling, Ohio University, 2004 **C/VW:** Harrison Freewell Baptist Church; Mount Hope Bible Camp, Focusing on the Family **A/S:** She attributes her success to the mentorship she received from others in the profession. **B/I:** She became involved in her profession because when she was 15 she worked as a camp counselor and a child came to her that was being abused. She wanted to help and make a difference. **H/O:** The highlight of her career was being the first person to be involved in the investigation of abuse occurring at the Department of Youth Services.

ROSEMARY D. KOLDE
Director of Professional Services (Retired),
Senior Physical Therapist
Casa Colina for Rehabilitation
255 E. Bonita Avenue
Pomona, CA 91767 United States
http://www.cambridgewhoswho.com

BUS: Physical Rehabilitation **P/S:** Healthcare **MA:** Southern California **EXP:** Ms. Kolde's expertise is in physical therapy. **H/I/S:** Bowling, Signing in Choir, Walking, Traveling, Gardening **EDU:** Coursework in Physical Therapy, Children's Hospital School of Los Angeles **A/A/S:** American Physical Therapy Association **C/VW:** American Heart Association, American Cancer Society, American Lung Association, Billy Graham, Arise **A/S:** She attributes her success to her hard work and drive and to always staying current. **B/I:** She became involved in this profession because she became intrigued while studying biology. **H/O:** The highlight of her career was opening a new facility and being one of the members who got it started. After it opened, they honored her as a VIP member of the board.

DONNA W. KOLOSKY, MBA
Executive Assistant
School of Engineering and Computer Science - University of Denver
2050 E. Iliff #228E
Denver, CO 80208 United States
dkolosky@du.edu
http://www.cambridgewhoswho.com

BUS: University **P/S:** University, Education **MA:** National **EXP:** Ms. Kolosky's expertise is in business administration. **D/D/R:** Assisting the Dean **H/I/S:** Reading, Traveling **EDU:** Master of Business Administration, Regis University **C/VW:** American Diabetes Association, American Cancer Society **A/S:** She attributes her personal and professional success to her hard work, diligence and determination. **B/I:** She became involved in the profession because she always had an interest in the field and enjoys working in the university setting. **H/O:** The most gratifying aspect of her career is her personal success while being a single mother.

TAMI L. KONIECZNYM, OTR/L, CBIS, CKT
Clinical Specialist
Children's Hospital of Philadelphia
3405 Civic Center Boulevard
Philadelphia, PA 19104 United States
konieczny@email.chop.org
http://www.chop.org

BUS: Hospital **P/S:** Children's Hospital Care, Research, Teaching **MA:** Local **D/D/R:** Acting as a Clinical Specialist, Training, Administering Medical Care for Brain Injuries, Burns, Chronic Pain and Spinal Cord Injuries, Supervising Six to Seven Staff Members, Developing Programs, Instituting Patient Care, Giving National Presentations **H/I/S:** Running, Playing Ultimate Frisbee, Attending Broadway Shows **EDU:** Master of Science in Occupational Therapy; Bachelor of Science in Occupational Therapy; Bachelor of Science in Biology; Coursework, D'Youville College; Coursework, Mount Union College **A/A/S:** CBIS; CBIT; CKT; Occupational Therapist

MICHELLE KOOPMANS
Registered Nurse, Student
PRN Health Services
5325 Wall Street
Madison, WI 53718 United States
micletts@centurytel.net
http://www.cambridgewhoswho.com

BUS: Staffing Agency **P/S:** Healthcare Staffing **MA:** Local **EXP:** Ms. Koopmans' expertise is in substance abuse. **EDU:** Pursuing Registered Nurse Diploma **CERTS:** Licensed Practical Nurse **C/VW:** Methodist Church, Local Community Charitable Works **A/S:** She attributes her personal and professional success to her drive and supportive family. **B/I:** She has always had an interest in the field and a desire to help others. **H/O:** The highlight of her career was working in a methadone clinic.

GABRIELA KORN
Executive Director
Kids World New York, Inc.
327 Deer Park Avenue
Dix Hills, NY 11746 United States
kidsworldnyinc@aol.com
http://www.cambridgewhoswho.com

BUS: Nursery School **P/S:** Nursery School that Offers Bilingual Education for Students Ages 10 Months to 4 Years **MA:** Local **D/D/R:** Creating Educational and Nutritional Programs for the Children, Supervising Teachers **H/I/S:** Traveling, Tennis, Spending Time with Family **FBP:** New York Times; Parenting Magazine **EDU:** Bachelor's Degree in Education, Minor in Business, Universidad De San Andren in Bolivia **CERTS:** Licensed Teacher, State of New York **A/A/S:** Childcare Council, National Association for the Education of Young Children **C/VW:** Donates Clothes and Supplies to the Community, Scholarship Fund for Children Attending the School, Teaching Parenting Seminars **A/S:** She attributes her success to the relationships she has developed with the parents and children. **B/I:** She was prompted to enter her profession because she enjoys working with children. **H/O:** The most gratifying aspect of her career is seeing the children learn and progress.

MICHELE M. KOSTERETZ, RN, BSN, CCRC, CRA
Clinical Research Associate
GlaxoSmithKline
4230 N. Oakland Avenue, 320
Shorewood, WI 53211 United States
michele.m.kosteretz@gsk.com
http://www.mygsk.com

BUS: Pharmaceutical Company **P/S:** Pharmaceuticals **MA:** International **EXP:** Ms. Kosteretz's expertise is in clinical pharmaceutical trials. **D/D/R:** Clinical Pharmaceutical Trials **H/I/S:** Ballet Dancing, Leading the Dance Ministry at her Church, Gardening, Spending Time with her Family and her Dog **FBP:** Research Practitioner; The Monitor **EDU:** Bachelor of Science in Education, University of Wisconsin at Milwaukee; Registered Nurse, University of Wisconsin-Milwaukee **A/A/S:** Association of Clinical Research Professionals **C/VW:** Leader of the Dance Ministry, Eastbrook Church, ELIM Retreat Ministries **A/S:** She attributes her personal and professional success to her faith in Jesus Christ. **B/I:** She became involved in the healthcare industry after her child was born into a neonatal intensive care unit and she admired the quality of treatment the nurses provided. **H/O:** The highlight of her career was when she became a Certified Research Coordinator and, more recently, serving as a speaker at a conference.

DONALD W. KOUBA
Coordinator of Photographic Studies, Photography Instructor
Prairie State College
202 S. Halsted Street
Chicago Heights, IL 60411 United States
dkouba@prairiestate.edu
http://www.prairie.cc.il.us

BUS: College **P/S:** Higher Education **MA:** Regional **EXP:** Mr. Kouba's expertise is in panoramic and digital photography. **D/D/R:** Instructing, Coordinating, Developing the Curriculum, Processing Films, Conducting Programs **H/I/S:** Water Skiing, Running, Swimming, Watching Videos **FBP:** Photoshop User **EDU:** Master's Degree in Photography, Rhode Island School of Design (1976) **A/A/S:** Art Institute of Chicago; Columbia College Alumni Association; Friends of Photography, CA; Museum of Contemporary Photography, Chicago, IL; National Association of Photoshop Professionals **A/H:** U.S. Embassies Exhibit Award **C/VW:** Society for Photographic Education **SP:** Barbara **CHILD:** Allison, Heather

MR. JEFFREY S. KOWALCZYK
Investment Consultant
LaSalle Street Consulting
30 N. LaSalle Street
Suite 2700
Chicago, IL 60602 United States
jeffrey.kowalczyk@raymondjames.com
http://www.raymondjames.com

BUS: Finance Consulting Agency **P/S:** Leader in Providing Institutional Investment Consulting for Clients **MA:** National **D/D/R:** Specializing in Financial Consulting Including Union and Municipal Pension Plans and Investment **EDU:** Bachelor's Degree in Economics, Illinois State University (1990) **A/A/S:** Founding Member, Association of Minor League Umpires; Collective Bargaining Unit for Minor League Umpires; Professional Baseball Umpire (1991-2000)

SHARON KAY KRAFT
Owner
American Maid
821 Illinois Street
Sheridan, WY 82801 United States
ammaid@ccorb.com
http://www.cambridgewhoswho.com

BUS: Home Cleaning Agency **P/S:** Cleaning Services **MA:** Regional **D/D/R:** Overseeing Business Operations Including Crisis Management, Security Issues for All Employees, Ensuring Customer Satisfaction, Managing the Staff and Equities **H/I/S:** Traveling, Camping, Riding her Harley Davidson, Spending Time with her Family **EDU:** High School Diploma **A/S:** She attributes her success to her hard work and passion for her profession. **B/I:** She became involved in her profession through a natural progression of opportunities. **H/O:** The highlight of her career was celebrating her company's 20th anniversary in 2007. **I/F/Y:** In five years, Ms. Kraft hopes to increase her business by thirty percent.

MR. KEITH A. KRAPF
Assistant Professor, Life Science Department Chair
John A. Logan College
700 Logan College Road
Carterville, IL 62918 United States
keithkrapf@jalc.edu
http://www.jal.cc.il.us

BUS: Community College **P/S:** Higher Education **MA:** Regional **D/D/R:** Teaching Life and Biological Sciences, Anatomy and Physiology **H/I/S:** Farming, Traveling with his Family, Reading about Home Improvements, Building and Constructing **FBP:** The Chronicle of Higher Education; Scientific American; National Geographic **EDU:** Master of Science in Biological Sciences, Southern Illinois University; Bachelor of Science in Education, Southern Illinois University **A/A/S:** Illinois Community College Biology Teachers Association; President, University of Illinois Council, Tri Beta Honor Society; Volunteer, Board of Directors, Fireworks at the Dam Program; Treasurer, Local Church

MARCIA L. KRAUSE
President
KRAUSE Consulting
1829 W. John Street
Champaign, IL 61821 United States
marcia@wolfram.com
http://www.cambridgewhoswho.com

BUS: Consulting Company **P/S:** Training, Research, Forensic Document Analysis **MA:** Regional **D/D/R:** Supplying Computer Support for Companies, Training, Editing Training Materials, Conducting Training Seminars **H/I/S:** Listening to Music, Golfing **FBP:** Business 2.0 **EDU:** Master's Degree in Curriculum and Instruction, University of Wisconsin, Madison (1982); Master's Degree in Linguistics, Indiana University, Bloomington (1965) **A/A/S:** Society for Technical Communication; International Association of Forensic Linguists

Ms. Patricia M. Kremel
Investment Advisor
Wells Fargo
S27 W. 29197 Jarmon Road
Waukesha, WI 53188 United States
tisha12281@wi.rr.com
http://www.cambridgewhoswho.com

BUS: Finance Company **P/S:** Financial Services Including Retail and Mortgage Banking, Multi-Family Lending, Community Lending and Investment, Commercial Real Estate and Specialty Mortgage Services **MA:** Local **EXP:** Ms. Kremel's expertise is in accounts, mortgage lending and investments. **D/D/R:** Overseeing Customer Service, Advising Clients on Investment **EDU:** Master of Business Administration, University of Wisconsin-Whitewater (2007); Bachelor's Degree in Business Management, Carroll College (2003) **A/A/S:** National Honors Society, Elite (2007); WaMu Elite Group (2006); Financial Management Association National Honor Society **DOB:** January 22, 1981

Terri L. Kretzinger
Fifth Grade Teacher
Prescott Community School
813 First Street
Prescott, IA 50859 United States
tkretzinger@aea14.k12.ia.us
http://www.cambridgewhoswho.com

BUS: Elementary Education **P/S:** Education **MA:** Local **D/D/R:** Teaching Mathematics, Reading and General Subjects to Elementary School Students **H/I/S:** Farming with her Two Children **EDU:** Bachelor's Degree in Elementary Education, Northwest Missouri College **A/A/S:** Teacher of The Year (2 Years) **C/VW:** St. Jude Children's Research Hospital, Jump Rope for the American Heart Association, Pony Express **A/S:** She attributes her success to loving children. **B/I:** She chose this profession because she knew in junior high school that she wanted to be a teacher. **H/O:** The highlight of her career was receiving an award for Teacher of the Year.

SUSAN A. KROCIAN, RN, BSN, CSN
School Nurse, District Head Nurse
Public School 5
5401 Hudson Avenue
West New York, NJ 07093 United States
skrocian@wnyschools.net
http://www.wnyschools.net

BUS: Public School **P/S:** Elementary Education **MA:** Regional **EXP:** Ms. Krocian's expertise is in intensive, critical care and school nursing. **D/D/R:** Supervising 10 Nurses, Liaising Between the School Board and Nurses throughout the District, Ensuring Compliance According to State Laws **H/I/S:** Color Guard Training, Scrapbooking, Reading **FBP:** Advance for Nurses; Nursing Spectrum; Advances in Critical Care **EDU:** Bachelor of Science in Nursing, New Jersey City University (2000) **CERTS:** Certified School Nurse, New Jersey City University (2001) **A/A/S:** New Jersey Education Association; New Jersey State School Nurses Association; Hudson County School Nurse Association; Bergen County School Nursing Association

MS. ELAINE S. KRONLUND
Director, Owner
Piano Masters
114 Depot Road
Westford, MA 01886 United States
http://www.cambridgewhoswho.com

BUS: Private Music Education Company **P/S:** Teaching All Levels of Classical and Contemporary Music and Performance to Students of All Ages **MA:** Regional **D/D/R:** Offering Contemporary Music Instruction Courses for Beginners, Intermediate and Advanced Students, Overseeing Bi-Annual Recitals, Teaching Technical Classical Music and Music Theory **H/I/S:** Collecting Dolls and Antiques, Attending the Theater **EDU:** Coursework in Education and Music, Los Angeles City College **A/A/S:** New England Piano Teachers Association; Concord Area Music Schools Association; National Vice Presidents, National Society of the Daughters of the American Revolution; National Society of New England Women; Boston University Women's Club **C/VW:** Choir, Church; Girl Scouts and 4-H Clubs

LYNN M. KROUTH
Vice President, Excess and Surplus Manager
Northern States Agency
2145 Ford Parkway
Saint Paul, MN 55116 United States
lkrouth@nsa-mga.com
http://www.nsa-mga.com

BUS: Insurance Agency **P/S:** Insurance Services Including Transportation Risk Management, Commercial and Public Automotive, Special Types, Garage and Excess, Surplus Lines, General Liability, Errors and Omissions and Property Insurance **MA:** National **D/D/R:** Managing Excess and Surplus Product Lines, Overseeing a Staff of Seven **H/I/S:** Watching Football and Baseball, Walking with her Dog **FBP:** American Agent & Broker **EDU:** Continuing Education Coursework **C/VW:** The Humane Society of the United States

MARGARET MARY KRUSE
Guidance Counselor
Girls Division
Regis Jesuit High School
6300 S. Lewiston Way
Aurora, CO 80016 United States
mkruse@regisjesuit.com
http://www.regisjesuit.com

BUS: High School **P/S:** Secondary Education **MA:** Regional **EXP:** Ms. Kruse's expertise includes academic, personal, social, college and career counseling, program development for college application process and mental health. **H/I/S:** Sewing, Baking, Traveling to Europe **FBP:** Industry-Related Publications **EDU:** Master's Degree, University of Northern Colorado, Greeley, Colorado (1983); Bachelor's Degree in German Language, Minor in French (1973) **A/A/S:** Rocky Mountain Association for College Admissions Counseling; Colorado School Counselor Association; American School Counselor Association; National Association of College Admissions Counselors; Former President, Delta Kappa Gamma, Lambda Chapter; Former President, PEO Chapter EK; Former President, The Friends of Littleton Library and Museum **B/I:** She became involved in her profession because she always wanted to become a teacher.

JUDITH E. KUCZMARSKI
Registered Nurse
Fort Sanders Regional Medical Center
Patricia Neal Rehabilitation Center, 1901 Clinch A
Knoxville, TN 37916 United States
judykuczmarski@yahoo.com
http://www.cambridgewhoswho.com

BUS: Healthcare **P/S:** Acute Healthcare Facility **MA:** Local **D/D/R:** Offering Spiritual Guidance to Patients, Nursing in the Parish **H/I/S:** Camping, Spending Time with her Children **FBP:** American Journal of Nursing **EDU:** Associate Degree in Nursing, Trocaire College **A/A/S:** Special Minister of Holy Communion, Catholic Church; International Parish of Nurses; Nurse Preceptor, Deaconess Parish Nurse Ministries, LLC **C/VW:** Local Church, Catholic Charities **A/S:** She attributes her success to having a strong faith. **B/I:** She became involved in her profession because she felt she could contribute spiritually as well as physically to her patients. **H/O:** The highlight of her career is the ongoing satisfaction derived from meeting with patients.

LINDA D. KUDELKA
Postmaster
United States Postal Service
1344 Samaria Road
Samaria, MI 48177 United States
http://www.cambridgewhoswho.com

BUS: United States Post Office **P/S:** Stamps, Postage, Retail Items, Mail Distribution **MA:** Local **D/D/R:** Identifying Customers' Needs **H/I/S:** Reading and Researching Information about Making Post Office Buildings Historical Landmarks **FBP:** People; Biographies **EDU:** Pursuing Associate Degree in Business, Monroe County Community College **A/A/S:** National Association for Female Executives; National League of Postmasters of the United States; National Association of Postmasters of the United States; Bedford Business Association; USPS Lifelong Learning Award; USPS Photo/Narrative Award **C/VW:** National Coalition Against Domestic Violence; United Way **A/S:** She attributes her success to her faith in God, positive thinking, always staying current and being a contributor. **H/O:** The highlight of her career was earning her current position.

SUSAN A. KUGEL
Owner
The Flamingo Card Company
33025 Peach Tree Lane
Lewis, DE 19958 United States
susankugel@yahoo.com
http://www.cambridgewhoswho.com

BUS: Sole Proprietorship **P/S:** Personalized Cards in 3D Including Beach, Wedding, Ladybug, Holiday, Special Occasion, Travel, Tourism and Children's Themes **MA:** Regional **EXP:** Ms. Kugel's expertise is in business development. **D/D/R:** Ensuring Customer Satisfaction **H/I/S:** Making Crafts, Traveling, Swimming, Riding Motorcycles, Caring for her Dog and Cat, Performing Community Service **FBP:** Kappan **EDU:** Master's Degree in Administration and Leadership, Plus 45, University of Delaware; Bachelor of Arts in Education **CERTS:** Certification in School Administration **A/A/S:** National Education Association; Phi Delta Kappa; Who's Who in Education; Who's Who in the East **A/H:** State Awards for Adult Education **C/VW:** Events Chairwoman, Local Community; Educational Consultant, Classroom Management and Discipline **DOB:** February 16, 1946 **POB:** Providence **SP:** Norman **CHILD:** J. Adam, Jason, Andrew **A/S:** She attributes her success to her hard work and supportive parents. **I/F/Y:** In five years, Ms. Kugel plans on enjoying her retirement by spending a lot of time relaxing on the beach.

DEBORAH A. KUHN
Registered Nurse
Excella Health
121 West Second Avenue
Latrobe, PA 15650 United States
kuhneclan@aol.com
http://www.cambridgewhoswho.com

BUS: Community Hospital **P/S:** Healthcare **MA:** Local **EXP:** Ms. Kuhn's expertise is in public relations. **H/I/S:** Writing, Scrap Booking, her Children **FBP:** American Journal of Nursing **EDU:** Associate Degree in Nursing, West Moreland Community College **A/A/S:** American Nurses Association **C/VW:** Life Way Pregnancy Crisis Center **A/S:** She attributes her success to hard work, determination, and especially prayer. **B/I:** She chose the profession because she started out as a medical assistant for 12 years, and then went back to school for nursing. **H/O:** The highlight of her career is when a patient or a family member shows appreciation.

David Kulasiewicz
Management Consultant
J.R. Mannes Defense Services Corp.
22 W. Glebe Road
Alexandria, VA 22305 United States
kulasiewicz@comcast.net
davidkay61@yahoo.com
http://www.chenegafederal.com

BUS: Veteran Owned Small Business **P/S:** Supplies the Government with the Talented Services of Exceptional Professionals Dedicated to the Defense of the United States of America, Security **MA:** International **D/D/R:** Specializing in Counter-Intelligence, Counter-Terrorism and Counter-Espionage, Budgeting, Collecting Data and Information from Over 25 Locations **H/I/S:** Restoring Classic Cars, Hunting, Fishing **EDU:** Master of Arts in Human Relations, The State University of New York (2006); Bachelor of Arts in Science, The State University of New York (1997) **A/A/S:** Veterans of Foreign Wars; Association of Former Air Force Officers of Special Investigations

Abraham A. Kumar, CIO
Chief Information Officer
Contemporary Services Corporation
17101 Superior Street
Northridge, CA 91325 United States
akumar@contemporaryservices.com
http://www.contemporaryservices.com

BUS: Event Management Company **P/S:** Sports and Entertainment Event Management Services **MA:** International **EXP:** Mr. Kumar's expertise is in software architecture design, training and security consulting. **H/I/S:** Listening to Music **EDU:** Master's Degree in Information Technology, Keller Graduate School of Management, DeVry University; Master of Business Administration, Keller Graduate School of Management, DeVry University **C/VW:** Various Churches **A/S:** He attributes his success to his self motivation and persistence. **B/I:** He became involved in his profession because he always wanted to make a difference in others lives. **H/O:** The highlight of his career was designing the key software workforce management tool.

BRENDA S. KUNNEMAN
Pastor
Lord of Hosts Church
5351 S. 139 Plaza
Omaha, NE 68137 United States
loh@lohchurch.org
bkunne@lohchurch.org
http://www.ovm.org

BUS: Religious Organization **P/S:** Reaching the Community and the Region with the Gospel, Training and Equipping Believers to be Effective Christians through Anointed and Uncompromising Messages **MA:** International **EXP:** Pastor Kunneman's expertise is in spiritual guidance. **D/D/R:** Counseling, Writing, Coordinating Material, Articles and Teaching Courses, Preaching, Acting as a Chief Financial Officer, Overseeing the Directional Decisions of the Ministry, Holding and Attending Conferences, Delivering Public Speeches **H/I/S:** Home Decorating **FBP:** Charisma **EDU:** College Coursework **CERTS:** Bible Course Program **B/I:** She became involved in her profession because she felt that it was her calling. **H/O:** The most gratifying aspect of her career is seeing peoples' lives changed for the good. **I/F/Y:** In five years, Pastor Kunneman hopes continue the work of the Lord, to find more opportunities to improve people's lives and brining them to Christ.

MR. WILLIAM L. KURTZ, MPA
Administrative Associate
State Fair Community College
Sedalia, MO 65301
http://sfcc.cc.mo.us

BUS: Community College **P/S:** Higher Education, Associate of Applied Science Degrees, Professional Certificates in Nearly 30 Programs, Vocational and Technical Degrees, Associate of Arts Degrees **MA:** Regional **D/D/R:** Overseeing Record Keeping, Assisting Students in TRIO Programs, Aiding Students with Global Educational Opportunities, Writing Government Grants, Managing College Records, Handling Paperwork **H/I/S:** Traveling **FBP:** Forbes; The Wall Street Journal; Barrons **EDU:** Master of Arts in Public Administration, University of Missouri (1964); Bachelor of Arts in Business Administration, University of Missouri (1950) **A/A/S:** Phi Gamma Delta; Board Member, Treasurer, Local Chapter, American Red Cross; Board Member, Treasurer, Mid America Chapter, Post-Polio Syndrome Support Group; Alpha Delta Sigma

GARY KUYKENDALL, RHIA, CTR
Cancer Registrar
University Medical Center
2390 W. Congress
Lafayette, LA 70596 United States
gkuyke@lsuhsc.edu
http://www.cambridgewhoswho.com

BUS: Healthcare Provider **P/S:** Cancer Data Management **MA:** Local **D/D/R:** Taking Cancer Histories and Reporting them to a Team of Doctors, Submitting Cancer Patient Histories for Cancer Statistical Studies **H/I/S:** Spending Time Outdoors, Listening to Music, Spending Time with Family, Playing and Watching Sports **EDU:** Bachelor of Science in Health Information Systems, University of Louisiana at Lafayette **CERTS:** Certified Tumor Registrar **A/A/S:** National Cancer Registrars Association **C/VW:** Louisiana Cancer Registrars Association **A/S:** He attributes his success to being around people who are able to teach him how to better do his job. **B/I:** He became involved in his profession after being forced to change jobs as a result of a health issue. **H/O:** The highlight of his career was receiving his CRT certification.

LOIS G. LA DELLE DALY
Quality Assurance Coordinator
Redwood Children's Services, Inc.
237 E. Gobbi Street
Ukiah, CA 95482 United States
ladelledalyl@rcs4kids.org
http://www.cambridgewhoswho.com

BUS: Nonprofit Organization **P/S:** Behavioral Health Services to Children **MA:** Local **EXP:** Ms. Daly's expertise is in configuration management. **D/D/R:** Banking, Engineering, Overseeing Quality Assurance, Operating Furnaces, Conducting Internal Audits, Managing Operations **H/I/S:** Bowling, Playing Softball and Tennis, Golfing, Swimming, Hunting, Quad Riding, Motorcycling, Fishing **FBP:** Quality Progress **EDU:** Associate of Arts in Liberal Arts, California State Polytechnic University; Associate of Science in Health Services, Sonoma State University, CA; Associate of Arts in Biological Sciences **CERTS:** Certified Quality Assurance Manager **A/A/S:** Associated Society of Quality

CATHERINE F. LaBERTA
Professor of Mathematics and Computer Science
Erie Community College
6205 Main Street
Williamsville, NY 14221 United States
labertac@aol.com
http://www.ecc.edu

BUS: Community College that is Part of the 64-Campus State University of New York System, Offering Associates Degrees and Specialized Certificates in Over 60 Programs **P/S:** Education, Athletics, Student Clubs and Organizations, Campus Activities, Personal, Academic and Career Counseling, Credit Transfer, Child Care, Disability Services **MA:** Regional **D/D/R:** Teaching Mathematics, Computer Science, Web Development and Web Design, Employment Training and Workforce Development **H/I/S:** Snow Skiing, Sailing, Boating, Golfing **EDU:** Coursework in Computer Science, University at Buffalo (1984); Master's Degree in Mathematics Education, Buffalo State University (1976) **A/A/S:** Worked on National Science Foundation Grant on Web Development; Former Chairwoman of the Mathematics and Computer Science Department (1983-1985); Director of Title III Grant on Computer Implementation into the Curriculum (1985-1988)

RAMONA KAY LACEY LPN
Licensed Practical Nurse, Office Nurse
Riverside Medical Center, Peotone Community Health Center
611 S. Division Street
Peotone, IL 60468 United States
rmlacey@comcast.net
http://www.riversidehealthcare.org

BUS: Medical Center **P/S:** Healthcare Services **MA:** Regional **EXP:** Ms. Lacey's expertise includes internal medicine, geriatric and pediatric nursing. **H/I/S:** Traveling, Flower Arranging, Walking, Bicycling, Baking and Decorating Cakes **FBP:** RN; American Journal of Nursing; LPN **CERTS:** Licensed Practical Nurse, School of Practical Nursing, Kankakee Community College **A/A/S:** Mayo Clinic Association; American Cancer Society; Juvenile Diabetes Foundation; Volunteer, American Red Cross; Assistant Sunday School Teacher, Local Church; Former Assistant, Local 4H Club **DOB:** August 20, 1950 **SP:** Michael **CHILD:** Kelly Marie, Michelle Lynn **W/H:** Licensed Practical Nurse, Local Hospital (1969); Licensed Practical Nurse, Local Nursing Home; Licensed Practical Nurse, Riverside Medical Center; Office Nurse, Peotone Community Health Center

MR. DAVID A. LACY
Fire Chief
Zanesville Fire Department
332 South Street
Zanesville, OH 43701 United States
zfd1@coz.org
http://www.coz.org/pubs_fire.cfm

BUS: Fire Department with 58 Fire Fighters **P/S:** Emergency Services to the Citizens of Zanesville **MA:** Regional **D/D/R:** Performing Administrative Duties, Protecting the Community from Fires **FBP:** Forbes **CERTS:** Certified in Hazardous Materials; Certified in Emergency Medical Services; Certified in Fire Safety Inspection **A/A/S:** International and Ohio State Fire Chiefs Associations; National Fire Protection Association; International Code Commission

JEANENE M. LAEGREID, MS, PT, PCS
Physical Therapist
Children's Therapy Center, Inc.
10811 S.E. Kent Kangley Road
Kent, WA 98030 United States
jlaegreid@aol.com
http://www.childrenstherapyctr.com

BUS: Nonprofit Organization **P/S:** Physical and Occupational Therapy, Aquatic Therapy, Speech, Communication and Feeding Therapy, Hippotherapy, Early Education and Playgroups, Dynamic Orthotics and Group and Individual Therapy for Children Ages 0-21 **MA:** Regional **D/D/R:** Acting as a Pediatric Clinical Specialist, Working with Children on an Outpatient Basis, Performing Physical Therapy for Motor Development Enhancement, Treating Feeding Problems with Orthotic Molds, Collaborating in Occupational and Speech Therapy **H/I/S:** Skiing, Gardening, Singing, Crocheting, Kayaking **FBP:** PT Magazine **EDU:** Master of Science in Physical Therapy, University of Southern California (1985) **CERTS:** Certified Advanced Pediatric Clinical Specialist, American Physical Therapy Association (2004) **A/A/S:** Seattle Women's Chorus; Neuro-Developmental Treatment Association; American Physical Therapy Association

DENEL O. LaFLEUR
Risk Management, PI, JCAHO
Acadian Medical Center
3501 Highway 190 E.
Eunice, LA 70535 United States
denel.lafleur@lpnt.net
http://www.cambridgewhoswho.com

BUS: Full-Service Hospital **P/S:** Healthcare **MA:** Local **EXP:** Ms. LaFleur's expertise is in performance improvement. **H/I/S:** Reading, Traveling **FBP:** Nursing Management; Perspective **EDU:** Master's Degree in Health Science Administration, University of St. Francis, Joliet, IL **A/A/S:** Mercy Award, 2006 **C/VW:** American Cancer Society, Special Olympics **A/S:** She attributes her success to her supportive home and work environment. **B/I:** She became involved in her profession because she wanted to make a difference and be part of policymaking. **H/O:** The highlight of her career was receiving the Mercy Award for exemplary service in 2006.

BARBARA B. LAHR
Senior Technical Specialist
Penn State Milton S. Hershey Medical Center
500 University Drive
Hershey, PA 17033 United States
timbala@aol.com
http://www.hmc.psu.edu

BUS: Medical Center **P/S:** Healthcare **MA:** Statewide **EXP:** Ms. Lahr's expertise is in laboratory medicine. **H/I/S:** Reading, Making Crafts, Walking **EDU:** Bachelor's Degree in Medical Technology, Millersville University of Pennsylvania **A/A/S:** American Society for Clinical Pathology; Bethesda Mission **A/S:** She attributes her success to the support she receives from her supervisors and mentors. **B/I:** She became involved in her profession because of her love for science. **H/O:** The most gratifying aspect of her career is working in her current position and the gratitude she receives from her staff.

JASPER CHUN-PING LAI
Real Estate Agent
U.S. Giants Real Estate
2585 Wallingford Road
San Marino, CA 91108 United States
laibowl@hotmail.com
http://www.jasperlai.com

BUS: Real Estate Brokerage **P/S:** Residential and Commercial Brokerage and Mortgage Services **MA:** Regional **D/D/R:** Selling Residential and Commercial Real Estate **H/I/S:** Playing Tennis, Investing in the Stock Market **FBP:** Barron's; Investor's Business Daily **EDU:** Coursework, La Sierra University **C/VW:** Buddhist Compassion Relief Tzu Chi Foundation; American Red Cross **A/S:** He attributes his success to King Fang Lai and Yei Chu Yeh Lai. **B/I:** He became involved in his profession because of his family background.

DONALD E. LAKE III
JD, Trial Attorney
Pryor Johnson Carney Karr Nixon, PC
5619 DTC Parkway
Suite 1200
Englewood, CO 80111 United States
dlake@pjckn.com
http://www.cambridgewhoswho.com

BUS: Law Firm **P/S:** Trial Attorneys Offering Defense Services for Healthcare Professionals **MA:** Regional **D/D/R:** Specializing as a Trial Attorney, Defending Medical Negligence and Insurance Coverage Issues **H/I/S:** Skiing, Bicycling **EDU:** JD, University of Denver; Bachelor's Degree in Political Science, The University of Oklahoma **A/A/S:** Colorado Bar Association; American Bar Association; Leadership Program, ADL **C/VW:** Children's Hospital; Multiple Sclerosis Foundation

EVA LaMANTIA
Realtor
Grove Realty
http://www.groverealtors.com

BUS: Real Estate **P/S:** Commercial and Residential Real Estate Sales **MA:** Local **EXP:** Ms. LaMantia's expertise is in residential real estate. **H/I/S:** Spending Time with her Children, Bowling, Swimming, Organizing **FBP:** Realtor **EDU:** Coursework in Hotel Management, Climate Control Institute **A/A/S:** Woodridge Chamber of Commerce; Downers Grove Chamber of Commerce; Illinois Association of Realtors **C/VW:** American Veterans, Goodwill **A/S:** She attributes her success to being goal oriented, having a positive attitude and caring about her clients. **B/I:** She was prompted to enter her profession because she had an interest in the field. **H/O:** The highlight of her profession was being the top agent last year.

KATHERINE T. LAMBERT
Social Worker
Katherine T. Lambert, Licensed Social Worker
25 Hurd Street, Suite 1
Lowell, MA 01852 United States
klambert226@comcast.net
http://www.cambridgewhoswho.com

BUS: Sole Proprietorship **P/S:** Social Work Including Psychiatric and Addiction Treatment **MA:** Local **EXP:** Ms. Lambert's expertise is in dual diagnosis and mental health assistance. **H/I/S:** Spending Time with her Family, Quilting, Traveling, Reading **FBP:** Psychotherapy Networker **EDU:** Master's Degree in Social Work, Salem State College **CERTS:** Licensed Independent Clinical Social Worker; Certified Clinical Alcohol, Tobacco and Other Drugs Social Worker; Dual Diagnosis and Addictions Certification, Boston University **A/A/S:** National Association of Social Workers; National Association of Alcohol and Drug Abuse Counselors; Academy of Certified Social Workers **A/H:** Employee of Excellence, Lowell General Hospital **C/VW:** Local Church; Organizations that Assist Disabled Children and their Families **A/S:** She attributes her success to her determination and ability to understand addictions and disease processes. **H/O:** The most gratifying aspect of her career is inspiring clients to seek recovery from substance abuse, mental health and health issues through caring rather than through guilt and shame.

WENDY L. LAMINACK, CRRN
Care Manager, Registered Nurse
1500 N. Ritter Avenue
Indianapolis, IN 46219 United States
yasmeen33@sbcglobal.net
http://www.ecommunity.com

BUS: Healthcare System **P/S:** Healthcare Services Including Primary Care, Cardiac Care, Fast Emergency Treatment, Innovative Surgical Services, Rehabilitation and Home Health Services **MA:** Regional **EXP:** Ms. Laminack's expertise is in rehabilitation and medical-surgical nursing. **D/D/R:** Overseeing the Non-License Group of 170 Members and Clinical Options, Working as a Clinical Manager for the Resource Department **H/I/S:** Family Gatherings **EDU:** Bachelor of Science in Nursing, Ball State University (1994) **CERTS:** Certified Rehabilitation Registered Nurse (2000) **A/A/S:** Association of Rehabilitation Nurses **SP:** Karim **CHILD:** Samantha, Sarah, Yusuf **A/S:** She attributes her success to the support she receives from her family and professionals. **H/O:** The most gratifying aspect of her career is working at her current position.

SISTER MARY KRISTEN LANCASTER
Administrative Representative,
Administrator of Transitional Care Unit
St. Joseph's/Candler Health System
11705 Mercy Boulevard
Savannah, GA 31419 United States
kristens@sjchs.org
http://www.cambridgewhoswho.com

BUS: Health System **P/S:** Healthcare **MA:** Local **EXP:** Sister Lancaster's expertise is in risk management. **D/D/R:** Overseeing Administrative Duties, Nursing **H/I/S:** Spending Time at the Beach, Gardening, Spending Time Outdoors **FBP:** Modern Healthcare; The Wall Street Journal **EDU:** Master of Health Administration, Saint Louis University, MO (1983); Master of Science in Nursing, The Catholic University of America, Washington, DC (1963); Bachelor of Science in Nursing, Mount Saint Agnes College, Baltimore, MD (1958); Coursework, Sisters of Mercy of Baltimore, MD (1948) **CERTS:** Registered Nurse, Mercy Medical Center, Baltimore, MD (1947); Licensed Nursing Home Administrator **A/A/S:** Community Advisory Committee, Institutional Review Board, Sigma Theta Tau International **A/H:** Woman of the Year Award, American Biographical Institute (2006) **DOB:** March 13, 1926 **W/H:** Risk Manager, Saint Joseph's Hospital, Savannah, GA (1996-2002); Coordinator, Performance and Risk Manager, Childcare, Saint Joseph's Hospital, Savannah, GA (1989); Vice President, Quality Assurance Coordinator, Risk Manager, Saint Joseph's Hospital, Savannah, GA (1983-1992); Administrative Assistant, Saint Joseph's Hospital, Savannah, GA (1980-1981); Consultant, Coordinator of Services for the Aged, Catholic Social Services, Inc. (Now Catholic Charities Atlanta, Inc., Archdiocese of Atlanta, Inc.) (1978-1980); Assistant Administrator, Saint Joseph's Infirmary, Atlanta, GA (1973-1977); Director, School of Nursing, Saint Joseph's Infirmary, Atlanta, GA (1963-1973); Director, Department of Nursing, Saint Joseph's Infirmary, Atlanta, GA (1963-1966); Administrator, Stella Maris Hospice, Baltimore, MD (1961-1962); Supervisor, St. Martin de Porres, Mobile, AL (1960-1961); Nurse, Saint Joseph's Infirmary, Atlanta, GA (1950-1961)

MICHAEL W. LANDERS
Chief Executive Officer, President
Integrity Development Group, LLP
3020 Highlands Parkway S.E., Suite C
Smyrna, GA 30082 United States
mlanders@integritydevgroup.com
kvasquez@integritydevgroup.com
http://www.integritydevgroup.com

BUS: Real Estate Acquisition and Development Company **P/S:** Real Estate Acquisition and Land Development **MA:** Regional **EXP:** Mr. Landers' expertise is in management. **D/D/R:** Overseeing Administration, Managing Land Acquisition and Development **H/I/S:** Spending Time with his Children, Writing, Observing Architecture **FBP:** Atlanta Business Chronicle **EDU:** Industry-Related Training and Experience **A/H:** Build Georgia Award (2007); Apple Of Our Eye Award; Beautification Award **C/VW:** The Watchtower Bible and Tract Society **POB:** Decatur, Alabama **A/S:** He attributes his success to his honesty and entrepreneurial spirit. **B/I:** He became involved in his profession because of his entrepreneurial spirit. **H/O:** The most gratifying aspect of his career is successfully completing his projects.

MR. MARSHALL R. LANDESMAN
Property Manager
Grubb & Ellis Management Services, Inc.
20600 Chagrin Boulevard
Suite 180
Beachwood, OH 44122 United States
marshall.landesman@grubb-ellis.com
http://www.grubb-ellis.com

BUS: Commercial Real Estate Firm **P/S:** Complete Ranges of Transactions, Management and Consulting Services **MA:** International **D/D/R:** Overseeing Daily Operations, Handling the East and West Sides of Cleveland, Managing Budgeting, Staff Members and Tenant Relations, Leasing, Preparing Finances for Owners **H/I/S:** Traveling by Motorcycle, Bowling, Participating in Church Activities **FBP:** Crane's Cleveland Business **EDU:** College Coursework; Coursework, Institute of Real Estate Management **CERTS:** Licensed in Real Estate, State of Ohio **A/A/S:** Former Member of the Board of Trustees, Northeastern Ohio Apartment Association

DEBBIE LANE, LCSW
School Social Worker, Licensed Clinical Social Worker
LaSalle Elementary School
1165 Saint Vincents Avenue
LaSalle, IL 61301 United States
dlane@lphs.net
http://www.cambridgewhoswho.com

BUS: Public Elementary School **P/S:** Education **MA:** Local **D/D/R:** Offering Services for Behavior Modification, Crisis Intervention, Child Welfare System-Foster Care, Drug and Alcohol Assessments, Working with the Child Welfare System as a School Social Worker, Handling Bullying, School and Domestic Violence and Sexual Assault Issues **H/I/S:** Reading, Hiking, Sports **FBP:** NASW Journal **EDU:** Master of Social Work, Aurora University (2002); Bachelor's Degree in Social Work, MacMurray College (1999) **CERTS:** Licensed Clinical Social Worker (2004) **A/A/S:** National Association of Social Workers; School Social Work Association of America

SHERYL L. LANE, M.ED.
Support Specialist
Cairo Elementary School
Ontario School District
195 S.W. Third Avenue
Ontario, OR 97914 United States
slane@ontario.k12.or.us
http://www.ontario.k12.or.us

BUS: School District **P/S:** Primary Education **MA:** Regional **D/D/R:** Developing the Curriculum, Instructing Students, Teaching Behavior Management and Special Education to Kindergarten through 12th-Grade Students, Planning Lessons **H/I/S:** Attending Dog Shows **FBP:** Educational Leadership; CEC Journal **EDU:** Master of Education in Educational Leadership, University of Idaho (2004) **A/A/S:** National Education Association **A/H:** Outstanding Trio Alumni Award, Idaho State University (1990); Student of the Year Award, Idaho State University (1988) **C/VW:** United Cerebral Palsy Association **A/S:** She attributes her success to her passion for her profession. **B/I:** She became involved in her profession because she always wanted to become an educator. **H/O:** The highlight of her career was being a part of Ohio State Alumni Association.

JULIA A. LANG
Special Education Teacher
Basalt High School
Roaring Fork School District
600 Southside Drive
Basalt, CO 81621 United States
jull@rfsd.k12.co
http://www.rfsd.k12.co.us

BUS: Public Education **P/S:** School Programs for Ninth to Twelfth Grade Students, Honor Classes as well as All Core Academics **MA:** Regional **D/D/R:** Teaching High School Students with Mild to Moderate Disabilities, Using the Block System by Seeing the Students Once a Day or Every Other Day Depending on their Needs, Running the Literacy Lab in Basic English and Mathematics, Teaching Time Management, Organizational, Study and Academic Skills to the Resource Class **H/I/S:** Traveling, Reading, Spending Time with her Family and Friends **EDU:** Master's Degree in Special Education, Seton Hall University (2001) **A/A/S:** National Educator's Association; Council for Exceptional Children

MS. JERALDINE CATHERINE LANGE, RN
Registered Nurse (Retired)
Lucille Packard Children's Hospital
1472 London Circle
Benicia, CA 94510 United States
jeraldinecatherine.lange@cwwemail.com
http://www.lpch.org

BUS: Nonprofit Hospital **P/S:** Medical Care for Babies, Children, Adolescents and Expectant Mothers **MA:** Regional **D/D/R:** Caring for Ventilated Intensive Care Infants, Cardiac Babies and Post-Operative Patients, Working In Neonatal Intensive Care Unit **H/I/S:** Exercising, Running, Spending Time with her Friends, Cooking, Going to the Health Club, Traveling **FBP:** NurseWeek **EDU:** Bachelor's Degree, St. Mary's College, Moraga, CA; Post-Graduate Coursework, Operating Room, Stanford Medical Center; Coursework in Liberal Arts **CERTS:** Registered Nurse, Indiana and Alameda County Medical Center, Saint Mary's College, Oakland (1967) **W/H:** Flight Attendant, Flying Tiger Airline (1980-1981, 1990-1992); Registered Nurse, Lucille Packard Children's Hospital (Retired); Bed-Side Nurse, Stanford Medical Center (Retired)

EDWARD HAROLD LANSBERRY, CCT/CVT, CNA
Monitor Technician, Unit Coordinator
Altoona Regional Health Systems
2500 Seventh Avenue
Altoona, PA 16602 United States
edcctcna@aol.com
http://www.cambridgewhoswho.com

BUS: Hospital **P/S:** Healthcare **MA:** Local **EXP:** Mr. Lansberry's expertise is in cardiology . **H/I/S:** Playing the Organ at Church **EDU:** Associate Degree **A/A/S:** Alliance of Cardiovascular Professionals; Cardiovascular Credentialing International **A/S:** He attributes his success to hard work and self drive. **B/I:** He chose the profession because he lost his brother in a car accident, and after seeing the care he received in the emergency room, she decided to pursue the field. **H/O:** The most gratifying aspect of his career is setting goals and meeting them.

CANDACE C. LARKIN
President
EZ Pro Delivery, Inc.
300 Ames Street
Saginaw, MI 48602 United States
candace@ezprodelivery.com
http://www.ezprodelivery.com

BUS: Courier Service Agency **P/S:** Delivery of Dry Ice, Infectious and Diagnostic Medical Items, X-Ray Equipment, Legal Documents and Lab Specimens **MA:** National **D/D/R:** Bidding on Jobs, Supervising 31 Employees, Developing the Business, Traveling, Overseeing the Company as the Chief Executive Officer, Packing and Shipping Medical Specimens, Selling Dry Ice Pellets for Packaging and Shipping Purposes **H/I/S:** Golfing, Reading **FBP:** Books by John Grisham **EDU:** Coursework in Business; High School Education **A/A/S:** Local Chamber of Commerce; Better Business Bureau **H/O:** The most rewarding aspects of her job is saving lives and knowing that she's making a difference. **I/F/Y:** In five years, Ms. Larkin would like to sell franchises and expand her business to reach a greater share of the market.

BARBARA L. LARSEN, MFT
Marriage and Family Therapist
Barbara Larsen, MFT
39791 Paseo Padre Parkway
Suite C
Fremont, CA 94538 United States
larsenbl@comcast.net
http://www.cambridgewhoswho.com

BUS: Psychotherapy Practice **P/S:** Psychotherapy, Energy Therapy, Therapeutic Meditation **MA:** Local **D/D/R:** Administering Psychotherapy, Healing Touch Energy and Therapeutic Meditation Therapy **H/I/S:** Gardening, Listening to Music, Reading, Hiking **EDU:** Master of Science in Counseling, California State University, Sacramento (1972); Bachelor of Arts in Psychology and Philosophy, University of California, Davis (1965) **A/A/S:** California Association of Marriage and Family Therapists; Association for Comprehensive Energy Psychology; Healing Touch International **DOB:** January 17, 1944 **A/S:** She attributes her success to her understanding of the concept of oneness. **B/I:** She became involved in her profession after her college advisor recommended it to her. **H/O:** The most gratifying aspect of her career is being able to make an impact in the lives of others through her work.

SUSAN K. LARSON, LPN
Licensed Practical Nurse
HCR Manor Care
7850 W. College Drive
Palos Heights, IL 60463 United States
cubfans037@aol.com
http://www.cambridgewhoswho.com

BUS: Rehabilitation Center **P/S:** Healthcare, Long Term, Rehabilitation **MA:** Local **D/D/R:** Caring for 30 Residents, Monitoring and Assessing Patients, Dispensing Medications **H/I/S:** Downhill Skiing, Reading **FBP:** Nursing2009; Nursing Spectrum **EDU:** Pursuing Bachelor of Science in Nursing, Saint Xavier University **CERTS:** Licensed Practical Nurse, Joliet Township High School; Certified in Geriatric Nursing **A/A/S:** First Licensed Practical Nurse at her Job to Receive her Certification in Geriatric Nursing **C/VW:** Cerebral Palsy Foundation, Cornerstone Services **A/S:** She attributes her success to her desire to see people get better as a result of her care. **B/I:** She became involved in this profession because she always wanted to help others in the healthcare field. **H/O:** The highlight of her career was setting a new school record for her score on the mock board exam.

JOYCE E. LaRUE
Co-Owner, Secretary, Treasurer
Premium Elks, Inc.
10713 State Highway 149
Unionville, MO 63565 United States
larulj@nemr.net
http://www.premiumelk.com

BUS: Food Processing and Sales Company **P/S:** Elk Meat and Products **MA:** National **D/D/R:** Overseeing Daily Operations and Public Relations, Packing and Shipping Orders **H/I/S:** Reading, Sewing, Cooking, Baking, Hunting, Fishing **FBP:** North American Elk **CERTS:** Certified Nurse Aide, State of Missouri **A/A/S:** President, Missouri Elk Farmers Association; Rocky Mountain Elk Foundation; North American Elk Breeders Association **C/VW:** Volunteer Firefighter, Liberty Township Fire Department, Omaha, MO; First Responder, Liberty Township Fire Department; American Legion Auxiliary; Veterans of Foreign Wars **DOB:** August 16, 1941 **POB:** Iowa City **SP:** Loyd **CHILD:** Doreen, Ferlin, Leslie, Melody **A/S:** She attributes her success to her hard work, quality products and people skills. **B/I:** She became involved in her profession after deciding to raise elk. **H/O:** The most gratifying aspects of her career are going to shows and meeting and greeting people.

MARTHA M. LATHAM, CDM, CFPP
Tray Line and Storeroom Supervisor,
Certified Food Protection Professional, CDM
DCH Regional Medical Center
809 University Boulevard.
Tuscaloosa, AL 35401 United States
mlatham@dchsystem.com
http://www.cambridgewhoswho.com

BUS: Hospital **P/S:** Healthcare **MA:** Local **EXP:** Ms. Latham's expertise is in patient food service and supply. **H/I/S:** Camping, Fishing, Hunting, Cross-stitching **FBP:** Food and Restaurant Management Magazine **CERTS:** Certified in Dietary Management, University of Florida; Certified Food Safety Instructor **A/A/S:** Dietary Manager Association; National Restaurant Association; Instructor, DCH Health System **C/VW:** St. Jude's; Alzheimer's Association, March of Dimes **A/S:** She attributes her personal and professional success to her hard work and dedication. **B/I:** She became involved in the food services industry after working as a dishwasher in a nursing home and enjoying the patient care the facility offered. **H/O:** The highlight of her career is the patient appreciation for her services and becoming certified as a Dietary Manager in 1996.

VIRGINIA C. LATTA
Commercial Line Supervisor, Office Manager
North County Insurance
350 W. Ninth Avenue, Suite 106
Escondido, CA 92025 United States
vlatta@northcountyinsurance.com
http://www.northcountyinsurance.com

BUS: Insurance Company **P/S:** Property, Casualty, Life and Health Insurance, Disability and Bond Services **MA:** Regional **EXP:** Ms. Latta's expertise is in bond services and insurance. **D/D/R:** Managing Large Accounts and Property, Casualty, Life, Health and Disability, Supervising, Overseeing Compliance and Regulations, Managing Operations, Ensuring Good Customer Service, Managing the Office **H/I/S:** Walking, Golfing, Spending Time with her Family, Traveling **CERTS:** Certified Insurance Service Representative; Registered Bond Person, The Travelers Companies, Inc.; Licensed Insurance Agent

NANETTE DIANN LAURITSEN
Caregiver
802 E. First Street
Pella, IA 50219 United States
nannet@netzero.com
http://www.cambridgewhoswho.com

BUS: Sole Proprietorship **P/S:** Caregiving Services for Elderly People **MA:** Local **EXP:** Ms. Lauritsen's expertise is in elderly care. **D/D/R:** Feeding and Bathing Elderly Patients, Administering Medications **H/I/S:** Reading, Writing Poem, Cooking, Playing Tennis **FBP:** BusinessWeek **EDU:** Coursework in Secretarial Studies, Des Moines Area Community College (1982) **A/A/S:** Cambridge Who's Who **C/VW:** Domestic Violence; Animal Shelter **DOB:** September 10, 1949 **POB:** Des Moines, IA **A/S:** She attributes her success to her persistence. **B/I:** She became involved in her profession because she always wanted to take care of her family. **H/O:** The most gratifying aspect of her career is having the ability to work with people.

MS. KELLI LAVAS JOHNSON
Attorney
Kelli Lavas Johnson, PLLC
728 N. Fielder Road
Arlington, TX 76012 United States
law.kjohnson@yahoo.com
http://www.kellijohnsonlaw.com

BUS: Law Firm **P/S:** Legal Services **MA:** Regional **EXP:** Ms. Johnson's expertise is in probate and estate planning. **D/D/R:** Practicing Personal Bankruptcy and Family Law **H/I/S:** Baking, Attending Dance Classes **EDU:** JD, Texas Wesleyan School of Law (2004); Bachelor of Science in Political Science, Texas Christian University (2001) **CERTS:** License in Law, State Bar of Texas (2006) **A/A/S:** Tarrant County Bar Association; Tarrant County Probate Bar Association; Tarrant County Young Lawyers Association; American Bar Association; National Association of Consumer Bankruptcy Attorneys

TROY LAVIGNE
Massage Therapist
Imagine Massage Therapy Inc.
1011 Walnut Street
Suite 201
Boulder, CO 80302 United States
troy_jesse@hotmail.com
http://www.cambridgewhoswho.com

BUS: Massage Therapy **P/S:** Massage, Reiki **MA:** Regional **D/D/R:** Performing Therapeutic, Neuro-Structural Integration Technique, Orthopedic, Sports, Swedish and Reiki Massages **H/I/S:** Competitive Soccer, Hiking, Cooking **CERTS:** Certified Massage Therapist, Boulder College of Massage Therapy (2005); Certified Reiki Master (2002) **A/A/S:** American Massage Therapy Association; Chairman, Boulder College Alumni **C/VW:** Kick Start My Heart **A/S:** He attributes his success to his love for his work and the fact that he enjoys bringing knowledge to his clients. **B/I:** He became involved in his profession because his father was a massage therapist and got him interested in a high level of aromatherapy and healing others. **H/O:** The highlight of his career was becoming an official massage therapist for Colorado Rapid Reserves.

EMMA R. LAWLER, RN, BSN, CM-DN, CLNC

Registered Nurse, Director of Nursing Services
RCM of Washington
900 Second Street N.E., Suite 8
Washington, DC 20002 United States
emmlaw@msn.com
emma.lawler@cwwemail.com
http://www.ytbtravel.com/emanee

BUS: Assisted Living Company **P/S:** Healthcare **MA:** Local **D/D/R:** Ms. Lawler's expertise includes case management, medical-surgical and legal nurse consulting and education. **H/I/S:** Working Out, Rollerskating **FBP:** American Journal of Nursing **EDU:** Bachelor of Science in Nursing, University of the District of Columbia; Registered Nurse **CERTS:** Certified Legal Nurse Consultant; Certification in Case and Disease Management **A/A/S:** Washington DC Nurses Association; Coalition for Developmental Disability; American Nurses Association **C/VW:** Volunteers of America; Believers Worship Center; United Way of America; The Salvation Army; Goodwill Industries International **A/S:** She attributes her success to her time management skills. **B/I:** She became involved in her profession because she always wanted to help people. **H/O:** The highlight of her career was the critical care course in 1996.

DONNA GRACE LAWSON

Academic Coach, Teacher
Clarksville-Montgomery County Schools
3705 Trenton Road
Clarksville, TN 37040 United States
donnas_arbonne@bellsouth.net
http://www.cambridgewhoswho.com

BUS: School **P/S:** Education **MA:** Local **D/D/R:** Educating Kindergarten through Eighth-Grade Students **H/I/S:** Reading, Traveling, Quilting **EDU:** Master's Degree in Administration and Supervision, Trevecca Nazarene University **A/A/S:** Association for Supervision and Curriculum Development **C/VW:** United Way, Diabetes Association, March of Dimes **A/S:** She attributes her success to hard work and passion. **B/I:** She became involved in her profession because as a student she enjoyed school very much and decided to pursue a career in education. **H/O:** The most gratifying aspect of her career is when former students return to thank her.

HELEN V. LAZERATION, BSN, CRNI
Registered Nurse, Vice President of
Alastan Mining and Development
Fairbanks Memorial Hospital
1650 Cowles Street
Fairbanks, AK 99701 United States
skyline@alaska.net
http://www.cambridgewhoswho.com

BUS: Hospital **P/S:** Healthcare **MA:** Local **EXP:** Ms. Lazeration's expertise is in infection control. **H/I/S:** Traveling, Gardening, Photography, Quilting **EDU:** Bachelor of Arts in Science, University of Portland; Registered Nurse **A/A/S:** Infusion Nurses Society; Association for Vascular Access; Association for Professionals in Infection Control and Epidemiology **C/VW:** Fairbanks Memorial Hospital Foundation; United Way **A/S:** She attributes her success to her determination and self-motivation. **B/I:** She became involved in her profession because of her desire to help people. **H/O:** The highlight of her career was earning her current position.

CORALEE LEAB
Owner, Accountant
Leab's Accounting, LLC
10360 Cool Hollow Road
Greencastle, PA 17225 United States
leabsaccounting@comcast.net
http://www.cambridgewhoswho.com

BUS: Accounting Firm **P/S:** Accounting Services Including Bookkeeping, Tax and Payroll Preparation, QuickBooks Management and Consulting Services **MA:** Pennsylvania, Maryland **EXP:** Ms. Leab's area of expertise is in public accounting. **H/I/S:** Camping, Spending Time with her Family, Cross Stitching, Traveling, Collecting Antiques **FBP:** My Business **EDU:** Pursuing Bachelor's Degree, Frostburg State University; Associate Degree in Accounting and Computers, Hagerstown Business College **A/A/S:** Maryland Association of Certified Public Accountants; Pennsylvania Society of Public Accountants; President, Mercersburg Area Swim Club **A/H:** Biltmore Who's Who (2008) **C/VW:** Local Church; Brandts Church of the Brethren; National Wildlife Federation **A/S:** She attributes her success to her knowledge and work experience. **B/I:** She became involved in this profession because she always had an interest in accounting and bookkeeping. **H/O:** The most gratifying aspect of her career is generating profit and loss reports for her clients. **I/F/Y:** In five years, Ms. Leab hopes to expand her business.

JERRY P. LEARY
President
Lawn Pro
4876-118 Princess Anne Road
Suite 410
Virginia Beach, VA 23456 United States
jerryleary@lawnpro.org
http://www.cambridgewhoswho.com

BUS: Landscaping Firm **P/S:** Landscaping Services Including Installation of Landscaping Devices **MA:** Local **EXP:** Mr. Leary's expertise is in landscape design. **H/I/S:** Fishing **FBP:** Portfolio **EDU:** Bachelor of Business Administration, St. Edward's University **A/A/S:** Virginia Beach Division, Hampton Roads Chamber of Commerce; Better Business Bureau **SP:** Karen **CHILD:** Mark, Ryan **A/S:** He attributes his success to his passion for his profession. **B/I:** He became involved in his profession because he had an interest in landscaping. **H/O:** The most gratifying aspects of his career are overseeing his own business and being in the landscaping profession, which he loves.

MR. DAVID J. LeBEAU
W. New England Representative
Bonhams Auctioneer and Appraisers
119 S. Main Street
PO Box 398
Sheffield, MA 01257 United States
djlebeau@verizon.net
http://www.appraisalbylebeau.com

BUS: Auction House **P/S:** Auctioning of Fine Art and Antiques, Paintings, Motor Cars and Cycles, Books, Porcelain, Contemporary Ceramics, Jewelry and Rivercraft **MA:** International **D/D/R:** Working with Antiquarian Generalists **H/I/S:** Volunteer at the Arts Center **FBP:** American Society of Appraisers Online Newspaper **EDU:** Master of Fine Arts, Carnegie Institute of Technology **A/A/S:** ASA; Boy Scouts Council; Cancer Society

KATHERINE J. LEBLANC
Director of Materials Management
Providence Alaska Regional Medical Center
3200 Providence Drive
Anchorage, AK 99508 United States
kleblanc@provak.org
http://www.cambridgewhoswho.com

BUS: Nonprofit Acute-Care Medical Center **P/S:** Healthcare **MA:** Local **D/D/R:** Specializing in Supply Chain Management, Purchasing Products and Equipment **H/I/S:** Snowmobiling, Reading, Working in her Yard, Spending Time Outdoors **FBP:** Materials Management Purchasing Guide **EDU:** Coursework in Administration, National Materials Management Society **A/A/S:** Association for Healthcare Resource & Materials Management; Professional Women's Association; Carols Management Society **C/VW:** Various Local Charities; St. Jude Children's Research Hospital **A/S:** She attributes her success to her determination. **B/I:** She became involved in her profession through a natural progression of opportunities.

DEBRA ROPER LEDFORD, AA
Owner, Director
Kids Corner Child Care
168 Upper Peachtree Road
Murphy, NC 28906 United States
debbieledford2@hotmail.com
http://www.cambridgewhoswho.com

BUS: Child Care Center **P/S:** Morning and after School Program for Children **MA:** Local **D/D/R:** Managing Administrative Duties and Contracts, Overseeing Staff Members and Children, Demonstrating Effective Leadership and Working with Children on Life Skills **H/I/S:** Spending Time with her Husband, Friends and Family, Volunteering, Reading, Spending Time Outdoors **FBP:** Ladies' Home Journal **EDU:** Associate Degree in Early Childhood Education, Tri-County Community College, NC (1997) **A/A/S:** National Association for the Advancement of Colored People **A/H:** Four Star Rating **C/VW:** The Boy Scouts of America; Child Guarding Programs; Smart Start Program; Special Olympics **A/S:** She attributes her success to her determination and to the support she receives from her family. **B/I:** She became involved in her profession because she always wanted to help and work with children. **H/O:** The most gratifying aspect of her career is running her business successfully. **I/F/Y:** In five years, Ms. Ledford hopes to receive a certification to work with special needs children.

REV. CYNTHIA A. LEE
Minister of Discipleship
Shadygrove United Methodist Church
8209 Shadygrove Road
Mechanicsville, VA 23111 United States
cindylee@shadygroveumc.org
http://www.shadygroveumc.org

BUS: Church **P/S:** Program Planning **MA:** Local **D/D/R:** Specializing in Christian Education and Formation **H/I/S:** Singing, Sewing, Reading, College Football Games **FBP:** Leader Magazine in Christian Educational and Ministries **EDU:** Master of Arts Degree in Christian Education, Scarritt College for Christian Workers; Bachelor of Science in Clothing, Textile and Related Arts, Virginia Polytechnic Institute and State University **A/A/S:** National Christian Education Association Fellowship; Virginia Conference Christian Education Fellowship **C/VW:** Mission Work at Gulf Coast, Soup at Monroe Park Methodist Church, Congregations around Richmond to Create Affordable Shelters **A/S:** She attributes her success to her personality, being a good listener and having a good grasp on education. **B/I:** She became involved in this profession because she has a passion for the field and has always been recruited for all her positions. **H/O:** The highlight of her career is working with children and watching them grow and change.

HERB M. LEE JR.
Executive Director
Pacific American Foundation
629 Kailua Road
Suite 208
Kailua, HI 96734 United States
herblee@thepaf.org
http://www.thepaf.org

BUS: Nonprofit Organization **P/S:** Life Improvement Services for Citizens of the United States Who Can Trace their Ancestry to the Indigenous Settlers **MA:** National **EXP:** Mr. Lee's expertise is in administration and communication. **H/I/S:** Listening to Music **FBP:** Fund Development Journals **EDU:** Master of Arts, University of Hawaii **A/A/S:** International Association for Public Participation **A/S:** He attributes his success to his ability to connect well with people on many different levels. **B/I:** He became involved in his profession because he wanted to connect with the community. **H/O:** The highlight of his career was when his organization became the new model for Hawaiian culture-based curriculum.

LORI A. LEE, RN
Registered Nurse, Emergency Room Manager
Christus St. John Hospital
18300 St. John Drive
Nassau Bay, TX 77058 United States
lori.lee@christushealth.org
http://www.cambridgewhoswho.com

BUS: Hospital **P/S:** Healthcare **MA:** Local **D/D/R:** Nursing **FBP:** Journal of Emergency Nursing **EDU:** Pursuing Degree in Business Management, University of Phoenix; Associate Degree in Nursing, Lamar University **A/A/S:** Emergency Nurses Association **C/VW:** Church **A/S:** She attributes her personal and professional success to her quality patient care. **B/I:** She became involved in the profession because she always had a passion for nursing. **H/O:** The most gratifying aspect of her career is the quality patient care she provides.

STEPHEN M. LEE
Buyer
Lear Siegler Logistics International
1070 Arian Circle
Suite 150
San Antonio, TX 78216 United States
stephenmlee2005@yahoo.com
http://www.cambridgewhoswho.com

BUS: Defense Contract Supplier **P/S:** Procurement **MA:** International **D/D/R:** Managing a Supply Chain, Contracting **H/I/S:** Golfing **FBP:** Forbes; Smart Money **EDU:** Master of Science in Business Administration, University of Phoenix, San Antonio; Bachelor of Science in Business Management, University of Phoenix, San Antonio **A/A/S:** National Black MBA Association; National Defense Industrial Association **C/VW:** Free Masons **A/S:** He attributes his personal and professional success to his supportive family and his drive to excel. **B/I:** He became involved in his profession after working in the field for 22 years in the Air Force. **H/O:** The highlight of his career was earning his master's degree.

DOLORES LEE LORENZEN
Owner
D& D Realty
7944 S.E. Foster Road
Portland, OR 97206 United States
dolores.leelorenzen@cwwemail.com
http://www.cambridgewhoswho.com

BUS: Real Estate Agency **P/S:** Real Estate Services **MA:** Local **EXP:** Her expertise is in financial operations management. **H/I/S:** Golfing, Traveling **FBP:** Oregonian Newspaper **EDU:** Bachelor of Arts in Business Finance, Clark College **C/VW:** Queen of Roses; Our Lady of Sorrow; Society of St. Vincent de Paul; St. Augustine Church **SP:** Donald

PAUL H. LeFevre II, M.Ed.
Reading Specialist
East Rochester School District
773 Portland Street
East Rochester, NH 03868 United States
plefevre@metrocast.net
http://www.cambridgewhoswho.com

BUS: School District **P/S:** Education Including Special Programs, Literacy Programs, Athletics and Extracurricular Activities and Special Education **MA:** Regional **D/D/R:** Teaching Special Education, Literature, Reading, Vocabulary and Comprehension Education, Directing Drama and Art **EDU:** Master of Science in Education, University of New England, Biddeford, Maine (2001); Bachelor of Science in Elementary Education, Norwich University (1977); Associate Degree in Art and Drama, Vermont College (1975) **CERTS:** Certification in Special Education and Learning Disabilities, Rivier College **A/A/S:** Association for Supervision and Curriculum Development; International Reading Association

CATHERINE A. LEFTIN
Assistant Vice President
TD Banknorth Inc.
650 Elm Street
Floor One
Manchester, NH 03103 United States
catherine.leftin@tdbanknorth.com
http://www.tdbanknorth.com

BUS: Commercial Bank **P/S:** Financial Services Including Investment Planning, Wealth Management, Insurance and Personal Banking **MA:** International **D/D/R:** Accounting, Underwriting Loans, Reviewing Financial Statements **H/I/S:** Volunteering for the Community, Dancing, Traveling, Attending Church **FBP:** The Wall Street Journal **EDU:** Master's Degree in Accounting, Southern New Hampshire University (2006); Bachelor of Science in Business Studies and Accounting, Minor in Finance, New Hampshire College (1992) **CERTS:** Graduate Certification in Taxation (2004) **C/VW:** New Hampshire Minority Health Coalition; Christian Research Institute

BRENDA THOMAS LEGAUX
Pharmacist
Pharmacy
CVS/pharmacy
125 De Lasalle Drive
New Iberia, LA 70560 United States
lyn1bren2@yahoo.com
http://www.cvs.com

BUS: Pharmaceutical and Retail Company **P/S:** Retail Merchandise, Pharmacy Services **MA:** Regional **D/D/R:** Managing All Areas of the Pharmacy Department, Processing Prescriptions, Entering Patient Medication Data, Educating and Counseling Patients **H/I/S:** Participating in All Outdoor Sports, Water Sports, Singing in the Choir, Attending Gospel Events **FBP:** Pharmacist's Letter **CERTS:** Registered Pharmacist, College of Pharmacy, Xavier University (1992); Certified Paralegal **A/A/S:** American Pharmaceutical Association **A/H:** Excellent Status, CVS/Pharmacy (2007); Miss JFK (1976); Lemon Award; Top 10 in the Class; CVS Wall of Fame **C/VW:** Historic Saint James African Methodist Episcopal Church, New Orleans, LA; Television Ministries; Veterans for America; Goodwill Industries International, Inc. **DOB:** April 28, 1958 **POB:** New Orleans, LA **SP:** Lynwood **CHILD:** Shea, Lacey **A/S:** She attributes her success to her hard work, experience and faith. **B/I:** She became involved in her profession because it was her father's dream for her to own a pharmacy just as his father did. **H/O:** The highlight of her career was becoming a VIP member of the Cambridge Who's Who Registry.

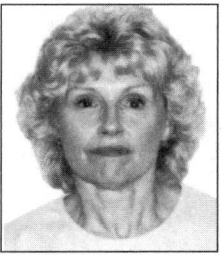

SHARON D. LEHMAN, RN, BSN, CCRN
Staff Nurse
Endoscopy and Gastroenterology Department
Wesley Medical Center
550 N. Hillside Street
Wichita, KS 67214 United States
bclehman@southwind.net
http://www.cambridgewhoswho.com

BUS: Medical Center **P/S:** Healthcare **MA:** Regional **D/D/R:** Gastroenterology Nursing, Overseeing the Pediatric Intensive Care Unit **H/I/S:** Scuba Diving, Running, Bicycling **FBP:** Critical Care Nurse **EDU:** Bachelor of Science in Nursing, Bethel College **CERTS:** Pursuing Certification in Critical Care Nursing **A/A/S:** Professional Practice Council; American Association of Critical-Care Nurses **A/H:** Excellence in Caring Award, Endoscopy Department, Wesley Medical Center (2006) **DOB:** August 27, 1952 **SP:** Barry **CHILD:** Chad, Cory, Christina **W/H:** Data Collection Assistant, Ribavirin and Respiratory Syncytial Virus Study (1989) **A/S:** She attributes her success to her love for people and her ability to treat her patients as her own. **B/I:** She became involved in her profession because of her interest in nursing. **H/O:** The highlight of her career was being nominated by her peers for the Excellence in Care Award in 2006.

JULIAN B. LEISERSON
Production Manager, Stage Manager
San Francisco Lyric Opera
631 O'Farrell Street, Suite 1604
San Francisco, CA 94109 United States
sflyricopera@hotmail.com
http://www.sflyricopera.org

BUS: Entertainment **P/S:** Opera Performances, Children's' Outreach Program **MA:** Local **D/D/R:** Managing Office and Backstage Production **H/I/S:** Unicycling **FBP:** The American Journal of Sociology **EDU:** Bachelor of Science in Sociology, Concentration in Criminology, University of San Francisco **A/A/S:** Free Battered Women

MR. PAUL DEAN LeMAIRE
Chief Executive Officer
Florida Medically Needy Foundation, Inc.
4020 Seashell Circle
Suite 34
Orlando, FL 32804 United States
fmnf32804@yahoo.com
http://www.fmnf.tripod.com

BUS: Nonprofit Organization **P/S:** Healthcare for the Needy **MA:** Statewide **EXP:** Mr. LeMaire's expertise is in business management and mentoring. **H/I/S:** Spending Time with his Son **EDU:** Coursework in Business Administration; Coursework in Hotel and Restaurant Management; Coursework in Photography, Seattle Filmworks School **CERTS:** Certification in Customizing Cars; Captain's License for 100 Turn Off Shore Oil Rig **A/A/S:** Honorary Chairman, Republican Council; United States Marine Corps; Business Advisory Council; Church; Sabers Police Association; Florida Association of State Troopers **A/S:** He attributes his success to his determination and will power. **B/I:** He became involved in his profession because he always wanted to help others. **H/O:** The most gratifying aspect of his career is being able to accomplish Impossible goals.

DEE LEMKE
Owner
Lemke Enterprises
8537 Duchess Court W.
Boynton Beach, FL 33436 United States
mermaid0320@msn.com
blueseamist0320@yahoo.com
http://www.cambridgewhoswho.com

BUS: Consulting Firm **P/S:** Consulting Services **MA:** Southern Florida **EXP:** Ms. Lemke's expertise is in operations management and administration. **H/I/S:** Reading, Solving Puzzles, Playing the Piano **EDU:** Associate Degree in Theatre Arts, MiraCosta Community College (1981)

MR. TOM LENCZYCKI
Senior Store Manager
Mattress Discounters
443 Amherst Street
Nashua, NH 03063 United States
tlenz150@yahoo.com
http://www.cambridgewhoswho.com

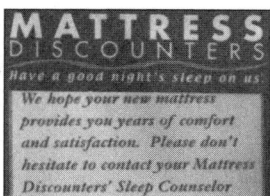

BUS: Largest Mattress Retailer in the United States **P/S:** Manufacture and Distribution, Retail and Discount Mattress Sales **MA:** International **D/D/R:** Management **H/I/S:** Traveling, Reading, Cooking **FBP:** PC World **EDU:** Bachelor's Degree, Saint Anselm College (1973) **A/A/S:** Order of the Arrow; Senior District Executive, Boy Scouts of America **A/H:** Compton's Who's Who (2005); Contemporary Who's Who (2005); Recipient, Contear Sirs **C/VW:** American Red Cross; Civil Air Patrol **SP:** Kathryn Lenczycki (Married 30 Years) **CHILD:** John **W/H:** Senior Store Manager, Mattress Discounters (1997-Present); Sales Consultant, New York Carpet World (1995-1997); Assistant Store Manager, Traveling Manager, Namco; Manufacturers Representative, Canko/Benda (1990-1992); Sales Team Leader, W.M.B. Reilly Co. (1989-1990); District Sales Manager, Sales Representative, John Danais Co. (1985-1989); Senior District Executive, Boy Scouts of America (1980-1985) **C/A:** Taken Two Stores Through Remolding; Worked through the Introduction of a New Store Culture as well as Two Chain Buyouts and a Successful Completion of Chapter 11 Proceedings; Obtained and Excelled in the Knowledge of Chemistry, Mechanics, and Changing Product Knowledge; First Independent Representative to Complete the Corporate Training Program for R.R. Streets Co.; Recognition as a Cubmaster, Troop Leader, and Professional Scouter; Inductee, Scouting Honor Society, The Order of the Arrow; Acknowledgement, Introduction and Promotion of Scouting for the Handicapped in the Northeast

SYBILLA B. LENZ
Owner
Insurance Services
8 Mountain View Terrace
Tunkhannock, PA 18657 United States
rsybil@epix.net
http://www.positivelivingbydesign.com

BUS: Insurance, Finance **P/S:** Annuities, Long Term Care, Life Insurance **MA:** Regional **D/D/R:** Planning for Retirements, Estates and Long-Term Care, Selling, Consulting **H/I/S:** Pottery, Studying Feng Shui **CERTS:** Life Underwriter Training Council Fellow; Certified Senior Advisor **A/A/S:** National Association of Women Business Owners; National Association of Insurance and Professional People; Life Underwriters Training Council; Million Dollar Roundtable; Speaker on Feng Shui

JANE LEONARD
Registered Nurse, Quality/Risk Manager, Operating Room Director,
House Supervisor
United Medical Centers
2525 Veterans Boulevard
Eagle Pass, TX 78852 United States
jleonard.umc@tachc.org
http://www.cambridgewhoswho.com

BUS: Hospital **P/S:** Healthcare **MA:** Regional **D/D/R:** Nursing, Managing the Operating Rooms, Following Staffing Procedures, Purchasing and Maintaining Equipment, Training Staff, Scheduling, Reporting to the Chief Nurse Officer on Patient Services and Care throughout All Hospital Areas **H/I/S:** Horseback Riding, Reading, Traveling, Rescuing Animals **FBP:** The Wall Street Journal; Organic Farming **EDU:** Associate of Applied Science in Nursing, Cambrian College, Ontario, Canada **C/VW:** County Animal Shelter, Meals on Wheels **A/S:** She attributes her success to her perseverance. **B/I:** She chose the profession because she enjoys nursing. **H/O:** The highlight of her career is when she knows she has helped others.

TERRI A. LEPTO
Certified Ombudsman Specialist
Area Agency on Aging
1550 Corporate Woods Parkway
Suite 100
Uniontown, OH 44685 United States
tlepto@services4aging.org
http://www.services4aging.org

BUS: Nonprofit Organization **P/S:** Long-Term Care Management Services Including Family Caregiver Support Programs, Consumer Protection and Education **MA:** Local **D/D/R:** Investigating Complaints in Long-Term Care Facilities, Advocating for Residents' Rights **H/I/S:** Dancing **EDU:** Bachelor's Degree in Medical Technology, West Virginia University **A/A/S:** MTA; West Virginia University Alumni Association **C/VW:** Redeemer Christian School **A/S:** She attributes her success to her desire and passion to help others. **B/I:** She became involved in her profession because she was influenced to help the elderly after caring for her sick mother. **H/O:** The most gratifying aspect of her career is being appreciated by her clients.

MR. DAMON L. LESTER
President of Operations
National Association of Minority Automobile Dealers
8201 Corporate Drive
Suite 190
Lanhan, MD 20795 United States
dmnlester@msn.com
http://www.namad.com

BUS: Nonprofit Automobile Dealer **P/S:** Automobile Services **MA:** National **D/D/R:** Assisting Minorities to Become New Automobile Dealers **H/I/S:** Golfing **FBP:** Time; Newsweek **EDU:** Bachelor's Degree in Business Administration and Accounting, Temple University **A/A/S:** National Association of Black Accountants; National Automobile Dealers Association; Society for Human Resource Management; National Coalition of Black Meeting Planners **A/S:** He contributes his success to his ability to deal with many types of people and hard work. **B/I:** He became involved in this profession because he felt it was a good transition after being an auditor. **H/O:** The most gratifying aspect of his career is his current position..

BARBARA K. LETCHER
Attorney
Newhouse, Prophater and Letcher, LLC
3040 Riverside Drive
Suite 103
Columbus, OH 43221 United States
bletcher@npllawyers.com
http://www.npllawyers.com

BUS: Law Firm **P/S:** Employment Law, Nonprofit Organizations, Small Business, Legal Services **MA:** Local **D/D/R:** Specializing in Labor and Employment Law, Insurance Coverage Disputes and Small Business Work **H/I/S:** Reading, Cooking **EDU:** JD, Ohio State University, Michael E. Moritz College of Law **CERTS:** Certified Labor and Employment Law Specialist, Ohio State Bar Association **A/A/S:** Columbus Bar Association; Ohio State Bar Association; Human Resources Association of Central Ohio; Society for Human Resource Management

SUE H. LEVAN
Accounting Manager
TQM Roofing Inc.
3646 Taylorsville Highway
Statesville, NC 28625 United States
sue@tqmroofing.com
http://www.cambridgewhoswho.com

BUS: Contracting and Construction Company **P/S:** Roofing Construction **MA:** Local **D/D/R:** Overseeing Accounting Management and Administration **H/I/S:** Reading, Listening to Music **FBP:** The Wall Street Journal **EDU:** Degree in Business Accounting, Mitchell College **C/VW:** St. Jude Children's Research Hospital

DEE DEE LEVERETT
Program Coordinator
Office of Homeland Security
Texas A&M University System Health Science Center
301 Tarrow Street, 7th Floor
College Station, TX 77840 United States
leverett@tamhsc.edu
http://www.tamhsc.edu/homeland

BUS: University **P/S:** Higher Education **MA:** Regional **D/D/R:** Organizing Programs, Teaching in Specific Security Courses and Offering a Disaster Life Support Course **H/I/S:** Golfing, Riding her Motorcycle **FBP:** Homeland Defense Journal; Early Bird **A/A/S:** Defense Institute for Medical Operations **A/H:** Recognition Award for Training Public Health Service

Mr. Robert M. LeVine

Founder, Director
Pathways to Personal Excellence
7320 Fifth Avenue N.W.
Bradenton, FL 34209 United States
roblpte1@aol.com
http://www.4pte.com

BUS: Integrated Systems for Increasing Intellect, Energy and Focus Creative Pattern to a Better Life for Children at Risk **P/S:** Motivational Speaking, Personal Improvement, Videos, Animations **MA:** International **D/D/R:** Motivating Positive Life Choices, Working with Children at Risk and Adults Seeking Life Changes **H/I/S:** Training, Traveling, Hiking **FBP:** The Wall Street Journal **EDU:** JD, University of Chicago School of Law; Bachelor of Science in Psychology **A/A/S:** National Real Estate Investors; Edison Academic Board of Directors; Sarasota Boxing Club Board of Directors **C/VW:** Children at Risk **H/O:** The highlights of his career were publishing a law book in 1980 and giving a speech in Toronto.

Carol E. Levy

Owner, President
Carol E. Levy Real Estate
211 Central Park W.
New York, NY 10024 United States
carol@carolelevy.com
http://www.carolelevy.com

BUS: Real Estate Agency **P/S:** High-End Residential Real Estate Sales and Investments **MA:** Local **D/D/R:** Overseeing Residential Real Estate Sales **H/I/S:** Spending Time with her Family, Traveling, Dancing, Going to the Theater, Watching Movies, Swimming, Going to the Beach, Reading **FBP:** The New York Times **EDU:** Bachelor's Degree in Theater, Columbia University **CERTS:** Licensed Broker, State of New York **A/A/S:** Real Estate Board of New York **C/VW:** United Jewish Federation; National Council of Jewish Women; Museum of Natural History; Central Park Conservancy; The Children's Museum **A/S:** She attributes her success to her unparalleled expertise and knowledge of real estate, her passion for her work, always setting the highest standards and exceeding her clients' highest expectations. **B/I:** She became involved in the profession, even though she was a successful actress, because of her love of real estate and superb interpersonal skills, which inspired her to change careers. **H/O:** The highlight of her career was becoming the premier independent broker in New York.

PATRICIA K. LEWALLEN
Realtor
West Realty
N. 24113 Highway 101
Hoodsport, WA 98548 United States
yourbid@hctc.com
http://www.westrealtyonline.com

BUS: Real Estate **P/S:** Residential Land Sales **MA:** International **D/D/R:** Specializing in Real Estate Sales **H/I/S:** Master Gardener, Playing Bridge **FBP:** Realtor **EDU:** Associate Degree in Dental Assistant, Los Angeles City College **A/A/S:** Washington State Board of Realtors; National Association of Realtors; Washington Association of Realtors; Mason County Realtors **A/S:** She attributes her success to her perseverance and hard work. **B/I:** She became involved in this profession because her personal experience triggered her interest in the profession. **H/O:** The highlight of her career is the challenge of each new and different situation she encounters on a daily basis.

EMILY A. LEWIS, MSW
TFC Case Manager/Coordinator
Lutheran Social Services
3003 A N. Richmond Street
Appleton, WI 54911 United States
elewis@lsswis.org
http://www.lsswis.org

BUS: Multi-Service Agency **P/S:** Social Services **MA:** Regional **D/D/R:** Facilitating Treatment Foster Care **H/I/S:** Reading, Making Jewelry **FBP:** Social Work Today **EDU:** Master's Degree in Social Work of Direct Practice, University of Wisconsin, Oshkosh; Bachelor of Science in Social Work, Minor in Human Services, Magna Cum Laude, University of Wisconsin, White Water **A/A/S:** Alpha Delta Mu, Beta Zeta Chapter, Honor Society for Social Work; President, Outreach Director and Committee Member, Social Work Student Organization **C/VW:** Breast Cancer; Police Association; Donates Jewelry Creations to Charities and Fundraisers **A/S:** She attributes her success to her strong supportive family and their encouragement. **B/I:** She became involved in her profession because she wanted to work one-on-one with people. **H/O:** The highlight of her career was getting her Master's Degree while working full time.

MARIANNE E. LEWIS
Director of Nurses
Presentation Nursing and Rehabilitation Center
10 Bellamy Street
Brighton, MA 02135 United States
marianne_lewis@kindredhealthcare.com
http://www.cambridgewhoswho.com

BUS: Healthcare Center **P/S:** Healthcare Including Rehabilitation Services, Long Term Care, Wound Care, Nutritional Counseling, Online Dental, Optometry, Podiatry and Intergenerational Programs, Alzheimer's Counseling **MA:** Regional **EXP:** Ms. Lewis' expertise is in wound and pain management. **D/D/R:** Overseeing Administrative Duties, Managing Rehabilitation Services and Tracheotomy Care, Performing Intravenous Therapy, Public Speaking **H/I/S:** Exercising, Boating, Camping, Spending Time Outdoors **EDU:** Bachelor of Science in Nursing, Framingham State College (1998) **A/A/S:** Director of the Year Award (2005); Nurse Executive Leadership Program; Leadership Class Lecturer, Framingham State College; National Association Directors of Nursing Administration/Long Term Care; Sigma Theta Tau **A/H:** Director of Nursing of the Year Award (2005) **DOB:** August 17, 1955 **SP:** Scott **CHILD:** Amy, Mark

TRACEY D. LEWIS, RTR
Radiologic Technologist, Applications Training Specialist
Dextrys
201 Edgewater Drive
Suite 225
Wakefield, MA 01880 United States
xraytech@hotmail.com
http://www.dextrys.com

BUS: Manufacturing Company **P/S:** Speech and Imaging Solutions **MA:** National **EXP:** Ms. Lewis' expertise is in radiography, diagnostic imaging, patient care, training and working with voice, speech and text applications. **H/I/S:** Ballroom Dancing, Listening to Music, Reading **FBP:** Trade-Related Journals; RT Image; Advance; RT-News **EDU:** Associate Degree in Radiography, Williamsport Area Community College **A/A/S:** The American Registry of Radiologic Technologists **A/S:** She attributes her success to the respect she receives from giving her patients excellent care. **B/I:** She became involved in her profession because she was driven by the death of her father, who was killed in an accident. **H/O:** The highlight of her career was traveling to 15 states with reputed professionals. **I/F/Y:** In five years, Ms. Lewis hopes to have earned her radiology imaging informatics credentials.

DANSHI LI
Senior Research Investigator
Bristol-Myers Squibb
311 Pennington Rock Hill Road
Pennington, NJ 08534 United States
danshi.li@bms.com
http://www.cambridgewhoswho.com

BUS: Pharmaceutical Company **P/S:** Medicines for Cancer, Cardiovascular and Metabolic Disorders, Infectious Diseases, Including HIV/AIDS and Serious Mental Illness **MA:** National **D/D/R:** Training, Performing Medical Research, Conducting Research on Cardiovascular Disease **H/I/S:** Badminton, Listening to Classical Music, Reading Novels **FBP:** Scientific Journals; Nature; Science **EDU:** Ph.D. in Cardiology, University of Tasmania (1997); MD, Kunming Medical College (1984) **A/A/S:** Heart Rhythm Society; Cardiac Electrophysiology Society; American Heart Association **A/H:** Young Investigator Award, North American Society of Pacing and Electrophysiology (1999-2000); Research Award Winner, Heart and Stroke Scientific Research Corporation of Canada (1999-2000); Equity and Merit Scholarship Winner, Australian International Development Assistance Bureau (1993-1997)

BRANDIE L. LIBBETT
Client Services Manager, Marketing Director,
Human Resources Manager
Law Offices of John D. Laughton
215 W. Franklin Street, Suite 411
Monterey, CA 93940 United States
brandie@estateplan-lawyers.com
http://www.estateplan-lawyers.com

BUS: Law Firm **P/S:** High Quality Legal Services for Clients, Estate Planning, Wills and Trusts, Trust Administration **MA:** Monterey County, San Benito County **H/I/S:** Horseback Riding **FBP:** National Notary Association Magazine **EDU:** Coursework in Legal Studies, University of California at Santa Cruz **CERTS:** Certified Notary Public **A/A/S:** California Advocates for Nursing Home Reform; American Academy of Estate Planning Attorneys; National Notary Association; Neighbors Abroad; Second Harvest Foodbank

MRS. CATHRYN W. LIBERSON, PH.D.
Clinical Director (Retired)
Hollywood Pavilion
1201 N. 37th Avenue
Hollywood, FL 33021 United States
http://www.cambridgewhoswho.com

BUS: Hospital **P/S:** Healthcare, Clinical Psychology **MA:** International **D/D/R:** Directing Clinical Psychology **H/I/S:** Swimming **FBP:** EMG; Clinical Neurophysiology **EDU:** Ph.D. in Clinical and Medical Psychology, Loyola University; Master's Degree in Clinical Psychology, The University of Oklahoma; Coursework, University of Chicago, IL **A/A/S:** Florida Psychological Association; Associate Professor of Psychiatry, College of Osteopathic Medicine, Nova Southeastern University; Associate Editor, The International Medical Journal **C/VW:** Florida Council of Fire Fighters; Florida Association of State Troopers; Police Family Survivor Fund; Memorial Sloan-Kettering Cancer Center; March of Dimes; Easter Seals; American Lung Association **A/S:** She attributes her career success to her natural intelligence, hard work and brilliant husband. **B/I:** She became involved in her profession after serving as a volunteer at a Veteran's Administration hospital. **H/O:** The highlights of her career were being the first author to correlate the differences between heart attacks in men and women, which she later presented at a national convention and being the project psychologist for the first female astronaut candidates. She attended the hearing of the Committee on Science and Astronauts at the United States House of Representatives' 87th congress.

JAMES M. LIEBLER
Vice President of Corporate and Legal Affairs
Opex Corporation
305 Commerce Drive
Moorestown, NJ 08057 United States
jliebler@opex.com
http://www.opex.com

BUS: Manufacturing **P/S:** High-Speed Automated Mail Sorter Manufacturing **MA:** International **D/D/R:** Handling Contracts, Labor, Employment and General Corporate Matters **H/I/S:** Sports, Writing, Poetry **EDU:** JD, Capitol University **A/A/S:** American Bar Association; New Jersey Bar Association; American Corporate Council Association **A/S:** He attributes his personal and professional success to his solid people skills.

MARY HENRY LIGHTFOOT
Program Coordinator, Regional Interpreter of Education Center
Department of Interpretation
Gallaudet University
800 Florida Avenue N.E.
Washington, DC 20002 United States
mary.lightfoot@gallaudet.edu
http://www.gallaudet.edu

BUS: University **P/S:** On-Campus and Online Courses, Distance Learning Programs **MA:** International **D/D/R:** Researching, Teaching Online and On-Campus Courses for the Deaf, Specializing in Video Technology and Video Interpretation, Researching on Video Communication Usage in Education, Tracking Usage of Video Conferencing Technology for General Usage, Improving Performance **H/I/S:** Spending Time with her Family, Traveling, Reading **FBP:** Journal of Interpreting **EDU:** Pursuing Master of Science in Instructional Design for On-Line Learning, Capella University; Bachelor of Arts in Speech and Hearing Science, Temple University, Cum Laude (1978) **CERTS:** Certification in Interpreting and Translating **A/A/S:** Potomac Chapter, RID; National Association of Black Interpreters; Former Chair, Speaker, Registry of Interpreters, Deaf Video Interpreting Committee, Asbury Park; Video ID Video Interpreting Committee Experts Group **A/H:** NJ Hall of Fame Inductee (2007); Innovator of the Year Award (2004) **C/VW:** Religious Volunteer Work, Video ID Video Interpreting Committee Experts Group

GAIL A. LIMING
University of Nebraska-Lincoln
13th R.
Lincoln, NE 68588 United States
gliming@unlnotes.unl.edu
http://www.cambridgewhoswho.com

BUS: University **P/S:** Higher Education Including the Research, Development and Writing of Creative Books, Poems, Novels and Prose **MA:** National **D/D/R:** Writing Books and Overseeing Library Duties **H/I/S:** Gardening, Walking, Writing **EDU:** Coursework in English, University of Nebraska-Lincoln **A/S:** She attributes her success to her ability to stay focused. **B/I:** She became involved in her profession because of the opportunity that came her way.

CAROL LINDER-SPIEGEL
Administrative Intensive Cares Services
Jackson South Hospital
9333 S.W. 152nd Street
Palmetto Bay, FL 33157 United States
cspiegel@jhsmiami.org
http://www.jhsmiami.com

BUS: Member of the Largest Nonprofit Healthcare Organization in South Florida **P/S:** Variety of Health Care Services Including Emergency Services, Addiction Treatment, Home Care Services, Pediatrics, Pregnancy and Childbirth, Oncology, Cardiology, Rehabilitation, Women's Health Care, Diabetes Services, Critical Care **MA:** International **D/D/R:** Organizing Meetings, Planning, Scheduling, Recruiting and Interviewing Critical Care Physicians, Performing Statistical Charting **H/I/S:** Collecting Antique Dolls and Elephant Figurines, Going to the Gym, Football **EDU:** Degree in Nursing, SUNY Albany **A/A/S:** WPN **DOB:** April 18, 1938 **SP:** Richard **CHILD:** Robin, Charles **A/S:** She attributes her career success to her compassion, hard work and dedication.

KAREN A. LINDNER, MS, MSHSA, BSN, RN
Personal Care Nurse, Mental Health Nurse
Adams County Health and Human Services
108 E. North Street
Friendship, WI 53934 United States
klindner@co.adams.wi.us
http://www.cambridgewhoswho.com

BUS: Healthcare Center **P/S:** Healthcare, Psychiatric Treatment **MA:** Regional **EXP:** Ms. Lindner's expertise is in surgical, acute and geriatric care nursing. **D/D/R:** Supervising the Staff, Caring for Patients, Working with the Clinical and Mental Health Departments **H/I/S:** Photography, Artwork **FBP:** Nursingmatters; Mental Health **EDU:** Master of Science in Health Services Administration, University of St. Francis (2003); Bachelor of Science in Nursing, Edgewood College, Madison, WI (1989) **A/A/S:** Wisconsin Personal Services Association; Wisconsin Psychiatric Association

JANICE M. LINDSEY
Infection Controller
Hamot Medical Center
201 State Street
Erie, PA 16550 United States
jan.lindsey@hamot.org
http://www.hamot.org

BUS: Medical Center **P/S:** Healthcare Services Including Cardiopulmonary, Neuroscience, Orthopaedic, Trauma, Women and Child Health and Case Management **MA:** Regional **EXP:** Her expertise is in trauma nursing, neuroscience, neurosurgery and patient advocacy. **H/I/S:** Outdoor Sports **FBP:** Journal of Neuroscience Nursing; RN; Nursing2009 **EDU:** Bachelor of Science in Nursing, Gannon University (2000) **CERTS:** Certification in CPR; Certification in Neuroscience Nursing; Certified Medical-Surgical Nurse **A/A/S:** Sigma Theta Tau; American Association of Neuroscience Nurses

MR. RICHARD M. LINDVALL
Minister, Chaplain
Tinley Park Community Church
11136 S. Whipple Street
Chicago, IL 60655 United States
sharon6163@msn.com
http://www.cambridgewhoswho.com

BUS: Community Church **P/S:** Worship Counseling, Community Service, Church Services **MA:** Illinois **D/D/R:** Offering Counseling, Community and Outreach Services **H/I/S:** Reading, Traveling, Performing Community Service **FBP:** Journal of Pastoral Care **EDU:** Coursework in Divinity, Judson University, Northern Seminary, Chicago Theological Seminary; Coursework in Arts and Education **A/A/S:** Association of Professional Chaplains; National Organization of Congregational Christian Churches

ANN LINGUITI PRON, MSN, CRNP
Assistant Professor, Pediatric Nurse Practitioner
PHMC Health Connection
Temple University
1035 W. Berks Street
Philadelphia, PA 19122 United States
alpron@temple.edu
http://www.temple.edu

BUS: Comprehensive Public Research University **P/S:** Degree Programs in Two Associate Degree Areas, 130 Bachelor's Degree Areas, 110 Master's Degree Areas, 50 Doctoral Degree Areas and Five First Professional Degree Areas **MA:** National **D/D/R:** Offering Pediatric Primary Care Nursing **H/I/S:** Singing, Reading, Water Exercising **FBP:** Medical and Nursing Journals **EDU:** Master of Nursing in Nurse Practitioner Studies, University of Pennsylvania (1986); Bachelor of Science in Nursing, University of Pennsylvania (1971) **CERTS:** Certified Pediatric Nurse Practitioner (1975) **A/A/S:** National Association of Pediatric Nurse Associates and Practitioners; American Nurses Association; Sigma Theta Tau; National Nursing Centers Consortium; Unitarian Church

LAURA J. LINSDAY
Pre Production Materials and Services Supervisor
Dakkata
1875 Holloway Drive
Holt, MI 48842 United States
laura.linsday@dakkotasystems.com
http://www.cambridgewhoswho.com

BUS: Assembly and Sequencing **P/S:** Automotive, Interior of Cars **MA:** International **D/D/R:** Specializing in Material Planning **H/I/S:** Cooking, Traveling, Camping **FBP:** Association for Operations Management Magazine **EDU:** Pursuing Bachelor's Degree in Business Management, University of Phoenix Online **A/A/S:** Association for Operations Management **C/VW:** Children's Miracle Network **A/S:** She attributes her success to diligence and hard work. **B/I:** She chose the profession because she enjoys moving up in her career.

KAREN M. LIPSEY
Loan Funder
Texas First State Bank
4900 Sanger Avenue
Waco, TX 76710 United States
kmlipsey1@yahoo.com
http://www.cambridgewhoswho.com

BUS: Bank **P/S:** Financial Services **MA:** Local **EXP:** Ms. Lipsey's expertise is in loan funding and loan documents. **H/I/S:** Cooking, Making Arts and Crafts, Watching Football, Spending Time with her Husband and Friends **C/VW:** Toys for Tots; Susan G. Komen for the Cure **DOB:** March 26, 1959 **POB:** Waco, TX **SP:** Billy **A/S:** She attributes her success to her ability to adapt within different areas of the field and stay current with changes. **B/I:** She became involved in the profession because a friend encouraged her to enter the field. **H/O:** The highlight of her career was earning her current position.

BRENDA L. LISA
Resident Care Management Director
Randolph Health and Rehabilitation
230 E. Presnell Street
Asheboro, NC 27203 United States
mcgruders@hotmail.com
http://www.cambridgewhoswho.com

BUS: Leader in Healthcare Services **P/S:** Long-Term Healthcare for Geriatric Patients **MA:** Regional **D/D/R:** Assessing Resident Profiles, Coordinating Care Teams, Promoting Social Activities and Therapies, Processing Medicaid Claims **H/I/S:** Reading, Working on Needlepoint **FBP:** Nursing Spectrum **EDU:** Associate Degree in Nursing, Empire State College **CERTS:** Registered Nurse; MDS Certification; AANAC Credentials **A/A/S:** CRAN; RAC-C

PAULA S. LISTER
Licensed Professional Counselor
Counseling Services
Byte & Associates, LLC
411 W. Chickasha Avenue
Chickasha, OK 73018 United States
nannysuel@yahoo.com
http://www.cambridgewhoswho.com

BUS: Counseling Agency **P/S:** Mental Health Counseling Services for Individuals and Families **MA:** Regional **D/D/R:** Offering Counseling for Crisis Intervention and Violence Prevention, Working with Children **H/I/S:** Spending Time with her Grandchildren **FBP:** Journal of Counseling Psychology; Developmental Psychology; Psychology Today **EDU:** Master's Degree in Education, Major in Counseling, Southwestern Oklahoma State University, Weatherford; Bachelor of Arts in Sociology, University of Science and Arts of Oklahoma **CERTS:** Licensed Professional Counselor **A/A/S:** American Counseling Association **C/VW:** Supervisor, Local Mental Health Group, Grady County, OK

LYNNE TATUM LITTLE, RDH
Dental Hygienist, Consultant
LTL Consulting
7845 Colony Road
Suite C4-259
Charlotte, NC 28226 United States
ltlittle@bellsouth.net
http://www.cambridgewhoswho.com

BUS: Dentistry **P/S:** Consulting **MA:** National **D/D/R:** Professional Speaking, Demonstrating Organizational Efficiency in Dental Hygiene and Technology-Focused Dentistry **H/I/S:** Golfing **EDU:** Associate of Applied Science in Dental Hygiene; Coursework in Physics, Appalachian State University **A/A/S:** North Carolina Dental Hygiene Association; American Dental Hygienists' Association **C/VW:** American Dental Hygienists' Association Oral Health Institute, Various Community Arts Organizations **A/S:** She attributes her success to her positive attitude and willingness to learn. **B/I:** She became involved in the profession because she has loved dentistry since she was in fifth-grade. **H/O:** The most gratifying aspect of her career is the people she has met and the opportunities she has had.

LYNDA LITTLE CRABILL, GRI
Associate Broker
Century 21 A1A Realty
611 N. Summit Street
Crescent City, FL 32112 United States
lynda.crabill@century21.com
lflc1223@gbso.net
http://www.bgso.net

BUS: Real Estate Agency **P/S:** Real Estate **MA:** Regional **D/D/R:** Specializing in Residential, Commercial, New Construction and Land Real Estate Sales **H/I/S:** Studying Genealogy, Volunteering at Civil Organizations, Working as a Private Investigator, Reading **FBP:** National Genealogical Association Publications **EDU:** Associate Degree in English and Art, Saint John's River Community College **CERTS:** Graduate Realtor Institute **A/A/S:** National Association of Realtors; Florida Association of Realtors; Virginia Association of Realtors; Blue Crab Festival Women's Business Group; Chairwoman, Historical Society; Palatka Pilot Club; Save Central Academy; T-Shirt Chairman, Blue Crab Festival; Palatka Pilot Women's Business Group **CHILD:** Mark, Justin, Garrett **A/S:** She attributes her success to understanding her clients' needs. **B/I:** She became involved in her profession because she was looking for a home and the sales manager at one of the homes was looking for a hostess so she took the job. It was the beginning of her career in real estate. **H/O:** The most gratifying aspect of her career is seeing that her clients are happy with what she has done for them.

CELIA A. LIVINGSTON
Library Automation Coordinator
Jefferson Community College
1220 Coffeen Street
Watertown, NY 13601 United States
clivingston@sunyjefferson.edu
http://www.sunyjefferson.edu

BUS: College **P/S:** Higher Education **MA:** Regional **D/D/R:** Handling the Library Management System and Electronic Database, Managing Inter-Library Loan and Service Programs Utilized by SUNY, Helping Students Work Online, Promoting a Research Sharing Program **H/I/S:** Supporting the New York Yankees, Traveling, Spending Time with her Grandchildren **FBP:** American Library Association Journal of Technology **EDU:** Bachelor of Arts in Liberal Arts, Utica College (1985) **A/A/S:** East New York Chapter, Association of College and Research Librarians; SUNY Library Association; American Library Association

ALINE C. LLEWELLYN
Classroom and Reading Teacher (Retired)
District of Columbia Public Schools
825 N. Capitol Street N.E.
Washington, DC 20002 United States
http://www.k12.dc.us

BUS: Public School District **P/S:** Education, Special Education Services, Specialized Reading Programs **MA:** Local **D/D/R:** Teaching Reading, Special Education and Elementary Education **H/I/S:** Gardening, Reading, Traveling, Enjoying Entertainment **FBP:** All Industry-Related Journals and Publications **EDU:** Master's Degree in Special Education, Howard University **A/A/S:** International Reading Association; Various Charitable Organizations in the Community; First Baptist Church of Hiland Park

GERALDINE LOCKARD
Executive Director, Training Materials Developer
Keys to Learning Power
5515 Littleneck Parkway
Littleneck, NY 11362 United States
gerrylockard@yahoo.com
nidgonzalez@optonline.net
http://www.qcc.cuny.edu

BUS: Educational Institution **P/S:** Consulting and Implementing for Special Projects to Improve Cognitive Functioning of Individuals and Groups **MA:** New York City, Long Island **EXP:** Ms. Lockard's expertise is in education and personal development. **D/D/R:** Improving the Performance of Students and Teachers, Training the Staff, Developing an Interactive Class and Advisement System, Utilizing Cognitive Behavior to Promote Effective Learning Methods, Assisting Students and Staff, Consulting **H/I/S:** Watching Movies, Painting, Writing **FBP:** Fortune; Kappan **EDU:** Master's Degree in Administration and Supervision, Pace University (1979); Master's Degree in Mathematics Education, CUNY Queens College (1968); Bachelor's Degree in Physics, Hunter College (1951) **CERTS:** Certification in Advanced FIE (2004) **A/A/S:** Trainer, Instrumental Enrichment Program (1999-2006); Presenter, Symposium on Education for 21st Century, American Association for the Advancement of Science (1998); Queens Association for Exceptionally Gifted Children; Phi Delta Kappa (1978); Phi Beta Kappa (1951); College Discovery Program **A/H:** Honoree, Who's Who in American Education (2005-2007) **CHILD:** Jeremy, Adrienne, Dierdre **W/H:** Facilitator, College Discovery, Staff Development, FIE Training, City University of New York (2000-2006); Mathematics Adjunct, Queensborough Community College (1995-2005); Mathematics Adjunct, York College (1996-1998); High School Mathematics Teacher, New York City Board of Education (1965-1992); Acting Supervisor, Mathematics and Science Department (1984-1988); Educational Advisor (1982-1984); Head Teacher, After-School Peer Tutoring Program (1981-1984); Technical Assistant, Switching Systems Development (1953-1956); Psychiatric Aide (1951-1952)

BARBARA LOCKBAUM
Chief Human Resources Division
Guthrie Ambulatory Health Care Clinic
11050 Mount Belvedere Boulevard
Fort Drum, NY 13602 United States
barbara.lockbaum@amedd.army.mil
barbara.lockbaum@us.army.mil
http://www.cambridgewhoswho.com

BUS: Department of Defense Healthcare Organization **P/S:** Healthcare Including Human Resources, Clinical, Marketing, Military Healthcare Advocacy Services **MA:** Regional **EXP:** Ms. Lockbaum's expertise is in personnel Support services. **D/D/R:** Strategic Planning for Staffing Effectiveness, Overseeing Process Improvement for Operational Human Resource Function Including Evaluations, Awards, Time Cards and Labor Relations for Military Personnel and Civilian Employees, Ensuring Compliance with Joint Commission Standards in All Human Resource Functions and Hospital Systems, Managing Quality, Ensuring Comprehensive Health Care Services and Medical Readiness for Developing Leaders, Soldiers and the Healthcare Team **H/I/S:** Spending Time with her Children and Grandchildren, Walking her Rescued Dogs, Watching her Rescued Cats Play, Reading, Making Pottery, Crocheting, Knitting, Painting, Praying **FBP:** Association of the United States Army Publications; HR; Military Doctrine Publications **EDU:** Pursuing Master's Degree in Counseling Psychology, Phoenix University; Master's Degree in Human Relations, The University of Oklahoma (1995); Bachelor of Arts in Liberal Arts, Minor in Psychology and Military Science, Northwestern University (1991) **A/A/S:** Association of the United States Army; Society for Human Resource Management **A/H:** Army Achievement Medals; Army Commendation Medals; Meritorious Service Medals; German Proficiency Badge for Physical Fitness and Marksmanship **C/VW:** Animal Rescue **DOB:** January 21, 1962 **POB:** Bremen **CHILD:** Jennifer, Cristofer **A/S:** She attributes her success to her perseverance, commitment, and balance. **B/I:** She became involved in her profession through a natural progression of opportunities made available to her through her career in the United States Army. **H/O:** The highlight of her career was being a company commander for soldiers in training and soldiers recovering from injuries. This was a challenging position but it was rewarding. **I/F/Y:** In five years, Ms. Lockbaum plans to retire from the military to work as a counselor for soldiers returning from war and their families. She also plans to work as a consultant for human resource management and military healthcare.

LINDA LOCKWOOD ELROD, RN
Registered Nurse, Owner
Professional Referral Services
2613 Terwilleger Boulevard
Tulsa, OK 74114 United States
lindylee8@aol.com
http://www.cambridgewhoswho.com

BUS: Healthcare **P/S:** Locating Participants for Drug Studies and Research **MA:** Regional **D/D/R:** Acting as a Liaison between Patients and Physicians **H/I/S:** Horseback Riding, Reading, Traveling **FBP:** Archaeological Digest **EDU:** Registered Nurse Diploma, St. John's School of Nursing **A/A/S:** Miss Oklahoma Sorority; Christian Athletes of America **C/VW:** Local Violence Charities and Cancer Charities through Mary Kay

VICTORIA ANN LOFGREN
Owner, Operator
Connecting Threads Sewing Studio
943 W. Congress Street
Tucson, AZ 85745 United States
victoriaann.lofgren@cwwemail.com
http://www.cambridgewhoswho.com

BUS: Fashion Design Company **P/S:** Sewing, Custom Seamstress **MA:** Regional **D/D/R:** Custom Designing, Teaching Sewing and Quilting **H/I/S:** Scrapbooking, Reading, Gardening **EDU:** Coursework in Spanish; High School Diploma **C/VW:** American Red Cross; Local Schools **A/S:** She attributes her success to her work ethic and desire for learning. **H/O:** The highlights of her career were helping a child to win a quilting contest and being thanked by her customer when she wears a dress designed by her.

MRS. KAREN L. LOGAN, BSN, RN
Quality Improvement Manager
Albert Einstein Medical Center
Jefferson Health System
5501 Old York Road
Philadelphia, PA 19141 United States
cplfresh@aol.com
http://www.cambridgewhoswho.com

BUS: Healthcare-Hospital **P/S:** Quality Management and Performance Improvement **MA:** Regional **D/D/R:** Developing, Implementing, Directing and Monitoring the Department of Medicine's Quality Management and Performance Improvement Programs **H/I/S:** Attending Nursing Symposiums, Conferences, Seminars and Health Fairs, Reading, Exercise and Travel **FBP:** Nursing Spectrum; Advance for Nurses **EDU:** Bachelor of Science in Nursing, La Salle University; Associate Degree, Focus on Business Administration, Community College of Philadelphia **CERTS:** Certification in Ventilators and Tracheotomies **A/H:** Gold Coin Recognition for Business Excellence **C/VW:** American Red Cross; Philabundance; United Way of America **A/S:** She attributes her personal and professional success to her hard work and dedication. **B/I:** She became involved in the nursing profession because she had always had an interest in the field and a desire to make a difference in the lives of others. **H/O:** The most gratifying aspect of her career is being a patient's advocate.

DAY ANN LOGUE, BSN, MSHA
President, Chief Executive Officer
Day A. Hopes and Associates, PA
2412 Saint Andrews Boulevard, Suite 16
Panama City, FL 32405 United States
dayannlogue@yahoo.com
http://www.cambridgewhoswho.com

Day A Hopes & Associates, PA

Proactive Risk Prevention Strategies
for ambulatory healthcare

Day Ann Logue, BSN, MSHA
Licensed Healthcare Risk Manager
2412 St. Andrews Boulevard, #16
Panama City, Florida 32405
(850)319-7757
day.annlogue@y.ahoo.com

BUS: Healthcare Consulting **P/S:** Risk Prevention Strategies **MA:** Florida **D/D/R:** Quality Outcome Management **H/I/S:** Cooking, Walking the Beach, Fishing, Reading **EDU:** Pursuing Ph.D. in Healthcare Administration, Kennedy-Western University; Master of Science in Healthcare Administration, University of Alabama at Birmingham (1989) **A/A/S:** Florida Hospital Association; Florida Society for Healthcare Risk Management and Patient Safety **C/VW:** YMCA; Rotary International; Panama City Rotary Club; Cystic Fibrosis Foundation

REGINA MARIE LoMAGLIO, RN
Registered Nurse
Golisano Children's Hospital at Strong
1325 Mount Hope Avenue
Rochester, NY 14620 United States
regina_lomaglio@urmc.rochester.edu
http://www.cambridgewhoswho.com

BUS: Hospital **P/S:** Healthcare **MA:** Regional **EXP:** Ms. LoMaglio's expertise is in pediatric care. **D/D/R:** Overseeing the Neonatal Intensive Care Unit **H/I/S:** Caring for her Pets **FBP:** Journal of Neonatal Nursing **EDU:** Pursuing Bachelor of Science in Nursing; Bachelor of Science, Utica College of Syracuse University; Associate of Science in Nursing, Monroe (2003) **A/A/S:** National Association of Neonatal Nurses; The Academy of Neonatal Nursing

BEATRICE K. LONG, LPN
Licensed Practical Nurse
Partners National Health Plans
5460 University Parkway
Winston-Salem, NC 27116 United States
elfhaven13@yahoo.com
http://www.partnershealth.com

BUS: Healthcare **P/S:** Innovative Healthcare Products and Services that Promote Good Physical and Mental Health and Manages the State's Premier Medicare Advantage Government Program **MA:** Regional **D/D/R:** Specializing in Congestive Heart Failure and Chronic Obstructive Pulmonary Disease, Offering Health Education, Diabetic Education and Instruction **H/I/S:** Gardening, Cooking **FBP:** American Journal of Nursing **EDU:** Pursuing Bachelor of Science in Nursing **CERTS:** Licensed Practical Nurse, Region IV School of Practical Nursing (1990) **A/A/S:** Concerned Nurses of West Virginia; North Carolina Board of Nursing **C/VW:** United Way of America; Precise County Court Volunteers; St. Steven's Indian Mission; American Heart Association

MS. LINDA LONG
Sole Proprietor
Linda Long Costal Cardiac
PO Box 2190 Ventnor
Ventnor, NJ 08406 United States
cottontale7@comcast.net
http://www.cambridgewhoswho.com

BUS: Patient Care Facility **P/S:** Mobile Cardiac Ultrasound **MA:** Local **D/D/R:** Specializing in Non-Invasive Cardiology, Reviewing the Hospital and Offices for Safety and Compliance **H/I/S:** Walking and Spending Time with her Two Granddaughters **FBP:** Money **EDU:** Associate Degree in Education, Atlantic Cape Community College **CERTS:** Certification in CCI **C/VW:** American Society for the Prevention of Cruelty to Animals

RITA M. LONG
Owner
Longview Farm
388 Cemetery Road
Meyersdale, PA 15552 United States
http://www.cambridgewhoswho.com

BUS: High-Quality Farm **P/S:** Raising Beef Cattle **MA:** Regional **D/D/R:** Farming, Making Business Decisions, Overseeing All Administrative Aspects of the Farm **H/I/S:** Music **FBP:** The Wall Street Journal **EDU:** Master of Education, University of Pittsburgh (1960); Bachelor of Science in Education, Juniata College (1955) **A/A/S:** Garden Club; Pennsylvania Farm Bureau; Church Organist; Juniata Alumni Association; University of Pittsburgh Alumni Association; Pennsylvania Retired Teachers Association

SHERYL M. LONGSWORTH
Independent Project Analysis Consultant
Third District PTA
10748 Olson Drive
Rancho Cordova, CA 95670 United States
sheryl6663@yahoo.com
http://www.3rddistrictpta.com/Home.html
https://www.edline.net/pages/Mitchell_MS

BUS: Nonprofit Organization **P/S:** Promotion of the Welfare of Children and Youth in Homes, Schools, Communities and Places of Worship, Raising of the Standards of Home Life, Creation of Adequate Laws for the Care and Protection of Children and Youth to Bring into Closer Relation the Home and School so that Parents and Teachers may Cooperate Intelligently in the Education of Children and Youth, Development Between Educators and the General Public to Secure for All Children and Youth the Highest Advantages in Physical, Mental, Social and Spiritual Education **MA:** Regional **EXP:** Ms. Longsworth's expertise is in process improvement. **D/D/R:** Assisting Individual School Parent-Teacher Association Organizations, Working with Provided Information and Materials **H/I/S:** Traveling, Watching Basketball, Camping, Attending Cultural Events, Concerts and Museums **FBP:** Fast Company; Entrepreneur; BusinessWeek **EDU:** Master of Business Administration, Grand Canyon University (2007); Bachelor of Science in Business Administration, University of Phoenix (2001) **A/H:** Delta Mu Delta (2007); National Dean's List (2001); Club Rev Award, Packard Bell NEC; Numerous Atta Girl Awards, American Canyon Middle School, Intel Corporation **C/VW:** Former President, Former Treasurer, Parent Teacher Association, Mitchell Middle School; Church Volunteer; Participant, Community Leadership Programs and Councils **DOB:** June 6, 1963 **POB:** Redwood City, CA **CHILD:** Hristo **W/H:** Third District Parent Teacher Association (2008-Present); Sacramento Municipal Utility District (2006); Advanced Concepts and Mission Systems (2001-2005); Packard Bell NEC, Inc. (1995-1999); Intel Corporation (1989-1995) **A/S:** She attributes her career success to her education, strong work ethic and tenacity. **H/O:** The most gratifying aspect of her career was helping a youth-oriented organization like Third District PTA improve its ability to serve its region by helping to improve its use of technology and software to be more effective.

CHERYL A. LOPEZ
Sales Associate
Weichert Realtors, Sun, Sand, Sea Homes
522 Mandalay Avenue
Clearwater, FL 33767 United States
chelopez@juno.com
http://www.sunsandseahomes.com

BUS: Largest Privately Owned Real Estate Company in the United States **P/S:** Real Estate Services **MA:** Local **D/D/R:** Specializing in Residential and Rental Real Estate, Managing Properties and Hotels **H/I/S:** Performing as a Stand-Up Comedian, Dancing, Spending Time with her Family and Friends **EDU:** College Coursework; High School Education **CERTS:** Real Estate License (2000) **A/A/S:** National Association of Realtors; Pinellas County Realty Board; New Jersey Association of Realtors; Weichert Million Dollar Sales Club; Muscular Dystrophy Funds

MS. LIDIA A. LOPEZ
907 Roxanne Drive
Hemet, CA 92543 United States
lidialopez25@hotmail.com
http://www.cambridgewhoswho.com

BUS: Sole Proprietorship **EXP:** Ms. Lopez's expertise includes public speaking and pediatric and adolescent care. **H/I/S:** Caring for her Dogs, Visiting Animal Shelters, Helping People **EDU:** Registered Nurse (2008); Associate Degree in Behavioral Science and Psychology, San Diego Community College (2004) **CERTS:** Certified in Advanced Cardiac Life Support **DOB:** July 15, 1976 **W/H:** United States Navy (1994-2004)

LAURA M. LOPEZ-MARINO, MS
Special Education Teacher
Plainview-Old Bethpage CSD
1191 Round Swamp Road
Old Bethpage, NY 11804 United States
lmlopez680@yahoo.com
http://www.pob.k12.ny.us

BUS: Educational Facility, Elementary School **P/S:** Excellent Teaching Services **MA:** Regional **D/D/R:** Teaching Second-Grade, Specializing in Special Education for Grades One through Six **H/I/S:** Music, Computers, Volleyball **EDU:** Master of Science in Special Education, Adelphi University (2004); Bachelor's Degree in Elementary Education, C.W. Post Campus, Long Island University **A/A/S:** Phi Beta Kappa; Parent Teacher Association; Who's Who Among American Teachers (2006)

JENNIFER L. LORENZ
Owner
LJ's Note Investors
11993 Belsay Road
Grand Blanc, MI 48439 United States
regintl21@cs.com
http://www.cambridgewhoswho.com

BUS: Finance **P/S:** Helping People Who Hold Contracts or Need to Cash Out Promissory Notes **MA:** National **D/D/R:** Writing and Cashing Out Promissory Notes, Searching for Grants on Behalf of the Company **H/I/S:** Spending Time with the Family **EDU:** Coursework in Business, Baker College **C/VW:** South Baptist Church, Clean Up Flint **A/S:** She attributes her success to the support she receives from her son. **B/I:** Her desire to be home to spend time with her son and still make money for her family motivated her to pursue her current career. **H/O:** The highlight of her career was closing a deal which helped a woman to pay for her daughter's wedding.

GLORIA SCOTT LORNE
Ambulatory Clinical Nurse
Reynolds Army Community Hospital
4301 Moway Road
Fort Sill, OK 73503 United States
http://www.cambridgewhoswho.com

BUS: Hospital **P/S:** Healthcare, Treatment for Active Duty Soldiers, Retired Soldiers and Dependents **MA:** National **D/D/R:** Handling All Aspects of Nursing Including Internal Medicine and Neurology **H/I/S:** Fishing, Spending Time with her Grandchildren, Going to Church **FBP:** Spiritual Writings **CERTS:** Licensed Practical Nurse, Great Plain Vocational Technical School **C/VW:** Church **A/S:** She attributes her success to her compassion. **B/I:** She became involved in her profession because she was inspired by her mother.

BONNIE LOU C. GEORGE
Patient Care Manager
Hospice of the Comforter
480 W. Central Parkway
Altamonte Springs, FL 32714 United States
blc500198@aol.com
http://www.hospiceofthecomforter.org

BUS: Leading Home Care Hospice Center **P/S:** Superb End of Life Care **MA:** Local **D/D/R:** Enabling Patients to Carry on an Alert, Pain-Free Life and to Manage Other Symptoms so that their Days May be Spent with Dignity and Quality, at Home or in a Home-Like Setting with Quality Hospice Care **H/I/S:** Biking, Motorcycling, Listening to Music, Singing, Reading, Spending Time with her Daughter **FBP:** Nursing2009; American Journal of Nursing; American Journal of Hospice and Palliative Medicine **EDU:** Pursuing Master of Science in Nursing, Specialty in Education, Walden University; Bachelor of Science in Nursing, with Honors, Deaconess Chamberlain College of Nursing (Now Chamberlain College of Nursing) (2006); Registered Nurse (1968); Nursing Diploma, Mountainside Hospital School of Nursing **A/A/S:** Florida Nurses Association; The National Hospice and Palliative Care Organization; Calvary Assembly Church

Ms. Ronda L. Love
Director of Operations
Blue Moon Works
3773 Cherry Creek Drive N.
Suite 985
Denver, CO 80209 United States
ronda.love@bluemoonworks.com
http://www.bluemoonworks.com

BUS: Marketing Agency **P/S:** Online Strategy Development, Natural Search Engine Optimization, Pay-Per-Click Advertising Management, e-mail Marketing Optimization, Customer Segmentation, Online Profile, Website Usability **MA:** International **EXP:** Ms. Love's expertise is in e-mail marketing, project management, ensuring quality, budgeting and staying updated with the trends in the business. **H/I/S:** Golfing **FBP:** eCommerce **EDU:** Bachelor of Arts in Sociology, Philosophy and Religion, Illinois College (1979)

Linda J. Lovett
Teacher Trainer
Rodeo Institute for Teacher Excellence
3535 Briarpark Drive
Suite 110
Houston, TX 77042 United States
lovett@ritemail.com
http://www.cambridgewhoswho.com

BUS: Nonprofit Training Program for Teachers **P/S:** Education, Direct Instruction **MA:** Local **D/D/R:** Training Teachers to Work with At-Risk Students from Grades Three to Six and Children with Difficultly in Reading, Teaching in the Summer Institute Training Workshop, Using a Script, Motivating Students **H/I/S:** Reading, Boating, Babysitting her Grandchildren **FBP:** International Reading Association Publications; John Grisham Publications **EDU:** Bachelor of Science in Education, Prairie View A&M University (1972) **CERTS:** Certification in Kindergarten (1975) **A/A/S:** Congress of Teachers **C/VW:** Star of Hope Women's Center; Lakewood Church; Volunteer, Information Center at Lakewood Church **A/S:** She attributes her success to her experience in the classroom and the rapport she has with her students, their parents and the administration. **B/I:** She became involved in her profession because she was a classroom teacher who loved reading and was offered the opportunity to apply her skills further. **H/O:** The highlight of her career was earning her current position.

LAURA R. LOWE
Financial Director
Lighthouse Mobile Ministries
125 N. Parkside Street
Suite 103
Colorado Springs, CO 80909 United States
lighthousemobile@gmail.com
http://www.cambridgewhoswho.com

BUS: Religious Ministry Dedicated to Humane Services **P/S:** Food, Clothing and Shelter to the Homeless, Needy and Inner-City Children **MA:** Regional **D/D/R:** Working as the Budget Board's Treasurer, Handling the Bookkeeping and Budgeting of the Ministry, Focusing on Outreach Programs in the Philippines and Colorado **H/I/S:** Cooking, Billiards **EDU:** High School Education **DOB:** June 3, 1967 **SP:** Jeff **CHILD:** Nathan, Rose

TAMMY E. LOWERY
Lab Co-Manager
Intermed Oncology Associates
17901 Governors Highway
Homewood, IL 60430 United States
telowery11462@earthlink.net
http://www.cambridgewhoswho.com

BUS: Hematology and Oncology Laboratory **P/S:** Laboratory Tests **MA:** Cook County **D/D/R:** Managing the Lab, Running Blood Tests, Scheduling, Hiring Employees, Meeting with Sales Representatives **H/I/S:** Reading **EDU:** Bachelor's Degree, Governors State University **A/S:** She attributes her success to her love of the healthcare field, because there is something new to see every day. **B/I:** She became involved in her profession through a career class, where she was introduced to laboratory work for the first time and loved it. **H/O:** The highlight of her career has been her position as a manager.

ANNE L. MOTTEK LUCAS
President
Black Star Trading Company
PO Box 22511
Flagstaff, AZ 86002 United States
info@blackstartrading.com
http://www.blackstartrading.com

BUS: International Gemstone Trading Company **P/S:** Gemstones, Gem Clippers, Drusy Gemstones, Gemstone Display Stands, Precious Beads **MA:** International **D/D/R:** Selling Gemstones and Gemstone Accessories **H/I/S:** Hiking, Listening to Music, Dancing **FBP:** Colored Stone **EDU:** Master of Arts in Sociology, Emphasis on Research, Northern Arizona University; Bachelor of Science in Forestry, Northern Arizona University **CERTS:** Certified in Diamonds, Gemological Institute of America **A/A/S:** Gemological Institute of America; Forestry Honor, Xi Sigma Pi; Freshman Honor, Phi Eta Sigma; Phi Kappa Phi Esteemed Honor Society **A/H:** Flag of Learning Liberty Award **C/VW:** YMCA; American Cancer Society; Greater Flagstaff Forest Partnership Monitoring and Research Team **A/S:** She attributes her success to her persistence. **B/I:** She became involved in her profession because she wanted to have her own business and had the connections from previous positions to help her succeed. **H/O:** The highlight of her career was having the Carnegie Museum of Natural History buy 200 Gem Clippers from her for their Gem Stone Collection.

NICOLE J. LUCAS, RN, BSN
Charge RN
Forbes Regional Campus
West Penn Allegheny Health System
2570 Haymaker Road
Monroeville, PA 15146 United States
campriishe@aol.com
http://www.cambridgewhoswho.com

BUS: Health System **P/S:** Healthcare **MA:** National **EXP:** Ms. Lucas' expertise is in intravenous therapy and the application of peripherally inserted central catheters. **H/I/S:** Spending Time Outdoors, Camping, Hiking, Reading **EDU:** Bachelor of Science in Nursing, Edinboro University **CERTS:** Certificate in Forensic Science and Law, Duquesne University; Certified in Peripherally Inserted Central Catheter Lines; Certified in Advanced Cardiac Life Support; Certified in Basic Life Support **A/A/S:** League of Intravenous Therapy Education **A/H:** Nick Cardello Award (1997); Youth of the Year Award **C/VW:** Camp Director and Camp Nurse, Camp 'R'; Catholic Youth Association **A/S:** She attributes her success to continuing her education. **B/I:** She became involved in her profession because she always wanted to serve people and has a number of family members in the healthcare field.

CRYSTAL M. LUCKENBACH, RN
Registered Nurse
Warren Hospital
185 Roseberry Street
Phillipsburg, NJ 08865 United States
CML2@enter.net
http://www.cambridgewhoswho.com

BUS: Hospital **P/S:** Healthcare **MA:** Local **D/D/R:** Specializing in Telemetry **H/I/S:** Spending Time Outdoors, Shooting Guns, Fishing **FBP:** Critical Care Nurse **EDU:** Associate Degree in Nursing, Raritan Valley Community College **A/S:** She attributes her personal and professional success to her upbringing. **B/I:** After losing her parents at a very young age, she decided to become involved in medicine. **H/O:** The highlight of her career was obtaining her RN degree.

CHRISTINE CORAGGIO LUDLOW
Certified School Nurse
Essex County Vocational Technical Schools
christinecoraggio.ludlow@cwwemail.com
http://www.cambridgewhoswho.com

BUS: School District **P/S:** Education **MA:** Regional **EXP:** Ms. Ludlow's expertise is in pediatric and psychiatric nursing. **D/D/R:** Working with Handicapped Children **H/I/S:** Interior Decorating, Reading, Traveling, Dancing, Artwork **FBP:** Nursing Spectrum **EDU:** Bachelor's Degree in Psychology, Caldwell College **CERTS:** Registered Nurse, Mountainside Hospital School of Nursing **A/A/S:** Mountainside Hospital Alumnae Association; Essex County School Nurses Association; American Psychological Association; Psi Chi; Alpha Sigma Lambda **A/H:** Genesis Education Award **C/VW:** Nurses for Divine Mercy **A/S:** She attributes her success to her ability to adapt to multicultural backgrounds. **B/I:** She became involved in her profession through a natural progression of opportunities. **H/O:** The highlights of her career were working in the neonatal intensive care unit at St. Barnabas Hospital and receiving gratitude from her patients.

I. JUDITH LUGO
Business Owner
J&J Lugo Services
2489 Mission Street, Suite 37
San Francisco, CA 94110 United States
jlugo89@sbcglobal.net
http://www.cambridgewhoswho.com

BUS: Income Tax Translations and Consulting Company **P/S:** Immigration Consulting **MA:** Regional **D/D/R:** Immigration Consulting, Preparing Taxes, Assisting Immigrants with Procedures, Translating Latin, Assisting in Courtrooms **H/I/S:** Caring for her Two Dogs and Two Birds **EDU:** High School Graduate **CERTS:** Certified Consultant of Immigration, State of California **A/A/S:** California Association of Immigration Consultants; California Society of Tax Consultants **C/VW:** American Red Cross **A/S:** She attributes her success to her referrals from clients and friends. **B/I:** She became involved in the profession because she wanted to help Latinos. **H/O:** The most gratifying aspect of her career is learning from others and helping others learn from her.

MRS. PAMELA S. LUKACHEK, RN
Registered Nurse, Head Nurse
Waterville Family Physicians
900 Waterville Monclova Road, Suite A
Waterville, OH 43566 United States
luka5501@sbcglobal.net
http://www.cambridgewhoswho.com

BUS: Medical Center **P/S:** Healthcare **MA:** Local **EXP:** Mrs. Lukachek's expertise is in geriatric and family practice nursing. **H/I/S:** Bicycling, Reading, Antiquing, Cooking, Spending Time with her Grandchildren **CERTS:** Diploma in Nursing, Mercy Hospital, Toledo (1973) **A/A/S:** Mercy Alumni Association **C/VW:** Hope United Methodist Church, Whitehouse, Ohio; Nurse, Annual Church Camp; Lucas County City Medical Reserve Corps; Volunteer, Annual Medical Mission Trip to Mexico **A/S:** She attributes her success to her faith in God and desire to help people. **B/I:** She became involved in her profession because she wanted to be a nurse since she was a child. **H/O:** The most gratifying aspect of her career is working in her current position.

Cynthia A. Lumpcik, RN, BSN, CLNC
Registered Nurse, BSN, CLNC
Foundation Legal Nurse Consulting
1014 College Drive S.E.
New Philadelphia, OH 44663 United States
http://www.cambridgewhoswho.com

BUS: Medical Consulting Company **P/S:** Nurse Consulting **MA:** Local **D/D/R:** Specializing in Coronary Care **H/I/S:** Gardening **FBP:** Industry-Related Publications **EDU:** Bachelor of Science in Nursing, The University of Akron **A/A/S:** American Association of Critical-Care Nurses **C/VW:** Big Brothers Big Sisters **A/S:** She attributes her success to her ambition and passion for nursing. **B/I:** She became involved in her profession because she has always wanted to be a nurse. **H/O:** The most gratifying aspect of her career is making people feel better.

Ms. Nora J. Luna
Vice President of Imports
World Commerce Forwarding, Inc.
16102 Air Center Boulevard
Houston, TX 77032 United States
nora.luna@worldcommfwd.com
http://www.worldcommfwd.com

BUS: Import and Export Freight Forwarders **P/S:** Freight Forwarding, Imports and Exports Merchandise to and from the United States **MA:** International **D/D/R:** Importing, Managing a Staff of Six in the Input Department, Acting as a Customs Broker, Working with US Customs to Clear Imports and Exports **H/I/S:** Fishing, Bowling, Going to her Son's Travel Baseball Tournaments **FBP:** The Trade Center **EDU:** College Coursework **A/A/S:** Freight Forwarders Association; National Freight Motor Traffic Association; Air Freight Association **C/VW:** Church Activities **B/I:** She was prompted to enter her profession because it's a family business. **H/O:** The highlight of her career is being able to help clients.

VICTORIA R. LUNDQUIST
President, Owner
1) Victoria's Chocolate Fountain 2) All Pro Cleaning Service
5532 Golden Willow
Fort Collins, CO 80528 United States
vlundquist77@msn.com
http://www.cambridgewhoswho.com

BUS: 1) Chocolate Fountain and Dipping Delights 2) Cleaning Service **P/S:** 1) Chocolate Delights 2) Cleaning Service for Residential and Commercial Properties **MA:** 1) Colorado 2) Regional **D/D/R:** Producing and Selling Specialty Chocolate Delights, Offering Cleaning Services **H/I/S:** Spending Time with her Four Children, Skiing, Going to the Beach **EDU:** High School Education **A/A/S:** Longmont Chamber of Commerce **C/VW:** African Girl; Global Ministries; Church; Recovering Addicts; Promotions for School Team; Resurrection Fellowship **A/S:** She attributes her career success to her diligence, marketing skills, integrity and faith in God. **B/I:** She became involved in entrepreneurial pursuits through her husband's and her love of special events.

GERALDINE F. LUNDY
Realtor
Century 21 America's Choice
13860-8 Wellington Trace
Wellington, FL 33414 United States
geraldine.lundy@gowpb.com
http://www.cambridgewhoswho.com

BUS: Real Estate Agency **P/S:** Residential and Commercial Real Estate **MA:** Wellington, Royal Palm Beach, Loxahatchee, Acreage **D/D/R:** Specializing in Residential Sales **H/I/S:** Singing, Walking, Sewing **EDU:** Industry-Related Training and Experience **A/A/S:** National Association of Realtors; Palm Beach Board of Realtors **C/VW:** Florida State Troopers; United Way of America; Hospice of Palm Beach County **A/S:** She attributes her personal and professional success to her faith in God. **B/I:** She became involved in the real estate industry after deciding to come out of retirement. **H/O:** The highlight of her career is being able to make her clients' dreams come true.

KAREN A. LURIA, EdS, IFDA, IIDA (AF), MA
President, Interior Designer
Karen Luria Interior Identity, Inc
5901 Mount Eagle Drive
Suite 711
Alexandria, VA 22303 United States
KarenLuria@interioridentity.com
http://www.interioridentity.com

BUS: Interior Design and Consultation Company **P/S:** Interior Design **MA:** VA, MD, Washington D.C. **D/D/R:** Specializing in Residential and Commercial Interior Design **H/I/S:** Scuba Diving, Skydiving, Professional Skiing **FBP:** I.D. **EDU:** Educational Specialist Degree, George Washington University; Master of Arts in Behavioral Sciences, George Washington University; Bachelor of Arts in Social Sciences, Long Island University **A/A/S:** International Furnishings and Design Association; International Interior Design Association; Associate, Interior Design Society; Better Business Bureau **C/VW:** NSO **B/I:** She became involved in this profession due to her familial background, which has given her an interest in design. **H/O:** The highlights of her career were being published in Home and Design and her nomination as secretary for the International Furnishings and Design Association.

SUSAN A. LUTTER
Broker, Owner
Gulf Waters Realty, LLC
15661 San Carlos Boulevard
Fort Myers, FL 33908 United States
sue@gulfwatersrealty.com
http://www.gulfwatersrealty.com

BUS: Full Service Real Estate Brokerage and Management Company **P/S:** Residential Property Services for Primary Residencies, Vacation Homes and Investment Properties, Property Management Services for Annual Rentals, Vacation Rentals, Vacation Rental Property Management, and Long-Term Rental Property Management **MA:** Southwest Florida **D/D/R:** Working with Homeowners, Buyers, Investors and Developers, Finding or Listing Properties, Residential Real Estate Condominiums, Townhouses and Single Family Homes, Keeping Clients Updated with Current Marketplace Sales **H/I/S:** Reading, Sports, Supporting the Everyblades Hockey Team **EDU:** College Coursework **A/A/S:** Greater Fort Myers Beach Realtors Association; Florida Association of Realtors; National Association of Realtors; Advisory Board, Lee County Business Women's Association; Lee County Chamber of Commerce **C/VW:** Volunteer Ombudsman, United States Senator John C. Stennis **W/H:** Contractor, Department of the Navy **A/S:** She attributes her success to her love for her profession. **H/O:** The highlight of her career was starting her own company. **I/F/Y:** In five years, Ms. Lutter plans to continue working in real estate.

WOLFGANG LUTZ, D.SC., PH.D.
Chancellor, Professor, Dr. Med Habil
Dublin Metropolitan University
12 Bramerton 213-215 Willesden Lane
London, NW6 7YT United Kingdom
http://www.cambridgewhoswho.com

BUS: University **P/S:** Higher Education **MA:** International **EXP:** Mr. Lutz's expertise is in writing books on nutritional problems due to carbohydrate consumption. **H/I/S:** Reading Scientific Papers, Writing Articles and Books on Low Carbohydrate Diets **FBP:** Scientific American; The Lancet; New Scientist; Time **EDU:** Ph.D., Dublin Metropolitan University, Ireland; Coursework in Internal Medicine, University of Vienna, Austria; Coursework in Medicine, University of Innsbruck, Austria **CERTS:** Venia Legendi, University of Vienna (1943) **A/H:** Distinguished Professor, Dublin Metropolitan University (2008); Doctoral Life Fellow, The Institute of General Management (2008); Freedom of the City of London Award (2007); Certificate, World Center for Optimal Nutrition, Poland (2004) **DOB:** May 27, 1913 **SP:** Helen **C/A:** Professor Emeritus (2005)

KATHLEEN J. LYLE
Adjunct Faculty, Registered Nurse Program
Tulsa Community College
909 S. Boston
Tulsa, OK 74119 United States
mooselyle@cox.net
http://www.cambridgewhoswho.com

BUS: Education **MA:** Local **D/D/R:** Nursing **H/I/S:** Traveling, Playing Sports with her Children **EDU:** Bachelor of Science in Nursing, Avila College **C/VW:** Church **A/S:** She attributes her success to her nursing education. **B/I:** She chose the profession because always had an interest in science.

Ms. Meghan B. Lynch
New York Office Assistant Manager
Specialty Transport, Inc.
55 Sandy Point Drive
Brick, NJ 08723 United States
twostep703@aol.com
http://www.cambridgewhoswho.com

BUS: Transportation Company **P/S:** Transportation Services Including Lending Cars to Actors for their Commercial Use **MA:** National **EXP:** Ms. Lynch's expertise is in loaning and transporting cars for commercial use, issuing press releases, conducting press conferences, publishing newspapers and marketing. **D/D/R:** Transporting Approximately One Million Dollars in Cars, Supplying Free Gasoline **H/I/S:** Sunbathing, Boating **FBP:** Car and Driver **EDU:** Pursuing Bachelor's Degree; Coursework in Interior Design, Rhodec International **A/A/S:** International Motor Press Association

Maria E. Lynn
Owner, Executive Chef
Catering by Maria
3 Avondale Lane
Aberdeen, NJ 07747 United States
cateringbymaria@optonline.net
http://www.cateringbymaria.com

BUS: Catering Company **P/S:** Food Service, Event Planning **MA:** Tri-State Area **D/D/R:** Planning Menus, Preparing Foods, Setting Up, Coordinating Events **H/I/S:** Cooking, Spending Time with her Family **FBP:** Catering; Gourmet **CERTS:** Professional Chef (with High Honors), Institute of Culinary Education, New York City (2004) **A/A/S:** International Special Events Society; ABC; Women Chefs and Restaurateurs; Chamber of Commerce **C/VW:** Ovarian Cancer Research Foundation, Robert Wood Hospital Johnson Foundation **SP:** Bob **CHILD:** Matthew, Alyssa **A/S:** She attributes her success to giving 110 percent of herself to her profession as well as her creativity and personal touch. **B/I:** She became involved in this profession because, after 12 years in the airline industry, she decided to attend culinary school to pursue her dream. **H/O:** The highlight of her career was participating in L'Oreal of Paris Fundraiser for the Ovarian Cancer Foundation by donating her food and services for two events.

DEBBIE LYONS
Associate Broker
Prudential Carruthers Realtors
11001 Manklin Creek Lane
Ocean Pines, MD 21811 United States
debbie.lyons@comcast.net
http://www.lyonsdev.com

BUS: Real Estate Agency **P/S:** Commercial and Residential Real Estate Exchange **MA:** National **EXP:** Ms. Lyons' expertise is in the sale of residential, executive homes, oceanfront, new construction and gulf homes. **H/I/S:** Raising Labrador Retrievers **FBP:** Coastal Living **EDU:** MD, Towson University; Bachelor of Science in Secondary Mathematics Education **CERTS:** Licensed Real Estate Broker, States of Maryland and Virginia **A/A/S:** Virginia Association of Realtors; Maryland Association of Realtors; National Association of Realtors

JOY E. LYTTLE, MSM, BA, RN
Director of Nursing
University Hospital of the West Indies
Kingston, Jamaica
joylylttle@yahoo.com
http://www.cambridgewhoswho.com

BUS: Hospital **P/S:** Healthcare **MA:** Local **D/D/R:** Specializing in Obstetrics, Utilizing Strategic Operations of Human Resources and Fiscal Activities Relating to All Nursing Staff, Caring for Patients, Educating Nurses, Lecturing **H/I/S:** Attending the Theater, Walking, Watching Television, Participating in Community Activities **FBP:** Nursing2009; Journal of Health Administration **EDU:** Master's Degree in Healthcare Management, St. Thomas University; Bachelor of Arts in General Studies, University of the West Indies **A/A/S:** Nurses Association of Jamaica; Nursing Education Special Interest Group; Women's Networking International **C/VW:** Local Education and Sports Committees, Accrediting Association of Seventh-day Adventist **A/S:** She attributes her success to her love for what she does as well as to her experience and motivation. **H/O:** The highlight of her career was receiving her regional accreditation and being on the task force for that.

JAMES A. MACALUSO
President
Legend Mechanical Corporation
85 Air Park Drive, Unit One
Ronkonkoma, NY 11779 United States
jmacaluso@legendhvac.com
http://www.cambridgewhoswho.com

BUS: Mechanical Company **P/S:** Industrial Design Building, Planning and Specifications, Heating, Ventilation and Air Conditioning **MA:** Local **D/D/R:** Designing, Managing the Company, Offering Heating, Ventilation and Air Conditioning Service and Installations, Estimating Supplies and Sales **H/I/S:** Golfing, Boating, Snowmobiling **FBP:** Forbes **EDU:** High School Diploma **A/A/S:** Local 355 **C/VW:** A Mother's Kiss **A/S:** He attributes his success to his dedication and persistence. **B/I:** He became involved in his profession because his family was in the industry. **H/O:** The highlight of his career was becoming the president of a successful business.

BARRY E. MacDONALD
Owner, Photographer
POG Images
3868 S. Fraser Street
Aurora, CO 80014 United States
barrry@live.com
http://www.pogimages.com

BUS: Photo Studio **P/S:** Photography of Nature, Creation of Fantasy Portraits with Images of Children, Fine Art Photography Including Mushrooms, Floral, Butterflies, Tree Roots and Trees, Fall Aspens, Weathered Trees, Mountain Scenes and Mountain Streams, Waterfalls, Nineteenth Century Cabins and Wagons, Christmas Scenes and Architecture **MA:** Regional **EXP:** Mr. MacDonald's expertise is in photographing children and nature settings, incorporating the images together and adding fairy wings photographed from butterflies or dragonflies to the children to create fantasy portraits, and mixing images of other subjects of nature into some aspect of fantasy to create new forms of nature. **H/I/S:** Weight Lifting, Hiking, Scuba Diving **FBP:** Popular Photography **EDU:** Associate of Arts in Ministerial Studies (1976) **A/H:** Dual Recipient, First Place Award; Recipient, Second Place Award, Best Photographer

TINA MACELI, DDS
Periodontist
Dr. Tina Maceli
45 Route 25A, Suite E1
Shoreham, NY 11786 United States
tmtdds@optonline.net
http://www.cambridgewhoswho.com

BUS: Private Practice **P/S:** Periodontal Care Including Dental Implant Surgery **MA:** Local **EXP:** Dr. Maceli's expertise is in periodontics, dental implant surgery, overseeing operations including caring for patients and supervising employees. **H/I/S:** Reading Novels and Biographies, Solving Crossword Puzzles, Building Toy Ships, Reading, Exercising, Practicing Yoga, Spending Time with her Family **EDU:** Doctor of Dental Surgery, Stony Brook University; Coursework in Specialty Training in Periodontology, University of Medicine and Dentistry of New Jersey **A/A/S:** American Dental Association; American Academy of Periodontology **C/VW:** Catholic Mission; Christian Children's Fund **DOB:** September 11, 1961 **POB:** Bronx, NY **SP:** Joseph **CHILD:** Joseph Paul, Ava **A/S:** She attributes her success to her desire for professional excellence. **B/I:** She became involved in her profession because of her interest in biology and dentistry. **H/O:** The most gratifying aspect of her career is helping people with periodontal ailments.

IDALIA M. MACHUCA-NUÑEZ
Bilingual Teacher
The Audubon School, P.S. 128 Manhattan
560 W. 169th Street
New York, NY 10032 United States
idaliamac@yahoo.com
http://www.nycaudubon.org

BUS: Elementary School Facility Dedicated to Excellence in Regular and Special Education **P/S:** Regular and Special Education Core Curriculum Including Reading, Numbers, Spelling, Art, Music, Physical Education **MA:** Local **D/D/R:** Specializing in Bilingual First Grade Education and Bilingual Special Education, Teaching Health **H/I/S:** Bicycling, Reading, Watching Movies, Spending Time with her Three Young Children **FBP:** American Teacher **EDU:** Pursuing Master's Degree in Administration and Supervision of Schools; Master's Degree in Special Education and Bilingual Special Education, Fordham University, NY (1999); Bachelor's Degree in Psychology, Fordham University, NY (1997) **CERTS:** Licensed in K-6 Bilingual and Monolingual

MR. RUBEN MACIAS
Sales Manager
LL & L, Inc.
131 Terminal Court, Suite C
South San Francisco, CA 94080 United States
http://www.cambridgewhoswho.com

RUBEN MACIAS
Hm. Telephone (707) 427-8045
Pager: (888) 874-5241
Cell: (707) 761-0553

LL&L Inc.
"Formerly Banana King Louie"
Produce Brokers

GOLDEN GATE PRODUCE TERMINAL
South San Francisco, CA 94080
Office Phone: (650) 583-7712 * Fax: (650) 583-3185

BUS: Produce Broker **P/S:** Year-Round Watermelon and Hard Squash Sales **MA:** Regional **D/D/R:** Selling to Wholesalers and Jobbers, Buying from Growers and Other Companies All Year Round **H/I/S:** Football, Baseball, Basketball, Golfing **FBP:** The Produce News; The Packer **EDU:** Diploma, Jefferson High School (1973) **A/A/S:** Arizona-California Watermelon Association **SP:** Lori **CHILD:** Jessica, Natalie

PHYLLIS DODGEN MACKE
Air Traffic Controller
Department of Defense, United States Army
phyllis@macke2000.com
http://www.cambridgewhoswho.com

BUS: Government Agency **P/S:** Air Traffic Services, Defense **MA:** National **D/D/R:** Working as an Air Traffic Controller **H/I/S:** Caring for her Parents, Boating and Water Sports **EDU:** Air Traffic Control Degree, FAA Academy **A/A/S:** Professional Women Controllers; Women in Aviation **A/S:** She attributes her success to her hard work. **H/O:** The highlight of her career was receiving recognition as the Professional Women Controller of the Year in 2006.

JEANNE A. MacLEAN
Owner
Warroad Aviation
PO Box T
Warroad, MN 56763 United States
fletcherlake@xpolrnet.com
http://www.fletcherlake.com

BUS: Fly-in Fishing Resort **P/S:** Hospitality **MA:** National **D/D/R:** Managing Three Businesses **H/I/S:** Traveling **EDU:** Diploma, Warroad High School **A/S:** She attributes her success to her hard work. **B/I:** She became involved in her profession because of her work experience in resorts at a young age. **H/O:** The most gratifying aspect of her career is meeting new people.

STACY E. MacNELLY
Teacher
Hereford Middle School
5834 Gladfelters Station Road
Seven Valleys, PA 17360 United States
smacnelly@bcps.org
http://www.cambridgewhoswho.com

BUS: School **P/S:** Middle School Education **MA:** Local **D/D/R:** Teaching Mathematics **H/I/S:** Reading, Scrapbooking, Spending Time Outdoors **FBP:** NEA Publications **EDU:** Bachelor's Degree in Elementary Education, Villa Julie College (Now Stevenson University); Pursuing Master's Degree in Mathematics, Loyola College **A/A/S:** Association of Childhood Education International; National Education Association; National Council of Teachers of Mathematics **C/VW:** UNICEF; United Way of America **A/S:** She attributes her personal and professional success to her determination and exceptional mentors. **B/I:** She has always had an interest in the field and a desire to give back to the community. **H/O:** The highlight of her career was getting a teaching job in her district directly out of school.

Ms. Gay L. Madden, RN
Vice President of Management Information Systems
The Hospice of the Florida Suncoast
6351 Second Palm Point
Saint Petersburg, FL 33706 United States
gaymadden@thehospice.org
http://www.thehospice.org

BUS: Hospice **P/S:** Services for Clients Living with Advanced Illnesses or Conditions, Caregiver Services, Assistance for Those Bereaved **MA:** Regional **D/D/R:** Combining Nursing, Information Specialist Skills and Dedicated Leadership Skills, Serving All Aspects of the Network System for 1,300 Staff Members **H/I/S:** Spending Quality Time with her Family **EDU:** Bachelor of Science in Nursing, University of Oklahoma; Registered Nurse, University of Oklahoma **A/A/S:** Healthcare Information and Management Systems Society; Public Speaker, National Hospice and Palliative Care Organization; Public Speaker, Computer World Conferences **C/VW:** Hospice of the Florida Suncoast **CHILD:** Chris, Jessica, Valerie **A/S:** She attributes her success to her commitment and focus on the needs of the patients and their families. **B/I:** She became involved in her profession after being influenced by the personal healthcare experiences she had as a child, and her personal commitment to the technology side of nursing that would allow patients to stay in their homes and receive care. **H/O:** The most gratifying aspect of her career is the number of patients and their families who have shared with her the difference she has made in their lives.

Jackie Madrigal
Latin Formats Editor
Radio and Records
5055 Wilshire Boulevard
Sixth Floor
Los Angeles, CA 90036 United States
jmadrigal7@aol.com
http://www.radioandrecords.com

BUS: Preeminent Information Company with a Radio and Music Trade Publication **P/S:** Broad Line of Print, Internet, Research, Convention and Seminar Products Offering Radio- and Record-Industry Executives with Access to Critical Research Information **MA:** International **D/D/R:** Editing, Writing a Weekly Column, Staying Current in the Latin Radio and Music Industry **H/I/S:** Watching Movies, Traveling, Playing Tennis **FBP:** Radio and Records; Time **EDU:** Bachelor of Arts in Music Business Management, Columbia College Chicago **A/A/S:** National Association of Hispanic Journalists; National Academy of Recording Arts and Sciences **C/VW:** St. Jude Children's Research Hospital

MR. RICHARD SEAN MAGBUAL, MD
Hospitalist, Internal Medicine
Kaiser Permanente
10800 Magnolia Avenue
Riverside, CA 92505 United States
tmbd@hotmail.com
http://www.kaiserpermanente.org

BUS: Healthcare Center and Health Insurance Company **P/S:** Health Insurance Plans for Employers, Families, and Individuals, Consulting, Imaging, Information Technology, Laboratory Science, Mental and Behavioral Health, Nursing, Pharmacy, Physical and Occupational Therapy **MA:** Local **D/D/R:** Working as a Hospital Doctor and On-call Emergency Room Doctor **H/I/S:** Basketball, Snowboarding, Reading, Running **FBP:** Annals of Internal Medicine Magazine **EDU:** Doctor of Medicine, New York Medical College (2000) **A/A/S:** American Medical Association; American College of Physicians

TRICIA E. MAGGI
Mathematics Teacher
Sewanhaka Central High School District
500 Tulip Avenue
Floral Park, NY 11001 United States
tmag7shsmath@aol.com
http://www.cambridgewhoswho.com

BUS: Unique School District with a Board of Regents Certified Evening High School Program **P/S:** Comprehensive High School Education Program for All School-Aged Children in Nassau County with a Rigorous Curriculum Supplemented by Enrichment Courses and Programs to Meet the Unique Needs of Every Youngster in the School System **MA:** Regional **D/D/R:** Teaching Ninth and Tenth-Grade Mathematics, Coaching the High School Rockettes **H/I/S:** Crafting, Crocheting **EDU:** Master of Arts in Mathematics Education, Adelphi University (1999); Bachelor of Arts in Mathematics Education, Molloy College **CERTS:** Licensed Administrator **A/A/S:** Nassau County Mathematics Teachers Association

CHRISTINE E. MAGNUS, RN, BSN, CPON
Registered Nurse, BSN, CPON
Children's Hospital of Orange County
455 S. Main Street
Orange, CA 92868 United States
cmagnus1@cox.net
http://www.choc.org

BUS: Regional Pediatric Healthcare Hospital **P/S:** Preventive Medical Care, Education and State-of-the-Art Pediatric Biomedical Research **MA:** Regional **D/D/R:** Nursing, Charge Nursing in the Pediatric Oncology Intensive Care Unit, Overseeing the Unit, Offering Direct Patient Care, Ensuring Resources for Nurses, Scheduling, Conducting Evaluations, Running Leadership Projects **H/I/S:** Participating in Beach Activities, Kayaking, Swimming, Pilates **FBP:** Journal of Pediatric Oncology; Working Nurse **EDU:** Bachelor of Science in Nursing, Registered Nurse, Azusa Pacific University (1988) **CERTS:** Nationally Certified Pediatric Oncology Nurse (2006) **A/A/S:** Association of Pediatric Oncology Nurses **A/H:** Featured, Working Nurse Magazine; Featured, Nursezone.com; Excellence in Writing Award, Azusa Pacific University (1988) **C/VW:** Board Member and Mentor, 'Working Against Cancer'; Liaison, Children's Hospital and Working Against Cancer Organization; Volunteer, Mariners Church

DR. VIDHYANAND MAHASE
Pharmacist
Safeway Pharmacy
7551 Forbes Boulevard
Lanham, MD 20706 United States
vickmahase@hotmail.com
http://www.safeway.com

BUS: Proven Leader Among Retail Grocery and Pharmacy Services **P/S:** Pharmacy Services, Online Shopping, Beauty and Healthcare Products, Photo Department, Gifts **MA:** Regional **D/D/R:** Specializing in Medical Therapeutic Management, Profiling Drug Interactions, Counseling Patients, Consulting with Doctors and Insurance Companies **H/I/S:** Football, Cricket, Teaching Indian Music to Children **FBP:** The Wall Street Journal; Rx Consultant **EDU:** Doctor of Pharmacy, Howard University, Department of Pharmaceutical Sciences (2005) **A/A/S:** Hult Alumni; Maryland Pharmaceutical Association; AIA **SP:** Francine

CHRISTINE MAHONEY-SCHNEIDER, CCC-SLP, MA
Speech Pathologist
New York City Board of Education, Public School 77
4211 14th Avenue
Brooklyn, NY 11219 United States
cmah7476@hotmail.com
http://www.cambridgewhoswho.com

BUS: Public School **P/S:** Education **MA:** New York City **D/D/R:** Working with Autistic Children **H/I/S:** Spending Time with her Children **EDU:** Master of Education in Special Education with a Concentration in Autism, Long Island University, C.W. Post Campus; Master of Arts in Speech-Language Pathology, St. John's University **A/A/S:** American Speech-Language Hearing Association; New York State Academy for Teaching and Learning **C/VW:** Make-A-Wish Foundation **A/S:** She attributes her success to her son and love of seeing children succeed. **B/I:** She became involved in her profession after seeing how speech therapy helped her disabled niece to communicate. She wanted to help other children the same way. **H/O:** The highlight of her career was being inducted into the New York City Academy for Teaching and Learning by her peers.

JENNIFER N. MAHONY
Transaction Coordinator
Realty Executives
10707 Town Center Drive, Suite 110
R. Cucamonga, CA 91730 United States
jennifer@realtyexecutives.com
http://www.realty@erealtyexecutives.com

BUS: Real Estate Company **P/S:** Contract Administration Services **MA:** Local **D/D/R:** Specializing in Residential Contracts **H/I/S:** Playing the Piano, Reading and Watching Movies **FBP:** Realtor **EDU:** Pursuing Bachelor's Degree in Finance and Business Law, Minor in Real Estate, California State Polytechnic University at Pomona **CERTS:** Licensed Real Estate Agent **A/A/S:** Board of Realtors; National Association of Realtors; California Association of Realtors **A/H:** President's Award **C/VW:** Local Church, St. Jude Children's Research Hospital **A/S:** She attributes her success to her mother who was her mentor. She also feels that her education and the skills she has learned add to her success. **H/O:** The highlight of her career is becoming more involved in her career and learning new things.

EMILIE S. MAIER, RMA
RMA and Medical Assistant Coordinator
Western Family Physicians, Inc.
2450 Kipling Avenue, Suite 108
Cincinnati, OH 45239 United States
auntlee@gmail.com
http://www.cambridgewhoswho.com

BUS: Family Medical Practice Dedicated to Excellence in Healthcare **P/S:** Adult Medicine Including Prevention, Health Maintenance, Care of Acute and Chronic Illness, Pediatrics including Vaccines, Children with ADHD, Women's Health Including Obstetrics, Gynecology, Colonoscopy, Incontinence, Geriatrics, Minor Surgery, Sports Medicine and Pre-Participation Exams, Annual Exams and Physicals, Counseling **MA:** Regional **D/D/R:** Managing the Office, Scheduling **H/I/S:** Cross-Stitching, Exercising **FBP:** JAMA Journal **CERTS:** RMA Certificate **A/A/S:** AAMA; Ohio CMAs; AMT

CHARLENE K L MAJERSKY, PH.D.
Department Head of Administrative Services
Naval Health Research Center
United States Navy
140 Sylvester Road
San Diego, CA 92106 United States
drinouye2001@yahoo.com
http://www.cambridgewhoswho.com

BUS: Government Organization **P/S:** Defense Including Healthcare Education and Military Training, Navy Medicine **MA:** National **D/D/R:** Overseeing Healthcare Administration **H/I/S:** Traveling, Reading, Watching Sports, Making Crafts **FBP:** Journal of Healthcare Management; Health Care Management Review **EDU:** Ph.D., Capella University **A/A/S:** Medical Service Corps; Naval Reserve Association **C/VW:** Fundraiser, Local Charitable Organizations; Local Geriatric Population; Child Development Center; Feed the Homeless; Alzheimer's Association **A/S:** She attributes her success to her positive values, integrity, open-mindedness, self-motivation and diligent work ethic. **B/I:** She became involved in her profession because she wanted to serve her country. **H/O:** The most gratifying aspect of her career is having the opportunity to collaborate and share her knowledge with others.

MR. MIKE J. MAKER
Trainer
Makerstable
7908 Stonemeadow Drive
Louisville, KY 40218 United States
makerstable@netzero.com
http://www.cambridgewhoswho.com

BUS: Racing **P/S:** Racing Horses **MA:** Regional **D/D/R:** Training, Overseeing Management of Horse Racing, Stable of Horses and 26 Staff Members

HELEN BERENICE MALDONADO, PA-C
California Area Diabetes Consultant
Indian Health Service
United States Department of Health and Human Services
650 Capitol Mall, Room 7100
Sacramento, CA 95814 United States
helen.maldonado@ihs.gov
http://www.cambridgewhoswho.com

BUS: Department of Health and Human Services **P/S:** General Health and Consulting Services **MA:** California **D/D/R:** Attending and Presenting at Seminars and Conferences, Overseeing Administration, Program Development, Organizing Programs in California and Consulting for Tribal Programs **H/I/S:** Making Jewelry, Swimming, Spending Time with her Grandchildren **FBP:** Journal Watch **CERTS:** Certified Physician Assistant **A/A/S:** The American Academy of Physician Assistants

Mr. Lee Mallatratt
Clinical Research Coordinator
Duke University Medical Center
Erwin Road
Durham, NC 27710 United States
malla001@mc.duke.edu
http://www.cambridgewhoswho.com

BUS: Medical Center **P/S:** Healthcare **MA:** International **D/D/R:** Coordinating Clinical Trials **H/I/S:** Gardening, Listening to Music, Art, Animal Protection and Rescue **EDU:** Bachelor of Science in Nursing, Villanova University (1978) **A/A/S:** Sigma Theta Tau; SOCRA **C/VW:** APS; Make-a-Wish; Breast Cancer Awareness **A/S:** She attributes her success to her independence, mentors and ability to be a responsible self-starter. **B/I:** She became involved in the profession because she always wanted to research. **H/O:** The most gratifying aspect of her career is helping patients and families on a daily basis.

Rachel M. Raru Maloney
Accounting Manager
George Washington University Hospital
2131 K Street N.W.
Suite 610
Washington, DC 20037 United States
rmaloneycpa@yahoo.com
http://www.cambridgewhoswho.com

BUS: Hospital **P/S:** Healthcare **MA:** Eastern Coast **D/D/R:** Accounting, Financing **EDU:** Master's Degree in Accounting, Strayer University **A/A/S:** American Institute of Certified Public Accountants **C/VW:** Children International; Christian Children's Fund **A/S:** She attributes her success to her hard work, drive and determination. **B/I:** She became involved in the profession because she enjoys working with numbers and training students. **H/O:** The most gratifying aspects of her career are earning respect from her staff and seeing former interns return to express their gratitude.

JOY C. MAMARIL
Realtor, Vice President
Platinum Business Group
2938 Avon Square Road
San Jose, CA 95121 United States
jmamaril@platinumbg.com
http://www.platinumbg.com

BUS: Real Estate **P/S:** Provide Residential and Commercial Real Estate and Mortgages **MA:** National **D/D/R:** Specializing in Residential Properties **H/I/S:** Tennis, Reading **FBP:** Time **EDU:** Bachelor's Degree in Mass Communications **A/A/S:** National Board of Realtors; Santa Clara Board of Realtors **C/VW:** St. Francis of Assisi Catholic Church **A/S:** She attributes her personal and professional success to her hard work and patience. **H/O:** The highlight of her career was being named Top Producer for 4 years.

JUDITH G. MANCIL, CCC
Deputy Clerk
Atkinson County Board of Commissioners
201 S. Main Street
Pearson, GA 31642 United States
judith_g_mancil@yahoo.com
http://www.cambridgewhoswho.com

BUS: Local Government **P/S:** Community Services **MA:** Local **D/D/R:** Accounting, Purchasing, Coordinating Safety Programs **H/I/S:** Fishing, Driving Four-Wheelers, Farming **CERTS:** Certified County Clerk; Certified Finance Officer, Level I; Certified Safety Coordinator **A/A/S:** Association of County Commissioners; Association of County Clerks of Georgia

MONICA C. MANERING, RN, BSN, PHN
Registered Nurse
Kaiser Permanente KP on Call
herb-moni@cox.net
http://www.cambridgewhoswho.com

BUS: Healthcare Facility **P/S:** Call Center, Ambulatory Care, Inpatient, Long-Term Care, Home Health, Adult Medicine, and Pediatric Care, Advanced Information Technology, Effective Protocols, and Extensive Clinical Knowledge Critical Care **MA:** National **D/D/R:** Nursing in the Urgent Care, Emergency Room, Intensive Care, Triage and Critical Care Departments, Doing In-services on Critical Care, Precepting New Nurses **H/I/S:** Horseback Riding, Reading, Motorcycles, Bike Riding, Swimming, Walking on the Beach **FBP:** Critical Care Nurse **EDU:** Bachelor of Science in Nursing, University of Phoenix (2006); Associate Degree in Nursing, Grossmont College (1997)

SHARON MANGOSING-GUTIERREZ
Assistant Vice President
Bank of America
208 Harristown Road
Fourth Floor
Glen Rock, NJ 07452 United States
snagutierrez@yahoo.com
http://www.bankofamerica.com

BUS: Banking Institution **P/S:** Financial Services and Assistance **MA:** Regional **D/D/R:** Financial Planning, Mortgages, Credit and Investment, Portfolio Management Series 6 and 63, Life and Health **H/I/S:** Traveling **FBP:** BusinessWeek; Forbes; Money **EDU:** Master of Business Administration in Management, Fairleigh Dickinson University (2001) **CERTS:** Series 6 and 63 (1999); Life and Health License (1998)

BARBARA MANKOWSKI, RN, BSN, CNOR
Registered Nurse, Assistant Nurse Manager of Orthopedics
Winthrop University Hospital
259 First Street
Mineola, NY 11501 United States
nursebasia@aol.com
http://www.cambridgewhoswho.com

BUS: Hospital **P/S:** Healthcare **MA:** Local **D/D/R:** Medical, Surgical and Operating Room Nursing **H/I/S:** Reading, Polish-American Activities **FBP:** Association of periOperative Registered Nurses Publications **EDU:** Bachelor's Degree in Nursing, Adelphi University **A/A/S:** Association of perioperative Registered Nurses **A/H:** Nurse of Excellence Award **A/S:** She attributes her success to her upbringing and hard work. **B/I:** She became involved in her profession because she enjoys helping people and making a difference. **H/O:** The highlight of her career was receiving the Nurse of Excellence Award.

MARY ELIZABETH (BETH) MANVILLE
Special Education Teacher
Gregory-Portland Intermediate School
4200 Wildcat Avenue
Portland, TX 78374 United States
bmanville@g-pisd.org
http://www.cambridgewhoswho.com

BUS: Education **P/S:** Mathematics **MA:** Local **D/D/R:** Special Education **H/I/S:** Scrapbooking, Making Crafts **FBP:** Educational Leadership **EDU:** Bachelor of Science in Early Childhood Education, Angelo State University **C/VW:** Girls Scouts of America **A/S:** She attributes her success to her hard work and the support she receives from her family. **B/I:** She became involved in her profession because she wanted to make a difference for other children. **H/O:** The most gratifying aspect of her career is seeing the progress that students make.

RUTH ELIZABETH MANZANO
Realtor
Long and Foster Realtors
1910 William Street
Fredericksburg, VA 22401 United States
ruth.manzano@longandfoster.com
http://www.lizmanzano.com

BUS: Leader in the Real Estate Industry **P/S:** Selling Real Estate **MA:** Central Virginia **D/D/R:** Land Listings and Sales, Selling Real Estate **H/I/S:** Soccer, Dancing, Gardening, Traveling **EDU:** Bachelor of Arts in Business, York College, New York **A/A/S:** Presidential Diversity Board, University of Mary Washington; Lifetime Member, Multi-Million Dollar Club; Chairman's Club; Hispanic Chamber of Commerce **A/H:** National Service Award, Realty Alliance Award (1997, 2005)

ROOHI G. MANZOOR
Realtor
World Properties International, Rubicon Crossings
105 E. Center Street
Manchester, CT 06040 United States
room@rubiconcrossings.com
http://www.wpirealty.com/room

BUS: Real Estate, Mortgages, Insurance **P/S:** Real Estate **MA:** National **D/D/R:** Realtor and Mortgage Officer **H/I/S:** Traveling, Visiting Historical Places **FBP:** Newsweek **EDU:** Bachelor's Degree in Computer Science, University of Kingston, England **A/A/S:** Metro Hartford Alliance; Greater Hartford Association of Realtors; National Association of Realtors; Connecticut Association of Realtors **A/S:** She attributes her success to being a people and service oriented person. **B/I:** She became involved in her profession because she was out of work from an injury and took that opportunity to enter the real estate field.

LINDA G. MARC, SC.D., MPH
Science Officer
Behavioral Science International, LLC
20 Charlesgate W., Suite 301
Boston, MA 02215 United States
lmarc@behavioralscienceintl.com
http://www.behavioralscienceintl.com

BUS: Consulting Company **P/S:** Consulting, Health Services, Research Design, Methodological Assessment **MA:** International **EXP:** Dr. Marc's expertise is in consulting with pharmaceutical and health-related companies, statistical analysis of health data including public health, extensive international public speaking in prestigious venues and developing health questionnaires for illiterate populations. **EDU:** Postdoctoral Research in Mental Health, Weill Cornell Medical College; Doctor of Science, Harvard School of Public Health; Master of Public Health, Yale School of Public Health **A/A/S:** American Public Health Association; Board Member, Chairwoman, Alumni Association, Yale School of Public Health; Haitian-American Association of Engineers and Scientists; Chairwoman, HIV/AIDS Special Interest Group, International Society for Quality of Life Research **A/S:** She attributes her success to her determination and perseverance.

BEVERLY MARCOGLIESE
Sales Associate
ReMax Village Square
9 Sloan Street
South Orange, NJ 07079 United States
bmarcogliese@hotmail.com
bmarcogliese@remax.net
http://www.bmarcogliese.remax-nj.com

BUS: Real Estate Agency **P/S:** Residential and Commercial Real Estate Exchange **MA:** Regional **D/D/R:** Overseeing All Residential Real Estate, Relocations, Repossessions, Foreclosures, Appraisals and Real Estate Exchanges, Covering All of Essex, Pasic, Union and Bergen Counties **H/I/S:** Traveling **FBP:** Realtor **EDU:** Coursework in Early Childhood Development, Montclair State University **CERTS:** Licensed Real Estate Agent (1981) **A/A/S:** Multiple Listing Service; National Association of Realtors

JOSETTE MARIA, MD
Physician, Owner
Maria Medical Center
800 Susan Tart Road
Dunn, NC 28334 United States
josettemaria@earthlink.net
http://www.cambridgewhoswho.com

BUS: Physician's Office **P/S:** Highest Quality of Healthcare and Patient Care, Internal Medicine **MA:** Regional **H/I/S:** Soccer **EDU:** MD, Hahnemann University of Philadelphia (1996) **CERTS:** Board Certified in Geriatrics and Internal Medicine; Licensed in New York, North Carolina, and Tennessee **A/A/S:** American Medical Association; American Society of Addiction Medicine; Association of Air Medical Services; American Academy of Urgent Care Medicine; American College of Physicians; American Geriatrics Society; APC; Southern Medical Association; Harnett Medical; North Carolina Medical Society; Diplomate, American Board of Internal Medicine; Diplomate, American Board of Geriatric Medicine

VICKIE L. MARION
Practice Manager
St. Thomas Radiology Associates
vmarion@stthomasrad.com
http://www.cambridgewhoswho.com

BUS: Radiology Center **P/S:** Full Service Diagnostic Imaging, Patient Care and Assessment **MA:** Local **EXP:** Ms. Marion's expertise is operations and human resources management, radiology, overseeing accounts payable and receivable, managing inventory control, purchasing, contract negotiation and administering post-acute care services. **H/I/S:** Traveling, Exercising, Dancing **A/A/S:** Radiology Business Management Association **EDU:** Bachelor's Degree in Management, Nichols College, MA (1990) **C/VW:** Relay for Life, American Cancer Society; American Red Cross

MS. CYNTHIA A. MARKEY
51 High Point Road
Tavernier, FL 33070 United States
cmarkey@keysso.net
http://www.keysso.net

MA: Local **D/D/R:** Specializing in Law Enforcement, Managing Public Protection and Crime Prevention **H/I/S:** Fishing, Scuba Diving, Boating, Boat Racing, Women's Professional Tackle Football, Florida Stingrays **EDU:** Bachelor of Science in Criminal Justice Administration, University of Phoenix (2007); Associate Degree in Criminal Justice, Broward Community College (1987) **A/H:** Dean's List, Florida Keys Community College **C/VW:** Girl Scouts of the United States of America **DOB:** April 8, 1967 **POB:** North Miami Beach, FL **W/H:** Parts Manager, Assistant Bookkeeper, Markey's Marine Service; Detention Deputy, Road Patrol, Detective, Court Deputy, Airport Deputy, Monroe County Sheriff's Office

DEBRA J. MARKS, M.ED.
Special Education Teacher
W.T. Clarke Middle School, East Meadow School District
740 Edgewood Drive
Westbury, NY 11590 United States
mom4marks@aol.com
http://www.eastmeadow.k12.ny.us/clarkems

BUS: Middle School **P/S:** Instruction and Curriculum **MA:** Regional **D/D/R:** Teaching Sixth, Seventh and Eighth-Grade Students in Self-Contained Classrooms, Developing Learning Styles for Students, Developing Social Skills and Self-Confidence, Participating in the Service Learning Program Including All Students of the School **H/I/S:** Reading, Traveling, Golfing **FBP:** American Teacher **EDU:** Master's Degree in Elementary Education, C.W. Post Campus, Long Island University (1973) **CERTS:** Special Education Certification, Hofstra University (1998) **A/A/S:** Parent-Teacher Association; Board of Education and New Special Education Teachers **C/VW:** Founders Day Award

LINDA LEE MARLOWE
Kindergarten Teacher, Owner, Teacher
Marlowe's Playful Bears Home Preschool
Isaac School District
Tempe, AZ 85282 United States
IIIdesertdwellers@highstream.net
http://www.cambridgewhoswho.com

BUS: Preschool **P/S:** Early Childhood Education **MA:** Statewide **D/D/R:** Encouraging Energy and Creativity, Teaching Children to Read **H/I/S:** Race Walking, Children's Literature, Puppetry, Cooking **EDU:** Master of Elementary Education, Northern Arizona State University **CERTS:** Credential, National Childcare Association (Equivalent to National Board Certification in Early Childhood Education); ESL Endorsement; Reading Endorsement K-12; Early Childhood Endorsement **A/A/S:** Arizona National Association of Teachers; Arizona Teachers Association **C/VW:** Breast Cancer; Local Child Abuse Prevention Organizations; American Leukemia Society; Reading is Fundamental; Read Across America; Rad Kids **A/S:** She attributes her success to prayer and determination. **B/I:** She chose the profession after being influenced by her father, who was a history teacher. **H/O:** The highlight of her career was putting together the campaign for Read Across America.

MR. STEPHEN WALTER MARQUARD
Network Specialist for the IBM/ITDA
Consulting
CDI Business Solutions
Saint Louis, MO 63110 United States
smarguard@charter.net
http://www.bign.com/sdmarquard

BUS: Professional Services Company **P/S:** Tailored Business Solutions to Clients in a Variety of Industries Worldwide through Four Integrated Operating Units **MA:** International **D/D/R:** Specializing in Advising System Administration Teams and Team Leadership **H/I/S:** Camping, Leather Crafting, Hunting, Sculpting, Walking, Traveling with Family on Vacations, Golfing **FBP:** Success **EDU:** Associate Degree in Computer Science, St. Louis Community College; Associate Degree in Industrial Arts, Jefferson College **A/A/S:** Eagle Scout; Phi Theta Kappa; Missouri State Teachers Association; Union and Cisco Network Group **A/H:** Deans List; Several Awards for Excellent Service for Duties Performed, Missouri Air National Guard **C/VW:** Church; AA Program; Team National; Santa for Several Community Events **A/S:** He attributes his success to the military and their teachings of electronics. **B/I:** He became involved in his profession first through college courses then again through military training and opportunities. **I/F/Y:** In five to ten years he sees himself more involved with church and community happenings.

MARY C. MARRIS
Training Manager, Project Manager
Department of Training and Technology
Eagle Systems and Services
6221 W. Gore Street
Lawton, OK 73505 United States
mmarris@esascorp.com
http://www.esas.com

BUS: Contracting Firm **P/S:** Training, Training Development, Logistics, Project and Program Management **MA:** National **EXP:** Ms. Marris' expertise is in program and policy development and implementation, instructional systems design and development, multimedia courseware design, team building, coaching and organization development consulting. **FBP:** PMI Network; PM Journal; TenStep PM Newsletters; Chief Learning Officer; Training & Development; ATSD; The Buzz Newsletter; IEEE Spectrum; Tech Republic Newsletters **EDU:** Master's Degree in Training and Development; Bachelor of Applied Arts and Sciences Degree in Public Administration and Political Science, Midwestern State University, Wichita Falls, TX **CERTS:** Certification in AAS Instructor Technology, Community College of Air Force; Six Sigma Green and Black Belt Certification, Villanova University **A/A/S:** American Society for Training & Development; Institute of Electrical and Electronics Engineers; Project Management Institute; Disabled American Veterans Association

CHERYL A. MARRS
Teacher
Elementary School
8475 Hannary Drive
Tallahassee, FL 32312 United States
camarrs@yahoo.com
tracksidehomes@nycap.rr.com
http://www.cambridgewhoswho.com

BUS: Elementary School **P/S:** Primary Education **MA:** National **D/D/R:** Teaching Kindergarten through Sixth-Graders and Special Education for Prekindergarten Students, Overseeing the Program in Information Technology, Desktop Publishing **H/I/S:** Bicycling, Singing, Walking, Volunteering, Writing Poetry **FBP:** Phi Delta Japan; Journal of Research on Technology in Education **EDU:** Master of Arts in Elementary Education, University of West Florida; Bachelor of Arts in Music Education, Florida State University **CERTS:** Certified Mentor/Assessor for New Teachers; National Board Certified Teacher **A/A/S:** Alumni Association, Florida State University; Phi Delta Kappa **A/H:** National Honor Roll's Outstanding American Teachers (2006); Parents Choice Educator of the Year (2003); Who's Who in Education (1988); Outstanding Woman of the Year Award (1975); Standout Award in Community **C/VW:** Habitat for Humanity **A/S:** She attributes her success to her determination, perseverance and the support she receives from her parents and administrators. **B/I:** She became involved in her profession because she was inspired by her teacher and church choir director. **H/O:** The most gratifying aspect of her career is seeing her students succeed.

ARLENE NEWMAN MARSHALL
President
Calhoun County Economic Development Corp.
2300 N. Highway 35
Port Lavaca, TX 77979 United States
amarshall@calhounedc.org
http://www.calhounedc.org

BUS: Economic Development **P/S:** Sustaining and Enhancing Quality of Life in Calhoun County by Promoting Area Resources to Effectively Maintain Diversity and Expand Economic Base of Calhoun County **MA:** Regional **D/D/R:** Networking **H/I/S:** Reading, Entertaining, Traveling **EDU:** Bachelor of Art in Music, University of Houston **A/A/S:** Texas Economic Development Council; Work Force Board; Delta Zeta **C/VW:** President, Rotary Club; Board Member, Victoria College Foundation **A/S:** She attributes her success to her drive, determination and desire to see things happen. **B/I:** She became involved in her profession because she became politically involved in the community when she moved to the area in 1983. **H/O:** The highlight of her career has been being elected County Judge for four years.

LISA J. MARSHALL
Teacher, Coach, Advisor
Chuckey-Doak High School
365 Ripley Island Road
Afton, TN 37616 United States
marshall@greenek12.org
http://www.cambridgewhoswho.com

BUS: High School **P/S:** Education **MA:** Local **D/D/R:** Advising Future Business Leaders of America and the Yearbook Staff, Teaching Keyboarding, Coaching Volleyball **EDU:** Bachelor of Science in Secondary Education, Kansas State University **A/A/S:** Future Business Leaders of America; National Business Education Association **C/VW:** March of Dimes **A/S:** She attributes her success to the support and encouragement of her mother. **B/I:** She became involved in the profession because she always wanted to work with children. **H/O:** The highlight of her career was being recognized as the Tennessee Advisor of the Year for Future Business Leaders of America in the 2005-2006 school year.

TIMOTHY SCOTT MARSHALL
Director
Toshiba Business Solutions
6401 Nob Hill Road
Tamarac, FL 33321 United States
kduke@tbsfltoshiba.com
http://www.cambridgewhoswho.com

BUS: Electronic Imaging Company **P/S:** Sales and Acquisition of Office Equipment, Software and Business Solutions **MA:** International **D/D/R:** Managing Company Sales **H/I/S:** Lifting Weights, Traveling **EDU:** Bachelor's Degree in Marketing and Entrepreneurship, Florida Atlantic University **A/H:** Number One Sales in the World, Toshiba Business Solutions **C/VW:** Kids in Crisis **A/S:** He attributes his career success to remaining consistent in his work, being people-oriented, working hard and being self-motivated. **B/I:** He became involved in marketing after working in the field after graduating from school and finding he loved the work. **H/O:** The most gratifying aspect of his career is being able to maintain his success rate.

MARY I. MARSHALL-CARTER
Chief Executive Officer
Marshall-Carter & Carter, LLC
429 S.E. 13th Terrace
Gainesville, FL 32641 United States
info@mmccllc.net
http://www.mmccllc.net

BUS: Transition Organization, Career Consultant Service **P/S:** Providing Hope and Direction for Families in Transition from Welfare to Work and to Families who have been Displaced by Natural Disasters, Career Placement Agent **MA:** Regional **D/D/R:** Planning and Organizing **H/I/S:** Watching her Son Play Tennis, Listening to Music, Dancing, Spending Quality Time with her Family, Helping Others **FBP:** Black Enterprise; Forbes **EDU:** Associate of Applied Science in Business Administration; Extensive Industry-Related Experience **CERTS:** Certified in Business Management and Human Resource Management, Santa Fe Community College; Certificate in Allied Health Surgical Technology **A/A/S:** Board Member, HIPPY of Gainesville, Florida, Williams Temple Church of God and Christ **C/VW:** Sister Hayzel Angels of Mercy **A/S:** She attributes her success to having a positive attitude and to never giving up. **B/I:** She became involved in her profession she saw an opportunity to offer hope to individuals willing to go through trials to make it. **H/O:** The highlight of her career is helping people to be supportive and provide for their families.

ANGELA MARTELLE
Business Analyst
McKesson Corporation
700 Locust Street
Dubuque, IA 52001 United States
angie_martelle@hotmail.com
http://www.mckesson.com

BUS: Healthcare Services Company **P/S:** Healthcare **MA:** National **EXP:** Ms. Martelle's expertise is in information technology, managing information systems, process streamlining, processing and procedures documentations for outstanding organizations, hospitals and pharmacies. **H/I/S:** Bowling, Watching Chicago Bears, NASCAR Racing **FBP:** CIO; Fortune **EDU:** Master's Degree in Business Administration, Regis University (2006); Bachelor of Arts in Finance and Management Information Systems, Loras College (2004) **CERTS:** Certification in Six Sigma Black Belt, Villanova University (2005)

CARIN BESSETTE MARTER, NREMT-P
Director of Clinical Programs
Southwest Ambulance
708 E. Baseline Road
Mesa, AZ 85201 United States
carinaz@aol.com
http://www.cambridgewhoswho.com

BUS: Private Ambulance Provider **P/S:** Ambulance Services **MA:** International **H/I/S:** Traveling, Mountain Climbing, Photography, Biking **FBP:** Forbes; Money **EDU:** Bachelor's Degree in Law, American International College; Associate Degree in Paralegal Studies, University of Arizona **CERTS:** Certified in Advanced Cardiac Life Support Instructor; Certified in Pediatric Advanced Life Support Instructor; International Critical Incident Stress Foundation; National Registry of Emergency Medical Technicians; Certified International Association of Basic Trauma Life Support Instructor; Certified Paramedic, States of Arizona and New Mexico **A/A/S:** National Flight Paramedic Association; National Registry of Emergency Medical Technicians; National Association of EMS Educators **C/VW:** South American Charities; Osano Foundation; Make-A-Wish Foundation **A/S:** She attributes her career success to the ethics her father taught her and to her love of her profession. **B/I:** While in high school, she traveled with the police, emergency health and fire departments and found that she was very interested in the field of emergency services. **H/O:** She feels that receiving the award for field employees in 2004 has been the highlight of her career.

DENISE S. MARTIN
Emergency Medical Services Program Director, Faculty
Oakland Community College
2900 Featherstone Road
Auburn Hills, MI 48326 United States
dsmartin@oaklandcc.edu
http://www.oaklandcc.edu/emt

BUS: Community College **P/S:** Educational Services for Students **MA:** Local **D/D/R:** EMT and Paramedic Initial and Continuing Education **H/I/S:** Spending Quality Time with her Children **FBP:** National Geographic; Journal of Emergency Medical Services **EDU:** Master of Science, Ferris State University; Bachelor's Degree in Emergency Medical Services Studies **A/A/S:** Society of Michigan EMS Instructor Coordinators **C/VW:** Veterans Associations; The Salvation Army; National Kidney Foundation; United Way of America

FRANCES MARTIN
Director, Respiratory Therapy Department
Wellstar Hospital (Kennestone)
677 Church Street
Marietta, GA 30060 United States
http://www.cambridgewhoswho.com

BUS: Healthcare **P/S:** Respiratory Therapy **MA:** Regional **D/D/R:** Directing the Respiratory Therapy Department **H/I/S:** Reading, Scuba Diving, Aerobic Walking and Spending Time with her Family **EDU:** Bachelor of Science in Health Service Administration, University of Central Florida; Bachelor's Degree in General Studies and Computers, Minor in Law, University of Central Florida **A/A/S:** American Association of Respiratory Care; Georgia Society of Respiratory Care; National Board of Respiratory Care **C/VW:** American Heart Association; American Lung Association; Volunteer, Asthma Camp **A/S:** She attributes her success to her determination, flexibility and supportive family. **B/I:** She became involved in her profession because she wanted to get involved in the patient care aspect of healthcare. **H/O:** The highlight of her career is having three children in college who are accomplished in their own right.

KANDACE K. MARTIN
Zone Coordinator
Prairie Lakes Area Education Agency
501 Bank Street
Webster City, IA 50595 United States
martinkandace@hotmail.com
http://www.teachersurvivaltips.com

BUS: Education Agency **P/S:** Education **MA:** Regional **EXP:** Ms. Martin's expertise is in administration and consulting in general and special education. **H/I/S:** Reading, Traveling, Gardening **FBP:** Educational Leadership **EDU:** Master's Degree in Educational Administration, Iowa State University; Bachelor of Arts in English, Iowa State University **CERTS:** Superintendent Endorsement, University of Northern Iowa **A/A/S:** Association for Supervision and Curriculum Development; Iowa Association for Middle Level Education; National Middle School Association **C/VW:** Habitat for Humanity; Hurricane Relief in Mississippi; Meals on Wheels **H/O:** The highlight of her career was seeing her student walking across the stage at graduation.

MAUREEN K. MARTIN
Director
Dubard School for Language Disorders, University of Southern
Mississippi
118 College Drive, Suite 10035
Hattiesburg, MS 39406 United States
maureen.martin@usm.edu
http://www.usm.edu/dubard

BUS: Educational Facility-University **P/S:** Education, Communication Disorder Services **MA:** National **D/D/R:** Specializing in Speech Language Pathology and Teacher of the Deaf and Hard of Hearing, Overseeing Full-Time Enrollments, 4 to 15-Year-Old Children, Out-Client Therapy and Evaluation Program, Resource Referral Program, Teaching University Students 'Association Method' Technique, Developing Research Programs, Sending Quality Instructions to Other Sites to Teach the 'Association' Method-Traveling Throughout Other States, Developing Distance Learning Course Online for Teachers Speech Language, Special Education Instructions in Private and Clinical Practices, Consulting School District to Utilize Method they use, International Training **H/I/S:** College Football, Art, Traveling, Gardening **EDU:** Ph.D. in Ireland, Europe; Master's Degree in Speech and Hearing Sciences, University of Southern Mississippi; Bachelor's Degree in Speech and Hearing Sciences, University of Southern Mississippi **A/A/S:** American Speech Language Hearing Association; International Dyslexia Association; AG Bell Association for the Deaf

PAULA J. MARTIN, RN
Relief Charge Nurse, Staff Nurse
Milford Campus
Bayhealth Medical Center
W. Clarke Avenue
Milford, DE 19963 United States
seaspray@bwave.com
http://www.cambridgewhoswho.com

BUS: Medical Center **P/S:** Healthcare, Acute Care **MA:** Local **EXP:** Ms. Martin's expertise is in medical and surgical nursing, orthopedics and oncology. **H/I/S:** Participating in Outdoor Activities **FBP:** American Journal of Nursing; Nursing2009 **EDU:** Associate of Science in Nursing, Dell Tech College **C/VW:** United Way of America; American Legion Auxiliary

SALLY MARTIN RODRIGUEZ, RN, BSN, PHN
Director of Nurses, Registered Nurse, Public Health Nurse, BSN
1) Central Health Services Center Project DEIR
1) California Department of Corrections and Rehabilitation
2) Chuckawalla Valley State Prison
861 Cypress Lane, Blythe, CA 92225 United States
sally.rodriguez@cdcr.ca.gov
http://www.cambridgewhoswho.com

BUS: 1) Government Agency 2) Correctional Institution **P/S:** 1) Rehabilitation and Correctional Services Including Law Enforcement 2) Correctional Services Including Quality Long-Term Housing and Medical Services for Inmates **MA:** 1) Regional 2) Regional **EXP:** Ms. Martin Rodriguez's expertise is in trauma nursing, flight nursing, overseeing medical staff, implementing and maintaining new policies and procedures to improve the quality of inmate and patient care and training staff. **H/I/S:** Spending Time with her Family, Reading **FBP:** RN **EDU:** Bachelor of Science in Nursing, California State University, Chico (1980); Coursework in Public Health Nursing, California State University, Chico **A/A/S:** California Correctional Supervisors Organization **SP:** Eddie **A/S:** She attributes her success to her determination and the support she receives from her mentors. **H/O:** The most gratifying aspects of her career are making a difference by educating other nurses and maintaining the quality of patient care.

DANIEL G. MARTINELLI
Owner, Operator
D. Martinelli Plumbing, Heating and Air Conditioning
3456 Old Bethlehem Pike
Coopersburg, PA 18036 United States
danmart@epix.net
http://www.cambridgewhoswho.com

BUS: One of Pennsylvania's Top Plumbing, Heating and Air Conditioning Companies **P/S:** Installation and Repair for Residential Homes, Commercial Accounts **MA:** Regional **D/D/R:** Residential Service New Construction, Residential Work, Remodeling, Additions, Gas Work, Well Tanks, Heating, Ventilation and Air Conditioning Change Outs, Water Filtration Systems **H/I/S:** Supporting the Philadelphia Eagles **FBP:** Entrepreneur Magazine **EDU:** Bachelor of Science in Business Administration, Kutztown University (1993) **CERTS:** Certification for Tankless Water Heaters (2007); Master Plumbers License (2002); Residential Heating, Ventilation and Air Conditioning License (1998) **A/A/S:** Home Builders' Association of Buck's and Montgomery County

ELISA MARTINEZ
Legal Assistant
Law Office of Jeff D. Rago
1100 Montana, Suite 202
El Paso, TX 79902 United States

BUS: Law Office **P/S:** Professional Legal Services **MA:** Local **D/D/R:** Assisting in Criminal, Real Estate, Probate, Personal Injury, Civil Law **H/I/S:** Spending Time with her Family **FBP:** NALS **EDU:** Continuing Legal Education, El Paso Community College **A/A/S:** El Paso Paralegal Association, National Association of Legal Professionals

Ms. Gladys R. Martinez, D.O., FACP
Physician
Royal Palm Internist
7086 Brunswick Circle
Boynton Beach, FL 33472 United States
drgladysmartinez@aol.com
http://www.cambridgewhoswho.com

BUS: Primary Care Facility **P/S:** Full Primary Care Practice With An Interest in Preventative Medicine and Women's Health **MA:** Local **D/D/R:** Practicing Internal Medicine, Treating Diabetes, Offering Guidance on Women's Issues **H/I/S:** Reading, Biking, Summer Sports **FBP:** American Journal of Medicine **EDU:** Doctor of Osteopathy, Nova Southeastern University; Bachelor of Science in Chemistry, Psychology and Biology, University of Miami **A/A/S:** American College of Psychology; American Medical Association; American Medical Women's Association; Florida Osteopathic Medical Association **C/VW:** Battered Women's Association; St. Jude Children's Hospital, Mission Honduras International **B/I:** She has been helping people since she was a child. **H/O:** She feels that being able to have a good rapport with her patients, and creating an understanding that she cares and they will come back is the highlight of her career.

Mr. Leo Martinez
Owner
LM Networking
2695 Vista Linda
Fairfield, CA 94534 United States
leomartinez001@yahoo.com
http://www.cambridgewhoswho.com

BUS: Interpretation and Translation company **P/S:** Administrative Services, Court Interpreting **MA:** Northern California **D/D/R:** Simultaneous Interpretations, Translating Documents **H/I/S:** Reading, Golfing, Coaching Soccer **EDU:** Bachelor of Business Administration, Peru; Bachelor of Business Administration, California State University at Sacramento; Coursework in International Business **A/A/S:** Founder, Hispanic Chamber of Commerce; Police Activity League **C/VW:** Hurricane Katrina Fund **A/S:** He attributes his success to the enjoyment he receives from working with others. **B/I:** He became involved in his profession after translation for the Immigration and Naturalization Service and for the commissioner. **H/O:** The most gratifying aspect is being able to translate simultaneously.

RAY ANTONIO MARTINEZ
Fleet Manager
Merck & Co., Inc.
ramon_martinez@merck.com
http://www.merck.com

BUS: Pharmaceutical Company **P/S:** Pharmaceuticals **MA:** Puerto Rico, Caribbean, South America **EXP:** Mr. Martinez's expertise is in fleet purchasing, maintenance, allocations and security. **H/I/S:** Motorcycling, Restoring Cars **FBP:** Caribbean Business News; Forbes **EDU:** Bachelor of Arts in Business Management, Universidad de Este de Puerto Rico

LUCY MARTINO SCOTT, RN, CCM, CLNC, CHCQN, FAIHQ
Nurse Case Manager, Owner
Legal Medical Services, Inc.
1080 Christmas Place
Greensboro, NC 27410 United States
lucy_m_scott@uhc.com
http://www.cambridgewhoswho.com

BUS: Healthcare **P/S:** Case Management, Medical Record Reviews **MA:** National **D/D/R:** Life Care Planning, Helping Patients Manage Benefits and Understand their Needs, Reviewing Medical Records, Interviewing Patients for Medical Legal Cases, Managing Cases **H/I/S:** Taking Care of her Dogs **EDU:** Associate Degree in Nursing, SUNY Farmingdale (1973); Registered Nurse (1973) **CERTS:** Case Management Certification (2006); Legal Nurse Consultant Certification (2000) **A/A/S:** Fellow, American Institute of Health Care Quality; American Board of Quality Assurance and Review; American Board of Nurse Case Managers **C/VW:** March of Dimes; American Heart Association; Infant Mortality Causes within Guilford County; American Cancer Society; Volunteer, Nurse's Health Study, Harvard University

BRUCE ALLYN MARTS, DO

Doctor of Osteopathy, Emergency Physician
Walnut Creek Medical Center, Kaiser Permanente
1425 S. Main Street
Walnut Creek, CA 94596 United States
docmarts@yahoo.com
http://www.permanente.net/homepage/doctor/marts
http://www.kaiserpermanente.org

BUS: Medical Center **P/S:** Healthcare Including Preventive Care, Well-Baby and Prenatal Care, Immunizations, Emergency Care, Screening Diagnostics, Hospital and Medical Services, Pharmacy Services, Assistance for the Uninsured and Special Populations, Training New Health Professionals, Introducing New Delivery Methods into the Healthcare Field **MA:** Regional **EXP:** Mr. Marts' expertise is in emergency medicine. **H/I/S:** Traveling, Watching Movies, Cooking, Exercising **FBP:** Emergency Medicine Reports **EDU:** Residency in Emergency Medicine, St. Barnabas Hospital; Doctor of Osteopathy, New York College of Osteopathic Medicine, New York Institute of Technology; Master of Science, Georgetown University; Bachelor's Degree, University of Notre Dame **A/A/S:** Osteopathic Physicians & Surgeons of California; American Osteopathic Association; American College of Osteopathic Emergency Physicians

PATRICIA E. MARVIN

Teacher
Tri-North Middle School
1000 W. 15th Street
Bloomington, IN 47404 United States
pmarvin@mccsc.edu
http://www.mccsc.edu

BUS: Middle School **P/S:** Education **MA:** Local **D/D/R:** Teaching Language Arts Including Literature, Reading, Writing, Grammar, Listening and Speaking Skills to Seventh and Eighth-Graders **H/I/S:** Reading, Gardening, Spending Quality Time with her Children, Playing Sports **FBP:** NCTE Journals **EDU:** Master's Degree in Secondary Education, Indiana University **A/A/S:** National Council of Teachers of English; Phi Delta Kappa **A/H:** I Make a Difference Award **C/VW:** Spending Time at School with Extra-Curricular Activities, Local Cancer Societies **A/S:** She attributes her career success to her commitment to her profession and to her true care and dedication to her students. **B/I:** After majoring in English and journalism while in college, she was encouraged by her mother to pursue a career in education and she found that she loved the field. **H/O:** She feels that being a teacher leader, a mentor to her students, and being trusted by her corporation to be involved in the accreditation process are the highlights of her career.

Rosalie A. Mashtalier, RN, BSN
Senior Clinical Nurse
United States Public Health Service
8901 S. Wilmont Road
Tucson, AZ 85706 United States
rmashtalier@bop.gov
http://www.cambridgewhoswho.com

BUS: Government Agency **P/S:** Public Health Services **MA:** National **D/D/R:** Offering Correctional Medical Services **H/I/S:** Traveling, Studying Astrology **EDU:** Pursuing Master's Degree; Bachelor of Science in Nursing, Loma Linda University; Emergency and Disaster Relief Coursework, Touro University **A/A/S:** Drug Enforcement Administration; Federal Bureau of Investigation; United States Customs; Commissioned Officers Association

Susan M. Mason
Teacher
Springdale Elementary School
560 Walton Court
Macon, GA 31204 United States
masonss@cox.net
http://www.bibb.k12.ga.us

BUS: Elementary School **P/S:** Elementary Education Including After School Tutoring Programs for Students **MA:** Regional **EXP:** Her expertise is in teaching fourth-grade language arts and mathematics. **H/I/S:** Watching Movies, Tennis, Walking, Exercising, Biking, Reading, Entertaining **FBP:** Educational Leadership **EDU:** Educational Specialist Degree in Middle Grades, Valdosta State University and Georgia Southern University; Master of Science in Middle Grades, Valdosta State University and Georgia Southern University; Bachelor of Science in Middle Grades, Valdosta State University and Georgia Southern University; Coursework in Special Education, Georgia Southern University (2003) **A/A/S:** National Education Association; Georgia Association of Educators; Phi Delta Kappan **A/H:** Teacher of the Year Award, State of Georgia (1999); My Teacher is Tops Award, Bibb County (2004)

KATHRYN I. MASSARO, MS
Teacher
Saint Agatha Academy
244 S. Main Street
Winchester, KY 40391 United States
kathrynmassaro@yahoo.com
kmassaro@cdlex.org
http://www.cambridgewhoswho.com

BUS: Catholic Elementary and Middle School **P/S:** Primary Education **MA:** Kentucky **D/D/R:** Teaching Academics, Virtues and the Catholic Faith to Third-Grade Students, Designing Programs **FBP:** The Reading Teacher **EDU:** Master's Degree in Reading and Literacy, Walden University (2006); Bachelor of Arts in Elementary Education, Bowling Green State University, OH (1995) **C/VW:** Volunteer, Children's Sunday School **DOB:** January 31, 1973 **POB:** Painesville, OH **SP:** Chris **CHILD:** Lauren, Caroline **W/H:** Teacher, Saint Agatha Academy; Teacher, Little Lambs Learning Center; Teacher, Grace Christian Child Care Center **A/S:** She attributes her success to her desire to learn and ability to work well with people. **B/I:** She became involved in her profession because she always wanted to teach children, and discovered how much she enjoyed working with small children when she and her husband moved to Kentucky. **H/O:** The highlight of her career was successfully implementing her reading and literacy program into her preschool curriculum. **I/F/Y:** In five years, Ms. Massaro hopes to enrich the lives of third-grade students.

EBONI NICOLE MASSEY
Director, Owner
Jump Start Educational Services, CCS
3215 Varrene Street
Fayetteville, NC 28303 United States
ebonimassey@aol.com
http://www.cambridgewhoswho.com

BUS: Educational Services Company **P/S:** Teaching, Tutoring and Special Workshops **MA:** Local **D/D/R:** Teaching Reading, Writing and Mathematics to Kindergarten through Sixth-Grade Students **H/I/S:** Reading, Watching Movies, Dining Out **FBP:** Instructor; Entrepreneur **EDU:** Bachelor's Degree in Elementary Education **A/A/S:** National Education Association **C/VW:** American Red Cross **A/S:** She attributes her success to her passion for teaching. **B/I:** She became involved in the profession because she wanted to make a difference in peoples lives. **H/O:** The most gratifying aspect of her career is enjoying what she does.

MR. ROGER D. MASTERS
Research Professor
Dartmouth College
53 Lyme Road
Apartment 21
Hanover, NH 03755 United States
roger.d.masters@dartmouth.edu
http://www.dartmouth.edu

BUS: University **P/S:** Higher Education, Scientific Research **MA:** International **D/D/R:** Consulting, Political Philosophy, Working with Toxins and Toxic Chemicals Effecting Behavior, Connecting Biology and Human Behavior **H/I/S:** Walking **FBP:** Science **EDU:** Ph.D., University of Chicago (1961) **A/A/S:** American Political Science Association; Association for Politics and the Life Sciences; American Academy of Environmental Medicine

MRS. PATTI A. MATAXEN
University of Phoenix
mataxen@yahoo.com
pmataxen@email.phoenix.edu

BUS: University **P/S:** Education **MA:** International **EXP:** Ms. Mataxen's expertise is in diabetes education, case management and grant writing. **D/D/R:** Teaching Online Healthcare Courses, Labor and Delivery Nursing **H/I/S:** Hunting, Fishing, Crocheting, Drawing **FBP:** The Wall Street Journal; American Journal of Nursing; PC World **EDU:** Master's Degree in Health Care Administration; Master of Science in Nursing, University of Phoenix; Bachelor of Science in Nursing, Wesleyan University **CERTS:** Certificate in Public Health Nursing, University of Colorado Health Sciences Center; Certification in Core Competencies for Public Health Professionals **A/A/S:** Texas Nurses Association; American Nurses Association; National Council of Nurse Administrators **A/H:** Sigma Theta Tau International Nursing Honor Society **C/VW:** Local Fundraisers; Local Charities **DOB:** October 30, 1954 **POB:** Dallas, TX **W/H:** University of Phoenix; Nursefinders; St. Croix Tribal Health Department; Burnett Medical Center **A/S:** She attributes her success to her hard work, education and the support she receives from her family. **B/I:** She became involved in her profession because she was encouraged by her co-worker. **H/O:** The highlight of her career was becoming a professor. **I/F/Y:** In five years, Ms. Mataxen will still be teaching and hopes to have earned her Ph.D. in health administration.

KRYSTAL L. MATESIC
Physical Therapist
In Home Rehab/H.C. Solutions
24811 Notre Dame
Dearborn, MI 48124 United States
southpaw18@wowway.com
http://www.cambridgewhoswho.com

BUS: Healthcare Services Provider **P/S:** High Quality Physical and Occupational Therapy Services for the Geriatric Population within Assisted and Independent Living Facilities and Home Care in the Community **MA:** Regional **D/D/R:** Working Closely with the Geriatric Population and their Rehabilitation Needs **H/I/S:** Softball, Volleyball **EDU:** Master's Degree in Physical Therapy, Wayne State University (1998); Bachelor of Science in Allied Health (1996)

MS. JENNIFER P. MATHIS-FISHER, MS
Personal Counselor
Center for Counseling and Psychological Services
Barry University, Miami Shores, Florida
11300 N.E.Second Avenue, Miami Shores, FL 33161 United States
jmathis-fisher@mail.barry.edu
http://www.barry.edu/counselingservices.com
http://www.barry.edu/dvtaskforce.com

BUS: International University **P/S:** Educational Services including Individual and Group Psychotherapy, Consulting, Psychological Testing and Community Outreach Regarding Mental Health Concerns with University Students **MA:** International **EXP:** Ms. Mathis-Fisher's expertise is in individual and group psychotherapy and community outreach. **D/D/R:** Counseling, Educating, Studying Family of Origin Work, Relationship Difficulties, Anxiety and Depression, Sexual Orientation Concerns **H/I/S:** Reading, Swimming, Jewelry Making, Cooking **FBP:** American Psychologist; Monitor on Psychology; Counseling Today **EDU:** Master's Degree in Clinical Psychology, Valdosta State University, GA (2005); Bachelor's Degree in Communications, Kennesaw State University, GA (2000) **A/A/S:** Professional Member, American Psychology Association; American Counseling Association; American College Counseling Association; Kappa Delta Pi Honor Society; Psi Chi Honor Society **A/H:** Elected Democratic Committee Woman of Precinct X048, Broward County, FL **C/VW:** The Leukemia and Lymphoma Society; Relay for Life; American Cancer Society **DOB:** October 4, 1977 **POB:** Rome, GA **SP:** George **A/S:** She attributes her success both personally and professionally to her steadfast determination, faith, and resilience to face life's challenges. **B/I:** She became involved in the profession because she had the skills and a strong belief that her purpose is to help others create personal changes within their lives. **H/O:** The highlight of her career was co-facilitating an initiative to create an awareness to prevent local violence.

JACQUELINE MATOS
Mathematics Chairperson, Summer School Principal,
Assistant Principal Community School
Freeport High School
50 S. Brookside Avenue
Freeport, NY 11520 United States
jacqueline.matos@cwwemail.com • jmatosny@msn.com
http://www.freeportschools.org

BUS: High School **P/S:** Secondary Education **MA:** Local **D/D/R:** Teaching Mathematics, Staffing, Developing Curriculum, Scheduling, and Responsible for Professional Development **H/I/S:** Cycling, Reading **FBP:** Mathematical-Models-Related Publications **EDU:** Master's Degree in Mathematics Education, Plus 45, Columbia University (2004); Bachelor's Degree in Mathematics, Columbia University (1999) **CERTS:** Pursuing Certification in Bilingual Education **A/A/S:** National Council of Teachers of Mathematics; AANYS; Kappa Delta Pi

PATTY A. MATTEO
Associate Broker
Hope Realty
1980 Dominion Way
Suite 101
Colorado Springs, CO 80918 United States
pattymatteo93@msn.com
http://www.cambridgewhoswho.com

BUS: Real Estate Company **P/S:** Residential Real Estate **MA:** Local **D/D/R:** First Time Home Buyers **H/I/S:** Working Out, Gardening, Running, Drawing and Painting **CERTS:** Licensed Broker **A/A/S:** National Association of Realtors **C/VW:** Teacher, Catholic Church; Donates Food to Local Charity **A/S:** She attributes her success to hard work, and her personable attitude. **B/I:** She chose the profession because she wanted supplemented income. **H/O:** The highlight of her career is finishing real estate studies while working a full time job.

CYNTHIA D. BURRELL MATTHEWS
French Teacher
Sacopee Valley High School
115 S. Hiram Road
Hiram, ME 04041 United States
burrellcyn@aol.com
http://www.sad55.k12.me.us
http://www.sad55.org

BUS: High School **P/S:** Education, Foreign Language, Gifted and Talented Program, French Club, Athletics, Clubs and Organizations, Food Services, Health Services, Personal Counseling Services **MA:** Local **D/D/R:** Teaching Foreign Languages Including Spanish, Advising the French and International Club, Tutoring Japanese, Overseeing the Gifted and Talented Program, Speaking French, Japanese, Spanish and English **H/I/S:** Singing with an Renaissance Music Trio, Attending and Performing in Theaters, Competing in Triathlons **FBP:** Educational Leadership; National Bulletin; American Association of French Teachers Publications **EDU:** Master's Degree in Education, University of Southern Maine (2000); Bachelor of Arts in International Relations, Tufts University; Bachelor of Music, New England Conservatory of Music; Coursework in Franco-American Studies **CERTS:** Certified French and Social Studies Teacher **A/A/S:** Maine Geographic Alliance; Foreign Language Association of Maine; American Association of Teachers of French; Board Member, Japan America Society of Maine; The Maine-Aomori Sister State Advisory Council; Maine Coalition for Citizen Diplomacy; World Affairs Council of Maine **C/VW:** Local Church; Caring Unlimited **DOB:** October 26, 1968 **POB:** Portland, ME **SP:** Troy **CHILD:** Maximilian **A/S:** She attributes her success to her ability to her ability to connect with her students, hard work and perseverance. **B/I:** She became involved in her profession because she was always interested in the French language and culture, and wanted to teach. **H/O:** The most gratifying aspect of her career is seeing her students succeed, especially in their fourth year as they take the national French exam. **I/F/Y:** In five years, Ms. Matthews plans on continuing her Franco-American studies and start working on her Ph.D.

KRISTIE K. MATTISON
Firefighter, Emergency Medical Technician
Bargersville Community Fire Department, Whiteland Fire Department
89 S. Baldwin Street
Bargersville, IN 46106 United States
kmattison@insightbb.com
http://www.bcfd.net

BUS: Fire Department **P/S:** Saving Lives, Protecting Property, Training, Education **MA:** Local **D/D/R:** Special Extraction Training **H/I/S:** Horseback Riding, Playing Softball **FBP:** Fire Engineering **CERTS:** Emergency Medical Technician, C9 Certification; Firefighter Certification I and II, Hazardous Materials Certification, Whiteland Fire Department **A/A/S:** Indiana Volunteer Fire Association; Whiteland Fire Department; Elected Chairwoman, Board of Directors, Whiteland Fire Department; Public Broadcasting Association; Lungs for Life; Indiana University Medical Center

KATHLEEN M. MAURER
Assistant Professor and Performing Artist
Ball State University School of Music
kmmaurer@bsu.edu
http://www.cambridgewhoswho.com

BUS: University **P/S:** Higher Education, Recitals and Concerts **MA:** U.S. Midwest Region **D/D/R:** Teaching Voice Classes **H/I/S:** Crafts and Coaching her Daughter in Singing **FBP:** NATS Journal of Singing **EDU:** Master's Degree in Music, Bowling Green State University; Doctor of Musical Art, ABD Status **A/A/S:** National Association of Teachers of Singing; College Music Society; Phi Kappa Phi; Pi Kappa Lambda **C/VW:** American Diabetes Association, Local Food Banks, American Heart Association **A/S:** She attributes her success to hard work, self discipline, organizational skills and talent. **B/I:** She became involved in her career because of her love of music.

LESLIE J. MAY, PH.D.
Senior Management Consultant
The Sinclair Group
10655 Six Pine Drive, Suite 130
The Woodlands, TX 77380 United States
ljmay@houston.rr.com
http://www.cambridgewhoswho.com

BUS: Consulting Company **P/S:** Consulting on Manufacturing Excellence **MA:** International **D/D/R:** Leading Innovation **H/I/S:** Bicycling **FBP:** Fast Company **EDU:** Doctor of Philosophy and Chemistry, Indiana State University **A/A/S:** American Chemical Society **C/VW:** National Multiple Sclerosis Society **A/S:** She attributes her career success to her hard work and dedication to her career. **B/I:** She has always had an interest in the sciences, and as there are very few women in her industry, she felt that it was the right profession for her. **H/O:** She feels that being nominated by her colleagues for the Genesis Award, or the People Development Award has been the highlight of her career.

JOCELYN A. MAYFIELD
Owner, Physical and Occupational Therapist
Gulf Coast Rehabilitation, Inc.
1706 Bienville Boulevard
Ocean Springs, MS 39564 United States
jmay0328@cs.com
http://www.cambridgewhoswho.com

BUS: Rehabilitation Center **P/S:** Drug Rehabilitation Including Outpatient Therapy, Direct Patient Care **MA:** Local **EXP:** Ms. Mayfield's expertise is in pediatric rehabilitation. **D/D/R:** Educating and Supporting Groups, Schools, Various Organizations on Sensory Processing Disorder, Interacting with 15 to 20 Physicians Per Day, Assisting Children with Autism and Asperger's Syndrome, Treating Patients with Sensory Integration Disorder, Helping the Physically Challenged Return to their Greatest Mobility Potential and Medical Services **H/I/S:** Running, Golfing **FBP:** PT Magazine **EDU:** Master's Degree in Physical Therapy, The University of Alabama (2002); Bachelor of Science in Occupational Therapy, Louisiana Medical Center (1987) **CERTS:** Certified Sensory Integration Therapist (2004) **A/A/S:** American Physical Therapy Association; The American Occupational Therapy Association; Mississippi Physical Therapy Association; Board Member, Together Enhancing Autism Awareness in Mississippi

CHERYL F. MAYO, LPC
Coordinator
Mother to Mother Ministry
722 W. Eighth Street
Pittsburg, KS 66762 United States
cherylmayo515@hotmail.com
http://www.cambridgewhoswho.com

BUS: Nonprofit Organization **P/S:** Community Services **MA:** National **EXP:** Ms. Mayo's expertise is in counseling. **H/I/S:** Reading, Photography, Caring for Animals **FBP:** Journal of Counseling and Development; Family Fun **EDU:** Master of Science in Counseling, Pittsburg State University, KS **A/A/S:** Association for Play Therapy; American Counseling Association **C/VW:** The Humane Society of the United States; The American Society for the Prevention of Cruelty to Animals **A/S:** She attributes her success to her personal fortitude and the support she receives from her family and friends. **B/I:** She became involved in her profession because of her desire to help others. **H/O:** The most gratifying aspect of her career is receiving gratitude from different families.

STEPHANI A. MAZURKIEWICZ

Sales Consultant
Novartis Pharmaceuticals Corporation
1 Health Plaza
East Hanover, NJ 07936 United States
mcclurgs5@aim.com
http://www.cambridgewhoswho.com

BUS: Pharmaceutical Corporation **P/S:** Cardiovascular and Diabetic Medicine, Pharmaceuticals **MA:** International **D/D/R:** Overseeing Pharmaceutical Sales **H/I/S:** Running Marathons, Riding her Harley Davidson **FBP:** Fortune; Forbes **EDU:** Bachelor's Degree in Business Economy, Minor in Marketing, Indiana University **A/A/S:** Republican Women's Group; Mishawaka Educational Foundation; Daughters of the American Revolution **C/VW:** International Diabetes Association; Relay for Life; American Red Cross **A/S:** She attributes her success to being disciplined and working well with a team. **B/I:** She became involved in her profession because she was always interested in the medical field.

MARY REBECCA U. MBAH, RN

Registered Nurse
Sharon Care Center
8167 W. Third Street
Los Angeles, CA 90048 United States
ibuchim2000@yahoo.com
http://www.cambridgewhoswho.com

BUS: Healthcare **P/S:** High Quality Healthcare Services to those in Need **MA:** Local **D/D/R:** Working in Geriatrics **H/I/S:** Playing Tennis, Reading, Playing Basketball **EDU:** Pursuing Bachelor of Science in Nursing, University of Phoenix; Registered Nurse, University of Nigeria **CERTS:** Certified Medical-Surgical Nurse **A/A/S:** Daughters of Divine Living

KATHRYN M. MCATEER
Special Education Teacher
Penn Delco School District
2881 Pancoast Avenue
Aston, PA 19014 United States
kmcateer1@verizon.net
http://www.cambridgewhoswho.com

BUS: Public School **P/S:** Education **MA:** Local **D/D/R:** Working with Students who Have Emotional Difficulties **H/I/S:** Practicing Karate **EDU:** Bachelor's Degree in Business Administration and Management, Eastern College; Master's Degree in Multi-Cultural Education, Eastern College **CERTS:** Certificate, Elementary Education; Certificate, Special Education **C/VW:** Priests of the Sacred Heart **A/S:** She attributes her success to her determination and motivation. **B/I:** She became involved in her profession because of her son's disability. **H/O:** The highlight of her career has been her interaction with emotionally disturbed students and watching them succeed.

VICKIE MCBRIDE, MBA, RN, BSN
Owner
Evergreen Styles
vickiemcbride@charter.net
http://www.cambridgewhoswho.com

BUS: Consulting Firm **P/S:** Healthcare Consulting Services **MA:** Regional **D/D/R:** Overseeing Compliance and Regulations, Consulting **H/I/S:** Shopping, Golfing **FBP:** Woundostomy; American Journal of Nursing **EDU:** Master of Business Administration, Baldwin Wallace College (1986); Bachelor of Science in Nursing, Marycrest College (1966) **CERTS:** Certified Nutraceutical; Certified Wound Care Specialist; Certified Legal Nurse Consultant **A/A/S:** National Association Directors of Nursing Administration in Long-Term Care; Fellow, Academy of Nursing Administration

MONICA J. MCCABE, RN, OCN
Project Manager
PPD, Inc.
3772 Old Maco Road N.E.
Leland, NC 28451 United States
momccabe@bellsouth.net
http://www.cambridgewhoswho.com

BUS: Contract Research Organization **P/S:** Clinical Trials **MA:** International **EXP:** Ms. McCabe's expertise is in oncology and hematology nursing and clinical research. **H/I/S:** Traveling **EDU:** Pursuing Master of Science in Nursing Management, Regis University **A/A/S:** Oncology Nursing Society; American Society of Clinical Oncology **C/VW:** Casa De La Cos Ninos; Southern Arizona Oncology Nursing Society; Cancer Survivor Celebration; American Diabetes Association; American Red Cross **A/S:** She attributes her success to her perseverance and determination. **B/I:** She became involved in her profession after realizing the need for quality care.

PATSY MCCALL
Realtor, Office Manager
Georgia Carolina Premier Properties Inc., Attn. Patsy McCall
430 N. Main Street
Hiawassee, GA 30546 United States
prmmccall@alltel.net
http://www.georgiacarolinapremierproperties.com

BUS: Real Estate Company **P/S:** Listing and Selling Properties in the Georgia Mountains **MA:** Local **H/I/S:** Yard Work, Swimming, Golfing **FBP:** Real Estate Publications **A/A/S:** Former Board Member, Former Chairperson, Towns County Hospital Authority; President, Hospital Auxiliary **C/VW:** Hospital Auxiliary **A/S:** She attributes her success to her honesty, hard work and personality. **B/I:** She became involved in her profession because a friend recommended it to her. **H/O:** The highlight of her career was earning her position.

Dr. Yvonne McCallum Peters

Associate Professor
Medgar Evers College, The City University of New York
1650 Bedford Avenue
Room 2038A
Brooklyn, NY 11225 United States
ypeters@mec.cuny.edu
http://www.mec.cuny.edu

BUS: College **P/S:** School of Business, School of Liberal Arts and Education, School of Science, Health and Technology and the School of Professional and Community Development **MA:** Regional **D/D/R:** English Composition, Advising Students, Special Curriculum Development **H/I/S:** Writing Poetry **FBP:** Time; The Chronicle of Higher Education **EDU:** Doctoral Degree, Columbia University (1999) **A/A/S:** National Youth Administration; Board Member, Nonprofit Academic Planning Committee; NYARE; National Council of Teachers of English **C/A:** Co-Author of a Textbook

Anna Louise McCarthy, RN

Registered Nurse (Retired)
Sunbury Community Hospital
Sunbury, PA 17801 United States
http://www.sunburyhospital.com

BUS: Hospital **P/S:** Emergency Room, Cardiology, Family Practice Offices, Gastroenterology, General Surgery, Gynecology, Hematology, Internal Medicine, Laboratory, Oncology, Ophthalmology, Orthopedic Surgery, Pathology, Podiatry, Psychiatry, Radiology, Sleep Laboratory, Urology and Vascular Surgery **MA:** Local **D/D/R:** Nursing, Administering Intravenous Therapy and Cardiac Services, Working as a Charge Nurse **H/I/S:** Spending Time with her Animals, Reading **FBP:** Nursing2009; The Herald **EDU:** Registered Nurse (1985); Diploma in Nursing, Geisinger Medical Center **CERTS:** Certified in Chemotherapy **DOB:** August 17, 1945 **W/H:** Registered Nurse, Sunbury Community Hospital

LAUREN T. MCCARTHY
Director
Agency Channel Marketing
Prudential Annuities
1 Corporate Drive
Shelton, CT 06484 United States
lauren.mccarthy@prudential.com
http://www.cambridgewhoswho.com

BUS: Insurance Company **P/S:** Insurance Services **MA:** International **D/D/R:** Marketing, Overseeing Strategic Planning, Product Launching, Brand Management, Quality Management, Managing Public Relations, Working on New Initiatives, Organizing Events and Sales Promotions **H/I/S:** Equestrian Sports, Painting, Gardening **FBP:** Boomer Market Advisor **EDU:** Bachelor of Fine Arts, Syracuse University **C/VW:** Habitat for Humanity; American Diabetes Association **A/S:** She attributes her success to her hard work and her education. **B/I:** She became involved in her profession because of her interest in the marketing field. **H/O:** The highlight of her career was earning her current position.

DOROTHY McCAULEY, RN, BSN, CDE
Nurse Consultant
Diabetes Resource Center
825 Yosemite Court
Lincoln, CA 95648 United States
diabetes3@surewest.net
http://www.cambridgewhoswho.com

BUS: Resource Center **P/S:** Services for Seniors and Children, Programming **MA:** International **EXP:** Ms. McCauley's expertise is in intensive management of diabetes and educating healthcare professionals on diabetes. **H/I/S:** Traveling **EDU:** Bachelor of Science in Nursing, London University **CERTS:** Certified Diabetes Educator **A/A/S:** American Diabetes Association; American Association of Diabetes Educators **A/H:** Nominee, Diabetes Educator of the Year (1986) **C/VW:** Local Children's Hospitals

LAURA K. McCLAIN
Principal
M.R. Weaver Elementary
520 Saint Maurice Lane
Natchitoches, LA 71457 United States
lmcclain@nat.k12.la.us
http://www.cambridgewhoswho.com

BUS: Elementary School **P/S:** Education for Students in Pre-Kindergarten through Third-Grade **MA:** Regional **D/D/R:** Managing School, Interacting with Parents of Students, Addressing Disciplinary Problems **H/I/S:** Traveling **FBP:** Educational Leadership **EDU:** Master's Degree in Educational Leadership, Northwestern State University (2005) **A/A/S:** Association for Supervision and Curriculum Development; International Reading Association; Louisiana Reading Association; Louisiana Association of School Principals; National Association of Elementary School Principals

KARIN McCLEERY
Manager, Sales Engineering
T-Mobile
60 Wells Avenue
Newton, MA 02459 United States
kjmccleery@charter.net
http://www.t-mobile.com

BUS: Telecommunications Company **P/S:** Telecommunication, Consulting and Integration Services **MA:** International **EXP:** Her expertise is in wireless data integration, mobile data solutions, managing sales and consulting. **H/I/S:** Reading, Hiking, Cooking, Mountain Biking **FBP:** Wireless Week; RCN News; Cooking Light **EDU:** Bachelor of Science in Magazine Journalism, Syracuse University (1989) **CERTS:** Certified Project Manager

JENNIFER E. McCLURE
Executive Director
Society for New Communications Research
2625 Middlefield Road
Suite 662
Palo Alto, CA 94306 United States
jmcclure@sncr.org
http://www.sncr.org

BUS: Global Nonprofit Think Tank and Proven Leader in Media, Marketing and Public Relations **P/S:** Advanced Study of New Communication Tools, Technologies and Emerging Modes of Communication and their Effect on Media, Professional Communications, Business and Society, Research, Publications, Events and Educational Offerings **MA:** International **D/D/R:** Participating in Internet Publishing, Offering Consulting Services for Marketers, Offering Public Relations and Media and Consulting Services for Organizations Looking to Improve Internal and External Communications, Speaking at Conferences for Media and Marketing, Promoting Public Relations Industry Education **FBP:** The Wall Street Journal; Advertising Age; MediaPost; Wired; PR Week; Industry-Related Blogs **EDU:** Master's Degree in Liberal Arts, Stanford University (2007); Bachelor's Degree in Liberal Arts, Sarah Lawrence College (1985) **A/A/S:** Public Relations Society of America; The Future of Work; Speaker, HDI Executive Forum; Co-Producer; Speaker, New Communications Forum; Speaker, Ragan Communications

YVONNE D. McCLUSKY
Executive Director
North Utica Senior Citizens Community Center, Inc.
40 Riverside Drive
Utica, NY 13502 United States
yvonne@thenucc.com
http://www.nucc.com

BUS: Community Center **P/S:** Senior and Children Services, Childcare and Senior Services and Programming **MA:** Local **D/D/R:** Presenting on Design and Implementing Intergenerational Programs Daily **H/I/S:** Camping, Canoeing **FBP:** The Wall Street Journal **EDU:** Bachelor's Degree in Human Services and Administration, Empire State College **A/A/S:** Your Neighbor; Chamber of Commerce **A/H:** Crystal Award Winner (2005) **C/VW:** Rotary Club

MARY K. MCCOLLUM
English Teacher
Dallas Independent School District, Skyline Center
7777 Forney Road
Dallas, TX 75227 United States
mkmc@ont.com
http://www.cambridgewhoswho.com

BUS: High School **P/S:** Regular Curriculum including English, Mathematics, Science, Social Studies, Art, Music, History, Physical Education **MA:** Regional **D/D/R:** Teaching Sheltered English, Reading and History **H/I/S:** Traveling, Playing Bridge, Reading **FBP:** Journal of English **EDU:** Master's Degree in Reading, Western Michigan University; Bachelor's Degree in History and English, Texas Technical College (1969) **A/A/S:** American Federation of Teachers; Parent-Teacher Association; Former Member, National Education Association; Texas Education Association; Former Member, National Teachers Association; National Council of Teachers of English

MRS. AMANDA J. MCCOY
Registered Nurse
Deaconess Hospital
613 Mary Street
Evansville, IN 47747 United States
hohna@my.iecc.edu
http://www.marykay.com/amccoy5263

BUS: Hospital **P/S:** Specialized in Rehabilitation, Geriatric Care, Acute Cardiac Care, Acute and Chronic Care of Renal Failure **MA:** Regional **D/D/R:** Overseeing Wound and Patient Care and Treatments, Directing the Staff, Completing Patient and Resident Assessments, Training, Educating, Specializing in Cardiac and Renal Care, Dispensing Medication **H/I/S:** Biking, Fishing, Doing Outdoor Activities, Playing with Dogs **FBP:** American Journal of Nursing; Nursing2009; Nursing Made Incredibly Easy **EDU:** Registered Nurse, Wabash Valley College (2005); Licensed Practical Nurse, Wabash Valley College (2004) **A/A/S:** Who's Who of American High School Students **DOB:** October 5, 1983 **SP:** Brian **CHILD:** Austin

MR. LARRY B. McCoy
President
McCoy Contracting, Inc.
307 Woodall Farm Lane
Princeton, NC 27569 United States
mccycorp@aol.com
http://www.cambridgewhoswho.com

BUS: Proven Leader in the Construction Industry **P/S:** Wide Variety of High Quality Construction Services to Clients including Commercial Site Development **MA:** Regional **D/D/R:** Bidding, Estimating, Billing, Overseeing All Aspects of the Business **H/I/S:** Loves Baseball, Coaching Son's Teams **FBP:** The Wall Street Journal; Blue Book **EDU:** College Coursework **A/A/S:** Better Business Bureau; Local Board, Education Steering Committee for Bonds; Active in Church and on Pastor's Council

MARIE A. McCREARY, RN
Registered Nurse
Hoag Memorial Hospital Presbyterian
1 Hoag Drive
Newport Beach, CA 92663 United States
http://www.hoaghospital.org

BUS: Acute Care, Nonprofit Hospital **P/S:** Cancer Center, Heart and Vascular Institute, Neuroscience Institute, Orthopedic Services, Women's Healthcare, Anesthesiology, Breast Care Center, Diabetes Education Center, End of Life Care, Epilepsy Center, Palliative Care, Rehabilitation **MA:** Orange County **D/D/R:** Orthopedic Nursing **H/I/S:** Traveling, Volunteering at Homeless Shelters **FBP:** RN; Nursing2009; Orthopaedic Nursing **EDU:** Diploma in Registered Nursing, St. Elizabeth School of Nursing **CERTS:** National Orthopedic Nurse Certification (2005) **A/A/S:** SNAC; Unit Practice Council; Magnet; Church

DORA LEE MCCULLOUGH
Public Relations Professional
50041 257th Street W.
Lancaster, CA 93536 United States
http://www.cambridgewhoswho.com

BUS: Public Relations Organization **P/S:** Public Relation Services **MA:** Southern California **EXP:** Ms. McCullough's expertise includes the development of programs within the school system and public relations. **H/I/S:** Spending Time with her Family, Reading, Sewing, Publishing Volumes of Genealogy **FBP:** Industry-Related Publications; Time; U.S. News & World Report **EDU:** Bachelor's Degree in Public Relations **A/A/S:** Epsilon Sigma Alpha International **A/H:** Honoree on Lawrence Welk Show **C/VW:** Founder, Bereaved Parents Program; Bible School Teacher, Auxiliary for Social Action, Grandview Presbyterian Church, Burbank, CA; Chairwoman of Professional Education, American Cancer Society; Committee Chairwoman, Resource Officer Project, Glendale Police Department; Coordinating Council, Parent Teacher Association; Charter Member, Glendale Citizens for Law and Order; Optimist Children's Home; Glendale Community Coordinating Council; Glendale Community Foundation; Glendale Emergency Preparedness Foundation; American Heart Association **DOB:** September 18, 1930 **POB:** Danville, IL **SP:** Charles (Deceased) **CHILD:** Rodger, Maureen, Michael, Rodney (Deceased) **W/H:** Liaison, Board of Education and Volunteers, Los Angeles City Schools; Assistant to the Executive Director, Glendale Community Foundation, CA; Chairman of Professional Education, American Cancer Society, Los Angeles County, CA **A/S:** She attributes her success to her perseverance and problem-solving skills. **B/I:** She became involved in her profession after her father developed cancer and the American Cancer Society helped her family with major cancer-related necessities before he passed away. She began answering phones and progressed naturally from there. **H/O:** The most gratifying aspect of her career is being able to share her writings and opinions with others. **I/F/Y:** In five years, Ms. McCullough intends to write one book about her life experiences and another based on the life of her deceased 20-year-old son.

ANNETTE CORRADO MCCUTCHAN, RN
Registered Nurse
New York City Department of Health
124 Worth Street
New York, NY 10013 United States
http://www.cambridgewhoswho.com

BUS: City Health Agency **P/S:** Public Health Services **MA:** Regional **D/D/R:** Administering Nursing Care for Students, Maintaining Records, Hands on Care for Students, Preventative Diseases **H/I/S:** Traveling, Reading **FBP:** RN **EDU:** Associate of Science in Nursing, City University of New York, Kingsborough Community College **A/A/S:** Union 436 Local DC37 **C/VW:** American Cancer Society, American Diabetes Organization **A/S:** She attributes her success to having the ability to adapt easily to every situation and being willing to continue to learn in an ever-changing position. **B/I:** She became involved in this profession because she was a volunteer for the American Red Cross and became interested in nursing through them. **H/O:** The most gratifying aspect of her career is being able to have a career in the nursing profession for as long as she has.

BEVERLY MARIE McDONALD
Volunteer
Manatee County Democratic Committee
Cortez Road
Bradington, FL United States
bevcd7@earthlink.net
http://www.cambridgewhoswho.com

BUS: Nonprofit Agency **P/S:** Political Party Elections **MA:** National **D/D/R:** Keeping Track of All Members, Distributing Welcome Packages, Personally Greeting Members **H/I/S:** Spending Time with her Grandchildren and Family, Swimming, Going to the Beach, Reading **FBP:** Health **EDU:** Bachelor of Science in Labor Relations and Human Services, Empire State College **CERTS:** Certified Occupational Therapist **A/A/S:** President, Public Profession Employees Association; National Democratic Committee; Parrish County Democratic Committee **C/VW:** St. Joseph's Church, National Democratic Committee; St. Francis Wildlife Association; American Cancer Society; Multiple Sclerosis Foundation **A/S:** She attributes her career success to her determination, her ability to work full-time while attending college and holding the position of President of the Employees Association. **B/I:** After working as a teacher for several years, she was offered the position of president of her condominium owners' association, before working for the commitment social services. **H/O:** She feels that being a great organizer of people and heading the Public Professional Employees Association is the highlight of her career.

CASSANDRA McDONALD
Chief Executive Officer, Founder
C.A.S.S. Productions
PO Box 1461
Zanesville, OH 43702 United States
cassproduction@gmail.com
http://www.cassandramcdonald.com

BUS: Nonprofit Summer and Afterschool Music Programs **P/S:** Music Education and Entertainment for Underserved Ethnic Populations in the United States and its Territories **MA:** International **H/I/S:** Sewing, Painting, Creating Art, Designing **FBP:** Black Enterprise **EDU:** Master's Degree in Music Education, University of Michigan **A/A/S:** ZCA; Ohio Arts Council **A/H:** Business Woman of the Year (1997); Vocal Net Ovation Award for Outstanding Soloist **C/VW:** Girl Scouts of America; Church

JULIE A. MCDONALD
Education Consultant
Calhoun Intermediate School District
20850 E. Avenue N.
Battle Creek, MI 49017 United States
mcdonalj@calhounisd.org
http://www.calhounisd.org

BUS: Intermediate School District Dedicated to Developing, Coordinating and Providing Quality Educational Services and Experiences in an Innovative and Responsive Manner **P/S:** Curriculum Development, No Child Left Behind, Library and Media Services, Special Education, Career and Technical Programs, Social Services **MA:** Regional **D/D/R:** Educational Leadership for 13 Districts, Legislative Updates, Professional Development, Offering Guidance to the Regional Center, Area Training, Consulting, School Improvement **FBP:** Educational Leadership **EDU:** Pursuing Doctor of Educational Leadership for Grades K-12, Michigan University **A/A/S:** Association for Supervision and Curriculum Development

MADA YVONNE MCDONALD
Community Activist, Public Relations Consultant
MM Public Relations
PO Box 514
Baton Rouge, LA 70821 United States
madamcd@msn.com
http://www.cambridgewhoswho.com

BUS: Leader in Public Relations Consulting **P/S:** Public Relations Specialties for Various Groups and Organizations **MA:** Local **D/D/R:** Working as an Advocate in the Public Relations Industry, Motivational Speaking, Ministering to Children, Youth and Parents in the Baton Rouge Community **H/I/S:** Participating in Church Activities, Cooking, Reading, Writing, Hosting Garage Sales, Decorating, Gardening, Working with Youth and Children, Window Shopping, Collecting Pictures, Designing Flower Arrangements, Decorating, Practicing Music, Aromatherapy **FBP:** Essence; Black Enterprise; DiversityInc.; Ebony; Smithsonian; Diversity **EDU:** Bachelor's Degree in Child Development, Southern University and A&M College, Baton Rouge, LA **A/A/S:** Board of Trustees, Camphor Memorial United Methodist Church; Baker/Zachary Alumnae Chapter, Delta Sigma Theta Sorority; Incorporated Member, Southern University Laboratory School Alumni Association; Louisiana Association of Minority Criminal Justice Workers; National Association for the Advancement of Colored People **A/H:** Recognized by the National Association of Female Executives (2004-2005 Edition) **W/H:** Drug Prevention Specialist, Teacher's Aide, North Baton Rouge Tutorial Program; Probation Officer, Families in Need of Services Program; Publicist, Journalist and Writer; Radio Talk Show Host

LINDA LEIGH McDONNELL-WOODS
Reading First Literacy Coach
Boronda Meadows Elementary School
840 S. Main Street
Salinas, CA 93901 United States
lindawlwoods@aol.com
http://www.cambridgewhoswho.com

BUS: Public Elementary School **P/S:** Education **MA:** Local **D/D/R:** Coaching the Reading First Literacy Program **H/I/S:** Producing Art as a Professional Artist **FBP:** O, the Oprah Magazine **EDU:** Bachelor of Arts in Spanish, San Jose State University **CERTS:** Bilingual Certificate of Competence, Target Language, Spanish **A/A/S:** California Teachers Association **A/H:** Lighthouse for Literacy Award, Monterey County Reading Association (1999) **C/VW:** Church, Old Mission San Juan Bautista **A/S:** She attributes her success to her passion for what she does. **B/I:** She became involved in her profession because she wanted to make a difference in the community.

CHRISTINE E. McEACHEN
Teacher
Pasco School District, Whittier Elementary School
616 N. Wehe
Pasco, WA 99301 United States
cmceachen@msn.com
http://www.cambridgewhoswho.com

BUS: Elementary School **P/S:** Education **MA:** Local **D/D/R:** Teaching Kindergarten through Eighth-Grade and Teaching English as a Second Language **H/I/S:** Spending Time with her Family **FBP:** Teaching K-8 **EDU:** Bachelor of Arts in Education, Washington State University; Master's Degree in Professional Development, Heritage University **A/A/S:** Washington Education Association; National Education Association **A/S:** She attributes her success to her passion for teaching. **B/I:** She became involved in her profession through the influence of her mother, who was a teacher. **H/O:** The most gratifying aspect of her career is when former students return to thank her.

LYN A. McELROY
Educator
Warren Central High School
9500 E. 16th Street
Indianapolis, IN 46229 United States
mcelroy_l@msn.com
http://www.cambridgewhoswho.com

BUS: High School **P/S:** Secondary Education **MA:** Local **D/D/R:** Imparting Vocational Education to Disabled Students, Teaching English and Mathematics **H/I/S:** Wine Tasting, Sports, Traveling, Hiking, Spending Time Outdoors, Exercising **EDU:** Pursuing Master's Degree; Bachelor's Degree in Health and Physical Education, Indiana University (1990); Associate Degree in Broadcasting and Sports Medicine **CERTS:** Pursuing History Endorsement, with Minor in Geography **A/A/S:** Indiana University Alumni Association

KATHERINE D. McFARLAND
Special Education Teacher
Waco Independent School District, University Middle School
1820 Irving Lee Street
Waco, TX 76711 United States
kmcfarland@wacoisd.org
http://www.cambridgewhoswho.com

BUS: Education **P/S:** Education **MA:** Local **D/D/R:** Teaching Severely Emotionally Disturbed and Autistic Students **H/I/S:** Doing Volunteer Work, Reading, Singing **FBP:** Advocate **EDU:** Bachelor of Science Degree, Education, Baylor University, Waco, TX **A/A/S:** Delta Kappa Gamma; Texas State Teachers Association; National Education Association **C/VW:** Ladies of Shrine; Daughters of the Nile **H/O:** The highlight of her career was helping a severely abused student to learn to read and move on to high school.

MRS. JENNIFER ANNE McGARVEY, M.ED.
Special Education Teacher
Newton Early Childhood Program
100 Walnut Street
Newtonville, MA 02460 United States
jennifer_mcgarvey@newton.k12.ma.us
http://www.newton.k12.ma.us

BUS: Preschool Program **P/S:** Education of Preschool Children, Developmental Programs **MA:** Regional **D/D/R:** Presenting Activities through a 'Total Communication' Approach to Support Both Verbal and Non-Verbal Learners, Integration of Augmentative Devices, Sensory Integration Supports and Visuals to Increase Motor Planning and Play Skill Development. **H/I/S:** Scrap Booking, Spending Time with the Family, Designing and Creating Theme-Based Curriculum Games to Increase Student's Learning **FBP:** MTA Magazine; Exceptional Child **EDU:** Master's Degree in Special Education, Pre-K through Ninth-Grade, and Early Childhood, Pre-K through Third-Grade, Lesley University (2000) **A/A/S:** Newton Teachers Association; Massachusetts Teachers Association **A/H:** Honoree, Cambridge Who's Who Among American Teachers (2006-2007) **C/VW:** Saint Jude Children's Hospital **DOB:** December 10, 1971 **POB:** Newton, MA **SP:** Stephen **CHILD:** Jessica, Allison, Kaitlyn, Emily **W/H:** Special Education Teacher, Newton Early Childhood Program (1992-Present)

MEGAN K. McGEE
Education Analyst, Instructional Designer
Wilmington Trust Corporation
1100 N. Market Street
Wilmington, DE 19801 United States
mmcgee@wilmingtontrust.com
http://www.cambridgewhoswho.com

BUS: Financial Institution **P/S:** Customized Wealth Advisory, Corporate Client and Regional Banking Services **MA:** International **D/D/R:** Consulting Internally, Conducting Professional Development Analysis and Training Including Classroom and Online Design, Overseeing Facilitation **H/I/S:** Running Marathons, Coaching Sports **FBP:** Fortune **EDU:** Bachelor's Degree in Psychology and Writing, Loyola College **CERTS:** Certified Trainer, AchieveGlobal **A/A/S:** American Society for Training Development; American Management Association **C/VW:** Leadership Council Member, American Breast Cancer Association

CHRISTY L. MCGILL
Physical Therapist Assistant
Appalachian Therapy Center
829 E. Lamar Alexander Parkway
Maryville, TN 37801 United States
cmcgill@appalachiantherapy.com
http://www.cambridgewhoswho.com

BUS: Therapy Center **P/S:** Physical Therapy **MA:** Tennessee **EXP:** Ms. McGill's expertise is in practicing orthopedic medicine. **H/I/S:** Spending Time with her Children **FBP:** Physical Therapy **EDU:** Associate of Science, Knoxville Business College, TN **A/A/S:** American Physical Therapy Association **A/S:** She attributes her success to her compassion. **B/I:** She became involved in her profession because she saw her friends who were in need of physical therapy and decided to study science. **H/O:** The most gratifying aspect of her career is seeing her patients recover.

GERRI E. MCGINNIS
President
Gerri's Construction and Trucking, Inc.
556 Telegraph Road
Winlock, WA 98596 United States
http://www.cambridgewhoswho.com

BUS: Trucking Company **P/S:** Common Carrier Transportation Services for Meat and Vegetable Shippers **MA:** California, Washington **D/D/R:** Running a Company **H/I/S:** Oil Painting, Sewing, Reading, Polishing her Tractor **FBP:** Trucking News; Overdrive **EDU:** High School Diploma (1955); West Coast Trade School **A/A/S:** Owner, Operator, Independent Drivers Association; National Federation of Independent Business

Mr. Jack D. McGowan, MD
Physician, Co-Director of Newborn Services
Conroe Regional Medical Center
504 Medical Center Boulevard
Conroe, TX 77316 United States
jmcgo53334@aol.com
http://www.conroeregional.com

BUS: Comprehensive Regional Tertiary Referral Center **P/S:** Cancer Center, Heart Care Center, Hospital Imaging Services, Lake Area Imaging Center, Outpatient Rehabilitation, Women's Services and Wound Care **MA:** Regional **D/D/R:** Neonatology **H/I/S:** Reading, Gardening **FBP:** AAP Journal **EDU:** MD, Indiana University School of Medicine **CERTS:** Board Certified in Neonatal and Perinatal Medicine and Pediatrics **A/A/S:** American Academy of Pediatrics; Texas Pediatrics Society **C/VW:** American Red Cross; March of Dimes

Sharon M. McGrath
Special Education Teacher
South Plainfield Board of Education
200 Lake Street
South Plainfield, NJ 07080 United States
sharmc8@earthlink.net
http://www.cambridgewhoswho.com

BUS: Public School **P/S:** Education **MA:** Local **D/D/R:** Teaching in Resource Room **H/I/S:** Playing Tennis, Spending Time with Family and Friends, Shopping **EDU:** Bachelor of Science in Education, Seton Hall University; Master's Degree in Learning Disabilities, Kean University **A/A/S:** Kappa Delta Phi; National Education Association; New Jersey Education Association **C/VW:** Church, Special Olympics Coach **A/S:** She attributes her success to being highly organized, hardworking and determined. **B/I:** She became involved in her profession because she always knew she wanted to be a teacher. **H/O:** The most gratifying aspect of her career was being nominated by her peers for Teacher of the Year.

WANETTA A. McGRIFF, RN, BSN
Registered Nurse, Assistant Manager
Kaiser Permanente
124 Lippizan Drive
Vallejo, CA 94591 United States
nettamcgriff@comcast.net
http://www.cambridgewhoswho.com

BUS: Healthcare Facility **P/S:** Healthcare **MA:** Local **D/D/R:** Offering Nursing in Emergency Oncology, Dialysis and Medical Telemetry, Overseeing Case Management and Utilization Management **H/I/S:** Spending Time with her Children and Grandchildren, Traveling, Relaxing, Going to the Spa **FBP:** RN **EDU:** Bachelor of Science in Nursing, University of Phoenix; Associate Degree in Nursing **CERTS:** Certified in Pediatric Advanced Life Support, Basic Life Support, Advanced Cardiac Life Support, Solano Community College **C/VW:** Feed the Children **A/S:** She attributes her success to her morals and her parents influence. **B/I:** She became involved in the profession because there are many nurses in her family. **H/O:** The highlight of her career was attending school for a bachelor of science in nursing while caring for her two small children.

MOIRA G. McGUIRE
Managing Partner
The Research Partners, LLC
5837 Ashton Lake Drive
Sarasota, FL 34231 United States
mmcguire@theresearchpartners.com
http://www.theresearchpartners.com

BUS: Research Company **P/S:** Market Research **MA:** International **D/D/R:** Managing Operations, Consulting, Medical Researching and C-Level Researching within Fortune 1000, Acting as the Managing Partner **H/I/S:** Cooking, Fine Dining, Art, Fine Wine, Reading, Spending Time with her Family **FBP:** The Wall Street Journal; The Economist; Forbes; Entrepreneur; BusinessWeek; National Restaurant Review **EDU:** Graduate Studies, University of Pennsylvania; Bachelor of Fine Arts, New York School of Interior Design; Associate of Arts in Restaurant and Culinary Arts, Restaurant School at Walnut Hill College **A/A/S:** National Restaurant Association; Marketing Research Association **C/VW:** Church **A/S:** She attributes her success to her upbringing and education. **B/I:** She became involved in her profession after working in market research and finding a mentor in her former employer. **H/O:** The highlight of her career was starting her own business.

GINGER L. MCILVANIE
Teacher
Riverside Christian School
731 Keys Road
Yakima, WA 98901 United States
glmcilv@charter.net
http://www.riversidechristianschool.com

BUS: School **P/S:** Education **MA:** Local **EXP:** Ms. McIlvanie's expertise is in junior high school science education. **D/D/R:** Teaching Science to Fifth-Grade Students in a Self-Contained Classroom, Offering Quality, Informative and Fun Education on Various Subjects to Students **H/I/S:** Gardening, Decorating, Photography, Reading **EDU:** Master's Degree in Education, Whitworth College; Bachelor's Degree in Education, Whitworth College; Principal Credentials, Whitworth College **A/A/S:** Washington Science Teachers Association; National Science Teachers Association **A/H:** Award, Who's Who Among American Teachers **B/I:** She became involved in her profession after working as a nurse for several years and deciding to pursue a career where she could reach more people on a daily basis.

BARBARA A. MCINTYRE
Registered Nurse
1) Thomas B. Finan Center 2) Willow Valley Housing
10102 Country Club Road
Cumberland, MD 21502 United States
daylightrn@pennswoods.net
http://www.cambridgewhoswho.com

BUS: 1) Psychiatric Hospital 2) Congregate Housing **P/S:** 1) Psychiatric Healthcare 2) Delegation Nursing **MA:** 1) Local 2) Local **D/D/R:** Managing the Unit and 22 Patients, Overseeing Medication Disbursements, Admissions, Discharges and Reports, Completing Rounds, Training New Medication Technicians within the Standards of the Maryland Board of Nursing **H/I/S:** Traveling, Reading, Animals, Watching Football **FBP:** Nursing2009; American Journal of Nursing **EDU:** Associate Degree in Nursing, Allegheny College; Coursework in Psychology and Ethics, St. Joseph's College **CERTS:** Board Licensed Nail Technician **A/A/S:** Instructor, Cardiopulmonary Resuscitation; Instructor, Medication Technician Instructor; Instructor, Master Prevention and Management of Aggressive Behavior **C/VW:** Breast Cancer Research; Animal Welfare Society; Teacher, Free Neighborhood and Community Cardiopulmonary Resuscitation Instruction Classes, Allegheny College **A/S:** She attributes her success to her desire to always do her best for her patients, great mentors, the support of her family and her hard work. **B/I:** She became involved in her profession because she always wanted to be a nurse. **H/O:** The most gratifying aspect of her career is helping others to feel better on a daily basis.

HELEN S. MCKENNA
Site Supervisor
Designer Medical Group, Kistler Clinic
175 S. Wilkes Barre Boulevard
Wilkes-Barre, PA 18702 United States
hmckenna@geisinger.edu
http://www.geisinger.org

BUS: Clinic **P/S:** Healthcare **MA:** Local **D/D/R:** Pediatric Nursing **H/I/S:** Spending Time with her Family, Traveling **FBP:** Nursing Journals; Web MD **EDU:** Diploma of Nursing, Scranton State General Hospital **C/VW:** Geisinger Children's Miracle Network; Breast Cancer Awareness; American Heart Association

MS. GERALDINE DAVIDSON MCKENZIE
Nursing Supervisor
Mountview Retirement Residence
2640 Honolulu Avenue
Montrose, CA 91020 United States
Linden-McKeesy@juno.com
http://www.cambridgewhoswho.com

BUS: Residential Healthcare Facility **P/S:** Independent Living and Assisted Services **MA:** Local **EXP:** Ms. McKenzie's expertise is in caring for geriatric patients, administering wound care, treating cases of dementia, acting as a liaison between doctors, hospitals and family members, works with home health care agencies to provide services for her residence, overseeing staff and ministerial services. **H/I/S:** Participating in Religious Activities, Preaching **EDU:** Coursework in Business Management **CERTS:** Licensed Vocational Nurse, Glendale Career College, CA (2000) **A/A/S:** Home Healthcare-Geriatric Organizations, Hospice; The American Nurses Association **C/VW:** Alzheimer's Foundation of America; Cardiovascular Research Foundation; Friends of the Police; Mothers Against Gun Violence **A/S:** She attributes her success to her mentor and her love for her profession. **B/I:** She became involved in her profession because of her love for helping others. **H/O:** The highlight of her career was earning her current position.

MARGARET McKINNEY-DEAN, MS, LSW
Licensed Social Worker
Regency Manor
2000 Regency Manor Circle
Columbus, OH 43207 United States
mmcdean0622@aol.com
http://www.cambridgewhoswho.com

BUS: Nursing Facility **P/S:** Rehabilitation, Dialysis Center, Mental Health Secured Units **EXP:** Ms. McKinney-Dean's expertise is in patient advocacy. **D/D/R:** Acting as a Liaison between Staff and Family, Discharge and Care Planning and Variety of Assessments **H/I/S:** Collecting Dolls, Reading, Watching Movies, Journaling **FBP:** Psychology Today **EDU:** Master's Degree in Counseling, University of Dayton (2002); Bachelor of Science in Social Work, Middle Tennessee State University (1986) **A/A/S:** Volunteer, Local Church

GORDON D. McLAREN
Associate Professor of Medicine
University of California, Irvine
5901 E. Seventh Street (11/111-H)
c/o VA Long Beach Healthcare System
Long Beach, CA 90822 United States
gordon.mclaren@med.va.gov
http://www.cambridgewhoswho.com

BUS: University **P/S:** Higher Education, Medical Research and Clinical Training Programs **MA:** Local **EXP:** Dr. McLaren's areas of expertise include internal medicine, hematology, oncology, iron metabolism disorders and medical education and research. **D/D/R:** Supervising Trainees, Caring for Patients, Teaching, Overseeing Clinical and Laboratory Research **H/I/S:** Playing Tennis, Bird-watching, Enology **FBP:** Blood; The Journal of the American Society of Hematology **EDU:** MD, Stanford University (1970); Diplomate in Internal Medicine, Hematology, and Medical Oncology **A/A/S:** Fellow, American College of Physicians; Board of Directors, Iron Overload Diseases Association, Inc; American Society of Clinical Oncology; American Society of Hematology; International BioIron Society; American Association for the Advancement of Science; American Federation for Medical Research; Western Association of Physicians **DOB:** July 1, 1943 **SP:** Christine **CHILD:** Graham

THERESA M. McLEAN, BSN
Registered Nurse
St. Francis Hospital
Five Bell Lane
Levittown, NY 11756 United States
http://www.cambridgewhoswho.com

BUS: High-Quality Medical Facility **P/S:** Abdominal Stenting, Ambulatory Surgery, Arrhythmias, Cardiac Catheterization, Rehabilitation, Cardiac Noninvasive Services, Cardiac Pacing, Cardiac Resynchronization Therapy, Cardiovascular Research, Care Management, Clinical Laboratory, Community Education Programs, Device Occlusion, Diabetic Care, Endoscopy, General Surgery, Heart Failure, Intensive and Critical Care, Interventional Cardiology Procedures, Interventional Radiology, Lung Cancer Screening, Orthopedics, Pain Management, Physical Therapy, Radiology, Vascular Surgery, Volunteer Programs, Women's Healthcare Center **MA:** Regional **D/D/R:** Utilizing her Expertise as a Registered Nurse and Ambulatory Out-Patient Assistant Head Nurse **H/I/S:** Bowling, Camping **EDU:** Bachelor of Science in Nursing, Adelphi University (1984) **A/A/S:** AACCRN

SALLY J. McMAHON, RN, BSN
Registered Nurse
St. Luke's Regional Medical Center
27220 Stone Park Boulevard
Sioux City, IA 51104 United States
mcbalt479@juno.com
http://www.stlukes.org

BUS: Hospital **P/S:** Healthcare Services **MA:** Regional **D/D/R:** Emergency Nursing **H/I/S:** Running, Biking, Gardening, Reading, Crocheting **EDU:** Pursuing Coursework in Family Nurse Practitioner (2007); Bachelor's Degree in Nursing, Briarcliff College **A/A/S:** Emergency Medical Services Conference Planning Committee; Church; Volunteer Paramedic

FRANCES CHARLENE BIGGS MCMANAWAY
Licensed Practical Nurse
Beaver County Memorial Hospital
212 E. Eighth
PO Box 640
Beaver, OK 73932 United States
frances@ptsi.net
http://www.cambridgewhoswho.com

BUS: Hospital **P/S:** Healthcare **MA:** Local **D/D/R:** Administering Emergency Medical Care **H/I/S:** Reading, Listening to Country Music, Puzzles, Camping, and Spending Time with Adopted Children **FBP:** Nursing2009 **C/VW:** Head Start, First Baptist Church **A/S:** She attributes her success to determination and loving her job. **B/I:** She chose the profession because she always wanted to become a nurse. **H/O:** The highlight of her career is delivering babies.

JAMIE F. MCMANUS
Chairman of Medical Affairs, Health Sciences and Education
Shaklee Corporation
4747 Willow Road
Pleasanton, CA 94588 United States
welldoc@sbcglobal.net
http://www.cambridgewhoswho.com

BUS: Distribution Company **P/S:** Healthcare and Natural Nutrient Products **MA:** International **EXP:** Dr. McManus' expertise is in wellness and prevention education and women's health. **H/I/S:** Exercising, Running, Hiking, Traveling **EDU:** Residency in Family Practice, University of California Davis Medical Center; MD, University of California, Davis; Master of Science in Virology and Microbiology, University of California, San Francisco; Bachelor of Science in Biological Science, University of California, Davis **A/A/S:** American Academy of Family Physicians; Vice President, Board of Directors, Alumni Association, University of California, Davis School of Medicine; American Medical Women's Association; Senior Scientific Advisory Council for the Council for Responsible Nutrition **A/H:** Woman of Distinction Award (2008) **C/VW:** Compassion International **A/S:** Dr. McManus attributes her success to her perseverance and her passion for helping people take control of their health. **B/I:** She became involved in her profession because of her interest in science and her desire to help people.

GLEN E. McMILLIAN
Executive Director of Transportation
Blue Springs School District
1809 N.W. Vesper Street
Blue Springs, MO 64015 United States
gmcmillian@bssd.net
http://www.cambridgewhoswho.com

BUS: School District **P/S:** Education **MA:** Local **D/D/R:** Recruiting and Supervising Bus Drivers, Crossing Guards, Secretaries and Assistants **H/I/S:** Golfing, Fly-Fishing, Bicycling **FBP:** School Bus Fleet **EDU:** Bachelor of Science in Wildlife Biology, University of Central Missouri **A/A/S:** Kansas City Pupil Transportation Association; Missouri Association for Pupil Transportation; National Association for Pupil Transportation **A/S:** He attributes his success to his management skills. **B/I:** He became involved in his profession because of his work experience in a bus company. **H/O:** The most gratifying aspect of his career is being respected by his community.

SHEILA KATHLEEN McNALLY
Registered Nurse
Kaiser Permanente
10350 E. Dakota Avenue
Denver, CO 80220 United States
skmn@comcast.net
http://www.cambridgewhoswho.com

BUS: Outpatient Clinic **P/S:** Mental Illness Healthcare **MA:** Regional **D/D/R:** Psychiatric Illness and Treatment **H/I/S:** Spending Time with her Family, Participating in Politics and Advocacy Activities, Traveling, Swimming, Meditating **FBP:** Colorado Nurses Association Publications **EDU:** Bachelor of Science in Nursing, Regents University, Denver, Colorado **A/A/S:** Colorado Nurses Association; Colorado Advocacy Nurses Group; Colorado Critical Incident Response Service **A/S:** She attributes her success to her easygoing personality and her willingness to always put the patient's needs first. **B/I:** She worked as a nurses aid in her teenage years and realized how much she liked it.

REGINA FORNACI MCNAMARA, RN, MSN, MPH
President
Kelsco Consulting Company
1035 S. Main Street
Cheshire, CT 06410 United States
rfmcnamara@aol.com
http://www.kelsco.com

BUS: Healthcare Consulting Company **P/S:** Consulting in Home Health Care, Hospices, Hospitals **MA:** National **H/I/S:** Gardening, Swimming, Hiking, and Spending Time with her Pets **FBP:** Harvard Business Review **EDU:** Master of Science in Public Health, Yale University; Master of Science in Nursing, Yale University; Bachelor of Science in Nursing, Villanova University; Fellowship for Nurse Executives, Wharton College **CERTS:** Certified Nurse Practitioners **A/A/S:** National Home Care Association; National Association of Women Executives; Connecticut Women in Healthcare **C/VW:** Local Library; Humane Society; Multiple Sclerosis Foundation; AIDS Research **A/S:** She attributes her success to creativity and persistence. **B/I:** She chose the profession because she loves the sciences and nursing.

DAWN M. MCNEIL
Office Administrator
Northridge Dental Group
9801 Balboa Boulevard
Northridge, CA 91325 United States
anklesmcneil@aol.com
http://www.northridgedentalgroup.com

BUS: Proven Leader in the Healthcare Industry, Dental Office **P/S:** Highest Quality of Dental Services to Patients Including, General, Cosmetic, Periodontal Dentistry **MA:** Local **D/D/R:** Servicing Patients, Handling Treatment Plans and Financial Arrangements **H/I/S:** Motorcycles, Volleyball **FBP:** Forbes; Dental Town **EDU:** Vocational Training and Dental Assisting, Simi Valley Adult School (1985) **A/A/S:** American Association of Dental Office Managers

GINA MCNELLIS, RHIA, CTR, CHP
Program Chair
Health Information Technology Program
ITT Technical Institute
1400 International Parkway
Lake Mary, FL 32746 United States
gina.mcnellis@hcahealthcare.com
http://www.cambridgewhoswho.com

BUS: Educational Institution **P/S:** Healthcare Education **MA:** Local **D/D/R:** Keeping Medical Records, Maintaining Confidentiality and Privacy, Writing the Curriculum for Educational Institutions and Education in Regards to Health Information and Cancer Registry **H/I/S:** Spending Time with her Family, Traveling, Reading, Bowling, Cooking and Baking **FBP:** For The Record; Advance **EDU:** Pursuing Master's Degree in Health Informatics and Information Management; Bachelor of Science in Health Administration, York College **A/A/S:** NCRA; Florida Health Information Management Association; American Health Information Management Association; CFHIMA **C/VW:** United Way of America; Give Kids the World; The Ronald McDonald House; American Cancer Society

TRACY M. MCNUTT
Registered Nurse
Baptist Hospital of East Tennessee
752 Whippoorwill Circle
Seymour, TN 37865 United States
tmnutt1@earthlink.net
http://www.cambridgewhoswho.com

BUS: Charitable, Nonprofit Healthcare Organization **P/S:** Heart, Cancer Care, Gamma Knife, Eye, Sleep, Women's Healthcare, Seniors, Homecare, Rehabilitation, Therapy Center **MA:** Regional **D/D/R:** Nursing in Sub-Acute Care and for Patients with Strokes, Pneumnonia, Thoracic Surgery and Neuroespiratory Disorders **H/I/S:** Basketball **FBP:** American Journal of Nursing **EDU:** Bachelor's Degree in Liberal Arts, University of Tennessee (1996); Associate Degree in Nursing, Walter State Community College (1994) **A/A/S:** Tennessee Nursing Association

DAN S. MCQUAY
President, Chief Executive Officer
Business Information Technology Solutions, Inc dba BITS, Inc
1934 Old Gallows Road
Suite 350
Vienna, VA 22182 United States
dmcquay@thebitsgroup.com
http://www.thebitsgroup.com

BUS: Information Technology Consulting Firm **P/S:** Program Management, Project Management, Change Management, ERP Implementation Design, Packaged Solutions, Internet Solutions, Infrastructure, High Availability, Operations Management, Information Insurance and Security, Oracle Product Solutions **MA:** National **D/D/R:** Acting as a Chief Architect for the Director of Operations, Managing and Implementing Enterprise Human Resource Applications Globally, Overseeing Enterprise Architecture and Financial and Medical Systems **H/I/S:** Spending Time with his Family, Sports, Hunting, Fishing **FBP:** BusinessWeek; The Wall Street Journal **EDU:** Master's Degree in Information Technology, Naval Post Graduate School (1995); Bachelor's Degree in Business, University of Maryland **A/A/S:** Project Management Institute **W/H:** United States Marine Corps (1978-1998) **A/S:** He attributes his success to his hard work and tenacity. **B/I:** He became involved in his profession because of the experience he gained in technology while working with the U.S. Marine Corps **H/O:** The most gratifying aspect of his career is managing his own business. **I/F/Y:** In five years, Mr. McQuay hopes to continue managing his business.

DONNA G. MCVEY, RN, BSN, BS
Registered Nurse
Jackson Oncology Associates, PLLC
2331 Twin Lakes Circle
Jackson, MS 39211 United States
emcvey@mbhs.org
http://www.cambridgewhoswho.com

BUS: Healthcare Center **P/S:** Healthcare **MA:** Regional **EXP:** Ms. McVey's expertise is in oncology and researching. **H/I/S:** Exercising, Reading, Watercolor and Pastel Painting **FBP:** Industry-Related Publications **EDU:** Bachelor of Science in Nursing, University Medical Center (1980); Bachelor of Science in Biology and Chemistry, University of Mississippi (1978) **A/A/S:** Local Breast Cancer Society; Delta Delta Delta **C/VW:** Former Member, Junior League; American Heart Association; American Cancer Society **A/S:** She attributes her success to her passion for her profession. **B/I:** She became involved in her profession because of her interest in the healthcare field and her desire to help others. **H/O:** The most gratifying aspect of her career is working with oncology patients.

DAWN L. MEAD, LMSW
Director of Foster Care and Adoption
Child and Family Services
4287 Five Oaks Drive
Lansing, MI 48911 United States
mead.dawn@childandfamily.org
http://www.cambridgewhoswho.com

BUS: Human Service Agency **P/S:** Foster Care, Adoption Services **MA:** Local **EXP:** Ms. Mead's expertise is in education, counseling and training. **H/I/S:** Traveling **CERTS:** Licensed Master Social Worker, Eastern Michigan University **A/A/S:** National Association of Social Workers; Federation of Private Agencies **C/VW:** The Leaven Center **A/S:** She attributes her success to being open to changes and new ideas. **B/I:** She became involved in her profession because of her desire to change the world. **H/O:** The most gratifying aspect of her career is being able to change people's lives.

ORLANDA L. MECKLEY
Elementary Teacher
Shaler Area School District, Burchfield Elementary School
1500 Burchfield Road
Allison Park, PA 15101 United States
meckleyo@sasd.k12.pa.us
http://www.sasd.k12.pa.us

BUS: Proven Leader in the Education Industry **P/S:** High Quality Educational Services to Students as well as Extracurricular Activities **MA:** Regional **D/D/R:** Following the Regular Curriculum, Writing Science and Mathematics Curriculum for the District in Conjunction with State Standards, Working with Asset Training **H/I/S:** Scrapbooking, Reading **FBP:** The Mailbox **EDU:** Master's Equivalency in Education; Graduate Coursework, Wilkes College; Bachelor of Arts in Education, Slippery Rock University (1974) **A/A/S:** National Education Association; Pennsylvania State Education Association; Shaler Area Education Association; Who's Who Among American Teachers **DOB:** November 23, 1952

Virginia Medina
Avon
1929 Old Oak Drive
Stockton, CA 95206 United States
virginiamedina_avon@comcast.net
http://www.youravon.com/vmedina

BUS: Cosmetics Company **P/S:** Beauty Products, Fragrance, Jewelry, Gift Items, Clothing, Lingerie, Shoes, Men's Products, Products for Teens and Kids **MA:** Local **D/D/R:** Leading the Sales Team, Selling Products **H/I/S:** Bicycling, Swimming, Reading, Spending Time with her Grandchildren **FBP:** Guideposts **EDU:** Associate Degree in Business Administration, Ventura Junior College (1979) **C/VW:** Volunteer, Local Church; Teacher, Faith Tabernacle Pentecostal Church; Volunteer, Avon Diversity Day Committee **DOB:** May 29, 1958 **POB:** Santa Paula, CA **SP:** Albert **CHILD:** Mark, Jonathan, Rebekah **B/I:** She became involved in her profession because she was a loyal Avon customer, and her friend suggested that she should work for them. **H/O:** The highlight of her career was being inducted into the Avon President's Club because of her high sales volume.

Lynda Marie Meheula
Owner, Director
Sharing and Caring Childcare
124 S.W. 313th Street
Federal Way, WA 98023 United States
llmeheula@comcast.net
http://www.cambridgewhoswho.com

BUS: Daycare Center **P/S:** Childcare Services **MA:** Regional **D/D/R:** Managing Business Operations, Working with Special Need Children from Low-Income and Non-Traditional Families, Admitting Students from Birth to 12-Years-Old, Mentoring Community College Students who are Studying Early Childhood Care **EDU:** Associate of Arts in Early Childhood Education, Highline Community College (2007) **CERTS:** Certified Child Development Associate **A/A/S:** National Association for Family Child Care

CINDY M. MEHLHAFF, RN, PA

Registered Nurse, Physician Assistant
cindy76082@yahoo.com
http://www.cambridgewhoswho.com

P/S: Healthcare Support and Awareness **MA:** Local **D/D/R:** Registered Nurse, Healthcare, Family Practice, Teaching and Caring for Others **H/I/S:** Gardening, Exercising, Attending Church, Mission Trips, Volunteer Work, Providing for the Underprivileged **FBP:** The Wall Street Journal; The Times World News; The Professional Physicians Assistant News **EDU:** Registered Nurse Studies, University of South Dakota at East Grand Forks (1978); Associate of Science in Nursing, University of South Dakota; Physician Assistant Degree, University of North Dakota at East Grand Forks **CERTS:** Physician Assistant Certification **A/A/S:** American Academy of Physicians Assistants **C/VW:** Actively Supporting Our Troops; Breast Cancer; Cystic Fibrosis; Support for Local Fire Department and Police; National Multiple Sclerosis Society; St. Jude Children's Research Center

SARAH D. MEINHARDT

Owner, Founder, Occupational Therapist
Fargo-Moorhead Pediatric Therapy
3507 Evergreen Road N.E.
Fargo, ND 58102 United States
meinhardt2001@msn.com
http://www.usana.com

BUS: Occupational Therapy-Healthcare Facility **P/S:** Occupational Therapy with a Specialty in Pediatrics, USANA Nutritionals **MA:** Regional **D/D/R:** Specializing in Occupational Therapy, Neurodevelopmental Treatment for Children with Disabilities **FBP:** OT Practice **EDU:** Bachelor of Science in Occupational Therapy, University of Illinois Medical Center, Chicago, IL (1981) **A/A/S:** American Occupational Therapy Association; NDOTA; USANA; AIMF

JOSE A. MEJIA
Cosmetologist, Owner
Freddy's Beauty Salon
4814 Huntington Drive S.
El Sereno, CA 90032 United States
http://www.cambridgewhoswho.com

BUS: Full-Service Beauty Salon **P/S:** Cosmetic Services **MA:** Local **EXP:** Mr. Mejia's expertise is in cosmetology. **D/D/R:** Managing Business Operations, Working with Customers **H/I/S:** Traveling, Reading, Surfing the Internet, Eating at Nice Restaurants **EDU:** Delstinos Beauty College **B/I:** He became involved in his profession because he wanted to make people look beautiful. **H/O:** The most gratifying aspect of his career is seeing his clients' satisfaction with his work.

STACY J. MELDRUM
Chief
Customer Service
Francis Tuttle Technology Center
12777 N. Rockwell Avenue
Oklahoma City, OK 73142 United States
smeldrum@francistuttle.com
http://www.francistuttle.com

BUS: Training and Development Company **P/S:** Training and Development Services **MA:** National **D/D/R:** Overseeing Events, Customer Services, Media Relations, Recruitment, Corporate Communications, Marketing and Public Relations **H/I/S:** Creating Custom Greeting Cards, Spending Time with her Family **FBP:** Fortune **EDU:** Master of Education, University of Central Oklahoma (2001); Bachelor of Science in Public Relations, University of Central Oklahoma (1999); Bachelor of Science in Education, University of Central Oklahoma (1999) **A/A/S:** Public Relations Society of America; American Marketing Association; American Business Women's Association; Oklahoma City Ad Club; National School of Public Relations Association; Oklahoma Association of Career and Technology Education; Leadership Oklahoma City; Board Member, Youth Women Children Association; Oklahoma Association of Minorities in Career and Technology Education **C/VW:** Community Literacy Foundation; Special Olympics; Mentor, National Association for the Education of Young Children **A/S:** She attributes her success to her faith and perseverance. **H/O:** The most gratifying aspect of her career is helping people.

THERESA A. MELTZ
Physician Assistant
Twin County Medical Association
67 Prospect Avenue
Hudson, NY 12534 United States
terrymeltz@msn.com
http://www.cambridgewhoswho.com

BUS: Medical Practice **P/S:** Multi-Specialty Family Practice Outpatient Clinic, Pulmonology, Nephrology, Cardiology, Surgery **MA:** Local **D/D/R:** Treating Chronic Issues **H/I/S:** Running, Cooking, Reading **FBP:** New England Journal of Medicine **EDU:** Master's Degree in Physician Assistant Studies, University of Nebraska; Associate of Science in Chemistry, Columbia Green Community College; Bachelor of Arts in Business, SUNY Oneonta; Associate of Science in Nursing, Columbia Memorial Hospital Nursing Program **A/A/S:** National Guard; Albany Medical College Alumni Association **C/VW:** 4-H Club Leader; Church; The Salvation Army; Team Diabetes **A/S:** She attributes her success to relying on her gut feelings, trusting her instincts and the support of her family. **H/O:** The highlights of her career were her tour in Iraq and the humanitarian work she got to do in helping the locals.

SAMIA A. MEMON
President
RABIA Corporation
294 McHenry Road
Wheeling, IL 60090 United States
rabana1@hotmail.com
http://www.cambridgewhoswho.com

BUS: Convenience Store **P/S:** Day to Day Basic Needs and Products, Retail, Sandwiches **MA:** Local **D/D/R:** Helping Customers, Maintaining Inventory, Ordering, Managing Two Stores **H/I/S:** Reading Mystery Books, Spending Time with her Children, Painting, Cosmetics **EDU:** Bachelor's Degree in Computer Science, University of Karachi, Pakistan (1995) **A/A/S:** Chamber of Commerce **C/VW:** Independence Day Parade; Local Charities **B/I:** She became involved in her profession because she worked in an office setting and did not like it, so she decided to open her own business because it gave her the freedom she desired. **H/O:** The highlight of her career was becoming a successful business owner.

ROSEMARY MENKE, MD
MD, FACOG
3643 Russell Avenue
Cincinnati, OH 45208 United States
rmenke1574@aol.com
http://www.cambridgewhoswho.com

BUS: Private Medical Practice Committed to Excellence in Women's Health Care through All Stages of Life **P/S:** Obstetrics and Gynecology, Office and Outpatient Care, Labor and Delivery, Major and Minor Surgical Procedures Including Laparoscopic Surgery **MA:** Regional **D/D/R:** Specializing in Obstetrics and Gynecology **H/I/S:** Gourmet Cooking, Making Jewelry, Reading Mysteries and Cookbooks **FBP:** Obstetrical & Gynecological Survey **EDU:** Bachelor's Degree (1989); MD (1986) **A/A/S:** American Medical Association; Fellow, American College of Obstetricians and Gynecologists; North American Society for Pediatric and Adolescent Gynecology; ODK

REV. TIMOTHY JAMES MERCALDO
Associate Pastor
Gateway Cathedral
200 Boscombe Avenue
Staten Island, NY 10309 United States
revtimothyj@aol.com
http://www.gateway2music.com

BUS: Evangelical Church **P/S:** Church Ministry **MA:** New York, New Jersey **D/D/R:** Teaching the Word of Jesus Christ from the Gospel, Fulfilling the Emotional, Physical and Spiritual Needs of Parishioners, Performing Music **H/I/S:** Spending Time with his Family, Watching Football and Baseball, Golfing, Traveling, Listening to Music, Reading **FBP:** Christianity Today; Leadership **EDU:** Bachelor of Arts in Theology, Moody Bible Institute, Chicago, Illinois; Coursework in History, Theology, Greek Studies, Kings College, Briarcliff Manor, New York **CERTS:** Licensed Minister, Evangelical Church Alliance **A/A/S:** South Shore Rotary Club, Staten Island; National Association of Evangelicals **C/VW:** The Salvation Army

PHYLLIS K. MEREDITH, RN, BSN, ACLS, PALS
Registered Nurse
Margaret Mary Community Hospital
321 Mitchell Avenue
Batesville, IN 47006 United States
pkm68@nalu.net
http://www.cambridgewhoswho.com

BUS: Hospital **P/S:** Healthcare, Emergency Medical Services **MA:** Local **D/D/R:** Medical-Surgical, Critical Care and Clinical Nursing **H/I/S:** Going to the Movies, Community Activities, Traveling, Spending Time with Friends and Family **FBP:** Home and Garden; CCRN Magazine **EDU:** Bachelor of Science in Nursing, Indiana Wesleyan University **CERTS:** Certified in Human Services, Pediatric Advanced Life Support, Advanced Cardiac Life Support and CPR Instruction **C/VW:** Relay for Life, American Cancer Society, American Heart Association **A/S:** She attributes her success to the support of her family and to her perseverance and faith. **B/I:** She became involved in her profession because she always wanted to be in a helping profession. **H/O:** The highlight of her career has been being able to help others.

ESTHER MERLING
Psychologist (Retired)
Lawrence Public High School
Valley Stream Public Schools
11705 Curzon Road
Richmond Hill, NY 11418 United States
esther.merling@cwwemail.com
http://www.cambridgewhoswho.com

BUS: School District **P/S:** Secondary Education, Psychological Testing, Counseling and Evaluations for High School Level Students in Public and Parochial Schools **MA:** Local **EXP:** Ms. Merling's expertise is in hypnotherapy, family and couple therapy and utilizing emotional stress relief techniques. **D/D/R:** Managing Help Groups Including Grief Topics, Behavioral and Substance Abuse, Treating Pediatric Patients **H/I/S:** Jogging, Playing Tennis, Writing **FBP:** In-Mind; Health; Scientific American **EDU:** Master's Degree in School Psychology, Queens College (1976); Master's Degree in General Psychology, Hunter College **A/A/S:** American Psychotherapy Association **DOB:** October 28, 1933 **A/S:** She attributes her success to her positive attitude.

DAYNA MERRYMAN
Psychotherapist
Hoffman Homes, Inc.
815 Orphanage Road
Littlestown, PA 17340 United States
dayna71@hotmail.com
http://www.hoffmanhomes.com

BUS: 24-Hour Residential Therapeutic Facility for Children Ages 5-18 **P/S:** Treatment for Aggressive and/or Self-Harmful Behaviors **MA:** National **D/D/R:** Treating Adolescent Girls Ages 14 to 18 **H/I/S:** Spending Time with her Three Children, Attending Church, Mission Work **FBP:** Behavioral Health **EDU:** Master of Social Work, Temple University; Master of Divinity, Gettysburg Lutheran Theological Seminary **C/VW:** Church, Mission Work **A/S:** She attributes her success to her faith in God. **B/I:** She became involved in the profession because she always had an interest in the field and a desire to help others. **H/O:** The most gratifying aspect of her career is successfully discharging children.

MELISSA J. MESSNER
Clinical Nurse Specialist
Smith and Nephew, Inc.
150 Minuteman Road
Andover, MA 01810 United States
melissa.messner@smith-nephew.com
http://www.smith-nephew.com

BUS: Manufacturing Company **P/S:** Gynecology and Women Surgery Devices **MA:** National **EXP:** Ms. Messner's expertise is in educating patients. **EDU:** Bachelor of Science in Nursing, William Carey College **CERTS:** Certified Nurse Practitioner in Women's Health Care; Certified Nurse Operating Room **B/I:** She became involved in her profession because she was always interested in the medical field. **H/O:** The highlight of her career was completing her high school education.

LEAH G. METTLER
Realtor
Prudential California Rose Marie
1 N. Cherokee Lane
Lodi, CA 95240 United States
agentleah@hotmail.com
http://www.prucalifornia.com

BUS: Real Estate Company **P/S:** Residential, Commercial, Farms, Ranches and Income Investments **MA:** Northern California **D/D/R:** Farms, Ranches, Income Producing Investments, Residential Real Estate **H/I/S:** Caring for her 12 Horses **FBP:** Realtor; American Quarter Horses Journal **EDU:** Associate Degree in Business, Delta NUOP **CERTS:** Certification, EE; Real Estate License **A/A/S:** National Association of Realtors; California Association of Realtors; Lodi Association of Realtors **A/H:** Three-Time Recipient, Circle Award **C/VW:** Lodi House, Women's Shelter **A/S:** She attributes her success to the influence of her wonderful manager, Rose Marie. **B/I:** She became involved in her profession after working in property management. She felt that her clients were not making enough on their investments and with her assistance they began to do well. **H/O:** The highlight of her career has been working with her manager and receiving the benefit of her knowledge, talent and drive.

JEANNIE L. MEYER, RN
Registered Nurse, Certified Nurse Assistant Instructor
Phoenix Shanti Group, Inc.
2345 W. Glendale Avenue
Phoenix, AZ 85021 United States
http://www.shantiaz.org

BUS: Healthcare and Education **P/S:** Housing, Education and Direct Client Services to Individuals, Families and Loved Ones Infected with and Affected by HIV and AIDS, Introducing Healthcare through the Clinic and Educational Certified Nurse Assistant Programs **MA:** National **D/D/R:** Specializing in Healthcare, Teaching Students Long-Term Care, Assisting in the Daily Care of Clients and Patients **H/I/S:** Reading, Traveling **FBP:** RN; NurseWeek **EDU:** Diploma in Nursing, St. Joseph's Hospital **CERTS:** Certified Nurse Assistant Program, American Board of Nursing Specialties

Tanya L. Meyer, RN

Registered Nurse
Luther Hospital
1221 Whipple Street
Eau Claire, WI 54701 United States
tlcon130@yahoo.com
http://www.cambridgewhoswho.com

BUS: Community Hospital **P/S:** Healthcare **MA:** Local **D/D/R:** Cardiovascular and Critical-Care Nursing **H/I/S:** Playing the Piano, Painting, Golfing, Traveling **FBP:** AACN Journal **EDU:** Associate of Science in Nursing, Chippewa Valley Technical College **A/S:** She attributes her success to her hard work and desire to help others. **B/I:** She became involved in this profession because her entire family is involved in nursing. **H/O:** The highlight of her career is her consulting nurse position.

John A. Micciola

Senior Investment Specialist
National Securities Corporation
3663 US Highway Nine
Old Bridge, NJ 08857 United States
jmicciola@nationalsecurities.com
http://www.nationalsecurities.com

BUS: Brokerage Firm **P/S:** Security Brokerage and Retirement Planning Services **MA:** International **D/D/R:** Assisting Clients with High-Growth Investments, Implementing Retirement Plans, Preserving Capital, Managing Assets, Ensuring Customer Satisfaction **H/I/S:** Bicycling, Cross-Training, Traveling, Playing Tennis **FBP:** The Wall Street Journal **EDU:** Coursework, DeVry Technical Institute; Diploma, Edward R. Murrow High School **CERTS:** Licensed in Series 7; Licensed in Series 63 **A/A/S:** Advisory Board Member, Black River Wealth Management; Board Member, Lasso Key Technologies **C/VW:** Feed The Children; Alzheimer's Association; Children's Cancer Association; Autism Awareness Association; Scleroderma Foundation **DOB:** October 7, 1966 **POB:** NY **SP:** Lisa **CHILD:** Jonathan, Julia **A/S:** He attributes his success to his customer service skills, honesty and integrity. **B/I:** He became involved in his profession because of his helping nature. **H/O:** The most gratifying aspect of his career is helping his clients to achieve their goals. **I/F/Y:** In five years, Mr. Micciola hopes to grow professionally.

ALEXIS D. MICHAELIAN
Teacher
St. Mary and All Angels
7 Pursuit
Aliso Viejo, CA 92656 United States
alexis.michaelian@smaa.org
http://www.smaa.org

BUS: Non-denominational Christian School **P/S:** Education **MA:** Local **D/D/R:** Elementary Education **H/I/S:** Biking, Reading, Outdoor Activities, Going to the Beach **EDU:** Master of Arts in Teaching, Chapman University; Bachelor of Arts in Liberal Studies, California State University at Fullerton **A/A/S:** Gamma Phi Beta; First Elementary School Teacher Sent to Milan in an Exchange Teaching Program, International School of Milan **A/S:** She attributes her success to her determination, keeping up with her studies and being versatile in teaching each child and their needs. **B/I:** She became involved in this profession because she always wanted to teach. **H/O:** The highlight of her career is being the first elementary school teacher to be sent to Milan on an exchange teaching program at the International School of Milan.

BARBARA P. MICKLE
Realtor
Howard Hannah Real Estate
437 Theatre Drive
Johnstown, PA 15904 United States
barbmickle@aol.com
http://www.heritagesold.com

BUS: Residential and Commercial Real Estate Agency **P/S:** Buying, Selling and Listing Real Estate Properties **MA:** Local **D/D/R:** Specializing in Residential Real Estate, Assisting First-Time Home Buyers, Interacting with Clientele by Giving the Highest Possible Level of Customer Service **H/I/S:** Spending Time with her Family, Reading **FBP:** USA Today; Realtor **EDU:** Diploma, Richland Township High School (1954) **CERTS:** Licensed Realtor (1994); Accredited Buyer Representative **A/A/S:** National Association of Realtors; Rebac

JACQUELINE NICOLE MIDDLEBUSHER, RN
Registered Nurse Team Leader
Jane Phillips Medical Center
3500 E. Frank Phillips Boulevard
Bartlesville, OK 74006 United States
jnrbusher@sbcglobal.net
http://www.jpmc.org

BUS: Medical Center **P/S:** Healthcare **MA:** Local **EXP:** Ms. Middlebusher's expertise is in caring for her patients, supervising staff, overseeing rehabilitation nursing and endoscopy emergency room. **H/I/S:** Spending Time with her Family **FBP:** American Journal of Nursing **EDU:** Associate Degree in Nursing, Oklahoma Wesleyan University (1996) **A/A/S:** Emergency Nurses Association; Trauma Registry **A/H:** Nominated for Nurse of the Year (2005) **A/S:** She attributes her success to her education and the support she receives from her family and mentors. **B/I:** She became involved in her profession because she always wanted to help others. **H/O:** The highlight of her career was having a leadership role in the emergency room.

CHERYL M. MIELBRECHT, PA-C
Certified Physician Assistant
Family Medicine
Mattawa Community Medical Center
210 Government Road
Mattawa, WA 99349 United States
miel2670@pacificu.edu
http://www.pacificu.edu

BUS: Nonprofit Rural Community Health Clinic **P/S:** Healthcare **MA:** Local **D/D/R:** Performing Adult and Pediatric Exams **H/I/S:** Spending Time with her Three Parrots, Hiking, Camping, Travelling, Amateur Photography **FBP:** Journal of American Association of Physicians Assistants; Advance Magazine for PAs **EDU:** Master's Degree in Science of Physician Assistant Studies, Pacific University School of Physician Assistant Studies (2007); Bachelor's Degree in Psychology, University of Washington (1994) **CERTS:** Certified Physician Assistant (2007) **A/A/S:** AAPA; WAPA **A/H:** Who's Who Among American Students (1985) **C/VW:** Veteran's Administration; Local Charities **POB:** Seattle, WA **W/H:** Group Health-Medical Assistant (1997-2007) **A/S:** She attributes her success to her supportive peers who are very knowledgeable and have great positive attitudes. **B/I:** She became involved in her profession because she was a medical assistant for 10 years and decided to do something more challenging. **H/O:** The most gratifying aspect of her career is working with patients one-on-one. **I/F/Y:** In five years, Ms. Mielbrecht plans to remain in her current position.

DENISE J. MIKITA
Executive Director
Colorado Association of Certified Veterinary Technicians
191 Yuma Street
Denver, CO 80223 United States
denise.mikita@cwwemail.com
http://www.cacvt.com

BUS: Nonprofit Organization **P/S:** Healthcare for Animals **MA:** Regional **EXP:** Mr. Mikita's expertise is in supervising all activities, overseeing the executive board and utilizing his leadership skills. **H/I/S:** Playing Sports, Photography, Reading, Traveling, Yard Work **FBP:** Veterinary Technician **EDU:** Master's Degree in Physiology, The Pennsylvania State University (1991); Bachelor of Science in Biology, Colorado State University (1989) **CERTS:** Certified Veterinary Technician **A/A/S:** Colorado Society of Association Executives; National Association of Veterinary Technicians in America; American Animal Hospital Association; Colorado Veterinary Medical Association; Metro Denver Shelter Alliance

LYDIA MILARS
Real Estate Investor
Bardon Miller Property Group
6558 Barton Avenue
Los Angeles, CA 90038 United States
lmilars@sbcglobal.net
http://www.cambridgewhoswho.com

BUS: Real Estate Firm **P/S:** Real Estate Investments Services **MA:** National **EXP:** Her expertise is in investing in properties, applying and teaching about make-up techniques, selling skin care and nutritional supplements. **H/I/S:** Gardening, Hiking **EDU:** Bachelor's Degree in Bioesthetics (1977) **CERTS:** Licensed Cosmetologist, Arizona High School (1975) **W/H:** Make-Up Department Head, Film 'Shopgirl' (2005); Make-Up Department Head, Film 'Raise Your Voice' (2004); Make-Up Department Head, Film 'A Cinderella Story' (2004); Make-Up Department Head, Film 'Cheaper by the Dozen' (2003); Assistant Make-Up Department Head, Film 'Seabiscuit' (2003); Make-Up Department Head, Film 'Big Fat Liar' (2002); Make-Up Department Head, Film 'Homeward Bound' (2002); Make-Up Artist, Film 'The Center of the World' (2001); Key Make-Up Artist, Film 'One Nigh at McCool's' (2001); Key Make-Up Artist, Film 'Dude, Where's My Car?' (2000); Make-Up Artist, Film 'Panic' (2000); Make-Up Artist, Film 'Anna Karenina' (1997); Key Make-Up Artist, Film 'American Strays' (1996); Key Make-Up Artist, Film 'Box of Moon Light' (1996); Key Make-Up Artist and Hair Stylist, Film 'Sydney' (1996); Make-Up Artist, Film 'The Four Diamonds' (1995); Key Make-Up Artist, Film 'Lieberman in Love' (1995); Make-Up Artist, Film 'The Client' (1994); Make-Up Artist, Film 'The Hudsucker Proxy' (1994); Make-Up Artist, Film 'Sliver' (1993); Key Make-Up Artist, Film 'That Night' (1992); Make-Up Artist, Film 'And Then She Was Gone' (1991); Make-Up Supervisor, Film 'To Save a Child' (1991); Assistant Make-Up Artist, Film 'Mannequin: On the Move' (1991) **A/S:** She attributes her success to her perseverance and her positive attitude.

MR. GLENN MILLAR
Capability Programmers Engineering Integration Senior Section Leader
BAE Systems
Warton Aerodrome (W310B)
Warton Preston
Lancashire, PR4 1AX United Kingdom
glenn.millar@baesystems.com
http://www.baesystems.com

BUS: Aerospace Company **P/S:** Manufacturing Aircraft, Munitions and Naval Systems **MA:** International **EXP:** Mr. Millar's expertise is in jet aircraft engineering. **D/D/R:** Supervising Integration Senior Section, Designing Tornado Ids and Adv Variants, Aircraft Multi-Systems Engineering, Working on Expensive Military Aircraft Platforms, Planning and Estimating **H/I/S:** Traveling, Golfing, Renovating his Home, Walking, Four-Wheeling **FBP:** IET Journal **EDU:** Coursework, Licentiateship of the City and Guilds of London Institute; Diploma in Aeronautical Engineering; Diploma in Technical Authorship **A/A/S:** Institute of Engineering & Technology; Institute of Leadership & Management; Institute of Scientific & Technical Communicators; Engineering Council **A/H:** Chairman's Bronze Award, BAE Systems (2003); Recipient, British Aerospace Chairman's Bronze Award (1999); Queen's Birthday Honors List (1983, 1985) **DOB:** March 27, 1954 **SP:** Julie **CHILD:** Amanda, Graham **W/H:** Technician, Roevin (1997-2000); Chief Technician, Royal Air Force (1970-1997); Commendation Group, Air Officer Commanding 18 Group; Commander-in Chief Operations, Royal Air Force, Germany

CHERYL A. MILLER
Executive Administrator, Personal Assistant
Walton Street Capital, L.L.C.
900 N. Michigan Avenue
Suite 1900
Chicago, IL 60611 United States
millerca@waltonst.com
http://www.cambridgewhoswho.com

BUS: Private Equity Real Estate Investment Firm **P/S:** Investment and Wealth Management Services **MA:** International **EXP:** Ms. Miller's expertise is in operations management. **H/I/S:** Relaxing, Shopping, Spending Time with her Family **FBP:** In Style; Health; Crain's Chicago Business; Chicago **EDU:** Diploma, Elmwood Park High School, IL **A/H:** Employee of the Month, World Dryer Corporation (1988) **C/VW:** Best Friends Animal Society; Pets Are Worth Saving **A/S:** She attributes her success to her love for her profession, organizational skills, drive to successfully complete all tasks and strive for perfection. **B/I:** She became involved in her profession because it allowed her to combine her interpersonal and organizational skills. **H/O:** The highlight of her career was having the opportunity to work with Neil Bloom.

CINDY MILLER
President
Pulse Fitness Systems
612 E. Glenoaks Boulevard
Glendale, CA 91207 United States
cmiller850@aol.com
http://www.lifestylesforhealth.com

BUS: Gym, Personal Training and Education Company **P/S:** Strength, Flexibility, and Heart Zones Training, Nutritional Consultations, Balanced Exercise Program, Custom Coaching, Personal Training, Health and Wellness in the Workplace Education, Studio Cycling **MA:** International **D/D/R:** Fitness Coaching for Specific Athletic Events, Working One-On-One with Athletes to Prepare their Body, Mind, and Nutritional Balance, Working as a Fitness Trainer in Self-Owned Studio as well as on the Internet, Implementing a Total Fitness System **H/I/S:** Sprinting, Participating in Triathlons **EDU:** Teaching Degree, Long Beach College (1972) **A/A/S:** IDEA; ACE

CRAIG A. MILLER
President
Craig Miller Trucking, LLC
PO Box 427
Wayne, OH 43466 United States
c.miller5@yahoo.com
http://www.cambridgewhoswho.com

BUS: Transportation Service Provider **P/S:** Transportation and Hauling Services **MA:** Local **D/D/R:** Leading as an Excellent Service Provider among his Competitors **H/I/S:** Playing Poker, Watching College Football, Watching NASCAR, Spending Time with his Wife **FBP:** Land Line Magazine **EDU:** Associate Degree in Business Management, Owens Community College **A/A/S:** Owner-Operator Independent Drivers Association **SP:** Melissa

EUGENIA H. MILLER, MS
Adjunct Professor
The College of New Rochelle
515 North Avenue
New Rochelle, NY 10801 United States
bibistory@aol.com
http://www.cnr.edu

BUS: Proven Leader in the Education Industry **P/S:** High Quality Educational Services **MA:** Local **D/D/R:** Multi-Cultural Education, Supervising Student Teachers, Working in Peer Mediation and Conflict Resolution **H/I/S:** Reading, Exercising **FBP:** Teaching Tolerance **EDU:** Master's Degree, College of New Rochelle **A/A/S:** Delta Sigma Theta; National Alliance of Black School Educators; President, Westchester Alliance of Black School Educators; Board President, New Rochelle Day Nursery

JEAN K. MILLER
Staff Nurse, Charge Nurse
Britthaven, Inc. Wilson N.C.
3164 Buffalo Road
Smithfield, NC 27577 United States
http://www.cambridgewhoswho.com

BUS: Proven Leader Committed to Excellence in Nursing and Assisted Living Services **P/S:** Patient Activities, Clinical Laboratory, Dental, Dietary, Housekeeping, Nursing, Occupational Therapy, Pharmacy, Physical Therapy, Physician, Social Work, Speech/Language Pathology and Diagnostic X-Ray Services **MA:** Regional **D/D/R:** Practicing Skilled, Staff and Charge Nursing in All Departments, Offering Personal Care, Dispensing Medications, Administering Treatments, Assessing Patient Needs, Meeting with Patient Families, Assisting with Doctors' Care, Offering Patients Information, Carrying Out Orders, Practicing Emergency Room and Intensive Care Unit Nursing, Working as a Medical Officer for the State of Virginia **H/I/S:** Dancing, Reading, Listening to Music, Reading Newspapers **EDU:** Diploma, Raleigh School; Diploma, Mary Elizabeth Hospital School of Nursing; Coursework, Mary Elizabeth Hospital School of Nursing (1951) **CERTS:** Licensed Nurse, State of Virginia (1969-1997); Licensed, State of North Carolina (1955)

KIM L. MILLER, LPN

Licensed Practical Nurse, Camp Nurse
Doubling Gap Center, East Pennsylvania Conference
1550 Doubling Gap Road
Newville, PA 17241 United States
ksmill91@verizon.net
http://www.cambridgewhoswho.com

BUS: Conference Camp Center **P/S:** Conference and Summer Camp Center **MA:** National **D/D/R:** Licensed Practical Nurse **H/I/S:** Reading, Completing Crafts, Spending Quality Time with her Family, Hiking, Walking **CERTS:** Licensed Practical Nurse, State of Pennsylvania **C/VW:** Fund Drives, California Research; American Heart Association **A/S:** She attributes her career success to her passion, love of her work and dedication. **B/I:** She became involved in nursing because of her love of the profession. **H/O:** The highlight of her career was working in hospice care.

LINDA A. MILLER, BSN, RN, CPN, CPST

Registered Nurse, CPN, CPST, BSN
Children's Mercy Hospital and Clinics, South Campus
5808 W. 110th Street
Overland Park, KS 66211 United States
lamiller@cmh.edu
http://www.cambridgewhoswho.com

BUS: Hospital, Clinic **P/S:** Pediatric Medical Care **MA:** Local **D/D/R:** Pediatric Nursing **H/I/S:** Scrapbooking, Reading and Bicycle Riding **FBP:** RN; Nursing2009 **EDU:** Associate of Arts in Pre-Nursing, Western Oklahoma State College; Bachelor's Degree in Nursing, Avila University **CERTS:** Certified Pediatric Nurse; Child Passenger Safety Technician **A/A/S:** Safekids USA **C/VW:** United Way of America; Facilitator, American Lung Association; Basic Life Support Instructor, American Heart Association; Volunteers as a Child Passenger Safety Instructor for Mid-America Nazarene University, Safekids USA **A/S:** She attributes her success to her love of education, particularly pediatric education. She enjoys educating new parents and learning new things.

MARTHA J. MILLER, NBCT
Fourth-Grade Educator
Valleyview Elementary School
Polk County Schools
2900 E. State Road, 540-A
Lakeland, FL 33813 United States
maggie.miller@polk-fl.net
http://www.polk-ft.net/Valleyview

BUS: Elementary School **P/S:** Primary Education **MA:** Local **EXP:** Ms. Miller's area of expertise is in first through sixth-grade elementary education. **H/I/S:** Gardening and Portrait Photography **FBP:** Writer's Digest; International Reading Association Magazine **EDU:** Bachelor's Degree in Psychology and Education, Florida Southern College **CERTS:** Nationally Board Certified **A/A/S:** International Reading Association; Who's Who Among American Teachers **A/H:** Southwest Area Teacher of the Year, Polk County, Florida (2006); Two-Time Recipient, The Disney Teacherrific Award **C/VW:** Well Fund; Band Boosters, Lakeland High School **DOB:** June 9, 1967 **POB:** Lake Wales, FL **SP:** Bobby **A/S:** She attributes her success to her personal drive. **B/I:** She became involved in her profession because she always had an interest in the field and a desire to educate others. **H/O:** The highlight of her career is making a positive impact on others.

MARY BETH MILLER
Special Education Teacher
Whispering Pines Elementary School
9090 Spanish Isles Boulevard
Boca Raton, FL 33428 United States
marybeth_98@hotmail.com
http://www.cambridgewhoswho.com

BUS: Elementary School **P/S:** Education **MA:** Boca Raton **D/D/R:** Teaching Inclusion and Self-Contained Classes **H/I/S:** Cooking, Exercising **EDU:** Master's Degree in Special Education, College of New Rochelle **A/A/S:** National Education Association; Classroom Teachers Association **H/O:** The highlight of her career is one day teaching vocational training and helping young adults.

PATRICIA S. ALSOBROOKS MILLER
Licensed Practical Nurse
OB/GYN Northwest AL; Dr. S.M. Chappel
2407 Helton Drive
Florence, AL 35630 United States
http://www.cambridgewhoswho.com

BUS: Gynecological Care Office **P/S:** Women's Healthcare **MA:** Local **D/D/R:** Nursing in Post-Menopausal Women's Health **H/I/S:** Reading, Gardening, Lawn Work, Supporting NASCAR **CERTS:** Licensed Practical Nurse, Northwest State College **A/S:** She attributes her success to family support and being the best that she can be. **B/I:** She became involved in the profession because she always wanted to be. **H/O:** The highlight of her career is being able to make a living and still have a passion for what she is doing.

ROSIE MILLER
Vice President of Development
Girl Scouts of Citrus Council
341 N. Mills Avenue
Orlando, FL 32803 United States
rmiller@citrus-gs.org
http://www.citrus-gs.org

BUS: Nonprofit Service Organization **P/S:** Quality Programs and Experiences **MA:** National **D/D/R:** Specializing in Fundraising and Community Relations **H/I/S:** Spending Time with the Family, Going to Theme Parks **FBP:** Newsweek; Orlando Business Journal; Hispanic Business Journal **EDU:** Bachelor of Science in Finance, St. Peter's College **A/A/S:** Chamber of Commerce; Rotary Club; President, Reserve Officer Training Corps Unit **C/VW:** Heart of Florida; United Way of America; Local Schools **A/S:** She attributes her success to the support of her family and co-workers. **H/O:** The highlight of her career was when she was asked to speak at the National Girl Scouts Conference for the last four years.

SHARON MCMAHON MILLER
Professor of Dental Hygiene
Erie Community College, School of Dental Hygiene
6205 Main Street
Williamsville, NY 14221 United States
miller@ecc.edu
http://www.cambridgewhoswho.com

BUS: College **P/S:** Dental Hygiene Education **MA:** Local **D/D/R:** Educating People on Dental Hygiene, Directing Programs for Individuals with Disabilities, Caring for Patients with Disabilities, Teaching Students about Being a Dental Hygienist **H/I/S:** Camping, Boating, Reading, Writing **FBP:** Access **EDU:** Master's Degree in Community Health Education, SUNY at Buffalo **A/A/S:** American Dental Hygienists' Association; State and Local Campaigns; New York State Educators Association **C/VW:** Lancaster Presbyterian Church **A/S:** She attributes her success to always giving 100 percent, as well as to her self-motivation, creativity and faith. **B/I:** She became involved in her profession because she loves people and was looking for a way to reach out to people and provide them with total body wellness. **H/O:** The highlight of her career was directing the program 'Special Care Day' which educates special needs children in a fun and creative way.

TIM MILLER
Chairman
Flatsigned
3415 W. End Avenue
Suite 1101
Nashville, TN 37203 United States
timmiller@flatsigned.com
http://www.flatsigned.com

BUS: Retail Publishing Company **P/S:** Limited Edition Books, Rare Autographed Books, First Edition Books, Books Signed by the Author, Directly on the Title Page without being Inscribed to Strangers, Signed Limited Numbered Editions **MA:** International **D/D/R:** Sales, Contacts, First Editions, Autographed Books, Lecturing Internationally **H/I/S:** Poker, Travel **FBP:** Autograph Collector Magazine **EDU:** Bachelor of Science in Speech Communications, Austin Peay State University (1982) **A/A/S:** International Society of Appraisers; Manuscript Society; Universal Autograph Collectors Club; Better Business Bureau

VIRGINIA FAYE MILLER, LPN
Licensed Practical Nurse, Charge Nurse
Pleasantview Home
Kalona, IA 52247 United States
ginnymillerlpn@yahoo.com
http://www.cambridgewhoswho.com

BUS: Geriatric Home **P/S:** Healthcare, Geriatric Care **MA:** Local **D/D/R:** Geriatric Care Facility **H/I/S:** Traveling, Reading, Renovating a New Home **CERTS:** Licensed Practical Nurse Certification, Kirkwood Community College; Medical Aid Certification; Nursing Assistant Certification **A/S:** She attributes her success to caring and giving all residents the best care she can. **B/I:** She became involved in her profession after working as a CNA. **H/O:** The highlight of her career has been getting her LPN certification in elder care.

PAMELA S. MILLER-SHAW, LPN
Licensed Practical Nurse, Charge Nurse
Colonial Manor
Pamela.MillerShaw@cwwemail.com
http://www.cambridgewhoswho.com

BUS: Nursing Home **P/S:** Long-Term Healthcare, Rehabilitation Services **MA:** Local **EXP:** Ms. Miller-Shaw's expertise is in geriatrics. **H/I/S:** Spending Time with her Daughter, Swimming, Skating **FBP:** Industry-Related Publications **CERTS:** Licensed Practical Nurse **C/VW:** Local Church **A/S:** She attributes her success to her hard work and dedication. **B/I:** She became involved in her profession because she always wanted to be a nurse. **H/O:** The most gratifying aspect of her career is helping her patients to recover.

BETTY JO MILNER
Broker and Realtor
805 W. Jefferson Street
Suite A
Shorewood, IL 60404 United States
gowithbettyjo@comcast.net
http://www.cambridgewhoswho.com

BUS: Real Estate Agency **P/S:** Purchase and Sales of Residential and Commercial Properties, Land Development, Mortgage Assistance **MA:** Regional **D/D/R:** Focusing on Clients who Need Handicapped Accessibility, Buying and Selling Farmland, Residential, Commercial and Investment Properties **H/I/S:** Swimming, Gardening **FBP:** Realtor; Fortune 500 **EDU:** College Coursework **A/A/S:** Illinois Association of Realtors; Grungy County Land Use Committee, Illinois Headwaters RCD; National Association of Realtors **C/VW:** Local Cancer Society

ELIZABETH SWEENEY MINASSIAN, MS, M.Ed., RN, BC
Field Representative/Surveyor
The Joint Commission
1 Renaissance Boulevard
Oakbrook Terrace, IL 60181 United States
eminassian@jointcommission.org
http://www.cambridgewhoswho.com

BUS: Healthcare **P/S:** Healthcare **MA:** National **D/D/R:** Accreditation Services **H/I/S:** Attending the Theater, Traveling, Spending Time at Plum Island Summer Home and with her Four Grandchildren **FBP:** Sigma Theta Tau Journal **EDU:** Master's Degree in Maternal and Child Health, Boston University; Master's Degree in Guidance and Counseling, Boston State College; Bachelor of Science in Nursing, Boston State College **CERTS:** Certified in Education and Staff Development, American Nurses Association, Credentialing Division **A/A/S:** Sigma Theta Tau; Visiting Nurses Association; American Nurses Association; Medical Reserve Corporation; The Visiting Nurse Association of Eastern Massachusetts; American Nurses Association **C/VW:** Volunteer, Emergency Task Force, Homeland Security, Town of Winchester; Sisters of the Poor; Rosie's Place; American Red Cross **A/S:** She attributes her success to her love of her job. **B/I:** She became involved in the profession because it was of great interest to her. **H/O:** The highlight of her career is teaching.

MINETTA MINNICK
Owner
Fauxbulous Finishes
1760 Inchcliff Road
Columbus, OH 43221 United States
minettam@faux-bulousfinishes.com
http://www.fauxbulousfinishes.com

BUS: Interior Design Company **P/S:** Faux Finishing, Painting and Interior Decoration **MA:** Local **EXP:** Ms. Minnick's expertise is in interior designs, creating faux finishes, painting murals, stenciling, ledge merchandising, real estate staging, color consulting, floral arrangement, hand painting on furniture, designing floor plans and window treatments. **H/I/S:** Attending the Theater, Listening to Music, Playing the Violin, Belly Dancing, Baking, Cake Decoration **FBP:** Interior Design and Stage Solutions; Window Treatments **EDU:** Pursuing Bachelor's Degree **CERTS:** Pursuing Certification in Interior Design, American Society of Interior Designers **A/A/S:** Powell Area Chamber of Commerce **C/VW:** Shedd Aquarium; Franklin Park Conservatory, Columbus **A/S:** She attributes her success to her passion for design, creativity and hard work. **B/I:** She became involved in her profession because she was inspired by her uncle and her father who were in the painting and remodeling business. **H/O:** The highlight of her career was opening her own business.

ROSEMARY MADRID MINORI
Realtor
RE/MAX Gold, SSB Realtors
1949 W. Kettleman Avenue
Lodi, CA 95242 United States
rosemary.madrid@norcalgold.com
http://www.cambridgewhoswho.com

BUS: Real Estate Sales Company **P/S:** Real Estate Sales **MA:** Local **D/D/R:** Listing and Selling Residential Properties **H/I/S:** Reading, Exercising **FBP:** Realtor; Health Magazines; Inspirational Magazines **EDU:** Real Estate Coursework; Industry-Related Training and Experience **A/A/S:** National Association of Realtors **C/VW:** Multiple Charitable Organizations **A/S:** She attributes her personal and professional success to her faith, hope and the support of her children. **B/I:** She became involved in the real estate profession because of a desire to help people. **H/O:** The highlight of her career is being able to help clients realize their dreams.

CARMEN M. MIRANDA
Senior Administrative Assistant
Pfizer Global Manufacturing
99 Jardines Street
Caguas, PR 00725 United States
carmen.miranda@pfizer.com
http://www.pfizer.com

BUS: Manufacturing Company **P/S:** Pharmaceutical Products **MA:** International **D/D/R:** Working with New Products and Technologies **H/I/S:** Listening to Music, Dancing, Sewing, Knitting, Bicycling **FBP:** Office Pro; Diversity Inc. **EDU:** Bachelor's Degree in Business Administration, Columbia College **A/A/S:** Secretary, Caguas Chapter, International Association of Administrative Professionals **C/VW:** La Cuna San Cristobal **A/S:** She attributes her success to the support she receives from her mentors and instructors. **B/I:** She became involved in her profession because she has been in the field since high school and wanted to progress further. **H/O:** The most gratifying aspects of her career are working in a team environment and establishing interpersonal skills.

SVETLANA ANTONOV MISKEVICH
Owner, Manager
Svetlana Herbs Ayurvedic Inc.
7907 Santa Monica Boulevard
West Hollywood, CA 90046 United States
onega35@gmail.com
http://www.svetlanaherbs.com

BUS: Alternative Health **P/S:** Personalized and Detailed Customer Service **MA:** Local **EXP:** Ms. Miskevich's expertise is in store management. **D/D/R:** Managing, Working with People to Better their Health, Consulting **H/I/S:** Spending Time with the Family, Traveling, Painting, Singing, Writing Books, Poetry, Learning **FBP:** Health Magazines **EDU:** Coursework, College and Vocal School, Russia; High School Education **A/A/S:** Disabled Veterans Association **A/S:** She attributes her success to being open-minded and curious.

BONNIE E. MITCHELL
Public Adjuster, Debt Relief Specialist
MetroPublic Adjustment, Inc.
2401 Reach Road
Suite 213
Williamsport, PA 17701 United States
debt.terminator@comcast.net
http://www.cambridgewhoswho.com

BUS: Insurance, Advocacy **P/S:** Representing Property Owners to Make Sure they Get their Due Settlements from Insurance Companies Regarding Property Damage, Opening Debt Relief and Settlement Programs **MA:** National **H/I/S:** Gardening, Caring for her Horses and Pets **C/VW:** Williamsport Chamber of Commerce; Local Community; Children International **A/S:** She attributes her success to going after things aggressively and not giving up. **H/O:** The highlight of her career is the satisfaction she feels when she makes a difference in the lives of others.

PAULA L. MITCHELL
Sub-Contractor
Tom Keith and Associates
121 S. Cool Spring Street
Fayettville, NC 28301 United States
appraisal.lady@usa.com
http://www.cambridgewhoswho.com

BUS: Real Estate Company **P/S:** High Quality Real Estate Services **MA:** North Carolina **D/D/R:** Working with Lenders, Insurance and Individuals for Developing Opinions about their Property **H/I/S:** Reading, Traveling, Skiing, Hiking **EDU:** Bachelor of Arts in Speech Communications and Public Relations, Appalachian State University **CERTS:** Certified in Residential Appraisal **A/A/S:** North Carolina Association of Professional Appraisers

TRACIE Y. MITCHELL, CPP
Director of Payroll
Windsor HR Services, Inc.
8000 Warren Parkway
Suite 103
Frisco, TX 75034 United States
tracie@windsorhr.com
http://www.windsorhr.com

BUS: Professional Employer Organization **P/S:** Payroll and Human Resource Services **MA:** Regional **D/D/R:** Payroll and Human Resources **H/I/S:** Reading, Bowling, Exercising **FBP:** HR; PayTech **EDU:** Bachelor of Science in Political Science, Virginia State University **A/A/S:** American Payroll Association **C/VW:** Breast Cancer Foundation; Diabetes Foundation; Susan G. Komen Breast Cancer Foundation **A/S:** She attributes her success to team work, her co-workers and her mentors. **B/I:** She became involved in this profession because she relocated to Texas after college and she had banking experience. **H/O:** The highlight of her career is passing the CPP Exam in 2003.

MR. ANTHONY EWART MITTON, LMT
Owner
Tony Mitton, LMT
6525 Alan A Dale Trail
Tallahassee, FL 32309 United States
mittont@nettally.com
http://www.cambridgewhoswho.com

BUS: Therapy Center **P/S:** Massage Therapy **MA:** Regional **EXP:** Mr. Mitton's expertise is in performing massage therapy. **H/I/S:** Reading History, Fishing **FBP:** Massage Today **EDU:** Master's Degree in Economics and Modern Languages, Cambridge University, England **CERTS:** Licensed Massage Therapist, Drake School of Massage, Tallahassee, FL **A/A/S:** American Massage Therapy Association; Birmingham City Council, UK **C/VW:** Findhorn Foundation **W/H:** Chairman, Flowstream International, Ltd, UK; Operations and Management Consultant, Florida Department of Corrections **A/S:** He attributes his success to his faith in God. **B/I:** He became involved in his profession because of his desire to help people.

MR. CHAD A. MIYATA
President
Apparel Projects Express Finishing, Inc.
2901 E. 12th Street
Los Angeles, CA 90023 United States
cmiyata@apparelprojectsexpress.com
http://www.apparelprojectsexpress.com

BUS: Distribution Company **P/S:** Sportswear, American Apparel Clothing, Shirts, Jeans **MA:** International **D/D/R:** Managing Operations Including Finance and Staff **H/I/S:** Playing Baseball **EDU:** Bachelor's Degree in Physical Education, California Lutheran University (1996) **A/H:** Salute to Small Business Award (2005) **DOB:** February 25, 1972

MARTHA K. MIZE, RN, BSN
Registered Nurse
Methodist Children's Hospital
7700 Floyd Curl Drive
San Antonio, TX 78229 United States
kathiemize@msn.com
http://www.cambridgewhoswho.com

BUS: Full-Service Children's Hospital **P/S:** Healthcare **MA:** Regional **D/D/R:** Neonatal Intensive Care **H/I/S:** Enjoying Sports, Reading, Spending Time with her Two-Year-Old Foster Son **FBP:** RN; Nursing2009 **EDU:** Bachelor of Science in Nursing, Arkansas State University (2004) **A/A/S:** Vice President, Association of perioperative Registered Nurses **CHILD:** Malaki **A/S:** She attributes her career success to her excellent coworkers and the mentorship she has received from her head nurse in the surgery intensive care. **B/I:** She became involved in nursing after having her appendix removed and being inspired by the nurses who assisted her.

BROOKE M. MOBLEY
Educator
Fort Oglethorpe High School
1850 Battlefield Parkway
Fort Oglethorpe, GA 30742 United States
bmobley.cso@catoosa.k12.ga.us
http://www.cambridgewhoswho.com

BUS: Education **P/S:** Education **MA:** Local **D/D/R:** Teaching Science and Mathematics for Grades Six through 12 **H/I/S:** Mountain Biking, Playing the Violin, Camping **EDU:** Master's Degree, University of Tennessee **A/A/S:** Tennessee Association of School Counselors; Georgia Association of Educators; National Educators Association; National Science Teachers Association; Georgia Association of Educators; National Educators Association; National Science Teachers Association **C/VW:** Kiwanis Club **A/S:** She attributes her success to her passion. **B/I:** She became interested in her profession because she tutored students and enjoyed it. **H/O:** The highlight of her career has been watching her students graduate.

MS. KATHERINE S. MODIC, BS
Theology Teacher
Cleveland Central Catholic High School
6550 Baxter Avenue
Cleveland, OH 44105 United States
kmodic687@earthlink.net
http://www.centralcatholichs.org

BUS: High School **P/S:** Secondary and Spiritual Education **MA:** Local **EXP:** Ms. Modic's expertise is in religion and music. **D/D/R:** Teaching Theology, Morality, Christian Lifestyle and Church History **H/I/S:** Singing in the Church Choir, Knitting, Solving Sudoku and Jigsaw Puzzles **FBP:** Catholic Universe Bulletin **EDU:** Bachelor of Science in Elementary Education, Cleveland State University (1978) **CERTS:** Certification in Theology Education, Diocese of Cleveland **C/VW:** Local Church **DOB:** January 30, 1955 **POB:** Cleveland, OH **A/S:** She attributes her success to her ability to teach and her faith in God. **B/I:** She became involved in her profession because of her interest in teaching. **H/O:** The most gratifying aspect of her career is receiving gratitude from her students. **I/F/Y:** In five years, Ms. Modic hopes to grow professionally and continue teaching high school students.

GREG W. MOELLER
Registered Nurse
Memorial Hermann-Texas Medical Center
6411 Fannin Street
Houston, TX 77030 United States
http://www.cambridgewhoswho.com

BUS: Full-Service Hospital **P/S:** Healthcare **MA:** Local Houston Texas **D/D/R:** Cardiac Nursing **H/I/S:** Gardening, Restoring Old Homes **FBP:** Industry-Related Publications **EDU:** Lee Community College **A/A/S:** Former Committee Member, Memorial Hermann-Texas Medical Center **A/S:** He attributed his success to his family. **B/I:** He became involved in his profession because he loved to help people. **H/O:** The highlight of his career was helping his patients.

RENA MOHAMMED
President, Chief Executive Officer, Chef
Remo's Catering
850 N.E. 212th Street
Terrace 4
North Miami Beach, FL 33179 United States
myboy8@bellsouth.net
http://www.cambridgewhoswho.com

BUS: Culinary Services Company **P/S:** Catering, Food Services, Hospitality **MA:** Regional **D/D/R:** Cooking Local and International Dishes, Catering Home and Corporate Parties, Working as a Head Chef **FBP:** Entrepreneur **EDU:** Bachelor's Degree in Food Service Management, Florida International University (2006); Associate of Science in Culinary Arts, Johnson & Wales University (2004) **A/A/S:** Former President, Florida Restaurant and Lodging Association (2002-2006); Chairperson, Education and Training, Committee Florida Restaurant and Lodging Association (2004-2006); Board of Directors, Academy of Hospitality and Tourism; Board of Directors, Florida Restaurant and Lodging Association; Board of Directors, Academy of Travel and Tourism; President, Homeowner's Association; Admission Representative, Johnson & Wales University **A/H:** Shining Star Award, Johnson & Wales University (1999, 2001-2002) **C/VW:** United Way of America; National Association for the Advancement of Colored People

CINDY J. MOHLER
Finance and Insurance Business Manager
Hallmark Volkswagen at Cool Springs
620 Bakers Bridge Avenue
Franklin, TN 37067 United States
cjmohler@comcast.net
cj@hallmarkauto.com
http://www.hallmarkauto.com

BUS: Automotive Company **P/S:** Car Manufacturing and Distribution **MA:** International **D/D/R:** Managing Sales and Finance, Marketing, Ensuring Customer Satisfaction **H/I/S:** Horseback Riding, Breeding Tennessee Walking Horses, Playing Classical Piano **EDU:** Bachelor of Business Administration, Concentration in Marketing, University of Kentucky **CERTS:** Licensed in Real Estate, State of Kentucky; Licensed Medical Billing and Claims Specialist **A/A/S:** Tennessee Walking Horse Breeders' and Exhibitors' Association **C/VW:** Christian Children's Fund **POB:** Glascow, KY **SP:** Tony **CHILD:** Cameron, Gordon **W/H:** Customer Service Representative, RR Donnelley and Sons; Customer Service Manager, Williams Printing Company, Atlanta, GA; Account Manager, Billing Specialist, Nashville Electrographics Company; Digital Film Supplier **A/S:** She attributes her success to her experience. **B/I:** She became involved in her profession through a natural progression of opportunities. **H/O:** The highlights of her career were attaining her current position and experiencing promotional opportunities within the organization.

DEB A. MOLES
Interior Designer
Deb Moles Designs
2104 Dixon Road
Frederick, MD 21704 United States
moles5@dixonrd.com
http://www.cambridgewhoswho.com

BUS: Design **P/S:** Interior Design **MA:** Regional **D/D/R:** Interior Design for Residential and Commercial Properties **H/I/S:** Golfing, Crafts **EDU:** College Coursework in Accounting and Computer Science, Florida Community College **CERTS:** Licensed Real Estate Agent; Certified in Interior Design **A/A/S:** Former Member, Officer's Wife Club **C/VW:** Children's Organizations; Parent-Teacher Association; Linganore Urbana Youth Athletic Association; Police Department **A/S:** She attributes her success to her determination and hard work. **H/O:** The most gratifying aspect of her career is finishing a project.

IBOLYA MOLNAR
Registered Nurse
Advocate Lutheran General Hospital
1775 Dempster Street
Park Ridge, IL 60068 United States
molnar16ibolya@yahoo.com
http://www.cambridgewhoswho.com

BUS: Hospital **P/S:** Level One Trauma Center and Teaching Hospital **MA:** National **D/D/R:** Surgical and Trauma Nursing **H/I/S:** Reading, Exploring her Interest in Mind Control **FBP:** Alternative Medicine **EDU:** Associate Degree, Nursing, Harper College; Pursuing Bachelor's Degree, Nursing, Amherst College; Master's Degree, Law and Business, Hungary **C/VW:** Local Nursing Home **A/S:** She attributes her success to the faith she has in herself and to always pushing for something new. **H/O:** The highlight of her career is not slowing down despite her age.

DANIELLE S. MONCLOVA
Veterinary Nurse
Herbst Veterinary Hospital
1376 S. Main Street
Boerne, TX 78006 United States
dmonclova@hotmail.com
http://www.cambridgewhoswho.com

BUS: Veterinary Hospital **P/S:** Animal Care Including General Health Surgery and Boarding for Pets **MA:** Local **EXP:** Ms. Monclova's expertise is in head X-ray technology. **D/D/R:** Assisting Veterinarians, Following Test Procedures, Ensuring Safety and Overseeing Intensive Care Services **H/I/S:** Gardening, Photography, Admiring Nature **EDU:** Pursuing Bachelor's Degree in Biology, The University of Texas at San Antonio; Associate of Arts in Animal Care Sciences; Coursework in Veterinary Medicine, Northwest Vista College, San Antonio, TX **C/VW:** Hill County Animal League **A/S:** She attributes her success to her hard work and determination. **B/I:** She became involved in her profession because of her interest in the veterinary field and desire to care for animals. **H/O:** The most gratifying aspect of her career is watching animals regain their health.

PATRICIA A. MONGIANO
Physical Therapy Director
Healing Touch Rehab, Inc.
43845 10th Street W., Suite 2D
Lancaster, CA 93534 United States
pacmon@aol.com
http://www.cambridgewhoswho.com

BUS: Healthcare Center **P/S:** Physical Therapy and Rehabilitation Assistance **MA:** Local **EXP:** Ms. Mongiano's expertise is in orthopedic and occupational therapy. **H/I/S:** Reading, Traveling, Skiing **FBP:** Industry-Related Publications **EDU:** Bachelor's Degree in Physical Therapy, Board of California **A/A/S:** American Counselors Association **C/VW:** Police Athletic League; American Cancer Society **SP:** Daniel **CHILD:** Lionel, Stephanie **A/S:** She attributes her success to her caring nature, persistence and passion for her profession.

DR. CRAIG MONROE
Dean, College of Communication
Rowan University
201 Mullica Hill Road
Glassboro, NJ 08028 United States
monroe@rowan.edu
http://www.rowan.edu

BUS: Extraordinary Comprehensive Institution Combining Liberal Education with Professional Preparation from the Baccalaureate through the Doctorate **P/S:** Collaborative, Learning-Centered Environment in which Highly Qualified and Diverse Faculty, Staff, and Students Integrate Teaching, Research, Scholarship, Creative Activity, and Community Service **MA:** Delaware Valley **D/D/R:** Specializing in Higher Education, Overseeing Five Departments and Eight Academic Programs **H/I/S:** Fishing, Gardening **EDU:** Ph.D., University of Nebraska (1976); Bachelor of Arts, University of Central Oklahoma (1964) **A/A/S:** International Communication Association; Eastern Communication Association; Executive Team Responsible for University Policies **C/A:** Published Four Books and 20 Articles

MARIO MONTEZ
Training Officer
Harlingen Fire Department
3510 E. Grimes Street
Harlingen, TX 78550 United States
firecrewm@aol.com
http://www.cambridgewhoswho.com

BUS: Fire Department **P/S:** Fire Services **MA:** Local **D/D/R:** Training Officers, Firefighting, Emergency Nursing, Working with Hazardous Materials **H/I/S:** Hunting, Fishing **FBP:** Fire Rescue **EDU:** College Coursework **A/A/S:** Harlingen Youth Football League **C/VW:** Harlingen Youth Football League **A/S:** He attributes his success to his mentors and past fire chiefs. **B/I:** He became involved in this profession because he always had a desire to be a firefighter. **H/O:** The highlight of his career is becoming a training officer and teaching in the fire academy and community college.

JANET C. MONTGOMERY
Computer Science Educator
St. John's College Preparatory School
72 Spring Street
Danvers, MA 01923 United States
janmont@stjohnsprep.org
http://www.stjohnsprep.org

BUS: All Boys College Preparatory School **P/S:** Education **MA:** Local **D/D/R:** Specializing in Technology Education **H/I/S:** Golfing, Playing the Piano, Skiing, Taking Care of her Six Grandchildren **EDU:** Pursuing Ph.D.; Master of Science in Information Systems, University of Maine; Master of Education in Computer Education, Lesley University, Cambridge, Massachusetts; Bachelor of Science **A/A/S:** International Society of Technology in Education; Massachusetts Computer Using Educators; Association for Supervision and Curriculum Development **A/S:** She attributes her success to her personal goals and to constantly striving to surpass expectations. **B/I:** She became involved in her profession because of her love of children and her love of teaching. **H/O:** The most gratifying aspect of her career is being able to do her job well and see students grow as a result.

EUGENIA MONTGOMERY-FRANKLIN
Resource Specialist
Los Angeles Unified School District
1419 W. 179th Street
Gardena, CA 90248 United States
efrank1@lausd.k12.ca.us
http://www.lausd.k12.ca.us

BUS: High Quality Educational Facility **P/S:** Enriching Primary and Secondary Level Schooling for Students in the Community including General Studies, Arts, Language, Music, Physical Education, Special Education and After-School Programs **MA:** Regional **D/D/R:** Teaching and Improving the Lifestyle of Special Education Students, Leading Conferences, Mentoring and Networking with Other Special Education Teachers, Resourcing the Latest Advancements for Student Body Educators **H/I/S:** Reading, Traveling, Sports **EDU:** Master's Degree in Special Education, University of Illinois (1973) **A/A/S:** National Association for the Advancement of Colored People; Los Angeles Unit other Resources; UTLA; CARS

DEBORAH A. MOODY
Wedding Consultant
Bronze Bouquet Wedding Consulting and Event Planning
122 Destry Court
San Jose, CA 95136 United States
info@bronzebouquet.com
http://www.bronzebouquet.com

BUS: Wedding Consultations **P/S:** Wedding Consulting Service **MA:** Local **CERTS:** Certified Wedding Consultant, Association of Certified Professional Wedding Consultants **A/A/S:** Association of Certified Professional Wedding Consultants; Association for Wedding Professionals International **C/VW:** Local Church **H/O:** The highlight of her career was receiving full certification.

NOELEEN M. MOOHAN
Director of Patient Care Services
Radiology
New York Presbyterian Hospital
97 Eton Road
Bronxville, NY 10708 United States
moohann@nyp.org
http://www.nyp.org

NewYork-Presbyterian
The University Hospital of Columbia and Cornell

BUS: Hospital **P/S:** Healthcare Including Special Care to the Newborns, Comprehensive Primary Care, Complex Cardiothoracic Surgery **MA:** Regional **EXP:** Ms. Moohan's expertise is in medical-surgical nursing, intensive care nursing, INR, IR and general radiology nursing. **H/I/S:** Hiking, Sewing, Dancing, Interior Decorating, Gardening **FBP:** Journal of AHRA; Journal of Radiological Nursing: American Journal of Nursing **EDU:** Pursuing Master of Science in Nursing; Coursework in Medical-Surgical Nursing, Neurology Module, American Nurses Association (1988); Associate Degree in Nursing, Royal City of Dublin Hospital, School of Nursing (1984) **CERTS:** Certification in Basic and Advanced Cardiac Life Support (2004); Certification in Intravenous Therapy (1993); Certified Critical Care Nurse, American Nurses Association (1987); Certification in Respiratory Therapy, American Nurses Association **A/A/S:** Radiological Society of North America; American Healthcare Radiology Administrators **DOB:** December 26, 1960 **W/H:** IR and INR Manager, General Radiology Nurse Manager, New York Presbyterian Hospital (1998-2005); Patient Care Coordinator, Interventional Neuroradiology Department (1994-1998); Patient Care Coordinator, Nuclear Cardiology Department, Columbia University Medical Center (1992-1993); Staff Nurse, Telemetry, Intensive Care and Cardiac Care Units, Lawrence Hospital (1987-1993); Staff Nurse, Neurosurgical Unit, Emergency Room, St. Barnabas Hospital (1985-1986); Staff Nurse, Cardiothoracic Unit, Royal City of Dublin Hospital, Ireland (1984-1985)

SHARON ELIZABETH MOON
Speech-Language Pathologist
Special Kids in Pre-School
2101 Sixth Avenue
Rock Island, IL 61201 United States
semoon@mchsi.com
http://www.cambridgewhoswho.com

BUS: Speech-Language Pathology for Developmentally Delayed Children **P/S:** Speech-Language Pathology **MA:** Local **D/D/R:** Speech-Language Pathology for Developmentally Delayed Pre-Schoolers and Augmentative Communication **H/I/S:** Reading, Tennis and Church **FBP:** ASHA Journal; Augmentative Communication **EDU:** Master's Degree, Western Illinois University **A/A/S:** QCSHA; American Speech-Language Hearing Association **C/VW:** American Cancer Society; American Heart Association; United Way of America; American Lung Association **A/S:** She attributes her success to her passion for her profession. **B/I:** She became involved in her profession because of the needs of her family. **H/O:** The highlight of her career has been finding every child's ability to communicate.

CHERYL D. MOORE
Technical Consultant MT
Trover Foundation/Regional Medical Center
900 Hospital Drive
Madisonville, KY 42431 United States
cdmoore@trover.org
http://www.cambridgewhoswho.com

BUS: Medical Services **P/S:** Hospital and Clinic Labs **MA:** Local **D/D/R:** Overseeing Laboratory Services and the Blood Bank **H/I/S:** Reading **FBP:** Industry Related Publications **EDU:** Master's Degree in Management, Oakland City University **C/VW:** Church **A/S:** She attributes her personal and professional success to God and her supportive family and mentors. **B/I:** She has always had an interest in medicine, particularly in Biology.

DONNA MOORE, MA, BS
Teacher
Winters High School
603 N. Height Street
Winters, TX 79567 United States
djtmoore@verizon.net
http://www.cambridgewhoswho.com

BUS: Elementary School **P/S:** Highest Quality of Educational Services to Students from Ninth to Twelfth-Grade Including Programs for After-School Activities **MA:** Local **D/D/R:** Teaching Special Education and Reading to Students in Ninth through Twelfth-Grade, Working with Intellectually Deficient Students, Speaking Proficiently **H/I/S:** Reading, Working on Cross Stitch Patterns, Crocheting **EDU:** Doctor of Education in Teacher Leadership, Walden University (2008); Master of Art Degree in Education and Reading, University of Texas (2003); Bachelor's Degree in Education (1987) **A/A/S:** International Reading Association; Association for Supervision and Curriculum Development

EVELYN M. MOORE, M.ED.
Reading Coordinator
Accelerated Interdisciplinary Academy
12825 Summit Ridge
Houston, TX 77085 United States
emm-july@houston.rr.com
http://www.cambridgewhoswho.com

BUS: Proven Leader in the Education Industry **P/S:** High Quality Educational Services to Students **MA:** Local **D/D/R:** Reading Coordinator, Phonics, Building a Strong Foundation for Reading, Testing for All Students in Kindergarten through Fifth-Grade **H/I/S:** Movies, Sewing, Listening to Books on Tapes **FBP:** Reading Teacher **EDU:** Master of Education in Reading Curriculum and Instruction, University of Houston; Bachelor of Business Administration, Philander Smith College **A/A/S:** International Reading Association; Urban League; Pan Atlantic Council

JOYCE DARLENE MOORE
Medical Transcriptionist
Health Information Management Department
Kosciusko Community Hospital
2101 E. Dubois Drive
Warsaw, IN 46580 United States
djmoore@rtcol.com
http://www.cambridgewhoswho.com

BUS: Hospital **P/S:** Healthcare **MA:** Regional **EXP:** Ms. Moore's expertise is in medical transcription. **H/I/S:** Genealogy, Reading, Attending the Church, Writing a Local Newspaper Column **CERTS:** Industry-Related Training **A/A/S:** Chief Transcriptionist, Kosciusko Community Hospital, Warsaw, IN **C/VW:** Local Church; Shop with a Cop; Vietnam Veterans; Polycystic Kidney Disease Foundation **DOB:** April 24, 1950 **POB:** Rochester, IN **SP:** Charles **CHILD:** Christopher, Colin **W/H:** Medical Transcriptionist, Kosciusko Community Hospital, Warsaw, IN; Medical Transcriptionist, Woodlawn Hospital, Rochester, IN; Medical Transcriptionist, Local Neurology Office; Medical Transcriptionist, General Surgeon; Author, Local Newspaper **A/S:** She attributes her success to her love for people. **H/O:** The highlight of her career was earning her current position.

NETTIE M. MOORE, RN
Registered Nurse
Methodist University Hospital
1300 Wesley Drive
Memphis, TN 38104 United States
nettienellie@bellsouth.net
http://www.cambridgewhoswho.com

BUS: Healthcare **P/S:** Hospital Providing Direct Patient Care **MA:** Regional **D/D/R:** All Aspects of Medical and Surgical Nursing, IV Therapy **H/I/S:** Attending Church Activities, Traveling and Reading **FBP:** Chicken Soul for the Nurse's Soul **EDU:** Associate of Science in Nursing, Southwest Tennessee Community College **A/H:** Nursing Excellence Award, Baptist Memorial Hospital; Top 100 Nurse Excellence in Memphis Nurse Alliance **C/VW:** Middle Baptist Health Ministry, St. Jude Children's Research Hospital **A/S:** She credits her career success to her passion for her career. **B/I:** She wanted to pursue a career in nursing because she loves helping others. **H/O:** She feels that being able to use CPR to restore a person's life is the highlight of her career.

SANDRA F. MOORE, ED.D.
Director of Fully Employed Programs
Pepperdine University, Graziadio School of Business
6100 Center Drive
West Los Angeles, CA 90045 United States
sandra.moore@pepperdine.edu
http://www.pepperdine.edu

BUS: Independent, Medium-Sized University **P/S:** Comprehensive Undergraduate and Graduate Curriculum **MA:** Regional **D/D/R:** Organizational Management **H/I/S:** Exercising, Fitness **FBP:** Journal of Management **EDU:** Doctor of Education in Organizational Leadership, Pepperdine University, Graduate School of Education (2007) **A/A/S:** Beta Gamma Sigma; Pepperdine Alumni Association; Toastmasters International; Former President, Associated Women for Pepperdine

CLARICE M. MOORE-GRANTT
Interventionist
P & C Enterprise
7828 Rogue River Trail
Fort Worth, TX 76137 United States
claricemarlene@sbcglobal.net
http://www.cambridgewhoswho.com

BUS: Counseling, Trainer, Coach **P/S:** Pre-Marital Counseling, Professional Adult Education **MA:** Local **D/D/R:** Consulting **H/I/S:** Studying, Gardening, Reading the Bible, Studying, Research **FBP:** The Master's Advocate; Journal of Psychological Practice; Entrepreneurial Women's Center; Entrepreneur.com **EDU:** Pursuing Ph.D. in Higher Education Leadership, Capella University; Master's Degree in Counseling Psychology, University of Central Texas; Diploma in Advanced Hypnotherapy (2006) **CERTS:** Nationally Certified Psychologist **C/VW:** Closer Walk Home for Homeless Alcohol/Drug Individuals in Fort Worth; Parenting Center **A/S:** She attributes her success to hard work, persistence and a love of learning. **B/I:** She became involved in counseling because she is a natural adviser and has the ability to help people. **H/O:** The most gratifying aspect of her career is working in her current position.

LAWRENCE A. MORA, MD
Physician
Lawrence A. Mora, MD
6221 Wilshire Boulevard
Suite 416
Los Angeles, CA 90048 United States
lawrencemora458@msn.com

BUS: Healthcare Private Practice **P/S:** Family Practice **MA:** Local **D/D/R:** Working as a Practicing Family Physician, Medical Detoxification, Chemical Dependency **FBP:** AMA Journal; AAFP Journal **EDU:** University of New Mexico, University of Texas at Houston, MD, Internship and Residency **A/A/S:** American Academy of Physicians

DEIRDRE D. MORAES
Clinical Trainer
Massachusetts Behavioral Health Partnership
150 Federal Street
Third Floor
Boston, MA 02110 United States
deirdremoraes@yahoo.com
http://www.masspartnership.com

BUS: Behavioral Health Partnership Dedicated to Ensuring Members Receive Clinically Appropriate, High-Quality, Accessible Healthcare **P/S:** Crisis Intervention and Screening, Medication Management, Individual, Group and Family Counseling, Inpatient and Outpatient Services, Substance Abuse Programs, Observation, Detoxification Services **MA:** Regional **D/D/R:** Clinical Social Work in Behavioral Health, Quality Management, Facilitating Software In-Training for New Hires and Large Groups, Writing All Policies and Procedures, Overseeing Semi-Annual Audit Process for Each Employee, Arranging for Continuing Education for Employees **H/I/S:** Working Out, Biking **FBP:** NASW Newsletter **EDU:** Master of Social Work, Boston College, Chestnut Hill (1989) **A/A/S:** American Massage Therapy Association; National Association of Social Workers

ESTER M. MORALES, FACDOL
Commander
Newark Recruiting Company, United States Army
60 Park Place
Suite 204
Newark, NJ 07102 United States
facdol@msn.com
http://www.army.mil

BUS: United States Army Recruiting Station **P/S:** Combat Service Support **MA:** Regional **D/D/R:** Supervising Recruiters, Maintaining Jurisdiction over Six Stations in the Newark Metro Area **H/I/S:** Running, Working Out, Spending Time Outdoors **FBP:** Fitness **EDU:** Bachelor of Science in Biology, Interamerican University, Puerto Rico (1997) **A/A/S:** United States Army

ALISA WOOD MORAN
Teacher
Silver Valley Elementary School
11161 E. Old Highway 64
Lexington, NC 27292 United States
amoran001@triad.rr.com
http://www.cambridgewhoswho.com

BUS: Public School **P/S:** Education **MA:** Local **D/D/R:** Teaching Elementary Education **H/I/S:** Playing the Piano for her Church **EDU:** Bachelor of Arts in Elementary Education, High Point University, Magna Cum Laude **CERTS:** Kindergarten through Sixth-Grade Certification **A/A/S:** National Education Association **A/H:** Teacher of the Year (2003) **B/I:** She became involved in the profession because she wanted to teach. **H/O:** The highlight of her career was being named Teacher of the Year in 2003.

ROSEMARY MORAN, M.ED.
Special Education Teacher
Kofa High School
Yuma Union High School District 70
3100 S. Avenue A
Yuma, AZ 85364 United States
rosiem525@yahoo.com
http://www.cambridgewhoswho.com

BUS: School District **P/S:** Secondary Education **MA:** Regional **EXP:** Ms. Moran's expertise is in teaching special education, English, reading and writing. **D/D/R:** Teaching **H/I/S:** Spending Time with her Family **FBP:** The Atlantic **EDU:** Master of Education in Special Education, Northern Arizona University; Bachelor of Science in General Studies, Gonzaga University **CERTS:** Certified in Special Education, State of Arizona and Washington; Certified Diving Instructor; Certified Reading Specialist **A/A/S:** Council for Exceptional Children; Markums Tae Kwon Do **C/VW:** Boy Scouts of America; Sunday School Teacher **A/S:** She attributes her success to her personal drive and to the support she receives from her son. **H/O:** The most gratifying aspect of her career is helping students and watching them succeed.

Mr. Brett A. Moreau, RN
Registered Nurse, Charge Nurse
Emergency Department, Education Department
Our Lady of Lourdes Regional Medical Center
205 Belle Grove Boulevard
Lafayette, LA 70506 United States
moreaubmsl@aol.com
http://www.lourdes.net

BUS: Faith-Based Medical Center **P/S:** Full-Service Healthcare Facility Accommodating Inpatients and Outpatients in the Community, Including a Diabetes Center, Community Outreach Programs **MA:** Regional **D/D/R:** Nursing, Supervising Eight Registered Nurses Per Shift, Instructing Doctors and Registered Nurses on Advanced Cardiac Life Support **H/I/S:** Hunting, Fishing, Water Sports, Bicycling, Cooking **FBP:** RN; Nursing2009 **EDU:** Bachelor of Science in Nursing, University of Southwestern Louisiana (1984) **CERTS:** Certified Emergency Nurse **A/A/S:** Sigma Theta Tau; Emergency Nurses Association **A/H:** Outstanding Graduate, The University of Southwestern Louisiana (1984) **DOB:** March 13, 1961 **SP:** Myra **CHILD:** Shelly, Logan **W/H:** Registered Nurse, Charge Nurse, Our Lady of Lourdes Regional Medical Center (1982-1984, 1986-Present); Registered Nurse, Doctors Hospital of Opelousas (1985-1986); Registered Nurse, Iberia Medical Center (1984-1985)

Julia N. Moreno
Club Owner
Scorpion Night Club
908 Indiana Avenue
Wichita Falls, TX 76301 United States
justbusiness@hotmail.com
http://www.cambridgewhoswho.com

BUS: Dance Club **P/S:** Entertainment **MA:** Local **D/D/R:** Managing All Aspects of the Club **H/I/S:** Sewing, Gardening, Fishing, Reading, Camping **C/VW:** Church **A/S:** She attributes her success to her determination and support from her family. **B/I:** She became involved in this profession because she always dreamed of being a club owner. **H/O:** The most gratifying aspect of her career is being a successful businesswoman.

MR. DREW T. MORGAN
President
DKM Financial Corp.
219 Mineola Boulevard
Mineola, NY 11501 United States
dkmfinancial@optonline.net
http://www.cambridgewhoswho.com

BUS: Finance **P/S:** Insurance Investments, Financial Advising **MA:** New York, New Jersey **D/D/R:** Wealth Planning **H/I/S:** Spending Time with his Family, Golfing **FBP:** Industry-Related Publications **EDU:** Million Dollar Round Table **A/S:** He attributes his success to his work ethic. **B/I:** He became involved in the profession because he liked working with numbers. **H/O:** The highlight of his career was starting his own company.

KAREN G. MORGAN, RN
Registered Nurse, Community Health Nurse
Burns Paiute Tribe Wadatika Health Center
133 S. Fairview Avenue
Burns, OR 97720 United States
karen.morgan@cwwemail.com
http://www.cambridgewhoswho.com

BUS: Medical Center **P/S:** Healthcare **MA:** Regional **EXP:** Ms. Morgan's expertise is in working for tribes, non-tribes, insurance agents, employees and local doctors, working in a local clinic and public speaking on diabetes, obesity, hypertension and other general issues. **D/D/R:** Lecturing, Public Speaking on Diabetes, Teaching Certified Nursing Assistants **H/I/S:** Attending the Theater, Participating in Choir Activities, Caring for Guide Dogs **FBP:** RN **EDU:** Registered Nurse, Oregon Health & Science University (1963)

MICHELLE K. MORGAN
Teacher
Germantown Elementary
1411 Cedar Park Road
Annapolis, MD 21108 United States
curlymissy200@yahoo.com
http://www.cambridgewhoswho.com

BUS: Education **P/S:** All Aspects of K-5 Education **MA:** Local **D/D/R:** Third-Grade, Axis Program **H/I/S:** Reading, Exercising, and Cooking **EDU:** Master's Degree, Reading Specialist, Loyola College **CERTS:** Certificate in Administration **A/A/S:** National Education Association; Who's Who Among American Educators **A/S:** She attributes her success to her love of children.

FIONA MORGAN-NEWBURY, RN, BSN
Registered Nurse
Meridian Health
1945 Route 33
Neptune, NJ 07753 United States
jfnewbs@optonline.net
http://www.cambridgewhoswho.com

BUS: Hospital **P/S:** Healthcare **MA:** Local **D/D/R:** Medical Intensive Care and Coronary Care **H/I/S:** Spending Time at the Beach, Reading, Exercising **FBP:** Nursing and Allied Health Research Guide; Sigma Theta Tau Publications **EDU:** Bachelor of Science in Nursing, Seton Hall University **A/A/S:** Sigma Theta Tau **A/S:** She attributes her success to perseverance and loving what she does. **H/O:** The highlight of her career was becoming a member of Sigma Theta Tau.

JOHN F. MORIGEAU
Equipment Operator
Flathead Irrigation
http://www.cambridgewhoswho.com

BUS: Irrigation Service **P/S:** Water Delivery **MA:** National **D/D/R:** Maintaining the Irrigational Canal, Excavations **H/I/S:** Hiking, Fishing, Horseback Riding **C/VW:** American Cancer Society **A/S:** He attributes his success to his father and his bosses. **B/I:** He became involved in his current profession because his grandfather was in the industry. **H/O:** The highlight of his career is excelling in his profession.

C. STEVE MORRIS
Technical Training Specialist
Eastman Kodak Health Group
6200 Tennyson Parkway
Plano, TX 75024 United States
cstevemorris@aol.com
http://www.cambridgewhoswho.com

BUS: Healthcare Education **P/S:** Health Imaging, Dry View X-Ray Laser Imaging **MA:** Southwest United States **D/D/R:** Training, Development and Presentation **H/I/S:** Helping Extended Family with Computer Questions and Problems, Building Computers and Networks **EDU:** Coursework in Mathematics and Physics, University of Texas at El Paso **CERTS:** Certified in CompTIA CTT+ **A/A/S:** American Society for Training and Development **C/VW:** River Parks Authority in Tulsa, Oklahoma **A/S:** He attributes his success to his ability to present the material he is teaching in an entertaining way. **B/I:** After being selected for a training position at a previous job he found that he had a talent for it and continued to pursue his career in training. **H/O:** The highlight of her career was working in his position at American Airlines where he created a virtual tour of the facilities by accessing the security camera feeds and putting them into the presentation.

VERNITA TRINNETTE MORRIS
National Professional Development Manager
Leapfrog Schoolhouse
6401 Hollis Street
Suite 100
Emeryville, CA 94608 United States
tmorris@leapfrog.com
http://www.leapfrog.com

BUS: Leading Designer, Developer and Marketer of Innovative, Technology-Based Educational Products and Related Proprietary Content **P/S:** Products that will Provide the most Engaging, Effective Learning Experience for All Ages **MA:** National **D/D/R:** Professionally Developing Schools, Businesses and Struggling Leaders, Overseeing a Staff of 55, Speaking at National Conferences and Presentations **H/I/S:** Cooking, Traveling, Shopping, Fishing, Reading **EDU:** Ph.D. in Organizational Leadership (2007); Master's Degree in Educational Leadership, Nova Eastern University (2004) **A/A/S:** Association for Supervision and Curriculum Development (ASCD); National Education Association (NEA); IRA

DONALD MORRISON, MSGT.
Broker, Realtor
Morrison Property Management LLC & US1 Realty
591 T. Johnson Road
Carthage, NC 28327 United States
morrisonpm@esc.wireless.com
http://www.us1realty.com

BUS: Property Management and RE Sales **P/S:** Real Estate **MA:** Pinehurst/Southern Pines/Aberdeen/Moore Co **D/D/R:** Realtor, Broker, Relocation Services for Residential (Homes/Houses) Land, Commercial Re in Moore Co **H/I/S:** Spending Time with the Family and Pets, Hiking, Walking, Camping **FBP:** The Wall Street Journal **EDU:** Associate of Applied Science in Aviation Operations; Associate of Applied Science in Avionic Systems Technical Southern College **C/VW:** Kiwanis Club Member **A/S:** She attributes her success to honesty and enjoying working with people.

MARGUERITE MORRISON
Director
M and F Morrison
84 Gosselin Road
Manchester, NH 03103 United States
http://www.cambridgewhoswho.com

BUS: Retail, Distribution of Nutritional Products **P/S:** Shaklee Nutritional Products **MA:** Local **D/D/R:** Wellness Nutritional Products **H/I/S:** Bicycling, Conducting Nutritional Research, Spending Time with her Family and Grandchildren **FBP:** Shaklee Newsletter **EDU:** Industry Related Experience **CERTS:** Dietary Consultant Certification **A/S:** She attributes her career success to her ability to represent a high-quality product from Shaklee.

LIZ MORROW
Sales Associate
Century 21 Lois Laur Realty Redlands Office
1998 Orange Tree Lane
Redlands, CA 92374 United States
lizmorrow@loislauer.com
http://www.loislaver.com

BUS: Real Estate **P/S:** Representing Clients **MA:** San Bernardino and Riverside Counties **D/D/R:** Helping Clients Purchase or Sell Homes **H/I/S:** Traveling, Snorkeling, Scuba Diving, Bicycling **FBP:** Century 21 Newsletter **EDU:** Associate Degree, San Bernardino College; Registered Nurse, San Bernardino College **A/A/S:** Soroptomist International; San Bernardino Assistant League **C/VW:** Tree Designer for Santa Claus Inc. **A/S:** She attributes her success to being optimistic and continually trying to succeed. **B/I:** She became involved in this profession because she loves looking at property and helping people. **H/O:** The highlight of her career was finding a million dollar home for a buyer.

DIANE M. MORSE
Project Manager
First Data Corporation
10910 Mill Valley Road
Omaha, NE 68154 United States
diane.morse@firstdatacorp.com
dianemorse@cot.net
http://www.firstdatacorp.com

BUS: e-Commerce Company **P/S:** Credit Card Processing and Financial Transactions **MA:** International **D/D/R:** Overseeing New Business Start-Ups, Managing Business with Certain Centers Moving to Other Countries, Offering Outsourcing, Opening International Call Centers, Processing Visa and MasterCard Transactions, Facilitating Electronic Commerce, Overseeing Contracts with the Treasury Department **EDU:** College Coursework

WALDRON A. MOSBY, SPHR
Senior Human Resource Representative
Entergy Operations, Inc.
7003 Bald Hill Road
Port Gibson, MS 39150 United States
wmosby@entergy.com
http://www.entergy.com

BUS: Energy Firm **P/S:** Producing and Distributing Electric Power **MA:** MS, LA, AR, TX, NY, VT and MA **D/D/R:** Managing Employee Relations, Quality Assurance and Control, Overseeing Human Resource Generalists Functions and Employees **H/I/S:** Golfing, Reading, Hunting, Fishing, Traveling **FBP:** HR; DiversityInc; Nuclear Plant Journal **EDU:** Bachelor of Science in Mechanical Engineering Technology, Southern University and A&M College (1984) **CERTS:** Certified Senior Professional in Human Resources (2006)

MONICA MOSES
Executive Director of Product Innovation
Star Tribune
425 Portland Avenue
Minneapolis, MN 55488 United States
mmoses@startribune.com
http://www.startribune/monicamoses.com

BUS: Publishing **P/S:** News and Information Products **MA:** Regional **D/D/R:** Charge Leadership, Innovation and Design **H/I/S:** Reading, Painting **FBP:** BusinessWeek; The Economist; The Week **EDU:** Master of Arts Degree, Communications, University of Minnesota **A/A/S:** New Media Federation; Newspaper Association of America **C/VW:** Person to Person; United Way of America **A/S:** She attributes her success to having a great work ethic, loving a good challenge and having the ability to make people consider challenging questions. **B/I:** She became involved in her profession because she was interested in what the media industry had to offer and enjoyed the challenge involved in the profession. **H/O:** The highlight of her career has been obtaining her current position at the Star Tribune.

HAROLD D. MOSS
Correctional Sergeant
Shawangunk Correctional Facility
New York State Department of Correctional Services
PO Box 700
Wallkill, NY 12589 United States
harold.moss@cwwemail.com
http://www.cambridgewhoswho.com

BUS: Governmental Agency **P/S:** Correctional Services **MA:** New York **EXP:** Mr. Moss' expertise is in security management, critical incident stress debriefings and consulting. **D/D/R:** Overseeing Other Correctional Officers and All of the Inmates, Managing the Emergency Response Team and the Blood Emergency Response Team, Critical Incident Stress Debriefings and Consulting on the Employee Assistance Program Committee **H/I/S:** Collecting Antique Classic Cars, Hunting, Gardening **EDU:** College Coursework in Labor Relations, Mohawk Valley Community College, Utica College **CERTS:** Certified Correctional Officer, American Correctional Association; Certification, American Correctional Association **A/A/S:** American Correctional Association; Corrections and Youth Services Association; Corrections Emergency Response Team **C/VW:** COPS Care; Former Volunteer, Scout Leader, Boy Scouts of America; Volunteer Fireman; Former Member, Election of Union Steward **POB:** Ilion, NY **A/S:** He attributes his success to the support he receives from his supervisors and co-workers.

KAREN MOULDER
Owner, Operator, Breeder
Ambleside Farm, LLC
469 South Street
Middletown Springs, VT 05757 United States
ambleside@vermontel.net
http://www.freewebs.com/amblesidefarmvt

BUS: Ranch **P/S:** Breeding Sport Horses Including American Warmbloods, North American Llamas, Labrador Retrievers and Exotic Birds **MA:** National **EXP:** Ms. Moulder's expertise is in instructing horseback riding. **D/D/R:** Breeding Horses and Other Exotic Animals **H/I/S:** Riding Horses, Skiing **FBP:** Equus; Practical Horseman; Dressage Today **EDU:** College Coursework, United States; College Coursework, Bermuda **A/A/S:** Green Mountain Horse Association; Professional Horsemen's Association of America; ESEF; ESDF; CVDA **DOB:** May 18, 1949 **SP:** Andrew **CHILD:** Deirdre, Jamison, Travis, Jared, Sidley, Zoe **W/H:** Owner, Operator, Breeder, Ambleside Farm; Equine Reproduction Specialist, Dr. Sherilyn Allen, VMD, PA; Assistant, Dr. Nancy Brown, Plymouth Veterinary Hospital, PA; Barn Manager, Riding Instructor, Here and There Farm, Spring House, PA; Veterinarian Technician, Dr. E. Barclay Rile, VMD, Blue Bell, PA; Freelance Accountant; Accounting Officer, Butterfield Fund Services, Bermuda; Curator, Bermuda Society of Arts, City Hall, Hamilton, Bermuda; Choreographer, Bermuda; Serendipity Stores, Hamilton, St. George, Bermuda **A/S:** She attributes her success to her caring nature for animals and her ability to select the best characteristics of animals for breeding. **B/I:** She became involved in her profession because of her on-site training from veterinarian Dr. E. Barclay Rile in 1973, who had a legacy of horseman skills to his credits. **H/O:** The most gratifying aspect of her career is watching the birth and development of a newborn foal.

KRISTINA G. MOZSARY
Residential Real Estate Broker, Investment Advisor
Kristina Mozsary Real Estate
1630 N. Main Street
Walnut Creek, CA 94596 United States
kmozsary@gmail.com
http://www.cambridgewhoswho.com

BUS: Real Estate **P/S:** Real Estate **MA:** Local **D/D/R:** Residential Properties **H/I/S:** Traveling, Learning About New Cultures **EDU:** Bachelor's Degree in Molecular Biology, San Francisco University **C/VW:** Disabled American Veterans **A/S:** She attributes her success to her hard work and determination.

BARBARA J. MUELLER
President
Mueller Therapy, Inc.
N546 Schroeter Drive
Random Lake, WI 53075 United States
cbmueller11@juno.com
http://www.cambridgewhoswho.com

BUS: Therapy Center **P/S:** Rehabilitation Services **MA:** Regional **EXP:** Ms. Mueller's expertise is in occupational therapy and staff oversight. **H/I/S:** Boating, Spending Time with her Family **FBP:** AOPT Journal **EDU:** Bachelor's Degree in Science, Mount Mary College (1988) **A/A/S:** Wisconsin Occupational Therapy Association; American Occupational Therapy Association **SP:** Charles **CHILD:** Krista, Carli, Nicholas

BEVERLY MUHAMMAD
Executive Assistant
Union County College
Union, NJ 07083 United States
evictoria5@aol.com
http://www.ucc.edu

BUS: College **P/S:** Higher Education Including Courses in Allied Health Services, Biology, Business, Chemistry, Economics, Government, History, English, Fine Arts, Modern Languages, Mathematics, Nursing and Medical Affiliates, Physics, Engineering, Technology, Practical Nursing, Psychology and Sociology **MA:** Local **D/D/R:** Working as a Departmental Webmaster, Coordinating Projects, Conducting Meetings, Planning, Researching, Updating Software, Scheduling Staff **H/I/S:** Gardening, Playing Football **FBP:** The Chronicle of Higher Education **EDU:** Bachelor of Arts in Business Administration, Bloomfield College, NJ (1973) **CERTS:** Certified Notary Public **A/A/S:** National Notary Association

MR. ROBERT J. MULLEN
Senior Pastor, Motivational Speaker
Word of Life Ministries
5038 E. Washington Street
Stockton, CA 95215 United States
wotwfm@aol.com
http://www.churchofstockton.com

BUS: Church **P/S:** Religious Services, Life Development Compact Discs, Consultations, Christian Education **MA:** International **D/D/R:** Offering Spiritual and Life Consulting Services, Helping and Educating Individuals to Reach their Potential, Encouraging and Motivating People in the Ministry **H/I/S:** Golfing, Playing Football and Baseball **EDU:** Bachelor of Arts, Bible College, San Bernardino; Associate of Arts, Bible College, San Bernardino **A/S:** He attributes his success to his faith in God and the support he receives from his wife.

BOBBIE G. MULLINS
School Nurse, Parish Nurse (Retired)
http://www.cambridgewhoswho.com

BUS: Nursing **P/S:** Church and Community Nursing **MA:** Local **D/D/R:** Senior and Teen Healthcare **H/I/S:** Singing in a Choir, Reading **FBP:** Ebony; Jet; Essence **EDU:** Certified Operating Room Technician **C/VW:** Local Church **A/S:** She attributes her success to her desire to help people. **B/I:** She became involved in the profession because she had a strong desire to help others.

MYRNA N. MUMM, PH.D.
Speech Language Pathologist
Columbus Public Schools
321 E. State Street
Columbus, OH 43215 United States
mmumm7607@wowway.com
http://www.cambridgewhoswho.com

BUS: Public Schools **P/S:** Providing Special Education in Public School for Prekindergarten Through Twelfth Grade **MA:** Local **D/D/R:** Diagnostic Service in Speech and Language Disorders, Major Interest in Autistic Children **FBP:** American Speech-Language Association Journal **EDU:** Ph.D. in Speech and Language, Ohio State University **CERTS:** Certification in Principal, Superintendent, and Supervisor in Special Education **A/A/S:** American Speech and Hearing Association; Ohio Speech and Hearing Association; School Speech and Hearing Association **C/VW:** President, Ohio State University Women's Club **A/S:** She attributes her career success to her love of attending school, and to her fascination with the field of education. **B/I:** She has wanted to be a teaching since the career was recommended to her by a friend as a child.

MR. FELIX R. MUNIZ JR., MBA
Investment Professional
New York Life Insurance Company
116 Laurens Street S.W.
Aiken, SC 29801 United States
frmunizjr@yahoo.com
http://www.newyorklife.com

BUS: Insurance Company **P/S:** Insurance Services Including Investment Strategy, Insurance and Financial Planning Services **MA:** National **EXP:** Mr. Muniz's expertise is in asset allocation, protection planning, employee and tax benefits, tax reduction strategies, private medical practices, business protection issues, asset management and deferred compensation. **H/I/S:** Playing the Bass Guitar, Golfing, Spending Time with his Wife, Reading, Caring for his Pet Dogs **FBP:** The Wall Street Journal; Barron's; Advisor Today; Round Table Review **EDU:** Master of Business Administration, University of Phoenix; Bachelor's Degree in Biology and Chemistry, Minor in Economics, University of Illinois **CERTS:** Certified Financial Planner; Certified Option Trader **A/A/S:** Million Dollar Round Table; Latin American Chamber of Commerce; Hitchcock Foundation; Greater Aiken Chamber of Commerce, SC **A/H:** Mutual Fund Sales Leader (2008); President's Council of New York Life Insurance Company (2007); Member of Annuity Champion Program, New York Life Insurance Company (2007) **C/VW:** Volunteer, Translator, Local Charitable Organizations; Habitat for Humanity

MS. MARY F. MUNOZ, RN
President, Registered Nurse, Massage Therapist
Massage and Nutrition Center
631 E. Sunset Avenue
Santa Maria, CA 93454 United States
marynoz45@aol.com
http://www.cambridgewhoswho.com

BUS: Healthcare Center **P/S:** Wellness, Healing and Therapeutic Services **MA:** National **EXP:** Ms. Munoz' expertise is in nutritional consulting and performing massage therapy. **D/D/R:** Using Emotional Freedom, Aromatherapy and Supplementation Health Techniques **H/I/S:** Gardening, Cooking, Traveling, Sewing, Crocheting, Interior Decorating, Golfing **FBP:** Massage and Bodywork **CERTS:** Certification in Clinical Nutrition (2007); Certification in Humanistic Psychology, American Institute of Holistic Health and Wellness (2006); Training Course Graduate, Women's Economic Ventures, Santa Barbara County (1998); Registered Nurse, Metropolitan School of Nursing, Ontario, Canada (1967) **A/A/S:** Alliance Institute for Integrative Medicine (2006); American Holistic Nurses Association **A/S:** She attributes her success to the support she receives from Dr. Lester Bryman.

DOUGLAS B. MURDOCK
Lead Medic
First Care (previously Devine EMS)
1195 Parrish Avenue
Hamilton, OH 45011 United States
triad@fuse.net

BUS: Healthcare EMS **P/S:** Medical Transport **MA:** Local **D/D/R:** Medical Administration **H/I/S:** Reading Sci-Fi, Swimming, Home Improvement **FBP:** EMS Magazine **CERTS:** Nationally Registered Paramedic, Licensed and Certified **A/A/S:** YMCA, Deacon Baptist Church

MS. DAWN A. MURPHY
President
Western Mass Environmental, LLC
PO Box 1295
16 Ponders Hollow Road
Westfield, MA 01086 United States
dawnm@westernmassenv.com
http://www.westernmassenv.com

BUS: Environmental Construction Service Company **P/S:** Environmental Contracting, Emergency Response, Hazardous Waste Clean Up **MA:** Regional **D/D/R:** Human Resources, Account Managing Accounts Payable, Accounts Receivable, Invoicing, Collections **H/I/S:** Camping, Riding Motorcycles **EDU:** High School **C/VW:** DARE, Mothers Against Drunk Driving **A/S:** She attributes her success to working together with her husband to start the business. **H/O:** The highlight of her career was starting and running her business with her husband.

GAIL ANN MURPHY, RN, BSN
Registered Nurse, BSN, RN II
Carilion Roanoke Memorial Hospital
PO Box 13727
Roanoke, VA 24036 United States
gailmurphy@hotmail.com
http://www.cambridgewhoswho.com

BUS: Hospital **P/S:** Healthcare **MA:** Regional **D/D/R:** Specializing in Cardiac Critical Care, Psychiatric Nursing and Vascular Intensive Care, Caring for Patients with Serious Vascular Disease and Conditions, Abdominal Aorta Aneurysms, Carotid Diseases, Surgeries, Ruptured Aneurysms, Amputations Due to Vascular Diseases **H/I/S:** Scuba Diving, Traveling **EDU:** Bachelor of Science in Nursing, Jefferson College of Health Sciences; Associate of Science Degree **CERTS:** Certified in Advanced Cardiac Life Support; Certified in Basic Life Support **C/VW:** Board Review Program; CAT Program; The Sara Program **B/I:** She became involved in her profession because she wanted to be a nurse since eighth-grade. **H/O:** The most gratifying aspect of her career is helping others.

Patti Murphy
Realtor
Davis & Davis Associates
6151 Fair Oaks Boulevard
Carmichael, CA 95608 United States
pmurphy9@sbcglobal.net
http://www.cambridgewhoswho.com

BUS: Real Estate **P/S:** Residential and Commercial Sales and Leasing **MA:** Local **D/D/R:** Sales and Retail, Office Leasing, Real Estate **H/I/S:** Boating, Sports Events, Wine Tasting, Softball, Traveling **FBP:** Success Magazine; Comstock **EDU:** Industry Related Training and Experience, Army Reserves **A/A/S:** National Association of Realtors; Carmichael Association of Realtors **C/VW:** Great Race; Timberlake Association; March of Dimes; Susan G. Komen Breast Cancer Foundation **A/S:** She attributes her success to persistence. **B/I:** She was prompted to enter her profession because she enjoys a challenge. **H/O:** The highlight of her career is accomplishing her goals.

Michelle Murphy-Rozanski, Ph.D.c, MSN, RN
Ph.Dc, MSN, RN, Certified Registered Nurse Practitioner
Temple Health System Northeastern Hospital School of Nursing
2301 E. Allegheny Avenue
Philadelphia, PA 19114 United States
mmurphy822@aol.com
http://www.cambridgewhoswho.com

BUS: Healthcare **P/S:** Teaching Emergency Medicine **MA:** Local **D/D/R:** Clinical Care, Critical-Care Nursing Instruction **FBP:** Industry Related Publications **EDU:** Ph.D.c, Educational Leadership, Drexel University; Master of Science in Nursing, Hahnemann University; Bachelor of Science in Nursing, Hahnemann University; Associate of Science in Nursing, Hahnemann University **CERTS:** Certified Registered Nurse Practitioner **A/A/S:** Sigma Theta Tau; American Nurses Association **A/S:** She attributes her success to determination, support and education. **B/I:** She became involved in her profession because she always wanted to be in the medical field. **H/O:** The highlight of her career has been becoming a leader in her field.

MR. TROY C. MURRAY
Facilities Manager
The Hartford
One Park Place
300 S. State Street
Syracuse, NY 13202 United States
tmurray1979@yahoo.com
http://www.tnutz-inc.blogspot.com

BUS: Insurance **P/S:** Fortune 100 Company that Provides All Aspects of Insurance, Including Life, Auto, Short and Long Term Disability, as well as Investment Products. **MA:** International **D/D/R:** Facilities Operations, Support **H/I/S:** Art, Watching Movies, Listening to Music, Supporting the NY Mets, Syracuse College Basketball **EDU:** Bachelor's Degree in Graphic Design, SUNY Oswego**A/A/S:** Sigma Chi Fraternity, Kappa Nu Chapter **A/H:** Perfect Attendance Award for all 4 years of High School **C/VW:** Ronald McDonald House Charity **A/S:** He attributes his success to hard work, and good work ethics.**H/O:** The highlight of his career in excelling in his current position, as Facilities Manager.

VIVIAN R. MURRAY-TILLER
Certified Nursing Assistant
vivmrrytll@earthlink.net
http://www.cambridgewhoswho.com

BUS: Healthcare **P/S:** Healthcare **MA:** Local **D/D/R:** Residents **H/I/S:** Sports **EDU:** Extensive Industry Related Training and Experience **A/A/S:** American Nurses Association **A/S:** She attributes her success to her mother. **B/I:** She became involved in her profession because she always had an interest in the medical field.

Ms. Danielle S. Musumeci
Project Engineer
Blach Construction Company
469 El Camino Real, Suite 120
Santa Clara, CA 95050 United States
danielle.musumeci@blach.com
http://www.blach.com

BUS: Construction Company **P/S:** Project Management, General Contracting **MA:** Local **EXP:** Ms. Musumeci's expertise is in budget management and client relations. **H/I/S:** Professional, Modern and Jazz Dancing, Instructing Color Guard **FBP:** Civil Engineer **EDU:** Master's Degree in Engineering Management, Santa Clara University; Bachelor's Degree in Civil Engineering, Santa Clara University **CERTS:** Engineering Training Certificate **A/A/S:** American Society of Civil Engineers; U.S. Green Building Council

Karara Muwanjiku Muhoro
Researcher
USA Kenya Scientific Research Organization
854 W. Glenway Drive, Apartment 9
Inglewood, CA 90302 United States
kmuwanjiku@netzero.com
http://www.cambridgewhoswho.com

BUS: Research Organization **P/S:** Deoxyribonucleic Acid Research **EXP:** Mr. Muwanjiku Muhoro's expertise is in deoxyribonucleic acid research breakthrough in physical chemistry. **D/D/R:** Researching on Physical Chemistry Including Nuclear Magnetic Resonance and Spectroscopy **H/I/S:** Jogging, Exercising, Listening to Classical Music, Writing **EDU:** Master of Science in Chemistry, California State University, Los Angeles **A/A/S:** Screen Actors Guild; American Chemical Society **I/F/Y:** In five years, Mr. Muwanjiku Muhoro hopes to pursue his Ph.D. and plans to present his research to the National Institute of Health.

ALICE M. MYERS
Clinical Education Specialist
Burdette Tomlin Memorial Hospital
2 Stone Harbor Boulevard
Cape May Court House, NJ 08210 United States
amyersrnmsn@verizon.net
http://www.cambridgewhoswho.com

BUS: Nonprofit Hospital **P/S:** Acute Care Healthcare **MA:** Local **D/D/R:** Clinical Education **H/I/S:** Spending Time with the Family, Crocheting **FBP:** Sigma Theta Tau Publications **EDU:** Master of Science in Nursing, University of South Alabama; Bachelor of Science in Nursing, University of Delaware, Magna Cum Laude **A/A/S:** Sigma Theta Tau; Association of Women's Health, Obstetric and Neonatal Nurses; American Nurses Association; South Jersey Nurses Association **C/VW:** New Jersey Workforce Initiative Program; Mentoring Nursing Students **A/S:** She attributes her success to her ability to create trust and build on the patients' strengths. **B/I:** She became involved in her profession because she had always wanted to be a nurse. **H/O:** The highlight of her career was mentoring graduate nurses and seeing them succeed.

LINDA S. MYERS
Assistant Vice President Branch Manager, Senior Escrow Officer
First American Title Insurance
475 E. Cottonwood Lane
Casa Grande, AZ 85222 United States
lmyers@firstam.com
http://www.firstam.com

BUS: Finance Company **P/S:** Escrow and Title Settlement Services **MA:** National **EXP:** Ms. Myers' expertise is in utilizing first American title insurance. **D/D/R:** Managing Buyer and Seller Transactions in any Denomination **H/I/S:** Hiking, Walking, Reading Spiritual Magazines, Biking **EDU:** High School Diploma **A/A/S:** Elks Lodge; American Cancer Society; Rotary Association; Escrow Association **A/H:** Top Fund-Raiser Award, March of Dimes, Pinal County

MR. WILLIAM KEVIN MYLES
Global Converting Technology Owner
Family Care
The Procter & Gamble Company
6105 Center Hill Avenue, Box M4
Cincinnati, OH 45224 United States
myleswk@netscape.net
http://www.pg.com

BUS: Dynamic Global Company which Provides Branded Products and Services of Superior Quality and Value that Improve the Lives of the World's Consumers **P/S:** Consumer Packaged Goods, Research and Development, Personal and Beauty Products, House and Home Products, Health and Wellness Products **MA:** International **D/D/R:** Engineering, Capacity Engineering, Managing Controls and Information Systems **H/I/S:** Running, Listening to Music, Stamp Collecting **FBP:** Black Enterprise; Kiplinger's Personal Finance **EDU:** Bachelor's Degree in Electrical Engineering, Purdue University **A/A/S:** National Society for Black Engineers; SPE; EIT **DOB:** June 30, 1973 **SP:** Keiya **CHILD:** Keyanna

MRS. TRACEY G. MYRICK
Clinical Trials Administrator
Comprehensive Care Center, Clinical Studies Unit
University of Alabama at Birmingham
2001 Third Avenue S., Suite 301
Birmingham, AL 35233 United States
tracey.myrick@ccc.uab.edu
http://www.ccc.uab.edu

BUS: University, Cancer Information and Research Center **P/S:** Caring for Cancer Patients, Diagnosis, Treatment and Prevention of Cancer **MA:** International **EXP:** Mrs. Myrick's expertise is in regulatory, quality control and data management. **D/D/R:** Overseeing Regulatory Submission of Cooperative Group Clinical Trials Presented to the Institutional Review Board for Approval, Managing Data, Supervising Eight, Clinical Trials as a Specialist, Monitoring Quality Assurance of Institutional Research Studies, Collecting Information of Patients Participating in Oncology and Hematology Clinical Trials, Utilizing Good Clinical Practice Guidelines and Regulations **H/I/S:** Traveling, Bowling, Making Crafts **FBP:** The Monitor **CERTS:** Certified Clinical Research Professional (1996) **A/A/S:** Central Alabama Chapter, Association of Clinical Research Professionals; Society of Clinical Research Associates; Association of Clinical Research Professionals **C/VW:** Order of the Eastern Star **DOB:** March 1, 1964 **POB:** Columbus, OH **SP:** Daniel **W/H:** Clinical Trials Administrator, Project Coordinator, Coordinator of Data Collection, Carraway Methodist Medical Center, Cancer Center (1992-1997); Data Coordinator, Comprehensive Cancer Center, Clinical Studies Unit, University of Alabama at Birmingham (1985-1992); Comprehensive Cancer Center, Clinical Studies Unit, University of Alabama at Birmingham; Data Collections Coordinator, Copy Manager

DIANA K. NACKORD, RN III, CEN
Registered Nurse III, Certified Emergency Nurse
Doctors Medical Center
Florida Avenue
Modesto, CA 95382 United States
ditzybird007@yahoo.com
http://www.dmc-modesto.com

BUS: One of the Largest Full-Care Hospitals in the Central Valley, Licensed for 398 Beds **P/S:** California Cancer Center, California Neurological Sciences Center, Central California Diabetes Center, Central California Heart Center, Emergency and Trauma Services and Transport, Nuclear Medicine, Pediatrics, Stanislaus Family Medicine Residency Program, Women and Children's Center **MA:** Local **D/D/R:** Caring for Patients Including Critical Care, Trauma, Emergency Medicine, Advanced Cardiac Life Support, Pediatric Advanced Life Support, Basic Life Support, Hazardous Material, Precepting **H/I/S:** Traveling, Golfing, Gardening, Music **FBP:** RN; American Journal of Nursing; Advance Nursing; Nurses Week **EDU:** Associate Degree, Modesto Junior College (1985) **CERTS:** Trauma Nursing Course Certified; Emergency Nursing Pediatric Coursework; Certified Emergency Nurse **A/A/S:** Emergency Nurses Association; Professional Women's Club; HAZMAT Team, Medical Center; Program with Fire Department and Staff, Trained on Procedures

MR. PAUL A. NALIWAJEK
Equipment Manager, Process Improvement and Support
American Red Cross
825 John Street
West Henrietta, NY 14586 United States
naliwajekp@usa.redcross.org
http://www.donatebloodnow.org

BUS: Nonprofit Charitable Organization **P/S:** Blood Services, Emergency Preparedness Training and Assistance, Emergency Crisis Care, Youth Services, Community Services **MA:** International **EXP:** Mr. Naliwajek's expertise is in process improvement and equipment management. **D/D/R:** Overseeing Process Improvement and Support, Starting a Completely Eco-Friendly Bed and Breakfast and Educational Facility Catering to Retired Individuals Wishing to Learn more about Green Buildings **H/I/S:** Classic Cars **FBP:** BusinessWeek **EDU:** Industry-Related Training and Experience; Coursework in Electronics; High School Education **A/A/S:** Former Member Brockport Kiwanis **C/VW:** American Red Cross Disaster Service Volunteer

LINDA J. NAPIER
Registered Nurse
University of New Mexico Hospital
2211 Lomas
Albuquerque, NM 97106 United States
ljnapier@att.net
http://www.cambridgewhoswho.com

BUS: Healthcare **P/S:** Hospital Healthcare **MA:** New Mexico, Arizona **D/D/R:** Emergency, Labor and Delivery Nursing, Training, Cardiac **H/I/S:** Spending Time with the Family, Quilting, Stained Glass, Porcelain Dolls **FBP:** Emergency Room Nurses; Labor and Delivery **EDU:** Bachelor of Science in Nursing, University of New Mexico; Pursuing Master of Science in Nursing, University of New Mexico **CERTS:** Certified Trauma Nurse; Certified Emergency Room Nurse; Certified in Pediatric Advanced Life Support; Certified in Adult Cardiac Life Support; Certified in Neonatal Resuscitation; Certified Basic Life Support Instructor **C/VW:** Church **A/S:** She attributes her success to family support. **B/I:** She was prompted to enter her profession because she always wanted to be a nurse. **H/O:** The highlight of her career is the daily reward of making a difference in the life of a patient and their families.

ROSEANN NAPOLITAN
Strategic Resources Manager
Novelis Corporation
6060 Parkland Boulevard
Mayfield Heights, OH 44124 United States
roseann.Napolitan@novelis.com
http://www.cambridgewhoswho.com

BUS: Manufacturing **P/S:** Rolled Can Sheet Aluminum, Metal Fabrication Conversion **MA:** International **D/D/R:** Financial Analysis and Procurement **H/I/S:** Gardening, Making Home Improvements **FBP:** Fraud Magazine; The Wall Street Journal **EDU:** Bachelor's Degree in Accounting, Youngstown State University **CERTS:** Certified in Management Accounting, Institute of Management in Accountants; Registered Financial Consultant, Kaplan College **A/A/S:** CMA; RFC

Lynda Nardone-Dabrowski, RN, BSN, LN
Risk Manager, Healthcare
Maryland Medicine Comprehensive Insurance Program
11 S. Paca Street
Suite 200
Baltimore, MD 21201 United States
legalnurselynn.1@juno.com
http://www.cambridgewhoswho.com

BUS: Healthcare, Medical-Acute Care, Legal Medical Malpractice **P/S:** Risk Management, Professional Liability, Physician Med-Mal, Nursing **MA:** Statewide **D/D/R:** Legal Nurse Consultant, Nursing **H/I/S:** Cross Country Skiing, Dancing, Spending Time with her Four Children **FBP:** Harvard Business Review; New England Journal of Medicine **EDU:** Bachelor of Science in Nursing, University of Maryland; Advanced Practice Degree in Legal Nurse Consulting, Minor in Paralegal Studies, Kaplan College; Registered Nurse, State of Maryland and California **A/A/S:** American Association of Legal Nurse Consultants; Delta Epsilon Tau; American Society of Health Care Risk Management **C/VW:** St. Jude Children's Research Hospital; St. Joseph's Parish; Feed the Children **A/S:** She attributes her success to her hard work, dedication, constant positive attitude and her continuing education. **B/I:** She became involved in this profession because healthcare and medicine have always been interesting to her and she had the opportunity to receive training as a teenager. **H/O:** The highlight of her career was when she had to stop working in 2001 to care for various family members and her husband supported her to go back to school.

Jennifer C. Nastri, RN
Registered Nurse
Connecticut Hospice
100 Double Beach Road
Branford, CT 06417 United States
blsm44@aol.com
http://www.hospice.com

BUS: Hospice **P/S:** Setting the National Standard for Home and Inpatient Hospice Care and Nursing, Serving Anyone in Need Regardless of Ability to Pay, Providing Care that Empowers the Dying to Live their Final Days in Dignity and Comfort **MA:** Regional **D/D/R:** Specializing in Geriatrics, Giving Patients their Daily Medications, Fulfilling the Day-To-Day Needs of the Elderly and Disabled with Patience and Compassion **H/I/S:** Basketball, Church **FBP:** American Journal of Nursing **EDU:** Registered Nurse, Hospital of St. Raphael of New Haven (1975) **A/H:** Teacher of the Year Award, Wal-Mart

John P. Naughton, MD

Professor and Interim Chairman Interim Chair,
Dept of Physical Medicine and Rehabilitation
University at Buffalo-School of
Medical and Bio Medical Sciences
3435 Main Street, Room 128, Farber Hall
Buffalo, NY 14214 United States
jpn@buffalo.edu • http://www.smbs.buffalo.edu

BUS: Educational Facility, College, Medical School **P/S:** Teaching, Advising and Career Preparation **MA:** Regional **D/D/R:** Helping Patients Return to Work, Started Field of Cardiac Rehabilitation, Performance Physiology, Served as Dean and President of Health Sciences **H/I/S:** Swimming, Jogging and Exercise **EDU:** MD, University of Oklahoma (1958); Residency, University of Oklahoma and George Washington University **A/A/S:** Fellow, American College of Physicians; Fellow, American College of Cardiology

Gloria E. Nazario

Teacher
Plainview Elementary School
10819 Plainview Avenue
Tujunga, CA 91042 United States
gnazar2@lausd.net
http://www.lausd.k12.ca.us

BUS: Public Elementary School **P/S:** Elementary Education **MA:** Local **D/D/R:** Teaching Technology **H/I/S:** Reading, Traveling **FBP:** Edutopia; The Journal of Computer Assisted Learning **EDU:** Master of Arts in Education and Technology, Pepperdine University **A/A/S:** National Education Association; California Teachers Association; International Society for Technology in Education; Computer-Using Educators, Inc.; Chair, United Teachers of Los Angeles **C/VW:** Feed the Children; Operation HOPE

ANGELA V. NEALE, CNT
Nursing Technician
Mount Washington Pediatric Hospital
1708 W. Rogers Avenue
Baltimore, MD 21209 United States
e.neale24@yahoo.com
http://www.cambridgewhoswho.com

BUS: Hospital **P/S:** Healthcare **MA:** Local **D/D/R:** Nursing **H/I/S:** Traveling, Reading, Swimming **EDU:** Pursuing Associate Degree in Nursing, Catonsville Community College **CERTS:** Certified Nurse Technician, Howard Community College **C/VW:** Volunteers at Nursing Home; University of Maryland Hospital Volunteer **A/S:** She attributes her success to her desire to help people. **B/I:** She chose the profession because she wanted to help others.

SUSAN J. NEEL
Director of Electric Market Operations
Center Point Energy
1111 Louisiana Street
Houston, TX 77002 United States
susan.neel@centerpointenergy.com
http://www.centerpointenergy.com

BUS: One of the Nation's Largest Combined Electricity and Natural Gas Delivery Companies with Approximately 5 Million Metered Electric and Natural Gas Customers **P/S:** Pipeline Operations, Power Delivery Services, Energy Services, Electric Transmission and Distribution, Natural Gas Distribution **MA:** Regional **D/D/R:** Overseeing Electric TCU Transaction Management, E-Commerce, Retail Marketing and Process and System Design, and Risk Management, Resolving Credit Issues, Teaching 'Electric 101' at the Electric Liability Council of Texas **H/I/S:** Antiques **FBP:** Forbes **EDU:** Bachelor's Degree in Business Administration, LeTourneau University (2001) **A/A/S:** Alpha Gamma Lambda **C/VW:** United Way of America; March of Dimes; Juvenile Diabetes

JUDITH A. NEILAN, MS, MA
Educator
Pioneer Junior and Senior High School
417 S. Chicago Street
Royal Center, IN 46978 United States
http://www.pioneer.k12.in.us

BUS: Leader in Education **P/S:** High Quality Educational Services for Students **MA:** Regional **D/D/R:** Publications Advisor, Working with Students in Istep Program Student Travel, Teaching English and Journalism, Teaching Writing at Community College, Adjunct Professor at the University of Phoenix and Ivy Tech Community College, Teaching English **H/I/S:** Family Activities, Cooking, Traveling, Reading **FBP:** Education Week **EDU:** Master's Degree in Journalism, Ball State University (1999); Master of Education in French, Minor in English, Indiana State University (1976); Bachelor's Degree in French and German, Indiana State University (1970) **A/A/S:** Indiana High School Press Association; Former President, White County Economic Development Committee; American Association of Teachers of French; Indiana Teachers of Foreign Language; National Scholastic Press Association; Journalism Educators Association; Delta Kappa Gamma; Delta Theta Tau; Deaconess, Monticello Christian Church **A/H:** Journalism Advisor of the Year, Indiana High School Press Association (2005)

BARBARA ANN NELSON, RN, MSN
Nursing Supervisor
Lee Memorial Health System
2676 Cleveland Avenue
Fort Myers, FL 33901 United States
barbaraann.nelson@cwwemail.com
bobbenurse@aol.com
http://www.leememorial.org

BUS: Healthcare Center **P/S:** Healthcare, Rehabilitation Services, Wound Care, Kidney Transplant Surgery, Obstetrics and Treatment for Cardiovascular Diseases, Cancer Treatments, Care for Trauma and Neurological Disorders **MA:** Local **EXP:** Ms. Nelson's area of expertise is in nursing management. **D/D/R:** Overseeing Residential Healthcare, Emergency and Critical Care Nursing **H/I/S:** Sailing, Swimming, Reading **FBP:** Home Healthcare Nurse; American Journal of Nursing **EDU:** Master's Degree in Nursing, The Ohio State University **CERTS:** Certification in CPR; Certified Emergency Nurse **A/A/S:** Cornwallis Association **A/H:** Professional Achievement Award, Barry University; Certificate of Appreciation for the Development of SAFE, Lee Memorial Health System **C/VW:** Susan G. Komen for the Cure; Children's Hospital of Southwest Florida; Cape Coral Police Department **A/S:** She attributes her success to her passion for her profession and her ability to face challenges. **B/I:** She became involved in this profession because she always wanted to be a nurse. **H/O:** The highlight of her career was helping in the development of a rape and sexual assault education center within the hospital called SAFE.

MEREDITH R. NELSON
Financial Administrator
First Baptist Church of Stewart
1831 Palm City Road, C501
Stewart, FL 34994 United States
merrinelson@gmail.com
http://www.cambridgewhoswho.com

BUS: Proven Leader in the Field of Religion and Spiritual Services, Truly Wonderful Congregation Committed to Lives of Lived Faithfulness **P/S:** Quality Religious and Spiritual Services to People **MA:** Regional **D/D/R:** Managing Building, Facilities and Financial Aspects, Accounts Receivable, Accounts Payable **FBP:** NACBA Ledger; Church Law and Tax **EDU:** Graduate, Dublin High School (1973) **A/A/S:** National Association of Church Business Administration

MR. WAYNE M. NELSON, MS
Chief Executive Officer, President
WWBC & Fitness
3022 Hingston Avenue
Egg Harbor Township, NJ 08234 United States
waawb@comcast.net
http://www.cambridgewhoswho.com

BUS: Leading Fitness Facility **P/S:** Fitness and Personal Training, Boxing Conditioning and Training, Published Fitness Book, Fitness DVD Release **MA:** National **D/D/R:** Motivational Speaking, Personal Training, Offering One-On-One Instruction, Boxing Training and Conditioning **H/I/S:** Attending Boxing Competitions, Traveling, Working Out, Coaching **FBP:** Men's Health; Men's Fitness; AAH-PERD; Referee **EDU:** Master of Science in Criminal Justice, Kennedy Western University (1996) **A/A/S:** American College of Christian Counselors; American College of Sports Medicine **H/O:** The highlight of his career was winning the 2005 Ringside World Amateur Boxing Championship (Master Division) at 201 lbs.

SHARON R. NELSON-LONG
Educator
Tice Elementary School
The School District of Lee County
4524 Tice Street
Fort Meyers, FL 33905 United States
smlcats@embarkmail.com
http://www.lee.k12.fl.us/schools/tic

BUS: Elementary School **P/S:** Education **MA:** Regional **EXP:** Ms. Nelson-Long's expertise is in teaching mathematics, reading and exceptional student education. **D/D/R:** Working with Learning and Speech Disability Students **H/I/S:** Sports **FBP:** International Reading Association Publications **EDU:** Master's Degree in Elementary Reading Diagnosis, Eastern Illinois University (1981); Bachelor of Science in Education, Eastern Illinois University **A/A/S:** Teaching Association of Lee County; National Education Association; International Reading Association; Delta Kappa Gamma

JOYCE A. NERDIG
Special Education Teacher
Cartwright School District
3733 N. 75th Avenue
Phoenix, AZ 85033 United States
jnerdig@estr.cartwright.k12.az.us
http://www.estr.cartwright.k12.az.us

BUS: Education **P/S:** Public School System **MA:** Local **D/D/R:** Special Education **H/I/S:** Antiquing, Gardening, Relaxing **EDU:** Bachelor of Science in Elementary Education and Special Education, Culver-Stockton College **A/A/S:** Alpha Delta Kappa **C/VW:** Ronald McDonald House, Mingus Mountain County Academy for Girls, Sojurner Center **A/S:** She attributes her career success to her students and to the challenges she faces and overcomes on a daily basis. **B/I:** She was inspired to pursue a career in special education by a friend of her mother. **H/O:** She feels that being able to work with special education students for as long as she has without burning out is the highlight of her career.

LISA M. NESS, BS
Kindergarten Teacher, ECFE Coordinator and Child Instructor
Rothsay Public School
123 Second Street N.W.
Rothsay, MN 56579 United States
lness@rothsay.k12.mn.us
http://www.rothsay.k12.mn.us

BUS: Education **P/S:** Elementary Education **MA:** Local **D/D/R:** Kindergarten Teacher, Early Childhood Education, Elementary Education **H/I/S:** Spending Time with the Family and her Twin Fraternal Boys, Ceramics, Scrapbooking, Reading **FBP:** The Mailbox **EDU:** Bachelor of Science in Elementary Education, Minnesota State University, Morehead, Minnesota **C/VW:** Church and Sunday School **A/S:** She attributes her success to excellent mentors and her network. **B/I:** She became involved in this profession because she always had the goal of being an educator since a young age. **H/O:** The highlight of her career is seeing the children's eyes light up when they understand something.

ELIZABETH M. NETZBAND
Teacher
Waterville Central School District
381 Madison Street
Waterville, NY 13480 United States
enetzband@watervilleschools.org
http://www.watervilleschools.org

BUS: School District **P/S:** Educational Services for Students **MA:** Regional **D/D/R:** Teaching English and Creative Writing, Teaching Advanced Placement English to Eighth-Grade Students **H/I/S:** Golfing, Traveling, Reading Fiction and Historical Literature **EDU:** Master's Degree in Teaching, Master's Degree in Literature, SUNY Binghamton; Bachelor's Degree in English Literature, SUNY Geneseo **A/A/S:** Daughters of the American Revolution **A/H:** Nominee, Who's Who Among American Teachers

STEVEN K. NEUENSCHWANDER
Realtor
Zip Realty, Inc.
9301 Vancouver Drive N.E.
Lacey, WA 98516 United States
steveneuen@aol.com
http://www.cambridgewhoswho.com

BUS: Real Estate Agency **P/S:** Buying, Selling and Listing Real Estate Services, Home Values, Resale, New Construction, Land, Acreage, Waterfront Homes, Relocation Advice and Assistance **MA:** Western Washington **EXP:** Mr. Neuenschwander's expertise is in residential and waterfront properties exchange, managing property sales and site relocations. **D/D/R:** Working with All Aspects of Residential Sales and Commercial Properties Exchange **H/I/S:** Golfing, Working with the Thurston County Homeless Planning Workgroup, Participating in Charity Golf Events **FBP:** Realtor **EDU:** Associate Degree in Business and Law, International Business College, Fort Wayne, IN; Coursework, Indiana Institute of Technology; Coursework, Vincennes University; Coursework, Community College of the Air Force; Coursework, University of Maryland, Manheim; Coursework, Earned in Germany; Coursework, Seoul, Earned in South Korea **A/A/S:** Thurston County Realtors Association; Christian Real Estate Network; Washington Realtors Association; Veterans of Foreign Wars; American Legion; National Association of Realtors; Veteran, United States Army **W/H:** Veteran, Final Rank E-7, United States Air Force; Magistrate, United States Army; Educator, Claims and Tort Litigation, Air Force Judge Advocate Generals School

LINDA A. NEUMANN, RN, SA
Registered Nurse (Retired), Surgical Assistant
Southwest General Health Center
18697 Bagley Road
Middleburg Heights, OH 44130 United States
x61393@aol.com
http://www.swgeneral.com

BUS: Hospital **P/S:** Healthcare **MA:** Regional **D/D/R:** Obstetric and Gynecological Nursing, Plastic Surgery Nursing, End Surgical Assistance **H/I/S:** Raising African Violets **EDU:** Associate Degree in Surgical Assistant Studies, Cuyahoga Community College; Registered Nurse Diploma, Fairview Park Hospital School of Nursing; Diploma, Parma Senior High School **A/A/S:** Participant, First Laparoscopic Gallbladder Surgery, Southwest General Health Center **B/I:** She became involved in healthcare through her talent and calling for the work. **H/O:** The highlight of her career was participating in the first laparoscopic gallbladder surgery performed at the health center.

MR. DAVID NEWAJ
Chief Architect
County of San Joaquin
24 S. Hunter Street
Room 5
Stockton, CA 95202 United States
dnewaj@sjgov.org
http://www.sjgov.org

BUS: County Government **P/S:** Delivering the Services Mandated by the State and Federal Governments, including Health, Welfare, Criminal Justice, Elections, Recording of Documents, Weights and Measures, Agricultural Enforcement, Infrastructure, Governed by a Five-Member Board of Supervisors that Sets Policy, Enacts Ordinances and Regulations and Oversees Activities of County Departments **MA:** Regional **D/D/R:** Designing Network and Storage Infrastructure, Maintaining Services Functions and Overall Responsibility for All Matters Involving the Network and Storage Infrastructure of the County **H/I/S:** Basketball, Football, Sports **FBP:** BusinessWeek; InformationWeek **EDU:** Bachelor of Arts in Computer Science, California State University at Chico (1985) **A/A/S:** Association for Computing Machinery; Institute of Electrical and Electronics Engineers

ROBYN F. NEWCOMB, RN
Registered Nurse
Carilion Clinic
2013 S. Jefferson Street
Roanoke, VA 24014 United States
rcaldwell@carilion.com
http://www.carilion.com

BUS: Clinic **P/S:** Healthcare, Level One Trauma Care **MA:** Regional **EXP:** Ms. Newcomb's expertise is in radiation oncology, CyberKnife and stereotactic radiosurgery. **D/D/R:** Coordinating and Implementing Treatments with Doctors and Patients, Overseeing Nurses Duties and Medications, Working with All Aspects of Radiation Oncology at the Cancer Center Including 24 People in the Different Units and Four Physicians, Consulting with Other Physicians **H/I/S:** Singing, Making Crafts, Renovating her Home **FBP:** American Journal of Nursing; Journal of Neuroscience **EDU:** Associate Degree in Nursing, West Ark University **CERTS:** Certification in Advanced Cardiac Life Support; Certification in Basic Life Support; Certification in Procedural Sedation **A/A/S:** CyberKnife Society; Virginia Nurses Association; American Nursing Association **C/VW:** Girl Scouts of the United States of America **A/S:** She attributes her success to her will to succeed and passion for her profession. **B/I:** She became involved in her profession because she loves working with people and enjoys taking care of others. **H/O:** The highlight of her career was earning her current position.

MS. CAROL R. NEWMAN
Attorney
cnewman@ffic.com
http://www.cambridgewhoswho.com

BUS: Legal Consulting **P/S:** Consulting on Law and Insurance **MA:** National **D/D/R:** Insurance Regulation and Compliance, Regulating Insurance Policies, Complex Litigating, Conducting Transaction Work, Handling Bankruptcy, Setting Strategic Direction on Asbestos Books, Trying to Eliminate Liability and Maximize Recovery, Playing Regulatory Role, Overseeing Methodology and Execution on Risk Assessments, Studying Emerging Trends **H/I/S:** Reading, Traveling, Spending Time with her Husband and Children **FBP:** Corporate Legal Times **EDU:** JD, University of Illinois (1980) **CERTS:** Licensed Real Estate Broker, State of Illinois and California **A/A/S:** American Bar Association; Illinois Bar Association; California Bar Association; Former Chair on Board of Insurance Regulatory Examiner Society Foundation; Association of Corporate Council **A/H:** Distinguished Graduate Award, University of Illinois College of Law (2003-2004) **SP:** Bradley **CHILD:** Clayton, Spencer, Dylan

MRS. KAREN K. NEWMAN
Histotechnologist (Retired)
10896 Singletree Trail
Dewey, AZ 86327 United States
aknew@commspeed.net
http://www.cambridgewhoswho.com

BUS: Hospital Facility **P/S:** Anesthesia Services, Birthing Center, Cancer Center, Critical Care and Emergency, Nutrition Therapy, Outpatient Center, Patient Relations, Radiology, Rehabilitation Center, Surgical Services, Histology Laboratory, Medical Examinations **MA:** Regional **D/D/R:** Microtoming (Human Tissue Cells), Special Staining, Writing Manuals, Working as a Temporary Technician across the Country **H/I/S:** Reading, Gardening, Traveling **EDU:** Training in Histology, West Nebraska General Hospital, Scottsbluff, NE; Diploma, Bridgeport High School, NE **A/A/S:** Founding President, Arizona Chapter, National Society for Histotechnology **DOB:** September 23, 1939 **SP:** Arthur **CHILD:** Susan, Jeri **W/H:** Maricopa County Medical Examiners Office, Phoenix, AZ; St. Francis Hospital, Wilmington, DE; Yale University, New Haven, CT; Good Samaritan Hospital, Mt. Vernon, IL; St. Luke's Hospital, Sioux City, IA **A/S:** She attributes her success to her parents and her dedication to the field. **B/I:** She became involved in her profession because she always had an interest in the medical field. **H/O:** The most gratifying accomplishment in her career was founding the Arizona chapter of the Society for Histotechnology in the early 1970's.

JAMEY NEWSTED
President
Next Step Strategies, LLC
Muskegon, MI 49444 United States
jnewsted@nextstepstrategies.org
http://www.nextstepstrategies.org

BUS: Leader in Resourcing and Training Churches **P/S:** Making Available All Materials Created and Used in the Church Setting including All Lessons, Devotional Books, and Training Materials **MA:** National **D/D/R:** Developing Middle School and High School Curriculum, Material, and Programming, Training Small Group Leaders, Developing a Small Group Program in the Church **H/I/S:** Football, Softball, Reading ESPN The Magazine **FBP:** Leadership **EDU:** Pursuing Master's Degree in Leadership, Regent University, Virginia Beach **A/A/S:** Pastor, Calvary Church; Football Coach, Fruitport High School; Toastmasters International

IRENE JOHN NGATENA
Registered Nurse
Holy Cross Hospital
1500 Forest Glen Road
Silver Springs, MD 20705 United States
irenejn@hotmail.com
http://www.cambridgewhoswho.com

BUS: Hospital **P/S:** Healthcare **MA:** Local **D/D/R:** Critical Care Nursing, Telemetry, Quality Assurance **H/I/S:** Swimming, Reading **EDU:** Bachelor's Degree in Nursing, University of Maryland **A/S:** She attributes her success to her family. **H/O:** The most gratifying aspect of her career is being able to help others.

MARTHA A. NICHOLS
President
MAGN Ltd. Design
133 Victory Hills
Coatesville, IN 46121 United States
magnltd@yahoo.com
http://www.cambridgewhoswho.com

BUS: Multi-faceted Designs, Interior and Exterior **P/S:** Highest Quality Interior and Exterior Design Services to Clients such as Conceptual Design, and Morganthorn Designs **MA:** Regional **D/D/R:** Conceptual Design, Budgeting, Forecasting for Projects, General Contracting **H/I/S:** Spending Time with the Family, Outdoor Activities **FBP:** Interior Design Journal; Architectural Digest **EDU:** Coursework in Fine Arts, Stephens College and Ohio State University, Cincinnati **A/A/S:** Central Indiana Real Estate Investors Association

KAREN NICHOLSON
Senior Support Specialist
Neptune Technology Group, Inc.
2222 W. Spring Creek Parkway 212
Plano, TX 75023 United States
knicholson@neptunetg.com
http://www.cambridgewhoswho.com

BUS: Leading Provider of Utility Software Automation Systems **P/S:** Service Orders, Meter Reading, Routing, Electric and Gas Utility Groups **MA:** National **D/D/R:** Working in Arcs Software **H/I/S:** Reading **EDU:** Coursework, Indiana Vocational Technical College (1980)

JUNE NICKENS, ES
Convergence Systems Engineer
North American Communication Resource, Inc.
june.nickens@cwwemail.com
http://www.avaya.com

BUS: Telecommunication Company **P/S:** Converged Infrastructure, Intelligent System and Network Management, MultiVantage Communication Services, MultiVantage Telephony Applications, Consulting and Integration, Business Communication Consulting **MA:** National **EXP:** Ms. Nickens' expertise is in network design, implementation and integrated management. **D/D/R:** Configuring Networks for Mid-Range to Large Corporations, Testing Technology for New Applications **H/I/S:** Walking, Weight Lifting, Traveling, Watching Football, Supporting Webster Junior Warriors **EDU:** Pursuing Master's Degree; Bachelor's Degree in Telecommunications, Rochester Institute of Technology **A/A/S:** Secretary of the Board, Webster Junior Warriors Football (2006-2008)

NATALIE NIEKRO-WOOSLEY
Vice President of Marketing and Advertising
Pure Fitness Clubs
1126 N. Scottsdale Road
Tempe, AZ 85281 United States
natalie@purefitnessclubs.com
http://www.purefitnessclubs.com

BUS: Proven Leader Committed to Excellence in the Fitness Industry **P/S:** Quality Certified Training Staff, Fitness Assessment, Personalized Training Program, Equipment including Treadmills, Ellipticals, Cross Trainers, Recumbent Bikes, Lifecycles, Stair Masters, Rowing Machines, Six Complete Lines of Circuit Training Equipment including Hammer Strength, Pre-Cor, Life Fitness, Keiser, Flex and Free Motion **MA:** National **D/D/R:** All Advertising Relating to Logo in Media, Television Commercials, Handling Graphic Design Issues, Marketing and Advertising, Leadership and Strategizing for Growth **H/I/S:** All Sports **FBP:** The Business Journal **EDU:** Bachelor's Degree in Advertising and Psychology, Florida Southern College (1994) **A/A/S:** President, Local Chapter of Leukemia Society; Board Member, John C. Lincoln Hospitals

PATTY A. NIEVEEN, LPN
Licensed Practical Nurse
Bryan LGH Medical Center
2300 S. 16th Street
Lincoln, NE 68502 United States
http://www.cambridgewhoswho.com

BUS: Adolescent Psychiatric Hospital **P/S:** Healthcare **MA:** Nebraska **D/D/R:** Adolescent Psychology **H/I/S:** Spending Time with her Granddaughter, Crossword Puzzles, Reading **FBP:** RN; Relive **CERTS:** Licensed Practical Nurse Diploma, Southeastern Community College **A/H:** Recognized for 35 Years of Service, Bryan LGN Medical Center (2006) **C/VW:** Hospital, Children's Home, American Veterans Associations **A/S:** She attributes her success to her genuine concern for others. **B/I:** She became involved in her profession because she always knew she wanted to be a nurse. **H/O:** The highlight of her career is her current position.

PRACHAYA NITICHAIKULVATANA
Medical Doctor
Bassett Healthcare
1 Atwell Road
Cooperstown, NY 13326 United States
oakni@yahoo.com
http://www.cambridgewhoswho.com

BUS: Hospital **P/S:** Healthcare **MA:** Local **D/D/R:** Internal Medicine **H/I/S:** Playing Tennis, Kayaking **EDU:** MD, Earned in Thailand; Master's Degree in Dermatology, Boston University **A/A/S:** American Medical Association; American College of Physicians **A/S:** She attributes her success to her family, for supporting her through medical school, and to her good mentors. **B/I:** She became involved in her profession to eventually bring her knowledge of American medicine back to her home country of Thailand. **H/O:** The most gratifying aspect of her career is being affiliated with a large hospital.

BARBARA NOËL, DO
Physician
William F. Ryan Health Center
110 W. 97th Street
New York, NY 10025 United States
yes2noel@hotmail.com
http://www.cambridgewhoswho.com

BUS: Healthcare **P/S:** Quality Care and Support for Patients **MA:** Statewide **D/D/R:** Obstetrics and Gynecology, Prenatal Care, Patient Education, Gynecological Surgery **H/I/S:** Traveling, Playing Tennis, Dancing **FBP:** New England Journal of Medicine **EDU:** Doctor of Osteopathic Medicine, New York College of Osteopathic Medicine **A/A/S:** American Medical Association; American Osteopathy Association; American Congress of Obstetrics and Gynecology **C/VW:** World Medical Mission **A/S:** She attributes her success to the very good mentors that inspired her. **B/I:** She became involved in her profession because she loves helping others. **H/O:** The highlight of her career was being able to practice medicine.

TRACY E. NOLAN
Chief Wireless Operations Officer, Senior Vice President
ACN, Inc.
13620 Reese Boulevard E.
Building XII, Suite 400
Huntersville, NC 28078 United States
tracyenolan@yahoo.com
http://www.acninc.com

BUS: Telecommunication Company **P/S:** Telecommunications Products and Services Including Digital Phone, Local Calling, Long Distance, Wireless Services, High Speed Internet and Satellite Television **EXP:** Ms. Nolan's expertise is in operations management. **D/D/R:** Overseeing Employee Development, Business Strategy and Company-To-Company Partnership Development, Setting Strategic Directions **H/I/S:** Playing Water Sports, Making Crafts, Spending Time with her Friends, Volunteering **FBP:** Wireless Week; The Wall Street Journal; IT **EDU:** Bachelor of Science in Marketing Research and Management Information Systems, Clarkson University (1986) **A/H:** 40 Under 40 Most Influential Executives; Today's Young Executives

BRIDGET M. NORE, RN, BSN
1) Registered Nurse Specialist 2) Jewelry Consultant
1) Good Samaritan Hospital 2) Premier Designs
10 E. 31st Street
Kearney, NE 68847 United States
noreb1@rcom-ne.com
http://www.premierdesigns.com

BUS: 1) Regional Medical Center with an Excellent Trauma Center 2) Jewelry **P/S:** 1) Healthcare Services 2) Direct Sales **MA:** 1) Local 2) International **D/D/R:** Wound Care, Ostomy and Continence Nursing, Nurse Education, Selling Fashion Accessories **FBP:** Journal of Wound Care; Ostomy and Continence Nursing **EDU:** Bachelor of Science in Nursing, University of Nebraska Medical Center **A/A/S:** Wound, Ostomy and Continence Nurses Society **C/VW:** American Cancer Society; Veterans of America; St. Jude Children's Research Hospital; United Way of America

BRIDGET D. NORMAN-MALME, MD, FACOG
Physician
Kaiser Permanente
7373 W. Lane
Stockton, CA 95210 United States
brdgdwnrn@yahoo.com
http://www.cambridgewhoswho.com

BUS: Nonprofit Healthcare Organization **P/S:** Healthcare **MA:** National **EXP:** Ms. Norman's expertise is in obstetrics and gynecology. **D/D/R:** Performing Obstetrics and Gynecological Examinations **H/I/S:** Traveling, Listening to Music, Playing the Piano, Spending Time Outdoors, Hiking, Biking **FBP:** JAMA **EDU:** MD, University of California, Davis; Bachelor of Arts in Human Biology, Stanford University **CERTS:** Diplomate, American College of Obstetricians and Gynecologists **A/A/S:** Fellow, American College of Obstetricians and Gynecologists; American Medical Association; Canadian Medical Association **C/VW:** Southern Poverty Law Center **A/S:** She attributes her success to her high self-esteem and determination. **B/I:** She became involved in her profession because of her interests in science, psychology and sociology. **H/O:** The highlight of her career was completing the board diplomate fellowship.

MR. BENJAMIN P. NORRIS
Case Manager, Youth Specialist
BPN Development Solutions, Wedgwood Christian Services
3580 Burton Ridge Road S.E. Apartment J
Grand Rapids, MI 49546 United States
benjamin.norris@yahoo.com
http://www.bpndevelopmentsolutions.com

BUS: Private Franchising **P/S:** Entrepreneurship, Leadership, Business Consultant, Mentoring, Counseling, Social Work **MA:** International **D/D/R:** Business Development, Mentoring, Teaching Life Skills, Case Management **H/I/S:** Reading, Traveling, Mentoring **FBP:** Business 2.0; Forbes **EDU:** Bachelor's Degree in Psychology, Hope College **A/A/S:** Psi Chi Honor Society; National Scholars Honor Society; International Scholar Laureate Program; Wedgwood Christian Services; Children International **A/H:** National Dean's List (2002-2005); Chancellor's List (2004-2005); Psi Chi Regional Research Award (2004, 2005); Hope Sigma Xi Senior Research Award; Leadership Honors Bootcamp

FRANCES D. NORRIS
Realtor
RE/MAX International, Inc.
2333-A W. March Lane
Stockton, CA 95207 United States
francesnorris@remax.net
http://www.remaxrealestate.com

BUS: Real Estate Company **P/S:** Residential and Commercial Real Estate Exchange Including Real Estate Investment and Relocation Services **MA:** International **D/D/R:** Managing Residential, Commercial and Relocation Real Estate **H/I/S:** Traveling, Collecting Antiques, Spending Time with her Family, Cooking **FBP:** Realtor; Real Estate; Property Lines **EDU:** Master's Degree in Curriculum and Instruction, University of the Pacific; Bachelor's Degree in Education, University of the Pacific **CERTS:** Licensed Real Estate Agent, State of California **A/A/S:** Central Valley Association of Realtors; California Association of Realtors; National Association of Realtors **C/VW:** Breast Cancer Foundation, RE/MAX **A/S:** She attributes her success to her energy, love for her profession, and people management skills. **B/I:** She became involved in her profession because she always had an interest in real estate and decided to pursue her career in real estate after her retirement from teaching. **H/O:** The highlight of her career was tripling her production in her second year.

HANNAH E. NORTON, RN
Registered Nurse
Lakeland Healthcare
31 N. St. Joseph Avenue
Niles, MI 49120 United States
hephzibah83@juno.com
http://www.lakelandhealth.org

BUS: Hospital **P/S:** High-Quality, Customer-Oriented, Compassionate Health-Related Services **MA:** Southwestern Michigan **EXP:** Ms. Norton's expertise is in obstetrics nursing and labor and delivery. **H/I/S:** Participating in Outdoor Activities, Camping, Rock Climbing **EDU:** Associate Degree in Nursing, Lake Michigan College **A/H:** Berrien County Medical Society Scholarship; DAR Scholarship; LMC Divisional Health Science Scholarship **C/VW:** World Gospel Mission **DOB:** December 10, 1983 **SP:** Jared **A/S:** She attributes her success to her faith in Jesus Christ as her Lord and Savior as well as support from her family. **B/I:** She became involved in this profession because she was reading the biography of Dr. Ida Scutter, who practiced in India, and it prompted her to get into the medical field. **H/O:** The highlight of her career was passing the state boards and receiving her nursing license.

JUDITH FLETCHER NORWOOD, RN, BS
Registered Nurse, Senior Cosmetologist
Sinai Hospital
2401 W. Belvedere Avenue
Baltimore, MD 21158 United States
d.c.norwood@worldnet.att.net
http://www.cambridgewhoswho.com

BUS: Trauma Hospital **P/S:** Healthcare **MA:** Regional **D/D/R:** Operating Room Nursing **H/I/S:** Reading, Playing the Guitar and Piano **FBP:** Advance for Nurses; Nursing Spectrum; American Journal of Nursing **EDU:** Bachelor of Science in Nutrition, Stafford University; Registered Nurse, Mountain Sanitarium School of Nursing (1963) **CERTS:** Certified in Swedish Massage; Certified Bodywrap Technician; Advanced Cardiac Life Support, Fletcher, North Carolina **A/A/S:** Association of perioperative Registered Nurses **C/VW:** Seventh-Day Adventist Church; American Diabetes Association; American Heart Association; Nursing Homes; Local Church; Mission Program; Sponsors a Child in India **A/S:** She attributes her success to her hard work, desire to help others and to growing up with good values. **H/O:** The most gratifying aspect of her career is reaching her goals and making people happy.

DONNA NOTO
Realtor
Ebby Halliday
1201 W. Green Oaks
Arlington, TX 76013 United States
donnanoto@ebby.com
http://www.ebby.com

BUS: Real Estate Agency **P/S:** Real Estate **MA:** Dallas and Fort Worth Metroplex **D/D/R:** Handling Residential Home Sales Valued at $250,000 and Above **H/I/S:** Traveling, Shopping, Participating in Church Activities, Attending her Daughter's Cheerleading Competitions **FBP:** Realtor **EDU:** Bachelor of Science in Education, University of North Texas (1985) **A/A/S:** Arlington Board of Realtors; Texas Association of Realtors; National Association of Realtors; Arlington Women's Connection; Arlington Chamber of Commerce **A/H:** Miss Texas Hemisphere (1982); National Twirling Champion (1981); Platinum Achiever, Diamond Circle **C/VW:** Focus on the Family; St. Paul Lutheran Church; Katrina Victims; American Red Cross; Arlington Night Shelter; Disabled Veterans; Toys for Tots; Boys and Girls Club; Junior League; Sponsor, Guatemalan Child; Texas Real Estate Political Action Committee; Smile Club; Ft. Worth City Club; Arlington Museum Society **A/S:** She attributes her success to her business ethics, integrity and discipline. **B/I:** She became involved in this profession because her father was in real estate. **H/O:** The most gratifying aspect of her career is managing her own team.

DAVID K. NOVICK, PH.D.
Department Head
Science
Gann Academy, The New Jewish High School of Greater Boston
333 Forest Street
Waltham, MA 02452 United States
dnovick@gannacademy.org
http://www.gannacademy.org

BUS: High School **P/S:** Secondary Education **MA:** Local **EXP:** Mr. Novick's expertise is in biology and science instruction. **D/D/R:** Supervising and Developing the Science Curriculum, Maintaining the Science Facility, Supervising and Mentoring Science Teachers **H/I/S:** Spending Time with his Family, Teaching **FBP:** Science; Educational Leadership; NSTA Journals; Scientific American **EDU:** Ph.D. in Biology, Tufts University; Bachelor of Science in Biology, Union College, with Honors **A/A/S:** National Science Teachers Association; National Association of Biology Teachers; American Association for the Advancement of Science; Association for Supervision and Curriculum Development; Sigma Xi **A/H:** Lemelson-MIT InvenTeam Grant Recipient (2007-2008); Excite Award Teacher, Massachusetts Institute of Technology (2007); Tufts Service Citation Award (1995) **A/S:** He attributes his success to his commitment, education, passion for science and people management skills. **B/I:** He became involved in his profession because of his experience in teaching biology. **H/O:** The most gratifying aspect of his career is making an impact on students' lives.

JULIANA M. NOWAK
Consultant Pharmacist
Magee-Women's Hospital
301 Halket Street
Pittsburgh, PA 15213 United States
jjcnowak@aol.com
http://www.cambridgewhoswho.com

BUS: Full-Service Women's Hospital Recently Expanded to Include a Range of Services to Men and Women **P/S:** Comprehensive Medical-Surgical Care to the People of Western Pennsylvania and the Surrounding Region **MA:** Local **D/D/R:** Practicing Geriatric Medicine, Working with Long-Term Patients, Reviewing Charts, Training New Nurses **H/I/S:** Reading, Traveling, Gardening, Spending Time with her Pets **EDU:** Bachelor's Degree in Pharmacy **A/A/S:** Board of Directors, Allegheny County Pharmaceutical Association; American Society of Consultant Pharmacists **C/VW:** Local Catholic Grade School

STEPHENYE ANGELIC NOYLES-BURNETT
Registered Nurse
Health Care Services
State of California
630 Bercut Drive
Sacramento, CA 95814 United States
casualocks2021@sbcglobal.net
http://www.cambridgewhoswho.com

BUS: Public Health Care Provider **P/S:** Licensure and Certification of Nurses, Health Care Management Programs **MA:** Statewide **EXP:** Ms. Noyles-Burnett's expertise is in patient advocacy. **D/D/R:** Evaluating Nurses, Overseeing Health Facilities **H/I/S:** Shopping for Real Estate Properties **FBP:** American Journal of Nursing **EDU:** Pursuing Master's Degree in Family Practice, University of Phoenix; Bachelor of Science in Nursing, Loma Linda University Adventist Health Sciences Center **A/H:** The Award of Perseverance, United States Army **A/S:** She attributes her success to her supportive and loving family. **B/I:** She became involved in her profession because she wanted a stable job that would allow her to make a difference in people's lives. **H/O:** The most gratifying aspect of her career is knowing that her hard work placed her in her current position.

VIRGINIA E. NUSS
Owner
East Coast Signs and Designs
476 Sheephill Road
Newmanstown, PA 17073 United States
vnuss@comcast.net
http://www.cambridgewhoswho.com

BUS: Vinyl Graphics **P/S:** Business Truck Lettering and Design **MA:** Local **D/D/R:** Creating Vinyl Graphics, Signs **H/I/S:** Traveling, Reading **FBP:** SignCraft Magazine **EDU:** Extensive Industry Related Training and Experience **C/VW:** Mount Etna Bible Church; Donates Projects to the Foundation for Keri Martin; Youth for Christ **A/S:** She attributes her success to her constant drive to improve the quality of work. **B/I:** She became involved in her profession because her experience in manufacturing. **H/O:** The highlight of her career is owning her own business.

NANCY E. NYHUS
Drama Teacher
Hamilton Middle School
8600 E. Dartmouth Avenue
Denver, CO 80231 United States
nancy_nyhus@dpsk12.org
http://www.cambridgewhoswho.com

BUS: Middle School **P/S:** Education **MA:** Regional **EXP:** Ms. Nyhus' expertise is in the implementation of drama and theater movement techniques. **D/D/R:** Creating and Teaching Theater Courses to Sixth through Eighth-Grade Students **H/I/S:** Cycling, Reading, Participating in Community Theatre **FBP:** Dramatics **EDU:** Master's Degree in Aesthetic Education, University of Denver (1997) **A/A/S:** Colorado International Teachers Exchange League; Educational Theatre Association; Alliance For Colorado Theatre **A/H:** Elementary Level Theatre Teacher of the Year (2005) **C/VW:** Volunteer Reader for the Blind and Dyslexic, Rocky Mountain Center **DOB:** October 19, 1967 **POB:** Denver, CO **W/H:** Fifth Grade Teacher; Elementary Theater Teacher; Middle School Theater **A/S:** She attributes her success to the support she receives from her coworkers. **H/O:** The most gratifying aspect of her career is watching the faces of her student actors during a curtain call. **I/F/Y:** In five years, Ms. Nyhus intends to continue teaching.

KATHLEEN O'CONNELL
School Counselor, Addictions Counselor,
Licensed Alcohol and Drug Counselor
Storey County School District
PO Box C
Virginia City, NV 89440 United States
windsongserenity@yahoo.com
http://www.storey.k12.nv.us

BUS: School District **P/S:** Education Including Alcohol Drug Addiction Counseling Services **MA:** Regional **EXP:** Ms. O'Connell's expertise is in alcohol and drug abuse counseling. **D/D/R:** Counseling on Conflict Resolution and Anger Management for School Students **H/I/S:** Gardening, Walking, Meditating **FBP:** American Journal of Psychotherapy **EDU:** Master's Degree in Counseling, University of Nevada (1979) **CERTS:** Certified Counselor, American Board of Professional Counselors **A/A/S:** Diplomat, American Psychotherapy Association

ERIN REBECCA O'DELL
Senior Logistics Specialist
Global Component Repair Services
Rolls-Royce Corporation
2001 S. Tibbs Avenue
Indianapolis, IN 46241 United States
eo007@aol.com
http://www.rolls-royce.com

BUS: Power Systems Manufacturer **P/S:** Aerospace Systems, Civil and Defense Aerospace, Marine, Energy **MA:** International **D/D/R:** Specializing in Logistics, Helping Customers **H/I/S:** Reading, Traveling, Volunteering **EDU:** Master's Degree in Communications, Purdue University (2000); Bachelor of Arts in Communications, Purdue University (1993) **A/A/S:** Association for Women in Communications; Purdue Alumni **C/VW:** Make A Wish Foundation; The Humane Society of the United States **A/S:** She attributes her success to her drive and motivation. **B/I:** She became involved in the profession because was presented with a good opportunity. **H/O:** The highlight of her career was earning her current position.

KAY W. O'DONNELL, BSN
Clinical Resource Manager
Forum-Health Trumbull Memorial Hospital
1350 E. Market Street
Warren, OH 44483 United States
http://www.forumhealth.org

BUS: Hospital **P/S:** Healthcare **MA:** Regional **D/D/R:** Caring for Patients, Medical-Surgical Nursing **H/I/S:** Hiking, Painting **EDU:** Bachelor of Science in Nursing, The Pennsylvania State University **C/VW:** American Cancer Society **A/S:** She attributes her success to the fact that she remains current in her field, enjoying the clinical and managerial atmospheres. **B/I:** She became involved in her profession because she wanted to be a nurse. **H/O:** The most gratifying aspect of her career was being a surgical practitioner assistant, because it gave her the experience and knowledge to be successful.

PATRICK J. O'GRADY
Assistant Service Manager
Henderson Chevrolet
240 N. Gibson Road
Henderson, NV 89014 United States
pat@hendersonchevy.com
http://www.hendersonchevy.com

BUS: Automotive Company **P/S:** High Quality Professional New Automotive Sales and Services, Warranties, Parts and Accessories **MA:** Regional **D/D/R:** Managing Operations, Overseeing Administrative Duties, Processing Payroll, Supervising Staff, Ensuring Customer Satisfaction and Hiring **H/I/S:** Playing the Drums, Golfing **EDU:** Coursework in Electrical Engineering; High School Diploma **CERTS:** Certified Master Technician, National Institute for Automotive Service Excellence **A/A/S:** Chevrolet Master Technician, Advisory Council (1997) **A/H:** Platinum Award, Automotive Advanced Engine Performance Specialist, GM Mark of Excellence; Award, GM Service Challenge; GM Top 50 CSI Positive Impact **DOB:** November 14, 1962 **SP:** Mary **CHILD:** Kristyn, Stephen **W/H:** Valley Park Motors, CA; Canoga Park Motors, CA; Findlay Oldsmobile, Inc; Findlay Subaru Henderson, NV; Henderson Chevrolet, Henderson, NV; Team Leader for 6 Technicians; Shop Foreman; Assistant Service Manager

RYAN S. O'LEARY
Senior Research Scientist
Personnel Decisions Research Institutes, Inc.
1300 N. 17th Street
Suite 100
Arlington, VA 22209 United States
ryan.oleary@pdri.com
http://www.pdri.com

BUS: Premier Research and Consulting Firm in the Field of Industrial and Organizational Psychology **P/S:** Designs, Develops, and Implements Human Resource Systems Based Upon Recent Advances in the Behavioral Sciences and the Highest Principles of Professional Practice, Consulting Services **MA:** National **D/D/R:** Selection and Performance Management, Human Resource Consulting Services, Leadership Training **H/I/S:** Golfing, Skiing **FBP:** Harvard Business Review; Journal of Applied Psychology **EDU:** Ph.D. in Industrial Psychology from Auburn University (2004); Master of Science in Industrial Psychology, Auburn University (2001); Bachelor of Science in Psychology, Emory University (1998) **A/A/S:** APA; APS; SIOP; PTCMW

MISS ALEXIS D. O'NEIL
Specialty Sales Representative
North Pacific Group, Inc.
287 S. Main Street
Concord, NH 03301 United States
aoneil@northpacific.com
lexydanielle@hotmail.com
http://www.northpacific.com

BUS: Distribution Company **P/S:** Wholesale Distribution of Specialty Products Including DriCore Sub Flooring Systems, Hardwood Lumber, Vortec House Wrap, JM Insulation, Bluwood, CertainTeed's Fiber Cement Siding, Restoration Millwork and Panorama Railing **MA:** North Shore Boston, Pittsburgh, New Hampshire **EXP:** Miss O'Neil's expertise is in securing sales and ensuring customer satisfaction. **H/I/S:** Traveling, Skiing, Boating **FBP:** Green Builder; The Journal of Light Construction **EDU:** Bachelor's Degree in Communications and Management, Keene State College **C/VW:** Make-A-Wish; American Cancer Society **A/S:** She attributes her success to her ability to be an asset to a great company, her organizational skills, detail-oriented nature, knowledge about her product lines and to her positive attitude. **B/I:** She became involved in her profession because of the experience she gained by selling radio along with her friend Selene Telles. **H/O:** The highlight of her career was working on the Extreme Makeover: Home Edition Project 514 in Manchester, New Hampshire. **I/F/Y:** In five years, Miss O'Neil hopes to be in a higher management position.

Teresa M. O'Neill

Senior Research Specialist, Quality Assurance
University of Illinois at Chicago, Toxicology Research Laboratory
808 S. Wood Street
M/C 868
Chicago, IL 60612 United States
toneill1@uic.edu
http://www.uic.edu/labs/tox/trlt.html

BUS: Good Laboratory Practices Pre-Clinical Contract Laboratory **P/S:** Pharmacology and Toxicology Research **MA:** Regional **D/D/R:** Specializing in Quality Assurance, Research and Toxicology **H/I/S:** Reading, Traveling **FBP:** Quality Assurance Journal **EDU:** Bachelor of Science in Biology, University of St. Francis (1984) **A/A/S:** Society of Quality Assurance; Midwest Chapter; Affiliate Member, Society of Quality Assurance

Patricia A. O'Rourke

Director, Retail Service Center
Tiffany & Company
15 Sylvan Way
Parsippany, NJ 07054 United States
patricia.orourke@tiffany.com
http://www.tiffany.com

BUS: Retail Store **P/S:** Jewelry, Diamonds, Watches, Crystal, Gifts and Accessories, Wedding Registry, Business Gifts **MA:** International **D/D/R:** Specializing in Distribution **H/I/S:** Traveling, Reading **FBP:** Women's Wear Daily **EDU:** Master of Business Administration, Caldwell College; Bachelor's Degree in Business Administration, Caldwell College

STEPHEN J. O'TOOLE
General Manager, Board of Directors
Print House Ltd
142 Kent Street
Hamilton, INTL 2001 New Zealand
steve@phprint.co.nz
http://www.phprint.co.nz

BUS: Printing Company **P/S:** Commercial Printing and Printing Consulting Services **MA:** International **D/D/R:** Overseeing the Staff, Production and Operations, Utilizing his Experience in Leadership Management for Strategic Planning Review of Finances **H/I/S:** Sports, Squash, Running **FBP:** The New Zealand Printer Magazine; Industry Related Publications **CERTS:** Advance Trade Certificate in Offset Printing, New Zealand Qualifications Authority **A/A/S:** Advisor, Printing Industries Training Council; Local Squash Association

MARY C. OBERC, RN, BSN, MSN
Clinical Nurse
McDonald Army Health Center
Building 576 Fort Eustis
Newport News, VA 23604 United States
http://www.cambridgewhoswho.com

BUS: Healthcare Center **P/S:** Healthcare **MA:** Local **D/D/R:** Practicing Pediatrics, Adult Medical-Surgical Nursing **H/I/S:** Reenacting the History of Colonial Williamsburg as Brigadier General Francis Marion, the 'Swamp Fox' During the Civil War **FBP:** American Journal of Nursing; Kiplinger's Personal Finance **EDU:** Master of Science in Nursing, Oral Roberts University; Bachelor of Science in Nursing, Villanova University **CERTS:** Certified in Advanced Cardiac Life Support; Certified in Pediatric Advanced Life Support **A/A/S:** American Nurses Association; Virginia Nurses Association; Sigma Theta Tau; Lieutenant Colonel, United States Army Reserve; Reserve Officers Association **C/VW:** Volunteer, St. Charles Lwanga House; Catholic Charities Care Center **A/S:** She attributes her success to her prior experience and willingness to learn. **B/I:** She became involved in her profession because she always liked the healthcare field and wanted to work closely with others. **H/O:** The most gratifying aspect of her career is working at the McDonald Army Health Center.

AMANDA K. OBERMARK
Human Resource Manager
Rehab Care Group
7733 Forsyth Boulevard
Clayton, MO 63105 United States
aobermark@hotmail.com
http://www.cambridgewhoswho.com

BUS: Healthcare **P/S:** Therapy Management, Contracting with Various Hospitals and Nursing Homes **MA:** National **D/D/R:** Human Resources **H/I/S:** Reading, Spending Time with the Family, Watching NASCAR **EDU:** Bachelor of Science in Business Management, Central Missouri State University **C/VW:** Washington High School; St. Francis Borgia **A/S:** She attributes her success to the strong foundation she received from previous employers. **H/O:** The highlight of her career is her current position.

JONNA K. OCAMPO, CSCS
Owner
Streetwear and Urban Apparel Outfitter
Jonna Ocampo
4130 Proton Drive, Suite 26A
Addison, TX 75001 United States
jonna.ocampo@yahoo.com
http://www.jonnaocampo.com

BUS: Health and Fitness Center **P/S:** Conditioning Programs with a Fitness Assessment, Individual and Group Personal Training **MA:** International **EXP:** Ms. Ocampo's expertise is in creating strength and conditioning programs and training athletes, power lifters and boxers. **H/I/S:** Boxing, Photography **EDU:** Bachelor's Degree in Music and Business Management, Fairleigh Dickinson University, with Honors (1991) **A/A/S:** Who's Who in American Colleges and Universities (1989-1990); Johnson Space Center; Texas Aerospace Scholar, National Aeronautics and Space Administration (2004); National Strength and Conditioning Association **A/H:** Aerospace Education Excellence Award, Civil Air Patrol (2004); Volunteer Award, New Jersey Superior Court (1993-1996); Who's Who in American High Schools (1987); First Place, United States World Championships, Norway **C/VW:** Civil Air Patrol **A/S:** She attributes her success to being focused, self-motivation, self-drive, education and to the support she receives from her husband. **B/I:** She became involved in her profession after participating in athletic activities at a young age. **H/O:** The highlight of her career was competing in the 48-kilogram weight class in the last year's World Championships and obtaining ninth place.

CATHERINE ODDO
Owner/Designer
Catherine Oddo Interior Design
13669 Summerwood Drive
Sterling Heights, MI 48312 United States
coidgtudio@yahoo.com
http://www.cambridgewhoswho.com

BUS: Interior Design **P/S:** Draperies, Furniture, Accessories **MA:** Local **D/D/R:** Draperies and Hard Window Treatments **H/I/S:** Traveling, Reading, Spending Time with the Family **EDU:** Industry Related Training and Experience; Continuing Education Programs **A/A/S:** Allied ASID **C/VW:** Local Community **A/S:** She attributes her personal and professional success to her design selections. **H/O:** The highlight of her career is the gratitude of her clients.

SANDRA M. ODOM
Vice President
Vita International Products
PO Box 43067
Los Angeles, CA 90043 United States
vitaintlproducts@comcast.net
http://www.cambridgewhoswho.com

BUS: Retail Store **P/S:** Jewelry, T-shirts, DVDs, Travel Accessories and Gift Items **MA:** International **D/D/R:** Selling Natural Stone and Native American Jewelry and Other Items **H/I/S:** Skiing, Practicing Tai Chi **EDU:** Bachelor's Degree in Business Administration and Management, California State University (1981); Master's Degree **A/A/S:** The Council of Black Administrators; Washington Committee for Women, Democratic National Committee; U.S. Women's Chamber of Commerce **C/VW:** Local Charitable Organizations; Birth Month Ministry, West Angeles Church of God in Christ; Kingdom Worship Arts

SUE M. OFFERDAHL
Owner
Northland Feed and Seed
209 E. Third Street
Park Rapids, MN 56470 United States
sueofferdahl@hotmail.com
http://www.cambridgewhoswho.com

BUS: Agricultural Retail Store **P/S:** Selling Grain, Feed, Seed, Pet Products, Lawn, Garden **MA:** Regional **D/D/R:** Selling Pet Food **H/I/S:** Spending Time with the Family and her Grandchildren, Fishing

MICHAEL F. OGNOSKY
Superintendent of Schools
Montrose Area School District
80 High School Road
Montrose, PA 18801 United States
mognosky@masd.info
http://www.cambridgewhoswho.com

BUS: School District **P/S:** Education **MA:** Regional **EXP:** Mr. Ognosky's expertise is in leadership development and supervision. **D/D/R:** Managing the Union, Delegates and Human Resource Division, Ensuring Quality Treatments and Rights of Employees and Newly Hired Employees, Negotiating Labor Issues **H/I/S:** Refereeing College Basketball Games, Spending Time with his Family **EDU:** Master's Degree in Educational Administration, The University of Scranton; Bachelor's Degree in Secondary Education, Bloomsburg University **A/A/S:** Eastern College Athletic Conference; Pennsylvania Interscholastic Athletic Association; Pennsylvania School Boards Association; Pennsylvania Association of School Administrators; American Association of School Administrators; National School Board Association; Phi Delta Kappa **A/H:** Leadership Award, School District (2007); Technology Award, School District (2007) **A/S:** He attributes his success to his personal drive. **B/I:** He became involved in his profession because he always wanted to become a teacher and was inspired by his high school social studies teacher. **H/O:** The highlight of his career was becoming the superintendent of schools in Montrose.

ALICE OHANESIAN

Owner
Piggy Bank Productions
332 N. Sycamore Avenue
Los Angeles, CA 90036 United States
alice_ohanesian@hotmail.com
http://www.cambridgewhoswho.com

BUS: Consulting **P/S:** Professional and Quality Consulting such as Human Potential and Technology Services **MA:** Regional **D/D/R:** Specializing in Business and Technological Consulting, Overseeing Clients and Customers Needs Including Technical Requirements, Bringing Together Teams from Midsize Corporations to Achieve Goals of the Business **H/I/S:** Yoga, Horseback Riding, Listening to Live Music **EDU:** Bachelor of Arts in Business Administration, California State University at Fullerton (1983) **A/A/S:** World Affairs Council

ROLAND O. OKUNGBOWA, CRNA

Certified Registered Nurse Anesthetist, Clinical Coordinator
River West Medical Center
59355 River West Drive
Plaquemine, LA 70764 United States
rokungbowa@cox.net
http://www.cambridgewhoswho.com

BUS: Medical Center **P/S:** Healthcare **MA:** Regional **EXP:** Mr. Okungbowa's expertise is in anesthesia and administering epidurals. **H/I/S:** Playing Tennis, Reading, Traveling **EDU:** Master's Degree in Nursing, Concentration in Anesthesia, Louisiana State University Head Science Center; Bachelor of Science in Nursing, Southern University and A&M College, Baton Rouge, Louisiana; Bachelor of Science in Biology, Earned in Nigeria **A/A/S:** American Association of Nurse Anesthetists; Louisiana Association of Nurse Anesthetists **B/I:** He became involved in his profession because of his interest in healthcare. **H/O:** The most gratifying aspect of his career is knowing all the people he has helped in his career.

EDEN P. OLARTE, RN, BSN
President, Administrator, Registered Nurse
Compassionate Home Care, Inc.
11118 S. Kedzie Avenue
Chicago, IL 60655 United States
compassionatehomecare2006@yahoo.com
eden_olarte@comcast.net
http://www.cambridgewhoswho.com

BUS: Healthcare **P/S:** High Quality Home Healthcare for those in Need **MA:** Cook County **D/D/R:** Nursing, Performing Administrative Duties, Marketing, Caring for Patients **H/I/S:** Gardening, Reading, Ballroom Dancing **EDU:** MD, University of the Philippines (1987); Bachelor's Degree in Nursing, Philippines (1975) **A/A/S:** Illinois Nurses Association; American Nurses Association; Philippines Nurses Association; Philippines Medical Association **A/H:** Most Outstanding Nurses Award for Excellence in Patient Care, Columbia (1996, 1997) **C/VW:** Various Charities **A/S:** She attributes her success to her dedication, sincerity and caring nature. **B/I:** She became involved in this profession after working as a doctor in the Philippines and moving to the United States. **H/O:** The most gratifying aspect of her career is having patients thank her and show their appreciation.

ALISA BETH OLIN, MS, BME, OTR/L
Registered and Licensed Occupational Therapist, Private Practitioner
Cranford Board of Education
700 Brookside Place
Cranford, NJ 07016 United States
aliolinotr@gmail.com
http://www.cambridgewhoswho.com

BUS: Cranford Township Public Schools **P/S:** Registered and Licensed Occupational Therapy for Children Ages 3 through 18 with Varying Degrees of Disabilities, Teaching Experience with Master's Level Occupational Therapy Students **MA:** Regional **D/D/R:** Specializing in Sensory Integration, Autism, **H/I/S:** Golfing, Opera Performance **FBP:** American Journal of Occupational Therapy (AJOT); Pediatrics Specialty Newsletter **EDU:** Pursuing Doctoral Degree in Education Administration, Walden University; Master's Degree in Biomedical Engineering, New Jersey Institute of Technology; Bachelor of Science in Occupational Therapy, Sargent at Boston University **CERTS:** Pursuing Supervisory Certificate in Administration in Education, Kean University; Certified Provider of the Listening Program **A/A/S:** New Jersey Occupational Therapy Association; American Occupational Therapy Association; National Council of Jewish Women **A/H:** Recognized, 'Highly Successful' Office of Alumni Affairs, Boston University **C/VW:** Chairwoman, Goodies for the Good Guys; NCJW; AOTA; NJOTA; Hadassah **A/S:** She believes that her inner drive and teamwork, and her love of watching children progress have helped her to become successful in her career. **H/O:** She feels that being able to teach at a college level, while maintaining clinical practice as an occupational therapist have added to her growth as a professional. In addition, her ability to serve as a supervisor and mentor to both her public school based students and future colleagues have allowed her to earn recognition amongst her professional peers. This along with her pursuit of her hobbies have left her well rounded and ready to face exciting challenges everyday.

Joseph M. Olive, Ph.D.
Chief Executive Officer
Mount of Olives
10990A Creek Road
Ojai, CA 93023 United States
joeolive@ojai.net
http://www.foundationoffice.org

BUS: Time-Honored Leader in Mental Healthcare **P/S:** Helping Families, Married Couples, Single-Parent Families and Singles Adapt to the Demands, Concerns and Issues of Daily, Ordinary Life through Counseling and Therapy **MA:** National **D/D/R:** Specializing in Family Psychology, Working as a Diabetic Specialist in the Medical Field **H/I/S:** Photography **FBP:** New England Journal of Medicine **EDU:** Ph.D. in Psychology, New York University (1963); MD, New York University (1962); Internship, Sao Paulo, Brazil **A/A/S:** Family Life Foundation

Patrick Oliver-Kelley, Ph.D., FRSA
Managing Director
Falcon Financial Advisors
355 S. End Avenue
Suite 18F
New York, NY 10280 United States
falconcinl@gmail.com
http://www.falconfinl.com

BUS: International Merchant Banking Group **P/S:** Financial and Strategic Advisory Services for Growing Companies and Entrepreneurs, Principal Investments, Connecting Strategic Partners to Projects **MA:** International **D/D/R:** Raising International Capital, Maintaining Working Relationships with over 4,000 Institutions Internationally **H/I/S:** Participating in Equestrian Events, Dressage, Practicing Yoga, Playing Chess, Poetry **FBP:** The Economist **EDU:** Ph.D. in International Finance, Buxton University (2000) **A/A/S:** Phi Beta Kappa; Fellow, The Royal Society, United Kingdom; Dante Society of America; Air Force Association

CAREN D. OLSEN
Teacher
Thelma Bedell Elementary School
Santa Paula Elementary School District
1305 Laurel Road
Santa Paula, CA 93060 United States
olsenc@vcss.k12.ca.us
http://www.cambridgewhoswho.com

BUS: Elementary School **P/S:** Primary Education **MA:** Ventura County **D/D/R:** Organizing After-School Programs for At-Risk Students, Teaching Bilingual Education Including English as a Second Language to Fourth through Sixth-Grade Students, Coordinating Educational Programs for Gifted and Talented Students **H/I/S:** Horseback Riding, Playing Tennis, Swimming, Sewing, Painting, Artwork, Making Crafts **FBP:** Instructor **EDU:** Bachelor of Arts in Spanish, Minor in Music, University of California, Santa Barbara (1969) **CERTS:** Certification in Elementary and Secondary Education **A/A/S:** California Textbook Adoption Committee; Bilingual, Gifted and Talented Education Committee; Teachers Union, Santa Paula Elementary School District **C/VW:** Ojai Community Chorus; Ventura County Saddle Club

DEANNA L. OLSON
Psychiatric and Marketing Liaison
North Valley Hospital
8451 Pearl Street
Thornton, CO 80229 United States
http://www.northValleyrehab.com

BUS: Acute Care Hospital **P/S:** Acute Care Hospital Including In-Patient Psychiatric Services **MA:** Statewide **D/D/R:** Completion of Psychiatric Evaluations for In-Patient Hospitalization **H/I/S:** Reading, Traveling, Writing Poetry and Short Stories **FBP:** The American Journal of Psychiatry; National Board Certified Counselors Publication **EDU:** Master's Degree in Counseling Psychology; Counselor Education, Marriage and Family Field, University of Colorado at Denver Campus; Bachelor's Degree in Psychology, University of Colorado at Denver **A/A/S:** American Counseling Association **C/VW:** Alzheimer's Association; Big Brothers, Big Sisters; Good Will; American Red Cross **A/S:** She attributes her career success to her very intense work ethic, and to her love of her profession. **H/O:** She feels that being contacted by the Dr. Phil Show as a resource on the show has been the highlight of her career.

SHELIA KAY OLSON
Paralegal
State of Alaska Attorney General's Office
1031 W. Fourth Avenue, Suite 200
Anchorage, AK 99501 United States
shelia.olson@alaska.gov
http://www.law.state.ak.us

BUS: Government Organization **P/S:** Legal Services Including Civil Law for Child Protection **MA:** Regional **D/D/R:** Finalizing Pleadings, Faxing, Preparing Summonses, Managing Multiple Tasks, Filing Caseload for Four Attorneys, Supervising Legal Assistants, Processing Petitions from Social Workers and Coordinating Files for Court Updates **H/I/S:** Painting, Reading Poetry, Snowmobiling, Photography **FBP:** Reader's Digest **EDU:** Bachelor's Degree in Justice, University of Alaska (2003); Associate of Arts in Accounting, Matanuska-Susitna College, University of Alaska (1996) **CERTS:** Online Certification in Crime Scene Investigation, Kaplan University (2005); Notary Public **C/VW:** Handbell Choir, St. John's Lutheran Church

MELANIE ONYETT, PHR
Human Resources, Benefits
Kehe Food Distributors, Inc.
900 N. Schmidt Road
Romeoville, IL 90446 United States
melanie.onyett@sbcglobal.net
http://www.cambridgewhoswho.com

BUS: Food Distribution **P/S:** Sales, Marketing, Distribution of Ethnic and Gourmet Foods **MA:** National **H/I/S:** Reading, Pets, Swimming, Gardening **FBP:** HR **EDU:** Bachelor's Degree, Psychology and Human Resources, Lewis University, Illinois **A/H:** PHR Certificate (2005) **C/VW:** Best Friends Animal Society **A/S:** She attributes her personal and professional success to her positive attitude and motivation. **B/I:** She has always had an interest in the field and feels it is her calling to help others. **H/O:** The highlight of her career was earning her PHR Certificate.

CYNTHIA C. OPATZ, RN
Owner, Registered Nurse, Co-Executive Administrator, Nursing
Administrator
Special Potential, LLC
15633 S.W. 37th Circle
Ocala, FL 34473 United States
opatzrn@msn.com
http://www.cambridgewhoswho.com

BUS: Leader in the Healthcare Industry, Group Home **P/S:** Wide Variety of High Quality Healthcare Services to those Residing in Group Homes **MA:** Regional **D/D/R:** Nurse for the Medically Fragile and Developmentally Disabled, Specializing in Perinatal Intensive Care Nursing, Patient Care, Handling All Medications and Treatments, Working with Patients 21-Years-Old and Up **H/I/S:** Sewing, Cooking, Crocheting **FBP:** Florida Nurse; Advanced Nursing **EDU:** Bachelor of Science Degree in Nursing, Southwest University (2002)

PAUL G. ORBON, DO
Physician
Cardiovascular Medical Associates
975 Stewart Avenue
Garden City, NY 11530 United States
porbon@cmadoctors.com
http://www.cmadoctors.com

BUS: Medical Clinic **P/S:** Healthcare **MA:** Regional **EXP:** Mr. Orbon's expertise is in acting as a internist and patient care. **H/I/S:** Woodworking, Playing Basketball, Golfing, Traveling **EDU:** Doctor of Osteopathic Medicine, New York School of Osteopathy; Bachelor of Science in Biology, Columbia University **A/A/S:** American Medical Association; American Osteopathic Association **A/S:** He attributes his success to his work ethic, upbringing, commitment and caring nature. **B/I:** He became involved in his profession because of his interest in the medical field. **H/O:** The highlight of his career was completing his residency program from the medical school.

CLARA B. ORDUZ
Spanish Teacher
Grand Meadow Public Schools, Independent School District 495
710 Fourth Avenue N.E.
Grand Meadow, MN 55936 United States
blackorduz@hotmail.com
http://www.cambridgewhoswho.com

BUS: Public High School **P/S:** Education **MA:** Local **D/D/R:** Teaching Spanish to High School Students **EDU:** Bachelor of Arts in Teaching Spanish, Universidad Pedagógica Nacional; Bachelor of Arts in Psychology, Universidad Nacional de Colombia **A/A/S:** National Education Association **C/VW:** Local Fire and Police Department **A/S:** She attributes her success to her dedication, believing in what she does and to focusing on her students. **B/I:** She became involved in her profession because she loves language and wanted to make education fun and interesting for her students. **H/O:** The most gratifying aspect of her career is knowing that the students enjoy her teaching and continue to learn.

RITA C. ORGAN
Executive Director
Indiana Museum of African American History
39 W. Jackson Place
Suite 75
Indianapolis, IN 46225 United States
ro_imaah@sbcglobal.net
http://www.cambridgewhoswho.com

BUS: Museum **P/S:** Museum **MA:** Local **D/D/R:** Start-Up Museums **H/I/S:** Cooking, Bicycling **FBP:** History News **EDU:** Bachelor of Arts in Interdisciplinary and Ethnic Art Studies, California College of the Arts; Masters Coursework **A/A/S:** American Association of Museums; Association of African American Museums; Association of Midwest Museums **C/VW:** United Way of America **B/I:** She was encouraged by several mentors to pursue a career in history. **H/O:** She feels that the work she has done to open and maintain the National Underground Railroad Freedom Center has been the highlight of her career.

PETER S. ORLANDO
President and Founder
Quality International Systems Company, LLC
22931 Industrial Drive W.
St. Clair Shores, MI 48080 United States
peter.orlando@qisco.net
http://www.qualityinternationalsystems.com

BUS: Total Quality Management, Consulting **P/S:** International Quality Management and Warehousing, Dimensional Verification **MA:** International **D/D/R:** Manufacturing Quality, Engineering and Logistics, International Warehousing and Distribution **H/I/S:** Reading, Culinary Arts, International Cuisine, Church Activities **FBP:** Leadership; Christianity Today **EDU:** Associate Degree in Christian Studies, Sure Foundation Theological Institute **CERTS:** Licensed Minister **C/VW:** Operation Mobilization, India **A/S:** He attributes his success to a calling from God. **B/I:** He became involved in this profession because he saw the need for internationally produced products to be qualified in this country. **H/O:** The highlight of her career is building relationships with people across the world.

VIRGINIA K. ORSINO-BOEHLERT
Special Education Teacher
Conkling School
Utica City School District
Mohawk Street
Utica, NY 13501 United States
vkb1954@aol.com
http://www.cambridgewhoswho.com

BUS: School District **P/S:** Education **MA:** Local **EXP:** Ms. Orsino-Boehlert's expertise is in special education and multi-disciplinary team teaching. **D/D/R:** Teaching Special Education and Inclusion Classes **H/I/S:** Reading, Cross-County Skiing, Snowshoeing **EDU:** Master's Degree in Special Education, Plus 60, Syracuse University; Bachelor's Degree in Education, SUNY Potsdam **CERTS:** Certification in Special Education (K-12) **A/A/S:** Mohawk Valley Writing Project, Learning Disabilities Association; National Teachers Association; Council for Exceptional Children **C/VW:** Parent-Teacher Association **SP:** Gregory **CHILD:** Gregory, Tessa, Emily **A/S:** She attributes her success to her love for children and her work experience. **B/I:** She became involved in her profession because she wanted to become a teacher or a social worker. **H/O:** The most gratifying aspect of her career is seeing her students' accomplishments. **I/F/Y:** In five years, Ms. Orsino-Boehlert hopes to do consulting and continue teaching.

JEANNE OSHEL
Registered Nurse
Greater Regional Medical Center
1700 W. Townline Street
Creston, IA 50801 United States
jeanneo@mchsi.com
http://www.cambridgewhoswho.com

BUS: Regional Medical Center **P/S:** Healthcare **MA:** Local **D/D/R:** Offering General OB/GYN Care, Labor, Delivery, Post Partum Services and Medical-Surgical Care **H/I/S:** Bowling, Boating **FBP:** RN **EDU:** Associate of Science in Nursing, Southwestern Community College **C/VW:** Donor, Various Local Charities **A/S:** She attributes her success to determination and always working harder, better and learning on the job. **H/O:** The highlight of her career is all the accreditations she has received. She is amazed at having gotten them, especially since she never thought she would be a nurse.

GISSELE OSPINA
Director of the Hispanic Division
The Green Agency
1620 Drexel Avenue
Miami Beach, FL 33139 United States
gissele@greenagency.com
http://www.greenagency.com

BUS: Model and Talent Agency **P/S:** Model and Talent Services **MA:** International **EXP:** Ms. Ospina's expertise is in talent identification. **D/D/R:** Managing Operations, Introducing Hispanic Talent to the American Television and Film Industry **H/I/S:** Painting, Reading, Watching Movies, Speaking English, Spanish and Basic Italian **EDU:** Bachelor's Degree in Interior Design, School of Arts and Letters, Jorge Tadeo Lozano University **A/A/S:** Screen Actors Guild; Miami Film Commission; American Federation of Television & Radio Artists; Association of Hispanic Advertising Agencies; National Association of Latino Independent Producers **C/VW:** Volunteer, Hands on Miami; Fundraiser, Los Niños del Campo **POB:** Bogota **A/S:** She attributes her success to her hard work, consistency, the support she receives from her colleagues and her ability to find great new talent. **B/I:** She became involved in her profession after having the good fortune to work with the Green Agency in an administrative capacity, which allowed her to learn the business from the best. **H/O:** The most gratifying aspect of her career is being able to place talented people in a position where they can shine.

FREDERICK W. OTT, MD
Assistant Professor of Neuroradiology, Neuroradiologist
Radiology
University of Minnesota
420 Delaware Street S.E., Department M
Minneapolis, MN 55455 United States
ottxx014@umn.edu
http://www.med.umn.edu

BUS: University **P/S:** Higher Education, Allied Health Programs, Basic Science and Clinical Science **MA:** National **D/D/R:** Teaching Radiology and Neuroradiology to Residents, Fellows and Medical Students, Performing Cerebral Angiography Procedures, Cerebral Intra Arterial Chemotherapy, Blood Brain Barrier Disruptions and Spinal Procedures **H/I/S:** Exercising, Spending Time with his Family, Working on Automobiles **FBP:** American Journal of Neuroradiology **EDU:** Residency in Radiology, University of Minnesota (1999-2004); Fellowship in Neuroradiology, University of Minnesota (2004-2005); MD, University of Minnesota (1999); Bachelor of Science in Pharmacy, University of Minnesota (1981) **CERTS:** Certified Neuroradiologist, The American Board of Radiology (2006); Certification in Diagnostic Radiology, The American Board of Radiology (2004) **A/A/S:** American Society of Spine Radiology; American Society of Neuroradiology; Radiological Society of North America; American College of Radiology; Association of University Radiologists; Minnesota Medical Association; Alpha Omega Alpha **A/H:** Award for Academic Excellence, American Society for Clinical Pathology (1997) **A/S:** He attributes his success to his hard work and commitment. **B/I:** He became involved in his profession because while working in pharmaceuticals he acquired a passion for radiology. **H/O:** The most gratifying aspect of his career is teaching residents who will become radiologists.

DANIEL OUELLETTE
Executive Director
Salisbury Housing Authority
23 Beach Road
Salisbury, MA 01952 United States
dan@salisburyhousing.org
http://www.salisburyhousing.org

BUS: Public Housing Authority **P/S:** Leader in Providing Subsidized Housing, Affordable Housing **MA:** Regional **D/D/R:** Specializing in Public Housing Negotiations, Administration and Public Relations **H/I/S:** Skiing, Water Skiing and Carpentry **FBP:** Industry Journal NAHRO Monitor **EDU:** Master of Science in Human Services, University of Massachusetts (2000); Bachelor's Degree, Boston College (1982) **A/A/S:** National Association of Housing and Redevelopment Officials, Massachusetts; Vice President, Housing Authority for Massachusetts National Association of Housing and Redevelopment Officials; Workforce Board

JAMIE L. OWEN HILYER, MSN, RN, CNAA-BC
Coordinator, Women's Wellness Center
Choctaw Health Center
United States Public Health Service Commissioned Corps
210 Hospital Circle
Choctaw, MS 39350 United States
jhilyer@excite.com • nana39365@dishmail.net
http://www.choctaw.org/government/health.htm

BUS: Ambulatory Healthcare Clinic **P/S:** Preventive Healthcare Services for Women and Children **MA:** Regional **D/D/R:** Specializing in Nurse Management **H/I/S:** Spending Time with Grandchildren and Family, Reading, Sewing, Home Renovation Projects, College Football, Traveling **FBP:** Journal of Public Health; Nursing Management **EDU:** Master of Science in Nursing, University of Phoenix (2002); Bachelor of Science in Nursing, Birmingham Southern College (1985) **CERTS:** Certification in Nursing Administration, American Nurses Credentialing Center (2006) **A/A/S:** American Nurses Association; Federal Nurses Association; Mississippi Nurses Association; Sigma Theta Tau-Omicron Delta Chapter; Commissioned Officers Association; Military Officers Association of America

ANGELA OWUSU-ANSAH, PH.D.
Director of Assessment
Samford University
800 Lakeshore Drive
Birmingham, AL 35229 United States
aoowusu@samford.edu
http://www.cambridgewhoswho.com

BUS: University **P/S:** Higher Education **MA:** Regional **D/D/R:** Conducting Educational Research, Developing Programs, Overseeing Four Staff Members **H/I/S:** Painting, Reading, Traveling **FBP:** Forum on Public Policy; The Journal of the Oxford Round Table; Educational Evaluation and Policy Analysis; Educational Researcher; The College Mathematics Journal **EDU:** Bachelor of Science in Psychology, Minor in Sociology, University of Ghana (1989); Ph.D. in Educational Administration, Research and Instructional Technology, The University of Southern Mississippi; Master's Degree in International Administration and Supervision, Rutgers, The State University of New Jersey **CERTS:** Certification in Grant Writing **A/A/S:** American Statistical Association; The Mathematical Association of America; Executive Board Member, Regional Research Laboratory for Education **A/H:** Oxford Round Table **C/VW:** Christian Children's Fund **A/S:** She attributes her success to her Christian faith, dedication, perseverance and the support she receives from her family. **B/I:** She became involved in her profession because the department chair of her doctoral program believed in her abilities by hiring her as a visiting professor the month she graduated. **H/O:** The most gratifying aspect of her career is having the opportunity to create and implement innovative ideas and programs.

CAROL REBECCA 'BECKY' PACE
Lead Teacher
Dana Road Elementary School
1247 Dana Road
Vicksburg, MS 39180 United States
bpace@vwsd.k12.ms.us
countrygirlorange@yahoo.com
http://www.vwsd.k12.ms.us

BUS: Elementary School **P/S:** Primary Education **MA:** Local **EXP:** Ms. Pace's expertise is in curriculum development. **D/D/R:** Acquiring Support Materials for Teachers, Overseeing 40 Staff Members, Grading Students, Assisting Teachers, Teaching **H/I/S:** Reading, Running, Metal Detecting, Sewing, Homemaking, Cooking, Making Arts and Crafts, Hiking, Collecting Antiques **FBP:** Educational Leadership **EDU:** Educational Specialist Degree in Educational Leadership, Mississippi College (2008); Master's Degree in Elementary Education, Mississippi College (1998); Bachelor of Arts in Elementary Education, University of Mississippi (1982); Associate of Arts in Elementary Education, Jones County Junior College (1980) **CERTS:** Certified Kindergarten through Eighth-Grade Teacher; Certified College-Level Instructor; Certified Building Principal **A/A/S:** Vicksburg Warren Association of Educators; Mississippi Association of Educators; National Council of Teachers of English; National Education Association; International Reading Association; Ole Miss Alumni Association **A/H:** Site Supervisor of the Year, AmeriCorps (2006); Who's Who Among American Teachers (1994, 1998, 2005-2008); Going the Extra Mile Award, AmeriCorps (2005); Teacher of the Year, Sherman Avenue Elementary (2001) **C/VW:** Various Charitable Organizations; Local Church Charity; American Cancer Society; Pennies for Patients, The Leukemia & Lymphoma Society; Relay for Life, American Cancer Society; American Lung Association; Volunteer, AmeriCorps **DOB:** March 9, 1960 **POB:** Tokyo **SP:** George **A/S:** She attributes her success to her persistence, hard work and parents, who made sure she received an education. **B/I:** She became involved in her profession because she always wanted to work with children. **H/O:** The most gratifying aspect of her career is the gratitude she receives from her successful students. **I/F/Y:** In five years, Ms. Pace plans to continue being a part of the educational process.

LORRAINE M. PADILLA
Managing Partner
New England Wealth Strategies
50 Charles Lindbergh Boulevard
Uniondale, NY 11553 United States
lorrainempadilla@yahoo.com
http://www.newenglandwealthstrategies.com

BUS: One of New York's Oldest and Largest Financial Firms Providing a Broad Range of Services and Products Specifically Designed to Meet the Financial Needs of the Community **P/S:** Annuities, Disability Income Insurance, Long-Term Care Insurance, Retirement Analysis, Life Insurance, Business Loan Protection, Executive Benefits **MA:** Regional **D/D/R:** Managing Almost 100 Personnel, Life Insurance and Retirement Investment Specialist **H/I/S:** Spending Quality Time with the Family **EDU:** Bachelor's Degree in Mathematics (1973) **A/A/S:** General Agents and Managers Association; National Association of Insurance and Financial Advisors

CINDY V. PADRE, MD
Doctor, Partner
Ruben A. Padre, MD and Cindy V. Padre, MD
200 N. Middletown Road
Pearl River, NY 10965 United States
cvpadre@yahoo.com
http://www.cambridgewhoswho.com

BUS: Private Medical Practice Committed to Excellence in Patient Care **P/S:** Comprehensive Healthcare Services **MA:** Local **D/D/R:** General Pediatrics **H/I/S:** Traveling, Listening to Music, Playing the Violin **FBP:** Contemporary Pediatrics **EDU:** Residency, The Brooklyn Hospital Center; Medical Degree, Saint George's University (2001)

CATHERINE L. PAGE
Professor
Rio Hondo Community College
3600 Workman Mill Road
Whittier, CA 90601 United States
cpage@riohondo.edu
http://www.cambridgewhoswho.com

BUS: Community College **P/S:** Healthcare **MA:** Local **D/D/R:** Gerontology, Neurology, Wound Care, Ostomy Care, Teaching in the Classroom and Hospital **H/I/S:** Participating in Girl Scouts Activities, Stamping, Beading **EDU:** Master of Science in Nursing, University of Southern California **A/A/S:** American Nurses Association; California Nurses Association; Wound, Ostomy and Continence Nurses Society **C/VW:** Parent-Teacher Association; Girl Scouts of the United States of America **A/S:** She attributes her success to constantly being challenged and achieving her goals. **B/I:** She became involved in her profession because she had always wanted to be a nurse and there were a lot of opportunities for teaching.

E. MARIA PAHUANA
Nurse Internship Administrator
Luther Woods Convalescent Center
313 W. County Line Road
Hatboro, PA 19040 United States
emaria.pahuana@cwwemail.com
http://www.cambridgewhoswho.com

BUS: Nursing Home **P/S:** Healthcare Including Long-Term Care **MA:** Local **EXP:** Ms. Pahuana's expertise is in geriatric care. **H/I/S:** Reading, Gardening **FBP:** RN; American Journal of Nursing; AGS Journal; ACHCA Journal; Advance for Providers of Post-Acute Care **EDU:** Pursuing Master's Degree, Andrew Jackson University; Bachelor of Arts in Behavioral and Social Gerontology, Gwynedd-Mercy College, PA; Associate Degree in Biological and General Studies, Montgomery County Community College, Blue Bell, PA; Coursework in Healthcare Administration, Saint Joseph's University, Philadelphia, PA **CERTS:** Certified Nursing Home Administrator, Saint Joseph's College of Maine; Certified Gerontologist, Montgomery County Community College; Certification in Paralegal Studies **A/A/S:** American College of Nursing Home Administrators; The American Geriatrics Society **C/VW:** Volunteer, Meals on Wheels

CYNTHIA L. PALABRICA, MD
President
HLS Medical Services SC
2350 N. Lake Drive
Suite 404
Milwaukee, WI 53211 United States
cpmd_1@ameritech.net
http://www.cambridgewhoswho.com

BUS: Medical Office **P/S:** Obstetric and Gynecological Healthcare **MA:** Local **EXP:** Dr. Palabrica's expertise includes obstetrics and general and adolescent gynecology. **H/I/S:** Sailing, Hiking, Sewing **FBP:** Journal of Obstetrics and Gynecology **EDU:** MD, Creighton University; Master's Degree; Bachelor's Degree **A/A/S:** Wisconsin Medical Society; American Medical Association; American College of Obstetricians and Gynecologists **C/VW:** Saint Robert School **A/S:** She attributes her success to her strong family values. **B/I:** She became involved in her profession because of her family background, as both her father and sister were physicians. **H/O:** The highlight of her career was starting a business that is family friendly for both her and her employees.

Dr. Richard P. Palazzolo

President, Chief Executive Officer
Together Forever Ministries
19803 Breezy Cove Court
Tomball, TX 77375 United States
tfministries1317@sbcglobal.net
http://www.togetherforeverministries.com

BUS: Ministry **P/S:** Ministry Services Including Anger Management, Individual, Marriage, Family, Depression, Alcohol, Substance Abuse and Pediatric Counseling **MA:** National **EXP:** Dr. Palazzolo's expertise is in marriage, family, drug and alcohol, grief, divorce recovery and teenage counseling. **H/I/S:** Watching Football, Listening to Music, Spending Time with his Family, Exercising **EDU:** Ph.D. in Family Counseling, Trinity College (2004); Master's Degree in Ministerial Studies, Global University (2001); Bachelor of Arts in Psychology and History, Wagner College (1973) **A/A/S:** American Association of Christian Counselors **DOB:** March 10, 1951 **SP:** Cindy **CHILD:** Eric, Paul

Betty W. Palmer, RN

Registered Nurse
Park Ridge Medical Center
2333 McCallie Avenue
Chattanooga, TN 37404 United States
runpalmer@bellsouth.net
http://www.cambridgewhoswho.com

BUS: Hospital **P/S:** Healthcare **MA:** Local **D/D/R:** Psychiatric Nursing **H/I/S:** Sewing, Gardening, Reading **FBP:** American Journal of Nursing **EDU:** Diploma in Nursing, Erlanger Medical Center **C/VW:** Church, American Cancer Society, Humanitarian Causes, Paralyzed Veterans of America **A/S:** She attributes her career success to her spiritual beliefs.

MARY A. PALMER
Owner
Isanti Auto Parts
38459 Highway 65
Stanchfield, MN 55080 United States
http://www.isantiautoparts.com

BUS: Proven Leader in the Auto Parts Industry **P/S:** Auto Parts, Recycling of Used Auto Parts **MA:** National **D/D/R:** Overseeing Accounting, Managing Inventory, Promoting Auto Part Sales **H/I/S:** Fishing **FBP:** The Wall Street Journal **EDU:** Coursework in Computer Science, Anoka Ramsey Community College (1974) **A/A/S:** Better Business Bureau; ARMS

EILEEN P. PALUMBO, RN, BSN
Registered Nurse
Eileen Palumbo, Nursing Consultant
95 High Street
Newton, NJ 07860 United States
epbish25@aol.com
http://www.cambridgewhoswho.com

BUS: Healthcare Center **P/S:** Healthcare **MA:** Local **EXP:** Ms. Palumbo's expertise is in working with head injury patients, physical therapy, performing surgery and rendering home care. **H/I/S:** Finding Antiques and Collectibles, Traveling, Boating, Volunteering **FBP:** Country Living; RN; Nursing Spectrum **EDU:** Bachelor of Science in Nursing, Minor in Psychology, Fairfield University, CT (1977) **A/A/S:** Columbiettes, Women's Auxiliary, Knights of Columbus **A/H:** Nurse of the Year Award, Bergen Nursing Team (1993) **C/VW:** Volunteer, American Red Cross (2003) **DOB:** February 25, 1955 **POB:** Brooklyn, NY **SP:** Michael

DALLAS PANCOAST JR.
Assistant Power Plant Manager
Aquila, Inc.
105 S. Victoria Avenue
Pueblo, CO 81003 United States
dallas.pancoast@aquila.com
http://www.cambridgewhoswho.com

BUS: Public Utility **P/S:** Electric Power Production **MA:** National **D/D/R:** Overseeing and Maintaining the Power Plant **H/I/S:** Hunting, Slot Car Racing, RC Trucks **EDU:** Coursework, Pueblo Community College **A/A/S:** Executive Board Member, MBA **C/VW:** United Way of America; Pregnancy Center **A/S:** He attributes his personal and professional success to his hard work and strong work ethic. **B/I:** He became involved in the profession because he enjoys the challenge of the job. **H/O:** The most gratifying aspect of his career is his ability to successfully accomplish a major task within his given budget.

EUGENE R. PANTANGCO, MD
President, Physician
Gastrointestinal and Liver Diseases of Newport
PO Box 8329
Newport Beach, CA 92658 United States
epgimd@gmail.com
http://www.cambridgewhoswho.com

BUS: Private Medical Practice Specializing in Gastroenterology **P/S:** Highest Quality of Care to Patients with Digestive Disorders and Liver Disease **MA:** Local **D/D/R:** Offering a Full Range of Health Care Services to Patients in the Treatment of Gastrointestinal Ailments **H/I/S:** Playing Golf and Tennis **EDU:** MD, The University of Vermont College of Medicine (1998); Residency, Yale University; Fellowship, University of Southern California at Los Angeles **A/A/S:** ASG; American Gastroenterological Association; American Medical Association; American College of Gastroenterologists; American College of Physicians

ANGELA ROSE PAPSODERO, RN
Group Facility Administrator
DaVita Inc.
802 N. John Young Parkway
Kissimee, FL 34741 United States
angela.papsodera@davita.com
http://www.gambrohealthcare.com

BUS: Largest International Dialysis Provider **P/S:** Dialysis Services **MA:** International **D/D/R:** Acting as Clinic Director and Administrator, Team Building, Financial Manager, Nursing Management, Quality Assurance **H/I/S:** Dancing **FBP:** The Wall Street Journal; Nephrology Nursing Journal **EDU:** Pursuing Master of Business Administration; Bachelor's Degree in Business Administration, Colorado Technical University; Registered Nurse, Associate in Applied Sciences, Elizabeth General Medical Center, Union College **A/A/S:** American Nephrology Nurses Association; Treasurer, Local Chapter of American Nephrology Nurses Association **C/VW:** Various Charity Work through the Church; Food Drives; American Red Cross; Second Harvest

CINDY S. PARIS
Technical Training Coordinator
Pella Corporation
102 Main Street
Pella, IA 50219 United States
csparis@pella.com
http://www.cambridgewhoswho.com

BUS: Manufacturing Company **P/S:** Windows and Doors **MA:** National **D/D/R:** Training, Mentoring **H/I/S:** Reading **EDU:** Associate of Arts in Business Administration, Colorado Technical University Online (2007) **CERTS:** Certified Medical Inspector, American Society for Quality; Certified Quality Technician, American Society for Quality; Certified Quality Auditor, American Society for Quality; Certified Instructor, United States Army **A/A/S:** American Society for Quality; Iowa Chapter, American Society for Training and Development **C/VW:** The American Legion; Disabled American Veterans; Juvenile Diabetes Research Foundation; Various Charities and Fundraisers through Pella Corporation **DOB:** August 7, 1963 **POB:** Ottumea, IA **SP:** Randy **CHILD:** Chelsea, Lindsea, Nichole **W/H:** United States Army **A/S:** She attributes her success to being a people person. **B/I:** She became involved in her profession while serving in the army. **H/O:** The most gratifying aspect of her career is seeing students implement her teachings.

SUNG DUK PARK
Registered Nurse
Jesse Brown VA Medical Center
820 S. Damen Street
Chicago, IL 60612 United States
sungduk.park@cwwemail.com
http://www.cambridgewhoswho.com

BUS: Hospital **P/S:** Healthcare for Veterans and their Dependents **MA:** Regional **EXP:** Ms. Park's expertise is in oncology and medical-surgical nursing. **H/I/S:** Traveling **EDU:** Coursework in Nursing, Earned in South Korea **A/A/S:** Korean American Nurses Association **A/H:** Asian-American Hall of Fame (2008) **C/VW:** Various Charitable Organizations **A/S:** She attributes her success to her hard work and love for her profession. **B/I:** She became involved in her profession through a natural progression of opportunities.

ANITA PHILLIPS PARKER
Teacher
Kannapolis Middle School
1445 Oakwood Avenue
Kannapolis, NC 28081 United States
Parkera@kannopolis.k12.nc.us
http://www.kannapolis.k12.nc.us

BUS: Education **P/S:** Education **MA:** Local **D/D/R:** Teaching Eighth-Grade Science **H/I/S:** Singing, Shopping **EDU:** Bachelor of Science in Biology, Radford University, Radford, Virginia **A/A/S:** Alpha Delta Kappa; North Carolina Science Teachers Association **C/VW:** Church; American Heart Association **A/S:** She attributes her success to her dedication and accuracy. **H/O:** The highlight of her career was earning Teacher of the Year for her school building and Teacher of the Year for the school system.

DEBORAH W. PARKER
Real Estate Broker Associate
RE/MAX Signature Properties
150 W. McPherson Church Road
Fayetteville, NC 28303 United States
deborahwparker@nc.rr.com
http://www.cambridgewhoswho.com

BUS: Real Estate **P/S:** Real Estate Sales **MA:** International **D/D/R:** Representing Sellers and Buyers, Researching and Finding a Home Perfect for her Clients' Needs **H/I/S:** Spending Quality Time with her Husband and Grandchildren **EDU:** Pursuing Degree in Real Estate; PLYS Continuing Education Courses for All Phases of Real Estate **A/A/S:** Fayette Board of Realtors; North Carolina National Board of Realtors **A/H:** President's Award for High Sales Recognition **C/VW:** The Children's Network **A/S:** She attributes her career success to the support and backing that her husband offers her. **B/I:** She became a realtor because she loves working with people. **H/O:** She feels that being able to help buyers find the home of their dreams is the highlight of her career.

JANET A. PARKER
Licensed Vocational Nurse II, Staff Developer, Assistant Nurse
Manager
Sutter Amador Hospital
200 Mission Boulevard
Jackson, CA 95642 United States
parkerja@sutterhealth.org
http://www.cambridgewhoswho.com

BUS: Healthcare, Hospital **P/S:** Healthcare Education **MA:** Local **D/D/R:** Rehabilitation, Skilled Nursing, Wound Care, Educating Certified Nursing Assistants **H/I/S:** Traveling, Spending Time in Mexico, Visiting Vineyards and Orchard Farms, Needlework, Spending Time with her 10 Grandchildren **FBP:** LPN 2006; RN **EDU:** Pursuing Registered Nurse Diploma; Associate of Arts in Nursing, Sacramento City College **CERTS:** Staff Developer Certification **C/VW:** Volunteer, March of Dimes; The Salvation Army; Goodwill **A/S:** She attributes her success to her motivation to get ahead. **B/I:** She became involved in this profession because she had an interest in the medical field and she comes from a family in the medical profession. **H/O:** The highlight of her career was getting her staff developing certification.

PAMELA L. PARKER
Chaplain
United States Army
Redstone Arsenal
Huntsville, AL 35898 United States
majorpam@bellsouth.net
http://www.cambridgewhoswho.com

BUS: Government **P/S:** Chaplain/Pastoral Counseling, Preaching, Teaching **MA:** International **D/D/R:** Specializing in Defense and Religious Guidance **H/I/S:** Spending Time with her Friends and Family **EDU:** Master of Science in Education, Samford University; Master of Divinity, Southern Baptist Theological Seminary **A/A/S:** Military Order of the World Wars **C/VW:** Samford University; Federal Campaign **A/S:** She attributes her success to doing her best. **B/I:** She became involved in her profession because it was a calling from God. **H/O:** The highlight of her career was the time she spent in Europe with the Army.

STELLA L. PARKS
Board Director
Beaumont-Cherry Valley Water District
560 Magnolia
Beaumont, CA 92223 United States

BUS: Water District Service Provider **P/S:** Water District **MA:** Local **D/D/R:** Directing the Board, Managing Public Relations **H/I/S:** Animals, Reading, Shopping **EDU:** College Coursework **A/A/S:** Republican Women; Order of the Eastern Star; Cherry Valley Chamber of Commerce; President, Cherry Growers Association **C/VW:** Food Baskets for the Elderly

MICHAEL T. PARRA, MD
President, Medical Doctor
Colorado Hematology-Oncology
401 W. Hampden Place
Suite 250
Englewood, CO 80110 United States
mtparramd@msn.com
http://www.denvercancercare.com

BUS: Healthcare Center **P/S:** Healthcare Including Oncology, Hematology **MA:** Colorado **EXP:** Mr. Parra's expertise is in oncology. **H/I/S:** Fencing, Playing Volleyball and Tennis **FBP:** Journal of Clinical Oncology **EDU:** Coursework in Medical Studies, Clayton State University (1984) **A/A/S:** Board of Medical Oncology; American Board of Internal Medicine

CHERRYL Y. T. PARRISH, CPM
Police Lieutenant
District of Columbia Police Department
cheryl.trotter-parrish@dc.gov
http://www.dc.gov

BUS: Public Service **P/S:** Enforcing Laws, Maintaining Peace **MA:** Local **D/D/R:** Administration, Managing the Patrol Service Area **H/I/S:** Traveling, Attending Gospel Shows, Reading, Writing, Typing, Proofreading **EDU:** Associate of Arts in Legal Secretarial Studies, Strayer College **CERTS:** Certified Public Manager **A/A/S:** Mid-Atlantic Association of Women in Law Enforcement; International Association of Women Police; National Council of Negro Women; National Organization of Black Law Enforcement **C/VW:** Children's Cancer Society; Alzheimer's Association

PERRY K. PARSONS, LCSW, CADC, LADAC
Life Strategies Counseling Inc.
1217 Stone Street
Jonesboro, AR 72401 United States
easylistener72401@yahoo.com
http://www.cambridgewhoswho.com

BUS: Clinic **P/S:** Family-Based Out-Patient Therapy **MA:** Regional **EXP:** Ms. Parsons' areas of expertise are in substance abuse therapy and play therapy. **D/D/R:** Making Diagnoses, Offering Daily Therapy to Individuals, Families and Groups **H/I/S:** Surfing the Internet, Driving Hot Rods, Playing the Guitar **FBP:** Journal of Social Work **EDU:** Master of Social Work, The University of Tennessee **CERTS:** Licensed Alcohol and Drug Abuse Counselor; Certified Alcohol and Drug Counselor **A/A/S:** National Association of Social Workers; National Association of Alcoholism and Drug Abuse Counselors **DOB:** October 3, 1958 **A/S:** He attributes his success to his endeavors to relate to his patients. **B/I:** He became involved in his profession because he enjoyed helping people with their problems and his mentor encouraged him to pursue the career. **H/O:** The most gratifying aspect of his career working to help save patients' lives. **I/F/Y:** In five years, Mr. Parsons will have earned his doctorate degree and operate in a clinic.

MRS. GEORGIA A. PASQUALONE, RN, MSPS, MSN, CEN
Forensic Nurse Consultant
Winchester Hospital
41 Highland Avenue
Winchester, MA 01890 United States
ltcgeorgia@msn.com
http://www.cambridgewhoswho.com

BUS: Hospital **P/S:** Healthcare **MA:** Regional **EXP:** Ms. Pasqualone's expertise is in forensic nurse consulting. **H/I/S:** Photography, Reading **FBP:** American Journal of Nursing **EDU:** Master's Degree in Forensic Sciences, University of New Haven; Master's Degree in Forensic Nursing, Fitchburg State College; Bachelor of Science in Nursing, Boston University **CERTS:** Certified Forensic Nurse; Certified Emergency Nurse; Diplomate, American College of Forensic Examiners **A/A/S:** Emergency Nursing Association; Sigma Theta Tau International **A/H:** Leadership Award in Nursing; Pioneer in Nursing Award, Sigma Theta Tau; Virginia A. Lynch Pioneer Award, International Association of Forensic Nurses **A/S:** She attributes her success to her determination, desire to preserve justice and her faith in God. **B/I:** She became involved in her profession because of her love for mysteries and solving criminal investigations and her desire to work in law and nursing. **H/O:** The most gratifying aspect of her career is being able to continually set and achieve goals. **I/F/Y:** In five years, Ms. Pasqualone hopes to increase her case load and continue reading records.

ELIZABETH PASSAGE JUDD
Education Program Specialist
United States Department of Education
400 Maryland Avenue S.W.
Washington, DC 20202 United States
elizabeth.judd@ed.gov
http://www.ed.gov

BUS: Department of Education **P/S:** Education, Establishing Policies on Federal Financial Aid for Education, Distributing Funds, Surveying and Disseminating Research **MA:** Local **EXP:** Ms. Passage Judd's expertise is in teaching English as a second language. **FBP:** Education Week; The Economist **EDU:** Master's Degree in Education, with Concentration on Curriculum Instruction, George Mason University **A/A/S:** Alumni Association, George Mason University; Alumni Association, The University of Texas, El Paso; Manassas Park City Schools; Association for Supervision and Curriculum Development **C/VW:** Volunteer, Horton's Kids; McLean Bible Church **A/S:** She attributes her success to being goal-oriented. **B/I:** She became involved in her profession through a natural progression of opportunities. **H/O:** The highlight of her career was obtaining her master's degree.

AMY BETH PATAKY
Pre-School Manager
Patti's All American-Gym-N-Learn
1530 Joliet Street
Dyer, IN 46311 United States
mpataky@sbcglobal.net
http://www.arbonne.com

BUS: Preschool and Fitness Center **P/S:** Education, Fitness Training **MA:** Local **D/D/R:** Specializing in Early Childhood Education and Business Management, Helping to Initiate Programs and Lessons, Managing Trial Classes, Communicating with Parents and Families **H/I/S:** Collecting Teddy Bears, Raising a Family, Shopping **EDU:** Bachelor's Degree in Elementary Education, Purdue University **CERTS:** Certification in First Aid and CPR; Certification in Gymnastics Safety; Certification, Kindergarten Endorsement Program; Kinder Accreditation for Teachers Program, Preschool FUNdamentals **A/A/S:** National Catholic Educational Association; National Council of Private Educators **C/VW:** March of Dimes; Kohl's Care for Kids **SP:** Michael **A/S:** She attributes her success to being raised in a family in which education was highly valued. **B/I:** She became involved in her profession because she comes from a family of educators. **H/O:** The highlight of her career was being able to start her own nursery program.

JAIMINI PATEL
Pharmacist
Wal-Mart Stores, Inc.
50 N. Macdade Boulevard
Glenolden, PA 19036 United States
jaymipatel@verizon.net
http://www.cambridgewhoswho.com

BUS: Retail Store **P/S:** Individualized Customer Service, Pharmaceuticals, Retail Merchandise **MA:** Local **D/D/R:** Managing the Pharmacy, Educating Patients **H/I/S:** Playing Chess, Traveling **FBP:** Forbes; Pharmacy Times **EDU:** Bachelor of Science in Pharmacy, Long Island University **A/A/S:** Indo-American Association; Indian Association **A/H:** Customer Service Award, Wal-Mart Stores, Inc. **C/VW:** Children's Miracle Network; Disabled American Veterans; Volunteer, Indian Earthquake Relief; Diabetes Camps, American Diabetes Association **A/S:** She attributes her success to her hard work, determination and dedication to her job. **B/I:** She became involved in her profession because she wanted to help others.

SUDHA D. PATEL, BS, RDMS
Multi-Competent Technologist
UMDNJ, Robert Wood Division Medical School, Pediatric Cardiology
1 Robert Wood Johnson Place
New Brunswick, NJ 08903 United States
ultrasdp@aol.com
http://www.cambridgewhoswho.com

BUS: Medical School **P/S:** Healthcare **MA:** Statewide **D/D/R:** Specializing in Pediatric and Fetal Echocardiography, Patient Education and In-service Orientation to New Students **H/I/S:** Traveling, Crafts, Arranging Community Cultural Events, Organizing Dance Performances **FBP:** Journal of the American Society of Echocardiography **EDU:** Bachelor of Science in Biology, India **CERTS:** Ultrasound Echo and Cardiovascular Certification; Certified in Pediatrics Fetal and Adult Echocardiography, Vascular, Abdomen and OB/GYN Studies **A/A/S:** ARDMS; ASOEC; Board of Directors, PCA of USA

ANTONELLO C. PATRONE
Business Unit Executive
IBM
6300 Oak Tree Boulevard
Cleveland, OH 44147 United States
http://www.cambridgewhoswho.com

BUS: Technology Solutions **P/S:** Computer Sales **MA:** International **D/D/R:** Sales Management, Sales Development **H/I/S:** Golfing, Outdoor Activities, and Spending Time with his Family **FBP:** The Wall Street Journal **EDU:** Master of Arts in Business Administration, Youngstown State University **A/A/S:** AMA; BMA **C/VW:** United Way of America, St. Jude Children's Research Hospital, American Cancer Society, Multiple Sclerosis Foundation **A/S:** He attributes his success to diligence. **B/I:** He chose the profession because of the international opportunities. **H/O:** The highlight of his career is his current position.

SHERRY L. PATTERSON, LPN
LPN, Medical Necessity Coordinator
Grady Memorial Hospital, Five Oaks, Medical Group
2220 Iowa
Chickasha, OK 73013 United States
http://www.cambridgewhoswho.com

BUS: Hospital **P/S:** Patient Care **MA:** Local **D/D/R:** Coordinate Doctor's Diagnosis, Decode Lab Reports, Bookkeeping, Distribution **H/I/S:** Playing the 12 String Guitar, Gardening, Landscaping **EDU:** Nursing Degree **C/VW:** Singing at Nursing Homes **A/S:** She attributes her success to hard work and dedication. **B/I:** She was prompted to enter her profession because she always wanted to be a nurse. **H/O:** The highlight of her career is helping people.

SHEILA A. PATTON, DTR
Dietetic Technician
Excela Health-Latrobe Hospital
121 W. Second Avenue
Latrobe, PA 15650 United States
spatton@excelahealth.org
http://www.cambridgewhoswho.com

BUS: Healthcare Center **P/S:** Healthcare **MA:** Regional **EXP:** Ms. Patton's expertise is in the oversight of computer-based food service and software administration. **H/I/S:** Bowling, Making Crafts, Scrapbooking, Reading **FBP:** Journal of the American Dietetic Association **EDU:** Associate Degree in Clinical Nutrition, Westmoreland Community College (1995) **A/A/S:** American Dietetic Association **C/VW:** United Way of America **A/S:** She attributes her success to her hard work and persistence. **H/O:** The highlight of her career was being an administrator with Latrobe Hospital.

JENNIFER S. PATZOLD
Chief Information Officer
Neptune Management Corporation
888 E. Las Olas Boulevard, Suite 300
Fort Lauderdale, FL 33301 United States
jpatzold@comcast.net
jpatzold@neptunesociety.com
http://www.neptunesociety.com

BUS: Funeral Home **P/S:** Cremation, Funeral Services **MA:** National **EXP:** Ms. Patzold's expertise is in information technology and technology services. **H/I/S:** Spending Time Outdoors, Water Sports, Scuba Diving **FBP:** The Wall Street Journal **EDU:** Bachelor of Science in Speech-Language Pathology, University of Washington **CERTS:** Certification in Online Information Technology; Six Sigma Certification, Microsoft Operations Board, Society for Information Management **A/A/S:** Six Sigma **A/S:** She attributes her success to her determination and persistence. **B/I:** She became involved in her profession because of her passion for technology. **H/O:** The highlight of her career was obtaining her current position.

Mr. Thomas A. Paulhus
Vice Principal
Blessed Sacrament School
277 Sixth Avenue
Paterson, NJ 07524 United States
thomas.paulhus@cwwemail.com

BUS: Proven Leader in the Education Industry **P/S:** High Quality Educational Services **MA:** Local **D/D/R:** Mentoring, Leading, Substituting, Teaching Social Studies, Religion and Language Arts, Acting as the Dean of Discipline and Student Council Coordinator **H/I/S:** Reading, Golf **FBP:** Educational Leadership **EDU:** Master's Degree in Educational Administration, Seton Hall University (2002); Bachelor's Degree History and Secondary Education Heidelberg College, Ohio (1975) **CERTS:** New Jersey Principal Certificate-2004; New Jersey Teaching Certificate-1994 **A/A/S:** Association for Supervision and Curriculum Development; Kappa Delta Pi **C/VW:** CCD at Church

Margaret Pawson
Owner
Mar-Go Limousine Service, LLC
91 Townsend Road
Hopewell Junction, NY 12533 United States
margolimo@aol.com
http://www.cambridgewhoswho.com

BUS: Transportation Company **P/S:** Transportation Services **MA:** Regional **D/D/R:** Managing Bookings, Budgeting, Advertising, Marketing, Dispatching, Scheduling **H/I/S:** Horseback Riding, Reading, Traveling **EDU:** High School Diploma **A/A/S:** Better Business Bureau; Little League **C/VW:** American Cancer Society **A/S:** She attributes her success to her hard work and determination. **B/I:** She became involved in her profession because of her personal experience. **H/O:** The most gratifying aspect of her career is establishing her own business.

MARGARET L. PAYNE, MD
Pediatrician, Managing Partner
Payne Pediatrics, Ltd, LLP
1213 Hermann Drive 770
Houston, TX 77004 United States
mpnpoint@sbcglobal.net
http://www.cambridgeswhoswho.com

BUS: Healthcare, Pediatrics **P/S:** Pediatric Medicine and Treatment **MA:** Local **D/D/R:** Pediatrics, Immunization **H/I/S:** Needlepoint **EDU:** MD, University of Texas; Bachelor of Arts, University of California **CERTS:** Board Certification, Texas Pediatric Society **A/A/S:** AAP; TMA, Texas Pediatric Society; Harris Court Medical Society **A/H:** Five Top Immunization Awards; Best Doctor in America, Nominated Twice

MICHELE BETH PAYUK
Florida Real Estate Sales Associate
Sales Department, All Florida GMAC Real Estate
1648 S.E. Port St. Lucie Boulevard
Port Saint Lucie, FL 34952 United States
shelby777@earthlink.net
http://www.team3floridarealestate.com
http://www.e-real-estate.com/michelepayuk

BUS: Real Estate Agency **P/S:** Real Estate Exchange for Condominiums, Vacant Land, Golf Communities, Residential, New Construction, Commercial and Property Management Service **MA:** St. Lucie County, Martin County, Indian River County, Brevard County, Charlotte County, Lee County, Hernando County, Citrus County, Hendry County, Highlands County, Polk County, Sumter County, Marion County, Putnam County **D/D/R:** Negotiating Contracts, Marketing, Representing Sellers, Buyers, Investors, Bookkeeping, Overseeing New Construction, Community Operations and Property Management Services **H/I/S:** Remodeling, Making Crafts, Walking, Dancing, Bicycling **FBP:** Realtor; Florida Realtor; Money; New York **EDU:** Coursework in Accounting, La Salle Extension University (1975); Coursework in Import and Export Trade (1972); Coursework in Marketing and Design (1967) **CERTS:** Licensed Real Estate Sales Associate, State of Florida; HouseValues Certified Professional; Certified 1031 Exchange Agent, Starker Services, Inc. **A/H:** Top Producer Award; Top Agent of the Month Award; Most Helpful Agent Award; First Annual ACE Award, Accounting Department, National Relocation, PHH; Honored Member, Manchester Who's Who Registry of Executives and Professionals; Elected Member, The Republican Town Committee, Bethel, CT **C/VW:** Disabled American Veterans; Veterans of Foreign Wars; Florida Highway Patrol; American Red Cross; Muscular Dystrophy Association; Florida Sheriffs Youth Ranches; Special Olympics **DOB:** September 5, 1948 **POB:** Danbury, CT **CHILD:** Kristi, Beth, Robert **A/S:** She attributes her success to her honesty, work ethic, desire for learning, organizational skills and being goal-oriented. **H/O:** The most gratifying aspect of her career is receiving gratitude from her clients.

MICHELE PEARL ELLISON, ACSW, M.DIV.
Owner, Principal
Michele Pearl Ellison Consulting
PO Box 53117
Pittsburgh, PA 15219 United States
michelepearle@yahoo.com
http://www.cambridgewhoswho.com

BUS: Human Service Company **P/S:** Education and Training Services, Program Evaluations, Motivational Speaking, Public Speaking, Consultations, Publications **MA:** International **D/D/R:** Performing Social Work, Offering Grief, Anger, Addiction and Violence Intervention and Prevention, Utilizing Social Welfare Policies, Integrating Christian Values **H/I/S:** Bicycling, Writing Poetry, Visiting Museums **FBP:** Smart Money; Fortune; The Wall Street Journal **EDU:** Pursuing Doctorate Degree, Howard University, School of Social Work; Master of Social Welfare, SUNY Stony Brook University; Master of Divinity, Virginia Union University; Bachelor of Social Work and Human Services, Empire State College; Coursework, South Oaks Institute of Alcoholism and Addictive Behavior Studies; Coursework, The Lutheran Church Year, Lutheran House of Studies **CERTS:** Certification in Clinical Pastoral Education, The HealthCare Chaplaincy; Certification in Hospital Chaplaincy, The HealthCare Chaplaincy; Certification, Academy of Certified Social Workers; Certification in Clinical Pastoral Education; Certification in Alcoholism Counseling; Certified Associate In Ministry, Evangelical Lutheran Church in America; Ordination, Providence Harvest International; Ordination, Council of Women Ministers of Greater Washington **A/A/S:** National Association of Social Workers; Leadership Pittsburgh Inc.; Former President, Local Chapter, National Association of Black Social Workers; North American Association of Christians in Social Work; Secretary, Council of Women Ministers of Greater Washington; Secretary, Male Support Arm; International Who's Who of Professionals; Who's Who Among Human Services Professionals **A/H:** Alumni of the Year, Long Island Lutheran High School; Outstanding Service Award, Council of Churches of the City of New York; Award, PEO International **C/VW:** Coalition Against Local Violence; Planning Council, Black Political Empowerment Project, Pittsburgh, PA; Election Protection, Pittsburgh, PA; Volunteer, Voter Registration; Monitor, The Racial Equity Monitoring Project; Forum Participant, Pennsylvania Education Policy Forum; Participant, Institute of Politics, Pittsburgh, PA; Facilitator, Creating a Culture of Peace; Allegheny County Hunger and Homeless Advisory Committee; Participant, Allegheny County Mental Retardation/Mental Health Advisory Council; Christian-Jewish Dialog, American Jewish Committee, Pittsburgh, PA; National Speaker, American Bible Society; Participant, Fact-finding Delegation, Egypt **DOB:** November 1, 1954 **POB:** Queens, NY **A/S:** She attributes her success to her faith in God, focus, perseverance and desire to help others. **B/I:** She became in her profession because her father was in politics and her mother was deeply involved in community work. **H/O:** The most gratifying aspects of her career are being involved in ecumenical, interfaith and international dialogue that impacts the daily lives of people. **I/F/Y:** In five years, Ms. Pearl Ellison sees herself as an author and businesswoman whose thoughts and work will have impacted the majority of the world's inhabitants.

MICHELLE R. PEARSON
Teacher
Janesville School District
527 S. Franklin Street
Janesville, WI 53548 United States
mpearson@janesville.k12.wi.us
http://www.janeville.k12.wi.us

BUS: Education **P/S:** All Levels of Education **MA:** Local **D/D/R:** Special Education **H/I/S:** Riding with her Husband on their Motorcycle, Spending Time with her Dog, Reading **EDU:** Bachelor's Degree in Education, Learning Disabilities and Emotional Disorders, University of Wisconsin; Master's Degree in Curriculum and Institution, National-Louis University **C/VW:** United Way of America; National Multiple Sclerosis Society; Church **A/S:** She attributes her success to her relationship with her students. She also has great communication skills. **B/I:** She became involved in the profession because of her brother, who had a learning disability. His disability triggered her interest. **H/O:** The highlight of her career is having had a student nominated for Who's Who Among American Students. The same student has gone on to work in the special education field.

DR. DONNA B. PEAVEY
Assistant Professor of Christian Education,
Keynote Speaker at Educational Conferences
New Orleans Baptist Theological Seminary
3939 Gentilly Boulevard
New Orleans, LA 70126 United States
dpeavey@nobts.edu
http://www.nobts.edu

BUS: Ministry, School **P/S:** Seminary Education, Educational Consulting **MA:** Local **EXP:** Ms. Peavey's expertise is in childhood education. **H/I/S:** Reading, Watching Movies, Spending Time with the Family **FBP:** Leadership; Discipleship Journal; Christian Education Journal **EDU:** Ph.D., New Orleans Baptist Theological Seminary; Master of Religious Education, New Orleans Baptist Theological Seminary; Master of Theology, New Orleans Baptist Theological Seminary; Bachelor of Science, University of Southern Mississippi **A/A/S:** Baptist Association of Christian Educators; North American Professors of Christian Education; National Association for the Education of Young Children **C/VW:** Baptist Seminary; First Baptist Church of New Orleans; Hope Ministry of Greater New Orleans **A/S:** She attributes her success to determination to follow what she believes is God's calling for her. **H/O:** The highlight of her career was being elected to a tenured faculty position. The most gratifying aspect of her career is having the opportunity to interact with the students.

GAIL PEDESCLEAUX-MUCKLE
Owner, Creative Consultant
KGM Design
54 Rainford Road
Edison, NJ 08820 United States
pedymuck@msn.com
http://www.cambridgewhoswho.com

BUS: Consulting Firm **P/S:** Consulting Services **MA:** National **EXP:** Ms. Pedescleaux-Muckle's expertise is in creative arts. **D/D/R:** Consulting with Creative Arts and Writing Professionals, Marketing, Advertising, Negotiating Contracts, Designing Greeting Cards, Writing and Motivational Speaking **H/I/S:** Jazzercise, Attending the Theater, Listening to Music, Gardening **EDU:** Bachelor of Arts in English, Central Michigan University (1971) **CERTS:** Certification in Creative Arts **A/A/S:** Multiple Sclerosis Association of America; American Ballet Theater **C/VW:** Women Helping Women **POB:** Cleveland, OH **SP:** Kirk **A/S:** She attributes her success to her hard work and to the support she received from her husband.

MR. JAMES V. PEGUESE, CCE
Assistant Commissioner, Security
Maryland Department of Public Safety, Division of Corrections
6776 Reisterstown Road
Baltimore, MD 21215 United States
jpeguese@dpscs.state.md.us
http://www.dpscs.state.md.us

BUS: Department Working to keep Maryland Communities Safe **P/S:** Adult Corrections, Security Management and Adult Offenders **MA:** Regional **D/D/R:** Responsible for the Maintenance of 27 Institutions/Facilities, Develops and Oversees the Implementation of Security Procedures, Reviews Security Procedures from Other Jurisdictions Locally as well as Nationally to Determine Best Practices, Maintains the Emergency Operations/Continuance of Operations Plans and Ensures Readiness, Managing the Special Response Team, Hostage Negotiation Team, Critical Incident Stress Management Team, Contraband Interdiction Team and K-9 Team **H/I/S:** Riding Bikes **FBP:** Corrections Today **EDU:** Bachelor of Arts Degree in Criminal Justice, Columbus University (2000) **A/A/S:** American Correctional Association; National Association of Wardens and Superintendents; Maryland Criminal Justice Administrative Association; National Association for the Advancement of Colored People; Masonic Lodge **C/VW:** American Cancer Society **SP:** Cheryl

ANN C. PELITERA
Special Education Teacher
Alden Central School
13250 Park Street
Alden, NY 14004 United States
apelitera@alden.wnyric.org
http://www.cambridgewhoswho.com

BUS: Education **P/S:** Public Middle School **MA:** Local **D/D/R:** Teaching in the Blended Inclusion Special Education Program for Students in Sixth through Eighth-Grades **H/I/S:** Exercising, Reading, Shopping, Spending Quality Time with her Children **EDU:** Master's Degree in Education, Buffalo State College; Bachelor's Degree in Elementary Education, SUNY Fredonia **A/A/S:** School Board **C/VW:** Church; Volunteer Swim Coach **A/S:** She attributes her career success to the positive role models she has had in her life and the love of her work and the children she teaches. **H/O:** The most gratifying aspect of her career is keeping in contact with former students and being able to see them become successful.

ELIZABETH A. PELLETIER, RN, CCRN
Registered Nurse, Critical Care Registered Nurse
Berkshire Medical Center
P. O. Box 2401
Pittsfield, MA 01202 United States
epelle@msn.com
http://www.berkshirehealthsystems.com

BUS: Nonprofit Community Hospital **P/S:** Comprehensive Healthcare Services to Residents of and Visitors to Berkshire County and Surrounding Communities **MA:** Regional **D/D/R:** Nursing, Intensive Care, Critical Care, Staff Nurse, Charge Nursing, Caring for Patients with Compassion and Understanding **H/I/S:** Golfing, Hiking, Bicycling, Gardening, Canning Vegetables, Drying Herbs, Tennis, Skiing, Cooking, Scuba Diving, Traveling **EDU:** Associate of Arts in Registered Nursing, Holyoke College **A/A/S:** American Association of Critical Care Nurses; Springside Greenhouse

DR. WILLIAM PENA
President
Return 2 Wellness, LLC
520 N.E. 38th Street
Suite 13
Miami, FL 33137 United States
drpena@return2wellness.com
http://www.return2wellness.com

BUS: Wellness Health Center **P/S:** Wellness, Nutrition, Health and Chiropractic Care **MA:** Local **D/D/R:** Neurology **H/I/S:** Martial Arts, Scuba Diving, Spending Time with his Family, Bike Riding, Editing Film on his Computer **FBP:** Time; Entrepreneur **EDU:** Pursuing Doctor of Chiropractic Medicine, Palmer College; Master's Degree in Information Technology, American Intercontinental University **A/A/S:** Former Vice-President and President, American Chiropractic Association **C/VW:** Catholic Church; Habitat for Humanity; Youth Groups; Feed the Homeless; Runs a Clinic to Work with the Needy to Provide Free Treatment at a Halfway House **A/S:** He feels that his tenacity and determination have helped him to achieve success in his career. **B/I:** Although he worked in the surgical field for ten years, he has always had an interest in alternative medicine, so after he was injured and treated by alternative methods, he decided to pursue a career in chiropractics.

NANCY PENCHEREK-JACKSON
Real Estate Broker
Home Hunters USA, Inc.
1415 Colonial Boulevard
Fort Myers, FL 33907 United States
jacksonnancy@msn.com
http://www.homehuntersusa.com

BUS: Real Estate Agency **P/S:** Real Estate Exchange **MA:** Local **EXP:** Her expertise is in commercial, residential listings and sales. **D/D/R:** Assisting in Building Homes and Duplexes, Managing Investment Properties, Corporate Relocations and Analyzing Market Strategy **H/I/S:** Traveling, Oil Painting, Dancing, Volunteering Missionary Services **FBP:** Realtor **EDU:** Associate Degree in English and Communications, Edison Junior Community College **CERTS:** Certified Instructor of Real Estate; Certified Notary Public **C/VW:** Lyons International Christ Community Church

MS. MARYANN PENN, PH.D.
Nurse Manager
USC Healthcare Network
2829 S. Grand Avenue
Los Angeles, CA 90007 United States
mapenn@lacusc.org
http://www.womenariseministries.org

BUS: Los Angeles County Healthcare Network **P/S:** Healthcare, Education, Ministering **MA:** National **D/D/R:** Medical-Surgical and Public Health Nursing, Administration and Biblical Counseling **H/I/S:** Traveling, Attending Plays and Concerts **FBP:** American Journal of Nursing; American Educator; Journal of Nursing Scholarship; Nurses World; Nursing2009; Christian Journals **EDU:** Doctorate in Biblical Counseling, Friends International Christian University (2000); Master of Science in Nursing, California State University at Dominguez Hills (1992); Bachelor of Science, Nursing California State University at Los Angels; ASN, Los Angeles Southwest Community College (1984) **CERTS:** Vocational Education Teaching Credential, State of California (1999); Public Health Nurse Licensure (1988); Quality Assurance Certificate (1992) **A/A/S:** Sigma Theta Tau; Southwest Nurses Alumni Association **A/H:** Community Service and Appreciation Awards **C/VW:** Foreign Missions; Feed the Children; World Vision; Negro College Fund; City of Hope; United Way of America **A/S:** She attributes her success to her faith in her personal Lord and Savior Jesus Christ and to acting on the word of God. **B/I:** She became involved in her profession because she felt nursing was her calling and ministry. **H/O:** The highlight of her career was completing nursing school.

DUDA PENTEADO
Fine Artist
Duda Penteado Fine Arts, Inc.
33-35 Westervelt Place
Jersey City, NJ 07304 United States
duda@dudapenteado.com
http://www.dudapenteado.com

BUS: Fine Art Company **P/S:** Fine Art **MA:** International **D/D/R:** Art, Lecturing, Presenting Workshops **H/I/S:** Golfing, Reading, Traveling **A/A/S:** Chairman, Art Certification Board **A/H:** The Key Jersey City Award **C/VW:** Hope Center Visual and Performing Arts, Dress for Success, Latinia Ecology Center **A/S:** He attributes his success to his perseverance. **B/I:** He became involved in his profession because he had a passion for art. **H/O:** The highlight of his career was receiving the Key to Jersey City award.

IDA MARIE PERA
Teacher
Yokayo Elementary School
Ukiah Unified School District
790 S. Dora Street
Ukiah, CA 95482 United States
mpera@pacific.net
http://www.uusd.net

BUS: School District **P/S:** Primary Education **MA:** Local **EXP:** Ms. Pera's expertise is in integrating arts into curriculum. **H/I/S:** Artwork **FBP:** American Artist **EDU:** Bachelor of Liberal Studies in History and Art, California State University, East Bay, Hayward; Bachelor of Arts in Studio Art, California State University, East Bay, Hayward; Associate of Arts in Early Childhood Studies, Ohlone College, Fremont, CA; Associate of Arts in Fine Arts, Ohlone College **A/A/S:** Technology Trek Coordinator, Former President, Ukiah Branch Library; Olive Hyde Art Gallery; Mendocino Art Center; Mendocino County Arts Association; Fremont Art Association; Former Presenter, The California Arts Project; Former Co-Coordinator, Redwood Arts Project, Region I, CA **A/H:** Grant Award, American Association of Women (2006); Teacher of the Year Award **C/VW:** Mission Outreach Committee, First Presbyterian Church, Ukiah; Former Chairwoman, Education Committee, Fremont Methodist Church **W/H:** Art Mentor, Ukiah Unified School District **A/S:** She attributes her success to her helping nature. **B/I:** She became involved in her profession because of her love for working with children. **H/O:** The highlight of her career was being recognized by the local parent-teacher association.

ELIZABETH PEREZ
Broker Associate
Prudential Florida WCI Realty
825 Arthur Godfrey Road
Miami Beach, FL 33140 United States
eperezhomes@gmail.com
http://www.sellingcastlesinthesky.net

BUS: Real Estate Agency **P/S:** Commercial and Residential Real Estate Exchange **MA:** International **D/D/R:** Managing Operations Including Marketing, Acquiring New Clients, Maintaining Relationships with Prior Clients and Selling Real Estate Properties **H/I/S:** Dancing, Traveling **FBP:** Florida Association of Realtors Publications; SmartMoney **EDU:** Associate Degree in Business Administration, Grace Commercial College (1979) **CERTS:** Certified International Property Specialist; Transnational Referral Certification **A/A/S:** National Association of Realtors; Real Estate CyberSpace Society **C/VW:** Volunteer, Big Brothers Big Sisters of America

TAMMY L. PEREZ
Special Education Teacher
Chattanooga Valley Middle School
847 Allgood Road
Flintstone, GA 30725 United States
tammy@perez1.com
http://www.walkerschools.org/cvm

BUS: Middle School **P/S:** Public Education **MA:** Local **D/D/R:** Teaching Special Education, Offering Teacher Support, Heading up the Department **H/I/S:** Spending Time with her Family, Reading **EDU:** Pursuing Master's Degree in Educational Leadership, Grand Canyon University (2008); Bachelor's Degree in Special Education, University of Tennessee at Chattanooga **A/A/S:** National Education Association; Georgia Association of Education **A/H:** Teacher of the Year (2006-2007) **C/VW:** Child Sponsor, World Vision; Community Program Volunteer

LUIS A. PÉREZ DELGADO
Engineering Manager
St. Jude Medical
Caguas West Industrial Park
Lot 21
Caguas, PR 00725 United States
Lperez@sjm.com
http://www.sjm.com

BUS: Medical Device Manufacturer **P/S:** Manufacturer of Medical Devices such as Heart Valves and Vascular Closure Devices **MA:** International **D/D/R:** Mechanical Engineering of Healthcare Products, Developed the First Custom Made Vision Inspection System Used Worldwide for Packaging **H/I/S:** Playing Basketball, Golfing, Motorcycling, Traveling **EDU:** Bachelor's Degree in Mechanical Engineering, University of Puerto Rico **A/A/S:** Engineering Association of Puerto Rico **C/VW:** Helping Needy Families Locally by Cleaning and Building Homes and Neighborhoods **A/S:** He attributes his success to being responsible and giving 100 percent effort to his job. **B/I:** He became involved in this profession because as a young boy he was always fascinated by cars and machines and how they work. **H/O:** The highlight of his career is developing the vision inspection system for packaging.

WILLIAM PERKINS III
Fire Chief, Assistant Director of Public Safety
University of Connecticut Health Center Fire Department
62 Mines Road
Bristol, CT 06010 United States
perkins@uchc.edu
http://www.firedept.uchc.edu

BUS: Fire Department **P/S:** Fire Suppression/Prevention, EMS **MA:** Local **D/D/R:** Overseeing Incident Command and Tactical Medicine, Protecting against Weapons of Mass Destruction and Terrorism **H/I/S:** Golfing, Hunting, Swimming **FBP:** Fire Chief **EDU:** Industry-Related Training and Experience **A/A/S:** National Fire Protection Association; HFMA; National Tactical Officers Association; International Association of Fire Chiefs **C/VW:** Police; American Heart Association; American Association for Cancer Research **A/S:** He attributes his personal and professional success to his values and role models.

DEBBIE A. PERRAULT, RN
Registered Nurse, Nursing Supervisor
Central Washington Family Medicine
debbie@cwfm.net
http://www.cambridgewhoswho.com

BUS: Nursing **P/S:** Family Practice Residency **MA:** Local **D/D/R:** Supervisor of 17 Nurses **H/I/S:** Reading, Knitting, Church **FBP:** RN **EDU:** Associate Degree in Nursing **C/VW:** March of Dimes; Memorial Bible Church; American Cancer Society; Parkinson's Foundation **A/S:** She attributes her personal and professional success to her compassion. **B/I:** She has always had an interest in the field and a desire to help others.

CINDY A. PERRY, RHIT
Manager, Consultant
Trail's End Studio
950 W. 42nd S.
Mountain Home, ID 83647 United States
cperry113@msn.com
http://www.cambridgewhoswho.com

BUS: Recording Studio **P/S:** Studio Giving Artists a Relaxed and Affordable Place to Record, Write Songs and Perform **MA:** National **D/D/R:** Marketing, Advertising, Managing Websites, Songwriting and Singing Including Folk, Country and Blues, Consulting and Managing Existing and New Singing Teams **H/I/S:** Skiing, Mountain Biking, Spending Time Outdoors **FBP:** American Health Information Management Association Journal **EDU:** Associate Degree in Applied Science, Rose State College, OK (1991) **CERTS:** Regional Health Information Technician (1993) **A/A/S:** American Health Information Management Association

M. LYNNE PERRY
Office Manager
J.R. Polgar, Inc.
2650 Enterprise Road
Clearwater, FL 33763 United States
lynne.perry@jrpolgars.com
http://www.cambridgewhoswho.com

BUS: Furniture Repair, Restoration and Building **P/S:** Furniture Repair and Restoration **MA:** Regional **D/D/R:** Managing Incoming and Outgoing Business **H/I/S:** Collects and Restores Cabbage Patch Dolls **EDU:** Extensive Industry Related Training and Experience **C/VW:** St. Vincent DePaul **A/S:** She attributes her success to her eagerness to learn.

MS. DENISE PERSOHN
Teacher
Parkway Central High School
Special School District
12110 Clayton Road
Ballwin, MO 63011 United States
dpersohn@parkway.k12.mo.us
http://www.cambridgewhoswho.com

BUS: School District **P/S:** Education **MA:** Local **D/D/R:** Working with Handicapped Children and Children with Learning Disabilities and Mental Retardation, Teaching Direct Reading to Disabled Students in Pre-Kindergarten through 11th-Grade **H/I/S:** Genealogy, Scrapbooking, Reading **EDU:** Master's Degree in Special Education **A/A/S:** Delta Phi

MAYA PESOK
Owner, Broker
1st Premier Mortgage Company, LLC
45 Sunrise Hill Road
Norwalk, CT 06851 United States
Maya@1stPremier.org
http://www.1stPremier.org

BUS: Mortgage Company **P/S:** Finance and Mortgage Services, Home Equity Lines of Credit, Credit Repair, Refinancing, Debt Consolidation, Home Improvement, Customer Service **MA:** Local **D/D/R:** Specializing in Customer Relations, Assisting Customers to Obtain Mortgages that Meet their Individual Needs, Ensuring Quality and Customer Satisfaction, Educating Clients Regarding Finances and Credit **FBP:** Mortgage Originator **CERTS:** Licensed Broker, State of Connecticut

KATHLEEN M. PETERS, RN, BSHS, CCM
Manager Case Management
Qualis Health
10700 Meridian Avenue N.
Seattle, WA 98133 United States
kmp54@comcast.net
http://www.qualishealth.org

BUS: Private, Nonprofit Organization **P/S:** Care Management, Quality Improvement and Assessment, and Health Services Research Services **MA:** Washington, Idaho, Alaska **D/D/R:** Specializing in Orthopedics, Rehabilitation and Case Management **FBP:** The Case Manager **EDU:** Bachelor's Degree, Human Service, University of Phoenix (2007); Registered Nurse Diploma, Middletown State Hospital **A/A/S:** Washington Medical Case Management Association; National Case Management Society of America; Lifelong AIDS Alliance; Southwest Youth

EVELYN H. PETERSEN
Vice President, Chief Executive Officer
VIP Construction, Inc.
3048 E. Baseline Road
Suite 102
Mesa, AZ 85204 United States
evelyn@viphomes.com
http://www.viphomes.com

BUS: Construction Company **P/S:** Construction Services Including Customized Construction, Sales of Residential and Commercial Properties **MA:** Regional **EXP:** Ms. Petersen's expertise is in operations management and land acquisition oversight. **H/I/S:** Traveling, Gourmet Cooking **FBP:** National Home Builder **EDU:** Coursework in Cosmetology, Trade School **CERTS:** Registered Contractor **A/A/S:** National Association of Home Builders; Better Business Bureau; Women's Relief Society **C/VW:** Local Church **A/S:** She attributes her success to her people management skills and to the support she receives from her family. **B/I:** She became involved in her profession because it was her family business. **H/O:** The most gratifying aspects of her career are interacting with people and running a profitable company.

ANGELA PETERSON, CST
Certified Surgical Technologist
Surgical Service Department
McLeod Health
555 E. Cheves Street
Florence, SC 29506 United States
sofball18@aol.com
http://www.mcleodhealth.org

BUS: Medical Center **P/S:** Healthcare **MA:** Regional **D/D/R:** Arranging Equipment and Supplies for Surgical Procedures, Caring for Preoperative Patients, Assisting Surgeons during Surgical Procedures, Dressings and Cleaning Post-Operative Patients, Assisting Physicians on Gynecological and General Surgery **H/I/S:** Playing Softball, Traveling, Gardening, Cooking, Making Crafts, Watching Sports **FBP:** Black Enterprise; The Surgical Technologist; Industry-Related Publications **CERTS:** Pursuing Registered Nurse Program; Certified Surgical Technologist, Florence-Darlington Technical College **A/A/S:** Board of Directors, South Carolina State Assembly of Surgical Technologists **A/H:** National Minority Award (2000); Recipient, Bruce and Lee Allied Health Scholarship (2000); National Award Winner; Dean's List **C/VW:** Former Volunteer, American Red Cross; McLeod Health Foundation; March of Dimes; United Way of America Foundation **POB:** Florence County, SC **A/S:** She attributes her success to her love for humanity and faith in God. **B/I:** She became involved in her profession because of her interest in the medical field. **H/O:** The most gratifying aspect of her career is knowing at the end of the day that she helped to improve someone's quality of life whether it's a minor procedure or an organ transplant to someone who's been desperately awaiting for a second chance at life.

KARLA J. PETERSON
Real Estate Broker
ComeHome2Minnesota Realty, Inc.
26189 Galen Drive
Wyoming, MN 55092 United States
karla@ch2mn.com
http://www.ch2mn.com

BUS: Leading Providers of Real Estate Services **P/S:** Local, Family-Owned Real Estate Company Designed to Help Clients Prepare to Sell their House, Find a New One or Build their Dream Home **MA:** Regional **D/D/R:** Specializing in Real Estate, Co-Owner of this Residential Real Estate Brokerage, Utilizing a more Personal Format for Helping their Clients While Maintaining the Ease and Convenience of the Internet, Marketing, Analysis, Relocations **H/I/S:** Gardening, Traveling **FBP:** Cosmopolitan **CERTS:** Broker's License (1989); Realtor's License (1981) **A/A/S:** Minnesota Association of Realtors; St. Paul Area Association of Realtors; National Association of Realtors

PAMELA JO PETERSON
Owner
Target Safety and Training
413 S. Main Street
Pima, AZ 85543 United States
wmwoman_2000@yahoo.com
http://www.cambridgewhoswho.com

BUS: Safety and Training Center **P/S:** Safety Training and Instruction **MA:** Local **D/D/R:** Emergency Medicine **H/I/S:** Traveling **FBP:** Emergency Medicine Journal **EDU:** Associate Degree in Nursing, Eastern Arizona College **A/A/S:** National Safety Council; Arizona Peace Officer Standards and Training Board **C/VW:** American Heart Association; Volunteer, Fire Department **A/S:** She attributes her success to her hard work. **B/I:** She became involved in this profession because she wanted to be involved in emergency medicine. **H/O:** The highlight of her career was owning her own company.

SUSAN E. PETERSON, LMT, NCTMB
President, Massage Therapist
Bodywright, Inc. dba Loosen Up
3050 Bristol Street
Costa Mesa, CA 92626 United States
loosenup92626@aol.com
http://www.loosenupmassagecenter.com

BUS: Therapy Center **P/S:** Massage Therapy Including Swedish, Sports Reflexology, Deep Tissue Massage Therapies, Spa Treatments Using Aromatherapies and Moist Heat **D/D/R:** Teaching Massage Therapists, Treating Patients with Neck and Back Problems Including Chronic Headaches, Fatigue, Circulation Improvement and Tightness Problems, Practicing Massage and Spa Treatments and Building Client Relationships **H/I/S:** Practicing Thai Chi **FBP:** Massage **EDU:** Coursework, Massage Therapy School, Western Institute of Neuromuscular Therapy (1996); Bachelor of Science in English, Suffolk University, Boston (1980) **CERTS:** Licensed Massage Therapist, American Massage Therapy Association, Irvine and Costa Mesa; Certified Vocational Teacher **A/A/S:** North American Vodder Association of Lymphatic Therapy

LISA M. PETRILLO
Teacher
Howell Board of Education
Howell, NJ 07751 United States
lmpetrillo@optonline.net
http://www.cambridgewhoswho.com

BUS: Public Middle School **P/S:** Education **MA:** Local **EXP:** Ms. Petrillo's expertise is in special needs education. **H/I/S:** Playing Competitive Volleyball, Coaching Basketball, Spending Time with the Family, Coaching Girls Lacrosse **EDU:** Bachelor of Arts in Special Education, Lynchburg College **CERTS:** Certified in Special Education; Certified in Elementary Education **C/VW:** Central Jersey Blood Bank **DOB:** October 7, 1961 **POB:** NJ **CHILD:** PJ, Mike, Kate, Joe **A/S:** She attributes her success to her passion for her profession. **B/I:** She became involved in her profession because she always had an interest in the field and a desire to teach.

ROENA SLOAN PETTIJOHN, CRNA
Certified Registered Nurse Anesthetist
Anesthesiology
Anesthesiologists Associates, P.C.
2341 McCallie Avenue
Parkridge Plaza III, Suite 402, P.O Box 3549
Chattanooga, TN 37409 United States
rspettijohn@aol.com • http://www.cambridgewhoswho.com

BUS: Private Healthcare Facility **P/S:** Anesthesia Services **MA:** Regional **D/D/R:** Specializing in All Aspects of Anesthesia **H/I/S:** Traveling, Hiking **EDU:** Coursework in Nursing, Topeka, KS (1956) **CERTS:** Pursuing Registered Nurse Anesthetist Recertification, Anesthesia School, Memorial Mission Hospital, North Carolina (1968); Certification in Basic Life Support; Certification in Advanced Cardiac Life Support; Certification in Pediatric Advanced Life Support **A/A/S:** Former President, Tennessee Association of Nurse Anesthetists; National Association of Nurse Anesthetists **A/H:** Certified Registered Nurse Anesthetist of the Year, Tennessee Association of Nurse Anesthetists (2006) **DOB:** November 29, 1935 **CHILD:** Patrick **B/I:** She became involved in her profession because of her life-long interest in the medical field.

MARGARET K. PETZOLD
President
Sunshine Packaging, Inc.
1136 S. Vail Avenue
Montebello, CA 90640 United States
sunshinepkginc@aol.com
http://www.cambridgewhoswho.com

BUS: Packaging and Distribution **P/S:** Janitorial Supplies for Clients on the West Coast **MA:** West Coast **D/D/R:** Specializing in Sales and Purchasing **H/I/S:** Reading **FBP:** BusinessWeek; Trucking **EDU:** Industry-Related Experience **A/A/S:** Montebello Chamber of Commerce **A/S:** She attributes her success to her hard work and determination. **B/I:** She became involved in her profession because she was referred to a trucking company and enjoyed the business. **H/O:** The highlight of her career has been starting her own business.

CARLETTA PFIRRMAN
Owner
Casino World, LLC
701 W. Deer Valley Road, Suite A3
Phoenix, AZ 85027 United States
carletta@casinoworldaz.com
http://www.casinoworldaz.com
http://www.casinodealing.net

BUS: Casino **P/S:** Special Events, Retail Gaming Supply Store, Home Play Gaming Products, Custom-Built Tables and Accessories **MA:** Regional **D/D/R:** Fundraising, Organizing Corporate Events and Private Home Parties, Designing Custom-Built Gaming Tables, Overseeing Sales **EDU:** Diploma, Edison High School, NJ **CERTS:** Pursuing Business License, State of Nevada; Business License, State of Arizona; Gaming License, State of Arizona; Casino Gambling License, State of California **A/A/S:** Arizona Chamber of Commerce; Phoenix Chamber of Commerce; National Federation of Independent Business; Better Business Bureau **C/VW:** Various Hospitals and Community Organizations; American Cancer Society; Make-A-Wish Foundation **A/S:** She attributes her success to her perseverance, hard work, fortitude and her ability to convert an idea into an achievement. **B/I:** She became involved in her profession because it was her husband's business. **H/O:** The most gratifying aspect of her career is being able to meet many interesting people. **I/F/Y:** In five years, Ms. Pfirrman would like to open a gaming dealer's academy and a portable state-of-the-art car wash.

MR. ROBERT J. PHARO, OTR
Director of Rehabilitation
Arbor Glen of Bridgewater
100 Monroe Street
Bridgewater, NJ 08807 United States
rjpharo@aol.com
http://www.arborglen.org

BUS: Healthcare Facility in a Retirement Community **P/S:** Retirement Community, Sub-Acute Rehabilitation Services **MA:** Tri-State Area **D/D/R:** Gerontology, Physical Disabilities, Running the Sub-Acute Rehabilitation Services of the Center **H/I/S:** Golfing, Traveling, Spending Time with his Wife and Daughter **FBP:** American Journal of Occupational Therapy **EDU:** Bachelor of Science in Occupational Therapy, Dominican College, Orangeburg, New York **A/A/S:** New Jersey Occupational Therapy Association; American Occupational Therapy Association **C/VW:** Special Olympics

KRISTINE H. PHELPS
Owner, Trainer
Crescendo Training Centre, Limited Liability Company
155 Quarry Road
288 S. Fairmont Road
Leola, PA 17540 United States
kphelps@dejazzd.com
http://www.crescendotrainingcentre.com

BUS: Service **P/S:** Training Horses, Giving Riding Lessons, Judging Horses **MA:** Regional **D/D/R:** Training Instruction, Judging Horses **H/I/S:** Gardening, Reading **FBP:** Stable Management **EDU:** Bachelor of Arts in Photography, Grand Valley State University **A/A/S:** District Director of Pennsylvania Arabian Horse Association, South Central District: Coach of Pennsylvania Arabian Youth Judging **A/H:** Executive Committee East Coast Arabian Championship; Multi-Regional Championships **A/S:** She attributes her success to her quest for knowledge. **B/I:** She chose the profession because she always wanted to work with horses. **H/O:** The highlight of her career is being able to give back to the children.

LYNDA ANN PHILIPS
Licensed Practical Nurse
Land O'Frost
911 Hastings Avenue
Searcy, AR 72020 United States
lphilips@landofrost.com
http://www.cambridgewhoswho.com

BUS: Food Industry **P/S:** Lunch Meat Production **MA:** International **D/D/R:** Occupational Nursing **H/I/S:** Gardening, Flowers, Cattle Farming **FBP:** Nursing2009 **CERTS:** Licensed Practical Nurse, Searcy Technical School **C/VW:** Kids Network; Children's Hospital; The Humane Society; Arkansas Cattleman's Beef Association **A/S:** She attributes her success to being able to make a difference in people's lives and caring for people knowing she can make a difference.

JOHN D. PHILLIPS JR.
Emergency Management Strategic Healthcare Group Central District
Manager, Program Support Assistant
Veterans Affairs Medical Center
1310 24th Avenue S.
Nashville, TN 37212 United States
john.phillips3@med.va.gov
http://www.1.va.gov/directory/guide/facility.asp?id=95

BUS: Hospital **P/S:** Dental, Dermatology, Infectious Disease, Neurology, Post Traumatic Stress, Neuropsychiatric Testing, Laser Surgery, Open Heart Surgery, Ophthalmology, Retinal Screening, Diabetic Education, Otolaryngology, Pain Clinic, Photopheresis, Cardiac Catheterization, Dialysis, Head and Neck Surgery, Major Orthopedic Surgery, Organ Transplantation and Peripheral Vascular Surgery **MA:** National **D/D/R:** Helping All Members within the District, Maintaining Contact with Management Assistants, Overseeing Different Programs **H/I/S:** Avid Bike Rider **FBP:** Government Executives; Federal Computer Week **EDU:** Bachelor's Degree in Business and E-Business, University of Phoenix **A/A/S:** American Legion; National Association of Executive Secretaries and Administrative Assistants **C/VW:** Raising Money for Multiple Sclerosis, MS150 Bike Club **SP:** John

LYNDA B. PHILLIPS
Registered Nurse
St. Joseph Hospital
5665 Peatree Dunwoody Road
Atlanta, GA 30392 United States
gagasnurse@yahoo.com
http://www.cambridgewhoswho.com

BUS: Healthcare **P/S:** Coordinating Outpatient Surgery and Nursing Staff **MA:** Local **D/D/R:** Operating Room Nursing **H/I/S:** Singing, Reading, Walking, Scuba Diving, Motorcycle Riding **FBP:** AORN Journal **CERTS:** Certified Registered Nurse, Georgia Baptist School of Nursing **A/A/S:** Association of perioperative Registered Nurses **C/VW:** Church; The Humane Society; Muscular Dystrophy Association; Children's Hospital of Atlanta **A/S:** She attributes her success to her faith and her desire to help people when they are most vulnerable. **B/I:** She became involved in this profession because she has always wanted to be a nurse and to help people and make a difference. **H/O:** The highlight of her career is successfully performing CPR.

Barbara A. Phillips-Cole, MD
Emergency Medicine Physician
Christus St. Frances Cabrini Hospital
3301 Masonic Drive
Alexandria, LA 71301 United States
drbaphillips@yahoo.com
http://www.cambridgewhoswho.com

BUS: Healthcare **P/S:** Medical Services **MA:** Local **D/D/R:** Practicing Family and Emergency Medicine **H/I/S:** Playing the Piano, Gardening, Cooking, Traveling, Reading, Skiing, Horseback Riding **EDU:** MD, Autonomous University of Guadalajara; Residency, University of Connecticut; Master of Social Work, University of Michigan; Bachelor of Arts in Social Work, University of New Hampshire **CERTS:** Board Certified in Family Medicine **C/VW:** American Medical Association; American Red Cross; American Heart Association; March of Dimes; Local Churches; American Cancer Society **A/S:** She attributes her personal and professional success to her persistence and hard work. **B/I:** She has always had an interest in the field and a desire to help others. **H/O:** The highlight of her career was teaching Behavioral Sciences at the University of Guadalajara.

Kristen M. Piccerelli
Implementation and Training Coordinator
Lighthouse MD, Caretracker Technologies
70 Royal Little Drive
Providence, RI 02806 United States
kpiccerelli@caretracker.com
http://www.cambridgewhoswho.com

BUS: Medical Management **P/S:** Caretracker Medical Management Software **MA:** National **D/D/R:** Training Individuals on the Company's Software Programs, Developing the Help System **H/I/S:** Reading **EDU:** Bachelor's Degree in Psychology and Education, University of Rhode Island **C/VW:** Katie Brown Educational Program **A/S:** She attributes her success to being a well-rounded person, a hard worker and always completing tasks that she begins. **B/I:** She became involved in the profession because she was a teacher and needed a change of pace. She wanted to work more and have more responsibilities. **H/O:** The highlight of her career is completing the HELP System.

MARCI N. PICKELL
Occupational Therapy
Petaluma Care and Rehab
115 B Street
Petaluma, CA 94952 United States
marcipickell@yahoo.com
http://www.cambridgewhoswho.com

BUS: Healthcare **P/S:** Physical Therapy, Outpatients, Out Billing, Occupational Therapy **MA:** Local **D/D/R:** Offering Speech and Physical Therapy **H/I/S:** Hiking, Biking **EDU:** Bachelor of Science, Minor in Psychology, Dominican University of California **A/A/S:** American Occupational Therapy Association; Psi Chi Honor Society of Psychology; Honor Society of Dominican University

YVONNE PICKERING CARTER
Curator, Owner
Gallery Cornelia
90 Cannon Street
Charleston, SC 29403 United States
gallerycornelia@bellsouth.net
http://www.cambridgewhoswho.com

BUS: Art Gallery **P/S:** Fine Art, African-American Art History, Exhibitions Featuring Female Artists **MA:** Regional **EXP:** Her expertise is in writing and the creation of visual performance art. **D/D/R:** Watercolor Painting, Working on Paper, Writing Narratives, Costume Designing, Curator for Exhibitions, Selecting Artists **H/I/S:** Gardening, Landscaping, Traveling **FBP:** Art News; Arts and Antiques **EDU:** Master's Degree in Fine Arts and Painting, Howard University; Bachelor's Degree in Art, Howard University **CERTS:** Certified Interior Designer, Trap Hagen School of Design **A/A/S:** Women's Caucus of Art; College Art Association; Ex-Chair, Department of Art, University of DC; Professor Emeritus, University of DC **C/VW:** Art Volunteer, Summer Programs After School Youth Program **A/S:** She attributes her success to her ability to find a way to continue to grow, her hard work and the support she receives from her family. **B/I:** She became involved in her profession because she has always been drawn to artistic expression and design. **H/O:** The highlight of her career is her performance pieces. **I/F/Y:** She aspires to have her poetry published.

DAME ISABEL H. PICZEK
Artist, Monumental Arts
Construction Art Center
2228 Echo Park Avenue
Los Angeles, CA 90026 United States
cambridge@cambridgewhoswho.com
http://www.cambridgewhoswho.com

BUS: Excellency in Fine Art **P/S:** Large Mural Paintings, Mosaic Art, Stained Glass **MA:** International **D/D/R:** Creating Murals on Plaster and Large Murals **H/I/S:** Traveling, Reading, Physics **EDU:** Master's Degree in Art, Budapest, Hungry (1955); Master's Degree in Physics **A/A/S:** Board of Directors, EM Star

GERRI PIENTA
Merchandise Manager
Drug Fair Group, Inc.
800 Cottontail Lane
Somerset, NJ 08873 United States
gpienta@drugfairgroup.com
http://www.drugfair.com

BUS: Distribution Firm **P/S:** Prescription Refills, Cosmetics, Fragrances, Professional Hair Care Accessories, Vitamins and Nutritional Supplements, Toys, Automotive Supplies, Greeting Cards, Gift Wrap and Seasonal Merchandise **MA:** Statewide **D/D/R:** Merchandising Cosmetics, Fragrance, Upscale Bath Products, Professional Hair Care Products, Ethnic Hair Care and Hair Accessories **H/I/S:** Reading, Walking **FBP:** Drug Store News; Mass Market Retailers; Retail Merchandiser; Beauty Fashion; Chain Drug Review; Beauty Store Business **EDU:** Bachelor of Arts in Elementary Education, Kean University (1974) **A/A/S:** National Association for Female Executives **A/H:** Glammy Award, Best Cosmetic Promotion for Regional Drug Chain, L'Oreal 'Elements of Success' (1999); Glammy Award, Best Cosmetic Promotion for Regional Drug Chain, Revlon Totally Revolutionary Simply Outrageous ColorStay (1995); Glammy Award Honorable Mention, Best Cosmetic Promotion for Regional Drug Chain (1994) **DOB:** December 12, 1952 **W/H:** Assistant Buyer, Cosmetic Buyer, Community Distributor, Store Level, Drug Fair of New Jersey (1969-1977); Second and Third-Grade Class Teacher (1974-1975)

PAULA K. PIERCE, HTL, HT
President
Excalibur Pathology
630 N. Broadway Street
Moore, OK 73160 United States
contact@excaliburpathology.com
http://www.excaliburpathology.com

BUS: Medical **P/S:** Ophthalmic Pathology **MA:** National **D/D/R:** Utilizing Histotechnology, Processing and Sustaining Tissue **H/I/S:** Spending Time with the Family **FBP:** Histonet **EDU:** Bachelor's Degree in Natural Science and Mathematics, Thomas Edison State College **A/A/S:** American Society of Clinical Pathologists; SSTA **C/VW:** Feed the Children **A/S:** She attributes her success to loving her job. **B/I:** She became interested in pathology when it was introduced as a new program at her college and sparked her interest. **H/O:** The highlight of her career was developing a fixative and procedure to prevent retinal detachment for her previous employer six years ago.

MS. AGNES PIERRE-LOUIS
Owner, Partner
CPL 700 Holding, LLC
271 Rockaway Street
Islip Terrace, NY 11752 United States
witak@hotmail.com
http://www.cambridgewhoswho.com

BUS: Real Estate Agency **P/S:** Real Estate Exchange **MA:** National **EXP:** Ms. Pierre-Louis' expertise is in real estate investment management. **D/D/R:** Overseeing Bookkeeping, Working with Small Law Firms, Handling Taxes, Accounting **H/I/S:** Reading, Painting **FBP:** Entrepreneur **EDU:** Bachelor of Arts in Business Administration and Finance, Kaplan University; Associate Degree in Business Administration, Toronto School of Business **C/VW:** American Association for Cancer Research; The Leukemia & Lymphoma Society; Children International

Tamara Pierson
Intervention Specialist
Barberton City Schools
555 Barberton Road
Barberton, OH 44203 United States
tellithorp@barberton.summit.k12.oh.us
http://www.cambridgewhoswho.com

BUS: Education **P/S:** Special Education Services **MA:** Local **D/D/R:** Conducting Interventions for Students with Cognitive Disabilities **H/I/S:** Swimming, Camping, Fishing **EDU:** Master's Degree in Education, Marygrove College **C/VW:** Various Programs for the Handicapped **A/S:** She attributes her success to caring about the children and wanting them to succeed. **B/I:** She became involved in her profession after volunteering in nursing homes and finding the type of work rewarding. **H/O:** The most gratifying aspect of her career is seeing the children progress.

Susan Morganelli Pignato
Educator
Forest Hills Elementary School
3200 N.W. 85th Avenue
Coral Springs, FL 33065 United States
susan.pignato@browardschools.com
http://www.browardschools.com

BUS: Elementary School K-5 **P/S:** Education **MA:** Local **D/D/R:** Teaching Reading and Mathematics, Technology Training for Both the School and the District **H/I/S:** Traveling **EDU:** Master's Degree in Education, Long Island University **A/A/S:** International Reading Association; AFT; National Education Association; Florida Education Association; Broward Teachers Union **C/VW:** DEC, Democratic Club **A/S:** She attributes her personal and professional success to her perseverance and dedication. **B/I:** She has always had an interest in the field and a desire to educate others. **H/O:** The highlight of her career is seeing the progress of children.

LOUISE M. FOTI PILLITIERI
Registered Professional School Nurse
M.J. Fletcher Elementary School
301 Cole Avenue
Jamestown, NY 14701 United States
l.pillittier@jamestown.wnyric.org
http://www.cambridgewhoswho.com

BUS: Healthcare, Education **P/S:** Healthcare **MA:** Local **D/D/R:** Pediatric Nursing and Mental Health Nursing **H/I/S:** Exercising, Playing Golf and Tennis, Gardening, Reading, Enjoying Music, Spending Time with her Grandchildren **FBP:** RN; Forbes **EDU:** Registered Nurses Degree, Women's Christian Association Hospital and School **A/A/S:** Women's Christian Association Alumni; JCC Alumni Association; Beta Sigma Phi; Parent Teacher Association; APWC; Marvin House; New York State Nurses Association; St. James Alter and Rosary Society **C/VW:** American Cancer Society; American Heart Association **A/S:** She credits her career success to her dedication to her profession. **B/I:** She has always wanted to be a nurse. **H/O:** She feels that being able to help someone get well is the highlight of her career.

MS. RUTH Z. PIÑA
Director, Staffing and Employee Services
Valero Energy Corp.
One Valero Way
San Antonio, TX 78249 United States
ruth.pina@valero.com
http://www.valero.com

BUS: Refining Company **P/S:** Extensive Refining System with a Capacity of Approximately 3.3 Million Barrels per Day **MA:** International **D/D/R:** Acting as a Human Resource Generalist, Dealing with Employee Relations, Employment Policies and Procedures and Company Policies **H/I/S:** Traveling **FBP:** HR; Fortune **EDU:** Bachelor's Degree in Management and Economics, Our Lady of the Lake University (1990) **A/A/S:** Society of Human Resource Management **DOB:** April 3, 1957 **SP:** Edward **CHILD:** Jennifer, Nicholas

CHERYL B. PINES, E-PRO, QSC
Realtor
Prudential Magnolia Realty
131 Cedar Lane, RR 8
Tupelo, MS 38801 United States
cpine@prumag.com
http://www.prudentialrealty.com

BUS: Real Estate Firm **P/S:** Real Estate Services Including New Construction, Multi-Family Dwellings, Condominiums, Rentals, Relocations, Commercial Brokerage Services, Mortgage Services **MA:** Regional **D/D/R:** Offering Real Estate Services, Ensuring Customer Satisfaction, Utilizing Integrated Technologies **H/I/S:** Cooking, Photography, Swimming, Golfing, Playing Tennis, Snow Skiing **FBP:** Realtor **EDU:** Bachelor of Science in Medical Technology, University of Pennsylvania (1971) **CERTS:** Pursuing Buyer's Representative Accreditation; Pursuing Certification, Realtors Institute; Quality Service Certification (2005); Licensed Realtor, Mississippi (2002); e-Pro Certification **A/H:** Leading Edge Prudential Award (2007); Tupelo Civilian of the Year (2004-2005) **SP:** James **CHILD:** Kimberly

TERRA N. PITTS-ELSENG
Senior Department Administrator
Bowe Bell and Howell
760 S. Wolf Road
Wheeling, IL 60090 United States
telseng@bowebellhowell.com
http://www.bowebellhowell.com

BUS: Manufacturing **P/S:** Mail Sorting Equipment **MA:** International **D/D/R:** Handling Micromanagement, Administration, Coordination, Scheduling **H/I/S:** Spending Quality Time with her Three Sons **FBP:** NAFE Publications **EDU:** Pursuing Degree in Business Management, Kaplan University; Associate Degree in Criminal Justice, Kaplan University **CERTS:** ISO Internal Audit Certification **A/A/S:** National Association for Female Executives **A/H:** Achievement Award (2004, 2005) **C/VW:** Mississippi Schools Affected by Hurricane Katrina Relief **A/S:** She attributes her career success to her determination. **B/I:** She pursued a career in manufacturing because she wanted to help others. **H/O:** She feels that her continuing education throughout her employment has been the highlight of her career.

HERNANDO J. PIZARRO
Realtor, Pastor
The Bob Denny Team
3292 Crain Highway
Waldorf, MD 20601 United States
hernando.pizarro@gmail.com
http://www.bobdennyteam.com

BUS: Real Estate **P/S:** Provide Real Estate and Commercial Sales/Spiritual Growth, Guidance and Teaching **MA:** International **D/D/R:** Marketing **H/I/S:** Watching NASCAR, Enjoying Motorsports, Reading **FBP:** Fortune 500 **EDU:** Bachelor's Degree in Theology, Canada Christian College **A/A/S:** National Association of Realtors; Maryland Association of Realtors; Southern Maryland Association of Realtors; Pinecrest Ministerial Fellowship **A/S:** He attributes his success to his diligence. **H/O:** The highlight of his career is being self-employed and being able to support his family.

MARIANNE PLOGER
Director, Instructor
Institute for Musical Perception,
Lecturer at the University of Michigan
10332 M-52
Manchester, MI 48158 United States
mploger@aol.com
http://www.marianneploger.com

BUS: Musical Communication **P/S:** Workshops, Publications and Private Instruction **MA:** Local **D/D/R:** Specializing in Musical Perception, Aural Musicianship, Musical Science, Composing, Playing the Piano **H/I/S:** Traveling **FBP:** Psychology Today **EDU:** Master's Degree, University of Michigan (1980); Bachelor's Degree in Piano Performance, St. Louis Conservatory of Music (1976)

RONALD J. POBLETE
Physician
Niccollai Medical Practice
219 Patterson Avenue
Little Falls, NJ 07424 United States
docrjp@aol.com
http://www.cambridgewhoswho.com

BUS: Healthcare Facility Committed to Excellence in Patient Care **P/S:** Family Medicine, Total Healthcare Services for Individuals and Families **MA:** Regional **D/D/R:** Diagnosing and Treating a Wide Range of Ailments for All Ages, Internal Medicine and Infectious Diseases **H/I/S:** Tennis, Golfing **EDU:** MD, Cebu Institute of Medicine, Philippines (1985) **A/A/S:** ASM; American College of Physicians; American Medical Association; Infectious Diseases Society of New Jersey

DOUGLAS A. PODRAZA
Aftermarket Support and Project Manager
Atlas Copco AB
3700 E. 68th Street
Commerce City, CO 80022 United States
doug.podraza@us.atlascopco.com
http://www.atlascopco.com

BUS: Industrial Manufacturing Company **P/S:** Construction and Mining Equipment, Industrial Tools and Assembly Systems **MA:** International **EXP:** Mr. Podraza's expertise lies in aftermarket systems. **H/I/S:** Participating in Outdoor Activities, Running, Golfing, Bicycling, Playing the Guitar **FBP:** Popular Science **EDU:** Bachelor's Degree in Mechanical Engineering, South Dakota School of Mines and Technology (2003) **A/A/S:** American Society of Mechanical Engineers International

THERESA E. POIRIER
Purchasing Supervisor
Engineered Sinterings and Plastics
1611 Litchfield Road
Watertown, CT 06795 United States
tpoitirt@engsint.com
http://www.engsint.com

BUS: Manufacturing **P/S:** Precision Powdered Metal, Thermoset, and Thermoplastic Component Parts and Assemblies **MA:** International **D/D/R:** Supervising the Purchasing Department **H/I/S:** Gardening, Crocheting **EDU:** Education, Watertown High School **A/A/S:** St. John the Evangelist Church; Young Republican Wives **C/VW:** American Red Cross

BRYAN A. POLEE
Owner
ZMP Enterprise, Inc
1062 N.W. Kelly Place
Oak Harbor, WA 98277 United States
bpolee33@msn.com
http://www.ezaggle.net

BUS: e-Commerce Retail **MA:** International **D/D/R:** Entrepreneur, Specializing in Making Start up Businesses Supersede their Earning Potential **FBP:** Rolling Stone; Entrepreneur Magazine **EDU:** Master of Business Administration in Organizational Leadership, Chatman University; Bachelor of Arts in Social Science **A/A/S:** NAACP; Boys and Girls Club

MR. LEO JOSEPH POLK
Owner, Band Leader
Polk Entertainment
16310 Saint Helena Way
Houston, TX 77053 United States
lpolk21792@aol.com
http://www.cdbaby.com/cd/leopolk

BUS: Entertainment Company **P/S:** Booking Bands, Music for Weddings, Bar Mitzvahs, Quinceaneras **MA:** National **D/D/R:** Performing Vocals, Operating Five Bands, Serving as Lead Vocalist, Playing the Trumpet, Emulating Louis Armstrong and Luther Vandross, Acting as Louis Armstrong in an Off-Broadway Production, Performing Voice-Overs, Appearing in a Walt Disney Movie **H/I/S:** Music, Sports, Playing Basketball **FBP:** International Music **EDU:** Coursework in Liberal Arts, Carnegie Mellon; Coursework in Business, Marketing, Minor in Music Education, Texas Southern University **A/A/S:** International Musicians; All Saints Church; Willowridge Band Booster Club; International Trumpet Guild; American Federation of Musicians; Southern Christian Leadership Conference; NWACP

PIRO A. POLOSKA
Realtor, Relocation Specialist
Sel-Fast REO Management
34931 US Highway 19N
Palm Harbor, FL 34684 United States
poloskap@aol.com
http://www.sel-fast.com

BUS: Real Estate Agency **P/S:** Real Estate **MA:** Tampa Bay Area **EXP:** Ms. Poloska's area of expertise is in relocation. **H/I/S:** Reading, Computers, Going to the Beach, Traveling, Playing Volleyball **FBP:** Physics-Related Publications **EDU:** Master's Degree in Physics Education, University of Tirana, Albania; Master's Degree in Mathematics and Physics Education, Miami University, Oxford, OH **A/A/S:** Pinellas Association of Realtors; National Association of Realtors **A/S:** He attributes his success to his hard work, motivation and desire to help people. **H/O:** The most gratifying aspect of his career is helping people better their lives.

KERRI E. PONIATOWSKI
Teacher
Saint Cyril and Methodius School
607 Sobieski Street
Lemont, IL 60439 United States
gothiccaddy@comcast.net
http://www.cambridgewhoswho.com

BUS: Catholic School **P/S:** Education **MA:** Local **D/D/R:** Teaching Sixth-Grade Science, Social Studies and Religion **H/I/S:** Gardening, Spending Time with her Family **EDU:** Bachelor of Arts Degree in Elementary Education and Special Education, Lewis University **A/A/S:** Phi Delta Kappa; Phi Alpha Beta **A/S:** She attributes her success to family support and team work. **B/I:** She became involved in her profession because she was inspired by her teachers. **H/O:** The highlight of her career has been getting to work with children and seeing them progress.

LAYNE M. POPERNIK, ABR
Realtor, Accredited Buyer Representative
Crye-Leike Realtors
6525 Quail Hollow
Memphis, TN 38120 United States
lpopernik@crye-leike.com
http://www.layne.crye-leike.com

BUS: Real Estate **P/S:** Buying, Selling and Listing of Residential, Commercial and Vacant Land Properties **MA:** National **D/D/R:** Commercial and Residential Sales, Working with Buyers and Sellers **H/I/S:** Antiquing, Boating, Water Skiing **FBP:** Architectural Digest **CERTS:** Accredited Buyer Representative, National Association of Realtors **A/A/S:** National Association of Realtors; Tennessee Association of Realtors; Memphis Area Association of Realtors; Real Estate Buyers Accreditation Council **C/VW:** The Leukemia & Lymphoma Society; St. Jude Children's Hospital

Ms. Victoria Christine Poploski
Interior Designer
Morgan House Interiors
44 Main Street
Clinton, NJ 08809 United States
vicki@morganhouseinteriors.com
http://www.morganhouseinteriors.com

BUS: Interior Design Company **P/S:** Services for All Aspects of Interior Design **MA:** Regional **D/D/R:** Specializing in Residential Interior Design Including Baths, Kitchens and the Overall Home **H/I/S:** Traveling **FBP:** Design New Jersey **EDU:** Bachelor of Science in Interior Design, Endicott College (2006) **A/A/S:** International Interior Design Association; National Kitchen & Bath Association **A/S:** She attributes her success to her determination, high standards and goal-oriented strategies. **B/I:** She became involved in her profession because she enjoyed color and was interested in the concept of its strategic placement within various spaces. She was also influenced by her art teacher, who recommended that she go into interior design. **H/O:** The most gratifying aspect of her career is being trusted and respected by her superiors.

Miss Yuliana E. Porras
Chemical Engineer
Bureau of Reclamation
PO Box 25007
Denver, CO 80225 United States
yporras@do.usbr.gov
http://www.usbr.gov

BUS: Largest Wholesaler of Water in the Country and the Second Largest Producer of Hydroelectric Power in the Western United States, Contemporary Water Management Agency **P/S:** Brings Water to more than 31 Million People, Offers Numerous Programs, Initiatives and Activities that will Help the Western States, Native American Tribes and others Meet New Water Needs **MA:** Regional **D/D/R:** Working in the Lab and Out in the Field Conducting Research and Engineering of Water Treatment Systems, Modifying Surfaces of Membranes for Decontamination **EDU:** Pursuing Master's Degree, Colorado School of Mines, Environmental Engineering; Bachelor's Degree in Chemical Engineering, Colorado School of Mines (2003) **A/A/S:** National Affairs Committee Chairwoman, Society of Hispanic Professional Engineers **A/H:** President's Award (2004, 2005)

Dr. Carla J. Porter
Podiatrist
Gerber Bromley, DPM P.C.
22 Fairmont Avenue
Poughkeepsie, NY 12603 United States
doctorporter@aol.com

BUS: Healthcare **P/S:** Podiatric Medicine and Surgery, Wound Care **MA:** Local **D/D/R:** Podiatric Medicine and Surgery **H/I/S:** Indoor and Outdoor Sports **EDU:** Doctor of Podiatric Medicine, New York College of Podiatric Medicine **A/A/S:** American College of Podiatric Surgeons **C/VW:** American Red Cross **A/S:** She attributes her success to being dedicated to people. **B/I:** She became involved in this profession because she wanted to help people. **H/O:** The highlight of her career is having the opportunity to help people.

Melissa Christine Porter
Hairstylist
Best Cuts
Route 130, Suite 440
East Windsor, NJ 08520 United States
bella2784@comcast.net
http://www.cambridgewhoswho.com

BUS: Hair Services **P/S:** Cosmetology and Hair Styling **MA:** Local **D/D/R:** Hair Styling **EDU:** Associate of Applied Science Degree, General Business, Mercer College Community College **A/S:** She attributes her success to hard work. **H/O:** The highlight of her career has been being able to do what she loves.

JOSEPH PORTERA, MA
Managing Director
Mackay Shields Financial LLC
9 W. 57th Street
New York, NY 10019 United States
portera_joseph@hotmail.com
http://www.mackayshields.com

BUS: Investment Management **P/S:** Investment Management **MA:** International **D/D/R:** Managing Global Fixed Income **H/I/S:** Spending Quality Time with his Children **EDU:** Master of Arts in International Political Economy and Development, Fordham University; Bachelor of Arts in Soviet Studies, Fordham University **C/VW:** Fordham Graduate Committee **A/S:** He attributes his career success to his hard work. **B/I:** He felt a natural calling to pursue a career in finance, and through hard work and dedication to his position, he has moved up in the business. **H/O:** He feels that the highlight of his career is yet to come.

SHELLEY POSS, GRI
Realtor Estate Agent
Lang Realty, Inc.
2901 Clint Moore Road, Suite 9
Boca Raton, FL 33496 United States
murphy515@aol.com
http://www.shelleyposs.com

BUS: Real Estate Agency **P/S:** Property Sales **MA:** International **EXP:** Ms. Poss' expertise is in selling properties including high end, new and existing residential homes, country club and waterfront properties. **FBP:** Realtor Association Newsletter **EDU:** Bachelor of Education, Temple University **CERTS:** Graduate, Realtors Institute (2006); e-Pro Certification (2005) **A/A/S:** PBRA; Women's Council of Realtors; Florida Association of Realtors; Realtor Institute; National Association of Realtors **C/VW:** Soroptimist

REV. DENNIS E. POSTELL SR.
Senior Pastor
Abundant Life Ministries Assemblies of God
1500 Cooper Street
Punta Gorda, FL 33950 United States
pastor@ab-life.org
http://www.ab-life.org

BUS: Congregation **P/S:** Women's, Honor Bound Men's and Youth Ministry, Fellowships, Community Outreach, Boy's and Girl's Club **MA:** Regional **EXP:** Rev. Postell's expertise is in advanced critical incident stress management and psychological and mental wellness for dispatchers dealing with tragedies. **D/D/R:** Responding to the Accidents Where People Suffer from Critical or Fatal Injuries, Visiting Correctional Institutions to Inform Inmates of Deaths in the Family, Working with the Charlotte County Sheriff's Office **H/I/S:** Fishing **FBP:** Monthly Newsletter from the International Conference of Police Chaplains **EDU:** Master of Ministry, Chesapeake Bible College & Seminary, Ridgely, MD; Bachelor's Degree, Southeastern University, Lakeland, FL (1995) **CERTS:** Certified Senior Chaplain, Charlotte County Sheriff's Office **A/A/S:** Board of Directors, Division of Juvenile Justice; International Conference of Police Chaplains; Board of Directors, Campbell County Memorial Hospital

BOBBY W. POSTON JR.
Volunteer Firefighter
Chester Township New Burlington Volunteer Fire Department &
Massey Township Volunteer Firefighter
51 Mound Road
Wilmington, OH 45177 United States
bpostonjr@msn.com
http://www.cambridgewhoswho.com

BUS: Fire Department **P/S:** Fire and Rescue Services **MA:** Local **EXP:** Mr. Poston's expertise is in fire fighting, rescue and emergency medical services. **D/D/R:** Instructing New Firefighters in Fire Fighting Techniques, Auto Extraction and Rip Training, Structure Awareness, Taking Care of the Critically Ill People **H/I/S:** Fishing, Walking, Swimming, Spending Time with his Children **CERTS:** Certified Emergency Medical Technician; Certified Rescue Diver **A/S:** He attributes his success to his training he gained from his profession and keeping up with other firefighters through seminars and schooling. **B/I:** He became involved in his profession because he always wanted to help the community and loves the profession.

DR. MARK A. POTTINGER
Assistant Professor, Department Chairman
Department of Fine Arts
Manhattan College
mark.pottinger@manhattan.edu
http://www.manhattan.edu

BUS: College **P/S:** Higher Education **MA:** Regional **D/D/R:** Hiring and Supervising Employees, Developing Curriculum, Assisting Students, Lecturing at Various Universities, Consulting, Teaching, Planning, Teaching Nineteenth Century French **H/I/S:** Traveling **FBP:** Journal of the American Mathematical Society; Cambridge Opera Journal **EDU:** Ph.D. in Musicology, The Graduate Center, CUNY (2005); Master of Music, University of Leeds, United Kingdom **A/A/S:** National Committee Member, Cultural Diversity; American Musicology Society; College Art Association; College Music Society **C/VW:** Board of Directors, Education Committee, The Rotary Club of Inwood **H/O:** The most gratifying aspect of his career is being able to maintain good relationships with his students. **I/F/Y:** In five years, Dr. Pottinger hopes to publish his books.

MARK POURMANAFZADEH
Owner, Hair Stylist
Hair By The Guys
15826 Hamden Circle
Austin, TX 78717 United States
markp1123@sbcglobal.net
http://www.cambridgewhoswho.com

BUS: Hair Salon **P/S:** Hair Care Including Hair Cutting, Coloring, Perms and Styling **MA:** Local **EXP:** Mr. Pourmanafzadeh's expertise is in hair care. **D/D/R:** Working with Male and Female Clients, Visiting Nursing Homes and Hospitals, Acting as a Mentor for Middle School Students **H/I/S:** Motorcycling **A/A/S:** National Harley Owners Group **C/VW:** Local Charitable Organizations

CHARLOTTE G. POWELL
Founder, Chief Executive Officer
Gourmet Punch Ready to Serve and More
1945 W. 25th Street
Jacksonville, FL 32209 United States
Charlotte@gourmetpunch.net
http://www.gourmetpunch.net
http://www.blackshoppingchannel.com

BUS: Catering Agency **P/S:** Catering Services for Events and Functions Including 30 Flavors of Punch, Party Fountains, Champagne Fountains, Party Bags and Baskets, Punch Distributions to Jenkins Quality Barbecue **MA:** International **EXP:** Ms. Powell's expertise is in finance management and utilizing her creative skills for her business. **H/I/S:** Bowling, Spending Time at the Church **FBP:** Gourmet News **EDU:** Ph.D. in Christian Psychology, Truth Bible College; Master of Arts in Christian Psychology, Truth Bible College; Bachelor of Arts in Biblical Studies, Jacksonville Theological Seminary **A/A/S:** Chief Executive Officer, Roundtable, Jacksonville; Women's Celebration of North Florida; African-American Chamber of Commerce; American Beverage Association **A/H:** Small Business Leader Award, Jacksonville Regional Chamber of Commerce Northwest Area Council **C/VW:** Truth for Living Ministries **B/I:** She became involved in her profession because of her interest in beverages and punches and her father introduced her to the field, who worked for Frank Soda pop. **H/O:** The most gratifying aspect of her career is preparing punch.

JUDY POWELL, BS, BA
Financial Analyst
Saint Thomas Health Services
4220 Harding Road
Nashville, TN 37205 United States
jcfifty@bellsouth.net
http://www.stthomas.org

BUS: High Quality Hospital Dedicated to Providing Excellent Services to Patients and Community **P/S:** Wide Range of Medical Services, Heart, Neuroscience, Rehabilitation, Cancer Services, Support Groups, Orthopedic Services **MA:** Local **D/D/R:** Acting as a Medical Technologist and Laboratory Financial Analyst, Handling Compliance Costs, Control Costs and Auditing, Coordinating, Purchasing Inventory Control for Laboratory Supplies for the Faculty **H/I/S:** Traveling, Reading **FBP:** Advanced Laboratory Science **EDU:** Bachelor of Science in Medical Technology, Lipscomb University (1968); Bachelor of Arts in Accounting, Tennessee State University

PAULETTE MARTA POWELL
Divisional Vice President, Department of Human Resources
Nestle
800 N. Brand Boulevard
Glendale, CA 91203 United States
paulette.powell@us.nestle.com
http://www.nestle.com

BUS: Manufacturing Company **P/S:** Food and Beverage Products Including Chocolates, Cereals, Creamers, Powdered Milk, Frozen Prepared Foods, Coffee Products and Butter **MA:** International **D/D/R:** Managing Human Resources, Overseeing Sales, Organizational Redevelopment and Employee Life Cycle, Working with Seniors, Conducting Talent Reviews, Training Sessions and Internal Presentations **H/I/S:** Soccer, Golfing, Water Sports **FBP:** Harvard Business Review **EDU:** Bachelor of Business Administration, University of Phoenix (2002)

MR. TROY E. POWELL
Director of Facilities
Dauphin Way Baptist Church
3661 Dauphin Street
Mobile, AL 36608 United States
troy@dwbc.org
http://www.cambridgewhoswho.com

BUS: Church **P/S:** Spiritual Services **MA:** Local **EXP:** Mr. Powell's expertise is in overseeing housekeeping procedures. **D/D/R:** Managing Operations, Supervising 12 Employees, Assisting Senior Citizens **H/I/S:** Painting **FBP:** Worship Facilities **EDU:** Coursework in Aviation, Alabama Aviation and Technical College **A/A/S:** National Association of Church Facilities Managers **A/S:** He attributes his success to his upbringing. **B/I:** He became involved in his profession because he was inspired by his father, who was a preacher. **H/O:** The most gratifying aspect of his career is being able to manage the church operations on a limited budget.

CARLA L. POWERS, RN
Registered Nurse
Canonsburg General Hospital
100 Medical Boulevard
Canonsburg, PA 15054 United States
http://www.wpahs.org/cgh

BUS: Community Hospital **P/S:** Medical, Surgical and Diagnostic Services, Ambulatory Care Center, Emergency Services, Cardiac Catheterization Services, Home Care, Occupational Programs **MA:** Regional **D/D/R:** Specializing in Intensive Care Nursing, Treating Cardiac and Respiratory Diseases and Ailments, Monitoring All Equipment and Patient Care, Administering Medications, Meeting with the Families of Patients **H/I/S:** Riding Motorcycles, Reading **EDU:** Registered Nurse, Ohio Valley Hospital **A/H:** Two-Time Nominee, Tradition of Caring; Two-Time Nominee, Cameo of Caring

RAYMOND A. POZZIE
Supervisor Team Leader
Shell Chemical Company, Ltd.
5900 Highway 225
Deer Park, TX 77536 United States
rpozzie@aol.com
http://www.cambridgewhoswho.com

BUS: Chemical Plant and Refinery **P/S:** Benzene, Toluene, and Xylenes **MA:** International **D/D/R:** Supervising Operations and Expert in the Sulfolane Extraction of Aromatics, Mainly Benzene **H/I/S:** Spending Time with his Family, Traveling, Classic Cars, Woodworking, Coin Collecting **EDU:** Coursework, Texas Bible College **A/A/S:** C.O.P. Ministry Elim Church **A/H:** 99 Champions of Excellence Award **C/VW:** Cal Farley's Ranch; Disabled Veterans; The Harbor; Elim Church; The 100 Club **A/S:** He attributes his success to the support of his wife, family and church. **B/I:** He became involved in the profession because he had a strong interest in the field and the opportunities and rewards offered. **H/O:** The highlight of his career was receiving the 99 Champions of Excellence award, which is only given to 2,000 individuals in the industry.

ROY E. PRASCHIL
Director of Operations
National Association of State Mental Health Program Directors
66 Canal Center Plaza
Suite 302
Alexandria, VA 22314 United States
roy.praschil@nasmhpd.org
http://www.nasmhpd.org

BUS: Representing the Fifty States Mental Health Facilities **P/S:** Five Divisions of State Mental Health Programs: Children, Family, Geriatrics, Forensic, Legal and Adults, Medical Directors Council **MA:** National **D/D/R:** Administration for the Five Divisions, Handling Daily Operations **H/I/S:** Golfing, Motorcycling **EDU:** Master of Arts in Psychology, University of Maryland **C/VW:** Foundation Fighting Blindness **A/S:** He attributes his success to the collaboration with individuals staff and the members.

LaDONNA M. JONES PRATT
Principal
Texas City Independent School District
1401 Ninth Avenue N.
Texas City, TX 77590 United States
lpratt1@houston.rr.com
http://www.cambridgewhoswho.com

BUS: School District **P/S:** Education **MA:** Local **D/D/R:** Teaching Special Education **H/I/S:** Reading, Spending Time with her Family **FBP:** Educational Journals **EDU:** Master of Science and Education Management, University of Houston-Clear Lake **A/A/S:** President, Gamma Gamma Omega Chapter, Alpha Kappa Alpha; Texas Association of Secondary School Principals **C/VW:** President, Alpha Kappa Alpha Inc. **A/S:** She attributes her success to her supportive parents. **B/I:** She became involved in her profession because she wanted to teach special education.

LAURIE E. PRESCOTT
Director
Rebekah Assembly of California
100 Ledyard Street
San Francisco, CA 94124 United States
laurieespinoza@hotmail.com
http://www.caioof.org

BUS: Membership Organization **P/S:** Member Representation, Community Services **MA:** Regional **D/D/R:** Managing Lodges' Issues **H/I/S:** Photography **FBP:** The Wall Street Journal **EDU:** Bachelor's Degree in Broadcasting, San Francisco State University (1965) **A/A/S:** Ladies Oriental Shrine of North America; San Mateo County Historical Society; Roseville Historical Society; San Francisco Historical Society; Daughters of the American Revolution; National Society United States Daughters of 1812; Descendants of the Colonial Clergy **A/H:** Outstanding Student Award, City College of San Francisco **C/VW:** Lions Clubs International; West Portal Lutheran Church; Order of the Eastern Star **DOB:** May 22, 1943 **POB:** San Francisco, CA **A/S:** She attributes her success to her interpersonal and people management skills. **B/I:** She became involved in her profession through a natural progression of opportunities. **H/O:** The highlight of her career was being elected as the president of the state office. **I/F/Y:** In five years, Ms. Prescott hopes to become the president of the organization.

MR. MARTY G. PRESSEY
Senior Project Manager
Info Reliance Corp.
9990 Lee Highway
Suite 450
Fairfax, VA 22030 United States
marty.pressey@inforeliance.com
http://www.inforeliance.com

BUS: Web-Based Software Company **P/S:** Custom Web-Based Software Solutions, Programming and Security Services, Project Management, Business Case Analysis, Infrastructure Support, Web Design, Certification, Accreditation **MA:** National **D/D/R:** Specializing in Database Management, Mainframe Programming and Project Management, Working as the Project Manager for the Marine Corps Training Information Management System, Meeting with Customers, Planning Work Priorities for the Marine Corps Training Information Management System Team, Recommending Hardware and Software Purchases, Assisting with Certification and Accreditation of Marine Corps Training Information Management System, Coordinating Interfaces with External Information Systems **H/I/S:** Leading and Participating in Various Church Ministries **FBP:** Oracle; PM Network **EDU:** Bachelor of Science in Computer Information Management, Park University (2003) **CERTS:** Oracle9i Oracle Certified Professional; Certified Project Management Professional, Project Management Institute, Inc. **A/A/S:** Building Expansion Project Manager, North Stafford Church of Christ **A/H:** Senior NCO of the Year, Defense Finance and Accounting Service (1996); Meritorious Service Medal; Joint Service Commendation Medals; Navy Commendation Medal; Navy Achievement Medals **DOB:** September 9, 1963 **SP:** Tonya **CHILD:** Christopher **W/H:** Englebrecht's Orchard; Marine Corps; Bellman; Warehouseman, Sunbeam Plastics; InfoReliance Corp. **A/S:** He attributes his success to his reliance on God and the power of prayer. **B/I:** He became involved in his profession after leaving the Marines to become a COBOL programmer. **H/O:** The highlight of his career was successfully guiding his team through the Y2K conversion of the Marine corps' pay and personnel system. **I/F/Y:** In five years, Mr. Pressey hopes to continue to help the Marine corps with various information system projects. He also plans to continue working in many other ministries for the church.

NATASHA PRETTY
Case Manager
Crystal Run Village, Inc.
601 Stony Ford Road
Middletown, NY 10941 United States
natasha_pretty@crvi.org
http://www.cambridgewhoswho.com

BUS: Human Services **P/S:** Services for Mentally and Developmentally Disabled Persons **MA:** Regional **D/D/R:** Case Management **H/I/S:** Taking Care of her Son, Reading, Shopping **FBP:** Psychology Today **EDU:** Pursuing Master's Degree, Long Island University, New York; Bachelor's Degree in Psychology, Mount St. Mary University, New York **A/A/S:** American Counseling Association; Psi Chi Honor Society for Psychology Majors **C/VW:** AIDS Walk; Gay Men's Health Crisis **A/S:** She attributes her success to the love and support she received from her family as well as to her faith. **H/O:** The highlight of her career was getting things done.

ALICE G. PRICE
Secretary
Faulkner's Drugs
215 E. Jefferson Street
Monroe, NC 28112 United States
monroealice4@aol.com
http://www.cambridgewhoswho.com

BUS: Pharmacy **P/S:** Healthcare Products, Prescriptions **MA:** Local **D/D/R:** Overseeing Accounts Payable and Receivable, Using Durable Medical Equipment, Billing Medicaid and Medicare **H/I/S:** Reading, Gardening **FBP:** Forbes **EDU:** Industry-Related Training and Experience

JO PRICE, RN, PH.D.
Registered Nurse in Emergency Services,
Mental Health and Juvenile Crisis Unit
Vista Lee Health Center
2989 Ortiz Avenue
Fort Meyers, FL 33905 United States
drjoprice@embarqmail.com
http://www.cambridgewhoswho.com

BUS: Behavioral Center **P/S:** Crisis and Stabilization Psychiatric Patient Care **MA:** Local **EXP:** Ms. Price's expertise is in psychiatric nursing, reiki treatment and private investigation. **D/D/R:** Handling Patient Admissions and Assessments **H/I/S:** Performing Yoga and Reiki, Meditating, Swimming **EDU:** Ph.D., Missouri College of Naturopathic Physicians; Master's Degree in Criminal Justice, University of Detroit Mercy; Bachelor's Degree in Social Science and Criminal Justice, Madonna University **CERTS:** Licensed Private Detective, Miami, FL **A/A/S:** Navy Nurse Corps Association; Lifetime Member, American Legion, Disabled American Veterans; Coordinator, Southwest Florida Alliance for Retired Americans **A/S:** She attributes her success to her life experiences that prepared her for the position. **B/I:** She became involved in the profession after being diagnosed with cancer and researching alternative medicine. **H/O:** The highlights of her career were serving as a Navy nurse during the Korean conflict and being promoted as a sheriff. **I/F/Y:** In five years, Ms. Price hopes to continue in her profession.

REV. WAYNE S. PRICE SR.
Executive Director
Center for True Justice and Healing
7212 Hawthorne Street
Landover, MD 20785 United States
revprice@ctjh.org
http://www.cambridgewhoswho.com

BUS: Community Based Ministry **P/S:** Grief Support for Victims, Services through Courts, Charities NFP **MA:** Regional **D/D/R:** Offering Grief Counseling **H/I/S:** Golfing, Vacationing in Hawaii **FBP:** Psychology Today **EDU:** Coursework, Salisbury State University **A/A/S:** Board of Roper Victims System Academy; Board of Local Violence Interfaith Conference

ROSINA P. PRIMO, CRS, GRI, ABR, BSN
Sales Vice President
William Raveis Real Estate
49 W. Putnam Avenue
Greenwich, CT 06870 United States
primor@raveisre.com
http://www.raveis.com

BUS: Real Estate Agency **P/S:** Real Estate Exchange **MA:** Regional **EXP:** Ms. Primo's expertise is in market analysis. **D/D/R:** Overseeing Exceptional Properties, New Construction and Corporate Relocation, Condominium Management, Assisting First-Time Home Buyers **H/I/S:** Golfing, Sailing **FBP:** The Wall Street Journal; The New York Times **EDU:** Bachelor of Science, St. Joseph's College, Maine; Coursework in Italian Studies, New York University, Florence, Italy **CERTS:** Registered Nurse, Presbyterian Hospital, University of Pittsburgh; Certified Residential Specialist, Graduate Realtor Institute; Accredited Buyer Representative **A/A/S:** Chairwomen, Greenwich Committee; Connecticut Association of Realtors; Multiple Listing Service; Consolidated Multiple Listing Service; American Association of University Women; National Association of Realtors **A/H:** Top Producer Award; Top Lister Award; Excellence in Customer Service Award; Top Selling Associate Award; Platinum Elite Member Award; Million Dollar Status Award; Sales Vice President Award; Top 200 Agents from 1700 Company **C/VW:** Montefiore Children's Hospital Greenwich Committee; American Ballet Theater; Overseas Press Club Foundation **A/S:** She attributes her success to her perseverance and customer services skills. **B/I:** She became involved in her profession because she started her career in the media industry and branched into real estate. **H/O:** The highlight of her career was becoming the vice president of sales in 2002.

DEBORAH A. PRIOR REINSMITH
Museum Financial Officer
Mobile Museum of Art
4850 Museum Drive
Mobile, AL 36608 United States
artmuseumaccounting@cityofmobile.org
http://www.mobilemuseumofart.com

BUS: Nonprofit Museum of Fine Arts **P/S:** Preservation and Display of Multi-Cultural Arts, Art Education Programs and Special Exhibits **MA:** National **D/D/R:** All Forms of Bookkeeping, Financial Reporting, Tax Accounting, General Deposits, Budget Composition and Financial Issues Concerning the Museum, Creative Real Estate Acquisition and Investing, Entrepreneurialism, Information Technology, Building Databases, Web Designing and Development, Specializing in International, Governmental, Corporate, Private and Nonprofit Accounting **H/I/S:** Gardening, Real Estate Investing, Web Designing **FBP:** Inc.; Entrepreneur **EDU:** Technical Business College Coursework; Hands-On Training **A/A/S:** Bookkeepers Association

RHONDA LEA PRITT
Photographer, Artist
R.P. Rose Photography
HC 64 Box 34
Hillsboro, WV 24946 United States
rprosell@frontiernet.net
http://www.cambridgewhoswho.com

BUS: Photography **P/S:** Photography and Art **MA:** National **D/D/R:** Photographing Weddings, Senior Portraits, Individuals, Families and Landscapes **H/I/S:** Exercising, Traveling, Gardening, Taking Pictures **FBP:** American Photo; Shutterbug **EDU:** Bachelor's Degree in Commercial Art and Advertising, Concord College, Athens, West Virginia **A/A/S:** Business and Professional Women's Club; NE Waugh Photography and KPearlman Photography-Fredericksburg, VA; Professional Photographers of West Virginia **C/VW:** St. Jude Children's Research Hospital **A/S:** She attributes her success to perseverance and hard work. **B/I:** She became involved in the profession because she loves photography. **H/O:** The highlight of her career is the traveling she gets to do. She is often requested to travel long distances to photograph the true essence and personality of people.

TERRI PROBERT
Childcare Teacher
Developmental Learning Center
7491 Far Hills Avenue
Centerville, OH 45459 United States
tap1971@earthlink.net
http://www.cambridgewhoswho.com

BUS: Privately Owned Day Care **P/S:** Childcare, Preschool and After School Care for Children Two and 1/2 to Ten Years Old **MA:** Local **D/D/R:** Working with Two-And-A-Half to Five-Year-Old Children **H/I/S:** Reading, Spending Time with her Family **FBP:** Variety **EDU:** Associate of Arts in Early Childhood Education, Sinclair Community College **A/A/S:** Who's Who Among American Teachers (2005, 2006) **C/VW:** Kettering Assembly of God **A/S:** She attributes her success to her hard work, motivation and general love for children. **B/I:** She became involved in her profession because she has always enjoyed working with children and decided to turn her love into a career after graduating from high school. **H/O:** The highlight of her career has been finding her profession to be very rewarding.

DAVID M. PROK
Professor Emeritus
Baldwin-Wallace College
2161 Dover Center Road
Westlake, OH 44145 United States
daveprok@aol.com
http://www.bw.edu

BUS: College **P/S:** Higher Education Including Athletic Programs **MA:** International **D/D/R:** Teaching Urban Sociology and Sex Education **H/I/S:** Biking, Artwork **FBP:** Professional Trade Journals **EDU:** Master of Arts in Sociology, Kent State University (1972); Bachelor of Arts in History, Minor in Sociology and English, Kent State University (1961); Coursework, REM Institute; Coursework in Theological Studies, Concordia Theological Seminary **CERTS:** Certified Sex Educator **A/A/S:** North Central Sociological Association; Center on Urban Poverty and Social Change; American Association of Sexuality Educators, Counselors and Therapists; Alpha Kappa Delta; Chairman, Sex and Gender Diversity, Educational Institute

JOYCE M. PROTO, GRI, CSP
Realtor
Keller Williams Realty
6272 Lake Osprey Drive
Sarasota, FL 34240 United States
jmproto@yahoo.com
http://www.cambridgewhoswho.com

BUS: Real Estate **P/S:** Commercial and Residential Real Estate **MA:** National **D/D/R:** Selling Residential and Commercial Real Estate with the New Home Advantage Team **H/I/S:** Playing Tennis, Continuing her Education, Fitness, Spending Time with the Family **FBP:** BusinessWeek; The Real Estate Book; Collection Homes **EDU:** College Coursework **CERTS:** Graduate Realtor Institute; CSP Certification **A/H:** RE/MAX Presidential Club Award **C/VW:** American Cancer Society; St. Jude Children's Research Hospital; Catholic Charities; United Way of America **A/S:** She attributes her success to her follow-up skills and her diligence to her clients. **B/I:** She became involved in this profession because she has always enjoyed working with people. **H/O:** The highlight of her career is gaining her own brokerage.

DANIEL L. PROVENCHER, CFP
President, CEO
Tourmed Assistance, Inc
4630 N. University Drive, Suite 411
Coral Springs, FL 33067 United States
tourmed2000@aol.com
http://www.cambridgewhoswho.com

BUS: Insurance Company **P/S:** Travel Insurance **MA:** International **D/D/R:** Cost Containment, Administration, Oversight of Daily Operations **H/I/S:** Fishing, Skiing, Golf **FBP:** Fortune; The Wall Street Journal; The New York Times

PAMELA PARSONS PRUITT
Educator
Patuxent Valley Middle School
Howard County Public School System
10910 Route 108
Ellicott City, MD 21042 United States
wareagle001@comcast.net
http://www.cambridgewhoswho.com

BUS: School District **P/S:** Education **MA:** Local **D/D/R:** Teaching French and Spanish to Sixth through Eighth-Grade Students **H/I/S:** Knitting, Reading, Gardening, Walking, Needleworking, Writing Fiction, Traveling **EDU:** Ph.D. in Romance Languages, University of Georgia (1984); Master of Arts in French, University of Georgia (1973); Bachelor of Arts in French, University of Georgia (1971) **A/A/S:** American Council on the Teaching of Foreign Languages; American Association of Teachers of French; National Education Association; Maryland Foreign Language Association **C/VW:** American Cancer Society; Vestry, Christ Episcopal Church **SP:** Shannon **CHILD:** Meghan **A/S:** She attributes her success to her love for her profession. **B/I:** She became involved in her profession because she wanted to make an impact on children's education. **H/O:** The most gratifying aspects of her career are making an impact in students' lives and the gratitude she receives from them.

Carol M. Ptasinki
Senior Associate Director
Joint Commission on Accreditation of Healthcare Organizations
1 Renaissance Boulevard
Oakbrook Terrace, IL 60181 United States
cptasinski@hotmail.com
http://www.cambridgewhoswho.com

BUS: Healthcare **P/S:** Joint Commission of Healthcare Organizations **MA:** National **D/D/R:** Standards Interpretation **H/I/S:** Vacationing **FBP:** American College of Executives Publications **EDU:** Bachelor of Science in Nursing, DePaul University; Master of Science in Nursing, St. Xavier University; Master of Business Administration, St. Xavier University **A/A/S:** American College of Healthcare Executives; Sigma Theta Tau **A/S:** She attributes her success to her motivation and to the fact that she is always willing to learn and keeps her education current. **B/I:** She became involved in her profession because she had always been interested in the field. **H/O:** The highlight of her career was earning her current position.

Judith Lynn Pugh, MD
Associate Pathologist
Children's Hospital of Birmingham
1600 Seventh Avenue S.
Birmingham, AL 35233 United States
judy.pugh@chsys.org
http://www.chsys.org

BUS: Hospital Dedicated to Excellence in Children's Healthcare **P/S:** Comprehensive Range of Clinical Services for Children, Leading Pediatric Hematology and Oncology Center, Stem Cell Transplant Programs, Provides Diagnosis for Children's Tissue-Based Diseases **MA:** Regional **D/D/R:** Treating Gastrointestinal Diseases, Practicing Pediatric Pathology **H/I/S:** Reading Mysteries, Hiking in the Southwest, Traveling **FBP:** American Journal of Surgical Pathology; American Journal of Clinical Pathology; Pediatric and Developmental Pathology **EDU:** Pediatric Nephrology Residency, Children's Medical Center (1991-1994); Pediatric Residency, University of New Mexico Hospital (1988-1991); MD, Texas Technology School of Medicine (1988) **A/A/S:** American Society of Clinical Pathology; College of American Pathologists; United States and Canadian Association of Pathologists; Gastrointestinal Pathology Society

Dr. Patricia Pullen
Pastor
Greater Deliverance Temple
960 Country Lane
Indiana, PA 15701 United States
pullen26@adelphia.net
http://www.cambridgewhoswho.com

BUS: Ministry **P/S:** Teaching and Empowering Others **MA:** International **D/D/R:** Motivational Speaking, Counseling, Hosting a Television Program **H/I/S:** Floral Arranging, Spending Quality Time with her Family **FBP:** Charisma **EDU:** Doctor of Divinity, Sacramento, California **A/A/S:** United States Ambassador for Peace **C/VW:** Assisting the Homeless, Unwed Teen Mothers and Teen Abstinence Programs **A/S:** She attributes her career success to her love of people and to her desire to help others spiritually. **B/I:** She has always felt called to pursue a career in ministry. **H/O:** She feels that achieving fulfillment from the work that she does and her ability to empower others through faith is the highlight of her career.

Ms. Darlyn G. Purdie
Kindergarten Teacher
Bladen County Schools, Plain View Primary School
1963 Chicken Foot Road
Baldenboro, NC 28320 United States
dgpurdie@bladen.k12.nc.us
http://www.bladen.k12.nc.us

BUS: Public School District **P/S:** Challenging Curriculum, Dedicated Faculty and Staff, Athletic Teams, Spelling Bee, Battle of the Books, Science Fair, Bridge Building Competition, Science Olympiad, Scholarships **MA:** Regional **D/D/R:** Teaching Kindergarten Students, Offering Expertise in Language Arts and Mathematics **H/I/S:** Reading, Watching Sports, Walking, Shopping, Listening to Gospel Music **FBP:** Jet; Essence; Ebony **EDU:** Bachelor of Arts in Education, UNCP (2005); Bachelor of Arts in Criminal Justice and Teaching, University of North Carolina at Pembroke (1981) **CERTS:** Certified Pre-Kindergarten and Kindergarten Educator **A/A/S:** National Association of Colleges and Employers; University of North Carolina at Pembroke Alumni Association **A/H:** Balden County Teacher of the Year (2006); Recipient of the Reverend James C. Bellamy, Senior Board Member of the Year Award (1983)

WILLIAM GUY PURDY
Director of Adult Basic Education
Northwest Mississippi Community College
4975 Highway 51 N.
Senatobia, MS 38668 United States
gpurdy@northwestms.edu
http://www.northwestms.edu

BUS: Educational Facility, Community College Dedicated to Excellence in Education **P/S:** Teaching Services and Adult Basic Education **MA:** Local **D/D/R:** Teaching Basic Skills, General Equivalency Diploma, Supervising, Staff Development, Curriculum Development **H/I/S:** Golfing, Fishing **FBP:** Pre-Employment Training Manual; Mississippi Journal; DeSoto County Workforce 2000 **EDU:** Bachelor's Degree in Engineering Technology, Mississippi State University (1993); Associate of Engineering Technology Degree, State Technical Institute at Memphis (1988) **A/A/S:** Who's Who Among American Teachers; Golden Key National Honor Society; Phi Theta Kappa; MAACE **A/H:** Supervisor of the Year, North Mississippi (2005-2006)

HOLLY PURVIS, NCSP
School Psychologist
Spencer County Public Schools
207 W. Main Street
Taylorsville, KY 40071 United States
holly.purvis@spencer.kyschools.us
http://www.cambridgewhoswho.com

BUS: School District **P/S:** Education **MA:** Regional **H/I/S:** Jazzercise **FBP:** Psychological Review **EDU:** Education Specialist Degree in School Psychology, University of Kentucky **CERTS:** National Certified School Psychologist **A/A/S:** Kentucky Association for Psychology in the Schools; National Association of School Psychologists

SUSANNE A. QUALLICH
Andrology Nurse Practitioner
Department of Urology
University of Michigan Health System
1500 E. Medical Center Drive
Ann Arbor, MI 48109 United States
quallich@umich.edu
http://www.cambridgewhoswho.com

BUS: Healthcare Facility **P/S:** Healthcare for Men **MA:** Regional **D/D/R:** Nursing Andrology, Specializing in Male Infertility, Sexual Health and Testosterone Replacement **H/I/S:** Traveling, Reading, Exercising, Cooking **FBP:** Gourmet; Food & Wine **EDU:** Bachelor of Science in Nursing, Case Western Reserve University (1994); Bachelor's Degree in Biology, John Caroll University (1993); Master of Science in Nursing, Case Western Reserve University **CERTS:** Certification in Urology (2000) **A/A/S:** American Society for Reproductive Medicine; American Academy of Nurse Practitioners; Society of Urologic Nurses and Associates **C/VW:** Various Charities **SP:** Leonard **CHILD:** Danielle, Brianna, Luke **B/I:** She became involved in her career because she always had an interest in the field and took advantage of the opportunities presented to her. **H/O:** The highlight of her career was being appointed to the editorial board of the Urology Nursing Journal.

BARBARA J. QUIGLEY
Teacher
Outlook Elementary School
Sunnyside School District No. 201
3800 Van Belle Road
Outlook, WA 98938 United States
barbara.quigley@cwwemail.com
http://www.sunnyside.wednet.edu

BUS: School District **P/S:** Education **MA:** Local **D/D/R:** Teaching First-Grade Students **H/I/S:** Reading, Traveling, Spending Time with her Family **FBP:** Industry-Related Publications; Delta Kappa Gamma Journals; Money **EDU:** Master's Degree in Early Childhood Development and Literature, Central Washington University, Ellensburg, WA **A/A/S:** Delta Kappa Gamma; Former Member, American Association of University Women **A/H:** Teacher of the Year Award, Wal-Mart (2007); Everyday Hero Award, Kiwanis Club (2007); 14-Time Nominee, Who's Who Among American Teachers; Educator of the Year Award, Sunnyside Chamber of Commerce; Golden Apple Award; Christa McAuliffe Award for Outstanding Performance **C/VW:** American Cancer Society; Disabled American Veterans; United Service Organizations; Outlook Booster Club; United Good Neighbors; Kiwanis Club **DOB:** August 17, 1935 **POB:** Wenatchee, WA **SP:** Keith **CHILD:** Michael **A/S:** She attributes her success to her positive attitude and learning skills. **B/I:** She became involved in her profession because she was inspired by her aunt who was a professor. **H/O:** The most gratifying aspect of her career is the gratitude she receives from her students.

DENISE A. QUINN
Brewery Plant Manager
Miller Brewing Company
2525 Wayne Madison Road
Trenton, OH 45067 United States
quinn.denise.a@mbco.com
http://www.millerbrewing.com

BUS: Second Largest Brewery in the US, Seven Major Breweries Located across America **P/S:** Full Manufacturing Services and Brews, Bottles and Markets the Highest Quality Beer and Malt Beverages **MA:** International **D/D/R:** Managing Overall Operations of the Plant, Production, Shipping, Financials **H/I/S:** Reading, Bowling **EDU:** Bachelor of Arts in Biology, Le Moyne College (1978) **A/A/S:** Master Brewers Association of the Americas; Butler County Port Authority; Board, Hamilton Chamber of Commerce; Government Affairs Committee

DEANNA D. QUINTANO, BA, MS
Elementary Special Education Teacher
Apple Valley Unified School District,
Desert Knolls Elementary School
18213 Symeron Road
Apple Valley, CA 92307 United States
mrsq@charter.net
http://www.avusd.org

BUS: Elementary School **P/S:** Education for Students in Kindergarten through Fifth Grade **MA:** Local **D/D/R:** Special Education for Kindergarten through Fifth-Grade **H/I/S:** Working on her New House, Decorating, Reading, Piano **FBP:** Harvard Mental Health Letter **EDU:** Master's Degree in Special Education, Western Oregon State College; Coursework, Chapman College **A/A/S:** Orange County Disability Association **A/H:** Apple Valley Teacher of the Year **C/VW:** United Way of America

REV. LAURA W. RABBITT
Ordained Minister
Compassion in Action
3 E. Main Street
Pawling, NY 12564 United States
laurarabbitt@earthlink.net
http://www.cambridgewhoswho.com

BUS: Nonprofit Organization **P/S:** Spiritual Services, Counseling **MA:** National **EXP:** Her expertise is in stress reduction, energy healing and spiritual counseling. **H/I/S:** Spending Time with her Children, Reading, Knitting, Traveling **EDU:** Bachelor of Science in Holistic Ministries, American Institute of Holistic Theology (2000) **C/VW:** United Nations Association of the United States of America; International Critical Incident Stress Foundation; Doctors Without Borders; Capoeira Arts Foundation **A/S:** She attributes her success to her caring nature and desire to help others. **H/O:** The most gratifying aspect of her career is helping others and making a difference in their lives.

JYLL M. RADEMACHER
Operations Manager
Microsoft
1600 Aspen Commons
Suite 950
Middleton, WI 53562 United States
jrademacher1@gmail.com
http://www.smackshopping.com

BUS: Software Company **P/S:** Software Products and Services **MA:** International **EXP:** Ms. Rademacher's expertise is in protect management. **D/D/R:** Managing Daily Operations, Overseeing Sales, Technology and Accounting Departments, Handling Business Development and the Strategic Vision of Research and Development Products **H/I/S:** Participating in Outdoor Activities, Playing Softball and Basketball, Rowing, Running **EDU:** Master of Business Administration, University of Wisconsin (2008); Bachelor's Degree in Conservation Biology, University of Wisconsin (2000)

DIANE RADVANSKI
Research Teaching Specialist
Robert Wood Johnson Medical School
University of Medicine and Dentistry of New Jersey
1 RWJ Place, MEB Room 484
New Brunswick, NJ 08903 United States
dradvanski@aol.com
http://www.rwjms.umdnj.edu

BUS: University Medical School **P/S:** Clinical Research, Patient Care, Medical Education, Continuing Education, Post-Doctorate Fellows Programs **MA:** Regional **D/D/R:** Conducting Research on Chronic Pain and Illness, Educating Patients **H/I/S:** Singing in the Choir, Volunteering with the Local Church, Basketball, Tennis, Softball **FBP:** Clinical Psychology: Science and Practice **EDU:** Master of Science in Allied Health Studies, College of Mount Saint Vincent (2003) **A/A/S:** Applied Association for Psychophysiology and Biofeedback; Allied Health Professional Section, ACR; Psi Chi; Alpha Sigma Mu

TANYA EVA WOLF RAGIR
Sculptor, Owner
Tanya Ragir Studio
3587 Ocean View Avenue
Los Angeles, CA 90066 United States
tanyaevawolf.Ragir@cwwemail.com
tanya@tanyaragir.com
http://www.tanyaragir.com

BUS: Sculpture Studio **P/S:** Public and Residential Art, Sculptures in Bronze, Ceramic, Stainless Steel and Aluminum, Broad Range of Sculptures Range for Tabletops and Walls **MA:** National **EXP:** Ms. Ragir's expertise is in figurative sculpturing in bronze, ceramic, stainless steel and aluminum. **H/I/S:** Spending Time with her Children **FBP:** The Artful Home; Guild Sourcebooks; The Guild Sourcebook of Architectural & Interior Art; Encyclopedia of Living Artists; Smithsonian **EDU:** Bachelor of Fine Arts, University of California, Santa Cruz **A/A/S:** Women in Business; National Association of Women Artists; American Society of Contemporary Artists; International Sculpture Center **A/H:** Silver Medal, National Sculpture Society, John Cavanaugh Memorial Award, NSS 2000 Annual Exhibition, Brookgreen Gardens, SC and NY (2000); John Cavanaugh Memorial Award for Figurative Sculpture, North American Sculpture Exhibition, Foothills Art Center, Golden, CO (1996); Award, 'California Small Works,' California Museum of Art, Santa Rosa, CA (1991); Grand Prize, 'Museum Without Walls,' Juried Exhibition, Pacific Garden Mall, Santa Cruz, CA (1976) **C/VW:** Venice Family Clinic; St. Joseph's Center; Dream Street Foundation; Center Theater Group; Los Angeles Music Center **CHILD:** Sophie, Jonah **W/H:** Group Exhibition, The Gordon Pass Gallery, Naples, FL, 'The Year of the Chimera 3.2,' Glass Garage Gallery, W. Hollywood, CA, Decker Studios Bronze, Varnish Fine Art, San Francisco, CA (2007); Group Exhibition, 'A Twisted Christmas,' BGH Gallery, Santa Monica, CA (2005); Solo Exhibition, Fresh Paint, Culver City CA (2004); Group Exhibition, BGH Gallery, Santa Monica CA (2004); Solo Exhibition, Bakersfield Museum of Art, Bakersfield, CA (2003); Solo Exhibition, BGH Gallery, Santa Monica, CA (2003); Group Exhibition, 'Contemporary Realism,' Mesa Arts Center, Mesa, AZ, 'The Sculptors,' Gallery 835, Los Angeles, CA, North American Sculpture Exhibition, Golden, CO, BGH Gallery, Bergamot Station, Santa Monica, CA, 'The Human Plane,' Glass Garage Fine Art Gallery, Los Angeles, CA (2002); Group Exhibition, National Sculpture Society Annual Exhibition, Americas Tower, New York, NY (2000-2001); Los Angeles County Museum of Art Exhibition Gallery, Los Angeles, CA (2000); Solo Exhibition, 'Interiors,' The Artists' Gallery, Santa Monica, CA (2000); Group Exhibitions, Valerie Miller Fine Art Gallery, Palm Desert, CA (1997); Solo Exhibition, Burbank Contemporary Art Center, Burbank, CA (1995); Group Exhibitions, Orange County Center for Contemporary Art, Santa Ana, CA (1995); Group Exhibitions, Rachele Lozzi Gallery, Los Angeles, CA, Hundai Gallery, Seoul, Korea, Artyard, Denver, CO (1995); Group Exhibitions, Platt Gallery, University of Judaism, Los Angeles, CA, Total Museum of Contemporary Art, Seoul, Korea (1993); Solo Exhibitions, 'The Feminine Landscape,' Heritage Gallery, Los Angeles, CA (1992); Group Exhibitions, California Sculpture Alliance Show, Whittier Museum, Whittier, CA (1990) **A/S:** She attributes her success to her perseverance and high standards. **B/I:** She became involved in her profession because she was always artistically gifted and was inspired by a teacher to pursue a career in art.

Judith A. Raia, MA, CCC-SLP

Speech-Language Specialist
Paramus Board of Education
145 Spring Valley Road
Paramus, NJ 07656 United States
jraia@paramus.k12.nj.us
http://www.paramus.k12.nj.us

BUS: Education **P/S:** Public School Education, Private Therapy **MA:** Local **D/D/R:** Speech and Language Difficulties in Children, Language, Articulation **H/I/S:** Traveling, Cooking, Skiing **FBP:** Advance for Speech-Language Pathologists & Audiologists **EDU:** Master of Arts in Speech-Language Pathology, Montclair State University; Coursework, Speech Communications, Special Education and Elementary Education, William Patterson University; Bachelor of Arts in Speech-Language Pathology, Montclair State University **A/A/S:** American Speech-Language-Hearing Association; New Jersey Speech-Language-Hearing Association; Bergen County Speech-Language-Hearing Association; Paramus Education Association; Bergen County Education Association; New Jersey Education Association **C/VW:** Bergen County Laryngectomy Association **H/O:** The most gratifying aspect of her career is helping children with unique and special cases over the years.

Mr. Rick E. Rainey

Controller
Bar-S Foods Co.
100 Bar-S Drive
Elk City, OK 73644 United States
rrainey@bar-s.com
http://www.cambridgewhoswho.com

BUS: Food Industry **P/S:** Hot Dogs, Bologna, Bacon, Lunch Meats Manufacturer **MA:** National **D/D/R:** Inventory **H/I/S:** Golfing, Spending Time with the Family **EDU:** Bachelor of Science in Accounting, Oklahoma State University **A/A/S:** American Institute of Certified Public Accountants **B/I:** He became involved in his profession because he took bookkeeping in high school and enjoyed it. **H/O:** The highlight of his career was his promotion to tax manager.

KATHRYN I. RALEY
Special Educator
Hawthorne Elementary School
125 Kingston Road
Baltimore, MD 21220 United States
kraley@bcps.org
http://www.cambridgewhoswho.com

BUS: Public School **P/S:** Education **MA:** Local **D/D/R:** Working with Emotionally Challenged Students **H/I/S:** Reading, Playing Music, Running **EDU:** Pursuing Master's Degree in Supervision and School Improvement, Goucher College; Bachelor of Arts in Special Education, Goucher College **CERTS:** Certification in Crisis Prevention and Intervention **A/A/S:** Maryland State Teachers Association **C/VW:** Working in Schools **A/S:** She attributes her success to her good educational foundation and her mentors. **B/I:** She always wanted to be a teacher, and as a senior in high school she worked with mentally handicapped students. This experience encouraged her to go into special education. **H/O:** The highlight of her career has been succeeding with all levels and age groups.

CESIA A. RAMIREZ
Teacher
The Island School PS188
Department of Education
442 E. Houston Street
New York, NY 10002 United States
cesiales@aol.com
http://www.cambridgewhoswho.com

BUS: Public School **P/S:** Education Services **MA:** Local **D/D/R:** Promoting Literacy in Reading, Teaching Reading and Writing Workshops **H/I/S:** Reading, Creating Art, Crafting, Going Out **FBP:** Instructor; Teaching K-8 **EDU:** Master's Degree in Literacy, Touro College (2005); Bachelor of Science, Touro College

MIGUEL A. RAMIREZ
Senior International Manager
The Scoular Company
250 Marquette Avenue
Suite 1050
Minneapolis, MN 55401 United States
mramirez@scoular.com
http://www.scoular.com

BUS: Trading Company **P/S:** Food and Feed Commodities **MA:** International **D/D/R:** Utilizing his Expertise with International Business **H/I/S:** Running **FBP:** BusinessWeek; The Wall Street Journal **EDU:** Master's Degree in Economics, Michigan State University; Bachelor's Degree, Michigan State University **A/A/S:** American Agricultural Economics Association; American China International Business Association **A/H:** Excellent Scholar Award, Institute of Food Technologists (2000) **C/VW:** Volunteer, Christian Group **A/S:** He attributes his career success to his hard work. **B/I:** He became involved in his profession because he enjoys the fast pace of the business and the many different people he meets. **H/O:** The highlight of his career was being promoted to senior international manager.

VICTORIA L. RAMOS
Administrative Executive Director
The Cupo Companies
50 Mount Prospect Avenue
Clifton, NJ 07013 United States
viki.r@cupo.com
http://www.cupo.com

BUS: Property Management and Development, Insurance and Real Estate Company **P/S:** Properties, Insurance, Real Estate **MA:** Eastern Sea-board, Tri-State Area **D/D/R:** Assisting the Chief Executive Officer and President, Troubleshooting, Deploying Acquisitions, Overseeing Office Equipment, Computers and Software Problems, Managing Human Resources **H/I/S:** Spending Quality Time with her Children, Going to Yankee Games, Shopping, Relaxing, Spending Time with Friends **EDU:** Industry-Related Training and Experience **C/VW:** Local Violence Prevention Program **A/S:** She attributes her success to her willingness to take on anything. **B/I:** She became involved in her profession because she wanted a career with opportunity for advancement.

NORMAN V. RANCOURT
Teacher
Norwalk Public School District, Kendall School
57 Fillow Street
Norwalk, CT 06850 United States
drnvrancourt@hotmail.com
http://www.cambridgewhoswho.com

BUS: School **P/S:** Education **MA:** Local **D/D/R:** Specializing in Elementary Education **H/I/S:** Volleyball, Golfing, Hiking, Hunting, Fishing **FBP:** Education Law Association Journal **EDU:** Doctor of Education, University of Bridgeport; Master's Degree in Elementary Education, University of Bridgeport; Master of Arts in Special Education, Fairfield University; Bachelor's Degree in Special Education, Southern Connecticut State University; Degree in Educational Management, Sacred Heart University, Fairfield, Connecticut **A/A/S:** Association for Supervision and Curriculum Development; Education Law Association; National Science Teachers Association; Council for Exceptional Children **A/H:** Nominee, Dissertation of the Year; Outstanding Thesis, Sacred Heart University **A/S:** He attributes his personal and professional success to his perseverance and desire to succeed. **B/I:** He became involved in the profession because he always had an interest in the field. **H/O:** The highlight of his career was receiving an award for dissertation of the year in educational law.

DELORES Y. RANDOLPH
1) Captain 2) Founder, Owner
1) Petersburg Bureau of Police (Retired)
2) Chesterfield Security Training Academy, Inc.
PO Box 2709
Petersburg, VA 23804 United States
csta-1@verizon.net
http://www.cambridgewhoswho.com

BUS: 1) Police Bureau 2) Security Training Academy **P/S:** 1) Law Enforcement 2) Security Training **MA:** 1) Local 2) Regional **EXP:** Ms. Randolph's expertise is in law enforcement. **D/D/R:** Running the Training School, Instructing Classes **H/I/S:** Genealogy, Reading **EDU:** Bachelor's Degree in Criminology, Minor in Philosophy, Saint Leo University **CERTS:** Certificate of Completion, Administrative Officers Management Program, North Carolina State University **A/H:** Purple Heart; Meritorious Duty Award; Expert Firearm Award; 12 Progress Awards; 11 Safe Driving Awards; Chief's Special Recognition Award **C/VW:** Make-A-Wish Foundation; Special Olympics **A/S:** She attributes her success to her education and training. **B/I:** She became involved in this profession because she was always interested in law enforcement and had a desire to help people. **H/O:** The most gratifying aspect of her career is being able to touch so many people's lives.

NATARAJAN RANGANATHAN, PH.D.
Senior Vice President of Research and Development
Kibow Biotech, Inc.
4629 W. Chester Pike
Newton Square, PA 19073 United States
rangan@kibowbiotech.com
http://www.kibowbiotech.com

BUS: Biotechnology and Pharmaceutical Company **P/S:** Developing New Technology and Therapeutic Products to Provide Symptomatic Relief and to Slow the Progression of Both Chronic and End-Stage Kidney Disease **MA:** International **D/D/R:** Specializing in Biotechnology, Overseeing the Business Including Research and Development, Supervising 12 Researchers **H/I/S:** Music **FBP:** Renal Business **EDU:** Ph.D. in Medical Research, Temple University (1976) **A/A/S:** American Society of Artificial Internal Organs; American Chemical Society; American Society of Nephrology; International Society of Nephrology; IPA

SUSIE M. RANSOM
Author, Poet, Teacher (Retired)
139 Jericho Road
Essex Junction, VT 05452 United States
lrboomer@aol.com
http://www.cambridgewhoswho.com

BUS: Sole Proprietorship **P/S:** Writing, Teaching **MA:** Regional **EXP:** Ms. Ransom's expertise is in synchronized swimming, choreography, education, literature and poetry. **H/I/S:** Reading, Working on Computers, Writing, Quilting, Coloring **FBP:** Time; National Geographic **EDU:** Bachelor of Science in Elementary Education, Minor in English, Castleton State College (1970); Coursework in Executive Secretary Studies **CERTS:** Certified Lay Speaker **A/A/S:** National Society Daughters of the American Revolution; Ladies Auxiliary Fire Department; Ladies Auxiliary Veterans of Foreign Wars **C/VW:** Grace United Methodist Church

LINDA E. RAPPAPORT, ESQ.
Partner, Chairman of Executive Compensation and Employee Benefits
Private Clients Practice Group
Shearman & Sterling, LLP
599 Lexington Avenue
New York, NY 10022 United States
lrappaport@shearman.com
http://www.shearman.com

BUS: Martindale-Hubbell AV-Rated Law Firm Committed to Excellence in the International Legal Industry **P/S:** Legal Services include Antitrust, Asset Management, Bankruptcy, Corporate Governance, Criminal, Environmental, Executive Compensation, Finance, Intellectual Property, International Arbitration, International Trade, Litigation, Mergers and Acquisitions, Private Clients, Property, Sports, Tax **MA:** International **D/D/R:** Specializing in Executive Compensation and Employee Benefits, Overseeing Operations of the Firm and 1000 Lawyers Globally, Performing Managerial Duties **EDU:** JD, New York University School of Law (1977); Bachelor of Arts in English Literature and Music, Magna Cum Laude, Wesleyan University, Connecticut **A/A/S:** International Partner of the Firm (1985); Federal Clerkship (1979); ACOEBL Honorarium; Legal Aid Board; Board Member, Mannes College of Music; Former Board Member, The New York Women's Foundation; Fellow, American College of Employees Benefits Council **A/H:** Received the Burton Award for a Published Article

MAHMOUD RASHIDI
Doctor of Medicine, Neurosurgeon
Bakersfield Neuroscience and Spine Institute
2601 Oswell Street
Suite 100
Bakersfield, CA 93306 United States
mrashidi@bnsi.org
http://www.bnsi.org

BUS: Healthcare Center **P/S:** Healthcare Including Group Practice, Neurosurgery and Spine Services **MA:** California **D/D/R:** Performing Cranial and Spinal Neurosurgery and Assuring Patients with Excellent Healthcare **H/I/S:** Watching Television, Hiking, Practicing Martial Arts, Spending Time at the Beach **FBP:** Forbes; Fortune; Money **EDU:** Fellowship in Pediatric Neurosurgery, The Hospital for Sick Children, University of Toronto (2002); Residency in Neurosurgery, University of Toronto (2001); Internship in Medicine, Earned in Iran (1991); MD, Earned in Iran (1991); Bachelor of Science, Earned in Iran (1986) **A/A/S:** Fellow, Royal College of Physicians and Surgeons of Canada; Congress of Neurological Surgeons; American Association of Neurological Surgeons; American Medical Association **A/H:** First Rank, Medical School, Iran

NANCY M. RATHJE
Corporate Technical Services Manager
Case Ready
Cargill, Inc.
511 W. North Avenue
Fresno, CA 93706 United States
nancy_rathje@cargill.com
http://www.cargill.com

BUS: Food Services Company **P/S:** Case Ready Steaks, Pork, Poultry and Veal **MA:** National **D/D/R:** Working with Technical Services, Food Safety and Product Quality **H/I/S:** Playing and Watching Volleyball, Watching College Football **FBP:** Meat & Poultry; Consumer Reports **EDU:** Bachelor of Science in Animal Science, University of Nebraska **A/A/S:** North American Meat Processors Association; American Meat Institute; National Meat Association; American Meat Science Association **C/VW:** Charity Walks; United Way of America; The Lord's Diner; Soup Kitchen **A/S:** She attributes her success to her upbringing, hard work and determination. **B/I:** She became involved in her profession after meeting a judge who helped in opening many doors for her while she was in college. **H/O:** The highlight of her career was earning her current position.

DOROTHY J. RAU
Director of Social Service
Carmel Richmond Healthcare and Rehabilitation Center
88 Old Town Road
Staten Island, NY 10304 United States
drau@chcsnet.org
http://www.chcsnet.org

BUS: Healthcare **P/S:** Long-Term Healthcare **MA:** National **D/D/R:** Geriatrics **H/I/S:** Collecting Antiques **FBP:** NASW Press Publications **EDU:** Master's Degree in Social Work, New York University **A/A/S:** National Association of Social Workers; Instructor, New York University **C/VW:** Chinese Representative, National Association of Social Workers (2005) **A/S:** She attributes her success to loving what she does. **H/O:** The highlight of her career was getting her master's.

DR. PRASAD S. RAVI
Scientist
Degussa Chem Corporation
8300 W. U.S. Highway 24
Mapleton, IL 61547 United States
prasad_ravi@msn.com
http://www.cambridgewhoswho.com

BUS: Manufacturing Facility **P/S:** Organic Specialty Chemicals Including Oleo Chemicals and Surfactants, Education, Organic Chemistry **MA:** Local **D/D/R:** Performing Applied Research, Process Development, Implementing New Products in Production, Plant Troubleshooting **H/I/S:** Listening to Music, Traveling, Weightlifting, Jogging, Bicycling, Swimming **FBP:** Chemical & Engineering News **EDU:** Ph.D. in Organic Chemistry, Synthesis, Isolation and Identification of Natural Products (1978) **A/A/S:** American Chemical Society

FLOEY E. RAY, MS
Teacher
Washington Elementary School
1930B Street N.E.
Miami, OK 74354 United States
nannyflow@hotmail.com
http://www.cambridgewhoswho.com

BUS: Elementary School **P/S:** Primary Education **MA:** Local **D/D/R:** Teaching Special Education to Third-Grade Students, Working with Handicapped Children and Organizing After-School Programs **H/I/S:** Spending Time with her Family **EDU:** Master's Degree in Special Education; Master's Degree in Education, Pittsburg State University, KS; Bachelor of Science in Elementary Education **A/A/S:** Oklahoma Education Association; National Education Association **A/H:** Third-Grade Teacher of the Year Award (2001); Teacher of the Year Award for the District (2000) **SP:** Fred **CHILD:** Greg, Cyndi **A/S:** She attributes her success to her passion for her profession. **B/I:** She became involved in her profession because of her experience and love for teaching. **H/O:** The most gratifying aspect of her career is being recognized in the teaching field.

SANDRA KAY RAYBUCK, BSED.
Science Instructor
Jefferson County-DuBois Area Vocational-Technical School
576 Vo Tech Road
Reynoldsville, PA 15851 United States
raybuck@jefftech.us
http://www.jefftech.us

BUS: Comprehensive Vocational-Technical High School **P/S:** Education and Training in Various Areas, Information Technology Education **MA:** Regional **D/D/R:** Teaching Physics, Implementing Programs for Teenage Health and Wellness, Utilizing Unique Audio and Visual Teaching Methods to Help Students Learn **H/I/S:** Creating Native American Drums, Collecting Memorabilia, Teaching Native American Dance and Music, Sewing, Reading, Learning **FBP:** Popular Science; Popular Mechanics **EDU:** Bachelor of Science in Education, Clarion University of Pennsylvania (1990); Bachelor of Arts in Physical Science and Geology, Clarion University of Pennsylvania (1990); Coursework in Science Education **A/A/S:** Pennsylvania Science Teachers Association; National Science Teachers Association **A/H:** Great Teacher of the Year Award (2007)

JOHN CHARLES REAGAN SR.
Owner
J.C. Reagan, Inc.
4474 Summer Haven Boulevard S.
Jacksonville, FL 32258 United States
johnreag@aol.com
http://www.cambridgewhoswho.com

BUS: Residential and Commercial Mortgage Company **P/S:** Residential and Commercial Mortgages, Refinancing Loans **MA:** Florida **D/D/R:** Mortgage Financing **H/I/S:** Traveling, Golfing, Watching Sports **FBP:** The Wall Street Journal **EDU:** Industry-Related Training and Experience **A/A/S:** Northeast Florida Board of Realtors; Northeast Florida Mortgage Association; Northeast Florida Builders Association; Chamber of Commerce; Florida Mortgage Brokers Association **C/VW:** Local Charities **A/S:** He attributes his success to being very good at what he does. **B/I:** He chose the profession because he enjoys helping others. **H/O:** The highlight of his career was obtaining his current position.

DENNIS J. REANIER

Pastor
Valley Christian Fellowship
1205 Cardinal Drive
Belgrade, MT 59714 United States
dreanier@revivalcry.com
http://www.revivalcry.com

BUS: Church **P/S:** Ministry **MA:** National **D/D/R:** Communicating with People, Worshiping God, Overseeing Ministry Network **H/I/S:** Spending Time with Family and Friends, Traveling, Watching Movies, Football and Basketball, Skiing **FBP:** The Wall Street Journal **EDU:** Master's Degree in Theology **A/A/S:** District Superintendent, Montana; Revival Crime Ministries; Board Member, Montana Bible Churches **C/VW:** Be a Hero, Orphanages Overseas

ANN M. RECKELBERG

Family and Consumer Science Educator
Luxemburg-Casco School District
619 Church Avenue
Casco, WI 54205 United States
areckelberg@luxcasco.k12.wi.us
http://www.cambridgewhoswho.com

BUS: School District **P/S:** Education **MA:** Local **D/D/R:** Teaching Family and Consumer Sciences to Seventh and Eighth-Grade Students **H/I/S:** Managing her Farm **EDU:** Bachelor of Science in Family and Consumer Science, University of Wisconsin **A/A/S:** Junior Chamber of Commerce **A/S:** She attributes her success to her community as well as her students and their parents. **B/I:** She became involved in her profession because her experiences with the 4-H club inspired her to pursue a career in teaching. **H/O:** The highlight of her career was being nominated for the Golden Apple Award for 2005-2006.

LISA REDDEL
Psychiatric Nurse
Federal Medical Center
Rochester, MN 55951 United States
lisareddell@hotmail.com
http://www.cambridgewhoswho.com

BUS: Federal Medical Center **P/S:** Nursing **MA:** Local **D/D/R:** Psychiatric Nursing **H/I/S:** Cross Stitching **FBP:** Nursing2009 **EDU:** Associate Degree in Psychiatric Nursing, Northeast Iowa Community College **A/A/S:** Phi Theta Kappa **A/S:** She attributes her success to her hard work, late nights of studying and her family's support. **B/I:** She became involved in her profession because she wanted more of a career and always was interested in the medical field.

PAMELA MARIANI REECE, CAS, MS
Director
Utica Teacher Center
Utica City School District
1203 Hilton Avenue
Utica, NY 13501 United States
preece@uticaschools.org
http://www.uticaschools.org

BUS: Professional Learning Center **P/S:** Education **MA:** Local **D/D/R:** Educating Teachers, Professional Training, Coordinating the School Mentoring Program, Overseeing New Teacher Orientations and In-Service Credit Programs **H/I/S:** Running, Traveling, Reading **FBP:** Educational Leadership; Phi Delta Kappan **EDU:** Master of Science, Educational Foundations; Bachelor of Arts in Sociology and Biology, Hamilton College **CERTS:** Certificate of Applied Science in School District Administration, SUNY Cortland **A/A/S:** Phi Delta Kappa; Association for Supervision and Curriculum Development **A/H:** Teacher Excellence Award; Teacher of the Month, Board of Education (1997) **C/VW:** American Heart Association; Saint Anthony's Church **A/S:** She attributes her success to her educational background. **B/I:** She became involved in the profession because she always enjoyed helping others. **H/O:** The highlight of her career was when the Board of Education elected her as Outstanding Teacher of the Year in 2001.

CYNTHIA D. REED, RN
Charge Nurse
Helen Keller Hospital
1745 Ashton Street
Tuscumbia, AL 35674 United States
jhns980@aol.com
http://www.helenkeller.com

BUS: Hospital **P/S:** Healthcare Including Treatment for Sleep Disorders, Lifesteps Weight Management and Smoking Cessation Programs **MA:** Regional **EXP:** Ms. Reed's areas of expertise include oncology and pediatric nursing. **D/D/R:** Managing Nurses and Nursing Assistants, Overseeing the Hospital Floor, Filling Chart Orders, Overseeing the Infusion Clinic **H/I/S:** Reading, Traveling, Making Jewelry, Football **FBP:** American Journal of Nursing; Oncology Forum; RN **EDU:** Registered Nurse, El Centro College (1991); Bachelor's Degree in Interior Design, The University of North Alabama (1980); Associate Degree in Nursing, El Centro College **CERTS:** Certification in Chemotherapy; Certification in Advanced Cardiac Life Support; Certified Pediatric Advanced Cardiac Life Support Instructor **A/A/S:** Alabama State Nurses Association; American Nurses Association; Secretary, Local Chapter, Oncology Nurses of Northwest Alabama; Oncology Nursing Society; American Cancer Society **C/VW:** Team Captain, Relay for Life **I/F/Y:** In five years, Ms. Reed hopes to be a travel nurse.

ANN M. REEDER, LPN
Licensed Practical Nurse Supervisor
Beverly Living Center
740 Dual Highway
Hagerstown, MD 21740 United States
reeder@innernet.net
http://www.cambridgewhoswho.com

BUS: Elder Care Facility **P/S:** Healthcare **MA:** Local **D/D/R:** Supervising the Evening Shift and Nurses, Personally Interacting with Residents to Meet All Resident Needs **H/I/S:** Knitting, Crocheting, Spending Quality Time with her Two Grandchildren **EDU:** Pursuing Registered Nurse Degree **CERTS:** Licensed Practical Nurse, Fulton County Area Vocational Technical School **A/A/S:** Local Church

JUDY L. REEVES
Office Manager
Orange County Drainage District
8081 Old Highway 90
Orange, TX 77630 United States
jcr@pnx.com
http://www.cambridgewhoswho.com

BUS: Government **P/S:** Drainage for Orange County **MA:** Regional **D/D/R:** Overseeing Office Operations **H/I/S:** Traveling, Reading, Scrapbooking **EDU:** Associate Degree in Computer Science, Lamar University **A/S:** She attributes her success to her hard work and dedication. **B/I:** She became involved in the profession because she enjoyed working with the government. **H/O:** The highlight of her career was earning her current position.

MARIE CHRISTINE REGAN-BEHRENS
Nursing Instructor (Retired)
Robert Morgan Institute
5172 S.W. 5 Terrace
Coral Gables, FL 33134 United States
mcrmia@aol.com
http://www.rmec.dadeschools.net

BUS: Two Year School **P/S:** Education, Vocational Programs **MA:** Regional **D/D/R:** Educating and Instructing Nursing Students in Public Health and Clinical **H/I/S:** Golfing, Aerobics **FBP:** Nursing Journal **EDU:** Master's Degree in Health Education, Nova Southeastern University (1983); Bachelor of Science, University of Maryland (1965) **A/A/S:** Greenway Golf Association; Women's Golf Association, Country Club Coral Gables; Military Order of World Wars; Reserve Officers Association

BARBARA A. REGLAND
Special Education Teacher
Hughesville High School
349 Cemetary Street
Hughesville, PA 17737 United States
bregland@elsd.org
http://www.elsd.org

BUS: High School **P/S:** All Facets of Student Guidance and Educational Services **MA:** Pennsylvania **D/D/R:** All Aspects of the Autistic Population **H/I/S:** Sewing, Gardening, Walking, Spending Time with the Family **EDU:** Master of Special Education, Mansfield University **A/A/S:** Council for Exceptional Children; TASH **C/VW:** Special Olympics **A/S:** She attributes her success to being people oriented, creative, resourceful and ambitious. **B/I:** She became involved in this profession because she has always had an affinity toward this profession. **H/O:** The highlight of her career is helping the children every day.

LEAH R. REICH
Public Information Officer
San Rafael City Schools
310 Nova Albion Way
San Rafael, CA 94960 United States
http://www.cambridgewhoswho.com

BUS: Communications, Education **P/S:** Communications and Public Relations for the School District **MA:** Local **D/D/R:** Media Relations, Spokesperson for the District, Newsletters **EDU:** Bachelor's Degree in English and Journalism, University of the Pacific **A/A/S:** Public Relations Society of America **C/VW:** Environmental Organizations; School Foundations **A/S:** She attributes her success to her passion for her job. **B/I:** She became involved in her profession because she loves children and had family members in the field who inspired her. **H/O:** The highlight of her career was having students thank her.

JOANNE R. REID
Vice President of Educational Services, President, Co-Owner
Corporate Development Associates, Inc., CDA Publishing, Inc.
2201 S. Highland Avenue
Lombard, IL 60148 United States
jrreid@corpdevelopmentassoc.com
http://www.corpdevelopmentassoc.com

BUS: Consulting Firm **P/S:** Educational and Consulting Services **MA:** National **EXP:** Ms. Reid's expertise is in education. **H/I/S:** Attending Air Shows, Golfing **FBP:** Discover; Scientific American; US News & World Report **EDU:** Doctoral Degree in Education, Northern Illinois University; Master's Degree in Education, Northern Illinois University; Bachelor's Degree in Chemistry, Northeastern University, Boston **A/A/S:** Kappa Delta Phi; American Society for Training and Development; Association of American University Presses; American Association for the Advancement of Science **C/VW:** American Humanist Association; Secular Humanist Society of Chicago; Center for Inquiring; Church of Scientific Humanism **A/S:** She attributes her success to her determination. **B/I:** She became involved in her profession because of her interest in working with computers. **H/O:** The most gratifying aspect of her career is publishing her last textbook entitled 'Auto CAD 2005 for Beginners.'

PHYLLIS T. REID
Motivational Speaker, Psychotherapist
PhilMar Foundation for Purposeful Living
PO Box 381881
Miami, FL 32338 United States
philmar@philmar2000.com
http://www.philmar2000.com

BUS: Counseling Services **P/S:** Career Coaching, and Motivational Speaking which Presents Messages in a Captivating, Motivating, Inspiring and Hope Building Way **MA:** Regional **D/D/R:** Conducting Spiritual Seminars, Motivational Workshops and Individual Coaching, Working as Trauma Specialist for Adults and Children **H/I/S:** Writing **FBP:** Unity Magazine; Science of Mind; Psychology Today **EDU:** Master's Degree in Counseling and Social Work, Barry University (2001); Bachelor's Degree, Barry University (1997) **A/A/S:** Metaphysical New Thought

THERESA S. REID-PAUL
Radiology Regional Program Director
Keiser University
1500 N.W. 49th Street
Fort Lauderdale, FL 33309 United States
terryr@keiseruniversity.edu
http://www.keisercollege.edu

BUS: Institute of Higher Learning **P/S:** Business Administration, Human Resources Management, International Business, and Marketing, Criminal Justice, Management Information Systems, Nursing, Elementary Education, Aquatic Engineering Technology, Computer Graphics and Design, Computer Animation and Design, Video Game Design, Computer Networking and Security Management **MA:** Regional **D/D/R:** Radiology Program Development, Overseeing 12 Campuses, Working as the Resource for Program Directors, Heading-Up Meetings Yearly, Taking Suggestions and Distributing them to Office of the Chancellor, Working on Reviews of Textbooks for a Publishing Company **H/I/S:** Long Walks, Traveling with her Husband, Spending Time with her Daughter **FBP:** Radiologic Science **EDU:** Master's Degree in Business Administration and Healthcare Management, University of Phoenix (2003) **A/A/S:** Broward Society of Radiology Technologists; American Society of Radiology Technologists; American Educators of Radiologic Sciences; American Registry of Radiologic Technologists

BYRON E. REILLY
Agricultural Marketing Specialist
Federal Agricultural Agencies
7 Riva Ridge Lane
Stafford, VA 22556 United States
bereilly@adelphia.net
http://www.cambridgewhoswho.com

BUS: Agricultural Specialist Company **P/S:** Facilitation of the Marketing of Grains and Related Agricultural Products **MA:** International **D/D/R:** Working with the Private Sector and Government Officials to Understand United States Marketing Systems and Facilitate Trade, Helping to Develop Agricultural Quality Control Systems for Grain and Pulses Worldwide **H/I/S:** Building Computers, Studying Gemology, Collecting Coins and Stamps, Gardening **FBP:** Feedstuffs; Technical Computer Literature **EDU:** Bachelor of Science in Agronomy, Delaware Valley College of Science and Agriculture, Doylestown, PA (1976) **A/A/S:** President Elect, Agricultural Commodity Certification Association (2007) **A/H:** Received Several Awards in Recognition of Efforts to Harmonize Testing Methods in Other Countries; Award for Input on Contract Specifications Leading to the Export of about Two Million Tons of United States Grain to Iraq; Honorary Indiana State Trooper **W/H:** Agricultural Commodity Inspector, IN; Representative, Public Relations; International Marketing **C/A:** Published Technical Papers on Harmonization of Inspection Methods for Grain **A/S:** He attributes his success to his passion for his profession. **B/I:** He became involved in his profession because he grew up on a family farm and loved science.

SCOTT R. REINERS
Veterinarian
Mountain View Equine Hospital
309 Old B and O Road
Steeles Tavern, VA 24476 United States
http://www.mveh.com

BUS: Full Service Horse Hospital **P/S:** Horse Care **MA:** Regional **D/D/R:** Performing Equine Surgeries, Treating Lameness **H/I/S:** Riding Horses, Sky Diving **FBP:** Veterinary Surgery; AJVR; Internal Veterinary Medicine **EDU:** Bachelor of Science, South Dakota State University; Doctor of Veterinary Medicine, Kansas State University; Internship, Ohio State University; Surgery Residency, Oklahoma State University **A/A/S:** Diplomat, American College of Veterinary Surgeons; American Veterinary Medical Association; American Veterinary Surgery Association; National College Association **C/VW:** Horse Rescue **A/S:** He attributes his success to persistence and hard work. **B/I:** He became involved in his profession because he was raised on a farm. **H/O:** The highlight of his career was finishing his research project on tendon grafting in horses.

MS. SUSAN G. REISS
Enterprise Systems Quality Engineer
Molecular Quality
Becton Dickinson Diagnostics Systems
54 Loveton Circle
Sparks, MD 21152 United States
Sue_Reiss@bd.com
http://www.bd.com

BUS: Medical Technology Manufacturer **P/S:** Medical Diagnostics, Medical Supplies, Devices, Laboratory Equipment and Diagnostic Products **MA:** International **D/D/R:** Overseeing Business Processes, Managing Six Sigma and Lean Practices, Ensuring Quality Assurance and Quality Control **H/I/S:** Reading, Gardening, Outdoor Sports, Hiking, Bicycling, Photography **FBP:** Fortune **EDU:** Bachelor's Degree in Science, University of Hartford (1987) **CERTS:** Certified Six Sigma Green Belt **A/S:** He attributes his success to paying attention to details, driving for results and desire to learn in a team or individual environment. **B/I:** She became involved in her profession through a natural progression of opportunities. **H/O:** The most gratifying aspect of her career is improving how things get done, whether it is improving a manufacturing process flow or implementing a business system. **I/F/Y:** In five year, Ms. Reiss hopes work in a mid-management level business process position.

Elizabeth A. Reiter, DDS

Doctor
Harmony Dental
1825 Village Center Circle, Suite 150
Las Vegas, NV 89134 United States
info@lvharmonydental.com
http://www.lvharmonydental.com

BUS: High Quality Oral Healthcare Services **P/S:** Adult-Focused Preventative, Restorative and Aesthetic Dentistry **MA:** Local **D/D/R:** Specializing in Preventative Services as well as Aesthetic Restorative Dentistry **H/I/S:** Gardening, Golfing, Tennis, Swimming, Scrapbooking **FBP:** Women's Dental Journal **EDU:** Doctor of Dental Surgery, University of Southern California School of Dentistry (1986) **A/A/S:** American Dental Association **C/VW:** Music Teachers Association; Children's Museum; Las Vegas Philharmonic **A/S:** She attributes her success to her passion for dentistry and continuous studies on the advances in her field and incorporating them into her practice. **B/I:** She became involved in her profession because she was inspired by her orthodontist when she was younger. **H/O:** The most gratifying aspect of her career is working in a beautiful environment that has helps patients get high-quality services in a relaxed and comfortable setting.

Linda L. Reitzel

Licensed Practical Nurse
Midwest Community Health Association
442 W. High Street
Bryan, OH 43506 United States
kdbeitzel@aol.com
http://www.cambridgewhoswho.com

BUS: Private Practice and Medical Clinic **P/S:** Health Care Services, Family Practices, Primary Health Care, Internal Medicine, Women's Health, Specialty Care and Disease Prevention **MA:** Regional **D/D/R:** Aiding the Doctors with Scheduling Patients, Performing Electrocardiograms, Examinations, Immunizations, Inoculations and Overall Care for Patients **H/I/S:** Spending Time with her Three Children and Three Grandchildren, Decorating Cakes **FBP:** Nursing **CERTS:** Licensed Practical Nurse, Buckeye School of Practical Nursing (1976) **A/A/S:** Women's Organization, St. Peter's Lutheran Church; Numerous Committees, Midwest Community Health Association; Compassionate Healthcare Free Clinic

DONNA A. RENNAKER
Emergency Medical Services Department Head
Marcus Daly Ambulance Service
1200 Westwood Drive
Hamilton, MT 59840 United States
drennaker@mdmh.org
http://www.cambridgewhoswho.com

BUS: Emergency Medical Services **P/S:** Ambulance Transports **MA:** National **D/D/R:** Emergency Medical Services, Lead Instructor **H/I/S:** Scrapbooking, Camping **EDU:** College Coursework **CERTS:** Certified in Advanced Stroke Life Support; Certified in Pre-Hospital Trauma Life Support **A/A/S:** Fetal Infant and Child Mortality Study; Board Member, 911 Advisory; Emergency Medical Services Council **A/S:** She attributes her success to hard work. **H/O:** The highlight of her career was getting her paramedics certification.

LINDA A. REPPUCCI
Registered Nurse
Boston Medical Center
850 Harrison Avenue
Boston, MA 02118 United States
http://www.cambridgewhoswho.com

BUS: Healthcare **P/S:** Quality Healthcare **MA:** Local **D/D/R:** Primary Care in Five Outpatient Clinics, Primary Care Clinic, International Clinic, Infectious Disease, Pulmonary Clinic, Geriatrics, Cardiology, Teaching, Counseling **H/I/S:** Playing the Keyboard and Percussion Instruments, Singing **EDU:** Bachelor's Degree in Drama and Music Education, Emerson College **CERTS:** Certification in Nursing **A/A/S:** National Audubon Society **C/VW:** The Salvation Army **A/S:** She attributes her career success to the grace of God, to her ability to forgive others and to her patience for helping others. **B/I:** She has always felt called to help others so she pursued a career in nursing. **H/O:** She feels that working with the nurses in primary care is the highlight of her career.

MARYLORETTO R. RESING
Counselor
Holmes Junior and Senior High School
2500 Madison Avenue
Covington, KY 41014 United States
mlresing@fuse.net
http://www.cambridgewhoswho.com

BUS: High School **P/S:** Secondary Education and Guidance Counseling **MA:** Local **EXP:** Ms. Resing's expertise is in child and family counseling. **H/I/S:** Spending Time with her Family, Traveling, Reading, Antiquing **FBP:** Kentucky Counseling Association Journal **EDU:** Master's Degree in School Counseling, Xavier University; Master of Arts in Community and Agency Counseling, Xavier University; Master of Arts in Religious Studies; Bachelor of Arts in Elementary Education, Thomas Moore College **A/A/S:** President, Kentucky Counseling Association; Former President, Northern Kentucky Association **C/VW:** Veterans Affairs; Native American Association; Special Olympics; The United Way of America **A/S:** She attributes her success to her faith in God. **B/I:** She became involved in her profession because of her interest in helping children. **H/O:** The most gratifying aspect of her career is seeing the children succeed.

MARGO REYES
Comptroller
Mister Sparky, Inc.
2064 Canton Road
Marietta, GA 30066 United States
mpr3302@gmail.com
http://www.cambridgewhoswho.com

BUS: Electric Company **P/S:** Residential and Commercial Electrical Services **MA:** Regional **D/D/R:** Specializing in Financial Analysis, Maintaining the Budget, Overseeing All Aspects of the Company's Financial Operations **H/I/S:** Exercising Including Pilates, Traveling **FBP:** CFO **EDU:** Accounting Degree, University of Texas, Austin **C/VW:** Volunteer, YMCA; The Salvation Army; Battered Women's Shelter of Warner Robin, GA

LINDA S. REYMANN, RN, MS, NCC

Associate Dean, Director of Wellness Center
Villa Julie College
1525 Greenspring Valley Road
Stevenson, MD 21153 United States
f-reyman@mail.vjc.edu
http://www.vjc.edu

BUS: Education **P/S:** Private College Offering All Degree Programs **MA:** International **D/D/R:** Promoting Health and Wellness **H/I/S:** Walking, Tennis **FBP:** ACA Journals; Nursing2009; APA Journal **EDU:** Doctoral Degree in Counseling, Loyola College; Master's Degree in Nursing, University of Maryland; Master's Degree in Pastoral Counseling, Loyola College **CERTS:** National Certification Corporation for the Obstetric, Gynecologic and Neonatal Nursing Specialties **A/A/S:** Sigma Theta Tau; American Counseling Association; American College Health Association; Association of University and College Counseling Center Directors **C/VW:** Make-A-Wish Foundation; United Way of America; Catholic Church **A/S:** She attributes her personal and professional success to her perseverance, a positive outlook and personal motivation. **B/I:** She has always had an interest in the field and a desire to help others. **H/O:** She considers working with college students to be the highlight of her career.

DONNA REYNOLDS, GRI

Realtor
Century 21 Peterson Real Estate
1000 S. Springfield Avenue
Bolivar, MO 65613 United States
donnareynolds@century21.com
http://www.century21.com

BUS: Real Estate Agency **P/S:** Buying and Selling Residential Real Estate Properties Including Land Sales, Farm Sales, Rentals, Relocations **MA:** National **EXP:** Ms. Reynolds' expertise is in residential real estate, farmland and land sales. **H/I/S:** Golfing, Spending Time Outdoors, Hunting, Fishing **FBP:** Realtor; Broker Agent **CERTS:** Certified Realtor, Graduate Realtor Institute (1995); Licensed Real Estate Agent (1993) **A/A/S:** The Springfield Board of Realtors; Missouri Association of Realtors; National Association of Realtors; Multiple Listing Service; Million Dollar Club

VICKI REYNOLDS
LPN
Hillside Family Practice
238 W. 22nd Street
Erie, PA 16502 United States
vreynolds@madbbs.com
http://www.selectmedicalcorp.com

BUS: Long-Term Acute Care Specialty Hospital **P/S:** High-Risk Respiratory Patients Needing Care Coordination Services between Doctors, Nurses, Patients and Patients' Families **MA:** National **D/D/R:** Responsible for 15-25 Patients for Weaning Program on Ventilators, Staff Training, Assessing Patients, Respiratory Nursing **H/I/S:** Creating Crafts, Needleworking, Sports **FBP:** AARC Times **EDU:** Associates in Allied Health Care, California College for Health Sciences (1994) **CERTS:** Certified in Advanced Cardiac Life Support (2004); Registered Respiratory Therapist (1993); Registered Licensed Practical Nurse (1976); Certified Nurse's Aid (1975) **A/A/S:** American Association for Respiratory Care; National Board for Respiratory Care; Community Theater Group; Pennsylvania and New York Chapters, LRC; Lambda Beta National Honor Society (1994) **A/H:** Highest Academic Achievement, Erie School District School of Practical Nursing (1976)

ROSA L. RHAMES, RN, CNRN, CCRN
Registered Nurse (Retired)
Kings County Hospital Center
647 Albany Avenue, Apartment 6L
Brooklyn, NY 11203 United States
rosarhames@aol.com
http://www.cambridgewhoswho.com

BUS: Hospital **P/S:** Healthcare **MA:** Regional **EXP:** Ms. Rhames' expertise is in surgical and neurosurgical nursing. **H/I/S:** Arts, Making Crafts, Home Improvement, Scrapbooking, Basket Making **FBP:** Fortune 500 **EDU:** Bachelor of Science in Nursing, Hunter College (1975); Associate of Science in Nursing, Bronx Community College (1971); Master of Science in Nursing, Plus 18, St. Joseph's College **CERTS:** Certification in Surgery, Neurosurgery, Trauma and Critical Care **A/A/S:** Chi Eta Phi **A/H:** Nurse of Distinction Award, Kings County Hospital, NY (1990); National Queen of Sales Award, Mary Kay **C/VW:** Friendship Baptist Church **CHILD:** Franklin

MICHAEL J. RHEINGOLD, AIA
Senior Architect
Design and Construction Services
New York State Office of General Services
Corning Tower, Empire State Plaza, 33rd Floor
Albany, NY 12242 United States
michael.rheingold@ogs.state.ny.us
http://www.usroute20.com

BUS: Government State Agency **P/S:** Design and Construction Services for Institutional Work **MA:** Statewide **EXP:** Mr. Rheingold's expertise is in architectural design and review. **H/I/S:** Restoring his Home, Working on the Route 20 Website, Restoring a 1956 Oldsmobile, Baseball **FBP:** The AIA Journal of Architecture; Architectural Record **EDU:** Bachelor's Degree in Architecture, University of Notre Dame **CERTS:** Certified New York State Building Code Enforcement Official, National Council of Architectural Registration Boards **A/A/S:** American Institute of Architects; Former Board Member, Route 20 Association **C/VW:** Local Charitable Organizations; Alzheimer's Association **DOB:** June 13, 1954 **POB:** Albany, NY **A/S:** He attributes his success to his hard work, dedication and willingness to learn new things. **B/I:** He became involved in his profession because he had an interest in the architectural field. **H/O:** The highlight of his career was being nominated for various design awards.

MR. BROOKE RHODES
Realtor
CentralPaHomeValues.com
RE/MAX A-1 Realty, Inc.
126 W. Harrisburg Street
Dillsburg, PA 17019 United States
brookerhodes@remax.net • brooke@PaHotListings.com
http://www.pahotlistings.com

BUS: Proven Leader in the Real Estate Industry **P/S:** Investment Property, Residential and Commercial Sales and Residential Resale, New Construction, Relocations, Land Sales **MA:** National **D/D/R:** Wide Range of Real Estate Services and Utilizes the most Current Technology, Processes and Systems to Assist Clients with All of their Home Buying and Home Selling Needs, Information on Home Buying, Home Selling, Financing and Owning Real Estate **H/I/S:** Sports, Golfing, Skiing, Spending Quality Time with his Wife and Four Children **FBP:** Realtor **EDU:** Degree in Automotive Engineering, New Zealand (1986); Art, French History and English Coursework **CERTS:** Licensed Realtor in Pennsylvania (2000); Licensed Builder and Construction, New Zealand (1992); Certification, University of New Zealand (1982); Licensed in International Law; Homes.com Certified Agent; Just Listed.com Certified; Foreclosure Agent **A/A/S:** National Association of Realtors; Pennsylvania Association of Realtors; Greater Harrisburg Association of Realtors; Real Estate Certified Society; Real Estate Cyber Space Society **A/H:** Selling Agent of the Year (2006)

DIANE M. RICCI
Performer, Dance Instructor, Choreographer
Under the Veil
8667 Herrick Avenue
Sun Valley, CA 91352 United States
caiporacat@aol.com
http://www.ancientjourney.com

BUS: Interpretive Belly Dance **P/S:** Performances, Belly Dancing **MA:** Local **D/D/R:** Belly Dancing **H/I/S:** Writing Poetry, Fencing **EDU:** Industry-Related Training and Experience **C/VW:** Greenpeace International **A/S:** She attributes her personal and professional success to her love for her work. **B/I:** She became involved in this profession because she was always interested in the field and came from a family of performers. **H/O:** The most gratifying aspect of her career is seeing her students succeed.

JONATHAN M. RICHARDS
School Media Specialist
Woodward Academy
951 E. Lafayette Avenue
Detroit, MI 48207 United States
jrichards@woodwardpsa.com
http://www.woodwardpsa.com

BUS: Educational Institution **P/S:** Scholastic Development, Progressive Teaching Methods and Personalized Education **MA:** Regional **D/D/R:** Handling Reference Inquires, Teaching Kindergarten through Eighth-Grade Students how to Utilize the Library, Assisting Teachers and Students, Holding Four Classes, Writing Grants, Fundraising, Troubleshooting, Offering Resources and Answers for Reference Questions and Media and Advertising Inquiries, Researching **H/I/S:** Japanese Artwork, Swimming, Horseback Riding, Traveling **FBP:** Kiplinger's; Money; PC World; The Week **EDU:** Coursework, Madonna University, Livonia, Michigan (2001); Bachelor of Arts in History and English, William Tyndale College, Farmington Hills, Michigan (2000) **CERTS:** Certificate in Teaching, State of Michigan **A/A/S:** International Federation of Library Associations and Institutions; Michigan Reading Association; American Library Association; Historical Commission, Special Libraries Association; Michigan Association for Media in Education **H/O:** The most rewarding aspect of his career is watching students take over their learning independently. **I/F/Y:** In five years, Mr. Richards hopes to help increase funding for the library and teach students how to read.

DAWN H. RICHARDSON
Owner, President, Chief Executive Officer
Dawn H. Richardson, Inc. dba Subway 40271
4930 Highway 52 W.
Suite 16
Dothan, AL 36305 United States
dawnterry@graceba.net
http://www.cambridgewhoswho.com

BUS: Restaurant Chain **P/S:** Submarine Sandwiches **MA:** National **D/D/R:** Managing the Crew, Adhering to Timelines and Deadlines, Working with Contractors, Maintaining and Overseeing All Phases of Restaurant Operations **H/I/S:** Playing the Guitar, Painting **FBP:** News Weekly **EDU:** Associate Degree in Biology, Valdosta Technical College (1979) **CERTS:** Certified Physician Assistant (1984); Certified Physical Therapist (1984); Licensed and Certified Contractor **W/H:** LABCORP (2000-2006); Quality Assurance Officer, Pathology Department (1984-2006); Cancer Registrar, State of Alabama

PAULINE RICHARDSON, RN, BSN, MSN
Registered Nurse, BSN, MSN
The Brooklyn Hospital Center
121 DeKalb Avenue
Brooklyn, NY 11201 United States
prichrn@aol.com
http://www.tbh.org

BUS: Healthcare Center **P/S:** Acute Rehabilitation Center, Cancer Resources, Emergency Medicine, Gastroenterology, Gynecological Oncology, Visiting Nurse Service, Internal Medicine, Occupational Therapy, Outpatient Services, Rehabilitation Medicine, Security Command Center, Women's Health Center **MA:** Regional **D/D/R:** Practicing Pediatric Emergency Nursing, Serving as an Adjunct Professor at New York City College of Technology, Acting as a Clinical Instructor **H/I/S:** Traveling **FBP:** American Journal of Nursing **EDU:** Master of Science in Nursing, SUNY Downstate Medical Center (2005); Bachelor of Science in Nursing, Medgar Evers College (1998); Registered Nurse, Jamaica, West Indies (1983) **A/A/S:** New York State Nurses Association

ESTELLA L. RICHARDSON-WILLIAMS, RN, BSN, MSN
Retired Nurse, Church Volunteer
250 Aldebaran Avenue
Lompoc, CA 93436 United States
leuniq1@comcast.net
http://www.cambridgewhoswho.com

BUS: Healthcare Center **P/S:** Healthcare Including Obstetrics, Pediatrics, Medical Surgery, General Medicine Services **MA:** Regional **EXP:** Ms. Richardson-Williams' expertise is in medical-surgery, obstetrics and pediatric nursing. **D/D/R:** Nursing for Navy Family Members, Supervising Surgical Unit and Vocation Recovery Room **H/I/S:** Traveling, Crocheting, Solving Puzzles, Shopping, Reading, Sewing, Cooking, Learning, Volunteering **EDU:** Master of Science in Nursing, California State University (1973); Bachelor of Science in Nursing, California State University (1966) **CERTS:** Registered Nurse, School of Nursing, Albert Einstein Medical Center (1956) **A/A/S:** Life Member of the 5th Episcopal Missionaries, Southern California Conference Lay Organization; Life Member of the 5th Episcopal District, Southern California Conference Lay Organization; Life Member, California Teachers Association; American Nurses Association; National Education Association **A/H:** Crystal Apple Award; Outstanding Contribution Award, Senior Citizen Nutrition Program; International Who's Who of Women in Education Award **C/VW:** Volunteer, African Methodist Episcopal Church; The Mission Society **DOB:** August 10, 1925 **POB:** Boston **SP:** Elvin **W/H:** Sun Clothing Manufacturer; Welder, World War II; Nursing Professor, Rio Hondo College **A/S:** She attributes her success to her education and work experience. **B/I:** She became involved in her profession because of her education in nursing. **H/O:** The highlight of her career was receiving her master's degree in 1973. **I/F/Y:** In five years, Ms. Richardson-Williams hopes to grow professionally.

LORETTA M. RICHNER
Principal
Pakanasink Elementary School
1953 Route 302, Renton Road
Circleville, NY 10919 United States
lrichner@pb.ouboces.org
http://www.cambridgewhoswho.com

BUS: Elementary School Committed to Excellence in Education **P/S:** Regular Curriculum including Literacy, Reading, Writing, Science, Art, Mathematics, Social Studies, Music and Physical Education **MA:** Regional **D/D/R:** Offering Instructional Leadership, Ensuring Teachers Have All Available Resources, New York State Assessments and Screenings, Holding Faculty Meetings for Staff Development, Overseeing Entire School, Facilitating All School Musical Reviews, Running the School's Building Team for Collaboration between Teachers and Parents **H/I/S:** Golfing, Tennis, Bridge, Enjoying her Three Grandchildren **FBP:** ASCD Publications **EDU:** Master's Degree in Education, SUNY New Paltz (1978); Bachelor's Degree in Elementary Education, Parsons College, Fairfield, Iowa (1968) **CERTS:** Certification in Advanced Studies, Administration Degree, SUNY New Paltz (1988) **A/A/S:** Parent Teacher Association; School District Leadership Team **A/H:** Excellence in Administration Award, Mid-Hudson Schools Study Council

DENISE M. RIDDICK JOHNSON
Practice Manager
Suffolk Psychiatric Group
2470 Pruden Boulevard
Suffolk, VA 23434 United States
dmarjoi50@aol.com
http://www.cambridgewhoswho.com

BUS: Psychiatric Practice **P/S:** Mental Healthcare **MA:** Local **D/D/R:** Handling Registration and Office Staff, Overseeing Hospital Billing and Accounting **H/I/S:** Playing Football and Basketball, Reading, Gourmet Cooking, Home Interior Decorating **FBP:** Fortune **EDU:** Bachelor's Degree in Healthcare, McDermott College; Bachelor's Degree in Business, Sojourner-Douglass College **A/A/S:** American Academy of Professional Coders; CPQ

ANGELA C. RIDLEY
Artist, Creator, Owner
Artlogic
9900 E. Greenbelt Road
Lanham, MD 20706 United States
aridley@artlogicstudio.com
http://www.artlogicstudio.com

BUS: Art **P/S:** Large-Scale Murals, Faux Paintings, Portraits and Furniture **MA:** National **D/D/R:** Creating Large-Scale Murals and Faux Painting **H/I/S:** Spending Time with her Husband and Four Children **FBP:** Home Decor and Home Improvement Magazines **A/A/S:** Artist Circle, Carpenter's Union **C/VW:** Goodwill **A/S:** She attributes her personal and professional success to her passion, hard work and supportive family. **B/I:** She became involved in her profession because after working in property management, her family helped her reinvent herself and pursue her dream. **H/O:** The most gratifying aspect of her career is having her children share in her pursuit of her dream.

DIANA P. RILEY
Teacher
Clara Cardwell Elementary and Middle School
616 Quincy Street
Brooklyn, NY 11221 United States
dr967663@aol.com
http://www.cambridgewhoswho.com

BUS: Elementary and Middle School Dedicated to Excellence in Education **P/S:** Regular Curriculum including English, Mathematics, Science, Social Studies, Art, Music, Physical Education, History **MA:** Regional **D/D/R:** Teaching All Regular Subjects, Teaching Inclusion, Writing Curriculum **H/I/S:** Outdoor Activities, Traveling **FBP:** Education **EDU:** Master's Degree in Special Education and General Education, Touro University (2005); Master's Degree in Teaching and Learning, Nova Southeastern University (2004)

TERI J. RILEY
Homebound Teacher
Brazosport Independent School District
301 W. Brazoswood Drive
Clute, TX 77531 United States
j_riley@sbcglobal.net
http://www.cambridgewhoswho.com

BUS: Public School District **P/S:** Kindergarten through 12th Grade Instruction for Students Out of School **MA:** Local **D/D/R:** Diversified Home Teacher **H/I/S:** Family, Playing the Piano **FBP:** Ladies' Home Journal; Better Homes and Gardens **EDU:** Bachelor's Degree in Elementary Education, Lamar University **C/VW:** American Society for the Prevention of Cruelty to Animals; Operation Christmas **A/S:** She attributes her personal and professional success to her love for her work. **B/I:** Since she was a child, she has always had an interest in teaching. **H/O:** The highlight of her career is seeing her students move on successfully.

LaTanya Ringer Williams, MPAS

Physician Assistant, MPAS
Stateville Correctional Facility
16300 Route 53
Crest Hill, IL 60403 United States
his1rib@comcast.net
http://www.idoc.state.il.us

BUS: Corrections Department **P/S:** Correctional Services **MA:** Local **D/D/R:** Correctional Medicine, Primary Care, Patient Education **H/I/S:** Bowling, Golfing, Tennis, Hiking, Camping, Motorcycle Riding with her Daughter, Spending Time Outdoors **FBP:** Black Enterprise **EDU:** Master's Degree in Physician Assistant Studies, University of Nebraska (2006) **A/A/S:** National Commission on Certification of Physician Assistants; American Academy of Physician Assistants; Illinois Academy of Physician Assistants; New Faith Baptist Church **SP:** Anthony **CHILD:** Amber, Leah, Joshua, Chyna

Scott W. Ringuette

Buyer Agent, Sales Associate
Michiana Online Realty
220 E. Bristol Street
Elkhart, IN 46514 United States
scott@michianaonlinerealty.com
http://www.cambridgewhoswho.com

BUS: Real Estate Brokerage **P/S:** Residential Real Estate Transactions **MA:** Local **D/D/R:** Helping Buyers with Real Estate and Investments **FBP:** Realtor **EDU:** Bachelor's Degree, English, Kalamazoo College **A/A/S:** National Association of Realtors **A/S:** He attributes his success to an excellent mentor and being able to think outside the box. **H/O:** The highlight of his career is the satisfaction he sees with the first time home buyers.

ROSE M. RIOS
Paralegal Specialist
Office of Disability Adjudication and Review
3505 Lake Lynda Drive
Orlando, FL 32817 United States
roserios@ssa.gov
http://www.cambridgewhoswho.com

BUS: Government Organization **P/S:** Public Services Including Administration Services for Disability Claims and Case Management Services **MA:** National **D/D/R:** Writing Cases and Decisions **H/I/S:** Cooking, Working on Computers **EDU:** Associate Degree in Secretary Science, Puerto Rico (1975) **C/VW:** St. Jude Children's Research Hospital **A/S:** She attributes her success to her hard work and dedication. **B/I:** She became involved in her profession because of her interest in reviewing cases and her desire to help people. **H/O:** The most gratifying aspect of her career is working for the government.

MRS. HILDA M. RISI, MS
Special Education Teacher
New York City Department of Education
Tottenville High School
100 Luten Avenue
Staten Island, NY 10312 United States
hrzalman@hotmail.com
http://www.cambridgewhoswho.com

BUS: High School **P/S:** Secondary Education **MA:** Local **D/D/R:** Teaching Special Education, Having Experience with Mainstream, Self-Contained, Resource Room, Inclusion, Collaboration and Team Teaching **H/I/S:** Reading, Needlepoint, Hiking, Spending Time in Outdoor Activities, Traveling **EDU:** Master's Degree in Special Education, CUNY Hunter College **A/S:** She attributes her success to her ambition and the support from others. **B/I:** She became involved in her profession because she loves working with children. **H/O:** The highlight of her career was helping a young man with cerebral palsy learn to write a question mark.

DORIS LEE RITCHIE
Retired Volunteer Consultant
dl-ritchie@sbcglobal.net
http://www.cambridgewhoswho.com

BUS: Volunteering **P/S:** Fundraising **MA:** Local **D/D/R:** Working with Institutes and Agencies Using Volunteers **H/I/S:** Playing Bridge, Dancing, Antiques, Reading **FBP:** Architectural Digest **EDU:** Bachelor of Arts in Social Science and Education, Elmhurst College; Master of Science in Education, Northern Illinois University; Doctor of Education, Northern Illinois University **A/A/S:** Phi Kappa Phi; Kappa Delta Pi; Pi Lambda Theta; Association for Volunteer Administrators; Founder, California State University at San Marcos; Scarce Irish Belleek International Collector's Society **A/H:** Community Award, Daughters of the American Revolution (2001) **C/VW:** Country Friends; Hospice of the North Coast; Carlsbad High Noon Rotary Club; Carlsbad Housing Commission, California State University, San Marcos **A/S:** She attributes her success to liking people and acting on something when she sees a need for it. **B/I:** She became involved in her profession because her family has a history of volunteering that has been passed on through the generations. **H/O:** The highlight of her career was being one of the founders for the University of California in San Marcos.

BARBARA ANN RITCHWOOD, RN
Senior Staff Nurse
New York Presbyterian Hospital
Weil Cornell Memorial Center Burn ICU
525 E. 68th Street
New York, NY 10021 United States
britchwood@hotmail.com
http://www.cambridgewhoswho.com

BUS: Leading Provider in the Healthcare Industry **P/S:** Hospital Medical Center with a Burn Intensive Care Unit and Medical and Nursing Services **MA:** Regional **D/D/R:** Specializing in Burn Intensive Care Nursing, Precepting In-Services, Offering Patient Care, Promoting Staff Development, Nursing, Encouraging Healthcare Administration and Leadership in Nursing Services and Management, Offering Forensic Services and Funeral Services **H/I/S:** Shopping, Spending Time with the Family **FBP:** Nursing Spectrum; Critical Care Nurse; Jar; Burn Care and Rehabilitation; RN; Mortuary Science **EDU:** Master of Science in Health Administration, New Jersey City University; Bachelor of Science in Nursing, New Jersey City University; Associate Degree in Funeral Services, North Hampton County Community College **CERTS:** Certified Sexual Assault Nurse Examiner; Certified in Advanced Cardiac Life Support; Certified in Pediatric Advanced Life Support; Certified in Advanced Burn Life Support; Registered Nurse Degree, Christ Hospital School of Nursing (1989); Instructor, Basic Cardiac Life Support **A/A/S:** American Burn Association; Forensic Nurses Society; International Association of Forensic Nurses **CHILD:** Kevin

LINDA A. RIVARD, RN, BSN
Cardiac Nurse
University of Connecticut Health Center
263 Farmington Avenue
Farmington, CT 06030 United States
ishopathome@cox.net
http://www.cambridgewhoswho.com

BUS: Healthcare Center **P/S:** Healthcare **MA:** Local **EXP:** Ms. Rivard's expertise is in cardiovascular nursing. **H/I/S:** Collecting and Restoring Antique Watches and Clocks **FBP:** Critical Care Nurse; American Journal of Nursing **EDU:** Bachelor of Science in Nursing, The State University of New York (1997) **A/A/S:** Connecticut Society for Cardiac Rehabilitation; Preventative Cardiovascular Nurses Association; American Association of Critical-Care Nurses; American Nurses Association **A/S:** She attributes her success to her education.

JESSICA DAWN RIVERA
Director of Admissions and Marketing
West Texas Centers for MHMR
319 Runnels
Big Spring, TX 79720 United States
http://www.cambridgewhoswho.com

BUS: Mental Health Center **P/S:** Mental Healthcare **MA:** West Texas **H/I/S:** Arts and Crafts, Mary Kay Consulting **EDU:** Bachelor of Arts in Human Ecology, University of Texas, TX **A/A/S:** Phi Beta Kappa, TAS **A/H:** Featured in Vascular Flora of Howard County Texas **C/VW:** Church Senior Center **POB:** Big Spring, TX **SP:** Lance **A/S:** She attributes her success to her education and training. **B/I:** She became interested in her profession while looking to start a new path in life. **H/O:** The most gratifying aspect of her career is being able to give people encouragement to get better.

ELAYNE-DANYELE RIVERS
President, Chief Executive Officer
Toonzworld Management Inc.
1925 McGraw Avenue
Suite 7D
Bronx, NY 10462 United States
tltoonz@aol.com
http://www.tltoonz.com

BUS: Artist Management **P/S:** Management, Marketing, Public Relations **MA:** Regional **D/D/R:** Personal Management **H/I/S:** Playing Pool, Bowling, Watching Movies, Writing, Reading, Playing Basketball **FBP:** The Source; Right On; Sister2Sister; Blender; Vibe; Complex; XXL; **EDU:** Associate Degree in Marketing, Katharine Gibbs School; Associate Degree in Liberal Arts and Physical Education, Fulton Montgomery Community College **C/VW:** freethestemcells.org; care.org **A/S:** She attributes her success to her hard work, drive and determination. **B/I:** She became involved in her profession because she wanted to make a difference.

SUZIE RIVO SOLENDER
President
Solender Services
48 Foxpoint Drive W.
Williamsville, NY 14221 United States
grantsbysuzie@yahoo.com
http://www.solenderservices.com

BUS: Nonprofit Organization **P/S:** Fundraising Assistance and Grant Writing Services **MA:** International **D/D/R:** Writing Grants and Proposals, Fundraising, Consulting Via Phone and E-Mail **H/I/S:** Knitting, Needlepointing, Football, Hockey **FBP:** The Chronicle of Philanthropy **EDU:** Associate Degree in Dental Hygiene, Erie Community College (1964); Micro-Master of Business Administration, University at Buffalo; Bachelor's Degree in Business, University at Buffalo **A/A/S:** Associate, Foundation Center; Amherst Area Chamber of Commerce; Board Member, Business Resource Council; Business and Professional Women of Madison **A/H:** Madison Who's Who **C/VW:** Advisory Board, Stakeholder, American Cancer Society; Board of Trustees, Temple Beth Zion **POB:** Buffalo, NY **SP:** Peter **A/S:** She attributes her success to the support she receives from her husband who works with her. **B/I:** She became involved in her profession because of her experience in writing grants pro bono for the advisory boards. **H/O:** The highlight of her career was receiving research assistance from her two children and their spouses. **I/F/Y:** In five years, Ms. Solender intends to continue writing grants.

DEBORAH M. RIZZO, RN
Clinical Director of Southwest Surgery Center
Southwest Medical Associates
2720-5 N. Tenaya Way
Las Vegas, NV 89128 United States
http://www.smalv.com

BUS: Nevada's Largest Medical Group **P/S:** Outpatient Clinic Services, Including Primary Care Specialists, Surgery, Thirteen Clinics, An Ambulatory Center, 2500 Employees **MA:** Statewide **D/D/R:** Processing Improvement, Quality, Compliance, Education, Staff Development, Running the Largest Free Standing Ambulatory Center, in Charge of Financials, and Staff Development, Second in Command to the Administrator **H/I/S:** Reading, Spending Time Outdoors, Boating, Riding ATVs, Crafts **FBP:** American Journal of Nursing; RN **EDU:** Pursuing Master's Degree in Healthcare Administration, Kennedy Western University; Bachelor's Degree in Healthcare Administration, Kennedy Western University; Associate Degree in Nursing, Cumberland County College **A/A/S:** National Association for IV Nurses; Southern Nevada Continuity of Care Association **C/VW:** March of Dimes

MARY ROBACK, LPN
Licensed Practical Nurse
Department of Nursing
Rockland Psychiatric Center
140 Old Orangeburg Road
Orangeburg, NY 10962 United States
psychroback@verizon.net • meroback@verizon.net
http://www.cambridgewhoswho.com

BUS: Psychiatric Center **P/S:** Psychiatric Healthcare **D/D/R:** Caring for Patients with Psychiatric and Psychosocial Disorders **H/I/S:** Collecting, Making Crafts **FBP:** Industry-Related Publications **EDU:** Bachelor's Degree in Psychology, Kean University; Bachelor's Degree in Science, Mercy College **CERTS:** Certified Applied Behavioral Analysis Therapist (1997); Diploma in Specialized Clinical Technology, Star Technical Institute, with Honors (1995); Certificate of Completion in Regulations on Bloodborne Pathogens, Occupational Safety and Health Administration (1994); Licensed Practical Nurse, Mercer County Vocational School **A/H:** Recognition Award for ECG Technique, Burdick (1994); Dean's Honor Roll, Mercer County Community College (1993-1994) **A/S:** She attributes her success to her caring nature and commitment to helping her disabled mother. **B/I:** She became involved in her profession because she was always interested in the medical field and wanted to help others. **H/O:** The most gratifying aspect of her career is seeing her patients recover. **I/F/Y:** In five years, Ms. Roback hopes to earn her RNASN degree and practice in the field of psychiatry.

MR. RICHARD E. ROBBINS
Property Manager
NASA, Marshall Space Flight Center
9001 Rideout Road
Huntsville, AL 35812 United States
richard.e.robbins@nasa.gov
http://www.nasa.gov

BUS: Space Research Center **P/S:** Special Projects, Aeronautics, Exploration Systems, Science, Space Operations **MA:** International **D/D/R:** Conducting Computer Based Training, Training Module, Special Projects, Supplying Equipment and Furniture Moving, Assisting NASA Professionals **H/I/S:** Reading, Building Custom Furniture, Woodworking **FBP:** Government Executive; Government Computer News; eWeek **EDU:** Master's Degree in Administrative Sciences, University of Alabama (1980) **CERTS:** Certified Property Manager, National Property Management Association **A/A/S:** National Property Management Association; Civitan International; Arab Christian Center; Angel Food Ministries; National Guard **C/VW:** Disabled American Veterans; Habitat for Humanity

MS. MICHELLE D. ROBERT
Attorney at Law
Law Offices of Michelle D. Robert
839 Saint Charles Avenue. Suite 312
New Orleans, LA 70130 United States
mdrobert@neworleanslawyer.com
http://www.neworleanslawyer.com

BUS: Law Firm **P/S:** Legal Services for Motor Vehicle Accidents, 18-Wheeler Accidents, Wrongful Death, Pedestrian and Bicycle Accidents, Under-Insured Motorists Claims, Traumatic Brain Injury, Railroad Accidents, Nursing Home Negligence, Products Liability, Slip and Falls, Worker's Compensation, Offshore, Maritime, River Accidents and Traffic Violations **MA:** Regional **EXP:** Ms. Robert's expertise is in personal injury litigation. **EDU:** JD, Tulane University (1993); Bachelor of Arts, Tulane University (1987)

BEVERLY C. ROBERTS
Registered Nurse
Kings County Hospital Center
451 Clarkson Avenue
Brooklyn, NY 11230 United States
broberts5@aol.com
http://www.cambridgewhoswho.com

BUS: Hospital **P/S:** Healthcare Including Acute Care **MA:** Local **EXP:** Ms. Roberts' area of expertise is in pediatric nursing. **H/I/S:** Attending Church, Reading, Cooking, Sewing **FBP:** American Journal of Nursing **EDU:** Associate of Science in Nursing, Helene Fuld College of Nursing **A/A/S:** New York State Nurses Association **C/VW:** The Brooklyn Tabernacle **A/S:** She attributes her success to her determination and hard work. **B/I:** She became involved in her profession because she wanted to help people. **H/O:** The most gratifying aspect of her career is receiving gratitude from her patients.

JEANMARIE ROBERTS
Registered Nurse, Certified Addictions Nurse
University Psychiatric Associates
8320 University Executive Park Drive
Suite 104
Charlotte, NC 28262 United States
jmrupa@bellsouth.net
http://www.cambridgewhoswho.com

BUS: Outpatient Psychiatry **P/S:** Healthcare, Psychiatric Mental Health Therapy, Outpatient and Drug and Alcohol Detox Programs **MA:** Regional **D/D/R:** Addictions Nursing **H/I/S:** Playing Pool, Weight-Training, Swimming **FBP:** Journal of Addictions Nursing; Journal of Nursing Scholarship; Sigma Theta Tau Publications **EDU:** Pursuing Master's Degree in Psychiatric Mental Health Nursing, University of North Carolina at Charlotte (2007); Bachelor of Science in Nursing, Holy Family College **A/A/S:** Pennsylvania State Nurses Association; American Nurses Association; International Nurses Society on Addictions; North Carolina Nurses Association; Sigma Theta Tau International; American Psychiatric Nurses Association; Metrolina Coalition of Nurse Practitioners **A/H:** Army National Guard Certificate of Appreciation (1998) **C/VW:** Katrina Relief; Literacy Tutor **A/S:** She attributes her success to being open-minded and not being afraid to make a change in her life. **B/I:** After both of her parents became ill and passed away, she realized she wanted to help people in a direct, emotional manner and decided to go to school to become a nurse. **H/O:** The highlight of her career was having the courage to go back to school and make a big change in her life.

MS. KIM ROBERTS, RN, BSN, CRRN
Registered Nurse
Rehabilitation
St. Joseph's Regional Medical Center
14460 Old-Trace Court
Granger, IN 46530 United States
nightengalekmr@sbcglobal.net • robertsk@sjmed.com
http://www.cambridgewhoswho.com

BUS: Medical Center **P/S:** Diagnostic Services, Emergency Department, Obstetrics, Oncology, Cancer, Orthopedics, Radiation Therapy, Rehabilitation, Cardiac and Surgical Services and Women's Clinical Center **MA:** Regional **D/D/R:** Managing 35 Employees, Offering Clinical Supervision and Admissions Coordinating, Overseeing Employee Time Cards, Scheduling, Coordinating Patient Care, Assisting Doctors, Collaborating with the Rehabilitation Unit **H/I/S:** Spending Time Outdoors, Camping, Fishing, Antiquing, Boating, Shopping **FBP:** Rehabilitation Nursing Journal; Nursing2009 **EDU:** Bachelor of Science Degree in Nursing, Indiana State University (2002) **CERTS:** Certified Rehabilitation Nurse **A/A/S:** Magnet Status Committee; Customer Service Committee; Policy and Procedures Committee; Education Committee; Committee to Plan Conferences; Brain Injury Association of Indiana; Sigma Theta Tau; National Nursing Honor Society; Association of Rehabilitation Nurses **SP:** Bernard **W/H:** Admissions Coordinator, Rehabilitation Unit, St. Joseph's Regional Medical Center; Supervisor, St. Joseph's Regional Medical Center **A/S:** She credits her success to her husband and mother. They have been her biggest supporters. She has a great family who have always cheered her success. She also feels gratitude to her employer, Saint Joseph's Regional Medical Center, for the opportunity she has received that has helped her advance in her nursing career.

MARCY D. ROBERTS, RN
Chief, Quality Services Division
Womack Army Medical Center
2817 Reilly Road
Fort Bragg, NC 28310 United States
marcy.roberts@us.army.mil
http://www.wamc.amedd.army.mil

BUS: Military Hospital **P/S:** Healthcare, Acute Care Facility and Out-Patient Care **MA:** Regional **D/D/R:** Working with Healthcare Quality Management, Joint Commission Accreditation, Performance Improvement, Case Management, Discharge Planning, Patient Safety and Risk Management **H/I/S:** Needlework, Reading, Hunting **EDU:** Master's Degree in Human Resources Management, Northeast Missouri State University (Now Truman State University) (1981); Bachelor's Degree in Nursing, Northeast Missouri State University (Now Truman State University) (1974) **A/A/S:** National Association of Healthcare Quality; Board of Directors, North Carolina Association of Healthcare Quality; American Association of Managed Care Nurses; Former Member, Association of Operating Room Nurses; Former Member, American Nurses Association **W/H:** Director of Nursing, Director of Perioperative Services, Chief of Utilization Management, Assistant Supervisor, Head Nurse, Staff Nurse, Operating Rooms, Emergency Rooms, Medical and Oncology Nursing Facilities **C/A:** Implemented Numerous New Programs, Including Policies and Procedures

SHERMAN L. ROBERTS SR.
Foreman, Electrician
International Brotherhood of Electrical Workers
15811 Jewel Avenue
Flushing, NY 11365 United States
profslr@aol.com
http://www.cambridgewhoswho.com

BUS: Labor Union for Electricians **P/S:** Employee Management for New Construction and Renovations **MA:** Manhattan, Brooklyn, Queens, The Bronx and Staten Island **D/D/R:** Managing High and Low Voltage Connections, Control Wiring and Installing Fire Alarm for Residential and Commercial Properties **H/I/S:** Playing the Piano and the Organ, Playing Handball and Pool, Bowling, Exercising **EDU:** Coursework in Electromechanical Technology, New York City College of Technology **A/A/S:** Hampton University Ministers' Conference and Choir Directors' Organists' Guild Workshop **C/VW:** Local Charitable Organizations **A/S:** He attributes his success to his determination, hard work and determination. **H/O:** The most gratifying aspect of his career is receiving reference from his clients.

PENNY ROBERTSON, RN, BSN, M.ED.
Nursing Teacher
Lanier Technical College
2990 Landrum Education Drive
Oakwood, GA 30566 United States
proberts@laniertech.edu
http://www.cambridgewhoswho.com

BUS: College **P/S:** Higher Education **MA:** Local **D/D/R:** Teaching Fundamentals, Medical-Surgical Nursing and Oncology **H/I/S:** Camping, Reading **FBP:** Nursing Made Incredibly Easy **EDU:** Master of Education, North Georgia College & State University (1974); Bachelor of Science in Nursing, Brenau University (1991) **A/A/S:** Sigma Theta Tau

MR. ANDREW L. ROBINSON
Middle School Principal
Monte Vista Christian School
2 School Way
Watsonville, CA 95076 United States
andyrobinson@mvcs.org
http://www.mvcs.org

BUS: School **P/S:** Education to Middle School and High School Students, Training Them Mentally, Physically, Socially and Spiritually, Developing Problem Solving and Critical Thinking Skills **MA:** Local **D/D/R:** Overseeing the Operation of Middle School Academic Programs, Scheduling and Evaluating Teachers **H/I/S:** Collecting Sports Memorabilia, Hot Air Ballooning, Attending Sporting Events **EDU:** Master's Degree in Education Administration, Pensacola Christian College, Pensacola, FL (1989); Bachelor's Degree in Christian Education, Western Baptist College, Salem, OR (1972) **CERTS:** Certified Master Teacher, Intel Teach Program **A/A/S:** Accreditation Chairman, Association of Christian Schools International and Western Association of Schools and Colleges Teams; District Representative, Association of Christian Schools International; Western Association of Schools and Colleges **SP:** Elda **CHILD:** Samuel **W/H:** Physical Education Instructor, Shepherds, Inc. Union Grove, WI; Fifth to Eighth-Grade Teacher, Community Christian School, Red Bluff, CA; Fifth to Eighth-Grade Teacher, Principal, Paradise Christian School, Paradise, CA **A/S:** He attributes his success to his hard work, desire to learn, people management skills and his ability to face difficult situations. **H/O:** The highlight of his career was being instrumental in the commencement of a laptop program for the Monte Vista Christian School, that has been developed from an inception to a viable technology program for the middle and high school students. **I/F/Y:** In five years, Mr. Robinson hopes to be in the field of education as a principal or an administrator where he will be able to utilize his talents acquired over the years and would like to work for the educational development of the students.

BECKY ROBINSON
Owner
BR Construction
4340 N.W. First Street
Des Moines, IA 50313 United States
brconstruction@networkiowa.com
http://www.cambridgewhoswho.com

BUS: Commercial Construction **P/S:** Construction **D/D/R:** Commercial Construction, Accounting, Estimating **H/I/S:** Traveling, Fishing, Gardening, Being Outdoors **EDU:** Bachelor of Science in Accounting, Grand View University (2000) **A/S:** She attributes her success to her determination and ability to move from residential construction to commercial. **B/I:** She became involved in this career because her father was involved in construction.

DALTON A. ROBINSON
Adjunct Professor
Essex County College and Kean University
303 University Avenue
Newark, NJ 07102 United States
drobinson864@yahoo.com
http://www.cambridgewhoswho.com

BUS: College, University **P/S:** Associate Degrees and Certificates, Undergraduate and Graduate Degrees **MA:** Regional **D/D/R:** Teaching College Composition, British American Literature, Effective Speech and Technical Writing **H/I/S:** Reading, Soccer, Drama **FBP:** Car and Driver; Health and Prevention; Popular Science; National Geographic; College English **EDU:** Post Graduate Diploma, International Institute for Aerospace Survey and Earth Sciences, Enschede, Netherlands; Master of Arts, Liberal Studies, Kean University; Bachelor of Science, The University of the West Indies **A/A/S:** KUAFF-AFT; National Council of Teachers of English; NTE **DOB:** March 1, 1952 **SP:** Dorothy **CHILD:** Aldeen, Ava, Patti-Rae, Averoy **W/H:** Adjunct Professor, Essex County College; Adjunct Professor, Kean University; Teacher, Lady Liberty Charter School; Regional Manager, Community Relations, National Housing Development Corporation, Jamaica; Physical Planner, Jamaican Government

ELAINE C. ROBINSON
Licensed Child Care Provider
Hearts of Love
4408 Harvest Road
Temple Hills, MD 20748 United States
elaine2robinson@verizon.net
http://www.cambridgewhoswho.com

BUS: Childcare Company **P/S:** Public Childcare Service **MA:** Regional **D/D/R:** Caring for Children Six Weeks to 12-Years-Old **H/I/S:** Reading, Exercising, Going to the Movies **FBP:** Childcare Books **EDU:** Diploma, Woodson Senior High School (1988) **CERTS:** Certified Childcare Provider; Childcare Specialist Level Three Credentials **C/VW:** Ebenezer African Methodist Episcopal Church; American Red Cross; Local High School; Community Service **A/S:** She attributes her success to helping children achieve self-esteem and motivation through education. **B/I:** She became involved in the profession because she worked in Montgomery Public Schools for 15 years and she really enjoys teaching children. **H/O:** The most gratifying aspect of her career is assisting with the success of each student.

LEAH ROBINSON
Licensed Vocational Nurse III
Human Touch Home Health
8939 S. Sepulveda Boulevard
Suite 400
Los Angeles, CA 90045 United States
http://www.cambridgewhoswho.com

BUS: Home Health Nursing Service **P/S:** Visiting Nurse Services **MA:** Local **D/D/R:** Geriatrics, Wound Care, General Nursing Duties **H/I/S:** Reading, Playing Bingo, Going to Amusement Parks **FBP:** American Journal of Nursing **EDU:** College Coursework **A/A/S:** FDCA; National Wildlife Federation; Youth Organization, Local Police Department **C/VW:** Save the Whales; Volunteer, Local Church; American Society for the Prevention of Cruelty to Animals; Police Children Fund; Save the Wildlife; Various Environmental Causes **A/S:** She attributes her success to her compassion and her ability to nurture others. **B/I:** She became involved in her profession after originally wanting to be a veterinarian. She decided to pursue a career in nursing because of her proficiency in wound care and her desire to help others. **H/O:** The highlight of her career was saving a pair of twins who were born three months early.

REV. MARRIE ROBINSON, M.ED., LMT
Director
Universal Healing Centers & Relief Shelters
3956 N.W. Seventh Place
Gainesville, FL 32607 United States
marrier007@aol.com
corderoc59@yahoo.com
http://www.cambridgewhoswho.com

BUS: Comprehensive Healing and Relief Centers **P/S:** Healing Services Including Holistic Modalities for the Mind, Body and Spirit **MA:** International **EXP:** Ms. Robinson's expertise is in management. **D/D/R:** Directing, Managing and Assisting with Healthcare Services, Contributing to Health, Healing and Spiritual Development, Growing Environmentally-Sound Food **H/I/S:** Dancing, Playing Volleyball, Participating in Outdoor Activities, Helping People **EDU:** Master's Degree in Sports Medicine, Temple University; Master's Degree in Exercise Physiology, Temple University; Bachelor's Degree in Physical Anthropology, University of Florida; Bachelor's Degree in Exercise Science, University of Florida **CERTS:** Ordained Alliance of Divine Love Minister; Licensed Massage Therapist; Certified Energy Medicine Practitioner; Certifications in 12 Different Areas of Massage; Certifications in First Aid, American Red Cross; Certification in Emergency Response, American Red Cross; Certified in CPR, National Safety Council **A/A/S:** American College of Sports Medicine; Associated Bodywork & Massage Professionals **C/VW:** Local Charitable Organizations **DOB:** August 14, 1958 **POB:** Orange, CA **C/A:** Founder, First All-Volunteer Cooperative Health Club in the United States; Founder, First Community-Supported Agricultural Program, Brevard County; Developer, Numerous Techniques of Body Work to Eliminate Pain and the Necessity for Surgeries of the Spine, Hips, Carpel Tunnel Syndrome and Many Conditions under the Umbrella of Fibromyalgia **A/S:** She attributes her success to her hard work and helpful nature. **B/I:** She became involved in her profession because of her passion for helping relieve people from their pain. **H/O:** The most gratifying aspect of her career is watching her patients recover. **I/F/Y:** In five years, Ms. Robinson hopes to open healing centers and relief shelters around the world.

SHIRLEY ROBINSON
Virginia Outreach Worker
Oxford House Inc.
1010 Wayne Avenue
Suite 400
Silver Spring, MD 20910 United States
shirleyjr2@cox.net
http://www.cambridgewhoswho.com

BUS: Social Services **P/S:** Social Services **MA:** Statewide **D/D/R:** Helping Individuals Recovering from Alcohol and Drug Addiction **H/I/S:** Singing **FBP:** Time; USA Today **EDU:** Industry-Related Experience **A/H:** Call to Service Award, President Bush **C/VW:** Louden County Community Shelter **A/S:** She feels that she has achieved success in her career by keeping a positive attitude. **B/I:** She is herself a recovering addict, and has lived in Oxford House. **H/O:** She feels that her current position is the highlight of her career.

FAY ROBINSON (BROWN)
Parish Health Nurse
South Florida Baptist Hospital, St. Joseph's-Baptist Health Care
301 N. Alexander Street
Plant City, FL 33566 United States
frobins9@tampabay.rr.com
http://www.sjbhealth.org

BUS: Private, Nonprofit Hospital Offering all of the High-Tech Services of an Acute Care Hospital, but in a Small, Warm and Friendly Environment Designed for Personal Attention and Compassionate Care **P/S:** Diagnostic Services, Surgery, Rehabilitation, Adult Acute and Intensive Care Units, Radiology, Pediatric and Adolescent Services, Sub-Acute Skilled Nursing Facility, Obstetrics **MA:** Regional **D/D/R:** Nursing Services, Caring for Individuals in Need, Body and Spiritual Healing and Wellness, Operating through the Church as Community Service for Patients of All Denominations, Counseling, Education **H/I/S:** Reading History Novels, Traveling **EDU:** Master's Degree in Community Health Management with an Emphasis on Healthcare Management, University of Liverpool, England (1979); Bachelor of Science in Nursing Exempt, University of the State of New York and University of Liverpool, England (1971-1977); Diploma in General Nursing, Registered Nurse, United Kingdom (1955) **CERTS:** Certificate in Teacher Training for Primary Health Care, Liverpool School of Tropical Medicine, University of Liverpool, England (1979); Certificate in Tropical Community Medicine and Health, Liverpool School of Tropical Medicine, University of Liverpool, England (1974); Certificate in Nursing Administration, Advanced Nursing Education Unit, University of West Indies, Jamaica (1968); Certificate, Health Visitor, West Indies School of Public Health, Jamaica (1962); Certificate, Part I, Registered Certified Midwife, Mount Pleasant Hospital, Swansea, South Wales; Part II, Cardiff District Midwifery Service, Cardiff, South Wales (1962); Numerous Certificates in Education, Administration and Nursing, Community Health and Development, Program Plan and Design, University of North Carolina, Chapel Hill **A/A/S:** American Nurses Association; Florida Nurses Association; American Public Health Association; Association of Nurses in AIDS Care; Friend of the International Parish Nurse Center; Royal Society of Health, United Kingdom; School of Nursing-West Indies University and University of the West Indies at Kingston, Jamaica (Lecturer); UNFPA Fellowship (1979); 3M Nurses Fellowship, Nurses Association of Jamaica Nominee for the International Council of Nursing (1976) **A/H:** Guinness Overseas Award for Outstanding Service in Nursing (1974); Jamaican Government Scholarship (1967) **W/H:** Parish Nurse, South Florida Baptist Hospital, Plant City, FL (2001-Present); Senior Community Health Nurse, Nurse Case Manager, HRS-Hillsborough County Public Health Unit, Tampa, FL, Program for Substance-Abused Newborns, Supervisor, Healthy Start Outreach Field Staff, Nursing Assessment, Counseling and Education of Patients with HIV/AIDS (1989-1998); Senior Registered Nurse Specialist, Department of Community Mental Health, Florida Mental Health Institute, University of South Florida, Tampa, FL (1988-1989); Psychiatric Staff Nurse, Hillsborough County Hospital, Tampa, FL (1985-1988); Curriculum Development, Lecturer, Community Health Education and Family Health, Courses to Medical Undergraduates and Post-Graduates, Students in the Diploma in Public Health and Community Health Programs (1979-1985); Nursing Tutor, Coordinator, Department of Nursing Education, University Hospital of the West Indies, Jamaica (1972-1977); Head Nurse, St. Barnabas Hospital, Bronx, New York (1971-1972); Public Health Nurse, Ministry of Health, Jamaica (1962-1967); University Hospital of the West Indies; Ministry of Health, Jamaica; Consultant, Nurses Association of Jamaica; Consultant, Nursing Education Department, The University Hospital of the West Indies; Advisor, The University on Health Matters

ROBYN A. ROCCO
Principal
Eco-Spaces, LLC
8251 Liriope Loop
Lehigh Acres, FL 33936 United States
eco_spaces@yahoo.com

BUS: Interior Design Consulting **P/S:** Design Build, Interior Design, Custom Decorating **MA:** National **D/D/R:** Designing Eco-Friendly Interior and Twinkey Projects **H/I/S:** Biking **FBP:** Metropolitan Magazine; Architectural Digest **EDU:** International Academy of Design, Bachelor of Fine Arts in Interior Design **A/A/S:** ASID; Florida Greenbuilding Coalition

SHERRI ROCK
Registered Nurse, Case Manager
Yukon Kuskokwim Health Corporation
700 Chief Eddie Hoffman Highway
Bethel, AK 99559 United States
sherri_rock@ykhc.org

BUS: Healthcare **P/S:** Healthcare **MA:** Local **D/D/R:** Listening to Patients and Satisfying their Needs to the Best of her Ability Utilizing All the Resources at her Disposal, HIV Case Management, Chronic Pain Management **H/I/S:** Physical Fitness, Outdoor Activities, Decorative Art, Spending Time with her Family, Playing with her Dogs **FBP:** Oxygen; RN **EDU:** Bachelor of Science in Nursing, Southern Nazarene University **CERTS:** Pursuing Certification in Pain Management, Pain Education and Case Management **A/A/S:** Former Member, American Nurses Association; Alumni, Southern Nazarene University **C/VW:** Sponsors a Child through Compassion International; Church; Tender Women's Center; Mary Kay Ash Charitable Foundation **A/S:** She attributes her success to her hard work and love of what she does. **B/I:** She became involved in this profession because she was always interested in nursing and helping people. **H/O:** The highlight of her career is receiving recognition from patients and healthcare providers for a job well done.

ANGELA F. RODDY
Owner
For Creative Sake
117 Glenside Avenue
Ponca City, OK 74601 United States
forcreativesake@sbcglobal.net
http://www.cambridgewhoswho.com

BUS: Graphic Design Firm **P/S:** Graphic Designing, Printing of Brochures, Flyers, Newspapers and Magazines, Logo Designing for Print and Web **MA:** WV, IL, AZ, TX, CA and OK **EXP:** Ms. Roddy's expertise is in graphic design, print media including newspapers and magazines. **D/D/R:** Ensuring Client Satisfaction, Printing, Designing **H/I/S:** Collecting Antiques, Quilting **EDU:** Bachelor's Degree in Graphic Design, Point Loma Nazarene University (1988) **C/VW:** Board Secretary, Brookfield Wesleyan Church; Various Outreach Groups **DOB:** November 24, 1964 **POB:** Eugene, OR **A/S:** She attributes her success to her ability in graphic designing, good work ethic, listening to people and their needs. **H/O:** The highlight of her career was being able to start her own business. **I/F/Y:** In five years, Ms. Roddy hopes to expand her clientele globally.

MR. RODNEY L. RODERICK, CPA
Controller
Varel International
1434 Patton Place
Suite 106
Carrollton, TX 75007 United States
rroderick@varelintl.com
http://www.varelintl.com

BUS: World's Largest Independent Manufacturer and Supplier of High-Quality Drill Bits **P/S:** Oil and Gas Products including Tough Drill PDC Bits, Nomenclature, PDC Bits, Specialty Bits, Features, PDC Bits, Challenger Motor Series, Challenger Jet Air Bits, VB Series, Navigator Bits, Hole Opening Bits, Geosciences, and Mining and Industrial Products including Ridgeback and Ridgeback Marathon **MA:** International **D/D/R:** Cost Accounting, Certified Public Accounting that Works in the Field, Following Procedures for Drill Bits for Oil Companies **H/I/S:** Spending Time with his Children, Football **FBP:** Journal of Accounting **EDU:** Master of Business Administration Candidate; Bachelor of Business Administration in Accounting, Southwest Texas State University (1991) **A/A/S:** Texas Society of CPAs; American Institute of CPAs

DIANA RODRIGUEZ
Second-Grade Teacher
J.Z. Leyendecker Elementary School
Laredo Independent School District
2420 Santa Maria Avenue
Laredo, TX 78040 United States
drodriguez@elisd.org

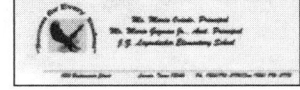

BUS: Elementary School Dedicated to Excellence in Education **P/S:** Primary Education Following a Regular Curriculum for Reading, Mathematics, Art, Music, Social Studies and Physical Education **MA:** Regional **D/D/R:** Teaching Second-Grade Students All Subjects **H/I/S:** Bowling, Dancing, Traveling **EDU:** Bachelor of Arts in Elementary Education, Laredo State University (1980) **CERTS:** Certification in Bilingual Studies (1981) **A/A/S:** Phi Delta Kappa; San Martin Porras Church **A/H:** Women's Hall of Fame in Education (2002); Tiger Legends (2002) **C/VW:** Parent-Teacher Association

PAMELA K. RODRIGUEZ, RN
Trauma Nurse Coordinator
Eastern New Mexico Medical Center
405 W. Country Club Road
Roswell, NM 88201 United States
pam_rodriguez@chs.net
http://www.enmmc.com

BUS: Level II Trauma Center **P/S:** Healthcare **MA:** Local **D/D/R:** Emergency Nursing **H/I/S:** Reading, Playing Videogames **FBP:** RN; American Journal of Nursing **EDU:** Bachelor of Science in Biology and Chemistry, Eastern New Mexico University; Bachelor of Science in Nursing, Eastern New Mexico University **A/A/S:** Society for Trauma Nurses; Emergency Nurses Association **C/VW:** American Red Cross; Muscular Dystrophy Lockup **A/S:** She attributes her success to loving what she does. **B/I:** She chose the profession because she wanted to focus on healthcare. **H/O:** The highlight of her career is knowing she is helping people.

VANESSA DEL S. RODRIGUEZ
Owner
VS Rodriguez & Associates
1752 Calle Budapest
College Park, PR 00921 United States
vsrodassoc@onelinkpr.net
http://www.cambridgewhoswho.com

BUS: Consulting Firm **P/S:** Consulting Services Including Engineering and Environmental Consulting Services **MA:** Regional **EXP:** Ms. Rodriguez's expertise is in environmental engineering, geological assessments and project management. **H/I/S:** Playing Tennis, Reading, Spending Time with her Family **FBP:** Forbes **EDU:** Bachelor's Degree in Civil Engineering, Polytechnic University of Puerto Rico; Bachelor's Degree in Geology, University of Puerto Rico, Mayaguez **CERTS:** Registered Environmental Manager (2004) **A/A/S:** Geological Society of Puerto Rico; Secretary, Former President, Women's Civil Engineering Society **C/VW:** American Cancer Society **A/S:** She attributes her success to her passion for her profession, hard work and desire to learn. **B/I:** She became involved in her profession because she always had an interest in construction, geology and protecting the environment. **H/O:** The most gratifying aspects of her career are working in her current position and being able to protect the environment.

MARY J. ROEPKE
Teacher
Our Savior First Lutheran Church and School
10125 Lasaine Avenue
Northridge, CA 91325 United States
mjrrom828@hotmail.com
http://www.osflcs.com

BUS: Christian Church, School with a Thorough Christ-Centered Education **P/S:** Religious Services, Kindergarten through Sixth Grade, Licensed Preschool Education **MA:** Regional **D/D/R:** Teaching Second-Grade, Reading, Developing Curriculum **H/I/S:** Reading, Walking, Swimming **FBP:** Educational Research **EDU:** Master's Degree in Curriculum Development and Reading, Concordia University (2002)

DIANNE L. ROGERS, RN
Screening Center Registered Nurse
Warren General Hospital
2 Crescent Park W.
Warren, PA 16365 United States
dianne.rogers@cwwemail.com
http://www.cambridgewhoswho.com

BUS: Hospital **P/S:** Healthcare **MA:** Regional **EXP:** Ms. Rogers' expertise is in mammography screenings and following-up after treatments. **H/I/S:** Reading, Traveling, Spending Time with her 11 Grandchildren, Crocheting, Philately, Writing Poetry **FBP:** Nursing2009; RN **EDU:** Associate Degree in Nursing, Jamestown Community College **CERTS:** Licensed Practical Nurse (1985); Certified Nurse Consultant **C/VW:** Moose Club; Local Charitable Organizations **A/S:** She attributes her success to her education. **B/I:** She became involved in her profession because she always wanted to become a nurse. **H/O:** The most gratifying aspect of her career is receiving gratitude from the patient's family members.

JO ALICE (JODIE) ROGERS, RN
Certified Registered Nurse
Senior Health Properties, Inc.
2600 Sagebrush Drive
Flower Mound, TX 75028 United States
jabrcats@aol.com
http://www.cambridgewhoswho.com

BUS: Long Term Care **P/S:** Nursing **MA:** Local **D/D/R:** Geriatrics **H/I/S:** Gardening, Animals, Spending Time with the Family **EDU:** Associate Degree in Nursing, Eastern New Mexico University; Pursuing Bachelor's Degree in Healthcare Administration, Century University **CERTS:** Certified in Occupational Safety and Health Administration; Certified Gerontological Nurse **C/VW:** American Cancer Society; Lubbock Children's Home; 4-H **A/S:** She attributes her personal and professional success to her wonderful bosses. **B/I:** She has always had an interest in the field and a desire to help others. **H/O:** The highlight of her career is providing quality care to her patients.

KATHRYN I. ROGERS
Owner and Supervisor
KAS Homecare
630 N. Valencia Place
Chandler, AZ 85226 United States
krogers_2@msn.com
http://www.cambridgewhoswho.com

BUS: Habilitation and Independent Home Living, Co-Owner of Arizona Quality Home Providers **P/S:** Life Skill for Disabled Adults, Housing and Independent Living **MA:** Local **D/D/R:** Supervision, Helping People with Disabilities to be Independent and Live on their Own **H/I/S:** Traveling **EDU:** Medical Assisting, Crestwood Career Academy **A/A/S:** The Arc of Arizona; Monday Night Drama Group **C/VW:** Monday Night Drama Group **A/S:** She attributes her success to hard work and dedication. **B/I:** She became involved in this profession because her brother was born with down syndrome and she enjoyed spending time with him and teaching him how to be more independent which led to her current career. **H/O:** The highlight of her career is when she sees shy individuals overcome shyness and perform on stage.

V. VAN ROGERS
Owner, President
Vastreck, Inc.
806 S. 1040 W.
Suite B
Payson, UT 84651 United States
vrogers@vastreck.com
http://www.vastreck.com

BUS: Engineering, Drafting **P/S:** Drafting Services **MA:** National **D/D/R:** Designing Commercial Cabinets **H/I/S:** Spending Time with his Family **FBP:** Industry-Related Publications **EDU:** Bachelor's Degree in Design Engineering, Brigham Young University (1986) **C/VW:** Church of Jesus Christ of Latter Day Saints

DAWN MARIE ROLAND
Administrative Support
Danville State Hospital
200 State Hospital Drive
Danville, PA 17721 United States
pondqueen@hotmail.com
http://www.cambridgewhoswho.com

BUS: Hospital **P/S:** Healthcare for the Mentally Handicapped **MA:** Central Pennsylvania Region **D/D/R:** Overseeing Operations, Repairs and Functionality of the Buildings and Grounds, Performing Administrative Duties, Multitasking **H/I/S:** Making Crafts, Gardening, Traveling throughout the United States, Writing Articles **FBP:** Kiplinger's **EDU:** Associate Degree in Secretarial Science, Pennsylvania College of Technology (1973) **A/A/S:** Mooresburg Bicentennial 200th Anniversary Committee (2006); American Federation of State, County and Municipal Employees **C/VW:** Volunteer, Local Fire Department; Co-Administrator Board, Mooresburg United Methodist Church; Union Member, American Federation of State, County and Municipal Employees **DOB:** August 27, 1954 **POB:** Williamsport, PA **SP:** Gale **CHILD:** Mandie, Bradley **A/S:** She attributes her success to her upbringing, hard work and desire to help others. **B/I:** She became involved in her profession because of her desire to help the community. **H/O:** The highlights of her career were working with the Brighter Christmas Fund and being asked to assist the design committee for the Pennsylvania State Careerlink offices. **I/F/Y:** In five years, Ms. Roland hopes to be traveling internationally.

F. NICOLE ROLLE
Program Specialist
ESE
201 W. Burleigh Boulevard
Taveres, FL 32778 United States
fnrolle@yahoo.com
http://www.cambridgewhoswho.com

BUS: Education **P/S:** Education **MA:** Local **D/D/R:** Working as a Special Education Specialist **H/I/S:** Reading, Traveling **FBP:** Education Week **EDU:** Master's Degree in Leadership, Nova Southeastern University **A/A/S:** Alpha Delta Kappa **C/VW:** Church, The Special Olympics **A/S:** She attributes her career success to the support and love her family offers her. **B/I:** She has always felt a drive to help educate children, so she pursued a career in education. **H/O:** She feels that her current position as a program specialist is the highlight of her career.

SUZANNE J. ROMANO
Latin Teacher, National Honor Society Class Advisor
Academy of Allied Health Science
2325 Heck Avenue
Neptune, NJ 07753 United States
s_romano@aahs.mcvsd.org
http://www.cambridgewhoswho.com

BUS: Secondary High School **P/S:** Education **MA:** North and Central New Jersey **D/D/R:** Teaching Latin, Class Club Advisement, Portfolio Assessment, Advising the Class of 2010 World Language Program **H/I/S:** Reading, Collecting Dolls **EDU:** Master of Arts in Education, Rutgers, The State University of Njew Jersey **CERTS:** Certificate in Supervision, New Jersey State **A/A/S:** Association for Supervision and Curriculum Development; National Honor Society; New Jersey Classical League; ACL **A/H:** Best of the Best Award for Outstanding Teachers, Association of Supervision and Curriculum Development; Best of the Best Award in Education **C/VW:** Oceans Action; Giving Christmas Gifts to the Crisis Intervention Center; Hats for the Homeless; Fundraising; The Salvation Army; Holiday Express **A/S:** She attributes her success to being driven and a life-long learner. **B/I:** She became involved in her profession after taking Latin as a child in parochial school. She enjoyed it so much that she got a bachelor's degree in Latin and English. **H/O:** The highlight of her career was receiving an award from the Association for Supervision and Curriculum Development. Ten of the best high schools are selected in the United States and hers was one of the winning schools.

SUE A. ROMIG
Supervisor
Trailblazer Health Enterprises
3101 S. Woodlawn Boulevard
Denison, TX 75020 United States
sue.romig@trailblazerhealth.com
http://www.trailblazerhealth.com

BUS: Wholly-Owned Subsidiary of BlueCross BlueShield of South Carolina, Leader in the Administration of the Medicare Program **P/S:** Quality Service to Medicare Beneficiaries and Healthcare Professionals, Low-Cost, High-Quality, Customer-Focused Service to the Centers for Medicare and Medicaid Services (CMS), and to Medicare Beneficiaries and Providers **MA:** Local **D/D/R:** Supervising Staff of 16 in the Call Center, Dealing with Providers, Physicians who Have Questions Regarding Coverage, Working One-On-One with Staff **H/I/S:** Scuba Diving, Water Skiing, Motorcycle Riding, Softball **FBP:** Scuba Divers **EDU:** Customer Service Coursework; Business Writing Coursework, Trailblazer Health Enterprises **A/A/S:** Lion's Club

DEBRA T. ROOKE
Police Officer
Springfield Police Department
Springfield, MA United States
http://www.cambridgewhoswho.com

BUS: Police **P/S:** Police Department **MA:** Local **H/I/S:** Reading, Going to the Health Club, Spending Time with her Three Daughters **EDU:** Bachelor of Science in Criminal Justice, Westfield Community College; Associate Degree in Law, Holyoke Community College **A/H:** Recognition for Aiding the Fire Department in a Rescue **C/VW:** Foster Program; Parent-Teacher Organization; Father Flanigan Boys and Girls Home; Multiple Sclerosis Society **A/S:** She attributes her success to her attitude and seeing the good in people. **B/I:** She became involved in this profession because she grew up in Springfield, in a tough area, and joined the police Explorer club in high school. **H/O:** The most gratifying aspects of her career are the times when she helps people, specifically delivering a baby or saving someone's life through CPR.

CLAIRE ROSACCO
Vice President of Government Affairs and Community Outreach
Cuyahoga Community College
700 Carnegie Avenue
Cleveland, OH 44115 United States
claire.rosacco@tri-c.edu
http://www.tri-c.edu

BUS: College **P/S:** Higher Education Including Certificate and University Transfer Programs, Off-Campus Credit Courses, Online Education, Non-Credit Workforce and Professional Development Courses **MA:** Regional **D/D/R:** Researching Opportunities for Funding from Sources Other than the State, Offering Community Outreach, Coordinating Major Events Involving Community Partnerships **H/I/S:** Listening to Music, Attending the Theater **EDU:** Bachelor's Degree in Journalism, Minor in Political Science, The Ohio State University (1979) **A/A/S:** City Club of Cleveland; Leadership Cleveland; Alumni Association, The Ohio State University **A/H:** National Council of Marketing and Public Relations Award for Best Government and Community Relations Program for Community Colleges (2006) **C/VW:** United Way of America of Greater Cleveland; Cuyahoga Community College Foundation

MRS. SOPHIA N. ROSARIO, BS
Director of Special Projects
Record Aircraft Parts, Corp.
8786 N.W. 18th Terrace
Miami, FL 33172 United States
srosario@recordair.com
http://www.cambridgewhoswho.com

BUS: Aviation Company **P/S:** Aircraft Parts **MA:** Local **EXP:** Mrs. Rosario's expertise is in project management. **D/D/R:** Overseeing 40 Staff Members, Managing Accounts, Overseeing Brokerage Services **H/I/S:** Watching Basketball, Playing Volleyball, Practicing Karate, Spending Time with her Family, Reading **FBP:** Criminal Profiling **EDU:** Bachelor of Science in Criminology, Barry University

OLIVIA ROSE
President
Archer International
2822 E. Coolidge Street
Long Beach, CA 90805 United States
curliecuerose@yahoo.com
http://www.cambridgewhoswho.com

BUS: Real Estate Agency **P/S:** Commercial and Residential Real Estate Exchange and Investments **MA:** Regional **D/D/R:** Managing Real Estate Investments, Assisting First Time Buyers and Consulting **H/I/S:** Snowboarding, Horseback Riding, Camping, Fishing, Reading, Watching Movies **FBP:** Fortune; Money **EDU:** Associate Degree in General Studies, Cerritos College (2000)

JULIE A. ROSELLI-RAYA, MSN, CRNA
Certified Registered Nurse Anesthetist
JRR Anesthesia Service Inc.
PO Box 190
Weaverville, CA 96093 United States
julie_rr@hotmail.com
http://www.cambridgewhoswho.com

BUS: Healthcare Association **P/S:** Anesthesia Dispensation **MA:** Northwest California **D/D/R:** Administering Anesthesia, Directing the Operating Room at Mountain Creek Medical Services Trinity Hospital, Acting as Director of Anesthesia at Trinity Hospital, Overseeing Staffing Nurses and Surgical Technicians **H/I/S:** Golfing, Biking, Hiking, Skiing, Boating, Water Sports, Needleworking, Reading, Learning Italian **FBP:** American Association of Nurse Anesthetists Journal; Survey of Anesthesiology **EDU:** Master of Science in Nursing in Anesthesia, University of Texas Health Science Center, San Antonio; Bachelor of Science in Nursing, Regis University **A/A/S:** California Association of Nurse Anesthetists; American Association of Nurse Anesthetists **C/VW:** Disabled American Veterans; Iraq Veteran Charities **A/S:** She attributes her success to always finishing what she starts and to her training in the Armed Forces. **B/I:** She became involved in the profession while working for a cardiologist, training in the area and finding an interest in anesthesiology. **H/O:** The most gratifying aspect of her career is working in her current position and offering anesthesia to patients in rural areas.

DR. SUSAN B. ROSENTHAL
First Vice President, Wealth Management Advisor
Merrill Lynch
3211 Shannon Road, Suite 200
Durham, NC 27707 United States
susan_rosenthal@ml.com
http://www.fa.ml.com/susan_rosenthal

BUS: Financial Management Company **P/S:** Financial Management Consulting Services **MA:** National **D/D/R:** Assisting Clients in Investment Retirement Plans, Estate Planning, Scheduling, Explaining Products and Services to Clients, Ensuring Customer Satisfaction, Consulting **H/I/S:** Swimming, Golfing, Hiking **FBP:** IMCA Journal; Journal of Financial Planning **EDU:** Ph.D. in Special Education, The University of North Carolina at Chapel Hill; Master of Education in Special Education, The University of North Carolina at Chapel Hill, Bachelor of Arts in French, The University of North Carolina at Chapel Hill **CERTS:** Certified Financial Planner; Certified Investment Management Analyst; Chartered Retirement Planning Counselor; Certified Special Needs Advisor **A/A/S:** Federal Emergency Management Agency **A/H:** Barron's Top 100 Women Financial Advisors List (2006, 2007, 2008); Registered Representative, America's Top 50 Advisors List (2004) **C/VW:** Board of Visitors, The University of North Carolina at Chapel Hill; Agape' Corner Boarding School, NC **POB:** New Orleans, LA **SP:** Michael **CHILD:** Johnny **A/S:** She attributes her success to her perseverance and listening to her clients. **B/I:** She became involved in her profession because she always wanted to work with people. **H/O:** The highlight of her career was being honored by Barron's as one of the Top Women Financial Advisors for three consecutive years.

BETH T. ROSNER, DDS, FAGD
Doctor of Dental Surgery
1414 Montauk Highway
Watermill, NY 11975 United States
drbethrosner@optonline.net
http://www.cambridgewhoswho.com

BUS: Private Practice **P/S:** Wide Variety of High Quality Dental Care Services Including General Dentistry and Cosmetic Dental Procedures **D/D/R:** Working as a Doctor of Dental Surgery, Researching, Working with Case Studies, Practicing Research Investigating at New York University **H/I/S:** Equestrian **EDU:** Doctor of Dental Surgery, New York University (1982); General Residency, Columbia Presbyterian Hospital **A/A/S:** Fellow, Academy of General Dentistry; Fellow, IACDFA

JUANITA MARCELLA ROSS, BA, MS
Review Chemist (Retired)
Food and Drug Administration
5600 Fishers Lane
Rockville, MD 20852 United States
juanitamarcella.ross@cwwemail.com
http://www.cambridgewhoswho.com

BUS: Government Agency **P/S:** Researching and Approving Drugs **MA:** National **EXP:** Ms. Ross' expertise is in reviewing chemical data for drug approval. **H/I/S:** Swimming, Researching Biblical History **FBP:** Time **EDU:** Master of Science in Chemistry, Major in Organic Chemistry, American University; Bachelor's Degree in Biology, Minor in Chemistry, Catholic University **A/A/S:** American Chemical Society **A/H:** Outstanding Performance Award, United States Government **C/VW:** Alumni Association for American and Catholic Universities **A/S:** She attributes her success to her hard work and perseverance. **B/I:** She became involved in her profession because of her interest in science. **H/O:** The highlight of her career was earning her current position.

FLORENCE E. ROST
Clinical Administrator
Maine General Medical Center
6 E. Chestnut Street
Augusta, ME 04330 United States
florence.rost@mainegeneral.org
http://www.cambridgewhoswho.com

BUS: Healthcare **P/S:** Healthcare **MA:** Local **D/D/R:** Management, Emergency Room Nursing, Trauma Medicine, Nursing Management, Emergency Nursing **H/I/S:** Reading, Gardening, Traveling **FBP:** Conservation and Wildlife Journals **EDU:** Registered Nurse, Central Maine General Hospital (Now Central Maine Medical Center); Coursework in Nursing Leadership in Excellence, Nursing Law, Case Management, Nursing Executive Relations, Human Resource Management, Infection Control, Self-Defense, Non-Violent Management of Escalating Behavior **A/A/S:** Former Member, Board of Directors, The Kennebec Valley Federal Credit Union; Former Member, Finance and Stewardship Committee, Highland Avenue Methodist Church; President and Administrative Council Member, United Methodist Women, Highland Avenue Unit **C/VW:** Habitat for Humanity; National Wildlife; Free Community Suppers **A/S:** She attributes her success to her Canadian upbringing and common sense. **B/I:** She became involved in her profession because she always liked helping people.

JONATHAN A. ROTH
President
Document Imaging Group, Inc.
6-A Pearl Court
Allendale, NJ 07401 United States
jroth@docigroup.com
http://www.docigroup.com

BUS: System Integration **P/S:** Document Imaging **MA:** Regional **D/D/R:** Sales, Overseeing All Aspects of the Company **H/I/S:** Playing and Coaching Basketball, Fishing **FBP:** Advanced Imaging Magazine **EDU:** Bachelor of Arts in Business Management, Fairleigh Dickinson University **CERTS:** Certified in Emergency Medical Services **C/VW:** Volunteer, Ambulance Corps **A/S:** He attributes his success to his ability to build relationships and his knowledge of the industry. **B/I:** He became involved in his profession through a natural progression of opportunities. **H/O:** The most gratifying aspect of his career is his current position.

KATHRYN M. ROTHER, MSA

Associate Head of School for Curriculum and Instruction
Salpointe Catholic High School
1545 E. Copper Street
Tucson, AZ 85719 United States
krother@salpointe.org
https://salpointe.org

BUS: Secondary School **P/S:** Secondary Education, College Preparatory Education **MA:** Local **EXP:** Ms. Rother's areas of expertise are in professional development and curriculum development. **H/I/S:** Hiking in Sedona, Arizona, Reading **FBP:** ASCD Newsletter; NCEA Momentum **EDU:** Master's Degree in Administration, University of Notre Dame; Master's Degree in Educational Leadership, Northern Arizona University **CERTS:** Certification in Secondary Education; Certification in Humanities; Certified Secondary Principal **A/A/S:** National Catholic Educational Association; Association for Supervision and Curriculum Development; Arizona School Administrators Association **A/H:** The Leonardo da Vinci Award; The National Society of High School Scholars **C/VW:** CTSO Local Charity

ANN M. ROULINAVAGE, RN

Cardiac Surgical Follow-Up Nurse
Wilkes-Barre General Hospital
375 N. River Street
Wilkes-Barre, PA 18702 United States
http://www.wvhcs.org

BUS: Hospital **P/S:** Healthcare **MA:** National **D/D/R:** Follow up Nursing and Post Operative Care **H/I/S:** Crafts, Playing Bridge, Spending Time with Grandchildren and Great Grandchildren **FBP:** RN **EDU:** Nursing, St. Joseph's Medical Center, Reading, Pennsylvania **C/VW:** American Red Cross; St. Jude Children's Research Hospital; Local Churches **A/S:** She attributes her success to loving what she does. **B/I:** She became involved in the profession because she always wanted to be a nurse. It was her calling. **H/O:** The highlight of her career is working with cardiac surgeons. She found the work interesting and that cardiac surgeons appreciate nurses.

PATRICIA M. ROWLAND, RN
Registered Nurse
South Nassau Communities Hospital
1 Healthy Way
Oceanside, NY 11572 United States
pattym64@optonline.net
http://www.southnassau.org

BUS: Hospital **P/S:** Healthcare Including Cancer, Cardiac and Mental Healthcare, Maternity Services, Pain Management, Pediatric and Orthopedic Surgery, Physical Rehabilitation and Sports Medicine **MA:** Local **EXP:** Ms. Rowland's expertise is in electrophysiology and troubleshooting. **D/D/R:** Performing Cardiac Catheterization Lab Work, Preparing the Lab, Installing Pacemakers, Educating Patients and their Families, Admitting and Discharging Patients **H/I/S:** Swimming, Reading Novels, Gardening, Riding on her Husband's Motorcycle, Traveling **FBP:** American Journal of Nursing **EDU:** Associate Degree in Nursing, Edna McConnell Clark School of Nursing **CERTS:** Certification in Basic Life Support; Certification in Advanced Cardiac Life Support **A/A/S:** Police Benevolent Association; Organ Donor Network of Long Island; American Association of Critical-Care Nurses **C/VW:** Local Police and Fire Department; The Leukemia & Lymphoma Society; Mothers Against Drunk Driving **A/S:** She attributes her success to her love for her profession. **B/I:** She became involved in her profession because she always wanted to become a nurse. **H/O:** The highlight of her career was teaching the staff members.

NANCY L. ROY
Owner
JMN, LLC.
3530 Robin Road
Tallahassee, FL 32305 United States
jmndrywall@yahoo.com
http://www.cambridgewhoswho.com

BUS: Proven Leader in Construction **P/S:** Commercial and Residential Drywall Hanging and Plastering **MA:** National **D/D/R:** Plastering, Overseeing Crew for Cleaning, Working at Citizens Insurance Company as a Reporting Specialist **EDU:** Registered Nurse, Concord Career Institute (1990) **DOB:** February 7, 1968 **SP:** Javier **CHILD:** Melissa

MARCIA T. ROZEMAN, RN

Registered Nurse
Caddo Parish School System
5800 W. 70th Street
Shreveport, LA 71107 United States
http://www.cambridgewhoswho.com

BUS: School District **P/S:** Education **MA:** Local **D/D/R:** School Nursing **H/I/S:** Spending Time with the Family, Reading, Gardening **EDU:** Bachelor of Science in Nursing, Northwestern State University **A/A/S:** Louisiana State Nurses Association; American Nurses Association; Louisiana School Nurses Organization **C/VW:** St. Jude Children's Research Hospital; Church; Shreveport Opera; Shreveport Symphony; Little Theatre **A/S:** She attributes her success to her love for children and playing a very large part in their lives. **H/O:** The highlight of her career is being in the same capacity for 50 years.

LINDA A. RUBECK

Teacher
Pioneer Middle School
Old Olean Road
Yorkshire, NY 14173 United States
lrubeck@pion.wnyric.org
http://www.pion.wnyric.org

BUS: Middle School **P/S:** Education **MA:** Local **D/D/R:** Teaching Family and Consumer Sciences to Grades Five through Eight **H/I/S:** Scrapbooking **EDU:** Master of Science Degree in Home Economics, Buffalo State Teachers College (1975) **A/A/S:** Family, Career and Community Leaders of America; Delta Kappa Gamma; American Association of Family and Consumer Sciences **A/H:** Alumni Achievement Award, Family, Career and Community Leaders of America (2002); Teacher of the Year Award, State Education Department, New York State (2002)

KATHLEEN E. RUCKDESCHEL
Houston, TX 77046 United States
Kathleen.Ruckdeschel@cwwemail.com
http://www.cambridgewhoswho.com

BUS: Investments **P/S:** Investment Planning **MA:** International **D/D/R:** Specializing in Retirement Plans and Marketing **H/I/S:** Physical Fitness, Traveling, Reading, Walking **FBP:** The Wall Street Journal; Boomer Magazine; Money; Registered Rep. **EDU:** Master of Business Administration, Our Lady of the Lake University **C/VW:** Leukemia & Lymphoma Society **A/S:** She attributes her success to her ability to focus and pay attention to detail. **H/O:** The highlight of her career is her current position.

BRIAN W. RUDDELL, JD
Member
Husch, Blackwell and Sanders, LLP
401 Main Street
Suite 14
Peoria, IL 61602 United States
brianruddell@huschblackwell.com
http://www.huschblackwell.com

BUS: Law Firm **P/S:** Legal Services Including Business Litigation, Product Liability and Toxic Torts, Land Use and Development, Tax and Estate Planning, Corporate and Financial Transactions, Specialized Legal Services in Labor and Employment, Construction, Environmental and Regulatory, Health Law, Insolvency, Intellectual Property and Technology, Franchise Law and International Law **MA:** Regional **EXP:** Mr. Ruddell's expertise is in corporate and employee benefits law. **H/I/S:** Traveling, Spending Time with his Grandchildren, Family and Friends **FBP:** The Wall Street Journal; BusinessWeek **EDU:** JD, Notre Dame College, Magna Cum Laude; Bachelor's Degree in Economics, University of Illinois, Magna Cum Laude **A/A/S:** Board of Trustees, Peoria Public Library; Former Board Member, YMCA; Former Board of Trustees, Crime Stoppers **CHILD:** Jessica, Benjamin **A/S:** He attributes his success to his ability to build positive relationships with his clients and the support he receives from his parents. **B/I:** He became involved in his profession because of his interest in the practical rules that govern society. **H/O:** The highlights of his career were earning the respect of his peers and being placed into a position of responsibility. **I/F/Y:** In five years, Mr. Ruddell hopes to become more involved with his community.

PAULA L. RUDE
Executive Assistant
Coy and Associates
5700 Smetana Drive
Suite 110
Minnetonka, MN 55343 United States
paula@coyandassociates.com
http://www.coyandassociates.com

BUS: Accounting **P/S:** Financial Turnaround and Management **MA:** National **D/D/R:** Consulting Services, Office Management **H/I/S:** Spending Quality Time with her Family, Dancing, Listening to Live Music **C/VW:** St. Raphael Parish **A/S:** She attributes her career success to her excellent organizational skills and to her hard work and dedication. **B/I:** She was drawn to the field of secretarial work by unforeseen circumstances. **H/O:** She feels that her current position is the highlight of her career.

TANYA RUDSTROM
ASD Special Education Teacher
Barry Elementary School
970 Klamath Lane
Yuba City, CA 95993 United States
tanyarudstrom@sbcglobal.net
http://www.cambridgewhoswho.com

BUS: Education **P/S:** K-8 Public Mainstream and Special Education **MA:** Local **D/D/R:** Teaching Autistic Spectrum Disorder Special Education Classes **H/I/S:** Painting, Spending Time with her Children **EDU:** Bachelor of Arts in Communications and Graphic Art, California State University at Chico; Pursuing Multiple Subjects at Chapman University **C/VW:** Children's Cancer Society **A/S:** She attributes her success to family support. **B/I:** She was prompted to enter her profession because she always had an interest in special needs children. **H/O:** The highlight of her career was obtaining her current position.

DANIEL RUGG
Family Services Coordinator
Wayland-Cohocton Central Schools
2350 Route 63
Wayland, NY 14572 United States
drugg@rochester.rr.com
http://www.cambridgewhoswho.com

BUS: Public School **P/S:** Counseling and Education **MA:** Local **D/D/R:** Marriage, Family and Child Psychology **H/I/S:** Bicycle Riding, Walking, Reading, Watching Movies and Exercising **EDU:** Master's Degree in Psychology, John F. Kennedy University **H/O:** The highlight of his career is his current position.

SARA RUNGE-PULTE, ED.D.
Assistant Professor
Northern Kentucky University College of Education and Human
Services
Nunn Drive, BEP-251
Newport, KY 41099 United States
rungesa@nku.edu
http://www.uky.edu

BUS: University **P/S:** Higher Education **MA:** International **EXP:** Ms. Runge-Pulte's expertise is in literacy, working with undergraduate and graduate students, evaluating first year interns and coordinating the international student teaching placements. **H/I/S:** Spending Time with her Family **FBP:** Newsweek **EDU:** Doctor of Education, University of Cincinnati (1997); Master's Degree in Elementary Education, Major in Reading and Writing, Northern Kentucky University (1991); Bachelor's Degree in Elementary Education, Northern Kentucky University (1989) **A/A/S:** International Reading Association; American Reading Forum; National Council of Teachers of English; Association of Supervision and Curriculum Development

LYN R. RUSHING
Fifth-Grade Mathematics and Science Teacher
Julia P. Bryant Elementary School
400 Donnie Simmons Way
Statesboro, GA 30458 United States
lyn.rushing@gmail.com
http://www.cambridgewhoswho.com

BUS: Elementary School **P/S:** Education **MA:** Local **EXP:** Ms. Rushing's expertise is in reading education. **D/D/R:** Teaching Mathematics and Science **H/I/S:** Conducting Computer Technician Training Courses for Teachers, Traveling, Reading, Spending Time with her Family **FBP:** Educational Leadership; Industry-Related Journals **EDU:** Pursuing Ph.D. in Leadership, Union Institute & University; Master's Degree Reading Specialist, Georgia Southern University **CERTS:** Certified in Educational Leadership; Certified Teacher Support Specialist **A/A/S:** Professional Association of Georgia Educators; National Association of Elementary School Principals; Association of Supervision and Curriculum Development; Content Advisory Committee in Reading, Georgia Assessments for the Certification of Educators **A/H:** Teacher of the Year (2001); Statesboro Bulloch County Recreational Volunteer of the Year (2000) **C/VW:** Volunteer, Catastrophe Relief; Volunteer, Women's Shelter; Girl Scouts of America; Relay for Life, American Cancer Society; American Diabetes Association; United Way of America **DOB:** May 10, 1954 **POB:** Atlanta, GA **SP:** John **CHILD:** Jennifer, Darby **A/S:** She attributes her success to her continuous education and students' achievements. **B/I:** She became involved in her profession because she always enjoyed working with children. **H/O:** The highlight of her career was being nominated for Who's Who Among American Teachers. **I/F/Y:** In five years, Ms. Rushing hopes to retire.

JENNIFER L. RUSSELL, MA
Music Teacher, Chorus Director
James L. Mulcahey Middle School
28 Clifford Street
Taunton, MA 02780 United States
jenmark@rcn.com
http://www.cambridgewhoswho.com

BUS: Education **P/S:** Education for Fifth through Eighth Grades **MA:** Local **D/D/R:** Music Education, Chorus Direction, Elementary Education **H/I/S:** Playing the Trumpet, Enjoying Outdoor Activities, Painting, Cooking **EDU:** Master's Degree in Educational Leadership, Bridgewater State College; Bachelor's Degree in Elementary Education and Music, Bridgewater State College **A/A/S:** Massachusetts Teachers Association **C/VW:** Holy Family Church, Holy Rosary Church, Relay for Life **A/S:** She attributes her career success to her hard work and to the support she receives from her family, her coworkers and from her students. **B/I:** She pursued a career in education because she enjoys working with children and with music. **H/O:** She feels that being able to watch her students' progress is the highlight of her career.

BARBARA E. RUSSI, BSN, CCM, CRRN
Rehabilitation Case Manager
Kaiser Foundation Rehabilitation Center
975 Sereno Drive
Vallejo, CA 94589 United States
barb.russi@comcast.net
http://www.cambridgewhoswho.com

BUS: Healthcare **P/S:** Acute Rehabilitation Center **MA:** Northern California **D/D/R:** Certified Case Manager, Certified Rehabilitation Registered Nurse **H/I/S:** Reading, Gardening, Caring for her Two Dogs **EDU:** Bachelor of Science in Nursing, San Jose State University **CERTS:** Certified Rehabilitation Nurse; Certified Case Manager **A/A/S:** Case Management Society of America; Association of Rehabilitation Nurses **C/VW:** Goodwill **A/S:** She attributes her personal and professional success to her hard work and determination. **B/I:** She became involved in this profession because she has always had an interest in the field and a desire to help others. **H/O:** The most gratifying aspect of her career is seeing improvement in the lives of others.

MICHELLE DIANE RUTH, BSN
Charge Nurse
Vanderbilt University Medical Center
1211 22nd Avenue S.
Nashville, TN 37232 United States
michelle.pearson@vanderbilt.edu
http://www.cambridgewhoswho.com

BUS: Healthcare **P/S:** Healthcare, Hospital **MA:** National **D/D/R:** Charge Nurse, Medical-Surgical Floor **H/I/S:** Riding Horses, Spending Time Outdoors **FBP:** Nursing Magazines and Journals **EDU:** Bachelor of Science in Nursing, Middle Tennessee State University **CERTS:** Certified Advanced Cardiac Life Support **C/VW:** Animal Shelters **A/S:** She attributes her success to her love of helping people and loving to see her patients get well and go home. **H/O:** The highlight of her career is seeing patients get better.

LYLA M. RUTLEDGE
President
ASC Solutions, LLC
2604 S.W. 102nd Street
Oklahoma City, OK 73159 United States
lrutledgeascs@att.net
http://www.cambridgewhoswho.com

BUS: Consulting Company **P/S:** Consulting Services for Ambulatory Surgical Centers **MA:** National **D/D/R:** Developing Surgical Hospitals and Surgery Centers **H/I/S:** Spending Time with her Husband and Family, Golfing **FBP:** Ambulatory Surgical Center Magazine; Federated Ambulatory Surgery Association Publications **EDU:** Diploma in Nursing Development, North Dakota School of Forestry **CERTS:** Registered Nurse, St. Andrew's School of Nursing **A/A/S:** Association of Operating Room Nurses; Oklahoma Nurses Association **C/VW:** Local Retired Law Enforcement Agencies; Child Safety Programs **A/S:** She attributes her success to her commitment, perseverance and enjoyment of her job. **B/I:** She became involved in her profession after gaining many years of experience as a surgical nurse and she was asked by a physician to help him to develop the business. **H/O:** The most gratifying aspects of her career are maintaining good relationships with all the physicians and the rapport she has developed with them through the years.

CAROL A. RYAN
Registered Nurse, Intensive Care Nurse (Retired)
Hewitt Health & Rehabilitation Center
45 Maltby Street
Shelton, CT 06484 United States
carol-ryan@sbcglobal.net
http://www.cambridgewhoswho.com

BUS: Hospital **P/S:** Long-Term Care and Subacute Rehabilitation Services **MA:** Local **EXP:** Ms. Ryan's expertise is in infection control. **D/D/R:** Coordinating Wound Care Services and Caring for Patients **H/I/S:** Reading, Cooking, Traveling **FBP:** Nursing2009; American Journal of Nursing **EDU:** Bachelor's Degree in Public Health, Southern Connecticut State University **CERTS:** Registered Nurse, St. Elizabeth's Hospital **A/A/S:** Infection Control Nurses of Connecticut; Association for Professionals in Infection Control and Epidemiology **C/VW:** Special Olympics **A/S:** She attributes her success to her hard work, determination and caring nature. **B/I:** She became involved in her profession through a natural progression of opportunities. **H/O:** The highlight of her career was obtaining her degree while raising eight children.

GARY W. RYAN
President, Chief Executive Officer
Securacom GPS, LLC dba GPS Anyplace, Inc.
2010 Orange Tree Drive
Edgewater, FL 32141 United States
garyryan@securacomgps.com
http://www.gpsanyplace.com

BUS: GPS Vehicle Location and Fleet Management Systems Company **P/S:** Global Positioning System Manufacturing and Distribution, Wireless Asset Management **MA:** International **EXP:** Mr. Ryan's expertise is in global positioning system application and integration, and vehicle and tracking solutions. **D/D/R:** Overseeing Operations and Product Sales, Inputting of Design and Functionality, Internet-Based Fleet Management **H/I/S:** Fishing, Boating **EDU:** Business Law and Engineering Degree, Portland State University **A/A/S:** Tau Kappa Epsilon Fraternity; Sports Car Club of America

CYNTHIA JO RYLANDS
Director of Professional Practice and Business Requirements
Medco Health Solutions
100 Parsons Pond Drive
Franklin Lakes, NJ 07417 United States
cinryl@nauticom.net
http://www.medco.com

BUS: Leading Pharmacy Benefit Manager with the Nation's Largest Mail-Order Pharmacy Operations **P/S:** Moderates Cost and Enhances the Quality of Prescription Drug Benefits, Ensures Access to Affordable, High Quality Prescription Healthcare **MA:** Regional **D/D/R:** Overseeing Operations, Training, Managing Mail-Service Prescriptions **H/I/S:** Following Pittsburgh Steelers and Pittsburgh Penguins Sports Teams, Researching Genealogy, Practicing Photography **EDU:** Master's Degree in Human Resource Management, La Roche College (1993); Bachelor of Science, Ducane University (1981) **A/A/S:** American Pharmaceutical Association **C/VW:** National Multiple Sclerosis Society

HELEN M. SACCO, MS.ED.
College Instructor (Retired)
Broome Community College
261 Academy Drive
Vestal, NY 13850 United States
msacco@stny.rr.com
http://www.cambridgewhoswho.com

BUS: Educational Facility **P/S:** Higher Learning Services **MA:** Local **D/D/R:** Effective Speaking and Speech Communication, Consultant for Communications and Presentations, Private Tutoring **H/I/S:** Traveling, Gardening, Reading, Volunteering, Community Service **EDU:** Master's Degree in Administration and Supervision, St. Bonaventure University (1972); Bachelor's Degree in Education, SUNY Fredonia (1968) **A/A/S:** Binghamton Professional Women's Association **A/H:** Nominated Twice for Who's Who Among American Teachers **SP:** Michael **CHILD:** John, Thomas

MR. RUBEN SAENZ, M.ED.
Assistant to the Vice President of Student Development
Brookhaven College
Dallas County Community College District
3939 Valley View Lane
Farmers Branch, TX 75244 United States
rsaenz87@Sbcglobal.net
http://www.dcccd.edu

BUS: College District **P/S:** Higher Education **MA:** Regional **EXP:** Mr. Saenz's expertise is in student development. **H/I/S:** Reading, Spending Time with his Family **EDU:** Master of Education in Administration, St. Mary's University (1975) **CERTS:** Certification in Nonprofit Management, Sate of Texas (2006) **A/A/S:** Executive Director, Santa Elena Foundation

MR. GARY STEVEN SAGGESE
Owner
Gary's Catering
8 Lisa Lane
Saugus, MA 01906 United States
saggese7193@comcast.net
http://www.cambridgewhoswho.com

BUS: Proven Leader in the Food Industry **P/S:** High Quality, Fresh Cooked, Mobile Catering Services to Clients **MA:** Regional **D/D/R:** Variety of Different Specials, Visiting Construction Sites, Italian Fare **H/I/S:** Baseball, College Football **FBP:** Food & Wine Magazine **EDU:** Graduate, Chelsea High School (1979)

CHERYL Y. SAILER, OTR
Occupational Therapist
Cambridge Medical Center
701 S. Dellwood
Cambridge, MN 55008 United States
cheryl.sailer@allina.com
http://www.cambridgewhoswho.com

BUS: Hospital **P/S:** Healthcare **MA:** Local **D/D/R:** Occupational Therapy **EDU:** Bachelor of Science in Occupational Therapy, Grand Forks University **A/A/S:** American Occupational Therapy Association; Minnesota Occupational Therapy Association **C/VW:** Mothers Against Drunk Driving **A/S:** She attributes her success to the support of her manager, co-workers and family. **B/I:** She became involved in the profession because she always wanted to work in the healthcare field and occupational therapy gave her the ability to help others return to their normal functions. **H/O:** The highlight of her career was earning her current position and feeling the satisfaction of helping her patients.

ELIZABETH A. SALADA, MD
Medical Doctor
Palomar Medical Group
12630 Monte Vista Road
Suite 209
Poway, CA 92064 United States
lizmd@cox.net
http://www.rbinc.com

BUS: Medical Center **P/S:** Healthcare, Including Internal Medicine, and Media and Medical Presentations **MA:** Regional **D/D/R:** Caring for Patients Including Offering Skin Care Treatments with Laser Botox and Chemical Peels, Practicing Women's Healthcare, Internal, Integrated, Wellness and Preventive Medicine **H/I/S:** Spending Time with her Family, Reading, Jogging, Cooking, Attending Cultural Events **FBP:** The New England Journal of Medicine; The Journal of the American Medical Association **EDU:** MD, Wake Forest University (1993); Master's Degree in Public Health, The University of North Carolina at Chapel Hill (1989); Bachelor's Degree in Biology, University of California, San Diego (1987) **A/A/S:** American College of Physicians; National Association of Medical Communicators; American Medical Women's Association **DOB:** August 8, 1965 **CHILD:** Benjamin, Gabriel, Sofia

MR. JOSE A. SALAZAR
Emergency Medical Services Battalion Chief
Loudoun County Fire and Rescue
16600 Courage Court
Leesburg, VA 20175 United States
jsalazar@loudoun.gov
http://www.loudoun.gov

BUS: County Fire and Rescue Department **P/S:** Fire and Rescue Services for the Community, Emergency Management, Volunteer Recruitment, Special Events Planning and Hurricane and Tornado Preparedness Services **MA:** Local **D/D/R:** Overseeing the Educational Delivery of All Programs and Training, Managing a Staff of Professional Trainers **H/I/S:** Fishing, Woodworking **FBP:** JEMS **EDU:** Master's Degree in Public Health, New York Medical College (1993); Bachelor's Degree in Community Health Education, Queens College (1990) **A/A/S:** National Association of Emergency Medical Services Educators; National Association of Emergency Medical Technicians

CHRISTY A. SALDIVAR, M.ED.
Special Education/Dyslexia Teacher
Juan Linn Elementary
PO Box 1759
Victoria, TX 77902 United States
saldivar@suddenlook.net
http://www.cambridgewhoswho.com

BUS: Public Elementary School **P/S:** Education **MA:** Local **D/D/R:** Special Education and Dyslexia **H/I/S:** Church Choir, Listening to Music, Crafts **FBP:** Bible **EDU:** Master's Degree in Education, University of Houston; Bachelor's Degree in Education, Texas A&M University **A/A/S:** Texas Teachers Classroom Association; School Committees, Math, Reading Curriculum **C/VW:** Church; Local Charities; Relay for Life; Susan G. Komen for the Cure; Cancer Awareness **B/I:** She became involved in her profession because she had a family member with a learning disability. **H/O:** The highlight of her career is seeing her students graduate from High School.

WENDY L. SALIGER, RN
Office Nurse
Heartland Regional Medical Center
5325 Faraon Street
St. Joseph, MO 64506 United States
wendy.spoonemore@mail.heartland-health.com
http://www.heartland-health.com

BUS: Medical Center **P/S:** Healthcare Including Skilled Nursing Services, Family Medicine, Urology, Care for Children with Special Needs, Endocrinology, Acute Rehabilitation, Wound Care, Emergency and Trauma Center, Gastroenterology, Physician Practices, Health Plans **MA:** Regional **EXP:** Ms. Saliger's expertise is in emergency room nursing. **D/D/R:** Working with Wound Care Doctors, Treating Diabetics, Performing Triage **H/I/S:** Reading, Walking, Spending Time with her Children **FBP:** Gastroenterology Nursing; American Family Physician; Emergency Nurses Association Publications **EDU:** Pursuing Bachelor of Science in Nursing **CERTS:** Pursuing Certification in Nurse Practitioner Program; Registered Nurse, Metropolitan Community College, Penn Valley (2006); Certified LP10 Vent Trauma Nurse; Certified Sexual Assault Nurse Examiner; Certification in Continuous Positive Airway Pressure and Bilevel Positive Airway Pressure; Certification in Advanced Cardiovascular Life Support; Certification in Pediatric Advanced Life Support; Certification in Basic Life Support **A/A/S:** President, Parent-Teacher Association; Phi Theta Kappa **A/H:** National Dean's List **A/S:** She attributes her success to her faith in God and to the support she receives from her family. **B/I:** She became involved in her profession because she was hospitalized when she was young and was inspired by the nurse. **I/F/Y:** In five years, Ms. Saliger hopes to work in a rural practice and pursue her Ph.D.

MS. DEBRA L. SALVADOR
Supervisor
United States Postal Service
PO Box 36254
Tucson, AZ 85740 United States
vrodbikerchick@hotmail.com
http://www.thebabyboomerstucson.com

BUS: Government Agency **P/S:** Postal Services **MA:** International **D/D/R:** Ensuring Quality Customer Service **H/I/S:** Riding her Harley-Davidson Motorcycle **FBP:** Newsweek **A/A/S:** Harley Owners Group; National Association of Postal Supervisors **C/VW:** Local Charitable Organizations; St. Jude Children's Research Hospital; Combined Federal Campaign for Federal Employees; Toastmasters International **DOB:** March 6, 1956 **POB:** Biddeford, ME **CHILD:** Joseph, Eric **W/H:** Letter Carrier, United States Postal Service; Political Liaison, National Association of Letter Carriers **A/S:** She attributes her success to her positive attitude. **B/I:** She became involved in her profession after reading an article about a postal mail carrier in a magazine. **H/O:** The highlight of her career was becoming a supervisor of customer service. **I/F/Y:** In five years, Ms. Salvador would like to be a station manager in Tucson or a postmaster of a small town in the surrounding area.

MARY E. SALZ
Owner
MES Embroidery
128 N. Chestnut Street
Wenona, IL 61377 United States
m_salz98@yahoo.com
http://www.cambridgewhoswho.com

BUS: Proven Leader in the Field of Embroidery **P/S:** Highest Quality of Embroidery Services and Heat Pressing Items, Committed to Providing Quality Products and Services **MA:** Regional **D/D/R:** Embroidery and Heat Pressing Items, Does Appliqués for Bags, Carpets, Clothing and Pillows; Embroidering any Personalized Item on any Fabric that can be Sewn **H/I/S:** Swimming, Reading, Sewing **FBP:** Stitches Magazine **EDU:** High School Education **A/A/S:** Wenona Junior Women's Club; Chamber of Commerce; National Network of Embroidery Professionals; EMB Forum

PATRICIA A. SAMSON
Counselor
Integrative Counseling Services, Morrisville State College
S.W. Cayuga Street
Oswego, NY 13126 United States
PattieSamson@aol.com
http://www.cambridgewhoswho.com

BUS: Mental Health **P/S:** Nonprofit Human Services **MA:** State **D/D/R:** Performing Play Therapy **H/I/S:** Meditation, Reading **FBP:** Industry **EDU:** Master's Degree in Counseling and Psychological Services, State University of New York at Oswego; Bachelor's Degree in Psychology, State University of New York at Oswego **A/A/S:** Phi Kappa Phi; Oswego County Mental Health Association; New York Chapter, Association for Play Therapy; American Counseling Association **A/S:** She attributes her success to her life experiences. **B/I:** She became involved in this profession because she wanted to be in a profession where she could help others. **H/O:** The highlight of her career is receiving her master's degree.

STEPHANIE L. SAN PAOLO, BS
Administrative Assistant
Walton Construction
2932 E. Pythian Street
Springfield, MO 65802 United States
stephaniesanpaolo@waltonbuilt.com
http://www.waltoncci.com

BUS: Construction **P/S:** High Quality Commercial Construction **MA:** Regional **D/D/R:** Contract Administrator **H/I/S:** Volunteering at the Fine Arts Center **FBP:** NAWC Images **EDU:** Bachelor of Science in Administrative Management, Southwest Missouri State University **CERTS:** Certified Construction Industry Administrator **A/A/S:** Springfield Contractors Association; National Association of Women Contractors; Woman in Construction Under 10 Years **A/H:** Outstanding Woman of the Year Award **C/VW:** National Multiple Sclerosis Society **A/S:** She attributes her success to the support she receives from her co-workers as well as from the Women's Association. **H/O:** The highlight of her career is winning the Outstanding Woman of the Year Award.

KIERSTEN B. SANCHEZ, BSN, RN
Registered Nurse
The Commons at Sousrrel Hall
2025 Wightman Street
Pittsburgh, PA 15217 United States
mistressoblivion@hotmail.com
http://www.cambridgewhoswho.com

BUS: Healthcare **P/S:** Healthcare **MA:** Local **D/D/R:** Psychiatric Nursing, Geriatric and Rehabilitation Nursing **H/I/S:** Practicing Yoga, Reading Non-Fiction **FBP:** American Journal of Nursing; Geriatric Nursing **EDU:** Master's Degree in Library Science, University of Pittsburgh; Bachelor of Science in Nursing, University of Pittsburgh **A/S:** She attributes her career success to her ability to remain current in her industry. **B/I:** She has always had an interest in the human body and diseases, so she pursued a career in nursing. **H/O:** She feels that helping a young adolescent girl recover from a mental illness that was preventing her from joining the military has been the highlight of her career.

DR. GLADYS E. SÁNCHEZ-BELLO
Counselor and Therapist
Brower College
728 Riverside Drive
Coral Springs, FL 33071 United States
Sextxcounseling@att.net
http://www.sexlifemd.com

BUS: Education **P/S:** Counseling and Sex Therapy, English and Spanish Speaking Capabilities, Treating Gay, Lesbian, Bisexual and Transsexual Clients **MA:** Regional **D/D/R:** Helping Gay, Lesbian, Bisexual and Transgendered People, Specializing in Local Violence and Cross-Cultural Issues, Giving Couples, Individual and Family Sessions, Teaching Psychology **H/I/S:** Traveling, Music **FBP:** Marriage and Family Therapy; Psychology Today; Psychology Publications **EDU:** Ph.D., Critical Psychology, Maimonides University (2004); Master's Degree in Marriage and Family Therapy, Carlos Albizu University (2002) **A/A/S:** American Association of Sex Educators, Counselors and Therapists; American Psychological Association; American Association for Marriage and Family Therapy; Society for the Scientific Study of Sexuality

ANN NARINIAN SANDERS, R.PH.
Consultant Pharmacist
Pharmacy Department
Tampa General Hospital
PO Box 1289
Tampa, FL 33061 United States
anns@usa.com
http://www.linkenin.com/innnsanders

BUS: Hospital, University **P/S:** Healthcare, Education **MA:** Regional **D/D/R:** Pharmacy Consulting, Geriatrics, Trauma Medicine **H/I/S:** Photography, Collecting Rocks and Minerals, Making Jewelry and Designs, Traveling **EDU:** Pursuing Master of Business Administration in Healthcare Administration and Risk Management, New York Institute of Technology (2008); Bachelor of Science in Pharmacy Studies, Minor in Hospital and Retail Pharmacy, Massachusetts College of Pharmacy and Health Sciences (1986); Associate Degree in Business Management, Fisher College (1985) **A/A/S:** American Pharmaceutical Association; American Society of Consultant Pharmacists; Florida Pharmacy Association; Florida Society of Health-System Pharmacists; Downtown Women's Club **C/VW:** Society of Individual Leaders **A/S:** She attributes her success to her desire to make a difference. **B/I:** She became involved in the profession because her father was a professor of pharmacy and her mother was a nurse. **H/O:** The highlight of her career was earning her current position as regional manager of the eastern seaboard for OMN Medical Services.

JO ANN SANDERS
Real Estate Broker
Baldwin Crest Realty
3409 W. 43rd Street
Los Angeles, CA 90008 United States
jazzy823@aol.com
http://www.cambridgewhoswho.com

BUS: Private Company Committed to Excellence in the Real Estate Industry **P/S:** Buying and Selling Residential and Commercial Properties, Rentals, Resales, First Time Home Buyers, Agent Services **MA:** Regional **D/D/R:** Working as an Agent for Residential Sellers and Buyers **H/I/S:** Reading, Traveling **FBP:** Realtor **EDU:** Master's Degree in Business Administration, California State University at Dominguez Hills (1981); Bachelor's Degree in Business Administration, Pepperdine University (1979) **A/A/S:** National Association of Realtors; California Association of Realtors; Multiple Listing Service Los Angeles Real Estate; Beverly Hills Multiple Listing Service; BOR

THERESA J. SANDERS
Office Manager
East Coast Service, LLP
3571 Flat Creek Rd
Darlington, SC 29540 United States
eastcoastc@bellsouth.net
http://www.cambridgewhoswho.com

BUS: Third Party Moving Service **P/S:** Moving Service **MA:** Local **D/D/R:** Overseeing Administration, Billing and Filing **H/I/S:** Gardening **EDU:** Diploma, Hartsville High School **A/S:** She attributes her success to her father who was instrumental in instilling a strong work ethic in her. **B/I:** She became involved in her profession because her husband's friend was involved in the industry and started his own company.

ERIC SANDLER
President
Sigma Six Corp.
8 Reith Street
Copiague, NY 11726 United States
esandler@sigma6corp.com
http://www.sigma6corp.com

BUS: Management Consulting Company **P/S:** Business Development and Marketing Consulting, Acquisitions and Divestures, ISO-9000/AS-9100/ISO-14000, ISO-13485, ISO-16949, and TL9000 Certifications, Compliance Matters Including Product STCs and PMAs, Lean Manufacturing and Six Sigma Implementation, Manufacturing and Process Planning, and Materials Chain Management Programs **MA:** International **EXP:** Mr. Sandler's areas of expertise include aviation research and development, and logistics and statistical process management. **H/I/S:** Soccer, Boating, Flying **FBP:** Aviation News; Vertical Magazine; Industry News; Maxim; Wired **EDU:** Bachelor of Science in Electrical Engineering, Fairleigh Dickinson University (1975) **CERTS:** Six Sigma Master Black Belt; ISO/AS 9000 Certified Internal Auditor **A/A/S:** American Society for Quality; Institute of Electrical and Electronics Engineers, Inc.; American Society of Mechanical Engineers; Long Island Forum For Technology; Lean Manufacturing Champion; Director of Business Development, Innovative Power Solutions

MR. JAMES A. SANDS
Owner, Founder, Chief Executive Officer
James A. Sands & Associates, LLC, dba Safety First Homes
3000 Blue Heron Drive
Suite G
Kissimmee, FL 34741 United States
safetyfirsthomes@yahoo.com
http://www.safetyfirsthomes.net

BUS: Construction Company **P/S:** Constructing Affordable Hurricane, Fire Proof, Energy Efficient Homes **MA:** National **EXP:** Mr. Sands' expertise is in designing and building hurricane proof concrete homes. **H/I/S:** Designing Homes **FBP:** U.S. News & World Report **EDU:** Bachelor of Arts in Building Construction, Pratt Institute **A/A/S:** Better Business Bureau; National Association of Home Builders **C/VW:** Special Olympics; Habitat for Humanity **A/S:** He attributes his success to his hard work and desire to improve his methods of building new homes. **H/O:** The most gratifying aspects of his career are receiving a great deal of business and recognition throughout his field.

CAROL SANFORD
Chief Executive Officer
InterOctave Development Group, Inc.
3712 N.E. 187th Street
Seattle, WA 98155 United States
carolsanford@interoctave.com
http://www.interoctave.com

BUS: Publishing and Consulting **P/S:** Speaking, Consulting, Author **MA:** International **D/D/R:** Consulting on the Human Consciousness Factor in Business Development **H/I/S:** Reading, Yoga, Writing **FBP:** Fortune; Fast Company; Ethical Business **EDU:** Master's Degree in Business, San Jose State University; Master's Degree in Urban Planning, San Jose State University; Bachelor's Degree in Public Law, University of California at Berkeley **A/A/S:** National Speakers Association; American Electronics Association; Athena International Foundation; Board Member, Jessica's Love **C/VW:** Board of Creative Grandparenting

Karen L. Sanner, LPN
Home Healthcare Nurse
Ambercare Home Health Company
2129 Osuna Boulevard
Albuquerque, NM 87113 United States
balloon_gal@yahoo.com
http://www.cambridgewhoswho.com

BUS: Medical Service **P/S:** Homecare **MA:** Home Healthcare **D/D/R:** Nursing **H/I/S:** Camping, Making Crafts, Volunteering **FBP:** Emergency Medicine **CERTS:** Licensed Practical Nurse in Critical-Care Nursing, Technical Vocational School **A/A/S:** NAPLE **C/VW:** Alzheimer's Association **A/S:** She attributes her success to home care and finding out about patients on a personal level. **B/I:** She became involved in the profession after working as nurse's assistant and acknowledging that she has had a desire to help people since she was young. **H/O:** The most gratifying aspect of her career is working in the emergency room where she can make a difference by providing premium nursing care.

Christina A. Santana, Ph.D.
Bilingual, English as a Second Language Director
Universal Academy
2616 N. MacArthur Boulevard
Irving, TX 75062 United States
achristis@tx.rr.com
http://www.universalacademy.com

BUS: School **P/S:** Education **MA:** Local **D/D/R:** Language Acquisition, General Administration, Leadership, Curriculum Development, Staff Development, Advisor for Student Organizations, Supervise Teachers, Train Staff on Current Trends in Education, Research on Language Acquisition, Budgeting, Choose Textbooks, Teaching Spanish, Eels, and Technology **H/I/S:** Playing the Piano **FBP:** Education Week **EDU:** Ph.D. in Education and Administration, Jackson State University, Jackson, Mississippi (1998); Master of Science in Leadership from Jackson State University (1997); Bachelor of Science in Industrial Engineering, Polytechnical University, El Salvador (1984) **A/A/S:** ASCD **C/VW:** Volunteer Family Support Group in New Orleans for US Army Families **SP:** Louis

MR. RUBÉN DAVID SANTIAGO
President
Independent Claims Adjusters, Inc.
12925 S.W. 132 Street, Suite 3
Miami, FL 33186 United States
dsantiago@ica4ins.com
http://www.ica4ins.com

BUS: Insurance Company **P/S:** General Insurance and Insurance Claims **MA:** Regional **EXP:** Mr. Santiago's expertise is in residential and commercial property, auto and risk management and liability investigation. **D/D/R:** Consulting for Carriers, Assisting the Insured to Mitigate their Damages, Appraising Damages, Answering Phone Calls, Overseeing Employees **H/I/S:** Bicycling, Attending the Gym, Participating in Community Activities **EDU:** Coursework in Engineering, University of Puerto Rico **CERTS:** Certified Insurance Adjuster, States of Florida, North Carolina, Texas, Minnesota and Oklahoma **A/A/S:** Board of Directors, Valencia Home Owners Association; Association of Property Casualty Claims Professionals **C/VW:** St. Richards Catholic Church; Volunteer Work, St. Monica Catholic Church **CHILD:** Jennifer, Jason

MS. OVEDIA M. SANTOS
Account Executive
HUB International Limited
40 E. Alamar Avenue
Santa Barbara, CA 93105 United States
ovedia.santos@hubinternational.com
http://www.us.hubinternational.com

BUS: Insurance Brokerage Company **P/S:** Brokerage Services Including Risk Management and Investment Services, Property, Casualty, Life, Health and Workers' Compensation Insurance, Reinsurance and Employee Benefits **MA:** International **D/D/R:** Selling Commercial Insurance, Managing Workers' Compensation Insurance, Conducting Seminars, Safety Programs and Gatekeeper Programs, Dealing with Insurance Claims and Empowering Business Owners **H/I/S:** Golfing, Singing in the Church Choir **EDU:** Bachelor's Degree in Sociology, University of South Florida (1974) **A/A/S:** Lecturer, Simi Valley Days Committee; Write 4 Hope; Conejo Valley Days; Daughters of the American Revolution

CONNIE J. SARAUER
Registered Nurse Consultant, QA, DON
Pathway Health Services
2025 Fourth Street
White Bear Lake, MN 55110 United States
connie.sarauer@pathwayhealth.com
http://www.cambridgewhoswho.com

BUS: Healthcare **P/S:** Healthcare **MA:** National **D/D/R:** Consulting, Quality Assurance, Acting as the Director of Nursing, Management **H/I/S:** Traveling, Spending Time with her Children, Camping **EDU:** Associate Degree, Nursing, Chippewa Falls Technical College **CERTS:** Certified, Cardiopulmonary Resuscitation **C/VW:** Senior Center; Cancer Research; Veterans; Police Department; Sheriff's Department; Diabetes Foundation **A/S:** She attributes her success to the support and inspiration from her mother. **B/I:** She became involved in her profession because she always knew she wanted to be in healthcare. **H/O:** The highlight of her career has been making a difference in her patients' lives.

ANDREA SAROTTE
Operations Director
Robbins Gioia, LLC
26555 Evergreen
Suite 880
Southfield, MI 48076 United States
andrea.sarotte@robbinsgioia.com
http://www.robbinsgioia.com

BUS: Consulting Firm **P/S:** Program Management Consulting Services **MA:** National **D/D/R:** Creating New Businesses, Overseeing Information Technology Staffing and Portfolio Management for Workers and Companies, Developing Information Technology Strategies, Working as a Business Consultant, Promoting Record Management **H/I/S:** Golfing, Fishing **FBP:** CIO; Crain's Detroit Business **EDU:** Bachelor's Degree in Business Marketing, University of Phoenix **A/A/S:** Project Management Institute; ARMA International; Association for Information and Image Management

HEATHER M. SASKI
Director of Social Work
Carthage Area Hospital
1001 West Street Road
Carthage, NY 13619 United States
http://www.carthageareahospital.com

BUS: Acute Care Hospital with 78 Beds Located in Jefferson County of Northern New York State, Federally Designated as a Sole Community Provider **P/S:** Cardiology, Critical Care, Acute Care, Emergency Services, Financial Referrals, Obstetrics, Ambulatory Surgery, Acute Rehabilitation, Skilled Nursing, Medical-Surgical Pediatrics **MA:** Regional **D/D/R:** Dealing with Alcohol, Drug Abuse, and Addiction Referral, Crisis Management, Behavior Management, Local Violence, Mental Health Evaluation, Child Abuse and Neglect, Elder Abuse, Psycho-Social Assessment, Liasing for the Community and Outreach Clinics and Programs, Coordinating Nursing Admissions **H/I/S:** Mountain Biking, Down Hill Skiing, ATV Riding, Camping **FBP:** Social Work Today **EDU:** Master's Degree in Social Work, Specializing in Individuals, Families and Groups, Syracuse University (2004) **CERTS:** Certificate of Advanced Studies in Women's Studies; Certificate in Gerontology **A/A/S:** National Association of Social Workers (2002-Present); Phi Alpha Honor Society, Zeta Gamma Chapter (2003); Golden Key International Honour Society (2002-Present); National Society of Collegiate Scholars (2002-Present); Phi Theta Kappa International Honor Society (2001-Present); Phi Kappa Phi (2002); Who's Who Among Students in American Universities and Colleges (2002) **A/H:** Rhonda B. Cohen Prize in Gerontology (2003, 2004); Chancellor's Scholar (2001) **DOB:** August 9, 1978 **W/H:** Hospice of Jefferson County

GERALD SAUNDERS JR.
Educator, Research
Logos Intelligent
PO Box 70076
Washington, DC 20024 United States
tramasterkey@hotmail.com
http://www.cambridgewhoswho.com

BUS: Biomedical Research Facility **P/S:** Biomedical Education and Research **MA:** International **EXP:** Mr. Saunders' areas of expertise are in real estate, education, biotechnical studies, college-level medical writing and clinical research. **H/I/S:** Photography, Reading Science Fiction, Fishing, Technology **EDU:** Master's Degree in Biology, The University of Arizona; Bachelor's Degree, The University of North Carolina at Chapel Hill; Coursework, Georgetown University School of Medicine **CERTS:** Certification in Engineering **A/A/S:** American Association for the Advancement of Science; Phi Delta Kappa International; Association for Supervision and Curriculum Development; The Woodrow Wilson National Fellowship Foundation **C/VW:** DC Central Kitchen; Local Food Pantry; Sherwood Recreation Center; Various Children's Organizations; World Vision **A/S:** He attributes his success to his vision and faith in God. **H/O:** The highlight of his career was conducting clinical trials on AZT with the National Institute of Health.

KIMBERLY SAVERANCE
Pharmacist
CVS
1746 Heckle Boulevard
Rock Hill, SC 29732 United States
ksaver55@yahoo.com
http://www.cambridgewhoswho.com

BUS: Retail/Pharmacy **P/S:** Medication **MA:** Local **D/D/R:** Pharmacist **EDU:** Pharm. D., University of South Carolina, College of Pharmacy **A/A/S:** SCPA **C/VW:** Church; St. Jude Children's Research Hospital **A/S:** She attributes her success to the support and encouragement of friends and family. **H/O:** The highlight of her career has been graduating with her Pharm. D.

ROBERTA SAVO
Pharmacist, Clinical Assessor
Keystone Mercy Health System
200 Stevens Drive
Philadelphia, PA 19113 United States
PJRS17@gmail.com
http://www.cambridgewhoswho.com

BUS: Healthcare System for Medication Assessment **MA:** National **D/D/R:** Clinical Judgment **H/I/S:** Traveling, Sports, Reading **EDU:** Doctor of Pharmacy, University of the Sciences in Philadelphia: College of Pharmacy **A/A/S:** American Pharmaceutical Association; American Society of Health System Pharmacists **C/VW:** St. Jude Children's Research Hospital **B/I:** She became a pharmacist because she wanted to make a difference in the way patients receive their medication. **H/O:** She feels that being accepted into her current position has been the highlight of her career to date.

CATHERINE DIANN SAYLOR
Assistant Clinical Professor
School of Dentistry
University of Missouri, Kansas City
650 E. 25th Street
Kansas City, MO 64108 United States
cdsfg4@umkc.edu
http://www.dentistry.umkc.edu

BUS: University **P/S:** Higher Education, Dentistry Education **MA:** Local **D/D/R:** Working as Registered Dental Hygienist, Assisting the Clinical Professor **H/I/S:** Playing Sports Including Softball, Training for Triathlons **FBP:** Access; Journal of Dental Hygiene **EDU:** Pursuing Master's Degree in Education, University of Missouri, Kansas City (2008); Bachelor's Degree in Dental Hygiene, University of Missouri, Kansas City (2005) **A/A/S:** American Dental Hygienists Association; Kansas City Alumni Association, University of Missouri; Sigma Phi Alpha; Junior League of Kansas City, Missouri **A/H:** Clinical Instructor of the Year (2006); Student of the Year (2005) **A/S:** She attributes her success to her desire to teach others and passion for education. **B/I:** She became involved in her profession because she wanted to teach and enjoys working in the dental-medical environment. **H/O:** The highlight of her career was being named the Student of the Year in 2005.

ANTONIA ERNA SCANTERBURY
Senior Staff Nurse
Maimonides Medical Center
4802 10th Avenue
Brooklyn, NY 11219 United States
lady-tonia@hotmail.com
http://www.cambridgewhoswho.com

BUS: Medical Healthcare Center **P/S:** Serving Community with the Best Healthcare, Cardiac Institute, Religion **MA:** Regional **D/D/R:** Utilizing Expertise in Medical-Surgical Nursing, Specializing in Pastoral Care **H/I/S:** Traveling, Listening to Music, Reading, Playing Sports with her Son **FBP:** Newsweek **EDU:** Registered Nurse; Associate Degree in Nursing, School of Nursing, Trinidad and Tobago; Bachelor of Science in Health Administration, St. Joseph's College **CERTS:** Ordained Elder, Westminster Presbyterian Church; Medical-Surgical Nurse Certification, American Nurses Credentialing Center **A/A/S:** Polk Education Association; Republican Senatorial Inner Circle; Vice President, University of Women, State of Maryland **A/H:** Woman of the Year (2001); Distinguished Graduate Award, Delta Gamma Sigma Honor Society (2006); Key to the City for Volunteerism, Lakeland, Florida **C/VW:** Church; President, Parent Teacher Fellowship; Head of Nurses, Mission **A/S:** She attributes her success to her faith in God, her hard work and diligence. **B/I:** She became involved in her profession because she has a love and compassion to help others.

GWEN K. SCHAAR
Practice Administrator
Barrington Obstetrics and Gynecology Associates, Ltd.
27790 W. IL Route 22
Suite 32
Barrington, IL 60010 United States
gwenkschaar@aol.com
http://www.barringtonobgyn.com

BUS: Private Obstetrics and Gynecology Practice **P/S:** Pelvic Examinations, Fertility Testing and Treatment, Contraception Counseling, Menopause Therapy, Breast Disease Screening and Mammography, Abnormal Pap Smear Evaluation, Second Opinions and Consultations, Normal and High-Risk Obstetrics, Vaginal Birth after Cesarean Section, Amniocentesis, In-Office Ultrasound **MA:** Regional **D/D/R:** Overseeing Two Practice Locations, Administrating Staff, Finance, Coding, Billing, Ensuring HIPAA Compliance **H/I/S:** Sewing, Reading, Crocheting **FBP:** The Journal of Medical Practice Management **CERTS:** Pursuing Medicare and Public Aid Specialist Certification, ISME; Certified Coding Specialist, PHACom (2005); Certified in Practice Administration, Medical Management Institute (2004) **A/A/S:** Medical Management Institute; Former Emergency Medical Technician **C/A:** Establishing a Practice for Practice Administrators

MR. STEPHEN M. SCHAEFFER
Director
Ethree Center
216 W. Somerset Street
Philadelphia, PA 19133 United States
daphantom@earthlink.net
http://www.congreso.net

BUS: Nonprofit **P/S:** Youth Development **MA:** Philadelphia **D/D/R:** Specializing in Urban Education **H/I/S:** Spending Time with the Family, Golfing, Playing Tennis **FBP:** Youth Today **EDU:** Master's Degree in International Peace and Conflict Resolution, Arcadia University; Bachelor's Degree in Film Making, C.W. Post Long Island University **A/S:** He attributes his success to the support from the organization and being able to think outside the box while meeting the needs of the children and being creative. **H/O:** The highlight of his career is the first time he was recognized for Who's Who Among American Teachers.

RUTH M. SCHAFER
Family and Consumer Science Educator
Family and Consumer Science Department
Wisconsin Heights School District
10173 US Highway 14
Mazomanie, WI 53560 United States
rschafer@wisheights.k12.wi.us
http://www.wisheights.k12.wi.us

BUS: School District **P/S:** Education Including Curriculum for Middle and High School Students **MA:** Regional **D/D/R:** Teaching Economics, Family Care and Consumer Education to Sixth through Eighth-Grade Students Including Food Preparation Techniques, Overseeing Child Development Classes **H/I/S:** Sewing, Reading **FBP:** Teaching Today **EDU:** Bachelor of Science in Home Economics and Science Education, University of Wisconsin (1992); Bachelor of Science in Clothing Textile Design Industry, University of Wisconsin (1981); Bachelor of Science in Fashion Merchandising, University of Wisconsin (1981) **CERTS:** Certified Food Manager; Certified Driver's Education Teacher **A/A/S:** Wisconsin Family and Consumer Educators; American Association of Family and Consumer Sciences **A/H:** Nominee, Kohl's Teacher Award (2003); Outstanding Employee, Sears; Outstanding Employee, Shoney's Restaurant; Outstanding Employee, Holiday Inn; Outstanding Employee, Phar-Mor **C/VW:** Evangelical Lutheran Church in America **DOB:** December 10, 1958 **POB:** Eau Claire, WI **SP:** Bruce **CHILD:** Christopher **W/H:** Teacher, Fall Creek School District; Teacher, North High School, Eau Claire School District; Teacher, Red Wing High School, Red Wing, MN; Teacher, Appleton School District, Appleton, WI; Teacher, Loyal School District, Loyal, WI; Teacher, Wisconsin Heights School District, Mazomanic, WI **A/S:** She attributes her success to her work experience. **B/I:** She became involved in her profession through a natural progression of opportunities. **H/O:** The most gratifying aspect of her career is receiving gratitude from her students' parents.

SARAH K. SCHARF, MS, CCC-SLP
Speech-Language Pathologist
University Settlement
184 Eldridge Street
New York, NY 10002 United States
scharfnfish@att.net
http://www.universitysettlement.org

BUS: Nonprofit Organization **P/S:** Mental Health Services, Conducting Youth Programs and Community Programs, Early Childhood Education **MA:** Local **D/D/R:** Caring for Babies and Working with Adults **H/I/S:** Reading, Traveling **EDU:** Master of Science in Speech-Language Pathology, University of Nebraska, Lincoln **A/A/S:** American Speech-Language-Hearing Association; Nebraska Speech-Language-Hearing Association; New York State Speech-Language-Hearing Association **C/VW:** Animal Rescue **A/S:** She attributes her success to her passion for her profession. **H/O:** The most gratifying aspect of her career is making a difference in people's lives.

Dr. Stephanie A. Schatzle-Sprague

Pharm.D.
Pharmacy
Winn Dixie 1461
8601 Siegen Lane
Baton Rouge, LA 70810 United States
drsaschat@cox.net
http://www.cambridgewhoswho.com

BUS: Pharmaceutical Company **P/S:** Pharmaceuticals **MA:** National **D/D/R:** Selling Pharmaceutical Products, Overseeing All Functions of Company **H/I/S:** Gardening, Spending Time with her Family **FBP:** Drug Topics; Industry-Related Publications **EDU:** Doctor of Pharmacy, Xavier University **C/VW:** The National Arbor Day Foundation; Most Blessed Sacrament Catholic Church; St. Jude Children's Research Hospital **POB:** LA **SP:** Bret **CHILD:** Sean, Andy, Hannah, Ritchie, Stephen, Katie, Carolyn **W/H:** Retail Management, Hospital Management **A/S:** She attributes her success to her faith in God. **B/I:** She became involved in her profession through a natural progression of opportunities. **H/O:** The most gratifying aspect of her career is meeting and helping people.

Mrs. Laura S. Schaumberg, PAHM

Senior Consultant
FlexTech, Inc.
445 Butternut Drive
Holland, MI 49424 United States
lschaumberg@flextech.com
http://www.flextech.com

BUS: IT Consulting Firm Dedicated to Supporting the Business and Technical Requirements of Managed Care Organizations **P/S:** Systems Implementation, Consulting, Offers a Full Spectrum of Managed Care Information System Support Services Including Implementation, Integration, and Customization **MA:** International **D/D/R:** Business to Systems and Integration Configuration, Medicare and Medicaid Payer Requirements, Health Insurance Payer Business Best Practices, Clinical Editing Best Practices, Document Business Requirements, Develop Technical Specifications for Client-Specific Software Enhancements **H/I/S:** Scuba Diving, Kenpo Karate **FBP:** Journal of Health Affairs **EDU:** Master of Arts in Public Administration from the University of Missouri, Kansas City; Bachelor of Science in Biology with Minor in Chemistry from the University of Missouri, Kansas City **CERTS:** Missouri Licensed EMT, Basic **A/A/S:** NAFE **W/H:** FlexTech, Inc. (2004-Present); Axiom-Systems, Inc (2001-2004); Blue Cross, Blue Shield of Kansas City (1997-2001); Children's Mercy Hospital (1995-1997); Gold Cross Ambulance, AMR (1994-1995)

THERESA A. SCHEKIRKE
President, Chief Executive Officer
Ferrel Capital
444 W. 47th Street
Kansas City, MO 64112 United States
tas@ferrellcapinc.com
http://www.ferrellcapinc.com

BUS: Financial **P/S:** Energy Banking, Real Estate **MA:** Diversified Holding Company **D/D/R:** Managing Active and Passive Portfolios **FBP:** The Wall Street Journal **EDU:** Bachelor's Degree Plus 30 in Geography, University of Nebraska; Post Graduate Coursework in Finance **CERTS:** Certified Bank Manager **A/A/S:** Chairwoman of the Board, Kearney Commercial Bank; ImmediaDent, LLC; Board Member, College of Saint Benedict, Business School **C/VW:** Board Member, Midwest Ear Institute **A/S:** She attributes her success to her internal motivation and hard work. **H/O:** The highlight of her career is obtaining her current position and being able to make a significant difference.

CARMEN L. SCHERUBEL, SRES
Realtor
ERA J. Tidwell & Associates
4468 Phelan Road
Phelan, CA 92371 United States
realtor.carmen@yahoo.com
http://www.highsedert-homes-land.com

BUS: Real Estate Company **P/S:** Professional Real Estate Services for the Sale of Land, Residential Homes, Commercial Properties and Investments **MA:** Statewide **D/D/R:** Representing Sellers for Residential, Land and Investments **H/I/S:** Flying Gliders, Volunteer Work **FBP:** Realtor; Broker Agent News **CERTS:** Real Estate License, State of California; Seniors Real Estate Specialist; Accredited Land Consultant Candidate **A/A/S:** Phelan Chamber of Commerce; Pinon Hills Chamber of Commerce; National Association of Realtors; California Association of Realtors; Victor Valley Association of Realtors; Realtors Land Institute; Greater Antelope Valley Association of Realtors **A/H:** Top 5 Percent of Local Real Estate Board **C/VW:** Friends of the Library Serrano Branch; Muscular Dystrophy Association; Susan G. Komen Breast Cancer Foundation; Fraternal Order of Police **A/S:** She attributes her success to her perseverance and continuing education. **B/I:** She became involved in her profession because she was referred into real estate by a friend and once she was in, loved it. **H/O:** The highlight of her career was being known and recognized in the community.

LINDA Y. SCHILLER
Clinical Professor, Psychotherapist
Boston University School of Social Work
98 Channing Road
Watertown, MA 02472 United States
schiller-robins@rcn.com
http://www.lindayaelschiller.com

BUS: University **P/S:** Higher Education **MA:** Regional **D/D/R:** Developing New Theories that Apply the Relational Model of Psychological Development to Group Work, Energy Medicine, Trauma Therapy and Dreamwork **H/I/S:** Gardening, Hiking, Practicing Yoga **FBP:** The Networker **EDU:** Master of Social Work **CERTS:** Certified Hypnotherapist; EMOR Certified Professional **A/A/S:** Association for the Advancement of Social Work with Groups; National Association of Social Workers; International Association for the Study of Dreams; New England Society for the Treatment of Trauma and Dissociation

KELLY K. SCHIRBER SAVOIA
Owner
Professional Employer Network, Inc.
7220 Trade Street
San Diego, CA 92121 United States
kelly@penpeo.com
http://www.penpeo.com

BUS: Outsourcing Company **P/S:** Flexible Payroll Schedule, Workers' Compensation Administration, Employee Earning Records, Market Placement, Direct Deposits, Administration of Monthly, Quarterly, Annual, and Final Audits, Garnishments, Certificate Requests and Processing, Claims Management, Human Resources Services, Loss Run Requests, New Hire Reporting Service, All Carrier Correspondence, Check Signing, Federal and State Monthly and Quarterly Filings, Annual Returns, Tax Services, Internet Timesheets and Reports and Employee Online Access **MA:** National **EXP:** Ms. Savoia's expertise is in insurance services. **H/I/S:** Spending Time with her Children **FBP:** Insurance Journal **EDU:** Coursework in Interior Design, Interior Designers Institute **A/A/S:** San Diego Christian Worship Center **A/S:** She attributes her success to her hard work, dedication and her faith in God. **B/I:** She became involved in her profession because she was inspired by her husband who owned a retail insurance company. **H/O:** The most gratifying aspect of her career is watching her company expand.

CATHY S. SCHLUP
Licensed Practical Nurse
Oxford Healthcare
1701 W. 26th Street
Sapling, MO 64803 United States
cathysue58@yahoo.com
http://www.cambridgewhoswho.com

BUS: Healthcare **MA:** Regional **D/D/R:** Geriatric and Pediatric Nursing **H/I/S:** Surfing the Internet **CERTS:** Licensed Practical Nurse, Nevada Vocational Technical **A/S:** She attributes her success to learning something new everyday. **B/I:** She chose the profession because she has always wanted to be a nurse. **H/O:** The highlight of her career is her current position.

VICKIE ANN SCHMERSAHL
Multifunctional Facilities Maintenance Supervisor, Electrical
Supervisor
Lockeed Martin Corporation
13800 Old Gentilly Boulevard
New Orleans, LA 70129 United States
vicki.a.schmersahl@lmco.com
http://www.lmco.com

BUS: One of the World's Largest Aerospace and Aviation Organizations **P/S:** Aeronautics, Air Mobility Support, Aircraft and Logistics Centers, Center For Innovation, Corporate Headquarters, Enterprise Information Systems, Finance Corporation, Information Technology, Integrated Systems and Solutions, Knolls Atomic Power Laboratory, Missiles and Fire Control, MS2, Sandia National Laboratory, Simulation, Training and Support, Space Operations, Space Systems Company, Systems Integration, Owego, Systems Management, Technical Operations, Technology Ventures, Transportation and Security Solutions **MA:** International **D/D/R:** Supervising more than 16 Maintenance Electricians, Carpenters, Painters, Sheet Metal, and Different Crews, Weekly Safety Meetings **H/I/S:** Tennis **FBP:** Plant Engineering **EDU:** Pursuing Bachelor's Degree in Business Administration, Touro University; Electronics Coursework **A/A/S:** National Space Society; National Association of Female Executives **C/VW:** Rebuilding after Katrina

MRS. DEBRA M. SCHMIDT, RN, BSN
1) Public Health Nurse 2) Health Promotion and Wellness Specialist
1) Ozaukee County Public Health Department 2) Aurora Healthcare
121 W. Main Street
Port Washington, WI 53074 United States
dschmidt@co.ozaukee.wi.us
http://www.co.ozaukee.wi.us/PublicHealth

BUS: Healthcare **P/S:** 1) Public Health Nursing 2) Total Health and Wellness Health Screening Professional **MA:** Local **D/D/R:** Working with Maternal/Child Health, Immunizations, Communicable Disease, Adult Health Screenings, Emergency Preparedness, Working with Aurora Health Care, Health Risk Assessments, Preventive Health and Wellness Instruction, Employee Presentations, Health Coaching **H/I/S:** Walking, Making Jewelry, Crafts, Reading, Volunteering at Church, Activities within the Parish Youth Center, Cooking, Baking, Spending Time with Family and Friends **FBP:** Nursing2009; Today's Christian Woman **EDU:** Bachelor of Science in Nursing, University of Wisconsin-Oshkosh (1983) **A/A/S:** Sigma Theta Tau National Honor Society of Nursing, Eta Pi Chapter; University of Wisconsin-Oshkosh College of Nursing Honor Society; Wisconsin Association for Perinatal Care Nutrition Committee, Infant and Family Committee; Wisconsin Oral Health Coalition; March of Dimes Education Committee **DOB:** February 2, 1961 **SP:** James **CHILD:** Jennifer, John, Joseph **W/H:** Aurora Health Care (2006-Present); Ozaukee County Public Health Department (1987-Present); St. Alphonsus Hospital, Port Washington, WI (1983-1987)

LYNELLE L. SCHMIDT
Senior Retail Auditor
Jo-Ann Fabric and Craft Stores
5555 Darrow Road
Hudson, OH 44236 United States
lynells@cox.net
http://www.jo-annstores.com

BUS: Retailer **P/S:** Fabric and Craft Necessities **MA:** National **D/D/R:** Asset Protection, Assisting Operational Controls, Inventory Observation, Employee Training **H/I/S:** Hiking **FBP:** Internal Auditor **EDU:** Associate Degree in Marketing and Retail, Waukesha County Technical College **A/S:** She attributes her success to being motivated and learning through experience and education to achieve her goals. **B/I:** She became involved in her profession through a natural progression of opportunities. **H/O:** The highlight of her career was being promoted to senior retail auditor.

KRISTIN MICHELLE SCHNEIDER
Computer Teacher
East Buchanan
100 Smith Street
Gower, MO 64452 United States
Flutebud@aol.com
http://www.cambridgewhoswho.com

BUS: Education **P/S:** Children from Low Income Families **MA:** Local **D/D/R:** Specializing in Early Childhood Education and Computer Education **H/I/S:** Playing the Piano and Flute, Writing Poetry **EDU:** Bachelor of Science in Early Childhood Education and Elementary Education, Central Missouri State University **A/A/S:** Missouri State Teacher Association; International Reading Association **A/S:** She attributes her success to having very powerful teachers, her family, educational and staff support. **H/O:** The highlight of her career has been being hired for the job at Neely because the area is very competitive.

JOELLE J. SCHNIRCH
Case Manager, Registered Nurse
Spectrum Home Health
2915 Strong Avenue
Kansas City, KS 66106 United States
r_schnirch@yahoo.com
http://www.cambridgewhoswho.com

BUS: Private Facility Dedicated to Excellence in Home Health Care **P/S:** Nursing Care, Infusion, Diabetic Care, Wound Care with ET Specialist, Physical Therapy, Occupational Therapy, Speech Therapy, Social Work Services as well as Home Health Aide Services **MA:** Regional **D/D/R:** Nursing Cardiac and Respiratory Patients at Home, Internal Training **H/I/S:** Scrapbooking, Spending Time with the Family and her Two Sons **FBP:** Nursing News **EDU:** Associate Degree in Nursing, Kansas City Community College (1979); Associate Degree in Nursing, Donnelly College (1977) **A/H:** Outstanding Associate Award, Kansas City Regional Home Care Association (2005)

TRICIA SCHOENKE
Inventory Control Manager
Air Liquide Electronics U.S. LP
13546 N. Central Expressway
Dallas, TX 75243 United States
tricia.schoenke@airliquide.com
http://www.us.airliquide.com

BUS: Distribution Firm **P/S:** Production and Supply of All Industrial Products, Electronics, Healthcare Gases and Chemicals Including Ultra Pure Gases, Liquids and Advanced Molecules Used in the Fabrication of Silicon Chips for Semiconductor Manufacturing, State-of-the-Art Analytical and Laboratory Services **MA:** International **EXP:** Ms. Schoenke's expertise is in quality control and inventory management of chemicals and gases. **D/D/R:** Publishing Technical and Internal Papers **H/I/S:** Making Crafts, Playing Softball and Volleyball, Sewing **EDU:** Bachelor of Science in Chemistry, University of Houston (1978) **A/A/S:** Association for Operations Management; The American Chemical Society **C/VW:** Still Creek Ranch **I/F/Y:** In five years, Ms. Schoenke hopes to become a director of electronics division or any other division within the company.

MR. PAUL SCHOMAKER
Manager of Production Systems
ChoicePoint Public Records Group
3540 Conference Way S.
Boca Raton, FL 33431 United States
paul.schomaker@choicepointprg.net
http://www.choicepoint.com

BUS: Proprietary Public Record Database **P/S:** Decision-Making Intelligence to Businesses and Government through the Identification, Retrieval, Storage, Analysis and Delivery of Data **MA:** National **D/D/R:** Specializing in Development, Programming and Troubleshooting **H/I/S:** Watching Hockey **EDU:** Bachelor of Science in Computer Science, Indiana University (1982) **A/A/S:** PAL

LYNETTE R. SCHOONOEVER, RN, BSN
Department Manager
East Houston Regional Medical Center
1311 East Freeway
Houston, TX 77015 United States
lynette.schoonover@hcahealthcare.com
http://www.cambridgewhoswho.com

BUS: Healthcare **P/S:** Full Range of Services **MA:** Regional **D/D/R:** Medical-Surgical, Management and Administration of Post-Op Surgery Department **H/I/S:** Gardening **FBP:** RN Magazine; Nursing2009; American Journal of Nursing **EDU:** Bachelor of Science in Nursing, University of Texas Medical Branch; ADN, Lee College **A/A/S:** American Medical Surgical Nurses Association; Academy of Medical-Surgical Nurses **C/VW:** American Cancer Society **A/S:** She attributes her success to hard work and integrity. **H/O:** The highlight of her career is seeing patients get well and go home.

RHONDA G. SCHREIBER
Phlebotomist
Saint Alexius Medical Center
1555 Barrington Road
Hoffman Estates, IL 60194 United States
rhondaschre@aol.com
http://www.cambridgewhoswho.com

BUS: Healthcare Provider **P/S:** Laboratory Services **MA:** Regional **D/D/R:** Overseeing Laboratory Productions **H/I/S:** Boating **FBP:** AJCP **EDU:** Master's Degree in Phlebotomy, Elgin Community College; Bachelor's Degree, Bryman College; Medical Assistant Diploma, Bryman College **A/A/S:** American Society of Clinical Pathologists **A/S:** She attributes her success to her understanding husband. **B/I:** She became involved in the profession because she enjoys helping others. **H/O:** The most gratifying aspect of her career is being able to put people at ease.

MRS. LINDA J. SCHROEDER

President, Owner
Document Direct Services, Inc.
2838 Rice Road
Joshua Tree, CA 92252 United States
ddirectservices@aol.com
http://www.cambridgewhoswho.com

BUS: Marketing and Venture Capital Firm **P/S:** Plasma Waste Converters for the Conversion of Waste Materials Marketing, Raising Venture Capital for Initial Public Offerings, Brokering Business Ventures **MA:** International **D/D/R:** Marketing, Maintaining Customer Relationships, Overseeing Business Operations **H/I/S:** Horseback Riding, Participating in Aquatic and Boating Activities, Racing Sports Cars **FBP:** The Wall Street Journal; The New York Times; Los Angeles Times; Animal-Related Publications **EDU:** Diploma, Royal Oak High School (1972) **A/A/S:** Back Country Horsemen of America; Ethical Trading Initiative; Corvette Club of America **C/VW:** Horse Rescue Foundations; Local Charitable Organizations; International Charitable Organizations **DOB:** January 13, 1954 **POB:** Los Angeles, CA **SP:** Ronald (Deceased) **A/S:** She attributes her success to her determination, work ethic, upbringing, common sense and to her ability to treat others in a way she wanted to be treated. **B/I:** She became involved in her profession after the death of her husband who was a venture capitalist. **H/O:** The most gratifying aspect of her career is the varied and wonderful individuals she has met along her career path. **I/F/Y:** In five years, Mrs. Schroeder aspires to have a center for abused children and battered women.

MARY CATHERINE SCHUELKE, MT, ASCP

Medical Technologist
Clinton Hospital
201 Highland Street
Clinton, MA 01510 United States
barginbasement54@yahoo.com
http://www.cambridgewhoswho.com

BUS: Hospital **P/S:** Healthcare **MA:** Local **D/D/R:** Running the Laboratory **H/I/S:** Gardening, Volunteering **FBP:** Industry-Related Publications **EDU:** Bachelor's Degree in Medical Technology, Michigan State University, MI; Associate Degree in Medical Laboratory Technology, Midwestern State University, TX **CERTS:** Certified Medical Technologist, American Society of Clinical Pathologists; Certified Medical Technologist, American Medical Technologists **A/A/S:** American Society of Clinical Pathologists **A/H:** Air Force Accommodation Medal of Honor (1981) **C/VW:** Volunteer, Massachusetts Organization for Addiction Recovery; Volunteer, New England SERVE **A/S:** She attributes her success to support from her family. **B/I:** She became involved in this profession because she used to work in the military. **H/O:** The most gratifying aspect of her career is seeing her patients get well and go home.

EVERETT D. SCHULTZ
Executive Vice President of General Services
Metro One Telecommunications, Inc.
11200 S.W. Murray Scholls Place
Beaverton, OR 97007 United States
everett@arschccb.com
http://www.cambridgewhoswho.com

MetroOne

BUS: Telecommunication Company **P/S:** Telecommunication and Business Process Outsourcing Services **MA:** National **EXP:** Mr. Schultz' expertise is in asset and warehouse management, construction, designing and building infrastructure, records management and overseeing logistics and trade shows. **H/I/S:** Hunting, Fishing, Boating, ATVing, Youth Sports Mentoring **FBP:** BusinessWeek **EDU:** Pursuing Coursework, University of Phoenix; Associate Degree in Accounting and Business Administration, Portland Community College **CERTS:** Certification in Professional Skills Training and Management **A/A/S:** Construction Contractors Board; Wilderness Unlimited; Rocky Mountain Elk Foundation; Madison Who's Who; International Facility Management Association **DOB:** January 23, 1961 **SP:** Mary Lou **CHILD:** Tyler, Travis **W/H:** Owner, Contractor, ARSCH Consulting and Construction Business (1999-2006); Assistant Vice President, General Services (1998-2006); Director, General Services (1993-1998); Controller, Metro One Hello Pages and Metro One Telecommunications (1991-1993); Credit and Collections, AVIA; Accounts Receivable and General Ledger Manager, LaCie Ltd (1989-1991); Foreman, Galvinizers Steel, Portland (1981-1989); Manager, Nuedlmens Formal Wear (1979-1981); Busboy and Host, Stuart Anderson's Cattle Company (1976-1981)

KRISTEN L. SCHULZE
Managing Chef
Eurest Dining Services, Compass Group
16211 La Cantara Parkway
San Antonio, TX 78256 United States
kristen.schulze@compass-usa.com
http://www.cgnad.com

BUS: Restaurant **P/S:** High Quality Food Service **MA:** Regional **D/D/R:** Marketing, Training, Development, Overseeing Day-To-Day Operations **H/I/S:** Organic Gardening, Knitting **FBP:** Entrepreneur **EDU:** Bachelor's Degree in Hospitality Management, University of Houston **C/VW:** Food Bank; The Leukemia & Lymphoma Society

TERESA A. SCHWALLER
Registered Nurse, Assisted Living Coordinator
Holy Spirit Retirement Home
1701 W. 25th Street
Sioux City, IA 51103 United States
tschwaller@iw.net
http://www.cambridgewhoswho.com

BUS: Senior Living Community **P/S:** Assisted Living and Skilled Nursing Services Including Residential Long-Term and Medical Therapy **MA:** Local **D/D/R:** Managing 35 Residents, Prescribing Medications, Handling Purchase Orders, Caring for Patients, Assisting the Social Worker in Assessing Consumers, Hiring, Overseeing Staff Discipline and Dementia Specific Unit **H/I/S:** Reading, Cooking, Gardening, Sports, Spending Time Outdoors **FBP:** RN Magazine **EDU:** Bachelor's Degree in Nursing, Western Iowa Tech Community College (1999); Associate Degree in Nursing, Western Iowa Tech Community College (1984); Registered Nurse **A/A/S:** Iowa Center for Assisted Living; National Center for Assisted Living **DOB:** March 31, 1959

PROF. LIA SCHWARTZ
Distinguished Professor, Executive Officer
The Graduate Center
365 Fifth Avenue
New York, NY 10016 United States
lschwartz@gc.cuny.edu
http://www.gc.cuny.edu

BUS: Educational Institution **P/S:** High Quality Educational Services to Students as well as Offering Over 30 Doctoral Programs and Six Master's Programs in the Humanities, Social Sciences and Sciences **MA:** International **D/D/R:** Teaching Spanish and Comparative Literature, Overseeing the Ph.D. Program **H/I/S:** Listening to Music, Ballet Dancing **FBP:** New Literacy History; New York Review Book; The Inquirer **EDU:** Ph.D., University of Illinois (1971) **A/A/S:** Modern Language Association; International Association of Hispanists

LAURA SCHWEITZER-TOBOLASKI
Vice President
Argo Summit Supply Company
5539 S. Archer Road
Summit, IL 60501 United States
laura@argosummitsupply.com
http://www.argosummitsupply.com

BUS: Plumbing and HVAC Wholesaler **P/S:** Faucets, Fixtures, Valves and Radiant Heat **MA:** Regional **D/D/R:** Overseeing Company Operations, Employee Training, Managing Sales Team **H/I/S:** Gardening, Knitting, Playing with her Children **FBP:** ASA **EDU:** Bachelor of Science in Biology, Northern Illinois University; Bachelor of Science in Anatomy and Physiology, Andrews University; Master of Science in Physical Therapy, Andrews University; Various Continuing Education Classes **CERTS:** Certificate in Business Management, Turner Construction **C/VW:** P.E.O. **A/S:** She attributes her personal and professional success to her hard work and determination.

CHRISTINE A. SCOTT
Escrow Officer
Stewart Title of Missoula County, Inc.
320 W. Broadway Street
Missoula, MT 59802 United States
christine@stewartmt.com
http://www.stewartmt.com

BUS: Real Estate Services **P/S:** Buying and Selling of Properties, Title Insurance, Escrows **MA:** National **D/D/R:** Closings, Buying and Refinancing Homes, Overseeing All Paperwork Processing, In-Depth Knowledge of Residential and Commercial Properties, Customer Service **H/I/S:** Horseback Riding, Caring for her Quarter Horses, Reading People Magazine **EDU:** High School Education; Industry-Related Experience

HEATHER L. SCOTT
Human Resource Manager
1020 Commanders Way N.
Annapolis, MD 21409 United States
heatherlscott73@comcast.net
http://www.cambridgewhoswho.com

D/D/R: Coordinating Benefit Programs, Managing Human Resource Department, Budgeting, Policy Writing and Employee Issues **H/I/S:** Watching Movies, Playing Football, Spending Time with her Family and Friends, Caring for her Dog **FBP:** HR **EDU:** Master's Degree in Human Resources and Management, Webster University (1998); Bachelor of Arts in English, University of South Carolina (1995) **A/A/S:** Society for Human Resource Management; Anne Arundel Society for Human Resource Management **CHILD:** Bella **A/S:** She attributes her success to her determination, self-motivation and to the support she receives from her family. **H/O:** The most gratifying aspect of her career is being able to interact with her employees.

LINDA A. SCOTT
Supervising Coordinator of the Blood Conservation Program
Geisinger Medical Center
100 N. Academy Avenue
Danville, PA 17822 United States
lscott@geisinger.edu
http://www.cambridgewhoswho.com

BUS: Medical Center **P/S:** Healthcare **MA:** Regional **EXP:** Ms. Scott's expertise is in blood conservation. **D/D/R:** Interacting with Physicians in Reviewing Laboratory Values and Placing Recommendations for Anemia Management **H/I/S:** Reading, Crocheting, Gardening, Camping, Traveling **FBP:** RN **EDU:** Diploma in Nursing, The Reading Hospital School of Nursing, PA **A/A/S:** Society for the Advancement of Blood Management **C/VW:** National Multiple Sclerosis Society **DOB:** November 20, 1949 **POB:** Shamokin, PA **SP:** Walter **CHILD:** Dawn, Amber, Kristin **C/A:** Developed and Implemented a Blood Conservation Program **A/S:** She attributes her success to her dedication and the support she receives from her family. **B/I:** She became involved in her profession because of her desire to care for others. **H/O:** The most gratifying aspect of her career is watching blood conservation programs develop and gain national attention in the medical field. **I/F/Y:** In five years, Ms. Scott would like to retire speak about blood conservation at conferences.

SHONNIE B. SCOTT
Teacher
Wasatch Elementary School
30 R Street
Salt Lake City, UT 84103 United States
scott@chapman.com
http://www.wasatch.slc.k12.ut.us

BUS: Caring and Innovative Elementary School Educational Environment **P/S:** Coursework to Engage Students' Intellect, Build Self-Confidence, Inspire Students to Develop their Creative Voice in Drama, Dance, Music, and Visual Arts and Encourage Them to Positively Impact the Communities in which They Live **MA:** Regional **D/D/R:** Teaching Kindergarten, Helping Refugee Children from Africa, Asia and the Middle East to Receive an Education through Music, Organizing Medical and Welfare Assistance **H/I/S:** Hiking, Tennis, Reading **EDU:** Master's Degree in Education; Bachelor of Science in Elementary Education, Brigham Young University (1971); Coursework in Child Development and Social Work Studies **A/A/S:** National Education Association; Utah Education Association; Founder, Arts Program at School (1994) **A/H:** Recipient, Teacher of the Week, KSL Radio (2005)

MR. DEBRA A. SCRANDIS, RN
Assistant Professor
University of Maryland School of Nursing
655 W. Lombard Street
Baltimore, MD 21201 United States
dscra001@son.umaryland.edu
http://www.nursing.umaryland.edu

BUS: One of the Leading Research Institutions in the Nation **P/S:** Undergraduate, Graduate and Doctoral Nursing Education **MA:** International **D/D/R:** Family Practice and Perinatal Mood Disorders **H/I/S:** Reading **EDU:** Ph.D. in Nursing, Barry University; Master of Science in Nursing, Boston College; Bachelor of Science in Nursing, Fitchburg State College **A/A/S:** American Nursing Association; American Women's Health Organization of Obstetrics and Neonatal Nursing; Southern Nursing Research Institute **C/VW:** Volunteer, Women's Health Clinic, University of Maryland

PATSY ANN SEABOLT, RN, BSN
Registered Nurse
Charleston Area Medical Center
3200 MacCorkle Avenue
Charleston, WV 25306 United States
patsy5@verizon.net
http://www.cambridgewhoswho.com

BUS: Hospital **P/S:** Healthcare Including Trauma, Cancer and Ambulatory Care **MA:** Greater Charleston Area **EXP:** Ms. Seabolt's expertise is in radiology. **H/I/S:** Sewing, Genealogy **FBP:** RN; The Wall Street Journal **EDU:** Coursework in Paralegal Studies, Marshall University; Bachelor of Science in Nursing, Mountain State University (2008); Associate Degree in Nursing, Morris Harvey College (Now University of Charleston) **C/VW:** Volunteer, Hospice Center; Creek Baptist Church, GA **CHILD:** Roberta

MS. BRENDA C. SEAY
Owner
1) Seay Truck Repair 2) Seay Transportation
2510 32nd Street
Gulfport, MS 39501 United States
seaTransportation@cableone.net
http://www.cambridgewhoswho.com

BUS: 1) Truck Repair Company 2) Transportation Company **P/S:** 1) Truck Repair 2) Transportation Services **MA:** 1) National 2) International **D/D/R:** Overseeing Business Operations **H/I/S:** Traveling, Golfing, Spending Time with her Family **FBP:** Who's Who Magazine **EDU:** High School Education **A/A/S:** Local Chamber of Commerce; Better Business Bureau **DOB:** December 19, 1950 **SP:** Bill **A/S:** She attributes her success to her hard work and work ethic. **B/I:** She became involved in her profession because she was inspired by her husband. **H/O:** The most gratifying aspect of her career is seeing the growth of her business. **I/F/Y:** In five years, Ms. Seay hopes to expand her business.

AMIR F. SEDHOM
Owner
Laria Corp dba Amir's Caterers and Laria Foods
29 Germania Street
Building H
Jamaica Plain, MA 02130 United States
amir.sedhom@cwwemail.com
http://www.cambridgewhoswho.com

BUS: Food Production Company **P/S:** Natural Food Products and Catering Services **MA:** National **EXP:** Mr. Sedhom's expertise is in ethnic cuisine. **H/I/S:** Swimming, Playing Tennis **FBP:** Industry-Related Publications **EDU:** Coursework in Accounting **C/VW:** Bible Meetings; Peace Organizations **A/S:** He attributes his success to his passion for his profession. **B/I:** He became involved in his profession because of his love for cooking. **H/O:** The highlight of his career was earning his current position.

SANDY J. SEELEY, RN
Registered Nurse, Clinical Analyst
The Methodist Hospital
6565 Fannin Street
Houston, TX 77030 United States
sjseeley@tmh.tmc.edu
http://www.methodisthealth.com

BUS: Private, Adult Teaching Hospital **P/S:** Cardiovascular Surgery, Treatment of Cancer and Epilepsy, Obstetrics and Gynecology, Nephrology and Kidney Disease, Endoscopic Surgery, Otolaryngology, Neurology and Neurosurgery, Organ Transplants, Orthopedics, and Urology **MA:** National **D/D/R:** Using the Michael De Bakey Method, Building a Support System with Hospital on Electronic Charting System, Working in Cardiovascular Surgery **H/I/S:** Enjoying NASCAR Racing, Supporting Jeff Gordon **EDU:** Associate Degree in Nursing, Kaskaskia College, Centralia, Illinois (1978) **A/A/S:** Local UHC, Patient Safety Electronic Charter **C/VW:** Habitat for Humanity; Volunteer, Local Schools, Church and Community

JOYCE M. SEIB
Workers' Compensation Claims Specialist
West Bend Mutual Insurance Company
1900 S. 18th Avenue
West Bend, WI 53095 United States
seibjoyce@yahoo.com
http://www.wbmi.com

BUS: Insurance Company **P/S:** Insurance Services Including Property and Casualty Insurance **MA:** WI, MN, IL, IA, IN and MO **D/D/R:** Overseeing Insurance Services, Handling Workers' Compensation Claims in Wisconsin and Minnesota, Investigating and Ensuring Claims are Correct, Training New Associates, Underwriting **H/I/S:** Cooking, Sewing, Reading, Exercising, Playing Tennis **EDU:** Pursuing Master of Business Administration, Mount Mary College; Bachelor's Degree in Mathematics, Northern Illinois University (1975) **CERTS:** Certified Associate in Insurance Services; Certified, Associate in Claims; Certified, Associate in Management; Certified, Workers Compensation Claim Law Associate **A/A/S:** Milwaukee Insurance Adjusters Association **A/H:** Award for Outstanding Compliance Program, Wisconsin Department of Workforce Development (2007); National Dean's List **SP:** Donald **CHILD:** Kara, Derek

GARY F. SEITZ, JD
Partner
Rawle and Henderson, LLP
300 Delaware Avenue
Suite 1015
Wilmington, DE 19899 United States
gseitz@rawle.com
http://www.rawle.com

BUS: Law Firm **P/S:** Comprehensive Legal Services to Creditors including Banks, Businesses and Corporations, Practice Areas including Commercial Bankruptcy, Corporate Litigation, Corporate Law, Partnership, Business Trust and Limited Liability Company Law, Professional Services Including Trial and Appellate Litigation in State and Federal Courts, Business Planning, Legal and Business Counsel, Maritime Transportation, Over 90 Attorneys **MA:** Regional and National **D/D/R:** Representing Clients in Commercial Bankruptcy, Admiralty and Maritime Law and Commercial Litigation, Handling Maritime and Non-Maritime Related Bankruptcy Matters for Creditors, Asset Purchasers and Trustees, Overseeing Admiralty and Maritime Litigation and Transactions with Particular Emphasis on Troubled Businesses **H/I/S:** Sailing, Hiking, Spending Quality Time with the Family **FBP:** ABI Journal; National Association of Bankruptcy Trustees Journal **EDU:** Master's Degree in Maritime Law, Tulane University (1988); JD, College of Law, University of Iowa (1986); Coursework, East China Normal University (1984); Bachelor's Degree, Buena Vista University, Magna Cum Laude (1983); Taipei Language Institute (1981) **A/A/S:** 'Fundamentals of Bankruptcy Litigation,' Continuing Legal Education Seminar, Delaware State Bar Association (2005); 'Fundamentals of Bankruptcy Litigation,' Delaware Supreme Court Bridging the Gap Seminar (2005); 'Ten Things Every Environmental Lawyer Should Know about Bankruptcy,' Continuing Legal Education Seminar, Delaware State Bar Association (2005); 'An Introduction to Bankruptcy Reorganization in America,' Taiwan-American Chamber of Commerce Conference, Taipei, Taiwan (2003); 'An Introduction to Some of the Legal Risks of Running a Nonprofit School,' Third Annual Conference, Chinese School Association of the United States, Washington D.C. (1999); 'Year 2000 and its Legal Impact on the Maritime Industry,' American Society for Testing and Materials Conference (1998); 'A Ship Owner's Right to Redemption Under Admiralty Rule E,' Admiralty Committee, Young Lawyers Division, American Bar Association (1998); Philadelphia Maritime Association; Maritime Exchange for the Delaware River and Bay; Maritime Law Association of the United States; National Association of Bankruptcy Trustees; Transportation Lawyers Association; American Bankruptcy Institute; Eastern District of Pennsylvania Bankruptcy Conference; Delaware Bankruptcy Inns of Court; Delaware State Bar Association; Iowa State Bar Association; Louisiana State Bar Association; New Jersey State Bar Association; Pennsylvania Bar Association; Washington State Bar Association; American Bar Association **W/H:** Recent Developments Reporter, International Litigation Quarterly, International Law Division, American Bar Association (1991-Present); Jackson v. Egyptian Navigation Co. (2004); In re J & L Structural (2004); In re AxisTel Communications, Inc. (2004); Fahnsestock v. Reeder (2002); In re Eagle Geophysical, Inc. (2001); In re Eagle Enterprises, Inc., and Liberty Recovery Systems, Inc. (2001); Reardon v. Hahn Yelena Corp. (2001); In re Vessel Club Med (2000); Johnson v. Chester Hous. Auth. (2000); Recent Developments Reporter, International Litigation Quarterly, International Law Section, American Bar Association (1991-1999) **C/A:** Co-author, 'Enforcing Ship Mortgages in Default,' Meeting, National Marine Banker's Association (2000); Author, 'A Bibliography of Useful Materials When Determining the Legal Ramifications of Intermodal Transportation,' Continuing Lawyers Education Program, Annual Convention, American Bar Association (1995); Co-author, 'Limit of Amount Insured,' Tort and Insurance Practice Section, American Bar Association (in Cooperation with the Maritime Law Association), United States

CAROL SELJESETH, M.ED., BS, BA
Science Teacher
Redemmer Lutheran High School
6501 N.W. 23rd
Bethany, OK 73008 United States
csejeseth@cox.net
http://www.edmond.k12.ok.us/north

BUS: High School **P/S:** Education and Curriculum, Activity Center **MA:** Regional **D/D/R:** Teaching Physics at Different High School Levels to 109 Students **H/I/S:** Reading **FBP:** Science Teacher **EDU:** Master of Education, University of Central Oklahoma (1975); Bachelor of Science in Biology and German, Minnesota State University (1965); Bachelor of Arts in German and Biology, Minnesota State University (1965) **A/A/S:** National Science Teachers Association; QuarkNet, High Energy Particle Physics **CHILD:** Chad, Malla **C/A:** Enlarged the Physics Program at Putnam City High School From Two to Seven Sections Each School Year; Built a Cosmic Ray Telescope at Quarket that can be Used in the Classroom; Founded 'Physics Day at Frontier City' for Three High Schools in Putnam City School District

FRANCES 'JOLENE' SELTZER, RN
Registered Nurse, Education Coordinator
Florida Surgical Center
3480 Hull Road
Gainesville, FL 32611 United States
seltzf@shands.ufl.edu
http://www.floridasurgerycenter.com

BUS: Healthcare Center **P/S:** Healthcare **MA:** Regional **EXP:** Ms. Seltzer's expertise is in perioperative nursing and conscious patient sedation. **D/D/R:** Coordinating Staff Education Including Development and Maintenance of Staff Competencies for High and Low Volume Professional Responsibilities, Coordinating Ambulatory Surgery Orientation and Rotations for Students in Nursing Practicum and Surgical Scrub Technical Students, Instructing Basic Life Support, Supporting the Administrative Clinical Coordinator **H/I/S:** Kayaking, Listening to Music **FBP:** AORN Journal **EDU:** Associate Degree in Nursing, Santa Fe Community College **CERTS:** Registered Nurse **A/A/S:** Association of perioperative Registered Nurses

ADRIANA M. SEMINARA
Owner
Now and Forever
477 Morris Drive
Valley Stream, NY 11580 United States
siciliane@aol.com
http://www.cambridgewhoswho.com

BUS: Invitations, Party Favors and Gifts **P/S:** Customized Invitations, Party Favors and Gifts **MA:** Local **D/D/R:** Creating Invitations and Favors **H/I/S:** Spending Time with the Family **EDU:** Bachelor of Arts in International Studies and Italian, Minor in Spanish, Long Island University, C.W Post Campus, Long Island University **A/S:** She attributes her success to her parents' support. **H/O:** The highlight of her career is the recognition she gets from her customers.

PATTY CLAUDSON SENESKI, RN
Registered Nurse
Banner Desert Medical Center
1400 S. Dobson Road
Mesa, AZ 85202 United States
patty.seneski@bannerhealth.com
http://www.cambridgewhoswho.com

BUS: Healthcare **P/S:** Healthcare **MA:** Local **D/D/R:** Training in Emergency Nursing, Forensics and Disaster Preparedness **EDU:** Diploma in Nursing, Presbyterian Medical Center **CERTS:** Certificate of Instruction in Clinical Aromatherapy, Denver, Colorado **A/A/S:** Emergency Nurses Association; Former President and Lifetime Member, International Association of Forensic Nursing **A/S:** She attributes her success to hard work. **B/I:** She became involved in the profession because she has wanted to be a nurse since she was three years old. She loves helping people. **H/O:** The highlight of her career is the quality of care she gives to her patients. They always come back to thank her for what she does for them while they are in the hospital and under her care.

JUANITA J. SENTER, LPN, CL III
Licensed Practical Nurse, CL III
Warren Memorial Hospital
1000 Shenandoah Avenue
Front Royal, VA 22630 United States
http://www.cambridgewhoswho.com

BUS: Hospital **P/S:** Healthcare **MA:** Local **D/D/R:** Working in Emergency Room Medicine, Intensive Care Unit Nursing **H/I/S:** Caring for her Neighbor **FBP:** News Now **CERTS:** Licensed Practical Nurse, Dowell J. Howard Center (1979) **C/VW:** Assembly of God Church; Former Chief Vice President, Little League; Women's Care Group; Project Homeless Connect; Family Giving **A/S:** She attributes her success to her love of people. **B/I:** She became involved in the profession because her father suffered from heart attacks and spent a lot of time in the hospital, where many of the nurses inspired her to also become a nurse. **H/O:** The most gratifying aspect of her career is when people come in and request her specifically.

TONY R. SERRANO
Loan Officer
Excellence Funding
8745 Whittier Boulevard
Second Floor
Pico Rivera, CA 90660 United States
tony@xfunding.net
http://www.tonyserrano.org

BUS: Mortgage Home Loans **P/S:** Excellent, Fast Efficient Service for People in Need of Home Loans **MA:** Local **D/D/R:** Conventional Residential Loans, Commercial Loans, Representing Borrowers **H/I/S:** Producing Music, Traveling **FBP:** The Wall Street Journal **EDU:** Associate of Arts in Business Administration, Cerritos College **A/A/S:** National Board of Realtors; California Board of Realtors; Montebello District Board of Realtors; National Association for Hispanic Real Estate Professionals **C/VW:** Calvary Chapel, Bienvenidos Youth Group Program **A/S:** He attributes his personal and professional success to his hard work and ability to provide quality service. **B/I:** He became involved in the profession because he was inspired by his mother. **H/O:** The highlight of his career was helping a single mother qualify for a loan.

DR. SANGEETA SETHI
Pediatric Dentist
Greenwich Sethi Dental
5 Edgewood Avenue
Greenwich, CT 06831 United States
Cavityfreebabi@yahoo.com
http://www.cambridgewhoswho.com

BUS: Healthcare **P/S:** Comprehensive Oral Care **MA:** Local **D/D/R:** Orthodontic Care, All Phases of Pediatric Dentistry **H/I/S:** Writing Poetry, Painting, Reading **EDU:** Doctor of Dental Surgery, New York University **A/A/S:** American Dental Association; Indian Dental Association **C/VW:** Hospital **A/S:** She attributes her success to determination and her love of working with children. **B/I:** She became involved in her profession because her father was a dentist.

CAROLYN A. SEVARIO
Teacher
Doyle Elementary School
Livingston Parish School Board
13909 Florida Boulevard
Livingston, LA 70754 United States
asevario@bellsouth.net
http://www.lpsb.org

BUS: Elementary School **P/S:** Primary Education **MA:** Regional **EXP:** Ms. Sevario's areas of expertise include general and special education, and total inclusion. **H/I/S:** Arts, Playing the Piano, Making Crafts, Gardening, Horseback Riding **FBP:** Educational Technology Journals **EDU:** Bachelor's Degree in Elementary Education, Belhaven College (1985) **A/H:** Dean's List, Belhaven College **C/VW:** Friendship United Methodist Church

KATHLEEN S. SEVERANCE
English Teacher
Canon City Middle School
1215 Main Street
Canon City, CO 81212 United States
severak@ris.net
http://www.canoncityschools.org

BUS: Middle School **P/S:** Education **MA:** Canon City **D/D/R:** Teaching English, Grammar and Literature **H/I/S:** Traveling, Reading, Attending her Son's Tennis Matches and Soccer Games **EDU:** Master's Degree in Reading, University of Northern Colorado; Bachelor's Degree in Secondary Education and Speech, Minor in English, University of Northern Colorado **A/A/S:** National Education Association; Colorado Education Association; American Association of University Women; International Reading Association **C/VW:** Leukemia & Lymphoma Society; The American Cancer Society **SP:** George **CHILD:** Charlie, Alex

JERRI A. SEWELL, RDH
Registered Dental Hygienist
jjts03@cox.net
http://www.cambridgewhoswho.com

BUS: Dentistry **P/S:** Dental Hygiene **MA:** Local **D/D/R:** Assisting Patients with Dental Hygiene **H/I/S:** Spending Time with the Family **FBP:** Journal of Dental Hygiene **EDU:** Associate Degree in Dental Hygiene, Amarillo College **C/VW:** Church **A/S:** She attributes her success to her enjoyment in helping others. **B/I:** She became involved in her profession because she wanted to help others. **H/O:** The most gratifying aspect of her career is seeing people smile after she helps them.

BEVERLEY A. SEYMOUR
Building Manager
Dale Poe Real Estate Company
5706 Corsa Avenue
Suite 200
Westlake Village, CA 91362 United States
mikenbev1@msn.com
http://www.cambridgewhoswho.com

BUS: Real Estate Company **P/S:** Real Estate Exchange **MA:** Local **D/D/R:** Overseeing Building Construction Works **H/I/S:** Exercising **EDU:** High School Diploma **C/VW:** Dare to Dream Foundation; Local Schools; Local Church; Celebrate Recovery Program, Calvary Community Church **A/S:** She attributes her success to her love for her profession. **B/I:** She became involved in her profession because she had a passion for meeting and helping people. **H/O:** The most gratifying aspect of her career is being able to provide a quality customer service.

SHIDEH AZITA SHADFAR, PHARM.D.
Clinical and Staff Pharmacist
Orlando Regional Medical Center
1414 Kuhl Avenue
Orlando, FL 32806 United States
s1_shadfar@hotmail.com
http://www.cambridgewhoswho.com

BUS: Level 1 Trauma Center and Teaching Hospital **P/S:** Healthcare **MA:** Regional **D/D/R:** Working in the Pharmacy **H/I/S:** Tennis, Latin Dancing, Swimming **EDU:** Doctor of Pharmacy, University of Minnesota; PGY-1 Pharmacy Residency, Mayo Clinic; Bachelor of Science in Pharmacology, University of Alberta **A/A/S:** American Journal of Health-System Pharmacy; American Society of Health-System Pharmacists; American Pharmaceutical Association; Alumni, Mayo School of Health Sciences; Florida Society of Health-System Pharmacists; Northeast Society of Health-System Pharmacists **A/S:** She attributes her success to family support, dedication, hard work and enjoying her work. **B/I:** She was prompted to enter her profession because she wanted more contact with patients. **H/O:** The highlight of her career is knowing that she is helping people.

THERESA MARIE SHAFFER, RN
Registered Nurse
Licking Memorial Hospital
1320 W. Main Street
Newark, OH 43055 United States
theresashaffer1976@yahoo.com
http://www.lmhealth.org

BUS: Hospital **P/S:** Healthcare **MA:** Local **D/D/R:** Overseeing Critical Care Nursing and Assisting in Outpatient Surgeries **H/I/S:** Playing Bingo **FBP:** American Journal of Nursing **EDU:** Associate Degree in Nursing, Central Ohio Technical College **A/A/S:** American Nurses Association; American Diabetes Association **A/S:** She attributes her success to her passion for her profession. **H/O:** The most gratifying aspect of her career is seeing her patients recover.

ROBERT B. SHANNER
Owner
Shanner and Shanner
3200 Fourth Avenue
Suite 203
San Diego, CA 92103 United States
rbshanner@yahoo.com
http://www.cambridgewhoswho.com

BUS: Business Bankruptcy **P/S:** Law Services **MA:** Regional **D/D/R:** Law **H/I/S:** Gardening, Sailing **EDU:** Bachelor of Laws,, California Western University; Bachelor of Arts in Journalism and English, University of New Mexico **A/A/S:** San Diego County Bar Association **C/VW:** Church, English Speaking Union **B/I:** He became involved in his profession because it was a family profession. **H/O:** The most gratifying aspect of his career is being able to help others.

ROBERT A. SHAPIRO
Director of Corporate Legal Affairs
Casio, Inc.
128 Robinhood Road
Clifton, NJ 07013 United States
bshapiro@casio.com
http://www.casio.com

BUS: Manufacturing Company **P/S:** Consumer Electronics **MA:** International **D/D/R:** Managing Legal Affairs and Compliance **H/I/S:** Photography, Skiing **FBP:** Fast Company; Wired; Technology; Business 2.0; Inc.com **EDU:** Master's Degree in Business and Information Systems, Goddard College (1980); Bachelor of Arts in Biology and Chemistry, Montclair State University, Summa Cum Laude (1972) **A/A/S:** New Jersey State Policemen's Benevolent Association; National Contract Management Association; Electronic Industries Alliance; Homeland Security Industries Association

---

MR. VIVEK SHARMA
Network Administrator
Viking Range Corporation
PO Box 956
Greenwood, MS 38935 United States
vsharma@vikingrange.com
http://www.vikingrange.com

BUS: Manufacturer and Marketer of Professional and Commercial Kitchen Appliances for the Home **P/S:** Kitchen Appliances, Ventilation, Refrigeration, Kitchen Clean Up, Outdoor, Counter-Top Appliances, Cookware and Cutlery Accessories **MA:** National **D/D/R:** Overseeing Network Administration, Exchange Administration and the Microsoft Active Directory, Networking, Offering Information Technology and General Troubleshooting on a Level 3 or 4, Working with Cisco, Microsoft and Oracle **H/I/S:** Coaching Daughter's Soccer Team, Spending Time with the Family **FBP:** Network World **EDU:** Bachelor of Science in Electrical Engineering, Northrop University (1989) **CERTS:** Cisco Certified Network Associate **A/A/S:** Institute of Electrical and Electronics Engineers Computer Society; Presenter, Clients; Presenter, Nuclear Regulatory Commission

MR. ABRAHAM A. SHARPER
President, Chief Executive Officer
Save Our Future West Africa Project, Inc.
940 Riverside Avenue
Trenton, NJ 08618 United States
sharper3@verizon.net
http://www.cambridgewhoswho.com

BUS: Nonprofit Organization **P/S:** Community Services Including Relief and Educational Assistance to Vulnerable Children in the United States and West Africa **MA:** International **EXP:** Mr. Sharper's expertise is in operations management. **D/D/R:** Fundraising, Caring for Children, Building Relationships, Promoting Child Welfare **H/I/S:** Reading the Holy Bible, Participating in Church Activities, Playing Volleyball **C/VW:** Deacon, Grace Cathedral Fellowship Ministries; Media Ministry; Local Church

TERI E. SHAVER
Instructional Consultant
Region 18 Education Service Center
2811 LaForce Boulevard
Midland, TX 79711 United States
tshvaer@esc18.net
http://www.cambridgewhoswho.com

BUS: Education **P/S:** Instructional Services to Kindergarten through 12th Grade Educators Including Workshops and Technical Assistance to School Districts **MA:** Regional **D/D/R:** Managing Discipline and Behavior **H/I/S:** Reading, Swimming **FBP:** CEC Publications **EDU:** Master of Education, Plus Hours in Special Education, Sul Ross State University; Bachelor of Science in Physical Education, University of Texas of the Permian Basin **CERTS:** Certified Reading Specialist; Endorsements and Certifications in Elementary and Special Education **A/A/S:** Council for Exceptional Children **C/VW:** Special Olympics, Father Flanagan's Boys and Girls Town, American Cancer Society, The Living Bank **A/S:** She attributes her career success to her thirst for learning, to her empathy for the less fortunate, and to her desire to help others achieve their goals. **B/I:** She has always wanted to work with handicapped youth, and she loves her current position. **H/O:** She feels that being able to work with her children in the classroom setting has been the highlight of her career.

MARGARET MARIE SHAW
Senior Training Specialist
State Street Corporation
200 Newport Avenue Extension
North Quincy, MA 02171 United States
mmshaw02125@hotmail.com
http://www.cambridgewhoswho.com

BUS: Investment Management Company **P/S:** High Quality Financial and Retiree Services **MA:** International **EXP:** Ms. Shaw's expertise is in skills training. **D/D/R:** Meeting with Managers in a Group Setting, Determining their Needs, Creating and Designing Training Programs for Managers Based on Skill Sets **H/I/S:** Working at Fenway Park Baseball Concession Stands **FBP:** Training and Development **EDU:** Bachelor of Science in Management, Concentration in Accounting, University of Massachusetts, Boston **A/A/S:** American Society of Training and Development; National Honor Society **A/H:** Friendly Fenway Achiever Award (1996); Dean's Award for Service in College Management **C/VW:** St. Anthony Shrine, Boston, MA

DENISE M. SHEEHAN
Vice President, Industry Events
National Glass Association
8200 Greensboro Drive, Suite 302
McLean, VA 22102 United States
denise@glass.org
http://www.glass.org

BUS: Trade Association **P/S:** Representing nearly 4,000 Member Companies and Locations, and Producing the Industry's Leading Events and Publications **MA:** National **D/D/R:** Coordinating Annual Trade Shows and Events, Offering Information and Education, as well as Promoting Quality Workmanship, Ethics, and Safety in the Architectural, Automotive and Window and Door Glass Industries **H/I/S:** Cooking, Going to the Beach **FBP:** Trade Show Weekly **EDU:** Bachelor of Science in Education, Major in Speech Pathology, James Madison University (1976) **A/A/S:** Atlanta Customer Advisory Board; IAEM; ASAE **C/VW:** Breast Cancer Society

ELIZABETH A. SHEELY, RN, BSN, CN III
Registered Nurse, Charge Nurse, Clinical Nurse III
Duke University Medical Center
Erwin Road
Durham, NC 27713 United States
lizsheely@verizon.net
http://www.cambridgewhoswho.com

BUS: Healthcare Center **P/S:** Healthcare **MA:** Local **D/D/R:** Recovering Patients from Anesthesia and Overseeing the Post Anesthesia Care Unit **H/I/S:** Playing the Violin, Skiing, Exercising **EDU:** Bachelor of Science in Nursing, University of North Carolina **C/VW:** Habitat for Humanity; Special Olympics; Breast Cancer Walk; American Red Cross **A/S:** She attributes her success to her persistence and love for her patients. **B/I:** She became involved in her profession because she always had an interest in medicine and she was inspired to pursue a career in nursing by her mother, who was a nurse. **H/O:** The most gratifying aspect of her career is watching the health improvement of her patients.

MR. CHARLES D. SHELDEN
Owner
Classic School and Office Supply
60155 Turquoise Road
Bend, OR 97702 United States
cshelden@classicsupplies.net
http://www.classicsupplies.net

BUS: Educational and Office Supply Distribution Company **P/S:** Supplying School and Office Supplies to Area Businesses, Professionals, Schools, Government and Individuals, Special Purchasing Plans, Wholesale Distribution **MA:** National **D/D/R:** Maintaining Communication with Schools, Vendors, Local Schools, Education Facilities, and Daycare Centers **H/I/S:** Fishing, Camping, Spending Quality Time with the Family **FBP:** 1B Magazine **EDU:** Bachelor of Arts in Business, Ashford University (2005); Associate of Arts in General Business, Ashford University (1999) **A/A/S:** School Home Office Products Association; Chamber of Commerce **DOB:** October 22, 1970 **SP:** Lisa **CHILD:** Austin, Spencer, Cierra, Lydia

JANIS L. SHELLINGTON
Executive Assistant
Northern Virginia Community College
7630 Little River Turnpike
Suite 812
Annandale, VA 22003 United States
jshellington@nvcc.edu
http://www.nvcc.edu

BUS: Community College **P/S:** Higher Education **MA:** Regional **D/D/R:** Overseeing Office Operations for the Vice President Including Scheduling Appointments, Organizing Meetings, Reconciling Three Budgets, Managing Workforce Development Projects and Overseeing Grants Awarded to the Department **H/I/S:** Watching Tennis, Basketball and Baseball, Supporting the Washington Redskins **FBP:** Workforce Management **EDU:** CSC Degree in Business Management Principles, Northern Virginia Community College (2004); Associate of Applied Science in Business Management (2004); CSC Degree in Business Information Technology (2004) **A/A/S:** Co-Chair of Commencement, Northern Virginia Community College (2003-2008); Board Member, Classified Staff Leadership Academy (2007); United States Achievement Academy **A/H:** Collegiate Award (1996); National Commemorative Certificate **C/VW:** Volunteer, Northern Virginia Community College Annual Service Awards (2004-2008) **DOB:** February 24, 1947 **POB:** Washington, DC **SP:** Gil **W/H:** Northern Virginia Community College; International Business Machine, Washington Metropolitan Area; United States Department of Treasury, DC; Prince George's County Public Schools, MD **A/S:** She attributes her success to her attention to detail, professionalism and willingness to help others. **B/I:** She became involved in her profession through a natural progression of opportunities. **H/O:** The highlight of her career was being nominated to the Northern Virginia Community College Classified Staff Leadership Academy in 2007. **I/F/Y:** In five years, Ms. Shellington intends to retire and spend quality time with her family.

MARY Y. SHEN, MS(ASCP), CLS
Clinical Laboratory Scientist
Torrance Memorial Medical Center
3330 Lomita Boulevard
Torrance, CA 90505 United States
ShenYee@aol.com
http://www.cambridgewhoswho.com

BUS: Hospital **P/S:** Clinical Laboratory Blood Tests **MA:** Local **D/D/R:** Practicing Hematology **H/I/S:** Reading, Cooking **FBP:** ASCP Lab Medicine **EDU:** Master's Degree in Clinical Lab Sciences **A/A/S:** American Society of Clinical Pathologists **C/VW:** Church **A/S:** She attributes her success to her hard work, perseverance and enjoyment of studying. **B/I:** She became involved in her profession because she was a chemistry major and loved science. She used to work in a blood bank and enjoys helping people. **H/O:** The highlight of her career as going into hematology after working in the blood bank.

PAUL R. SHEPARD
President
Doctors Choice Dental Laboratory
31 S.E. 24th Avenue
Pompano Beach, FL 33062 United States
kyeot7a@bellsouth.net
http://www.cambridgewhoswho.com

BUS: Dental Laboratory **MA:** Regional **D/D/R:** Assisting Physicians, Offering Medical Legal Consulting, Setting Contracts with Medical Facilities, Meeting with Providers, Scheduling and Accepting Certain Rates of Pay **H/I/S:** Camping, Baseball **EDU:** Bachelor's Degree in Health **A/A/S:** American Academy of Professional Coders

STORMY A. SHEPHERD
Licensed Practical Nurse
Self Employed
9390 Ellen Court
Thornton, CO 80229 United States
http://www.cambridgewhoswho.com

BUS: Healthcare **P/S:** Healthcare **MA:** Local **D/D/R:** Nursing **H/I/S:** Reading, Crocheting, Knitting **FBP:** American Journal of Nursing **EDU:** Associate Degree in Liberal Arts, Red Rocks Community College **CERTS:** License in Nursing, Beth Israel Practical School of Nursing **C/VW:** March of Dimes; The Salvation Army; Helping the Needy **A/S:** She attributes her success to her love for her job. **H/O:** The most gratifying aspect of her career is making a patient smile.

ESTHER S. SHERMAN, RN, BSN, M.ED.
Registered Nurse (Retired), Educator,
President, Chief Executive Officer
Enterprising Paradigms of South Florida, Inc.
PO Box 26222
Jacksonville, FL 32226 United States
shrmesth@comcast.net
http://www.cambridgewhoswho.com

BUS: Consulting and Contracted Service Company **P/S:** Art Exhibitions, Framing, Glamour Product Retail Sales **MA:** National **D/D/R:** Overseeing Art Sales **H/I/S:** Sewing, Gardening **FBP:** Industry-Related Publications **EDU:** Master's Degree in Education, Florida Atlantic University; Bachelor of Science in Nursing, Florida A&M University **CERTS:** Certification in Basic Fitness, Florida Atlantic University; Certification in Facilitative Leadership, Barry University; Certification in Assisting Change in Education, Barry University **A/A/S:** Phi Delta Kappa; American Cancer Society **A/H:** Proclamation, House of Representatives; Outstanding Achievement in Breast Cancer Awareness Award, American Cancer Society; Award, Greater Palm Beaches Business; Award, Greater Palm Beaches Business and Professional Women Club; Recognition of Noteworthy Contributions and Service to the Community in the Area of Health Science Award, Florida A&M University Alumni Association; Who's Who Among Women in Education; Nominee, Woman of the Year in Health Care, School Board, Palm Beach County; Certificate of Recognition, Outstanding Educator, School Board; Certificate of Recognition for Outstanding Service to the Sickle Cell Association; First Annual Award for Health Education and Counseling Services, Sickle Cell Association, Palm Beach County, FL; Certificate of Recognition, Delta Sigma Theta **C/VW:** Board of Directors, Riviera Beach Family Resource Center, Palm Beach County, FL; Cultural Arts Advisory Committee, Riviera Beach, FL; Victoria's Life Ministry; Chartered Member, Sickle Cell Foundation, Palm Beach County; Board of Directors, Comprehensive Aids Program, Palm Beach County Juvenile Justice Commission; Palm Beach County Health Care Task Force; Board of Directors, Mental Health Association, Palm Beach County; Sickle Cell Foundation, Palm Beach County; Pleasant City Heritage Gallery, Palm Beach County, FL; Florida State School Health Advisory Council; Breast Cancer Task Force, American Cancer Society **DOB:** July 19, 1943 **POB:** Blakely, GA **W/H:** President, Chief Executive Officer, Enterprising Paradigm of South Florida (1997-2007); Docent, Sales Associate, Educator, Artist Showcase of the Palm Beaches, Palm Beach County, FL (1999-2003); Consultant, Florida Resource Center for Women and Children, Palm Beach County, FL (2002); Sales Associate, African American Art Gallery, Palm Beach County, FL (1998-2000); Nurse, Health Educator, Children Home Society, Palm Beach County, FL; Outreach Educator, Comprehensive AIDS Center, Palm Beach County, FL (1998-1999); Retiree (1996-1997); Health Occupations Education Specialist, School District of Palm Beach County, FL (1993-1996); School-Based Nurse, Royal Palm Exceptional Education Center, School District of Palm Beach County, FL (1992-1993); Occupational Health Nurse, School District of Palm Beach County, FL (1990-1992); School Health Services Specialist, School District of Palm Beach County, FL (1978-1990) Nursing Instructor, Palm Beach Community College, Palm Beach County, FL (1972-1978); Health and Drug Prevention Education Resource Teacher, School District of Palm Beach County, FL (1969-1972): Community Health Nurse, Palm Beach County Public Health Department, Palm Beach County, FL (1965-1969); Adjunct Professor, Personal Health and Fitness, Palm Beach Community College; Nurse, Presidential Women Center, Palm Beach County, FL; Per Diem Nurse, Lakeview Psychiatric Hospital and Adolescent Treatment Center, Palm Beach County, FL; Per Diem Nurse, Glenbeigh Adolescent Hospital, Palm Beach County, FL; Per Diem Nurse, Good Samaritan Medical Center, Palm Beach County, FL; Per Diem Nurse, St. Mary's Medical Center, Palm Beach County, FL

BEVERLEY V. SHIELDS, RN, BSN, BS
Assistant Head Nurse (Retired)
Queens Hospital Center
8268 164th Street
Jamaica, NY 11432 United States
beverleyshields@aol.com
http://www.cambridgewhoswho.com

BUS: Hospital **P/S:** Healthcare **MA:** Regional **D/D/R:** Nursing, Working in the Chemical Dependency Unit, Educating Patients, Supervising and Mentoring New Nurses **H/I/S:** Traveling, Gardening, Reading, Exercising, Taking Computer Classes **EDU:** Bachelor of Science in Nursing, York College (1992); Bachelor of Science in Community Health, York College (1988); Registered Nurse, Earned in England (1970) **CERTS:** Certified Midwife, London, England (1972) **A/A/S:** New York State Nurses Association; American Nurses Association; International Nurses Society on Addictions; Delegate, American Nurses Association **C/VW:** Paralysis Charities; American Heart Association **DOB:** September 19, 1942 **POB:** Kingston **CHILD:** Howard, Jake **A/S:** She attributes her success to her helping nature. **B/I:** She became involved in her profession because of her passion for helping people. **H/O:** The highlight of her career was becoming a nurse.

BOBBIE SHIER
Director of Credit Services
Windsor Foods
4200 E. Concours, Suite 100
Ontario, CA 91764 United States
bobbie.shier@windsorfoods.com
http://www.cambridgewhoswho.com

BUS: Leading Manufacturer and Marketer of Frozen Ethnic Foods, Appetizers, and Specialty items **P/S:** High-Quality Frozen Foods for the Consumer Market, Commercial Restaurants, and Foodservice Operations **MA:** International **D/D/R:** Overseeing Credit Services **H/I/S:** Traveling, Antiquing **FBP:** The Wall Street Journal **EDU:** Coursework in Administration of Justice, Riverside Community College; Coursework in Night Academy, Riverside Police Department **A/A/S:** National Association of Credit Management **C/VW:** Susan G. Komen Breast Cancer Foundation; American Society for the Prevention of Cruelty to Animals **DOB:** July 31, 1952

LISA SHINDLE, MSN, CRNP
Nurse Practitioner
Hospital for Special Surgery
535 E. 70th Street
New York, NY 10021 United States
shindlel@hss.edu
http://www.hss.edu

BUS: Hospital-Based Medical Practice **P/S:** Patient Care **MA:** International **D/D/R:** Treating Metabolic Bone Disease **H/I/S:** Traveling, Cooking **FBP:** Industry-Related Journals **EDU:** Master's Degree in Family Nurse Practitioner, Johns Hopkins University **CERTS:** Certified Family Nurse Practitioner **A/A/S:** Sigma Theta Tau **A/S:** She attributes her career success to her determination and family drive to succeed. **B/I:** Having always had an interest in the medical field, she became a doctor because she wanted to share direct contact with her patients. **H/O:** She feels that her work in starting the Smoking Sensations Program with Johns Hopkins Hospital and the fact that the program was picked up be the World Health Organization have been the highlights of her career.

ALEXIS SHIPLEY-BARTON
Certified Clinical Research Professional (Retired), Registered Nurse
(Retired)
Indiana Oncology and Hematology Consultants
1 N. Illinois Street
Indianapolis, IN 46204 United States
alexis.shipley@cwwemail.com
http://www.cambridgewhoswho.com

BUS: Hospital **P/S:** Cancer-Focused Healthcare **MA:** Regional **D/D/R:** Conducting Clinical Research, Collecting Data and Consulting **H/I/S:** Biking, Swimming, Weightlifting, Spending Time with her Grandchildren **FBP:** Nursing Spectrum; INBA; Nursing Focus **EDU:** Bachelor's Degree in Mathematics, Indiana University; Bachelor's Degree in Nursing, University of Indianapolis; Coursework in Legal Consulting **CERTS:** Certified Clinical Research Professional, University of Indianapolis; Certified Clinical Research Associate, Society of Clinical Research Associates (1990); Certification in Clinical Research, Association of Clinical Research Professionals (1990) **A/S:** She attributes her success to her work ethic and to the support she receives from her father. **B/I:** She became involved in her profession because of her interest in mathematics and research. **H/O:** The highlight of her career was being a part of the clinical auditing committee, where she managed data across the county.

MR. EDWARD SHKOLNIKOV, ESQ.
Esquire
Law Office of Edward Shkolnikov
468 N. Camden Drive, Suite 304N
Beverly Hills, CA 90210 United States
shkolnikov_esq@yahoo.com
http://www.cambridgewhoswho.com

BUS: Law Office **P/S:** Law Services **D/D/R:** Litigating DUI, Murder and Capital Cases, Public Speaking **H/I/S:** Skiing, Playing Hockey, Spending Time with his Family **FBP:** BusinessWeek; Newsweek; People **EDU:** JD, Abraham Lincoln University School of Law (2004); Bachelor's Degree in Nursing, Novosibirsk Medical School (1989) **A/A/S:** Beverly Hills Bar Association; Los Angeles County Bar Association; California Bar Association; American Bar Association; California Criminal Justice Organization

DR. JoAnna Burley Shore
Assistant Professor
Marketing and Finance
Frostburg State University
101 Braddock Street
Frostburg, MD 21532 United States
jbshore@frostburg.edu
http://www.frostburg.edu

BUS: State University **P/S:** Information Systems Education for the College of Business for Future Managers **MA:** Statewide **D/D/R:** Teaching about Information Systems, Higher Education, Technology in the Classroom and Small Businesses Technology Adoption, Promoting the Benefits that Frostburg State has to Offer **H/I/S:** Spending Time with her Two Sons, Watching and Coaching her Children's Soccer Games, Golfing, Weight Lifting, Preparing to Send her Sons to College **FBP:** The Wall Street Journal; Management Information Systems Quarterly; JBIT **EDU:** Doctoral Degree in Information Systems, Argosy University; Master's Degree in Educational Technology, Frostburg State University; Bachelor's Degree in Business, Frostburg State University **A/H:** Outstanding Marylander with a Disability **C/VW:** Mineral County Food Bank; Children with Disabilities Mentor **CHILD:** Harrison, Christopher **B/I:** She became involved in her profession as a GA because she was asked to teach at the university after graduating with a high GPA. **H/O:** The highlights of her career were publishing five articles with her husband Dr. Mark A. Shore in Mathematics and Computer Education and one article each in The Journal of Business and Information Technology. She also had abstracts published in Russian Journals over the past 3 years. **I/F/Y:** In five years, she hopes to become the chairwoman of her department.

JERRI L. SHRADER
Owner, Artist
Sleeping Bear Studio
291 Olympic View Avenue
Ocean Shores, WA 98569 United States
sleepingbearstudio@msn.com
http://www.jerrishrader.com

BUS: Fine Arts **P/S:** Fine Arts **MA:** Local **D/D/R:** Portraits, Native American Art **H/I/S:** Photography **FBP:** Consumer Reports **EDU:** Associate Degree in Art **A/A/S:** President, Association of the Arts of Ocean Shores **C/VW:** American Red Cross; Progressive Animal Welfare Society; American Association of Retired Persons **A/S:** She attributes her success to the support she receives from her family. **B/I:** She became involved in her career because of her love of drawing. **H/O:** The highlight of her career was being commissioned to draw and paint a portrait of a fallen firefighter.

Brenda L. Shults
Manager
Addison Pilot Shops
4653 Westgrove Drive
Addison, TX 75001 United States
addisonpilotshop@sbcglobal.net
http://www.cambridgewhoswho.com

BUS: Aviation **P/S:** Aviation Parts, Supplies, Novelties and Materials, Newest and Most Innovative and Unique Products **MA:** National **D/D/R:** Managing Purchasing and Marketing **H/I/S:** Breeding Mini-Dachshunds, Horse Training, Attending her Children's Sporting Events **FBP:** Aviation **EDU:** Associate Degree in Telecommunications, United States Army **A/A/S:** Honorary Chairperson, National Republican Committee **C/VW:** Former Chairperson, ACES of Denton County **A/S:** She attributes her success to her customer service skills. **B/I:** She became involved in her profession because of her family's experience in aviation and her own experience with aviation while she was in the Army. **H/O:** The highlight of her career has been finding and researching new products and seeing the customers' satisfaction.

E. Hope Shupp
Teacher, Service Consultant
Berks County Intermediate Unit
111 Commons Boulevard
Reading, PA 19605 United States
scubahope@yahoo.com
http://www.dhsinternational.com

BUS: Wholesale and Retail Distribution on the Internet **P/S:** Education **MA:** Local **D/D/R:** Working with Multiple Disabilities on Land and Water **H/I/S:** Traveling, Scuba Diving, Running her Online Business **FBP:** Educational Journals **EDU:** Master's Degree in Special Education, Alvernia College; Master's Degree in Adult Distance Education, University of Phoenix **CERTS:** Certified in Elementary and Special Education; Certified Scuba Diving Instructor (Disabled/Non-Disabled) **A/A/S:** Phi Lambda; Lambda Pi Eta **C/VW:** Easter Seals, Special Olympics, Ocean Conservatory; Swimming Instructor, American Red Cross **A/S:** She attributes her success to patience and understanding that everyone learns differently. **B/I:** She became involved in her profession because she took advantage of an opportunity. **H/O:** The highlight of her career has been seeing the smiles on the faces of both students and parents.

DR. CLAIRE V. SIBOLD
Professor, School of Education
Biola University
13800 Biola Avenue
La Mirada, CA 90639 United States
claire.sibold@biola.edu
http://www.biola.edu

BUS: Private Christian University **P/S:** Academic Programs, Doctoral Degrees to Bachelor's Degrees, In-service and Workshops in Literacy and Children's Literature **MA:** National **D/D/R:** Preparing Teachers, Comprehensive Exams and Literacy Initiatives **H/I/S:** Reading, Swimming, Hiking, Researching **FBP:** Journal of Adolescent & Adult Literacy **EDU:** Ph.D. in Secondary Curriculum with Corollaries in Research and Reading Education, Arizona State University (1984); Master of Arts in Education with Emphases in Curriculum Development and Literacy, University of Washington (1978); Bachelor of Arts in English, University of Washington (1971) **A/A/S:** International Reading Association (1972); Chairwoman of Two Committees, Biola University; Phi Delta Kappa (1983); Orange County Reading Professors' Network (1999); California Reading Initiative (1999); California Reading Association; Who's Who in Education; Presenter, Oxford Round Table, Oxford **A/H:** Distinguished Volunteer Service Award, Local School (2000) **C/VW:** Volunteer, Animal Rescue Organization **DOB:** April 25, 1950 **POB:** Seattle, WA **SP:** Jon **CHILD:** Genoa, Bryn **W/H:** Professor, Department of Education, Biola University, La Mirada, CA (1987-Present); Editor, Project Director, New Product Development CTB/McGraw-Hill, Monterey, CA (1987-1988); Visiting Assistant Professor, Department of Reading Education, Arizona State University, Tempe, AZ (1986-1987); Adjunct Professor, Department of Secondary Education, Arizona State University, Tempe, AZ (1984-1986); Instructor, Graduate Assistant, Center for Reading Education, Arizona State University, Tempe, AZ (1980-1984); Secondary Teacher, Judson Private School, Scottsdale, AZ (1984-1985); Secondary Teacher, Reading Consultant, Shoreline High School, Seattle, WA (1979-1981); Substitute Teacher, Seattle Public Schools, Seattle, WA (1976-1977); Secondary Teacher, North Kitsap High School, Poulsbo, WA (1971-1976); Secondary Teacher, South Kitsap High School, Port Orchard, WA (1972-1973); Student Teaching, Nathan Eckstein Junior High School, Seattle, WA (1971) **C/A:** Author of Articles Published in Professional and Christian Journals and Books; Recently Published a Book on Context Clues for Creative Teaching Press

---

MISTY L. SIEGRIST, LPN
Licensed Practical Nurse
Maxim Home Healthcare
124 Nora Street S.E.
Grand Rapids, MI 49548 United States
siegrist124@comcast.net
http://www.spectrum-health.org

BUS: Home Healthcare Center **P/S:** Home Healthcare Including Pediatric Consultation and Referral Service, Rehabilitation Services, Home Care Nursing, In-Home Care, Foster Care, Programs for Patients with Brain Injuries and Physically Impaired **MA:** National **EXP:** Ms. Siegrist's expertise is in rehabilitation. **D/D/R:** Coordinating the Pediatric Home Ventilator Program, Caring for Patients with Brain Injuries and Assisting their Families **H/I/S:** Gardening, Reading, Writing Poetry **FBP:** American Journal of Nursing **CERTS:** Licensed Practical Nurse, Grand Rapids Community College (1999) **C/VW:** Volunteer, Miracle Network Fundraising **POB:** Grand Rapids, MI **A/S:** She attributes her success to her caring nature and her ability to make a difference in the lives of others.

ANNE KELLEY SILANSKAS
Director of East Coast Operations
Dillstar Productions, Inc.
10281A Trademark Street
Rancho Cucamonga, CA 91730 United States
annekelley@dillstarproductions.com
http://www.comedywedding.com

BUS: Comedy Theater **P/S:** Joey and Maria's Comedy Italian Wedding, The Soprano's Last Supper, Maria's Bachelorette Party, The Wake of Matty O'Malley, Jimmy and Jenny's Wacky Western Wedding, Nick and Zita's Funny Fat Greek Wedding, as well as Three other Dinner Theater Productions, Promotional Appearances and Fundraising Events **MA:** National **D/D/R:** Specializing in Directing, Coordination, Sales, Marketing and Hands-On Management of Nine Locally Based Interactive Dinner Theater Shows, Overseeing All Casting and Supervision of over 160 Performers on the East Coast **H/I/S:** Acting, Scriptwriting, All Forms of Film and Theater Involvement **FBP:** Industry-Related Publications Journals **EDU:** Coursework, Actor's Workshop of Boston **A/A/S:** Assistant Director, Genesius Arts Project; Co-Founder, Women In Art **A/H:** Enact Award for Stage Management (1992)

MARIA C. SILVEIRA
Realtor
North Shore
Century 21 Citywide
680 Broadway
Everett, MA 02149 United States
msilveira@compresuacasa.com
http://www.cambridgewhoswho.com

BUS: Real Estate Company **P/S:** Residential Properties, Financial Services, Relocations, Listings, First Time Home Buyers **MA:** Regional **D/D/R:** Handling Sales, Working Mostly with Spanish Speaking Customers **EDU:** Coursework in Real Estate; Coursework, Earned in Brazil **A/A/S:** Broker's Association; Massachusetts Association of Realtors; National Association of Realtors

DR. ERNEST D. SIMELA
President
Simela Medical Arts PC
Hempstead, NY 11550 United States
esimela@aol.com
http://www.cambridgewhoswho.com

BUS: Healthcare **P/S:** Health and Allied Services **MA:** New York **D/D/R:** Working in Pediatrics **H/I/S:** Reading, Traveling, Photography **EDU:** MD in Pediatrics, Albert Einstein College of Medicine; Bachelor of Science in Chemistry and Biology, Hamline University **A/A/S:** President, Mthwakazi Foundation Inc.

LELAND L. SIMMONS, ED.D., CCC-SLP
Speech and Language Pathologist, Educator
Pomona Unified School District
800 S. Garey Avenue
Pomona, CA 91769 United States
leland2@earthlink.net
http://www.cambridgewhoswho.com

BUS: School District **P/S:** Education **MA:** Local **EXP:** Mr. Simmons' expertise is in speech and language pathology in childhood and geriatric neurological disorders. **D/D/R:** Teaching Comparative and Special Education in Graduate Seminars, Offering Language, Speech and Hearing Services in Schools **H/I/S:** Playing Classical Music **EDU:** Doctor of Education in Organizational Leadership, Pepperdine University (2004); Master of Science in Education, with a Concentration in Computer Science, Pepperdine University; Bachelor's Degree in Liberal Arts, California State University, Los Angeles (1985) **CERTS:** Certified Speech, Language and Hearing Pathologist; Certification in Clinical Competence in Speech and Language **A/A/S:** Chapman University College; President, Mount St. Antonio Chapter, Phi Delta Kappa; American Speech-Language-Hearing Association; National Education Association; CATA **A/S:** He attributes his success to his personal drive and the encouragement he receives from his parents. **B/I:** He became involved in his profession because he wanted to do something different as an undergraduate student.

MR. CHAD J. SIMON
Field Supervisor
Farmers Mutual Hail Insurance
6785 Weston Parkway
West Des Moines, IA 50266 United States
chads@fmh.com
http://www.fmh.com

BUS: Insurance Company **P/S:** Hail and MPCI Insurance Services for Farmers and Claims Management Services **MA:** Local **EXP:** Mr. Simon's expertise is in marketing and crop supervision. **H/I/S:** Bowling, Playing Softball **EDU:** Associate of Arts in Business Administration, Northeast Community College

JACQUELINE C. SIMON, MA, BS, BA
President, Chief Executive Officer
JCS Ventures Business Development Consulting Firm
3315 San Felipe Road, Suite 144
San Jose, CA 95135 United States
jacqueline3@tmo.blackberry.net
http://www.jcs-ventures.com

BUS: Consulting Firm **P/S:** Business Development, Financial Investment Planning, Joint Venture Partnerships, Bonding and Insurance, Contract Procurement, Small Business Certification, Grant Development, Leadership, Assertiveness and Diversity Training **MA:** International **D/D/R:** Educating Clients, Handling Financing and Global Marketing **H/I/S:** Golfing, Traveling, Reading, Writing **FBP:** The Wall Street Journal **EDU:** Master's Degree in Business and Personnel, San Jose State University **A/A/S:** Heritage Society; Women and Business Executives, California; International Institute; First Female Branch Director, North County Fire Protection, District of Monterey County; SVC Resource Development Group **C/VW:** St. Jude Children's Research Hospital; Fisher Foundation; Girls Inc., Katrina Victim Relief; Boys and Girls Club of America; Church; Simon & Delavega International Fundraiser **A/S:** She attributes her success to her mentors and being able to grasp and understand concepts learned from others. **B/I:** She became involved in this profession because her parents were very philanthropic and she saw what others accomplished as a result of their help. **H/O:** The highlight of her career was working with Colin Powell.

DEBRA S. SIMONS
Photographer
Moments in Time
5869 Myra Drive
Mansfield, TX 76063 United States
dsimons@hughes.net
http://www.cambridgewhoswho.com

BUS: Photography **P/S:** Portraits **MA:** Local **D/D/R:** Photographing Children and Families **H/I/S:** Photography **EDU:** Bachelor's Degree in Education, Southwestern University **A/A/S:** Texas Professional Photography Association; Professional Photography Association **A/S:** She attributes her success to her level of client service. **B/I:** She became involved in her profession because she has always had an interest in photography.

MS. JACQUELINE J. SIMPKINS
Investigative Social Worker
Child Protection
District of Columbia Child and Family Services Agency
6115 W. Hil Mar Circle
District Heights, MD 20747 United States
missjsimpkins@aol.com
http://www.cfsa.dc.gov/cfsa

BUS: Government Agency **P/S:** Child Protective and Supportive Family Services **MA:** Regional **EXP:** Ms. Simpkins' expertise lies in the investigation of abuse, neglect and emergency child removal cases. **D/D/R:** Conducting Hospital Visits and Interviews, Attending Court Trials **H/I/S:** Reading, Playing Basketball, Cooking **FBP:** Black Enterprise **EDU:** Master's Degree in Social Work, Howard University (1997); Bachelor of Science, North Carolina Central University (1991) **A/A/S:** National Association of Social Workers

AMY M. SIMPSON
Business Teacher
Portageville High School
904 King Avenue
Portageville, MO 63873 United States
asimpson@portageville.k12.mo.us
http://www.cambridgewhoswho.com

BUS: High School **P/S:** Education for High School Students **MA:** Local **D/D/R:** Personal Finance **H/I/S:** Watching Movies **EDU:** Pursuing Master's Degree in Education Technology, Southeast Missouri State University; Bachelor's Degree in Entertainment Management, Missouri State University (2002) **A/A/S:** Association for Career and Technical Education; Missouri Business Education Association **C/VW:** American Cancer Society **A/S:** She attributes her success to her family support. **B/I:** She became involved in the profession because she was always interested in education. She started in entertainment management, but the traveling requirements for the job proved to be too difficult. She chose to teach after substitute teaching. **H/O:** The highlight of her career was gaining confidence and determination after her first year of teaching.

BETTY MICHELLE SIMS
Owner, Founder
Urban Betty
1206 W. 38th Street
Suite 1201
Austin, TX 78705 United States
chelle@urbanbetty.com
http://www.urbanbetty.com

BUS: Hair Salon **P/S:** PureOlogy, Wella System Professional, and Bumble & Bumble, Highlighting, Hair Coloring, Waxing, and Cutting **MA:** Austin, Cedar Park, Round Rock, Texas **D/D/R:** Highlighting, Coloring, Cutting Hair **H/I/S:** Shopping, Reading, Caring for her Dogs **FBP:** American Salon; Modern Salon; Salon Today **EDU:** High School Education; Coursework in Cosmetology **A/H:** KVUE Winner, Salons in the City (2007); Best Salon in Austin and Best Highlights, austin.citysearch.com (2007); Second Place, Nationwide Wella Hair Colorist **C/VW:** Seton Fund; Women's Chamber of Commerce; Free Haircuts, Locks of Love **DOB:** March 15, 1977 **POB:** Seymour, TX **SP:** Clinton **W/H:** Salon 505, Arboretum; Bella Salon; Independent Contractor; Salon Owner **A/S:** She attributes her success to her supportive friends and family. **B/I:** She became involved in her profession because she was motivated by her friends and family. **H/O:** The highlight of her career was opening Urban Betty in 2005. **I/F/Y:** In five years, she hopes to expand Urban Betty into a full spa and possibly branch out into a second location.

ELIZABETH A. SIMS
Network Coordinator, Observation and Outpatients in Beds, Care
Management
Community Health Network
1500 N. Ritter Avenue
Indianapolis, IN 46219 United States
easims@ecommunity.com
http://www.ecommunity.com

BUS: Leading Nonprofit Health System Dedicated to the Health and Well-Being of Individuals in Central Indiana **P/S:** Quality, Cost-Effective Healthcare Services Including Nursing, Business Care and Management Coordination **MA:** Regional **D/D/R:** Working as a Liaison for Four Hospitals within Indianapolis, Seeing over 8,000 Patients Annually, Observing Patient Care and Outpatients in Beds, Coordinating Financing, Overseeing Case Managers and Clinical Staff, Changing Existing Processes by Improving Revenues, Adopting Four Other Positions for Inpatients, Mentoring Individuals, Maintaining Compliance, Creating New Charges to Improve the Financial System, Increasing her Revenues by 10 Million Dollars **H/I/S:** Playing Women's League Golf, Running **EDU:** Bachelor of Science in Nursing, Indiana University School of Nursing (1994); Bachelor of Science in Education, Illinois State University (1987) **CERTS:** Pursuing Certification in Nursing Administration and Leadership, Association of Critical Care Nurses (2007) **A/A/S:** Sigma Theta Tau International; American Association of Critical Care Nurses; Board Member, Central Indiana Chapter, Association of Critical Care Nurses; Presenter, National Observation Patient Conference

MS. ROSE M. SIMS, LVN
Licensed Vocational Nurse
North Texas State Hospital
Vernon, TX 76384 United States
simsdrwmn@aol.com
http://www.cambridgewhoswho.com

BUS: Hospital **P/S:** High Quality Healthcare Services for Patients **MA:** Local **D/D/R:** Psychiatric Nursing, Interacting with Nurses and Doctors; Assessing and Educating Patients **H/I/S:** Traveling, Reading, Live Theater, Symphony **FBP:** American Nursing Journal **CERTS:** Licensed Vocational Nurse Degree, Vernon College (1999)

PEGGE L. SINES
Owner
Dream Haven LLC
233 E. Morrison Street
Edgerton, OH 43517 United States
special_72@hotmail.com

BUS: Senior, Elderly Living **P/S:** Nursing Home Alternative **MA:** Northwest Ohio, Northeast Indiana, Southwest Michigan **D/D/R:** Administrating Services for Alzheimer's and Dementia Patients **H/I/S:** Spending Time with her Family, Speaking at Organizations, Helping Children and the Elderly **FBP:** Senior Living **CERTS:** Certified Activity Director for Elderly, Owens Community College and Northwest Ohio Community College; Tested Nursing Assistant, State of Ohio; Nationally Certified Activity Professional **A/A/S:** Chamber of Commerce; District Representative, Resident Activity Professionals Northwest Ohio; NADA **A/H:** Resident Activities Professionals Media Award **C/VW:** Ministerial Group **A/S:** She attributes her personal and professional success to her perseverance and determination. **B/I:** She has always had an interest in the field and enjoys working with the elderly. **H/O:** The highlight of her career was the success of her care of the residents.

VEDPRAKASH SINGH, MD
Gynecologist
Angelsea Women's Specialists
PO Box 228
Thackeray Street
Hamilton, 2001 New Zealand
vpsing2@xtra.co.nz
http://www.cambridgewhoswho.com

BUS: Private Practice Dedicated to Providing Quality, Comprehensive Women's Healthcare Services **P/S:** General Gynecology, Endometriosis Surgery, Pelvic Floor Surgery, Laparoscopic Surgery, Assisted Reproduction Services **D/D/R:** Endometriosis Surgery, Pelvic Floor Surgery, in Vitro Fertilization **H/I/S:** Playing Cricket **FBP:** Industry-Related Publications **EDU:** MD; Coursework, University of Bombay **A/A/S:** Australian Gynecological Endoscopy Society; The Federation of Obstetric and Gynecological Societies of India; Local Lecturer; Fellow, Royal Australia and New Zealand College of Obstetrics and Gynecology; Perinatal Society of Australia and New Zealand

CHRISTIE DIANNE CHILDERS SINGLETON, BA, LPN
Registered Psychological Technician
Psychological Services of Oklahoma
Route 1 Box 161C
Eufaula, OK 74432 United States
cdcs24@cox.net
http://www.cambridgewhoswho.com

BUS: Counseling for Children, Family and School Services **P/S:** Counseling Services **MA:** Local **D/D/R:** Conducting Psychological, Educational and Achievement Testing, Counseling **H/I/S:** Traveling, Golfing, Gourmet Cooking, Sewing, Spending Time with her Family **FBP:** American Counseling Association Journal **EDU:** Master's Degree in Education; School Counselor, School Psychometrist, School Psychologist at East Central University; Bachelor's Degree in Psychology, Minor in Sociology, Northeastern State University **CERTS:** Pursuing LPC **A/A/S:** American Counseling Association; Oklahoma Nurses Association **C/VW:** Christian-Disciples of Christ **A/S:** She attributes her success to her father who believed in her.

TISA C. SINGLETON
Chief Executive Officer
Singleton Developmental Centers
1400 Summit Avenue
Greensboro, NC 27405 United States
tisasingle@aol.com
http://www.cambridgewhoswho.com

BUS: Child Care Center **P/S:** Child Care Services **MA:** Regional **D/D/R:** Hiring New Directors, Submitting Grant Information, Processing Payroll, Overseeing Properties, Conducting Interview for the Certified Nursing Assistant Program, Overseeing Operations, Managing Real Estate Properties, Managing 40 Employees Including Directors, Teachers and Property Managers **H/I/S:** Swimming **FBP:** O The Oprah Magazine **EDU:** Bachelor's Degree in Business Management, John Wesley College, Cum Laude (2005) **A/A/S:** Founder, Children of Deaf Adults; Chairwoman, Early Childhood Education Advisory Committee, Guilford Technical Community College; National Self Employee Association; Phi Beta Kappa **A/S:** She attributes her success to her faith in God. **H/O:** The most gratifying aspects of her career are meeting new people and visiting the babies. **I/F/Y:** In five years, Ms. Singleton hopes to franchise her training centers and get involved in volunteering services.

MS. PAMELA B. SIREN
Vice President
Neighborhood Health Plan
253 Summer Street
Boston, MA 02210 United States
pam_siren@nhp.org
http://www.nhp.org

BUS: Healthcare Management Company **P/S:** Healthcare Insurance Services **MA:** Local **D/D/R:** Overseeing Quality Management and Compliance **H/I/S:** Collecting Antiques, Photography **FBP:** Health Affairs **EDU:** Master of Science in Public Health, Boston University School of Public Health (1998); Bachelor of Science in Nursing, Widener University (1979) **A/A/S:** Healthcare Compliance Association; Association of Community Affiliated Plans; American Association of Internal Auditors; American Society of Quality Professionals **C/VW:** Regional Medical Response Team; Boston Healthcare for the Homeless; Rosie's Place; The Pine Street Inn **A/S:** She attributes her success to her desire to help people. **B/I:** She became involved in her profession because she enjoys helping others.

MR. GLENN P. SIVAK
High School Teacher
Boardman High School
7777 Glenwood Avenue
Boardman, OH 44512 United States
glennsivak@sbcglobal.net
http://www.boardman.k12.oh.us

BUS: High School Dedicated to Excellence in Education **P/S:** Secondary Education, English, Mathematics, Science, Social Studies, History, Athletics, Industrial Technology Educational Programs **MA:** Local **D/D/R:** Instructing in Wood Technology, Overseeing the Wood Technology Department **H/I/S:** White Water Rafting, Biking, Hiking, Outdoor Sports **FBP:** Woodlinks Magazine; Woodsmith; Popular Woodworking **EDU:** Master's Degree in Exercise and Sports Science, Ashland University, Ohio (2001) **A/A/S:** American Health Physical Education and Recreation Program; International Technology Education Association

DR. WALTER E. SKERRITT
Minister, Director
Global Missions Ministry
19346 Sorrento Street
Detroit, MI 48235 United States
revdoc6@yahoo.com
http://www.cambridgewhoswho.com

BUS: Independent Ecclesiastical Church Ministry Servicing the Caribbean and Africa with a Focus on the Republic of Liberia **P/S:** Discourse on the Gospel of Truth, Community Social Services Including Feeding of the Hungry, Housing, Clothing and Counseling **MA:** International **EXP:** Rev. Skerritt's areas of expertise include missionary work, social and government services. **D/D/R:** Guiding the Development of the Global Missions Ministry, Recruiting Individual Members and Partner Organizations Including Churches, Clubs and Civic Groups, Communicating Internationally with Individuals, Groups and Organizations, Establishing a Committee to Launch a New School in Liberia **H/I/S:** Traveling, Swimming, Soccer, Cricket, Basketball **EDU:** Advanced Disability Training (1994); Section 3 Regulations and Initiative Training (1994); Affordable Housing Act Training (1993); Community Housing Resource Boards Training (1993); Title 8 Investigations Training (1993); Doctor of Divinity, International Bible Institute and Seminary, Orlando, FL (1985); Master Community Development Block Grant Program (1985); FH&EO Monitoring of the Rental Rehabilitation and UDAG Programs (1985); Computer Literacy Training (1984); Monitoring Community Housing Resource Boards (1984); Personal Career Development (1982-1983); of Theology, International Bible Institute and Seminary, Orlando, FL (1983); Housing Counseling Program Administration (1982); Making Meetings Work (1981); Management Introduction and Seminar (1981); Supervisory Seminar I (1981); A Housing Seminar on Structural Revision in Government, Wayne State University (1981); Labor Relations Briefing (1980); EEO Responsibilities of Supervisors (1980); Monitoring and Evaluation of the Housing Counseling Program (1980); Neighborhood Self-Help Development Program (1980); Performance Appraisal Counseling and Feedback (1980); Management of Neighborhoods, Voluntary Associations and Consumer Protection Programs (1979); Government Technical Representative Training (1979); Basic EEO Counseling (1979); Personnel Management for EEO Counselors (1979); Coordination of Projects with Other Organizations, Strategies and Techniques for HUD Managers (1978); Housing and Human Services for the Elderly (1976); Public Relations Workshop (1976); Advanced Community Services (1975); Program Planning and Coordination of Social Services (1975); Basic Staffing and Placement (1975); Position Classification and the Management Process (1974); Management by Objective (1974); Grant Administration and Control (1974); Middle Management Institute (1973); Task Analysis and Job Restructuring (1973); The Management of Change (1973); Bachelor of Theology, Clarskville School of Theology, TN (1966); Coursework in Theology, Manhattan Bible Institute, NY (1963); Diplomate of Theology, Caribbean Wesleyan College, Bridgetown, Barbados, West Indies (1954); High School Diploma, St. Kitts Grammar School, St. Kitts, West Indies (1948) **CERTS:** Certified Counselor, United Association of Christian Chaplains and Counselors International (1985) **A/A/S:** Founding Member, Basseterre Wesleyan Holiness Church (1988); Founder, Trinity Wesleyan Church, Hartford, CT (1985); Founder, Great Salvation Church, Detroit, MI (1985); National Association of Human Rights Workers (1973); Founder, Two Churches, St. Kitts-Nevis (1949-1950); United Methodist Churches; American Baptist Churches; Progressive National Baptist Convention **A/H:** Man of the Year, American Biological Institute (1991); Certificate of Merit, Michigan State Senate (1986); Spirit of Detroit Award, Detroit City Council (1982, 1986); State Seal, Michigan State Senate; Honorary Appointment, Research Board of Advisors, The American Biographical Institute **C/VW:** Easter Seals; The Salvation Army **DOB:** June 3, 1931 **POB:** Sandy Point **CHILD:** Shirley, Eardley, Corinee, Dwight, Zachary, Janine, Cornel

OSWALD E. SKINNER
Technical Specialist of Molecular Diagnostics
James A. Haley Veterans' Administration Hospital
13000 Bruce B. Downs Boulevard
Department Plains 113
Tampa, FL 33612 United States
ozzie.skinner@med.va.gov
http://www.visn8.ed.va.gov/tampa

BUS: Veterans' Hospital **P/S:** Veterans' Healthcare Including Patient Care, Molecular Testing **MA:** National **EXP:** Mr. Skinner's expertise is in molecular pathology and diagnosis. **D/D/R:** Mentoring **H/I/S:** Traveling, Reading **FBP:** New England Journal of Medicine **EDU:** Master's Degree in Organizational Management, University of Phoenix; Bachelor of Arts in Health Service Management, Saint Leo University **A/A/S:** American Association for Clinical Chemistry; Association Médicale Mondiale; American Medical Technologists **C/VW:** Local Church; Fundraiser, Local Charitable Organization; American Red Cross **A/S:** He attributes his success to his excellent communication and networking skills. **B/I:** He became involved in his profession after working in the military, he took up an aptitude test in which the results showed that science and medical field would be a good fit for him. **H/O:** The highlight of his career was setting up a clinical laboratory in Honduras.

BRUCE A. SKOLNICK, MD
MD, Cardiologist
Cardiology Center of North Jersey
1030 Clifton Ave
Clifton, NJ 07013 United States
skolnick@aol.com
http://www.cambridgewhoswho.com

BUS: Cardiology Center **P/S:** Extending Interventional Cardiology Services to Those in Need **MA:** Local **D/D/R:** Specializing in Interventional Cardiology **H/I/S:** Traveling, Skiing, Playing Tennis **FBP:** The New England Journal of Medicine **EDU:** MD, University of Medicine and Dentistry of New Jersey School of Medicine; Bachelor's Degree in Zoology, University of Maryland **CERTS:** Board Certified Interventional Cardiologist **A/A/S:** Fellow, American College of Cardiologists; American Medical Association; American College of Physicians **A/S:** He attributes his success to being willing to work hard, remain committed and reach his goals. **B/I:** He became involved in this profession because he was always interested in medicine throughout high school. **H/O:** The highlight of his career is treating people in acute distress with emergency procedures that provide immediate relief making a dramatic improved difference in their condition.

LINDA K. F SKYLAR
Science and Mathematics Teacher
The Winston School
5909 Royal Lane
Dallas, TX 75229 United States
linda_skylar@winston-school.org
http://www.winston-school.org

BUS: School **P/S:** Education for Children with Atypical Learning Styles **MA:** Local **D/D/R:** Teaching Science and Mathematics, Coaching Volleyball and Tennis **H/I/S:** Coaching Volleyball and Tennis, Needleworking **EDU:** Master's Degree in Education, Texas Woman's University; Bachelor of Science in Chemistry, East Texas State University **A/A/S:** National Science Teachers Association; Center for Applied Special Technology; American Chemical Society; United States Tennis Association **C/VW:** American Cancer Society; Church; The Winston School; American Society for the Prevention of Cruelty to Animals; World Wildlife Fund; Heifer International; Susan G. Komen Breast Cancer Foundation **A/S:** She attributes her personal and professional success to her love of chemistry. **H/O:** The most gratifying aspect of her career is every time one of her students succeeds in college.

CAROL M. SLATIN
Chairwoman, Special Education Department
Prince George's County Public Schools, Parkdale High School
6001 Good Luck Road
Riverdale, MD 20737 United States
cslatin@pgcps.org
http://www.cambridgewhoswho.com

BUS: Public High School **P/S:** Ninth through 12th Grade Education **MA:** Local **D/D/R:** Teaching Special Education Students **H/I/S:** Skiing, Traveling, Visiting the Ocean and Mountains, Reading, Hiking, Practicing Yoga **FBP:** The Smithsonian Magazine **EDU:** Bachelor's Degree in Psychology, Boston University; Master's Degree in Special Education, Rutgers, The State University of New Jersey **A/A/S:** Council for Exceptional Children **C/VW:** Folklore Society of Greater Washington **B/I:** She became involved in her profession because she always felt a need to help the mentally challenged and received her bachelors degree in psychology. **H/O:** The most gratifying aspect of her career is her ability to persevere in her field.

EILEEN F. SLIMM, LPN
Licensed Practical Nurse
Plastic Surgery Arts & Spa
78 Easton Avenue
New Brunswick, NJ 08901 United States
eileennurse@msn.com
http://www.psanj.com

BUS: Healthcare Center **P/S:** Healthcare and Plastic Surgery **MA:** Local **EXP:** Ms. Slimm's expertise is in cosmetic plastic surgery nursing. **H/I/S:** Traveling, Sailing, Exercising **FBP:** Cosmetic Times **CERTS:** Certification in Injectable Materials of Collagen, Inamed; Certified Cosmetic Surgery Nursing in Botox and Allergan; Licensed Practical Nurse, Salem County Hospital **A/A/S:** American Society of Plastic and Reconstructive Surgical Nurses; American Society of Skin Care Specialists **C/VW:** American Society for Breast Cancer; Susan G. Komen for the Cure **A/S:** She attributes her success to the support she receives from her mentors. **B/I:** She became involved in her profession because of the experience she gained as a nurse.

MS. THERESA RENEE SLOAN
Teacher, Owner
Sloan's Education Station
Statesville, NC United States
theresasloan@hotmail.com
http://www.cambridgewhoswho.com

BUS: Educational Center **P/S:** Education for Children with and without Special Learning Needs **MA:** Local **D/D/R:** Teaching Special Education to Kindergarten through 12th-Grade Students, Conducting After-School Programs, Modifying Instructions for Students with Disabilities **H/I/S:** Playing Tennis, Walking, Traveling, Solving Puzzles and Crossword, Gardening **EDU:** Master of Arts in Special Education, North Carolina Central University, Durham; Bachelor of Arts in Elementary Education, Livingstone College, Salisbury, NC **CERTS:** Certified Elementary Education Teacher (K-6); Certified Special Education Teacher (K-12) **A/A/S:** North Carolina Association of Educators; National Association for the Advancement of Colored People; Delta Sigma Theta **DOB:** June 12, 1966 **A/S:** She attributes her success to the support she receives from her grandmother and her college professor Dr. Maxine McLanahan. **B/I:** She became involved in her profession because of her love for children and desire to make a positive difference in their lives. **H/O:** The most gratifying aspect of her career is the gratitude she receives from her students.

ANITA L. SLUSHER, MA, LPC
Counselor
Westport Growth Center
4104 Central
Kansas City, MO 64111 United States
anitaslusher@sbcglobal.net
http://www.cambridgewhoswho.com

BUS: Private Practice **P/S:** Counseling **MA:** Local **D/D/R:** Counseling Children and Adults **H/I/S:** Reading, Watching Movies, Doing Yard Work **EDU:** Master of Arts in Counseling and Guidance, University of Missouri, Kansas City; Bachelor's Degree in Psychology, Adams State College **CERTS:** Licensed Professional Counselor **A/A/S:** American Counseling Association **A/S:** She attributes her success to her hard work. **B/I:** She became involved in this profession because she always had an interest in the field.

CAROLE R. SMARR, RNG, GC-C
Case Manager
Multicare Regional Maternal-Fetal Medicine
314 Martin Luther King Junior Way
Suite 402
Tacoma, WA 98405 United States
preciouspregnanciesheavyhearts@msn.com
http://www.cambridgewhoswho.com

BUS: Medical Center **P/S:** Healthcare, Maternal-Fetal Medicine **MA:** Regional **EXP:** Ms. Smarr's expertise is in bereavement counseling and maternal-child nursing. **D/D/R:** Offering Quality Care in Prenatal Diagnosis and High-Risk Pregnancies, and Support to High-Risk Pregnancy Patients and their Families **H/I/S:** Quilting, Traveling, Shopping for Antiques, Visiting Early 20th Century Bed and Breakfasts **FBP:** Journal of Perinatal & Neonatal Nursing; Contemporary OB/GYN; American Journal of Obstetrics & Gynecology **EDU:** Registered Nurse, Tacoma General Hospital School of Nursing and Tacoma Community College (1973) **CERTS:** Certification in Death and Grief Studies, American Academy of Grief Counselors (2005); Certification in Inpatient Obstetrical Nursing, National Certification Corporation for the Obstetric, Gynecologic and Neonatal Nursing Specialties **A/A/S:** American Academy of Grief Counselors; Elder, DuPont Community Presbyterian Church

JANICE M. SMATT
Owner
Janyce African Wear, Inc.
PO Box 590872
Fort Lauderdale, FL 33359 United States
sjshabach@aol.com
http://www.cambridgewhoswho.com

BUS: Retail Clothing Company **P/S:** African Clothing for Men and Women, Footwear, Jewelry, Accessories **MA:** International **D/D/R:** Selling African Clothing, Jewelry and Accessories, Procuring Stock from Ghana, Kenya, South Africa and the United States **H/I/S:** Rollerskating, Rollerblading, Cooking, Baking, Photography **FBP:** Essence; Jet **EDU:** College Coursework **CERTS:** Licensed Practical Nurse, McFatter Technical Center (1990) **C/VW:** Greater Fort Lauderdale New Testament Church of God; Missionary, Africa, The Philippines **DOB:** June 3, 1968 **POB:** Trelawny **W/H:** Licensed Practical Nurse (1990-Present); Certified Nursing Assistant (1989-1990); Retail Worker (1987-1988); Dietary Aide (1986-1987); Factory Worker (1985-1986) **A/S:** She attributes her success to her faith in God and belief in herself. **H/O:** The most gratifying aspect of her career is knowing that her faith contributes to her success. **I/F/Y:** In five years, Ms. Smatt hopes to be an entrepreneur.

RITA SMILKSTEIN, PH.D.
Invited Faculty
Western Washington University, Seattle Urban Campus
9600 College Way
Seattle, WA 98103 United States
rsmilkst@sccd.ctc.edu
http://www.borntolearn.net

BUS: Premier Public Comprehensive University **P/S:** Research Applications and Training **MA:** National **D/D/R:** Brain-Based Teaching, Consulting, Training **H/I/S:** Reading, Writing **FBP:** Educational Leadership **EDU:** Doctoral Degree in Educational Psychology, University of Washington **A/A/S:** College Reading and Learning Association; National Association for Developmental Education; American Society for Curriculum and Development; Delta Kappa Gamma Society; Phi Delta Kappa; American Civil Liberties Union **A/H:** International Educator's Award (2004); Robert Griffin Award; Elected as Fellow, American Council of Developmental Education Associations (2006) **C/VW:** Donations to Cancer Research

AMY CORINNE SMITH
Senior Vice President
Lehman Brothers
155 Linfield Drive
Menlo Park, CA 94025 United States
acsmith@barclayscapital.com
http://www.cambridgewhoswho.com

BUS: Investment Banking **P/S:** Corporate Finance Advisory Services **MA:** International **EXP:** Ms. Smith's area of expertise is in investment banking coverage of alternative energy companies. **H/I/S:** Spending Time Outdoors, International Travel **FBP:** The Wall Street Journal; Financial Times **EDU:** Bachelor's Degree in Business, University of California at Santa Barbara **A/A/S:** Advisory Board Member, Clean Technology and Sustainable Industries Organization **A/S:** She attributes her success to her upbringing and hard work. **B/I:** She became involved in her profession because she enjoys learning, mathematics and business. **H/O:** The highlight of her career is being a powerful and respected woman in her field.

BARBARA R. SMITH, MED.

Program Specialist
Redlands Unified School District
20 W. Lugonia Avenue
Redlands, CA 92374 United States
barb_smith@redlands.k12.ca.us
http://www.redlands.k12.ca.us

BUS: School District **P/S:** Education **MA:** Regional **D/D/R:** Working with Families, Schools and the Department of Behavioral Health, Working with Student's with Behaviors that Interfere with their Success in School and Life, Training Teachers, Teaching, Counseling, Assessing Behavior in Students, Administrating Meetings **H/I/S:** Traveling, Boating, Swimming, Reading **EDU:** Master's Degree in Counseling, University of Redlands (1999); Bachelor of Science, University of Redlands (1978) **CERTS:** Certification, Therapeutic Behavioral Services (2007); Pupil Personnel Services Credential for the Education of the Gifted and Talented (1993); Teaching Credential, University of Redlands (1988) **A/A/S:** California Association of School Counselors; Alpha Theta Pi Sorority, Inc. **C/VW:** Young Women's Christian Association **DOB:** September 7, 1956 **POB:** Redlands, CA **SP:** Walter **CHILD:** Nate, Meggi **W/H:** District Counselor (2004-Present); Site Counselor (1999-2004); Elementary and Middle School Teacher (1988-1999); Various Positions, Financial Industry (1978-1981) **A/S:** She attributes her success to her firm belief that all students have potential and are good at heart. **B/I:** She became involved in her profession because the field of education allowed her to spend time with her family that other professions would not. **H/O:** The most gratifying aspect of her career is seeing her students succeed. **I/F/Y:** In five years, Ms. Smith hopes to expand programs for the emotionally challenged. She would also like to establish a clear support network for students and their families that will continue after graduation.

CARLYLE T. SMITH

Professor of Psychology
Trent University
2151 E. Bank Drive
Department of Psychology
Peterborough, Ontario K9L 1A1 Canada
csmith@trentu.ca
http://www.trentu.ca

BUS: University Dedicated to Providing the Intellectual Tools and Social Awareness to become a Successful Professional and an Active Citizen of the World **P/S:** Undergraduate and Graduate Degree Programs, International Programs, Continuing Education, Research, Athletics, Personal, Academic and Career Counseling, Student Clubs and Organizations, Library and Media Services **MA:** International **D/D/R:** Specializing in Higher Education, Researching, Knowledgeable in All Aspects of Sleep, Dreams and Memory, Behavior, Offering Leadership in Research **H/I/S:** Downhill Skiing, Hockey, Curling **FBP:** The Journal of Sleep Research; Sleep; Dreaming **EDU:** Ph.D. in Biopsychology, University of Waterloo; Bachelor of Science in Chemistry, University of Manitoba; Post-Doctorate in Sleep Behavior with Michele Jouvet, University of Claude-Bernard, Lyon, France **CERTS:** Licensed Registered Clinician **A/A/S:** Canadian Sleep Society; Associated Professional Sleep Societies; Sleep Research Society; Association for the Study of Dreams; World Federation of Sleep Research and Sleep Medicine Societies

CAROLYN SMITH, RN
Registered Nurse
Huntsville Hospital
101 Sivley Road S.W.
Huntsville, AL 35701 United States
pccaroly@hhsys.com
http://www.cambridgewhoswho.com

BUS: Healthcare **P/S:** Patient Care in a Hospital Setting **MA:** Local **D/D/R:** Caring for Orthopedic Spine Patients **H/I/S:** Reading **FBP:** Reader's Digest; Home Journal **EDU:** Associate Degree, Calhoun Community College **C/VW:** United Way of America **A/S:** She attributes her personal and professional success to her ability to listen to others. **B/I:** She became involved in the healthcare industry through a strong desire to help others. **H/O:** The highlight of her career was being appointed as a charge nurse.

CHRISTINA M. SMITH
Senior Marketing Mgr
Business Marketing Group
AT&T
20205 N. Creek Parkway
Bothell, WA 98011 United States
cs9894@att.com • christie.m.smith@cingular.com
http://www.cingular.com

BUS: Wireless Service Provider **P/S:** Wireless Services, Tones and Graphics, Multimedia Messaging, Text Messaging, Mobile Email, Video, Games, Compatible Phones and Accessories **MA:** National **D/D/R:** Specializing Information Technology, Enterprise Security, Acquisitions and Mergers **H/I/S:** Baseball, Softball **FBP:** PM Network **A/A/S:** Project Management Institute

CYDYA SMITH, HHC, AADP, IAC
Lifestyle Coach, Health Counselor
Xuberant Life
167 E. 107th Street, Suite 7
New York, NY 10029 United States
cydya@xuberantlife.com
http://www.xuberantlife.com

BUS: Healthcare Counseling Company **P/S:** Counseling and Coaching for Individuals and Groups on Proper Nutrition to Enhance Physical, Mental, Emotional and Spiritual Well Being **MA:** International **D/D/R:** Creating and Delivering Presentations and Workshops to Corporations and Member Organizations on the Topics of Nutrition, Health, Time Management and Stress Management, Maintaining a Private Health Counseling and Lifestyle Coaching Practice in Person or by Telephone, Implementing and Defining 'The Divine Alchemy of Collaboration' with her Clients to Help them Achieve their Birthright, which is a Healthier, Happier Life, Helping Clients to Determine what Inspires their Hearts and Stimulates their Minds, Integrating the Best of her Client's Heart and Mind Inspirations and Visions into their Daily Lives, Focusing on Strategies and Forming Solutions that Will Provide Desired Outcomes, Helping Clients to Adapt Better Nutrition and Healthier Eating Habits, Examining Career and Vocation Choices, Exploring Relationships, Implementing Daily Physical Exercises with Realistic Goals, Teaching Meditation **H/I/S:** Writing, Rhyming, Cooking, Dancing, Listening to Music **FBP:** Ode; Spirituality & Health **EDU:** Coursework, Institute for Integrative Nutrition **CERTS:** Certification in Second Degree Reiki; Board Certification, American Association of Drugless Practitioners; Certified Holistic Health Counselor, Teachers College, Columbia University **A/A/S:** Physicians Committee for Responsible Medicine; The Center for Educational Outreach and Innovation; Business Network International; International Association of Counselors & Therapists **A/H:** Distinguished Service Award, American Airlines **C/VW:** Oxfam International **DOB:** August 25, 1946 **POB:** Detroit, MI **A/S:** She attributes her success to her determination and personal drive. **H/O:** The most gratifying aspect of her career is creating a healthier lifestyle for people and their families.

DIANNE SMITH
President
DCS Trucking, Inc.
7935 S. State Road 39
Clayton, IN 46118 United States
dtwohappy@tds.net
http://www.cambridgewhoswho.com

BUS: Transportation Company **P/S:** Transportation Services **MA:** Regional **D/D/R:** Dispatching Trucks, Processing Payroll, Overseeing Staff, Hiring **H/I/S:** Horseback Riding **FBP:** Business Journal; Heavy Duty Trucking **EDU:** High School Diploma **A/S:** She attributes her success to the support she receives from her husband and children.

ELEANOR MARIE SMITH, RN
Registered Nurse (Retired)
Lovelace Sandia Medical Center
335 62nd Street N.W.
Albuquerque, NM 87105 United States
EleanorMarie.Smith@cwwemail.com
http://www.cambridgewhoswho.com

BUS: Medical Center **P/S:** Healthcare **MA:** Regional **D/D/R:** Supervising, Working with Doctors and Patients, Assisting with Minor Surgeries and Procedures, Leading the Team, Conducting Meetings **H/I/S:** Exercising, Reading **EDU:** Associate Degree in Nursing, St. Mary Elizabeth Nazareth College (Now Saints Mary and Elizabeth Medical Center) (1952) **A/A/S:** New Mexico Indian Nursing Association; Peak Busters; Native American Ministries; Pilgrimage for Vocation; Queen of Angels; Kateri Tekakwitha Circle, National Tekakwitha Conference **A/H:** Recipient, Award, Native American Indian Running (1989); Recipient, Professional Nurse Award for Excellence (1993)

H. MARIE SMITH, RN
Director of Nurses
Tower Day Surgery
1044 S.W. 44th Street
Oklahoma City, OK 73109 United States
msmith@ortho-ok.com
http://www.orthopedichealthsystems.com

BUS: Medical-Surgical Services **P/S:** Risk Management, Quality Improvement **MA:** Statewide **D/D/R:** Maintaining the In-Service for Staff, Overseeing 10 Nurses Per Shift, Working with the Budget Committee, Solving All Human Resource Issues, Writing, Reviewing and Revising Policy Procedures **H/I/S:** Spending Time with her Grandchildren, Watching Football **FBP:** Association of Perioperative Registered Nurses Journal **EDU:** Registered Nurse Diploma, Latrobe Area Hospital School of Nursing (1969) **A/A/S:** Association of perioperative Registered Nurses

HELEN M. SMITH
Program Coordinator for Art, Theater and Dance
Montgomery County Public Schools
850 Hungerford Drive
Rockville, MD 20850 United States
helen_smith@mcpsmd.org
http://www.mcps.k12.md.us

BUS: Public School District **P/S:** Regular Core Curriculum Including Reading, Mathematics, English, Social Studies, Art, Music, Science, Physical Education, History **MA:** Regional **D/D/R:** Overseeing Developmental Curriculum on the Secondary Level, Working with Staff, Making Assessments, Handling Instruction in Art, Theater and Dance, Coordinating Lead Level of County-Wide Development, Collaborating with Other Offices, Writing Reports and Plans Programs **H/I/S:** Riding Horses, Painting, Reading **FBP:** Educational Leadership **EDU:** Master's Equivalency in Art and Education, Montgomery County Public Schools (1984); Coursework, Catholic University of America **A/A/S:** National Art Education Association; Association for Supervision Curriculum Development; Montgomery County Association of Administrative and Supervisory Personnel; Maryland Art Education Association Carter Art Educator

JANET W. SMITH
Special Education Teacher
Great Bridge High School
301 Hanbury Road W.
Chesapeake, VA 23322 United States
janet.smith14@worldnet.att.net
http://www.cambridgewhoswho.com

BUS: High School **P/S:** Education **MA:** Local **D/D/R:** Educating Mentally Challenged Students **H/I/S:** Reading, Church, Section for Youth Department **FBP:** Spirit Led Woman; Spiritual Reading **EDU:** Master's Degree in General Education, Dominion University at Norfolk **A/A/S:** National Education Association **C/VW:** Purple Heart **A/S:** She attributes her success to patience, love for her work and kids expectations. **B/I:** She was prompted to enter her profession because she wanted to be able to help children. **H/O:** The highlight of her career was working with a student and being able to teach her all that she now knows.

MR. JEREMY T. SMITH
Business Manager
Partners and Resources for Operational Safety
7401 Martin Luther King Boulevard
Denver, CO 80207 United States
jeremy.smith@pros-aviationservices.com
http://www.pros-aviationservices.com

BUS: Independent Business Unit within Aviation Research Group/US, Inc. **P/S:** Airline Safety and Consulting **MA:** International **D/D/R:** Overseeing Airline Operational Safety and Security **H/I/S:** Camping, Fishing **EDU:** Pursuing Master of Business Administration, University of Phoenix; Bachelor of Science in Information Technology, University of Phoenix **CERTS:** Certified, Quality Auditor; Certified, ISO 9000 Auditor, International Auditor and Training Certification Association **A/A/S:** American Society for Quality **C/VW:** American Cancer Society

KAREN ELAINE SMITH, MT
Medical Technologist
American Red Cross
25 Church Street
Wilkes Barre, PA 18702 United States
smithkmo@aol.com
http://www.redcross.org

BUS: Nonprofit Organization **P/S:** Healthcare Cancer Services, Women's Health Services, Surgery, Counseling, Mental Health and Psychiatry Services, Radiology, Rehabilitation **MA:** International **D/D/R:** Managing the Blood Bank **H/I/S:** Reading, Hiking, Spending Time with her Family **FBP:** Laboratory Medicine **EDU:** Bachelor of Science in Biology and Medical Technology, Wilkes University **A/A/S:** American Society of Clinical Pathologists; Westminster Presbyterian Church **C/VW:** Church **A/S:** She attributes her success to her hard work and determination. **H/O:** The most gratifying aspect of her career is working with the American Red Cross.

KYLE E. SMITH
Sales Consultant
RE/MAX Platinum
28301 Tomball Parkway, Suite 600
Tomball, TX 77375 United States
homegirl1@hotmail.com
http://www.har.com/kylesmith

BUS: Real Estate Agency **P/S:** Real Estate Services **MA:** Local **D/D/R:** Overseeing Residential and Commercial Real Estate Exchanges **H/I/S:** Traveling, Boating, Playing Tennis, Golfing **FBP:** Realtor; Premier Homes **CERTS:** Licensed Real Estate Salesperson (1995) **A/A/S:** Tomball Area Chamber of Commerce; National Association of Realtors; RE/MAX International **A/H:** Top Listed Agent (2006); Second Top Producer (2006) **C/VW:** Children's Miracle Network **DOB:** February 24, 1952 **POB:** Dayton, OH **SP:** Harry **CHILD:** Harry, Matthew, Kimberly

LEATRICE KATHRYN WAITE SMITH
Registered Nurse (Retired)
Vassar Brothers Hospital
Poughkeepsie, NY United States
http://www.cambridgewhoswho.com

BUS: Hospital **P/S:** Healthcare **MA:** Regional **D/D/R:** Nursing, Recovery Room Nursing Was her Specialty **H/I/S:** Traveling, Reading, Doing Needlework **FBP:** Life Extension; Health and Wellness **EDU:** Coursework in Nursing, SUNY New Paltz **A/S:** She attributes her success to loving her profession. **B/I:** She became involved in her profession because she felt it was her calling.

MR. MARC A. SMITH
Meter Revenue Technician
Xcel Energy
243 Lipan Street
Denver, CO 80223 United States
marc.smith@xcelenergy.com
http://www.xcelenergy.com

BUS: Natural Gas and Electricity Distribution Company **P/S:** Comprehensive Portfolio of Energy-Related Products and Services **MA:** CO, MI, MN, NM, ND, SD, TX, WI **D/D/R:** Working with Technical Support of Automated Meter Reading to Ensure Correct Billing for Customers, Performing Demonstrations, Training **H/I/S:** Football, Basketball, Bicycling, Reading **EDU:** Coursework, Colorado State University

MARY L. SMITH
President
Kevin M. Rice Memorial Cancer Fund, Inc.
35 Wesley Drive
Jackson, KY 41339 United States
maryccm1@wmconnect.com
http://www.cambridgewhoswho.com

BUS: Nonprofit Cancer Fund **P/S:** Provision of a Tote Bag for Every Patient, Filled with Approximately Thirty Items Needed as they Receive Cancer Treatments, Funding for Medical and Travel Expenses **MA:** Regional **EXP:** Ms. Smith's area of expertise is in fundraising. **H/I/S:** Reading, Spending Time with her Family and Three Grandchildren, Writing Poetry, Publishing her Work **FBP:** Cure **EDU:** Industry-Related Training and Experience **CERTS:** Church-Commissioned Community Worker, Stamford, CT (2002) **C/VW:** Executive Director, Community Youth Center; Support Group, Happiness Even After Loss **DOB:** August 8, 1953 **POB:** Jackson, KY **SP:** James **CHILD:** Kevin, Jeremy, Jennifer **A/S:** She attributes her success to her faith in the Lord. **B/I:** She became involved in her profession because her son died of cancer. Because he was such an inspiration to others, she wanted to honor him by starting the foundation in his name. **H/O:** The most gratifying aspect of her career is letting people know that she cares through this foundation. **I/F/Y:** In five years, Ms. Smith hopes the cancer fund will continue to grow so that it can expand its services.

Nancy J. Smith, LPN II
Licensed Practical Nurse II
UMC Hospital Medical Center
1769 E. Russel Road
Las Vegas, NV 89119 United States
fireladyXII@aol.com
http://www.umc-cares.org

BUS: Teaching Hospital **P/S:** Comprehensive Healthcare Including a Burn Care Facility, Adult Emergency Center, Laboratory Services, Nutrition, Pharmacy, Radiology and Rehabilitation **MA:** Regional **D/D/R:** Working in the Pediatrics Unit, Being Responsible for the Admissions Process, Assessing and Checking Patient Vitals, IV's, Emergency Care and Medicine, Treating Minor Problems, Monitoring and Transferring Patients to a Hospital for Major Medical Conditions, Acting as a Mentor and Teaching Other Nurses **H/I/S:** Music, Dancing, Football, Baseball **EDU:** Pursuing Bachelor's Degree in Nursing, University of Phoenix; Associate Degree in Vocational Nursing, South Plains College (1981)

Ms. Rebecca A. Smith, APNC, CCNS, CCRN
Clinical Nurse Specialist in Emergency and Critical-Care
Our Lady of Lourdes Medical Center
1925 Pacific Avenue
Atlantic City, NJ 08401 United States
harbec44@aol.com
http://www.cambridgewhoswho.com

BUS: Tertiary Care Hospital **P/S:** Healthcare Services **MA:** Local **D/D/R:** Treating Critical Care Patients **H/I/S:** Boating, Building a Log Cabin **FBP:** Clinical Nurse Specialist **EDU:** Master of Science in Nursing, Widener University **CERTS:** Certified Clinical Nurse Specialist; Certified Critical Care Nurse **A/A/S:** Sigma Theta Tau; National Association of Clinical Nurse Specialists; American Association of Critical-Care Nurses; New Jersey State Nursing Association; American Nursing Association **C/VW:** Habitat for Humanity **H/O:** The highlight of her career is being a clinical nurse specialist and having exposure to different areas.

RHONDA L. SMITH, LPN
Licensed Practical Nurse
HCR Manor Care
309 E. Springfield Avenue
Champaign, IL 61801 United States
rls_1951@yahoo.com
http://www.cambridgewhoswho.com

BUS: Healthcare **P/S:** Geriatric Nursing **MA:** Local **D/D/R:** Supervising a Staff of Six, Dispensing Medications, Offering Treatments **H/I/S:** Traveling and Spending Time with her Family **EDU:** Associate Degree in Nursing, Parkland College **A/A/S:** Former President, Nursing Unit, Mt. Olive Baptist Church; Baptist Nurses Health Unit **C/VW:** Local Church **B/I:** She became involved in the profession because as a child she cared for her grandmother and decided to make caring for people a career. **H/O:** The highlight of her career is being in the medical surgery unit.

ROBIN I. SMITH
Real Estate Professional
Award Realty
3015 South Jones Boulevard
Las Vegas, NV 89146 United States
robin@smithteamlasvegas.com
http://www.smithteamlasvegas.com

BUS: Full Service Real Estate **P/S:** Real Estate Sales **MA:** Local **D/D/R:** Selling Residential Real Estate **H/I/S:** Traveling, Spending Time with the Family **EDU:** Associate Degree in Merchandising and Design, Fashion Institute of Design and Merchandising **CERTS:** Licensed Real Estate Agent; Pursuing Certification in Real Estate; New Home Sales Professional **A/A/S:** National Association of Realtors; Greater Las Vegas Board of Realtors **A/S:** She attributes her success to her ability to keep an open mind to opportunities no matter how they present themselves. **H/O:** The highlight of her career is working with first time home buyers.

RONDA S. SMITH, RN
Registered Nurse, Hospital Night Supervisor
Kootenai Medical Center
2003 Lincoln Way
Coeur d'Alene, ID 83814 United States
rssmith2761@yahoo.com
http://www.cambridgewhoswho.com

BUS: Hospital **P/S:** Full Medical Center for All Aspects of Healthcare Services **MA:** Local **D/D/R:** Pediatric Nursing, Supervising the Hospital Overnight **H/I/S:** Gardening, Hiking, Playing with her Dogs **FBP:** Nursing2009 **EDU:** Associate Degree in Nursing, Tulsa Junior College **C/VW:** Volunteers of America; Paralyzed Veterans of America **A/S:** She attributes her success to having a great preceptors in her experiences, as well as using common sense along with her experiences and education. **H/O:** The highlight of her career is being selected to be the hospital supervisor at night.

TERESA E. SMITH
Realtor
1st Choice Realty
1513 Solano Street
Corning, CA 96021 United States
teresa.smith04@cwwemail.com
http://www.cambridgewhoswho.com

BUS: Real Estate Agency **P/S:** Real Estate Services **MA:** Local **D/D/R:** Managing Sales and Listings, Overseeing Property Management and Notarial Services **H/I/S:** Traveling, Caring for her Pets **EDU:** Coursework in Business, Real Estate and Mortgage Loans **A/A/S:** California Association of Realtors; Tehama County Association of Realtors; California Association of Notaries; National Education Association; National Notary Association **C/VW:** Heifer International Foundation; Local Charitable Organizations **A/S:** She attributes her success to her honesty and integrity. **B/I:** She became involved in her profession because she was influenced by her friend. **H/O:** The most gratifying aspect of her career is receiving gratitude from her customers.

TINA JEAN SMITH
President
Roof Repair Specialties, Inc.
6008 Centerhill Church Road
Loganville, GA 30052 United States
princessindian72@aol.com
http://www.cambridgewhoswho.com

BUS: Construction **P/S:** Roofing, Copper, Installations **MA:** Local **D/D/R:** Specializing in Slate, Copper, Tile Installation, Roofing Construction, Setting-Up and Estimates, Financing, Manufacturing **H/I/S:** Playing Horseshoes, Spending Time with her Daughter **EDU:** High School Education **A/A/S:** Home Builders Association of Georgia **C/VW:** 4-H Groups; Cancer Societies **A/S:** She attributes her success to hard work. **B/I:** She became involved in this profession because she grew up in construction. **H/O:** The highlight of her career is having happy customers.

MRS. LISA SMITH-DENNIS, BS
Owner
Smith Dennis Tax Service
2396 McEldery Street
Baltimore, MD 21286 United States
lisasanick@aol.com
http://www.cambridgewhoswho.com

BUS: Sole Proprietor **P/S:** Tax and Finance Services **MA:** Statewide **D/D/R:** Preparing Tax Returns **H/I/S:** Traveling, Reading, Relaxing **EDU:** Bachelor of Science in Psychology, Morgan State University **C/VW:** The Salvation Army; Goodwill; United Way of America **A/S:** She attributes her success to her parents. **B/I:** She chose the profession because she comes from a family of tax accountants. **H/O:** The highlight of her career is providing quality services at reasonable prices.

BONNIE L. SMYTHE
Research and Development Manager
Nature's Path Foods, Inc.
2220 Natures Path Way
Blaine, WA 98230 United States
bsmythe@naturespath.com
http://www.naturespath.com

BUS: Distribution Firm **P/S:** Whole Grain, Organic Cereals and Products including Granola and Energy Bars, Toaster Pastries, Frozen Bread and Waffles **MA:** International **D/D/R:** Managing the New Product Development Department, Launching Six to 12 New Products Per Year, Overseeing Product Runs, Labels and Procedures, Assisting with Co-Packaged Products, Creating Recipes **H/I/S:** Horseback Riding, Traveling, Gardening **FBP:** Prepared Foods **EDU:** Bachelor of Science in Food Science, University of Manitoba (1979) **A/A/S:** Institute of Food Technologists

CYNTHIA A. SNEED, BSN
Nurse Supervisor III
North Carolina Correctional Institution for Women
1034 Bragg Street
Raleigh, NC 27610 United States
scao5@doc.state.nc.us
http://www.cambridgewhoswho.com

BUS: Correctional Institution **P/S:** Correctional Psychiatric Nursing **MA:** Local **D/D/R:** Scheduling Meetings, Internal Audits, Overseeing Records, Supervising a Nursing Staff of 29 Full-Time and Part-Time Workers **H/I/S:** Attending Horse Shows **FBP:** American Journal of Nursing **EDU:** Bachelor of Science in Nursing, University of North Carolina **C/VW:** Church **A/S:** She attributes her career success to being able to treat others fairly and with respect. **B/I:** She was inspired by her grandmother, who was a nurse, to pursue a career in nursing. **H/O:** She feels that having her office voted as the office with the best records nationally after a commission audit is the highlight of her career.

CARMEN M. SNIDER
Senior Account Manager
CDS Global
1901 Bell Avenue
Des Moines, IA 50515 United States
cmsnider@hotmail.com
http://www.cds-global.com

BUS: Consulting **P/S:** Fulfillment and Circulation Services **MA:** Regional **EXP:** Ms. Snider's expertise is in operations management. **D/D/R:** Maintaining Client Relations, Consulting **H/I/S:** Golfing, Reading **EDU:** Bachelor of Arts in Accounting and Finance, Graceland University; Diploma, Lincoln High School **C/VW:** United Way of America **A/S:** She attributes her success to her mentors and ability to work well with a team. **B/I:** She became involved in her profession by taking advantage of an opportunity that was presented to her. **H/O:** The most gratifying aspect of her career is serving as the instrumental contact for a new client.

MS. REGINA Y. SNOW
Writer, Novelist
RYS Corporation LLC
1551 Ben Sawyer Boulevard, Penthouse 2-H
Mount Pleasant, SC 29464 United States
spiritsnow@aol.com
regina.snow@cwwemail.com
http://www.cambridgewhoswho.com

BUS: Publishing Company **P/S:** Publications Including Books, Novels **MA:** International **D/D/R:** Brainstorming Ideas for her Writing, Forming a Layout, Planning for the Design of the Publication, Collaborating with the Editor, Marketing the Material, Releasing the Material, Writing Mainstream Novels and Short Stories **H/I/S:** Bicycling, Spending Time at the Beach, Attending Cultural Events, Exercising **EDU:** Master of Business Administration, West Virginia State University **C/VW:** Meals on Wheels; Special Olympics; Local Missionaries **A/S:** She attributes her success to her faith, determination and personal drive. **H/O:** The highlight of her career was being in the top 10 of 30,000 women in a Fortune 500 construction company.

SUSAN P. SNYDER
Instructor, Teacher
Antelope Valley College
3401 W. Avenue K
Lancaster, CA 93536 United States
ssnder@avc.edu
http://www.avc.edu

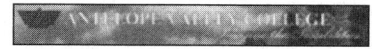

BUS: Comprehensive Community College **P/S:** Sixty-Two Degrees and Certificate Programs, Academic Divisions Include Arts and Letters, Business, Computer and Media Arts, Health Sciences, Physical Education and Athletics, Mathematics and Science, Social and Behavioral Science and Family and Consumer Education, and Technical Education **MA:** Regional **D/D/R:** Teaching Nursing, Fundamentals and Chronic Illness **FBP:** HAW; Nursing2009 **EDU:** Bachelor of Science Degree in Liberal Arts, Colorado Christian University (1997); Bachelor of Science Degree in Nursing, California State University (1991) **A/A/S:** American Association of Critical-Care Nurses; Pi Lambda Theta International Honor Society

MR. MARK SOBEL, PH.D.
Executive Officer
American Society for Investigative Pathology
9650 Rockville Pike
Bethesda, MD 20814 United States
http://www.asip.org

BUS: Nonprofit Educational Organization Involving a Society of Biomedical Scientists who Investigate Mechanisms of Disease **P/S:** Promote the Process of Education in the Principles of Pathobiology, Uses a Variety of Structural, Functional, and Genetic Techniques and Ultimately Applies Research Findings to the Diagnosis and Treatment of Diseases **MA:** National **D/D/R:** Overseeing Science Administration Policies, Planning Meetings, Organizing National Panels to Orchestrate the Society in Excelling in Inventive Investigations **FBP:** AJCP; The Journal of Molecular Diagnostics **EDU:** MD, Mount Sinai School of Medicine (1975); Bachelor of Arts in Classical Music and History, Brandeis University (1970); Ph.D., City University of New York **A/A/S:** President, Association for Molecular Pathology; American Society for Biochemistry and Molecular Biology; American Association for the Advancement of Science; AMP; American Association for Cancer Research; AAHARP; Alpha Omega Alpha, Mt. Sinai School of Medicine (1995) **A/H:** The Saul J. Horowitz Jr. Memorial Award, Mt. Sinai School of Medicine (1991); The Public Health Commendation Medal (1989)

DANIELA SOKOLOSKI, RN, MS
Medical Policy and Benefit Administrator
University of Michigan, M-Care
2301 Commonwealth Boulevard
Ann Arbor, MI 48105 United States
dsokolos@mcare.med.umich.edu
http://www.cambridgewhoswho.com

BUS: Health Insurance **P/S:** Medical Benefit Coverage **MA:** Regional **D/D/R:** Determining Medical Coverage Policies **H/I/S:** Swimming, Exercising, Reading **FBP:** Managed Care Magazine **EDU:** Master's Degree in Healthcare Administration, University of Michigan **A/A/S:** American Nurses Association **C/VW:** Church; Walk for Diabetes; Sponsors Needy Families at Christmas; Helps Local Schools with Tutoring; Supports Worthy Causes through her Business **A/S:** She attributes her success to her positive attitude and to seeing change as an opportunity. **B/I:** She became involved in her profession because she was a hospital nurse and wanted to branch out. **H/O:** The highlight of her career was being able to balance work and home life.

DEBORAH B. SOLIMAN
Coding Specialist
Stringfellow Memorial Hospital
301 E. 18th Street
Anniston, AL 36207 United States
dbsoliman@bellsouth.net
http://www.cambridgewhoswho.com

BUS: Public Healthcare Organization **P/S:** Healthcare **MA:** Local **D/D/R:** Coding, Ensuring Quality Assurance for Physicians **H/I/S:** Going to the Beach, Traveling to the Caribbean **EDU:** Bachelor's Degree in Nursing, Jacksonville State University (1976) **CERTS:** Certified Coding Specialist **C/VW:** Susan G. Komen Breast Cancer Foundation **A/S:** She attributes her success to good leadership skills. **B/I:** She became involved in her profession through a natural progression of opportunities. **H/O:** The highlight of her career was serving as director of utilization review and good services.

DAVID M. SOLOMON, RN
Patient Care Coordinator
Catawba Valley Medical Center
810 Fairgrove Church Road
Hickory, NC 28602 United States
davidsol@embarqmail.com
http://www.cambridgewhoswho.com

BUS: Hospital **P/S:** Emergency Care Services **MA:** Local **D/D/R:** Emergency Nursing **H/I/S:** Spending Quality Time with his Two Sons, Golfing, Baseball, Building Model Airplanes, Fishing **FBP:** Journal of Emergency Medicine **EDU:** Bachelor's Degree in Nursing, Lenoir Rhyne College **CERTS:** Certificate in Nursing **A/A/S:** Emergency Nurses Association **C/VW:** The Salvation Army **A/S:** He attributes his success to hard work and support from family and friends. **B/I:** He became involved in the profession after he came out of the military having worked in communications. **H/O:** The highlight of his career was attaining his certification.

ROHAN SOMAR, MD, FACEP, FAAEM
Chairman, Chief Executive Officer
Emergency Medicine
Saint Clare's Health System
PO Box 1246
Denville, NJ 07834 United States
rsomar@saintclares.org
http://www.epscdocs.com

BUS: Hospitals System **P/S:** Healthcare Including Women's Healthcare, Maternal-Child, Emergency, Pediatric, Cardiovascular Care, Weight Loss Surgery, Cancer Treatment and Behavioral Therapy **MA:** Regional **D/D/R:** Managing Operations Including Recruiting, Processing Payroll and Billing **H/I/S:** Playing Cricket, Dancing **FBP:** Medical-Related Publications **EDU:** Residency in Emergency Medicine, Mount Sinai School of Medicine and Beth Israel Medical Center (1993); Internship, Columbia University and St. Luke's Roosevelt Hospital Center (1991); MD, Mount Sinai School of Medicine (1990) **A/A/S:** American College of Emergency Physicians; Health Executive, Physicians Association; American Medical Association **C/VW:** Board of Directors, Godley; Charitable Organizations, Guyana; Charitable Organizations, Ghana

GARY SONNENBERG, CFO
Chief Financial Officer
Martin Luther College
1995 Luther Court
New Ulm, MN 56073 United States
sonnengl@mlc-wels.edu
http://www.mlc-wels.edu

BUS: College Serving the Ministerial Needs of the Wisconsin Evangelical Lutheran Synod **P/S:** Courses of Study Qualifying Men for Entrance into Wisconsin Lutheran Seminary, Where they will Continue their Preparation for the Pastoral Ministry of the Wisconsin Evangelical Lutheran Synod, Courses of Study for the Preparation of Qualified Educators for the Teaching Ministry in Preschools, Elementary and Secondary Schools **MA:** Regional **D/D/R:** Overseeing Staff, Human Resources, Financial Aid Records and Administration, Accounting, Managing the Maintenance Staff **H/I/S:** Sailing, Spending Time with the Family **FBP:** NACUBO Publications **EDU:** High School Education **A/A/S:** President, of Rotary Club (2003); President, Rotary Club (1997); National Association of College and University Business Officers; Treasurer, Minnesota Bed & Breakfast Association; Treasurer, City Library, New Ulm, Minnesota

JEAN CAROL SOONG, RN, BSN
Information Systems Project Leader for Clinical Systems
Good Samaritan Hospital
1225 Wilshire Boulevard
Los Angeles, CA 90017 United States
jsoong@goodsam.org
http://www.goodsam.org

BUS: World-Class Academic Medical Center **P/S:** Cardiology, Cardiac Surgery, Radiology, Ear, Nose and Throat Services, Emergency, Oncology, Ophthalmology and Retinal Medicine, Orthopedics, Podiatry, Physical and Pulmonary Medicine, Respiratory Care Radiation Oncology, Surgery, Women's Health and Newborn Services, Urology **MA:** Local **D/D/R:** Performing Clinical Analysis **H/I/S:** Spending Time with her Family, Golfing, Tennis **FBP:** Healthcare IT News **EDU:** Bachelor of Science in Nursing, California State University **CERTS:** Six Sigma Foundation Training (2002) **A/A/S:** Healthcare Information and Management Systems Society; American Nursing Informatics Association **H/O:** The most gratifying aspect of her career is making a difference in her current position.

GLORIA K. SORRELS
Special Teacher
Krebs Public Schools
20 S.W. Fifth Street
Krebs, OK 74554 United States
gsorrels@krebs.k12.ok.us
http://www.cambridgewhoswho.com

BUS: Public Elementary School **P/S:** Education **MA:** Local **D/D/R:** Teaching Special Education Classes **H/I/S:** Riding, Horses, Camping, Spending Time with her Grandchildren **EDU:** Master's Degree in Special Education, South Eastern University; Bachelor's Degree in Education, Southeastern University **C/VW:** Girl Scouts; FFA; Church; Camp Plea; 4-H **A/S:** She attributes her success to the love for the kids, and wanting to see them succeed.

MR. PAUL E. SOSENKO
Study Coordinator, Practice Manager
Daniel A. Warner, MD, PA, Consultive Medicine
1630 Mason Avenue, Suite C
Daytona Beach, FL 32117 United States
consultivemed@aol.com
http://www.cambridgewhoswho.com

BUS: Medical Clinic **P/S:** Healthcare **MA:** Regional **EXP:** Mr. Sosenko's expertise is in HIV and AIDS consultation and care. **D/D/R:** Working as a Clinical Care Technician, Overseeing Clinic Operations **H/I/S:** Photography, Participating in Water Sports, Gardening **EDU:** Associate Degree in Medical Management, Keiser University, Daytona Beach, FL (2000); Associate of Science in Accounting, Onondaga Community College (1992) **C/VW:** Broadway Cares/Equity Fights AIDS; Arch Angels; Special Olympics, FL; The Humane Society of the United States; Volunteer, American Heart Association

MARGARET L. SOTTOSANTI
Teacher of Gifted and Talented Children
Wesley Lakes Elementary School
685 McDonough Parkway
McDonough, GA 30254 United States
mikki_ksu@charter.net
http://www.msottosanti@henry.k12.ga.us

BUS: School **P/S:** Education **MA:** Local **D/D/R:** Encouraging Creativity in Children **H/I/S:** Spending Time with her Grandson, Reading, Gardening **FBP:** NEA Today **EDU:** Master of Arts in Teaching, Piedmont College; Bachelor of Science in Education, Kent State University **A/A/S:** Georgia Association of Educators; Georgia Association of Gifted Children **A/H:** Wesley Lakes Elementary Teacher of the Year (2004); Henry County Finalist, Teacher of the Year (2004); Nominee, Disney American Teacher of the Year Award **C/VW:** A Friend's House; Community Service; Haven House; Blessing Thrift Shop **A/S:** She attributes her success to her strong work ethic, care and compassion for her students. **B/I:** She became involved in her profession because she had a wonderful teacher who was a role model for her. **H/O:** The highlight of her career was being a finalist in the county Teacher of the Year competition.

MARLENE M. SOUPIR
Technology Teacher
Tracy Area Elementary School
700 S. Fourth Street
Tracy, MN 56175 United States
soupirm@tracy.k12.mn.us
http://www.tracy.k12.mn.us

BUS: Elementary School **P/S:** Primary Education **MA:** Local **D/D/R:** Teaching Technology to Students in Kindergarten through Sixth-Grade **H/I/S:** Spending Time with her Children **EDU:** Bachelor of Science in Elementary Education **A/A/S:** International Reading Association; MNRC; Parent-Teacher Association **C/VW:** Local Church **A/S:** She attributes her success to her perseverance and working with good people. **B/I:** She became involved in her profession because she wanted to make a difference.

SHEILA DENISE SOUTHALL
Special Education Teacher
San Jacinto Elementary School
2615 Virginia
Baytown, TX 77520 United States
sheild616@aol.com
http://www.cambridgewhoswho.com

BUS: Public Elementary School **P/S:** Education **MA:** Local **D/D/R:** Special Education **H/I/S:** Fishing, Collecting Angels, Spending Time with her Family **EDU:** Master's Degree in Curriculum and Instruction, University of Houston; Bachelor's Degree, Texas A&M University **A/A/S:** Texas Classroom Teachers Association **C/VW:** United Way of America **A/S:** She attributes her success to her rapport with the students. **B/I:** She became involved in her profession because she had an uncle who was learning disabled and wanted to be able to help others in his position. **H/O:** The highlight of her career was helping a child who could not walk.

KATHLEEN M. SOWELL
Income Tax Preparer
Kathleen M. Sowell
5729 W. Cinnabar Avenue
Glendale, AZ 85302 United States
http://www.cambridgewhoswho.com

BUS: Taxes, Accounting **P/S:** Tax Preparations **MA:** Local **D/D/R:** Preparing Taxes, Interior Design/Decoration, Floor Plans, Landscaping, Seamstress **H/I/S:** Landscaping, Interior Decorating, Oil Painting **EDU:** Coursework, Indiana State University College of Business **A/H:** Blue Ribbon Award; Honor Roll; Honor Society **C/VW:** St. Jude Children's Hospital; Disabled Veterans; Boys and Girls Club **A/S:** She attributes her career success to her ability to remain active despite having suffered a stroke, cancer, and double bypass surgery at the age of 83, and to her positive attitude and drive to perform. **B/I:** She became involved in her profession because after working for General Electric for 25 years, she realized her love of accounting and decided to start her own business. **H/O:** She feels that being able to help others while looking back on her success throughout her career, and the connections and relationships she has formed over the years are the highlights of her career.

DAWN M. SPADER, RN
Registered Nurse
BayHealth Medical Center
640 S. State Street
Dover, DE 19901 United States
dnr1856@yahoo.com
http://www.cambridgewhoswho.com

BUS: Hospital **P/S:** Healthcare **MA:** Local **D/D/R:** Nursing in Orthopedics **H/I/S:** Softball, Horseback Riding **EDU:** Associate Degree in Nursing, Delaware Technical & Community College **A/A/S:** American Association of Student Nurses **C/VW:** March of Dimes; American Cancer Society **A/S:** She attributes her personal and professional success to her personal drive and passion for helping others. **B/I:** She has always had an interest in the field and a desire to help others. **H/O:** The highlight of her career is the rewarding nature of her profession.

BRIANNE L. SPALDING
Marketing Director
Crawford & Bangs, LLP
1290 E. Center Court Drive
Covina, CA 91724 United States
bspalding@builderslaw.com
http://www.cambridgewhoswho.com

BUS: Law Firm **P/S:** Construction Litigation **MA:** Regional **D/D/R:** Event Planning, Managing Databases, Marketing **H/I/S:** Reading, Arts and Crafts **FBP:** The Wall Street Journal **EDU:** Bachelor of Science in Business Administration and Marketing and Management, California State Polytechnic University, Pomona **A/A/S:** Legal Marketing Association; Golden Key International Honour Society; Treasurer, Southern California Chapter, Legal Marketing Association **C/VW:** Christian Children's Fund **A/S:** She attributes her success to her continued education and ability to learn quickly. **B/I:** She became involved in the profession because she enjoyed the field. **H/O:** The most gratifying aspect of her career is expanding the firm through marketing.

PENNY L. SPARKS
Security Title
Comtemporary Service Corporation
3710 N. Meridian Street
Apartment 906
Indianapolis, IN 46208 United States
sparks-p@sbcglobal.net

BUS: Sports Facility **P/S:** Crowd Management and Security Services **MA:** Local **D/D/R:** Communicating with People **EDU:** Coursework, Purdue University; Coursework, Indiana University; Coursework, Trade School **CERTS:** Computer Technician Certificate

POLLY D. SPEARS
Activity Coordinator
Bethel Missionary Baptist Church, Bethel Towers
224 N. Martin Luther King Jr. Boulevard
Tallahassee, FL 32301 United States
http://www.bethelmissionarybaptist.com

BUS: Proven Leader in the Healthcare Industry, Independent Living Facility **P/S:** Wide Variety of High Quality Healthcare Services to Residents and the Community **MA:** Regional **D/D/R:** Coordinating the Activity Program at Bethel Tuners, Offering Spiritual, Social, Educational and Health-Related Programs, Co-Hosting a Radio Show on Weal 1450 AM Titled 'A Chosen Generation' which Focuses on the Elderly Population **H/I/S:** Swimming, Reading, Walking, Spending Time with her Four Wonderful Daughters, Five Grandchildren and Three Great-Grandchildren **EDU:** Master of Arts Degree in Adult Nursing, Emphasis on Orthopedics, University of North Carolina at Chapel Hill (1982); Bachelor of Science in Nursing, Tuskegee University (1962); Diploma, Brewster Hospital School of Nursing (1953) **A/A/S:** Delta Sigma Theta; Chi Eta Phi; Sigma Theta Tau; Board of Directors, American Cancer Society; Board of Directors, Elder Care Services; Board of Directors, Elder Affairs; Board of Directors, Foster Grandparents; Advisory Board, Health South Community; Adjunct Professor, Florida A&M University School of Nursing

JANET SMITH WILSON SPEECHLEY, AS, BS
Licensed Practical Nurse (Retired)
Still Hopes Episcopal Retirement Center
West Columbia, SC 29160 United States
mimi1948@windstream.net
http://www.cambridgewhoswho.com

BUS: Retirement Center **P/S:** Healthcare **MA:** Local **EXP:** Ms. Speechley's expertise is in geriatric nursing. **H/I/S:** Continuing her Education, Spending Time with her Grandchildren, Reading, Karaoke **FBP:** American Journal of Nursing **EDU:** Bachelor's Degree in Social Work, University of South Carolina; Associate Degree in Science and Business, University of South Carolina; Associate of Science in Nursing, Midlands Technical College **CERTS:** Licensed Practical Nurse, Midlands Technical College **A/A/S:** Pearl S. Buck Foundation **C/VW:** American Red Cross; Board Member, Southern Baptist Mission Board **DOB:** October 4, 1948 **POB:** NC **CHILD:** Richard, Kathleen **W/H:** Nurse (1983-2008); Administrative Assistant; University of South Carolina; College of Charleston; Probation Officer **A/S:** She attributes her success to treating each patient as a human being and family member. She also provides a personal touch along with respect and dignity. **B/I:** She became involved in this profession because nursing provided her with an opportunity to be of service to her fellow man.

CAROL J. SPENCER
Director
Resident Management Institute
30438 Mattson Road
Culdesac, ID 83524 United States
rmi@residentmanagementinstitute.com
http://www.residentmanagementinstitute.com

BUS: Vocation Education **P/S:** Property Management **MA:** California **D/D/R:** Student Council, Administration **H/I/S:** Scuba Diving, Fly Fishing **FBP:** Inc. **EDU:** Extensive Industry Related Training and Experience **A/A/S:** Certification, Western Mobile Home Park Association **C/VW:** Catholic Charities; Working with the Homeless **A/S:** She attributes her success to her hard work and determination. **B/I:** She became involved in her profession because of her husband.

MR. THOMAS T. SPENCER
Special Education Teacher
McKinley Primary Center
228 N. Greenlawn Avenue
South Bend, IN 46615 United States
tspencer@sbcsc.k12.in.us
http://www.cambridgewhoswho.com

BUS: Public School **P/S:** Elementary Education **MA:** Local **D/D/R:** Teaching Special Education **H/I/S:** Playing the Drums, Collecting, Antiquing **FBP:** New Yorker **EDU:** Ph.D. in American History, University of Notre Dame; Master's in Education, Indiana University, South Bend **A/A/S:** Association for People with Severe Handicaps; Organization of American Historians **A/H:** Elementary Teacher of the Year (1991); Learning Magazine's Top 25 Professionals **C/VW:** Volunteer, Local Hospice and Homeless Shelter; Habitat for Humanity; St. Vincent de Paul

PAMELA J. SPERRY
Realtor
RE/MAX Powerhouse
4200 Tamiami Trail
Port Charlotte, FL 33952 United States
ilovepuntagorda@comcast.net
http://www.isellpuntagorda.com

BUS: Leader in Real Estate **P/S:** Selling Luxury Homes, Residential and Commercial Real Estate, Property Management **MA:** Regional **D/D/R:** Assisting Buyers and Sellers with Upscale Properties, Luxury Homes and Condominiums **H/I/S:** Boating, Cooking **FBP:** Florida Realtor **EDU:** College Coursework, Syracuse University **CERTS:** Real Estate License, States of Florida and Kentucky **A/A/S:** Women's Council of Realtors; National Association of Realtors; Isles Yacht Club **A/H:** Top Producer, RE/MAX; Top Realtor in Southwest Florida **C/VW:** Volunteer, Team Punta Gorda; Greyhound Adoption Program **C/A:** Published in Six Newspapers

KATHLEEN M. SPILLMAN
Secretary, Bookkeeper (Retired)
Calmar-Festina-Spillville Catholic School
302 S. Maryville Street, PO Box 815
Calmar, IA 52132 United States
dbqu05sec@arch.pvt.k12.ia.us
ks_cfs@yahoo.com
http://www.arch.pvt.k12.ia.us

BUS: Private Catholic School **P/S:** High Quality Educational Services for Preschool Students and Kindergarten through Eighth Graders **MA:** Regional **D/D/R:** Performing Secretarial Work, Bookkeeping, Recording Absentees, Paying All Bills for All Programs, Preparing Payroll for Accountants, Keeping Track of Records and Typing **H/I/S:** Reading Novels by Nora Roberts, Quilting, Dirt Track Racing, Watching NASCAR Races, Surfing the Internet, Spending Time with her Family **EDU:** Coursework in Secretarial Studies, Northeast Iowa Community College (1980) **A/A/S:** St. Aloysius Rosary Society; Former Leader, 4-H Club **DOB:** February 1, 1946 **W/H:** Rockwell Collins, Cedar Rapids, IA (1968-1972); Admiral Corp., Harvard, IL (1965-1967); C & S Clothing, Manchester, IA (1962-1963); Secretary, Decorah Women's Bowing Association

SHERRIE LYNN SPITLER, ADRN
Registered Nurse
Rockingham Memorial Hospital
235 Cantrell Avenue
Harrisonburg, VA 22801 United States
sherriespit@adelphia.net
http://www.rmhonline.com

BUS: Hospital **P/S:** Healthcare **MA:** Local **D/D/R:** Medical-Surgical Nursing, Working in Orthopedics, Neurosurgery, Labor and Delivery Departments, Psychiatric Nursing **H/I/S:** Camping, Cross Stitching, Swimming, Spending Time with her Family **FBP:** RN **EDU:** Associate Degree in Nursing, Blue Ridge Community College **A/H:** Youth Advisor, Church **A/S:** She attributes her success to the support she receives from her family and to her church. **B/I:** She became involved in her profession because she liked helping people and she always wanted to be a nurse. **H/O:** The most gratifying aspect of her career is bringing newborn babies into the world and then knowing there is hope.

KAY L. SPRIGGS, M.ED.
Inclusion English Teacher
Opelika High School
1700 Lafayette Parkway
Opelika, AL 36801 United States
kayspriggs@bellsouth.net
http://www.cambridgewhoswho.com

BUS: High School **P/S:** Education **MA:** Local **D/D/R:** Teaching English and Special Education Classes to High School Students, Consulting, Presenting at Seminars **H/I/S:** Decorating, Reading **EDU:** Master of Education in Learning Disabilities, Auburn University **A/A/S:** Alpha Delta Kappa **C/VW:** Former State President and Local President, Emblem Club **A/S:** She attributes her success to her flexibility and focus on the children. **B/I:** She became involved in the profession because she was influenced by her parents, who were both educators. **H/O:** The highlight of her career is hearing positive stories from her former students.

DR. DEBORAH H. SPROTT
Dentist/Director
The Smile Dental Group
13319 E. Freeway at Uvalde
Houston, TX 77015 United States
dhsprott@sbcglobal.net
http://www.cambridgewhoswho.com

BUS: Group Dental Practice **P/S:** General Dentistry, Cosmetic Dentistry, Bridges, Bonding, Tooth Veneers, Implants, Whitening, Crowns, Fillings, Extractions, Root Canals, Orthodontics **MA:** Regional **D/D/R:** Performing Cosmetic and General Dental Procedures **H/I/S:** Music, Reading **FBP:** Dental Economics; Contemporary Esthetics and Restorative Practice **EDU:** Doctor of Dental Surgery in Dentistry (1979) **A/A/S:** American Dental Association; Texas Dental Association; Greater Houston Dental Society

EVAGELIA SPYRATOS
Registered Nurse
MinuteClinic
8625 South Harlem Street
Bridgeview, IL 60455 United States
eva-spyratos@juno.com
http://www.cambridgewhoswho.com

BUS: Medical Facility **P/S:** Medical Ambulatory and Community Services **MA:** Regional **D/D/R:** Working in the Surgical Intensive Care Unit, Handling Surgically and Medically Unstable Patients, Home Health and Community Nursing **H/I/S:** Gardening, Traveling, Camping **FBP:** Critical Care Nurse; American Journal of Critical Care; The Nurse Practitioner **EDU:** Master's Degree in Nursing, DePaul University (2006); Diploma in Nursing, St. Francis Hospital School of Nursing (1996); Bachelor of Science in Psychology, University of Illinois at Chicago (1993) **A/A/S:** Illinois Nurses Association; American Association of Critical-Care Nurses; American Academy of Nurse Practitioners **A/H:** 10 Years of Service Award, Resurrection Health Care **C/VW:** American Cancer Society; Arthritis Foundation

MICHAEL E. ST. GEORGE, ESQ.
Owner, Attorney at Law
Law Offices of Michael E. St. George P.C.
440 E. Southern Avenue
Tempe, AZ 85282 United States
stgeorge@stgeorgelaw.com
http://www.stgeorgelaw.com

BUS: Legal Services **P/S:** Providing Quality Legal Representation and Consulting Services **MA:** Local **D/D/R:** Litigating in General Business, Entrepreneurial Representation, Mergers and Acquisitions **H/I/S:** Playing the Guitar, Piano, Upright Base and Mandolin **FBP:** Forbes **EDU:** JD, Arizona State University **A/A/S:** State Bar Association of Texas; State Bar Association of Arizona **C/VW:** Local Church

MARY ANN STACK
Associate Broker
Prudential Fox and Roach Realtors
1 W. Main Street
Moorestown, NJ 08057 United States
maryannstack@comcast.net
http://www.moorestownestate.com

BUS: Real Estate Brokerage **P/S:** All Facets of Residential, Commercial and Land **MA:** National **D/D/R:** Specializing in Business Management, Negotiating, Acting as a Fine Home Specialist and Relocation Specialist **H/I/S:** Golfing, Dancing, Traveling **FBP:** Success **EDU:** Industry Related Training and Experience **A/A/S:** National Association of Realtors; New Jersey Association of Realtors

JOHN STADTMILLER
Owner, President
Republic Broadcasting Network
1015 S. Mays Street, Suite 100
Round Rock, TX 78664 United States
john@republicbroadcasting.org
http://www.rbnlive.com

BUS: Proven Leaders in Radio Broadcasting **P/S:** All Talk and News Radio Station Heard All Throughout the Country and the World **MA:** International **D/D/R:** Hosting an International Talk Show from 4-6 PM Central Standard Time, Managing, Marketing and Promoting the Radio Station **H/I/S:** Riding Harley Davidson Motorcycles **A/A/S:** National Federation of Independent Business

JENNIFER GRETH STAHL, R.PH.
Pharmacy Manager
Tops Pharmacy
301 Meadow Drive
North Tonawanda, NY 14120 United States
jenjesben@aol.com
http://www.cambridgewhoswho.com

BUS: Pharmacy **P/S:** Medication, Heatlhcare Products **MA:** Regional **D/D/R:** Filling Prescriptions, Counseling Customers, Managing the Inventory, Consulting with Physicans **H/I/S:** Cub Scout Den Leader, Photography, Quilting, Crafting **FBP:** Drug Topics **EDU:** Bachelor of Science in Pharmacy, SUNY, University at Buffalo **C/VW:** The ADA; Arthritis Foundation; Children's Foundation; American Diabetes Association; Sjögren's Syndrome Foundation, Inc.; Lupus Foundation, Inc. **A/S:** She attributes her career success to her sincere concern for her patients' well-being. **H/O:** She feels that the return visits that she receives from grateful patients are the highlights of her career.

NICOLE M. STALNAKER
Information Technology Operations Manager
McKee Nelson, LLP
One Battery Park Plaza
New York, NY 10004 United States
nstalnaker@mckeenelson.com
http://www.mckeenelson.com

BUS: Entrepreneurial Law Firm **P/S:** Specializes in Structured Finance, Tax Litigation, Tax Planning and White Collar Investigations for Fortune 200 Business and Major Underwriters **MA:** Local **D/D/R:** Managing the Help Desk, Overseeing Day to Day Support, Handling Deployment, Introducing New Technologies to the Firm **H/I/S:** Playing Billiards, Reading Mysteries **FBP:** Law Technology News **EDU:** Bachelor's Degree in Computer Information Systems, Kent State University (2001)

ARLEEN B. STANDIFORD
Consultant
Educational Consulting Services
6601 Tennysone, Suite 3303
Albuquerque, NM 87111 United States
arleen.standiford@gmail.com
http://www.cambridgewhoswho.com

BUS: Educational Consulting **P/S:** Montessori, Charter Schools, Intensive Phonics **MA:** Regional **D/D/R:** Educational Consulting, Teaching Elementary School **H/I/S:** Playing the Piano **FBP:** Montessori Life **EDU:** Master's Degree in Educational Leadership, Mexico State University **A/A/S:** Association for Supervision and Curriculum Development; AMS; IMS; IMC **C/VW:** Church; Boy Scouts of America; Jefferson Educational Freedom Association **A/S:** She attributes her personal and professional success to her inner drive and ability to set goals. **B/I:** She has always had an interest in the field and a love for education.

DON STANLEY
Realtor
RE/MAX Realty Services
15020 Shady Grove Road
Rockville, MD 20850 United States
donstanley@mris.com
http://www.my-next-house.com

BUS: Residential Home Services **P/S:** Sales and Purchases of Residential Properties **MA:** International **D/D/R:** Selling Residential Real Estate **H/I/S:** Canoeing, Kayaking, Fishing **FBP:** Realtor **EDU:** Bachelor's Degree in Business Administration and Psychology, Salisbury State College; Associate Degree in Arts, Montgomery Community College **A/A/S:** National Association of Realtors; Maryland Association of Realtors **A/H:** RE/Max Hall of Fame **C/VW:** Children's Miracle Network; Make-A-Wish Foundation **A/S:** He attributes his success to his hard work and effort. **B/I:** After working with a realtor title search company in college he made a natural progression to his current position. **H/O:** The highlight of his career was receiving the RE/MAX Hall of Fame Award.

PATRICE L. STANLEY
Teacher
Keystone School
119 E. Craig Place
San Antonio, TX 78212 United States
pstanley@keystoneschool.com
http://www.keystoneschool.com

BUS: Academically Accelerated Private School **P/S:** Private School Education **MA:** Local **D/D/R:** Offering a General Elementary Science Education, Coaching **H/I/S:** Traveling, Coaching Sports, Volunteering **FBP:** AIMS Publications **EDU:** Dual Bachelor's Degree s in Special Education and Elementary Education, University of Iowa **A/A/S:** University Interscholastic League; Local Chapter, Academic and Curriculum Development Group; Who's Who Among American Teachers

TERI R. STANSELL, RN
Director of Nursing
Support Solutions of the MidSouth
5909 Shelby Oaks Drive, Suite 100
Memphis, TN 38134 United States
teristansell@Supportsolutionsms.com
http://www.cambridgewhoswho.com

BUS: Healthcare Company **P/S:** Wide Variety of Healthcare and Patient Care Services **MA:** Statewide **D/D/R:** Developing Health Plans, Dispensing Medications, Following through on Doctor's Orders, Acting as a Pharmaceutical Liaison, Consulting on Nursing with Private Firms, Offering Healthcare and Patient Care Services to Needy and Mentally Retarded People **H/I/S:** Boating **FBP:** Journal of Nursing in Intellectual and Developmental Disabilities **EDU:** Associate Degree in Nursing, University of New York (1999) **CERTS:** Certification in Mental Retardation and Developmental Disabilities; Certified Instructor for Unlicensed Personnel, Tennessee State-Approved Medical Administration; Certified Instructor, American Red Cross **A/A/S:** Developmental Disabilities Nurses Association **DOB:** February 21, 1958 **SP:** Rick **CHILD:** Rick Jr., Chad, Shane, Mandy, Michael

MARCI STAR
Owner, Creative Director
Star Looks, LLC
PO Box 29284
Los Angeles, CA 90029 United States
marci@star-looks.com
http://www.starlooks.com

BUS: Cosmetics and Entertainment Company **P/S:** Professional, Organized, Affordable and Creative Face and Body Artistry Whenever and Wherever it is Needed **MA:** Regional **D/D/R:** Working as a Makeup Artist, Managing 20 Artists, Offering Services for Events, Films, Commercials, Television, Weddings, Graduations and Proms, Handling All Marketing and Advertising through Bridal Shows and Conferences **H/I/S:** Listening to Music **EDU:** Bachelor's Degree in Communication and Business, Colorado University of Boulder (2003)

JENNIFER L. STARRETT, JD, CRPC
Licensed Financial Advisor, Franchise Owner
Ameriprise Associated Franchise
Ameriprise Financial, Inc.
830 Crescent Centre Drive, Suite 400
Franklin, TN 37067 United States
jennifer.l.starrett@ampf.com
http://www.ameriprise.com

BUS: Finance Company **P/S:** Financial Services **MA:** Regional **D/D/R:** Offering Retirement Plans, Overseeing Cash Reserve, Preparing Tax Returns, Estate Planning, Managing Operations **H/I/S:** Scuba Diving, Traveling, Reading **FBP:** Financial Advisor **EDU:** JD, University of Tennessee College of Law (1998); Bachelor of Science in Pre-Law, Middle Tennessee State University (1995) **CERTS:** Certified Chartered Retirement Planning Counselor; Licensed Agent, States of Indiana, Texas, Tennessee, Kentucky and Florida **A/A/S:** Chamber of Commerce **A/H:** The Mercury Award (2005); First Year Top Achiever Award, Company Conference (2006)

CYNTHIA A. STASKUNAS
Clinical Leader
Kindred Hospital of Boston
1515 Commonwealth Avenue
Brighton, MA 01534 United States
cstaskunas@comcast.net
http://www.cambridgewhoswho.com

BUS: Healthcare **P/S:** Acute Care Hospital **MA:** Local **D/D/R:** Critical-Care Nursing **H/I/S:** Gardening, Art **A/A/S:** American Nurses Association; Massachusetts Nursing Association; National Association for Sport and Physical Education; American Heart Association **C/VW:** American Cancer Association; Breast Cancer Foundation; Devereux Foundation **A/S:** She attributes her success to her openness to learning. **B/I:** She became involved in this profession because she always wanted to help people.

KATHERINE STAVRIANOPOULOS, PH.D.
College Counselor
John Jay College of Criminal Justice
445 W. 59th Street
New York, NY 10019 United States
stavros@jjay.cuny.edu
http://www.jjay.cuny.edu

BUS: College **P/S:** Higher Education **MA:** Local **D/D/R:** Counseling Adolescents, Families and Couples **H/I/S:** Hiking, Biking, Skiing, Yoga **FBP:** The Networker **EDU:** Ph.D. in Educational Psychology, Fordham University **CERTS:** Licensed Mental Health Counselor **A/A/S:** American Psychological Association; American Association for Marriage and Family Therapy; Boy Scouts of America

LEANNE WADDING STEARNS
Owner
Stearns Garage and Machine Shop
5271 Pittsburgh Road
Harrisville, PA 16038 United States
wstearns@zoominternet.net
http://www.cambridgewhoswho.com

BUS: Machinery, Repair **P/S:** Repair of Automobiles, Small Trucks, Tractors, Lawn Mowers, Garage and Machine Shop **MA:** Regional **D/D/R:** Managing Business Operations and Administration **H/I/S:** Reading, Crocheting **FBP:** National Federation of Independent Business Small Business **EDU:** Coursework in Graphic Arts, Lawrence County Vocational Technical School **A/A/S:** County Government; Parliamentary Procedures Club **C/VW:** The Salvation Army; Volunteer Activities in the Community **A/S:** She feels that she has attained success in her career through her persistence and determination to never give up.

KATHERINE T. STEIN, LMT
Licensed Massage Therapist
Spa Terre
4 Grove Isle
Miami, FL 33133 United States
ktsbillie@aol.com
http://www.cambridgewhoswho.com

BUS: Spa **P/S:** Indonesian Style Massage Therapy **MA:** Local **D/D/R:** Specializing in Shiatsu, Deep Tissue, Swedish, Reflexology and Hot-Stone Massages **H/I/S:** Swimming, Traveling, Dancing **CERTS:** Licensed Massage Therapist, Educating Hands School of Massage **A/A/S:** Florida State Massage Therapy Association; Women in Networking; Vietnam Veterans **C/VW:** The Humane Society of the United States

SHARIE L. STELZEL
Teacher, English as a Second Language Coordinator
CG Sivells Elementary School
1605 N. Alabama Road
Wharton, TX 77488 United States
tstelzel@sbcglobal.net
http://www.cambridgewhoswho.com

BUS: Public Elementary School **P/S:** Education **MA:** Local **D/D/R:** Specializing in English as a Second Language, Supporting Technology for School, Teaching First Grade **H/I/S:** Spending Time with the Family, Traveling, Reading Karen Kingsbury Books **FBP:** The Advocate; Tech Edge; Delta Kappa Gamma Journal **EDU:** Bachelor of Education in Elementary Education and Music, Frostburg State University **CERTS:** Certified in English as a Second Language, University of Houston **A/A/S:** Delta Kappa Gamma; International Society for Women Educators; Delta Omicron; Texas Computer Education Association; First Baptist Church of Wharton **C/VW:** American Red Cross; Church; American Cancer Society; American Diabetes Association; Handbell Choir **SP:** Harvey **A/S:** She attributes her success to support from her family and peers. **B/I:** She became involved in her profession because she always had an interest in science and wanted to have a positive impact on students. **H/O:** The most gratifying aspect of her career is being a positive influence for her students.

MS. ELIZABETH M. STEPHAN
Owner
USA Realty Help
6682 Paul Mar Drive
Lake Worth, FL 33462 United States
elizabeth_stephan@yahoo.com
http://www.mycmsite.com/sites/beth1
http://www.bethinks.blogspot.com

BUS: Real Estate Company **P/S:** Residential Real Estate Exchange Services **MA:** Local **D/D/R:** Overseeing Foreclosures and Lease Options **H/I/S:** Reading, Golfing, Participating in her Children's Activities **FBP:** Kiplinger's Personal Finance **EDU:** Bachelor's Degree in Economics and Finance, Drake University **CERTS:** Registered Communication Distribution Designer **A/A/S:** ITWomen; Executive Women's Golf Association; Women's Chamber of Commerce of Palm Beach County; eWomenNetwork; Women in Technology International; Building Industry Communications Society International **A/H:** Art Communication Award, Belden CDT (2005) **C/VW:** Multiple Sclerosis Society; Board of Governors, Chancellor Charter School, Lantana, FL; Toastmasters International **A/S:** She attributes her success to her self belief. **B/I:** She became involved in her profession because she saw the potential in real estate. **H/O:** The most gratifying aspect of her career is running her business successfully.

DORIS LaRee STEPHENS, BSN, RN, COHN-S

Registered Nurse, Staff Nurse
Tyson Fresh Meats
1500 Plum Creek Parkway
Lexington, NE 68850 United States
larce_stephens@yahoo.com
http://www.cambridgewhoswho.com

BUS: Meat-Packing Plant **P/S:** Meat Products **MA:** International **D/D/R:** Practicing Occupational Health, Dealing with Injuries and Illness Issues, Conducting Annual Hearing Tests, Acting as a Liaison for Doctors and Physical Therapists **H/I/S:** Shopping, Traveling **FBP:** RN **EDU:** Bachelor of Science in Nursing, Nebraska Medical Center, Carney **CERTS:** Certified Occupational Health Nurse **A/A/S:** Nebraska Association for Occupational Health Nurses; American Association of Occupational Health Nurses; American Nurses Association; Nebraska Off Highway Vehicle Association **C/VW:** American Red Cross **A/S:** She attributes her career success to her hard work, dedication and excellent teachers. **B/I:** She became involved in nursing through her desire to care for others in an active setting. **H/O:** The highlight of her career was receiving her certification in occupational health nursing.

MARK A. STEPHENS, PH.D.

Chairperson, Professor
Economics, Finance and Marketing
Tennessee Tech University
1105 N. Peachtree Avenue
Cookeville, TN 38505 United States
mstephens@tntech.edu
http://www.tntech.edu

BUS: Public, Co-Educational and Comprehensive University **P/S:** Leadership and Outstanding Programs in Engineering, the Sciences, and Related Areas as well as Strong Programs in the Arts and Sciences, Business, Education, Agriculture and Human Ecology, Nursing, Music, Art and Interdisciplinary Studies **MA:** International **D/D/R:** Leading, Supervising and Administering Instruction in General and International Economics Courses, Teaching Undergraduate and Graduate Classes **H/I/S:** Playing Golf **FBP:** American Economic Review; The Economist **EDU:** Ph.D. in Economics, University of Tennessee (1985); Bachelor's Degree in International Trade and Finance, Louisiana State University (1975) **A/A/S:** American Economics Association

MS. TERESA L. STEPHENSON
Reading Coach, Teacher
Waterville Community Elementary School
Bradley County Board of Education
800 S. Lee Highway
Cleveland, TN 37311 United States
tstephenson@bradleyschools.org
http://www.cambridgewhoswho.com

BUS: Board of Education **P/S:** Education **MA:** Local **D/D/R:** Teaching Reading, Coordinating Reading Recovery Programs, Developing Children's Interest in Reading **H/I/S:** Traveling, Reading, Attending the Church, Listening to Music **FBP:** The Journal of Reading Recovery; Literacy Teaching and Learning **EDU:** Master's Degree in Education, Plus 45, The University of Tennessee at Chattanooga **A/A/S:** Bradley County Education Association; Tennessee Education Association; National Education Association; National Reading Recovery Association; International Reading Association **C/VW:** Local Church **A/S:** She attributes her success to her leadership skills and her love for children. **B/I:** She became involved in her profession because she was inspired by her aunty who was a teacher. **H/O:** The most gratifying aspect of her career is the gratitude she receives from her students and their parents.

MR. BERNARD STERN
Chemist
570 Grand Street, Suite H1105
New York, NY 10002 United States
berniestern@msn.com
http://www.cambridgewhoswho.com

BUS: Self-Employed **P/S:** Analytical Chemistry, Compliance Reviews, Drug Testing; DDR: Monitoring Drugs by the NDA and ANDA, Evaluating Food, Fresh Produce and Herbs for Pesticides and Filth, Ensuring Sanitary Food Conditions **MA:** International **D/D/R:** Analytical Chemistry, Food and Drug Analysis **H/I/S:** Music, Enjoying New Technological Innovations Such as HDTV, Virtual Reality, 3D Innovations **FBP:** PC Magazine; Popular Science; Facts; Smithsonian **EDU:** Master of Arts in English; Master of Science in Information Science, Pace University; Bachelor of Science in Chemistry **A/A/S:** American Chemical Society; Atomic Energy Commission

LAURI L. STETTLER
Owner
Holmen Locker and Meat Market, LLC
412 Main Street
Holmen, WI 54636 United States
llstettler@centurytel.net
http://www.holmenmeatmarket.com

BUS: Retail Meat and Food Processing Company **P/S:** Babcock Premium Pork, Bacon, Ham, Hot Dogs, Ring Bologna, Summer Sausage, T-Bones, Rib Eye, Chuck Roast, Ground Beef, Bacon Wrapped Sirloin, Pork Chops, Spare Ribs, Country Style Ribs, Pork Loin Roast, Fresh Ham, Chicken Breasts, Meat Bundles, Cheeses, Butters, Salsas, Syrups, Mustards, Dressings, Marmalade, Spices, Salt-Free Products, Sauces, Preserves, Organic Spices **MA:** Statewide **D/D/R:** Coordinating the Entire Meat Process from Slaughter to Retail, Handling Office Administration, Overseeing Wholesale Sales **H/I/S:** Reading **FBP:** Meatingplace **EDU:** College Coursework **A/A/S:** Former President, Holmen Area Civic and Commerce Association **A/H:** State Champion, Cured and Smoked Beef **C/VW:** Various Charitable Organizations **B/I:** She became involved in her profession because her husband was a meat cutter and she wanted to start her own business.

KATHY R. STEVENS
Cage and Credit Manager
Isle of Capri Casino Resort Biloxi
151 Beach Boulevard
Biloxi, MS 39530 United States
kathy.stevens@islecorp.com
http://www.islecorp.com

BUS: Casino **P/S:** Gaming, Hospitality, Entertainment, Beauty and Food Services **MA:** Local **D/D/R:** Managing Finance, Overseeing Staff, Management and Compliance of Gaming Commission, Working with Opening Team on Opening New Properties and Setting up Policies and Procedures **H/I/S:** Playing Tennis, Spending Time with her Family, Caring for her Dogs **A/A/S:** Former President, Gulf Coast Cage Credit Association **C/VW:** American Red Cross; YMCA; Foster Parent, Safe Houses **A/S:** She attributes her success to her supportive father and excellent mentors. **B/I:** She became involved in her profession because of the experience she gained working in the banking industry. **H/O:** The highlight of her career was acting as a liaison at the corporate office.

WILLIAM J. STEVENS
Associate Vice President
The Guardian Life Insurance Company of America
7 Hanover Square
New York, NY 10004 United States
wjstevens@glic.com
william.stevens00@cwwemail.com
http://www.cambridgewhoswho.com

BUS: Insurance Company **P/S:** Life and Health Insurance, Investments and Financial Services **MA:** National **D/D/R:** Managing Distribution Growth and Productivity **H/I/S:** Golfing, Coaching Youth Soccer and Lacrosse, Traveling, Reading Self-Help Books **FBP:** GAMA International Journal **EDU:** Master's Degree in Financial Services, The American College, PA **CERTS:** Chartered Financial Consultant, The American College; Chartered Life Underwriter, The American College **A/A/S:** GAMA International; Society of Financial Service Professionals; National Association of Insurance and Financial Advisors **A/H:** Lifetime Field Service Award (2006) **C/VW:** United Way of America; American Cancer Society **A/S:** He attributes his success to his work ethic, mentors and passion for his profession. **B/I:** He became involved in this profession because he wanted to help people and always had an interest in finance. **H/O:** The highlight of his career was receiving the lifetime field service award in 2006.

MELISSA R. STEVENSON, ABR
Realtor
Newcastle Realty
8843 N. Knoxville Avenue
Peoria, IL 61615 United States
Got_House@sbcglobal.net
http://www.GotHousePeoria.com

BUS: Real Estate **P/S:** Residential and Commercial Sales **MA:** Local **D/D/R:** Representing Residential First-Time Buyers and Sellers **H/I/S:** Playing Softball, Spending Time with her Friends, Walking her Dogs **EDU:** Bachelor of Science in Recreation and Park Administration, Illinois State University **CERTS:** Accredited Buyer Representative **A/A/S:** National Association of Realtors; Illinois Association of Realtors; Peoria Area Association of Realtors **C/VW:** Moss-Bradley Residential Association **A/S:** She attributes her career success to the high quality of service she provides to her clients, and to the referrals she receives from her clients' satisfaction. **B/I:** While looking for a career change she found that she really enjoys sales and helping people, and she feels that real estate allows her to combine the two. **H/O:** She feels that hitting the Million Dollar Mark in 2005 has been the highlight of her career.

CARL D. STEWART
Production Engineer
Authentec, Inc.
709 S. Harbor City Boulevard
Suite 400
Melbourne, FL 32901 United States
carl.stewart@authentec.com
http://www.authentec.com

BUS: Biometrics **P/S:** Finger Print Sensors **MA:** Worldwide **D/D/R:** Engineering Production Tests **H/I/S:** Massage Therapy **FBP:** Massage Therapy Journal **EDU:** Master's Degree in Engineering Management, University of South Florida; Bachelor's Degree in Engineering Technology, University of Central Florida **A/S:** She attributes her success to her determination. **B/I:** She became involved in her profession because she is interested in hardware and software systems. **H/O:** The highlight of her career is speaking at the Torridon User Group.

JOSLYN E. STEWART, MS.ED., MS
Teacher of the Deaf and Hard of Hearing
Earl B. Wood Middle School
Montgomery County Public Schools
14615 Bauer Drive
Rockville, MD 20853 United States
joslyn_stewart@mcpsmd.org
http://www.montgomeryschoolsmd.org

BUS: Public Middle School **P/S:** Secondary Education **MA:** Local **D/D/R:** Teaching Science to Sixth through Eighth-Grade Hearing Impaired and Learning-Disabled Students **H/I/S:** Collecting Star Wars Paraphernalia, Singing in a Choir, Spending Time with her Chow-Chow, Chewy **FBP:** Industry-Related Publications **EDU:** Master's Degree in Science and Mathematics, Johns Hopkins University (1998); Master's Degree in Deaf Education, Western Maryland College (1992) **A/A/S:** MCEA; National Association of Special Education Teachers; National Education Association; Maryland State Teachers Association; Council for Exceptional Children; Parent Teacher Association; Montgomery County for Hearing Impaired Children **C/VW:** Mount Pisgah Church; Goodwill; Local Charitable Organizations **A/S:** She attributes her success to her hard work and her ability to change the materials to meet the needs of the children. **B/I:** She became involved in her profession because she was inspired as a child. **H/O:** The most gratifying aspect of her career is seeing the progress of her students.

SHARON C. STEWART
Human Resources Manager
Chenega Integrated Systems, LLC
1509 Saint Andrews Boulevard
Panama City, FL 32405 United States
sharon.stewart@cis-llc.net
http://www.cis-llc.net

BUS: Manufacturing Company **P/S:** Electrical Assembly, Standard Bench Test Equipment, Automated Wire Processing, Metal Fabrication, Vertical Milling Machines and Sheet Metal Brakes **MA:** International **EXP:** Ms. Stewart's expertise is in counseling, recruiting, hiring, terminating employees, implementing policies, supervising, managing and training employees. **H/I/S:** Horseback Riding, Golfing, Swimming, Boating **EDU:** Coursework, University of South Carolina (1989) **CERTS:** Certified Notary Public, State of Florida **A/A/S:** Society for Human Resource Management; Vice President, Bay County Human Resource Management Association; President, Bay County Leadership Network **A/H:** National Dean's List

MR. WILLIAM T. STEWART JR.
National Account Manager
Inventive Health
200 Cottontail Lane
Somerset, NJ 08873 United States
wstewart@inventivehealth.com
http://www.cambridgewhoswho.com

BUS: Consulting Firm **P/S:** Consulting Services for Pharmaceuticals **MA:** International **D/D/R:** Overseeing the United States Marketing and Development of New Products, Directing and Working Internationally **H/I/S:** Golfing, Listening to Jazz **FBP:** Pharmaceutical Executives **EDU:** Bachelor's Degree in Chemistry, University of Arkansas (1978) **CERTS:** Harvard Financial Management Program (2004); Harvard Advanced Negotiations Skills Program (1994) **A/A/S:** Omega Psi Phi; American Society of Health-System Pharmacists

CYNTHIA A. STEWART-MCDUFFIE, MJA, BS
Information Security Specialist
United States Joint Forces Command
116 Lake View Parkway
Suffolk, VA 23435 United States
c.stewart-mcduffie@att.net
http://www.cambridgewhoswho.com

BUS: United States Government Military **P/S:** Security **MA:** National **D/D/R:** Overseeing Security Office Affairs, Offering Security at Military Complex Buildings, Protecting the Security of Classified Information **H/I/S:** Reading **FBP:** Newsweek **EDU:** Master's Degree in Justice Administration, Norwich University (2006); Bachelor's Degree in Criminal Justice, Park University (2001) **A/A/S:** National Court Appointed Special Advocate Association **C/VW:** Breast Cancer Research Foundation; Susan G. Komen Breast Cancer Foundation **A/S:** She attributes her success to her Air Force training and the guidance she received. **B/I:** She became involved in her profession because of a suggestion from her father. **H/O:** The highlight of her career has been the success she achieved during her military service.

MR. MARC L. STIEHR
Senior Director of Network Technology
YMCA of Metropolitan Chicago
801 N. Dearborn Street
Chicago, IL 60610 United States
mstiehr@ymcachgo.org
http://www.ymcachgo.org

BUS: Nonprofit Organization **P/S:** Fitness and Wellness Programs, Child Care, Housing and Counseling Services, Job Preparation Training, Recreational Activities, Value-Based Programming **MA:** Regional **EXP:** Mr. Stiehr's expertise is in needs assessment, project planning, hardware and software acquisition, regulation of departmental policies and procedures and the evaluation of emerging technologies. **D/D/R:** Overseeing Corporate Technology, Establishing Strategy and Ensuring Network Operations, Managing Technical Help Desk, Managing Voice Communications, Technology Licensing, Systems Security and Wireless Mobile Technologies **H/I/S:** Singing **FBP:** CIO; CIO Insight **EDU:** Bachelor of Science in Economics and Urban Planning, The University of Wisconsin Oshkosh **A/A/S:** Association of Information Technology Professionals **A/H:** Computerworld Smithsonian Award **SP:** Bari **CHILD:** Matthew, Kristin **B/I:** He became involved in his profession because he started his career in the city programming and planning field.

LaVerne J. Stigall, BBA, MBA
Realtor Associate, MBA
Coldwell Banker, Hoffman Properties
1709 Kirby Parkway, Suite 2
Memphis, TN 38120 United States
stigall10@netzero.com
http://www.cambridgewhoswho.com

BUS: Real Estate **P/S:** Real Estate Purchases and Sales **MA:** Local **D/D/R:** Working with Residential Property, Representing Buyers and Sellers **H/I/S:** Playing Bridge, Going to Couple's Clubs and Ladies' Clubs, Traveling **FBP:** Architectural Digest; Smart Money; U.S. News and World Report **EDU:** Master of Business Administration, University of Arkansas; Bachelor of Business Administration, University of Memphis **A/A/S:** American Association of University Women; National Association of Realtors; Tennessee Association of Realtors; Memphis Area Association of Realtors; National Association of Retired Federal Employees; University of Memphis Alumni **C/VW:** Christ United Methodist, Kingswood Sunday School; The Salvation Army Women's Auxiliary **B/I:** She was in the U.S. Navy for thirty years, and after retiring she wanted to keep busy and to help others, so she began a second career. **H/O:** She feels that her work as an administrative assistant to thirteen Admirals while in the U.S. Navy was the highlight of her career.

Mr. Craig J. Stiles
Assistant Vice President
Global Wealth Management
Merrill Lynch
2501 Coolidge Road, Suite 500
East Lansing, MI 48823 United States
c_stiles@ml.com
http://www.fa.ml.com/smithstilesgroup

BUS: Financial Adviser **P/S:** Wealth Management, Mutual Funds, Concentrated Stock Positions (NSO/ISO Analysis), Executive Advisory Services, Cash Management Services **MA:** International **EXP:** Mr. Stiles' expertise is in finance. **D/D/R:** Advising Concentrated Stock Positions, Managing Cash, Disciplined Investment Strategies and Implementation **H/I/S:** Spending Time with his Family, Playing Basketball, Golfing **FBP:** The Wall Street Journal; Worth **EDU:** Master of Business Administration in Finance, Hayworth College of Business, Western Michigan University; Bachelor of Science in Industrial Engineering, Arizona State University **CERTS:** Certified Financial Manager; Accredited Wealth Management Adviser **A/A/S:** Williamston Theatre; Rotary Club of Lansing **C/VW:** St. Vincent Catholic Charities; Williamston Area Beautification Fund; St. Mary Parish of Williamston **DOB:** February 9, 1973 **POB:** Kalamazoo, MI **SP:** Stephanie **CHILD:** Michaela, Christian, Charlie, Miriam, Peyton **W/H:** GTX Corporation; Parker Hannifin Corporation **A/S:** He attributes his success to his family. **B/I:** He became involved in his profession when he was asked to become a partner and form a team to focus on providing wealth management services to individuals seeking discipline, advice and honesty with transparency. **H/O:** The highlight of his career is watching his clients and knowing that he played a part in their success. **I/F/Y:** In five years, Mr. Stiles hopes to hit the company's $1 billion objective.

JEANNE ANN STING
Teacher
Keystone Oaks School District, Myrtle Avenue Elementary
3724 Myrtle Avenue
Pittsburgh, PA 15234 United States
jmstingers@comcast.net
http://www.kosd.org

BUS: Public Elementary School **P/S:** Primary Education **MA:** Local **D/D/R:** Teaching First Grade **H/I/S:** Gold Wing Motorcycling, Quilting, Playing Tennis **FBP:** Newsweek; National Geographic **EDU:** Master's Degree, Plus 60, University of Wisconsin-Platteville **CERTS:** Certification in Reading **A/A/S:** Delta Kappa Gamma; Former President, Western Pennsylvania Primary Educators

DEBORAH L. STOBAUGH
Clinical Consultant
DeBecc & Associates
3385 Pony Tracks
Colorado Springs, CO 80922 United States
drstobaugh@yahoo.com
http://www.cambridgewhoswho.com

BUS: Consulting **P/S:** Clinical Consulting **MA:** International **D/D/R:** Pharmaceutical Healthcare **H/I/S:** Golfing, Crocheting **FBP:** Forbes **EDU:** Doctor of Pharmacy, University of Kansas; Master's Degree in Business Administration, Baker University **A/A/S:** Kansas Pharmaceutical Association; American Society of Healthcare Professionals; American Society of Hospital Pharmacists **C/VW:** St. Jude Children's Research Hospital; Shriners Hospitals **A/S:** She attributes her success to her ability to assess situations quickly. **B/I:** She was prompted to enter her profession because she had an interest in the field. **H/O:** The highlight of her career is the impact she has on patients.

DR. LORI A. STOCK
Doctor of Chiropractic
L.A.S. Chiropractic
4101 Mexico Road
Saint Peters, MO 63376 United States
drstock@att.net
http://www.cambridgewhoswho.com

BUS: Private Practice **P/S:** Healthcare Including Chiropractic Services **MA:** Regional **D/D/R:** Answering Phone Calls, Practicing Spine Chiropractic and Applied Kinesiology Techniques, Performing Acupuncture, Overseeing Administrative Duties, Managing Finance, Treating Joint Motion and Muscular Disorder Patients, Bookkeeping, Scheduling **H/I/S:** Sports, Participating in Track Events, Playing Softball, Baseball and Football **FBP:** Chiropractic Economics **EDU:** Doctor of Chiropractic, Logan College of Chiropractic (2005) **A/A/S:** Vice President, New Melle Lions Club; Missouri State Chiropractic Association; American Chiropractic Association

MAXINE V. STOEHR, RN
Manager
Claim Pend Unit
Humana, Inc.
500 W. Main Street
Louisville, KY 40202 United States
twobasket@hotmail.com
http://www.humana-military.com

BUS: Insurance Company **P/S:** Health Insurance Services **MA:** National **D/D/R:** Supervising Registered Nurses and Staff, Dealing with Health and Commercial Insurance Claims **H/I/S:** Horse Racing, Traveling **EDU:** College Coursework **CERTS:** Registered Nurse, DePaul University (1970)

W. ANN STOKES
Associate Professor
Bloomsburg University of Pennsylvania
400 E. Second Street
Bloomsburg, PA 17815 United States
astokes@bloomu.edu
http://www.bloomu.edu

BUS: Musical Educational Facility **P/S:** Leader in Higher Education for those Wishing to Enrich their Learning **MA:** Regional **D/D/R:** Teaching Music Education and String Instruments Including the Violin, Viola and the Piano **H/I/S:** Swimming **FBP:** MENC Journal **EDU:** Ph.D. in Music Education, Northwestern University (1990) **A/A/S:** Music Educators National Conference

MR. E. CARL STONE IV
District Business Manager
United States Global Sales
Merck & Company, Inc.
6109 Laura Lane
Crozet, VA 22932 United States
carl_stone@merck.com

BUS: Global Research-Driven Pharmaceutical Company **P/S:** Pharmaceutical Products and Sales, Discovery, Development and Deliverance of Novel Medicines and Vaccines **MA:** International **D/D/R:** Developing Leadership, Managing Talent, High Performance Team-Building, Coaching and Mentoring Programs, Promoting Employee and Customer Engagement, Business Acumen, Presentation and Facilitation Skills, Franchise Ownership, Forecasting and Strategic Planning, Overseeing Performance Management, Executing Strategies **H/I/S:** Family Activities, Reading, NCAA Athletics **FBP:** Gallop Management Journal; The Economist; Harvard Business Review **EDU:** Master's Degree in Educational Leadership and Business Administration, Old Dominion University; Bachelor's Degree in Physical Education, East Carolina University **A/A/S:** Kiwanis; Rotary; National Advisory Board, Scholastic Coach Magazine **C/VW:** Virginia Beach Volunteer Rescue Squad; Naval Special Warfare Foundation; Committee Member, Allen Stone Memorial Races **DOB:** August 25, 1961 **POB:** Durham, NC **W/H:** Assistant Baseball Coach, NCAA; Athletic Director, Assistant Principal, High School Teacher, Head Coach, Pharmaceutical Sales Representative, Pharmaceutical Professional Development Trainer, Pharmaceutical District Business Manager **A/S:** He attributes his career success to his passion for personal growth and development combined with unique abilities for directly and indirectly motivating the successful growth and development of others. **H/O:** The most gratifying aspect of his career is assisting and observing the long-term growth and success of former players, employees and mentees. Because his leadership philosophy is based on 'Leading to be Succeeded', he is blessed with many individual and team career highlights.

KAYE L. STONEKING
Registered Nurse, Certified Nurse Operating Room
Akron General Medical Center
400 Wabush Avenue
Akron, OH 44307 United States
stoneking63090@aol.com
http://www.cambridgewhoswho.com

BUS: Level I Trauma Center **P/S:** Healthcare **MA:** Statewide **D/D/R:** Specializing in Ophthalmics **H/I/S:** Gardening, Reading, Fishing **FBP:** AORN Journal; American Journal of Nursing **CERTS:** Pursuing Certificate of Operating Room Nurse **A/A/S:** Association of Operating Room Nurses; Ohio Nurses Association **A/H:** Recipient of the Joan Ashley EFIC Award (1988) **A/S:** She attributes her success to enjoying what she does. **B/I:** She chose the profession because it has been her long time dream. **H/O:** The highlight of her career was receiving the Joan Ashley Award.

BARBARA D. STOUT, LPN
LPN
Blossom Nursing and Rehabilitation Center
109 Blossom Lane
Salem, OH 44460 United States
http://www.royalmanorhealthcare.com

BUS: Skilled Nursing Home **P/S:** Nursing Care and Rehabilitation Care **MA:** Statewide **D/D/R:** Generalized Nursing **H/I/S:** Reading, Dog Breeding and Racing **FBP:** Industry-Related Publications **CERTS:** Licensed Practical Nurse, Hannah E. Mullins School of Practical Nursing **C/VW:** Relay for Life; Easter Seals **A/S:** She feels that her patience and understanding have helped her to become successful in her career. **B/I:** She saw nursing as a way to help others.

FRANCES M. STRACQUALURSI, BSN
Coordinator of Special Diabetes Program for Indians
Rapid City Service Unit
3200 Canyon Lake Drive
Rapid City, SD 57702 United States
frances.stracqualursi@ihs.gov
http://www.cambridgewhoswho.com

BUS: Government Organization **P/S:** Healthcare **MA:** Regional **D/D/R:** Overseeing Clinical, Wellness and Prevention Divisions, Handling 17 Staff, Coordinating Activities and Interrelationships of the Three Divisions **H/I/S:** Camping, Sewing, Traveling **FBP:** Diabetes Care **EDU:** Bachelor of Science in Nursing, St. Mary's University (1974); Bachelor of Arts in Education, St. Mary's University (1972) **CERTS:** Registered Nurse, St. Mary's University (1974) **A/A/S:** American Diabetes Association; American Association of Diabetes Educators

MARGARITA STRAND
Senior Manager, Data Management
Data Management and Biostatistics
DOV Pharmaceutical, Inc.
150 Pierce Street
Somerset, NJ 08873 United States
mstrand1978@yahoo.com
http://www.dovpharm.com

BUS: Biopharmaceutical Company **P/S:** Discovery, Acquisition, Development and Commercialization of Novel Drug Candidates for the Central Nervous System and Disorders which Involve Alternations in Neuronal Processing **MA:** International **EXP:** Ms. Strand's expertise is in clinical data management in the pharmaceutical industry. **D/D/R:** Overseeing the Data Management Department, Leading Study-Specific In-House Data Management Activities from Study Start-Up to Database Lock, Coordinating and Overseeing Ongoing Clinical and Laboratory Data Cleaning, Medical Coding and Quality Assurance Activities of the Project Team, Managing Vendor and CRO Proposal Reviews, Negotiating Budgets, Reconciling Invoices, Interacting with the Vendor's Project Team to Ensure Proper and Timely Delivery of Services in Compliance with Contractual Obligations, Offering Input into Internal Departmental Budget Planning and Allocation of Resources **H/I/S:** Traveling, Listening to Music, Jogging, Walking, Playing Badminton and Tennis **FBP:** Applied Clinical Trials; DIA Today; Bio-IT World **EDU:** Bachelor's Degree in Economics and Management, Specializing in Financial Management and Bank Affairs, South Ural State University, Chelyabinsk, Russia (2001) **A/A/S:** Drug Information Association **A/H:** Excellence Award for Superior Performance, DOV Pharmaceutical, Inc. (2006); Recognition of Five Years of Dedicated Service, DOV Pharmaceutical, Inc. (2005) **A/S:** She attributes her success to her determination and to the support and inspiration she receives from her mentors.

TINA M. STRASHEIM, SPHR
Human Resources Manager
AgustaWestland Bell, LLC
11700 Plaza America Drive
Suite 900
Reston, VA 20190 United States
tstrasheim@hotmail.com
http://www.cambridgewhoswho.com

BUS: Aerospace **P/S:** Helicopters, Aerospace Program Management **MA:** International **D/D/R:** Executive Coaching, Managing Human Resources, Employee Relations and Strategic Development, Overseeing 100 Employees **H/I/S:** Volunteering in her Community, Traveling **FBP:** HR; Fortune; Financial Times; BusinessWeek **EDU:** Master's Degree in Industrial and Labor Relations, Cornell University (2000); Bachelor's Degree in Environmental Policy and Planning, Cornell University (1998) **CERTS:** Certified Senior Professional in Human Resources (2006) **A/A/S:** Society for Human Resource Management; Human Resource Leadership Forum; Human Capital Institute; American Helicopter Association; Army Aviation Association of America; Phi Pheta Kappa; Treasurer, Dallas Chapter, Society of Human Resource Management **C/VW:** Church **A/S:** She attributes her success to her perseverance and determination. **B/I:** She became involved in her profession after working for a power plant and realizing that she enjoyed changing bylaws. **H/O:** The highlight of her career has been setting up the HR Function at Agusta Westland Bell.

MR. JAMES H. STREET JR.
President, Business Manager
Elesy Manor, Inc.
4010 Buckingham Road
Gwynn Oak, MD 21207 United States
jsstreet@verizon.com
http://www.cambridgewhoswho.com

BUS: Assisted Living Home for Seniors **P/S:** Senior Healthcare, Assisted Living **MA:** Regional **D/D/R:** Overseeing the Complete Operation of Patients, Nurses and Administrative Staff, Implementing Complete Compliance and Knowledge of All Geriatric Medical Issues and Concerns **H/I/S:** Watching NFL Games, Supporting the Philadelphia Eagles **EDU:** Master's Degree in Management and Supervision, Central Michigan University (1984); Bachelor's Degree in Business Administration, Oakwood College, AL (1965) **A/A/S:** American Institute of Certified Public Accountants

MARY ALICE STREUBEL
Educator
Self-Employed
1204 W. Third Street
Grandview, WA 98930 United States
revstrube@aol.com
http://www.cambridgewhoswho.com

BUS: Nonprofit Preschool **P/S:** Education **MA:** Local **D/D/R:** Specializing in Reading and Literacy, Homeschooling her Son **H/I/S:** Spending Time with her Family, Enjoying Outdoor Activities, Working Out **EDU:** Master's Degree in Reading and Literacy, Walden University (2004); Bachelor's Degree in Elementary Education, Concentration English as a Second Language, Northwest University (1998) **CERTS:** Ham Radio License **A/A/S:** Former Member, Whatcom Community College Teachers Association; Home School Cooperative, Community Theater **C/VW:** Volunteer Work, Catholic Family Services **A/S:** She attributes her success to God and the support she receives from her husband. **H/O:** The highlight of her career was obtaining a master's degree, which she is fully utilizing.

MS. JUDITH A. STRONG
Owner
Judith A. Strong, No Time to Grieve
2550 S. Ellsworth Road, Unit 758
Mesa, AZ 85209 United States
judystrong758@hotmail.com
http://www.notimetogrieve.com

BUS: Entrepreneur **P/S:** Communications, Education, Public Speaking, Literary Works **MA:** National **EXP:** Ms. Strong's area of expertise lies in her understanding of the impact that grief, loss, and adversity have on the individual. **D/D/R:** Helping People Deal with Grief and Loss Issues, Offering Life Balance Training, Helping to Rebuild Life after Loss, Journeying, Writing, Updating and Maintaining the Website, Developing an Online Business to Reflect Issues of Grief and Comfort and Encourage Moving Forward with Intention and Courage **H/I/S:** Quilting, Singing, Participating in Outdoor Activities, Bicycling **FBP:** Writer's Digest; The Economist **EDU:** Bachelor of Arts in Theology and Biblical Studies, Minor in Social Science, Crown College **A/A/S:** Scottsdale Society of Women Writers; Society of Southwestern Authors; National Association Women Writers **A/H:** Writers Notes Book Award (2005) **C/VW:** Local Church; Arizona Blankets for Kids; The Hospice Movement **DOB:** August 16, 1940 **POB:** Milwaukee, WI **SP:** Donald **CHILD:** Jennifer, Amy, Greg, Mark **W/H:** Classroom Teacher, Kindergarten through 12th-Grade (2001-2002); Art Publisher, Producer and Distributor (1993-2001); Preschool Teacher (1986-1993); Writer, Educator for Grief Loss and Recovery **A/S:** She attributes her success to her persistence, first-hand experience, being a good listener and her excellent research skills. **B/I:** She became involved in her profession because of her experiences as a widow with children still at home and the need for guidance to integrate the emotional and practical aspects of grief and loss.

KIMBERLY R. STUART
Shareholder
Crain Caton & James
1401 McKinney Street, Suite 1700
Houston, TX 77010 United States
kstuart@craincaton.com
http://www.craincaton.com

BUS: Full-Service Law Firm Serving Clients from Around the World **P/S:** Administrative Services, Admiralty, Appellate Law, Banking, Bankruptcy and Creditors' Rights, Commercial Litigation, Corporate Law and Business Planning, Employment and Labor Law, Energy Law, Environmental Law, Estate Planning, Fiduciary Litigation, Financial Services Law, Insurance and Personal Injury Law **MA:** International **D/D/R:** Practicing General Civil Litigation, Employment and Labor Law, Consultation and Litigation, Products Liability, Premises Liability and Toxic Tort Litigation, Settling Contractual Disputes **H/I/S:** Skiing, Growing Roses, Raising Money for the Muscular Dystrophy Association and the American Cancer Society **FBP:** Texas Lawyer **EDU:** JD, Cum Laude, South Texas College of Law (1996); Bachelor of Arts in Communications and Political Science, H. Sophie Newcomb Memorial College Institute, Tulane University (1991) **A/A/S:** National Association for Female Executives; United Way of America Young Leaders; Downtown Houston Alliance Emerging Leaders; South Texas Law Review **A/H:** Texas Rising Star, Texas Monthly Magazine (2005, 2006) **C/A:** Published in South Texas Law Review

---

CURTIS STUBBS
Realtor
Century 21 Real Estate LLC
56 N. Main Street
Pittsford, NY 14534 United States
curtis.stubbs@century21.com
http://www.century21.com

BUS: Real Estate Agency **P/S:** Real Estate Exchange **MA:** National **EXP:** Mr. Stubbs' expertise is in real estate sales. **D/D/R:** Managing the Sale of Residential Properties, Finance and Relocation, Assisting First Time Home Buyers and People Facing Foreclosure **H/I/S:** Construction, Mechanics **FBP:** BusinessWeek; Forbes **EDU:** Master's Degree in School Counseling, SUNY, University at Buffalo (1970); Master's Degree, SUNY, University at Buffalo (1963) **CERTS:** Licensed Chemical Dependency Counselor; Licensed Technology Teacher **A/A/S:** Department of Homeland Security, Auxiliary Coast Guard; Army Reserve Association; American Association of Retired Persons; National Association of Realtors **A/H:** Most Honest Man, Burgard Vocational High School (1958) **C/VW:** Leader, Blood Donation Drive **DOB:** June 22, 1939 **POB:** Buffalo, NY **SP:** Maxine (Deceased) **CHILD:** Estella **C/A:** Highest Rank of Major Promotable, U.S. Army Reserve

MAJ. TINA STUMP
Director of Crisis Management
Maryland Division of Correction
6776 Reisterstown Road, Suite 214
Baltimore, MD 21215 United States
tstump@dpscs.state.md.us
http://www.dpscs.state.md.us

BUS: Public Safety, Emergency Preparedness and Correctional Services **P/S:** Works to Keep Maryland Communities Safe and Provides Services to the Victims of Crime, Also Provides Criminal Justice and Law Enforcement Agencies with Timely Access to Accurate Information about Defendants and Offenders **MA:** Regional **D/D/R:** Handling Emergency Preparedness and Crisis Management, Overseeing 27 Correctional Facilities in the State of Maryland, Managing Audits, Exercises, Special Response Team and K-9 Units, Working at Local Detention Centers by Request **H/I/S:** Reading, Gardening **FBP:** Homeland Defense Journal **EDU:** Pursuing Master's Degree in Management, Johns Hopkins University; Bachelor's Degree in Management, Johns Hopkins University (2006) **A/A/S:** Phi Theta Kappa; American Correctional Association

POLLY JEAN STURGEON
Owner, Operator
Beckner Trucking, LLC
789 E. U.S. Highway 52
Rushville, IN 46173 United States
pjsturgeon@yahoo.com
http://www.cambridgewhoswho.com

BUS: Logistics Firm **P/S:** Transporting Logs, Lumber, Agriculture Grain **MA:** IN, WI, MI, OH, PA, KY and IL **D/D/R:** Transporting Logs **H/I/S:** Spending Time with her Family **FBP:** Industry-Related Publications **CERTS:** Industry-Related Training **DOB:** February 22, 1951 **CHILD:** Karen, Kristine **B/I:** She became involved in her profession because of the experience and inspiration she received from her father. **H/O:** The most gratifying aspect of her career is driving around and seeing new places.

DR. MARIA NOWAKOWSKA STYCOS
Visiting Senior Lecturer (Retired)
Cornell University
Romance Studies
Morrill Hall 303
Ithaca, NY 14853 United States
mns2@cornell.edu
http://www.arts.cornell.edu/romance/spanishfaculty/stycos.html

BUS: University **P/S:** Higher Learning Services in a Range of Degree Programs, Facility where many Undergraduates Participate in a Wide Range of Interdisciplinary Programs, Original Research and Study **MA:** International **D/D/R:** Specializing in 20th Century Spanish and Spanish-American Poetry and Works by Women, Supervising Teaching Assistants **H/I/S:** Listening to Music, Enjoying Art, Visiting Galleries and Museums, Gardening, Attending the Opera, Traveling, Reading **FBP:** The New Yorker **EDU:** Ph.D. in Hispanic Literature, Cornell University (1977); Master's Degree in Spanish Literature, Cornell University (1967) **A/A/S:** Alumni Association, Cornell University; Modern Language Association; Latin American Studies Program, Cornell University; Faculty Advisory Committee, Herbert F. Johnson Museum of Art, Cornell University; Charter Member, Museum for Women in the Arts; Metropolitan Opera Guild **A/H:** Winner, NEH Competition **C/VW:** Internal Rescue Committee; American Red Cross; CISPES

DESIREE SUAZO
Director
Sweet Home Care Service, Inc.
75 N. Main Street
Freeport, NY 11520 United States
shc3762@hotmail.com
http://www.cambridgewhoswho.com

BUS: Healthcare **P/S:** High Quality Healthcare Services **MA:** Regional **D/D/R:** Handling Administration, Coordinating Services, Offering Home Health Attendants, Personal Care Attendants, Registered Nurses and Licensed Practical Nurses to Patients **H/I/S:** Swimming, Cross Stitching, Reading **EDU:** Pursuing Master's Degree in Nursing (2007); Bachelor of Arts Degree in African American Studies and Economics, Syracuse University (2006)

MR. JOHN FRANCIS SUBERO
President, CEO
JCI Distributors, Inc.
13155 S.W. 42nd Street, Suite 108
Miami, FL 33175 United States
jcidistr@msn.com
http://www.cambridgewhoswho.com

BUS: Distributor **P/S:** Airport Equipment and Aviation Products **MA:** International **D/D/R:** Handling Airport Equipment Sales and the Distribution of Airport Terminal Equipment, Selling to Latin America and the Caribbean Market, Developing Airport and Air Facilities for Aircraft **H/I/S:** Softball, Swimming, Exercising **FBP:** ATW **EDU:** Bachelor of Arts in Business Administration, University of South Florida (1992) **A/A/S:** American Management Association

SUSAN L. SUESSMANN, RN-BC
Home Care Coordinator, Visiting Nurse
Valley Home Care
15 Essex Road
Paramus, NJ 07652 United States
sl_suess@hotmail.com
http://www.Valleyhealth.com

BUS: Home Healthcare **P/S:** Visiting Nursing Services, Home Healthcare **MA:** Local **D/D/R:** Coordinating Home Care, Working as a Visiting Nurse **H/I/S:** Gardening, Traveling **FBP:** Industry-Related Publications **EDU:** Bachelor of Science in Nursing, Seton Hall University **CERTS:** Board Certified, American Nurses Credentialing Center; Certified in Home Health **C/VW:** Journeys Program **A/S:** She attributes her success to her determination to get an education, continually learning and evolving within her profession. **B/I:** She became involved in her profession because she has always wanted to help others. She was even in the Future Nurses of America in the eighth-grade.

DR. A. E. SULLIVAN JR.
Bishop, Chief Apostle
The Gospel Truth Global Apostle Network
PO Box 1627
Harrisburg, PA 17105 United States
apostlesullivan@yahoo.com
http://www.cambridgewhoswho.com

BUS: Ministry **P/S:** Religious Services **MA:** International **D/D/R:** Preaching, Teaching, Training, Counseling, Pastoring **H/I/S:** Spending Time with his Family, Traveling, Reading, Exercising **FBP:** Gospel Today; New Man **EDU:** Doctorate, Grace Bible College and Seminary; Master of Ministry; Bachelor of Science **A/A/S:** Interdenominational Ministers' Conference of Greater Harrisburg; Pennsylvania State Pastor's Conference; National Association for the Advancement of Colored People

STACY M. SULLIVAN
Vice President
Family Office Wealth Management Consulting Service
1127 Edgewater Drive
Orlando, FL 32804 United States
ssullivan@familyofficeinfo.com
http://www.familyofficeinfo.com

BUS: Finance Consulting **P/S:** Trust Advisors **MA:** Local **D/D/R:** Managing Trust and Foundation Wealth **H/I/S:** Spending Time with her Dog, Going to the Gym, Reading **FBP:** Trusts and Estates **EDU:** Bachelor's Degree in Accounting, University of Phoenix **A/A/S:** Institute of Certified Bankers

BETH L. SUMNICK
Chief Executive Officer
Business Life Solutions
1115 Sweet Breeze Drive
Valrico, FL 33594 United States
bethyvonnes@aol.com

BUS: Business Management, Consulting and Financial Advisement **P/S:** Business Development, Financial Advisement, Investment and Life Insurance Services **MA:** National **D/D/R:** Consulting with Business Owners, Writing Policies and Procedures, Creating a Fun, Profitable Organization, Managing a Staff of Client's Businesses **H/I/S:** Exploring Artistic Design, Building, Painting, Sewing, Cheerleading, Coaching Youth Sports, Swimming, Traveling **EDU:** Bachelor's Degree in Business Management, University of Phoenix (2003); Top Graduate, Dental Assistant Program, American Red Cross (1991); High Honor Graduate, Brevard Community College; High Honor Graduate, University of Phoenix **CERTS:** Licensed Agent in Health Insurance, Annuities and Life Insurance, State of Florida (2007); Public Notary, State of Florida (2006); Nationally Certified Dental Assistant (1995) **DOB:** September 8, 1973 **SP:** Michael

MR. THOMAS V. SUNNYCALB
President, Chief Executive Officer
Shield Training Company
962 S. Hoagland Boulevard
Kissimmee, FL 34741 United States
shieldfla@earthlink.net
http://www.shieldtrainingcompany.com

BUS: Security **P/S:** Full Training for Security Officers, Private Instruction in Self-Defense **MA:** Florida **D/D/R:** Teaching Law Enforcement Firearms, Emergency Medical Services **H/I/S:** Raising German Shepherds, Spending Quality Time with his Wife **EDU:** Associate Degree in Criminal Justice, Ashworth College; Diploma in Police Science, Police Science Institute; Trained in Terrorism Response, National Republican Congressional Committee **CERTS:** State Licensed Firearm Certified Instructor, PI Instructor, Bilingual Instructor and Kick Boxing for Women's Self Defense **A/A/S:** International Foundation for Protection Officers; Patron Member, National Rifle Association; International Association of Law Enforcement Firearms Instructors Inc.; American Society of Law Enforcement Trainers; Florida Sheriffs Association; Osceola County Sheriff's Association **A/H:** Congressional Order of Merit (2007) **C/VW:** American Red Cross **SP:** Sherry

Ms. Jennifer 'Josephi' H. Susser
Sales Representative, Curriculum Specialist
Pearson
112 S. Gate Road
Charleston, WV 25314 United States
jennifer.susser@pearson.com
http://www.pearson.com

BUS: International Media Company **P/S:** Education, Business Information and Consumer Publishing **MA:** West Virginia and Virginia **EXP:** Ms. Susser's expertise is in managing sales. **D/D/R:** Managing Service and Technology for Teachers, Offering Consulting Services on Elementary School Textbooks, Training in West Virginia and Virginia **H/I/S:** Boating, Reading, Traveling, Gardening, Spending Time with her Daughter **EDU:** Master's Degree in Reading and Education Administration, College of Graduate Studies, West Virginia University; Bachelor of Science in Early Childhood and Elementary Education (PreK-8), University of Charleston **A/A/S:** Alpha Omega Pi; West Virginia Teachers Association; West Virginia Reading Association; West Virginia Mathematics Association **A/H:** Morris Harvey History Research Award (1979); Golden Apple Teacher Award; President's Sales Goal Award **C/VW:** Local Church; Local Charitable Organizations **DOB:** May 3, 1955 **POB:** Albuquerque, NM **W/H:** Sales Representative, Pearson Scott Foresman, WV, VA (1997-2008); Educational Consultant, Scott Foresman, Duluth, GA (1992-1997); AGS Representative, Pearson Learning Group, WV **A/S:** She attributes her success to her work ethic and passion to do her best for the children and teachers of her state. **B/I:** She became involved in her profession because she wanted to expand her horizons while teaching. **H/O:** The most gratifying aspects of her career are knowing that students are benefiting by using the company's educational products and teachers have learned they can depend on her.

Dr. Glenda J. Sutton
Advice Nurse, Minister
Kaiser Permanente, Mid-Atlantic
2101 E. Jefferson Street
Box 6190
Rockville, MD 20849 United States
gs_5s@cox.net
http://www.kaiserpermanente.org

BUS: Proven Leader in the Healthcare Industry **P/S:** High Quality Healthcare Services **MA:** National **D/D/R:** Nursing, Receiving Calls from Members, Advising and Referring **H/I/S:** Reading Christian Based Material, Spending Time with her Family **FBP:** Charisma; RN **EDU:** Master's Degree in Healthcare Administration, Webster University, St. Louis (2000); Master's Degree in Nursing Administration, University of Maryland, Baltimore (1987); Registered Nurse Studies (1970); Ph.D. in Christian Education and Philosophy, Faith Christian University, Washington, DC **A/A/S:** California Nurses Association; Minister of Healing; Mount Pleasant Baptist Church; Board of Directors, Faith Christian University

THE PSYCHIC SUZ
Clairvoyant
The Psychic Suz
PO Box 4549
Long Beach, CA 90804 United States
thepsychicsuz@aol.com
http://www.cambridgewhoswho.com

BUS: Consultancy **P/S:** Lectures on Psychic Abilities **MA:** National **D/D/R:** Psychometry, Dream Analysis, Clairvoyance, Readings, Personal Parties **EDU:** College Coursework in Social and Behavioral Science **A/S:** She attributes her success to her gift and caring about her clients. **H/O:** The most gratifying aspect of her career is her ongoing ability to help people and assist in their lives.

MRS. DONNA D. SWAFFAR
Director of Marketing
Saint Francis Health System
6161 S. Yale Avenue
Tulsa, OK 74136 United States
ddswaffar@saintfrancis.com
http://www.saintfrancis.com

BUS: Integrated, Medically-Based Health System **P/S:** All Specialties and Services Including Bariatrics, Cancer, Children's Health, Heart, Mental Health, Surgery, Women's Health, Primary Care, Rehabilitation, Transplants **MA:** Regional **D/D/R:** Specializing in Public Relations and Marketing, Handling All Publications and Corporate Communications, Planning Company Retreats, Overseeing All Event Planning, Serving on the Mission Committee, Producing All Collateral Material, Directing All Advertising, Overseeing Hiring and Training of New Staff Members, Managing Issues **H/I/S:** Gardening, Dancing, Composing Music **FBP:** Harvard Business Review; Tulsa World **EDU:** Master's Degree in Music, University of Kentucky; Bachelor's Degree in Music, University of Tulsa **A/A/S:** Public Relations Society of America; American Marketing Association; Tulsa Metropolitan Chamber of Commerce

CHRISTOPHER G. SWAYDEN, DMD
Dentist
Tri Care Dental
1719 S. Loop 288, Suite 110
Denton, TX 76205 United States
swaydogg77@hotmail.com
http://www.cambridgewhoswho.com

BUS: Dental Clinic **P/S:** Dental Care **MA:** Statewide **D/D/R:** Performing Cosmetic Dentistry, Dentures and Endodontics, Fitting Braces, Making Extractions **H/I/S:** Spending Time Outdoors **FBP:** Journal of the American Dental Association; Men's Fitness; Travel and Leisure **EDU:** Doctor of Medical Dentistry, Nova Southeastern University (2004); Bachelor's Degree in Biology, University of Texas (2000) **A/A/S:** American Dental Association; American Orthodontic Society **C/VW:** High Plains Children's Home, Amarillo, TX

SUZANNE M. SWEET
Department Manager
Eastman Kodak Company
1669 Lake Avenue
Rochester, NY 14652 United States
suzanne.sweet@kodak.com
http://www.kodak.com

BUS: Distribution Company **P/S:** Photographic Products and Services **MA:** International **D/D/R:** Managing a Staff of 120, Assuring Quality, Strategic and Production Planning, Implementing New Techniques, Budgeting, Coaching on Lean, Six Sigma and Heijunka Principles and Techniques, Overseeing Forecasting Services, People Development and Diversity Issues, Working with Teams of People to Promote Continuous Improvement and Excellence in the Operations Such as Dealing with Human Resource Issues, Quality Issues and Process Improvements **H/I/S:** Playing Volleyball, Golfing, Sewing, Making Crafts **EDU:** Bachelor of Science in Chemistry, Oswego State College (1980) **CERTS:** Certified Six Sigma Black Belt Professional (2000) **A/A/S:** The Women's Forum of Kodak Employees **DOB:** May 10, 1958 **SP:** Lawrence **CHILD:** Rachel, Rebecca **W/H:** Manager, Film Sensitizing Department (2004-Present); Administrative Assistant, Manager, Vice President, Imaging Chemicals, WW Color Paper (2003-2004); Manager, Finishing Department (2001-2002); Finishing Technical Director (1998-2001); Finishing Technical Manager (1997-1998); Quality Excellence Manager (1997); Acting Department Manager (1996-1997); Team Advisor (1995-1996); Senior Product Engineer Manager (1992-1995); Administrative Assistant (1991-1992); Process Engineer (1987-1989); Manufacturing and Development Engineer, Eastman Kodak (1980-1987) **A/S:** She attributes her success to being a change agent within the company, open to new opportunities to execute strategic and tactical plans. **B/I:** She became involved in her profession because she had a background in chemistry. **H/O:** The most gratifying aspect of her career is helping others develop skill sets so that they are successful in their jobs. **I/F/Y:** In five years, Ms. Sweet hopes to work from a management position of the manufacturing area.

LUCILLE Y. SWEETING
Chief Executive Officer
Sweeting's Family Day Care
1549 Silver Beach Road
Riviera Beach, FL 33404 United States
lucilley.sweeting@peoplepc.com
http://www.cambridgewhoswho.com

BUS: Private Childcare Facility Committed to Caring for Children in a Safe and Friendly Environment **P/S:** Day Care Services **MA:** Local **D/D/R:** Managing Operations, Offering Day Care Services to Nine Children, Budgeting, Feeding the Children, Caring for Children for 12 Hours **H/I/S:** Reading, Computers, Volunteering at the VA Medical Center of West Palm Beach **FBP:** Parenting **EDU:** Master's Degree in Early Childhood Development, Nova Southeastern University (1979); Bachelor's Degree in Early Childhood and Elementary Education, Nova Southeastern University (1978) **A/A/S:** National Association for Continuing Education; Palm Beach Childcare Association; American Legion Auxiliary of Riviera Beach **DOB:** April 9, 1940 **SP:** Joseph **CHILD:** Charlotte, Vanessa, Jennifer, Felicia

DIANE M. SWEZEY, BSN, MSN, C-ANP
Nursing Administrator, Clinical Supervisor,
Adult Nurse Practitioner
diane-quogue@msn.com
http://www.cambridgewhoswho.com

BUS: Healthcare **P/S:** Hospital Healthcare **MA:** International **D/D/R:** Adult Critical-Care Nursing **H/I/S:** Spending Time with her Family at her Cabin in the Catskill Mountains, Camping, Breeding and Raising Golden Retrievers **FBP:** Nurse Practitioner Journal; Nursing Spectrum; Nursing2009; American Medical Association Catalog **EDU:** Master's Degree in Adult Health, Concentration in Critical-Care, SUNY at Stony Brook; Bachelor of Science in Nursing, SUNY, Stony Brook University **CERTS:** Licensed Nurse Practitioner **A/A/S:** Long Island Nurse Practitioner Association; American Nurse Practitioner Association **C/VW:** Goodwill; Long Island Clothing Drive; Local Food Pantries **A/S:** She attributes her success to a great education that emphasized patient advocacy and the strength of the nurse's role. **B/I:** She became involved in her profession because she was always drawn to helping people. **H/O:** The highlight of her career has been gaining the respect of her fellow nurses and the doctors she has worked with.

MARY EVA SWIGAR, MD

Director of Psychiatry
Robert Wood Johnson Medical School
University of Medicine and Dentistry of New Jersey
CINCL Academic Boulevard
Suite 2200, 125 Paterson Street
New Brunswick, NJ 08901 United States
swigar@umdnj.edu • http://www.cambridgewhoswho.com

BUS: State University of Health Sciences **P/S:** Undergraduate, Graduate, Postgraduate and Continuing Education for Health Professionals and Scientists **MA:** Mid-Atlantic Region **D/D/R:** Studying Medically-Oriented Psychiatry, Therapy, Evaluation and Psychopharmacology **H/I/S:** Traveling, Reading, Mushroom Hunting **EDU:** MD, Temple University School of Medicine; Internship, Bryn Mawr College; Residency, Yale University **A/A/S:** New York Academy of Sciences; FINCA International; Save the Children Fund; American Lung Association; American Arthritis Association

MARGARET A. SYVERSON

Elementary Education Teacher
Tracy Area Elementary School
700 Fourth Street S.
Tracy, MN 56175 United States
anniesyverson2001@yahoo.com
http://www.cambridgewhoswho.com

BUS: Public Elementary School **P/S:** General Education to Children Grades Kindergarten to Sixth **MA:** Tracy **D/D/R:** Teaching All Subjects to Fourth-Grade Students **H/I/S:** Swimming, Reading, Playing the Piano **FBP:** Newsweek **EDU:** Bachelor's Degree in Education, Southwest Minnesota State University; Master's Degree in Elementary Education, Southwest Minnesota State University **A/A/S:** President, Teachers Union; Education Minnesota; President, Tracy Education Association **A/H:** Teacher of the Year Award (2003) **C/VW:** Mentor Student Teachers, Southwest State University **A/S:** She attributes her success to her mother who encouraged her to get a good education.

THERESA I. SZUCS, BSN
Administrative Nursing Supervisor
St. Joseph Regional Medical Center
85 S. Powder Mill Road
Morris Plains, NJ 07950 United States
treesz@optonline.com
http://www.stjosephshealth.org

BUS: Medical Center **P/S:** Healthcare **MA:** Regional **D/D/R:** Assessing Staff Nurses, Ensuring Nurses Adhere to Policies and Procedures, and State Mandates, Maintaining Safety, Supervising, Managing Clinical Issues, Codes, Traumas, Policies and Procedures, Overseeing Nurses, Reviewing Quality Management Regulations and Critical Care Management **H/I/S:** Golfing **EDU:** Pursuing Master of Science in Nursing, Walden College; Bachelor of Science in Nursing, William Paterson University (1977) **A/A/S:** American Nurses Association

HAMID R. TABRIZI, DMD
President
Tabrizi Dental Associates, Inc.
389 Main Street, Suite 404
Malden, MA 02148 United States
hrtdada@aol.com
http://www.cambridgewhoswho.com

BUS: Dentistry Practice **P/S:** Periodontal Procedures, Consultations, Oral Care, Dental Hygiene **MA:** Regional **D/D/R:** Performing General Dental Procedures, Periodontal Work, Teeth Cleaning, Extractions, Implants, and Offering Oral Care **H/I/S:** Playing Chess, Listening to Classical Music **FBP:** Jada Magazine **EDU:** Doctor of Dental Medicine, Boston University (1992) **A/A/S:** American Dental Association; Massachusetts Dental Association; Academy of General Dentistry

RACHEL E. TAIT, MAT, MA
Assistant Director of Educational Services
Eden Institute
1 Eden Way
Princeton, NJ 08540 United States
info@edenservices.org
http://www.edenservices.org

BUS: Educational Institute **P/S:** Lifespan Services for Individuals with Autism **MA:** New Jersey **D/D/R:** Specializing in Educational Leadership, Overseeing Curriculum and Behavioral Management **H/I/S:** Running, Bicycling, Traveling, Spending Time with her Dogs **EDU:** Master's Degree in Special Education, Ryder University; Bachelor's Degree in Elementary Education, Elizabethtown College **A/A/S:** New Jersey Private Education Centers; Connecticut Association of Private Special Educators; National Association of Private Special Education Centers **C/VW:** Special Olympics **A/S:** She attributes her career success to her hard work and determination. **B/I:** She became involved in special education while studying to become a teacher. **H/O:** The most gratifying aspect of her career is being able to watch her students progress every day.

TRACIE L. TALIAFERRO, MS, CADC
Owner, Founder, Program Director
Back to Basics Counseling Services, LLC
227 Saint Ann Street, Suite 101
Owensboro, KY 42303 United States
backtobasics1@bellsouth.net
http://www.cambridgewhoswho.com

BUS: Counseling Center **P/S:** Substance Abuse Counseling and Treatment, Anger Management Counseling **MA:** Local **EXP:** Ms. Taliaferro's expertise is in counseling. **D/D/R:** Counseling Families and Married Couples **H/I/S:** Traveling, Playing Softball and Basketball **EDU:** Master's Degree, Western Kentucky University (2001) **A/A/S:** Chamber of Commerce; Professional Business Women's Association; North American Dog Agility Council **A/S:** She attributes her success to her passion for counseling and her ability to help and motivate others.

ANGELA L. TALTON
Divisional Vice President of Inbound Services
and Operations-Home Services
Sears Holding Corporation
3333 Beverly Road
Hoffman Estates, IL 60179 United States
atalton@searshc.com
http://www.searshc.com

BUS: Nation's Third-Largest Broad Line Retailer Committed to Providing Quality Products and Services **P/S:** Lawn and Garden Maintenance Services, Home Electronics, Automotive Repair and Maintenance, Apparel, Home Accessories and Products **MA:** National **D/D/R:** Offering Post-Sale Assistance, Managing a Call Center with 2,000 People, Hiring Employees, Planning and Forecasting, Overseeing Project Management, Offering Excellent Customer Services, Encouraging Team Motivation, Mentoring, Pursuing Career Development **H/I/S:** Playing Chess, Reading, Golfing, Walking **EDU:** Master of Business Administration, Northwestern University, Kellogg Graduate School of Management (2006); Bachelor's Degree, University of North Carolina at Chapel Hill (1986) **A/A/S:** Lecturer, Presenter, Business Conferences

DR. EUGENE M. TANGUILUT
Doctor of Osteopathy and Endovascular Surgery
The Well Group
3700 W. 203rd Street
Olympia Fields, IL 60461 United States
drtanguiliet@yahoo.com
http://www.cambridgewhoswho.com

BUS: Healthcare Company **P/S:** Healthcare, Endovascular Surgery, General Surgery **MA:** National **D/D/R:** Performing General, Vascular and Endovascular Surgery, Operating on Patients, Lecturing Other Physicians, Working with Residents **H/I/S:** Snow Skiing, Waterskiing, Spending Time with his Family **FBP:** Journal of Vascular Surgery; New England Journal of Medicine **EDU:** MD in General Surgery, Cornell University; MD in Vascular Surgery, The Cleveland Clinic; MD in Endovascular Surgery, The Cleveland Clinic **A/A/S:** Illinois Osteopathic Association; American College of Osteopathic Medicine; American Osteopathic Association **C/VW:** St. Michaels Church **A/S:** He attributes his success to his passion for the profession and dedication to his patients. **B/I:** He became involved in the profession because he wanted a challenging career. **H/O:** The most gratifying aspect of his career is helping wheelchair-bound patients walk again.

RAUL H. TAPIERO
Chief Technology Officer, Vice President, Broker Dealer
Banco Santander
45 E. 53rd Street
New York, NY 10022 United States
rtapiero@optonline.net
http://www.gruposantander.com

BUS: Financial Institution **P/S:** Financial Services for Individuals, Companies and Institutions **MA:** International **D/D/R:** Managing Global Projects, Overseeing Network Infrastructure and Telecommunications, Working with Wintel and Unix, Processing Transactions Including Equity, Stocks and Fixed Income **H/I/S:** Scuba Diving, Reading, Attending the Theater and the Opera **FBP:** eWeek; InformationWeek; Redmond; Network Computing **EDU:** Master's Degree in Technology Management, Polytechnic University (2004); Master's Degree in Systems Analysis, University of Buenos Aires (1987) **A/A/S:** Institute of Electrical and Electronics Engineers **A/H:** Dow Jones Achievement Award (2004) **DOB:** June 22, 1957 **I/F/Y:** In five years, Mr. Tapiero hopes to start his own consulting firm.

ZINAIDA TARAN
Assistant Professor
Siena College
515 Loudon Road
Loudonville, NY 12211 United States
ztaran@gmail.com
http://www.siena.edu

BUS: College **P/S:** Higher Education **MA:** Local **EXP:** Ms. Taran's expertise is in brand strategy analysis. **D/D/R:** Conducting Research on Brand Equity and Marketing, Teaching Consumer Behavior, Marketing and Advertising Techniques **H/I/S:** Dancing, Reading, Hiking **FBP:** Journal of Marketing Research **EDU:** Ph.D. in Marketing Management, Rutgers, The State University of New Jersey (2001); Master of Business Administration (2000); Coursework in Mathematical Economics, Earned in Russia (1990) **A/A/S:** Academy of Marketing Science; Academy of Marketing Studies; Marketing Research Association; American Marketing Association **H/O:** The most gratifying aspects of her career are ensuring students understand the subject and being innovative in her approach.

MELISSA A. TARGETT, LEED AP
Sustainable Design Consultant
El Taller Collaborative, PC (ETC)
550 Broad Street, Fifth Floor
Newark, NJ 07102 United States
mtargett@etcpc.com
http://www.etcpc.com

BUS: Design, Construction, Architecture **P/S:** Minority Owned Business Providing Architecture, Mechanical Engineers, Plumbing, Construction Management for Both Commercial and Individual Projects **MA:** Local **D/D/R:** Performing Full-Service Architectural Functions **H/I/S:** Hiking, Reading, Spending Time Outdoors **FBP:** ECO Structure; Environmental Design and Structure; Environmental Business **EDU:** Bachelor's Degree, Environmental Policy, Green Mountain College **A/A/S:** United States Green Building Council **C/VW:** Nature Conservancy **A/S:** She attributes her success to passion for the field. **B/I:** She chose the profession because she was highly concerned about environmental issues. **H/O:** The highlight of her career is her current position.

MS. JANET L. TATE
Manager
Benchmark Title Agency, Inc.
5915 Memorial Highway
Tampa, FL 33615 United States
jtate8@Tampabay.rr.com
http://www.cambridgewhoswho.com

BUS: Title Insurance Agency **P/S:** Title Services for Commercial and Residential Real Estate Transactions **MA:** Florida **EXP:** Ms. Tate's expertise is in title and abstract insurance. **D/D/R:** Teaching and Training, Closing Real Estate Transactions **H/I/S:** Spending Time Outdoors, Spending Time with her Grandson **FBP:** LandAmerica Commonwealth Publications **CERTS:** Licensed Notary Public; License in Title Closing **A/H:** Executive Award, LandAmerica Financial Group (2005) **C/VW:** Founder, Community Clothing Pantry **A/S:** She attributes her success to her desire to constantly learn more about her company. **B/I:** She became involved in her profession because she was encouraged by her friend to explore in the field of title insurance. **H/O:** The highlight of her career was earning her current position.

SHELIA ANN TATROE
Registered Nurse, Phlebotomist,
Laboratory Technician, Supervisor, Office Manager
surseygao15@aol.com
http://www.cambridgewhoswho.com

MA: Local **D/D/R:** Cardiology Nursing, Tracheotomy Care, Teaching Families, Referring Patients to Agencies, Processing Insurance Information, Medications, Hospice Nursing, Cancer Nursing **H/I/S:** Reading, Spending Time with her Family **FBP:** Medical and Sports Literature **EDU:** Degree in Nursing, State of New York and North Carolina **CERTS:** Registered Nurse, States of New York and North Carolina**A/A/S:** Hospice; Community Service for the Aging; Mentally Challenged Children and Adults **C/VW:** Church; Community Missions; Soup Kitchens **A/S:** She attributes her success to her son, family support and drive to succeed. **B/I:** She became involved in the profession because she took care of her own siblings and family members and always wanted to help others. **H/O:** The most gratifying aspect of her career is having a passion for her profession.

CANDY A. TAULTON
Legal Advocate
Family Counseling & Children's Services
220 N. Main Street
Adrian, MI 49221 United States
ruthies_cat2@yahoo.com
http://www.cambridgewhoswho.com

BUS: Nonprofit Human Services Organization **P/S:** Community Family and Children's Services **MA:** Local **D/D/R:** Working as a Legal Advocate in Local Violence Cases **H/I/S:** Spending Time with the Family, Practicing Martial Arts **EDU:** Bachelor of Arts in Human Services, Siena Heights University **A/S:** She attributes her success to the support of her agency and her ability to develop relationships within the community. **B/I:** She became involved in her profession because she had a desire to help women get the respect they deserve. **H/O:** The highlight of her career has been her ability to organize and facilitate team meetings and educate the community.

BECKY L. TAYLOR
Owner
Cedars Restaurant
6522 Statesboro Highway
Sylvania, GA 30467 United States
bgeorgia@planters.net
http://www.cambridgewhoswho.com

BUS: Leading High Quality Family Restaurant **P/S:** Family Buffets, Steaks, Seafood with an Emphasis on Customer Satisfaction **MA:** Regional **D/D/R:** Training the Staff, Overseeing Billing, Accounts Payable and Receiveable, Customer Service and Public Relations **H/I/S:** Playing Bridge and Tennis **EDU:** Coursework, Dominion College

EVELYN D. TAYLOR
Executive Director
Parents Challenge
115 N. Union Boulevard
Colorado Springs, CO 80909 United States
edt@theschuckcorporation.com
http://www.parentschallenge.org

BUS: Nonprofit **P/S:** Educational Advocacy for Low-Income Families, Scholarships **MA:** Local **D/D/R:** Offering Written and Oral Communications, Motivational Counseling **H/I/S:** Music, Reading Nonfiction, Watching Science Fiction **FBP:** Black Enterprise **EDU:** Master of Arts in Journalism, Northern Illinois University **A/A/S:** Black Alliance for Educational Options; Colorado Nonprofit Leadership Program **C/VW:** African-American Youth Leadership Conference; Harrison School District Superintendent's Advisory; United Way of America; Northern Illinois University Foundation; Emanuel Missionary Baptist Church; AIDS Foundation, Chicago **A/S:** She attributes her success to the support she receives from her family and community. **B/I:** She became involved in her profession because of her passion to help the underserved educational community and make a difference in the lives of others.

Laurie L. Taylor
Support Unit Supervisor
City of Forest Grove Police Department
2102 Pacific Avenue
Forest Grove, OR 97116 United States
ltaylor@ci.forest-grove.or.us
http://www.ci.forest-grove.or.us

BUS: Police Department **P/S:** Public Safety **MA:** Local **D/D/R:** Obtaining Training, Accreditation, Planning and Researching Grants **H/I/S:** Traveling, Reading, Crafts **EDU:** Associate of Applied Science in Business Administration, Portland Community College **CERTS:** Accredited for Law Enforcement Agencies **A/A/S:** Vice President, Oregon North West Police Accreditation Coalition **A/H:** Employee of the Year (2003) **C/VW:** Bonnie L. Hays Animal Shelter; The Humane Society of the United States; Susan G. Komen for the Cure; Relay for Life **A/S:** She attributes her success to being organized, to her time management skills and to her hard work. **B/I:** She became involved in her profession because she had an interest in law enforcement and was looking for a change. **H/O:** The highlight of her career is being responsible for the accreditation of the police department.

Ms. Mary Jane Taylor, RN, BSN
Telemetry Staff Registered Nurse
Saint Bernadine Medical Center
2101 N. Waterman Avenue
San Bernardino, CA 92404 United States
mjstory@aol.com
http://www.cambridgewhoswho.com

BUS: Healthcare **P/S:** Healthcare Services Including a Treatment Facility for Cardiac Patients **MA:** Local **D/D/R:** Nursing, Treating Patients **H/I/S:** Writing Poetry, Singing **FBP:** Newsweek; National Geographic **EDU:** Bachelor's Degree in Nursing, Loma Linda University Medical Center School of Nursing **CERTS:** Certified in Advanced Cardiac Life Support; Certified in Advanced Electrocardiograms **A/S:** She attributes her personal and professional success to her ability to set goals and work towards them. **H/O:** The highlight of her career is seeing her positive impact on the lives of patients.

RENEÉ J. TAYLOR
Claims Representative
State Farm Insurance
10451 N.W. 117th Avenue
Miami, FL 33178 United States
mjtyrt1@aol.com
http://www.cambridgewhoswho.com

BUS: Insurance Company Helping People Manage the Risks of Everyday Life, Recover from the Unexpected and Realize their Dreams **P/S:** Insurance, Banking, Mutual Funds, Retirement Planning, College Planning **MA:** National **D/D/R:** Handling Claims for Fires, Automobiles and Catastrophic Accidents **H/I/S:** Reading, Listening to Jazz Music **FBP:** BusinessWeek; Black Enterprise **EDU:** Master of Business Administration, Nova Southeastern University (2004); Bachelor of Science in Professional Management, Nova Southeastern University (1989) **A/A/S:** National Black MBA Association **A/H:** Officer of the Year, Alpha Kappa Psi (2004)

SOON-WY M. TAYLOR, CRCST
Medical Supply Technician
Hopi Health Care Center
PO Box 4000
Polacca, AZ 86042 United States
soon-wy.taylor@ihs.gov
http://www.ihs.gov

BUS: Healthcare Center **P/S:** Healthcare, Medical Supplies for Native American Civilians and Veterans **MA:** National **EXP:** Ms. Taylor's expertise is in supply management. **D/D/R:** Overseeing Sterile Processing and Material Management, Maintaining the Quality of Patient Care, Managing Distribution, Procurement and Central Supply Services **H/I/S:** Reading, Spending Time with her Family, Spending Time Outdoors, Doing Farm Work, Participating in Church Activities **FBP:** IAHC-SMM Communique; Healthcare Purchasing News; Infection Control Today **EDU:** Coursework, Purdue University **CERTS:** Certified Central Service Technician; Certified Nursing Assistant; Veteran Affairs Level One Training **A/A/S:** Grand Canyon Chapter, International Association of Healthcare Central Service Material Management **C/VW:** Disabled American Veterans **A/S:** She attributes her success to the support she receives from her mother. **B/I:** She became involved in her profession because of her experience in nursing. **H/O:** The most gratifying aspect of her career is mentoring and teaching others about what she has learned and experienced.

ZENN TAYLOR
Vice President
Energy Quest Resources, Inc.
3601 W. Sahara Drive
Suite 208
Las Vegas, NV 89102 United States
energyquest.inc@gmail.com
http://www.cambridgewhoswho.com

BUS: Oil and Gas Exploration **P/S:** Oil and Gas Exploration and Production **MA:** National **D/D/R:** Marketing, Managing Business Operations **FBP:** The Wall Street Journal **EDU:** Master's Degree in Marketing, Pepperdine University **C/VW:** Church; Charitable Organizations **A/S:** He attributes his success to constant education, drive, determination and lots of hard work. **B/I:** He became involved in his career because grew up in North Texas, around the industry where he developed an interest. **H/O:** The highlight of his career was in 1982, when he owned his own oil company.

DONALD L. TEAHON
Staff Nurse
Banner Good Samaritan Medical Center
1111 E. McDowell Road
Phoenix, AZ 85006 United States
1teabag@cox.net
http://www.cambridgewhoswho.com

BUS: Medical Center **P/S:** Healthcare, Emergency Medical Care **MA:** Local **EXP:** Mr. Teahon's expertise is in emergency and trauma nursing. **H/I/S:** Biking, Running Marathons **EDU:** Diploma in Nursing, St. Francis School of Nursing, NE **C/VW:** Special Olympics; Basilica of the National Shrine of the Immaculate Conception, Washington, DC **A/S:** He attributes his success to his work ethic, upbringing and to the support he receives from his mother. **B/I:** He became involved in his profession because he wanted to fulfill his late mother's dream of having at least one of her children in the medical field. **H/O:** The most gratifying aspects of his career are educating the public and being a daily advocate for patients.

MICHELE MARIE TECARRO
Rehabilitation Program Coordinator
New Jersey Veterans Memorial Home at Menlo Park
132 Evergreen Road
Edison, NJ 08837 United States
michele.tecarro@njdmava.state.nj.us
http://www.cambridgewhoswho.com

BUS: Healthcare Center **P/S:** Healthcare Services for Veterans **MA:** New Jersey **EXP:** Ms. Tecarro's expertise is in restraint management. **D/D/R:** Overseeing Rehabilitation Services, Caring for Wounded Patients **H/I/S:** Swimming, Traveling **FBP:** Journal of Rehabilitation Medicine **EDU:** MD, Earned in Philippines; Bachelor's Degree in Physical Therapy, Earned in Philippines; Bachelor of Science in Nursing, Earned in Philippines **CERTS:** Certified Assisted Living Administrator **A/A/S:** American Academy of Certified Public Managers; American Cancer Society; Soroptimist International **A/S:** She attributes her success to her caring nature. **B/I:** She became involved in her profession because she was interested in physical therapy and was looking for a career change. **H/O:** The most gratifying aspect of her career is conducting programs.

VALERIE E. TEETS
Owner, Manager
Apollo Gymnastics
12700 Apollo Drive
Woodbridge, VA 22192 United States
teetsgirl@aol.com
http://www.cambridgewhoswho.com

BUS: Gymnasium **P/S:** Gymnastics Instruction **MA:** Local **D/D/R:** Specializing in Developmental Program Involving Strength, Flexibility and Gymnastic Skills **H/I/S:** Watching her Daughter and Husband Drag Race **EDU:** High School Education **A/A/S:** Chamber of Commerce; Better Business Bureau **A/S:** She attributes her career success to her hard work and the family support she receives. **B/I:** She became involved in gymnastics instruction through her desire to help the children of her neighborhood. **H/O:** The most gratifying aspect of her career is seeing the children smile.

DEBBIE L. TEMAN
1) Office Manager 2) Travel Agent
1) Soquel Dental Office 2) YourGlobalTravelStore.com
2515 Porter Street
PO Box 559
Soquel, CA 95073 United States
debbie.teman@sbcglobal.net
http://www.yourglobaltravelstore.com

BUS: 1) Dental Practice 2) Travel Business **P/S:** 1) Dentistry 2) Hospitality **MA:** 1) Statewide 2) Statewide **D/D/R:** Managing the Office, Accounting **H/I/S:** Spending Time with the Family, Gardening, Riding Horses, Traveling **CERTS:** Pursuing California State Real Estate License; Registered Dental Assistant, Clayton Career College, San Jose; Certified Referring Travel Agent **A/A/S:** Women's Crisis Center; American Society for the Prevention of Cruelty to Animals **DOB:** July 20, 1963 **CHILD:** Tyler

LOWELL G. TENSMEYER, PH.D.
Research Scientist (Retired)
Eli Lilly and Company
35 W. 59th Street
Indianapolis, IN 46208 United States
ltensmeyer@sbcglobal.net
http://www.lilly.com

BUS: Worldwide Leading, Innovation-Driven Corporation Committed to Excellence in the Pharmaceutical Industry **P/S:** Spectroscopy **MA:** International **D/D/R:** Researching Sufra Red and Ramon Spectroscopy, Molecular Structure, and Crystals, Teaching at Utah State University and Ohio University, Helping Other Scientists with Structural Problems, Helping Determine which New Molecules Would Meet Pharmaceutical Needs **H/I/S:** Enjoying his Grandchildren and Great Grandchildren, Gardening **FBP:** Journal of the American Chemical Society; Journal of Biblical Literature; Journal of Physical Chemistry **EDU:** Ph.D. in Physical Chemistry, University of Utah (1957) **A/A/S:** American Chemical Society; American Physical Society; Phi Beta Kappa; Alpha Eta Sigma; Alpha Chi Sigma

DANA L. TERRELL
English Department Chair, English Teacher
Kingfisher High School
1500 South 13th
Kingfisher, OK 73750 United States
gdterrell@pldi.net
http://www.kingfisher.k12.ok.us/khs

BUS: Proven Leaders in Public Education **P/S:** Secondary Level General Studies, Arts, Music, Computer Science, Physical Education, Special Education and After-School Programs **MA:** Regional **D/D/R:** Working as the English Department Chair and as an Advanced Placement Teacher, Sponsoring the National Honor Society, Junior Civic Club, Junior Class, and the Rural Civic Club, Specializing in Preparing Students for Future Speaking and Communicating, Assisting them with the P.A.S.S. Test, Teaching English, Advanced Placement English and Business **H/I/S:** Cooking, Reading, Going to Baseball Games, Watching all Student and Family Sports Events **FBP:** English Journal **EDU:** Bachelor of Arts in English with High Honors, Northwest Oklahoma State University (1973); Additional 45 Hours, Oklahoma State University and the University of Central Oklahoma **A/A/S:** Delta Kappa Gamma; Kappa Kappa Iota; Epsilon Sigma Alpha; American Association of University Women; National Education Association; Oklahoma Education Association

---

DIANE FRANCES A. TESALONA
Sales Associate
Nordstrom Rack
45575 Dulles Eastern Plaza
Sterling, VA 20166 United States
dtesalon@gmu.edu
diane.tesalona@nordstrom.com
http://www.cambridgewhoswho.com

BUS: Retail Store **P/S:** Clothing **MA:** National **D/D/R:** Overseeing Business Administration, Managing the Office and Expenses **H/I/S:** Playing the Violin and Piano, Rowing **EDU:** Bachelor of Science in Government and International Politics, Minor in Business, George Mason University **CERTS:** Certification in Customer Service **A/A/S:** Asian Pacific American Heritage Association; Filipino Cultural Association; Zeta Tau Alpha; Alpha Lambda Delta National Honor Society; The National Society of Collegiate Scholars **C/VW:** Lupus Foundation of America; Susan G. Komen for the Cure; St. Jude Children's Research Hospital; United Way of America **A/S:** She attributes her success to her family values and work ethic. **B/I:** She became involved in her profession after starting as a sales associate. **H/O:** The highlight of her career was being asked to become a manager after only six months.

DR. CHARLES N. TETZLAFF
Scientist
Sequenom
189 Wells Avenue
Newton, MA 02459 United States
ctetzlaff@sequenom.com
http://www.sequenom.com

BUS: Proven Leader in the Biotechnology Industry **P/S:** Genomics, Proprietary MassARRAY System, Research, The Best Genetic Analysis Products that Translate Genomic Science into Superior Solutions for Molecular Medicine **MA:** International **D/D/R:** Supporting Customers and Scientists, Conducting Genetic Analysis, Liaising between the Company, Academia and Government Agencies, Researching on Genetic States and Diseases **H/I/S:** Martial Arts, Wine Tasting **FBP:** Nature; Science; Nature Biotechnology **EDU:** Post-Doctoral Coursework in Biochemistry, Brown University; Ph.D., Tufts University (2001) **A/A/S:** ACS

DR. KURT THAW
Director
Center for Health, Appetite and Nutrition
1701 N. State Street
Jackson, MS 39210 United States
thawak@millsaps.com
http://www.cambridgewhoswho.com

BUS: Nutritional Health and Research Center **P/S:** Training and Certification for Counselors Interested in Being Personal Wellness Consultants Using Only Scientifically-Supported Techniques, Research on Obesity, Weight Loss and Eating Behaviors, Seminars for Businesses on the Benefits of Weight Loss for Companies and Employees **MA:** National **EXP:** Dr. Thaw's area of expertise is in weight management, scientific research and leadership skills using an integrative approach to improve health and wellness. **H/I/S:** Outdoor Activities, Sports, Fitness, Traveling, Music **FBP:** Behavioral Neuroscience; Physiology and Behavior; Journal of Obesity **EDU:** Post Doctorate Research and Training, University of Virginia, Cornell Medical College (1994-1998); Ph.D. in Neuroscience, Florida State University (1994); Bachelor of Science in Psychology, Georgia Southern University (1987) **A/A/S:** Mississippi Academy of Sciences; Society for Neuroscience; Society for the Study of Ingestive Behavior; Association for Chemoreception Sciences; Society for Neuroscience; Association for Chemoreception Sciences **DOB:** April 1, 1965 **SP:** Melanie **CHILD:** Chelsea **W/H:** Millsaps College (1998-Present); Cornell Medical College (1997-1998); Sweet Briar College (1996-1997); University of Virginia (1994-1996) **A/S:** He attributes his success to his appreciation of knowledge and his desire to understand complex behaviors and cognitions. **B/I:** He became involved in his profession after his frustration with false claims and promises that have no long-term benefits. fostered his desire to offer people something that really worked. **H/O:** The highlight of his career was the successful implementation of his program with 40 clients, all of whom had sustained success and improved health.

MR. WAYNE B. THELWELL, LVN
Licensed Vocational Nurse
Salinas Valley State Prison
Soledad, CA United States
waynethelwell@mail2world.com
http://www.cambridgewhoswho.com

BUS: Correctional Institution **P/S:** Correctional Services Including Healthcare **MA:** Regional **EXP:** Mr. Thelwell's expertise is in pediatric, telemetry and intensive care nursing. **D/D/R:** Monitoring Vitals and Patients' Feedings, Administering Mediation, Teaching **H/I/S:** Photography, Spending Time Outdoors **FBP:** RN; LPN **EDU:** Coursework in General Education **CERTS:** Licensed Vocational Nurse, Military (1993)

TAMMY C. THERIOT, ABR, NHSS
Realtor
Covenant Realty
1850 W. Lake Houston Parkway
Kingwood, TX 77339 United States
tammytheriot@earthlink.net
http://www.tammytheriot.com

BUS: Full-Service Real Estate Agency **P/S:** Real Estate Exchange Services **MA:** Northeast and Central Texas **EXP:** Ms. Theriot's expertise includes new home sales, negotiation and investment. **H/I/S:** Traveling, Gambling **FBP:** Realtor **EDU:** Bachelor's Degree in Medical Record Science, University of Southwestern Louisiana (Now University of Louisiana at Lafayette) **CERTS:** Licensed Real Estate Agent, State of Texas; Accredited Buyers' Representative; New Home Sales Specialist; Real Estate Investment Specialist **A/A/S:** Women's Council of Realtors; Houston Association of Realtors; Texas Association of Realtors; National Association of Realtors; Texas Notary Public Association **DOB:** August 10, 1958 **SP:** Mitchell **CHILD:** Dustin, Casey **A/S:** She attributes her success to her motivation. **B/I:** She became involved in her profession when she transferred to Texas, saw that the real estate market was booming and decided to change careers. **H/O:** The most gratifying aspect of her career is seeing her clients happy after a closing.

ALFRED F. THOBEN
Partner
D'Arcangelo & Co., LLC
3000 Westchester Avenue
Purchase, NY 10577 United States
athoben@darcangelo.com
http://www.darcangelo.com

BUS: Accounting Firm **P/S:** Accounting Services Including Auditing, Corporate and Individual Tax Preparation, Estate Tax, Financial Planning, Consulting **MA:** Regional **D/D/R:** Auditing, Preparing Tax Returns **FBP:** BusinessWeek **EDU:** Master's Degree in Accounting, New York University; Bachelor's Degree in Economics, St. Francis College **CERTS:** Certified Public Accountant, State of New York **A/A/S:** American Institute of Certified Public Accountants; New York State Society of Certified Public Accountants **A/S:** He attributes his success to his dedication and hard work. **B/I:** He became involved in his profession because of his interest in accounting. **H/O:** The most gratifying aspect of his career is being able to help his clients with various financial issues.

ANCY SUSAN THOMAS, PT, MA
Center Manager
Kessler Rehabilitation Center
33-00 Broadway
Fair Lawn, NJ 07410 United States
athomas@selectmedicalcorp.com
http://www.cambridgewhoswho.com

BUS: Healthcare **P/S:** Hospital with a Separate Clinic for Occupation, Speech and Physical Therapy **MA:** Local **D/D/R:** Performing Physical Therapy, Working with Patients on Exercise Development, Marketing for the Clinic, Handling the Budget, Ordering Products, Overseeing 12 Employees **H/I/S:** Reading, Volunteering at Church, Creating Pottery, Painting, Spending Time with the Family **FBP:** US News & World Report; Time **EDU:** Master of Arts in Developmental Disabilities and Physical Therapy; New York University; Bachelor of Science in Physical Therapy, New York University **A/A/S:** American Physical Therapy Association **C/VW:** Volunteering with the Youth Program, Church **A/S:** She attributes her success to her passion for the field and her hard work. **B/I:** She became involved in her profession because she loves helping people. **H/O:** The highlight of her career was being made supervisor.

B.J. Thomas
Realtor
Exit Realty Canyon Lake
13201 SM 306
Canyon Lake, TX 78133 United States
bj@canyonlaketexashomes.com
http://www.canyonlaketexashomes.com

BUS: Proven Leader in the Real Estate Industry, Leader in Comal County Texas Real Estate **P/S:** Residential Real Estate, Commercial Real Estate, Resort Properties, Waterfront Properties, Land Sales **MA:** National **D/D/R:** Listing and Selling Properties, Working with Buyers and Sellers, Investors, Developers and Builders, Holding Office Meetings, Training New Agents **H/I/S:** Spending Time with her Grandson, Dancing, Shopping, Reading **FBP:** Real Estate Publications **EDU:** High School Education **A/A/S:** Founder and Former President, Canyon Lake Women in Business; Former President, Chamber of Commerce; New Braunfels-Canyon Lake Association of Realtors; Women's Council of Realtors, Canyon Lake United Methodist Church; Heritage Museum of the Texas Hill Country; Hochheim Prairie of Comal County; Chamber of Commerce **A/H:** Top Producer (2008); A-List Top Lister (2008)

Ms. Cristy M. Thomas, APRN, BC
Advanced Practice Registered Nurse, Nurse Practitioner
Dept. of Surgery; Division of Trauma/Critical Care
University of Nevada School of Medicine
2040 W. Charleston Boulevard, Suite 302
Las Vegas, NV 89102 United States
cthomas@medicine.nevada.edu
http://www.unr.edu/med

BUS: University, Hospital **P/S:** Healthcare **MA:** Regional **EXP:** Ms. Thomas' expertise is in trauma nursing. **D/D/R:** Coordinating Trauma Care, Teaching Trauma Surgery to Residents and Medical Students **H/I/S:** Traveling **EDU:** Master of Science in Nursing, University of Nevada, Las Vegas, with Honors; Bachelor of Science in Nursing, University of Michigan, with Honors **CERTS:** Certified Professional Legal Nurse Consultant, National Center for Legal Nursing Consultants (2007) **A/A/S:** Sigma Theta Tau; Phi Kappa Phi; Anti-Aging Medicine Society; American Academy of Nurse Practitioners; Society of Trauma, Nurse Practitioners for the State of Nevada **A/S:** She attributes her success to the support of her peers and family and to her self-motivation. **H/O:** The highlight of her career was having the honor of working as an advanced practice in-trauma nurse.

HERMAN ANDRE THOMAS
Founder, Chief Executive Officer
Wireless Ingenuity, LLC
2018 156th Avenue N.E., Suite 100
Bellevue, WA 98007 United States
andre@wirelessingenuity.com
http://www.wirelessingenuity.com

BUS: Venture Capital and Development Firm and Limited Liability Corporation **P/S:** Venture Capital Advisory Services **MA:** International **D/D/R:** Overseeing Strategic Planning, Offering Venture Capital Funding **H/I/S:** Traveling Internationally, Philanthropy, Skiing **EDU:** Master of Business Administration, Harvard Business School **A/A/S:** Overlake Christian Church; Jack and Jill of America, Inc. **A/H:** Recipient, Wall Street Journal Fellow Award

LINDA J. THOMAS, PH.D.
Division Chairwoman
Department of Nursing
Madisonville Community College
750 Laffoon Street
Madisonville, KY 42431 United States
linda.thomas@kctcs.edu
http://www.madcc.kctcs.edu

BUS: Community College **P/S:** Higher Education **MA:** International **EXP:** Ms. Thomas' expertise is in educational leadership, curriculum development and faculty evaluation. **D/D/R:** Overseeing Administration and Supervision, Budgeting, Developing Programs **H/I/S:** Gardening, Sewing, Making Crafts, Basket Weaving **FBP:** Journal of Nursing Education; Nurse Education Today **EDU:** Ph.D. in Educational Leadership, University of Louisville, Western Kentucky University; Master of Science in Nursing, University of Evansville (1985); Bachelor of Science in Nursing, The University of Kansas (1969) **A/A/S:** Treasurer, Kentucky Nurses Foundation; Kentucky Nurses Association; Vice Chairwoman, Hopkins County Community Clinic; American Nurses Association; Phi Kappa Phi; Sigma Theta Tau **C/VW:** Kentuckian Girl Scout Council; Board Member, Young Men's Christian Association **SP:** Robert **CHILD:** Stephanie, Bryan

MARREA N. THOMAS
Procedures and Training Specialist
Daiichi Sankyo Pharma Development
399 Thornall Street
Edison, NJ 08837 United States
mthomas@dsvs.com
http://www.daiichisankyo-us.com

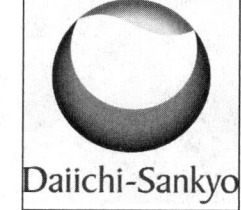

BUS: Pharmaceutical Company **P/S:** Pharmaceutical Products Including WelChol, Benicar, Benicar HCT, Floxin Otic, Evoxac **MA:** International **D/D/R:** Monitoring Training Program, Mapping Out Responsibilities and Requirements for Each Employee, Accessing which Standard Operating Procedure to be Trained In, Working with Outside Manufacturers for Training for 205 Employees **H/I/S:** Drawing, Painting, Cooking **EDU:** Master's Degree in Project Management, Colorado Technical University (2006) **CERTS:** Certified in Constructional Design (2007); Certifications in Change Management, Business Management and Project Management **A/A/S:** Parenteral Drug Association; American Society of Quality Control

MICHAEL B. THOMAS
Director of Radiology
Methodist Sugar Land Hospital
16655 S.W. Freeway
Sugar Land, TX 77479 United States
mthomas@tmh.tmc.edu
http://www.methodisthealth.com

BUS: New-Generation Hospital Providing Quality Services in a Home-Like Setting **P/S:** Express Diagnostics and Imaging Services, Medical Treatment, Surgery, Birthing Center, Emergency Care Center, Intensive Care Unit/Clinical Decision and Treatment Unit (ICU/CDTU), Physician Offices **MA:** Regional **D/D/R:** Participating in Health Fairs within the Community, Overseeing Radiology **H/I/S:** Outdoor Sports, Horses **EDU:** Bachelor's Degree in Health Administration, Warren National University (previously Kennedy-Western University) WY (2007); Associate Degree in Radiology, Houston Community College (1982) **A/A/S:** American Healthcare Radiology Administrators; American Registry of Radiologic Technologists

SHARON G. THOMAS
Region Office Manager
Civil Service Employees Association
120 Pineview Drive
Amherst, NY 14228 United States
sgthomaswny@yahoo.com
http://www.cambridgewhoswho.com

BUS: Labor Union **P/S:** Protecting and Improving Members' Quality of Life **MA:** Western New York **D/D/R:** Assisting the Region President and Region Director **H/I/S:** Theater, Concerts, Going to the Gym, Reading **FBP:** Time; Prevention; Forbes; National Geographic **EDU:** College Coursework **CERTS:** Sunday School Teaching Certificate **C/VW:** American Cancer Society; Literacy Volunteer; St. John Baptist Church; Veterans

VIOLET L. THOMAS-HICKS
Realtor, Notary Public
Century 21 Success
2501 Cherry Avenue, Suite 150
Signal Hill, CA 90755 United States
violetthomashicks@msn.com
http://www.violetthomashicks.com

BUS: Real Estate Company **P/S:** Real Estate Sales **MA:** Regional **D/D/R:** Facilitating Real Estate Sales, Refinancing, Offering Traveling Notary Services **H/I/S:** Reading **FBP:** Realtor **EDU:** Coursework in Business Administration, California State University, Los Angeles **CERTS:** Licensed Real Estate Agent, State of California; Licensed Notary Public, State of California **A/A/S:** California Association of Realtors; National Association of Realtors; National Notary Association; The National Black Nurses Association, Inc. **A/S:** She attributes her career success to the support she receives from her family and friends. **B/I:** She became involved in her profession because she felt that it was important to educate the consumer about the products they purchase. **H/O:** The most gratifying aspect of her career is helping her clients find their dream homes.

CHAMEL LYNN THOMPSON, RN
Registered Nurse
New York Hospital Queens
156-04 134th Avenue
Jamaica, NY 11434 United States
Clynnt80@yahoo.com
http://www.cambridgewhoswho.com

BUS: Hospital **P/S:** Healthcare **MA:** Local **D/D/R:** Caring for Patients and Newborns, Assisting Patients during Labor and Delivery, Working on the Shared Governance Committee **H/I/S:** Reading, Word Search Puzzles **FBP:** Nursing2009; Journal of Maternal Child Nursing; Advance for Nurses **EDU:** Bachelor of Science in Nursing, Molloy College (2003) **A/A/S:** Association of Women's Health, Obstetric and Neonatal Nurses **C/VW:** United Negro College Fund **A/S:** She attributes her success to her hard work and her faith in God. **B/I:** She became involved in her profession because of her caring nature. **H/O:** The most gratifying aspect of her career is seeing her patients being happy.

MR. DOUGLAS ALLAN THOMPSON, MS
New Teacher Mentor
Howard-Suamico School District
2700 Lineville Road
Green Bay, WI 54313 United States
dougthom@hssd.k12.wi.us
http://www.hssd.com

BUS: School District **P/S:** Education **MA:** Local **D/D/R:** Familiarizing Teachers with New Standards and Curriculum, Coordinating the Gifted and Talented Programs for Grades Six through Eight, Developing and Implementing Curriculum to Meet the State's Standards **H/I/S:** Fishing, Camping, Traveling **FBP:** Educational Leadership **EDU:** Master's Degree in Curriculum and Instruction, University of Wisconsin, Milwaukee; Bachelor's Degree in Education, University of Wisconsin, University of Wisconsin-Superior **A/A/S:** Association for Supervision and Curriculum Development; Wisconsin Education Association; National Education Association **A/H:** Outstanding Educator Certificate, Wisconsin Center For Academically Talented Youth (1993); Who's Who Among American Teachers (1995, 2006) **C/VW:** Society of St. Vincent de Paul, Inc.; American Cancer Society **A/S:** He attributes his success to his efforts to work with and learn from his students, and from being able to share his knowledge with others. **B/I:** He became involved in his profession because he always enjoyed education. **H/O:** The most gratifying aspects of his career are seeing students return to see him and remembering specific ways that he has impacted their lives.

IDETTE R. THOMPSON
Captain
24 Wolcott Hill Road
Wethersfield, CT 06109 United States
dragonflyer64@aol.com
http://www.ct.gov/doc

BUS: Correction Center **P/S:** Law Enforcement, Correction Services **MA:** Connecticut **EXP:** Ms. Thompson's expertise is in operations management. **D/D/R:** Ensuring the Safety and Security of Personnel, Male and Female Inmates **H/I/S:** Reading, Traveling, Spending Time with her Family **FBP:** Fortune 500; Forbes **EDU:** Pursuing Bachelor's Degree in Criminal Justice, with a Concentration in Homeland Security; Associate Degree in Criminal Justice, Ashworth College, GA **A/H:** Dean's List (2004); Ribbon of Distinction, Department of Corrections (1996) **C/VW:** Local Church

KARYN M. THOMPSON
Medical Esthetician, Owner
Rejuveness
2118 Halleck Avenue S.W.
Seattle, WA 98116 United States
karyntce@yahoo.com
http://www.cambridgewhoswho.com

BUS: Health and Beauty Spa **P/S:** Personal Skin Care, Education, Sale of Beauty Care Products **D/D/R:** Consulting with Plastic and Cosmetic Surgeons, Marketing New Handheld Devices Including the Wrinkle Iron for in-Home Treatments, Performing Skin Care Treatments Including Skin Protection Procedures **H/I/S:** Exercising, Spending Time at the Beach, Traveling **EDU:** Coursework, Euro Institute of Skin Care **CERTS:** Licensed Esthetician, States of California and Washington **C/VW:** Local Charitable Organizations

LORI J. THOMPSON
Certified Sign Agent, Notary Public
1372 Goldeneagle Drive
Corona, CA 92879 United States
ljtnotary@sbcglobal.net
http://www.cambridgewhoswho.com

BUS: Notary Services **P/S:** Notary Services **MA:** Local **H/I/S:** Wine Tasting, Traveling **EDU:** Industry Related Training and Experience **CERTS:** Certified Signing Agent **A/A/S:** California Notary Association **C/VW:** Local High School **A/S:** She attributes her success to drive and determination. **B/I:** She was prompted to enter her profession because she had an interest in the field. **H/O:** The highlight of her career is the flexibility it allows.

NATALIA THOMPSON
Teacher
Georgia Brown Elementary of Paso Robles Public Schools
525 36th Street
Paso Robles, CA 93446 United States
natnbob@aol.com
http://www.cambridgewhoswho.com

BUS: Public Elementary School **P/S:** Elementary Education **MA:** Local **D/D/R:** Teaching Bilingual Education, Tutoring Students before and after School **H/I/S:** Reading, Traveling **FBP:** CABE Newsletter **EDU:** Master's Degree in Educational Administration, California State University, Fullerton **A/A/S:** California Association for Bilingual Education; American Cancer Society

WENDELL R. THOMPSON
District Sales Manager
Sysco Food Service
1977 The Oaks Boulevard
Kissimmee, FL 34746 United States
thompson.wendell@cfl.sysco.com
http://www.sysco.com

BUS: Food Service Company **P/S:** Food Products, Ingredients Needed to Prepare Meals, Numerous Ancillary Preparation and Serving Items **MA:** International **D/D/R:** Supervising Sales Representatives, Ensuring Customer Satisfaction, Managing Sales of Food and Supplemental Food Products **H/I/S:** Golfing **FBP:** Food & Wine **EDU:** Coursework, Culinary College **A/A/S:** Chamber of Commerce; Central Florida Hotel & Lodging Association

JACQUELINE M. THORNE-FIGUEROA
School Counselor
Board of Education, PS 123M, Mahalia Jackson School
301 W. 140th Street
Manhattan, NY 10030 United States
jthornef@schools.nyc.gov
http://www.nycboe.net

BUS: Proven Leader in the Education Industry, Kindergarten through Sixth Grade Learning Institution **P/S:** Atmosphere Conducive to Learning which Includes Programs and Services that Address Strengthening the Needs of Students, Provides a Learning Environment which Encourages Self-Esteem and Attempts to Create Independent Learners by Building on the Individual Strengths of Students **MA:** Regional **D/D/R:** Offering Solution-Based Counseling, Anger Management Therapy, Coordinating the Word of the Day Activity for the Entire School and the Character Education Program **H/I/S:** Reading, Watching Movies, Walking **FBP:** Counseling; ASCA School Counselor Journal **EDU:** Master's Degree in Psychology, Fordham University (1993) **CERTS:** Anger Management Certification (2005); Special Education Certification, New York City Board of Education (1995) **A/A/S:** American Psychological Association; American School Counselor Association; Association for Supervision and Curriculum Development

ANN M. THREADGILL
Teacher, Department Chairwoman, Finance Officer (Retired)
Thomas Jefferson High School
7501 Mayland Drive
Richmond, VA 23294 United States
http://www.cambridgewhoswho.com

BUS: Public High School **P/S:** Basic Educational Subjects, Career and Technical Education, Media Center, International Languages **MA:** Regional **D/D/R:** Teaching Mathematics and Computer Science **H/I/S:** Golfing **FBP:** U.S. News & World Report **EDU:** Bachelor of Science in Mathematics, Virginia Commonwealth University (1971) **A/A/S:** National Council of Teachers of Mathematics

DOROTHEA L. THURNER
Child Welfare Supervisor
Baca County Department of Social Services
772 Colorado Street
Springfield, CO 81073 United States
dorothea.thurner@state.co.us.com
http://www.semhs.org

BUS: Nonprofit Organization **P/S:** Healthcare Including Out-Patient and In-Patient Services to Chronically and Persistently Mentally-Ill Patients **MA:** Baca County **EXP:** Ms. Thurner's expertise is in family care services. **H/I/S:** Cooking, Horseback Riding **FBP:** Psychology Today **EDU:** Pursuing Ph.D. in Counseling and Psychology, Walden University; Master's Degree in Human Behavior, American University **CERTS:** Clinically Certified Forensic Counselor, American College of Certified Forensic Counselors **A/A/S:** Local Safety Program; Child Protection Team, Baca County; Senate Bill 94 Committee; National Association of Forensic Counselors; American Psychological Association

HOLLI A. TICKNOR
Consultant Account Manager
Roche Diagnostics Corporation
9115 Hague Road
Indianapolis, IN 46250 United States
holli.ticknor@roche.com
http://www.roche.com

BUS: Healthcare Company with a Uniquely Broad Spectrum of Innovative Solutions, Active in the Discovery, Development, Manufacture and Marketing of Novel Healthcare Solutions **P/S:** Diagnosis and Treatment of Manifest Diseases, Offering Ways of Identifying and Targeting Diseases Early, Diabetes Care and Medical Diagnostics **MA:** National **D/D/R:** Selling Hospital Blood Glucose Monitors and Outpatient Blood Glucose Monitors, Public Speaking Dealing with Diabetes and Diabetes Education **H/I/S:** Traveling, Golfing, Gardening, Tennis **EDU:** Bachelor of Science in Biology and Chemistry, University of Texas (1987) **A/A/S:** Board of Governors, Dominim Country Club; Board of Directors, Camp Independence; American Association of Diabetes Educators; Girl Scout Leader; Daughters of the American Revolution **CHILD:** Ryan, Rachel

CHARLES EDWIN TIFT, LMSW
Social Worker
Serenity House Personal Care Home, Inc.
36 Coates Road
Hinesville, GA 31313 United States
tift@clds.net
http://www.shpch.com

BUS: Personal Care Center **P/S:** Social Services, Counseling **MA:** Regional **EXP:** His expertise is in substance abuse counseling. **H/I/S:** Playing Basketball **FBP:** Industry-Related Publications **EDU:** Master of Social Work, Savannah State University (1999); Bachelor of Business Administration, Albany State University (1977) **CERTS:** Licensed Master Social Worker, State of Georgia **C/VW:** Feed the Children; Seattle Union Gospel Mission; Young Life Ministries; Youth With a Mission **A/S:** He attributes his success to his self-motivation and his desire to help others. **H/O:** The highlight of his career was being an independent contractor with the department of human services.

APRIL A. TILTON, PA-C
Physician Assistant
Aging and Geriatric Research
University of Florida
PO Box 112610
Gainesville, FL 32610 United States
atilton@aging.ufl.edu
http://www.ufl.edu

BUS: Major, Public, Comprehensive, Land-Grant, Research University, State's Oldest, Largest and Most Comprehensive University, Among the Nation's most Academically Diverse Public Universities **P/S:** More than 100 Undergraduate Majors, 16 Colleges and More than 100 Research, Service and Education Centers, Bureaus and Institutes, Professional Degree Programs Include Dentistry, Law, Medicine, Pharmacy and Veterinary Medicine **MA:** Local **D/D/R:** Specializing in Family Practice Medicine, Acting as a Prescriptive Authority for All Non-Scheduled Drugs, Geriatrics, Overseeing Clinical Care of Geriatric Patients and Assisting in the Department of Aging and Geriatric Research **H/I/S:** Walking, Gardening, Reading, Watching Movies, Fishing **FBP:** JAAPA **EDU:** Bachelor of Science in Biological Science, University of Osteopathic Medicine (1989); Bachelor of Arts in Chemistry, Gustavus Adolphus College (1987) **A/A/S:** American Academy of Physician Assistants; Florida Association of Physician Assistants

DORIS TIMM, RN, BSN
Director of Nursing
Bristol Manor
96 Parkway
Rochelle Park, NJ 07662 United States
doristimm@yahoo.com
http://www.cambridgewhoswho.com

BUS: Healthcare **P/S:** Long Term Healthcare **MA:** Statewide **D/D/R:** Directing Gerontology **H/I/S:** Playing the Piano, Gardening, Reading, Making Crafts, Spending Time with her Children and Pets **EDU:** Bachelor of Science in Nursing, Gwyneth Mercy College, Summa Cum Laude **A/A/S:** National Association of Directors of Nursing **C/VW:** American Cancer Society; Vietnam Veterans Association **A/S:** She attributes her success to her mother who was great role model. **B/I:** She chose the profession because she wanted to be a nurse from a very young age. **H/O:** The highlight of her career is her current position.

MARYLOU TINER
Substitute Teacher
Mariposa County Unified School District
PO Box 8
Mariposa, CA 95338 United States
mltiner@mailstation.com
http://www.cambridgewhoswho.com

BUS: School District **P/S:** Education **MA:** Regional **D/D/R:** Substitute Teaching for Elementary School Classes, Special Education and All Subjects **H/I/S:** Sending Encouraging Cards and Notes to her Friends, Family and Students **FBP:** Reader's Digest; Child Evangelism Magazine **EDU:** Bachelor's Degree in Early Childhood Education, California State University (1976); Graduate, Addictions Program, Reformers Unanimous **CERTS:** Certified Teacher, State of California **A/A/S:** Director, Release Time Christian Education, Mariposa County; Board Member, Child Evangelism Fellowship **C/VW:** Jail Ministry; AARP Tax Aide **DOB:** May 14, 1930 **POB:** Wilmar, CA **SP:** Henry (Deceased) **CHILD:** Timothy, Greg, David, Raafat **W/H:** Covina-Valley Unified School District, CA (1980-1986); Mariposa Unified School District, CA **A/S:** She attributes her success to Jesus. **B/I:** She became involved in her profession because of her experience teaching Bible study when she was young and her love for teaching. **H/O:** The most gratifying aspects of her career are working with children in evangelism classes and teaching children in a religious atmosphere.

MS. DEBRA J. TINKLER-SUTTON, RN, BS
Registered Nurse, Home Health Field Nurse, Case Manager
Accentra Home Healthcare
4350 Will Rogers Parkway, Suite 500
Oklahoma City, OK 73108 United States
djt1227@sbcglobal.net
http://www.accentrahealthcare.com

BUS: Healthcare Center **P/S:** Home Healthcare Including Physical Therapy, Occupational Therapy, Speech Therapy **MA:** Regional **EXP:** Ms. Tinkler-Sutton's expertise is in home healthcare and wound care. **D/D/R:** Following up with Doctors, Administering Antibiotics, Starting Up IV Lines, Helping Patients who Require Home Assistance **H/I/S:** Water Skiing, Gardening, Artwork, Making Crafts, Reading **FBP:** Nursing2009; American Journal of Nursing; Success in Home Care **EDU:** Pursuing Coursework in Pain Management Resource; Bachelor's Degree in Family Studies and Gerontology, Southern Nazarene University (2000); Associate Degree in Nursing, Seminole State College (1980)

TERRI LYNN TIPTON
Assistant Principal
Greenville Middle School
1250 Terrell Street
Greenville, GA 30222 United States
thediamondt@gmail.com
http://www.cambridgewhoswho.com

BUS: Public School **P/S:** Education **MA:** Local **D/D/R:** Instructing, Working as a Mist Coordinator, Visionary Team Member and Gaps School Trainer, coordinating Safety, Testing and Reading Endorsements **H/I/S:** Playing the Piano, Performing in Dramas, Creating Computer Picture Albums, Working with Arts and Crafts, Spending Time with her Two Nephews, Taking Care of Two Dogs and Two Cats **FBP:** Educational Leadership **EDU:** Master of Educational Administration, Troy State University; Bachelor of Science in Elementary Education, University of Alabama at Birmingham **A/A/S:** Association for Supervision and Curriculum Development; PAGE **A/H:** Outstanding Young Woman of America (1997); Teacher of the Year for Manchester Elementary School (1998); Meriwether County Teacher of the Year (1999); Atlanta Journal Constitution Honor Teacher Awards Nominee (2000) **C/VW:** Compassion International; Various Charitable Organizations **B/I:** She became involved in her profession because she wanted an opportunity to make a difference and help her students learn and achieve. **H/O:** The most gratifying aspect of her career is her ability to make a difference in her students' lives and guide them toward becoming leaders.

JANET M. TITUS
First Grade Teacher
Buffalo Elementary School
306 S. Bluff Street
Buffalo, IN 47925 United States
jtitus@nwhite.k12.in.us
http://www.cambridgewhoswho.com

BUS: Elementary School **P/S:** Education **MA:** Local **D/D/R:** Specializing in Early Childhood Education, Teaching Reading and Language Arts **H/I/S:** Golfing, Swimming, Reading **FBP:** The Mailbox **EDU:** Master of Education, Ball State University (1982); Bachelor's Degree in Elementary Education, Ball State University **A/A/S:** Delta Kappa Gamma; Reading Association; Indiana State Teachers Association; North White Classroom Teachers Association **C/VW:** Buffalo Christian Church **A/S:** She attributes her success to her positive attitude, her sense of humor and her determination. **B/I:** She became involved in her profession because she loves children. **H/O:** The most gratifying aspect of her career is when former students return to visit her to say thank you and share their successes.

TERI D. TOBIN
Asset Manager
National Community Renaissance
9065 Haven Avenue, Suite 100
Rancho Cucamonga, CA 91730 United States
ttobin@nationalcore.org
dentistobin@aol.com

BUS: House Preservation Service **P/S:** Preservation of At-Risk Affordable Housing **MA:** National **D/D/R:** Managing Risk and Property, Community Relations **H/I/S:** Singing, Songwriting, Salsa Dancing, Aerobics **CERTS:** AHM; TaCCs **A/A/S:** Chapter 106, Institute for Real Estate Management; Hope Through Housing Foundation; Afro-Academic, Cultural, Technological, and Scientific Olympics; Urban League

MR. CHARLES H. TODD
Owner
Todd Ranch
205 N. Ninth Street
Onida, SD 57564 United States
toddranch@venturecomm.net
http://www.cambridgewhoswho.com

BUS: Ranch **P/S:** Cattle Breeding Including Agricultural Seed Sales, Farming and Consulting Services **MA:** Regional **D/D/R:** Cattle Farming, Managing Sales, Consulting **H/I/S:** Raising Horses, Waterskiing, Speed Boat Racing **FBP:** Successful Farming **EDU:** Master of Science in Theology, Grace University (1975); Bachelor of Science in Agricultural Economics, South Dakota State University (1974) **CERTS:** Certified Crop Advisor **A/A/S:** International Certified Crop Advisory Program **C/VW:** Local Church **SP:** Nancy **CHILD:** Charles, Michael, Timothy

JULIE A. TOLAR
Pub and Restaurant Manager
Rogue Regency Inn
2300 Biddle Road
Medford, OR 97504 United States
julie@rogueregency.com
http://www.rogueregency.com

BUS: Hotel **P/S:** Hospitality and Food Services **MA:** Regional **D/D/R:** Managing Operations Including Sports Bar and Liquor Orders, Overseeing Employees, Scheduling and Handling Human Relations Functions, Overseeing Food, Beverage, Karaoke and Comedy Shows, Ensuring Customer Satisfaction **H/I/S:** Playing Football and Baseball, Fishing, Wine Tasting **FBP:** Cheers **EDU:** Coursework in Political Science, Rockland Community College **C/VW:** Susan G. Komen for the Cure; Local Charitable Organizations

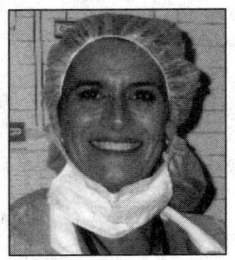

KATHLEEN TOMÉ-LATTIG, RN
Registered Nurse
Staten Island University Hospital
Seaview Avenue
Staten Island, NY 10305 United States
kathleentomelattig@aol.com
http://www.cambridgewhoswho.com

BUS: Level I Trauma and Magnet Hospital with Outstanding Medical Services **P/S:** Healthcare **MA:** National **D/D/R:** Operating Room Nursing with an Emphasis on Orthopedics and Total Joint Replacement **H/I/S:** Traveling, Dancing, Fitness, Pilates, Enjoying Music **FBP:** AORN Publications; NYSNA Publications **EDU:** Associate Degree Plus 40 in Nursing, Morris County Community College **CERTS:** Certified Operating Room Nurse, Association of Perioperative Registered Nurses **A/A/S:** New York State Nurses Association; Association of Operating Room Nurses **C/VW:** Covenant House **A/S:** She attributes her success to being willing to do whatever she has to do in order to help others.

JANE I. TOMLINSON
AA Teacher
Central Bucks School District
Weldon Way
Doylestown, PA 18901 United States
jatomlin1@comcast.net
http://www.cbsd.org

BUS: Education **P/S:** Education **MA:** Local **D/D/R:** Teaching 10th to 12th-Grade Students **H/I/S:** Painting, Photography **EDU:** Master's Degree in Education, Temple University; Bachelor of Arts in AA Education, Trenton State University **A/A/S:** Pennsylvania State Education Association; James A. Mitchner Art Museum **C/VW:** James A. Michener Art Museum, Bucks County Historical Society **A/S:** She attributes her success to her passion and love for children. **B/I:** She became involved in her profession because she loves education and people and wanted to combine all of these.

MRS. JANA TOMSKY, MD
Medical Doctor
Clayton Valley Medical Group
1520 Kirker Pass Road
Clayton, CA 94517 United States
janatomsky@yahoo.com
http://www.cambridgewhoswho.com

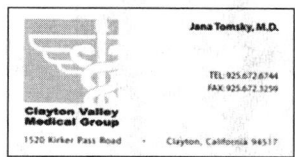

BUS: Family Medical Practice **P/S:** Healthcare **MA:** Local **EXP:** Mrs. Tomsky's areas of expertise are in women's healthcare and pediatrics. **D/D/R:** Overseeing Family Practice Services **H/I/S:** Dancing, Skiing, Playing the Piano, Spending Time with her Family **FBP:** Journal of Family Practice **EDU:** Residency in Family Practice, Methodist Hospital of Sacramento, CA (2004); Internship, Creighton University, Omaha, NE (2002); MD, Prague, Earned in Czech Republic **A/A/S:** American Academy of Family Physicians; Vice Chairwoman, Faculty Practice Department, John Muir Medical Center, Walnut Creek, CA **DOB:** May 19, 1966 **W/H:** Mercy Methodist Hospital and Clinic, Sacramento, CA (2002-2004); Creighton University, Omaha (2001-2002); Teacher, Medical Assistant, Electrocardiogram Technician (1998-2001) **A/S:** She attributes her success to her abilities to make her patients happy and produce positive results. **B/I:** She became involved in her profession because her college professor suggested that she should go to medical school. **H/O:** The most gratifying aspect of her career is helping people to lead healthier lives.

MS. LENA SUE TOOLE
Chief Operating Officer
Administration
Jefferson County Clerk's Office
527 W. Jefferson Street, Suite 105
Louisville, KY 40202 United States
stoole@jeffersoncountyclerk.org
http://www.jeffersoncountyclerk.org

BUS: Government Organization **P/S:** Public Services, Legal Records Recording, Motor Vehicle Registration, Professional Licenses, Delinquent Tax Collection, Tax Certifications, Billing and Collections, Elections **MA:** Regional **EXP:** Ms. Toole's expertise lies in her interaction with all levels of agency personnel to offer guidance and directions. **D/D/R:** Offering Directions to Legal Records, Motor Vehicles, Facilities and Finance Divisions of the Agency, Maintaining the Agency Fee Budget, Creating a Company Overview, Reviewing and Managing Funds, Collecting Funds at Point of Sale Transactions, Distributing Monies, Processing Payroll, Purchasing, Managing Health Benefits Administration for 324 Employees **H/I/S:** Traveling, Dining Out, Reading, Dancing **FBP:** Regulatory and Compliance Issues; Leadership and Communication Publications **EDU:** Associate Degree in Applied Science and Accounting, Jefferson Community College **A/A/S:** Former Treasurer, Business and Professional Women, River City; Former Vice President of Finance, Former President, American Society of Women Accountants **A/H:** Award of High Distinction for Academic Achievement, Jefferson County College **C/VW:** Former Member, Session of Presbyterian Church; Chairwoman, Various Local Committees **A/S:** She attributes her career success to her hard work, accountability and loyalty to her employees. **B/I:** She became involved in her profession because she enjoys working with people, numbers and has a great attention to detail. **H/O:** The highlight of her career was obtaining her current position.

JOYCE C. TORELLI
Realtor, Consultant
Prudential Prime Properties
2 S. Bolton Street
Marlborough, MA 01752 United States
jtorelli@comcast.net
http://www.joycetorelli.com

BUS: Real Estate Agency **P/S:** Residential Real Estate Exchange **MA:** International **D/D/R:** Relocating Properties, Overseeing Land Development, New Construction, Condominiums and Residential Property Exchanges **H/I/S:** Reading, Horseback Riding, Traveling, Spending Time with her Children **FBP:** Realtor; Fortune **EDU:** Coursework, Quinsigamond Community College (1982) **CERTS:** Licensed Real Estate Agent (1986); Accredited Seller Representative; Certified Buyer Representative; Senior Real Estate Specialist; Certified Relocation Specialist **A/H:** Top Agent Award (2005-2006); Ranked Top 25, State of Massachusetts

AMY K. TORKOMIAN
Realtor
Fidelity Financial Bancorp
2525 N. Lake Avenue, Suite 8
Altadena, CA 91001 United States
amy@ffbancorp.com
http://www.ffbancorp.com

BUS: Financial Services **P/S:** Financial and Real Estate Sales **MA:** National **D/D/R:** Selling Residential Real Estate **H/I/S:** Playing with her Puppy, Working Out, Running, Painting, Traveling **FBP:** Realtor **CERTS:** Licensed Real Estate Agent and Loan Officer, State of California **A/A/S:** National Association of Realtors; California Association of Realtors **C/VW:** Goodwill; The Salvation Army **A/S:** She attributes her success to her professionalism and exposure. **B/I:** she became involved in this profession because she started as a loan officer and continued on to get her real estate license. **H/O:** The highlight of her career is getting referrals from clients and making them happy.

MS. MARIA LEONORA C. TORRES
Chief Executive Officer, President
MLT Enterprises
9107 Wilshire Boulevard, Suite 450
Beverly Hills, CA 90210 United States
mariatorres@mltenterprise.com
http://www.mltenterprise.com

BUS: Manufacturing, Wholesale, Retailer **P/S:** Cookware, Houseware, Kitchenware **MA:** International **D/D/R:** Designing, Marketing **H/I/S:** Ballroom Dancing, Aerobics, Painting, Designing Apparel, Interiors, Decorating the Home, Handicrafts, Fencing **EDU:** Bachelor of Science in Business Administration, Fashion Institute of the Phillipines, Fashion Designing and Marketing, Fashion Careers International, USA **A/A/S:** Founder and President, Katawang Pinoy Foundation; Rotary Club

SUSANA ZADUNAISKY TORRES
Owner, Director
Susana Torres Translations
6132 Carew Street
Houston, TX 77074 United States
sutotr@sbcglobal.net
http://www.torrestranslations.com

BUS: Translations **P/S:** Translations in All Languages **MA:** National **D/D/R:** Technical and Medical Translations **H/I/S:** Music **EDU:** Bachelor of Science in Clinical Chemistry, University of Buenos Aires, Argentina; Bachelor of Science in Pharmacy, University of Buenos Aires **A/A/S:** Houston Minority Business Council **A/H:** Leadership Award, Minority Business Development Agency (2001); Business Woman of the Year Award, Ft. Wayne Hispanic Chamber of Commerce (2004) **C/VW:** Houston Symphony **A/S:** She attributes her success to her passion for writing, establishing relationships with her clients and her honesty.

HERMIONI TOTO
Dentist
Toto Dental Associates
124 S. N.W. Highway
Palatine, IL 60074 United States
toothcrew@msn.com
http://www.cambridgewhoswho.com

BUS: Dentist **P/S:** Quality Dental Services, Patient Care, Friendly Environment, General Dentistry **MA:** Local **D/D/R:** Practicing General Family Dentistry **H/I/S:** Golfing **FBP:** Journal of Prosthetic Dentistry; Compendium **EDU:** Doctor of Dental Surgery, Loyola University (1978) **A/A/S:** Academy of General Dentistry; American Dental Association **C/VW:** American Cancer Society; American Lung Association; Children's Wish

HEIDI R. TRACY, RN

Registered Nurse
American Traveler
1387 W. 1200 N., Unit A
West Bountiful, UT 84087 United States
preemiesrn@yahoo.com
http://www.cambridgewhoswho.com

BUS: Travel Nursing **P/S:** Quality Nursing to Anyone in Need Without Regard to Age, Race or Creed **MA:** National **D/D/R:** Nursing in Neonatal Intensive Care **H/I/S:** Scrapbooking, Crafts and Reading **FBP:** RN **EDU:** Associate Degree in Nursing, Weber State University; Associate Degree in General Studies, Weber State University **B/I:** She became involved in her profession because she wanted to be a nurse since she was a child. **H/O:** The highlight of her career has been seeing babies improve daily.

CINDY L. TRAMMELL

Account Manager
Coram Specialty Infusion Service
Apria Healthcare
1680 Century Center Parkway, Suite 12
Memphis, TN 38134 United States
lookinupward@aol.com
http://www.cambridgewhoswho.com

BUS: Healthcare Center **P/S:** Home Infusion Services, Distribution of Specialty Pharmaceuticals **MA:** National **D/D/R:** Overseeing Sales and Giving Presentations **H/I/S:** Listening to Music, Playing Tennis, Reading, Spending Time Outdoors, Sports, Basketball, Supporting the Grizzlies **FBP:** The Wall Street Journal **EDU:** Bachelor's Degree in Business, Indiana Wesleyan University

TINA M. TREFFERT
1) Office Manager 2) Office Manager
1) Jeffery Kraig, DDS 2) JTL Trucking and Repair
145 S. Marr Street
Fond Du Lac, WI 54935 United States
jtltrucking@sbcglobal.net
http://www.cambridgewhoswho.com

BUS: 1) Dental Clinic 2) Automotive Company **P/S:** 1) Dental Care 2) Automotive Service and Repair **MA:** 1) Regional 2) Regional **D/D/R:** Managing the Office, Quarterly Reports, Accounts Payable and Receivable, Repair Services Billing and Patient Scheduling, Processing Payroll **H/I/S:** Cooking, Baking, Exercising **FBP:** Marketplace **EDU:** Bachelor's Degree in Criminal Justice, University of Wisconsin (2000)

JUDITH C. TREGO
Human Resource Director
U.S. Army, Letterkenny Army Depot
1 Overcash Avenue
Chambersburg, PA 17201 United States
judith.c.trego@us.army.mil
http://www.cambridgewhoswho.com

BUS: Federal Government **P/S:** Defense Department, Services and Products to Soldiers in the Field **MA:** Regional **D/D/R:** Managing Human Resources, Revitalizing the Work Force the Army Recruitment Plan **H/I/S:** Reading, Cars **FBP:** US News & World Report **EDU:** Industry Related Training and Experience **A/A/S:** National Association of the Deaf **C/VW:** Church; The Salvation Army; Cancer Society; Lung Society; Chambersburg Hospital **A/S:** She attributes her success to her honesty and integrity. **B/I:** She became involved in her profession because she enjoys seeing people progress on their job. **H/O:** The highlight of her career was when she was nominated for Woman of the Year.

MONICA M. TREPAGNIER
Ambassador, Advanced Tutor
University of Mississippi Medical Center School of Nursing
2500 N. State Street
Jackson, MS 39216 United States
smit6052@bellsouth.net
http://www.umsmed.edu

BUS: Healthcare **P/S:** Higher Education **MA:** Local **DDR:** Conducting Advanced Tutoring for the School of Nursing **H/I/S:** Traveling **FBP:** American Journal of Nursing **EDU:** Bachelor of Science in Biology, Millsaps College **A/A/S:** Mississippi Association of Student Nurses **C/VW:** St. Jude Children's Research Hospital; Habitat for Humanity **A/S:** She attributes her success to her strong supportive instructors. **B/I:** She chose the profession after she gave birth to her son. **H/O:** The most gratifying aspect of her career is having the ability to help people.

NEVYANA TRIFONOVA
Real Estate Agent
Prudential Americana Group
5625 Mohagany Run Place
Las Vegas, NV 89122 United States
ntrifonova2001@yahoo.com
http://www.cambridgewhoswho.com

BUS: Premier Real Estate Association **P/S:** Residential Real Estate Sales and Purchases **MA:** Regional **D/D/R:** Working with Buyers, Sellers and Renters **H/I/S:** Playing the Classical Violin **EDU:** Master's Degree in Marketing and Management, International University of National and World Economy, Bulgaria (2001) **A/H:** Student of the Year (2002)

CHERYL L. TRINKAUS
Registered Nurse
Department of Veteran Affairs
10000 Brecksville Road
Brecksville, OH 44141 United States
http://www.cambridgewhoswho.com

BUS: Healthcare Services **P/S:** Healthcare for Local Residents **MA:** Regional **D/D/R:** Rehabilitation Nursing **H/I/S:** Gardening **FBP:** American Journal of Nursing **EDU:** Associate Degree in Nursing, SUNY, Upstate Medical University **C/VW:** Selera Derma Foundation **A/S:** She attributes her success to having a great repertoire with her patients, veterans and their families. She feels that communication is essential. **B/I:** She became involved in nursing because her mother once said, 'Why don't you become a nurse,' and she did.

SARA RAINE TROFEO
Owner
Trofeo Fine Custom Framing and Photography
3601 Woodland Park Avenue N.
Seattle, WA 98103 United States
trofeoseattle@gmail.com
http://www.trofeo.biz

BUS: Custom Framing **P/S:** Custom Framing, Fine Art, Portrait Photography, Archival Custom Framing, Designing Elegant Interesting Frame Packages, Artistic Portraiture **MA:** Local **D/D/R:** Designing Elegant Archival, Unique Framing and Artistic Portraiture **H/I/S:** Hiking, Mountain Biking, Bicycling **FBP:** Aperture; Elle Decor **EDU:** Bachelor's Degree in Fine Arts, Alfred University **A/A/S:** Former Member, Professional Photography Association; National Association for the Self-Employed **C/VW:** Various Charitable Associations, Poncho **H/O:** The highlight of her career is having an anniversary show at the shop rotating gallery.

LORETTA TROTMAN, MA
Technology Teacher
Public School 95
New York State Department of Education
345 Van Sicklen Street
Brooklyn, NY 11223 United States
ltrotman2003@yahoo.com • ltsaved@earthlink.net
http://www.cambridgewhoswho.com

BUS: School **P/S:** Education **MA:** Local **EXP:** Ms. Trotman's expertise is in technology and religious education. **D/D/R:** Teaching her Students, Working at her Church, Caring for her Mother **H/I/S:** Attending Church Services, Creating Websites, Playing Basketball, Fixing Things, Working in the Prayer Room at her Church **FBP:** Believer's Voice of Victory; Spirit Led Woman; Charisma **EDU:** Master of Science in Instructional Technology, New York Institute of Technology; Bachelor of Science in Data Systems Management; Associate Degree in Computer Programming **A/H:** Dean's List **C/VW:** Beulah Church of God Hospital Ministry **POB:** Brooklyn, NY **CHILD:** Regina **W/H:** Typist, Programmer, Analyst, Public School Teacher, Bible School Teacher **A/S:** She attributes her success to her faith in the Lord Jesus Christ. **B/I:** She became involved in her profession because she wanted to be a teacher since high school. **H/O:** The highlight of her career was having a student come back years later and tell her that without her, he would not be the man he is today. **I/F/Y:** In five years, Ms. Trotman hopes to be working to bring more people to Jesus Christ, visiting the sick and helping those in need of God's love.

SHIRLEY TROWBRIDGE
Registered Nurse, Independent Consultant
Arbonne International
shirleytrow@adelphia.net
http://www.dynamicnetwork.myarbonne.com

BUS: Distribution Company **P/S:** Health and Wellness Personal Care Products **MA:** International **D/D/R:** Educating on Health, Wellness and Disease Prevention, Creating Multiple Streams of Income by Building a Network of Consumers of Pure, Safe and Beneficial Swiss Products, Representing and Focusing on an Array of Health and Wellness Personal Care Products **H/I/S:** Caring for Orchids and Bonsais, Collecting Seashells **EDU:** Registered Nurse **A/S:** She attributes her personal and professional success to her desire to help others to be informed of the importance of their health. **B/I:** She has always had an interest in the field and a desire to help others.

CYNTHIA TRUESDELL, RN
Night Supervisor
Countryside Care Center
41861 State Highway 10
Delhi, NY 13753 United States
randctrue@localnet.com
http://www.co.delaware.ny.us

BUS: Healthcare Center **P/S:** Healthcare **MA:** Regional **EXP:** Ms. Truesdell's expertise is in nursing home room supervision and staff management. **D/D/R:** Supervising up to 160 Residents, Updating Care Plans, Handling All Problems or Emergencies that May Arise during the Night **H/I/S:** Reading, Weight Lifting, Body Building, Watching Videos at Home, Flower Gardening, Swimming, Caring for her Pet Birds, Outdoor Bird-Watching, Riding Tractors with her Husband **EDU:** Coursework, Vassar Brothers Medical Center, School of Nursing (1970); Coursework, Dutchess Community College **A/H:** Third and Fifth-Place Trophies, Natural Body Building Contest, New York City, NY (2008); Finalist, EAS Body for Life Challenge (2002, 2003); Employee of Distinction Award **C/VW:** Relay for Life; American Cancer Society **DOB:** February 3, 1950 **POB:** Catskill, NY **SP:** Robert **W/H:** Assistant Director of Nursing, Stamford Community Hospital (1970-1986); Staff Nurse, Night Supervisor, Infection Control Nurse, Cardiac Care Nurse, Stamford Community Hospital

ANN MARIE M. TRUPIANO, RN, BSN, CMC
Registered Nurse, Case Manager
University Medical Center of Southern Nevada
1800 W. Charleston
Las Vegas, NV 89102 United States
annetrupiano@umsn.com
http://www.cambridgewhoswho.com

BUS: Acute Care Hospital, Level One Trauma and Burn Center **P/S:** Healthcare **MA:** Local **D/D/R:** Critical-Care Nursing, Case Management **H/I/S:** Etching, Silversmithing **FBP:** Time **EDU:** Bachelor of Science in Nursing, University of Nevada at Las Vegas; Associate Degree in Nursing, University of Nevada at Las Vegas **CERTS:** Certified in Advanced Cardiac Life Support **A/H:** Dean's List **C/VW:** American Heart Association; American Stroke Association

DEANNE LEE J. TRYON, ME
Teacher of the Visually Impaired
Hallsville Independent School District
PO Box 810
Hallsville, TX 75650 United States
dtryon@hisd.com
http://www.hisd.com

BUS: Public School **P/S:** Education **MA:** Local **D/D/R:** Teaching Special Education, College Presentations, Private Tutoring **H/I/S:** Playing Softball, Reading, Running, Caring for her Foster Children **EDU:** Master's Degree in Special Education and Visual Impairment, Texas Tech University; Bachelor's Degree in Psychology; Bachelor of Arts in Psychology and Kinesiology, LeTourneau University **CERTS:** Certification in Special Education, University of Texas at Tyler **A/A/S:** Kappa Delta Phi; Council for Exceptional Children; Who's Who Among American Teachers **C/VW:** Foster Parent; American Heart Association **A/S:** She attributes her success to having a family that supports her. **B/I:** She became involved in this profession because of her experiences caring for her niece when she was 16 years old. Her niece learned and progressed over that time, and she, in turn, fell in love with the profession. **H/O:** The most gratifying aspect of her career is seeing what the children can acquire even when others think that they can not do it. Their accomplishments become her achievements.

CYNTHIA A. TSERKIS
English Teacher, Coach
Boonton Middle School
306 Lathrop Avenue
Boonton, NJ 07005 United States
cassandra21174@optonline.net
http://www.cambridgewhoswho.com

BUS: Middle School **P/S:** Secondary Education **MA:** Local **D/D/R:** Teaching Language Arts and Reading, Coaching Field Hockey **H/I/S:** Participating in Outdoor Activities, Coaching, Spending Time with Children **FBP:** Discovery **EDU:** Bachelor of Science in Education, East Stroudsburg University, PA **A/A/S:** National Council of Teachers of English; National Education Association; United States Field Hockey Association **C/VW:** Special Olympics **A/S:** She attributes her success to her determination. **B/I:** She became involved in her profession because she always wanted to be a teacher. **H/O:** The most gratifying aspect of her career is helping and seeing her students succeed.

JAN TUCKER
Broker
ERA Lakeside Realty
200 Lakeside Plaza
Loudon, TN 37774 United States
jan.tucker@era.com
http://www.jan-tucker.com

BUS: Real Estate Agency **P/S:** Residential, Executive, Lake Front, New Construction, Townhouse, Golf Homes, Senior Homes and Gated Homes Sales and Listings **MA:** National **D/D/R:** Listing and Selling Residential Properties **H/I/S:** Golfing, Boating, Reading, Listening to Music, Traveling **FBP:** Realtor **CERTS:** Accredited Buyer Representative; e-PRO Internet Professional Designation **A/A/S:** East Tennessee Broker Council; Tennessee Association of Realtors; National Association of Realtors **A/H:** Top Twenty-Five Percent Nationwide, ERA Realty (2005); ERA Beyond Excellence; ERA Leader's Circle; Top Selling Broker, ERA Realty

KAROLE L. TUDOR, MS
Second-Grade Teacher
Princeton City Schools
11850 Conrey Road
Cincinnati, OH 45249 United States
ktudor@princeton.k12.oh.us
http://www.princetoncityschools.edu

BUS: School **P/S:** Education **MA:** Local **D/D/R:** Inclusion Instruction with All Areas of Curriculum, Specializing in Writing and Science **H/I/S:** Gardening, Reading, Traveling **FBP:** Instructor Magazine **EDU:** Master's Degree Plus 20 in Elementary Education, Miami University; Bachelor of Science in Elementary Education, Miami University **A/A/S:** Ohio Education Association; National Education Association **C/VW:** Relay for Life; Local Hospice; American Red Cross **A/S:** She attributes her success to always looking for new ways to reach the children. **B/I:** She became involved in her profession because she had a long time desire to work in education. **H/O:** The highlight of her career was being nominated for teacher of the year for her school.

PALMIRA R. TURBETTI-MOTTO
7282 E. Cherokee Road
Stockton, CA 95215 United States
palmira.1@netzero.net
http://www.cambridgewhoswho.com

BUS: Sole Proprietorship **EXP:** Ms. Turbetti-Motto's expertise is in piano, accordion and voice instruction. **D/D/R:** Teaching Music Privately, Facilitating Music Lessons for Various Church Services **H/I/S:** Writing Music, Baking Italian Biscotti Cookies, Spending Time with her Family and Friends **EDU:** Pursuing Bachelor's Degree in Music Education, Pacific University; Associate Degree in Humanities, Delta College; Associate Degree in Liberal Arts, Delta College **A/A/S:** National Association of Pastoral Musicians; International Poets Society **C/VW:** Volunteer Musician, Local Church **DOB:** August 23, 1959 **POB:** Stockton, CA **SP:** Melvin **A/S:** She attributes her success to her strong faith in God, supportive family and friends, persistence, future-oriented attitude and optimistic outlook on life. **B/I:** She became involved in her profession by working in retail while pursuing her bachelor's degree. **H/O:** The highlight of her career has been constantly learning and growing. **I/F/Y:** In five years, Ms. Turbetti-Motto hopes to obtain her bachelor's degree and a position as a music teacher, and write music or poetry.

JEAN L. TURKOVICH, RN
Registered Nurse, Case Manager
UPMC Health Plan
One Chatam Center
112 Washington Place
Pittsburgh, PA 15219 United States
turkolyn@yahoo.com
http://www.cambridgewhoswho.com

BUS: Healthcare **P/S:** Medical Insurance **MA:** Regional **D/D/R:** Medicare **H/I/S:** Reading, Crocheting, Spending Time with her Family **EDU:** Diploma in Nursing, Sewickley Valley Hospital, Sewickley, PA **C/VW:** St. Titus Catholic Church of Aliquippa, PA; American Cancer Society **A/S:** She attributes her success to her desire to help people and do well for herself and her patients. **B/I:** She became involved in the profession because of her need to care for people. It gives her great satisfactions to help others. **H/O:** The highlight of her career is having her children be proud of her and what she does for her patients.

EDNA L. TURNER, LCSW
Licensed Clinical Social Worker
Merced County Mental Health Department
480 E. 13th Street
Merced, CA 95341 United States
tmerced45@aol.com
http://www.cambridgewhoswho.com

BUS: Healthcare Center **P/S:** Mental Healthcare **MA:** Local **D/D/R:** Counseling Victims of Spousal Abuse, Performing Individual Therapy for Women who Suffer from Childhood Molestation **H/I/S:** Traveling, Spending Time at the Beach **FBP:** Jet **EDU:** Master of Social Work, Fresno State University **C/VW:** Local Church **A/S:** She attributes her success to her desire to help people. **B/I:** She became involved in her profession because she wanted to help people. **H/O:** The highlight of her career was having a good educational background.

KARYN RENEE TURNER
Elementary Education Teacher
New York City Department of Education
65 Court Street
Brooklyn, NY 11201 United States
mskturner@netzero.com
kturner5@schools.nyc.gov
http://www.cambridgewhoswho.com

BUS: School District **P/S:** Education **MA:** Local **EXP:** Ms. Turner's expertise is in social studies education. **D/D/R:** Offering Support for 10 to 12 Elementary and Middle Schools in the Areas of Attendance Improvement and Educational Neglect Intervention, Assisting in Offering School-Related Services for Students Living in Shelters and Temporary Housing **H/I/S:** Collecting Josephine Baker Memorabilia and African American Historical Artifacts, Attending the Theater and Ballet, Traveling, Shopping, Fine Dining **FBP:** Teaching K-8; Psychology Today; NEA Magazine; American Educator; Education Week **EDU:** Master's Degree in Elementary Education and Special Education, Touro College; Bachelor's Degree in Culture and Society, Empire State College **CERTS:** Certified School Attendance Teacher; Certified Social Studies Teacher; Certification in Elementary Education Grades 1-6; Certification in Secondary Education **A/A/S:** American Federation of Teachers; United Federation of Teachers; Black Educators United; Association of Black Educators in New York; National Association for the Advancement of Colored People **A/H:** Former Miss Black Staten Island; Ford Foundation Scholarship Award; Essay Award, American Cancer Society; Brotherhood Award, B'Nai B'Rith **C/VW:** Kevin Turner Memorial Scholarship Foundation; The Unity Games; Project Hospitality, Island Voices Organization **DOB:** September 7, 1954 **POB:** New York, NY **CHILD:** Chad **W/H:** Fist Legislative Assistant, Staten Island Assemblywoman Elizabeth A. Connelly; Receptionist, Proskauer & Rose, New York, NY; International Fashion Model; Disc Jockey, Sicily, Italy; Executive Assistant, WNET TV Channel 13; School Aide, Department of Education; Paraprofessional, Department of Education; Teacher, Department of Education **A/S:** She attributes her success to her dedication, focus, strong belief in God and the insurmountable support she receives from her family. **H/O:** The most gratifying aspect of her career is seeing the positive impact she has made on children and their families when she sees them later in life. **I/F/Y:** In five years, Ms. Turner hopes to continue to work with children and their families with whatever social issues are affecting them at the time.

MARIE A. TURNER
Realtor Associate
Better Homes New Jersey, URI Realty
811 Church Road
Cherry Hill, NJ 08002 United States
Turner4821@aol.com
http://www.cambridgewhoswho.com

BUS: Real Estate **P/S:** Real Estate **MA:** National **D/D/R:** Selling Residential and Commercial, Relocation and Land Investment Properties to First-Time Homebuyers **H/I/S:** Reading, Gardening, Traveling **FBP:** Realtor; Forbes **CERTS:** Licensed in Medical Technology; Licensed Realtor, State of New Jersey; Pursuing Brokerage License, Burlington County College **A/A/S:** National Association of Realtors; New Jersey Association of Realtors; Who's Who of Intellectuals; Phi Theta Kappa **C/VW:** Volunteer, Church Youth Groups; Speaker, NSA; Goodwill

SCOTT C. TURNER, LMT
Professional Massage, Injury Management Therapist
Arizona Health Care Practitioner
1719 W. Wood Bridge Court
Tucson, AZ 85746 United States
a1massagelmt@aol.com
http://www.cambridgewhoswho.com

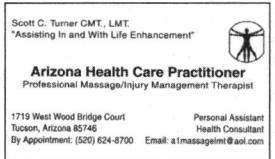

Scott C. Turner CMT., LMT.
"Assisting In and With Life Enhancement"
Arizona Health Care Practitioner
Professional Massage/Injury Management Therapist
1719 West Wood Bridge Court   Personal Assistant
Tucson, Arizona 85746   Health Consultant
By Appointment: (520) 624-8700   Email: a1massagelmt@aol.com

BUS: Healthcare, Alternative Healing **P/S:** Health Consulting, Massage Therapy and Injury Management **MA:** Local **D/D/R:** Assisting in and with Life Enhancement **EDU:** Coursework, Cortivas Desert Institute of the Healing Arts; Clinical Training, Tucson Medical Center; Coursework in Sports Therapy, University of Arizona **A/A/S:** American Massage Therapy Association **A/H:** Recognition for Substantial Community Outreach **B/I:** He became involved in his profession because while he was employed at Canyon Ranch Resort, he saw the healing benefits massage therapy offered. He also had a desire to help others and channel energy in a positive way to relieve ailments. **H/O:** The most gratifying aspect of his career is seeing the positive outcome of his patients and knowing his work has truly benefited them.

MRS. NOCAMAGU TUSWA, R.PH.
Pharmacist, SP
Swan Pharmacy, Inc.
650 Franklin Avenue
Brooklyn, NY 11238 United States
swanrx@optonline.net
http://www.cambridgewhoswho.com

BUS: Pharmacy **P/S:** Drugs Prescription, Drug Counseling, Customer Service **MA:** Regional **D/D/R:** Filling Prescriptions, Managing Insurance Claims, Drug Counseling, Diabetes and Blood Pressure Testing, Supervising Two Technicians and One Pharmacist, Offering HIV and Hepatitis C Counseling **H/I/S:** Solving Crossword Puzzles, Watching Basketball, Making Crafts **FBP:** U.S. Pharmacist; Drug Topics **EDU:** Coursework in HIV and Hepatitis C; Bachelor's Degree in Pharmacy, Arnold and Marie Schwartz College of Pharmacy, Long Island University (1985) **CERTS:** Certification in HIV and Hepatitis C, The New York Academy of Medicine (2006) **A/A/S:** Pharmacists Society of the State of New York **CHILD:** Yolisa

JUDY A. TUTTLE, RN
Telephonic and Concurrent Review Care Manager, Registered Nurse
Health Net
22085 Queen Street
Castro Valley, CA 94546 United States
judith.x.tuttle@healthnet.com
http://www.healthnet.com

BUS: Healthcare Center **P/S:** Healthcare Including Health Insurance, Healthcare Products Related to Prescription Drugs, Healthcare Product Coordination for Multi-Region Employers, Administrative Services for Medical Groups and Self-Funded Benefits Programs **MA:** Regional **EXP:** Ms. Tuttle's expertise is in case management. **D/D/R:** Reviewing On-Site Member Cases **H/I/S:** Singing, Scrapbooking **FBP:** Nursing2009 **EDU:** Associate of Arts; Registered Nurse **CERTS:** Certified Nurse, Samuel Merritt College School of Nursing (1981) **SP:** Peter **CHILD:** Bryan, Sarah **W/H:** Health Net (2004-Present); San Ramon Regional Medical Center, Inc. (1999-2004); Golden State Rehab (1991-1999); Samuel Merritt Hospital (1981-1991)

KERRY SUE TYLER
President
1) Hunting Done Homes, LLC
1668 S. 1100 W.
Ogden, UT 84404 United States
swwtsue@hotmail.com
http://www.cambridgewhoswho.com

BUS: Fence Company **P/S:** Fences **MA:** Regional **EXP:** Ms. Tyler's expertise is in concrete resurfacing and design, bookkeeping, tax and office management. **H/I/S:** Crocheting, Decorating Cakes, Genealogy, Photography **EDU:** Bachelor of Arts in English, University of Texas **A/A/S:** Local Chamber of Commerce

PATTI TYSON
Realtor
Keller Williams Lifestyle
3540 E. Baseline Road, Suite 120
Phoenix, AZ 85042 United States
ptyson55@hotmail.com
http://www.cambridgewhoswho.com

BUS: Real Estate Agency **P/S:** Commercial and Residential Real Estate Exchange **MA:** Regional **D/D/R:** Managing the Sales of Lands and Residential Properties **H/I/S:** Golfing **EDU:** Bachelor's Degree in Business Studies, Glendale Community College (1975)

MR. RICHARD D. UDINE
Senior Vice President of Wealth Management
Citigroup-Smith Barney
3000 Atrium Way, Suite 500
Mount Laurel, NJ 08054 United States
richard.d.udine@smithbarney.com
http://www.fa.smithbarney.com/209/udine

BUS: Full-Service Brokerage and Investment Company **P/S:** Portfolio Management, Equities, Mutual Funds, Annuities, Wealth Management and Personal Financial Analyses, Retirement Planning **MA:** National **D/D/R:** Acting as a Financial Advisor, Managing Portfolios for High-Net-Worth Individuals, Assisting Clients with Equity and Fixed Income Investments **H/I/S:** Golfing, Traveling, Playing Poker, Spending Time with his Four Children, Participating in Charity Work **FBP:** Barron's; Fortune **EDU:** Bachelor of Science in Marketing and Advertising, Fairleigh Dickinson University (1977) **A/A/S:** Former President, Gibbsboro-Voorhees Athletic Association; Former Member, South Jersey Business Association; Chairman's Council, Smith Barney **C/VW:** United Way of America; Ronald McDonald House

KAREN J. ULRICH
Senior Specialist in Store Marketing
Target
1000 Nicollet Mall, Suite TPS2980
Minneapolis, MN 55403 United States
karen.ulrich@target.com
http://www.target.com

BUS: Retail Discount Department Store **P/S:** Men, Women and Children's Clothing, Bed and Bath, Kitchen, Electronics, Baby Registry, Photo, Pharmacy, Optical, Portrait Studio and Super Recipes **MA:** National **EXP:** Ms. Ulrich's expertise is in construction, brand signing and in-store marketing. **D/D/R:** Using Computerized Designs, Constructing In-Store Displays, Overseeing a Remodeling Team **EDU:** Associate of Arts in Psychology **A/A/S:** Board of Directors, Nonprofit Youth Performance Company **A/S:** She attributes her success to her passion for her profession. **B/I:** She became involved in her profession because of her desire to work with Target. **H/O:** The most gratifying aspect of her career is developing her store.

MR. DEAN J. UMINSKI, CEcD
Executive
Crowe Chizek and Company, LLC
330 E. Jefferson Boulevard
South Bend, IN 46601 United States
duminski@crowechizek.com
http://www.crowechizek.com

BUS: Consulting Firm **P/S:** Auditing and Tax Consulting **MA:** National **D/D/R:** Selecting Sites, Negotiating Incentives, Presenting Projects to State and Local Officials **H/I/S:** Sailing, Spending Time with his Family, Traveling **FBP:** CFO; Forbes **EDU:** Bachelor of Science in Business, Indiana University (1978) **CERTS:** Certified Economic Developer **A/A/S:** Policy and Issues Committee, International Economic Development Council; Certified Member, Community Economic Development Center; Economic Development Association; Indiana Chamber of Commerce; Vision 2010 Committee **C/VW:** Local Charitable Organizations; Local Schools **A/S:** He attributes his success to having a knack for presenting projects to state and local officials. **B/I:** He became involved in his profession because he wanted to help America and his community remain stable, including the work force. **H/O:** The highlight of his career was making an impact in the economic development field.

FAYE UNDERHILL NICHOLS, CACII, SAP
Deputy Director
Behavioral Health Services of Pickens County
309 E. Main Street
Pickens, SC 29671 United States
fayeun@bellsouth.net

BUS: Healthcare Facility **P/S:** Counseling Services to Children and Adolescents for Alcoholism and Substance Abuse **MA:** Local **D/D/R:** Overseeing the Staff in Three Departments and Three Supervisors, Managing Care for Outpatients, Adolescents and Children **H/I/S:** Reading, Shopping, Spending Quality Time with the Family **FBP:** Psychology Today **EDU:** Pursuing Master's Degree in Counseling, Liberty University; Bachelor of Arts in Religious Education, Gardner Webb University (1979) **A/A/S:** Clinical Addiction Counselor II; South Carolina Council for Alcohol and Drug Abuse; Secona Baptist Church, Secretary of the Board for Mary House

VICTORIA R. UNDERWOOD, BSN, RN
Registered Nurse
Aureus Medical Group
11825 Q Street
Omaha, NE 68137 United States
vrunderwood@yahoo.com
http://www.kumc.edu

BUS: Healthcare **P/S:** Hospital, Agency and Travel Nursing **MA:** Regional **D/D/R:** Orthopedics and Medical/Surgical, Telemetry **H/I/S:** Music, Watching Movies, Fitness **FBP:** Fitness; Oxygen; Trauma Nursing **EDU:** Bachelor of Science in Nursing, Kansas University School of Nursing; Associate of Science in Nursing, Seward County Community College **CERTS:** Certified in Basic Life Support **A/A/S:** Sigma Theta Tau International **C/VW:** Relay for Life; American Heart Association **A/S:** She attributes her personal and professional success to her outgoing personality, honesty, and patients. **B/I:** She has always had an interest in the field and a desire to care for others. **H/O:** The highlight of her career was joining Sigma Theta Tau International.

JAMES J. UNGVARSKY, PSY.D., MPA
Senior Vice President, Chief Operating Officer
University of the Rockies
555 E. Pikes Peak Avenue
Suite 108
Colorado Springs, CO 80903 United States
jim.ungvarsky@rockies.edu
http://www.rockies.edu

BUS: University **P/S:** Higher Education **MA:** International **EXP:** Dr. Ungvarsky's expertise is in statistics and research design. **D/D/R:** Practicing Psychology, Marriage and Family Therapy, Conducting Financial Planning and Classes **H/I/S:** Practicing Martial Arts, Collecting Stamps **FBP:** APA Publications **EDU:** Doctor of Psychology, Colorado School of Professional Psychology; Master's Degree in Public Administration, San Jose State University; Master in Psychology, Chapman University; Bachelor's Degree in Psychology, Cleveland State University **A/A/S:** Former President, Board of Directors, Mental Health America, Pikes Peak Region; Leadership Pike Peak; Former Board of Directors, Crime Stoppers; American Psychology Association **C/VW:** Local School; Local Church; Kiwanis **B/I:** He became involved in his profession after working as a financial advisor while his wife was in the military.

CHRIS URLING
Executive Director
Northern California Drywall Contractors Association
2051 Junction Avenue, Suite 200
San Jose, CA 95131 United States
chris@drywallca.com
http://www.cambridgewhoswho.com

BUS: Nonprofit Organization **P/S:** Insulation, Metal Stud Frames, Gypsum Board, Acoustic Ceilings, Finish Trimming, Plastering **MA:** Northern California **EXP:** Mr. Urling's expertise is in the oversight of operations, labor and management. **H/I/S:** Working with Leaded Glass, Restoring Cars, Bowling, Making Crafts, Water and Snow Skiing **FBP:** Popular Mechanics **EDU:** College Coursework **A/A/S:** Association of the Wall and Ceiling Industries International; ASA **C/VW:** Boy Scouts of America; Habitat for Humanity **CHILD:** Amy, Eric **A/S:** He attributes his success to his honesty and networking skills. **B/I:** He became involved in his profession because he always wanted to help others and solve their problems. **H/O:** The most gratifying aspect of his career is setting and achieving goals.

BONNIE LOU UZZELL
Special Education Teacher
Vigo County Schools, Terre Haute South Vigo School
3737 S. Seventh Street
Terre Haute, IN 47802 United States
bluz52@hotmail.com
http://www.cambridgewhoswho.com

BUS: School **P/S:** Special Education, Functional Living and Vocational Skills for Adult Life **MA:** Vigo County **D/D/R:** Teaching Children with Multi-Categorical Handicaps, Teaching Social and Living Skills, Reading, Mathematics, Cooking, Banking, Letter Writing, Fundamental Living Skills **H/I/S:** Sewing, Cooking, Attending Sporting Events, Basketball, Interior Decorating, Crafts **FBP:** NEA Publications; CEC Publications **EDU:** Bachelor's Degree in Mental Retardation, Indiana State University; Master of Science in Learning Disabilities and Emotional Disabilities, Indiana State University **A/H:** Recipient, Technology Grant; Nominee, Golden Apple Award **C/VW:** Missionary Work, Church of Christ; United Way of America; Various Charitable Organizations; Mental Health Association; American Red Cross **A/S:** She attributes her success to always being interested in learning, helping her students, always attending meetings to keep current and networking.

ROCHELLE L. VALASEK
Executive Director
Reflecting Excellence
PO Box 1562
Clemmons, NC 27012 United States
rochelle@reflectingexcellence.com
http://www.reflectingexcellence.com

BUS: Ministry **P/S:** Bible Study of The Ruby Legacy, Devotionals and Frazzled Moms' Devotions to Go **MA:** International **EXP:** Ms. Valasek's expertise is in women's ministries. **D/D/R:** Public Speaking on Christianity, Studying the Scripture of Proverbs for Woman, Sharing Spiritual Giftedness and Friendship, Hosting Ministry Teas, Writing and Encouraging Spiritual Health **H/I/S:** Reading, Scrapbooking, Spending Time with her Family, Camping, Hiking **EDU:** Coursework in Children and Teen Literature, Institute of Children's Literature **CERTS:** Certified in Magazine Publishing and Creative Writing **A/A/S:** Evangelist, Minister, American Red Cross; American Veterans Organizations; Co-Founder, Former Sister 2 Sister 4 Christ Ministries; Co-Host, Internet and Podcast Show, Sister 2 Sister Moments **SP:** Tony **A/S:** She attributes her success to her faith in God. **B/I:** She became involved in her profession because she felt it was her calling. **H/O:** The most gratifying aspect of her career is helping others in her community.

LILIAN X. VALENCIA, MSW
School Based Therapist
Intercommunity Child Guidance Center
10155 Colima Road
Whittier, CA 90605 United States
lvalencia@intercommunity.org
http://www.intercommunity.org

BUS: Mental Health **P/S:** Mental Health Agency for Children and Their Families, Nonprofit **MA:** Regional **D/D/R:** Offering Individual and Family Sessions to Adolescents Ages Three to 18, Interacting with Schools and Social Services **FBP:** NASW Publications **EDU:** Master of Social Work, University of Southern California **CERTS:** Certified in Preventive Management of Assaultive Behavior **A/A/S:** National Association of Social Workers; National Association of School Social Workers **A/S:** She attributes her success to her perseverance, to her passion for helping clients and to her ability to continue to refine her expertise within the field.

STEPHEN W. VALENTA
President, Chief Executive Officer
Offix
10222 Battleview Parkway
Manassas, VA 20109 United States
svalenta@offix.com
http://www.offix.com

BUS: Office Retail Store **P/S:** All Products and Services for Manufacturing Companies Including Canon Copiers, HP, Ricoh and KIP **MA:** Regional **D/D/R:** Developing the Business, Examining Market Trends to Admit New Manufacturers **EDU:** Associate Degree in Electronic Technology, ECPI College of Technology **CERTS:** Certified, ATSP **A/A/S:** Better Business Bureau **H/O:** The highlight of his career was starting his own business. **I/F/Y:** In five years, Mr. Valenta hopes to open six more stores.

KATHERINE VALENTINE
Owner
The Sewing School
3633 Fairlane Street
High Point, NC 27265 United States
thesewingteacher@thesewingschool.org
http://www.thesewingschool.org

BUS: School Specializing in Sewing Instruction **P/S:** Sewing Education, Fashion Design, After School Programs, Summer Camp, Fashion Shows **MA:** North Carolina **D/D/R:** DDR: Teaching Sewing Classes for Children and Adults, Participating in After-School Programs **FBP:** Threads **CERTS:** Martha Pullen Licensed Instructor **A/A/S:** Professional Association of Custom Clothiers; American Sewing Guild; HAS

LIZ M. VAMBELL-WIRTH
Accounts Manager
Family Medical Practitioners
1147 Independence Boulevard
Virginia Beach, VA 23455 United States
deizzzard@aol.com
http://www.cambridgewhoswho.com

BUS: Multi-Disciplinary Medical Practice **P/S:** High-Duality Healthcare Services **MA:** Local **D/D/R:** Accounting, Billing, Coding, Offering Personal Interaction with Patients, Assisting them with Financial Aspects **H/I/S:** Adopting Special-Needs Animals, Supporting the New York Yankees, Enjoying Sports, Fishing, Reading, Spending Quality Time with her Family and Pets **FBP:** Newsweek; The New York Times; The New York Post **EDU:** College Coursework **A/H:** Award for Fundraising Activities **C/VW:** American Society for the Prevention of Cruelty to Animals; Memorial Sloan-Kettering Cancer Center; American Red Cross; Bone Marrow Donor; American Cancer Society; Wildlife Foundation **DOB:** September 7, 1962 **POB:** Norfolk, VA **SP:** Mike **A/S:** She attributes her success to her employers. **B/I:** She became involved in medical accounting because of her personal experience in the field and her love of her work. **H/O:** The highlight of her career was the recognition she received from independent contractors in her field and her 90 percent or higher positive collection rate.

MR. DIRK VAN GORP
Business Unit Manager
Atpharma, Inc.
100 Overlook Center
Princeton, NJ 08540 United States
dvgorp@atpharmainc.com
http://www.atpharmainc.com

BUS: Proven Leader in the Consulting Industry **P/S:** Regulatory Services, Adding Real Value to Businesses in the Pharmaceutical, Veterinary, Medical Device and Healthcare Industries **MA:** International **D/D/R:** Overseeing Operations and Management, Consulting, Managing Sales, Field Employees and Clients, Ensuring Validation and Regulatory Compliance **H/I/S:** Spending Time with his Children, Soccer **FBP:** Pharmaceutical Engineering; Technology **EDU:** Bachelor of Science in Chemistry, Belgium (1995) **A/A/S:** International Society of Pharmaceutical Engineers

JUDITH M. VAN NATTER
Director of Volunteer Services
Hope Hospice
611 N. Walnut Ave
New Braunfels, TX 78130 United States
jvannatter@hopehospice.net
http://www.cambridgewhoswho.com

BUS: Healthcare, Nonprofit **P/S:** Providing End of Life Care **MA:** Local **D/D/R:** Volunteering, Recruiting, Training, Overseeing Retention and Recognition **H/I/S:** Listening to All Types of Music, Reading, Playing the Piano **FBP:** Volunteer Management **EDU:** Industry-Related Experience **A/A/S:** 'Reach to Recovery,' American Cancer Society **C/VW:** Christian Research Institute **A/S:** She attributes her career success to her respect and appreciation for the feelings of others. **H/O:** The highlight of her career is being able to work with the volunteers.

RUTH VAN OTTEREN
Chief Executive Officer
Van Otteren Cereal Company
136 Worth Court S.
West Palm Beach, FL 33405 United States
rahvo@bellsouth.net
http://www.cambridgewhoswho.com

BUS: Manufacturer **P/S:** Nutritional Cereal **MA:** Local **D/D/R:** Nutritional Cereal for Campers, Available in a Tube **H/I/S:** Cooking **EDU:** Bachelor of Arts, University of Michigan **C/VW:** Church; Community Outreach; Numerous Worthy Causes for the Local Community **A/S:** She attributes her success to her family support. **B/I:** She became involved in the profession because she loves cooking and wanted to create something new. **H/O:** The most gratifying aspect of her career is her cereal.

Ms. Heidi L. VanAmburgh-Buol

Corporate Fitness and Wellness Director
Ocean Edge Resort
2907 Main Street
Brewster, MA 02631 United States
heidi.vanamburgh@oceanedge.com
http://www.oceanedge.com

BUS: Resort, Residential, Corporate, Fitness, and Recreation Programs **P/S:** Hospitality, Fitness and Wellness **MA:** International **D/D/R:** Fitness and Wellness Consulting, Conducting Recreational Programs, Designing and Building Gym Resorts **H/I/S:** Skiing, Snowboarding, Hiking **FBP:** Fitness; Recreation Management; The Wall Street Journal **EDU:** Bachelor's Degree, University of Massachusetts **A/A/S:** American Council on Exercise; AAAI; ISMA **C/VW:** City of Hope; Walk for Heart; American Breast Cancer Society **A/S:** She attributes her success to her caring for people and desire to help people maintain their wellness. **B/I:** She became involved in her profession because she wanted to work in hospitality as a corporate consultant. **H/O:** The highlights of her career were working for MTV for five years as a fitness trainer and coaching a high school dance team to perform at a Boston Celtics game.

Kathleen L. Vande Sande

Executive Administrator
Strategy and Business Development
BancTec, Inc.
2701 E. Grauwyler Road
Irving, TX 75061 United States
kathleen.vandesande@banctec.com • k_vandesande@yahoo.com
http://www.banctec.com

BUS: Outsourcing Company **P/S:** Outsourcing Services for All Business Types and Industries through Electronic Payment, Document and Content Processing Services **MA:** International **D/D/R:** Overseeing Company Administration **H/I/S:** Reading, Traveling **FBP:** Smithsonian; The New York Times; The Wall Street Journal; Forbes; The McKinsey Quarterly **CERTS:** Industry-Related Training **A/A/S:** Executive Women International **C/VW:** March of Dimes; American Heart Association; United Way of America **A/S:** She attributes her success to her detail-oriented nature.

LISA D. VANDERMEULEN
Sales Counselor
Westbrook Homes
2837 Carretas Court
Las Cruces, NM 88007 United States
lisar@elprr.com
http://www.westbrookhomes.com

BUS: Construction Company **P/S:** Real Estate, New Home Construction **MA:** Regional **D/D/R:** Specializing in Residential Home Sales **H/I/S:** Snorkeling, Cooking, Writing Short Stories, Poetry, Spending Time with her Family **FBP:** Su Casa **EDU:** Coursework in Business, El Paso Community College **CERTS:** Licensed Real Estate Agent, State of New Mexico (2004) **A/A/S:** Las Cruces Association of Realtors; Realtors Association of New Mexico; National Association of Realtors

THERESA M. VANNIER
Reserve Advisor
U.S. Air Force
217 Warrior Street
Cresview, FL 32536 United States
theresav22@cox.net
http://www.cambridgewhoswho.com

BUS: Government Organization **P/S:** Defense Services **MA:** National **EXP:** Ms. Vannier's expertise is in budget management. **D/D/R:** Mobilizing Individuals, Overseeing Administrative Duties, Developing Policies, Ensuring Proper Training **H/I/S:** Golfing, Needlework **FBP:** Logistics Officers Association Journal **EDU:** Bachelor's Degree in Biology and Law Enforcement, Minor in German, Jacksonville State University, Alabama (1977) **A/A/S:** Reserve Officers Association; Logistics Officers Association **C/VW:** Combined Federal Campaign **W/H:** Lieutenant Colonel, United States Air Force (2005) **A/S:** She attributes her success to her self-confidence and leadership skills. **B/I:** She became involved in her profession because of her desire to serve people. **H/O:** The highlight of her career was attaining the rank of Squadron Commander 2x. **I/F/Y:** In five years, Ms. Vannier hopes to take over the position as deputy chief in Germany.

MR. RALPH VARCHETTO
Performance Coach, Trainer, Owner
Advance Training Solutions Performance Center
200A Whitehead Road
Hamilton, NJ 08619 United States
rvarchetto@advancetrainingsolutions.com
http://www.cambridgewhoswho.com

BUS: Performance Training Center **P/S:** Youth Performance Training **MA:** Local **EXP:** Mr. Varchetto's expertise is in performance coaching and speed and agility training. **H/I/S:** Hosting Agility and Performance Training Clinics and Camps **FBP:** Strength and Conditioning Journal **EDU:** Bachelor of Science in Exercise Science, William Paterson University **CERTS:** Certified Personal Fitness Trainer **A/A/S:** National Strength and Conditioning Association; American College of Sports Medicine; IDEA Health & Fitness Association; International Youth Conditioning Association **A/S:** He attributes his success to his self-drive, desire to do the work he loves and enjoys. **B/I:** He became involved in his profession because he saw a need for children to receive supervised training. **H/O:** The highlight of his career was opening his business and watching it grow.

MS. MARIA E. VARGAS-MONTALVO, ESQ.
President and GM
La Taza De Oro Restaurant
96 Eighth Avenue
New York, NY 10011 United States
http://www.cambridgewhoswho.com

BUS: Restaurant **P/S:** Breakfast, Lunch and Dinner **MA:** Local **D/D/R:** Making Family Recipes, Serving Authentic Puerto Rican Cuisine and Cafe au Lait **H/I/S:** Athletics, Listening to Music, Dance, The Arts **EDU:** JD, University of Puerto Rico **A/A/S:** New York State Bar Association

ANI V. VARTABETIAN
Chief Executive Officer
Anso Realty, Inc.
2005 Prairie Street, Suite 100
Chatsworth, CA 91311 United States
toani@aol.com
http://www.ansorealty.com

BUS: Residential, Commercial and Industrial Real Estate **P/S:** Recruiting Agents, Quality Control, Advertising **MA:** Local **D/D/R:** Working as a Real Estate Broker **H/I/S:** Skiing, Car Racing, Watching Movies **FBP:** Car and Driver **EDU:** Bachelor of Arts in Urban Studies and City Planning, California State University at Northridge **A/A/S:** National Association of Realtors; California Association of Realtors **A/H:** Recipient, Outstanding Graduating Senior Award; Honors Graduate **C/VW:** California State University **A/S:** She attributes her success to her determination and motivation. **B/I:** She became involved in her profession because of her passion for real estate.

GLORIA G. VAUGHT
Environmental Protection Specialist
Federal Law Enforcement Training Center
1300 W. Richey
Artesia, NM 88210 United States
gloria.vaught@dhs.gov
http://www.cambridgewhoswho.com

BUS: Training Federal Agents **P/S:** Keeping Environmental Programs in Compliance of All State and Federal Regulations **MA:** International **D/D/R:** Environmental Safety **H/I/S:** Hiking, Camping, Reading **EDU:** Coursework in General Studies, University of Arkansas **C/VW:** Eagles Auxiliary **A/S:** She attributes her success to her hard work. **B/I:** Her desire to work in the environmental field motivated her to pursue her current career. **H/O:** The highlight of her career was obtaining her current position.

RICHARD D. VEENSTRA, PH.D.
Professor
Department of Pharmacology
SUNY Upstate Medical University
750 E. Adams Street
Syracuse, NY 13210 United States
veenstrr@upstate.edu
http://www.upstate.edu

BUS: University **P/S:** Higher Education **MA:** International **D/D/R:** Researching on Cardiovascular Electrophysiology, Ion Channels and Gap Junctions **H/I/S:** Running, Riding his Bicycle, Cross Country Skiing, Sports, Attending the Theater, Watching Movies **FBP:** Biophysical Journal; The Journal of Physiology; Circulation Research; American Journal of Physiology; Cardiovascular Research **EDU:** Ph.D. in Physiology and Biophysics, The University of Iowa (1983); Bachelor's Degree in Zoology, Iowa State University (1977) **A/A/S:** Hamilton White Society; Biophysical Society; Society of General Physiologists; Iroquois Chapter, Sierra Club Earth Day Cleanup; The American Physiological Society; League of American Bicyclists; The American Society for Cell Biology **A/H:** Finalist, Louis N. Katz Basic Science Research Prize for Young Investigators, American Heart Association (1986) **C/VW:** Executive Board, Onondaga Cycling Club; Nature Conservancy; American Heart Association; League of American Bicyclists; United Way of America; World Wildlife Fund **DOB:** June 2, 1955 **POB:** Des Moines, IA **W/H:** Associate Professor, Department of Pharmacology, SUNY Upstate Medical University (1992-2006); Assistant Professor, SUNY Upstate Medical University (1986-1992); Research Associate, Department of Anatomy and Cell Biology, Emory University School of Medicine (1986); Postdoctoral Fellow, National Institute of Health, Emory University (1984-1986) **C/A:** First Cardiac Gap Junction Channel Recording (1986) **A/S:** He attributes his success to his desire to learn, self-motivation and his ability to utilize the opportunities that came his way. **H/O:** The highlight of his career was being featured in the journal 'Science' which vaulted him to his first and only faculty appointment.

STEPHANIE O. VELUZ
Compliance/Project Manager
Horizon Blue Cross Blue Shield of New Jersey
3 Penn Plaza
Newark, NJ 07105 United States
densteph4@yahoo.com
http://www.cambridgewhoswho.com

BUS: Insurance Company **P/S:** Health Insurance **MA:** National **D/D/R:** Specializing in Medical Compliance, Project Management, Program Development and Implementation, Quality Management, Wound Care, Preventive Care, Process Improvement, Regulatory and Accreditation Submissions, Auditing, Reporting, Developing Databases **H/I/S:** Spending Time with her Family, Traveling **FBP:** Nursing Spectrum **EDU:** Bachelor's Degree in Nursing, Seton Hall University **CERTS:** Certification in Project Management **A/A/S:** Former Member, American Association of Managed Care Nurses **C/VW:** Vietnam Veterans of America **A/S:** She attributes her success to remaining current in her field. **B/I:** She became involved in her profession because she was recruited to develop a program for Horizon. **H/O:** The highlight of her career was developing and implementing member-focused diabetes and wound care programs.

CATHY ANN VENEZIA, MSEd
Owner, Founder, Behavior Therapist
Little Spirits, LLC
10 E. 38th Street, Third Floor
New York, NY 10016 United States
lspirits@yahoo.com
http://www.littlespirits.com

BUS: Therapeutic Learning Center **P/S:** Center for Children with Special Needs **MA:** Local **D/D/R:** Directing Behavioral Therapy **H/I/S:** Traveling, Going to the Beach **EDU:** Master's Degree in Special Education and Developmental Disabilities, College of New Rochelle **C/VW:** Little Spirits Foundation, Inc. **A/S:** She attributes her success to her love of her profession. **B/I:** She became involved in her profession because she had summer jobs working with autistic children and wanted to continue to make a difference.

RUBERTA VERA
Mayor of Natalia
City of Natalia
300 Third Street
Natalia, TX 78059 United States
con06@sbcglobal.net
http://www.nataliatexas.com

BUS: Government Facility **P/S:** Leadership and Service, Organization **MA:** Regional **D/D/R:** Specializing in Leadership and Organization, Working with Grants and Infrastructure in Place for New Businesses and New Homes for the Community, Ensuring Excellence in Water, Sewer, Schools and Government Services, Mentoring and Volunteering **H/I/S:** Reading, Gardening **EDU:** Coursework in Management, San Antonio College (1970); Diploma, Natalia High School (1966) **A/A/S:** Review Board for Alamo Area Council of Governments; Chairman, Economic Development and Environmental Review Board; President, Interstate 35 South Economic Development Council; Ambassador, Congressional District 23 **C/VW:** Former Co-Chair, Medina County Relay for Life; Public Speaker, American Cancer Society; Chair, Cancer Preventative Care

JEANMARIE VERCHOT-LUBICZ, PH.D.
Associate Professor
Oklahoma State University
127 Noble Research Center
Stillwater, OK 74078 United States
verchot.lubicz@okstate.edu
http://www.okstate.edu

BUS: State University Providing World-Class Education to All Students in Undergraduate and Graduate Programs **P/S:** Programs in Health Sciences, Engineering and Architecture, Agricultural and Natural Sciences, Education and Human Environmental Sciences, Online Classes, Athletics, Student Organizations, Research Programs, Campus Residence **MA:** National **D/D/R:** Teaching Graduate and Doctoral Degree Students, Teaching Virology, Editing Journals **H/I/S:** Running, Needlework, Swimming **FBP:** Science Journals **EDU:** Fellowship to Cambridge University; Ph.D. in Microbiology, Texas A&M University (1995) **A/A/S:** International Society for Molecular Plant-Microbe Interactions; American Association for the Advancement of Science; American Society for Virology; American Society of Plant Biologists; Fellowship to Cambridge University; Sigma Xi, The Scientific Research Society

THOMAS A. VERDUSCO, RN
Operating Room Nurse
Presbyterian Intercommunity Hospital
12401 Washington Boulevard
Whittier, CA 90602 United States
tommyboyrecords@msn.com
http://www.cambridgewhoswho.com

BUS: Hospital **P/S:** Healthcare, Acute Care **MA:** Regional **EXP:** Mr. Verdusco's expertise is in operating room nursing. **H/I/S:** Traveling **FBP:** AORN Journal **EDU:** Associate of Science in Nursing, Rio Hondo College (1979) **A/A/S:** Association of Operating Room Nurses **C/VW:** American Cancer Society **A/S:** He attributes his success to his compassionate nature and his passion for his profession. **B/I:** He became involved in his profession because of his experience as a medic in the United States Navy. **H/O:** The most gratifying aspect of his career is helping people get better on a daily basis.

JONNIE J. VERMILLION
Massage Therapist
An Essential Touch
5320 N. Vincent Road
Newman Lake, WA 99025 United States
jonnie5150@comcast.net
http://www.cambridgewhoswho.com

BUS: Massage Therapy **P/S:** Full Service Wellness Salon Specializing in Massages **MA:** Local **D/D/R:** Deep Tissue Therapy **H/I/S:** Traveling, Playing Softball, Camping, Participating in Outdoor Activities with her Family, Gardening, Massaging **FBP:** American Massage Therapy Journal **CERTS:** Massage Certification, Inland Massage Therapy Institute **A/A/S:** American Massage Therapy Association **C/VW:** St. Jude Children's Research Hospital **A/S:** She attributes her success to her children who are her driving force as well as the support and encouragement she receives from her husband, family and friends. **B/I:** She became involved in this profession because she was encouraged by her husband to take a massage therapy course. **H/O:** The highlights of her career were completing her certification as a former single parent and opening and maintaining a successful business.

KRISTINE M. VERSAGGIO
Director of Human Resources
Avis Budget Group
10000 Bessie Coleman Drive
Chicago, IL 60666 United States
kristine.versaggio@cendant.com
http://www.cambridgewhoswho.com

BUS: One of the World's Largest Car Rental Operators Comprised of Avis and Budget Care Rentals **P/S:** Over 6,000 Car and Truck Rental Locations in the Americas, Australia, New Zealand and the Caribbean **MA:** Regional **D/D/R:** Working as a Director of Human Resources, Working with the Area Vice President on Strategic Issues, Heading Mergers and Acquisitions, Encouraging the Direction of the Midwest Area, Performing Labor Negotiations, Overseeing Employee Relations, Managing a Staff of Nine **H/I/S:** Enjoying Outdoor Activities, Skiing, Bicycling **FBP:** Harvard Business Review **EDU:** Master of Arts in Human Resources and Sociology, Our Lady of the Lake University, Texas (1999) **CERTS:** Certified Senior Professional in Human Resources **A/A/S:** Society for Human Resource Management

MARLENE M. VETUSTO
Sales Agent
Northnagle Realtor
516 Titus Avenue
Rochester, NY 14617 United States
mvetusto@frontiernet.net
http://www.cambridgewhoswho.com

BUS: Real Estate **P/S:** Residential Real Estate Sales **MA:** Local **D/D/R:** Offering Quality Personalized Service **H/I/S:** Spending Time with her Family, Traveling, Bowling **FBP:** Consumer Reports; Money **CERTS:** Graduate Realtor Institute **C/VW:** American Heart Association; American Cancer Society; American Diabetes Association; Church Volunteer **A/S:** She attributes her success to being able to relate well with others. **H/O:** The highlight of her career is being known in the community.

MARTIN E. VICKERS
1) Master Counselor 2) Counselor
1) Eckerd Youth Alternatives, Inc. 2) Camp E-Kel-Etu
19186 N.E. 13th Street
Silver Springs, FL 34488 United States
martin_ethan2002@yahoo.com
http://www.cambridgewhoswho.com

BUS: 1) Nonprofit Organization 2) Government Organization **P/S:** 1) Community Services 2) Legal Services **MA:** 1) Regional 2) Regional **D/D/R:** Overseeing Treatment of At-Risk Children, Supervising Counselors and Clients, Administering Medication **H/I/S:** Traveling, Hiking, Canoeing **FBP:** Popular Mechanics **EDU:** Bachelor's Degree in Anthropology, Sociology and Criminal Justice, Valdosta State University **A/S:** He attributes his career success to his positive attitude and consistency. **B/I:** He became involved in his profession because he enjoys working with children and teaching the fundamentals of life. **H/O:** The most gratifying aspect of his career is being able to work with children.

WANDA L. VIERA
President
Universal Tax Service Inc.
PO Box 155
Eustis, FL 32727 United States
universaltax2@embarqmail.com
http://www.universaltaxserviceinc.com

BUS: Taxation Company **P/S:** Tax Services for Mortgage Companies and Banks to Prevent Fraudulent Loans by using 4506T Form, Verifying Social Security Numbers Directly through the Social Security Administration **MA:** International **D/D/R:** Assisting Clients, Delivering Tax Verification Services in 24 Hours, Submitting Information to the Internal Revenue Service and Social Security Administration **H/I/S:** Spending Time with her Children, Enjoying Motocross with her Son, Working with her Husband's Custom Autobody and Paint Business **EDU:** College Coursework **C/VW:** Volunteer, Teen Court Systems **DOB:** August 9, 1970 **POB:** Homestead, FL **SP:** Sebastian **CHILD:** Michael, Devon, Enzo **A/S:** She attributes her success to her customer service skills. **H/O:** The most gratifying aspects of her career are running a successful business and receiving positive feedback from her clients. **I/F/Y:** In five years, Ms. Viera hopes to develop her company into one of the largest tax verification service company and to help stabilize the economy.

MR. DOMINICK A. VIETRI
43 Southgate Avenue
Annapolis, MD 21401 United States
dvietri@vericomtech.com
http://www.vericomtechnologies.com

BUS: Fleet Management and Vehicle Security Company **P/S:** Monitoring Vehicle and Driver Activity, Allowing Businesses to Measure Performance and Minimize Risk, Resulting in Decreased Costs and Increased Profits **MA:** National **EXP:** Mr. Vietri's expertise is in customer care and equipment management. **D/D/R:** Overseeing Operations, Sales and Marketing **H/I/S:** Traveling, Golfing **FBP:** Fleet Management Transport **EDU:** Associate Degree in Computer Services, RCA Technical Institute (1969)

MR. ERIC J. VIEU
Owner
Gold Star Restorations, Inc.
1200 Millbury Street
Worcester, MA 01607 United States
goldstars895@yahoo.com
http://www.goldstarrestoration.com

BUS: Cleaning Company **P/S:** Mold Removal, Air Duct Cleaning, Heating, Ventilation, Air Conditioning for Residential and Industrial Properties **MA:** Regional **D/D/R:** Managing Operations and Business Activities **H/I/S:** Golfing, Four-Wheeling **FBP:** The Wall Street Journal **EDU:** Industry-Related Training and Experience **A/A/S:** Chamber of Commerce; Better Business Bureau **C/VW:** Fire Department, Schools **A/S:** He attributes his success to his determination and ability to build a team. **B/I:** He became involved in the profession after working in the field with another company and finding the confidence to open his own business. **H/O:** The most gratifying aspect of his career is owning his own successful business.

SANDRA M. VILLALBA
Speech-Language Pathologist
Independent School District
9600 Sims Drive
El Paso, TX 79925 United States
http://www.cambridgewhoswho.com

BUS: Education **P/S:** Public School Education **MA:** Local **D/D/R:** Offering Speech Therapy Services **H/I/S:** Gardening, Sewing **FBP:** Advance **EDU:** Master of Science in Communication Disorders, Our Lady of the Lake University **A/A/S:** American Speech-Language-Hearing Association; Marquis Who's Who in American Education; National Education Association; Texas State Teachers Association **A/S:** She attributes her success to patience. **B/I:** She chose the profession because she loves helping people. **H/O:** The highlight of her career is the gratitude expressed by the students.

AMY SOCORRO VILLAROYA
Director, ED/ICU/CCU, Nursing Supervisor
Doctors Hospital of Manteca
1205 E. North Street
Manteca, CA 95336 United States
amy.villaroya@tenethealth.com
http://www.tenethealth.com

BUS: 73-Bed Rural Community Hospital Dedicated to Providing an Environment for the Provision of Quality Nursing, Diagnostic and Therapeutic Services on both an Inpatient and Outpatient Basis to the Surrounding Community **P/S:** Community Programs, Expanded and Enhanced Imaging Services, Emergency Services, Pharmacy Services, Physical Therapy, Intensive Care and Coronary Care Unit, Obstetrical Services, Occupational Medicine **MA:** Local **D/D/R:** Offering Critical Care and Emergency Services, Overseeing General Operations and a Staff of 70 Employees, Cardiovascular Nursing **H/I/S:** Reading, Traveling, Spending Time with her Family **FBP:** Nurse Management **EDU:** Bachelor of Science in Nursing, Cebu State College School of Nursing, Philippines (1979) **CERTS:** Certified Critical Care Nurse (1985) **A/A/S:** ACCN; MSA; Medical Relief Foundation

LISA A. VINCENT
Administrator
Gumpoint Christian School
10340 Schultz Road
Branch, LA 70516 United States
gumpointschool@aol.com
http://www.gumpoint.com

BUS: Leader in Education **P/S:** Education for Pre-Kindergarten to Twelfth Grade **MA:** Statewide **D/D/R:** Ensuring Academic Achievement, Overseeing Statewide Administration of the Distance Learning Students Program, Offering a Progressive Education, Working at her Brother's Law Office, Compiling Financial Reports **H/I/S:** Traveling, Reading, Computers **FBP:** Alpha Omega Publications **EDU:** Bachelor of Science in Microbiology, Louisiana State University **A/A/S:** Golden Key National Honor Society; 4-H; Student Council; Youth Choir Director, Gum Point Church

DENISE VINES
President, Chief Executive Officer
LaShaye Enterprises, LLC
40 Adams Street, Suite One
Irvington, NJ 07111 United States
lasuave_entreprises@msn.com
dayjavu@msn.com
http://www.cambridgewhoswho.com

BUS: Parent Company of One Financial and Development Company **P/S:** Property Management, Real Estate Sales, Title Search, Financial Training, Project Management, Business Management Training **MA:** National **D/D/R:** Training and Networking with New Business Owners on how to Run their Businesses, Advising People on Buying Homes **H/I/S:** Collecting Sports Cars **FBP:** Carlton Sheets; Entrepreneur; Business News **EDU:** College Coursework **A/A/S:** Executive Board Member, Newark Technical High School

CAROL VINSON LEA
Minister of Christian Education, Disciple Division Director
Mount Calvary Baptist Church
1735 Enterprise Drive, Suite 3
Fairfield, CA 94533 United States
cvlea@mountcalvarychurch.org
http://www.mountcalvarychurch.org

BUS: Church **P/S:** Spiritual Services, Christian Education **MA:** Regional **EXP:** Ms. Lea's expertise is in Christian education, ministry and discipleship. **H/I/S:** Traveling, Reading, Singing **EDU:** Master's Degree in Christian Counseling, California Graduate School of Theology; Bachelor of Science in Electrical and Computer Engineering, Pacific Union College; Coursework, Golden Gate Baptist Theological Seminary **A/A/S:** National Association for the Advancement of Colored People; Baptist Association of Christian Educators; American Association of Christian Counselors; National Council of Negro Women **C/VW:** American Red Cross; Solano County Mental Health Services **DOB:** October 19, 1944 **POB:** Paducah, KY **SP:** (Deceased) **CHILD:** Francis, Claybon **A/S:** She attributes her success to her love and passion for helping people. **B/I:** She became involved in her profession because she always had an interest in teaching and in the learning process. **H/O:** The highlight of her career was seeing the church grow numerically and spiritually, while the ministry expanded locally and internationally. **I/F/Y:** In five years, Ms. Lea hopes to retire from the local church and travel to do consulting.

GILBERT S. VITALA
Surveyor, Forester, Owner
GSV Surveying and Land Services, Inc.
229 Middle River Road
Greenbush, ME 04418 United States
gsv@midmaine.com
http://www.cambridgewhoswho.com

BUS: Land Surveying Company **P/S:** Survey and Forestry Services **MA:** Local **EXP:** Mr. Vitala's expertise is in land surveying. **H/I/S:** Fishing **EDU:** Bachelor of Science in Forestry, University of Maine **A/A/S:** Maine Society of Land Surveyors; Society of American Foresters; American Congress of Mapping Cadastral **C/VW:** American Forests

MR. RAYMOND J. VIVACQUA, MD
Medical Director of Transfusion Services at Crozer Center
Associates in Hematology-Oncology
1 Medical Center Boulevard
Upland, PA 19013 United States
rewplt@comcast.com
http://www.cambridgewhoswho.com

BUS: Private Medical Practice **P/S:** Hematology, Medical Oncology, Chemotherapy **MA:** Regional **D/D/R:** Overseeing the Clinical Screening Programs, Setting up Educational Programs for Patients and Physicians, Treating Cancer and Blood Diseases **H/I/S:** Sailing, Carpentry, Photography **FBP:** Journal of Clinical Oncology **EDU:** Residency, Philadelphia Veterans Administration Hospital; MD, Thomas Jefferson University, Jefferson Medical College **A/A/S:** American Society of Clinical Oncology; American Society of Hematology; American Association of Blood Banks; Board Member, Community of Hematology and Oncology Consortium

SUSAN F. VOLLE, RN, BSN
Registered Nurse
Arvada Health Center
6121 W. 60th Avenue
Arvada, CO 80003 United States
suevolle@yahoo.com
http://www.cambridgewhoswho.com

BUS: Nursing Home **P/S:** Healthcare, Geriatrics **MA:** Local **D/D/R:** Rehabilitation Nursing **H/I/S:** Hiking, Biking, Swimming, Participating in Outdoor Activities **FBP:** American Journal of Nursing **EDU:** Bachelor of Science in Nursing, Loretto Heights College **CERTS:** Certified Registered Rehabilitation Nurse **A/A/S:** Eden Associate **A/H:** AMR Angel Award (1998) **C/VW:** Crossroads of Denver; Samaritan's Purse **A/S:** She attributes her success to her love of nursing and her belief that nursing is her calling. **B/I:** She became involved in nursing through her exposure to geriatrics. Her grandmother worked as an administrator at a nursing home, and she has always wanted to be a geriatric nurse. **H/O:** The highlight of her career was receiving her certificate as an Eden Associate in August 2006.

HOLLY VON SEGGERN
Director
Marketing and Brand Development
Whitsons Culinary Group
1800 Motor Parkway
Islandia, NY 11749 United States
vonseggernh@whitsons.com
http://www.whitsons.com

BUS: Food Service Company **P/S:** A Wide Range of High-Quality Dining Services to Public and Private Sector Clients in a Variety of Industries **MA:** National **D/D/R:** Developing the Business, Marketing, Preparing Proposals and Client Presentations, Handling Public Relations, Communications and Advertising, Merchandising for Corporate Standards, Offering On-Site Training, Planning for Community Events and Programs **H/I/S:** Reading, Composing Stained Glass, Serving as a Sunday School Assistant Superintendent **FBP:** FoodService Director; Food Management; Nation's Restaurant News; Restaurants & Institutions **EDU:** Bachelor's Degree in Marketing and Management, Binghamton University (1990) **A/H:** Spirit of Whitsons Award **C/VW:** Planning Committee, The Shepherd's Ball, SCO Family of Services; Volunteer, Madonna Heights Services, SCO Family of Services; Volunteer Sunday School Teacher; The Salvation Army

CARA S. VOSS
President
Community Hope International
354 Judsville School Road
Dobson, NC 27017 United States
community01@surry.net
http://www.communityhopeint.org

BUS: Nonprofit **P/S:** Nonprofit Church Organization Connecting Communities through Technology **MA:** National **D/D/R:** Offering Presentations, Training Workshops, Public Speaking and Marketing **H/I/S:** Listening to Music **EDU:** Master's Degree in Theology, Vintage Bible College and Seminary; Bachelor's Degree in Christian Education, Vintage Bible College and Seminary; Honorary Doctorate, World Christianship Ministries; Pastoral Degree, World Christianship Ministries **C/VW:** Church, Community Hope International **A/S:** She attributes her success to her experience and God. **B/I:** She became involved in the profession because she was visited by God. **H/O:** The highlight of her career is helping people.

JAMES E. VOWELL
Owner
The Editing Company
jevowell@editingcompany.com
http://www.editingcompany.com

BUS: Editing Company **P/S:** Professional Proofreading and Editing Services, Book, Magazine and Newspaper Designing **MA:** International **D/D/R:** Designing, Composing and Editing Books **H/I/S:** Skiing, Playing Tennis, Golfing, Traveling **FBP:** Editor & Publisher; Columbia Journalism Review **EDU:** Master of Business Administration, University of California, Los Angeles; Bachelor's Degree in Journalism, The University of Texas at Austin **A/A/S:** Board of Directors, Wildwood Canyon Park **C/VW:** Sierra Club; The American Society for the Prevention of Cruelty to Animals **SP:** Codette **A/S:** He attributes his success to his honesty. **B/I:** He became involved in his profession because he wanted to work in journalism. **H/O:** The highlights of his career were being the founding editor of the Los Angeles Reader and hiring Matt Groening, the creator of the television show, 'The Simpsons,' as an editor.

CYNTHIA A. WACHNER
CEO
Creations, Inc.
PO Box 587
Visalia, CA 93279 United States
creationsinc2006@sbcglobal.net
http://www.cambridgewhoswho.com

BUS: Fine Art, Creation, Marketing **P/S:** Fine Art, Writing, Marketing Company, Painting Watercolor and Oil **MA:** National **D/D/R:** Teaching, Creating, Writing, Fine Art **H/I/S:** Spending Time with the Family, Traveling, Beach, Animals **FBP:** HR; Artist Magazine; Fine Art Connoisseur; Watercolor Magic **EDU:** Master's Degree in Human Resources, Chapman University; Bachelor of Science in Organizational Behavior, University of San Francisco **CERTS:** Teaching Credentials, State of California; Professional Clearance in Adult Education; Certified in Business Management, Certified in Small Business Development; Certified in English as a Second Language; delete elementary secondary basic skills, english social science life sciences including general science; Cross-Cultural Language and Academic Development Certificate **A/A/S:** Society for Human Resource Management; National Society and Tulare Kings County Chapters, Alliance for California Artists, Visalia Art League **C/VW:** First Presbyterian Church **A/S:** She attributes her success to her perseverance.

KIMBERLY L. WADDELL, MA
Case Manager for Special Education
Klein Independent School District
6700 N. Klein Circle Drive
Houston, TX 77088 United States
kimwaddell@usa.net
http://www.cambridgewhoswho.com

BUS: Education **P/S:** Education for Kindergarten through 12th Grade **MA:** Local **D/D/R:** Special Education and Management, Managing All Special Education Programs, Admissions Review, Conducting Dismissal Meetings, Assisting with Discipline for Special Education Students, Assessment Leadership **H/I/S:** Traveling, Attending Social Events, Enjoying Art and the Theater **FBP:** Various Educational Journals and Publications **EDU:** Master's Degree in Elementary Education, Sam Houston State University; Bachelor of Science in Special Education, Ball State University, Indiana **CERTS:** Certification in Middle Management; Supervisor Certification **A/H:** Outstanding Performance Teacher, Board of Education (1993) **C/VW:** Christian Appalachian Volunteer, Working with Houston Homeless; Stephen Ministry at Cypress Christian Church Spring Project; Tutor, Huntington Learning Center; Principal Administrator, Private International American School in Venezuela (2001-2004) **A/S:** She attributes her success to her love of the profession and efforts to make a difference in the lives of her students. **H/O:** The most gratifying aspect of her career is successfully teaching students with learning disabilities.

SANDRA L. WADE, ABR, SRES
Realtor
Coldwell Banker, Danforth
15112 45th Avenue N.W.
Gig Harbor, WA 98332 United States
harborsales@comcast.net
http://www.gigharborrelocation.com

BUS: Leader in Real Estate **P/S:** Full Representative of Buyers and Sellers in Real Estate Transactions **MA:** South Sound, Key Peninsula **D/D/R:** Selling Undeveloped Land, Residential and Commercial Real Estate, Specializing in International Aviation and the Senior Market **FBP:** NW MLS Website; Realtor **C/VW:** The Humane Society of the United States; Pierce County Fire Department; Pierce County Association of Police and Sheriff's Department

MR. ARTHUR J. WAGNER
Assistant Principal, Athletic Director
Tempe Union High School District, McClintock High School
1830 E. Del Rio Drive
Tempe, AZ 85282 United States
awagner9@cox.net
http://www.cambridgewhoswho.com

BUS: High School **P/S:** General Secondary Curriculum, Arts, Music, Physical Education, Foreign Language Instruction, Learning Resources, Student Support Services, Athletics, Extracurricular Activities, Student Clubs and Organizations **MA:** Local **D/D/R:** Specializing in Athletic Direction, Coordinating Athletic Activities **H/I/S:** Golfing, Attending Church **FBP:** Athletic Management **EDU:** Master's Degree in Educational Leadership, Northern Arizona University; Master's Degree in Special Education, Northern Arizona University **A/A/S:** Association for Supervision and Curriculum Development; ASA; Arizona Interscholastic Athletic Administrators Association

DONNA G. WAGNER, RN
Registered Nurse
Lavaca Medical Center
1400 N. Texana Street
Hallettsville, TX 77964 United States
dwagner_rn@yahoo.com
http://www.cambridgewhoswho.com

BUS: Hospital **P/S:** Acute Care and Emergency Health Services **MA:** Local **D/D/R:** Nursing **H/I/S:** Gardening, Fishing, Reading, Cross-Stitching **FBP:** Consumer Reports **EDU:** Associate of Applied Science in Nursing, Victoria College **C/VW:** St. Rose Catholic Elementary School; Sacred Heart High School; Blood Drives **A/S:** She attributes her success to her personal desire to be the best she can be. **B/I:** She became involved in the profession because her mother was a nurse. **H/O:** The most gratifying aspect of her career is when patients tell her she saved their lives.

STEPHANIE LYNN WAGNER, RN
Chief Executive Officer, Registered Nurse
The CPR Lady, LLC
156 Magnolia Lane
Middletown, NJ 07748 United States
thecprlady1@yahoo.com
http://www.cambridgewhoswho.com

BUS: Leader in the Healthcare Industry **P/S:** Quality Healthcare Services Including Cardiopulmonary Resuscitation, Child Safety Information Classes, Baby Proofing Homes and the Heimlich Maneuver **MA:** Regional **D/D/R:** Teaching Young Adults how to Protect their Children, Stressing the Importance of Child Safety, Supplying Informational Pamphlets, Instructing for the American Heart Association, Administering Cardiopulmonary Resuscitation and the Heimlich Maneuver, Offering Infant, Child and Adult Health Services **H/I/S:** Spending Time with her Children and Husband **FBP:** RN **EDU:** Associate of Science in Nursing, SUNY, University at Albany (1998) **CERTS:** Certified Cardiopulmonary Resuscitation Instructor; Pursuing Certification in First Aid and Safety Instructor **A/A/S:** American Safety and Health Institute

MELODY F. WAINIO
Registrar
Bryant & Stratton College
27557 Chardon Road
Willoughby Hills, OH 44092 United States
mfwainio@bryantstratton.edu
mwainio@ameritech.net
http://www.bryantstratton.edu

BUS: America's Premiere Private Career College **P/S:** Offers 15 Degree Programs which Provide Cutting Edge Skills as Well as Real World Experience, Giving a Decided Advantage in Fields with Exciting Futures, Student Education Services, Teaching, Research **MA:** Local **D/D/R:** Instructing, Advising Being Responsible for All Registration Processes, Room Assignments, Graduation, Orientation, Transcripts, Maintaining Student Records, Supervising Advising **H/I/S:** Traveling, Cooking, Collecting Cookbooks, Sewing **FBP:** National On-Campus Report; The Successful Registrar **EDU:** Master's Degree in Education, Capella University (2002); Bachelor's Degree in Technical Education, University of Akron (1987) **A/A/S:** NACADA; Association for Supervision and Curriculum Development

JILL M. WAKABAYASHI
Physical Therapist Assistant Program Director
Kapi'olani Community College
4303 Diamond Head Road
Honolulu, HI 96816 United States
jwakabay@hawaii.edu
http://www.kcc.hawaii.edu

BUS: College **P/S:** Higher Education Including Practical Nursing Programs, Business and Liberal Arts **MA:** International **EXP:** Ms. Wakabayashi's expertise is in health science and physical therapy rehabilitation, specific muscle movement function, long-term aging process and neurology. **D/D/R:** Overseeing and Advising Students, Handling Public Relations for Programs and the Campus, Teaching Five Classes, Lecturing, Working in the Laboratory **H/I/S:** Making Crafts **EDU:** Master's Degree in Public Health, University of Hawaii (1996) **A/A/S:** Local Chapter, Parkinson's Disease Association; American Physical Therapy Association; Physical Therapy Assistants Group **A/H:** Outstanding Parent-Teacher Association Program Education Award (2006)

Kari Westly Waldhaus, CRSP
Owner
The Entrepreneur's Source
PO Box 550
Baker City, OR 97814 United States
kwaldhaus@e-sourceconsulting.biz
http://www.theesource.com/kwaldhaus

BUS: Business Coaching, Career Coaching and Consulting Company **P/S:** Business Coaching, Career Coaching and Consulting Services **MA:** National **EXP:** Ms. Waldhaus' area of expertise is in career coaching. **D/D/R:** Aiding People in Establishing Businesses **H/I/S:** Traveling, Performing Real Estate Services, Interior Designing **FBP:** Entrepreneur **EDU:** College Coursework **CERTS:** Life, Accident and Health Licenses; Series 7, 6, 63 and 66; Licensed Health Insurance Agent; Certified Retirement Services Professional; Certified Retirement Administrator; Certified Retirement Counselor **A/A/S:** President, Rotary Club of Baker City; Board Member, Baker County Economic Development Council; Treasurer, Baker County Chamber of Commerce and Visitors Bureau; Board Member, Baker Enterprise Growth Initiative **A/H:** Financial Advisor of the Year, States of Hawaii and Alaska (2004) **C/VW:** Women in Search of Excellence; Relay For Life, American Cancer Society **DOB:** April 30, 1958 **POB:** Honolulu, HI **SP:** Jack **CHILD:** Kirstin, Aaron **A/S:** She attributes her success to her hard work, open-mindedness and genuine concern for her clients. **H/O:** The highlight of her career was establishing her own business. **I/F/Y:** In five years, Ms. Waldhaus hopes to expand her business.

Mr. Jerry A. Waliszewski
Agent
Jerry Waliszewski Insurance Agency
1852 Dale Douglas Drive
El Paso, TX 79936 United States
jaws1@whc.net
http://www.jerrysagency.com

BUS: Family-Owned Insurance Agency **P/S:** Insurance Services and Related Products for Automotive, Home, Business, Life, Health, Bonds and Financial Planning **MA:** Regional **D/D/R:** Selling Personal, Property and Casualty Insurance, Assisting in Financial Planning **H/I/S:** Working on Cars, Traveling **FBP:** Discover **EDU:** Master of Business Administration, Webster University (1977) **A/A/S:** Independent Insurance Agents and Brokers of America; Chamber of Commerce **DOB:** July 13, 1943 **SP:** Mary **CHILD:** Jerry, Lisa, David

CAROLYN J. WALKER
Librarian
Northwest Georgia and Lookout Valley Baptist Associations
63 Pin Oak Drive
Rock Springs, GA 30739 United States
libraryg@aol.com
http://www.cambridgewhoswho.com

BUS: Library **P/S:** Books, Videos, DVDs, Books on Tape and CD, Study Kits **MA:** Local **D/D/R:** Librarian, Processing Book Selections **H/I/S:** Antique Cars, Traveling, Spending Time with Family and Friends **FBP:** Southern Living **EDU:** Industry-Related Training and Experience **A/A/S:** Teacher, Southern Baptist Convention; President, Chickamauga Women's Club; Newsletter Editor, Antique Car Club **C/VW:** Volunteer, Chickamauga Public Library; Historian, Friends of the Library Organization; Chickamauga Women's Club Charity Events **A/S:** She attributes her success to her drive, passion for reading and wanting to work with people. **B/I:** She was prompted to enter her profession when her pastor thought she would be the right person to set up the church library. **H/O:** The highlight of her career was the first time the Southern Baptist Convention called to have her teach on a national level.

DEE A. WALKER
Sales Associate
Marsh Landing Realty
4200 Marsh Landing Boulevard, Suite 100
Jacksonville Beach, FL 32250 United States
deeannawalker@aol.com
http://www.cambridgewhoswho.com

BUS: Real Estate Company **P/S:** Listings, Buying and Selling Homes, Marketing, Mortgage Assistance **MA:** Regional **D/D/R:** Working with Listings, Selling High-End and Exclusive Homes in Up-Scale Communities **H/I/S:** Golfing, Walking, Jogging **FBP:** The Water's Edge **EDU:** College Coursework, Kentucky Westland College **A/A/S:** Executive in the Sales and Marketing Council, Home Builder's Association **A/H:** Voted Best in Customer Satisfaction, Builders Magazine (2005-2006)

JILL M. WALKER
Hospice Social Worker, Social Work Consultant
Vitas Innovative Hospice Care
1845 Business Center Drive, Suite 120
San Bernardino, CA 92408 United States
jillwalker@adelphia.net
http://www.vitas.com

BUS: The Nation's Largest and Leading Provider of Hospice Services **P/S:** Palliative Care, Hospice Care, End of Life Care **MA:** Nationwide **D/D/R:** Performing Individual, Group and Family Therapy, Offering Pediatric Hospice and End of Life Care, Treating Abused and Neglected Children, Skilled Nursing, Social Work Consulting **H/I/S:** Participating in Girl and Cub Scout activities, Baseball, Horseback Riding, Camping **FBP:** Journal of NASW; End of Life Journals **EDU:** Associate of Arts, Loma Linda University; Bachelor of Arts, Loma Linda University; Master of Science in Social Work, Loma Linda University (2001) **CERTS:** Licensed Clinical Social Worker (2005) **A/A/S:** Phi Alpha Honor Society; National Association of Social Workers; National Hospice and Palliative Care Organization **A/H:** Vitas Social Worker of the Year Award (2004)

PATRICIA HINTON WALKER
1) Vice President 2) Chief Executive Officer
1) Uniformed Services University of the Health Sciences
2) Stepping-Stones Consulting and Coaching
4301 Jones Bridge Road, Suite A-2025
Bethesda, MD 20814 United States
phintonwalker@comcast.net
http://www.cambridgewhoswho.com

BUS: 1) Training Center 2) Consulting Firm **P/S:** 1) Healthcare Education 2) Coaching and Consulting Services **MA:** 1) International 2) International **D/D/R:** Teaching Health Sciences in Master's and Doctorate Programs, Following Health and Public Policies, Organizational Consulting and Life Coaching, Managing Accreditations **H/I/S:** Golfing, Listening to Music **FBP:** Industry-Related Publications; Business Literature **EDU:** Ph.D. in Higher Education Administration, University of Mississippi (1984); Master of Science in Nursing, University of Mississippi (1978); Bachelor of Science in Nursing, University of Kansas (1966) **CERTS:** Fellow, American Academy of Nursing; Fellow, National Academy of Practice **A/A/S:** American Nurses Association; Co-Chairwoman, Nursing Academy, American Academy of Nursing; American Medical Informatics Association; National Academies of Practice; Sigma Theta Tau

SHIRLEY A. WALKER
Associate Professor
University of Mary Hardin-Baylor
900 College Street
Belton, TX 76513 United States
shirley.walker@umhb.edu
http://www.shirleywalker.net

BUS: Christ-Centered University Providing a Quality Higher Education for Qualified Students from Diverse Geographic, Ethnic, Socioeconomic, and Religious Backgrounds **P/S:** Bachelors and Masters Degree Programs, Athletics, Personal and Academic Counseling, Residence Life, Spiritual Life, Clubs and Organizations, Health Services **MA:** Local **D/D/R:** Adviser for Basics, In-services for the Nursing Home **H/I/S:** Bowling, Tennis, Reading **FBP:** Health and Social Work **EDU:** Master's Degree in Social Work, Ohio State University (1973) **A/A/S:** North American Association of Christians in Social Work; Society for Social Work Leadership in Health Care; National Association of Social Workers **A/H:** Social Worker of the Year, National Association of Social Workers, Texas Chapter, Central Counties Branch (2006)

VIRGINIA WALKER, RN
Health Educator, Registered Nurse
South Central Foundation
Alaska Native Medical Center
4201 Diplomacy Drive, Second Floor
Anchorage, AK 99508 United States
vwalker@scf.cc
http://www.anmc.org

BUS: Medical Center **P/S:** Healthcare **MA:** Regional **D/D/R:** Consulting on Health Education Issues Including Smoking Cessation, Pain Relief, Breast and Cervical Health and Car Seat Installation **H/I/S:** Reading, Flying **EDU:** Pursuing Master's Degree in Public Health, University of Alaska; Bachelor of Science in Nursing, Alaska Methodist University (1973) **A/A/S:** American Society for Circumpolar Health; Former Member, National Education Association

Mr. Michael C. Wall
Owner
Mike Wall and Associates
941 E. Lake Shore Drive
Allyn, WA 98524 United States
treasurehunt4u98118@yahoo.com
http://www.mikewallandassociates.com

BUS: Proven Leader Dedicated to Excellence in the Appraisal Industry **P/S:** Retirement Home and Charities Liquidations, Appraisal Events, Personal Property Appraisals, Estate Appraisal Services **D/D/R:** Consulting on Art and Antiques, Appraising Fine Art and Estates, Overseeing Estate Liquidations, Including Personal Property and Antiques **H/I/S:** Landscaping **FBP:** Antiques Magazine; Smithsonian **EDU:** Coursework in Art History, University of Washington **A/A/S:** Association of Personal Property

Gwenevere U. Wallace
Fourth and Fifth-Grade Special Education Teacher
Marion Intermediate School
410 Forest Hill Drive
Shelby, NC 28150 United States
http://www.cambridgewhoswho.com

BUS: Public School **P/S:** Special Education Instruction **MA:** Local **D/D/R:** Teaching **H/I/S:** Walking, Enjoying Nature **EDU:** Bachelor of Science in Early Childhood Education and Science, Pfeiffer University **C/VW:** The American Society for the Prevention of Cruelty to Animals; Habitat for Humanity **A/S:** She attributes her success to showing respect to the children and reaching out to them on all levels. **B/I:** She chose the profession because she has always wanted to be a teacher, especially because she had such tremendous teachers.

Lois M. Walling
Senior Army Instructor
Rhea County Board of Education
305 California Avenue
Dayton, TN 37321 United States
lmwalling@aol.com
http://www.cambridgewhoswho.com

BUS: High School **P/S:** Secondary Education **MA:** National **D/D/R:** Teaching Junior Reserve Officers' Training Corps and Social Studies **H/I/S:** Traveling, Spending Time at the Beach, Spending Time with her Family **FBP:** Army Times **EDU:** Bachelor's Degree in Business and Personal Management, University of Maryland; Bachelor's Degree in Psychology, Plus 20 Credits in Social Studies, History and Government, University of Maryland **CERTS:** JROTC Certification **A/A/S:** American Legion; Veterans of Foreign Wars; Who's Who Among American High School Teachers; Kiwanis Club; Senior Army Instructor for Seventh Brigade, WV, KY, TN, OH **A/H:** Bronze Star for Combat; Teacher of the Year for Third District, Eastern TN; Award, Order of Saint George **C/VW:** Parish Committee, Local Church; Veterans Organizations **A/S:** She attributes her success to having worked with great leaders and mentors. **B/I:** She became involved in her profession because she always wanted to help children. **H/O:** The highlight of her career was receiving the Order of Saint George Award.

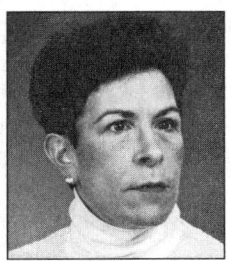

Ms. Claudia M. Walsh, RN
Registered Nurse
Nursing and Patient Care Services
Catholic Health Systems, Buffalo Mercy Hospital
565 Abbott Road
Buffalo, NY 14220 United States
http://www.cambridgewhoswho.com

BUS: Hospital **P/S:** Healthcare **MA:** Regional **D/D/R:** Caring for Pre- and Post-Craniotomy and Laminectomy Patients, Helping Patients who Have Undergone Surgery for Hip and Knee Replacement and Cervical Fusion, Conducting Patient Education in Various Areas Including Wound Care, Transfer and Positioning, Helping Hemodialysis and Renal Transplant Patients Pre- and Post-Operation, Caring for Patients Undergoing Surgery for Vaginal Hysterectomy, Assisting Cancer Patients in Various Areas Including Chemotherapy and Radiation, Treating Insulin Dependent Diabetes Patients, Scheduling Diagnostic Tests and Surgical Procedures, Working as a Medical and Surgical Floor Nurse, Precepting New Employees, Fulfilling Charge Nurse Duties, Distributing Medication, Starting Intravenous Treatments, Checking Vital Signs, Working with Patients with Developmental Disabilities Including Those who are Profoundly Retarded, Working with Medically Fragile Patients **H/I/S:** Reading, Decorative Gardening **EDU:** Diploma, Mount Mercy Academy, Buffalo, NY, with Honors; Bachelor of Arts in Biology, Canisius College, Buffalo, NY (1976); Diploma in Nursing, The Buffalo General Hospital School of Nursing, NY (1982) **A/A/S:** Nurses United **W/H:** Emergency Room, Buffalo Mercy Hospital

ROSALIE M. WALSH
Nutritionist, Consultant (Retired)
Nutritional Consultant
87-73 95th Street
Woodhaven, NY 11421 United States
http://www.cambridgewhoswho.com

BUS: Nutrition, Consulting **P/S:** Consulting, Mentoring, Education on Nutrition and Food Management **MA:** National **D/D/R:** Managing Food Services **H/I/S:** Reading, Walking the Dog, Traveling, Pet Therapy **FBP:** ADA Journal **EDU:** Master's Degree in Nutrition, Hunter College; Bachelor of Science in Home Economics and Nutrition, Queens College **A/A/S:** American Dietetic Association **A/S:** She attributes her success to her determination, tenacity and hard work. **B/I:** She became involved in her profession because she had her own nutritional issues growing up and wanted to get involved in a field where she could help others. **H/O:** The highlight of her career is that the field allows her to continually grow as a person.

MARK W. WALTON
Physician
Expresscare Plus
2141 Academy Circle
Colorado Springs, CO 80909 United States
mark.walton@cwwemail.com
http://www.cambridgewhoswho.com

BUS: Healthcare Center **P/S:** Healthcare **MA:** Colorado Springs **D/D/R:** Practicing Family Medicine **H/I/S:** Listening to Music, Attending the Theater, Watching Musical Comedy Movies **FBP:** Industry-Related Publications; Time; Newsweek; Reader's Digest **EDU:** Doctor of Osteopathy, Chicago College of Osteopathic Medicine **A/A/S:** Colorado State Medical Society; El Paso County Medical Society; American Osteopathic Association **C/VW:** The American Society for the Prevention of Cruelty to Animals; Feed the Children; Mission Springs; World Wildlife Fund **A/S:** He attributes his success to his caring nature. **B/I:** He became involved in his profession because he was inspired by his father who was a doctor. **H/O:** The most gratifying aspect of his career is being able to help patients who are in need.

SUSAN WALTZ
Associate Professor of Nursing,
Nursing Program Chairwoman
Ivy Tech Community College of Indiana
4475 Central Avenue
Columbus, IN 47203 United States
swaltz@ivytech.edu
http://www.ivytech.edu/columbus

BUS: Statewide Open-Admissions Community College that has Grown into the Second-Largest Post-Secondary Institution in Indiana **P/S:** Programs Leading to Two-Year Associates Degrees and One-Year Technical Certificates, Quality Education Services, Teaching, Learning, Research **MA:** National **D/D/R:** Recruiting and Educating Nurses, Advising Students **H/I/S:** Playing the Piano, Scrapbooking, Designing Jewelry, Digital Photography **FBP:** Nursing Magazine; American Journal of Nursing; Nursing Management **EDU:** Pursuing Doctor of Nursing; Master of Science in Nursing, Ball State University (2002); Bachelor of Science in Nursing, Indiana University (1989) **A/A/S:** Sigma Theta Tau, Alpha Chapter; Epsilon Sigma Alpha International; Former State President, Delta Delta Chapter; Fundraising, ESL Sorority **A/H:** ESA Woman of the Year **SP:** Michael **CHILD:** Mark, Katie, Paige, Parker **W/H:** Acute Care Nurse, Nurse Supervisor, Nurse Educator, Obstetrics, Pediatrics

LYNDA WANGSGARD
Teacher
Davis School District, Creekside Elementary School
275 W. Mutton Hollow Road
Kaysville, UT 84037 United States
lwangsgard@dsdmail.net
http://www.cambridgewhoswho.com

BUS: Elementary School **P/S:** Education **MA:** Local **EXP:** Ms. Wangsgard's expertise is in first grade education, curriculum development and public relations. **H/I/S:** Needlepoint, Reading, Researching Family Histories, American History and the History of the Church of Jesus Christ of Latter-Day Saints **EDU:** Master of Education, Brigham Young University **CERTS:** Early Childhood Education Certification; English as a Second Language Certification **A/A/S:** International Reading Association; Utah Council of Teachers of Mathematics; DCIRA **C/VW:** Church of Jesus Christ of Latter-Day Saints Museum of Church History; Parent-Teacher Association; Utah Council, Teachers of Mathematics; Davis County Chapter, International Reading Association **A/S:** She attributes her success to her love for people and desire to do her best. **B/I:** She became involved in her profession because of her love of children and learning. **H/O:** The most gratifying aspect of her career is teaching reading and mathematics to her first grade students.

James J. Warburton Jr.
Broker, Associate
RE/MAX 1st Choice
980 Reservoir Avenue
Cranston, RI 02910 United States
warburtongroup@aol.com
http://www.remax.com

BUS: Real Estate Agency **P/S:** Residential and Commercial Real Estate, Luxury Homes, Property Search, Moving Assistance, Mortgage Assistance, Financial Services **MA:** Rhode Island **EXP:** Mr. Warburton's expertise is in residential and commercial sales. **H/I/S:** Golfing **FBP:** The Wall Street Journal **EDU:** Bachelor of Business Arts, Bryant College (1962) **CERTS:** Licensed Broker, State of Rhode Island; Certified Residential Specialist; Accredited Buyer Representative; Certified Buyer Representative **A/A/S:** Graduate Realtor Institute; National Association of Realtors; Rhode Island Association of Realtors

Dorothy Ward
Licensed Massage Therapist
Dorothy Ward, LMT
1185 E. Putnam Avenue
Riverside, CT 06878 United States
molly02@optonline.net
http://www.cambridgewhoswho.com

BUS: Healthcare **P/S:** Therapeutic Massage **MA:** International **D/D/R:** Offering Rehabilitation and Preventative Therapy **H/I/S:** Spending Time with the Family, Traveling, Gardening, Horseback Riding, and Playing Tennis **CERTS:** Licensed Massage Therapist, Connecticut Center for Massage Therapy **A/A/S:** American Association of Massage Therapy **C/VW:** Hospice **A/S:** She attributes her success to her love of people and always wanting to help others. **B/I:** She chose the profession because she enjoys working with people. **H/O:** The highlight of her career has yet to come.

SANDRA WARD
Teacher
New York City Department of Education
65 Court Street
Brooklyn, NY 11201 United States
ward11465@msn.com
http://www.cambridgewhoswho.com

BUS: Educational Facility **P/S:** Leading Secondary School **MA:** Local **D/D/R:** Teaching Seventh and Eighth-Grade Special Education, Educating Students in Mathematics, Literacy, Science and Social Studies **H/I/S:** Baseball, Cricket **FBP:** Readers Digest **EDU:** Master of Science in Special Education, Adelphi University (1995) **A/A/S:** School Leadership Team; Clerk, St. Mary's Episcopal Church

MS. CHRISTINE M. WARNE
Environmental Services Manager
West Coast Gynecologic Oncology
1005 Pinellas Street
Clearwater, FL 33756 United States
cplenskewarne@aol.com
http://www.cambridgewhoswho.com

BUS: Hospital **P/S:** Healthcare **MA:** Local **D/D/R:** Managing Insurance and Billing **H/I/S:** NASCAR Racing, Caring for Animals, Shopping, Listening to Music, Attending the Concerts, Participating in Church Activities **CERTS:** Certified Medical Technician **C/VW:** Street Ministry for the Homeless; Joshua House, Migrant Workers; Cypress Meadows Community Church **H/O:** The most gratifying aspect of her career is meeting the demands of the employees.

WINDY K. WARNER
Executive Life Coach
ProCoach, Inc.
6405 Chevy Chase
Dallas, TX 75225 United States
windy@coachwindy.com
http://www.coachwindy.com

BUS: Consulting Company **P/S:** Executive Coaching for Technology Professionals and Attorneys to Increase Career Success, Eliminate Burn-Out, Rediscover Passions and Build and Sustain Thriving Businesses **MA:** National **D/D/R:** Offering Services for Small Business Growth, Specializing in Business Vision, Property Management, Interpersonal Communication, Behavioral Styles, Work and Life Balance, Traveling to Seminars to Conduct Presentations **H/I/S:** Skiing, Hiking, Traveling, Watching Movies **FBP:** Fast Company; Inc.; Time **EDU:** Graduate, Coach University (2001); Bachelor's Degree in Mathematics, University of California at Berkeley (1972) **A/A/S:** Leadership Texas Alumni; International Coach Federation; Alumni Group, University of California, Berkeley

DONNA E. WARREN, MS
Teacher
Mainland Preparatory Academy
319 Newman Road
La Marque, TX 77568 United States
dwarren@mainlandprep.org
http://www.mainlandprep.org

BUS: Community-Based Facility **P/S:** Innovative Curriculum for Children from Prekindergarten through Eighth Grade that is Designed to Meet Children and Adolescents' Individual Needs through a Structured Program **MA:** Regional **D/D/R:** Specializing in Elementary Education, Teaching Language Arts and Spelling to Fourth and Fifth-Graders, Teaching the Eighth-Grade Research and Paper Writing Class, Running a Math Camp for Exceptional Children and the Eighth Grade Honor Society, Tutoring after School and in the Summer **H/I/S:** Gardening, Reading, Writing Poems, Exercising **FBP:** Education Today **EDU:** Master's Degree in Elementary Education with Early Childhood Specialization, Texas Southern University (1982); Bachelor's Degree in Elementary Education, Northeast Louisiana University (Now University of Louisiana at Monroe) (1970) **CERTS:** Certified Kindergarten Teacher **A/A/S:** McKinley United Methodist Church; Qualified Daycare Director

MR. MICHAEL J. WARREN, RN, CCRN
Registered Nurse, Critical-Care Registered Nurse, Shift Manager
Doctors Medical Center
1441 Florida Avenue
Modesto, CA 95350 United States
michael1.warren@tenethealth.com
http://www.dmc-modesto.com/CWSContent/dmc-modesto

BUS: Hospital **P/S:** Healthcare, Surgical Intensive Care **MA:** Regional **D/D/R:** Critical-Care Nursing **H/I/S:** Traveling, Snow Skiing **FBP:** Critical Care Nurse **EDU:** Pursuing Bachelor's Degree in Nursing, California State University at Dominguez Hills; Associate Degree in Nursing, Brookdale Community College **CERTS:** Certified Critical Care Registered Nurse **A/A/S:** American Association of Critical Care Nurses

CHERYL A. WARRICK
Senior Engineer
Lockheed Martin
199 Bortons Landing Road
Moorestown, NJ 08057 United States
cheryl.a.warrick@lmco.com
http://www.lockheedmartin.com

BUS: Advanced Technology Company **P/S:** Research, Design, Development, Manufacture and Integration of Advanced Technology Systems, Products and Services, Organized Around Core Business Areas, Aeronautics, Electronic Systems, Information and Technology Services, Integrated Systems and Solutions, Space Systems **MA:** International **D/D/R:** Facilitating Government Contracting, Specializing as a Thermal Analyst and Project Leader **H/I/S:** Hiking, Reading **FBP:** American Society of Mechanical Engineers Publications **EDU:** Bachelor's Degree in Mechanical Engineering, Drexel University (1990) **A/A/S:** Society of Women Engineers

MR. WILLIAM B. WASHBURN
Supervisor of Engineering Support
Union Switch and Signal, Inc.
645 Russell Street
Batesburg, SC 29006 United States
wbwashburn@switch.com
http://www.switch.com

BUS: Leader in the Design, Manufacture and Service of Signaling, Automation and Control Equipment Systems for the Railroad and Mass Transit Industries **P/S:** Wide Range of Components for the Railroad and Rail Transit Markets, Wayside Control Products, Range of Carborne Products, Wayside and Carborne Technology **MA:** International **D/D/R:** Liasing for Manufacturing and Engineering, Signaling on Railways, Training and Orienting New Employees, Overseeing of a Staff of 15 **H/I/S:** Music, Golfing **FBP:** BusinessWeek; Business 2.0 **EDU:** Pursuing Master's Degree; Bachelor's Degree in Business Administration, Southern Wesleyan University **A/A/S:** Association of American Railroads; Federal Railroad Administration

CAROLYN L. WASHINGTON
Registered Nurse, BSN, Geriatric Case Manager
Home Stretch
1231 Vuelta Olivos
Suite 4
Fremont, CA 94539 United States
wcarolyn16@yahoo.com
http://www.cambridgewhoswho.com

BUS: Home Health Case Management Firm **P/S:** Home Healthcare Including Post-Operative Care, Post Hospital Care and Monitoring **MA:** Regional **D/D/R:** Overseeing the Care of Geriatric Patients, Advocating for Seniors, Acting as a Liaison between Patients and Doctors **H/I/S:** Writing, Sea Kayaking, Practicing Yoga, Playing the Guitar and Percussion Instruments, Studying Politics and History, Spending Time with her Two Dachshunds **EDU:** Nursing/MD Residency in Virology, HIV/AIDS, University of California, San Francisco (1996); Bachelor of Science in Nursing, San Francisco State University (1988); Associate of Arts in Licensed Psychiatric Technician Studies, Mission College (1985) **CERTS:** Registered Nurse, State of California; Public Health Nurse, State of California; Staff IV Certification, Stanford University Medical Center **A/A/S:** California Nurses Association; Emily's List; Democratic Party **A/H:** Nominee, Art of Caring Award, Stanford University Medical Center **C/VW:** Various Local Charitable Organizations **DOB:** November 8, 1951 **POB:** South Charleston, WV **C/A:** Published Article, Nurse's Voice, Fourth Quarter Edition (2008); Published Article, NurseWeek (2008) **A/S:** She attributes her success to the support she receives from her co-workers and the satisfaction she gets from helping people who are ill. **B/I:** She became involved in her profession because she comes from a family of nurses.

DR. RALEIGH B. WASHINGTON
President
The Road to Jerusalem
1530 Josephine Street
Denver, CO 80206 United States
raleighw@roadtojerusalem.org
http://www.roadtojerusalem.org

BUS: Religious Organization **P/S:** Spiritual Service, Encourage Gentile Believers in Jesus Christ to Embrace the Messianic Jewish Community **MA:** International **D/D/R:** Preaching, Managing Religious Conferences, Coordinating Tours to Israel and Teaching Seminars to Leaders **H/I/S:** Golfing **FBP:** Charisma Network; Christianity Today; Across The Nation **EDU:** Four Honorary Doctoral Degrees; Master's Degree in Divinity, Trinity International University (1983) **A/A/S:** Board of Trustees, Azusa Pacific University **C/VW:** Toastmasters International

K. MARTIN WATERS JR.
Chairman
Waters Incorporated
301 S. McDowell Street, Suite 210
Charlotte, NC 28204 United States
waters30@watersincorporated.com
http://www.watersincorporated.com

BUS: Real Estate and Property Management Company **P/S:** Real Estate Exchange Including Brokerage and Management of Commercial Real Estate **MA:** North and South Carolina **EXP:** Mr. Waters' expertise is in operations and insurance management and investments. **D/D/R:** Selling Commercial Real Estate Property, Maintaining Client Relationships **H/I/S:** Golfing **FBP:** Forbes; Fortune **EDU:** Bachelor of Science in Physics and Business, Davidson College (1948) **CERTS:** Certified Commercial Investment Member **A/A/S:** Charlotte Region Commercial Board of Realtors; North Carolina Association of Realtors; Accredited Management Organization; Former Director, Mutual Savings and Loan Association; Phi Beta Kappa; National Association of Realtors; Former Director, Charlotte Board, First Union National Bank **C/VW:** Presbyterian Church; New Church Development Commission, Presbytery; Director, Sharon Towers Retirement Center; Former Director, Shepherd Center; Former Director, Nalle Clinic; Former President, Charlotte Rotary Club **POB:** Charlotte, NC **SP:** Dorothy **CHILD:** Robin

MR. MATTHEW W. WATKINS
Managed Services Coordinator
Agil IT
66 Industry Court, Suite C
Troy, OH 45373 United States
matthew-watkins@woh.rr.com
http://www.cambridgewhoswho.com

BUS: Information Technology Company **P/S:** Managed Services Using N-Able Platform, Microsoft Products, Cisco Products, 3COM Products **MA:** International **EXP:** Mr. Watkins' expertise is in information technology systems design and administration. **D/D/R:** Engineering and Implementing Comprehensive Monitoring Systems, Managing and Maintaining Business Systems across All Business Demographics, Responding to Failures in a Timely Manner, Ensuring Highest Degree of Availability to the Clients, Utilizing Microsoft Products Including Windows Server, Structured Query Language and Exchange **H/I/S:** Attending the Theater, Watching Opera Shows and Broadway Movies, Hunting, Boating, Reading, Interacting with People **EDU:** Associate Degree in Telecommunications, Hocking College (1991); Associate Degree in Broadcasting, Hocking College (1991) **CERTS:** Certification, Hewlett Packard; Certification, IBM; National Certified First Responder **A/A/S:** Leadership Troy (2004); Republican Party; President, Student Senate, Hocking College (1990); Fundraising Chairman, Student Senate, Hocking College (1989) **C/VW:** Parade Chairman, Troy Strawberry Festival; First Lutheran Church **DOB:** November 4, 1969 **POB:** Troy, OH **SP:** Lynn **CHILD:** Jaclyn, Colleen, Connor, Ronan **W/H:** Manager, District Manager, Pocket Change; Manager, OSI Systems; Engineer, Ford Motor Company; Network Administrator, Information Technology Director, Panasonic **A/S:** He attributes his success to his tenacity, honesty and his love for his profession. **B/I:** He became involved in his profession because of his interest in the technology-driven objects and computers. **H/O:** The highlight of his career was working as a network administrator at Panasonic in Troy. **I/F/Y:** In five years, Mr. Watkins aspires to continue in the information technology filed and become the head of the department of engineers.

JANET A. WATSON, RN
Clinical Manager
At Your Service Home Care
4701 N. Keystone Avenue, Suite 400
Indianapolis, IN 46205 United States
jwatson@vnsi.org
http://www.cambridgewhoswho.com

BUS: Leader in Home Care Services **P/S:** In-Home Skilled Nursing and Personal Care, Tender Care, Home Matters and Emotional Support to the Patient in the Comfort of their Own Home **MA:** Regional **D/D/R:** Geriatrics, Responsible for the Staff and well Being of the Patients, Preceptor for Student Nurses, Overseeing Admissions and Staff Members, Ensuring Proper Patient Care, Precepting Student Nurses, Conducting At-Home Assessments **H/I/S:** History, Reading **FBP:** American Journal of Nursing **EDU:** Registered Nurse Diploma, St. Elizabeth School of Nursing (1973) **A/A/S:** National Geographic Society

BARBARA WATSON-CLARK
Business Manager
Park Place Surgery Center
2450 Maitland Center Parkway
Maitland, FL 32751 United States
b.clark@earthlink.net
http://www.cambridgewhoswho.com

BUS: Outpatient Surgery Center **P/S:** Medical Care **MA:** Local **D/D/R:** Managing the Business, Overseeing Scheduling, Human Resources, Accounts Payable and Receivable and 15 Employees **H/I/S:** Writing Poetry, Writing a Novel **CERTS:** Licensed Practical Nurse **C/VW:** Veterans' Associations; Homeless Shelters; Make-A-Wish Foundation **A/S:** She attributes her career success to her ability to balance her work and personal life. **B/I:** She became involved in medical management after she began working for an orthopedic office. **H/O:** The most gratifying aspect of her career is receiving positive feedback from her clients.

ANGELA E. WATTS, CRRN, RN
Certified Rehabilitation Registered Nurse
Centura Health Saint Anthony Central Hospital
4231 W. 16th Avenue
Denver, CO 80204 United States
http://www.cambridgewhoswho.com

BUS: Hospital **P/S:** Level I Trauma Center, Direct Patient Care, 389 Beds **MA:** Regional **D/D/R:** Offering Restorative Medicine **H/I/S:** Hiking, Health and Wellness Exercising **FBP:** Nursing2009 **EDU:** Associate Degree in Nursing, Community College of Denver **CERTS:** Certification in Rehabilitation Nursing **A/A/S:** American Nursing Association; American Rehabilitation Association **A/H:** Nurse of the Year, Rehabilitation Unit, Centura Health (2003) **A/S:** She attributes her success to her continued education and passion for her profession. **B/I:** She became involved in this profession because she always wanted to become a nurse. **H/O:** The highlight of her career was being selected as Nurse of the Year in 2003.

JENNIFER WEATHERSBEE
Dental Hygienist
Augusta Dental Associates
1218 Augusta W. Parkway
Augusta, GA 30909 United States
jennyjay459@yahoo.com
http://www.cambridgewhoswho.com

BUS: Dental Office **P/S:** General Dentistry **MA:** Local **D/D/R:** Ensuring Proper Dental Hygiene **H/I/S:** Attending Church, Spending Time with Family and Friends, Traveling **EDU:** Bachelor of Science in Dental Hygiene, Medical College of Georgia (2004); Associate of Science in General Studies, Georgia Military College (2002) **A/S:** She attributes her success to her parents, her graduation from college and her drive and determination. **B/I:** She became involved in her profession because she grew very fond of her dentist and wanted to follow in his footsteps. **H/O:** The most gratifying aspect of her career is her current position, helping her patients maintain good dental hygiene.

BRENDA B. WEAVER
Teacher (Retired)
Washington Middle School
1277 Martin Luther King Jr. Public Middle School
Cairo, GA 39828 United States
weav9569@alltel.net
http://www.cambridgewhoswho.com

BUS: Public Middle School **P/S:** Educational Services **MA:** Local **D/D/R:** Teaching Science to Sixth through Eighth-Grade Students **H/I/S:** Making Arts and Crafts, Fishing **FBP:** AARP; Art Magazines **EDU:** Master's Degree in Education, Valdosta State University; Bachelor's Degree in Secondary Education, Florida State University **A/A/S:** National Education Association; Georgia Association of Educators **C/VW:** Relay for Life; American Heart Association

BUS: Retail **P/S:** Unusual Gift Shop **MA:** Local **D/D/R:** Selling Unusual Gifts **H/I/S:** Music, Art, Reading, Antiques **FBP:** Cooks **A/A/S:** Historical Guild of Early American Decorators **C/VW:** Wild Flower Society; Animal Rescue League; Audubon Society **A/S:** She attributes her success to her humility and working with others as equals. **B/I:** She became involved in this profession because she has always been interested in retail.

BUS: Church **P/S:** Religious Services **MA:** Local **D/D/R:** Helping People **H/I/S:** Reading, Spending Time with the Grandkids **FBP:** Religious Publications **EDU:** Bachelor's Degree, Little Rock Campus, Park University **A/A/S:** Rotary Club

HERBERT J. WEBER III
Manager (Retired)
Strategic Planning, Facility Management Division
Ford Motor Company
7704 Glenfield Drive
Monroe, MI 48161 United States
hweber52@hotmail.com
http://www.cambridgewhoswho.com

BUS: Manufacturing Company **P/S:** Automotive Products **MA:** International **D/D/R:** Supervising Staff, Overseeing United Auto Workers Skilled Trades, Project and Property Management **H/I/S:** Networking, Golfing **EDU:** Master of Business Administration, Baker College (2005); Bachelor of Business Administration, Baker College (2001); Associate of Science in Mathematics, Monroe County Community College (1994) **A/A/S:** Society of Automotive Engineers; American Welding Society **C/VW:** Diabetes Research Foundation; Multiple Sclerosis Society; United Way of America **A/S:** He attributes his success to his education and his ability to face challenges. **B/I:** He became involved in his profession because he started his career in the construction field and wanted a more stable career. **H/O:** The highlight of his career was obtaining an opportunity to work as a team player with different people.

SHARON D. WEBER
Realtor
Best Realty Inc, GMAC
1925 Central Avenue
Billings, MT 59102 United States
weber6776@bresnan.net
http://www.cambridgewhoswho.com

BUS: Real Estate **P/S:** Real Estate **MA:** Local **D/D/R:** Working with First-Time Homebuyers **H/I/S:** Entertaining and Spending Time with her Pets **EDU:** Industry Related Training and Experience **A/A/S:** Montana Association of Realtors; National Association of Realtors **C/VW:** American Red Cross; American Cancer Society **A/S:** She attributes her success to exceptional customer service. **B/I:** She chose the profession because her husband was in construction and she was involved with new homes. **H/O:** The highlight of her career is great customer satisfaction.

MR. SCOTT A. WEEDEN
Owner
Weeden Consultants, Inc.
522 S. Hunt Club Boulevard
Suite 225
Apopka, FL 32703 United States
sweeden@weeden-consultants.com
http://www.weeden-consultants.com

BUS: Freight and Distribution Company **P/S:** Time Sensitive and Specific Freight, AT&T and Select Costco Products Road Show Distribution, Insurance for High Value Freight, Logistics, Warehousing **MA:** International **D/D/R:** Operating Transportation and Logistics, Managing and Handling Multiple Distributions for Major Organizations and Companies Including Tat, Costco and Blue Cross and Blue Shield, Making Time Specific Deliveries **H/I/S:** Playing Basketball **FBP:** Entrepreneur **EDU:** Bachelor of Science in Business Management, Saint Peter's College, NJ (1993) **A/A/S:** West Essex Diamond Club, NJ; Speaker, Salem Middle School Career Days, Lithonia, GA; Florida Diversity Council; National Minority Council; FC Barcelona **C/VW:** Apopka Little League; Habitat for Humanity, Orlando, FL

JaLyn Weeks
Owner and Head Teacher
ABC/123 Preschool
165 N. 100 W.
Malad, ID 83252 United States
jweeks83@yahoo.com
http://www.cambridgewhoswho.com

BUS: Early Childhood Education **P/S:** Pre-School Servicing Forty-Plus Children **MA:** Local **D/D/R:** Specializing in Early Childhood Education and Development and Reading **H/I/S:** Spending Time Outdoors **FBP:** Family Fun **EDU:** Bachelor of Arts Degree in Elementary Education and Early Childhood Education and Development, Idaho State University **C/VW:** Various Charitable Organizations; Oneida Youth Council **A/S:** She attributes her career success to particular programs and networking that allow her to reach each individual child's needs, while fully equipping them with the necessary knowledge to succeed in kindergarten. **B/I:** She has always had a love for children, and she has always wanted to make a difference in children's lives. **H/O:** She feels that the knowledge that her students are prepared for what lies ahead of them in kindergarten is the highlight of her career.

BARBARA WEIDENBACH
Chief Executive Officer, President
Glo Bees, LLC
38242 La Loma Avenue
Palmdale, CA 93551 United States
globees@globeesllc.net
http://www.globeesllc.net

BUS: Window Covering Manufacturer and Distributor **P/S:** Glow in the Dark Window Treatments, Window Coverings, Commercial, Signage, RV, Marina, Printed Blinds and Shades **MA:** International **D/D/R:** Fabricating and Manufacturing Window Treatments, Coverings and Components, Inventing, Managing and Designing Intellectual Property, Supervising Daily Operations **A/H:** International Invention Award (2004) **I/F/Y:** In five years, Ms. Weidenbach hopes to be the Oprah Winfrey of window coverings.

ELLEN K. WEILER, MA
Speech-Language Pathologist
Kansas Rehabilitation Hospital
1504 S.W. Eighth Avenue
Topeka, KS 66606 United States
ekweiler@yahoo.com
http://www.cambridgewhoswho.com

BUS: Hospital **P/S:** Hospital, Healthcare **MA:** Local **D/D/R:** Working with Patients with Swallowing Disorders, Neurological Disorders and Diseases, Rehabilitating Patients **H/I/S:** Spending Time with the Family **EDU:** Master's Degree in Speech-Language Pathology, Wichita State University **A/A/S:** American Speech-Language-Hearing Association; Kansas Speech-Language-Hearing Association **C/VW:** Lutheran Church **A/S:** She attributes her success to the support of her family. **B/I:** She became involved in her profession because she became interested in helping others with speech problems after working in a daycare with someone who had speech problems. **H/O:** The highlight of her career has been staying current in her field and watching her patients make progress.

CYNTHIA M. WEIMER
Director of Laboratory Services
Havasu Regional Medical Center
101 Civic Center Lane
Lake Havasu City, AZ 86403 United States
cweimer@npgcable.com
http://www.havasuregional.com

BUS: Dynamically Expanding Hospital with 138 Beds, Offering a Wide Variety of Services and Specialized Treatment Options **P/S:** Diagnostic Imaging, Oncology, Surgical Services, Twenty-Four Hour Emergency Care, Labor and Delivery, Trauma and Critical Care **MA:** Local **D/D/R:** Ensuring Compliance with Laboratory Medical Technology, Overseeing 30 Personnel, Managing Finances of the Laboratory **H/I/S:** Playing Video Games, Playing the Guitar **FBP:** ASCP Publications; MNO Publications **EDU:** Pursuing Master's Degree, University of Phoenix (2007); Bachelor's Degree in Medical Technology, Ball State University (1979) **A/A/S:** American Society of Clinical Pathologists; American Society for Microbiology; Clinical Laboratory Management Association; American Society for Clinical Laboratory Science

MRS. DVORA L. WEINRAUB, MS, OTR/L
Senior Occupational Therapist
New York City Department of Education
1131 Beach 12th Street
Far Rockaway, NY 11691 United States
dvl36@aol.com
http://www.cambridgewhoswho.com

BUS: Department of Education **P/S:** Education **MA:** Local **EXP:** Mrs. Weinraub's expertise is in occupational therapy services for children with various disabilities including cerebral palsy, mental retardation, down syndrome, attention deficit and hyperactivity disorders, autism, prematurity, microcepherly and PDD. **D/D/R:** Working with Children in Home, School and Community Settings on a One-On-One Basis, Consulting with Other Disciplines **H/I/S:** Bike Riding, Swimming, Traveling, Running, Baking, Spending Time with Family and Friends **FBP:** SI Focus **EDU:** Master of Science in Occupational Therapy, Touro College; Bachelor's Degree in Health Science, Touro College **CERTS:** Certified FIPT **A/A/S:** The Feingold Association; New York State Occupational Therapy Association; American Occupational Therapy Association; International Association of Yoga Therapists; International Association of Yoga Therapists; World Federation of Occupational Therapy **A/H:** Highest Clinical Achievement Award; Highest Academic Achievement Award; Occupational Therapy Program Scholarship Award **A/S:** She attributes her success to her motivation and desire to help children to succeed. **B/I:** She became involved in her profession because her younger sibling was affected with infantile stroke and she wanted to help others suffering with the same. **H/O:** The most gratifying aspect of her career is watching her students succeed.

BRENDA L. WEISS
Owner
Weiss Design Group, Inc.
7935 N.W. 110th Drive
Park Land, FL 33076 United States
weissdesg@aol.com
http://www.weissdesigngroup.net

BUS: Interior Design Firm **P/S:** Commercial, Residential, Healthcare and Hospitality Interior Design Services **MA:** National **D/D/R:** Designing Healing Environments for Hospitals, Assisted Living Facilities, Psychiatric Units, Medical Spas, Commercial and Residential Properties, Specializing in Color Selection **H/I/S:** Watercoloring **FBP:** Florida Decor; Florida Design Magazine; Parkland Life; South Florida Hospital News **EDU:** Bachelor's Degree in Education and Psychology, University of Pennsylvania (1993); Bachelor's Degree in Interior Design, Florida International University (1992); Master of Science in Counseling, Boston University (1975) **CERTS:** Certification in Healthcare Design, Harvard University Graduate School of Design **A/A/S:** American Society of Interior Designers; Environmental Design Research Association; International Association of Color Consultants **C/VW:** Various Charitable Organizations **SP:** Michael **CHILD:** Seth, Eric, Austin, Rachelle

DORIS A. WELBORN
Diabetes Coordinator
Chatham Hospital
PO Box 649
Siler City, NC 27344 United States
dwelborn@chathamhospital.org
http://www.cambridgewhoswho.com

BUS: Hospital **P/S:** Healthcare **MA:** Local **D/D/R:** Certified Diabetes Educator, Certified Insulin Pump Trainer, Diets **H/I/S:** Reading, Spending Time with the Family, Riding a Goldwing Motorcycle with her Husband, Snow Skiing, Swimming, Camping, Traveling **FBP:** Diabetes Educator **EDU:** Master's Degree in Nutrition, University of North Carolina; Bachelor's Degree in Nutrition, University of North Carolina **CERTS:** Registered Dietician; Certified Diabetes Educator; Certified Insulin Pump Trainer **A/A/S:** American Dietetic Association; American Association of Diabetic Educators **C/VW:** Youth Sponsor, Church; American Cancer Society; Relay for Life; People to People International Program **A/S:** She attributes her personal and professional success to God and her continued growth. **B/I:** She became involved in the profession because she has many family members who are diabetic. **H/O:** The highlight of her career was being named Nutritional Delegate for the People to People Committee in November 2005.

GLORIA A. WELCH
Realtor
Real Estate III
1045 Carrington Place
Charlottesville, VA 22901 United States
gloriawelch@realestateiii.com
http://www.cambridgewhoswho.com

BUS: Real Estate **P/S:** Real Estate **MA:** Local **D/D/R:** Selling Real Estate, Managing Listings **H/I/S:** Dancing **EDU:** Industry-Related Training and Experience **A/A/S:** National Association of Realtors; Diamond Club **C/VW:** Various Worthy Community Causes **A/S:** She attributes her success to doing the best job possible and staying in contact with her clients. **B/I:** After taking some real estate courses with her daughters, she found she liked the field and decided to pursue her current career. **H/O:** The most gratifying aspect of her career is meeting new people and making connections with them.

VICTORIA WELLINGTON, MA, RN
Executive Director
Primetime Health Associates, Ltd.
PO Box 283
Granville, OH 43023 United States
vickey_wellington@windstar.net
roynvic@alltel.net
http://www.americannurses.com

BUS: Health Education Facility **P/S:** Continuing Education for Nurses and Social Workers **MA:** National **D/D/R:** Practicing as a Registered Nurse **H/I/S:** Sailing, Gardening, Playing Bridge **FBP:** American Journal of Nursing **EDU:** Bachelor's Degree in Nursing, Michigan State University (1956); Master's Degree in Management and Supervision, Central Michigan University **A/A/S:** Nursing Instructor, Central Ohio Technical College (2003); American Nurses Association; Ohio Nurses Association; Knox Licking District Nurses Association; Department of Homeland Security **A/H:** Heart of Nursing Award, KLDNA (1996)

MS. CAROL A. WELLS, M.A.ED.
Program Manager
Chapman University
1 University Drive
Orange, CA 92866 United States
cwells@chapman.edu
http://www.chapman.edu

BUS: University **P/S:** Higher Education **MA:** National **EXP:** Ms. Wells' expertise includes sales and marketing. **D/D/R:** Recruiting, Managing Programs, Hiring and Managing Adjunct Professors, Developing Schedules, Advising Students, Participating in Community and Business Outreach Programs **H/I/S:** Traveling, Swimming, Reading, Sewing, Knitting, Scrapbooking, Crafting Jewelry, Spending Time with her Family and Friends, Photography **FBP:** The Chronicle of Higher Education **EDU:** Master of Arts in Education, Concentration in Institutional Technology, Chapman University; Bachelor of Arts in Social Science, Chapman University **CERTS:** Pursuing Certification in Gerontology **A/H:** 15 Year Achievement Award, Security Pacific Bank; 15 Year Achievement Award, Chapman University; Award for Amateur Photography **C/VW:** Sponsor, Coordinator, American Red Cross; Victorville First Assembly of God Church; High Desert Resource Network; Developer, Rebecca Britt Foundation **DOB:** August 14, 1948 **POB:** Mt. Cisco, NY **SP:** Robert **CHILD:** Brian, Shelley **W/H:** Program Manager, Counselor, Chapman University (1993-Present); Administrative Assistant to the Principal, First Assembly of God Church dba Victor Valley Christian School (1983-1993); New Accounts Representative, Security Pacific Bank (1968-1983) **A/S:** She attributes her success to her experience in marketing, growth and retention, loyalty, integrity, honesty and customer service skills. **B/I:** She became involved in her profession through a natural progression of opportunities. **H/O:** The most gratifying aspect of her career is using her university position and home-based business to teach clients and students how to become successful. **I/F/Y:** In five years, Ms. Wells intends to work part-time at her home-based business, travel and spend time with her family and friends.

THEDA BARA E. WELLS
Supervisor, Credential Secretary and Historian
Department of Women
Church of God in Christ
8465 Sherman Oaks Drive
Germantown, TN 38139 United States
wicmemcogic@aim.com
http://www.cogic.org

BUS: Proven Leader in the Religion and Spiritual Services Industry **P/S:** High Quality Spiritual Services to Members of the Church, Religious Instruction and Charitable Outreach **MA:** Regional **D/D/R:** Completing Historical Research on Women Nationally in the Church of God in Christ, Working as the Licensing and Certification Clerk for Women Appointees **H/I/S:** Writing, Knitting, Crocheting **FBP:** Ebony; Reader's Digest **EDU:** Bachelor's Degree in Bible Philosophy, American Bible Institute, Kansas City, Missouri (1979); Diploma, Christian Writing Institute, Wheaton, Illinois **CERTS:** Certificate, 20th Century Bible Course, Portland, Oregon **A/A/S:** Secretary, Parent-Teacher Association; International Women Examination Board **A/H:** First Prize, 'Letter to Young Americans', Tennessee's Nationwide Poetry Contest, USPS; Germantown, Tennessee Theda B. Wells Day (August 27, 1997) **DOB:** March 18, 1919 **SP:** Booker **CHILD:** Booker, Vanessa, Davene

KAREN M. WENDLING, DM
Dietary Manager
Greenewood Manor Nursing Home
711 Dayton-Xenia Road
Xenia, OH 45385 United States
http://www.cambridgewhoswho.com

BUS: Nursing Home **P/S:** Long-Term Care **MA:** Local **D/D/R:** Specializing in Food Services **H/I/S:** Playing Computer Games **FBP:** Restaurant and Institutions Magazine **CERTS:** Certified Dietary Manager, Sinclair College **A/S:** She attributes her success to perseverance. **H/O:** The highlight of her career is holding her current position and having made all the upgrades in the kitchen.

MR. CLIFFORD H. WERNER
Special Education Teacher
Norwood Elementary School
Miami-Dade County Public Schools
19810 N.W. 14th Court
Miami, FL 33169 United States
buzzwerner@hotmail.com
http://www.dadeschools.net

BUS: School District **P/S:** Education **MA:** Regional **D/D/R:** Working with Profoundly Mentally and Physically Handicapped Children, Managing Individualized Education Plans for a Class of Six Students, Incorporating a Physical Therapy-Based Curriculum with Adaptive Equipment to Support the Student's Weight **H/I/S:** Riding Motorcycle **FBP:** NEA Newsletter **EDU:** Master of Science in Exceptional Student Education, Barry University (1994) **A/A/S:** Council for Exceptional Children; United Teachers of Dade; National Education Association

BETH ANN WESEL
Teacher Consultant
Edwardsburg Public Schools
69410 Section Street
Edwardsburg, MI 49112 United States
bwesel@remc11.k12.mi.us
http://www.cambridgewhoswho.com

BUS: Public School (K-7) **P/S:** Regular and Special Education for Kindergarten through 7th Grade Students; DDR: Scheduling and Facilitating Teacher Assistance Team Meetings,Completing Academic Evaluations, Developing Behavior Intervention Plans **MA:** Local **D/D/R:** Special Education **H/I/S:** Gardening, Pets, Crafts **FBP:** Exceptional Children **EDU:** Master's Degree in Learning Disabilities, Indiana University; Bachelor of Science, Western Michigan University, Coursework in Emotionally Impaired K-12 and Elementary Education, Mathematics K-9 **A/A/S:** Indiana University of Excellence in Graduate Education for Special Education **C/VW:** American Cancer Society **A/S:** She attributes her success to her patience. **B/I:** She became involved in her profession because she has always enjoyed working with children. **H/O:** The highlight of her career is when her students are successful.

ANNETTE M. WEST, PH.D.
Chief Executive Officer
West Business and Computer Solutions
1180 Briarbend Drive
Sumter, SC 29154 United States
wbcs@sc.rr.com
http://www.wbcs2k.com

BUS: Consulting Company **P/S:** Business Management Solutions, Human Resources Training and Development, Office Start-Up and Development Solutions, Consulting Services **MA:** Regional **D/D/R:** Conducting Seminars for New Companies, Offering Human Resource and Management Services, Training Courses and Computer Consultations **H/I/S:** Reading, Writing, Sewing, Riding Motorcycles **FBP:** SHRM Journal; Minority MBA Journal **EDU:** Ph.D. in Business Management, Argosy University (2005); Master's Degree in Management and Human Resources, Troy University (2001); Bachelor of Business Administration, Morris College (2000) **CERTS:** Ordained Minister (1998) **A/A/S:** Alumni Representative, Argosy University; Society for Human Resource Management; Minority MBA Association; Phi Beta Lambda; AACC **C/VW:** Living Word Outreach Ministry (2002); Volunteer, Nursing Home; Volunteer Chaplain, Local Prisons and Hospitals

GREGORY N. WEST, ESQ.
Associate Dean
Fire and EMS Training
Waukesha County Technical College
800 Main Street, Apartment S-232
Pewaukee, WI 53072 United States
gwest@wctc.edu
http://www.wctc.edu

BUS: College **P/S:** Higher Education **MA:** Regional **EXP:** Mr. West's areas of expertise include fire suppression and prevention, emergency medical services and higher education management. **D/D/R:** Hiring and Terminating Employees, Scheduling, Budgeting, Resolving Disputes **EDU:** JD, Concord University School of Law (2006); Bachelor of Science in Fire Science Management, Southern Illinois University (1998); Bachelor of Science in Industrial Engineering, Marquette University (1996) **CERTS:** Nationally Registered Emergency Medical Technician-Paramedic; Certified Emergency Medical Technician-Paramedic, Wisconsin Department of Health Services; Certified WTCSB Firefighter II; Certified WTCSB Driver/Operator-Pumper; Certified WTCSB Driver/Operator-Aerial; Certification in Federal Emergency Management Agency Courses I-700, 100, 200, 300 and 400 **A/A/S:** National Fire Protection Association; The International Association of Fire Chiefs; Wisconsin EMS Association; Wisconsin Society of Fire Service Instructors; International Association of Fire Service Instructors; National Association of EMS Educators; National Association of Fire Investigators; Wisconsin State Firefighters Association; National Council on Readiness and Preparedness; The State Bar of California; State Bar of Wisconsin; American Bar Association **C/VW:** Tess Corners Volunteer Fire Department **W/H:** Higher Education Administrator; Fire Serviceman

MS. LINDA W. WEST, ABR, CRS, GRI
Realtor, ABR, CRS, GRI
Old Dominion Realty, Inc.
2340 S. Main Street
Harrisonburg, VA 22801 United States
Homes@lindawest.net
http://www.lindawest.net

BUS: Real Estate Agency **P/S:** Full-Service Real Estate Sales **MA:** Regional **EXP:** Ms. West's expertise is in residential, land, commercial, new construction and consulting sales. **D/D/R:** Staying Abreast of the Real Estate Market, Making Appointments with Clients, Creating Marketing Campaigns for Clients, Showing Properties, Following up with Clients and Customers, Serving on Several Committees, Liaising between the Mortgage Industry, Attorneys and Settlement Firms to Strive for Worry-Free Transactions between All Parties Involved in Real Estate Transactions **H/I/S:** Raising Butterflies, Teaching, Spending Time with her Family, Hiking, Swimming, Golfing, Motorcycling **FBP:** Commonwealth; Realtor; Residential Specialist; Shenandoah Valley Guide; Virginia Living; Shenandoah Living; Discovery Magazine **CERTS:** Pursuing Broker Certification; Diploma in Secretarial Skills, Kings College **A/H:** Multi-Million Dollar Producer, Multiple Years, Harrisonburg-Rockingham Association of Realtors **C/VW:** Butterfly Week; American Lung Association; Box Lunch for Golf Tournament; Dayton Police Department; Hike for Special Olympics; American Cancer Society; March of Dimes; Relay for Life **W/H:** VIP Representative, Referrals and Relocations, Smart Moves **A/S:** She attributes her success to her ability to keep up with market trends and offer excellent customer service, strong marketing skills, technology savvy, good communication skills and dedication to everything she does. **B/I:** She became involved in her profession because she had been in real estate administration in the 1980s before she went into computer application training and was encouraged by her mother to get her license. **H/O:** The most gratifying aspect of her career is being the exclusive agent on a large development project of 143 new construction homes and duplexes.

WANDA M. WESTCOTT, RN, ASDN
Intravenous Immunoglobulin Nurse
Maxim Healthcare Services
1900 Powell Street, Suite 440
Emeryville, CA 94608 United States
wandawestcott@yahoo.com
http://www.maximhealthcare.com

BUS: Medical Staffing Company **P/S:** Medical and Clinical Staffing Including Nurse Employment, Homecare, Wellness Services, Preventative Health and Education, Immunizations, Vaccinations at Corporate Settings and Public Venues **MA:** National **EXP:** Ms. Westcott's expertise is in high tech infusion therapy, freelance nursing. **D/D/R:** Nursing Patients with Autoimmune, Coronary and Alzheimer's Disease **H/I/S:** Reading, Watching Movies, Skiing, Water Skiing, Traveling, Working on Computers **FBP:** Nursing2009; Budget Living **EDU:** Associate Degree in Nursing, Pacific Union College **CERTS:** Certified Critical Care Nurse **A/A/S:** American Association of Critical Care Nurses; American Heart Association **C/VW:** Local Church **A/S:** She attributes her success to her longevity, fortitude, work ethic and her ability to learn from her family members. **B/I:** She became involved in her profession because she was inspired by her father who was an educator in the medical field. **H/O:** The highlight of her career was working in cardiac rehabilitation for 10 years. **I/F/Y:** In five years, Ms. Westcott aspires to earn more certifications and undergo many trainings.

ELIZABETH D. WETHERHOLT, MA
Intervention Specialist
Karrer Middle School
Dublin City Schools
7245 Tullymore Drive
Dublin, OH 43016 United States
kwetherholt8277@wowway.com
http://www.dublin.k12.oh.us

BUS: School District **P/S:** Education **MA:** Local **D/D/R:** Teaching Learning Disabled Children in Kindergarten, Overseeing Intervention Services **H/I/S:** Indulging Politics, Reading, Singing with a Choral Group **EDU:** Master's Degree in Special Education; Bachelor's Degree in Music Education, Ohio State University **CERTS:** Certification in Learning Disabilities, Ohio State University; License in Elementary Education **A/A/S:** National Education Association; Ohio Education Association; Secretary, Dublin Educators' Association **C/VW:** Broad Street Presbyterian Church **POB:** Columbus, OH **SP:** Karl **CHILD:** Jane, David **A/S:** She attributes her success to her love for children and her education. **B/I:** She became involved in her profession because she wanted to help students with learning disabilities. **H/O:** The highlight of her career was watching the improvements in disabled students.

LYNDANNE M. WHALEN
Senior Counsel, Patents and Licensing
Bayer Material Science, LLC
100 Bayer Road
Pittsburgh, PA 15205 United States
whalenl1@lycos.com
http://www.cambridgewhoswho.com

BUS: Chemical Company **P/S:** Intellectual Property Law and Licensing **MA:** International **D/D/R:** Prosecuting Patent Applications, Licensing Agreements and Counseling **H/I/S:** Making Crafts, Singing **FBP:** American Bar Association Publications; Court Reports; The United States Patent Quarterly **EDU:** JD, Dickinson University School of Law **A/A/S:** American Intellectual Property Law Association; Pittsburgh Intellectual Property Law Association; American Bar Association **C/VW:** Choir, Saint Gregory Church **A/S:** She attributes her success to her sense of humor. **B/I:** She became involved in the profession because she loves chemistry but did not find laboratory work to her liking. **H/O:** The highlight of her career was earning her current position.

EDNA WHARTON, RN
Registered Nurse
Wingate at Beacon
10 Hastings Street
Beacon, NY 12508 United States
mayleenwharton@yahoo.com
http://www.cambridgewhoswho.com

BUS: Long Term Sub-Acute Facility **P/S:** Healthcare **MA:** Local **D/D/R:** General Nursing, Midwifery **H/I/S:** Studying the Bible, Walking, Gardening **FBP:** RN **EDU:** Pursuing Bachelor of Science in Nursing; Associate of Science in Nursing, Rush Green Hospital, England; Master's Degree in Nursing **CERTS:** Registered Midwife **C/VW:** Feed the Children; World Vision United States; Various Charitable Organizations **A/S:** She attributes her success to her love of caring for people. **B/I:** She became involved in nursing because she has always been interested in nursing and caring for people. **H/O:** The highlight of her career has been observing the needs of her patients and making recommendations to the doctors she works with.

BARBARA JANE WHEDBEE, RN
Registered Nurse
McDonough District Hospital
525 E. Grant Street
Macomb, IL 61455 United States
bjwhedbee@mdh.org
http://www.cambridgewhoswho.com

BUS: Hospital **P/S:** Healthcare Services **MA:** Regional **D/D/R:** Managing Emergency Services **H/I/S:** Gardening, Traveling **FBP:** Jems **EDU:** Associate Degree, Carl Sandburg College, Illinois **A/A/S:** Emergency Nurses Cancel Alcohol Related Emergencies; Emergency Community County Board; Local Emergency Planning Committee

MS. RHONDA R. WHEELER
Owner
Wheeler Investments
316 Mitzi Lane
Van Buren, AR 72956 United States
rwhee3248@aol.com
http://www.cambridgewhoswho.com

BUS: Real Estate Agency **P/S:** Commercial and Residential Property Sales **MA:** Southeastern United States **D/D/R:** Buying Real Estate, Leasing, Offering Individual Primary Care **H/I/S:** Four Wheeling, Horseback Riding, Reading Romantic Novels **FBP:** U.S. News & World Report **EDU:** Master of Science in Nursing, University of Arkansas **CERTS:** Licensed Nurse Practitioner

JEANETTE C. WHITACRE
Owner
Jett Mechanical, LLC
1535 W. Wetmore Road, Suite A
Tucson, AZ 85705 United States
jettmechanical_llc@hotmail.com
http://www.jettmechanicalonline.com

BUS: Southern Arizona's Comfort Specialists **P/S:** Residential and Commercial HVAC Service, Installations **MA:** Regional **D/D/R:** Handling All Administrative Responsibilities for the Company, Marketing and Advertising, Accounting, Recruiting, Working as an Escrow and Mortgage Loan Processor, Handling Customer Service Issues **H/I/S:** Photography, Personal Training, Art **EDU:** High School Education **A/A/S:** United States Chamber of Commerce; Better Business Bureau; Southern Arizona Home Building Association **SP:** Larry **CHILD:** Aaron, Amanda

PEGGY W. WHITAKER
Owner
Fre-Jan's
116 W. Main Street
Colquitt, GA 39837 United States
whitakerp@bellsouth.net
http://www.cambridgewhoswho.com

BUS: Ladies and Children's Apparel **P/S:** Ladies and Children's Apparel **MA:** Local **D/D/R:** Managing Business Operations **H/I/S:** Golfing, Fishing, Horseback Riding **EDU:** Associate Degree in Nutrition **C/VW:** American Cancer Society, Relay for Life; St. Jude Children's Research Hospital **A/S:** She attributes her success to her hard work and dedication.

GAIL L. WHITE
Fiscal Manager
Sacramento Employment and Training Agency
925 Del Paso Boulevard
Suite 100
Sacramento, CA 95815 United States
glwhite@delpaso.seta.net
http://www.seta.net

BUS: Powers Agency of the City and County of Sacramento **P/S:** Connecting People to Jobs, Business Owners to Quality Employees, Education and Nutrition to Children, Assistance to Refugees, and Hope to many Sacramento Area Residents **MA:** Regional **D/D/R:** Managing and Initiating the New Payroll System, Overseeing General and Annual Audits, Monitoring Accounts and Grants, Maintaining the General Ledger **H/I/S:** Swimming, Horseback Riding **EDU:** JD in Law, Golden Gate University, San Francisco (1978) **A/A/S:** Government Finance Officers Association; MENSA **C/VW:** Step Ministry

LEONA M. WHITE
Secretary
Second Baptist Church
319 W. Church Street
Bowling Green, MO 63334 United States
srbalw@sbcglobal.net
http://www.cambridgewhoswho.com

BUS: Church **P/S:** Religious Services **MA:** Local **D/D/R:** Writing Newsletters and Letters, Filing, Answering Phones, Creating Bulletins, Working on a Project Contributing to the Synopses of Portions of the Bible **H/I/S:** Reading, Sewing, Traveling **EDU:** Diploma, Bowling Green High School **C/VW:** Second Baptist Church **A/S:** She attributes her success to the encouragement and support she received from her boss and others around her. **B/I:** She became involved in the profession after being inspired by a neighbor who was a court secretary. **H/O:** The most gratifying aspects of her career are helping people feel good about themselves and assisting her boss in accomplishing various tasks.

MICHELE R. WHITE, MBA
Administrative Coordinator to Executive Pastor
Ginghamsburg United Methodist Church
6759 S. County Road 25A
Tipp City, OH 45371 United States
mwhite@ginghamsburg.org
http://www.ginghamsburg.org

BUS: Church **P/S:** Worship Services, Quarterly Class Guides for Adult Classes **MA:** Local **D/D/R:** Organizing Adult Discipleship and Service Events, Maintaining Contact with Teachers **H/I/S:** Working at an English Camp in the Czech Republic, Theater, Doing Aerobics **EDU:** Master of Business Arts, University of Phoenix **C/VW:** Darfur Sudan Project, World Vision **A/S:** She attributes her success to her organizational skills and her natural abilities within her field. **B/I:** She became involved in her profession after considering a career in healthcare. She was drawn, instead, to her current profession and excelled. **H/O:** The highlight of her career was when over 80 percent of the congregation attended a class.

NORMA LaNELL WHITE
Realtor
Coldwell Banker
504 Tower Drive
Moore, OK 73160 United States
lanellwhite@aol.com
http://www.cambridgewhoswho.com

BUS: Real Estate Agency **P/S:** Residential Real Estate Exchange **MA:** Oklahoma **D/D/R:** Buying and Selling Residential Real Estate Properties **H/I/S:** Walking, Reading, Spending Time with her Family, Listening to Music **FBP:** Realtor **EDU:** Master's Degree in Speech Communication, Southern Nazarene University **A/A/S:** Oklahoma City Metro Association of Realtors; National Association of Realtors **A/S:** She attributes her success to her self-motivation and to her organizational skills. **B/I:** She became involved in her profession because of her interest in working with the public and making more money by helping others find their perfect home. **H/O:** The most gratifying aspect of her career is helping first time home buyers find their right home.

ROBERT E. WHITE JR.
President
First Professionals Insurance Group, Inc.
1000 Riverside Avenue
Suite 800
Jacksonville, FL 32204 United States
white@fpic.com
http://www.fpic.com

BUS: Insurance Firm **P/S:** Professional Liability Insurance for Healthcare Providers **MA:** Regional **D/D/R:** Managing Operations and Administrative Duties **H/I/S:** Traveling, Playing Softball, Reading, Hiking, Biking **FBP:** Best's Review **EDU:** Bachelor of Arts in Business Administration, San Francisco State University, Magna Cum Laude (1974) **C/VW:** United Way of America **A/S:** He attributes his success to his work ethic. **H/O:** The highlight of his career was helping his company regain its 'A Best's Financial Strength Rating.'

WILLIE A. WHITE
Pastor
Zara Grove Church
1648 Highway 469 Simpson
Harrisville, MS 39082 United States

BUS: Church **P/S:** All-Inclusive Religious Services **MA:** Local **D/D/R:** Preaching, Teaching, Visiting the Sick and Inmates **H/I/S:** Spending Time with the Family, Traveling, Basketball, Reading, Singing **FBP:** The Good Stuff; Ministries Today **EDU:** Bachelor of Arts in Sociology, Jackson State University; Master of Divinity, New Orleans Theological Seminary; Doctor of Ministries, Andersonville Seminary **A/A/S:** UTS in Louisiana

THOMAS M. WHITELAW
Realtor
Exit Realty All Stars
3600 US Highway 27 N.
Sebring, FL 33870 United States
tmwhitelaw@comcast.net
http://www.cambridgewhoswho.com

BUS: Real Estate Company **P/S:** Real Estate Services Including Open Houses, Marketing and Listing for Residential Properties **MA:** Local **D/D/R:** Listing and Selling Homes, Specializing in Residential Real Estate, Selling Land and Single Family Homes, Offering Relocation Services, Utilizing her Expertise in 1031 Exchanges **H/I/S:** Fishing, Golfing **FBP:** Florida Realtor; Realtor **EDU:** Coursework in Art and Science, Indiana University; Coursework in Accounting **CERTS:** Real Estate License (2005) **A/A/S:** Greater Tampa Association of Realtors; Florida Association of Realtors; National Association of Realtors; Realtor.com

CONSTANCE D. WHITFIELD
Realtor, Broker Associate
Keller Williams Success Realty
2316 W. 23rd Street
Panama City, FL 32405 United States
connie@liveinpc.com
http://www.liveinpc.com

BUS: Real Estate Agency **P/S:** Residential and Commercial Real Estate Exchange Including Financial Services **MA:** Panhandle, Bay City, Washington, Gulf Countries, Panama City and Panama City Beach, FL **D/D/R:** Assisting Buyers and Sellers with Residential and Commercial Real Estate Transactions **H/I/S:** Reading Science Fiction, Writing, Listening to Music, Gardening, Creative Designing **FBP:** Realtor **EDU:** Master's Degree in Music Education and Clarinet Performance, Auburn University (1977); Bachelor's Degree in Music Education, Auburn University (1976); Postgraduate Coursework, Florida State University **CERTS:** Licensed Real Estate Broker, State of Florida; e-Pro Certification, National Association of Realtors **A/A/S:** Bay County Chamber of Commerce; Auburn Alumni Association; Fleet Reserve Association; Florida Association of Realtors; National Association of Realtors; Florida Home Builder's Association; Newsletter Chairman, Kappa Kappa Gamma **A/H:** Ruby Award for Sales Achievement, Century 21; Gold Club Award, Bay County Association of Realtors **W/H:** Officer, United States Navy **H/O:** The most gratifying aspect of her career is seeing her clients happy in their new homes. **I/F/Y:** In five years, Ms. Whitfield would like to expand her business and customer base.

CHERYL L. WHITMORE
Resource Specialist
Tempe Elementary District 3
3205 S. Rural Road
Tempe, AZ 85282 United States
cwhitmor@tempeschools.org
http://www.cambridgewhoswho.com

BUS: Elementary School District **P/S:** Education **MA:** Regional **D/D/R:** Working in All Aspects of Special Education **H/I/S:** Reading, Yardwork **EDU:** Master of Science in Curriculum, Emporia State University; Educational Specialist Degree in Leadership and Policy Studies, Arizona State University **C/VW:** United Way of America **A/S:** She attributes her career success to her desire to help children, and to improve the lives of those less fortunate. **B/I:** She began her career as a registered nurse, and transitioned her career into education so that she could help children. **H/O:** She feels that the return visits she receives from former students to thank her have been the highlight of her career.

MAUREEN WHITNEY, ABR, GRI
Senior Sales Vice President, ABR, GRI
Star One Realtors
9722 Montgomery Road
Cincinnati, OH 45242 United States
mkwhitney@fuse.net
http://www.starone.com

BUS: Proven Leader in the Real Estate Industry **P/S:** Quality Real Estate Services to Clients, Such as Designing Private Custom Homes, and Buying and Selling Homes **MA:** Regional **D/D/R:** Listing, Buying and Selling Residential Properties **H/I/S:** Horseback Riding, Swimming, Reading, Gardening **FBP:** Broker News **EDU:** Coursework, Wright State University (1982-1983); Coursework, University of Cincinnati (1975-1976) **CERTS:** Accredited Buyer Representative (2006); Graduate Realtor Institute (2003); Real Estate License (1989) **A/A/S:** National Association of Realtors; Cincinnati Area Board of Realtors; Ohio Association of Realtors

Laura Lee Whitten
Certified Vision Rehabilitation Therapist
Alabama Department of Rehabilitation Services
2419 Gordon Smith Drive
Mobile, AL 36617 United States
WBluredvision@aol.com
http://www.rehab.state.al.us

BUS: Rehabilitation of the Blind and Visually Impaired **P/S:** Educating the Blind and Visually Impaired in Independent Living Skills and Job Readiness Skills **MA:** Regional **D/D/R:** Visiting Visually Impaired Individuals in their Homes and Educating them on how to Become Independent, Developing Braille Reading and Writing Skills, Preparing Clients for the Work Place, Training Clients in Assistive Technology, Managing Clients in Four Counties Assessing Independent Living Skills, Evaluating for and Dispensing Low-Vision Devices, Evaluating the Work Place for Assistive Technology Requirements, Teaching Braille, Supervising Rehabilitation Interns and Human Service Aides **H/I/S:** Traveling, Horseback Riding, Bowling, Assisting with Beepball, Softball for the Blind **FBP:** Blind Rehabilitation News **EDU:** Master of Arts in Blind Rehabilitation Teaching for the Blind and Visually Impaired, Emphasis in Low Vision Therapy, Western Michigan University (1986); Bachelor of Science in Special Education for the Visually Impaired, Minors in Elementary Education and Creative Arts, Western Michigan University (1984) **A/A/S:** Alabama Rehabilitation Association; Former President, President Elect and Secretary, Division of Certified Vision Rehabilitation Therapists; Association for the Education and Rehabilitation of the Blind and Visually Impaired; Former Member, The Federation for the Blind and the American Council for the Blind; Former Secretary and Treasurer, Community Action for Student Handicappers (1983-1984); American Beep Ball Association (1982-1986); Women's International Bowling Congress (1982-1986) **A/H:** Rehabilitation Teacher of the Year Award (1995) **C/VW:** American Federation for the Blind (1982-1987); Blind Bowling League of Kalamazoo Michigan (1982-1986); Participant, Goal Ball for the Blind (1982-1986); Participant, Braille Literacy Empowerment Project, American Federation for the Blind **DOB:** February 6, 1961 **POB:** Tawas, MI **W/H:** Certified Vision Rehabilitation Therapist, Alabama Department of Rehabilitation Services, Mobile, Al (1987-Present); Ken-O-Sha Elementary School Teacher for the Blind and the Visually Impaired, Grand Rapids, MI (1984-1985); Counselor for Handicapped Adults, Combined Health Services, Marquette, MI (1985); Unit Leader, Michigan Metro Girl Scouts, Ortonville, MI (1983); Teacher and Teacher Assistant, Woodward Elementary School, Kalamazoo, MI (1983); Reading Clinic Tutor, Western Michigan University, Kalamazoo, MI (1982); Teacher and Teacher Assistant, Comstock Elementary Schools, Comstock, MI (1982); Rehabilitation Teacher Intern

Hazel May Whittick-White, RN
Representative, Registered Nurse (Retired)
N2K Trading Academy
16912 S.W. 119th Court
Miami, FL 33177 United States
maywhittick@aol.com
http://www.n2ktradingacademy.com

BUS: Investment Firm **P/S:** Financial Services Including Stock Options, Training, Education and Recruitment **MA:** National **D/D/R:** Training People in Stock Options, Offering Information on the Benefits of the Academy, Managing Training Classes and Updating Information **H/I/S:** Reading, Singing in Church Choir **FBP:** Nursing Spectrum **CERTS:** Registered Nurse, Earned in England (1967); Certification in Midwifery; Certificate in Public Health; Certification in Community Health Nursing **A/A/S:** Glendale Baptist Church; Local Charitable Organizations

PEGGY E. WICKER
Teacher
Riverdale Elementary School
Orange Unified School District
1401 N. Handy Street
Orange, CA 92867 United States
peggy.wicker@sbcglobal.net
http://www.cambridgewhoswho.com

BUS: Elementary School **P/S:** Primary Education **MA:** Local **D/D/R:** Teaching Elementary School, Mentoring Teachers in United States and World Geography **H/I/S:** Traveling, Taking Cruises, Reading, Playing Cards, Surfing the Internet **FBP:** NEA Today; AARP: The Magazine **EDU:** Master of Science in Education, California State University, Fullerton; Bachelor's Degree, Santa Clara University **CERTS:** Certified Teacher, San Jose State University **A/H:** The 'Who' Award for Helping Develop a Computerized Elementary Report Card, Orange Unified Education Association; Hats Off Master Teacher Award, Orange Unified School District; Teacher of the Year, Riverdale Elementary School **C/VW:** National Osteoporosis Foundation; American Cancer Society; American Lung Association; Juvenile Diabetes Research Foundation **A/S:** She attributes her success to always maintaining a positive attitude and working hard. **B/I:** She became involved in her profession because a friend suggested that she leave her job and pursue a career in education. **H/O:** The most gratifying aspect of her career is not only having her master's degree in education, but also mentoring other teachers.

LOIS M. WIDNER, RN
Registered Nurse
Mt. Graham Regional Medical Center
1600 S. 20th Avenue
Safford, AZ 85546 United States
lois.widner@cwwemail.com
http://www.cambridgewhoswho.com

BUS: Medical Center **P/S:** Healthcare **MA:** Local **EXP:** Ms. Widner expertise is in critical care nursing. **H/I/S:** Quilting, Crafting, Traveling, Participating in Church Activities **EDU:** Bachelor's Degree in Nursing, University of Phoenix; Associate Degree in Nursing Science, Lakeland Community College **A/A/S:** American Association of Critical Care Nurses **C/VW:** Local Teen Fair **B/I:** She became involved in her profession because of the personal experience she faced with her grandparents who were critically injured in a car accident, which influenced her to be in the healthcare field. **H/O:** The most gratifying aspect of her career is being respected within her community.

SANDRA WIECZOREK
Realtor
Prudential Connecticut Realty
441 N. Main Street
Southington, CT 06489 United States
swieczorek@prudential.com
http://www.cambridgewhoswho.com

BUS: Real Estate Company **P/S:** Condominium and Residential Real Estate Exchange **MA:** Greater Hartford, CT **D/D/R:** Meeting One-On-One with Clients, Answering Phone Calls, Answering E-Mails, Consulting and Lecturing Occasionally, Acting as a Guest Speaker for the Company, Acquiring more Repeat and Referral Business who are Looking to Move up or Find a Different Style, Buying and Selling Condominiums and Residential Properties, Helping Senior Citizens and First Time Home Buyers **H/I/S:** Spending Time with her Family, Cooking, Boating, Gardening, Reading **FBP:** Realtor **EDU:** Master of Science in Reading, Central Connecticut State University; Bachelor of Science in Elementary Education **A/A/S:** Connecticut Association of Realtors; National Association of Realtors; Mid-State Association of Realtors **A/H:** Mid-State Top Producer Award (2007) **C/VW:** Chairwoman, The Sunshine Kids **A/S:** She attributes her success to hard work and perseverance. **I/F/Y:** In five years, Ms. Wieczorek hopes to become a trainer for new real estate agents.

NORMA JEAN WIEDL, RN
Staff Nurse
Memorial Hospital of Salem County
310 Woodstown Road
Salem, NJ 08079 United States
silverfoxy34@verizon.net
http://www.mhschealth.com

BUS: Hospital **P/S:** Healthcare **MA:** Regional **D/D/R:** Nursing, Overseeing the Labor and Delivery Unit, Assisting Patients **H/I/S:** Golfing, Traveling **EDU:** Associate Degree in Nursing, Rowan University (1974) **CERTS:** Industry-Related Training, Citizens General Hospital (1955) **A/A/S:** Former Chairwoman, Septemberfest Committee **A/H:** Employee of the Year Award (1984)

CLINTON C. WIESE
Assistant Controller
New Country Auto Center
1200 Carbon Junction
Durango, CO 81301 United States
clintaz@gobrainstorm.net
http://www.newcountryautocenter.com

BUS: Car Dealership **P/S:** New and Used Car Repair, Service and Accessories **MA:** Local **D/D/R:** Automotive Accounting, Reviewing Statements, Reconciling Bank Records **H/I/S:** Golfing, Boating, Waterskiing, Snow Skiing **FBP:** Automotive News **EDU:** Bachelor's Degree in Accounting, The University of Arizona **A/A/S:** Association of Certified Financial Examiners **A/S:** He attributes his success to his personal pride, integrity and wanting to do things correctly. **B/I:** He became involved in this profession because he has always been involved in public and private accounting and auditing since college. **H/O:** The highlight of his career was attaining his current position.

REBECCA J. WIGGENHORN
Professor of Business and Applied Technologies Division
Business and Applied Technologies Division
Clark State Community College
570 E. Leffel Lane
Springfield, OH 45505 United States
wiggenhornr@clarkstate.edu
http://www.clarkstate.edu

BUS: College **P/S:** Higher Education **MA:** Regional **D/D/R:** Teaching Online Programs, Working with Traditional and Non-Traditional Students, Advising Business and Internship Coordination, Teaching Office Administration and Medical Office Administration **H/I/S:** Walking, Reading, Collecting Antiques **FBP:** Journal of Business Communication; Office Solutions; Computer World; Business Communication Quarterly **EDU:** Master of Arts in Management and Supervision, Central Michigan University (1987); Bachelor of Science in Business Education, Wright State University (1980) **A/A/S:** Association for Business Communication; The Chair Academy International **A/H:** Exemplary Leadership Award (2006); Professional Excellence Award (1992, 2000); Who's Who Among America's Teachers Award **A/S:** She attributes her success to the support she receives from her mother who was a teacher.

MRS. EDNA S. WIKER
Owner, Certified Tax Professional
Edna S. Wiker
284 W. Rosa Drive
Green Valley, AZ 85614 United States
ewiker@cox.net
http://www.cambridgewhoswho.com

BUS: Private Practice **P/S:** Accounting, Tax Preparation Services **MA:** AZ, CA, KS and CO **EXP:** Mrs. Wiker's expertise is in income tax return preparation. **H/I/S:** Knitting, Exercising, Bowling, Bicycling **FBP:** The Wall Street Journal **EDU:** Coursework, University of Michigan **CERTS:** Certified Tax Professional (1993) **A/A/S:** Treasurer, Estates Homeowners Association, Pueblo **DOB:** October 10, 1933 **SP:** Neil **W/H:** Tax Preparer, Hilderbrand & Associates, P.C., Colorado Springs, CO (1985-1992); Co-Owner, Leo R. Smentowski & Associates, CPA Firm, Colorado Springs, CO (1977-1985); Tax Preparer, Touche Ross & Associates, Colorado Springs, CO (1971-1977); Head Accountant, Vicon Industries, Colorado Springs, CO (1962-1970); Office Bookkeeper, Daniels Chevrolet, Colorado Springs, CO (1960-1961); Office Personnel, Michigan Dairy Producers, Adrian, MI (1954-1960)

MS. THERESA A. WILCOX
Advanced Practice Registered Nurse
Theresa A. Wilcox, APRN, BC
14 Erin Way
South Weymouth, MA 02190 United States
tawpmhcnsbc@verison.net
http://www.cambridgewhoswho.com

BUS: Healthcare Center **P/S:** Healthcare **MA:** Regional **EXP:** Ms. Wilcox's expertise is in the treatment of sexually abused patients, child therapy and psychology education. **H/I/S:** Practicing Martial Arts, Spending Time with her Grandchildren **EDU:** Master's Degree in Psychiatric Nursing, Boston College (1978) **A/A/S:** EMDR Institute; American Nurses Credentialing Center; International Social Survey Program **CHILD:** Jaina, Jon **A/S:** She attributes her success to the support she receives from her family.

GAYLE WILDER, CPC
Principal
G. Wilder and Associates
4423 S. 313th Street
Auburn, WA 98001 United States
gayle.wilder@comcast.net
http://www.gwilderandassociates.com

BUS: Recruiting Firm **P/S:** Recruiting Professionals for Commercial Real Estate Needs **MA:** Statewide **D/D/R:** Interviewing, Recruiting, Referencing for Commercial Real Estate, Directing Commercial Real Estate Development, Managing Portfolio Managers, Lease Administrators and Assistant Property Managers **H/I/S:** Fishing with her Husband in Alaska, Collecting Fenton Glass **FBP:** Seattle Times; Architectural Digest **EDU:** College Coursework **CERTS:** Secretarial Certificate; Certified Personnel Consultant **A/A/S:** Former Publicity Chairperson and Board Member, Commercial Real Estate Women; Membership and Publicity Committees, Puget Sound Rental and Housing Association **A/H:** Recruiter of the Year, Employee of the Year **C/VW:** Jubilee House for Abused Women; Sponsor, Nicaraguan Child **SP:** Larry **CHILD:** Ashley, Troy, Tammy, Terri **C/A:** Nationally Recognized Certified Personnel Consultant (1984); Started Recruiting Firm (2001) **A/S:** She attributes her success to her love for her job, her commitment to it and having good mentors throughout her career. **B/I:** She became involved in her profession because of her interest in recruiting. **H/O:** The most gratifying aspects of her career are the national recognition she has received as well as opening up her own firm and seeing it grow.

ROY S. WILENSKY, PSY.D., LCP, PLLC
Doctor
Sterling Behavioral Health Services, Ltd.
20905 Professional Plaza
Suite 220
Ashburn, VA 20147 United States
drwilensky@gmail.com
http://www.cambridgewhoswho.com

BUS: Healthcare Center **P/S:** Healthcare Including Clinical and Forensic Psychology **MA:** Local **D/D/R:** Counseling Adults, Families and Couples, Practicing Clinical Hypnosis and Forensic Psychology, Teaching Relaxation Techniques, Conducting Psychological and Forensic Tests **H/I/S:** Listening to Music, Traveling, Reading, Exercising, Speaking Spanish **EDU:** Ph.D. in Clinical Psychology, American School of Professional Psychology, Argosy University; Postdoctoral Master of Science in Clinical Psychopharmacology, California School of Professional Psychology, Alliant International University; Master of Social Work, Virginia Commonwealth University; Bachelor of Arts in Anthropology, Minor in Philosophy, The George Washington University **CERTS:** Licensed Clinical Psychologist, States of Virginia and Maryland **A/A/S:** Virginia Psychological Association; Virginia Academy of Clinical Psychologists; Co-Chairman, Outreach Committee, Northern Virginia Society of Clinical Psychologists; American Psychological Association; National Association of Social Workers **A/H:** Public Service Award, State of Virginia (2004) **C/VW:** Doctors of the World, USA; Asylum Network; Amnesty International USA **A/S:** He attributes his success to his self-motivation, intelligence and intellectual curiosity. **B/I:** He became involved in his profession because he was always interested in human nature and wanted to combine that interest with his ability to help people. **H/O:** The highlight of his career was receiving an award from the state of Virginia in 2004.

MS. CAROL THERESA WILEY
Registered Nurse
Alief Independent School District
8150 Howell Sugar Land Road
Houston, TX 77083 United States
carol.wiley@aliefisd.net
http://www.aliefisd.net

BUS: School District **P/S:** Elementary, Middle and High School **MA:** Regional **D/D/R:** Preparing State Mandated Health Screenings and Reports, Registering Students, Scheduling Parent Meetings, Ensuring All Students Receive Necessary Immunizations, Offering General Healthcare, Routine and Level II Nursing, Working with Ventilator-Dependent Infants, Dispensing Medications, Facilitating Parent Communications, Working in the Ambulatory Care Unit **H/I/S:** Playing with and Walking her Dogs, Visiting her Parents and Friends, Spending Time on the Farm **FBP:** RN **EDU:** Pursuing Bachelor of Science, Texas Womens' University; Registered Nurse, Warton County Junior College (1990); Bachelor's Degree in Business, University of Houston (1980) **CERTS:** Nursing License, State of Texas (1990) **A/A/S:** Texas Association of School Nurses; National Association of School Nurses; Public Speaker, School of Healthcare **A/H:** District School Nurse of the Year, Alief Independent School District (2006-2007) **C/VW:** Volunteer, House of Amos **DOB:** September 8, 1958 **POB:** Kingsville, TX **SP:** Chester **CHILD:** Derek **W/H:** Oak Bend Medical Center; Alief ISD, Richmond State School; Gastroenterology Consultants **A/S:** She attributes her success to her ability to see the broad picture of each situation and her relationship with her parents. **B/I:** She became involved in her profession because of her brother and the concern for his illness. **H/O:** The highlight of her career was helping develop the teaching materials for the new computer system. **I/F/Y:** In five years, Ms. Wiley hopes to have her master's degree in nursing.

DR. JILL CARLTON WILKENS
Medical Director
Colonnade Imaging Center
100 Fulford Avenue
Bel Air, MD 21014 United States
pedirad@comcast.net
http://www.cambridgewhoswho.com

BUS: Diagnostic Center **P/S:** Diagnostic Imaging Services Including Radiology, Nuclear, Computed Axial Tomography Scan and Mammography **MA:** Regional **D/D/R:** Overseeing a Staff of Approximately 30 Employees and Women's Imaging and Pediatric Care Services, Consulting with Referring Physicians, Performing Radiological Procedures, Interpreting a Multitude of Cases on a Daily Basis, Marketing, Lecturing and Organizing Events to Promote Business **H/I/S:** Traveling, Needlepointing, Horseback Riding, Spending Time with her Children **FBP:** Architectural Digest **EDU:** MD in Radiology, Albert Einstein Medical Center **C/VW:** Pro Bono Resource Center, MD; Baltimore County Poll **A/S:** She attributes her success to her hard work, dedication, determination and perseverance. **H/O:** The highlight of her career was earning her current position.

MAXINE A. WILKINS
Teacher
Greater Johnstown School District
1091 Broad Street
Johnstown, PA 15906 United States
mwilkins48@hotmail.com
http://www.gjsd.net

BUS: School District **P/S:** Education, Special Education, Curriculum Development, Music and Arts Programs, Guidance Counseling, Transportation Services, Extracurricular Activities, Food Services, Library, Media, Technology **MA:** Regional **EXP:** Ms. Wilkins' expertise is in early childhood education. **H/I/S:** Horseback Riding **EDU:** Coursework in Elementary Education, The Pennsylvania State University; Bachelor's Degree in Education, Slippery Rock University **A/A/S:** Slippery Rock University Alumni Association; American Quarter Horse Association **A/H:** Superintendent's Outstanding Achievement Award

CARRIE A. WILLENBORG
Owner Operator, Master Electrician
E-Quality Electric, LLC
632 19th Avenue S.W.
Cedar Rapids, IA 52404 United States
msparkette@yahoo.com
http://www.cambridgewhoswho.com

BUS: Electrical Wiring **P/S:** Electrical Contracting **MA:** Local **D/D/R:** New Residential Wiring **H/I/S:** Woodworking, Small Beading, Arts and Crafts, Fishing, Camping, Spending Time with her Children **CERTS:** Licensed Master Electrician **A/A/S:** American Builders and Contractors Association **A/S:** She attributes her success to hard work and being able to progress quickly in her trade. **H/O:** The highlight of her career was doing the hard wiring in a $1,000,000 home that won an award.

BARBARA A. WILLIAMS
Part Time Adjunct Instructor
Allied Health Science
Community College of Philadelphia
1700 Spring Garden Street
Philadelphia, PA 19130 United States
williamsbar@aol.com
http://www.cambridgewhoswho.com

BUS: College **P/S:** Higher Education Including Nursing, Regular Nutrition and Latest Nutritional Courses **MA:** International **D/D/R:** Teaching Nutrition to Nursing Students and Allied Health Professionals **H/I/S:** Shopping, Reading, Traveling **FBP:** EBONY; Industry-Related Publications **EDU:** Master's Degree in Counseling, with a Concentration in Diversity, University of Bridgeport (1989); Bachelor's Degree in Food and Nutrition, West Virginia University **CERTS:** Registered Dietitian; Dietetic Technician, Registered **A/A/S:** Vice President, Cliveden Hills Association; Former President, Philadelphia Dietetic Association; Zeta Phi Beta **C/VW:** Teacher, Local Church; Treasurer, Grace Baptist Church of Germantown

CAROL STERDIVANT WILLIAMS, RN, COHN-S
Occupational Health Product Manager (Retired)
Federal Occupational Health
United States Department of Health and Human Services
100 Alabama Street, Suite 3R8
Atlanta, GA 30303 United States
iam4carol@bellsouth.net
http://www.cpsc.gov

BUS: Government Healthcare Center **P/S:** Occupational Healthcare Services **MA:** International **EXP:** Ms. Williams' expertise is in critical care and coronary care nursing, project management, oversight of the step down, intensive care and burn units, consulting, and quality assurance review of healthcare facilities. **D/D/R:** Managing Occupational Health Products, Raising Awareness on HIV and Aids, Training with an Emphasis on Law Enforcement, Maintaining Occupational Safety and Health Administration Records, Training for Stress Management, Teaching Health Education to Family Caregivers and Nurses **H/I/S:** Reading, Gardening **FBP:** Occupational Health & Safety; American Journal of Nursing; RN; Nursing Spectrum **EDU:** Associate of Science in Nursing, Meridian Junior College **CERTS:** Certified Occupational Health Nurse Specialist **A/A/S:** American Association of Occupational Health Nurses; Who's Who in American Nursing **A/H:** Region IV Special Service Award, Department of Health and Human Services; Gold Shield Award, Jackson, Mississippi Police Department; Certificate of Appreciation, Powder Springs Community Task Force **C/VW:** Volunteer, American Cancer Society; Volunteer, American Heart Association; Presenter, Panelist, Association for the Improvement of Minorities in the Internal Revenue Service; Special Olympics; Community Literacy Program Conference; Boys Scouts of America; Volunteer, Paralympic Games; Powder Springs Community Task Force; Cobb Literacy Council; Nurses Guild, Turner Chapel AME Church **W/H:** Registered Nurse, University of MS Medical Center (1970-1980) **A/S:** She attributes her success to her hard work and love for her profession. **B/I:** She became involved in her profession because she had a desire to help people and provide compassionate care to the ill. **H/O:** The highlight of her career was running training programs on blood-borne pathogens. **I/F/Y:** In the next five years, Ms. Williams hopes to retire.

CONNIE L. WILLIAMS
1) Owner 2) Chief Executive Officer
1) Integrated Payment Solutions 2) Scent-Sations
120 Morris Drive, Milam, TX 75959 United States
connie@integratedpaymentsolutions.net
conniescandleshop@yahoo.com
http://www.integratedpaymentsolutions.net
http://www.conniescandleshop.com

BUS: 1) Payment Processing Company 2) Candle Retailer **P/S:** 1) Processing Payments from Credit Cards 2) Mia Bella Scented Candles, Bath and Body Products, Fundraisers **MA:** 1) National 2) National **EXP:** Ms. Williams' area of expertise is in the distribution of terminals and pin pads. **D/D/R:** Overseeing Electronic Check Processing, Bookkeeping, Filing Paperwork, Ensuring Customer Satisfaction **H/I/S:** Fishing, Making Crafts, Quilting, Sewing **FBP:** Home Business Connection; Digital Transactions **EDU:** Diploma, St. Anthony High School **A/A/S:** Angel Society; Sabine County Chamber of Commerce; Knights Templar **A/H:** Award, Evo Merchant Service **C/VW:** Miliam Settlers Day; Milams Fire Department **DOB:** June 7, 1945 **POB:** Owensboro, KY **SP:** Williams **CHILD:** Dawn, Bobbi, Scott, Rodney, Shelly, Ashley **A/S:** She attributes her success to her hard work and ambition. **B/I:** She because involved in her profession because her son got her interested in credit card processing. **I/F/Y:** In five years, Ms. Williams hopes to have accumulated a sizable amount of wealth.

MR. DAVID A. WILLIAMS, MS.ED.
Director of Student Activities
Elmira College
1 Park Place
Elmira, NY 14901 United States
dwilliams@elmira.edu
http://www.elmira.edu

BUS: Private College Dedicated to Excellence in Higher Education **P/S:** Graduate and Undergraduate Programs, Higher Education **MA:** National **D/D/R:** Working in the Residence Life Department, Offering his Skills as a Liaison between the Business, Academic and Alumni Relations Offices, Creating Contracts, Serving as a Legal Agent for Elmira College, Conducting Fall Freshmen Orientation, Arranging Speakers, Bands and Lecturers **H/I/S:** Volleyball, Wallyball, Reading, Traveling, Debating **FBP:** The Chronicle of Education; American College Personnel Association Journal; The Intercollegiate Review **EDU:** Pursuing Master's Degree in General Management, Elmira College; Master of Science in Adult Education and Human Resources Management and Development, Elmira College (2004); Bachelor's Degree in English Literature and Psychology, Elmira College (2002) **CERTS:** CPR/AED Certified; First Aid Certified **A/A/S:** Chair, Selection Committee, Who's Who Among College Students; American College Personnel Association; National Association of Campus Activities; National Orientation Directors Association; Omicron Delta Kappa National Leadership Honor Society; National Campus Media Advisors; Founding Member, Sigma Etz Chapter, The National Residence Hall Honorary **A/H:** Outstanding Graduate, Elmira College (2002) **C/VW:** United Way of America; Urban League of Rochester; Church

DIANE R. WILLIAMS
Associate Broker
Windermere Real Estate
44-530 San Pablo Avenue, Suite 101
Palm Desert, CA 92260 United States
dianewilliams@dc.rr.com
http://www.dianewilliams.com

BUS: Leading Real Estate Company in the West **P/S:** Residential Sales, Investment Properties **MA:** International **D/D/R:** Specializing in Real Estate, Residential Sales, High End, Upscale Residential Homes on Golf Courses and Gated Communities **H/I/S:** Golfing **EDU:** Coursework in Business, DePaul University (1981) **CERTS:** USGA Course Rated Certified Trainer **A/A/S:** Who's Who in Marketing; California Association of Realtors; National Association of Realtors; California Desert Association of Realtors; United States Golf Association

EARL WILLIAMS
Counselor, Therapist
Earl Williams, LCSW
10101 Slater Avenue
Fountain Valley, CA 92708 United States
ewilcsw@pacbell.net
http://www.positiverelationshipsorangeco.com

BUS: Private Practice **P/S:** Counseling, Psychotherapy **MA:** Regional **D/D/R:** Counseling, Volunteering for Social Work **H/I/S:** Reading, Traveling **FBP:** NASW Press **EDU:** Master of Social Work, California State University, Fresno **C/VW:** Local Church **A/S:** He attributes his success to his hard work and fortune. **H/O:** The most gratifying aspect of his career is helping others and owning his business.

GAYLYN R. WILLIAMS
Chief Executive Officer
Success Builders International
PO Box 63383
Colorado Springs, CO 80962 United States
gaylyn@successbooks.info
http://www.successbooks.info/index.php

BUS: Publishing and Training Company **P/S:** Training on Communication Skills and Stress and Conflict Management **MA:** International **D/D/R:** Writing and Publishing Books on Communication Skills and Stress and Conflict Management **H/I/S:** Reading, Hiking **FBP:** Colorado Springs Business Journal **EDU:** Bachelor of Arts in Linguistics, Dallas Bible College; Coursework in Neuro-Linguistic Programming, International Training Partners **A/A/S:** Colorado Springs Association of Real Estate Investors; Colorado Association of Real Estate Investors; Better Business Bureau **A/S:** She attributes her success to her faith in God and belief in herself. **B/I:** She became involved in her profession by recognizing the importance of training others in interpersonal skills. **H/O:** The highlights of her career have been her speaking engagements and the books that she has written.

JACKIE CRAFT WILLIAMS
Clinical Specialist
University of Memphis, Integrated Microscopy Center
3774 Walker Avenue
Memphis, TN 38152 United States
jcraft@memphis.edu
http://www.cambridgewhoswho.com

BUS: University **P/S:** Research, Clinical Electron Microscopy **MA:** International **D/D/R:** Specializing in Clinical Electron Microscopy **H/I/S:** Reading, Gardening **FBP:** Scientist **CERTS:** Licensed Practical Nurse, Crowleys Ridge Vocational Technical School **A/A/S:** American Society of Clinical Pathologists **A/S:** She attributes her success to her concern for the patients. **B/I:** She became involved in her profession because she was a licensed practical nurse and wanted a change. **H/O:** The highlight of her career was saving an infant's life.

KAREN WILLIAMS
Freelance Weather Producer
Allbritton Communications
1100 Wilson Boulevard
Arlington, VA 22209 United States
kwillswxdiva@aol.com
http://www.cambridgewhoswho.com

BUS: Television **P/S:** Off-Air Weather Producer and Weathercaster **MA:** Regional **D/D/R:** Producing Weather Graphics **H/I/S:** Going to the Theater and Concerts **FBP:** Black Enterprise; Time **EDU:** Bachelor of Arts in Communications, Temple University; Pursuing Degree in Meteorology, Mississippi State Learning Program **A/A/S:** National Weather Association; American Meteorology Association; National Association of Black Journalists **C/VW:** DataStre Project, American Meteorology Society **A/S:** She attributes her personal and professional success to her hard work, determination and prayers. **B/I:** She has always had an interest in the weather and mechanics of the earth. **H/O:** The highlight of her career was being given the opportunity to start as Master Controller Operator.

LAURIE WILLIAMS
Owner
Laurie Williams Services
6 Automation Lane
Suite 115
Albany, NY 12205 United States
laurie@lwilliamscb.net
http://www.lwilliamscb.net

BUS: Accounting Firm **P/S:** Accounting Including Bookkeeping **MA:** National **EXP:** Ms. Williams' expertise is in operations management. **D/D/R:** Consulting on Software, Lecturing for Business Associations, Conducting Seminars, Training Accounting Firms Including Bookkeepers to Use the Software and Other Products, Enterprising Solutions, Helping Business Owners Follow their Finance, Assisting Clients in Creating and Maintaining a Healthy, Efficient Bookkeeping System, Creating Accurate Financial Statements and Reports, Delivering a Clean Set of Books to their Accountant at Tax Time **H/I/S:** Composing Music, Singing, Playing Percussion Instruments **FBP:** General Ledger **CERTS:** Certified Bookkeeper, American Institute of Professional Bookkeepers (2003); Certified Advanced QuickBooks ProAdvisor **A/A/S:** American Institute of Professional Bookkeepers (2004) **H/O:** The most gratifying aspects of her career are demonstrating clients how to use the software and how essential it is, watching people running their own individual businesses and keep control of their finance and feel more secure knowing they have financial support.

Mr. Michael R. Williams Jr.

Bishop, Senior Pastor
Bethel Christian World Outreach Ministries, Inc.
2729 Westmoor Court S.W.
Olympia, WA 98502 United States
bishop@bethelcwom.org
http://www.bethelcwom.org

BUS: Church **P/S:** Organizational Structure, Leader Development **MA:** International **D/D/R:** Overseeing 79 Churches in Washington and Overseas, Counseling Pastors, Developing Curriculum and Communication Projects **H/I/S:** Playing Chess and Golf **FBP:** The Week **EDU:** Graduate Degree in Theological Studies, Friendship Christian University **A/A/S:** Founder, Nonprofit Omega Community Development Association

Ray Williams Jr.

Owner
Williams Vending Machines
16440 N.W. 22nd Court
Miami Gardens, FL 33054 United States
wiwandawil@bellsouth.net
http://www.cambridgewhoswho.com

BUS: Retail Store **P/S:** Vending Machines for Law Firms, Schools and other Organizations **MA:** Local **D/D/R:** Managing Operations **H/I/S:** Traveling, Fishing, Caring for People **C/VW:** Local Church; Save the Children; United Way of America; Special Olympics **A/S:** He attributes his success to his ability to convert his dream into reality. **B/I:** He became involved in his profession because he was inspired by his friend. **H/O:** The most gratifying aspect of his career is owning his own vending machines.

RUTH S. WILLIAMS
Owner
RSW Ventures, Inc.
1786 S.W. Sixth Street
Loveland, CO 80537 United States
ums@mailstation.com
http://www.cambridgewhoswho.com

BUS: Retail Store **P/S:** Sale and Resale of Precious Gems, Metals and Ironworks **MA:** Regional **EXP:** Ms. Williams' expertise is in commodity research. **D/D/R:** Purchasing Quality Products for Specific Customer Needs **H/I/S:** Skiing, Spending Time with her Family **FBP:** Gemstones **EDU:** Associate Degree in Business Studies, Utica Business College (1970) **A/H:** Donor of the Year Award, Veterans of America (2006-2007) **C/VW:** Volunteer, Feed the Children; Council Member, Sioux Indian Tribe (2006); Volunteer, American Indians Charitable Organizations

THELMA A. WILLIAMS
Technical Trainer
Imagescan-Financial Consulting
4411 Forbes Boulevard
Lanham, MD 20706 United States
http://www.iscanit.com

BUS: Finance and Banking **P/S:** Software Development, Payment Processing, Complete Suite of Scalable PC-Based Products for Standalone or Fully-Integrated Wholesale and Retail Lock-Box Processing, High-Speed Remittance Processing, and Whole-Tail Processing **MA:** International **D/D/R:** Technical Training in Information Technology **FBP:** Smart Money; Forbes; Black Enterprise; Success (Home Business) **EDU:** College Courses in Information Systems Studies **CERTS:** Certified Life Insurance Producer **A/A/S:** National Association for Female Executives; Blacks in Government; International Church of Christ, Landover, Maryland

MS. WILHELMINA M. WILLIAMS
Teacher
Cass Technical High School
2501 Second Avenue
Detroit, MI 48201 United States
wmwilhel@hotmail.com
http://www.cambridgewhoswho.com

BUS: High School **P/S:** Education **MA:** Local **D/D/R:** Information Processing **H/I/S:** Traveling to Germany, Hawaii and Brazil, Exercising **EDU:** Master's Degree in Education Plus 30, Specialty in Guidance Counseling, University of Maryland **A/A/S:** MCCAW; Business Professionals Association; Michigan Education Association; Michigan Business Education Association; Association for Supervision and Curriculum Development **C/VW:** Local Church; Various Charities **A/S:** She attributes her success to her parents and husband. **B/I:** She became involved in her profession through a natural progression of opportunities. **H/O:** The highlight of her career was being selected to teach at Cass Technical School.

MARGARET GAYLENE WILLIAMS-CLOUGH, RNC, NNP
Licensed Practical Nurse, Ministry
The First Gnostic Church of Tucson
Tucson, AZ 85710 United States
singbbshop@aol.com
http://www.cambridgewhoswho.com

BUS: Church **P/S:** Sermons, Baptisms, Communion, Weddings, Funerals, and Spiritual Teachings and Counsel **MA:** Local **D/D/R:** Conducting Spiritual Teachings **H/I/S:** Traveling, Listening to Music, Reading Sylvia Brown Novels, Spending Time with her Family and her Adopted Dog **EDU:** Doctor of Theology, Horizon Church (2006) **CERTS:** Ordained (1996); Licensed Practical Nurse, Lincoln Technical College (1972); Certification in Past Life Regression **C/VW:** Disabled American Veterans; Christian Appalachian Project; The Humane Society of the United States **A/S:** She attributes her career success to her inner drive and to her desire to help others. **B/I:** After she retired from nursing, she felt a calling from God to help people on a more spiritual level, and she has found that this career has offered her the most fulfillment of her life.

DORIS L. WILLIAMSON
Owner, President
Business Promotion and Services
4511 Yale Street
Amarillo, TX 79109 United States
doris1951@suddenlink.net
http://www.cambridgewhoswho.com

BUS: Proven Leader in the Marketing and Promotion Industries **P/S:** Services to Not Only Increase Traffic and Sales, but to Help Reduce Costs and Increase Employee Satisfaction **MA:** Texas and New Mexico **D/D/R:** Marketing, Advertising, Overseeing Sales Administration **H/I/S:** Reading, Photography **FBP:** Industry-Related Publications **EDU:** General Equivalency Diploma **A/A/S:** Chamber of Commerce

JEAN WILLIAMSON SMITH
Reading First Coach
Dewitt Elementary School
PO Box 9
Dewitt, KY 40930 United States
jean.williamson-smith@knox.kyschools.us
http://www.cambridgewhoswho.com

BUS: Elementary School **P/S:** Primary Education **MA:** Local **D/D/R:** Teaching Reading, Coaching Kindergarten through Third-Grade Students **H/I/S:** Traveling, Collecting Antiques, Riding Motorcycles **FBP:** Industry-Related Publications **EDU:** Master's Degree in Elementary Education, Plus 45; Bachelor's Degree in Special Education, Union University; Coursework in Supervision and Principalship, Union University **CERTS:** Certified Reading Specialist **C/VW:** Beacon Baptist Church **SP:** Gary **A/S:** She attributes her success to the support she receives from her family and her interpersonal skills. **B/I:** She became involved in her profession because she was inspired by her grandfather and she always wanted to be a teacher. **H/O:** The most gratifying aspects of her career are receiving commendations from her former students and finding her profession to be challenging. **I/F/Y:** In five years, Ms. Williamson Smith hopes to continue helping children.

DEIRDRE A. WILLIS
President
D&C Power, Inc.
8685 State Road 64 W.
Ona, FL 33865 United States
deirdre@dandcpower.com
http://www.cambridgewhoswho.com

BUS: Manufacturing Company **P/S:** DC Power Products and Turnkey Power Systems **MA:** National **EXP:** Ms. Willis's expertise is in the oversight of administration, processing payroll and insurance billings. **H/I/S:** Cruising **EDU:** College Coursework **C/VW:** Local Charitable Organizations; Hands in Arcadia **A/S:** She attributes her success to the support she receives from her husband. **B/I:** She became involved in the profession because of her family background and she always enjoys flexibility in her profession. **H/O:** The most gratifying aspect of her career is running a successful business for four years.

MR. GEORGE H. WILLIS
Grand Chef De Gare
La Societe Des Quarente
777 N. Meridan Street
Indianapolis, IN 46204 United States
gjwilllis@telpage.net
http://www.cambridgewhoswho.com

BUS: Volunteer Veterans Organization **P/S:** Veterans Services **MA:** National **D/D/R:** Advising on Benefits and Programming, Working as the Assistant Manager **H/I/S:** Cooking, Dancing, Enjoying the Outdoors **EDU:** Master's Degree in Business Administration **CERTS:** Master Chief Petty Officer **A/A/S:** Instructor at Navy School of Health Science; Fleet Marine Force Corpsman; American Legion; Veterans of Foreign Wars; Disabled American Veterans; Woodmen of the World; Forty and Eight; Marine Corps League **A/H:** Outstanding Volunteer for Community Services, Woodmen of the World; Outstanding Ruritan Club **C/VW:** County Manager, American Red Cross; Veterans Administration Volunteer Services; Local Fundraisers for Cancer Patients; Project Graduation; Veterans Organizations in VISN-6; Former State Commander, North Carolina American Legion; American Veterans, Fleet Marine Force Corpsman; American Legion; Veterans of Foreign Wars; Disabled American Veterans; Woodmen of the World; Forty and Eight; Marine Corps League

GREGOREESE M. WILLOCKS-GONZALEZ

Forensic Drug Chemist
Office of the Attorney General
U.S. Virgin Islands Department of Justice
9034 Little Princesse
St. Croix, VI 00823 United States
gwillocks@usvidoj.vi
http://www.cambridgewhoswho.com

BUS: Government Organization **P/S:** Public Services Including Forensic Chemistry, Simple and Complex Litigation and Legal Defense **MA:** Regional **D/D/R:** Working in Forensic Drug Chemistry, Analyzing Physical Evidence and Utilizing Chemical, Microscopic, Chromatographic and Comparative Techniques and Instrumentation to Examine, Identity and Evaluate Controlled Substances **H/I/S:** Traveling, Trying New and Adventurous Activities Including Extreme Sports **EDU:** Pursuing Master's Degree in Forensic Science; Bachelor of Science in Biology, with a Minor in Chemistry, Florida A&M University (2001) **CERTS:** Certificate in Forensic Chemistry, College of Pharmacy & Pharmaceutical Sciences, Florida A&M University; Certificate in Forensic Chemistry, U.S. Drug Enforcement Administration **A/A/S:** American Chemical Society

ANN VERONICA WILSON

New York City School Teacher (Retired)
annvwilson@aol.com
http://www.cambridgewhoswho.com

BUS: Education **P/S:** New York City Public Schools **MA:** Local **D/D/R:** Teaching English, Writing Poetry **H/I/S:** Traveling within the United States and Europe, the Middle East, East Africa, Canada and Mexico, Writing Poetry, Caring for her Flame Point Siamese Cat **FBP:** Poetry Today **EDU:** Bachelor's Degree in Education, Notre Dame College for Women, Staten Island, NY (1964); Master's Equivalency in Social Sciences, Fordham University, Saint Mary's College, Walnut Creek, CA **A/A/S:** The International Library of Poetry and Noble House **C/VW:** Missionary Oblates; Society of the Little Flower; Sacred Heart League **A/S:** She attributes her success to her hard work and perseverance despite adversity. **B/I:** She became involved in her profession because her paternal ancestry includes a long line of teachers. **H/O:** The highlight of her career was writing, directing and producing a play for her first grade students entitled, 'A Snow White Christmas.'

DONNA L. WILSON, JD

Attorney
Wilson Law, PLC
461 McLaws Circle
Suite 2
Williamsburg, VA 23185 United States
donna@wilsonlawplc.com
http://www.wilsonlawplc.com

BUS: Legal Services **P/S:** Estate Planning, Education, Design and Implementation, Using a Team Approach to Best Serve Client's Needs, Asset Protection, Real Estate **MA:** Local **D/D/R:** Conducting One-on-One Consultations with Clients, Educating Clients **H/I/S:** Traveling, Reading, Skiing **FBP:** Lawyers Weekly; ABA Journal; Virginia Lawyer; Probate & Property **EDU:** JD, Regent University; Master of Science in Education, Old Dominion University; Bachelor of Science in Education, James Madison University **A/A/S:** Business Professionals Networking Group; Virginia State Bar Association; Virginia Trial Lawyers Association; American Bar Association; Women's Professional Business Networking **C/VW:** Court Appointed Public Defender **A/S:** She attributes her success to her hard work and to having a vision. **B/I:** She became involved in her profession because she wanted to get involved in law and be able to help people. **H/O:** The highlight of her career is having the opportunity to truly make a difference in people's lives.

MR. JEFFREY D. WILSON

Funeral Director
Nardolillo Funeral Home, Inc.
1278 Park Avenue
Cranston, RI 02910 United States
nardo@nardolillo.com
http://www.nardolillo.com

BUS: Private Company Dedicated to Excellence in Funeral Services **P/S:** Funeral Preparation, Arrangements, Directing Services **MA:** National **D/D/R:** Overseeing Family Needs, Organizing Funeral Arrangements, Conducting Funeral Ceremonies, Assisting in the Removal Process, Preparing, Dressing and Casketing Bodies, Managing Finances, Writing Obituaries, Coordinating Services Including Music, Reading, Funeral Mass, Cemetery Arrangements **H/I/S:** Antiquing, Attending the Theater **FBP:** The Director **EDU:** Pittsburgh Institute of Mortuary Science (1978) **CERTS:** Licensed Funeral Director, State of Rhode Island and Pennsylvania **A/A/S:** Rhode Island Funeral Director's Association; Board of Governors, National Funeral Director's Association; Kiskiminetas Lodge 617 **A/H:** Golden Eagle Award (2004); Five-Time Recipient, Eagle Award

JULEEN A. WILSON
Staff Nurse
Geisinger Medical Center
100 N. Academy Avenue
Danville, PA 17822 United States
jawilson@geisinger.edu
http://www.geisinger.edu

BUS: Healthcare **P/S:** Healthcare **MA:** Regional **D/D/R:** Offering Pediatric Intensive Care **H/I/S:** Reading, Gardening, Cross Stitching **EDU:** Associate Degree in Nursing, Pennsylvania College of Technology; Bachelor's Degree in Missions, Penn View Bible Institute **A/S:** She attributes her success to her upbringing and parental support as well as her perseverance. **B/I:** She became involved in the profession because her mom and aunt are both nurses and her uncle was a doctor. She wanted to be a nurse since she was young. **H/O:** The highlight of her career is using her skills in foreign countries as well as helping kids and families during illnesses.

RUBY SULLIVAN WILSON
Principal (Retired)
Sausalito Marin City School District
630 Nevada Street
Sausalito, CA 94965 United States
rswilson138@sbcglobal.net
http://www.cambridgewhoswho.com

BUS: Public School **P/S:** Education for Grades Kindergarten Through Eighth **MA:** Local **D/D/R:** Educating and Motivating 200 Kindergarten through Eighth-Grade Students **H/I/S:** Reading, Traveling, Crocheting **FBP:** Ebony; Time; Black Enterprise; Leadership **EDU:** Master's Degree in Elementary Education, University of San Francisco; Master's Degree in Administration, University of San Francisco; Bachelor's Degree in Biology, Howard University **A/A/S:** Association of California School Administrators; Delta Sigma Theta; Delta Kappa Gamma **A/H:** Marin City Educator Mother of the Year (2001) **C/VW:** National Council of Negro Women; National Association for the Advancement of Colored People; United Nations Educational, Scientific and Cultural Organization; AMVETS; Habitat For Humanity; Catholic Charities; Volunteer, Marlin County School; Adults with Delayed Development

SUSAN WILSON
Independent Distributor
Advocare
923 Bevan Street
Akron, OH 44319 United States
kickboxersw@sbcglobal.net
http://www.advocare-nutrition.com

BUS: Health and Wellness Consulting Firm **P/S:** Person to Person Skincare and Nutrition Counseling **MA:** National **D/D/R:** Wellness Consulting **H/I/S:** Gardening **EDU:** High School Graduate **C/VW:** The Salvation Army **A/S:** She attributes her success to her hard work. **B/I:** She became involved in her profession through a natural progression of opportunities.

TAN V. WILSON, PMP
President
Entellect, LLC
11304 Dockside Circle
Reston, VA 20191 United States
tanwilson@entellectllc.com
http://www.entellectllc.com

BUS: Consulting Firm **P/S:** Business Development, Technical Writing, Program and Proposal Management Services **MA:** National **EXP:** Mr. Wilson's expertise is in strategic business development. **D/D/R:** Managing Public Relations, Marketing and Corporate Assets, Procuring Federal Initiatives, Reviewing Plans to Evaluate Reports for Contractors, Assisting the Government in Implementing Federal Programs, Assisting Small Firms Entering into the Federal Sector with Business Intelligence, Generating Leads **H/I/S:** Practicing Yoga, Traveling, Shopping **FBP:** Washington Technology **EDU:** Bachelor of Science in Chemistry and Political Science, Albright College (1993) **CERTS:** Certification in Management, Project Management Institute (2007) **A/A/S:** Project Management Institute; National Contract Management Association; Association of Proposal Management Professionals **DOB:** December 19, 1970 **W/H:** Mabbett & Associates, Inc (2007-2008); MasiMax Resources (2003-2007); QC Laboratories, Inc (2002-2003); Wastex Industries, Inc (2001-2002); Lancaster Laboratories, Inc (1993-2001) **A/S:** She attributes her success to her mentors and networking skills. **H/O:** The highlight of her career was starting her own business as an entrepreneur.

W. Michael Wilson
Operations Manager
Naturally Fresh, Inc.
1000 Naturally Fresh Boulevard
Atlanta, GA 30349 United States
mwilson@naturallyfresh.com
wils741@comcast.net
http://www.naturallyfresh.com

BUS: Food Manufacturing and Distribution Company **P/S:** Food Manufacturing and Distribution Services **MA:** National **EXP:** Mr. Wilson's expertise includes research development and quality control. **D/D/R:** Overseeing Plant Manufacturing, National Distribution, Freight Logistics and Purchasing, Coordinating and Analyzing Budgets and Capital Expenditures **H/I/S:** Baseball, Football, Hockey, Basketball **FBP:** Business Watch **EDU:** Bachelor's Degree in Accounting and Business Administration, High Point University (2000) **A/H:** Manager of the Year; Employee of the Year **C/VW:** Local Charitable Organizations **DOB:** May 17, 1978 **POB:** Media, PA **SP:** Sabrina **CHILD:** Madison, Sean **A/S:** He attributes his success to his hard work, determination and ability to find and implement solutions.

Edwina Uilani Wilson-Snyder
Principal
St. Anthony Junior-Senior High School
PO Box 892
Wailuku, HI 96793 United States
esnyder@sasmaui.org
http://www.sasmaui.org

BUS: School **P/S:** Education **MA:** Regional **D/D/R:** Overseeing Educational Administration and Fiscal Responsibilities Fiscal Responsibilities **H/I/S:** Going to the Beach, Spending Time Outdoors and in the Mountains, Spending Time with Family and Friends, Traveling **FBP:** Inc.; Smithsonian **EDU:** Bachelor's Degree in Education and Sociology, Whittier College; Graduate, St. Anthony Junior-Senior High School **A/A/S:** National Catholic Educational Association; National Association of Secondary School Principals; Hawaii Association of Independent Schools; County Police Commissioner **C/VW:** Relay for Life; American Cancer Society **A/S:** She attributes her success to her strong work ethic, taking risks and having a passion for her work. **B/I:** She became involved in this profession because she always had a calling for teaching. **H/O:** The highlight of her career was being the deputy superintendent for the Maui district for eight years.

Mr. Bruce M. Winchell, Esq.
Senior Attorney
Sandia National Laboratories
1155 University Boulevard S.E.
Albuquerque, NM 87106 United States
bmwinch@sandia.gov
http://www.sandia.gov

BUS: Government Organization **P/S:** Nuclear Weapons, Energy and Infrastructure Assurance, Nonproliferation, Defense Systems and Assessments, Homeland Security, Science-Based Technology Research, Community Leadership, Educational and Business Partnerships, Environmental Protection Services **MA:** National **EXP:** Mr. Winchell's expertise is in intellectual property and government contract law. **D/D/R:** Negotiating Government Contracts, Assisting Clients on Case Preparation, Teaching Business and Intellectual Property Law **H/I/S:** Cross-Country Skiing **EDU:** JD, The University of Akron (1974); Bachelor of Science in Chemistry; Bachelor of Arts in Speech **CERTS:** Registered Patent Attorney; Registered Patent Agent, Earned in Canada; Certified Licensing Professional, Licensing Executives Society **A/A/S:** Licensing Executives Society; American Chemical Society; American Intellectual Property Law Association

Amy M. Wineka, RN, BHCS
Adena Health System, Main Site
55 Centennial
Chillicothe, OH 45601 United States
awineka@adena.org
http://www.adena.org

BUS: Healthcare Provider **P/S:** Urgent Care **MA:** Regional **D/D/R:** Proffering Specialty Care Including Intensive Care, Surgery and Emergency Medicine **H/I/S:** Making Crafts, Attending County Fair Craft Shows, Reading, Traveling **FBP:** RN; Nursing Magazine **EDU:** Bachelor's Degree in Healthcare Management, University of Phoenix; Registered Nurse Diploma, Mount Carmel School of Nursing **A/A/S:** Junior Leadership Program **C/VW:** Calvary Baptist Church of Chillicothe; March of Dimes; American Cancer Society; Big Brothers Big Sisters

MR. GARY L. WINK
President, Chief Executive Officer
Golden Chamber of Commerce
1010 Washington Avenue
Golden, CO 80401 United States
info@goldencochamber.org
http://www.goldencochamber.org

BUS: Nonprofit Organization **P/S:** Public Services Including Business, Service and Products of the Golden Area, Promotion of the Commercial, Industrial and Civic Interests of the Members **MA:** National **D/D/R:** Working with Volunteers to Achieve a Difference, Managing a Staff and 75, Working at the Visitors' Center **H/I/S:** Gardening, Yard Work **FBP:** ColoradoBiz **EDU:** Coursework in Agriculture and Business, Iowa State University (1963) **A/A/S:** United States Chamber of Commerce; Jefferson Economic Council; Distant Industry Advisory Council

ERMA A. WINSLOW
Administrator and Guidance Counselor (Retired)
City Board of Education
http://www.cambridgewhoswho.com

BUS: Department of Education Committed to Providing Quality, Comprehensive Elementary, Middle and High School Education **P/S:** Education, Special Education, Guidance and Counseling, Curriculum Development, Recreation, Library and Media Services **MA:** Local **D/D/R:** Counseling Junior High School and High School Students, Assisting Students in Meeting their Educational, Academic, Personal and Social Needs, Continuing to Work with Young Adults for the Betterment of the Community **H/I/S:** Listening to Music, Writing **FBP:** Endangered Values; Religious Books **EDU:** Master's Degree in Health Education, Columbia University; Master's Degree in Guidance and Counseling, Fordham University (1972); Bachelor's Degree in Health and Recreation, Talladega College, Alabama (1958) **C/VW:** Counselor and Assistant to Principal at Joan of Arc Junior High School; Guidance Counselor at Junior High School 258; Guidance Counselor at Richmond Hill High School; Founder and Chair, Bedford Stuyvesant Community Block Association, Brooklyn, New York **A/H:** Community Service Award; Guidance Counselor Award

SHIRLEY WINTERHALTER
Vice President of Sales
Family Savings Magazine
shirley@familysavingonline.com
http://www.cambridgewhoswho.com

BUS: Direct Mail/Advertising **P/S:** Advertising **MA:** Regional **D/D/R:** Overseeing Print Advertising, Management and Sales **H/I/S:** Running, Kickboxing, Golfing, Gardening, Spending Time with her Family **EDU:** Bachelor of Science in Business Education, Wright State University **C/VW:** Woman and Man of the Year Fundraiser for Leukemia and Lymphoma Society; American Heart Association, The Leukemia and Lymphoma Society; American Heart Association; New Optimist **A/S:** She feels that the positive working relationships that she has built with her employees, and the efforts that she puts forth into making sure that they are happy have helped her to build a successful business. **B/I:** She took advantage of an opportunity and began her career. **H/O:** She feels that her work in increasing circulation by one hundred thousand since she began with the company has been the highlight of her career.

DENISE A. WINTZ
Information Technology, Director of Customer Support
Safe Horizon
2 Lafayette Street, Third Floor
New York, NY 10007 United States
dawintz1@verizon.net
http://www.safehorizon.org

BUS: Nonprofit Organization **P/S:** Information Technology Support for Staff who Provide Assistance, Prevents Violence, and Promotes Justice for Victims of Crime and Abuse, their Families, and Communities **MA:** Regional **D/D/R:** Managing the Information Technology Department for Victims of Local Violence, Survivors of Homicide, Mourning Victims of Violent Homes, Covering All Five Boroughs, Support, Offering Onsite Desktop Support **H/I/S:** Golfing, Tennis, Traveling **FBP:** Success **EDU:** Coursework, Fordham University **A/A/S:** National Coalition of 100 Black Women; Corporate Woman's Network; National Society of Black Engineers; National Association for Female Executives **C/VW:** Mentoring Adults and Young Children, Annual Baptist Church

ARNITA A. WISE
Owner
Metro Hair Station
1480 Addison Road S.
Capitol Heights, MD 20743 United States
awise1@verizon.net
http://www.cambridgewhoswho.com

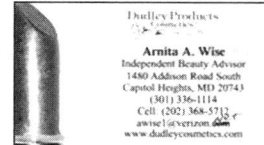

BUS: Beauty Salon **P/S:** Dudley Products, Hair Styling, Makeup Application **MA:** Local **D/D/R:** Hair Styling, Offering Beauty and Makeup Services **H/I/S:** Spending Time with her Four Grandchildren **FBP:** Salon Today; Modern Salons **EDU:** Bachelor of Arts in Psychology, University of the District of Columbia (1987); Associate of Arts in Psychology, American University (1985); Coursework in Cosmetology, Cardozo Beauty Academy **A/A/S:** National Cosmetology Association; Prince George's Chamber of Commerce; Trustee Board Member, Metrotone Baptist Church; Distributor, Dudley Products, Inc **A/H:** Humanitarian Award, Eunice Dudley (2004); Best Business in Capital Heights Award **C/VW:** Millwood/Waterford Civic Association; Breast Cancer Awareness; Local Schools **A/S:** She attributes her success to being consistent, believing in what she is doing and finishing what she starts. **B/I:** She became involved in her profession because she has always been interested in helping women look beautiful. **H/O:** The highlights of her career were receiving the Humanitarian Award from Eunice Dudley and the National Community Service Award from the President's Council on Service and Civic Participation.

MARY B. WISNIEWSKI
Artist, Writer
Mary's Mud Babies
PO Box 443
Bryant, AL 35958 United States
mary.wisniewski@cwwemail.com
http://www.cambridgewhoswho.com

BUS: Sole Proprietorship **P/S:** Artwork, Writing **MA:** National **D/D/R:** Painting Portraits, Making Sculptures of Children and Animals, Working with Stained Glass **H/I/S:** Gardening, Traveling, Caring for Animals, Spending Time with her Children **FBP:** Craft Report; Sunshine Artist **EDU:** Bachelor of Science in Art and Literature, Southern College (1965) **A/H:** Best Recreational Worker, State of Tennessee **C/VW:** Tyner Methodist Church; Local Animal Rescue Shelters; The Humane Society of the United States **CHILD:** Ann, Joseph, Janie, Jean **A/S:** She attributes her success to her positive attitude and determination. **B/I:** She became involved in her profession because she was inspired by her family. **H/O:** The most gratifying aspect of her career is being able to enjoy performing her professional duties.

MR. PATRICK A. WITCIK
Retail Pharmacist
Walgreen Co.
2325 W. Monroe Street
Springfield, IL 62704 United States
p.witcik@yahoo.com
http://www.walgreens.com

BUS: Pharmaceutical Company **P/S:** Prescriptions, Over-the-Counter Medications **MA:** National **D/D/R:** Counseling Doctors and Patients, Consulting, Filling Prescriptions, Advising Patients on Over-the-Counter Medications, Handling Vaccinations, Monitoring Drug Interactions **H/I/S:** Bicycling, Skiing, Reading **FBP:** Drug Topics **EDU:** Bachelor of Science in Pharmacy, North Dakota State University (1976) **CERTS:** Registered Pharmacist **A/S:** He attributes his success to his perseverance. **B/I:** He became involved in his profession through a natural progression of opportunities. **H/O:** The most gratifying aspect of his job is helping people. **I/F/Y:** In five years, Mr. Witcik hopes to continue working in his current position.

GINA WITHROW
Business Owner
Alaska Asphalt Services
maxwithrow@aol.com
http://www.cambridgewhoswho.com

BUS: Asphalt Paving **P/S:** Paving, Excavation **MA:** Local **D/D/R:** Supporting Contractors **H/I/S:** Working Out, Outdoor Activities, Spending Time with her Two Children **C/VW:** Catholic Social Services; The Father's Heart Street Ministry **A/S:** She attributes her success to being self-motivated and goal oriented, full of energy and driven to succeed. **B/I:** She became involved in her profession after managing a bank for 12 years. She wanted a profession where she could still be with her children as much as possible, so she opted for a career change. **H/O:** The highlight of her career has been working in an industry that does not typically have many females. She has a good reputation and stands behind her work.

SUZANNE L. WITTENSCHLAEGER
Counselor
South Lakes High School
11400 S. Lakes Drive
Reston, VA 20191 United States
switten@aol.com
http://www.fcps.edu/SouthLakesHS

BUS: High School **P/S:** Educational Services for Students **MA:** Local **D/D/R:** Counseling for All Students, Specializing in Emotionally Disabled and Mentally Retarded Students **H/I/S:** Running **FBP:** American School Counselor Journal **EDU:** Pursuing Ph.D. in Psychology, Capella University; Master's Degree in Counseling; Bachelor's Degree in Psychology; Associate Degree in Physical Education and Recreation, Marymount University **CERTS:** Certification in Sports Psychology Consulting **A/A/S:** Association for the Advancement of Applied Sport Psychology; National Strength and Conditioning Association; American School Counselors Association; American Counseling Association; American Psychological Association **C/VW:** National Multiple Sclerosis Foundation; American Cancer Society; Team Captain for Friends and Family, Bicycle Group Fundraiser to Raise Awareness for Multiple Sclerosis

LISA LAUBACKER WOJCIK, BS, MT, ASCP, CLS
Laboratory Manager
Sheehan Memorial Hospital
425 Michigan Avenue
Buffalo, NY 14203 United States
smhlab@smhhealth.org
http://www.cambridgewhoswho.com

BUS: Hospital **P/S:** Full Healthcare **MA:** Local **D/D/R:** Working in the Laboratory with Clinical Chemistry and Hematology **H/I/S:** Reading Historical Books, Volunteering at her Children's School **EDU:** Bachelor of Science in Medical Technology, St. Bonaventure University **CERTS:** Certified Clinical Laboratory Scientist, National Credentialing Agency **A/A/S:** American Society of Clinical Pathologists **C/VW:** St. Aloysius Gonzaga; Breast Cancer Foundation; American Cancer Society **A/S:** She attributes her personal and professional success to her care for the well-being of her patients. **B/I:** She has always had an interest in the field and enjoys the investigation aspect of laboratory work. **H/O:** The highlight of her career is having the ability to change the course of the treatment of her patients.

BETTY WOLF
Owner
Wolf's Day Care Center
181 N. Drive
Saugerties, NY 12477 United States
betty-bob@msn.com
http://www.cambridgewhoswho.com

BUS: Child Care Center **P/S:** Infant and Toddler Programs, Preschool Programs, Half-Day and Before and After School Programs **MA:** Regional **D/D/R:** Overseeing Staff of Seven People, Instructing Cardiopulmonary Resuscitation Professionals, Caring for Children and Infants, Managing Operations, Overseeing Before- and After-School Programs **H/I/S:** Gardening, Sewing, Making Handicrafts **FBP:** Young Children; National Education Association Journal; Association of Edison Illuminating Companies Publications **EDU:** Bachelor's Degree in Early Childhood Education, University of Westford, England; Associate Degree; Coursework in Dispensing Medication **CERTS:** Licensed Beautician, State of New York (1963); Certified Child Development Associate **A/A/S:** New York State Association for the Education of Young Children; National Education Association **A/H:** Award, Citation for Exemplary Day Care Service, President Clinton; Award, Commendation, Congressman Maurice Hinchey; Two-Time Recipient, National Businesswoman of the Year Award, National Republican Congressional Committee; Ronald Reagan Medal of Honor

KENNETH R. WOLFE
Professor Emeritus
University of Toledo
8627 Augusta Lane
Holland, OH 43528 United States
kwolfe2029@sbcglobal.net
http://www.utoledo.edu

BUS: University **P/S:** Higher Education **MA:** International **D/D/R:** Teaching Engineering and Applied Mathematics, Developing Optimized and Heuristic Models for Various Industries **H/I/S:** Exercising, Working with Computers, Bicycling, Reading **FBP:** Informs **EDU:** Ph.D. in Chemical Engineering, Minor in Mathematics, Georgia Institute of Technology (1956); Bachelor's Degree in Chemical Engineering, Georgia Institute of Technology **A/A/S:** Acting Chairman, Ph.D. Systems Program; Operations Research Society of America; Tau Beta Phi; American Institute of Chemical Engineering; American Society of Engineering Educators; American Institute of Industrial Engineering; Ohio Society of Professional Engineers; Sigma Xi Scientific Research Society; Phi Lambda Upsilon; Phi Kappa Phi Honor Society; Institute for Operations Research and the Management Sciences **A/H:** Outstanding Undergraduate Professor (1995); Outstanding Teacher Award, University of Toledo (1994)

FRED WOLSKI
Vice President
Barnhart Press
2600 Farnam Street
Omaha, NE 68131 United States
fred@barnhartpress.com
http://www.cambridgewhoswho.com

BUS: Commercial Printing Company **P/S:** Complex Premium Printing **MA:** Regional **D/D/R:** Overseeing High-End Printing Projects and Corporate Sales **H/I/S:** Playing Hockey, Listening to Music, Exercising **EDU:** Bachelor of Arts in Journalism, University of Nebraska, Omaha (1988) **A/A/S:** Omaha Federation of Advertising; American Marketing Association **A/S:** He attributes his success to his gregariousness. **B/I:** He became involved in his profession because he had an interest in the printing field. **H/O:** The highlight of his career was earning his current position.

CHRISTINA WONG
Student
Colgate University
13 Oak Drive
Hamilton, NY 13346 United States
cwong@colgate.edu
http://www.colgate.edu

BUS: University **P/S:** Higher Education **MA:** Local **D/D/R:** Studying Organic Chemistry **H/I/S:** Traveling, Spending Time with Friends and Family, Playing Soccer and Volleyball, Swimming **FBP:** The Economist **EDU:** Pursuing Bachelor of Arts in Chemistry, Colgate University, Hamilton, New York **A/A/S:** Phi Eta Sigma; Cultural Organizations **C/VW:** Susan G. Komen Breast Cancer Foundation

JULIA H. WOOD, RNC
Registered Nurse
Morristown Memorial Hospital
100 Madison Avenue
Morristown, NJ 07960 United States
woodnj@optonline.net
http://www.morristownmemorialhospital.org/en/morristown

BUS: Healthcare Facility, Hospital **P/S:** Excellent Health and Patient Care Services **MA:** Regional **D/D/R:** Working in the High Risk Delivery Unit, Nursing and Labor and Delivery Patient Care **H/I/S:** Soccer **FBP:** Journal of Perinatal and Neonatal Nursing **EDU:** Bachelor of Science in Nursing, Skidmore College (1981) **CERTS:** Certified in In-House Obstetrics and Fetal Monitoring **A/A/S:** Sigma Theta Tau; Association of Women's Health, Obstetric and Neonatal Nurses

BRINDA CARROL WOODALL, BSN, RN
Registered Nurse
Contract Travel Nurse
http://www.cambridgewhoswho.com

BUS: Travel Nursing **P/S:** Nursing **MA:** National **D/D/R:** Intensive Care Unit Nursing, Emergency Room Nursing, Perioperative Nursing, Gastroenterology Laboratory Nursing, Critical Care Nursing **H/I/S:** Reading, Watching Sports **FBP:** RN **EDU:** Bachelor of Science in Nursing, Henderson State University **A/A/S:** Arkansas Nurses Association; Association of Critical Care Nurses; Association of perioperative Registered Nurses; Emergency Room Nurses Association; Former Member, Fire Department

PATRICK L. WOODEN SR.
Pastor, President
Upper Room Church, Inc.
3300 Idlewood Village
Raleigh, NC 27614 United States
pwooden@nc.rr.org
http://www.cambridgewhoswho.com

BUS: Church **P/S:** Religious Services **MA:** International **D/D/R:** Preaching the Word of God

MICHELLE L. WOODS
Owner
Michelle's Aerobics, Fitness and Personal Training
1108 Greenwood Avenue
Jackson, MI 49203 United States
fitdiva410@sbcglobal.net
http://www.cambridgewhoswho.com

BUS: Fitness Company **P/S:** Personal Fitness Training, Individual and Group Classes **MA:** Regional **D/D/R:** Personal Training, Developing Workout Programs, Consulting on Diet Programs and Nutritional Products, Group Spinning, Kickboxing, Offering Step Classes, Gliding Classes, Body Pump Classes, Zumba Classes and Drums Alive Classes **H/I/S:** Bicycling, Rollerskating, Running, Working Out **FBP:** ACE Journal **EDU:** College Coursework **CERTS:** Certified Group Exercise and Personal Trainer, National Exercise Training Association, American Council on Exercise; Appointed Member, Michigan Board of Nursing, Governor of the State of Michigan; Chairwoman, Disciplinary Subcommittee, Michigan Board of Nursing **A/A/S:** National Exercise Training Association; Young Men's Christian Association; American Council on Exercise; Zumba Fitness **DOB:** October 1, 1955 **CHILD:** Christopher, Ryan **A/S:** She attributes her success to her passion for her profession. **B/I:** She became involved in her profession because fitness was a hobby of hers.

DR. WILL W. WOODS
Pastor
Altona Baptist Church, Inc.
PO Box 548
Christiansted, VI 00821 United States
revwwwoods@aol.com
http://www.cambridgewhoswho.com

BUS: Church **P/S:** Religion and Spiritual Services Including Dynamic Worship, Spiritual Counseling, Opportunities for Spiritual Growth and Development, Family Counseling, Weddings, Spiritual Leadership **MA:** Regional **EXP:** Mr. Woods' expertise is in pastoral ministry. **D/D/R:** Offering Guidance, Spiritual Leadership and Human Services to the Community **FBP:** Time; Christian Counseling Today **EDU:** Doctor of Divinity **A/A/S:** American Christian Counseling Association; Baptist General Conference **C/VW:** American Red Cross

TRICIA K. WOODWARD
Registered Nurse, Orthopedic Nurse
Unity Health System
1550 Long Pond Road
Rochester, NY 14626 United States
triciahollister@yahoo.com
http://www.unity.com

BUS: Hospital **P/S:** Healthcare **MA:** Local **D/D/R:** Nursing, Caring for Patients, Assisting Doctors, Overseeing Recovery Room Operations and Staff, Practicing General Surgery, Mentoring Interns **H/I/S:** Spending Time with her Family, Traveling, Baking, Gardening **FBP:** RN; American Journal of Nurses **EDU:** Bachelor of Science in Nursing, SUNY Brockport **CERTS:** Certified Orthopedic Nurse **A/A/S:** American Association of Critical-Care Nurses; National Association of Orthopaedic Nurses; National League for Nursing **C/VW:** American Heart Association **A/S:** She attributes her success to her dedication and work ethic. **B/I:** She became involved in her profession because she always wanted to help people. **H/O:** The highlight of her career was receiving her certification in orthopedics.

ROSEMARY J. WOOL
Director, Chief Executive
Prison Healthcare Practitioners
Wicken House
105 Weston Road
Aston Clinton, HP22 5EP United Kingdom
wool1@gotadsl.co.uk
http://www.prisonhealthcarepractitioners.com

BUS: Membership Organization, Prison Healthcare Association **P/S:** Consultant in Prison Healthcare **MA:** International **D/D/R:** Working with Senior Government and Prisoners, Psychiatry, Drug and Alcohol Addictions **H/I/S:** Singing, Listening to Music, Church Activities **FBP:** The Economist **EDU:** FRC, Psychology (1986); Coursework, University of London (1974); MD, University of London (1960); MRC, Psychology **A/A/S:** BMA; Royal College of Psychiatry; Advisory Board Member, The International Centre of Drug Policy **DOB:** July 19, 1935 **W/H:** Director of Legal Affairs, Council of Europe (1996-Present); Family Practitioner (1963-1970); Director of Healthcare, Prison Service of England and Wales (1989-1996); Head of Education in Department of Addictions, St. George's Hospital Medical School (1996-2004); Psychiatrist Specializing in the Treatment of Drug and Alcohol Misuse (1998-2004) **C/A:** Prison Reviews Published by the Council of Europe

JOHANNA D. WOOLMAN, MS
Clinical Therapist, Owner
Dragonfly Essentials
10632 S.W. 100th Street
Miami, FL 33176 United States
Jdw@dragonflytherapies.com
http://www.dragonflytherapies.com

BUS: Holistic Therapies **P/S:** Therapies Reaching Physical, Emotional and Mental Difficulties and Complementing Traditional Medicine with an Alternative Herbal Approach **MA:** Regional **D/D/R:** Specializing in Marriages between Eastern and Western Modalities and Applying the Best Approach to the Needs of Each Client **H/I/S:** Traveling, Reading **FBP:** Industry-Related Publications **EDU:** Pursuing Doctorate in Psychological Forensics, Carlos Albizu University; Master's Degree in Clinical Psychology, Specialty in Forensics, Carlos Albizu University; Master's Degree in Criminal Justice, Specialty in Behavioral Science, Nova Southeastern University **CERTS:** Certified Reiki Master **A/A/S:** Agency for Aromatherapy Medicines; Notary Republic; Reiki Worldwide Association; American Psychological Association **C/VW:** Congregation Bet Breira

TAMMY E. WORKMAN, RN
Registered Nurse
Palm Beach Pediatrics
12955 Palms West Drive
Loxahatchee, FL 33470 United States
tammyworkman@adelphia.net
http://www.cambridgewhoswho.com

BUS: Healthcare **P/S:** Medical Care **MA:** Regional **D/D/R:** Pediatrics **H/I/S:** Watching Professional Sports Games **FBP:** Nursing2009 **EDU:** Pursuing Bachelor of Science in Nursing, Florida Atlantic University; Associate Degree in Science, Palm Beach Community College; Associate of Science in Nursing, Palm Beach Community College **CERTS:** Licensed Emergency Medical Technician **C/VW:** Susan G. Komen Breast Cancer Foundation **A/S:** She attributes her personal and professional success to her dedication to the profession. **B/I:** She became involved in the profession because she has always wanted to help others. **H/O:** The most gratifying aspect of her career is working in her current position as a triage nurse.

ROSELAND LOWE WORRELL
Marketing and Sales Counselor
Lake Prince Woods
100 Anna Goode Way
Suffolk, VA 23434 United States
worrells@gtcinternet.com
http://www.cambridgewhoswho.com

BUS: Senior Care Center **P/S:** Continuing Care, Healthcare **MA:** International **EXP:** Ms. Worrell's expertise is in marketing, sales counseling and the oversight of new cottage building projects. **H/I/S:** Spending Time with her Family, Reading **FBP:** CIO; Paper Loop **EDU:** Master of Business Administration, University of Arkansas, Monticello (1996); Bachelor's Degree in Organizational Management, Saint Paul's College (1994) **A/A/S:** Lifetime Member, Parent-Teacher Association; Director, Family Life Education; Veterans Affairs Team Leader, City of Suffolk **A/H:** Outstanding Young Woman of America Award, City of Suffolk **C/VW:** Volunteer, Local Charitable Organizations; Deacon, Holy Neck Christian Church

ELEANOR M. W WORTHY
Nurse Practitioner
OB/GYN
Baylor College of Medicine, Teen Family Planning Clinic
5656 Kelley Street
Houston, TX 77026 United States
eleanor2308@earthlink.net
http://www.cambridgewhoswho.com

BUS: College, Family Planning Clinic **P/S:** Healthcare, Medical Research, Education **MA:** Regional **D/D/R:** Practicing Women's Health, Obstetrics and Gynecology **H/I/S:** Working Out, Driving, Swimming, Horseback Riding, Caring for her Cats, Driving her Porsche **FBP:** Journal of Nurse Practitioners; Royal College of Midwives **EDU:** Master of Science in Nursing, University of Texas Medical Branch **A/A/S:** President Elect, Galveston Coalition of Advanced Practice Nurses (2007-2008); Sigma Theta Tau; Phi Kappa Phi; Women's Healthcare Nurse Practitioners Association; American Academy of Nurse Practitioners; Branch Representative, Royal College of Midwives; Royal College of Midwives Representative, English Board **A/H:** Dean's Award for Outstanding Academic Achievement (2007); Honoree, Who's Who Among Students in American Universities and Colleges (2007) **DOB:** August 11, 1962 **SP:** Thomas **CHILD:** Alexander **W/H:** Part-Time Clinical Instructor, University of Texas Medical Branch (2006-2007); In Vitro Fertilisation Nurse, Center for Reproduction and Women's Health (2004-2006); Clear Lake Regional Medical Center (2004); Recovery Nurse, Center of Reproductive Medicine (2001-2004); Registered Nurse, Clear Lake Regional Medical Center (2000-2001) **A/S:** She attributes her success to her passion for women's health, enthusiasm and a constant desire to learn. **B/I:** She became involved in the profession because she wanted to help others and make her own path in life. **H/O:** The most gratifying aspect of her career is her decision to work in women's health.

BETTY M. WRIGHT
Owner
BMW Associates
7221 S. Land Park Drive
Sacramento, CA 95831 United States
bmw90@sbcglobal.net
http://www.cambridgewhoswho.com

BUS: Consulting Firm **P/S:** Consulting Services, Human, Personal and Financial Services for Incompetent Individuals and Disabled Veterans **MA:** Local **D/D/R:** Managing Finances, Social Services and Special Programs, Counseling on Leadership Guidance for Children, Mentally Impaired and Elderly Individuals **H/I/S:** Reading, Traveling **FBP:** NASW Journal **EDU:** Master of Social Work, University of Sacramento; Bachelor of Arts in Psychology, California State University, Fresno **CERTS:** Private Fiduciary Certification; CPG Certification **A/A/S:** Delta Sigma Theta; National Coalition of 100 Black Women; Former Chairwoman, In-Home Support Services Advisory Committee; Vice Chairwoman, The Sacramento County Adult and Aging Commission

DIAN WRIGHT, RN, MSN, FNP, MBA
Family Nurse Practitioner
Corner Care Clinics
2125 State Street
New Albany, IN 47150 United States
diannp07@insightbb.com

BUS: Immediate Care Clinic **P/S:** Healthcare **MA:** Southern Indiana, Louisville KY **D/D/R:** Offering First-Line Services to a Patients in a Clinical Setting **H/I/S:** Shopping, White Water Rafting, Fine Dining, Enjoying Nature, Bicycling **FBP:** Advance for Nurse Practitioners **EDU:** Master's Degree of Science, Indiana Wesleyan University; Master of Business Administration, Indiana Wesleyan University; Bachelor of Science in Nursing, U.S. Army Madisonville TN **A/A/S:** Sigma Theta Tau, Chapter 188; American Academy of Nurse Practitioners **C/VW:** Volunteer, American Red Cross; Health Fairs; Community Service **A/S:** She attributes her success to her mother's support and her desire to overcome rough experiences. **B/I:** She became involved in the profession after taking psychology and sociology courses and found she had a natural aptitude to help people. **H/O:** The most gratifying aspect of her career is being able to give back to others.

MARILYN 'NIA' WRIGHT, RN
Endoscopy Department Head
Washington Hospital Center
110 Irving Street N.W.
Washington, DC 20010 United States
m.nia.wright@medstar.net
http://www.whcenter.org

BUS: Hospital, Acute Care Level 1 Trauma Center **P/S:** Anesthesiology, Cardiology, Gastroenterology, Dermatology, Geriatrics and Long-Term Care, General Internal Medicine, Interventional Radiology, Neuroscience, Infectious Diseases, Medical Imaging, Nephrology, Neurosurgery, Neurology, Pharmacy, Gynecologic Oncology, Obstetrics and Gynecology, Pathology and Laboratory Medicine, Ophthalmology and Otolaryngology **MA:** Local **D/D/R:** Operating Room Nursing, Managing Endoscopy Management **H/I/S:** Drama Ministry, Singing in the Special Events Choir, Working with the Local Boy Scout Troop **FBP:** AORN Journal; CenterNurse Journal **EDU:** Bachelor of Science in Nursing, University of the District of Columbia; Bachelor of Arts in Psychology, University of the District of Columbia **CERTS:** Certified Nurse Operating Room **A/A/S:** Association of perioperative Registered Nurses; American Organization of Nurse Executives; The Society of Gastroenterology Nurses and Associates; New Life Worship Center; Life Today International **A/H:** Nurse Educator of the Year, DC-Baltimore Area, Nursing Spectrum

NATHAN L. WRIGHT, BA
Accounts Payable Service Assistant
Forest City Enterprises
50 Public Square, Suite 1200
Cleveland, OH 44113 United States
nathanwright@forestcity.net
http://www.forestcity.net

BUS: Real Estate and Construction **P/S:** Housing **MA:** National **D/D/R:** Managing Accounts Payable **H/I/S:** Bowling, Spending Time with Family and Friends **FBP:** Industry Related Publications **EDU:** Bachelor's Degree, Sociology, Cleveland State University **C/VW:** The Cleveland Clinic; The American Red Cross **A/S:** He attributes his personal and professional success to his parents. **B/I:** He has always had an interest in the field and enjoys the challenge of the profession. **H/O:** The highlight of her career is his community involvement with the Cleveland Clinic.

SUSAN WRIGHT
Chief Executive Officer
The Criterion Group, Inc.
4842 Sylmar Avenue
Sherman Oaks, CA 91423 United States
susan@criteriongroup.com
http://www.criteriongroup.com

BUS: Below the Line Production Agency **P/S:** Film Production **MA:** National **D/D/R:** Overseeing Management **H/I/S:** Traveling, Gardening, Hiking, Dining with Friends **FBP:** Daily Variety; Hollywood Reporter; Vanity Fair **EDU:** Bachelor of Arts in Journalism, California State University, Northridge **A/A/S:** United States Actors Guild; Signatory, Writers Guild; Patron, American Film Institution

PEGGY WURM, DDS
Director of Dentistry
1199 National Benefit Fund
330 W. 42nd Street
New York, NY 10036 United States
drpeggywurm@cs.com
http://www.cambridgewhoswho.com

BUS: Health Benefit Fund **P/S:** Healthcare **MA:** National **D/D/R:** Directing the Dentistry Health Fund **H/I/S:** Playing the Piano, Swimming, Traveling **EDU:** Doctor of Dental Surgery, Stony Brook University; Master's Degree in Business and Health Administration, New York University; Bachelor's Degree in Biology, Stony Brook University **A/A/S:** Fellow, American College of Dentistry; American Academy of Oral Medicine; American Association of Consultants; Clinical Dental Network; Academy of General Dentistry; American Public Health Association; Diplomat, American Board of Quality Assurance and Utilization Review **C/VW:** Volunteer, Local Hospital **A/S:** She attributes her success to having a deep sense of caring, a desire to be the best she can be and her ability to deal with others. **B/I:** She became involved in dentistry because she was always interested in medicine and always liked the dental field. **H/O:** The highlight of her career was serving on the Employee International Union for 11 years and building the diagnostic and treatment planning facility, which was a brand new concept at the time.

GLENDA S. WYLIE
Director of Technical Marketing
Halliburton
10200 Bellaire Boulevard
Houston, TX 77072 United States
glenda.wylie@halliburton.com
http://www.halliburton.com

BUS: Energy Firm **P/S:** Oil Field Services Including Exploration and Development, Drilling, Abandonment, Oil Field Maintenance, Conversion and Refining Services, Oil Field Operations, Oil Production, Aid in Community Relations and Infrastructure Development, Formation Evaluation, Production Optimization and Landmark Dividing **MA:** International **EXP:** Ms. Wylie's expertise is in oil field technology and assets and developing new oil field products. **FBP:** Money; Forbes; The Wall Street Journal **EDU:** Master's Degree, University of Alaska Anchorage (1991); Bachelor of Science in Chemical Engineering, Texas A&M University (1979); Bachelor of Science in Chemistry (1975) **CERTS:** New Product Development Professional (2004) **A/A/S:** AAQHA; CFWA; Director, Municipal Utility District No. 36; Drilling Engineering Association; IBC; American Petroleum Institute; American Association of Drilling Engineers; National Association for Female Executives **A/H:** HARTS Award, Executive Management Committee **C/VW:** American Red Cross

KAY KATHERINE YADAO GALVAN, LVN
Licensed Vocational Nurse
Lodi Memorial Hospital
975 S. Fairmont Avenue
Lodi, CA 95240 United States
goddesssexybabydoll@hotmail.com
http://www.lodihealth.org

BUS: Nonprofit Hospital that Strives to Improve the Quality of Life in the Community it Serves **P/S:** Quality and Timely Healthcare Services, Ranging from Health Promotion and Education to Diagnostics, Acute-Inpatient Care, Rehabilitation Services and Home Care Services **MA:** Regional **D/D/R:** Pediatric and Geriatric Medical and Surgical Nursing **H/I/S:** Reading, Writing, Singing, Dancing **EDU:** Pursuing Associate of Arts **CERTS:** Registered Nurse Studies (2007) **A/H:** Elementary School Valedictorian; State Scholar, High School

ANTHONY K. YAMAMOTO, LCSW
Director
Social Work Department
Children's Hospital Central California
9300 Valley Children's Place
Madera, CA 93638 United States
ayamamoto@childrenscentralcal.org
http://www.childrenscentralcal.org

BUS: Hospital **P/S:** Healthcare for Seriously Ill and Injured Children **MA:** Regional **EXP:** Mr. Yamamoto's expertise is in medical social work. **D/D/R:** Overseeing Psychiatric Work for Children and Adults, Working with Nonprofit Organizations, Treating Child Abuse Victims and Injuries, Counseling Families and Groups, Teaching Clinical and Management Courses in Asian American Studies **H/I/S:** Traveling, Reading, Wrestling **EDU:** Master of Social Work, University of California, Los Angeles (1976) **CERTS:** Licensed Clinical Social Worker, State of California **A/A/S:** Society of Social Work Leaders in Healthcare **A/H:** Outstanding Healthcare Social Worker Award, Mendibury Foundation (2006); Outstanding Young Men of America Award; Who's Who Historical Society (1988) **C/VW:** Volunteer, Sexual Assault Field of Madera County, CA; Easter Seals; The Leukemia & Lymphoma Society **A/S:** He attributes his success to the support he receives from his family. **B/I:** He became involved in his profession because of his desire to help people and make a positive difference in their lives. **H/O:** The highlight of his career was starting an inpatient psychiatric unit at the Children's Hospital Central.

JANET M. YAMRON
Professor of Music, Music Education, Associate Dean
Boyer College of Music and Dance
2001 N. 13th Street
Philadelphia, PA 19122 United States
jyamron@temple.edu
http://www.temple.edu/boyer

BUS: Performing Arts College Offering a Wide Array of Degree Programs in Music and Dance **P/S:** Undergraduate and Graduate Degree Programs in Music and Dance, Professional Training, Excellent Performing Opportunities **MA:** International **D/D/R:** Overseeing the Entire Undergraduate Program, Developing the Curriculum, Advising Students and Faculty, Teaching Conducting and Choral Group Methods, Working as a Local, Regional and National Adjudicator **H/I/S:** Going to the Theater, Singing **FBP:** Choral Journal; Music Educators Journal **EDU:** Master's Degree Plus in Performance History and Literature, Temple University (1957); Bachelor's Degree in Choral Conducting, Boyer College of Music and Dance, Temple University (1954) **A/A/S:** American Choral Directors; Chair of Various Committees for Bi-Centennial Celebration (1976)

MICHELE A. YARBROUGH, MPA
Comptroller
Mobile County District Attorney's Office
205 Government Street
C-501
Mobile, AL 36606 United States
michele_yarbrough@mobile_da.org
http://www.marykay.com/myarbrough13

BUS: Law Services **P/S:** Payroll, Financial Grant Administration **MA:** Regional **D/D/R:** Managing Payroll, Human Resources, Hiring and Firing **H/I/S:** Watching Rugby **EDU:** Master of Public Administration, University of South Alabama **A/A/S:** American Society of Public Administration; Family Council Nursing Home **C/VW:** Little Flower Catholic Church, Battleship Rugby Club **A/S:** She attributes her success to her family. **B/I:** She chose the profession after completing an internship at the district attorney's office and was offered a position. **H/O:** The highlight of her career was receiving her master's degree.

CINDY YATES
Regional Management Trainer
GEICO
4201 Spring Valley Road
Dallas, TX 75244 United States
cyates@geico.com
http://www.cambridgewhoswho.com

BUS: Insurance Company **P/S:** Automobile Insurance **MA:** National **D/D/R:** Designing Courses, Conducting Classes, Coaching, Developmental Training, Managing Supervisory Services **H/I/S:** Reading, Camping, Sports, Spending Quality Time with her Family and Friends **EDU:** Bachelor's Degree in Human Resources Management, University of North Texas **A/A/S:** American Society for Training and Development **A/H:** Recognized as an Outstanding Course Leader, American Institute for Chartered Property Casualty Underwriters **C/VW:** Christian Community Action; United Way of America

MR. RODNEY NEIL YAWN
Critical Care Paramedic, Instructor for Disabled Services
American Medical Response
124 W. Park Drive
Birmingham, AL 35211 United States
cmosnuffy@aol.com
http://www.cambridgewhoswho.com

BUS: Transportation Company **P/S:** Ambulatory Services **MA:** Local **EXP:** Mr. Yawn's expertise is in critical care nursing. **D/D/R:** Instructing Emergency Medical Technicians **H/I/S:** Golfing, Stargazing, Hunting, Fishing **FBP:** Journal of Emergency Medical Services **EDU:** Bachelor's Degree, University of Alabama at Birmingham; Associate Degree in Emergency Medical Technician Studies, Northwest-Shoals Community College **A/A/S:** National Association of EMS Educators; National Response Plan; National Association of Emergency Medical Technicians; International Star Trek Fan Association **C/VW:** Birmingham Zoo; Volunteer, Brookside Fire Department **A/S:** He attributes his success to his hard work. **H/O:** The highlight of his career was being promoted as a training officer. **I/F/Y:** In five years, Mr. Yawn hopes to continue in the same field and would also like to teach.

CARL E. YEAGER
Site Manager, OSS
Shell Oil Company
701 Poydras Street
New Orleans, LA 70139 United States
carl.yeager@shell.com
http://www.shell.com

BUS: Energy Firm **P/S:** Oil and Gas Services **MA:** New Orleans, Los Angeles **EXP:** Mr. Yeager's expertise is in architectural design. **H/I/S:** Golfing, Playing Softball, Coaching Children's Recreational Sports **FBP:** Facility Management **EDU:** Bachelor's Degree in Architectural Technology, The University of Southern Mississippi (1982) **A/A/S:** National Fire Protection Association; American Society for Information Science and Technology; International Facility Management Association

CHRISTINE MARY YEARBURY
Owner and Manager
Riverview Villa Rest Home
22A Wolfe Street
Whangarei, New Zealand
c-bird@xtra.co.nz
http://www.cambridgewhoswho.com

BUS: Senior Residence **P/S:** Nursing Services, Palliative Care, Social Services, Spiritual Counseling, Beauty Services, Pain Management, Short and Long-Term Care **MA:** Regional **D/D/R:** Managing a Rest Home with 14 Residents, Handling Daily Operations, Overseeing Patient Care and Patient Education, Managing a Staff of Seven Care Assistants **H/I/S:** Listening to Rock 'n' Roll **CERTS:** Registered Nurse, New Zealand (2000) **A/A/S:** New Zealand Nurses Organization

ERICKA YEGER
Accounting Manager
Senior Services Associates, Inc.
101 S. Grove Avenue
Elgin, IL 60120 United States
eyeger@mchsi.com
http://www.seniorservicesassoc.org

BUS: Senior Services Charitable Organization **P/S:** Senior Services to Help Older Adults Preserve their Independence and Mental and Physical Wellness **MA:** Local **D/D/R:** Managing Accounting **H/I/S:** Gardening and Traveling **EDU:** Associate Degree in Business Management and Marketing, College of Dupage; Pursuing Bachelor of Arts, University of Phoenix **C/VW:** Senior Services Associates **A/S:** She attributes her success to motivation and striving to advance. **B/I:** She chose the profession because she always liked accounting. **H/O:** The highlight of her career is her current position.

REGINA M. YENTSCH, RN, BSN
Intake Coordinator
Columbia Montour Home Health and Hospice
410 Glenn Avenue, Suite 200
Bloomsburg, PA 17815 United States
tailswaggin@hotmail.com
http://www.cmhhh.org

BUS: Home Health Agency **P/S:** Comprehensive Home Health Services **MA:** Regional **D/D/R:** Staff Nursing, Managing Cases, Overseeing the Cardiac Care Unit, Hospice Caring, Preaching through Puppetry Ministry to the Community, Nursing Homes, Individual Homes and Team Approach through the Church **H/I/S:** Preaching through Puppetry Ministry, Making Crafts **FBP:** American Journal of Critical Care **EDU:** Bachelor of Science in Nursing, Bloomsburg University of Pennsylvania (1998) **CERTS:** Registered Nurse, Ashland State General Hospital School of Nursing (1975); Certified CPR Instructor **A/A/S:** American Association of Critical Care Nurses; Puppet Ministry, American Heart Association **C/VW:** Local Church **A/S:** She attributes her success to her faith in God. **B/I:** She became involved in her profession because of her caring nature. **H/O:** The highlight of her career was receiving her bachelor's degree in nursing.

LAURIE E. YORK, RN, CNOR
Director OR/SPD/Laser
Elliott Hospital
One Elliott Way
Manchester, NH 03103 United States
elyork@elliott-hs.org
http://www.sss.elliott-hs.org

BUS: Healthcare **P/S:** Hospital Addressing the Medical Needs of the Community **MA:** Local **D/D/R:** Operating Room Nursing **H/I/S:** Motorcycle Riding, Playing in the Pool League, Spending Time with her Grandchildren **FBP:** AORN **EDU:** Pursuing Master of Science Degree, Regis University; Registered Nurse Diploma, Eastern Maine Medical School of Nursing **CERTS:** Certified CNOR **A/A/S:** New Hampshire Nursing Association; IASPMN; AORN **C/VW:** United Way of America; Special Olympics; March of Dimes; Elliott Hospital Foundation **A/S:** She attributes her success to her communication skills. **B/I:** She became involved in her profession because she was born to be a nurse. **H/O:** The highlight of her career is improving relations between hospital staff and physicians and providing improved patient care.

LINDA K. YOUNG
Infection Control Nurse, President
MD Transcriptions
The Centers
5664 S.W. 60th Avenue
Ocala, FL 34474 United States
ly39@emborgmail.com
http://www.thecenters.us

BUS: Mental Healthcare Center **P/S:** Healthcare, Acute Care Services **MA:** Marion and Citrus County **EXP:** Ms. Young's expertise is in psychiatric evaluations and transcriptions, dispensing medication, ambulatory surgery, medical transcription, psychiatric and substance abuse, infection control and intensive care nursing. **D/D/R:** Developing Individual Treatment Plans, Orienting New Employees **H/I/S:** Reading, Traveling, Gardening, Fishing **FBP:** RN **EDU:** Coursework in Pharmacology, National Association for Practical Nurse Education and Service **CERTS:** Certified Infection Control Nurse, Western Schools (1999); Licensed Practical Nurse, Akron School of Practical Nursing (1979); Certified Medical Transcriptionist, Canton College (1974) **A/H:** Nurse of the Year Award (1997)

RENEE YOUNG
Physical Therapist II
Renee Young, PT
1842 Olympus Loop Drive
Vista, CA 92081 United States
drytherapy@msn.com
http://www.cambridgewhoswho.com

BUS: Physical Therapy Practice **P/S:** Healthcare **MA:** Local **D/D/R:** Performing Physical Therapy with a Focuse on Orthopedics **H/I/S:** Natural Body Building **FBP:** American Physical Therapy Association Journals **EDU:** Master's Degree, University of California at Northridge **A/H:** Gold Medal Recipient, Natural Olympiad **C/VW:** Veterans Administration; The Salvation Army; Girls Scouts of the United States of America; Boys Scouts of America **A/S:** She attributes her success to enjoying the medical field. **H/O:** The most gratifying aspect of her career are the recognition she receives from her peers and mentoring new graduates.

WILSON YOUNG, MD
MD
Mount Sinai Medical Center
1 Gustav Levy Place
New York, NY 10029 United States
wyhadley@hotmail.com
http://www.nymc.edu

BUS: Hospital **P/S:** Healthcare **MA:** Regional **EXP:** Dr. Young's expertise is in internal medicine, cardiology and pharmacology. **D/D/R:** Performing Internal Medicine Research on Cardiac Stem Cell Differentiation **H/I/S:** Shooting Pool **EDU:** Pursuing Ph.D., New York Medical College; MD, New York Medical College (2007); Master of Science, New York Medical College (1999); Bachelor of Arts, Columbia University, Columbia College (1995) **A/A/S:** New York Academy of Sciences; Medical Society of the State of New York; American Medical Association; Berson Society **DOB:** March 7, 1973 **I/F/Y:** In five years, Dr. Young hopes to be working in academia as well as practicing and researching cardiology.

BRENDA C. YOUNGS
Spanish Medical Interpreter, Legal Assistant
Hart, Sheth, Boedefeld, Gervich
1420 Cave Springs Estate Drive
St. Peters, MO 63376 United States
salsapr1958@aol.com
http://www.cambridgewhoswho.com

BUS: Healthcare **P/S:** Interpreters for Hospital and All Types of Law Services **MA:** Missouri **D/D/R:** Spanish and Medical Interpreting **H/I/S:** Ballroom Dancing **EDU:** Bachelor of Science, University of Puerto Rico **A/A/S:** Board Member, Puerto Rican Society **A/H:** St. Louis Star Ball Bronze Medal Championship

JENNIFER M. ZABEL
Teacher
The Department of Defense Education Activity
Lyman Hall Elementary
631 Smiley Street
Hinesville, GA 31313 United States
jennifer.zabell@am.dodea.edu
http://www.cambridgewhoswho.com

BUS: Government Office **P/S:** Education **MA:** Local **D/D/R:** Teaching Elementary Education, Creating Curriculum **H/I/S:** Watching her Children's Soccer Games, Watching Movies **FBP:** The Mailbox; Education Weekly **EDU:** Master of Arts in Education, Concentration in Curriculum Instruction, University of Phoenix (2005) **A/A/S:** Professional Association of Georgia Educators **C/VW:** St. Jude Children's Research Hospital **SP:** Charles **CHILD:** Chandler, Addsyn **A/S:** She attributes her success to her ability to understand her students.

Ms. Cynthia E. Zachary, RN, MSN
Registered Nurse
All Care Family Practice
10636 Bitterroot Way
Knoxville, TN 37932 United States
cynthiabsn2001@comcast.net
http://www.fsregional.com

BUS: Hospital **P/S:** Maternity Services, Advanced Cardiac Technology, Critical Care Units, Day Surgery Unit, Emergency Medicine, Gastroenterology, Gynecology, Joint Replacement Center, Pulmonary Care, Full Service Acute-Care Hospital and Regional Referral Center with 541 Beds **MA:** Local **EXP:** Ms. Zachary's expertise is in emergency room nursing, coding, neonatal intensive care nursing and family practice nursing. **H/I/S:** Reading, Traveling **EDU:** Master of Science in Nursing, The University of Tennessee (2006); Bachelor of Science in Nursing, The University of Tennessee (2001) **A/A/S:** American Nurses Association; Tennessee Nurses Association; Sigma Theta Tau; Gamma Chi Chapter

Magaly Zapata
Microbiology Lab Technician
Department of Biology
Universidad de Puerto Rico, Recinto de Mayagüez
PO Box 9012
Mayaguez, PR 00681 United States
magasata@yahoo.com
http://www.uprm.edu

BUS: University **P/S:** Higher Education Including Microbiology **MA:** Local **D/D/R:** Instructing and Coordinating General Microbiology Laboratory Activities **H/I/S:** Photography, Writing Poems, Traveling, Reading History **FBP:** Microbiology and Biotechnology Literature **EDU:** Bachelor of Science in Agricultural Science, Mayaguez Campus, University of Puerto Rico (1980); Diploma, Guayanilla High School (1975) **A/A/S:** Honorary Member, Society for Industrial Microbiology; Puerto Rican Chapter, American Society of Microbiology **DOB:** April 27, 1958 **CHILD:** Gabriel **W/H:** Microbiology Laboratory Technician, Coordinator, General Microbiology Laboratory, Biology Department, University of Puerto Rico, Mayagüez Campus (1987-2007); Quality Control Supervisor, Mayaguez Dairy, Inc. (1982-1986); Quality Control Technician, Cooperativa de Ganaderos, Inc. (1980-1981)

Karen Zapka, RN, BSN, CDE
Registered Nurse
Baystate Health
3300 Main Street, Suite 3A
Springfield, MA 01107 United States
karen.zapka@bhs.org
http://www.baystatehealth.com

BUS: Top 100 most Highly Integrated Healthcare Networks **P/S:** Baystate Regional Cancer Program, Cardiac Services, Hip and Knee Replacement, Minimally Invasive Surgery and Women's Services **MA:** National **D/D/R:** Outpatient Diabetes Instruction, Education on Type I and Type II Diabetes, Teaching Self-Management **H/I/S:** Reading, Hiking, Making Home Crafts **EDU:** Bachelor of Science in Nursing, Elms College; Diploma in Nursing, Bay State Medical School of Nursing (1978) **A/A/S:** American Association of Diabetes Educators **C/VW:** American Diabetes Association; Leukemia and Lymphoma Society; Children's Wish Foundation; Dana-Farber Cancer Institute; Jamaica Cancer Society

Jolanta J. Zasadna
Realtor, Owner, Broker
Jolanta Realty Inc.
3816 104th Avenue N.
Clearwater, FL 33762 United States
info@jolantarealty.com
http://www.jolantarealty.com

BUS: Real Estate **P/S:** Sales and Management of Real Estate **MA:** Regional **D/D/R:** Specializing in Residential, Commercial and Industrial Real Estate **H/I/S:** Swimming, Going on Cruises, Water Sports **FBP:** Realtor **EDU:** Master's Degree in Law and Administration, Wroclaw University, Poland (1975); Bachelor's Degree in Law **A/A/S:** National Association of Realtors; Florida Association of Realtors; Polish American Engineers of Florida; President, Polish Center **C/VW:** Polish Local Radio Program; The President Polish Center; The Polish Church **A/S:** She attributes her success to her love for what she does and the enjoyment she gets from helping others. **H/O:** The highlight of her career was securing four acres of property and two buildings for the Polish Society.

MARK S. ZECCA
Senior Director of Information Technology
Mitchell 1, LLC, A Snap-On Company
14145 Danielson Street
Poway, CA 92064 United States
mark.zecca@mitchell1.com
http://www.mitchell1.com

BUS: Automotive Repair Information and Software Development **P/S:** Software Development and Applications, Websites and Web Based Information **MA:** National **D/D/R:** System Engineering **H/I/S:** Sailing **FBP:** PC Magazine; Network World **EDU:** Doctor of Business Administration and Communications, Letourneau University of Texas **A/A/S:** San Diego Software Information Systems Council; Hembach Professional Project Management Association; Association of Date Providers; Automotive Aftermarket Industry Association; Institute of Electrical & Electronics Engineers **C/VW:** Knights of Columbus, Board Member, St. Pasquale Academy; Supports a Branch of Mentally Disabled Adults **A/S:** He attributes his success to never settling and always looking for the next thing to learn and try. **H/O:** The highlight of his career is being a mentor and inspiring women to enter the field. He eventually hopes to teach in a classroom setting.

GINGER LYNN ZEMPEL
Owner
Caring Hands, LLC
N. 1833 County Road K
Waupaca, WI 54981 United States
caringhands18@yahoo.com
http://www.caringhandsllc.com

BUS: Nursing-Based Staffing and Recruitment Firm **P/S:** Non-Medical Elder Care, Certified Nursing Assistants, Companions for In-Home Elder Care to Assist with Personal and Everyday Needs **MA:** Wapaca County, Washara County **D/D/R:** Offering Nursing Home Alternatives and Quality In-Home Care Services, Promoting Independent Living **H/I/S:** Reading, Playing with her Ferrets and Hedgehog, Spending Quality Time with her Two Nephews and Niece **FBP:** NASE Publications **EDU:** Coursework, Tennessee Temple University **CERTS:** Certified Nursing Assistant **C/VW:** Church; Fostering Animals, The Humane Society of the United States **A/S:** She attributes her success to her honesty, hard work, drive and love of helping others. **B/I:** She became involved in healthcare because she had experience in the field and a desire to provide patients with care and assistance. **H/O:** The highlight of her career was building a family-like company with employees that she loves and is proud of.

FABIAN ZEVALLOS
President, Owner
Florida Lien Search, Inc.
10301 S.W. 107th Street
Miami, FL 33176 United States
fabian@floridaliensearch.com
http://www.floridaliensearch.com

BUS: Real Estate Consulting Firm **P/S:** Lien Search Specialists, Real Estate Consulting Services **MA:** Florida **D/D/R:** Managing Public Relations, Troubleshooting, Overseeing Accounts Payable and Receivable, Managing Clientele Work Issues **H/I/S:** Traveling, Playing Soccer **A/A/S:** Coach, Local Children's Soccer Team; Miami Project; Better Business Bureau **C/VW:** Walk for Autism; American Cancer Society **A/S:** He attributes his success to his customer service skills and his ability to complete projects. **B/I:** He became involved in his profession because he was always interested in real estate and wanted to work for himself.

JACQUELYN M. ZIELINSKI
Operating Room Supervisor
Divine Savior Healthcare
Portage, WI 53901 United States
jzielinksi@dshealthcare.com
http://www.cambridgewhoswho.com

BUS: Hospital **P/S:** Healthcare, Providing Quality Service for Sick and Injured Patients **MA:** Local **D/D/R:** Supervising the Operating and Recovery Rooms, Assisting in Endoscopy and Day Surgery **H/I/S:** Reading, Musician, Music Ministry **FBP:** AORN Magazine **EDU:** Associate Degree in Nursing, Madison Technical College **C/VW:** Head of Music Ministry for Portage Assembly of God; Travels to Churches; Speaker at Women's Conferences **A/S:** She attributes her success to having a great support system. **B/I:** She became involved in her profession after working as a surgical technologist and returning to school. **H/O:** The highlight of her career has been being able to take care of her patients.

NADINE ZIMMER
District Technology Coordinator
Covington Exempted Village Schools
28 Grant Street
Arcanua, OH 45318 United States
zimmern@covingtonk12.org
http://www.covington.k12.oh.us

BUS: Education K-12 **P/S:** All Aspects of Education **MA:** Local **D/D/R:** Coordinating Technology, Business and Mathematics **H/I/S:** Traveling, Reading, Learning New Technology **EDU:** Bachelor's Degree in Education, Wright State University, Dayton, OH **C/VW:** Church; Various Community Civic Causes; School Fundraisers; United Way of America **A/S:** She attributes her success to her dedication to completing a job well. **H/O:** The highlight of her career was when she worked as a systems analyst and as an educator.

SHARON L. ZIMMERMAN
Chief Executive Officer, Vice President
Ernest R. Kimball, Inc.
506 Pineview Drive
Webster, NY 14580 United States
bigbadmamaz@yahoo.com
http://www.cambridgewhoswho.com

BUS: Trucking Company **P/S:** Trucking Services Including Hauling of Earth Materials **MA:** Local **EXP:** Ms. Zimmerman's expertise is in operations and finance management. **H/I/S:** Four-Wheeling, Gardening, Collecting Rocks **FBP:** Harbor Freight Tools **EDU:** High School Diploma **C/VW:** Volunteer, Local Charitable Organizations

GEORGE ZORBALAS
Design and Research Development Engineer (Retired)
RCA Corporation
gzorbalas@worldnet.att.net
http://www.cambridgewhoswho.com

ZORBALAS CONSULTING SERVICES, INC.
Solutions in Motion Control, Filters, Communications

GEORGE S. ZORBALAS

12 Pebble Lane   Tel. (856) 667-3309
Cherry Hill, NJ 08002-1554   Fax (856) 667-5420
E-Mail: gzorbalas@worldnet.att.net

BUS: Entertainment Firm **P/S:** Entertainment Services Including Video Recording and Design **MA:** International **D/D/R:** Formatting Phase Lock Techniques and Network Synthesis **H/I/S:** Listening to Music, Playing Tennis **EDU:** Doctorate in Electrical Engineering, Stanford University **A/A/S:** Former Member, Institute of Electrical and Electronics Engineers **A/H:** Achievement Award for Outstanding Contribution to the TR-600 Program, RCA Broadcast Systems (1975) **C/VW:** Local Church **DOB:** August 12, 1933 **POB:** Chalkis **SP:** Katina **CHILD:** Spiros, Paul, Steven **A/S:** He attributes his success to his dedication and passion for his profession. **B/I:** He became involved in his profession because he was always interested in mathematics, engineering and design. **H/O:** The most gratifying aspects of his career were formatting phase lock techniques and facilitating linear-phase network synthesis.

MARIO ZUCCARELLO
Physician
University of Cincinnati, Department of Neurosurgery
231 Albert Sabin Way
Cincinnati, OH 45267 United States
auccarm@uc.edu
http://www.uc.edu

BUS: University Neurosurgery Department **P/S:** Neurosurgery **MA:** International **D/D/R:** Treating Vascular Disease of the Brain and Spinal Cord **H/I/S:** Tennis, Listening to Music **FBP:** Journal of Neurosurgery; New England Journal of Medicine **EDU:** MD, University of Padua, Italy **A/A/S:** Congress of Neurological Surgeons; Society of Neurological Surgeons; ISS; New York Academy of Sciences **C/VW:** BAF; American Heart Association **A/S:** He attributes his success to hard work. **B/I:** He became involved in his profession because he was interested in neurology and surgery. **H/O:** The highlights of his career were being recognized as one of the best doctors in America and being chosen as a keynote speaker for several international meetings.

PHYLLIS R. ZUCKERMAN
Reading Specialist
Catapult Learning
Jersey City, NJ 07306 United States
phyllis.zuckerman@cwwemail.com
http://www.cambridgewhoswho.com

BUS: Education Company **P/S:** Education for Pre-Kindergarten through Eighth Grade Students **MA:** Local **D/D/R:** Teaching Reading and Language Arts **H/I/S:** Reading, Attending the Theater, Watching Movies, Teaching Piano and Keyboard **FBP:** Reading Teacher **EDU:** Bachelor of Arts in Elementary Education, Minor in Music, New Jersey City University **A/A/S:** Phi Delta Kappa; International Reading Association **C/VW:** Channel 13 PBS; American Cancer Society; National Multiple Sclerosis Society **A/S:** She attributes her success to her hard work and the support she receives from her students and parents. **B/I:** She became involved in her profession because she was inspired by a former teacher and wanted to work with children. **H/O:** The highlight of her career was being nominated for Who's Who Among American Teachers.

LAURA ZURL, GRI
Realtor
Century 21 New Millennium
PO Box 1635 13350 H.G. Truman Road
Solomons, MD 20688 United States
laura.zurl@c21nm.com
http://www.marylandhomerealestate.com

BUS: Real Estate **P/S:** Real Estate Needs, Residential, Commercial, Land, New Build, Pre-Owned **MA:** National **D/D/R:** Interior Designing for Residential Properties, Staging **H/I/S:** Helping Others, Boating, Reading, Traveling, Vacations **FBP:** Realtor; Architectural Digest; Southern Accents **EDU:** Interior Decorating Diploma with Highest Honors **CERTS:** Graduate of Southern Maryland Association of Realtors **A/A/S:** Maryland Association of Realtors; National Association of Realtors; Solomons Yacht Club; Solomons Business Association **C/VW:** Race for Life **A/S:** She attributes her success to her sphere of influence, referrals, word of mouth, repeat business and the relationships she builds. **B/I:** She became involved in her profession after a neck injury prevented her from continuing in her profession. She had a love for home interior design and found it was a perfect fit for her. **H/O:** The highlight of her career has been the smiles on her clients faces once they have the finished product.

MR. STUART ZWEBEN
Associate Dean of Academic Affairs and Administration
Computer Science and Engineering
Ohio State University, College of Engineering
2070 Neil Avenue
Columbus, OH 43210 United States
zweben.1@osu.edu
http://www.osu.edu

BUS: Proven Leader in the Field of Higher Education **P/S:** High Quality Undergraduate and Graduate Programs as well as Professional Programs in a Wide Array of Subjects of Study **MA:** International **D/D/R:** Supporting the Dean, Computing Education and Work Force Technology, Doing Research Involving Software Engineering, Testing Software and Quality, Handling Faculty Related Issues, Promotions and Tenures, All Research, Budgets and Space, Giving Guest Lectures, Attending Conferences and Professional Meetings **H/I/S:** Team Sports **FBP:** IEEE; Computers; Software; Engineering Transactions; CHE; ACM: Communications **EDU:** Ph.D., Purdue University (1974); Master's Degree in Statistics and Computer Science, Purdue University (1971); Bachelor of Science in Mathematics, CUNY City College (1968) **A/A/S:** Association for Computing Machinery; Institute of Electrical and Electronics Engineering; American Association of University Professors

LORELEI A. ZWIERNIKOWSKI
Elementary Music Director
South Lyon Community Schools
lorezski@sbcglobal.net
http://www.cambridgewhoswho.com

BUS: School **P/S:** Education for Children with Cognitive Impairments **MA:** Local **D/D/R:** Teaching Elementary Music **H/I/S:** Traveling, Reading, Gardening **FBP:** Missionary Journal **EDU:** Master's Degree in Music Education, University of Michigan **A/H:** Teacher of the Year Award, Oakland County, MI **C/VW:** Local Church; Michigan Association of County Veterans Counselors **DOB:** November 5, 1955 **POB:** Howell, MI **W/H:** Music Director, Recruitment Director, High School Band Director, Elementary Music Director, South Lyon Community Schools, South Lyon, MI (1979-Present); Praise and Worship Instructor, Central Bible College, Detroit (1997); K-12 Music Director, Whitmore Lake Schools, Whitmore Lake, MI (1978-1979); Organist, St. Joseph Catholic Church, South Lyon, MI; Private Piano Teacher; Wind Instrument Teacher, Wind Section Instructor, High School Band; Computer Instructor, South Lyon Adult Education; Music Instructor, South Lyon Martin Luther Home **A/S:** She attributes her success to the support she receives from her community. **B/I:** She became involved in her profession because she was inspired by her second-grade teacher who taught her how to play the piano. **H/O:** The highlight of her career was being nominated for Teacher of the Year for Oakland County.

Featured Members

2008–2009

Cristy R. Abadie
Title: Nurse **Company:** Sunrise Pediatrics **Address:** 3116 6th Street, Metairie, LA 70002 United States **BUS:** Healthcare Clinic **P/S:** Pediatric for Children Ages Newborn to 18 Years **MA:** Local **EXP:** Ms. Abadie's expertise includes immunizations and diagnostic tests. **CERTS:** Licensed Practical Nurse, Louisiana Technical College **A/A/S:** Habitat for Humanity, St Jude Children's Research Hospital
Email: info@CambridgeWhosWho.com

Sharilyn Sue Abbajay
Title: Founder **Company:** Abbajay and Associates, LLC **Address:** 7114 Lois Lane, Lanham, MD 20706 United States **BUS:** Consulting Company **P/S:** Consulting Services Including Beauty Care **MA:** National **D/D/R:** Assisting Managers and Owners, Answering Phone Calls **H/I/S:** Practicing Yoga and Pilates, Weightlifting, Hiking **EDU:** Coursework in Arts and Science, University of Maryland **A/A/S:** Board Member, Executive Committee, International Spa Association; Cosmetic Executive Women; Maryland Salon Association; The Day Spa Association **C/VW:** Local Charitable Organizations
Email: sabbajay@hotmail.com

Omaran A. Abdeen, MD
Title: Partner, Physician **Company:** Kidney Consultants Medical Group **Address:** 11550 Indian Hills Road, Suite 371, Mission Hills, CA 91345 United States **BUS:** Nephrology Center **P/S:** Neurologic Care **MA:** Regional **EXP:** Dr. Abdeen's expertise is nephrology. **D/D/R:** Managing the Operations of the Hospital and Dialysis Care Unit, Consulting, Overseeing Administrative Duties at Affiliate Hospitals **H/I/S:** Running **EDU:** Fellowship, University of California, San Diego; Residency, University of California, San Diego; MD, University of California, San Diego; Bachelor's Degree in Chemistry, California State Polytechnic University **A/A/S:** National Kidney Foundation; Fellow, American Society of Nephrology; American College of Physicians; American Society of Hypertension; Former Member, American Heart Association
Email: abdeen@yahoo.com
URL: http://www.cambridgewhoswho.com

Norma E. Abele
Title: Teacher **Company:** Quartz Hill High School **Address:** 6040 W. Avenue L, Lancaster, CA 93536 United States **BUS:** School **P/S:** Education **MA:** Local **D/D/R:** Teaching Life Sciences and Health Education **H/I/S:** Traveling, Camping, Reading **EDU:** Master of Arts in Education, Claremont Graduate University; Bachelor of Science in Biology, Fort Lewis College **A/A/S:** National Education Association; California Teachers Association; Antelope Valley Teachers Association **C/VW:** American Cancer Society
Email: nabele@verizonmail.com
URL: http://www.qhhs.org

Janice S. Abelove
Title: Teaching Assistant, Supervisor for Pre-Student Teachers **Company:** The Pennsylvania State University **Address:** 1730 Bristol Avenue, Apt. 501, State College, PA 16801 United States **BUS:** University **P/S:** Education **MA:** Local **D/D/R:** Supervising, Teaching, Conducting Seminars **H/I/S:** Sports, Traveling, Reading, Listening to Music, Theater, Art **EDU:** Bachelor of Science in Elementary and Kindergarten Education, The Pennsylvania State University (1970) **A/A/S:** Former Officer, Parent Teacher Association; Former President, Pennsylvania State Education Association; Delta Kappa Gamma; Pennsylvania State Alumni Association; Nittany Lion Club; Lecturer; Pennsylvania State Education Association; Bellefonte Education Foundation; Former President, South Funded Healthcare Trust
Email: janabelove@aol.com
Email: janabelove@verizon.net
URL: http://www.cambridgewhoswho.com

Ms. Kimberly A. Abey
Title: President **Company:** Spotlight Creative, LLC **Address:** 11702 B Grant Road, Suite 426, Cypress, TX 77429 United States **BUS:** Visual Enhancement Corporation **P/S:** Graphic Design, Visual Communications, Marketing, Advertising Campaigns **MA:** International **D/D/R:** Running the Business, Designing Websites, Offering Customer Service, Supervising the Staff, Overseeing Human Resources, Accounts Payable and Receivable, Managing Payroll, Acquiring New Accounts, Offering Visual Communications, Mid-Market Corporate Branding, Internal and External Corporate Communications and Professional Sports Client Services **H/I/S:** Scuba Diving **EDU:** Bachelor of Fine Arts, Youngstown State University, OH (1987) **A/A/S:** National Association of Photoshop Professionals; Advisory Board, Kingwood Community College; International Association of Business Communicators; Graphic Artist Guild; Better Business Bureau
Email: kim@spotlightcreative.com
URL: http://www.spotlightcreative.com

Christine Abood
Title: Teacher **Company:** Carleton Elementary School **BUS:** Elementary School **P/S:** Primary Education for Students in Kindergarten through Fifth-Grade **MA:** Regional **D/D/R:** Teaching Core Curriculum in an Urban Setting to First and Second-Grade Students **H/I/S:** Cooking, Calligraphy **EDU:** Master of Arts in Elementary Education, Oakland University (1977) **A/A/S:** Board of Directors, Arts & Scraps; Metropolitan Detroit Reading Council **A/H:** District Teacher of the Year (1991)

Nicholas J. Abraczinskas
Title: Mergers and Acquisitions Senior Associate **Company:** Taylor Companies **Dept:** Investment Banking Department **Address:** 1128 16th Street N.W., Washington, DC 20036 United States **BUS:** Consulting Firm **P/S:** Mergers and Acquisitions, Investment, Synergy Analysis, Corporate Development, Oil and Gas Energy Consulting Services **MA:** International **EXP:** Mr. Abraczinskas' expertise includes mergers and acquisitions, divestitures, corporate development, finance, business management, sales and strategic consulting. **H/I/S:** Reading, Golfing, Traveling **EDU:** Master of Business Administration, The George Washington University School of Business; Bachelor of Science in Chemical Engineering, North Carolina State University **A/H:** Leadership Excellence Award, ExxonMobil (2005); Downstream Sales Excellence Award, ExxonMobil (2002) **C/VW:** American Cancer Society; ExxonMobil Employees Favorite Charities Campaign
Email: nicholas.abraczinskas@gmail.com
URL: http://www.cambridgewhoswho.com

Rosamma Abraham
Title: Nursing Administrator **Company:** North Shore-Long Island Jewish Forest Hills Hospital **Address:** 27005 76th Avenue, New Hyde Park, NY 11040 United States **BUS:** Hospital **P/S:** Healthcare **MA:** Local **D/D/R:** Critical-Care Nursing, Supervising and Managing Nurses **H/I/S:** Reading **EDU:** Master of Science in Nursing, Columbia University (1999) **CERTS:** Acute Care Nurse Practitioner, Columbia University (1999); Critical Care Registered Nurse **A/A/S:** American Nurses Association **A/H:** Nominee, Leadership Award (2006) **C/VW:** American Cancer Society; St. Jude Children's Research Hospital; American Red Cross; Food for the Poor; March of Dimes
Email: rosamma378@hotmail.com
URL: http://www.cambridgewhoswho.com

Beatrice B. Abrams
Title: Executive Director in Clinical Research **Company:** Novartis Pharmaceuticals Corporation **Address:** 1 Health Plaza, East Hanover, NJ 07936 United States **BUS:** Pharmaceutical Manufacturer **P/S:** Pharmaceuticals **MA:** International **EXP:** Ms. Abrams' expertise is in clinical research regarding dermatology. **H/I/S:** Tap Dancing, Photography **EDU:** Ph.D. in Plant Development, University of California at Irvine **A/A/S:** Dermatology Leadership Foundation; American Academy of Dermatology; Drug Information Association **C/VW:** Planned Parenthood, United Way, Local Women's Shelters
Email: abrambe1@earthlink.net
URL: http://www.cambridgewhoswho.com

Dr. Jeffrey S. Abrams
Title: Director **Company:** Princeton Orthopaedic & Rehabilitation Associates **Address:** 325 Princeton Avenue, Princeton, NJ 08540 United States **BUS:** Healthcare Center **P/S:** Healthcare Including Orthopaedic Surgery and Sports Medicine **MA:** Regional **D/D/R:** Managing 15 Physicians **H/I/S:** Golfing, Playing Tennis, Skiing **EDU:** MD, Upstate Medical Center **A/A/S:** American Academy of Orthopaedic Surgeons
Email: rxbonz@aol.com
URL: http://www.princetonorthopaedic.com

Luzia D. Abranches
Title: Director of Operations **Company:** All Granite and Marble, Inc. **Address:** 1909 N. Washington Boulevard, Sarasota, FL 34234 United States **BUS:** Granite and Quartz Fabricator and Installer **P/S:** Granite and Quartz Fabrication **MA:** National **D/D/R:** Directing Operations **H/I/S:** Traveling, Reading **EDU:** Coursework, Completed in Brazil **CERTS:** Pursuing Certification in Housing Adjustments **A/A/S:** Notary Public
Email: lucyallgranitemarble@gmail.com
URL: http://www.allgranitemarbleinc.com

Yolanda P. Acebo
Title: School Director **Company:** Dade Medical Institute **Address:** 3401 N.W. Seventh Street, Miami, FL 33125 United States **BUS:** Medical Institute **P/S:** Education on General Radiological Technologist, Massage Therapy, Medical Assistants, Diagnostic Medical Ultrasound, Magnetic Resonance Imaging **MA:** Regional **D/D/R:** Leadership, Management, Creative **H/I/S:** Traveling, Oil Painting **EDU:** Master's Degree in Health Administration, University of Miami **CERTS:** Radiology and Mammography Technician **A/A/S:** Atlantic Assisted Reproductive Therapies; Southern Florida Sonography Society **C/VW:** American Cancer Society
Email: yacebo@aol.com
URL: http://www.dademedicalinstitute.com

Peter Achuonjei
Title: President, Chief Executive Officer **Company:** Spartan Healthcare Staffing Services of Michigan, Inc. **Address:** 4572 S. Hagadorn Road, Suite 1E, East Lansing, MI 48823 United States **BUS:** Healthcare Staffing Agency **P/S:** Supplemental Staffing for Hospitals, Nursing Homes and Home Healthcare **MA:** Regional **D/D/R:** Coordinating Contracts, Developing Relationships with Hospitals and Insurance Companies, Reviewing Staff Performance, Resolving Issues, Conducting the Final Interview of All Prospective Staff, Advertising, Overseeing Accounting, Invoicing, Marketing **H/I/S:** Playing Soccer, Basketball and Football **EDU:** Ph.D. in Agriculture, Michigan State University (1996); Master's Degree in Agriculture, University of Wisconsin (1985); Bachelor's Degree in Business Economics, SUNY Plattsburgh (1982) **A/A/S:** Association for International Agriculture and Extension Education
Email: achuonjei.peter@spartancare.com
URL: http://www.spartancare.com

Altagracia Acosta
Title: Assistant Principal **Company:** High School for Health Careers and Sciences **Address:** 2385 Barker Avenue, Apartment 6R, Bronx, NY 10467 United States **BUS:** High School **P/S:** Education, Education for Children Interested in Science **MA:** Regional **D/D/R:** Supervising the Science, Foreign Language and Guidance Departments, Assisting Teachers and Professional Guidance Counselors, Participating in Study Groups with Teachers, Attending Conferences with Teachers, Parents and Students, Hiring and Firing Educators, Assisting in the Planning of High School Curriculum, Participating in School Functions, Working with Columbia Presbyterian College and the Bronx Zoo **H/I/S:** Reading **EDU:** Master's Degree in Administration and Supervision, Mercy College (2003); Master's Degree in Secondary Education, Mercy College (2001); Bachelor's Degree in Biology and Chemistry, Earned in the Dominican Republic (1985)
Email: haroniz@aol.com

Mr. Juan C. Acosta
Title: Vice President, Chief Financial Officer **Company:** MTV Latin America **Address:** 1111 Lincoln Road, 6th Floor, Miami Beach, FL 33139 United States **BUS:** Entertainment **P/S:** Cable Distribution **MA:** International **D/D/R:** Directing the Financial Function, Offering Advice and Guidance on all Financial, Operations and Strategic Matters Across all Latin American Operation, Overseeing Accounting and Financial Reporting, Annual Budget Coordinator, Treasury and Tax Reporting, Investment and Financial Options, Internal Control Management and Audit **H/I/S:** Traveling, Music, Spending Time with his Family **EDU:** Master's Degree in Business Administration, Florida International University (2005); Bachelor's Degree in Accounting, Florida International University, Summa Cum Laude (2001) **CERTS:** Certified Public Accountant **A/A/S:** Florida Institute of Certified Public Accountants
Email: juancarlosla@aol.com
URL: http://www.mtvla-media.com

Nancy M. Adamczyk
Title: Paralegal **Company:** Jones Day **Address:** 901 Lakeside Avenue, Cleveland, OH 44114 United States **BUS:** Global Firm with More than 2,200 Lawyers **P/S:** Legal Services in All Areas of Practice, for All Levels of Industry, with 30 Offices Worldwide **MA:** International **EXP:** Ms. Adamczyk's expertise includes securities and the investigation of white collar crimes. **D/D/R:** Handling Cases from Beginning to End, Pleadings, Gathering Facts, Conducting Depositions and Interviews, Coordinating Exhibits, Assisting at Trials **H/I/S:** Running, Bike Riding **CERTS:** Certified Paralegal, State of Ohio **A/A/S:** Cleveland Association of Paralegals; Paralegal Section, Cleveland Bar Association
Email: nmadamczyk@jonesday.com
URL: http://wwww.jonesday.com

Adrienne M. Adams
Title: Owner **Company:** Tia Adrianas Bed and Breakfast **Address:** 7 Via Delfin, Sayulita, Mexico **BUS:** Local Bed and Breakfast **P/S:** Ten Room Bed and Breakfast in a Small Village Allowing Guests Access to Local Beaches and Other Local Sites **MA:** Local **D/D/R:** Taking Guests on Local Tours, Overseeing Activities, Preparing Meals **H/I/S:** Sewing, Gardening, Watching Events that her Grandchildren are Involved In **EDU:** Coursework, University of California, Los Angeles **A/A/S:** Indian Tribe Support, Mexico **A/H:** Featured as a Top Mexico Get-A-Way, Seventeen Magazine
Email: tia@tiaadrianas.com
URL: http://www.tiaadrianas.com

Amelia Hope Adams
Title: Counsel **Company:** Reed Smith, LLP **Address:** 1301 K Street N.W., Suite 1100 East Tower, Washington, DC 20005 United States **BUS:** Law Firm **P/S:** Legal Representation for Areas Including Advertising Technology and Media, Advocacy, Antitrust, Regulatory Litigation, Arbitration, Banking, Commercial Restructuring, Capital Markets, Class Action Defense, Communications, Construction, Employment, Energy, Environmental Law, Financial Services, Fraud, Government Relations, Healthcare, Homeland Security, Immigration, Information Technology, Intellectual Property, Life Sciences, Mergers and Acquisitions, Pro Bono, Real Estate, Risk and Liability, Tax, Trusts and Estates **MA:** Regional **D/D/R:** Practicing Investment Management and Corporate Law **EDU:** JD, Campbell University, North Carolina; Master of Laws in Taxation, University of Florida (1993) **A/A/S:** American Bar Association
Email: hadams@reedsmith.com
URL: http://www.reedsmith.com

Cathy D. Adams
Title: Physical Education Teacher **Company:** Edward A. Upthegrove Elementary School **Address:** 280 N. Main Street, Labelle, FL 33935 United States **BUS:** Elementary School **P/S:** Primary Education, Core Curriculum Including Reading, Mathematics, English, Science, Social Studies, Music, History, Art and Physical Education **MA:** Regional **D/D/R:** Teaching Kindergarten Through Fifth-Grade Students and After-School Mathematics for Fifth-Grade Students Twice a Week, incorporating different activities into physical education classes for fun, movement with brain function skills, overseeing sensory motor integration learning environment laboratory and increasing brain function. **H/I/S:** Sports, Playing Volleyball, Watching Football, Reading, Traveling **EDU:** Master's Degree in Education, Concentration in Curriculum and Instruction, Florida Gulf Coast University (2004); Bachelor of Science in Exercise and Sports Science, University of Florida (1996); Bachelor of Science in Psychology, Minor in Biology, Palm Beach Atlantic College (1994) **A/A/S:** Public Speaker, Circles of Care Conference on Early Childhood Development; Florida Alliance for Health, Physical Education, Recreation, Dance and Sport
Email: cathyd_70@yahoo.com
URL: http://www.hendry-schools.org

Gwendolyn J. Adams
Title: Realtor **Company:** Keller Williams Real Estate **Address:** 40 S. Cedar Crest Boulevard, Allentown, PA 18104 United States **BUS:** Real Estate Company **P/S:** Real Estate Services Including Buying and Selling Residential and Commercial Property **MA:** Regional **D/D/R:** Selling Residential and Commercial Properties, Organizing Open House Events, Listing Homes **CERTS:** Licensed Real Estate Agent, State of Pennsylvania (1978) **A/A/S:** Council of Residential Specialists
Email: gjadams@bellsouth.net
URL: http://www.kw.com

Janet D. Adams
Title: Chief Nurse Executive **Company:** San Antonio State School **Address:** 6711 S. New Braunfels, Suite 500, San Antonio, TX 78223 United States **BUS:** Division of the Department of Aging and Disability **P/S:** Residential Facility for People with Mental Retardation **MA:** Statewide **EXP:** Ms. Adams' expertise includes clinical nursing and administration. **H/I/S:** Training Dogs for Pet Therapy **EDU:** Master of Science in Nursing, Texas Tech University; Bachelor of Science in Nursing, University of Texas at Austin **A/A/S:** Texas Tech Honor Society **A/H:** Research Award in Nursing
Email: janet.adams2@dads.state.tx.us

Johnny R. Adams Sr.
Title: Ret. Court Reporter/Ordained Min **Address:** 2405 CR 1550, Warren, TX 77664 United States **BUS:** Retired Court Reporter **P/S:** Ordained Minister **MA:** Regional **EXP:** Mr. Adams expertise is in photography. **H/I/S:** Gardening and Photography Studio **CERTS:** Ordained Deacon, Southern Baptist Church (1995) **C/VW:** Singer, Preacher, Bethel Baptist Church, Minister to Inmates, Tyler County Justice Center
Email: info@CambridgeWhosWho.com

Lori S. Adams
Title: Teacher **Company:** Iberia Parish School Board, Center Street Elementary **Address:** 1520 Center Street, New Iberia, LA 70560 United States **BUS:** Elementary School **P/S:** Education **MA:** Regional **D/D/R:** Teaching All Subjects to First Grade Students **H/I/S:** Competitive Bowling, Collecting Antique Bottles and Angels **EDU:** Bachelor of Arts Degree in Education, University of Southern Mississippi (1984) **CERTS:** Licensed Dance Instructor **A/A/S:** National Education Association; Louisiana Education Association; Louisiana Association for the Education of Young Children **A/H:** Reigning Ms. Classic, Southern American Dream (2007); Mrs. Iberia (2005); Ms. Thibeaux (2004)
Email: angeleyes6119@cox.net
URL: http://www.oncoursesystems.com

Sheila B. Adams
Title: Private Practice Owner, Licensed Massage Therapist **Company:** Massage for Health **BUS:** Private Healthcare Practitioner **P/S:** Therapeutic Massage Services **MA:** Regional **D/D/R:** Performing Swedish and Deep Tissue Massages, Reiki, Aroma Therapy, Assisting with Stress Alleviation, Running the Daily Operations of the Practice, Marketing **H/I/S:** Traveling, Reading, Learning **EDU:** Associate Degree in General Studies, California State University-Monterey Bay (1985) **CERTS:** Nationally Board Certified Massage Therapist **A/A/S:** American Massage Therapy Association
Email: massage4health@netscape.net
URL: http://www.cambridgewhoswho.com

Frances C. Adams-Dallas
Title: Route Sales Merchandiser **Company:** Merchant's Distributors, Inc. an Alex Lee Co. **Address:** 169 Eastwyck Circle, Decatur, GA 30032 United States **BUS:** Distributor **P/S:** Food Sales, Distribution, Free Lance Writing and Cooking **MA:** National **EXP:** Ms. Adams-Dallas' expertise includes catering and food sales. **H/I/S:** Baking, Travel, Reading, Calligraphy **EDU:** Bachelor of Arts in Science and Business Marketing, Troy University, Troy, AL; Bachelor of Science in Business Administration and Marketing **A/A/S:** Long Ridge Writer's Group
Email: msfadams_dallas@bellsouth.net

Carolyn S. Adamson
Title: Administrative Assistant III **Company:** Children's Mercy Hospital & Clinics **Dept:** Gastroenterology **Address:** 2401 Gillham Road, Gastroenterology Department, Kansas City, MO 64108 United States **BUS:** Healthcare Facility **P/S:** Pediatric Services, Outpatient Services, Emergency and Liver Care Services, Community and Outreach Clinics, Hygiene Coordination **MA:** Regional **D/D/R:** Coordinating Attendants, Assisting Physicians, Overseeing the Pediatric and Liver Care Centers, Scheduling Educational Conferences with Speakers from Across the Country, Managing Patient Correspondence, Maintaining Physicians' Licenses and Community and Outreach Clinics, Helping Establish New Community Medical Practices **H/I/S:** Running, Exercising, Sewing, Traveling, Home Decorating **EDU:** Pursuing Bachelor's Degree in Human Resource Management, Ottawa University **CERTS:** Certified Paralegal, Rockhurst University (2005); Certification in Advanced Dental Hygiene, The University of Missouri-Kansas City, Dental Assistant **A/A/S:** American Business Women's Association; The Executive Secretary Society; Volunteer, Hurricane Katrina Relief; National Association of Executive Secretaries and Administrative Assistants
Email: cadamson@cmh.edu
URL: http://www.childrens-mercy.org

Joseph A. Adebayo
Title: Youth Coordinator **Company:** Christ Apostolic Church of Illinois **Address:** 8157 S. Exchange Avenue, Chicago, IL 60617 United States **BUS:** Nonprofit Organization **P/S:** Christian Services **MA:** International **D/D/R:** Coordinating Youth Programs **H/I/S:** Reading **EDU:** Bachelor's Degree, Earned in Nigeria; Elementary Education Diploma in Practical Theology, International Seminary of Florida **C/VW:** Church
Email: akanjiade57@yahoo.com

Ayotunde S. Adelusola
Title: Owner **Company:** Everjoy, LLC dba Tim Horton's **Address:** 3475 Cleveland Avenue, Columbus, OH 43224 United States **BUS:** Restaurant Establishment **P/S:** Food, Beverages, Baked Goods **MA:** Local **D/D/R:** Managing Two Restaurants, Overseeing Marketing **H/I/S:** Jogging, Reading, Watching Documentaries **EDU:** Master's Degree in Divinity, United Theological Seminary (2001); Master of Arts Degree in Religious Communication, United Theological Seminary (2001); Bachelor of Arts Degree in Economics, University of Central Missouri (1985) **A/A/S:** YC21 Social Club; Yoruba Club
Email: blkfire@juno.com
URL: http://www.everjoy@sbcglobal.net

Bobby R. Adkins
Title: Nationally Certified Activity Director, Community Coordinator **Company:** Developmental Services of Dickson County **Address:** 511 Pleasant Valley Drive, Dickson, TN 37055 United States **BUS:** Community-Based Organization **P/S:** Support for Physically and Mentally Challenged Individuals and their Families **MA:** Regional **EXP:** Mr. Adkins' expertise includes the utilization of memory enhancement techniques to treat patients affected by Alzheimer's disease and dementia. **D/D/R:** Consulting, Tracking Clients Financial Records, Scheduling Appointments for Patients, Developing Programs **H/I/S:** Artwork, Listening to Music **CERTS:** Certified Activity Director, National Certification Council for Activity Professionals **A/H:** Second Place Award, Team Leader for Development Services (2007); First Place Award, Development Services Professional, State of Tennessee, Nashville (2006) **C/VW:** Fundraising Events
Email: spoiltbratt13@aol.com
URL: http://www.cambridgewhoswho.com

Kevin R. Adkins
Title: Owner, Piano Technician **Company:** Ye Olde Piano Shoppe **Address:** 126 W. Mountain Creek Church Road, Greenville, SC 29609 United States **BUS:** Musical Instrument Repair Shop **P/S:** Piano Tuning and Repair Services **MA:** Local **D/D/R:** Overseeing Piano Sales, Tuning and Repairing Pianos **H/I/S:** Playing the French Horn, Listening to Music, Sports, Playing Racquetball, Spending Time with his Wife, Traveling, Dining Out **EDU:** Master of Music in Church Music, Bob Jones University (2008); Coursework, American School of Piano Tuning (1988); Bachelor of Arts in Church Music, with a Concentration in French Horn, Bob Jones University (1984) **A/A/S:** Piano Technicians Guild **C/VW:** Local Church
Email: musicmankev@juno.com
URL: http://www.adkinspianotuningrepair.com

Esther Adler
Title: Owner **Company:** Relaxation and Health **Address:** Springfield, NJ 07081 United States **BUS:** Health and Wellness Company **P/S:** Pilate's, Yoga, Thai Yoga, Massage, Relaxation Education **MA:** Regional **D/D/R:** Offering Health and Wellness Services Including Pilate's and Yoga Classes, Relaxation Techniques **H/I/S:** Attending the Regional Ballet, Theater Dancing and Performing, Reading Books by Dr. Demartini and Dr. Wayne W. Dyer **EDU:** College Coursework **CERTS:** Certified Fitness Instructor; Certified Yoga Instructor; Certified Pilates Instructor
Email: estheradler@estheradler.com

Josepha L. Advincula, RN, BSN
Title: Registered Nurse **Company:** Englewood Hospital and Medical Center **Address:** 350 Engle Street, Englewood, NJ 07631 United States **BUS:** Major Medical and Academic Institution **P/S:** Anesthesiology, Critical Care, Cancer Care, Cardiology, Diabetes, Emergency, Gastroenterology, Gynecology, Healing and Relaxation Therapies, Heart and Vascular Institute of New Jersey, Home Health, Hyperbaric Oxygen Therapy, Laboratory, Mental Health and Maternity **MA:** Regional **EXP:** Mr. Advincula's expertise includes cardiopulmonary, telemetry and general patient care. **H/I/S:** Shopping, Traveling **EDU:** Bachelor of Science in Nursing, Fairleigh Dickinson University (2002)
Email: jadvincuka02@hotmail.com
URL: http://www.englewoodhospital.com

Crystal M. Aerts
Title: International Product and Marketing Specialist **Company:** Appleton **Dept:** International **Address:** 825 E. Wisconsin Avenue, P.O. Box 359, Appleton, WI 54912 United States **BUS:** Manufacturing Company **P/S:** Production of Carbon-less, Thermal, Security and Packaging Products **MA:** International **D/D/R:** Overseeing Opportunities in Global Marketing, Consulting with Clientele, Researching **H/I/S:** Reading, Running, Biking, Teaching Spinning and Yoga **EDU:** Bachelor of Business Administration Degree in Marketing, University of Wisconsin in Oshkosh (2002); Bachelor of Arts Degree in Spanish, University of Wisconsin in Oshkosh (2002) **A/A/S:** PULSE; Young Professionals Networking Organization; Young Professionals Networking Association **A/H:** Chairman's Award for Growth, International Division (2005-2006) **C/VW:** Volunteer on the United Way Campaign Committee for Appleton
Email: caerts@appletonideas.com
Email: crohde79@yahoo.com

Viktoria E. Agaronnik, PT, PC
Title: Physical Therapist **Company:** Viktoria Agaronnik PT, PC **Address:** 1851 E. 18th Street, Brooklyn, NY 11229 United States **BUS:** Private Practice **P/S:** Physical Therapy Treatments, Evaluations, Pediatric Physical Therapy **MA:** Regional **D/D/R:** Offering Pediatric Physical Therapy in Home Care Settings, Working in a Private Practice, Independent Contracting **H/I/S:** Yoga **EDU:** Pursuing Ph.D.; Bachelor of Science Degree in Physical Therapy, New York University (1992); Bachelor of Arts Degree in Music, St. Petersburg, Russia (1987) **A/A/S:** American Physical Therapy Association; Neurodevelopmental Treatment Association; **A/H:** Who's Who Among Students in American Colleges and Universities (1991-1992)
Email: yevge7@aol.com

Kathleen Marie Agovino
Title: Owner, Dance Instructor **Company:** Kathi's Dance Studio **Address:** 1 S. Morton Avenue, Morton, PA 19070 United States **BUS:** Dance Center **P/S:** Dance Instruction **MA:** Local **D/D/R:** Teaching Tap, Ballet, Hip Hop, Lyrical, Jazz, Ballroom and Break Dancing, Aerobics, Senior Aerobics, Overseeing Business Operations, Performing Dance Workshops **H/I/S:** Scrapbooking, Dance, Cooking, Designing, **CERTS:** Certified in Aerobics, American Aerobics Association **C/VW:** Juvenile Diabetes Research Foundation, Benefit Performances for Charity
Email: kathidancestudio@rcn.com
URL: http://www.kathisdancestudio.com

Robert Aguilar, Ed.D.

Title: Chief Executive Officer, President **Company:** International Group, Inc. **Address:** 1100 W. Main Street, Visalia, CA 93291 United States **BUS:** Consulting Firm **P/S:** Educational Workshops, Seminars, Management Teams **MA:** Regional **EXP:** Mr. Aguilar's expertise includes student mentorship and grant writing. **D/D/R:** Training Managers, Chief Executive Officers and the Board of Directors in Leadership and Management, Hiring Executives for Corporations and Superintendents for Schools, Overseeing Employees **H/I/S:** Golfing, Attending Youth Sporting Events, Spending Time with his Family **EDU:** Doctor of Education, University of the Pacific, Stockton **A/A/S:** Visalia Chamber of Commerce **A/H:** Community Leader Award; Giant Award, Community College **C/VW:** Board Member, United Way
Email: raguilar@internationalgroup.us
URL: http://www.cambridgewhoswho.com

Jayne Ahearn

Title: Director of Liturgy **Company:** Saint Raphael the Archangel Church **Address:** 830 S. Westhaven Drive, Oshkosh, WI 54904 United States **BUS:** Roman Catholic Church **P/S:** Worship, Charity, Education **MA:** Local **D/D/R:** Preparing Worship Services, Performing Clerical Work **H/I/S:** Hiking, Swimming **EDU:** Ph.D. in Developmental Genetics, Arizona State University (1983); Master of Arts, University of Notre Dame (1991); Bachelor of Arts in Zoology, University of Wisconsin (1966) **A/A/S:** National Association of Pastoral Musicians; Liturgy Network
Email: healohaakua@yahoo.com

Daniel P. Ahlers

Title: Business Owner **Company:** Video Plus & Jabberwock Coffee and Books **Address:** 507 Hwy 77 Suite E, Dellrapid, SD 57022 United States **BUS:** Video/Coffee Retail Store **P/S:** Video Sales, Rentals, Coffee Books and Music **MA:** Local **EXP:** Mr. Ahler's expertise is in small business entrepreneurship. **H/I/S:** Basketball. Camping **EDU:** Bachelor of Arts in Government and Internatinal Affairs, Augustana College **A/A/S:** The Haven, State Legislature Historical **C/VW:** Local Charities
Email: info@CambridgeWhosWho.com

Sarah T. Ahmed

Title: Speech-Language Pathologist **Company:** Poway Unified School District **Address:** 14614 Garden Road, Poway, CA 92064 United States **BUS:** School District **P/S:** Education **MA:** Local **D/D/R:** Teaching, Working with Children with Autism and Learning Disabilities, Utilizing Innovative Teaching Methods **H/I/S:** Reading, Cooking, Housekeeping **EDU:** Ph.D. in Communication Sciences and Disorders, University of Florida **A/A/S:** California Speech-Language-Hearing Association; American Speech-Language-Hearing Association **C/VW:** Habitat for Humanity, American Breast Cancer Society
Email: sarah_tahira@hotmail.com
URL: http://www.cambridgewhoswho.com

Amy S. Aiken Masters

Title: Educator **Company:** Onsted Middle School **Address:** 10109 Slee Road, Onsted, MI 49265 United States **BUS:** Middle School **P/S:** Education **MA:** Local **D/D/R:** Teaching Middle School **H/I/S:** Coaching Varsity Volleyball, Coaching Travel Softball **EDU:** Master's Degree in School Counseling, Siena Heights University **C/VW:** American Red Cross, Relay for Life
Email: amya@wildcat.onsted.k12.us
URL: http://www.cambridgewhoswho.com

Gerard James Aitken IV

Title: President **Company:** Aitken International **Address:** 330 Laymon Road, Swan Lake, NY 12783 United States **BUS:** Energy Firm **P/S:** Research and Development of Alternative Energy **MA:** National **EXP:** Mr. Aitken's expertise includes the research and development of alternative energy products. **D/D/R:** Raising Funds **H/I/S:** Spending Time with his Family, Swimming, Playing Poker **EDU:** Bachelor's Degree in Business Development, The Pennsylvania State University **C/VW:** St. Jude Children's Research Hospital; Cystic Fibrosis Foundation; Fundraiser, Prototypes
Email: gerardjaitkeniv@yahoo.com
URL: http://www.lumeloid.com
URL: http://www.quensor.com

Mr. Alan M. Akerson

Title: Master Carpenter **Company:** Wooden Workman **Address:** P. O. Box 173, Stetson, ME 04488 United States **BUS:** Privately Owned Company Committed to Excellence in the Construction Industry **P/S:** Building, Remodeling, Carpentry **MA:** Regional **D/D/R:** Remodeling, Installing, Painting, Applying Dry Wall, Paneling, Landscaping **H/I/S:** Church, Nature, Writing Poetry **EDU:** Two-Year Trade Degree in Building and Construction and Masonry, Northern Maine Vocational Technical Institute (1966); Two Years of Bible Studies, Transylvania Bible School (1980) **CERTS:** Ordained Minister, Calvary Grace Church of Faith
Email: info@CambridgeWhosWho.com
URL: http://www.cambridgewhoswho.com

Victoria Akins

Title: Technology Adviser **Company:** Tidewater District Congress of Parents and Teachers **Address:** 1405 Suffield Circle, Virginia Beach, VA 23456 United States **BUS:** Volunteer Child Advocacy Association **P/S:** Educational Resources **MA:** Regional **EXP:** Ms. Akins' expertise is in technology. **D/D/R:** Compiling Plans and Reports, Generating Fliers and Other Media for Schools, Making Certificates, Keeping Track of Legislation Tallies **H/I/S:** Watching Baseball, Basketball and Ice Hockey **EDU:** Pursuing Degree in Integrated Science and Technology, James Madison University **A/A/S:** Virginia Biotechnology Association; Sigma Alpha Lambda; The National Society of Collegiate Scholars
Email: revadalby@aol.com
URL: http://www.vapta.org

Arlene F. Akker

Title: Teacher **Company:** Muskegon High School **Address:** 80 W. Southern Avenue, Muskegon, MI 49441 United States **BUS:** High School **P/S:** Education **MA:** Local **D/D/R:** Teaching Global Issues, History and Government Courses **H/I/S:** Reading, Traveling, Browsing the Internet **EDU:** Master of Arts in Reading, Western Michigan University; Bachelor of Arts in English and Social Science, Hope College **A/A/S:** National Education Association; Michigan Education Association; National Council for the Social Studies; National Council of Teachers of English **C/VW:** Alumni of Western Michigan University, Alumni of Hope College, Western Michigan Christian High School, American Cancer Society, Alzheimer's Association
Email: aakker@mpsk12.net
URL: http://www.muskegonpublicschools.org/schools/muskegon

Mr. Rashed A. Al Hatllan

Title: Director for Security, Safety and Loss Prevention **Company:** Aramco Services Company **Dept:** Department of Security and Loss Prevention **Address:** 9009 West Loop S., Houston, TX 70096 United States **BUS:** Oil Production and Manufacturing Company **P/S:** Oil, Petroleum, Gas **MA:** International **D/D/R:** Overseeing Industrial Security, Safety and Loss Prevention **H/I/S:** Diving, Golfing **EDU:** Bachelor of Science in Criminal Justice, Texas A&M University **A/A/S:** American Society for Industrial Security; FIAT; EPBL **C/VW:** United Way; American Cancer Society; Charities for Battered and Abused Children
Email: rashed.hatllan@aramcoservices.com
URL: http://www.cambridgewhoswho.com

Victoria Alaimo

Title: Department Head of Music and Art **Company:** Valley Stream Central High School **Address:** 320 Fletcher Avenue, Manhasset, NY 11030 United States **BUS:** High School **P/S:** Education **MA:** Local **EXP:** Ms. Alaimo's expertise is in music education. **H/I/S:** Traveling **EDU:** Master of Education in Music, Columbia University **CERTS:** Post-Master's Certification **A/A/S:** Kappa Delta Pi; MENC: The National Association for Music Education; Long Island String Festival Association
Email: valaimo1@aol.com

Brenda Marie Alarcon, CRS, CCIM

Title: Realtor **Company:** CPS Homes & Lands **Address:** 3209 Cleveland Avenue, Santa Rosa, CA 95403 United States **BUS:** Real Estate Agency **P/S:** Real Estate Services **MA:** National **EXP:** Ms. Alarcon's expertise includes commercial and residential real estate sales. **H/I/S:** Gardening, Exercising **CERTS:** Certified Residential Specialist **A/A/S:** California Association of Realtors; National Association of Realtors
Email: balarconsellsre@hotmail.com
URL: http://www.balarcon.com

Karen Juncker Albert

Title: Director of Early Childhood Education **Company:** Temple Bat Yahm **Address:** 1011 Camelback Street, Newport Beach, CA 92660 United States **BUS:** School **P/S:** Religious Studies Including Early Childhood Education for Infants and Toddlers, Full-Inclusion Preschool Program for Children with Disabilities **MA:** Regional **D/D/R:** Developing the Curriculum and a Full-Inclusion Program, Educating Parents, Supervising and Training the Staff **H/I/S:** Classical Ballet Dancing, Yoga, Reading, Attending Musical and Opera Theater, Spending Time with her Grandchildren **EDU:** Master of Education, with a Concentration in Guidance Counseling, Bowling Green State University (1970); Bachelor of Science in Home Economics, Purdue University (1966) **CERTS:** Certification in Human Development, Pacific Oaks College and Children's School (1986); Certification in Nursery School Administration, Fullerton College (1983) **A/A/S:** Early Childhood Educators of Reform Judaism; Council for Exceptional Children; Oxford Round Table; President, Orange County Association for the Education of Young Children; Vice President, California Association for the Education of Young Children; President, National Jewish Early Childhood Network; National Association of Temple Educators; National Jewish Early Childhood Network; National Association for the Education of Young Children; Association for Childhood Education International **A/H:** Woman of the Year Award for Community Service, Temple Bat Yahm
Email: kjalbert@tby.org
URL: http://www.cambridgewhoswho.com

Diane Lynn Albert-Haynes

Title: Uniform Control Manager **Company:** Resort At Squaw Creek **Address:** 400 Squaw Creek Road, Box 3333, Olympic Valley, CA 96146 United States **BUS:** All-Season Mountain Resort **P/S:** Mountain Home Experience with Four Diamond Luxury and Full Service Amenities **MA:** Regional **D/D/R:** Planning Events, Purchasing Uniforms, Performing Inventory Control for Banquets and Conferences **H/I/S:** Enjoying Football and Traveling **EDU:** High School Education **A/A/S:** Soroptimist International of the Americas; PEAK, Peak University **A/H:** Associate of the Month (2004); Associate of the Year (2004) **C/VW:** Lance Armstrong Foundation; Susan G. Komen For the Cure; Lee National Denim Day for Breast Cancer Awareness
Email: dhaynes@destinationhotels.com
URL: http://www.squawcreek.com/resort-overview.php

Martha Albrecht

Title: Surgical Education Coordinator **Company:** St. John's Health Care Center **Address:** 1235 East Cherokee, Springfield, MO 65804 United States **BUS:** Healthcare **P/S:** Level 1 Trauma Center **MA:** Regional **D/D/R:** Overseeing Orientation of New Employees to the Surgical Area, Overseeing Three Area Technical Schools, Taking Students into the Operating Room for their Clinical Experience, Planning and Presenting In-Service Programs Bi-Monthly for the Operating Room Staff, Scheduling and Facilitating Staff Meetings, Overseeing CPR Certification for the Operating Room Staff, Researching and Updating Policy Changes **H/I/S:** Hiking, Bicycling **EDU:** Bachelor of Science in Nursing, Gordon Keller School of Nursing Hillsboro Community College (1972) **CERTS:** Pending Operating Room Nursing Certification **A/A/S:** Association of Peri Operative Registered Nurses; Former Member, Association of Holistic Nurses; Former Member, Post Anesthesia Nurses Association
Email: freewoman@peoplepc.com

Lisa E. Alcala

Title: Assistant Principal **Company:** Grace Yokley Middle School **Address:** 2947 S. Turner Avenue, Ontario, CA 91761 United States **BUS:** Middle School **P/S:** Education **MA:** Regional **D/D/R:** Overseeing Administrative Duties, Coaching School Sports **H/I/S:** Running, Skiing, Outdoor Sports **EDU:** Master's Degree in Education and Computer Technology, California State Polytechnic University, Pomona (1996); Master's Degree in Administration, California State University, San Bernardino (2003) **A/A/S:** Association for Supervision and Curriculum Development
Email: lisa-alcala@mtnview.k12.ca.us
URL: http://www.mtnview.k12.ca.us

Veronica Flores Aldaco

Title: Sixth-Grade Teacher **Company:** Porterville Unified School District **Address:** 600 W. Grand Avenue, Porterville, CA 93257 United States **BUS:** School District **P/S:** Education **MA:** Local **D/D/R:** Teaching English Language Learners **H/I/S:** Attending her Son's Soccer Games, Reading, Gardening **EDU:** Bachelor's Degree in Liberal Studies, Supplemental Credential in English, California State University at Bakersfield, 2000 **A/A/S:** California Association for Bilingual Education; Association of Mexican-American Educators; California Teachers Association; National Education Association **A/H:** WalMart Teacher the Year Award (2005-2006) **C/VW:** St. Jude Children's Research Hospital
Email: valdaco@porterville.k12.ca.us

Viola Claire Goby Alderete

Title: Store Manager **Company:** Corey's Jewelry Box **Address:** 29101 Rymal, Roseville, MI 48066 United States **BUS:** Retail Jewelry Store **P/S:** Retail Jewelry Store **MA:** Local **EXP:** Ms. Alderete's expertise includes public relations, sales and management. **H/I/S:** Playing with her Grandchildren, Spending Time with her Family **EDU:** Associate Degree, McComb Community College; Coursework in Business Management, Wayne State University; Madonna College
Email: info@CambridgeWhosWho.com

Terri Sue Aldridge-Russell

Title: President, Chief Executive Officer **Company:** Breakaway Consulting Group, Inc. **Address:** 714 Riggins Road, Tallahassee, FL 32308 United States **BUS:** Consulting Company **P/S:** Consulting Services Including Resource Assessment Services and Training on Alcohol Prevention **MA:** Regional **D/D/R:** Strategic Planning, Curbing Drug Abuse, Organizing Signature Events **H/I/S:** Spending Time with her Child, Reading, Writing, Scrapbooking, Cycling **EDU:** Bachelor of Science in Political Science and Religion, Florida State University (1999) **C/VW:** Leon County Community Traffic Safety Team; Chairwoman, Asthma Walk, American Lung Association (2008)
Email: terrisue@breakawayconsultinggroup.com
URL: http://www.breakawayconsultinggroup.com

Roberta A. Aleem
Title: Quality Assurance Supervisor **Company:** Advance Die Casting Co/A Division of Rollcast, LLC **Dept:** Quality **Address:** 8020 West Townsend St, Milwaukee, WI 53222 United States **BUS:** Aluminum and Zinc Manufacturers **P/S:** Aluminum and Zinc Casting, Gage Trainer, Blueprints, Supervising Inspectors, Also CMM-Layout and ISO Certified, Die Castings **MA:** Local **EXP:** Ms. Aleem's expertise is in product quality assurance. **H/I/S:** Bowling **EDU:** UMC, Process Control, Engineering, Geometric **A/A/S:** ASQ
Email: raa@adcmfg.com

Elena Aleteanu
Title: Owner **Company:** California Skin Care and Day Spa **Address:** 6180 Jarvis Avenue Ste R, Newark, CA 94560 United States **BUS:** Spa **P/S:** Skin Care Services and Day Spa **MA:** National **D/D/R:** Administering Facial Toning and Peels **H/I/S:** Traveling Worldwide **CERTS:** Licensed Cosmetologist; Herbal, Chemical, Acid and Peel Licensed
Email: elena@cadayspa.com
URL: www.cadayspa.com

Dr. Charlotte Alexander
Title: Associate Professor of English **Company:** The City University of New York **Dept:** College of Staten Island **Address:** 2808 Victory Boulevard, Staten Island, NY 10314 United States **BUS:** University **P/S:** Higher Education **MA:** National **D/D/R:** Teaching Women's Studies and Poetry **H/I/S:** Reading, Traveling, Walking **EDU:** Ph.D. in American Literature, Indiana University; Master of Arts in Education, Indiana University; Bachelor of Science in Education, Indiana University **C/VW:** Citymeals-on-Wheels; God's Love; We Deliver; City Harvest
Email: charlotte.alexander@cwwemail.com
URL: http://www.cambridgewhoswho.com

Cynthia L. Alexander
Title: AP Government Teacher **Company:** McAllen Memorial High School **Address:** 101 E. Hackberry Avenue, McAllen, TX 78501 United States **BUS:** High School Facility Dedicated to Excellence in Education **P/S:** Regular Core Curriculum Including Reading, Mathematics, English, Science, Social Studies, Art, Music, History, Physical Education, Language Arts and Computers **MA:** Regional **D/D/R:** Teaching Advanced Placement Government to Twelfth-Grade and U.S. History and Social Studies to the Eleventh-Grade, Coaching Varsity Tennis **EDU:** Pursuing Master's Degree in History; Bachelor of Arts, University of Texas (1991) **A/A/S:** Public Speaking at Local Service Centers; American Federation of Teachers
Email: calexander@rgv.rr.com
URL: http://www.memorial.mcallenisd.org

Joyce Alexander
Title: Producer, Psychotherapist **Company:** Alexander Productions **Address:** P.O. Box 48271, Los Angeles, CA 90048 United States **BUS:** Therapeutic Company **P/S:** Seminars, Individual and Group Therapy **MA:** Local **EXP:** Ms. Alexander's expertise includes bereavement, stress management and life coaching. **H/I/S:** Travel, Friends **EDU:** Master's Degree in Clinical Psychology, Antioch University **A/A/S:** American Psychological Association; California Marriage and Family Therapy Association
Email: joycealexander@yahoo.com
URL: http://www.joycealexander.com

Mrs. Antoinette Yvonne Alexander Mills
Title: Senior Marketing Manager and Business Development Manager **Company:** IBM **Dept:** Global Technology Services **Address:** 3039 Cornwallis Road, Research Triangle Park, NC 27709 United States **BUS:** Technology and Consulting Corporation **P/S:** Development of Technology and Infrastructure Solutions. **MA:** International **EXP:** Mrs. Alexander Mills' expertise includes sales and channel enablement, market intelligence and account and project management. **D/D/R:** Developing Solutions, Planning and Executing Global Go-To-Market Strategies, Managing Global Marketing **H/I/S:** Skydiving, Playing Softball, Rock Climbing, Web Designing, Playing the Piano and Guitar, Sketching, Cooking, Exercising **EDU:** Bachelor of Business Administration in Marketing, University of Georgia (1994); Master's Degree in International Business, Mercer University (1997); Bachelor of Science in Computer Information Systems, DeVry University (2001) **A/A/S:** National Black MBA Association; Delta Sigma Phi Business Fraternity; Alpha Sigma Lambda Honor Society; Delta Phi Epsilon Honor Society; Vice-Chairwoman of IBM Black Diversity Network Group (2003-2007) **A/H:** Joint Recipient, Beacon Award (2006); Recipient of Cisco Alliance Excellence Award (2004) **C/VW:** Habitat for Humanity; Hands On Atlanta; American Cancer Society
Email: alexanda@us.ibm.com

Derrick J. Alford
Title: Owner **Company:** DSOUL Designs **Address:** 100 Metropolitan Avenue, Brooklyn, NY 10019 United States **BUS:** Design Company **P/S:** Movie Set Design **MA:** National **D/D/R:** Working with Art Directors on Movie Production, Creating Sets **H/I/S:** Cycling, Spending Time with his Family **A/A/S:** Local 52 **C/VW:** Volunteer, Son's School
Email: dalford1@nyc.rr.com
URL: http://www.dsouldesigns.com

Nathalie Alfred
Title: Marketing Communication Director **Company:** MediaEdge CIA **Address:** 825 7th Ave, New York, NY 10019 United States **BUS:** Communications Media Company **P/S:** Planning and Buying, Media Agency **MA:** Local **EXP:** Ms. Alfred's expertise is in corporate communications. **H/I/S:** Reading, Traveling, Soccer, Movies, Theatre **A/A/S:** AAAA
Email: Nathalie.Alfred@MECGlobal.com
URL: www.MECglobal.com

Khalillah S. Ali
Title: Chief Executive Officer, Owner, Nurse Practitioner **Company:** Supreme Wisdom Family Health Clinic **Address:** 4907 Spring Avenue, Dallas, TX 75210 United States **BUS:** Family Health Clinic in Medically Underserved Community **P/S:** Health Care **MA:** Local, Regional **D/D/R:** Working with Geriatric, Adolescents and Pediatric Patients and 225 Home Health Patients, Making House Calls **H/I/S:** Jazz, Art, Decorating **EDU:** Master's Degree in Nursing Practitioner Studies, SUNY Stonybrook (2004); Associate Degree in Nursing, Farmingdale State University (2002); Bachelor of Science in Nursing, SUNY Stonybrook (2001) **A/A/S:** Association of Nurse Practitioners; Sigma Theta Tau
Email: ness62_99@yahoo.com

Syed Wasim Ali
Title: Manager, Software Development **Company:** Neustar, Inc **Address:** 46000 Center Oak Plaza, Sterling, VA 20166 United States **BUS:** Telecommunications Service Provider **P/S:** Voip Peering Exchange, Wireless Messaging **MA:** International **EXP:** Mr. Ali's expertise includes software development and architectural design. **H/I/S:** Golf, Spanish, Martial Arts **EDU:** Bachelor's Degree in Engineering
Email: syed.ali@neustar.biz
URL: www.neustar.biz

Duran Alicea
Title: Disc Jockey, Marketer **Company:** Against All Odds **Address:** 30 Congress Drive, Moonachie, NJ 07071 United States **BUS:** Retail, Entertainment **P/S:** Promotion for Record Signings, Celebrity Appearances and Grand Openings **MA:** National **D/D/R:** Deejaying, Entertaining, Marketing **H/I/S:** Playing Basketball, Playing Video Games
Email: deejayran@netzero.net
URL: http://www.deejayran.com

Carol M. Aljets
Title: Teacher **Company:** Nelson Elementary School **Address:** 708 St. Lewis Street, Edwardsville, IL 62025 United States **BUS:** Public School **P/S:** Certified K through Ninth-Grade, Regular Education for 420 Students **MA:** Regional **D/D/R:** Teaching all Curriculum Areas to Gifted and Special Needs Children, Hosting Teaching Candidates **H/I/S:** Racing Sailboats, Riding a Harley Davidson **EDU:** Master's Degree in Education, Southern Illinois University (1996); Specialist Degree in Reading Diagnostics
Email: ckohlfeld@ecusd7.org

Robert Everett Allari
Title: Owner **Company:** Tredere Custom Golf and Design Studios **Dept:** Management **Address:** 304 Carnation Avenue, Corona Del Mar, CA 92625 United States **BUS:** Golf Club and Design Studio **P/S:** Design, Restoration and Manufacture of Classic Golf Clubs **MA:** International **D/D/R:** Managing Professional Golf Club Products, Designing Golf Clubs, Overseeing Sales Transactions, Participating in Golf Tournaments, Managing Charity Golf Tournaments **H/I/S:** Collecting Old and Rare Golf Clubs and Artifacts, Spending Time with his Family, Vacationing, Playing Golf and Tennis **EDU:** Bachelor of Business Administration, Pacific University **A/A/S:** Autism Society of America; American Saddle Horse Museum; Professional Golfers' Association; International Professional Association of ClubFitters; Robert Trent Jones Society **C/VW:** Pathways Hospice; Autism Society of America; Desert Cities Junior Miss Scholarship Program; WorldStrides
Email: robertallari@gmail.com
URL: http://www.cambridgewhoswho.com

Barbara A. Allen
Title: Executive Sales Consultant **Company:** RE/MAX Greater Atlanta **Address:** 5163 Roswell Road, N.E., Atlanta, GA 30342 United States **BUS:** Real Estate Services **P/S:** Commercial Properties, Luxury Homes, Residential Properties, Investment Properties, First Time Home Buyers, Condominiums **MA:** Local **D/D/R:** Selling Residential Real Estate and Investment Properties, Managing Sales and Loan Operations, Helping Customers Find their Dream Home at Reasonable Costs, Advising Clients on All Home-Buying Details, Suggesting Various Monthly Payment Options and Loan Prequalification Plans **H/I/S:** Traveling, Reading, Theater, Tennis, Golfing **EDU:** Bachelor of Arts in Elementary Education, Harris Teachers College (1974) **A/A/S:** The Atlanta Board of Realtors; The National Association of Realtors
Email: badaja@gmail.com
URL: http://www.barbarainatlanta.com

Benjamin F. Allen
Title: Owner **Company:** Ben Allen's Pest Control Company, Inc. **Address:** 567 Rockdale Circle, Dublin, GA 31021 United States **BUS:** Pest Control Company **P/S:** Silverfish, Ant, Rat and Mice Control **MA:** Local **D/D/R:** Overseeing Pest Control Services for Residences, Corporations, Restaurants, Apartments, Hotels and Condominiums **H/I/S:** Fishing, Deer Hunting, Participating in Church Activities **EDU:** High School Diploma **A/A/S:** Georgia Pest Control Association
Email: benfallen@bellsouth.net

Denise L. Allen
Title: Early Childhood Special Education Teacher **Company:** Chicago Board of Education, Stevenson Elementary School **Address:** 8010 S. Kostner Avenue, Chicago, IL 60652 United States **BUS:** Elementary School **P/S:** Education **MA:** Local **D/D/R:** Teaching Special Education Students **H/I/S:** Reading, Showing Tourists around Chicago Sites, Mentoring Young Teachers **EDU:** Master of Science in Education Plus 45, National-Louis University; Bachelor of Arts in Education, Chicago State University (1978) **CERTS:** National Board Certification; Certified in English as a Second Language, National Board of Professional Teaching; Certified Teacher, National Board for Professional Teaching Standards **A/A/S:** Alumni of Erickson Institute; NASA **C/VW:** United Negro College Fund
Email: jodekr@aol.com

Jerry L. Allen
Title: Senior Program Manager **Company:** City of Beaverton **Address:** 4755 S.W. Griffith Drive, Beaverton, OR 97005 United States **BUS:** Local Government **P/S:** Code Services, Neighborhood Programs, Dispute Resolutions, Auxiliary Service, Be Safe Program **MA:** Regional **D/D/R:** Organizational Managing, Improving Processes, Managing Products, Implementing Software **H/I/S:** Golfing **EDU:** Bachelor's Degree in Economics, Portland State University
Email: jerrylallen@comcast.net
URL: http://www.beavertonoregon.gov

Jonathan W. Allen, MD, FACC
Title: Medical Doctor **Company:** Malama Pono **Address:** 135 S. Wakea Avenue, Suite 101, Kahului, HI 96732 United States **BUS:** Private Cardiology Practice **P/S:** Cardiology Care Services **MA:** Regional **EXP:** Dr. Allen's expertise is in cardiology. **D/D/R:** Managing Operations, Reviewing Electrocardiograms, Interpreting Stress Tests, Making Clinical and Hospital Calls **H/I/S:** Aerobics, Attending Church **EDU:** Fellowship in Cardiology, Columbia University; Residency in Internal Medicine, Columbia University; MD in Cardiology, Boston University Medical Center (1987); Postgraduate Coursework, Columbia University; Bachelor's Degree in English, Major in American Literature, Harvard University, Cum Laude (1983) **CERTS:** Recertification in Cardiology, American College of Cardiology **A/A/S:** Board Member, American Board of Internal Medicine
Email: jonathanallenmd@aol.com

Mr. Martin Allen
Title: Account Manager **Company:** Airgas North Central **Address:** 601 C Avenue N.E., Cedar Rapids, IA 52401 United States **BUS:** Distributor of Industrial, Medical, Specialty Gases and Related Equipment **P/S:** Safety Supplies, Welding Products and Services **MA:** National **D/D/R:** Managing Account Information, Developing New Business Relationships, Establishing New Business Accounts **H/I/S:** Watching Chicago Bears Football and University of Iowa Hawkeyes Basketball, Exercising, Spending Time with his Children **EDU:** High School Education **A/H:** Outstanding Sales Person of the Year Award (2006-2007); President's Award, Sales Growth (2006)
Email: martin.allen@airgas.com
URL: http://www.airgas.com

Pastor Roger L. Allen
Title: Pastor **Company:** Common Grand Community Church **Address:** 3725 Towne Pint Road, Port Smith, VA 23703 United States **BUS:** Religion, Spiritual Services **P/S:** A Small Southern Baptist Church **MA:** Local **D/D/R:** Starting Southern Baptist Churches **EDU:** Cedarville College, BS **A/A/S:** AACC
Email: comngrnds@msn.com

Rodney Allen, MS
Title: Trainer, Teacher **Company:** Raleigh County Board of Education **Address:** 105 Adair Street, Beckley, WV 25801 United States **BUS:** Board of Education **P/S:** Education **MA:** Countywide **D/D/R:** Training, Teaching Injury Prevention, Preparing Students for Games **H/I/S:** Traveling **EDU:** Master's Degree in Strategic Management, Mountain State University; Bachelor of Science in Education, Specialty in Health, Physical Education and Library Science, Concordia University **A/A/S:** Pastor, New Life Baptist Church **C/VW:** Handicapped Organizations, Special Olympics
Email: info@CambridgeWhosWho.com
URL: http://www.cambridgewhoswho.com

Sonya J. Allen
Title: Controller **Company:** Dorian Studio, Inc **Address:** 1161 South Post, Spokane, WA 99201 United States **BUS:** Photography Studio **P/S:** School Photographs **MA:** National **D/D/R:** Managing All Financial Aspects of Company Including Financial Statements and Closing Entries, Overseeing Cash Management and Human Resources **H/I/S:** Gardening, Piano, Travel, **EDU:** Bachelor's Degree in Engineering, Whitworth College, State of Washington (1990) **CERTS:** Certified Public Accountant (1992) **A/A/S:** WSCPA,AICPA, Red Hat Society, Poodle Club of America, **C/VW:** Chairman for MDA at Dorian Studio; United Way of America; Local Church; Red Hat Society
Email: sallen@dorianstudio.com
URL: www.dorianstudio.com

Tammy L. Allen
Title: Training Coordinator **Company:** Eastern Kentucky Childcare Coalition **Address:** 247 South Hwy 123 Apt 53, Corbin, KY 40701 United States **BUS:** Nonprofit Childcare Agency **P/S:** Training, Resource and Referral Service **MA:** Local **EDU:** Bachelor of Science in Music, Cumberland University **C/VW:** Church
Email: tammyallen@ekcc.org

Wanda E. Allen
Title: Cancer Coalition Coordinator **Company:** City of Trenton, Division of Health **Address:** 218 N. Broad Street, Trenton, NJ 08608 United States **BUS:** Government Healthcare Agency **P/S:** Free Healthcare Services **MA:** Regional **D/D/R:** Coordinating the Health Van, Traveling through the City Offering Services to the Public Including HIV Testing, Diabetes Screening, Breast and Prostate Cancer Screening, Working with Other Agencies to Form Partnerships to Spread the Word of Prevention and Healthy Lifestyles **H/I/S:** Running, Reading **EDU:** Master's Degree in Administration, Concentration in Human Resource Management, Central Michigan University (2001); Bachelor of Science in Law and Justice, College of New Jersey (1998); Pursuing Doctorate in Health Administration, Central Michigan University **A/A/S:** American Public Health Association; Governors Evaluation Task Force Evaluation Committee; Office of Cancer and Control Prevention Gynecological Work Group; Office of Cancer and Control Prevention Advocacy Work Group; Horizon New Jersey Health Advisor Committee, Trenton Crusade Against Cancer Education Task Force; New Jersey Cancer Education and Early Detection Coalition, Susan G. Komen For the Cure Educational Advisory Committee
Email: wallen@trentonnj.org
URL: http://www.trentonnj.org

Elnora P. Allen-Evans
Title: Medical Records Clerk, Certified Nurse Assistant, Licensed Minister **Company:** Hospice of Southern West Virginia **Address:** P.O. Box 1472, Beckley, WV 25802 United States **BUS:** Hospice **P/S:** Healthcare **MA:** Local **EXP:** Ms. Allen-Evans' expertise is in business administration. **D/D/R:** Directing School Programs **H/I/S:** Traveling, Reading, Decorating **EDU:** Associate Degree, Fort Hayes Career Center, Columbus, OH **CERTS:** Licensed Minister; Licensed Phlebotomist; Licensed Certified Nurses Assistant **C/VW:** Local Church; Salvation Army; Volunteers of America; Homeless Shelters; United Way
Email: barakell88@yahoo.com
URL: http://www.cambridgewhoswho.com

Carolina M. Allende
Title: Veterinary Student **Company:** Washington State University **Address:** 308 N.W. Webb Street, Pullman, WA 99163 United States **BUS:** University **P/S:** Veterinary Services **MA:** Statewide **D/D/R:** Studying Pathology and Neuroscience **H/I/S:** Rock Climbing, Reading, Traveling **EDU:** Bachelor's Degree in Biology and Zoology, Southern Utah University; Pursuing Doctor Veterinary Medicine
Email: kaddy_did@yahoo.com
URL: http://www.cambridgewhoswho.com

Kelli S. Alligood
Title: Pediatric Nurse Practitioner **Company:** Southeast Pediatrics **Address:** 8415 Goodwood Boulevard, Suite 104, Baton Rouge, LA 70806 United States **BUS:** Hospital **P/S:** Pediatric Healthcare **MA:** Local **EXP:** Ms. Alligood's expertise is in general pediatric nursing. **H/I/S:** Spending Time with her Husband and Daughter **EDU:** Master of Science in Nursing, Focus on Pediatrics, University of South Alabama **CERTS:** Advanced Practice Registered Nurse; Certified Pediatric Nurse Practitioner **A/A/S:** Louisiana Association of Nurse Practitioners; National Association of Pediatric Nurse Practitioners **C/VW:** Children's Miracle Network
Email: kelli.alligood@ololrmc.com
URL: http://www.ololrmc.com

Janet Marie Allison
Title: Office Manager, Reception **Address:** 124 Clyde Street, Beckley, WV 25801 United States **BUS:** Healthcare Industry **P/S:** Wide Range of Medical Services **MA:** Regional **D/D/R:** Working in the Hospital, Performing Administrative and Clerical Duties **H/I/S:** Cooking, Singing at Church, Playing Volleyball and the Piano **EDU:** Bachelor of Arts in Health Studies, Mountain State University; Pursuing Associate Degree, Medical Assistant, Mountain State University (Expected 2007) **A/A/S:** National Honors Society; American Association of Medical Assisting **C/VW:** Teacher, Sunday School
Email: pa2be@netphase.net
URL: http://www.cambridgewhoswho.com

Amada C. Galvan de Almanzar
Title: Secondary Mathematics Teacher **Company:** Classical High School **Address:** 770 Westminster Street, Providence, RI 02903 United States **BUS:** High School **P/S:** Secondary Education **MA:** Local **D/D/R:** Teaching Business Mathematics and Algebra **H/I/S:** Reading, Traveling **EDU:** Master of Economics, Earned in Mexico; Master of Education; Bachelor's Degree in Economics, Earned in the Dominican Republic **CERTS:** Certifications in Secondary Mathematics, Spanish and Leadership **A/A/S:** Rhode Island Mathematics Teachers Association; Providence Teachers Union; American Federation of Teachers **C/VW:** Boy Scouts of America; Community Volunteer
Email: acgalvan18@yahoo.com
URL: http://www.providenceschools.org

David L. Almerigi
Title: President **Company:** David Almerigi & Associates **Address:** P.O. Box 407, Seahurst, WA 98062 United States **BUS:** Aerospace Company **P/S:** Xframe (Finite Element Analysis) **MA:** Local **EXP:** Mr. Almerigi's expertise includes programming and management. **H/I/S:** Country Western Dancing **EDU:** Bachelor of Science in Aeronautics and Astronautical Engineering, University of Michigan **CERTS:** Licensed Professional Engineer, State of Washington
Email: dalmerigi@msn.com

Manette D. Aloba
Title: Director of Human Resources **Company:** Barrington Broadcasting **Address:** 2500 W. Higgins Road, Suite 155, Hoffman Estates, IL 60169 United States **BUS:** Broadcasting Company **P/S:** Network Television **MA:** Local **EXP:** Ms. Aloba's expertise is in human resources. **H/I/S:** Traveling to Japan **EDU:** Bachelor of Business Administration and Management, Columbia College
Email: maloba@barringtontv.com
URL: http://www.barringtontv.com

Kevin W. Alspach
Title: Owner/Operator **Company:** The Damarus Quentin Corp/Quentin Reupholstering Center **Address:** 215 1/2 West Galen Street, Bucyrus, OH 44820 United States **BUS:** Demolition/Upholstery Sole Proprietor **P/S:** Building Demolition and Debris Removal, All Aspects of Reupholstery **MA:** Local **EXP:** Mr. Alspach's expertise is in demolition. **H/I/S:** Hiking, Exploring, Basketball **EDU:** Coursework in Business Management, Ohio University-Lancaster; Apprenticeship in Furniture Upholstery **A/A/S:** Landlords Association, Ohio Association Chiefs of Police Inc, Boystown
Email: damarcusquentin@yahoo.com

Benjamin A. Alston
Title: President **Company:** Elite Enquiries **Address:** 5 Centre Street, Floor 2, Hempstead, NY 11550 United States **BUS:** Private Investigation Firm **P/S:** Investigation Services **MA:** National **EXP:** Mr. Alston's expertise is in surveillance. **D/D/R:** Overseeing Bail Recovery Services, Insurance Fraud and Witness Investigation **H/I/S:** Reading, Watching Baseball **EDU:** Master's Degree in Sociology, New York University (1984); Bachelor of Arts in Sociology, Minor in Criminal Justice, Long Island University (1974) **CERTS:** Licensed Private Investigator, State of New York **A/A/S:** Purple Art Association; Society of Professional Investigators; Associated Licensed Detectives of New York State; National Fraternal Order of Police **C/VW:** Veterans of Foreign Wars; The American Legion; Disabled American Veterans
Email: eliteenquiries@aol.com

Lucy Altagracia Sardonia
Title: Social Worker **Company:** Abdereen Adult Care **Address:** 5 Prospect Street, Lakewood, NJ 08071 United States **BUS:** Retirement Facility **P/S:** Healthcare for Seniors **MA:** National **EXP:** Ms. Altagracia Sardonia's expertise is in social work. **H/I/S:** Rollerblading, Biking, Doing Aerobics **EDU:** Bachelor of Social Work, Syracuse University (1983) **CERTS:** Certified Social Worker, State of New Jersey (1995) **A/A/S:** League of United Latin American Citizens
Email: lucysard@optonline.net
Email: lsardonia@mediahealth.com

Kenneth C. Althiser
Title: GIS Analyst **Company:** ACS at the City of Riverside **Address:** 38920 Newberry Street, Cherry Valley, CA 92223 United States **BUS:** Government Organization **P/S:** Information Technology and Geographic Information System Services to the City of Riverside **MA:** Regional **D/D/R:** consulting, conducting analysis, overseeing cartography and database design and maintaining the database for local government applications. **H/I/S:** Playing Volleyball, Reading **EDU:** Bachelor's Degree in Geology, Chapman University (1977)
Email: kalthiser@riversideca.gov
URL: http://www.riversideca.gov

Ailene Altman Mitchell
Title: Principal **Company:** Department of Education, The Park Slope Education Complex **Address:** 544 7th Avenue, Brooklyn, NY 11215 United States **BUS:** School System **P/S:** Primary and Secondary Education for Students **MA:** Regional **EXP:** Ms. Altman Mitchell's expertise includes literacy and reading education. **D/D/R:** Restructuring Schools, Developing Curricula and Data **H/I/S:** Biking, Hiking, Reading **EDU:** Master's Degree in Education, Pace University **A/A/S:** Teach For America; Association for Supervision and Curriculum Development; Phi Delta Kappa
Email: amitch2@schools.nyc.gov

Richard A. Altstaetter
Title: President **Company:** Colonial Forge Appraisal Service **Address:** 65 Partridge Lane, Stafford, VA 22556 United States **BUS:** Appraisal Company **P/S:** Real Estate Appraisals **MA:** National **D/D/R:** Conducting Residential Appraisals and Physical Inspections of Homes, Managing a Staff of Appraisers, Reviewing Work, Communicating with Clients, Working with Mortgage Companies to Refinance or Buy Homes **H/I/S:** Golfing, Playing Football **EDU:** Bachelor's Degree **A/A/S:** Foundation of Real Estate Appraisers; Dulles Area Association of Realtors
Email: appraisals@colonialforge.net
URL: http://www.colonialforge.net

Alma L. Alvarez
Title: Property and Casualty Underwriter **Company:** State Farm Insurance **Address:** 12010 Lake Mead Lane, Humble, TX 77346 United States **BUS:** Insurance Company **P/S:** Insurance **MA:** Texas **EXP:** Ms. Alvarez's expertise includes property and casualty insurance. **H/I/S:** Traveling, Cooking, Shopping **EDU:** Bachelor of Science in Mathematics, University of Texas; Bachelor of Arts (1984) **A/A/S:** Chartered Property Casualty Underwriter **C/VW:** United Way, Mexican American National Association
Email: alma.alvarez.a5n4@statefarm.com

Beth E. Alvarez
Title: Orchestra Director **Company:** Glendale-River Hills School District **Address:** 5515 N. Navajo Avenue, Glendale, WI 53217 United States **BUS:** Public School District **P/S:** General Primary and Secondary Curriculum, Arts, Music, Orchestra, Physical Education, Foreign Language Instruction, Learning Resources, Student Support Services, Athletics, Extracurricular Activities, Student Clubs and Organizations **MA:** Regional **D/D/R:** Teaching String Courses to Fifth through Eighth-Grade Orchestra Students, Planning Lessons for 120 Students **H/I/S:** Distance Running, Playing the Cello, Performing at Nursing Homes and Community Events **EDU:** Master's Degree in Music Performance, University of Wisconsin (2005); Bachelor's Degree in Music Education, Minor in German, University of Wisconsin (2000) **A/A/S:** Wisconsin Education Association Council
Email: bethalvarez77@yahoo.com
URL: http://www.glendale.k12.wi.us

Hugo V. Alvarez, JD
Title: Managing Partner **Company:** Alvarez, Paz, and Barbara, LLP **Address:** 2701 South Bayshore Drive Suite 605, Miami, FL 33133 United States **BUS:** Law Firm **P/S:** Law Firm **MA:** Local **EXP:** Mr. Alvarez's expertise is in real estate litigation. **H/I/S:** Reading, Traveling, Sports **EDU:** Tulane University, JD **A/A/S:** DCBA, CABA, LBA, BASF
Email: alvarez@apblaw.com
URL: www.apblaw.com

Nancy Alvarez
Title: Lieutenant **Company:** Monroe County Sheriff's Office **Dept:** Special Investigations Division **Address:** 5525 Junior College Road, Key West, FL 33040 United States **BUS:** Government Organization **P/S:** Law Enforcement **MA:** Local **D/D/R:** Working with Homeland Security and Intelligence Agencies **H/I/S:** Watching NASCAR Races, Gardening **EDU:** Bachelor of Arts in Criminal Justice, Union Institute & University
Email: nalvarez@keysso.net
URL: http://www.keysso.net

Rodney A. Alves

Title: International Advisor **Company:** Manatt, Phelps & Phillips, LLP **Address:** 11355 W. Olympic Boulevard, Los Angeles, CA 90064 United States **BUS:** Consulting Company **P/S:** Law and Business Consulting Services **MA:** International **D/D/R:** Overseeing International Transactions Including Antitrust Matters and Mergers and Acquisitions, Assisting Brazilian and Multinational Companies with Corporate and Business Transactions, Practicing International Corporate Law, Advising Clients **H/I/S:** Spending Time with his Family, Hiking, Biking, Surfing, Playing Volleyball and Soccer **EDU:** JD, Mackenzie University; Master of Law, Los Angeles School of Law, University of California **A/A/S:** Board Member, International Association of Young Lawyers; Director, Brazil-California Business Council; Coordinator, Instituto Brasileiro de Direito Empresarial, CA **A/H:** Marquis Who's Who in American Law (2003-2004); Marquis Who's Who in the World (2005) **C/VW:** The Place Adventist Fellowship
Email: ralves@manattjones.com
URL: http://www.manattjones.com

Harold T. Amaker, Ph.D.

Title: Director of Community Relations **Company:** BMW-MINI of Sterling **Address:** 21826 Pacific Boulevard, Sterling, VA 20166 United States **BUS:** Automobile Dealership **P/S:** New and Previously Owned Automobiles, BMWs, MINI Coopers, Financing, Repair Services, Parts and Accessories **MA:** Regional **D/D/R:** Recruiting Future Automotive Industry Professionals, Offering Internship Opportunities, Designing Programs **EDU:** Ph.D. in Business Administration, La Salle University (2000); Master of Business Administration, Golden Gate University; Master of Science in Business Management, Central Michigan University; Bachelor's Degree in Business Administration, Virginia State University (1961) **CERTS:** Graduate Certificate in Government Information, American University; Graduate Certificate in Public Relations, American University **A/A/S:** National Association for the Advancement of Colored People; Lifetime Member, Kappa Alpha Psi (1989-Present); Alumni Association, Virginia State University; Booster Club, Virginia State University **A/H:** Rookie of the Year Award, Mercedes-Benz International (1987); Athletic Hall of Fame, Virginia State University; Star Sales Consultant with Mercedes Benz
Email: hamaker@verizon.net
URL: http://www.bmwofsterling.com

Kelly Anne Amato

Title: English Teacher **Company:** Rossi Intermediate School **Address:** 2572 Palermo Avenue, Vineland, NJ 08361 United States **BUS:** School **P/S:** Education for Grades Sixth through Eighth **MA:** Local **D/D/R:** Teaching English to Seventh and Eighth-Grade Students **H/I/S:** Reading, Traveling, Coaching Cheerleading **EDU:** Bachelor of Science in Elementary Education, University of Delaware **A/A/S:** New Jersey Education Association; National Education Association; Vineland Education Association **C/VW:** American Diabetes Association
Email: kamato@vineland.org

Betty J. Ambrose

Title: Assistant Program Manager, District 1 Central **Company:** State of Arizona **Dept:** Department of Economic Security FAA **Address:** 215 E. McDowell Street, Phoenix, AZ 85007 United States **BUS:** Government Organization **P/S:** Professional Development, Human Services **MA:** Regional **D/D/R:** Monitoring Quality Control and Evaluation Methods, Developing Research Methodologies and Strategies in Office Operations, Interpreting Statistical Reports, Resolving Issues, Presenting Agency Services to Customers and Community Partners, Analyzing Operations for Improvements, Regulating Public Assistance Programs, Ensuring Customer Satisfaction **H/I/S:** Working on Computers, Sewing **CERTS:** Certification in Counseling of Chemically Dependent **A/A/S:** Lifetime Member, Black Theater Troupe; Booster Club **A/H:** Certificate of Appreciation, State of Arizona Emergency Response Team (2006); Employee of the Quarter, State of Arizona, FAA, Glenrosa Local Office (2005); Outstanding Teamwork Award, Maricopa County, DOME (1998); Valuable Service Award, Family Affair Project (1998); Certificate of Achievement, Maricopa County, DOME (1997); Certificate of Recognition, Maricopa County, DOME (1996); Valuable Service Award, Hip Hop Drama Playhouse, City of Phoenix (1996); Employee of the Month, Maricopa County, DOME (July 1996, August 1996); Certificate of Appreciation, Sir Lantz Entertainment Company (1995)
Email: bambrose@azdes.gov
Email: bambrose6@cox.net
URL: http://www.azdes.gov/faa.gov/faa/default.asp

Donna R. Ambrose, MS

Title: Special Education Teacher **Company:** Public School 111, Seton Falls Elementary **Address:** 3740 Baychester Avenue, Bronx, NY 10466 United States **BUS:** Primary Education Services for Students **P/S:** Excellence in All Core Academic Subjects, Wide Variety of Enrichment and Specialized Learning Programs, Services, Charitable Events, Supportive Teacher Staff and Administration **MA:** Regional **D/D/R:** Teaching Emotionally and Physically Challenged Students in a Self-Contained Classroom, Instructing All Core Courses Including Language Arts, Social Studies, Mathematics and Reading to Nine through 12-Year-Old Children, Modifying Lesson Plans Using Different Modalities **H/I/S:** Reading **EDU:** Master of Science in Education and Psychology, Mercy College, New York (2004) **CERTS:** Certification in Regular Education, K-12; Certification in Special Education, K-6 **A/A/S:** The United Federation of Teachers **A/H:** Attuning the Students Award Certificate of Completion (2007)
Email: Donnaamb@verizon.net
URL: http://www.cambridgewhoswho.com

Sandra L. Ames

Title: Library Media Specialist **Company:** Olathe Unified School District 233 **Dept:** Heatherstone Elementary School **BUS:** School District **P/S:** Education **MA:** Local **D/D/R:** Teaching, Consulting with Teachers and Lecturers, Lecturing, Managing Facilities for Learning Environments **H/I/S:** Traveling, Reading, Water Sports **EDU:** Master's Degree in Reading, Concentration in Undergraduate Library Media, Plus 60, University of Nebraska; Bachelor of Arts in Elementary Education and Library Science, The University of South Dakota (1972) **CERTS:** National Board Certified Teacher **A/A/S:** Olathe National Education Association; President, National Board for Professional Teaching Standards; National Education Association; American Library Association; International Reading Association; Former President, Delta Kappa Gamma **A/H:** Semi-Finalist, Master Teacher Award **C/VW:** Metropolitan Lutheran Ministry
Email: sameshn@olatheschools.com
URL: http://www.cambridgewhoswho.com

Terry J. Ammons

Title: Owner **Company:** Granny's Treasures **Address:** 7450 Highway 60, Ekron, KY 40117 United States **BUS:** Retail Thrift Shop **P/S:** Footwear, Clothing, Furniture, Antiques Products, Glass Wear, Books **MA:** Regional **EXP:** Ms. Ammon's expertise is in customer service. **H/I/S:** Bowling, Bingo, Spending Time with Grandchildren **EDU:** High School Education **A/A/S:** Bingo Hall; Pet Protection; Children's Cancer Research
Email: granny@bbtel.com

Miss Angelica Amor

Title: Bartender, Trainer **Company:** Pappadeaux Seafood Kitchen **Address:** 3520 Oak Lawn Avenue, Dallas, TX 75219 United States **BUS:** Restaurant **P/S:** Seafood, Beverages **MA:** Local **D/D/R:** Serving Guests, Training New Employees, Ensuring Customer Satisfaction **H/I/S:** Acting **EDU:** Pursuing Bachelor's Degree in Finance, Southern Methodist University; Associate Degree, Navarro College (2007) **CERTS:** License, Texas Alcoholic Beverage Commission **C/VW:** Habitat for Humanity
Email: jelliebean722@hotmail.com
Email: aamor@smu.edu
URL: http://www.pappadeaux.com

Barbara A. Amos

Title: Staff Pharmacist **Company:** CVS Pharmacy **Address:** 550 N. Franklin Street, Christiansburg, VA 24073 United States **BUS:** Retail Pharmacy **P/S:** Retail Pharmacy **MA:** National **D/D/R:** Monitoring Drug Interactions, Administering Immunizations, Educating Patients about Medications **H/I/S:** Reading, Walking **EDU:** Doctor of Pharmacy, Shenandoah University, 2004 **A/A/S:** Phi Chio; Kappa Epilso; APHA
Email: bamospharmd@verizon.net

Veronica L. Ampey, ATC

Title: cert athletic trainer Coordinator for High School Healthcare **Company:** Georgetown Day School **Address:** 4200 Davenport Street, N.W., Washington, DC 20016 United States **BUS:** Coeducational Day School **P/S:** Education for Prekindergarten through 12th-Grade Students, Healthcare Services Including Sports Medicine **MA:** Local **EXP:** Ms. Ampey's expertise is in sports medicine. **D/D/R:** Managing Health Services, Overseeing Students and Faculty, Performing Administrative Duties **H/I/S:** Scuba Diving, Spending Time with Family **EDU:** Master's Degree in Sports Medicine, United States Sports Academy; Bachelor's Degree in Health and Fitness (1985) **CERTS:** Certified Athletic Trainer (1986) **A/A/S:** The National Athletic Trainers' Association; Chairwoman, National Committee, Mid-Atlantic Athletic Trainers' Association; Delta Sigma Theta; National Association of Black Scuba divers
Email: vampey@gds.org
URL: http://www.gds.org

Jeffrey E. Amundson

Title: Master Carpenter **Company:** JAM Carpentry **Address:** 6251 Laurene Avenue, Lino Lakes, MN 55014 United States **BUS:** Home Improvement Company **P/S:** Home Improvement Services and Custom Wood Work **MA:** Local **EXP:** Mr. Amundson's expertise is in carpentry. **D/D/R:** Modeling Cabinetry Designs, Repairing, Managing Contracts **H/I/S:** Freshwater Fishing, Camping, Spending Time Outdoor **EDU:** Coursework, Vocational School **CERTS:** Certification in Cabinet Making, St. Paul Technical College (1990)
Email: jamcarpentry@yahoo.com

Maria E. Anaya

Title: ESOL Teacher & Tutor **Company:** Ayuda, Inc. **Address:** 7118 Byron Avenue, Miami Beach, FL 33141 United States **BUS:** Nonprofit Counseling Agency **P/S:** Family Empowerment and Parents Now Programs **MA:** Regional **EXP:** Ms. Anaya's expertise includes counseling and education. **H/I/S:** Swimming, traveling **EDU:** Bachelor of Science in Education, Equivalency by Josef Silny and Associates, 2001 **A/H:** Certificate of Appreciation, Early Literacy Training, Happy Kids ABC (2004) **C/VW:** Ayuda, Inc.
Email: intralan@netscape.com
URL: http://www.cambridgewhoswho.com

Cathy A. Anderkin

Title: Clinic Manager **Company:** Aurora Sheboygan Clinic **Address:** 2414 Kohler Memorial Drive, Sheboygan, WI 53081 United States **BUS:** Nonprofit Healthcare Provider and Clinic **P/S:** Multiple Specialty Healthcare **MA:** Regional **D/D/R:** Overseeing Four Satellite Offices, Orienting the Staff, Supervising Seven Departments and 110 employees **EDU:** Bachelor of Science in Healthcare Administration, Kennedy Western University (2005) **A/A/S:** ALTRUSA
Email: cathy.anderkin@aurora.org
URL: http://www.aurora.org

Judith C. Andersen, MD

Title: Director, Center for Bleeding Disorders and Thrombosis **Company:** Karmanos Cancer Institute **Address:** 4100 John R Street, Detroit, MI 48201 United States **BUS:** Cancer Institution **P/S:** Healthcare Including Research and Development for Cancer Treatment **MA:** National **D/D/R:** Treating Bleeding Disorders and Thrombosis Patients, Supervising Nurses and Staff Members, Collecting Research Data, Conducting Training for Medical Students, Residents, Fellows and Junior Faculty Members **H/I/S:** Cooking, Hiking, Gardening, Traveling **EDU:** MD, Jefferson Medical College, Philadelphia; Bachelor's Degree in Chemistry, Wellesley College **A/A/S:** American Society of Hematology; International Society on Thrombosis and Haemostasis **C/VW:** Hemophilia Foundation of Michigan; Animal Rescue Society; American Cancer Society
Email: andersen@karmanos.org
URL: http://www.karmanos.org

Suzette Louise Andersen

Title: Senior Case Manager **Company:** Fairfax County Government, Community Services Board **Address:** 12011 Government Center Parkway, Suite 300, Fairfax, VA 22035 United States **BUS:** Government **P/S:** Case Management, Monitoring, Coordinating and Counseling Clients, Alcohol and Drug Services, Victim Assistance Network, Mental Health Services **MA:** Regional **EXP:** Ms. Andersen's expertise is in case management. **D/D/R:** Working with Mentally Retarded and Impaired Individuals, Facilitating Employment for the Homeless, Locating Housing, Overseeing Interdisciplinary Work **H/I/S:** Writing, Cooking, Mentoring Family Members, Photography for Pleasure and Profit, Studying Spanish History, Basketball **EDU:** Master of Social Work, Virginia Commonwealth University (2002); Master's Degree in Counseling and Guidance, The University of Montana (1983); Bachelor's Degree in Youth Leadership and Recreation Management, Minor in Sociology, Minor in Psychology, Brigham Young University (1981) **A/A/S:** American Counseling Association; Qualified Mental Retardation Professional, **C/VW:** Church
Email: suzyandersenmt@verizon.net
URL: http://www.fairfaxcounty.gov

Andy Anderson

Title: President **Company:** Tazz Man, Inc. **Address:** 3101 E. Abram Street, Arlington, TX 76120 United States **BUS:** Proven Leader in the Entertainment Industry **P/S:** Blackjack Table, Beverages, Pool Table, Adult Entertainment, Restaurant **MA:** International **D/D/R:** Managing 26 Businesses and Employees **H/I/S:** Ultimate Fighting **EDU:** Doctor of Theology, University of Dayton (1985) **A/A/S:** National Republican Party; Mason
Email: hander5053@aol.com
URL: http://www.hardbodys.org

Ms. Charmaine N. Anderson
Title: Mathematics Teacher **Company:** East New York Family Academy **Address:** Brooklyn, NY United States **BUS:** School **P/S:** Education **MA:** Local **D/D/R:** Teaching Mathematics to Sixth and Seventh-Grade Students **H/I/S:** Camping, Hiking **EDU:** Master's Degree in Mathematics Education, Nova Southeastern University, FL **A/A/S:** The United Federation of Teachers; American Federation of Teachers **C/VW:** Boys & Girls Clubs of America; Girls & Boys Town
Email: charm_anderson@msn.com
URL: http://www.cambridgewhoswho.com

Cindi K. Anderson
Title: Secretary, Treasurer **Company:** New Beginnings Church of God **Address:** 8125 Highway 69A, Big Sandy, TN 38221 United States **BUS:** Nonprofit Organization **P/S:** Church, Youth Community Center **MA:** Local **H/I/S:** Quilting, Making Murals **EDU:** College Coursework **C/VW:** Ministerial Alliance
Email: nbc@bentoncountycable.net
URL: http://www.cambridgewhoswho.com

Eva Anderson
Title: Administrator **Company:** Eva's Residential Care Facilities **Address:** 2500 8th Avenue, Los Angeles, CA 90018 United States **BUS:** Nonprofit Organization **P/S:** Social Services, Finding Homes for the Disabled, Catering to the development of Disabled People **MA:** Local **EXP:** Ms. Anderson's expertise is in social services. **D/D/R:** Overseeing all Administrative Work, Caring for the Disabled **H/I/S:** Playing Tennis, Watching Movies **EDU:** College Coursework **A/A/S:** WAHA; Historical Society
Email: classyeva@aol.com
URL: http://www.cambridgewhoswho.com

James C. Anderson
Title: Independent RELIV Distributor, Educational Specialist **Company:** RELIV **Address:** 517 S. Murray Street, Gainesboro, TN 38562 United States **BUS:** Food Supplement Manufacturing Company **P/S:** RELIV Food Supplements and Food Nutrients, Marketing, Distribution, Research **MA:** Local **D/D/R:** Supervising Students for General Education and Development **H/I/S:** Walking, Sports **EDU:** Master's Degree in Education, University of Colorado at Boulder (1961); Bachelor of Science, Tennessee Tech University (1954) **CERTS:** Certified Educational Development Specialist, Tennessee Technological University (1991); Certified Flying Instructor **A/A/S:** American Nuclear Society; Phi Delta Kappa; Lieutenant, Reserve Officer Training Corps, Korea; Public Speaker, Peaceful Applications of Nuclear Atomic Energy
Email: jcarl.anderson@yahoo.com

Joyce L. Anderson
Title: Director of Curriculum, Testing and Guidance **Company:** Stephenville Independent School District **Address:** 2655 W. Overhill Drive, Stephenville, TX 76401 United States **BUS:** Public School District **P/S:** Education **MA:** Local **EXP:** Ms. Anderson's expertise includes curriculum development and educational administration. **H/I/S:** Reading, Gardening **EDU:** Doctorate in Educational Administration, Texas A&M Commerce University (2006) **A/A/S:** Texas Staff Development Council; Association for Supervision and Curriculum Development; Association of Texas Technology Education; UCEA; NASST; TWSCE **C/VW:** American Cancer Society
Email: joyce.anderson@sville.us
URL: http://www.stephenville.k12.tx.us

Kathleen Rita Anderson
Title: Gyrokinesis, Gyrotonic, Pilates and Yoga Instructor **Company:** Serene Yoga **Address:** 4 Varney Street, Jamaica Plain, MA 02130 United States **BUS:** Physical Fitness Center **P/S:** Gyrokinesis, Gyrotonic, Pilates and Yoga Instruction **MA:** Greater Boston Area **D/D/R:** Teaching Gyrokinesis, Gyrotonic, Pilates, Tai Chi, Aqua Aerobics, Yoga and Flamenco Dancing **H/I/S:** Traveling, Hiking, Dancing **EDU:** Master's Degree in Dance Movement Therapy, Antioch University New England, Keene, NH **A/A/S:** MassYoga Network **C/VW:** The Leukemia & Lymphoma Society
Email: kathleen@yogawithkathleen.com
URL: http://www.yogawithkathleen.com

Nancy J. Anderson
Title: Senior Systems Training Specialist **Company:** Kindred Healthcare **Address:** 640 S. 4th Street, Louisville, KY 40202 United States **BUS:** Long-Term Acute Hospitals and Nursing Centers **P/S:** Long-Term Healthcare **MA:** National **D/D/R:** Training in Clinical Information Systems **EDU:** Bachelor's Degree in Occupational Therapy, Ohio State University **A/A/S:** American Society for Training and Development
Email: nancy_anderson@kindredhealthcare.com
URL: http://www.kindredhealthcare.com

Rebecca S. Anderson
Title: Licensed Practical Nurse **Company:** Alvin Nursing Center **Address:** 416 N. Shirley Street, Alvin, TX 77511 United States **BUS:** Nursing Home **P/S:** Healthcare **MA:** Local **D/D/R:** Managing Nursing Assistants and Residents, Teaching College Students **H/I/S:** Skiing, Ice Skating, Gymnastics, Playing Basketball **CERTS:** Licensed Vocational Nurse; Licensed Practical Nurse
Email: rebecca.anderson@cwwemail.com

Robert D. Anderson
Title: Owner **Company:** Anderson's Taxidermy **Address:** 2156 Collier Road, Springfield, OH 45506 United States **BUS:** Taxidermy **P/S:** Taxidermy **MA:** Ohio **D/D/R:** Preparing Game Heads **H/I/S:** Traveling with his Wife, Fishing, Hunting, Spending Time Outdoors, Biking **EDU:** High School Graduate; Coursework in Taxidermy, Northwestern School of Taxidermy **A/A/S:** Pheasants Forever; National Wild Turkey Federation; Buckeye Buck Association for Taxidermists **A/H:** Best Overall Division of Reptiles (2005); Best Overall in Master Division in Fish (2004) **C/VW:** Church

Suzanne R. Anderson
Title: Sergeant of Corrections (Retired) **Company:** Texas Department of Correction-Institutional Division **Address:** 1916 N. Highway 36 Bypass N., Gatesville, TX 76596 United States **BUS:** Women's Correctional Facility **P/S:** Rehabilitation for Adult Female Offenders, Custody Maintenance **MA:** Regional **D/D/R:** Supervising Rehabilitation Services for Inmates **H/I/S:** Bowling, Dancing, **EDU:** College Coursework Completed in Continuing Education, Computers and On-the-Job Training; Coursework in Foundation Studies, Central Texas College; High School Education
Email: suzianderson9591@htcomp.net
URL: http://www.cambridgewhoswho.com

Walter J. Anderson
Title: Terminal Supervisor **Company:** Polman Transfer, Inc. **Address:** 63425 Highway 10 W., Wadena, MN 56482 United States **BUS:** Trucking Company **P/S:** Trucking Services **MA:** National **D/D/R:** Purchasing Parts and Equipment, Overseeing All Mechanical Problems **H/I/S:** Auto Racing; Watching NASCAR Race **EDU:** Coursework in Vocational Training, Central Lakes College **A/A/S:** Secretary, Minnesota Maintenance Council
Email: wally@polmantransfer.com
URL: http://www.polmantransfer.com

Melissa A. Anderson-Seeber
Title: Chief Local Public Defender **Company:** Waterloo Juvenile Public Defender Office **Address:** 229 E. Park Avenue, 3rd Floor, Waterloo, IA 50703 United States **BUS:** Law Office **P/S:** Legal Representation for Indigent Adult and Juvenile Clients **MA:** Regional **D/D/R:** Representing Juvenile and Adult Clients at Trial **H/I/S:** Golfing, Cooking **EDU:** JD, Drake University Law School (1991) **A/A/S:** National Association of Criminal Defense Lawyers; Iowa Public Defenders Association
Email: maseeber@mchsi.com
URL: http://spd.iowa.gov

Rita Andino
Title: Painter, Interior Designer, Author **Company:** Rita Andino Interiors **Address:** 8233 Harding Avenue, Apartment 205, Miami Beach, FL 33141 United States **BUS:** Art Studio **P/S:** Fine Arts **MA:** Local **EXP:** Ms. Andino's expertise is in the creation of impressionistic art pieces. **H/I/S:** Traveling, Swimming, Reading, Writing **EDU:** Coursework in Accounting, Bookkeeping, Painting, Photography, Drawing, Print Making, Italian Language and Jewelry Designing **A/A/S:** Honorary Member, Florida Sheriffs Association **C/VW:** Local Church; Miami Rescue Mission; The Salvation Army
Email: ritaandino@webtv.com
URL: http://www.ritaandino.com

Mrs. Sheri L. Andreason
Title: Executive Office Specialist **Company:** CH2M-WG Idaho, LLC (CWI) **Address:** 2525 N. Fremont Avenue, P. O. Box 1625 MS 5108, Idaho Falls, ID 83415 United States **BUS:** Environmental Cleanup Industry **P/S:** Idaho Cleanup Project **MA:** Regional **D/D/R:** Overseeing Executive Office Management, Executing, Coordinating and Disseminating Information Relating to Project Business Functions, Practices and CWI Policies, Mentoring and Guiding Other Administrative Personnel throughout CWI, Communicating Effectively and Interface with CWI Senior Staff, DOE, Corporation and Staff, Working with the State of Idaho **H/I/S:** Spending Time with Family, Scrapbooking, Reading, Hiking, Camping in the Great Outdoors **EDU:** Coursework, University of Idaho; Degree, Mackay High School, Mackay, Idaho **CERTS:** Medical Coding Specialist **A/A/S:** International Association of Administrative Professionals; Member, National Parent Teacher Association; Idaho National Laboratory Employee Association; United Way; Christmas for Families; CARE Committee
Email: andreasl@icp.doe.gov
URL: http://www.cambridgewhoswho.com

Andrena K. Andrews
Title: Licensing Brand Manager **Company:** Sean John **Address:** 1710 Broadway, New York, NY 10019 United States **BUS:** One of the Leading Fashion Designers of Men's and Women's Clothing **P/S:** Designer Apparel, Outerwear, Specialty Jeans, Women's Wear, Men's Wear, Casual Sportswear **MA:** International **D/D/R:** Managing All Licensees, Acting as a Company Liaison, Advertising **H/I/S:** Reading, Traveling **EDU:** JD, New York Law School (2002) **A/A/S:** Alpha Kappa Alpha
Email: aandrews@seanjohn.com
URL: http://www.seanjohn.com

Nettie M. Andrews
Title: Elementary Teacher **Company:** Tucson Unified School District, Fort Lowell Elementary School **Address:** 5151 E. Pima Street, Tucson, AX 85712, Tucson, 85712 **BUS:** School **P/S:** Education **MA:** Local **D/D/R:** Teaching Students **H/I/S:** Arts and Crafts **EDU:** Master of Science in Education, Earned in the Republic of Panama; Master of Science in Bilingual Education, Arizona State University **A/A/S:** Tucson Education Association **C/VW:** Local Community Organizations

Stacy L. Andrews
Title: Vice President **Company:** Mobility Transport, Inc. **Address:** P.O. Box 697, Elma, WA 98541 United States **BUS:** Nonprofit Transportation Company **P/S:** Medical Taxi Services **MA:** Regional **D/D/R:** Creating Transportation Alternatives to Medical Appointments, Overseeing Human Resources for Employees, Coordinating New Contracts with Hospitals, Clinics and Physicians, Managing Grants, Transporting Patients **H/I/S:** Reading, Camping, Quad Trail Riding **EDU:** Associate of Science in Business Administration, Western International University, with Honors (2006); Associate of Science in Gemology, Gemological Institute of America, Santa Monica, California (1992); Associate of Science in Horology, South Seattle Community College, West Seattle (1991) **A/A/S:** Community Action Transit; National Write Your Congressman
Email: ctw@centurytel.net

Barbara E. Andrus
Title: Teacher **Company:** Ava Middle School **Address:** P.O. Box 338, Ava, MO 65608 United States **BUS:** Public School **P/S:** Education **MA:** Local **D/D/R:** Teaching Social Studies and Ancient Civilization to Students in Sixth-Grade, Tutoring **H/I/S:** Raising her Grandson, Gardening, Farming, Riding Horses, Swimming, Hiking, Hunting, Camping **EDU:** Master's Degree in Elementary Education, Southwest Missouri State University **CERTS:** Certification in Elementary Education, Emphasis on Early Childhood Education, Learning Disabilities K-9, Middle School Social Studies and Language Arts **A/A/S:** Delta Kappa Gamma **C/VW:** Literacy Council
Email: teachld57@yahoo.com
URL: http://www.avabears.net

Cherry A. Ang
Title: Office Manager, Research Coordinator **Company:** Pediatric Pulmonology, LLC **Address:** 32 Strawberry Hill Court, Suite 11, Stamford, CT 06902 United States **BUS:** Pediatric Office **P/S:** Diagnosis and Treatment of Children with Diseases and Respiratory Disorders **MA:** Regional **D/D/R:** Researching on Premature Birth, Managing the Office **H/I/S:** Exercising, Traveling **EDU:** Bachelor of Science in Human Development and Family Studies, University of Connecticut (2001)
Email: cang@stamhealth.org

Jane A. Angel
Title: Realtor **Company:** Coldwell Banker Real Estate LLC **Address:** 68 Malaga Cove Plaza, Palos Verdes Estates, CA 90274 United States **BUS:** Real Estate Agency **P/S:** Commercial and Residential Real Estate Exchange **MA:** California **D/D/R:** Managing Commercial and Residential Property Exchange, Assisting Clients in Establishing Homes, Aiding First-time Buyers, Relocating Properties, Consulting **H/I/S:** Playing the Piano, Swimming, Exercising **EDU:** Bachelor of Science in Business Management, The Ohio State University (1979) **CERTS:** Licensed Realtor (2000) **A/A/S:** Local Board of Realtors; Palos Verdes Peninsula Association of Realtors; California Association of Realtors **A/H:** Top Five Percent in the Nation for Sales Representing Buyers and Sellers, International Presidency League (2008) **C/VW:** Local Schools
Email: janeaangel@aol.com
URL: http://www.californiamoves.com

Kathe D. Angell
Title: Owner, Operator **Company:** The Healing Place **Address:** 110 E. Granada Boulevard, Suite 205, Ormond Beach, FL 32176 United States **BUS:** Massage Therapy Center **P/S:** Massage Reflexology Services, Reiki Healing Technique, Cranio-Sacral, PreNatal Massage; Reiki Certification Classes for Children and Adults; Aqua-Chi Detox Footbath **MA:** Regional **D/D/R:** Utilizing Massage Reflexology and Reiki Relaxation Techniques, Treating Obese, Elderly and Disabled Patients **H/I/S:** Creating Native American Dream Catchers, Scrapbooking, Walking on the Beach, Feeding the Birds, Writing Poetry, Spending Time with her Granddaughters **EDU:** Coursework in Reflexology, International Institute of Reflexology (1998); Diploma, Mainland Senior High School (1969); Alenta Firewoman (1998) **CERTS:** Atlantic Academy of Massage (1995); Reiki Training (1991-93); Ordained in the Order of Melchizedek (1996); Hotline Representative for the Domestic Abuse Council (1989-1993) **A/A/S:** IMA, Sanctuary of the Beloved; Sierra Club; Audubon Society, Humane Society, North Shore Animal League, WWF; National Parks Conservation Association; National Arbor Day Foundation; WMFE; Doris Day Animal League; St. Mary's Episcopal Church; Best Friends Animal Society; Wildlife Land Trust; Unity Church; National Wildlife Federation; NRDC **A/H:** National Register's Who's Who (2000)
Email: kangell7@bellsouth.net

Carol M. Anglemyer
Title: Owner **Company:** Carol's Professional Tax Service **Address:** 26661 County Road 38, Goshen, IN 46526 United States **BUS:** Finance Company **P/S:** Tax Preparation for Small Businesses and Individuals **MA:** Regional **EXP:** Ms. Anglemyer's expertise is in the preparation of tax returns. **H/I/S:** Reading, Walking, Traveling, Sewing, Attending Musical Concerts, Orchestras, Gardening **EDU:** Coursework, Bethel College, Mishawaka, IN; Coursework, Indiana University South Bend; Diploma, Bourbon High School (1947) **C/VW:** Beulah Missionary Church, Goshen, IN
Email: anglemyergc@aol.com
URL: http://www.cambridgewhoswho.com

Roger L. Angus
Title: Fire Chief **Company:** Spencer Volunteer Fire Department **Address:** 101 E. Main Street, Spencer, NE 68777 United States **BUS:** Emergency Rescue Service **P/S:** Fire Suppression, Fire Prevention, Public Education, Vehicle Extraction, Emergency Rescue, Weather Alerts **MA:** Regional **D/D/R:** Fighting Structure Fires and Wildfires, Overseeing Department Operations **H/I/S:** Hunting, Fishing **CERTS:** Certified Fire Fighter; Emergency Medical Technician **A/A/S:** Nebraska State Volunteer Firefighters Association

Mohamad A. Annan
Title: Principal **Company:** Annan and Associates **Address:** 783 N Marion, Clovis, CA 93611 United States **BUS:** Structural Analysis **P/S:** Provides Professional Services in Structural Engineering, Works with Professional Architects and Developers **MA:** Local **EXP:** Mr. Annan's expertise includes residential and commercial structural engineering. **H/I/S:** Traveling **EDU:** Bachelor of Science in Civil Engineering, Fresno State University (1995) **CERTS:** Licensed, Certified Professional Civil Engineer, State of California **A/A/S:** ASCE; Professional Member, ICC
Email: m-annan@sbcglobal.net

Mr. William Annis
Title: Executive Director **Company:** Marshall Internal and Family Medicine **Address:** 14900 Old US 27 N., Marshall, MI 49068 United States **BUS:** Healthcare **P/S:** Directing Operation Practice Management **MA:** Regional **D/D/R:** Managing Physician Practices **EDU:** Master's Degree in Hospital and Healthcare Administration, Xavier University (1992); Bachelor's Degree in Marketing, Franklin University (1987) **A/A/S:** American College of Healthcare Executives
Email: bill@annis.net

Michelle J. Anschutz
Title: Construction Engineer **Company:** Kansas Department of Transportation **Address:** 1686 First Avenue E., Horton, KS 66439 United States **BUS:** Transportation, Engineering **P/S:** State-Government Construction of Highway and Bridges **MA:** Regional **EXP:** Ms. Anschutz expertise is in management. **D/D/R:** Overseeing Construction **EDU:** Bachelor of Science in Civil Engineering, University of Kansas **A/A/S:** Lions Club
Email: info@CambridgeWhosWho.com
URL: http://www.cambridgewhoswho.com

Donna L. Antaya
Title: Respiratory Therapist **Company:** Sacred Heart Medical Center **Address:** 101 W. Eighth Avenue, Spokane, WA 99204 United States **BUS:** Medical Center **P/S:** Healthcare Including Respiratory Therapy Services **MA:** Local **EXP:** Ms. Antaya's expertise is in neonatal care. **H/I/S:** Fabricating Gold and Silver Jewelry **EDU:** Associate of Applied Science, Spokane Community College **A/A/S:** Spokane Community College
Email: breathzda@hotmail.com
URL: http://www.cambridgewhoswho.com

Erika Y. Anthony
Title: Street Outreach Coordinator **Company:** Long Island Crisis Center **Address:** 2740 Martin Avenue, Bellmore, NY 11710 United States **BUS:** Nonprofit Organization **P/S:** Coordinating Street Outreach Projects for Troubled Youth **MA:** Nassau County **D/D/R:** Coordinating Awareness Workshops and Self-Empowerment Groups, Individual Client Intervention within At-Risk Communities and Schools **H/I/S:** Reading, Traveling **EDU:** Bachelor's Degree in Social Work, Molloy College **A/A/S:** National Honor Society; NSLS **C/VW:** Volunteer Counselor, Long Island Crisis Center
Email: eanthony@longislandcrisiscenter.org
URL: http://www.longislandcrisiscenter.org

Joseph Antignani
Title: President **Company:** Green Mountain Lines, LLC **Address:** 432 South Street, Suite C-11, Bennington, VT 05201 United States **BUS:** Charter and Tour Company **P/S:** Motor Coach Transportation **MA:** National **D/D/R:** Performing Office Duties, Ensuring Customer Service, Driving, Writing Contracts **H/I/S:** Reading, Traveling, Golfing **A/A/S:** UMCA; ABA **C/VW:** Elks Lodge
Email: grnmtnbus@comcast.net

Michael R. Antón
Title: Project Architect **Company:** Stater Bros. **Address:** 375 De Berry Street, Colton, CA 92324 United States **BUS:** Retail Store **P/S:** Commercial Products **MA:** Southern California **EXP:** Mr. Anton's expertise includes building design and construction. **H/I/S:** Teaching at Junior College, Fishing **EDU:** Bachelor of Science in Architecture, California Polytechnic State University, San Luis Obispo **A/A/S:** Construction Specifications Institute; American Institute of Architects; International Code Council
Email: michael.anton@starterbros.com
URL: http://www.staterbros.com

Debra E. Antonio
Title: Membership, Marketing **Company:** Girl Scouts Wagon Wheel Council **Address:** 3535 Parkmoor Village Drive, Colorado Springs, CO 80917 United States **BUS:** Nonprofit Organization **P/S:** Service Young Girls Across the Country **MA:** National, statewide **D/D/R:** Overseeing Human Resources, Interviewing Potential Members, Conducting Orientations, Explaining the Application Process, Marketing the Program, Assigning Girls to Troops **H/I/S:** Boating, Camping, Reading, Traveling, Spending Time with her Family **EDU:** Master of Business Administration, Emphasis in Human Resources, American InterContinental University (2006) **A/A/S:** Girl Scouts of the USA
Email: dantonio1956@msn.com
Email: dantonio@girlscouts-wwc.org
URL: http://www.girlscouts-wwc.org

Alice A. Aparis
Title: Postal Worker (Retired) **Company:** United States Postal Service **BUS:** United States Postal Service **MA:** National **D/D/R:** Delivering the Mail, Offering Customer Service **H/I/S:** Enjoying Art, Reading, Camping in her Recreational Vehicle **EDU:** Coursework in Business Administration, Palomar College **C/VW:** Volunteer, Senior Center
Email: aliceaparis@verizon.net
URL: http://www.cambridgewhoswho.com

Patricia Apostolides
Title: Realtor **Company:** Century 21 APD and Associates **Address:** 5500 N. Desert, El Paso, TX 79912 United States **BUS:** Real Estate Firm **P/S:** Real Estate **MA:** National **D/D/R:** Selling Commercial and Residential Real Estate, Assisting First-Time Home Buyers **H/I/S:** Archeology, Indian Myths, Hiking, Photography, Videos, History of Texas **EDU:** Master's Hours in Foreign Language and Spanish, University of Texas at El Paso; Bachelor's Degree in Sociology, University of Texas (1969) **A/A/S:** El Paso Archaeological Society; National Association of Realtors; Texas Association of Realtors; Heritage Community of Girl Scouts Rio Grande; Advisory Board El Paso Sheriff's Association; Operation Santa Claus; El Paso Native Plant Society; Ambassador Program People to People in China (2007)
Email: patti.apostolides@sbcglobal.net
URL: http://www.cent21apd.com

Kenneth P. Appel
Title: District Manager **Company:** Allied Barton Security Services **Address:** 50 Jackson Avenue, Syosset, NY 11791 United States **BUS:** Government Organization **P/S:** Security Guard Services Including Access Control, Vehicle Control and Perimeter Control, Reception Services, Gate House Services, Emergency Medical Technician First Responder Services, Control Room Operations **MA:** Regional **D/D/R:** Overseeing the Protective Service Department, Managing and Supervising Individuals **EDU:** Master of Arts in Criminal Justice, John Jay College of Criminal Justice, New York (1984); Bachelor of Science in Police Science, John Jay College of Criminal Justice (1984) **A/A/S:** American Society for Industrial Security
Email: kenneth.appel@alliedbarton.com
URL: http://www.alliedbarton.com

Candace M. Appl
Title: Teacher **Company:** St. Joseph Middle School **Address:** 606 E. Peters Drive, P.O. Box 409, St. Joseph, IL 61873 United States **BUS:** School **P/S:** Education **MA:** Local **D/D/R:** Teaching Sixth-Grade **H/I/S:** Gardening, Scrapbooking, Spending Time with her Dogs, Exercising **EDU:** Master's Degree in Advanced Studies, Education, Emphasis in Reading, Eastern Illinois University **A/A/S:** Phi Beta Kappa
Email: cmappl@stjoe.k12.il.us
URL: http://www.stjoe.k12.il.us

Jennifer L. April
Title: Senior Associate, Auditor **Company:** Pricewater House Coopers, LLP **Address:** 2001 Market Street, Suite 1700, Philadelphia, PA 19103 United States **BUS:** Accounting Firm **P/S:** Financial Services **MA:** International **EXP:** Ms. April's expertise is in client service. **H/I/S:** Traveling, Practicing Yoga, Exercising, Spending Time with Family **EDU:** Bachelor of Science in Accounting and Business Administration, Neumann College **CERTS:** Pursuing Certified Public Accountant **A/A/S:** Pennsylvania Certified Public Accountants; Neumann College Alumni Association **C/VW:** Volunteer of the Year, Neumann College, 2007
Email: jennifer.l.april@us.pwc.com
URL: http://www.cambridgewhoswho.com

Dr. Peter P. Aran
Title: Doctor of Gastroenterology and Internal Medicine **Company:** Gastroenterology Specialists, Inc. **Address:** 6565 S. Yale Avenue, Suite 1200, Tulsa, OK 74136 United States **BUS:** Medical Practice **P/S:** Healthcare Services Including Gastroenterology, Cancer Unit, Digestive Diseases and Internal Medicine **MA:** Regional **D/D/R:** Referring Patients, Treating Eating Disorders and Bladder Disease, Consulting with Clientele **H/I/S:** Running, Tennis, Spending Time with his Children **EDU:** MD, University of Iowa (1987); Fellowship, University of Chicago (1987); Coursework in Internal Medicine, University of Iowa (1984) **CERTS:** Certified in Specialized Internal Gastrointestinal Medicine **A/A/S:** American Gastroenterological Association; American Medical Association; American Association for the Study of Liver Diseases
Email: gihepardoc@aol.com

Mr. Sergio Aranguren
Title: Product Specialist **Company:** Agilent Technologies **Address:** 7891 W. Flagler Street, PBM 600, Miami, FL 33144 United States **BUS:** World Leading Provider of Instrumentation, Systems, Supplies, Software, Services and Support to Life Science and Chemical Analysis **P/S:** Capillary Electrophoresis, DNA Microarrays, Gas Chromatography, ICP-MS, Lab-on-a-Chip, Liquid Chromatography, Mass Spectrometry, UV-VIS **MA:** International **D/D/R:** Manufacturing and Servicing Chemical Analysis Instruments for Chromatography and Mass Spectrometry **H/I/S:** Reading, Traveling **EDU:** Bachelor of Science Degree in Chemistry and Computers, Venezuela (1978) **A/H:** Published in Journals, Presenter, Various Seminars
Email: searangu@hotmail.com
URL: http://www.agilent.com

Jorge E. Arce, DDS
Title: Doctor of Dental Surgery **Company:** Dental Implants Center **Dept:** Dentistry **Address:** 1932 Manhattan Beach Boulevard, Suite A, Redondo Beach, CA 90278 United States **BUS:** Dental Practice Devoted to Restoring and Enhancing the Natural Beauty of Original Missing Teeth **P/S:** Dental Implants, State-of-the-Art Procedures, Comprehensive Treatment Planning, Reconstructive and Implant Dentistry to Achieve Optimal Dental Health **MA:** Regional **EXP:** Mr. Arce's expertise is in oral reconstructive surgery. **D/D/R:** Administering Bone and Soft Tissue Grafting Procedures, Replacing Damaged Teeth with Dental Implants **H/I/S:** Going to the Beach, Volleyball **EDU:** Doctor of Dental Surgery, Universidad Autonoma de Manizales, Columbia (1992) **CERTS:** Certification in Oral Surgery (1996) **A/A/S:** Diplomate, American Board of Oral Implantology and Implant Dentistry; Public Speaking
Email: drarce@dentalimplantscenter.com
URL: http://www.dentalimplantscenter.com

Linda L. Archambault, Ed.S.
Title: Principal **Company:** R. O. Gibson Middle School **Address:** 3900 W. Washington, Las Vegas, NV 89107 United States **BUS:** Middle School Education **P/S:** Regular Middle School Curriculum, Administration, Teaching **MA:** Regional **D/D/R:** Overseeing the Curriculum, Staffing, Teacher Morale, Facilities, Safety Issues and the At-Risk Special Education Program **H/I/S:** Involved with Horses, Horseback Riding, Playing Bridge, Spending Time with her Grandchildren **EDU:** Master's Degree in Secondary Education, Indiana University (1983); Pursuing Ph.D. in Business Administration, Kennedy Western University **CERTS:** Certification, Education Specialist, Nova University (1992) **A/A/S:** Association for Supervision and Curriculum Development; National Association of Secondary School Principals; Clark County Association of School Principals
Email: linda_archambault@interact.ccsd.net
URL: http://ccsd.net/schools/gibsonms

Analea D. Archibald
Title: Owner **Company:** Analea's Stitch and Design **Address:** 7400 Camelia Drive, Hanover Park, IL 60133 United States **BUS:** Embroidery Company **P/S:** Unique Personalized Embroidery **MA:** Local **EXP:** Ms. Archibald's expertise is in professional design. **H/I/S:** Baking **A/A/S:** National Network of Embroidery Professionals
Email: analeas@comcast.net

Iris Arden
Title: Chief Executive Officer **Company:** Ramon International Insurance Brokers, Inc. **Address:** 142 Mineola Avenue, Suite 3D, Roslyn Heights, NY 11577 United States **BUS:** Insurance **P/S:** Cargo, Commercial Insurance **MA:** International **D/D/R:** Overseeing Sales, Marketing and Promotions **H/I/S:** Creative Writing, Traveling, Participating in Summer Sports **EDU:** Bachelor's Degree in Business Administration, New York Institute of Technology; Coursework in Insurance, College of Insurance **A/A/S:** Insurance Underwriters **C/VW:** Various Causes
Email: irisarden@ramonins-usa.com
URL: http://www.ramonins-usa.com

Ovidio Arevalo, MS, CSCS
Title: Teacher and Strength Trainer **Company:** Falfurrias High School **Address:** 1004 N. Portscheller Street, Falfurrias, TX 78355 United States **BUS:** High School **P/S:** Education for Students in Ninth through 12 Grade **MA:** Regional **EXP:** Mr. Arevalo's expertise is in education. **D/D/R:** Consulting with Other Schools about the Benefits of Strength and Conditioning for Student Athletes **H/I/S:** Learning about History **EDU:** Master of Science in Kinesiology, Texas A&M University, Kingsville (2003) **A/A/S:** Texas High School Coaches Association; International Sports Sciences Association; National Strength and Conditioning Association; USA Weightlifting Federation
Email: ocoacha@yahoo.com

Sara R. Argueta
Title: Immigration Consultant **Company:** Latin American Immigration Service **Address:** 6172 Whittier Boulevard, Los Angeles, CA 90022 United States **BUS:** Immigration, Notary, Translation Service Company **P/S:** Immigration, Notary, Translation Services **MA:** Regional **EXP:** Ms. Argueta's expertise includes immigration consulting and tax preparation. **H/I/S:** Reading **C/VW:** Church
Email: latinamerican@sbsglobal.net
URL: http://www.cambridgewhoswho.com

A. May Ariss
Title: French Teacher **Company:** Sylvania Franciscan Academy **Dept:** Language Department **Address:** 5335 Silica Drive, Sylvania, OH 43560 United States **BUS:** High School **P/S:** Secondary Education **MA:** Local **D/D/R:** Teaching French **H/I/S:** Traveling, Playing Tennis, Cooking **EDU:** Pursuing Master of Arts in French; Bachelor of Arts in French, The University of Toledo (1998) **A/A/S:** Alliance Francaise **C/VW:** Sylvania Franciscan Academy
Email: ariss2@msn.com
URL: http://www.sylvania-franciscan-academy.net

Jerry S. Arkin
Title: President **Company:** Arkin Insurance Agency **Address:** 390 Augusta Place, Clarksville, TN 37043 United States **BUS:** Insurance Company **P/S:** Insurance Services **MA:** National **D/D/R:** Overseeing Health, Life, Disability, Vision and Dental insurance **H/I/S:** Exercising, Sports, Boating **EDU:** Bachelor of Science in Optometry, Pennsylvania College of Optometry (1979); Bachelor of Arts in Psychobiology, Temple University (1976) **A/A/S:** Brentwood Chamber of Commerce; Cool Springs Chamber of Commerce; Nashville Chamber of Commerce; Better Business Bureau; Agency for Healthcare Research and Quality **A/H:** Million Dollar Sale Award (2006) **C/VW:** Volunteer, High School Band
Email: jarkin@charter.net
URL: http://www.jarkin.ahcpgroup.com

Ronald Armenti, DPM, FACFAS
Title: Doctor Podiatric Medicine **Company:** New Jersey Foot and Ankle Association **Address:** 1553 Highway 27, Suite 2300, Somerset, NJ 08873 United States **BUS:** Medical Facility **P/S:** Taking Care of Medical Related Problems Including Surgery, Ailments of the Foot and Ankle **MA:** Local **EXP:** Mr. Armenti's expertise includes foot and ankle surgery. **EDU:** Doctor of Podiatric Medicine, New York College of Medicine (May 1996) **A/A/S:** New Jersey Podiatric Medicine Society; American College of Foot and Ankle Surgery, Diplomat, American Board of Podiatric Medicine
Email: ronxnj@yahoo.com
URL: http://www.cambridgewhoswho.com

Angela R. Armes-Thomas
Title: Occupational Therapist **Company:** Eye Care Center **Address:** 1013 Morris Drive, Richmond, KY 40475 United States **BUS:** Healthcare Optometrists **P/S:** Work With Optometrists in the Areas of Low Vision, Adaptive Equipment, Vision Training **MA:** Local **EXP:** Ms. Armes-Thomas expertise is in pediatrics. **H/I/S:** Camping, Being a Mom **EDU:** Eastern Kentucky University **CERTS:** Graduate Level Pediatrics Certificate **A/A/S:** Educational Presentations in Schools; Sunday School Teacher, Local Church; Volunteer, Continuing Education Programs: Special Olympics; Lions Club International; Medfrest
Email: rathomas@eyepro.net

C. Jayne Armstrong
Title: President **Company:** Greener Products for a Better World, Inc. **Address:** 3173 Payne Avenue, Apartment 4, San Jose, CA 95117 United States **BUS:** Online Retail Store **P/S:** Skincare and Spa Products Including Anti-Aging and Anti-Cellulite Products **MA:** International **D/D/R:** Working with Aesthetics, Designing Websites, Writing about Cancer Survival and Support **H/I/S:** Snowboarding, Walking, Playing the Guitar, Taking part in Frisbee Competitions **EDU:** Associate of Arts in Computer Administration, Computer Learning Center **C/VW:** Sierra Club; The Humane Society of the United States; National Wildlife Federation; Action Network; The Rainforest Foundation; Ovarian Cancer Research Foundation; American Cancer Society
Email: jayne@shoppingkharma.com
URL: http://www.shopkharmaestore.com

Dennis L. Armstrong
Title: Orthopedic Surgeon **Company:** Dennis L. Armstrong, MD, PC **Address:** 6553 E. Baywood, Suite 101B, Mesa, AZ 85206 United States **BUS:** Medical Office **P/S:** Healthcare **MA:** Regional **EXP:** Mr. Armstrong's expertise includes orthopedic surgery and joint replacement. **H/I/S:** Raising Animals, Golfing **EDU:** MD, Wayne State University, 1971; Residency in Orthopedic Surgery, Henry Ford Hospital; Bachelor of Arts, Michigan State University, 1967 **A/A/S:** American Medical Association; American Academy of Orthopaedic Surgeons **C/VW:** Humane Society, Animal Welfare League
Email: darmst4425@aol.com

Frances Armstrong
Title: Hair Salon Owner **Company:** Salon 403 LLC **Address:** 11747 Jefferson Avenue Suite 3C, Newport News, VA 23606 United States **BUS:** Cosmetics/Beauty Salon **P/S:** Full Service Hair Salon **MA:** Local **EDU:** Bachelor's Degree, Norfolk State University
Email: salon403@gmail.com
URL: www.myspace.com/salon403

Marilyn A. Armstrong
Title: Publisher, Editor in Chief **Company:** Best of St. Pete, Inc. **Address:** 200 Second Avenue, Suite 149, St. Petersburg, FL 33701 **BUS:** Magazine **P/S:** Magazine **MA:** St. Petersburg **EXP:** Ms. Armstrong's expertise is in publishing. **H/I/S:** Writing **EDU:** Associate Degree in Human Services, St. Petersburg College, Florida; Associate Degree in Art, Santa Fe College, Gainesville, Florida; Coursework in Nursing **A/H:** Three-Time Nominee, Businesswoman of the Year **C/VW:** Fundraisers, Cultural, Social and Political Causes in St. Petersburg
Email: marilyn@bestinstpete.com
URL: http://www.bestinstpete.com

W. Maye Armstrong
Title: Teacher of the Handicapped **Company:** Pemberton Township High School **Address:** 148 Arneys Mount Road, Pemberton, NJ 08068 United States **BUS:** Public High School **P/S:** Education and Curriculum **MA:** Regional **D/D/R:** Supporting and Teaching Special Needs Students **H/I/S:** Reading, Traveling **EDU:** Master's Degree in Education, Philadelphia Biblical College (1999); Bachelor's Degree in Biblical Studies, Philadelphia Biblical College (1997)
Email: warmstro@msn.com
URL: http://www.pemberton.k12.nj.us/pths/home/pthsedit_ed.htm

Carolyn M. Arndt
Title: Special Education Teacher (Retired) **Company:** Midd-West School District **Dept:** Special Education **Address:** 540 E. Main Street, Middleburg, PA 17842 United States **BUS:** School District **P/S:** Education **MA:** Regional **EXP:** Ms. Arndt's expertise is in transition coordination. **D/D/R:** Teaching Special Education, English and Mathematics to 11th and 12th-Grade Students, Ensuring Standard Classroom Settings and Accompanying Students to Regular Education Classroom **H/I/S:** Traveling, Reading Murder Mysteries, Quilting, Scrapbooking, Watching Baseball and Football **EDU:** Bachelor of Science in Special Education and Regular Education for Grades Kindergarten through Eight, Bloomsburg State Teachers College (Now Bloomsburg University) (1973) **CERTS:** Certified Teacher, Kindergarten through Eighth-Grade, State of Pennsylvania **A/A/S:** Former Vice President, Mid-West Education Association; Middleburg Kiwanis; Former Advisor, Key Club; President, Snyder County Historical Society; Secretary, Richfield Fire Company Auxiliary; Susquehanna Valley Civil War Round Table; Juniata Mennonite Historical Society; Mt. Pleasant Mills Fire Company; Richfield Ambulance League; Pennsylvania State Education Association; National Education Association
Email: arndtgar@countryilink.net
Email: arndtgar@earthlink.net
URL: http://www.cambridgewhoswho.com

Ann C. Arnold, MD
Title: Medical Director **Company:** Medical Center of Plano **Address:** 3901 West 15th Street, Plano, TX 75075 United States **BUS:** 425-Bed Hospital and Healthcare Center **P/S:** Healthcare **MA:** Local **D/D/R:** Overseeing the Operations of the Medical Center and 900 Physicians, Practicing Geriatric and Internal Medicine **H/I/S:** Golfing, Spending Time with her Dogs and her Husband **EDU:** MD, University of Arkansas; Bachelor's Degree, University of Arkansas **A/A/S:** The United States Foreign Service (1975); Texas Medical Association; American Medical Association **A/H:** Alliance Compassionate Physician Award for Leading a Large Mission to Kenya, Veterans of Foreign Wars of America; One of the Best Doctors in Dallas, D Magazine; One of the Best Doctors in Texas, Texas Monthly; One of Best Doctors in America in Internal Medicine; Fellow, American College of Physicians **C/VW:** Leader, Mission to Kenya
Email: elmaca@aol.com
URL: http://www.cambrigdewhoswho.com

Lisa M. Arnold
Title: Administrative Assistant, Paralegal **BUS:** Law Firm **P/S:** Legal Services for Driving Under the Influence, Driving while Intoxicated, Drug Crimes, Post Conviction, Violent Crimes and White Collar Crimes **MA:** Regional **EXP:** Ms. Arnold's expertise is in telecommunications. **D/D/R:** Managing Clients, Handling Accounts Payable and Receivable, Scheduling Appointments and Hearings, Preparing Legal Documents, Assisting Lawyers **H/I/S:** Bowling, Spending Time with her Husband and Children **EDU:** Associate Degree in Microcomputer Operations, Star Technical Institute (1993) **CERTS:** Certified Paralegal; Licensed Notary Public **A/A/S:** Pennsylvania Association of Notaries **C/VW:** LEE National Denim Day (2007)
Email: larnold@ezlinx.net
URL: http://www.cambridgewhoswho.com

Vickie M. Arnold
Title: Clinical Director **Company:** Roanoke Valley Center for Sight **Address:** 438 W. Main Street, Salem, VA 24153 United States **BUS:** Healthcare Center **P/S:** Healthcare, Ophthalmology Services **MA:** Local **D/D/R:** Overseeing and Managing the Operations of the Ambulatory Surgery Center, Assisting Doctors in Ophthalmic Surgery **H/I/S:** Camping, Gardening **EDU:** Associate of Applied Science in Nursing, Virginia Western Community College **A/A/S:** Association of periOperative Registered Nurses; Ambulatory Surgery Center Association; American Society of Ophthalmic Registered Nurses **C/VW:** Virginia Association of Volunteer Rescue Squads
Email: ornurse54@cox.net

Miguel A. Arocho
Title: Director of Consulting Services **Company:** Evertec, Inc. **Address:** Carre 176 KM 1.3, San Juan, PR 00926 United States **BUS:** Transaction Resource Company, Outsourcing Services **P/S:** Transaction Resource for Banking, Government and Financial Institutions **MA:** Puerto Rico **EXP:** Mr. Arocho's expertise is in business development. **D/D/R:** Designing New Innovative Technology Products **H/I/S:** Bicycling, Golfing, Traveling, Spending Time with his Two Children **EDU:** Master of Business Administration, University of Dallas, Texas, 1984; Bachelor of Business Administration, University of Puerto Rico, Magna Cum Laude, 1982 **A/A/S:** Former Member, ICCP; TPMA; DPMA **C/VW:** American Cancer Society
Email: marocho@evertecinc.com
URL: http://www.evertecinc.com

Michelle L. Arreola
Title: Customer Service Manager **Company:** San Diego Fluid System Technologies **Address:** 6350 Nancy Ridge Drive, Suite 101, San Diego, CA 92121 United States **BUS:** Manufacturing Company **P/S:** Sales and Service for Swagelok Fluid Handling Components **MA:** Regional **EXP:** Ms. Arreola's expertise is in sales analysis. **D/D/R:** Gathering and Analyzing Information, Analyzing Profit Margins, Managing and Training the Customer Service Team, Overseeing Purchasing **H/I/S:** Spending Time with Husband, Watching Movies, Reading, Shopping **EDU:** Bachelor of Arts in Psychology, San Diego State University (2002); Graduated with Distinction, San Diego State University, Magna Cum Laude **A/A/S:** Phi Beta Kappa; San Diego State University Alumni Association
Email: marreola@sdfst.com
URL: http://www.swagelok.com

Teresa K. Arriaza
Title: Office Operations Manager **Company:** State Farm Insurance, Doug Auzat's Agency **Address:** 4421 W. Riverside Drive, Suite 100, Burbank, CA 91505 United States **BUS:** Insurance Company **P/S:** Automobile, Home and Life Insurance, Financial Services **MA:** Local **D/D/R:** Overseeing Operations, Writing Policies, Selling Insurance **H/I/S:** Singing, Watching Events, Freestyle Motor Cross, Drag Racing, Riding her Quad, Offroading, Camping, Reading 'How to Score from the Red Zone' **EDU:** Pursuing Bachelor of Arts in Sociology, California State University
Email: teresa@dougauzat.com
URL: http://www.dougauzat.com

Patricia Arriola
Title: Broker/Owner **Company:** Century 21 Gables Gate Realty **Address:** 815 Ponce De Leon Suite 100, Coral Gables, FL 33134 United States **BUS:** Real Estate **P/S:** Residential, Executive, Hi End, Beach Front, Condos on Water, New Construction, Golf Homes Gated **MA:** National **D/D/R:** Selling Residential and High-End Properties **H/I/S:** Skiing **EDU:** Bachelor of Science in Geriatrics, University of Cornienlet, Argentina; Bachelor of Science in Economics and Finance, Fordham University **A/A/S:** Florida Association of Realtors, National Association of Realtors
Email: gablesgate@century21.com
URL: www.gablesgaterealty.com

Susan Arrowood
Title: Therapist/Owner **Company:** Arrowood Consulting Inc **Address:** 404 C West Fleming Drive, Morganton, NC 28655 United States **BUS:** Healthcare Company **P/S:** Offering Mental Health Services and Consulting to Community **MA:** Local **D/D/R:** Treating Adults, Children and Adolescents with Mental Health Issues **H/I/S:** Spending Time with Daughter, Flower Arrangements **EDU:** Master's Degree, Gardener University **A/A/S:** American Counseling Association
Email: susann714@hotmail.com

John Artale
Title: Owner **Company:** INSITE Home Inspections **Address:** Port Jefferson Station, NY 11776 United States **BUS:** Real Estate **P/S:** Home Inspections **MA:** Local **D/D/R:** Conducting Residential Home Inspection Reports, Identifying Shortcomings, Offering Renovation and Remodeling Services **H/I/S:** Spending Time with Family, Going on Vacation, Performing Yard Work, Researching the Internet **CERTS:** Licensed Home Inspector, State of New York, NRI (2000)
Email: sarge52j@netscape.net

James T. Arthur
Title: Professional Engineer, Realtor **Address:** PO Box 780890, Wichita, KS 67278 United States **BUS:** Engineering, Real Estate, Consultant, Project Development **P/S:** Residential, Commercial, Industrial **MA:** Local **D/D/R:** Consulting **H/I/S:** Fishing, Golfing **EDU:** Bachelor of Science in Engineering, University of Kansas(1958) **CERTS:** Leadership Certificate, Kansas
Email: info@CambridgeWhosWho.com

Rebecca L. Arwine
Title: Office Manager **Company:** Partners-N-Concrete, Inc. **Address:** 1706 Silver Street, Anderson, IN 46012 United States **BUS:** Concrete Company **P/S:** Construction **MA:** Central Indiana **EXP:** Ms. Arwine's expertise is in operational management. **EDU:** Associate Degree in Business Administration, Indiana Business College, 2005 **A/A/S:** Anderson Chamber of Commerce; Madison County Women-to-Women Business Association
Email: rebeccapartnersnconcrete@yahoo.com
URL: http://www.partners-n-concrete.com

Takashi Asayama
Title: Managing Director **Company:** Global Tax Advisory Office **Address:** 631 N. De Sales Street, San Gabriel, CA 91775 United States **BUS:** Financial Consulting **P/S:** Global Tax Advisory Consulting **MA:** International **D/D/R:** Transferring Prices to Automobile Manufacturers **EDU:** Bachelor of Arts in Economics, Yoko Hama National University in Japan **A/A/S:** the AICPA
Email: takashi.asayama@hotmail.com

Pedro R. Asencio
Title: President **Company:** Validation and Automation Group Consulting, Inc./VA Group **Dept:** Administration **Address:** P.O. Box 5075, PMB 299, San German, PR 00683 United States **BUS:** Engineering Service Company **P/S:** Validation, Automation and Project Management of Pharmaceutical and Medical Devices **MA:** Puerto Rico **EXP:** Mr. Asencio's expertise includes computer and information systems, validation engineering and project management. **D/D/R:** Overseeing Daily Operations **H/I/S:** Traveling, Golfing, Spending Time with his Family, Listening to Jazz, Playing Jazz **EDU:** Master of Business Administration, Bridgeport University, Bridgeport, CT; Bachelor of Science in Mathematics and Engineering, InterAmerican University of Puerto Rico and University of Puerto Rico **CERTS:** Executive Program Certification, Wharton School of Business, University of Pennsylvania; Certification in Project Management, Bortech Technology Institute, Puerto Rico **A/A/S:** American Society for Quality; American Management Association; Puerto Rico Manufacturers Association; ISPE; TOPS100 **C/VW:** Local Baptist Church
Email: pedro_asencio@hotmail.com
URL: http://www.vagroup-pr.com

Catherine A. Ashanky
Title: Vocal Music and Choral Director, Teacher **Company:** 1) Grove Hill Elementary School 2) Stanley Elementary School **Address:** 306 Aylor Grubbs Avenue, Stanley, VA 22851 United States **BUS:** Elementary School **P/S:** Primary Education **MA:** Regional **D/D/R:** Teaching General Music and Vocal Performance, Directing Choral Groups of Fifth through Seventh-Grade Students **H/I/S:** Caring for her Pets, Shopping, Attending the Church **EDU:** Bachelor of Music Education, James Madison University, VA(1975) **A/A/S:** Music Educators National Conference **A/H:** Who's Who Among American Teachers (2003); Who's Who Among American Teachers (1998) **C/VW:** Local Church
Email: cashanky@pagecounty.k12.va.us
URL: http://www.pagecounty.k12.va.us

Robin D. Asher
Title: College Campus Chairwoman **Company:** University of Phoenix, Springfield Campus **Address:** 1343 E. Kingsley Street, Suite C, Springfield, MO 65804 United States **BUS:** University **P/S:** Higher Education **MA:** Regional **D/D/R:** Counseling Students **H/I/S:** Reading, Riding Motorcycles **EDU:** Master of Business Administration, Southwest Baptist University; Master of Science in Health Service Administration, Southwest Baptist University; Bachelor's Degree in Psychology, Minor in Business Administration, Southwest Baptist University **A/A/S:** National Association of Financial Aid Administrators; Missouri Association for Financial Aid Administrators; Worship Leader, Treasurer, Forest Avenue Assembly of God Church; President, Springfield North Kiwanis International Club **C/VW:** Spring Northside Kiwanis International Club, Forest Avenue Assembly of God Church
Email: robin.asher@phoenix.edu

Glenda Manley Ashley
Title: Physician, Medical Doctor **Company:** Newport Medical Associates **Address:** 2310 York Street, Blue Island, IL 60406 United States **BUS:** Medical Practice **P/S:** Healthcare **MA:** Chicago **EXP:** Ms. Ashley's expertise includes pediatrics and rehabilitation. **H/I/S:** Reading, Traveling, Collecting Art **EDU:** MD in Pediatrics, Physical Medicine and Rehabilitation, Howard University; Bachelor of Science in Biology, CUNY Brooklyn College **A/A/S:** Chicago Pediatrics Society; American Medical Association; Chicago Medical Association **C/VW:** American Red Cross, The Links, Chicago Pediatrics Society
Email: glenbillash@comcast.net
URL: http://www.cambridgewhoswho.com

Mr. Jeremy H. Ashley
Title: Student **Company:** Texas Technical University Health Sciences Center **Address:** 3601 4th Street, Lubbock, TX 79430 United States **BUS:** Pharmacy School **P/S:** Education **MA:** National **D/D/R:** Learning Pharmacy **H/I/S:** Basketball, Tennis, Football **EDU:** Three-Year Pharmacy Student **A/A/S:** Phi Delta Chi; Phi Lambda Sigma; Christian Pharmacy Fellowship International
Email: jeremy.ashley@ttuhsc.edu
URL: http://www.ttuhsc.edu

Sharon A. Ashley
Title: Medical Doctor, MPH **Company:** Sheridan Healthcorp, Inc. **Address:** 1613 N. Harrison Parkway, Suite 200, Sunrise, FL 33323 United States **BUS:** Healthcare Center **P/S:** Healthcare **MA:** Local **EXP:** Ms. Ashley's expertise is in pediatric anesthesiology. **D/D/R:** Treating Infants and Children, Caring for Sick Patients, Consulting, Lecturing **H/I/S:** Exercising, Swimming, Traveling, Spending Time with her Grandchildren **EDU:** Fellowship, Children's Hospital of Los Angeles; Residency in Pediatrics, Martin Luther King Jr. Hospital, Los Angeles; MD, Hahnemann University Hospital, PA **A/A/S:** Society of Regional Anesthesiology; Society of Pediatric Anesthesiology; National Medical Association; American Society of Anesthesiology; American Medical Association **C/VW:** Local Charitable Organizations
Email: sashley128@aol.com
URL: http://www.cambridgewhoswho.com

Miss Ashley N. Asklof
Title: sales and service **Company:** Bank of America **Dept:** banking **Address:** 604 W. Union Avenue, Bound Brook, NJ 08805 United States **BUS:** Bank **P/S:** Money Management **MA:** Local **D/D/R:** Overseeing Operations **H/I/S:** Playing Tennis, Traveling, Writing, Working with Money **EDU:** Diploma, Homeschooling
Email: french4th@mail.com

Vittorio Assante
Title: Owner, President **Company:** Da Umberto Restaurant **Address:** 107 W. 17th Street, New York, NY 10011 United States **BUS:** Restaurant **P/S:** Food and Beverages, Italian Cuisine **MA:** New York **D/D/R:** Overseeing Restaurant Operations **H/I/S:** Spending Time With his Family **C/VW:** Local Church
Email: vassante@nyc.rr.com
URL: http://www.cambridgewhoswho.com

Kristi Assiran
Title: Realtor **Company:** Prudential Fox & Roach **Address:** 763 W. Lancaster Avenue, Bryn Mawr, PA 19010 United States **BUS:** Real Estate Agency **P/S:** Real Estate Services **MA:** Regional **D/D/R:** Aiding in the Sale and Purchase of Luxury Homes **H/I/S:** Traveling **EDU:** Coursework in Business Management, Upsala College **C/VW:** The Prudential Reading Club for Inner City Children
Email: kassiran@comcast.net
URL: http://www.cambridgewhoswho.com

Matthew Astin
Title: Resident Physician **Company:** Pitt County Memorial Hospital **Address:** Greenville, NC 27858 United States **BUS:** Hospital **P/S:** Healthcare **MA:** Local **EXP:** Mr. Astin's expertise is in cardiac life support. **H/I/S:** Sports, Attending Sporting Events, Attending the Theater **EDU:** MD, Mercer University, Macon, GA (2006)
Email: zo0654@yahoo.com

Dawne Astride
Title: Attorney **Company:** Law Offices D. A. Casselle **Address:** 1415 Gail Ave, Allentown, PA 18103 United States **BUS:** Law **P/S:** Family Law, Legal Services **MA:** Local **EXP:** Ms. Astride's expertise is in family law. **H/I/S:** Swimming and Gardening **EDU:** University of California at Los Angeles, BA Political Science
Email: info@CambridgeWhosWho.com
URL: www.cassellelaw.com

Ethel B. Atchison
Title: Dressmaker **Company:** Ethel's Fashion and Design Shopp **Address:** 395 Sycamore Street, Jemison, AL 35085 United States **BUS:** Clothing Store **P/S:** Uniforms, Robes, Wedding Dresses **MA:** National **D/D/R:** Designing and Producing Wedding Gowns and Church Robes **CERTS:** Licensed Dressmaker, International Correspondence School **A/A/S:** Chamber of Commerce **C/VW:** Local Youth Department, Mental Health Center
Email: ethatchis@aol.com

Mr. Gregory W. Atkins
Title: Funeral Director, Embalmer, Owner **Company:** Baker Funeral Homes, LLC dba Whitted Williams Funeral Home & Baker Williams Mortuary **Address:** 5500 Foothill Boulevard, Oakland, CA 94605 United States **BUS:** Funeral Parlor **P/S:** Funeral and Cremation Services **MA:** Regional **D/D/R:** Overseeing Mortuary Services and Operations, Managing Finances, Supervising Employees, Embalming, Offering Major and Minor Restorations, Extending Compassion to Grieving Families **H/I/S:** Playing Football and Basketball, Watching the Olympic Games, Swimming, Listening to Music, Dining Out **EDU:** Bachelor of Science in Biology, Minor in Chemistry, Lincoln University, Jefferson City, MO (1974) **CERTS:** Certificate, Mortuary School (1977); **A/A/S:** California Funeral Directors Association
Email: WhittedWilliams@sbcglobal.net

Shanna R. Atkins
Title: Evening Shift Coordinator **Company:** Piedmont Geriatric Hospital **Address:** P.O. Box 427, Burkeville, VA 23922 United States **BUS:** Hospital **P/S:** Healthcare, Geriatrics and Psychiatric Care **MA:** Regional **D/D/R:** Managing Staff and Patients, Coordinating Admissions, Conducting Staff Meetings, Counseling **H/I/S:** Collecting Stamps, Gardening, Scrapbooking, Spending Time with her Daughter, Participating in Church Activities **EDU:** Bachelor's Degree in Nursing, Virginia Commonwealth University (2002)
Email: msred4d@hotmail.com

Helen Atkinson
Title: Retired Engineer, Writer, Water Colorist **Company:** Helen L. Atkinson **Address:** 666 11th Avenue, Apartment 103, Fairbanks, AK 99701 United States **BUS:** Fine Arts Sole Proprietorship **P/S:** Water Color Paintings, Writing **MA:** International **EXP:** Ms. Atkinson's expertise includes civil engineering, freelance writing, water coloring and professional journalism. **H/I/S:** Golfing, Traveling, Reading, Theatre **EDU:** Ph.D. in Civil Engineering, University of Alaska Fairbanks; JD (2003); Bachelor of Arts in Civil Engineering, University of Alaska, Fairbanks (2006) **A/A/S:** Library Board; Alaska University Foundation **A/H:** Outstanding Alumni Award, Colleges of Engineer and Mining (1936); Golden Nugget Award
Email: h.lynx@alaska.net
URL: http://www.newhorizongallery.com

Elizabeth A. Auclair
Title: Director, Teacher, Holistic Health Counselor **Company:** Martha Graham Dance Company **Address:** 316 E. 63rd Street, New York, NY 10065 United States **BUS:** Dance and Performing Arts Studio **P/S:** Dance and Performing Arts Instruction **MA:** International **D/D/R:** Leading Rehearsals **H/I/S:** Yoga, Reading **C/VW:** Sierra Club; Planned Parenthood; Various Cancer Research Programs
Email: elizauclair@gmail.com

Jared Augello
Title: National Accounts Manager **Company:** Reckitt Benckiser **BUS:** Packaged Goods Manufacturing Company **P/S:** Consumer Goods, Household Cleaning Products, Healthcare Products, Personal Care Products, Food **MA:** International **D/D/R:** Selling to Retailers, Launching New Products, Creating Customized Marketing Plans **H/I/S:** Golfing, Skiing **EDU:** Master of Business Administration, Concentration in Marketing, Emory University (2003); Bachelor's Degree in Government, Dartmouth College (1997)
Email: jraugello@yahoo.com
URL: http://www.reckittbenckiser.com

Tamika C. Auguste
Title: Staff Physician **Company:** Washington Hospital Center **Address:** 110 Irving Street N.W., 5B-18, Washington, DC 20010 United States **BUS:** Hospital **P/S:** Healthcare **MA:** Local **EXP:** Ms. Auguste's expertise includes obstetrics and gynecology and medical simulation. **H/I/S:** Traveling **EDU:** MD, Georgetown University, 2000; Bachelor of Science in Biology, University of Miami, 1995 **A/A/S:** Association of Professors of Gynecology and Obstetrics
Email: tamika.c.auguste@medstar.net

Aubrie G. Augustus
Title: Vice President, Clinical Excellence and Outcomes Management **Company:** East Jefferson General Hospital **Address:** 4200 Houma Boulevard, Metairie, LA 70006 United States **BUS:** Acute Care Hospital **P/S:** Healthcare, Cardiovascular and Rehabilitation Services, Diabetes Management, Emergency Medicine, Cancer Center **MA:** Regional **D/D/R:** Overseeing Organization and Staff Performance, Managing Social Services and Infection Control, Ensuring Clinical Effectiveness, Management and Review **H/I/S:** Reading **EDU:** Master's Degree in Healthcare Administration, Trinity University, San Antonio, Texas (2002) **A/A/S:** National Association for Healthcare Quality
Email: aaugustus@ejgh.org
URL: http://www.eastjeffhospital.com

Patricia L. Aulds
Title: Cluster Nurse Manager **Company:** University of Texas-Medical Branch Correctional Care **Address:** University Boulevard and Sixth Street, Galveston, TX 77550 United States **BUS:** Healthcare Facility **P/S:** Healthcare for Inmates in Correctional Facilities **MA:** Texas **EXP:** Mr. Aulds' expertise is in administration. **H/I/S:** Spending Time with her Family **EDU:** Master's Degree in Nursing, Texas Woman's University; Bachelor of Science, University of Texas Medical Branch **A/A/S:** Sigma Theta Tau **C/VW:** Local Church
Email: patrn70@yahoo.com
URL: http://www.utmb.edu

Kurt A. Aurand
Title: Owner **Company:** K.A. Construction **Address:** 68 Beagle Club Road, Lewisburg, PA 17837 United States **BUS:** Construction Company Serving Residents of Lewisburg **P/S:** Additions, Remodeling and New Construction Services **MA:** Regional **D/D/R:** Overseeing Business Operations, Working on Several Projects in Progress Including Interior and Exterior Work **H/I/S:** Attending Children's Sports Activities Including Football, Baseball and Soccer, Coaching Sports Teams, Camping with his Family **EDU:** High School Education **CERTS:** Certified in Plumbing, Heating and Air Conditioning, Trade School; Certified in Home Inspection
Email: kurt32@dejazzd.com

Cheryl H. Austin
Title: Registered Nurse **Company:** Moses Cone Health System **Dept:** Annie Penn Hospital **Address:** 618 S. Main Street, Reidsville, NC 27320 United States **BUS:** Nonprofit Hospital **P/S:** Healthcare, Orthopedic Surgery, General Medicine, Gastroenterology, Ophthalmology and Podiatry Services **MA:** Regional **EXP:** Ms. Austin's expertise includes obstetric and gynecological medical-surgical nursing. **D/D/R:** overseeing intensive care and pediatric units as well as assisting nurses. **H/I/S:** Singing in the Choir **CERTS:** Registered Nurse, Rockingham Community College (1972) **A/H:** Nursing Excellence Award (2008) **C/VW:** Vice President, Women's Missionary Society; African Methodist Episcopal Church
Email: cherylaustin@bellsouth.com
URL: http://www.mosescone.com

Patricia A. Austin, C.Ht., CNHP
Title: Clinical Hypnotherapist, Owner **Company:** Matthews Hypnosis Center **Address:** 1805 Sardis Road N., Suite 138, Charlotte, NC 28270 United States **BUS:** Hypnosis Center **P/S:** Hypnosis Therapy, NLP **MA:** Local **D/D/R:** treating addictive personalities including alcohol and drug addictions and ending negative behavior patterns using hypnosis and NLP. **H/I/S:** Horseback Riding, Gardening, Reading **EDU:** Ph.D., Breyer State University **CERTS:** Certified Naturopathic Physician, Clayton College of Natural Health; Certified Natural Health Practitioner, University of Natural Health **A/A/S:** Institute of Professional Psychologists; American Board of Hypnotherapy; American Hypnosis Association; National Board of Professional and Ethical Standards; National Guild of Hypnotists; International Association of Counselors & Therapists **C/VW:** Best Friends Animal Society; Volunteer, Local Charitable Organizations
Email: patriciaaustin@matthewshypnosis.com
URL: http://www.matthewshypnosis.com

Allie L. Authement
Title: Owner **Company:** Allie's Figure & Day Spa **Address:** 200 Point Street, Houma, LA 70360 United States **BUS:** Day Spa **P/S:** Women's Health and Fitness Club, Facials, Body Wraps, Massage and Treatment Rooms for Men and Women, Permanent Makeup, Airbrush Tanning, Tattoo Removal, Scar Revision, Synergie, Image Skin Care, Hair Salon, Laser Hair Therapy, Cellulite Reduction Treatments **MA:** National **D/D/R:** Performing Aesthetic Treatments, Managing Daily Business Operations, Overseeing the Fitness Center and Spa, Marketing, Hiring Employees **H/I/S:** Fishing, Knitting, Crocheting, Exercising **EDU:** Coursework in Fitness; Coursework in Nutrition **CERTS:** Certification in Aesthetics; Licensed in Permanent Cosmetics Application; Certified Endomologist
Email: alliesspa@comcast.net
URL: http://www.alliesspa.com

Mr. Hugh Avant
Title: Fire Chief, Safety Instructor **Company:** Total Safety **Address:** 1101 South First, Artesia, NM 88210 United States **BUS:** Government Organization **P/S:** Safety Education, Fire Prevention and Fire Suppression **MA:** Regional **D/D/R:** Teaching Classes on Safety Primarily to People in the Oil Field Industry, Volunteering as Fire Chief, Actively Involved in Fire Prevention and Suppression, Handling On-Site Automobile Accidents and Oil Field Incidents on an On-Call Basis, Inspecting Equipment Including Fire Extinguishers, Air and Breathing Equipment, Monitoring Equipment and High-Angle Rescue Services **H/I/S:** Hiking, Bicycling **EDU:** Coursework in Music, Centenary College, Hackettstown, NJ **A/A/S:** International Association of Fire Chiefs; Southeastern New Mexico Firefighters Association; New Mexico State Firefighters Association
Email: hsbavant@plateautel.net
URL: http://www.cambridgewhoswho.com

Marinda M. Avera
Title: Professor (Retired) **Company:** Sandhills Community College **Address:** 3395 Airport Road, Pinehurst, NC 28374 United States **BUS:** Community College **P/S:** Associate Degree Programs, Certificate Programs, Local University Matriculation **MA:** International **D/D/R:** Performing Business Administration Duties and Medical Office Technical Services **H/I/S:** Singing with an Adult Ensemble, Playing Bridge, Antiquing **EDU:** Master of Business Administration, East Carolina University **CERTS:** Certified Myers-Briggs Type Indicator Practitioner; Certified Zengermiller Facilitator; Licensed Real Estate Broker **C/VW:** Good Samaritan Hospital; Southern Pines First Church; United Way; Susan G. Komen Breast Cancer Foundation
Email: averam@sandhills.edu
URL: http://www.sandhills.edu

Maria E. Avila
Title: Educator **Company:** Ysleta Independent School District **Address:** 11649 Bunkey Henry Lane, El Paso, TX 79936 United States **BUS:** Public School District **P/S:** Education for Prekindergarten through 12th-Grade Students **MA:** Regional **D/D/R:** Teaching Reading to First through Third-Grade Students, Coordinating After-School Programs, Managing Self-Contained Classrooms **H/I/S:** Reading **EDU:** Master's Degree in Instructional Specialist and Reading, The University of Texas (1979); Bachelor of Science in Reading The University of Texas (1972) **CERTS:** Certified Bilingual Teacher Grades 1-8, State of Texas **A/A/S:** Ysleta Teachers Association; International Reading Association; NEA
Email: avilamea@earthlink.net
URL: http://www.yisd.net

Joanne L. Avilla, RN, BSN
Title: Registered Nurse **Company:** Kaiser Permanente **Address:** 1425 S. Main Street, Walnut Creek, CA 94596 United States **BUS:** Hospital **P/S:** Healthcare **MA:** Regional **D/D/R:** Offering Women's Health and Perinatal Services **H/I/S:** Hiking, Reading, Movies, Spending Time with Family **EDU:** Bachelor of Science in Nursing, University of San Francisco; Associate of Arts in Speech Communications; Associate of Arts in Liberal Arts, West Valley College **CERTS:** Public Health Nurse; Neonatal Resuscitation Provider **A/A/S:** Sigma Theta Tau International Honor Society of Nursing; Golden Key National Honor Society **C/VW:** Feed the Children; American Cancer Society
Email: avjoii@sbcglobal.net

Suman Awasthi, RN, BSN
Title: Registered Nurse **Company:** Long Island Jewish Medical Center **Address:** 27005 76th Avenue, New Hyde Park, NY 11040 United States **BUS:** Teaching Hospital **P/S:** Healthcare **MA:** Local **D/D/R:** Practicing Operating Room Nursing **H/I/S:** Reading **EDU:** Bachelor of Science in Nursing, SUNY Stony Brook **A/A/S:** Association of Operating Room Nurses
Email: write2suzzi@yahoo.com

Jill J. Axelson
Title: Construction Coordinator **Company:** Quiring Corporation **Address:** 5118 E. Clinton Way, Suite 201, Fresno, CA 93727 United States **BUS:** General Contractor **P/S:** General Contracting, Construction **MA:** Regional **EXP:** Ms. Axelson's expertise is in business administration. **EDU:** Bachelor's Degree in Business Administration, University of Phoenix (2005); Associate Degree in Building Safety Code Administration, Fresno City College (2003); Associate Degree in Physical Education, College of Sequoias (2001) **A/A/S:** Phi Theta Kappa Society Induction March 2002
Email: jaxelson@quiring.com
URL: http://www.quiring.com

Carol J. Axten
Title: Plans, Program and Control Lead **Company:** Naval Air Systems Command **Address:** Building 3259, Patuxent River, MD 20670 United States **BUS:** Government **P/S:** Naval Aviation, Aerospace **MA:** International **EXP:** Ms. Axten's expertise includes program management and system engineering. **H/I/S:** Spending Time with her Family, Traveling, Recreational Sports **EDU:** Master's Degree in Engineering, Pennsylvania State University; Master's Degree in Business Administration, Temple University; Master's Degree in International Relations, Salve Regina University; College of Naval Command and Staff, Naval War College **CERTS:** Capitol Hill Fellowship/Certificate in Legislative Affairs, Georgetown University; **A/A/S:** National Defense Industrial Association; Women in Defense Organization
Email: carol.axten@navy.mil
URL: http://www.cambridgewhoswho.com

Miroslava Ayala
Title: Vice President **Company:** Document Duplication Services **Address:** 626 Wilshire Boulevard, Suite 920, Los Angeles, CA 90017 United States **BUS:** Copy Services Company **P/S:** Document Copying Services **MA:** Regional **D/D/R:** Managing Operations Including Production and Sales, Ensuring Customer Satisfaction, Delivering Orders **H/I/S:** Playing Soccer, Dancing, Traveling **EDU:** College Coursework
Email: miros@dds-imaging.com

Leigh A. Ayers
Title: Flexography Teacher Company: South Mecklenburg High School, Charlotte NC Address: 8900 Park Road, Charlotte, NC 28210 United States BUS: Public High School Serving Residents of Charlotte P/S: Public Secondary Education for Local Students MA: Local D/D/R: Teaching Flexographic Printing H/I/S: Volunteering at a local raptor rehabilitation center. EDU: Associate Degree in Graphic Arts Management, Central Piedmont Community College (1996) A/A/S: Flexographic Technical Association; Printing Industries of the Carolinas; International Graphic Arts Education Association; Graphic Arts Technical Foundation; Classroom Teachers Association
Email: l.ayers@cms.k12.nc.us
URL: http://pages.cms.k12.nc.us/layers/

Paula K. Ayers, RHIA
Title: Medical Staff Coordinator Company: St. Edwards Mercy Medical Center Address: 7301 Rogers Avenue, Fort Smith, AR 72903 United States BUS: General Acute Care Hospital Licensed for 349 Beds P/S: Medical Services MA: Regional D/D/R: Processing Applications for Physicians, Dentists and Allied Health Professionals for Hospital Affiliation. Managing the Staff, Monitoring Reappointments, Updating Credential Files, Supporting Committee Work H/I/S: Reading, Piano EDU: Bachelor of Science in Health Information Administration, University of Texas, Medical Branch, Galveston, Texas (1976) CERTS: Certified Professional Credentialing Specialist (2007); Registered Health Information Administrator (1976) A/A/S: American Health Information Management Association; Arkansas Association of Medical Staff Services
Email: payers@ftsm.mercy.net
URL: http://www.stedwardmercy.com

Marie M. Ayoub
Title: Hospital Staff and Community Pharmacist Company: Stamford Hospital Address: 185 Franklin Street, Stamford, CT 06901 United States BUS: Hospital P/S: Medical, Diagnostic and Support Services MA: Regional D/D/R: Collaborating with Physicians and Nurses, Overseeing Outpatient Safety by Offering Drug Information to Healthcare Professionals, Monitoring Drug Therapy. Supervising and Assessing the Appropriateness of the Patient Drug Regimen, Revising the Drug Regimen According to Guidelines and Recent Literature, Documenting Patient Interventions H/I/S: Soccer, Reading EDU: Doctor of Pharmacy, University of Connecticut (2006); Bachelor of Science in Molecular and Cell Biology, University of Connecticut (2004); Bachelor of Science in Pharmacy Studies, University of Connecticut (2003) A/A/S: Regulatory Affairs Professionals Society; Student National Pharmaceutical Association; Connecticut Pharmacist Association; American Society of Health-System Pharmacists; American Pharmaceutical Association
Email: marieayoub@hotmail.com
URL: http://www.stamfordhospital.org

Mr. Labid A. Aziz
Title: Founder, Chief Executive Officer Company: Two Rams Entertainment Address: 1 Neil Circle, Natick, MA 01760 United States BUS: Media Company P/S: Film Production, Documentaries, Media-Based Content MA: National D/D/R: Setting up Media Production and Development Products, Producing TV Content, Feature-Length Films and Documentaries, Helping Clients Create Media Campaigns Used for Education, Awareness, Advocacy, Fundraising and Marketing on the East Coast, Working on 2 Television Shows, 10 Films, 5 Documentaries and a Media Campaign Addressing the Elderly, Elder Care and Healthcare Policies in Maine H/I/S: Playing Basketball and Soccer, Golfing EDU: Bachelor of Arts Degree in Psychology, Brandeis University (1999) A/A/S: National Association for the Advancement of Colored People; The American Civil Liberties Union C/VW: United Way; Boys and Girls Clubs of America
Email: labid@tworams.com
URL: http://www.tworams.com

Michael J. Azzato
Title: Broker Associate Company: Century 21 Address: 45 Soundcrest Ave, Northport, NY 11768 United States BUS: Real Estate Broker P/S: Residential Real Estate MA: Local EDU: Queens College, FIT, MA, BA, AA A/A/S: Long Island Association of Realtors; National Association of Realtors
Email: michaelazzato@aol.com

Tama L. Babcock
Title: Facility Security Officer Company: Praxis, Inc. BUS: Government Contractor P/S: Research and Development MA: International EXP: Ms. Babcock's expertise is in security. H/I/S: Antiquing, Traveling EDU: Associate Degree in Security and Human Resources, University of Maryland A/A/S: NCMS, United States Army A/H: Two Outstanding Performance Awards C/VW: Volunteer, Church
Email: t.babcock@yahoo.com
URL: http://www.pxi.com

Jane E. Babinsky
Title: Owner, President Company: K9 Piper's Place Ltd. Address: 7331B N. Aurora Road, Aurora, OH 44202 United States BUS: Dog Day Care and Training Facility P/S: Safe, Dog-Friendly Environment for Dogs to Play and Socialize In, Obedience or Advanced Training MA: Local D/D/R: Teaching Obedience to Problem Puppies, Selling Dog Supplies H/I/S: Showing Dogs, Playing the Bagpipes, Creating Artwork and Photography, Writing History EDU: Coursework in Recreational Therapy, Heidelberg College (1978) A/A/S: Writer, Pet Editor, Heart of Lake County Magazine
Email: k9pipersplace@yahoo.com
URL: http://www.k9pipersplace.com

Salvatore Bacarella
Title: President Company: Garden Works Address: 43-35 157th Street, Flushing, NY 11355 United States BUS: Landscaping Company P/S: Landscaping MA: Local EXP: Mr. Bacarella's expertise includes landscape contracting, design and management. EDU: Bachelor's Degree in Business Management, CUNY Queensborough Community College CERTS: ITPI Certification A/A/S: United States Department of Agriculture; NSLA
Email: gardenworks.sal@gmail.com
URL: http://www.landscapenyc.com

Tiffany Hong Bach
Title: Pharmacist Company: Huntington Beach Hospital BUS: Hospital P/S: Healthcare MA: Local EXP: Ms. Bach's expertise is in infectious disease treatment. H/I/S: Swimming, Playing Sports, Playing Piano EDU: Doctor of Pharmacy, Western University of Health Sciences A/A/S: California Society of Health-System Pharmacists; American Pharmacists Association; HOPA/ASH
Email: tbach@westernu.edu

Lindsay Bachlechner
Title: Special Education Teacher Company: Trumbull Board of Education Address: 6254 Main Street, Trumbull, CT 06611 United States BUS: School District P/S: Education MA: Local D/D/R: Teaching Reading and Mathematics to Special Education Students H/I/S: Reading, Listening to Music EDU: Master of Arts in Special Education and Elementary Education, University of Connecticut A/A/S: Council for Exceptional Children; National Education Association
Email: bachlecl@trumbullps.org

Joanne E. Backofen, MD
Title: Medical Doctor Company: Anesthesia and Pain Consultants Address: 4305 Summerfield Drive, Piney Flats, TN 37686 United States BUS: Private Group Practice P/S: Anesthesiology Consultation and Services MA: Regional EXP: Ms. Backofen's expertise includes anesthesiology and pediatrics. H/I/S: Reading, Sewing, Gardening EDU: MD, Cornell University (1976); Degree in Pediatric Anesthesiology, Johns Hopkins University (1982) A/A/S: American Society of Anesthesiologists; Society for Pediatric Anesthesia; Society of Ambulatory Anesthesia
Email: backofen@charterbn.com

Hermie L. Bacus
Title: Broker/Owner Company: Intero Real Estate Evergreen Address: 4055 Evergreen Village Square Suite 220, San Jose, CA 95135 United States BUS: Real Estate Broker P/S: Residential, Executive, Hi End, Lake Front, New Construction, Condos, Golf Homes, Senior, Gated MA: National D/D/R: Selling Residential, Commercial and Investment Properties H/I/S: Snowboarding EDU: Bachelor of Science in Civil Engineering, CIT A/A/S: California Association of Realtors, National Association of Realtors
Email: hermie@interoevergreen.com
URL: www.interoevergreen.com

Shawky Z.A. Badawy
Title: Chairman, Professor Company: SUNY Upstate Medical University Dept: Department of Obstetrics and Gynecology Address: 736 Irving Avenue, Syracuse, NY 13210 United States BUS: Upstate Medical University P/S: Education, Healthcare, Research MA: National D/D/R: Teaching Reproductive Endocrinology, Infertility, Obstetrics and Gynecology H/I/S: Traveling, Playing Tennis, Entertaining EDU: Fellow, Rockefeller University, New York; MD, AIN Shams University College of Medicine, Cairo, Egypt; Residency in Obstetrics and Gynecology, SUNY Upstate Medical University, Syracuse, NY A/A/S: American College of Obstetricians and Gynecologists; American Society of Reproductive Medicine; International College of Surgeons; American College of Surgeons; American Association of Reproductive Health; Royal Society of Medicine C/VW: Leukemia and Lymphoma Society; American Cancer Society; American Diabetes Society; Local Fire Department; Mothers Against Drunk Driving
Email: badawys@upstate.edu
URL: http://www.cambridgewhoswho.com

Gretell Báez
Title: Audit Director, Certified Public Accountant Company: Puerto Rico Telephone Company Address: Roos. 1513, 10th Floor, Guaynabo, PR 00969 United States BUS: Telecommunications P/S: Wireless Communications MA: Regional D/D/R: Ensuring Compliance, Offering Disclosure, Reporting Directly to the Board of Directors, Participating on the Audit Committee, Handling Executive Hiring H/I/S: Theater, Music, Art EDU: Bachelor's Degree in Administration and Accounting, University of Puerto Rico, with Honors (1998) A/A/S: American Institute of Certified Public Accountants (2006); Puerto Rico Society of Certified Public Accountants (2003)
Email: gbaez@prtcmail.prtc.net
URL: http://www.telefonicapr.com

Steve Baghoomian
Title: Broker Company: Midland Real Estate Address: 201 Santa Monica Blvd, Suite 640, Santa Monica, CA 90401 United States BUS: Real Estate Broker P/S: Real Estate MA: National EXP: Mr. Baghoomian's expertise is in brokerage. H/I/S: Working as a Life Coach EDU: Bachelor's Degree in Mechanical Engineering, Carwley Tech, 1979 A/A/S: National Association of Realtors; California Association of Realtors; AAR; CISC; ICSE C/VW: American Relief, Local Police and Sheriff Departments
Email: steve@midland-realestate.net
URL: http://www.midland-realestate.net

Susan M. Bahe
Title: Science Teacher Company: Lakota High School Address: 500 Main Street N., Lakota, ND 58344 United States BUS: High School P/S: Education MA: Local D/D/R: Teaching Science to High School Students EDU: Bachelor of Science in Biology, Wartburg College; Diploma, Sherwood High School A/A/S: National Science Teachers Association
Email: sue.bahe@sendit.nodak.edu

Mrs. Annie Pearl Bailey
Title: Music Teacher, Poet Company: Novi Community School District, Orchard Hills Elementary School Address: 41900 Quince Drive, Novi, MI 48375 United States BUS: Elementary School P/S: Education MA: Local D/D/R: Overseeing the Music Department, Teaching Vocal, Instruments and General Music, Arranging Choral Music, Composing H/I/S: Poetry, Composing Music, Traveling, Reading, Conducting Research, Playing the Piano EDU: Master of Science in School Leadership, Concord University, 2007 A/A/S: Detroit Musicians Association; Former Board Member, Rochester Symphony Orchestra; Novi Board of Educators; MENC: The National Association for Music Education A/H: Music Award for 36 Years of Service, School District; Award, Michigan Education Association; Award, Detroit Music Association C/VW: Church, Meditation Outreach of Detroit
Email: abailey@novi.k12.mi.us
URL: http://www.cambridgewhoswho.com

Judy K. Bailey
Title: Sixth-Grade Mathematics Teacher Company: Washington Middle School, El Dorado School District 15 Address: 601 Martin Luther King Avenue, El Dorado, AR 71730 United States BUS: Middle School P/S: Education MA: Local D/D/R: Teaching Pre-Advanced Placement Mathematics and Regular Mathematics H/I/S: Ceramics, Volunteering with Church EDU: Bachelor of Science in Education, Oklahoma Christian College; 18 Plus Hours in Middle School Curriculum, South Arkansas University CERTS: Certification in Elementary Education 1-6 Grade, State of Arkansas; Certification in Middle School Mathematics 1-8 Grade, State of Arkansas A/A/S: National Education Association; Arkansas Education Association; Classroom Teachers Association C/VW: Hillsboro Street Church of Christ
Email: jbailey123@suddenlink.net
URL: http://www.wms.scsc.k12.ar.us

Patricia R. Bailey, BSM
Title: Practice Administrator Company: Prince William OBGYN Associates Address: 8640 Sudley Road, Suite 303, Manassas, VA 20110 United States BUS: Healthcare Center P/S: Healthcare MA: Regional D/D/R: Managing Human Resources, Accounts Payable and Insurance Contracts EDU: Bachelor's Degree in Business Management, National Lewis University (1993) A/A/S: Professional Association of Healthcare Office Managers C/VW: Breast Cancer Foundation
Email: pattib@pwobgyn.com
URL: http://www.pwobgyn.com

Thelma A. Bailey
Title: Supervisor Company: Bronx Center for Rehabilitation and Healthcare Address: 1010 Underhill Avenue, Bronx, NY 10472 United States BUS: Hospital P/S: Healthcare Including Rehabilitation Services MA: Local D/D/R: Supervising Critical and Intensive Care Services, Coordinating Programs, Teaching H/I/S: Reading, Playing Basketball and Volleyball EDU: Bachelor of Science in Healthcare Administration, CUNY Brooklyn College (1981) C/VW: Local Church
Email: thelma.bailey@cwwemail.com

William Clint Bailey
Title: Senior Systems Analyst **Company:** Interstate Batteries **Address:** 12770 Merit Drive, Suite 400, Dallas, TX 75251 United States **BUS:** Battery Company **P/S:** Batteries **MA:** International **D/D/R:** Analyzing Enterprise Resource Planning Systems **H/I/S:** Traveling, Playing Tennis **EDU:** Bachelor's Degree in Accounting, Louisiana Technical University **A/A/S:** Delta Sigma Phi; Information Systems Audit and Control Association; IAA **C/VW:** Big Brothers Big Sisters of America; United Way
Email: clint.bailey@pnmresources.com
URL: http://www.cambridgewhoswho.com

Priscilla Bailey Stout
Title: Owner **Company:** 1) Stout Trucking 2) Beauti Control **Address:** 2380 Nathan Roberson Road, Jamesville, NC 27846 United States **BUS:** 1) Trucking Company 2) Beauty Products and Spa **P/S:** 1) Truck Deliveries 2) Beauty Products **MA:** National **D/D/R:** Delivering Hazardous Materials, Offering Spa Treatments **H/I/S:** Sewing, Embroidery, Spending Time with her Grandchildren **EDU:** High School Graduate **C/VW:** Local Church
Email: pstout2961@aol.com
URL: http://www.beautipage.com/mkuponthego

Donna Bernhardt Bainbridge
Title: 1) Research Project Director 2) Global Advisor **Company:** 1) The University of Montana Rural Institute 2) Fun Fitness and Fitness Programming for the Special Olympics, Inc. **Address:** 1) 52 Corbin Hall, Missoula, MT 59870 **BUS:** 1) Consultation 2) Programming Development, Research **P/S:** 1) Education 2) Reduce Health Disparities for People with Intellectual Disabilities and to Advocate for Equality and Inclusion **MA:** 1) National 2) International **EXP:** Ms. Bainbridge's expertise includes educational consultation and the development of fitness and wellness programs. **H/I/S:** Gardening, Reading, Fly Fishing **EDU:** Doctor of Education, Boston University **A/A/S:** American Association on Intellectual and Developmental Disabilities; APTA; APHA **C/VW:** Alzheimer's Association; Clinic Volunteer, Injured and Disabled Veterans
Email: dbridge@montana.com
URL: http://www.cambridgewhoswho.com

Sandra A. Baines-Taggart
Title: Owner **Company:** Anderson's Candles and Such **Address:** 204 Dunn Street, Cincinnati, OH 45215 United States **BUS:** Retail Industry **P/S:** Candles, Religious Items **MA:** Regional **H/I/S:** Walking, Reading, TV **CERTS:** Licensed Practical Nurse, Claude V. Carter School of Practical Nursing **A/A/S:** Mission House of Prayer
Email: sandi_bt@hotmail.com
URL: http://www.cambrigdewhoswho.com

Elizabeth A. Bajor
Title: Nursing Supervisor (Retired) **Company:** Niagra Falls Memorial Medical Center **BUS:** Hospital **P/S:** Healthcare **MA:** Local **EXP:** Ms. Bajor's expertise includes nursing administration and management. **H/I/S:** Spending Time with Family, Volunteering in the Healthcare Industry, Traveling, Golfing **EDU:** Bachelor of Science in Nursing, SUNY at Buffalo; Master's-Level Coursework Completed in Nurse Management, SUNY at Buffalo **A/H:** New York State Outstanding Nurse Award; Nurse of Distinction, Memorial Center **C/VW:** Volunteer, Grief and Family Support Group, Niagara Falls Memorial Medical Center; Volunteer, Senior and Retiree Groups
Email: edrojab@roadrunner.com
URL: http://www.cambridgewhoswho.com

Alex Baker
Title: Marketing and Information Technology Specialist **Company:** Daihen, Inc. **Address:** 1400 Blauser Drive, Tipp City, OH 45371 United States **BUS:** Manufacturing Company **P/S:** Cutting Equipment, Welding Robotic Systems **MA:** International **D/D/R:** Multimedia Programming, Implementing Marketing Strategies, Developing Information Technology **H/I/S:** Playing the Drums, Mountain Biking, Traveling **EDU:** Bachelor of Science in Computer Science, Minor in Japanese, Ohio University **A/H:** Outstanding Performer Award (2005-2007); Quality Award (2005-2006)
Email: alexbaker@creativeremake.org
URL: http://www.daihen-usa.com

Barbara J. Baker
Title: Registered Nurse **Company:** Department of Veterans Affairs **Address:** 1301 W. Frank Avenue, Lufkin, TX 75904 United States **BUS:** Hospital **P/S:** Serving Veterans with Medical Services **MA:** Regional **D/D/R:** Nursing, Managing Cases, Assessing Lab Reports, Recruiting Medical Staff for the Army **H/I/S:** Fishing, Swimming, Spending Time Outdoors **EDU:** Bachelor of Science in Nursing, Wichita State University (1990) **CERTS:** Licensed Registered Nurse, States of Texas and Kansas; Army International Registered Nurse
Email: bj.baker@us.army.mil

C. Darlene Baker
Title: Director of Finance and Administration **Company:** Planned Parenthood of East Central Illinois **Address:** 302 E. Stoughton, Champaign, IL 61820 United States **BUS:** Healthcare **P/S:** Women's Reproductive Health and Advocacy **MA:** Local **EXP:** Ms. Baker's expertise is in finance. **H/I/S:** Bowling
Email: dbaker@ppeci.org
URL: http://www.ppeci.org

Clora Mae Baker
Title: Associate Professor **Company:** Southern Illinois University, Carbondale **Address:** 212 Pulliam Hall, Carbondale, IL 62901 United States **BUS:** Higher Education **P/S:** Baccalaureate, Master's and Doctoral Education **MA:** International **H/I/S:** Gourmet cooking, gardening, reading **EDU:** Ph.D. in Curriculum and Instruction in Professional Development in Business and Vocational Education, Ohio State University **A/A/S:** Phi Delta Kappa, National V.P., Delta Pi Epsilon
Email: cmbaker@siu.edu
URL: http://www.cambridgewhoswho.com

Gary C. Baker
Title: Teacher, Strength Coach, Personal Trainer **Company:** Boonville School District **Address:** 700 Main Street, Boonville, MO 65233 United States **BUS:** Public School District **P/S:** Fitness and Health Living Education **MA:** Regional **EXP:** Mr. Baker's expertise is in personal training. **D/D/R:** Incorporating Strength Training and Healthy Living in Programs, Coordinating with Head Coaches throughout the School District, Working with Students in Sixth through 12th-Grade **H/I/S:** Power Lifting, Football, Baseball, Basketball **EDU:** Bachelor of Science in Physical Education, Central Methodist University (2002); Bachelor of Science in Recreational Administration, Central Methodist University (2002) **CERTS:** Certified in Personal Training, American Fitness Training of Athletics (2003) **A/A/S:** National Strength Coaches Association; Missouri State Teachers Association; National Strength and Conditioning Association; American Fitness Training of Athletics
Email: garybaker28@hotmail.com
URL: http://www.boonville.k12.mo.us

Joe C. Baker
Title: Owner **Company:** Triad Premium Water Company **Address:** 1703 Helen Road, Greensboro, NC 27405 United States **BUS:** Water Company **P/S:** Water Delivery and Storage **MA:** Regional **D/D/R:** Delivering Water to Homes and Businesses **H/I/S:** Traveling **EDU:** High School Education **A/A/S:** International Sanitary Supply Association **C/VW:** Local Red Cross
Email: triadpremwater@aol.com

King Baker
Title: Owner **Company:** JK Ranch Trust **Address:** 6329 Road 7, Orland, CA 95963 United States **BUS:** Sand, Gravel and Farming Company **P/S:** Sand, Gravel, Farming **MA:** Regional **D/D/R:** Flying Planes, Running the Business **H/I/S:** Air Transport Pilot **EDU:** Coursework, California State University at Chico; Coursework, Sierra School of Aeronautics **C/VW:** Various
Email: kingbaker@hughes.net

Mr. Mike L. Baker
Title: General Manager **Company:** PrimeFlight Aviation Services (St. Paul Airport-Minneapolis) **Address:** 4300 Glumack Drive, Suite E-1190, Saint Paul, MN 55111 United States **BUS:** Aviation **P/S:** Electric Carts, Handicapped and Wheelchair Assistance, Skycaps for Baggage Level **MA:** National **D/D/R:** Assisting Passengers with Electric Carts, Wheelchairs, Skycaps and Baggage Handlers **H/I/S:** Remodeling Cars and Trucks, Spending Time with Family, Auto Racing **EDU:** Diploma, St. Teresa Academy, Texas (1999) **A/H:** Eagle Scout, Boy Scouts of America
Email: mspmbaker@primeflight.com
URL: http://www.primeflight.com

Susan E. Baker
Title: Registered Nurse **Company:** John Muir Health **Address:** 1601 Ygnacio Valley Road, Walnut, CA 94598 United States **BUS:** Hospital **P/S:** Healthcare **MA:** Local **EXP:** Ms. Baker's expertise includes emergency and operating room nursing. **H/I/S:** Traveling **EDU:** Bachelor's Degree in Nursing, California State University, Chico **A/A/S:** AORN; CNOR
Email: nursebaker123@yahoo.com
URL: http://www.cambridgewhoswho.com

Tsambika Bakiris
Title: Speech Language Pathologist **Company:** Progressus Therapy **Address:** P.O. Box 202333, Austin, TX 78720 United States **BUS:** Therapy Center **EDU:** Master's Degree in Communication; Bachelor's Degree in Social Psychology **A/A/S:** Texas Speech-Language Hearing Association; American Speech-Language-Hearing Association
Email: tsambika@hotmail.com
URL: http://www.cambridgewhoswho.com

Rebecca Balch
Title: Sales Manager **BUS:** Advertising Sales **MA:** National **EXP:** Ms. Balch's expertise is in healthcare marketing. **H/I/S:** Photography **EDU:** Bachelor of Science in Marketing, West Chester University of Pennsylvania
Email: rebecca.balch@comcast.net

Felicia Ann Baldonado
Title: Center Manager **Company:** Telecris Plasma Resources **Address:** 2502 E. Pikes Peak Avenue, Colorado Springs, CO 80909 United States **BUS:** Plasma Industry **P/S:** Plasma Collection **MA:** International **D/D/R:** Running an FDA Compliance Center **H/I/S:** Spending Time with her Children, Going to Competitive Dance Competitions with her Daughter **EDU:** Associate of Science in Criminal Justice, Pikes Peak Community College **A/A/S:** Phi Beta Kappa **C/VW:** Broadmoor Community Church
Email: felicia.baldonado@talecrisplasma.com
URL: http://www.talecrisplasma.com

Kaye B. Baldwin
Title: Kindergarten Teacher **Company:** Blount County Board of Education, Locust Fork Elementary **Address:** 155 School Road, Locust Fork, AL 35097 United States **BUS:** Public Elementary School **P/S:** Education for Kindergarten through Sixth-Grade Students **MA:** Local **D/D/R:** Teaching All Subjects, Implementing Alabama Reading Initiative Programs **H/I/S:** Spending time with her Grandson **EDU:** Master's Degree in Early Childhood Education, University of Alabama at Birmingham (1988)
Email: kbaldwin@yahoo.com
URL: http://locustforkes.blount.k12.al.us

Vicki L. Baldwin
Title: Marketing Coordinator **Company:** WideLite **Address:** 1611 Clovis R. Barker Road, San Marcos, TX 78666 United States **BUS:** Manufacturing Company **P/S:** Commercial Lighting Systems **MA:** International **EXP:** Ms. Baldwin's expertise includes graphic design and technical writing. **H/I/S:** Reading, Painting, Gardening **EDU:** Bachelor of Fine Arts, Minor in Industrial Arts, University of North Texas **C/VW:** United Way of Hays County; Local Charitable Organizations
Email: vic-b-1283@yahoo.com

Mrs. Ann Balistreri
Title: Distributor **Company:** Magic Kids USA **Address:** 711 Oriole Drive, Streamwood, IL 60107 United States **BUS:** Retail Clothing Company **P/S:** Name-Brand Children's Clothing at Discount Prices **MA:** National **EXP:** Ms. Balistreri's expertise is in sales. **H/I/S:** Listening to Italian Music, Spending Time with her Grandchild, Cooking Italian Food **C/VW:** United Way, Breast Cancer Association
Email: annabalistreri@wowway.com

Amy Ball
Title: Owner **Company:** K9 Country Club **Address:** 1298 Reading Road, Mason, OH 45040 United States **BUS:** Pet Care Center **P/S:** Training and Grooming **MA:** Local **D/D/R:** Overseeing Day Care for Canines, Caring for Animals with Special Needs, Grooming, Training, Managing Daily Operations **H/I/S:** Caring for Dogs **EDU:** High School Diploma, Palisades High School (1988) **CERTS:** Pursuing Trainer Certification; Certified Groomer
Email: amyball@4kpclub.com
URL: http://www.4k9club.com

Kelly M. Ball
Title: Optometrist **Company:** Bentz Eye Center **Address:** 4820 Okeechobee Boulevard, West Palm Beach, FL 33417 United States **BUS:** Private Ophthalmology Practice **P/S:** Eye Health, Examinations, Lasik Surgery, Contacts, Glasses **MA:** Local **D/D/R:** Treating Ocular Disease, Fitting Contact Lenses, Removing Foreign Substances from the Eye, Examining Patients **H/I/S:** Running, Traveling **EDU:** Optometry Degree, Illinois College of Optometry (2003) **A/A/S:** American Optometry Association; CLCS; Palm Beach Optometry Association
Email: eyedoc7@hotmail.com

Linda Ballard
Title: Professor **Company:** Dyersburg State Community College **Address:** 385 Plantation Road, Munford, TN 38058 United States **BUS:** College **P/S:** Higher Education **MA:** Local **D/D/R:** Teaching Accounting and Business Courses, Assisting Students **H/I/S:** Conducting Research in Genealogy, Traveling, Crocheting **EDU:** Master of Business Administration, University of Memphis; Bachelor of Arts in Accounting, University of Memphis; Associate in Applied Sciences, Shelby State Community College **CERTS:** Certified Public Accountant **A/A/S:** Tennessee Society of Certified Public Accountants; American Institute of Certified Public Accountants
Email: lllb1122@bigriver.net
URL: http://www.dscc.edu

Vonda L. Ballard
Title: Physical Therapy Assistant **Company:** Daybreak Venture **Address:** Arlington, TX **BUS:** Nursing and Rehabilitation Center **P/S:** Long-Term Care, Rehabilitation **MA:** National **D/D/R:** Assisting with Geriatrics, Psychiatry and Return-to-Work Programs **H/I/S:** Reading, Rollerblading, Watching Movies **EDU:** Associate of Applied Science, Tarrant County Community College **A/A/S:** American Physical Therapy Association **C/VW:** American Diabetes Association
Email: balyar@aol.com

Carolyn O. Baltazar
Title: Research Scientist II **Company:** Neurogen Corporation **Address:** 195 Stevenson Road, New Haven, CT 06515 United States **BUS:** Small Molecule Drug Discovery and Development Company **P/S:** Targeting of New Drug Candidates to Improve the Lives of Patients Suffering from Pain, Insomnia, Inflammation, Depression and Obesity **MA:** Local **D/D/R:** Overseeing Research and Development for Large-Scale Protein Expressions and Production of FF9 Insect Cells, Researching the Baculovirus Expression System, Studying Flow Cytometry, Troubleshooting, Applying Protocols, Ensuring the Laboratory is Running Adequately, Managing DNA Sequencing Research for the First Stages of Drug Development **H/I/S:** Running, Salsa Dancing, Volleyball, Volunteering **EDU:** Bachelor of Arts in Biological Science, Mount Holyoke College (1994) **A/A/S:** Society for In Vitro Biology; Bonsai Society of Greater New Haven; Team Developer, Community Dining Room; Board of Directors, Distressed Children International
Email: cobaltazar@comcast.net
URL: http://www.neurogen.com

Amory S. Balucating
Title: Registered Nurse **Company:** Advocate Good Sheppard Hospital **Address:** 450 Highway 22, Barrington, IL 60010 United States **BUS:** Hospital **P/S:** Critical Care Nurse Caring for Neurologically and Humodynamically Impaired Patients, ICU, Trauma Time Sensitive Part of the Nursing Profession **MA:** National **EXP:** Mr. Balucating's expertise is in critical care nursing. **H/I/S:** Basketball, Playing and Watching Football, Hiking **EDU:** Bachelor of Science in Nursing, Saint Xavier University of Illinois **CERTS:** Certified Critical Nurse, American Association of Critical Care Nurses; Certified CPR Instructor **A/A/S:** American Association of Critical Care Nurses, American Heart Association
Email: Balucanting@comcast.net

Linnette Banchs
Title: Contractor for Federal Government **Company:** Ruchman & Associates **Address:** 8221 Preston Court, Suite A, Jessup, MD 20794 United States **BUS:** Government Organization **P/S:** Business Support Solutions **MA:** International **EXP:** Ms. Banchs' expertise includes on-site supervision and administrative work. **H/I/S:** Traveling, Sports, Cooking, Sightseeing, Playing Tennis, Skating, Reading **EDU:** Pursuing Bachelor of Arts in Business Administration, Universidad Interamericana de Puerto Rico (2009) **A/A/S:** Board of Directors, La Mansion; Legal Committee
Email: linnette_banchs@msn.com
URL: http://www.ruchman.com

Laura Carr Bandrowski
Title: President **Company:** Laura Carr Fine Arts, LLC **Address:** 188 E. 64th Street, Apartment 706, New York, NY 10065 United States **BUS:** Art Gallery **P/S:** 20th Century Paintings, Sculptures, Works on Paper, Consulting with Clients Regarding Sales and Purchases of Major Art Work, Art Appraisals **MA:** Local **EXP:** Ms. Bandrowski's expertise is in 20th century post-war art. **EDU:** Bachelor of Fine Arts, CUNY Queens College **CERTS:** Certified Art Appraiser, American Society of Appraisers **A/A/S:** American Society of Appraisers
Email: lartful@aol.com
URL: http://www.cambridgewhoswho.com

Mr. Niloy Banerjee
Title: Senior Manager of Technical Program Management **Company:** NVIDIA Corporation **Address:** 4650 Cushing Parkway, Fremont, CA 94538 United States **BUS:** Manufacturing Company **P/S:** Semiconductors, Graphics Processing Unit **MA:** International **EXP:** Mr. Banerjee's expertise includes the management of systems software, hardware projects, quality assurance, subcontracts, competence, resources and implementation. **D/D/R:** Strategic Planning, Releasing Software Drivers for the Graphics Processing Unit **H/I/S:** Swimming, Painting **EDU:** Master of Business Administration, University of Phoenix; Bachelor of Science in Electronic Engineering, University of Pune **A/A/S:** Gold Member, Institute of Electrical and Electronics Engineers; Silicon Valley Software Process Improvement Network, The Indus Entrepreneurs
Email: nbanerjee@yahoo.com
URL: http://www.linkedin.com/in/niloy

Cheryl A. Banks
Title: Preschool Teacher **Company:** Sunrise Christian Academy **Address:** 18400 N.W. 68th Avenue, Hialeah, FL 33015 United States **BUS:** Academic Institution **P/S:** Daycare Education for 4 Year Olds **MA:** Local **D/D/R:** Teaching Preschool **H/I/S:** Reading, Swimming **CERTS:** Certificate in Secretarial Studies, Earned in Britain **C/VW:** Local Church, Bible Society Various Local Charities
Email: info@CambridgeWhosWho.com
URL: http://www.cambridgewhoswho.com

Joseph E. Banks III
Title: Executive Director **Company:** Southside Community Services, Inc **Address:** 4001 S Anthony Blvd, Fort Wayne, IN 46806 United States **BUS:** Nonprofit Organization **P/S:** Tutoring and Mentoring at Risk Children **MA:** Local **EXP:** Mr. Banks' expertise includes education, administration and fundraising. **H/I/S:** Singing, Golf, Bowling **EDU:** MD, University of Del Noreste; Residency, New York Medical **A/A/S:** Adjunct Professor, Grace College and Seminary
Email: conjobanks@earthlink.net

Yvonne B. Banks
Title: Supervisor of Community Residences **Company:** Alcohol and Drug Dependency Services, Inc. **Address:** 200 Albany Street, Buffalo, NY 14213 United States **BUS:** Nonprofit **P/S:** Substance Abuse Rehabilitation **MA:** Regional **EXP:** Ms. Banks' expertise is in women's issues. **H/I/S:** Scuba Diving, Hiking, Watching Birds **EDU:** Bachelor of Science in Human Services, Medaille College **CERTS:** Certification in Trauma Counseling **A/H:** Joan Levine Award, Women's Focus Inc. **C/VW:** Church
Email: ybb717@verizon.net

Marie O. Banner
Title: Teacher **Company:** Saint Ann School **Address:** 314 E. 110th Street, New York, NY 10029 United States **BUS:** Private School **P/S:** Education **MA:** Local **D/D/R:** Teaching Language Arts and Mathematics **H/I/S:** Shopping, Reading **EDU:** Bachelor of Science in Elementary Education, York College; Plus 30 Credits, CUNY Brooklyn College **C/VW:** Pallotti Alumni of New York, St. Jude Children's Research Hospital

Patricia A. Banville
Title: Teacher (Retired) **Company:** Parma City Schools **Address:** 765 Camden Lane, Brunswick, OH 44212 United States **BUS:** Public School System **P/S:** Primary and Secondary Regular and Special Education **MA:** Regional **D/D/R:** Teaching Seventh through 12th-Grade English, Maintaining Discipline, Monitoring the Halls, Developing Course Materials, Preparing for State Testing **H/I/S:** Cross-Stitching, Reading **EDU:** Master's Degree in Supervision, Baldwin-Wallace College (1991) **A/A/S:** National Education Association **A/H:** Person of the Month, Cox Cable; Martha Holden-Jennings Scholar

Michael L. Baranik, LAC, ACRPS
Title: Executive Director **Company:** The Shepherd's House Recovery Ministry, Inc. **Address:** 1422B Guillot Drive, Jennings, LA 70546 United States **BUS:** Faith-Based Recovery Program **P/S:** Prevention and Treatment Services for Adolescents with Drug and Alcohol Problems **MA:** Local **D/D/R:** Running Outpatient Treatment Programs, Working with Five Counselors, Treating Children **H/I/S:** Studying Etymology **EDU:** Bachelor's Degree in Psychology and Business, Liberty University **CERTS:** Advanced Certified Relapse Prevention Specialist, Applied Science Center (2003); Licensed Addiction Counselor, United States Navy (1998); Certified Career Counselors, Department of Labor **A/A/S:** International Committee, Red Cross; ICACD
Email: polite1@charter.net

Elisabeth M. Barbaria
Title: Marketing Manager **Company:** Optimedica **Address:** 3130 Coronado Drive, Santa Clara, CA 95054 United States **BUS:** Manufacturer of Eye Treatment Instruments **P/S:** Development and Manufacturing Services of Lasers for the Ophthalmology Industry **MA:** International **D/D/R:** Marketing, Advertising, Overseeing the Sales Force and Promotions, Promoting Events and Trade Shows **H/I/S:** Kayaking, Traveling **EDU:** High School Diploma **A/A/S:** Medical Marketing Association Meeting Planners International; Trade Show Exhibition Association; OWL
Email: ebarbaria@optimedia.com
URL: http://www.optimedia.com

Linda M. Barber
Title: Managing Director **Company:** Navigant Consulting, Inc. **Address:** 1009 Lenox Drive, Suite 101, Lawrenceville, NJ 08648 United States **BUS:** Insurance and Reinsurance Company **P/S:** Insurance and Reinsurance Services, Arbitration, Consulting **MA:** National **EXP:** Ms. Barber's expertise is in insurance. **H/I/S:** Scuba Diving, Gardening **EDU:** JD, Temple University **CERTS:** Certified Arbitrator, AIDA Reinsurance and Insurance Arbitration Society **A/A/S:** AIDA Reinsurance and Insurance Arbitration Society
Email: lbarber@navigantconsulting.com
URL: http://www.navigantconsulting.com

Monica L. Barberi
Title: High School Mathematics Teacher **Company:** Chino Hills High School **Address:** 16150 Pomona Rincon Road, Chino Hills, CA 91709 United States **BUS:** High School **P/S:** Secondary Education **MA:** Local **D/D/R:** Instructing High School Students, Teaching Algebra and Level 1 Spanish Courses **H/I/S:** Reading, Relaxing, Spending Time with her Family **EDU:** Master's Degree, University of La Verne (2004) **CERTS:** Certified Administrator **A/A/S:** National Education Association; The California Association of Directors of Activities; Association for Supervision and Curriculum Development
Email: moinca_barberi@chino.k12.ca.us
URL: http://www.chinohillshigh.com

Mr. David Thomas Barchanowicz
Title: Owner, Operator **Company:** Prague Trucking **Address:** P. O. Box 69, Pine Level, AL 36065 United States **BUS:** Transportation Company **P/S:** Hauling Frozen Commodities and Fresh Food to Stores or Warehouses, Working with Brokers **MA:** Regional **D/D/R:** Delivering Products on Terms, Overseeing Operations and Management **H/I/S:** Football, Auto Racing, Family Time with his Six Children, 14 Grandchildren and 3 Great Grandchildren **EDU:** High School Graduate
Email: chichi@mon.cre.net
URL: http://www.cambridgewhoswho.com

Louis R. Barfield, MD, FASCRS
Company: Baton Rouge Colon Rectal Associates, LLC **Address:** 7777 Hennessy Boulevard, Suite 206, Baton Rouge, LA 70808 United States **BUS:** Private Practice **P/S:** Healthcare Including Colon and Rectal Surgeries **MA:** Regional **D/D/R:** Treating Patients with Colon, Rectal and Anal Disease, Performing Colon Cancer Screenings, Screening and Diagnostic Cloudscapes, Treating Colon and Rectal Cancer, Performing Colon and Rectal Resections, Laparoscopies, Benign and Inflammatory Colon and Rectal Disease and Invasive Surgeries **H/I/S:** Exercising, Sports, Playing the Guitar **EDU:** Residency, Ochsner Medical Center (2003); MD, Louisiana State University Health Sciences Center, New Orleans (1997) **CERTS:** Diplomate, American Board of Surgery; Diplomate, American Board of Colon and Rectal Surgery **A/A/S:** Piedmont Society of Colon and Rectal Surgeons; American Society of Colon and Rectal Surgeons; American College of Surgeons; Society of American Gastrointestinal and Endoscopic Surgeons **A/H:** Aesculapius Society Intern of the Year Award, Louisiana State University Health Sciences Center (1998); Gratis Professor of Surgery Award, Louisiana State University Health Sciences Center
Email: lrbarfieldb@aol.com

Mr. Darran M. Barhaugh, Esq.
Title: Principal, Attorney **Company:** Law Offices of Darran M. Barhaugh **Address:** 81 Bunting Lane, Naperville, IL 60565 United States **BUS:** Legal **P/S:** Private Practice Law Firm **MA:** DuPage, Kane, Kendall, Will and Cook Counties **D/D/R:** Dealing with Family Law, DUI Cases, Divorce and Child Custody Matters **H/I/S:** Golfing, Spending Time with his Family **EDU:** JD, John Marshall Law School, Chicago, Illinois (2005) **A/A/S:** National College of DUI Defense; Illinois State Bar Association; Chicago Bar Association; Du Page County Bar Association; American Bar Association; Illinois Trial Lawyer Association
Email: darran@dmblegal.com
URL: http://www.darranbarhaughlaw.com/
URL: http://www.dmblegal.com

Loretta M. Barkell
Title: Executive Chief **Company:** Sheriff's Office, Maricopa County **Address:** 100 W. Washington Street, Phoenix, AZ 85003 United States **BUS:** Law Enforcement Agency **P/S:** Law Enforcement, Detention Services **MA:** Local **EXP:** Ms. Barkell's expertise includes finance and budgeting. **H/I/S:** Hiking, Gardening, Traveling **EDU:** Bachelor's Degree in Business Administration, University of Maryland **A/A/S:** Society for Human Resource Management; AAC **C/VW:** United Way, Society of St. Vincent de Paul
Email: lbarkell@cox.com

Irene S. Barker
Title: Owner **Company:** Treasure Chest **Address:** 401 S. Summit Street, Crescent City, FL 32112 United States **BUS:** Thrift Store **P/S:** Gently Used Items Including Furniture, Appliances, Clothing, Baby Items **MA:** Local **D/D/R:** Managing Operations, Ensuring Consumer Satisfaction **H/I/S:** Gardening, Spending Time with her Family **A/A/S:** Eagles **C/VW:** St. Jude Children's Research Hospital; Shriners Hospitals for Children; Disabled American Veterans
Email: irenebarker1003@yahoo.com
URL: http://www.cambridgewhoswho.com

Mrs. Marcia S. Barker, BS

Title: Executive Director, Founder **Company:** Adoption Information Services, Inc. **Address:** 558 Dovie Place, Lawrenceville, GA 30045 United States **BUS:** Adoption Consultancy **P/S:** Adoption Consultation Services **MA:** National **D/D/R:** Assisting with Infant Adoptions **H/I/S:** Singing, Playing Baseball **EDU:** Bachelor of Science in Human Services Administration, Mercer University (1982) **A/A/S:** Resolve
Email: aismarcia@comcast.net
URL: http://www.adoptioninfosvcs.com

Mary E. Barko

Title: Accounts Receivable Reviewer **Company:** Med 3000 **Address:** Cleveland, OH 44101 United States **BUS:** Healthcare Management and Technology Company **P/S:** Healthcare Management Services Including Medical Billing and Coding Services **MA:** Local **D/D/R:** Overseeing Medical Assistance Services and Medical Billing and Coding **H/I/S:** Reading **EDU:** Master's Degree in Adult Education, University of Phoenix (2004); Bachelor of Arts in Communications, Baldwin-Wallace College **A/A/S:** American Association of Medical Assistants **C/VW:** St. Jude Children's Research Hospital; Multiple Sclerosis Society
Email: marybethb@netscape.com
URL: http://www.cambridgewhoswho.com

Antionette L. Barnes

Title: Safety Specialist General Assembly **Company:** Hyundai Motor Manufacturing Alabama **BUS:** Motor Manufacturing Operation, Hyundai's First Assembly and Manufacturing Plant in the United States **P/S:** Stamping Facility, Paint Shop, Vehicle Assembly Shop, Two-Mile Test Track, Engine Shop **D/D/R:** Managing Safety and Environmental Issues, Investigating Accidents, Responding to Personal Issues of Workers **H/I/S:** Singing **EDU:** Bachelor of Science in Manufacturing, Concentration in Industrial, Safety and Environmental Compliance, Georgia Southern State University (2002) **A/A/S:** Omicron Delta Kappa; Society of Manufacturing Engineers; Sigma Gamma Rho; American Society of Safety Engineers
Email: abarnes@hmmusa.com
URL: http://www.hmmausa.com

Dawn Dorsey Barnes

Title: Case Manager **Company:** Woman's Hospital of Texas (HCA) **Address:** 7800 Fannin Street, Suite 402, Houston, TX 77054 United States **BUS:** Leading Healthcare Providers **P/S:** High-Quality and Cost Effective Medical Services **MA:** Regional **D/D/R:** Case Management, Specializing in Neonatology **H/I/S:** Working as a Praise Director at Church, Breeding Rottweilers **EDU:** Master's Degree in Business Administration, Texas Southern University (2003) **CERTS:** NCC Certification **A/A/S:** Instructor in Neonatal Resuscitation Program
Email: dawn.barnes@hcahealthcare.com

Jeanette A. Barnes

Title: Chief Executive Officer **Company:** Fur & Furless Children **Address:** 3375 Kings Creek Road, Hayes, VA 23072 United States **BUS:** E Commerce **P/S:** Educational Wooden Toys by Anatex Durable and Non Toxic, Develops Motor Skills and Learning, Dog Products Including Coats, Rain Jackets, Books, Outfits, Carriers, Sabine Hunter Thai-Ridgeback Dogs, Largest Kennel in US, All Four Colors Available Including Fawn, Blue, Black and Red **MA:** Regional **EXP:** Ms. Barnes' expertise is in sales management. **H/I/S:** Running, Biking, Fishing, Kids **EDU:** Master's Degree in Environmental Management; Bachelor of Science in Microbiology and Chemistry, University of Wisconsin **A/A/S:** US Army Chem Officer (1998-2005); NASE; ATRA
Email: jeanette_husman@yahoo.com
URL: www.furandfurlesschildren.com

Kellie Mengel Barnes

Title: President, Owner **Company:** Southern Landscapes of Louisiana **Address:** 1613 Highland Avenue, Metairie, LA 70001 United States **BUS:** Landscaping Contractor **P/S:** Landscape Installation and Maintenance **MA:** Local **EXP:** Ms. Barnes' expertise is in business management. **H/I/S:** Sewing, Teaching Third-Grade Girls to Sew **EDU:** Master of Arts in Library and Information Sciences, Louisiana State University; Bachelor of Arts in Journalism, Southeastern Louisiana University **A/A/S:** Secretary, New Orleans Horticultural Society **C/VW:** New Orleans Botanical Gardens City Park; The Krew of Shanghai Community; Crossroads of Louisiana
Email: kelliembarnes@cox.net

Lisa Barnes

Title: Reading, Language Arts, Social Studies Teacher, Seventh-Grade Department Leader **Company:** Chute Middle School **Address:** 1400 Oakton Street, Evanston, IL 60202 United States **BUS:** Middle School **P/S:** Secondary Education Including Regular Core Curriculum **MA:** Local **EXP:** Ms. Barnes' expertise is in professional development. **D/D/R:** Dealing with Discipline and Academic issues of At-Risk Students, Developing the Curriculum, Processing, Facilitating Monthly Meetings, Creating Reward programs for students for their accomplishments and mentoring. **H/I/S:** Running, Tennis, Aerobics, Reading **EDU:** Master of Arts in Educational Leadership, Northeastern Illinois University, Summa Cum Laude (2006); Bachelor of Science in Computer Science, Northeastern Illinois University (1993); Bachelor of Science in Elementary Education, Minor in Social Work and Mathematics **A/A/S:** American Association of Childhood Educators International; Chapter Secretary, Northeastern Illinois University
Email: mrslbarnes@aol.com
URL: http://www.chutemiddleschool.com

Sherry B. Barnes

Title: Licensed Practical Nurse **Company:** Laurel Manor Healthcare **Address:** 902 Buchanan Road, New Tazewell, TN 37825 United States **BUS:** Long-Term Nursing and Rehabilitation Center **P/S:** Skilled Nursing and Rehabilitation Services **MA:** Southeast United States **EXP:** Ms. Barnes' expertise includes wound care services and staff development. **H/I/S:** Reading, Hiking **CERTS:** Pursuing Certification in Wound Care; Licensed Practical Nurse, Lee County Vo-Tech School, Ben Hur, VA **A/H:** Award, Laurel Manor Health Care **C/VW:** Local Church; Local Youth Organizations; Relay For Life; March of Dimes
Email: docbarnes78@yahoo.com
URL: http://www.cambridgewhoswho.com

Linda K. Barnett

Title: Volunteer Coordinator **Company:** Amenity Hospice **Address:** 211 First Avenue S.E., Cedar Rapids, IA 52401 United States **BUS:** Hospice **P/S:** Healthcare, End-of-Life Care **MA:** Local **D/D/R:** Recruiting, Developing the Volunteer Program **H/I/S:** Traveling, Reading, Spending Time with Family, Collecting Art and Pottery **EDU:** High School Diploma; College Coursework **CERTS:** Certified in Volunteer Management **A/A/S:** Leadership in Volunteerism **C/VW:** Child Protection Center
Email: cdrvol@amenityhospice.com
URL: http://www.amenityhospice.com

Linda L. Barnette, BA, MS, M.Ed.

Title: Assistant Principal **Company:** The Albany School, Public School No. 91 **Address:** 532 Albany Avenue, Brooklyn, NY 11203 United States **BUS:** Public School **P/S:** Education **MA:** Local **EXP:** Ms. Barnette's expertise is in educational administration. **H/I/S:** Serving as Minister **EDU:** Master of Science in Special Education, CUNY Brooklyn; Master of Science in Administration and Supervision, CUNY Brooklyn **A/A/S:** Association for Supervision and Curriculum Development; Brooklyn Reading Council; Council of Supervisors and Administrators **A/H:** Honored, The Native Black American Woman Inc.; Honored, Church, Police Department **C/VW:** Church, Salvation Army
Email: lbarn51190@aol.com

Vicki J. Barnhill

Title: Facilitator **Company:** Plato Learning **Address:** 321 Watson Road S.W., NAVSUPPACT, Ste. 147, Naval Anacost Annex, DC 20373 United States **BUS:** Educational Technology Company **P/S:** Prescriptive, Personalized Instruction, Technology-Based Teaching Tools and Standards-Driven Assessment and Data Management to Facilitate Continuous Academic Improvement **MA:** International **D/D/R:** Facilitating Education **H/I/S:** Golfing, Traveling, Sailing **EDU:** Pursuing Master of Public Administration, Georgetown University; Master's Degree in Cellular Molecular Biology, University of Virginia **A/A/S:** Delta Gamma **C/VW:** American Cancer Society
Email: vjbarnhill@verizon.net
URL: http://www.cambridgewhoswho.com

Gerard P. Baroffio

Title: VP **Company:** Amerikoltc Mining, Inc **Address:** 202 Sunset Dr, Butler, PA 16001 United States **BUS:** Retail **P/S:** Bituminous Coal **MA:** Local **EXP:** Mr. Baroffio's expertise includes sales and management. **EDU:** Bachelor of Arts, Boston College **A/A/S:** Catholic Church, PCC, CACA, WACC
Email: info@CambridgeWhosWho.com

Carol A. Barone Smith

Title: Teacher **Company:** Perkins Local Schools **Address:** 3714 Campbull St, Sandusky, OH 44870 United States **BUS:** School **P/S:** Public School Education Provider **MA:** Local **D/D/R:** Teaches Business law, Key Boarding, Accounting and social studies to grade 9-12 **H/I/S:** Spending Time with Grandchildren **EDU:** Master's Degree in Education, Bowling Green University **A/A/S:** Business Education Association; Toastmasters; Founder, Promise Foundation
Email: jupe1938ca@aol.com
Email: /csmith@perkins.k-12.ch.us

George B. Barr Jr.

Title: Vice President **Company:** Desparte & Associates, Inc. **Address:** 4 S. 100 N. Route 59, Suite 13A, Naperville, IL 60563 United States **BUS:** Construction Company **P/S:** Commercial Construction Services, Glass Panels, Doors and Frames Installation Services **MA:** Regional **D/D/R:** accounting, overseeing operations including glass and glazing industry representation, working with architects, developers and designers. **H/I/S:** Golfing **EDU:** Bachelor of Arts in History and Economics, Duke University **A/A/S:** The American Institute of Architects; Manufacturers' Agents National Glass Association; National Glass Association **C/VW:** Morning Star Mission
Email: gbatdesparte@aol.com
URL: http://www.cambridgewhoswho.com

Rudolph Barr

Title: President, Chief Executive Officer **Company:** Barr and Drayton Relocation Specialists **Address:** 26-19 Casher Drive, Decatur, GA 30034 United States **BUS:** Relocation and Moving Company **P/S:** Moving Services **MA:** Regional **D/D/R:** Networking, Adding Additional Exposure and Credibility for the Company, Training Engineers, Troubleshooting, Welding **H/I/S:** Golfing **EDU:** General Equivalency Diploma **A/A/S:** Van Line Moving Lines **C/VW:** Glory to God Ministry, Christ's Tabernacle
Email: barr470@bellsouth.net
URL: http://www.cambridgewhoswho.com

Cynthia R. Barrett, M.Ed.

Title: Fourth-Grade Classroom Teacher **Company:** Jack Anderson Elementary School **Address:** 250 Shute Lane, Hendersonville, TN 37075 United States **BUS:** Elementary School Facility Dedicated to Excellence in Education **P/S:** Regular Core Curriculum Including Accelerated Reading and Mathematics Programs, Two Levels of Resource Classrooms, Computers, Special Education Department, Enhanced Learning Program, Extended Resource Classroom, 4-H Club, Search Program for Gifted Children **MA:** Regional **D/D/R:** Teaching in Self-Contained Classrooms **H/I/S:** Gardening her 116 Rose Bushes, Supporting the Predators Hockey Team **EDU:** Master's Degree in Education Plus 61 Hours post-grad in Education, Curriculum and Instruction for Grades 1-12, National-Louis University, Heidelberg, Germany (1995); Bachelor's Degree in Finance and Economics, University of Tennessee, Chattanooga (1984) **A/A/S:** United States Achievement Academy, President, Local School Band, The People to People Program
Email: barrfam1@bellsouth.net
URL: http://www.barrettc2@k12tn.net

Nancy Barrett Howes, M.Ed., BS

Title: Reading Specialist **Company:** Orange Elementary School **Address:** 218 E. Main Street, Orange, VA 22960 United States **BUS:** Elementary School Dedicated to Excellence in Primary Education **P/S:** Elementary Education, Food Services, Library Services, Guidance Services, Homework Hotline **MA:** Regional **D/D/R:** Working with Students to Develop their Reading Skills, Running the Breakfast Reading Club **H/I/S:** Playing the Flute, Hand bells and Keyboard **EDU:** Master of Education, Reading Specialty, James Madison University (2002); Bachelor of Science in Elementary Education, Madison College (1974) **A/A/S:** Speaker, Virginia State Reading Association (2002); Flutist, Hand Bell Player, Orange Baptist Church **A/H:** Who's Who Among American Teachers; Who's Who Among American Women
Email: nhowes@ocss-va.org
URL: http://www.ocss-va.org/schools/oes/index.htm

Barbara M. Barron

Title: Managing Member **Company:** Barron, Newburger, Sinsley and Wier, PLLC **BUS:** Law Firm **P/S:** Legal Services **MA:** National **D/D/R:** Managing Law Firm, Offering Bankruptcy, Commercial and Consumer Law **EDU:** JD, University of Texas; Master of Business Administration, Columbia University Graduate School of Business; Bachelor of Arts, Barnard College, Magna Cum Laude with Honors in Economics **C/VW:** Representative, Synagogue; YMCA; Chairwoman, Seniors Branch of Autism; Metropolitan Board, Bankruptcy, Executive President, Austin Bar Association
Email: bbarron@bnpwlaw.com
URL: http://www.bnswlaw.com

Mrs. Stephanie Barrows

Title: Teacher **Company:** Gables Elementary School **Address:** 1680 Becket Avenue, Columbus, OH 43235 United States **BUS:** Public Elementary School **P/S:** Primary Education **MA:** Regional **D/D/R:** Offering Early Childhood Education, Teaching All Core Subjects in a Self-Contained Classroom with the Aid of a District Created Reading Program **H/I/S:** Reading, Listening to Music **EDU:** Master's Degree in Education, Mary Grove College (2000); Bachelor of Arts in Elementary Education, Mount Vernon Nazarene College (1995) **CERTS:** Certification in Elementary Education, K-8, Mount Vernon Nazarene College, NY (1995) **A/A/S:** Alpha Chi; Ohio Education Association; Columbus Education Association; National Education Association **A/H:** Educator of the Year Award, Parent-Teachers Association (2006-2007) **C/VW:** The United Way
Email: schoolteacher30@hotmail.com
URL: http://www.columbus.k12.oh.us/gables/

Lois Y. Barry, MBA, OTR

Title: Outpatient Clinical Director **Company:** Warm Springs Rehabilitation System dba Post Acute Medical, LLC **Dept:** Rehabilitation Services **Address:** 5101 Medical Drive, San Antonio, TX 78229 United States **BUS:** Rehabilitation Center **P/S:** Rehabilitation Services **MA:** Local **EXP:** Ms. Barry's expertise includes occupational therapy and rehabilitation services. **D/D/R:** Overseeing the Operations of a Hospital-Based Rehabilitation Outpatient Clinic **H/I/S:** Traveling, Photography, Caring for her Pets, Spending Time with her Niece and Nephew, Walking, Swimming, Reading **EDU:** Master of Business Administration in Healthcare Management, Our Lady of the Lake University, San Antonio; Bachelor of Science in Occupational Therapy, Texas Woman's University **CERTS:** Certification in the Treatment of Adult Hemiplegia, Bobath Three-Week Training Course **A/A/S:** Texas Occupational Therapy Association; American Occupational Therapy Association; National Association for Female Executives; Delta Mu Delta **A/H:** Therapist of the Year, Warm Springs Rehabilitation (2002); International Who's Who Award (2000); National Dean's List (1986) **C/VW:** American Diabetes Association; World Wildlife Fund; American Heart Association
Email: lbarry@satx.rr.com

Teresa A. Barry

Title: Director of Client Services **Company:** The Madison **Address:** 577 Chestnut Ridge Rd, Woodcliff Lake, NJ 07677 United States **BUS:** School **P/S:** Educational Consulting, E-Learning and Professional Development **MA:** Local **EXP:** Ms. Barry's expertise is in client services. **EDU:** Bachelor's in Accounting, Minor in Economics and Minor in French, Fairfield University
Email: tbarry@themadisoninstitute.com
URL: www.themadisoninstitute.com

Decolynne-Jo Barteski

Title: Executive Assistant **Company:** Kinder Morgan Canada, Inc **Address:** Suite 2700, 300-5th Avenue SW, Calgary, T2P 5J2 Canada **BUS:** Energy Marketing **P/S:** Energy Transportation, Storage and Distribution **MA:** International **D/D/R:** Marketing and Shipper Services, Business Developing **CERTS:** Professional Legal Assistant **A/A/S:** IAAP, Toastmasters
Email: jo_barteski@kindermorgan.com
URL: www.kindermorgan.com

Aaron Bartholomew

Title: Owner, Operator **Company:** T & A Earthworks **Address:** 1872 State Route 487, Orangeville, PA 17859 United States **BUS:** Landscaping and Hardscaping Company **P/S:** Landscaping **MA:** Local **EXP:** Mr. Bartholomew's expertise includes conservation and paver installation. **H/I/S:** Spending Time Outdoors **EDU:** Associate Degree, Pennsylvania College of Technology **A/A/S:** ICTI **C/VW:** Children's Museum, Chesapeake Bay Foundation
Email: arnstoneman@aol.com

Mel Bartholomew

Title: President **Company:** Square Foot Gardening Foundation **Address:** 3615 Wolf Creek Drive, Building 1107, Eden, UT 84310 United States **BUS:** Fully Credited, Agricultural, Nonprofit Organization **P/S:** Teaching, Demonstrating and Propagating Gardening Technique **MA:** International **D/D/R:** Using Unconventional Agriculture Techniques, Inventing, Motivational Speaking, Hosting a PBS Television Show, Working on Radio and Internet, Assisting with World Hunger **H/I/S:** Gardening, Traveling **EDU:** Bachelor of Science in Civil Engineering, Georgia Institute of Technology (1953) **A/H:** Author, Largest-Selling Gardening Book in America, 'Square Foot Gardening' and Five other Books
Email: melbartholomew2002@yahoo.com
URL: http://www.squarefootgardening.com

Peter W. Bartlett

Title: Consultant, Trainer **Company:** Golden Rule Enterprises **Address:** 1950 E. Mary Lue Street, Inverness, FL 34453 United States **BUS:** Insurance Consulting Company **P/S:** Training, Consulting, Expert Witness Testimony **MA:** Regional **D/D/R:** Insurance Training, Consulting, Serving as an Expert Witness, Publishing Educational Brochures, **H/I/S:** Spending Time with his Family, Horses and Animals, Writing Poetry **EDU:** Ph.D., Cosmopolitan University **C/VW:** Community Ad Hoc Charity, Prison and Hospital, Church
Email: pbartle16@tampabay.rr.com
URL: http://www.badcollisionrepair.com

Verajane Bartlett

Title: Teacher's Assistant **Company:** Lighthouse Learning Center **Address:** 10 S. Alton Street, Freeburg, IL 62243 United States **BUS:** Child Care Center **P/S:** Childcare, Early Childhood Education **MA:** Local **D/D/R:** Working with Children, Drawings, Games **H/I/S:** Spending Time with her Friends, Shopping, Babysitting **EDU:** Associate of Science in Early Childhood Development, South Western Illinois College (2007) **A/A/S:** ISB of E; Gamma Delta Literary Society, Illinois College; Phi Theta Kappa Honor Society, Southwestern Illinois College **C/VW:** Franklin Neighborhood Community Association
Email: jane_lighthouse@yahoo.com

Lori Kay Barton

Title: Psychologist **Company:** Hope Counseling Center **Address:** 2300 Dogwood Road, Dover, PA 17315 United States **BUS:** Counseling Center **P/S:** Mental Healthcare **MA:** Local **EXP:** Ms. Barton's expertise includes individual and family psychotherapy. **D/D/R:** Spiritual Patient Counseling, Managing Operations Including Assessment and Consultation, Offering Mental Health Services for Adolescents and Adults **H/I/S:** Reading, Hiking, Walking **EDU:** Master of Science in Clinical Psychology, Millersville University (1987); Bachelor's Degree in Psychology, Indiana University of Pennsylvania (1985) **CERTS:** Licensed Psychologist, Pennsylvania Psychological Association; Certified Spiritual Director, Oasis Ministries **A/A/S:** National Spiritual Direction Conference **C/VW:** Local Schools; Local Charitable Organizations
Email: lorikb@verizon.net
URL: http://www.cambridgewhoswho.com

Susan E. Barton

Title: Hi-Tech Registered Nurse **Company:** Professional Home Care **Address:** 4401 Vestal Parkway E., Vestal, NY 13850 United States **BUS:** Residential Care Center **P/S:** Home Healthcare Services **MA:** Regional **D/D/R:** Overseeing Wound Care Nursing, Utilizing Intravenous Therapy **H/I/S:** Gardening, Needle Pointing, Spending Time at the Beach **EDU:** Bachelor of Science in Healthcare Management, Saint Joseph's College **CERTS:** Registered Nurse (2007); Diploma in Nursing, Robert Packer Hospital School of Nursing **C/VW:** Breast Cancer Association; Alzheimer's Association Memory Walk; Various Charitable Organizations
Email: sbarton@stny.rr.com
URL: http://www.cambridgewhoswho.com

Cynthia J. Baryames

Title: Realtor **Company:** ReMax Real Estate Professional **Address:** 1673 Haslett Road, Haslett, MI 48890 United States **BUS:** Real Estate **P/S:** Residential, Lake Front, Water Front, New Construction, Luxury, Condos, Vacant Land **MA:** National **D/D/R:** Residential Properties, Relocation is a New Construction Specialist **H/I/S:** Power Walking **EDU:** Ph.D. in Fine Art, Michigan State University; Bachelor of Science in Business Law **A/A/S:** Michigan Association of Realtors, National Association of Realtors
Email: cj@yourhomepros.com
URL: www.cjbaryames.com

Dorothy E. Basham

Title: Owner **Company:** D + B Property Rentals **Address:** 205 Tobacco Road Suite 2, Bowling Green, KY 42101 United States **BUS:** Real Estate **P/S:** Rental Properties, Improving Community **MA:** Local **EXP:** Ms. Basham's expertise is in cost control. **H/I/S:** Video Games with Grand Kids **A/A/S:** Alliance Club; Bowling Green Little League
Email: info@CambridgeWhosWho.com

Afzal Bashir

Title: Information Technology Manager **Company:** Dunkin Brands', Inc. **Address:** 130 Royall Street, Mailstop 1W, Canton, MA 02021 United States **BUS:** Food and Beverage Industry **P/S:** Coffee, Donuts, Ice Cream **MA:** International **EXP:** Mr. Bashir's expertise is in information technology. **EDU:** Coursework in Technical Auto, Apex Trade School
Email: afzalb@att.net
Email: afzal.bashir@cwwemail.com
URL: http://www.cambridgewhoswho.com

Margaret Shaw Baskette

Title: Executive Assistant **Company:** Capital One Services, Inc. **Address:** 3316 Cartwright Court, Richmond, VA 23233 United States **BUS:** Global Diversified Financial Services Provider **P/S:** Financial Services, Credit Cards, Banking Services, Auto Loans, Home Loans, Personal Loans, Healthcare Finance **MA:** International **D/D/R:** Coordinating Events, Monitoring the Department's Budget, Assisting and Supporting the Managing Vice President of the Corporate Real Estate Department and the Vice President of Strategy, Planning and Analysis, Scheduling Travel Plans, Internet Research, Leading Team of 10 Assistants, Chairing of Administrative Development Committee, Sits on the Administrative Council **H/I/S:** Listening to Music **EDU:** Bachelor of Science in Marketing, Minor in Economics, University of Richmond (1973) **CERTS:** Certification in Event Coordination (2004); Certification in Project Management (2003); Certification in General Insurance (1993) **A/A/S:** International Association of Administration Professionals
Email: peggy.baskette@capitalone.com
URL: http://www.capitalone.com

Patricia R. Bass

Title: Chief Executive Officer **Company:** Comprehensive Communications Systems **Address:** 5405 Louden Lane, Madison, WI 53716 United States **BUS:** Consulting and Communications **P/S:** Conflict Management, Consulting, Coaching **MA:** National **D/D/R:** Consulting **H/I/S:** Indianapolis 500 Formula Racing **CERTS:** Graduate Certificate in Conflict Management, Marquette University; Graduate Certificate in Paralegal Studies, Paralegal Institute of Phoenix **A/A/S:** Wisconsin Association of Mediators; Life Member, Association of Family Court Conciliators; Institute for the Study of Conflict and Transformation; NOOWBO
Email: midwestadr@yahoo.com
URL: http://www.comprehensive_communications_systems.com

Ms. Joan P. Bassett

Title: Published Writer **Address:** 525 Meadow Sweet Circle, Osprey, FL 34229 United States **BUS:** Published Writer **P/S:** Screen Writing, Poetry, Children's Fiction **MA:** Local **D/D/R:** Writing Poetry, Musicals and Screen Plays **H/I/S:** Listening to Music, Walking **EDU:** Coursework in Music and Business, Ursuline College, Cleveland; Coursework in Radio and Television Sociology, John Carrol University; Coursework in Early Childhood Education, Cuyahoga Community College, Cleveland; Coursework in Writing, University of Cincinnati **A/A/S:** National Association for the Education of Young Children; Former Member, Council on Human Relations; Former Member, Cleveland Campfire Girls
Email: jbpatt@verizon.net

Rosemary C. Basson

Title: Occupational Therapy Assistant, COTA/L **Company:** Genesis Health Care Rehab Services at Hathaway Manor **Address:** 863 Hathaway Road, New Bedford, MA 02740 United States **BUS:** Geriatric Short- and Long-Term Rehabilitation Facility **P/S:** Geriatric Short- and Long-Term Care and Rehabilitation **MA:** National **EXP:** Ms. Basson's expertise includes geriatric rehabilitation and reiki therapy. **H/I/S:** Art, Speaking Portuguese as a Second Language **EDU:** Associate Degree in Health and Science, Mount Ida College (1995); Completed Coursework, Dominican College; Coursework, Swain School of Design **CERTS:** Certified Licensed Occupational Therapy Assistant (1995) **A/A/S:** National Board for Certification in Occupational Therapy **C/VW:** Hospice Volunteer
Email: basson.inc1@hotmail.com
URL: http://www.cambridgewhoswho.com

Adell Batchelor-Walker

Title: President, Chief Executive Officer **Company:** Angel Village **Address:** 6709 La Tijera Blvd Suite 245, Los Angeles, CA 90045 United States **BUS:** Education **P/S:** Consulting, Advocating, for Minority Parents, Exchanging Their Skills with Their Children's Education **MA:** National **D/D/R:** Motivating, Educating and Training Clients **H/I/S:** Traveling **EDU:** Master of Science in Early Childhood Education, Atlanta University; Bachelor of Science in Elementary Education, Savanna State University **A/A/S:** National Reading Association, National Teachers Association of English and Mathematics
Email: angelvillage@aol.com
Email: jazz4azz@aol.com

Mildred W. Bates

Title: Kindergarten Teacher **Company:** Deamude Seventh-day Adventist Christian School **Address:** 1765 W. 2100 S., Ogden, UT 84401 United States **BUS:** Private School **P/S:** Education **MA:** Local **D/D/R:** Teaching Kindergarten Students, Special Education **H/I/S:** Quilting, Playing Pinochle **EDU:** Bachelor of Arts in Education, Weber State University **CERTS:** Certification in Special Education, Utah State University (1985) **A/A/S:** Phi Delta Kappa; Beta Sigma Phi; Utah Retired Teachers Association **A/H:** Huntsman Award (2001)
Email: mildred.bates@cwwemail.com

Juan F. Batlle

Title: Medical Director **Company:** Edificio Centro Láser **Address:** Calle Fantino Falco 3, Naco, Santo Domingo, Dominican Republic **BUS:** Ophthalmology Medical Center **P/S:** Eye Care Services **MA:** Caribbean **D/D/R:** Training 25 Residents Per Year from Around the World in the Art of Ophthalmologic Laser Surgery and Implants **H/I/S:** Horseback Riding, Golfing, Traveling **EDU:** MD, Specialization in Ophthalmology, Duke University **A/A/S:** American Academy of Ophthalmology; Dominican Academy of Ophthalmology; The American Society of Cataract and Refractive Surgery; International Society of Refractive Surgery; Lions Club; Founder, Laser Center **C/VW:** MMI
Email: jbatlle01@codetel.net.do
URL: http://www.centrolaser.net

Bryan L. Batten

Title: President **Company:** Palmetto Precision Machining, Inc. **Address:** 517 Camson Road, Anderson, SC 29625 United States **BUS:** Manufacturing Company **P/S:** Modification of Automotive Parts and Machinery **MA:** National **D/D/R:** Managing Finance and Operations, Ensuring Customer Satisfaction, Overseeing Sales **H/I/S:** Traveling **EDU:** Bachelor of Science in Mechanical Engineering, Clemson University **C/VW:** Local Church
Email: bryan@palmettoprecision.com
URL: http://www.palmettoprecision.com

Chanel N. Battle

Title: Realtor **Company:** McColly Real Estate **Address:** 5773 U.S. Highway 6, Portage, IN 46368 United States **BUS:** Real Estate Agency **P/S:** Representing Buyers and Sellers of Real Estate **MA:** Regional **D/D/R:** Negotiating the Purchase and Sale of Residential and Commercial Properties, Assisting Clients from Beginning through the Closing, Writing Sales Contracts, Analyzing Reports **H/I/S:** Jogging, Sewing, Writing Poetry **EDU:** Pursuing Bachelor's Degree in Business Management, Davenport University; Associate Degree in Business Management, Davenport University (2006) **CERTS:** Realtors License, State of Indiana (2006)
Email: cbattle@mccolly.com
URL: http://www.chanelbattle.com

Rebecca L. Battles

Title: Liaison Manager **Company:** Kenexa **Address:** 1755 N. Collins Boulevard, Richardson, TX 75080 United States **BUS:** Recruitment Company **P/S:** Staffing **MA:** International **D/D/R:** Hiring and Retaining Quality Employees, Managing Accounts and Projects **H/I/S:** Traveling, Participating in Church Activities **EDU:** Bachelor's Degree in Public Relations and Human Resources, Baylor University **A/A/S:** Baylor Woman's Alumni Association **C/VW:** American Red Cross, United Way, Veterans Administration
Email: baylor1013@yahoo.com
URL: http://www.cambridgewhoswho.com

Rose G. Baublitz

Title: Professional Instructor **Company:** Ashland University **Address:** 1900 E. Dublin-Granville Road, Columbus, OH 43036 United States **BUS:** University **P/S:** Education **MA:** Local **EXP:** Ms. Baublitz's expertise includes curriculum and instruction. **D/D/R:** Addressing Issues in Education, Managing the Classroom, Developing Effective Teaching Methods **H/I/S:** Traveling, Gardening, Cooking **EDU:** Educational Specialist Degree in Curriculum and Instruction; Associate Degree in Business Law, Dyke College (Now David N. Myers College); Bachelor's Degree in Education, Findlay College (Now University of Findlay); Master's Degree, University of Toledo, Specialist Degree Ashland University **A/A/S:** National Education Association, Ohio ASCD, National ASCD **C/VW:** Church, Neighborhood and Community Events
Email: rgbaublitz@insight.rr.com
URL: http://www.cambridgewhoswho.com

Sherman R. Bauer

Title: Data Systems Manager **Company:** Champaign Community Unit School District 4 **Address:** 703 S. New Street, Champaign, IL 61820 United States **BUS:** School District **P/S:** Education **MA:** Local **D/D/R:** Overseeing the Data Management Systems, Managing Student Software Systems and the UNIX Database Operating System, Troubleshooting, Managing Finances and Data-Related Requests, Writing Queries, Generating Business and Student Reports **H/I/S:** Collecting Coins, Golfing **EDU:** Master's Degree in Management Information Systems, Warren National University (2004); Bachelor of Science in Statistics, University of Illinois (1986)
Email: bauersh@champaignschools.org
URL: http://www.champaignschools.org

Debra Baughman, RN, BSN

Title: Registered Nurse, School Nurse **Company:** Valley Local School District **Address:** 1821 State Route 728, Lucasville, OH 45648 United States **BUS:** School District **P/S:** Education **MA:** Regional **D/D/R:** treating ill and injured students, administering medications, reviewing immunization records, screening for scoliosis, hearing and vision, instructing on CPR for seventh and ninth-grade students and utilizing her first aid and CPR assistance experience. **H/I/S:** Reading **EDU:** Bachelor of Science in Nursing, University of Kentucky (1982) **CERTS:** Certified School Nurse, Ohio University, Ohio Department of Education **A/A/S:** Chairwoman, Wellness Policy, Yearly Health Fair **A/H:** Governor's Buckeye Best Healthy Schools (2005-2006) **C/VW:** American Heart Association
Email: dbaughman12@yahoo.com
URL: http://www.valley.k12.oh.us

Mr. James A. Baumann

Title: Doctoral Student **Company:** Bowling Green State University **Address:** 302 W. Hall, Bowling Green, OH 43402 United States **BUS:** University **P/S:** Higher Education **MA:** Regional **EXP:** Mr. Baumann's expertise is in emerging technology. **D/D/R:** conducting research on digital and high definition television. **H/I/S:** Football, Basketball, Watching Formula One Racing **EDU:** Doctoral Degree in Communication Studies, Concentration on New and Emerging; Master's Degree in Communication, Indiana State University (2002) **A/A/S:** National Communication Association; Central State Communications Association **A/H:** Cambridge Who's Who of Executives and Professionals (2007-2008); Graduate Scholarship and Assistantship, Bowling Green State University (Fall 2005, Spring 2006,2007); Graduate Scholarship and Assistantship, Indiana State University (Fall 2000,2001 Spring 2001,2002); Dean's List (Fall 1999, Spring 1999,2000); Elizabeth M. and Gene O. Cameron Speech Communication Award (1999); Computer Plus Award (1998)
Email: jbauman@bgsu.edu
URL: http://www.bgsu.edu

Michelle S. Baumgartner

Title: Accounting Assistant **Company:** San Diego Imaging Medical Group, Inc. **Address:** 8745 Aero Drive, Suite 200, San Diego, CA 92123 United States **BUS:** Medical Diagnostic Group **P/S:** Medical Diagnosis, Radiology **MA:** Local **D/D/R:** Accounting, Payroll, Expense Accounts, Retirement Plans, Handling 21 Bank Accounts, Setting Up and Closing Line of Credits **H/I/S:** Spending Time with her Son and Daughter, Sports **EDU:** High School Graduate; Coursework in Accounting and Computers **A/A/S:** American Payroll Association **C/VW:** Children's Hospital San Diego
Email: mbaumgartner@sandiegoimaging.com
URL: http://www.sandiegoimaging.com

Nancy Bauser

Title: Brain-Injured Peer Counselor, Life Coach **Company:** NSB Group **Address:** 4260 Wabeek Lake Drive S., Bloomfield Hills, MI 48302 United States **BUS:** Counseling, Modeling and Support Company **P/S:** Support for Brain-Injury Survivors **MA:** Southeastern Michigan **D/D/R:** Acting as a Model for Recovery **H/I/S:** Exercising, Walking **EDU:** Master of Social Work, University of Wisconsin-Madison, 1976; Bachelor of Science in Education, University of Michigan, 1973 **CERTS:** Board Certified in Traumatic Stress and Disability Trauma **A/A/S:** National Association of Social Workers; Academy of Certified Social Workers; American Academy of Experts in Traumatic Stress
Email: nancy@survivoracceptance.com
URL: http://www.survivoracceptance.com

Dr. Bruce A. Baxter

Title: Director **Company:** Mission Clinic, West Indies **Address:** 167 Washburn Road, Tallmadge, OH 44278 United States **BUS:** Clinic **P/S:** Healthcare **MA:** International **D/D/R:** performing podiatric surgery and wound care treatment. **EDU:** Externship in Vascular Medicine, Cleveland Clinic (1989); Doctor of Podiatric Medicine, The Ohio College of Podiatric Medicine; Coursework in Clerkship, Surgery Department, St. Elizabeth Hospital, Youngstown, OH **CERTS:** Board Certified, American Board of Podiatric Orthopedics and Primary Podiatric Medicine **A/A/S:** Masonic Lodge **A/H:** Dr. Carl Bergmann Award (1990)
Email: bbaxter3@neo.rr.com

Lynn M. Baxter

Title: Program Technician **Company:** University of Arkansas **Dept:** Department of Agriculture, Cooperative Extension **Address:** 2301 S. University Avenue, Little Rock, AR 72204 United States **BUS:** University **P/S:** Higher Education Including Agricultural Programs **MA:** Arkansas **D/D/R:** Managing Pesticide Applications, Overseeing Precision Agriculture and Drift Management **H/I/S:** Flying Airplanes, Hunting, Fishing, Landscaping, Spending Time with her Children **EDU:** Bachelor of Science in Agricultural Business, Arkansas State University **CERTS:** Certified Analyst, SAFE Foundation; Certification, Private Pilot Single-Engine Land, Federal Aviation Administration **A/A/S:** WRK of Arkansas **C/VW:** Morgan Nick Foundation; The One Campaign
Email: lynnwalker55@hotmail.com
URL: http://www.cambridgewhoswho.com

Sheila R. Baxter

Title: Commanding General of Army Medical Center **Company:** Madigan Army Medical Center **BUS:** Military Hospital **P/S:** Healthcare **MA:** Regional **D/D/R:** overseeing healthcare administration and medical logistics. **H/I/S:** Reading, Sports, Spending Time Outdoors **EDU:** Pursuing Master of Divinity, International Theological Center, Atlanta, GA; Master's Degree in Health Services Management, Webster University, Saint Louis, MO (1983); Bachelor's Degree in Health Education and Physical Education, Virginia State University (1977) **A/A/S:** Alpha Kappa Alpha; United States Army **A/H:** Community Service Award, Government of Pirmasen, Germany (2002) **C/VW:** Destiny Ministries; Prison Fellowship Ministries
Email: sheila.baxter@us.army.mil

Lisa Bays, JD

Title: Vice President, General Counsel **Company:** CL Frates and Company **Address:** 5005 N Lincoln, Oklahoma City, OK 73105 United States **BUS:** Insurance **P/S:** Insurance, Third Party Administration for Insurance Agencies **MA:** National **D/D/R:** Insurance Law, Corporate Law, Administrative Law, Insurance and ERISA **H/I/S:** Attending Dance Recitals, Soccer and Football Games **EDU:** JD, Oklahoma City University School of Law **A/A/S:** Oklahoma Bar Association, Society of Professional Benefited Administrators
Email: lbays@clfrates.com
URL: http://www.clfrates.com

Vasiliki Bazos, DDS

Title: Doctor **Company:** Bazos Dental **Address:** 2545 Via Campesina, Suite 302, Palos Verdes Estates, CA 90274 United States **BUS:** Cosmetic Dental Practice **P/S:** Holistic Approach to Oral Healthcare Services, In-House Laboratory, Hygienist and Orthodontist on Staff **MA:** International **D/D/R:** Seeing Eight Patients Daily, Color Matching **H/I/S:** Playing Piano, Ballet Dancing, Swimming, Basketball **EDU:** Doctor of Dental Surgery in General Dentistry, University of California at Los Angeles (1996)Bachelor of Arts in Biology, American International College (1993) **A/A/S:** California Dental Association; American Dental Association **A/H:** Nominee, Pierre Fauchard Academy Award
Email: vbazos@hotmail.com

Sharlet A. Beach

Title: Certified Occupational Therapy Assistant **Company:** Coliseum Medical Center **Address:** 108 Crestwood Road, Warner Robins, GA 31093 United States **BUS:** Medical Center **P/S:** Rehabilitation, Healthcare, Acute Care **MA:** Regional **D/D/R:** Offering Occupational Therapy to Hospital Patients with Neurological and Orthopaedic Diagnoses Including Stroke, Back Pain, Hip Surgery and Head Injuries **H/I/S:** Swimming, Reading, Bodybuilding **EDU:** Associate Degree in Art, Green River Community College, Washington (1991); Associate Degree in Applied Science, Green River Community College, Washington (1991) **A/A/S:** American Occupational Therapy Association; Georgia Occupational Therapy Association **A/H:** Outstanding Occupational Therapist Award (2005) **C/VW:** Speaks Publicly for Support Groups for Parkinson's Disease in Seattle
Email: imabeach2000@yahoo.com
URL: http://www.coliseumhealthsystem.com

Olga J. Beale

Title: President, Chief Executive Officer **Company:** Beale Water Works, Inc **Address:** 578 East Filmore Ave, McAlester, OK 74501 United States **BUS:** Bottled Water Agra and Food Production **P/S:** Bottled Water Pure Artesian Well Water for Individuals **MA:** Regional **D/D/R:** manufacturing and Marketing **H/I/S:** Dogs **EDU:** Bachelor of Arts in Music, Oklahoma College for Women; Master's Degree in Education, South Eastern University **CERTS:** Superintendent Certification, Oklahoma University
Email: jazzpurr@swbell.net

Anthony L. Bean

Title: AODA Counselor **Company:** Birds of a Feather, Inc. **Address:** Kenosha, WI 53143 United States **BUS:** Healthcare Center **P/S:** Mental Health and Substance Abuse Care **MA:** Local **D/D/R:** Counseling on Traditional Living **H/I/S:** Coaching Basketball, Volunteering **EDU:** Pursuing Bachelor's Degree in Human Services, Upper Iowa College; Associate Degree in Human Services, Gateway Technical College, University of Wisconsin **A/A/S:** American Red Cross **C/VW:** Young Men's Christian Association; American Red Cross
Email: Anthony.Bean@cwwemail.com
URL: http://www.birdsofafeatheragency.org

Amy W. Beard

Title: Mathematics Teacher, Softball Coach **Company:** Prince William County Schools **Dept:** Brentsville District High School **Address:** 12109 Aden Road, Nokesville, VA 20181 United States **BUS:** School District **P/S:** Education **MA:** Regional **D/D/R:** Teaching Algebra I and II and coaching softball and the middle school volleyball team. **H/I/S:** Spending Time with Family, Working on her Farm, Coaching, Playing Softball, Hunting **EDU:** Bachelor of Arts in Secondary Education, Major in Mathematics Endorsement, Minor in History, West Virginia Wesleyan College **A/H:** Northwestern District Softball Coach of the Year (2006); Bull Run District Softball Coach of the Year (2003); PWCS Staff Recognition Teaching Award, Brentsville District **C/VW:** Care Kids
Email: beardax@pwcs.edu
URL: http://www.brentsvillehs.groupfusion.net

Ralph Waldo Beard

Title: Owner **Company:** R & D Cement Work, Inc. **Address:** 4730 Jeffersonville Road, Macon, GA 31217 United States **BUS:** Construction Company **P/S:** Construction Services **MA:** Local **D/D/R:** overseeing concrete work for parking lots, sidewalks for towns and streets. **EDU:** High School Diploma
Email: RalphWaldo.Beard@cwwemail.com

Kathy D. Bearden-Colbert
Title: Principal **Company:** General George S. Patton School **Address:** 13700 S. Stewart Street, Riverdale, IL 60827 United States **BUS:** Public School **P/S:** Pre-Kindergarten through Eighth-Grade Classes, Instruction and Curriculum **MA:** Local **D/D/R:** Building Leaders, Making Decisions, Offering Instructional Staff Leadership, Analyzing Data, Involving the Community, Developing the Curriculum **H/I/S:** Dancing, Reading **EDU:** Master's Degree in Educational Leadership, Governor State University (1997); Master's Degree in Counseling, Ohio State University (1980) **A/A/S:** Illinois Principals Association; National Association of Secondary School Principals; Delta Sigma Theta; Association for Supervision and Curriculum Development
Email: katcolbe@aol.com
URL: http://www.district133.org

Kecia H. Beasley
Title: Teacher **Company:** Roosevelt School District **Address:** 7000 S. Southern Avenue, Phoenix, AZ 85040 United States **BUS:** School District **P/S:** Education **MA:** Local **D/D/R:** Teaching Bilingual Education, Translating Spanish **H/I/S:** Jogging, Basketball, Gardening **EDU:** Master's Degree in Spanish, Arizona State University **A/A/S:** Black Student Union; Dance Club **C/VW:** St. Agnes Church
Email: khbdec4@aol.com

Roy W. Beasley
Title: Christian Broadcaster **Company:** Restoration Radio Network International, Inc. **Address:** 417 Welshwood Drive, Nashville, TN 37211 United States **BUS:** Broadcasting Radio **P/S:** Religious Broadcaster **MA:** International **EXP:** Mr. Beasley's expertise is in program production. **H/I/S:** Construction **EDU:** Davie Lipscomb College, Harding Grad School, MA **A/A/S:** Rotary, NAR
Email: rbeasley@juno.com
URL: www.restorationradio.com

Beverly Sue Beaty
Title: Foreign Language Teacher **Company:** Uinta County School District 1 **Dept:** Western Wyoming Community College **Address:** 638 Harrison Drive, Evanston, WY 82930 United States **BUS:** School District **P/S:** Middle School, High School and Community College Curriculum **MA:** National **EXP:** Ms. Beaty's expertise includes education and translation. **D/D/R:** Teaching Spanish and French for High School, Middle School and Community College Students **H/I/S:** Playing the Piano, Singing, Watching Baseball and Football **EDU:** Bachelor of Arts in Foreign Language, Oklahoma State University (1972) **A/A/S:** Wyoming Foreign Language Teachers Association; American Teachers Association; PEO; American Translators Association; National Education Association
Email: bbeaty@uinta1.k12.wy.us
URL: http://www.uinta1.k12.wy.us

Sara Michele Beaty
Title: Attorney **Company:** Tobin and Grifferty, PC **Address:** 678 Troy Schenectady Road Suite 303, Latham, NY 12110 United States **BUS:** Law Office **P/S:** Legal Services **MA:** Local **EXP:** Ms. Beaty's expertise includes real estate, nonprofit corporation and family law. **H/I/S:** Working in a Jewelry Store, Reading **EDU:** Utica College, Syracuse University, Albany Law School, BS, JD **A/A/S:** New York State Bar Association; American Bar Association; Humane Society; North Shore Animal Shelter
Email: sbeaty@tobgrif.com

Lillie S. Beaudoin
Title: Owner **Company:** The Hidden Gate Gift Shop and Restaurant **Address:** 2117 S. Fleisher Avenue, Tyler, TX 75701 United States **BUS:** Retail Store and Restaurant **P/S:** Retail Gifts, Food Services **MA:** Local **D/D/R:** Managing the Gift Shop and Restaurant, Overseeing Two Business Locations, Cooking, Baking, Making Sales **H/I/S:** Reading, Making Arts and Crafts, Painting, Sewing **A/A/S:** Former Member, American Business Women's Association; Lifetime Member, The International Order of the Rainbow for Girls; National Honor Society; Better Business Bureau; Tyler Chamber of Commerce **A/H:** Poet of the Year, Library of Congress

Guadalupe M. Beauvec
Title: Licensed Vocational Nurse **Company:** Wedgewood Nursing Rehabilitation **Address:** 6330 Dan Danciger Road, Fort Worth, TX 76028 United States **BUS:** Private Facility Committed to Excellence in the Healthcare Industry **P/S:** Hispanic and Bilingual Staffing Services for Geriatric Patients **MA:** Regional **D/D/R:** Staff Nursing, Overseeing 22 to 24 Geriatric Patients Including Total Medical Care, Completing All Insurance Issues **H/I/S:** Bowling, Music, Walking **EDU:** Nursing Degree, University of Texas, Brown, Texas (1971) **A/A/S:** President, Licensed Vocational Nursing Association of Texas (1988-1994); First Vice President, National Licensed Vocational Nursing Association of Texas (1990-1994)
Email: info@CambridgeWhosWho.com
URL: http://www.cambridgewhoswho.com

Aaron Becenti
Title: Owner, Founder **Company:** Aaron Becenti Design, Inc. **Address:** 1141 S. Van Ness Avenue, Santa Ana, CA 92707 United States **BUS:** Graphic Design Company **P/S:** Graphic Design, Photography, Product Marketing, Convention and Exhibit Planning **MA:** Regional **D/D/R:** Graphic Designing, Overseeing Daily Business Operations, Managing All Designs and Creations, Marketing, Planning Conventions and Exhibits, Creating Brochures and Business Cards **H/I/S:** Cycling, Collecting Cars **EDU:** Bachelor of Fine Arts, California State University (2004) **A/A/S:** American Institute of Graphic Arts
Email: aaron@studiobecenti.com
URL: http://www.studiobecenti.com

Andrew M. Beck III
Title: AVP Marketing Manager **Company:** BB+T-KDC Insurance Services, Inc **Address:** 433 East Center Street, Kingsport, TN 37660 United States **BUS:** Insurance Company **P/S:** Commercial Insurance **MA:** Local **EXP:** Mr. Beck's expertise is in commercial risk management. **H/I/S:** College Football, Racing **EDU:** University of Georgia, Bachelor's in Business Administration, Specialty in Insurance and Risk Management **A/A/S:** CIC, Arm Associate Risk Management of Insurance Institute
Email: drew.beck@bbandt.com
URL: www.bbt.com

Rev. Douglas Beck
Title: Director of International Ministries **Company:** Mobile Baptist Association **Address:** 605 Texas Place, Mobile, AL 36603 United States **BUS:** Religious Center **P/S:** Spiritual Services **MA:** International **EXP:** Rev. Beck's expertise includes English, Uzbek and the management of Asian missions. **D/D/R:** Proclaiming the Gospel of Jesus to Seafarers, Refugees, Local Residents, Students, Non-English Speaking Patients in Local Hospitals and Inmates in Jail, Performing Follow-Up Ministries for More than 133 Nationalities in Any Language **H/I/S:** Running, Photography, Gardening **EDU:** Master of Divinity, Southwestern Baptist Theological Seminary (1997); Bachelor of Arts in Religion, Baylor University, Waco, TX (1992) **A/A/S:** Port Ministries International **C/VW:** Foster Care Associates
Email: imc@mobilebaptists.org
URL: http://www.mobilebaptists.org/imc_wp.htm

Patricia Beck
Title: Territory Manager **Company:** U.S. Food Service, Oklahoma Division **Address:** 1346 77th Place, Pauls Valley, OK 73705 United States **BUS:** Food and Beverage Distributors **P/S:** Broadline Food Service, Wholesale Distribution **MA:** National **D/D/R:** Supplying Food and Beverages for Oklahoma Casinos, Visiting Sites Daily, Showing New Products, Presenting Options for the Best Products at the Best Price **H/I/S:** Photography **EDU:** High School Education **C/VW:** Public Speaking on Safety Issues and Foodborne Illnesses
Email: patty.beck@usfood.com
URL: http://www.usfood.com

Brandon E. Becker
Title: Chairman, Musical Theatre Department **Company:** Appomattox Regional Governor's School for the Arts and Technology **Address:** 512 W. Washington Street, Petersburg, VA 23803 United States **BUS:** School **P/S:** Education **MA:** Statewide **D/D/R:** Teaching Performing Arts and Musical Theatre, Choreographing, Directing **H/I/S:** Performing, Choreography, Directing **EDU:** Master of Fine Arts, Virginia Commonwealth University; Bachelor of Fine Arts, University of Utah **A/A/S:** Virginia Music Educators Association; Phi Kappa Phi **C/VW:** Make-A-Wish Foundation
Email: brandonearlbecker@yahoo.com
URL: http://www.cambridgewhoswho.com

Mrs. Michelle Y. Becker
Title: Exceptional Children Teacher **Company:** Lakeshore Middle School **BUS:** Middle School **P/S:** Education **MA:** Local **D/D/R:** Working with Sixth through Eighth-Grade Severely Mentally Disabled Children, Creating an Individual Education Plan for Each Student Including Mainstream Students, Teaching Physical Education and Life, Communication and Job skills to Non-Verbal Students, Developing the Curriculum, Planning **H/I/S:** Caring for her Pets, Traveling **EDU:** Pursuing Master's Degree in Curriculum and Instruction, University of Phoenix; Bachelor's Degree in Psychology, Salem College (2001) **CERTS:** Certified Disabled Education Teacher (K-12); Certified Adapted Curriculum Education Teacher (K-12)
Email: mbecker@iss.k12.nc.us

Kristi M. Beckman
Title: Realtor **Company:** Re/Max Elite **Address:** 3125 S Price Road Suite 120, Chandler, AZ 85248 United States **BUS:** Real Estate Broker **P/S:** Residential, Executive, Hi End, Town Homes, Condos, New Construction, Gulf Homes, Senior, Gated **MA:** Local **EXP:** Ms. Beckman's expertise is in the sale of golfing properties. **D/D/R:** Selling High-End Residential Properties **H/I/S:** Spending Time with Grandchildren, Likes To Travel **A/A/S:** Arizona Association of Realtors, National Association of Realtors
Email: kbeckman1@cox.net
URL: www.kristibeckman.com

Camey Bedell
Title: Chief Executive Officer **Company:** Envision Resources, Inc. **Address:** 2210 San Joaquin Street, Fresno, CA 93721 United States **BUS:** Software Development and Consulting Company **P/S:** Patient Assistance Programs, Software Development, Consulting Services to Patients and Healthcare Providers, Reimbursement Programs, Manufacturer Assistance Applications, Generic and Therapeutic Searches **MA:** National **D/D/R:** Developing Software Programs, Overseeing Business Operations, Managing Employees, Developing Drug Recovery Programs in a Variety of Healthcare Settings **H/I/S:** Motorcycle Racing, Camping, Knitting, Reading Historical Novels and Harry Potter **EDU:** Coursework in Law, SUNY Plattsburgh, New York; College Coursework, Fresno Junior College, California **A/A/S:** American Society of Health-System Pharmacists
Email: cbedell@envisionresources.com
URL: http://www.envisionresources.com

Sharon J. Bednar, GS12
Title: Special Assistant to Vice Chairman (Retired) **Company:** Surface Transportation Board **Address:** 395 E. Street S.W., Washington, DC 20423 United States **BUS:** Government Economic Regulatory Agency **P/S:** Regulatory Jurisdiction over Railroad Rates and Service Issues **MA:** Nationwide **D/D/R:** Acting as the Executive Assistant to the Vice Chairman, Handling All Day-to-Day Aspects of the Office, Overseeing Executive Managerial Leadership **H/I/S:** Traveling, Sewing, Making Arts and Crafts, Practicing Yoga, Meditating **EDU:** Diploma, Patricia Stevens Career College, IL (1964) **A/A/S:** Former Member, The International Association of Administrative Professionals; Former Member, Architecture Committee, Homeowners' Association; Former Member, Library Advisory Committee **C/VW:** Y-ME National Breast Cancer Organization
Email: losh@fedweeknet.com
Email: losh@fedweeknet.com
URL: http://www.stb.dot.gov

Mr. Alexander R. Beeber
Title: Chief Information Officer, Owner **Company:** Intelitech, LLC **Address:** 36 Swan Drive, Portsmouth, RI 02871 United States **BUS:** Consulting Company **P/S:** Software Consulting Services **MA:** International **EXP:** Mr. Beeber's expertise includes technical, software and office equipment consulting. **D/D/R:** assisting clients and conducting training programs on software systems. **H/I/S:** Fishing, Golfing, Scuba Diving **EDU:** Bachelor's Degree in Marketing, Salve Regina University (2001); Bachelor's Degree in Information Systems, Salve Regina University (2001); Associate Degree in Law, Salve Regina University (2001) **A/A/S:** National Speakers Association
Email: ageonat@yahoo.com
URL: http://www.cambridgewhoswho.com

W. Louis Beecher
Title: Attorney **Company:** Beacher Law Firm **Address:** 620 Lafayette, Waterloo, IA 50704 United States **BUS:** Law Firm **P/S:** Legal Services **MA:** Local **EXP:** Mr. Beecher's expertise is in general law. **H/I/S:** Collecting Race Cars **EDU:** Law Degree, University of Iowa **A/A/S:** County Bar
Email: info@CambridgeWhosWho.com

Lana K. Beerhalter
Title: Vocal Director **Company:** Little Axe High School **Address:** 2000 168th Avenue N.E., Norman, OK 73086 United States **BUS:** High School **P/S:** Education **MA:** Local **D/D/R:** Teaching Vocal Music **H/I/S:** Traveling, Photography, Scrapbooking, Collecting Antiques **EDU:** Master's Degree in Vocal Performance, Emporia State University **A/A/S:** Connecticut Music Educators Association; Delta Kappa Gamma; Tau Beta Sigma; Kappa Kappa Psi; OFA; LATA; Tri-M Music Honor Society **C/VW:** Church
Email: labeer@sbcglobal.net

Diana L. Beeson, CRS
Title: Realtor **Company:** Greg Garrett Realtors **Address:** 6502 Slide Road, Suite 202, Lubbock, TX 79424 United States **BUS:** Real Estate Broker **P/S:** Marketing and Sales of Real Estate **MA:** National **H/I/S:** Golf **A/A/S:** Texas Association of Realtors, National Association of Realtors
Email: beesongroup@ntsonline.net
URL: www.greggarrettrealtors.com

Paul Beets
Title: Software Engineer **Company:** Harman/Becker Automotive Systems **Address:** 39001 W. Twelve Mile Road, Farmington Hills, MI 48331 United States **BUS:** Automotive Systems Company **P/S:** Audio Electronics, Automotive Sound Systems **MA:** National **EXP:** Mr. Beets' expertise is in software engineering. **D/D/R:** Designing Software, Managing Paperwork, Scheduling **H/I/S:** Golfing **EDU:** Bachelor of Science in Telecommunications and Network Technology, Purdue University (2003) **A/H:** Eagle Scout, Boy Scouts of America
Email: pbeets@harmanbecker.com
URL: http://www.cambridgewhoswho.com

Marianna H. Begay
Title: Administrative Officer, Acting Superintendent Company: Bureau of Indian Affairs, Laguna Address: P.O. Box 1448, Laguna, NM 87026 United States BUS: Government Agency P/S: Educational Administrative Services MA: Local D/D/R: Assisting the Principal with Administrative Functions, Maintaining Records, Managing Human Resources and Contracts, Budgeting H/I/S: Reading, Sewing EDU: Coursework, Parks Business College, Denver, CO A/H: Annual Performance Award, Bureau of Indian Affairs, Laguna Agency C/VW: Oak Canyon Rodeo Club Email: marianna.begay@bia.gov
URL: http://www.cambridgewhoswho.com

Pinky Deborah Begnaud
Title: Owner, Licensed Practical Nurse Company: Simple Health, LLC Address: 313 General Mouton, Lafayette, LA 70501 United States BUS: Healthcare Facility P/S: Alternative Technologies, Ionic Foot Spa, Nikken and Nature's Sunshine MA: Regional D/D/R: Conducting Detoxification, Offering Pain Management, Nutrition and Environmental Wellness, Working with Mentally and Physically Challenged Children H/I/S: Traveling CERTS: Licensed Practical Nurse, Gulf Area Vocational-Technical School (1984)
Email: pinkybmagic5@aol.com
URL: http://www.mynikken.com/pinky

Ralph F. Behner
Title: Special Agent Company: Western-Southern Financial Group Address: 1207 Delaware Avenue, Marion, OH 43302 United States BUS: Insurance Company P/S: Life Insurance MA: Local D/D/R: Preparing Annuities for Senior Citizens, Organizing the Life Underwriter Training Council H/I/S: Collecting Antique Cars EDU: Coursework in Aviation Technology, Ohio State University CERTS: Certified Boating Safety Instructor A/A/S: Local Insurance Association; Life Underwriter Training Council Fellow; National Association of Insurance and Financial Advisors; United States Power Squadrons; Financial Services Specialist A/H: Humanitarian Award; Outstanding Senior Citizen Award C/VW: Civitan International; Gideon's International
Email: pdcralph@gmail.com
URL: http://www.cambridgewhoswho.com

Stephen A. Behr
Title: Retail Supervisor Company: Sodexho Campus Services at the College of St Catherine Address: 2004 Randolf Avenue, St Paul, MN 55105 United States BUS: College P/S: Food Service MA: Local D/D/R: Food Services, Preparation, Stocking, Custom Service H/I/S: Music, Bongos, Model Rail Roading CERTS: Certificate in Serve Safe, Food and Handling A/A/S: Land Stewardship Program
Email: info@CambridgeWhosWho.com

Ms. Diana E. Beiler, MFTI
Title: Clinical Social Worker I Company: Yuba County Victim Witness Program Address: 4240 Dan Avenue, Olivehurst, CA 95961 United States BUS: County Counseling Center P/S: Counseling for Victims of Crimes MA: Regional EXP: Ms. Beiler's expertise includes marriage and family therapy. H/I/S: Working Out, Swimming, Spending Time Outdoors, Going on Short Road Trips, Visiting Museums, Traveling EDU: Master of Science in Marriage and Family Counseling, University of Phoenix (2003); Bachelor of Science in Social Work, Pacific Union College (1994)
Email: dyzeemae2@aol.com

Meri D. Bekirovik, Ph.D.
Title: Business Manager Company: Michael T. Colletti, DDS BUS: Private Dental Practice P/S: Dental Services MA: Local D/D/R: Overseeing Practice Scheduling, Insurance, Purchasing Supplies, Accounts Payable and Receivable and Customer Service, Compiling Production and Collection Reports H/I/S: Gardening, Swimming, Practicing Fitness EDU: Ph.D. in Pediatric Dentistry, University of Macedonia (1998)
Email: mdbekirovik@yahoo.com

Justine M. Belanger
Title: Executive Secretary Company: Memorial Hospital of Rhode Island Address: 111 Brewster Street, Pawtucket, RI 02860 United States BUS: Hospital P/S: Healthcare MA: Regional D/D/R: Coordinating Functions and Events, Purchasing, Maintenance, Budgeting, Supervising H/I/S: Cooking, Gardening, Spending Time with her Children EDU: Coursework in Business Administration; Diploma, Lincoln High School A/A/S: Blood Drive Coordinator, Pawtucket Community
Email: justine_belanger@mhri.org
Email: jcricket1111@aol.com
URL: http://www.mhri.org

Colleen V. Belcher
Title: Realtor Company: Wagner Realty Address: 5215 State Road 64 East, Bradenton, FL 34208 United States BUS: Residential and Commercial Real Estate P/S: Working with Buyers and Sellers of Residential Properties, Commercial and Investments, Relocation, Marketing and Staging Homes for the Best Price in All Markets MA: Manatee County D/D/R: Coordinating Relocation Listings and Investments, Marketing H/I/S: Marathoner, Golfer, Dogs EDU: Northern Michigan University CERTS: Certified Residential Specialist; E-Pro, National Association of Realtors; Real Estate License (1992) A/A/S: National Association of Realtors; Florida Association of Realtors; President, Women's Council of Realtors (2005) A/H: CRS District Representative Award (2003)
Email: colleen@colleenbelcher.com
URL: http://www.ColleenBelcher.com

Lori Ellen Belenzon-Anderson
Title: Spanish Teacher Company: Temecula Valley High School Address: 45826 Corte Carmillo, Temecula, CA 92592 United States BUS: Public High School P/S: Education MA: Regional D/D/R: Teaching Spanish Levels One to Four, Heading the Study Abroad Program in Madrid H/I/S: Personal Training, Traveling, Spending Time with her Family EDU: Bachelor of Arts in Spanish, California State University, San Diego (1988) A/A/S: California Foreign Language Teachers Association
Email: lbelenzon@trusd.k12.ca.us
URL: http://www.cambridgewhoswho.com

Regina G. Belknap
Title: Educator Company: Sequatchie County Board of Education Address: 7079 State Route 28, Dunlap, TN 37327 United States BUS: School P/S: Education MA: Local EXP: Ms. Belknap's expertise is reading education. H/I/S: Reading, Traveling EDU: Bachelor's Degree in Elementary Education and Reading Instruction, University of Tennessee A/A/S: Chairwoman, Reading Committee
Email: nbelknap@sequatchie.k12.tn.us

Brian T. Bell
Title: 1) Public Adjuster 2) Owner 3) Co-Owner Company: 1) Metro Public Adjustment, Inc. 2) Self-Employed 3) Quick Wit Warehouse, LLC Address: 3551 Bristol Pike, Bensalem, PA 19020 United States BUS: 1) Public Adjusting Company 2) Self-Employed Business 3) Entertainment Company P/S: 1) Public Adjusting, Homeowner Assistance, Policy Reviews 2) Computer Repair and Design Work 3) Entertainment Products MA: Southern New Jersey D/D/R: Public Adjusting, Reviewing Policies, Repairing Computers, Designing H/I/S: Traveling, Skiing, Watching Football EDU: Degree in Computer Repair and Networks/Technology A/A/S: Kiwanis Club; Chamber of Commerce, Hammonton, NJ
Email: briant.bell@comcast.net

Donald R. Bell
Title: Senior Staff Engineer (Retired) Company: 1) Hughes Aircraft Company 2) Raytheon Company Address: 1065 Lomita Boulevard, Harbor City, CA 90710 United States BUS: 1) Aviation Company 2) Distribution Firm P/S: 1) Aviation Services 2) Intelligence and Information Systems Such as Satellite, Laser and Radar Program Services for the Government MA: International EXP: Mr. Bell's expertise is in aerospace engineering. H/I/S: Relaxing, Traveling, Reading, Fishing, Hunting EDU: Coursework, United States Naval Academy C/VW: Veterans of Foreign Wars; The American Legion
Email: donald.bell@cwwemail.com

Frances M. Bell
Title: Retired Mathematics and Reading Teacher Company: OPS BUS: School P/S: Elementary Education MA: Local EXP: Ms. Bell's expertise is in mathematics education for kindergarten through third-grade students. H/I/S: Knitting, Cooking, Reading EDU: Middletons Business College, Three Years of College
Email: info@CambridgeWhosWho.com

Jennifer G. Bell
Title: Director of Marketing Company: Millennium BUS: Construction Company P/S: Landscaping Maintenance, Roofing, Molding, Decks MA: Southern California EXP: Ms. Bell's expertise includes business development and sales. H/I/S: Fashion Designing for Mode Clothing EDU: Bachelor's Degree in Marketing, University of Phoenix; Bachelor's Degree in Business Management, University of Phoenix A/A/S: South Coast Apartment Association; Greater Inland Empire Chapter, Community Associations Institute C/VW: Volunteer, Local Animal Shelter
Email: jbell@rgsservices.com
URL: http://www.rgsservices.com

Maureen J. Bell
Title: Group Leader Company: Catalent Pharma Solutions Address: 14 Schoolhouse Road, Somerset, NJ 08873 United States BUS: Contract Manufacturing, Pharmaceutical Development Company P/S: Pharmaceutical Development MA: International EXP: Ms. Bell's expertise includes leadership and training. D/D/R: Auditing Notebook Documents and Laboratories, Reviewing Investigations, Currently, Developing and Monitoring the change control program H/I/S: Going to the Beach, Spending Time with her Family and Friends, Exercising EDU: Bachelor of Science Degree in Nutrition, Rutgers University, 1998 CERTS: Certified Quality Auditor-2004 A/A/S: American Society for Quality C/VW: Revlon Run/Walk, Breast Cancer Organizations, Multiple Sclerosis Society
Email: mobell04@aol.com

Susanne M. Bell
Title: Certified Athletic Trainer Company: Oakwood Healthcare, Inc. Address: 15777 Northline Road, Southgate, MI 48195 United States BUS: Sports Medicine P/S: Healthcare, Athletic Training MA: High School D/D/R: Athletic Training for High School Students H/I/S: Keeping Fit, Hiking, Camping EDU: Master of Science in Health and Human Performance with a Concentration in Advanced Athletic Training, University of Tennessee at Chattanooga A/A/S: National Athletic Trainers' Association; Michigan Athletic Trainers' Association
Email: sbell@divinechild.pvt.k12.mi.us

Vickie K. Bell
Title: Senior Accountant Company: Farmers Mutual Hail Insurance Company of Iowa Address: 6785 Westown Parkway, West Des Moines, IA 50266 United States BUS: Insurance Company P/S: Excellence in Crop Insurance Services MA: International D/D/R: Creating Financial Statements, Ledger Items and the Bank Reconciliation Quarterly H/I/S: Reading CERTS: Two-Year Certificate in Accounting and Programming, Northeast Missouri State University A/A/S: Insurance Accounting & Systems Association, Inc.
Email: vickie@fmh.com
URL: http://www.cambridgewhoswho.com

Mr. Glenn J. Bellamy
Title: Registered Nurse, Professional Sales Representative Company: Schering-Plough Address: 30 Murray Avenue, Goshen, NY 10924 United States BUS: Pharmaceutical Company P/S: Respiratory Products, Licenses, Science-Based Medicines, Healthcare, Allergy and Asthma Products MA: International D/D/R: Introducing Pharmaceutical and Respiratory Products to Physicians, Communicating with More than 10 Physicians Daily, Nursing Critical Care Patients, Overseeing Emergency Room Department, Managing Administrative Duties Critical Care Administration, ENT H/I/S: Fishing, Boating, Swimming, Outdoor Activities, Reading Boating Magazines, Field and Stream and Sports Afield EDU: Bachelor's Degree in Healthcare Administration, Empire State College (1980); Associate Degree, Pace University (1975) CERTS: Registered Nurse
Email: glenn.bellamy@spcorp.com
URL: http://www.schering-plough.com

Susan J. Bellor
Title: Spanish Teacher, Coordinator of International Baccalaureate Program Company: Massena Central School District Address: 19 Churchill Avenue, Massena, NY 13662 United States BUS: Public School District P/S: Education, Basic Primary and Secondary Curriculum Programs, Special Education, Art, Music, Physical Education, Language Arts, Athletics, Extracurricular Activities MA: Regional D/D/R: Teaching College-Level Spanish Courses, Coordinating Disciplines for Teachers, Performing Internal Assessments, Developing Lesson Plans, Updating Curriculum, Overseeing Daily Operations H/I/S: Golfing, Exercising, Collecting Antiques EDU: Master's Degree in Reading, SUNY Potsdam (1978); Bachelor's Degree in Spanish, SUNY Potsdam (1973) A/A/S: Adjunct Professor, St. Lawrence University; American Association of Teachers of Spanish and Portuguese; New York State Association of Foreign Language Teachers; American Association of University Women; St. Lawrence County Business and Professional Women
Email: sbellor1@twcny.rr.com
URL: http://www.mcs.k12.ny.us

Dennis C. Belotti
Title: Co-Publisher, Executive Editor Company: Unwind Magazine, LLC Address: P.O. Box 151, Lincoln Park, NJ 07035 United States BUS: Magazine P/S: Entertainment and Leisure Information MA: New York, New Jersey EXP: Mr. Belotti's expertise includes sales, marketing and operations management. D/D/R: Managing Daily Operations and Accounting, Approving All Printed Materials, Meeting Printing Deadlines, Selling Premier Advertising Space, Gathering Classy Leisure Event Information for a Monthly Publication H/I/S: Golfing, Traveling EDU: Associate Degree in Business Administration, Essex County Community College A/A/S: Don's 21 Executive Club
Email: unwindmag@yahoo.com
Email: viperman06@aol.com
URL: http://www.unwindmag.net

Renee M. Belvis
Title: English for Speakers of Other Languages Teacher **Company:** John F. Kennedy Middle School **Address:** 1660 Palmetto Street, Clearwater, FL 33755 United States **BUS:** Public Middle School **P/S:** Education **MA:** Local **D/D/R:** Teaching English to Speakers of Other Languages **H/I/S:** Salsa Dancing **EDU:** Bachelor of Arts in Psychology, York College **A/A/S:** Teachers of English to Speakers of Other Languages; Kappa Delta Psi; World Language Teachers Association; Sunshine State Teachers of English to Speakers of Other Languages; National Association of Teachers of English **C/VW:** Teacher, Adult English for Speakers of Other Languages; United Corporate Ministries of Methodist Church
Email: ebrb1@aol.com
URL: http://www.cambridgewhoswho.com

Angela Benard
Title: Medical Esthetician **Company:** Laser and Medical Spa **Address:** 1425 N. McLean Boulevard, Suite 100, Elgin, IL 60123 United States **BUS:** Medical Spa **P/S:** Personal Patient Care through Special Technology **MA:** Regional **EXP:** Ms. Benard's expertise is in micro-pigmentation. **H/I/S:** Riding Horses, Dancing **EDU:** Associate Degree in Applied Science, Bellville College **CERTS:** Licensed Esthetician, Hanover Park **C/VW:** Women's Magazine
Email: mtkghani1@aol.com

Aaron Bender
Title: Psychoanalyst **Company:** Aaron Bender, Ph.D. **Address:** 1011 Abington Road, Cherry Hill, NJ 08034 United States **BUS:** Therapy Practice **P/S:** Healthcare **MA:** Regional **EXP:** Mr. Bender's expertise is in psychotherapy. **H/I/S:** Playing Scrabble, Swimming, Writing Poetry **EDU:** Ph.D. in Social Studies, Concentration in History, New York University; Master's Degree in Social Studies, Concentration in History, New York University; Bachelor's Degree in Economics, CUNY Brooklyn College; American Psychotherapy Diplomate **A/A/S:** National Association for the Advancement of Psychoanalysis
Email: aaronbender98@yahoo.com

Kena Louise Bendsten
Title: Registered Nurse **Address:** Apollo College, 1001 Menaul Boulevard N.W., Albuquerque, NM 87107 United States **BUS:** Healthcare Facility **P/S:** Wide Range of Medical Services **MA:** Local **EXP:** Ms. Bendsten's expertise is in pediatrics. **D/D/R:** Nursing, Teaching, Immunizing, Rehabilitating **H/I/S:** Arts and Crafts, Crocheting, Embroidery **EDU:** Pursuing Master's Degree from Vol Phoenix in Nursing Education; Associate Degree in Nursing, Eastern New Mexico College, Roswell; Bachelor of Science in Nursing, University of New Mexico **A/A/S:** I-Care Foundation **A/H:** National Dean's List

Amy S. Benedict
Title: District Sales Manager **Company:** Pfizer **BUS:** Pharmaceutical Company **P/S:** Pharmaceuticals **MA:** International **EXP:** Ms. Benedict's expertise is in sales management. **H/I/S:** Traveling, Attending the Theater, Athletics **EDU:** Master of Science in Organizational Leadership, Miami University **A/A/S:** Delta Gamma; Phi Beta Kappa **C/VW:** United Way
Email: amy.benedict@cwwemail.com
URL: http://www.cambridgewhoswho.com

Leon H. Benek
Title: President and Owner **Company:** Benek Financial Group, Inc. **Address:** 300 Deschutes Way S.W., Suite 319, Tumwater, WA 98501 United States **BUS:** Finance Company **P/S:** Financial Planning, Investment Advisory Services **MA:** Regional **D/D/R:** Estate Planning, Executive Compensation Planning, Income and Estate Tax, Asset Protection, Strategies Planning, Financial Advisory and Consulting for High Net Worth Business Owners more than (10 Million) **H/I/S:** Golfing, Softball, Spending Time with his Grandchildren **EDU:** Bachelor of Education, Western Washington University **CERTS:** Certified Estate Planner; Registered Financial Consultant **A/A/S:** National Association of Insurance and Financial Advisors **C/VW:** Special Olympics
Email: leonbenek@comcast.net
URL: http://www.benekfinancialgroup.com

Kathleen M. Benites
Title: Teacher **Company:** Charlotte Elementary School **Address:** 168 Watson Avenue, Charlotte, TX 78011 United States **BUS:** Public Elementary School **P/S:** Education for Students in Prekindergarten through Fifth-Grade **MA:** Regional **D/D/R:** Teaching Language Arts to Fourth and Fifth-Grade Students Math **H/I/S:** Working Out at the Gym, Reading **EDU:** Bachelor of Science in Elementary Education, New Mexico State University (1999) **CERTS:** Certification in Education 1-8
Email: kbenites@charlotte.k12.tx.us
URL: http://www.charlotte.k12.tx.us

Astrid Benjamin
Title: President **Company:** Full Circle Financial Service **Address:** 1108 Rutland Road 2nd Floor, Brooklyn, NY 11212 United States **BUS:** Insurance Services **P/S:** Commercial and Personal Insurance, Tax Preparation, Mortgages **MA:** Regional **EXP:** Ms. Benjamin's expertise includes business and personal insurance. **H/I/S:** Going to the Gym and Beaches **CERTS:** P and C New York State Broker License
Email: astridfcfserv@optonline.net

Lotti B. Benker
Title: Founder, President **Company:** Help Animals Lives Today **Address:** 6625 Massachusetts Drive, Kingman, AZ 86409 United States **BUS:** Animal Rescue and Adoption Agency **P/S:** Pet Welfare **MA:** Arizona, Nevada, California **EXP:** Ms. Benker's expertise is in animal behavior modification. **H/I/S:** Writing Poetry, Reading, Traveling, Walking Dogs **EDU:** Master's Degree in Business Administration and Psychology, SUNY Brockport **A/A/S:** Society of Animal Welfare Administrators; Chamber of Commerce; International Poetry Association; American Society of Women Accountants Facility; Mental Health Administrators
Email: lottibnkr@citlink.net
URL: http://www.haltaz.org

Amanda M. Bennett
Title: Certified OT Assistant **Company:** Trinity Rehabilitation, Inc **Address:** 13 Northtown Drive Suite 110, Jackson, MS 39211 United States **BUS:** Rehabilitation Center **P/S:** Rehab Services **MA:** Local **EXP:** Ms. Bennett's expertise is in geriatrics. **H/I/S:** Crochet, Beach, Cats **EDU:** Pearl River College, AOTA **A/A/S:** MOTA
Email: amandabennett@bellsouth.net

Courtney P. Bennett
Title: Pastor **Company:** Boston's United Pentecostal Church **Address:** 73 Brooks Street, Brighton, MA 02135 United States **BUS:** Church **P/S:** Preaching, Teaching, Counseling, Religion, Spiritual Services **MA:** Massachusetts **D/D/R:** Counseling, Preaching, Teaching **H/I/S:** Traveling **A/A/S:** United Pentecostal Church International
Email: bostonupc@netscape.net
URL: http://www.bostonupc.net

Jamie E. Bennett
Title: Pharmacist **Company:** CVS **Dept:** Pharmacy **Address:** 115 S Piney Street, Chester, MD 21619 United States **BUS:** Retail **P/S:** Selling Personal Products, Everyday Home Items, Pharmaceuticals **MA:** National **EXP:** Ms. Bennett's expertise includes individual and direct patient care. **H/I/S:** Traveling, Hiking, Biking, Outdoor Activities **EDU:** Doctorate in Pharmacy, Shenandoah University; Bachelor of Science in Biology, Limestone College **A/A/S:** Kappa Epsilon
Email: jbennett@su.edu
URL: http://www.cvs.com

Marilyn K. Bennett
Title: Associate Director of Bands, Head Director of the Junior High **Company:** Palacios Independent School District **Address:** 1209 12th Street, Palacios, TX 77465 United States **BUS:** Public High School **P/S:** Education **MA:** Local **D/D/R:** Directing the Band **H/I/S:** Cooking, Reading, Needlecrafting **EDU:** Master of Music Education, Midwestern State University; Bachelor of Arts in Music Education, Midwestern State University **A/A/S:** Texas Music Educators Association; Association of Texas Small School Bands; National Association for Music Education; WBDI; Mu Phi Epsilon; Delta Kappa Gamma
Email: marilynb@palacios.k12.tx.us
URL: http://www.cambridgewhoswho.com

Stephanie C. Bennett
Title: Chief Operations Officer of Nurs **Company:** Med Care Pediatric Group **Address:** 12371 S Kirkwood, Stafford, TX 77477 United States **BUS:** Pediatric Office **P/S:** In-Home Medical Care for Children **MA:** Local **EXP:** Ms. Bennett's expertise is in pediatrics. **H/I/S:** Animals Reading Traveling **EDU:** Bristol Community College-Fall River, MA, AS-Nursing
Email: stephanie@medcarepro.com
URL: www.medcarepro.com

Catherine Orndorff Benson
Title: City Clerk, Master Municipal Clerk **Company:** City of Safety Harbor **Address:** 750 Main Street, Safety Harbor, FL 34695 United States **BUS:** Government Organization **P/S:** Public Services **MA:** Local **EXP:** Ms. Benson's expertise is in public administration. **D/D/R:** Supervising Municipal Elections, Managing Records **H/I/S:** Scuba Diving, Traveling, Training Dogs, Conducting Dog Shows **EDU:** Coursework in Accounting, Old Dominion University, Norfolk, VA; Coursework in Business **CERTS:** Association of Records Managers and Administrators **A/A/S:** Pinellas County Municipal Clerks Association; Florida Association of City Clerks; The Association of Records Managers and Administrators; International Institute of Municipal Clerks **C/VW:** Daughters of the American Revolution; Relay For Life, American Cancer Society
Email: cbenson@cityofsafetyharbor.com
URL: http://www.cityofsafetyharbor.com

Lisa G. Benson
Title: Clinician **Company:** Northeast Parent and Child Society **Address:** 454 Warren Street, Hudson, NY 12534 United States **BUS:** Nonprofit Organization **P/S:** Residential, Special Education, Family Foster Care, Children's Mental Health, Family Preservation and Career Development Programs, Foster Care, Mentoring, Child Guidance Center, Sexual Abuse Treatment, After-School Children's Shelter, Children's Group Homes, Independent Living **MA:** Regional **D/D/R:** Traveling to Low-Income Families' Homes to Provide Therapy, Handling Case Management, Assisting Families with Therapy Treatment **H/I/S:** Traveling, Shopping **EDU:** Master of Education in Marriage and Family Therapy, Springfield College (2002) **A/A/S:** American Association for Marriage and Family Therapy
Email: bensonl@parsoncenter.org

Craig Bentley
Title: Project Manager **Company:** National Salvage and Service Corp **Address:** PO Box 300, Clear Creek, IN 47426 United States **BUS:** Demolition Construction **P/S:** Project Management **MA:** National **EXP:** Mr. Bentley's expertise is in project management. **H/I/S:** Hunting, Fishing **EDU:** Bachelor's in Economics, Purdue University **A/A/S:** Project Management Institute
Email: info@CambridgeWhosWho.com

Henry Benton
Title: Retired **Address:** 917 Ashfield Avenue, Pomona, UT 91767 United States **BUS:** Evangelist **P/S:** Preacher **MA:** Local **D/D/R:** Evangelizing, Preaching **H/I/S:** Fishing, Shopping, Sewing, Spending Time with her Grandchildren, Nieces and Nephews **EDU:** Jackson, High School
Email: info@CambridgeWhosWho.com

Mr. Windell Benton Jr.
Title: Store Manager **Company:** Gibson's Discount Store **Address:** 111 W. Main Street, Kerrville, TX 78028 United States **BUS:** Retail Store **P/S:** Sporting Goods, Toys, Jewelry, Clothing, Housewares, Food Products, Plants, Recreational Vehicle and Hardware **MA:** Regional **D/D/R:** Managing Operations **H/I/S:** Skydiving, Skiing, Water Skiing, Hunting **EDU:** Diploma, Junction High School **CERTS:** Management Training **A/A/S:** Former Member, Christian Motorcycle Association
Email: rockhound0122@yahoo.com
URL: http://www.cambridgewhoswho.com

Ronald T. Benz
Title: Physician, Otolaryngologist **Company:** Sharp Rees-Stealy Medical Group **Address:** 8933 Activity Road, San Diego, CA 92126 United States **BUS:** Medical Company **P/S:** Healthcare **MA:** Local **EXP:** Mr. Benz's expertise includes otolaryngology and general pediatrics. **H/I/S:** Watching Sports, Umpiring at Baseball Games **EDU:** MD; Bachelor of Science **CERTS:** Certified Otolaryngologist **A/A/S:** Children's Hospital and Medical Center, San Diego; Marquette Medical School; American College of Surgeons
Email: ronald.benz@sharp.com
URL: http://www.cambridgewhoswho.com

Linda C. Bequette
Title: Teacher **Company:** St. Augustine of Canterbury School **Address:** 1900 W. Belle Street, Belleville, IL 62226 United States **BUS:** School **P/S:** Education **MA:** Local **EXP:** Ms. Bequette's expertise is in elementary education. **H/I/S:** Reading, Playing Piano **EDU:** Bachelor of Science in Special Education, Southern Illinois University, Edwardsville, Illinois **CERTS:** Certified in Special Education and Elementary Education **C/VW:** Children International
Email: squeekygirl2@yahoo.com

Ketevan Berekashvili
Title: Research Coordinator **Company:** Beth Israel Medical Center **BUS:** Hospital **P/S:** Healthcare **MA:** Regional **D/D/R:** Preparing for the Opening of Four New Spine Institutes, Writing Protocol for the Institute Review Board, Completing Analysis of the Spine Institutes Database, Researching for the Spine Institutes, Preparing the Necessary Documentation Needed to Approve Each Study **H/I/S:** Flamenco Dancing, Playing the Piano **EDU:** Master's Degree in Epidemiology, Columbia University (2006) **A/A/S:** American Public Health Association
Email: kkb47@columbia.edu
URL: http://www.wehealny.org

Ms. Catherine Anne Berg
Title: Poet **Address:** 1600 Bulevar Menor, Pensacola Beach, FL 32561 United States **BUS:** Self-Employed **P/S:** Poetry **MA:** Regional **D/D/R:** Writing Poetry on Topics Including Colors, Death and Babies **EDU:** Master's Degree, University of Texas at Dallas (2005) **A/A/S:** National Association of Women Writers
Email: bergblane@aol.com
URL: http://www.dallasartsrevue.com

Toni A. Berg

Title: School Nurse, Educator **Company:** Albuquerque Public Schools, New Future School **Address:** 5400 Cutler Avenue N.E., Albuquerque, NM 87110 United States **BUS:** School **P/S:** Education **MA:** Local **D/D/R:** Teaching Health and Parenting Education, Lactation Consulting **H/I/S:** Gardening, Spending Time with her Grandchildren **EDU:** Bachelor of Science in Nursing, University of New Mexico; Master of Science in Health Education, University of New Mexico **CERTS:** Registered Nurse Diploma, University of New Mexico; ICEA Certified Childbirth Educator; Licensed Health Educator, IBCLC **A/A/S:** Association of Women's Health Obstetric and Neonatal Nurses; Steering Committee, New Mexico Immunization Coalition; Sigma Theta Tau; International Childbirth Education Association; International Lactation Consultants Association **C/VW:** Program Planning Committee, New Mexico Breast Feeding Task Force; Albuquerque Biological Park, Rio Grande Zoo
Email: taberg@thuntek.net
URL: http://www.aps.edu

Dr. John Berger III

Title: Director of Cardiac Intensive Care **Company:** Children's National Medical Center **Address:** 111 Michigan Avenue N.W., Washington, DC 20010 United States **BUS:** Medical Center **P/S:** Healthcare **MA:** Regional **EXP:** Mr. Berger's expertise includes pediatric cardiology and critical-care medicine. **EDU:** MD, Washington University, St. Louis **A/A/S:** Society of Critical Care Medicine; American College of Cardiology; American Academy of Pediatrics; Pediatrics Cardiac Intensive Care Unit
Email: jberger@cnmc.org

Suzannah M. Berger-Koob

Title: Manager **Company:** Kaiser Permanente **Address:** 611 S. Milpitas Boulevard, Milpitas, CA 95035 United States **BUS:** Health Maintenance Organization **P/S:** Healthcare **MA:** National **D/D/R:** Managing Optical Services **H/I/S:** Gardening, Collecting Antiques **CERTS:** Certified, American Board of Opticianry **A/A/S:** American Board of Opticianry **C/VW:** American Diabetes Association; American Heart Association; Special Olympics; The Leukemia & Lymphoma Society
Email: makineyez@yahoo.com
URL: http://www.cambridgewhoswho.com

Susan J. Bergman

Title: Social Studies Teacher **Company:** Todd Beamer High School **Address:** 35999 16th Avenue S., Federal Way, WA 98003 United States **BUS:** High School **P/S:** Education **MA:** Local **D/D/R:** Teaching History to High School Students **H/I/S:** Coaching the Swim Team, Practicing Photography, Skiing, Boating **EDU:** Master of Education in Administration, Plus 60, University of Puget Sound, WA; Bachelor's Degree in Education, University of Portland **CERTS:** Pursuing National Board Certification **A/A/S:** Association for Supervision and Curriculum Development; National Education Association; Phi Delta Kappa; National Civic Government **C/VW:** Relay for Life, American Cancer Society; University of Portland Alumni Association
Email: sbergman@fwps.org

Jennette Bergstrom

Title: Director Medical Surgical **Company:** Exempla Saint Joseph **Address:** 1835 Franklin Street, Denver, CO 80218 United States **BUS:** Hospital **P/S:** Hospital **MA:** Local **EXP:** Ms. Bergstrom's expertise is in nursing leadership. **H/I/S:** Yoga Instructor, Skiing, Golfing **EDU:** Master of Science in Nursing, University of Colorado, Health and Science Center **A/A/S:** American Organization of Nursing Executives **C/VW:** Girl Scouts of the USA, Local Church
Email: j-bergstrom@comcast.net
URL: http://www.cambridgewhoswho.com

Joanne Berlingieri

Title: Broker **Company:** Margolis and Associates **Address:** 118 E. 28th Street, Suite 805, New York, NY 10016 United States **BUS:** Insurance Services **P/S:** Group and Individual, Medical and Life **MA:** Regional **EXP:** Ms. Berlingieri's expertise includes group and individual insurance. **H/I/S:** Spending Time with her Nieces and Nephews, Painting **EDU:** Bachelor of Science in Production Management and Textiles, Fashion Institute of Technology
Email: jberlingieri@aol.com
URL: http://www.cambridgewhoswho.com

Rafaela Bermudez, LPC

Title: Licensed Professional Counselor **Company:** Theracare and Alliance Associates **Address:** 2527 E. Ann Street, Philadelphia, PA 19134 United States **BUS:** Mental Healthcare and Education Organization **P/S:** Developmental, Educational and Evaluation Services for Children **MA:** Regional **D/D/R:** Working with Children with Emotional Problems, Making Assessments, Supervising Youth, Offering Drug and Alcohol Therapy, Offering Individual and Group Therapy, Overseeing Crisis Intervention **H/I/S:** Crafting **EDU:** Master's Degree in Human Services, Lincoln University (2000) **A/A/S:** Pi Gamma Mu; Executive Board Member, Hallahan High School
Email: danfae@verizon.net
URL: http://www.cambridgewhoswho.com

Mr. D. Douglas Bernard

Title: Owner, President **Company:** Tropical Commodities Inc. **Address:** 9230 N.W. 12th Street, Miami, FL 33172 United States **BUS:** Importation Company Specializing in Fresh Produce **P/S:** Fresh Produce and Chili Peppers **MA:** International **D/D/R:** Overseeing Importing **H/I/S:** Auto and Go Cart Racing, Owning and Running Pavos Sa in El Salvador to Grow, Process and Market Turkeys **EDU:** Master's Degree in International Commerce, Thunderbird School of Global Management (1968); Bachelor of Arts in Languages, Sociology, History and Economics, Wilmington Ohio College (1967) **A/A/S:** Peace Corps (1962, 1964)
Email: douglas@tropicalcommodies.com
URL: http://www.tropicalcommodities.com

Marla S. Bernard, RN, BSN, OCN

Title: Registered Nurse Case Manager **Company:** McKesson Health Solutions **Dept:** Disease Management Division **Address:** One Post Street, San Francisco, CA 94104 United States **BUS:** Managed Healthcare Facility **P/S:** Healthcare Benefits **MA:** National **D/D/R:** Practicing Oncology Nursing, Building Relationships with Patients, Coordinating Care and Home Health Services, Consulting, Training Staff Members **H/I/S:** Scrapbooking, Reading, Traveling **EDU:** Pursuing Master's Degree in Nursing, Northern Illinois University; Bachelor's Degree in Nursing, Rockford College; Registered Nurse, Rockford College; Diploma, White Station High School **CERTS:** Certified Oncology Nurse; **A/A/S:** Oncology Nursing Society; Faith Center **C/VW:** Volunteer Parish Nurse, Faith Center
Email: mochab3@aol.com

Donald Bernardin

Title: Co-Founder **Company:** Major Alliances **Address:** 4809 Avenue N., Suite 203, Brooklyn, NY 11234 United States **BUS:** Consulting Firm **P/S:** Consulting Services Including Teaching Tax Strategies and Incentives **MA:** Local **D/D/R:** Educating and Empowering Others Regarding Finance, Mentoring and Helping Others with Starting Businesses, Developing Strategies and Goals **H/I/S:** Traveling, Watching Movies, Playing Basketball and Football, Golfing **EDU:** Coursework, Queensborough Community College, St. John's University **CERTS:** Certified Emergency Medical Technician **A/A/S:** Manhattan Chamber of Commerce; Caribbean-American Chamber of Commerce; Leaders of Tomorrow
Email: donald@majoralliances.com
URL: http://www.majoralliances.com

Susanne M. Bernier

Title: Buyer **Company:** Archer Daniels Midland Company Cocoa (ADM) **Address:** 12500 W. Carmen Avenue, Milwaukee, WI 53225 United States **BUS:** One of the World's Largest Processors of Soybeans, Corn, Wheat, Cocoa, World Leader in Bioenergy **P/S:** Leading Manufacturer of Biodiesel, Ethanol, Soybean Oils and Meal, Corn Sweeteners, Flour and Other Value Added Food and Feed Ingredients **MA:** International **D/D/R:** Handling Sales, Customer Service and Traffic Coordination for Domestic and International Destinations **H/I/S:** Cooking, Baking, Gardening, Bowling, Walking her Eight-Year-Old Purebred Beagle **EDU:** High School Graduate (1981) **CERTS:** Certificates: One Day Course on Word for Windows (1997-2000); Attended Five Day Course in Fenton, Missouri; Mayflower/United to Learn Computer System (1997-98); Business Writing, One Day Course (2006)-Certificate Presented by Skillpath; Certificate of Completion, OTR Truck drivers Course (1997); Certificate 1977-78 WCTC Technical College for Floral Arranging **A/H:** First Place Chorus Ribbons, Medals and Awards, High School (1997-1981); First Place, DECA Speech Course (1981)
Email: susanne_bernier@admworld.com
URL: http://www.admworld.com

David W. Bernstein

Title: Partner **Company:** Clifford Chance US, LLP **Address:** 31 W. 52nd Street, New York, NY 10019 United States **BUS:** Law Firm **P/S:** Legal Services **MA:** International **EXP:** Mr. Bernstein's expertise includes mergers and acquisitions, securities and corporate governance. **EDU:** LLP, Harvard Law School, Magna Cum Laude; Bachelor's Degree in Economics, Harvard University **A/A/S:** Board of Trustees, International Preschools Incorporated; Board of Governors, Inwood Country Club **C/VW:** American Friends of Sadler's Wells, International Preschools Incorporated, Harvard University, Harvard Law School
Email: info@CambridgeWhosWho.com
URL: http://www.cambridgewhoswho.com

Kimberley Berridge

Title: Teacher **Company:** Colton Joint Unified School District **Address:** 1212 Valencia Drive, Colton, CA 92324 United States **BUS:** School District **P/S:** Education **MA:** Local **D/D/R:** Teaching Fifth-Grade Students **H/I/S:** Spending Time with her Family **EDU:** Bachelor's Degree in Education, The California State University **A/H:** Nation's Most Respected Teacher Award, Who's Who Among America's Teachers (2005-2006)
Email: Kimberley.Berridge@cwwemail.com
Email: jsducke@aol.com
URL: http://www.cambridgewhoswho.com

Franklin G. Berry

Title: President **Company:** Proseperity Expansion Group, LLP **Address:** 141 Fernery Road C4, Lakeland, FL 33809 United States **BUS:** Real Estate **P/S:** Real Estate Transactions **MA:** International **EXP:** Mr. Berry' expertise is in investment services. **H/I/S:** Swimming, Gardening **EDU:** D.Min, Rolent Wesleyan College **A/A/S:** USMC
Email: fberry2@gmail.com
URL: www.superiorelectricblankets.com

Martha Lynn Berry, RN, M.Div.

Title: Registered Nurse **Company:** HCA Johnston-Willis **Dept:** Chippenham **Address:** 2424 New Berne Road, Richmond, VA 23228 United States **BUS:** Hospital **P/S:** Healthcare **MA:** Regional **D/D/R:** Consulting with Patients, Interacting with Family People, Monitoring Patients, Generating Reports, Overseeing Psychiatric Care Nursing **H/I/S:** Horseback Riding, Swimming, Shooting Range, Listening to Music, Artwork, Reading **EDU:** Master's Degree in Theology, Virginia Theological Seminary (1976) **CERTS:** Registered Nurse (2004); Certification in CPR **A/A/S:** Honor Society; NRA
Email: marthalynn.berry@cwwemail.com

Joseph C. Berti Sr.

Title: Director of Operations **Company:** Premier Aviation, LLC **Address:** 312 Sassafras Street, Brown Mills, NJ 08015 United States **BUS:** Aviation Company **P/S:** Air Ambulance Transportation Service **MA:** National **D/D/R:** Managing and Overseeing Flight Operations for an FAR Part 135 Air Carrier **H/I/S:** Flying, Camping, Spending Time Outdoors, Sports **EDU:** Master in Business Administration, TUI University; Bachelor of Science in Aeronautics, Saint Louis University **CERTS:** Airline Transport Pilot Certification in Fixed Wing and Rotor Wing Aircraft, Federal Aviation Administration; Five Flight Instructor Ratings; Three Ground Instructor Ratings **A/A/S:** US Airline Pilots Association; National Association of Flight Instructors; Airborne Law Enforcement Association; National Guard Association of the United States; Air Force Association; Experimental Aircraft Association; Aircraft Owners and Pilot Association **C/VW:** Youth Group; Local Church
Email: jbertisr@aol.com
URL: http://www.cambridgewhoswho.com

Bobbi J. Berton

Title: Administrator **Company:** RGM Medical Management, Inc. **Address:** 500 Rugh Street, Greensburg, PA 15601 United States **BUS:** Healthcare Center **P/S:** Healthcare Including Weight Loss Services **MA:** National **D/D/R:** Overseeing Administrative Duties **H/I/S:** Horseback Riding **EDU:** Associate of Arts in Business, Western School of Health & Business Careers (Now Sanford-Brown Institute) **C/VW:** Local Church
Email: drbobs@wvdsl.net
URL: http://www.cambridgewhoswho.com

Mr. Perry P. Berube

Title: Owner **Company:** Berube's Diesel Repair **Address:** 33708 150 Street S.W., Euclid, MN 56722 United States **BUS:** Automotive Business **P/S:** Diesel Repair and Sales **MA:** North America **D/D/R:** Engine Rebuilding and Repairing Transmissions on Tractors and Trucks, Handling All Administrative Responsibilities, Training of Hired Students, with Close to 30 **H/I/S:** Riding and Training Quarter Horses, Fishing **EDU:** Mechanics Degree, North Dakota State School of Science (1978)
Email: berubediesel@wiktel.com
URL: http://www.cambridgewhoswho.com

James Louis Besier, Ph.D.

Title: Barcode Medication Administrator **Company:** Health Alliance **Address:** 914 Cedarpark Drive, Cincinnati, OH 45233 United States **BUS:** Healthcare Center **P/S:** Healthcare **MA:** Regional **D/D/R:** Directing Pharmacy and Residency Programs **H/I/S:** Swimming, Biking **EDU:** Ph.D. in Organizational Behavior, Union Institute & University (2004); Coursework, University of Cincinnati College of Nursing **A/A/S:** Adjunct Professor, The James L. Winkle College of Pharmacy, University of Cincinnati; American Association of Colleges of Pharmacy **A/H:** Fellow, American Society of Health-System Pharmacists
Email: jim.besier@healthall.com
URL: http://www.cambridgewhoswho.com

Doris Y. Best

Title: Owner **Company:** Dory Enterprises, LLC **Address:** 9410 Thorpe Road, Berlin Heights, OH 44814 United States **BUS:** Tax Preparation Firm **P/S:** Accounting, Tax Preparation **MA:** Local **D/D/R:** accounting, processing payroll and IRS audits. **H/I/S:** Making Crafts, Sewing **CERTS:** Enrolled Agent (1994) **A/A/S:** Ohio State Society of Enrolled Agents; National Association of Enrolled Agents
Email: dorytaxbob@aol.com
URL: http://www.cambridgewhoswho.com

Mary Sue Best

Title: President **Company:** Best Speakers **Address:** 5402 Washington Boulevard, Indianapolis, IN 46220 United States **BUS:** Sole Proprietorship **P/S:** Writing, Speaking Engagements, Organizing Classes, Seminars and Biographies of Patriots **MA:** National **D/D/R:** writing, public speaking, teaching writing and early American history. **H/I/S:** Gardening, Caring for her Pets **EDU:** Master's Degree in English, The University of Mississippi **A/A/S:** President, Indianapolis Women's Club; National Society of Arts and Letters; President, Fortnight Lee Literary Club; American Association of University Women; National League of American Pen Women; The International Platform Association
Email: davidmarysue@earthlink.net
URL: http://www.cambridgewhoswho.com

Sommer M. Bethel

Title: Dean of Studies **Company:** St. Genevieve High School **Address:** 13967 Roscoe Boulevard, Panorama City, CA 91402 United States **BUS:** Public High School **P/S:** Secondary Education **MA:** Local **D/D/R:** Conducting Interviews, Hiring New Teachers as a Human Resources Director, Overseeing the Student Panel Interviewing Teachers, Spearheading Online Learning, Heading Up Curriculum and Development **H/I/S:** Cheerleading, Dancing **EDU:** Master's Degree in Education, National University, San Diego, CA (2005) **A/A/S:** Dancer, Universal Dance Academy
Email: sommerbethel@hotmail.com
URL: http://www.valiantspirit.com

Mr. Frank W. Bettencourt

Title: Dance Orchestra Leader and Arranger (Retired) **Company:** Frank Bettencourt Orchestra **Address:** 3521 Belle Meade Lane, Birmingham, AL 35223 United States **BUS:** Music **P/S:** Big Band Leader, Arranger **MA:** Local **H/I/S:** Swimming, Spending Time with his Family **EDU:** College Degree in Music, San Jose State University (1937) **A/A/S:** Phi Mu Alpha

Dr. Sandra J. Bevacqua

Title: Owner, President **Company:** World Integrated Systems in Health **Address:** 4627 N. 1st Avenue, Suite 2, Tucson, AZ 85718 United States **BUS:** Health Education Consultation Company **P/S:** Health Education, Helping Individual with Blood Chemistry **MA:** International **D/D/R:** Teaching, Nutrition, Food Science, Balancing Blood Chemistry through Diet and Lifestyle **H/I/S:** Skiing, Horseback Riding, Medication, Playing Ju-Jitsu Karate **EDU:** Ph.D. in Molecular Biology, University of Arizona Medical Center (1989); Bachelor of Science in Biology and Marine Science, Pennsylvania State University (1977) **A/A/S:** Phi Beta Kappa; Board Member, American Society for Cell Biology; American Association for the Advancement of Science
Email: wish2@cox.net
URL: http://www.wish4life.com

Dr. David L. Bevett

Title: Clinical Psychologist **Company:** Dr. David Bevett **Address:** Honolulu, HI **BUS:** Private Practice **P/S:** Healthcare **MA:** Local **EXP:** Dr. Bevett's expertise includes marital, family, adolescent, child, substance abuse and dependence therapy, treating post-traumatic stress, stress management counseling and consultation. **D/D/R:** Lecturing at the University **H/I/S:** Singing, Playing Conga and the Bongo Drums, Composing Music, Practicing Martial Arts, Dancing **EDU:** Ph.D. in Clinical Psychology, Rutgers University; Post-Doctorate Degree in Medical Psychology, Uniformed University of Health Sciences; Master of Social Work, Rutgers University; Master of Clinical Psychology, Rutgers University; Bachelor of Science in Biology and English, Seton Hall University **CERTS:** Licensed Psychologist, States of Hawaii and Colorado; Certification of Professional Qualification in Psychology; Diploma in Marriage and Family Counseling **A/A/S:** Association of State and Provisional Psychology Boards; Oahu Hawaii Native American Warrior Circle Dancing Group; American Psychology Association; National Indian Educational Association **A/H:** Fellow, The Academy of Family Psychology **C/VW:** Local Charitable Organizations; Veterans of Foreign Wars
Email: shawnee161@hotmail.com

Debra Beye-Barwick

Title: Chief Executive Officer, Treas **Company:** The Florida Research Institute for Equine Nurturing, Development and Safety Inc.A/K/A F.R.I.E.N.D.S., INC. **Address:** 1840 N.E. 65th Court, Fort Lauderdale, FL 33308 United States **BUS:** Nonprofit 501 3 (C) Horse Rescue for Horses Afflicted with EIA **P/S:** Horse Rescue Current Herd 56 Head of Horses **MA:** International **D/D/R:** Maintaining a Safe Haven for Horses Infected with Equine Infectious Anemia, Working with Various Researchers to Find a Cure or Vaccine for Equine Infectious Anemia, Collaborating with the USDA, the State of Florida and the University of Kentucky **H/I/S:** Caring for Horses Freelance Equine Photography **CERTS:** Certified Equine Science Instructor **C/VW:** FRIENDS., Inc.
Email: horserescuer@comcast.net
URL: http://www.eiahorses.org

Thad L. Beyle

Title: Professor Emeritus **Company:** University of North Carolina Chapel Hill **Dept:** Political Science Department **Address:** Hamilton Hall, Chapel Hill, NC 27599 United States **BUS:** University **P/S:** Higher Education **MA:** National **D/D/R:** Teaching Political Science to College Students **H/I/S:** Playing Tennis, Golfing, Spending Time at the Beach, Reading **EDU:** Ph.D. in American Government (1963); Master's Degree in Russian Studies, Syracuse University (1959); Bachelor of Arts in Political Science, Syracuse University (1956) **A/A/S:** Former Board Member, Midwest Political Science Association; Former Board Member, Southern Political Science Association; The American Political Science Association; Public Administration Association **C/VW:** Local Charitable Organizations
Email: beyle@email.umc.edu
URL: http://www.umc.edu

Avneesh K. Bhai

Title: Medical Doctor **Company:** Kaiser Permanente **Address:** 12001 W. Washington Boulevard, Los Angeles, CA 90066 United States **BUS:** Hospital **P/S:** Healthcare **MA:** California **EXP:** Ms. Bhai's expertise includes acupuncture and family medicine. **H/I/S:** Listening to Music, Traveling **EDU:** MD in Family Medicine; Residency, California Hospital Medical Center **A/A/S:** Mentor, University of California at Los Angeles **A/H:** National Diabetes Association Award (2007)
Email: akbhai@kp.org

Amit Bharat

Title: Partner **Company:** Lees Management, LLC **Address:** 2903 Hamilton Street, West Hyattsville, MD 20782 United States **BUS:** Hospitality Management Company **P/S:** Hospitality Services Including Restaurant, Bar and Liquor Store **MA:** Local **EXP:** Mr. Bharat's expertise is in operations management. **H/I/S:** Playing Table Tennis and Chess **EDU:** Master of Business Administration in Finance, University of Delhi
Email: amitbharat4u@yahoo.com
Email: amitbharat4u@aol.com
URL: http://www.onebaltimore.com

Bianca L. Biagioni

Title: President, Chief Executive Officer, Producer **Company:** B.A.D. Entertainment, Inc. **Address:** 4151 Prospect Avenue, Suite 140, Los Angeles, CA 90027 United States **BUS:** Production Company, Entertainment Industry **P/S:** Films, Television Programs **MA:** National **D/D/R:** Producing, Directing, Writing and Co-Directing Films and Television Programs **EDU:** Bachelor's Degree in Communications, University of Miami (2004)
Email: biancabiagioni@badentertainment.com

John N. Biasi

Title: Real Estate Broker **Company:** Prudential Rand Realty **Address:** 2 Corporate Drive, Suite 201, Central Valley, NY 10917 United States **BUS:** Real Estate Agency **P/S:** Real Estate **MA:** Local **EXP:** Mr. Biasi's expertise includes the relocation and the negotiation of residential, commercial and investment properties. **H/I/S:** Golfing, Motorcycling **EDU:** High School Education **A/A/S:** National Association of Realtors; New York State Association of Realtors; Chamber of Commerce **A/H:** Prudential Chairman Award (Five Times); Top Agent in Seven Offices
Email: john.biasi@prudentialrand.com
URL: http://www.prudentialrand.com

Beverly S. Biben

Title: Owner **Company:** A Class Act **Address:** 7009 Heatherhill Road, Bethesda, MD 20817 United States **BUS:** Gift Baskets, Gourmet Foods, Fine Gifts for All Occasions **P/S:** Customized Hand-Created Gifts and Gift Baskets for Both Individual and Corporate Giving **MA:** International **EXP:** Ms. Biben's expertise includes the creation of corporate and personal gifts and gift baskets. **H/I/S:** Golf, Tennis, Gardening **EDU:** George Washington University **A/A/S:** The Business Resource Network Group; Woodmont Country Club; President Auxiliary of Medical Society of District of Columbia **A/H:** Annual Award, Metropolitan Washington Public Health Association (1989); Benjamin Nickols Award, Medical Society of Washington, D.C.(1989)
Email: aclassact@comcast.net
URL: http://www.a-class-act.com

Rebecca Susan Bickham

Title: Assistant Principal **Company:** Crescent Elementary and Junior High School **Address:** 62575 Bayou Road, Plaquemine, LA 70764 United States **BUS:** Elementary and Junior High School **P/S:** Education **MA:** Local **D/D/R:** ensuring discipline, counseling, monitoring and managing administrative and enrollment programs. **H/I/S:** Gardening, Scuba Diving, Fishing **EDU:** Master's Degree in Educational Administration and Supervision, Plus 30 (1987); Bachelor of Arts in Health and Physical Education, Southeastern University (1972) **CERTS:** Certification in Health, Physical Education, Science, Mathematics and Adult Education **A/A/S:** Louisiana Association of Principals; Louisiana Association of Administrators
Email: becbic@cox.net
Email: bickhamb@jpsb.net

William J. Bieker

Title: Funeral Director, Coordinating Manager **Company:** DO McComb and Sons Funeral Home **Address:** 1140 Lake Avenue, Ft Wayne, IN 46805 United States **BUS:** Funeral Home **P/S:** Embalming, Funerals, Transportation **MA:** National **EXP:** Mr. Beiker's expertise includes embalming and cosmetology. **H/I/S:** Auto Racing **EDU:** Associate in Mortuary Sciences, Indiana College of Mortuary Service
Email: biercr@aol.com

Paul Big Bear

Title: Entertainer **Company:** The Party Continues **Address:** PO Box 332, Abington, PA 19001 United States **BUS:** Entertainment Provider **P/S:** Singing, Acting, Comedy, Fundraising **MA:** International **D/D/R:** Acting, Singing, Directing, Comedy **H/I/S:** Reading, Traveling, Writing **EDU:** Bachelor of Science in Horticulture, Pennsylvania State University; Doctor of Divinity, Ambassador College, CA **A/A/S:** BMI, ASCAP, SAG, Chamber of Commerce, Golden Heart
Email: paulbigbear@aol.com
URL: www.thepartycontinues.net

Lenore M. Bilinski

Title: Teacher of Physical Education and Health **Company:** Auburn High School **Address:** 250 Lake Avenue, Auburn, NY 13021 United States **BUS:** Public High School **P/S:** Public Secondary Education **MA:** Regional **D/D/R:** Teaching Physical and Health Education to Secondary Education, Coaching Junior Varsity Hockey, Basketball, Volleyball and Softball, Overseeing the Aquatic Program for a Boys Summer Camp **H/I/S:** Traveling **EDU:** Master's Degree in Health Education, SUNY Cortland (2003); Bachelor's Degree in Physical Education, SUNY Cortland (2001) **A/A/S:** AAFERD
Email: lisunbum@aol.com

Janelle S. Billings

Title: EMT Instructor **Company:** South Texas College **Address:** 909 Palmetto Drive, Mission, TX 78574 United States **BUS:** College **P/S:** Training, Emergency Medical Responders **MA:** Local **D/D/R:** Teaching Emergency Medical Technician Courses as a Clinical Instructor **EDU:** Associate of Arts in Emergency Medical Technician Studies, South Texas College **A/A/S:** National Association of EMS Instructors
Email: billings@southtexascollege.edu

Margery P. Bilskie

Title: Infection Control Specialist **Company:** Herman Family Dental **Address:** 706 S 15th Street, Vincennes, IN 47591 United States **BUS:** Dental Office **P/S:** Sterilize Instruments **MA:** Local **D/D/R:** Overseeing Administrative Duties **H/I/S:** Fishing, Grand Children **EDU:** Lincoln, High School
Email: info@CambridgeWhosWho.com

Louise A. Binette

Title: Owner **Company:** Custom Draperies **Address:** 33 Oxford Street, Sanford, ME 04073 United States **BUS:** Custom Drapery Company **P/S:** Drapes-Blind Shades **MA:** Local **EXP:** Ms. Binette's expertise is in window treatments. **H/I/S:** Skiing **EDU:** Champlain College, One Year of College in Accounting **A/A/S:** Chamber of Commerce
Email: info@CambridgeWhosWho.com

Deborah L. Bird

Title: Owner **Company:** Bird and Associates **Address:** P.O. Box 27418, San Diego, CA 92198 United States **BUS:** Consulting Firm **P/S:** Business, Medical and Information Technology Consulting **MA:** Regional **D/D/R:** Addressing Staff Complaints, Injury Cases, Medical Malpractice **EDU:** Pursuing Ph.D. in Nursing; Master of Science in Nursing, University of Phoenix **CERTS:** Registered Nurse **A/A/S:** Rehabilitation Nurse Coordinators Network; American Association of Lutheran Churches; VVNPT; Sigma Theta Tau **C/VW:** Veterans of Foreign Wars; Daughters of the American Revolution
Email: admin@birdassoc.com
URL: http://www.birdassoc.com

Brenda L. Birdow

Title: Computer Science Staff IV **Company:** United Space Alliance **Address:** 1150 Gemini, Houston, TX 77058 United States **BUS:** Space Shuttle Program **P/S:** Aerospace **MA:** International **EXP:** Ms. Birdow's expertise is in configuration management. **D/D/R:** Assisting the Space Shuttle Program **H/I/S:** Reading, Solving Cross Word Puzzles **EDU:** Master's Degree in Criminology, University of Houston at Clearlake **C/VW:** Volunteer, Juvenile Probation Center; United Way, Hurricane Katrina Fund
Email: blbirdow@aol.com

David Matthew Birr
Title: President **Company:** Synchronous Energy Solutions, Inc. **Address:** 329 Woodview Road, Apt. D, Lake Barrington, IL 60010 United States **BUS:** Energy and Environmental Engineering Company **P/S:** Energy and Environmental Engineering **MA:** Regional **EXP:** Mr. Birr's expertise is in energy performance contracting. **H/I/S:** Playing Tennis **EDU:** Bachelor of Science in Industrial Engineering, Northwestern University; Graduate Coursework **A/A/S:** National Accreditation Committee; National Association of Energy Service Companies
Email: davebirr@aol.com
URL: http://www.cambridgewhoswho.com

Sherri L. Bischoff
Title: Office Manager **Company:** Partnership for Excellence **Address:** 620 Southpointe Court, Colorado Springs, CO 80906 United States **BUS:** Dentists Office **P/S:** Family Dentistry, Implants, Bone Grafting **MA:** Local **D/D/R:** Managing the Organization **H/I/S:** Traveling, Hiking **EDU:** Bachelor of Science in Organizational Management, Colorado Christian University **A/A/S:** American Dental Association **C/VW:** Better Health Naturally, Health Advocate
Email: sherri@johnsondds.com
URL: http://www.cambridgewhoswho.com

April Bishop
Title: Director of Spiritual Care, Deaconess **Company:** Lutheran Social Services of the South **Address:** 5638 Medical Center Drive, Katy, TX 77494 United States **BUS:** Social Services Organization **P/S:** Social Services **MA:** Local **EXP:** Ms. Bishop's expertise is in theology. **H/I/S:** Horseback Riding **EDU:** Bachelor's Degree in Theology, Concordia University **A/A/S:** Phi Beta Kappa **C/VW:** Community Outreach Programs
Email: aprillynnkaty@yahoo.com
URL: http://www.cambridgewhoswho.com

Mr. Robert M. Bishop
Title: Client Services Administrator **Company:** United States Air Force **Dept:** 28th CES/CERW **Address:** 2103 Scott Drive, Ellsworth Air Force Base, SD 57706 United States **BUS:** United States Military **P/S:** Combat Aircrafts, Airlifts, Refueling Services, Reconnaissance, Developing Airmen, Technology-to-Warfighting **MA:** International **D/D/R:** Maintaining the Network for the Base and 350 Computer Systems, Installing and Maintaining Software, Offering Project Management **H/I/S:** Playing Computer Games and Softball, Bowling, Reading **EDU:** Master of Business Administration, National American University (2007); Bachelor's Degree in Information Technology and Networking, National American University (2005); Bachelor's Degree in Professional Aeronautics, Embry Riddle Aeronautical University (1997) **A/A/S:** Former Vice Commander, American Legion POST 315 **A/H:** Who's Who in American Colleges and Universities (2006)
Email: robert.bishop@ellsworth.af.mil
URL: http://www.af.mil

Wanda A. Bittues
Title: Human Resource Director **Company:** Ca-Par Electric, Inc. **Address:** P.O. Box 1323, Kenner, LA 70063 United States **BUS:** Electrical Company **P/S:** Electrical Utilities, High Voltage Cable System Analysis and Design, Hypot and Engineering Services, Industrial Services, New Construction and Repair, Switchgear and Distribution Voice, Data and Video, Security Systems, Fire Alarms, Data Wiring **MA:** Regional **D/D/R:** Managing Employees, Finance Management, General Human Resources **H/I/S:** Gardening, Spending Time with her Family **EDU:** Associate Degree Plus 90 Credits in Office Management, Houghton College **A/A/S:** Associated Builders and Contractors; Women in Construction; Women in Business Entrepreneurs New Construction **C/VW:** Carriere Baptist Church; Goodwill
Email: w.bittues@ca-par.com
URL: http://www.ca-par.com

Jonathon T. Bixler
Title: Manager **Company:** OHC Environmental Engineering, Inc. **Dept:** Asbestos Project **Address:** 5118 N. 56th Street, Suite 215, Tampa, FL 33610 United States **BUS:** Environmental Consulting Company **P/S:** Environmental Consulting Services Including Construction, Project Management, Industrial Hygiene Programs, Laboratory Services, On-Site Training, Asbestos Projects, Facility Surveys and Assessment and Indoor Air Quality Assessments **MA:** Regional **D/D/R:** managing asbestos, leading projects, environmental consulting, collecting and monitoring samples. **H/I/S:** Working on Computers **EDU:** Bachelor of Science in Civil Engineering, Tri-State University (1995) **CERTS:** Certified Hazardous Materials Manager **A/A/S:** American Society of Civil Engineers; Institute of Hazardous Materials Management
Email: jbixler@tampabay.rr.com
URL: http://www.ohcnet.com

Laura Anne Bjorgo
Title: Accounts Manager **Company:** City's Best Marketing **Address:** 10740 Lyndale Avenue S., Bloomington, MN 55420 United States **BUS:** Marketing and Advertising Agency **P/S:** Marketing Strategies, Sales Promotion, Direct Response Advertising **MA:** Twin Cities Metropolitan Area **D/D/R:** Overseeing Sales, Marketing, Advertising, Managing Client Accounts **EDU:** Bachelor of Arts in Advertising and Journalism, South Dakota State University **A/A/S:** Board of Directors, Bloomington Chamber of Commerce; Former Member, Rotary Club of Bloomington
Email: laurab@c-b-m.com
URL: http://www.c-b-m.com

Doug Black
Title: Retail Buyer **Company:** Steinmart **Address:** 1200 Riverplace Boulevard, Jacksonville, FL 32207 United States **BUS:** Department Store **P/S:** Full-Service Department Store **MA:** National **EXP:** Mr. Black's expertise is in home décor. **H/I/S:** Soccer, Traveling, Spending Time with Sons **EDU:** Bachelor's Degree in Business, Harrogate University **C/VW:** Humane Society, Habijack
Email: dougblack67@yahoo.com
URL: http://www.cambridgewhoswho.com

Monica M. Black
Title: Laboratory Shift Supervisor **Company:** Upper Chesapeake Health **Address:** 501 S. Union Avenue, Harve De Grace, MD 21078 **BUS:** Hospital **P/S:** Healthcare **MA:** Local **D/D/R:** Overseeing Laboratory Medical Technologists **H/I/S:** Traveling, Reading **EDU:** Bachelor of Science in Medical Technology, University of Santo Thomas **CERTS:** Certified, American Society of Clinical Pathologists **A/A/S:** American Society of Clinical Pathologists **C/VW:** Community Organizations
Email: labh.moba@mt.uchs.org
URL: http://www.cambridgewhoswho.com

Susan W. Black
Title: Owner/Receptionist/Manager **Company:** Silver Memories/John B Harrison, DDS, MSc **Address:** 545 4th Avenue S, St Petersburg, FL 33701 United States **BUS:** Dental Office **P/S:** Healthcare, Orthodontics, Beautiful Smiles, Jewelry Maker **MA:** Local **D/D/R:** Interacting with People **H/I/S:** Jewelry Making, Bead Work, Silver Smithing **EDU:** Orange County Community College **A/A/S:** Sun Coast Gem and Mineral Association, PARC, CASA
Email: sueblack@tampabay.com

Sharon E. Blackford
Title: Teacher of Functional Skills **Company:** Central Noble Middle and High School **Address:** 302 Cougar Court, Albion, IN 46701 United States **BUS:** High School **P/S:** Secondary Education **MA:** Local **EXP:** Ms. Blackford's expertise is in special education. **D/D/R:** organizing career guidance programs for high school students. **H/I/S:** Gardening, Landscaping, Spending Time with her Family **EDU:** Master of Arts in Special Education
Email: blackfords@centralnoble.k12.in.us

Diane L. Blackmon
Title: Program Coordinator for Kenosha eSchool **Company:** Kenosha Unified School District **Dept:** Kenosha eSchool **Address:** 3600 52nd Street, Kenosha, WI 53144 United States **BUS:** Public School District Serving Residents of Kenosha **P/S:** Empowerment for All Students through Diverse and Challenging Opportunities to Learn through the Collaborative Efforts of Students, Families, Community and Staff **MA:** Regional **D/D/R:** Handling Online Programming Projects, Teaching Mathematics, Counseling Students **H/I/S:** Enjoying Music **EDU:** Master's Degree in Educational Computing, Cardinal Stritch University (1993) **A/A/S:** Wisconsin Charter School Association; North American Council for Online Learning
Email: dblackmo@kusd.edu
URL: http://www.eschool.kusd.edu

Philicia J. Blacknall
Title: Executive Administrator **Company:** Bethel Christian Center **Address:** 99 Catherine Street, Red Bank, NJ 07701 United States **BUS:** Church **P/S:** Serving People, Love for God, Family Oriented **MA:** Local **D/D/R:** Scheduling Pastors, Making Appointments, Ensuring Peace and Harmony in the Church **H/I/S:** Travel, Reading Magazines, Crossword Puzzles **EDU:** Some College, High School Diploma **A/A/S:** Family Day Care Facility; Love Inc; Aslan Youth Ministry
Email: pblacknall@aol.com

Lois Butler Blackstone
Title: Owner, Director **Company:** Kinder Kastle Child Care **Address:** 1709 W. Jefferson Street, Quincy, FL 32351 United States **BUS:** Private Facility Committed to Excellence in Education and Day Care **P/S:** Teaching Children Ages 1-12 **MA:** Regional **D/D/R:** Teaching Social Skills to 1-4 Year Olds, Working with and Caring for 30 Children, Preparing the Curriculum for Preschool Focusing on Social Skills and the Alphabet, Overseeing the Older Children, Serving Breakfast, Lunch and Snacks **H/I/S:** Music, Playing Guitar, Playing Piano, Watching the Dallas Cowboys **EDU:** Bachelor of Science in Early Childhood Education, Northwestern International University (2006) **CERTS:** National Child Development Associate Credentials, Council for Professional Recognition (2004); Child Development Specialist Credentials; Director Credentials, Department of (2003) **A/A/S:** National Association of Early Childhood Educators **A/H:** Bronze Business Member, Florida Sheriff's Association; Small Business Service Award, Florida A&M University (2004)
Email: leonblack28@netscape.com
URL: http://www.cambridgewhoswho.com

Mickey J. Blackwell
Title: Owner **Company:** Pro Construction **Address:** 303 W. Clark Street, Hiawatha, IA 52233 United States **BUS:** Construction Company **P/S:** Construction Services **MA:** Regional **D/D/R:** Remodeling Kitchens, Bathrooms and Basements, Installing Windows and Sheetrock **H/I/S:** Golfing, Fishing, Traveling **A/A/S:** National Association of Home Builders
Email: mickey306215@aol.com

Ms. Wendy A. Blackwell
Title: Buyer **Company:** Costco Wholesale **Address:** 1901 West 22nd Street, Second Floor, Oak Brook, IL 60523 United States **BUS:** Wholesale Company **P/S:** Selling Quality Products for the Best Prices with Discount, High Quality Brands in Food, Jewelry, Electronics, Caskets **MA:** National **D/D/R:** Managing Over 46 Locations Nationally and Regionally, Finding New Items in the Food Sector, Overseeing 350 Million in Sales and Inventory Control **H/I/S:** Watching Hockey, Sewing, Baking, Fastball **EDU:** Bachelor's Degree in Elementary Education, Bridgewater State College (1991) **C/VW:** Fundraiser, Children's Hospital
Email: wblackwell@costco.com

Georgia W. Blaha
Title: Dietitian **Company:** AD Medical Supply **Address:** 8148 Clarendon Hills Road, Willowbrook, IL 60527 United States **BUS:** Home Health Agency **P/S:** Medical Nutrition Therapy, Medical Equipment **MA:** Local **EXP:** Ms. Blaha's expertise includes diabetes and enteral feeding management. **H/I/S:** Working Out, Gardening **EDU:** University of Illinois at Chicago, BS **A/A/S:** Past Member, American Dietetic Association
Email: eggplant100@comcast.net

Karen Elaine Blair
Title: Faculty Professor **Company:** The Pennsylvania State University **Address:** 315 Health and Human Development East Building, University Park, PA 16802 United States **BUS:** University **P/S:** Higher Education **MA:** Statewide **EXP:** Ms. Blair's expertise includes healthcare administration and health sciences. **D/D/R:** Teaching Science, Health and Human Development, Healthcare Administration and Community Development, Working with International Programs and Local and State Governments **H/I/S:** Traveling, Playing Tennis, Sailing, Running **EDU:** Ph.D., The Pennsylvania State University (1999); Master of Education, The Pennsylvania State University (1996); Bachelor of Science, Respiratory Care, Indiana University of Pennsylvania (1987) **CERTS:** Licensed Registered Care Practitioner, Certified Pulmonary Function Technologist **A/A/S:** ADA Sigma Gamma; American Association for Respiratory Care; Vice President, Main Street Program, Pennsylvania Downtown Center; Board of Directors, Moshannon Valley Economic Development Partnership; The Pennsylvania Centre Orchestra; The English Speaking Union of the United States Central Pennsylvania Branch; Counselor, The Atlantic Council of the United States; The Rowland Theatre Inc.; ALTRUSA International; Kiwanis International; University Women's Club; American Association of Respiratory Care; American Alliance for Health, Physical Education, Recreation and Dance; Former Member, Critical Care Society **C/VW:** Board Member, The Pennsylvania Centre Orchestra
Email: keb166@psu.edu
URL: http://www.cambridgewhoswho.com

Betty J. Blair-Klemensich
Title: Elementary Teacher **Company:** Babbitt-Embarrass School District 2142 **Address:** 30 South Drive, Babbitt, MN 55706 United States **BUS:** School District **P/S:** Education **MA:** Local **D/D/R:** Teaching **H/I/S:** Playing Saxophone in a Band **EDU:** Master's Degree in Reading, University of Minnesota **A/A/S:** International Reading Association; Minnesota Reading Association
Email: bettyreads3@yahoo.com
URL: http://www.cambridgewhoswho.com

Phil Blake, MD
Title: Urologist Company: Lake Jackson Urology Address: 188 Abner Jackson Parkway, Lake Jackson, TX 77566 United States BUS: Medical Practice P/S: Adult and Pediatric Urological Care MA: Local EXP: Mr. Blake's expertise is general urology. H/I/S: Reading, Camping, Spending Time with Family EDU: MD, The Johns Hopkins Medical School BA, Princeton University A/A/S: Texas Medical Association; American Medical Association; Fellow American College of Surgeons C/VW: Church, Community Service
URL: http://www.ljurology.com

Jessica L. Blakeney
Title: Office Manager, Team Leader Company: TMC Orthopedic, LLP Address: 1000 S. Loop, W. Suite150, Houston, TX 77054 United States BUS: Orthopedic Company P/S: Orthotics and Prosthetics MA: Local D/D/R: Managing Five Locations, Assuring Quality, Fitting Braces, Precertifying Incoming Patients, Verifying Insurance, Coding, Billing H/I/S: Playing Sports EDU: Bachelor of Science in Athletic Training, University of Alabama (2001) CERTS: Certified Athletic Trainer A/A/S: Golden Key National Honor Society
Email: bamajlb@aol.com
URL: http://www.tmcortho.com

Sharon A. Blancarte
Title: Administrator Company: Dr Blancarte, MD Address: 1701 W Ben White Blvd Suite 140, Austin, TX 78704 United States BUS: Private Practice P/S: Internal Medicine Practice MA: Local D/D/R: Overseeing Business Operations Including Purchasing H/I/S: Sewing EDU: Bachelor of Arts in Microbiology, University of Texas, Austin; Bachelor of Science in Medical Technology A/A/S: Former Member, Travis County Medical Alliance
Email: sharon@drblancarte.com
URL: www.drblancarte.com

Marlene Carol Blanchard
Title: Owner Company: Court Street Dairy Lunch Address: 347 Court Street N.E., Salem, OR 97301 United States BUS: Restaurant P/S: Fresh Homemade Food Including Muffins and Soups, Carefully Chosen Produce MA: Regional D/D/R: Serving Breakfast and Lunch H/I/S: Working with Computers, Reading EDU: Coursework in Home Economics and Bookkeeping, Johnson High School, Saint Paul, MN
Email: leanmeanbaby2@aol.com
URL: http://www.cambridgewhoswho.com

Leah Y. Blanchfield
Title: Assistant to the Vice President for Student Development Company: North Park University Address: 3225 W. Foster Avenue, Chicago, IL 60625 United States BUS: University P/S: Higher Education MA: International EXP: Ms. Blanchfield's expertise is in time management. H/I/S: Reading, Cooking A/A/S: American Student Government Association C/VW: Save the Children
Email: lblanchfield@northpark.edu
URL: http://www.northpark.edu

Mirna D. Blanco
Title: Teacher Company: New York City Department of Education Address: 3050 Webster Avenue, Bronx, NY 10467 United States BUS: Public Education P/S: Instruction and Curriculum MA: Local D/D/R: Teaching English as a Second Language, Mathematics and Science, Practicing Exceptional Classroom Management, Offering Excellent Communication and Relation Skills for Both Students and Parents H/I/S: Dancing, Reading EDU: Pursuing Master's Degree in Teaching English as a Second Language, Mercy College; Bachelor of Science in Elementary Education, Baruch College (1999) A/A/S: National Council of Teachers of English as a Second Language; Bilingual Association of Teachers
Email: reddalia55@aol.com
URL: http://schools.nyc.gov/default.aspx

Mabel R. Bland
Title: Founder, Owner Company: M. Bland Billing Service Address: P.O. Box 1234, Bronx, NY 10466 United States BUS: Medical Billing Company P/S: Insurance and Patient Billing for Family Practitioners, Internists and Pediatricians MA: Local EXP: Mrs. Bland's expertise includes the management of administrative duties and marketing. D/D/R: Overseeing Claim Submissions, Posting Payments and Claims Inquiries, Managing Patient Follow-Ups and Billing, Overseeing Appeals, Processing Claims for Private Practices H/I/S: Spending Time with her Family, Reading, Enjoying Nature EDU: New York State Regents Diploma in Medical Claims and Billing Specialist Studies, The Bronx High School of Science A/A/S: Wildlife Conservancy Society A/H: Outstanding Graduate of the Year, Weston Distance Learning, Inc. (2007)
Email: mbbs@optonline.net
URL: http://www.cambridgewhoswho.com

Todd D. Blank
Title: Principal Company: Todd Blank Design Address: 1539 Filbert Street, San Francisco, CA 94123 United States BUS: Design and Communications Company P/S: Corporate ID Design and Branding MA: Regional EXP: Mr. Blank's expertise includes user-experienced interaction and design and Websites. H/I/S: Bicycling, Playing Guitar EDU: Bachelor of Arts in Graphic Design, Rhode Island School of Design A/A/S: AIGA; GAG A/H: Usabitlity Awards, Nielsen Norman Group; International Web Page Award (Four Times); Web Awards, Web Marketing Association (Twice); Advertising Awards, London International (Twice); Site of the Month, Digital Threads C/VW: Friends of Urban Forest
Email: todd@toddblankdesign.com
URL: http://www.toddblankdesign.com

Robert M. Blanks
Title: EcoLab Route Company: Ecolab Inc. Address: 370 Wabasha Street N., St. Paul, MN 55102 United States BUS: Hotel and Food Service Support Company P/S: Food Service Sanitation, Technical Support, Hotel Maintenance and Food MA: International D/D/R: Selling Ecolab Cleaning Products and Equipment, Advising, Collecting Bills, Managing Customer Restaurant Accounts, Offering Technical Services and Repairs H/I/S: Playing Music EDU: Coursework, Northern Virginia Community College; Industry-Related Training, United States Navy. A/A/S: XanGo, LLC C/VW: Navy Memorial; Fire Chiefs Association; Sheriffs Association
Email: r.blanks@verizon.net
URL: http://www.cambridgewhoswho.com

Mr. Christopher W. Blastos
Title: Officer Company: Milford Police Department Address: 19 Garden Street, Milford, NH 03055 United States BUS: Police Department P/S: Public Safety and Law Enforcement MA: Local D/D/R: training co-workers on special operations and firearms instruction and overseeing patrol duties. H/I/S: Traveling, Spending Time with his Children, Reading Dave Grossman's Books EDU: Bachelor of Arts in Psychology, Plymouth State University (1990) CERTS: Certification in Special Weapons And Tactics Instruction
Email: christopherw.blastos@cwwemail.com
Email: cblastos@milford.nh.gov
URL: http://www.cambridgewhoswho.com

Janet Lavada Blazer
Title: Christian Counselor Company: Family First Christian Counseling Address: 1103 South Street, Harrisonville, MO 64701 United States BUS: Counseling Services P/S: Psychotherapy MA: Local D/D/R: Counseling for Families, Children and Mentally Handicapped People in Parenting Skills, Human Development, Abuse, Neglect, Poor Attachment, Relationship Building, Children at Risk, Anger Management, Oppositional and Defiant Juveniles H/I/S: Traveling, Attending Church Programs, Spending Time with her Grandchildren, Reading, Writing, Quilting EDU: Master's Degree in Psychology, Southern Nazarene University (2000) CERTS: Certified in Crisis Prevention Education; Certified to Train Para-Professionals and the Mentally Disabled; Certified Case Manager for the Aggressive and Non-Aggressive A/A/S: American Association of Christian Counselors; American Counseling Association; Christian Association for Psychological Studies; North American Association of Masters in Psychology; Psi Ch A/H: Distinguished Achievement Award in Family Studies and Gerontology C/VW: Local Church; Therapy for Handicapped People; Special Olympics; Sponsor, Youth Summer Camps; Workers Rap Conference
Email: janetlblazer@embarqmail.com
URL: http://www.cambridgewhoswho.com

Mary Ann Adrian Bleish
Title: Business Manager, Owner Company: Animal Clinic of Platte County Address: 10123 N.W. 45 Highway, Parkville, MO 64152 United States BUS: Veterinary Hospital P/S: Pet Supply Retail, Veterinary and Small Animal Medicine MA: Platte County EXP: Ms. Bleish's expertise is in client relations. D/D/R: Managing Personnel, Administrative Duties Including Financials, Inventory and Web Design H/I/S: Photography, Genealogy, Traveling EDU: Master of Business Administration in Finance, Park University C/VW: Local Church
Email: marybleish@aol.com
URL: http://www.animalclinicofplattecounty.com

Denise J. Blevins, LSW
Title: Resource Family Development Specialist Company: Latah County Youth Services Address: 522 S. Adams Street, Room 201, Moscow, ID 83843 United States BUS: Government Agency P/S: Foster Home Recruitment, Training, Licensure and Recertification, Reports to the County Commissioners, Program Development, Early Intervention, Prevention of the Escalation of Criminal Behavior, Detention, Community Service MA: Regional D/D/R: Conducting Background Checks and Home Study Programs, Recruiting, Training and Verifying Eligibility of Potential Foster Parents H/I/S: Reading, Traveling, Listening to Music, Singing, Photography, Caring for her Cats EDU: Bachelor of Arts in Sociology, University of Idaho (1983) A/A/S: Idaho Juvenile Justice Association; Idaho Juvenile Justice Commission; Chairwoman, Grants Committee; Ethics Committee A/H: Government Award
Email: dblevins@latah.id.us
URL: http://www.latah.id.us/dept/ys_main.htm

Lorie E. Blevins, MS
Title: Instructor, Business Technical Coordinator Company: Shawnee Mission North High School Address: 7401 Johnson Drive, Overland Park, KS 66202 United States BUS: High School Facility Dedicated to Excellence in Education P/S: Regular Core Curriculum including Reading, Math, English, Science, Social Studies, Art, Music, History, Physical Education, Languages, Computers MA: Regional D/D/R: Teaching Computer Skills, Advanced Computer Training, On-the-Job Training Programs, Business Technology, Interviewing Skills and Portfolio Development, Giving In-service H/I/S: Traveling EDU: Master of Science in Business Education, Emporia State University (1991) A/A/S: Running BPA Club on State Competition
Email: lorieblevins@smsd.org
URL: http://smsd.org

Brandon Blickenstaff
Title: Associate Broker Company: Coldwell Banker Partners Real Estate Address: 109 S. Burlington Dr., Pueblo West, CO 81007 United States BUS: Real Estate Agency P/S: Transfer of Real Estate, Residential Real Estate, Executive Properties, Lake View Properties, New Construction, Condominiums, Golf Properties MA: National EXP: Mr. Blickenstaff's expertise is in residential properties. H/I/S: Riding Motorcycles EDU: Coursework in Sociology and Criminal Justice, Colorado State University A/A/S: National Association of Realtors; Colorado Association of Realtors
Email: brandon@brendablickenstaff.com
URL: http://www.brendablickenstaff.com

Sheila L. Bliss
Title: Home and Hospital Teacher Company: Mt. Diablo Unified School District Address: 1936 Carlotta Drive, Concord, CA 94519 United States BUS: School District P/S: Education MA: Regional D/D/R: teaching all subjects to children, creating curriculum and instructing English and Spanish in China and Taiwan. H/I/S: Learning Russian Language, Ukrainian Cross Stitching, Quilting, Knitting, Traveling EDU: Master's Degree in Curriculum Development, University of Southern California (1971); Bachelor's Degree, United States International University, San Diego, CA CERTS: Certified Teacher K-9
Email: slmbliss@sbcglobal.net

Richard H. Block
Title: Partner Company: Dreier LLP Address: 499 Park Avenue, New York, NY 10022 United States BUS: Private Law Firm P/S: Legal Services MA: National EXP: Mr. Block's expertise includes labor and employment law. H/I/S: Traveling EDU: Bachelor of Arts, Princeton University; JD, Hofstra University A/A/S: Law Fellows; American Bar Foundation; Simon Wiesenthal Center
Email: rblock@dreierllp.com
URL: http://www.dreierllp.com

Brenda Blood
Title: Title 1 Mathematics Teacher Company: Yellow Branch Elementary School Address: 377 Dennis Riddle Drive, Rustburg, VA 24588 United States BUS: School P/S: Education MA: Local D/D/R: Teaching Mathematics, Building Self-Confidence in Students H/I/S: Reading, Traveling EDU: Bachelor's Degree in Elementary Education, Liberty University A/A/S: Clark County Education Association; Virginia State Education Association C/VW: Thomas Road Baptist Church
Email: bblood@campbell.k12.va.us
URL: http://www.campbell.k12.va.us/ybes

Lisa R. Bloom
Title: Owner **Company:** Ms. Lisa's Little Wildcats **Address:** 201 N. Cherokee Ford Road, Blacksburg, SC 29702 United States **BUS:** Preschool, Day Care **P/S:** Childcare Services **MA:** Local **D/D/R:** Caring for and Ensuring the Well-Being of Children Ages 6 Weeks to 12, Provides Services for up to 25 children, Teaches on the Preschool level, Offers the Benefits of teaching early educational skills and development, Provides various educational field trips, 4 fulltime staff, PALS and CPR certified, Started a sleep apnea program of checking the children during sleep time, placing monitors in each infants crib for sleep apnea, **H/I/S:** Reading, Cooking, Spending Time with her Own Children **CERTS:** Certified Nursing Assistant, Isothermal Community College-1997; **A/A/S:** Eastside Baptist Church; Junior Women's Club **A/H:** Volunteer of the Year Award from Blacksburg Elementary School-2008 **C/VW:** Special Olympics, Relay for Life, Various Local Fundraisers for Dance Competitions and School
Email: abloom@bellsouth.net

Valerie Bloomfield-Ambrose, MFA
Title: Artist **Address:** 9809 S.W. Malibu Terrace, Palm City, FL 34990 United States **BUS:** Freelance Artistry in Portraiture and Sculpture **P/S:** Commissioned Portraits of Well-Known and Prestigious Political Figures and University Leaders **MA:** National **D/D/R:** Lecturing on Anatomy and Life Drawing, Paintings and Sculptures **EDU:** Master of Fine Arts Degree, American University, Washington D.C. (1982); Bachelor's Degree, Glasgow School of Art (1957) **A/A/S:** Palm City Artists Association; Salmagundi Club, New York, NY; Hibiscus Children's Center **A/H:** First Place, Arts Council Show
Email: johnambrose@supranos.com
URL: http://www.cambridgewhoswho.com

Ann Blossfeld
Title: Design Partner **Company:** Searl Blossfeld Design **Address:** 500 N Dearborn Suite 950, Chicago, IL 60610 United States **BUS:** Architecture & Design **P/S:** Architecture and Interior Design **MA:** Local **EXP:** Ms. Blossfeld's expertise includes restoration and interior design. **H/I/S:** Traveling, Skiing Roller Blading **EDU:** Master of Arts, University of Illinois at Urbana-Champaign; Bachelor of Arts, Michigan State University **A/A/S:** Museum of Contemporary Art, AIA
Email: info@CambridgeWhosWho.com
URL: www.searlarch.com

Mrs. Claudette D. Blot
Title: Director of Summer Transition Education Program, Program Coordinator **Company:** Bentley College **Dept:** Multicultural Center, Student Affairs Division **Address:** 175 Forest Street, Student Center 360, Waltham, MA 02452 United States **BUS:** University **P/S:** Education **MA:** Local **D/D/R:** Recruiting, Advising Students, Designing Programs and Workshops, Coordinating, Intervention, Mediating **H/I/S:** Conducting Workshops for Students **EDU:** Bachelor of Science in Biology and Pre-Medical Studies, Wilberforce University **A/A/S:** National Association for Financial Aid and Admissions Counselors; National Association of Admissions and Registrar; Speaking Guild of Massachusetts; Board Member, Higher Education Resource Center of Brockton **A/H:** National Award for Community Partners
Email: cblot@bentley.edu

Margaret W. Blue
Title: Chairwoman, Business Technology Department **Company:** Biloxi High School **Address:** 1845 Richard Drive, Biloxi, MS 39532 United States **BUS:** High School **P/S:** Education **MA:** Local **D/D/R:** Teaching Business to High School Students **H/I/S:** Reading **EDU:** Master of Education in Business, William Carey College; Bachelor's Degree in Business Education, University of Southern Mississippi **A/A/S:** Mississippi Business Education Association; Southern Business Education Association; National Business Education Association **C/VW:** Church
Email: margaret.blue@biloxischools.net
URL: http://www.biloxischools.net

Phillip Bly
Title: Director of Risk Management **Company:** Crescent Heights of America, Inc. **Address:** 2200 Biscayne Boulevard, Miami, FL 33137 United States **BUS:** Real Estate Development Company **P/S:** Residential Condominium Development, Internet Commercial Real Estate **MA:** International **EXP:** Mr. Bly's expertise includes risk management and insurance. **H/I/S:** Traveling, Music, Theatre **EDU:** Bachelor of Science in Mathematics, Kent State University (1970) **A/A/S:** Police and Sheriff Association; Rights and Insurance Society **C/VW:** Blood Drives
Email: pbly@cresentheights.com
URL: http://www.crescentheights.com

Mark R. Boast
Title: Chief Executive Officer **Company:** Camelspit, Inc. **Address:** 93202 W. Hanks Road, Prosser, WA 99350 United States **BUS:** Consulting and Agricultural Firm **P/S:** Agricultural and Consulting Services **MA:** National **D/D/R:** Restoring Agricultural Machinery, Farming, Consulting, Raising Apples and Wine Grapes **H/I/S:** Restoring Agricultural Machinery, Riding his Harley-Davidson Motorcycle, Traveling **EDU:** Coursework, Arizona Automotive Institute **A/A/S:** United States Air Force; Elks Club
Email: camelot@bentonrea.com
Email: camelspit@rosahills.com
URL: http://www.rozahills.com

Michael P. Bobic, Ph.D.
Title: Director, Pre-Law Program **Company:** Emmanuel College **Address:** 181 Springs Street, Franklin Springs, GA 30639 United States **BUS:** Institution of Higher Education **P/S:** Top Quality Higher Education **MA:** Regional **D/D/R:** Teaching Constitutional Law, International Law, Introduction to United States History, Courses One and Two, Director of Institutional Research, As Director, Administering 3000 Evaluations Each Semester with Student Participation, Generating Reports and Doing all the Analysis, For Pre-Law Courses, Helping to Design the Curriculum, Administering Sample LSAT's and Increased the Success Rate of the LSAT's by 27 Percent, Involved with Graduate Senior and Alumni Surveys **H/I/S:** Fencing **EDU:** Ph.D. in Political Science, University of Tennessee (1996); Bachelor's Degree in Political Science (1985) **A/A/S:** Phi Kappa Phi, Berea College; Chair, Panelist, Discussionist, National Conventions; Western Political Science Association; Midwest Political Science Association; Southern Political Science Association; Phi Gamma Mu, Faculty Sponsor; Writer, Three to Four Articles for the American Political Science Association **A/H:** Published Articles in the Journal of Public Administration and Journal of Research on Public Policy and Administration
Email: mbobic@eclions.net
URL: http://www.home.eclions.net

Kathleen Bocella
Title: Supervisor Care Management **Company:** Independence Blue Cross **Address:** 1901 Market Street, Philadelphia, PA 19103 United States **BUS:** Health Insurance Company **P/S:** Health Insurance Policies **MA:** Regional **D/D/R:** Overseeing and Evaluating the Nursing Staff, Reviewing Cases, Auditing **H/I/S:** Polish Folk Dancing **EDU:** Coursework in Nursing, Gwynedd-Mercy College **CERTS:** Certified Case Manager; Registered Nurse, Villanova University **A/A/S:** Case Management Society of America
Email: kathleen.boccella@ibx.com

Barbara Lee Boden, MA, CPCC
Title: President, Chief Executive Officer **Company:** Leading Attitudes, Inc. **Address:** 2317 Michael Road, Suite 201, Myersville, MD 21773 United States **BUS:** Consulting Firm **P/S:** Leadership Coaching and Consulting Services **MA:** Statewide **D/D/R:** coaching women in personal leadership development and transformation. **EDU:** Master's Degree in Organizational Transformation, Vermont College **CERTS:** Certified Professional Co-Active Coach; Certified Coach, International Coach Federation **A/A/S:** Leader, Coaches Training Institute
Email: barbara@leadingattitudes.com
URL: http://www.leadingattitudes.com

Christine M. Bodi
Title: Registered Nurse **Company:** Huntington Hospital **Address:** 270 Park Avenue, Huntington, NY 11743 United States **BUS:** Nonprofit Community Hospital **P/S:** Cancer Center, Surgical Services, Emergency Services, Neurosciences, Obstetrics and Gynecology, Orthopedic Services, Pediatrics, Psychiatric Services, Cardiology, Oncology, Women's and Children's Services **MA:** Regional **D/D/R:** Operating Room Nursing, Pre- and Post-Operative Nursing, Cardiac and Intensive Care Unit Nursing **H/I/S:** Sailing, Walking **EDU:** Associate Degree in Nursing, State University of New York (1981) **A/A/S:** Association of PeriOperative Registered Nurses
Email: lockercb1212@aol.com
URL: http://www.huntingtonhospital.com

Richard M. Bodinizzo
Title: Clinical Marketing Manager **Company:** MedImmune, Inc. **Address:** 1 MedImmune Way, Gaithersburg, MD 20878 United States **BUS:** Biotechnology Company **P/S:** Biotechnology Sales, Specializing in Pediatric Infectious Diseases and Immunology **MA:** International **D/D/R:** Leading the Business Unit, Hospital Consulting, Serving as the Business Unit Leader **H/I/S:** Cooking, Golfing, Traveling, Softball League **EDU:** Bachelor of Science in Environmental Science, East Stroudsburg University, 1996
Email: bodinizzor@medimmune.com

Brandy Boeckeler
Title: Reading Specialist **Company:** Bruce Guadalupe Community School **Address:** 1028 S. Ninth Street, Milwaukee, WI 53204 United States **BUS:** Charter School **P/S:** Education **MA:** Local **H/I/S:** Reading **EDU:** Master's Degree in Reading Education, University of Wisconsin-Oshkosh **A/A/S:** Wisconsin State Reading Association; International Reading Association; Teacher of the Year, 2006-2007
Email: bboeckeler@yahoo.com

Janet J. Boes
Title: Staff Nurse (Retired) **Company:** Tipton County Hospital **Address:** 1000 S. Main Street, Tipton, IN 46072 United States **BUS:** Hospital **P/S:** Healthcare **MA:** Local **EXP:** Ms. Boes' expertise is in long-term rehabilitation. **D/D/R:** Caring for the Elderly **H/I/S:** Playing the Piano and Organ, Photography **EDU:** Bachelor of Science in Nursing, Indiana Wesleyan University **CERTS:** Licensed Practical Nurse **A/A/S:** Military Order of the Purple Heart; Officer, Order of Eastern Star **C/VW:** Church
Email: bonesbb@hotmail.com
URL: http://www.cambridgewhoswho.com

Brian J. Bogart
Title: Certified Financial Planner, Senior Vice President of Investments **Company:** Ferris, Bakes, Watts, Inc/Bogart Financial Group **Address:** 7601 Lewinsville Road Suite 203, McLean, VA 22102 United States **BUS:** Finance Management **P/S:** Financial Planning, Investment Management **MA:** Local **D/D/R:** Planning for Retirement, Managing Investments **H/I/S:** Golf, Tennis, Travel, Reading **EDU:** MBA, National University of California **A/A/S:** FPA
Email: bbogart@fbw.com
URL: http://www.fbw.com/bogartfinancialgroup/index.html

Anastasia Bogdanova
Title: Director of Graphic Design, Partner, Creative Director **Company:** CBT, Type Sync Studio **Dept:** Graphic Design **Address:** 9 Park Road, Bedford, MA 01730 United States **BUS:** Professional Graphic Design Firm **P/S:** Architecture, Urban Design, Site Planning and Interior Design **MA:** International **EXP:** Ms. Bogdanova's expertise includes graphic design and marketing. **EDU:** Bachelor's Degree in Graphic Design, Art Institute of Boston (2003) **A/A/S:** AIGA; Directors Club; Boston Chamber of Commerce
Email: anastasia@typesync.com
URL: http://www.typesync.com

Jo B. Boggs
Title: Owner **Company:** Boggs Jewelry **Address:** 4845 Sun City Center Blvd, Sun City Center, FL United States **BUS:** Jewelry Retail **P/S:** Clock and Watch Repair as well as Jewelry Sales **MA:** Local **EXP:** Mr. Boggs' expertise includes business operations and customer service. **EDU:** High School Graduate
Email: info@CambridgeWhosWho.com

Helen M. Bohannon
Title: President **Company:** Bohannon Ranch, Inc. **Address:** 23282 US Highway 301 N., Lawtey, FL 32058 United States **BUS:** Retailer **P/S:** Manufacturing Health Food Products, Massage Therapy **MA:** International **D/D/R:** Overseeing Operations **H/I/S:** Horseback Riding, Spending Time with her Family **CERTS:** Industry-Related Training **A/A/S:** SOHO **C/VW:** Highland First Baptist Church
Email: helen@bohannonranch.com
URL: http://www.bohannonranch.com

Jeanne T. Boisvert
Title: Education Coordinator, Senior Nurse III of Step Down Unit in Cardiovascular-Unit Program **Company:** Children's Hospital Boston **Address:** 300 Longwood Avenue, Boston, MA 02115 United States **BUS:** Children's Hospital **P/S:** Pediatric Cardiology **MA:** National **D/D/R:** Coordinating Education for Staff, Coordinating Staff Nurse Orientation, Nursing **H/I/S:** Swimming, Reading, Traveling **EDU:** Bachelor of Science in Nursing, Fitchburg State College **A/A/S:** Northeast Pediatric Cardiology Nurses Association; Society of Pediatric Nurses
Email: jeanne.boisvert@childrens.harvard.edu

Ann B. Bolden
Title: Manager **Company:** Speedway Internet **Address:** P.O. Box 05447, Detroit, MI 48205 United States **BUS:** Internet Services Firm **P/S:** Dial Up and 5X DSL Speed Internet Service **MA:** Statewide **EXP:** Ms. Bolden's expertise is in business management. **EDU:** Coursework in Business Law, Wayne State University; Coursework in General Studies, University of Munich, Germany **C/VW:** North Shore Animal League America; Society of St. Vincent de Paul, Inc.; The Salvation Army
Email: annb.bolden@yahoo.com

Ardis M. Boldenow
Title: Teacher **Company:** Goldenrod Hills Head Start **Address:** 1401 Pine Street, Dakota City, NE 68731 United States **BUS:** School **P/S:** Education **MA:** Regional **EXP:** Ms. Boldenow's expertise is in early childhood education. **D/D/R:** , teaching Spanish, supervising teacher aides, planning lessons and coaching students. **H/I/S:** Running, Reading, Sewing, Spending Time with her Family **EDU:** Bachelor of Arts in Education, Wayne State University **A/A/S:** Nevada Head Start Association; National Education Association; National Association for the Education of Young Children **C/VW:** American Cancer Society; Lutheran Church; CMN
Email: aboldeno1@yahoo.com
URL: http://www.ghhs.com

Angela C. Boley
Title: Vice President, Treasurer **Company:** Boley Cattle Inc. **Address:** 10540 FM 932, Jonesboro, TX 76538 United States **BUS:** Cattle Ranch **P/S:** Pet Grooming, Livestock Grooming, Boarding and Kennel Services **MA:** North Central Texas **D/D/R:** Raising, Breeding and Selling Registered Black Angus and American Quarter Horses **H/I/S:** Riding Horses, Training Dogs **EDU:** Coursework in Geology, University of Houston, North Harris **A/A/S:** ACA **C/VW:** Pet Grooming for Pet Shelters
Email: abc02@htcomp.net

Susette LaFlesche Bollard
Title: Assistant Superintendent **Company:** Orange North Supervisory Union **Address:** 111B Brush Hill Road, Williamstown, VT 05679 United States **BUS:** School District **P/S:** Education **MA:** Local **D/D/R:** Overseeing School Curricula and Instruction **H/I/S:** Reading Books by Richard Elmore, Richard Dufour and Roland Barth **EDU:** Master of Education, Trinity College of Vermont; Bachelor of Arts in Music, Augustana College **A/A/S:** American Foundation for Suicide Prevention; Association for Supervision and Curriculum Development; National Council of Teachers of Mathematics
Email: sboilard@onsu.ed
URL: http://www.fc.onwsu.org

Stephen A. Bollinger
Title: President **Company:** Pervasis Therapeutics **Address:** 6 Lauren Lane, Mansfield, MA 02048 United States **BUS:** Medical Devices **P/S:** Development of Cell-Based Therapies to Induce Repair and Regeneration in a Wide Array of Tissues **MA:** National **D/D/R:** Using Medical and Biological Devices, Developing Clinical Operations, Overseeing Business Development, Dealing Directly with Physicians and Hospitals, Fundraising **H/I/S:** Fencing, Fitness, Medieval Armor Build and Collect it. **EDU:** Master's Degree in Business Administration, Oklahoma City University (1994); Bachelor of Science in Mechanical Engineering, United States Military Academy, West Point-1987 **A/A/S:** Local and National Speaker, Medical and Biological Devices Cardiovascular, OB/Gyn, General Surgery and Plastics and Reconstructive Surgery; Captain in Oklahoma, Gulf War, Airborne Ranger, United States Army
Email: sbollinger@pervasistx.com
URL: http://www.pervasistx.com/Home.html

Ms. Ana Bolt
Title: Dance Director and Instructor **Company:** Miami-Dade County Public Schools **Address:** 4301 N. Michigan Avenue, Miami Beach, FL 33179 United States **BUS:** Public School District **P/S:** Education **MA:** Miami Beach, FL **D/D/R:** Teaching Dance, Coaching the Middle School Track Team **H/I/S:** Drawing, Painting **EDU:** Bachelor of Fine Arts, New World School of the Arts **A/A/S:** Dance Now Ensemble; Dade County Dancers Association **A/H:** Teacher of the Year, Nautilus Middle School (2008) **C/VW:** Relay for Life, American Cancer Society; Health and Expo Fitness Convention
Email: anabolt@dadeschools.net

Erin M. Bolton
Title: Marketing Manager **Company:** Acredo Technologies, Inc. **Address:** 2906 A Harrison Ave, Panama City, FL 03240 United States **BUS:** Global Telecommunications Business **P/S:** Total Business Communication Solutions, Voice-Over-Internet Protocols, Instant Messaging, E-mail, Faxing, Press Management **MA:** International **D/D/R:** Organizing Monthly Presentations, Managing Marketing **H/I/S:** Exercising, Dancing, Going to the Beach **EDU:** Pursuing Master of Business Administration, Florida State University; Bachelor's Degree in Journalism and Mass Media Studies, Rutgers University, New Jersey **A/A/S:** Gulf Coast Media Marketing Association; Chamber of Commerce; Existing Industry Committee; Industry Appreciation Committee; Bay Area Young Professionals Network; Cystic Fibrosis Foundation **A/H:** Best in Class', Acredo Technologies, Inc. (2007); Operation Noble Eagle, United States Air Force; Airman of the Fourth Letter of Recognition, United States Air Force (2004)
Email: ebolton@acredo.us
URL: http://www.acredo.us

Mark Bomberg
Title: Research Professor **Company:** Syracuse University **Address:** 149 Link Hall, Syracuse, NY 13244 United States **BUS:** University **P/S:** Higher Education, Research, Building Energy and Environmental Systems Laboratory **MA:** International **D/D/R:** Studying Heat, Air and Moisture Transfer in Buildings **H/I/S:** Swimming, Skiing **EDU:** Ph.D. in Technology, Earned in Sweden; Ph.D. in Science and Engineering, Earned in Poland **A/A/S:** American Society for Testing and Materials; American Society for Heating, Refrigerating and Air-Conditioning Engineers; International Organization for Standardization
Email: markbomberg@gmail.com
URL: http://beesl.syr.edu

Pauline A. Bonaventura
Title: Director of Medical Affairs **Company:** Interfaith Medical Center **Address:** 1545 Atlantic Avenue, Brooklyn, NY 11231 United States **BUS:** Multisite Community Teaching Healthcare System **P/S:** 300 Beds Facility with 331 Physicians and 25 Allied Health Professionals **MA:** Regional **D/D/R:** Credentialing, Conducting Thorough Investigations of Medical Professionals on Staff, Background Checking, Licensing, Ensuring Proper Codes of Conduct Are Followed **H/I/S:** Crocheting, Handicrafting, Volunteer Guide, Central Park Zoo and World Trade Center **EDU:** High School Education **A/A/S:** National Association of Medical Staff; New Jersey Association of Medical Staff Services **C/VW:** Volunteer, 9/11 Families Memorial; Central Park Wildlife Center
Email: pbonaventura@interfaithmedical.com
URL: http://www.interfaithmedical.com

Ms. Mary J. Slem Bond
Title: Educator (Retired) **Company:** Norwalk City School District **Address:** 134 Benedict Avenue, Norwalk, OH 44857 United States **BUS:** School **P/S:** Education **MA:** Regional **D/D/R:** Teaching Students with Learning Disabilities, Teaching Elementary Education, Reading, Language Arts and English **H/I/S:** Reading, Gardening Flowers, Walking, Traveling, Spending Time with her Grandchildren **EDU:** Master of Education, Ashland University, 2000; Bachelor's Degree in Education, University of Rio Grande of Ohio, 1966 **A/A/S:** National Education Association; Ohio Education Association; Red Hats Society **C/VW:** Feed the Children; Missionary Committee, Calvary Baptist Church

Ms. Doris P. Bondi
Title: President **Company:** In Balance Training **Address:** 11701 Villa Malaparte Avenue, Las Vegas, NV 89138 United States **BUS:** Health and Wellness **P/S:** Fitness, Rehabilitation, Healthcare Services **MA:** Regional **D/D/R:** Offering Health and Wellness Training, Instructing Balance, Yoga, Pilates and Strength-Training Classes, Administering Rehabilitation Therapy, Treating Senior Citizens, Stroke Victims, Multiple Sclerosis and Parkinson's Disease Patients, Utilizing Body Sculpting and Stability Ball Work Techniques **H/I/S:** Singing, Movies, Museums, Live Theater **EDU:** Bachelor's Degree in Business, California State University (1979) **CERTS:** Certified Fitness Trainer; Certified Adapted Movement Professional; Certified Exercise Movement Practitioner **A/A/S:** International Dance Exercise Association; Guide Dogs of America; Multiple Sclerosis Society; Lions Club of Summerlin; Women's Club of Summerlin; National Arthritis Foundation; Les Marraines; Blind Children's Center in California
Email: inbalancetrainin@aol.com

Mr. Brian T. Bonekemper
Title: Account Executive **Company:** Kenmark Optical **Dept:** Pennsylvania Sales Department **Address:** 260 Cannon Street, Green Island, NY 12183 United States **BUS:** Distribution Firm **P/S:** Optical Frames **MA:** National **EXP:** Mr. Bonekemper's expertise is in sales management. **D/D/R:** Managing Account and Customer Support, Selling the Latest Styles in Eye Wear, Overseeing Account Services for Independent Businesses and Doctors Offices **H/I/S:** Traveling, Golfing **EDU:** Bachelor of Arts in Business Management and Criminal Justice, DeSales University **A/A/S:** Chairman, Board of Auditors, Milford Township **C/VW:** Fundraiser, Local Cancer Organizations; Relay for Life, American Cancer Society
Email: bbonekemper@comcast.net
URL: http://www.cambridgewhoswho.com

James J. BonGiorno
Title: Owner/President **Company:** Jim's Hauling and Clean Up Division **Address:** 719 Broad Avenue Extension, Duncansville, PA 16635 United States **BUS:** Sanitation Service Provider **P/S:** Curbside Service, Roll-Off, Commercial **MA:** Local **H/I/S:** Singing **EDU:** Pennsylvania, College
Email: jimshaulinginc@hotmail.com

Jesus R. Bonilla
Title: Office Assistant/Certified Braille Transcriber **Company:** Education Service Center, Region 20 **Dept:** Braille Services **Address:** 1314 Hines Avenue, San Antonio, TX 78208 United States **BUS:** Educational Service Agency **P/S:** Braille Transcription, Reproduction of Educational Materials **MA:** International **EXP:** Mr. Bonilla's expertise is in Braille transcription. **H/I/S:** Restoring Classic Cars, Owner of a 1957 Chevrolet, Bel Air and a 1946 Ford Pick Up, Building Model Gas and Electric Airplanes. Flying vintage/classic airplanes. **EDU:** Pursuing Bachelor's Degree in Business Administration with a Minor in Aviation Flight Technology, Wayland Baptist University **CERTS:** Certified in Braille Transcription, National Library of Congress (2005); Certified Drug and Alcohol Counselor (1994); Licensed Private Airplane Pilot (1977) **A/A/S:** Retired United States Army Sergeant First Class **A/H:** Member, Honorable Order of Kentucky Colonials, Presented by the Governor of Kentucky, Martha L. Collins (1984) **C/VW:** St. Jude Children's Research Hospital; Texas State Troopers Association; Paralyzed Veteran's Association
Email: jrbonilla@gmail.com

Bernard L. Bonin
Title: Manager, Accountant **Company:** Desai Holdings, LLC **Address:** 2421 Clearview Parkway, Metairie, LA 70001 United States **BUS:** Hotel **P/S:** Hospitality, Food Service **MA:** Local **D/D/R:** Managing Hotel Operations, accounting, ordering, analyzing data and collecting revenues. **H/I/S:** Collecting Stamps **EDU:** Bachelor of Arts in Accounting, University of New Orleans **A/H:** Who's Who in American Business (2006-2007); Who's Who American Junior Colleges (1971)
Email: blb_70460@hotmail.com
URL: http://www.cambridgewhosewho.com

David R. Bonola
Title: Funeral Director/Embalmer **Company:** D'Esopo Funeral Chapel **Address:** 277 Folly Brook Blvd, Wethersfield, CT 06109 United States **BUS:** Mortuary **P/S:** Prepartion of the Departed for Viewing and Burial, Responsible for Embalming, Sanitation, Make Up and Dressing the Deceased, Consistent Contact with the Families, Following Through with Their Wishes, Prepares for the Viewing and Services, as Director he also Performs the Service, Oversees the Regulatory Paper Work and Obtains all Necessary Information from Vital Statistics **MA:** International **H/I/S:** Traveling, Boating, Beaches, Loves the Sun **EDU:** Associate of Science in Mortuary Science, Bryerwood College, CT; Bachelor of Arts in Political Science, Central Connecticut State University, CT **CERTS:** Certified Funeral Service Professional **A/A/S:** First Class Petty Officer, United States Navy Reserve
Email: lymetavern@yahoo.com

Joseph Booker Jr.
Title: MD **Address:** 503 Brookstone Circle, Madison, MS 39110 United States **BUS:** Healthcare **P/S:** Gynecology/Women's Health **MA:** Local **EXP:** Mr. Booker's expertise is in gynecology. **H/I/S:** Poetry **EDU:** MD **A/A/S:** International Society of Poets
Email: info@CambridgeWhosWho.com

Allen L. Boorstein
Title: President **Company:** Amber Blocks, Ltd **Address:** 535 Park Avenue, NYC, NY 10021 United States **BUS:** Strategic Planning and Consulting Company **P/S:** Strategic Planning and System Dynamics **MA:** National **EXP:** Mr. Boorstein's expertise includes management and strategic planning. **H/I/S:** Photography **EDU:** Harvard Business School, MBA **A/A/S:** Dynamics Society
Email: info@CambridgeWhosWho.com

James M. Booth
Title: Area Manager **Company:** Nalco **Address:** 1601 W. Diehl Road, Naperville, IL 60563 United States **BUS:** Chemical Manufacturing **P/S:** Chemicals, Machinery, Consulting **MA:** International **EXP:** Mr. Booth's expertise is in maintenance. **D/D/R:** Managing and Training a Staff of Five, **H/I/S:** Golfing **EDU:** Bachelor of Science in Chemical Engineering, The University of Missouri-Columbia (1998) **A/A/S:** American Institute of Chemical Engineering
Email: jmbooth@nalco.com
URL: http://www.nalco.com

Patricia Ann Booth
Title: Supportive Service Coordinator, Social Worker **Company:** American Hellenic Educational Progressive Association **Address:** 4370 Community Drive, West Palm Beach, FL 33409 United States **BUS:** Apartment Complex **P/S:** Low-Income Independent Housing for Elderly and Disabled Persons **MA:** National **EXP:** Ms. Booth's expertise is in social work. **D/D/R:** Offering Social Services and Bereavement Counseling for Residents **H/I/S:** Swimming, Singing with her Church Choir **EDU:** Pursuing Doctorate Degree; Master of Social Work, Barry University; Master of Arts in Religious Education and Pastor Ministry, St. John's University; Bachelor's Degree in Philosophy, Molloy College **CERTS:** Licensed Clinical Social Worker **A/A/S:** National Association of Social Workers; International Social Work **C/VW:** Faith and Light Ministry
Email: dreamrlty2@aol.com

Ms. Peggy Boothe

Title: Owner **Company:** JMB Business Supplies, Inc. **Address:** 1691 Town Center Street, Suite 105, Aurora, IL 60504 United States **BUS:** Business Supply Store **P/S:** Retail Office Supplies, Furniture, Paper Products, Art, Drafting and School Supplies, Healthcare Supplies, Computers and Electronics, Printing Services **MA:** Regional **D/D/R:** Price Competitive Office Supplies, Operations and Management, Printing, Office Furniture, Next Day Free Delivery, Offering Travel Agent Services Including Discount Airfare, Hotel Packages, Cruises, Car Rental and Vacations **H/I/S:** Traveling **EDU:** College Courses at Waubonsee Community College **CERTS:** Las Vegas Certified Travel Consultant **A/A/S:** Professional Travel Network
Email: pboothe@jmbbiz.com
URL: http://www.jmbbiz.com

Rodolfo E. Bordoni

Title: Medical Doctor **Company:** Georgia Cancer Specialists **Address:** 340 Kennestone Hospital Boulevard, Suite 100, Marietta, GA 30060 United States **BUS:** Medical Center **P/S:** Healthcare **MA:** Local **EXP:** Dr. Bordoni's expertise includes cancer education and lung cancer treatment. **H/I/S:** Playing Soccer, Reading, Watching Opera **EDU:** MD, National University of Rosario, Santa Fe, Argentina; Coursework, British Hospital for Internal Medicine, Argentina **CERTS:** Medical Oncology Training Program, Emory University, GA **A/A/S:** Chairman, Founder, Georgia Group for Lung Cancer; East Gasco; Chairman, Founder, Annual Lung Cancer Symposium, Atlanta; Chairman, Professional Education, Georgia Cancer Foundation; American Society of Clinical Oncology; American Society of Hypertension; American Medical Association **A/H:** National Award; Research Career Development Award, Veterans Health Administration **C/VW:** Local Oncology Program; Chairman, Performance Improvement Committee, WellStar Kennestone Hospital
Email: rodolfo.bordoni@gacancer.com
URL: http://www.gacancer.com

William A. Borello

Title: President, Owner **Company:** W. Borello Enterprises, Billy B's Restaurant & Bar **Address:** 9922 Holmes Rd, Kansas City, MO 64131 United States **BUS:** Bar **P/S:** Restaurant, Bar **MA:** Local **H/I/S:** Music, Theater, Having a Good Time **EDU:** Bachelor of Science in Business Administration, University of Missouri
Email: wbarello@msn.com

Mary Pat Borgess, MD

Title: Medical Doctor, Medical Director of Breast Imaging **Company:** Methodist Hospital **Address:** 3525 Olentangy River Road, Columbus, OH 43014 United States **BUS:** Hospital **P/S:** Radiology, Breast Imaging **MA:** Regional **EXP:** Ms. Borgess' expertise is in breast imaging. **H/I/S:** Cooking, Hiking, Running, Kayaking **EDU:** MD, Ohio State University College of Medicine **A/A/S:** Society of Breast Imaging; Radiological Society of North America; American Roentgen Ray Society; Columbus Medical Association; Ohio State Radiological Society; American Medical Association **C/VW:** Local Schools Booster; Church; Habitat for Humanity; Defenders of Wildlife; Park Conservation; Medical Mission Volunteer, Heart to Honduras
Email: mborgess@riversiderad.com
URL: http://www.riversiderad.com

John M. Bornschein

Title: Senior Director **Company:** National Day of Prayer, Focus on the Family **Address:** 8605 Explorer Drive, Colorado Springs, CO 80920 United States **BUS:** Prayer Organization **P/S:** Organizing Events for the National Day of Prayer **MA:** National **EXP:** Mr. Bornschein's expertise includes marketing and communications. **H/I/S:** Playing Golf, Reading **EDU:** Pursuing Master of Divinity, Bethany Baptist College; Bachelor's Degree in Biblical Studies, Ambassador Bible College **A/A/S:** Toastmasters; Vice President, School District Parent-Teacher Organization **C/VW:** Colorado Springs Rescue Mission, American Cancer Society
Email: john.bornschein@fotf.org
URL: http://www.nationaldayofprayer.com

Ms. Patricia N. Borrelli

Title: Medical Technician/Office Manager **Company:** Laura L. Fisher, M.D. **Address:** 1385 York Avenue, New York, NY 10021 United States **BUS:** Private Medical Practice **P/S:** Internal Medicine **MA:** Regional **D/D/R:** Vitals, Medical Technician Care, EKGs, Venipuncture, Lab Results, Office Management, Payroll **H/I/S:** Jogging, Swimming **EDU:** Bachelor of Science in Pre-Med, Fairfield University (1997) **CERTS:** Pursuing Registered Nurse Certification, Fairfield University
Email: patricia_borrelli2@hotmail.com

Joan M. Bortolon

Title: Assistant Human Resource Director **Company:** Illinois Department of Human Services **Address:** 57 Country Place, Springfield, IL 62703 United States **BUS:** Government Organization **P/S:** Public Services **MA:** Local **EXP:** Ms. Bortolon's expertise is in human resource management. **H/I/S:** Reading, Traveling, Stained Glass Painting **EDU:** Master's Degree in Political Science, Illinois State University **C/VW:** Ronald McDonald House Charities
Email: jmb4604@aol.com

Phillip P. Borup

Title: President, Chief Executive Officer **Company:** Stonehurst Securities, Inc. **Address:** 101 Parkshore Drive, Suite 100, Folsom, CA 95630 United States **BUS:** Financial Services Company **P/S:** Financial Services, Investment Sales, Financial Planning, Private Placement Offerings, Business Development Focusing on Moneymaking Assets **MA:** National **EXP:** Mr. Borup's expertise is in investment management. **H/I/S:** Writing Music, Participating in Community Theater with his Son **EDU:** Bachelor of Science in Business Management, Almeda University **A/A/S:** National Association of Securities Dealers **C/VW:** Boy Scouts of America, Church
Email: phillip.borup@stonehurstsecurities.com
URL: http://www.stonehurstsecurities.com

Rhondda Bosanquet, BA, MS

Title: Teacher **Company:** Elder W. Diggs Elementary School **Address:** 250 W. Cragmont Drive, Indianapolis, IN 46208 United States **BUS:** Elementary School **P/S:** Primary Education **MA:** Local **D/D/R:** Teaching basic skills to disabled students **H/I/S:** Sculpting Clay, Watercolor Painting **EDU:** Master's Degree in Secondary School Administration, Plus 12, Butler University; Bachelor of Arts in Special Education, Indiana University **A/A/S:** Alpha Lambda Delta
Email: rhondda.bosanquet@cwwemail.com

Douglas J. Bosma

Title: Perfumer **Company:** Mane USA **Address:** 60 Demerast Road, Wayne, NJ 07470 United States **BUS:** Fragrance and Flavor Design Company **P/S:** Personal and Household Fragrances, Specializing Using and Creating Natural Essential Oils **MA:** Worldwide **D/D/R:** Creating Fragrances and Oils for Household Use and Personal Care by Utilizing Client Ideas and Suggestions **H/I/S:** Golf, Traveling **EDU:** Bachelor's Degree in Biochemistry and Business Management, Minor in Mathematics, Seton Hall University (2003) **A/A/S:** Brazilian American Chamber of Commerce
Email: douglas.bosma@mane.com
URL: http://www.mane.com

Brian A. Bossart

Title: President **Company:** Shear Comfort Landscape, Inc. **Address:** 2245 Warner Road S.E., Canton, OH 44707 United States **BUS:** Landscaping Company **P/S:** Landscape Design, Building and Installing Brick Patios and Water Features **MA:** Local **EXP:** Mr. Bossart's expertise is in landscape design. **D/D/R:** Hiring Employees, Organizing Staff, Estimating Costs **H/I/S:** Playing Pool, Golfing, Four-Wheeling **EDU:** Associate Degree, Start Technical College (1989)
Email: bbossart@neo.rr
URL: http://www.cambridgewhoswho.com

Bruce Bossow

Title: President **Company:** Premier Commercial Realty **Address:** 9225 S III Route 31, Lake in the Hills, IL 60156 United States **BUS:** Real Estate Broker **P/S:** Selling, Leasing, Consulting **MA:** Local **EXP:** Mr. Bossow's expertise is in commercial real estate brokerage. **H/I/S:** Fishing, Pilot, Hunting, Travel, Scuba **EDU:** John Stratton School of Commercial RE, Partridge and Associates Comm Franchise, Broker **A/A/S:** NASDE, NIACR, Rotary-Past President, Chamber of Commerce, Founder of Fox River Waterway Management Agency
Email: bbossow@premier-comm.com
Email: info@premier-comm.com
URL: www.premier-comm.com

Mr. Barry C. Boston, BSN, MSA

Title: Certified Registered Nurse Anesthetist **Company:** Anesthesia Medical Group **Address:** 29th Avenue, Suite 301, Nashville, TN 37203 United States **BUS:** Private Medical Practice Consisting of Anesthesiologists, Nurse Anesthetists and Other Professional Staff and the Largest Anesthesia Group in Nashville **P/S:** Anesthesia Team Services **MA:** Regional **EXP:** Mr. Boston's expertise includes anesthesia for orthopedics and obstetrics and gynecology. **H/I/S:** Spending Time with his Family and New Baby **EDU:** Bachelor of Science in Nursing Degree, University Tennessee at Knoxville; Master's Degree in Anesthesia, Middle Tennessee School of Anesthesia (2000) **A/A/S:** Tennessee Association of Nurse Anesthetists
Email: thebostons@comcast.net
URL: http://www.amg-group.com

Kevin D. Botelho

Title: Owner, Chef **Company:** Botelho, LLC **Address:** 79 Main Road, Tiverton, RI 02878 United States **BUS:** Restaurant **P/S:** Food and Beverage Services Including Seafood and Portuguese Food **MA:** Local **EXP:** Mr. Botelho's expertise includes business management and culinary arts. **H/I/S:** Exercising, Sports, Spending Time with his Family
Email: kbbotelho@cox.net
URL: http://www.cambridgewhoswho.com

Janice K. Botkin

Title: Director of Maternal Child Services **Company:** Augusta Medical Center **Address:** 78 Medical Center Drive, Fishersville, VA 223939, Fishersville, **BUS:** Hospital **P/S:** Obstetrics, Gynecology **MA:** Local **D/D/R:** Managing a Staff of 66, Buying Equipment, Budgeting **H/I/S:** Golfing, Skiing **EDU:** Master of Science, James Madison University; Bachelor of Science in Nursing, Radford University **A/A/S:** Association of Women's Health, Obstetric and Neonatal Nurses **C/VW:** Goodwill, United Way
Email: jbotkin@augustamed.com
URL: http://www.cambridgewhoswho.com

Elisabeth Boucher

Title: Owner **Company:** La Chouchoute Internationale **Dept:** Film Production Division **Address:** 13603 Marina Pointe Drive, Apartment D315, Marina Del Rey, CA 90292 United States **BUS:** Production Company **P/S:** Feature Films Production **MA:** Regional **D/D/R:** Writing, Directing and Producing Movies **H/I/S:** Writing, Dancing, Listening to French Music **EDU:** Bachelor's Degree in Liberal Arts, Columbia College Chicago (1990)
Email: elisabethboucher@yahoo.com
URL: http://www.cambridgewhoswho.com

Claudia Marie Boudreaux

Title: President **Company:** Shoulders to Lean On, Inc. **Address:** 208 Kraemer Street, Houma, LA 70364 United States **BUS:** Nonprofit Organization **P/S:** Support for Families of Inmates, Helping with Visitation Processes and Court Trials, Working with Prisoners to Help them Land Jobs After they are Released Through Mock Interviews and Basic Skills Classes **MA:** Regional **D/D/R:** Overseeing All the Functions of the Company, Working with Families of Inmates **H/I/S:** Sewing, Cooking, Reading **A/H:** Published Author, Louisiana Cure Newsletter and the International Cure Newsletter **C/VW:** Louisiana Lifers Association
Email: carouselhourse55@bellsouth.net

Jon R. Bouffard

Title: Paramedic **Company:** DHART **Address:** Medical Center Drive, Lebanon, NH United States **BUS:** Paramedic **P/S:** Advanced Response Medical Services **MA:** Local **EXP:** Mr. Bouffard's expertise includes adult and pediatric acute and pre-hospital care. **EDU:** Vermont Technical School, Associates in Engineering **A/A/S:** International Association of Flight Paramedics, National Association of EMT's, National Association of EMS Educators
Email: jon@nesec.biz
URL: www.dhnc.org//dept//dhart

Keith E. Boulware

Title: Building Inspector **Company:** City of New Bern **Address:** P.O. Box 1129, New Bern, NC 28563 United States **BUS:** Municipal Government Office **P/S:** Municipal Government **MA:** Local **D/D/R:** Inspecting Government Buildings, Including Plumbing, Heating, Air Conditioning, Mechanical, Electrical and Structural Safety for Buildings Up to Level Three **H/I/S:** Collecting Coins and Stamps, Traveling, Participating in Town Cultural Events **EDU:** Master's Degree in Engineering Management, Air Force Institute of Technology; Bachelor's Degree in Mechanical Engineering, Georgia Institute of Technology **CERTS:** Certified Building Inspector for Plumbing, Mechanical, Electrical and Structural Safety, to Level Three, North Carolina Code Officials Qualification Board **A/A/S:** Planning Board, City of River Bend; International Association of Electrical Inspectors; North Carolina Building Inspectors' Association **C/VW:** Missions Committee
Email: keboulware1@juno.com
URL: http://www.cambridgewhoswho.com

Dr. John R. Bourdette

Title: Professor Criminal Justice, Director Dependency Program **Company:** Western New Mexico University **Address:** P.O. Box 447, Silver City, NM 88062 United States **BUS:** Public University Serving Students Nationally **P/S:** Public Higher Education **MA:** National **D/D/R:** Teaching All Chemical Dependency Courses for Future Counselors **H/I/S:** Horseback Riding **EDU:** Ph.D. in Sociology, Oklahoma State University (1974) **A/A/S:** National Association of Alcohol and Drug Abuse Counselors; International Coalition for Addiction Studies Education; American Sociological Association; Academy of Criminal Justice Sciences
Email: bourdettej@wnmu.edu
URL: http://www.wnmu.edu

Karen M. Bourgoin

Title: Registered Dental Hygienist **Company:** Oxford Hills Dental Associates **Address:** 230 Main Street, Norway, ME 04268 United States **BUS:** Dental Care Center **P/S:** Dental Care **MA:** Regional **EXP:** Ms. Bourgoin's expertise is in oral cancer screenings. **D/D/R:** scaling, root planing, polishing teeth, taking and evaluating x-rays, educating patients **H/I/S:** Bicycling, Hiking, Reading **EDU:** Associate of Science in Dental Hygiene, Magna Cum Laude, The University of Augusta, Bangor Campus (2005) **A/A/S:** American Dental Association
Email: karen.bourgoin@cwwemail.com

Gregory T. Boutsikaris
Title: Subject Matter Expert Company: Sungard Availability Services Address: 15 Exchange Place, Jersey City, NJ 07302 United States BUS: Disaster Recovery and Hosting Service P/S: Disaster Recovery MA: International EXP: Mr. Boutsikaris' expertise is in advanced recovery services. H/I/S: Singer/Songwriter/Composer EDU: Master of Arts, Drew University; Bachelor of Arts, Seton Hall University, New Jersey A/A/S: Seton Hall Athletic Hall of Fame C/VW: Various Charities Email: greg@gtbouts.com
URL: http://www.gtbouts.com

Miles Bowen
Title: President Company: Miles Restorations, Inc. Address: 117 McCall Street, Bennington, VT 05201 United States BUS: Painting, Decorating and Historic Restoration Company P/S: Professional, Distinctive Paint Finishes and Unique Surface Restoration Services for Sophisticated Residential Clients MA: Regional D/D/R: Overseeing Business Operations, Offering Consultations H/I/S: Participating in a Local Ministry EDU: Bachelor's Degree in Theater Arts, Massachusetts College of Liberal Arts A/A/S: National Association of Professional Painters; Historic New England Chapter, Painting and Decorating Contractors of America
Email: milesrestoration@yahoo.com
URL: http://www.milesrestorations.com

Dr. Fay L. Bower
Title: Chairwoman Company: Holy Names University Dept: Department of Nursing Address: 1457 Indianhead Circle, Clayton, CA 94517 United States BUS: University P/S: Higher Education MA: International EXP: Dr. Bower's expertise includes evidence-based practices and community healthcare. D/D/R: Conducting Healthcare Research H/I/S: Gardening, Traveling, Spending Time with her Family, Watching Baseball EDU: Ph.D. in Nursing, University of California, San Francisco (1979); Master of Science, University of California, San Francisco (1966); Bachelor of Science in Nursing, San Jose State University (1965) A/A/S: Fellow, American Academy of Nursing; American Nurses Association; National League for Nursing; Sigma Theta Tau C/VW: Veterans of Foreign Wars (2004); Rotary Club of Oakland; National Council for Disabled Children; American Cancer Society
Email: fbower1@sbcglobal.net
Email: bower@hnu.edu
URL: http://www.hnu.edu

Sylvia L. Bowerman
Title: Administrative Assistant, Human Resources Staff Company: Herbruck Poultry Ranch Address: 6425 Grand River Avenue, Saranac, MI 48881 United States BUS: Poultry Ranch for Egg Production P/S: Eggs, Four Million Chickens MA: National D/D/R: Performing Administrative Duties, Overseeing Human Resources, Accounts Receivable, Inventory and Distribution Orders H/I/S: Crocheting, Auto Racing EDU: Bachelor of Arts in Business Administration, Northwood University; Associate Degree in Labor Relations and Personnel Management, Lansing Community College A/A/S: Phi Theta Kappa C/VW: Walk for Life; Local Medical Assistance Fundraisers; Platinum Supporter, Ionia County Free Fair; Relief After Violent Encounter
Email: c40@iserv.net

Elizabeth A. Bowers
Title: Teacher Company: Spruce Creek Elementary Address: 642 Taylor Road, Port Orange, FL 32127 United States BUS: School P/S: Education MA: Port Orange, Florida EXP: Ms. Bowers' expertise is in elementary education. H/I/S: Reading EDU: Bachelor's Degree in Elementary Education, University of Central Florida CERTS: Pursuing National Board Certification A/A/S: American Federation of Teachers C/VW: Local Church
Email: happyasred@aol.com

Raymond Bowler II
Title: Lieutenant, Fire Inspector Company: Littleton Fire and Rescue Address: 230 W. Main Street, Littleton, NH 03561 United States BUS: Fire and Emergency Medical Service P/S: Fire, Rescue, Emergency Medical Services, Public Safety MA: Local EXP: Mr. Bowler's expertise includes fire code inspection and enforcement. H/I/S: Working on his House EDU: Bachelor's Degree in Occupational Safety and Health, Keane State College A/A/S: National Fire Protection Association C/VW: Volunteer, Wanakee Methodist Center Summer Program; United Way
Email: rbowler@littletonfirerescue.org
URL: http://www.littletonfirerescue.org

Ms. Dana L. Bowling
Title: Medical Transcription Manager Company: Miami Valley Cardiologists, Inc. Address: 122 Wyoming Street, Dayton, OH 45409 United States BUS: Cardiology Practice P/S: Healthcare Services MA: Local EXP: Ms. Bowling's expertise includes medical transcription and management. H/I/S: Running, Traveling EDU: Coursework, Sinclair Community College C/VW: Foundation Fighting Blindness, American Heart Association
Email: dana414@netzero.com
URL: http://www.cambridgewhoswho.com

Arthur Thomson Bowman
Title: Former Vice President, Chief Financial Officer Company: Bowmans, Inc. Address: 326 N. Main Street, Kaysville, UT 84037 United States BUS: Retail Food Establishment P/S: Food Service MA: Local D/D/R: Overseeing Accounting and Cash Management H/I/S: Golfing, Traveling EDU: Master of Business Administration, University of Utah A/A/S: Rotary Club C/VW: Local Charities
Email: artbow61@msn.com

Elena Dorothy Bowman
Title: Software Engineer (Retired) Company: Elena Dorothy Bowman Address: 3 Julio Street, Chelmsford, MA 01824 United States BUS: Sole Proprietorship P/S: Writing Science Fiction, Mystery and Romance Novels MA: International EXP: Ms. Bowman's expertise includes software engineering and writing. H/I/S: Listening to Music, Watching Movies, Dancing EDU: Bachelor of Science in Engineering, Fitchburg State College A/A/S: President, Merrimack Valley Branch, National League of American Pen Women
Email: elenadb@comcast.net
URL: http://www.elenadb.home.comcast.net

Patricia A. Bowman
Title: President Company: Silent Voices Address: 65 Tall Pine Drive, Lewiston, Lewiston, ME 04240 United States BUS: Publishing Company P/S: Writing Poetry and Publishing Books MA: Regional EXP: Ms. Bowman's expertise is in writing memoirs. H/I/S: Skiing, Kayaking, Reading, Making Crafts, Spending Time with her Grandchildren, Litigating, Camping CERTS: Certified Medical Assistant; Certified Teaching Assistant; Certified Special Education Teacher A/A/S: Brain Injury Society; Malibu Handicap Ski Association A/H: Editor's Choice Award for Poetry (2007); Recipient, Editors Award for Poetry, International Society of Poetry (2005); Volunteer of the Year Award, NERA; Don Leader Award
Email: patsilentvoices@aol.com

Bernita Boyce
Title: Assistant Principal Company: Bayard Elementary School Address: 5 Henry Street, Wilmington, DE United States BUS: Large Elementary School with Over 1,100 Students and 110 Staff Members P/S: Helping Students Develop and Maintain their Academic and Social Skills on a Primary Level of Schooling MA: Regional D/D/R: Assisting in the Daily Operations of the School, Contacting Parents and Monitoring Students Attendance, Coordinating Staff Development Programs, Meeting with Colleagues in the District, Overseeing Enrollment in Summer School, Conducting Orientation for Students and Faculty, Formerly Acting as Principal of Powell Elementary School H/I/S: Traveling, Vegetarian, Cooking, Reading EDU: Doctor of Education in Innovation and Leadership, Wilmington College (2007); Education Specialist in Education Administration, University of Alabama at Birmingham (1999); Master's Degree in Elementary Education, University of Alabama at Birmingham (1986); Bachelor's Degree in Elementary Education, University of Alabama at Birmingham (1979) A/A/S: Association of School Curriculum and Development; National Geographic Society; Delaware Association of School Administrators
Email: bermosley3@aol.com
URL: http://www.christina.k12.de.us/bayard/

Laura E. Boyd
Title: Owner Company: La Risa Cafe, LLC Address: HC 72 Box 97, Ribera, NM 87560 United States BUS: Restaurant P/S: Northern New Mexican Cuisine, Homemade Breads and Desserts, Beverages, Catering MA: Local D/D/R: baking, cooking, training staff, bookkeeping and managing daily operations. H/I/S: Horseback Riding, Hosting High School Exchange Programs EDU: College Coursework
Email: jasonrocks2@netscape.net
URL: http://www.larisacafe.com

Carrie L. Boyer
Title: Primary Literacy Coordinator Company: Youngstown City Schools Dept: West Elementary School Address: 310 S. Schenley Avenue, Youngstown, OH 44509 United States BUS: School District P/S: Primary Education MA: Regional D/D/R: Coordinating Primary Literacy and Education Programs H/I/S: Playing Volleyball EDU: Master of Administration, Grand Canyon University A/A/S: Delta Kappa Gamma C/VW: Local Church
Email: clj314@aol.com
URL: http://www.cambridgewhoswho.com

Marilyn Boyer
Title: Author Company: The Learning Parent Address: 2430 Sunnymeade Road, Rustburg, VA 24588 United States BUS: Educational Institution P/S: Christian Parenting Education Including Homeschooling Products MA: International EXP: Ms. Boyer's expertise includes writing, curriculum development and public speaking. H/I/S: Reading, Scrapbooking, Swimming EDU: College Coursework A/A/S: Home School Legal Defense Association; Home Educators Association of Virginia; National Home Education Research Institute C/VW: Josh Boyer Memorial Benefit Concert; Leukemia Foundation; Make-A-Wish Foundation
Email: boyers@thelearningparent.com
URL: http://www.thelearningparent.com

Ms. Stephanie J. Boykin
Title: Realtor Company: RE/MAX Real Estate Professionals Address: 1401 Rucker Boulevard, Enterprise, AL 36330 United States BUS: Real Estate Agency P/S: Innovative Real Estate Services MA: International D/D/R: Assisting in Military Relocations, Selling New Construction Real Estate and Land, Working as a Residential Specialist and Buyer's Agent H/I/S: Singing in a Choir, Gardening EDU: Industry-Related Training and Experience CERTS: Licensed (2004) A/A/S: Lions Club; National Association of Realtors; Alabama Association of Realtors C/VW: Volunteer Lion's Club
Email: urrealtor4life@roadrunner.com
URL: http://www.StephanieBoykin.com

Melanie L. Boyles
Title: Registered Nurse, Course Coordinator Company: Sentara School of Health Professionals BUS: Medical School P/S: Healthcare Education MA: Hampton Roads EXP: Ms. Boyles' expertise is in critical-care nursing. D/D/R: Assisting Patients with Critical Health Issues, Coordinating Programs for New Nurses, teaching all aspects of medical and surgical contents. H/I/S: Quilting, Reading, Studying Medieval History EDU: Bachelor of Science in Nursing, Virginia School of Nursing, Virginia Commonwealth University Medical College CERTS: Registered Nurse, Portsmouth General Hospital School Of Nursing A/A/S: Plank Owner, Naval Medical Center Portsmouth (2005); American Association of Critical Care Nurses C/VW: Children's Hospital of The King's Daughters Health System; Children's Miracle Network
Email: boylesrn@cox.net
URL: http://www.cambridgewhoswho.com

Mary F. Boze
Title: Owner, Manager Company: Boze Properties Address: 925 Robinhood Court, Maitland, FL 32751 United States BUS: Rental Agency P/S: Real Estate Rentals MA: Local D/D/R: Finding Properties H/I/S: Appreciating Art EDU: Industry-Related Training and Experience C/VW: Community Outreach
Email: chamchambo@yahoo.com
URL: http://www.cambridgewhoswho.com

Marney E. Braasch
Title: Senior Compensation Analyst Company: Interstate Hotels & Resorts Address: 4501 N. Fairfax Drive, Suite 500, Arlington, VA 22203 United States BUS: Hotel Chain P/S: Managing Major Hotel Chains, Hospitality MA: National EXP: Ms. Braasch's expertise includes compensation and human resources. H/I/S: Working Out at the Gym, Spending Time Outdoors, Hiking, Walking, Running, Watching Movies, Dining, Traveling EDU: Bachelor of Science in Speech Communication, Minor in Human Resource Development, Concentration in Public Relations and Organizational Communications, James Madison University C/VW: Catholic Church
Email: braascme@yahoo.com
URL: http://www.ihrco.com

Robert Guy Brach
Title: Development Services Engineer Company: Bexar County, Texas Address: 233 N. Pecos La Trinidad, San Antonio, TX 78240 United States BUS: Government Organization P/S: Community Services Including County Infrastructure Development and Growth Control MA: Bexar County, Texas EXP: Mr. Brach's expertise is in civil engineering. H/I/S: Home Remodeling EDU: Bachelor of Science in Civil Engineering, The University of Texas, El Paso, TX (1986) A/A/S: American Society of Civil Engineers; Chi Epsilon C/VW: Autism Research Institute
Email: rbrach@bexar.org
URL: http://www.cambridgewhoswho.com

Brenda L. Bracy
Title: Legal Assistant Company: Schuering Zimmerman Scully Tweedy & Doyle, LLP Address: 400 University Avenue, Sacramento, CA 95825 United States BUS: Law Firm P/S: Medical Malpractice, Insurance Defense, Dental Malpractice MA: Regional D/D/R: Assisting Attorneys, Typing, Managing Calendars EDU: Coursework, Technical School
Email: brendabracy@hotmail.com

Liz Bradford
Title: President **Company:** Bradford Public Relations, Inc. **Address:** 4140 Emerson Avenue, Suite 4, Dallas, TX 75205 United States **BUS:** Public Relations Firm **P/S:** Public Relations **MA:** National **EXP:** Ms. Bradford's expertise is in public relations for small to large-sized corporations. **H/I/S:** Traveling **EDU:** Bachelor of Journalism, University of Texas at Austin **A/A/S:** Dallas Chamber of Commerce
Email: lbradford@bradfordpr.com
URL: http://www.bradfordpr.com

Shanna K. Bradford
Title: Sixth-Grade Mathematics Teacher **Company:** Lafayette School Corporation, Sunnyside Middle School **Address:** 2600 Cason Street, Lafayette, IN 47904 United States **BUS:** Middle School **P/S:** Education **MA:** Local **EXP:** Ms. Bradford's expertise is in administration. **D/D/R:** Teaching Gifted Students **H/I/S:** Gardening, Camping, Biking, Participating in Outdoor Activities, Attending Church Events **EDU:** Master's Degree in Administration and Curriculum Supervision, Purdue University **A/A/S:** National Education Association; Indian State Teachers Association; Lafayette Education Association; International Council of Mathematics; Phi Delta Kappa; Kappa Delta Pi; Indiana Reading Association; Association for Supervision and Curriculum Develop **C/VW:** Crestview United Brethren Church, National Wildlife Association
Email: sbradford@lsc.k12.in.us

Jean E. Bradley, RD
Title: Clinical Dietitian (Retired) **Company:** Kingsbrook Jewish Medical Center **Address:** 585 Schenectady Avenue, Brooklyn, NY 11203 United States **BUS:** Medical Center **P/S:** Healthcare **MA:** Regional **EXP:** Ms. Bradley's expertise is in nutrition education. **D/D/R:** conducting nutrition assessments, consulting with patients and their families and organizing workshops on nutrition and diet. **H/I/S:** Singing, Writing, Sewing **EDU:** Bachelor of Science in Food and Nutrition, Southern University and A&M College **C/VW:** Food Bank For New York City; American Dietetic Association
Email: jean.bradley@cwwemail.com
URL: http://www.kingsbrook.org

Pearl Larue Bradley
Title: Bishop/Pastor/Ambassador **Company:** University Holy Ghost Theology Outreach Mission, Inc **Address:** 6912 S Central Avenue, Los Angeles, CA 90001 United States **BUS:** Church **P/S:** Outreach Ministry with an Emphasis on Community Service **MA:** National **D/D/R:** Teaching and Preaching, Echelon Counseling **H/I/S:** Traveling, Reading **EDU:** Ph.D. **A/A/S:** ASCAT
Email: info@CambridgeWhosWho.com

Ian Bradshaw
Title: President **Company:** Ian Bradshaw Photography, Ltd. **Address:** 51 Cedar Lane, Dover, PA 17315 United States **BUS:** Photography **P/S:** Photography on Location **MA:** International **EXP:** Mr. Bradshaw's expertise is in photography. **D/D/R:** Lecturing **H/I/S:** Golfing, Teaching College Photography Classes, Consulting **EDU:** Coursework in Mathematics, Earned in England **A/H:** World Press Photo Award; Various Industry-Related Awards of Recognition
Email: ian@ianbradshaw.com
URL: http://www.ianbradshaw.com

Jennifer Brady
Title: Intern Pharmacist **Company:** Eckert **Address:** Pittsburgh, PA **BUS:** Drug Store **P/S:** Pharmaceuticals **MA:** Pittsburgh, Pennsylvania **D/D/R:** Filling Prescriptions **H/I/S:** Dancing **EDU:** Pursuing Doctor of Pharmacy, Duquesne University, Pittsburg, Pennsylvania
Email: jennb1384@hotmail.com

Sherrie J. Brady
Title: Co-Owner **Company:** Brady's Auto Service **Address:** 9377 E. Commerce Drive, Churubusco, IN 46723 United States **BUS:** Repair and Service Firm **P/S:** Repairing All Domestic and Foreign Automobiles **MA:** Local **EXP:** Ms. Brady's expertise is in operations management. **D/D/R:** bookkeeping, ordering new automotive parts, answering calls, processing payroll and preparing paperwork. **H/I/S:** Remodeling Cars **EDU:** High School Diploma **A/A/S:** Chamber of Commerce
Email: sherries67ss@verizon.net

Katherine Bragg
Title: Owner/Director **Company:** TransOutsource, Inc **Address:** PO Box 25095, London, N6C6A8 Canada **BUS:** Computer Software Education **P/S:** Software **MA:** International **H/I/S:** Reading, Gardening, Learning **EDU:** Coursework in Technology Computer Software, Professor **A/A/S:** Psychology, Human Resources
Email: info@CambridgeWhosWho.com
URL: www.tranoutsource.com

Mr. Henry H. Braithwaite
Title: Chief Financial Officer **Company:** Reynolds Exteriors, Inc. **Address:** 4870 Haygood Road, Suite 102, Virginia Beach, VA 23455 United States **BUS:** Contracting, Remodeling **P/S:** High End Home Remodeling Products **MA:** Regional, Hampton Roads **D/D/R:** Overseeing Financing, Payroll, Taxes, Monitoring Contractors, Dealing with Vendors **H/I/S:** Tennis, Painting, Video Games, Cooking, Wine Collecting **EDU:** Bachelor of Arts in French and Business, Emory University (2002)
Email: thepsych@aol.com
URL: http://www.cambridgewhoswho.com

Karen D. Branan
Title: Vice President, Banking Centers **Company:** Bank of America **Address:** 6390 Ten Oaks Road, Clarksville, MD **BUS:** Bank **P/S:** Banking Services **MA:** National **EXP:** Ms. Branan's expertise includes human resources, banking operations, sales and customer service. **H/I/S:** Reading Mystery Novels, Spending Time with her Family **EDU:** High School Graduate **A/A/S:** Chamber of Commerce **C/VW:** Order of the Eastern Star, Baltimore Cedarettes
Email: kdbangel@aol.com
URL: http://www.bankofamerica.com

Stephanie Branch
Title: Office Administrator **Company:** Sonnett and Associates **Address:** 333 S. Grand Avenue, Suite 3550, Los Angeles, CA 90071 United States **BUS:** General Civil Practice **P/S:** Products Liability, General Tort Liability and Business Litigation, Practicing in All State and Federal Courts **MA:** Regional **D/D/R:** Managing All Administrative Aspects of the Office, Accounting, Training and Overseeing Staff, Troubleshooting **H/I/S:** Golfing, Yoga, Traveling **EDU:** Associate Degree in Paralegal Studies, Watterson College (1996) **A/A/S:** Association of Legal Administrators
Email: sbranch@asonnettlaw.com
URL: http://www.asonnettlaw.com

Gary Allen Brandon
Title: Applications Engineer **Company:** Technical Training Aids **Address:** 2076 Valleydale Terrace, Birmingham, AL 35244 United States **BUS:** Selling an Expanded Array of Products and Services and Software to Satisfy All of the Technical Training Needs of Educators **P/S:** Comprehensive Line of Training Aids Ranging from Career Exploration Labs for Middle School Students to Sophisticated, Curriculum-Based Learning Units for Community College and University Students **MA:** National **D/D/R:** Working as an Autodesk Software Trainer and Instructor, Designing and Writing Online Tutorials for Instructors, Offering Software Expertise to Professors, Teachers, Architects and Mechanical Engineers, Creating Blueprints with Software **H/I/S:** Watching All Sports **EDU:** Bachelor of Science in Computer-Aided Drafting; Associate Degree in Animation, Virginia College (1994) **A/A/S:** Autodesk User Group International
Email: gbran10656@aol.com
URL: http://www.ttaweb.com

Milena I. Brankova
Title: Vice President, Regional Director **Company:** CEGEDIM Strategic Data USA, LLC **Address:** 10 Exchange Place, Jersey City, NJ 07302 United States **BUS:** Pharmaceuticals and Biotechnology Marketing Research Company **P/S:** Research, Pharmaceuticals **MA:** International **EXP:** Ms. Brankova's expertise includes biotechnology and pharmaceutical marketing research. **H/I/S:** Spending Time with her Family **EDU:** Master of Business Administration, Rutgers University **A/A/S:** PBIRG; European Pharmaceutical Marketing Research Association **C/VW:** Various Charitable Organizations
Email: mbrankova@yahoo.com
URL: http://www.cegedimstrategicdata.com

Jeannie Brannan
Title: Speech-Language Pathologist **Company:** South Texas Regional Medical Center **Address:** Highway 97, Jourdanton, TX 78026 United States **BUS:** Hospital **P/S:** Healthcare **MA:** Local **EXP:** Ms. Brannan's expertise includes rehabilitation and speech therapy. **EDU:** Master's Degree in Science and Communication Disorders, Baylor University **A/A/S:** American Speech-Language-Hearing Association
Email: jeannie_weir@hotmail.om
URL: http://www.cambridgewhoswho.com

Edward R. Brannigan
Title: President **Company:** New Jersey Fraternal Order of Police **Address:** 108 W. State Street, Trenton, NJ 08608 United States **BUS:** Law Enforcement Organization **P/S:** Representation for Law Enforcement Officers through Education, Legislation, Community Involvement and Employee Representation **MA:** National **EXP:** Mr. Brannigan's expertise includes labor and legislation and administration. **D/D/R:** Overseeing Finances and Labor Relations, Maintaining Legislation Contracts, Politics and Contacts with State Officials **H/I/S:** Golfing, Vacationing, Cruising **EDU:** High School Education **CERTS:** Certified Police Instructor; Certified Fire Arm Instructor **A/A/S:** Advisory Board, United States Department of Labor **C/VW:** Special Olympics; Police Memorial Fund; Easter Seals
Email: njfoppreserb@aol.com
URL: http://www.njfop.org

Gunnar Branson
Title: Principal **Company:** Branson Powers, Inc. **Address:** 4228 N. Paulina Street, Chicago, IL 60613 United States **BUS:** Strategic Marketing Company **P/S:** Consulting Services **MA:** National **EXP:** Mr. Branson's expertise is marketing. **H/I/S:** Reading, Writing **EDU:** Bachelor of Fine Arts, University of North Carolina
Email: gbranson@bransonpowers.com
URL: http://www.bransonpowers.com

Lisa Marie Brantley
Title: Supervisor **Company:** Butterfield Oxygen and Medical **Address:** 1161 S. U.S. Highway 1, Fort Pierce, FL 34950 United States **BUS:** Medical Equipment and Supplies **P/S:** Respiratory, Diabetes and Orthotic Equipment **MA:** Regional **D/D/R:** Supplying Medicare and Medical Equipment, Medical Billing **H/I/S:** Playing Softball **CERTS:** Certified Phlebotomist and Certified Lab Technician, Indian River Community College, Florida; Emergency Medical Technician
Email: librant03@yahoo.com

Patricia A. Braski
Title: Nurse Practitioner **Company:** William Beaumont Hospital **Address:** 3601 W. 13 Mile Road, Royal Oak, MI 48073 United States **BUS:** Hospital **P/S:** Healthcare **MA:** Local **EXP:** Ms. Braski's expertise is in nursing. **H/I/S:** Traveling **EDU:** Master's Degree in Nursing and Pediatrics, Wayne State University **A/A/S:** National Association of Pediatric Nurse Associates and Practitioners; National Association of Neonatal Nurses **C/VW:** The Humane Society
Email: patbrask@yahoo.com
URL: http://www.cambridgewhoswho.com

Nicole T. Braswell
Title: Owner **Company:** N & D Beauty Supplies **Address:** 3602 Salem Road, Covington, GA 30016 United States **BUS:** Beauty Supply Retailer **P/S:** Hair and Skin Products **MA:** Regional **D/D/R:** Managing Daily Operations Including Finances, Controlling Inventory, Keeping Abreast of Industry Changes **H/I/S:** Walking, Running, Swimming **EDU:** Bachelor's Degree in Business, Online University (2006)
Email: niyosbeautysupply@bellsouth.net

Andrei Calin Brateanu
Title: Physician **Company:** Huron Hospital, Cleveland Clinic Health System **Address:** 13951 Terrace Road, Cleveland, OH 44112 United States **BUS:** Hospital **P/S:** Healthcare **MA:** Local **EXP:** Mr. Brateanu's expertise includes internal medicine and pain management. **H/I/S:** Listening to Music, Swimming **EDU:** MD, Romania University of Medicine and Pharmacy **A/A/S:** American College of Physicians; American Medical Association; AAMA; Association of Program Directors in Internal Medicine
Email: abrateanu@hotmail.com

Amy Braun
Title: Clinical Pharmacist II **Company:** Harris County Hospital District **Address:** 1602 Garth Road, Baytown, TX 77520 United States **BUS:** Hospital **P/S:** Healthcare **MA:** Local **EXP:** Ms. Braun's expertise is in ambulatory care. **H/I/S:** Traveling, Reading **EDU:** Doctor of Pharmacy, University of Texas at Austin; Bachelor of Science in Biochemistry; Bachelor of Arts in French **A/A/S:** American College of Clinical Pharmacy; American Pharmacy Association; American Society of Health-System Pharmacists
Email: u2Amy@yahoo.com
URL: http://www.cambridgewhoswho.com

Anna A. Bravo
Title: Teacher **Company:** Somerton School District **Address:** 3200 County 16½ Street, Somerton, AZ 85350 United States **BUS:** Public School System **P/S:** Educating Students in Kindergarten through Eighth-Grades **MA:** Regional **D/D/R:** Teaching Reading and Comprehension, Mathematics and History to First Grade Students Following State Standards, Acting as First Grade Team Leader, Technology Coach **H/I/S:** Softball **EDU:** Bachelor's Degree in Education, Northern Arizona University (2002) **CERTS:** Certification in Education
Email: abravo@somerton.k12.az.us
URL: http://www.somerton.k12.az.us

Dr. Timothy Bray
Title: Doctor **Company:** Lakeview Medical Group **Address:** 7600 Lakeview Parkway, Suite 200, Rowlett, TX 75088 United States **BUS:** Hospital **P/S:** Medicine, Healthcare **MA:** Regional **D/D/R:** Managing Patients, Consulting **H/I/S:** Golfing, Spending Time Outdoors **EDU:** MD, University of North Texas, Fort Worth; D.O., University of North Texas Health Science Center at Fort Worth, University of Mary Hardin-Baylor
Email: tbray@lakeviewmedicalgroup.com

Christina D. Brazier
Title: Nursing Instructor **Company:** West Central Technical College **Address:** 179 Murphy Campus Boulevard, Waco, GA 30185 United States **BUS:** College **P/S:** Technical Higher Education **MA:** Local **D/D/R:** Teaching Nine Students in Clinics and at Hospitals **H/I/S:** Spending Time with her Family, Reading Medical Mystery Novels **EDU:** Master of Science in Nursing Education, University of West Georgia; Bachelor of Science in Nursing, University of West Georgia **CERTS:** Registered Nurse, Floyd College **A/A/S:** International Society of Psychiatric-Mental Health Nurses **C/VW:** American Diabetes Association
Email: cbrazier@westcentraltech.edu
URL: http://www.westcentraltech.edu

Mr. Ricardo A. Breceda
Title: Sculptor, Designer **Company:** Perris Jurassic Park **Address:** 1209 W. Perry Street, Perris, CA 92571 United States **BUS:** Metal Sculptor **P/S:** Imaginative Artistry in Metal **MA:** National **D/D/R:** Creating Custom Metal Sculptures, Creating Dinosaurs, Horses, Eagles, Large and Small Animals from Sheet Metal, Using Photographs and Clients' Designs **H/I/S:** Playing Sports **EDU:** Bachelor's Degree in Education, Escuela Normal Del Estado, Mexico (1982)
Email: info@perrisjurassicpark.com
URL: http://www.perrisjurassicpark.com

Rose A. Bredlau
Title: Associate Director **Company:** AT&T **Address:** 2000 W. AT&T Center Drive, Hoffman Estates, IL 60192 United States **BUS:** Telecommunications Company **P/S:** Telecommunications **MA:** International **EXP:** Ms. Bredlau's expertise includes leadership and sales. **D/D/R:** Marketing, Creating Strategies for Two Flagship Programs, Developing Business, Consulting, Training, Coaching **H/I/S:** Traveling, Reading, Spending Time with Family **EDU:** Master of Business Administration in Leadership and Change Management, DePaul University (2001); Bachelor's Degree in Business, Emphasis on e-Commerce and Marketing, National Louis University, 1998 **A/A/S:** Women of AT&T; Board of Directors, Homeowners Association **A/H:** Employee of the Year, President's Award **C/VW:** United Way, American Cancer Society, Women In Need of Growing Stronger
Email: rosebredlau@yahoo.com
URL: http://www.cambridgewhoswho.com

Darlene J. Breedlove
Title: Owner, Operator **Company:** Jimni Logistics **Address:** P.O. Box 189, Silver Springs, NV 89429 United States **BUS:** Transportation Company **P/S:** Transportation Logistics for Moving Household Goods Internationally **MA:** International **D/D/R:** Overseeing Domestic and International Logistics and Relocations **H/I/S:** Exercising, Bike Riding, Walking Dog, Motorcycle Riding with Husband, Hiking, Camping, Fishing, Tap Dancing **EDU:** Coursework in National Resource Science, Delta College **A/A/S:** Soroptimist International; Senior Citizens Group **A/H:** Dale Carnegie Outstanding Performance Award (February 1997); **C/VW:** Fundraising for Cancer Centers Sylvan Learning Centers and Various charities
Email: Jimni7@att.net
URL: http://www.cambridgewhoswho.com

Mrs. Megan R. Brehmer
Title: Interior Designer **Company:** HFS Concepts 4 **Address:** 1826 E. Bassett Way, Anaheim, CA 92805 United States **BUS:** Interior Designer Specializing in High-end Hospitality Design and High-end Residential Kitchen and Bath Design **P/S:** Renovation and New Construction of High-End Bathrooms and Kitchens **MA:** Domestic and International **H/I/S:** Spending Time with Family and Friends, Traveling with her Husband **EDU:** Associate of Arts in Interior Design, Brooks College (2002) **A/A/S:** National Kitchen & Bath Association
Email: ldmrb131@yahoo.com
URL: http://www.cambridgewhoswho.com

Laura Deeley Bren
Title: President **Company:** Atlantic/Smith, Cropper & Deeley, LLC. **Address:** 7171 Bent Pine Road, Willards, MD 21874 United States **BUS:** Insurance Company **P/S:** Insurance **MA:** Regional **D/D/R:** Insuring Commercial Lines, Managing Business Insurance, Managing Workers Compensation, Property Insurance and General Liability, Specializing in Commercial Properties and Overseeing Business Operation **H/I/S:** Spending Time with her Son **EDU:** Bachelor of Arts in Philosophy, Salisbury University **A/A/S:** SCIC; NAPSLO; IAB of Maryland; ASLI Designation **C/VW:** Believe in Tomorrow Foundation; Atlanta General Hospital
Email: lbren@ascd.net
URL: http://www.ascd.net

Jane H. Brenenstahl
Title: Tax Preparer, Bookkeeper **Company:** Brenenstahl's Bookkeeping and Taxes **Address:** 4465 Pensacola Street, Shasta Lake, CA 96019 United States **BUS:** Accounting Firm **P/S:** Tax Preparation, Bookkeeping and Payroll Services **MA:** Regional **EXP:** Ms. Brenenstahl's expertise is in accounting. **D/D/R:** Preparing Tax Returns for Individuals and Small Businesses **H/I/S:** Backpacking, Reading, Traveling **EDU:** Associate of Arts in Bookkeeping, Shasta Community College **A/A/S:** California Tax Education Council; Jehovah's Witnesses
Email: jjsmith@aol.com
URL: http://www.cambridgewhoswho.com

Catharine V. Brennan
Title: Director, Teacher **Company:** Discovery School **Address:** 1701 S.W. Collins, Topeka, KS 66604 United States **BUS:** Montessori Preschool **P/S:** Education **MA:** Local **EXP:** Ms. Brennan's expertise includes Montessori philosophy and methodology. **H/I/S:** Spending Time with her Family, Reading, Watching Movies, Gardening **EDU:** Master's Degree, North American Montessori Training Center; Bachelor of Arts, Wilson College **A/A/S:** Kansas Association for the Education of Young Children; National Association for the Education of Young Children; Texas Association for the Education of Young Children; CPCCK
Email: dsatopeka@att.net
URL: http://www.discoveryschooltopeka.org

Patricia A. Brennan
Title: Teacher **Company:** Franklin School **Address:** 2401 Manor Lane, Park Ridge, IL 60068 United States **BUS:** School **P/S:** Education **MA:** Local **D/D/R:** Teaching Reading and Mathematics Inclusion Classes **H/I/S:** Jogging, Tennis, Golfing, Horses **EDU:** Master of Arts in Educational Leadership, Xavier University **A/A/S:** National Education Association, Illinois Education Association; PREA **C/VW:** Church, ACS, Susan G. Komen for the Cure
Email: pbrennan@d64.k12.il.us
URL: http://www.cambridgewhoswho.com

Mark A. Brester
Title: Territory Manager **Company:** The W.I. Clark Company **Address:** 132 Dayl Drive, Kensington, CT 06037 United States **BUS:** Industrial, Construction and Forestry Company **P/S:** John Deere Construction **MA:** Northeastern Connecticut **D/D/R:** Production, Managing the Accounts in the Area **H/I/S:** Kayaking, Hiking, Biking **A/A/S:** United States Soccer; NISOA **C/VW:** Fidelco
Email: mbrester@wiclark.com
URL: http://www.cambridgewhoswho.com

Ina L. Brewer
Title: President **Company:** Brewer and Sons, Inc. **Address:** 7026 Nundy Avenue, Gibsonton, FL 33534 United States **BUS:** Mobile Home Park Firm **P/S:** Mobile Home Park Services **MA:** Regional **D/D/R:** Billing, Managing Operations for Seven Mobile Home Locations around Gibsonton **H/I/S:** Traveling, Spending Time with her Family **EDU:** Master of Science in Learning Disabilities, Eastern Michigan University; Bachelor of Science in Education, Capitol University **A/A/S:** Florida Mobile Home Park Owners and Managers; Manufacturers Association of Florida **C/VW:** Baptist Church
Email: ina.brewer@cwwemail.com

Ellen S. Brewood
Title: Realtor **Company:** Realty Executives of Kansas City **Address:** 11401 Ash Street, Leawood, KS 66111 United States **BUS:** Real Estate Company **P/S:** Residential and Commercial Real Estate, Bank Foreclosures, Corporate-Owned Property, Relocation Services, Mortgage Services **MA:** Local **H/I/S:** Traveling, Movies, Theater **EDU:** Coursework, Kansas State College, Pittsburgh, Kansas **A/A/S:** American Board of Realtors; Leneta Christian Center, Volunteer Work; NRBA; KCRAR; National Association of Realtors
Email: kcreosales@aol.com
URL: http://www.cambridgewhoswho.com

Sharie L. Brick
Title: Team Supervisor **Company:** American Red Cross **Address:** 7747 N. Kings Highway, Myrtle Beach, SC 29572 United States **BUS:** Nonprofit Organization **P/S:** Blood Services, Community Service **MA:** International **D/D/R:** Nursing, Handling All Aspects of Management for Mobile Blood Collecting Units **H/I/S:** Walking, Running Marathons to Raise Funds **EDU:** Associate Degree in Nursing, Inver Hills Community College, Minnesota, 1975 **A/A/S:** Church; American Nurses Association **C/VW:** Multiple Sclerosis Society, Church
Email: bricks@usa.redcross.org

Cheryl Bridges
Title: Registered Dental Hygienist **Company:** Dr. Dunn's Office **Address:** 12251 West Avenue, San Antonio, TX 78216 United States **BUS:** Dental Office **P/S:** Dentistry **MA:** Local **EXP:** Ms. Bridges' expertise is in periodontal therapy. **H/I/S:** Teaching Yoga, Making Jewelry **EDU:** Associate Degree in Dental Hygienist Studies, Del Mar College (1984) **A/A/S:** American Dental Association; President, San Antonio District Hygienist Society; American Dental Hygienist Association; Texas Dental Hygienist Association
Email: cbrdh00@aol.com
URL: http://www.cambridgewhoswho.com

Samantha M. Bridges
Title: Interpreter **Company:** Weatherford Independent School District **Address:** 1301 Charles Street, Weatherford, TX 76086 United States **BUS:** Independent School District **P/S:** Education for Students in Prekindergarten through High School, Courses for Advanced Students, Special Needs Students, Gifted and Talented Courses **MA:** Texas **D/D/R:** Translating from English to American Sign Language in French Word Order, Communicating with Deaf and Hard-of-Hearing Children **H/I/S:** Arts, Crafts, Dancing **EDU:** Pursuing Bachelor's Degree; BEI License (2005) **CERTS:** Certification in Communications, Tarrant County College, Northwest Campus (2001)
Email: sammbridges@yahoo.com
URL: http://www.weatherfordisd.com

Andrew J. Brienza
Title: Major Account Exercise **Company:** Careerbuilder.com **Address:** 6 Hudson St, West Winsor, NJ 00550 United States **BUS:** Human Capitol Retail **P/S:** Online Recruitment and Talent Acquisition **MA:** National **EXP:** Mr. Brienza's expertise is in sales. **H/I/S:** Physical Fitness and Earning Money **EDU:** West Chester University, BS
Email: andrew.brienza@careerbuilder.com

Wendy C. Briggs
Title: Secretary, Treasurer **Company:** Crystal Clean Distributing, Inc. **Address:** 2136 Sumter Street, Columbia, SC 29072 United States **BUS:** Maintenance Company **P/S:** Janitorial Services Including Floor Care Maintenance, Market Machinery, Repairing Services **MA:** Regional **D/D/R:** Consulting with Clientele, Training Franchise Companies and Janitorial Companies **H/I/S:** Hiking **EDU:** College Coursework Completed; High School Education Completed
Email: wbriggsccd@bellsouth.net

Sarah Scriven Bright
Title: Evangelist **Company:** Sarah Scriven Bright **Address:** 148 SW 13th Ave, Ocala, FL 34474 United States **BUS:** Ministry Human Resources **P/S:** Ministry, Outreach **MA:** International **EXP:** Ms. Bright's expertise is in evangelism. **H/I/S:** Aerobics, Walking **A/A/S:** Pentecostal Assemblies of the World
Email: info@CambridgeWhosWho.com

Theresa A. Brill
Title: Registered Nurse **Company:** Chestnut Hill Hospital **Address:** Trevose, PA 18350 United States **BUS:** Hospital **P/S:** Healthcare **MA:** Regional **EXP:** Ms. Brill's expertise includes perinatology, high-risk pregnancy case management, antenatal and genetic testing. **H/I/S:** Walking, Swimming, Listening to Music, Reading, Watching Movies **EDU:** Bachelor of Science in Health Arts **CERTS:** Certified Third Trimester Limited Obstetric Ultrasound **A/A/S:** Association of Women's Health, Obstetric and Neonatal Nurses; CMBS **A/H:** Outpatient Nursing Choice Award (2007) **C/VW:** Trevose Town Watch; Former Director, Bensalem Township School District
Email: usafavmom@aol.com
URL: http://www.cambridgewhoswho.com

Reed N. Brimhall
Title: Vice President, Controller, CAO **Company:** URS Corporation **Address:** 600 Montgomery Street, Suite 2500, San Francisco, CA 94111 United States **BUS:** Engineering and Construction Company **P/S:** Engineering Services **MA:** International **EXP:** Mr. Brimhall's expertise is in accounting. **H/I/S:** Fishing, Writing, History, Riding ATVs **EDU:** Bachelor of Business Administration in Accounting, Idaho State University **A/A/S:** American Institute of Certified Public Accountants; OSCTA; Idaho Society of Certified Public Accountants **C/VW:** Board Member, Idaho Virtual Academy
Email: reed_brimhall@urscorp.com
URL: http://www.urscorp.com

Brian B. Brinker
Title: Assistant Manager for Used Car **Company:** Airport Ford **Address:** 8001 Burlington Pike, Florence, KY 41042 United States **BUS:** Automotive Company **P/S:** Car Sales **MA:** National **EXP:** Mr. Brinker's expertise includes the refurbishment and sale of used cars. **D/D/R:** Managing Online Remarketing of Vehicles, Updating a Portion of the Website, In Charge of Pricing and Presentation and Weekly Updates **H/I/S:** Sports, Collecting Baseball Memorabilia, Playing Classical Music and Classic Rock on the Piano **EDU:** Bachelor's Degree in Accounting, Northern Kentucky University
Email: mrred27@hotmail.com
URL: http://www.airportford.com

John D. Brinkley
Title: President **Company:** JB Marketing **Address:** 1115 Loraine Avenue, Plainfield, NJ 07062 United States **BUS:** Marketing **P/S:** Marketing Advice and Services to Small Businesses and Nonprofit Organizations **MA:** Regional **D/D/R:** Creating Marketing Plans, Performing Market Research, Developing Websites, Understanding and Addressing Specific and Unique Aspects of a Client's Business, Managing Projects **H/I/S:** Golfing, Jazz and World Music **EDU:** Master's Degree in Education, Rutgers, The State University of New Jersey (1975)
Email: jbrmarketing@comcast.net
URL: http://www.caribbeanunseen.com

Maria D. Briones, MD
Title: Doctor **Company:** Maria Briones, MD, PC **Address:** 344 Main Street, Suite 103, Mount Kisco, NY 10549 United States **BUS:** Private Practice **P/S:** Healthcare, Internal Medicine, Weight Loss Program **MA:** Regional **EXP:** Ms. Briones' expertise is in internal medicine. **D/D/R:** performing knee and hip replacement surgery, managing private practice and assisting on weight loss and weight management. **H/I/S:** Swimming, Traveling **EDU:** MD, Autonomous University of Central America, Costa Rica (1986) **A/A/S:** Diplomat, American Board of Internal Medicine; American Medical Association; American College of Physicians; American Society of Bariatric Physicians
Email: mariabri@optonline.net
URL: http://www.mariabrionesmd.com

Tina C. Briscoe
Title: Teacher **Company:** Crowley Independent School District, Dallas Park Elementary School **Address:** 8700 Viridian Lane, Fort Worth, TX 76123 United States **BUS:** Elementary School **P/S:** Education **MA:** Local **D/D/R:** Teaching First Grade, Teaching English as a Second Language **H/I/S:** Reading, Traveling **EDU:** Bachelor of Science in Spanish, Austin College, Sherman, Texas; Master's Degree in Elementary Education, Austin College **A/A/S:** United Education Association
Email: tbriscoe@crowley.k12.tx.us

Ms. Beatriz Brito-Ferrer
Title: Principal, Educator **Company:** Brito Miami Private School **Address:** 2732 S.W. 32nd Avenue, Miami, FL 33133 United States **BUS:** School **P/S:** Education **MA:** International **D/D/R:** overseeing administrative duties, teaching mathematics including algebra, trigonometry and geometry, counseling students, teachers and parents. **H/I/S:** Dancing, Watching Movies, Collecting Spoons and Safety Matches **EDU:** Bachelor of Psychology, Florida International University **A/A/S:** National Honor Society; Interact **A/H:** Teacher of the Year Award; Principal of the Year Award, Day Care Center **C/VW:** American Cancer Society
Email: beatriz@britomiamiprivate.com

Ms. Linda Y. Britt
Title: Medical Transcriptionist **Company:** George Washington University Hospital **Address:** 900 23rd Street N.W., Washington, DC 20037 United States **BUS:** Hospital **P/S:** Healthcare **MA:** Local **EXP:** Ms. Britt's expertise includes the medical transcription of radiology and pathology. **H/I/S:** Exercising, Jogging **CERTS:** Certified Medical Technologist
Email: lbritt7307@aol.com
URL: http://www.cambridgewhoswho.com

Diane M. Brobst
Title: Substitute Teacher, Retired Teacher **Company:** Blue Mountain School District **Address:** 675 Red Dale Road, Orwigsburg, PA 17961 United States **BUS:** Elementary School Facility **P/S:** Regular Core Curriculum Including Reading, Mathematics, English, Science, Social Studies, Art, Music and History **MA:** Regional **D/D/R:** Teaching Mathematics, Organizing the Curriculum **H/I/S:** Reading, Horse Riding, Caring for her Cats and Dogs **EDU:** Master's Degree in Elementary Education, Kutztown University (1994); Bachelor's Degree in Elementary Education, Kutztown University (1970) **A/A/S:** St. Paul's Lutheran Church; Christian Children's Fund
Email: brobst@myfam.com
URL: http://www.schools-data.com/schools/Blue-Mountain-East-El-Sch-Orwig

Patricia A. Brock
Title: Kindergarten Teacher **Company:** Leon County Schools, Springwood Elementary School **Address:** 3801 Fred George Road, Tallahassee, FL 32303 United States **BUS:** School **P/S:** Education **MA:** National **D/D/R:** Teaching Early Childhood Education **H/I/S:** Playing Piano, Listening to Music, Traveling, Antique Shopping, Helping Others, Writing Children's Books **EDU:** Bachelor of Arts in Elementary Education and Early Childhood Education, Florida State University, 1971 **CERTS:** National Board Certified Teacher **A/A/S:** International Reading Council **A/H:** District Teacher Award **C/VW:** Weekend Supervisor, Ronald McDonald House
Email: patbrock2000@yahoo.com

Joy L. Broda
Title: Fourth-Grade Teacher **Company:** Tacoma School District **Address:** 4110 Nassau Avenue N.E., Tacoma, WA 98422 United States **BUS:** Public School District for Tacoma Residents **P/S:** Public Education for Local Students **MA:** Local **D/D/R:** Teaching Fourth-Grade Subjects to 25 Students Including Reading, Mathematics, Science, Art and Social Studies, Working with Children with Emotional Issues, Meeting with Parents **H/I/S:** Art **EDU:** Bachelor's Degree in Sociology and Elementary Education, University of Washington (1984) **A/A/S:** Tacoma Education Association; National Education Association; Washington Education Association
Email: joy@brodas.com
URL: http://www.cambridgewhoswho.com

Dr. Charles Edward Brodine
Title: Physician (Retired) **Company:** Dr. Charles Edward Brodine **Address:** 211 Russell Avenue, Apartment 57, Gaithersburg, MD 20877 United States **BUS:** Healthcare Center **P/S:** Healthcare **MA:** National **EXP:** Dr. Brodine's expertise is in hematology,. **D/D/R:** practicing environmental health, preventative and internal medicine, conducting medical research, educating patients, managing projects on research regarding frozen blood and trauma. **H/I/S:** Photography, Traveling **EDU:** MD, Washington University, Saint Louis (1953); Bachelor of Science, Iowa State University (1949) **A/A/S:** Navy Bureau of Medicine and Surgery Policy Council; Board of Consultant, Surgeon's General of the Armed Forces; Board of Directors, Gorgas Memorial Institute of Tropical and Preventive Medicine, Panama; Commanding Officer, Advisory Committee, National Sickle Cell Disease; U.S. Navy Medical Research and Development Command; National Research Council; National Academy of Sciences; Hematology Research Study Section, National Institutes of Health; Board of Directors, Academy of Medicine, Washington, DC; Medical Advisory Board; Executive Committee, National Council on International Health; Committee of Biomedical Research US-Egypt Working Group; White House Working Group on International Health **A/H:** Award, Navy's Legion of Merit for Medical Research Project in Vietnam; Outstanding Performance Award, Legion of Merit Commander of NMRDC; Navy Meritorious Service Medal; Charles Dexter Conrad Award, United States Secretary of the Navy; Superior Honor Award, United States Department of State; Outstanding Achievement Award, United States Department of State; Who's Who in the World Award; Award, Who's Who in Medicine; Award, Who's Who in Science and Engineering; Award, Who's Who in America **C/VW:** American Red Cross
Email: chuckandlois@gmail.com
URL: http://www.cambridgewhoswho.com

Erica N. Brogan
Title: Registered Nurse, Charge Nurse **Company:** Washington Regional Medical Center **Address:** 3229 W. Mica Street, Fayetteville, AR 72704 United States **BUS:** City Hospital **P/S:** Healthcare **MA:** Regional **EXP:** Ms. Brogan's expertise is in operating room nursing. **D/D/R:** Caring for Patients, Overseeing Nurses, Expediting Schedules **H/I/S:** Gardening, Cooking **EDU:** Bachelor of Science in Nursing, University of Arkansas, 2003 **CERTS:** Certified Operating Room Nurse; Certification in Advanced Cardiac Life Support; Certified Charge Nurse **A/A/S:** Association of periOperative Registered Nurses, Sigma Theta Tau
Email: enbrogan@gmail.com

Robert E. Brooker
Title: Superintendent **Company:** Plum Lake Golf Club **Address:** 3160 Club House Road, Sayner, WI 54560 United States **BUS:** Golf Course **P/S:** Golfing **MA:** Local **EXP:** Mr. Brooker's expertise is in turf management. **H/I/S:** Golfing, Fishing, Hunting, Traveling **EDU:** Bachelor of Arts in Turf Management, University of Massachusetts, Amherst **A/A/S:** Golf Course Superintendents Association of America; Wisconsin Turf Association; Wisconsin State Golf Association; Northern Great Lakes Golf Course Superintendents Association **C/VW:** Lions Club
Email: brooker@nnex.net
URL: http://www.cambridgewhoswho.com

Helen E. Brooks
Title: Nurse Practitioner, Adjunct Faculty **Company:** University of North Carolina at Greensboro **Dept:** School of Nursing **Address:** 409 Sunset Drive, Greensboro, NC 27402 United States **BUS:** Institution of Higher Learning Dedicated to Excellence in Education **P/S:** Full Array of Graduate, Undergraduate and Programs, School of Nursing, Teaching, Research, Patient Care **MA:** Regional **EXP:** Ms. Brooks' expertise includes cardiology and adult health. **H/I/S:** Skiing, Traveling, Gardening **EDU:** Master of Science Degree in Nursing, University of North Carolina, Greensboro (2001); Pursuing Doctorate in Acute and Clinical Care, University of Tennessee at Memphis (Expected 2009) **A/A/S:** AANP; NCGNP; ACC; NCNA; Sigma Theta Tau
Email: jbrooks47@triad.rr.com
URL: http://www.uncg.edu

Mercedes Brooks, LPN
Title: Unit Manager, Licensed Practical Nurse **Company:** Genesis Health **Address:** 101 Pocono Trail, Hopatcong, NJ 07843 United States **BUS:** Proven Leader in the Healthcare Industry **P/S:** Healthcare, Long Term Care **MA:** Regional **D/D/R:** Overseeing a Unit for a 24-Bed Facility, Managing the Area, Dispensing Medication, Promoting Patient Care, Treating Patient Needs, Supervising the Staff, Consulting with Doctors Regarding Patient Care **H/I/S:** Reading, Traveling **CERTS:** Licensed Practical Nurse, Denville Vocational Technical School (1987) **A/A/S:** Featured, Front Cover, 'LPN Advance' Magazine
Email: info@CambridgeWhosWho.com
URL: http://www.genesishealth.com

Tamara S. Brooks
Title: Teacher **Company:** Moulton-Udell Community School **Address:** 305 E. 8th Street, Moulton, IA 52572 United States **BUS:** Community School Facility **P/S:** Regular Core Curriculum including Reading, Math, English, Science, Social Studies, Art, Music, History, Language Arts, Physical Education, Computers **MA:** Regional **D/D/R:** Teaching Title I Reading and 7th and 8th-Grade Literature **H/I/S:** Alzheimer's Care and Issues, Church, Reading, History **EDU:** Master's Degree in Special Education Multi-Categorical K-8, Morningside College (1993); Bachelor's Degree in Elementary Education with a Minor in Sociology, Upper Iowa University (1977) **A/A/S:** National Education Association; ISEA; Delta Kappa Gamma **A/H:** Outstanding Young Women of America Award; Who's Who Among America's Teachers
Email: brotam@iowatelecom.net
URL: http://www.moulton-udell.k12.ia.us

Paulette C. Brookshire
Title: Owner **Company:** BBM Cosmetics, LLC **Address:** Rock Hill, SC United States **BUS:** Privately Owned Beauty and Supplies Manufacturing Company **P/S:** Private Label Wholesale Products, E-Commerce, Eye Shadow, Foundation and Lipstick **MA:** International **D/D/R:** Manufacturing Natural Mineral Cosmetics, Selling a Wholesale Private Label Skincare Line, Contracting for Mixing Services, Checking Emails, Filling Orders, Handling Payroll and Bookkeeping, Overseeing Website Maintenance, Selling Cosmetic Supplies, Handling Search Engine Registration, Filling Contracts **H/I/S:** Selling Mineral Cosmetics **EDU:** Associate Degree in Business, York Technical College (1971); Coursework in Computers, Winthrop University **CERTS:** Licensed in Life and Casualty Personal Property Insurance (1972) **A/A/S:** Woodmen of the World
Email: bbmcosmetics@comporium.net
URL: http://www.bbmcosmetics.com

Mr. Mark D. Bross
Title: Computer Simulation Technology Specialist **Company:** CST of Montgomery County, Inc. **Address:** 1001 Sterigere Boulevard, Suite 6, Norristown, PA 19401 United States **BUS:** Nonprofit Organization **P/S:** Surveys, County Housing Programs, Community Residential Rehabilitation **MA:** Local **D/D/R:** Interviewing, Communication Skills **H/I/S:** Spending Time Outdoors, Camping, Hiking **EDU:** Associate Degree in Liberal Arts, Montgomery County Community College
Email: mark.bross@cwwemail.com
URL: http://www.cambridgewhoswho.com.

Douglas A. Broughton
Title: Info Management Specialist **Company:** U.S. Department of Transportation **Dept:** Federal Highways **Address:** 228 Walnut Street, Room 508, Harrisburg, PA 17101 United States **BUS:** Government Organization **P/S:** Transportation Services **MA:** National **EXP:** Mr. Broughton's expertise includes information management and technology, administration, procurement, purchasing, web casting and telecommunications. **H/I/S:** Golfing **EDU:** Pursuing Bachelor's Degree in Organizational Management, Ashford University (2008); Associate Degree in Administrative Management, Community College of the Air Force (1991)
Email: irish56be8@hotmail.com
URL: http://www.fhwa.dot.gov

Mary R. Brouillette

Title: Business Teacher **Company:** Bellows Free Academy of Saint Albans **Address:** 71 South Main Street, St. Albans, VT 05478 United States **BUS:** High School **P/S:** Regular Core Curriculum Including Reading, Mathematics, English, Science, Social Studies, Art, Music, History, Language Arts, Computers, Physical Education and Business Courses **MA:** Local **D/D/R:** Teaching Career Exploration, Sports Marketing and Entrepreneurial Classes, Offering Leadership Training Classes in the Dale Carnegie Model, Counseling, Advising, Running a Mentor Program **H/I/S:** Golfing, Biking, Kayaking, Playing Softball **EDU:** Pursuing Master's Degree in Sports Management; Bachelor's Degree in Business, St. Michael's College, Plus 45 (1988) **A/A/S:** Vermont Business Teachers Association; Virginia Shooting Sports Association
Email: mbrouillette@bfasta.net
URL: http://www.bfasta.net

Tina L. Broussard

Title: Maintenance Planner **Company:** FilmTec Corporation **Address:** 5400 Dewey Hill Road, Edina, MN 55439 United States **BUS:** Light Industrial Manufacturer **P/S:** Light Manufacturing **MA:** International **D/D/R:** Planning Maintenance Activities **H/I/S:** Riding Motorcycles, Golfing, Fishing, Hunting **C/VW:** Training Therapy Dogs
Email: tinabc085@yahoo.com

Deborah Sue Brower

Title: Histologist **Company:** Ohio Valley General Hospital **Address:** 25 Heckel Road, McKees Rocks, PA 15136 United States **BUS:** Hospital **P/S:** Healthcare **MA:** Local **EXP:** Ms. Brower's expertise is in histology. **H/I/S:** Making Crafts, Creating Centerpieces **EDU:** Bachelor of Arts in Biology, Washington and Jefferson College **CERTS:** Certified, American Society for Clinical Pathology **A/A/S:** National Society for Histotechnology
Email: info@CambridgeWhosWho.com
URL: http://www.cambridgewhoswho.com

Barbara Ann Brown

Title: Retired Children's Librarian **Company:** The Chicago Public Library-Legler Branch **Address:** 115 South Pulaski, Chicago, IL 60624 United States **BUS:** Public Library Information System **P/S:** Book Lending, Newspapers, Magazines, Computer Resources, On-Line Catalog Search, Volunteer Engaged **MA:** Local **D/D/R:** Offering Reference Advisory Services to the General Public Including Children's Programs, Exhibits, Enriched Education Services for Schools, Churches and Other Community Organizations **H/I/S:** Reading, Writing **EDU:** Bachelor of Science Degree in Elementary Education; Master's Work in Library Sciences and Management and Supervision **A/A/S:** Tutoring; Foster Parenting; Church Nursing
Email: info@CambridgeWhosWho.com

Mr. Brian W. Brown

Title: Patent Agent **Company:** Morgan & Finnegan, LLP **Address:** 1775 I Street N.W., Suite 400, Washington, DC 20006 United States **BUS:** Intellectual Property Law Firm **P/S:** Legal Services Relating to Evaluating, Selling or Licensing Intellectual Property, Conducting Due Diligence, Dealing with Antitrust Issues and Structural Transactions **MA:** International **EXP:** Mr. Brown's expertise is in patent law. **D/D/R:** Drawing and Securing Foreign and Domestic Patents for Inventors, Consulting and Collaborating with Attorneys, Managing Validity Searches and Opinions **H/I/S:** Photography, Astronomy, Genealogy **EDU:** Bachelor's Degree in Physics, Northern Arizona University (1981) **A/A/S:** American Intellectual Property Law Association
Email: bwcsbrown@comcast.net
URL: http://www.morganfinnegan.com/index.html

Christine L. Brown

Title: Credit Manager **Company:** Arvco Container Corp **Address:** 845 Gibson Street, Kalamazoo, MI 49001 United States **BUS:** Financial **P/S:** Accounts Receivable **MA:** Regional **D/D/R:** Generating Revenue **H/I/S:** Fishing, Archery, Bocce Ball **EDU:** Two Years of College **A/A/S:** Boy Scouts, Girl Scouts, Veterans
Email: cbrown@arvco.com
URL: www.arvco.com

Crystal B. Brown

Title: Systems Analysis Manager **Company:** National Board of Medical Examiners **Address:** 3750 Market Street, Philadelphia, PA 19104 United States **BUS:** Academic and Educational Research Company **P/S:** Academic and Educational Research, Medical Education, Credentialing **MA:** National **D/D/R:** Maintaining Quality Control for Test Data Systems **H/I/S:** Reading, Jogging, Cooking **EDU:** Master's Degree, The Johns Hopkins Bloomberg School of Public Health; Bachelor's Degree in Spanish, Haverford College, Haverford, PA **A/A/S:** American Educational Research Association
Email: crsbelcher@comcast.net
URL: http://www.nbme.org

Dr. Dennis W. Brown

Title: Director of Secondary Education **Company:** Fremont Unified School District **Address:** 4210 Technology Drive, Fremont, CA 94538 United States **BUS:** Public School District **P/S:** Education for Kindergarten through 12th-Grade Students **MA:** Local **EXP:** Dr. Brown's expertise is in education. **D/D/R:** Offering Instructional Leadership, Managing the Curriculum **H/I/S:** Traveling, Playing Sports, Listening to Jazz Music, Collecting Art **EDU:** Doctor of Education in Educational Administration, University of Southern California (1994); Master's Degree in Public Administration, Roosevelt University (1978); Master of Science in Special Education (1975); Bachelor of Science in Education, Chicago State University (1969) **A/A/S:** 100 Black Men of America, Inc.; Kappa Alpha Psi **C/VW:** United Way; United Negro College Fund
Email: dbrown@fremont.k12.ca.us
URL: http://www.fremont.k12.ca.us

Eleanor S. Brown

Title: Owner **Company:** E.S. Brown and Associates **Address:** 949 Aberdeen Avenue N.E., Renton, WA 98056 United States **BUS:** Consulting and Family Therapy Company **P/S:** Consulting for Businesses and Organizations **MA:** National **D/D/R:** Offering Family Therapy and Consulting Services Including Organizational Assistance, Advising, Writing, Teaching Computers, Offering Systems Consulting **H/I/S:** Participating in Political Activism **EDU:** Master's Degree in Psychology; Whole System Design **A/A/S:** Member, Mensa International; Developer, Mapping of the Moon; President, Condominium Owners Association
Email: eaglegazer1@gmail.com

Evan E. Brown

Title: Owner, Manager **Company:** Forever Green Lawn Maintenance **Address:** P.O. Box 4361, Naperville, IL 60567 United States **BUS:** Lawn Maintenance Company **P/S:** Lawn Maintenance **MA:** Local **D/D/R:** Managing Daily Operations **H/I/S:** Watching Sports, Visiting Friends and Family **C/VW:** Church
Email: ebrwon@aol.com
URL: http://www.cambridgewhoswho.com

Halbert Brown Jr.

Title: Owner, Chief Executive Officer **Company:** Universal Nursing Services of Texas **Address:** 2379 N.E. Loop 410, Suite 10, San Antonio, TX 78217 United States **BUS:** Healthcare Agency **P/S:** Home Healthcare, Skilled Nursing, Physical Therapy, Occupational Therapy, Speech Therapy **MA:** Regional **D/D/R:** Coordinating with the Director, Administering Home Infusions, Managing Accounts, Assigning Nurses to Field Locations, Offering Social Services **H/I/S:** Traveling, Golfing **EDU:** Master of Business Administration, Embry-Riddle Aeronautical University (2003) **CERTS:** Master's Level Certificate in Leadership and Management in Healthcare Services **A/A/S:** Texas Association for Home Care; Business Networking International; Greater San Antonio Chamber of Commerce; Alumni, Quality Home Care Council; National Black Chamber of Commerce; Chairman, Alamo Area Chamber of Commerce; Chairman, Alamo City Black Chamber of Commerce
Email: hbrown1458@aol.com

James C. N. Brown

Title: Owner **Company:** James C.N. Brown, MD **Address:** 432 E. Bloomington Street, Iowa City, IA 52245 United States **BUS:** Medical Practice **P/S:** Healthcare **MA:** Local **EXP:** Mr. Brown's expertise includes the treatment of affective disorders, substance abuse and related health issues. **EDU:** Bachelor of Medicine, Bachelor of Surgery, Bachelor of the Obstetric Arts, National University of Ireland; Master of Science in Psychiatry, State University of Iowa **A/A/S:** Johnson County Medical Society; Johnson County Delegate, Iowa Medical Society (1983-2003); Iowa State Medical Society; American Medical Association; Iowa Psychiatric Society; Distinguished Fellow, American Psychiatric Association
Email: jcnbrown@aol.com

Jashana Brown

Title: Home Health Nurse **Company:** Saint Barnabas Medical Center **Address:** 22 Old Short Hills Road, Livingston, NJ 07039 United States **BUS:** Medical Center **P/S:** Healthcare **MA:** National **EXP:** Ms. Brown's expertise is in home healthcare nursing. **D/D/R:** Supervising the Staff **H/I/S:** Reading, Exercising **EDU:** Bachelor of Science in Nursing, Bloomfield College (2007) **A/A/S:** New Jersey State Nurses Association **C/VW:** Local Church
Email: jgodsprincess@aol.com
URL: http://www.cambridgewhoswho.com

Joan M. Brown

Title: Teacher **Company:** Oneonta City Schools **Address:** 27605 State Highway 75, Oneonta, AL 35121 United States **BUS:** School District **P/S:** Education **MA:** Local **D/D/R:** Overseeing the Science Department for Sixth through Eighth-Grade Students, Teaching Sixth-Grade Science **H/I/S:** Hiking, Gardening **EDU:** Bachelor of Science in Elementary Education, University of Alabama at Birmingham **A/A/S:** Alabama Science Teachers Association; Vice President, Oneonta Educators Association; NEA **C/VW:** St. Jude Children's Research Hospital, Cancer Foundation
Email: jbrown@oneonta.k12.al.us

Mrs. Karen Jayne Brown

Title: Professional Interior Designer **Company:** 1) Tools of the Trade, LLC 2) Brown's Bay Interior Design, LLC 3) Diamond Architectural Rendering, LLC 4) Designer Draperies, LLC **Address:** 901 Griffing Park Road, Buffalo, MN 55313 United States **BUS:** Design Firm **P/S:** Commercial and Residential Interior Design **MA:** International **EXP:** Mrs. Brown's expertise includes high-end residential interior design and architectural rendering. **D/D/R:** Managing Operations **H/I/S:** Listening to Music, Attending the Concerts, Treasure Hunting **EDU:** Bachelor of Science in Interior Design, University of Minnesota (1991); Associate of Arts, North Hennepin Community College (1987) **CERTS:** Certification, National Council for Interior Design Qualification (1997) **A/A/S:** American Society of Interior Designers; International Furnishings and Design Association; Interior Design Society; International Interior Design Association **A/H:** Citation of Excellence Award, Buildings Magazine (2007); Recipient, NeoCon (2007); Citation of Excellence Award, Designer Draperies (2007); Innovation Award **C/VW:** Saint Matthew's Churches
Email: brownbox@usfamily.net
URL: http://www.karenbrownasid.com
URL: http://www.diamondrendering.com

Leondra Brown

Title: Program Director **Company:** Boys & Girls Club of Delaware **Address:** 19 Lambson Lane, New Castle, DE 19720 United States **BUS:** Nonprofit Organization **P/S:** Youth Activities **MA:** National **EXP:** Ms. Brown's expertise is in finance. **D/D/R:** Helping Children **H/I/S:** Reading **EDU:** Master's Degree in Organization Management and Leadership, Springfield College
Email: lbrown@bgclubs.org
URL: http://www.bgclubs.org

Malinda B. Brown

Title: Prekindergarten Teacher **Company:** Ben Hazel Primary School **Address:** 628 Railroad Avenue W., Hampton, SC 29924 United States **BUS:** School **P/S:** Education **MA:** Local **D/D/R:** Teaching Pre-Kindergarten **H/I/S:** Taking Care of a 3-Year-Old, Decorating Cakes **EDU:** Master's Degree Plus 30 in Early Childhood Education, University of South Carolina; Bachelor's Degree in Early Childhood Education, Clemson University **A/A/S:** South Carolina Early Childhood Association **C/VW:** American Cancer Society
Email: mbbrown@hampton1.k12.sc.us
URL: http://bhp.hampton1.org

Meredith R. Brown

Title: Faculty **Company:** The Lamplighter School **Address:** 11611 Inwood Road, Dallas, TX 75229 United States **BUS:** Education **P/S:** Early Childhood Education **MA:** Local **EXP:** Ms. Brown's expertise is in early childhood education. **H/I/S:** Family **EDU:** Bachelor's Degree, Southern Methodist University
Email: info@CambridgeWhosWho.com

Neujia-Patricia M. Brown

Title: Writer, Poet, Design Consultant **Company:** Creations by Neujia **Address:** P.O. Box 200847, Anchorage, AK 99520 United States **BUS:** Poetry, Consulting, Design, Marketing, Public Speaking **P/S:** Poetry, Public Speaking, Consulting, Design, Community Organization **MA:** Local **D/D/R:** Writing Poetry, Public Speaking, Consulting, Designing, Organizing the Community **H/I/S:** Enjoying Nature, Brooks and Mountains **EDU:** Master of Science in Psychology and Sociology, Minor in English, University of Alaska; Combination of Academic Employment and Community Involvement Equal to a Master's Level **A/A/S:** National Association for the Advancement of Colored People; American Civil Liberties Union; Professional Businesswomen of Anchorage, Alaska **A/H:** Various Awards for Poetry and Charity **C/VW:** American Red Cross
Email: iceoldster@webtv.net

Ms. Patricia Brown

Title: Owner **Company:** Keeling Company **Address:** 1551 Williamsbridge Road, Apt. 1C, Bronx, NY 10461 United States **BUS:** Residential/Commercial Real Estate and Finance Company **P/S:** Real Estate, Financial Services **MA:** Local **EXP:** Ms. Brown's expertise includes research and project development. **H/I/S:** Reading, Playing Tennis, Renovating, Playing Sports **EDU:** College Coursework Completed, Indiana State University **C/VW:** Local Soup Kitchens
Email: keelingco25@yahoo.com

Miss Rachel E. Brown

Title: Special Education Teacher **Company:** North Kansas City School District **Dept:** Crestview Elementary **Address:** 4327 N. Holmes, Kansas City, MO 64116 United States **BUS:** North Kansas City School District **P/S:** Special Education **MA:** Regional **D/D/R:** Working with Special Education Students **H/I/S:** Studying the Arts and painting **EDU:** Bachelor of Science in Special Education with a minor in Art, From the University of the Ozarks **A/A/S:** Missouri State Teachers Association **C/VW:** Christian Foundation of Children and aging
Email: rbrown3092@kc.rr.com
Email: rbrown@nkcsd.k12.mo.us
URL: http://www.nkesd.k12.mo.us/cres/

Robert H. Brown

Title: Film Editor **Company:** Footpath Productions, Inc. **Address:** 5945 Donna Avenue, Tarzana, CA 91356 United States **BUS:** Film Editing **P/S:** Editing Films **MA:** International **D/D/R:** Interfacing with Directors, Producers and Writers **H/I/S:** Golfing, Reading, Traveling **EDU:** High School Graduate **A/A/S:** Academy of Motion Picture Arts and Sciences
Email: bhb3501@sbcglobal.net
URL: http://www.cambridgewhoswho.com

Shelly-Ann L. Brown

Title: Home School Instructor **Company:** Brown's Tutoring **Address:** 524 Shoemaker Road, West Point, GA 31833 United States **BUS:** Elementary School Facility Dedicated to Excellence in Education **P/S:** Regular Core Curriculum Including Reading, Math, English, Science, Social Studies, Music, Art, History, Physical Education **MA:** Regional **D/D/R:** Teaching Physical and Health Education **H/I/S:** Aquatic Director, Boy Scouts of America **EDU:** Bachelor's Degree in School Health, University of Florida (2004); Pursuing Master's Degree in Early Childhood Education, Columbus State University **A/A/S:** National Teachers Association; Georgia Association of Educators; St. Peter's Catholic Church; USAA
Email: shellydg98@yahoo.com
URL: http://wres.troup.k12.ga.us

Tara-Jo Brown

Title: Accountant **Company:** The Kuskokwim Corporation **Address:** 4300 B Street, Suite 207, Anchorage, AK 99503 United States **BUS:** Village Corporation **P/S:** Passive Investments, Contracting and Construction Services **MA:** National **D/D/R:** Accounting, Maintaining Journal Entries and Payroll, Auditing, Managing Human Resources **H/I/S:** Fishing, Hunting **EDU:** Bachelor of Science in Accounting, Tulsa College (1995) **A/A/S:** Society for Human Resources Management
Email: RockandTara@aol.com
Email: tjb@kuskokwim.com

Tonia R. Brown

Title: Teacher **Company:** South Delta High School **Address:** 303 S. Parkway Avenue, Rolling Fork, MS 39159 United States **BUS:** High School **P/S:** Education **MA:** Local **D/D/R:** Teaching Mathematics to High School Students **H/I/S:** Reading, Traveling, Working on the Computer **EDU:** Bachelor's Degree in Mathematics Education, Delta State University **A/A/S:** National Education Association; National Council of Teachers of Mathematics **C/VW:** Church
Email: b_tonia@hotmail.com
URL: http://www.cambridgewhoswho.com

Verna L. Brown

Title: RMC, RMM **Company:** Amos Medical Service **Address:** 7350 Van Dusen Road Suite 320, Laurel, MD 20707 United States **BUS:** Internal Medicine **P/S:** Management, Medical Billing, Internal Medicine **MA:** Local **EXP:** Ms. Brown's expertise includes medical billing, coding and management. **H/I/S:** Raising 5 Year Old Daughter as well as Being Support to Two Older Sons and Being a Loyal Wife **EDU:** Harristown College, 1 Year **A/A/S:** Association of Registered Health Care Professionals, Director of Children's Church, Mount Calvary Baptist Church
Email: govlb2@aol.com

Celina M. Brown Balcos, DMD

Title: General Dentist **Company:** Signature Dental, LLC **Address:** 2750 Owens Drive suite B, Conyers, GA 30094 United States **BUS:** Dental Clinic **P/S:** Oral Healthcare **MA:** Regional **D/D/R:** Practicing General and Pediatric Dentistry, Performing Fillings, Extractions, Root Canal Surgery and Cleanings, Fixing Crowns, Partials, Bridges, Veneers and Fixed Partial Dentures, Whitening Teeth **H/I/S:** Traveling **EDU:** Doctor of Medical Dentistry, Medical College of Georgia (1999); Bachelor of Science in Biology, Georgia State University (1995) **A/A/S:** Georgia Dental Association; American Dental Association **C/VW:** health fairs
Email: cbalcos@bellsouth.net

Patricia D. Brown-Moten

Title: Teacher of Social Studies **Company:** Stratford Board of Education, Samuel Yellin School **Address:** 111 Warwick Road, Stratford, NJ 08084 **BUS:** Public School **P/S:** Education **MA:** Local **D/D/R:** Teaching Social Studies **H/I/S:** Spending Time with her Children, Gardening, Reading **EDU:** Master of Arts in Student Personal Services, Rowan University; Bachelor of Arts in History, Trenton State College **A/A/S:** Stratford Education Association
Email: pbmoten@hotmail.com

Teddy Joan Browne

Title: Owner/Barber **Company:** Best Little Barber Shop in Redlands **Address:** 461 Tennessee Suite N, Redlands, CA 92373 United States **BUS:** Barber **P/S:** Hair Cutting **MA:** Local **EXP:** Mr. Brown's expertise is in men's hair cuts. **H/I/S:** Reading, Spending Time with Grandkids **EDU:** American Barber College **A/A/S:** St. Joseph's Church
Email: lhestermike@aol.com

Stephanie L. Brownlee

Title: Auditor **Company:** Defense Contract Audit Agency **Address:** 801 E. Campbell Road, Richardson, TX 75081 United States **BUS:** Government Organization **P/S:** Audit, Accounting and Financial Advisory Services **MA:** International **D/D/R:** Auditing and Representing the Department of Defense **H/I/S:** Traveling, Playing the Clarinet **EDU:** Master of Arts in Accounting, Texas A&M University-Commerce (2006) **A/A/S:** Student Member, Texas Society of Certified Public Accountants
Email: stephanie.brownlee@dcaa.mil
URL: http://www.dcaa.mil

Renata Brubaker

Title: Claims Processor **Company:** Hartford Claim Center **Address:** 4130 E. Alta Vista Road, Phoenix, AZ 85042 United States **BUS:** Insurance Claims Center **P/S:** Insurance Claims Services **MA:** International **D/D/R:** Processing Automobile Accident Claims **H/I/S:** Reading **EDU:** Bachelor of Arts in Business Management, Arizona State University
Email: recalvoso@gmail.com

Cindy M. Bruce

Title: Owner **Company:** Southwest Cellular **Address:** 1123 E. Davis Avenue, Weatherford, OK 73096 United States **BUS:** Retail Cellular Store **P/S:** Cellular Service Plans, Cellular Telephone Equipment and Accessories, Tanning, UPS Services, Home Decor, Jewelry **MA:** Regional **EXP:** Ms. Bruce's expertise is in cellular services. **H/I/S:** Horseback Riding, Reading **EDU:** Coursework in Computers, Southwestern Oklahoma State University **C/VW:** American Cancer Society
Email: swcell@sbcglobal.net
URL: http://www.cambridgewhoswho.com

LaTayne Bruce-Simpson

Title: Marketing and Campaign Specialist **Company:** Nationwide Insurance **Address:** 11000 Richmond Avenue, Houston, TX 77083 United States **BUS:** Insurance and Financial Service Company **P/S:** Full Range of Insurance Products and Financial Services for Home, Car, Family and Financial Security **MA:** National **D/D/R:** Overseeing the Regional Budget, Working with Affiliate Partners, Organizing Community Involvement **H/I/S:** Playing All Sports **EDU:** MBA, LaTourneau University (2007); Bachelor's Degree in Business Management, LaTourneau University (2002) **CERTS:** Licensed Adjuster **A/A/S:** National Black MBA Association; Houston Citizen Chamber of Commerce; Houston Works Board
Email: brucel@nationwide.com
URL: http://www.nationwide.com

Sara D. Brumbeloe, RN

Title: Nurse Practitioner **Company:** East Alabama Medical Center **Address:** 2000 Pepperell Parkway, Opelika, AL 36801 United States **BUS:** Community Hospital **P/S:** Healthcare **MA:** Regional **EXP:** Ms. Brumbeloe's expertise is in critical-care nursing. **D/D/R:** Teaching Pre-Specialty Students, Assessing Patients, Ordering Medications, Consulting with Physicians, Lecturing **H/I/S:** Caring for her Dog, Making Jewelry, Teaching Aerobics, Exercising **EDU:** Pursuing Master's Degree in Adult Nurse Practitioner Studies, Concentration in Forensic Nursing, Vanderbilt University (2007) **CERTS:** Certified Trauma Nurse; Certification in Pediatric Advanced Life Support; Registered Nurse, Auburn University **A/A/S:** Sigma Theta Tau International Honor Society of Nursing; Phi Kappa Phi; Tennessee Nurses Association **C/VW:** East Alabama Medical Center Foundation; Cornerstone Foundation
Email: saradean@bellsouth.net
URL: http://www.eamc.org

Thad Brumfield Jr., USAF

Title: Budget Analyst **Company:** Booz Allen Hamilton **Address:** 8283 Greensboro Drive, McLean, VA 22102 United States **BUS:** Technology Consulting **P/S:** IT Consulting Services **MA:** International **EXP:** Mr. Brumfield's expertise is in budgeting. **H/I/S:** Physical Fitness **EDU:** Jackson State University, Park University, MS **A/A/S:** Air Force Association; Military Officers, Association of America; The American Legion
Email: tbaumfield_99@yahoo.com

Olivia M. Brune

Title: Police Officer **Company:** Jacksonville Police Department **Address:** 200 W. Douglas Avenue, Jacksonville, IL 62650 United States **BUS:** Law Enforcement Agency **P/S:** Community Policing and Public Safety **MA:** Regional **D/D/R:** Patrolling, Conducting Investigations, Handling Sexual Abuse and Assault Cases, Working as a Field Training Officer **H/I/S:** Dirt Track Racing, Motorcycle Riding, Racquetball, Golfing **EDU:** Associate Degree in Law Enforcement Administration, Lincoln Land Community College (1998) **A/A/S:** Lodge 125; Fraternal Order of Police
Email: obrune@jacksonvilleil.com
URL: http://www.jacksonvillepd.com

Kimberly A. Bruning

Title: Title I Reading Teacher **Company:** Norton City Schools **Dept:** Norton Cornerstone Elementary School **Address:** 4138 Cleveland Massillon Road, Norton, OH 44203 United States **BUS:** School District **P/S:** Education **MA:** Local **D/D/R:** Teaching Reading to First through Fourth-Grade Students, Mentoring **H/I/S:** Practicing Karate, Watching Movies, Motorcycling, Walking, Gardening, Reading, Home Remodeling, Boating **EDU:** Master of Education in Teaching, Marygrove College, Detroit, MI; Bachelor of Science in Elementary Education, The University of Akron, OH **A/A/S:** Ohio Education Association; National Education Association **A/H:** Teacher of the Month Award (2007); Recipient, Blakney Foundation Award (2004); Nominee, Disney Teacher of the Year Award (1993 and 1996); Black Belt, Taekwondo Oh Do Kwan (1982) **C/VW:** Akron Children's Hospital; Ronald McDonald House Charities; Goodwill Industries International; United Way; The Salvation Army; Harvest for Hunger; Hattie Larlham
Email: kepproperties@neo.rr.com
URL: http://www.cambridgewhoswho.com

Linda M. Bruno

Title: Commissioner **Company:** Atlantic 10 Conference **Address:** 230 S. Broad Street, Philadelphia, PA 19102 United States **BUS:** Athletic Organization **P/S:** College Sports Services for Men and Women Including Basketball, Baseball, Field Hockey, Golf, Lacrosse, Rowing, Soccer, Softball, Swimming, Tennis, Track and Field and Volleyball, Academic Honors, Championships, Ticketing **MA:** National **EXP:** Ms. Bruno's expertise is in athletic administration. **EDU:** Master's Degree in Education, Iona College (1979); Bachelor of Arts, Iona College (1976)
Email: lbruno@atlantic10.org
URL: http://www.atlantic10.org

Jasmin Brunson-Dyett

Title: Pharmacist **Company:** Walgreens **Address:** 10191 S.W. 21st Street, Miramar, FL 33025 United States **BUS:** Pharmaceutical Store **P/S:** Pharmaceutical Products **MA:** National **EXP:** Her expertise is in customer counseling. **D/D/R:** Dispensing Prescription Drugs **H/I/S:** Reading, Watching Movies **EDU:** Doctor of Pharmacy, Florida A&M University (2007)
Email: jbrunsondyett@yahoo.com
URL: http://www.walgreens.com

Terry R. Brust

Title: Funeral Director/Owner **Company:** Banks and Brust Funeral Home/Newkirks Funeral Home **Address:** 400 N Court Street, Sullivan, IN 47882 United States **BUS:** Funeral Service Provider **P/S:** Funeral Services/Help Troubles Families **MA:** National **D/D/R:** Counseling Grieving Families **H/I/S:** Travel **EDU:** Bachelor of Science, Indiana State University; Coursework in Teaching and Mortuary Science, Bensons University **A/A/S:** Elk/Shrine
Email: banksandbrust@verizon.com

André Bryan

Title: Electrical Engineer **Company:** City of Miami **Address:** 444 S.W. Second Avenue, Eighth Floor, Miami, FL 33130 United States **BUS:** Government Organization **P/S:** Public Services **MA:** Local **EXP:** Mr. Bryan's expertise is in project management. **H/I/S:** Playing Table Tennis, Listening to Music **EDU:** Bachelor of Science in Electrical Engineering, University of Florida **C/VW:** Habitat For Humanity
Email: abryam@ci.miami.fl.us
URL: http://www.ci.miami.fl.us

Dr. Edna Bryan, RN
Title: Pastor **Company:** The Joy of The Lord Prayer Clinic and Counseling Center **Address:** 19445 N.W. 19th Court, Miami Gardens, FL 33056 United States **BUS:** Ministry **P/S:** Ministry Services, Ministry Protocol Education **MA:** Local **EXP:** Dr. Bryan's expertise is in ministerial counseling. **H/I/S:** Reading, Traveling, Spending Time with her Two Children and Six Grandchildren **EDU:** Ph.D. in Divinity, School of Practical Theology, 2007; Master of Arts in Healthcare Management, St. Thomas University, 1983; Bachelor of Arts in Behavioral Science, Mercy College, 1978 **CERTS:** Registered Nurse, New York State Board of Nursing, 1972; Registered Nurse, Britain Board of Nursing, England, 1961 **A/A/S:** American Association of Christian Counselors; Proclamation, Miami-Dade County Office of the Mayor; Board of County Commissioners **A/H:** Certificate of Special Congressional Members of the U.S. Congress (2007); Outstanding and Invaluable Service to the Community **C/VW:** Volunteer, Prison System
Email: ednabryan@bellsouth.net
URL: http://www.cambridgewhoswho.com

Rita J. Bryan
Title: Owner **Company:** Romance By Rita **Address:** 990 Wilburns Mill Road, Troutdale, VA 24378 United States **BUS:** Privately Owned Company Committed to Excellence in Crafts **P/S:** Making Quilts, Crafts, Jewelry **MA:** Regional, National **D/D/R:** Cross-Stitching, Making Quilts, Jewelry and Crafts **H/I/S:** Reading **EDU:** Mental Health Technology Courses, Wytheville Community College (1984)
Email: ritajjtb@yahoo.com
URL: http://www.cambridgewhoswho.com

Freda A. Bryant
Title: President/Owner **Company:** Bryant Burton Healthcare **Address:** 7027 England Street, Houston, TX 77021 United States **BUS:** /Mental Wellness/Therapy **P/S:** Therapy **MA:** National **D/D/R:** Ensuring Mental Wellness for All Patients **H/I/S:** Reading **EDU:** Coursework, Southern University **A/A/S:** National Notary Association
Email: bryantburton@aol.com

Leah P. Bryant
Title: Family Support Specialist **Company:** Youth Advocate Programs, Inc. **Address:** 1029 Birch Street, Laurys Station, PA 18059 United States **BUS:** Nonprofit Organization **P/S:** Drug and Alcohol Counseling for All Ages Including Family Intervention for Addiction **MA:** Local **EXP:** Ms. Bryant's expertise includes drug and alcohol counseling. **H/I/S:** Learning about Different Cultures and Languages, Reading **EDU:** Bachelor of Science in Psychology, Minor in Biology, DeSales University, Center Valley, PA (2003) **CERTS:** Certified Nursing Assistant, Bethlehem Vocational-Technical School; Certified Medical Administrative Assistant
Email: l-p-bryant@hotmail.com
URL: http://www.cambridgewhoswho.com

Melissa Ann Bryant
Title: Certified Massage Therapist, Owner **Company:** All In Knots **Address:** 8375 Jumpers Hole Road, Millersville, MD 21108 United States **BUS:** Massage Therapy **P/S:** Massage Therapy **MA:** Local **EXP:** Ms. Bryant's expertise includes alternative therapy and deep tissue massages. **H/I/S:** Horseback Riding **EDU:** Massage Therapy License, Baltimore School of Massage **A/A/S:** American Massage Therapy Association
Email: all_in_knots@hotmail.com
URL: http://www.aikmassage.com

Juanita Bryant-Bell
Title: Principal **Company:** Grand Avenue Elementary School **Address:** 711 School Drive, North Baldwin, NY 11510 United States **BUS:** Elementary School **P/S:** Education **MA:** Local **EXP:** Ms. Bryant-Bell's expertise is in educational leadership. **H/I/S:** Traveling, Playing Tennis, Working Out, Singing, Dancing **EDU:** Professional Diploma in Administration and Supervision, CUNY Queens College, 1986 **A/A/S:** Association for Supervision and Curriculum Development; National Association of School Principals; National Association of Elementary School Principals
Email: jbryant-bell@uniondaleschools.org
URL: http://www.gas.unionschools.org

Janice M. Bryant-Knight
Title: Professional School Counselor **Company:** Eliot Middle School **Address:** 1830 Constitution Avenue N.E, Washington, DC 20002 United States **BUS:** Middle School **P/S:** Education, Group Therapy **MA:** Local **EXP:** Ms. Bryant-Knight's expertise includes group, individual, adult and youth counseling. **H/I/S:** Crocheting, Swimming **EDU:** Master's Degree, Plus 60, Trinity College; Master of Science in Counseling (1985) **A/A/S:** Association for Supervision and Curriculum Development; American School Counselor Association **C/VW:** Volunteer, Local Hospitals
Email: jbrk50@verizon.net
URL: http://www.cambridgewhoswho.com

Felicia Doris Buadoo-Adade
Title: Director, **Company:** Government of the District of Columbia Department of Health **Dept:** DC Breast and Cervical Cancer Early Detection **Address:** 825 N. Capitol Street N.W., Third Floor, Washington, DC 20002 United States **BUS:** Government Healthcare Agency **P/S:** Public Health Services **MA:** International **D/D/R:** Overseeing Nutrition, Administration, Women's Health and Cancer **H/I/S:** Traveling, Cooking, Sewing, Reading, Music **EDU:** Ph.D., The Graduate School, Howard University, Washington D.C.; Master of Public Health in Women's Health, College of Medicine, Howard University; Bachelor of Science in Medical Dietetics, Howard University; Master of Science in Human Nutrition and Food, The Graduate School, Howard University; Bachelor of Science in Microbiology, Howard University; Associate of Science in Education, Northern Virginia Community College, Alexandria, VA; Associate of Science in Biology, Northern Virginia Community College **A/A/S:** American Public Health Association; American Dietetic Association; DC Metropolitan Area Dietetic Association; Board of Dietetic Practice, State of Maryland **C/VW:** Bike for the World, American Diabetic Association; American Heart Association; Disabled American Veterans
Email: felicia.buadoo-adade@dc.gov
URL: http://www.cambridgewhoswho.com

Candice R. Buchanan
Title: Registered Nurse **Company:** U.S. Nursing **Address:** Chicago, IL 60613 United States **BUS:** Travel Nursing Company **P/S:** Healthcare **MA:** National **EXP:** Ms. Buchanan's expertise includes neurosurgical and intensive care nursing. **H/I/S:** Photography, Painting **EDU:** Associate Degree in Nursing, St. Louis Community College **A/A/S:** American Association of Neuroscience Nurses **C/VW:** American Lung Association
Email: crbuchanan2001@yahoo.com

Charlotte Z. Buchmann
Title: Psychologist **Company:** Self-Employed **Address:** 38-24 Leslie Place, Fairlawn, NJ 07410 United States **BUS:** Psychological Diagnostics **P/S:** Psychology, Custody Evaluations **MA:** Local **D/D/R:** Participating in Clinical and School Psychology **H/I/S:** Reading **EDU:** Master of Arts in Psychology, New York University; Bachelor of Arts in Psychology, Drew University **A/A/S:** New Jersey Psychological Association; New York State Psychological Association; American Psychological Association; National Education Association; Bergen County Education Association of New Jersey
Email: czbuc@hotmail.com
URL: http://www.cambridgewhoswho.com

Debbie Sue Buck
Title: Assistant Principal **Company:** Fernando R. Ledesma High School **Address:** 12347 Ramona Boulevard, El Monte, CA 91732 United States **BUS:** High School **P/S:** Secondary Education **MA:** Local **D/D/R:** Working with At-Risk Children, Developing the Curriculum, Budgeting, Overseeing Teachers, Organizing Activities **H/I/S:** Watching Movies, Gardening, Reading Leadership Magazine **EDU:** Master of Education, Chapman University; Bachelor's Degree in Theater Arts, California State University; Associate Degree in Business, Citrus College **CERTS:** Certified Teacher; Certified Administrator **A/A/S:** Association of California School Administrators
Email: dbuck@emuhsd.k12.ca.us
URL: http://www.cambridgewhoswho.com

Kathleen C. Buckingham
Title: Educator **Company:** Naches Valley Middle School **Address:** 27 Shafer Avenue, Naches, WA 98937 United States **BUS:** Public Intermediate School **P/S:** Educating Students in Grades Five through Eight **MA:** Regional **D/D/R:** Educating Children, Counseling Students on Performance, Developing their Study Skills for all Subjects, Conducting Labs, Utilizing Smart Boards and Information Technology in Class **H/I/S:** Camping, Hiking **EDU:** Bachelor of Arts Plus 90 in Education, Major in Physical Education, Minor in History, Central Washington University (1972) **A/A/S:** National Education Association; Washington Education Association; President, Naches Valley Education Association; Volunteer, Central Lutheran Church **A/H:** Who's Who Among American Teachers
Email: kbuckingham@charter.net
URL: http://www.naches.wednet.edu/Nachesvalley/nvms/index.htm

Cheryl J. Buckley
Title: Owner **Company:** Cheryl's Little River Café **Address:** 290 Main Street, Little River, KS 67457 United States **BUS:** Family Dining Restaurant **P/S:** Home Cooking **MA:** Local **D/D/R:** Managing All Operations of the Restaurant, Cooking, Waitressing, Cleaning, Budgeting, Purchasing, Coordinating Weekly Town Historical Meetings **H/I/S:** Cooking, Spending Time with her Children, Interior Design **EDU:** Diploma, St. Mary's of the Plains High School

Tom C. Buckthorpe
Title: President **Company:** T-Buck Technical Services, Inc. **Address:** 5818 Drexel Avenue, Little Rock, AR 72209 United States **BUS:** Mechanical Cost Estimating **P/S:** Mechanical Cost Estimating **MA:** National **EXP:** Mr. Buckthorpe's expertise includes mechanical estimation, engineering and construction. **H/I/S:** Pistol Shooting
Email: info@CambridgeWhosWho.com
URL: http://www.cambridgewhoswho.com

Sunita D. Buddhu
Title: President, Owner **Company:** Lotus Consulting Service **Address:** 958 Broad Street, Apt. C-2, Hartford, CT 06106 United States **BUS:** Financial Consulting Company **P/S:** Tax Preparation, Starting New Businesses, Financial Services **MA:** Connecticut **D/D/R:** Starting New Businesses, Handling Scholarships, 401(K) and IRA Paperwork **EDU:** Pursuing Bachelor of Arts in Business Administration, Albertus Magmus College
Email: lotusconsulting@hotmail.com

Holly A. Buechler
Title: General Manager **Company:** JL Properties, Inc. **Address:** 3900 C Street, Suite 140, Anchorage, AK 99503 United States **BUS:** Real Estate Firm **P/S:** Real Estate Exchange and Property Management **MA:** Regional **D/D/R:** Managing Residential and Commercial Properties **H/I/S:** Bicycling, Playing Basketball, Caring for her Dogs, Hiking, Kayaking, Playing the Guitar **EDU:** Bachelor's Degree in Justice, University of Alaska (1996) **A/A/S:** Institute of Real Estate Management
Email: holly@jlproperties.com
URL: http://www.auroramilitaryhousing.com

Andrew D. Buffalino
Title: Mechanical Engineer **Company:** Sunpower, Inc. **Address:** 182 Mill Street, Athens, OH 45701 United States **BUS:** Research and Development Company **P/S:** Alternative Power **MA:** National **EXP:** Mr. Buffalino's expertise is in alternative energy. **D/D/R:** Designing Work for Power and Alternative Energy **H/I/S:** Cooking, Making Stained Glass **EDU:** Bachelor's Degree in Mechanical Engineering, Rose-Hulman Institute of Technology **A/A/S:** Society of Automotive Engineers; American Society of Mechanical Engineers
Email: buffad01@hotmail.com
URL: http://www.sunpower.com

Carmella BugBee
Title: Executive Assistant **Company:** Ron Sachs Communications **Address:** 114 S. Duval Street, Tallahassee, FL 32301 United States **BUS:** Public Relations Company **P/S:** Communications Services, Media Consulting **MA:** Statewide **D/D/R:** Performing Administrative Duties **H/I/S:** Football, Baseball, walking, swimming **EDU:** Associate Degree in Business Administration, Tallahassee Community College
Email: carmella@ronsachs.com
URL: http://www.ronsachs.com

Tara Victoria Bugman, Pharm.D.
Title: Supervising Pharmacist **Company:** Rite Aid **Address:** 2318 W. Genesee Street, Syracuse, NY 13219 United States **BUS:** Retail Drugstore **P/S:** Over-the-Counter and Prescription Pharmacy Services, Household Items, Greeting Cards, Film Development, Online and On-Site Services **MA:** National **D/D/R:** Running the Daily Operations of the Pharmacy, Overseeing Staff Members, Filling Prescriptions, Educating, Consulting and Assisting Customers with their Prescription and Over-the-Counter Medication Needs **EDU:** Doctor of Pharmacy, Albany College of Pharmacy **A/A/S:** American Pharmacists Association
Email: drtara2006@yahoo.com
URL: http://www.eckerd.com

Tom Bui
Title: Director **Company:** Bui Quality Construction Inc **Address:** 5645-A General Washington Drive, Alexandria, VA 22312 United States **BUS:** Construction **P/S:** Business Builder **MA:** Regional **D/D/R:** Designing Commercial Buildings, Renovating **H/I/S:** Fishing, Family Sports **CERTS:** Plumbing and Contractors License **A/A/S:** NFPA, Church, Community Outreach
Email: TomBui007@yahoo.com

Glenn R. Bulgrien
Title: Owner, Operator **Company:** Bulgrien Trucking **Address:** 5592 Peck Street, P.O. Box 193, Peck, MI 48466 United States **BUS:** Trucking Company **P/S:** Transportation **MA:** Regional **D/D/R:** Hauling Steel, Dirt, Machines and Flatbed Loads, Finding and Delivering Trucking Loads on Schedule and Safely **H/I/S:** Golfing, Camping, Spending Time with Grandchildren **EDU:** High School Education **C/VW:** Church
Email: rrjack@greatlakes.net
URL: http://www.cambridgewhoswho.com

Christina L. Bullmer

Title: Juvenile Court Officer, Social Worker **Company:** 30th Judicial Circuit Court **Address:** Ingham County, Lancing, MI United States **BUS:** Circuit Court **P/S:** Office of Court Services and a Probation Department **MA:** Regional **D/D/R:** Handling Juvenile and Family Cases, Making Recommendations for Investigations, Working with Schools, Helping Foster Agencies to Determine a Child's Needs, Coordinating Appropriate Services **H/I/S:** Painting, Golfing, Listening to Music, Spending Time with her Family **EDU:** Master's Degree in Social Work, Western Michigan University (2006); Bachelor's Degree in Psychology, Michigan State University (2000); Associate Degree in Arts, Kalamazoo Valley Community College (1998) **C/VW:** Child Benefit Fund
Email: christinabullmer@yahoo.com

Karyn D. Bullock

Title: President **Company:** 2 Blue Chip Professional, LLC **Address:** 4414 Marriotsville Road, Owings Mill, MD 21117 United States **BUS:** Finance **P/S:** State Compliance Examinations **MA:** National **D/D/R:** Training, Consulting, Offering Mortgages **H/I/S:** Swimming **EDU:** Bachelor's Degree, University of Phoenix **A/A/S:** Maryland Association of Mortgage Brokers, National Association of Mortgage Brokers
Email: kdbullock@2bluechippro.com

Ryan Bullock

Title: Partner, President **Company:** ESBAMF Distributors, LLC **Address:** 1000 N. Hamilton Street, Suite A1, Chandler, AZ 85225 United States **BUS:** Manufacturing and Distribution Company **P/S:** Mexican Food Distribution, Manufacturing Fresh Salsa **MA:** National **EXP:** Mr. Bullock's expertise includes new business development, marketing and operations management. **D/D/R:** Forecasting, Overseeing Finance and Sales **H/I/S:** Spending Time with his Family, Spending Time Outdoors, Boating, Fishing **CERTS:** Industry-Related Training **A/A/S:** Better Business Bureau **A/H:** Salesman of the Year Award **C/VW:** The Church of Jesus Christ of Latter-Day Saints
Email: ryan@elsolmexicanfood.com
URL: http://www.elsolmexicanfood.com

Darlene M. Bultemeier

Title: Distributor **Company:** XanGo, LLC **Address:** 427 S. Walnut Street, Princeville, IL 61559 United States **BUS:** Distribution Company **P/S:** Health Drinks, Fruit Juices **MA:** International **D/D/R:** Managing Sales, Promoting XanGo Products, Caring for Autistic Children **H/I/S:** Spending Time with her Child **EDU:** Coursework in Business (1970); Diploma, Iaccoa Falls High School
Email: darbult@mchsi.com
URL: http://www.darlene123.com

Joanna Bunch

Title: Licensed Optician **Company:** Sam's Club Optical **BUS:** Professional Optical Services Company **P/S:** Contact Lens and Eyeglass Fittings **MA:** Regional **D/D/R:** Managing All Aspects of Customer Prescriptions Including Eyeglass Frame Selection and Instruction for Contact Lens Insertion and Removal, Developing and Manufacturing Lenses **H/I/S:** Crafting Quilting, Gardening **CERTS:** Licensed Realtor (2000); Licensed Optician (1982) **A/A/S:** Former Board Member, Tennessee Dispensing Opticians Association; American Board of Optometry; National Contact Lens Examiners
Email: joannabunch@comcast.net
URL: http://www.samsclub.com

Lana Bunis

Title: Dentist, Owner **Company:** Ave U Dental Healthcare, P.C. **Address:** 2415 Avenue U, Brooklyn, NY 11229 United States **BUS:** Dental Office **P/S:** Dentistry Services Including Cosmetic Dentistry, Implants, Orthodontics **MA:** Local **D/D/R:** Performing General and Cosmetic Dentistry, Including Root Canals and Oral Surgery **H/I/S:** Playing Tennis, Reading Magazines **EDU:** Doctor of Dental Surgery, College of Dentistry, New York University (2002); Master's Degree in Biology, New York University (1998); Bachelor's Degree in Biology, New York University (1997) **A/A/S:** American Academy of Cosmetic Dentistry; American Academy of General Dentistry; Second District Dental Society; American Dental Association **C/VW:** Local Charities
Email: lbunis@hotmail.com
URL: http://www.aveudental.com

Cynthia Bunnell

Title: President **Company:** Designs by CHB, Inc. **Address:** 36031 Bunnell Lane, Eustis, FL 32736 United States **BUS:** Construction Design Firm **P/S:** Construction Drawings and Custom Designs for Residential Houses **MA:** Regional **EXP:** Ms. Bunnell's expertise is in computer aided design. **D/D/R:** Overseeing Operations, Creating Designs for Contractors **EDU:** Coursework, La Salle University, Chicago (1971); Diploma, Boone High School (1954) **A/A/S:** National Youth Equine Association for Kids Eight and Younger
Email: designsbychb@yahoo.com

Deborah A. Buonocore

Title: Realtor **Company:** Prudential Connecticut Realty **Address:** 97 Whitney Avenue, New Haven, CT 06512 United States **BUS:** Real Estate Company **P/S:** Real Estate Purchase and Sales Real Estate **MA:** Regional **D/D/R:** Offering Customer, Internet Relocation and Notary Public Services, Working as an Internet Lead Specialist **H/I/S:** Traveling **EDU:** Degree in Interior Design **CERTS:** Licensed Real Estate Specialist (1989) **A/A/S:** Greater New Haven Association of Realtors; Connecticut Association of Realtors; Notary Public, State of Connecticut; National Association of Realtors **A/H:** Quarterly Achievement Awards; Top Producer; Number One Agent, Listings and Residential Sales; President's Circle; Recognition Award, Founders Club
Email: debbiebuonocore@prudentialct.com
URL: http://www.prudentialct.com

Aimee L. Burch

Title: BSN, Certified Medical-Surgical Registered Nurse **Company:** Mary Lanning Memorial Hospital **Address:** 715 N. Saint Joseph Avenue, Hastings, NE 68901 United States **BUS:** Hospital **P/S:** Healthcare **MA:** Regional **EXP:** Ms. Burch's expertise is in medical-surgical nursing. **H/I/S:** Spending Time with her Family, Reading **EDU:** Pursuing Master of Science in Nursing, Creighton University; Bachelor of Science in Nursing, Creighton University **CERTS:** Certified Medical-Surgical Nurse **A/A/S:** Sigma Theta Tau; Omicron Delta Kappa; American Medical-Surgical Nurses Association **C/VW:** The Heartland Pet Connection
Email: cornhusker_red@yahoo.com
URL: http://www.mlmh.org

Heidi M. Burcher

Title: Managing Director of Real Estate Finance, Executive Vice President **Company:** Alpha Risk Management, Inc. **Address:** 24 William Street, Farmingdale, NY 11735 United States **BUS:** Consulting Firm **P/S:** Consulting Services Including Risk Management Consulting **MA:** International **D/D/R:** Managing Real Estate Finance **H/I/S:** Traveling, Reading **EDU:** Bachelor of Arts in English, The City College of New York
Email: hbucher@alphariskmanagement.com
URL: http://www.alphariskmanagement.com

Karri A. Buresh

Title: Optometrist **Company:** Berner Eye Clinic **Address:** 250 East 300 S., Salt Lake City, UT 84111 United States **BUS:** Optometry Practice **P/S:** Primary Eye Care **MA:** Regional **EXP:** Ms. Buresh's expertise includes optometry, pediatrics and vision therapy. **H/I/S:** Scuba Diving, Skiing, Hiking, Traveling **EDU:** Doctor of Optometry, Southern College of Optometry **A/A/S:** Utah Optometric Association; Board Member, Special Olympics Utah; Utah Optometric Association **A/H:** Young Optometrist of the Year Award (2007) **C/VW:** P.E.O. International, Church
Email: bernereyeclinic@yahoo.com
URL: http://www.visionsource-bernereyeclinic.com

Agnes Burger

Title: Registered Nurse **Company:** HHC Woodhull Hospital **Address:** 760 Broadway, Brooklyn, NY 11206 United States **BUS:** Hospital **P/S:** Pediatric Healthcare, Special Care Unit **MA:** Local **D/D/R:** Caring for Pediatric Patients, Working with Special Care Unit, Monitoring Beds **H/I/S:** Reading, Gardening, Cooking **EDU:** Associate of Arts in Nursing, Registered Nurse, CUNY Borough of Manhattan Community College **CERTS:** Certified Pediatric Nurse **A/A/S:** Phi Theta Kappa **C/VW:** Search and Rescue Dogs, American Society for the Prevention of Cruelty to Animals, North Shore Animal League

Celeste Burgess, MA

Title: Assistant Principal of Health and Physical Education Department **Company:** Martin Van Buren High School **Address:** 230-17 Hillside Avenue, Queens Village, NY 11427 United States **BUS:** High School Facility Dedicated to Excellence in Education **P/S:** Regular Core Curriculum Including Reading, Math, English, Science, Social Studies, Art, Music, History, Language Arts, Computers, Physical Education **MA:** Regional **D/D/R:** Overseeing the Department, Curriculum and Units, Motivating Students, Overseeing the Newly Mandated Testing Program for 9th-Graders **H/I/S:** Bowling, Bowling Tournaments, Scrapbooking **EDU:** Master's Degree in Health Science and Safety, San Diego State University (1978); Master's Degree in Administration and Supervision, Long Island University (1985) **A/A/S:** New York City Association of Assistant Principals for Health and Physical Education
Email: msapbee@aol.com
URL: http://www.mvbhs.com

Robin L. Burgess

Title: Mental Health Supervisor **Company:** East Bay Mental Health **Address:** 610 Wampanoag Trail, Riverside, RI 02915 United States **BUS:** Mental Health Facility **P/S:** Healthcare **MA:** Local **D/D/R:** Supervising the CASSP Department, Helping Parents with Behaviorally Disabled Children, Funding Programs to Aid in Education and Mental Health Counseling **H/I/S:** Reading, Antiquing, Walking **EDU:** Master's Degree in Agency Counseling, Rhode Island College (2004) **A/A/S:** Involved in Native American, Ecology and Anthropology Work
Email: rburgess@eastbay.org
URL: http://www.cambridgewhoswho.com

Linda J. Burgin

Title: Research Analyst VI **Company:** Oregon Department of Education **Address:** 255 Capitol Street N.E., Salem, OR 97310 United States **BUS:** State Education Department **P/S:** Education for Kindergarten through 12th-Grade Students **MA:** Oregon **EXP:** Ms. Burgin's expertise includes statistics and demographics. **H/I/S:** Spending Time with her Grandchildren, Reading, Playing Tennis, Exercising **EDU:** Pursuing Master of Science in Public Administration, Portland State University and Lewis & Clark College; Bachelor of Science in Business Administration, Oregon State University **A/A/S:** Service Employees International Union
Email: linda.burgin@state.org.us
URL: http://www.ode.state.or.us

Amanda Lynne Burke

Title: Assistant Director of Residence Life **Company:** Adrian College **Address:** 110 S. Madison, Adrian, MI 49221 United States **BUS:** College **P/S:** Accounting, Business Art and Design, Biology, Chemistry, Communication Arts and Sciences, Earth Science, Economics, English, Environmental Science/Studies, Exercise Science and Physical Education, History, Interior Design, International Studies, Mathematics, Modern Languages and Cultures, Music, Philosophy/Religion, Physics, Political Science, Psychology, Sociology, Social Work and Criminal Justice, Teacher Education, Theatre, Art History, Computer Information Systems, Public Relations, Women's Studies **MA:** Regional **D/D/R:** Overseeing Judicial Services, Reviewing Cases, Holding Meetings with Individuals in Violation, Managing the Student Staff, Planning School Events and Programs and Arts and Crafts **H/I/S:** Marathon Runner **EDU:** Pursuing Master's Degree in Leadership in Higher Education, Sienna Heights University; Bachelor's Degree in Communications, Adrian College (2004) **A/A/S:** Homecoming Committee; Adrian Chamber of Commerce Town and Gown; Public Speaker, Local Banquets and Meetings
Email: aburke@adrian.edu
URL: http://www.adrian.edu

Debby Burke

Title: Counselor **Company:** Gateway Technical College **Address:** 1001 S. Main Street, Racine, WI 53403 United States **BUS:** Technical College **P/S:** Higher Education, Business Education Counseling, Training, Leadership, Technological Resources **MA:** Local **D/D/R:** Working with Students on Program Selection and Class Scheduling, Handling Admissions for Transfer Students, Training the Local Workforce **H/I/S:** Quilting, Traveling, Attending Theater **EDU:** Master's Degree in Guidance and Counseling, University of Wisconsin-Whitewater (1987); Bachelor of Education Degree, University of Wisconsin-Whitewater (1967) **A/A/S:** American Association of University Women; National Education Association; Association for Career and Technical Education; Wisconsin Education Association Council; Licensed Professional Counselor for the State of Wisconsin **C/VW:** United Way; Easter Seals
Email: burked@gtc.edu
URL: http://www.gtc.edu

J. Clark Burke Jr.

Title: Manger of Therapeutic Activities **Company:** Summit Oaks Hospital **Address:** 19 Prospect Street, Summit, NJ 07901 United States **BUS:** Hospital **P/S:** Healthcare **MA:** Regional **D/D/R:** Managing Recreational Therapy and Anger and Stress Management **H/I/S:** Whitewater Rafting; Playing Tennis; Volleyball; Hiking; Volunteering; Horseback Riding; Ping Pong; Snow Sports **EDU:** Master's Degree in Recreation and Parks Administration, Fairleigh Dickinson University (1987); Bachelor of Arts in Psychology, Marietta College (1977) **A/A/S:** ELKS; Former Vice Chairman and Board Member, Plainfield Young Men's Christian Association; Former Vice Chairman, Local Residential and Shelter Committee; Susan G. Komen for the Cure
Email: clark.burke@psysolutions.com
URL: http://www.psysolutions.com

Kristyn T. Burke

Title: School Psychologist **Company:** Jersey City Board of Education **Address:** 48 W. 45th Street, Bayonne, NJ 07002 United States **BUS:** Education **P/S:** Education **MA:** Local **EXP:** Ms. Burke's expertise is in school psychology. **H/I/S:** Traveling **EDU:** Professional Diploma in School Psychology, New Jersey City University **CERTS:** Pursuing Graduate Certification in Applied Behavior Analysis; Master of Arts in Educational Psychology, New Jersey City University **A/A/S:** Psi Chi Honor Society
Email: kristynb628@verizon.net

Sandra G. Burkes
Title: Secretary IV (Retired) **Company:** University of Illinois **Address:** Chicago, IL **Dept:** School of Public Health **BUS:** University **P/S:** Higher Education **MA:** International **EXP:** Ms. Burkes' expertise is in database access. **D/D/R:** Performing Secretarial Duties and Database Entry, Formatting Reports for Faculty, Sending Monthly Reports, Supplying Secretarial Support Services for Sending Out Election Ballots, Updating Budget Sheets, Working on Computers **H/I/S:** Collecting Toy Dragons **EDU:** High School Education **A/H:** Sunburst Special Recognition Award, University of Illinois at Chicago School of Public Health (1989); Outstanding Service Award; Who's Who Among Executive and Professional Women; International Book of Honor; International Who's Who of Women; Directory, Distinguished Americans
Email: hueyb4259@sbcglobal.net
URL: http://www.cambridgewhoswho.com

Ms. Catherine A. Burkhardt
Title: Director of Underwriting **Company:** Insurex **Address:** 1666 Souvenir Drive, El Cajon, CA 92021 United States **BUS:** Commercial Insurance Brokerage Agency **P/S:** Commercial Lines **MA:** National **EXP:** Ms. Burkhardt's expertise is in marketing. **H/I/S:** Traveling, Gardening, Movies, Reading, Cooking **A/A/S:** CISR, SDIW, PWI
Email: cathy@insurex.com
Email: cattwoman@cox.net
URL: http://www.insurex.com

Galen C. Burkholder
Title: Co-Owner, Manager **Company:** WSM Media Services **Address:** 185 Chamberlin Road, Shippensburg, PA 17257 United States **BUS:** Publishing Company **P/S:** Desktop Publishing, Design and Layout **MA:** National **EXP:** Mr. Burkholder's expertise includes quality assurance, desktop publishing, design and layout. **H/I/S:** Singing, Writing Lyrics and Books **EDU:** Bachelor of Arts in Education, Mathematics and Physics, Shippensburg University (1971) **A/A/S:** Associate Secretary, Shippensburg Lions Club; Pennsylvania Southern Gospel Music Association; Friends of Old Main, Shippensburg University; Melvin Jones Fellow, Lions Club International **C/VW:** Volunteer, Lions Club International; Relay for Life; American Cancer Society
Email: wsm-ms@kuhncom.net

Andrew L. Burks
Title: Instrumentation/Electrical Technician II **Company:** Valero **Address:** 16151 Craigen Road, Beaumont, TX 77705 United States **BUS:** Petroleum Refinery **P/S:** Premium, Environmentally Clean Products including Reformulated Gasoline, California Air Resources Board Phase II Gasoline, Low-Sulfur Diesel and Oxygenates **MA:** Regional **D/D/R:** Overseeing Electrical and Control Schemes, Working on Modifications for Capital Projects and Refinery-Associated Repairs, Maintaining Closed Circuit Televisions and Cameras, Phone Systems and Plant Radio Systems, Conducting Safety Meetings **H/I/S:** Fishing, Spending Time with his Three Children **EDU:** College Coursework Completed **A/A/S:** NACE International
Email: andrew.burks@valero.com

Deidra D. Burleson
Title: Parent Involvement and Social Service Specialist **Company:** Scurry Community Services **Address:** 2800 Second Street, Snyder, TX 79549 United States **BUS:** Childcare Facility **P/S:** Childcare Programs, Head Start, Early Head Start, Prenatal Programs, Day Care, Disability Programs **MA:** Local **D/D/R:** Caring for Children, Meeting with Parents **H/I/S:** Traveling **EDU:** Bachelor of Science in Occupational Education, Wayland Baptist University, 2006 **A/A/S:** Community Resource Coordination Groups **C/VW:** Church
Email: deidra_burleson@yahoo.com

Ora A. Burley
Title: Owner **Company:** Golden Star Management **Address:** 12911 Stillington Drive, Houston, TX 77051 United States **BUS:** Performing Arts Provider **P/S:** Provide Guidance and Management Services to Models, Actors and Fashion Designers **MA:** Local **D/D/R:** Performing Administrative Duties **H/I/S:** Traveling **EDU:** Associate Degree in Fashion Design, The Art Institute of Dallas **A/A/S:** Associate Member, Jack and Jill of America Inc.
Email: orabronzebeauty@hotmail.com
URL: www.missora.com

Misti D. Burms
Title: Office Manager **Company:** Michael S. Mayron, MD, PSC **Address:** 110 3rd Street, Suite 370, Henderson, KY 42420 United States **BUS:** Healthcare **P/S:** Neurology **MA:** Local **EXP:** Ms. Burms' expertise is in medical billing. **H/I/S:** Spending Time with her Husband, Hiking, Fishing, Enjoying the Outdoors **CERTS:** Certified Emergency Medical Technician
Email: katzeyec@netscape.net

Willie M. Burnett
Title: Director, Alumni Affairs **Company:** Tuskegee University **Address:** 320 Kresge Center, Tuskegee, AL 36088 United States **BUS:** University **P/S:** Education/Fundraising **MA:** National **D/D/R:** Fundraising, Implementing Programs **H/I/S:** Watches Sports **EDU:** Master of Science in Student Personnel Services and Guidance Counseling; Bachelor's Degree in English, Tuskegee University **A/A/S:** American Counseling Association, National Fundraising Association
Email: burnett@tuskee.edu
URL: www.tuskee.edu

Erica L. Burnham
Title: Managing Director **Company:** Parkland Title, LLC **Address:** 11555 Heron Bay Boulevard, Suite 200, Coral Springs, FL 33076 United States **BUS:** Title Insurance and Real Estate Company **P/S:** Insurance Services **MA:** National **D/D/R:** Facilitating Real Estate Closings, Selling Title Insurance **H/I/S:** Reading, Spending Time with her Children **A/A/S:** Coral Springs Chamber of Commerce; Board of Directors, City of Tamarac; Volunteer, Local School Events
Email: eburnham@parklandtitleusa.com
URL: http://www.parklandtitleusa.com

Deborah L. Burns
Title: Interrelated Special Education Teacher **Company:** Prairie View High School, East Central Kansas Special Education Cooperative **Address:** 13731 Kansas Highway 152, Lacygne, KS 66040 United States **BUS:** Public High School **P/S:** High School Education, Academic Curriculum, Classes in Art, Music, Band, Foreign Language, Drama, Vocational Agriculture, Desktop Publishing, Journalism and Multimedia Productions **MA:** Regional **D/D/R:** Teaching Mathematics, Science, Basic English Skills and World History to Special Students in a Self-Contained Classroom, Supervising After-School Activities **H/I/S:** Gardening, Yard Work, Quilting, Spending Time with her Three Grandchildren **EDU:** Pursuing Master's Degree in Special Education; Bachelor of Science in Special Education, Emporia State University (2005) **CERTS:** Certified Special Education Teacher; Certification in Business **A/A/S:** National Education Association; Kansas Education Association; Coach, Special Olympics; Junior Class Sponsor, Prairie View High School
Email: debbieb@pv362.org
URL: http://www.pv362.org/pvhs

Dr. James E. Burns Jr.
Title: 1) Teacher (Retired) 2) Representative 3) Health Insurance Sales **Company:** 1) Albert M. Greenfield Elementary School 2) ACN Telecommunications Company 3) Benefit Consulting Group **Address:** 2200 Chestnut Street, Philadelphia, PA 19103 United States **BUS:** 1) Elementary School 2) Telecommunications Company 3) Consulting Company **P/S:** 1) Primary Education 2) Telecommunication Systems 3) Health Insurance Services **MA:** Local **D/D/R:** Teaching, Assisting in Telecommunication Services, Offering Health Insurance Plans **H/I/S:** Golfing **EDU:** Ph.D. in Urban Education, Temple University; Master's Degree in Counseling Education, West Chester University of Pennsylvania; Bachelor's Degree in Economics, Lafayette College **CERTS:** Certified Teacher (K-8); Certification in Counseling Education (K-8) **A/A/S:** Philadelphia Federation of Teachers; Pennsylvania State Education Association **C/VW:** United Negro College Fund; American Cancer Society; The American Society for the Prevention of Cruelty to Animals
Email: boourns007@comcast.net

Katrina N. Burns
Title: Microbiology and Molecular Genetics Class Laboratory Preparation Supervisor **Company:** Michigan State University **Address:** East Lansing, MI 48824 United States **BUS:** University **P/S:** Education **MA:** National **D/D/R:** Teaching Multiple Levels of Microbiology Laboratory Experiments, Reviewing Experiments with Faculty to Ensure Success, Managing a 12-Person Staff **H/I/S:** Part-Time Writer and Screen Writer **EDU:** Bachelor's Degree in Microbiology, University of Michigan; Certified in Molecular Biology **A/A/S:** Former Member, Toastmasters; Board of Directors, United Nations **A/H:** Winner, Alpha Kappa Alpha Sorority Writing Contest; Valedictorian, Cooley High School; 'Best of 1981' Local Commercial Spots **C/VW:** Lansing Area United Nations
Email: bkatrina@comcast.net

Mark W. Burns
Title: Analyst, Staff Officer **Company:** Department of Defense **BUS:** Government Organization **P/S:** Defense Services **MA:** International **EXP:** Mr. Burns' expertise is in logistics management. **H/I/S:** Personal Development **EDU:** Pursuing Master's Degree, George Mason University **C/VW:** Heritage Foundation
Email: etool1@msn.com
URL: http://www.cambridgewhoswho.com

Carole Anne Burns-Donoghue
Title: Owner **Company:** Personalized Service Insurance Agency **Address:** 143 Shaker Road Buliding E, East Longmeadow, MA 01028 United States **BUS:** Insurance Company **P/S:** Superior Property and Casualty Insurance Services **MA:** International **D/D/R:** Offering Insurance Policies, Overseeing Operations and Management, Training **H/I/S:** Antique Cars **CERTS:** Licensed in Property and Casualty Insurance, State of Massachusetts **A/A/S:** National Association of Insurance Agents; Massachusetts Association of Insurance Agents; Notary Public; Board of Director, Hampton County Independent Insurance Agents **A/H:** Strathmore Who's Who
Email: carole9999@aol.com
URL: http://www.cambridgewhoswho.com

Peggy L. Burr
Title: Business Manager, Development Associate **Company:** Harriman-Jewell Series **Address:** 500 College Hill, Box 1015, Liberty, MO 64068 United States **BUS:** Performing Arts Company **P/S:** Performing Arts Presentations **MA:** Local **D/D/R:** Recording All Donations and Deposits, Accounting, Fundraising **H/I/S:** Reading, Traveling, Beading **EDU:** Bachelor of Science in Accounting, University of Saint Joseph, Missouri **A/A/S:** Fundraising Committee, University of St. Joseph **C/VW:** ADA, Council on Philanthropy, Multiple Sclerosis Society, Susan G. Komen Race for the Cure
Email: burrpeg@harriman-jewell.org
URL: http://www.harriman-jewell.org

Pamela Burrell
Title: Executive Secretary, Accounts Payable, Payroll **Company:** Robot Coupe U.S.A., Inc. **Address:** 264 S. Perkins Street, P.O. Box 16625, Ridgeland, MS 39157 United States **BUS:** Equipment Manufacturing **P/S:** Commercial Food Processors and Vegetable Preparation Units **MA:** Local **D/D/R:** Reconciling Accounts Payable, Screening Calls, Making Appointments, Arranging Travel, Typing Letters, Processing New Hires, Ensuring Administrative Efficiency **H/I/S:** Gardening, Working on her Yard **EDU:** Diploma, Jim Hill High School (1978)
Email: pam@robotcoupeusa.com
URL: http://www.robotcoupeusa.com

Edward Burrier
Title: President, Owner **Company:** Ed Burrier & Associates **Address:** 6817 Briar Ride Circle, Roanoke, VA 24108 United States **BUS:** Consulting Company **P/S:** Rail Road Consultation Services, Locomotive Service Work **MA:** International **D/D/R:** Repairing Locomotives, Traveling Globally, Coordinating Contacts, Overseeing Operation of Locomotives **H/I/S:** Golfing **EDU:** Bachelor's Degree in Business Administration, Ashland University (1991); Associate Degree in Electro Mechanics, Ishawnee State University (1985) **A/A/S:** Locomotive Maintenance Officers Association
Email: eburrier@aol.com

Mr. Ivan Burris
Title: Broker, Owner **Company:** Vegas Realty, LLC **Address:** 8010 W Sahara Ave Ste260, Las Vegas, NV 89117 United States **BUS:** Real Estate Broker **P/S:** Residential, Executive homes, New Construction, Condos, Town Homes, Senior, Gated, Golf Homes, Senior **MA:** National **EXP:** Mr. Burris' expertise is in commercial properties. **D/D/R:** Supervising 15 Agents **H/I/S:** Golf **CERTS:** Real Estate License (1985) **A/A/S:** National Association of Realtors; Nevada Association of Realtors; Society of Las Vegas Exchanges
Email: ivanburris@aol.com

Austin L. Burruss
Title: Air Traffic Controller, Realtor **Company:** Federal Government **Address:** 273 N.W. Main Boulevard, Lake City, FL 32055 United States **BUS:** Real Estate Firm **P/S:** Wide Range of Real Estate Services, Land Sales **MA:** Regional **EDU:** Bachelor's Degree in Business Administration, St. Leo University **A/A/S:** Lake City Board of Realtors; Florida Board of Realtors; National Board of Realtors **A/H:** National Dean's List; Who's Who Among High School Students
Email: austinL738@hotmail.com
URL: http://www.cambridgewhoswho.com

Georgia Burt Presnell
Title: Administrative Assistant **Address:** 1545 River Park Drive Suite 107, Sacramento, CA 95815 United States **BUS:** Bank **P/S:** Banking and Credit Services **MA:** Local **D/D/R:** Performing Administrative Duties **H/I/S:** Line Dancing, Writing Poetry and Music, Playing the Organ and Piano by Ear, Reading, Family get togethers **EDU:** Weber High School, Weber College, High School Diploma, 2 Years of College **A/A/S:** President, Soroptimist International of Sacramento; Chair, March of Dimes, Northern California; Vice President, Easter Seal Society **A/H:** California's Outstanding Senior, Worker, Rotarian Outstanding Senior Citizens (2006); Volunteer of the Year; Woman of Distinction **C/VW:** Volunteer, Ronald Mc Donald House; Make a Wish Foundation; Walk for the Cure
Email: ffpgbp@aol.com
URL: www.riverbank.com

Evelyn W. Burton
Title: Retired Teacher **Company:** Cleveland Public Schools **Address:** 48 Lansdowne Blvd, Youngtown, OH 44506 United States **BUS:** School **P/S:** Provide Education to Young Children **MA:** Local **EXP:** Ms. Burton's expertise includes ministry and early childhood education. **H/I/S:** Singing **EDU:** Master's Degree, Case Western Reserve University; Bachelor of Science, Wilbur Forest University **A/A/S:** National Council of Negro Women
Email: info@CambridgeWhosWho.com

Monique Busch, MSW, ACSW, Ph.D.
Title: President **Company:** Performance Solutions Unlimited, LLC **Address:** 9475 Timber View Drive, Indianapolis, IN 46250 United States **BUS:** Consulting Firm **P/S:** Human Services, Consulting, Training, Coaching **MA:** National **EXP:** Dr. Busch's expertise includes quality improvement, evaluation, leadership development, performance enhancement, accreditation and staff and board retreats. **H/I/S:** Golfing, Running, Gourmet Cooking **EDU:** Ph.D., Indiana University School of Social Work (2006); Master of Social Work, Portland State University (1996) **A/H:** Espirit Award for Academic Excellence; Outstanding Associate Faculty Award (2004-2006)
Email: moniquebusch@psu-llc.org
URL: http://www.psu-llc.org

Linda Stone Bush
Title: Realtor **Company:** Prudential Texas Realty **Address:** 115 Wild Basin Road, West Lake Hills, TX 78746 United States **BUS:** Real Estate Agency **P/S:** Residential Real Estate **MA:** Local **EXP:** Ms. Bush's expertise is in relocation. **H/I/S:** Traveling, Playing Bridge, Interior Design and Marketing **EDU:** Bachelor of Science in Accounting, Louisiana State University; Coursework in Prelaw Studies, University of Houston **CERTS:** Certified Residential Specialist; Accredited Buyer Representative **A/A/S:** Graduate Realtor Institute; Board Member, Austin Symphony; Board Member, Austin Opera Lyric; American Association of University Women; Austin County Club Board; Burton Creek County Club **A/H:** Most Referred Realtor; Top 5 Percent of Producers Nationwide (2001); Number Two Agent in Houston (1988); **C/VW:** Austin Symphony
Email: brainybush@aol.com
URL: http://www.prudentialtexasrealty.com/lindabush

Patti Bush
Title: Medial Specialist, Director **Company:** Dr. William H. (Bob) Bailey Middle School **Address:** 2500 N. Hollywood Boulevard, Las Vegas, NV 89156 United States **BUS:** Middle School **P/S:** Secondary Education **MA:** Local **EXP:** Ms. Bush's expertise is in grant writing. **D/D/R:** Overseeing Administration, Curriculum and Development **H/I/S:** Traveling, Going on Cruises, Reading, Needlework, Making Crafts **EDU:** Master's Degree in Curriculum, Plus 40, University of Nevada **A/A/S:** Clark County School District; National Education Association; National Literacy Association **C/VW:** Local Hospital; American Foundation for the Blind; American Red Cross; Salvation Army
Email: pattib@yahoo.com
Email: pattib50@yahoo.com
URL: http://www.ccsd.net/schools/bailey

Helen D. Bush-Topp
Title: 1) Owner, Consultant 2) Independent Beauty Consultant **Company:** 1) Easy of Mind 2) Mary Kay **Address:** P.O. Box 952, Frenchtown, MT 59834 United States **BUS:** 1) Consulting Company 2) Retail Beauty Company **P/S:** 1) Early Education Consulting for Parents 2) Skincare Products Including Cosmetics and Fragrances **MA:** Regional **D/D/R:** Consulting on Early Childhood Education, Assisting Parents in Finding a Suitable Education Program for their Child, Beauty Consulting, Improving Women's Self-Esteem **EDU:** Bachelor's Degree in Liberal Studies; College Coursework Completed, The University of Montana, Missoula, Montana (2002)
Email: hbtopp@centric.net
URL: http://www.marykay.com

Mary A. Buss
Title: Store Manager **Company:** NAPA Auto Parts **Address:** 1141 Main Street, Chipley, FL 32428 United States **BUS:** Automotive Company **P/S:** Automotive Spare Parts **MA:** National **EXP:** Ms. Buss' expertise is in operations management. **H/I/S:** Traveling, Spending Time with her Grandchildren **EDU:** High School Diploma **A/A/S:** Advisory Board, Washington County Technical Center **A/H:** Triple Crown Award (2005) **C/VW:** Local Church; Florida State Troopers, VFW, Salvation Army, Young Explorers, Sacred Heart Hospital
Email: missmary20@hotmail.com
URL: http://www.cambridgewhoswho.com

Maria Bustillo, MD
Title: MD **Company:** South Florida Institute for Reproductive Medicine **Address:** 6850 SW 115th Street, Miami, FL 33156 United States **BUS:** Healthcare Endocrinologist **P/S:** Reproductive Center **MA:** Local **EXP:** Mds. Bustillo's expertise is in conception assistance. **H/I/S:** Racquetball, Traveling **EDU:** University of Wisconsin Medical School, MD **A/A/S:** ASCRM, Reproduction of American Association
Email: mbustillo@sfirm.org

Antolina Floramar Valdez Caluya Butalid
Title: Social Worker, Professional Counselor **Company:** Ohio Department of Mental Health **Address:** 1756 Sagamore Road, Northfield, OH 44067 United States **BUS:** Government Organization **P/S:** Healthcare Services **MA:** Local **D/D/R:** Counseling Mentally Ill Patients and their Families **H/I/S:** Traveling, Reading **EDU:** Master of Arts in Education, University of Hawaii (1972); Bachelor of Science in Psychology, University of Santo Tomas, Manila, Philippines (1960) **A/H:** Outstanding Professional Award, National Alliance on Mental Illness (2005); Humanitarian of the Year Award **C/VW:** Diocese of Cleveland; American Foundation to Aid the Poor
Email: butalida@mh.state.oh.us
URL: http://www.cambridgewhoswho.com

Carla W. Butler
Title: Teacher **Company:** South Marshall Elementary School **Address:** 102 Cambridge Drive, Murray, KY 42071 United States **BUS:** Public Elementary School **P/S:** Primary and Intermediate Education **MA:** Regional **D/D/R:** Teaching Primary Mathematics, Writing and Other Subjects to Fourth-Grade Students, with an Emphasis on Organizational and Practical Living Skills **H/I/S:** Bowling, Doing Church Work **EDU:** Master of Arts in Education, Union University (2003); Bachelor of Arts in General Education (1998) **A/A/S:** Kentucky Education Association; National Education Association; Youth Director at Church **A/H:** Who's Who Among American Teachers (2004-2007)
Email: cbutler27@hotmail.com
URL: http://www.marshall.k12.ky.us/smes/

Gayle Carter Butler
Title: First-Grade Teacher **Company:** Oak Knoll Elementary School **Address:** 23 Bodine Avenue, Williamstown, NJ 08094 United States **BUS:** Elementary School **P/S:** Primary Education **MA:** Williamstown, NJ **EXP:** Ms. Butler's expertise is in education. **H/I/S:** Reading, Traveling **EDU:** Master's Degree in Reading and Literacy, Walden University (2007); Bachelor's Degree in Elementary Education and Sociology, Rowan University **A/H:** Gloucester County Teacher of the Year Award (2007); Wal-Mart Teacher of the Year Award (2006); Mercer County Teacher of the Year Award (1999) **C/VW:** Shiloh Apostolic Church
Email: gayle_btlr@yahoo.com
URL: http://www.cambridgewhoswho.com

Michael Butler
Title: Rep. Phlebotomy Services II CA **Company:** Quest Diagnostics **Address:** 2519 Milvia Street, Berkeley, CA 94702 United States **BUS:** Medical Laboratory **P/S:** Medical Laboratory Testing **MA:** National **EXP:** Mr. Butler's expertise is in venipuncture. **H/I/S:** Playing the Keyboard **EDU:** Associate of Arts, Contra Casta College **A/A/S:** American Society of Phlebotomy Technicians
Email: mikeshoneylove@aol.com
URL: http://www.cambridgewhoswho.com

Mr. Willie J. Butler, MA
Title: Research Associate **Company:** Radiant Development **Address:** 515 N. State Street, Chicago, IL 60610 United States **BUS:** Clinical and Contract Research Organization **P/S:** Healthcare, Pharmaceutical Products, Clinical Trials **MA:** National **EXP:** Mr. Butler's expertise includes clinical research and data management. **H/I/S:** Reading, Walking and Listening to Light Jazz **EDU:** Master of Arts in Applied Professional Studies, DePaul University (2004); Bachelor of Arts in Business, DePaul University (2002); Associate of Arts in Computer Studies, The Center for Degree Studies (1998) **A/A/S:** Golden Key International Honour Society; Clinical Research Professionals; International Biopharmaceutical Association; ICHGCP **C/VW:** United Negro College Fund
Email: wbutler850@sbcglobal.net
URL: http://www.cambridgewhoswho.com

Melissa Butterworth
Title: President of Healthcare Division **Company:** Advanced Strategic Partners **Address:** 16850 Collins Avenue, Suite 116, Sunny Isles Beach, FL 33160 United States **BUS:** Laboratory **P/S:** Laboratory Diagnostic Testing **MA:** National **EXP:** Ms. Butterworth's expertise includes sales, marketing and mergers and acquisitions of laboratory operations. **H/I/S:** Traveling, Exercising **EDU:** Bachelor of Science in Management, University of North Florida, Jacksonville; Bachelor of Science in Marketing, University of North Florida **A/A/S:** Toast Master International; Board American Medical Labs **C/VW:** National Multiple Sclerosis Foundation
Email: m18butterworth@comcast.net
URL: http://www.lucianodesigns.com

Shirley K. Buttram, Ed.S.
Title: Coordinator of Developmental Studies **Company:** Northeast Alabama Community College **Address:** P. O. Box 159, Rainsville, AL 35986 United States **BUS:** Community Colleges **P/S:** Higher Education, Certification Programs **MA:** Regional **D/D/R:** Assisting with Necessary Duties **H/I/S:** Writing, Poetry, Painting, Amateur Artist in Oils, Gardening, Hiking, Exercising **EDU:** Bachelor of Science; Master of Arts; Education Specialist **A/A/S:** National Education Association; Alabama Education Association; National Association of Developmental Education; Alabama Association of Developmental Education; Lecturer **A/H:** Who's Who Among America's Teachers; Most Influential Teacher; Published Poetry in 1995
Email: buttrams@nacc.edu
URL: http://www.nacc.edu

Marilynn Buxton, BS
Title: Gifted and Talented Teacher **Company:** Waverly-Shell Rock Schools-Washington Irving Elementary School **Address:** 216 Sixth Street S.W., Waverly, IA 50677 United States **BUS:** Public School **P/S:** Education, Athletics, Extracurricular Activities **MA:** Local **D/D/R:** Teaching Gifted and Talented Students in Grades Four through Six **H/I/S:** Swimming, Singing, Playing Sudoku **EDU:** Bachelor of Science, Iowa State University (1973) **A/A/S:** Sweet Adeline's International Singers; Iowa State Education Association; National Education Association; Iowa Talented And Gifted Association; Gifted Endorsement
Email: buxtonm@waverly-shellrock.k12.ia.us
URL: http://www.waverly-shellrock.k12.ia.us

Tara M. Buzan
Title: Owner **Company:** A Taste of Britain with Easy Elegance **Address:** 40 Berkley Road, Devon, PA 19333 United States **BUS:** British Themed Tea Shop/Restaurant Caterer **P/S:** Tea Lunch Shop, Catering for All Occasions, Buffets, Sit Down Dinners, Cookouts, Featuring Gourmet British Foods and Teas, Sandwiches, Salads, Desserts and Specialty Main Dishes, Gifts Shipped Nationally British Goods and Scones shipped Nationally **MA:** Local **D/D/R:** Overseeing Business Operations, Hosting Children's Parties, Teaching Etiquette, Catering Parties in Customers' Homes **H/I/S:** Horseback Riding, Cooking **EDU:** Bachelor's Degree in Hotel, Restaurant and Travel Management, University of Massachusetts **A/H:** Best of County Line Magazine, Tea Shop (2004-6) Best of Main Line Times Magazine, Tea Shop (2004-6)
Email: meals@easyelegance.net
URL: http://www.easyelegance.net

Ms. Eslyn B. Byarm
Title: Certified Clinical Coordinator **Company:** Horizon Blue Cross Blue Shield of New Jersey **Address:** 3 Penn Plaza E., Newark, NJ 07105 United States **BUS:** Insurance Agency **P/S:** Health Insurance **MA:** Regional **EXP:** Ms. Byarm's expertise is in case management. **D/D/R:** Reviewing Insurance Claims for Physical and Occupational Therapy **H/I/S:** Walking, Traveling **EDU:** Bachelor of Science in Nursing, Columbia Union College **CERTS:** Certified Case Manager **A/A/S:** Case Management Society of America; Customer Relationship Management Association **C/VW:** Local Healthcare Center; Local Music Ministry; Living Faith Christian Center
Email: eslyn.byarm@cwwemail.com

Sara L. Byerley
Title: Owner, Independent Consultant **Company:** SecWitch Consultants, LLC **Address:** 2314 Belmar Drive, Jeffersonville, IN 47130 United States **BUS:** Consulting Company **P/S:** Independent Consultant, SAP and Other Application Security **MA:** National **D/D/R:** Implementing Business Programs, Overseeing SAP Security for Human Relations Applications, Designing Security Systems, Evaluating Security, Conducting Disaster Recovery Planning for Small, Medium and Large Companies, Using Computer and Network Systems **EDU:** Master's Degree in Computer Data Management, Webster University (1984); Bachelor's Degree in Business Administration, Indiana University Southeast (1980) **A/A/S:** Certified Information Systems Security Professional, JANS Network Institute
Email: slbyerley@insightbb.com
URL: http://www.cambridgewhoswho.com

Richard N. Byers
Title: Senior Buyer **Company:** Continental Maritime of San Diego **Address:** 1995 Bay Front Street, San Diego, CA 92113 United States **BUS:** Ship Repair Contractor Company **P/S:** Master Ship Repair **MA:** International **D/D/R:** Purchasing Repair Products for U.S. Navy Ships **H/I/S:** Model Trains and Railroads, Spending Time with his Wife and Family **EDU:** High School Diploma **CERTS:** Certification in Computers, University of California; Certification in Lean Manufacturing, San Diego State University **A/A/S:** Former Assignment, U.S. Naval Security Group Command
Email: rnbyers@cox.net

Dena M. Byersdorf
Title: President Company: Gig Harbor Motorsports Address: 3818 Grandview Street, Gig Harbor, WA 98335 United States BUS: Retail Auto Sales Company P/S: Retail and Wholesale Car Sales MA: Washington D/D/R: Overseeing All Operations, Financing Vehicles for Customers, Advertising, Marketing, Ensuring Customer Satisfaction H/I/S: Cooking, Boating, Spending Time with her Family EDU: Coursework in Communications, University of Washington A/A/S: Washington State Auto Dealers Association; Peninsula School District C/VW: American Cancer Society, Susan G. Komen for the Cure
Email: dena521@comcast.net
URL: http://www.gigharborms.com

Ms. Tyrone Bynoe
Title: Assistant Professor of Education Company: University of the Cumberlands Address: 7192 College Station Drive, Williamsburg, KY 40769 United States BUS: Higher Education Institution P/S: Majors and Minors in Art, Biology, Chemistry, Accounting, Business Administration, Communications, Theater Arts, English, Modern Foreign Language, Military Science, Psychology, Human Services, Social Work MA: International D/D/R: Teaching Graduate Education Courses, Researching, Presenting Papers at Conferences H/I/S: Golfing, Exercising, Reading EDU: Doctor of Education Administration, Curriculum, Finance, Teachers College Columbia University (2004); Master's Degree in American History, SUNY University at Albany (1992); Master's Degree in Education Administration and Policy Studies, SUNY University at Albany (1990); Master's Degree in European History, SUNY University at Albany (1985); Bachelor of Arts in American History Education, SUNY University at Albany (1978) A/A/S: National Council for the Social Studies; National Center for Education Statistics; American Education Finance Association; Association for Supervision and Curriculum Development; International Society for Technology, Education and Other Professional Associations
Email: tbynoe@ucumberlands.edu
URL: http://www.ucumberlands.edu

Elaine P. Byrd
Title: Deputy District Director Company: US House of Representatives Address: 503 West 83rd Place, Merriville, IN 46410 United States BUS: Constituent Services Government P/S: Constituent Services MA: Local EXP: Ms. Byrd's expertise is in customer service. H/I/S: Fishing, Traveling EDU: NW, College A/A/S: Lake County Women's Club
Email: lainybyrd@hotmail.com

Kimberly Byrd
Title: President Company: The Byrd's Nest Weddings and Events Address: 13503 Copper Canyon Road, Pine City, MN 55063 United States BUS: Event Management Company P/S: Weddings, Corporate Events, Parties and Social Events MA: Local D/D/R: Creating and Planning Festivities for All Occasions H/I/S: Farming, Spending Time with her Kids, Reading CERTS: Certified Catering and Gourmet Chef, Penn Foster Career School; Certified Food Safety Manager, University of Minnesota; Certified Event Planner, US Event Guide C/VW: Volunteer, St. Mary's Catholic School
Email: the_byrdsnest@msn.com

Jennifer Lynne Byrne
Title: Director Company: Riverside Publishing Company Address: 3208 Mandina Court, McKinney, TX 75070 United States BUS: Software Company P/S: Information Technology Including Programming, Software and Databases MA: National D/D/R: Overseeing Account Management H/I/S: Reading Biographies and Fiction, Traveling EDU: Bachelor's Degree, University of North Texas A/A/S: Association of Supervision and Curriculum Development; Jimmy V Celebrity Golf Classic
Email: byrnej1@tx.rr.com

Michelle M. Byrne
Title: Senior Information Technology, Consultant for Corporate Security Company: Polaroid Address: 1265 Main Street W2-2D, Waltham, MA 02451 United States BUS: Manufacturing Company P/S: Consumer Electronics MA: International EXP: Ms. Byrne's expertise is in project management. D/D/R: Maintaining Customer Support Applications, Managing Content and Web Support H/I/S: Traveling, Reading, Spending Time with her Family, Riding her Motorcycle EDU: Bachelor's Degree in Psychology, with a Concentration in Theology and Computer Science, Boston College A/A/S: ASIS A/H: Certificate of Excellence, Polaroid Operations (2005) C/VW: Team Captain, Multiple Sclerosis Society Walk; Vice President, Stoneham Pop Warner Board of Directors; Stoneham High School Booster Club
Email: michelle.byrne@polaroid.com
URL: http://www.polaroid.com

Cynthia C. Cabadas
Title: Owner Company: Up Front Letterpress, LLC Address: 110 Stadium Drive, Arlington, TX 76010 United States BUS: Printing Company P/S: Custom Embossing, Foil Stamping, Brochures and Greeting Cards MA: Regional D/D/R: Overseeing Custom Dying of Cut Foils, Embossing Stamps H/I/S: Reading EDU: Diploma, Monterey High School (1973)
Email: cynthia.cabadas@cwwemail.com

Valori B. Cable
Title: Critical Care Registered Nurse Company: Kingman Regional Medical Center Dept: ICU/CCU Address: 3213 Stockton Hill Road, Kingman, AZ 86409 United States BUS: Nonprofit Medical Center P/S: Acute Patient Care MA: Regional D/D/R: Nursing Patients in the Intensive Care and Critical Care Units, Educating Critical Trauma Patients and their Families H/I/S: Participating in the Community Orchestra EDU: Bachelor's Degree in Nursing, University of Wyoming (2006) CERTS: Certified Registered Nurse; Certified Critical Care Registered Nurse
Email: vbc@frontiernet.net

Selena Cabral
Title: Spanish Teacher Company: Fox Lane Middle School Address: Route 172, Bedford, NY 10506 United States BUS: Middle School P/S: Education MA: Local D/D/R: Teaching Spanish H/I/S: Singing, Dancing EDU: Master of Arts in Educational Communication and Technology, New York University; Bachelor of Science in Spanish Education, New York University A/A/S: Bedford Teachers Association; Kappa Delta Pi
Email: selenacabral@yahoo.com
URL: http://www.cambridgewhoswho.com

Marilou Cabusao
Title: Registered Nurse, BSN, CCRN Company: Sharp Grossmont Hospital Address: 5555 Grossmont Center Drive, La Mesa, CA 91942 United States BUS: Hospital P/S: Healthcare MA: Local EXP: Ms. Cabusao's expertise is in intensive-care nursing. H/I/S: Traveling, Reading EDU: Bachelor of Science in Nursing, University of Santo Tomas, Philippines A/A/S: American Association of Critical-Care Nurses
Email: marilou-rn@cox.net
URL: http://www.sharp.com

Sister Philip Dolores Cacciatore
Title: Teacher, Book Store Manager Company: Cardinal Spellman High School Address: One Cardinal Spellman Place, Bronx, NY 10466 United States BUS: College Preparatory School P/S: Academic and Religious Studies MA: Regional D/D/R: Teaching Mathematics, Managing and Selling Items in the Book Store H/I/S: Bowling, Enjoying Basketball, Volleyball, Reading, Solving Crossword Puzzles EDU: Master's Degree in Education and Supervision, Seton Hall University; Professional Diploma in Education and Supervision, Fordham University A/A/S: National Education Association
Email: info@CambridgeWhosWho.com
URL: http://www.spellman.com

Velma Cadaveira
Title: Office Manager Company: Premier Physical Therapy of Rockland LLC Address: 100 Route 59, Suite 103, Suffern, NY 10901 United States BUS: Physical Therapy Facility P/S: Physical Therapy and Rehabilitative Services MA: Local EXP: Ms. Cadaveira's expertise is in office management. D/D/R: Offering Insurance Coverage, Entering Data and Payments, Marketing H/I/S: Gardening, Taking Care of her Foster Children
Email: vanny042@verizon.net
URL: http://www.ptpremier.com

Eddy Cadet
Title: Salesman Company: 4 Life Research Address: 9850 South 300 West, Sandy, UT 84070 United States BUS: Healthcare Marketing P/S: Transfer Factor-Rio VidaJuice with TF MA: National D/D/R: Marketing, Accounting H/I/S: Tennis, Basketball, Soccer EDU: Schooled in Haiti, High School
Email: info@CambridgeWhosWho.com
URL: www.professionalnetworker.com

Lawrence F. Cafero, Ed.D
Title: Connecticut State Marshal Company: CT State Marshal Commission Address: 60 Rampart Road, Norwalk, CT 06854 United States BUS: State Marshal Government P/S: State Marshal Commission MA: Local D/D/R: Processing Legal Documents H/I/S: Collecting Coins EDU: Doctorate of Education, Nova University A/A/S: Retired Secondary School Principal, NEA, National Association of Secondary Principals
Email: info@CambridgeWhosWho.com

R. Craig Cagle
Title: Sales Manager, Nutrisentials Division Company: Kelly Foods Corporation Address: 3337 Medina Road, Medina, OH 44256 United States BUS: Food Corporation P/S: Foods, Animal Health Products MA: National EXP: Mr. Cagle's expertise is in sales. H/I/S: Golfing EDU: Bachelor of Arts in Marketing, Western Carolina University A/A/S: Lambda Chi Alpha
Email: craig.cagle@butlerahs.com

Michael W. Cahill
Title: Interior Designer Company: Michael W. Cahill Designs Address: 7 Partners Trace, Poughkeepsie, NY 12603 United States BUS: Interior Design Company P/S: Complete Interior Design MA: Duchess County, Westchester, Manhattan D/D/R: Creating Classic Formality with a Touch of Contemporary Flair in Residential Homes, Catering to High-End Clients H/I/S: Gardening, Auctions, Playing Tennis, Cooking, Classic Cars EDU: Associate in Social Science, Duchess Community College-1985; Associate in Fine Arts, Fashion Institute of Technology 1989 A/A/S: American Society of Interior Designers C/VW: Children's Cancer Research, Alzheimer's Research
Email: cahillmw@msn.com

Eddie G. Cain
Title: Owner Company: B & C Tree, Inc. Address: 30007 Old Highway 395, Escondido, CA 92026 United States BUS: Landscaping Company P/S: Lawn Care, Palm Trees MA: National EXP: Mr. Cain's expertise includes landscape design and operations management. D/D/R: Overseeing Residential and Commercial Projects H/I/S: Golfing, Traveling EDU: Diploma, Orange Glenn High School
Email: ekcain@msn.com
URL: http://www.bandctree.com

Bonnie Caird
Title: Certified Six Sigma Black Belt Company: Mercury Marine Address: W6250 W. Pioneer Road, Fond Du Lac, WI 54935 United States BUS: Manufacturer P/S: Marine Manufacturing MA: Local D/D/R: Managing the Supply Chain H/I/S: Spending Time with her Family Outdoors, Camping, Hiking EDU: Bachelor of Science in Operational Management, Marian College; Associate Degree in Accounting, Moraine Park Technical College CERTS: Certified Six Sigma Black Belt, American Society for Quality A/A/S: Women in Management; American Society for Quality C/VW: Girl Scouts of the USA, United Way, Local Church
Email: bonnie_caird@mercmarine.com

Frank J. Calandruccio, SRES
Title: Realtor/Owner Company: Remax Country Address: 76 S Main Street, Milltown, NJ 08850 United States BUS: Real Estate Broker P/S: Residential, Executive, HiEnd, Lake Front, New Construction, Condos, Gulf Homes MA: National D/D/R: Overseeing 22 Agents, Selling Real Estate H/I/S: Surfing EDU: Bachelor of Science in Business Management, Johnson and Wales College, RI A/A/S: New Jersey Association of Realtors, National Association of Realtors
Email: frankcaland@remax.net
URL: www.frankcal.com

Betty Ann P. Caldwell
Title: Senior Civil Engineer/Project Manager Company: Bluewater Design Group Address: 2500 Via Cabrillo Marina, San Pedro, CA 90731 United States BUS: Civil Engineering Consulting P/S: Engineering, Planning and Program Management MA: International EXP: Ms. Caldwell's expertise includes civil engineering and management. H/I/S: Golf and Tennis EDU: Bachelor of Science, North Carolina State University A/A/S: American Society of Civil Engineers, Member of Engineering Fraternity Theta Tau
Email: info@CambridgeWhosWho.com

Ms. Priscilla Caldwell
Title: Clerk of Court Company: Floyd County Magistrates Court Address: Three Government Plaza, Suite 227, Rome, GA 30161 United States BUS: Magistrate Court P/S: Addresses Small Claims, Public Services, Law Enforcement MA: Local D/D/R: Coordinating Mediation, Supervising Deputy Clerks, Interns and Judge Assistants H/I/S: Collecting Elvis Memorabilia and Antique Cups and Saucers EDU: Bachelor of Science in Secretarial Science, Floyd College (1984)
Email: caldwellp@floydcountyga.org
URL: http://www.georgiacourts.org

Mr. Trevor Caldwell
Title: Owner, Registered Agent Company: RTC, LLC Address: 3360 Highway 70 Bypass, P.O. Box 909, Camden, TN 38320 United States BUS: Transportation Trucking Company P/S: Transportation Services for Private Businesses MA: National D/D/R: Overseeing Accounting and Finances, Managing, Ensuring Customer Satisfaction, Briefing Drivers, Evaluating Performances H/I/S: Golfing, Spending Time with his Family EDU: Pursuing Master of Business Administration, Union University; Bachelor of Science in Business Administration, Emphasis in Economics and Finance, Minor in Management and Marketing, The University of Tennessee at Martin (1995); Associate of Science in Business Administration, Jackson State Community College (1992) A/A/S: Former President, Rotary Club of Camden (2002-2004) C/VW: St, Jude's Children's Hospital
Email: trevorc_ttinc@bellsouth.net

Darlene L. Calhoun, BS, MS, MET
Title: Director of Educational Technology Company: Computer Tots & Computer Explorers Address: 5825 Spinnaker Pointe, Parkville, MO 64152 United States BUS: Computer School P/S: Technology Education for Children and Adults MA: International EXP: Ms. Calhoun's expertise is in computer peripherals. H/I/S: Collecting Tiffany Lamps, Reading EDU: Master of Educational Technology, Wesley University; Master's Degree in Elementary Education, SUNY New Paltz; Bachelor's Degree in Physical Education, SUNY Cortland
Email: ctotskc@yahoo.com
URL: http://www.computertots.com/189

Ms. Melissa S. Calhoun, RN
Title: Registered Nurse Company: Advocate Christ Medical Center and Hope Children's Hospital Address: 4440 W. 95th Street, Oak Lawn, IL 60453 United States BUS: Hospital P/S: Healthcare Services MA: Local D/D/R: Neonatal Nursing for Premature and Term Infants with Birth Defects Including Cardiac, Lung and Other Diseases H/I/S: Traveling, Creating Handcrafted Work, Home Remodeling EDU: Associate Degree in Nursing, Moraine Valley Community College (2004) C/VW: St. Jude Children's Research Hospital
Email: nicurn19@yahoo.com
URL: http://www.cambridgewhoswho.com

Ellen M. Call
Title: Front Office Manager Company: Stonebridge Hospitality Address: 4301 Credit Union Drive, Anchorage, AK 99503 United States BUS: Hotel P/S: Service Provider MA: Local D/D/R: Ensuring Customer Satisfaction EDU: Coursework, University of Alaska Anchorage
Email: higanchfom@sbcos.com

Richard L. Callaghan
Title: President Company: Association For Intelligence Officers Dept: New Mexico Chapter Address: 672 La Viveza Court, Santa Fe, NM 87501 United States BUS: Nonprofit Educational Organization P/S: Education, Consulting MA: Local EXP: Mr. Callaghan's expertise is in espionage. D/D/R: Consulting for Government Agencies H/I/S: Hunting, Fishing EDU: Master of Business Administration A/A/S: UDT-SEAL Association; Life Member of the UDT Seal Association
Email: richard.callaghan@cwwemail.com

Nelda A.B. Callard
Title: Teacher (Retired) Company: Royalton Hartland Central School District Address: State Street, Middleport, NY 14105 United States BUS: Public Elementary School P/S: Education MA: Local D/D/R: Teaching Elementary Education H/I/S: Reading, Singing in Choir, Gardening, Walking EDU: Master's Degree in Education, State University of New York, Buffalo; Bachelor's Degree in Education, State University of New York, Geneseo A/A/S: American Federation of Teachers; Royalton Hartland Teachers Association C/VW: Financial Consultant Service Team; Girl Scouts of the United States America
Email: dbcnbc50@hotmail.com
URL: http://www.cambridgewhoswho.com

Bonita D. Calloway
Title: Certified School Nurse Company: Edison Township Board of Education Dept: John Marshall Elementary School Address: 15 Cornell Street, Edison, NJ 08817 United States BUS: School District P/S: Primary Education MA: Local D/D/R: Teaching Health Issues, Managing Administrative Duties, Ensuring the Health and Welfare of Students and Faculty H/I/S: Collecting Stamps EDU: Pursuing Doctoral Degree, Walden University; Master of Science, Long Island University; Master of Business Administration, Long Island University; Master of Business Administration, Arnold & Marie Schwartz College of Pharmacy and Health Sciences; Bachelor of Science in Nursing, Long Island University CERTS: Registered Nurse, Long Island University A/A/S: National Association of School Nurses; Girl Scout of United States of America
Email: bonita.calloway@edison.k12.nj.us
URL: http://www.edison.k12.nj.us

Maria T. Camacho
Title: Medical Doctor, Medical Director Company: Valley Baptist Medical Center Address: 102 N. Nueces Park Lane, Harlingen, TX 78552 United States BUS: Nonprofit Health System P/S: Health Services, Educational Services Including Spiritually-Based Health Education, Community Outreach Programs MA: Local D/D/R: Treating Patients, Directing Treatment in the Pediatric Critical Care Unit H/I/S: Fishing EDU: MD, Universidad Mayor de San Andres, Bolivia (1987) A/A/S: American Academy of Pediatrics; Society of Critical Care Medicine
Email: mateguia@aol.com
URL: http://www.valleybaptist.net

Alexander Cameron
Title: Program Coordinator Company: Arcturus Waldorf Teacher Education Program Address: 6531 N. Lakewood Avenue, Chicago, IL 60626 United States BUS: Teacher Certification Program P/S: College Education MA: Citywide D/D/R: Using Transformative Learning Techniques, Teaching Adult Education, Educating Using the Waldorf Method H/I/S: Skiing, Traveling, Kayaking, Hiking, Camping EDU: Ph.D., California Institute of Integral Studies, 2005; Master of Arts in Education, Emphasis on Secondary Social Studies, Reed College, 1976; Bachelor of Arts in Psychology, Dartmouth College, 1968 CERTS: Certified Waldorf Teacher A/A/S: Transformative Educational Society C/VW: Anthroposophical Society in America
Email: alxndr@hotmail.com
URL: http://www.arcturus.info

Jennifer Nichole Cameron
Title: DoD Consultant Company: Booz Allen Hamilton Dept: Acquisition Management USN Address: 1615 Murray Canyon Road, San Diego, CA 92108 United States BUS: Government Services firm P/S: Global Strategy and Technology Consulting for the United States Navy MA: National D/D/R: Managing Acquisitions, Defense Consulting for Various United States Military Branches H/I/S: Traveling, Rock Climbing and Cooking EDU: Pending Bachelor of Science in Global Business Management, University of Phoenix C/VW: Global Volunteers (globalvolunteers.org); Juvenile Diabetes Research Foundation (JDRF) Johnson and Johnson
Email: J_Cameron05@yahoo.com
URL: http://www.boozallen.com

Karen L. Camp
Title: Administrative Director of Patient Services Company: Yale-New Haven Hospital Address: 20 York Street, T118, New Haven, CT 06504 United States BUS: Healthcare, Hospital, Academic Medical Center P/S: Medical Services, AIDS Care Program, Geriatric Care, Surgical Services, Critical Care MA: Regional EXP: Ms. Camp's expertise includes healthcare administration and leadership, critical care and management. H/I/S: Music, Travel EDU: Executive Master of Business Administration, University of New Haven; Bachelor of Nursing, Quinnipiac University; Diploma in Nursing, St. Luke's Hospital A/A/S: American Association of Critical Care Nursing; Society of Critical Care Medicine; American Nurses Association; American Trauma Society; American Organization of Nurse Executives
Email: kacee3259@aol.com
URL: http://www.ynhh.org

Ashley Jean Campbell
Title: Kindergarten Teacher Company: Montrose Christian School Address: 5100 Randolph Road, Rockville, MD 20852 United States BUS: School P/S: Education MA: Local EXP: Ms. Campbell's expertise is in primary education. D/D/R: Adjusting the Curriculum, Offering Piano Lessons H/I/S: Exercising, Playing Hockey, Tennis, Soccer and Basketball, Coaching Local Softball Team EDU: Bachelor of Science in Elementary Education, Messiah College (2006) CERTS: Accredited Christian Certificate, Association of Christian Schools International; Certification in Teaching, Pennsylvania and Maryland
Email: acampbell@montrosechristian.org
URL: http://www.montrosechristian.org

Connie B. Campbell
Title: Chief Executive Officer, Founder Company: I Think Smart Solutions, Inc Address: 5830 W Kesler Street, Chandler, AZ 85226 United States BUS: ERP Consulting P/S: ERP Implementation and Project Management MA: Local D/D/R: Managing Projects, Installing Software and Applications H/I/S: Traveling, Skiing EDU: Coursework, Arizona State University A/A/S: Project Management Institute
Email: connie@ithinksmart.org
URL: www.ithinksmart.org

Denise H. Campbell
Title: Special Education Teacher Company: White Pine County School District Address: White Pine County School District, Ely, NV 89301 United States BUS: School P/S: Education MA: Local D/D/R: Coordinating Literature Programs, Teaching Special Education and Reading Classes H/I/S: Reading, Quilting, Doing Needlework, Spending Time with her Family EDU: Pursuing Doctor of Education in Educational Leadership, Walden University; Master of Science in Special Education, Western Oregon State College A/A/S: National Education Association; International Reading Association C/VW: The Church of Jesus Christ of Latter Day Saints, President Relief Society
Email: denise6309@sbcglobal.net
URL: http://www.cambridgewhoswho.com

Janet Campbell
Title: Founder, Chairman, Chief Executive Officer Company: Seno Medical Instruments Address: 3838 Medical Drive, Suite 101, San Antonio, TX 78229 United States BUS: Medical Device Manufacturer P/S: Opto-Acoustic Medical Devices for Cancer Detection MA: International D/D/R: Overseeing Operations H/I/S: Spending Time with her Pets, Bicycle Riding, Snow Skiing, Walking, Sailing EDU: MBA in Finance, The Johns Hopkins University A/A/S: The Griffins Society; Board Member, Texas Hall of Fame A/H: Alumni of the Year, University of Missouri School of Arts and Sciences (2005) C/VW: The Griffins Society
Email: jcampbell@senomedical.com
URL: http://www.cambridgewhoswho.com

Joe W. Campbell
Title: Regional Director Company: Sam's Club Dept: Human Resources Address: 608 S.W. Eighth Street, Bentonville, AR 72712 United States BUS: Wholesale Store P/S: Consumer Goods and Office Supplies MA: International D/D/R: Recruiting Staff on a Regional Level, Overseeing Managers, Strategic Planning and Employee Relations H/I/S: Motorcycling, Sports EDU: Coursework, Southern Illinois University; High School Diploma A/A/S: Society for Human Resource Management
Email: joe.campbell@samsclub.com
URL: http://www.samsclub.com

Matthew K. Campbell
Title: History Teacher Company: Brockton Public Schools, West Junior High School BUS: Junior High School P/S: Education for Sixth through Eighth-Grade Students MA: Local D/D/R: Teaching Social Studies to Seventh-Grade Students, Teaching History, Geography and World Economics, Organizing Comparative Government and Multidisciplinary Projects H/I/S: Reading History, Sports EDU: Master's Degree in History, University of Massachusetts, Boston (2007); Bachelor's Degree in Criminal Justice and Multidisciplinary Studies, Stonehill College (2003) CERTS: Certified History Teacher, 5-8, 9-12 A/A/S: The National Scholars Honor Society; Phi Alpha Theta
Email: soupde@aol.com

Olevia L. Campbell
Title: Manager Patient Financial Services Company: Jamaica Hospital Medical Center BUS: Hospital Facility P/S: Full Array of Healthcare Services MA: Regional D/D/R: Handling All Insurance Areas, Medicare, HMOs and Blue Cross Blue Shield Billing Follow-Ups, Following Criteria for All Financial Transactions, Offering Managed Care, Overseeing Outpatient and Inpatient Claims with Diagnosis and Procedure Codes H/I/S: family EDU: Associate in Science Degree, Queensborough Community College (2004) A/A/S: Mount Moriah AMF Church A/H: Recognition From the Hospital for her Numerous Years of Dedication
Email: ocampbel@jhmc.org
URL: http://www.jhmc.org

Susana Inés Campbell
Title: Teacher Company: Springdale Public Schools Address: 1879 E. Robinson Avenue, Springdale, AR 72764 United States BUS: Public School District P/S: Education MA: International D/D/R: Teaching English as a Second Language and Spanish H/I/S: Reading, Traveling EDU: Master's Degree in Teaching English as a Second Language, University of Piura, Peru A/A/S: Board Member, PALMS program; JOKM 'Schools to Watch' committee. A/H: Teacher of the Year, JOKM School C/VW: Church
Email: scampbell@sdale.org

Rev. Joseph G. Campellone, OSFS
Title: President Company: Father Judge High School Address: 3301 Solly Avenue, Philadelphia, PA 19136 United States BUS: High School P/S: Education MA: Local EXP: Rev. Campellone's expertise is in educational administration. D/D/R: Running Capital Campaigns, Community Development, Overseeing Initiatives Dealing with Violence, Drugs, Alcohol, Abuse and Diversity H/I/S: Reading, Sports, Coaching, Reading EDU: Master of Theology, DeSales Theological Center; Bachelor of Arts in Oncology, Desales University; Master of Oncology, DeSales Theological Center, DC A/A/S: Philadelphia Union League; Chamber of Commerce; Board Member, DeSales Theological Center; Mayfair Community Development Corporations; Sports and Spiritually Committee A/H: Mayfair DC Commitment to Youth Award; Man of the Year, Philadelphia New Gleaner (1999); Apostle of Youth Award, Arch Diocese Of Philadelphia; Who's Who Among American Teachers (Five Times); Who's Who in College and University Students; Leadership Award, Community College of Philadelphia
Email: jcampellone@father judge.com
URL: http://www.fatherjudge.com

Karen D. Campf
Title: Director of Education Company: Alliance Community Hospital Address: 200 State Street, Alliance, OH 44601 United States BUS: Healthcare P/S: Full Service Hospital MA: Local D/D/R: Offering Specialized Patient Care H/I/S: Reading, Knitting EDU: Bachelor's Degree in Nursing A/A/S: American National Nurse Association; American Heart Association
Email: kcampf54@yahoo.com
URL: http://www.achosp.org

Luis Canari

Title: President **Company:** Limac **Address:** 16756 Simonds Street, Granada Hills, CA 91344 United States **BUS:** Hotel Engineering **P/S:** Expert of Aeronautic Products to South America, Hotel South America, Structural Engineering **MA:** International **EXP:** Mr. Canari's expertise is in structural engineering. **H/I/S:** Hiking **EDU:** Bachelor of Science in Structural Engineering; Master's Degree in Engineering **A/A/S:** Founder, Minority Engineering Association
Email: lcanari4@aol.com

Sylvana C. Candela, MS

Title: President **Company:** Earthly Mama Herbals, Inc. **Address:** 12132 Marshall Street, Culver City, CA 90230 United States **BUS:** Herbal Treatment Center **P/S:** Ayurvedic Herbal Remedies Including Nutritional Supplements, Herbal Formulas, Acupuncture, Organic Herbal Coffee Blends **MA:** National **EXP:** Ms. Candela's expertise includes oriental and traditional Chinese medicine. **D/D/R:** Supervising, Teaching, Performing Acupuncture, Treating Fertility Problems, Overseeing Sales of Nutritional Supplements, Conducting Research on Obesity and Chronic Illnesses **H/I/S:** Writing Children's Books, Composing Music **EDU:** Doctoral Degree in Acupuncture and Oriental Medicine; Master's Degree in Traditional Chinese Medicine, Yo San University, Los Angeles (2000) **A/A/S:** Wildlife Society; American Civil Liberties Union; Union of Concerned Scientists
Email: polarbear8553@yahoo.com
URL: http://www.earthlymama.com
URL: http://www.sylvanacandela.com

Dena L. Cannada

Title: Spanish Teacher **Company:** Stafford County Public Schools, North Stafford High School **Dept:** World Languages **BUS:** Public High School Serving the Needs of District Residents **P/S:** Public Education for Students Regarding Other Cultures **D/D/R:** Teaching High School Spanish, Teaching Students to Explore and Understand Different Cultures, Discussing Literature, Teaching English, Grading Papers and Exams **H/I/S:** Dancing, Watching Movies, Reading, Working on Arts and Crafts, Spending Time with her Dog **EDU:** Pursuing Master's Degree in Education, University of Phoenix; Bachelor of Arts in Spanish and English Education, Ball State University (1998); Semester and Summer Abroad in Mexico; Summer Abroad in England **A/A/S:** Head Coach, School Dance Team **A/H:** Who's Who in Teaching (Three Times)
Email: tinydancer9401@hotmail.com
URL: http://www.staffordschools.net

Barbara Cannon

Title: Emergency Medical Technician, Firefighter **Company:** Junction City Fire and Ambulance **Address:** 707 N. Main Street, Junction City, AR 71749 United States **BUS:** Emergency Medical Services **P/S:** Rescue Services, Fire Protection **MA:** Regional **H/I/S:** Quilting, Raising Orchards **EDU:** Coursework, South Arkansas Community College **CERTS:** Licensed National Registry Emergency Medical Technician and Firefighter **A/A/S:** American Heart Association
Email: bdandfrun@yahoo.com

Curtis P. Cannon

Title: Community Development Director **Company:** City of Oxnard **Address:** 305 W. Third Street, Oxnard, CA 93030 United States **BUS:** Government Organization **P/S:** Economic Development and Public Administration Services **MA:** Local **D/D/R:** Overseeing Economic Development and Redevelopment **H/I/S:** Spending Time with his Family, Golfing, Playing Basketball, Softball and Baseball **EDU:** Master of Science in Public Administration, California State University, Northridge; Bachelor of Science in Public Administration, University of La Verne; Associate of Science in Business Management, Citrus College **A/A/S:** Community Redevelopment Agency; California Association for Local Economic Development; ICSC **C/VW:** Executive Secretary to the Bishop, The Church of Jesus Christ of Latter-day Saints
Email: curtis.cannon@ci.oxnard.ca.us
URL: http://www.cambridgewhoswho.com

George Q. Cannon III

Title: Salesman **Company:** Kaeser & Blair, Inc. **Address:** 4236 Grissom Drive, Batavia, OH 45103 United States **BUS:** Advertising **P/S:** Promotional Items **MA:** Local **D/D/R:** Advertising, Selling Promotional Items **H/I/S:** Gardening, Stamp Collecting **C/VW:** Church
Email: info@CambridgeWhosWho.com
URL: http://www.cambridgewhoswho.com

Mary 'Arlene' Cannon, RN

Title: Registered Nurse **Company:** Presbyterian Hospital of Greenville **Address:** 4215 Joe Ramsey Boulevard, Greenville, TX 75401 United States **BUS:** Hospital **P/S:** Nursing, Healthcare Services, Inpatient Services, Intensive Care Unit, Maternity Center, Medical Unit, Rehabilitation Center, Surgical Center, Transitional Care, Outpatient Services, Cardiopulmonary, Cardiac Rehabilitation, Diabetes Management Center **MA:** Regional **D/D/R:** Offering Cardiac Rehabilitation Nursing and Education about Risk Factors for Heart Disease, Cholesterol, Hypertension and Diabetes, Teaching Patients How to Set and Achieve New Goals and Make Lifestyle Changes to Assure a Healthy Heart **H/I/S:** Spending Time with her Grandchildren, Scuba Diving, Scrapbooking **CERTS:** Registered Nurse, Grayson County College (1991) **A/A/S:** Eastern Star; American Association of Cardiovascular and Pulmonary Rehabilitation; Exercise Special Population Instructor, Cooper Aerobic Institute (1996); Family Fellowship of Greenville, Texas **A/H:** Greatest 100 Nurses Award in the Dallas-Fort Worth Area (2003) **C/VW:** American Heart Association, Carl's Boys Home, TX
Email: arlenecannon@prodigy.net
URL: http://www.hmhd.org

Steve P. Cannon

Title: Executive Director **Company:** Gwinnett Environmental and Heritage Center **Address:** 2020 Cleanwater Drive, Buford, GA 30519 United States **BUS:** Educational Center **P/S:** Environmental Education **MA:** Southeastern United States **D/D/R:** Overseeing the Environmental Center **H/I/S:** Sail boating **EDU:** Bachelor of Science in Environmental Planning, Georgia State University **A/A/S:** Golden Key International Honour Society; Blue Key Honor Society; Georgia Water Wise Council; Metropolitan North Georgia Water Planning District; Georgia Association of Water Professionals; Southeast Association of Museums; American Association of Museums; Mortar Board **C/VW:** American Cancer Society; Rotary International; The Episcopal Church of St. Mary and St. Martha of Bethany
Email: steven.cannon@gwinnettcounty.com
URL: http://www.gwinnettehc.com

Mr. Michael L. Cantor

Title: Chief Operating Officer, General Counsel **Company:** Allegro Realty Advisors **Address:** 8111 Rockside Road, Suite 250, Cleveland, OH 44125 United States **BUS:** Consulting Firm **P/S:** Consulting Services Including Corporate Real Estate Services, Tenant Representation, Site Selection, Development and Management Consulting Services **MA:** International **EXP:** Mr. Cantor's expertise includes corporate real estate services, management consulting, strategic planning, tenant representation, real estate and economic development. **D/D/R:** Overseeing Client Service Delivery, Managing and Training the Staff, Risk Management, Managing Other Business Functions **H/I/S:** Spending Time with his Family, Artwork, Music, Writing, Running, Cross-Country Skiing **EDU:** JD, Cleveland-Marshall College of Law, Cleveland State University (2000); Bachelor of Science in Business, Miami University (1991); Bachelor of Arts in English, Miami University (1991) **CERTS:** Licensed Real Estate Broker, State of Ohio **A/A/S:** Board Member, Ohio/Kentucky Chapter of CoreNet Global; Government Affairs Council, Greater Cleveland Partnership; Cleveland Metropolitan Bar Association; Ohio State Bar Association; Ohio Environmental Committee; American Bar Association
Email: mcantor@allegrorealty.com
URL: http://www.allegrorealty.com

Yolanda R. Cantu

Title: Owner **Company:** McAllen Stained Glass **Address:** 1200 E. Jasmine Avenue, McAllen, TX 78501 United States **BUS:** Stained Glass Studio **P/S:** Stained Glass, Art Glass **MA:** National **D/D/R:** Designing, Manufacturing and Exhibiting Stained Glass Panels **H/I/S:** Going to the Beach with her Daughters **EDU:** Pursuing Studio Art Degree; Bachelor's Degree in Bilingual and Bicultural Education, Endorsement in Early Childhood; University of Texas-Pan American, 1980; Endorsement in Kindergarten **A/A/S:** Art Glass Association **C/VW:** VAMOS!
Email: mcallenstglass@aol.com

Mr. Tuan A. Cao

Title: Architectural Designer **Company:** AT Home Design, Principal **Dept:** Architecture **Address:** 1616 Tenaka Place, Sunnyvale, CA 94087 United States **BUS:** Architectural Design Company **P/S:** Custom Designing Services for Commercial and Residential Properties **MA:** Regional **EXP:** Mr. Cao's expertise is in architectural design. **D/D/R:** Collaborating with Structural Engineers, Consultants, Plumbers and Electricians, Overseeing Scheduling, Managing Company Finances **H/I/S:** Collecting Watches, Building 3-D Models **EDU:** Bachelor of Arts in Architecture, Berkeley University (1998); Architectural Degree, Earned in Vietnam (1978) **A/A/S:** American Institute of Architects
Email: archituan@sbcglobal.net

Ms. Audrey L. Capers-Credle

Title: Teacher **Company:** Tacoma Public Schools, Roosevelt Elementary School **Address:** 3550 E. Roosevelt Avenue, Tacoma, WA 98404 United States **BUS:** Public Elementary School **P/S:** Education for Students in Headstart Programs through Fifth-Grade, English as a Second Language, Special Education, Music **MA:** Local **D/D/R:** Teaching Students Fourth-Grade Students **H/I/S:** Bowling, Playing Games, Listening to Jazz Music **EDU:** Bachelor of Arts in Elementary Education, Minor in Music, University of Puget Sound (1981) **A/A/S:** National Association for the Advancement of Colored People; National Urban League
Email: audreycredle@msn.com
URL: http://www.tacoma.k12.wa.us/schools/es/roosevelt/index.asp

Theresa A. Caples

Title: Charge Nurse, Licensed Practical Nurse **Company:** Jefferson City Manor Care Center **Address:** 1720 Vieth Drive, Jefferson City, MO 65109 United States **BUS:** Skilled Nursing Facility **P/S:** Healthcare Services **MA:** Local **D/D/R:** Practicing Long-Term Geriatric Care **H/I/S:** Hiking, Bird Watching, Spending Time Outdoors, Writing, Photography **CERTS:** Practical Nursing License, Nichols Care Center; Intravenous Certified; Clinical Nursing Supervisor **A/A/S:** American Automobile Association; River Bluffs Audubon Society; Midweek Trekkers; National Wildlife Federation; Runse Nature Center; Hiking Club; MOSALPN **A/H:** Who's Who Among Rising Young Americans (1993); Employee of the Month (April 1997)
Email: info@CambridgeWhosWho.com
URL: http://www.cambridgewhoswho.com

Jack Capone Jr.

Title: Realtor **Company:** J-D Realty **Address:** 367 Bantam Road, Litchfield, CT 06759 United States **BUS:** Real Estate Broker **P/S:** Residential, Executive, Hi End, Lake Front, New Construction, Town Homes, Condos, Golf Homes, Senior Gated **MA:** National **EXP:** Mr. Capone's expertise is in commercial dry cleaning. **H/I/S:** Golf **A/A/S:** Connecticut Association of Realtors, National Association of Realtors
Email: info@CambridgeWhosWho.com

Keith E. Capps

Title: Revenue Cycle Coordinator **Company:** Baptist Regional Medical Center **Address:** 1 Trillium Way, Corbin, KY 10701 United States **BUS:** Medical Provider **P/S:** High Quality Healthcare and Patient Care to those in Need **MA:** Regional **EXP:** Mr. Capps' expertise is in billing. **H/I/S:** Water Sports **EDU:** Bachelor of Science in Computer Science, Cumberland College (1988) **A/A/S:** American Heart Association
Email: kcapps@bhsi.com
URL: http://www.baptistregional.com

Maxine H. Caprioli-Hight

Title: Owner **Company:** Artistically Yours **Address:** 111 S. Taylor Street, Fallon, NV 89406 United States **BUS:** Art Gallery **P/S:** Local and International Exhibitions of Art Including Picture Frames, Lithographs, Prints, Crafts and Miniatures **MA:** Regional **D/D/R:** Framing Historical Art, Painting Western Landscapes and Wildlife, Creating Portraits, Working with Acrylics **H/I/S:** Watching Equestrian Sports **EDU:** Associate Degree in Art and Commercial Art **A/A/S:** Cider Painters; Professional Picture Framers of America **A/H:** Artist of the Year, Reno Rodeo (2007); Exhibitor, Smithsonian institute, Washington, DC
Email: himax@oasisol.com
URL: http://www.artisticallyyours.com

Mr. Vincenzo G. Caraglia

Title: Owner **Company:** Caraglia, Inc. **Address:** 978 Saratoga Street, East Boston, MA 02128 United States **BUS:** Deli, Restaurant and Catering Company **P/S:** Food Services **MA:** Local **EXP:** Mr. Caraglia's expertise is in business management. **D/D/R:** Managing Company Operations and Finances **H/I/S:** Traveling, Photography **EDU:** Pursuing Bachelor's Degree, Suffolk University; Associate Degree in Business Management and Operations, North Shore Community College
Email: vcaraglio@netscape.net

Sandra Patricia Carbone

Title: Assistant Manager **Company:** Innomax **Address:** 530 W. Elk Place, Denver, CO 80216 United States **BUS:** Wholesale and Retail Supplier of Bedroom Sleep Systems **P/S:** Sleep Systems, Heirloom-Quality American-Made Furniture, Bedroom Linens **MA:** International **H/I/S:** Traveling, Collecting Antiques, Frank Sinatra Memorabilia and Clowns, Enjoying Music, Musicals, Plays, Ballets, Opera, Dancing **EDU:** College Coursework **A/A/S:** St. Anthony's Society; American Business Women's Association **A/H:** Top Sales Employee of the Year (2003); Employee of the Month Award, Innomax (More Than 25 Times); **C/VW:** Colorado Christian Home; St. Anthony's Society, Various Walkathons
Email: sandycarbone@innomax.com
URL: http://www.innomax.com

Marilyn P. Cardello
Title: Pain Management Nurse Coordinator Company: Healthcare Associates Address: 1099 Targee Street, Staten Island, NY 10304 United States BUS: Healthcare Facility P/S: Pediatric and Adult Neurology, Pain Management MA: Local D/D/R: Managing Pain, Performing Administrative Duties, Ordering Equipment, Administering Intravenous Therapy H/I/S: Playing Tennis, Attending Broadway Theater, Walking
Email: mpc2107@aol.com
URL: http://www.hca-si.net

James V. Cardito
Title: Vice President of Sales Company: Margarita International Address: 144 Home Street, Malverne, NY 11565 United States BUS: Manufacturing Company P/S: Footwear Including Athletic Shoes and Sandals MA: International D/D/R: Selling Footwear Manufactured in the Dominican Republic to United States Retailers H/I/S: Golfing, Coaching Little League EDU: Bachelor of Science in Business, Minor in Economics, SUNY Oswego (1977)
Email: jimcardito@optonline.net
URL: http://www.margaritaindustries.com

Connie L. Carey
Title: Director of Student Health Company: Sterling College Address: 125 W. Cooper Street, Sterling, KS 67579 United States BUS: College P/S: Education, Wellness and Health Intervention MA: Local EXP: Ms. Carey's expertise is in proactive preventative healthcare. H/I/S: Quilting, Painting, Reading, Attending Church, Gardening, Spending Time with her Family, Cooking, Singing in Various Choirs CERTS: Registered Nurse, Bethel Deaconess Hospital School of Nursing A/A/S: American College Health Association C/VW: Salvation Army, Disaster Programs, Pro-Life Organizations, Girl Scouts of America, American Red Cross
Email: ccarey@sterling.edu
URL: http://www.sterling.edu

Mary Lou Carey
Title: Owner Company: Carey and Associates Address: 5300 Rivers Edge Drive, Fallon, NV 89406 United States BUS: Proven Leader in the Business Industry P/S: Wide Variety of High Quality Business Management Solutions to Clients MA: National D/D/R: Consulting, Operational Auditing, Analyzing Forensics, Managing Solutions and Resolutions, Developing Procedures and Processes H/I/S: Football EDU: Bachelor of Business Management, University of Nevada (2000) A/A/S: APEX
Email: mlcarey100@yahoo.com
URL: http://cambridgewhoswho.com

Jennifer H. Cargal
Title: Real Estate Agent Company: Keller Williams of Greater Cleveland Address: 8500 Station Street, Mentor, OH 44060 United States BUS: Real Estate Company P/S: Real Estate Exchange for Residential Properties MA: National EXP: Ms. Cargal's expertise is in residential sales. EDU: Coursework in Business Management, Sullivan University, KY A/A/S: Cleveland County Association of Realtors; National Association of Realtors
Email: jcargal2@earthlink.net
URL: http://www.howardhanna.com

Marguerite Carideo
Title: Artist Company: Studio 527 Artworks Address: 25 Evergreen Way, Pawling, NY 12564 United States BUS: Aquamedia and Ink on Paper and Canvas P/S: Fine Art Paintings MA: National D/D/R: Creating Artwork Including Silver Jewelry, Stained Glass and Acrylic Painting H/I/S: New York Yankees fan EDU: High School Education A/A/S: Board Member, Oriental Brush Artists Guild, North Salem, NY (1996-2004) Instructor, Introduction to Oriental Brush Painting, Croton/Cortlandt Center for the Arts, Cortlandt Manor, NY. A/H: Eight Awards for Miniature Acrylic Painting, National Miniature Shows; Accepted Artist, Over Fifty National and International Juried Art Shows C/VW: Miles of Hope Breast Cancer Foundation
Email: margueritecarideo@yahoo.com

Ms. Jenny S. Carleo
Title: Agricultural Agent Company: Rutgers University Address: 4 Moore Road, Cape May Court House, NJ 08210 United States BUS: University P/S: Research, Higher Education MA: National D/D/R: Studying Plant Biology and Agricultural Science H/I/S: Spending Time with Family, Sewing EDU: Master of Science in Plant Biology, Rutgers University (2003); Bachelor's Degree in Agricultural Science, Cook College at Rutgers University (1999) A/A/S: Chairwoman, Education Committee, Director, NJAA; New Jersey Beekeepers Association; Agricultural Agents Association of New Jersey; National Association of County Agricultural Agents; New Jersey Christmas Tree Growers Association C/VW: Hope Community Foundation, ARK for Christ
Email: carleo@rce.rutgers.edu
URL: http://www.cambridgewhoswho.com

Nikki R. Carlino
Title: Production Manager Company: Nikki Carlino Address: 355 Eighth Avenue, Suite 12E, New York, NY 10001 United States BUS: Production Company P/S: Entertainment Services MA: Local D/D/R: Managing the Creative Staff, Budgeting, Overseeing the Payroll, Bookkeeping H/I/S: Writing, Volunteering, Attending the Theater, Spending Time with her Friends EDU: Associate Degree in Theater Arts, CUNY Borough of Manhattan Community College A/A/S: Academy of Television Arts and Sciences; Department of Cultural Affairs A/H: Citation for her 'Cultural Efforts Vitality for the Borough of Manhattan,' City of New York C/VW: The Humane Society, Local Hospitals
Email: ncarlino@netzero.net

Ingrid Carlo
Title: Senior Payroll Analyst System Company: Associated Press BUS: Business Data Processing Company P/S: Human Resources, Outsourcing, Financial Services, Benefits Administration, Payroll Management, Screening and Selection Services MA: International D/D/R: Implementing Products Used for Payroll and Benefits Processing H/I/S: Reading, Exercising, Playing Softball EDU: Bachelor's Degree in Management and Accounting, Fordham University (2003) A/A/S: Beta Alpha Psi; Society for Human Resource Management
Email: ingcar027@yahoo.com
URL: http://www.adp.com

Barbara Carlson
Title: Realtor Company: Barbara Carlson, LLC, Coldwell Banker Address: 81 Woodland Avenue, Ocean View, DE 19970 United States BUS: Real Estate Company Serving Residents of Ocean View P/S: Luxury Real Estate Properties MA: Local D/D/R: Working with Clients to Find Highland Properties, Previewing the Market with Clients EDU: Associate Degree in Advertising, Pennsylvania Academy of the Fine Arts (1980) A/A/S: Chamber of Commerce; Recipient, Award for her Volunteer with Cottage Tour, Governor of Delaware
Email: barbaracarlson@cbmove.com
URL: http://www.cbmove.com/barbara Carlson

Holly R. Carlson, RN
Title: Registered Nurse Company: Hematology & Oncology Center Address: 95 University Avenue, Des Moines, IA 50314 United States BUS: Healthcare Center P/S: Oncology Healthcare MA: Regional D/D/R: Offering Oncology Care H/I/S: Spending Quality Time with her Husband and Pets, Gardening EDU: Pursuing Master of Science in Nursing; Bachelor of Science in Nursing, University of Iowa; Associate Degree in Nursing, College of Health Services (2006); Associate of Science in Liberal Arts, Des Moines Area Community College (2004); Associate Degree in General Science, Des Moines Area Community College (2004) A/A/S: Oncology Nursing Society C/VW: American Heart Association
Email: spicemonkey41@yahoo.com
URL: http://www.cambridgewhoswho.com

Ms. Lisa J. Carlson, CP
Title: Public Assistance, Program Analyst Company: Federal Emergency Management Agency Dept: Response and Recovery Division Address: 800 N. Loop 288, Denton, TX 76209 United States BUS: Government Agency P/S: Disaster Response and Recovery MA: National D/D/R: Administering Disaster Response and Recovery for State and Local Governments, Working as a Public Assistance Emergency Management Specialist, Serving as the Reports Specialist for the Public Assistance Branch, Conducting Technical Reviews of Appeals, Writing, Editing and Approving Federal Emergency Management Agency Responses, Completing Closeouts of Disaster Public Assistance Programs H/I/S: Reading, Mountain Biking, Spending Time with her Family EDU: Coursework in Paralegal Studies (2005); Bachelor of Arts in American Studies, Baylor University (1987) CERTS: Certified Paralegal, Concentration in Contracts, Real Estate and Administrative Law, National Association of Legal Assistants(2006) A/A/S: Team Member, Denton County Community Emergency Response; Dallas Area Paralegal Association; Paralegal Division, State Bar of Texas; American Society of Notaries; National Association of Legal Assistants A/H: Ms. Carlson has held multiple positions with the Federal Emergency Management Agency since 2001. She started out working as an intern with a political action committee as well as with congressman Steve Bartlett of Dallas. She then worked in various legal positions before becoming a program specialist. She resides in Denton, Texas with Buster Douglas Carlson, the world's most handsome cat. She also loves spending time with her niece, Emily, 'Tiny E.' Ms. Carlson aspires to be a mountain biker and is an avid kayaker. C/VW: Humane Society; Dallas Volunteer Attorney Program; National Multiple Sclerosis Society
Email: lisa.carlson@dhs.gov
URL: http://www.dhs.gov/fema

Roberta Carlson, CHT
Title: Technical Program Manager Company: Fresenius Medical Care Dept: Technical, Biomedical Address: 1410 W. 25th Street, Melrose Park, IL 60160 United States BUS: Medical Center P/S: Healthcare Services Including Dialysis MA: International D/D/R: Overseeing Technical Operations, Maintaining Equipment and Water Systems in the Dialysis Department, Monitoring Quality H/I/S: Camping, Gardening, All Terrain Vehicles EDU: College Coursework CERTS: Certified Hemodialysis Technician (1975)
Email: roberta.carlson@fmcna.com

Mary Katherine Carlton
Title: Owner Company: MKIllustrations Address: 6388B 101st Street, Ewa Beach, HI 96706 United States BUS: Illustration Studio P/S: Medical Illustrations for Physicians, Pharmaceutical Companies, Foundations, Health Clinics and Journals MA: National D/D/R: Designing Medical Illustrations, Animation and PowerPoint Presentations, Utilizing General Anatomy Subjects for Designing Promotional Material H/I/S: Running Marathons EDU: Master of Science in Medical Illustration, Medical College of Georgia, Augusta (2003); Bachelor of Arts, Tulane University (2001) CERTS: Certified Medical Illustrator, The Association of Medical Illustrators (2005) A/A/S: The Association of Medical Illustrators
Email: marykate@mkillustrations.com
URL: http://www.mkillustrations.com

Dana L. Carly
Title: Registered Nurse Company: Sharon Regional Health System Address: 740 E. State Street, Sharon, PA 16146 United States BUS: Hospital P/S: Healthcare MA: Regional EXP: Ms. Carly's expertise includes direct and intensive patient care nursing. H/I/S: Reading, Listening to Music EDU: Pursuing Bachelor's Degree in Nursing CERTS: Registered Nurse, Jameson School of Nursing
Email: dana121@hotmail.com

Rick L. Carmichael
Title: Chief of Police (Retired) Company: Fairbury Police Department Address: 1811 G Street, Fairbury, NE 68352 United States BUS: Police Department P/S: Law Enforcement Including Drug Investigations and Enforcing Laws MA: Regional D/D/R: Investigating Methamphetamine Laboratories, Working with the Local Sheriff, Interrogating Individuals for Drug Investigations, Enforcing Local Laws H/I/S: Fishing, Woodworking EDU: Coursework in Business Management and Law Enforcement, Plus 3000 CERTS: Certified Police Officer (1979); Certified Methamphetamine Lab Technician
Email: rcarmichael68352@yahoo.com
URL: http://www.usacops.com/ne/p68352/index.html

Idella Carn
Title: Widow, Mother, Pastor Company: Holy Anchor of Faith Church Address: 519 N Harrison Street, Wilmington, DE 19805 United States BUS: Church P/S: Delivering the Word of God MA: Local D/D/R: Preaching, Spreading God's Prophetic Word H/I/S: Enjoys Spending Time with 5 Children and 6 Grandchildren, Loves to Sing and Cook Cakes EDU: Dr Howard D Jamison School of Ministries, Clerical School
Email: idellacarn1@aol.com

Jeannette A. Carney
Title: Community Health Nurse Company: First Care Home Health of South Eastern Nebraska Address: 301 Centennial Mall S., Lincoln, NE 68509 United States BUS: State Agency P/S: Healthcare MA: Statewide D/D/R: Offering Public and Preventative Health Services Including a Breast Cancer Early Detection Program for Low-Income Women, Nursing in Community Health Programs H/I/S: Gardening, Home Projects, Photography, Reading EDU: Master's Degree in Nursing, Nebraska Wesleyan University (2003); Bachelor's Degree in Nursing, Nebraska Wesleyan University (2001) A/A/S: Sigma Theta Tau C/VW: Capital Human Society
Email: jcarney2001@windstream.net
URL: http://www.cambridgewhoswho.com

Roxana Carolina Fernandez, OTR/L
Title: Chief Executive Officer Company: Grecos World, Inc Address: 5761 Buckingham Parkway, Culver City, CA 90230 United States BUS: Healthcare P/S: Pediatric Rehabilitation Services MA: Local H/I/S: Traveling EDU: Bachelor's Degree, University of Southern California A/A/S: AOTA
Email: roxiefdez@aol.com

Adrienne C. Carpenter
Title: Esthetician, Owner Company: Aesthetics Within Address: 2412 Astron Drive, Colorado Springs, CO 80906 United States BUS: Home Based Beauty Salon/Day Spa P/S: Skin Nutrition using Sanitas, Skin Care, Brow Waxing, Facials, Bodywaxings, Eyelash and Eyebrow Tinting MA: Regional D/D/R: Offering Facials, Body Waxing and Eyebrow Tinting, Scheduling Appointments and Bookkeeping, Overseeing Entire Company H/I/S: Boating, Hunting EDU: Bachelor of Arts Degree in Business Administration, Stephen's College, Columbia, Missouri (1996)
Email: acarpm@aol.com

Elizabeth B. Carpenter
Title: Registered Nurse, Clinical Education Coordinator **Company:** DCH Regional Medical Center **Address:** 809 University Boulevard E., Tuscaloosa, AL 35401 United States **BUS:** Medical Center **P/S:** Healthcare **MA:** Local **EXP:** Ms. Carpenter's expertise is in medical-surgical nursing. **H/I/S:** Softball, Boating, Swimming, Going to the Beach **EDU:** Bachelor of Science in Nursing, University of Alabama **A/A/S:** HEAL; Healthcare Educators of Alabama; Sigma Theta Tau International **C/VW:** American Red Cross, American Cancer Society
Email: bcarpenter@dchsystem.com
URL: http://www.dchsystem.com

Robin Reneé Carpenter
Title: Senior Program Analyst **Company:** U.S. Department of Commerce **Address:** 14th and Constitution Avenue, Washington, DC 20230 United States **BUS:** Government Agency **P/S:** Federal Government Services **MA:** International **EXP:** Ms. Carpenter's expertise includes project management and contracting. **EDU:** Master of Arts in Public Administration, Bowie State University; Bachelor's Degree in Political Science, Frostburg State University **CERTS:** Certified Project Manager, Management Concepts **A/A/S:** American Business Women's Association **C/VW:** Order of the Eastern Star
Email: carpenterhoushold@comcast.net

Mr. Kenneth L. Carper, Jr., CSP, CRS
Title: Associate Broker **Company:** Gateway Realty, Inc **Address:** 120 North Pointe, Suite 200, Lancaster, PA 17601 United States **BUS:** Real Estate Brokerage **P/S:** New Construction Homes **MA:** National **H/I/S:** Snow Skiing
Email: kenjr@gatewayworthinc.com
URL: www.gatewayrealty.com

Candice Y. Carr
Title: Pharmacist **Company:** Regional Oncology Center **Address:** 1688 W. Granada Boulevard, Ormond Beach, FL 32174 United States **BUS:** Medical Center **P/S:** Pharmacy, Heart Institute, Organ Transplant, Neuroscience, Orthopedics, Cardiology and Oncology Units **MA:** Regional **D/D/R:** Interning for Medical Center Pharmacy, Training in Pharmaceutical Computer Systems and Information Input, Checking Chemotherapy Orders, Making Blood Product Orders **EDU:** Doctorate of Pharmacy, Albany College of Pharmacy (2007) **CERTS:** Certification in Immunization (2005); License, Florida and Pennsylvania **A/A/S:** The Rho Chi Society; American Pharmacists Association **A/H:** Rho Chi Award (2007)
Email: candice.carr@cwwemail.com
Email: candace.carr@hmc.org
URL: http://www.halifax.org

Kathleen Rae Carr
Title: Wedding Photographer **Company:** Kathy's Portraits **Address:** 33800 Beverly Drive, Hemet, CA 92545 United States **BUS:** Privately Owned Photography Company **P/S:** Wedding Photographer **MA:** National **D/D/R:** Offering Wedding, Family Portraits, Engagements, Candid and Couple Photography Services **H/I/S:** Horses, Jet Skiing, Bicycling **A/A/S:** Professional Photographers of California, Worldwide International Professional Photographers
Email: katway@juno.com

Constance Carr-Shepherd
Title: 1) Psychotherapist 2) College Professor **Company:** 1) Riverside Church Counseling Center 2) College of New Rochelle **Address:** 2 Washington Square Village, New York, NY 10012 United States **BUS:** 1) Healthcare 2) Education **P/S:** 1) Counseling 2) Undergraduate and Graduate Programs **MA:** Regional **D/D/R:** Teaching, Offering Marriage and Family Therapy, Counseling **H/I/S:** Reading, Yoga, Thai Chi **EDU:** Master of Arts in Psychology, New York University (1965) **CERTS:** Licensed in Marriage and Family Therapy **A/A/S:** American Association for Marriage and Family Therapy
URL: http://www.cnr.edu

Mariann Brown Carrasco
Title: Wildlife Biologist **Company:** Fisher Consulting Services **Address:** P.O. Box 108, Acme, WA 98220 United States **BUS:** Environmental Consulting Firm **P/S:** Wildlife Biology, Professional Expertise and Consulting on Wetlands, Environmental Education, Fish Surveys, Biological Assessments **MA:** National **D/D/R:** Consulting on Terrestrial and Marine Mammals **H/I/S:** Horseback Riding, Boating **EDU:** Bachelor of Science in Wildlife Management, Humboldt State University, CA **A/A/S:** The Wildlife Society; Society of Wetlands Scientists; Coordinator, Marine Mammal Stranding Network, Whatcom County **C/VW:** Northwest Wildlife Rehabilitation Center; Standing Network Coordinator, Whatcom County Marine Mammal Resources
Email: mariannkbrown@aol.com
URL: http://www.fisherconsultingservices.com

Nicole A. Carrera
Title: 1) Materials Planner 2) Owner **Company:** 1) Avon Products, Inc. 2) Imagination Invitations **Address:** 12310 Sinnett Street, Huntley, IL 60142 United States **BUS:** 1) Manufacturing Company 2) Stationery Shop **P/S:** 1) Cosmetic Products 2) Invitations and Stationery Products **MA:** International **D/D/R:** Planning, Comparing Prices, Designing Invitations, Selling Wedding Stationery Products **H/I/S:** Making Crafts, Scrapbooking, Designing Invitations **EDU:** Bachelor of Arts in Business Administration and German, Augustana College, IL (2001)
Email: niki.carrera@comcast.net

Leslie A. Carrico
Title: Senior Marketing Manager **Company:** Avaya, Inc. **Address:** 1300 W. 120th Avenue, Room D1-D33, Westminster, CO 80234 United States **BUS:** Telecommunications Company **P/S:** Telecommunications Products and Services Including Messaging and Contact Centers, Internet Provider IP Telephony **MA:** International **D/D/R:** Making Presentations to Customers and Partners, Conducting Educational Training For Sales, Creating New Tools, Overseeing Business Marketing **H/I/S:** Traveling, Scuba Diving, Caring for her Pets **EDU:** Bachelor of Arts in Business Administration, University of Denver (1992) **CERTS:** License in Series 6 and 63; Life Insurance License **A/A/S:** Advisory Board; Devereux Cleo Wallace; Victims Assistance Law Enforcement Academy; Golden Key International Honour Society **C/VW:** Local Charitable Organizations
Email: lcarrico@avaya.com
URL: http://www.avaya.com

Amanda M. Carrillo
Title: Marketing Analyst **Company:** State Farm Insurance Company **Address:** 1 State Farm Drive, Frederick, MD 21709 United States **BUS:** Insurance Company **P/S:** Insurance Services, Mutual Funds, Financial Services **MA:** National **D/D/R:** Assisting Field Agents, Keeping up with the Market, Giving Representatives Tools for Use in Sales, Analyzing Demographics, Networking with Other Market Analysts, Lecturing **H/I/S:** Dancing, Volleyball, Outdoor Activities **EDU:** Bachelor of Arts Degree in Finance, Minor in Insurance, Illinois State University (2003) **A/A/S:** Toastmasters; Alumni of Illinois State University Association; Pi Sigma Epsilon
Email: amanda.carrillo.nwaz@statefarm.com
URL: http://www.statefarm.com

Ms. Cynthia L. Carroll
Title: 1) Owner, Certified Funding Specialist 2) Scopist, Transcriptionist **Company:** 1) WhyWaitToRelax 2) Carroll Transcription Services, Inc. **Address:** 2440 Romaine Creek Road, Fenton, MO 63026 United States **BUS:** 1) Travel Agency 2) Transcription Service Company **P/S:** 1) Travel Packages, Tourism, Cruises, Hotels and Rental Vehicles 2) Legal Transcription and Scoping Services **MA:** International **EXP:** Ms. Carroll's expertise includes financial management and verbatim transcription. **D/D/R:** Assisting Clients, Transcribing Orally Recorded Legal Proceedings, Scoping Court Reporters, Preparing Legal Documents, Working with Nonprofit Organizations, Conducting Research **H/I/S:** Country Line Dancing, Reading, Socializing with People **EDU:** Coursework, Hickey Business School; Coursework, Meramec Community College; Diploma, Oakville Senior High School, **CERTS:** Certified Fundraising Specialist; Certified Travel Agent **A/H:** Carnival Cruise Lines Award; Team Gateway Award; Passport2Giving Award; Certificate of Appreciation, Memorial Sloan-Kettering Cancer Center; Personal Computer Institute Award; Datamax Office Systems Award **C/VW:** Sunshine Ministries; St. Jude Children's Research Hospital; Women's Another Chance; The Leukemia & Lymphoma Society; Memorial Sloan-Kettering Cancer Center; National Wildlife Federation; American Heart Association
Email: cynthia.carroll@sbcglobal.net
URL: http://www.cambridgewhoswho.com

Herbert Geoffrey Carroll
Title: Procurement Oversight Specialist **Company:** Government National Mortgage Association **Address:** 550 12th Street S.W., 3rd Floor, Potomac Center So **BUS:** Government Corporation **P/S:** Mortgage-backed Securities; Multi-class Securities; and Reverse Mortgages (2007) **MA:** National **D/D/R:** Contracting, **H/I/S:** Classical Pianist; Cufflinks Collector; and Melodizer of scripture verses in the Bible. **EDU:** Master of Arts Degree in Management, National University; and Bachelor of Science Degree in Business Administration, Claflin College **CERTS:** Certified Level III Acquisition Professional; Certified Contracting Officer's Technical Representative **C/VW:** The National Prayer Chapel
Email: hgcarroll_777@msn.com
URL: http://www.ginniemae.gov

Ms. LaDonna E. Carroll
Title: Office Specialist **Company:** Robert C. Schwartz Jr., MD, PA **Address:** 3878 Oak Lawn Avenue, Suite 625, Dallas, TX 75219 United States **BUS:** Mental Healthcare Service **P/S:** Mental Healthcare **MA:** Regional **EXP:** Ms. Carroll's expertise is in administration. **H/I/S:** Spending Time with her Three Children **EDU:** Associate Degree in Liberal Arts, Trinity Valley Community College **A/A/S:** Girl Scouts of the United States of America; Boy Scouts of America; Awana Clubs International
Email: ladonnatx@aol.com
URL: http://www.cambridgewhoswho.com

Max Carroll
Title: Funeral Director **Company:** Cherokee Memorial Park and Funeral Home **Address:** PO Box 1000, Lodi, CA 95241 United States **BUS:** Mortuary **P/S:** Funeral Services and All Preparation **MA:** Local **D/D/R:** Embalming, Directing Funerals **H/I/S:** Tennis, Theater **CERTS:** Certified Funeral Director, Cincinnati College of Mortuary Sciences, with Honors **A/A/S:** National Funeral Directors Association
Email: mmc3939@aol.com

Treva J. Carroll
Title: Assistant General Manager **Company:** Dayton Place **Address:** 1950 South Dayton, Apt. 118, Denver, CO 80247 United States **BUS:** Healthcare Marketing **P/S:** Geriatric Home Healthcare **MA:** Local **D/D/R:** Marketing **EDU:** Associate Degree in Bible Studies, Jacksonville Theological Seminary **A/A/S:** Southwestern Coalition **A/H:** Top Retirement Community in Denver, Denver Business Journal; Top Retirement Community in Colorado, Business and Beyond
Email: info@CambridgeWhosWho.com

Melissa J. Carson
Title: President **Company:** Carson Reporting & Associates **Address:** 4600 Greenville Avenue, Suite 110, Dallas, TX 75206 United States **BUS:** Freelance Court Reporting Firm **P/S:** Legal Court Reporting Services **MA:** Regional **D/D/R:** Overseeing Court Reporting Duties for Proceedings Including Depositions, Meetings, Arbitrations, Executive Interviews, Civil Service Hearings and Town Hall Meetings, Overseeing Business Operations **H/I/S:** Traveling, Decorating **EDU:** Associate Degree in Court Reporting, Dallas Court Reporting College (1981) **A/A/S:** Texas Court Reporting Association; National Court Reporting Association
Email: mcarson@carsonreporting.com
URL: http://www.cambridgewhoswho.com

Natasha I. Cartagena
Title: Vice President, Branch Manager **Company:** Shelter Mortgage Company, Subsidiary **Address:** Garente Bank, Suite 102, Melbourne, FL 32940 United States **BUS:** Banking and Lending Company **P/S:** Residential Mortgages **MA:** National **D/D/R:** Lending to Residential First-Time Home Buyers **H/I/S:** Traveling Once a Year, Reading, Swimming **EDU:** Bachelor of Arts in Sociology, University of Miami; Bachelor of Arts (1996) **A/A/S:** National Home Builders and Contractors Association; Local Home Builders and Contractors Association; Brevard, Polk County and Gulf Coast **A/H:** Management Award (2006-2007) **C/VW:** March of Dimes
Email: natasha.cartagena@cwwemail.com
URL: http://www.shelter.mortgage.com

Byron K. Carter
Title: President, Chief Executive Officer, Owner, Founder **Company:** Pretty Quick Delivery **Address:** 11000 Kinghurst Street, Houston, TX 77099 United States **BUS:** Transportation Company **P/S:** Transportation Services Including Delivery of Hazardous Materials, Medical Field Products, Construction Items, Machinery and Field Equipments **MA:** National **D/D/R:** Overseeing Business Development, Administration and Customer Services **H/I/S:** Spending Time with his Family, Fishing **EDU:** Master of International Business, LeTourneau University **A/A/S:** Houston Minority Business Council; City of Houston; Port of Houston Authority **C/VW:** Christian Chamber of Commerce
Email: prettyquick@sbcglobal.net
URL: http://www.prettyquick-delivery.com

Cindy D. Carter
Title: Media Production Specialist **Company:** Long Hollow Baptist Church **Address:** 1080 West Main St Suite 1304, Hendersonville, TN 37075 United States **BUS:** Church **P/S:** Provide Baptist Church Services to Parishioners **MA:** Local **EXP:** Video. **H/I/S:** Hanging out with family **EDU:** Bachelor of Science, University of Texas at Arlington
Email: cindy.carter@longhollow.com

Gwendolyn U. Carter
Title: 1) Administrative Coordinator 2) Director of Nurses **Company:** 1) Capital Health System 2) City of Trenton **Address:** 750 Brunswick Avenue, Trenton, NJ 08618 United States **BUS:** 1) Medical Center 2) City of Trenton, NJ **P/S:** 1) Health Care Services 2) Healthcare Services **MA:** Local **D/D/R:** Offering Critical and Trauma Care, Managing Operations, Staffing, Public Health Nursing, Writing Policy and Procedures, Management, Sexual Assault Nurse Examinations **H/I/S:** Playing Tennis, Traveling, Spending Time with her Grandchildren **EDU:** Master's Degree in Nursing, Holy Family University, Philadelphia, PA **A/A/S:** National Black Nurses Association; Nursing Honor Society, Sigma Theta Tau International **C/VW:** American Red Cross; Operation Smile
Email: gvc18@aol.com
URL: http://www.cambridgewhoswho.com

Herbert Latham Carter
Title: Founder-President **Company:** Omni Church-Museum Association, Inc. **Address:** 5225 Summer Ave, Memphis, TN 38122 United States **BUS:** Religion Advancement of Religious Message **P/S:** Nonprofit Living Bible Museum IRS 501 c 3 Florida Chapter: September 8, 1987 **MA:** International **D/D/R:** Religious Writing, Also Works with the Vice President, Patrick S. Collins, and Secretary Treasurer, John S. Jobe **H/I/S:** Research of Scriptures, Videos, Outdoor Activities **EDU:** Florida State University, College **A/A/S:** Originator of Living Bible Museum American Legion, Masonic Lodge of Florida, Order of the Mystic Shrine
Email: info@cambridgewhoswho.com

Lynette I. Carter
Title: Teacher **Company:** New York City Department of Education **Address:** 65 Court Street, Brooklyn, NY 11201 United States **BUS:** School District **P/S:** Education **MA:** Local **D/D/R:** Tutoring, Teaching Special Education and Religion **H/I/S:** Traveling, Reading, Watching Movies, Socializing **EDU:** Master's Degree Plus 30 in Special Education, Adelphi University, 1985 **A/A/S:** United Federation of Teachers
Email: lynetteski915@yahoo.com
URL: http://www.cambridgewhoswho.com

Natalie R. Carter
Title: Gifted and Talented Specialist **Company:** Florence Hill Elementary **Address:** 4425 Rosedale Drive, Grand Prairie, TX 75052 United States **BUS:** Elementary School **P/S:** General Elementary Curriculum, Arts, Music, Physical Education, Special Education, Gifted and Talented Program, Learning Resources, Support Services, Athletics, Extracurricular Activities, Student Clubs and Organizations **MA:** Regional **D/D/R:** Overseeing Gifted and Talented First through Fifth-Grade Students, Creating Special Programs and Curriculum to Challenge Students, Organizing Educational Field Trips, Utilizing the Pull-Out Program for Gifted Students **H/I/S:** Reading, Watching Movies, Studying Genealogy **EDU:** Bachelor's Degree in Elementary Education, Cameron University (1984) **CERTS:** Certification in Gifted and Talented Education, Texas A&M University-Commerce (Formerly East Texas State University) (1992) **A/A/S:** Texas Association for the Gifted and Talented; Grand Prairie Association of Gifted and Talented Children; National Association for Gifted Children; Texas Classroom Teachers Association
Email: robin.carter@gpisd.org
URL: http://florencehill.gpisd.org

Ryan K. Carter
Title: Product Manager **Company:** Emhart Teknologies **Address:** 50 Shelton Technology Center, Shelton, CT 06484 United States **BUS:** Manufacturing Company **P/S:** Mechanical Fasteners Including Screws, Bolts, Nuts, Threaded Rods, Power Tools, Hand Tools and Cutting Tools **MA:** International **D/D/R:** Managing Business Operations Including Marketing and Sales **EDU:** Master of Science in Finance, Rensselaer Polytechnic Institute; Bachelor of Science in Mechanical Engineering, Iowa State University
Email: ryan.k.carter@gmail.com

Susan D. Carter
Title: General Manager **Company:** Home Depot **Dept:** Fuel Store **Address:** 2480 Meadow Crest Road, Greensboro, GA 30642 United States **BUS:** Retail Store **P/S:** Hardware for Home Construction and Gardening **MA:** National **D/D/R:** Managing Business Operations **EDU:** Coursework in CPU Programming, Athens Technical School **A/H:** Outstanding Store Manager Award (1996-2001); Finalist, Ray Kroc Award, McDonald's **C/VW:** Youth Minister, Bogart First Baptist Church
Email: suzcarter714@hotmail.com
URL: http://www.cambridgewhoswho.com

Tawana L. Carter
Title: Dir. of Executive Affairs **Company:** Florida Bankers Association **Address:** 10001 Thomasville Road Suite 201, Tallahassee, FL 32303 United States **BUS:** Banking Finance **P/S:** Lobbyist/Lobbying Service **MA:** Local **EXP:** Ms. Carter's expertise includes accounting and administration. **H/I/S:** Family **EDU:** Bachelor of Science in Business Administration, Flager College **C/VW:** Volunteer, Community Centers/Christian Heritage Church
Email: info@CambridgeWhosWho.com

Victoria L. Carter
Title: Associate Broker **Company:** Genesis Real Estate and Property Management **Address:** 5013 Pacific Highway, East Fife, WA 98424 **BUS:** Real Estate Agency **P/S:** Real Estate Service and Sales **MA:** National **D/D/R:** Consulting with Residential Clients **EDU:** College Coursework Completed **A/A/S:** Girl Scouts of the USA; Boy Scouts of America; Ballroom Dance Group
Email: vikkicarter@genesisrealestate.com
URL: http://www.genesisrealestate.com

Beatrice L. Carter-Jones
Title: Primary Teacher **Company:** Argomer Elementary School **Address:** 1 CMR 470, APO AE, 09165 United States **BUS:** Elementary School **P/S:** Primary Education **MA:** International **D/D/R:** Teaching Elementary Education **H/I/S:** Writing Poetry, Sewing, Needlepointing, Exercising, Reading **EDU:** Master of Education, University of Virginia (1973); Bachelor of Science in Elementary Education, St. Paul's College (1969) **A/A/S:** National Education Association; Alpha Kappa Alpha; La Roca Foundation International
Email: Beatrice.CarterJones@cwwemail.com

Erin E. Cartwright, Esq.
Title: Associate Attorney **Company:** Chausow Shafer, P.C. **Address:** 734 Central Avenue, Suite 200, Highland Park, IL 60034 United States **BUS:** Law Firm **P/S:** Legal Services Including Family and Criminal Law **MA:** Regional **D/D/R:** Practicing Family and Criminal Law with a Specialization in Divorce, Adoption, Guardianship, Domestic Battery and Automobile Cases, Handling Domestic Violence Issues, Orders of Protection, Child Support and Parentage Cases **H/I/S:** Traveling, Horseback Riding **EDU:** JD, Thomas M. Cooley Law School (1999); Bachelor of Arts in Anthropology and Sociology, Minor in Business, Saint Mary's College (1995) **A/A/S:** American Bar Association; Illinois State Bar Association; King County Bar Association; Lake County Bar Association; Kane County Bar Association
Email: cartwright@chausowshafer.com
URL: http://www.chausowshafer.com

Phyllis A. Carullo-Miller
Title: Teacher **Company:** Mission Meadows Elementary School **Address:** 5657 Spur Avenue, Oceanside, CA 92057 United States **BUS:** Provider of Quality Education to Oceanside, California Area **P/S:** General Studies Curricula, Dedicated Faculty and Staff, Athletics Activities, Extracurricular Activities **MA:** Local **D/D/R:** Teaching Kindergarten through Tenth-Grade Students, Organizing, Implementing and Reviewing Skills in Reading, Writing and Mathematics **H/I/S:** Writing Children's Books, Playing with Dogs **EDU:** Master's Degree in Education, CUNY Hunter College, New York (1979); Bachelor's Degree in English and Education, CUNY Hunter College, New York (1974); Magna Cum Laude **A/A/S:** Board Member, Bonsall Community Sponsor Group; School Site Council; Teacher Association Representative; Panel Member, Juvenile Justice System; Board Member, Guajome Park Academy (Charter School); Author of Children's Books **A/H:** Kelly Gold Medal, Methods of Teaching; John F, Kennedy Award, Highest Academic Average and Service to Hunter College
Email: phyllisanncarullo@cox.net

Iris Carver Silvers
Title: Director **Company:** Maggie Methodist Preschool **Address:** 4192 Soco Road, Maggie Valley, NC 28751 United States **BUS:** Daycare Center **P/S:** Child Care Services, Education **MA:** Regional **D/D/R:** Teaching Pre-School, Planning Lessons, Advertising **H/I/S:** Nascar, Fishing and Family Time **EDU:** Bachelor of Science in Child Development, Western Carolina University (1993); Bachelor of Science in Birth through Kindergarten, Western Carolina University (2005)
Email: james_silvers@bellsouth.net

Dr. Valarie C. Cascadden
Title: Licensed Marriage and Family Therapist **Address:** 14156 Magnolia Boulevard, Suite 105, Sherman Oaks, CA 91423 United States **BUS:** Private Practice **P/S:** Counseling with Marriage and Family Therapy **MA:** Regional **D/D/R:** Counseling on Marriage, Relationships and Mid-Life Transitions **H/I/S:** Gardening, Wine Tasting, Participating in Opera, Fine Arts, Attending the Theater **EDU:** Ph.D., Pacifica Graduate Institute (2007); Master's Degree in Counseling Psychology, National University **A/A/S:** Brain Longevity Center; The Sherman Oaks Chamber of Commerce; Tarzana Chamber of Commerce; California Association of Marriage and Family Therapists; Glendale Area Mental Health Professional Association; Association for Humanistic Psychology; San Fernando Valley Chapter, American Association for Marriage and Family Therapy **C/VW:** Local Radio Station; Better Business Bureau, CA; Alley Cats Allies; The Humane Society of the United States; KUFC
Email: valarie@journeyguide.net
URL: http://www.journeyguide.net

Joseph P. Cascio
Title: Landscape Architect **Company:** Cascio Dezine Solutions **Address:** 1645 W Indianola Ave, Phoenix, AZ 85015 United States **BUS:** Architecture and Design Company **P/S:** Landscape Architecture/Design/Install/Master Planning **MA:** National **EXP:** Mr. Cascio's expertise is in landscape architecture. **H/I/S:** Traveling, Photography, Reading **EDU:** Queensland College, BS Landscape Architecture
Email: dezinesolutions@cox.net

Geraldine Case
Title: Insurance Agent **Company:** Gerri Case and Associates **Address:** 26314 Cathedral, Redford, MI 48239 United States **BUS:** Insurance **P/S:** Annuities, Trusts, Disability, Reverse Mortgages **MA:** Regional **D/D/R:** Marketing **H/I/S:** Spending Time with Grandchildren **A/A/S:** Chamber of Commerce
Email: gerricase@yahoo.com

Jessi Ann Casella
Title: Housing Manager/Minister **Company:** West-In-Arms/Family Christian Church **Address:** Apollo, PA 15613 United States **BUS:** Church **P/S:** Hud Housing of Ministry **MA:** Local **D/D/R:** Working with Disabled Adults, Offering Care and Compassion **H/I/S:** Travel, Time With Friends, Movies, Reading **EDU:** Coursework, Clarion College, PA; Coursework, Rhena Bible School **CERTS:** Ordained Minister **A/A/S:** Rhena Bible School, Family Christian Church
Email: info@CambridgeWhosWho.com

Christina M. Casey
Title: Vice President **Company:** Chelsea Property Group **Dept:** Human Resources **Address:** 105 Eisenhower Parkway, Roseland, NJ 07068 United States **BUS:** Real Estate Firm **P/S:** Real Estate Development and Management Services **MA:** International **EXP:** Ms. Casey's expertise is in employment law. **D/D/R:** Developing and Managing Premium Outlet Shopping Centers, Handling Human Resource Benefits, Recruiting, Policies and Procedures **H/I/S:** Collecting Antiques, Hiking, Walking, Reading **EDU:** Master of Science in Social Work, Bryn Mawr College; Bachelor of Arts in Sociology, Villanova University **C/VW:** Mary Cooney & Edward Essl Foundation, Inc.; American Cancer Society
Email: ccasey@cpgi.com
URL: http://www.cpgi.com

Patrick Casey
Title: Director **Company:** The Regional Municipality of York **Address:** 17250 Yonge Street, New Market, L3Y 6Z1 Canada **BUS:** Government **P/S:** Government Communications **MA:** International **H/I/S:** Spending Time With Family **EDU:** Humber College, Journalism Diploma with Honors
Email: patrick.casey@york.ca

Thomas Cash
Title: Program Administrator **Company:** City of Redmond **Address:** 18080 NE 76th Street, Redmond, WA 98052 United States
Email: rockymtneducatr@comcast.net

Robert A. Casillo
Title: Program Administrator **Company:** Coosa Valley Youth Services **Address:** 4625 McClellan Rd, Anniston, AL 36207 United States **BUS:** Correctional Facility **P/S:** Juvenile Corrections **MA:** National **D/D/R:** Leadership Development and Educational Services **H/I/S:** Sports and Travel **EDU:** Bachelor's Degree in Healthcare Administration, University of Phoenix **A/A/S:** United Way Representative, National Institute of Corrections
Email: pmcasillo@cvys.net
URL: www.cvys.net

David P. Casper
Title: Vice President of Nutrition **Company:** Agri-King, Inc. **Address:** 18246 Waller Road, Fulton, IL 61252 United States **BUS:** Distribution Firm **P/S:** Livestock Nutrition Products, Product Research and Development **MA:** International **EXP:** Mr. Casper's expertise is in nutritional consulting. **H/I/S:** Golfing, Collecting Model Trains **EDU:** Ph.D. in Dairy Nutrition, South Dakota State University (1989); Master's Degree in Dairy Science (1985) **A/A/S:** American Registry of Professional Animal Scientists; American Society of Animal Science; American Dairy Science Association **A/H:** Richard M. Hoyt Award for Dairy Research
Email: david.casper@agriking.com
URL: http://www.agriking.com

Vida M. Castaneda
Title: Court Analyst **Company:** Administrative Office of the Courts **Address:** 455 Golden Gate Avenue, San Francisco, CA 94102 United States **BUS:** Court Services Department **P/S:** Court Services **MA:** Local **EXP:** Ms. Castaneda's expertise is in child welfare. **H/I/S:** Traveling, Reading, Spending Time with Family **EDU:** Master's Degree in Social Welfare, University of California at Berkeley; Bachelor's Degree in Sociology and American Indian Studies, San Diego State University **A/A/S:** National Association of Counsel for Children
Email: vldamsw@sbcglobal.net

Josephine Castillo
Title: Owner **Company:** Josie's Tax Service **Address:** 1128 Ameluxen Avenue, Hacienda Heights, CA 91745 United States **BUS:** Taxation Company **P/S:** Tax Preparation Services **MA:** Local **D/D/R:** Managing Individual and Rental Taxes and Audits **H/I/S:** Snow Skiing, Playing Scrabble, Reading the Bible **EDU:** Diploma, Almani High School (1995) **A/A/S:** Notary Public
Email: castilj@yahoo.com

Brady Castleberry
Title: Dispatcher **Company:** Mesa Airlines **Address:** 400 N. 44th Street, Phoenix, AZ 85203 United States **BUS:** Airline **P/S:** Regional Air Service **MA:** Regional **D/D/R:** Pre-Planning for Flights Including Fuel Loads and Weather Conditions, Overseeing all Mechanical Concerns of Long Flights **H/I/S:** Traveling, Working on his Car, Shopping, Cooking, Reading **EDU:** Bachelor of Science in Commercial Aviation, Delta State University **C/VW:** Mesa Angels Foundation
Email: brady.castleberry@cwwemail.com
URL: http://www.mesa-air.com

Dawnmarie T. Castro
Title: Vice President **Company:** Citibank **Address:** 388 Greenwich Street, New York, NY 10013 United States **BUS:** Bank **P/S:** Financial Services **MA:** International **EXP:** Ms. Castro's expertise includes general and project management. **H/I/S:** Skiing, Traveling, Cooking **EDU:** Bachelor of Science in Bank and Finance, Wilmington College **A/A/S:** Women's Council **C/VW:** Safe Horizons, March of Dimes
Email: dawnmarie.castro@citi.com
URL: http://www.cambridgewhowho.com

Lucy F. Castro
Title: Realtor **Company:** Century 21 Classic Properties **Address:** 713 East Lake Avenue, Watsonville, CA 95076 United States **BUS:** Real Estate Broker **P/S:** Residential and Commercial Sales **MA:** National **D/D/R:** Selling Mobile Homes and Commercial Land **CERTS:** Board Certified Realtor **A/A/S:** Board of Realtors in California
Email: info@CambridgeWhosWho.com

Ann G. Cata
Title: LD Resource Teacher **Company:** Robert Nathanial Dett Elementary School **Address:** 2306 W. Maypole Street, Chicago, IL 60612 United States **BUS:** School **P/S:** Teaching **MA:** Local **EXP:** Ms. Cata's expertise is in case management. **H/I/S:** Gardening **A/A/S:** CTU Delegate, Green Leaching Networking
Email: anncata23@yahoo.com

Mr. Jeffrey E. Catancio
Title: Paralegal **Company:** Morrison & Foerster, LLP **Address:** 425 Market Street, Floor 35, San Francisco, CA 94105 United States **BUS:** Comprehensive Legal Services in Business and Litigation **P/S:** Antitrust and Competition Law, Communications and Media Law, Employment and Labor, Trade Secrets, Employment Class Actions, Sarbanes-Oxley and Whistle blowing, Discrimination and Other Employment Litigation, Labor Relations, International Employment Law, Advice, Counseling and Training, Energy Law, Energy Litigation, Energy Regulation, Energy Transactions, International Energy Arbitration, Entertainment Law, Environmental Law, Compliance and Transactions, Environmental Litigation, Financial Services Law, Land Use and Natural Resource Law **MA:** International **D/D/R:** Overseeing Litigation Cases for Big Corporations, Collecting and Processing Documents, Organizing Cases, Managing and Maintaining Evidence for Cases **H/I/S:** Tennis, Hockey, Camping **EDU:** Associate of Arts Degree in Paralegal Studies, Skyline College (2004)
Email: jcatancio@sbcglobal.net
URL: http://www.mofo.com

Thomas J. Cathers Sr.
Title: Owner/President **Company:** Thomas J Cathers Consultant **Address:** 23 N Whitesbog Road, Browns Mills, NJ 08015 United States **BUS:** Vehicle Maintenance Training Consultant **P/S:** Evaluate Assess, Recommend and Construct and Instruct Vehicle Maintenance Training Programs **MA:** International **D/D/R:** Managing Vehicle Maintenance Training Centers, Conducting Employment Placement for Students **H/I/S:** Cross Continent Motorcycle Endurance Competition, Freelance Photography, Freelance Writing, Astronomy, Woodworking and General Outdoor Activities **EDU:** Master's Degree in Business Administration, Central MI **A/A/S:** Toastmasters International, Society of Automotive Engineers, National Automotive Technicians Educational Foundation, Automotive Service Excellence, Kappa Delta Pi **A/H:** Who's Who in Americas Best Teachers
Email: canis_lupusl@comcast.net

Donald Preston Cato
Title: Director **Company:** Donald P. Cato **Address:** 7415 35th Avenue, Jackson Heights, NY 11372 United States **BUS:** Art and Film-Making Company **P/S:** Art and Films **MA:** International **D/D/R:** Overseeing the Direction of Films, Editing and Telling Stories through Film, Teaching Film Direction **H/I/S:** Playing Rugby, Photography, Reading, Painting, Creating Sculptures **EDU:** Master's Degree in Landscaping, University of Oregon (1976) **A/A/S:** National Television Academy; University of Oregon
Email: dcato@nyc.rr.com

Dr. Nancy S. Catterall
Title: Director of Audiology **Company:** Thomas Jefferson University **Dept:** Jefferson Center for Balance and Hearing **Address:** 925 Chestnut Street, 6th Floor, Philadelphia, PA 19107 United States **BUS:** University Medical Center **P/S:** Comprehensive Diagnostic and Rehabilitative Hearing Healthcare, Higher Education **MA:** National **D/D/R:** Directing the Clinic, Managing Protocol **H/I/S:** Skiing **EDU:** Doctor of Audiology (2006) **A/A/S:** Committee Member, Thomas Jefferson University; American Speech-Language-Hearing Association; American Academy of Audiology; Pennsylvania Speech Language Hearing Association; American Board of Audiology
Email: nancy.catterall@jefferson.edu
URL: http://www.jefferson.edu

Mr. Edward J. Cavaliere, M.Ed.
Title: Special Education Teacher, Learning Behavior Specialist **Company:** Chicago Board of Education **Address:** 2728 S. Kostner Avenue, Chicago, IL 60623 United States **BUS:** School **P/S:** Education for Special Education Students in Preschool to Age 21 **MA:** Regional **D/D/R:** Teaching Special Education to Children with Behavioral and Learning Problems **H/I/S:** Speech, Acting in Community Theater, Reading, Volunteering, Watching Movies, Mentoring, Attending the Theatre **EDU:** Master of Education Plus 48, Louis University; Bachelor of Science in Special Education, Speech and Theater, Chicago State University **A/A/S:** Council for Exceptional Children; The Chicago Teachers Union **A/H:** Volunteer Service Recognition Award (1989-1992); Nominated, Disney Hand Teacher Award (2005); Outstanding Performance and Best Teacher Award (1992-1993); Certificate of Appreciation (1995-1999) **C/VW:** United Charities
Email: cavaej@aol.com
URL: http://www.cambridgewhoswho.com

Yasmin Cavallo
Title: Unit Manager **Company:** Mellon Financial **Address:** 135 Santilli Highway, Everett, MA 02149 United States **BUS:** Finance **P/S:** Investment Management, Trust and Custody, Foreign Exchange, Securities Lending, Performance Analytics, Fund Administration, Stock Transfer, Proxy solicitation, Treasury Management, Banking Services **MA:** International **D/D/R:** Managing Mutual Funds and Wealth **H/I/S:** Exercise, Family, Church **EDU:** Bachelor's Degree in Business, Bachelor's Degree in Management Information Systems
Email: cavallo.y@mellon.com

Floretta E. Cavazos
Title: Salon Owner, Cosmetologist **Company:** Hair Dynamix **Address:** 1629 Pollasky Avenue, Suite 105, Clovis, CA 93612 United States **BUS:** Hair Salon **P/S:** Hair Services, Hair Products **MA:** Local **D/D/R:** Styling Hair, Offering Beauty Treatments **H/I/S:** Exercising, Reading, Art, Making Crafts **EDU:** College Coursework; Bible College; Victory Training Center **CERTS:** Licensed Cosmetologist, Federico's School of Cosmetology **A/A/S:** Clovis Better Business Bureau; Business Advisory Board **A/H:** National Leadership Award 2007 **C/VW:** Faith Summit Church; Children's Ministry
Email: floretta.cavazos@cwwemail.com

Gloria H. Caves
Title: Owner, Voice Teacher **Company:** Gloria's Studio of Voice **Address:** 614 Mount Pleasant Church Road, Broxton, GA 31519 United States **BUS:** Vocal School **P/S:** Private Vocal Training, Events Training **MA:** Regional **D/D/R:** Basic and Advanced-Level Vocal Training for Competitions **H/I/S:** Traveling in her Recreational Vehicle **EDU:** Coursework and Vocal Training Under a Master Voice Teacher, Valdosta, Georgia; Church Choir Vocal Training; Home Study **C/VW:** Teen Challenge, Dublin, Georgia
Email: gloria13@bellsouth.net

Ms. Lindsay H. Caye
Title: Marketing Communications Coordinator **Company:** The Golf Club of Georgia **Address:** Alpharetta, GA 30005 United States **BUS:** Proven Leader in the Sports and Recreation Industry **P/S:** Golf **MA:** Regional **D/D/R:** Designing, Presenting and Marketing Membership Material, Layout and Content, Working with the Business Communication Department in Public Relations
Email: lcaye@golfclubofgeorgia.com
URL: http://www.golfclubofgeorgia.com

Nancy Carolyn Cech
Title: Army Officer **Company:** United States Army **Address:** Fort Campbell, KY United States **BUS:** Army **P/S:** United States Security **MA:** International **EXP:** Ms. Cech's expertise is in leadership management. **H/I/S:** Spending Time Outdoors, Caring for her Three Dogs **EDU:** Bachelor of Arts in History and Psychology, University of San Diego (2001) **CERTS:** Licensed Sailor; Licensed in SCUBA **A/A/S:** Intelligence College; Veterans of Foreign Wars of the United States **A/H:** Army Commendation Medal and Army Achievement Recipient (Two Times); National Defense Service Medal; Global War on Terrorism Expeditionary Medal; Global War on Terrorism Service Medal; Army Service Ribbon; Overseas Service Ribbon; Combat Action Badge; Army Valorous Unit Award **C/VW:** Veterans of Foreign Wars; American Society for the Prevention of Cruelty to Animals
Email: nancy.cech@us.army.mil
Email: nancy.cech@cwwemail.com
URL: http://www.cambridgewhoswho.com

Ms. Phyllis C. Cedola
Title: Secretary, Attendance Officer **Company:** South Orange Maplewood Board of Education **Address:** 70 N. Ridgewood Road, S. Orange, NJ 07079 United States **BUS:** Public Education **P/S:** Instruction and Curriculum **MA:** Local **D/D/R:** Performing Secretarial Duties, Overseeing Attendance Records **H/I/S:** Gardening, Knitting **EDU:** Diploma, Orange High School **A/A/S:** Italian-American New Jersey Heritage Commission; Chairman, Italian Festival; Chairman PNC Art Center; Treasurer, Federation of Italian-American Society
Email: pccedola@nac.net
URL: http://www.somsd.k12.nj.us

Mickey Cekovic
Title: 1) Senior Labor Relations Specialist 2) Government Relations Specialist **Company:** 1) Pitta and Dreier, LLP 2) Pitta, Bishop, DelGiarno & Dreier, LLP **Address:** 499 Park Avenue, New York, NY 10022 United States **BUS:** Law Firm **P/S:** Legal and Government Relations, Labor and Employee Benefits Legal Services **MA:** Regional **D/D/R:** Practicing Labor and Employment Law, Consulting, Interacting with the Government, Lobbying **H/I/S:** Golfing **EDU:** Bachelor of Arts in History, Minor in Business, Sequence in Pre-Law, Marist College **A/A/S:** Registered Lobbyist, New York State Commission on Lobbying; New York City Clerk **C/VW:** The Daytop Organization
Email: mcekovic@pittadreier.com
URL: http://www.pittadreier.com

Helena Cence
Title: Vice President **Company:** Coldwell Banker Pacific Properties **Address:** 4211 Wailae Avenue, Honolulu, HI 96816 United States **BUS:** Real Estate Agency **P/S:** Residential Real Estate Sales **MA:** Island of Oahu **D/D/R:** Selling Residential Real Estate, Counseling **H/I/S:** Traveling, Reading, Opera, Spending Time with her Grandchildren **EDU:** MBA, Lund University, Sweden **CERTS:** Certified International Property Specialist **A/A/S:** Rotary Club **C/VW:** Rotary Club
Email: helena@cence.net
URL: http://www.cence.net

Dante L. Cerchio
Title: President **Company:** DC Logistics **Address:** 8117 SVL Box, Victorville, CA 92395 United States **BUS:** Trucking Company **P/S:** Carrier and Broker of Liquid Chemicals **MA:** National **EXP:** Mr. Cerchio's expertise is in customer service. **H/I/S:** Sandrails, Boating, Golfing **EDU:** College Coursework **A/A/S:** Transportation Association; Department of Transportation
Email: dclogistics@sbcglobal.net
URL: http://www.cambridgewhoswho.com

Nina E. Cerfolio
Title: Medical Doctor **Company:** Nina E. Cerfolio, MD, PC **Address:** 2 Fifth Avenue, Suite 5, New York, NY 10003 United States **BUS:** Private Psychiatry Practice **P/S:** Mental Healthcare **MA:** International **D/D/R:** Working with Ovarian Cancer Patients **H/I/S:** Competing in Triathlons and Ultramarathons **EDU:** Post-Doctoral Work, New York University; MD, Chicago Medical School **A/A/S:** Distinguished Fellow and Executive Board Member, American Psychiatric Association; Academy of Psychiatric Medicine; Former Chairwoman, New York Chapter, Women's Psychiatric Association; Board Member, Channel 13 **C/VW:** Pro Bono Psychiatric Care, Fundraising for Children in Chechnya, The Achilles Club, Iraq War Veterans Organization
Email: ninacerf@nyc.rr.com

Christine M. Ceron
Title: Senior Vice President, Wealth Services Manager **Company:** SunTrust Banks, Inc. **Address:** 515 E. Las Olas Boulevard, Fort Lauderdale, FL 33301 United States **BUS:** Bank **P/S:** Private Wealth Investment Management Services **MA:** Regional **D/D/R:** Managing and Overseeing a Team of Seven, Coordinating Regional Meetings, Assisting Individuals with Investment Goals **H/I/S:** Professional Cycling, Spending Time in Miami Beach, Rowing **EDU:** Bachelor of Arts in Political Science and Economics, Fordham University (1982) **CERTS:** Certified Financial Planner; Licensed in Series VII, LXIII and LXXIV; Licensed Insurance Agent, State of Florida **A/A/S:** Senior Leaders of Brown County
Email: christine.ceron@suntrust.com
URL: https://www.suntrust.com

Garrett P. Cerulli
Title: Manager of Program Management, New England **Company:** SAVVIS, Inc. **Address:** 1 First Avenue, Waltham, MA 02451 United States **BUS:** Information Technology Firm **P/S:** Information Technology Utility Services, Infrastructure, Outsourcing, Professional Services, Web Hosting, Infrastructure **MA:** International **D/D/R:** Managing Technical Projects, Hosting Websites, Networking Infrastructure **H/I/S:** Traveling, Reading, Diving **EDU:** Bachelor's Degree in Political Science, Boston College; Bachelor of Arts (1989) **CERTS:** Certified ITIL; Certified in Cisco Systems **A/A/S:** Project Management Institute **C/VW:** Rosie's Place; American Cancer Society; American Red Cross
Email: garrett.cerulli@savvis.net
URL: http://www.savvis.net

Ms. Christine M. Cesar
Title: Registered Nurse Case Manager **Company:** Amerigroup, Inc. **Address:** 22 Century Boulevard, Suite 310, Nashville, TN 37214 United States **BUS:** Health Insurance Company **P/S:** Insurance, Medicaid **MA:** Regional **D/D/R:** Managing Pediatric and Geriatric Medical Cases, Treating Patients with Catastrophic Spinal and Neurological Injuries **H/I/S:** Watching Sports, Reading, Watching Movies, Crafting, Attending the Theater, Hiking, Listening to Music, Playing Piano **EDU:** Bachelor of Science in Nursing, Columbia College of Nursing, Wisconsin (1988) **CERTS:** Certification in Case Management **A/A/S:** Case Management Society of America
Email: gergie00@hotmail.com

Victoria Chabolla
Title: Renal Dietitian, Licensed Dietitian **Company:** DaVita, Inc. **Address:** 2000 S. Llewellyn Avenue, Dallas, TX 75224 United States **BUS:** Medical Center **P/S:** Nutritional Consultation Service, Kidney Dialysis Services **MA:** Local **D/D/R:** Consulting for Diet and Nutrition, Evaluating Patients, Conducting Laboratory Tests, Administering Medications, Collaborating with Physicians, Educating Patients on Nutrition, Demonstrating Healthy Eating Habits **H/I/S:** Camping **EDU:** Bachelor of Science in Clinical Dietetics, University of Texas Southwestern Medical Center at Dallas (2003) **CERTS:** Registered and Licensed Dietitian, State of Texas **A/A/S:** Council on Renal Nutrition; NORTEX; Food Bank
Email: Victoria.Chabolla@cwwemail.com
Email: vchabolla@aol.com

Tresa B. Chakkalakkal, MD, FAAP
Title: Medical Doctor, FAAP **Company:** Sunshine Valley Pediatrics **Address:** 653 N. Town Center Dr., Las Vegas, NV 89144 United States **BUS:** Private Practice **P/S:** Child Healthcare **MA:** Local **D/D/R:** Performing Pediatric Outpatient Office and Clinic Work, Making Nursery Rounds at Two Hospitals **H/I/S:** Listening to Music, Reading **EDU:** MD in Pediatrics, Brookdale Hospital Medical Center **A/A/S:** Fellow, American Academy of Pediatrics; Diplomate, American Board of Pediatrics
Email: tresabindu@yahoo.co.uk

Barbara Chamberlain
Title: Writer **Company:** Fantastix Studios, Ink **Address:** 123 Merideth Court, Aptos, CA 95003 United States **BUS:** Storytelling Network **P/S:** Storytelling Seminars, Creative Writing Classes **MA:** Regional **D/D/R:** Telling Stories, Conducting Seminars, Instructing Creative Writing Courses **H/I/S:** Gardening, Walking, Swimming **EDU:** Master's Degree in Library Information Science, San Jose State University, California (1992); Bachelor's Degree in American Colonial History and California History, University of California at Santa Cruz **A/A/S:** National League American Pen Women; Jack London Society; William Saroyan Society; National Storytelling Association
Email: carousel21@hotmail.com
URL: http://www.fantastixstudios.com

Lynne Chamberlain
Title: Owner **Company:** Pre-Paid Legal Services, Inc. **Address:** 120 Grenada Street, Carpentersville, IL 60110 United States **BUS:** Law Firm **P/S:** Legal Services **MA:** National **D/D/R:** Offering Legal Services to Small Businesses and Individuals **H/I/S:** Traveling, Cross-Stitching, Sewing, Arranging Flowers **EDU:** Associate Degree in Business, Rockford Business College; Associate Degree in Accounting, Rockford Business College; Associate Degree in Clerical Studies, Rockford Business College; Associate Degree in Medical Assistant Studies, Rockford Business College **A/A/S:** American Association of Medical Assistants **C/VW:** Veterans of Foreign Wars, The American Legion
Email: lynnechamberlain@prepaidlegal.com
URL: http://www.prepaidlegal.com/go/lynnechamberlain

Lisa M. Chambers
Title: Vice President **Company:** Steven C. Investments, Inc. **Address:** 2600 Denali Street, Anchorage, AK 99503 United States **BUS:** Real Estate Agency **P/S:** Buying and Selling Investment Properties **MA:** Local **EXP:** Ms. Chambers' expertise is in property management. **H/I/S:** Golfing, Horseback Riding, Playing the Piano **EDU:** College Coursework **CERTS:** Real Estate Certification (1996) **A/A/S:** Building Owners and Managers Association International **C/VW:** Children International; Boys & Girls Clubs of America; Alaska Peace Officers Association; Special Olympics; Local Police Department
Email: ilvice@aol.com

V. Ginger Chamness
Title: Owner **Company:** GC/RLC & Associates, Inc. **Address:** 22504 Cedar Road, Poteau, OK 74953 United States **BUS:** Transportation Company **P/S:** Transportation Services through Freights **MA:** United States, Canada **D/D/R:** Managing Daily Operations, Accounting, Processing Payroll, Keeping Records, Filing Licenses **H/I/S:** Dancing, Caring for her Airdale Terriers, Having Fun with her Red Hat Group the 'Hats on a Hot Tin Roof' **EDU:** Diploma, Sacramento Senior High School; Industry-Related Coursework **C/VW:** Local Children's Organizations; The Red Hat Society; American Cancer Society, Fundraiser, Education TV
Email: gingerc@shiputs.net
URL: http://www.cambridgewhoswho.com

Richard Francis Champigny
Title: Parochial Vicar (Priest) **Company:** St. Jude Catholic Church **Address:** 21689 Toledo Road, Boca Raton, FL 33433 United States **BUS:** Church **P/S:** Spiritual Service Including Spiritual Direction and Guidance **MA:** National **D/D/R:** Preaching, Overseeing Ministry Work and Spiritual Guidance **H/I/S:** Playing Tennis, Bicycling, Conducting Karaoke Shows for the Elderly **EDU:** Master's Degree in French, Fordham University (1969); Master's Degree in Theology, Earned in Italy (1965); Bachelor of Arts Degree in Philosophy, St. Bonaventure University (1961) **A/A/S:** Former Member, Kiwanis Club; Former International Coordinating Priest, World Wide Marriage Encounter Movement; Former International Coordinator; Fraternity of Priests
Email: champcarm@yahoo.com
URL: http://www.stjudeboca.com

Hazel I. Champlin
Title: Director of Nursing **Company:** Senior Living Properties, Inc. **Address:** P.O. Box 1389, Grapevine, TX 76051 United States **BUS:** Long-Term Care Facility **P/S:** Healthcare **MA:** Local **D/D/R:** Overseeing the Nursing Staff, Caring for Patients **H/I/S:** Traveling **EDU:** Bachelor of Science in Nursing, Baylor University **C/VW:** Local Church
Email: hazell.champlin@cwwemail.com
URL: http://www.cambridgewhoswho.com

Ms. Lucia Chan
Title: Project Manager **Company:** Faithful & Gould **Address:** 655 Montgomery Street, Suite 1710, San Francisco, CA 94111 United States **BUS:** Project Management and Cost Management Firm **P/S:** Project Management, Cost Management, Construction Management and Cost Estimation **MA:** International **D/D/R:** Overseeing Construction, Contract Administration, Project Management and Design **H/I/S:** Traveling **EDU:** Master's Degree in Civil and Structural Engineering, Widener College **A/A/S:** American Society of Civil Engineers; Project Management Institute; Association for Advanced of Cost Engineering
Email: lucia.chan@fgould.com
URL: http://www.fgould.com

Bobbi Chandler
Title: Owner **Company:** Marine Upholstery **Address:** 1000 Seventh Street, Parker, AZ 85344 United States **BUS:** Manufacturing Company **P/S:** Boat Upholstery, Biminis, Truck and Car Seat Repair, Custom Hatch Cover Repair, Rebuilding of Seats, Wood Boat Repair **MA:** Local **D/D/R:** Overseeing Business Operations and Repair Work, Creating Upholstery, Managing Client Relationships, Purchasing and Marketing **H/I/S:** Reading, ATVing, Shooting **EDU:** Coursework in Business, University of Phoenix (2003) **A/A/S:** Local Chamber of Commerce; National Federation of Independent Businesses
Email: marine_upholstery@yahoo.com
URL: http://www.marine-upholstery.com

Maudie Sue Chandler
Title: Realtor **Company:** Century 21 Select Real Estate, Inc. **Address:** 409 Century Park Drive, Yuba City, CA 95991 United States **BUS:** Real Estate Agency **P/S:** Residential and Commercial Real Estate Exchange **MA:** International **D/D/R:** Selling Residential Real Estate, Supporting First-Time Buyers **H/I/S:** Traveling, Spending Time with her Grandchildren **EDU:** Diploma, Marysville High School **CERTS:** Licensed Realtor (1986) **A/A/S:** California Association of Realtors; Sutter-Yuba Association of Realtors; Local Chamber of Commerce; Network Professionals; Centurion Honor Society; Sacramento Board of Realtors; National Association of Realtors **C/VW:** Easter Seals; American Cancer Society
Email: maudiesue@realtor.com
URL: http://www.maudiesue.com

Angelica H. Chang
Title: Patient Representative **Company:** Palm Beach Gardens Medical Center **Address:** 3360 Burns Road, Palm Beach Gardens, FL 33410 United States **BUS:** Medical Center **P/S:** Healthcare **MA:** Regional **EXP:** Ms. Chang's expertise includes patient care, insurance and counseling services and patient registration. **H/I/S:** Traveling, Studying Different Cultures **EDU:** Bachelor's Degree in Health Administration, Florida Atlantic University (2006) **A/A/S:** Healthcare Financial Management Association; Phi Beta Kappa
Email: gelichang@yahoo.com
URL: http://www.pbgmc.com

Jennifer K. Chang
Title: Global Marketing Manager **Company:** Baxter Healthcare **Address:** 95 Spring Street, New Providence, NJ 07974 United States **BUS:** Global Healthcare Company **P/S:** Assists Healthcare Professionals and their Patients with Treatment of Complex Medical Conditions Including Hemophilia, Immune Disorders, Kidney Disease, Cancer, Trauma and Other Conditions, Manufacturer of Plasma-Based and Recombinant Proteins, also Provides IV Nutrition Solutions, Containers and Compounding Systems and Services, General Anesthetic Agents and Critical Care Drugs, Contract Manufacturing Services and Drug Packaging and Formulation Technologies **MA:** International **D/D/R:** Managing Global Molecular Marketing, Overseeing Product Management, Supporting Promotional Sales and Sales Objective Pricing **EDU:** Bachelor of Arts Degree in Public Relations, Southern Methodist University (1995) **A/A/S:** Healthcare Marketing and Communications Council, Inc.
Email: JennNJ1@aol.com
URL: http://www.baxter.com

Phoua Chang
Title: Registered Nurse **Company:** Saint Mary's Hospital **Address:** 1216 Second Street S.W., Rochester, MN 55902 United States **BUS:** Hospital **P/S:** Healthcare **MA:** Nation **EXP:** Ms. Chang's expertise is in cardiology nursing. **H/I/S:** Spending Time with her Family **EDU:** Bachelor of Science in Nursing, Viterbo College (Now Viterbo University) (1994) **C/VW:** Local Schools
Email: chang.phoua@mayo.edu

Alice Chao
Title: Pediatric Dentist **Company:** Alice Chao, DDS **Address:** 107 Stelton Road, Piscataway, NJ 08854 United States **BUS:** Pediatric Dental Office **P/S:** Pediatric Dental Care **MA:** Regional **EXP:** Ms. Chao's expertise is in pediatric dentistry. **H/I/S:** Traveling, Playing Tennis, Teaching and Tutoring Young Children Mathematics **EDU:** Doctor of Dental Surgery, Ohio State University; Certificate in Pediatric Dentistry, University of Medicine and Dentistry of New Jersey **A/A/S:** American Academy of Pediatric Dentistry; New Jersey Dental Association; Diplomat, American Board of Pediatric Dentistry; American Board of Pediatric Dentistry **C/VW:** The Smile Train
Email: alice_chao_dds@yahoo.com

Deborah A. Chaplin
Title: Library Media Specialist **Company:** Valley Elementary School **Address:** 98 Panther Drive, Hot Springs, VA 24445 United States **BUS:** Elementary School **P/S:** Education **MA:** Local **D/D/R:** Managing Library Services, Instruction and Materials **H/I/S:** Reading, Quilting, Scrapbooking **EDU:** Master's Degree in Library Science, Longwood University **A/A/S:** Virginia Educational Media Association; Shenandoah Valley Reading Council; Bath Education Association; Virginia Education Association; National Education Association **C/VW:** Bath Lions Club, Bath Book Buddies, Reading is Fundamental
Email: dchaplin@tds.net
URL: http://www.bath.k12.va.us

Dr. Dennis S. Chapman
Title: Equine Dental Practitioner **Company:** Stable 2 Stable Equine Dental Practice P.C. **Address:** 120 Clear Creek Road, Langhorne, PA 19047 United States **BUS:** Equine Dentistry and Surgery **P/S:** Equine Dental Treatment and Surgery **MA:** Regional **EXP:** Dr. Chapman's expertise is in equine dentistry. **H/I/S:** Riding his Thoroughbred **EDU:** Ph.D. in Organizational Leadership, University of Phoenix; Doctor of Equine Dentistry, American School of Equine Dentistry; Master of Business Administration, St. Joseph's University; Bachelor's Degree in Political Science and Business Administration, Pennsylvania State University **CERTS:** Certified Equine Dentist, Professional Grade III, Academy of Equine Science **A/A/S:** International Association of Equine Dentistry; Academy of Equine Dentistry; Federal Law Enforcement Officers Association; Federal Criminal Investigators Association; American College of Forensic Examiners; Chapel of Four Chaplains; Legion of Honor **C/VW:** Last Chance Ranch Equine Rescue, Special Equestrians Therapeutic Riding Program, Pegasus Riding Academy, St. Jude Children's Research Hospital, Women in Transition
Email: dchap32989@aol.com

Jessica Gene't Chapman
Title: Speech Therapist **Company:** Waco Independent School District **Address:** 501 Franklin Avenue, Waco, TX 76701 United States **BUS:** School District **P/S:** Education **MA:** Local **EXP:** Ms. Chapman's expertise is in speech therapy for pre-kindergarten through twelfth-grade students. **H/I/S:** Traveling, Photography, Playing Baseball and Softball **EDU:** Bachelor of Arts in Communication Disorders, Baylor University **A/A/S:** Delta Kappa Gamma **C/VW:** American Cancer Society; Goodwill; The Salvation Army
Email: jchapman@wacoisd.org

Rosetta A. Chapman
Title: Teacher **Company:** Brevard Academy **Address:** 2910 Flat Creek Valley Road, Lake Toxaway, NC 28747 United States **BUS:** Charter School **P/S:** Instruction and Curriculum **MA:** Regional **EXP:** Ms. Chapman's expertise is in elementary education. **D/D/R:** Teaching First, Third and Fifth-Grade Students **H/I/S:** Crocheting, Reading, Softball **EDU:** Bachelor's Degree in Elementary Education, Mars Hill College (2003)
Email: chapbreva@citcom.net
URL: http://www.brevardacademy.org

Tori Chapman
Title: Regional Director, Vice President **Company:** Licensing International **Address:** 8426 Clint Drive, Suite 139, Belton, MO 64012 United States **BUS:** Corporate Trademark Licensing Company **P/S:** Marketing, New Product Development **MA:** National **D/D/R:** Fortune 500 Brands and Trademarks, New Brand Concepts **H/I/S:** Spending Time with her Horses **EDU:** Master's Degree in Marketing **A/A/S:** Institute of Trade Mark Attorneys; International Licensing Industry Merchandisers' Association **C/VW:** Church, Christian Broadcasting Network
Email: torichampman@licensingint.com
URL: http://www.cambridgewhoswho.com

Kathy E. Chappell
Title: Special Assistant, Office Manager **Company:** Immigration & Customs Enforcement, Detention & Removal Operations **Address:** 1545 Hawkins Boulevard, El Paso, TX 79925 United States **BUS:** Federal Law Enforcement Agency **P/S:** Detention and Removal of Unlawful Aliens **MA:** National **D/D/R:** Managing Office Operations **H/I/S:** Reading, Solving Crossword Puzzles, Mahjong, Bowling, Bible Study **EDU:** Associate Degree in Business Management, El Paso Community College; Accounting Degree, International Business College; Executive Secretary Degree, Gadsden Business College **A/A/S:** Phi Theta Kappa **C/VW:** American Red Cross, Salvation Army, March of Dimes, West Texas Food Bank, Breast Cancer Awareness
Email: keccha@aol.com

Bridget S. Charles
Title: Teacher **Company:** Rafael Hernandez School **Address:** 26 Kenz Terrace, West Orange, NJ 07052 United States **BUS:** Public Elementary School **P/S:** General Elementary Education for Students in Prekindergarten through Eighth-Grade, Special Education, Bilingual Studies Program, Reading Redemption Programs, Connected Mathematics Program, Computer Technology Study Program, Independent Software Instruction, Arts, Music, Physical Education, Learning Resources, Student Support Services, Athletics, Extracurricular Activities **MA:** Regional **D/D/R:** Overseeing the Scholastic Reading 180 Program, Teaching Literacy and Social Studies to Seventh and Eighth-Grade Students, Helping Struggling Readers to Reach Eighth-Grade Assessment Level, Guiding Group Reading Sessions, Mentoring New Teachers, Conducting Faculty Workshops **H/I/S:** Writing, Attending her Daughter's Sporting Events **EDU:** Master's Degree in Curriculum and Instrument, Caldwell College (2004); Bachelor's Degree in Psychology, Caldwell College (2000); Bachelor's Degree in Education, University of the West Indies (1981) **CERTS:** Post Master's Degree Supervisory Certification (2007) **A/A/S:** Newark Teachers Union; Eighth-Grade Advisor, Rafael Hernandez School
Email: bpsamchar@hotmail.com
URL: http://www.nps.k12.nj.us/hernandez/index.htm

Ofelia F. Charles
Title: Teacher, Reading Leader **Company:** South Hialeah Elementary School **Address:** 265 E. Fifth Street, Hialeah, FL 33010 United States **BUS:** School **P/S:** Education **MA:** Local **D/D/R:** Serving as the School's Reading Leader, Preparing Students for Creative Writing and Critical Thinking **H/I/S:** Reading, Traveling **EDU:** Pursuing Doctorate **CERTS:** Certification in Elementary Education **A/A/S:** Parent-Teacher Association; International Reading Council **C/VW:** Youth Leader, Church
Email: ocharles@dadeschools.net

Rev. Linda V. Charley
Title: 1) Pastor 2) Sleep Technician **Company:** 1) St. Luke Independent Church 2) EM Regional Medical Center 3) Kingdom Ministry, Inc. **Address:** 1050 E. Patterson Street, Alliance, OH 44601 United States **BUS:** 1) Church 2) Medical Center **P/S:** 1) Religious Services 2) Healthcare **MA:** International **D/D/R:** Preaching, Teaching, Treating Patients with Sleep Disorders **H/I/S:** Walking, Motorcycling, Exercising, Spending Time with her Family **EDU:** Master of Arts in Christian Ministry Studies, Ashland Theological Seminary **CERTS:** Pursuing Board Certification in Sleep Techniques; Licensed Cosmetologist, State of Ohio; Certified Teacher, Wheaton College; Diploma in Theology, McCreary Center for African American Religious Studies **A/A/S:** Elyria High School; Black History Club of Alliance, OH **A/H:** National Honor Society **C/VW:** Advisory Board Member, Salvation Army Church; The Salvation Army
Email: lcharley@oh.rr.com
URL: http://www.cambridgewhoswho.com

Jacqueline P. Charter-Holley
Title: Music Teacher **Company:** P.S. 92, Brooklyn **Address:** 601 Parkside Avenue, Brooklyn, NY 11226 United States **BUS:** School District **P/S:** Education **MA:** Local **D/D/R:** Giving Guitar Lessons, Teaching Music and Movement **H/I/S:** Crocheting, Reading **EDU:** Master of Education, New York University; Bachelor of Arts, Queens College **A/A/S:** Music Educators Association of New York City **C/VW:** St. George's Episcopal Church
Email: brwnfrenchhrnldy@yahoo.com
URL: http://www.cambridgewhoswho.com

Carol E. Chase, CNA, CMA
Title: CNA, Nursing Home Medicine Aide **Company:** Trans Health Fort Washington Rehabilitation **Address:** 7300 Sheffield Drive, Temple Hills, MD 20748 United States **BUS:** Nursing Home Facility **P/S:** Nursing Home Services **MA:** Regional **D/D/R:** Dispensing Medications According to Federal, State and Local Guidelines, Handling General Patient Care **H/I/S:** Reading **EDU:** Graduated High School **CERTS:** Certified Nursing Assistant, Clinton Nursing Home (1968)
Email: carollechase@yahoo.com

Mrs. Ruthann B. Chase
Title: English As A Second Language Teacher **Company:** Laconia High School **BUS:** Public High School **P/S:** Education for Students in Ninth through Twelfth-Grade, Mathematical and Scientific Processes and Concepts, Critical and Creative Problem Solving, Creativity through Fine Art, Technologies **MA:** Regional **D/D/R:** Teaching Mathematics and English as a Second Language, Implementing Applied Mathematical Skills into Basic Core Classes, **H/I/S:** Gardening, Travel, **EDU:** Specialist Degree in Computer Education, Southwestern University (1992); Master's Degree in Guidance Counseling, University of Miami (1989); Bachelor's Degree in Elementary Education, Florida Southern College (1967) **A/A/S:** Alpha Delta Kappa; New Hampshire Executive Board of Education for the Humane Society; **C/VW:** American Cancer Society
Email: tchase@worldpath.net
URL: http://www.pmhschool.com

Mr. Phillip R. Chatwood Sr.
Title: Teacher **Company:** National Trail Local Schools **Address:** 4943 Fox Road, Greenville, OH 45331 United States **BUS:** Middle and High School Facilities **P/S:** Regular Core Curriculum including Reading, Math, English, Science, Social Studies, Art, Music, History, Physical Education, Language Arts, Computers **MA:** Regional **D/D/R:** Teaching Middle School Science, Counseling Students **EDU:** Master of Arts Degree in Science, Wright State University (1977) **A/A/S:** Phi Delta Kappa; National Trail Teachers Association; Board of Odaka County; Volunteer Recovery Association; Ohio Educational Association; LEA **A/H:** Published in Ohio Science Academy Magazine
Email: philchatwood@wcoil.com
URL: http://www.cambridgewhoswho.com

Lupita Chavarria
Title: Publisher **Company:** Enlace Latino **Address:** P.O. Box 56378, Little Rock, AR 72215 United States **BUS:** Spanish Newspaper **P/S:** News and Advertisements Geared for the Hispanic Community **MA:** Regional **D/D/R:** Writing Articles for the Spanish Community, Marketing, Handling the Sales Department **H/I/S:** Writing Poetry, Heading a Folklore Dance Group **EDU:** Bachelor of Arts in Marketing and Business Administration, Instituto Escolar, Chiguagua, Mexico **A/A/S:** National Association of Hispanic Journalists; Coalition for Comprehensive Immigration Reform; Grupo Enlace; President, Alianca Hispana **C/VW:** La Casa, Amigos de las Mujeres de Juarez, Local Church
Email: lupitachavarriag@yahoo.com
URL: http://www.enlacelatino.net

Sandra L. Chavez
Title: Assistant Professor of Military Science **Company:** United States Army **Address:** 11200 S.W. 8th Street, Miami, FL 33199 United States **BUS:** Military **P/S:** National Defense and Protection **MA:** National **EXP:** Ms. Chavez's expertise is in public administration. **D/D/R:** Teaching American Military History and Science **H/I/S:** Spending Time Outdoors, Going to the Gym, Running, Walking, Sports **EDU:** Teaches Military History and Science, University of Miami and FIU; Master of Arts in Public Administration, University of Colorado, Colorado Springs-2005; Bachelor of Science in Political Science, Illinois Institute of Technology-1997 **C/VW:** Volunteer, Fundraising Events for Alzheimer's Disease and Breast Cancer; Charity Walks
Email: chavezs@fiu.edu
URL: http://fiu.edu/~armyrotc

DeLois Duvonya Chavis
Title: Pharmacist **Company:** Eckerd **Address:** 12216 N. NC Highway 150, Winston-Salem, NC 27127 United States **BUS:** Retail Pharmacy **P/S:** Pharmacy **MA:** National **D/D/R:** Managing Medications **H/I/S:** Buying Real Estate, Creating Crafts, Sewing, Painting **EDU:** Pursuing Doctor of Pharmacy, Idaho State University; Bachelor's Degree in Zoology, University of North Carolina at Chapel Hill; Bachelor's Degree in Pharmaceutical Studies, University of North Carolina at Chapel Hill
Email: chavisdd1413@as.com

Suzanne L. Chawk
Title: Vice President of Sales **Company:** AIG VALIC **Address:** 1 Barons Court, Saginaw, MI 48603 United States **BUS:** Financial Planning Agency **P/S:** Financial Planning, Retirement Planning, Insurance, Portfolio Management, Risk Management, Cash Management, Education Planning, Investment Strategies, Annuities, IRAs, Mutual Funds **MA:** Regional **D/D/R:** Financial and Retirement Planning, Assisting New Businesses, Social Services, Education Agencies and Nonprofit Organizations with Business Development Strategies, Consulting **H/I/S:** Skiing, Exercising, Reading **EDU:** Master of Business Administration, Barry University, Miami, Florida (1987); Bachelor of Science in Nursing, Florida International University (1977) **A/A/S:** National Association of Securities Dealers
Email: suzanne_chawke@aigvalic.com
URL: http://www.aigvalic.com

Andraya M. Cheers
Title: Teacher **Company:** Memphis City Schools **Address:** 1602 Dellwood Avenue, Memphis, TN 38116 United States **BUS:** School District **P/S:** Education **MA:** Regional **D/D/R:** Teaching Kindergarten through Eighth-Grade Students **H/I/S:** Reading, Creating Webquests, Traveling, Riding her Motorcycle **EDU:** Master's Degree in General Education, Cumberland University; Master's Degree in Instruction and Curriculum Technology, Grand Canyon University; Bachelor's Degree in Education, Austin Peay State University **A/A/S:** Memphis Education Association; Tennessee Education Association; Delta Sigma Theta; Alpha Phi Omega; Pinnacle, Cumberland University; Kappa Delta Phi; National Education Association **A/H:** Chancellor's List; Dean's List
Email: cheersandrayam@mcsk12.net
URL: http://www.toostrong.net/acheers

Alexander Chemelekov
Title: Optometrist **Company:** Sam's Club # 6608 **Dept:** Optical **Address:** 1525 W. Bell Rd, Phoenix, AZ 85023 United States **BUS:** Optometry Practice **P/S:** Optometry **MA:** Local **D/D/R:** Offering Optometric Services **H/I/S:** Being a Professional Bridge Player, Photography, Sculpting **EDU:** Doctor of Optometry, New England College of Optometry
Email: alex.chem@gmail.com
URL: http://www.cambridgewhoswho.com

Hsiang-Cheng Alex Chen
Title: MD and Ph.D. Student **Company:** Duke University **Address:** 595 La Salle Street, Durham, NC 27710 United States **BUS:** University **P/S:** Education **MA:** National **D/D/R:** Autoimmune Diseases, Osteoarthritis, Linkage, Genetic Mapping for complex diseases **EDU:** MD, Earned in Taiwan; Pursuing Ph.D. in Autoimmune Diseases, Osteoarthritis, Linkage and Genetic Mapping
Email: hsiangcheng.chen@duke.edu
URL: http://www.cambridgewhoswho.com

Pin Chen
Title: Music Director **Company:** West Adams Preparatory School **Address:** 3710 Del Mar Heights Road, San Diego, CA 92130 United States **BUS:** School **P/S:** Education **MA:** Local **D/D/R:** Directing the Orchestra and Instrumental Music Department, Overseeing Staff and Students, Teaching the Guitar and Violin **H/I/S:** Acting, Fencing **EDU:** Bachelor's Degree in Music, Northwestern University, Chicago, IL (2003) **A/A/S:** California Chapter, Music Educators National Conference; California Teachers Association; Southern California School Band and Orchestra Association; American Teachers String Association **C/VW:** Local Charitable Organizations; Local School
Email: pinlet@alumni.northwestern.edu
URL: http://www.cambridgewhoswho.com

Teresa Ping-Ping Chen
Title: Artist **Company:** American International Culture Arts **Address:** 5543 1/2 Santa Anita Avenue, Temple City, CA 91780 United States **BUS:** Freelance Artist **P/S:** Art, Oil Paintings, Silk Paintings **MA:** International **EXP:** Ms. Chen's expertise is in silk painting. **H/I/S:** Singing, Painting **EDU:** Painting Classes, The Catholic University of America, Washington, District of Columbia; Bachelor of Arts in Administration Management, Taiwan **A/H:** Golden Award for 10 Greatest Artists in China (2007)
Email: pingruchen@hotmail.com
URL: http://www.cambridgewhoswho.com

James Chenevert Jr.
Title: Manager **Company:** Genex Cooperative, CRI **Address:** 2288 Gourrier Avenue, Baton Rouge, LA 70820 United States **BUS:** Bovine Artificial Insemination Company **P/S:** Bovine Artificial Insemination for Import and Export Purpose **MA:** International **D/D/R:** Overseeing Management **H/I/S:** Raising Cattle, Hunting **EDU:** Diploma, Livonia High School **A/A/S:** National Cattlemen Beef Association; National Association of Animal Breeders; American Brahman Breeders Association; Louisiana Cattlemen Association **C/VW:** St. Jude Children's Research Hospital, St. Francis Cabrini Catholic Church
Email: jchenevert@crinet.com

Susan J. Cheppa
Title: Realtor **Company:** Long & Foster **Address:** 2333 Baltimore Blvd, Finksburg, MD 21048 United States **BUS:** Real Estate Broker **P/S:** Home Sales **MA:** National **D/D/R:** Working with First-Time Home Buyers **H/I/S:** Soccer Mom **A/A/S:** Maryland Association of Realtors, National Association of Realtors
Email: susancheppa@mris.com
URL: www.longandfoster.com

Rachel Hall Cherry
Title: Registered Nurse Supervisor (Retired) **Company:** Roanoke Memorial Hospital, Cherry and Associates **Address:** 2998 Comers Rock Road, Elk Creek, VA 24326 United States **BUS:** Healthcare, Organic Vegetables and Berries **P/S:** Healthcare **MA:** National **D/D/R:** Teaching Electrocardiogram Reading to Specialists, Consulting, Conducting Electric Cardiography Workshops **H/I/S:** Reading, Traveling, Canning Natural Grown Wild Plants, Berries and Vegetables **EDU:** Diploma in Cardiology, Roanoke Memorial Hospital; Training in Respiratory Intensive Care, Duke University Hospital **A/A/S:** American Association of Critical-Care Nurses; American Heart Association; Virginia Nurses Association; National Nursing League; American College of Cardiology Teaching Faculty **A/H:** International EKG Readings Award (1973) **C/VW:** American Red Cross, CPR Classes, Free Local Healthcare

Nemalen Chetty
Title: Mechanical Engineer **BUS:** Engineering **P/S:** Product Development **D/D/R:** Consulting with Engineers **H/I/S:** Reading, Fishing, Playing Tennis, Exercising, Watching Soccer and Football, Tutoring **EDU:** Bachelor of Science in Mechanical Engineering, University of Michigan **CERTS:** Board Certified Engineer, National Council of Engineering and Surveying **A/A/S:** University of Michigan Alumni Association; American Society of Mechanical Engineers; National Council of Examiners for Engineering and Surveying **C/VW:** Purple Heart
Email: nemalen@sbcglobal.net

Timothy M. Chewing, EMT
Title: EMS Educator **Company:** Catawba Valley Community College **Address:** 2550 Hwy 70 SE, Hickory, NC 28602 United States **BUS:** College **P/S:** Community College **MA:** Local **D/D/R:** Performing Emergency Medical Services **H/I/S:** Hiking, Walking **EDU:** Bachelor's Degree, Bowling University **A/A/S:** National Association of EMS Educators
Email: info@CambridgeWhosWho.com

Dr. Donald L. Chicavell
Title: Adjunct Professor **Company:** National University of La Joya California **Address:** 211 Rhododendron Drive, Sequim, WA 98382 United States **BUS:** University **P/S:** Higher Education **MA:** National **D/D/R:** Teaching Graduate-Level Education Courses, Motivating Teachers and Educators to Complete their Master's Degrees and Administrative Certification Requirements, Supervising Administrative Interns and Students in Obtaining Certifications and Master's Degrees in Research Projects **EDU:** Ph.D. in Educational Administration, The University of Santo Thomasa, Philippines (1977) **A/A/S:** National Education Association; Association of Secondary School Principals; National Association of Elementary School Principals; Keynote Speaker, The Philippines Psychological Association; The National Science Foundation; The University of Alaska
Email: donc@olympus.net
URL: http://www.nu.edu

Karen Child
Title: Family and Marriage Therapist **Company:** Karen Child, MFT **Address:** 2900 Bristol Street, Suite A207, Costa Mesa, CA 92626 United States **BUS:** Counseling Center **P/S:** Therapy Classes, Counseling **MA:** Local **D/D/R:** Counseling on Sexual Addiction and Premarital Issues **EDU:** Pursuing Ph.D.; Master's Degree in Marriage and Family Therapy, University of San Diego **A/A/S:** California Association of Family and Marriage Therapists; American Association for Marriage and Family Therapy; Christian Therapists Association
Email: karenchildma@yahoo.com
URL: http://www.cambridgewhoswho.com

Patricia Childress-Jones
Title: Manager **Company:** Woodgrain Distribution **Dept:** Human Resources **Address:** 80 Shelby Street, Montevallo, AL 35115 United States **BUS:** Distribution Company **P/S:** Moldings, Building Materials **MA:** National **D/D/R:** Managing Human Resources **H/I/S:** Reading, Spending Time at the Beach **EDU:** Associate Degree in Business, Alverson Draughn Business College (1967) **A/A/S:** Society for Human Resource Management
Email: pjones@woodgrain.com
URL: http://www.woodgraindistribution.com

Catherine Chin
Title: LMT **Company:** Keep in Touch Licensed Massage Therapy **Address:** 4513 Little Neck Parkway, Little Neck, NY 11362 United States **BUS:** Healthcare Service Provider **P/S:** Works Mainly with Post Surgical Patients **MA:** Local **EDU:** Benjamin Cardozo High School, College Coursework in Physical Therapy **A/A/S:** Health Care Provider Organization
Email: catherinechinlmt@yahoo.com

Leonardo Chin
Title: President, Chief Executive Officer **Company:** Digitek, Inc. **Address:** 2130 Oakdale Avenue, San Francisco, CA 94124 United States **BUS:** Printing Services Company **P/S:** Printing, Graphics and Direct Mailing Services **MA:** National **D/D/R:** Managing Operations **H/I/S:** Traveling **EDU:** College Coursework **C/VW:** AIDS Foundation; American Cancer Society
Email: leonard@digiteksf.com
URL: http://www.digitekonline.com

Cynthia H. Ching
Title: Owner, Stylist **Company:** Tangerine Hair Studio **Address:** 119 Paseo de San Antonio, San Jose, CA 95112 United States **BUS:** Hair Salon **P/S:** Hair Styling, Facials, Haircuts, Shampoos, Blow-Dries, Deep Conditioning, Flat Ironing, Perm Straightening, Perms, Hair Extensions, Braiding, Color Touch-Up, Full Color, Partial Highlights, Full Highlights, Combo Color, Color Toning and Extra Color, Ink Work, Chemical Relaxer, Permanent Straightener, Paul Mitchell Products **MA:** Regional **D/D/R:** Styling Hair, Managing Nine Staff Members, Ordering Products, Applying Make-Up, Overseeing Business Operations **H/I/S:** Snowboarding, Playing the Piano **EDU:** Associate of Arts Degree in General Education, Orange Coast College (2001) **CERTS:** Cosmetology License, Paul Mitchell (2003)
Email: tangerinehs@yahoo.com
URL: http://www.tangerinehairstudio.com

Warren A. Chiodo
Title: Student Doctor **Company:** New York College of Podiatric Medicine **Address:** 1800 Park Avenue, New York, NY 10035 United States **BUS:** College **P/S:** Healthcare, Podiatric Medicine **MA:** Regional **D/D/R:** Performing Foot and Ankle Surgery **H/I/S:** Watching Movies, Spending Time with his Fiancee, Watching Football **EDU:** Bachelor's Degree in Biology, Iona College **A/A/S:** American Diabetes Association; American Academy of Podiatric Sports Medicine; American Podiatric Medical Students Association; American College of Foot & Ankle Orthopedics & Medicine **C/VW:** New Jersey Special Olympics
Email: wchiodo@nycpm.edu
URL: http://www.nycpm.edu

Brett John Chisholm
Title: Owner **Company:** Brett Chisholm Photography **Address:** 1304 Malone, Houston, TX 77007 United States **BUS:** Commercial Photography Studio **P/S:** Commercial Fashion Photography **MA:** International **EXP:** Mr. Chisholm's expertise is in fashion photography. **H/I/S:** Photography **EDU:** College Coursework **A/A/S:** Professional Photographers of America; Professional Photographers Guild of Houston; Chamber of Commerce; Best Photographer, Houston City Search **C/VW:** SNAPS; American Advertising Federation
Email: brett@brettchisholm.com
URL: http://www.brettchisholm.com

Carrie K. Chitsey
Title: President **Company:** 1) Client Services Customer Care 2) Red Leaf Capitol Professional Service and Healthcare **Address:** 2415 S. Austin Avenue, Suite 103, Denison, TX 75020 United States **BUS:** 1) Call Center, Outsourcing Company 2) Financial Service Consulting Company **P/S:** 1) Financial Services 2) Healthcare Benefits, Financial Service Consultation **MA:** National **D/D/R:** Managing Customer Relations **H/I/S:** Playing Texas Hold 'Em **EDU:** Bachelor's Degree in Business, University of Texas **A/A/S:** Women Owned Businesses Organization; Board Member, Pension Downtown Alliance **C/VW:** Board Member, Boys & Girls Club of America
Email: carrie@redleafcapitol.com
URL: http://www.redleafcapitol.com

Lynn M. Chiu
Title: Special Education Teacher **Company:** B.L. Miller Elementary School **Address:** 506 W. Virginia Avenue, Sebring, OH 44672 United States **BUS:** Elementary School **P/S:** Primary Education **MA:** Local **D/D/R:** Teaching Sign Languages, Life and Language Skills to Learners with Multiple Needs **H/I/S:** Spending Time with her Family **EDU:** Master's Degree in Early Childhood Special Education, Malone College (1994); Bachelor's Degree in Liberal Arts, Wittenberg University **CERTS:** National Board Certification, Reading Continuing Education Units **A/A/S:** Ohio Education Association; National Education Association **C/VW:** Local Church; Local Schools
Email: lmc1966@zoominternet.net
URL: http://www.cambridgewhoswho.com

Ms. Sung In Cho
Title: Public Relations Manager **Company:** Samsung Electronics America **Address:** 105 Challenger Road, Ridgefield Park, NJ 07030 United States **BUS:** Electronics Company **P/S:** Consumer Electronics **MA:** National **D/D/R:** Managing Public Relations **H/I/S:** Reading, Watching Movies **EDU:** MBA, New York University; Bachelor of Arts in Japanese Language and Literature, Pomona College **C/VW:** Phillips Exeter Academy
Email: castlesung@yahoo.com
URL: http://www.cambridgewhoswho.com

Liza Chobrutskaya
Title: Director **Company:** Claim Expert, Inc. **Address:** 1402 W. 4th Street, Apt. C5, Brooklyn, NY 11204 United States **BUS:** Medical Coding **P/S:** Medical Billing and Coding **MA:** Local **D/D/R:** Overseeing Business Operations **H/I/S:** Reading **EDU:** Bachelor's Degree in Computer Science, Brooklyn College **CERTS:** Certified in Medical Billing; Coding Specialist, Brooklyn College **A/A/S:** American Association of Billers; National Health Carrier Association
Email: claimexpert4md@aol.com
URL: http://www.cambridgewhoswho.com

Ivylee E. Choloply
Title: Assistant Director of Nursing **Company:** Manor Care **Address:** 14 Lincoln Avenue, Yeadon, PA 19050 United States **BUS:** Rehabilitation Facility **P/S:** Rehabilitation **MA:** Local **EXP:** Ms. Choloply's expertise is in long-term nursing care. **H/I/S:** Reading **EDU:** Diploma in Nursing; Pursuing Bachelor of Arts
Email: info@CambridgeWhosWho.com
URL: http://www.cambridgewhoswho.com

Bridget M. Chow
Title: Claims Analyst **Company:** Midwest Employers Casualty Company **Address:** 14755 N. Outer Forty, Suite 300, Chesterfield, MO 63017 United States **BUS:** Claims, Excess Workers Compensation **P/S:** Insurance **MA:** National **D/D/R:** Claims Analyst, Overseeing Case Load for Excess Workers Compensation, Catastrophic Cases, Senior Cases, Visiting Clients, Mediation, Trial **H/I/S:** Golfing, Traveling **EDU:** Bachelor of Science in Business Administration, Cheney University of Pennsylvania
Email: bmbc624@yahoo.com
URL: http://www.mwecc.com

Rina Chowdhury
Title: Vice President Company: Citigroup Address: 68 S. Service Road, Suite 400, Melville, NY 11747 United States BUS: Collaboration Engineering Group P/S: Certify Enterprise Collaboration Tools, Microsoft Office 2007 with Vista, Microsoft Sharepoint, Instant Messaging MA: International D/D/R: Managing Technology Infrastructure Projects for Applications between Business Clients and Technology Organizations, Ensuring Applications Meet Compliance Standards H/I/S: Camping, Traveling EDU: Pursuing Bachelor's Degree in Business Management, Dowling College CERTS: Pursuing Project Management Certification
Email: rina.chowdhury@citigroup.com
URL: http://www.citigroup.com

Brenda G. Chrisman
Title: Operations Manager Company: Heritage Title, LLC Address: 136 General Drive, suite 100, Luray, VA 22835 United States BUS: Real Estate Agency P/S: Real Estate Sales, Title Insurance MA: Statewide D/D/R: Underwriting, Marketing, Supervising All Staff Members and Closings H/I/S: Traveling, Gardening EDU: Page County High School Graduate CERTS: Licensed in Title Insurance Underwriting A/A/S: Virginia Land Title Association; Page, Rockingham and Shenandoah County Chambers of Commerce
Email: bchrisman@htitlecom
URL: http://www.heritagetitlellc.net

Lori Christensen
Title: Director of Social Services Company: The Salvation Army Address: 1310 S Woodruff Avenue, Idaho Falls, ID 83404 United States BUS: Nonprofit Human Services Agency P/S: Social Services Support Programs MA: Local D/D/R: Offering Social Services to Battered Women, At-Risk Youth and Individuals with Autistic Disorders H/I/S: Family, Reading EDU: Associate Degree, Brigham Young University
Email: thebaby1@localnet.com

Ms. Terry L. Christensen
Title: Licensed Massage Therapist Company: TLC Massage Address: 279 E. Third N., Soda Springs, ID 83276 United States BUS: Therapeutic Center P/S: Massage Therapy Including Bodywork Therapy and Health Balancing MA: Regional EXP: Ms. Christensen's expertise includes operations management and deep tissue and Swedish therapy. D/D/R: Performing Deep Tissue and Swedish Therapy, Scheduling Appointments H/I/S: Practicing Yoga EDU: Associate Degree in Physical Therapy, Idaho State University (1998) A/A/S: American Massage Therapy Association
Email: scruffins@hotmail.com
URL: http://www.cambridgewhoswho.com

Mrs. Tana Hartman Christian, RN
Title: Registered Nurse Company: Wakemed Address: 3000 New Bern Avenue, Raleigh, NC 27614 United States BUS: Private, Nonprofit Medical Facility P/S: Wide Range of High Quality Medical Services MA: Statewide D/D/R: Working as a Staff Nurse in the Children's Emergency Room H/I/S: Exercise EDU: Associate Degree in General Education, Mattatuck Community College; Diploma in Nursing, St. Mary's Hospital School of Nurses (1987)
Email: tana_rn2@yahoo.com
URL: http://www.wakemed.org

Angela D. Christie
Title: Chief Executive Officer, President Company: AC Counseling and Consultant, Inc. Address: 5610 S.E. Second Street, Ocala, FL 34480 United States BUS: Counseling Company P/S: Counseling At-Risk Children, Consulting MA: Local D/D/R: Overseeing Company Activities, Counseling Families, Individuals, Groups and Children with Behavioral Disorders EDU: Master's Degree in Counseling and Psychology, Webster University A/A/S: American Psychotherapy Association; The Florida Accreditation Program
Email: achristie56@aol.com
URL: http://www.cambridgewhoswho.com

Rodney Christner
Title: President Company: Rodney's Concrete and Construction Address: 2994 Hwy. 1, Washington, IA 52353 United States BUS: Construction Company P/S: Decorative Concrete and Contracting Services MA: Regional D/D/R: Overseeing Daily Operations, Budgets, Contracts, Accounts Receivable and Payable, Contracting, Advertising and Marketing H/I/S: Restoring Old Cars, Fishing, Boating, Outdoor Activities with Family EDU: High School Graduate A/A/S: Better Business Bureau
Email: rodneys@iowatelecom.net

Keith A. Christopherson
Title: Business Acct/Financial Secretary Company: Heat and Frost Industries and Asbestos Workers Local #34 Address: 95 Empire Drive, St Paul, MN 55103 United States BUS: Mechanical Insulation Customer Service P/S: Industrial and Commercial Mechanical Insulation MA: Regional EXP: Mr. Christopherson's expertise is in management. H/I/S: Hunting EDU: Two Years of Coursework, Technology College
Email: keithins34@eschelon.com

Tata E. Chuneo
Title: Retired Company: Chuuk State Government FSM Address: 417 E Lanikaula, Hilo, HI 96720 United States BUS: Real Estate P/S: Commercial Real Estate MA: Local H/I/S: Movies, Reading, Watching TV EDU: Master's Degree, University of Southern Maine
Email: debbijeam2000@yahoo.com

Martha S. Chupp
Title: Owner, President Company: Chupp Jewelers, Inc Address: 662 Main St, Lafayette, IN 47901 United States BUS: Jewelry, Retail P/S: All Types of Sterling Silver Jewelry, Clock and Watch Repairs MA: Local D/D/R: Conducting Insurance and Quick Sales Appraisals, Caring for Customers H/I/S: String Beads, Football, Basketball, NASCAR EDU: Graduate, Medican Beauty College, Logansport, IN (1961)
Email: myrcchupp@aol.com

Mr. Ryan C. Chuston
Title: President Company: Lymphedema and Wound Care Institute Address: 10023 S. Main Street, Suite C-8, Houston, TX 77025 United States BUS: Healthcare P/S: Physical Therapy, Medical Equipment, Medical Services MA: National D/D/R: Administrating More Than Three Outpatient Rehabilitation Facilities, Attending Hearings, Conducting Audits, Appealing to Insurance Companies on Behalf of Patients, Ensuring Patients are Protected and Getting the Benefits to which They are Entitled H/I/S: Jogging, Mountain Biking, the Outdoors EDU: Bachelor's Degree in Legal Law, University of Houston (1992); Coursework, Loyola Law School A/A/S: National Republican Congressional Committee; Star Drug Committee A/H: Republican of the Year (2006); Congressional Medal of Distinction (2006) C/VW: Aids Foundation, Houston; American Cancer Society; Volunteer, Houston Institute of Attitude and Healing; Juvenile Diabetes Foundation
Email: ryanchuston@aol.com
URL: http://www.lymphedemainstitute.org

Rita C. Cicchinelli
Title: Classroom Teacher Company: Mohonasen Central School District Address: 2719 Hamburg Street, Schenectady, NY 12303 United States BUS: School District P/S: Education MA: International D/D/R: Teaching Second-Grade Students H/I/S: Reading, Traveling, Country Line Dancing EDU: Master's Degree in Reading for the Classroom Teacher, SUNY at Albany A/A/S: New York State Education Association; National Education Association
Email: rcicchinelli@mohonasen.org

Perry Cichanowicz
Title: Registered Nurse, Corporate Chief Executive Officer Company: RN Associates, CBRF Address: 10941 W. Saint Martins Road, Franklin, WI 53132 United States BUS: Nonprofit Group Homes for the Developmentally Disabled P/S: Residential Care for the Mentally Ill, Blind, Autistic and Physically Disabled Adults Suffering from Chronic Mental Illness MA: Regional D/D/R: Practicing Psychiatric Nursing for Adolescent, Adult and Geriatric Patients, Offering Long-Term Care for the Developmentally Disabled, Helping Release Patients from an Institutional Setting to a Group Home Setting H/I/S: Weight-Lifting, Fishing, Hunting, Running, Camping, Hiking, Traveling EDU: Master's Degree in Nursing, Cardinal Stritch University; Bachelor of Science in Nursing, University of Wisconsin-Milwaukee A/A/S: Public Speaker, Mental Health Advocacy
Email: info@CambridgeWhosWho.com
URL: http://www.cambridgewhoswho.com

Jerry P. Cigarran
Title: President Company: Classic Carpet Dyers Inc. Address: 11310 U.S. Highway 301 N., Thonotosassa, FL 33592 United States BUS: Time-Honored Carpet Service Company P/S: Restoring, Cleaning, Repairing and Dyeing Carpets MA: Regional D/D/R: Cleaning and Repairing Carpets, Managing Two Locations with 34 Employees, Overseeing All Operations for the Commercial and Residential Business, Training Staff Members H/I/S: Fishing, Camping, Hunting EDU: Associate Degree in Business Management, Hillsborough Community College (1989) A/A/S: Bay Area Apartment Association
Email: ccd1981@aol.com

Nicholas G. Ciminera
Title: Staff Nurse Company: Warminster Hospital Address: 7 Suzanne Court, Richboro, PA 18954 United States BUS: Suburban Hospital P/S: Healthcare Services MA: Local D/D/R: Monitoring the Progressive Care Unit, Offering Wound Care, Conducting Professional Assessments, Communicating with Patients H/I/S: Reading, Watching Football EDU: Bachelor of Science in Nursing, Holy Family University, PA (2006) CERTS: Pursuing Certified Registered Nurse Practitioner, La Salle University; Registered Nurse, National Council of State Board of Nursing (2007) A/A/S: Lecturer and Recruiter, American Nurses Association
Email: nciminera@gmail.com
URL: http://www.cambridgewhoswho.com

Jeffrey W. Ciolino
Title: Occupational Therapist Company: Lifelong Therapeutics, Inc Address: 143 Chardonnay Drive, East Quogue, NY 11942 United States BUS: Rehabilitation Center P/S: Occupational Therapy for Seniors MA: Local EXP: Mr. Ciolino's expertise includes geriatric management and rehabilitation. H/I/S: Wrestling Coach EDU: Bachelor of Science, Syracuse University
Email: lifelong@optonline.net

Charles T. Ciravolo
Title: Managing Director Company: Center for Wealth Preservation Address: 6800 Jericho Turnpike, Suite 202W, Syosset, NY 11791 United States BUS: Financial Management Agency P/S: Financial Planning, Long-Term Investment Services, Estate Planning, Business Solutions, Personal Solutions, Education Planning, Retirement Planning MA: Regional EXP: Mr. Ciravolo's expertise includes financial planning and management. D/D/R: Overseeing Estate Planning and Long-Term Investment Services, Recruiting, Selecting and Training New Associates H/I/S: Boating EDU: Bachelor of Science in Business Marketing, SUNY Plattsburgh (1989) CERTS: Licensed Health, Life and Automobile Insurance Agent in Series 7, 24, 6 and 63, States of NY, FL and PA A/A/S: Chairman, South Huntington Educational Foundation; Advisory Board Member, C.W. Post Campus, Long Island University
Email: cciravolo@finsvcs.com
URL: http://www.cwpmetro.com/new/cwpmetro

Cecilia Cisneros
Title: Teacher Company: Turlock United School District, Osborn School Address: 201 N. Soderquist Road, Turlock, CA 95380 United States BUS: School P/S: Education MA: Local D/D/R: Teaching English to Spanish Speaking Children H/I/S: Reading, Spending Time with Family EDU: Bachelor of Arts in Education, California State University A/A/S: California Teachers Association; Turlock Teachers Association A/H: Teacher of the Year 2006-2007 C/VW: Church
Email: ccisneros@turlock.k12.ca.us

Norma Jean Cisneros
Title: Owner Company: Southern Underground Services, LLC Address: 151 N. Broad Street, Winder, GA 30680 United States BUS: Energy Firm P/S: Distributing Electricity MA: Regional D/D/R: Managing Administrative Duties H/I/S: Spending Time with her Family, Watching Movies, Cooking, Exercising C/VW: Jehovah's Witnesses
Email: njcnjc@bellsouth.net

Mrs. Tiffany A. Claassen, RDH
Title: Registered Dental Hygienist Company: Blakeney Dental Center Address: 9335 Blakeney Professional Drive, Charlotte, NC 28277 United States BUS: Private Practice Dental Office P/S: General Dentistry and Cosmetics MA: Local D/D/R: Sterilizing Tools, Treating and Educating Patients H/I/S: Photography and Scrapbooking EDU: Bachelor of Science in Biology, Wingate University, North Carolina CERTS: Registered Dental Hygienist, Central Piedmont Community College, North Carolina A/A/S: Alpha Chi (1998-2001) A/H: Student of the Year in Dental Hygiene (2006); Biology Student of the Year (1998) C/VW: Local Church, Youth Leader
Email: jeffntiffany@andersonrepublic.com
URL: http://www.cambridgewhoswho.com

Ronald K. Claiborne
Title: President Company: King James Publication and Consulting Services, LLC Address: 1095 Green Level Road, Scottsburg, VA 24589 United States BUS: Consulting Firm P/S: Consulting Services MA: National D/D/R: Conducting Motivational Leadership Workshops, Working with Small Business Owners H/I/S: Writing, Reading EDU: Doctoral Degree in Organizational Leadership and Management, University of Phoenix; Master of Business Administration, University of Phoenix (2004); Bachelor of Science in Accounting, Saint Paul's College C/VW: Local Church
Email: kjpcs2004@yahoo.com
URL: http://www.cambridgewhoswho.com

Edward F. Clapp
Title: Senior Test Technician **Company:** Coherent, Inc. **Address:** 1280 Blue Hills Avenue, Bloomfield, CT 06002 United States **BUS:** Manufacturing Company **P/S:** Laboratory Analytical Instruments Includes Carbon Dioxide Laser Head Systems **MA:** International **D/D/R:** Overseeing Production Alignment **H/I/S:** Playing Soccer **EDU:** Pursuing Bachelor's Degree in Engineering
Email: ed.clapp@coherent.com
URL: http://www.coherent.com

Carlyn A. Clark
Title: Teacher **Company:** Daughtry Elementary School **Address:** 150 Shiloh Road, Jackson, GA 30233 United States **BUS:** Elementary School **P/S:** Education **MA:** Local **D/D/R:** Reading, Writing, Increasing Literacy **H/I/S:** Hiking, Knitting, Reading, Ice Skating **EDU:** Bachelor's Degree in Human Learning, Tennessee Wesleyan College **A/A/S:** Phi Delta Kappa; Georgia Reading Association; Professional Association of Georgia Educators Support for Teachers; Macintosh Reading Council **C/VW:** Afterschool Care, Boys Book Club, Relay for Life
Email: ilivetoteachkids@yahoo.com
URL: http://www.cambridgewhoswho.com

Dr. Christy F. Clark
Title: President **Company:** CFC Enterprises **Address:** 1201 Island Place East, Memphis, TN 38103 United States **BUS:** Privately Consulting Company **P/S:** Counseling, Leadership, Equal Employment Compliance and Appeals, Training **MA:** Regional, National **EXP:** Dr. Clark's expertise is in human resources administration. **H/I/S:** Walking, Interior Designing, Reading **EDU:** Ph.D. in Education and Leadership, University of Memphis (2003); Coursework, Madison University, Gulfport, Mississippi **A/A/S:** Leadership Memphis; Soror of the Year, Alpha Kappa Alpha Sorority; Alumnus of the Year, LeMoyne-Owen College; Meritan, Vice President, Board of Directors, Life Member, NAACP; Ashanti Literary Guild
Email: cfcenterprises@earthlink.net

Dorothy M. Clark
Title: Retired respiratory therapist **Address:** 1008 Vanderbilt Circle, Pflugerville, CO 78660 United States **BUS:** Healthcare, Medical Services **P/S:** Respiratory therapy services **MA:** Local **EXP:** Ms. Clark's expertise includes geriatrics and asthma education. **H/I/S:** Sewing **EDU:** Master of Science, Jackson State University; Bachelor of Arts, LSU Medical School; Associate of Arts, Foothill College **A/A/S:** AARC, AEA
Email: granch@aol.com

Harry E. Clark
Title: Chief Executive Officer, Pharmacist **Company:** Clark Health Care **Address:** 330 Broad Street, Waverly, NY 14892 United States **BUS:** Pharmacy **P/S:** Surgical Supports **MA:** Local **D/D/R:** Selling Hearing Aids **H/I/S:** Photography **EDU:** Bachelor of Science, University of Albany **A/A/S:** Church
Email: info@CambridgeWhosWho.com

Jan W. Clark
Title: Exceptional Children's Instructor **Company:** Cherryville High School **Address:** 313 Ridge Avenue, Cherryville, NC 28021 United States **BUS:** High School **P/S:** High School Education, Core Curriculum Including Reading, Math, English, Science, Social Studies, Art, Music, History, Language Arts, Physical Education to Mentally Retarded and Handicapped Students **MA:** Regional **D/D/R:** Teaching Life and Job Skills, Shadowing Students in Work, Teaching All Core Subjects to Mentally Retarded and Handicapped Students **H/I/S:** Reading, Spending Time with her Grandchildren **EDU:** Bachelor's Degree, Sacred Heart College (1978) **A/A/S:** Professional Educators of North Carolina; Teacher of the Year (2003-2004
Email: janclark@gatson.k12.nc.us
URL: http://www.gatson.k12.nc.us

Julie L. Clark
Title: Regional Account Executive **Company:** Horizon Settlement Services, Inc. **Address:** 6 Garvins Falls Road, Concord, NH 03301 United States **BUS:** Title Company **P/S:** Title Insurance Sales **MA:** Regional **D/D/R:** Marketing **H/I/S:** Horseback Riding, Running, Writing, Spending Time at the Ocean Shore, Yoga, Eating Nutritional Foods **EDU:** Associate of Science, New Hampshire Technical Institute; Paralegal Degree, New Hampshire Technical Institute **A/A/S:** Home Builders and Remodelers Association of New Hampshire; New Hampshire Mortgage Bankers and Brokers Association; Concord Board of Realtors; Women's Council, New Hampshire Association of Realtors **C/VW:** Salvation Army, Horizons Kitchen of New Hampshire, Muscular Dystrophy Association, Boys & Girls Clubs of America, March of Dimes, Walk for Hunger, Society for the Protection of the Tress, American Cancer Society
Email: jclark@horizonsettlement.com

Laurie Clark
Title: Chief Executive Officer **Company:** LA CC Childcare Academy **Address:** 16619 Wyoming Street, Detroit, MI 48221 United States **BUS:** Pre School **P/S:** Safe Childhood Care and Education for Children Ages 2-13 Years and Children with Special Needs 24 Hours Care Available **MA:** Local **EXP:** Ms. Clark's expertise is in educational management. **H/I/S:** Racquet Ball **EDU:** Bachelor of Arts in Early Education, Union University; Master's Degree Coursework, Mary Grove College **A/A/S:** NAACP, 4C'S
Email: laurielorine@sbcglobal.net

Marjorie C. Clark
Title: Owner **Company:** American Drapery and Design **Address:** P.O. Box 4302, Casper, WY 82604 United States **BUS:** Interior Design Company **P/S:** Interior Design for Residential and Commercial Applications, Window Coverings **MA:** Local **D/D/R:** Designing Interiors, Window Coverings, Extensive Color Backgrounds and Historical Furnishings, Contracting, Preparing Bids, Overseeing Operations and Management **H/I/S:** Floral Designing, Reading Art History and Foreign Cultures **EDU:** Bachelor of Arts in Interior Design, Brigham Young University **CERTS:** Certified Hardiness Trainer, Hardiness Institute **A/A/S:** City of Casper Board of Adjustment; Parent Teacher Association, Paradise Valley Elementary School (1981-1991) **A/H:** Partners in Education Award (1992-1993) **C/VW:** Volunteer, Local School; Local Charitable Organizations; Church of Jesus Christ of Latter-day Saints
Email: marjorie.clark00@cwwemail.com
URL: http://www.americandraperydesign.com

Perry L. Clark
Title: Design Engineer **Company:** Pacific Satellite Connection **Address:** 1629 S Street, Sacramento, CA 95814 United States **BUS:** Broadcast, Service Provider **P/S:** Broadcast Industrial Service Provider **MA:** Western United States **EXP:** Ms. Clark's expertise includes broadcast design and operations engineering. **H/I/S:** Playing in One of Three Bands **EDU:** Five Years of Coursework in Music, California State University at Sacramento **A/A/S:** Society of Broadcast Engineers **C/VW:** Veterans, National Multiple Sclerosis Society
Email: olympicboys@mac.com
URL: http://www.pacsat.com

Roxanne L. Clark, MPA, FAAMA
Title: Chief Financial Officer **Company:** Great Lakes Cancer Management Specialists **Address:** 19229 Mack Avenue, Suite 24, Grosse Pointe Woods, MI 48236 United States **BUS:** Private Practice **P/S:** Healthcare, Diagnosis, Treatment **MA:** Local **EXP:** Ms. Clark's expertise includes strategic planning, finance and cancer program development. **H/I/S:** Sailing **EDU:** Master of Public Administration, University of Michigan **A/A/S:** ACCC; ACE; MHOS; AAMA **C/VW:** United Way, American Cancer Society, Hospice of Southeast Michigan
Email: rclark@greatlakescms.com
URL: http://www.greatlakescms.com

Traci L. Clark
Title: Owner **Company:** Finial **Address:** 2590 Copper Ridge Drive, Steamboat Springs, CO 80487 United States **BUS:** Interior Design **P/S:** High-End Residential and Commercial Interior Designs **MA:** International **D/D/R:** Consulting with Clients to Correctly Represent their Style and Uniqueness **H/I/S:** Riding Horses, Traveling, Spending Time with her Pets **EDU:** Bachelor's Degree in Interior Design, University of Tennessee of Martin **C/VW:** Christian Youth Program, Youth Life, Weiner Sports Club, Come Let's Dance, Whiteman School
Email: finialdesigns@yahoo.com
URL: http://www.finialdesigns.com

Alisan P. Clarke
Title: Owner **Company:** A. Clarke Studio **Address:** 2907 Stratford Drive, Austin, TX 78746 United States **BUS:** Art Studio **P/S:** Art Therapy and Education **MA:** National **D/D/R:** Working with Geriatric, Bipolar and Depressed Patients, Healing through Art **EDU:** Bachelor of Fine Arts, The University of Texas at Austin **CERTS:** Registered Nurse, University of Pennsylvania **A/A/S:** Austin Parks Foundation **C/VW:** Executive Board Member, Local Women Printmakers Associations
Email: alisanclarke@yahoo.com
URL: http://www.cambridgewhoswho.com

Laurie Ann Clarkson
Title: Teacher **Company:** Sacred Heart School **Address:** 110 Thompson Drive, Troy, MO 63379 United States **BUS:** Catholic School **P/S:** Education **MA:** Local **D/D/R:** Teaching Elementary Education **H/I/S:** Traveling, Spending Time with Family, Scrap Booking, Photography **EDU:** Pursuing Master's Degree in Education, Missouri Baptist University; Bachelor of Science in Elementary Education, Missouri Baptist University; Pursuing Reading Specialist Credential, Missouri Baptist University **A/A/S:** Missouri State Teachers Association; American Society of Curriculum Development; National Christian Educators Association; National Catholic Educators Association **C/VW:** Relay for Life, St. Vincent de Paul, Christian Charities
Email: ibew1@centurytel.net
URL: http://www.cambridgewhoswho.com

Mr. Charles J. Clausen
Title: Vice President **Company:** Builder Direct Blinds **Address:** 659 Auburn Avenue N.E., Suite 401, Atlanta, GA 30312 United States **BUS:** Window Covering Wholesaler **P/S:** Custom Window Coverings to Enhance a Home's Comfort, Appearance and Feel through Blinds and Plantation Shutters **MA:** Regional **D/D/R:** Overseeing Builder Development, Expanding the Company to Work with New Home Builders, Training, Promoting Sales **H/I/S:** Golfing, Reading, Traveling **EDU:** Coursework, University of Georgia **A/A/S:** National Association of Home Builders; Atlanta Association of Home Builders
Email: chad@bdblinds.com
URL: http://www.bdblinds.com

Theodore R. Clay Jr.
Title: Owner **Company:** Clay's Painting **Address:** 1293 Watson Road, Hollandale, MS 38748 United States **BUS:** Painting, Dry Wall Installation **P/S:** Residential, Commercial and Industrial Improvements **MA:** Local **D/D/R:** Spraying, Brushing, Installing Drywall **H/I/S:** Writing Poetry and Short Stories **EDU:** Bachelor's Degree in Education, Mississippi Valley State University; Coursework in Journalism, University of Kansas **A/A/S:** American Legion; Veterans Association **C/VW:** Disabled American Veterans
Email: xclay-19@aol.com
URL: http://www.cambridgewhoswho.com

James T. Clayton
Title: Superintendent of Maintenance **Company:** Kansas City Area Transportation Authority **Address:** 1200 E. 18th Street, Kansas City, MO 64108 United States **BUS:** Transit Agency **P/S:** Development, Management and Coordination of Public Transportation **MA:** Regional **D/D/R:** Overseeing the Maintenance and Repair Departments, Managing Environmental Affairs **H/I/S:** Fishing, Hunting **EDU:** College Coursework
Email: jclayton@kcata.org
URL: http://www.kcata.org

Linda Clegg
Title: School Nurse Manager **Company:** Taunton Public Schools **Address:** 50 Williams Street, Taunton, MA 02780 United States **BUS:** School District **P/S:** Education **MA:** Local **D/D/R:** Supervising Over 20 Nurses, Staffing Full-Time and Part-Time Nurses, Maintaining and Implementing State Policies, Treating Asthma, Diabetes and Allergies **H/I/S:** Walking, Eating Healthy Food, Exercising **EDU:** Master of Science in Health Services Management, Lesley University (1998); Bachelor of Science in Nursing, Northeastern University (1985) **A/A/S:** National Association of School Nurses
Email: lclegg@tauntonschools.org
Email: linda.clegg@cwwemail.com
URL: http://www.cambridgewhoswho.com

Mr. Steven A. Clemens
Title: Managing Member **Company:** Cowest Insurance Associates, LLC **Address:** P. O. Box 101387, Denver, CO 80250 United States **BUS:** Proven Leader Dedicated to Excellence in the Commercial Insurance Industry **P/S:** Commercial Insurance Brokerage Services **MA:** International **D/D/R:** Analyzing Customer Risks, Formulating Insurance Rates, Forming Solutions, Overseeing Customer Safety, Insurance Services for Oil and Gas Industries, Mining Companies, Athletic Clubs and Social Service Organizations **H/I/S:** Collector's Cars **EDU:** Bachelor of Arts Degree in Liberal Arts and English Literature with a Minor in Broadcast Production, University of Texas (1970) **A/A/S:** Professional Independent Insurance Association; Certified Insurance Counselors
Email: steve@cowest.com
URL: http://www.cowest.com

Ruben J. Clement
Title: President, Chief Executive Officer **Company:** Sierra View Contractors, Inc. **Address:** P.O. Box 2733, Rancho Cordova, CA 95741 United States **BUS:** California-Licensed Residential Remodeling Corporation **P/S:** High Quality Contracting, Renovations, Remodeling, Window and Door Replacement, Residential Services **MA:** Northern California **D/D/R:** Managing Contracts and Crews, Supervising and Coordinating Projects **H/I/S:** Playing Basketball, Water Sports, Riding Motorcycles, Playing Poker **EDU:** Bachelor of Science in Business Management, Golden Gate University (1992) **A/A/S:** Rancho Cordova Chamber of Commerce; Building Trades Association
Email: sierraviewrj@sbcglobal.net
URL: http://www.cambridgewhoswho.com

Heather D. Clements
Title: First Grade Teacher **Company:** Hermitage Springs School, Tompkinsville Elementary School **Address:** 1522 Clementsville Road, Red Boiling Springs, TN 37150 United States **BUS:** Public School **P/S:** Education for Prekindergarten through 12th-Grade Students **MA:** Regional **D/D/R:** Teaching All Subjects to First Grade Students **H/I/S:** Sports **EDU:** Master of Arts Plus 30 in Elementary Education, Tennessee Technology University (1994) **A/A/S:** Who's Who Among America's Teachers
Email: heather.clements.monroe@kyschools.org
URL: http://www.clay-lea.k12.tn.us

Keith A. Clements
Title: Owner **Company:** Keith Clements Enterprise **Address:** 8014 Mango Avenue, Apt. 48, Fontana, CA 92336 United States **BUS:** Merchandising Company **P/S:** Bobble Heads **MA:** National **D/D/R:** Advocating for Renters **H/I/S:** Writing Screenplays **EDU:** Bachelor's Degree in Communication Studies, University of California at Santa Barbara **A/A/S:** Kiwanis Club of Fontana **C/VW:** American Cancer Society's Relay for Life, Agade House
Email: keclem923@aol.com
URL: http://www.cambridgewhoswho.com

Yolanda A. Clements
Title: Director of Rehabilitation, Physical Therapist **Company:** Senior Living Concepts **Address:** 3880 Via Lucero, Santa Barbara, CA 92311 United States **BUS:** Healthcare Facility **P/S:** Healthcare, Rehabilitation **MA:** Local **D/D/R:** Treating Geriatric and Joint Replacement Patients, Supervising Restorative and Clinical Instruction, Administering Hands-On Therapy **H/I/S:** Hiking, Walking her Dogs, Arranging Flowers, Gardening, Spending Time with Family **EDU:** Bachelor of Science in Physical Therapy, University of California at North Ridge **CERTS:** License of Cosmetology **C/VW:** World Vision, Habitat for Humanity, Church, WWF, Sierra Club
Email: yolandac@nwbeccorp.com
URL: http://www.cambridgewhoswho.com

Clara L. Clerkley
Title: Supervisor of the Department of Women **Company:** Lighthouse Church of God in Christ **Address:** 2127 S. Corinth Street, Dallas, TX 75227 United States **BUS:** Church, Human Services **P/S:** Religion **MA:** Local **D/D/R:** Training, Mentoring, Life Coaching, Counseling on Motherhood **H/I/S:** Reading **EDU:** Diploma, W.W. Wilson High School **A/A/S:** Church of God in Christ **C/VW:** Outreach Ministries, Local Hospital, Local Nursing Homes
Email: michael_cl_c@sbcglobal.net
URL: http://www.cambridgewhoswho.com

Theresa N. Clevenger
Title: Director of Vocal Music **Company:** Switzerland of Ohio School District **Address:** 304 Mill Street, Woodsfield, OH 43793 United States **BUS:** School District **P/S:** Education **MA:** Regional **D/D/R:** Teaching Music Education **H/I/S:** Teaching Music Lessons, Playing Tennis **EDU:** Pursuing Master's Degree in Education, Muskingum College; Bachelor of Arts in Music Education, West Liberty State College
Email: theresaclevenger@yahoo.com
URL: http://www.cambridgewhoswho.com

Patricia L. Clifford
Title: Registered Nurse **Company:** Blake Medical Center **Address:** 2020 59th Street W., Bradenton, FL 34207 United States **BUS:** Rehabilitation Center **P/S:** Rehabilitation Services **MA:** Local **EXP:** Ms. Clifford's expertise includes subacute care, charge nursing and wound care. **H/I/S:** Traveling, Antiquing **EDU:** Associate of Arts in Education, Manatee Community College **CERTS:** Registered Nurse, Manatee Community College **A/A/S:** American Association for Respiratory Care; Psi Beta **C/VW:** First Baptist Church
Email: pclifford7@yahoo.com
URL: http://www.cambridgewhoswho.com

Marie T. Climaldi-Brand
Title: Registered Nurse, Ombudsman **Company:** Florida's Long-Term Care Ombudsman Program **Dept:** Elder Affairs **Address:** 4040 Esplanade Way, Tallahassee, FL 32399 United States **BUS:** Nonprofit Organization **P/S:** Advocacy Services for the Elderly People who Need Long-Term Care Facility **MA:** Local **D/D/R:** Litigating for the Elderly **H/I/S:** Gardening, Traveling, Cruising **CERTS:** Registered Nurse, Misericordia Hospital School of Nursing, States of Florida, Pennsylvania and New Jersey; Certified Nursing Administrator, National League for Nursing **A/A/S:** Top Speaker, Withlacoochee Speakers Bureau; Chairwoman, The Sumter County Elder Advisory Committee; Former President, Homeowners' Association **A/H:** Golden Choice Award, Department of Elder Affairs, FL; Nominated, Council, Ombudsman (2007) **C/VW:** St. Timothy Catholic Church, Lady Lake
Email: mtb203@embarg.com

Martina R. Cline, MS
Title: Registered Nurse, CMS Member Services Liaison **Company:** Pediatric Primary Care Children's Medical Services Network **Dept:** Member Services Liaison **Address:** 1515 East Silver Spring Blvd, Suit 213, Ocala, FL 34470 United States **BUS:** 1) Healthcare for Children with special needs. 2) Music Writer, Vocalist and Performer. **P/S:** 1) Children's Medical Services Network (CMSN) is a managed system of care for children with special healthcare needs (medical, behavioral, or developmental). 2) Writing and Performing original music, Member of Taxi, GoGirls, America's Singer's and SongWriters Of America and SonicBids **MA:** 1) Florida 2) International **D/D/R:** 1) Pediatric care coordination services, Gastroenterology, Oncology and Internal Medicine. 2) Writing music and performing **H/I/S:** Caring for her Animals, Writing Music Lyrics and Melodies, Performing her Music, Gardening. **EDU:** Associate Degree in Nursing, Santa Fe Community College, Gainesville, Florida, 1998 **A/A/S:** Phi Beta Kappa **A/H:** International Songwriting Competition Finalist, Singers and Songwriters Of America **C/VW:** Breast Cancer Awareness, American Cancer Society
Email: atinynurs@aol.com
URL: http://www.broadjam.com/bunbun

Mark R. Clinkscales
Title: Teacher **Company:** Leesville Road High School **Address:** 8409 Leesville Road, Raleigh, NC 27613 United States **BUS:** High School Dedicated to Excellence in Education **P/S:** High School Instruction and Curriculum **MA:** Local **D/D/R:** Earth Science Teacher for the Ninth-Grade High School Students, Teaching Three Classes a Day, Approximately 30 Students in Class, Teaching in Class Resource as well as the Freshman Academy, Coaching Baseball and Football at School **H/I/S:** Hunting, Fishing, Football **EDU:** Master of Arts in Teaching, University of North Carolina, Chapel Hill (2001) **A/A/S:** North Carolina High School Coaches Association
Email: mclinkscales2@wcpss.net
URL: http://www.leesville.org

Dexanne B. Clohan
Title: Senior Vice President, Chief Medical Officer **Company:** HealthSouth Corporate **Address:** 1 HealthSouth Parkway, Birmingham, AL 35243 United States **BUS:** Healthcare Service Provider **P/S:** Healthcare **MA:** National **D/D/R:** Administrative Medicine, Physical Medicine, Rehabilitation **H/I/S:** Skiing **EDU:** MD, The George Washington University School of Medicine **A/A/S:** American Medical Association; American Academy of Physical Medicine and Rehabilitation; Alabama Society of Physical Medicine and Rehabilitation; Medical Association of the State of Alabama **C/VW:** Arthritis Foundation, Cerebral Palsy; United Way
Email: dexanne.clohan@healthsouth.com
URL: http://www.healthsouth.com

Christy L. Clouse
Title: Educator, Varsity Cheerleading Coach **Company:** Coffee County Central High School **Address:** 593 Big Oak Drive, Manchester, TN 37355 United States **BUS:** Public High School **P/S:** Secondary Level Education **MA:** Regional **D/D/R:** Sixteen, Teaching Honors Level Physics, Physical Science and Psychology, Coaching the Varsity Cheerleading Team **H/I/S:** Reading, Enjoying Sports **EDU:** Master's Degree in Administrative Leadership, Tennessee Tech University (2006); Bachelor's Degree in Physics, Middle Tennessee State University (1990) **A/A/S:** Treasurer, State Cheerleading Coaches Association; National Education Association; Tennessee Education Association
Email: clousec131@aol.com
URL: http://www.coffeecountyschools.com/chs/

Douglas N. Cloutier
Title: Drafter, Designer **Company:** Apollo Professional Services **Address:** 31 Pelham Road, Salem, NH 03079 United States **BUS:** Contracting Company **P/S:** Contracting Services **MA:** National **D/D/R:** Drafting, Designing, Creating Educational and Commercial Facilities, Designing Layouts **H/I/S:** Public Speaking **EDU:** Coursework, Roger Williams University; Coursework, Porter and Chester Institute **CERTS:** Dale Carnegie Course **C/VW:** Connecticut Public Television; Toastmasters International
Email: dnclout@msn.com
URL: http://www.cambridgewhoswho.com

Miles Lee Clyde
Title: Owner **Company:** MLC Consulting Services, LLC **Address:** 7245 W Emile Zola Avenue, Peoria, AZ 85381 United States **BUS:** Engineering Consulting **P/S:** Failure Mechanics, Failure Analysis **MA:** National **D/D/R:** Metallurgical Failure Analysis **H/I/S:** Glamour Photography, Building, Running, Car Restoration **EDU:** Oxford University, Doctorate in Mechanical Engineering, Licensed **A/A/S:** Society of Automotive Engineers, American Society of Mechanical Engineering, ASM International, National Society of Professional Engineering
Email: mclyde2@cox.net

Amanda Bulette Coakley, Ph.D., RN
Title: Nurse Scientist, Staff Specialist **Company:** Massachusetts General Hospital **Address:** 55 Fruit Street, Boston, MA 02114 United States **BUS:** Hospital **P/S:** Healthcare **MA:** Local **D/D/R:** Nursing Administration, Researching, Educating **EDU:** Ph.D., Boston College School of Nursing; Master of Science in Nursing, Northeastern University; Bachelor of Science in Nursing, Northeastern University; Associate Degree in Nursing, Lasell Junior College **A/A/S:** North American Nursing Diagnosis Association; Eastern Nursing Research Society; International Association for Human Caring; Sigma Theta Tau **C/VW:** Church
Email: mandicoakley@comcast.net

Nelson E. Coates
Title: Film Production Designer **Address:** 4225 Klump Avenue, Studio City, CA 91602 United States **BUS:** Entertainment Firm **P/S:** Film Production Such as Motion Picture **MA:** National **D/D/R:** Creating Visual Effects, Overseeing Settings and Costumes **H/I/S:** Traveling **EDU:** Bachelor of Mass Communication, Abilene Christian University (1984) **A/A/S:** Academy of Motion Picture Arts and Sciences; Academy of Television Arts & Sciences; Art Directors Guild
Email: necoates@pacbell.net
URL: http://www.cambridgewhoswho.com

Alicia M. Cobb, RD, LDN, CDE
Title: Clinical Dietitian **Company:** Compass Group-Morrison **Address:** 9542 Kings Parade Boulevard, Charlotte, NC 28273 United States **BUS:** Leader in the Healthcare Industry **P/S:** Quality Healthcare Services to those in Need **MA:** Regional **D/D/R:** Treating Patients for High Cholesterol, Diabetes, Hypertension and Obesity **H/I/S:** Lifting Weights, Running, Practicing Zumba, Cooking **EDU:** Bachelor of Science in Human Nutrition, Winthrop University (1997) **CERTS:** Certificate of Training in Adult Weight Management **A/A/S:** Charlotte Dietetic Association; North Carolina Dietetic Association; American Dietetic Association; Nutritionist of the Year, Women Infant and Children, North Carolina (2000)
Email: alicia.cobb@carolinashealthcare.org
URL: http://www.carolinashealthcare.org

Rita Cobb
Title: Payroll Manager **Company:** Benson Industries, LLC **Address:** 14179 S. W. Walnut Lane, Tigard, OR 97223 United States **BUS:** Commercial Glass Company **P/S:** System Design, Unitized Curtainwall, Monumental Storefronts, Custom Skylights, Stone Support Systems, Metal Plate Cladding, Engineering, Shop and Fabrication Drawings, Production Orders, Structural Calculations, Prototype Testing, Air and Water Resistance, Structural Wind Loading, Seismic Racking, Thermal Performance, Sound Transmission, Quality Assurance, Project Management, Field Installation, Fabrication and Assembly **MA:** International **D/D/R:** Overseeing Payroll for 500 Employees in Several States, Distributing Payments to Contractors, Managing Employee Benefit Programs **H/I/S:** Hiking, Swimming, Tennis, Bicycling **EDU:** Associate Degree in Social Services, Mid-Plains Community College
Email: razgy4him@yahoo.com
URL: http://www.bensonglobal.com

Claudia N. Coburn
Title: Teacher **Company:** Teacher Rockwall ISD, Nebbie Williams Elementary School **Address:** 350 Dalton Road, Rockwall, TX 75087 United States **BUS:** School **P/S:** Education **MA:** Local **D/D/R:** Teaching Sixth through Tenth-Grade Students, Writing Books **H/I/S:** Reading, Gardening, Writing Children's Books **EDU:** Master's Degree in Media Technology, Texas A&M University; Bachelor of Science in Science, Texas A&M University **CERTS:** Certified Science Educator **A/A/S:** Texas State Teachers Association; Association of Texas Professional Educators **A/H:** Elementary Teacher of the Year Award 2002 **C/VW:** Church, Habitat for Humanity
Email: ccoburn@rockwallisd.org
URL: http://www.cambridgewhoswho.com

Theresa A. Cocheran
Title: Title I Teacher **Company:** Boone County Schools **Address:** 69 Avenue B, Madison, WV 25130 United States **BUS:** School **P/S:** Education **MA:** Local **D/D/R:** Reading Specialist **H/I/S:** Woodworking, Crocheting, Reading **EDU:** Master of Arts Plus 63 in Reading, Marshall University **A/A/S:** Association for Supervision and Curriculum Development; Delta Kappa Gamma; West Virginia Reading Association; International Reading Association; American Federation of Teachers **C/VW:** Susan G. Komen Breast Cancer Foundation
Email: tacteaches@hotmail.com
URL: http://www.cambridgewhoswho.com

Ms. Diana G. Cochran, BFA

Title: President, Owner **Company:** Vann Jernigan Florist, Inc. **Address:** 1529 Piedmont Avenue N.E., Suite C, Atlanta, GA 30324 United States **BUS:** Retail Florist **P/S:** Floral Vase Arrangements for Large Companies, Parties, Birthdays, Weddings and Funerals **MA:** Local **D/D/R:** Designing Floral Vases for Corporate Offices and Events Including Weddings **H/I/S:** Photography, Drawing **EDU:** Bachelor of Fine Arts, The Cleveland Institute of Art (1991) **CERTS:** Certified Master Florist
Email: vannjernigan@bellsouth.net
URL: http://www.vjflorist.com

Annette Cockrell

Title: State Public Assistance Coordinator for the Governor's Office Homeland Security **Company:** James Lee Witt and Associates, Cockrell Consultants **BUS:** Nonprofit Organization **P/S:** Public Assistance, Global Emergency Personnel and Consultants, Disaster Recovery Services **MA:** International **D/D/R:** Coordinating Public Assistance, Rebuilding Infrastructures, Global Options for Emergency Management, Coordinating Management Teams, Working for Relief from Natural Disasters **H/I/S:** Traveling **EDU:** Bachelor of Science in Emergency Management, Arkansas Technical University (2004); Bachelor of Arts in Sociology, Arkansas Technical University (2004) **A/A/S:** Emergency Management Association; Governor's Earthquake Council
Email: annettec565@msn.com
URL: http://www.wittassociates.com

Lisa A. Cocola

Title: Second-Grade Teacher **Company:** Van Rensselaer Elementary School **Address:** 25 Van Rensselaer Drive, Rensselaer, NY 12144 United States **BUS:** Elementary School **P/S:** Primary Education **MA:** Local **D/D/R:** Teaching Language Arts, Mathematics, Science, Social Studies and Grammar for Second-Grade Students **H/I/S:** Bowling, Reading, Making Crafts, Spending Time at the Church, Lecturing, Reading the Liturgy, Planning all Holiday Masses **EDU:** Master of Education, The College of Saint Rose; Bachelor of Science in Elementary Education, The College of Saint Rose, Associate Degree in Early Childhood Education, Hudson Valley Community College **CERTS:** Certification in Early Childhood Education **A/A/S:** New York State United Teachers **A/H:** President's List; Recipient, Service and Appreciation Award for Education **C/VW:** Local Church; Local Police League; Fire Fighters Association; Special Olympics; American Cancer Society
Email: bellafem2002@yahoo.com

Dona L. Coffey

Title: Teacher (Retired) **Company:** Albany County School District 1 **Dept:** Beitel Elementary **Address:** 811 S. 17th Street, Laramie, WY 82070 United States **BUS:** School District **P/S:** Education **MA:** Regional **D/D/R:** Teaching Kindergarten Students **H/I/S:** Reading, Spending Time with her Grandchildren, Caring for her Dogs, Growing Flowers, Stained Glass Art **EDU:** Master's Degree in Early Childhood and Elementary Education, University of Wyoming; Bachelor's Degree in Elementary Education, Hastings College **A/A/S:** Wyoming Education Association; National Education Association **A/H:** Teacher Achievement Award, Arch Coal (2001) **C/VW:** Local Charitable Organizations; Wyoming Territorial Park; Laramie Plains Museum
Email: dcoffey@wyoming.com
URL: http://www.cambridgewhoswho.com

Larry Dean Coffey

Title: Laboratory Technician, Quality Assurance Professional **Company:** The George E. Failing Company **Dept:** Quality Assurance **Address:** 2215 S. Van Buren Street, Enid, OK 73703 United States **BUS:** Manufacturing Company **P/S:** Portable Drilling and Special Order Rigs **MA:** International **D/D/R:** Inspecting Drilling Rigs, Calibrating Gauges and Measuring Tools **H/I/S:** Playing Softball, Volleyball and Basketball, Bicycling, Traveling, Spending Time with his Family, Reading History, Photography **CERTS:** Industry-Related Training **C/VW:** Hope Outreach; Caring 4 Kids Foundation; United Way of America; American Red Cross
Email: duke_coffey@yahoo.com
Email: calibrate@gefco.com
URL: http://www.cambridgewhoswho.com

Susan Cogan

Title: Vice President **Company:** Brodies Pub Inc. **Address:** 3262 East Main Street, Mohegan Lake, NY 10547 United States **BUS:** Restaurant **P/S:** Restaurant, Special Occasions **MA:** Local **D/D/R:** Financial Operations, Customer Relations **H/I/S:** Traveling and Gardening **EDU:** Bachelor of Arts in Fine Arts, Chestnut Hill College, PA **A/A/S:** Westchester Association of Women Business Owners **C/VW:** Fundraiser, St. Jude Children's Research Hospital
Email: BroPub@optonline.net
URL: www.brodiespubny.com

Norma L. Coghill

Title: Account Manager **Company:** Arthur J. Gallagher and Co. **Address:** 505 N. Brand Boulevard, Suite 600, Glendale, CA 91203 United States **BUS:** Insurance Company **P/S:** Insurance Services **MA:** International **D/D/R:** Overseeing Professional Liability Management **H/I/S:** Hiking, Cooking, Baking, Bowling **EDU:** College Coursework
Email: norma_coghill@ajg.com
URL: http://www.ajg.com

Heather A. Cohen

Title: Human Resources Manager **Company:** Weiser, LLP **Address:** 135 West 50th Street, New York, NY 10020 United States **BUS:** CPA **P/S:** CPA Firm which Provides Accounting Services to the Public **MA:** Regional **D/D/R:** Scheduling of Audit Engagements, Recruiting New Hires, Generalist **H/I/S:** Baseball Games, Traveling, Reading **EDU:** Bachelor's Degree in Accounting, SUNY Albany; Master's Degree in Human Resources, NYU **A/A/S:** New York State Society of CPA's, Society for Human Resource Management, American Cancer Society, American Heart Association, New Jersey State Society
Email: hcohe@weiserllp.com

Judy F. Cohen

Title: Faith Based Counselor **Company:** Positive Inspiration Faith Based Counseling **Address:** 17045 El Camino Real, Suite 218, Houston, TX 77058 United States **BUS:** Counseling Center **P/S:** Faith Based Counseling, Discovering the Root of Emotions by Studying the Mind, Body, Soul and Spirit **MA:** Regional **D/D/R:** Premarital and Marriage Counseling, Counseling Victims of Domestic Violence and Clients Suffering from Depression, Chemical Dependence and Self-Esteem Issues, Anger Management **H/I/S:** Cooking **EDU:** Pursuing Master's Degree; Bachelor's Degree in Biblical Counseling, Ashwood University (2005) **A/A/S:** Faith Based Counselor Training Institute; Mental Health Association of Greater Houston
Email: elderjjjudy@yahoo.com

Mr. Stan Cohen, JD

Title: Owner **Company:** Private Law Office **Address:** 41 Park Avenue, Suite 17F, New York, NY 10016 United States **BUS:** 1) Private Law Practice 2) Your Hampton Home Real Estate Company **P/S:** 1) Legal Services for Residents of New York 2) Sales of Real Estate **MA:** New York City, Hamptons **D/D/R:** Practicing Corporate Real Estate Litigation, General and Divorce Law Litigation as a Solo Attorney in the States of New York, New Jersey, Florida and Washington D.C., Building Luxury Homes in the Hamptons with an Emphasis on Green Homes **H/I/S:** Playing Tennis, Swimming, Spending Time with his Puppy **EDU:** JD, New England School of Law (1976) **A/A/S:** Public Speaker at United Nations; World Future Society; Board Member, Parish Museum Business Council; USA Club of Rome; Past President, Board Member, The Earth Society; NGO Committee on Human Settlements (2002-2006) **A/H:** Editor and publisher of turn around management assoc of NY TMANY newsletter (4x year) Earth society journal contributor; published story and honeymoon Manhattan bride magazine; Report on rising coast of energy and effects on economy 1974; written manuscripts for plays and movies. **C/VW:** Board Member of The Group Center
Email: s@stancohen.com
URL: http://www.yourhamptonhome.com

Elizabeth Carol Cohoon

Title: Teacher **Company:** Cornersville High School **Address:** 323 S. Main Street, Cornersville, TN 37047 United States **BUS:** High School **P/S:** Education **MA:** Local **D/D/R:** Teaching Eighth-Grade English and Language Arts **H/I/S:** Reading, Writing, Traveling, Tennessee Walking Horses, Extreme Adventures **EDU:** Pursuing Degree in Administration and Supervision, Middle Tennessee State University; Master's Degree in Curriculum and Instruction, Middle Tennessee State University; Bachelor of Art in English, Middle Tennessee State University **A/A/S:** National Education Association; Tennessee Education Association; Marshall County Education Association; Middle Tennessee State University Phi Kappa Phi; Cornersville Church of Christ; National Council of Teachers of English **C/VW:** American Cancer Society
Email: cohoonc@k12tn.net
URL: http://www.cambridgewhoswho.com

Gina Coker

Title: Insurance Specialist **Company:** Department of Veterans Affairs, Philadelphia VAROIC **Address:** 5000 Wissahickon Avenue, Philadelphia, PA 19144 United States **BUS:** Federal Government Agency **P/S:** Government Life Insurance **MA:** National **D/D/R:** Life Insurance for Veterans **H/I/S:** Bowling, Reading, Swimming, Traveling, Spectator Sports such as Boxing, Football, Gymnastics, Track and Field **EDU:** Coursework, University of Pennsylvania; Coursework, Carnegie Mellon University **CERTS:** Certificate of Proficiency in Qualitative Research, Burke Institute; Certificate of Completion in Instructor Training Development, Veterans Benefits Academy **A/A/S:** Vice President, Mount Zion Willing Workers Ministry **A/H:** Silver Medal, Excellence in Government Awards (2006); Bronze Medal, Excellence in Government Awards (2005); Extra Step Awards; Examiner Carey Award Program **C/VW:** Action Aids, Inc.
Email: gina.coker@va.gov
URL: http://www.insuranceva.gov

Ms. Margaret C. Colavito

Title: Artist, Director, Owner **Company:** Upstairs Art Gallery, Inc. **Address:** 896 Bergen Avenue, Jersey City, NJ 07306 United States **BUS:** Art Gallery **P/S:** Painting Classes, Art Framing Services, Fine Art Sales, Art Exhibitions, Education **MA:** Regional **D/D/R:** Teaching Oil Painting, Managing Administrative Duties, Accounts Receivable and Payable, Ensuring Customer Satisfaction, Framing Artwork, Overseeing Gallery Operations **H/I/S:** Painting, Playing Tennis, Collecting Antiques **EDU:** Associate Degree in Liberal Arts, Jersey City Junior College (1955); Coursework in Art, New York University; Coursework, Seton Hall University; Coursework, Fairleigh Dickinson University **A/A/S:** The Jimmy King Civic Association; Jersey City 9-11 Memorial Committee; Chairman, Treasurer, Former President, The Hudson Artists of New Jersey; League of Women Voters; Salmagundi Art Club; New Jersey Chapter, American Artists Professional League; Westfield Art Association **A/H:** Artist of the Year Award
Email: upstairsartgalleryinc@netzero.net
URL: http://www.cambridgewhoswho.com

Bev Colbert

Title: Board Secretary, Business Manager **Company:** Highland Community Schools **Address:** 1715 Vine Avenue, P.O. Box B, Riverside, IA 52327 United States **BUS:** School District **P/S:** Education **MA:** Regional **D/D/R:** Finance Budgeting and Compiling the Certified Annual Report **H/I/S:** Master Gardner **EDU:** Bachelor of Arts in Business Administration, University of Iowa **CERTS:** Certified, Iowa School **A/A/S:** Iowa Association of School Business Officials; Association of School Business Officials International, Golden Keeper National Honor Society **C/VW:** Relay for Life
Email: bcolbert@highland.k12.ia.us
URL: http://www.highland.k12.ia.us

Deborah P. Cole

Title: Project Consultant **Company:** The DCH Group **Address:** 2477 Spring Garden Cove, Cordova, TN 38016 United States **BUS:** Consulting Company **P/S:** Hospitality Consulting **MA:** International **D/D/R:** Developing Projects, Marketing, Hospitality Consulting, Counseling Adolescents, Adults, Groups and Individuals **H/I/S:** Gardening, Swimming, Reading, Traveling **EDU:** Bachelor's Degree in Psychology and Education, East Carolina University; Coursework in Education, Psychology and Leadership Studies **A/A/S:** Network of Memphis; Eating Disorders Coalition of Tennessee **C/VW:** Former Director, Transformation Center for Women
Email: dpcole56@yahoo.com
URL: http://www.thedchgroup.com

Jeanie R. Cole

Title: Test Department Leader **Company:** OSI Electronics **Address:** 2385 E. Pleasant Valley Road, Camarillo, CA 93012 United States **BUS:** Contract Manufacturing Company **P/S:** Medical, Aerospace, Military and Telecommunications Product Manufacturing **MA:** International **D/D/R:** Supervising 20 People, Overseeing Products that Flow through the Test Department, Analyzing Feedback, Customer Service **H/I/S:** Reading, Shopping, Painting, Ceramics **EDU:** Associate Degree in Science, ITT Technical Institute (1998)
Email: jcole@osielectronics.com
URL: http://www.osielectronics.com

Augodelia P. Coleman

Title: Teacher **Company:** Rivermont Elementary School, Hamilton County Department of Education **Address:** 3330 Hixson Pike, Chattanooga, TN 37415 United States **BUS:** Public Elementary School **P/S:** Education for Students in Kindergarten through Fifth-Grade **MA:** Regional **D/D/R:** Teaching all Subjects to Kindergarten Students **H/I/S:** Singing, Theater, Arts and Crafts, Spending Time with her Children and Husband **EDU:** Master's Degree in K-12 Arts and Education, Tusculum College (2001); Bachelor of Science in Early Childhood Education and Elementary Education, Knoxville College (1992) **CERTS:** Certified Urban Teacher Specialist **A/A/S:** National Education Association; Tennessee Education Association; International Reading Association; Zeta Phi Beta; Tennessee Mathematics Teachers Association; Hamilton County Education Association
Email: augodelia@hotmail.com
URL: http://www.hcschools.org/rivermont

Jennifer C. Coleman

Title: Owner **Company:** Pinnacle Appraisal Group **Address:** 7310 Harvest Hill Drive, Rewlett, TX 75089 United States **BUS:** Real Estate Appraiser **P/S:** Appraisal **MA:** Local **D/D/R:** Customer Service **H/I/S:** Gardening **A/A/S:** COFC, PTA
Email: jcoleman@pinnacleappraisalgroup.com
URL: www.pinnaclehomeappraisal.com

Dr. Samantha Coleman

Title: Chiropractic Physician **Company:** Chiropractic Solution Center **Address:** 287 Independence Blvd, Suite 311, Virginia Beach, VA 23464 United States **BUS:** Healthcare Chiropractor **P/S:** Chiropractic Care, Consulting, Clinical Biomechanics of Posture **MA:** Virginia **D/D/R:** Chiropractic Care, Clinical Biomechanics of Posture, Consulting **H/I/S:** Running, Kickboxing, Swimming, Working Out **EDU:** Doctor of Chiropractic **A/A/S:** International Chiropractic Association, Florida Chiropractic Association CBP, Nonprofit
Email: chirosolutions@verizon.net

Tammi D. Coleman, BS

Title: Fifth-Grade English-Language Arts Teacher **Company:** Apex Academy **Address:** 16005 Terrace Road, E. Cleveland, OH 44112 United States **BUS:** Primary Charter School Serving Almost 600 Students **P/S:** Rigorous Academic Program Using Open Court Reading and Saxon Mathematics **MA:** Local **D/D/R:** Teaching Language Arts and Reading, Mentoring, Overseeing Summer School **H/I/S:** Reading, Music, Jazz **EDU:** Bachelor of Science in Elementary Education, Baptist Bible College and Seminary (1982) **CERTS:** Certified in Language Arts and Reading
Email: 64tcoleman@nationalheritageacademies.com
URL: http://www.cambridgewhoswho.com

Donald E. Coles

Title: Architect **Company:** Dharma Graphics **Dept:** Environmental Design **Address:** 607 S. Third Street, Apartment Three, Philadelphia, PA 19147 United States **BUS:** Architectural Firm **P/S:** Computer-Aided Design, Planning Documents for Permits **MA:** Regional **D/D/R:** Designing, Creating Computer-Aided Documents, Managing Retail and Commercial Plans **H/I/S:** Practicing Yoga, Teaching Transcendental Meditation, Exercising, Dancing Salsa, Merengue and Bachata **EDU:** Coursework, California State University at Berkley (1980); Coursework in Design, California College; Bachelor of Arts in Environmental Design, California State University, Berkley; Diploma, William Tennent High School (1966) **A/A/S:** The World Peace Government **C/VW:** Mother Bethel African Methodist Episcopal Church
Email: donald_coles@yahoo.com
URL: http://www.servicemagic.com

Ruth C. Collado

Title: Reading Coach **Company:** St. Lucie County School Board **Address:** 516 S.E. Nome Drive, Port St. Lucie, FL 34984 United States **BUS:** School District **P/S:** Education **MA:** Regional **D/D/R:** Analyzing and Discussing Immediate Intervention Strategies, Coaching Teachers in the Implementation of New Reading Methods and Strategies **H/I/S:** Woodworking, Scrapbooking **EDU:** Master of Elementary Education, Plus 30, University of Massachusetts (1991); Bachelor's Degree in Elementary Education, University of Puerto Rico (1972) **CERTS:** Certified Teacher, Endorsement in Reading and English for Speakers of Other Languages, State of Florida; Certified Literacy Coordinator, Lesley University, Boston, MA (2000) **A/A/S:** International Reading Association; St. Lucie County Reading Council **A/H:** Distinguished Educator of the Year Award; Floresta Elementary School, FL (2004)
Email: ruthccollado@bellsouth.net

Nancy J. Colletti, M.Ed.

Title: Teacher **Company:** Rowland Unified School District **Address:** 19500 Nacora Street, Rowland Heights, CA 91748 United States **BUS:** School **P/S:** Education **MA:** Local **D/D/R:** Teaching Music, Performing as Choral Director, Facilitating the Education of the Gifted and Talented Students **H/I/S:** Enjoying Music, Practicing Vocal Development, Participating in European Study Tours in Fine Arts, Taking Care of his Cocker Spaniels **EDU:** Graduate Coursework, University of South California, University of California Los Angeles, Film and Entertainment Chapman College, Pepperdine University, University of San Diego, University of LaVerne; Master of Music Education, Whittier College; Bachelor of Arts in Music, Whittier College; Elementary, Secondary Credential in Music and Math **A/A/S:** Los Angeles Philharmonic; American Society of Composers; American Film Institute; Roger Wagner Chorale; William Hill Chorale; Association of Rowland Educators; California Teachers Association; National Education Association; President, Phi Beta; American Guild of Musicians Association; Lifetime Member, California Scholarship Federation; Film Music Society; American Association of University Women **A/H:** Who's Who Among America's Teachers (Seven Times); Recognized Scholar, Whittier College; California Honorary Service Award; Teacher of the Year, Shelyn School; Bank of America Award in Fine Arts **C/VW:** Kayne West Foundation; Benefit Sponsor, UNICEF Snowflake Ball; Schepens Eye Center; Crystal Cathedral; Patron, Music Matters, Los Angeles Philharmonic
Email: info@CambridgeWhosWho.com
URL: http://www.cambridgewhoswho.com

Lori Collie-Rodriguez

Title: Office Manager **Company:** Gurney F Pearsall, MD, PA **Address:** 7900 Fannin Street, Suite 3200, Houston, TX 77054 United States **BUS:** Healthcare Center **P/S:** Pediatrics **MA:** Local **EXP:** Ms. Collie-Rodriguez's expertise is in nursing. **EDU:** Bachelor of Science in Nursing, Houston Baptist University **CERTS:** Registered Nurse **A/A/S:** Medical Office Management Association; Professional Association of Healthcare Office Management
Email: ldcollie@hotmail.com
URL: http://www.cambridgewhoswho.com

Kenneth L. Collier

Title: Chief Executive Officer **Company:** From the Heart Records, LLC **Address:** PO Box 583, Stone Mountain, GA 30086 United States **BUS:** Music Distributor **P/S:** Music Production, Distribution **MA:** National **D/D/R:** Producing **H/I/S:** Baseball, Basketball, Music **EDU:** Associate Degree in Communications, United States Navy **A/A/S:** ASCAP
Email: eyecfth@yahoo.com
URL: www.myspace/eyecfth

Deborah A. Collins

Title: Registered Sales Assistant **Company:** First Citizens Investor Services **Address:** 520 Westwood Shopping Center, Fayetteville, NC 28314 United States **BUS:** Investment Financial **P/S:** Full Service Brokerage Firm **MA:** Local **D/D/R:** Placing Trades, Mutual Funds, Equity Trades, Full Service of Clients and Organizing **H/I/S:** Reading and Movies **EDU:** Bachelor' s Coursework in TheologyTrue Vine Ministry World Outreach Fellowship, Family Bible College of Fayetteville
Email: dctom1@embarqmail.com

Hattie M. Collins

Title: Behavior Health Registered Nurse **Company:** Little Company of Mary Hospital **Address:** 9501 S. California Avenue, Evergreen Park, IL 60620 United States **BUS:** Nonprofit Catholic Community Hospital **P/S:** Healthcare Services Including Inpatient and Outpatient Care, Oncology Center, Emergency Room Services and Orthopedics **MA:** Local **D/D/R:** Serving in the Adolescent Psychiatry Ward, Supervising Nursing Staff, Discharging Patients, Consulting with Patients **H/I/S:** Walking, Bowling, Sewing, Shopping **EDU:** Pursuing Ph.D., Loyola University; Master of Science in Health Services Administration, University of St. Francis (1998); Bachelor of Science in Liberal Arts, University of St. Francis (1988) **A/A/S:** Illinois Nurses Association; American Nurses Association; Black Nurses Association
URL: http://www.lcmh.org

Kathleen Kaufman Collins

Title: Fourth-Grade Teacher **Company:** Clark Shawnee Local School District **Dept:** Reid School **Address:** 3640 E. High Street, Springfield, OH 45505 United States **BUS:** Elementary and Middle School Facilities **P/S:** Regular Core Curriculum Including Reading, Math, English, Science, Social Studies, Art, Music, History, Physical Education, Language Arts, Computers **MA:** Regional **D/D/R:** Teaching All Core Subjects in Title I School to Grades One through Eight, Mentoring Students, Tutoring After School, Ensuring Open Communication **H/I/S:** Gardening, Reading, Traveling, Authoring a Book **EDU:** Master's Degree in Mentoring and Teacher Leading, Wright State University (1987); Bachelor of Arts in Education, Wittenberg University (1973) **CERTS:** Certified K-8; Certified K-12 Special Education and Gifted and Talented; Certification in Mental Health; Certification in Severe Behavioral Disorders **A/A/S:** LPCD; Phi Delta Kappa; Ohio Education Association; Arts Alive; Arts Advisory Council; National Education Association; Kappa Delta Epsilon; Council for Arts in the Classroom; Strong Advocate, Arts in the Classroom
Email: cs_kcollin@k12server.mveca.org
URL: http://www.clark-shawnee.k12.oh.us

Michael B. Collins

Title: President **Company:** Michael Collins & Company, Inc **Address:** P.O. Box 125, Finchville, KY 40022 United States **BUS:** Landscape Contracting Company **P/S:** Residential and Commercial Property Lawn Maintenance **MA:** Local **D/D/R:** Landscaping **H/I/S:** Working Out **EDU:** Coursework in Business Management, University of Louisville
Email: milelawncare@bellsouth.net
URL: http://www.mcclawns.com

Ruth A. Collins

Title: Administrative Leader **Company:** Faribault Public Schools **Dept:** Roosevelt Elementary School **Address:** 925 Parshall Street, Faribault, MN 55021 United States **BUS:** Public School **P/S:** Education **MA:** Local **EXP:** Ms. Collins' expertise includes educational leadership in regular and special education. **D/D/R:** Conducting Early Childhood Special Education Testing and Assessments, Developing Programs for Autism and other Several Developmental Disabilities, Coordinating Administrative Duties **H/I/S:** Gardening, Quilting, Spending Time with her Children, Hunting Elk, Deer and Duck, Fishing **EDU:** Master of Special Education in Early Childhood Education, Minnesota State University, Mankato; Bachelor of Science in Elementary Education, Minnesota State University, Mankato **CERTS:** Licensed Principal; Licensed Special Education Director **A/A/S:** Minnesota Elementary School Principals' Association; Minnesota Association of School Administrators; Minnesota Administrators for Special Education; National Association of Elementary School Principals
Email: tnrranch@hotmail.com
URL: http://www.faribault.k12.mn.us

Thomas R. Collins Jr.

Title: Mechanical Designer **Company:** K & L Microwave, Inc. **Address:** 2250 Northwood Drive, Salisbury, MD 21801 United States **BUS:** Manufacturing Company **P/S:** Communication Equipment, Microwave Filters and Associated Products **MA:** International **D/D/R:** Developing Mechanical Solutions, Detail and Assembly Compliance Documentation, Training Drafters **H/I/S:** Browsing on the Computer, Spending Time with his Family, Participating in Church Activities, Building Street Rods **EDU:** Bachelor of Science in Applied Science, University of Maryland, College Park (19780 **C/VW:** Church
Email: trcollinsjr@msn.com

Kenneth E. Collis

Title: Special Education Teacher **Company:** Fairfax County Public Schools **Dept:** Robinson Secondary School **Address:** 5035 Sideburn Road, Fairfax, VA 22032 United States **BUS:** School District **P/S:** Special Education **MA:** Regional **EXP:** Mr. Corliss' expertise includes special education and curriculum development. **H/I/S:** Photography, Reading History **EDU:** Bachelor of Science in Psychology, George Mason University (2001) **CERTS:** Licensed Teacher (2005) **C/VW:** Council for Exceptional Children
Email: kenny.collis@fcps.edu
URL: http://www.fcps.edu

Ms. Desiree Colomina

Title: Chief Operating Manager **Company:** Sweet Dreams Cakes **Address:** 5220 N.W. 109th Avenue, Doral, FL 33178 United States **BUS:** Bakery **P/S:** Cakes, Deserts and Other Baked Foods **MA:** Local **EXP:** Ms. Colomina's expertise includes business management and decorating cakes. **D/D/R:** Overseeing Operations **H/I/S:** Traveling, News Reporting **EDU:** Bachelor of Arts in Broadcast Communication Studies, Minor in Journalism, Barry University, Miami Shores, FL **A/A/S:** National Association of Hispanic Journalists; National Association of Broadcasters; National Organization of Entertainment Journalism **C/VW:** America Developing Smiles; St. Jude Children's Research Hospital
Email: desiree@sweetdreamscakes.net
URL: http://www.sweetdreamscakes.net

Victor M. Colon

Title: President **Company:** VC Health Staffing Corporation **Address:** 17620 N.W. 67th Avenue, Apartment 1123, Hialeah, FL 33015 United States **BUS:** Healthcare Staffing Agency **P/S:** Nurse Recruitment and Medical Staffing for Hospitals **MA:** Local **D/D/R:** Consulting, Recruiting Spanish-Speaking Medical Staff, Managing Business Operations **EDU:** Bachelor of Arts in Accounting, Finance and Human Resources, Universidad Interamericana de Puerto Rico
Email: victor-colon@hotmail.com
URL: http://www.cambridgewhoswhos.com

Mr. Richie Colonna

Title: Project Manager **Company:** Piazza Construction, Ltd. **Address:** 4431 W. Crawford Street, Denison, TX 75020 United States **BUS:** General Contracting and Construction Company **P/S:** Construction **MA:** Regional **D/D/R:** Project Management, Field Supervision, Supervising Subcontractors and In-House Laborers **H/I/S:** Fishing, Fly-Fishing, Spending Time with his Children **A/A/S:** Knights of Columbus **C/VW:** Church
Email: richie@piazza-construction.com
URL: http://www.piazza-construction.com

Carla Amy Colunga
Title: Coordinator of Sales Opportunities **Company:** Verizon Wireless **BUS:** Wireless Network Service **P/S:** Wireless Voice and Data Services **MA:** International **D/D/R:** Working in All Sales Departments, Multitasking, Acting Support Person for the Retail Team, Managing Relations with Retailers Including Best Buy, Wal-Mart and Costco **EDU:** Coursework in Computers, Cumberland County College **A/A/S:** Former Member, Women of the World; President, Women's Ministry, Chestnut Assembly of God; Former Youth Leader, Chestnut Assembly of God
Email: carla.colunga@verizonwireless.com
URL: http://www.verizonwireless.com

Nedra LaQuawn Colvin
Title: Real Estate Appraiser **Company:** Nedra L. Colvin Appraisals Services **Address:** 501 Salt Flat Road, Lewiston, CA 96052 United States **BUS:** Real Estate Agency **P/S:** Real Estate Appraisals **MA:** Regional **EXP:** Ms. Colvin's expertise is in real estate appraisal services. **D/D/R:** Conducting Real Estate Appraisals, Reviewing Market Values, Interacting with Realtors, Consulting with Clients **H/I/S:** Reading, Traveling **EDU:** Coursework, Contra Costa College **CERTS:** Certified Real Estate Appraiser **A/A/S:** California Association of Realtors; Appraisal Institute; National Association of Realtors
Email: nedraandfrank@com-pair.net
URL: http://www.cambridgewhoswho.com

Ariadne K. Comas
Title: 1) Mental Health Clinical Social Worker 2) Independent Consultant **Company:** 1) Louisiana Department of Health and Hospitals 2) Private Counseling **Address:** 1519 S. Allen Street, State College, PA 16801 United States **BUS:** 1) Hospital System 2) Sole Proprietorship **P/S:** 1) Healthcare Services 2) Counseling Services Including Marriage and Family Counseling **MA:** Regional **D/D/R:** Overseeing Clinical Mental Health Services, Performing Individual and Group Therapy **H/I/S:** Traveling, Reading **EDU:** Master of Social Work, Tulane University (1970); Bachelor's Degree in Sociology, Upsala College, NJ (1968) **A/A/S:** National Association of Social Workers **C/VW:** Local Charitable Organizations; Director, Young Men's Christian Association
Email: acoma116@gmail.com
URL: http://www.cambridgewhoswho.com

Dorothy M. Combs
Title: Educator, Producer **Company:** Dorothy Combs and InPraise **Address:** 9715 S. Forest Avenue, Chicago, IL 60628 United States **BUS:** Sole-Proprietorship **P/S:** Religious Services **MA:** National **EXP:** Ms. Combs' expertise is in writing lyrics. **H/I/S:** Jazzercize, Playing Tennis, Playing the Piano and the Alto Saxophone **EDU:** Bachelor of Science in Education, Jackson State University; Coursework in Counseling, Roosevelt University **A/A/S:** American Society of Composers; WTTW **C/VW:** American Red Cross; Lincoln Center for the Performing Arts
Email: combs291@aol.com
URL: http://www.cambridgewhoswho.com

Sally Combs-Elliott
Title: Director of Women's Athletic Promotions (Retired) **Company:** Purdue University **Dept:** Women's Athletics **Address:** Mackey Arena, West Lafayette, IN 47906 United States **BUS:** University **P/S:** Higher Education **MA:** Regional **D/D/R:** Developing Curriculum, Conducting Athletic Programs **H/I/S:** Golfing, Decorating Home, Shopping, Reading **EDU:** Master of Science in Health Education, Indiana University; Bachelor's Degree in Physical Education and English, Indiana University **A/A/S:** President's Council, Purdue University **C/VW:** Volunteer, John Purdue Club; Trinity-by-the-Cove Episcopal Church
Email: scomes122@aol.com

Joyce A. Comer
Title: Special Education Teacher, Teacher of English to Speakers of Other Languages **Company:** Albuquerque Public Schools **Address:** 6400 Uptown Boulevard, Suite 115, East Albuquerque, NM 87111 **BUS:** Public School District **P/S:** Education **MA:** Local **D/D/R:** Teaching Special Education and English to Speakers of Other Languages, Academic Therapy **H/I/S:** Traveling, Gourmet Cooking, Mountain Biking, Walking **EDU:** Master of Art in Education and Multicultural Special Education, College of Santa Fe; Bachelor of Art in Sociology and Business, University of New Mexico **A/A/S:** Council for Exceptional Children; Southwest Literacy Association
Email: casheljoyce@msn.com

Neil J. Como
Title: Field Sales Manager **Company:** QSP, Reader's Digest **Address:** 107 Wildflower Lane, Middletown, CT 06457 United States **BUS:** Fundraising Company **P/S:** Publishing School Fundraising **MA:** Local **D/D/R:** School and Nonprofit Fundraising **H/I/S:** Traveling, Golfing **EDU:** Bachelor of Arts in Sports Administration Business, Springfield College, Massachusetts
Email: neil.como@rd.com

Charley E. Compton
Title: Vice President of Sales **Company:** Universal Business Equipment **Address:** 120 Porter Street, Bridgeport, CT 06606 United States **BUS:** Office Supplies and Technology Retailer **P/S:** Office Supplies, Furniture and Technology Products **MA:** Regional **D/D/R:** Creating New Business Opportunities, Collaborating with Office Suppliers and Furniture Manufacturers, CAD Program to help Customers Design their Office Furniture **H/I/S:** Playing the Guitar, Basketball, Attending Church **EDU:** Bachelor of Science in Psychology and Sociology, Evangel University (1978) **A/A/S:** Bridgeport Chamber of Commerce; Bridgeport Regional Business Council; Milford Chamber of Commerce; Trumbull Business Network
Email: charleyc@universal-business.com
URL: http://www.universal-business.com

Gina L. Comstock
Title: Physical Education and Swimming Teacher **Company:** East Junior High School **Address:** 831 Gobel Street, Rock Springs, WY 82901 United States **BUS:** Elementary and Middle School Facilities Dedicated to Excellence in Education **P/S:** Regular Core Curriculum including Reading, Math, English, Science, Social Studies, Art, Music, History, Physical Education, Language Arts, Computers **MA:** Regional **D/D/R:** Teaching Physical Education, Health and Swimming to First, Second, Third and Eighth-Grade Students **H/I/S:** Volleyball, Basketball, Softball, Bowling, Chasing Children **EDU:** Bachelor of Science Degree for K-12, University of Wyoming (1988) **C/VW:** Volunteer Coach, Soccer and T-Ball Little League
Email: info@CambridgeWhosWho.com
URL: http://www.sw1.k12.wy.us/schools/ejhs

Carolina Conde-Perry
Title: Director, Owner **Company:** El Pequeño Artista, LLC **Address:** 249 20th Street, Brooklyn, NY 11215 United States **BUS:** Bilingual Arts Center for Child **P/S:** Education in Language Arts for Children from 5 Months to 8 Years Old, Ballet, Salsa, Dance, Yoga, Art, Cooking, Music and Spanish Lessons **MA:** Local **D/D/R:** Teaching Cooking Courses, Directing the Studio, Creating the Curriculum and Lesson Plans, Marketing and Advertising **H/I/S:** Cooking, Scuba Diving, Pilates **EDU:** Master's Degree in Bilingual Education, Columbia University (1998) **A/H:** Outstanding Latino of the Year
Email: elpequenoartista@gmail.com
URL: http://www.elpequenoartista.com

Judy Starr Confer
Title: Executive Director **Company:** River of Time Museum **Address:** 12901 N. La Montana Drive, Fountain Hills, AZ 85268 United States **BUS:** Museum **P/S:** Historical Monuments Including History of the Lower Verde River Valley of Arizona and the Importance of Water in the Sonoran Desert **MA:** Local **EXP:** Ms. Confer's expertise is in petroglyphs. **D/D/R:** Studying Cultural Heritage, Overseeing Daily Operations **H/I/S:** Art **EDU:** Bachelor of Science in Spanish, Education and History, University of Illinois (1962) **A/A/S:** Museum Association of Arizona; Central Arizona Museum Association
Email: director@riveroftimemuseum.org
URL: http://www.riveroftimemuseum.org

Carolyn Patton Conley
Title: Certified Public Accountant **Company:** Carolyn P. Conley, CPA **Address:** 2916 W. 21st Street, Wichita, KS 67203 United States **BUS:** Accounting Firm **P/S:** Accounting Services for Income and Nonprofit Organizations **MA:** National **D/D/R:** Taxes, Nonprofit Audits **H/I/S:** Attending the Theater, Quilting **EDU:** Master's Degree in Accounting, Wichita State University (1967); Bachelor's Degree in Business Administration, Wichita State University (1966) **A/A/S:** American Institute of Certified Public Accountants; Leadership Wichita; Leadership Kansas; Leadership America; White House Conference on Small Business **C/VW:** Church; YWCA; Wichita Historical Museum; Old Cowtown Museum
Email: carolynconley@sbcglobal.net
URL: http://www.cambridgewhoswho.com

Mr. Michael P. Conley-Kuhagen
Title: Graduate **Address:** 6710 Elmwood Avenue, Apartment 306, Middleton, WI 53562 United States **BUS:** Higher Education Facility **P/S:** Graduate Studies **MA:** Regional **D/D/R:** Acting as a Social Worker **H/I/S:** Cooking, Bowling, Traveling **EDU:** Pursuing Master's Degree in Counseling, University of Wisconsin; Bachelor's Degree in Human Services, Emphasis on Social Work, Upper Iowa University (1999) **CERTS:** Certified Social Worker, State of Wisconsin (1999) **A/A/S:** Program Manager for Technical Work; Goodwill
Email: mconleykuhagen1@yahoo.com

Cynthia Lorraine Connell-Johnson
Title: Data Processor **Company:** Hillsborough County Public Schools **Address:** 901 E. Kennedy Boulevard, Tampa, FL 33602 United States **BUS:** School District **P/S:** Education **MA:** Tampa Bay **D/D/R:** Entering Statistical Data, Analyzing and Reporting Findings, Processing State Compliance **H/I/S:** Spending Time with her Family **A/A/S:** National Association of Educational Office Professionals **C/VW:** Relay for Life
Email: cindy.johnson@sdhc.k12.fl.us

Ms. Shryl L. Conner
Title: Trade Show Manager **Company:** Domestic Environmental Corp. **Address:** 2000 N. Andrews Avenue Ext., Pompano Beach, FL 33069 United States **BUS:** Marine Air Conditioning Manufacturer **P/S:** Air Conditioning for Boats **MA:** International **D/D/R:** Trade Show Planning, Production and Presentation **H/I/S:** Traveling, Cooking, Spending Time with Friends and Family **EDU:** Coursework in Marketing, Pennsylvania State University **A/A/S:** American Boat and Yacht Council; National Marine Manufacturers Association; **A/H:** Best in Show (2006)
Email: shryl.conner@dometicusa.com

Billie Kathrene Tussey Conrad
Title: Sixth-Grade Mathematics Teacher **Company:** Phillip A. Sharp Middle School **Address:** 35 Wright Road, Butler, KY 41006 United States **BUS:** Middle School **P/S:** Education **MA:** Pendleton County **D/D/R:** Teaching Sixth-Grade Math **H/I/S:** Reading, Spending Time with her Grandchildren, Traveling, Making Crafts **EDU:** Master's Degree in Music Education, Morehead State University; Bachelor's Degree in Music Education, Morehead State University **CERTS:** Rank I Certification, University of Kentucky **A/A/S:** Kentucky Education Association; National Education Association; National Council of Teachers of Mathematics; Kentucky Council of Teachers of Mathematics **C/VW:** St. Jude Children's Research Hospital, Mathalon, Berlin Baptist Church
Email: billieconrad@aol.com
URL: http://www.pendleton.kyschools.us

Angela Conrad-Francis
Title: President **Company:** Isas, Inc. **Address:** 5 Claridge Court, Greensboro, NC 27407 United States **BUS:** Multi-Service Professional **P/S:** Furnishing Consultation, Laundry Service, Volunteer Consulting, Human Resource Management **MA:** International **D/D/R:** Traveling to and Consulting for Furniture Manufacturers and Furniture Industry Professionals, Human Resource Management Services, Working with the Homeless, Training and Educating Employees **EDU:** College Coursework in Nursing **CERTS:** Furniture Appraising **C/VW:** Various Charities in the U.S. and South America
Email: sklar29@aol.com
URL: http://www.cambridgewhoswho.com

Bianca M. Constance
Title: Executive Assistant **Company:** Securities Industry and Financial Markets Association **Address:** 360 Madison Avenue, New York, NY 10017 United States **BUS:** Financial Market Trade Association **P/S:** Facilitating a Link Between Investors and Issuers Locally and Globally to Create Economic Growth and Financial Security **MA:** International **D/D/R:** Administration, Asset Management Group Work **H/I/S:** Reading, Completing Cross Stitch Patterns, Theater **EDU:** Bachelor of Arts in Opera, Virginia Commonwealth University (1981) **A/A/S:** International Association of Administrative Professionals; Public Speaker **A/H:** Published with Honors and Awards
Email: bconstance@sifma.org
URL: http://www.sifma.org

Sylvia J. Contreras
Title: Library Volunteer Coordinator **Company:** Santa Maria Public Library **Address:** 420 S. Broadway, Santa Maria, CA 93454 United States **BUS:** Public Library, Nonprofit Group **P/S:** Public Service, Information **MA:** Regional **D/D/R:** Fundraising, Public Relations **H/I/S:** Reading, Spending Time with Grandchildren **EDU:** Associate Degree in Business, Rancho Domingas Long Beach City College **CERTS:** Notary Public **C/VW:** Friends of the Libraries USA
Email: timeswelivein@hotmail.com

Alberto Convers
Title: Medical Doctor **Company:** Radiology Associates of South Florida **Address:** Miami, FL United States **BUS:** Private Practice Radiological Group **P/S:** Radiological Services, 50-55 Radiologists **MA:** South Florida **D/D/R:** General Radiology, Breast Imaging, Mammograms, Ultrasound Testing and Procedures **H/I/S:** Spending Time with his Family **EDU:** MD, Javeriana University, Bogota, Colombia (1973); Specialization in Radiology, Mount Sinai Hospital, Miami, FL **A/A/S:** American College of Radiology; Florida Radiological Society **C/VW:** Various Local Charities
Email: alconvers@yahoo.com

Mamie Louise Conway

Title: Deputy Director (Retired), Ordained Elder **Company:** 1) South Brooklyn Health Center 2) The African Methodist Episcopal Church **Address:** Aiken, SC 29803 United States **BUS:** 1) Medical Center 2) Church **P/S:** 1) Healthcare 2) Religious Services **MA:** Regional **D/D/R:** Establishing Administrative Policy and Procedure, Developing Community and School Health Programs, Establishing Open Door Prayer Ministry for the Community **H/I/S:** Traveling, Studying, Reading, Sewing, Cooking **EDU:** Master's Degree in Healthcare Administration, Long Island University (1979) **CERTS:** Registered Nurse, Mercy-Douglass Hospital School of Nursing, Philadelphia (1953) **A/A/S:** Board of Directors, Aiken Area Council on Aging; Aiken Outreach Ministry; Christian Educators Department for Youths and Adults **C/VW:** Prison Ministry; ACOM; Cumberland AME Church; Aiken Area Council on Aging
Email: revmamie@bellsouth.net
URL: http://www.cambridgewhoswho.com

Angela Michelle Cook

Title: Budget Analyst **Company:** United States Department of Agriculture **Dept:** Natural Resources Conservation Service **Address:** 143 Glenwood Drive, Monticello, AR 71655 United States **BUS:** Government Organization **P/S:** Public Services Including Agricultural Regulations **MA:** National **EXP:** Ms. Cook's expertise includes finance management, accounting and information systems. **H/I/S:** Playing Basketball, Exercising, Reading, Spending Time with her Children **EDU:** Master of Business Administration in Accounting and Global Information Technology (2003) **A/A/S:** Alpha Kappa Alpha; Phi Gamma Delta **C/VW:** Sweet Hope Missionary Baptist Church
Email: angela.cook@wdc.usda.gov

David Cook Jr.

Title: Chief Investigator (retired) **Company:** Contra Costa County District Attorneys Office **BUS:** Law Enforcement Agency **P/S:** Protecting and Serving **MA:** National **EXP:** Mr. Cook's expertise includes polygraphy and law enforcement. **H/I/S:** Collecting Coins, Fishing, Bowling **EDU:** Bachelor's Degree in Police Science, Emphasis on Criminology, California State University **A/A/S:** President, Polygraphy Association; United States Navy
Email: info@cambridgewhoswho.com

Gail Ann Cook

Title: Bookkeeper, Bartender **Company:** Heidelberg Lounge and Casino **Address:** 27 Division Road, Great Falls, MT 59404 United States **BUS:** Casino **P/S:** Recreation Including Food and Beverage Services and Gaming **MA:** Regional **D/D/R:** Bartending, Bookkeeping, Managing the Casino **EDU:** High School Education **A/A/S:** Montana Tavern Association; Cascade County Tavern Association **C/VW:** Special Olympics; MDA
Email: heidelberg@imt.net

Janet C. Cook

Title: Owner **Company:** Janet's Memories, Bridal and Formal Wear **Address:** 45 S. Maple Street, Hohenwald, TN 38462 United States **BUS:** Retail **P/S:** Formal Wear for Men, Women and Children **MA:** Regional **D/D/R:** Managing Company, Marketing Formal Wear for Men, Women and Children, Overseeing Sales and Rentals, Creating Wedding Gowns **H/I/S:** Swimming, Fishing, Oil Painting **EDU:** CSA, St. Mary's Technical School(1982) **A/A/S:** Chamber of Commerce; Sponsor, American Coed Pageant
Email: janetsmemories@bellsouth.net

Karen L. Cook

Title: President **Company:** EECOM **Address:** 1505 Columbia Drive NE, Albuquerque, NM 87106 United States **BUS:** Consulting **P/S:** Consulting Services, Public Policy and Programs **MA:** National **EXP:** Ms. Cook's expertise is in sustainable economic development. **D/D/R:** Operations; Assisting Corporations and Government in embracing sustain-ability; create analysis of Individual situations and a plan forward; Helping message and create policy and see to its implementation. **H/I/S:** Traveling **A/A/S:** National Association of Realtors; Lead AP; USGBC **A/H:** Awarded NAIOP Presidents Award for Excellence, 2001 Founding President of USGBC, New Mexico Chapter Awarded EPC Community Award for Excellence, 1997
Email: karen@eecominc.com
URL: http://www.eecom.com

Renay Cook

Title: Elementary Instructor **Company:** Prospect School **Address:** 5305 Terrace Road, East Cleveland, OH 44112 United States **BUS:** School **P/S:** Elementary School Dedicated to Excellence in Education **MA:** Regional **D/D/R:** Kindergarten Teacher, Teaching Entire Curriculum to Students, Having Students for a Full Day, Teaching Writing, Letter Writing and Math, Among Other Subjects, Mentoring, Private Tutoring, Consulting **H/I/S:** Walking, Traveling, Reading **EDU:** Master of Science Degree in Elementary Education, University of Akron (1979) **A/A/S:** Delta Sigma Theta Sorority, Inc.; Ohio Education Association; East Cleveland Education Association
Email: rcook3dst@msn.com

Dr. Stephen A. Cook

Title: Periodontist **Address:** 2114 Scott Street, Lafayette, IN 47904 United States **BUS:** Private Periodontist Practice **P/S:** Periodontal Work, Reconstructive Dentistry **MA:** Regional **D/D/R:** Performing Reconstructive Surgical Procedures, Maintaining Teeth and Dental Implants and Treating Periodontal Diseases **H/I/S:** Golfing **EDU:** Doctor of Dental Surgery, Indiana University (1978); Master of Science in Dentistry, Indiana University (1984) **A/A/S:** American Dental Association; American Academy of Periodontology; Indiana Dental Association; American College of Dentists
Email: scookdds@choiceonemail.com

Linda M. Cooke

Title: Dermatologist **Company:** Hannibal Clinic **Address:** 100 Medical Drive, Hannibal, MO 63401 United States **BUS:** Medical Clinic **P/S:** Healthcare **MA:** Regional **D/D/R:** Practicing General Medical Dermatology and Surgical Dermatology Including Treating Patients with Skin Cancer, Aesthetic, Cosmetic Dermatology, Overseeing Botox, Chemical Peels, Fillers and Laser Treatments, Working with Multispecialty Groups **H/I/S:** Traveling, Jogging, Spending Time with her Family **EDU:** MD, Uniformed Services University of the Health Sciences **A/A/S:** Missouri State Medical Association; Maryland Dermatology Society; American Academy of Dermatology; American Society of Cosmetic Dermatology and Aesthetic Surgery **A/H:** Award for America's Top Physician, Clinical Research Group (2004-2007) **C/VW:** Local Church; Shriners; March of Dimes; The Salvation Army
Email: delmcooke@rallstech.com
URL: http://www.hannibalclinic.com

Walter Cooks Jr.

Title: Senior Pastor **Company:** New Hope Missionary Baptist Church **Address:** 1567 S. Reservoir Street, Pomona, CA 91766 United States **BUS:** Church **P/S:** Spiritual Services **MA:** Regional **D/D/R:** Scheduling Church Activities, Directing Head Start Programs **H/I/S:** Playing Baseball **EDU:** Doctor of Theology, Reed College (1983); Master's Degree in Philosophy, Chapman University (1972) **A/A/S:** Civilian Conservation Corps; Former President, National Association for the Advancement of Colored People
Email: walter.cooks@cwwemail.com

Corey D. Cooley

Title: Vice President **Company:** Jesse E Cooley Jr Funeral Services Inc **Address:** 1830 S Fruit Avenue, Fresno, CA 93706 United States **BUS:** Funeral Home **P/S:** Provide Funeral Services at There Locations Throughout the San Joaquin Valley **MA:** Regional **D/D/R:** Embalmer and Funeral Director, Helping Families Through a Grieving Time **H/I/S:** Traveling **EDU:** Degree in Mortuary Sciences, Gupton Jones, Atlanta, GA **A/A/S:** Masonic Lodge, National Funeral Home Directors Association
Email: jecoojr@aol.com

Mr. Ryan B. Cooling

Title: Athletic Director **Company:** Presentation High School **Address:** 2281 Plummer Avenue, San Jose, CA 95125 United States **BUS:** Private All-Girls High School **P/S:** Regular Core Curriculum Including Reading, Mathematics, English, Science, Social Studies, History, Economics, Physical Education, Language Arts and Computers **MA:** Regional **D/D/R:** Managing All Sports Teams and Summer Camps, Overseeing Budgeting, Traveling, Hiring and Firing Employees, Working with the City on Renting City Facilities **H/I/S:** Volleyball **EDU:** Master of Business Administration, Phoenix University (2002) **A/A/S:** Public Speaker, Local Schools; National Federal High School Coaches Association; California State Athletic Director Association; National Interscholastic Athletic Administrators Association
Email: rcooling@pres-net.com
URL: http://www.pres-net.com

Angel Jo Coons

Title: Owner **Company:** With Help From Angel **Address:** 37756 Sutton Drive, Purcellville, VA 20132 United States **BUS:** Personal Assistance Business **P/S:** Personal Assistance, Cooking, Cleaning, Running Errands, Catering **MA:** Local **D/D/R:** Domestic Duties, Catering **H/I/S:** Reading, Cooking, Making Silk Flower Arrangements and Wreaths, Decorating her Home, Spending Time with her Children **A/A/S:** Eagles Club **C/VW:** Mountain View Elementary School, Parent-Teacher Organization
Email: angeljocoons@aol.com
URL: http://www.cambridgewhoswho.com

Claire Cooper

Title: Caregiver **Company:** Santa Barbara County **Address:** Santa Maria, CA 93454 United States **BUS:** Home Healthcare and Assisted Living Facility **P/S:** Assisted Living Services, Home Healthcare **MA:** Local **D/D/R:** Offering Home Healthcare Services Including Running Errands, Cooking Meals, Taking Patients to Doctor Appointments and on Outings, Offering Cleaning Services **H/I/S:** Spending Time with her Friends, Surfing the Internet, Reading, Playing with her Cats **CERTS:** Certificate in Medical Billing, Santa Barbara Business College (1999) **A/A/S:** Vineyard Church of Santa Maria, California
Email: angelical@yahoo.com

Gladys K. Cooper, RN

Title: Registered Nurse Program Director **Company:** Quantum Management **Address:** 12035 Milldale Road, Zachary, LA 70791 United States **BUS:** Full-Service Human Resources Company **P/S:** Effective Recruitment Solutions **MA:** National **D/D/R:** Administration, Charge Nursing, Caring for Patients, Quality Compliance **H/I/S:** Playing Piano **EDU:** Bachelor of Science in Nursing, Loyola University (1993) **A/A/S:** Association of Ambulatory Behavioral Health; Greater Baton Rouge Mental Health Board
Email: happynotes@cox.net
URL: http://www.quantum.ca

Laretha A. Cooper

Title: Child Care Specialist **Company:** Self-help Community Services, Inc. **Address:** 520 Eighth Avenue, Suite 5, New York, NY 10018 United States **BUS:** Home Care Agency **P/S:** Home Healthcare Management, Social Services, Home Childcare Services, Care of Disabled and Disadvantaged Children, Home Health Aide Services, Community and Guardian Law Services **MA:** Regional **D/D/R:** Conducting Field Visits, Ensuring Quality of Services, Supervising Home Health Aides, Overseeing Safety and Child Development, Customer Care and Solutions **H/I/S:** Swimming, Horseback Riding, Photography, Outdoor Sports **EDU:** Master of Science in Human Resource Management, The New School, NY (1998); Bachelor of Arts in Business Administration, St. Augustine's College, NC (1989) **CERTS:** Certification in Career Planning and Development, The New School, NY **A/A/S:** National Association for the Advancement of Colored People; National Coalition of 100 Black Women
Email: lanestle@aol.com

Molly Cooper

Title: Director of Safety and Technical Services **Company:** Vertical Technology Services, LLC **Address:** 20140 Scholar Drive, Hagerstown, MD 21742 United States **BUS:** Technology Company **P/S:** Erection, Maintenance and Repair of Towers and Antennas, Safety Training **MA:** National **EXP:** Ms. Cooper's expertise includes direction of the installation, maintenance and repair of communication towers. **D/D/R:** Installing, Maintaining and Repairing Communication Towers, Directing Safety Training **H/I/S:** Studying Medieval History, Making Home Improvements **EDU:** Associate Degree in Criminal Justice, Hagerstown Community College **CERTS:** Anritsu; OSHA 500; Crosby Rigging Trainer; Miller/Troll Trainer
Email: molly@verticalts.com
Email: aerin@myactv.net
URL: http://www.verticalts.com

Wilbur L. Cooper

Title: President, Owner **Company:** C&S Truck Services, Inc. **Address:** 2130 Lucerne Park Road, Winter Haven, FL 33881 United States **BUS:** Trucking Company **P/S:** Transportation, Trucking Tanker and Produce **MA:** Eastern United States **D/D/R:** Dispatching, Driving, Maintenance **H/I/S:** Drag Racing his '67 Dodge Dart, High-Performance Cars **EDU:** Diploma, Winter Haven High School
Email: info@CambridgeWhosWho.com
URL: http://www.cambridgewhoswho.com

Bobby L. Copeland Jr.

Title: Owner **Company:** AHI Construction **Address:** 21588 Coral Rock Lane, Wildomar, CA 92595 United States **BUS:** Construction Company **P/S:** Drywall, Painting, Framing, Tile, Decorative Concrete, Plumbing, Electrical, Roofing, Windows, Doors, Patio Covers, Room Additions and More **MA:** Local **D/D/R:** Building Homes, Remodeling Existing Homes Including Bathrooms and Kitchens **H/I/S:** Riding Harley Davidson Motorcycles **EDU:** High School Graduate **CERTS:** B License; Home Improvement Certification; Asbestos Certification **A/A/S:** Better Business Bureau; RSB
Email: ahibobbuilder@aol.com
URL: http://www.admirablehomeimprovements.com

John T. Copeland

Title: Principal **Company:** Hillsborough County School District, Memorial Middle School **Address:** 4702 N. Central Avenue, Tampa, FL 33603 United States **BUS:** Middle School **P/S:** Education **MA:** Regional **D/D/R:** School Administration **H/I/S:** Golfing, Spending Time with his Family **EDU:** Master's Degree in Education, University of La Verne; Bachelor's Degree in Sociology, University of California at Davis; Diploma, Booker T. Washington High School **A/A/S:** Association for Supervision and Curriculum Development; American Federation of School Administrators; Vietnam Veteran, United States Army **C/VW:** United Negro College Fund
Email: john.copeland@sdhc.k12.fl.us
URL: http://www.cambridgewhoswho.com

Keith W. Copeman
Title: Firefighter, Paramedic, Instructor, Educator **Company:** City of Arlington Fire Department **Address:** 620 W. Division Street, Arlington, TX 76011 United States **BUS:** Dynamic Fire and Rescue Organization Serving a Dynamic and Growing Arlington **P/S:** Neighborhood Fire Prevention Activities and Emergency Response Services **MA:** International **D/D/R:** Driving for the Fire Department, Overseeing the Truck and Engine Maintenance and Repairs, Performing All Duties Including Pumping Water, Truck Functions, Rescue and Cutting Utilities **H/I/S:** Scuba Diving, Snow Skiing **CERTS:** Licensed Paramedic; Certified Trainer for Advanced Cardiac Life Support; Certified Trainer for Pediatric Life Support; Certified Emergency Medical Technician **A/A/S:** Educator in Paramedic Studies, Tarrant County College; International Association of Fire Fighters; Lecturer, County of Qatar; Educator in Emergency Medical Services and Rescue, Royal Saudi Air Force
Email: klcopeman@verizon.net

Mr. Steven R. Coppenbarger
Title: President **Company:** AAK Mechanical, Inc. **Address:** 1410 E. Jefferson Street, Clinton, IL 61727 United States **BUS:** Installation Company **P/S:** Stainless Steel Piping, Residential Concrete and Welding Services **MA:** National **D/D/R:** Overseeing Food Industry and Personal Care Services for Kraft Foods, Bunge, ACH Food Companies, Conair and PlastiPac, Mechanical Contracting, Installing Equipment and Stainless Steel Piping, Ensuring Customer Satisfaction **H/I/S:** Playing Football, ATV Riding **EDU:** High School Education **A/A/S:** American Welding Society
Email: aakmechanical05@hughes.net
URL: http://www.cambridgewhoswho.com

Ms. Beth Ann Copsey
Title: Principal, Broker **Company:** The B-Hive Sales & Marketing **Address:** 2470 Saint Rose Parkway, Suite 305, Henderson, NV 89074 United States **BUS:** Real Estate and Marketing Agency **P/S:** Marketing for Resorts and Second Homes, Real Estate, Consultations for Developers, Community Launches **MA:** National **D/D/R:** Marketing, Selling Real Estate **H/I/S:** Traveling, Diving, Skiing **EDU:** Bachelor of Science in Communications, Eastern New Mexico University **A/A/S:** Greater Las Vegas Association of Realtors **A/H:** Division Sales Person of the Year Award (2004) **C/VW:** American Society for the Prevention of Cruelty to Animals, No-Kill Animal Shelters
Email: beth@bhive.com
URL: http://www.bhive.com

Donna Jo Corday
Title: Service and Repair Manager **Company:** Homecare Medical **Address:** 5665 S. Westridge Drive, New Berlin, WI 53151 United States **BUS:** Home Medical Supplier **P/S:** Respiratory, Home Medical Equipment and Rehabilitation Products, Enthral **MA:** Local **D/D/R:** Servicing and Repairing Company and Client Units **H/I/S:** Gardening, Car Racing, Attending Country Music Concerts, Bowling, Deer Hunting **EDU:** Associate of Arts in Business Management, University of Phoenix (2008) **A/A/S:** Traffic Club
Email: cordaydonna@aol.com
URL: http://www.homecaremedical.com

Thomas D. Cordell
Title: Office Manager **Company:** The Law Offices of Leonard C. Goodman **Address:** 53 W. Jackson Boulevard, Suite 1220, Chicago, IL 60604 United States **BUS:** Law Firm **P/S:** Federal, Criminal and Civil Legal Representation **MA:** Regional **EXP:** Mr. Cordell's expertise includes negotiation and conflict resolution. **D/D/R:** Performing Administrative Duties, Dealing with Clients, Opposing Councils and Prosecutors, Investigating Complaints, Monitoring Interviews, Working with Offenders, Dealing with Computer Professionals, Telephone Companies and Website Designers, Accounting, Resolving Disputes Regarding Payments **H/I/S:** Playing Racquetball, Traveling, Going on Road Trips **EDU:** Master of Public Administration, University of Illinois at Chicago; Bachelor of Science in Political Science, Concentration in Law, Minors in Public Administration and Military Science, Lewis University **CERTS:** Certified Mediator (2008) **A/A/S:** Veterans of Foreign Wars; The American Legion
Email: tcord007@gmail.com
URL: http://www.susanecox.com

Linda S. Cordial
Title: Special Education Teacher **Company:** Central Elementary School **Address:** 400 Clinton Street, Ottawa, IL 61350 United States **BUS:** Public Elementary School **P/S:** Education **MA:** Local **D/D/R:** Instructional Support, All Areas of Special Education **H/I/S:** Reading, Interior Designing, Floral Arranging **EDU:** Master's Degree Equivalent, 63 Graduate Hours; Bachelor's Degree in Supervision, Northern Illinois University; Trained and Supervised Student Teachers from Northern Illinois University and Illinois State University **A/A/S:** Ottawa Elementary Education Association; Starved Rock Reading Council; Illinois Education Association; National Education Association; Illinois Reading Council; Reddick Mansion Association of Ottawa **A/H:** Who's Who Among American Teachers (2005) **C/VW:** James Cordial Merit Scholarship
Email: lcordial@mtco.com

Anna M. Cordova
Title: Vice President **Company:** FILMLOOK, Inc. **Address:** 2917 W. Olive Avenue, Burbank, CA 91505 United States **BUS:** Post-Production Facility **P/S:** Entertainment, Post-Production Services **MA:** International **D/D/R:** Marketing **H/I/S:** Walking, Writing, Reading, Listening to Music **EDU:** Bachelor of Arts in Manufacturing, California Polytechnic University **A/A/S:** Women in Film, American Film Institute, IDA **C/VW:** Veterans of Foreign War
Email: anna@filmlook.com
URL: http://www.filmlook.com

Leslie Cordova
Title: Speed, Strength and Conditioning Coach, Chief Executive Officer **Company:** Xplosive Strength and Speed **BUS:** Corporation **P/S:** Sports Performance Training and Education for Athletes, Coaches and Parents **MA:** Southern California **D/D/R:** Youth and Team Training **H/I/S:** Playing Tennis, Bike Riding, Traveling, Reading **EDU:** Master's Degree in Sports Administration, California State University; Master's Degree in Education, Loyola Marymount University; Bachelor's Degree in Exercise Science, University of New Mexico **A/A/S:** National Strength and Conditioning Association; International Youth Conditioning Association
Email: leslie@xplosivestrength.com
URL: http://www.xplosivestrength.com

Michael A. Corey, Ph.D.
Title: Chief Researcher **Company:** Goldilocks Universe **Address:** 2 Port View Drive, Charleston, WV 25311 United States **BUS:** Templeton Speaker for all Associated Occasions, Chief Theological Researcher, Writer, First to Prove the Existence of God Using Science Alone **P/S:** Consultation and Research on the Origin of Life through Science and Religion **MA:** International **D/D/R:** Exploring the Origin of Life, Debating Theories, Internet Consulting, Alternative Medicine Consulting, Writer and Publisher of Ten Books **H/I/S:** Playing Guitar **EDU:** Ph.D. in Science and Religion, Union Institute & University (1996) **A/A/S:** American Association for the Advancement of Science; Speaker, John Templeton Foundation
Email: michaleanthonycore@gmail.com
URL: http://www.michaelacorey.com/

Jodie Cornelius
Title: Speech and Language Pathologist **Company:** Self Employed Individual Contractor **Address:** 5725 Fairway Circle, Haltom City, TX 76117 United States **BUS:** Private Practice of Speech and Language, Healthcare and Rehabilitation Services **P/S:** Speech and Dysphagia Therapy, Long-Term Care and Rehabilitation **MA:** Regional **D/D/R:** Promoting Dysphagia and Dementia Therapy **H/I/S:** Reading **EDU:** Master of Science in Speech Language Pathology, Texas Christian University (1985) **A/A/S:** Public Speaker
Email: Jlc3339@cs.com

Cheryl Corr
Title: Director of Equipment and Controls **Company:** Great Atlantic and Pacific Tea Company **Address:** 2 Paragon Drive, Montvale, NJ 07645 United States **BUS:** Supermarket **P/S:** General Foods and Merchandise **MA:** Local **D/D/R:** Purchasing of all Capital Equipment for Use in Old, New and Remodeled Stores **EDU:** Bachelor of Science in Business Administration, Montclair State University **A/A/S:** FMI, the A and P Bergen County March of Dimes
Email: corr@aptea.com
URL: www.aptea.com

Jose P. Correia
Title: President **Company:** Jay's Meats and Provisions **Address:** 91 Brook Avenue, Dorchester, MA 02125 United States **BUS:** Distribution Firm **P/S:** Meat and Provisions **MA:** Regional **D/D/R:** Managing Sales, Ensuring Customer Satisfaction **H/I/S:** Fishing, Traveling
Email: g9bostonrob@mac.com

Mr. George Corrie
Title: Park Ranger **Company:** National Park Service **Dept:** Interior Service **Address:** Mammoth Cave National Park, P.O. Box 7, Mammoth Cave, KY 42259 United States **BUS:** World's Largest Cave, Government **P/S:** Hiking Trails, Camp Grounds, Hotels, Cottages **MA:** Regional **D/D/R:** Presenting 11 Different Types of Tours, Supervising 17 Tour Guides, Training Tour Guides **H/I/S:** Camping, Hiking **EDU:** Bachelor of Science in Natural Resource Management, University of Kentucky (1969) **A/A/S:** Sons of American Revolutions; Board of Directors, Lost River Cave and Valleys; Published in Six Journals
Email: george_corrie@nps.gov
URL: http://www.nps.gov

Mr. Robert R. Corson Jr.
Title: Owner **Company:** Corson Custom Graphics **Address:** 53 Corson Lane, Canonsburg, PA 15317 United States **BUS:** Advertising Company **P/S:** Information Science, Banners, Street Signs, Personal Signs, Flyers, Business Cards **MA:** Regional **D/D/R:** Graphic Design, Producing Commercial Vinyl and Aluminum Signs for Businesses, Hospitals, Pennsylvania Department of Transportation, Managing All Aspects of Daily Operations of the Company **H/I/S:** Flying his Hot Air Balloon **EDU:** Associate Degree in Graphic Design, Pittsburgh Technical Institute (1999)
Email: corsoncustomgraphic@msn.com

Michelle Cortes
Title: Social Worker **Company:** University of Medicine and Dentistry of New Jersey **Dept:** Eric B. Chandler Health Center **Address:** 277 George Street, New Brunswick, NJ 08901 United States **BUS:** University and Healthcare Center **P/S:** Higher Education, Healthcare, Childcare **MA:** Local **EXP:** Ms. Cortes' expertise includes family dynamics and child development. **H/I/S:** Exercising, Spending Time with Children **EDU:** Master of Social Work, Fordham University **CERTS:** Licensed Social Worker, States of New Jersey and New York **C/VW:** AIDS Walk New York
Email: kianosmom@aol.com
URL: http://www.cambridgewhoswho.com

Joel S. Corvera, MD
Title: Physician **Company:** Emory University **Dept:** Division of Cardiothoracic Surgery **Address:** 1365 Clifton Road N.E., Atlanta, GA 30322 United States **BUS:** University Hospital **P/S:** Higher Education **MA:** International **D/D/R:** Performing Cardiac Surgery **H/I/S:** Playing Tennis, Watching Basketball **EDU:** MD, Vanderbilt University, Nashville, Tennessee; Coursework in Pre-Medical Studies, Columbia University, NY; Coursework in Economics and Mathematics, Duke University **A/A/S:** American College of Surgeons; The Society of Thoracic Surgeons **C/VW:** American Cancer Society; Susan G. Komen
Email: jscorve@emory.edu

Aundria Camille Cosby
Title: Clinical Research Coordinator, RN, BSN **Company:** The Center for Rheumatology and Bone Research **Address:** 6100 Grenfell Loop, Bowie, MD 20720 United States **BUS:** Pharmaceutical Company **P/S:** Research, Development of New Pharmaceuticals **MA:** International **D/D/R:** Coordinates Research Studies, Liaison Between Pharmaceutical Companies, the Physicians and the Subjects in the Studies, Handles Compliance with the FDA, Schedules Meetings **H/I/S:** Shopping, Traveling **EDU:** Bachelor of Science in Nursing, Florida A&M University (1997) **A/A/S:** National Nurses Association
Email: aundriacosby@hotmail.com

Joseph A. Cosenza
Title: Editor **Company:** Marblehed Entertainment **Address:** 1122 E. 31St Street, Brooklyn, NY 11210 United States **BUS:** Video Production Company **P/S:** Films and Music Videos Production, Video Editing **MA:** Local **D/D/R:** Editing Music Videos, Overseeing Camera Work and Lighting, Logging Videos on the Computer **H/I/S:** Exercising **EDU:** Diploma, James Madison High School (2005)
Email: dfilley@marblehed.com
URL: http://www.marblehed.com

Arlet M. Cossetta
Title: Owner **Company:** Cossetta's Cleaning **Address:** 2419 Wimbledon Bay, Saint Paul, MN 55125 United States **BUS:** Cleaning Center **P/S:** Commercial and Residential Cleaning Services **MA:** Local **D/D/R:** Overseeing Operations Including Cleaning, Polishing Furniture, Ensuring Customer Satisfaction, Recruiting, Training **H/I/S:** Volunteering at Nursing Homes, Helping Elderly People
Email: cosettascleaning@hotmail.com

Christine M. Costamagna
Title: Vice President, Assistant Secretary **Company:** Bank of America **Address:** 555 California Street, Eighth Floor, San Francisco, CA 94104 United States **BUS:** Bank **P/S:** Financial Services Including Savings Accounts, Deposits, Credit Cards, Mortgages, Home Equity, Investments, Wealth Management and Insurance **MA:** International **D/D/R:** Drafting Resolutions, Conducting Board Meetings, Business Consulting Regarding Transactions, Managing Finance **H/I/S:** Playing Tennis **EDU:** Bachelor's Degree in English, University of California, Davis (1988) **A/A/S:** Society of Corporate Secretaries and Governance Professionals; United States Tennis Association
Email: christine.m.costamagna@bankofamerica.com
URL: http://www.bankofamerica.com

Erica L. Costello
Title: Chorus Teacher **Company:** Cleveland Middle School **Address:** 6910 Natalie Avenue N.E., Albuquerque, NM 87110 United States **BUS:** Public Middle School **P/S:** Middle School Education **MA:** Regional **D/D/R:** Teaching the Art of Choral Music with an emphasis on Adolescent Voices, Teaching Sixth-Grade General Music, Piano Laboratory Classes, Managing the DYNAMICS Show Choir **H/I/S:** Bowling, Photography **EDU:** Pursuing Master of Arts in Music Education, The University of New Mexico; Bachelor of Arts in Music Education, The University of New Mexico (1998) **A/A/S:** Related Arts Chairwoman, Instructional Council Representative; New Mexico Symphony Orchestra Chorus; Music Teachers National Association; NMMEA; ACDA; MENC; Alpha Delta Kappa, **A/H:** Who's Who Among American Teachers and Educators (2005-2006, 2006-2007); Nominee, Disney Hand Teacher Award for Excellence and Creativity in Teaching (2003-2004, 2004-2005, 2005-2006)
Email: costello_e@aps.edu
URL: http://www.cambridgewhoswho.com

Dr. Mary Ann Costello
Title: Assistant Superintendent **Company:** Frontier Central School District **Address:** 5120 Orchard Ave, Hamburg, NY 14075 United States **BUS:** Education **P/S:** Education, School District **MA:** Local **D/D/R:** Curriculum Instruction, Information Tech **H/I/S:** Golf, Photography **EDU:** Ed.D, St University of Buffalo; Master of Science in Secondary Education Canisius College; Bachelor of Science in Spanish, St. University College at Buffalo **A/A/S:** NASSP; Phi Delta Kappa; Delta Kappa Gamma; Phi Delta Kappa
Email: mcostello@frontier.wnyric.org
Email: drmac4432@aol.com

Rebecca L. Cothern
Title: Curriculum Resource Teacher **Company:** East Elementary School **Address:** 27050 Fairway Drive, Punta Gorda, FL 33982 United States **BUS:** Elementary School **P/S:** Education **MA:** Regional **D/D/R:** Curriculum Resource Education **H/I/S:** Spending Time with her Family, Reading, Scrapbooking **EDU:** Specialist Degree in Educational Leadership, Nova Southeastern University, 2007; Master's Degree in Curriculum and Instruction, Florida Gulf Coast University, 1998 **C/VW:** Church
Email: becky_cothern@ccps.k12.fl.us

Andrea Cottman
Title: President **Company:** Gemini 2 **Address:** Sag Harbor, NY 11963 United States **BUS:** Gallery **P/S:** Fine Art and Collectibles **MA:** Regional **D/D/R:** Attending Gallery Openings and Showings to Convince Clients and Collectors to Catalog their Art for Insurance or Personal Purposes, Putting Together Critiques of Artwork, Cataloging Artist Portfolios, Selling Fine Art **H/I/S:** Collecting Art **EDU:** Master's Degree in Special Education and Educational Administration, City University of New York **CERTS:** Pursuing Certified Appraiser, New York University **A/A/S:** National Alliance of Black School Educators, Association for Dyslexia; Art Hall Houses **C/VW:** The High Tea Society
Email: andreacottman@hotmail.com
URL: http://www.cambridgewhoswho.com

Pamela K. Coughlin
Title: Owner **Company:** A Stitch in Time **Address:** 1623 S. Castor Road, Midland, MI 48640 United States **BUS:** Tailor Company **P/S:** Bridal, Heirloom Sewing, Quilting, Victorian Reproductions **MA:** International **D/D/R:** Bridal Alterations and Custom Work, Victorian Reproductions **H/I/S:** Reading, Spending Time with her Grandchildren **A/A/S:** Professional Association Custom Clothiers; Michigan Quilt Network; American Quilter's Society **C/VW:** Michigan 4-H Foundation
Email: stitchintime@hotmail.com
URL: http://www.cambridgewhoswho.com

Connie M. Coulson
Title: Coding Specialist **Company:** Lancaster General **Address:** 555 N. Duke Street, P.O. Box 3555, Lancaster, PA 17604 United States **BUS:** Hospital, Trauma Center **P/S:** Healthcare **MA:** Local **D/D/R:** Chargemaster, Coordinator, Managing Compliance Issues, Coordinating Resources **H/I/S:** Reading **EDU:** Bachelor's Degree in Sociology, Millersville University **CERTS:** Certified Professional Coder, American Association of Professional Coders **A/A/S:** American Association of Professional Coders
Email: info@CambridgeWhosWho.com
URL: http://www.cambridgewhoswho.com

Mr. Thomas Coulter
Title: Financial Planner **Company:** Coulter's Creative Financial Planning **Address:** 5 W. Main Street, Elmsford, NY 10523 United States **BUS:** Financial Planning Company **P/S:** Financial Advisory Services for Seriously Ill and Divorce Mediation **MA:** Local **D/D/R:** Offering Divorce Mediation Services and Financial Advice to the Seriously Ill **H/I/S:** History **CERTS:** Licensed Stockbroker in Series 7, 63 and 65; Licensed in Life Insurance, Health, Properties and Entities; Licensed Affording Care Master; Certified Senior Advisor; Certified Divorce Financial Analyst **A/A/S:** Freemasonry **A/H:** Rockland County Shield; Orange County Shield; Rockland County Police Emerald **C/VW:** Chapter 333, Vietnam Veteran of America
Email: ccfpinc@aol.com

Samuel C. Courbis
Title: Chemist II **Company:** Shire **Address:** 11200 Gundry Lane, Owings Mills, MD 21117 United States **BUS:** Bio pharmaceutical Company **P/S:** Specialty Pharmaceuticals Including Adderall, Carbatrol and Elapses **MA:** International **D/D/R:** Developing Testing Methods for Raw Materials, Training Employees Regarding Method Usage **H/I/S:** Skeet Shooting, Sporting Clays **EDU:** Pursuing Master's Degree in Chemistry, University of Maryland, Baltimore; Bachelor of Science in Chemistry, Millersville University (2001) **CERTS:** Pursuing Post-Bachelor's Certification in Regulatory Issues in Biotechnology **A/A/S:** American Chemical Society
Email: dfupby12@yahoo.com
URL: http://www.shire.com

Judith E. Courteaux
Title: Owner **Company:** Vida of New Orleans, Inc. **Address:** 2101 Alamo Avenue, Harvey, LA 70058 United States **BUS:** Proven Leader in the Beauty Industry **P/S:** Manufacturing Beauty Supplies, Hair and Skin Products, Acne Kits, Body Lotions, Scrubs and Shampoos **MA:** National **D/D/R:** Handling Administration and Operational End of Business, Managing Operations **H/I/S:** Reading, Traveling, Art **EDU:** Associate of Arts in Business, Santa Rosa Junior College, California (1969)
Email: vida@vidaofneworleans.nocoxmail.com
URL: http://www.vidaofneworleans.org

Rosemary D. Courtney
Title: Health Science Technology Instructor, Dental Hygienist **Company:** High School for Health Professions **Address:** Harlingen, TX United States **BUS:** High School **P/S:** Teaching Students Dental Hygiene, Dentistry, Health Science, Anatomy, Physiology **MA:** Local **D/D/R:** Teaching Dental Science, Anatomy and Physiology Classes **H/I/S:** Reading, Long Distance Bicycling **EDU:** Associate Degree in Dental Hygiene, Indiana University (1979); Bachelor's Degree in Political Science, Indiana University (1974) **CERTS:** Teaching Certificate (2005) **A/A/S:** American Dental Hygienist Association; Former President, Texas State Dental Hygienist Association
Email: rcourtney@rgv.rr.com
URL: http://www.cambridgewhoswho.com

Katherine Ann Couto
Title: Manager for Environmental Services **Company:** Sodexo **Address:** 9950 Slater Avenue, Fountain Valley, CA 92708 United States **BUS:** Environmental Cleaning Company **P/S:** Environmental Cleaning Services **MA:** National **EXP:** Ms. Couto's expertise is in housekeeping. **H/I/S:** Reading, Watching Soccer, Attending Church **EDU:** Bachelor of Science in Hotel Management, University of Nevada, Las Vegas **C/VW:** Girl Scouts of the United States of America
Email: kar.reynolds@gmail.com
URL: http://www.sodexo.com

Keri L. Couzens
Title: Office Manager **Company:** Bob Beron State Farm Insurance **Address:** 3232 Governor Drive, Suite C, San Diego, CA 92122 United States **BUS:** Insurance Company **P/S:** Personal, Commercial, Automobile, Health, Life, Long Term Insurance **MA:** National **D/D/R:** Selling Property, Casualty, Commercial, Automobile, Health, Life and Long Term Insurance, Marketing and Service, Taking Home Owner Pictures for Marketing through Other Company Leads **H/I/S:** Music, Going to the Beach, Bicycling **EDU:** Bachelor of Science in Economics, University of Arizona (2003) **CERTS:** Licensed for Insurance Sales in Arizona (2003); Licensed for Insurance Sales in California (2005)
Email: keri.l.couzens.nm1x@statefarm.com
URL: http://www.bobberon.com

Elizabeth Grace Covington
Title: Owner **Company:** GC Luxury Homes, LLC **Address:** 9716 Sunset Hill Circle, Lone Tree, CO 80124 United States **BUS:** Construction Company **P/S:** Luxury Speculation, Construction of New and Custom Homes **MA:** Regional **EXP:** Ms. Covington's expertise is in business management. **D/D/R:** Collaborating with the National Association of Home Builders **H/I/S:** Snow skiing, Water skiing, Riding her Motorcycle, Boating, Mountain Biking, Hiking **EDU:** Bachelor's Degree in English, Minor in Political Science, Colorado State University (1999)
Email: gcluxuryhomes@comcast.net

Mr. Darrell L. Cowan II
Title: Chief Financial Officer, Owner **Company:** Independent National Security **Address:** 1442 E Lincoln, Suite 332, Orange, CA 92865 United States **BUS:** Independent Security Contracting Services **P/S:** Armed and Unarmed Patrol, On-Site Security, Alarm Response and Access Control Systems, Camera Monitoring Products, Parking Enforcement Services **MA:** California **D/D/R:** Serving the Public as the Former Chief of Police, Working as a Security Contractor **H/I/S:** Instructing Firearm Classes **EDU:** Police Officer Standards and Training, Fullerton College, CA; Police Officer Standards and Training, Western Nevada College, with Honors **A/A/S:** Community Association Institute; Apartment Association of Southern California Cities; Apartment Association of Orange County; Apartment Association of the Greater Inland Empire; Crime Free Multi-Unit Housing; Crime Free Business Association; California Association of Community Managers; California Apartment Owner's Association; California Association of Licensed Security Agencies; National Rifle Association
Email: dcowan@independentnational.net
URL: http://www.independentnational.net

Timothy F. Cowans Sr.
Title: Pastor **Company:** Brookfield Church of God **Address:** 131 Elliot Drive, Wilmington, NC 28405 United States **BUS:** Church **P/S:** Ministry of the Gospel **MA:** Local **H/I/S:** Bowling, Traveling **CERTS:** Ordained Bishop **A/A/S:** Church of God Head Quarters, Youth, Sports, Men and Women Ministries
Email: brookfieldcog@aol.com

Mr. Richard J. Cowell
Title: 1) Service Technician 2) Entrepreneur **Company:** 1) Tricomm Services, Inc. 2) Dynamite DJ & Dance **Address:** 637 Schiller Avenue, Trenton, NJ 08610 United States **BUS:** 1) Communications Company 2) Entertainment Company **P/S:** 1) Computer Installation, Service and Repair 2) DJ and Dance Entertainment **MA:** Regional **D/D/R:** Managing Fiber Optics Technology, Infrastructure Cabling for Computers and Phones, Data Networking, Troubleshooting, Offering DJ and Dance Services for Special Events, Fitness Instruction **EDU:** Associate Degree in Accounting, Mercer County Community College (1977) **A/A/S:** Holy Cross Lutheran Church
Email: cccowell@aol.com

Michael H. Cowley
Title: Owner **Company:** Cowley's Siding and Remodeling **Address:** 2801 W. 63rd Avenue, Merrillville, IN 46410 United States **BUS:** Construction Company **P/S:** Home Exterior Specialty Construction, Installation, Remodeling, Renovations and Repairs **MA:** Regional **D/D/R:** Overseeing the Business and Five Crews for Siding, Exterior Remodeling and New Construction Projects, Installing Siding, Windows and Doors, Making Home Repairs, Sofets, Fascias **H/I/S:** Hunting, Fishing, Enjoying the Outdoors **EDU:** High School Education **C/VW:** Cedar Lake Eagles
Email: cowleyssid@comcast.net

Brian W. Cox
Title: Firefighter, NREMT-B **Company:** Livingston Parish Fire Protection District #5 **Address:** 8098 Hwy 190, Denham Springs, Louisiana, 70726, **BUS:** Fire Department **P/S:** Fire Protection, Emergency Medicine **MA:** Local **D/D/R:** Firefighting, Emergency Medical Services, DRT (Dive Recovery Team) **H/I/S:** Scuba Diving, Traveling, Landscaping, camping **EDU:** Associate Degree in Business Administration, American InterContinental University (2006) **A/A/S:** Dive Recovery Team, Fire Inspector, NREMT-B, Hazmat
Email: bcox9111@cox.net
URL: http://www.cambridgewhoswho.com

Mr. D. J. Cox
Title: Owner, Graphic Designer **Company:** Dragonflyte Designworks **Address:** 2531 Commercial Avenue, Madison, WI 53704 United States **BUS:** Commercial Art and Design **P/S:** Logo Types, Graphic Design and Photography, Graphic Illustration, Bumper Sticker Design, Model Portfolio, Portrait, Nature, Wedding Photography, Signage, Compact Disc Covers, Designs for Posters, Stickers and Business Cards **MA:** Regional **D/D/R:** Preparing Logotypes, Original Fonts and Calligraphy for Genealogical Archiving, Designing Clock faces from Original Acrylic Paintings, Designing Art for Individual and Commercial Logos, Commercial Art, Fine Art **H/I/S:** Fine Art Tutoring, Painting, Swimming, Biking, Traveling, Outdoor Summer Activities, Astronomy, Music Appreciation, Animals **EDU:** Associate Degree in Commercial Art, Madison Area Technical College (1976)
Email: dragonflyte@sbcglobal.net
URL: http://www.dragonflyte.net

Jane B. Cox
Title: Personal Assistant to Former President **Company:** Shell Oil **Address:** 2001 Kirby Drive, Suite 1004, Houston, TX 77019 United States **BUS:** Global Group of Energy and Petrochemical Companies **P/S:** Extraction and Deliverance of Oil and Gas in Environmentally and Socially Responsible Ways **MA:** International **D/D/R:** Working as the Executive Assistant to the Former Chief Executive Officer of the Company, Acting as a Liaison to the Board of Directors, Handling All Domestic and International Travel Arrangements, Coordinating Meetings **H/I/S:** Traveling, Attending Church Group Seminars **CERTS:** Executive Secretarial Certification, Zorn Business College (1957) **A/A/S:** Member, Second Baptist Church
Email: jcox1963@yahoo.com

Mrs. Lisa C. Cox
Title: President **Company:** Carreras Technologies, Inc. **Address:** P.O. Box 1643, Chesterfield, VA 23832 United States **BUS:** Identification Printers and Custom Plastic Card Distributor **P/S:** Distribution Services for Photo Identification Equipment and Supplies, Printing Services for Business Cards, Photo Identification Badges and Membership Cards **MA:** Regional **D/D/R:** Overseeing All Operations, Offering Quality Services and Customer Satisfaction to Ensure Repeat Business, Photo ID Equipment and Supplies, IDs and Memberships for Businesses that don't Have Printing Equipment **H/I/S:** Golfing **EDU:** Bachelor's Degree in Business Administration, Minor in Computer Science, Barton College (1984)
Email: sales@carrerastech.com
URL: http://www.carrerastech.com

Susan Jean Cox
Title: Intervention Specialist **Company:** Olentangy Local Schools **Address:** 813 Shanahan Road, Lewis Center, OH 43035 United States **BUS:** School District **P/S:** Education **MA:** Local **D/D/R:** Teaching English, Intervention **H/I/S:** Traveling, Reading, Spending Time with her Family **EDU:** Bachelor's Degree in Comprehensive English, Ohio State University **CERTS:** Certified in Mild Learning Disabilities K-12 **A/H:** Teacher of the Year (2006-2007) **C/VW:** Habitat for Humanity, All Saints Lutheran Church
Email: sue_cox@olentangy.k12.oh.us
URL: http://www.cambridgewhoswho.com

Kent A. Coxe
Title: Attorney **Company:** Van Osdol, Magruder, Erickson & Redmond, P.C. **Address:** 911 Main Street, Suite 2400, Kansas City, MO 64105 United States **BUS:** Law Firm **P/S:** Business and Litigation, Estate Planning, Health Law, Intellectual Property, Labor and Employment, Real Estate, Commercial, Construction, Criminal Defense, Family Law, Health Care **MA:** Regional **D/D/R:** Offering All Legal Services for Small and Medium-Sized Businesses, Acting in a Timely, Responsible and Cost-Effective Manner to Client Services **H/I/S:** Outdoor Activities, Gardening **EDU:** JD, University of Iowa (1987); Master of Laws in Tax, University of Missouri, Kansas City **A/A/S:** Kansas City Metropolitan Bar Association; Missouri Bar Association; Missouri Hospital Association; Greater Kansas City Society of Healthcare Attorneys; Johnson County Bar Association; Director and Former Chairman, The Authorized Foundation of Western Missouri; Board Member, American Stroke Foundation **A/H:** Super Lawyer of the Year, Kansas, Missouri (2005)
Email: kcoxe@vomer.com
URL: http://www.vomer.com

Heather Coyle
Title: Senior Vice President, Management Supervisor **Company:** Cline Davis & Mann **Address:** 302 Carnegie Center, Suite 103, Princeton, NJ 08540 United States **BUS:** Pharmaceutical Advertising Agency **P/S:** Pharmaceutical Advertising **MA:** International **D/D/R:** Making Strategic Plans **H/I/S:** Golfing, Traveling, Spending Time with her Family **EDU:** Master of Business Administration, Wharton School of the University of Pennsylvania **C/VW:** Primary Cancer Organizations
Email: bmeriger@clinedavis.com
URL: http://www.cambridgewhoswho.com

Robin T. Cozzolino
Title: Early Intervention Family Specialist **Company:** Multnomah Educational Service District **Address:** 14030 N.E. Sacramento Street, Portland, OR 97230 United States **BUS:** Education **P/S:** Home-Based Education, Counseling, Massage Therapy **MA:** Regional **D/D/R:** Counseling Families with Children with Disabilities, Offering Home-Based Education to Families, Giving Child Massages **H/I/S:** Water Sports, Massage **EDU:** Master's Degree in Special Education and Early Intervention, Santa Clara University (1992); Bachelor's Degree in History, San José State University (1983); Pursuing MA in Licensed Professional Counseling, Capella University **A/A/S:** Council for Exceptional Children; Oregon Toddler Mental Health Association; World Association for Infant Mental Health
Email: cmsrobin9@comcast.net
URL: http://www.mcsd.k12.or.us

Kathy D. Crabtree
Title: Collection Representative **Company:** Internal Revenue Service **Address:** 3659 Old Greenbrier Pike, Springfield, TN 37172 United States **BUS:** Government Organization **P/S:** Financial Services **MA:** National **D/D/R:** Ensuring Customer Satisfaction, Answering Telephones, Handling Collections **H/I/S:** Making Crafts **EDU:** Pursuing Bachelor's Degree in Accounting, Tennessee State University (2008); Associate Degree in Accounting, Volunteer State Community College, Gallatin, Tennessee (2000); Bachelor's Degree in Human Relations, Trevecca Nazarene University (2001)
Email: crabtree03@comcast.net
URL: http://www.irs.com

Rhoda L. Craghead
Title: Case Manager III **Company:** Department of Human Services **Address:** HC 61 Box 20, Sallisaw, OK 74955 United States **BUS:** Social Services Company **P/S:** Programs and Services for Developmentally Disabled Individuals **MA:** Regional **D/D/R:** Case Management **H/I/S:** Reading **EDU:** Bachelor of Arts in Education, North Eastern State (1984)
Email: rhoda.craghead@okdhs.org
URL: http://www.cambridgewhoswho

Susan Craig Shore
Title: President, Owner, Interior Designer **Company:** Seashore Floors & More, LLC **Address:** 1212 E. Pass Road, Gulfport, MS 39507 United States **BUS:** Interior Design Company **P/S:** Hardwood Flooring, Carpet, Tile, Laminate, Design Service, Flooring Studio, Discounted Products, Blinds, Granite Counter Tops **MA:** Regional **EXP:** Ms. Craig Shore's expertise includes the design of floor and window coverings. **D/D/R:** Performing Daily Business Operations, Assisting Clients with Product Selections and Estimates, Overseeing Commercial Bids **H/I/S:** Snorkeling **EDU:** Associate Degree in Design, Gulf Coast Community College (1985) **A/A/S:** Better Business Bureau; Home Builders Association; Chamber of Commerce
Email: seashorefloor@bellsouth.net

Thomas Crainer
Title: General Manager **Company:** RBC Bearings, Inc. **Address:** 1 Tribology Center, Oxford, CT 06478 United States **BUS:** Manufacturing **P/S:** Ball, Roller, Needle and Spherical Bearings **MA:** International **D/D/R:** Operations Management, Team Building **H/I/S:** Working Outdoors **EDU:** Master of Business Administration, University of Phoenix
Email: tcrainer@rbcbearings.com
URL: http://www.rbcbearings.com

Rodney D. Crampton
Title: Project Manager **Company:** Krieger and Stewart, Inc. **Address:** 3602 University Avenue, Riverside, CA 92501 United States **BUS:** Consulting, Engineering Company **P/S:** Consulting and Engineering, Water and Waste Water Management **MA:** Regional **D/D/R:** Water and Waste Water Managing **H/I/S:** Hunting, Fishing **EDU:** Master of Science, Civil Engineering, Concentration in Hydraulics, University of Nebraska; Bachelor of Science in Civil Engineering, University of Nebraska; Diploma, Bartley High School **A/A/S:** American Society of Civil Engineers; Professional License in Project Management in Nevada and California **C/VW:** Riverside Optimist Club
Email: carolcrampton@sbcglobal.net
URL: http://www.cambridgewhoswho.com

Patricia A. Crane
Title: Severe Profound Multi-handicapped Program Facilitator for Durham Public Schools **Company:** Durham Public Schools, E.K. Powe Elementary School **Address:** 915 Ninth Street, Durham, NC 27705 United States **BUS:** Public School System **P/S:** General Elementary and Secondary Curriculum, Special Education, Exceptional Children Program, Arts, Music, Physical Education, Foreign Language Instruction, Learning Resources, Student Support Services, Athletics, Extracurricular Activities, Special Programs, Student Clubs and Organizations **MA:** Local **D/D/R:** Teaching Special Education, Assisting Children with Physical and Mental Handicaps, Creating Education Goals and Lesson Plans, Overseeing Multi-handicapped and Profoundly Handicapped Programs, Offering Case Management and Curriculum Support to Special Education Teachers, Offering Strategies to Use with Exceptional Children, Assisting with Curriculum Selection and Lesson Plans, Training and Mentoring New Teachers, Reviewing Children's Records for IEP Compliance **H/I/S:** Swimming, Reading **EDU:** Master's Degree in Multi-Handicapped Education, The University of Alabama (1983); Bachelor's Degree in Learning and Behavior Disorders, University of Kentucky (1981)
Email: cranesden@msn.com
URL: http://www.dpsnc.net

Roger O. Cranville, OBE
Title: Senior Vice President **Company:** Allegheny Conference on Community Development **Dept:** Global Marketing **Address:** 425 Sixth Avenue, Suite 1100, Pittsburgh, PA 15219 United States **BUS:** Economic Development Organization **P/S:** Global Business Development **MA:** International **D/D/R:** Managing Global Marketing for the Pittsburgh Region, Improving the Global Competitiveness of Companies in the Pittsburgh Region **H/I/S:** Cooking, Reading **EDU:** Bachelor's Degree in Electrical Engineering (1971) **A/A/S:** President, British American Business Council; Deputy Secretary, Pennsylvania International Business Development; Co-Chairman, Pittsburgh Region, International Transition Team
Email: rcranville@alleghenyconference.org
URL: http://www.alleghenyconference.org

Mary Hellen Craven
Title: Teacher **Company:** Daingerfield-Lone Star Independent School District **Address:** 200 Tiger Drive, Dangerfield, TX 75638 **BUS:** School District **P/S:** Education **MA:** Dangerfield, Texas **D/D/R:** Teaching Elementary Students **H/I/S:** Sewing, Making Crafts, Genealogy, Scrapbooking **EDU:** Master of Education, Sul Ross State University, 1978; Bachelor's Degree in English, The College of the Southwest, Hibbs, New Mexico, 1974 **A/A/S:** District Committee, Texas Classroom Teachers Association **C/VW:** Girl Scouts of the USA, Boy Scouts of America, The Church of Jesus Christ of Latter-Day Saints, Kidney Foundations, Texas Patrol Officers
Email: hellen224@aol.com

Charolette V. Crawford
Title: Teacher **Company:** Terrebonne Parish School Board **Address:** 201 Stadium Drive, Houma, LA 70364 United States **BUS:** School District **P/S:** Education **MA:** Local **D/D/R:** Teaching English and Language Arts **H/I/S:** Singing with her Church Choir **EDU:** Bachelor's Degree in Elementary Education, Harding University **A/A/S:** National Education Association; Louisiana Education Association **C/VW:** Church of Christ, Children's Homes
Email: jcrawford8@hotmail.com
URL: http://www.tpsb.org

Dianne M. Crawford
Title: President, Chief Executive Officer **Company:** Inter-First Company, LLC **Address:** 3450 N. Rock Road, Suite 703, Wichita, KS 67226 United States **BUS:** Aviation Company **P/S:** Fasteners for Aerospace **MA:** National **EXP:** Ms. Crawford's expertise is in finance management. **H/I/S:** Traveling, Golfing, Horse Racing **EDU:** Bachelor of Science in Education, McGill University; Diploma, Lake Mountain High School **C/VW:** American Cancer Society; Disabled American Veterans; Local Church
Email: dianne@inter-first.aero
URL: http://www.inter-first.aero

Norman P. Crawford
Title: Owner **Company:** Leaning Tree Enterprises **Address:** 177 Locktown-Flemington Road, Flemington, NJ 08822 United States **BUS:** Synthetic Lubricants Retail/Commercial **P/S:** Synthetic Lubricants Sales, Commercial **MA:** National **A/A/S:** National Health
Email: ncrawfor@aol.com

Pauline G. Cray
Title: Owner **Company:** Back Inn Time Bed & Breakfast, Park Cafe **Address:** 68 Fairfield Street, Saint Albans, VT 05478 United States **BUS:** Hotel **P/S:** Hospitality Services Including Catering, Private Retreats, Tea Parties, Mystery Weekends, Wedding Receptions and Halloween Haunted Houses **MA:** Regional **EXP:** Ms. Cray's expertise is in business operations management. **D/D/R:** Managing Operations, Gardening, Interior Designing, Decorating, Supervising Employees, Catering, Preparing Menu, Purchasing, Maintaining Inventory Controls **H/I/S:** Tennis, Listening to Music, Reading, Hiking **EDU:** College Coursework **C/VW:** Local Teen Center; Make-A-Wish
Email: eaglespirit0804@yahoo.com
URL: http://www.cambridgewhoswho.com

Denise L. Creacy, MSW
Title: Social Worker **Company:** Casey Family Services **Dept:** Foster Care **Address:** 789 Reservoir Avenue, Bridgeport, CT 06606 United States **BUS:** Nonprofit Organization **P/S:** Child Advocacy Including Foster Care and Post-Adoption Services **MA:** Local **EXP:** Ms. Creacy's expertise is in behavior management. **D/D/R:** Working Closely with Foster Care Services **H/I/S:** Traveling, Reading, Spending Time with her Family **EDU:** Master's Degree, Springfield College (2008); Bachelor's Degree in Social Work, Morgan State University, MD **A/A/S:** Certified Trainer, The Mandt System, National Association of Social Workers **C/VW:** Advisory Board Member, Salvation Army
Email: dcreacy@caseyfamilyservices.org
URL: http://www.caseyfamilyservices.org

Linda Credit

Title: Chief Executive Officer **Company:** Braids Your Way **Address:** 3126 W Manchester Blvd, Inglewood, CA 90305 United States **BUS:** Salon **P/S:** Full Service Hair Boutique **MA:** Local **D/D/R:** Braiding, Extensions, Weaving, Etc **H/I/S:** Traveling, Reading Novels **EDU:** Master of Arts in Public Administration, University of Southern California **A/A/S:** Jack and Jill of America, National Braiding Association, Donates to Local Shelters, Children's Hospitals, Toy Drives
Email: lfcredit@verizon.net

Gayle Creed

Title: Content Mastery Teacher **Company:** Boswell High School **Address:** 5805 W. Bailey Boswell Road, Fort Worth, TX 76179 United States **BUS:** Public High School **P/S:** Education **MA:** Local **D/D/R:** Special Education **H/I/S:** Waterskiing, Spending Time with Family, Reading **EDU:** Bachelor of Arts in Liberal Arts and Political Science, University of Texas, Arlington, 1985 **A/A/S:** Association of Texas Professional Educators; Delta Kappa Gamma **C/VW:** Central Texas Conference Youth in Mission
Email: chevelle2@aol.com
URL: http://www.emsisd.com/boswell

Noraida Crespo

Title: Office Manager **Company:** Riverside Pediatric Group **Address:** 4201 New York Avenue, Union City, NJ 07087 United States **BUS:** Pediatric Medical Office **P/S:** Primary Pediatric Healthcare **MA:** Regional **D/D/R:** Business Administration, Office Management **H/I/S:** Spending Time with Family **EDU:** High School Graduate **C/VW:** Local Church
Email: noraidac@aol.com
URL: http://www.riversidepediatricgroup.com

Debbie Crews

Title: Benefit Manager **Company:** Pacific Coast Companies, Inc. **Address:** 10600 White Rock Rd., Ste 100, Rancho Cordova, CA 95670 United States **BUS:** Consulting **P/S:** Retail Wholesale **MA:** West Coast **D/D/R:** Benefit Administration, Supervising 3 employees **H/I/S:** Spending Time with her Family, Reading **EDU:** Business Management Coursework, Southern State College **A/A/S:** SHRM, SAHRA, SAHUA, NAHU
Email: debbie.crews@paccoast.com
URL: http://www.pcbp.com

Julie Lynn Crider

Title: Biology Teacher **Company:** Red Bank High School **Address:** 640 Morrison Springs Road, Chattanooga, TN 37415 United States **BUS:** High School **P/S:** Secondary Education Including Vocational Programs **MA:** Regional **D/D/R:** Teaching Advanced Placement Biology, Anatomy, Physiology, Health and 12 Basic Laboratory Procedures, Utilizing Lecturing Techniques for Advanced Placement Classes to Prepare Students for College, Tutoring, Home Schooling, Coaching the Track Team, Healthcare **H/I/S:** Writing Poetry, Running, Supporting the Tennessee Titans and Nashville Predators **EDU:** Bachelor of Science in Biology, Union University, TN (2003) **CERTS:** Certification in Biology and Science Education 7-12, State of Tennessee **C/VW:** Various Local Charitable Organizations
Email: crider_julie@hcde.org
URL: http://www.hcde.org

Carol I. Crimi

Title: Social Services Consultant **Company:** Sunset Shores Adult Day Health Center **Address:** 720 Barnum Avenue Cutoff, Stratford, CT 06614 United States **BUS:** Adult Day Care **P/S:** Day Care for Adults **MA:** Local **D/D/R:** Geriatric Counseling, Individual and Group Counseling with Clients and Family Caregivers. Behavioral Therapy, Assist with entitlement programs, Clinical assessments, Counseling with Loss and Grief, Coping Skill workshop/ **H/I/S:** Gardening, Creative Writing **EDU:** Master of Science in Counseling and Human Resources, University of Bridgeport **CERTS:** Licensed Professional Counselor **A/A/S:** Connecticut Counseling Association, Group Leader of Conn. Chapter of National Alzheimer's Association. Connecticut Mental Health Counselors, American Gerontology Society **C/VW:** Fundraising, National Alzheimer's Association; Fundraising, American Diabetes Association
Email: fcc@peoplepc.com
URL: http://www.cambridgewhoswho.com

Rosann F. Crismore

Title: Office Manager **Company:** Law Offices of Kurt Boyd **Address:** 5850 Conoga Avenue, Suite 400, Woodland Hills, CA 91367 United States **BUS:** Law Office **P/S:** Legal Representation for Personal Injury and Defense Court Cases **MA:** Regional **D/D/R:** Managing All Office Operations Including Administration **H/I/S:** Cooking, Baking, Traveling, Horseback Riding
Email: rosann@boydlawyer.com
URL: http://www.boydlawyer.com

Shari R. Crist

Title: Teacher **Company:** Jefferson County Public Schools **Address:** 1829 Denver West Drive, Golden, CO 80401 United States **BUS:** School District **P/S:** Education **MA:** Local **D/D/R:** Teaching English as a Second Language **H/I/S:** Reading, Watching Movies, Graphic Arts **EDU:** Master's Degree in Curriculum and Instruction, English as a Second Language and Bilingual Education, University of Colorado, Health Sciences Center **A/A/S:** National Association of Geoscience Teachers; Jefferson County Education Association; National Education Association; National Association for Bilingual Education; California Association for Bilingual Education
Email: scristbr@jeffco.k12.co.us

Robin Critchfield

Title: Controller **Company:** Environmental Professional Associates **Address:** 1441 Garden Highway, Yuba City, CA 95991 United States **BUS:** Utility Line Clearance Company **P/S:** Utility Line Clearance, Tree Trimming, Vegetation Control **MA:** Statewide **D/D/R:** Accounting **H/I/S:** Spending Time with Family, Gardening, Reading **EDU:** Bachelor of Business Administration in Accounting, California State University at Sacramento **C/VW:** Moose Lodge, LeTip International
Email: rcrab2@yahoo.com
URL: http://www.provco.net

Mr. David Crockett

Title: Sales Manager **Company:** Mayr Corporation **Address:** 25 Crossover Lane, Taunton, MA 02780 United States **BUS:** Manufacturing Company **P/S:** Safety Clutches, Shaft Couplings, Safety Brakes, Electromagnetic Clutches and Brakes **MA:** National **D/D/R:** Sales Management, Setting-Up Quantity Pricing, Determining Applications, Calling Clients and Waste-Water Industry Professionals **H/I/S:** Building Model Railroads, Traveling **EDU:** Bachelor of Science in Management, University of Phoenix (2006); Associate in Applied Science, Middlesex County College (1992) **A/A/S:** American Society of Mechanical Engineers; Water Environment Federation; State University Business Officers Association
Email: mayrsales@aol.com
URL: http://www.mayrcorp.com

Terri Crone

Title: 1) Lab Supervisor, Medical Technologist 2) Consultant **Company:** 1) LabCorp 2) Mary Kay **Address:** 2525 E. Royalton Road, Broadview Heights, OH 44147 United States **BUS:** 1) Laboratory 2) Skin Care and Color Cosmetic Company **P/S:** 1) Clinical Testing 2) Beauty Consultant **MA:** National **D/D/R:** Supervising a Technical Lab, Offering Technical Consultations **H/I/S:** Mary Kay Consulting **EDU:** Bachelor of Science in Biology, Cleveland State University **CERTS:** Certification in Medical Technology, University Hospital (1993) **A/A/S:** American Society for Clinical Pathologists **C/VW:** American Cancer Society; Relay for Life
Email: momcrone@aol.com
Email: tcrone1@marykay.com
URL: http://www.labcorp.com

Jean M. Crosby

Title: President **Company:** Prudential Crosby Realtors **Address:** 551 N. Mulford Road, Rockford, IL 61107 United States **BUS:** Real Estate Agency, Law and Policy, Licensed Law, Ethics and Arbitration **P/S:** Sales and Development **MA:** National **D/D/R:** Regulatory Knowledge **H/I/S:** Spending Time with her Seven Grandchildren, Traveling, Reading **EDU:** Two Years of Coursework **CERTS:** Certified Residential Broker; Certified Residential Specialist; Graduate Realtor Institute **A/A/S:** National Association of Realtors; Illinois Association of Realtors; Past Director of Real Estate, State of Illinois **C/VW:** Volunteer through the National Association of Realtors and Illinois Association of Realtors
Email: jean_crosby@yahoo.com
URL: http://www.prudentialcrosby.com

Beth R. Cross-Wilhelm

Title: Corporate, Securities Paralegal **Company:** Woods Oviatt Gilman LLP **Address:** 700 Crossroads Building, Rochester, NY 14614 United States **BUS:** Securities Paralegal Securities Paralegal **P/S:** Paralegal **MA:** Local **D/D/R:** Legal Services **H/I/S:** Travel, Reading, Gardening **EDU:** Bachelor's in Business Administration from Ohio University **A/A/S:** Affiliate Member of Monroe County Bar Association
Email: songbirds2@frontier.net

Cindy A. Crouch

Title: Office Manager **Company:** Joe T. Powell, MD **Address:** 6818 Austin Center Boulevard, Austin, TX 78731 United States **BUS:** Medical Office **P/S:** Healthcare **MA:** Regional **D/D/R:** Management, Accounting **H/I/S:** Owning a Flower Shop, Wedding Planning, Riding her Harley-Davidson **EDU:** Bachelor of Science in Human Resource Management, Park University (2004) **CERTS:** Licensed Workers' Compensation Adjuster, State of Texas; Certification in Floral Design **A/A/S:** Harley-Davidson Organizations
Email: cindycrouch@yahoo.com
URL: http://www.cambridgewhoswho.com

Sharon D. Croucher

Title: Business Teacher **Company:** North Valley High School **Address:** 6741 Monument Drive, Grants Pass, OR 97526 United States **BUS:** High School **P/S:** Education **MA:** Local **D/D/R:** Teaching Business and Record Keeping Courses **H/I/S:** Reading, Bowling, Golfing, Traveling **EDU:** Master of Business Administration, Southern Oregon University **A/A/S:** National Business Education Association; Ohio Education Association **C/VW:** Relay for Life
Email: Sharon.Croucher@cwwemail.com
Email: kscroucher2@hotmail.com
URL: http://www.cavemanbowl.com

John D. Crow, CEO

Title: Chief Executive Officer **Company:** Crow Friedman Group, LLC **Address:** 5583 Murray Road, Memphis, TN 38119 United States **BUS:** Insurance Company **P/S:** Insurance, Professional Liability **MA:** National **D/D/R:** Training, Speaking for Continuing Education on Insurance Business for the Construction Industry **H/I/S:** Hunting, Fishing, Boating **EDU:** Bachelor of Arts, University of Houston **A/A/S:** American Institute of Architects; Tennessee Association of Professional Surveyors; Instructional Engineering Association; Board of Directors, International Association for Impact Assessment; Certified Founder and 30-Year Member, Playing Association **C/VW:** Heart Foundation of Memphis
Email: john@crowfriedman.com
URL: http://www.crowfriedman.com

Lyris R. Crowdy Peak

Title: Parent Involvement Coordinator **Company:** Omaha Public Schools Head Start **Address:** 5523 N. 34th Street, Omaha, NE 68111 United States **BUS:** Federally-Funded Educational Program **P/S:** Comprehensive Child Development Programs for Low-Income Families **MA:** National **D/D/R:** Working with Families Regarding their Children's Education, Nutrition, Encouraging Parent Involvement, Training Parents, Coordinating Family Activities **H/I/S:** Reading, Walking, Watching Movies, Music, Spending Time with Family **EDU:** Pursuing Master's Degree in Mental Health Therapy; Bachelor of Arts in Sociology and Psychology (1972) **CERTS:** Certified Social Worker, State of Nebraska **A/A/S:** Urban League; National Association of Social Workers; Former Executive Director, Family Resource Center Coalition of Nebraska
Email: lyris.peak@ops.org
URL: http://www.ops.org

Stacy Crowe-Simonson

Title: Executive Chef, Co-Owner **Company:** Chez Nous, La Cuisiniere **Address:** 217 S. Avenue G, Humble, TX 77338 United States **BUS:** French Restaurant, female chef clothing line **P/S:** French Cuisine, clothing line **MA:** Regional, national **D/D/R:** Food Preparation, Restaurant Management **H/I/S:** Gardening **EDU:** Chef Training, Chateau des Reynats; Coursework in Social Science Completed, Texas Tech University **A/A/S:** Confrerie de la Chaine des Rotisseurs **A/H:** Distinguished Restaurants of North America; Recognized by Zagat Survey
Email: echeznous@embarqemail.com
URL: http://www.cheznousfrenchrestaurant.com
URL: http://www.lacuisineierechefwear.com

Emily E. Crowell

Title: Analyst **Company:** JPMorgan **Address:** 277 Park Avenue, New York, NY 10172 United States **BUS:** Financial Services Firm **P/S:** Investment Banking, Financial and Government Institutions, Diversified Corporate Planning and Analysis Groups, Securities, Treasury Services, Government Mergers **MA:** International **D/D/R:** Organizing Presentations, Assessing Finances, Assessing Clients' Debt and Equity, Working Closely with the Chief Financial Officer **H/I/S:** Skiing **EDU:** Bachelor's Degree in Economics, Duke University (2004); Bachelor's Degree in History, Duke University (2004)
Email: emily.e.crowell@jpmchase.com
URL: http://www.jpmorgan.com

Malcolm P. Crowther

Title: Principal **Company:** Apartment Realty Advisors **Address:** 4520 Main Street Suite 1000, Kansas City, MO 64111 United States **BUS:** Real Estate Broker **P/S:** Brokerage and Advisory Services for Investors of Multi Family Properties **MA:** National **D/D/R:** Real Estate Investment Services, Working with Clients from finding properties to closing **H/I/S:** Fitness **EDU:** JD, University of Kansas **A/A/S:** Director, National Multi-Housing Conference
Email: crowther@arausa.com

Carlos James Crudup

Title: Medical Doctor **Company:** Advocate Health Care **Address:** 4901 W. 79th Street, Burbank, IL 60459 United States **BUS:** Healthcare Center **P/S:** Healthcare **MA:** Regional **EXP:** Dr. Crudup's expertise includes family and sports medicine. **H/I/S:** Playing Basketball, Skiing, Visiting Aquariums **EDU:** MD, Chicago Medical School (2001) **A/A/S:** American Medical Association **C/VW:** Board Member, Providence Hospital
Email: losmed@aol.com

Julie L. Cruise

Title: Director of Sales **Company:** Hampton Inn Seattle Southcenter **Address:** 7200 S. 156th Street, Tukwila, WA 98188 United States **BUS:** Hotel **P/S:** Hospitality **MA:** National **D/D/R:** Sales, Marketing **H/I/S:** Crafting, Quilting **EDU:** High School Graduate **A/A/S:** Education Committee, Chamber of Commerce **C/VW:** Volunteer, Children's Hospital
Email: julie_cruise@hilton.com
URL: http://www.cambridgewhoswho.com

Diane R. Crump

Title: Pre-Kindergarten Teacher **Company:** Fort Worth Independent School District **Dept:** George C. Clarke Elementary School **Address:** 3300 S. Henderson Street, Fort Worth, TX 76110 United States **BUS:** School District **P/S:** Primary Education **MA:** Local **D/D/R:** Teaching Prekindergarten Children and English as a Second Language **H/I/S:** Gardening, Sports, Golfing, Traveling **EDU:** Bachelor of Science in Education, Plus 30, The University of Kansas **A/A/S:** Fort Worth Education Association; Texas State Teachers Association; National Education Association **A/H:** Teacher of the Year Award (2004) **C/VW:** Parent-Teacher Association
Email: diane.crump@cwwemail.com

Flavia Cruz

Title: Teacher **Company:** Ansonia High School **Address:** 20 Pullasky Highway, Ansonia, CT 06401 United States **BUS:** School **P/S:** Education **MA:** Local **D/D/R:** Teaching Biology, Anatomy and Physiology to Sophomores and Seniors **H/I/S:** Playing Tennis, Knitting, Traveling, Reading, Running **EDU:** Master of Science in Education, University of New Haven; Bachelor of Science in Biology and Premed, University of New Haven **A/A/S:** National Science Teachers Association **C/VW:** Holy Rosary Church
Email: fcruz@ansonia.org
URL: http://www.cambridgewhoswho.com

Mayra V. Cruz

Title: President **Company:** Unified Service Agency Corp **Address:** 740 Newark Avenue, Elizabeth, NJ 07208 United States **BUS:** Legal Services Paralegal **P/S:** Paralegal Services/Taxes **MA:** Local **D/D/R:** Immigration, Taxes, Translator **H/I/S:** Singing, Reading, Exercise **EDU:** Associate Degree, American International Institute; Bachelor's Degree, Berkeley College **A/A/S:** NJSBA, ALA, NANP
Email: cruzromaro2001@yahoo.com

Virginia E. Cruz de Montoya

Title: Billing Clerk, Bilingual **Company:** Marie H. Reed Community Learning Center Elementary School **Address:** 2200 Champlain Street N.W., Washington, DC 20009 United States **BUS:** Premier Elementary School **P/S:** Top Quality Education **MA:** Regional **D/D/R:** Bilingual Billing and Clerking, Communicating with Parents on all Issues Affecting the School Including Meetings, Closings, Events and Sick Students, Handling all Correspondence In and Out of the Office for Teachers, Parents and Students **H/I/S:** Dance, Music **EDU:** Pursuing Bachelor of Science in Early Childhood Education, University of the District of Columbia **A/A/S:** Member, National Association for Education of Children **A/H:** Recipient, C.D.H. in Early Childhood (1991) **C/VW:** Volunteer, Community to Help Spanish Speaking Citizens with their English Catholic School; Volunteer, St. James Catholic Church; Teaching Saturdays at the Catholic School
Email: virginia.montoya@k12.dc.us
URL: http://www.k12.dc.us

Dennis Cruze

Title: Technical Engineering Manager **Company:** Motivating Graphics **Address:** 3100 Eagle Parkway, Fort Worth, TX 76177 United States **BUS:** Printing and Manufacturing Company **P/S:** Printing of Manuals and Boxes for the Telecommunications Industry, CD and DVD Replication **MA:** International **EXP:** Mr. Cruze's expertise includes package design and implementation. **H/I/S:** Hunting Birds, Boating, Skiing, Tubing, Spending Quality Time with his Family **EDU:** Bachelor of Science in Engineering, Oklahoma University (1997) **A/A/S:** Kiwanis Club **A/H:** Award for Technical Support, Fuji-Xerox (2001) **C/VW:** The Salvation Army; Holiday Volunteer, Meals for the Homeless
Email: dcruz@motivatinggraphics.com
URL: http://www.motivatinggraphics.com

Anthony Cucich

Title: Architect **Address:** 3702 Astoria Boulevard, Astoria, NY 11103 United States **BUS:** Sole Proprietorship **P/S:** Architectural Services Including Residential and Commercial Design **MA:** Regional **D/D/R:** Architectural Designing, Communicating with Clients, Overseeing Projects and Building Department Permits **H/I/S:** Playing Tennis **EDU:** Coursework in Architecture, New York University (1972); Coursework, Institute de Bramante, Italy (1960) **CERTS:** Licensed Architect, States of New York, New Jersey and Florida **A/A/S:** The American Institute of Architects **C/VW:** American Cancer Society; Local Charitable Organizations
Email: tony@a.cucich.com

Braulio Cuevas

Title: President **Company:** Braulio Cuevas HVAC, Inc. **Address:** 68 Derby Street, Valley Stream, NY 11581 United States **BUS:** Installation Service Company **P/S:** Heating, Ventilation, Air Conditioning, Refrigeration Sales, Repair and Installation Services **MA:** Regional **D/D/R:** Managing Equipment Sales, Troubleshooting **H/I/S:** Brazilian Jiu-Jitsu **CERTS:** Certifications in Heating, Ventilation, Air Conditioning and Refrigeration Design, Installation and Repair **C/VW:** Local Charitable Organizations
Email: brauliocuevas1@aol.com
URL: http://www.brauliocuevashvacinc.com

Ken R. Cullen

Title: Information Technology Director **Company:** Granger III and Associates, LLC **Address:** 16980 Wood Road, Lansing, MI 48906 United States **BUS:** Information Technology Company **P/S:** Waste Management, Renewable Energy **MA:** Local **D/D/R:** All Aspects of Information Technology **H/I/S:** Golfing, Playing Basketball **A/A/S:** Great Lakes Interactive Marketing Association **C/VW:** American Heart Association
Email: kcullen@grangernet.com
Email: ken.cullen@cwwemail.com
URL: http://www.grangernet.com

Barbara D. Culp, Ed.D.

Title: Principal (Retired) **Company:** R.N. Fickett Elementary School **Address:** P.O. Box 371061, Decatur, GA 30037 United States **BUS:** Public Elementary School **P/S:** Educating Students in Kindergarten through Fifth-Grade in All Core Subjects, Language Arts, French as a Second Language, Athletics, Saturday School for Extra Help, Afterschool Programs **MA:** Regional **D/D/R:** Managing the Daily Operations of the School, Supervising 72 Teachers, 36 Classified Staff Members and 947 Students, Analyzing Educators' Attitude toward Students, Consulting with Custodians Prior to School Opening, Leading by Example **H/I/S:** Traveling, Studying the Bible, Internet Surfing, Dining Out, **EDU:** Doctor of Education, Rhodes Scholar, Atlanta University (1988) **CERTS:** Completed Georgia Superintendent Professional Development Program **A/A/S:** Road Scholar; National Association of Elementary School Principals; Alpha Kappa Alpha; American Society of Poets; American Association of University Women
Email: bdculp@mindspring.com
URL: http://www.barbaraculp.com

Sandra Joy Cumbey

Title: Vice President of Global Business Partnership **Company:** American Express **Address:** 1365 Bent Creek Drive, Southlake, TX 76092 United States **BUS:** Preeminent Financial Services Company **P/S:** Global Commercial Cards and Travel Solutions **MA:** International **D/D/R:** Business Development, Marketing, Global Relationship Management, Driving Market Share **H/I/S:** Real Estate Investing, Running, Racquetball, Cooking, Wine Tasting **EDU:** Bachelor's Degree in Business, University of Phoenix (1987) **A/A/S:** National Association of Purchasing Management; American Production and Inventory Control Society; Budget Financial Committee Member for Carroll Independent School District
Email: joy.cumbey@yahoo.com
URL: http://www.citigroup.com

Janna Cummings

Title: Facility Director **Company:** The Coral Building, LLC **Address:** 2550 Coral Avenue N.E., Suite 229, Salem, OR 97305 United States **BUS:** Transitional Living Facility **P/S:** Transitional Living for Women **MA:** National **D/D/R:** Director of Administrations of Transitional Living for Women **H/I/S:** Gardening, Making Jewelry **EDU:** Associate Degree in Administration, Chemeketa Community College **CERTS:** Certificate of Completion by City of Salem Oregon Police Department, Landlord Training Program: Keeping Illegal Activity out of Rental Property; ARMS, Abuse Recovery Ministries and Services Training, Hillsboro, Oregon: Her Journey Leader **A/A/S:** Outstanding Leadership and Community Services and Abuse Recovery Ministry and Services: Her Journey Leader, Chemeketa Community College **C/VW:** Various Charitable Organizations
Email: jannainsalem@comcast.net

Lacey L. Cunill

Title: President, Chief Executive Officer **Company:** Graphic Express **Address:** 212 N. Main Street, Dayton, TX 77535 United States **BUS:** Graphic Design Firm **P/S:** Graphic Designing Services Including Screen Printing, Embroidery and Advertising Specialties **MA:** Regional **D/D/R:** Creating Graphic Art and Advertisements, Screen Printing, Embroidering, Billing, Marketing, Advertising, Working on Banners, Managing Operations and Staff **H/I/S:** Studying Graphic Design **EDU:** Coursework in Business, Dayton High School **CERTS:** Industry-Related Training **A/H:** Certificate of Participation, Graphic Design Program, Teen Workshop, Art Institute of Houston
Email: graphicexpress_ceo@yahoo.com
URL: http://www.graphicexpressonline.com

Carrie Lee Cunningham

Title: Vice President **Company:** Health Management Systems, Inc. **Address:** 401 Park Avenue S., New York, NY 10016 United States **BUS:** Financial Recovery Service **P/S:** Financial Recovery **MA:** National **D/D/R:** Managing Healthcare Operations, Business Development, the Sales Staff, Sales Goals and Budget and Forecasting Process, Decision Making Executive Team Member, Second Title Vice President of Software Services for a Secondary Business Manages IT and PNL Agenda of a Managed Health Benefits Delivery Care System **H/I/S:** Traveling, Camping, Reading, Movies **EDU:** Bachelor of Science in Business Management, University of Phoenix-1999 **CERTS:** Accredited Through the Health Insurance Association of America as Managed Care Professional-1998 **A/A/S:** Blue Cross Blue Shield Association; American Health Insurance Plan; Sits on PAC Board for HMS **C/VW:** Women of Faith
Email: ccunningham@hms.com
URL: http://www.hms.com

Kim M. Cunningham

Title: Registered Nurse **Company:** Southside Regional Medical Center **Address:** 801 S. Adams Street, Petersburg, VA 23803 United States **BUS:** Acute-Care Trauma Center **P/S:** Healthcare **MA:** Regional **D/D/R:** Intensive Care Nursing, Non-Invasive Vascular Lab Studies **H/I/S:** Gardening **CERTS:** Pursuing Registry in Non-Invasive Vascular Sonography; Registered Nursing Diploma, Southside Regional Medical Center School of Nursing **C/VW:** American Society for the Prevention of Cruelty to Animals
Email: misckimc@verizon.net

Samuel D. Cunningham Jr.

Title: Unit Manager **Company:** Allstate Financial Customer Contact Center **Address:** 536 Atrium Drive, Vernon Hills, IL 60061 United States **BUS:** Insurance Company **P/S:** Financial Services **MA:** National **D/D/R:** Management, Life Insurance and Annuities **H/I/S:** Participating in Community Outreach, Spending Time with his Family, Reading, Participating in Political Events, Watching Sports, Attending Concerts **EDU:** Bachelor's Degree in Marketing, Central State University (1989) **A/A/S:** Kappa Alpha Si; National Association of Life Underwriters; Toastmasters International; Relatively Speaking Club; Elected Official; Alderman City Council **C/VW:** Boys & Girls Club of Lake County; The Statesman House
Email: aldermancunningham@sbcglobal.net
URL: http://www.samcunningham.com

Jacki Curcio

Title: Skin Care Specialist, Owner **Company:** The Skin Center **Address:** 17557 Chatsworth Street, Granada Hills, CA 91344 United States **BUS:** Beauty Spa **P/S:** Body Care Treatments Including Skin Care, Facials, Hair Removal Services **MA:** Regional **D/D/R:** Working with Doctors, Performing Skin Care Treatments, Training, Handling Purchase Orders, Marketing, Advertising, Managing Sales and Business Operations **H/I/S:** Traveling, Listening to Music, Visiting Museum **EDU:** High School Education **A/A/S:** National Women's Business Council; The House Majority Trust; National Republican Congressional Committee's Business Advisory Council **A/H:** Business Woman of the Year Award, National Republican Convention Committee (2004-2006); Notable American Women Award; Who's Who Among Women of the Word (2000)
Email: jackicurcio@sbcglobal.net
URL: http://www.jackicurcio.com

Kara J. Curley

Title: Nurse Case Manager **Company:** Genesis Westford House **Address:** 3 Park Drive, Westford, MA 01886 United States **BUS:** Medical Care Facility **P/S:** Rehabilitation, Short-Term and Long-Term Nursing **MA:** Local **D/D/R:** Case Management, Marketing, Wound Care **H/I/S:** Golf, Playing Pool Competitively **CERTS:** Licensed Practical Nurse, Shawsheen Valley Technical High School **C/VW:** Relay for Life
Email: curleyk1@yahoo.com
URL: http://www.cambridgewhoswho.com

Barbette M. Curran

Title: Owner **Company:** Barbette's Healing Touch **Address:** 301 S. Bedford Street, Suite 210, Madison, WI 53703 United States **BUS:** Massage Therapy Company **P/S:** Massage Therapy, Diet and Exercise Consulting **MA:** Local **D/D/R:** Zero Balancing, Therapeutic Massage, Stone Therapy, Swedish Massage, Craniosacral Massage, Japanese Shiatsu, Lymphatic and Medical Massage, Zero Balancing **H/I/S:** Gardening, Cooking, Baking, Biking, Rollerblading, Dancing, Hiking, Practicing Yoga **CERTS:** Certified Massage Therapist; National Certification in Therapeutic Massage and Bodywork; Certification in Zero Balancing **A/A/S:** American Massage Therapy Association; Zero Balancing Health Association; Le Sette de Marquette Festival **C/VW:** Orton Park Festival, Atwood Community Center
Email: barbettec@sbcglobal.net

Charlotte C. Currie

Title: Co-Owner, Manager **Company:** Currie & Son **Address:** 900 Enterprise Boulevard, Lake Charles, LA 70601 United States **BUS:** Distribution Firm **P/S:** Feed, Farm, Lawn, Dog and Horse Supplies **MA:** Local **EXP:** Ms. Currie's expertise includes finance and operations management. **D/D/R:** Making Orders, Checking in, Ordering Merchandise, Pricing Products, Managing Finance Including Bookkeeping, Taxation **H/I/S:** Reading, Spending Time with her Grandchildren **EDU:** High School Diploma
Email: crcurrie@aol.com
URL: http://www.cambridgewhoswho.com

Scott Currie

Title: President **Company:** Electrical Management Group **Address:** 4017 Clay Avenue, Suite G, Fort Worth, TX 76117 United States **BUS:** Electrical Installation Company **P/S:** National electrical retail roll-outs and service **MA:** National **D/D/R:** Scheduling, Estimating, Project Coordination, Operations and Management **H/I/S:** Golfing, Traveling, Listening to Music, Reading Retail Magazines, Display and Design Ideas **EDU:** Coursework in Computer Science, Dallas County Junior College; IEC Studies, Various Trade Schools **A/A/S:** PRISM; Fellowship Church **C/VW:** Church
Email: scurrie@electricalmg.com
URL: http://www.electricalmg.com

Jo Curry

Title: Office Manager **Company:** Woodward County Farm Bureau **Address:** 301 E. Oklahoma Avenue, Woodward, OK 73801 United States **BUS:** Independent, Non-Governmental, Voluntary Organization **P/S:** Services for Farm and Ranch Families **MA:** Local **D/D/R:** Managing the Office, Offering Customer Service, Taking Care of Membership Needs, Coordinating Meetings **H/I/S:** Watching Basketball and Football, Gardening, Landscaping **EDU:** High School Education **A/H:** Secretary of the Year, Oklahoma Farm Bureau, Northwest Region (1993); Secretary of the Year, Oklahoma Farm Bureau, Northwest Region (1992)
Email: info@CambridgeWhosWho.com
URL: http://www.okfarmbureau.org/county/Default.aspx

Cindy Lou Curtice

Title: Owner, Operator **Company:** Island Pet Spa **Address:** 307 Love Point Road, Stevensville, MD 21666 United States **BUS:** Dog Grooming Business **P/S:** Dog Grooming Salon, Boutique and Daycare **MA:** Maryland **D/D/R:** Dog Grooming, Pet Training **H/I/S:** Spending Time with her Family and Friends **EDU:** College Coursework; Diploma, Dog Grooming School
Email: cindy1lou@aol.com
URL: http://www.cambridgewhoswho.com

Cristy Curtis

Title: Owner **Company:** Desert Tree Fitness Services, LLC **Address:** 44177 W. Palmen Drive, Maricopa, AZ 85238 United States **BUS:** Fitness Program **P/S:** Health and Fitness **MA:** Local **D/D/R:** Women's Fitness, Counseling, Personal Training **H/I/S:** Spending Time Outdoors, Hiking, Camping **EDU:** Associate Degree in Health and Exercise, Utah Career College **CERTS:** Certification, American Council on Exercise; Certification, National Exercise and Sports Trainers Association **C/VW:** Various Local Charities
Email: cristy@maricopabootcamp.com
URL: http://www.maricopabootcamp.com

Myrta Ellen Curtis

Title: Senior Secretary **Company:** South Suburban College, Business and Career Institute **Address:** 15800 S. State Street, South Holland, IL 60473 United States **BUS:** Public Higher Education Facility **P/S:** Wide Selection of Career Education and College Transfer Credit Programs **MA:** Regional **D/D/R:** Compiling Monthly Reports, Purchasing Orders, Answering Department Questions, Handling All Administrative Functions for the Business and Career Institute **H/I/S:** Reading, Working on Crafts **EDU:** Associate Degree in Office Administration and Technology, South Suburban College (2006) **A/A/S:** Phi Beta Kappa; Executive Board Member, Nazarene Missions International; Member, Local Church; Treasurer, Sunday School
Email: mcurtis@southsuburbancollege.edu
URL: http://www.southsuburbancollege.edu

Deborah Pratt Curtiss

Title: Artist, Writer **Company:** Deep See (DPC) **Address:** 5225 Green Street, Apt. 15, Philadelphia, PA 19144 United States **BUS:** Art Company **P/S:** Painting, Drawing, Literacy **MA:** National **D/D/R:** Visual Metaphors, Visual Literacy, Creating Art **H/I/S:** Spending Time with her Family **EDU:** Master's Degree in Art Education, University of the Arts (1983); Degree in Fine Arts, Yale University (1961) **A/A/S:** International Visual Literacy Association; College of Art Association; Artist Equity **C/VW:** International Visual Literacy Association, Green Tree Artist, Northwest Artist Collective
Email: debcurtiss@verizon.net
URL: http://www.inliquid.com

Mona A. Cushnie

Title: Realtor **Company:** Weichert Realtors **Address:** 128 E. Route 59, Nanuet, NY 10954 United States **BUS:** Real Estate Agency **P/S:** Real Estate Exchange **MA:** National **EXP:** Ms. Cushnie's expertise includes residential real estate and market analysis. **D/D/R:** Assisting Clients with Relocations, Selling Multi-Family Homes **H/I/S:** Performing at the Musical Theater **EDU:** Master of Science in Education, Lehman College, NY; Bachelor of Science in Elementary Education, Fisk University, TN **A/A/S:** New York Board of Realtors; National Association of Realtors **C/VW:** Grace Episcopal Church; Coordinator, Meals on Wheels
Email: mcushnie@weichert.com
URL: http://www.monacushnie.com

Rev. Ann Cutler

Title: President, Writer **Company:** Cutler Enterprises **BUS:** Conglomerate Company **P/S:** Rental Business, Monavie Distribution, Life Coaching and Property Rentals **MA:** Local **D/D/R:** Finding Rental Properties, Writing Articles on the Internet, Counseling on Deliverance and Healing, Conducting Real Estate Appraisals, Writing, Renting Properties **H/I/S:** Swimming, Boating **EDU:** Doctor of Divinity (2005); Bachelor of Arts in Speech and Communication, University of Cincinnati (1976) **CERTS:** Certification of Ordination (2005) **A/A/S:** National Association of Independent Landlords; International Association for Theophostic Ministry **C/VW:** Foundations for Life
Email: cutla4@tampabay.rr.com
URL: http://www.cambridgewhoswho.com

Vivian Cutrone, RN, CNOR

Title: Registered Nurse, Certified Nurse, Operating Room **Company:** North Shore-Long Island Jewish Health System **Dept:** Syosset Hospital **Address:** P.O. Box 389, Malverne, NY 11565 United States **BUS:** Hospital **P/S:** Healthcare Including Surgery **MA:** Regional **D/D/R:** Nursing, Assisting with Pediatric Surgical Procedures **H/I/S:** Reading, Needlework, Spending Time Outdoors, Listening to Music **EDU:** Diploma in Nursing, The Jewish Hospital and Medical Center of Brooklyn **CERTS:** Registered Nurse; Certified Operating Room Nurse
Email: 1ntrllyblonde@myway.com
URL: http://www.northshorelij.com

Norma Cypert

Title: Escrow Branch Manager **Company:** First American Title **Address:** 2260 S. Fourth Avenue, Yuma, AZ 85364 United States **BUS:** Real Estate Agency **P/S:** Real Estate and Mortgage Settlement Services **MA:** International **D/D/R:** Managing the Sale of Residential Property **H/I/S:** Traveling, Spending Time with her Children **EDU:** Coursework in Liberal Arts, University of San Francisco **A/A/S:** Big Brothers Big Sisters of America; Arizona State Escrow Association
Email: nfaudoa@firstam.com
URL: http://www.firstam.net

Mr. Tim Czilinger

Title: Owner **Company:** Road King Logistics **Address:** 21 Shady Lane, Lake Ariel, PA 18436 United States **BUS:** Trucking and Transportation **P/S:** Transportation Services, Logistics **MA:** International **D/D/R:** Business Management, Trade Show and High Value Transportation **H/I/S:** Baseball, Weekend Get-Aways, Fishing, Jazz Festivals
Email: transdogg@aol.com
URL: http://www.roadkinglogistics.com

Catherine D'Agnese

Title: Owner, Manager **Company:** CJ Management, LLC **Address:** 417 Queen Palm Drive, Davenport, FL 33897 United States **BUS:** Professional, Effective, Accurate and Efficient Property Management Services **P/S:** Full Service Property Management and Leasing Services for Owners of Rental Homes, Individual Rental Condominiums, Rental Apartments and Vacation Rental Property **MA:** National **D/D/R:** Property Manager for 100 Homes, Advertising Rentals, Managing Accounts, Overseeing Operations and Maintenance of Rental and Investment Properties for Two, Three and Four Bedroom Homes, Managing Staff of Five Contractors **H/I/S:** Boating, Crocheting **EDU:** Coursework in Banking, St. John's University **A/A/S:** Chamber of Commerce; Better Business Bureau; Central Florida Property Managers Association, Inc. **A/H:** Seal of Compliance (2006); Seal of Approval, Florida State (2007)
Email: cathy@cjmanagement.net
URL: http://www.cjmanagement.net

Ms. Angela M. D'Alessandro

Title: Continuity Management Consultant **Company:** Nationwide Mutual Insurance Company **Address:** 462 Burmont Road, Drexel Hill, PA 19026 United States **BUS:** Insurance Company **P/S:** Insurance Coverage **MA:** National **EXP:** Ms. D'Alessandro's expertise includes business continuity, disaster recovery, mainframe storage management, systems programming and change management. **H/I/S:** Democratic Politics, Reading **EDU:** Diploma, Upper Darby High School **CERTS:** Associate Business Continuity Professional **A/A/S:** Chairwoman, Local Democratic Committee; Elected Member, Pennsylvania Democratic Party **C/VW:** United Way of America
Email: dalessa@nationwide.com

Kathy D'Andrea

Title: Safety Manager **Company:** Western Nevada Supply Company **Address:** P.O. Box 1576, Sparks, NV 89432 United States **BUS:** Wholesale Distributor **P/S:** Waterworks, Plumbing, Irrigation, Heating, Ventilation and Air Conditioning, Fencing **MA:** NV, ID, CA, WY **EXP:** Ms. D'Andrea's expertise is in safety education. **H/I/S:** Golfing, Reading, Gardening **EDU:** Bachelor's Degree in Business, University of Nevada at Reno **CERTS:** Certification in Occupational Safety and Health Administration for OSHA **A/A/S:** AGC Safety Committee; National Safety Council **C/VW:** Special Olympics
Email: kdandrea@goblueteam.com
URL: http://www.blueteam.wns1.com

Mr. Nicholas H. D'Angelo

Title: Sales Executive **Company:** Bradco Supply Corporation **Address:** 286 Burnham Road, Lowell, MA United States **BUS:** Building Materials Distributor **P/S:** Residential Roofing, Siding, Windows, Commercial Roofing, Kitchens, Lumber **MA:** national **D/D/R:** Selling Home Improvement Products and new construction **H/I/S:** Skydiving **CERTS:** Certificate in Radio Broadcasting, Connecticut School of Broadcasting
Email: ndangelo@bradcosupply.com
URL: http://www.bradcosupply.com

Joan A. D'Urso

Title: Teacher **Company:** Patchogue-Medford Schools **Address:** 281 Medford Avenue, Patchogue, NY 11772 United States **BUS:** Public School District **P/S:** Public Education for Local Students **MA:** Regional **D/D/R:** Teaching Inclusion Third-Grade Science Classes, Working with an Autistic Population, Coordinating the Third-Grade Science and Technology Programs, Overseeing Website Updates, Teaching All Subjects, Conducting Student-Led Class Meetings, Teaching Manners and Life Lessons through a Whole Child Approach **H/I/S:** Traveling **EDU:** Master of Arts Plus15 in Special Education, Adelphi University (1983) **A/A/S:** National Education Association of New York; National Education Association
Email: jd'urso@pmschools.org
URL: http://www.pmschools.org

Sharan S. Dababnah

Title: Office Manager **Company:** Neonatology & Pediatric Acute Care Specialists, Inc. **Address:** 352 Second Street N.W., Suite 205, Hickory, NC 28601 United States **BUS:** Medical Practice **P/S:** Healthcare **MA:** National **EXP:** Ms. Dababnah's expertise is in operations management. **D/D/R:** Managing Accounts, Interacting with Patients, Preparing Bills **H/I/S:** Reading, Walking **EDU:** Associate Degree, Dabney S. Lancaster Community College, Virginia **A/A/S:** North Carolina Odyssey of the Mind
Email: sharan@charterinternet.com

Michelle M. Dabney

Title: Psychology Instructor **Company:** Cincinnati State Technical Community College **Address:** 3520 Central Parkway, Cincinnati, OH 45223 United States **BUS:** Community College **P/S:** Education **MA:** Local **D/D/R:** Domestic Violence Psychology, Rape Crisis Counseling **H/I/S:** Playing the Piano, Reading **EDU:** Master's Degree in Psychology, Cleveland State University (1994) **A/A/S:** American Psychological Association; NCBAA
Email: michelledabney4@aol.com
URL: http://www.cinstate.cc.oh.us

Lorrie Patricia Daggett

Title: Director **Company:** Activx Biosciences **Address:** 11025 N. Torrey Pines Road, La Jolla, CA 92037 United States **BUS:** Biopharmaceutical Company **P/S:** Biopharmaceutical Research, Target and Off-Target Activities of Drugs, Research on Protein Kinase and Protease Families **MA:** International **EXP:** Ms. Daggett's expertise is in project management. **D/D/R:** Managing Projects and Human Resources, Corporate Planning, Overseeing Scientific Research and Business Development, reviewing Intellectual Property Portfolio License Agreements, Accounting **EDU:** Pursuing Master of Business Administration, University of California, San Diego; Bachelor of Science in Psychology, University of California Los Angeles (1981) **C/VW:** National Multiple Sclerosis Society
Email: lorried@activx.com
URL: http://www.activx.com

Nadra Dahdah

Title: Broker Associate **Company:** Re/Max Execs **Address:** 1720 S Elena Avenue, Redondo Beach, CA 90277 United States **BUS:** Real Estate Broker **P/S:** Residential, Executive, Hi End, Beach Front Homes and Condos, New Construction, Golf Homes, Gated **MA:** Local **D/D/R:** Residential Properties and Investment Properties **H/I/S:** Martial Arts **EDU:** Long Beach State University **A/A/S:** California Association of Realtors; National Association of Realtors
Email: nadra@southbayca.com
URL: http://www.southbayca.com

Crystal A. Daigle, RDH

Title: Registered Dental Hygienist **Company:** A Beautiful Smile Dental Center, Heartland Dental Care Group **Address:** 16565 Vanderbilt Drive, Suite 2, Bonita Springs, FL 34134 United States **BUS:** Proven Leader in the Health Care Industry **P/S:** High Quality Dental Services for Patients including General Dental Services **MA:** Regional **D/D/R:** Periodontics, X-Rays, Routine Cleanings, Patient Education, Nutrition and Tobacco Consulting **EDU:** Associate of Science, University of Maine (1998) **A/A/S:** American Dental Hygiene Association; National Dental Hygiene Honor Society
Email: countygirl_3@hotmail.com
URL: http://cambridgewhoswho.com

Cindi C. Dailey-Richardson

Title: Corporate Compliance Officer **Company:** NMA Comprehensive Health Center **Address:** 446 26th Street, Suite 101, San Diego, CA 92102 United States **BUS:** Health Center **P/S:** Healthcare Facility **MA:** Local **D/D/R:** Coordinating Grants, Ensuring Compliance **H/I/S:** Traveling, Youth Group **EDU:** Bachelor of Arts in Business Management, Oakwood College **A/A/S:** Healthcare Compliance Association; Chemet Coalition; Statewide African American HIV-AIDS Coalition
Email: cdrichardson@sdhc.com
URL: http://www.cambridgewhoswho.com

Yognie Arjoon Daiowraj

Title: 1) Assistant Controller 2) Vice President **Company:** 1) Access Capital, Inc. 2) MO Auto Repairs, Inc. **Address:** 405 Park Avenue, New York, NY 10022 United States **BUS:** 1) Capital Lending Company 2) Automotive Service Company **P/S:** 1) Lending Services 2) Domestic and Foreign Cars Repair Service **MA:** 1) National 2) Local **EXP:** Ms. Daiowraj's expertise includes finance and operations management. **D/D/R:** Working with Foxpro Software, Managing Finance Including Accounts Payable **H/I/S:** Spending Time with her Children, Singing **EDU:** Associate Degree in Psychology, CUNY Brooklyn College
Email: barjoon@accesscapitalinc.com

Diane C. Dal Lago

Title: President **Company:** Diane Dal Lago, Ltd. **Address:** 6011 Benjamin Road, Suite 105, Tampa, FL 33634 United States **BUS:** Manufacturing Company **P/S:** Women's Apparel, Crystal Embellishments, Appliques, Bags, Bridal Accessories and Costume Design Services **MA:** National **EXP:** Ms. Dal Lago's expertise includes costume design and staff management. **D/D/R:** Managing Operations **H/I/S:** Spending Time with her Daughters **EDU:** Associate Degree in Merchandising, Bergen Community College, Paramus, NJ **CERTS:** Licensed Apparel Designer **A/A/S:** National Honor Society; Board Member, International Academy of Design and Technology **A/H:** Employer of the Year Award, Florida Metropolitan University (2007); Dean's List, Bergen Community College
Email: diane@dianedallagoltd.com
URL: http://www.racewayfashionista.com

Bernadette C. Dale

Title: President, Chief Executive Officer **Company:** Altima Healthcare Services, Inc. **Address:** 16890 West Maglitto Circle, Tomball, TX 77377 United States **BUS:** Home Health Care Company **P/S:** Home Health Care Services to the Elderly Including a Team of Nurses, Home Health Aids, Physical Therapists, Speech and Occupational Therapists, Giving Medication, Assisting with Eating and Bathing **MA:** Local **D/D/R:** Overseeing the Daily Operations, Assigning Staff to Designated Areas, Filling-In for Staff When Needed, Supervising Another Business in the Philippines **H/I/S:** Dancing, Writing, Basketball **EDU:** Master in Business Administration, Philippines (1980); Bachelor of Science in Business Administration, Philippines (1978) **A/A/S:** Texas Association for Home Care
Email: altimahealthcare@msn.com

Emily E. Dale

Title: Third-Grade Teacher **Company:** Wicomico County Board of Education **Address:** Salisbury, MD United States **BUS:** School **P/S:** Provides Public School Education from K through 12th-Grade **MA:** Local **D/D/R:** Teaches Math, Reading and Science, Using a Hands On Interactive Approach to Keep Kids Interested in Learning **H/I/S:** Fashion Design, Sewing **EDU:** Bachelor of Arts in Education, Douglas University **A/A/S:** Maryland Educator Association, Sigma Lambda Chi, seat on County Risk Management Board
Email: dale01@comcast.net
URL: www.wcboe.org

Alethia Daley

Title: Clinical Assistant **Company:** Children's Hospital Boston **Address:** 300 Longwood Avenue, Boston, MA 02115 United States **BUS:** Hospital **P/S:** Children's Healthcare **MA:** International **D/D/R:** Assisting Patients and their Families **H/I/S:** Creating Crafts, Cake Decorating **EDU:** Associate of Science in Nursing, Medway College **C/VW:** Church, Local Prisons
Email: alethiadaley@yahoo.com

Robert F. Daley

Title: Principal Attorney **Company:** Robert Peirce and Associates, PC **Address:** 2500 Gulf Tower, Pittsburgh, PA 15219 United States **BUS:** Law Firm **P/S:** Legal Services **MA:** Regional **D/D/R:** Litigating for Personal Injury Law, Representing Nursing Home Residents **H/I/S:** Golfing **EDU:** Coursework in Law, Duquesne University (1998)
Email: bdaley@peircelaw.com
URL: http://www.peircelaw.com

Mary J. Dall, RN

Title: Registered Nurse **Company:** Southwest Health Center **Address:** 808 S. Washington Street, Cuba City, WI 53807 United States **BUS:** Healthcare Center **P/S:** Healthcare, Long-Term Care **MA:** Regional **EXP:** Ms. Dall's expertise is in nursing. **H/I/S:** Gardening **CERTS:** Diploma in Nursing, St. Mary's College **C/VW:** St. Jude Children's Research Hospital
Email: mary.dall@cwwemail.com

Elias A. Dalloul

Title: Medical Doctor **Company:** Providence Medical Group **Address:** 2723 S. Seventh Street, Suite A, Terre Haute, IN 47802 United States **BUS:** Full-Services Medical Center **P/S:** Medical Care **MA:** Regional **D/D/R:** Practicing Interventional Cardiology, Seeing to Patients' Needs, Performing Healthcare Procedures **H/I/S:** Playing Tennis **EDU:** MD, Earned in Syria **CERTS:** Board Certification in Intervention Cardiology, United States **A/A/S:** American College of Cardiology; American College of Medicine; American Medical Association
Email: eadalloul@aol.com
URL: http://www.cambridgewhoswho.com

Hazel V. Dalton

Title: Assistant Professor **Company:** The University of Texas **Dept:** MD Anderson Cancer Center School of Health Science **Address:** 16335 Quail Place Drive, Missouri City, TX 77489 United States **BUS:** University, Cancer Center **P/S:** Higher Education Including Cancer Treatment and Training for Healthcare Professionals **MA:** International **EXP:** Ms. Dalton's expertise includes immunohistochemistry, lecturing and healthcare education such as teaching routine and special histological techniques. **D/D/R:** Interviewing Students, Managing Histotechnology Program, Performing Administrative Duties, Budgeting, Hiring, Firing, Overseeing Curriculum Changes, Maintaining Information Regarding Certifications **H/I/S:** Writing, Reading The Holy Bible, Storytelling **EDU:** Master of Science in Community Health, California College for Health Sciences (2005); Bachelor's Degree in Applied Behavioral Sciences, National College **A/A/S:** Educational Chairwomen, Texas Society for Histotechnology; Souls of My Sister; American Society for Clinical Pathology; Education Committee Member, National Society for Histotechnology **A/H:** Technologist of the Year Award
Email: hdalton@mdanderson.org
URL: http://www.mdanderson.org

Eileen A. Daly

Title: Assistant Broker **Company:** Prudential Land Realty **Address:** 95 S Middletown Road, Nanuet, NY 10954 United States **BUS:** Real Estate Broker **P/S:** Listing and Selling Foreclosures **MA:** Local **D/D/R:** Residential Foreclosures
Email: EDaly@aol.com

Sylvia M. Damato

Title: Realtor **Company:** Prodigy Home Services, Inc. **Address:** 2035 County Road D, Suite E, Maplewood, MN 55109 United States **BUS:** Real Estate Agency **P/S:** Finance, Real Estate, Mortgages, Credit Repair **MA:** Regional **D/D/R:** Selling Residential Real Estate **H/I/S:** Traveling, Reading **EDU:** Bachelor of Arts in Humanities, English and Archeology, North Central University **A/A/S:** Minnesota Air National Guard; National Association of Realtors; Minnesota Association of Realtors; Saint Paul Area Association of Realtors **C/VW:** Salvation Army
Email: jackyofalltrades@comcast.net
URL: http://www.cambridgewhoswho.com

Mary Aigner Dammann

Title: Director/Owner **Company:** Step Up Childcare and Pre School **Address:** 734 State Hwy 217, Tijeras, NM 87059 United States **BUS:** Childcare and Preschool Education **P/S:** Day Care, Pre School, Infants **MA:** Local **D/D/R:** Progressive Day Care, 3 Meals, Activities **H/I/S:** Hiking, Reading **EDU:** Coursework in Business Management, Alaska Business College **A/A/S:** New Mexico Association of Childcare and Early Childhood Development
Email: info@CambridgeWhosWho.com

Ann H. T. Dang

Title: Owner, Mortgage Broker **Company:** Clear Choice Mortgage Services **Address:** 2323 S. Voss Road,, Suite 120, Houston, TX 77057 United States **BUS:** Mortgage For Residential and Commercial Real Estate **P/S:** Financial Services **MA:** Regional **D/D/R:** Mortgage Financing, Manage Office With the Loan Officers, Originage Loans, Deals with Customer Service, Deals with Administration, HR Responsibilities, Administrate a Staff of 14, Attends Closings, Negotiates for her clients, marketing for the company, Rewarding Aspect-a buyer gets financing on his house or business, Future Goal-Expand business, **H/I/S:** Traveling **CERTS:** Licensed Realtor-2005, Licensed Mortgage Broker-2005 **A/A/S:** HAR, TAR, NAR
Email: ccms-ann@sbcglobal.net

Louis A. DAngeli

Title: President **Company:** BDCI Management **Address:** 1245 U.S. Highway 22, Lebanon, NJ 08833 United States **BUS:** Staffing Company **P/S:** Staffing **MA:** National **D/D/R:** Staffing Consultations **H/I/S:** Deep Sea Fishing, Shooting Competitively **EDU:** Bachelor of Science in Computer Science, University of Phoenix
Email: ldangeli@bdcius.com
URL: http://www.bdcius.com

Debra D. Daniels

Title: New Teacher Coach and Mentor **Company:** National Heritage Academies **Dept:** Buffalo United Charter School **Address:** 325 Manhattan Avenue, Buffalo, NY 14214 United States **BUS:** Elementary Charter School **P/S:** Preparing Students in Kindergarten through Seventh-Grade to Face the Challenges of a Progressive and Diverse Society while Embracing a No Excuses Policy to Learning **MA:** Regional **D/D/R:** Mentoring New Teachers with Guidance and Tools to Develop Lesson Plans and Teach in a Reflective Way, Overseeing Staff Development **H/I/S:** Playing Tennis, Going Fishing **EDU:** Master's Degree in Literacy, University of Buffalo (2003); Bachelor of Arts Degree in Sociology, D'Youville College, Buffalo, NY (1973) **A/A/S:** International Reading Association; Association for Supervision and Curriculum Development
Email: 48.ddaniels@heritageacademies.com
URL: http://www.heritageacademies.com

Mr. John Wesley Daniels Jr.

Title: New York State Commissioner of Jurors **Company:** The Oneida County Courthouse **Address:** 200 Elizabeth Street, Utica, NY 13501 United States **BUS:** Government Agency **P/S:** Jury Selection **MA:** Local **D/D/R:** Court Administration Overseeing All Matters Relating to Jurors **H/I/S:** Reading **EDU:** Master's Degree in Social Policy, Empire State College (2007); Bachelor of Arts in Political Science, Binghamton University (1998)
Email: jwesley060@att.blackberry.net
URL: http://www.co.oneida.wi.gov/county/

Mrs. Mary B. Daniels

Title: Administrative Assistant, Educator **Company:** Beaufort County Schools, St. Helen Early Learning Center **Dept:** Administration **Address:** 1031 Sea Island Parkway, St. Helena Island, SC 29920 United States **BUS:** Public School System **P/S:** Educating Students in Prekindergarten through 12th-Grade, Academics, Athletics, Computer Sciences, After School Programs **MA:** Local **EXP:** Mrs. Daniels' expertise is in educational administration. **D/D/R:** Assisting the Principal with Office Management, Participating in Student-Parent-Teacher Conferences, Managing Behavioral Problems, Planning Field Trips and Outings, Supervising Students, Emergency Substitute Teaching **H/I/S:** Walking, Reading, Watching Television, Traveling, Performing Volunteer Work **EDU:** Associate Degree in Early Childhood Education, Wheelock College (2005) **A/A/S:** Pine Grove Baptist Church Choir
Email: mpd9237@beaufort.k12.sc.us
URL: http://www.beaufort.k12.sc.us

Robin A. Daniels

Title: Teacher for the Deaf, Hard of Hearing and Regular Education **Company:** Kedron Elementary School **Address:** 100 Grandview Terrace, Fayetteville, GA 30215 United States **BUS:** Elementary School **P/S:** Education **MA:** Local **D/D/R:** Assessing and Evaluating Curriculum Needs, Creating Yearly Plans for Students, Managing Data, Supervising Activities of Students, Teaching Language Arts, Reading, Mathematics, Social Studies and Science to Third-Grade Students **H/I/S:** Reading, Traveling **EDU:** Specialization Degree in Educational Leadership, Lincoln Memorial University (2005) **A/A/S:** Association for Supervision and Curriculum Development; International Reading Association; Professional Association of Georgia Educators; Georgia Staff Development Council; Administrative Internship Program
Email: Robin.Daniels@cwwemail.com
Email: robin58@bellsouth.net
URL: http://www.peepleselementary.org
URL: http://www.kedvonknight.org

Polly A. Danielsen
Title: Teacher **Company:** Glendale Unified School District, Marshall Elementary School **Address:** 13413 Riverside Drive, Apartment A, Sherman Oaks, CA 91423 United States **BUS:** Public School for Students in Kindergarten through High School **P/S:** Basic Core Curriculum Including Reading, Writing, Speaking, Listening, Mathematics, Instruction in Science, History, Social Science and the Arts **MA:** Regional **D/D/R:** Teaching All Subjects to Elementary School Students **H/I/S:** Folk Dancing **EDU:** Bachelor's Degree in Elementary Education, San Jose State University (1962) **CERTS:** California State Certified **A/H:** Who's Who Among American's Teachers; Graduated with Honors
Email: shazampd2@roadrunner.com
URL: http://www.glendale.k12.ca.us/

Mr. Thomas C. Dant
Title: Realtor **Company:** RE/MAX 2000 **Address:** 12301 Old Columbia Pike, Suite 310, Silver Spring, MD 20904 United States **BUS:** Real Estate Agency **P/S:** Representing Buyers and Sellers of Properties **MA:** Regional **D/D/R:** Real Estate Investing and Negotiating, Determining Value of Homes, Dealing with Residential, Land, Commercial, Single-Family, Condominiums and Townhouses, Assisting Clients with Home Inspections, Titles Searches, Mortgages **H/I/S:** Golfing **EDU:** College Coursework **A/A/S:** Evangelist; Millionaires Club
Email: tomdant@mris.com
URL: http://www.tomdant.com

Ruth Dantis-Naval
Title: Staff Development Specialist **Company:** Advocate Health Centers **Address:** 2555 S. King Drive, Chicago, IL 60616 United States **BUS:** Nonprofit Healthcare Center **P/S:** Health and Consultation Services **MA:** Regional **EXP:** Ms. Dantis-Naval's expertise is in nursing. **D/D/R:** Overseeing Clinical Orientation of New Employees, Re-Certifying Staff in CPR, Teaching CPR, Continuing Education for Nurses and Clinical Staff, Promoting Clinical Healthcare Revisions, Trauma and Critical-Care Nursing **EDU:** Bachelor of Science in Nursing, Lewis University (2007) **CERTS:** Registered Nurse (1997) **A/A/S:** Illinois Nurses Association; Sigma Theta Tau
Email: ruth.dantis@advocatehealth.com
URL: http://www.advocatehealth.com/ahc

Denise L. Danzo
Title: Director **Company:** Danza Dance Academy **Address:** 4807 N. Industrial Way, Castle Rock, CO 80109 United States **BUS:** Dance Academy **P/S:** Teaching Ballet, Jazz, Tap and Hip-Hop Dance **MA:** Local **D/D/R:** Instructing Dance, Managing Operations, Hiring and Firing Employees, Billing, Scheduling Classes **H/I/S:** Spending Time Outdoors, Mountain Biking, Hiking **EDU:** Associate Degree, Community College of Aurora (1999) **A/A/S:** Colorado Dance Alliance
Email: denisedanzo@comcast.net
URL: http://www.danzadanceacademy.com

Paula K. Darling, MBA
Title: Chairman, Chief Executive Officer **Company:** Customer Solutions Online, Inc. **Address:** 1420 Spring Hill Road, Suite 600, McLean, VA 22102 United States **BUS:** Business Software and Systems Developer **P/S:** Powerful and Affordable On Demand Business Solutions **MA:** International **D/D/R:** Operations **H/I/S:** Teaching, Tennis, Golfing **EDU:** Pursuing Ph.D. in Statistics, Virginia Tech; Master of Business Administration, Averett College (1996); Bachelor of Arts in Business, Auburn University (1983) **A/H:** Everett College Outstanding Alumni Award; Pinnacle Capital Award, GE Capital (1992) **C/VW:** Local Hospital
Email: paula@4cso.com
URL: http://www.4cso.com

Joyce N. Dartez
Title: Administrative Secretary **Company:** City of New Iberia **Dept:** New Iberia Recreation Department **Address:** 300 Parkview Drive, New Iberia, LA 70563 United States **BUS:** Recreational Center **P/S:** Sports, Rentals, Events **MA:** Regional **D/D/R:** managing registration, rentals and deposits, performing administrative duties, checking all games, announcing the college football game weekly winners and handling gift certificates. **H/I/S:** Football, Basketball, Baseball **EDU:** High School Diploma **A/A/S:** American Legion Auxiliary
Email: jdartez@cityofnewiberia.com
URL: http://www.cityofnewiberia.com

Sal DaSilva
Title: President **Company:** JPS Collision, Inc. **Address:** 24 Foundry Street, Newark, NJ 07105 United States **BUS:** Automotive Body Shop **P/S:** Automobile Repair Services Including Detailing, Paint, Collision Work and Aerodynamic Kits **MA:** Local **D/D/R:** Overseeing Customer Relations, Estimating Labor Prices, Repairing Automobiles, Tracking Vehicles **H/I/S:** Golfing **EDU:** Coursework in Automobiles; Coursework in Estimating; High School Education **A/A/S:** Portuguese Chamber of Commerce; US Chamber of Commerce
Email: jpscars@aol.com
URL: http://www.jpscollision.com

Angel L. Daug
Title: Licensed Practical Nurse **BUS:** Healthcare Clinic **P/S:** Healthcare **MA:** Local **D/D/R:** Long-Term Healthcare and Methadone Clinic **H/I/S:** Reading **EDU:** Bachelor's Degree in Marketing Management, De La Salle University **CERTS:** Licensed Practical Nurse, Microtech Training Center; Pursuing Registered Nurse Diploma **A/A/S:** National League for Nursing, NAACP
Email: angel.daug@gmail.com
URL: http://www.cambridgewhoswho.com

Kimberly S. Daugherty
Title: President **Company:** Quickset Hair Salon, Inc. **Address:** 5627 North Henry Boulevard, Stockbridge, GA 30281 United States **BUS:** Full-Service Hair Salon **P/S:** Haircare **MA:** Local **D/D/R:** Net Weaving, Hair Extensions, Treating Cancer Patients and People who have Alopecia **EDU:** Master's Degree in Cosmetology, Metropolitan School of Hair, Stone Mountain, GA (1998)
Email: quicksetsalon@yahoo.com
URL: http://www.quicksetsalon.com

Carmelita H. Dausuel
Title: Chief Executive Officer **Company:** Creations by Carmelita **Address:** 22 Hamilton Road, Teaneck, NJ 07666 United States **BUS:** Fashion Retail **P/S:** Fashion and Interior Design **MA:** National **D/D/R:** Tailoring **H/I/S:** Traveling, Reading, Cooking and Former Member of Teaneck Tappers **EDU:** Coursework, FIT, New York, NY; Coursework, Bergen Community College; Internship, NJ Decorating Exchange **A/A/S:** ASID
Email: carmelitad076@yahoo.com

Mr. Brian A. Davenport
Title: Construction Coordinator **Company:** Arkansas Western Gas Company **Address:** 1811 E. Borick Drive, Fayetteville, AR 72703 United States **BUS:** Utility Company **P/S:** Natural Gas **MA:** Regional **D/D/R:** Mapping, Welding, Ensuring the Facility's Availability for New Construction, Promoting Gas Usage through Marketing and Appliance Sales to Increase Revenue, Inspecting and Planning the Repair of Damaged Facilities, Overseeing Personnel, Preparing Documents for New Services, Main Extensions and Replacements **H/I/S:** Golfing, Hunting, Fishing, Basketball **EDU:** Coursework, Southern Technical College **A/A/S:** National Rifle Association
Email: brian.davenport@sourcegas.com
URL: http://www.cambridgewhoswho.com

Rachel L. Davenport, Pharm.D.
Title: Clinical Pharmacist **Company:** Tanner Medical Center **Address:** 111 Danny Drive, Apartment F, Carrollton, GA 30117 United States **BUS:** Public Medical Hospital **P/S:** Medical Services for Residents of Carrollton, Georgia **MA:** Regional **D/D/R:** Specializing in Geriatric Pharmaceuticals, Pharmacokinetics, Drug Information and Medication Therapy Management **H/I/S:** Scrapbooking, Participating Outdoor Activities, Camping, Swimming **EDU:** Doctor of Pharmacy, College of Pharmacy and Health Sciences, Mercer University (2007); Pre-Pharmacy, University of West Georgia **A/A/S:** The Rho Chi Society; Phi Kappa Phi; Honor Council; American Pharmacist Association; National Community Pharmacists Association
Email: rachel03cw@yahoo.com

Alon David
Title: Kitchen Designer **Company:** Nola Design **Address:** 7152 Convoy Court, San Diego, CA 92111 United States **BUS:** Kitchen Construction Firm **P/S:** Custom Kitchen Design for Residential and Commercial Use **MA:** Local **EXP:** Mr. David's expertise is in kitchen and bath design. **A/A/S:** Local Synagogue
URL: http://www.noladesign.biz

Alecia Davidson
Title: Teacher **Company:** Unity Elementary School **Address:** 525 Park Avenue, LaGrange, GA 30240 United States **BUS:** Public Elementary School **P/S:** Education **MA:** Local **D/D/R:** Teaching Third-Grade Students in all Subjects, Working with Gifted and Talented Students **H/I/S:** Reading, Computers **EDU:** Elementary Education Specialist, Troy State University **A/A/S:** National Education Association; Georgia Education Association **C/VW:** World Vision
Email: davidsonas@troup.com
URL: http://www.cambridgewhoswho.com

James M. Davidson
Title: Chief Information Officer **Company:** Ferry County Public Hospital District 1 **Address:** 36 Klondike Road, Republic, WA 99166 United States **BUS:** Hospital **P/S:** Healthcare **MA:** Regional **EXP:** Mr. Davidson's expertise includes the maintenance of database administration and software and applications development. **H/I/S:** Biking **EDU:** Coursework in Accounting, Spokane Community College **CERTS:** A+ Microsoft Certified Professional **A/A/S:** Advisor, Socrates Technologies Corporation **C/VW:** Volunteer, Firefighter
Email: jdavidson@pwi.net
URL: http://www.fcphd.org

John A. Davidson, MD
Title: Physician, Director of Hyperbaric Medicine and Problem Wound Management, St. Luke's Hospital: Director of Wound Care Program, Kindred Hospital, Saint Louis **Company:** Saint Luke's Hospital **Dept:** Hyperbaric Medicine and Wound Management Division **Address:** 232 S. Woods Mill Road, Saint Luke's Hospital, Chesterfield, MO 63017 United States **BUS:** Hospital **P/S:** Inpatient and Outpatient Services Including Wound Care Unit **MA:** Regional **D/D/R:** Practicing Wound Care and Hyperbaric Medicine, Performing Legal Consulting **H/I/S:** Snorkeling, Camping, Swimming **EDU:** Master's Degree in Physiology, Southern Illinois University (1980); MD, Chicago Medical School (1977); Bachelor's Degree in Pre-medicine, Davidson College (1972) **A/A/S:** Undersea and Hyperbaric Medical Society; American Medical Association; Association for the Advancement of Wound Care; Diver's Alert Network
Email: john.davidson@stlukes-stl.com

Lisa A. Davidson, RN, BSN, CCRN
Title: Pediatric Clinical Educator **Company:** John C. Lincoln Deer Valley Hospital **Address:** 1457 E. Tremaine Avenue, Gilbert, AZ 85234 United States **BUS:** Hospital **P/S:** Healthcare **MA:** Regional **EXP:** Ms. Davidson's expertise is in clinical education. **D/D/R:** Educating Staff and Nurses, Caring for Pediatric Patients, Consulting, Lecturing, Developing Policies, Reviewing Medical Records, Overseeing the Pediatric Emergency and Critical Care Units **H/I/S:** Horseback Riding **EDU:** Pursuing Master's Degree in Bioethics, Midwestern University; Bachelor of Science in Nursing, Ohio State University (1987) **CERTS:** Certified Critical Care Registered Nurse **A/A/S:** Society of Trauma Nurses; American Bioethics Advisory Commission; American Association of Critical Care Nurses
Email: peosnurse2@cox.net
URL: http://www.jcl.com/content/deervalley

Helen I. Davies, MS, TCM, LAC
Title: Owner **Company:** Helen's Hands **Address:** 8351 Dove Ridge Way, Elizabeth, CO 80134 United States **BUS:** Equestrian Massage Therapy Center **P/S:** Acupuncture, Chinese Herbal and Massage Therapy for Horses and Riders **MA:** Regional **D/D/R:** Practicing Massage Therapy and Acupuncture, Treating Musculoskeletal Disease, Autoimmune Disease and Digestive Disorder, Managing Daily Business Operations **H/I/S:** Riding, Hiking, Camping **EDU:** Master of Science in Traditional Chinese Medicine, Colorado School of Traditional Chinese Medicine (2004) **CERTS:** Pursuing License in Acupuncture, State of Colorado (2008) **A/A/S:** Acupuncture Association of Colorado; Certification Commission for Acupuncture and Oriental Medicine
Email: larkemt@netzero.net

Tinamaria Davino
Title: Executive Assistant **Company:** Verizon **Address:** 175 Park Avenue, 2nd Floor, Madison, NJ 07940 United States **BUS:** One of the World's Leading Providers of Communication Services **P/S:** Offers a Quality Network, Reliable Service, a Great Value and a Partner Customers Can Trust **MA:** National **D/D/R:** Administration, Responsible for Calendar, Emails, Phone Calls and Travel Arrangements **H/I/S:** Dancing, Shopping, Reading **EDU:** Associate Degree (2005)
Email: tina.m.davino@verizon.com
URL: http://www22.verizon.com/

Allison Darby Davis
Title: Kindergarten Teacher **Company:** Cook Primary School **Address:** 1503 Patterson Street, Adel, GA 31620 United States **BUS:** Elementary School **P/S:** Education **MA:** Regional **D/D/R:** Facilitating Writing Activities, Encouraging Students to Write in Journals, Managing Literacy Centers and the Accelerated Reader Program, Phonetics, Reading Groups and Guided Reading, Teaching All Subjects Including Science, Mathematics and Social Studies, Overseeing Experiments **H/I/S:** Reading, Gardening, Walking **EDU:** Master's Degree in Early Education, Valdosta State University (1989) **A/A/S:** International Reading Association; Alpha Delta Kappa **A/H:** Teacher of the Year, Professional Association of Georgia Educators (1994)
Email: adavis@cook.k12.ga.us
URL: http://www.cook.k12.ga.us/users/cps

Annie R. Davis
Title: Pastor, Chief Executive Officer **Company:** Greater Emmanuel P.A. **Address:** 2425 W. Jefferson Street, Rockford, IL 61101 United States **BUS:** Nonprofit Church **P/S:** Religious Services, Counseling, Community Issues **MA:** Local **D/D/R:** Teaching Individuals about Religion, Counseling, Helping the Community **H/I/S:** Gardening, Sewing **EDU:** College Coursework **CERTS:** Ordained Minister
Email: davisannie53@aol.com

Carmen L. Davis
Title: Master Certified Service Advisor **Company:** Franklin Park Lincoln Mercury **Address:** 5272 Monroe Street, Toledo, OH 43623 United States **BUS:** Car Dealership **P/S:** Automobile Sales **MA:** Regional **D/D/R:** Offering Customer Service **H/I/S:** Traveling, Sports **CERTS:** Master Service Certification for Automobiles **A/H:** Gold Medallion Elite Award (2006)
Email: cdavis61@bex.net
URL: http://www.cambridgewhoswho.com

Cheryl L. Davis
Title: Department Head **Company:** Wilkes Middle School **Dept:** Physical Education **Address:** 11544 S. Gessner Drive, Houston, TX 77071 United States **BUS:** Middle School **P/S:** Education and Curriculum **MA:** Local **D/D/R:** Overseeing 300 Students and Seven Teachers, Following Lesson Plans, Planning Curriculum, Offering Evaluation **H/I/S:** Traveling **EDU:** Master's Degree in Education Management and Administration, Texas Southern University; Bachelor's Degree in Physical Education, Minor in Science Education, Prairie View A&M University **C/VW:** Local Church Missionaries; American Red Cross; American Heart Association; TAPHER
Email: cdavis@houstonisd.org
URL: http://www.houstonisd.org

Cynthia L. Davis
Title: Interior Designer, President **Company:** C Davis Interior Design and Luxury Lifestyle, Inc. **Address:** 95 Chastain Road, Suite 202, Kennesaw, GA 30144 United States **BUS:** Interior and Architecture Design Company **P/S:** Full-Service Residential and Commercial Design **MA:** National **D/D/R:** Creating Luxury High End Designs **H/I/S:** Jet Skiing, Water Skiing on the Lake, Horseback Riding, Enjoying All Outdoor Activities **EDU:** Bachelor's Degree, Jacksonville State University
Email: cdavislla@yahoo.com
Email: cdavis@cdavisinteriordesign.com
URL: http://www.luxurylifestylesatlanta.com
URL: http://www.cdavisinteriordesign.com

Ms. Darlene S. Davis
Title: Teacher (Retired) **Company:** Pittsburgh Independent School District **Address:** 204 Daphne Street, Pittsburg, TX 75686 United States **BUS:** School District **P/S:** Education **MA:** Regional **D/D/R:** Teaching All Subjects, Managing the Classroom **H/I/S:** Reading, Traveling, Sewing **EDU:** Master's Degree in Elementary Education, East Texas State University (1975) **A/A/S:** Texas state Teachers Association
Email: ddavis7255@aol.com

Dewey W. Davis
Title: Vice President **Company:** St. John Health System **Dept:** Property, Facilities Management **Address:** 1923 S. Utica Avenue, Tulsa, OK 74104 United States **BUS:** Healthcare Company **P/S:** Healthcare Services **MA:** Regional **EXP:** Mr. Davis' expertise is in administration. **D/D/R:** Managing property facilities, construction, renovations and maintenance of all health system properties, 4 major hospitals, 40 other outpatient facilities, 4 assisted living facilities, 3 nursing homes, overseeing a staff of 300 employees, budgeting, oversee operations, **H/I/S:** Golfing **EDU:** Bachelor of Science, Oklahoma State University (1973) **A/A/S:** Oklahoma Hospital Association; American Hospital Association; ASHRAE; National Fire Protection Association
Email: sdwdavis@aol.com
URL: http://www.sjmc.org

Dinah M. Davis
Title: Owner **Company:** JonChrisda Travel **Address:** 165 Highway 315, Columbiana, AL 35051 United States **BUS:** Travel Company **P/S:** Travel **MA:** National **D/D/R:** Booking Travel Arrangements, Recruiting Travel Agents, Training and Assisting People in Building their Own Home-Based Business **H/I/S:** Gardening, Making Crafts, Crocheting, Knitting **EDU:** Master's Degree in Elementary Education, University of Alabama
Email: dinahdavis@hughes.net
URL: http://www.ytb.com/dinahdavis

Gloria O. Davis
Title: Speech-Language Pathologist for Autistic Children, Autism Coach **Company:** Turner Elementary School **Address:** 1500 N.W. 49th Avenue, Lauderhill, FL 33313 United States **BUS:** School **P/S:** Education **MA:** Local **D/D/R:** Teaching Autistic Children **H/I/S:** Reading, Traveling, Entertaining **EDU:** Master of Science in Communication Disorders and Teaching the Deaf, University of Oklahoma; Bachelor of Science in Speech and Communication, Florida A&M University **A/A/S:** National Education Association; Local Autism Society; Alpha Kappa Alpha **A/H:** Minority Educator of the Year; First Runner-Up, Teacher of the Year **C/VW:** Local Church, Pro Bono Therapy for the Disabled, Instruction of Disabled and At-Risk Children
Email: gloriadavis@browardschools.com
URL: http://www.cambridgewhoswho.com

Jacqueline Ann Davis
Title: Administrative Secretary to the Unit Director **Company:** Delaware Psychiatric Center **Address:** 1901 N. Dupont Highway, New Castle, DE 19720 United States **BUS:** State-Operated Hospital **P/S:** Psychiatric Center, Continuous Treatment, Group Homes, Clinic-Based Services, Mental Health Counseling Services, Twenty-Four Hour Mobile Crisis Intervention **MA:** Regional **D/D/R:** Treating Mentally-Ill Patients, Alcohol and Drug Abuse, Patient Rehabilitation, Scheduling, Handling Clerical Work and Payroll, Tutoring, Working with Computers, Microsoft Excel **H/I/S:** Weight Training **EDU:** Diploma, Emily Bissell High School (1975) **CERTS:** Nursing Assistant Training (1996); Certification in Crisis Prevention
Email: jacqueline.davis@state.de.us
URL: http://www.dhss.delaware.gov/dhss/dsamh/dpc.html

Jimmy D. Davis
Title: Chaplain **Company:** Mississippi State Hospital **Address:** P.O. Box 157A, Whitfield, MS 39193 United States **BUS:** Hospital **P/S:** Healthcare Including Psychiatric Treatment **MA:** Local **D/D/R:** Overseeing Pastoral Duties **H/I/S:** Exercising **EDU:** Master of Divinity, Southwestern Baptist Theological Seminary **A/A/S:** Mississippi Chaplains Association **C/VW:** Crossgates Baptist Church
Email: davisjimy@netscape.net
URL: http://www.cambridgewhoswho.com

Judith D. Davis
Title: Kindergarten Teacher **Company:** Canterbury Elementary School **Address:** Canterbury, CT 06331 **BUS:** Public Elementary School **P/S:** Education **MA:** Local **D/D/R:** Elementary and Early Childhood Education, Teaching Kindergarten and Gifted and Talented Programs **H/I/S:** Reading **EDU:** Master's Degree in Reading, University of Connecticut; Master's Degree Plus 30 in Gifted Education, University of Connecticut **A/A/S:** Phi Delta Kappa
Email: jdavis023@sbcglobal.net
URL: www.canterburypublicschools.org

Kimberly T. Davis
Title: 1) Plant Operations 2) Owner **Company:** 1) Howard Community College 2) My Sweets & More **Address:** 1) 10901 Little Patuxent Parkway, 1) Columbia, MD 21044 **BUS:** 1) Community College 2) Food Service Company **P/S:** 1) Education 2) Baked Goods, Catering **MA:** 1) Local 2) Local **D/D/R:** 1) Maintenance 2) Baked Goods **H/I/S:** Cooking **EDU:** Associate Degree in Secretarial Sciences, Gulf Coast Community College **A/A/S:** Parent-Teacher Association; Veterans of Foreign Wars; United States Air Force **C/VW:** Save the Faith, Day Care
Email: morgan103@verizon.net
URL: http://www.cambridgewhoswho.com

Louise Marie Davis, CRS
Title: Associate Broker **Company:** Hometown GMAC Real Estate **Address:** 310 'D' Main Street, Pleasanton, CA 94566 United States **BUS:** Real Estate Broker **P/S:** Residential, Executive, Hi End, Condos, New Construction, Condos, Estates, Horse Properties **MA:** National **A/A/S:** California Association of Realtors
Email: louise@louisedavis.com
URL: www.louisedavis.com

Magnolia E. Davis, RN
Title: Registered Nurse **Company:** Methodist Hospital **Address:** 1305 N. Elm Street, Henderson, KY 42420 United States **BUS:** Hospital **P/S:** Healthcare **MA:** Local **EXP:** Ms. Davis' expertise includes rehabilitation, medical-surgical and senior care nursing. **H/I/S:** Traveling, Reading, Gardening, Photographing, Scrapbooking **EDU:** Associate of Science in Nursing, Henderson Community College (1975); Diploma, School of Practical Nursing (1972) **A/H:** Kentucky Colonel Award; Nominee, Methodist Hospital Mission Award (2005); Methodist Hospital Most Valued Partner of the Year Award (2004); Methodist Hospital Mission Award (2003); Nominee, Methodist Hospital Nurse Practice Award (2003); Montgomery Hospital Staff Nurse Recognition Award (1984, 1995, 1996); Gold Scissors Award, Owensboro School of Practical Nursing (1972) **C/VW:** American Cancer Society; Good Works Program; Make-A-Wish
Email: wmdavis@henderson.net

Nancy B. Davis
Title: President and Executive Trainer **Company:** Davis Executive Training **Address:** 7118 Lake Run Circle, Vestavia Hills, AL 35242 United States **BUS:** Executive Communication Training Specializing in Presentations Skills. **P/S:** Presentations Skills Training, In-House Workshops Improving Communication Skills in All Areas of Business, Using a Small Group Format, video feedback all in just four hours. 'No need pulling your employees out of the office for a full day.' Also available for guest speaking engagements with 'Building Better Communicators' **MA:** National **D/D/R:** training executives communication skills conducting an In-house four hour workshop. Plus 'Davis Executive Training' trains young people (not yet in the work force). Both four hour In-house workshops use: Feedback from the audience and video footage. Focusing on: Eye control, controlling anxiety, maximum impact from visuals or when to avoid them. What to do with your hands, how to keep in control during the question and answer part of your presentation, volume control **H/I/S:** Spending Time Outdoors, Hiking, Birding, Enjoying Nature, Organic Cooking, Spending Time with Friends and Family, Listening to Music **EDU:** Industry-Related Training; High School Education **A/A/S:** Founder, President, Davis Executive Training; Founder, President, Parent Watch; Member, Network Birmingham; BBB; National Audubon Society, Sierra Club, Ladies of Liberty Park, Gulf Specimen Marine Laboratory, Supporter, Teen Court of Alabama
Email: speakskills@aol.com
URL: http://www.davisexecutivetraining.com

O. Evell Davis
Title: Senior Pastor **Company:** United Pentecostal Church **Address:** Corsicana Hwy at McArthur Street, Athens, TX 75751 United States **BUS:** Church **P/S:** Ministry to Spiritual Needs to Community, Bi Lingual Church **MA:** Local **D/D/R:** Offering Ministerial Services **H/I/S:** Boating, Fishing **EDU:** Master's Degree in Christian Counseling, National Christian Council Association **CERTS:** Peace Officer Certificate **A/A/S:** Chaplain for Athens Police
Email: odavis4235@aol.com

Paula Ann Davis
Title: Microbiologist **Company:** Food and Drug Administration **Address:** 8301 Muirkirk Road, Laurel, MD 20708 United States **BUS:** Government Agency **P/S:** Research **MA:** National **D/D/R:** Researching Food Pathogens and New Discoveries in the Field **H/I/S:** Reading, Painting, Gardening **EDU:** Master of Science in Forensic Science, National University; Bachelor of Science in Biology, Minor in Chemistry, Shepherd University **A/A/S:** Alumni Association, Shepherd University **C/VW:** Chesapeake Search and Rescue; National Ataxia Foundation
Email: bloodhound2@comcast.net

Mr. Ronald W. Davis, MS
Title: Reference Librarian **Company:** Delaware State University **Address:** 1200 N. Dupont Highway, Dover, DE 19901 United States **BUS:** University **P/S:** Higher Education **MA:** International **D/D/R:** Serving as a Research Librarian and Online Teaching Expert **H/I/S:** Traveling, Quilting, Photography, Racquetball **EDU:** Master of Science in Library Sciences, Clark Atlanta University; Master of Science in Online Teaching, Cappella University; Bachelor of Science in Social Work, University of Alabama **A/A/S:** Delaware Library Association; American Red Cross
Email: rdavis@desu.edu
URL: http://www.desu.edu

Sheryl A. Davis
Title: Graduate Student Researcher **Company:** San Francisco Institute of Architecture **Address:** 5 Congress Street, Trimble, OH 45782 United States **BUS:** Architecture and Design **P/S:** Ecological Design and Historic Preservation **MA:** National **D/D/R:** Implementing Sustainable Design Principles in Historic Preservation, Rehabilitation/Adaptive Reuse, Restoration and Reconstruction, Promoting Traditional Building Methods as Standard Green Design Practice, Fusing Modern and Traditional Styles to Create a New and Sustainable Architectural Style, Advocating the Development of the 'Slow City' as the New Urbanism **H/I/S:** Travel, Musicianship, Writing, Photography, Interpreting Artistic Production, Horseback Riding, Basketball, Softball, Trying New Sports (the Latest Would be Polo? **EDU:** Bachelor of Arts in Imaging Consulting, Ohio University **A/A/S:** Historians of Eighteenth-Century Art and Architecture, The Institute of Classical Architecture & Classical America; U.S. National Architecture, The Institute of Classical Architecture & Classical America, U.S. National Committee of the International Council on Monuments and Sites, US Green Building Council Emerging Green Builder, Architects/Designers/Planners for Social Responsibility, Emerging Green Builder, Architects/Designers/Planners for Social Responsibility; International Network for Traditional Building; Architecture & Urbanism; Historic Preservation Professional Practice Network; American Society of Landscape Architects; Organization of Women Architects and Design Professionals
Email: sheryladavis@hotmail.com

Sue H. Davis
Title: Owner **Company:** S & R Professional Apparel **Address:** 525 W. Rochester Road, Ottumwa, IA 52501 United States **BUS:** Retail Store **P/S:** Uniforms for Medical Professionals, Nursing Students, Retirement Homes and Restaurants, Lab Coats, Scrubs, Aprons and Accessories **MA:** National **D/D/R:** Merchandising, Overseeing Employees **H/I/S:** Playing Tennis, Archery, Horseback Riding **EDU:** Bachelor's Degree in Biology, Goucher College, Baltimore, MD (1950) **CERTS:** Certified Medical Technologist, Charity Hospital, New Orleans (1960); Certification in Hematology **C/VW:** Board Member, The Humane Society of the United States; Board Member, Heartland Humane Society of Ottumwa
Email: sue.davis.uniforms@mchsi.com

Teresa J. Davis
Title: Teacher **Company:** Gardendale Christian Academy **Address:** 1800 Decatur Highway, Gardendale, AL 35071 United States **BUS:** Christian Academy **P/S:** Religious Education **MA:** Local **D/D/R:** Teaching All Subjects for First-Grade Students, Planning Lessons, Organizing Cheerleaders **H/I/S:** Reading, Arts, Making Crafts, Watching Sports **EDU:** Bachelor of Arts in Elementary Education, University of Alabama, Birmingham (1989)
Email: teresa.davis@cwwemail.com

Mr. Thomas E. Davis
Title: Owner **Company:** Omega Environmental Technologies **Address:** 10802 N. Stemmons Freeway, Dallas, TX 75220 United States **BUS:** Wholesale Distribution and Manufacturing Company **P/S:** Automotive, Heating, Ventilation and Air Conditioning Products **MA:** International **D/D/R:** Data Management **H/I/S:** Gardening **EDU:** Bachelor of Science in Business Administration in Accounting, University of Texas at Dallas **A/A/S:** APICS **C/VW:** Local Schools
Email: thom.davis@omega-usa.com
URL: http://www.omega-usa.com

Wilma Davis
Title: Owner **Company:** Belleview Valley Nursing Home, Inc. **Address:** 106 S. St. Mary's Street, Pilot Knob, MO 63663 United States **BUS:** Skilled Nursing Facility **P/S:** Healthcare, Rehabilitation **MA:** Regional **D/D/R:** Overseeing Nursing Home Operations **H/I/S:** Playing Bluegrass Music **CERTS:** Licensed Practical Nurse, Community School of Nursing, St. Louis, 1958 **A/A/S:** Missouri Healthcare Association **C/VW:** Order of the Eastern Star, Relay for Life, United Methodist Church, Marble Creek Baptist Church
Email: kellywilsonjr@yahoo.com

Tandra Davis-Phillips
Title: Owner **Company:** Care Medical of Georgia **Address:** 630 Highway 314, Suite 1003, Fayetteville, GA 30214 United States **BUS:** Medical Supply Company **P/S:** Medical Supplies **MA:** Georgia **EXP:** Ms. Davis-Phillips' expertise includes management and finance. **D/D/R:** Working with the Sales Team **H/I/S:** Playing Online Games **EDU:** Associate Degree in Business, Oklahoma State University **A/A/S:** Order of the Eastern Star
Email: tandraphillips@caremedicalofga.com
URL: http://www.caremedicalofga.com

Barbara G. Davisson
Title: Chairwoman, Nurse **Company:** Eastern Washington Cavalry Association **Address:** 1710 W. Borden Road, Spokane, WA 99224 United States **BUS:** Nonprofit Organization **P/S:** Historical Preservation **MA:** Local **D/D/R:** Historical Re-Enactments **H/I/S:** Scuba Diving, Taking Underwater Photographs, Graphic Design, Photo Editing **EDU:** Bachelor's Degree in Nursing, Columbia University; Master's Degree in Adult Education, Gonzaga University, Spokane, Washington **CERTS:** Licensed Massage Therapist **A/A/S:** Secretary, Chini High School Equestrian Team; Former President, Post Anesthetic Care Nurses Association; Partner, Oil Can Henry Franchise
Email: barb@14thvirginiacavalry.org
URL: http://www.14thvirginiacavalry.org

Carole Simone Davy
Title: Chief Operating Officer **Company:** Andrew M G Davy, MD, PC **Address:** 1513 Voorhies Avenue, Brooklyn, NY 11235 United States **BUS:** Healthcare **P/S:** Pain Medicine, Adults and Children, Chronic Pain **MA:** Regional **EXP:** Ms Davy's expertise includes protocol and policies. **H/I/S:** Tennis, Reading **EDU:** Bachelor of Science in Nursing, SUNY Brockport
Email: simdavy@hotmail.com

Agnes M. Dawana
Title: Senior Trading Operations Specialist **Company:** Wells Capital Management **Address:** 525 Market Street, 10th Floor, San Francisco, CA 94105 United States **BUS:** Asset Management Firm **P/S:** Asset Management, Hedging Products, Interest Rate Derivatives, Loan Offer Equities and Investment Advisory Services **MA:** Regional **D/D/R:** Overseeing Books, Interest Rates and Derivatives **EDU:** Bachelor's Degree in Business Studies, with a Concentration in Management, University of Phoenix (2005) **A/A/S:** Bloomberg
Email: agnes.dawana@wellsfarfgo.com
URL: http://www.wellscap.com

Zuleakha A. Dawoodjee
Title: Director of Investor Relations **Company:** Rentech **Address:** 10877 Wilshire Boulevard, Suite 710, Los Angeles, CA 90024 United States **BUS:** Alternative Energy Company **P/S:** Energy Independence Technologies Utilizing Domestic Resources to Produce Ultra-Clean Synthetic Fuels, Developers of Fischer-Tropsch Coal-to-Liquids and Gas-to-Liquids Technologies **MA:** International **D/D/R:** Overseeing Investor Relations **EDU:** Bachelor's Degree in Business and Finance, University of Southern California (1998)
Email: jddwoodjee@hotmail.com
URL: http://www.rentechinc.com

Mr. David R. Day
Title: Director of Information Technology **Company:** Keystone Aerial Surveys **Address:** City of Philadelphia Northeast Philadelphia Airport, 9800 Ashton Road, Philadelphia, PA 19114 United States **BUS:** Aerial Data Acquisition **P/S:** Aerial Imagery **MA:** National **D/D/R:** Managing Information Technology, Handling Storage and Programming **H/I/S:** Golfing, Farming, Sports (Eagles Fan) **EDU:** Bachelor of Science Degree, Philadelphia Biblical University, Langhorne, Pennsylvania (1991)
Email: dday@keystoneaerialsurveys.com
URL: http://www.keystoneaerialsurveys.com

Mr. Jared E. Day, MAT
Title: Teacher **Company:** Bristol Tennessee City Schools, Haynesfield Elementary **Address:** 615 Edgemont Avenue, Bristol, TN 37620 United States **BUS:** Elementary School **P/S:** Enrichment in All Academic Departments, Specialty Programs, Extracurricular and Fundraiser Events, Skilled Teachers and Administrative Staff, Online Reading Log and Curriculum Guide **MA:** Regional **D/D/R:** Teaching First Grade, Adapting Textbooks to Appropriate Reading Levels **H/I/S:** Biking **EDU:** Master's Degree in Elementary Education, East Tennessee State University (2002) **A/A/S:** Association for Supervision and Curriculum Development
Email: DayJ@btcs.org
URL: http://www.btcs.org/haynesfield/dayj

Collins L. Daye
Title: Horse Trainer **Company:** Mossy Oaks Farm, LLC **Address:** 639 McWhorter Drive, Athens, GA 30606 United States **BUS:** Equine Farm **P/S:** Horse and Riding Training **MA:** National **D/D/R:** Hunter Jumpers **H/I/S:** Family, Friends **EDU:** Bachelor's Degree, University of Georgia **A/A/S:** USEF, AHSA, GAHJA, CHJA
Email: info@CambridgeWhosWho.com

Dr. Pedro A. de Alarcón
Title: William H. Albers Professor, Chairman **Company:** University of Illinois College of Medicine at Peoria **Dept:** Department of Pediatrics **Address:** 530 N.E. Glen Oak Avenue, Peoria, IL 61603 United States **BUS:** University **P/S:** Higher Education **MA:** National **EXP:** Dr. de Alarcón's expertise includes hematology and pediatrics. **H/I/S:** Collecting Fountain Pens, Traveling, Playing Tennis, Squash **EDU:** Fellowship in Pediatric Hematology and Oncology, SUNY Upstate Medical University, Syracuse (1979); Residency in Pediatrics, Mary Fletcher Hospital, The University of Vermont (1976); Residency in Internal Medicine, Washington Hospital Center (1974); MD, The George Washington University **C/VW:** Children's Hospital of Illinois; International Outreach Programs; St. Jude Children's Research Hospital
Email: pdealarc@uic.edu
URL: http://www.uicomp.uic.edu

Clyde Emerson de Bourg
Title: Supervisor of the Publications Division, Secretary of the Textbook Committee (Retired) **Company:** Government of the Republic of Trinidad and Tobago **Dept:** Ministry of Education **BUS:** School **P/S:** Education, Textbook Reviews and Production **MA:** Trinidad and Tobago **D/D/R:** Reviewing Educational Textbooks **H/I/S:** Playing the Keyboard at Parties and Festivals, Conducting Church Services at Retirement Homes and Nursing Homes, Creating Art, Calligraphy **EDU:** Ph.D. in Education, Michigan State University **A/A/S:** Lay Minister, Broome County Council of Churches
Email: sudpoet@hotmail.com
URL: http://www.cambridgewhoswho.com

Duncan J. de Chastelain
Title: General Counsel CA **Company:** GE Money **Address:** 2300 Meadowvale Blvd, Mississauga, L5N5P9 Canada **BUS:** Consumer Finance General Partnership **P/S:** Credit Cards, Personal Loans, Mortgage **MA:** National **H/I/S:** Mountain Bike, Kayaking, Skiing **EDU:** Queens University, Osgoode Hall **CERTS:** LLB; LLM **A/A/S:** ONBAR, CABAR, Law Society of Canada
Email: duncan.dechastelain@ge.com
URL: www.ge.com

Daisy De Ganuza, MD
Title: Psychiatrist **Company:** Daisy De Ganuza, MD **Address:** 16554 N. Dale Mabry Highway, Tampa, FL 33618 United States **BUS:** Private Practice **P/S:** Mental Healthcare, Consulting **MA:** Regional **D/D/R:** Dr. De Ganuza's expertise is in Christian counseling, psychiatric evaluation and treating bipolar, attention deficit, eating, depression, post-traumatic stress, anxiety disorders and addiction. **H/I/S:** Traveling, Listening to Music, Playing Tennis, Dancing, Exercising, Practicing Tai Chi and Yoga **EDU:** Fellowship in Child and Adolescent Psychiatry, University of South Florida, Tampa (1978); Master's Degree, Cleveland Clinic (1977); MD, University of El Salvador (1971); Coursework, University of Florida, Gainesville **CERTS:** Certification, Educational Commission for Foreign Medical Graduates (1973) **C/VW:** The Friends of Israel Gospel Ministry
Email: DaisyGA16@verizon.net
URL: http://www.cambridgewhoswho.com

Gloria J. de la Cruz
Title: Charge Nurse (Retired) **Company:** Wadworth Veterans Hospital **Address:** Wilshire & Sawtelle Brods, Los Angeles, CA 90073 United States **BUS:** Hospital **P/S:** Healthcare Services **MA:** National **EXP:** Ms. de la Cruz's expertise includes diabetes and general medicine nursing. **H/I/S:** Swimming, Walking, Reading **EDU:** Diploma in Nursing, Manila, Philippines **CERTS:** Certification in Diabetes and Medical-Surgical Practices **A/A/S:** Philippines Nurses Association **A/H:** Nominee, Nurse of the Year Award (2005); Nominee, Seminarian Sponsorship **C/VW:** Cathedral Church, Los Angeles; American Diabetes Association; Volunteer, Local Charitable Organizations, Philippines
Email: de_la_cruz.gloria_j@west_la.med.va.gov
URL: http://www.cambridgewhoswho.com

Bernardo de la Garza
Title: Rancher **Company:** Randado Ranch **Address:** 3658 S. State Highway 16, Hebbronville, TX 78361 United States **BUS:** Ranch **P/S:** Cattle **MA:** Regional **D/D/R:** Ranching, Raising Cattle and Livestock, Preserving a Historic Ranch, **H/I/S:** Hunting **EDU:** Bachelor of Science in Agricultural Economics, Texas A&M University **A/A/S:** Knights of Columbus
Email: adlg221@sbcglobal.net

Carmen De La Rosa
Title: Bookkeeper **Company:** Battery Wave LLC **Address:** 1 Battery Park Plaza, New York, NY 10004 United States **BUS:** Restaurant and Catering Facility **P/S:** Catering to Weddings, Banquets, Proms, Dinners, Lunches, Customer Service **MA:** Local **D/D/R:** Bookkeeping, Managing Payroll and Revenue, Overseeing Staff **H/I/S:** Cooking, Cleaning **EDU:** Associate of Science in Nursing and Nutrition, Valedictorian, CUNY Bronx Community College (2002); Associate Degree in Nutrition, CUNY Bronx Community College (2002)
Email: crmndelarosa@yahoo.com
URL: http://www.batterygardens.com

Dr. Maria Isabel de la Torre
Title: President **Company:** Corporación RA **Address:** 220 W. Hillside Road, Suite 9, Laredo, TX 78041 United States **BUS:** Medical Products Supplier **P/S:** Contact Lenses and Medical Device Exportation to Mexico and South America **MA:** International **D/D/R:** Overseeing All Operations of the Business Including Sales, Inventory and Contracts **H/I/S:** Gardening **EDU:** MD in Ophthalmology, Universidad de la Salle, Mexico (1977) **A/A/S:** American Association of Ophthalmology; Republican Women of Texas Association
Email: corpra@stx.com
URL: http://www.corporacionra.com

Satiro de Oliveira
Title: Pediatrician **Company:** Children's Hospital Los Angeles **Address:** 4650 W. Sunset Boulevard, Los Angeles, CA 90027 United States **BUS:** Internationally Leading Hospital in Pediatric and Adolescent Health **P/S:** Pediatric Care for the Most Seriously Ill and Injured Children in Los Angeles **MA:** Regional **D/D/R:** Practicing Pediatric Healthcare, Pediatric Hematology and Oncology **H/I/S:** Running **EDU:** Medical Doctor of Pediatrics, Brazil (1995) **A/A/S:** American Society of Clinical Oncology; American Academy of Pediatrics
Email: satiro_oliveira@yahoo.com

Carol C. De Sena
Title: Proprietor **Company:** (Antonio's) Anthonio's inc. **Address:** 891 E. Palmetto Park Road, Boca Raton, FL 33432 United States **BUS:** Hair Salon **P/S:** Makeup artistry and master stylist **MA:** Boca Raton, Florida, United States **H/I/S:** Cars, Riding Horses, racing, boating, snorkeling, dancing traveling reading writing exercising and Living Life **A/H:** Best of Pembroke Pines New Concepts **C/VW:** Cancer Fast; BIB; CFF; DAV; PVA; VFW; MSKCC; AHA; HS
Email: cdesena2000@hotmail.com
URL: http://www.authorsden.com/diane

T. Lynne De Vrieze
Title: Teacher **Company:** Carthage Junior High School **Address:** 1322 E. Highland Avenue, Carthage, MO 64836 United States **BUS:** High School **P/S:** Secondary Education **MA:** Regional **D/D/R:** Teaching Mathematics for Seventh-Grade at-Risk Students **H/I/S:** Reading, Swimming, Bicycling **EDU:** Master's Degree in Technology and Education, Pittsburg State University, KS; Bachelor's Degree, Missouri Southern State University (2000) **A/A/S:** National Education Association; Association for the Advancement of Computing in Education
Email: devriezel@carthage.k12.mo.us
URL: http://www.cambridgewhoswho.com

Carol D. De Young
Title: Nurse Consultant (Retired) **BUS:** Sole Proprietorship **P/S:** Healthcare **MA:** Local **EXP:** Ms. De Young's expertise includes mental health nursing, outpatient care, home healthcare and mental health services for families and groups. **D/D/R:** Lecturing, Consulting on Mental Health and Family Therapy, Working with the Community Mental Health Center and a Group of Elderly People, Volunteering for a Library, Caring for her 96-Year-Old Mom **H/I/S:** Reading, Watching Tennis, Supporting the Colorado Rockies **EDU:** Master's Degree in Psychiatry and Public Health, University of Colorado; Bachelor's Degree, CUNY Hunter College; Diploma, Winchester School of Nursing **CERTS:** Certification in Home Health Nursing and Medicare **A/A/S:** Colorado Nurses Association; Aurora Mental Health Center; American Public Health Association; National League for Nursing **C/VW:** Local Mental Health Center; Democratic Party
Email: cdy2cats@comcast.net
URL: http://www.cambridgewhoswho.com

Amye Dean
Title: Medical Representative **Company:** Smith and Nephew **Address:** Memphis, TN United States **BUS:** Distribution Firm **P/S:** Medical Devices **MA:** North Mississippi, Northwest Alabama **D/D/R:** Selling Orthopedic Devices **H/I/S:** Spending Time with her Family, Playing Tennis **EDU:** Bachelor of Science in Nursing, Baptist College of Health Sciences, Memphis, TN
Email: adean13@comcast.net

Mr. David L. Dean
Title: Deputy Sheriff **Company:** Jefferson County Sheriff's Office **Address:** 200 Jefferson County Parkway, Golden, CO 80401 United States **BUS:** Law Enforcement **P/S:** Public Safety **MA:** Local **D/D/R:** Supervising Inmates **H/I/S:** Reading, Hiking, Weightlifting **EDU:** Pursuing Master's Degree in Crisis Management, Grand Canyon University, Phoenix; Bachelor of Science in Business Information Systems, University of Phoenix; Bachelor of Science in Criminal Justice, University of Phoenix; Associate Degree in Criminal Justice, Troy University, AL **A/A/S:** Fraternal Order of Police; Colorado Law Enforcement Officer's Association; Colorado Police Protective Association **C/VW:** Church; Promise Keepers
Email: dbadge6603@comcast.net

Ms. Susan Dean
Title: Teacher **Company:** Soaring Eagles Elementary School **Address:** 4710 Harrier Ridge Drive, Colorado Springs, CO 80916 United States **BUS:** Elementary School **P/S:** Education **MA:** Local **D/D/R:** Teaching Students with Special Needs **H/I/S:** Hiking, Reading, Sewing, Quilting **EDU:** Master of Integrated Sciences, Colorado College **A/A/S:** Harrison Education Association **C/VW:** Boy Scouts of America
Email: sdeanra@msn.com

Sally A. Deane
Title: Reading Teacher **Company:** Elmira City School District **Address:** 933 Hoffman Street, Elmira, NY 14905 United States **BUS:** School District **P/S:** Education **MA:** Local **D/D/R:** Teaching Reading, Developing Reading Programs **H/I/S:** Running, Reading, Golfing, Skiing **EDU:** Master of Education in Reading, Elmira College, Plus 30 Credits (2004); Bachelor of Arts in English, Elmira College (1997) **CERTS:** Certified Administrator **A/A/S:** Association for Supervision and Curriculum Development; Southern Tier Reading Council
Email: sdeane@stny.rr.com
URL: http://www.elmiracityschools.com

Veronica J. Deans
Title: Member Accounting Manager **Company:** 1st Advantage Federal Credit Union **Address:** 12891 Jefferson Avenue, Newport News, VA 23608 United States **BUS:** Credit Union **P/S:** Financial Services **MA:** National **D/D/R:** Automated Clearing Houses **H/I/S:** Traveling, Gardening **C/VW:** Community Activities, Ebenezer Baptist Church
Email: vdeans@1stadvantage.org
URL: http://www.1stadvantage.org

Dustin DeBoer
Title: Owner **Company:** Solid Rock Photography **Address:** 304 S. Main Street, Austin, MN 55912 United States **BUS:** Photography Studio **P/S:** Youth Ministry, Photography **MA:** Regional **D/D/R:** Expressing the Beauties of Nature while Hiking and Facilitating Youth Ministry through the Photography and Digital Imagery **H/I/S:** Reading, Hiking, Rock Climbing, Biking, Gardening, Photography, Participating in Outdoor Activities **EDU:** Master's Degree in Education, Concentration in Outdoor and Adventure, University of Minnesota, Twin Cities Campus; Bachelor of Science in Youth Ministry, Baptist College, Clarke Summit, Pennsylvania **A/H:** Roosevelt Award, City of Austin for his Photo of a Historic Bridge **C/VW:** Youth Dynamics
Email: dustin@solidrockphotography.org
URL: http://www.solidrockphotography.org

Francoise Debost
Title: Owner **Company:** West Coast Wellness **Address:** Metro Gateway Center, 1840 Gateway Blvd., San Mateo, CA 94404 United States **BUS:** Health and Wellness Company **P/S:** Nutritional Supplements, Cosmetics, massages **MA:** International **D/D/R:** Wellness Education, Massage, Marketing and management **H/I/S:** Fitness, Yoga, Skiing, Tennis, Reading **EDU:** MBA, Lyon University, France (1986); Bachelor's Degree in Mathematics and Science, Lycee Moliere, Paris, France (1981) **A/A/S:** IMA **C/VW:** Local Children's Schools
Email: frandebost@yahoo.com
URL: http://www.4nuu.com

Mr. Mark W. DeCarlo Jr.
Title: Christian Counselor **BUS:** Counseling Center **P/S:** Christian Counseling **MA:** Local **EXP:** Mr. DeCarlo's expertise includes biblical and theological studies in the original languages of Greek and Hebrew. **H/I/S:** Spending Time with his Family, Reading, Playing Paintball **EDU:** Pursuing Associate of Arts in Biblical Studies, Mon Valley Bible Institute **A/A/S:** Phi Theta Kappa; International Scholar Laureate Program **A/H:** National Dean's List **C/VW:** Television Editor, Morning Star Baptist Church
Email: markjr03@hotmail.com
URL: http://www.cambridgewhoswho.com

Renee DeChambeau Fraser, DDS
Title: Doctor of Dental Surgery **Company:** Drs. Delaney, Ralstrom, Makowski & Associates **Address:** 39400 Garfield Road, Suite 200, Clinton Township, MI 48038 United States **BUS:** Dental Practice **P/S:** Pediatric Dentistry **MA:** Regional **D/D/R:** American Board Certified, Dentistry Services for Children that are Physically or Mentally Compromised **H/I/S:** Tennis, Jogging **A/A/S:** American Dental Association; American Board of Pediatric Dentistry; Michigan Dental Association
Email: info@CambridgeWhosWho.com
URL: http://www.cambridgewhoswho.com

Carmelita L. DeCicco
Title: Teacher **Company:** Hudson City School District **Address:** 360 State Street, Hudson, NY 12334, Hudson, **BUS:** School District **P/S:** Elementary Education for Pre-K through Second-Grade **MA:** Local **D/D/R:** Teaching Kindergarten Students Reading and Math **H/I/S:** Outdoor Activities, Reading, Guitar, Singing **EDU:** Master of Science in Special Education, College of Saint Rose **C/VW:** Choir, Saint Mary's Church
Email: leta425@hotmail.com
URL: http://www.cambridgewhoswho.com

Mrs. Heidi Schloss Decker
Title: Art Resource Teacher **Company:** Baltimore City Public School System **Address:** 2800 Taney Road, Baltimore, MD 21209 United States **BUS:** School District **P/S:** Education **MA:** Regional **D/D/R:** Teaching Art Courses, Utilizing Interdisciplinary Teaching Methods, Teaching the Gifted and Talented **H/I/S:** Traveling, Reading, Drawing, Illustrating, Writing, Going to the Theater, Singing, Watching Films, Performing **EDU:** Master of Arts Equivalency in Art Education/Gifted and Talented Students, Goucher College Teachers' Institute, Towson University; Bachelor of Science in Art Education, Towson University, Cum Laude **A/A/S:** Maryland Art Education Association; Towson University Alumni Association; Red Hat Society; Baltimore Teachers' Union; Mentor, Maryland Institute College-Art; Baltimore City Public Schools; Pilot Program (2007) **A/H:** Outstanding Young Women of America (1984); Awarded for Developing ALL, a Gifted/Talented Program for Bay-Brook Elementary School; President's Volunteer Action Award (1984); PTI Technology Achievement Award, Mayor's Office Latchkey Program **C/VW:** Synagogue; Local Arts Organizations; Defends Animal Rights
Email: artmom7@comcast.net

Debra Ann DeCrescenzo
Title: Owner **Company:** Jackson Hewitt, Inc. **Address:** 2100 Central Park Avenue, Yonkers, NY 10710 United States **BUS:** Accounting Firm **P/S:** Accounting and Taxation Services **MA:** National **D/D/R:** Accounting, Bookkeeping, Preparing Tax Returns **H/I/S:** Horseback Riding, Kayaking, Spending Time Outdoors **EDU:** College Coursework **A/A/S:** Local Chamber of Commerce; American Business Women's Association
Email: decrescenzo@verizon.com
URL: http://www.jacksonhewitt.com

Mrs. Carly Jean DeDonder
Title: Special Education Teacher **Company:** Washburn Rural High School **Address:** 5900 S.W. 61st Street, Topeka, KS 66619 United States **BUS:** High School Dedicated to Excellence in Student Services **P/S:** Secondary Education, Teaching, Athletics, Clubs and Activities **MA:** Regional **D/D/R:** Teaches 9th-12th-Grade English, Science and Mathematics in a Self Contained Classroom to Students with Learning Disabilities and a Life Skills and Health Class, Started Program in Life Skills Class where Students Run their Own Restaurant Called 'Jr. Blues Cafe', Students Plan Menus, Go Shopping, Prepare Food, Send Invitations, Serve and Clean Up Afterwards, Teachers and Staff Pay to be Served Lunch, Created Clothing Exchange Program where Staff Donates Clothing and the Students can Take Out Something to Wear for the Day when they Dress Inappropriately-then Return it at the End of the Day, Life Skills Class Does the Laundry, Coaches Cheerleading Sophomores and Juniors, Has Taught Swimming to Special Needs Kids Since Age 15 **H/I/S:** Spending Time with Husband and Dogs, Attending Football and Basketball Games at the High School **EDU:** Bachelor of Science Degree in Science, Emporia University (2005) **CERTS:** Teaching Certification in Special Education and Health
Email: dedonder@usd437.net
URL: http://www.wrhs.net

John A. Deem
Title: Assistant Superintendent **Company:** Yazoo City Municipal School District **Address:** 1133 Calhoun Avenue, Yazoo City, MS 39194 United States **BUS:** School District **P/S:** Education **MA:** Regional **D/D/R:** Organizing Teacher's Meeting, Overseeing School Discipline, Managing the Operations of All Departments, Hiring Employees **H/I/S:** Reading, Golfing **EDU:** Specialist Degree in Administration, The University of Southern Mississippi (1974); Specialist Degree in Counseling, University of Southern Mississippi (1974)
Email: jdeem@yazoocity.k12.ms.us
URL: http://www.yazoocity.k12.ms.us

Kelly A. Deeter, RN
Title: Registered Nurse **Company:** Lebanon Veterans Medical Center **Address:** 1700 S. Lincoln Avenue, Lebanon, PA 17042 United States **BUS:** Proven Leader in the Healthcare Industry **P/S:** Wide Range of Medical Services, Healthcare Needs for the Veterans **MA:** Regional **D/D/R:** Neurological Trauma **H/I/S:** Volleyball, Active in Church Group, NASCAR Racing, Gardening, Landscaping **EDU:** Associate Degree, Luzerne County Community College **CERTS:** Registered Nurse; Licensed Practical Nurse Degree, Schuylkill Training and Technology Center **A/A/S:** Participates as a CPR Instructor, Red Cross; Professional Advancement Council **A/H:** Nursing Star Award (2003)
Email: kellydeeter@earthlink.net
URL: http://www.va.gov/lebanonVAMC

Danielle DeFazio, RN
Title: Registered Nurse **Company:** Pinnacle Dialysis **Address:** 2900 N. Military Trail, Suite 195, Boca Raton, FL 33431 United States **BUS:** Proven Leader in the Healthcare Industry **P/S:** Dialysis Unit, Nephrology **MA:** Regional **D/D/R:** Running a 26-Bed Dialysis Unit for Patients with Chronic Conditions who Need Continuous Dialysis **EDU:** Associate Degree in Science and Nursing, Broward Community College (2005)
Email: danielledefazio@bellsouth.net
URL: http://www.cambridgewhoswho.com

Prof. Jeanne M. Degatano
Title: 1) Professor 2) Owner 3) Librarian **Company:** 1) Drexel University 2) The Cape May Teddy Bear Company 3) Edison Township School District **Address:** 3141 Chestnut Street, Philadelphia, PA 19104 United States **BUS:** 1) University 2) Retail Shop 3) School District **P/S:** 1) Higher Education 2) Teddy Bears 3) Education **MA:** Local **D/D/R:** 1. Supervising Individuals, Students, Teachers, Conducting Workshops for Teachers for Classroom Management, Working in Shops, Designing Teddy Bears, Developing her Business, Sponsoring the Teddy Bear Tee's, Performing Activities, Ordering through Web Site, Managing Library Operations in School District at Edison Township, Teaching Research Study Skills, Overseeing the Technology-Driven Program, Teacher Preparation Courses and Administration Courses **EDU:** Coursework in Education and Technology, George Washington University (1997); Coursework in Educational Administration, Kean University (1989); Coursework in Library Media Services, Kean University (1985) **A/A/S:** New Jersey Association of School Librarians; American Library Association; National Education Association; Phi Kappa Phi
Email: jd336@drexel.edu
URL: http://www.drexel.edu/soe
URL: http://www.capemayteddybear.com

Barbara A. DeGennaro

Title: Owner **Company:** Night and Day Entertainment **Address:** 1241 Johnson Road, San Luis Obispo, CA 93401 United States **BUS:** Entertainment Company **P/S:** Entertainment Including Dance **MA:** Regional **D/D/R:** Ensuring Customer Satisfaction **H/I/S:** Walking, Cooking, Writing Poetry, Practicing Massage Therapy, Visiting Spas **EDU:** Coursework in Business Administration; High School Diploma **CERTS:** Certified Cosmetologist **A/H:** Woman of the Year Award **C/VW:** California Firefighters; Project Angels of Food; Performing Arts Center
Email: barbara.degennaro@cwwemail.com
Email: bdegennaro@charter.net

Christopher DeGracia

Title: Operations Manager **Company:** Seattle Opera **Address:** P.O. Box 9248, Seattle, WA 98109 United States **BUS:** Opera House **P/S:** Performances of Classic European and New American Opera Music **MA:** Regional **D/D/R:** Performing Administrative Duties, Maintaining Warehouse, Running Business Operations, Organizing Projects **H/I/S:** Photography, Arts, Woodworking **EDU:** Bachelor's Degree in Fine Arts, Carnegie Mellon University (1989) **A/A/S:** Taunton Association of Performance Arts **C/VW:** Northwest Harvest; Habitat for Humanity
Email: christopher.degracia@seattleopera.org
URL: http://www.seattleopera.org

Susan DeGregorio-Rosen

Title: Registered Nurse, Labor Relations **Company:** St. Barnabas Healthcare System **Address:** 94 Old Short Hills Road, Livingston, NJ 07039 United States **BUS:** Hospital **P/S:** Healthcare **MA:** Local **D/D/R:** Teaching Shared Governance in Labor Relations, Legal Nurse Consulting **H/I/S:** Oil Painting **EDU:** Bachelor of Arts in Healthology; Legal Nurse Consultant **A/A/S:** American Association of Legal Nurse Consultants; American Organization of Nurse Executives **C/VW:** Doctors Without Borders, St. Jude Children's Research Hospital
Email: sdegregorio-rosen@sbhcs.com
URL: http://www.cambridgewhoswho.com

Robert J. Dehney

Title: Partner, Bankruptcy Lawyer **Company:** Morris, Nichols, Arsht & Tunnell **Address:** 1201 N. Market Street, Wilmington, DE 19801 United States **BUS:** Law Firm **P/S:** Legal Services **MA:** National **D/D/R:** Corporate Restructuring, Bankruptcy, Acquisition of Assets **H/I/S:** Spending Time with his Family **EDU:** JD, Pace University; Bachelor of Arts in History and Economics, Dickinson College **A/A/S:** Connecticut Bar Association; New York State Bar Association; Delaware State Bar Association; Pennsylvania Bar Association; American Bankruptcy Institute; Turnaround Management Association **C/VW:** Board Member, The Brandywine Zoo, Delaware
Email: rdehney@mnat.com
URL: http://www.mnat.com

Francis J. Deisler

Title: Chief Executive Officer, President **Company:** National Association of Forensic Counselors **Address:** 1910 Saint Joe Center Road, Suite 53, Fort Wayne, IN 46825 United States **BUS:** Certification and Accreditation Board **P/S:** Mental Health and Forensic Certification and Accreditation **MA:** National **D/D/R:** Certifying Mental Health Professionals for the Treatment of Sociopaths and Sex Offenders, Consulting as an Expert Witness on Forensic Mental Health Cases **H/I/S:** Golfing, Fishing, Boating **EDU:** Ph.D. in Clinical Psychology, Stony Brook University (1982); Master's Degree in Psychology, Goddard College, VT (1976); Bachelor's Degree in Psychology, SUNY Albany (1971) **CERTS:** Licensed Clinical Psychologist; Licensed Clinical Social Worker; Licensed Marriage and Family Therapist **A/A/S:** American College of Certified Forensic Counselors; The Association for Addiction Professionals; National Association of Social Workers
Email: sneakerz@msn.com
URL: http://www.nationalafc.com

Toni M. DeJaco-McKee, M.Ed.

Title: English Teacher, Track and Cross Country Coach **Company:** Campbell County Public Schools **Address:** 137 Lake Street, Bellevue, KY 41073 United States **BUS:** Public School System **P/S:** Best Possible Education for All Students in a Safe Environment **MA:** Regional **D/D/R:** Teaching Adjunct Courses in Writing and Composition, Establishing and Following Curriculum Guidelines, Disciplining Students, Creating Lesson Plans, Counseling Referrals, Communicating with Administrators **H/I/S:** Reading, Sports **EDU:** Master's Degree in Secondary Education, Northern Kentucky University (2005) **A/A/S:** National Education Association
Email: toni.mckee@campbell.kyschools.us
URL: http://www.campbell.kyschools.us

María del Carmen Rodríguez, Ph.D., LPC, NCC

Title: Assistant Professor **Company:** Kean University **Dept:** Counseling **Address:** 1000 Morris Avenue, Union, NJ 07083 United States **BUS:** University **P/S:** Forty-Eight Undergraduate and 28 Graduate Degree Programs Serving 13,000 Students, Student-Centered Learning Environment Preparing Students for Rewarding Careers and Lifelong Learning **MA:** Regional **D/D/R:** Teaching Community, Practicum, Multicultural and Theories of Counseling Courses, Conducting Research on Spirituality and Trauma, Helping Students with Research, Working in School Committees, Consulting on Community Service **H/I/S:** Poetry, Singing, Practicing Yoga, Weight Lifting **EDU:** Ph.D. in Psychology, New York University (1985); Master's Degree in Psychology, University of Puerto Rico (1978); Bachelor's Degree in Psychology, University of Puerto Rico (1975) **CERTS:** Licensed Professional Counselor; National Certified Counselor **A/A/S:** American Counseling Association; American Federation of Teacher; President, Kean Federation of Teachers; Trustee, New Jersey National Alliance on Mental Illness; President, Labor Union, Kean University; National Board of Certified Counselors
Email: maril6@earthlink.net
URL: http://www.kean.edu

Rosalia N. Dela Soledad

Title: Associate Level 1 **Company:** NYC Transit-Power Engineering **Address:** 2 Broadway, New York, NY 10004 United States **BUS:** Engineering MTA **P/S:** Electrical Engineering for Subway Stations and Power **MA:** Local **D/D/R:** Rehabilitation and Modernization Designer of Subway Stations and GBH's **H/I/S:** Poetry Writing **EDU:** High School, Bad Krueznach, Germany
Email: rsoledad@aol.com

Michele D. DeLaGarza

Title: President **Company:** DLG Real Estate **Address:** 14440 JFK Blvd, Houston, TX 77032 United States **BUS:** Real Estate **P/S:** Sells Commercial Real Estate, Office Buildings, Shopping Centers, Medical Buildings, Sales and Leasing **MA:** National **D/D/R:** Selling Commercial Real Estate **H/I/S:** Volunteer Work, Yoga **EDU:** Montgomery Community College; Sam Houston State University **A/A/S:** Junior League of North Houston and South Montgomery Counties
Email: michele@dlgrealestate.com
URL: www.dlgrealestate.com

Donna M.C. Delaney

Title: Teacher (Retired) **Company:** Gloucester High School **Address:** 61 Appleton Street, Salem, MA 01970 United States **BUS:** School **P/S:** Education **MA:** Local **D/D/R:** Teaching, Advising, Educational Literacy Consulting **H/I/S:** Reading, Gardening, Poetry Sharing Group, Walking, Illustrating Children's Books, Recycling within the Community **EDU:** Master's Degree, Institute of Open Education; Master's Degree in Education, Antioch College, Massachusetts **A/A/S:** National Council of Teachers of English; Peabody Essex Museum, Salem; Smithsonian, Washington **C/VW:** Gay Straight Alliance, Saint Joseph Indian School, South Dakota
Email: rydermom2003@yahoo.com

Brian M. Delarm

Title: Sales Professional **Company:** Sanofi-Aventis Pharmaceuticals **Address:** 300 Somerset Corporate Boulevard, Bridgewater, NJ 08807 United States **BUS:** Pharmaceutical Company **P/S:** Pharmaceutical Products **MA:** Albany **EXP:** Mr. Delarm's expertise includes sales and management. **H/I/S:** Playing Soccer, Water Skiing **EDU:** Bachelor of Arts in Psychology, Siena College **A/A/S:** Show Directors Board Member, U.S. Water Ski Show Team **C/VW:** United States Water Ski Show Team, American Diabetes Association, American Cancer Society
Email: blax2020@yahoo.com
URL: http://www.uswaterskishowteam.com

Sherry A. DeLauder

Title: Fifth-Grade Teacher **Company:** Thurgood Marshall Elementary Montgomery County Public Schools **Address:** 12260 McDonald Chapel Drive, Gaithersburg, MD 20878 United States **BUS:** Elementary School Facility Committed to Excellence in Education **P/S:** Regular Core Curriculum Including Reading, Math, English, Science, Social Studies, Art, Music, History, Language Arts, Physical Education **MA:** Regional **D/D/R:** Teaching All the Disciplines, Reading, Writing, Spelling, Language Arts, Social Studies, Mathematics and Science, Social Studies, Mathematics and Science Liaison, State Testing Writer MSPAP, Writer for County Science Curriculum **H/I/S:** Designing Clothes **EDU:** Master's Equivalency in Early Childhood Education, University of Hood and Maryland (1990); Bachelor of Science Degree in Home Economics Education with a Minor in Physical and Social Sciences, University of Maryland (1968) **A/A/S:** National Education Association; Maryland State Education Association; Kappa Omicron Nu; Kappa Phi **A/H:** Award Entrance into the Governor's Academy for Mathematics and Science (1999)
Email: sherry_a_delauder@mcpsmd.org
URL: http://www.mcps.k12.md.us/schools/thurgoodmarshalles

Vicki Delgado

Title: Director of Health Information **Company:** Turquoise Lodge **Dept:** Department of Health **Address:** P.O. Box 80810, Albuquerque, NM 87198 United States **BUS:** Government Organization **P/S:** Healthcare **MA:** New Mexico **EXP:** Ms. Delgado's expertise includes health information management, overseeing the cancer registry and quality improvement services. **H/I/S:** Snowboarding, Spending Time with her Son, Reading, Solving Puzzles **EDU:** Pursuing Bachelor's Degree in Health Information Administration, University of Cincinnati; Associate Degree in Health Information Management, Albuquerque Technical Vocational Institute (2003) **CERTS:** Certified Tumor Registrar (2004) **A/A/S:** Secretary and Treasurer, New Mexico Medical Group Management Association
Email: vickia.delgado@state.nm.us

Anne P. DellaCamera

Title: Teacher, Consultant for Gifted Education **Company:** Southwood Middle School **Address:** 16301 S.W. 80th Avenue, Palmetto Bay, FL 33157 United States **BUS:** Public Middle School **P/S:** Education for Students in Sixth through Eighth-Grade, Visual and Performing Arts, Gifted Resource Program, Student Services, Summer Reading Programs, Sports **MA:** International **D/D/R:** Managing Gifted Education Programs Including Professional Training, Certifications and Curriculum Development, Teaching Gifted Resource and Advanced Geography Programs, Writing Curriculum for Gifted Programs **EDU:** Master of Science in Education and Social Sciences, Southern Connecticut State University (1973) **CERTS:** Nationally and Internationally Certified Consultant for Gifted Education, National and International (1973) **A/A/S:** Educational Advisory Association to the United Nations; People to People Ambassador Program; United Nations Association of Greater Miami; People of People Ambassador Program; Social Studies Delegation; US-Russia Joint Education Conference; Delegate the 2007 Global Peace Initiative Cairo Egypt **A/H:** Teacher of the Year, Southwood Middle School
Email: dellacamera@dadeschools.net
URL: http://southwood.dadeschools.net

Christopher Delmarsh

Title: District Sales Manager **Company:** AAA Auto Club South **Address:** 2200 Northlake Parkway, Tucker, GA 30084 United States **BUS:** Travel Company **P/S:** AAA Membership **MA:** Regional **D/D/R:** Marketing, Selling, Sales Manager Overseeing 45 Salesmen, Teach Salesmanship to Salesman both inside and outside the main office. **H/I/S:** Playing Golf and Tennis **EDU:** Bachelor of Arts in Finance, Florida State University (1993) **A/A/S:** Kiwanis Club; Chamber of Commerce; **C/VW:** H. Lee Moffitt Cancer and Research Institute
Email: cdelmarsh@aaasouth.com
URL: http://www.aaasouth.com/c.delmarsh

Keisha M. DeLoatch-Nandalal

Title: Teacher **Company:** Harford County Public Schools **Dept:** Fountain Green Elementary **Address:** 517 S. Fountain Green Road, Bel Air, MD 21015 United States **BUS:** School District **P/S:** Primary Education **MA:** Regional **D/D/R:** Teaching, Working with Special Needs Children, Giving Presentations on English as a Second Language to Other Teachers **H/I/S:** Reading, Traveling, Photography, Scrapbooking **EDU:** Master's Degree in Reading, with Concentration in English as a Second Language, Johns Hopkins University (2001); Master's Degree in Guidance and Counseling, Loyola College (1996) **CERTS:** Certified English as a Second Language Teacher; Certification in Elementary Education, State of Maryland **A/H:** Maryland's Most Beautiful People Award (1994)
Email: keisha.nandalal@hcps.org
URL: http://www.hcps.org

Wayne K. Deluz

Title: Owner **Company:** Big Island Motors **Address:** 1 Keaa Street, Hilo, HI 96720 United States **BUS:** Automotive Company **P/S:** Sales of Mazda, Subaru, Hyundai, Used Cars **MA:** Hawaii **EXP:** Mr. Deluz's expertise is in operations management. **H/I/S:** Golfing
Email: wdeluz@bigislandmotors.com
URL: http://www.bigislandmotors.com

Lynn DeMaria

Title: Owner/Operator **Company:** Box to be Fit, LLC (the boxing club-Pacific Beach) **Address:** 4190 Mission Blvd Suite 171, San Diego, CA 92109 United States **BUS:** Gym **P/S:** Boxing, Muay Thai, Jiu Jitsu **MA:** Local **D/D/R:** Management, Operations and Public relations **H/I/S:** Family, Working Out **CERTS:** Certified Medical Receptionist, Pacific College of Medical Dental Assistants **A/A/S:** Portuguese Society, WF Organization
Email: sboilme@sbcglobal.net
URL: www.theboxingclub.net

Kevin H. Demel
Title: Territory Manager **Company:** Yellow House Machinery Co. **Address:** 2121 E. Second Avenue, Odessa, TX 79761 United States **BUS:** Heavy Construction Company **P/S:** John Deere Industrial Construction Equipment, Oil, Gas **MA:** Regional **D/D/R:** Sales Consulting **H/I/S:** Scuba Diving, Water Sports, Theater **EDU:** Four Years of Coursework in Psychology and Sociology, Texas Tech University **A/A/S:** Odessa Economic Development Commission; Odessa City Planning and Zoning Commission; Permian Basin Theater Association **C/VW:** Performing Arts Theater, Private Christian School System
Email: kevind@yellowhouse.us
URL: http://www.yellowhouse.us

Michael P. Demetriou
Title: President, Chief Executive Officer **Company:** The Demetriou Group **Address:** 415 Madison Avenue, 13th Floor, New York, NY 10017 United States **BUS:** Insurance Company **P/S:** Insurance Services Including Liability, Automobile, Worker's Compensation and Business Insurance **MA:** National **D/D/R:** Overseeing Large Commercial Groups, Homeowners, Small and Medium Commercial Groups, Managing Financial Planning and Company Relationships, Overseeing Five Branches, Marketing to New Clients **EDU:** Bachelor of Science in Communications and Business Management, University of Massachusetts, Amherst (2000) **A/A/S:** Excess Line Association of New York; Professional Insurance Wholesalers Association of New York State; Independent Insurance Agents and Brokers of America; YIP; ITARI; National Association of Professional Insurance Agents; National Association of Professional Insurance Agents
Email: mdemetriou@demetriougroup.com
URL: http://www.demetriougroup.com

Sara R. DeMonbrun
Title: Founder, Director **Company:** Save Our Cats and Kittens, Inc. **Address:** 498 Carmel Drive, Fort Walton Beach, FL 32547 United States **BUS:** Animal Shelter **P/S:** Shelter for Cats and Kittens, Thrift Shop, Adoption Services **MA:** Local **D/D/R:** Fund Raising **H/I/S:** Reading, Collecting Cat Items, Bird Watching **EDU:** Master's Degree in Educational Leadership, University of West Florida, Pensacola **A/A/S:** Florida Retired Educators Association **C/VW:** The Humane Society
Email: cdemonbrun@cox.net
URL: http://www.myspace.com/saveourcatsandkittens

Rayna Marie Dempsey
Title: Fire Lieutenant **Company:** Fort Sam Houston Fire Department **Address:** 3830 Schofield, Fort Sam Houston, TX 78234 United States **BUS:** Government Fire Department **P/S:** Fire Emergency Service **MA:** Local **EXP:** Ms. Dempsey's expertise includes fire rescue and hazardous material mitigation. **H/I/S:** Riding her Harley Davidson, Exercising, Spending Time with her Family and Friends, Camping **CERTS:** Certified Emergency Medical Technician **A/A/S:** Former Vice President, Fire Association; Women in Fire Service; International Association of Fire Fighters
Email: fyrpwr15@yahoo.com
URL: http://www.cambridgewhoswho.com

Sherry L. Denenberg
Title: Staff Nurse **Company:** Medical Staffing Network **Address:** 3110 E. Market Street, York, PA 17402 United States **BUS:** Staffing Agency **P/S:** Healthcare Staffing **MA:** Local **D/D/R:** Medical-Surgical Nursing, Pediatrics **H/I/S:** Traveling, Reading **CERTS:** Licensed Practical Nurse, York Technical Institute; Pursuing Registered Nursing Degree, Harrisburg Area Community College **A/A/S:** Phi Theta Kappa **C/VW:** Make-A-Wish Foundation, March of Dimes
Email: sherrydenenberg@aol.com
URL: http://www.msnhealth.org

Diane M. Dennard
Title: Field Supervisor II **Company:** Department of Public Safety **Dept:** Division of Parole and Probation **BUS:** Government Organization **P/S:** Public Safety Including Probation and Parole Services **MA:** Local **D/D/R:** Supervising **H/I/S:** Bowling, Playing Tennis **EDU:** Master's Degree in Business Management, Morgan State University (1981) **A/A/S:** Alpha Kappa Alpha
Email: ddennard@dpscs.state.md.us

Roscoe J. Denney, III
Title: Teacher/coach **Company:** South Laurel High School **Address:** 201 South Laurel Road, London, KY 40744 United States **BUS:** School **P/S:** Teaching and Coaching, Public High School **MA:** Local **D/D/R:** Teaching Special Ed, Coaching Basketball **H/I/S:** Golf, Bowling, Travel **EDU:** Bachelor of Science in Education, Eastern Kentucky University **A/A/S:** KEA, NEA, KABC, Kiwanis
Email: roscoe_@yahoo.com

Candy Ann Dennis
Title: Director, Owner **Company:** Candy's Dance & Fitness Academy **Address:** 283 Cabot Street, Beverly, MA 01915 United States **BUS:** Dance Academy **P/S:** Dance Instruction Including Ballet and Point, Jazz, Tap, Lyrical, Hip-Hop, Modern, Ballroom and Latin Styles, Fitness Programs Including Pilates, Toning and Stretch Techniques, Kickboxing, Pageant Training, Dance Therapy **MA:** Local **EXP:** Ms. Dennis' expertise is in dance instruction. **D/D/R:** Instructing Dance, Performing Administrative Duties of Dance Therapy Treatment, Teaching Choreographing Routines and All Styles of Dance and Fitness Courses, Utilizing Social Services Therapy for Depression, Victims of Abuse and Life Issues **H/I/S:** Practicing Latin Ballroom Dancing, Spending Time with her Daughter **EDU:** Pursuing Coursework in Expressive Dance Therapy; Bachelor of Arts in Exercise Science, Salem State College, MA (2005); Bachelor's Degree in Dance and Fitness, School of Dance, Dean College (2002); Bachelor's Degree in Dance and Fitness, Salem State College **CERTS:** Certification, Aerobics and Fitness Association of America; Certification, Chicago National Association of Dance Masters; Certification in CPR, American Red Cross; Certification in Fist Aid **A/A/S:** Chicago National Association of Dance Masters; Aerobics and Fitness Association of America **C/VW:** American Red Cross
Email: candysacademy@yahoo.com
URL: http://www.candysdanceacademy.com

Melanie G. Dennis
Title: English Teacher **Company:** Richmond Community Schools, Richmond High School **Address:** 300 Hub Etchison Parkway, Richmond, IN 47374 United States **BUS:** School **P/S:** Education **MA:** Regional **D/D/R:** Teaching English **H/I/S:** Writing, Reading, Traveling **EDU:** Master's Degree in Education, Ball State University (1998); Bachelor of Arts in English, Lincoln University (1984) **A/A/S:** Who's Who Among American Teachers; Teacher of the Month; Teacher of the Week **C/VW:** Feed the Children, American Heart Foundation, Society for the Prevention of Cruelty to Animals, Breast Cancer Awareness
Email: info@CambridgeWhosWho.com
URL: http://www.cambridgewhoswho.com

Raymond A. Dennis
Title: Teacher, Minister **Company:** Gospel Mission MBC **Address:** 7301 SO Avalone Blvd, Los Angeles, CA 90003 United States **BUS:** Ministry **P/S:** Christian Religious Services **MA:** Local **D/D/R:** Biblical Studies **H/I/S:** Reading **EDU:** Bachelor's of Business Administration, University of Philippines **A/A/S:** WBSC, LADA
Email: felyday@sbcglobal.net

Ida Y. Dennis-Hunter
Title: Founder, Executive Director **Company:** El Shaddai Transitional Resource Agency **Address:** P.O. Box 27266, Detroit, MI 48227 United States **BUS:** Resource Agency **P/S:** Transitional Resources for Women and Children Going from Welfare to Workforce, Educational Resources and Agencies for Work Clothes, Food and Emergency Shelter **D/D/R:** Running the Organization, Supervising a Staff of Six Employees, Calling and Meeting with Other Agencies to Collaborate, Bringing In Funding, Seeking Volunteers, Working Actively in Community Service Organizations **H/I/S:** Enjoying the Arts, Producing and Directing Community Plays at Local Theaters **EDU:** Master's Degree in Social Work, Wayne State University (1993); Bachelor's Degree in Social Work, Wayne State University (1992); Associate Degree in Business Administration, Summa Cum Laude, Baker College (2006) **A/A/S:** Local Detroit Chapter, National Association for the Advancement of Colored People; Supervisory Community Chairwoman, Motown First Federal Credit Union; Advisory Committee, JFL Diversified Inc; Local Public Speaker **A/H:** Poet, Published The International Society of Poets; Highest Achievement Award, Dale Carnegie
Email: idennishunter@yahoo.com

Elva L. Denny
Title: Owner, Psychotherapist **Company:** A Place for Hope **Address:** 951 Southpoint Circle, Suite B, Valparaiso, IN 46385 United States **BUS:** Psychotherapy **P/S:** Mental Health Outpatient Services for Individuals, Couples and Families **MA:** Regional **D/D/R:** Psychotherapy **H/I/S:** Reading, Knitting, Gardening, Taking Short Trips, Arranging Flowers **EDU:** Master's Degree in Psychotherapy, Purdue University; Master of Arts in Counseling, 1981; Ph.D., Clinical Psychology, Walden University **A/A/S:** American Counseling Association; Psi Chi; American Association of Medical Hypnoanalysis; Society for Clinical Hypnosis; Sierra Club **C/VW:** Talltree Arboretum, National Preserves, National Wildlife Federation
Email: edenny@crown.net
URL: http://www.cambridgewhoswho.com

John L. Denson
Title: Operations Manager **Company:** Jess Munos Autobody **Address:** 7115 Jefferson Street, Albuquerque, NM 87109 United States **BUS:** Auto Body Shop **P/S:** Car Service and Repair **MA:** Albuquerque **EXP:** Mr. Denson's expertise is in operations management. **H/I/S:** Traveling, Rodeo Cowboy **A/A/S:** Board of Directors, New Mexico Rodeo Association **C/VW:** Boys' Ranch
Email: jdenson@munoscc.com
URL: http://www.munoscc.com

Brad J. Dentis
Title: Vice President of Operations **Company:** Rib Crib Corporation **Address:** 4535 S. Harvard Avenue, Tulsa, OK 74135 United States **BUS:** Restaurant **P/S:** Food Services, Hospitality, Customer Service **MA:** Regional **D/D/R:** Overseeing Restaurant Operations **H/I/S:** Golfing, Biking, Running, Playing Racquetball **A/A/S:** Tulsa's Young Professionals; Oklahoma Restaurant Association **C/VW:** Make-A-Wish Foundation, Cystic Fibrosis Foundation
Email: bdentis@ribcrib.com
URL: http://www.ribcrib.com

Robin G. Denton
Title: Teacher **Company:** Newport News Public Schools **Dept:** John Marshall Elementary School **Address:** 743 24th Street, Newport News, VA 23607 United States **BUS:** Outstanding Public Elementary School **P/S:** Quality, Appropriate Education for All Students in Kindergarten through Second-Grade, in a Safe and Inviting Environment **MA:** Regional **D/D/R:** Teaching Children All Subjects on the Primary Level with a Focus on Individualizing Each Child's Needs **H/I/S:** Art, Music, Poetry, Using Computers **EDU:** Bachelor of Science in Elementary Education, Liberty University (1977) **A/A/S:** People for the Ethical Treatment of Animals; Community Jazz Band and Orchestra
Email: rgd113@cox.net
URL: http://www.sbo.nn.k12.va.us

Arlotte J. DePoorter
Title: Licensed Vocational Nurse (Retired) **Company:** Bellwood General Hospital **Address:** 606 W. Maple Street, Edgerton, MN 56128 United States **BUS:** Hospital **P/S:** Healthcare Including Nursing Services, Emergency Room Services, Consultation Services **MA:** Local **D/D/R:** Overseeing the Maternity Ward, Treating Emergency Room Patients **CERTS:** Licensed Vocational Nurse, Cerritos College (1973) **C/VW:** Local Church; The American Legion; Minnesota Retirement Community
Email: arlotte.depoorter@cwwemail.com

Heather Derby
Title: Sales Executive **Company:** Communication Engineering Company **Address:** 405 Boyson Road, Hiawatha, IA 52233 United States **BUS:** Technology **P/S:** Business Network and Data Systems, IP Telephony, Technology, Innovation **MA:** National **D/D/R:** Business-to-Business Sales to Midsize Companies, Enterprise Solutions, Consulting, Disaster Recovery, Unified Communication **H/I/S:** Marketing and Promoting Local Live Music **EDU:** Bachelor of Arts in Communications, University of Iowa (1997)
Email: hderby@ceciowa.com
URL: http://www.ceciowa.com

Joseph Derenzis
Title: 1) Owner, Financial Consultant 2) Teacher **Company:** 1) HBW Insurance and Financial Services, Inc. 2) Avon Park High School **Address:** 3425 Mockingbird Drive, Sebring, FL 33875 United States **BUS:** 1) Financial Business 2) High School **P/S:** 1) Financial Services, Online Networking, Retirement Planning, Insurance, Annuities 2) Education for Ninth through Twelfth-Grade Students **MA:** National **D/D/R:** Analyzing Clients' Financial Portfolios, Offering Guidance to Clients, Teaching Algebra **H/I/S:** Golfing **EDU:** Bachelor of Arts in Marketing and Business, Pace University (1987) **CERTS:** Certified Teacher, State of Florida (2002) **A/A/S:** Better Business Bureau; United Way of America; Sebring Chamber of Commerce **A/H:** Voted Best Financial Advisor in 2006, 2007, in Highlands County. Also recognized in the local newspaper Highland Today and News-Sun. Joe was also Teacher of The Year in 2007. **C/VW:** Volunteers financial consulting at United Way.
Email: jandvhbw@embarqmail.com
URL: http://www.helpingbuildwealthonline.com

Arlene M. Deroy
Title: Senior Application Developer **Company:** Aetna, Inc. **Address:** 151 Farmington Avenue, Hartford, CT 06158 United States **BUS:** One of the Nation's Leading Diversified Healthcare Benefits Companies **P/S:** Health, Dental, Group, Life, Disability and Long-Term Care Benefits **MA:** National **D/D/R:** Working on Lead Claims Projects, Handling Production Problems, Enhancements, Research, Processing Systems for Medical Claims **H/I/S:** Soccer **EDU:** Bachelor's Degree in Computer Science, Alfred University (1995)
Email: veloceam@aetna.com
URL: http://www.aetna.com

Laura J. Desai
Title: Teacher **Company:** Crockett Middle School **Address:** 2631 Kuser Road, Hamilton, NJ 08619 United States **BUS:** Middle School **P/S:** Education, Foreign Language Education, Library, Athletics **MA:** Local **D/D/R:** Teaching Spanish to Students in Grades Six through Eight, Managing Daily Curriculum, Translating for Parents and Teachers **H/I/S:** Tennis, Traveling, Cooking, Crafting Silver Jewelry **EDU:** Bachelor of Science in Business, Bachelor of Science in Spanish, Minor in Human Resources, The College of New Jersey (2001) **CERTS:** Certification in K-12 Spanish Education, State of New Jersey; Alternate Route Program **A/A/S:** Foreign Language Educators of New Jersey; Spanish Honor Society; Spanish Club; Student Chapter, Society for Human Resource Management
Email: laurajdesai@aol.com
URL: http://www.hamilton.k12.nj.us

Francois X. Desaulniers
Title: Safety Coordinator **Company:** Paul Dinto Electrical Contractors **Address:** 121 Turnpike Drive, Middlebury, CT 06762 United States **BUS:** Electrician Contractor **P/S:** Electrical Contracting **MA:** Local **EXP:** Mr. Desaulniers' expertise is in safety management. **H/I/S:** Bowling, Golfing **EDU:** Associate Degree in Industrial Engineering, Paines Valley University
Email: feesdulnie@aol.com

Mr. Mark D. Deschner
Title: President **Company:** Deschner Enterprises **Address:** 509 Green Cedar Drive, League City, TX 77573 United States **BUS:** Automotive Specialty Aftermarket Company **P/S:** Automotive and Diesel Performance and Accessories, Modifications, Detailing **MA:** Local **D/D/R:** Overseeing Daily Operations, Submitting Bids and Quotes, Managing Contract Negotiations, Handling All Finances **H/I/S:** Traveling, Enjoying Music and Theater **EDU:** Bachelor of Science in Science, University of Phoenix (2005); Bachelor of Arts in Business Management **A/A/S:** Society of Auto Engineers; American Society of Mechanical Engineers
Email: mddeschner@comcast.net

Jeanette R. DeSimone
Title: Inside Sales Manager **Company:** H & C Tool Supply Corp. **Address:** 235 Mt. Read Boulevard, Rochester, NY 14611 United States **BUS:** Industrial Tool Distribution Company **P/S:** Industrial Tools, Safety Products, Abrasives, Fasteners, Sale of Tools and Customer Service **MA:** National **D/D/R:** Offering Customer Service, Quoting Prices, Selling Tools to Small Business Owners and Major Corporations Nationally, Cutting Tools, Overseeing All Orders Taken by Phone and Inside Sales Department **H/I/S:** Playing Pool, Shooting Darts, Bowling, Reading, Watching Movies **EDU:** Degree, Jefferson High School (1985)
Email: jeanette.desimone@hctoolsupply.com

Wendy C. DeSpain
Title: Coordinator for No Child Left Behind **Company:** Plano Independent School District **Address:** 2700 W. 15Th Street, Plano, TX 75075 United States **BUS:** School District **P/S:** Education **MA:** Regional **D/D/R:** Managing School Operations, Ensuring Quality Instruction in Every Classroom, Working as a Community Liaison between Educationally Disadvantaged Students and their Families, Helping Families with Food and Other Necessities, Helping to Create Lifelong Learners who are Positively Contributing Members of Society, Analyzing Statistical Issues **H/I/S:** Traveling, Spending Time with her Family, Camping, Reading, Scrapbooking **EDU:** Master of Education, Concentration in Elementary Education, University of North Texas (2000); Bachelor of Science in Interdisciplinary Studies, Stephen F. Austin State University (1995) **A/A/S:** Texas Elementary Principals and Supervisors Association; Former President, Plano Principals Association; National Association of Federal Education Program Administrators; Association for Compensatory Educators of Texas; Texas Association of School Administrators
Email: wendy.despain@pisd.edu
URL: http://www.pisd.edu/memorial

Joan Dessureau
Title: Owner **Company:** Joan Dessureau Antiques **Address:** 8206 Gladstone Road, Wyndmoor, PA 19038 United States **BUS:** Trade Show Sales **P/S:** Antiques, Collectibles **MA:** National **D/D/R:** Managing the Sale of American Art and Antique Pottery **H/I/S:** Listening to Music, Reading **EDU:** Master's Degree in Education, University of Pennsylvania (1968); Bachelor of Arts in Education, Temple University (1964) **A/A/S:** Board of Retirees, Philadelphia Federation of Teachers; Board Member, Delaware Valley Opera Co.; Board Member, American Art Pottery Association; Board Member, Women for Greater Philadelphia; Greater Delaware Valley Antiques Dealers' Association
Email: joanantiques@comcast.net
URL: http://www.cambridgewhoswho.com

John F. Detomaso
Title: Realtor **Company:** Morro Bay Realty **Address:** 805 Main St, Morro Bay, CA 93442 United States **BUS:** Real Estate Broker **P/S:** Residential, Executive, Hi End, Ocean Front Properties, New Construction, Condos, Golf homes, Gated **MA:** National **D/D/R:** Residential Properties **H/I/S:** Watches football/Baseball **EDU:** Bachelor of Arts in General Economics, University of San Francisco **A/A/S:** California Association of Realtors, National Association of Realtors
Email: johnd@morrobayrealty.com
URL: www.morrobayrealty.com

Julie A. Deuschle
Title: Sales Manager **Company:** Clarion Boards, Inc. **Address:** 143 Fiberboard Road, Shippenville, PA 16254 United States **BUS:** Manufacturing Company **P/S:** Manufacture High Density Fiber Board **MA:** National **D/D/R:** Developing Moisture Resistant, High Density Fiber Boards, Overseeing Logistics, Ordering Inventory **H/I/S:** Camping, Outdoors **EDU:** Bachelor of Science in Industrial Engineering, University of Pittsburgh, Pittsburgh, PA (1992)
Email: julie.deuschle@atcpanels.com

David James DeVargas
Title: Director of Marketing **Company:** Travelpride Gay Vacations **Address:** 710 N.E. 26th Street, Wilton Manors, FL 33305 United States **BUS:** Travel Agency **P/S:** Gay Cruise Charters and Tours, Personalized Luxury and Small Ships, Travel to International Destinations **MA:** International **D/D/R:** Marketing, Managing Communications, Advertising, Overseeing Online Advertising, Targeting Advertisements for Gay Audiences and Men over 45 Years Old, Establishing General Reservations, Evaluating Strategies **H/I/S:** Traveling, Listening to Classical Music **EDU:** Bachelor of Science in Advertising, University of Texas at Austin (1998) **A/A/S:** International Gay and Lesbian Travel Association
Email: david@travelpride.com
URL: http://www.travelpride.com

Edwin B. Devera
Title: Artist **Address:** 7837 Goode Street, San Diego, CA 92139 United States **BUS:** Freelance Artist **P/S:** Artwork **MA:** Regional **D/D/R:** Creating Artistic Expressions **H/I/S:** Running, Cycling, Swimming **EDU:** Diploma in Art, Stratford Career Institute (2006); Bachelor of Fine Arts, University of the Philippines, Manila **A/A/S:** Escondido Art Association

Regina Joy Devine
Title: Certified Pharmacy Technician **Company:** Wal-Mart **Address:** 484 State Route 949, Dunmor, KY 42339 United States **BUS:** National Retail Company **P/S:** Apparel, Electronics, Entertainment Products, Home Furnishings, Jewelry, Sports Equipment, Toys, Automotive Equipment and Services, Photo Equipment, Pharmacy Services **MA:** National **D/D/R:** Filling Approximately 350-500 Prescriptions Daily in Two Pharmacy Locations, Inputting Patient Data, Verifying Patient and Prescription Information with Physicians, Addressing All Insurance Issues for Insurance Plans **H/I/S:** Reading **EDU:** General College Coursework for Nursing Education Foundation, Purdue University (1993) **CERTS:** Certified Pharmacy Technician, Technical Institute of Gary Indiana (1998)
Email: joydevine@hotmail.com
URL: http://www.walmart.com

Alisa A. Devlin, MD
Title: Staff Psychiatrist **Company:** Franklin Square Hospital **Address:** 9105 Franklin Square Drive, Baltimore, MD 21237 United States **BUS:** Hospital Facility **P/S:** Inpatient and Outpatient Healthcare Services **MA:** Regional **D/D/R:** Psychiatric Diagnosis and Evaluations, Treating Patients with Bipolar Disorder, Performing Intake and Follow-Up Treatment, Performing Intake and Medication Management with Followup Treatment **H/I/S:** Watching Ice Hockey, Writing, Drawing **EDU:** MD, Hahnemann Medical College (1993) **A/A/S:** American Psychiatric Association; Maryland Psychiatric Society; American Clinical Society of Psychiatry for College; American Society of Clinical Psychopharmacology
Email: utzers@aol.com
URL: http://www.franklinsquare.org/

Ginger K. Dewitt
Title: Realtor **Company:** RE/MAX Performance Plus **Address:** 19400 108th Avenue S.E., Suite 202, Renton, WA 98055 United States **BUS:** Real Estate Company **P/S:** Commercial and Residential Real Estate Exchange **MA:** National **D/D/R:** Buying and Selling Residential Properties, Assisting Clients with Relocation **H/I/S:** Sports **EDU:** Coursework, Rockwell Institute **CERTS:** Licensed Realtor (2005) **A/A/S:** Washington Association of Realtors; National Association of Realtors
Email: gingerdewitt@remax.net
URL: http://www.gingerdewitt.com

Raymond J. DeWitt
Title: Owner, Operator **Company:** RJD Improvements **Address:** 10 Suffolk Avenue, Patchogue, NY 11772 United States **BUS:** Irrigation Company **P/S:** Outdoor Sprinkler Systems **MA:** Regional **D/D/R:** Designing and Installing Sprinkler Systems **H/I/S:** Golfing, Rollerblading, Skiing **EDU:** Industry-Related Training and Experience
Email: raydew1@optonline.net
URL: http://www.servicemagic.com

Rayne A. Dews
Title: President **Company:** Storm Computer Inc. **Address:** 21909 Brier Road, Brier, WA 98036 United States **BUS:** Personal Technology Solutions **P/S:** Personal Technology Solutions **MA:** National **D/D/R:** Business Coaching **H/I/S:** Reading Journals, Dancing, Exercise, Cooking, Spending Time with Family, Learning New Things, Politics and Nonprofits **EDU:** Bachelor of Science in Holistic Health, American Institute of Holistic Theology **A/H:** ULC Who's Who **C/VW:** Cystic Fibrosis Foundation, American Red Cross, Breast Cancer Society
Email: rayne@storm-computer.com
URL: http://www.shopstormcomputer.com

Jamie Di Bene-Gorger
Title: Science Teacher, Chairman Science Department **Company:** Louisville High School **Address:** 22300 Mulholland Drive, Woodland Hills, CA 91364 United States **BUS:** Private Catholic High School for Girls **P/S:** Education **MA:** Local **D/D/R:** Teaching Advanced Placement Biology for 10th and 11th-Grade Students **H/I/S:** Referring Soccer, Singing with the Church Choir **EDU:** Master of Science in Education, Mount St. Mary's College **A/A/S:** American Cancer Society; American Chemical Society; American Youth Soccer Organization; NMTA **C/VW:** Volunteer, Regional Referee Administrator
Email: jgorger@aol.com
URL: http://www.louisvillehs.org

Stephanie Di Palma Sears
Title: Coordinator of Sales and Marketing **Company:** Fidelity National Title Insurance Company **Dept:** Atlanta National Title Services **Address:** 200 Galleria Parkway S.E., Suite 2060, Atlanta, GA 30339 United States **BUS:** Insurance Company **P/S:** Commercial Insurance Polices for Office Buildings, Railroads, Forests and Industrial Facilities **MA:** International **D/D/R:** Marketing, Managing Client Relations, Coordinating Events, Organizing Real Estate Conferences **H/I/S:** Sports **EDU:** Bachelor's Degree in English Literature, Minor in Public Relations, Wittenberg University (2006) **A/A/S:** Commercial Real Estate Women; National Association of Industrial and Office Properties; International Council of Shopping Centers; Real Estate Investment Advisory Council **C/VW:** Canine Companions for Independence
Email: stephanie.dipalma@fnf.com
URL: http://www.fntic.com//ntsatlanta

Anabelle Dias
Title: Attorney in Criminal Law **Company:** Annabelle Dias and Associates, PA **Address:** 1226 E. Seventh Avenue, Tallahassee, FL 32303 United States **BUS:** Law Firm **P/S:** Legal Advice and Representation, Trials **MA:** Local **D/D/R:** Practicing Criminal Defense Law **H/I/S:** Traveling **EDU:** JD, Florida State University, 1998; Bachelor of Science in Accounting, Florida State University, 1994 **A/A/S:** National Association of Criminal Defense Lawyers; Florida Association of Criminal Defense Lawyers; Tallahassee Bar Association **C/VW:** Assisted Katrina Survivors
Email: anabellelaw@yahoo.com

Carlos G. Diaz
Title: Psychiatrist **Company:** Ponce Psychiatric Associates **Address:** 2431 Avenue Las Americas, Suite 303, Ponce, PR **BUS:** Psychiatric Practice **P/S:** Psychiatric Care **MA:** Local **D/D/R:** Treating Depression and Anxiety Disorders **H/I/S:** Traveling, Writing **EDU:** Doctor of Medicine in Psychiatry, University of Puerto Rico School of Medicine; Bachelor of Science in Biology, Georgetown University **A/A/S:** Academy of Psychiatry, Puerto Rico; College of Physicians-Surgeons of Puerto Rico; President-elect, Association de Psicologia de Puerto Rico **C/VW:** Iniciativa Comunitaria
Email: elgatoconbotas.carlos@gmail.com

Gina M. Diaz
Title: RRT, NPS **Company:** Twinkle Star Medical Services **Address:** 1536 West 25th Street, Suite 437, San Pedro, CA 90732 United States **BUS:** Healthcare Service Provider **P/S:** Respiratory Care **MA:** Local **D/D/R:** Neonatal and Pediatric Specialist, Sleep Studies, Advanced Level Practitioner **H/I/S:** Piano Music, Exercising, Spending Time Outdoors **EDU:** Bachelor of Arts in Science, Long Beach Paramedical College **A/A/S:** Instructor, American Heart Association, St. John Basco Boys Home
Email: info@CambridgeWhosWho.com
URL: http://cambridgewhoswho.com

Lourdes Diaz

Title: General Manager **Company:** Anti Fire of Puerto Rico, Inc. **Address:** P.O. Box 140219, Arecibo, PR 00614 United States **BUS:** Installation Service Company **P/S:** Fire Prevention Equipment Including Fire Extinguishers and Sprinkler Systems **MA:** Regional **D/D/R:** Accounting, Overseeing the Fire Sprinklers Department, Purchase orders, Overseeing Fire Alarm Installation **H/I/S:** Reading Inspirational Books **EDU:** Associate Degree in Marketing, Monroe Community College (1990) **A/A/S:** National Fire Prevention Agency
Email: lourdes@antifirepr.com
URL: http://www.antifirepr.com

Patricia Diaz

Title: Broker Associate **Company:** REMAX First Advantage **Address:** 260 Inman Avenue, Colinia, NJ 07090 United States **BUS:** Real Estate Agency **P/S:** Residential Real Estate Sales **MA:** Statewide **D/D/R:** Offering Local Real Estate Knowledge **H/I/S:** Bowling, Playing Softball, Walking **A/A/S:** New Jersey Association of Realtors; National Association of Realtors **A/H:** ReMax 110 Percent Clubs (1999-2005); One Million Dollar Club (1999-2001); Circle of Excellence (2002-05)
Email: patti_07066@yahoo.com
URL: www.remax.net

Teresa Diaz, MD

Title: MD **Company:** Oakcare Medical Group **Address:** 1411 E. 31st Street, Oakland, CA 94602 United States **BUS:** Healthcare **P/S:** County Clinic for Obstetrics and Gynecology **MA:** Local **D/D/R:** Working with the Poor, Under-Served and Uninsured Population, Utilizing her Experience as a Former Drug and HIV Counselor **H/I/S:** Salsa Dancing **EDU:** MD, University of Medicine and Dentistry, New Jersey (1999); Residency, University of Connecticut (2004) **A/A/S:** American Medical Association; National Medical Association; National Hispanic Medical Association
Email: laydtee@aol.com

Patricia DiBenedetto Barba

Title: Renal Nutritionist **Company:** Da Vita Healthcare **Address:** 3 Countryside Drive, Lincoln, RI 02865 United States **BUS:** Healthcare Service Provider **P/S:** Renal Dialysis Services **MA:** Local **D/D/R:** Renal Nutrition, Patient and Staff Education, Dosing of Medication **H/I/S:** Garden, Travel, Theater **EDU:** Master of Science in Health Science Education, University of Buffalo **A/A/S:** Former Chair, Renal Dietetic/Diabetic Education Council, American Dietetic Association; Founder, Renal Nutrition Group, National Kidney Association
Email: PattiBarba@verizon.net

Dino DiCianno

Title: Executive Director **Company:** Nevada Department of Taxation **Address:** 1550 College Parkway, Carson City, NV 89706 United States **BUS:** Government Organization **P/S:** Revenue Collection and Tax Payer Services **MA:** Regional **EXP:** Mr. DiCianno's expertise includes revenue management and the preparation of tax returns. **H/I/S:** Hunting, Fly-Fishing, Spending Time with his Family **EDU:** Master of Arts in Economics, Washington State University; Bachelor's Degree in Mathematics, Southern Oregon University
Email: dicianno@tax.state.nv.us
URL: http://www.tax.state.nv.us

Kathryn M. Dickerson

Title: Attorney **Company:** Dickerson Law **Address:** 705 Chickasawhay Street, Waynesboro, MS 39367 United States **BUS:** Law Private Practice **P/S:** Law Practice **MA:** Local **D/D/R:** Domestic and Property **EDU:** JD, Mississippi Law School **A/A/S:** American Bar Association, Women's Bar Association, Mississippi Sierra Club
Email: dickerson.katie@jamil.com

Theodore F. Dickman

Title: Engineer Tech III **Company:** Metropolitan District **Address:** 78 Willowbrook Road, East Hartford, CT 06118 United States **BUS:** Sewers **P/S:** Preventing Contamination of Water **MA:** Local **D/D/R:** Water, Sewers, Wastes Supervisor **H/I/S:** Writing Poetry
Email: info@CambridgeWhosWho.com

Deborah J. Dickson

Title: Director of Infrastructure **Company:** Rapid Solution Group **Address:** 4251 Bridger Road, Kansas City, MO 64111 United States **BUS:** Leader in the Marketing Industry **P/S:** Marketing Materials, Printing them for Financial, Insurance, Gaming and Recreational Companies **MA:** National **D/D/R:** Telecommunications and Infrastructure, the Company's Data Center, Phone Systems, the Network Between their Four Offices, Overseeing the Six Direct Reports Located in California, New York, Missouri and Illinois; Offering Education Training, Promoting Quality Assurance **H/I/S:** Hiking, Caring for Dogs **EDU:** Bachelor's Degree in Information Technology, University of Missouri **CERTS:** Certified Information Systems Security Professional **A/A/S:** Institute of Electrical and Electronics Engineers; Data Center Management
Email: ddickson@rapidsolutionsgroup.com
URL: http://www.rapidsolutionsgroup.com

Susan V. Dickson

Title: Coordinator **Company:** Riverside County Office of Education **Dept:** Teacher Support Center **Address:** 3939 13th Street, Riverside, CA 92501 United States **BUS:** School District **P/S:** Education **MA:** Local **D/D/R:** Overseeing the Professional Development of Beginning Teachers **H/I/S:** Traveling, Reading, Needlework **EDU:** Master of Arts in Education, San Diego State University; Bachelor of Arts in Education, Duke University **C/VW:** Temecula Valley Master Chorale; Gideons International
Email: sdickson@rcoe.us
URL: http://www.rcoe.us

Ms. Danette M. Dicristo

Title: President, Owner **Company:** Anclote Adventure Boat Rentals, Inc. **Address:** 7437 Chapel Avenue, New Port Richey, FL 34652 United States **BUS:** Travel and Recreation Company **P/S:** Boat Rentals to Anclote Key and Island Beaches **MA:** Regional **D/D/R:** Scheduling Reservations, Ensuring Safety for Boats, Cleaning Boats, Overseeing Sales and Management **H/I/S:** Collecting Antiques **EDU:** Associate Degree in Human Services and Recreational Leadership
Email: anclotedanette@yahoo.com
URL: http://www.ancloteadventure.com

Joan Diebold, DVM

Title: Owner, Veterinarian **Company:** Compassionate Care Veterinary Center **Address:** 1147 N. Main Street, Randolph, MA 02368 United States **BUS:** Hospital **P/S:** Veterinary Care, Surgery **MA:** Local **EXP:** Dr. Diebold's expertise includes small animal internal medicine, exotic medicine and dermatology. **EDU:** Doctor of Veterinary Medicine, University of Pennsylvania **A/A/S:** Local Chamber of Commerce; Association of Exotic Mammal Veterinarians; American Association of Feline Practitioners; American Animal Hospital Association; American Veterinary Medical Association
Email: jdiebold@compassionatecarevet.com
URL: http://www.compassionatecarevet.com

Dr. Irma G. Dietert

Title: Hospital and Homebound Teacher, Chaplain **Company:** Polk County School Board **Dept:** Instructional Services Division **Address:** 304 N. Fern Road, N.W. Area, ESE Office, Lakeland, FL 33801 United States **BUS:** School **P/S:** Education **MA:** Local **D/D/R:** Teaching Sick Children in their Homes and in the Hospital **H/I/S:** Gardening, Sports, Traveling, Reading, Singing, Playing the Piano, Listening to Music **EDU:** Doctorate in Ministry, Chicago Theological Seminary; Master of Divinity, Garrett Evangelical Theological Seminary; Bachelor's Degree in Christian Education, Florida Southern College **CERTS:** Certification in English as a Second Language; Certification in English Secondary Education **A/A/S:** American Association of University Women; National Federation of Republican Women; Polk Education Association; Inner Circle Member, National Republican Senatorial Committee; Former Vice President, University of Women in Florida State; National Education Association **C/VW:** Fundraiser, Hospice Exceptional School Education; No Child Left Behind; Foster Care; Elderhood Committee
Email: idietert@tampabay.rr.com

Elly Del Prado Dietz

Title: Partner **Company:** Duvall, Gruning & Dietz, PLLC **Address:** 112 N. LBJ Drive, San Marcos, TX 78666 United States **BUS:** Law Firm **P/S:** Legal Services **MA:** Local **EXP:** Ms. Dietz's expertise includes family law, general civil litigation, real estate law and property law. **H/I/S:** Swimming, Running, Spending Time Outdoors, Traveling **EDU:** JD, University of Texas at Austin (1988); Bachelor's Degree in Zoology, University of Texas (1985) **CERTS:** AV Rated, Martindale Hubble **A/A/S:** Caldwell County Bar Association; Hays County Bar Association; Texas State Bar Association; Western District of Texas, United States District Court **C/VW:** St. Mark's Episcopal Church
Email: edietz@dgdlawyers.com
URL: http://www.dgdlawyers.com

Elisa DiGennaro

Title: Special Education Teacher **Company:** Rocky Point Union Free School District **Address:** 90 Rocky Point-Yaphank Road, Rocky Point, NY 11778 United States **BUS:** Public School System **P/S:** Primary and Secondary Education **MA:** Local **D/D/R:** Teaching Students with Special Needs in a Self-Contained Classroom, Second-Grade Inclusion Classes, Lesson Planning, Monitoring One Resource Room Period, Tutoring Summer Classes **H/I/S:** Spending Time with her Husband, Taking Care of her Dog **EDU:** Master's Degree Plus 60 in Liberal Arts, Stony Brook University (2004)
Email: edigennaro@rockypoint.k12.ny.us
URL: http://www.rockypoint.k12.ny.us

Lisa M. DiGioia-Ross, Pharm.D.

Title: 1) Assistant Professor of Pharmacy Practice 2) Chief Financial Officer, Clinical Pharmaceutical Consultant 3) Per Diem Pharmacist Clinical and Staff **Company:** 1) University of Louisiana, Monroe 2) Robert D. Ross, MD, APMC 3) Ochsner Health System, Medical Center **Address:** 4224 Houma Boulevard, Suite 430, Metairie, LA 70006 United States **BUS:** 1) Public State University 2) Private Medical Practice 3) Acute Care Hospital, Teaching Institution **P/S:** 1) Professional Higher Education for Pharmacy Students 2) Patient Care and Education 3) Patient Care, Education and Research **MA:** Regional **D/D/R:** Lecturing 100 Students per Year, Overseeing an Average of 12 to 30 Students per Year, Managing All Financial Services, Offering Drug Consultations, Teaching Students, Patients and Staff, Forwarding Drug Information to Doctors, Dispensing Medication and Order Verification, Counseling Patients, Offering Drug Intervention Dissemination, Monitoring Patients' Medication **H/I/S:** Amateur Photography, Scrapbooking, Working Out, Spending Time with her Animals Including Exotic Parrots, Traveling, Volunteering with Junior League of New Orleans **EDU:** Residency, Ochsner Medical Center (1999); Doctorate of Pharmacy, Xavier University (1998); Bachelor of Science in Pharmacy, St. John's University (1991) **A/A/S:** Accepted, ASHP and Merck Competitive Traineeship in Asthma (2002); American College of Clinical Pharmacy; American Association of Colleges of Pharmacy; American Society of Health-System Pharmacists; American Pharmaceutical Association; Board Member, Louisiana Society of Health-System Pharmacists; Rho Chi Honor Society; Golden Key National Honor Society; Kappa Gamma Pi National; Catholic Graduate Honor Society; Junior League of New Orleans **A/H:** Louisiana Governor's Office Award for Anti-Coagulation Education to the Elderly (2000); Xavier University College of Pharmacy Award for Excellence-Highest Cumulative Average in Professional Curriculum, Valedictorian (1999); CVS Drug Store Community Service Award (1990); Dean's List, St. John's University (1986-1991); St. John's University Academic Grants (1986-1991)
Email: rossulmedu@cox.net

Margaret F. Dikel

Title: Webmaster **Company:** The Riley Guide **Address:** 11218 Ashley Drive, Rockville, MD 20852 United States **BUS:** Online Staffing Company **P/S:** Staffing, Career Information Analysis and Career Resources **MA:** National **D/D/R:** Consulting, Developing Career Evaluations and Career-Based Websites for Corporations, Government and Nonprofit Organizations, Searching the Internet, Evaluating Websites, Writing Books about Employment and the Use of the Internet for Job Searching **H/I/S:** Playing the French Horn, Gardening **EDU:** Master of Science in Library and Informational Science, Simmons College, Boston, MA **A/A/S:** American Library Association; National Career Development Association **C/VW:** Local Church; Maryland-National Capital Park and Planning Commission; Local Charitable Organizations
Email: webmaster@rileyguide.com
URL: http://www.rileyguide.com

Deborah L. DiLeo

Title: Administrative Assistant **Company:** JCG Development **Address:** 2223 El Cajon Boulevard, San Diego, CA 92104 United States **BUS:** Real Estate Development Firm **P/S:** Real Estate Development **MA:** National **D/D/R:** Troubleshooting, Presenting Monthly Reports **H/I/S:** Exercising, Reading **CERTS:** Notary Public, California
Email: debbie@jcgdev.com
URL: http://www.hampstead.com

Joy A. Dillard

Title: Owner **Company:** Joy's Joy Rides, LLC **Address:** 7028 Red Arrow Highway, Coloma, MI 49038 United States **BUS:** Automotive Dealer **P/S:** Pre-Owned Automobile Sales; Mechanic and repair shop on premises. **MA:** Statewide **D/D/R:** Attends auctions to obtain automobiles. Manages the repair shop and sales, financing automobiles **H/I/S:** Billiards, Scrapbooking, Spending Time with her Family **EDU:** Pursuing Bachelor's Degree in Accounting; Associate Degree in Accounting, Davenport University, Michigan (1987) **C/VW:** Local Police Department, Local Schools
Email: joysjoyridesllc@hotmail.com
URL: http://www.joysjoyridesllc.com

Brittany M. Dillier
Title: Operations Assistant **Company:** Blair Orthopedic Associates and Sports Medicine **Address:** 3000 Fairway Drive, Altoona, PA 16602 United States **BUS:** Orthopedists and Sports Medicine Physicians **P/S:** General and Subspecialty Orthopedic Care, Physical Medicine, Rehabilitation, Podiatry, In-House Physical Therapy and X-ray Services **MA:** Regional **D/D/R:** Supervising Daily Operations, Acting as a Customer Service Representative, Overseeing Many Functions of the Company, Coordinating the 2007 Health-A-Rama, Scheduling Physicians for the Local Conference, Designing and Coordinating the Website **H/I/S:** Reading, Cheerleading, Dancing **EDU:** Associate Degree in Business Administration, The Pennsylvania State University (2006) **A/A/S:** Local Chamber of Commerce
Email: brittanydillier@blairortho.com
URL: http://www.blairortho.com

Linda M. Dillon
Title: Owner **Company:** Blue Duck Bistro **Address:** 216 N Main, Hutchinson, KS 67504 United States **BUS:** Bistro Restaurant **P/S:** Service **MA:** Local **D/D/R:** Management Skills, Organizational Skills, Operations **H/I/S:** Climb Mountains, Scuba **A/A/S:** Chamber of Commerce, Downtown Revitalization Group
Email: blueduckbistro@aol.com
URL: www.blueduckbistro.com

Susan J. DiLorenzo
Title: Team Leader **Company:** Lahey Clinic North **Address:** 1 Essex Center Drive, Peabody, MA 01960 United States **BUS:** Teaching Hospital **P/S:** Inpatient and Outpatient Medical Treatment, Education, Research **MA:** Local **D/D/R:** Public Relations, Training Employees on Computer Systems, Troubleshooting, Customer Service, Handling Insurance Information **H/I/S:** Belly Dancing, Going to the Gym **EDU:** Coursework in Medical Terminology, Burdette College; High School Graduate **A/A/S:** Board Member, Portal to Hope; Northeast Belly Dance Association
Email: susan.j.dilorenzo@lahey.org
URL: http://www.lahey.org

Debbi DiMaggio
Title: Realtor **Company:** The Grubb Co **Address:** 1960 Mountain Blvd, Oakland, CA 94611 United States **BUS:** Residential Real Estate Agent Broker **P/S:** Marketing and Selling Real Estate **MA:** National **D/D/R:** Specialize in the Oakland, Berkeley and Piedmont Areas of the Bay Area and East Bay **H/I/S:** Tennis and Travel **EDU:** Bachelor of Science in Political Science, University of California, Berkeley **A/A/S:** 0
Email: debbi@debbidimaggio.com
URL: www.debbidimaggio.com

Eugene DiMariano Jr.
Title: Attorney **Company:** Law Office of Eugene DiMariano **Address:** 157 Portsmouth Avenue, Suite 101, Stratham, NH 03885 United States **BUS:** Law Firm **P/S:** Legal Services **MA:** National **D/D/R:** Practicing Personal Injury Law, Litigating for Workers' Compensation **H/I/S:** Sports, Reading **EDU:** JD, Pepperdine University; Bachelor of Arts in Political Science, University of Pennsylvania **A/A/S:** New Hampshire Bar Association; New Hampshire Trial Lawyers Association; American Bar Association; American Association for Justice; NHBLA **C/VW:** Local Church
Email: edimariano@verizon.net
URL: http://www.dimarianolaw.com

Adriana Maria Dimond
Title: District Sales Manager **Company:** Eli Lilly and Company **Address:** 448 E. 20th Street, Apartment 8A, New York, NY 10009 United States **BUS:** Pharmaceutical Company **P/S:** Research, Marketing, Pharmaceutical Sales **MA:** International **D/D/R:** Managing a Team of Sales Representatives, Coaching, Inspiring and Teaching about Products, Traveling with Each Representative Monthly, Personal Development, Interviewing and Hiring New Representatives, Working with Human Resources, Negotiating Salary and Moving Expenses, Overseeing Products **H/I/S:** Exercising, Running, Reading, Spending Time with her Family, Playing the Piano **EDU:** Bachelor of Science in Molecular Biology, University of Richmond (1998)
Email: dimond_adriana_m@lilly.com
URL: http://www.lilly.com

Tina M. Dingess
Title: Collections Manager **Company:** Ohio CAT **Address:** 3993 E. Royalton Road, Broadview Heights, OH 44147 United States **BUS:** Retail Sales Company **P/S:** Rental and Sales of Caterpillar Construction Equipment, Parts and Service for Caterpillar Engines **MA:** National **D/D/R:** Managing Collections, Credit and Accounts Receivable **H/I/S:** Spending Time with her Family, Caring for her Dalmatians, Traveling **EDU:** Bachelor of Science in Accounting, University of Phoenix **A/A/S:** National Association of Credit Management **C/VW:** Local Church; Local Charitable Organizations
Email: tdingess@ohiocat.com

Valerie A. DiNizio
Title: Senior Administrative Assistant **Company:** Ortho Women's Health & Urology **Address:** 1000 US Highway 202, Raritan, NJ 08869 United States **BUS:** Pharmaceutical Company **P/S:** Oral Contraceptives, Pharmaceuticals **MA:** National **D/D/R:** Performing Administrative Duties **H/I/S:** Spending Time with her Family **EDU:** Coursework in Secretarial Studies, Taylor Business Institute; Diploma, North Plainfield High School **A/A/S:** Our Lady of Mount Virgin; President, Homeowners Association **C/VW:** Religious Education Teacher, Our Lady of Mount Virgin; United Way
Email: vdinizio@ompus.jnj.com
URL: http://www.cambridgewhoswho.com

James M. Dinslage
Title: Registered Nurse **Company:** Kaiser Permanente **Address:** 1 Kaiser Plaza, Oakland, CA 94612 United States **BUS:** Hospital **P/S:** Cardiovascular and Critical Care, Healthcare **MA:** Regional **D/D/R:** Working with Cardiovascular Intensive Care Patients **H/I/S:** Outdoor Activities, Playing Volleyball, Basketball and Softball **EDU:** Bachelor of Arts in Biology, College of Saint Catherine, Minnesota
Email: jimmydinslage@hotmail.com

Ms. Edna P. Dinwiddie
Title: Owner (Retired) **Company:** Ruth's Coffee Shop **Address:** Yuma, AZ 86409 United States **BUS:** Coffee Shop **P/S:** Coffee and Food Services **MA:** Local **EXP:** Ms. Dinwiddie's expertise is in finance management. **D/D/R:** Managing Operations, Overseeing Employees, Cooking, Serving **H/I/S:** Reading, Solving Puzzles **EDU:** High School Diploma **A/A/S:** Board Chairman, Business and Professional Women's Network **C/VW:** Katherine Hindlick Senior Center
Email: edna.dinwiddie@cwwemail.com
URL: http://www.cambridgewhoswho.com

Christina B. Dior
Title: Owner **Company:** Triple Crown Mortgage, LLC **Address:** 10475 Park Meadows Drive, Suite 600, Lone Tree, CO 80124 United States **BUS:** Mortgage Company **P/S:** Residential Mortgage Lending, Referral Loans, Refinancing **MA:** Regional **EXP:** Ms. Dior's expertise is in mortgage brokering. **H/I/S:** Traveling, Cooking, Spending Time with her Family, Driving **EDU:** Bachelor of Arts in Psychology, Mount Saint Mary College, Maryland **A/A/S:** Better Business Bureau **C/VW:** Racing 2 Save Lives
Email: christinadior@triplecrownmtgllc.com
URL: http://www.triplecrownmtgllc.com

Sheryle M. Dirks
Title: Assistant Dean **Company:** Duke University: The Fuqua School of Business **Address:** 1 Tower View Drive, Durham, NC 27708 United States **BUS:** One of the Leading Business Schools in the World **P/S:** Highest Quality Education for Business and Academic Leaders, Promotion the Advancement of the Understanding and Practice of Management through Research **MA:** Regional **D/D/R:** Acting as the Managing Director of Career Management Center, Assisting Students with their Job Searches, Working with Companies to Employ Students, Assuring Quality Experience for Students, Meeting Student's Career Needs **H/I/S:** Hiking, Cooking, Reading **EDU:** Master's Degree in Human Resources, Iowa State University (1993)
Email: sheryle.dirks@duke.edu
URL: http://www.fuqua.duke.edu

Katharine B. DiSciorio
Title: Project Director **Company:** United Healthcare **Address:** 48 Monroe Turnpike, Trumbull, CT 06611 United States **BUS:** Healthcare System **P/S:** Healthcare Services Including Insurance **MA:** National **D/D/R:** Managing Call Center Technology **H/I/S:** Traveling, Reading, Golfing **EDU:** Bachelor's Degree in Accounting, Mercy College **A/A/S:** National Call Center Management Institute
Email: kdiscior@oxhp.com

JoMarie DiTata
Title: Media and Technology Specialist **Company:** Amsterdam High School **Address:** 140 Saratoga Avenue, Amsterdam, NY 12010 United States **BUS:** High School **P/S:** Education **MA:** Local **D/D/R:** Teaching Media and Digital Technology to High School Students, Professional Development for Teachers in Digital Learning and Technology **H/I/S:** Website and Wiki Building, Reading **EDU:** Master of Library Science, SUNY Albany Bachelor of Science in Education, College of St. Rose **A/A/S:** American Library Association **A/H:** Who's Who Among America's Teachers
Email: jmditata@gasd.org
URL: http://www.cambridgewhoswho.com

Cynthia Louise Dittman, M.Ed.
Title: Learning Support Teacher **Company:** School District of Lancaster **Dept:** Washington Elementary School **Address:** 545 S. Ann Street, Lancaster, PA 17602 United States **BUS:** Elementary School **P/S:** Excellence in All Core Curriculum, Enrichment and Leisure Subject Areas, High Quality and Caring Teaching Staff, Supportive and Comfortable Learning Environment **MA:** Regional **D/D/R:** Teaching First through Third-Grade Students with Learning Disabilities, Autism and Behavioral Problems, Tutoring Dyslexic Students **H/I/S:** Traveling, Reading, Spending Time with her Son **EDU:** Master's Degree in Education, Temple University (1990) **CERTS:** Certified Orton-Gillingham Practitioner **A/A/S:** Pennsylvania State Education Association; National Education Association; Ascension Lutheran Church
Email: ccdittman@lancaster.k12.pa.us
URL: http://www.lancaster.k12.pa.us

Ms. Maura E. DiTucci
Title: Business Development Manager **Company:** Greater Boston Chamber of Commerce **Address:** Greater Boston Chamber of Commerce, 265 Franklin Street, 12th Floor, Boston, MA 02110 United States **BUS:** Business Advocacy and Networking Organization **P/S:** Ensure the Long-Term Advancement of Greater Boston as One of the World's Great Metropolitan Regions **MA:** Professionals of all Levels Looking for High-Level Networking Opportunities and Strategic Ways to Build their Business **EXP:** Ms. DiTucci's expertise includes sales and business development. **H/I/S:** Playing Golf, Reading, Cheering on the Red Sox **EDU:** Bachelor of Arts, University of Hartford **A/A/S:** Boston Future Leaders 2007 Class **C/VW:** Cam Neely Foundation for Cancer, Wide Horizons for Children, United Way of America
Email: mditucci@bostonchamber.com
URL: www.bostonchamber.com

Elaine DiVeronica
Title: Clinical Manager **Company:** Genesys Regional Medical Center **Address:** One Genesys Parkway, 2 North/Oncology, Grand Blanc, MI 48439 United States **BUS:** 400-Bed Teaching Hospital **P/S:** Regionally Integrated Health Care Delivery System Comprised Of a Complete Continuum of Care with Services including Rehabilitation, Senior Care, Sleep Disorders, Women and Children, Pediatrics Orthopedics, Hospice and Home Services **MA:** National **D/D/R:** Working with Staff of Nearly 100 Employees, Experienced in a Variety of Settings including Medical Oncology, HIV/AIDS Care, HIV Clinical Research and as a Nurse Practitioner in a Private Practice Partnership **H/I/S:** Reading, Hiking, Horseback Riding, Animal Conservation **EDU:** Master of Science in Nursing, Florida International University (1997); Bachelor of Science in Nursing, Florida Atlantic University (1991); Associate of Arts in Liberal Arts, Broward Community College (1986) **CERTS:** Registered Nurse, State of Texas; Registered Nurse, State of Michigan; Advanced Registered Nurse Practitioner, State of Florida; Certification in Chemotherapy, Genesys Regional Medical Center (2004-Present); Certification in Basic Life Support; Certified Legal Nurse Consultant, American Academy of Medical Legal Nurse Consultants **A/A/S:** Phi Kappa Phi National Honor Society; Sigma Theta Tau Nursing Honor Society; Hospice and Palliative Nurses Association; Oncology Nursing Society; Florida Nurses Association; Association of Nurses in AIDS Care; Board Member, Nominating Committee, Association of Nurses in AIDS Care, Broward County Chapter (1997/1998) **A/H:** Recipient of the Carolyn Zaumeyer Research Award (1997)
Email: ediveronica@genesys.org
URL: http://www.genesys.org

Elizabeth 'Liz' Dixon
Title: Speech Improvement and Correction Coach, Drama Coach **Company:** Alfred and Elizabeth Dixon Speech Systems **Address:** 80 Madison Avenue, New York, NY 10016 United States **BUS:** Speech and Drama Coaching Company **P/S:** Coaching Services for Actors and Business Executives **MA:** National **D/D/R:** Coaching Business Executives and Young Professionals in Film and on Stage, Improving Communication and Diction Skills for Increased Speech Success, Writing Insturctional Literature **A/A/S:** Former Member, Actor's Equity Assoication
URL: http://www.alfredelizabethdixon.com

Laurie Vernelson Dixon
Title: Daycare and Preschool Director **Company:** Trinity Christian School and Preschool **Address:** 3111 Golden Road, Greenville, NC 27858 United States **BUS:** Preschool and Daycare Center **P/S:** Christian Child Care Education and Day Care Services **MA:** Local **D/D/R:** Teaching **H/I/S:** Singing **EDU:** Associate Degree in Office Administration, Pitt Community College, NC **A/A/S:** National Christian School Association
Email: tcsdaycare@embarqmail.com
URL: http://www.trinityfwbchurch.org

Sheila K. Dixon

Title: Chief Executive Officer **Company:** S&E Marketing Concepts **Address:** Chantilly, VA 20152 United States **BUS:** Marketing Company **P/S:** Marketing and Entrepreneurial Development Including Business Coaching **MA:** Regional **EXP:** Ms. Dixon's expertise is in marketing. **D/D/R:** Assisting Entrepreneurs with Marketing Plans, Ideas and Strategies, Advising, Suggesting and Assisting Clients with Analysis, Sales Campaigns and Strategies, Conducting Personal and Professional Workshops, Consulting and Lecturing **H/I/S:** Playing Tennis, Volunteering in her Community for Various Causes **EDU:** Bachelor of Science in Business, Duquesne University (1988) **A/A/S:** American Marketing Association; National Association for Female Executives
Email: results@verizon.net
URL: http://www.self-expressions.com

Dr. Joyce M. Dixon-Robinson

Title: President, Founder **Company:** Agape Love Bible College **Address:** 4716 West Lisbon Avenue, Milwaukee, WI 53208 United States **BUS:** Religious Institution **P/S:** Ministerial Guidance, Training and Instruction **MA:** International **D/D/R:** Teaching Oracle and Development, Ministry Training Program **H/I/S:** Giving Biblical Nutritional Seminars, Reading, Opening Christian Book Stores, Writing Short Stories, Poetry, Exercising, Singing **EDU:** Doctoral Degree in Divinity and Theology, Grace College and Seminary (2006); Bachelor's Degree in Theology; Bachelor's Degree in Divinity (1997) **C/VW:** The Brandon J. Knox Scholarship Fund
Email: agapelove@wi.rr.com
URL: http://www.agapelovebiblecollege.com

Karen Kim Dlugauskas

Title: Catastrophe Claims Coordinator **Company:** CGI **Address:** 9924 Westpark Drive, Benbrook, TX 76126 United States **BUS:** Insurance **P/S:** Insurance Outsourcing **MA:** Local **D/D/R:** Coordinator of Catastrophe Events within the United States. Set Up Teams of Adjusters and Oversee Storm Operations. Work Hand in Hand with Various Insurance Company Catastrophe Claims Units. **H/I/S:** Spending Time with Family
Email: kim.dlugauskas@cgi.com
URL: cgi.com

Ms. Nancy Ann Doak

Title: Mathematics Teacher **Company:** Lakewood High School **Address:** 855 Summerset Avenue, Lakewood, NJ 08701 United States **BUS:** Public High School **P/S:** Education for Ninth through 12th-Grade Students **MA:** Local **D/D/R:** Utilizing the Curriculum to Assist Students with Standardized Tests, Teaching Remedial and Advanced Placement Classes **H/I/S:** Reading, Exercising, Traveling **EDU:** Master of Arts in Education, Concentration in Mathematics, Arcadia University, Glenside, PA (2002); Bachelor of Science in Mathematics, Minor in Secondary Education, Millersville University **A/A/S:** New Jersey Education Association; National Education Association **A/H:** Teacher of the Year, Lakewood School District
Email: goldeneagle2m@verizon.net
URL: http://www.cambridgewhoswho.com

Patricia H. Dobbins

Title: Application Consultant **Company:** United States National Bank **Address:** 13327 S.E. Tumbleweed Court, Happy Valley, OR 97086 United States **BUS:** Banking Establishment **P/S:** Banking and Financial Services **MA:** International **D/D/R:** Supporting Two Web-Based Applications with T.C. Input and Web Input for Assisting Transfers and Stop Payments for Corporate Customers **H/I/S:** Reading **EDU:** Bachelor's Degree in Mathematics, Stillman College (1969) **A/A/S:** Alpha Kappa Alpha
Email: patricia.dobbins@usbank.com
Email: patricia.dobbins@cwwemail.com
URL: http://www.usbank.com

Julie Ana Dobo

Title: Owner **Company:** Curios **Address:** 155 Mercer Street, Brooklyn, NY 10012 United States **BUS:** Novelty Gifts Product Creator and Vendor **P/S:** Unique Objects Inspired by Great People, Places and Things **MA:** Local **D/D/R:** Production Management and Light Design **H/I/S:** Production Management and Light Design for Modern Dance. As well as inventing and producing electronic theatrical products **EDU:** Some College, High School Diploma **A/A/S:** Production Manager: Joyce Theater Foundation, Inc Joyce SoHo
Email: curios@gmail.com

Gregory S. Dobson

Title: Owner **Company:** Sportscard Center **Address:** 403 Radio City Drive, North Pekin, IL 61554 United States **BUS:** Retail Store **P/S:** Buying and Selling Sports Cards **MA:** Local **D/D/R:** Overseeing Operations and Management, Recruiting, Training **H/I/S:** Playing Softball, Stock Car Racing, Cruising in his 1959 Mustang, Reading Sports Magazines **EDU:** Bachelor's Degree in Business, University of Illinois (1986) **A/A/S:** National Federation of Independent Business; High School Booster Club
Email: gd3511@yahoo.com
URL: http://www.sportscardcenter.net

Gloria L. Dodd

Title: Doctor of Veterinary Medicine **Company:** Everglo-Natural Veterinary Services, Inc. **Address:** P.O. Box 1242, Gualala, CA 95445 United States **BUS:** Distribution Company **P/S:** Holistic Vet Products **MA:** International **EXP:** Ms. Dodd's expertise includes FDA-regulated homeopathic products and services, vibration medicine and overseeing 383 FDA approved homeopathic remedies. **H/I/S:** Horseback Riding, Artwork, Reading, Writing, Hiking, Wildlife Preserve Photography **EDU:** Doctor of Veterinary Medicine, University of California, UC Davis School of Veterinary Medicine (1959) **A/A/S:** American Holistic Veterinary Medical Association; International Association for Vegetation Science **C/VW:** People for the Ethical Treatment of Animals; Legal Defense League for Animals; Women in American Indian Society; National Mustang Association
Email: everglo@mcn.org
URL: http://www.holisticvetpetcare.com

Shelley A. Dodson

Title: Primary Patent Examiner **Company:** Department of Commerce, USPTO Patent and Trademeark Office **Address:** 11205 Prospect Hill Road, Glenn Dale, MD 20769 United States **BUS:** Government Agency **P/S:** Biochemical Intellectual Property Law, Patents and Trademarks **MA:** International **D/D/R:** Issuing Patents and Trademarks for Sunscreens, Antiperspirants and Cosmetic Applications, Training, Managing Customer Service **H/I/S:** Basketball, Golfing, Traveling **EDU:** Master's Degree in Biochemistry, Stanford University (1983); Bachelor's Degree in Biology, Stanford University (1980) **A/A/S:** American Society for Microbiology (1976-1983); Patent and Trademark Office Society
Email: stuff1958@aol.com
URL: http://www.uspto.gov

Erin A. Doherty-Helmers

Title: Senior Ad Coordinator **Company:** CMP Media, LLC **Address:** 600 Community Drive, Manhasset, NY 11030 United States **BUS:** Service Provider **MA:** International **H/I/S:** Cake Decorating **EDU:** Bachelor's Degree, Hofstra University **A/A/S:** P3, Women and Production, Phi Sigma
Email: ehelmers@cmp.com

Martha L. Doiron

Title: Referring Travel Agent **Company:** YTB Travel **Address:** 2011 Lakeridge Circle, Unit 101, Chula Vista, CA 91913 United States **BUS:** Travel Agency **P/S:** Travel and Tourism, Fundraising Cruises, Excursions, Flight and Hotel Reservations **MA:** National **D/D/R:** Booking Travel Arrangements, Managing Fundraising Cruises, Honeymoon Registries, Network Marketing and Direct Sales, Setting up Individuals with their Own Travel Business, Overseeing Travel Services for Cruises and Excursions, Planning Airline and Hotel Reservations **H/I/S:** Playing Ping Pong **EDU:** Bachelor of Science in Nursing, Columbia University (1957)
Email: marthadoiron@cox.net
URL: http://www.angelsdotravelonline.com

Nancy L. Dolan

Title: Director of Sales **Company:** InteliStaf Travel, A Medical Staffing Company **BUS:** Staffing Agency **P/S:** Supplemental Healthcare Staffing for Nurses and Other Health Professions **MA:** National **D/D/R:** Overseeing Recruiters for Travel Nurses, Managing the Contract Placement of Traveling Nurses and Allied Professionals, Training, Attracting New and Retaining Current Travelers, Ensuring Growth in the Division, Offering Project Management, Overseeing Process Flow **EDU:** Coursework in Healthcare Administration, Ithaca College (1988-1989)
Email: ndolan@intelistaf.com
URL: http://www.intelistaf.com

Mr. Bryan J. Doleshel

Title: Managing Director **Company:** Sharefest Community Development, Inc. **Address:** 3525 Lomita Boulevard, Suite 200, Torrance, CA 90505 United States **BUS:** Public Benefit Corporation **P/S:** Community-Wide Workday, Collaborating with Cities, School Districts, Churches and Charities, Building Homes, Fundraising, Landscaping Local Parks, Refurbishing Schools, Assisting Senior Citizens **MA:** Regional **D/D/R:** Managing a Public Benefit Corporation, Working with Cities and Schools, Mobilizing Communities to Meet the Needs of Schools, Collaborating with Vendors and Businesses to Ensure Appropriate Services **EDU:** Bachelor of Arts in Organizational Leadership, Biola University (2006)
Email: bryan@sharefestinc.org
URL: http://sharefestinc.org

Robert Frank Domaleski

Title: Certified Registered Nurse Anesthetist **Company:** University of Tennessee Medical Center **BUS:** Hospital **P/S:** Healthcare, Education, Research **MA:** Local **D/D/R:** Administering Anesthetics, Advanced Practice Nursing **H/I/S:** Playing Golf, Flying with His Daughter **EDU:** Master's Degree in Nursing, Medical College of Georgia; Master's Degree in Physiology, Medical College of Georgia **A/A/S:** American Association of Nurse Anesthetists; Past President, Graduate Nurses' Association **A/H:** National Collegiate Nursing Award; Clinical Excellence Award from Medical College of Georgia **C/VW:** All Saints Catholic Church, Knoxville, Tennessee
Email: rdomaleski@bellsouth.net
URL: http://www.cambridgewhoswho.com

Vicky C. Dominguez

Title: Professor **Company:** College of Southern Nevada **Address:** 3200 E. Cheyenne Avenue, North Las Vegas, NV 89030 United States **BUS:** College **P/S:** Higher Education **MA:** Regional **D/D/R:** Teaching Finance, Accounting, Computerized Accounting and Bookkeeping, Tax Services **H/I/S:** Traveling **EDU:** Doctorate in Business Administration, University of Phoenix; Master of Business Administration, Adamson University, Manila (1977) **A/A/S:** American Institute of Certified Bookkeepers; President, International Tax Specialists; JMJ Foundation
Email: vicky.dominguez@csn.edu
URL: http://www.ccsn.edu

Dr. Robert E. Donaghy

Title: 1) Optometrist 2) Owner **Company:** 1) Optic 2020 2) Reality Wall, Inc. **Address:** 300 Sunset Street, Greenriver, WY 82935 United States **BUS:** 1)Optometry Facility 2)Marketing Company **P/S:** 1) Refractive Glasses, Lenses, Dry Eye, Glaucoma 2) Marketing, Graphics **MA:** Local **D/D/R:** Tailor made Products **H/I/S:** Traveling, Scuba diving, Cooking, Photography, Playing Tennis, Spending Time with his Family **EDU:** MD, Inter American University of Puerto Rico, School of Optometry (2004); Master's Degree in Biology with Focus on Immunology, Greenwich University and Westchester University (1987); Bachelor of Arts in Microbiology and Chemistry, dual Major, University of Pennsylvania (1981) **A/A/S:** Laboratory Management Diplomat, American Society of Clinical Pathologists; Microscopy Society of America
Email: drdrmrod@yahoo.com
URL: http://www.cambridgewhoswho.com

Shayena Donaldson-Fortune

Title: Occupational Therapist **Company:** Metropolitan Jewish Geriatric Center, Adult Day Health Center **Address:** 855 Ocean Avenue, Apartment 6G, Brooklyn, NY 11226 United States **BUS:** Proven Leader Dedicated to Excellence in the Occupational Therapy Rehabilitation Industry **P/S:** Rehabilitation Services for Adults and Geriatric Patients with Physical and Mental Disabilities, Arthritis, Neurological Disorders, Fractures and other Acute Disabilities **MA:** Regional **D/D/R:** Geriatrics Patients with Multiple Sclerosis, CVA, Physical Disabilities, Cellulitis, Physical, Mental and Psychological Disorders, Sets Patient Goals, Evaluates and Screens Patients for Rehabilitation Eligibility, Performing Homecare for RCM Millennium Rehabilitation Services, Working with Geriatric Patients **H/I/S:** Bowling, Tennis, Shopping, Scrapbooking, Reading, Keeping Up-to-Date with Treatment Planning **EDU:** Master of Science in Occupational Therapy, American International College (2004) **A/A/S:** American Occupational Therapy Association **A/H:** Who's Who Among America's Colleges and Universities
Email: tallshy@hotmail.com
URL: http://www.cambridgewhoswho.com

Ms. Wilma Mosquebe Dondoy

Title: Owner **Company:** Royalty Realty & Mortgage Services **Address:** 1699 El Camino Real, Suite 101, Millbrae, CA 94030 United States **BUS:** Real Estate and Loan Company **P/S:** Real Estate and Loan Services **MA:** International **D/D/R:** Selling Residential and Commercial Properties, Homes and Buildings, Working with Investment Properties and Relocations, Assisting Clients in Achieving Financial Independence through Real Estate **H/I/S:** Golfing **EDU:** Associate Degree in Business, University of the Philippines **CERTS:** Licensed in Real Estate **A/A/S:** San Mateo County Association of Realtors; San Francisco Association of Realtors; California Association of Realtors; National Association of Realtors
Email: wdondoy@rrmtgcorp.com
URL: http://www.rrmtgcorp.com

Herbert A. Donham

Title: Manager, Funeral Director **Company:** Gardner-Brockman Funeral Home **Address:** 505 Main St, Vincennes, IN 47591 United States **BUS:** Funeral Home **P/S:** All Aspects of funeral arrangements and Pre-planning **MA:** Local **D/D/R:** Embalming, Directing Funerals **H/I/S:** Photography **EDU:** Associate Degree in Mortuary Science, Indiana College of Mortuary Science **A/A/S:** Indiana Funeral Directors, NFD
Email: info@CambridgeWhosWho.com

Corrine R. Donley

Title: Professor Emeritus, Behavior Analyst **Company:** University of Wisconsin Oshkosh **Dept:** Special Education **Address:** 1278 Elmwood Avenue, Oshkosh, WI 54901 United States **BUS:** University **P/S:** Education **MA:** Local **D/D/R:** Part-Time Consulting to Help Treat Clients with Inappropriate Behaviors **H/I/S:** Playing the Piano, Directing the Choir, Enjoying Cultural Events **EDU:** Doctor of Education, Teachers College, Columbia University; Master of Education in Music Education for the Disabled, Teachers College, Columbia University; Bachelor of Science, Ohio State University **A/A/S:** Association for Behavior Analysis; Council for Exceptional Children **C/VW:** Presbyterian Church; Southern Poverty Law Center; American Friends Service Committee
Email: cdonley@new.rr.com

Mr. Patrick B. Donnell

Title: President, Chief Executive Officer **Company:** Global Trade Base Company **Address:** 7305 Boulevard 26, Suite 205, North Richland Hills, TX 76180 United States **BUS:** Export Management Firm **P/S:** Exporting and Importing for Domestic Food Producers, Creating Packaging for Overseas Sales, Importing Camping Equipment and Biometrics **MA:** International **D/D/R:** Specializing in International Trade of Food Products and Agricultural Commodities, Recruiting, Marketing, Managing Shipping Logistics and Daily Operations **H/I/S:** Boating, Writing, Camping **EDU:** High School Education (1984) **A/A/S:** Eagle Scouts; Republican Party; Master Masons; Chairman, Founder, 501C-3 Eyes of Justice
Email: pbdonnell@globaltradebase.com
URL: http://globaltradebase.com

Patricia A. Donofrio

Title: Teacher **Company:** Prince George's County Public Schools **Address:** 12520 Kembridge Drive, Bowie, MD 20715 United States **BUS:** Public School **P/S:** Instruction and Curriculum, Extra Curricular Activities **MA:** Regional **D/D/R:** Elementary Teacher all Subjects, Co-Chair, School Board Management Team, Mentor of Student Interns from Maryland College Park **H/I/S:** Quilting, Traveling **EDU:** Master of Science, Brooklyn College (1970); Bachelor's Degree in Child Study and Social Sciences, St. Joseph's (1967) **A/A/S:** Phi Delta Kappa
Email: pvdonofrio@comcast.net
URL: http://www.pgcps.org

Michelle R E Donovan

Title: Attorney **Company:** Plunkett Cooney **Address:** 38505 Woodward Avenue, Suite 2000, Bloomfield Hills, MI 48304 United States **BUS:** Law Firm **P/S:** Legal Services **MA:** Local **D/D/R:** practicing real estate and title insurance law and litigating for fraud and identity theft cases **H/I/S:** Exercising, Traveling, Cooking, Teaching **EDU:** JD, Thomas M. Cooley Law School, Lansing, MI; Bachelor of Arts in English, University of Detroit Mercy, MI **CERTS:** Licensed Title Insurance Agent, United States District Court, Eastern District of Michigan **A/A/S:** Macomb County Bar Association; Legislative Committee, Michigan Land Title Association; Vice President, Thomas M. Cooley Alumni Board **C/VW:** Michigan Humane Society; The Humane Society of the United States; Former Member, Parish Council, Local Church
Email: mdonovan@plunkettcooney.com
URL: http://www.plunkettcooney.com

Roger Doody Sr.

Title: Vice-President **Company:** Stone Insurance, Inc. **Address:** 1502 W. Causeway Approach, Suite A, Mandeville, LA 70471 United States **BUS:** Insurance **P/S:** All Lines of Insurance **MA:** National **D/D/R:** Overseeing both Offices, Sixty Members, Property, Casualty, Health and Life Insurance, Bonds, Home Owners **H/I/S:** Fishing, Hunting **EDU:** Bachelor's Degree in Business Administration, The University of New Orleans (1965) **A/A/S:** Independent Insurance Agents Association
Email: roger.doody@stone-insurance.com
URL: http://www.stone-insurance.com

Marlene C. Doores

Title: Owner **Company:** Little Coffee Shop **Address:** 204 N. Main, Pavillion, WY 82523 United States **BUS:** Coffee Shop **P/S:** Serving Coffee and Food to Customers **MA:** Regional **D/D/R:** Cooking Breakfast and Lunch, Waitressing, Overseeing Marketing and Customer Service **H/I/S:** Volleyball, Basketball, Baseball, Fishing, Hunting **CERTS:** Executive Medical Secretary (1978) **A/A/S:** Writing a Cookbook Titled, 'Mom's Magic'
Email: mdoores@msn.com
URL: http://www.cambridgewhoswho.com

Janice M. Dorazio

Title: Director of Rehabilitation **Company:** Valerie Manor **Address:** 1360 Torringford Street, Torrington, CT 06790 United States **BUS:** Rehabilitation Center **P/S:** Acute, Short and Long-Term Rehabilitation Services **MA:** Connecticut, Rhode Island **D/D/R:** overseeing therapists, ordering equipment, monitoring documents, Medicare audits and appeals and directing interdisciplinary meetings **H/I/S:** Sewing, Making Crafts, Skiing **EDU:** Pursuing Master's Degree in Healthcare Administration, University of Phoenix; Bachelor of Science in Human Resources and Health Services, University of Connecticut; Associate Degree in Physical Therapy, Becker College **A/A/S:** American Physical Therapy Association; National Strength and Conditioning Association **C/VW:** Alzheimer's Association; Susan G. Komen for the Cure
Email: doraziorj@sbcglobal.net
URL: http://www.cambridgewhoswho.com

Gayle Dornhecker

Title: President **Company:** Hope Pet Grooming, Inc. **BUS:** Pet Care Center **P/S:** Pet Care Services Including Pet Grooming and Supplies **MA:** Regional **D/D/R:** Caring for Pets Including Grooming Dogs, Washing and Drying Pets Bed, Selling Natural Dog Food, Shampoo, Biscuits, Brushes and Combs **H/I/S:** Caring for her Pets **A/A/S:** New England Pet Grooming Professionals **C/VW:** Camp Hope; American Cancer Society
Email: hecker222@aol.com

Hollis Dorrough Jr.

Title: Deputy Police Chief for Field Op **BUS:** Law Enforcement **P/S:** Law Enforcement **MA:** International **D/D/R:** Law Enforcement Management, Police Training **H/I/S:** Autobiographies, Singing, Reading, Music Collection **EDU:** Bachelor's Degree in Law Enforcement and Management, St Josephs, Whiting, IN **A/A/S:** Member of Association of Chicago Police, Member of South Suburban Chief of Police, Member of Noble Association Black Enforcements
Email: hdorrough@aol.com

Elisabeth Alleyne Dorsey, Ed.M.

Title: President and Founder **Company:** E'quation Concepts **Address:** P.O. Box 231020, Boston, MA 02123 **BUS:** Arts, Education and Public Affairs **P/S:** Education, Performing Arts **MA:** Massachusetts, New York **D/D/R:** Performing Arts, Education, Consulting, Event Planning **H/I/S:** Acting, Dancing, Singing, Running, Visual Arts, Writing Song Lyrics, Cooking, Learning New Languages, Community Activities, Reading the Bible, Being With Children, Writing. **EDU:** Master of International Education, Harvard Graduate School of Education; Bachelor of Arts Degree in African Studies and International Affairs, Brown University **CERTS:** Former Certified Teacher in History, Mathematics and Literature, State of New York **A/A/S:** Leadership and Community Service Award for Film and Cultural Diversity, Harvard Graduate School of Education; Certificate of Achievement in Leadership, School Development Program, Yale University; Member of Cast of Children, Sesame Street, Sesame Workshop. **C/VW:** Community Volunteering, Church Service
Email: concepts4life@yahoo.com
URL: http://www.cambridgewhoswho.com

Cheryl A. Dosher

Title: Owner **Company:** Wine and Roses Florist **Address:** 620 N. Atlantic Avenue, Southport, NC 28461 United States **BUS:** High Quality Florist **P/S:** Full Service Florist, Weddings, Funerals, all Occasions **MA:** National **D/D/R:** Designing of Floral Arrangements, Running Business with Family, Handling all Problems or Concerns, Overseeing the Store **H/I/S:** Gardening **EDU:** High School Education (1974) **A/A/S:** Vice President, Garden Club, Chamber Member

Ms. Judith A. Dothage, CPNP

Title: CPNP (Retired) **Address:** Crestwood, MO 63126 United States **BUS:** Healthcare, Oncology **P/S:** Pediatric Neuron-Oncology Nursing **MA:** International **D/D/R:** Pediatric Neuro-Oncology Nurse, CNP, Consulting with other Health Professionals to Share her Expertise and Mentor Young and Upcoming Professionals **H/I/S:** Reading, Traveling, Gourmet Cooking, Photography, Exploring a Life of Retirement and Free Time **EDU:** Bachelor of Science Degree in Nursing, Drury College, MO **CERTS:** Certified Nurse Practitioner, Missouri State University **A/A/S:** National Association of Pediatric Nurse Practitioners
Email: judydot@aol.com

Mr. Mark David Dotson

Title: President, Chief Executive Officer **Company:** Western Utah Copper Company **Address:** 1208 South 200 West, Milford, UT 84751 United States **BUS:** Mining **P/S:** Copper, Widely Held Extraction **MA:** National **D/D/R:** Mining, Geology, Management **H/I/S:** Grandchildren, Hunting **EDU:** Master's Degree, University of Phoenix **A/A/S:** BLM-Business Line Management
Email: wucc@scinternet.net

Jaymie Dougan

Title: Kindergarten Teacher **Company:** San Carlos Unified School District, Rice Primary School **Address:** P.O. Box 207, San Carlos, AZ 85550 United States **BUS:** Elementary School **P/S:** Education **MA:** Local **D/D/R:** Teaching **H/I/S:** Phoenix Suns Fan, Landscaping, Reading, Spending Time with Friends and Family **EDU:** Bachelor's Degree, Arizona State University; Master's Degree, University of Texas at El Paso **A/A/S:** Christian Educators Association Internationa **A/H:** Teacher of the Year Award **C/VW:** World Vision
Email: jjaynot@gmail.com

Tasha R. Dougherty

Title: Freelance **P/S:** freelance graphic design, project management, marketing **MA:** National **D/D/R:** Overall Marketing Including Blanket Advertising, Community Publications, Dealer Networks and Campaigns, Designing Campaigns, Helping with Commercial Advertisements Yearly, Overseeing Money Management, Dealing with Community and Customer Relations **H/I/S:** Photography, Graphic Art **EDU:** Bachelor of Fine Arts in Visual Communications, Kutztown University (1991); Coursework in Marketing and Communications, Villanova University (1996)
Email: tasdoc@ptdprolog.net

G. Bruce Douglas, DDS

Title: Endodontist **Company:** Boulder Endodontics **Address:** 3100 Arapahoe Avenue Suite 300, Boulder, CO 80303 United States **BUS:** Healthcare Dentistry **P/S:** Endodontic **MA:** Local **D/D/R:** Endodontics **H/I/S:** Skiing, Hiking, Woodworking **EDU:** Bachelor of Science, Colorado State University; DDS, University of Detroit **CERTS:** Certificate of Endodontics **A/A/S:** American Dental Association, Diplomat with the American Association of Endodontics, American Association of Endodontics, Colorado Dental Association, Boulder Dental Association, Taught Endodontics While in the Air Force to the General Practice Residents
Email: boulder_endo@quest.net

Marjorie A. Douglas

Title: Photo Imager **Company:** Miles Kimball Company **Address:** 2155 S. Oakwood Road, Oshkosh, WI 54904 United States **BUS:** One of the Leading Catalog Companies in the Country **P/S:** Unique and Creative Photo Gifts for all Celebrations Including Holidays and Christmas, Weddings, Kitchen, Home, Outdoor, Desktop and Office, Apparel and Personal Care, Gifts and Collectibles, Children, Leisure, Travel and Auto and Pets **MA:** National, International **D/D/R:** Creating Photo Composition, Manipulating and Photo Painting Personalized Photo Products, Creating Gifts for New Products Using Photographs **H/I/S:** All Photography, Walking in Nature, Creating Stained Glass Artwork, Enjoying Symphonic Music, Completing Freelance Typesetting, Layout and Photography **EDU:** Bachelor of Arts Degree, Minor in Photography, University of Wisconsin, Oshkosh (1977) **A/H:** Star Award for New Product, The Home Market Place Catalog
Email: windowshispers@yahoo.com
URL: http://www.mileskimball.com
URL: http://www.exposuresonline.com

Alexandrina Douglas Robinson

Title: Chief Counsel **Company:** ING North America Insurance Corporation **Address:** 5780 Powers Ferry Road, Atlanta, GA 30327 United States **BUS:** Finance Insurance Services **P/S:** Insurance Products **MA:** National **D/D/R:** Intellectual Property/Information Technology, Latin American Communication **H/I/S:** Travel, Reading, Hiking, Fitness and Exercising **EDU:** MALD, Fletcher School; JD, Howard University **A/A/S:** Atlanta Bar Association, ITMA, Alpha Kappa Alpha Sorority Incorporation
Email: info@CambridgeWhosWho.com

Paul L. Dow

Title: Owner, President **Company:** Dow Construction **Address:** 258 S. Denny Hill Road, Paragon, IN 46166 United States **BUS:** Construction Company **P/S:** Commercial and Residential Construction **MA:** Regional **D/D/R:** Offering New Construction and Remodeling, Overseeing Work Crews, Performing Interior Finish Carpentry, Managing Financial and Business Policies **EDU:** Associate Degree in Construction Technology, Vincennes University (1990) **A/A/S:** Greater Morgan County Builders Association; Morgan County Fair Association; Morgan County 4-H Council

Mr. Bryan C. Dowd, MA, CRC
Title: Counseling Psychologist Company: U.S. Department of Veterans Affairs Regional Office Address: 1642 42nd Street N.E., Suite J, Cedar Rapids, IA 52402 United States BUS: Government Health Service for American Veterans and their Families P/S: Excellence in Patient Care, Veterans' Benefits and Customer Satisfaction MA: Regional D/D/R: Offering Rehabilitation Services for Service-Disabled Veterans, Working with the Administration of Monetary Benefits, Grant Compensation, Financial Benefits with Education, Burial Allowances, Assistance with Transition into a New Line of Work, Transportation, Safety and Job Searches, Assessing the Strengths of Veterans through the Development of Goals and Preparing for Employment, Reviewing Circumstances, Determining Program Eligibility H/I/S: Riding Motorcycles EDU: Master's Degree in Rehabilitation, University of Iowa (1992) CERTS: Certified Rehabilitation Counselor A/A/S: Former Member, National Rehabilitation Administration Association; Pi Lambda Theta; Former Member, Chi Sigma Iota; Former Member, Phi Delta Kappa International; American Counseling Association; Managerial Enhancement Program
Email: bryan.dowd@va.gov
URL: http://www.cambridgewhoswho.com

Pheobe S. Dowdell-White
Title: Curriculum Specialist Kindergarten through Third-Grade Company: E.B. Kennelly School Address: 180 White Street, Hartford, CT 06101 United States BUS: Elementary School P/S: Education MA: Local D/D/R: Coaching at Girls and Boys Town, Helping with the Behavioral Management of the Students, Assisting Teachers with Mathematics and Reading Objectives H/I/S: Spending Time with Family, Attending Church Activities EDU: Master's Degree in Elementary Education, Concentration in Learning Behavior Disorders, SUNY Fredonia; Bachelor of Arts in Elementary Education, SUNY Fredonia A/A/S: Xi Chapter; Lambda Kappa Mu; Coach, Girls and Boys Town C/VW: Star of Bethlehem Baptist Church in Ossining, NY
Email: rell71@hotmail.com

Joan V. Dowdy
Title: Utilization Management Registered Nurse Company: California Rehabilitation Center Dept: Department of Corrections Address: Western Street, Norco, CA 92860 United States BUS: Department of Corrections P/S: Healthcare MA: Local EXP: Ms. Dowdy's expertise is in rehabilitative nursing for individuals with drug dependencies. H/I/S: Swimming, Exercising, Growing Roses and Vegetables, Cooking, Reading EDU: Bachelor of Science in Nursing, University of Phoenix CERTS: Registered Nurse Diploma, Philadelphia Hospital School of Nursing A/A/S: Sigma Theta Tau C/VW: Greater Life Baptist Church; National Association for the Advancement of Colored People; United Negro College Fund
Email: jdowdy2639@aol.com

Lori D. Dowling
Title: Environmental Compliance Specialist Company: Quad Knopf Address: 5110 W. Cypress Avenue, Visalia, CA 93277 United States BUS: Engineering Consulting Firm P/S: Architecture, Environmental Planning, Biological Sciences, Geographic Information Systems, Landscape Architecture, Civil Engineering, Surveying, Land Development and GIS Knowledge Area Services MA: National D/D/R: Overseeing Environmental Compliance and Engineering H/I/S: Golfing, Traveling, Spending Time Outdoors EDU: Bachelor of Science in Drafting Technology; Associate of Science in Architectural Drafting, Central Missouri State University A/A/S: United States Green Building Council; International Erosion Control Association
Email: lorid@quadknopf.com
URL: http://www.quadknopf.com

Larry K. Downey
Title: Executive Director of the Office of Property and Corporate Service Company: Cushman & Wakefield, Inc. Address: 2525 E. Camelback Road, Suite 1000, Phoenix, AZ 85016 United States BUS: National and International Commercial Real Estate Agency P/S: Commercial, Industrial and Retail Properties MA: International D/D/R: Representing Tenants and Office Building Owners H/I/S: Fly-Fishing EDU: Bachelor of Arts in Business Administration, Northern Arizona University, 1979 A/A/S: NAIOP; CoreNET; Phoenix Community Alliance A/H: Top 40 in the Country, 2006; C/VW: Make-A-Wish Foundation, Salvation Army
Email: larry.downey@cushwake.com
URL: http://www.cushwake.com

Tracy Doyle
Title: 1) Corporate Chief Executive Officer 2) Registered Nurse Company: 1) Doyle's Masonry and Concrete, LLC Address: 5019 Pee Dee Highway, Conway, SC 29527 United States BUS: Construction and Masonry Company P/S: 1) Residential and Commercial Brick and Concrete Contracting 2) Medical Services MA: National D/D/R: Training New Employees, Overseeing Marketing, Public Relations and Advertising, Negotiating Deals, Clearing Construction Sites, Landscaping, Planning Residential Business H/I/S: Running a Strictly Business Raceteam EDU: Associate Degree in Nursing, Horry-Georgetown Technical College (1999) CERTS: Certified Nursing Assistant (1994); Licensed Practical Nurse (1994) A/A/S: Phi Beta Kappa Society; Oncology Nursing Society; American Nurses Association; Pianist, Local Church; Playwright, Local Church
Email: brick@sccoast.net
URL: http://www.cambridgewhoswho.com

Michael A. Dozier
Title: President, Chief Executive Officer Company: Unity Records Address: 4927 Fairmount Ave, Philadelphia, PA 19139 United States BUS: Record Label Company P/S: Professional Recording MA: Tristate D/D/R: Overseeing Management H/I/S: Watching Basketball A/A/S: Top Management C/VW: Christian Church
Email: unitymonopoly@yahoo.com
URL: http://www.cambridgewhoswho.com

Dragomir I. Draganov
Title: Senior Research Scientist Company: WIL Research Laboratories, LLC Address: 1407 George Road, Ashland, OH 44805 United States BUS: Contract Research Organization P/S: Scientific Research MA: International D/D/R: Directing Studies in Toxicokinetics, Pharmacokinetics and Metabolite Identification H/I/S: Fishing EDU: Ph.D. in Pharmacology and Toxicology, Military Medical Academy, Bulgaria; MD, Bulgarian Medical Academy A/A/S: American Association of Pharmaceutical Scientists; Bulgarian Toxicological Society; SOT C/VW: Volunteers at his Daughter's School
Email: ddraganov@wilresearch.com
URL: http://www.wilresearch.com

Michael Draska
Title: President Company: Draska Investment Services Address: 47504 S. Fork Drive Suite 4, Macomb, MI 48044 United States BUS: Investment Firm P/S: Stocks, Bonds, Mutual Funds, Annuities MA: National D/D/R: Developing and Diversifying Investment Portfolios to Individual and Small Business Owners H/I/S: Playing Softball EDU: Master's Degree in International Finance and Portfolio Development, Walsh College of Accountancy and Business Administration; Bachelor's Degree in Finance, Walsh College of Accountancy and Business Administration A/A/S: Former President, Walsh College Alumni Association; Lions Clubs International A/H: Various Financial Awards, Different Companies C/VW: Local Church; Treasurer, Quake on the Lake; Rainbow Connection
Email: mdraska@mfcmail.biz
URL: http://www.draskainvestmentservices.com

Adriane Drayton
Title: Executive Administrative Assistant Company: United States Army Address: 3000 Joint Staff Pentagon, J-3 Front Office, Washington, DC 20318 United States BUS: Military P/S: National Security MA: International D/D/R: Offering Support to Two and Three-Star Generals, Traveling, Handling Communications, Scheduling H/I/S: Traveling, Reading, Teaching Sunday School EDU: Master's Degree in Human Resource Management Development, National-Louis University, 2003 A/A/S: Society for Human Resource Management C/VW: Church, World Vision, Helping the Elderly
Email: aadrayton@comcast.net

Nomie Dreier
Title: Owner, Sole Proprietor Company: Absolutely Hair by Nomie Address: 1201 Falls Avenue E., Suite 38, Twin Falls, ID 83301 United States BUS: Hair and Beauty Salon P/S: Hair Styling Services MA: Local D/D/R: Performing Weaves, Haircuts, Permanents and Colorings, Ensuring that Clients Feel Appreciated and Important H/I/S: Working CERTS: Licensed Esthetician; Registered Cosmetologist A/A/S: Chamber of Commerce

Daniel D. Drew
Title: Production Supervisor Engineer Company: GAF Materials, Corp Address: 902 Old Richburg Rd, Chester, SC 29706 United States BUS: Roofing Manufacturer P/S: Fiberglass Roofing Materials MA: National D/D/R: Electrical Engineering H/I/S: Hockey, Soccer, Outdoors EDU: Bachelor of Science, Michigan State University
Email: drewdan1@gmail.com

Emily M. Drews
Title: Writer, Artist, Designer Company: Self-Employed Address: 709 Central Street, Oshkosh, WI 54901 United States BUS: Artistic Creations P/S: Art, Writing MA: Local D/D/R: Oil and Watercolor Painting, Designing Lamps, Clothing, Writing EDU: Bachelor of Arts in Art History and English, Bethany Lutheran College CERTS: Certified Teacher, State of Wisconsin
Email: fairiemoon@yahoo.com
URL: www.fairiemoon.com

Sally A. Driesel
Title: Licensed Veterinary Technician Company: Animal Emergency Services of Rochester BUS: Animal Hospital P/S: Emergency Services for Animals, Veterinary Surgery MA: Local D/D/R: Treating Animals, Animal Management, Anesthesia EDU: Associate Degree in Veterinary Technician Studies, Medaille College

Sandra J. Driskill
Title: Substitute High School Spanish Teacher, Tutor and Translator Address: 1488 FM 1293 Road, Kountze, TX 77625 United States BUS: School P/S: Education MA: Regional D/D/R: teaching Spanish to high school students, tutoring students and translating, Working for Translation Services on Receiving Calls H/I/S: Translating, Traveling, Singing, Working with Senior Citizens, Fishing, Solving Puzzles EDU: Master's Degree in Spanish, Murray State University; Bachelor of Arts in Spanish and English, Lamar University A/A/S: Muscular Dystrophy Association A/H: Who's Who among American Teachers Award (2000-2001) C/VW: Catholic Charities of Beaumont
Email: sandrad4242@att.net
URL: http://www.cambridgewhoswho.com

Luciano A. Driver
Title: Security Representative Company: Pennsylvania Department of Corrections BUS: Correctional Facility P/S: Public Safety, Law Enforcement MA: Regional D/D/R: Overseeing Public Safety Measures H/I/S: Reading CERTS: Certification in Private Investigation, Professional Career Development Institute C/VW: Bible League
Email: ldantonio77@hotmail.com
URL: http://www.cambridgewhoswho.com

Edna F. Droke
Title: English as a Second Language Teacher Company: Gustine Independent School District Address: 1151 County Road 182, Comanche, TX 76442 United States BUS: Public School District P/S: General Elementary and Secondary Curriculum, Special Education, English as a Second Language Program, Foreign Language Instruction, Arts, Music, Physical Education, Learning Resources, Student Support Services, Athletics, Extracurricular Activities, Student Clubs and Organizations MA: Regional D/D/R: Overseeing the English as a Second Language Program, Teaching English, Reading and Vocabulary to Kindergarten through 12th-Grade Students, Utilizing the Pull-Out and Reading Recovery Programs H/I/S: Crocheting, Painting, Playing Piano EDU: Bachelor of Science in Education, Tarleton State University (1983) CERTS: Certification in K-12 Education A/A/S: Kappa Delta Pi
Email: edroke@gustine.esc14.net
URL: http://www.gustine.esc14.net

Mr. Angelo Drosos
Title: Chief Executive Officer Company: Drosos & Associates, PC Address: 2 E. Blackwell Street, Suite 4, Dover, NJ 07801 United States BUS: Accounting and Consulting Firm P/S: Accounting Services, Payroll Services, Internal Revenue Service and State and Local Representation, Tax Services and Preparation, Financial Consulting MA: Regional D/D/R: Offering Tax Services for Individuals and Corporations, Performing Payroll Services, Consulting and Planning for Clients with Internal Revenue Service Issues H/I/S: Relaxing EDU: Bachelor's Degree in Accounting, Rutgers, The State University of New Jersey (1997) A/A/S: The National Society of Tax Professionals; American Bar Association; Association of Certified Fraud Examiners
Email: drososandassoc@verizon.net
URL: http://www.drososandassociates.com

Philip E. Drouin
Title: Vice President Company: Laptops for the Wounded Address: 42 Greenhurst Lane, East Hartford, CT 06118 United States BUS: Nonprofit Organization P/S: Laptops With Web Cams for Wounded Troops MA: International D/D/R: Rebuilding Laptops, Charity, IT Support Training H/I/S: Hunting, Golfing, Classic Cars, Customization A/A/S: North American Hunting Club; Buck Masters Member
Email: Helping4ltfw@yahoo.com
URL: http://www.laptopsforthewounded.com

Gini Dryer-Dow
Title: Funeral Director Company: Weeks' Dryer Mortuary Address: 220 134th Street South, Tacoma, WA 98444 United States BUS: Mortuary P/S: Funeral Service MA: Local D/D/R: Plan Funeral Service H/I/S: Reading, Quilting EDU: Master's Degree, University of Portland A/A/S: Board Member Washington State Funeral Director Association
Email: T.g.dow@comcast.net

Rina Du Toit

Title: Broker Associate **Company:** Koenig and Strey, GMAC Real Estate **Address:** 825 S. Waukegan Road, Lake Forest, IL 60045 United States **BUS:** Real Estate Firm Serving Clients in the Chicago Area **P/S:** Residential Real Estate **MA:** Regional **D/D/R:** Assisting International Clients with Relocation, Selling Luxury Properties to Foreign Governments **H/I/S:** Traveling, Interior Decorating, Gardening, Antiques **EDU:** Master of Science, University of the Orange Free State **A/A/S:** International Club of Lake Forest
Email: rdutoit@ksgmac.com
URL: http://www.rinadutoit.com

Gurpreet S. Dubb

Title: Chief Executive Officer **Company:** Greet Well, Inc., DBA X'Pressions **Address:** 732 N. Pastoria Avenue, Suite 734, Sunnyvale, CA 94085 United States **BUS:** Food **P/S:** Imports and Distribution **MA:** International **D/D/R:** Importing Food and Ethnic Products from India **H/I/S:** Going to the Gym, Music **EDU:** Master's Degree in Computer Application, Osmania University, India (1996)
Email: x_pressions@comcast.net
URL: http://www.cambridgewhoswho.com

Sally L. Dubensky

Title: Educator **Company:** Scottsdale Unified School District **Dept:** Pima Elementary School **Address:** 8330 E. Osborn Road, Scottsdale, AZ 85251 United States **BUS:** School District **P/S:** Education **MA:** Local **D/D/R:** Teaching Instrumental Music, Teaching Fourth to Six Grade Students, Playing the Piano and Bassoon, Mentor Teacher **H/I/S:** Camping, Walking, Reading **EDU:** Master's Degree in Educational Leadership, Northern Arizona University; Bachelor of Arts in Music, San Jose State University, 1976 **A/A/S:** National Education Association; Arizona Education Association; Music Educators National Conference **A/H:** Teacher of the Year Award (2004-2005)
Email: sdubensky@susd.org
URL: http://www.susd.com

Mr. Richard J. Dubois II

Title: Systems Analyst **Address:** P.O. Box 5182, Burlington, VT 05402 United States **BUS:** Independent Systems Analyst **P/S:** Non-Analytical Mathematics and Logic, Algebraic, Calculus and Writing **MA:** Regional **D/D/R:** Conducting Underwriting, Writing Books on Mathematics **H/I/S:** Making Watercolor Painting, Taking Road Trips to Florida, Enjoying NASCAR and Nextel Cup Racing, Reading in English, French and Greek **EDU:** Bachelor's Degree in Architecture, Rhode Island School of Design, Suma Cum Laude (1981); Coursework Completed in Advanced Mathematics, Brown University (1981); Degree in Architectural and Building Technical Engineering (1977) **A/A/S:** Former Executive Board Member, Howard Center for Human Services Adult Behavioral and Finance Committees; Delegate, National Science Youth Camp in Barto **A/H:** Who's Who Among High School Students (1975)

Ms. Debora L. Ducharme

Title: Art Teacher **Company:** Malone Central School **Dept:** Flanders Elementary School **Address:** 524 E. Main Street, Malone, NY 12953 United States **BUS:** Elementary School **P/S:** Education for Third through Sixth-Grade Students **MA:** Regional **EXP:** Ms. Ducharme's expertise is in art instruction. **D/D/R:** Teaching drawing, painting, sculpting and weaving to third through sixth-Grade students. She also has experience in lesson plan organization and student art shows **H/I/S:** Solving Puzzles, Reading, Gardening, Painting, Scrapbooking **EDU:** Master of Fine Arts, State University of New York, Buffalo (1984); Bachelor of Education, State University of New York, Buffalo (1978) **A/A/S:** New York State Art Teachers Association
Email: dducharme@malonecsd.org
URL: http://www.qube.malone.k12.ny.us

Cindy A. Duckworth

Title: Licensed Professional Counselor **Company:** MDS Counseling **Address:** 1355 S. Colorado Boulevard, Suite C-100, Denver, CO 80222 United States **BUS:** Counseling Center **P/S:** Counseling Services **MA:** Regional **D/D/R:** counseling traumatized children and adults **H/I/S:** Traveling **EDU:** Master's Degree in Psychology and Counseling Education, University of Colorado, Denver **A/A/S:** American Counseling Association; National Board for Certified Counselors; EMDRIA; MDIC **C/VW:** Local Charitable Organizations
Email: cindyduckworth@msn.com
URL: http://www.mdscounseling.org

Eileen Carroll Dudley

Title: Enterprise Solution Specialist **Company:** UNISYS Corporation **Address:** 1316 Mirror Terrace N.W., Winter Haven, FL 33881 United States **BUS:** Information Technology Consulting Services and Solutions Company **P/S:** Virtualization/Consolidation Across Industries in the Public Sector, Commercial and Transportation **MA:** International **D/D/R:** Offering Consolidation and Application Deployment, Pre-Sales Architect for Data Center and Overall, Managing Systems Integration, Overseeing Computer Hardware **H/I/S:** Enjoying Water Sports, Boating **EDU:** Bachelor of Arts in Mathematics, University of South Florida, St. Petersburg (1973) **CERTS:** Certified Novell Engineer; Microsoft Certified Systems Engineer; Enhanced Machine Controller
Email: eileen.dudley@unisys.com
URL: http://www.unisys.com

Ms. Sandra Dudley

Title: Front Office Manager **Company:** Embassy Suites Hotel **Address:** 4350 PGA Boulevard, Palm Beach Gardens, FL 33410 United States **BUS:** International Hotel Chain **P/S:** Guest Services, Rooms, Amenities, Pool, Shopping **MA:** International **D/D/R:** Managing All Aspects of the Front Office, Overseeing Emergency Situations **H/I/S:** Fishing, Dancing **EDU:** High School Education **A/H:** Spirit and Pride Award (2007-2008)
Email: sandyfree1127@aol.com
URL: http://www.embassysuites.com

Dr. Elizabeth A. Duewer

Title: Senior Lecturer **Company:** University of Wisconsin, Platteville **Address:** 1 University Plaza, Platteville, WI 53818 United States **BUS:** University **P/S:** Education **MA:** National **D/D/R:** Teaching Botany and Zoology **H/I/S:** Playing the Organ, Teaching Piano Lessons, Playing the Handbells, Singing in the Choir, Gardening, Traveling **EDU:** Bachelor of Science in Floriculture, University of Illinois; Master of Science in Botany, University of Illinois; Ph.D. in Botany, University of Arizona **A/H:** First Woman Accepted into the Ph.D. Program **C/VW:** Habitat for Humanity
Email: duewere@uwplatt.edu
URL: http://www.uwplatt.edu

Chanelle Duffard-Smith

Title: Client Representative **Company:** IBM **Address:** 1500 4th Avenue North 4th Floor, Nashville, TN 37219 United States **BUS:** Technology Retail **P/S:** A Variety of Business Machines and Other Technical Services, Marketing **MA:** International **D/D/R:** Specializing in Client Relationships and Generating New Business **H/I/S:** Football **EDU:** Bachelor of Science in Marketing, Louisiana State University **A/A/S:** Nashville Technology Council; Women in Technology
Email: duffard@us.ibm.com
URL: www.ibm.com

Mr. Frederick A. Duffy

Title: Principal (Retired) **Company:** Lake Forest School District **Address:** 7221 Cedar Creek Road, Lincoln, DE 19960 United States **BUS:** School District **P/S:** Regular Core Curriculum Reading, Math, English, Science, Social Studies, Art, Music, History, Physical Education, Language Arts, Computers **MA:** Regional **D/D/R:** Teaching Practicum II at the Wilmington College, Tutoring Students at the Local Elementary School **H/I/S:** All Sports Including Football, Track, Basketball **EDU:** Master's Degree Plus 60 Credits in Curriculum Development, University of Delaware (1984); Bachelor's Degree in Elementary Education, Delaware State University (1971) **A/A/S:** Deacon, Sunday School Director; Finance and Labor Committee; Van Driver, Mount Enron Baptist Church; Chairman, Canton-Sussex Industry Committee; Vice Chairman, Greater Milford Boys and Girls Club; Board of Directors, Felton Bank; Former Board of Directors, Senior Center; School Board for Dover Academy; Grand Lodge, State of Delaware; Grand Chapter, Eastern Star State of Delaware
Email: faduffy1109@comcast.net
URL: http://www.lakeforestsd.com

Diane Gail Dugan

Title: Owner, Redken Facilitator, Teacher **Company:** Total Concept Salon **Address:** 2231 Earl View Drive, Harrisburg, PA 17112 United States **BUS:** Salon **P/S:** Hair Cutting, Styling and Coloring **MA:** International **D/D/R:** Cutting and Styling Hair **H/I/S:** Sewing, Skiing **CERTS:** Licensed Cosmetologist, Empire Cosmetology School; Licensed Teacher; Industry-Related Training, Redken Color Academy, New York, NY; Industry-Related Training, Trevor Sorbie Salon, Europe
Email: dianegail.dugan@cwwemail.com

Mr. Arturo J. Duharte

Title: Credit and Collection Coordinator **Company:** Affinia Global Sales **Address:** 1667 W. 42nd Street, Hialeah, FL 33012 United States **BUS:** Proven Leader in the Auto Parts Industry **P/S:** Credit, Collection and Aftermarket **MA:** International **D/D/R:** Preparing Reports for Management, Working Hand in Hand with Management, Preparing Analysis Credit Lines **H/I/S:** Reading **EDU:** Bachelor of Science in Accounting, Barry University (2006)
Email: aduharte@hotmail.com

Gabrielle G. Dujué

Title: Project Manager **Company:** Hill International, Inc. **Address:** 144 W. State Street, Trenton, NJ 08608 United States **BUS:** Construction Management Firm **P/S:** Programs, Projects, Construction, Estimation and Cost Management, Troubled Project Turnaround, Contract Procurement, Administration, Worldwide Construction Consulting and Construction Claims **MA:** International **D/D/R:** Assisting Clients with Planning of Projects, Securing Services of Architects and Engineers, Overseeing Design Process and Construction, Assisting with Bids and Post-Occupancy Issues, Managing Commercial Institutional Projects **H/I/S:** Running **EDU:** Bachelor's Degree in Architecture, Pratt Institute, with Honors (1988) **CERTS:** Certification in Code Enforcement and Building Inspection (1990) **A/A/S:** American Institute of Architects
Email: gabrielledujue@hillintl.com
URL: http://www.hillintl.com

Michelle K. Duley

Title: Assistant Director, Fund raising Coordinator **Company:** Children's Christian Center **Address:** 21 Linwood Avenue, Bel Air, MD 21014 United States **BUS:** Education Institute **P/S:** Education and Healthcare for Children **MA:** Local **D/D/R:** working with children **H/I/S:** Reading, Scrapbooking **EDU:** Associate of Arts in Early Childhood Education, Hartford Community College (2004) **A/A/S:** National Honor Society **C/VW:** Kennedy Krieger Institute; Walk-A-Thon Services; Us Foundation
Email: shellbaby6573033@aol.com

Sharon L. Dull

Title: Owner, President **Company:** Rose of Sharon **Address:** 8666 Chatham Road, Medina, OH 44256 United States **BUS:** Greenhouse **P/S:** Plants, Fruits, Vegetables, Starting Seeds **MA:** Local **D/D/R:** Propagation, Gardening, Seeding, Growing Plants **H/I/S:** Fair Directing, Fishing **EDU:** Coursework, Akron University; Coursework, Tri-C **A/A/S:** Medina County Agricultural Society; Akron All Breed **A/H:** Best Gardener in Medina County (2006) **C/VW:** Forgotten Animal Shelter, Humane Society
Email: greenhouse347@aol.com
URL: http://www.cambridgewhoswho.com

Alicia Y. Dumas

Title: Tour Guide **Company:** Chicago Trolley **Address:** 615 W. 41st Street, Chicago, IL 60609 United States **BUS:** Transportation **P/S:** Tour and Charter Services, City Sightseeing **MA:** Local **D/D/R:** Guiding Tours for Private Charters, Offering Information on the City of Chicago **H/I/S:** Basketball **EDU:** College Coursework Completed in Business **CERTS:** Certified Nursing Assistant
Email: dumasalicia@yahoo.com
URL: http://www.chicagotrolley.com

Shannen L. Dumond

Title: Registered Nurse **Address:** 2208 Calumet Drive, Harker Heights, TX 76548 United States **BUS:** Nursing **P/S:** Medical Services **MA:** Regional **D/D/R:** Pediatric ICU Nurse, High Level Unit, Surgery **EDU:** Master's Degree in Counseling and Psychology, Troy State University (2006) **A/A/S:** Member of the American Association of Critical Care Nurses; Chi Sigma Iota Society; Gamma Beta Phi Society; Association of Preoperative Registered Nurses; Association of Clinical Research Professions
Email: shannen_dumond@hotmail.com
URL: http://www.sw.org

Anita D. Dunbar, CRS, SRES

Title: Realtor, Associate Broker **Company:** Montague, Miller & Co. **Address:** 500 Westfield Road, Charlottesville, VA 22901 United States **BUS:** Real Estate Brokerage Firm **P/S:** Residential and Commercial Real Estate Exchange Including Horse Properties, Mountain View, Executive and Luxury Properties, Condominiums, Lake-front and Golf Homes **MA:** Charlottesville, Albemarle, Central Virginia **EXP:** Ms. Dunbar's expertise includes residential and vacant land sales. **H/I/S:** Collecting Antiques, Traveling **CERTS:** Certified Residential Specialist, State of Virginia **A/A/S:** Board Member, Charlottesville Area Association of Realtors; The Virginia Association of Realtors; National Association of Realtors; Charlottesville Regional Chamber of Commerce; Leadership Charlottesville; Board of Directors, Literacy Volunteers of Charlottesville/Albemarle **A/H:** Certified Residential Specialist of the Year, State of Virginia (2006); Sales Associate of the Year, Charlottesville Area Association of Realtors (2005)
Email: adunbar@cfw.com
URL: http://www.anitadunbar-realtor.com

Mr. Tavarus J. Dunbar

Title: Morale, Welfare and Recreational Specialist **Company:** Marine Corps Community Services **Address:** 321 Joseph Boll Avenue, Las Vegas, NV 89081 United States **BUS:** Retail, Business Operations **P/S:** Support Equipment and Merchandise for Military Personnel, Air Shows and Open Houses, Birthday Ball, Commercial Sponsorship, Exceptional Family Member Program, Gifts, Marine Corps Family Team Building, Official Entertainment Fund, Personal Services, Retail/Services/Recreation Business, Semper Fit/Sports, Support Unit Funds, USA Practice/Uniform Resource Demonstration **MA:** Regional **D/D/R:** Overseeing Service and Retail Management **H/I/S:** Running, Shooting Pool, Basketball, Poker **EDU:** Master's Degree in Business Administration, University of Phoenix (2007)
Email: tavarusd@excite.com
URL: http://www.usmc-mccs.org

Mr. Luther H. Duncan

Title: President, Chief Executive Officer **Company:** Sure Shot Paintball, Inc. **Address:** 20835 Callaway Village Way, Unit 1, Callaway, MD 20620 United States **BUS:** Retail Store and Playing Field **P/S:** Sales and Services, Paintball Field **MA:** Local **D/D/R:** managing the communications department, ensuring customer satisfaction and overseeing operations **H/I/S:** Hunting, Fishing **CERTS:** Industry-Related Training **C/VW:** Eagle Scout, The Boy Scouts of America
Email: pbsureshot@yahoo.com
URL: http://www.pbsureshot.com

Nicco Duncan

Title: Founder, Chief Executive Officer **Company:** A Perfect Plan **Address:** P.O. Box 622, Woodstock, GA 30188 United States **BUS:** Consulting Company **P/S:** Consulting Startups and Business Planning **MA:** National **D/D/R:** Marketing, Business, Consulting **H/I/S:** Supporting the Atlanta Braves **EDU:** Bachelor's Degree in Marketing, Kennesaw State University **A/A/S:** Kennesaw Business Association; Canton Road Association; Cobb County Chamber of Commerce; Growbiz Georgia; WEDA; Acworth Business Association; Woodstock Business Association; National Women's Chamber of Commerce; Georgia Women's Chamber of Commerce **C/VW:** Women 2 Work, St. Jude Children's Research Hospital, Make-A-Wish Foundation
Email: nicco@aperfectplan.net
URL: http://www.aperfectplan.net

Tammy E. Duncan

Title: Registered Agent **Company:** Duncan's Mobile Automotive, LLC **Address:** 5065 New Road Extension, Hollywood, SC 29449 United States **BUS:** Automotive Repair Company **P/S:** Automobile Repairs and Service **MA:** Regional **D/D/R:** Customer Assistance, Following Up with Customers to Ensure their Satisfaction at the Completion of the Job, Handling Finances and Bookkeeping, Setting Up Website on E-Bay Featuring Automobiles and Parts for Purchase, One of the Few Automobile Repair Professionals Making House Calls **H/I/S:** Fishing, Automobiles **EDU:** Bachelor of Science Degree in Occupational Therapy, Medical University of South Carolina (1990) **A/A/S:** National Certified Occupational Therapy Board; American Occupational Therapy Association
Email: duncanhoward@netscape.com
URL: http://www.cambridgewhoswho.com

Kathryn R. Dungy, Ph.D.

Title: Assistant Professor **Company:** New College of Florida **Address:** 5800 Bay Shore Drive, Division of Social Science, Sarasota, FL 34243 United States **BUS:** Institution of Higher Education **P/S:** Liberal Arts, Research Based Education where Students and Faculty Mentors Design Personalized Programs of Classes, Honors College for the State of Florida University System, Nation's Number One Public Liberal Arts College **MA:** Regional **D/D/R:** Caribbean and Latin American History, Advisory Services, Does Emeritus Evaluative Instead of Grades **H/I/S:** Photography, Internet **EDU:** Ph.D. in History, Duke University (2003); Master's Degree in History, Duke University (2000); Bachelor's Degree in Sociology and History, Spelman College (1991) **A/A/S:** Delta Sigma Theta Sorority; Association of American Historians; Association of Caribbean Historians; Latin American Studies Association
Email: wahsupdoc@gmail.com
URL: http://www.ncf.edu

Patricia Kay Dunham

Title: President, Financial Advisor **Company:** First Wall Street Financial Advisors **Address:** 190 W. Huffaker Lane, Suite 405, Reno, NV 89511 United States **BUS:** Financial and Brokerage Firm **P/S:** Financial Advice **MA:** International **D/D/R:** Bookkeeping, Accounting, Staffing, Marketing, Retirement Services **H/I/S:** Reading, Exercising, Needleworking, Spending Time with her Granddaughter **EDU:** Coursework, Eastern Oregon State University, La Grande, OR **CERTS:** Licensed Series 7, Series 63, Series 65; Licensed in Life and Health Insurance
Email: kaydunham@firstwallstreet.net
URL: http://www.firstwallstreet.net

Susan Dunlap

Title: Customized Workforce Training Manager **Company:** Community College of Beaver County, Continuing Education Division **Address:** 1 Campus Drive, Monaca, PA 15061 United States **BUS:** Community College **P/S:** Education **MA:** Local **D/D/R:** Workforce Training, Developing Curriculum for Workforce Training, Serving as Grant Coordinator, Writing the Newsletter 'The Workforce and Beyond' **H/I/S:** Spending Time with her Husband and Six Grandchildren **EDU:** High School Graduate; Industry-Related Training and Experience **A/A/S:** Business Service Team, Pennsylvania Career League; Beaver County Women's Conference; Pennsylvania Women's Work Advisory Committee **C/VW:** Make-A-Wish Foundation, Autism Charities, Conservation District
Email: sue.dunlap@ccbc.edu
URL: http://www.ccbc.edu

Colleen Dunn

Title: Teacher of the Deaf **Company:** Reads **Address:** 351 Thelma Avenue, Somerset, MA 02726 United States **BUS:** Deaf Education Facility **P/S:** Quality Education **MA:** Regional **D/D/R:** Following Massachusetts Curriculum and Adapting it to the Classroom Environment **H/I/S:** Needlepoint, Home Decorating **EDU:** Master's Degree in Deaf Education, Boston University (2000) **A/A/S:** Member, MTA; Former Sunday School Teacher
Email: colleendunn@tmail.com
URL: http://www.cambridgewhoswho.com

Dennis G. Dunn

Title: Pastor **Company:** Fellowship Missionary Baptist Church **Address:** 8550 Saul Bell Road NW, Albuquerque, NM 87121 United States **BUS:** Church **P/S:** Christian Church with Multi-Cultural Membership **MA:** Local **D/D/R:** Ministry, Teaching, Counseling, Visionary **H/I/S:** Golf **A/A/S:** World Baptist Alliance, Southern Baptist Convention, National Baptist Convention
Email: info@CambridgeWhosWho.com
URL: www.fmbc-abq.org

Karen Dunn

Title: Registered Nurse **Company:** St. Elizabeth Health Center **Address:** 1167 Blue Sky Drive, New Castle, PA 16105 United States **BUS:** First Magnet Hospital in Ohio **P/S:** Medical Services **MA:** Local **D/D/R:** Working with Oncology and Dialysis, Kidney Transplant, Staff Nurse, Night Staff, Delegating Duties, Admissions **H/I/S:** Football, Piano, Reading, Traveling, Spending Time with Family **CERTS:** Registered Nurse Diploma, Trumble Memorial Hospital School of Nursing (1987)
Email: kdcasscam@msn.com

Rachelle C. Dunn

Title: Senior Staff Geologist **Company:** TRC Solutions **Address:** 1590 Solano Way, Suite A, Concord, CA 94520 United States **BUS:** Provider of Technical, Financial, Risk Management and Construction Services to Industry and Government Clients **P/S:** Creating and Implementing Sophisticated and Innovative Solutions to the Challenges Facing America's Energy, Transportation, Environment, Infrastructure and Infrastructure Security Markets **MA:** Local **D/D/R:** Setting Up for Jobs, Writing Reports, Project management, Evaluate information and submit reports, Liaison with state regulatory commission **H/I/S:** Bowling, Hiking, Square Dancing, Hand Work **EDU:** Bachelor of Science in Geology, California State University (2003)
Email: rdunn@trcsolutions.com
URL: http://www.trcsolutions.com

Denise Dunstan

Title: Licensed Vocational Nurse **Company:** MHMRA of Harris County **Address:** 3600 S. Gessner Road, Suite 245, Houston, TX 77063 United States **BUS:** Group Home **P/S:** Healthcare for Physically and Mentally Impaired Patients **MA:** Local **D/D/R:** Nursing **H/I/S:** Volunteering **CERTS:** Licensed Vocational Nurse, Hillcrest Vocation Nurses College **A/A/S:** American Rehabilitation Association; Lesbian Health Initiative **C/VW:** Lesbian Health Initiative; Caretaker for 80-Year-Old Woman, American Rehabilitation Nurses Association
Email: smilinghigh@hotmail.com
URL: http://www.cambridgewhoswho.com

Stephanie Anne Duplantis

Title: Project Superintendent **Company:** Premier Steel **BUS:** Construction Company **P/S:** Steel, Chemical, Refineries, Buildings, Repair, Installations **MA:** Local **D/D/R:** Supervising Construction, Running Crews **H/I/S:** Spending Time with her Two Children **EDU:** Bachelor's Degree in Business Administration and Industrial and Procurement Management, Madison University **CERTS:** Pursuing Certificate in Project Management, Boston University **A/H:** Cambridge Who's Who Executive and Professional Registry **C/VW:** Big Brothers Big Sisters of America
Email: cajunbaby75@yahoo.com
URL: http://www.cambridgewhoswho.com

Natalie C. DuPree

Title: Special Education Teacher **Company:** Booneville High School **Address:** 945 N. Plum Street, Booneville, AR 72927 United States **BUS:** High School **P/S:** Education **MA:** Regional **D/D/R:** Teaching Special Education to Students in Grades 10 through 12, Community-Based Instruction **H/I/S:** Spending Time with her Son, Scrapbooking, Golfing **EDU:** Bachelor of Science in Education, University of Ozarks
Email: natalie@bps.wsc.k12.ar.us

Mrs. Sandra M. Duquette

Title: Esthetician **BUS:** Day Spa **P/S:** Skin and Nail Care, Cosmetics, Bioelements and Environ Skincare Line **MA:** Regional **D/D/R:** Performing Skin Care, Clinical and Body Treatments Including Whole Body Waxing, Nails, Facials, Chemical Peels, Managing Payroll, Accounts Payable and Receivable, Selling Bioelements and Environ Skincare Products **H/I/S:** Reading, Music, Bowling, Dancing, Relaxing, Football **EDU:** General Equivalency Diploma **CERTS:** Certification in Recording Arts and Mass Communication; Certified Eustachian Specialist; Certified Nail Technician **A/A/S:** Plymouth Chamber of Commerce **C/VW:** Volunteer, Various Community Organizations
Email: lady_blue64@yahoo.com
URL: http://www.faciallyyours.com

Ms. Vicki M. Duran

Title: Senior Manufacturing Engineer **Company:** Washington Group International **Dept:** Engineered Product Division **Address:** 5301 Sierra Vista, Carlsbad, NM 88220 United States **BUS:** Manufacturing Company **P/S:** Fabrication and Maintenance of Nuclear Containment Vessels **MA:** International **D/D/R:** Developing, Evaluating and Improving Manufacturing Methods, On-the-Job Training to Personnel as Necessary to Ensure Manufacturing is Consistent with Approved Procedures and Protocols **H/I/S:** Making Pure Glycerin Soap, Singing at Oasis Fellowship Ministries **EDU:** Pursuing Bachelor's Degree in Business Management, Northwood University **A/A/S:** Minister, Oasis Christian Fellowship
Email: vmduran@hotmail.com

Lisa Jeanette Durben

Title: Assistant Nurse Manager **Company:** Children's Hospitals and Clinics of Minnesota **Address:** 9279 Braun Avenue S.E., Delano, MN 55328 United States **BUS:** Hospital **P/S:** Healthcare **MA:** Regional **D/D/R:** neonatal nursing, managing administrative duties and overseeing the intensive care unit, Working on the Vermont Oxford Network Program, Reviewing Clinical Projects **H/I/S:** Horseback Riding **EDU:** Master of Business Administration in Healthcare Management, Colorado Technical University (2007); Bachelor's Degree in Nursing, University of Minnesota (1982) **CERTS:** Critical Care Registered Nurse; Certified Neonatal Resuscitation Program Instructor; Board Certified Lactation Consultant **A/A/S:** Sigma Theta Tau **A/H:** The Champion of Children's Individual and Group Award (2001); The Champion of Children's Individual and Group Award (2006) **C/VW:** Children's Hospitals and Clinics of Minnesota
Email: lisa.durben@childrensmn.org
URL: http://www.childrensmn.org

Eldrenna Durham

Title: Director of Professional Development for School Administrators **Company:** Charlotte-Mecklenberg Schools **Address:** Charlotte-Mecklenberg Schools, Charlotte, NC 28262 United States **BUS:** Public Schools Serving Residents of Charlotte **P/S:** Public Education for Local Students **MA:** Regional **D/D/R:** Building a Standards Program, Training Principals to Create a Professional Learning Community **H/I/S:** Traveling, Playing Scrabble, Reading **EDU:** Doctorate in Educational Leadership, University of Sarasota (1999); Master's Degree in Curriculum Instruction, Michigan State University (1985); Master's Degree in Administration, University of North Carolina (1991) Add: Bachelor of Science Degree, Education, Johnson Smith University, Charlotte, NC, 1978 **CERTS:** Training Crucial Conversations and the Seven Habits of Highly Effective People **A/A/S:** The LINKS, Incorporated; Phi Delta Kappa; Sigma Gamma Rho Sorority, Inc.; Association for Supervision and Curriculum Development; Federal Managers Association
Email: drdream99@yahoo.com

Theresa Durham

Title: Owner, Office Manager **Company:** 1) D&M Trim, Inc. 2) David's Flowers Patch and Gifts **Address:** 1607 Lucas Avenue, Green Cove Springs, FL 32043 United States **BUS:** Wood Works **P/S:** Interior Wood Trim, High-Quality Work, Crown Molding, Oak Stairs, Picture Frames **MA:** Regional **D/D/R:** Managing, Customer Service, Cost Analysis **H/I/S:** Spending Time with her Grandchildren, Bow Hunting, Archery **EDU:** Coursework in Account Management; Coursework in Accounting, St. John River Community College **A/A/S:** National Archery Champion; Archery Hall of Fame
Email: dmtriminc@aol.com
URL: http://www.cambridgewhoswho.com

Linda F. Durning
Title: President **Company:** Comfort & Care of Wallingford, LLC **Address:** 80 S. Main Street, Suite 1, Wallingford, CT 06492 United States **BUS:** Non-Medical Home Care Company **P/S:** Professional Home Care Services Including Housekeeping and Laundry, Meal Preparation and Menu Planning, Medication Reminders, RESPITE Care, Shopping, Errands and Appointments, Place of Worship Needs, Telephone Reassurance and Money Management Services, Companion Services **MA:** Regional **D/D/R:** Overseeing Finances, Marketing, Advertising, Managing Employee Pay Scale, Directing the Human Resource Department, Developing the Company **H/I/S:** Volunteering **EDU:** Associate Degree in Geriatrics, Southern Connecticut State University (1981) **A/A/S:** Hamden Chamber of Commerce; Alzheimer's Association; Women in Engineering Leadership Institute; Killingworth Chamber of Commerce **A/H:** Athena Award, Athena International; Certificate of Achievement, Quinnipiac Chamber of Commerce **C/VW:** Volunteer, Alzheimer's Association; Volunteer, Connecticut Breast Cancer Association
Email: cmfrtcrwlfd@aol.com
URL: http://www.comfortandcareofwallingford.com

Roberta M. Duskin, RPh.
Title: Assistant Manager **Company:** Kindred Pharmacy Services **Address:** 5450 Riggins Court, Suite 4, Reno, NV 89502 United States **BUS:** Local Pharmacy Associated with a Long-Term Care Facility **P/S:** Pharmaceutical Services **MA:** National **D/D/R:** Overseeing a Staff of 12, Serving Approximately 450 Long-Term Facilities, Processing All Staff Paperwork Regarding Scripts and Compliance **H/I/S:** Spending Time with her Two Children, Gardening **EDU:** Bachelor of Science in Pharmacy, Oregon State University **A/A/S:** Nevada Humane Society

Patrick B. Duthie
Title: Educator, Coach **Company:** Farmington Public Schools **Address:** 32500 Shiawassee Road, Farmington Hills, MI 48336 United States **BUS:** School District **P/S:** Public Education **MA:** Local **D/D/R:** Teaching Physical Education, Coaching Swimming **H/I/S:** Traveling, Spending Time with Family **EDU:** Master of Science in Physical Education, Eastern Michigan University, Bachelor's Degree in Health and Physical Education, Bowling Green State University **A/A/S:** Omicron Delta Kappa **A/H:** Recipient, Academic Scholarship for Highest GPA Among Athletes **C/VW:** Shriners Hospitals for Children
Email: pbdiii@aol.com

William Duvall
Title: Owner **Company:** Duvall Farms **Address:** 1740 Hwy 1669, Worthville, KY 41098 United States **BUS:** Farm **P/S:** Breeding and Feeding **MA:** Local **D/D/R:** Beef Cattle
Email: info@CambridgeWhosWho.com

Brenda S. Dwiggins
Title: Kindergarten Teacher **Company:** East Milton Elementary School **Address:** 5156 Ward Basin Road, Milton, FL 32583 United States **BUS:** Public Elementary School **P/S:** Exceptional Student Education Applied Technology, Adult and Community Education, Alternative Academic Programs Curriculum Areas, Pre-K Programs Professional Development **MA:** Local **D/D/R:** Teaching Core Curriculum, Working with Autistic and Special Education Students, Reading Computer Programs, Teaching All Elementary School Subjects **H/I/S:** Riding Motorcycles and Horses **EDU:** Pursuing Master's Degree in Curriculum and Instruction, University of West Florida (Expected 2008) **A/A/S:** Road Runner Reading Club; Santa Rosa Professional Educators; Reading Council for Santa Rosa County
Email: dwigginsb@mail.santarosa.k12.fl.us
URL: http://www.santarosa.k12.fl.us/schools/eme/

Kevin J. Dworak
Title: President, Chief Executive Officer **Company:** Work Studio **Address:** 1605 Oakview Drive, Silver Spring, MD 20903 United States **BUS:** Architectural Firm **P/S:** Designing Residential, Religious and Urban Architecture **MA:** Regional **D/D/R:** Designing Custom High-End Architecture **H/I/S:** Working **EDU:** Master's Degree in Architecture, SUNY at Buffalo **A/A/S:** AIA
Email: kevindworak@yahoo.com

Karen A. Dwyer, AIC
Title: Claims Manager **Company:** FirstComp Insurance **Address:** 931 Jefferson Boulevard, Warwick, RI 02886 United States **BUS:** Insurance Company **P/S:** Insurance Services, Workers Compensation Insurance **MA:** Local **EXP:** Ms. Dwyer's expertise is in supervision. **H/I/S:** Quilting **EDU:** Bachelor's Degree, Quinsigamond Community College **A/A/S:** New Hampshire Adjuster's Association
Email: karen.dwyer@cwwemail.com
URL: http://www.cambridgewhoswho.com

Kevin L. Dye
Title: District Product Support Manager **Company:** JLG **Address:** 3 Quail Ridge Drive, Agency, MO 64401 United States **BUS:** Construction Equipment Manufacturing Company **P/S:** Manufacturing Aerial Work Platforms and Rough Terrain Forklifts **MA:** Regional **D/D/R:** Product Support Management, Training, Mechanical Services **H/I/S:** Golfing, Motorcycle Riding, Traveling, Spending Time with his Children **EDU:** College Coursework in Auto Mechanics, Technical College (1988)
Email: kldye@jlg.com
URL: http://www.jlg.com

Mrs. Kathleen M. Dyer
Title: Head Supervisor (Retired) **Company:** Bible Church Academy **Dept:** Education **Address:** 791 Cranor Road, Murfreesboro, TN 37130 United States **BUS:** Religious Institution **P/S:** Education Including an Accelerated Christian Curriculum **MA:** Regional **D/D/R:** Supervising, Scheduling, Assisting Teachers, Working One-on-One with Troubled Children **H/I/S:** Reading, Gardening, Sewing, Cooking, Caring for her Cat, Spending Time with her Grandson, Fishing, Attending Ball Games, Swimming, Boating, Camping **EDU:** Diploma, Tennessee Department of Education (1993) **CERTS:** Certification, Teacher Training Program, School of Tomorrow (2006); Certification in Supervision (1993, 1995) **A/A/S:** The Red Hat Society; Bible Study Groups **A/H:** Teaching Award **C/VW:** Ladies Auxiliary; Bible Church of Jesus; Volunteer, Visiting the Sick
Email: angelcat1968@comcast.net
URL: http://www.cambridgewhoswho.com

Andrea R. Dysart
Title: Fourth-Grade Teacher **Company:** Wayne Central School District, Freewill Elementary School **Address:** P.O. Box 155, Ontario Center, NY 14520 United States **BUS:** Elementary School **P/S:** Education for Students in Kindergarten through Fifth-Grade **MA:** Regional **D/D/R:** Teaching Fourth-Grade Students **EDU:** Master's Degree in Elementary Education, Nazareth College **A/A/S:** Who's Who Among American Teachers; New York State United Teachers; Wayne Teachers Association
Email: adysart@wayne.k12.ny.us
URL: http://www.wayne.k12.ny.us/

Lorri Odessa Dyson
Title: Second-Grade Teacher **Company:** Signal Hill Elementary School/Westgate Elementary School **Address:** 15427 Milton Hall Place, Manassas, VA 20112 United States **BUS:** School **P/S:** Education **MA:** Regional **D/D/R:** Second-Grade, Specializing in Reading **H/I/S:** Basketball, Volleyball, Softball **EDU:** M.Ed. in Curriculum and Instruction, Advanced Studies in Teaching and Learning, Literacy and Reading, George Mason University, Manassas, Virginia (2006); Bachelor of Arts in Early Childhood Education, Benedict College, Columbia, South Carolina (1988) **A/A/S:** National Association for the Advancement of Colored People; Delta Sigma Theta Sorority, Inc.; Mentors New Teachers and Students; Tutors Children; Parent-Teacher Organization; Implemented Students and Teachers Achieving Excellence Program; Trained New Teachers in Positive Discipline/Positive Instruction for Prince William County Schools **A/H:** Nominee, Disney Outstanding Teacher Award; Staff Award for Excellence
Email: dysonlo@pwcs.edu
URL: http://www.pwcs.edu

Stefanie L. Eads, RN
Title: Registered Nurse, Nurse Manager **Company:** Ende Medical Practice, LLP **Address:** 121 S. Market Street, Petersburg, VA 23803 United States **BUS:** Internal Medical Practice **P/S:** Internal Medicine, Healthcare **MA:** Local **D/D/R:** Medical-Surgical, Forensic and Home Health Nursing **H/I/S:** Bowling, Golfing **CERTS:** Registered Nurse, Southside Regional School of Nursing, Virginia **C/VW:** CARES
Email: seads49448@aol.com

Karen E. Eagleson
Title: Director **Company:** Johnson County Emergency Management **Address:** 122-A Hoyt Street, Warrensburg, MO 64093 United States **BUS:** Disaster Preparedness Management **P/S:** Disaster Preparedness, Response and Recovery from Natural and Man Made Disasters **MA:** Local **D/D/R:** Coordinator of Hazmat, First Response and Follow Up Throughout the County of Population Exceeding 50,000 **H/I/S:** Traveling, Motorcycle Traveling **CERTS:** Certificate of Achievement, From the Emergency Management Institute **A/A/S:** County Board of Salvation Army; Board Member, HELP
Email: jocoema@charterinternet.com
URL: www.jococourthouse.com

Mr. James L. Ealey
Title: Teacher, Dean of Discipline **Company:** Fiorello H. LaGuardia High School **Address:** 100 Amsterdam Avenue, New York, NY 10023 United States **BUS:** Specialized Public High School **P/S:** Secondary Education Offering Conservatory Training at the College Level **MA:** Local **D/D/R:** Teaching High School Mathematics, Managing Disciplinary Responsibilities for the School **H/I/S:** Basketball, Learning Guitar **EDU:** Master's Degree in Mathematics, City College of New York (1984) **A/A/S:** National Council of Teachers of Mathematics
Email: jl_ealey2@yahoo.com
URL: http://www.laguardiahs.org

Donna Corn Earl
Title: Broker Associate **Company:** Beverly-Hanks and Associates **Address:** 400 Beverly Hanks Center, Hendersonville, NC 28792 United States **BUS:** Real Estate Agency **P/S:** Real Estate **MA:** Local, Western North Carolina **D/D/R:** Interacting with Clients, Selling Residential and Commercial Real Estate, Condos and New Homes **H/I/S:** Spending Time with her Children, Horseback Riding **EDU:** Coursework in Commercial Real Estate **CERTS:** License in Real Estate, Columbia Institute; Certified Commercial Investment Member Institute; Certified New Home Specialist; Accredited Luxury Home Specialist **A/A/S:** CCIM; National Association of Realtors; Western North Carolina Regional MLS Guide **C/VW:** United Way, American Heart Association, Breast Cancer Research Foundation, Habitat for Humanity
Email: donna@donnaearl.com
URL: http://www.donnaearl.com

Annie Marie Earle
Title: Commercial Service Office Manager **Company:** Peterson Power Systems, Inc. **Address:** 2828 Teagarden Street, San Leandro, CA 94577 United States **BUS:** Energy Firm **P/S:** Power Generation and Engine Services Including Sales, Rentals and Repairing **MA:** Regional **D/D/R:** overseeing the maintenance work, Managing Office Operations Including Supervising Technicians, Sales Personnel, Enrolling Units for Prime Product Systems, Contacting Customers for Renewals, Scheduling Technicians for Attending Calls, Preparing Time Cards **H/I/S:** Exercising, Caring for her Birds **EDU:** Bachelor of Science in Business Management, University of Phoenix (1998) **C/VW:** Local Church
Email: amearle@petersonpower.com
URL: http://www.petersonpower.com

D. Laureen Earnest
Title: President **Company:** Carolina Algae Control, LLC **Address:** 1600 Long Grove Drive, Apartment 1316, Mount Pleasant, SC 29464 United States **BUS:** Algae Control & Pond Management Company **P/S:** Ultrasound Algae Control, Water Quality and Management Services **MA:** National **D/D/R:** Consulting, Writing and Speaking, Creating Environmentally-Friendly Water Management Programs for Residential, Commercial and Industrial Clients **H/I/S:** Traveling, Creative Writing, Observing Nature and Animals **EDU:** Associate Degree in Interior Design, Bauder College, Magna Cum Laude **A/A/S:** American Water Works Association; South Carolina Rural Water Association in Technology Distribution; Industry-Related Trade Shows and Associations; Gogreencharleston.org **C/VW:** Local Church; Federal Emergency Management Association
Email: laureen@carolinaalgaecontrol.com
URL: http://www.carolinaalgaecontrol.com

Amy R. Easley, BS, MT (ASCP) SM
Title: Microbiology Supervisor **Company:** North Mississippi Medical Center **Address:** 830 S. Gloster Street, Tupelo, MS 38801 United States **BUS:** Medical Center **P/S:** Healthcare Including Family Medicine, Internal Medicine and Specialty Clinics throughout 22 Countries **MA:** Regional **EXP:** Ms. Easley's expertise includes susceptibility testing and molecular pathology immunology. **D/D/R:** supervising microbiology department, identifying organisms **H/I/S:** Scrapbooking, Reading, Antiquing **EDU:** Bachelor's Degree **A/A/S:** American Society for Microbiology; American Society for Clinical Pathology
Email: beasley@nmhs.net
URL: http://www.nmhs.net

Darlene F. East
Title: Administrative Assistant **Company:** North Carolina A&T State University **Address:** 1601 E. Market Street, Greensboro, NC 27411 United States **BUS:** University **P/S:** Education **MA:** National **D/D/R:** Managing the Office Support Staff, Maintaining Public Relations, Budgeting, Procuring Funds, Performing Reviews, Writing Job Descriptions, Training New Hires, Writing Articles for A&T Today **H/I/S:** Volunteering as Coordinator for Prayer & Life Clinic **EDU:** Pursuing Master's Degree in Adult Education; Bachelor of Science in Journalism and Communication, Concentration in Public Relations; Associate Degree in Accounting, Allegheny County Community College **A/A/S:** Phi Kappa Phi; Kappa Tau Alpha; Golden Key Honour Society **C/VW:** Prayer and Life Clinic
Email: deast@ncat.edu
URL: http://www.ncat.edu

Ronald Easter Jr.
Title: Owner **Company:** Southern Tier Hood & Exhaust **Address:** 23 Maple Street, Addison, NY 14801 United States **BUS:** Grease Duct Cleaning Company **P/S:** Fire Prevention, Duct Grease Removal **MA:** Local **D/D/R:** Overseeing Cleaning Company Operations **H/I/S:** Spending Time with his Family **CERTS:** Certification, Certified Hood & Duct Cleaners Association **A/A/S:** Certified Hood & Duct Cleaners Association **C/VW:** New York State Police Fund, Local Schools
Email: sthoodexhaust@yahoo.com

Jane D. Easton
Title: Realtor, Commercial Specialist **Company:** RE/MAX Colonial Homes, Inc. **Address:** 500 Charles Street, La Plata, MD 20646 United States **BUS:** Real Estate Firm **P/S:** Buying and Selling Residential and Commercial Properties, Land Sales, Relocations, First Time Home Buyers, Mortgage Services, Investment Services and Single Family Homes **MA:** International **D/D/R:** Selling Residential, Commercial, Land and New Homes, Conducting Relocations **H/I/S:** Watching University of Maryland and Southern Illinois University Basketball and Washington Redskins Football **EDU:** Bachelor of Science in Business Administration, Southern Illinois University (1965) **A/A/S:** Greater Washington Scottish Terrier Club; American Association of Retired Persons; National Active and Retired Federal Employees Association; Lioness; Southern Maryland Association of Realtors; Maryland Association of Realtors; National Association of Realtors
Email: jde@olg.com
URL: http://www.remax.com

Sarah C. Eaves
Title: Sales Coordinator **Company:** Wayland Baptist University Bookstore **Address:** 1900 W. Seventh Street, Plainview, TX 79072 United States **BUS:** University Bookstore, Retailer **P/S:** Textbooks, Gifts **MA:** Local **D/D/R:** Buying for the Gift Store **H/I/S:** Owning her Business, 'Salligraphy,' Gardening, Cooking **EDU:** Bachelor of Science in Biology, Wayland Baptist University **CERTS:** ASCP Certification, Methodist Hospital **A/A/S:** PEO **C/VW:** Medical Missions, First Baptist Church, Plainview
Email: eavess@wbu.edu

Deborah Clark Ebel
Title: Psychiatric Nurse **Address:** 2719 Overbrook Avenue, Norfolk, VA 23513 United States **BUS:** Mental Healthcare Company **P/S:** Training, Pediatric and Adolescent Mental Healthcare **MA:** Regional **D/D/R:** Acting as Psychiatric Nurse Working with Children, Adolescents and Families Child Advocate in the Area of Child and Adolescent Mental Health **H/I/S:** Family History, Genealogy, Reading Nonfiction, Listening to Music, Surfing the Internet **EDU:** Pursuing Master's Degree in Psychology; Coursework in Child Welfare; Bachelor of Science in Psychology, Cum Laude; Associate of Arts in Nursing, Cum Laude **CERTS:** Registered Nurse, State of Virginia **A/A/S:** First Families of Tennessee; American Psychiatric Nurses Association; International Society of Psychiatric-Mental Health Nurses; National Alliance on Mental Illness **C/VW:** National Child Advocacy Center, Huntsville, Alabama
Email: debebel@cox.net
URL: http://www.debebel.com

Dr. Jeffrey J. Eberting
Title: Orthodontist **Company:** Eberting Orthodontics **Address:** 619 Smithview Drive, Maryville, TN 37803 United States **BUS:** Orthodontics Practice **P/S:** Orthodontics **MA:** Regional **EXP:** Dr. Eberting's expertise includes dentistry and orthodontics. **H/I/S:** Playing the Keyboard, Guitar and Bass, Singing, Listening to Music **EDU:** Doctor of Dental Medicine, Temple University; Master of Science in Orthodontics, Temple University; Bachelor of Arts in History, Duke University **A/A/S:** American Dental Association; Second District Dental Society, American Dental Association; Tennessee Dental Association; American Association of Orthodontists; Southern Association of Orthodontists; Tennessee Association of Orthodontists **C/VW:** Rotary Club of Maryville
Email: Jberting@eberting.com
URL: http://www.eberting.com

Philomena O. Ebo
Title: Registered Nurse **Company:** Prince George's County Board of Education **Address:** 9003 Eldon Drive, Clinton, MD 20735 United States **BUS:** Public School District, Board of Education **P/S:** General Primary and Secondary Curriculum, Special Programs, Arts, Music, Language Arts, Physical Education, Learning Resources, Student Support Services, Athletics, Extracurricular Activities, Student Clubs and Organizations, Health Services, Administrative Services **MA:** Local **D/D/R:** Dispensing Students' Medications, Treating Ill Children **H/I/S:** Exercising, Traveling **EDU:** Bachelor of Science in Nursing, George Mason University, Virginia **A/A/S:** Prince George's County Health Department; National Association of Nurses
Email: philoebo@msn.com
URL: http://www1.pgcps.org/board

Ms. Rose Echevarria
Title: Chief Executive Officer, Owner **Company:** Mom & Pops 76, Inc. **Address:** 11242 Ballico Avenue, Ballico, CA 95303 United States **BUS:** Convenience Store **P/S:** Grocery Store, Mexican Restaurant, Gas Station, Convenience Store Items **MA:** Regional **D/D/R:** Overseeing Business Operations, Subdividing Land for Building New Homes **EDU:** Associate of Arts Degree, Merced College, California **A/A/S:** Member, Hispanic Chamber of Commerce, Merced, California
Email: rosieballicostore@hotmail.com

Joralyn S. Echols
Title: Outreach and Public Relations Coordinator **Company:** Glencairn Museum **Address:** 1001 Cathedral Road, Bryn Athyn, PA 19009 United States **BUS:** Museum **P/S:** Preservation, Conservation and Restoration of Art Including Educational Programs using Art and Artifacts from Various Cultures **MA:** Local **D/D/R:** building public relationship, maintaining the web sites, working on the production of documentaries and conducting educational events and lectures **H/I/S:** Singing, Making Crafts, Participating in the Religious Activities **EDU:** Pursuing Master's Degree in Museum Studies; Bachelor of Arts in Education, Bryn Athyn College (2005) **A/A/S:** Professional Development Committee; American Association of Museums; PRAM
Email: joralyn.echols@glencairnmuseum.org
URL: http://www.glencairnmuseum.org

Stephan Eck
Title: Owner **Company:** Eck Logging **Address:** 2506 Canoe Run Road, Jersey Shore, PA 17740 United States **BUS:** Logging Company **P/S:** Logging, Timber Harvesting **MA:** Local **D/D/R:** Overseeing Company Operations **H/I/S:** Hunting **EDU:** Doctor of Business Administration **A/A/S:** National Rifle Association
Email: sec22@hughes.net
URL: http://www.cambridgewhoswho.com

Andrea D. Eckenroad
Title: Special Education Teacher **Company:** Daniel Boone Area School District **Dept:** Amity Intermediate Center **Address:** 200 Boone Drive, Douglassville, PA 19518 United States **BUS:** School **P/S:** Education **MA:** Local **D/D/R:** Monitoring and Instituting Remedial Measures for Special Education Programs **H/I/S:** Dancing **EDU:** Bachelor of Science in Education, West Chester University; Diploma, Wilson High School **A/A/S:** Pennsylvania State Education Association; Pi Lambda Theta **C/VW:** United Way
Email: eckenroa@dboone.k12.pa.us
URL: http://www.dboone.k12.pa.us

Heidi Elizabeth Eckert
Title: Lead Technician **Company:** CVS Pharmacy **Address:** 516 High Street, Mount Holly, NJ 08060 United States **BUS:** Large Retail Pharmacy Chain **P/S:** Pharmacy and Retail Household Items, Photo Processing **MA:** National **D/D/R:** Maintaining the Pharmacy, Scheduling, Performing Inventory Control, Hiring and Training Staff, Filling Prescriptions and Assisting Customers **H/I/S:** Country Line Dancing **EDU:** Coursework in Nursing, Burlington County College **A/A/S:** Among the First to Become a Nationally Certified Pharmacy Technician; American Pharmacy Association; National Pharmacy Technician Association
Email: seckert188@comcast.net
URL: http://www.cvs.com

Anne Edano
Title: Realtor, Mortgage and Foreclosure Specialist **Company:** RE/MAX Marquee Partners **Address:** 7920 W. Sunset Boulevard, Suite 100, Los Angeles, CA 90046 United States **BUS:** Real Estate Firm **P/S:** Commercial and Residential Real Estate Exchange Including Homes, Condos and Lofts **MA:** Regional **EXP:** Ms. Edano's expertise includes real estate management, mortgage and foreclosure. **H/I/S:** Practicing Kung Fu, Spiritual Healing, Capoeira **EDU:** Bachelor of Fine Arts, Chapman University (2004) **CERTS:** Certification in Bookkeeping; Certification in Teaching **A/A/S:** Capoeira Brazil
Email: anne.edano@hotmail.com
URL: http://www.financing.com

Vernon D. Edejer
Title: Financial Advisor **Company:** CAPITAL Asset Management Group **Address:** 4800 Montgomery Lane, Hampden Square M25, Bethesda, MD 20814 United States **BUS:** Financial Planning Company **P/S:** Investments, Insurance Planning **MA:** Regional **EXP:** Mr. Edejer's expertise includes retirement and financial planning. **H/I/S:** Watching and Playing Basketball, Spending Time and Traveling with his Family, Reading **C/VW:** Volunteer, Local School
Email: vedejer@comcast.net

Helen A. Edenfield
Title: Associate Broker **Company:** Re/Max 4 Executives, Inc **Address:** 3350 Northlake Parkway, Atlanta, GA 30345 United States **BUS:** Real Estate **P/S:** Residential, Executive Homes, Lake Front, New Construction, Condos, Golf Homes, Senior, Gated, Horse Properties **MA:** National **D/D/R:** Residential Properties, Top Producer **H/I/S:** Antiquing, Gardening **A/A/S:** Georgia Association of Realtors, National Association of Realtors
Email: sainthelen@yahoo.com

Ubong D. Edet (Dominic)
Title: Clinical Pharmacist, Staff Pharmacist **Company:** Kent General Hospital **Dept:** Bayhealth Medical Center **Address:** 640 S. State Street, Dover, DE 19901 United States **BUS:** Nonprofit Organization **P/S:** Inpatient and Outpatient Medical Services, Emergency Healthcare **MA:** Regional **D/D/R:** ensuring clinical pharmacy services to patients, Consulting Doctors, Monitoring Dosage Levels, Administering Intravenous Medications and Entering Data **H/I/S:** Playing and Watching Soccer, Golfing, Politics **EDU:** Doctor of Pharmacy, University of Maryland School of Pharmacy (2004) **A/A/S:** American Pharmacists Association; American Society of Health-System Pharmacists **C/VW:** Volunteer, Local Church
Email: uedet001@umaryland.edu
URL: http://www.bayhealth.org

Sharon A. Edmiston
Title: President **Company:** 1) Cruises, Inc. 2) Health is Precious **Address:** 5739 State Avenue, Sacramento, CA 95819 United States **BUS:** 1) Travel Agency 2) Marketing Agency **P/S:** 1) Cruises 2) Cosmetics **MA:** International **EXP:** Ms. Edmiston's expertise is in skincare rejuvenation. **D/D/R:** Reviewing Individual Customers' Needs and Matching Them with the Right Cruise Lines and Carriers, Handling Pharmanex BioPhotonic Scanner and Gavanix Spa System **H/I/S:** Traveling, Biking, Snorkeling, Hiking, Spending Time with her Family **EDU:** Bachelor's Degree in Early Childhood Education, California State University, Sacramento **CERTS:** Certified Teacher for Grades (K-9); Certified Celebrity and Carnival Cruise Line Specialist; Certified Specialist for All Cruise Lines, Cruise Line International Association, Inc. **A/A/S:** Ambassador, Metro Chamber; Roseville Chamber of Commerce; Rancho Cordova Chamber of Commerce; Small Business Committee; Sports Foundation; eWomenNetwork **C/VW:** Volunteer, Chamber of Commerces; Bayside California Church
Email: sharon@joyofcruises.com
Email: sharon@healthisprecious.com
URL: http://www.joyofcruises.com
URL: http://www.healthisprecious.com

Gail P. Edmonds
Title: District-Wide Visual Arts Coordinator (Retired) **Company:** Middletown Public Schools **Address:** 311 Hunting Hill Avenue, Middletown, CT 06457 United States **BUS:** Art Education **P/S:** Curriculum Design and Assessment, Professional Staff Development **MA:** Connecticut, New York, Massachusetts **D/D/R:** Experienced Art Educator, Coordinator and Exhibiting Artist, State Consultant for Arts, Curriculum Design and Assessment **H/I/S:** Advocating, Painting, Traveling, Photography, Attending the Theater **EDU:** Master's Degree in Arts and Liberal Studies, Wesleyan University; Bachelor's Degree, College of New Rochelle, New Rochelle, NY **CERTS:** Certificate of Advanced Study, Wesleyan University, Middletown, CT **A/A/S:** Connecticut Art Education Association; National Art Education Association; Connecticut Association of Arts Administrators **A/H:** Who's Who Among American Art Teachers (2007, 2005, 2004); Outstanding Supervisor/Administrator of the Year, Connecticut Art Education Association **C/VW:** American Cancer Society; Alzheimer's Association
Email: gpedmonds@yahoo.com
URL: http://www.cambridgewhoswho.com

Annette J. Edwards
Title: Realtor **Company:** Sand Castle Realty Group, Inc. **Address:** 2220 Venetian Court, Suite Two, Naples, FL 34109 United States **BUS:** Real Estate Company **P/S:** Residential Real Estate Including Homes, Condominiums and Land **MA:** Regional **D/D/R:** Representing Buyers and Sellers, Buying and Selling Investment and Waterfront Properties, Helping Clients Find the Best Property for them, Scheduling Open Houses and Property Viewings, Meeting the Relocation Needs of Clients, Assisting First-Time Buyers **H/I/S:** Spending Time Outdoors, Playing Rugby, Traveling, Boating, Working on Home Improvement Projects **EDU:** Licensed Real Estate Agent (2004); Bachelor's Degree in Hospitality Management, Kent State University (2003) **A/A/S:** Florida Association of Realtors **A/H:** Top Selling Agent of the Year, National Association of Realtors **C/VW:** Local Church
Email: annette@sandcastlepros.com
URL: http://www.sandcastlepros.com

Betty T. Edwards
Title: Title I Teacher **Company:** Gilbert Elementary School **Address:** 314 Main Street, Gilbert, SC 29054 United States **BUS:** Rural Elementary School **P/S:** Elementary Education **MA:** Regional **D/D/R:** Teaching Elementary and Middle School Students, Title I Teaching for Students with Reading Disabilities **H/I/S:** Reading, Spending Time with Family **EDU:** Bachelor of Arts in Elementary Education, University of South Carolina (1970)
Email: bedwards@lexington1.net
URL: http://www.gilbertelementary.com

David Wayne Edwards
Title: Shift Manager **Company:** Dana Corporation **Address:** 750 N. Black Branch Road, Elizabethtown, KY 42701 United States **BUS:** Automotive Company **P/S:** Truck Frame Stamping **MA:** National **D/D/R:** Production Supervision, Leadership **H/I/S:** Farming **A/A/S:** Kentucky Cattlemen's Association; Republican Party

Jennifer Oaige Edwards
Title: Library Media Specialist **Company:** Barksdale Elementary School, Plano Independent School District **Address:** 2015 Elmsted Drive, Allen, TX 75013 United States **BUS:** Public Elementary School **P/S:** Education for Students in Kindergarten through Fifth-Grade, Library, Art, Music, Physical Education **MA:** Local **D/D/R:** Teaching Library Skills to Students in Kindergarten through Fifth-Grade, Reading Stories to Students, Assisting Students with Using Library Resources **H/I/S:** Reading, Dancing, Watching Movies **EDU:** Master's Degree in Library Science, University of North Texas (2000); Bachelor's Degree in Early Childhood Education, Texas Tech University (1998)
Email: pedwards712@yahoo.com
URL: http://k-12.pisd.edu/Schools/Barksdale/Brksdle.htm

Marta E. Edwards
Title: Administrator, Owner **Company:** Mana for Children **Address:** 345 E. 1830 S., Orem, UT 84058 United States **BUS:** Nonprofit Organization **P/S:** Working with Children **MA:** Regional **D/D/R:** Teacher for Elementary Education, Nutrition and Safety Awareness, Reimbursing Day Care Providers for Partial Expenses for Breakfast and Lunch, in Charge of 480 People **H/I/S:** Tennis, Swimming **EDU:** Ph.D. in English, National Commercial School (1963); Ph.D. in Music, National Commercial School (1962); Bachelor of Science in Accounting, National Commercial School (1962) **A/A/S:** American Legion; National Conservatory of Music in Buenos Aires; Latin Business Women's Association; U.S. Army, Central Command of Commissaries
Email: martha.edwards@comcast.net
URL: http://www.cambridgewhoswho.com

Mr. Michael R. Edwards
Title: Draftsman, Designer, Estimator, Project Manager **Company:** Profusion **Address:** 3245 Tyrone Boulevard N., Saint Petersburg, FL 33710 United States **BUS:** Metalwork Design, Fabrication and Installation Business **P/S:** Architectural Customized Metalwork, Railings, Kitchens, Doors, Furniture, Gates, Handrails, Home Decor, Outdoor Items **MA:** Regional **D/D/R:** Metalworking, Performing Estimates and Inside Sales, Drafting, Designing Products, Managing Daily Operations **H/I/S:** Old Cars, Fishing **EDU:** Associate Degree in Architect Drafting and Design, Schuylkill Institute of Business & Technology (2004); Coursework in Welding, Welder Training and Testing Institute (1990) **A/A/S:** DMA
Email: hannahound13@aol.com
URL: http://www.profusionusa.com

Ronnie E. Edwards
Title: Owner, President, Head Appraiser **Company:** Action Fast Appraisal Service, Inc. **Address:** P.O. Box 768, Tracy, CA 95378 United States **BUS:** Real Estate Appraisal Firm **P/S:** Real Estate Appraisal Services **MA:** Local **D/D/R:** real estate consulting and overseeing appraisal services **H/I/S:** Fishing, Biking, Football **CERTS:** Licensed Appraiser, California State University, Stanislaus
Email: actionaprslservice@sbcglobal.net

Ms. Sonia P. Edwards
Title: Real Estate Sales Agent **Company:** EXIT Premier Realty **Dept:** Sales **Address:** 9701 Apollo Drive, Suite 101, Largo, MD 20774 United States **BUS:** Real Estate Company **P/S:** Real Estate Selling and Listing Services **MA:** Regional **D/D/R:** Specializing in Residential and Commercial Real Estate Sales, Day Trading, Introducing People to the Real Estate Business, Analyzing the Market, Handling Relocations and Investment Properties **H/I/S:** Spending Time with her Family **EDU:** Pursuing Bachelor's Degree; Associate of Applied Science, Kingsborough Community College **A/A/S:** Prince Georges County Association of Realtors; Maryland Association of Realtors; National Association of Realtors
Email: soniaedwards2004@aol.com
URL: http://www.soniaedwardsepr.com

Tony L. Edwards
Title: Pastor **Company:** Pelzer Church of God **Address:** PO Box 276, Pelzer, SC 29669 United States **BUS:** Church **P/S:** Balances his Pastoral Duties of Visiting the Sick and the Elderly, Detention Centers, Preparing and Holding Funeral Services, Weddings, Baptisms, Etc, Offers his Advice and Council for Married Couples, Premarital Couples, Spiritual Counseling for Congregation and Community as well as Bereavement Counseling when Necessary **MA:** International **D/D/R:** Preaching, Singer and Musician **H/I/S:** Time with his Family, Saving Souls, Singing, Music **EDU:** Diploma in Christian Education, South Carolina Church of God State Bible and Music Institute, SC **CERTS:** Certified Minister, International Church of God, Minister Internship Program
Email: tledwards51@aol.com

Mr. Clarence C. Edwards Jr.
Title: Manager, Nuclear Medicine **Company:** The New York and Presbyterian Hospital **Address:** 1700 Metropolitan Avenue, Bronx, NY 10462 United States **BUS:** One the Most Comprehensive University Hospitals in the World, with Leading Specialists in Every Field of Medicine Dedicated to Excellence in Healthcare **P/S:** Services Include Cancer Care, Digestive Diseases, Geriatrics, Heart, Orthopedics, Neuroscience, Pediatrics, Psychiatry, Transplantation, Vascular, Women's Health and Many Other Services **MA:** International **EXP:** Mr. Edwards' expertise includes nuclear medicine, diagnostic imaging and radiographic isotopes. **D/D/R:** Overseeing Operations Including Equipment and Testing, Scheduling, Payroll, Employee Hiring **H/I/S:** Keyboard, Piano **EDU:** MBA in Business, University of Phoenix (2005) **A/A/S:** Society of Nuclear Medicine
Email: tech99m@msn.com
URL: http://www.nyp.org

Kristine A. Effaldana
Title: Vice President **Company:** R.K. Dana Pest Control Corporation **Address:** 160 N. Liberty Drive, Stony Point, NY 10980 United States **BUS:** Pest Control Technology Company **P/S:** Environmentally Friendly Baits, Botanical Sprays and Gels, Pest and Termite Monitoring, New Home Preventative Set-up, General Pest Control, Rodent Service, Termite Inspections, Bat Elimination, Snake Repellents, Mosquito Treatments, Fully Insured, Bonded, Chemical-Free Service, Low Risk Pesticides **MA:** Regional **D/D/R:** Identifying Bugs, Retail Management and Supervision, Education of Greener Pesticides, Consulting with Restaurants and Hospitals on Pesticides and Green Pesticide Use **H/I/S:** Bike Riding, Quading, Stain Glass, Aquatic Ponds **EDU:** Bachelor's Degree in Business, Berkeley College (1985) **A/A/S:** National Pest Control Association; Better Business Bureau; North Rockland Business Alliance; Chamber of Commerce; New York State Pest Control Association
Email: rkdana6@aol.com
URL: http://www.danapestcontrol.com

Cheryle Egan
Title: Owner, President **Company:** Imagine That Boutique **Address:** 514 Penn Avenue, West Reading, PA 19611 United States **BUS:** Fashion Boutique **P/S:** Contemporary Clothing, Jewelry and Gifts **MA:** Regional **D/D/R:** Ordering Merchandise that is Original and Unique, Contacting Vendors, All Administrative Duties, Bookkeeping, Advertising, Marketing **H/I/S:** Spending Time with Her Two Children, Husband and Dogs **EDU:** Coursework Completed, East Stroudsburg State College **A/A/S:** Banking Officer for Meridian Bank; Chamber of Commerce of Redding, Pennsylvania
Email: gcegan@comcast.net
URL: http://www.imaginethatboutique.com

April A. Egbert
Title: Manager, Lender Division **Company:** First American Title Company **Address:** 2 First American Way, San Clemente, CA 92672 United States **BUS:** Real Estate **P/S:** Sales, Title Insurance **H/I/S:** Skiing, Sailing **EDU:** Bachelor of Arts in Sociology, University of Colorado (1987) **A/A/S:** SOS
Email: aegbert@firstam.com
URL: http://www.firstam.com/oc

Weldon C. Egerton
Title: Technology Teacher **Company:** Durham Public Schools **Address:** 4800 Old Chapel Hill Road, Durham, NC 27707 United States **BUS:** Proven Leader in the Education Industry **P/S:** Quality Student Education Services, Teaching, Learning, Special Programs, Research **MA:** Local **D/D/R:** Math, Science, Engineering, Research and Test Alternative Transportation **H/I/S:** Coaching Track and Field, Playing Guitar, Working on a CD of Singing and Playing the Guitar **EDU:** Bachelor's Degree in Technology Education, Elizabeth City State University **A/A/S:** Alpha Phi Omega; Ordained Minister; Elder, The Rebirth Deliverance Ministries
Email: weldon.egerton@dpsnc.net
URL: http://www.dpsnc.net

Marjean P. Ehlers
Title: Co-Director **Company:** Wesley Foundation **Address:** 549 W. Fourth Street, Maryville, MO 64468 United States **BUS:** Religious Organization **P/S:** Worship **MA:** International **D/D/R:** Counseling Young Adult and Students **H/I/S:** Spending Time with her Family, Artistically Designing Altars **EDU:** Doctor of Education in Leadership, University of Missouri; Master's Degree in Counseling, University of Iowa; Bachelor of Arts in Psychology and Sociology, Northwest Missouri State University **A/A/S:** Foundational Work, St. Paul School of Theology **C/VW:** Wesley Foundation, Mozambique Partnership with Seminary Students
Email: m500275@mwmissouri.edu

Janna M. Ehrke
Title: Minimum Data Set and Clinical Coordinator **Company:** Fort Atkinson Memorial Health Services **Address:** 611 Sherman Avenue, Fort Atkinson, WI 53538 United States **BUS:** Hospital **P/S:** Healthcare **MA:** Local **EXP:** Ms. Ehrke's expertise includes geriatrics and rehabilitation. **H/I/S:** Watching Sports, Spending Time with her Children **EDU:** Associate Degree in Nursing, Blackhawk Technical College **CERTS:** Certified Firefighter **C/VW:** Volunteer, Breast Cancer Awareness Program
Email: ehrkej@earthlink.net
URL: http://www.cambridgewhoswho.com

Laura A. Eickmeier, MA
Title: Curriculum Director, High School English Teacher **Company:** Pinewood School **Dept:** English **Address:** 26800 W. Fremont Road, Los Altos Hills, CA 94022 United States **BUS:** Nonprofit Private School **P/S:** Kindergarten through Twelfth-Grade, Rigorous Academics, Student Involvement and Athletic Programs, Scholarship Programs, Enriching Students with Critical Thinking, Writing, Reading, Speaking, Research and Organizational Skills, Small Class Sizes **MA:** Local **D/D/R:** Teaching 11th-Grade British Literature, Implementing School Curriculum, Teaching the Faculty **H/I/S:** Traveling, Antiques, Collecting Vintage Quilts, Music **EDU:** Master of Arts in Education, Oakland University (1979) **CERTS:** Certification in Secondary Education (1978) **A/A/S:** Association for Supervision and Curriculum Development
Email: leickmeier@pinewood.edu
URL: http://pinewood.edu

Dr. John E. Eiland
Title: Physician **Company:** Providence Centralia Hospital **Address:** 1000 S. Scheuber Road, Centralia, WA 98531 United States **BUS:** Hospital **P/S:** Healthcare and Medical Services Including Obstetrics and Gynecology **MA:** Regional **EXP:** Dr. Eiland's expertise includes obstetrics and gynecology. **H/I/S:** Golfing, Playing Tennis, Traveling **EDU:** MD, Western University of Health Services **A/A/S:** ACOBGYN; American Medical Association
Email: john.eiland@providence.org
URL: http://www.providence.org

Patricia I. Eimerl
Title: Teacher **Company:** Oakland Unified School District **BUS:** School District **P/S:** Education **MA:** Local **D/D/R:** teaching American civil war and American history **H/I/S:** Reading, Crocheting, Spending Time with her Family **EDU:** Bachelor of Arts in History, University of Redlands
Email: patricia.eimerl@cwwemail.com
Email: patriciaeimerl@comcast.net
URL: http://www.ousd.k12.ca.us

Christopher J. Eirich, CPCU
Title: President **Company:** Quality Adjustments, Inc **Address:** 950 1st Street, Winter Haven, FL 33880 United States **BUS:** Insurance Adjusting **P/S:** Adjustments Services **MA:** International **D/D/R:** General Adjuster **H/I/S:** Model Rail Roading 'O' Scale **EDU:** Master of Science in Insurance and Risk Management, NE University; La Salle University **A/A/S:** Roman Catholic, NAIA, CPCU, Knights of Columbus
Email: ceirich@qualityadjustments.com
URL: www.qualityadjustments.com

Janice Eisen
Title: Manager of Student Information Systems **Company:** Pearland Independent School District **Address:** 2316 Old Alvin Road, Pearland, TX 77581 United States **BUS:** Local Public School District Serving the Residents of Pearland **P/S:** Public Kindergarten through12th Education for the Students of Pearland **MA:** Local **D/D/R:** Overseeing Student Database Systems, Supervising a Team of Five Employees, Working with Computer Programming **EDU:** Bachelor's Degree in Speech, Oklahoma Christian University (1978) **A/A/S:** Founding Member, Women Leadership; Executive Board Member, United Way; Women's Leadership Society; Member, Habitat for Humanity
Email: wrjseisen@sbcglobal.net
URL: http://www.cambridgewhoswho.com

Cynthia M. Eismann
Title: Nurse Consultant **Company:** Omnicare Pharmacy Services **Address:** 2850 Milford Square Pike, Quakertown, PA 18951 United States **BUS:** Nursing Home **P/S:** Nursing Services, Long Term Care Facilities, Assisted Living and Pharmaceuticals **MA:** National **D/D/R:** Consulting, Developing Staff, Education, Training **H/I/S:** Gardening **EDU:** Certified Legal Nurse Consultant, College of Professional Studies (2003); Associate of Science in Medical Laboratory Technology, Biscayne Paramedical Institute (1976); Bachelor of Science in Health Services; Bachelor of Arts, Almeda University **A/A/S:** Pennsylvania Association of Directors of Nursing Administration; National League for Nursing **C/VW:** American Red Cross, VITA Tutoring Program
Email: cynthia.eismann@omnicare.com
URL: http://www.cambridgewhoswho.com

Amer El Souki
Title: Project Manager **Company:** Tech. Inc. **Address:** 9701 Philadelphia Ct, Suite E, Lanham, MD 20706 United States **BUS:** Telecommunications Company **P/S:** Telecommunications in Computers, Audio-Visual and Security Contractors **MA:** Regional **D/D/R:** Scheduling, Construction, Management **H/I/S:** Traveling, Basketball **EDU:** Master's Degree in Telecommunications, George Mason University **A/H:** National Dean's List **C/VW:** Various Charities
Email: aelsouki@yahoo.com
URL: http://www.cambridgewhoswho.com

Sherri L. Elam
Title: President, Owner **Company:** Millennium Mortgage Financial, Inc. **Address:** 4004 N. College Avenue, Suite J, Fayetteville, AR 72703 United States **BUS:** Residential and Commercial Lending Company **P/S:** Residential and Commercial Lending **MA:** Statewide **D/D/R:** lending and helping her clients achieve financial wellness **H/I/S:** Competing in a Women's Doubles Tennis League, Playing Piano **CERTS:** Certified Mortgage Broker; Certification in Identity Theft **A/A/S:** Chamber of Commerce; Business Network International; Public Speaker, Women in Victory; Single Parent Organizations **C/VW:** Single Parent Women's Organizations; Shelters; Churches
Email: sherri@millenniummortgage.biz
URL: http://www.millenniummortgage.biz

Betty Haynes Elder
Title: Teacher **Company:** Robert E. Lee High School **Address:** 411 E. Loop 323, Tyler, TX 75701 United States **BUS:** High School **P/S:** Counselors, Food Services, Library Services, Fine Arts, Athletics, Technology, Physical Education, Health Services, Mathematics, Science, Social Studies, English as a Second Language and English I through IV **MA:** Regional **D/D/R:** Teaching English, Art and Spanish to Students in Ninth to 12th-Grades, Offering English as a Second Language Course **H/I/S:** Reading, Sewing, Walking, Gardening, Traveling **EDU:** Bachelor of Arts in Education, Spanish and English, Minor in Art, Stephen F. Austin State University (1972) **A/A/S:** Texas Foreign Language Association; Texas State Teachers Association; National Education Association; Phi Delta Kappa
Email: beld7982@yahoo.com
URL: http://www.tylerisd.org/Schools/REL

Dorothy A. Eldreth, RN, MSN, CNA-BC
Title: Patient Care Manager **Company:** Bryn Mawr Hospital **Address:** 130 S. Bryn Mawr Avenue, Bryn Mawr, PA 19010 United States **BUS:** Nonprofit Health System **P/S:** Healthcare **MA:** Regional **D/D/R:** Mentoring, Overseeing Nursing Staff and Clinical Coordinator **H/I/S:** Cooking, Scrapbooking, Reading, Quilting, Spending Time with her Family **EDU:** Master of Science in Nursing, Wilmington College **A/A/S:** American Organization of Nurse Executives; Sigma Theta Tau
Email: deldreth@verizon.net
URL: http://www.cambridgewhoswho.com

Elizabeth Elgin-Disney
Title: English Teacher **Company:** Burleigh Manor Middle School, National Blue Ribbon School **Address:** 8612 Spruce Run Court, Ellicott City, MD 21042 United States **BUS:** Public Middle School **P/S:** Academics, Fine Arts and Enrichment Programs for All Students with Challenging, Rigorous and Appropriate Course of Studies **MA:** Regional **D/D/R:** Secondary English Education, Coordinating Service Learning, Developing and Implementing Curriculum, Teaching Research Technique to the Entire School **H/I/S:** Traveling, Reading **EDU:** Graduate Coursework in English, Loyola College (1993) **A/A/S:** Served as Curriculum Writer, Teacher and Director of the Saturday Program for Inner-City Children, Maryland Center for Thinking Studies, Baltimore, MD
Email: edisney@hcpss.org
URL: http://www.hcpss.org

Pamela A. Elisofon
Title: Attorney **Company:** Elisofon Law Office **Address:** 26 Court Street, Suite 2515, Brooklyn, NY 11242 United States **BUS:** Private Law Practice **P/S:** General Practice Law **MA:** Regional **D/D/R:** Working in Civil Litigation, Personal Injury, Negligence, Real Estate, Wills, Probate, Immigration, Contracts and Administrative Law with Individuals and Businesses, Handling All Human Resources, Accounting, Advertising and Employment Discrimination Law **H/I/S:** Tennis, Reading, Theater, Ballet **EDU:** JD, St. John's University Law School (1992); Bachelor's Degree in Business, Adelphi University (1988) **A/A/S:** Director, Brooklyn Bar Association; Co-Chairwoman, Employment and Labor Law Committee; Former Vice President, President (2008); Brooklyn Women's Bar Association; Arbitrator, Kings County Small Claims Court; Jewish Lawyers Guild; National Employment and Labor Law Association; Brooklyn Torah Club; Director, Hypothetical Theatre Company; Director, Brooklyn Chapter, St. John's Law School Alumni Association
Email: pelisofon@yahoo.com
URL: http://www.elisofonlawoffice.com

Ricky L. Elkins, RN, BSN
Title: Registered Nurse, BSN **Company:** American Nursing (Travel Nurse) **Address:** 3331 Lexington Road, Richmond, KY 40475 United States **BUS:** Nursing Company Dedicated to Excellence in Healthcare **P/S:** Nursing Services, Traveling Nursing Services, Emergency Room, Corrections **MA:** Regional **D/D/R:** Emergency Room, IV Fluids, Calculates Fluids, Assessment of Pain Levels for Patients **H/I/S:** Gliders **EDU:** Bachelor of Science Degree in Nursing, University of Kentucky (2000) **A/A/S:** Civil Air Patrol; Emergency Nurses Association
Email: eclipse2003@qx.net
URL: http://www.cambridgewhoswho.com

Monica R. Ellerbe
Title: Special Education Teacher **Company:** Dekalb County Board of Education **Address:** 3770 North Decatur Road, Decatur, GA 30034 United States **BUS:** Public Education **P/S:** Maximizes Students' Social and Academic Potential, Preparing Them to Compete in a Global Society **MA:** Regional **D/D/R:** Working with Special Education Students in Mathematics and Language Arts, Responsible for Individualizing Lesson Plans and Helping Administer Standardized Tests to Students, Teaching Kindergarten to Fifth-Grade within Pull Out Classes **H/I/S:** Reading, Swimming **EDU:** Pursuing Ph.D. in Special Education, Argosy University **A/A/S:** National Education Association; Georgia Association of Educators; Delta Sigma Theta Sorority International; New Birth Missionary Baptist Church
Email: mrealmondjay@bellsouth.net
URL: http://www.dekalb.k12.ga.us

Randall L. Ellington
Title: Consultant, President **Company:** Ellington Consulting, Inc. **Address:** 1540 Skyview Drive, Holts Summit, MO 65043 United States **BUS:** Computer Consulting Company **P/S:** Selection, Installation and Administration of Linux and Aix Systems **MA:** Midwest **D/D/R:** AIX Systems **H/I/S:** Camping, Hunting, Listening to and performing Music **EDU:** Associate Degree in Electronics Communications, Indiana Vocational Technical College **CERTS:** Certified IBM AIX Systems Administrator; Certified IBM AIX Installation and Recovery Specialist; Certified AIX Instructor **C/VW:** Open Arms Crisis Pregnancy Center, Children International, Missouri Narcotics Officer's Association, Missouri Sherrif's Association
Email: randye@ellingtonci.com
URL: http://www.ellingtonci.com

Barbara S. Elliott
Title: Choral Director **Company:** Heritage High School **Address:** 3020 Wards Ferry Road, Lynchburg, VA 24502 United States **BUS:** High School **P/S:** Music Education **MA:** Local **D/D/R:** Directing the Choir **H/I/S:** Reading **EDU:** Master's Degree in Special Education, Lynchburg College (1984) **A/A/S:** Music Educators National Conference
Email: albarjes3@aol.com
URL: http://www.cambridgewhoswho.com

Kathleen M. Elliott
Title: Licensed Practical Nurse **Company:** Lancia's Villa Royal **Address:** 1991 Crocker Road, Westlake, OH 44145 United States **BUS:** Nursing Home, Extended Care Unit **P/S:** Healthcare **MA:** National **D/D/R:** Geriatric Nursing **H/I/S:** Woodworking, Crocheting, Glass Painting **CERTS:** Licensed Practical Nurse, Bellaire School of Practical Nursing, State of Ohio **C/VW:** Alzheimer's Foundation of America

Raymond J. Elliott
Title: Instructor of Reading **Company:** St. Philip's College **Address:** 1801 Martin Luther King Drive, San Antonio, TX 78203 United States **BUS:** Community College **P/S:** Higher Education **MA:** Regional **D/D/R:** Teaching Reading Development to Students **EDU:** Master of Arts in Adult Education, University of the Incarnate Word (1994); Master of Business Administration, University of the Incarnate Word (1990) **A/A/S:** Texas Community College Teachers Association
Email: relliott@accd.edu
URL: http://www.accd.edu/

Bobbi F. Ellis, LPN
Title: Staff Nurse, Charge Nurse **Company:** Wesley Manor Retirement Community Healthcare Center **Address:** 1015 E. Manslick Road, Louisville, KY 40219 United States **BUS:** Healthcare **P/S:** Quality Long-Term Care **MA:** Local **D/D/R:** Handling Admissions, Administration, Staff, Dispensing Medication **H/I/S:** Yard Work, Reading **CERTS:** First Aid, CPR; Licensed Practical Nurse **C/VW:** Volunteers Time with her Daughter's School
Email: bossyb1126@insightbb.com

Jan L. Ellis
Title: Real Estate Professional **Company:** Remax **Address:** 405 S.W. Fedgwick Road, Suite 101, Port Orchard, WA 98367 United States **BUS:** Real Estate Agency **P/S:** Real Estate Exchange **MA:** Local **EXP:** Ms. Ellis' expertise is in real estate listing. **D/D/R:** Managing the Purchase and Sale of Properties, Assisting Clients, Reselling Homes Including Waterfront and Vacant Land **H/I/S:** Traveling, Photography **EDU:** Coursework, Washington State University **A/A/S:** Washington Association of Realtors; National Association of Realtors **C/VW:** Volunteer, Habitat for Humanity
Email: jan.ellis@cwwemail.com
Email: janellis16@hotmail.com
URL: http://www.cambridgewhoswho.com

Pamela J. Ellis
Title: Owner **Company:** Global Hands Fair Trade Shop, LLC **Address:** 252 Center Street, Lake Geneva, WI 53147 United States **BUS:** Retail, Fair Trade **P/S:** Supports Artisans and Farmers, Supplying Handcrafted Items From Around the World **MA:** International **D/D/R:** Spirituality, Horticulture, Forestry **H/I/S:** Endurance Exercising, Running, Swimming **EDU:** Associate Degree in Horticulture and Forestry, University of Wyoming; Coursework, Gateway Technical School **A/A/S:** Fair Trade Federation; Chamber of Commerce; Women's Groups
Email: marvls@tds.net

Suzanne Marie Ellis
Title: Doctor of Veterinary Medicine **Company:** Toms River Animal Hospital **Address:** 769 Route 37 W., Toms River, NJ 08755 United States **BUS:** Animal Hospital **P/S:** Veterinary Medicine **MA:** Local **D/D/R:** Caring for Cats and Dogs **H/I/S:** Cooking, Watching Football **EDU:** Doctor of Veterinary Medicine, Ross University **A/A/S:** American Veterinary Medical Association
Email: suzannedvm@comcast.net

Jeanie Ellison Connell
Title: Managing Director **Company:** Northern Trust **Address:** 2701 Kirby, Houston, TX 77098 United States **BUS:** Leader in Finance **P/S:** Asset Management, Trust Fiduciary Services **MA:** National **D/D/R:** Lending, Client Contacting, Administration, Managing a Portfolio of 90 Million Dollars **H/I/S:** Baseball, Houston Astros, Golfing, Running, Reading, Tennis, Volunteer Work **EDU:** Master's Degree in English, Sam Houston State University (1979); Bachelor's Degree in English, University of Texas (1969) **A/A/S:** Delta Gamma National Fraternity; Board of Trustees, Houston Grand Opera; Board Member, Memorial Park Conservatory
Email: jec3@ntrs.com
URL: http://www.northerntrust.com

Donna L. Ellsworth
Title: Group Sales Coordinator **Company:** Eastern States Exposition **Address:** 1305 Memorial Avenue, West Springfield, MA 01089 United States **BUS:** Nonprofit organization **P/S:** Development and Promotion of Agriculture, Education, Industry and Family Entertainment **MA:** National **D/D/R:** overseeing advanced ticket sales, group sales and motorcoach tours **H/I/S:** Reading, Cooking **EDU:** Coursework, High School of Commons (1969)
Email: groupsales@thebige.com
URL: http://www.thebige.com

Ms. Abigail Elowsky
Title: Manager **Company:** R.L. Polk **Address:** 26955 Northwestern Highway, Southfield, MI 48033 United States **BUS:** Automotive **P/S:** Automotive Information and Marketing Solutions to the Automotive World and its Related Industries **MA:** International **D/D/R:** Overseeing Project Management **H/I/S:** Playing Volleyball **EDU:** Bachelor of Arts, Chemistry and Biology, Kalamazoo College (1996)
Email: abigail_kirkwood@polk.com
URL: http://www.polk.com

Catherine A. Elwell
Title: Professor **Company:** 1) Saint Leo University 2) Walden University **Dept:** Department of Criminal Justice **Address:** 111 Halemaumau Street, Honolulu, HI 96821 United States **BUS:** University **P/S:** Higher Education **MA:** National **D/D/R:** teaching criminal justice and criminology, Writing her Dissertation **H/I/S:** Listening to Music, Sewing, Gourmet Cooking, Reading, Writing **EDU:** Doctoral Degree in Criminal Justice, Walden University, MN; Associate Degree **A/A/S:** Academy of Criminal Justice Sciences; American Society of Criminology; American Correctional Association; National Institute of Justice; National Criminal Justice Research and Science Association; Alpha Phi Sigma; Pi Sigma Alpha; Phi Theta Kappa **C/VW:** March of Dimes; American Breast Cancer Foundation; The Kidney Foundation
Email: elwellc@hawall.rr.com

Jean Anderson Embree
Title: 1) Author 2) Adjunct Professor of English **Company:** 1) Word Works Publishers 2) Evergreen Valley College **Address:** 4095 Yerba Buena Avenue, San Jose, CA 95121 United States **BUS:** 1) Publishing Company 2) College **P/S:** 1) College Textbooks 2) Higher Education **MA:** National **D/D/R:** teaching communication studies, writing sonnets and college textbooks **H/I/S:** Traveling, Reading, Spending Time with her Grandchildren **EDU:** Master of Arts in English Literature, San Jose State University; Bachelor of Arts in English Literature and Teaching, Minor in Psychology, University of California, Berkeley **CERTS:** Certified Online Educator **A/A/S:** Young Rhetoricians; International Association for the Fantastic in the Arts; Health Care for All; TYTO Association; FDA Union **C/VW:** Board Member, Unitarian Church; National Organization of Women; The Institute for Science and Technology
Email: jaembree@aol.com
URL: http://www.angelfire.com/poetry/jaembree

Patricia A. Emerson
Title: Licensed Marriage and Family Therapist **Company:** Patricia Emerson, Ph.D. **Address:** 41770 12th Street West, Suite C, Palmdale, CA 93551 United States **BUS:** Proven Leader in the Field of Counseling and Therapy **P/S:** High Quality Marriage and Family Therapy Services to Clients **MA:** Regional **D/D/R:** Individual and Couple's Counseling Regarding Divorce, Personality Disorders, Dissociation, Anxiety, Anger, Depression, Alcohol and Drug Dependency, Domestic Violence, Sexual Abuse and Incest **H/I/S:** Walking, Singing **EDU:** Ph.D. in Sociology, Specializations in Gender Studies and Marriage and Family Therapy, University of Southern California (2000); Master of Science in Community Counseling, Winona State University (1991); Master of Arts in Psychology and Sociology, Winona State University (1988) **A/A/S:** American Association of Marriage and Family Therapists; California Association of Marriage and Family Therapists; Association of Family and Conciliation Courts
Email: drpat@drpatriciaaemerson.com
URL: http://www.drpatriciaaemerson.com

Mary Kay Emery
Title: Special Education Teacher **Company:** Socorro Independent School District **Dept:** Myrtle Cooper Elementary School **BUS:** Elementary School **P/S:** Primary Education **MA:** Local **D/D/R:** educating medically fragile students, managing real estate sales and nursing, Assisting and Counseling Parents of Medically Fragile Students, Teaching Special Education, Caring for Medically Fragile Students **H/I/S:** Spending Time with her Family and Friends, Reading, Scuba Diving, Helping Others **EDU:** Bachelor of Science in Education, with a Concentration in Mental Retardation, The University of Texas at El Paso **A/A/S:** School Improvement Team; Delta Kappa Gamma **C/VW:** Local Church; March of Dimes; Special Olympics; Alzheimer's Association; American Cancer Society
Email: memery@sisd.net

D. Bart Emigh
Title: Team Leader **Company:** Pocatello Vet Center **Address:** 1800 Garrett Way, Pocatello, ID 83201 United States **BUS:** Readjustment Counseling Center **P/S:** Counseling Services for Combat Veterans **MA:** National **D/D/R:** Counseling War-Era United States Veterans **H/I/S:** Woodworking, Fishing **EDU:** Master of Arts in History, Santa Clara University; Master's Degree in Counseling, Santa Clara University **A/A/S:** Lifetime Member, Veterans of Foreign Wars
Email: bartemigh@msn.com

Rhea Emmer, C.S.A.
Title: Founder **Company:** The Center to Be **Address:** 53 Lenora Cresent, Fond Du Lac, WI 54935 United States **BUS:** Nonprofit Organization **P/S:** Spiritual Awareness and Education, Leadership Development **MA:** National **D/D/R:** Developing Spirituality Programs **H/I/S:** Traveling, Watching Football, Horse Back Riding **EDU:** Doctorate of Ministry, Spirituality, University of Creation Spirituality, Oakland, CA; Master of Arts in Spirituality, Creighton University, Omaha, NE; Bachelor of Science in Nursing, Marian College
Email: rheacsa@charter.net
URL: http://www.thecentertobe.org

Jimmy K. Emmons
Title: Owner, Founder **Company:** Circle E Farms **Address:** P.O. Box 56, Leedey, OK 73654 United States **BUS:** Farm **P/S:** Farming, Ranching **MA:** Local **EXP:** Mr. Emmons' expertise includes sales and marketing. **H/I/S:** Traveling, Car Riding **EDU:** Diploma, Leedey High School **A/A/S:** Fundraiser, President, National Young Farmer Educational Association; Dewey County Conservation District
Email: jimmyemmons@hotmail.com
URL: http://www.cambridgewhoswho.com

Dr. Robert A. Emry
Title: Professor in Human Communications **Company:** California State University at Fullerton **Address:** Fullerton, CA 92834 United States **BUS:** University **P/S:** Higher Education for Undergraduate and Graduate Students, Honor Programs, Internship Opportunities, Academic Scholarships, Athletic Scholarships **MA:** Regional **D/D/R:** Teaching Intercultural and Human Communications, Civic Engagement, Relations and Community Building **H/I/S:** Exercising **EDU:** Ph.D. in Speech Communications, The University of Kansas (1976) **A/A/S:** American Society for Training and Development; National Communication Association; Western State Communication Association
Email: remry@fullerton.edu
URL: http://www.fullerton.edu

Mr. Jason Blair Encinas
Title: Test Operator **Company:** Hewlett Packard **Address:** 2617 Marathon Drive, San Diego, CA 92123 United States **BUS:** Information Technology Company **P/S:** Information Technology Services **MA:** Regional **EXP:** Mr. Encinas' expertise is in information technology. **D/D/R:** Computer networking and Linux operating systems, Conducting Hardware Tests on Projects, Ensuring all Phases of Testing are Completed and its Functionality is Maintained after Each Test, Troubleshooting, Monitoring Network **H/I/S:** Golfing, Soccer **EDU:** Associate of Science in Information Technology Computer Networking System, ITT Technical Institute (2007) **A/A/S:** Free Software Foundation
Email: jason.encinas@gmail.com
URL: http://www.cambridgewhoswho.com

Ronald Eng
Title: Associate Agricultural Biologist **Company:** California Department of Food and Agriculture **Address:** 1220 N. Street, Room 341, Sacramento, CA 95814 United States **BUS:** State Department of Food and Agriculture **P/S:** Food and Agriculture Protection **MA:** California **D/D/R:** Controlling Vegetation in Three Counties, Test Management **H/I/S:** Flying Planes, Scuba Diving **EDU:** Bachelor's Degree in Biological Science, California State University at Sacramento **C/VW:** Local Church
Email: reng@cdfa.ca.gov

Dr. Pherbia Ann Engdahl
Title: Principal (Retired) **Company:** St. Johns County School District **Address:** 40 Orange Street, Saint Augustine, FL 32084 United States **BUS:** School District **P/S:** Education **MA:** Regional **EXP:** Dr. Engdahl's area of expertise is in theater arts. **D/D/R:** Developing curriculum and instruction programs **H/I/S:** Reading, Spending Time at the Beach, Caring for her Dog **EDU:** Ph.D. in Curriculum, Instruction and Administration, Andrews University; Educational Specialist Degree **CERTS:** Licensed Superintendent **A/A/S:** Association for Supervision and Curriculum Development; Pi Beta Phi **C/VW:** Local Church
Email: engdahp@stjohns.k12.fl.us
URL: http://www.cambridgewhoswho.com

William H. Engelleitner
Title: Consultant **Company:** AME Pittsburgh **Address:** 133 Tory Road, Moon Township, PA 15108 United States **BUS:** Environmental Consulting **P/S:** Metals, Minerals, Coal, Chemicals, Consulting in the Fields of Powder and Bulk Solids Size Enlargement, Agglomeration **MA:** International **D/D/R:** Size Enlargement by Agglomeration, Solids Processing **H/I/S:** Walking and Hiking, Reading, Music, Cooking **EDU:** Bachelor of Science in Mechanical Engineering, Technical University at Darmstadt; Coursework in Business Management, Penn State University **A/A/S:** Institute for Briquitting and Agglomeration, Publishes in Powder and Bulk Engineering, Center for Professional Advancement (Agglomeration Technology Course Director, 1994-2001)
Email: info@CambridgeWhosWho.com

Sharon Kay Enget
Title: Elementary Teacher **Company:** McKinley Elementary School **Address:** 1740 Constance Boulevard N.E., Andover, MN 55304 **BUS:** Elementary School **P/S:** Education **MA:** Local **D/D/R:** Teaching Kindergarten through First Grade Students **H/I/S:** Reading, Collecting Antique, Shopping, Spending Time with her Children, Preaching the Gospel **EDU:** Bachelor of Science in Education with Kindergarten Endorsement, St. Cloud State University, Minnesota (1978) **A/A/S:** Minnesota Education Association **C/VW:** Sharing and Caring Hands; Church and Youth
Email: sharon.enget@anoka.k12.mn.us

Candace A. K. English
Title: Team Leader Trauma **Company:** National Staffing Solutions **Address:** 1324 Lakeland Hills Boulevard, Lakeland, FL 33805 United States **BUS:** Staffing Agency **P/S:** Hiring, Recruiting and Staffing Services **MA:** Local **D/D/R:** Nursing, Overseeing the Trauma Team **H/I/S:** Swimming, Spending Time with her Children **EDU:** Associate Degree in Nursing, Polk Community College **CERTS:** Certification in Advanced Cardiac Life Support; Certified Trauma Nurse Core Curriculum Instructor; Certification, Emergency Nursing Pediatric Course **A/A/S:** Emergency Nurses Association; Florida Nurses Association **C/VW:** Local High School; Local Fire Department; United Way; American Cancer Society; Hardee Swim Association
Email: englishrn@embarqmail.com
URL: http://www.cambridgewhoswho.com

Patrick G. Engstrom
Title: Chairman, Founder **Company:** Knowledge Factor, Inc. **Address:** 1553 Platte Street, Suite 300, Denver, CO 80202 United States **BUS:** Online Career Training Institute **P/S:** Education Including ASP Learning, Confidence-Based Learning and Online Programs **MA:** National **EXP:** Mr. Engstrom's areas of expertise include general management and human resources. **D/D/R:** Managing the company management team, networking, **H/I/S:** Motorcycling **EDU:** Master's Degree in Engineering, California State University (1980); Bachelor's Degree in Engineering, Colorado State University (1963)
Email: pengstrom@knowlegefactor.com
URL: http://www.knowledgefactor.com

James V. Enoch
Title: Owner **Company:** James Enoch Cleaning Company **Address:** 2414 Bywood Road, Greensboro, NC 27405 United States **BUS:** Professional Cleaning Service Provider **P/S:** Professional Floor Cleaning **MA:** Local **D/D/R:** Cleaning Floors **H/I/S:** Golfing, Reading, Travel **EDU:** Associate Degree, Jefferson College
Email: enoch1793@bellsouth.net

Audrey W. Eoff
Title: Educational Consultant **Address:** 503 Dawson Street, Weslaco, TX 78596 United States **BUS:** Public Education **P/S:** Workshops for Teachers Using the Newspaper, Leadership Training Seminars Pre-K through College in All Subjects **MA:** Regional **D/D/R:** Teaching in Homes and Schools **H/I/S:** Crafts **EDU:** Post Graduate Work, University of Texas Pan American (1960-1965); Master of Arts in Elementary Education, Texas A&M International University; Bachelor of Arts in Elementary Education, Texas A&M International University **A/A/S:** Newspaper Association of America; World Association of Newspapers, Epsilon Sigma Alpha International; Tesan Editor of Texas Newspaper in Education; St. Pius the Tenth Literacy Committee; Music Ministry; Lector Ministry **A/H:** Texas Outstanding ESA'er (2005-2006)
Email: aeoff@rgv.rr.com
URL: http://www.cambridgewhoswho.com

Stewart Epstein
Title: Physician **Company:** Macomb Medical Clinic **Address:** 2405 E. 14 Mile, Sterling Heights, MI 48310 United States **BUS:** General Family Medical Practice **P/S:** Patient Care, Clinical Evaluations, Testing, Diagnosis, Weight Loss Programs, Internal Medicine, Addiction Medicine **D/D/R:** Teaching the Staff about Medical Practices **H/I/S:** Golfing **EDU:** Doctor of Osteopathic, College of Osteopathic Medicine (1969) **A/A/S:** American Medical Association; American Osteopathic Association; Macomb County Medical Society
Email: stew5660@comcast.net
URL: http://www.macombmedicalclinic.com

Steve Erchul
Title: Shareholder **Company:** Smith, Schafer & Associates, LTD **Address:** 6800 France Avenue S., Suite 555, Eclima, MN 55435 United States **BUS:** Accounting Firm **P/S:** Audit, Reviews and Compilation Services, Tax Planning and Preparation, Business Consulting, Bookkeeping, Business Succession Planning, Financial Forecasts and Projections, Business Valuations, Estate and Retirement Planning, Accounting Software Selection and Implementation, Financial Planning, Cash Flow and Budgetary Analysis **MA:** Local **D/D/R:** Tax Planning, Managing Tax Returns, General Business Planning **H/I/S:** Golfing, Biking, Soccer **EDU:** Master's Degree in Taxation, University of Minnesota (2001); Bachelor's Degree, North Dakota State University (1993) **A/A/S:** American Institute of Certified Public Accountants
Email: s.erchul@smithschafer.com
URL: http://www.smithschafer.com

Geneva O. Erdahl
Title: Psychotherapist **Company:** Marriage Family Child Therapy **Address:** 901 E. Tahquitz Canyon Way, Suite A201, Palm Springs, CA 92262 United States **BUS:** Mental Healthcare **P/S:** Multi-Cultural Counseling Services **MA:** Regional **D/D/R:** Managing Private Practice, Dealing with Foster Care and Group Home Individuals, Specializing in Adolescence Counseling and Family Therapy **H/I/S:** Swimming, Dancing **EDU:** Master's Degree in Clinical Psychology, Pepperdine University, Los Angeles, California (1971) **A/A/S:** California Association of Marriage and Family Therapists; American Association of Marriage and Family Therapists
Email: geneva.erdahl@cwwemail.com

Arlene M. Erickson
Title: 1) Public Health School Nurse 2) Geriatric Nurse **Company:** 1) Richfield Intermediate School, Centennial Grade School 2) Bloomington Healthcare & Rehabilitation **Address:** 100 S.W. 195th Avenue, Unit 105, Beaverton, OR 97006 United States **BUS:** 1) Public Schools 2) Nursing Home **P/S:** 1) Education 2) Skilled Nursing, Residential Healthcare **MA:** Regional **D/D/R:** Counseling Students and Parents, Monitoring 80-100 Students' Health, Training Nursing Staff, Director of Nurses for Castle Ridge Care Center **H/I/S:** Gardening, Reading, Knitting, Hand Quilting, Crocheting **EDU:** Bachelor of Science in Public Health Nursing, Minor in Education, Mounds-Midway School of Nursing; Bachelor of Science in Nursing, University of Minnesota (1965) **A/A/S:** Minnesota Nurses Association

Kelly L. Erickson
Title: Special Education Teacher **Company:** Central Bucks High School West **Dept:** Public High School **Address:** 375 W. Court Street, Doylestown, PA 18901 United States **BUS:** School **P/S:** Education for 10th through 12th-Grade Students **MA:** Local **D/D/R:** Teaching Special Education **H/I/S:** Tennis, Skiing, Traveling **EDU:** Master of Education in Elementary and Special Education, La Salle University; Bachelor of Arts, The University of Maryland **A/A/S:** Phi Lambda Beta; Council for Exceptional Children
Email: kerickson@cbsd.org

Jane M. Erickson-Linder
Title: Speech and Language Pathologist **Company:** South Washington County Schools **Address:** 1251 School Drive, Woodbury, MN 55125 United States **BUS:** Special Education **P/S:** Speech and Language in Early Childhood Development, Teaching Children How to Talk **MA:** Regional **EXP:** Ms. Erickson-Linder's area of expertise is in speech-language pathology. **D/D/R:** Speaking to Daycare Groups, Serving Asperger's and Autistic Population **H/I/S:** Winter Sports, Animals, Reading, Music, Spending Family Time **EDU:** Master of Education in Communication Disorders, University of Wisconsin (1984); Bachelor of Science in Education and Communication Disorders, St. Cloud State University **A/A/S:** American Speech-Language-Hearing Association
Email: jerickson@sowashco.k12.mn.us

Lauren A. Erlichman, M.Ed.
Title: Autism Specialist **Company:** Advocating for Autism **Address:** 21 E. Jefferson Circle, Pittsford, NY 14534 United States **BUS:** Educational Center **P/S:** Special Education **MA:** Regional **D/D/R:** training parents and teachers, overseeing administrative duties, scheduling for working with children and consulting with doctors about treatments **H/I/S:** Caring for her Pets **EDU:** Master's Degree in Special Education, Nazareth College (1993); Bachelor's Degree in Psychology and Speech Communications, SUNY New Paltz (1980) **A/A/S:** National Alliance for Autism Research
Email: lerlichman@spencerportschools.org

Lee Lillian Ernst
Title: Designer, Owner **Company:** Lee Ernst Designs, Inc. **Address:** 430 Perkins Extension, Memphis, TN 38117 United States **BUS:** Retail Store **P/S:** Stationery, Arts, Gifts **MA:** Memphis and Surrounding Areas **EXP:** Ms. Ernst's area of expertise is in the design of stationery. **D/D/R:** Creating Stationary, Cards, Gifts for Clients, Running both Businesses, Lee Ernst Designs and Menage **EDU:** Coursework in Education and Sociology, The University of New Orleans **C/VW:** The Hadassah Foundation; Women's Foundation for a Greater Memphis
Email: leeernst@bellsouth.net
URL: http://www.menage.com

Gail L. Errickson
Title: Employment Specialist **Company:** CPC Behavioral Healthcare **Address:** 1088 Highway 34, Aberdeen, NJ 07747 United States **BUS:** Behavioral Healthcare Center **P/S:** Human Services, Counseling Children, Adults and Families **MA:** Local **D/D/R:** Rehabilitation Counseling for Adults, Job Placement, Training **H/I/S:** Gardening, Walking, Spending Time with her Grandchildren **EDU:** Bachelor's Degree in Human Services, Concentration in Rehabilitation and Mental Health, Thomas Edison State College; Associate Degree in Education **A/A/S:** National Rehabilitation Association; Memorial United Methodist Church; APSE; DAR **A/H:** Good Citizen Award, High School
Email: g.errickson@gmail.com

Mr. David P. Erstling
Title: Credit Manager **Company:** Apparel Imports, Inc. dba Formal Wear International **Address:** 6604 N.W. 82nd Avenue, Miami, FL 33166 United States **BUS:** Manufacturer and Distributor **P/S:** Apparel **MA:** Local **D/D/R:** Credit **H/I/S:** Sports Enthusiast, Listening to Music, Spending Time with his Grandchildren **EDU:** Associate Degree in Business Management **A/A/S:** National Association of Credit Management **C/VW:** St. Jude Children's Research Hospital; American Diabetes Association
Email: derstling@jyfwi.com
URL: http://www.cambridgewhoswho.com

Shawna L. Erviti
Title: Charter Manager **Company:** 1) Out Island Development 2) Sky Limo Corp **BUS:** Real Estate and Vacation Rental Firm **P/S:** Hospitality and Concierge Services Including Private Transportation, Housing, Villa Rentals, Air Charters, Boat and Yacht Rental Services **MA:** International **EXP:** Ms. Erviti's area of expertise is in aircraft management. **D/D/R:** Overseeing VIP services including leisure and corporate travel, housing and leisure arrangements for clients, travel and tourism management, assisting clients and managing operations **H/I/S:** Traveling, Spending Time with her Family **EDU:** Associate Degree in Travel and Tourism Management, Johnson & Wales University (1999)
Email: shawna@skylimoaircharter.com
URL: http://outislanddevelopment.com

Andy Esbenshade
Title: Realtor, GRI, Accredited Buyer Representative **Company:** Coldwell Banker Homesale Services **Address:** 215 S. Centerville Road, Suite A, Lancaster, PA 17603 United States **BUS:** Real Estate Agency **P/S:** Real Estate Exchange **MA:** Local **D/D/R:** overseeing residential and commercial real estate exchange **H/I/S:** Sailing, Mountain Biking, Kayaking, Walking **CERTS:** Certified Realtor, Graduate Realtor Institute; Certified Buyer Representative **A/A/S:** Graduate Realtor Institute **C/VW:** Executive Board, Landis Valley Museum; Board Member, Lancaster Housing Opportunity Partnership; Board Member, Historic Preservation Trust of Lancaster County; Board Member, Economic Development Action Group, Lancaster Campaign; Hamilton Club, Lancaster
Email: andy@andyrealtor.com
URL: http://www.andyrealtor.com

Consejo O. Escrupolo
Title: Operating Room Staff Nurse (Retired) **Company:** St. John Macomb Hospital **Address:** 11800 E. 12 Mile Road, Warren, MI 48093 United States **BUS:** Hospital **P/S:** Healthcare **MA:** National **D/D/R:** Urology, Operating Room Nursing, Surgical Nursing, Orthopedics Focusing on the Hand **H/I/S:** Spending Time with Family **EDU:** Bachelor's Degree, Earned in the Philippians **A/A/S:** Association of periOperative Registered Nurses **C/VW:** First Baptist Church of Oak Park, Medical Missions, Bible Society
Email: con1936@yahoo.com

Raquel S. Eshleman
Title: Teacher **Company:** Paxton-Buckley-Loda Junior High School **Address:** 50 Panther Way, Paxton, IL 60957 United States **BUS:** Junior High School **P/S:** Education **MA:** Local **D/D/R:** Teaching Reading and Language Arts to Middle School Students **H/I/S:** Reading, Scrapbooking **EDU:** Bachelor's Degree in Elementary Education, Western Illinois University **A/A/S:** Illinois Reading Council; Kappa Delta Pi; IEA-NEA **A/H:** Outstanding Pre-Service Award
Email: reshleman@pbl.k12.il.us
URL: http://www.pblunit10.com

Paula D. Espada
Title: Registered Pharmacist **Company:** Consultant **Address:** 6433 Todd Court, Bensalem, PA 19020 United States **BUS:** Pharmaceutical Company **P/S:** Manufacturing and Packaging Services for Pharmaceutical, Biotechnology and Consumer Health Companies **MA:** International **D/D/R:** overseeing the clinical supply service department and acting as an operational liaison between Germany and England **H/I/S:** Salsa Dancing, Swimming, Basketball **EDU:** Coursework in Pharmaceutical Studies, Long Island University (1987) **CERTS:** License, States of New Jersey and Puerto Rico; Certified Quality Manager (2005); Certified Quality Analyst (2003); Registered Pharmacist (1989); Certified Manager and Auditor, American Society for Quality **A/A/S:** American Society for Quality; International Society for Pharmaceutical Engineering
Email: paulaespada@comcast.net
URL: http://www.catalent.com

Mr. Christopher J. Esper, DO
Title: Doctor of Osteopathy **Company:** University of Pittsburgh Medical Center, Horizon **Address:** 20000 Harvard Road, Warrensville Heights, OH 44122 United States **BUS:** Premier Health Care Delivery System **P/S:** Clinical Expertise in Primary Care Medicine, Cardiology, Oncology, Ophthalmology and Sleep Medicine **MA:** Annals of Surgery **D/D/R:** Performing Operations on a Daily Basis for General to Vascular Procedures, Overseeing Daily Responsibility of Staff, Preparing for Training in Vascular Surgery **H/I/S:** Soccer, Golf, Cooking **EDU:** Doctor of Osteopathy in Osteopathic Medicine, Lake Erie College of Osteopathic Medicine (2002); Bachelor of Science in Biology, Slippery Rock University (1998) **A/A/S:** American Osteopathic Association; American College of Surgeons; POMA
Email: chrisesper015@hotmail.com
URL: http://horizon.upmc.com

Flora Espino
Title: President **Company:** VCV Financial Services, Inc. **Address:** 1550 Broadway, Suite F, Chula Vista, CA 91911 United States **BUS:** Real Estate and Income Tax Company **P/S:** Real Estate Services **MA:** Local **EXP:** Ms. Espino's area of expertise is in finance. **H/I/S:** Traveling, Cycling **EDU:** Associate Degree, Mesa College Anthony Robbins Mastery University **A/A/S:** Board Member, National Latina Business Women Association **C/VW:** Anthony Robbins Foundation
Email: floravcvinc@yahoo.com
URL: http://www.vcvfinancialinc.com

Mrs. Sylvia Espinoza
Title: 1) Teacher 2) Prepaid Legal Independent Associate Small Business and Group Specialist **Company:** 1) Oceanside Unified School District **Address:** 1) 2111 Mission Avenue, 1) Oceanside, CA 92054 **BUS:** Public School System **P/S:** 1) Education 2) Legal Services **MA:** National **D/D/R:** Teaching Elementary Education, Reading, Prepaid Legal Services **H/I/S:** Walking, Jogging, Spending Time with Family and Friends **EDU:** Master of Science in Reading and Language Arts, National University; Bachelor of Arts in Education, San Diego State University **A/A/S:** National Education Association **A/H:** Who's Who Among American Teachers, 2005-2006; Teacher of the Year, 2005 **C/VW:** Various Charities
Email: silviaeppl@yahoo.com
URL: http://www.prepaidlegal.com/hub/silviae
URL: http://www.cambridgewhoswho.com

Tina L. Essex, RN
Title: Registered Nurse **Company:** Desert Regional Medical Center **Address:** 1150 N. Indian Canyon Drive, Palm Springs, CA 92262 United States **BUS:** Medical Center **P/S:** Healthcare Services Including Wound Care, Bariatric Surgery, Emergency Services, Transfusions and Hospice Care **MA:** Local **D/D/R:** travel nursing, oncology nursing, medical-surgical nursing, reporting patients' results to doctors, administering medication to patients, checking vitals and acting as an advocate for patients, families and doctors **H/I/S:** Reading, Hiking, Walking, Writing, Swimming **EDU:** Associate of Science, Columbus Technical Institute (Now Columbus State Community College) (1986) **CERTS:** Registered Nurse, Columbus Technical Institute (Now Columbus State Community College) **A/A/S:** Treasurer, Association of Rehabilitation Nurses, CA; Ohio Nurses Association; Practice Committee, Ohio Board of Nursing **C/VW:** Volunteer, Pregnancy Distress Center
Email: tinal.essex@yahoo.com
URL: http://www.desertmedctr.com

Beth R. Estes
Title: Vice President **Company:** Wesco Graphics, Inc. **Address:** 410 E. Grant Line, Road B, Tracy, CA 95376 United States **BUS:** Printing Firm **P/S:** Graphic Printing **MA:** Regional **D/D/R:** Offering Graphic Printing for Real Estate Companies, City Colleges and Various Publications, Overseeing the Production and Accounting Department, Promoting Customer Education **EDU:** Bachelor's Degree in Special Education, Newark State College (1974) **A/A/S:** PIA
Email: betty@weslographics.com
URL: http://www.weslographics.com

Jeannette C. Estrada
Title: Owner, Accountant **Company:** Account-On-Time **Address:** P.O. Box 161, Ferris, TX 75125 United States **BUS:** Accounting Firm **P/S:** Accounting Services Including Tax Preparation **MA:** Regional **EXP:** Ms. Estrada's areas of expertise include income tax return preparation, processing payroll and the generation of financial reports. **D/D/R:** Teaching **H/I/S:** Reading, Swimming **EDU:** Bachelor of Science in Accounting, Elmhurst College (1983) **A/A/S:** Downtown Business Association
Email: jeannette.estrada@cwwemail.com

Mila Etropolski

Title: Director, Clinical Leader **Company:** Johnson & Johnson Pharmaceutical Research and Development **Address:** 1125 Trenton-Harbourton Road, Titusville, NJ 08560 United States **BUS:** Pharmaceutical Manufacturer **P/S:** Developing Medicines and Pharmaceutical Products **MA:** International **D/D/R:** Clinical Research and Development **H/I/S:** Outdoor Sports **EDU:** MD in Internal Medicine **A/A/S:** ASA **C/VW:** American Heart Association, Goodwill
Email: mila_etropolski@hotmail.com

Charlotte A. Eubank

Title: Owner-Manager **Company:** Hamlin Electrical Construction LLC **Address:** 1406 Neptune Drive, Clinton, OK 73601 United States **BUS:** Power Lines Construction **P/S:** Power Lines and Pole Line Electrical Construction **MA:** Local **D/D/R:** Underground Lines, New Lines and Repair **H/I/S:** Reading, Travel **EDU:** High School, Quintin, OK
Email: kceubank@hotmail.com

Glenda R. Eubanks, M.Ed.

Title: Federal Program Director, Director of Curriculum and Assessment, Professional Development Coordinator **Company:** Homedale Joint School District **Dept:** Administration **Address:** 848 W. Locust Lane, Nampa, ID 83686 United States **BUS:** Public School **P/S:** Education for Students in Kindergarten through Twelfth-Grade, Mathematics, Language, Writing, Social Studies, Science, Reading, Health and Music **MA:** Regional **D/D/R:** teaching, Implementing Curriculum and Professional Development, Managing State and Federal Funds, Working with Faculty, Administering Reports **H/I/S:** Golfing, Traveling, Gardening, Listening to Music **EDU:** Master of Arts in Curriculum Instruction, Northwest Nazarene University (1992); Bachelor of Arts, Northwest Nazarene University (1972) **A/A/S:** Association for Supervision and Curriculum Development; Phi Delta Kappa; Idaho Association of School Administrators **A/H:** Teacher of the Year for Idaho (1998)
Email: gandjeubanks@yahoo.com
URL: http://www.homedaleschools.org

Judith L. Euritt

Title: Owner **Company:** E&E Search Consultants **Address:** 12828 Lake Avenue N.W., Poulsbo, WA 98370 United States **BUS:** Investigative Services Company **P/S:** Reuniting Individuals Separated by Adoption **MA:** National **D/D/R:** Confidential Intermediary, Counseling **H/I/S:** Traveling **EDU:** Bachelor of Science in Nursing, Olympic College, 1962 **CERTS:** Registered Counselor, State of Washington **A/A/S:** WINGS; Silverdale, Washington **C/VW:** Children of the Nation
Email: adoptionsearchwa@msn.com
URL: http://www.adoptionsearchwa.com

Benjamin Evans

Title: Graduate Assistant **Company:** West Virginia University **Address:** Morgantown, WV United States **BUS:** University **P/S:** Higher Education Including Graduate and Undergraduate Athletic Training **MA:** Regional **D/D/R:** assisting students with on-site injuries, Supervising Practices and Games **EDU:** Bachelor of Arts in Kinesiology, The Pennsylvania State University (2006) **A/A/S:** Penn State Alumni Association; National Athletic Trainers' Association
Email: benjamin.evans@cwwemail.com
Email: bfe103@yahoo.com
URL: http://www.cambridgewhoswho.com

Mr. Cody D. Evans

Title: Minister of Music Education **Company:** Regency Park Baptist Church **Address:** 1120 N.E. 8th Street, Moore, OK 73160 United States **BUS:** Cooperating Southern Baptist Church **P/S:** Spiritual Guidance and Services **MA:** Local **D/D/R:** Incorporating Themes into Worship to Engage Members Fully, Focusing on Encouragement and Education, Playing Piano, Saxophone and Operatic Singing **H/I/S:** Enjoying Opera, All Outdoor Sports **EDU:** Bachelor's Degree in Music, Major in Church Music, Oklahoma Baptist University (2003) **A/A/S:** Phi Mu Alpha; International Thespian Society; Singing Churchmen of Oklahoma
Email: musicminister@rpbc.info
URL: http://www.rpbc.info

Dawn Ranee Evans

Title: Senior Captain **Company:** Caterpillar **Address:** 1300 4 H Park Road, Pontiac, IL 61764 United States **BUS:** Industrial Manufacturer **P/S:** Manufacturing **MA:** International **D/D/R:** Security, Leading the Team **H/I/S:** Attending Church **EDU:** Bachelor of Science in Business Management, University of Illinois **CERTS:** Certified ISO 9000 Auditor **A/A/S:** American Society for Industrial Security **C/VW:** Church, Relay for Life
Email: evans_dawn_r@cat.com
URL: http://www.cambridgewhoswho.com

Gilbert Evans

Title: Hustle Dance Motivator **Company:** Keeping it Simple with Shorti Smoove **Address:** 8819 Stoepel Street, Detroit, MI 48204 United States **BUS:** Dance and Social Interaction Group **P/S:** Community Service, Wellness **MA:** Local **EXP:** Mr. Evans' expertise is in weight loss. **D/D/R:** Motivating People to Stay Healthy and Active **H/I/S:** Reading, Spending Time with her Friends and Family **EDU:** Coursework in Police Investigations and Criminal Justice, Wayne County Community College
Email: kisss4life@yahoo
URL: www.kiss4life@yahoo.com

Mr. Michael M. Evans

Title: Nursing Instructor **Company:** The Pennsylvania State University **Address:** 101 Clarkson Avenue, Apartment B, Jessup, PA 18434 United States **BUS:** University **P/S:** Undergraduate and Graduate Academic Programs, Outreach Programs, Research, Arts and Performance, Libraries, Athletics and Recreation, Student Support Services, Clubs and Organizations **MA:** Regional **D/D/R:** Teaching Clinics in Psychiatric, Pediatric and Medical-Surgical Settings, Adult Healthcare, Clinical Calculations, Fundamental Laboratories, Community Health and Men's Healthcare **EDU:** Pursuing Master's Degree in Adult Health, Clinical Nurse Specialist, Concentration in Nursing Education, College Misericordia; Bachelor of Science in Nursing, The Pennsylvania State University (2003) **CERTS:** Registered Nurse; Certified Medical Surgical Registered Nurse **A/A/S:** National Association of Clinical Nurse Specialists; American Diabetes Association; Phi Kappa Phi; Sigma Theta Tau; Academy of Medical-Surgical Nurses; American Nurses Association
Email: mme124@psu.edu
URL: http://www.psu.edu

Rebecca A. Evans

Title: Owner, Coach, Author, Public Speaker, President **Company:** Inner Element **Address:** P.O. Box 1477, Eagle, ID 83616 United States **BUS:** Coaching Center **P/S:** Coaching and Speaking Services to Maintain a Quality Life **MA:** National **D/D/R:** transformational coaching, motivational speaking and writing **H/I/S:** Traveling, Reading, Creating New Adventures and Projects for her Children **A/A/S:** Better Business Bureau; National Coaching Association; National Association of Women Business Owners **A/H:** Inspector General Award for Excellence in the Military; Mrs. Idaho Award (2004) **C/VW:** Ronald McDonald House Charities; Life's Little Solutions
Email: revans05@cableone.net
URL: http://www.inner-element.com

Ms. Sonja Evans

Title: Owner **Company:** Psychic Life Readings **Address:** 112 Hetzel Street, State College, PA 16801 United States **BUS:** Psychic Services **P/S:** Psychic Readings **MA:** International **D/D/R:** Reading Egyptian Tarot Cards, Making Homemade Candles, Dream Catchers, Incense, Oils, Crystals, Opened Up 3 Retail Shops Selling Crystals, oils, incense, candles, dream catchers, performs psychics readings using various modalities. **H/I/S:** Traveling, Grandchildren (3)
Email: mssallik05@yahoo.com

Mr. William D. Evans IV

Title: Director **Company:** No More Empty Shelves **Address:** 14170 Rideout Court, Fontana, CA 92336 United States **BUS:** Christian Ministry **P/S:** Food Services to Low Income Individuals, Homeless Individuals, the Needy and Seniors **MA:** Southern California **D/D/R:** Overseeing the Organization, Offering Human Services to those in Need **H/I/S:** Golfing, Reading the Bible **EDU:** Associate Degree in Real Estate, Los Angeles Trade Technical College (1978) **CERTS:** Certified Arborist
Email: nmes91766@sbcglobal.net
URL: http://www.cambridgewhoswho.com

Alison A. Everett

Title: Mathematics Teacher, Basketball Coach **Company:** Benjamin Franklin Middle School **Address:** 225 Middle School Road, Rocky Mount, VA 24151 United States **BUS:** Public Middle School **P/S:** Education **MA:** Local **D/D/R:** Teaching Math, Coaching Basketball **H/I/S:** Cooking, Solving Sudoku Puzzles **EDU:** Bachelor's Degree in Mathematics, Minor in Computer Science and Secondary Education, Ferrum College **A/A/S:** National Education Association; Virginia Education Association
Email: alison.everett@frco.k12.va.us

Willie Everett

Title: Medical Assistant **Company:** Self-Employed **Address:** 4210 Windtree Drive, Tampa, FL 33624 United States **BUS:** Medical Field **P/S:** Healthcare **MA:** Local **D/D/R:** Rehabilitation, Meeting Patients' Needs, Patient Education, Caring for the Physical Needs of the Patient **H/I/S:** Watching Movies, Traveling on Cruises **EDU:** College Coursework Completed, Concord Career Institute **C/VW:** Blood Donor, Tampa
Email: paraiso35@hotmail.com

June K. Everling

Title: Independent Healthcare Consultant, Wound Care Certified **Address:** 1800 N. Wabash Road, Marion, IN 46952 United States **BUS:** Nursing Home **P/S:** Long-Term Healthcare **MA:** Indiana **D/D/R:** regulating compliance and wound care **H/I/S:** Reading, Baking, Gardening **EDU:** Bachelor of Science in Nursing, Indiana Wesleyan University (1983) **A/A/S:** National Alliance of Wound Care
Email: jkeverling@juno.com
URL: http://www.cambridgewhoswho.com

Pamela J. Evers-Ragan

Title: Director of Nurses, Registered Nurse **Company:** Cedar County Memorial Hospital **Address:** 1401 S. Park Street, El Dorado Springs, MO 64744 United States **BUS:** Hospital **P/S:** Healthcare Including Emergency Room and Pharmaceutical Services **MA:** Regional **EXP:** Ms. Evers-Ragan's area of expertise is in the treatment of critical care patients. **D/D/R:** Overseeing Nursing Staff, Administering Nursing Services **EDU:** Bachelor of Science in Nursing, University of Wisconsin, Milwaukee (1993) **CERTS:** Registered Nurse **A/A/S:** Golden Key International Honour Society **A/H:** Young Women of America Award (1991)
Email: pamragan_1@msn.com
Email: ccmhdirector@yahoo.com
URL: http://www.cedarcountyhospital.org

Luann M. Evert

Title: 1) Advanced Registered Nurse Practitioner 2) Professor **Company:** 1) Valley View Regional Hospital 2) East Central University **Address:** 1) 430 N. Monta Vista 2) 1100 E. 14th Street, Ada, OK 74820 United States **BUS:** 1) Hospital 2) University **P/S:** 1) Healthcare 2) Education **MA:** 1) Local 2) Local **D/D/R:** Emergency Nursing, Family Practice Teaching Nursing **H/I/S:** Sports, Scuba Diving **EDU:** Master of Science in Nursing, Emphasis on Education and Family Practice, Fort Hays State University **CERTS:** Advanced Registered Nurse Practitioner **A/A/S:** Emergency Nurses Association; Oklahoma Nurses Association; American Nurses Association; Sigma Theta Tau **C/VW:** American Heart Association; American Cancer Society, Boy Scouts of America, Girl Scouts of the USA
Email: levert@ecok.edu

Ms. Jacqueline Darlene Ewans

Title: Veterinary Technician **Company:** Berwick Animal Clinic **Address:** 3272 Refugee Road, Columbus, OH 43232 United States **BUS:** Animal Clinic **P/S:** Medical Treatment and Surgery for Animals **MA:** Local **D/D/R:** Preparing and Assisting during Surgery **H/I/S:** Shopping, Watching Movies, Spending Time with her Family **EDU:** Associate Degree in Veterinary Technology, Columbus State University (2004)

Mr. Hall Edward Ewing II

Title: State Manager **Company:** Reverse Mortgage of America **Address:** 13843 W. Meeker Boulevard, Suite 117, Sun City West, AZ 85375 United States **BUS:** Reverse Mortgage Company **P/S:** Education for Senior Citizens, High Quality Reverse Mortgage Services, Financial Services, Real Estate Financing, Savings Products, Associated Services, Maintains an Active Leadership Role in Local, State and National Mortgage Banking Organizations **MA:** Regional **D/D/R:** Marketing, Managing Reverse Mortgages for Senior Citizens, Educating and Helping Customers, Working as a Reverse Mortgage Expert **H/I/S:** Horses, Playing Baseball, Playing Football **EDU:** Master's Degree in Physical Education for the Handicapped, University of South Florida (1972) **A/H:** First Person to Make One Million Dollars in Retail Sales (1985)
Email: hewing4102@aol.com
URL: http://www.reversemortgageofamerica.com

Ryan D. Eyer

Title: Director of Research and Development **Company:** Flowserve Corporation **Address:** 5215 N. OConnor Boulevard, Suite 2300, Irving, TX 75039 United States **BUS:** Manufacturing Company **P/S:** Industrial Pumps, Valves and Seals **MA:** International **EXP:** Mr. Eyer's expertise includes marketing, portfolio and project management and the oversight of research and project development. **D/D/R:** Training, Setting and Attending Appointments with International Employees **H/I/S:** Sports, Reading, Learning **EDU:** Master of Business Administration in Marketing and Operation Management, University of Illinois at Urbana-Champaign (2005); Master of Arts in Mechanical Engineering, Concentration in Combustion and Propulsion, University of Illinois at Urbana-Champaign (2004); Bachelor of Science in Physics and Business Management, Illinois Wesleyan University, Bloomington (2001) **CERTS:** Certified Six Sigma Black Belt **A/A/S:** Phi Gamma Delta **C/VW:** Volunteer, Dallas Cowboys
Email: ryeyer@flowserve.com
URL: http://www.flowserve.com

Mr. Kenneth C. Eynon

Title: Sr. Account Manager **Company:** CPACinc.com **Address:** 22700 Savi Ranch Parkway, Suite B, Yorba Linda, CA 92887 United States **BUS:** Technology Company **P/S:** Information Technology Hardware, Global Information Technology for Fortune 500 Companies **MA:** International **D/D/R:** Managing Accounts **H/I/S:** Mountain Biking **EDU:** Associate Degree in Business, Cuesta College; Coursework in International Management, California State University, Fullerton
Email: ken.eynon@keneynon.com
Email: keynon@cpacinc.com
URL: http://www.cpacinc.com

Joyce E. Ezaki

Title: Manager, Marketing and Client Services **Company:** American Realty Advisors **Address:** 801 N. Brand Boulevard, Suite 800, Glendale, CA 91203 United States **BUS:** Real Estate **P/S:** Innovative Real Estate Investment Solutions **MA:** National **D/D/R:** Overseeing Consultation Relations, Preparing All Request for Proposals, Advertising, Marketing, Conducting Collateral and Quality Assessment, Writing Two Direct Reports, Managing Client Services and Administrative Services **EDU:** Bachelor of Arts in Economics, University of California at Los Angeles (2000); Diploma, Thousand Oaks High School (1995) **A/A/S:** Asian American Community Service Association; Volunteered for 'Project by Project'
Email: jezaki@americanreal.com
URL: http://www.americanreal.com

Tina Gray Ezzell

Title: Career Development Manager **Company:** FAC Food Service Logistics **Dept:** Carrier Development **Address:** 1951 Centura Highway, Rocky Mount, NC 27804 United States **BUS:** Non Asset-Based Logistics Organization **P/S:** Safe and Efficient Transportation of Time-Sensitive Freight throughout the 48 Contiguous United States, Dedicated Food Transport, Food Consolidation, Food Service Logistics, Food Transportation, Freight Consolidation, Frozen Food Transportation, Frozen Freight Consolidation, Multi Stop Food Transport, Refrigerated LTL, Refrigerated Shipping, Refrigerated Transportation, Restaurant Deliveries, Small Food Shipments, Small Package, Temperature Controlled Shipping **MA:** National **D/D/R:** Handling Analysis, Building Truckloads, Auditing and Training for Freight, Negotiating for Costs and Profitability, Working Closely with Information Technology Department on New Software Programs, Creating Systems and Procedures, Consulting Services for Outside Companies in the Manufacturing and Food and Beverage Industry, Managing Carrier Contracts **H/I/S:** Owning Ezzell Farms, Breeding and Training American Quarter Horses, Enjoying Barrel Racing, Working Young Horses, Spending Time with her Son **EDU:** Associate Degree in Information Technology, Nash Community College (1999); Graduated Southwest High School (1979) **A/A/S:** Gamma Beta Society (1998-1999); National Barrel Horse Association **A/H:** Who's Who Among Students In American Junior Colleges (1998-1999)
Email: tezzell@faclogistics.com
URL: http://www.faclogistics.com

Maureen Fachler

Title: Speech-Language Pathologist, Consulting Supervisor **Company:** EBS Healthcare **Dept:** Theracare Rehab **Address:** P.O. Box 911, Concordville, PA 19331 United States **BUS:** Healthcare Services **P/S:** Rehabilitative Speech Pathology Services **MA:** Regional **D/D/R:** Practicing Speech Pathology, Working in Schools with Children in Pre Kindergarten through Fifth-Grade Requiring Speech Therapy, Working with Geriatric Patients Including Stroke Victims, Assisting with Language Therapy Using Verbal Exercises, Conducting Evaluations, Administering Swallow Treatments, Writing Individualized Education Plan Reports, Offering Care Plans **H/I/S:** Reading, Shopping **EDU:** Master's Degree in Speech Language Pathology, University of Pittsburgh (2004); Bachelor of Science in Speech-Language Pathology, University of Texas, Austin (2002) **CERTS:** Certification, American Speech-Language-Hearing Association (2004) **A/A/S:** California Speech-Language-Hearing Association; American Speech-Language-Hearing Association
Email: mfzukahealth@yahoo.com

Michelle S. Faedo

Title: Owner, Chef **Company:** Michelle Faedo's Sandwich Shop **Address:** 3609 N. 15th Street, Tampa, FL 33605 United States **BUS:** Restaurant **P/S:** Food Services **MA:** Regional **D/D/R:** serving homemade foods using fresh quality ingredients and devil crabs, Managing Operation of her Family and Restaurant, Serving Italian, Cajun, Spanish and American Foods **H/I/S:** Shopping, Hiking **EDU:** High School Education **A/A/S:** Better Business Bureau **C/VW:** Volunteer, Local Fire Department; Local Police Department; Local Schools; Cheerleader, University of Southern Florida
Email: michellefaedo@yahoo.com
URL: http://www.devilcrab.com

Carla S. Fahrni

Title: Activity Director **Company:** Canterbury Villa of Alliance **Address:** 1785 Freshley Avenue, Alliance, OH 44601 United States **BUS:** Nursing Home **P/S:** Healthcare, Geriatrics **MA:** Local **D/D/R:** Directing and Planning Activities and Programs, Teaching Dementia Care to Staff **EDU:** Coursework in Activity Direction, Diversified Education Solutions **CERTS:** Licensed Practical Nurse **C/VW:** Alzheimer's Association
Email: csflpn2@aol.com
URL: http://www.cambridgewhoswho.com

Cindy Fairchild, BSN

Title: Nursing Instruction **Company:** Antelope Valley Medical College **Address:** 44503 Denmore Avenue, Lancaster, CA 93535 United States **BUS:** School **P/S:** Maternal-Child Healthcare Education **MA:** Regional **D/D/R:** Teaching Parenting and Lactation Classes, Offering Neonatal Care, Working as a Part of the Neonatal Instructional Committee, Instructing Nurses on the Proper Care for Newborns and Lactation support **H/I/S:** Playing with Grandchildren, Going to Disneyland and traveling **EDU:** Pursuing Master's Degree in Nursing Education; Certified Public Health Nurse, State of California; Bachelor of Science in Nursing, University of Phoenix (2006) **CERTS:** International Board Certified Lactation Consultant **A/A/S:** International Lactation Consultant Association; Association of Women's Health, Obstetric and Neonatal Nurses; National Association of Neonatal Nurses; Childbirth and Postpartum Professional Association
Email: cjfairchild@verizon.net

Mr. Raymond G. Faldetta

Title: President, Owner **Company:** Total Care Insurance Repair, Inc. **Address:** 13733 N.W. 22nd Street, Sunrise, FL 33323 United States **BUS:** Fire and Water Restoration Company and Construction Industries **P/S:** Specializing in Emergency Catastrophe Response and Structural Repair 2)Offering Detailed and Itemized Property Damage Assessments with Forensic Reports, Expert Witness Services and Total Restoration and Reconstruction Services. 3) We Provide 24-hour Emergency Water Extraction and Dehumidification Services, as well as Indoor Air-Quality Testing, Board-Up Services, Infrared and Video Documentation and Total Reconstruction and Consulting Services **MA:** National **D/D/R:** Detailed Inspections and Professional Cost Analysis in the Reconstruction and or Full Restoration Services, caused by Fire, Water, Arson, Sink Hole and Natural Disasters for Residential, Historical, Commercial and Industrial Properties, Serving Insurance Companies, Independent Adjusting Firms, Public Insurance Adjusters, Attorney's and the General Public 2) Professional Property Damage Cost Assessments, Appraisals, Umpire Services. 3) Building and Renovations of Custom **H/I/S:** Kitchen and Bath Design, Cooking Italian, Baseball, Travel, World News and Current Events **CERTS:** State Certified General Contractor; Certified Windstorm Insurance Network Umpire (2007); Certified Mold Remediator, Indoor Air Quality Association, Inc. 02664, Washington D.C. (2002); Research Training Testing and Consulting, Baton Rouge, LA (2002) **A/A/S:** Better Business Bureau of South Florida and the Caribbean; Building Trades Association of South Florida; South Florida Claims Association; Windstorm Insurance Network; Property Loss Research Bureau; Florida Association of Public Insurance Adjusters
Email: totlcare@comcast.net
URL: http://www.totalcareinsurancerepair.com

Janet Faleski

Title: Managing Director **Company:** ThinkPanmure LLC **Address:** 31 West 52nd Street, New York, NY 10019 United States **BUS:** Financial Finance, Banking, Financial Services **P/S:** Investment Banking, Financial Services **MA:** National **D/D/R:** Marketing, Overseeing the corporate access department **H/I/S:** Spending Time With Family and Friends, Cooking, Traveling, Skiing, Reading **EDU:** Bachelor's Degree in Finance, University of Scranton
Email: janet.faleski@gmail.com
URL: www.thinkepanmure.com

Florence R. Falkowski, M.Ed.

Title: Second-Grade Teacher **Company:** A. Ward Spaulding Elementary School **Address:** 55 N. Stone Street, West Suffield, CT 06093 United States **BUS:** Proven Leader in the Education Industry **P/S:** High Quality Educational Services for Students as well as Extracurricular Activities **MA:** Regional **D/D/R:** Acting as Team Leader, Teaching Second-Grade Reading, Preparing Curriculum **H/I/S:** Practicing Calligraphy, Gardening, Traveling **EDU:** Master of Education in Elementary Education, Concentration in Reading, Westfield State College; Bachelor of Science in Early Childhood Education, Southern Connecticut State University **CERTS:** Certification in Kindergarten through Grade 6 **A/A/S:** Phi Kappa Phi
Email: flfalkonski@sbcglobal.net
URL: http://sp.suffield.org

Mario Fallone

Title: Owner, President **Company:** Cal 1st Mortgage **Address:** 45940 Corte Tobarra, Temecula, CA 92592 United States **BUS:** Finance and Equity Repositioning Company **P/S:** Mortgage, Home and Home Equity Loans **MA:** Regional **D/D/R:** Overseeing Daily Operations, Organizing Seminars and Presentations **H/I/S:** Golfing **CERTS:** Certified Mortgage Planner (2002); Certified Real Estate Agent, State of California (2006); Licensed in Life Insurance, State of California (2006) **A/A/S:** Southern California Board of Realtors; California Chamber of Commerce
Email: Mariofallone1@aol.com

Linyu Fan

Title: Teacher **Company:** IS 5 **Address:** 50-40 Jacobus Street, Elmhurst, NY 11373 United States **BUS:** Public School **P/S:** Education **MA:** Local **D/D/R:** Teaching English as a Second Language, Teaching English and Chinese **H/I/S:** Reading, Writing, Drawing, Spending Time with Friends, Keeping Fit, Practicing Tai Chi **EDU:** Master's Degree in English as a Second Language, New York University; Bachelor's Degree in English and Chinese, China
Email: lizfan0601@yahoo.com
URL: http://www.cambridgewhoswho.com

Mrs. Enza Fangio

Title: Screenwriter & Former Fifth-Grade Lead Teacher **Address:** 1401 Windsor Drive, McKinney, TX 75070 United States **BUS:** Film and Television Industry **P/S:** Screenwriting **D/D/R:** Screenwriting, Teaching Students, Mentoring Fellow Teachers, Developing Creative Curriculum **H/I/S:** Spending Family Time, Open Wheel Racing, Writing Screenplays **EDU:** Bachelor of Arts in History, Baylor University **A/H:** Disney Teacher of the Year Nominee (2005-2006) **C/VW:** Catholic Church, American Parkinson's Disease Association, American Cancer Society
Email: team-fangio@sbcglobal.net

Mrs. Patti Jo Fantozz, M.Ed.

Title: Vice President **Company:** Photomakers, LLC **Address:** 26290 Hull Prairie Road, Perrysburg, OH 43551 United States **BUS:** Private Company **P/S:** Retail Photography, Photography Studio and Lab **MA:** Regional **D/D/R:** Managing the Store, Scheduling, Hiring, Firing, Interviews, Maintaining Equipment, Ordering and Purchasing Supplies, Retail Sales, Also Owns a Baskin-Robbins Franchise and Tuffy Auto with her Husband **H/I/S:** All Sports **EDU:** Master's Degree in Education, Bowling Green State University (1986) **A/A/S:** Perrysburg School Foundation President; Dogs Foundation, Assistant
Email: pjfmusic@aol.com

Lauren B. Farber

Title: Second-Grade Teacher **Company:** Phillips Avenue School **Address:** 141 Phillips Avenue, Riverhead, NY 11901 United States **BUS:** Elementary School **P/S:** General Elementary Curriculum, Prekindergarten, Full-Day Kindergarten Program, Special Education Program, Reading, Arts, Music, Physical Education, Media Room, Extracurricular Activities, Athletics, Student Support Services, 21st Century Community Learning Center **MA:** Regional **D/D/R:** Teaching All Subjects to Second-Grade Students, Writing Grants for the 21st Century Community Learning Center, Organizing the Homework Club, Marine Wildlife Foundation Club, Art Program and Riverhead Library Partnership Program **H/I/S:** Golfing, Baseball, Planning her Upcoming Wedding **EDU:** Master's Degree in Liberal Studies in Education, Stony Brook University (2006); Bachelor's Degree in Elementary Education, SUNY Cortland (2001) **CERTS:** Certified Teacher, New York State **A/A/S:** Curriculum Mapping Committee, Riverhead Central School District
Email: lauren.farber@riverhead.net
URL: http://www.riverhead.net/HTML/Phillips.html

Gilda Farias-Healy

Title: Account Executive **Company:** Herbert L. Jamison and Co., LLC **Address:** 100 Executive Dr., West Orange, NJ 07052 United States **BUS:** Insurance **P/S:** Commercial and Fine Arts Insurance **MA:** National **D/D/R:** Casualty Insurance and Fine Arts Insurance **H/I/S:** Saint Catherine Church Choir and Music Ministry, Reading, Traveling, Classical Music **EDU:** Pursuing Master's Degree in Museum Professions, Seton Hall University; Bachelor's Degree in Psychology, Marymount Manhattan College, Cum Laude **CERTS:** Licensed NY State Property and Casualty Broker **A/H:** Dean's List, Marymount Manhattan College
Email: m.healy1@comcast.net
URL: http://www.cambridgewhoswho.com

Christine P. Farkas

Title: Senior Director **Company:** Merrill Lynch **Dept:** Equity Research Department **Address:** 4 World Financial Center, New York, NY 10080 United States **BUS:** Financial Management and Advisory Company **P/S:** Financial Advice and Investment Banking Services **MA:** National **EXP:** Ms. Farkas' expertise includes equity research for the beverage and tobacco industries. **H/I/S:** Spending Time with her Daughter, Playing the Piano **EDU:** Bachelor's Degree in Commerce, McGill University **A/A/S:** Chartered Financial Analyst, New York Society of Security Analysts
Email: c_farkas@ml.com
URL: http://www.cambridgewhoswho.com

Gina Farley
Title: Senior Copywriter Company: Hamilton Beach Brands, Inc. Address: 4421 Waterfront Drive, Glen Allen, VA 23060 United States BUS: Manufacturing and Distributing Company P/S: Distributing Small Kitchen Appliances MA: International D/D/R: Writing, Editing, Proofreading Advertising, Packaging, Collaterals, Website Copy H/I/S: Reading, Writing, EDU: Bachelor of Arts in Journalism, Marshall University, Huntington, WV (1986) A/A/S: American Marketing Association
Email: gina.farley@hamiltonbeach.com
URL: http://www.hamiltonbeach.com

Scott M. Farmer
Title: Exercise Physiologist, Strength Coach Company: Minnesota Health, Fitness and Sport Address: 1704 Boulder Drive, Sartell, MN 56377 United States BUS: Health, Wellness and Sports Company P/S: Sports Training for Outstanding Young Professionals MA: Regional EXP: Mr. Farmer's area of expertise includes health promotion and specific sport training. D/D/R: EFT Counseling, Working with Young Adults in all Sports and Groups, Conducting Tests and Evaluating the Performance of Students H/I/S: Reading, Coaching Hockey, Lecturing Youth Athletes on Disease Prevention EDU: Master of Science in Education, with a Concentration in Clinical Physiology, Old Dominion University; Bachelor of Science in Education, with a Concentration in Clinical Physiology, The University of Iowa CERTS: Certification, National Strength and Conditioning Association; Certification, American College of Sports Medicine A/A/S: National Strength and Conditioning Association; American College of Sports Medicine C/VW: Local High School; Local Charitable Organizations; United Way
Email: scott@mnhfs.com
URL: http://www.mnhfs.com

Duane N. Farney
Title: President, Chief Executive Officer Company: Farney Lumber Company Address: 7194 Brewery Road, Lowville, NY 13367 United States BUS: Manufacturing Company P/S: Manufacturing Lumber MA: Northeast United States D/D/R: Overseeing Company Operations H/I/S: Traveling EDU: Coursework in Hardwood, Lumber and Inspection, National Hardwood Lumber Association Trade School A/A/S: United States Chamber of Commerce C/VW: Local Church
Email: d_farney@frontiernet.net

Phyllis Farrar
Title: Program Consultant Company: Kansas State Department of Education Address: 120 S.E. 10th Avenue, Topeka, KS 66612 United States BUS: Department of Education P/S: Education MA: Local D/D/R: Teaching Foreign Languages H/I/S: Photography, Sailing, Hiking EDU: Master of Language Arts, The University of Kansas A/A/S: ACTFL; AATG; NCSSFL; TESAC; NEA; NABE; KEA; Central States Conference; National Network for Early Language Learning
Email: pfarrar@ksde.org

Ann M. Farrell
Title: President, Owner Company: Quantum Endeavors Address: 15721 Alsace Court, Winfield, IL 60190 United States BUS: Executive and Leadership Coaching Center P/S: Executive and Leadership Coaching MA: Regional D/D/R: Coaching, Assisting Business Owners in Creating a Better Business Plan H/I/S: Spending Time with her Family EDU: Bachelor's Degree in Finance, DePaul University, Chicago (1980) CERTS: Certified Professional Coach, International Coach Federation; Certified Public Accountant (2006) A/A/S: International Coaches Federation; National Association of Women's Business Federation
Email: ann@quantumendeavors.com

Sharon A. Farrell-Keckley
Title: Owner Company: Shaggy Dogs Pet Grooming, LLC Address: 940 Galloway Road, Galloway, OH 43119 United States BUS: Pet Care Center P/S: Pet Care and Dog Grooming Services for all Breeds, Clothing for Dogs MA: Local EXP: Ms. Farrell-Keckley's areas of expertise include pet grooming and pet care. D/D/R: Managing Operations, Cutting and Styling Dog's Fur, Dog Bathing, Caring for Pets, Consulting With Dog Owners on Pet Care H/I/S: Spending Time with her Family, Gardening, Reading, Caring for her Horse CERTS: Certified Dog Groomer, Ohio Academy of Pet Styling (2005) A/A/S: Better Business Bureau, OH; Angie's List C/VW: Local Animal Shelter
Email: shgds@sbcglobal.net
URL: http://www.cambridgewhoswho.com

Terrence L. Farrier
Title: President, Chief Executive Officer, Lieutenant Colonel Company: Consolidated and Personal Business Services Address: 1133 Pond Cypress Drive, Virginia Beach, VA 23455 United States BUS: Management and Consulting Company P/S: Consulting Services Including Business Management MA: Regional D/D/R: Developing Businesses through Leadership and Organizational Changes, Dealing with Contracts, Marketing, Handling Personnel and Budgets H/I/S: Practicing Martial Arts, Golfing, Jogging, Swimming EDU: Pursuing Ph.D., Regis University; Master's Degree in Strategic Studies (2005); Master's Degree in Business Administration, Regent University (2001) CERTS: Training Program, United States Army (2005) A/A/S: Academy of Business Administration; The American Legion C/VW: General Grand Chapter, Order of the Eastern Star; Grand Masonic Lodge
Email: cpbs_consulting@prodigy.net
URL: http://www.cambridgewhoswho.com

Judith L. Farris
Title: Opera and Concert Singer, Private Voice Instructor, Artist in Residence Company: Southeast Missouri State University, Department of Theater and Dance Address: 1 University Plaza, Cape Girardeau, MO 63701 United States BUS: Theater, Voice Instruction Programs P/S: Theater, Voice, Music MA: Local, New York City D/D/R: Opera, Concert Singing, Voice Instruction, Teaching Music EDU: Master's Degree in Music Training and Voice, Southeast Missouri State University A/A/S: Zonta International A/H: Woman of the Year, 2006
Email: info@CambridgeWhosWho.com
URL: http://www.cambridgewhoswho.com

Mary Farruggia Holt
Title: Chief Financial Officer Company: Safe Sedation, Inc. Address: 7475 Wisconsin Avenue, Suite 350, Bethesda, MD 20814 United States BUS: Healthcare Center P/S: Healthcare Including Anesthesia Services MA: Regional D/D/R: overseeing treatments for anesthesia patients, managing accounts, Medicare and Medicaid billing, assessment billing and procedures, maximizing and handling of billing H/I/S: Caring for her Pets, Spending Time Outdoor, Vacationing, Boarding Horses EDU: Pursuing Ph.D. in Healthcare Administration; Master's Degree in Accounting, University of Phoenix C/VW: Freedom Alliance; Fisher House; Locks of Love; Local Charitable Organizations
Email: zholtj@verizon.net

Phillip J. Farver
Title: Athletic Director Company: Indian Rocks Christian School Address: 12685 Ulmerton Road, Largo, FL 33774 United States BUS: School P/S: Education MA: Local D/D/R: Scheduling Games and Managing Transportation H/I/S: Golfing EDU: Bachelor of Science in Secondary Education, Maranatha Baptist Bible College (1978) A/A/S: Interscholastic Administrators Association
Email: philfarver@indianrocks.org

Frank Fasi II
Title: Account Executive Company: BNC Mortgage, Inc. Address: 700 Bishop Street, Suite 1701, Honolulu, HI 96813 United States BUS: Specialty Finance Company P/S: Mortgage Lending MA: Regional D/D/R: Overseeing Sales Agents Including Training, Supervision of All Internal Sales, Servicing Existing Accounts, Pursuing New Accounts H/I/S: Golfing, Hunting, Fishing, Spending Time with his Children EDU: Bachelor of Arts in Political Science, George Washington University (1987) A/A/S: National Association of Mortgage Brokers; Hawaii Association of Mortgage Brokers; Speaker, Statewide Sales Conferences
Email: ffasi@bncmortgage.com
URL: http://www.bncmortgage.com

Samuel Charles Faucette
Title: Director of Safety Compliance, Training and Recruiting Company: Old Dominion Freight Line, Inc. Address: 500 Old Dominion Way, Thomasville, NC 27360 United States BUS: Transportation Company P/S: Transportation Services, Less-Than-Truckload Transportation MA: National D/D/R: Safety Compliance, Training, Recruiting H/I/S: Golfing, Reading CERTS: Certified Director of Safety, North American Transportation Management Institute A/A/S: Vice Chairman, Safety Management Council; North Carolina Trucking Association C/VW: Local Business Club, Make-A-Wish Foundation
Email: faucetts@mebtel.net
URL: http://www.odfl.com

Deborah K. Faulkner
Title: Superintendent, Principal Company: Delphic Elementary School Address: 1420 Delphic Road, Montague, CA 96064 United States BUS: Elementary School P/S: Primary Education MA: Local D/D/R: overseeing budget, curriculum, students and faculty H/I/S: Traveling, Spending Time with her Husband EDU: Pursuing Master's Degree in Special Education, California State University, Chico; Bachelor's Degree in Psychology, California State University, Long Beach CERTS: Certification in Human Resources; Certification in Elementary Education A/A/S: Secretary, Alumni Association, National Football League; ACBA; SCBA
Email: dfaulkner6@socal.rr.com
URL: http://www.cambridgewhoswho.com

Michael Favre
Title: Coordinator, Strength and Conditioning Company: United States Olympic Committee Dept: Performance Services Address: Performance Services, 1 Olympic Plaza, Colorado Springs, CO 80909 United States BUS: National Sports Governing Body P/S: Physically Preparing Summer and Winter Athletes and Teams for Olympics and International Competition MA: National and International D/D/R: Enhancing the Physical Performance of Athletes in Greco-Roman Wrestling, Freestyle Wrestling, Judo, Tae Kwon Do, Fencing, Sprint Cycling, Weightlifting and Gymnastics, Lecturer and Published Author on Strength and Conditioning and Related Topics. H/I/S: Spending Time with Family, Hiking, Weightlifting, Power lifting, Reading EDU: M.Ed. in Sports Administration, Temple University (2001); Bachelor of Science in Exercise Science, Arizona State University (1997) CERTS: NSCA Certified Strength and Conditioning Specialist; USA Weightlifting Senior Coach; USA Track and Field Level 1 Coach; Accredited Strength and Conditioning Coordinator with the United Kingdom Strength and Conditioning Association A/H: Coach Practitioner Award
Email: mike.favre@usoc.org
URL: http://www.usolympicteam.com

Misty L. Fayard
Title: Treasurer Company: J&W Enterprises of Biloxi, LLC Address: 14115 Lorraine Road, Biloxi, MS 39532 United States BUS: Construction Company P/S: Constructing Commercial and Residential Buildings MA: Local D/D/R: overseeing administrative duties and job site, bookkeeping, processing payroll and managing finance H/I/S: Art, Photography EDU: Pursuing Bachelor of Arts in Graphic Design, Minor in Small Business, Tulane University College C/VW: St. Jude Children's Research Hospital
Email: jwseafood@aol.com

Karen A. Featherstone
Title: Information Technology Support Specialist Company: American Electric Power Address: 700 Morrison Road, Gahanna, OH 43230 United States BUS: Power Generation Company P/S: Generating and Transmitting Electricity MA: Local EXP: Ms. Featherstone's areas of expertise include technical support, application and workstation support and information technology. D/D/R: Supporting Personal Computers, Laptops, Desktops, Ordering Necessary Components, Troubleshooting Hardware and Software Problems CERTS: Cisco Certified Entry Network Technician; Microsoft Certified Systems Engineer C/VW: Minister, New Birth Christian Ministries
Email: kafeatherstone@aep.com
URL: http://www.aep.com/

John F. Fedie
Title: Architectural Sales Engineer Company: Johnson Screens Address: 1950 Old Highway 8 N.W., New Brighton, MN 55112 United States BUS: Manufacturing Architectural Metals P/S: Screen material used for wall cladding, column covers, lighting, drains, vents, sculptures and much more. Stainless steel and powder coated mild steel options. MA: North America D/D/R: Designing, Managing, Cost estimates H/I/S: Outdoor Activities EDU: Bachelor of Science in Engineering, University of Wisconsin (1999)
Email: jfedie@comcast.net

John R. Feehrer, Ph.D.
Title: Hardware Engineer Company: Sun Microsystems, Inc. Address: 1 Network Drive, Mailstop UBUR02-105, Burlington, MA 01803 United States BUS: Software Development Company P/S: Computer Components, Software Development and Information Technology Services MA: International D/D/R: creating the design and architecture of input and output subsystems H/I/S: Hiking, Running, Fishing EDU: Ph.D. in Electrical Engineering, University of Colorado (1995); Master's Degree in Electrical Engineering, University of Colorado (1991); Bachelor of Science in Electrical Engineering, Brown University (1986) A/A/S: Institute of Electrical and Electronics Engineers C/VW: Local Church; Habitat for Humanity
Email: john.feehrer@sun.com
URL: http://www.cambridgewhoswho.com

Mr. Michael A. Fehner
Title: Restaurant Manager **Company:** The Patina Group **Address:** 400 S. Hope Street, Los Angeles, CA 90071 United States **BUS:** Proven Leader Committed to Excellence in the Food and Beverage Industry **P/S:** Chain Restaurants, Catering, Special Events **MA:** National **D/D/R:** Overseeing Naples Restaurant Pizzeria, Managing the House Staff, Managing the Wines, Handling Cash Management, Sales and Marketing, Sommelier **H/I/S:** Walking, Racquetball, Arts and Theater, Photography **EDU:** Master's Degree in Architecture and Urban Planning, University of California Los Angeles (1974); Bachelor's Degree in Social and Behavioral Science with a Minor in Arts, University of California, Irvine (1972) **A/A/S:** Club 33
Email: maaf@flash.net
URL: http://www.patinagroup.com

Glenda Feilen
Title: President **Company:** Starquest, Inc. **Address:** 9859 Blossom Springs Road, El Cajon, CA 92021 United States **BUS:** Teaching the 'Law of Attraction', personal fashion design consultant **P/S:** Nutrition, Skin Care, Cosmetics, Fashion **MA:** National **D/D/R:** Assisting Clients in Personal Growth and Self-Improvement **H/I/S:** Traveling, Spending Time with her Grandchildren **EDU:** J.D. from Western Sierra School of Law, 2003; Bachelor of Arts in Russian and English, Brigham Young University; Naturopathic Doctor, School of Natural Healing **A/A/S:** Divine Design Fashion Division **C/VW:** Church, Local Schools
Email: info@CambridgeWhosWho.com
URL: http://www.AreAllYourPiecesInPlace.com

Heather C. Feiring
Title: Independent Sales Director **Company:** Mary Kay Cosmetics **BUS:** Cosmetic Company **P/S:** Skin Care, Body Care, Color Cosmetic Products **MA:** National **D/D/R:** Selling Skin Care, Body Care, Color Cosmetic Products, Men's Skin Care **H/I/S:** Spending Time with Family, Caring for her Dogs, Driving, Scrapbooking, Snow Skiing **EDU:** Bachelor of Science in Crop and Weed Science, North Dakota State University; Associate of Science in Farm and Ranch Management and Agricultural Sales and Service, Williston State College **A/A/S:** PAS Association; National FFA Alumni Association; Director, Queens Court of Sales; First Diamond, July 2005 **C/VW:** Fire Chief of Epping Rural Fire Department, Church Council
Email: cfeiring@nccray.com

Tonya B. Felder
Title: Executive Director **Company:** Associated General Contractors **Address:** 1707 S.W. Eighth Avenue, Amarillo, TX 79101 United States **BUS:** Nonprofit Organization **P/S:** Construction Services **MA:** Texas **D/D/R:** Executive Management, Forecasting Commercial Projects, Construction Legislation **H/I/S:** Reading, Traveling, Spending Time with her Family **EDU:** Associate Degree in Paralegal Studies, Southern Institute of Technology **A/A/S:** Amarillo Contractors Association; Construction Specifications Institute; Associated General Contractors of America
Email: agcama@suddenlinkmil.com
URL: http://www.agcamarillo.com

Pamella S. Felix
Title: President **Company:** Southeast Stone Company, Inc. **Address:** 316 Harrington Road, Rockingham, NC 28379 United States **BUS:** Stone Installation Company **P/S:** Stones **MA:** North Carolina, South Carolina **D/D/R:** Sales, Installations, Stone Veneer **H/I/S:** Swimming, Spending Time Outdoors, Four-Wheeling with her Grandsons **EDU:** High School Graduate **A/A/S:** Moore County Home Builders Association; Richmond County Home Builders Association
Email: southcaststone@arolina.rr.com
URL: http://www.southeasternstone.com

Karen M. Felon, M.Ed.
Title: Secondary Science Teacher **Company:** Cleveland Board of Education **Address:** 1380 E. Sixth Street, Cleveland, OH 44114 United States **BUS:** High School **P/S:** Education **MA:** Local **D/D/R:** Teaching Biology, Secondary Science **H/I/S:** Singing in the Southwest Community Chorus, Reading **EDU:** Master of Arts in Education Plus 30 in Instruction and Curriculum and Science, Cleveland State University, 1977; Bachelor of Science in Biology, Cleveland State University, 1972 **A/A/S:** Pi Lambda Theta; Phi Delta Kappa **C/VW:** Church
Email: k.felon20007@yahoo.com

David A. Felton, DDS, MS
Title: Doctor **Company:** University of North Carolina School of Dentistry **Dept:** Department of Prosthodontics **Address:** Department of Prosthodontics, Room 330 Bauer Hall CB 7450, Chapel Hill, NC 27599 United States **BUS:** College **P/S:** Allied Dental Education, Dental Ecology, Diagnostic Sciences and General Dentistry, Endodontics, Operative Dentistry, Oral and Maxillofacial Surgery, Orthodontics, Pediatric Dentistry, Periodontology, Prosthodontics **MA:** Regional **D/D/R:** Full Time Staff Member Teaching Pre-Dentistry to Clinical and Graduate Students, Private Dentistry Practice Includes Students and Residential Patients, Concentrating on Prosthodontics and Maxillofacial Services **H/I/S:** Golf **EDU:** DDS in Prosthodontics, University of North Carolina at Chapel Hill (1977); Master's Degree in Prosthodontics, University of North Carolina at Chapel Hill (1984); Bachelor of Science, Zoology, North Carolina State University, 1973 **A/A/S:** American College of Prosthodontics; American Dental Association; Academy of Prosthodontics; Greater New York Academy of Prosthodontics; International College of Dentists; International College of Prosthodontics; American Association of Dental Educators; Academy of Osseomtegration; American Association of Dental Research; Public Speaking, Locally, Nationally and Internationally on Prosthodontic Subjects; Published 40 Peer-Reviewed Publications and 120 Abstracts, Public Speaking Local, National, International
Email: dave_felton@dentistry.unc.edu
URL: http://www.dent.unc.edu

Michaela M. Felus
Title: Pediatric Physical Therapist **Company:** Children's Therapy Plus **Address:** 6504 E. 129th Avenue, Crown Point, IN 46307 United States **BUS:** Private Practice **P/S:** Pediatric Physical Therapy Services **MA:** Regional **D/D/R:** Hands-On Pediatric Physical Therapy **EDU:** Bachelor of Science in Physical Therapy, Daemen College; Diploma, Andrean High School; Certified Clinical Instructor; Center Coordinator **C/VW:** Local Community Charities, Children's Hospital
Email: mfelus@hotmail.com

Karen L. Fennell, MSNEd., CNNP
Title: Owner, Neonatal Nurse Practitioner, MSN **Company:** 1) University Monograms 2) Artistic Imprints and Apparel **Address:** 2527 Cocoon Run, Wingate, NC 28174 United States **BUS:** Retail Store **P/S:** Screen Printing and Embroidery Products Such as T-Shirts, Aprons, Bags and Totes, Athletic Apparel, Button Downs, Denim, Fleece Wear, Head Wear, Henleys, Ladies Apparel, Long Sleeve Shirts, Mock and Turtle Necks, Outerwear, Shorts, Sport Shirts, Toddler and Infant Wear, Towels and Robes **MA:** National **EXP:** Ms. Fennell's areas of expertise include embroidery, screen printing, vinyl lettering and the sale of promotional products. **H/I/S:** Caring for her Four Horses **EDU:** Master of Science Nursing, University of Phoenix (2007) **CERTS:** Certified Nurse Practitioner, Georgetown University (1996) **A/A/S:** Carolinas Association of Neonatal Nurse Practitioners; National Association of Neonatal Nurses
Email: artisticimprints@hotmail.com
URL: http://www.artisticimprints.net

Agnes C. Ferencz
Title: Senior Property Underwriter **Company:** Markerl Underwriting Managers, Inc. **Address:** 310 Highway 35 S., Red Bank, NJ 07701 United States **BUS:** Commercial Property and Package Underwriting Agency **P/S:** Commercial Insurance **MA:** Regional **D/D/R:** Property and Package Underwriting **H/I/S:** Playing Golf and Softball, Traveling, Reading **EDU:** Diploma, American Institute for Charter Property Casualty Underwriting **A/A/S:** National Association of Professional Surplus Lines Offices, Ltd. **C/VW:** Blood Drives; Temple
Email: aferencz@markelcorp.com
URL: http://www.cambridgewhoswho.com

Pat P. Fergerson
Title: Manager **Company:** Franklin Ridge Apartments **Address:** 213 W. Hartley Drive, High Point, NC 27265 United States **BUS:** Apartment Complex **P/S:** Apartment Rental, Property Management **MA:** Regional **D/D/R:** Managing **H/I/S:** Reading, Traveling **EDU:** High School Graduate **C/VW:** Triad Fraternal Order of Police
Email: pat1fergie@aol.com
URL: http://www.cambridgewhoswho.com

Kimberly B. Ferguson
Title: Realtor **Company:** Residential Properties **Address:** 1 Bowen's Wharf, Newport, RI 02840 United States **BUS:** Real Estate Agency **P/S:** Residential Real Estate Sales **MA:** Regional **D/D/R:** Listing and Selling Luxury Homes and Waterfront Properties, Creative Marketing **H/I/S:** Racing her Sailboat, Playing Tennis **EDU:** Bachelor of Science in Psychology, Tufts University **A/A/S:** National Association of Realtors; County Board of Realtors; Board Member, Conanicut Island Sailing Foundation **A/H:** First Female Appointed, Laser Master World, Brazil, 2005 **C/VW:** Conanicut Island Sailing Foundation
Email: kimferg@cox.net
URL: http://www.kimferguson.net

Rev. Malcolm W. Ferguson
Title: Pastor **Company:** Burnwell Baptist Church **Address:** 1509 Glover Road, Quinton, AL 35130 United States **BUS:** Baptist Church **P/S:** Spiritual Services **MA:** Local **D/D/R:** Preaching Gospel, Performing Community Services and Ministry Work, Preaching Gospel, Educating Congregation about the Work of Baptist Church **H/I/S:** Reading, Spending Time at the Church **EDU:** College Coursework
Email: malcolm.ferguson@cwwemail.com
URL: http://www.cambridgewhoswho.com

Stephanie R. Ferguson
Title: Project Manager **Company:** National Aeronautics and Space Administration **Address:** 100 University Drive, Fairmont, WV 26554 United States **BUS:** Government Organization **P/S:** Aerospace Technology and Research **MA:** International **EXP:** Ms. Ferguson's areas of expertise include project and Website management. **D/D/R:** , managing and validating of spacecraft critical software, IV and V management systems, managing records and analyzing ethical issues **H/I/S:** Snow Skiing **EDU:** Master's Degree in Management Information Systems, The George Washington University **A/A/S:** Project Management Institute; International Organization for Standardization **C/VW:** Local Charitable Organizations
Email: stephanie.r.ferguson@nasa.gov
URL: http://www.cambridgewhoswho.com

Zaydie F. Feria
Title: Assistant Professor of Nursing **Company:** Southwestern College **Address:** 8100 Gigantic Street, San Diego, CA 92154 United States **BUS:** College **P/S:** Higher Education **MA:** Local **D/D/R:** instructing on geriatrics and long-term care **H/I/S:** Reading, Photojournalism, Gardening **EDU:** Master of Science in Nursing, University of Phoenix **A/A/S:** Sigma Theta Tau **C/VW:** Local Charitable Organizations
Email: zferia@gmail.com
URL: http://www.cambridgewhoswho.com

Candida M. Fermin, MA
Title: Teacher **Company:** P.S. 75 Mayda Cortiella School **Address:** 95 Grove Street, Brooklyn, NY 11221 United States **BUS:** Elementary School **P/S:** Primary Education **MA:** Local **D/D/R:** teaching all core subjects for kindergarten through third-Grade students, developing curriculum and preparing students for their secondary level education **H/I/S:** Bowling, Attending the Orchestra, Listening to Violin Music **EDU:** Master's Degree in Early Childhood Education, The City College of New York (2003) **CERTS:** Certified General Education Teacher; Certified Elementary Education Teacher **A/H:** Teacher Recognition Award, New Life Day Care (1999-2000) **C/VW:** Volunteer, St. Jude Children's Research Hospital
Email: candytheteacher3@aol.com

Mrs. Brenda I. Fernandez, MA
Title: Assistant Principal, Elementary Instructional Specialist **Company:** Los Angeles Unified School District Alta Loma Elementary **Address:** 1745 Vineyard Avenue, Los Angeles, CA 91405 United States **BUS:** Elementary School **P/S:** Regular and Special Education Core Curriculum Including Reading, Math, English, Science, Social Studies, Art, Music, History, Physical Education **MA:** Regional **D/D/R:** In Charge of Special Education Program and General Education Program for 860 Students, Assisting with IEPs, Supervises the Inclusion Program, Monitors the Education Program and Various Students with Multiple Disabilities **H/I/S:** Reading, Education, Cooking, Baking, Entertaining **EDU:** Master's Degree in Educational Leadership, National University, California (2002) **A/A/S:** Associated Administrators of Los Angeles; Phi Lambda Theta; Association of California School Administrators
Email: taz1teach@aol.com
URL: http://www.lausd.k12.ca.us/schools/altaloma

Sandra Fernandez, CRS, GRI, PMN, TRC, CIPS, AHWD
Title: Broker, Associate **Company:** Realty World International Gateway **Address:** 7137 S.W. 117th Avenue, Miami, FL 33183 United States **BUS:** Real Estate Agency **P/S:** Residential Real Estate Exchange **MA:** Miami-Dade County **EXP:** Ms. Fernandez's area of expertise is in the management of residential property. **D/D/R:** Managing Residential Sales **H/I/S:** Traveling **EDU:** Diploma, Coral Gables High School **CERTS:** Transnational Referral Certified, Graduate Realtor Institute; Certified International Property Specialist **A/A/S:** President, Miami-Dade Chapter, Women's Council of Realtors; Chairwoman, Florida Chapter, Council of Residential Specialists; At Home With Diversity; Performance Management Network
Email: sandra@fernandezhomes.com
Email: fernandez5664@bellsouth.net
URL: http://www.fernandezhomes.com

Donna Ferrara
Title: LSA **Company:** Prudential Douglas Elliman **Address:** 1528 Old Northern Boulevard, Roslyn, NY 11576 United States **BUS:** Real Estate Company **P/S:** Real Estate Services **MA:** North Shore **D/D/R:** overseeing real estate services for the clients **H/I/S:** Walking, Gardening, Exercising **EDU:** High School Diploma **C/VW:** St. Jude Children's Research Hospital
Email: donna.ferrara@prudentialelliman.com
URL: http://www.prudentialelliman.com

Victoria Ferrarini
Title: President, Chief Executive Officer **Company:** Brianna Trucking, Inc. **Address:** 1725 N. New England Avenue, Chicago, IL 60707 United States **BUS:** Trucking Company **P/S:** Trucking Services, Transportation of Road Materials for Construction Sites **MA:** Regional **EXP:** Ms. Ferrarini's area of expertise is in project management. **D/D/R:** hiring and firing employees, Overseeing Operations, Bookkeeping, Completing Paperwork, Dispatching, Negotiating Contracts **H/I/S:** Listening to Music, Reading, Singing, Playing the Guitar, Playing Ice Skating **EDU:** Pursuing Master of Business Administration, Dominican University; Master of Social Work, Dominican University (2004) **C/VW:** Local Radio Show; National Association for Parents of Children with Visual Impairments
Email: victoriaferrarini@comcast.net
URL: http://www.briannatrucking.com

Deanna F. Ferrell
Title: Manager **Company:** Lowe's Home Improvement **Address:** 1350 Springdale Road, Rock Hill, SC 29730 United States **BUS:** Home Improvement Retail Store **P/S:** Home Improvement Contracting, Residential and Commercial Retail Sales **MA:** National **D/D/R:** Outdoor Power Equipment and Installation Services **H/I/S:** Hiking, Spending Time with Children, Jet Skiing **EDU:** Bachelor's Degree in Environmental Studies, Winthrop University **CERTS:** Certified in Power Equipment, Lowe's Home Improvement **C/VW:** Church
Email: info@CambridgeWhosWho.com
URL: http://www.lowes.com

Verna L. Ferrell
Title: Music Teacher **Company:** Reedy Creek Elementary School **Address:** 10801 Plaza Road Extension, Charlotte, NC 28215 United States **BUS:** Elementary School **P/S:** Primary Education **MA:** Local **EXP:** Ms. Ferrell's areas of expertise include music education for kindergarten through fifth-grade students utilizing the content management system. **D/D/R:** Offering Private Piano Lessons **H/I/S:** Reading, Studying Psychology, Dancing, Artwork, Making Crafts, Playing the Piano, Watching Basketball and Football **EDU:** Postgraduate Degree, Winthrop College, SC; Postgraduate Degree, The University of North Carolina, Charlotte; Postgraduate Degree, The University of North Carolina, Greensboro; Bachelor of Arts, University of Wisconsin-Eau Claire; Associate of Arts, Brevard College, NC **CERTS:** Level I Certified Orff-Schulwerk Teacher, Western Carolina University, Cullowhee **A/H:** National Honor Roll (2005-2006); Outstanding American Teacher Award for Performance in the Motivation and Empowerment of Today's Youth **C/VW:** Public Television; Arts and Science Council; United Way
Email: verna.ferrell@cms.k12.nc.us

David A. Ferrera
Title: Vice President, General Manager **Company:** MindFrame, Inc. **Address:** 26429 Rancho Parkway South, Suite 140, Lake Forest, CA 92630 United States **BUS:** Medical Company **P/S:** Medical Devices, Process Development for Medical Devices Focusing on Ischemic Stroke Intervention **MA:** National **D/D/R:** Developing Medical Devices, Overseeing all Aspects of the Company **H/I/S:** Traveling with his Family, Reading, Skiing, Ice Hockey **EDU:** Bachelor of Science in Plastic Engineering, University of Massachusetts Lowell **A/A/S:** American Society of Neuroradiology; World Federation of International and Therapeutic Neuroradiology; Society of Plastics Engineers **C/VW:** American Cancer Society
Email: davef@mindframeinc.com
URL: http://www.mindframeinc.com

David M. Ferro
Title: Manager of National Accounts **Company:** Hess Corporation **Address:** 1 Hess Plaza, Woodbridge, NJ 07095 United States **BUS:** Energy Firm **P/S:** Exploration and Production of Natural Gas, Electricity, Fuel and Oil **MA:** Local **EXP:** Mr. Ferro's areas of expertise include accounting and public relations management. **H/I/S:** Golfing, Watching Football **EDU:** Bachelor of Science in Mathematics, Ohio State University
Email: dferro@hess.com
URL: http://www.cambridgewhoswho.com

Rosanna M. Ferroggiaro
Title: Pharmacy Technician Supervisor **Company:** Children's Hospital of Central California **Dept:** Outpatient Pharmacy **Address:** 41169 Goodwin Way, Madera, CA 93636 United States **BUS:** Children's Hospital **P/S:** Pediatric Healthcare Services **MA:** Regional **D/D/R:** Offering Customer Service, Typing, Dispensing Medications, Compounding Medications for Pediatric Dosing, Consulting with Doctors Regarding Prior Authorizations and Diagnosis with Medical Justification for Medicaid Billing **H/I/S:** Bowling, Traveling, Scrapbooking **EDU:** Master's Degree in Education, National University (2008); Bachelor of Arts in Liberal Studies and Elementary Education, California State University, Fresno (2000)
Email: rferroggiaro@childrenscentralcal.org
URL: http://www.childrenscentralcal.org

Ms. Linda Fetterolf
Title: Owner **Company:** Fetts Construction **Address:** 2428 Old Bristol Road, Holland, PA 18966 United States **BUS:** Construction Company **P/S:** Residential and Commercial Building **MA:** Local **D/D/R:** Managing Estimates, Inspections and documentation **H/I/S:** Gardening
Email: linda@fettsconstruction.com
URL: http://www.fettsconstruction.com

Andrew P. Fey
Title: Assistant Chief **Company:** Pleasant Township Fire Department **Address:** 2925 Lancaster Thornville Road N.E., Lancaster, OH 43130 United States **BUS:** Fire Department **P/S:** Fire and Emergency Services **MA:** Local **D/D/R:** Leading the Fire Department **H/I/S:** Snow Skiing, Rock Climbing, Running with his Dogs **EDU:** Associate of Arts in Fire Service, Hocking College **A/A/S:** Pleasant Township Firefighters Association; International Association of Fire Fighters, Local 2818; Charter Member, Fraternal Order of Leatherheads Society **A/H:** Blue Code Award, Knights of Columbus, 2002
Email: feychief@yahoo.com
URL: http://www.pleasantfire.com

Anthony D. Fiacchino
Title: Chief Executive Officer **Company:** Aerostar Global Logistics Group **Address:** 824 S. Kay Avenue, Addison, IL 60101 United States **BUS:** Global Transportation and Logistics **P/S:** Supply Chain Management Solutions, Global Transportation **MA:** International **D/D/R:** Executive Management, Business Development **H/I/S:** Spending Time with his Family, Coaching Soccer, Riding his Harley-Davidson Motorcycle **EDU:** High School Graduate **A/A/S:** Italians of America Group; Department of Homeland Security; U.S. Customs and Border Protection **C/VW:** ALS Association, Organic Trade Association
Email: t.fiacchino@aerostarglobal.com

David E. Fiedler
Title: Project Manager **Company:** Sun City Electric **Address:** 4260 Wagon Trail Avenue, Las Vegas, NV 89118 United States **BUS:** Electric Company **P/S:** Electrical Contracting **MA:** Local **D/D/R:** Managing Projects **H/I/S:** Working with Computers, Spending Time Outdoors, Biking, Snowboarding, Skiing **EDU:** Bachelor of Science in Construction Management, Minor in Risk Control, University of Wisconsin, 2003 **C/VW:** Church
Email: dfiedler@suncityelectric.com
URL: http://www.suncityelectric.com

James B. Fields, STD, MA
Title: Pastor, Administrator **Company:** Cedar View Methodist Church and Christian School **Dept:** Kindergarten Through 12th-Grade **Address:** P.O. Box 143, Kingsport, TN 37662 United States **BUS:** Christian School **P/S:** Education Including Religious Studies **MA:** Regional **D/D/R:** pastoring the church, preparing sermons, managing administrative duties, overseeing teachers and students, conducting meetings with parents and editing evangelical magazine **H/I/S:** Golfing **EDU:** Ph.D. in Sacred Theology, with Honors (1988); Master's Degree in Theology and Bible, Manahath School of Theology (1975); Bachelor of Arts in Bible Studies (1984); Bachelor of Divinity, Bob Jones University **A/A/S:** Tennessee Association of Christian Schools; American Association of Christian Schools; American Council of Christian Churches; International Counsel of Biblical Churches; General Superintendent, Evangelical Methodist Church; National Office Chairman, Bible Methodist Missions; President, International Council of Bible Believing Churches
Email: cvcsseahawks@aol.com

Rory T. Fields
Title: Director **Company:** Primm Valley Casino Resorts **Dept:** Slot Operations Department **Address:** 31900 Las Vegas Boulevard S., Primm, NV 89019 United States **BUS:** Casino **P/S:** Slots, Players Club Services **MA:** Local **D/D/R:** managing slot operations and the players club, filling and fixing machines and training employees **H/I/S:** Supporting the Lakers, Spending Time with his Family **EDU:** Coursework in Industrial Technology and Management, Cheyney University of Pennsylvania (1984) **CERTS:** Graduate Leadership Program; Graduate Diversity Programs, MGM Corporation
Email: rfi7364634@aol.com
Email: rfields@terriblescasinos.com
URL: http://www.cambridgewhoswho.com

Dr. Adeline Fields-Goode
Title: Pastor **Company:** Saint Paul Memorial Holy Church **Address:** 2300 Burton Street, Richmond, VA 23223 **BUS:** Church **P/S:** Religious Services **MA:** Local **D/D/R:** mentoring, praying, aiding those in need, counseling and outreaching **H/I/S:** Sewing, Reading, Speaking with People **EDU:** Coursework in Special English, John Tyler Community College, Chester, VA; Coursework in Tailoring, Virginia Commonwealth University; Coursework, Virginia Bible Institute **CERTS:** Three Certifications in Sewing and Upholstery, John Tyler Community College **C/VW:** Former Worship Leader, St. Mark's Holy Church of America; Chairwoman, Missionary Department, St. Mark's Holy Church of America; Chairwoman, Extension Fund Department, St. Mark's Holy Church of America; Make-A-Wish; Disabled American Veterans; Local Police Department; Local State Troopers; Various Community Charitable Organizations
Email: adeline.fieldsgoode@cwwemail.com
URL: http://www.cambridgewhoswho.com

Edgar A. Figueroa, MD, FACS
Title: Doctor, Director of Trauma and Surgical Critical Care **Company:** University of Florida **Address:** 1317 Oak Street, Gainesville, FL 32611 United States **BUS:** University **P/S:** Higher Education **MA:** Regional **D/D/R:** performing trauma, hepato-pancreatic, vascular and oncological surgeries, overseeing surgical critical, trauma and laparoscopic care treatments **H/I/S:** Golfing, Deep Sea Fishing **EDU:** Residency, Puerto Rico (1992); MD, Universidad Central del Este, Dominican Republic (1980); Bachelor of Science, University of Puerto Rico (1976) **CERTS:** Licensed Trauma Surgeon, State of Florida (1988) **A/A/S:** American Medical Association; Political Action Group; Committee of Trauma Surgeons; Fellow, American College of Surgeons; Member, American College of Physicians Executives; Board Member, Hispanic Chamber of Commerce; Florida Medical Association; Florida Medical Association **A/H:** Cambridge Who's Who **C/VW:** Operation NOW; United Third Bridge; United Way; Make-A-Wish Foundation
Email: edgar.figueroa@health-first.org

Gayle M. Filantres
Title: Junior High Teacher of the Gifted **Company:** Mount Prospect School District 57 **Address:** 700 W. Lincoln Street, Mount Prospect, IL 60056 United States **BUS:** School **P/S:** Education **MA:** Local **D/D/R:** Teaching **H/I/S:** Ceramics, Reading, Horses **CERTS:** Certificate of Advanced Study, Northern Illinois University **A/A/S:** Illinois Education Association; National Education Association **C/VW:** American Lung Association
Email: gfilantres@lincoln.dist57.org

Marion C. Filippi
Title: President, Chief Executive Officer **Company:** Ballard's Inn **Address:** P.O. Box 1818, Block Island, RI 02807 United States **BUS:** Resort **P/S:** Hospitality, Food Service **MA:** National **D/D/R:** managing finance and overseeing business operations **EDU:** Master of Business Administration, Bryant University, Rhode Island; Master of Arts in Geography, University of Rhode Island; Bachelor of Arts in Geography, Vassar College, NY **A/A/S:** Bryant University Student Alumni Association; University of Rhode Island Alumni Association; Vassar College Alumni Association; National Fire Protection Association; Commissioner, Rhode Island Fire Safety
Email: marionfilippi@aol.com
URL: http://www.ballardsinn.com

Jerry A. Fincher
Title: Education Specialist **Company:** Holland Middle School **Dept:** Special Education Department **Address:** 4733 Landis Avenue, Baldwin Park, CA 91706 United States **BUS:** Middle School **P/S:** Education **MA:** Local **D/D/R:** managing resources for language arts, mathematics, pre-algebra and geometry department, accounting, computing and overseeing finance, Publishing, Mentoring New Teachers **H/I/S:** Renovating Homes, Carpentry, Gardening, Caring for his Dogs **EDU:** Educational Specialist Degree in Business and Special Education, California State Polytechnic University, Pomona **A/A/S:** Professional Development School
Email: jafincher749@bpusd.net

Eugene J. Fine
Title: Director of M. Donald Blaufox Laboratory of Molecular Research **Company:** Albert Einstein College of Medicine **Dept:** M. Donald Blaufox Laboratory of Molecular Research **Address:** 1825 E. Chester Road, Bronx, NY 10461 United States **BUS:** College of Medicine **P/S:** Medical Education and Research **MA:** National **D/D/R:** Nuclear Medicine **H/I/S:** Reading, Playing the Guitar and Piano, Listening to Music **EDU:** MD, SUNY Downstate Medical Center (1976); Master's Degree in Physics, University of Pennsylvania (1991); Bachelor of Arts in Physics, Queens College, CUNY (1968) **A/A/S:** American College of Nuclear Physics; Society of Nuclear Medicine; American College of Physicians; Nutrition and Metabolic Society
Email: efine@aecom.yu.edu
URL: http://www.aecom.yu.edu/rechargetrial

Anthony E. Fini
Title: Regional Manager **Company:** Nuance Communications **Address:** 394 Timber Ridge Drive, Bartlett, IL 60103 United States **BUS:** Business Solutions Company **P/S:** Speech Recognition Software, Design Solutions, Professional Services **MA:** International **D/D/R:** Designing Software Solutions to meet Client's Needs, Enterprise Selling of Hand Technology, Account Management **H/I/S:** Golfing, Sports **EDU:** Bachelor of Science in Education, Northern Illinois University (1978)
Email: tony.fini@nuance.com

Deborah A. Finke
Title: Licensed Professional Counselor **Company:** Rockford College **Address:** 5055 E. State Street, Rockford, IL 61103 United States **BUS:** University **P/S:** Accredited University Level Courses, Fewer than 20 Students Per Class, State-of-the-Art Wireless Internet, On-Campus Housing and Food Service **MA:** Regional **D/D/R:** Assisting Students with Career Transitions and Life Issues, Advising on Decisions Regarding Majors, Completing Resumes, Counseling and Stress Management **H/I/S:** Caring for Animals, Gardening, Enjoying Nature and Spirituality, Promoting Wellness **EDU:** Master of Science in Education, Concentration in Counseling, Northern Illinois University (2005); Bachelor of Science in Psychology, Rockford College (1998) **CERTS:** National Certified Counselor (April 2006) **A/A/S:** Illinois Counseling Association; American Counseling Association; Illinois Mental Health Counselors Association; American Psychological Association; National Career Development Association; Chi Sigma Iota; Kappa Delta Phi; District Creditional Counselor (November 2007)
Email: dafinke@sbcglobal.net
URL: http://www.rockford.edu

Pam Finley
Title: Loan Originator **Company:** Pulaski Mortgage **Address:** 2566 E. Joyce Boulevard, Suite 1, Fayetteville, AR 72703 United States **BUS:** Mortgage Company **P/S:** Loan Assistance, Federal Housing Administration and Alternative Loans **MA:** National **D/D/R:** Consulting People with Credit Problems and helping them to Qualify for Purchase of Homes, Mortgage Banking **H/I/S:** Spending Time with her Grandchildren, Horseback Riding **EDU:** Industry-Related Training; High School Education **CERTS:** Certification in Engineering **A/A/S:** BNI; Chamber of Commerce **A/H:** Million Dollar Producer, President's Club (2005, 2006)
Email: pfinley@pulaskimortgage.com
URL: http://www.cambridgewhoswho.com

Dr. Geraldine R. Finn
Title: Director of Gender Studies **Company:** The University of Findlay **Address:** 1000 N. Main Street, Findlay, OH 45840 United States **BUS:** University **P/S:** Higher Education for Students, Undergraduate and Graduate Degree Programs **MA:** Regional **D/D/R:** Teaching Gender Studies, Culture, History, Irish and American Immigration Classes, Directing Women's Study Program **H/I/S:** Traveling, Reading, Spending Time with Grandchildren **EDU:** Ph.D. in History and Ethnic Studies, Union Institute & University (1998) **A/A/S:** Phi Beta Delta; Phi Alpha Theta; University Representative, The University of Findlay; American Association of University Women
Email: finn@findlay.edu
URL: http://www.findlay.edu

Kenneth A. Finneran
Title: Vice President of Human Resources **Company:** Hellmann Worldwide Logistics, Inc. **Address:** 10450 N.W. 41st Street, Doral, FL 33178 United States **BUS:** International Freight Forwarding and Logistics Company **P/S:** Transportation and Logistics Services, Supply Chain Solutions **MA:** International **D/D/R:** overseeing employee development, strategic human resource development and evaluating staff performance **H/I/S:** Golfing, Playing Tennis and Basketball, Traveling **EDU:** Master's Degree in International Studies, Rheinische Friedrich-Wilhelms University, Bonn; Bachelor's Degree in International Studies, American University **A/A/S:** Junior Chamber International **C/VW:** March of Dimes; American Cancer Society
Email: kfinnera@us.hellmann.net
URL: http://www.hellmann.net

Mary E. Finocchi, Pharm.D.
Title: Emergency Department Clinical Pharmacist **Company:** Tampa General Hospital **Address:** P.O. Box 1289, Tampa, FL 33601 United States **BUS:** Hospital **P/S:** Emergency Services Including Trauma Care, Pediatrics, Childbirth, Orthopedics, Cardiac Care and Rehabilitation Center **MA:** Local **D/D/R:** managing patients medication including proper drug dosing and toxicology cases, educating staff registered nurses and doctors **H/I/S:** Running, Biking **EDU:** Doctor of Pharmacy, University of Minnesota (2005)
Email: mfinocchi@tgh.org
URL: http://www.tgh.org

Mariel Fiori
Title: Managing Editor **Company:** La Voz del Valle del Hudson (Bard College) **Address:** 30 Campus Road, Annandale on Hudson, NY 12504 United States **BUS:** Magazine **P/S:** Higher Education, Journalism **MA:** Hudson Valley **D/D/R:** Journalism **H/I/S:** Reading, Working Out, Cooking **EDU:** Bachelor of Arts in Spanish and Latin American Studies, Bard College; Bachelor of Arts in Journalism, Argentina University **A/A/S:** National Association of Hispanic Journalists
Email: marielfiori@hotmail.com
URL: http://www.lavozdelhudson.blogspot.com

Rachel E. Fischbein, LMT
Title: Licensed Massage Therapist **Company:** Sunflower Massage **Address:** 1 Irving Place, Apartment U22C, New York, NY 10003 United States **BUS:** Therapy Center **P/S:** Massage Therapy **MA:** Local **D/D/R:** Performing Swedish, Prenatal, Sports, Deep Tissue and Shiatsu Massages **H/I/S:** Swimming, Traveling, Photography **EDU:** Associate Degree in Massage Therapy, Swedish Institute (2006) **CERTS:** Certified Prenatal Massage Therapist **A/A/S:** American Massage Therapy Association **C/VW:** Greenpeace International
Email: info@sunflowermassage.net
URL: http://www.sunflowermassage.net

Lesley J. Fischer
Title: Owner **Company:** Sand Dunes Travel **Address:** 15721 260th Ave NW, Big Lake, MN 55309 United States **BUS:** Travel Service Provider **P/S:** Vacation Packages and Travel Accommodations **MA:** Local **EDU:** High School
Email: info@CambridgeWhosWho.com

Jeffrey M. Fish
Title: Property Manager **Company:** Morlin Asset Management, LP **Address:** 444 S. Flower Street, Suite 500, Los Angeles, CA 90071 United States **BUS:** Real Estate Company **P/S:** Commercial Real Estate Management **MA:** Northern and Southern California **D/D/R:** Managing Property and Facility **H/I/S:** Golfing, Painting **EDU:** Bachelor of Business Administration, DeVry University **A/A/S:** Institute of Real Estate Management; Building Owners and Managers Association International **C/VW:** Knights of Columbus
Email: j.fish@morlinmgmt.com
URL: http://www.morlinmgmt.com

Gia F. Fisher
Title: Director of Information Technology **Company:** Health Net, Inc. **Address:** 21281 Burbank Boulevard, Woodland Hills, CA 91367 United States **BUS:** Insurance Company **P/S:** Health Insurance Services **MA:** National **EXP:** Ms. Fisher's areas of expertise include network operations, applications and database technologies. **H/I/S:** Traveling **EDU:** Bachelor of Science in Business Management **A/A/S:** Project Management Institute **A/H:** Who's Who in Music **C/VW:** Malibu Rotary Club
Email: giafisher@aol.com

Marilyn Fisher
Title: Senior Financial Adviser **Company:** SIGNATOR Advisory Group **Address:** 1 Huntington Quadrangle, Melville, NY 11747 United States **BUS:** Financial and Estate Planning **P/S:** Account Management, Insurance, Annuities **MA:** Regional **D/D/R:** Specializing in Pensions, 401K, IRA Distribution, Rollover and Inheritance Rules **H/I/S:** Gardening, Practicing Yoga, Swimming, Bird Watching **EDU:** Bachelor's Degree in Illustration, Pratt Institute **CERTS:** CLU; ChFC; CFP; IAR **A/A/S:** Nassau County Estate Planning Council; The Financial Planning Association; The FPA Fee Advisor Group; Ed Slott's Master IRA Group; SFSP **C/VW:** United States of America Olympic; Defenders of Wildlife; The Ocean Conservancy; The National Wildlife Association
Email: mfisher@jhnetwork.com
URL: http://www.marilynfisher.signatorfinancial.com

Dr. Richard G. Fisher
Title: Doctor **Company:** Baylor College of Medicine **Address:** 1 Baylor Plaza, Houston, TX 77030 United States **BUS:** Medical School **P/S:** Healthcare, Education **MA:** Houston **EXP:** Dr. Fisher's area of expertise is in interventional radiology. **D/D/R:** Teaching and Practicing Radiology **H/I/S:** Sailing **EDU:** MD, The University of Texas Medical Branch; Bachelor of Arts in Chemistry, University of Connecticut **CERTS:** Certified in Interventional Radiology **A/A/S:** American College of Radiology; Houston Radiology Society; Texas Radiological Society; The Radiological Society of North America, Inc.; American Roentgen Ray Society; Society of Interventional Radiology; American Medical Association
Email: richard_fisher@hehd.tmc.edu
URL: http://www.cambridgewhoswho.com

Sondra L. Fisher
Title: Reading Specialist **Company:** Williamsport Area School District **Address:** 1500 Cherry Street, Williamsport, PA 17701 United States **BUS:** School **P/S:** Education **MA:** Local **D/D/R:** Reading Recovery **H/I/S:** Reading **EDU:** Master's Degree in Special Education, University of Pittsburgh; Reading Specialist Certification, State of California, University of Pennsylvania **CERTS:** Cooperative Education Certification, The Penn State University **A/A/S:** Reading Recovery; Pennsylvania State Education Association
Email: slfisher11@verizon.net

Susan P. Fisk
Title: Owner, Registered Nurse, LMT **Company:** Salubrious Massage, Inc. **Address:** 7304 Cottonwood, Suite 205, Midvale, UT 84047 United States **BUS:** Massage Center **P/S:** Healthcare **MA:** Local **EXP:** Ms. Fisk's area of expertise is in intuitive massage. **H/I/S:** Massaging, Boating, Reading **EDU:** Associate Degree in Nursing, Valencia Community College **CERTS:** Licensed Massage Therapist, Utah **A/A/S:** Association for Body and Massage Professionals **C/VW:** Volunteer, Hospice; Multiple Sclerosis
Email: sufis2005@gmail.com
URL: http://www.cambridgewhoswho.com

Wendy R. Fite
Title: Chief of Application Development Office **Company:** Administrative Office of the US Courts **Address:** One Columbus Circle NE, Suite 3-272, Washington, DC 20544 United States **BUS:** Government **P/S:** Information Technology **MA:** International **D/D/R:** IT Services **H/I/S:** Scuba, Distance Runner, Pilot **EDU:** St Norbert College, Central Michigan University, MS **A/A/S:** US Army; AADA; NMI; Habitat for Humanity
Email: wendy.fite@verizon.net

Mary Louise Fitzgerald
Title: Director **Company:** Mary Kay **BUS:** Retail Store **P/S:** Cosmetics and Skin Care Products **MA:** National **D/D/R:** overseeing skin care products sales **H/I/S:** Gardening, Sewing, Reading **EDU:** Bachelor of Science in Home Economics, The University of Tennessee **CERTS:** Certification in Teaching **A/A/S:** Zeta Tau Alpha; Education Honor Society **C/VW:** Volunteer, Cancer and Violence Program, Mary Kay
Email: mlpjf@aol.com
URL: http://www.marykay.com/mfitzgerald

Ms. Bridget Fitzpatrick
Title: Senior Principal Technical Consultant **Company:** Mustang Engineering **Address:** 16001 Park Ten Place, Houston, TX 77084 United States **BUS:** Consulting Company **P/S:** Automotive Consulting Including Chemical, Refining, Pharmaceuticals, Plastics and Utilities **MA:** International **EXP:** Ms. Fitzpatrick's areas of expertise include HMI and abnormal condition management. **H/I/S:** Visiting National Parks, Gardening, Home Remodeling **EDU:** Master of Business Administration, University of Phoenix; Bachelor's Degree in Chemical Engineering, Massachusetts Institute of Technology **A/A/S:** American Institute of Chemical Engineering; American Chemical Society; Industry Standard Architecture **C/VW:** Massachusetts Institute of Technology
Email: bridget.fitzpatrick@gmail.com
URL: http://www.cambridgewhoswho.com

Carly S. Fives
Title: Special Services Coordinator of Special Education and Gifted Services **Company:** 21st Century Cyber Charter School **Address:** 455 Boot Road, Downingtown, PA 19335 United States **BUS:** State-Accredited Diploma-Granting School Serving Pennsylvania Students in Grades 6 Through 12 **P/S:** Online Classes Using a School-Issued Computer and Program-Provided Software and Required Hardware, Textbooks, Email Accounts for Students and Parents, Technical Support and Dial-Up Internet Access **MA:** Regional **D/D/R:** Overseeing the Special Education and Guidance Department Administration, Overseeing IEP's, Taking Care of Legal Issues Related to the Programs, Coordinating All Services, Contracting Out Services, Acting Liaison Between All Third-Party Providers **EDU:** Master of Arts in Special Education, Pennsylvania State University (2007) **A/A/S:** Phi Delta Kappa International
Email: cfives@21cccs.org
URL: http://www.21cccs.org

Janet Elizabeth Flack
Title: Owner/Principal Interior Designer **Company:** Janet Flack Interiors, Inc **Address:** 280 Holden Street, Wyoming, PA 18644 United States **BUS:** Interior Design Corporation **P/S:** Interior Design (Commercial and Residential) **MA:** National **D/D/R:** Space Planning, Renovation, Interior Design **H/I/S:** Sculpting, Painting **EDU:** Bachelor's Degree in Illustration, Endicott College; Diploma in Interior Design, Harrington College of Design **A/A/S:** IIDA, AIA
Email: jfinterior@aol.com

Bonnie L. Flannery
Title: General Manager, Food Service Director **Company:** Compass Group USA **Dept:** Eurest Dining Services **Address:** 5188 W. Rowland Lane, Silver Lake, IN 46982 United States **BUS:** Food Service Company **P/S:** Hospitality and Food Services **MA:** International **D/D/R:** supervising three chefs, ordering supplies, accounting and overseeing administrative duties, Managing Operations of the Cafeteria, 21 Employees and Two Buildings, Serving Foods, Ensuring Customer Satisfaction **H/I/S:** Spending Time with her Family **EDU:** Diploma, Tippecanoe Valley High School **A/A/S:** President, Diamond Lake Conservation Club **A/H:** Emerald Who's Who
Email: bonflannery@yahoo.com
Email: bonflannery@netzero.com

Eileen M. Flavin
Title: Assistant Department Administrator for Central Service **Company:** Kaiser Permanente Hospital **Address:** 441 Lakeview Avenue, Anaheim, CA 92807 United States **BUS:** Hospital **P/S:** Anesthesiology, Internal Medicine, Neurosurgery, Behavioral Health, Internal Medicine, Cardiac Surgery, Interventional Radiology, Cardiology Laboratory, Physical Therapy and Many Other Services **MA:** Regional **D/D/R:** Ensuring Operating Room Back-Up Carts are Available, Replenishing Used Carts, Conducting Physical Therapy Traction Set-Ups on a Daily Basis, Handling Operating Room Instrumentation and Sterilization, Setting Up Individual Case Carts for Surgeons, Responding to All Codes for Crash Carts in the Hospital, Assembling Crash Cart Instruments and Supplies for Adult, Pediatric and Neonatal Patients, Training In-House **H/I/S:** Watching Basketball, Playing Piano, Cooking **EDU:** Bachelor of Science in Healthcare, University of California (1971) **CERTS:** Certified Registered Central Service Technician; Certified Central Service Technician **A/A/S:** Facilitative Committee for New Hospital; Board Member, Orange County, California Central Service Association; Instructor, International Hospital Association for Central Service and Materials Management **A/H:** Hero of the Year Award, MSAT (2006)
Email: eileen.m.flavin@kp.org
URL: http://www.kaiserpermanente.org

Jennifer L. Fleener
Title: Spanish Teacher **Company:** Pioneer Westfield High School **Address:** N7046 County Road CH, Westfield, WI 53964 United States **BUS:** Public High School **P/S:** High School Education, Foreign Language Education **MA:** Regional **D/D/R:** Educating Students, Teaching Spanish Level II to Middle School Preparatory Classes, Developing Curriculum **H/I/S:** Traveling, Scrapbooking, Enjoying Outdoor Activities **EDU:** Bachelor's Degree in Education, Concentration in Spanish, University of Wisconsin-Steven's Point (2004) **A/A/S:** American Association of Teachers of Spanish and Portuguese; Wisconsin Association of Foreign Language Teachers; National Education Association
Email: jlfleener@charter.net
URL: http://www.westfield.k12.wi.us/pwhs/pwhs_main.html

Randi Fleischman
Title: President **Company:** Happy Handbags **Address:** 810 Jennetty Court, Perth Amboy, NJ 08861 United States **BUS:** Cigar Box Handbag Company **P/S:** One-of-a-Kind Cigar Bo Handbags **MA:** Tri-State Area **D/D/R:** Creating Custom-Made Handbags **C/VW:** Breast Cancer Foundation
Email: randi@happyhandbags.info
URL: http://www.happyhandbags.info

Kerry L. Fleming
Title: Elementary School Counselor **Company:** Livingston Park Elementary School **Address:** 1128 Livingston Avenue, North Brunswick, NJ 08902 United States **BUS:** Public School **P/S:** Instruction and Curriculum **MA:** Regional **D/D/R:** Counseling Students with Problems Inside of School, Class Lessons, Behavior Plans **H/I/S:** Running and Fitness, Music, Art, Animals **EDU:** MB, Student Personnel Services, University of Delaware (2000) **CERTS:** Licensed Associate Counselor, Kean University (2005)
Email: kerleaflem@yahoo.com
URL: http://www.nbtschools.org/lpindex.html

Monique A. Fleming
Title: Research Assistant Professor **Company:** University of Southern California, Department of Psychology **Address:** Seeley G. Mudd Building, Room 501, Los Angeles, CA 90089 United States **BUS:** University **P/S:** Education, Psychology Research **MA:** International **D/D/R:** Social Psychology, Attitudes and Persuasion, Social Cognition **H/I/S:** Hiking, Walking on the Beach **EDU:** Ph.D. in Social Psychology, Ohio State University **A/A/S:** American Psychological Association; Association for Psychological Science; Society for Personality and Social Psychology; Social Psychology Network **C/VW:** Doctors Without Borders, Nature Conservancy, Oxfam
Email: mfleming@usc.edu
URL: http://fleming.socialpsychology.org

Holly Fleming-Pitre
Title: Esthetician **Company:** Bellissima Salon Spa **Address:** 210 Mystic Boulevard, Houma, LA 70360 United States **BUS:** Salon, Spa **P/S:** Full-Service Salon/Spa **MA:** Local **D/D/R:** Facials, Waxing, Microdermabrasions, Mud Wraps, Peels, eyelash extensions **H/I/S:** Spending Time with her Family **EDU:** Coursework in Elementary Education, Nicholls State University; Coursework in Elementary Education, Louisiana State Universit **CERTS:** State Board Certified Esthetician, Aveda Institute Neill Corporation **C/VW:** Goodwill
Email: hollypitre@myway.com
URL: http://www.cambridgewhoswho.com

Cheryl L. Fletcher
Title: Registered Nurse, Perinatal Nurse Educator **Company:** Unity Health System **Address:** 27 Lake Home Street, Rochester, NY 14612 United States **BUS:** Medical Center **P/S:** Healthcare **MA:** Regional **D/D/R:** obstetrics and gynecology nursing, educating perinatal nursing, hosting in-service workshops and orientations, conducting chart audits and inviting speakers **H/I/S:** Reading, Gardening **EDU:** Pursuing Master's Degree in Nursing; Bachelor of Science in Nursing, Roberts Wesleyan College (1994) **A/A/S:** Association of Women's Health, Obstetric and Neonatal Nurses
Email: cfletcher@unityhealth.org
URL: http://www.unityhealth.org

Lindsay Fletcher
Title: Special Education Teacher **Company:** W.G. Smith School **Address:** 1900 Wharton Street, Philadelphia, PA 19146 United States **BUS:** School **P/S:** Education **MA:** Local **D/D/R:** acting as a special education liaison in the school, teaching special education for children with learning disabilities and developmental disorders **H/I/S:** Traveling, Reading, Participating in Military Activities **EDU:** Master's Degree in Multicultural Education, Eastern University; Bachelor of Arts in History, George Mason University **CERTS:** Certification in Special Education, Eastern University; Certification in Elementary Education, Eastern University **C/VW:** Big Brothers Big Sisters of America
Email: lrfletcher@phila.k12.pa.us

Claudette Fletcher-Kennedy
Title: President, Director **Company:** Burnis Kennedy Scholarship Fund, Inc. **Address:** 6447 Rustic Ridge Trail, Grand Blanc, MI 48439 United States **BUS:** Scholarship Organization **P/S:** Scholarships for Underprivileged Youth **MA:** Local **D/D/R:** Overseeing and Conducting Business to Award Educational Scholarships to Underprivileged Youth **H/I/S:** Traveling, Cooking **EDU:** Associate Degree in Computer Data Control, Institute of Computer Management, Cleveland; Associate Degree in Business Management, Flint Community College **C/VW:** Flint Shelter, Big Brothers Big Sister of Flint
Email: claudette_k@yahoo.com
URL: http://www.cambridgewhoswho.com

Kathryn 'Ka' Flewellen
Title: Assistant Director AU/NTL Master's Degree Program **Company:** American University **Address:** 4400 Massachusetts N.W., Washington, DC 20016 United States **BUS:** University **P/S:** Higher Education **MA:** Local **D/D/R:** Overseeing Daily Operations of the Master's Degree Program in Organization Development Including Recruitment, Recruiting, Conducting Special Programs **H/I/S:** Writing Poetry, Painting and Making Jewelry **EDU:** Pursuing Ph.D., Fielding Graduate University, Santa Barbara, CA; Master of Science, American University (2000); Bachelor of Science, McCaluster College; Bachelor of Arts, McCallister College **A/A/S:** Organization Development Network; Academy of Management; National Association of University Women
Email: KaKathryn.Flewellen@cwwemail.com
Email: changestrategist@aol.com
URL: http://www.american.edu

Debbie H. Flint, LPN
Title: Licensed Practical Nurse **Company:** Fort Hudson Nursing Center, Inc. **Address:** 319 Broadway, Fort Edward, NY 12828 United States **BUS:** Nursing Center **P/S:** Long-Term Healthcare, Rehabilitation **MA:** Local **D/D/R:** Working with Geriatric Patients, Caring for Patients with Diabetes and Alzheimer's Disease **H/I/S:** Gardening **CERTS:** Two-Year Degree in Licensed Practical Nursing, BOCES Myers Education Center, Saratoga, New York **A/H:** Employee of the Month **C/VW:** Alzheimer's Walk for Life; Breast Cancer Research
Email: DebbieH.Flint@cwwemail.com

Erin M. Flitcroft, DVM
Title: Veterinarian **Company:** Companion Animal Hospital **Address:** 3720 Highway 431N, Phenix City, AL 36867 United States **BUS:** Private Practice of Veterinary Medicine **P/S:** Small Animals Care **MA:** Regional **D/D/R:** Teaching Laboratory Science in School, Specializing in Breeding **H/I/S:** Horseback Riding, Shows, Jumper (of Horses) **EDU:** Doctor of Veterinary Medicine, Tuskegee University School of Veterinary Medicine **A/A/S:** American Veterinary Association
Email: dvmmustanggirl@yahoo.com
URL: http://www.vin.com

Victoria K. Florek
Title: Lead Mathematics Teacher **Company:** Stratford Board of Education **Address:** 1000 E. Broadway, Stratford, CT 06615 United States **BUS:** Board of Education **P/S:** Education **MA:** Local **EXP:** Ms. Florek's area of expertise is in professional development. **D/D/R:** teaching mathematics, writing curriculum and working with elementary schools in the district **H/I/S:** Bicycling, Spending Time at the Beach **EDU:** Master's Degree in Elementary Education, University of Bridgeport (1977) **A/A/S:** National Council of Teachers of Mathematics **A/H:** PIMMS Award (1997) **C/VW:** Swim Across the Sound
Email: florekv@stratford.k12.ct.us

Joan A. Flores
Title: School Counselor **Company:** School District of Philadelphia, Tanner G. Duck Rey School **Address:** 1501 W. Diamond Street, Philadelphia, PA 19121 United States **BUS:** School **P/S:** Education **MA:** North Philadelphia **D/D/R:** Individual and Group Counseling **H/I/S:** Spending Time with her Children **EDU:** Master's Degree Plus 30 in Human Services, Lincoln University **A/A/S:** American Counseling Association; Pennsylvania Counseling Association **A/H:** Top Ladies of Distinction, Easter Star 2008 **C/VW:** Top Ladies of Distinction, March of Dimes
Email: jflores@phila.k12.pa.us
URL: http://www.cambridgewhoswho.com

Anne M. Florin
Title: Recognition Consultant **Company:** Wells Fargo **Address:** 1801 Park View Drive, Shoreview, MN 55126 United States **BUS:** Financial, Banking **P/S:** Finance, Bank **MA:** International **D/D/R:** Recognition of Employees, Formal and Informal **H/I/S:** Riding her Motorcycle, Skiing, Water Sports, Scrapbooking **EDU:** Coursework, Mankato State College (Now Minnesota State University, Mankato) **C/VW:** Local Humane Society; Co-Superintendent, Sunday School, Church; Abate Motorcycle Organization; Buddy Bears
Email: anne.m.florin@wellsfargo.com
URL: http://www.wellsfargo.com

Amy Flowers
Title: Realtor **Company:** The Flowers Team at Realty Executives Dillon **Address:** 2240 Otay Lakes Road, Suite 306, Chula Vista, CA 91915 United States **BUS:** Real Estate Company **P/S:** Residential, Executive, High-End, Oceanfront, Bayfront, New Construction, Condominium, Golf Home, Gated and Estate Real Estate **MA:** National **D/D/R:** Selling Residential Properties **H/I/S:** Spending Time with her Family, Snow Boarding **EDU:** Master of Science in Entrepreneurship, San Diego State University; Bachelor of Science in Marketing, Arizona State University **A/A/S:** California Association of Realtors; National Association of Realtors; Chula Vista Chamber of Commerce
Email: amy@amyflowers.com
URL: http://www.flowersteamonline.com

Larry Flowers
Title: Psychiatrist **Company:** Larry Flowers **Address:** 110 Cypress Station Drive, Suite 113, Houston, TX 77090 United States **BUS:** Private Psychiatric Practice **P/S:** Treatment of Major Depressive Disorders **MA:** Local **D/D/R:** Treating Mood Disorders and Chemical Dependency in Adults and Adolescents **H/I/S:** Playing Tennis, Jogging, Basketball **EDU:** Medical Degree in Psychiatry, Meharry Medical College (1982); Psychiatry Residency Training Program, Baylor College of Medicine (1986) **A/A/S:** American Psychiatry Association; American Medical Association; Texas Psychiatric Association **C/VW:** Catholic Charities; Young Men's Christian Association
Email: larry.flowers@sbcglobal.net
URL: http://www.cambridgewhoswho.com

Robert W. Flowers
Title: Chief Executive Officer **Company:** Saber 98 Technologies, LLC **Address:** 1026 W. Mount Gallant Road, York, SC 29745 United States **BUS:** Information Technology Company **P/S:** Information Technology Consulting **MA:** Local **D/D/R:** Overseeing Project Management and Software Development, Web Development **H/I/S:** Studying Computer Hardware, Enjoying Computer Gaming, Golfing **EDU:** Associate Degree in Computer Technology, York Technical College **A/A/S:** Charlotte Information Technology Users Group; Windows Information Technology User Group; Co-Founder, Carolina Computer Gaming Association **C/VW:** St. Jude Children's Research Hospital, Catawba United Methodist Church
Email: rflowers@saber98.com
URL: http://www.saber98.com

Mr. James A. Floyd Jr.
Title: Field Supervisor, Owner **Company:** Trexcon, LLC **BUS:** Privately Owned Company Committed to Excellence in the Construction Industry **P/S:** Excavating, Concrete Work, Construction **MA:** Regional **D/D/R:** Working with Concrete, Building Bases for Cell Phone Towers, Constructing Driveways, Excavating Services, Conducting Business via the Internet **H/I/S:** Deer Hunting, Fishing, Bird Hunting **EDU:** Associate Degree in Electronics, Red's Electronics (1984) **A/A/S:** Louisville Homebuilders Association
Email: bofloyd.trexcon@insightbb.com
URL: http://www.cambridgewhoswho.com

Natalie A. Floyd
Title: Adult Nurse Practitioner **Company:** Birmingham Veterans Administration Medical Center **Address:** 700 19th Street S., Birmingham, AL 35218 United States **BUS:** Medical Center **P/S:** Acute, Chronic and Long-Term Care **MA:** Local **D/D/R:** Nursing **H/I/S:** Traveling, Bowling, Playing Tennis, Reading **EDU:** Master's Degree in Nurse Practitioner Studies, University of Alabama, Birmingham **A/A/S:** American Diabetes Association; Sigma Theta Tau **A/H:** Cambridge Who's Who; Award, Sigma Theta Tau (2007)
Email: n.a.floyd@att.net

Carrie A. Flury
Title: Certified Physician Assistant **Company:** La Familia Care Center of Eastern New Mexico Medical Center **Address:** 712 W. Hobbs Street, Roswell, NM 88203 United States **BUS:** Family Medical Center **P/S:** Healthcare **MA:** Local **D/D/R:** Caring for Patients in Emergency Care Units, Geriatric Care, Managing Diabetes and High-Cholesterol Patients, DOT Physicals and Women's Health **H/I/S:** Hiking, Camping, Reading, Spending Time with her Family **EDU:** Master of Science in Advanced Physician Assistant Studies, Arizona School of Health Sciences (2000); Bachelor of Science in Physician Assistant Studies, Alderson-Broaddus College (1996) **A/A/S:** National Commission on Certification of Physician Assistants; American Academy of Physician Assistants; New Mexico Academy of Physician Assistants
Email: carrieflury@hotmail.com

Anthony Fodera
Title: Professional Photographer, Owner **Company:** Fodera Photography **Address:** 1138 Monroe Drive, Stewartsville, NJ 08886 United States **BUS:** Photography **P/S:** Photography **MA:** Regional **D/D/R:** Family and Children's Portraits, Weddings **H/I/S:** Collecting Model Trains, Collecting Mustangs **EDU:** Bachelor of Fine Arts, Pratt Institute **CERTS:** Certified by the Professional Photographers of America **A/A/S:** Professional Photography Association of New Jersey; Professional Photography Association of Pennsylvania; Society of Sports and Events Photographers **C/VW:** NILMDTS
Email: avfphoto@aol.com
URL: http://www.foderaphotography.com

Jessica Anne Fogas
Title: Marketing Manager **Company:** Adams County Winery **Address:** 251 Peach Tree Road, Orrtanna, PA 17353 United States **BUS:** Vineyard and Winery **P/S:** Wine Production **MA:** National **D/D/R:** Vineyard and Winery Management **H/I/S:** Reading, Fishing, Boating, Traveling, Spending Time with her Family **EDU:** Bachelor of Science in Business, Susquehanna University (2005) **A/H:** Double Gold Award, Keystone Wine Competition (2006) **C/VW:** American Heart Association; March of Dimes; Habitat for Humanity
Email: jessica@adamscountywinery.com
URL: http://www.adamscountywinery.com

Shelli R. Fohrman
Title: Sales and Leasing Specialist **Company:** Denny Hecker's Rosedale Hyundai **Address:** 2767 Long Lake Road, Roseville, MN 55113 United States **BUS:** Automotive Sales and Leasing **P/S:** Sale and Leasing of New and Used Cars **MA:** Regional **D/D/R:** Taking Customer Information, Preparing Customized Dealer Trades, Offering Accurate Information to Consumers, Ensuring Customer Satisfaction **H/I/S:** Painting, Volleyball, Softball, Drawing, Reading, Playing with her Children **EDU:** Industry-Related Training Coursework in Art **A/A/S:** Young Authors' Association
Email: sfohrman@comcast.net
URL: http://www.rosedalehyundai.com

Elaine R. Foley
Title: Data Management Assistant **Company:** Touro Infirmary **Address:** 1401 Foucher Street, New Orleans, LA 70115 United States **BUS:** Healthcare **P/S:** Infirmary **MA:** Local **D/D/R:** Assisting All Areas of Data Management **H/I/S:** Gardening, Dancing, Exercising, Enjoys spending tine with Grandchildren, Socializing, Watching TV **CERTS:** Multi Level Touro Certifications, Horizon Computer Institute **A/A/S:** ACORN
Email: foleye@turo.com

Christine L. Folmer
Title: Director **Company:** St. Andrew by the Bay Preschool **Address:** 701 College Parkway, Annapolis, MD 21409 United States **BUS:** Preschool **P/S:** Education **MA:** Local **D/D/R:** Teaching Children Aged Three to Five, Handling Curriculum Guide, School Budget and Calendar, Processing all Registration Applications and Health Inventory to Meet the Standards of Childcare Administration **H/I/S:** Traveling, Reading, Collecting American Historical Memorabilia **EDU:** Bachelor's Degree in Early Childhood Education, Towson University **A/A/S:** The Maryland Committee for Children; Arundel Childcare Connections **C/VW:** St. Andrew by the Bay
Email: CLFolmer@aol.com
URL: http://www.standrewbythebay.org

Christina K. Folsome
Title: Teacher, Registered Nurse **Company:** Alfred Ely Beach High School **Address:** 3001 Hopkins Street, Savannah, GA 31405 United States **BUS:** Public High School **P/S:** Secondary Education Including Athletics, Accelerated Programs, Special Education **MA:** Local **D/D/R:** Teaching Basic Medical and Nursing Skills, Healthcare Science and Medical-Surgical Nursing Courses, Teaching Healthcare Science Technology to High School Students, Mentoring New Teachers, Meeting other Department Leaders **H/I/S:** Sports, Listening to Music, Reading, Traveling **EDU:** Master's Degree in Biblical Science, Jacksonville Theological Seminary and Revelation Message Bible College **A/A/S:** Association for Career and Technical Education; Senate Committee, School Leadership Team **A/H:** National Honor Roll's Outstanding American Teachers; Teacher of the Year Award (2006); Who's Who Among American Teachers (2005-2006); Teacher Excellence Award, Savannah Morning News (2005-2006)
Email: christine.folsome@savannah.chatham.k12.ga.us
URL: http://www.savannah.chatham.k12.ga.us

Raymond Fong
Title: Chief Executive Officer, President **Company:** FSE, LLC **BUS:** Technology and Automotive Company **P/S:** Construction, Remodeling, Computer Rebuilding and Repair, Automotive Detailing, Customer Service **MA:** Regional **D/D/R:** Supervising Staff, Managing Business Policies and Procedures, Computer Rebuilding, Building Dual Processing Technology, Automotive Detailing for Exotic Cars, Real Estate Inventors **H/I/S:** Smoking Cigars, Boxing, Attending Car Shows, Going to the Beach, Sports Spectator **EDU:** Bachelor of Science in Business Management, University of Phoenix (1997) **A/A/S:** Jaguar Clubs of North America
Email: fongerelli@gmail.com

Hattie M. Fonville
Title: Research Clinical Nurse **Company:** National Institutes of Health **Address:** 1892 Champlain Drive, Severn, MD 21144 United States **BUS:** Government Healthcare Facilities **P/S:** Medical and Behavioral Research, Developing, Maintaining and Renewing Scientific Human and Physical Resources **MA:** National **D/D/R:** Charge Nurse for a 16-Bed Unit, Performing Clinical Research, Overseeing the Alcoholism Unit, Teaching Patients About Alcoholism **H/I/S:** Interior Decorating, Floral Arranging, Sewing, Jewelry Making, Antiques **EDU:** Associate Degree in Nursing, Craven Community College (1993) **A/A/S:** American Nurses Association
Email: hfonville@hotmail.com
URL: http://www.nih.gov

David B. Foose
Title: Speech-Language Pathologist **Company:** Howe Center **Address:** 7600 W. 183rd Street, Tinley Park, IL 60477 United States **BUS:** Department of Human Service **P/S:** Habitation Planning and Training for Developmental Disabled Adults and Intermediate Care Facility for Developmental Disabled Adults **MA:** Local **D/D/R:** Speech-Language Pathologist, Augmentative Communication and Swallowing Disorders **H/I/S:** Computer, Reading, Traveling **EDU:** Master's Degree in Speech-Language Pathologist, South Illinois University **A/A/S:** Illinois Speech and Hearing Association; American Speech and Hearing Association; United States Society for Alternative and Augmentative Communications
Email: davefoos@comcast.net
URL: http://www.cambridgewhoswho.com

Deborah H. Ford, MS, Ed.S.
Title: Assistant Principal, CTAE Director **Company:** Marion County High School **BUS:** High School **P/S:** Secondary Education **MA:** Local **D/D/R:** budgeting, managing finance, recruiting employees and developing curriculum, Working with the Department of Board of Education on Budgeting, Managing Business Operations, Assisting Parents, Addressing Discipline Issues, Consulting, Lecturing **H/I/S:** Visiting Historical Buildings **EDU:** Educational Specialist Degree, Troy University (1999); Master of Science, The University of Georgia (1987) **CERTS:** Congressional Certification **A/A/S:** Georgia Association of Secondary School Principals; Association for Career and Technical Education; American Association of Family and Consumer Sciences; Kappa Delta Gamma **A/H:** State Teacher of the Year Award
Email: dford@marion.k12.ga.us
URL: http://www.marion.k12.ga.us

Marvella E. Ford
Title: Associate Professor, Associate Director of Cancer Disparities **Company:** Medical University of South Carolina **Address:** 86 Jonathan Lucas Street, Charleston, SC 29425 United States **BUS:** University **P/S:** Education **MA:** Local **D/D/R:** Reducing Cancer Disparities and Health Disparities, Social Epidemiology **H/I/S:** Working **EDU:** Ph.D. in Psychology and Social Work, University of Michigan, 1992; Master's Degree in Psychology, University of Michigan, 1989; Master's Degree in Social Work, University of Michigan, 1987 **A/A/S:** American Psychological Association **C/VW:** Feed the Children, Hope International, American Cancer Society
Email: fordmar@musc.edu

Shirley A. Ford
Title: Reverend **Company:** Lincoln Church of God **Address:** 513 South Carter Street, Lincoln, AR 72744 United States **BUS:** Church **P/S:** Helping Others Find God **MA:** Regional **H/I/S:** Reading, Working, The Church, Taking Care of Family **A/A/S:** The Ministerial Alliance, The Gideons **C/VW:** Works with numerous churches and prison ministries
Email: mhuffaker@pgtc.com
URL: www.pgtc.com

Lisa Kay Fore
Title: Teacher **Company:** Forest Heights Middle School **Address:** 5901 Evergreen Street, Little Rock, AR 72205 United States **BUS:** Middle School Facility Dedicated to Excellence in Education **P/S:** Regular Core Curriculum including Reading, Math, English, Science, Social Studies, Art, Music, History, Languages, Computers, Physical Education **MA:** Regional **D/D/R:** Teaching 7th and 8th-Grade English, Currently Teaching 6th-Grade Health, 6 Classes Per Day for Approximately 250 Children, Also Teaching Social, Mental, Emotional and Physical Health, Is a Cheerleader Judge **H/I/S:** Reading, Gardening **EDU:** Master's Degree in Library Media and Technology, University of Central Arkansas (2007) **A/A/S:** Former Cheerleader Coach **A/H:** Teacher of the Year (2000); Who's Who Among America's Teachers
Email: lisa.fore@lrsd.org
URL: http://www.forestheightsmiss4.tripod.com

Janet L. Forgy
Title: District Sales Coordinator **Company:** Aflac **Address:** 6715 W. Beverly Road, Laveen, AZ 85339 United States **BUS:** Insurance Company **P/S:** Insurance Services **MA:** National **D/D/R:** Directing Sales, Marketing, Promoting Relationships, Managing Clients, Hiring, Recruiting **H/I/S:** Attending Theater, Listening to Music, Walking **EDU:** Master's Degree in Public Communications and Broadcasting, Western Illinois University **C/VW:** Greater Phoenix Chamber of Commerce; Northwest Phoenix Leeds Group
Email: janet_forgy@us.aflac.com
URL: http://www.aflac.com

Ian Formigle
Title: President **Company:** Clarus Property Ventures, Inc. **Address:** 1111 S.W. Broadway Avenue, Portland, OR 97205 United States **BUS:** Real Estate Agency **P/S:** Real Estate Sales, Asset Management, Space Acquisition and Disposition **MA:** International **EXP:** Mr. Formigle's areas of expertise include business development, overseeing acquisition and disposition analysis, marketing strategy and strategic alliance. **H/I/S:** Kayaking, Biking, Skiing **EDU:** Bachelor's Degree in Economics and Political Science, University of California, Berkley (1995) **A/A/S:** Sierra Club; Oregon Entrepreneurs Network **C/VW:** Healing Waters; Doernbecher Children's Hospital
Email: ian@claruspv.com
URL: http://www.claruspv.com

Jana F. Fornstrom
Title: Instructional Facilitator **Company:** Laramie County School District #2 **Address:** 5 E. Elm Street, Pine Bluffs, WY 82082 United States **BUS:** School District **P/S:** Education **MA:** Local **D/D/R:** Reading **H/I/S:** Reading **EDU:** Master of Education, University of Wyoming
Email: jfornstrom@aol.com
URL: http://www.cambridgewhoswho.com

Virginia E. Forris-Walker
Title: Registered Nurse **Company:** Wayne County Juvenile Detention Facility **Address:** 1326 Saint Antoine Street, Detroit, MI 48226 United States **BUS:** Government Organization **P/S:** Healthcare Including Pre Adjudicated Juvenile Corrections Services **MA:** Countywide **EXP:** Ms. Forris-Walker's areas of expertise include medical surgical and psychiatric nursing. **H/I/S:** Dancing, Teaching Children, Tutoring, Reading, Listening to Music **EDU:** Master of Science in Nursing, University of Phoenix (2000) **CERTS:** Certification in Critical and Intensive Care Nursing **A/A/S:** Sigma Theta Tau **C/VW:** Detroit Public Schools; Local Church
Email: vwa8534365@aol.com

Pamela A. Forster, USV

Title: Agent, Field Trainer, Investment Consultant **Company:** Bankers Life and Casualty **Dept:** Bankers Investment Network **Address:** 202 Montrose West Avenue, Suite 240, Copley, OH 44321 United States **BUS:** Insurance Company **P/S:** Insurance Services for Seniors through a Broad Portfolio of Quality, Competitive Insurance Products Including Long-Term Care, Life, Annuities and Medicare Supplement **MA:** National **D/D/R:** training new agents, ensuring customer satisfaction, overseeing and managing compliance issues, visiting clients, assessing and supplying clients' insurance needs, financial and retirement planning **H/I/S:** Gardening, Playing Ice Hockey, Motorcycling **CERTS:** Series 6 License (2006); Securities License; Certification in Life, Health and Accident Insurance (2004); Certified Medical Assistant, Kent State University (1988)
Email: pamela.forster@bankerslife.com
URL: http://www.bankerslife.com

James A. Forte

Title: Owner **Company:** Forte Overnight **Address:** 2903 Paula Drive, Clovis, CA 93612 United States **BUS:** Distribution Company **P/S:** Packaged Merchandise **MA:** National **D/D/R:** negotiating contracts, freight forwarding and overseeing operations **EDU:** Coursework in Architecture, English and Business Law, Columbia Basin College, Washington State University **A/A/S:** California State University, Fresno **C/VW:** St. Joachim's Roman Catholic Church; The American Society for the Prevention of Cruelty to Animals
Email: james.forte@cwwemail.com
URL: http://www.cambridgewhoswho.com

Maureen T. Fortin

Title: Teacher **Company:** Suffield Public Schools **Address:** 260 Mountain Road, Suffield, CT 06078 United States **BUS:** Public School System **P/S:** Primary and Secondary Level Education **MA:** Local **D/D/R:** Teaching All Subjects to K-6th-Grade Students and Tutoring an After-School Literacy Class **H/I/S:** Spending Time with Family **EDU:** Master's Degree in Counseling and Education, Salem State College (1984) **A/A/S:** Connecticut Education Association; National Education Association
Email: dfortin1@cox.net
URL: http://www.suffield.org

Cathleen Denise Forton

Title: Beautician, Owner **Company:** Golden Girls Hair Styling **Address:** 624 Grand River Avenue, Port Huron, MI 48060 United States **BUS:** Full-Service Hair Salon **P/S:** Beauty Care **MA:** Local **D/D/R:** Hairstyling, Perms, Nails, Updos, Applying Makeup, Assisting Elderly and Handicapped Customers **H/I/S:** Quilting, Making Crafts, Driving a School Bus **EDU:** College Coursework Completed **CERTS:** Licensed in Cosmetology, 1982 **A/A/S:** B4s **C/VW:** Local Charities, Orphanage
Email: forton@toast.net

Karen D. Foss

Title: Teacher **Company:** Midway Primary School **Address:** 5 Midway School Road, Silver Creek, GA 30173 United States **BUS:** School **P/S:** Elementary Education **MA:** Local **D/D/R:** Reading Instruction, Literacy Coaching **H/I/S:** Reading, Traveling, Singing in the Church Choir **EDU:** Master of Education in Educational Leadership, Kennesaw State University; Master of Education in Early Childhood Education, Berry College **A/A/S:** Professional Association of Georgia Educators; International Reading Association **C/VW:** Church, Homeless shelter
Email: kfoss@floydboe.net
URL: http://www.cambridgewhoswho.com

Andrew L. Foster

Title: President **Company:** Gulfstar Rental Solutions **Address:** 3425 W Cardinal Drive, Beaumont, TX 77705 United States **BUS:** Rental HVAC and Power Rental **P/S:** Ind. Power, Heating and Cooling **MA:** National **D/D/R:** Cooling, Power, Process and Heating **EDU:** Bachelor of Science in Criminal Justice and Business Management, Sam Houston College **A/A/S:** Better Business Bureau **C/VW:** Garth house charity for orphans
Email: andyfoster@gulfstarrental.com
URL: www.gulfstarrental.com

Mr. David A. Foster, M.Ed.

Title: Teacher **Company:** Pathway School **Address:** 2042 W. Main Street, Apartment 9, Jeffersonville, PA 19403 United States **BUS:** Unique Institution Known for a Multi-Sensory Approach to Instruction, Utilizing a Combination of Clinical, Behavioral and Educational Specialists to Meet Individual Learning and Behavior Needs **P/S:** Self-Contained Elementary Classes with a Single Instructor, Middle and Upper School Students Change Classes with a Variety of Instructors and Courses Including Basic Life Skill Instruction, a Residential Program, Academics, Technology, Career Education, Transition Services, Recreational Services and Athletics **MA:** Regional **D/D/R:** Monitoring Children's Behavior and Behavior Challenges, Teaching Science at a High School Level, Planning Specialized Instruction **H/I/S:** Reading Non-Fiction Biographies **EDU:** Master's Degree in Special Education, Pennsylvania State University (2001) **A/A/S:** Association for Supervision and Curriculum Development
Email: dfrost34@comcast.net
URL: http://www.pathwayschool.org

Kent Foster

Title: Plant Engineer **Company:** AMCOR PET Packaging **Address:** 401 Nestle Way, Lathrop, CA 95330 United States **BUS:** Manufacturing Company **P/S:** CSD, Water Bottles **MA:** International **D/D/R:** Facility Management and Production Support Systems, Project Management, Maintenance Management **H/I/S:** Golfing, Fishing, Camping **EDU:** Master's Degree in Business Administration, University of Redlands (1995) **CERTS:** Certificate in Project Management, Villanova University
Email: kent.foster@amcorpet.com
URL: http://www.cambridgewhoswho.com

Ronald F. Foster, ABR, QSC

Title: Broker, Owner **Company:** Ronald F. Foster Properties, Inc. **Address:** P.O. Box 66521, Houston, TX 77266 United States **BUS:** Real Estate Agency **P/S:** Real Estate Services **MA:** National **EXP:** Mr. Foster's area of expertise is in real estate. **D/D/R:** Managing and Overseeing the Sale of Residential and Commercial Properties, Market Analysis, Relocation, Leasing and Property Management **H/I/S:** Cooking, Traveling **EDU:** Bachelor of Business Administration, Texas Tech University **A/A/S:** Texas Association of Realtors; Houston Association of Realtors; Houston Independent Real Estate Brokers Association; National Association of Realtors
Email: ron@ronfosterproperties.com
URL: www.ronfosterproperties.com

William S. Foster

Title: Systems Programmer, Analyst **Company:** BWX Technologies **Address:** P.O. Box 785, Lynchburg, VA 24501 United States **BUS:** Government Contracting Company **P/S:** Naval Department **MA:** International **D/D/R:** Systems Programming, Analyzing **H/I/S:** Rock Climbing **EDU:** Master of Technology Management, University of Phoenix (2007); Bachelor of Science in Information Systems, University of Phoenix (2005) **A/A/S:** Non-Board Member of VA PTA/PTSA Technology Committee
Email: sfoster001@msn.com
URL: http://www.sfoster001.freespaces.com/index.htm

Susan G. Fotos

Title: President **Company:** Fotos Insurance **Address:** 2862 SE Calvin Street, Port St Lucie, FL 34982 United States **BUS:** Insurance **P/S:** Health and Life insurance, policies, aflac **MA:** Local **D/D/R:** Health Insurance Education and Sales **H/I/S:** Reading **EDU:** High School Graduate **CERTS:** Four Different Insurance Licenses with the State **A/A/S:** NAHU, IIABAI, Chamber of Commerce
Email: susan@fotosinsurance.net
URL: www.fotosinsurance.net

Jamie K. Fountain

Title: Resident **Company:** Cincinnati Children's Hospital Medical Center **Address:** 3333 Burnet Avenue, Cincinnati, OH 45229 United States **BUS:** Hospital **P/S:** Healthcare **MA:** International **D/D/R:** Pediatric Neurodevelopmental Disabilities **H/I/S:** Reading, Exercising **EDU:** MD, Albany Medical College (2006) **A/A/S:** American Academy of Pediatrics; American Medical Association; Christian Medical & Dental Associations **C/VW:** Local Church, Community Gospel Missions
Email: jkfountain@gmail.com

Samantha D. Foushee Lancaster

Title: Director of the Center for Survey Research **Company:** East Carolina University **Address:** 300 E. First Street, Greenville, NC 27858 United States **BUS:** University **P/S:** Higher Education, Survey Research **MA:** National **D/D/R:** organizational development training, overseeing research projects, methodology and administrative duties, budgeting, creating survey designs, analyzing data and reports, conducting workshops, training faculty with focus on group training, community development leadership and lecturing **H/I/S:** Reading, Listening to Music, Singing, Cooking **EDU:** Master of Arts in Industrial Organizational Psychology, East Carolina University **A/A/S:** President, Humane Society of Eastern Carolina; Society for Industrial and Organizational Psychology; Society for Industrial and Organizational Psychology, North Carolina; American Psychological Association **C/VW:** The Humane Society of the United States
Email: foushees@ecu.edu
URL: http://www.ecu.edu/rds/srl/srl.html

Dr. Brock L. Fowler

Title: Doctor of Clinical Psychology and Forensics **P/S:** Psychology **MA:** Local **D/D/R:** Clinical Psychology, Crisis Intervention, Cross-Cultural and Forensic Studies **H/I/S:** Watching Movies, Listening to Music, Spending Time with Friends, Bicycling, Wine Tasting **EDU:** Ph.D. in Psychology; Associate Degree in Psychology of Ethnic Minorities **A/A/S:** American Psychological Association; California Psychological Association; Association of Black Psychologists **C/VW:** American Cancer Society, Gilda's House, A Better Chance Inc., Martin Luther King Build the Dream
Email: docbrock5@aol.com
URL: http://www.cambridgewhoswho.com

Julaine Kathryn Fowler

Title: Lead Teacher **Company:** Penrose Head Start **Address:** 3200 New Hendersonville Highway, Pisgah Forest, NC 28768 United States **BUS:** Federal Government Services **P/S:** Western Carolina County Community Action, a Private Nonprofit Organization, Services for Low Income and Disadvantaged Children to Strengthen their Abilities to Cope with School and their Environment **MA:** Regional **D/D/R:** School Administration, Implementing Lesson Plans, Holding Presentations at Parent Meetings **H/I/S:** Gardening **EDU:** Associate Degree in Special Education, St. Petersburg Junior College (Now St. Petersburg College)(1973)
Email: info@CambridgeWhosWho.com
URL: http://www.cambridgewhoswho.com

Tammy Lynn Fowler Thornton

Title: Assistant Hall Director **Company:** University of North Texas **Address:** P. O. Box 307170, Denton, TX 76203 United States **BUS:** Student-Centered Public Research University with 11 Colleges and Schools **P/S:** 96 Bachelor's, 111 Master's and 50 Doctoral Degree Programs **MA:** Regional **D/D/R:** Overseeing Student Housing and Maintenance for the University, Managing Staff, Disciplining Students, Experience as a Residence Hall Director **EDU:** Master's Degree in Community Counseling, Stephen F. Austin State University (2007); Bachelor of Science in Psychology, Stephen F. Austin State University (2003) **A/A/S:** West Hall Association; Residence Hall Association; National Residence Hall Honorary Advisor
Email: pammy@unt.edu

Denise F. Fox

Title: Owner **Company:** Designs for Windows **Address:** 19 Westside Avenue, Bayshore, NY 11706 United States **BUS:** Window Treatments **P/S:** Window Treatments **MA:** Local **D/D/R:** Sewing **H/I/S:** Embroidering, Crocheting, Knitting, Painting, Sight Seeing, Reading
Email: sugarplum1560@aol.com

Jeri Lanette Fox

Title: National Project Coordinator **Company:** Fox Research, Inc. **Address:** 1405 W. Center Street, Suite 206, Greenwood, AR 72936 United States **BUS:** Market Research Company **P/S:** Test Projects, Market Research **MA:** National **D/D/R:** Coordinating Projects for Test Market Research, National Advertising **H/I/S:** Spending Time at the Beach, Traveling **EDU:** Bachelor of Arts in Political Science, University of Arkansas **A/A/S:** Market Research Association; Political Science Honor Society **C/VW:** St. Jude Children's Research Hospital; Breast Cancer Awareness
Email: jerifoxres@yahoo.com
URL: http://www.foxresearchinc.com

Marilyn Johnson Friedrich Fox

Title: Secondary School Teacher (Retired) **Company:** Kokomo-Center Schools **Dept:** Science **Address:** Kokomo, IN 46901 United States **BUS:** Public School System **P/S:** Education **MA:** Local **D/D/R:** Teaching Science, Chemistry, Physics, Earth Science, Physical Education and Health Classes **H/I/S:** Ballroom and Square Dancing with her Husband, Reading, Traveling, Boating, Fishing, Cross-Country Skiing, Journaling, Gardening, Remodeling **EDU:** Master of Arts in Education, Ball State University (1962); Bachelor of Arts in Education, University of Nevada, Reno (1955); Coursework, Indiana University, Kokomo **A/A/S:** Phi Delta Kappa; Delta Kappa Gamma; National Education Association; Indiana Retired Teachers Association; National Science Association; Psi Iota Xi; Lions Club **A/H:** Who's Who in American Education; Who's Who in the Midwest; International Who's Who of Intellectuals; Who's Who of American Women **C/VW:** Saint Anne's Church; American Red Cross; Psi Iota Xi
Email: lmfox@fourway.net
URL: http://www.cambridgewhoswho.com

Nancyjane Fox

Title: Packaging Specialist, Consultant **Company:** NJF Enterprises Specialty Packaging **Address:** 245 Westwind Circle, Osterville, MA 02655 United States **BUS:** Independent Packaging Contractor **P/S:** Industrial and Retail Packaging, Custom Design, Consultations; Smart Cycle Line; Stand up Pouches; Inlaid Label Containers **MA:** National **D/D/R:** Diversified in Industrial and Retail Specialty and Custom Packaging, Assisting Packaging Design. **H/I/S:** Walking, Boating **EDU:** Associate Degree in Retail Sales and Marketing, Chamberlain Junior College
Email: ncapecod1@aol.com

Lauren M. Foxworth

Title: Design Center Manager **Company:** Ryland Homes **Address:** 207 Regency Executive Suite 100, Charlotte, NC 28217 United States **BUS:** Contractor **P/S:** Home Decor and Management **MA:** Local **D/D/R:** Home/Wedding Decor **H/I/S:** Decorating
Email: laurenfoxworth@bellsouth.net

Sherrie Lynn Fraley
Title: Manager/Department of Psychiatry **Company:** Maricopa Integrated Health Care District (County Hospital) **Dept:** Psychiatry **Address:** 570 W. Brown Road, Mesa, AZ 85201 United States **BUS:** Legal Service Procedures **P/S:** Behavioral Healthcare **MA:** Statewide **D/D/R:** Offering Managerial Services, Performing Administrative Duties, Overseeing Special Projects, Hosting a Number of Wide-Ranging Programs and Initiatives for Both Administration and the Legal Services Segments, Acting as a Court Liaison, Handling New legal Procedural Modifications and Maintenance Issues, Addressing Admission Challenges and Concerns, Specializing in MIHS Admissions Procedures; Serving on Cross-Functional Team of Professionals to Help Ensure Total Customer Satisfaction **H/I/S:** Volunteering, Serving her Community, Gardening, Participating in Outdoor Sports Clubs, Supporting Two Very Active Sons **EDU:** Bachelor's Degree in Business Administration, Western International University (2006) **CERTS:** Notary, State of Arizona; Certification from Executive Development for Government Employees **A/A/S:** Arizona Dragon Boat Association; Secretary, Advisory School Board; Softball Coach, MIHS; National Association for Mental Illness; Dragon Boat Association; Teacher, Queen of Peace Catholic School; Advisory Board, Queen of Peace Catholic School **A/H:** Employee of the Month, 2008 **C/VW:** Team Member, MS Walk; Team Leader, American Diabetes Association (Past 10 Year); Team Leader, All Night Walk, American Cancer Society Relay for Life
Email: sherrie.fraley@hcs.maricopa.gov
URL: http://www.mihs.org

Barbara Francavilla, LPC, LCADL
Title: Student Assistance Counselor **Company:** Jefferson Township Board of Education **Dept:** Jefferson Township Middle School **Address:** 1000 Weldon Road, Oak Ridge, NJ 07438 United States **BUS:** Board of Education, School **P/S:** Education **MA:** Local **D/D/R:** Counseling Individuals and Groups, Developing Programs for At-Risk Students, Crisis Counseling, Grief Counseling **H/I/S:** Avid Reader **EDU:** Master's Degree in Counseling, Montclair State University; Bachelor of Science in Sociology, William Paterson University **A/A/S:** American School Counselors Association; American Mental Health Association
Email: bjf1118@aol.com

Ms. Keniesha P. Francis
Title: Behavioral Health Overlay Services Therapist **Company:** G4S Securicor, Hastings Youth Academy **Address:** 765 E. Saint John's Avenue, Hastings, FL 32145 United States **BUS:** Detention Center **P/S:** Juvenile Detention for Males Ages 14 through 19, Collaborative Treatment Services Including Educational and Medical Components **MA:** Regional **D/D/R:** Offering Mental Health and Substance Abuse Treatment, Organizing Cognitive Behavioral, Rational and Emotive Therapy Programs **H/I/S:** Singing in Church Choir **EDU:** Master's Degree in Rehabilitation and Mental Health Counseling, University of South Florida (2006) **CERTS:** Certification in Marriage and Family Therapy; Registered Mental Health Counselor, State of Florida **A/A/S:** American Counseling Association; American Association for Marriage and Family Therapy
Email: slimk032001@yahoo.com
URL: http://www.cambridgewhoswho.com

Veedra E. Francis
Title: Speech Language Pathologist **Company:** Rivers Bend Rehabilitation **BUS:** Rehabilitation Center **P/S:** Healthcare **MA:** Local **D/D/R:** Rehabilitating those with Traumatic Brain Injuries, Stroke, Neurological Disorders and Dysphagia **H/I/S:** Shopping **EDU:** Master's Degree in Speech-Language Pathology, Northwestern University **A/A/S:** Michigan Speech-Language-Hearing Association; Business and Professional Women Association
Email: afro.goddess@yahoo.com
URL: http://www.cambridgewhoswho.com

Maria Franco
Title: Broker **Company:** Fidelity Brokers **Address:** 130 w. 11th Street, Suite E, Tracy, CA 95376 United States **BUS:** Real Estate Agency **P/S:** Real Estate, Mortgages **MA:** Regional **D/D/R:** Listing Services **A/A/S:** National Notary Association; California Association of Realtors
Email: mafranco0055@yahoo.com
URL: http://www.cambridgewhoswho.com

Margarita Francois-Ottinot, Pharm.D.
Title: Pharmacy Manager **Company:** CVS Pharmacy **Address:** 17524 N.W. 61st Court, Miami, FL 33015 United States **BUS:** High Quality Pharmacy **P/S:** Prescription Medication **MA:** Regional **D/D/R:** Dispensing Prescriptions and Medications, Managing Inventory, Customer Service, Patient Needs and Counseling, Overseeing other Pharmacists **H/I/S:** Tennis, Racquetball, Biking, Reading **EDU:** Ph.D. in Pharmacology, Florida A&M University (2004) **A/A/S:** Florida Pharmacy Association
Email: maggy1908@hotmail.com
URL: http://www.cvs.com

Denise M. Franke
Title: Mathematics Teacher, Mathematics Department Head **Company:** Columbia Middle School **Address:** 739 Morse Avenue, Sunnyvale, CA 94085 United States **BUS:** Middle School **P/S:** Education **MA:** Local **D/D/R:** Teaching Mathematics to Middle School Students, Overseeing Mathematics Department Operations **H/I/S:** Scrapbooking, Vacationing **EDU:** Bachelor of Science in Mathematics, California Polytechnic State University San Luis Obispo; Teaching Credentials **A/A/S:** National Council of Teachers of Mathematics; California Mathematics Council; California League of Middle Schools
Email: dfranke@sesd.org
URL: http://www.cambridgewhoswho.com

Ivana M. Frankenberger
Title: 1) Planning Assistant, Board of Zoning Appeals Staff Advisor 2) Owner **Company:** 1) Town of Greece 2) Face, Etc. **Address:** Rochester, NY 14616 United States **BUS:** 1) Municipal Government Agency 2) Mineral Cosmetics Distributor **P/S:** 1) Zoning Ordinances 2) Cosmetics Consultations and Application **MA:** Regional **D/D/R:** 1) Zoning Codes for the Town of Greece, ZBA Staff Advisor 2) Licensed Esthetician **H/I/S:** Crafts, Crocheting, Cooking **EDU:** Associate Degree in Business, Empire State College (2003); Associate Degree in Marketing and Management, Rochester Business Institute (1987) **CERTS:** New York State Notary; New York State Licensed Esthetician
Email: anavi430@aol.com

Lonnie Franklin
Title: Production Supervisor **Company:** Canplast USA **Address:** 7104 Cessna Drive, Greensboro, NC 27409 United States **BUS:** Machinery Manufacturing, Production, Machinery, Edge Binding Facility **P/S:** Lonnie is the Supervisor of the Production Floor. He Oversees 15 Machine Operators, Does all the Scheduling and Daily Assignments. Lonnie is Also Responsible for the Inspection of all Machines, Ensuring They are Up to Code and Are Running Effectively. The Machines Produce PVC Edge Binding **MA:** International **D/D/R:** Machinery Inspection, Set-Up and Fixing of Defects, Management **H/I/S:** Spending Time with His Family, Basketball and Football **EDU:** Bachelor of Science in Accounting, Winston Salem State University, NC; Coursework in Electrical Engineering **A/A/S:** Church, Feed the Children
Email: info@CambridgeWhosWho.com

Helene Franklin Conyers
Title: Psychotherapist (Retired) **Company:** Private Practice Psychotherapy **BUS:** Private Practice **P/S:** Marriage and Family Counseling **MA:** Regional **D/D/R:** Using a Psychoanalytic Approach to Family and Marriage Counseling **H/I/S:** Solving Crossword Puzzles **EDU:** Master's Degree in Psychology, City University of New York (1969); Bachelor of Science in Psychology and Sociology, City University of New York (1965) **A/A/S:** American Psychological Association
Email: hfconyers@aol.com

Karen S. Franxman
Title: Designer, Member **Company:** Always and Forever Wedding Service, LLC **Address:** 1791 Whispering Trails, Union, KY 41091 United States **BUS:** Events Coordinator **P/S:** Invitations, Personal Stationery, Event Planning Services, Cosmetic Services **MA:** National **D/D/R:** Styling Hair, Applying Cosmetics, Coordinating Events, Teaching Bridal Etiquette **H/I/S:** Spending Time with her Daughters **CERTS:** Certified Cosmetologist, Vogue College of Hair Design (1982) **A/A/S:** National Honors Society, New York Stationery Show (2007); Bridal Education Expo (2005) **A/H:** Hall of Fame Award
Email: alwaysforever@zoomtown.com
URL: http://www.alwaysforever.com

Mark Franz
Title: Chef, Owner **Company:** 1) Farallon Restaurant 2) Water Bar 3) Nick's Cove and Cottages **Address:** 450 Post Street, San Francisco, CA 94102 United States **BUS:** Restaurant **P/S:** Hospitality and Food Services **MA:** California **EXP:** Mr. Franz's area of expertise is in operations management. **H/I/S:** Making Surf Boards, Fly Fishing **CERTS:** Industry-Related Training **A/A/S:** The Culinary Institute of America **C/VW:** Meals On Wheels Association of America; American Cancer Society
Email: mfranz@farallonrestaurant.com

Steven L. Fraser
Title: Director of U.S. Operations **Company:** EPIC Technologies **Address:** 200 Bluegrass Drive E., Norwalk, OH 44857 United States **BUS:** Manufacturing Company **P/S:** High-Mix, Medium-Volume Electronic Contracts **MA:** International **D/D/R:** Managing Operations, Engineering, Over seeing all Functions of the Company **H/I/S:** Boating, Engaging in Motorsports, Golfing **EDU:** Bachelor of Science in Electrical Engineering, Indiana State University **C/VW:** United Way
Email: steve.fraser@epictech.com
URL: http://www.epictech.com

Christine Anne Frayer
Title: Elementary Teacher **Company:** Mitchell Elementary School **Address:** 2713 Drexel Avenue, Racine, WI 53403 United States **BUS:** Public Elementary School **P/S:** Education for Kindergarten through Fifth-Grade Students **MA:** Regional **D/D/R:** Teaching Third-Grade Students, Tutoring **H/I/S:** Reading **EDU:** Master of Arts in Reading and Learning Disabilities, Cardinal Stritch University (2007); Bachelor of Arts in Elementary School Education, Cardinal Stritch University (2000) **CERTS:** Certified Teacher K-6, State of Wisconsin **A/A/S:** Racine Education Association; Kappa Delta Phi
Email: wfrayer@sbcglobal.net
URL: http://www.racine.k12.wi.us

Dana Michelle Frazier
Title: Programmer/Analyst **Company:** Rheem Manufacturing Company **Address:** 101 Bell Road, Montgomery, AL 36117 United States **BUS:** Manufacturing Company **P/S:** Waterheater Production, Products for the Home and Business **MA:** National **D/D/R:** Selling Financial Software, Pricing, Counting Costs, Overseeing the General Ledger Including Accounts Payable, Accounts Receivable, Check Reconciliation and Invoicing, Conducting In-House Training, Previously Worked at Software Company **H/I/S:** Reading, Attending Children's Ball Games, Spending Time with Family **EDU:** Associate Degree in Data Processing, Trenholm State Technical College (1990)
Email: dfrazier@rheem.com
URL: http://www.rheem.com
URL: http://www.rheemkless.com

Alice Frazier Champion
Title: Assistant Principal **Company:** Delk County School System, Miller Grove Middle School **Address:** 3770 N. Decatur Road, Decatur, GA 30281 United States **BUS:** School System **P/S:** Student Development, Education **MA:** Local **D/D/R:** Child Development, School Administration **H/I/S:** Reading, Biking **EDU:** Doctorate in Educational Leadership, Nova Southeastern University (2006) **A/A/S:** National Association of Assistant Principals **C/VW:** United Negro College Fund; Cancer Research Fund
Email: frazierc@nova.edu

Tobias J. Freccia
Title: Chief Executive Officer **Company:** Freccia Studios **Address:** 4 Sneckner Court, Menlo Park, CA 94025 United States **BUS:** Architectural Design Firm **P/S:** Architectural Services Including Art and Design Consultancy, Decorative Ornamentation, Custom Fabrication and Installation, Genuine and Metal Leaf Gilding Supplies, Retail Sales of Gold, Silver and Copper Leaf, Art and Design Education and Training, Architectural sourcing **MA:** International **D/D/R:** designing new building to historic preservation, exterior stone casting, ornamental plaster designing, fabrication and installation, gold leaf and decorative finishing, applications and training on art design **H/I/S:** Hiking, Backpacking **EDU:** Bachelor of Fine Arts, Parsons the New School of Design (1990) **A/A/S:** American Society of Interior Designers; The Congress of Residential Architecture
Email: design@frecciastudios.com
URL: http://www.frecciastudios.com
URL: http://www.artsparx.com

Betty-Jane Free
Title: Coordinator NMDP Donor Center **Company:** Southeastern Community Blood Center **Address:** 1731 Riggins Road, Tallahassee, FL 32308 United States **BUS:** Blood Bank, Bone Marrow Registry **P/S:** Blood Bank, Bone Marrow Registry **MA:** Regional **D/D/R:** Recruiting New Donors, Collecting Data for the National Marrow Donor Program, Following Entire Process Until Match is Made **H/I/S:** Church Activities, Choir, Sunday School, Teaching **EDU:** Bachelor of Science in Medical Technology, Florida State University **A/A/S:** National Marrow Donor Program; Florida Association of Blood Banks, American Society of Clinical Pathology-Medical Technologists; Thanks Badge; Thanks Badge II **A/H:** Member of the Year, Florida Blood Banks, 2002; Regional Handing You a Star Award, 2002 **C/VW:** Capitol City Christian Church, Girl Scouts
Email: bfree47554@aol.com
URL: http://www.cambridgewhoswho.com

Angela Freeman
Title: First-Grade Teacher **Company:** Harrah Public Schools **Address:** 20227 N.E. 10th Street, Harrah, OK 73045 United States **BUS:** School District **P/S:** Education **MA:** Local **EXP:** Ms. Freeman's areas of expertise is in education. **D/D/R:** teaching reading, mathematics, science and social studies to first-grade students, Managing Discipline, Educating First-Grade Department Staff, Implementing Reading Sufficiency Program **H/I/S:** Scrapbooking, Gardening, Caring for her Pets **EDU:** Bachelor of Science, University of Central Oklahoma **A/A/S:** Kappa Kappa Iota
Email: freemanabcm@cox.net
URL: http://www.harrahschools.com

Charles F. Freeman

Title: Chairman, President **Company:** Felburn Foundation **Address:** 5619 Main Street, Loris, SC 29569 United States **BUS:** Private Education Foundation **P/S:** Educational Grants to Local Libraries, Colleges, Universities **MA:** Regional **D/D/R:** Making Decisions **EDU:** Bachelor of Science in Political Science, Furman University **A/H:** Lifetime Achievement Award, Loris Chamber of Commerce

Ms. Judith D. Freeman

Title: Speech-Language Pathologist **Company:** Willowbrook Health Systems, Inc. **Address:** 1451 Elm Hill Pike, Suite 300, Nashville, TN 37210 United States **BUS:** Healthcare Center **P/S:** Full-Service Home Health Care, Outpatient Rehabilitation Services and Hospice Care to Traditional Acute-Care **MA:** Regional **D/D/R:** Overseeing Dining Hall, Teaching Communication, Evaluating Patients, Utilizing Various Treatment Techniques, Training Staff, Consulting with Families **H/I/S:** Needlepointing, Reading **EDU:** Master's Degree in Communication Sciences, Tennessee State University, Nashville (2001) **CERTS:** Certificate of Clinical, American Speech-Language-Hearing Association **A/A/S:** American Speech-Language-Hearing Association; Tennessee Association of Audiologists and Speech Pathologists **C/VW:** American red Cross
Email: willowbrookmrdd@bellsouth.com
URL: http://www.willowbrookhealth.com

Melissa O. Freeman

Title: Founder, Chief Executive Officer **Company:** M. Free Entertainment **BUS:** Entertainment Company **P/S:** Promotions, Marketing **MA:** National **D/D/R:** Networking **H/I/S:** Gourmet Cooking **EDU:** Bachelor of Science in Behavioral and Social Sciences, Major in Environmental Science and Policy, University of Maryland, College Park (1996) **C/VW:** Feed The Hungry
Email: purplepoetrylady@aol.com
URL: http://www.mfreeentertainment.com

William J. Freeman

Title: Branch Manager **Company:** Motion Industries, Inc. **Address:** 610 Beatty Road, Monroeville, PA 15146 United States **BUS:** Industrial Distribution Company **P/S:** Bearings and Power Transmission Components **MA:** International **D/D/R:** Applying his Skills as a Power Transmission Application Specialist **H/I/S:** Golfing **EDU:** Master of Business Administration, Indiana University of Pennsylvania **A/H:** Gold Award, Motion Industries President's Club (2004-2006)
Email: bill.freeman@motion-ind.com
URL: http://www.motion-ind.com

Helen B. Freeman-Ward

Title: Teacher (Retired) **Company:** Baltimore City Board of Education **Address:** 4849 Pimlico Road, Baltimore, MD 21215 United States **BUS:** School District **P/S:** Education **MA:** Local **D/D/R:** Managing Camp and Community Programs, Offering Day Care **H/I/S:** Reading, Participating in her Community, Bowling, Swimming, Rollerskating **EDU:** Master's Degree in Early Childhood Education and Special Education; Bachelor of Science in Education, Coppin University **A/A/S:** Iota Phi Beta **A/H:** Mother's Club; Mother of the Year (1982)

Amy E. Freigruber

Title: Professor **Company:** Rochester College **Address:** 800 W. Avon, Rochester Hills, MI 48309 United States **BUS:** College **P/S:** Education **MA:** Regional **D/D/R:** Teaching Psychology **H/I/S:** Photography, Gardening, Traveling, Camping **EDU:** Pursuing Ph.D. in Educational Leadership, Touro University; Bachelor of Arts in Psychology, University of Detroit Mercy; Master of Arts in Science and Psychology, Capella University **C/VW:** Susan G. Komen For the Cure, St. Jude Children's Research Hospital, Domestic Violence Shelter, Multiple Sclerosis Society
Email: psychgrad81973@yahoo.com

Corinna Freischlag

Title: President **Company:** Symka **Address:** 3107 W. Colorado Avenue, Suite 109, Colorado Springs, CO 80904 United States **BUS:** Company Specializing in the Manufacture and Distribution of Healthcare Machinery **P/S:** Continuous Passive Motion Machines Distributed in Colorado, New Mexico and Alaska **MA:** Regional **D/D/R:** Creating Intermittent Pneumatic Foot Pumps **H/I/S:** Water Activities, Playing Tennis **EDU:** Pursuing Master's Degree; Bachelor of Science in Physiology and Psychology, University of Northern Colorado (1989) **CERTS:** Certified Recreational Therapist
Email: cori@symka.com
URL: http://www.symka.com

Charles L. French Jr.

Title: Fire Captain **Company:** Tulsa Fire Department **Address:** 10302 E. 94th Place N., Owasso, OK 74055 United States **BUS:** Fire Department **P/S:** Public Safety Including Fire Rescue and Emergency Medical Services **MA:** Regional **D/D/R:** Training and Supervising Fire Crews, Acting as the District Chief **H/I/S:** Running, Golfing, Spending Time with her Children and Family **EDU:** Master of Science, Oklahoma State University (2002) **A/A/S:** Oklahoma Task Force 1; 'Oklahoma Fools' Fire Department Liaison, MDA
Email: station5tfd@yahoo.com
URL: http://www.cityoftulsa.org/PublicSafety/Fire

Paula P. French

Title: Teacher **Company:** Garden Grove Unified School District **Address:** 11303 Sandstone Avenue, Fountain Valley, CA 92708 United States **BUS:** Public School District **P/S:** Educational Programs Focusing on Student Achievement **MA:** Local **D/D/R:** Teaching Kindergarten Students Language/Vocabulary, Development, Critical Thinking Skills, Reading, Math, Problem Solving, Serving on the Leadership Committee, Faculty Advisory Committee, Acting as a Literacy Coach **H/I/S:** Reading, Kickboxing, Baking **EDU:** Master of Science in Curriculum and Instruction, Emphasis in Early Childhood Education, California State University at Fullerton (2002); Bachelor of Arts in Elementary Education, University of Arizona (1995) **A/A/S:** National Education Association; California Teachers Association; National Association for the Education of Young Children
Email: info@CambridgeWhosWho.com
URL: http://www.ggusd.k12.ca.us

Teresa R. French

Title: Reading Teacher **Company:** Victoria Independent School District **Dept:** Howell Middle School **Address:** 2502 Fannin Drive, Victoria, TX 77901 United States **BUS:** Middle School **P/S:** Secondary Education **MA:** Regional **D/D/R:** teaching English and reading for the gifted and talented **H/I/S:** Skiing, Reading, Traveling, Spending Time with her Family **EDU:** Bachelor of Arts in Elementary Education, The University of Texas at Tyler **A/A/S:** Texas Classroom Teachers Association; President, Victoria Chapter, Delta Kappa Gamma **C/VW:** Catholic Serra Club; American Cancer Society; National Honor Society
Email: teresa.french@visd.com

Lisa M. Frenkel

Title: Vice President, Chief Legal Officer **Company:** HCA **Address:** 7400 Fannin Street, Suite 650, Houston, TX 77054 United States **BUS:** Corporate Operator of Hospitals and Health Systems **P/S:** Hospitals, Surgery Centers and Healthcare-Related Services **MA:** Regional **D/D/R:** Overseeing Legal Issues and Compliance **H/I/S:** Reading, Spending Time with her Family, Enjoying the Arts, Watching Movies and Plays, Cooking, Shopping, Exercising, Hiking, Traveling **EDU:** Juris Doctorate, St. Mary's University School of Law; Bachelor of Arts in Psychology, Emery University **CERTS:** Board Certified in Health Law **A/A/S:** American Health Lawyers Association; American Bar Association; Vice Chairwoman, Health Law II

Tara M. Frey, DDS

Title: Dentist **Company:** The Smile Center **Address:** 200 Grayson Road, Suite 100, Virginia Beach, VA 23462 United States **BUS:** Dental Office **P/S:** Family and Cosmetic Dentistry **MA:** Regional **D/D/R:** General Dentistry Including Treatments for Children, Orthodontics, Oral Surgery and Cosmetic Dentistry, Handling Daily Operations, Managing Dental Office Staff **H/I/S:** Scuba Diving, Working Out **EDU:** Doctor of Dental Surgery, Medical College of Virginia (1999) **A/A/S:** Academy of General Dentistry; American Orthodontic Society; DOCS
Email: tara@thesmilecenter.info
URL: http://www.thesmilecenter.info

Erin Meyer Frick

Title: Owner, Vice President **Company:** J Lance Properties, Inc. **Address:** 4060 Peachtree Road, Suite D-355, Atlanta, GA 30534 United States **BUS:** Building, Developing **P/S:** Building, Developing **MA:** National **D/D/R:** Marketing, Business Development **H/I/S:** Spending Time with Family, Traveling **EDU:** Bachelor of Science in Corporate Journalism, Auburn University **A/A/S:** Greater Atlanta Home Builders Association, Society of Professional Journalists **A/H:** Featured in October 2007 Edition of Today's Custom Homes
Email: ehmf@alltel.net
URL: http://www.jlanceproperties.com

Sarah B. Friday

Title: President **Company:** Friday's Auto Sales, Inc. **Address:** 3181 Palm Beach Boulevard, Fort Myers, FL 33916 United States **BUS:** Used Automobiles Company **P/S:** Used Automobiles **MA:** Local **D/D/R:** Used Automobile Sales **H/I/S:** Traveling, Reading, Horseback Riding **EDU:** College Coursework Completed **A/A/S:** NATA **C/VW:** Volunteer, Christian Radio Station
Email: fridaysauto@aol.com
URL: http://www.cambridgewhoswho.com

Addam Friedl

Title: Principal **Company:** EYP Mission Critical Facilities, Inc. **Address:** 200 W. Adams Street, Suite 2750, Chicago, IL 60606 United States **BUS:** Engineering Consulting Firm **P/S:** Engineering Consulting **MA:** National and International **D/D/R:** Engineering Consulting, Managing the Electrical Department of the Chicago Office **EDU:** Bachelor of Science in Electrical Engineering, University of South Florida
Email: afriedl@eypmcf.com
URL: http://www.eypmcf.com

Kimberly Friedman O'Berry

Title: President/Independent Contractor **Company:** Affordable Courier and Transport Inc/Citrus Travel & Tours **Address:** 900 E Hartford Street, Hernando, FL 34442 United States **BUS:** Transportation Courier **P/S:** Luxury Transportation/Courier Service **MA:** National **D/D/R:** Working as a Travel Agent **H/I/S:** Traveling **EDU:** Davenport College
Email: kfriedman@tampa.rr.com

Mark Friesenhahn

Title: Owner **Company:** Frankenstein Computers **Address:** 3636 S. Ranch Drive, Ponca City, OK 74601 United States **BUS:** Computer Repair Company **P/S:** Computer Repair **MA:** Local **D/D/R:** Refurbishing and Repairing Computers **H/I/S:** Trains **A/A/S:** Volunteer Firefighter, Ponco City; Lincoln School Parent-Teacher Organization

Samuel Frimpong, Ph.D., P.Eng.

Title: Robert H. Quenon Endowed Chairman, Professor **Company:** Missouri University of Science's Technology **Dept:** Mining and Nuclear Engineering **Address:** 1870 Miner Circle, 226 McNutt Hall, Rolla, MO 65409 United States **BUS:** University **P/S:** Higher Education **MA:** United States, Canada, Mexico **EXP:** Dr. Frimpong's areas of expertise include oil sands extraction, energy and minerals economics, machine-formation interactions, machine dynamics and machine intelligence. **D/D/R:** surface mining, mine design engineering, petroleum production engineering, risks and safety engineering **H/I/S:** Sailing, Reading, Soccer, Basketball, Tennis, Playing Badminton, Listening to Music, Attending the Theater, Poetry **EDU:** Fellowship, University of Zambia (1988); Ph.D. in Mining Engineering, University of Alberta, Canada; Master of Science in Mining Engineering, University of Zambia; Bachelor of Science in Mining Engineering, University of Science and Technology, Ghana, with Honors; Post-Graduate Diploma, University of Science and Technology, Ghana, with Honors **A/A/S:** The Association of Professional Engineers, Geologists and Geophysicists of Alberta; Canada Foundation for Innovation, Ottawa; College of Reviewers Japanese Government's Research Council on CO2 Sequestration (1997-2000); American Association of Civil Engineers; Canadian Institute of Mining, Metallurgy and Petroleum; Mine Planning and Equipment Selection; Canadian Institute of Mining, Metallurgy and Petroleum; UNI, Peru; International Symposium on Environmental Issues, Waste Management in Energy and Mineral Production; Bulk Materials Handling; International Conference on Energy, Environment and Disasters; International Association of Science and Technology for Development; The Society for Modeling and Simulation International; Expert Member, Council on Emerging Energy Technologies, United Nations Educational, Scientific and Cultural Organization; Association of Professional Engineers; Society for Mining, Metallurgy and Exploration **A/H:** Distinguished Lecturer Award, CPI (1998-2002); Award of Distinction, World Mining Congress (1997); Patron Award, University of Science and Technology, Ghana; Grand Award, Northwest Mining Association (1989); United Nations Educational Award, Scientific and Cultural Organization Research Outstanding Graduate Award, University of Science and Technology, Ghana (1986) **C/VW:** Compassion International; Samaritan's Purse
Email: frimpong@umr.edu
URL: http://www.cambridgewhoswho.com

Audrey L. Frison

Title: Assist Dir for Patient Care Services **Company:** VA Northern Indiana Health Care System **Address:** 2121 Lake Avenue, Fort Wayne, IN 46805 United States **BUS:** Healthcare **P/S:** US Government Medical Center **MA:** Local **EXP:** Ms. Frison's area of expertise is in nursing management. **H/I/S:** Reading, Children's Sports Events, Travel, Church **EDU:** Bachelor of Science in Nursing, East Kentucky University; Master's Degree in Hospital Administration, Xavier University **A/A/S:** Sigma Feta Tau, ONE, NEINE, Aids Foundation, Healthcare Coalition
Email: info@CambridgeWhosWho.com

Jo-Ann M. Fritz

Title: Manager **Company:** America Title Services, LLC. **Address:** 10301 Wayzata Boulevard, Minnetonka, MN 55305 United States **BUS:** Title Insurance Company **P/S:** Titles, Escrow **MA:** Statewide **D/D/R:** Title Insurance, Overseeing Sixteen Entire Operations **H/I/S:** Traveling, Spending Time with her Family, Sailing **EDU:** Coursework for Master's, University of California at Irvine, Arizona State University and University of Minnesota; Bachelor of Science in Education, St. Cloud State College
Email: jfritz@americatitleservices.com
URL: http://www.americatitleservices.com

Carrie E. Sens Froebel

Title: Owner, Manager **Company:** Froebel Ranch **Address:** 2711 Beckendorff Road, Sealy, TX 77474 United States **BUS:** Cattle Ranch **P/S:** Cattle **MA:** National **D/D/R:** Maintaining and Operating a 600-Acre Cattle Ranch **H/I/S:** Traveling Abroad **EDU:** Diploma, Southwestern School of Business and Technical Careers **C/VW:** American Legion Auxiliary; Women of the Evangelical Lutheran Church in America; Food Pantry Coordinator; Altar Guild, Church

Michelle A. Fromhart-Dent

Title: Owner, Craniosacral Therapist **Company:** Center for Heart and Mind Communication and Integration **Address:** Baltimore, MD 21212 United States **BUS:** Healthcare Center **P/S:** Polarity Therapy **MA:** International **EXP:** Ms. Fromhart-Dent's areas of expertise include trauma therapy and re-training the mind. **H/I/S:** Ballroom Dancing, Crocheting **EDU:** MD, McDaniel College; Master of Arts in Education; Master's Degree in Language Development and Linguistic **CERTS:** Registered Craniosacral Therapist; Registered Polarity Therapist; Certified Message Therapist **A/A/S:** American Polarity Therapy Association; Craniosacral Therapy Association of North America; National Council for Massage Therapist
Email: mfromhart@aol.com

Mary Ann Frontzak

Title: Special Education Teacher, Transition Coordinator **Company:** Downer's Grove South High School **Address:** 1436 Norfolk Street, Downer's Grove, IL 60516 **BUS:** High School **P/S:** Education **MA:** Local **D/D/R:** Vocational Transition, Teaching Ninth through 12th-Graders, Preparing Individuals for Higher Studies and Helping Them Reach Their Goals and Become Productive Members in the Society **H/I/S:** Camping, Participating in Athletic Activities **EDU:** Master of Education, Northern Illinois University **A/A/S:** National Athletic Trainers' Association; Illinois Athletic Trainers' Association; Great Lakes Athletic Trainers' Association; Downer's Grove Education Association; National Education Association **C/VW:** St. Raphael Youth Football
Email: mfrontzak@csd99.org
URL: http://www.csd99.org

Steven P. Fruda

Title: Senior Product Manager **Company:** Travers Tool Company **Address:** 12815 26th Avenue, Flushing, NY 11354 United States **BUS:** Metalworking Tools and Industrial Supply Company **P/S:** Tool Distribution, Abrasives, Files, Deburring Tools, Adhesives, Paint, Sundries, Chemicals, Lubricants, Greases, Solid Carbide Cutting Tools, Carbide Indexable Cutting Tools, Electrical Equipment and Supplies, Fasteners, Fluid Power, Hand Tools, Power Tools, Machine Tool Accessories, Machinery, Material Handling Equipment, Measuring and Inspection Services, Safety and Hygiene, Stock Material, Storage and Workshop Equipment, Technical Reference and Software, Tooling Components, Welding and Soldering Equipment **MA:** International **D/D/R:** Overseeing Direct Mailings and Distribution, Selling Supplies to the Metalworking Industry, Managing Product Lines **H/I/S:** Music, Playing Drums **EDU:** Bachelor of Science in Communications, St. John's University, New York (1993) **A/A/S:** Young Executive Forum
Email: sfruda@nyc.rr.com
URL: https://www.travers.com

William R. Fry Jr.

Title: Owner, MBA **Company:** Unique Solutions Management Company, LLC **Address:** 497 W. Main Street, Batavia, OH 45103 United States **BUS:** Management Company **P/S:** Dental Office Management **MA:** Southwest Ohio **D/D/R:** Financial Operations **H/I/S:** Traveling, Fishing **EDU:** Master of Business Administration, Webster University; Bachelor's Degree in Business, Regents College; Associate of Science, Regents College **A/A/S:** Chamber of Commerce; Marine Corps League
Email: uniquesolutions@fuse.net
URL: http://www.cambridgewhoswho.com

Kimberly Frye

Title: Special Education Teacher **Company:** Manassas Park Middle School **Address:** 8202 Euclid Avenue, Manassas Park, VA 20111, Manassas Park, **BUS:** Middle School **P/S:** Education **MA:** Local **D/D/R:** Teaching Special Education, Middle School **H/I/S:** Reading, Traveling **EDU:** Master's Degree in Special Education, George Mason University **A/A/S:** National Education Association; Virginia Education Association **C/VW:** Women's Shelter, Muscular Dystrophy, Toys for Tots
Email: kim.simon@mpark.net
URL: http://www.mpark.net

Harriett M. Fudge

Title: Registered Nurse **Company:** Alaska Women's Health Service **Address:** 4115 Lake Otis Parkway, Anchorage, AK 99508 United States **BUS:** Women's Clinic **P/S:** Healthcare for Women **MA:** Local **D/D/R:** Managing Office Operations, Promoting Community Health and Wellness, Maternal Nursing **H/I/S:** Reading, Knitting, Crocheting **EDU:** Master of Science in Nursing, University of Phoenix (2005); Bachelor of Science in Nursing, University of Phoenix (1988) **CERTS:** Registered Nurse; Certified Obstetrics Practitioner Supervisor
Email: h.fudge@akwomenshealth.com
URL: http://www.akwomenshealth.com

Cheryl Fugate

Title: Regional Enrollment Manager **Company:** The Hartford **Address:** 2627 Naples Drive, Schererville, IN 46375 United States **BUS:** Insurance Company **P/S:** Life Insurance, Disability Insurance **MA:** Regional **D/D/R:** Enrollment **H/I/S:** Spending Time with her Children **EDU:** Associate of Arts, Robert Morris College **A/A/S:** LOMA
Email: cheryl.fugate@hartfordlife.com
URL: http://www.cambridgewhoswho.com

Selena L. Fuhrmann

Title: Administrative Secretary **Company:** Ministry Home Care dba Affinity Visiting Nurses **Address:** 816 W. Winneconne Avenue, Neenah, WI 54956 United States **BUS:** Medical Center **P/S:** Healthcare Including Hospice Services **MA:** Regional **D/D/R:** Processing Payroll, Invoicing, Ensuring Customer Satisfaction, Overseeing Statistics and Staff Nurses **H/I/S:** Tracing her Family's History, Crocheting **EDU:** Coursework in Accounting, Technical College (1978); High School Diploma **C/VW:** Fundraiser, Local Hospice; American Cancer Society
Email: selena.furhmann@cwwemail.com

Jeffrey J. Fujimoto, PT, DPT, OCS, CSCS

Title: Rehabilitation Director **Company:** San Antonio Community Hospital; Casa Colina Centers for Rehabilitation **Address:** 999 San Bernardino Road, Upland, CA 91786 United States **BUS:** Hospital **P/S:** Medical and Surgical Services **MA:** Regional **EXP:** Mr. Fujimoto's areas of expertise include orthopedic physical therapy, satellite occupational therapy and speech therapy. **D/D/R:** Overseeing Daily Operations **H/I/S:** Golfing **EDU:** Doctor of Physical Therapy, Azusa Pacific University (2003); Master's Degree in Physical Therapy, Azusa Pacific University (1999); Bachelor's Degree in Biological Sciences, University of California, Santa Barbara (1994) **A/A/S:** American Physical Therapy Association; National Strength and Conditioning Association; Handicap Chairman of the Local Group of the Southern California Golf Association **A/H:** Adjunct Professor at Azusa Pacific University, Consulting for San Antonio Community Hospital
Email: jfuji@excite.com
URL: http://www.sach.org

Kerry L. Fuldner Watts

Title: President, Owner **Company:** KLF Architectural Systems, Inc. **Address:** 4825 S. Sydney Avenue, Springfield, MO 65810 United States **BUS:** Construction Company **P/S:** Construction Services Including Aluminum Windows, Storefronts, Curtain Walls and Entry Doors **MA:** National **D/D/R:** Ensuring Customer Satisfaction, Public Speaking on all Aspects of the Aluminum Manufacturing Industry, Representing the Manufacturer, Supplying Information to Architects **H/I/S:** Running Marathons, Reading Harry Potter Novels, Cooking, Spending Time Outdoors **EDU:** Bachelor of Business Administration, Emphasis in Marketing, The University of Arizona, Tucson (2001)
Email: klfarch@mchsi.com

Sandra Kay Fullen

Title: Label Control Clerk **Company:** Dentsply International, Inc. **Address:** 608 Rolling Hills Drive, Johnson City, TN 37604 United States **BUS:** Dental Clinic **P/S:** Dental Care **MA:** International **D/D/R:** Fabricating, Branding, Ink Jet Printing **H/I/S:** Reading **CERTS:** Certification, American Production and Inventory Control Society
Email: ck111298@aol.com
URL: http://www.dentsply.com

Lynda M. Fuller

Title: Poet and Telecommunications **Company:** AT&T **Address:** 311 West Washington, Chicago, IL 60606 United States **BUS:** Phone Company **P/S:** Telecommunications **MA:** Statewide **D/D/R:** Poet and Telecommunications **H/I/S:** Movies, Exercising, Dancing, Singing, Horseback Riding **EDU:** Bachelor of Science in Telecommunications Systems Management, Richmond University **A/A/S:** President-Illinois Condo Association, Member-Phi Theta Kappa International Honor Society (2005)
Email: msmuzik1@sbcglobal.net

Connie M. Fullmer

Title: Dental Hygienist **Company:** Woods Family Dentistry **Address:** 1044 29th Street, Albany, OR 97321 United States **BUS:** Dentistry **P/S:** Dental Services **MA:** Local **D/D/R:** Dental Hygiene **H/I/S:** Riding Four-Wheelers **EDU:** Associate of Science in Dental Hygiene, Lane Community College **C/VW:** Volunteer Work
Email: conniefullmer@comcast.net

Marva D. Fulp

Title: Teacher **Company:** Hampton City Schools, Bassette Elementary School **Address:** 671 Bell Street, Hampton, VA 23661 United States **BUS:** Elementary School **P/S:** Education **MA:** Local **D/D/R:** Teaching Fifth-Grade Science **H/I/S:** Reading, Taking Classes **EDU:** Bachelor of Arts in Psychology and Sociology, Virginia Intermont College **A/A/S:** Virginia Education Association; Virginia Association Science Teacher; National Science Teacher Association **C/VW:** The Peninsula League of Women, Relay for Life
Email: mfulp@sbo.hampton.k12.va.us

Betty J. Funderburgh

Title: Co-Supervisor, Home-Based Family Preservation Counseling Program **Company:** Family Service of Central Indiana, Inc. **Address:** 615 N. Alabama Street, Suite 320, Indianapolis, IN 46204 United States **BUS:** Nonprofit Social Service Organization **P/S:** Counseling Services **MA:** National **D/D/R:** Bereavement, Sexual Abuse Counseling **H/I/S:** Traveling, Gardening, Reading, Playing with her Animals, Cooking **EDU:** Master's Degree in Counseling, Purdue University; Bachelor's Degree in Psychology, Purdue University **CERTS:** Licensed Clinical Social Worker **C/VW:** United Way
Email: bettyf@family-service-inc.org
URL: http://www.family-service-inc.org

Henry C. Fung

Title: Director, Stem Cell Transplant **Company:** Rush University Medical Center **Address:** 1725 W. Harrison Street, Suite 834, Chicago, IL 60612 United States **BUS:** Hospital **P/S:** Healthcare **MA:** Local **D/D/R:** Conducting Stem Cell Research for Multi Myeloma and Lymphoma, Teaching At Medical School-Internal Medicine, Oncology, Hematology, Stem Cell Procedures, Patient Care with Leukemia, Multi Myeloma, Lymphoma, **H/I/S:** Traveling, Reading, **EDU:** MD, Chinese University of Hong Kong, 1987, Residency-1988-1991-Internal Medicine and Hemotology; **A/A/S:** American Society of Hematology; American Society of Clinical Oncology; European Medical Association; Association of Clinical Research Professionals; FRCPE, European Society of Medical Oncology **C/VW:** Lymphoma Research Foundation
Email: henry_fung@rush.edu
URL: http://www.rush.edu

Mr. Wayne E. Funk

Title: President **Company:** WLF Packaging Enterprises, LLC **Address:** 6493 CR 17, Garrett, IN 46738 United States **BUS:** Industrial Packaging **P/S:** Packaging Consulting, Cost Reduction Strategies, Contracting, Design **MA:** International **D/D/R:** Managing Industrial Packaging **H/I/S:** Spending Time with his Children **EDU:** Master's Degree in Business, Indiana University (1991) **A/A/S:** International Organization of Packaging Professionals; International Standards Casting Association
Email: wfunk@locl.net
URL: http://www.wlfpackage.com

Brandy J. Funni

Title: Registered Nurse **Company:** University Hospitals **Address:** 11100 Euclid Avenue, Cleveland, OH 44106 United States **BUS:** University Hospital **P/S:** Higher Education, Healthcare **MA:** Cleveland **EXP:** Ms. Funni's areas of expertise include acute care and critical care nursing. **D/D/R:** Overseeing the Intensive Care Unit **H/I/S:** Spending Time with her Family, Reading, Exercising, Spending Time Outdoors **EDU:** Bachelor of Science in Nursing, The University of Akron **CERTS:** Certified Critical Care Registered Nurse
Email: blam1079@yahoo.com
URL: http://www.cambridgewhoswho.com

Michele V. Fuqua

Title: Registered Nurse **Company:** Sacred Heart Medical Center **Address:** 101 W. Eighth Avenue, Spokane, WA 99220 United States **BUS:** Medical Center **P/S:** Healthcare, Intensive Care **MA:** Regional **D/D/R:** Neurology, Trauma, Adult Intensive Care **H/I/S:** Hiking, Biking, Ballroom Dancing, Golfing, Spending Time with her Family **EDU:** Associate Degree in Nursing, Kent State University **CERTS:** Registered Nurse **A/A/S:** American Neurological Association; Spokane Neurological Association **C/VW:** American Cancer Society, Multiple Sclerosis Foundation

April M. Furnace

Title: Cosmetologist **Company:** New Image Hair Studio **Address:** 29800 Bradley Road, Menifee, CA 92586 United States **BUS:** Beauty Salon **P/S:** Beauty Services **MA:** Menifee, California **D/D/R:** African-American Hair Styling **EDU:** Coursework, Elegante Beauty College, 2001-2002
Email: amfurnace@yahoo.com
URL: http://www.cambridgewhoswho.com

Timothy L. Fuss
Title: First Sergeant **Company:** New Hanover County Sheriff's Office **Address:** 3950 Juvenile Center Drive, Castle Hayne, NC 28429 United States **BUS:** Government Agency **P/S:** Law Enforcement Services **MA:** Regional **D/D/R:** Overseeing Law Enforcement, Sanctioning Grants, Ensuring State Mandated Training for Employees, Conducting Background Investigations, Recruiting Employees, Teaching Law Enforcement **H/I/S:** Golfing **EDU:** Master of Public Administration, University of North Carolina Wilmington (2003); Bachelor of Arts in Criminal Justice, University of North Carolina Wilmington (1997) **CERTS:** Certification in CPR; Certification in Public Relations; Certified Detention Officer; Basic Law Enforcement Training **A/A/S:** The American Society of Criminology; American Correctional Association
Email: tfuss@nhcgov.com

Eddy Gaasbeek
Title: Director **Company:** Bhaktivedanta Archives **Address:** 1453 Tom Shelton Road, Sandy Ridge, NC 27046 **BUS:** Nonprofit Organization **P/S:** Bhaktivedanta Archives **MA:** Local **D/D/R:** Overseeing Management Staff **H/I/S:** Reading, Working Out, Taking Nature Walks **C/VW:** Food for Life, India
Email: eka108@gmail.com
URL: http://www.prabhupada.com

Michael M. Gabelli
Title: Vice President **Company:** Gabelli Group Capital Partners, Inc. **Address:** 140 Greenwich Avenue, Suite 4, Greenwich, CT 06830 United States **BUS:** Financial Advisory Firm **P/S:** Financial Services Including Asset Management, Merger Arbitrage, Value Investing, Sports Business and Entertainment Marketing **MA:** International **EXP:** Mr. Gabelli's area of expertise is in merger arbitrage. **D/D/R:** Managing Portfolios, Mutual Funds and Venture Capital, Marketing, Overseeing Financial Analysis and Private Equity Transactions **H/I/S:** Playing Softball, Flag Football and Basketball, Golfing, Watching Movies, Spending Time with his Family, Traveling, Food and Wine Tasting **EDU:** Master's Degree in Finance and Development, New York University (2005); Pursuing Master of Business Administration; Coursework in Sports Business **A/A/S:** National Italian American Foundation; Princeton Club of New York; Air Transport Association of America **C/VW:** Board Member, Gabelli Foundation; EM-6 Educational Foundation; The Columbus Citizens Foundation; Trustee, Air Force Association
Email: michaelg@gabelli.com
URL: http://www.gabelli.com

Ms. Rosemary B. Gabledon
Title: Beauty Consultant **BUS:** Consulting Firm **P/S:** Beauty Care Consultations **MA:** Ventura County, California **D/D/R:** Consulting on Self-Esteem and Self-Image Issues, Enhancing Personal, Social and Dining Etiquette Skills, Building Confidence, Training to Develop a Good Posture, Coordinating Programs to Enhance Style and Grooming Techniques **H/I/S:** Traveling, Reading, Dancing, Writing, Performing Arts **EDU:** Coursework in Business, Citrus College **CERTS:** Certified Esthetician, Elegante Beauty College **C/VW:** Alliance for the Arts; The Wellness Community
Email: rosemary120@verizon.net
URL: http://www.cambridgewhoswho.com

Dawn L. Gabriel
Title: Senior Director **Company:** Johnson and Johnson **Dept:** Research and Development Compliance **Address:** 185 Tabor Road, Morris Plains, NJ 07950 United States **BUS:** Pharmaceutical Firm **P/S:** Pharmaceuticals, Diagnostic, Therapeutic, Surgical and Bio-Technology Products **MA:** International **D/D/R:** Ensuring Quality, Managing Compliance **H/I/S:** Golfing, Exercising, Spending Time Outdoors **EDU:** Ph.D. in Pharmaceutical Sciences, University of Connecticut **A/A/S:** New Jersey Pharmaceutical Quality Control Association **A/H:** Innovators Circle Award (2006) **C/VW:** Volunteer, Various Charitable Organizations
Email: dgabriel@conus.jnj.com

Samuel V. Gadam
Title: Geriatric Psychiatrist **Company:** Kaiser Permanente **Address:** 1010 Pensacola Street, Honolulu, HI 96814 United States **BUS:** Medical Group **P/S:** Medical Services **MA:** National **D/D/R:** Geriatric Psychiatry **H/I/S:** Exercising, Going to the Beach, Traveling, Cooking, Photography **EDU:** MD in Geriatric Psychiatry, University of Hawaii at Manoa, John A. Burns School of Medicine **A/A/S:** American Association for Geriatric Psychiatry
Email: smgadam@hawaiiantel.net
URL: http://www.cambridgewhoswho.com

Mr. Richard Gade, MBA
Title: Account Manager **Company:** Integrated Production Service, LLP **Address:** 157 Lloyd Road, Lafayette, LA 70506 United States **BUS:** Service Company **P/S:** Wireline Services, Formation Evaluation **MA:** Regional **D/D/R:** Installing Wireline Cabling, Managing Various Accounts, Offering Service to the Southern Louisiana Petroleum Industry **H/I/S:** Snow Skiing, Traveling, Playing Tennis **EDU:** Master of Business Administration, Louisiana State University (2007); Bachelor of Science in Electrical Engineering, University of Colorado at Boulder (1990)
Email: rick_gade@yahoo.com

Mr. Jorge E. Gaeta
Title: Vice President **Company:** West Side Original, Inc. **Address:** 7379 Orange Thorpe, Unit C, Buena Park, CA 92841 United States **BUS:** Leading Wholesale Apparel Manufacturer **P/S:** Popular Style Clothing Lines Focusing on Silk Screening, T-Shirts, Products Geared for Today's Culture **MA:** International **D/D/R:** Management, Marketing and Sales, Warehouse Operations, Customer Relations, Overseeing Order Completion **EDU:** Coursework, Cyprus College and Fullerton College **CERTS:** Licensed in Life Insurance, Primerica **C/VW:** Registered Voters (Orange County) Alcoholics Anonymous Charities of (Orange County and Los Angeles) Victory Outreach
Email: wsoriginalmedia@gmail.com
URL: http://www.wsoriginalmedia.com

Cathy A. Gagnon
Title: 1) Professor, Clinical Coordinator, Adjunct Nursing Faculty 2) Nurse Educator, QI Coordinator **Company:** 1) Mount San Antonio College 2) Pasadena Fire Department **Address:** 1100 N. Grand Avenue, Walnut, CA 91789 United States **BUS:** 1) College 2) Government Organization **P/S:** 1) Education 2) Public Safety **MA:** Statewide **D/D/R:** Paramedic Teaching, Clinical Nursing, Coordinating Clinical and Field Internships, Negotiating Contracts, Scheduling, Maintaining Discipline, Nursing Education **H/I/S:** Gardening, Caring for her Pets, Reading **EDU:** Master of Science in Nursing, California State University, Dominguez Hills (2000); Bachelor of Science in Nursing, California State University, Dominguez Hills **A/A/S:** Emergency Nurses Association; American Heart Association; American Association of Critical-Care Nurses'; American Nurses Association
Email: cgagnon@mtsac.edu

Gina R. Gaither, CDM, CFPP
Title: Certified Dietary Manager, Certified Food Protection Professional **Company:** Community Nursing and Rehabilitation Centers **Address:** 212 Prairie Wind Boulevard, Stephenville, TX 76401 United States **BUS:** Nutrition Distribution, Education, Food Industry **P/S:** Supplies Students with Nutritious Meals **MA:** Local **D/D/R:** Maintaining Quality Control of Food, Nutrition Assessment **H/I/S:** Scrapbooking, Camping, Craftwork, Reading **EDU:** Bachelor's Degree in Human Science, Concentration in Child and Family Studies and Nutrition, Charleston State University (Expected 2008) **CERTS:** Certified Dietary Manager; Certified Food Protection Professional **A/A/S:** KOEN; Honor Society for Human Services Through University; Student Leadership Association; Trainer, Adult Girl Scouts of the USA; Hazard Analysis and Critical Control Points; Dietary Managers Association
Email: tnggaither@earthlink.com
URL: http://www.cambridgewhoswho.com

Daniel Galaburda
Title: Senior Attorney **Company:** National Grid **Address:** 25 Research Dr, Westborough, MA 01582 United States **BUS:** Utilities Distributor **P/S:** Energy Delivery, Private Utility holding company **MA:** Local **D/D/R:** Transmission Regulatory **H/I/S:** Running Marathons, Hiking, Pianist **EDU:** Bachelor of Arts, Boston College; JD, Georgetown University **A/A/S:** Legal Advisory for 'Environmental Protection' in the Caribbean
Email: dgalaburda@hotmail.com

Anca Galesanu
Title: Registered Nurse **Company:** Dearborn County Hospital **Address:** 600 Wilson Creek Road, Lawrenceburg, IN 47025 United States **BUS:** County Hospital **P/S:** Healthcare Services and Associated Services **MA:** Regional **D/D/R:** Pediatric and Adult Cardiology Nursing, Caring for Premature Babies **H/I/S:** Playing Volleyball, Tennis, Swimming, Soccer **EDU:** Pursuing Master's Degree Northern Kentucky University; Bachelor of Science in Nursing, Northern Kentucky University (2006) magna Cum laude; Law Degree, Earned in Romania, Cum Laude (1999) **A/A/S:** Board Member and Leadership Committee for Sigma Theta Tau; International Honor Society of Nursing and Vice President of Rho Checa chapter **A/H:** deans list, Presidents List **C/VW:** Church
Email: anca_galesanu@yahoo.com
URL: http://www.dch.org

Nancy E. Gallagher
Title: President Owner **Company:** Sandhill Residential Appraisals **Address:** 358 Nash Road, St Pauls, NC 28384 United States **BUS:** Real Estate Appraiser **P/S:** Real Estate Appraisals **MA:** Local **D/D/R:** Residential Appraisals **H/I/S:** Gardening, Watching HGTV **EDU:** University of South Florida, Tampa **A/A/S:** NC Appraisers Coalition
Email: info@CambridgeWhosWho.com

Elizabeth Gallaro
Title: Teacher of Nursing **Company:** New York City Department of Education **Address:** 52 Chambers Street, New York, NY 10007 United States **BUS:** Department of Education **P/S:** Educational Administration **MA:** New York City **D/D/R:** Career and Technical Education **H/I/S:** Making Arts and Crafts, Relaxing **EDU:** Master's Degree in Education, Adelphi University, New York **A/A/S:** Association for Curriculum and Development; National Education Association **C/VW:** Various Charitable Organizations
Email: egallaro@schools.nyc.gov

John J. Galli Jr.
Title: President **Company:** John Galli Jr., Inc. **Address:** 17614 Squaw Valley Drive, Dallas, TX 75252 United States **BUS:** Real Estate Agency **P/S:** Commercial and Residential Real Estate Exchange, General Contracting, Property Development and Construction Management **MA:** TX, FL **D/D/R:** Overseeing Foreclosures, Land Development and Mortgage Field Services **H/I/S:** Golfing, Skiing, Yachting, Sport Fishing, Vacationing **EDU:** Bachelor of Science, The State University of New York **CERTS:** Licensed Real Estate Broker, State of Texas; Licensed Contractor, State of Florida **C/VW:** Various Charitable Organizations
Email: jginc@prodigy.net

Miss Kay C. Gallinger-Crofoot
Title: Elementary Teacher **Company:** Howell Public Schools **Address:** 861 E. Sibley Street, Howell, MI 48843 United States **BUS:** School District **P/S:** Education **MA:** Local **EXP:** Ms. Gallinger-Crofoot's area of expertise is in elementary education. **H/I/S:** Reading, Volunteering, Researching Teacher Web Sites, Continuing her Education, Spending Time on a Weekly Basis with her 'Little Sister' **EDU:** Master's Degree in Elementary Education, Marygrove College; Bachelor of Science in Elementary Education, Central Michigan University **A/A/S:** Michigan Education Association; National Education Association **A/H:** Teacher of the Year Award (2006); Five-Time Nominee, Teacher of the Year **C/VW:** Big Brothers Big Sisters of America; The Salvation Army; Goodwill
Email: gallingek@howellschools.com
Email: kaygalli@yahoo.com
URL: http://www.howellschools.com

Ronald W. Galloway
Title: Project Officer **Company:** Aberdeem Area Indian Hlth Svc-Office of Tribal Activities **Address:** 115 4th Avenue SE Room 224, Aberdeem, SD 57401 United States **BUS:** Healthcare **P/S:** Health Services for 7 Tribes **MA:** Regional **D/D/R:** Working as a CHRPCC Data Specialist **H/I/S:** Running, Test **EDU:** Bachelor's in Healthcare Management, Belleview University **A/A/S:** NREMT; NNAEMSA
Email: info@CambridgeWhosWho.com

Susan Galloway Hepworth
Title: Registered Nurse **Company:** Cottonwood Women's Center Intermountain Healthcare **Address:** 5770 S. 300 E., Murray, UT 84107 United States **BUS:** Nonprofit Hospital **P/S:** Behavioral Health, Cancer Care Programs, Cardiology Services, Neonatal, Pediatrics, Women's Health **MA:** Regional **D/D/R:** Teaching Lamaze Courses, Coordinating Maternity and Childbirth Education, Nursing **H/I/S:** Dancing, Exercising, Researching on the Computer, Spending Time Outdoors with her Autistic Son **EDU:** Bachelor of Science in Nursing, Brigham Young University (1982) **CERTS:** Certified Lamaze Instructor; Certified Neonatal Resuscitation Program Instructor **A/A/S:** Lamaze International
Email: cwshepwo@ihc.com

Mr. David Gamache
Title: Interior Decorator **Company:** David Gamache Interiors **Address:** 13425 Reid Circle, Fort Washington, MD 20744 United States **BUS:** Interior Designing Company **P/S:** High Quality Interior Decorating Services to Clients in Residential and Commercial Interiors **MA:** National **D/D/R:** Residential and Commercial Designs, Handmade Draperies **H/I/S:** Music **EDU:** High School Graduate
Email: davidgamache@comcast.net
URL: http://cambridgewhoswho.com

Vivian R. Gamble
Title: Occupational Therapist **Company:** Marshfield Clinic **Address:** Marshfield, WI 54449 United States **BUS:** Clinic **P/S:** Registered Occupational Therapist **MA:** Local **D/D/R:** Lymphedema Therapy **H/I/S:** Speaking at Conferences on Cancer Care, Reading, Crafts, Walking, Gardening, Dancing **EDU:** Bachelor of Arts in Occupational Therapy, American Occupational Association **A/A/S:** National Lymphedema Network, American Cancer Society
Email: Gamblevivian@marshfieldclinic.com
URL: www.marshfieldclinic.com

Douglas P. Ganassi
Title: Certified Athletic Trainer **Company:** NovaCare Rehabilitation **Address:** 1133 Fourth Avenue, Elizabeth, PA 15037 United States **BUS:** Rehabilitation Center **P/S:** Rehabilitation, Occupational and Hand Therapy and Athletic Training **MA:** Regional **D/D/R:** Teaching and Assisting Patients with Rehabilitation, Working Part-Time with High School Students **H/I/S:** Swimming, Lacrosse, Soccer **EDU:** Master's Degree, Northeast Louisiana University (1990); Bachelor's Degree, Slippery Rock University of Pennsylvania (1986) **A/A/S:** National Athletic Trainers Association; Eastern Athletic Association; Pennsylvania State Education Association
Email: nluulmpensspirit@yahoo.com
URL: http://www.novacare.com

William H. Gandy Sr.
Title: President/Executive Director **Company:** Santa Rosa Professional Educators/Gandys Special Services **Address:** 5154 Santa Rosa Street, Milton, FL 32570 United States **BUS:** Education/Private Investigator Service Provider **P/S:** Education, Union Service, Activity **MA:** Local **D/D/R:** Education, Investigations, Negotiations, Leadership **H/I/S:** Football, Baseball, Hunting, Travel **EDU:** Bachelor of Arts, University of Arkansas; Master in Administration, Troy State University **CERTS:** Certified Private Investigator **A/A/S:** FEA, AFT, NEA, Relay for Life, Santa Rosa, Work Force Coalition, Horses of America, Juvenile Justice Council
Email: info@CambridgeWhosWho.com

Helaine G. Gann
Title: Consultant **Company:** Self-Employed **Address:** 1731 Pine Street, Martinez, CA 94553 United States **BUS:** Healthcare Consulting **P/S:** Community Resources **MA:** Local **D/D/R:** Planning, Training **EDU:** Bachelor of Arts in Science, USC
Email: info@CambridgeWhosWho.com

Harold T. Gantt
Title: Owner **Company:** GWG **Address:** 920 Mill Drive, Savannah, GA 31419 United States **BUS:** Construction Company **P/S:** Home Building and Repairs **MA:** National **D/D/R:** Contracting and Subcontracting Special Jobs **H/I/S:** Volunteering, Spending Time with his Wife **EDU:** Diploma, Rossville Tompkins High School **C/VW:** St. Paul's Missionary Baptist Church, Driver for the Elderly

Jie Gao
Title: Lecturer **Company:** CUNY LaGuardia Community College **Address:** 31-10 Thomson Avenue, Long Island City, NY 11101 United States **BUS:** Community College **P/S:** Education **MA:** Local **D/D/R:** Teaching English to Students of Other Languages, Teaching Chinese Literature **H/I/S:** Reading, Research, Translation **EDU:** Bachelor's Degree in Polish Literature and Polish Language, Beijing University **A/A/S:** English as a Second Language Council **A/H:** Who's Who Among American Teachers (2000, 2002, 2003)
Email: gaoji@lagcc.cuny.edu
URL: http://www.lagcc.cuny.edu/ELA

Jason S. Garber, CLT
Title: President **Company:** Envirotexx, LLC **Address:** 3531 Central Park Blvd, Louisville, TN 37777 United States **BUS:** Landscaping Service Provider **P/S:** Mowing, Full Grounds Maintenance **MA:** Local **D/D/R:** Business Management, Certified Landscape Professional **EDU:** One Year of College, Continuing Education Courses **CERTS:** Landscape Professional, ALKA **A/A/S:** Small Business Develop Center
Email: info@CambridgeWhosWho.com
URL: www.jasonenvirotexx.com

Amador Garcia Jr.
Title: Manager of Security Services **Company:** Seton Medical Center, Daughters of Charity Health System **Address:** 1900 Sullivan Avenue, Daly City, CA 94015 United States **BUS:** Medical Center **P/S:** Healthcare **MA:** Local **D/D/R:** Maintaining Public Relations, Overseeing Security, Serving as a Liaison between the Hospital and Security Agents **H/I/S:** Hot Rodding **EDU:** Associate of Science, Skyline College **A/A/S:** American Society for Industrial Security International
Email: amadorgarcia@dochs.org
URL: http://www.setonmedicalcenter.org

April Alysse Garcia
Title: Music Teacher **Company:** Notre Dame Catholic School **Address:** 907 Main Street, Kerrville, TX 78028 United States **BUS:** Catholic School **P/S:** Education **MA:** Local **D/D/R:** Teaching Music to Students **EDU:** Bachelor's Degree in Music, Schreiner University **A/A/S:** TMEA; TCDA
Email: alysse.garcia@notredameschool.cc
URL: http://www.notredameschool.cc

Daniela Garcia
Title: Chief Executive Officer **Company:** American Coast Insurance Services, Inc **Address:** 8020 Somerset Blvd, Paramount, CA 90723 United States **BUS:** Insurance Services **P/S:** Property and Casualty/Life/Income Tax Services **MA:** National **D/D/R:** Insurance Brokerage **H/I/S:** Reading, Traveling, Movies **EDU:** Bachelor of Science in Business Administration, California State at Long Beach **A/A/S:** NFIB
Email: americancoastins@sbcglobal.net

Eliot R. Garcia
Title: Mentally Ill Adult Case Manager **Company:** Monroe Community Mental Health Authority **Address:** 1001 S. Raisinville Road, Dundee, MI 48131 United States **BUS:** Community Mental Health Center **P/S:** Adult Mental Health Case Management **MA:** Local **D/D/R:** Assisting Senior Citizens and Patients with Alzheimer's, Substance Abuse and Mental Illnesses, Managing Paperwork, Meeting with Clients **H/I/S:** Exercising, Cooking **EDU:** Master of Arts in Research Psychology, San Jose University (1985); Master of Science in Clinical Psychology, San Jose University (1985); Bachelor's Degree in Psychology, San Jose University (1979) **CERTS:** Certification in CPR
Email: eliotandtia@aol.com

Lori Ann Garcia
Title: Graphic Artist **Company:** Graphics Etc, Inc **Address:** 10761 Wallflower Avenue, Las Vegas, NV 89135 United States **BUS:** Graphic Design/Media/Web Design Information Technology **P/S:** Graphic Services **MA:** National **D/D/R:** Publication Design and Production **H/I/S:** Traveling, Movies **EDU:** Diploma in Graphic Design, Long Island University; 2 Year Degree in Commercial Design, The Art Institute of Las Vegas
Email: graphicsetc@cox.net
URL: http://www.graphics-etc.com

Mrs. Maria L. Garcia
Title: English and Bilingual Teacher (Retired) **Company:** La Joya Independent School District **Dept:** English Language Arts **Address:** 2610 N. Moorefield Road, Mission, TX 78574 United States **BUS:** Independent School District **P/S:** Middle School Education **MA:** Local **EXP:** Mrs. Garcia's expertise includes bilingual and English education for sixth, seventh and eighth-grade students. **H/I/S:** Spending Time with her Daughter and Grandchildren **EDU:** Bachelor's Degree in Elementary Education, Minor in Reading, Minor in Bilingual Education, The University of Texas-Pan American (1991) **A/A/S:** American Federation of Teachers **C/VW:** Local Church; St. Williams Catholic Church
Email: m.garcia7@ljisd.com
URL: http://www.cambridgewhoswho.com

Melissa Garcia
Title: Teacher **Company:** United High School **Address:** 100 E. Aurora Street, Apartment 355, Laredo, TX 78041 United States **BUS:** High School **P/S:** Secondary Education **MA:** Local **D/D/R:** Teaching Ninth-Grade Science and Biology **H/I/S:** Reading **EDU:** Bachelor of Arts, The International University **CERTS:** Certification in Secondary Biology and General Science, Texas A&M University; Certification, The International University; Bachelor of Science in Biology, Texas A&M University (1999) **A/A/S:** Science Teachers Association of Texas
Email: mmagnon@hotmail.com

Rafael Suraez Garcia
Title: Co-Owner **Company:** Cafe Habana City **Address:** 911 Bertrand Drive, Lafayette, LA 70506 United States **BUS:** Cuban Restaurant **P/S:** Cuban Coffee and Sandwiches, Tamales, Beef, Chicken, Pork, Rice and Beans **MA:** Local **D/D/R:** Preparing Mojitos and Cuban Sandwiches, Marketing, Bookkeeping and Overseeing all Aspects of the Business, D Jays at the Restaurant on Fridays **H/I/S:** Art, Photography, Playing Baseball
Email: rafael.garcia@cwwemail.com
URL: http://www.cafehabanacity.com

Tony O.C. Garcia
Title: Tattoo Artist **Company:** A Different Image Tattoo Studio **Address:** 6212 SE 15th Street, Midwest City, OK 73110 United States **BUS:** Tattooing Studio **P/S:** Tattooing **MA:** Local **D/D/R:** Sterilizing, Customers, Comfortably, Procedure **H/I/S:** Drawing, Tattooing **EDU:** Graduate Degree in High School **A/A/S:** Toys for Tots, Raffle Drawing Certificate for National Leadership Award
Email: tony@adifferentimage.com
URL: www.adifferentimage.com

Dr. Fae Garcia Bush
Title: School Social Worker **Company:** Martin Luther King Elementary, Helen Keller elementary **Address:** 6010 Sapporo Drive, Colorado Springs, CO 80918 United States **BUS:** School District **P/S:** Education **MA:** Local **D/D/R:** Leadership, Helping Children with Emotional and Social Difficulties **H/I/S:** Spending Time in the Mountains, Traveling, Spending Time with her Two Dogs and Four Grandchildren **EDU:** Doctor of Education, Fielding Graduate Institute, 1982; Master of Social Work, University of Denver **CERTS:** Certified Sex Educator, 1979 **A/A/S:** National Association of Social Workers; Colorado Springs Education Association; American Association of Sex Educators, Counselors and Therapists; National Hispanic Schools **C/VW:** Hispanic Scholarship Fund, Latino Scholarship Organizations, Imagination Celebration
Email: bushfl@d11.org

Deborah A. Garcia-Sanchez, PMP
Title: Project Manager, Physical Scientist **Company:** U.S. Department of Energy **Dept:** Sandia Site Office **Address:** P.O. Box 5400, Albuquerque, NM 87185 United States **BUS:** Department of Energy **P/S:** Energy Distribution, Construction Project Management, Facilities **MA:** National **EXP:** Ms. Garcia-Sanchez's area of expertise is in project management. **D/D/R:** Overseeing the Construction of Commercial Buildings, Laboratories and Infrastructure **H/I/S:** Artwork, Making Crafts, Carving Gourds **EDU:** Pursuing Master's Degree in Industrial Engineering, New Mexico State University; Bachelor of Science in Environmental Science, College of Santa Fe (2006) **CERTS:** Certified Project Management Professional (2003) **A/A/S:** Project Management Institute **C/VW:** The Breast Cancer Research Foundation; Wildlife Restoration
Email: dgarciasanchez@comcast.net
Email: dgarcia-sanchez@doeal.gov

Ann S. Gardner
Title: Vice President of Marketing **Company:** Remodel Wrights **Address:** 15 Gooding Avenue, Bristol, RI 02809 United States **BUS:** Construction Company **P/S:** Design and Build Environmentally Friendly Homes **MA:** Regional **D/D/R:** Marketing Environmentally-Friendly Products, Web Marketing **H/I/S:** Spending Time Outdoor, Gardening, Reading **EDU:** Master of Science in Computer Science, Fitchburg University (1990); Bachelor of Science in Computer Engineering, Roger Williams University (1987) **C/VW:** Our Lady of Mount Carmel Church; Local Charitable Organizations
Email: office@remodelwrights.com
URL: http://www.remodelwrights.com

Linda L. Gardner
Title: Retail Buyer **Company:** Old Salem Museums & Gardens **Address:** 600 S. Main Street, Winston-Salem, NC 27101 United States **BUS:** Nonprofit Museum **P/S:** Early Southern Decorative Arts, Toys, Old Salem Children's Museum, Old Salem Toy Museum, Gardens of Salem, Gift Shop, Bakery, Events, Programs **MA:** Regional **D/D/R:** Purchasing Items for Historic Shops, Book and Merchant Shops and Visiting Centers, Selecting Materials for the Period Rooms and Galleries in the Museum, Reviewing Products, Contacting Vendors, Coordinating Book Signing Events, Serving as Liaison to the Accounting Department **H/I/S:** Heirloom Embroidering, Reading, Gardening, Traveling **EDU:** Pursuing Degree in Business and Marketing, Marshall University; Pursuing Associate Degree in Internet Studies, Forsyth Technical Community College **A/A/S:** American Booksellers Association, Southern Independent Booksellers Alliance
Email: lgardner@oldsalem.org
URL: http://oldsalem.org

Paula J. Gardner, M.S.Ed.
Title: School Psychologist **Company:** Southern Columbia Area School District **Address:** 802 Southern Drive, Catawissa, PA 17820 United States **BUS:** School District **P/S:** Education for Kindergarten through 12th-Grade **MA:** Regional **D/D/R:** Assessing Children with Learning Disabilities and Children who are Gifted, Counseling Students with Attention Deficit Hyperactive Disorder, Initiating and Maintaining Preschool Summer Programs for Children at Risk Prior to Entering Kindergarten **H/I/S:** Traveling, Hiking **EDU:** Master of Science in Education, Bucknell University (1985); Bachelor of Science in Individual and Family Studies, The Pennsylvania State University (1980) **A/A/S:** National Association of School Psychologists; Pennsylvania Association of School Psychologists; Board Member, Southern Columbia Community That Cares Program; Girl Scout Leader; St. Andrew's Episcopal Church
Email: pgardner@scasd.us
URL: http://www.scolumbiasd.k12.pa.us

Jarvis D. Garetson
Title: Partner Company: Garetson Brothers Address: 2394 120th Road, Copeland, KS 67837 United States BUS: Farm P/S: Growing Corn, Wheat, Cotton, Sorghum and Barley MA: National EXP: Mr. Garetson's area of expertise is in agriculture. D/D/R: Overseeing Irrigation and Nutrition Management, Applying Pesticides, Scheduling, Harvesting H/I/S: Football, Water Skiing EDU: Bachelor of Science, Kansas State University (1995) A/A/S: Kansas Farm Bureau; Southwest Kansas Irrigation Association; Kansas Milo Growers Association
Email: garetsonbros@yahoo.com

Phyllis J. Garhart
Title: Finance Director Company: Borough of Tyrone Address: 1100 Logan Avenue, Tyrone, PA 16686 United States BUS: Government Organization P/S: Public Service Including Budgetary Functions, Operational Programs and Public Fund Investments MA: Regional D/D/R: Educating Residents, Managing Finance for General, Special Revenues, Enterprise and Fiduciary Funds H/I/S: Making Crafts, Motorcycling, Sports EDU: Coursework in Information Technology and Finance, St. Francis College A/A/S: Alliance of Bikers Aimed Toward Education; Recording Secretary, Tyrone Borough Authority
Email: pgarhart@tyroneboropa.com
URL: http://www.tyroneboropa.com

Wanda L. Garland
Title: Bookkeeper, Comptroller Company: Deerfield Construction Group Address: 610 Professional Drive, Suite 210, Gaithersburg, MD 20879 United States BUS: Construction Company P/S: Construction Services MA: Maryland, Virginia and Washington, DC EXP: Ms. Garland's area of expertise is in operations management. D/D/R: Processing Payroll and Payroll Taxes, Managing Accounts Payable and Receivable, Overseeing Job-Costing Programs, Making General Ledger Entries and Preparing In-House Financial Reports H/I/S: Crocheting, Cross-Stitching, Beading EDU: Diploma, Hudsonville High School (1972) CERTS: Certificate of Training Excellence, Receptionist Guide to Front Desk Security, Computrain International; Certification, Microsoft Office; Certification, Quickbooks; Certificate of Facility Management Course Completion C/VW: Financial Secretary, Johnsville United Methodist Church
Email: wgarland@deerfieldcon.com

Tricia A. Garling
Title: Program Manager Company: Quest Software, Inc. Address: 14101 Sullyfield Circle, Suite 340, Chantilly, VA 20151 United States BUS: Information Technology Company P/S: Designing, Distributing Software Development Products for Packaged and Custom Software Applications and Associated Software Infrastructure Components such as Databases, Application Servers and Operating Systems MA: Regional D/D/R: Managing Federal Government Programs, Installing High-Speed Networks in the Washington, DC Metro Area H/I/S: Gardening, Downhill Skiing EDU: Master's Degree in Systems Management, University of Southern California (1985) CERTS: Registered Communications Distribution Designer A/A/S: Building Industry Consulting Services International (2002)
Email: tricia.garling@quest.com

Mrs. Ann H. Garner
Title: Teacher, Life Skills Program Company: Surry County Schools, Surry Central High School Dept: Exceptional Children Address: 716 SOUTH MAIN STREET, DOBSON, NC 27017 United States BUS: School P/S: Education MA: Local D/D/R: Teaching Exceptional and Mentally Handicapped Children, Teaching Life Skills H/I/S: Traveling, Spending Time with her Husband, Children and Grandchildren EDU: Educational Specialist Degree in Curriculum, Administration and Supervision, Appalachian State University; Master's Degree in Special Education and Learning Disabilities, Appalachian State University; Bachelor's Degree in Mental Disabilities, Appalachian State University CERTS: National Board Certification, 2000 A/A/S: National Education Association; North Carolina Education Association; Delta Kappa Gamma; ARC C/VW: Board Member, Residence Services Board for the Mentally Handicapped; Special Olympics; Local Art Gallery
Email: garnera@surry.k12.nc.us
URL: http://www.cambridgewhoswho.com

Jami Garner Werth, RRT
Title: Registered Respiratory Therapist Company: Pulmonary Management Services Address: 1628 Deerwood Drive, Rockwall, TX 75032 United States BUS: Private Practice P/S: Pulmonary Care MA: Local D/D/R: CPR Instructor, BLS Instructor H/I/S: Playing Softball, Watching Sports EDU: Associate of Science, Tyler Junior College A/A/S: National Board of Respiratory Care, American Heart Association
Email: jami_werth@sbcglobal.net

William K. Garr
Title: Senior Pastor Company: 7th Street Christian Church Address: 122 W 7th Street, Paris, KY 40361 United States BUS: Christian Church P/S: Spreading God's Gospel MA: Local D/D/R: Specializing in Educating Young Ministers and Spreading the Word of God to all, Including the Sick and Shut-In and Prison Ministry CERTS: Lay Ministry Licensed Certification, Lexington Theological Seminary A/A/S: The YMCA Black Achievers; Bourbon County Ministerial Association; Relay for Life
Email: info@CambridgeWhosWho.com

Jennifer E. Garretson
Title: Second-Grade Teacher Company: Wichita Public Schools Dept: Washington Elementary School Address: 424 N. Pennsylvania, Wichita, KS 67214 United States BUS: Elementary School P/S: Education MA: Local D/D/R: Teaching Second-Grade, Teaching English to Speakers of Other Languages, Teaching Inclusion Classes H/I/S: Reading, Traveling, Cooking, Playing Tennis EDU: Master of Education, Wichita State University (2004); Bachelor's Degree in Elementary Education, Wichita State University A/A/S: United Teachers of Wichita; Kansas Education Association; National Education Association
Email: jegarretson@sbcglobal.net

Carla J. Garrett
Title: Teacher (Retired) Company: Roff Public School Address: P.O. Box 157, Roff, OK 74865 United States BUS: School District P/S: Education MA: Local EXP: Ms. Garrett's area of expertise is in early childhood education. H/I/S: Landscaping, Traveling, Exercising, Rodeo EDU: Master's Degree in Reading, East Central University; Bachelor of Science in Elementary Education, East Central University A/A/S: Roff Classroom Teachers Organization C/VW: Methodist Church of Roff; East Central University Alumni Fund
Email: carla.garrett00@cwwemail.com
URL: http://www.cambridgewhoswho.com

Marilyn R. Garrett
Title: Business Representative Company: SDS, Smart Document Solutions Address: 120 Bluegrass Parkway, Alpharetta, GA 30005 United States BUS: Medical Records Service Provider P/S: Release of Health Information/Medical Records MA: International D/D/R: Health Information H/I/S: Church Treasurer, Cross Stitching A/A/S: Church of Nazarene
Email: mschooch00@aol.com

Jill A. Garripoli
Title: Pediatrician Company: Rutherford Pediatrics and Pulmonology Address: 338 Union Avenue, Rutherford, NJ 07070 United States BUS: Private Practice P/S: Healthcare MA: Local EXP: Ms. Garripoli's area of expertise is in general pediatrics. D/D/R: Treating Infants, Children and Adolescents H/I/S: Practicing Taekwondo EDU: Doctor of Osteopathy, School of Osteopathic Medicine, University of Medicine and Dentistry of New Jersey A/A/S: Junior Women's Club, Lyndhurst; American Academy of Pediatrics; American College of Osteopathic Pediatricians C/VW: American Lung Association
Email: jillgarripoli@yahoo.com

Jo Ann M. Garrison
Title: Legal Administrative Assistant Company: Thomas S. Cometa, Esquire Address: 250 Pierce Street, Suite 213, Kingston, PA 18704 United States BUS: Law Firm P/S: Legal Services, Family and Criminal Law MA: Local D/D/R: Meeting Clients, Maintaining Paperwork for Clients, Drafting Documents H/I/S: Playing Tennis, Bowling EDU: Associate Degree in Secretarial Science, Luzerne County Community College (1985) CERTS: Certified Notary Public A/A/S: Board of Directors, Kiwanis Club
Email: jojobyday@aol.com

Todd Garrow
Title: Coordinator Company: Southwest Florida Addiction Services, Inc. Dept: Human Resources Address: 2675 Winkler Avenue, Suite 180, Fort Myers, FL 33901 United States BUS: Rehabilitation Center P/S: Healthcare Including Substance Abuse Treatment MA: Local EXP: Mr. Garrow's expertise is in human resources management. H/I/S: Golfing, Exercising, Sports EDU: Bachelor's Degree in Business Management and Human Resource Management, Urbana University A/A/S: Society for Human Resource Management C/VW: United Way
Email: toddgarrow@yahoo.com
URL: http://www.cambridgewhoswho.com

Cheza Collier Garvin
Title: Program Director, Psychologist Company: Public Health, Seattle and King County Address: 401 Fifth Avenue, Suite 900, Seattle, WA 98104 United States BUS: Public Health P/S: Service and Education for Health Programs MA: Local D/D/R: Chronic Disease Prevention and Healthy Aging Administration and Research, Directing Diabetes and Health Promotion Programs with Special Emphasis on Program Development and Community Partnership H/I/S: Salsa and Liturgical Dancing, Reading, Music, Attending the Theater, Spending Time with her Husband EDU: Ph.D. in Clinical Psychology, University of Washington; Master of Public Health, University of California at Berkeley; Master of Social Work, University of California at Berkeley A/A/S: Washington State Psychological Association C/VW: Church, Bible Study, Health and Dance Ministry, Community Organizations
Email: drcgarvin@comcast.net
URL: http://www.metrokc.gov/health

Roman B. Gary
Title: Architect Company: Cohen Carnaggio Reynolds Architecture Address: 2720 First Avenue South, Birmingham, AL 35233 United States BUS: Architectural P/S: Commercial and Residential Design MA: Local D/D/R: Commercial and Residential Design H/I/S: Golf, Basketball, Poetry Writing, Reading EDU: Bachelor of Architecture
Email: rgary06@aol.com

Paula Garza
Title: Teacher Company: Lafourche Parish School Board Address: 177 W. 55th Street, Cut Off, LA 70345 United States BUS: School Board P/S: Education MA: Local D/D/R: Elementary Education H/I/S: Traveling, Watching Movies, Exercise EDU: Bachelor's Degree in Elementary Education, Nichols State University (1979) A/A/S: National Educators Association; Special Olympic Coach; Five Time World Game Coach; One National Games Coach A/H: State Special Olympics Coach of the Year Award (1999) C/VW: Special Olympics; Religion Teacher; Vacation Bible School Teacher
Email: pgarza.coes@lafourche.k12.la.us
URL: http://www.cambridgewhoswho.com

Marsha C. Garziano
Title: Business Manager Company: Pass Christian Public School District Address: 136 Eleanor Avenue, Pass Christian, MS 39571 United States BUS: Public School District P/S: Regular Core Curriculum Including Reading, Math, English, Science, Social Studies, Art, Music, History MA: Regional D/D/R: Accounting Services for the District Including Payroll, Accounts Receivable and Payable, Fixed Assets, Budgeting, Finance, Tax Issues Annually, Overseeing 4 Employees H/I/S: Reading EDU: Bachelor's Degree in Business Administration, University of Mississippi (1982); Master's Degree in Educational Administration, University of Mississippi (1998) A/A/S: MASBO; SASBO A/H: 1st MASBO Business Manager of the Year Award
Email: mgarziano@pc.k12.ms.us
URL: http://www.passchristianschools.com

Mr. Mark Gasparini
Title: Doctor Company: Mark Gasparini, D.P.M., P.C. Address: 119 New York Avenue, Massapequa, NY 11758 United States BUS: Podiatry Practice P/S: Podiatric Care MA: Local D/D/R: Podiatric Medicine, Surgery, Alleviating Pain and Discomfort H/I/S: Sports EDU: Doctor of Podiatry, New York College of Podiatric Medicine A/A/S: New York State Podiatric Medical Association; FAPA
Email: mcagg22@aol.com
URL: http://www.drgasparini.com

Julie A. Gasper
Title: Marketing Administrator, Production Coordinator Company: The Schemmer Associates, Inc. Address: 1044 N. 115th Street, Suite 300, Omaha, NE 68154 United States BUS: Engineering Company P/S: Architectural and Civil Engineering Services MA: Midwest D/D/R: Marketing EDU: Bachelor's Degree in Journalism, Midland Lutheran College A/A/S: American Marketing Association; Public Relations Committee, American Council of Engineering Companies; Construction Writers Association
Email: jgasper@schemmer.com
URL: http://www.schemmer.com

Kim K. Gates
Title: Teacher Company: Rockwell Elementary Address: 10183 Highway 31, Spanish Fort, AL 36527 United States BUS: Public School P/S: Education for Students in Kindergarten through Fifth-Grade MA: Regional D/D/R: Teaching Kindergarten, Second and Fourth-Grade Students, Teaching Disciplined Art and Theater Classes, Assisting Teachers with Technology Integration H/I/S: Collecting Raggedy Ann and Andy Items EDU: Bachelor's Degree in Elementary Education, University of South Alabama; Bachelor's Degree in Early Childhood Education, University of South Alabama A/A/S: Library Committee A/H: Teacher of the Year (2006)
Email: kgates@bcbe.org

Sheila I. Gates
Title: Seamstress, Special Effects Makeup Artist **Company:** Dan Lee Gates **Address:** 1711 W. Alameda Avenue, Apartment C, Burbank, CA 91506 United States **BUS:** Fashion Designs Firm **P/S:** Costume Design, Special Effects Makeup, Greeting Cards, Wedding Favors **MA:** International **D/D/R:** Designing Wedding Gowns, Favors and Greeting Cards, Creating Dolls, Special Effects with Makeup **H/I/S:** Sewing, Applying Cosmetics, Making Crafts **EDU:** Coursework in Business Administration and Mathematics, Prairie State College **A/A/S:** Nickelodeon; Playboy; Disney **C/VW:** Church; American Cancer Society
Email: sheila.gates@sbcglobal.net

Mr. Sean K. Gatison
Title: Financial Specialist **Company:** Robert Half International, Inc. **Dept:** Salaried Professional Service Division **Address:** 263 Tresser Boulevard, Stamford, CT 06901 United States **BUS:** Staffing and Consulting Company **P/S:** Consulting Services, Administrative Support for Information Technology Professionals, Financial Recruiting Services, Legal Support **MA:** Regional **EXP:** Mr. Gatison's areas of expertise include the analysis of financial statements, recruiting and client consultation. **D/D/R:** Managing Invoices, Overseeing Insurance Policies, Analyzing Financial Reports while utilizing SAP **H/I/S:** Watching Basketball, Golfing **EDU:** Master of Business Administration in International Management, Rensselaer Polytechnic Institute **CERTS:** Producer Life, Accident/Health **A/A/S:** National Association of Black Accountants; President, Omega Psi Phi Fraternity, Inc. Epsilon Iota Iota Chapter
Email: gat5@snet.net
URL: http://www.cambridgewhoswho.com

Barbara P. Gaudio
Title: Owner **Company:** Barbara P. Gauido, LMT, CH **Address:** 7A Maple Street, Chester, CT 06412 United States **BUS:** Therapy Center **P/S:** Hypnotherapy and Massage Therapy **MA:** Local **EXP:** Ms. Gaudio's area of expertise is in strategic development. **D/D/R:** Treating and Diagnosing Attention Deficit Hypertension Disorder, Managing Operations **H/I/S:** Needlework, Camping, Hiking **CERTS:** Certified Massage Therapist **A/H:** Nationwide Register's Who's Who
Email: shunyata@snet.net
URL: https://www.healatshunyata.com

Micheline Gauthier
Title: Purchasing **Company:** Astra Zeneca **Address:** 7171 Frederick-Banting, St Laurent, H4S 1Z9 Canada **BUS:** Healthcare Pharmaceuticals/Biotechnology **P/S:** Pharmaceutical Sales **MA:** International **D/D/R:** Purchasing, Global Projects **H/I/S:** Reading, Animals, Walking **A/A/S:** American Management Association
Email: miche.g@videotron.ca
URL: www.astrazeneca.com

Carolina E. Gautreaux
Title: Executive Manager **Company:** Cammon Steel Company, Inc. **Address:** 56 New Hutchinson Mill Road, La Grange, GA 30240 United States **BUS:** Manufacturing Company **P/S:** Steel Metal Roofing **MA:** Regional **D/D/R:** Overseeing Company Finances and Human Recourses **H/I/S:** Riding Motorcycles, Gardening, NASCAR Racing **CERTS:** Certification in Computerized Accounting and Management, Gretener Career College **A/A/S:** Better Business Bureau; Georgia Chamber of Commerce; Dunnam Bradstreet **A/H:** Number One in Sales Award, Cammon Steel Company **C/VW:** Volunteer, Paws and Claws
Email: cgautreaux@cammonsteel.com
URL: http://www.cammonsteel.com

Linda A. Gavin
Title: Owner **Company:** Barfield's of Cape Cod **Address:** 175 Main Street, Route 6A, Yarmouth Port, MA 02675 United States **BUS:** Family-Owned Retail Shop **P/S:** Selling Antique Lamps, Custom Made Shades **MA:** International **D/D/R:** Repairing and Converting Antiques into Lamps, Creating Hand-Painted Lamp Shades, Working Directly with Decorators and Designers, Handling Customer Service and Sales, Overseeing all Functions of the Business **H/I/S:** Hiking, Boating, Swimming **EDU:** Diploma, Braintree High School
Email: barfieldsofcapecodyp@yahoo.com

John D. Gay
Title: Regional Leasing Manager **Company:** Cisco Systems, Inc. **Address:** 500 Northridge Road, Suite 700, Atlanta, GA 30350 United States **BUS:** Finance Company **P/S:** Financial Services for Cisco Customers through a Combination of Lease Financing, Channel Financing and Remarketed Equipment **MA:** Regional **EXP:** Mr. Gay's areas of expertise include public sector and tax exempt financing. **D/D/R:** Acquiring Products and Services through Financing, Offering Financial Advice to State and Local Government Institutions **H/I/S:** Traveling, Reading, Hiking, Spending Time Outdoors **EDU:** Master's Degree in Finance, California State University (1980); Bachelor's Degree in Finance, San Diego State University (1972) **A/A/S:** The Association of Government Leasing & Finance; Equipment Leasing and Finance Association; Government Finance Officers Association
Email: jogay@cisco.com
URL: http://www.cisco.com

Steve S. Gayes
Title: Petroleum Territory Manager **Company:** Marathon Petroleum, LLC **Dept:** Brand Marketing **Address:** 539 S Main Street, Findlay, OH 45840 United States **BUS:** Petroleum Distribution **P/S:** Petroleum Energy/Oil **MA:** Regional **D/D/R:** Marketing **H/I/S:** Weight Lifting, Woodworking, Cycling **EDU:** Master's Degree in Business Administration, Roosevelt University **A/A/S:** Future Business Leaders of America
Email: stevegayes@comcast.net
URL: www.stevegayes.com

Lynn Ge-Zerbe, MD, MPH
Title: Endocrinologist, Physician **Company:** St. Luke's Clinic **Dept:** Snake River Endocrinology **Address:** 746 N. College Road, Genoa Building Suite A, Twin Falls, ID 83301 United States **BUS:** Healthcare **P/S:** Hormone Deficiencies, Thyroid, Diabetes **MA:** Local **D/D/R:** Offering Endocrinology and Epidemiology Services **H/I/S:** Traveling, Art, Painting **EDU:** Medical Doctor, Peking Union Medical College; Master of Public Health in Epidemiology, University of Pittsburgh **A/A/S:** American Association of Clinical Endocrinologists; Endocrine Society; American College of Physicians
Email: lynnge@mvrmc.org

Victoria R. Gearlds
Title: Pharmacist **Company:** Park Avenue Pharmacy **Address:** 131 Park Avenue, Glasgow, KY 42141 United States **BUS:** Pharmacy **P/S:** Pharmacy Services **MA:** Local **D/D/R:** Customer Service, Filling Prescriptions, Management **H/I/S:** Traveling, Spending Time with her Husband and Two Children **EDU:** Bachelor of Science in Pharmacy, Sanford School of Pharmacy **A/A/S:** American Pharmacists Association; APHA; Alpha Phi Omega Service Fraternity **C/VW:** Girl Scout Troop Leader, Alpha Phi Omega Service Fraternity, Community Activities
Email: victoriagearlds@yahoo.com

Douglas A. Gedestad, DMD
Title: President **Company:** Douglas A Gedestad DMD, Inc **Address:** 2409 L Street Suite 1, Sacramento, CA 95816 United States **BUS:** Healthcare Dentist **P/S:** Dental Care **MA:** Local **D/D/R:** General Dentistry **H/I/S:** Golf **EDU:** Bachelor of Science, University of California at Davis; DMD, University of Pennsylvania **A/A/S:** Sacramento District Dental Society, California Dental Society, American Dental Society
Email: drgedestad@sbcglobal.net

Lisa J. Geer
Title: Landscape Architect **Company:** LJ Geer Design **Address:** PO Box 14608-53708, Madison, WI 53708 United States **BUS:** Landscape Architect **P/S:** Landscape Architecture, Commercial, Institutional, Sustainable and Native Landscapes, Alternative Storm Water Design, Roof Top Gardens **MA:** Wisconsin **D/D/R:** Sustainable Site Design, Native Landscape **H/I/S:** Photography, Kayaking **EDU:** Bachelor's Degree in Landscape Architecture, University of Wisconsin-Madison (1986) **CERTS:** Licensed and Registered in Landscape Architecture, State of Wisconsin; Lead Accredited Professional; Trained in Wetland Delineation, University of Wisconsin-Lacrosse **A/A/S:** Gold Certification, United States Green Building Council, 2006; Landscape Architect, Wisconsin Department of Natural Resources Northeast Project, Howard, Wisconsin **C/VW:** Citizens for Natural Resources Association
Email: ljgeer@tds.net
URL: http://www.ljgeerdesign.com

Theresa C. Gehr
Title: Supervisor of Emergency Services **Company:** Moundbuilders Guidance Center **Address:** 65 Messimer Drive, Newark, OH 43055 United States **BUS:** Community Mental Health Center **P/S:** Emergency Mental Health and Drug and Alcohol Treatments **MA:** Local **D/D/R:** Overseeing Eight Counselors, Supervising Emergency Mental Health Department, Drug and Alcohol Crises Management, Post Traumatic Stress Disorder Treatments for Teenage Behavioral Disorders and Counseling for Families of Teenagers, Group, Individual and Emergency Counseling **H/I/S:** Camping, Traveling, Spending Time with her Family **EDU:** Master of Social Work, Grand Valley State University (1997); Bachelor of Social Work, Grand Valley State University (1996) **A/A/S:** National Association of Social Workers; FSO; Phi Alpha Honor Society
Email: tgehr01@moundbuildersguidance.org
URL: http://www.cambridgewhoswho.com

Debra S. Gehrt
Title: Auditor 1 **Company:** FHL Bank of Topeka **Address:** One Security Benefit Place, Topeka, KS 66606 United States **BUS:** Bank **P/S:** Loans and Banking Services for Commercial Banks, Thrifts, Credit Unions, Insurance Companies **MA:** National **D/D/R:** Finance, Item Processing, Audit, Lending, Accounting **H/I/S:** Being with her Grandchildren **EDU:** Bachelor of Business Administration in Finance, Washburn University **CERTS:** Investment Analyst Certificate, New York Institute of Finance; AIB Banking and Finance Diploma, American Banking Association **A/A/S:** ITIA; President Elect, Former Board Member, Ronald McDonald House Charities of Northeast Kansas
Email: debbie.gehrt@fhlbtopeka.com
URL: http://www.fhlbtopeka.com

Emily K. Geiler, LMT, RYT
Title: Massage Therapist, Yoga Instructor **Company:** Emily K. Geiler, LMT, RYT, NCTMB **Address:** St. Louis, MO 63129 United States **BUS:** Health and Wellness Services **P/S:** Healthcare, Fitness **MA:** Statewide **D/D/R:** Sports, Deep Tissue, Deep Relaxation, Pregnancy and Infancy Massaging, Teaching Yoga **H/I/S:** Rollerblading, Playing Volleyball, Traveling, Scuba Diving, Hunting **CERTS:** Pursuing Certification in Respiratory Therapy, Sanford-Brown College; Licensed Registered Yoga Instructor (2005); Massage Therapist, State of Missouri (2001); National Certification in Therapeutic Massage and Bodywork **A/A/S:** American Massage Therapy Association; Yoga Alliance **C/VW:** American Heart Association
Email: egeiler@mac.com

Joyce Geisel
Title: Licensed Hearing Aid Specialist, Certified Audiometric Technician **Company:** Hearing Healthcare Associates **Address:** 17 Sixth Avenue, Greenville, PA 16125 United States **BUS:** Audiology Center **P/S:** Hearing Correction, Hearing Aids, Diagnostic Audiological Assessments, Balance Screenings, Custom Fit Hearing Protection **MA:** Local **D/D/R:** Identifying Different Hearing Problems, Working with Ear, Nose and Throat Physicians, Working with Audiologists, Servicing All Makes and Models of Hearing Aids and Hearing Protection, Including Industrial, Improving Quality of Life for Patients **H/I/S:** Bowling, Hiking **EDU:** Associate of Science in Applied Business, Youngstown State University (1982) **A/A/S:** International Hearing Society
Email: hhea_gvh@yahoo.com
URL: http://www.hearinghealthcareassociates.com

Elizabeth Gellatly
Title: Resource Teacher, Administrative Designee **Company:** Sycamore Elementary School **Address:** 340 N. Main Street, Orange, CA 92868 United States **BUS:** Public Education **P/S:** Maintaining Academic Excellence for Students in Kindergarten through Third-Grade **MA:** Elementary **D/D/R:** Educating Students, Focus in Academic Excellence, Reading Specialist, Utilizing Montessori Background as a Foundation for Effective Learning **H/I/S:** Sailing, Hiking, Eating Raw Food **EDU:** Master of Arts in Curriculum and Instruction, Cleveland State University; Administrative Degree, California State University, Long Beach **CERTS:** Pursuing Certification in GLAD Strategies **A/A/S:** Association Montessori International; California Teachers Association; Orange County Reading Association; Phi Beta Kappa **C/VW:** Cancer Foundation, Veterans Association
Email: egellatl@earthlink.net
URL: http://www.cambridgewhoswho.com

Rosemary A. Gelormini
Title: Regional Sales Trainer **Company:** HSBC Mortgage Corp (USA) **Address:** 2929 Walden Avenue, Depew, NY 14043 United States **BUS:** One of the Top Ten Financial Services Companies in the United States **P/S:** Full Range of Personal and Commercial Banking Products and Services to Individuals, Corporations, Institutions and Governments, Products and Services is Offered through its Personal Financial Services, Mortgage Division, Private Banking, Commercial Banking and Corporate Investment Banking and Markets Segments **MA:** National, International **D/D/R:** All Levels of Corporate Training, Motivational Speaking, Corporate Sales Training, Training New Sales People throughout United States for Mortgage Division on Sales, Customer Service, Along with Conforming and Non-Conforming Mortgage Products, Utilizing Software Programs Including Loan Quest, Image Quick and Webloan **H/I/S:** Figure Skating, Playing Piano, Reading, Walking, Bicycling, Membership at GYM, Arts, Attending the Theater **EDU:** Graduate, Todd Duncan's High Trust Sales Academy, San Diego, California (2005); Associate Degree in Business Management, Central City Business Institute (1973) **CERTS:** Certified Trainer, HSBC **A/H:** Best in Customer Service Award, HSBC; Circle Of Excellence Award (2006)
Email: SalesTrainer89@aol.com
URL: http://www.us.hsbc.com

Cynthia L. Generazzo
Title: Occupational Therapy Assistant, Adapted Physical Education Teacher **Company:** South Coast Educational Collaborative **Address:** G.A.R. Highway, Swansea, MA 02777 United States **BUS:** Educational Programs **P/S:** Vocational Education Programs and Professional Development Programs and Services for their Member School Systems **MA:** Regional **D/D/R:** Offering Occupational Therapy with Special Needs Elementary Age Children, Working with Spectrum Disorders, Autism and Multiple Handicaps, Utilizing on Adapted Equipment and Assisted Technology Computers, Addressing Feeding Issues with Parents and Teachers, Teaching Classes through a Personally Adapted Physical Education Curriculum for All Elementary School Students **H/I/S:** Spending Time with her Family, Training as a Tri-Athlete, Playing Softball **EDU:** Bachelor of Science in Physical Education, Concentration in Adapted Physical Education, Bridgewater State College (1995); Associate Degree in Occupational Therapy, Bay State College (1998) **A/A/S:** American Occupational Therapy Association, Inc.; Massachusetts Association for Health, Physical Education, Recreation and Dance
Email: crazzo_99@yahoo.com

Alice Genon
Title: Personal Assistant **Company:** Hallandale Surgical Center **Address:** 815 SE 1st Avenue, Hallandale, FL 33021 United States **BUS:** Surgeon **P/S:** Surgical Procedures **MA:** Local **D/D/R:** Managing Office, Handling all Accountants, Bookkeeping, Insurance and Patient Information **H/I/S:** Traveling, Loves History **EDU:** Pursuing Bachelor's Degree; Associate Degree in Public Relations, Broward Community College **A/A/S:** Synagogue
Email: ag7895@aol.com

Sarah E. Gentry
Title: Registered Nurse **Company:** United States Navy **Address:** 825 E. Palomar Street, Apartment 1914, Chula Vista, CA 91911 United States **BUS:** Naval Branch of the United States Armed Services **P/S:** Maintaining, Training and Equipping Combat-Ready Naval Forces **MA:** National **D/D/R:** Oncology and Hematology Nursing, Administering Chemotherapy, Caring for Patients, Acting as Charge Nurse, Training Nursing Assistants, Performing Administrative Duties **H/I/S:** Hiking **EDU:** Bachelor of Science in Nursing, Indiana University (2004) **A/A/S:** Oncology Nursing Society; Sigma Theta Tau
Email: nursegentry@yahoo.com
URL: http://www.navy.mil

Christine George
Title: Owner **Company:** Christine George Design **Address:** 2720 Hale Court, Waldorf, MD 20603 United States **BUS:** Fine Art and Design Company **P/S:** Oil Paintings, Commissions, Open Edition Prints, Gifts, Photography, Graphic Design **MA:** Regional, National, International **D/D/R:** Oil Paintings, Focus on Equine Art, Did Painting of Barbaro, Kentucky Derby Winner, Passion for Painting Horses, Experienced in Graphic Corporate Branding Such as Logos from Packaging to Product Development, Had Oil Paintings Displayed at Women's Memorial in Arlington Cemetery, Faces of the Fallen and Galleries throughout the USA, Officially Licensed Photographer for the Kentucky Derby **H/I/S:** Horseback Riding, Snow Skiing, Water Skiing **EDU:** Bachelor's Degree in Fine Arts, Art Center College of Design, with Honors (1984) **A/A/S:** Work Published in Equine Images, Blood Horse, Horse Talk, Sidelines, Maryland Independent, Horses and Art **A/H:** Commissioned to do Portraits; Chamber of Commerce; Won Cleo and Two Addy Awards (1989)
Email: c@christinegeorge.com
URL: http://www.christinegeorge.com

Jonnie George
Title: Pharmacist, Manager **Company:** Mount Olive Pharmacy **Address:** 615 N. Breazeale Avenue, Mount Olive, NC 28365 United States **BUS:** Retail Pharmacy **P/S:** Prescription Services **MA:** Local **D/D/R:** Managing Operations, Filling Prescriptions **EDU:** Bachelor's Degree in Pharmacy, University of North Carolina at Chapel Hill **A/A/S:** American Pharmaceutical Association **C/VW:** American Heart Association; American Cancer Society; Local, Senior Citizens Projects
Email: coptergal@aol.com

Tania George
Title: Owner, Designer **Company:** Shabby to Chic Interiors **Address:** 2508 Persimmon Drive, Little Elm, TX 75068 United States **BUS:** Interior Design Company **P/S:** Furniture Design, Floral Designs, Draperies and Home Decor Accessories **MA:** Local **D/D/R:** Interior Design Services for Residential and Commercial Interior Spaces **H/I/S:** Playing Tennis, Traveling, Reading, Going to the Theater, Painting **EDU:** Bachelor of Arts, Texas A&M University **C/VW:** Church
Email: Tania_george1@yahoo.com
Email: shabbychictexas@hotmail.com

Ms. April L. Geraci
Title: Retail **Company:** Irving Oil Corporation **Address:** 73 Lafayette Road, North Hampton, NH 03862 United States **BUS:** Energy Firm **P/S:** Fuel Extraction **MA:** Eastern Canada and New England **D/D/R:** Delegating Duties to Employees, Ensuring Co-Workers are Aware of their Responsibilities, Managing Customer Service, Inventory Control and Cash Reconciliations, Processing Payroll, Utilizing her Leadership Skills **H/I/S:** Gardening, Camping, Spending Time with her Four Children **EDU:** Bachelor's Degree in Business Management, Franklin Pierce College, NH (2006) **CERTS:** Diploma in Medical Assistance, New Hampshire Community Technical College, Claremont (1991)
Email: dngrrnger@yahoo.com
URL: http://www.cambridgewhoswho.com

Chris C. Gerber
Title: President **Company:** Transolution **Address:** 4500 Transolution Lane, Missoula, MT 59804 United States **BUS:** Automotive Repair and Maintenance Facility **P/S:** General Automotive Company that Specializing in Automatic Transmissions, Reputation is Built on Honesty and Trust **MA:** Local **D/D/R:** Transmission Repairs, Managing Five Employees **H/I/S:** Drag Racing, Hunting, Hiking **CERTS:** Certified in Automotive Service Excellence; Certification, automotive Transmission Rebuilders Association; Research Student, Transgo; Various Industry-Related Certifications and Professional Development Instruction **A/A/S:** Automotive Transmission Rebuilders Association **C/VW:** Mentor, Willard School
Email: tranpro1@questoffice.net
URL: http://www.transolution.biz

David A. Gerdman
Title: Basin Engineer **Company:** Wisconsin Department of Natural Resources **Address:** 2220 E. County Road V, Mishicot, WI 54228 United States **BUS:** Government Organization **P/S:** Management and Maintenance of Air, Water and Land Resources, Outdoor Recreational Opportunities **MA:** Regional **D/D/R:** Managing Watersheds, Planning Wastewater Treatment Systems **H/I/S:** Running, Skiing **EDU:** Master's Degree in Civil Engineering, University of Wisconsin, Madison (1999); Bachelor's Degree in Civil Engineering (1997) **A/A/S:** American Society of Civil Engineers
Email: david.gerdman@wisconsin.gov
URL: http://www.dnr.wi.gov/org/water/wm

Nicholas J. Gerich
Title: Biological Sciences Technician **Company:** US Department of Agriculture, Forest Service **Address:** 810 Front Street, Leadville, CO 80461 United States **BUS:** Government **P/S:** Managing the National Forests **MA:** National **D/D/R:** Water Rights and Related Issues **H/I/S:** Riflery, Reloading, Gunsmithing, Hunting, Collecting Books and Movies **EDU:** Associate of Applied Science in Environmental Technologies, Colorado Mountain College
Email: ngerich@fs.fed.us

Elizabeth M. Gerleman
Title: Registered Nurse, Charge Nurse **Company:** Trinity Medical Center **Address:** 719 1/2 West 17th Street, Davenport, IA 52804 United States **BUS:** Medical Center **P/S:** Healthcare **MA:** Regional **D/D/R:** Cardiac Care Treatment, Burn Unit Care, Oncology, Medical and Surgical Intensive Care Unit, Cardiac Step Down Visiting Nurse **H/I/S:** Traveling, Reading, Gardening **EDU:** Bachelor of Science in Nursing, Marycrest College **A/A/S:** Decision Making Council, Trinity Medical Center
Email: cameo1097@mchsi.com
URL: http://www.cambridgewhoswho.com

Christine J. Gerogosian
Title: Office Service Manager **Company:** APICS The Association for Operations Management **Address:** 5301 Shawnee Road, Alexandria, VA 22312 United States **BUS:** Operations Management Company **P/S:** Management Including Production, Inventory, Supply Chain, Materials Management, Purchasing and Logistics **MA:** International **D/D/R:** Managing Print and CD-ROMs, Overseeing Production, Coordinating Offsite Classes, Purchasing, Offering Support **H/I/S:** Motherhood **EDU:** Woodbridge High School (1999) **A/A/S:** ASAE; The Center for Association Leadership
Email: cgerogosian@apics.org
URL: http://www.apics.org

Diana J. Gerrans
Title: Technical Associate III **Company:** Tyco Thermal Controls **Address:** 934 Charter Street, Redwood City, CA 94063 United States **BUS:** Manufacturing Company **P/S:** Heating Products **MA:** International **D/D/R:** Documenting, Internal Auditing, Product Installation Instructions, Manufacturing Specifications, Product Design, Photography for Reports, Approvals and Special Events **H/I/S:** Taking Digital Photography, Traveling, Jewelry Making **EDU:** Associate of Science in Liberal Arts, Yuba College
Email: dianajgerrans@sbcglobal.net
URL: http://www.cambridgewhoswho.com

Dr. Larry J. Gertler
Title: Holistic Practitioner **Company:** Center for Holistic Health **Address:** 5273 College Avenue, Suite 101, Oakland, CA 94618 United States **BUS:** Private Facility Dedicated to Excellence in Healthcare **P/S:** Holistic Health and Well Being, Biochemical and Biochemistry Nutrition **MA:** Regional **D/D/R:** Adjusting Extremities, Manipulating All Joints Except the Spine, Handling Applied Kinesiology, Conducting Statewide Seminars Monthly **H/I/S:** Pruning Trees, Tennis, Walking **EDU:** Chiropractic Degree, National Chiropractic College (1977) **A/A/S:** International College of Applied Kinesiology
Email: acc5273@pacbell.net
URL: http://www.drgertler.com

Tammy S. Gessner
Title: Pastor and Chaplain **Company:** Richfield United Church of Christ **Address:** PO Box 17, Richfield, PA 17086 United States **BUS:** Ministry **P/S:** Spreading the Word of God **MA:** Local **H/I/S:** Volunteering **EDU:** Bachelor's in Human Services, LaVerne Community College **CERTS:** Certified Chaplain and EMT **A/A/S:** ACPE
Email: holycow3@ptd.net

Christine A. Getter
Title: Senior Translation Specialist **Company:** Pfizer, Inc. **Address:** 50 Pequot Avenue, New London, CT 06320 United States **BUS:** Pharmaceutical Company **P/S:** Pharmaceuticals Including Medical Services, Research on New Drugs, Development of Medicines and Drug Information for Consumers and Healthcare Providers **MA:** International **EXP:** Ms. Getter's areas of expertise include linguistics and validation. **D/D/R:** Overseeing Patients' Recovery in All Therapeutic Areas, Ensuring the Quality of Products, Maintaining Historical Archives, Managing Contractors, Conducting Pilot Studies **EDU:** Associate Degree, Ocean State Business Institute, Rhode Island (1994) **A/A/S:** The e-PRO Evolution; Drug Information Association; Diagnostic Bioprobes S.R.L
Email: cgetter@cox.net
URL: http://www.pfizer.com

Jennifer R. Ghaemmaghami
Title: President **Company:** Lexington Intermodal, Inc. **Address:** 1331 Airport Freeway, Suite 308, Euless, TX 76040 United States **BUS:** Trucking Company **P/S:** Trucking and via Railroad Transportation Service **MA:** Regional **D/D/R:** Overseeing Daily Operations, Managing Finances, Scheduling and Dispatching Drivers, Preparing Payroll, Developing Business, Improving Sales, Subcontracting **H/I/S:** Indoor Soccer **EDU:** Diploma, MacArthur High School (1995)
Email: Jennifer@us1tx.com

Ashley D. Gholston
Title: Owner, Head Coach **Company:** Cheer Company Allstars Cheer & Dance **Address:** 2615B Capital Circle N.E., Tallahassee, FL 32308 United States **BUS:** Cheerleading and Competitive Dance **P/S:** Cheerleading **MA:** Local **D/D/R:** Teaching Students Cheerleading **H/I/S:** Cheerleading **EDU:** Bachelor of Arts in Hospitality, Florida State University
Email: ashley@thecheercompany.org
URL: http://www.thecheercompany.org

Donna M. Gianola
Title: Former Firefighter, Emergency Medical Technician Company: Coxsackie Hose Suite 3 Address: 218 Mansion Street, Coxsackie, NY 12051 United States BUS: Volunteer Fire and Rescue Service P/S: Fire Fighting MA: Regional D/D/R: Extraditions, Rescues, Resuscitation, Grant Writing, Coordinating the Fire Prevention Program H/I/S: Gardening, Photography, Playing Sports EDU: Associate of Applied Science in Medical Lab Technology, SUNY A/H: New York EMS Provider of the Year C/VW: Local Church
Email: aemt129791@aol.com

Sherry Ann Gibb
Title: Horse Trainer Company: Gibb Ranch Address: 5100 Grey Van Road, Reno, NV 89510 United States BUS: Horse Ranch P/S: Stallions Stud Services, Horse Sales, Equine Training, Show Horses, Events, Training, Lessons, Clinics, Boarding Services MA: International D/D/R: Riding Horses, Preparing Horses for Shows, Feeding and Cleaning Horses, Offering Riding Lessons H/I/S: Waterskiing, Snow Skiing CERTS: Certification in Equine Reproductive Management and Artificial Insemination (2002) A/A/S: American Paint Horse Association; American Quarter Horse Association; Pinto Horse Association of America; American Junior Rodeo Association; The American Professional Rodeo Association
Email: info@gibbranch.com
URL: http://www.gibbranch.com

Mr. David Gibbs
Title: General Foreman Company: North Houston Pole Line Dept: Major Underground Address: 15410 Henry Road, Houston, TX 77060 United States BUS: Underground Utility Construction Company P/S: Primary Electric Connections, Communications MA: OK, AZ, NM, TX EXP: Mr. Gibbs' expertise is in the installation of underground utilities. D/D/R: Working on New Construction with Engineers and Architects H/I/S: Hunting, Fishing EDU: Associate of Science in Business Administration, University of Texas
Email: dgibbs@nhplc.com
URL: http://www.nhplc.com

Elizabeth L. Giblin
Title: Owner Company: Spiritual Healings and Reading BUS: Spiritual Healing P/S: Parties, Events, Weddings, Memorial Services, Funerals, Christenings, Tarot Readings and Heeling's, Long Distance Heeling's and Readings. Available for Private Sessions, Classes and Services MA: Regional D/D/R: Spiritual Healing EDU: Certified Spiritual Healer, United Fellowship Chapel (1989); Spiritual Minister, United Fellowship Chapel (2004); Metaphysician, United Fellowship Chapel (2003)
Email: ebbit@cox.net

Christopher S. Gibson
Title: President Company: Infinity Construction Solutions, Inc. Address: 1400 Market Place Boulevard, Suite 154, Cumming, GA 30041 United States BUS: Telecommunications Company P/S: Wireless Development, Construction MA: Regional D/D/R: Telecom Construction Management, Consulting H/I/S: Waterskiing, Snow Skiing EDU: Pursuing MBA, University of Phoenix; Bachelor's Degree in Civil Engineering, Old Dominion University, 1998 A/A/S: Lambda Kai Alpha C/VW: Kentucky Colonels, American Red Cross
Email: cgibson@constructionsolutions-inc.com
URL: http://www.constructionsolutions-inc.com

Jean D. Gibson, LPN, RN
Title: Registered Nurse Company: Forest Hill Manor Address: 25 Bolduc Avenue, Fort Kent, ME 04743 United States BUS: Skilled Nursing Medical Center P/S: Long Term Care and Treatment MA: Local D/D/R: Supervising Nursing Home Staff, Admitting, Assessing and Treating Patients H/I/S: Knitting, Crocheting, Quilting, Cooking CERTS: Registered Nurse, Northern Maine Community College (1992); Licensed Practical Nurse (1955)
Email: jag22@fairpoint.net
URL: http://www.nmmc.org/foresthill.php

Michelle R. Gibson
Title: Assistant General Manager Company: Quality Inn, Mount Vernon Address: 1910 Freeway Drive, Mount Vernon, WA 98273 United States BUS: Limited Service Hotel P/S: Hospitality MA: Local D/D/R: Computer Operations H/I/S: Spending Time with her Family, Walking, Doing Needlepoint, Reading EDU: Associate Degree in Computer Information Systems C/VW: Goodwill
Email: mgibson@mvqi.com
URL: http://www.mvqi.com

Sharon K. Gibson
Title: Western Regional Claims Manager Company: Harrah's Entertainment, Inc Address: One Harrahs Court, Las Vegas, NV 89119 United States BUS: Casino P/S: Hotel/Casino-Claims Administration MA: International D/D/R: Property and Casualty Claims for 29 Properties in the Country H/I/S: Owns and Rides a Harley Davidson EDU: Diploma, Waynesburg Central High School CERTS: AIC Designation A/A/S: RIMS; Public Speaker, Conferences and Seminars
Email: info@CambridgeWhosWho.com

Wendell M. Gibson
Title: Funeral Director/Embalmer Company: King Funeral Home Address: 124 Davis Road, Martinez, GA 30907 United States BUS: Funeral Home P/S: Pre Need Services, Funeral Arrangements, Dedication to Families Needs MA: Local D/D/R: Funeral Director/Embalmer, Reconstruction, Financial Services, Care and Empathy H/I/S: Spending Time with Beautiful Wife Elizabeth CERTS: Certification in Mortuary Science, Gupton-Jones College of Mortuary Science A/A/S: Georgia Graduate Embalmers Organization
Email: info@CambridgeWhosWho.com

Kathleen M. Giesen-Cotter
Title: Clinical Care Manager, Registered Nurse, Certified Professional in Healthcare Quality Company: Virta at Work, Virta Health Address: 50 Lake Center Drive, Marlton, NJ 08043 United States BUS: Hospital P/S: Healthcare MA: Local EXP: Ms. Giesen-Cotter's expertise is in clinical nursing. H/I/S: Skiing, Reading, Biking EDU: Coursework, Helene Fuld School of Nursing A/A/S: Nursing Spectrum; Occupational Healthcare Management Services; National Association for Healthcare Quality; Association of Occupational Health Professionals in Healthcare C/VW: Local High School; Catholic Charities
Email: kgiesen@virtua.org
URL: http://www.cambridgewhoswho.com

Francesca Giglia
Title: Representative in Corporate Security Company: Consolidated Edison Company of New York, Inc. Address: 4 Irving Place, Room 749-S, New York, NY 10003 United States BUS: Renowned Utility Company P/S: Gas, Electric and Steam Services for Millions of Customers in Manhattan MA: Regional D/D/R: Securing Facilities and Resources, Working Closely with Law Enforcement, Fire Department and Emergency Management and Planning, Conducting Internal and External Investigations, Training Emergency Rescue Techniques at the In-House Facility as Medical Aid Rescue Squad H/I/S: Playing Tennis and Golf EDU: Bachelor of Science in Emergency Management and Planning and Homeland Security, SUNY Empire State CERTS: Certified Instructor in First Aid, CPR and AED, American Red Cross A/A/S: Women's Group of Consolidated Edison; Published Monthly Article in Metaphysical Magazine
Email: gigliaf@coned.com
URL: http://www.coned.com

Emily M. Gilbert
Title: President Company: Texas Lonestar Address: P.O. Box 131542, Houston, TX 77219 United States BUS: Real Estate Company Serving Residents of Houston P/S: Real Estate Properties, Investment Properties, Relocations MA: Regional D/D/R: Overseeing Property Management of Parking Lots and 16 Commercial Properties, Managing Employees, Bookkeeping EDU: College Coursework Completed
Email: luckytexan@gmail.com

Natalie J. Gilbert
Title: Human Resources Manager Company: Advantage Care Rehabilitation, Inc. Dept: Advantage Home Health Services Address: 500 Lewis Run Road, Suite 218, West Mifflin, PA 15122 United States BUS: Rehabilitation Center P/S: Rehabilitation and Home Healthcare Services MA: Regional D/D/R: Reorganizing Employee Information, Overseeing 150 Employees and Contractors' Files H/I/S: Spending Time with her Family, Caring for her Animals, Participating in Dancing Competition EDU: Associate Degree in Medical and Computer Programming CERTS: Pursuing Human Resource Management Certificate Program A/H: Chairman Star Award (2007-2008) C/VW: Pennsylvania Humane Society; American Cancer Society
Email: nat@advantagecarerehab.com
URL: http://www.cambridgewhoswho.com

Stacy L. Gilbert, CPA
Title: Partner, Certified Public Accountant Company: Rose, Dratch & Gilbert, PA Address: 175 Fairfield Avenue, Suite 4C-D, West Caldwell, NJ 07006 United States BUS: Accounting Firm P/S: Tax Preparation, Accounting Services, Financial Consulting, Income Tax Planning, Business Valuations, Forensic Accounting, Expert Testimony, Litigation Support Services, Installation, Implementation, Training and Modification of Accounting Software, Corporate and Personal Insurance Review, Assistance in Mandatory Filings with Regulatory Agencies, Estate and Trust Administration, Trustee and Executor Services, Design of Shareholder Agreements, Related Business Valuations and Periodic Updates MA: Regional D/D/R: Offering Accounting, Taxation and Financial Consulting, Assisting Clients in the Restaurant Industry, Advising Clients Regarding Operations and Management H/I/S: Watching Baseball EDU: Bachelor of Science in Accounting, CUNY Herbert H. Lehman College (1980) CERTS: Certified Public Accountant (1983) A/A/S: New Jersey Society of Certified Public Accountants; New York State Society of Certified Public Accountants; The American Institute of Certified Public Accountants
Email: sgilbert@rddgcpas.com
URL: http://www.rosedratchgilbert.com

April S. Gildehaus
Title: Owner, Massage Therapist Company: Massage for Your Health Address: 1011 Market Street, Hermann, MO 65041 United States BUS: Therapy Center P/S: Massage Therapy Services Including Swedish and Lymphatic Craniofacial Therapy, Lymphatic Drainage Massage MA: Local EXP: Ms. Gildehaus' expertise is in massage therapy. H/I/S: Practicing Yoga, Traveling, Reading CERTS: Certification in Massage Therapy, Saint Louis College of Health Careers A/A/S: National Certification Board for Therapeutic Massage & Bodywork; AMPA C/VW: Crusade Against Cancer, Relay For Life
Email: massageforyourhealth@yahoo.com
URL: http://www.massageforyourhealth.com

Grace Emily Gilgen
Title: Owner, Operator Company: The Cauldron Costume Shoppe Address: 3914 S. Main Street, Nibley, UT 84321 United States BUS: Costume Design Shop P/S: Costume Sales and Rentals MA: Local D/D/R: Designing Costumes H/I/S: Gardening, Fishing, Studying Genealogy CERTS: Certificate in Power Sewing Machine Operation, Utah Technical College A/A/S: Daughters of Utah Pioneers C/VW: Daughters of Utah Pioneers
Email: grace_gilgen@yahoo.com

Gail C. Gilkey
Title: Physical Therapist Company: TLC Health Care Services, Inc. Address: 22 Hilltop Avenue, Barrington, RI 02806 United States BUS: Healthcare Center P/S: Healthcare Including Physical Therapy MA: Local EXP: Ms. Gilkey's expertise is in physical therapy. H/I/S: Reading, Writing, Listening to Music EDU: Master of Science in Physical Therapy A/A/S: American Physical Therapy Association C/VW: The Humane Society of the United States; American Heart Association; American Cancer Society
Email: windyhillpress@cox.net
URL: http://www.cambridgewhoswho.com

Iris Bond Gill
Title: Senior Program Associate Company: American Youth Policy Forum Address: 1836 Jefferson Place N.W., Washington, DC 20036 United States BUS: Youth Organization P/S: Research and Professional Development MA: National D/D/R: Overseeing High School Reform H/I/S: Traveling EDU: Master's Degree in Public Policy and Management, Carnegie Mellon University; Bachelor's Degree in Economics, Arizona State University
Email: ibgill@aypf.org
URL: http://www.aypf.org

Susan J. Gillam
Title: Owner Company: Susie's at Seventh Street Address: 5002 C Camelot Drive, Columbia, TN 38401 United States BUS: Linens Retail P/S: Linens-Design Some of Their own Products MA: Local D/D/R: Offer Their 'Own' Label of Sheets H/I/S: Cooking, Exercising, Family Time EDU: qGeneral Diploma, Ashland High School A/A/S: Downtown Professional Association, Hope House
Email: linensupercenter@gmail.com

Katrin Gillespie
Title: Senior HR Manager Company: Four Seasons Hotel Atlanta Address: 75 14th Street NE, Atlanta, GA 30309 United States BUS: Hotel P/S: Hospitality MA: International D/D/R: Benefits, Recruitment, Customer Service H/I/S: Running, Traveling, Photography EDU: Master's in History, Oxford University; Bachelor's Degree in International Management, Oxford Brookes University
Email: katrin.gillespie@fourseasons.com
URL: www.fourseasons.com

Rosemary Gillett

Title: 1) Interior Designer 2) Visual Artist **Company:** 1) Rosemary Gillett Interior Design 2) Gillehart Studio **Address:** P.O. Box 1361, Winter Park, FL 32790 United States **BUS:** 1) Interior Design Firm 2) Visual Art Studio **P/S:** 1) Design Consulting Services, Custom Furniture Design 2) Post Minimal Art **MA:** International **D/D/R:** Creating Italian Contemporary Design and Visual Art **H/I/S:** Traveling, Creating Table Settings **EDU:** Coursework, Texas A&I University (Now Texas A&M University, Kingsville); Coursework, University of Saint Thomas; Coursework, Florida State University **CERTS:** Licensed Interior Designer, State of Florida; Registered Interior Designer, State of Florida **A/H:** National Honor Award, American Society of Interior Designers (1976); American Society of Interior Designers Awards (1976, 1977, 1985); Merit Award, Mid-Florida Chapter, The American Institute of Architects; Recognition Winner, Florida Architecture's Interior Design and Paintings **C/VW:** Winter Park Holiday Signet Project (2003-2005)
Email: rwgillett@earthlink.net
URL: http://www.rosemarygillett.com

J. Scott Gilliam

Title: Director of Training **Company:** DARE America **Address:** 9800 S. La Cienega Boulevard, Suite 401, Inglewood, CA 90301 United States **BUS:** Nonprofit Organization **P/S:** Drug Abuse Resistance Education **MA:** International **D/D/R:** Conducting Drug Abuse Resistance Education Training, Writing Curriculum **H/I/S:** Traveling **EDU:** Bachelor's Degree in Business Administration, California State University, Northridge **C/VW:** Elks Club
Email: scottgilliam411@sbcglobal.net
URL: http://www.dare.com

Roxanne Gilliland

Title: Office Manager **Company:** Dawson Development **Address:** P.O. Box 830, Gadsden, AL 35902 United States **BUS:** Professional Apartment Rental Firm **P/S:** Leasing Apartments and Homes, Apartment Management Services **MA:** Local **D/D/R:** Managing Operations Including Bookkeeping and Apartments, Overseeing Managers **H/I/S:** Cooking **C/VW:** Local Church; The Humane Society
Email: rgilliland@dawsonbuilding.com
URL: http://www.dawsondevelopment.com

Tami Gillmore

Title: Chief Financial Officer **Company:** NRG Media, LLC **Address:** 2875 Mount Vernon Road S.E., Cedar Rapids, IA 52403 United States **BUS:** Radio Station **P/S:** Operating 83 Radio Stations **MA:** Regional **EXP:** Ms. Gillmore's expertise includes finance management, cash flow statement preparation and budgeting. **D/D/R:** Working with Investors and Bankers **EDU:** Bachelor of Arts in Accounting, Mount Mercy College (1987) **A/A/S:** Broadcast Cable Financial Management Association
Email: tgillmore@nrgmedia.com
URL: http://www.nrgmedia.com

Cynthia Allison Gilmer, BSN

Title: Registered Nurse **Company:** Rush Medical Group, Inc. **Address:** 2269 Highway 496, Meridian, MS 39301 United States **BUS:** Medical Center **P/S:** Healthcare Services Including Audiology, Cardiology, Neurology, Pathology, Radiology, Urology, Ear, Nose and Throat Conditions, Orthopedic, Gastroenterology, Internal Medicine, General Surgery Including Cardiovascular, Head and Neck, Neuro and Vascular Surgery **MA:** Local **EXP:** Ms. Gilmer's expertise includes respiratory, oncology, pediatrics and obstetric care nursing. **D/D/R:** Administering Medication, Keeping Medical Records **H/I/S:** Reading, Singing **EDU:** Bachelor of Science in Nursing, The University of Southern Mississippi (1997) **CERTS:** Registered Nurse
Email: cindi@comcast.net
URL: http://www.rushhealthsystems.org

Deborah Kellerman Gilpin, MS

Title: Itinerant Hearing Support Teacher **Company:** Western Wayne School District **Address:** P.O. Box 220, South Canaan, PA 18459 United States **BUS:** School District **P/S:** Education **MA:** Local **D/D/R:** Working with Children with Hearing Loss, Teaching Transitional Skills **H/I/S:** Spending Time with her Son and her Two Greyhounds **EDU:** Master of Science in Education for the Heating Impaired, Bloomsburg University; Bachelor of Science in Elementary Education **A/A/S:** Alexander Graham Bell Association for the Deaf and Hard of Hearing **C/VW:** First State Greyhound Rescue; Aldenville Baptist Church
Email: debbiegilpin@hotmail.com
URL: http://www.westernwayne.org

Ila M. Gilstrap

Title: Director, Greenville Parent Center **Company:** Greenville Independent School District **Address:** 2526 Utilis Street, Greenville, TX 75401 United States **BUS:** Educational Center for Parents **P/S:** Helping Parents Teach their Children Life Skills **MA:** Local **D/D/R:** Acting as a Liaison between School and Parents **H/I/S:** Reading, Country Music **EDU:** Master's Degree in Elementary Education and English, New York University (1958); Bachelor of Science in Elementary Education, Texas College (1954) **A/A/S:** National Education Association; Texas States Teachers Association; Greenville Board of Libraries
Email: gilstrai@greenvilleisd.com
URL: http://www.greenvilleisd.com

Lourdes B. Ginn

Title: Realtor **Company:** Fortune International Realty **Address:** 1390 Brickell Avenue, Miami, FL 33131 United States **BUS:** Real Estate Agency **P/S:** International, Local, Residential and Commercial Real Estate **MA:** Local **D/D/R:** Residential Real Estate Sales **H/I/S:** Smoking Cigars **EDU:** Coursework in Criminal Justice, Miami-Dade Community College; High School Graduate **CERTS:** Licensed Realtor, 2003 **A/A/S:** Miami Dade Board of Realtors
Email: mlmjginn@bellsouth.net
URL: http://www.lourdesbginn.com

Norma M. Ginther

Title: Social Work Trainer and Consultant **Company:** Institute for Human Service **Address:** 1706 E. Broad Street, Columbus, OH 43203 United States **BUS:** Human Services **P/S:** Child Protection and Welfare **MA:** International **D/D/R:** Investigation and Assessment of Families, Conducting Conference and Training Groups Internationally **H/I/S:** Reading, Traveling **EDU:** Master of Social Work, Ohio State University; Bachelor's Degree in Psychology and Sociology **CERTS:** Licensed Independent Social Worker, State of Ohio **A/A/S:** American Professional Society on the Abuse of Children **C/VW:** King Avenue United Methodist Church, Equality Ohio
Email: nginther@ins-trainet.com
URL: http://www.ihs.com

Esther P. Giordano

Title: Speech-Language Pathologist **Company:** Totowa Public Schools, Memorial School **Address:** Totowa Road, Totowa, NJ United States **BUS:** Public School District **P/S:** Education for Prekindergarten through Second-Grade, Speech Therapy **MA:** Regional **D/D/R:** Offering Oral-Motor Therapy, Working with Autistic Children with Articulation Difficulties, Assisting Inclusion Teachers with Teaching Students with Language Problems **H/I/S:** Playing Guitar, Singing **EDU:** Master's Degree in Speech-Language Pathology, Kean University (1997) **CERTS:** Certificate of Clinical Competence in Speech-Language Pathology **A/A/S:** American Speech-Language-Hearing Association; New Jersey Speech-Language Hearing Association; Bergen County Speech-Language Hearing Association; Rocking Horse Rehab
Email: chickie3121@aol.com
URL: http://totowa.k12.nj.us

Meredith R. Girardi

Title: Elementary School Teacher **Company:** Gerwin jewish Nursing Rehabilitation Center **Dept:** Admissions Coordinator **Address:** 68 Hauppage Road, Commack, NY 11725 United States **BUS:** Rehabilitation Nursing Home **P/S:** Regular and Special Education Core Curriculum Including Reading, Mathematic, Science, Social Studies, Art, Music and History **MA:** Regional **D/D/R:** Teaching General and Special Education, Teaching Art to First Grade Students **H/I/S:** Reading **EDU:** Pursuing Master's Degree in Literacy and Cognition; Bachelor's Degree in Elementary Education, General and Special Education, Saint Joseph's College (2007)
Email: meredith96@msn.com

Ms. Kimberly A. Giroux

Title: Special Education Teacher, Case Manager **Company:** Raymond High School **Address:** 45 Harriman Hill Road, Raymond, NH 03077 United States **BUS:** High School **P/S:** Secondary Education Including Special Education, Promotion of Intellectual Growth, Fostering of Self-Esteem and Mutual Respect, Development of Interpersonal Skills, Encouragement of Individuals to Reach their Potential Pursuit of Learning **MA:** Regional **D/D/R:** Teaching Special Education, Reading and Science, Assisting Students in their Subjects Including Foreign Languages, Supporting Teachers and Special Education Students, Overseeing the Resource Room Activities and Caseload Management of 25 Students in Grades Nine through 12 **H/I/S:** Reading, Spending Time with her Family **EDU:** Bachelor's Degree in Interdisciplinary Studies, Notre Dame College (2002) **CERTS:** Certification in General Special Education (K-12); Certification in Elementary Education (K-8) **A/A/S:** New Hampshire Education Association; Workshops for Special Education Department **A/H:** Who's Who Among American Teachers; National Honor Roll's Outstanding American Teachers
Email: kagg@comcast.net
Email: k.giroux@sau33.com
URL: http://www.sau33.com

Rachel L. Gist

Title: Registered Nurse **Company:** Integrity Home Health **Address:** 3675 S. Noland Road, Suite 222, Independence, MO 64055 United States **BUS:** Home Healthcare Center **P/S:** Home Healthcare Services Including Inpatient and Outpatient Care for the Elderly and Developmentally Disabled, Rehabilitation Services **MA:** Regional **EXP:** Ms. Gist's expertise includes orthopedic, surgical, triage and field nursing, patient care management and patients' treatments. **D/D/R:** Visiting and Evaluating Patients in Nursing Homes and Rehabilitation Centers **EDU:** Associate Degree in Nursing, Penn Valley Community College (2004) **CERTS:** Registered Nurse
Email: rachel.gist@cwwemail.com
URL: http://www.integrityhc.com

Elizabeth Giustizia

Title: Partner **Company:** Noack, Mitchell & Company Certified Public Accountants **Address:** 5621 Strand Boulevard, Suite 305, Naples, FL 34110 United States **BUS:** Accounting Firm **P/S:** Taxation, Auditing and Consulting Services **MA:** Statewide **D/D/R:** Auditing Condominium Associations, Nonprofit Auditing **H/I/S:** Traveling **EDU:** Bachelor's Degree in Finance, Minor in Accounting, Florida Gulf Coast University, 2002 **A/A/S:** Florida Institute of Certified Public Accountants; American Institute of Certified Public Accountants **C/VW:** Alpha Chi Omega Foundation; J. Timothy Hogan Foundation
Email: liza@noackmitchellcpa.com
URL: http://www.noackcpa.com

Deborah D. Givens

Title: Hair Stylist **Company:** Jam Hair **Address:** 7836 La Tour Court, Rancho Cucamonga, CA 91739 United States **BUS:** Hair Salon **P/S:** Private, Personalized Service **MA:** Regional **D/D/R:** Hair Care and Styling, Precision Cuts, Flat Ironing, Color, Weaves, Extensions **H/I/S:** Painting, Drawing, Reading the Bible **EDU:** Associate of Arts in Interior Design, Chaffey College; Coursework, Dudley University and Marinello School of Beauty **CERTS:** Licensed, Board of Barbering and Cosmetology **A/A/S:** National Republican Committee; Business Advisory; Cultural Center of Rancho Cucamonga
Email: LaanDDeb@yahoo.com

Sheila R. Givens, M.Ed.

Title: Special Education Teacher **Company:** Virginia Beach City Public Schools **Address:** 4400 Virginia Beach Boulevard, Virginia Beach, VA 23462 United States **BUS:** Public School **P/S:** Education for Children with Special Needs **MA:** Local **D/D/R:** Working with Students with Severe Disabilities **H/I/S:** Traveling **EDU:** Pursuing Master of Education in Curriculum and Instruction, Grand Canyon University; Master of Arts in Severe Disabilities, Norfolk State University (1999); Bachelor of Arts in Special Education, Norfolk State University (1975) **A/A/S:** Virginia Beach Education Association; National Education Association **C/VW:** Goodwill Industries, The Salvation Army
Email: srgivens@vbschools.com
URL: http://www.vbschools.com

David Timothy Gladstone

Title: Senior Manager **Company:** NJVC **Address:** 8614 Westwood Center Drive, Vienna, VA 22182 United States **BUS:** Information Technology Company **P/S:** Information Technology Service and Support **MA:** Local **EXP:** Mr. Gladstone's expertise is in project management. **H/I/S:** Skiing, Playing Softball **EDU:** Bachelor's Degree in Political Science, Washburn University **C/VW:** St. Jude Children's Research Hospital
Email: david.t.gladstone.ctr@nga.mil

Emma J. Glasco

Title: President **Company:** My Son and I Cleaning Services, LLC **Address:** 214 Line Road, Kennett Square, PA 19348 United States **BUS:** Property Cleaning Company **P/S:** Interiors and Exteriors, Carpets, Hardwood Floors, Residential Property, Commercial Property, Windows, Ceiling Fans, One Time Cleaning, Weekly and Bi-Weekly Cleaning, Spring Cleaning, Move In and Move Out Cleaning, Monthly Cleaning, Specialized Services **MA:** Local, Statewide **D/D/R:** Residential and Commercial Cleaning **H/I/S:** Collection of Pigs, Reading Non-Fiction Books **EDU:** (Steven E. Glasco, Jr.) Bachelor of Science in Business Management, University of Phoenix; Supplies and Logistics, U.S. Army Quartermaster School, Fort Lee, Virginia **A/A/S:** Chamber of Commerce; Better Business Bureau; Second Baptist Church; Association of Residential Cleaning Professionals International, Local YMCA
Email: mysonandicln@aol.com
URL: http://www.mycleaning.net

Roy Glasgow Jr.

Title: Funeral Director, Embalmer **Company:** Rich & Thompson Funeral Service **Address:** 306 Glenwood Avenue, Burlington, NC 27215 United States **BUS:** Funeral Home **P/S:** Funeral and Cremation Services **MA:** Local **D/D/R:** Embalming, Preparing for Funerals, Coordinating with Families **H/I/S:** Hunting, Fishing **EDU:** College Coursework Completed **A/A/S:** Civitan International
Email: rzglasgow@bellsouth.net

Keecha R. Glass
Title: Financial Center Manager **Company:** Citibank **Address:** 6953 South Jefferey Blvd, Chicago, IL 60620 United States **BUS:** Bank **P/S:** Provide Financial Resources within the Auburn Grisham Community **D/D/R:** Banking Products, Life Insurance, Financial Planning **H/I/S:** Working Out, Shopping, Traveling **EDU:** Master of Business Administration, National Louis University
Email: keecha8@sbcglobal.net

Janelle L. Glaum
Title: Teacher **Company:** Monetvista Christian School **Address:** 181 Barnes Road, Aptos, CA 95003 United States **BUS:** Private Christian School **P/S:** Regular Core Curriculum Including Reading, Math, English, Science, Social Studies, Art, Music, History, Physical Education, Language Arts, Religion **MA:** Regional **D/D/R:** Teaching Bible Studies, Advising Girls in the Senior Class on Beauty and Identity Classes **H/I/S:** Baseball, Running **EDU:** Bachelor's Degree in Recreational Therapy and Administration, California State University (1978) **A/A/S:** Alumni, California State University at Chico, Chico, California; Art & Science Collaborations, Inc. **A/H:** Who's Who Among America's Teachers (2004-2007)
Email: jglaum@gmail.com
URL: http://www.mvcs.org

Cynthia A. Glaze
Title: Owner, Chief Financial Officer, Chief Executive Officer **Company:** Precision Combustion Technology, LLC **Address:** 2717 Ruby Street, Gonzales, LA 70737 United States **BUS:** Engineering and Industrial Contractor **P/S:** Emissions Reduction Strategies, Industrial Welding, Piping, Vessel Fabrication, Redesigned Fired Heat Equipment, Heat Exchanger Assessment and Re-boiler Heater **MA:** National **D/D/R:** Accounting, Managing the Operations of the Engineering and Procurement Departments, Overseeing Full-Time Employees, Training Employees in the Oil Refineries, Chemical Plants and the Fabrication of Industrial Piping Vessels **H/I/S:** Reading Genealogy and History Books, Painting, Sewing **CERTS:** Certificate in Accounting, Pittsburg State University, KS **A/A/S:** Gonzales Area Chamber of Commerce **C/VW:** Local Police and Sheriff's office
Email: cglaze@precisioncombustion.com
URL: http://www.precisioncombustion.com

Christopher M. Gleason
Title: Addiction Specialist, Evaluation Specialist **Company:** Centegra Health Systems **BUS:** Hospital **P/S:** Healthcare **MA:** Local **D/D/R:** Evaluating Addictions, Recommending Treatment Plans **H/I/S:** Spending Time with Family, Golfing **EDU:** Bachelor of Arts in Human Services, Judson College **C/VW:** Church, Various Organizations
Email: chrismaryabby@sbcglobal.net

Leah S. Glenn
Title: Accounting Director **Company:** Wentworth Energy, Inc. **Address:** 112 E. Oak Street, Suite 200, Palestine, TX 75801 United States **BUS:** Oil and Gas Exploration and Production **P/S:** Purchase and Development of Oil and Gas Properties Including Leasing, Drilling, Production and Marketing **MA:** Regional **D/D/R:** Knowledge of Oil and Gas Operations, Negotiations and Review of Contracts, Hiring and Training of Staff, Completing Various Other HR Responsibilities, Overseeing Management of Daily Operations and Procedures **H/I/S:** Any Outdoor Sports **EDU:** Bachelor's Degree in Business Administration, University of Texas (1992) **A/A/S:** Member, Alpha Chi Honor Society; Member, American Association of Professional Landman
Email: leah@wentworthenergy.com
URL: http://www.wentworthenergy.com

Amy Marie Glessing, A.uD.
Title: Educational Audiologist **Company:** Oswego County BOCES **Address:** 179 County Route 64, Building W. 450 Room 7, Mexico, NY 13114 United States **BUS:** Proven Leader in the Education Industry **P/S:** Educational Programs, Career and Technical Education, Alternative Programs, High School Learning Center, Program for Academic and Career Exploration, Adolescent Pregnancy Prevention Services, Academic Summer School, Families Accessing Naturalization Services, General Equivalency Diploma Program, Special Education **MA:** Local **D/D/R:** Instructing Teachers on how to Handle and Assist Students with Hearing Loss, Diagnostic Testing for Auditory Processing Disorders, Working with the County to Increase Awareness, Statewide Speaking to Nurses and Educators **H/I/S:** Singing, Cooking, Outdoor Sports **EDU:** Pursuing Doctorate Degree; Master's Degree in Audiology, SUNY Fredonia (1998); Bachelor's Degree in Speech and Hearing Impaired Education, SUNY Fredonia (1996) **A/A/S:** American Speech-Language-Hearing Association; Educational Audiology Association
Email: amyears@yahoo.com
URL: http://www.oswegoboces.org

Amanda Glover
Title: Owner, Property Manager **Company:** Midlands Investment Group, LLC **Address:** 2225 Highway 1 S., P.O. Box 10, Elgin, SC 29045 United States **BUS:** Real Estate Company **P/S:** Apartment Rentals **MA:** Regional **D/D/R:** Managing Property, Accounting, Rent Collection, Overseeing Finances and Mortgage, Addressing Problems Involving Legal Disputes **EDU:** Associate Degree in Business Management, Midlands Technical College (2004)
Email: amandapglover@yahoo.com

Cody W. Glover
Title: Designer **Company:** Circa Design Showroom, Wesley-Wayne Interiors **Address:** 233 Grand Avenue, Southlake, TX 76092 United States **BUS:** Home Furnishings Showroom and Design Studio **P/S:** Furnishings, Color, Drapery, Accessories for the Home, Management of Home Building and In-Home Design **MA:** Southlake, TX, Northern California **D/D/R:** Planning Space, Overseeing In-Home Design, Project Management and Model Home Staging, Managing Color and Specifications, Working Under and Meeting Deadlines **H/I/S:** Traveling, Cooking, Gardening **EDU:** Associate Degree in Interior Design and Retail Planning, Art Institute of Dallas **A/H:** Dream Home, Fort Worth, Texas Magazine (2006); WFAA Dream Home (2006); Dallas Designing Texas Dream Home (2006); Parade of Homes, Frisco, TX (2004); Nominee, 16th Annual ARTS Award
Email: cody@circadesignshowroom.com
URL: http://www.circadesignshowroom.com

Mrs. Kimberly L. Glover
Title: Special Education Teacher **Company:** Fair Plain West Elementary School **Address:** 1901 Fairplain Avenue, Benton Harbor, MI 49022 United States **BUS:** Elementary School **P/S:** Education for Kindergarten through Fifth-Grade Students **MA:** Local **D/D/R:** Teaching Special Education Including Children with Learning Disabilities **H/I/S:** Reading, Spending Time at Church **EDU:** Master of Education, Indiana University; Bachelor of Science, Ferris State University **A/A/S:** Zeta Phi Beta **C/VW:** United Way
Email: kimberly.glover@bhas.org

Brenda G. Glynn
Title: Teacher **Company:** Church Street Elementary School **Address:** 7013 Church Street, Riverdale, GA 30274 United States **BUS:** Elementary School **P/S:** Primary Education **MA:** Riverdale **EXP:** Ms. Glynn's expertise includes diagnostic and prescriptive reading instruction and strategy development. **H/I/S:** Reading, Writing, Traveling **EDU:** Master's Degree in Educational Counseling, Southeastern Louisiana University; Bachelor of Arts in Elementary Education, Southern University, Baton Rouge **CERTS:** Certified Hydro Colon Therapist; I-ACT Certification, Awareness Institute, Atlanta, GA; Certification in Early Childhood **C/VW:** Local Church
Email: bglynn@clayton.k12.ga.us

Joan M. Gobble
Title: Manager/Owner **Company:** The Irish Pub **Address:** 9155 E. Tangue Verde Road, Suite 177, Tucson, AZ 85749 United States **BUS:** Restaurant and Bar **P/S:** Food, Beer, Wine and Liquor **MA:** Local **D/D/R:** Managing Business Operations and Customer Service **H/I/S:** Traveling, Relaxing at Home **EDU:** Industry-Related Training

Mae Gochan-Efann
Title: Proprietor **Company:** Theodore Trading and Manufacturing **BUS:** Trading and Manufacturing Company **P/S:** Fashion Accessories **MA:** International **D/D/R:** Nursing **H/I/S:** Spending Time Outdoors **CERTS:** Registered Nurse, Velez College of Nursing (1978) **A/A/S:** Women's Club of Minnesota
Email: theodoretm@yahoo.com

Deborah R. Godes
Title: Vice President of Healthcare Industry Practice **Company:** Connect Your Care **Address:** 307 International Circle, Suite 200, Hunt Valley, MD 21030 United States **BUS:** Healthcare Center **P/S:** Healthcare **MA:** National **D/D/R:** Implementing, Managing Partners, Developing Healthcare Plans **H/I/S:** Spending Time with her Family, Cooking **EDU:** Master of Business Administration, Wharton School of the University of Pennsylvania
Email: deborah.godes@connectyourcare.com
URL: http://www.connectyourcare.com

Heather L. Godwin, M.Ed.
Title: Teacher, Business Owner **Company:** Indian Lake Schools **Address:** 4838 Township Road 127, Zanesfield, OH 43360 United States **BUS:** School District **P/S:** Education Including Reading, Mathematics, English, Science, Social Studies, Arts, Music, History and Physical Education **MA:** Regional **EXP:** Ms. Godwin's expertise is in classroom management. **D/D/R:** Planning Lessons, Teaching Science and Language Arts to Sixth-Grade Students, Overseeing the Operations of her Laundry and Tanning Business Including Advertising on the Radio and in Newspapers **H/I/S:** Exercising, Traveling **EDU:** Master of Education, Urbana University (2003)
Email: bwandtan@yahoo.com

Sally L. Goebel
Title: National Support Manager, Customer Triage Services **Company:** Siemens Medical Solutions **Address:** 110 MacAlyson Court, Cary, NC 27511 United States **BUS:** Medical Imaging Equipment Company **P/S:** Medical Imaging Technology **MA:** International **D/D/R:** Offering Technical Support **H/I/S:** Gardening, Needlepoint **EDU:** Bachelor of Science in Business Administration, Missouri Southern State University **A/A/S:** Board Member, North Carolina Biomedical Association; American College of Healthcare Services **C/VW:** American Cancer Society
Email: sally.goebel@siemens.com
URL: http://www.cambridgewhoswhos.com

Nancy Lyn Goettl
Title: Chief Executive Officer **Company:** Learning Opportunities **Address:** 300 Emerson Lane, Mankato, MN 56001 United States **BUS:** Book Distributor **P/S:** Distribution of Children's Books for Students in Kindergarten through 12th-Grade Including Titles from Major Publishers and Independent Presses, Customer Service, Books for Schools and Libraries **MA:** Regional **D/D/R:** Promoting Business, Selling Books to Schools and Public Libraries, Communicating with 200 Publishers, Scheduling Appointments with Schools, Showing Samples of Available Books, Inputting Orders **H/I/S:** Reading, Golfing, Singing, Listening to Music, Dancing Ballet, Acting **EDU:** Bachelor of Science in Business Administration, Minor in Economics, Minnesota State University, Mankato, Summa Cum Laude (1989) **A/A/S:** Omicron Delta Epsilon; Phi Kappa Phi
Email: nlgoettl@hickorytech.net
URL: http://www.learning-opp.com

Donald G. Goff
Title: Vice President, Government Relations **Company:** Elbit Systems of America **Address:** 4700 Marine Creek Parkway, Fort Worth, TX 76179 United States **BUS:** Leading Manufacturer of Aerospace Products **P/S:** High Performance Products and Sub-System Solutions Focusing on the Defense, Homeland Security and Commercial Aerospace Markets **MA:** United States Domestic Market **D/D/R:** Overseeing All Congressional Activities Including Lobbying, Managing All Responsibilities in the Executive Branch, Handling Branding Activities **H/I/S:** Golfing **EDU:** Master's Degree in Education, Duke University (1980); All-But-Dissertation Degree **A/A/S:** Representative, United States Chamber of Commerce; American Helicopter Society; Association of the United States Army; Army Aviation Association of America
Email: dgoff@elbitsystemsofamerica.com
URL: http://www.elbitsystemsofamerica.com

Tena S. Goff
Title: Evidence Custodian **Company:** Richland County Sheriff's Department **Address:** 5623 Second Notch Road, Columbia, SC 29223 United States **BUS:** Government Organization **P/S:** Law Enforcement **MA:** Regional **D/D/R:** Handling and Caring for Forensic Evidence, Managing and Supervising the Evidence Room, Overseeing the Retrieval and Storage of Evidence, Ensuring Evidence is Received by the Proper Standards, Maintaining a Chain of Custody of Evidence for the Local Courts, Managing and Transporting Seized Money to Banks, Updating the Policy and Procedure Manual **H/I/S:** Traveling, Horseback Riding **EDU:** College Coursework **CERTS:** Nationally Certified Property and Evidence Specialist (2004); Certified Search and Rescue Technician **A/A/S:** National Association For Search & Rescue; International Association for Property and Evidence
Email: tgoff@rcsd.net
URL: http://www.rcsd.net

Emil F. Gofourth
Title: General Manager **Company:** Quality Inn and Suites **Address:** 917 S. Huron Drive, Mackinaw City, MI 49701 United States **BUS:** Hotel **P/S:** Hospitality **MA:** National **D/D/R:** Customer Relations/Group Sales **H/I/S:** Traveling, Cooking **EDU:** College Coursework **CERTS:** Certified Chef **A/A/S:** American Culinary Foundation **C/VW:** American Cancer Society
Email: emil.gofourth@sbcglobal.net

Annika M. Goins
Title: Administrative Assistant **Company:** B & S Heating and Air **Address:** 3213 Leggett Road, Sale Creek, TN 37373 United States **BUS:** Heating and Air Conditioning Company **P/S:** Installing Heating and Air Conditioning Units in New Homes, Replacement Units for Businesses **MA:** Regional **D/D/R:** Working Part Time Answering Phones, Ordering Materials, Overseeing Other Office Work **H/I/S:** Traveling, Spending Time with her Children **EDU:** Bachelor's Degree in Business, The University of Tennessee at Chattanooga (1999)
Email: coygoins@bellsouth.net

Anthony Gojceta
Title: President **Company:** Regno Croatorum Tax Consulting, Inc. **Address:** 3281 46th Street, Long Island City, NY 11103 United States **BUS:** Consulting Firm **P/S:** Consulting Services Including Accounting **MA:** International **D/D/R:** Accounting, Translating, Interpreting, Banking, Organizing Taxes for People, Author Documents for Power of Attorneys Related to Property, Buying and Selling Properties, Consulting **H/I/S:** Traveling, Reading, Jogging, Playing Tennis and Soccer **EDU:** Bachelor's Degree in Business Management, American Institute of Banking, NY; Coursework in Accounting, Hunter College; Coursework, Zagreb School of Economics and Management, Croatia **CERTS:** Certified Professor at Etranger, Paris, France **A/A/S:** National Notary Association; Hunter College Alumni Association **C/VW:** American Red Cross; Local Church; Helping Friends in Need, Croatia; The Salvation Army
Email: regnocro@aol.com

Daniel P. Goldbeg, Esq.
Title: Partner **Company:** Kasowitz, Benson, Torres and Friedman, LLP **Address:** 1633 Broadway, New York, NY 10019 United States **BUS:** Law Firm **P/S:** Commercial Litigation **MA:** Local **EXP:** Mr. Goldberg's expertise is in commercial litigation. **H/I/S:** Sailing **EDU:** JD, School of Law, Pace University; Bachelor of Arts in Economics and Political Science, Trinity College **A/A/S:** New York State Bar Council; Federal Bar Association
Email: dgoldberg@kasowitz.com
URL: www.kasowitz.com

Anne B. Golden, CFP
Title: West Coast Regional Senior Managing Director **Company:** Trainer Wortham & Company, First Republic C. Investment Management **Address:** 111 Pine Street, San Francisco, CA 94111 United States **BUS:** Financial Investment Management Firm **P/S:** Diversified Domestic and International Portfolio Management, Registered Investment Advisor, Well-Defined Investment Process, Disciplined Risk Management, Monitoring and Accounting **MA:** National **D/D/R:** Working with High-Net-Worth Individuals, Managing Family Portfolios Including Third-Generation Clients, Handling Half-a-Billion Dollars for National Clients, Domestic, International and Real Estate **H/I/S:** Playing Tennis, Golf, Skiing, Spending Time with her Husband, Daughters and Granddaughters **EDU:** Bachelor of Arts in Asian Studies, University of Colorado (1964) **CERTS:** Certified Financial Planner (1983); Series 7, 63 and 65 Certification **A/A/S:** Former President, Financial Women's Association of San Francisco (1998); Chairwoman, Board of Regents, John F. Kennedy University (1990-1998)
Email: agolden@trainerwortham.com
URL: http://www.trainerwortham.com/

Morrisa Tialin Golden
Title: Lead Teacher **Company:** Freemont Elementary School **Address:** Stockton, CA 95206 United States **BUS:** School **P/S:** Education **MA:** Local **D/D/R:** Planning the Curriculum **H/I/S:** Traveling **EDU:** Master of Arts in Curriculum Instruction, California State University at Sacramento **A/A/S:** National Education Association; California Teachers Association **C/VW:** Salvation Army
Email: mtmgolden@aol.com

Stephanie H. Goldfarb
Title: Chef, President **Company:** Salt Kitchen & Fine Foods **Address:** 420 N. Orange Drive, Los Angeles, CA 90036 United States **BUS:** Food Service Company **P/S:** Food Services **MA:** Local **D/D/R:** Catering, Cooking **H/I/S:** Playing Tennis and Water Sports, Practicing Pilates, Running **EDU:** Graduate, Epicurean School of Culinary Arts (2000); Associate of Arts, Pierce College (1986) **A/A/S:** The Sirens Society **C/VW:** Best Friends Animal Society; Global Initiative
Email: stefchef1@hotmail.com
URL: http://www.saltkitchen.com

Diann Sara Goldstein
Title: Speech-Language Pathologist **Company:** Diann S. Goldstein, MA, CCC/SLP, MSPH **Address:** 10 Turell Road, Medford, MA 02155 United States **BUS:** Speech-Language Therapy **P/S:** Evaluation, Diagnosis and Treatment of Speech and Language Problems in Children and Adults **MA:** Regional **D/D/R:** Speech and Language Pathology and Cognitive Disabilities, Delays and Impairment from Stokes in Children and Adults, TBIs, Autism, Syndromes Diseases **H/I/S:** Spending Time with her Mother and Close Friends, Attending the Theater, Reading **EDU:** Master of Science in Public Health, Tufts University; Master of Arts in Speech-Language Pathology, New York University; Bachelor's Degree in Speech-Language Pathology, Boston University **CERTS:** Licensed Speech-Language Pathologist, State of Massachusetts; Certified to work in the Massachusetts Public School Systems. **A/A/S:** American Speech-Language-Hearing Association; Massachusetts Speech-Language-Hearing Association; American Public Health Association. **C/VW:** Merrill M. Goldstein, MD Memorial Scholarship Fund, Tufts University School of Medicine
Email: diannsg@comcast.net

Thomas J. Golson
Title: Web Master **Company:** TG and V Associates **Address:** 2308 Baileys Landing Drive, Raleigh, NC 27606 United States **BUS:** E-Commerce Internet **P/S:** Internet Store Fronts, Small Home Business **MA:** National **D/D/R:** Wireless Phone and Satellite TV **H/I/S:** Music, Traveling **EDU:** Technical Electronic School **A/A/S:** Disabled Veterans
Email: tgolson@localnet.com
URL: http://www.choice-wireless.net

Annette S. Gomez
Title: Owner, Vice President **Company:** Champ's Sports Bar and Club **Address:** 10651 N. Loop, Suites D, E, F, El Paso, TX 79927 United States **BUS:** Sports Bar, Restaurant **P/S:** Food, Beverages, Entertainment **MA:** Local **D/D/R:** Managing, Accounting, Sales **H/I/S:** Playing Cards **CERTS:** Licensed Real Estate Agent **A/A/S:** El Paso Association of Realtors
Email: champsbar8@yahoo.com

Gregory Gomez
Title: VP **Company:** Unitech Builders Corp **Address:** 16155 SW 117 Avenue Bay Suite 11, Miami, FL 33177 United States **BUS:** Construction Contractor **P/S:** Government Contract Commercial Builder **MA:** Local **D/D/R:** Management, Qualifier **H/I/S:** Spending Time with Son **CERTS:** Florida State Licenses, General Contractor, Roofing, Structural Masonry Inspection
Email: greggomez55@aol.com

Marisol Gomez, Esq.
Title: Trial Attorney **Company:** Gamba & Lombana, PA **Address:** 2701 Ponce de Leon Boulevard, Mezzanine, Coral Gables, FL 33134 United States **BUS:** Catastrophic Litigation Firm **P/S:** Catastrophic Litigation, Trial Law **MA:** Local **D/D/R:** Litigation **H/I/S:** Traveling **EDU:** JD, Saint Thomas University; Master's Degree in Corporate Finance, University of Miami **A/A/S:** Board of Directors, Florida Association for Women Lawyers, Miami Dade County; Cuban-American Bar Association; Puerto Rico Bar Association; Florida Board of Governors Young Lawyers Division **A/H:** Miami Dade Chapter Award 2007; Florida Legal Elites Up and Coming 2007 **C/VW:** Hands On Miami
Email: mgomez@gambalombana.com

Richard M. Gomez
Title: Vice President **Company:** TGSV Enterprises, Inc. **Address:** 1301 W. 68th Street, Hialeah, FL 33014 United States **BUS:** Construction Company **P/S:** General Contracting Services **MA:** Local **EXP:** Mr. Gomez's expertise is in construction management. **D/D/R:** Managing Business Operations, Client Acquisitions, Advertising, Dealing with Vendors and Sub-Contractors **H/I/S:** Writing, Biking **EDU:** Bachelor of Science in Construction Management, University of Florida **A/A/S:** University of Florida Alumni Association; The Associated General Contractors of America **C/VW:** Catholic Church
Email: rgomez@tgsv.com
URL: www.tgsv.com

Maria M. Gomez-Menendez, RDH
Title: 1) Office Administrator 2) Owner **Company:** 1) Gables Perfect Smile 2) PD Consulting **Address:** 295 Shore Drive E., Miami, FL 33133 United States **BUS:** 1) Dental Clinic 2) Consulting Firm **P/S:** 1) General Dentistry 2) Consulting Services for Office Administration **MA:** Regional **EXP:** Ms. Gomez-Menendez's expertise is in the management of administrative duties. **H/I/S:** Practicing Yoga **EDU:** Pursuing Bachelor of Arts in Business Management; Associate Degree in Dental Hygiene, Miami Dade College (2003); Associate of Arts, Miami Dade College (1998) **A/A/S:** American Dental Hygienist's Association
Email: mariamenendez75@aol.com
URL: http://www.professionaldentalconsulting.com

Jacqueline L. Goncher
Title: Human Resources Representative, Recruiter II **Company:** Concurrent Technologies Corporation **Address:** 100 CTC Drive, Johnstown, PA 15904 United States **BUS:** Independent Nonprofit Applied Research and Development Professional Services Organization **P/S:** Management and Technology-Based Solutions for a Wide Array of Clients Representing State and Federal Government and Private Sector Organizations **MA:** International **D/D/R:** Performing Human Resource Duties, Overseeing Technical Recruiting Including Immigration, Expatriation Recruitment and High Level Executive Management Recruiting, Attending Career Fairs and New Employers Orientation **H/I/S:** Spending Time with her Family **EDU:** Bachelor's Degree in Human Resources, Geneva College; Associate Degree in Specialized Business and Legal Administration, Cambria Rowe Business College **A/A/S:** Society for Human Resource Management; Pennsylvania Society for Human Resource Management
Email: goncher@ctc.com
URL: http://www.ctc.com

Donna Gonzaga Neely
Title: Clinical Case Manager **Company:** University of Nebraska Medical Center Physicians **Address:** 985540 Nebraska Medical Center, Omaha, NE 68198 United States **BUS:** Healthcare Facility **P/S:** Comprehensive Medical Care, Training Doctors and Ophthalmology Physicians, Preeminent Physician Group in the Region **MA:** Regional **D/D/R:** Running the Ophthalmology Clinic, Overseeing Diagnostic Testing and Clinical Research with Community Physicians **H/I/S:** Photography, Bicycling, Traveling **EDU:** Master's Degree in Business Administration, University of Nebraska at Omaha (2006); Bachelor of Science Degree, University of Nebraska at Omaha (1992) **A/A/S:** Joint Commission on Allied Health Personnel in Ophthalmology; Association of Technical Personnel in Ophthalmology
Email: dneely@unmc.edu
URL: http://www.unmc.edu

Jesse J. Gonzales
Title: Telecommunications Manager **Company:** Albuquerque Public Schools **Dept:** Telephone Repair and Maintenance **Address:** 915 Locust Street S.E., Albuquerque, NM 87106 United States **BUS:** Public School **P/S:** Education for Students in Kindergarten through Twelfth-Grade **MA:** Regional **D/D/R:** Managing All Phone Services for 145 Schools **H/I/S:** Golfing, Camping, Reading, Working on Custom Motorcycles **EDU:** Bachelor of Arts in Criminal Justice (1984); Associate of Arts in Construction Communications, El Paso Community College (1972); Coursework in Communications, United States Navy (1972) **A/A/S:** President, Avaya Users Group of New Mexico; Two-Term President, Colorado Chapter, Fraternal Order of Eagles **C/VW:** St. Labre Indian School, Northern Cheyenne and Crow Reservations, Ashland, MT; St. Joseph's Indian School, Chamberlain, SD; St. Bonaventure Indian Mission and School, Thoreau, NM
Email: jeskatcr@msn.com
URL: http://www.aps.com

Rachel Cazares Gonzales
Title: Physician Assistant **Company:** Department of Corrections **Address:** 8707 Chili Hill Road, Newcastle, CA 95658 United States **BUS:** Government Organization **P/S:** Detention Services **MA:** Local **EXP:** Ms. Gonzales' expertise is in emergency medicine management. **H/I/S:** Running **EDU:** Bachelor of Science in Physician Assistant Studies, Keck School of Medicine, University of Southern California **A/A/S:** American Academy of Physician Assistants; California Academy of Physician Assistants
Email: rcgmaya@hotmail.com

Claudia E. Gonzalez
Title: Physician **Company:** Naval Medical Center at Portsmouth **Address:** 620 John Paul Jones Circle, Portsmouth, VA 23708 United States **BUS:** Family Medical Center **P/S:** Healthcare **MA:** Local **EXP:** Dr. Gonzalez's expertise includes women's health and family medicine. **H/I/S:** Walking, Traveling, Spending Time with her Family **EDU:** MD, Wake Forest University **A/A/S:** American Academy of Family Physicians; Virginia Academy of Family Physicians **C/VW:** March of Dimes, Susan G. Komen for the Cure
Email: cgcoke@yahoo.com

Rev. Georgina Gonzalez
Title: Dean, Director **Company:** Vision Bible Institute & Adult Learning Center **Address:** 6324 Seventh Avenue, Brooklyn, NY 11220 United States **BUS:** Educational Institution **P/S:** Religious Education and Bible Studies **MA:** International **D/D/R:** Overseeing Administrative Duties Including Human Public Affairs, Managing Public Relations, Mentoring and Educating People to become Better Christians and Citizens **H/I/S:** Bowling, Playing Volleyball **EDU:** Master's Degree in Christian Counseling, Vision International Education Network, CA (2007); Bachelor's Degree in Christian Education, Vision International Education Network, CA **A/A/S:** Board Member, Bay Ridge Christian Academy, David City **A/H:** Who's Who Among American Teachers (2000)
Email: ggonzalez226@yahoo.com
Email: ggmzalez226@gmail.com
URL: http://www.cambridgewhoswho.com

Jose L. Gonzalez
Title: Registered Nurse, Emergency Room Charge Nurse **Company:** Baptist Health South Florida **BUS:** Hospital **P/S:** Healthcare **MA:** Regional **D/D/R:** Emergency Room Nursing **H/I/S:** Photography **EDU:** Associate of Science, Miami Dade College
Email: jlgonzorn@aol.com
URL: http://www.baptisthealth.net

Lorenza Gonzalez
Title: Public Service Dispatcher II, Avon Representative **Company:** California Highway Patrol **Address:** 1551 Benicia Road, Vallejo, CA 94591 United States **BUS:** Highway Patrol **P/S:** Highway Patrol Services **MA:** Local **D/D/R:** Dispatching **H/I/S:** Music, Dancing, Bowling, Playing Darts **C/VW:** Volunteer, Moose Lodge
Email: tcsrizzo@aol.com
URL: http://www.cambridgewhoswho.com

Marlene Gonzalez
Title: Associate Teacher **Company:** CAC **Address:** 1120 North G Street, Lompoc, CA 93436 United States **BUS:** Private School Facility Dedicated to Excellence in Education **P/S:** Regular Curriculum for Pre-School Children **MA:** Regional **D/D/R:** Overseeing 10 Children, Working on Lesson Plans, Activities, Paperwork and Computer Work, Corresponding with Parents **H/I/S:** Soccer **EDU:** Pursuing Associate Degree in Early Childhood Education, Alan Hancock
Email: mglene76@aol.com

Paula T. Gonzalez
Title: Healthcare Coordinator, RN, BSN **Company:** Sunrise of Lynnfield **Address:** 55 Salem Street, Lynnfield, MA 01940 United States **BUS:** Assisted Living Facility **P/S:** Senior Living and Healthcare **MA:** National **D/D/R:** Offering Geriatric Services, Specializing in Memory Impairment **H/I/S:** Golfing, Photography **EDU:** Bachelor of Science in Nursing, University of Rhode Island **C/VW:** Church
Email: lynnfield.hcc@sunriseseniorliving.com
URL: http://www.sunriseseniorliving.com

Gretel I. Gonzalez-Arroyo
Title: Internal Audit Director **Company:** COSVI **Address:** P.O. Box 363428, San Juan, PR 00936 United States **BUS:** Insurance Company **P/S:** Insurance **MA:** Local **D/D/R:** Performing Financial and Operational Audits **H/I/S:** Traveling, Bowling, Music, Singing, Playing the Saxophone **EDU:** Master of Business Administration in Human Resources, Inter American University of Puerto Rico; Bachelor of Business Administration in Accounting, University of Puerto Rico **A/A/S:** CPA Association; Institute of Internal Auditing
Email: gretel.gonzalez@cosvi.com

Rev. Peggy Warren Goochey
Title: Reverend (Retired) **Company:** United Methodist Church **Address:** 1480 Broadway, Unit 2523, San Diego, CA 92101 United States **BUS:** Online Store **P/S:** Biblical Vignette Scripts, Monologues, One-Act and Full-Length Plays, Creative Drama Sessions for Children in Religious Education, Drama Consultations for Church Theater Productions, Drama Ministry **MA:** National **D/D/R:** Writing Religious Dramas, Consulting with Church Theater Groups **H/I/S:** Genealogy, Cooking, Spending Time with Friends and Family, Reading by the Ocean **EDU:** Master's Degree in Religious Education, Southern Methodist University, Perkins School of Theology (1985); Bachelor of Arts in Speech and Theater, Oklahoma City University (1979) **CERTS:** Certified Minister in Christian Education **A/A/S:** Founder, The Olive Tree Players of Mission Valley; Order of Ordained Deacons, United Methodist Church; Christian Educators Fellowship; National Association of Female Executives; Christian Writer's Guild; Daughters of the American Revolution
Email: peggygoochey@churchdramacoach.com
URL: http://www.churchdramacoach.com

Teresa L. Good
Title: Front End Manager **Company:** Bloom **Address:** 14454 Lee Highway, Lot 285, Gainesville, VA 20155 United States **BUS:** Retail Store **P/S:** Grocery Products **MA:** National **D/D/R:** Ensuring Customer Satisfaction, Delivering Brand Positions to Associates and Customers, Overseeing, Leading and Motivating the Department Team, Preparing Feedback for the Store Manager, Executing Standard Practices and Other Policies, Assisting, Overseeing Business Operations and Employees, Participating in Quarterly Meetings, Creating Public Relationships, Training Associates, Managing Accounting Functions, Maintaining All Equipment **H/I/S:** Bowling, Playing Billiards **EDU:** Pursuing Bachelor of Arts in Business Administration, Colorado Technical University; High School Diploma
Email: teresa_good2002@yahoo.com
URL: http://www.shopbloom.com

Monica E. Goode
Title: Co-Owner **Company:** Goodes Welding **Address:** 301 S. Pine, Ponca City, OK 74601 United States **BUS:** Welding and Fabrication Company **P/S:** Hammermill Fitting and Welding, Custom Building Trailers **MA:** Regional **D/D/R:** Managing Human Resources and Accounts Payable and Receivable **H/I/S:** Scrapbooking, Cross-Stitching, Fishing, Playing Outdoor Sports with her Children **EDU:** Coursework, Kansas School of Cosmetology (1994); High School Education
Email: goodeswelding@poncacity.net

Mr. Robert D. Goodis
Title: Founder, President **Company:** Mason Dixon Darfur Alliance/Robert Goodis Charities **BUS:** Nonprofit Organization **P/S:** Charitable Fundraising **MA:** International **D/D/R:** Organizing Education and Awareness Events, Booking Guest Speakers, Lobbying for Action in Darfur **EDU:** Pursuing a Degree, Bard College
Email: masondixon_darfur_alliance@yahoo.com
Email: robert@robertgoodis.com
URL: http://www.robertgoodis.com

Beverly Sandra Goodman
Title: 1) Owner 2) Private Investigator Class 'CC' **Company:** 1) Bevv Sandra Creates 2) State of Florida **Address:** 1799 N. Highland Avenue, Unit I-123, Clearwater, FL 33755 United States **BUS:** 1) Art 2) Crime Prevention **P/S:** 1) Art 2) Crime Prevention **MA:** 1) National 2) Florida **D/D/R:** 1) Wild Animal Murals, Collage Art 2) Criminal Business Fraud **H/I/S:** Writing **EDU:** Coursework, City University of New York; Coursework, Florida Crime Prevention Training Institute **A/A/S:** National Rifle Association; Lake Worth Police Department, Florida; Author of 'Bits and Bulk by Bevy'; Award, Office of Attorney General Robert A. Butterworth (Department of Legal Affairs), 1992 **C/VW:** Salvation Army
URL: http://www.cambridgewhoswho.com

Melissa Goodman
Title: Financial Services Representative **Company:** Met Life **Address:** 11220 Elm Lane, Suite 202, Charlotte, NC 28227 United States **BUS:** Financial Services Company **P/S:** Insurance, Investments, Personal and Business Financial Analysis **MA:** International **EXP:** Ms. Goodman's expertise is in customer relations. **H/I/S:** Traveling, Reading **EDU:** Bachelor's Degree in Psychology, Minor in Criminal Justice, University of North Carolina at Charlotte **A/A/S:** Business Networking International; Women in Insurance and Financial Services; Belmont Chamber of Commerce **C/VW:** Don Trivette Memorial
Email: mgoodman1@metlife.com
URL: http://www.cambridgewhoswho.com

Elizabeth I. Goodrich
Title: Educator **Company:** Montgomery Central High School **Address:** 3955 Highway 48, Cunningham, TN 37052 United States **BUS:** High School **P/S:** Education for Ninth through 12th-grade Students **MA:** Local **D/D/R:** Teaching Second Language Acquisition Classes **H/I/S:** Spending Time with her Children **EDU:** Master of Arts in Education, Austin Peay State University (1993) **A/A/S:** AMC; American Council on the Teaching of Foreign Languages; Teaching Content Through a Foreign Language; The Nature Center for Environmental Activities; National Education Association; Friends of Historic Fort Royal; Boy Scouts of America **C/VW:** Agape
Email: beth.goodrich@cmcss.net

Judith W. Goodwich, MS
Title: Assistant Principal **Company:** Southwest Academy Magnet School **Address:** 17 Pinewood Farm Court, Owings Mills, MD 21117 United States **BUS:** Comprehensive Middle School **P/S:** Rigorous and Relevant Programs of Study **MA:** Regional **D/D/R:** Seventh-Grade Education, Overseeing All Necessary Construction and Work Orders for the Building, Observing and Assessing Teachers, Working with the Science Department and STEMS Program, Helping Students Keep Up to Date with Science, Technology and Computers **EDU:** Master's Degree Plus Credits in General Education, University of Notre Dame (1997); Bachelor of Science in Elementary Education, University of Maryland (1969) **A/A/S:** Association for Supervision and Curriculum Development; National Middle School Association; Volunteer in Nursing Homes
Email: jgoodwich@bcps.org
URL: http://www.bcps.org

Mr. Daniel P. Goodwin
Title: Fire Chief **Company:** Vienna Volunteer Fire Department **Address:** 609 28th Street, Vienna, WV 26105 United States **BUS:** Fire Department **P/S:** Fire Protection, Fire Investigation **MA:** Local **EXP:** Mr. Goodwin's expertise is in operations management. **D/D/R:** Teaching Firemanship Classes **H/I/S:** Golfing, Hunting, Fishing **EDU:** Associate Degree in Fire Services, West Virginia University at Parkersburg **CERTS:** Certified Fire and Explosion Investigator; Licensed Firefighter Level III **A/A/S:** National Fire Chiefs Association; Former President, West Virginia Firefighters **A/H:** Fireman of the Year Award, Vienna Volunteer Fire Department (1982) **C/VW:** Muscular Dystrophy Association
Email: vfd@vienna-wv.com
URL: http://www.vienna-wv.com

Jennifer L. Goodwin
Title: Principal **Company:** Jennifer L Goodwin, CPA **Address:** P.O. Box 21640, Concord, CA 94521 United States **BUS:** Accountant Accounting **P/S:** Accounting/Business Management, Financial Services **MA:** National **D/D/R:** Advisory Services, Financial Services, Marketing Management/Business Management **H/I/S:** Hiking, Photography, Sewing, Traveling **EDU:** Heald Business College, California State University, Associate Degree in Accounting, BA in Business Administration/Marketing **A/A/S:** AICPA, California Society of CPA's
Email: jgoodwin@jenniferlgoodwincpa.com
URL: www.jenniferlgoodwincpa.com

Renee Goodwin
Title: Assistant Band Director **Company:** Legacy High School **Address:** 3208 Fisher Court, Arlington, TX 76001 United States **BUS:** Secondary School **P/S:** Balanced Educational Curriculum, Music Education **MA:** Regional **D/D/R:** Teaching Band to Sixth through Twelfth-grade Students, Directing Band Performances, Leading School Music Department, Mentoring on Campus, Judging Band Contests, Organizing Band Clinics, Consulting with Other Music Teachers, Playing French Horn **H/I/S:** Reading, Shopping, Attending Church **EDU:** Bachelor of Arts, The University of Texas, Arlington (1988) **A/A/S:** Texas Music Educators Association; Texas Bandmasters Association; The National Association for Music Education
Email: goodva@mansfieldisd.org
URL: http://www.mansfieldisd.org/schools/thoward/our_school.htm

Carol A. Goral
Title: Teacher, Leader **Company:** School District of Philadelphia, Holme Elementary School **Address:** 9125 Academy Road, Philadelphia, PA 19114 United States **BUS:** Public School **P/S:** Education **MA:** Philadelphia **D/D/R:** Prior Teacher for Third to Eight Grade Students, Specializing in Staff Development, Supporting Teachers in Guided Reading and Mathematics Programs **H/I/S:** Reading, Sewing, Traveling **EDU:** Master's Degree in Education, West Chester University of Pennsylvania **A/A/S:** Association for Supervision and Curriculum Development; National Council of Teachers of Mathematics **C/VW:** National Multiple Sclerosis Society
Email: carolgoral@aol.com
URL: http://www.cambridgewhoswho.com

Lucille F. Gordon
Title: Owner **Company:** Grandma Knit Witt **Address:** 14000 Ludlow Street, Oak Park, MI 48237 United States **BUS:** Knitting **P/S:** Professional Knitting **MA:** International **D/D/R:** Unique New Knitting Idea to Share **H/I/S:** Gardening **A/H:** First Place in State

Mr. Robert M. Gordon
Title: Interface Analyst **Company:** Atlantic Health Systems **Address:** 1000 The American Road, Morris Plains, NJ 07950 United States **BUS:** Healthcare **P/S:** Pediatrics, Orthopedics, Cancer Care, Rehabilitation, Medicine, Women's Health, Cardiovascular Care, Neuroscience, Quovadx and Many Other Services **MA:** Local **D/D/R:** Ensuring that Communications between Servers is Maintained, Monitoring Lifeline of the System, Covering Three Hospitals with over 100 Connections, Consulting **H/I/S:** Playing Soccer, Practicing Photography **EDU:** Bachelor's Degree in Business and Information Systems, Iona; Associate in Data Processing, Norwalk Community College **A/A/S:** Northern Connecticut P.C. Connection
Email: robert.gordon@atlantichealth.org
URL: http://www.atlantichealth.org

Florida Lee Gordon Spearman
Title: Health Science Lecturer **Company:** Chicago City College-Harold Washington Campus **Address:** P.O. Box 4824, Chicago, IL 60680 United States **BUS:** World-Class Facility Dedicated to Excellence in Education **P/S:** Applied Science Department, Art Department, Business and Computer Information Systems Department, English/Speech Department, Foreign Language/English As A Second Language (ESL) Department, Humanities Department, Mathematics Department, Physical Science Department, Social Science Department, Theatre Department **MA:** Regional **D/D/R:** Teaching and Preparing Students for Bachelor's Program to Become Registered Nurses **H/I/S:** Reading, Pizzas **EDU:** Master's Degree in Management and Science, National Louis University; Master's Degree in Theology, Logos Bible Institute (1998)
Email: skip34@sbcglobal.net
Email: fspearman@ccc.edu

Paula S. Gordy
Title: Business Owner **Company:** Kirk and Gordy Associates, Inc **Address:** Route 1 Box 43C, Lancaster, MO 62548 United States **BUS:** Outpatient Mental Health Outpatient Mental Health **P/S:** Individual, Group, Child and Family Therapy **MA:** Local **D/D/R:** Performing Social Work **H/I/S:** Reading, Taking Walks, Enjoying Nature, Spending Time with her Family and Friends, Getting Involved with Local Church Youth Programs **EDU:** University of Missouri, MSW
Email: kirkgordyiow@telecom.com

Alex Gorodetsky
Title: President **Company:** Arttech Bath and Kitchen **Address:** 3340 Lawson Boulevard, Oceanside, NY 11572 United States **BUS:** Kitchens Constructions **P/S:** Home Improvement **MA:** Local **D/D/R:** Kitchen and Bath Design and Build **H/I/S:** Reading **EDU:** University of Odessa, MSCE **A/A/S:** NKBA
Email: arttech@arttech.us.com
URL: www.arttech-us.com

Philip J. Gosinski
Title: Senior Engineer **Company:** General Electric Aviation **Address:** 210 Columbian Avenue, Rutland, VT 05701 United States **BUS:** Manufacturer **P/S:** Manufacturing Jet Engine Airfoils **MA:** International **D/D/R:** Robotic Material Removal **H/I/S:** Downhill Skiing, Working on his House **EDU:** Bachelor of Science in Mechanical Engineering, University of Connecticut; Associate of Science in Mechanical Engineering, Waterbury Technical State College (Now Naugatuck Valley Community College) **C/VW:** GE Volunteers, Rutland Community Cupboard
Email: philip.gosinski@ae.ge.com

DeAnn Gossard
Title: Licensed Massage Practitioner **Company:** Healthy Applications **Address:** 620 N. Emerson Avenue, Suite 201, Wenatchee, WA 98801 United States **BUS:** Private Massage Therapy Practice **P/S:** National Massage and Healthcare Services to Improve Functions **MA:** Local **D/D/R:** Specializing in Injury Treatment, Practicing Massage Therapy, Utilizing Several Modalities, Receiving Referrals from Doctors **H/I/S:** Hiking, Fishing **EDU:** Associate Degree in Licensed Massage Practitioner Studies, Ashmead School of Massage, Fife, WA (2000) **A/A/S:** International Massage Association; National Certification Board for Therapeutic Massage and Bodywork
Email: healthyapplycation@hotmail.com

Robert A. Gottschalk
Title: Chief Operating Officer **Company:** K'oyitl'ots'ina LTD **Address:** 1603 College Road, Suite 2, Fairbanks, AK 99709 United States **BUS:** Facility Service Provider to U.S. Government **P/S:** Asset Management and Maintenance **MA:** National **D/D/R:** Engineering **H/I/S:** Snow Skiing, Golfing, Traveling, Playing Guitar **EDU:** Bachelor's Degree in Nuclear Engineering, SUNY Maritime College **A/A/S:** Naval Reserve Association
Email: bob.gottschalk@koyitlotsina.com

Chelsea E. Gouin
Title: Customer Service Sales Manager **Company:** Food Lion **Address:** 3740 Ashley Phosphate Road, North Charleston, SC 29418 United States **BUS:** Retail Grocery Chain **P/S:** Groceries **MA:** International **D/D/R:** Customer Service, Sales **H/I/S:** Reading, Traveling, Camping, Fishing, Hiking **EDU:** High School Graduate **C/VW:** Children's Miracle Network, Easter Seals, Camp Happy Days
Email: chlsboo@aol.com

Michele Gould
Title: Certified Nutritionist **Company:** Let's Get You Healthy **Address:** 215 Virginia Avenue, Unit 102, San Mateo, CA 94402 United States **BUS:** Nutrition **P/S:** Nutrition **MA:** Local **EXP:** Ms. Gould's expertise is in holistic nutrition. **H/I/S:** Hiking, Fly Fishing, Cooking, Writing, Baking, Taking Walks, Reading, Traveling **EDU:** Des Moines Community College, AS in Paralegal Studies **CERTS:** Account Specialist, Licensed Real Estate Agent **A/A/S:** National American Nutritionist Professionals, Sponsor for Save Children Foundation, American Cancer Society
Email: info@letsgetyouhealthy.net/gouldmichele@hotmail.co

Mr. Michael Edward Goulet
Title: Manager, Partner **Company:** Gaines Jewelers **Address:** G3310 Beecher Road, Flint, MI 48532 United States **BUS:** Retail Jewelry Company **P/S:** Retail Sales, Full Service Jeweler, Repairs **MA:** International **D/D/R:** Managing Business Operations, Overseeing the Buying and Selling of Jewelry Pieces, Performing Accounting Functions **H/I/S:** Golfing, Skiing, Spending Time with his Grandchildren **EDU:** High School Education (1969) **A/A/S:** West Flint Opt Club
Email: m.e.goulet@comcast.net
URL: http://www.gainesjewelry.com

Michelle L. Govan
Title: Chief Executive Officer **Company:** M.L. Govan Consultants **Address:** P.O. Box 193, Willow Grove, PA 19090 United States **BUS:** Consulting Firm **P/S:** Health-Related Workshops, Seminars, Motivational Speeches and Coaching **MA:** Nationwide **D/D/R:** Women and Teen Health Workshops **H/I/S:** Traveling **EDU:** Pursuing Bachelor's Degree in Medical Imaging, Concentration in Education, Bloomsburg University; Frontline Leadership Course **A/A/S:** Philadelphia Society of Radiologic Technologists; Pennsylvania Radiology Educators Society **C/VW:** Local Church
Email: info@mlgovan.com
URL: http://www.mlgovan.com

Jean Ann Grabowski
Title: Early Childhood Educator **Company:** Nesbit Elementary School **Address:** 500 Biddulph Way, Belmont, CA 94002 United States **BUS:** Elementary School **P/S:** Elementary Education **MA:** Local **D/D/R:** Teaching Early Childhood Education for Kindergarten Classes **H/I/S:** Traveling, Listening to Music, Tap Dancing, Attending Concerts, Caring for her Pet **EDU:** Master's Degree in Early Childhood Education, California State University, San Francisco; Bachelor of Science in Psychology, California State University, San Francisco **CERTS:** Early Childhood Education Specialist Credential, California State University, San Francisco **A/A/S:** National Education Association; San Mateo Reading Association; California Education Association **A/H:** Favorite Teacher Award **C/VW:** Animal Charities
Email: jgrabowski@belmont.k12.ca.us

Robin L. Grace
Title: Director of Operating Room **Company:** Cape Cod Hospital **Address:** 135 Red Berry Lane, Marstons Mills, MA 02648 United States **BUS:** Healthcare, Hospital **P/S:** Operating 14 Room in a Hospital **MA:** Local **D/D/R:** Running of the Operating Room Patients Entering to Leaving Hospital **H/I/S:** Gardening, Attending her Children's Ice Hockey Games **EDU:** Bachelor of Science in Nursing, Curry College **A/A/S:** AORN, MONE
Email: r.grace@capecodhealth.org

Heidi Graf
Title: Realtor, Sales Associate **Company:** Bozeman Broker Group **Address:** 1745 S. 19th Avenue, Suite 2, Bozeman, MT 59718 United States **BUS:** Real Estate Agency **P/S:** Residential, Commercial and Property Sales **MA:** Regional **D/D/R:** Keeping in Touch with Clients, Placing Ads in the Paper, Showing Properties, Handling Phone Calls, Keeping Abreast with Market Packets, Posting For-Sale Signs **H/I/S:** Downhill Skiing, Water-Skiing, Biking **EDU:** Bachelor of Arts in Elementary Education, Minor in Art, Montana State University (2000) **A/A/S:** Gallatin Association of Realtors; Montana Association of Realtors; National Association of Realtors; Chamber of Commerce; Bobcat Booster; Hawk Booster **A/H:** Rookie of the Year 2005,2006
Email: heidi@bozemanbrookers.com
URL: http://www.bozemanbrokers.com

James W. Gragg
Title: Owner **Company:** James Auto Upholstery **Address:** 3787 Hendersonville Road, Fletcher, NC 28732 United States **BUS:** Upholstery Company **P/S:** Upholstery Services for Cars, Planes, Boats, Motorcycles and Hot Rods **MA:** Local **EXP:** Mr. Gragg's expertise is in upholstery. **D/D/R:** Ensuring Customer Satisfaction **H/I/S:** Boating, Swimming, Skiing **A/A/S:** Local Chamber of Commerce; National Federation of Independent Businesses
Email: upman969@aol.com
URL: http://www.jamesautoupholstery.com

Darlene Graham
Title: Owner **Company:** Graham and Richardson Trucking Co **Address:** 206 Grenn Street, Brookhaven, MS 39601 United States **BUS:** Trucking Transportation Services and Logistics **P/S:** Trucking **MA:** International **D/D/R:** Relocator, Trailers, United States and Canada **H/I/S:** Cooking **EDU:** Popoha Lincoln Junior College, High School Diploma **CERTS:** Trucking Certificate **A/A/S:** Elk of World
Email: mompet@bellsouth.net

James C. Graham
Title: Associate Director **Company:** Colorado State University **Address:** 141F General Services, Fort Collins, CO 80523 United States **BUS:** University **P/S:** Education, Research **MA:** Local **EXP:** Mr. Graham's expertise includes radiation and safety. **H/I/S:** Hiking, Climbing **EDU:** Master's Degree in Health Physics, Colorado State University **A/A/S:** Health Physics Society **C/VW:** Local Schools
Email: jgram@colostate.edu
URL: http://www.cambridgewhoswho.com

Mary F. Graham
Title: District Sales Manager **Company:** Mueller Industries **Address:** 8285 Tournament Drive, Memphis, TN 38125 United States **BUS:** Manufacturing Company **P/S:** Domestic Copper Tube and Fittings, Plastic Fittings Other Source Products, Valves, Faucets, Plumbing Specialties, Brass Nipples and Fittings, Steel Nipples, Malleables **MA:** International **D/D/R:** Overseeing Product Line Sales for the Southern California Area, Low and High Desert and Los Angeles County, Showing Products to Wholesalers, Original Equipment Manufacturers, Retail Distributors **H/I/S:** Reading, Camping **EDU:** College Coursework **A/A/S:** California Plumbing and Mechanical Contractor Association
Email: mgraham@muellerindustries.com
URL: http://www.muellerindustries.com

Sherry Cottle Graham
Title: 1) Chief Executive Officer 2) Network Administrator **Company:** 1) Graham Marketing 2) Honda of America **Address:** 1) 1600 Valley Drive, 1) Marysville, OH 43040 **BUS:** 1) Nutritional Counseling Company 2) Automotive Company **P/S:** 1) Health, Beauty 2) Cars, Trucks **MA:** 1) International 2) International **D/D/R:** 1) Nutritional Counseling 2) Network Consulting **H/I/S:** Working with Stained Glass, Designing and Creating Jewelry, Gardening **EDU:** Bachelor of Science in Zoology, Ohio State University; Pursuing Master of Business Administration, Finley Community College; Associate of Science in Electrical Engineering, Rose Community College **A/A/S:** American Business Women's Association; Girl Scouts of the USA **C/VW:** Church
Email: sgraham6@columbus.rr.com
URL: http://www.theminteralgirls.com

Jeanine Graham-Bellamy
Title: Database and Infrastructure Software Support Manager **Company:** Royal Caribbean Cruises, LTD **Address:** 14700 Caribbean Way, Miramar, FL 33027 United States **BUS:** Cruise Line **P/S:** Travel and Cruise Accommodations and Assistance **MA:** International **D/D/R:** Managing a Group of 25 Employees, Overseeing Production Management, Making Changes in Applications, Managing Budgets and Contracts **H/I/S:** Traveling, Going to the Movies, Spending Time with her Two Daughters **EDU:** Bachelor of Science in Computer Engineering, University of Florida **A/A/S:** Oracle Users Group **C/VW:** St. Jude Children's Research Hospital
Email: jgraham@rccl.com

Timothy Francis Grainey
Title: Director of Research Operation **Company:** Maritz Research **Address:** 1740 Indian Wood Circle, Maumee, OH 43537 United States **BUS:** Market Research Company **P/S:** Customer Service, New Buyer Studies **MA:** International **D/D/R:** Maintaining Market Accounts for Construction, Heavy Trucks and Motor Sports **H/I/S:** Traveling, Playing Soccer **EDU:** Ph.D. Coursework, University of Minnesota **A/A/S:** American Marketing Association
Email: tim.grainey@maritz.com
URL: http://www.marltz.com

Maria E. Grajales
Title: Broker **Company:** Exit Unlimited Realty **Address:** 1471 Baldwin Street, Waterbury, CT 06706 United States **BUS:** Real Estate Company **P/S:** Residential, Executive Homes, Lake Front, Town Homes, Condos, Golf Homes, Gated and Horse Properties **MA:** National **D/D/R:** Supervising Six Agents, Selling Residential Properties **H/I/S:** Playing Basketball and Soccer with her Daughter **A/A/S:** Connecticut Association of Realtors; National Association of Realtors
Email: mariaexit@yahoo.com
URL: http://www.mariaexit.net

Susan F. Grammer
Title: Attorney at Law **Company:** Susan F Grammer **Address:** 2 Terminal Drive, Suite 17B, East Alton, IL 62024 United States **BUS:** Attorney **P/S:** Legal Services, General Practice, Contested Family Litigation, Estate Planning, Workers Comp **MA:** Local **D/D/R:** Collections, Adoption, Juvenile, Bankruptcy, Social Security, Disability **H/I/S:** Family **EDU:** JD, Washington University School of Law **A/A/S:** American Bar Association, American Association of Adoption, Illinois Bar Association

Myzsa Grandell
Title: Manpower Analyst **Company:** United States Air Force **Address:** 10108 Maronda Drive, Riverview, FL 33569 United States **BUS:** Military Component Dedicated to Defending the United States of America **P/S:** Excellence in Military Services, Flying and Fighting in Air, Space and Cyberspace, Development of Airmen, Technology-to-Warfighting, Integrating Operations, Air and Space Superiority, Global Attack, Rapid Global Mobility, Precision Engagement, Information Superiority, Agile Combat Support **MA:** Local **D/D/R:** Working as a Manpower Officer, 37-F Personnel, Verifying that the Maximum Effort and Manpower is Provided for Each Task **H/I/S:** Listening to Music, Watching Movies **EDU:** Bachelor of Science in Behavioral Science, United States Air Force Academy (2003)
Email: myzsa@hotmail.com
URL: http://www.af.mil

Kay B. Grandstaff
Title: Elementary Teacher **Company:** Harrisonburg City Public Schools **Dept:** Spotswood Elementary School **Address:** 400 Mountain View Drive, Harrisonburg, VA 22801 United States **BUS:** School District **P/S:** Education **MA:** Local **D/D/R:** Teaching English as a Second Language, Gifted and Talented Education to Students with Learning Disabilities and Adult Remediation for Nursing and Early Childhood Education, Reading, Language and Mathematics at the Community College Level **H/I/S:** Gardening **EDU:** Master of Science in Elementary Education, East Carolina University **CERTS:** Certified Gifted Education Specialist **A/A/S:** Former President, Phi Delta Kappa; Alpha Delta Kappa **C/VW:** American Heart Association; American Cancer Society; Big Brothers Big Sisters of America
Email: kgrandstaff@harrisonburg.k12.va.us
Email: kgrandstaff@comcast.net
URL: http://www.harrisonburg.k12.va.us

Richard C. Grangaard

Title: First Vice President, Wealth Advisor **Company:** Morgan Stanley **Address:** 505 Market Street, West Des Moines, IA 50266 United States **BUS:** Financial Advisory Firm **P/S:** Investments, Financial Services Including Trusts, Stocks and Bonds, Estate Planning, Insurance and Wealth Transfers **MA:** International **EXP:** Mr. Grangaard's expertise is in financial management. **D/D/R:** Assisting Clients of High Net Worth to Reach their Financial Goals **H/I/S:** Golfing, Boating, Cycling, Fishing, Traveling, Skiing **EDU:** Bachelor of Science in Psychology, The University of Iowa **C/VW:** Volunteer Teacher, Local Elementary School; Rotary Club
Email: richard.grangaard@morganstanley.com
URL: http://www.morganstanley.com

Earl B. Grant

Title: Program Director **Company:** Corrections Center of Northwest Ohio, Recovery Services of Northwest Ohio **Address:** County Road 24.25, Stryker, OH 43557 United States **BUS:** Recovery Center **MA:** Local **EXP:** Mr. Grant's expertise includes drug, alcohol, mental health and case management. **H/I/S:** Playing the Keyboard for a Blues Band, Traveling **EDU:** Bachelor's Degree in Social Work, University of Toledo **CERTS:** Licensed Independent Chemical Dependency Counselor, Ohio Chemical Dependency Professionals Board **A/A/S:** National Association of Social Workers **C/VW:** Cancer Society of Ohio
Email: recoveryservices.ccno@noris.org
Email: earl.grant@moris.org

Joi Odom Grant

Title: Mathematics Administrator **Company:** School District of Palm Beach County **Address:** 3300 Forest Hill Boulevard, West Palm Beach, FL 33406 United States **BUS:** Public School District **P/S:** Education for Kindergarten through 12th-grade Students, Educational Excellence, Academic Programs which Increase Literacy in Reading, Writing and Mathematics **MA:** Regional **D/D/R:** Overseeing the Mathematics Curriculum to Ensure that it Complies with Standards **H/I/S:** Going to the Beach, Spending Time with her Family **EDU:** Educational Specialist Degree in Educational Leadership, Nova Southeastern University (2006); Master's Degree in Elementary Education, Nova Southeastern University (1993); Bachelor of Science in Elementary Education, Bethune-Cookman University (1989) **A/A/S:** Palm Beach County Council of Teachers of Mathematics; National Education Association; Florida Education Association
Email: grantj@palmbeach.k12.fl.us
URL: http://www.palmbeach.k12.fl.us

Sarah J. Grant, MBA

Title: President Squire Hill Enterprises **Company:** Squire Hill Enterprises **Address:** 93 Seney Drive, Bernardsville, NJ 07924 United States **BUS:** Real Estate Development Firm **P/S:** Custom Designed Residential Construction Beginning at One Million Dollars and Up **MA:** Regional **D/D/R:** Designing and Building New Luxury Homes, Selecting Sites, Supervising All Aspects of Construction, Selecting and Working with Architects **EDU:** Master's Degree in Business Management, Indiana University (1956) **A/A/S:** New Jersey Association of Home Builders
Email: sarahgrant1313@yahoo.com

Norma Grassini Komara

Title: Owner **Company:** Pure Artisan **Address:** 14145 Creek Crossing, Orland Park, IL 60467 United States **BUS:** Gifts Entrepreneur **P/S:** Online Sales, Home Decor **MA:** Local **D/D/R:** Designing Rooms **H/I/S:** Traveling, Spending Time with her Family **EDU:** Master of Education
Email: sales@pureartisan.com
URL: www.pureartisan.com

Daisy W. Grate

Title: Bookkeeper **Company:** C.E. Murray High School **Address:** 108 Council Road, Salters, SC 29590 United States **BUS:** High School **P/S:** Secondary Education **MA:** Regional **D/D/R:** Overseeing Accounts Payable and Receivable, Handling the Purchasing Order for the Staff and All Incoming and Outgoing Funds, Contracting with Consultants, Overseeing 60 Employees, Interacting with Students **H/I/S:** Sewing, Making Crafts, Reading, Decorating **EDU:** Associate of Arts in Business Administration, Limestone College (2008) **A/A/S:** School Improvement Committee; Title I Team Committee; Homecoming Committee
Email: dopate@wcsd.k12.sc.us
URL: http://www.wcsd.k12.sc.us

Arlene R. Graver

Title: Owner **Company:** 1) Opossum Lake Treasures 2) Opossum Lake Accounting and Tax Services **Address:** 99 Campground Road, Carlisle, PA 17015 United States **BUS:** 1) Retail Shop 2) Accounting and Taxation Firm **P/S:** 1) Antiques and Collectibles 2) Accounting and Tax Services **MA:** Local **EXP:** Ms. Graver's expertise is in operations management. **H/I/S:** Volunteering **CERTS:** Certified Public Accountant, Commercial College **A/A/S:** Former Secretary, Pennsylvania Institute of Certified Public Accountants **C/VW:** Local Charitable Organizations
Email: graver99@comcast.net
URL: http://www.opossumlaketreasures.com

Melissa June Graves, BS

Title: Fourth-Grade Teacher **Company:** Mayfair Elementary School **Address:** 3305 E. Home Avenue, Fresno, CA 93703 United States **BUS:** Exceptional Elementary School **P/S:** High Quality Elementary Education, Student Services **MA:** Local **D/D/R:** Teaching Fourth-grade Students, Mathematics, Experience Teaching Grades One through Five **H/I/S:** Gardening, Construction, Riding Motorcycles **EDU:** Bachelor of Arts, California State University at Fresno (1979); K-12 Ryan Credential **A/A/S:** CMA; FARC; Mui Phi Epsilon; State Council, California Teachers Association
URL: http://www.fresno.k12.ca.us/schools/s032/sch032hp.htm

Andrew S. Gray

Title: Physical Education Teacher **Company:** York Village Elementary School **Address:** 124 York Street, York, ME 03909 United States **BUS:** School **P/S:** Education **MA:** Local **D/D/R:** Teaching Physical Education **H/I/S:** Golfing, Spending Time Outdoors **EDU:** Bachelor's Degree in Physical Education, Plymouth State College **A/A/S:** Maine Association of Health, Physical Education, Recreation and Dance; American Alliance for Health, Physical Education, Recreation and Dance **C/VW:** American Heart Association, American Cancer Society
Email: agray@yorkschools.org
URL: http://www.yorkschools.org/agray

Ellen L. Gray

Title: Second-Grade Teacher (Retired) **Company:** Buckatunna Elementary School **Address:** P.O. Box 60, Buckatunna, MS 39322 United States **BUS:** Elementary School **P/S:** Primary Education **MA:** Local **D/D/R:** Teaching Mathematics, Spelling, Reading, Elementary and Special Education **H/I/S:** Fishing, Gardening, Volunteering for Charitable Organizations, Attending the Church **EDU:** Bachelor's Degree in Elementary Education, Mississippi State University (1979) **CERTS:** Certification in Elementary Education (K-8) **A/A/S:** Mississippi Educational Associations
Email: ellen.gray00@cwwemail.com

Karen M. Gray

Title: Director **Company:** WriteLink **BUS:** Creative Writing and Consulting Services **P/S:** Copywriting, Editing, Journalism, Consulting **MA:** Regional **D/D/R:** Copywriting, Editorials, Screenplays, Novels, Consulting with Writers on Marketing and Rewrites of Manuscripts, Editing Manuscripts, Preparing Screenplays, Novels, Magazine Articles, Children's Books, Writing Copy for Marketing Products **H/I/S:** Watching NASCAR and Nextel Cup Racing, Crafting, Promoting Character Education for All Ages **EDU:** Associate Degree in English, University of Maryland (1979) **CERTS:** Certified Copywriter with American Writers and Artists; Certified in Public Relations with Maryland Smiles Program; Pursuing French Studies Degree **A/A/S:** American Writers and Artists Inc.; Freelance Screenwriters Forum; National Education Association; Freelance Writer for Parenting Publications
Email: WriteLink92@aol.com

Mary Gray

Title: Director, Advertising Sales **Company:** Sugar Publishing, Inc. **Address:** One Sutter Street, San Francisco, CA 94104 United States **BUS:** Online Media Company **P/S:** Entertainment, Advertising Sales **MA:** Regional **EXP:** Ms. Gray's expertise includes event sales and online and print advertising sales. **H/I/S:** Swimming, Traveling, Skiing **EDU:** Bachelor of Science in Biopsychology, Cognitive Science and Organizational Studies, University of Michigan (1999) **A/A/S:** Junior League of Oakland-East Bay, Inc.
Email: mary@sugarpublishing.com
URL: http://www.sugarpublishing.com

Ms. Sharon E. Gray

Title: Editor **Company:** Wycliffe Bible Translator **Address:** 2601 West Walnut Hill Lane Unit 204, Irving, TX 75038 United States **BUS:** Religion Religion/Spiritual Services **P/S:** Religion/Nonprofit **MA:** International **EXP:** Ms. Gray's expertise is in biblical translation. **H/I/S:** Reading, Freelance Editing, Singing in Church **EDU:** University of Sheffield, University of Cambridge, Received 2 MA Degrees **A/A/S:** SBAL
Email: hobnobkitkat@hotmail.com

Margaret A. Greason

Title: Pre-School Teacher **Company:** Kids Cottage **Address:** 206 S. Main Street, Bridgeville, DE 19933 United States **BUS:** Education **P/S:** Early Childhood Education **MA:** Local **D/D/R:** Painting, Cake Decorating **H/I/S:** Painting, Knitting, Crocheting, Gardening, Beaches **A/A/S:** Phi Pheta Kappa, National Association of the Education of Young Children
Email: eceteacher@mail.com

Chelsea G. Greek

Title: Counselor **Company:** School Board of Levy County **Address:** 480 Marshburn Drive, Bronson, FL 32621 United States **BUS:** Public Middle and High School **P/S:** Education/Counseling **MA:** Local **D/D/R:** Individual Counseling, Academic Advising, Career Counseling, Crisis Counseling **H/I/S:** Gardening, Landscape Design, Remodeling Homes **EDU:** Master's Degrees in School Counseling and Mental Health Counseling, Webster University; Bachelor of Arts, St. Leo College; Associate Degree, Santa Fe Community College **CERTS:** Florida State Licensure in Mental Health Board Certified in Professional Counseling **A/A/S:** American Psychotherapy Association, American Mental Health Counselors Association, **C/VW:** Various School Functions
Email: greekc@levy.k12.fl.us

Antoinette L. Green

Title: Owner **Company:** Greenleaf-Essences **Dept:** Sales, Marketing, Accounting **Address:** 1157 South Webb Rd, Unit 1097, Wichita, KS 67207 United States **BUS:** Retail/Wholesales Distributor **P/S:** Quality Essences, Oil Burners, Unscented Tea Light Candles Burning Oils **MA:** National **D/D/R:** Overseeing Daily Operations, Advertising, Marketing, Managing Finances, Creating Aroma Candles and Scented Oils **H/I/S:** Fishing, Family Photography, Crocheting **EDU:** Coursework in Psychology, University of California at Compton **C/VW:** Volunteer At Church, Breast Cancer Organizations
Email: agreen@greenleaf-essences.com
URL: http://www.greenleaf-essences.com

Diane C. Green, MS, M.Ed.

Title: Elementary Teacher **Company:** Hempstead Public Schools **Address:** 185 Peninsula Boulevard, Hempstead, NY 11550 United States **BUS:** Public School District **P/S:** Regular Core Curriculum Including Reading, Mathematics, English, Science, Social Studies, Art, Music, History, Physical Education **MA:** Regional **D/D/R:** Teaching All Core Subjects to Fifth-grade Students **H/I/S:** Golfing, Tennis, Volunteering within the Community **EDU:** Master's Degree in Administration, C.W. Post University; Master's Degree in School Counseling, Hofstra University (1974) **A/A/S:** Phi Delta Kappa **C/VW:** Civic Council of Hempstead
Email: yemaja1@aol.com
URL: http://www.hempsteadschools.org

George G. Green

Title: Senior Director **Company:** Mortgage Bankers Association **Address:** 1919 Pennsylvania Avenue N.W., Washington, DC 20006 United States **BUS:** Real Estate Financial Company **P/S:** Real Estate Financial Services **MA:** National **EXP:** Mr. Green's expertise is in the finance of commercial real estate. **H/I/S:** Listening to Jazz Music **EDU:** Master of Science in Real Estate Finance, The Johns Hopkins University; Bachelor of Science in Economics, Claremont McKenna College
Email: ggreen@mortgagebankers.org
URL: http://www.mortgagebankers.org

Jude O. Green

Title: Owner, Managing Partner **Company:** Wizard Constructors, Geco Engineering and Design **Address:** 6024 RR 2338, Suite 101, Georgetown, TX 78608 United States **BUS:** Consulting and Construction Company **P/S:** Commercial Design, Construction and Engineering **MA:** National **D/D/R:** Mechanical, Electrical and Plumbing Design Management **H/I/S:** Captaining his Ice Hockey and Football Teams **EDU:** Bachelor of Science in Mechanical Engineering, University of Texas **A/A/S:** Golden Key National Honor Society; Tau Beta Phi; Dean's List; Alpha Lambda Delta
Email: admin@wizardconstructors.com
Email: admin@gecoengineering.com
URL: http://www.gecoengineering.com
URL: http://www.wizardconstructors.com

Linda L. Green

Title: Heart Life Instructor **Company:** Programs of the Heart **Address:** 550 Mohawk Drive, Suite 500, Boulder, CO 80303 United States **BUS:** Educational Service Provider **P/S:** Personal Development Workshops and Courses **MA:** International **D/D/R:** Instructing Workshops and Courses in Personal Management **H/I/S:** Salsa Dancing, Traveling, Running, Skiing, Snorkeling **EDU:** Graduate Coursework in Trans Personal Psychology, Naropa University; Bachelor of Science in Engineering, Purdue University; Mastery of the Heart, 1997-1998; Heart of the Life Instructor Training, 1998 **A/A/S:** Former Board of Director, Programs of the Heart **C/VW:** Social Director, Unity Church of Boulder
Email: lindagreen@programsoftheheart.com
URL: http://www.programsoftheheart.com

Mr. Mike Green

Title: Owner **Company:** Innovative Grafix Signs & Apparel **Address:** 38372A Innovation Court, Suite 101, Murrieta, CA 92563 United States **BUS:** Printing and Production Company **P/S:** Screen Printing, Embroidery, Vinyl Stickers, Brochures, Business Cards **MA:** National **D/D/R:** Managing Operations, Marketing, Assisting Customers **H/I/S:** Boating, Off-Road Racing, Motorcycling **EDU:** College Coursework
Email: innovativegrafix@verizon.net
URL: http://www.innovativegrafix.com

Patricia A. Green
Title: Neurology Clinic Manager **Company:** Wishard Health Services **Address:** 1001 W. 10th Street, Indianapolis, IN 46202 United States **BUS:** Hospital **P/S:** Healthcare Education, Neurology Care and Clinical Services **MA:** Regional **D/D/R:** Overseeing Staff, Scheduling, Consulting with Patients, Training Employees, Conducting Orientation Programs **H/I/S:** Singing **EDU:** Nursing Diploma, Wishard General Hospital (1974) **A/A/S:** Gospel Music Workshop of America; Music Ministry; Women's Ministry **C/VW:** New Light Baptist Church
Email: greenp52@sbcglobal.net
URL: http://www.wishard.edu

Terri Ann Green
Title: Professional Land Surveyor **Company:** TEC Civil Engineering **Address:** 4115 Broad Street, Suite B11, San Luis Obispo, CA 93401 United States **BUS:** Civil Engineering and Land Surveying Company **P/S:** Land Surveying, Consulting, Civil Engineering Design **MA:** Regional **D/D/R:** Land Surveying, Managing Small to Large Multi-Unit Sites **H/I/S:** Gardening, Golfing, Spending Time with her Family **EDU:** Bachelor of Arts in Psychology, Chapman University; Licensed Professional Land Surveyor, CA **A/A/S:** California Land Surveyors Association
Email: tgreen@tecslo.com
URL: http://www.tecslo.com

Valyncia Sheon Green
Title: Clinical Pharmacy Specialist **Company:** University of Mississippi Medical Center **Dept:** Cardio Metabolic Clinic **Address:** 2500 N. State Street, c/o Cardio Metabolic Clinic, Jackson, MS 39216 United States **BUS:** Hospital **P/S:** Healthcare **MA:** Local **EXP:** Ms. Green's expertise includes clinical pharmacy and metabolic disorders. **D/D/R:** Practicing Internal Medicine **H/I/S:** Traveling, Shopping **EDU:** Doctor of Pharmacy, Xavier University, New Orleans, LA; Pharmacy Practice Residency, University of Mississippi Medical Center; Associate of Arts, Southwest Mississippi Community College; **A/A/S:** Mississippi Society of Health-System Pharmacists; Mississippi College of Clinical Pharmacy; Magnolia State Pharmaceutical Society American Society of Health-System Pharmacists
Email: valynciat@aol.com

Allen Leonard Greenberg, MD
Title: Director of Biological Therapies, Director of the Transfusion Committee **Company:** Memorial Cancer Institute **Address:** 1150 N. 35th Avenue, Suite 170, Hollywood, FL 33021 United States **BUS:** Medical Center **P/S:** High-Quality Treatment Facilities with an Emphasis on Prevention of Cancer, Early Diagnosis and Support Services **MA:** National **EXP:** Mr. Greenberg's expertise includes hematology, gene therapy, biological therapies of malignancies, immunology and coagulation, gene therapy, chemotherapy and biological therapy. **H/I/S:** Writing Poetry and Song Lyrics, Meteorology, Playing Baseball and Football **EDU:** MD, Mount Sinai School of Medicine (1974); Bachelor of Arts in Biology, Franklin and Marshall University (1970) **A/A/S:** Fellowship, American College of Physicians; American Society of Hematology; American Board of Internal Medicine; American Society of Blood and Marrow Transplantation
Email: agreenberg@mhs.net

Albertha Marie Greene
Title: Owner, Daycare Provider **Company:** Greene-Major-Daycare **Address:** 6128 Sabine Drive, Fayetteville, NC 28303 United States **BUS:** Private Daycare Facility **P/S:** Infant and Childcare for Military Children **MA:** Regional **D/D/R:** Offering 24-Hour Family Childcare for Military Children at Fort Brag, Creating and Running Extended Care Programs **H/I/S:** Cooking, Reading, Teaching **CERTS:** Licensed Daycare Provider, North Carolina Department of Health and Human Services (2002); Certification of Accreditation, National Association for the Education of Young Children **A/A/S:** North Carolina Chapter, Child Care Services Association **A/H:** Smart Start Childcare Solutions Award (2006); Fort Brag Childcare Award (2005)
Email: greenedaycare@aol.com

Elaine Greene
Title: Owner **Company:** Decorating Dilemma Doctor **Address:** 403 Washington Court, Canon City, CO 81212 United States **BUS:** Design Company **P/S:** Interior Decorating, Landscape Design **MA:** Regional **D/D/R:** Color Consulting, Room Design **H/I/S:** Gardening, Painting, Landscaping, Reading, Spending Time with her Children **CERTS:** Certification in Interior Design; Certification in Landscape Design
Email: e.h.greene@bresnan.net

Jerome D. Greene
Title: Oracle Application Developer and Analyst **Address:** 134 Jordan Court, Limerick, PA 19468 United States **BUS:** Information Technology **P/S:** Software Development and Analysis **MA:** Regional **D/D/R:** Using Oracle Tools and Operating Systems, Developing Programs, Analyzing Technology **EDU:** Bachelor of Science in Computer System Technology, The Spring Garden College (1986) **CERTS:** Certification in Website Technology, Lincoln Technical Institute (Formerly the Cittone Institute) (2003); Certification in Oracle Software **A/A/S:** Philadelphia Area Computer Society
Email: jperson19468@gmail.com

Mary E. Greene
Title: Visiting Professor **Company:** Bard College, Center for Environmental Policy **Address:** P.O. Box 5000, Annandale On Hudson, NY 12504 **BUS:** College **P/S:** Education, Environmental Law **MA:** Regional **EXP:** Ms. Greene's expertise includes environmental law and policy. **H/I/S:** Hiking, Traveling, Writing, Spending Time with her Children **EDU:** JD, University of Florida, Levin College of Law; Bachelor of Business Administration Emphasis on Economics, University of Florida (1987) **A/A/S:** American Bar Association; Florida Bar Association; Environmental Protection Agency **C/VW:** Habitat for Humanity, United Way, Bard College
Email: mgreene2@hvc.rr.com
URL: http://www.cambridgewhoswho.com

Linda S. Greenfield
Title: Owner, Health Coach **Company:** New Dawne Enterprises **BUS:** Natural Alternative Healthcare Company **P/S:** Natural Alternative Health, Hands-On Holistic Healing, Colon Therapy, Wellness Coaching, Nutritional Products **MA:** National **D/D/R:** Holistic Healing Including Cleansing and Detoxing, Performing Colonics, Utilizing Raindrop Techniques with Therapeutic Essential Oils, Treating Back Pain and Inflammation, Traveling to Help Clients **H/I/S:** Horseback Riding, Biking, Swimming **EDU:** College Coursework in Massage Therapy **CERTS:** Certification in Colonic Irrigation; Certification in Holistic Health Counseling
Email: lindag55@nyc.rr.com
URL: http://www.newdawne.com

Rob Greenstein
Title: Area Sales Manager **Company:** Automated Packaging Systems **Address:** 12130 Mora Drive, Suite 2, Santa Fe Springs, CA 90670 United States **BUS:** Bagging, Equipment and Flexible Packaging Manufacturer **P/S:** Packaging Machinery, Manufacturing **MA:** International **EXP:** Mr. Greenstein's expertise includes management and layout and equipment design. **D/D/R:** Managing Machinery Packaging **H/I/S:** Playing Roller Hockey and Tennis, Golfing **EDU:** Industry-Related Training and Experience **CERTS:** Certification in Sales Skills **A/A/S:** National Handling Management Society; Founders Club (2005, 2006, 2007) **A/H:** Sales Manager of the Year (2003, 2005) **C/VW:** American Cancer Society; Helen Woodward Animal Shelter
Email: rob.greenstein@autopkg.com
URL: http://www.autobag.com

Stacy M. Greenwood
Title: School Psychologist **Company:** Topeka Public Schools Unified School District 501 **Address:** 918 S.W. 10th Avenue, Topeka, KS 66604 United States **BUS:** Public School District **P/S:** Public Education for Students in Prekindergarten through 12th-grade **MA:** Regional **D/D/R:** Evaluating and Determining Which Students Qualify for Special Education, Working and Consulting with Teachers, Supporting Staff, Mental Health Needs of Students, Attending Meetings, Offering Academic and Behavioral Interventions **H/I/S:** Digital Photography **EDU:** Education Specialist in School Psychology, The University of Kansas (2004) **A/A/S:** National Association of School Psychologists; Kansas Association of School Psychologists
Email: sgreenwo@topeka.k12.ks.us
URL: http://www.topeka.k12.ks.us

Cristen D. Greer
Title: Teacher **Company:** Peoria Public School District **BUS:** School **P/S:** Education **MA:** Local **D/D/R:** Teaching All Subjects of Fifth-Grade **H/I/S:** Listening to Music, Bowling, Playing Pool **EDU:** Bachelor of Arts (2005) **A/A/S:** WAS; National Education Association; Illinois Educational Association; Who's Who Among American Teachers (2007) **C/VW:** Various Charities, Community Builders
Email: cristen.greer@psd150.org
Email: cristen.greer@tsdiso.org
URL: http://www.cambridgewhoswho.com

Elizabeth M. Greeson
Title: President **Company:** Supernatural Productions, Inc. **BUS:** Full Entertainment Service Company **P/S:** Public Music Performance, Corporate Parties, Public Speaking, Copy, Fiction and Non-fiction Writing, CD's, DVD's, Production and Marketing. Music Consulting **MA:** International **D/D/R:** Award Winning Singing, Music Performance, Education, Public Speaking and Writing, Song Writing and Recording, Writing non-fiction articles, Public Speaking on Music Appreciation, Blues History, Women's Role In the Blues, Songwriting, Aging In Public **H/I/S:** Traveling, Art, Cooking, Reading, French Culture, Walking **EDU:** Bachelor of Arts in Music, Columbia College (1996) **A/A/S:** Member, American Writers and Artists Institute; Member, Twilight Tales Readers Group **A/H:** Best Comedy/Novelty Song, International Songwriting Contest (2005); Voted Best Blues Singer in Chicago, 'He Left It in His Other Pants' (2005) **C/VW:** Donate to Public TV and Radio, Donate to The Salvation Army, Leukemia Foundation.
Email: liz@lizmandeville.com
URL: http://www.lizmandeville.com

Erin Gregg
Title: Kindergarten and First Grade Special Education Teacher **Company:** Holt Elementary School **Address:** Northport, AL 35473 United States **BUS:** Public Elementary School **P/S:** Education for Student in Prekindergarten through Fifth-Grade, Special Education, Support Services, Library, Writing Team, Technology Team, Student Council, Literacy Team, Parent-Teacher Organization **MA:** Regional **D/D/R:** Teaching Special Education in a Resource Room, Pulling Out Students from Classrooms and Teaching Remedial Mathematics, Reading and Writing, Educating Students about Life Skills, Assisting Learning Disabled Students, Implementing Reading Programs and Phonics Progression Programs **H/I/S:** Watching Football **EDU:** Bachelor's Degree in Early Childhood Special Education K-6, The University of Alabama (2005); Bachelor's Degree in General Education K-6, The University of Alabama (2005) **A/A/S:** Council for Exceptional Children; National Education Association; Alabama Educators Association
Email: erin.gregg.hes@tcss.net
URL: http://holt.tce.schoolinsites.com

Julannah L. Gregory, RN, BSN
Title: Registered Nurse **Company:** Department of Education **Address:** 790 East New York Avenue, Brooklyn, NY 11203 United States **BUS:** Public School Agency Dedicated to Excellence in Regular and Special Education **P/S:** Regular Core Curriculum Including Reading, Mathematics, English, Science, Social Studies, Art, Music, Physical Education **MA:** Local **D/D/R:** Health Assessments, Reviewing Physician's Notes, Working with Special Needs Children, Handling Counseling, Working on a Team with a Social Worker **H/I/S:** Playing Jazz Music **EDU:** Registered Nursing Degree, Kingsborough Community College (2000); Bachelor of Science in Nursing, Downstate Medical Center (2002); Pursuing Master of Science in Nursing Degree, Molloy College **A/A/S:** American Nurses Association
Email: jacemcgregor@aol.com

Ann Greiner
Title: Owner **Company:** Greiner Floor Covering **Address:** 2241 W. Johnson Road, Ludington, MI 49431 United States **BUS:** Floor Covering Company **P/S:** Sales and Installation of Floor Coverings **MA:** Local **D/D/R:** Designing, Managing Business Operations **H/I/S:** Gardening, Golfing, Canning, Cooking **EDU:** Associate Degree in Nursing, West Shore Community College **A/A/S:** Chamber of Commerce; Zonta International; Business Network International **C/VW:** The Humane Society, Nature Conservatory, American Cancer Society, Local Fire Department, Special Olympics
Email: ann@greinerfloorcovering.com
URL: http://www.greinerfloorcovering.com

Charlene A. Grendze
Title: Assessor, Office Manager **Company:** Webster Township **Address:** 5665 Webster Church Road, Dexter, MI 48130 United States **BUS:** Local Government **P/S:** Community Service **MA:** Local **D/D/R:** Community Service, Assisting in Tax Collection, Office Management, Certified Assessor, 1976 **H/I/S:** Spending Time with Family, Participating in Girl Scouts of America, Boating **EDU:** Industry Related Training and Experience **A/A/S:** Board of Directors, Girl Scouts of the U.S.A., Huron Valley Council **A/H:** Many Awards, Girl Scouts of America
Email: cgrendze@twp.webster.mi.us
URL: http://www.twp.webster.mi.us

Catherine L. Grider
Title: School Lead Teacher **Company:** Charles Wright Academy **Address:** 7723 Chambers Creek Road W., University Place, WA 98467 United States **BUS:** School **P/S:** Education **MA:** Local **EXP:** Ms. Grider's expertise is in early childhood education. **H/I/S:** Jogging, Painting **EDU:** Master's Degree in Educational Technology, City University **CERTS:** Certification in Special Education **A/A/S:** Washington Education Association **C/VW:** Children's Schools, Bikers Against Child Abuse
Email: cdgrider@comcast.net
URL: http://www.charleswright.org

Lynn Grier

Title: Educator **Company:** St. Gabriel School **Address:** 2550 41st Avenue, San Francisco, CA 94116 United States **BUS:** Catholic Elementary Education Facility **P/S:** Education for Students in Kindergarten through Eighth-Grade **MA:** Regional **D/D/R:** Teaching Social Studies and Literature to Seventh and Eighth-grade Students, Running the Student Council and the Academic Decathlon **H/I/S:** Reading **EDU:** Master's Degree in Education, University of San Francisco (1980); Credentialed in Administrative Services **A/A/S:** Published in Teachers Guide; National Catholic Educators Association; Board Member, YMCA
Email: lgrier714@aol.com
URL: http://www.stgabrielsf.com

Christopher J. Griffin

Title: President, Chief Executive Officer **Company:** Consultant **Address:** 2005 Franke Court, Suite D, Augusta, GA 30909 United States **BUS:** Consulting in Construction Industry **P/S:** Commercial and Residential Construction **MA:** National **EXP:** Mr. Griffin's expertise is in commercial construction. **H/I/S:** Spending Time with his Two Children, Flying Airplanes, **EDU:** High School Education **A/A/S:** Columbia County Chamber of Commerce, AOPA Aircraft Owners and Pilots Association **C/VW:** Coaching his Son's Ice Hockey Team
Email: cjgriffin@live.com

Jane Griffin

Title: Owner, Designer **Company:** Nikole Kasey Originals **Address:** 18836 Halyard, Cornelius, NC 28031 United States **BUS:** Women's Accessories Retail **P/S:** Women's and home Accessories, custom designs **MA:** National **D/D/R:** Making Unique Designs **H/I/S:** Needlepoint Knitting **EDU:** Santa Barbara College **A/A/S:** Lake Norman Art League, TNNA, Needlework Association
Email: sandi@nikolekasey.com
URL: www.nikolekasey.com

Maureen E. Griffin

Title: 1) Salon Owner 2) Licensed Real Estate Broker **Company:** 1) Life-Styles Salon, Inc. 2) MGM Real Estate Service **Address:** 556 Enfield Street, Enfield, CT 06082 United States **BUS:** 1) Personal Care Center 2) Real Estate Agency **P/S:** 1) Hair and Skin Care, Body Treatments 2) Real Estate Exchange, Consulting Services **MA:** Connecticut **D/D/R:** Offering Hair Care, Designing, Managing Business Operations, Purchasing Real Estate Properties **H/I/S:** Practicing Yoga and Jin Shin Jyutsu, Bicycling, Reading, Designing Jewelry, Praying **CERTS:** Licensed Realtor, State of Connecticut; Licensed Cosmetologist, State of Connecticut; Certification in Jin Shin Jyutsu **A/A/S:** National Cosmetology Association; Greater Hartford Association of Realtors; National Association of Realtors; Connecticut Assn of Realtors; National Association of Professional Women; Jin Shin Jyutsu **C/VW:** American Cancer Society; Look Good Feel Better Program; Disabled American Veterans
Email: melena50@sbcglobal.net
URL: http://mgmrealestate.ctmls.mlxchange.com

Stephanie L. Griffin

Title: Dental Hygienist **Company:** Dr. James P. Retzer, DDS, Family Dentistry **Address:** 2 Birch Road, Cedar Crest, NM 87008 United States **BUS:** Dental Office **P/S:** Family Dentistry **MA:** Local **EXP:** Ms. Griffin's expertise is in dental hygiene. **H/I/S:** Spending Time with Children **EDU:** Associate of Science in Dental Hygiene, University of New Mexico
Email: slgbe@aol.com
URL: http://www.cambridgewhoswho.com

Georgette B. Griffith

Title: Owner, Teacher, Mentor **Company:** The Woodland Brook Studio **Address:** Rural Route 1, Box 205E, Lost Creek, WV 26385 United States **BUS:** Art Studio **P/S:** Artwork and Graphic Designs such as Hat, Note Cards, Logo Designs and Education **MA:** National **D/D/R:** Creating Artwork Using Pencil and Ink, Watercolors, Acrylic and Oil Paints, Designing, Teaching **H/I/S:** Traveling, Fly Fishing **EDU:** Bachelor of Arts in Secondary Education, Plus 40, West Liberty State College; Coursework in Speech Therapy and Speech Arts, Plus 40, Hofstra University **A/A/S:** West Virginia Art Association; West Virginia Education Association; Alpha Delta Kappa **A/H:** Teacher of the Year Award (2003); Teacher of the Year Award (1997-1998); Teacher of the Year Award (1991) **C/VW:** Local Hospital; Sheriff's Department; HUGGED
Email: woodlandbrook@sunlitsurf.com
URL: http://www.cambridgewhoswho.com

Lisa Griffith, RN

Title: Patient Care Coordinator **Company:** Allen County Hospital **Address:** 101 S. Street, Iola, KS 66749 United States **BUS:** Hospital **P/S:** Healthcare **MA:** Iola, Kansas **D/D/R:** Managing the Staff, Emergency Room Department, Respiratory Therapy Department and Oncology Day Clinic, Coordinating Patient Care **H/I/S:** Spending Time with her Family **EDU:** Associate Degree in Applied Science and Nursing, Neosho County Community College **CERTS:** Certification in NACLS, Trauma Nursing Core Course, Pediatric Advanced Life Support, Advanced Cardiac Life Support and CPR **A/A/S:** Emergency Nurses Association **C/VW:** Board, Living Opportunities for the Handicapped; Tri-Valley Handicapped Association
Email: lisa.griffith@hcamidwest.com

Jay L. Griggs

Title: Event Director **Company:** IntegraSys **Address:** 2601 Network Boulevard, Frisco, TX 75034 United States **BUS:** Software Development Advertising, Marketing, Public Relations and Data Processing **P/S:** Software Development of Credit Union Software **MA:** National **D/D/R:** Marketing, Overall strategy and direction for conferences, trade shows, small client events. Has Staff to execute the direction **H/I/S:** Sports, Interior Design **EDU:** Howard Payne University, BBA-1990; **A/A/S:** Christian Church **C/VW:** Church, Habitat for Humanity
Email: jjay_puddin@yahoo.com

Ashot Grigoryan

Title: Senior Loan Consultant **Company:** First Capital Financial Resources, Inc. **Address:** 2727 W. Alameda Avenue, Burbank, CA 91505 United States **BUS:** Mortgage and Real Estate Company **P/S:** Mortgage and Real Estate Services **EXP:** Mr. Grigoryan's expertise includes real estate and mortgage management. **H/I/S:** Fishing, Playing Golf **EDU:** Master of Economics, University of Armenia (1999)
Email: ashotgrigoryan@yahoo.com
URL: http://www.firstcapital.com

Karen A. Grimley, MBA, RN, FACHE

Title: Director of Clinical Consulting **Company:** Broadlane, Inc. **Address:** 13737 Noel Road, Dallas, TX 75240 United States **BUS:** Healthcare Company Committed to Addressing Fundamental Provider Issues with New Business Approaches and Innovative Technologies **P/S:** High Quality Transformational Business Services, Capital Equipment Services, Clinical Services, Contracting Services, Information Services, Labor Services, Pharmacy Services, Purchasing Services, Operational Experts **MA:** International **D/D/R:** Healthcare Consulting, Improving Patient Outcome, Overseeing Clinical Requirements, Focusing on Patient Safety **H/I/S:** Golfing, Cooking **EDU:** Master of Business Administration, Anna Maria College **A/A/S:** American College of Healthcare Executives; American Organization of Nurse Executives
Email: karen.grimley@broadlane.com
URL: http://www.broadlane.com

Linda A. Grimm

Title: PT **Company:** Aurora Public School **Address:** 647 Laredo Street, Aurora, CO 80011 United States **BUS:** Education School **P/S:** Education **MA:** Local **D/D/R:** Teaching Special Needs Children **H/I/S:** Plays piano, violin, scrapbooks, photography, skiing, learning German **EDU:** University of Colorado, Bachelor's Degree in Physical Therapy **A/A/S:** University of Colorado Health Science Ambassador
Email: lindagrim@aol.com

James Robert Grimord

Title: Director of Learning Services **Company:** Quinebaug Valley Community College **Address:** 742 Upper Maple Street, Danielson, CT 06239 United States **BUS:** Community College **P/S:** Higher Education **MA:** Regional **D/D/R:** Overseeing all Student Services, Transfer Advising, Assisting the Disabled, Managing the Learning Center, Managing Students and their Activities **H/I/S:** Golfing, Riding his Motorcycling **EDU:** Master of Science in Education, Central Connecticut State University **A/A/S:** Governing Board Member, New England Transfer Association; P.G.K. Knights of Columbus; Association on Higher Education and Disability
Email: jgrimord@qvcc.commnet.edu
URL: http://www.qvcc.commnet.edu

Lilia M. Grinston

Title: Operator, Drafter (Retired) **Company:** AT&T **Address:** 3444 Penfield Road, Columbus, OH 43227 United States **BUS:** Communications Company **P/S:** Internet, Home Phone, Wireless, Digital Television Services **MA:** National **D/D/R:** Operating Phones, Drafting, Computer Data Entry **H/I/S:** Volunteering at Church Ministries, Reading **EDU:** Pursuing Coursework in Consulting **A/A/S:** Christ Memorial Baptist Church
Email: liliagrinston@yahoo.com
URL: http://www.att.com

Richard F. Groeber

Title: Weather Observer **Company:** Dick's Weather Service **Address:** 1452 North Limestone Street, Springfield, OH 45503 United States **BUS:** Meteorology **P/S:** Local Weather Data, Research **MA:** Regional **D/D/R:** Weather Reporting, Weather Services **H/I/S:** Walking, Movies, Baseball **EDU:** Associate Degree, Urbana University **A/A/S:** American Meteorological Society, National Weather Association
Email: dickswxq@aol.com
URL: http://www.dicksweatherservice.com

Terence Michael Grogan

Title: Supervising Physician **Company:** Aurora Medical Group **Address:** 980 S. Saint Augustine Street, Pulaski, WI 54162 United States **BUS:** Healthcare Company **P/S:** Healthcare **MA:** Local **EXP:** Mr. Grogan's expertise includes family medicine, mid-level supervision and osteopathic medicine. **H/I/S:** Playing Golf and Tennis, Playing the Guitar, Riding Motorcycles **EDU:** Doctor of Osteopathic Medicine, Philadelphia College of Osteopathic Medicine; Master of Electrical Engineering, Naval Postgraduate School, Monterey, California; Bachelor of Science in Psychology, Michigan State University **A/A/S:** American Osteopathic Association; American Academy of Family Physicians; American Academy of Osteopathy; Wisconsin Society of Family Practice; Wisconsin Association of Osteopathic Physicians & Surgeons; American Legion **C/VW:** Food Bank of Green Bay
Email: drtmgrogan@aol.com
URL: http://www.cambridgewhoswho.com

Elaine C. Grose

Title: Science Laboratory Manager, Assistant Professor **Company:** Neumann College **Address:** One Neumann Drive, Aston, PA 19014 United States **BUS:** College **P/S:** Higher Education **MA:** International **D/D/R:** Teaching Environmental Science **H/I/S:** Reading, Golfing **EDU:** Ph.D. in Environmental Toxicology, North Carolina State University; Master's Degree in Biology, North Carolina State University; Bachelor of Science in Education, SUNY Cortland **C/VW:** St. Vince DePaul
Email: grosee@neumann.edu
URL: http://www.neumann.edu

Becky L. Gross

Title: Senior Sales Representative **Company:** GlaxoSmithKline **Address:** 5 Moore Drive, Research Triangle Park, NC 27709 United States **BUS:** Pharmaceutical Company **P/S:** Respiratory, Neurology, Vaccine Pharmaceuticals **MA:** International **EXP:** Ms. Gross' expertise includes marketing and sales. **H/I/S:** Traveling, Reading, Writing Books, Waterskiing, Snow Skiing **EDU:** Bachelor of Science in Nursing, West Texas A&M University **A/A/S:** TBN **C/VW:** Junior League, Church
Email: gigi@suddenlinkmail.com

Mrs. Yvonne A. Gross, RN

Title: Director of Nursing **Dept:** Nursing Administration **Address:** 613 Hammonds Lane, Brooklyn Park, MD 21225 United States **BUS:** Nursing Home **P/S:** Healthcare Services Including Occupational and Physical Therapy **MA:** Local **D/D/R:** Overseeing Operations for a 129-Bed Facility **H/I/S:** Collecting Decorative Eggs and Troll Figurines **EDU:** Pursuing Bachelor of Science in Nursing, University of Phoenix; Associate Degree in Nursing, Baltimore City College (2006) **CERTS:** Pursuing ICD-9 Coding Certification **C/VW:** Genesis Foundation
Email: newer7@comcast.net

Dr. Saul B. Grossmann

Title: Distinguished Lecturer (Retired) **Company:** Temple University **Dept:** College of Education **Address:** 19 First Avenue, Haddon Heights, NJ 08035 United States **BUS:** University **P/S:** Higher Education **MA:** Local **D/D/R:** Consulting, Teaching Education Policy and Leadership Studies **H/I/S:** Exercising, Practicing Tai Chi, Gardening **EDU:** Doctor of Education in Educational Administration, Temple University (1974) **CERTS:** Letter of Superintendency, State of Pennsylvania; Principal Certification, State of Pennsylvania; Secondary Teacher Certification, State of Pennsylvania **A/A/S:** American Association of School Administrators; Association of School Business Officials International; American Educational Research Association; Phi Delta Kappa International **A/H:** Outstanding Alumnus, West Philadelphia High School (2002); Silver Beaver Award, Boy Scouts of America (1995); Award for his Commitment to Education, Schoolmen's Club of Philadelphia (1992); National Youth Services Award (1998); Merit Award, The Pennsylvania Horticultural Society (1985); Educator of Excellence (1983); Achievement Award, National Association for the Advancement of Colored People **C/VW:** Board of Directors, Stanfill Towers (2008); Vice President, United Synagogue, Mid-Atlantic Region (2002-2006); President, Temple Beth Sholom (1999-2001); Board of Directors, Children's Services, Inc. (1988-1999); Vice President, Liberty Council, Boy Scouts of America (1988-1997); President, Friends of Haddon Heights Public Library (1974-1976)
Email: saulmir@comcast.net
URL: http://www.temple.edu/education

Barbara P. Groth
Title: Social Services Project Coordinator, Nutritionist Company: City of Burbank Address: 1301 W. Olive Avenue, Burbank, CA 91506 United States BUS: Government Organization P/S: Public Service Including Organizing Summer Recreation and Nutrition Program Classes MA: Local D/D/R: Overseeing Administrative Ring Duties Including Organizing Nutrition Programs for the Elderly, Reviewing Products and Menus with Employees and Grant Writing H/I/S: Gardening EDU: Bachelor of Science in Nutrition, Notre Dame de Namur University, Belmont, CA, Magna Cum Laude (1976) A/A/S: Los Angeles District, American Dietetic Association; California Dietetic Association
Email: bgroth@ci.burbank.ca.us
URL: http://www.ci.burbank.ca.us

Mr. Brooks L. Grotte
Title: Credit Analyst Company: Bremer Financial Corporation Dept: Credit Department Address: 3100 S. Columbia Road, Grand Forks, ND 58201 United States BUS: Bank P/S: Banking and Financial Services MA: Wisconsin, Minnesota, North Dakota D/D/R: Underwriting, Performing Credit Analyses H/I/S: Fishing, Hunting EDU: Bachelor of Business Administration in Management, Banking, Finance and Economics, The University of North Dakota; Bachelor of Business in Finance, The University of North Dakota C/VW: United Way of America; Relay For Life, American Cancer Society
Email: blgrotte@bremer.com
URL: http://www.bremer.com

Janis E. Grubb
Title: Owner Company: Queen Anne's Garden Nursery Address: 845 Applegate Road, Atwater, CA 95301 United States BUS: Nursery P/S: Roses, Trees, Garden Arts, Perennials MA: Local D/D/R: Managing Business Operations H/I/S: Playing the Violin, Gardening, Collecting Charles Wysocki Art Prints and Honey Jars EDU: Diploma, Atwater High School A/A/S: California Association of Nurseries and Garden Centers; California Women for Agriculture; FFA; Merced County Farm Bureau C/VW: Local High School Programs; 4-H Club
Email: sgrubb@inreach.com

Monika Grudek
Title: Chief Executive Officer Company: BAK Research, Inc., Safe Hire Consulting, Inc. Address: 1320 Rock Cove Court, Hoffman Estates, IL 60192 United States BUS: Background Screening Company P/S: Background Checks, Court Records, Research MA: National D/D/R: Professional Background Screening, Pre-Employment Screening H/I/S: Reading, Traveling, Golfing EDU: Pursuing Bachelor's Degree in Business Administration, Harper College, IL A/A/S: National Association of Professional Background Screeners; Board of Directors Board Secretary, Polish-American Chamber of Commerce
Email: monika@safehireconsulting.com
URL: http://www.safehireconsulting.com

Pamela J. Grundstad
Title: Vocal Music Director Company: Boone Community School District Address: 500 Seventh Street, Boone, IA 50036 United States BUS: School District P/S: Education MA: Local D/D/R: Teaching Vocal Music H/I/S: Bird Watching, Quilting, Gardening EDU: Master of Arts in Music Education, Truman State University A/A/S: National Association for Music Education; American Choral Directors Association C/VW: Habitat for Humanity
Email: pgrundstad@boone.k12.ia.us
URL: http://www.cambridgewhoswho.com

Robert A. Grzelak
Title: Information Technology Business Consultant Company: John Hancock Address: 601 Congress Street, Boston, MA 02210 United States BUS: Finance and Insurance Company P/S: Financial Services and Products, Insurance and Annuities MA: Regional D/D/R: Running Information Technology Systems, Selling Financial Products H/I/S: Teaching Spin Class EDU: Bachelor's Degree in Actuarial Science, University of Illinois C/VW: Community Service
Email: bgrzelak@jhancock.com

Alma Dalia Guardian
Title: Teacher Company: Hebbronville Elementary School Address: 210 W. Lucille Street, Hebbronville, TX 78361 United States BUS: Public Elementary School Serving Residents of Hebbronville P/S: Public Elementary Education for Local Students MA: Local D/D/R: Practicing a Hands-On Approach to Teaching Very Young Children, Using Music to Encourage Children to Move Around, Using Books to Aid in Developing Vocabulary H/I/S: Reading, Spending Time with her Family EDU: Bachelor's Degree in Interdisciplinary Studies, Texas A&M International University (1996) CERTS: Pursuing Speech Therapist Assistant Certification, Texas A&M International University A/A/S: Texas Education Agency; Licensed Speech-Language Pathologist and Audiologist; Certified in Prekindergarten through 12th-Grade Education; Certified in Special Education for Prekindergarten through 12th-Grade; Certified Bilingual Educator in Prekindergarten, Kindergarten and Eighth-Grade Spanish
Email: almag.cantu@tamiu.edu

Cristina M. Guarneri
Title: Founder Company: Angel's Promise Address: West Paterson, NJ 07424 United States BUS: Publishing Company P/S: Children's Books with Profits to Benefit the Ministry MA: International D/D/R: Used to be a Guidance Counselor on High School Level in Paterson School District, Excels at Working with Students on all Levels from Academic, Social and Emotional with Angel's Promise, She Meets with Illustrators, Publishers and Books are Available Through Amazon, Barnes and Noble and Borders H/I/S: Reading, Authoring Books EDU: Seton Hall University, Mont Clair State University, Finishing Doctorate in Education, Post Master's Degree in Counseling, MA in Counseling and BA in Psychology CERTS: Certified School Counselor, Getting Licensed to do Private Counseling A/A/S: ACA, Kappa Delta Pi, National Honor Society for Education
Email: sunset1667@aol.com
Email: angelspromise@yahoo.net

Maureen C. Gubbels
Title: Registered Nurse Company: Methodist Hospital Address: 8511 W. Dodge Street, Omaha, NE 68114 United States BUS: Nonprofit Hospital P/S: Healthcare MA: Local EXP: Ms. Gubbels' expertise is in gerontology. H/I/S: Volunteering, Crocheting, Exercising, Cooking EDU: Bachelor of Science in Biology, Dana College; Bachelor of Science in Nursing, Creighton University CERTS: Pursuing Certification in Gerontology C/VW: Eastern Nebraska Office on Aging
Email: maureenc99@yahoo.com

Mr. Kyle R. Guelcher, Esq.
Title: Attorney Company: The Law Office of Kyle R. Guelcher Address: 1350 Main Street, Third Floor, Springfield, MA 01103 United States BUS: Private Law Firm P/S: Legal Services MA: Local D/D/R: Overseeing Debt Collection for Big and Small Businesses, Practicing General Litigation, Intellectual Property and Business Legal Services, Writing Wills, Conducting Estate Work, Practicing Identity Theft Law, Motor Vehicle Law and Entertainment Law H/I/S: Running, Soccer EDU: JD, Western New England College School of Law (2002) A/A/S: Omicron Delta Kappa; Commercial Law League of America; Boston Bar Association; At-Large Director, Massachusetts Bar Association's Young Lawyers Division
Email: attorneyguelcher@yahoo.com
URL: http://cambridgewhoswho.com

Jane Guenther
Title: Coordinator Company: Catholic Charismatic Renewal Address: 10909 Saint Henry Lane, Saint Ann, MO 63074 United States BUS: Nonprofit Organization P/S: Healing, Life in the Spirit Seminars, Religious Retreats, Teaching Programs, Spiritual Direction MA: Regional D/D/R: Spiritual Direction, Organizing Retreat, Healing Work Conferences H/I/S: Sailing EDU: Master's Degree in Divinity, Aquinas Institute of Theology; Bachelor of Science in Architecture and Education, Webster University A/A/S: The National Charismatic Renewal Committee C/VW: American Diabetes Association
Email: janeguenther@archstl.org
URL: http://www.stlcharismatic.org

Ms. Monique Guerrero
Title: Officer in Charge of Group S-3 Current Operations Company: The 4th Psychological Operations Group Address: 1911 Building D, Fort Bragg, NC 28310 United States BUS: Military P/S: Psychological Operations for Non-Conventional Global Military Units and Information Support Teams for American Embassy's Worldwide MA: International D/D/R: Managing Business Operations, Coordinating Travel Programs H/I/S: Skiing, Motorcycling, Traveling EDU: Master of Arts, University of Oklahoma (2001) A/A/S: The Veterans of Foreign Wars of the United States; Blue Knights International Law Enforcement Motorcycle Club
Email: guerrerm@soc.mil
URL: http://www.cambridgewhoswho.com

Teresita A. Guevarra, RN, BSN
Title: RN, BSN Company: Paterson Division of Health Address: 4 Hoxsey Place, Haledon, NJ 07508 United States BUS: Human Services Department of Health P/S: Public Health Nursing MA: Local EXP: Ms. Guevarra's expertise is in long-term care. H/I/S: Watching Television EDU: RN, BSN A/A/S: Filipino American Nurses Association

Mrs. Earline J. Guidry
Title: Owner Company: God Unlimited Store House Address: 1943 N. Redondo Drive, Baton Rouge, LA 70815 United States BUS: Health and Nutrition Product Retailer P/S: Holistic Healthcare Products Including Herbs selling information on outdoor weddings MA: International D/D/R: Marketing and Retailing Products, Recruiting Distributors H/I/S: Singing, Reading, Playing the Keyboard, Exercising, Gardening EDU: Associate Degree in Business Administration, Delta School of Business (1972); Associate Degree in Business Administration, Heald Business College (1971); Associate Degree in Business Administration, Southern University of Baton Rouge (1970)
Email: eguidry4@cox.net
URL: http://www.godsstorehouseunlimited.com

Nicole Guiliani
Title: Owner, Esthetician Company: Jezebelle Day Spa Address: 3242 Adams Avenue, San Diego, CA 92116 United States BUS: Day Spa P/S: Facials, Body Wraps, Waxing, Microdermabrasion MA: Local EXP: Ms. Giuliani's expertise is in skin care. H/I/S: Traveling EDU: Associate of Arts in Fashion Merchandising, Fashion Careers of California C/VW: Kids in Touch
Email: nicoleguiliani@hotmail.com
URL: http://www.jezebelledayspa.com

Ramona Guin
Title: Assistant Professor Company: Louisiana Tech University Dept: Division of Nursing Address: 305 Wysteria Street, Ruston, LA 71270 United States BUS: Selective-Admissions Teaching and Research University P/S: Bachelor's, Master's and Doctoral Degrees MA: Regional D/D/R: Nursing, Teaching Clinical Nursing, Team Teaching, Working with Students in Community Service Setting and Emergency Nursing H/I/S: Herbal Medicine, Riding Horses, Swimming EDU: Master of Science in Nursing, University of Phoenix (2002) CERTS: Sexual Assault Nurse Examiner, University of California at Riverside (2006); Certified Legal Nurse Consultant, Vicki Milazzo Training Institute (1997) A/A/S: Board Member, Louisiana State Nurses Association; Association of Forensic Nurse; National Organization for Associate Degree Nursing; Louisiana Organization for Associate Degree Nursing; Chairwoman, Clinical Practice Council, Louisiana State Nurses Association; Beta Chi Chapter, Sigma Theta Tau
Email: rguin@latech.edu
URL: http://www.latech.edu

Shaney M. Gulick
Title: Staff Nuclear Pharmacist Company: GE Healthcare Address: 7920 Elmbrook Drive, Suite 116, Dallas, TX 75247 United States BUS: Healthcare Manufacturing P/S: Nuclear Pharmacy, Medical Diagnostics, Diagnostic Imaging, Life Sciences, Medical Research and Development, Disease Management, Drug Testing and Screening, Biopharmaceutical Manufacturing MA: National D/D/R: Processing Radioactive Material, Preparing Material for use in Medical Imaging and Diagnostics Including X-Rays, Nuclear Medicines and Cancer Therapy, Maintaining Radioactive Material's Safety, Identifying and Adhering to All Rules and Regulations H/I/S: Spending Time with her Family, Enjoying Music, Scrapbooking EDU: Doctor of Pharmacy, Purdue University, Indiana (2003) A/A/S: Society of Nuclear Medicine; Adjunct Professor, Nuclear Medicine Technology Program, Baylor University
Email: shaney@gulick.com
URL: http://www.amersham.com/index.html

Ann E. Gulyas
Title: Inpatient Rehabilitation Professional Company: University Hospital Address: 150 Bergen Street, Newark, NJ 07103 United States BUS: Hospital P/S: Healthcare MA: National D/D/R: Managing Clinical Operations, Overseeing the Staff, Performing Administrative Duties H/I/S: Traveling, Horseback Riding EDU: Master's Degree in Speech-Language Pathology, Kent State University CERTS: Board Certified Specialist in Swallowing Disorders A/A/S: New Jersey Speech-Language Hearing Association; American Speech-Language-Hearing Association C/VW: Multiple Sclerosis Society; American Heart Association
Email: aegulyas@aol.com
URL: http://www.cambridgewhoswho.com

Julie R. Gunn, RN, CLNC
Title: Registered Nurse, Certified Legal Nurse Consultant, Owner Company: J.R. Gunn and Associates Address: P.O. Box 946, Greenwood, IN 46142 United States BUS: Medical and Legal Consulting Company P/S: Obstetrical, Gynecological and Infertility Services, Long-Term Care Nursing, Ambulatory Clinical Management, Certified Legal Nurse Consulting MA: National D/D/R: Consulting H/I/S: Playing the Piano, Singing as a Soloist in the Church Choir, Attending her Son's Sporting Events EDU: Diploma in Nursing, Marion County General Hospital School of Nursing (1974) CERTS: Certified Nurse Examiner, Planned Parenthood, East Central Indiana; Certified Breast Exam Instructor, American Cancer Society; Certified Legal Nurse Consultant A/A/S: National Alliance of Certified Legal Nurse Consultants; Greater Indianapolis Chamber of Commerce; Better Business Bureau C/VW: Missionary Work
Email: jewel53@comcast.net
URL: http://www.jrgunnandassociates.com

Jin Liang Guo
Title: Physician Assistant Company: US Healthworks Address: 4320 196th Street S.W., Suite D, Lynnwood, WA 98036 United States BUS: Healthcare Clinic P/S: Family Practice MA: National EXP: Mr. Guo's expertise are in work-related industries. H/I/S: Fishing, Snowboarding, Hiking EDU: Pacific University, MS-Physician Assistant A/A/S: AAPA, WAPA
Email: jlguo@pacificu.edu

Sandra Gupton

Title: Registered Nurse, Legal Nurse Consultant **Address:** P.O. Box 111, Kingston, TN 37763 United States **BUS:** Sole Proprietorship **P/S:** Healthcare Consulting Services **MA:** Local **EXP:** Ms. Gupton's expertise includes cardio-diagnostics and radiology. **D/D/R:** Managing Cattle Operations, Offering Consulting Services **H/I/S:** Horseback Riding, Spending Time with her Family **EDU:** Bachelor of Science in Biology, Ohio State University **CERTS:** Registered Nurse, Roane State Community College **A/A/S:** Tennessee Nurses Association; Who's Who Among Students In American Universities and Colleges; Gamma Beta Phi **C/VW:** Local Church; Local Charitable Organizations; Habitat for Humanity; International Myeloma Foundation
Email: sandygupton@yahoo.com

Robert C. Gussman

Title: Health, Safety and Environmental Manager **Company:** Baker Hughes **Address:** 2001 Rankin Road, Houston, TX 77073 United States **BUS:** Energy Firm **P/S:** Oil and Gas Extraction **MA:** Los Angeles, Texas, Oklahoma **D/D/R:** Dealing with Health, Safety and Environmental Affairs **EDU:** Bachelor's Degree in Industrial Engineering, Lamar University, Beaumont, TX; Coursework in Hazardous Materials Management, Institute of Hazardous Materials Management **A/A/S:** The American Society of Safety Engineers **C/VW:** Child Advocates, Houston; Habitat for Humanity
Email: robert.gussman@bakerhuges.com
URL: http://www.bakerhughes.com

Ms. Lori A. Gustin

Title: Owner, Operator, Locksmith, Security Officer **Company:** Gustin Security Services **Address:** P.O. Box 70, Arkansas City, KS 67005 United States **BUS:** Locksmith and Security Services **P/S:** Locksmith, Security Services **MA:** Local **D/D/R:** Locksmith; Security; Quality Control **H/I/S:** Reading, Gardening, Automobiles **EDU:** Associate Degree in Criminal Justice, Connor State College **A/A/S:** American Legion; North American Hunt Club; Handyman Club of America **C/VW:** Habitat for Humanity
Email: lgustin@cox.net
URL: http://www.cambridgewhoswho.com

Susan M. Guth

Title: Clinical Care Coordinator **Company:** The Coordinating Center **Address:** 8258 Veterans Highway, Suite 13, Millersville, MD 21108 United States **BUS:** Nonprofit Healthcare Coordination Company **P/S:** Services for Individuals with Disabilities **MA:** Regional **D/D/R:** Pediatrics, Coordinating Training **H/I/S:** Traveling **EDU:** Master of Social Work, Marywood University **CERTS:** Certified Advanced Social Work Case Manager **A/A/S:** National Association of Social Workers
Email: sguth@coordinatingcenter.org
URL: http://www.coordinatingcenter.org

Linda K. Guthrie

Title: Special Needs Teacher **Company:** Denver Public Schools **Address:** 3185 S. Willow Court, Denver, CO 80231 United States **BUS:** Public School District **P/S:** Education **MA:** Local **D/D/R:** Teaching Disabled and Multi-disabled Students in Kindergarten through Fifth-Grade, Consulting **H/I/S:** Going on Cruises, Traveling, Going to the Symphony, Enjoying the Fine Arts **EDU:** Bachelor's Degree in Education, University of Northern Colorado **A/A/S:** Who's Who Among American Teachers (2005-2006); Colorado Education Association; National Education Association **A/H:** Mile High Teacher Award, City County of Denver (2006-2007); Most Valuable Teacher Award, Denver Public Schools (2003-2004); Outstanding Volunteer Award, Colorado Symphony Orchestra (1998) **C/VW:** Special Olympics
URL: http://www.cambridgewhoswho.com

Travis B. Guthrie

Title: Executive Director **Company:** Aries Realty and Development Corporation **Address:** 1325 San Marco Boulevard, Suite 401, Jacksonville, FL 32207 United States **BUS:** Construction Company **P/S:** Home Restoration, Selling and Buying Residential and Commercial Property **MA:** Regional **D/D/R:** Overseeing Daily Operations, Managing Daily Activities and Transactions **H/I/S:** Running, Swimming **EDU:** Degree in Finance and Marketing, University of North Florida
Email: tguthrie@theipm.com

Gabriella V. Gutierrez

Title: Certified Pharmacy Technician **Company:** ShopKo Stores Operating Company, LLC **Address:** 1190 N. Sixth Street, Monmouth, IL 61462 United States **BUS:** Retail Store **P/S:** Retail Services **MA:** Regional **D/D/R:** Developing Pharmaceutical Products **H/I/S:** Listening to Music, Reading **EDU:** Associate of Science, Carl Sandburg College **CERTS:** Certified Pharmacy Technician **C/VW:** Mount Calvary Lutheran Church
Email: gvgutierrez@hotmail.com
URL: http://www.cambridgewhoswho.com

Michael G. Gutierrez

Title: Managing Director **Company:** Standard & Poor's **Address:** 55 Water Street, New York, NY 10041 United States **BUS:** Finance Company **P/S:** Financial Services Including Credit Rating **MA:** International **EXP:** Mr. Gutierrez's expertise includes operational risk analysis and ranking. **H/I/S:** Listening to Music, Reading **EDU:** JD, Columbia University **A/A/S:** Mortgage Bankers Association **A/H:** National Hispanic Corporate Achievement Award (2006)
Email: michael_gutierrez@sandp.com
URL: http://www.standardandpoors.com

Rachel Gutierrez

Title: Director of Radiology **Company:** Ben Archer Health Center **Address:** P.O. Box 370, Hatch, NM 87937 United States **BUS:** Family Practice Clinic **P/S:** Medical Services for Underprivileged Community Members **MA:** Local **EXP:** Ms. Gutierrez's expertise includes radiology, transcription and supervisory skills. **H/I/S:** Bowling **EDU:** Pursuing Bachelor's Degree in Healthcare Administration, University of Phoenix; Associate Degree in Radiology, New Mexico State University
Email: gutierrezrtr@msn.com

Kit Gutierrez-Vilano

Title: Director of Catering **Company:** Doubletree Hotel **Address:** 2 Civic Plaza Drive, Carson, CA 90745 United States **BUS:** Hotel **P/S:** Hospitality **MA:** International **EXP:** Ms. Gutierrez-Vilano's expertise includes sales and operations. **H/I/S:** Cooking, Spending Time with her Children **EDU:** Bachelor's Degree in Business Administration, St. Paul's College **A/A/S:** Chamber of Commerce; NASE; National Association of Catering Executives **C/VW:** Teaching Kids to Care
Email: kvilano@carsondoubletree.com
URL: http://www.carsondoubletree.com

Allen R. Guy

Title: President **Company:** AG Plastics Associates **Address:** 10 Augusta Lane, West Columbia, TX 77486 United States **BUS:** Consulting Company **P/S:** Plastic Consulting Services **MA:** International **D/D/R:** Working with Polyolefins, Offering Consulting Services for Plastic Industries, Lecturing **H/I/S:** Fishing, Golfing **EDU:** Bachelor's Degree in Physics and Mathematics, Fort Hays State University **A/A/S:** Society of Plastics Engineers; Technical Association of the Pulp and Paper Industry; Society of Plastics Engineers; Tappe
Email: allanrguy@embarqmila.com

Susan Guyer

Title: Assistant Professor **Company:** Springfield College **Address:** 263 Alden Street, Springfield, MA 01109 United States **BUS:** College **P/S:** Higher Education, Athletic Healthcare **MA:** National **D/D/R:** Higher Education, Teaching Courses in Prevention of Athletic Injuries, Therapeutic Exercise **EDU:** Doctor of Physical Education, Springfield College; Master's Degree in Athletic Training, Old Dominion University; Bachelor of Science in Physical Education, Castletown State College **A/A/S:** President-Elect, Massachusetts Chapter, National Athletic Trainers' Association **C/VW:** American Heart Association
Email: mguyer@spfldcol.edu
URL: http://www.cambridgewhoswho.com

Diana Elizabeth Guzman

Title: Owner **Company:** Guzman's Used Cars **Address:** 1502 N. Kaufman Street, Seagoville, TX 75159 United States **BUS:** Automobiles Retail **P/S:** Motor Vehicle Dealership **MA:** Local **H/I/S:** Horseback Riding, Jogging, Camping, Hiking **EDU:** High School, Graduate
Email: dianaguzman01@yahoo.com

Ronald J. Gwodz

Title: President, Senior Consultant **Company:** G Systems, L.P. **Address:** 135 Dawes Highway, Pompton Lakes, NJ 07442 United States **BUS:** Business Development Consulting Company **P/S:** Marketing, Sales, Contracts Management, Program and Product Management, Proposal Preparation, Negotiations, Financial Audits, Training, Controls, Regulatory Compliance, Budgets, Sourcing, Supply Chain Technology, Legal, Operations, Policies and Procedures, Team Building, Strategic Planning **MA:** Regional **EXP:** Mr. Gwodz's expertise includes business development, sales, contracts management, program and product management and proposals. **D/D/R:** Marketing, Negotiating Contracts, Team Building, Strategic Planning **EDU:** Master of Business Administration, Fairleigh Dickinson University (1977); Bachelor of Science in Marketing, University of Bridgeport (1971) **A/A/S:** Honorary Co-Chairman, Business Advisory Council, Bush Administration, Washington, DC (204-2008); American Management Association (1980-2008); National Contract Management Association (1980-2008); Course Instructor, Advanced Business Management, Rutgers University, Newark, NJ (1978)
Email: ronald.gwodz@cwwemail.com
Email: rgwodz@optonline.net
URL: http://www.cambridgewhoswho.com

Robin Haas

Title: Licensed Clinical Social Worker, Owner **Company:** Robin Haas, LCSW **Address:** 747 Pontiac Avenue, Cranston, RI 02910 United States **BUS:** Social Work Practice **P/S:** Assistance with Child and Family Issues **MA:** Local **EXP:** Ms. Haas' expertise includes individual and family work, trauma and depression, foster care and adoption. **H/I/S:** Swimming, Baking Bread, Stained Glass, Creating Recipes **EDU:** Master of Social Work, Simmons College, School of Social Work; Bachelor of Science in Elementary Education, Boston University **A/A/S:** National Association of Social Workers **C/VW:** Human Rights Campaign, GLADD
Email: robin.haas@att.net
URL: http://www.cambridgewhoswho.com

Sandra E. Hachey, RN

Title: Registered Nurse **Company:** Genesis Healthcare **Address:** 32 Hospital Hill Road, Gardner, MA 01440 United States **BUS:** Quality Healthcare Facility **P/S:** Long-Term and Short-Term Care, Alzheimer's Care, Assisted Living, Specialty Services, Rehabilitation Therapy, Ventilator Care, Private Duty Array for Home Care, Hospice Care **MA:** Regional **D/D/R:** Overseeing Geriatric Rehabilitation and Alzheimer's Care Departments, Creating Optimum Environments for Patients and their Families, Compassionate Patient Care **EDU:** Associate of Science in Nursing, Atlantic Union College, South Lancaster, Massachusetts (1996)
Email: usarmy1221@comcast.com
URL: http://www.genesishcc.com

Mr. Wendlin Joe Hacker

Title: Self-Employed **Address:** P.O. Box 118, Vega, TX 79092 United States **BUS:** Organic Food Company **P/S:** Ranching and Farming of Organic Whole Grains **MA:** Regional **D/D/R:** Farming and Ranching Organically-Grown Whole Grains Including Long, Medium and Short Grains, Rice, Soft Wheat, Oats, Millet, Corn and Hard Red and White Winter Wheat, Overseeing All Purchasing, Designing Packaging **H/I/S:** Golfing, Hunting, Football, Basketball, Baseball, Going to Church, Spending Time with his Family of Four Boys and Two Girls **EDU:** Bachelor of Science in General Business, Minor in Accounting and Agriculture, Eastern New Mexico University (1956) **A/A/S:** President, Hereford Athletic Booster Club (1982-1985); Boy Scouts of America; Former Member, National Food Grower's Association **A/H:** Silver Bearer Award Recipient, Boy Scouts of America **C/VW:** Feed the Children; Former Little League Baseball Coach; Former President, Kids Inc.; Sunday School Teacher, Deacon, Elder, Board Member, Local Church

Gina S. Hackett

Title: Pharmacist **Company:** Rite Aid Pharmacy Store 6378 **Address:** 1863 Everglade Avenue, Clovis, CA 93619 United States **BUS:** Retail Pharmacy **P/S:** Prescription Refills, Personal Care, Nutrition, Wellness and Household Products **MA:** Regional **D/D/R:** Filling and Dispensing Prescription Medications, Offering Customer Service, Communicating with Doctors, Patient and Drug Information Counseling **H/I/S:** Spending Time with Family **EDU:** Doctor of Pharmacy, University of the Pacific (2000) **A/A/S:** Mbda Kappa Sigma
Email: hackettfam@sbcglobal.net
URL: http://www.riteaid.com

Vicki L. Hackett

Title: Teacher (Retired) **Company:** Northgate High School **BUS:** High School **P/S:** Education **D/D/R:** Writing Curriculum, Mentoring New Teachers, Consulting **H/I/S:** Gardening, Reading **EDU:** Bachelor of Arts in Education, University of Florida, Gainesville, FL (1967) **A/A/S:** National Council of Teachers of English; Teacher of the Year Award, Mount Diablo Unified School District (1996)
Email: vickita7@aol.com
Email: vicki.hackett@cwwemail.com
URL: http://www.cambridgewhoswho.com

Cassandra J. Haddox, DO

Title: Resident **Company:** Allegheny General Hospital **Address:** 2620 Grandview Avenue, Pittsburgh, PA 15235 United States **BUS:** Public General Hospital **P/S:** Inpatient and Outpatient Healthcare **MA:** Regional **D/D/R:** Emergency Medicine, Assessing and Treating Patients, Managing Ten to Twelve Nurses and Three to Four Medics **H/I/S:** Volleyball, Basketball **EDU:** Doctor of Osteopathy, Kansas City University of Medicine and Biosciences (2006); Bachelor of Science in Chemistry, Truman State University (2002) **A/A/S:** Alpha Chi Sigma; American Osteopathic Association; Psi Sigma Alpha; Sigma Sigma Phi; Phi Kappa Phi; Society for Academic Emergency Medicine
Email: cjo_12@yahoo.com
URL: http://www.wpahs.org/agh

Deborah A. Hadley

Title: Speech-Language Pathologist **Company:** EBS Healthcare **Address:** P.O. Box 911, Concordville, PA 19331 United States **BUS:** Staffing Agency **P/S:** Recruitment Service for Speech Therapists, Psychologists and Psychiatrists **MA:** National **EXP:** Ms. Hadley's expertise is in speech-language pathology. **D/D/R:** Training Speech Pathologists Regarding Current Advances and Methods to Assist Autistic Children, Evaluating and Treating Language Disabilities and Disorders **H/I/S:** Playing Tennis, Shopping, Reading **EDU:** Master of Arts in Communication Disorders, Saint Louis University (1994); Bachelor of Science, Saint Louis University (1992) **CERTS:** Licensed Speech-Language Pathologist, States of Texas and Missouri **A/A/S:** Texas Speech-Language-Hearing Association; Houston Association for Communication Disorders; Neuropsychology Division, American Speech-Language-Hearing Association; Delta Sigma Theta Sorority
Email: dahadley63112@sbcglobal.net
URL: http://www.cambridgewhoswho.com

Theresa C. Hafele

Title: Spanish Teacher **Address:** 20 Cairo Junction Road, Catskill, NY 12414 United States **BUS:** Education **P/S:** Spanish Language Instruction **MA:** Local **D/D/R:** Teaching Spanish to Ninth through 12th-Grade Students **H/I/S:** Kayaking, Horseback Riding, Hiking **EDU:** Master's Degree in Reading K-12, SUNY Oneonta; Master's Degree in Spanish K-12, SUNY Oneonta; Master's Degree in Elementary Education, SUNY Oneonta **A/A/S:** New York State Association of Foreign Language Teachers
Email: t.hafele@att.net

Lisa P. Hagans

Title: Health Information Director **Company:** Lallie Kemp Medical Center **Address:** 126 Alida Street, Hammond, LA 70403 United States **BUS:** Healthcare Hospital **P/S:** Medical Records **MA:** Local **EXP:** Ms. Hagans' expertise is in medical records. **H/I/S:** Music, Tennis, Surfing the Net **EDU:** Louisiana Tech University, BS in Medical Record Science **A/A/S:** American Health Information Management Association
Email: lhagans@lsuhsc.edu

Lisa Hager-Ochs

Title: Mid-Level Medical Practitioner, Physicians Assistant **BUS:** Medical Practice **P/S:** Healthcare **MA:** Local **D/D/R:** Rural Healthcare, Pediatrics, Building Relationships with Patients, Keeping Patients' Morale High **H/I/S:** Photography, Swimming, Hiking **EDU:** Pre Med Coursework, University of Cincinnati **CERTS:** Certification in Physician Assistant Studies, Cattering College of Medical Arts **A/A/S:** American Association of Physician Assistants **C/VW:** American Cancer Society, Alzheimer's Society, American Red Cross
Email: lnpochs@yahoo.com
URL: http://www.cambridgewhoswho.com

Gail Blake Hagler

Title: Writer **Company:** Self-Employed **Address:** 909 Burnley Road, Charlotte, NC 28210 United States **BUS:** Self-Employed **P/S:** Books, Poetry, Short Stories **MA:** Local **D/D/R:** Writing Short Stories **H/I/S:** Writing, Cooking **A/H:** Who's Who Best Poet (1987)
Email: gailhagler@aol.com
Email: gbla@yahoo.com
URL: http://www.cambridgewhoswho.com

Joachim Hagopian

Title: Marriage and Family Therapist **Company:** D'Veal Family and Youth Services **Address:** 1845 N. Fair Oaks Avenue, Pasadena, CA 91103 United States **BUS:** Healthcare Center **P/S:** Mental Healthcare Including Social Services **MA:** Local **D/D/R:** Counseling Individuals and Couples, Performing Family Therapy, Caring for Adolescents **H/I/S:** Astrology, Hiking, Camping, Playing and Watching Basketball, Traveling, Writing **EDU:** Master of Science in Psychology, California State University, Los Angeles; Bachelor of Science in Public Affairs, United States Military Academy **C/VW:** Environmental Causes; AIDS Research; Planned Parenthood
Email: jhagopian@dveal.com
URL: http://www.dveal.com

Connie C. Hahn

Title: Counseling Psychology **Company:** Healthy Resolutions, PLLC **Address:** 135 McKinley Avenue, Kellogg, ID 83837 United States **BUS:** Psychosocial Rehabilitation Center **P/S:** Behavioral Healthcare **MA:** Local **EXP:** Ms. Hahn's expertise is in psychosocial rehabilitation for individuals. **D/D/R:** Expanding on Life Skills, Overseeing Services for Medicaid and Mentally Challenged Individuals **H/I/S:** Walking **EDU:** Ph.D. in Counseling Psychology, Walden University (2000); Master of Counseling Psychology, University of Idaho (1992); Bachelor of Science in Psychology, University of Idaho (1986) **A/A/S:** Phi Delta Kappa; Psi Chi; National Autism Association; NPAA **C/VW:** Local Catholic Church; Local Charitable Organizations
Email: healthyresolutions@verizon.net
URL: http://www.cambridgewhoswho.com

Mr. Larry T. Hahn

Title: Vice President of Strategic Partnerships **Company:** Achieve 3000 **Address:** 6507 Circo Drive, Granbury, TX 76049 United States **BUS:** Educational Institution **P/S:** Web-Based Educational Services Including Individualized Learning Solutions Scientifically Proven to Accelerate Reading Comprehension, Vocabulary, Writing Proficiency and Performance on High-Stakes Tests **MA:** National **D/D/R:** Selling Web-Based Literacy Programs, Configuring Reading Materials for Schools, Working with Educational Leaders, State Association Partners and Corporate Personnel **H/I/S:** Golfing, Playing Football **EDU:** Master's Degree in Educational Administration, Abilene Christian University, TX (1985); Bachelor's Degree in Elementary Education, Minor in Reading, Abilene Christian University, TX (1982) **CERTS:** Superintendent Certification, Sul Ross State University, TX (1998)
Email: larry.hahn@achieve3000.com
URL: http://www.achieve3000.com

Brenda G. Haight

Title: Teacher **Company:** Iron County School District **Address:** 2077 W. Royal Hunte Drive, Cedar City, UT 84720 United States **BUS:** Public Elementary School **P/S:** Education **MA:** Local **D/D/R:** Teaching Second-Grade with Endorsements in Reading and Working with the Gifted and Talented **H/I/S:** Cooking, Sewing, Gardening, Doing Crafts, Reading **EDU:** Pursuing Master's Degree; Bachelor's Degree in Southern Utah State University **A/A/S:** Iron County Educators Association; Utah Educators Association; National Educators Association; National Association of Gifted and Talented; Utah Association of Gifted and Talented; Science Teachers of Utah; National Council of Teachers of Mathematics **C/VW:** Church, School
Email: brenda.haigh@iron.k12.ut.us
URL: http://www.cambridgewhoswho.com

Bambi E. Haines

Title: Licensed Practical Nurse **Company:** Golden Living Center, Shippenville **Address:** 21158 Paint Boulevard, Shippenville, PA 16254 United States **BUS:** Long-Term Care Facility **P/S:** Long-Term Care **MA:** Local **D/D/R:** Offering Care for Alzheimer's Patients **H/I/S:** Participating in Activities with her Children **EDU:** High School Graduate **CERTS:** Licensed Practical Nurse, Clarion County Career Center
Email: sbhaines@usachoice.com
URL: http://www.cambridgewhoswho.com

Lola B. Haines

Title: Owner **Company:** Wilco Investments **Address:** 1795 Shepherd of the Hills Expressway, Branson, MO 65616 United States **BUS:** Construction Company **P/S:** Excavating, Utility Lines, Electrical Parts **MA:** Local **D/D/R:** Maintaining the Budget, Secretarial Duties **H/I/S:** Sewing, Working at Thrift Shops **EDU:** Coursework, Northeast Missouri College, Kirksville, Missouri

Enayat Hakim-Elahi, MD, MS

Title: MD **Company:** Elmhurst Hospital Center **Address:** 7901 Broadway, Room C-510, Elmhurst, NY 11373 United States **BUS:** Hospital **P/S:** Acute-Care, Long-Term Care, Emergency Room, Maternal and Child Healthcare Education **MA:** Regional **D/D/R:** Since 1972, Consulting Obstetrics and Gynecology Patients, Educating Medical Students in Operating Room **H/I/S:** Traveling, Swimming **EDU:** Master's Degree in Public Administration and Advanced Medical Management (2004); MD, Tehran University of Medical Science (1959) **CERTS:** Certified Obstetrician, Gynecologist (1979); Certification in Quality Assurance and Utilization Management **A/A/S:** The American College of Obstetricians and Gynecologists; American College of Surgeons; American Society for Colposcopy and Cervical Pathology
Email: hakime@nychhc.org
URL: http://nyc.gov/html/hhc/qhn/html/ehc.html

Todd M. Halacy

Title: District Urban Programs Manager **Company:** Virginia Department of Transportation **Address:** 1700 N. Main Street, Suffolk, VA 23434 United States **BUS:** Government Agency **P/S:** Transportation **MA:** Regional to Hampton ROADS **EXP:** Mr. Halacy's experience is in project management. **D/D/R:** Overseeing Multi-Million Dollar Projects in the Hampton Roads Region **H/I/S:** Boating **EDU:** Bachelor's Degree in Civil Engineering (2001) **CERTS:** 2007, Licensed Professional Engineer for the Commonwealth of Virginia **A/A/S:** American Society of Civil Engineers; American Society of Highway Engineers
Email: Todd.Halacy@vdot.virginia.gov
URL: http://www.virginiadot.org

Kristen Haldeman Kauffman

Title: Chief Executive Officer **Company:** Smooth Business Systems, Inc. **Address:** P.O. Box 202378, Denver, CO 80220 United States **BUS:** Management Consulting Firm **P/S:** Small Business Consultations, Designing Services, Marketing Business Plans, Implement Filing and Accounting Systems, Satellite Office, Installation Services **MA:** National **D/D/R:** Analyzing and Establishing Small Businesses, Marketing, Hiring Subcontractors, Managing Projects, Overseeing Design Efficiency, Implementing Strategic Plans **H/I/S:** White Water Rafting **EDU:** Master's Degree in Finance, University of Colorado at Denver (2003) **A/A/S:** Project Management Institute
Email: kristen@smoothbusinesssystems.com
URL: http://www.smoothbusinesssystems.com

Elaine D. Hale

Title: Circulation Manager, Typesetter **Company:** The Cash-Book Journal **Address:** 210 W. Main Street, Jackson, MO 63755 United States **BUS:** Publisher **P/S:** Community Newspaper and Newsletter **MA:** Regional **D/D/R:** Entering Data, Assisting Customers, Typesetting, Writing Obituaries, Engagement Announcements and Community News **H/I/S:** Reading, Writing, Restoring Old Homes, Campaigning **EDU:** High School Diploma **A/A/S:** Tea Society; Historical Society; Missouri Press Association; The Historical Association **C/VW:** Mothers Against Drunk Driving; Campaigning for Congresswoman Jo Ann Emerson
Email: keithlhale@charter.net
URL: http://www.cambridgewhoswho.com

Pamela A. Hale, RN, BSN

Title: Liver Transplant Coordinator **Company:** Tennessee Valley Healthcare System **Dept:** Nashville Campus VA Medical Center **Address:** 1310 24th Avenue S., Nashville, TN 37212 United States **BUS:** Government Agency **P/S:** Healthcare, Transplant Services **MA:** National **EXP:** Ms. Hale's expertise is in nursing. **D/D/R:** Arranging Liver Transplants, Scheduling Operating Rooms and Registered Nurses **H/I/S:** Scrapbooking, Selling Longaberger Baskets **EDU:** Bachelor of Science in Nursing, North Park University **CERTS:** Registered Nurse **A/A/S:** Association of periOperative Registered Nurses; American Association for the Study of Liver Diseases; Ducks Unlimited; Veteran, United States Military **C/VW:** Local Church, Tennessee Donor Services; American Liver Foundation; Women in Military Service Memorial
Email: pamela.hale@va.gov
URL: http://vaww.tvhs.med.va.gov/

Carol Haley

Title: Learning Disabilities Teacher **Company:** Nashville Grade School **Address:** 750 E. Gorman Street, Nashville, IL 62263 United States **BUS:** Public School **P/S:** Education **MA:** Local **D/D/R:** Teaching Early Elementary Education to Students with Learning Disabilities **H/I/S:** Reading, Solving Word Puzzles, Playing Sports with her Children **EDU:** Master's Degree Plus18 in Elementary Education, Southern University at Edwardsville; Bachelor's Degree in Special Education, MacMurray College **C/VW:** Church, Boy Scouts of America, Washington County Right to Life, American Cancer Society
Email: chaley@washington.k12.il.us
URL: http://www.cambridgewhoswho.com

Elaine M. Halka

Title: Registered Nurse **Company:** Metrowest Medical Center **Address:** 115 Lincoln Center, Framingham, MA 01702 United States **BUS:** Medical Center **P/S:** Healthcare **MA:** Local **D/D/R:** Her expertise is in overseeing medical surgical nursing. **H/I/S:** Photography, Gardening **EDU:** Bachelor of Science in Nursing, SUNY New Paltz **CERTS:** Diploma in Nursing, Bellevue and Mills Schools of Nursing (1964)
Email: elaine.halka@cwwemail.com

Barbara L. Hall

Title: Vice President of Commercial Claims **Company:** Marine Claims Services, Inc. **Address:** 4226 Coronado Avenue, Stockton, CA 95204 United States **BUS:** Third Party Claims Administrator Specializing in the Commercial and Recreational Marine Industry **P/S:** Complete Claims Management Solutions for Insurance Companies **MA:** National **D/D/R:** Handling Marine Claims Services Including Boat Repair, Marina Issues and Lending Boaters Assistance with Any Issues, Former President of Modesto Claims Association, Former Vice President of Claims Conference of Northern California **H/I/S:** Writing Articles for Marine Publications **EDU:** Industry Related Training and Experience **A/A/S:** Vintage Claims Association; Mid-Valley Claims Association; Board Member, Combined Claims Conference, Inc.; Claims Conference of Northern California; Claims Conference Security Committee
Email: barbara@mcsclaims.com
URL: http://www.mcsclaims.com

Mrs. Debbie G. Hall

Title: Owner **Company:** Debbie's Jewels **Address:** 125 S. Jefferson Street, Perry, FL 32347 United States **BUS:** Retail Gift Shop **P/S:** Sterling Silver and Pandora Jewelry, Vera Bradley Designs, Thymes, Woodwick Candles, Gift and Wedding Registries, Arthur Court Designs Including Aluminum Serving Pieces, Lenox casual dinnerware, Noritake Including Casual, Stemware and Formal Dinnerware, Flatware **MA:** Local **D/D/R:** Overseeing Customer Service, Offering Fine Gifts with a Personal Touch, Controlling Inventory, Managing Accounts Payable and Receivable, Overseeing the Staff, Advertising, Marketing **H/I/S:** Shopping, Antiquing, Going to the Beach, Family and Friends **EDU:** Bachelor of Arts in Fashion Merchandising and Marketing, Florida State University-1982 **A/A/S:** Better Business Bureau, Taylor County Chamber of Commerce, **C/VW:** Breast Cancer Research, Local Sports Organizations, Relay for Life
Email: debbiesjewels2000@yahoo.com

Donna E. Hall

Title: Teacher **Company:** Shivers Junior High School **Address:** P.O. Box 607, Aberdeen, MS 39730 United States **BUS:** High School **P/S:** Secondary Education **MA:** Local **EXP:** Ms. Hall's expertise includes special education and the organization of special classes. **H/I/S:** Traveling **EDU:** Bachelor's Degree in Elementary Education, Shorter College **A/H:** Distinguished Teacher Award **C/VW:** The Good Samaritan Center
Email: djhallz@yahoo.com
URL: http://www.cambridgewhoswho.com

Dr. Gary D. Hall

Title: Plastic Surgeon **Company:** Advanced Cosmetic Surgery **Address:** 11401 Nall Avenue, Suite 216, Leawood, KS 66211 United States **BUS:** Cosmetic Surgery Clinic **P/S:** Cosmetic Surgery, Liposuction, Breast Augmentation **MA:** Regional **D/D/R:** Plastic Surgery, Consulting **H/I/S:** Sailing, Dining, Biking **EDU:** MD, University of Kansas (1988); Bachelor's Degree in Pharmacy, University of Missouri-Kansas City School of Pharmacy (1984) **A/A/S:** American Society of Plastic Surgeons; The American Society for Aesthetic Plastic Surgery; Fellow, American College of Surgeons; Treasurer, Kansas City Plastic Surgery Society
Email: info@hallmd.com
URL: http://www.hallmd.com

Larry C. Hall

Title: Owner, Operator **Company:** L.C. Hall Express, LLC **Address:** 209 Giddings Avenue, Windsor, CT 06095 United States **BUS:** Trucking Company **P/S:** Trucking **MA:** Local **D/D/R:** Delivering Goods and Services **H/I/S:** Playing Billiards, Riding his Bike **EDU:** Associate Degree, Manchester Community College
Email: larry.hall@cwwemail.com
URL: http://www.cambridgewhoswho.com

Marcia E. Hall, Ph.D.

Title: Women's Health and Military Sexual Trauma Program Director **Company:** U.S. Department of Veterans Affairs **Address:** 913 Garden Valley Boulevard, Roseburg, OR 97471 United States **BUS:** Government Organization **P/S:** Healthcare Services for Veterans **MA:** Regional **EXP:** Ms. Hall's expertise includes trauma therapy and program coordination. **D/D/R:** Resolving Mental Health Issues with Female Veterans and their Families **H/I/S:** Gardening, Caring for her Dog, Swimming **EDU:** Ph.D., Walden University (2005); Master's Degree in Health and Human Performance, San José State University **A/A/S:** American Public Health Association; Nursing Network on Violence Against Women, International
Email: marciah@jeffnet.org
URL: http://www.cambridgewhoswho.com

Nancy Hall

Title: Practice Manager **Company:** Forsyth Comprehensive Neurology **Address:** 2025 Frontis Plaza Boulevard, Suite 120, Winston Salem, NC 27103 United States **BUS:** Company Composed of Board-Certified Neurologists, Physician Assistants, Registered Nurses and Certified Medical Assistants Working Together as a Team to Offer Comprehensive Care for Patients with Neurological Disease or Injury **P/S:** Excellent Care and Advanced Treatment of a Wide-Array of Neurological Diseases **MA:** Regional **D/D/R:** Practicing Management, Overseeing Coding and Compliance, Running the Office, Addressing Human Resources Including Personnel Matters, Payroll, Accounts Receivable and Payable, Working with the Budget and the End-of-Year Finances **H/I/S:** Spending Time with her Family, Traveling **EDU:** Bachelor of Science in Healthcare, Bienville University (2002) **A/A/S:** American Academy of Professional Coders; Academy of Health Information Professionals; American Health Information Management Association
Email: nmhall@novanthealth.org
URL: http://www.forsythcomprehensiveneurology.com

Olga V. Hall

Title: IT Portfolio Manager, Web Venues **Company:** CSC **Address:** Westford, MA 01886 United States **BUS:** Information Technology Consulting Firm **P/S:** Information Technology Outsourcing **MA:** International **EXP:** Ms. Hall's expertise includes e-commerce, program management and information technology. **H/I/S:** Going to the Theater, Reading, Studying the History of the Roman Civilization **EDU:** Master of Arts in Linguistics, Moscow State Linguistics University **CERTS:** Certified Project Management Professional, Project Management Institute **A/A/S:** Project Management Institute; New England Java Users Group **C/VW:** West NET, Giving Technical Grants to Teachers and Students
Email: olga.hall@sun.com
Email: o.v.hall@mac.com
URL: http://www.linkedin.com/in/olgahall

Regina Hall, RN, LMT

Title: Owner **Company:** Hands 'N Motion Therapeutic Massage Services **Address:** 1663 Drummond Lane, Lincoln, CA 95648 United States **BUS:** High Quality Massage Therapy Facility **P/S:** Professionally Trained and Certified Therapists, Large Selection of Massage Programs, Affordable Rates **MA:** Regional **D/D/R:** Performing Relaxation, Therapeutic, Deep Tissue and Swedish Massage, Working in Clients' Homes, Geriatric Massage, Chronic Pain Management, Studying Hydrotherapy, Hot Stone Therapy and Sports Massage Techniques **H/I/S:** Track and Field Events, Watching Soap Operas **EDU:** Associate Degree in Nursing, St. Louis Community College (1998) **CERTS:** Licensed Massage Therapist, Missouri College (2005); Certified Registered Nurse (1998)
Email: hands-n-motion@hotmail.com
URL: http://www.cambridgewhoswho.com

Thomas A. Hall

Title: Founder, Owner **Company:** The Thomas Network **Address:** 1220 18th Street N.E., Washington, DC 20002 United States **BUS:** Construction Company **P/S:** Home Maintenance, Consulting, Renovation, Audio Visual and Design Services **MA:** Regional **D/D/R:** Managing Projects and Marketing, Supervising Staff, Extensive Background in the Entertainment Industry **H/I/S:** Studio Engineering, Architectural Design, Stand-Up Comedy **EDU:** College Coursework, Howard University (1975-1978) **A/A/S:** Gold Record Award, 'Tommy Boy Records'; Publisher and Co-Founder, Bi-Weekly Newsletter, 'Monopoly of Sounds'; Recipient, American Institute of Architectural Scholarship; Bryant and Bryant Architects and Planners of Washington DC, Owner, Thomas Network
Email: tnwkava@yahoo.com

Vernon L. Hall

Title: Owner **Company:** Vern's AQ Cleaning Service **Address:** 1007 Thomas Avenue, Monroe, LA 71202 United States **BUS:** Janitorial Company **P/S:** Janitorial Services Including Maid, Commercial and Residential Cleaning Services **MA:** Regional **D/D/R:** Maintaining Floors, Overseeing Carpet Shampooing and Cleaning Services **H/I/S:** Playing Dominoes, Chess and Billiards **EDU:** Master's Degree in Sports Administration, Grambling State University (1989) **A/A/S:** Louisiana Home Builders Association
Email: shackhall3@bellsouth.net
URL: http://www.cambridgewhoswho.com

Brenda L. Hall-Dvorak

Title: National Signature Event Coordinator **Company:** Three Affiliated Tribes **Address:** 2963 Warwick Place, Bismarck, ND 58504 United States **BUS:** Tribal News and Updates Provider **P/S:** National Signature Event, Updates and News Events Concerning the Tribes **MA:** National **D/D/R:** Organizing Lewis and Clark National Signature Event, Planning for Bicentennial, Ensuring Cultural Propriety **H/I/S:** Personal Training **EDU:** Master's Degree in Management, University of Mary (2000); Master's Degree in American Indian Studies, University of Arizona, Tucson (1990) **A/A/S:** COTA; National Lewis and Clark Bicentennial Committee; Former Chairwoman, National Congress of American Indians
Email: ndbdvorak@hotmail.com
URL: http://www.mhanation.com

Scott E. Hallgren

Title: Physician **Company:** Florida Center for Gastroenterology **Address:** 8250 Bryan Dairy Road, Suite 200, Largo, FL 33777 United States **BUS:** Healthcare Center **P/S:** Healthcare, Gastroenterology Services **MA:** Regional **EXP:** Dr. Hallgren's expertise is in gastroenterology. **D/D/R:** Teaching Medical Students **H/I/S:** Golfing, Photography, Hiking **EDU:** Doctor of Osteopathic Medicine, University of Osteopathic Medicine and Health Science, Des Moines, IA (1980) **A/A/S:** Fellow, American College of Physicians; Florida Osteopathic Medical Association; Florida Gastroenterologic Society **C/VW:** Hospice; American Cancer Society
Email: ercpman@aol.com

Mrs. Tina Halpain

Title: Owner **Company:** Pro Plan It, Inc. **Address:** 335 Meadow View Drive, Lavon, TX 75166 United States **BUS:** Meeting Management Company **P/S:** Meeting Management **MA:** National **D/D/R:** Planning Large Corporate Meetings, International Consulting, Executive Strategy, Call Center Strategy and Contests, Promotional Items, **H/I/S:** Golfing, Skiing, Playing Volleyball **EDU:** Bachelor of Science in Marketing, Murray State University-1992; **C/VW:** Ronald McDonald House, Room to Read, Habitat for Humanity, Tarrant Area Food Bank Volunteer
Email: tinahalpain@proplanit.com
URL: http://www.proplanit.com

Antoinette M. Halton

Title: Owner, Chief Executive Officer **Company:** Breath of Life Ministry **Address:** P.O. Box 1083, Amherst, NY 14226 United States **BUS:** Religious Counseling and Broadcasting Company **P/S:** Bible-Based Answers to Life Issues **MA:** International **D/D/R:** Offering Child and Family Christian Counseling Services **H/I/S:** Traveling, Crafts **EDU:** Bachelor of Social Work, SUNY Empire State College **CERTS:** Certification in Life Counseling; Certification in Christian Counseling; Certified Professional Life Coach **A/A/S:** Child and Family Services **C/VW:** Child and Family Services; Church; Greater Faith Bible Tabernacle Ministries; Citywide Crusade; Facilitator, Early Childhood Centers
Email: dujue@aol.com
URL: http://www.churchfolkgetreal.com

Janet M. Hamann, Ph.D.

Title: Program Director of Secondary Education (Retired) **Company:** California State University at Bakersfield **Address:** 6647 El Colegio Road, Isla Vista, CA 93117 United States **BUS:** University **P/S:** Higher Education **MA:** Regional **D/D/R:** Directing the Credential Program, Ensuring Students Fulfill Correct Course Requirements, Mentoring and Educating Secondary Educational Professionals, Teaching Educational Philosophy **H/I/S:** Playing Tennis, Reading, Swimming **EDU:** Ph.D. in Educational Psychology, University of California, Los Angeles (1989) **A/A/S:** Association of Clinical Research Professionals
Email: janet.hamann@cwwemail.com
URL: http://www.csub.edu

Eric C. Hambrecht

Title: Executive Chef, Owner **Company:** Stage House Restaurant **Dept:** Tavern at the Stage House **Address:** 366 Park Avenue, Scotch Plains, NJ 07076 United States **BUS:** Restaurant **P/S:** Food and Beverages Including Tavern-Style American Cuisine **MA:** Local **D/D/R:** Overseeing Business Management and Fine Dining **H/I/S:** Spending Time with his Family, Home Remodeling, Landscaping **EDU:** Associate of Arts in Culinary Arts, Johnson and Wales University (1986) **C/VW:** Leukemia and Lymphoma Society; Founder, Chef's Night to Benefit Elijah's Promise, the Frog and the Peach
Email: eric@stagehouserestaurant.com
URL: http://www.stagehouserestaurant.com

Joyce T. Hamel

Title: Administrator **Company:** Rusin Maciorowski & Friedman, Ltd. **Address:** 10 S. Riverside Plaza, Suite 1530, Chicago, IL 60606 United States **BUS:** Law Firm **P/S:** Legal Services **MA:** Regional **EXP:** Ms. Hamel's expertise is in human resource management. **D/D/R:** Overseeing General Operations, Creating Company Policies, Reviewing the Budget, Interviewing, Hiring, Overseeing Employees, Managing the Facility **H/I/S:** Traveling, Reading, Sports **EDU:** Bachelor's Degree in English, National College of Education, Evanston, IL **A/A/S:** Association of Legal Administrators **C/VW:** Breast Cancer Society; National Parkinson Foundation; National Eating Disorders Association; National Down Syndrome Society; American Lung Association; American Heart Association; Lupus Foundation of America
Email: jhamel@rusinlaw.com
URL: http://www.rusinlaw.com

Danielle L. Hamilton

Title: Administrator **Company:** Associated Ophthalmic Specialists, Inc. **Address:** 7945 Wolf River Boulevard, Suite 240, Germantown, TN 38138 United States **BUS:** Healthcare **P/S:** Ophthalmology Practice **MA:** Regional **D/D/R:** Assisting the Physician in Surgeries, Scheduling, Working with Research Assistants **H/I/S:** Reading **EDU:** High School Education
Email: aoswood@aol.com

Mrs. Jataun Hamilton, BSN

Title: Administrative Supervisor **Company:** Mt. Sinai Hospital **Address:** 2750 W. 15th Street, Chicago, IL 60608 United States **BUS:** 432-Bed Teaching, Research and Tertiary-Care Facility **P/S:** Healthcare Services **MA:** Regional **D/D/R:** Acting as a Liaison between Staff, Patients and Family, Overseeing System Problems, Ensuring Adequate Staffing **H/I/S:** Being a Computer Buff **EDU:** Bachelor of Science in Nursing, Olivet Nazarene University (1993)
URL: http://www.sinai.org/who/who_msh.asp

Dr. Marilyn Hamilton
Title: Executive Director, Chief Executive Officer **Company:** Wholistic Counseling Services, Inc. **Address:** 4450 S. Wayside Drive, Suite 100B, Houston, TX 77087 United States **BUS:** Social Counseling Services **P/S:** Individual, Group and Family Sessions, Supportive and Intensive Outpatient Alcohol and Drug Abuse Counseling and Education, Anger Management Counseling and Education, Domestic Violence Program, Stress Management Counseling and Education, Parenting Skills Enhancement, Job Quest Training, HIV-AIDS and Sexually Transmitted Disease Prevention Counseling and Education, Substance Abuse Assessment and Evaluation **MA:** Regional **D/D/R:** Counseling Adults and Children on Issues including Domestic Violence, Anger Management, Parenting and Substance Abuse **H/I/S:** Entering Contests, Watching Movies, Playing with her Grandchildren **EDU:** Doctorate in Counseling, Texas Southern University (1988); Master of Science in Industrial Education (1983); Bachelor of Science in Drafting and Design Technology (1980) **A/A/S:** Texas Council on Family Violence; Phi Delta Kappa; Houston Council on Alcoholism and Drug Abuse; American Association for Counseling and Development; Co-Chairwoman, Advisory Board, Johnson-Phillip All Faiths Chapel; National Association for the Advancement of Colored People; Certificate of Appreciation, Faithful Service to Education; Annual Career Workshop Certificate, Zeta Phi Beta Sorority **C/VW:** Volunteer, Workshop Presenter and Facilitator, Center on Family, Texas Southern University (1993-1996); Outreach Counselor, Over the Hill (1991-1995)
Email: wcsi2@aol.com
URL: http://www.wholisticservices.com

Sarah E. Hamilton
Title: Customer Relations Manager **Company:** Harland Financial Solutions **Address:** 22722 29th Drive S.E., Suite 200, Bothell, WA 98021 United States **BUS:** Financial Organization **P/S:** Risk Management Solutions **MA:** National **EXP:** Ms. Hamilton's expertise includes mortgages and software. **H/I/S:** Bachelor of Science in Computer Science, Montana College of Mineral Science and Technology
Email: sarah.hamilton@harlandfs.com
URL: http://www.harlandfs.com

Donna Hamilton-Richards
Title: Registered Nurse, Certified Operating Room Nurse **Company:** Kaiser Permanente **Address:** 9961 Sierra Avenue, Fontana, CA 92335 United States **BUS:** Hospital **P/S:** Healthcare **MA:** Local **D/D/R:** Operating Room Nursing, Assisting Doctors during General Surgery Including Brain and Orthopedic Surgery **H/I/S:** Hula and Tahitian Dancing, Reading, Writing, Traveling, Watching Shirley Temple Movies, Attending the Theater **EDU:** Associate of Arts in Nursing, Mohave Community College **CERTS:** Certified Operating Room Nurse, Riverside Community College, CA **A/A/S:** Association of periOperative Registered Nurses
Email: tamc5c2@netzero.net

Angela M. Hamlet
Title: Project Coordinator **Company:** Chicago Public Schools **Address:** 125 S. Clark Street, Chicago, IL 60603 United States **BUS:** Public School System **P/S:** Comprehensive Education, High Quality Programs, Teaching, Learning, Development **MA:** Regional **D/D/R:** Performing Classroom Assessments, Creating and Analyzing Online Teacher Surveys, Improving and Maintaining the Website **H/I/S:** Shopping, Arts and Crafts, Reading **EDU:** Bachelor of Arts in Psychology, University of Illinois at Chicago (1999)
Email: amhamlet@cps.k12.il.us
URL: http://www.ecechicago.org

Christine E. Hamlyn, RN, BSN
Title: Registered Nurse **Company:** Floyd Memorial Hospital and Health Services **Address:** 1850 State Street, New Albany, IN 47150 United States **BUS:** Hospital **P/S:** Fulfilling Healthcare Needs **MA:** Regional **D/D/R:** Critical-Care Nursing, Charge Nurse, Case Management **H/I/S:** Watching Old Movies, Reading, Caring for the Animals on her Small Farm **EDU:** Pursuing Master of Business Administration; Bachelor of Science in Nursing, Indiana University **A/A/S:** American Heart Association; Relay for Life; American Diabetes Association
Email: ceham.lyn@hotmail.com
URL: http://www.floydmemorial.org

Janice A. Hammock, RN
Title: Registered Nurse **Company:** Kaleida Health System-Gates **Address:** 3 Gates Circle, Buffalo, NY 14209 United States **BUS:** Largest Health Care Provider in Western New York **P/S:** Education and Prevention, Home Care Services, Long Term Care, Pediatric Medical Services, Stroke Care Center, Support Services **MA:** Regional **D/D/R:** Critical Care Nursing, CAT SCANS, MRIs, Monitoring Critically Ill Patients on a Daily Basis **H/I/S:** Sewing, Gardening, Watching Football **EDU:** Associate Degree in Nursing, Highland Park Community College (1974) **A/A/S:** Pharmaceutical Society; CRC, Pharmaceutical Research Studies
Email: jahammock@adelphia.net
URL: http://www.kaleidahealth.org

Docenia Hammond
Title: Mathematics Teacher (Retired) **Address:** 516 Chavis Way, Raleigh, NC 27601 United States **BUS:** Sole Proprietorship **P/S:** Education for Ninth through 12th-grade Students **MA:** Local **D/D/R:** Teaching Algebra, Business and General Mathematics, Geometry and Computer Courses **H/I/S:** Traveling **EDU:** Bachelor of Science in Mathematics, Saint Augustine's College, NC (1958) **A/A/S:** President, Woman's Auxiliary; The North Carolina Council of Teachers of Mathematics; National Alumni Member, Saint Augustine's College; Alpha Kappa Alpha **C/VW:** Christian Faith Baptist Church
Email: docenia.hammond@cwwemail.com

Stephanie M. Hammonds
Title: Pharmacist **Company:** Target Corporation **Address:** 519 Gateway Drive, Brooklyn, NY 11239 United States **BUS:** Retail Store and Pharmacy **P/S:** Retail, Pharmacy **MA:** National **EXP:** Dr. Hammonds' expertise includes pediatrics and preventative care. **D/D/R:** Dispensing Prescription Medications **H/I/S:** Reading, Photography, Traveling, Running **EDU:** Pursuing Master's Degree in Public Health, The George Washington University; Doctor of Pharmacy, Purdue University **CERTS:** Licensed Pharmacist, States of New York, Pennsylvania and Maryland
Email: stephanie.hammonds@target.com
Email: mjb2345@gmail.com

Shirley A. Hampton
Title: Artist **Company:** Hampton Art **Address:** Maytowne Shoppes 118 North Jefferson Avenue, West Jefferson, NC United States **BUS:** Art Gallery **P/S:** Works are from her Imagination, Produces Original One of a Kind Pieces, Most of her work is Abstract Impressionistic, with a touch of Realism at Times, Plain Abstract, Abstracted People, Or Animals with no Rules or Restrictions. Being Original is very difficult especially when you are trying not to let other works by other artists style come into mind. **MA:** International **D/D/R:** All Work is a Creation of Imagination, One of a Kind, Sculptures and Absolutely No Rules in Art **H/I/S:** Animals, Shopping, Walking her Dog, Art is her Hobby, Her Sport and her First Love **EDU:** Coursework in Business and Art, Appalachian State University, FL
Email: hampton2c@skybest.com

Kathleen F. Hanawahine
Title: Registrar of Land Court, Ex-Officio Tax Appeal Court **Company:** State of Hawaii-Judiciary **Address:** 777 Punchbowl Street, Honolulu, HI 96813 United States **BUS:** Government Judiciary **P/S:** Land Registration, Taxes **MA:** Regional **D/D/R:** Real Property and Taxes, Running Statewide Programs, Only Court Administrator in Hawaii, Handling Registered Land, Tax Appeals, Income, Real Property, Tobacco, General Excise, All Taxes and Land Court Signs on Behalf of the Judge of the Land Court on Ex parte Petitions Based on Facts **H/I/S:** Crafts, Watching Football **EDU:** High School Coursework **A/A/S:** Spoke at Surveyors Convention on Land Court Systems; Published Article in Pacific Business News
Email: kathleen.f.hanawahine@courts.state.hi.us
URL: http://www.cambridgewhoswho.com

Michelle W. Hancock
Title: Owner, President **Company:** Mike Hancock Construction, Inc. **Address:** 105 B Harvest Moon Court, Jupiter, FL 33458 United States **BUS:** Construction Company **P/S:** Construction Services Including Interior Renovations **MA:** Regional **EXP:** Mr. Hancock's expertise is in business operations management. **H/I/S:** Dancing **EDU:** College Coursework **C/VW:** American Breast Cancer Foundation
Email: lilbitcountry99@aol.com
URL: http://www.cambridgewhoswho.com

Donna J. Handler
Title: Massage Therapist, Spa Owner **Company:** That Special Touch Spa & Health Center **Address:** 19600 E. Main Street, Parker, CO 80138 United States **BUS:** Health Center **P/S:** Health and Wellness **MA:** Local **EXP:** Ms. Handler's expertise is in massage therapy. **H/I/S:** Dancing, Playing Tennis **C/VW:** Landmark Education, Health Fair
Email: donna@thatspecialtouchspa.com
URL: http://www.thatspecialtouchspa.com

Lucinda F. Handshoe
Title: Language Arts Teacher **Company:** Artie Henry Middle School **Address:** 2702 Overview Street, Round Rock, TX 78681 United States **BUS:** Education **P/S:** English Literature/Journalism **MA:** Local **D/D/R:** Teaching Eighth-Grade Language Arts and Analytical Skills Including Symbolism, Metaphors, Themes and Ideas, Mentoring Students of All Levels Throughout the High School **EDU:** Bachelor of Arts in English, Concentration on Literature and Creative Writing, Minor in Journalism (Cum Laude), Texas Tech University **CERTS:** Certified in Reading, State of Texas; Certified in the New Jersey Writing Project **A/A/S:** SAC; Texas Classroom Teachers Association; Golden Key International Honor Society **A/H:** Outstanding Teacher of the Year, National Honor Roll
Email: ms.handshoe@sbcglobal.net
URL: http://www.lucindahandshoe.com

Kara Leigh Hanes, BA
Title: Director of Marketing **Company:** Brethren Retirement Community **Address:** 750 Chestnut Street, Greenville, OH 45331 United States **BUS:** Nonprofit Continuum Retirement Community **P/S:** Long Term Healthcare **MA:** Local **D/D/R:** Marketing and Public Relations, Handling All Administrative Duties as a Professional Officer, Public Speaker **H/I/S:** Spending Time with her Two Children **EDU:** Bachelor of Arts, Muskingum College, Ohio (1998) **A/A/S:** State Board Member, Business and Professional Women **A/H:** Ohio Young Careerist Award (2005); President Award, Rotary International (2003)
Email: kara.hanes@bhrs.org
URL: http://www.bhrs.org

Donna M. Hanford, MS, NCSP
Title: School Psychologist, Counselor, Therapist, Teacher **Company:** Gold Rush Home Study Charter School **Address:** 24055 S. Bear Clover Court, Sonora, CA 95370 United States **BUS:** Public Charter School **P/S:** Personalized Learning Plans, Tutoring, Elementary Education **MA:** Local **D/D/R:** Offering Home Therapy, Counseling, Problem Solving, Assisting Students in Coming to their Own Conclusions, Teaching Psychology, Critical Thinking and Concept Introduction, Using Visualization, Deep Breathing Exercises and Relaxation Techniques **H/I/S:** Reading, Spending Time with Family **EDU:** Master's Degree in Clinical School Psychology, California State University at Hayward (1985); Bachelor's Degree in Sociology with a Minor in Psychology, Santa Clara University (1973) **A/A/S:** National Association of School Psychologists; California Association of School Psychologists
Email: legardg@goldrush.com

Linda J. Hanks
Title: Assistant Office Administrator **Company:** McCurley Orsinger McCurley Nelson & Downing, LLP **Address:** 5950 Sherry Lane, Suite 800, Dallas, TX 75225 United States **BUS:** Law Firm **P/S:** Experienced Trial Lawyers, Dispute Resolution through Alternative Methods including Mediation and Arbitration, Consultations, Representation on Divorce, Child Related Issues, Paternity and Parental Rights, Pre and Post-Nuptial Agreements, International Disputes, Appeals, Alternate Dispute Resolution, Collaborative Law **MA:** National **D/D/R:** Overseeing all Paralegals and Associates, Preparing Accounting Spreadsheets, Administering Financial Services, Accounting and Reporting **H/I/S:** Tennis, Riding her Motorcycle **EDU:** Associate Degree in Accounting, Mansfield Business College (1991) **A/A/S:** Co-Chairwoman of Small Firm Section, Association of Legal Administrators
Email: lhanks@momnd.com
URL: http://www.momnd.com

Cathie Hanna
Title: Early Care Education Supervisor **Company:** John C. Lincoln Hospitals **Address:** 303 E. Eva Street, Phoenix, AZ 85020 United States **BUS:** Nonprofit Healthcare System **P/S:** Inpatient and Outpatient Services, Two Hospitals, Several Physician Practices and Outreach Programs **MA:** Regional **D/D/R:** Teaching Early Childhood Education, Supervising 355 Staff Members, Training Teachers, Developing Curriculum for in-Hospital Preschool and Kindergarten Programs **H/I/S:** Drawing, Art, Music, Hockey **EDU:** Pursuing Bachelor's Degree in Education, Ohio State University; Associate Degree in Childhood Development, Central Arizona College (1997) **A/A/S:** National Association for the Education of Young Children; Kiwanis International
Email: cathie.hanna@jcl.com
URL: http://www.jcl.com/content

Claudia P. Hannah
Title: Realtor **Company:** Weichert Realtors **BUS:** Real Estate Agency **P/S:** Residential Real Estate Properties **MA:** Montgomery County **D/D/R:** Selling Residential Properties **H/I/S:** Attending Concerts, Listening to Bach, Mozart and Bluegrass, Visiting Museums **EDU:** Bachelor's Degree in English Literature, Vassar College **C/VW:** Whitman-Walker Clinic; AIDS Research; Diabetes Organizations
Email: claudiahannah@mris.com
URL: http://www.weichert.com

Pamela K. Hannaman-Pittman, ND, MS
Title: Naturopathic Physician **Company:** Dr Pamela K Hannaman-Pittman, ND, MS, LLC **Address:** 13074 Fairway Lane, Ashland, VA 23005 United States **BUS:** Healthcare Consultant **P/S:** Natural Health Consultant, Naturopathic Physician **MA:** Local **D/D/R:** Naturopathic Medicine, Also a Writer Doing Articles for Magazines, Giving Lectures on Natural Treatment **H/I/S:** Reading, Movies, Playing Piano **EDU:** Mary Washington University, Medical College of Virginia, Basty University, BS, MS, ND **A/A/S:** Certified Medical Coder, American Association of Professional Coders, American Association of Naturopathic Physicians, Supports the Food Bank, Daily Planet Shelter, Church and other Local Charities
Email: n8urdoc@doctor.com
URL: www.hannaman-pittman.com

Ms. Katherine E. Hansell
Title: Accounting Manager, Consultant **Company:** San Diego Christian Foundation DBA Canyon Villas **Address:** 4282 Balboa Avenue, San Diego, CA 92117 United States **BUS:** Senior Retirement Community Living Center **P/S:** Assisted Living and Independent Living Services for Seniors **MA:** Regional **D/D/R:** Overseeing the Bookkeeping for Clients Including Auditing and Other Financial Aspects, Streamlining the Office Function, Cleaning Up the Accounts Payable and Receivable, Processing Insurance Claims, Creating a Better Functioning Facility, Training Employees to Take Over the Accounting Process After the Initial Consultation **H/I/S:** Creating Floral Arrangements for the Church, Working on Crafts, Skiing, Fishing **EDU:** High School Education **CERTS:** Certification in Bookkeeping, American Institute of Professional Bookkeepers (2007) **A/A/S:** American Institute of Professional Bookkeepers; Member, Local Church; Trainer, Local Bookkeepers
Email: mrswhisperk@yahoo.com

Erik T. Hansen
Title: Realtor **Company:** Keller Williams Advantage II Realty **Address:** 12301 Lake Underhill Road, Suite 111, Orlando, FL 32828 United States **BUS:** Real Estate Company **P/S:** Residential and Commercial Real Estate **MA:** Regional **D/D/R:** Selling Residential Real Estate to First Time Home Buyers, Finding Clients the Best Price and Value, Booking Appointments for Clients, Creating Leads Through the Internet **H/I/S:** Golfing, Supporting the New Orleans Saints, Relaxing on the Beach, Reading books on Real Estate investing **EDU:** Bachelor of Arts in Business Administration, University of Central Florida (2006); Licensed Realtor (2004) **A/A/S:** Neighborhood Homeowners' Association; Chamber of Commerce; National Association of Realtors; Florida Association of Realtors **A/H:** Bronze Award for Total Sales (2005, 2006)
Email: erikh@kw.com
URL: http://www.OrlandoAreaDreamHomes.com

Janet M. Hansen
Title: Teacher **Company:** Corcoran Unified School District **Address:** 1520 Patterson Avenue, Corcoran, CA 93212 United States **BUS:** School District Dedicated to High Quality Education **P/S:** Elementary and Secondary Education, Transportation, Testing, Resources **MA:** Regional **D/D/R:** Elementary Education, Teaching in a Self-Contained Classroom **H/I/S:** Traveling, Fishing, Hunting, Gardening **EDU:** Bachelor of Science in Child Development, California State University at Fresno **A/A/S:** Kappa Delta Pi; National Education Association; Beginning Teacher Support and Assessment Providers
Email: jhansen@king.k12.co.us
URL: http://www.corcoran.k12.ca.us

Pamela J. Hansen
Title: Intervention Specialist **Company:** Olmsted Falls Middle School **Address:** 27045 Bagley Road, Olmsted Falls, OH 44138 United States **BUS:** Middle School Facility Dedicated to Excellence in Regular and Special Education **P/S:** Regular and Special Core Curriculum Including Reading, Mathematics, English, Science, Social Studies, Art, Music, History, Physical Education, Foreign Language, Technology Education and Health **MA:** Regional **D/D/R:** Teaching Special Education to Sixth-Grade, Teaching Reading, English and Mathematics, Combining Sixth, Seventh and Eighth-Grades for a Special Reading Class, Building Rep for OFEA **H/I/S:** Tennis, Golfing **EDU:** Master of Science in Education as a Reading Specialist and Supervisor, University of Akron, Akron, Ohio **A/A/S:** Phi Delta Kappa; Kappa Delta Pi
Email: pjbhansen@yahoo.com
URL: http://www.ofcs.k12.oh.us/middle

Jillian R. Hanshew
Title: Kindergarten Teacher **Company:** Colonial Village Day Care **Address:** 7998 S. 775 E., Zionsville, IN 46077 United States **BUS:** Daycare Center, Early Childhood Education Center **P/S:** Early Childhood Education, Daycare **MA:** Local **D/D/R:** Early Childhood Education **H/I/S:** Starting her 'Welcome Baby' Gift Business **EDU:** Bachelor of Science in Psychology, Minor in Biology, Indiana University **C/VW:** Feed The Children, St. Jude Children's Research Hospital
Email: thehanshews@sbcglobal.net

Carol M. Hanson
Title: Owner, Manager **Company:** Sete Properties, LLC **Address:** 6372 Camino Largo, San Diego, CA 92120 United States **BUS:** Real Estate Agency **P/S:** Real Estate Exchange, Rental Holdings **MA:** Local **D/D/R:** Managing Rental Properties, Interviewing Tenants, Negotiating Leases and Sales, Overseeing the Work of her Two Employees and General Maintenance of the Building **H/I/S:** Volunteering, Cooking, Swimming, Reading, Attending the Quarter Horses Show, Attending the Theater **EDU:** Bachelor of Science in Business Administration, San Diego State University (1965) **CERTS:** Licensed Real Estate Agent **A/A/S:** Old Globe Theater; Gamma Phi Beta; Zoological Society of San Diego; Friends of East County Arts; Starlight Society; Vista Hill Foundation; Group Of Twelve; PR Club; Burnham Institute for Science and Research **A/H:** Nominee, Guildred of the Year **C/VW:** Salvation Army; Meals on Wheels
Email: cmmillsemail@aol.com
URL: http://www.cambridgewhoswho.com

Heidi Leigh Hanson
Title: Student of Costume Design **Company:** Yale University School of Drama **Address:** 222 York Street, New Haven, CT 06511 United States **BUS:** University **P/S:** Drama Education, Theater Design **MA:** Local **EXP:** Ms. Hanson's expertise includes theater design and entertainment. **H/I/S:** Drawing **EDU:** Pursuing Master of Fine Arts, Yale University School of Drama; Bachelor's Degree in Theater Arts, California State University, Long Beach **A/A/S:** Philadelphia Theater Alliance
Email: heidi.hanson@yale.edu
URL: http://www.cambridgewhoswho.com

Bethany A. Happe
Title: Assistant Principal **Company:** Holy Trinity Catholic School **Address:** 2922 Beaver Avenue, Des Moines, IA 50310 United States **BUS:** Elementary School **P/S:** Education **MA:** Local **D/D/R:** Overseeing Educational Administration **H/I/S:** Reading, Golfing **EDU:** Educational Specialist, Drake University **CERTS:** Licensed in Administration, Pre-Kindergarten through 12th-Grade **A/A/S:** Iowa Association for Supervision and Curriculum Development; Association for Supervision and Curriculum Development; National Catholic Educational Association **A/H:** Teacher of the Year (2001) **C/VW:** American Cancer Society; JDRS
Email: boogie723@yahoo.com
Email: bhappe@htschool.org
URL: http://www.htschool.org

Karen M. Harbison
Title: Special Education Teacher **Company:** Polk County Board of Education **Address:** P.O. Box A, Benton, TN 37307 United States **BUS:** Special Education **P/S:** Academics and Behaviors Education for Autistic Students **MA:** Local **D/D/R:** Identifying Behaviors in Autism **H/I/S:** Playing the Guitar, Reading **EDU:** Pursuing Master's in Psychology, Minor in Mathematics, Capella University; Bachelor of Arts in Special Education and General Education **A/A/S:** Phi Beta Kappa Sorority
Email: karen_harbison@hotmail.com

Barry S. Hardeman
Title: President, Owner **Company:** Tom Chitty and Associates **Address:** 802 Green Valley Road, Suite 100, Greensboro, NC 27408 United States **BUS:** Real Estate Agency **P/S:** Real Estate **MA:** Greensboro, High Point, Kernersville, Jamestown, Browns Summit **D/D/R:** Advertising **H/I/S:** Traveling, Attending the Theater **EDU:** Coursework, Ringling College Art and Design, Florida; Coursework, Guilford Technical Community College **C/VW:** Greyhound Friends, The Sunshine Kids
Email: barryhardeman@hotmail.com
URL: http://www.tomchitty.com

Hal Harder
Title: Licensed Massage Therapist **Company:** Muscular Therapy Associates **Address:** 955 Main Street, Suite 211, Winchester, MA 02180 United States **BUS:** Physical Healthcare **P/S:** Massage and Physical Therapy Services **MA:** Regional **D/D/R:** Offering Massage Therapy Using the Benjamin Method **H/I/S:** Car Collecting **EDU:** Associate Degree in Applied Sciences, Hudson Valley Community College (1981) **CERTS:** Muscular Therapy Institute (2007) **A/A/S:** American Massage Therapy Association; American Society of Radiologic Technologists
Email: hal.harder@comcast.net
URL: http://www.cambridgewhoswho.com

Freeman Hardin Jr.
Title: Realtor **Company:** Prudential California Realty **Address:** 14014 Bear Valley Road, Suite AB, Victorville, CA 92392 United States **BUS:** Real Estate Agency **P/S:** Residential and Commercial Real Estate **MA:** Statewide **D/D/R:** Buying and Selling Commercial and Residential Real Estate, Leasing **H/I/S:** Practicing Martial Arts, Shooting, Hiking, Fishing, Camping, Hunting, Playing Football and Baseball **EDU:** Industry-Related Experience and Training **CERTS:** Certified Residential Specialist **A/A/S:** California Association of Realtors; National Association of Realtors **A/H:** Top Agent Honors Award, 2007; No. 1 Agent, Prudential Realty, Victorville, 2007 **C/VW:** Church
Email: freemanhardin@msn.com
URL: http://www.extremefreeman.com

Chelf W. Hardwicke
Title: Owner **Company:** Bomar Synthetics **Address:** P.O. Box 16371, Jacksonville, FL 32245 United States **BUS:** Synthetic Lubricants **P/S:** Amsoil-The First in Synthetics **MA:** International **D/D/R:** Distribution of Amsoil Products, Handles Day to Day Operations **H/I/S:** Avid Motorcyclist, Travel **EDU:** Coursework in Data Processing, Virginia Commonwealth University; Coursework in Amsoil and Synthetic Lubricants, Amsoil University **A/A/S:** American Motorcycle Association, Goldwing Road Riders Association; Masonic Order, Loyal Order of Moose
Email: bomar_ent@yahoo.com
URL: http://www.amsoil.com

Katie A. Hardy
Title: Nail Technician **Company:** Queens Nails **Address:** P.O. Box 145, Seville, GA 31084 United States **BUS:** Nail Salon **P/S:** Manicures, Pedicures, Spa Services **MA:** Local **D/D/R:** Working as a Nail Technician, Overseeing Customer Satisfaction **H/I/S:** Spending Time with Her Family **EDU:** Pursuing Medical Billing and Coding Degree, Penn Foster; Coursework in Micro Computer Specialist, Georgia Institute of Technology **C/VW:** Various charities
Email: lowblow@planttel.net
URL: http://www.cambirdgewhoswho.com

Mr. Morris Hardy
Title: Owner **Company:** Boise CPR **BUS:** Instructional CPR and First Aid **P/S:** CPR, AED, First Aid **MA:** Local **D/D/R:** Rescuing People and Animals from Fires, Offering Emergency Medical Services, Teaching CPR to Local Town Residents **H/I/S:** Golfing, Doing Lawn Work **EDU:** High School Education **CERTS:** Instructional CPR Certification-1995 **A/A/S:** Idaho Mountain Search and Rescue
Email: cpr@biosecpr.com
URL: http://www.boisecpr.com

Leon Nathan Hare
Title: Executive Director **Company:** Community Action Organization of Erie County, Inc. **Address:** 70 Harvard Place, Buffalo, NY 14209 United States **BUS:** Nonprofit Organization **P/S:** Human Services **MA:** Local **D/D/R:** Executive Administration **H/I/S:** Bowling; Traveling **EDU:** Pursuing Master's Degree in Business Organization; Bachelor of Arts in Business Management, Medaille College **A/A/S:** Primary Care Development Association; Primary Care Development Association: Black Social Workers Association; New York State Community Action Association **C/VW:** Father's; National Head Start Association; Grace Manor
Email: inhare@caoec.org
URL: http://www.caoec.org

Stephanie D. Hargens
Title: Academic Administrator **Company:** K-12, Inc. **Address:** 900 N. Ford Road, Zionsville, IN 46077 United States **BUS:** Virtual Academy, Educational Management Company **P/S:** Marketing, Curriculum **MA:** Local **EXP:** Ms. Hargens' expertise includes research-based practices and administration. **H/I/S:** Cooking, Solving Sudoku and Crossword Puzzles, Spending Time with her Children **EDU:** Master of Arts in Educational Leadership and Policy Studies, California State University at Northridge, 2005 **A/A/S:** Phi Kappa Phi; National Association of Secondary School Principals
Email: shargens@sbcglobal.net

Maria Elaine Harkis
Title: Interior Architect, Owner **Company:** Medusa **Address:** 147 Mount Pleasant Avenue, West Orange, NJ 07052 United States **BUS:** Architectural Firm **P/S:** Architectural and Interior Designing Services Including Designing Kitchens and Baths **MA:** Local **D/D/R:** Designing, Selecting Stones and Mosaics, Creating Layouts, Drafting, Overseeing Faux Finishes and Window Treatments for High-End Homes **H/I/S:** Watercolor Painting, Sewing, Making Furniture, Cooking, Playing Volleyball, Fishing **EDU:** Master of Science in Architecture, New Jersey Institute of Technology (1996) **A/A/S:** Philoptochos Society
Email: mariamedusa@aol.com

Donna M. Harlow
Title: President **Company:** Harlow's Hair Design **Address:** 96 N. Main Street, Carver, MA 02330 United States **BUS:** Proven Leader in the Beauty Industry **P/S:** Variety of Quality Beauty Services Including Hair Cutting and Coloring, Waxing and Facials, Corrective Coloring, Foils **MA:** Regional **D/D/R:** Hair Coloring, Payroll, Ordering Supplies, Managing Employees, Hiring of Employees, Licensed Instructor of Cosmetology **H/I/S:** Relaxing **CERTS:** Licensed Cosmetologist, Henry O Peabody School, Norwood, Massachusetts (1974) **A/A/S:** Cranberry County Chamber of Commerce; People's Choice Award for Haircut of the South Shore
Email: beamer1996@aol.com
URL: http://www.cambridgewhoswho.com

Dana Marie Harmon
Title: Owner, Executive Chef **Company:** The Platter Restaurant and Motel **Address:** N8089 U.S. Highway 141, Crivitz, WI 54114 United States **BUS:** Restaurant, Hotel/Motel **P/S:** Hospitality, Lunch, Breakfast, Dinner **MA:** Regional **D/D/R:** Presenting Food in an Artistic Way with a Strong Attention to Detail **H/I/S:** Spending Time with her Mom and Family, Spending Time at Community Events **EDU:** Four-Year Degree, Indiana University **A/A/S:** WRA **C/VW:** Little League Baseball, Booster Club, Knights of Columbus, American Legion, Elks Club, Food Pantry
Email: littlemanvegas@yahoo.com

Henry Harms
Title: Owner **Company:** LA Fabricating and Machining Ltd **Address:** 9402 99 Street, LaCrete, T0H2H0 Canada **BUS:** Fabricating Manufacturing **P/S:** Fabrication and Welding **MA:** Local **D/D/R:** Welding **H/I/S:** Horses **CERTS:** Journey Man Welder
Email: lafab@tellusplanet.net

Rev. Angela C. Harpe
Title: Owner **Company:** Haley's **Address:** 1309 Harbor Landing, Roswell, GA 30076 United States **BUS:** Retail Shop **P/S:** Household Essentials, Inspirational, Bath and Body Products, Candles and Scents, Bulk Buys **MA:** International **EXP:** Rev. Harpe's expertise includes retail, small gifts and collectibles. **D/D/R:** Managing Operations, Consulting, Lecturing **H/I/S:** Spending Time with her Family, Writing and Publishing Church Curriculum, Reading, Researching, Traveling, Cooking Visiting with Friends and Family **EDU:** Doctorate of Ministry in Theology, Life Christian University (2008); Master of Theology, Summa Cum Laude, Life Christian University; Bachelor of Theology, River Bible Institute **CERTS:** Ordained Minister; Florida Workforce Professional Certification I, Dynamic Works Institute **A/A/S:** Founder, Executive Director, Women of God Ministries International, Inc.; Co-Founder, Managing Partner, Global Network Association of Christian Women Ministers; Board of Directors, Reality Live Ministries **A/H:** Workforce Florida Achievement Award **C/VW:** Sister in the Spirit, WGMI Inc.
Email: info@haleysonlinestore.com
Email: angelacw24@yahoo.com
URL: http://www.haleysonlinestore.com

Debbie K. Harper
Title: Vice President, Loan Officer **Company:** Mountain West Small Business Finance **Address:** 228 N. Orem Boulevard, Orem, UT 84057 United States **BUS:** Fixed Asset Financing Company **P/S:** Fixed Asset Financing for Small Businesses **MA:** Utah, Northern Arizona **D/D/R:** Originating Loans, Financing Commercial Properties for Small Businesses **H/I/S:** Reading, Cruising **EDU:** Bachelor of Science in Accounting, Brigham Young University, Utah **A/A/S:** NADCO
Email: dharper@mwsbf.com

Kenneth Harper
Title: Realtor **Company:** Weichert Realtors **Address:** 606 E. Baltimore Pike, Media, PA 19063 United States **BUS:** Real Estate Company **P/S:** Real Estate Services **MA:** Lower Southeastern Pennsylvania **EXP:** Mr. Harper's expertise is in residential property sales. **H/I/S:** Sports, Playing Football **EDU:** High School Education **A/A/S:** American Legion **C/VW:** Peace Council, Knights of Columbus
Email: kharper5@weichert.com
URL: http://www.weichert.com

Thomas Scott Harper
Title: Media Team Facilitator **Company:** Be in Health **Dept:** Media, Public Relations and Design **Address:** 4178 Crest Highway, Thomaston, GA 30286 United States **BUS:** Nonprofit Organization **P/S:** Outreach Ministry Services for Healing and Preventing All Biological and Psychological Diseases **MA:** Regional **D/D/R:** Sound Engineering, Facilitating Media, Teaching, Managing Operations, Organizing Conferences **H/I/S:** Photography, Listening to Music, DJing, Playing Volleyball, Spending Time with his Family **EDU:** Coursework, Gordon College **C/VW:** Pleasant Valley Church
Email: tsharper@beinhealth.com
Email: tsharper@mac.com
URL: http://www.beinhealth.com
URL: http://www.ctrlzyouth.com/

Charlene Harrell
Title: General Manager **Company:** Wendy's QSC Restaurants **Address:** 39 E. Broad Street, Bridgeton, NJ 08302 United States **BUS:** Food Restaurant **P/S:** Fast Food Wendy's Restaurant **MA:** Local **EXP:** Ms. Harrell's expertise is in human resource management. **H/I/S:** My Family, Reading, Music **EDU:** Associate Degree, Cumberland County College **A/A/S:** Alumni Trustee, Alpha Beta Gamma, SHRM, NAACP
Email: charrell@aol.com

Kate Harrienger, MS
Title: English Teacher **Company:** Watertown High School **Address:** 1335 Washington Street, Watertown, NY 13601 United States **BUS:** Public High School Facility Dedicated to Excellence in Education **P/S:** Regular Core Curriculum Including Reading, Mathematics, English, Science, Social Studies, Art, Music, History, Physical Education, Language Arts, Computers **MA:** Regional **D/D/R:** Teaching Six Classes of English to 9th and 10th-graders, Former Guest Speaker for the New Visions Program, Publishing Poetry **H/I/S:** Soccer, Reading, Spending Time with her Three Children **EDU:** Master of Science Degree in English, SUNY Potsdam (2000) **CERTS:** Certified in Secondary Education for Grades Seventh through 12 **A/A/S:** Graduated Summa Cum Laude; Dean's List; President's List; Honor Society for both Graduate and Undergraduate School; NCTE
Email: katharrienger@watertowncsd.org
URL: http://www.watertowncsd.org

Earnest Larry 'Doc' Harrington Sr.
Title: Head Athletic Trainer, Professor of Sports Medicine (Retired) **Company:** University of Southern Mississippi **BUS:** University **P/S:** Higher Education, Graduate and Undergraduate Studies, Research, Athletics **MA:** Regional **D/D/R:** Educating College Students in Sports Medicine, Serving as a Liaison between Universities and the Army, Training all Sports Including Tennis **H/I/S:** Spending Time with his Family, Fishing **EDU:** Ph.D. in Education, University of Southern Mississippi **CERTS:** Certified Corrective Physical Therapist **A/A/S:** Southwest Athletic Trainers' Association Hall of Fame; National Athletic Trainers' Association Hall of Fame
Email: earnest.harrington@cwwemail.com

Michael Harrington
Title: Senior Director of Customer Relations and Finance **Company:** Marriott Vacation Club International **Address:** 1200 Bartow Road, Lakeland, FL 33801 United States **BUS:** Timeshare Program **P/S:** Timeshares **MA:** International **EXP:** Mr. Harrington's expertise is in finance. **H/I/S:** Golfing, Weight Training, Running, Spending Time with his Family **EDU:** Bachelor of Business Administration, Medaille College **C/VW:** Junior League of Greater Lakeland, Local Parish
Email: michael.harrington@vacationclub.com
URL: http://www.vacationclub.com

Addie M. Harris
Title: Recovery Room Nurse, Minister (Retired) **BUS:** Healthcare Services Provider **P/S:** Healthcare **MA:** Local **D/D/R:** Offering Nursing and Community Services **H/I/S:** Studying the Bible, Ministering to Youth, Participating in Women's League Activities **CERTS:** Licensed Practical Nurse Diploma, Valdosta Technical College; Certification in CPR; Certification in Cardiac Life Support **A/A/S:** American Association of Nurse Anesthetists **C/VW:** Church, World Vision, Feed the Children
Email: h1609@mch51.com

Barbara L. Harris
Title: 1) Proprietor 2) Member **Company:** 1) Guys and Dolls Hair Studio 2) Harris Minimart, LLC **Address:** 148 State Route 202, Bennington, NH 03442 United States **BUS:** 1) Hair Studio 2) Convenient Store **P/S:** 1) Hair Salon 2) Grocery Store **MA:** 1) Local 2) Local **D/D/R:** 1) Styling 2) Accounting **H/I/S:** Snowmobiling, Riding Motorcycles **EDU:** Industry-Related Training and Experience
Email: topcat99@adelphia.net
URL: http://www.cambridgewhoswho.com

Charissa L. Harris
Title: Owner, Registered Massage Therapist **Company:** Massage Central **Address:** 4510 Stonewall Street, Greenville, TX 75401 United States **BUS:** Therapy Center **P/S:** Massage Therapy Including Deep Tissue, Sport, Reflexology, Swedish, Aromatherapy, Couples and Hot Stone Massage Services **MA:** Local **D/D/R:** Performing Swedish, Deep Tissue and Reflexology Massage Therapy, Overseeing Rehabilitation Units, Scheduling, Marketing and Advertising **EDU:** High School Diploma **CERTS:** Registered Massage Therapist, Hands on Therapy School of Massage (2003)
Email: charissa.harris@cwwemail.com

De Wayne Harris
Title: Pastor **Company:** New Salem Baptist Church **Address:** 4493 Old Turnpike Road, Kenton, TN 38233 United States **BUS:** Baptist Church **P/S:** Sunday school, 3 Services Per Week, Youth Ministry, choir, Outreach and Visitations, Vacation Bible School **MA:** Local **D/D/R:** Calling the Children His Congregation During Mass **H/I/S:** Family of 5, Hunting **A/A/S:** Kenton Ministerial Alliance

Geraldine C. Harris
Title: Education Specialist, Education Staff Development Nurse **Company:** Hackensack University Medical Center **Address:** 30 Prospect Avenue, Hackensack, NJ 07601 United States **BUS:** University Medical Center **P/S:** Higher Education, Healthcare, Acute Care Trauma Center **MA:** Local **D/D/R:** Nursing, Teaching Clinical Education, Staff Development **H/I/S:** Reading, Walking **EDU:** Parish Nurse Certification; Master's Degree in Administrative Nursing, New York University; Bachelor of Science in Nursing, Felician College; Associate Degree in Nursing, Felician College **A/A/S:** Nurses Service Organization; Chairwoman, Nurses Association; Local Church; Bergen County Partnership, Bergen County; Health Task Force **C/VW:** Church
Email: g.harris@humed.com
URL: http://www.humed.com

Jennifer L. Harris, RMT
Title: Registered Massage Therapist, Certified Reflexologist **Company:** Methodist Hospital P.T. **Address:** 26214 Lame Beaver, San Antonio, TX 78258 United States **BUS:** High Quality Medical Facility **P/S:** Wide Range of Medical Services, Including PostPartum Depression **MA:** Regional **EXP:** Ms. Harris' expertise includes reflexology and massage therapy techniques. **H/I/S:** Walking, Reading, Crafts for Decorative Additions to Clothing **CERTS:** State Certified Reflexologist (1998); Registered Massage Therapist (1999) **A/A/S:** International Institute of Reflexology
Email: tinyreflexologist@hotmail.com
URL: http://www.cambridgewhoswho.com

Lorrie A. Harris
Title: Vocal Teacher **Company:** Sunshine Entertainments **Address:** 25200 Carlos Bee Boulevard, Suite 116, Hayward, CA United States **BUS:** Entertainment **P/S:** Singing and Acting Lessons **MA:** National **D/D/R:** Singing and Acting Coach **H/I/S:** Exercising, Nature, The Beach, Anything Outdoors **EDU:** Foothill College
Email: hsag3652@aol.com

Monica Harris
Title: Owner, Editor **Company:** Monica Harris Mindolovich Editorial Services **Address:** 522 E. 20th Street, Apartment 6D, New York, NY 10009 United States **BUS:** Publishers Company **P/S:** Contemporary Women's Fiction and Non-Fiction **MA:** National **D/D/R:** Editorial Services, Professional Consulting for Publishing Houses and Writers **H/I/S:** Spending Time with Family, Participating in Family Activities **EDU:** Bachelor of Arts in Professional Writing, Carnegie Mellon University; Bachelor of Arts in Literature and Cultural Writing, Carnegie Mellon University **A/A/S:** Black Women in Publishing; Black Women Romance Writers of America **C/VW:** Habitat for Humanity, Dance Theater of Harlem
Email: mhm68@msn.com
URL: http://www.cambridgewhoswho.com

Paula J. Harris
Title: President **Company:** Penn Mill Enterprises **Address:** 73687 Penn Mill Road, Covington, LA 70435 United States **BUS:** Distribution Company **P/S:** Phone Directories **MA:** Local **EXP:** Ms. Harris' expertise is in business management. **H/I/S:** Fishing, Golfing, Traveling, Working on Computers **CERTS:** Diploma, Hattiesburg High School **C/VW:** Local Church
Email: granpapala@aol.com

Robert W. Harris
Title: Teacher, Student Teacher Supervisor (Retired) **Company:** Pearson **Dept:** National Accounts Division **Address:** 333 S. Beaudry Avenue, Carson, CA 90747 United States **BUS:** Publishing Company **P/S:** Educational Publications and Programs **MA:** National **EXP:** Mr. Harris' expertise is in account management. **D/D/R:** Contributing Social Studies Programs, Overseeing Accounts of States of California, Washington, Nevada and Oklahoma **H/I/S:** Reading **EDU:** Coursework, Long Beach, CA
Email: lvha869794@aol.com

Sara Harris
Title: School Psychologist **Company:** Illinois State University **Address:** DeGarmo 460 Psychology, Normal, IL 61790 United States **BUS:** University **P/S:** Education, Human Development **MA:** National **D/D/R:** Specializing in Early Childhood Psychology **H/I/S:** Spending Time Outdoors and with Family, Traveling, Reading **EDU:** Pursuing Ph.D. in School Psychology, Illinois State University; Bachelor of Arts in Psychology, Illinois College, 1999 **A/A/S:** American Psychological Association; National Association of School Psychologists; Illinois School Psychologists Association **C/VW:** Children's Discovery Museum
Email: sara22harris@netscape.net

Twila Y. Harris
Title: Attorney, Partner **Company:** Harris and Jones, LLC **Address:** 149 S. McDonough Street, Suite 215, Jonesboro, GA 30236 United States **BUS:** Law Firm **P/S:** Legal Services **MA:** Local **EXP:** Ms. Harris' expertise is in civil law. **H/I/S:** Reading **EDU:** Georgia State University, University of Tennessee College of Law, BBA, JD **A/A/S:** American Civil Liberties Union, NAACP, American Bar Association, Clayton County Bar Association, Georgia Association of Clinical Defense Lawyer, Association of Trial Lawyers of America, Kappa Alpha Psi, Golden Key National Society, Coach Mundy's Mill High School Mock Trial Competition
Email: twilaharris@excite.com
URL: www.harrisandjones.com

Ginger L. Harris-Pike
Title: Chairwoman of the Early Childhood Education Department Company: Central Carolina Community College BUS: Community College P/S: Education MA: Local EXP: Ms. Harris-Pike's expertise is in early childhood education. H/I/S: Traveling, Gardening EDU: Master's Degree in Early Childhood Education, University of North Carolina at Chapel Hill A/A/S: North Carolina Community College Faculty Association; National Association for the Education of Young Children C/VW: Partnership for Children
Email: glharrispike@hotmail.com

Corbit Harrison
Title: Director of Strategic Planning Address: 6009 Marsh Circle, Loveland, OH 45140 United States BUS: Marketing, Business Development and Sales Management P/S: Software MA: International D/D/R: Strategic Planning, Business and Sales Management EDU: Master of Business Administration, Suffield University
Email: corbith@gmail.com
URL: http://www.cambridgewhoswho.com

Jann Murray Harrison
Title: Artist, Owner Company: Jann Harrison Fine Art BUS: Art Gallery P/S: Art MA: International D/D/R: Writing, Oil Painting, Creating the Character Francois Fibian H/I/S: Participating in Political Activities EDU: Bachelor of Fine Arts, Minor in Art History, University of Tennessee at Knoxville; Studied with Joseph Sulkowski A/A/S: Phi Beta Phi C/VW: Vanderbilt Hospital, Nashville; Multiple Sclerosis Society, Kate duVin National Wine Auction Charity, Artrageous, Nashville Cares for HIV, Children's Charities
Email: jann@jannharrison.com
URL: http://www.jannharrison.com

Lucella T. Harrison
Title: Teacher, Administrator Company: West Contra Costa Unified School District Address: 1108 Bissell Avenue, Richmond, CA 94801 United States BUS: School District P/S: Education MA: Local D/D/R: Instruction H/I/S: Playing the Piano, Attending Church, Traveling EDU: Master of Arts in Creative Arts, San Francisco State University; Bachelor of Arts, San Francisco State University A/A/S: CTA; NEA; NAACP; Delta Theta National Alliance of Black School Educators C/VW: Saint Paul African Methodist Episcopal Church
Email: lucella@sbcglobal.net

Tamera L. Harrison
Title: Owner, Artist Company: Perm Makeup Salon and Spa Address: 4054 Mother Lode Drive, Shingle Springs, CA 95682 United States BUS: Skin Care, Day Spa, Permanent Makeup P/S: Permanent Makeup, Skin Care, Spa MA: Local EXP: Ms. Harrison's expertise includes permanent makeup, skin care and salon and spa services. H/I/S: Spending Time with Family, Sports, Dogs EDU: Coursework, American River College and Sierra College A/A/S: Society of Permanent Cosmetics Professionals C/VW: Breast Cancer Society, Make-A-Wish Foundation
Email: tamra@permmakeup.com
URL: http://www.permmakeup.com

Audrey J. Hart
Title: Owner, Proprietor Company: Miss Audrey's Human Connection Address: 1637 Atlantic Avenue, Atlantic City, NY 08401 United States BUS: Retail Store P/S: Thrift Shop, Boutique, Recycling MA: Regional D/D/R: Sewing H/I/S: Spending Time with her Family, Sewing, Politics C/VW: Local Charitable Organizations
Email: hart2305@hotmail.com

Claire E. Hart
Title: Kindergarten Teacher, Religion Coordinator Company: Saint Bernadette School Address: 20 Burr Street, New Haven, CT 06512 United States BUS: Catholic Elementary School P/S: Education, After School Program MA: Hartford, CT D/D/R: Teaching Kindergarten Using Multi-sensory Methods and Puppetry, Conducting Workshops on Teaching Methods H/I/S: Knitting, Collecting Bears, Writing, Meditating, Playing Musical Instruments EDU: Bachelor of Science in Education, College of Saint Mary of the Springs (Now Ohio Dominican College) A/A/S: National Catholic Educational Association; Catholic Education Award C/VW: Oblate Missions, Catholic Charities, Boys and Girls Village
Email: bumblesandpopsicle@netzero.net

Jenifer A. Hart
Title: Owner, Director Company: Designing Beauty Academy Address: 4625 W. 20th Street, Greeley, CO 80634 United States BUS: School of Cosmetology P/S: Education on Hair, Nails and Skin Care MA: Regional D/D/R: Managing Business, Teaching Classes, Encouraging and Coaching Students H/I/S: Spending Time with Family CERTS: Certification in Cosmetology; Licensed in Cosmetology A/A/S: American Association of Cosmetology Schools; Better Business Bureau
Email: jeni@dbastyle.com
URL: http://www.designingbeautyacademy.com

Kathryn B. Hart, Ph.D.
Title: Associate Director Company: Terros BUS: Nonprofit Organization P/S: Community Services Including Counseling on Mental Health, HIV and Substance Abuse Treatment, Education and Training Programs MA: Regional D/D/R: Managing Clinical and Front Office Operations, Hiring and Firing Employees, Supervising Staff, Conducting Assessments, Maintaining Medical Records, Overseeing Rehabilitation Services, Treating General Mental Illness and Substance Abuse Patients, Performing Administrative Duties H/I/S: Playing the Violin, Golfing, Playing Bridge EDU: Ph.D. in Health Service Administration, Walden University, MN (1995); Master of Science in Counseling, Winona State University, MN (1987) A/A/S: Board President, Mentally Ill Kids in Distress; Board of Directors, Secretary, East Valley Chapter, National Alliance on Mental Illness; American Counseling Association C/VW: Violinist, Tempe Symphony Orchestra
Email: kathhart1@prodigy.net
URL: http://www.terros.org

Stephanie L. Hart, MBA
Title: Business Manager Company: Virginia Commonwealth University Address: 1112 E. Clay Street, Richmond, VA 23298 United States BUS: University P/S: Higher Education MA: Regional EXP: Ms. Hart's expertise includes research administration and grants management. H/I/S: Traveling, Cooking EDU: Master of Business Administration, Babcock Graduate School of Management, Wake Forest University A/A/S: Society of Research Administrators; National Council of University Research Administrators; Who's Who Among Professional Women C/VW: Volunteer, Girl Scouts
Email: slhart@vcu.edu
URL: http://www.vcu.edu/idas

Tonya J. Hart
Title: Denver Engineering Division Manager Company: CTL Thompson, Inc. Address: 8848 S. Dudley Street, Littleton, CO 80128 United States BUS: Engineering and Consulting Firm P/S: Geotechnical Engineering and Consulting Services MA: Local D/D/R: Conducting Research on Expansive Soils H/I/S: Hiking, Camping, Hunting, Cooking EDU: Master's Degree in Science and Geotechnical Engineering, West Virginia University; Bachelor of Science in Engineering, with Concentration in Civil Engineering, Colorado School of Mines A/A/S: Colorado Association of Geotechnical Engineers; American Society of Civil Engineers
Email: thart@ctlthompson.com
URL: http://www.ctlt.com/

Robin L. Hartdegen
Title: Teacher Company: St. Ann School Address: 4921 Meadowdale Street, Metairie, LA 70006 United States BUS: Catholic Education Facility P/S: Instruction and Curriculum MA: Regional D/D/R: Teaching Sixth-grade Mathematics, Coordinating the Mathematics Committee H/I/S: Shopping, Playing Volleyball EDU: Master's Degree in Curriculum and Instruction, University of New Orleans (1995) A/A/S: National Council of Teachers of Mathematics; National Council of Middle School Teachers; Louisiana Teachers of Mathematics
Email: rhartdegen@cox.net
URL: http://www.stannschool.org/

Larry C. Hartfield
Title: Tennis Instructor, Owner Company: Stretch Tennis Address: Bronx, NY 10475 United States BUS: Coaching Center P/S: Tennis Instruction MA: Local D/D/R: Coaching Tennis H/I/S: Playing Tennis, Watching Sports EDU: Associate Degree, Media Arts Center A/A/S: Professional Tennis Registry; United States Tennis Association; American Tennis Association
Email: lchart50@peoplepc.com
URL: http://www.cambridgewhoswho.com

Amy E. Hartman
Title: Student, Candidate for Master of Arts Company: Naropa University Dept: Transpersonal Counseling Psychology BUS: Graduate Student D/D/R: Studying Transpersonal Counseling Psychology, Incorporating Spiritual Component into Psychology H/I/S: Hiking, Cooking, Playing Piano EDU: Pursuing Master of Arts Degree in Transpersonal Counseling Psychology, Naropa University; Bachelor of Arts Cum Laude in English and Women's Studies, University of Colorado (1999) A/A/S: American Counseling Association; Association for Spiritual, Ethical and Religious Values in Counseling; Colorado Counseling Association; Colorado Association for Spiritual, Ethical and Religious Values in Counseling; Colorado Licensed Professional Counselors Association; Association of Transpersonal Psychology
Email: amyandyh@hotmail.com
URL: http://www.cambridgewhoswho.com

Trina L. Hartman
Title: Owner Company: Shear Design Hair Studio Address: 3191 Rt 27, Franklin Park, NJ 08823 United States BUS: Beauty Spa P/S: Facial, Waxing, Hair Styling, Relaxers, Perms MA: Local D/D/R: Hair Cutting, Coloring, Styling H/I/S: Softball, Reading, Spending Time at the Beach EDU: Vocational Technical Program, Cosmetology Beauty School
Email: trinalhart@msn.com

Shawn M. Hartsock
Title: Director Of Operations Company: Shippensburg Area EMS Address: P.O. Box 69, Shippensburg, PA 17257 United States BUS: Emergency Medical Services Company P/S: Emergency Medical Care MA: Local D/D/R: Overseeing Operations, Risk Management, Financial Administration H/I/S: Restoring Old Cars EDU: Associate Degree in Business Administration, Hagerstown College (1993) A/A/S: National Registry of Emergency Medical Technicians; Pennsylvania Institute of Applied Health Sciences
Email: shawnhartsock@cwwemail.com
URL: http://www.cambridgewhoswho.com

Cheryl L. Hartwig
Title: Second-Grade Teacher Company: Flat Rock Community Schools Address: 28639 Division Street, Flat Rock, MI 48134 United States BUS: Elementary School P/S: Education MA: Local D/D/R: Teaching Children in Second-Grade H/I/S: Boating, Swimming, Gardening EDU: Master's Degree in Early Childhood Education, Eastern Michigan University; Bachelor of Arts in Social Sciences, Minor in Fine Arts, Michigan State University A/A/S: National Education Association; Michigan Education Association C/VW: Grosse Ile Presbyterian Church
Email: cheriehartwig@yahoo.com
URL: http://www.cambridgewhoswho.com

Linda L. Harveland
Title: Administrative Secretary Company: Hamilton International Middle School Address: 4400 Interlake Avenue N., Seattle, WA 98103 United States BUS: Middle School P/S: Public School Education MA: Local D/D/R: Organizational skills, Scheduling for Students, Teachers, Community programs, Budget analysis, Payroll and human resource. H/I/S: Spending Time with her Family, Reading, Baking EDU: Coursework in Business, Minot College of Business A/H: Outstanding Performance Award; Ministering Teacher Award C/VW: Board Member, Church; Ladies' Ministry, Church; Parent-Teacher Association
Email: lharveland@seattleschools.org
URL: http://www.cambridgewhoswho.com

Jennifer L. Harvey
Title: Vice President Company: ANW Builders, LLC Address: 11680 S.E. 64th Avenue, Runnells, IA 50237 United States BUS: Construction Company P/S: Residential and Commercial Construction MA: Local EXP: Ms. Harvey's expertise includes design and finance. H/I/S: Traveling EDU: Associate Degree A/A/S: RTA C/VW: Dollars for Scholars
Email: anwbuilders@msn.com

Keith Harvey
Title: Electric Distribution Supervisor Company: Public Service Electric and Gas Company Address: 900 W. Grand Street, Elizabeth, NJ 07202 United States BUS: Utility Company P/S: Electric, Gas and Appliance Services MA: Local D/D/R: Managing, Supervising H/I/S: Spending Time with Family, Watching Sports, Playing Billiards, Going to the Gym, Cooking EDU: Associate of Science in Business Management, Rutgers University; Management and Leadership Seminars, Skillpath Seminars; Coursework in Leadership and Management, American Management Association A/A/S: Association of American Blacks in Energy; Chairman, Minority Interchange A/H: Outstanding Member of the Year Award, Minority Interchange C/VW: National Black United Fund, Habitat for Humanity, March of Dimes
Email: keith.harvey@pseg.com
URL: http://www.pseg.com

Melissa Anne Harvey
Title: RN, CCM, CNLCP, MSCC, BSN Company: Utilization Management Address: 1200 Saint Ann Street, Jackson, MS 39202 United States BUS: Medical Care Management and Consulting Company P/S: Catastrophic Case Management, Life Care Planning, Expert Witness, Medicare Consulting MA: Local D/D/R: Coordinating Care for Catastrophically Injured and Geriatric Patients, Life Care Planning, Expert Witness Designation H/I/S: Sailing, Kayaking, Fishing, Gardening, Playing Bass Guitar EDU: Bachelor of Arts in Liberal Arts, University of Mississippi at Oxford; Bachelor of Science in Nursing, University of Mississippi at Jackson CERTS: Certified Case Manager; Certified Nurse Life Care Planner; Certified Medicare Set-Aside Consultant A/A/S: American Nurses Association; Mississippi Nurses Association; National Hospital Association; National Alliance Medicare Set-Aside Professionals A/H: Case Manager of the Year, 1992, 2002 C/VW: Lobbyist, Burn Center, Jackson, Mississippi; Blair Batson Hospital; American Cancer Society; Ronald McDonald House; Relay for Life
Email: melhar21@bellsouth.net

Carla Harvill
Title: Speech, Language Pathologist **Company:** East Newton Elementary School **Address:** 2286 Dixie Road, Covington, GA 30014 United States **BUS:** Elementary School **P/S:** Education **MA:** Local **D/D/R:** Offering Speech and Language Therapy **H/I/S:** Reading, Sports, Spending Time with her Grandchildren **EDU:** Master of Education, Concentration in Speech-Language Pathology, University of Georgia; Bachelor of Science in Speech-Language Pathology, University of Georgia **A/A/S:** American Speech-Language-Hearing Association; Georgia Speech-Language Hearing Association; Georgia Organization of School-Based Speech-Language Pathologists **C/VW:** Goodwill, Sunrise Prison Ministries
Email: chharvill@bellsouth.net
URL: http://www.cambridgewhoswho.com

Patricia Elaine Hasemann
Title: Licensed Clinical Social Worker **Company:** University of Illinois at Chicago **Address:** 1745 Corporate Crossing, O'Fallon, IL 62294 **BUS:** University **P/S:** Education **MA:** International **EXP:** Ms. Hasemann's expertise is in adolescent social work. **H/I/S:** Reading, Bike Riding **EDU:** Master of Social Work, Southern Illinois University at Edwardsville **A/A/S:** North American Association of Christians in Social Work; National Association of Social Workers **C/VW:** Church
Email: pehasema@uic.edu
URL: http://www.cambridgewhoswho.com

Mrs. Veronica Marie Hass
Title: Owner **Company:** PBVBrat Designs **Address:** 15707½ Larch Avenue, Lawndale, CA 90260 United States **BUS:** Production **P/S:** Hand-Sewn Greeting Cards, Photography, Jewelry **MA:** Local **D/D/R:** Arts and Crafts: Jewelry Making, Card Making, Crocheting, Memory Books for Reunions **H/I/S:** Walking, Bicycling, Going to the Beach, Watching Movies, Water Aerobics **EDU:** Industry-Related Training and Experience **A/A/S:** Venice High School Alumni Association **C/VW:** VHS Alumni Association
Email: veronica.hass@sbcglobal.net
URL: http://www.pbvbrat.blogspot.com
URL: http://www.printroom.com/pro/pbvbrat

Forrest N. Hassler
Title: Maintenance Worker **Company:** Wolf Mountain Conference Association **Address:** 16555 Jericho Road, Grass Valley, CA 95949 United States **BUS:** Nonprofit Organization **P/S:** Recreation and Spiritual Services **MA:** National **D/D/R:** Utilizing his Mechanical Skills, Training and Orienting Camp Leaders, Counselors and Employees **H/I/S:** Spending Time Outdoors, Camping, Riding his Motor Bike, Backpacking **EDU:** High School Diploma
Email: bluesky95949@sbcglobal.net
URL: http://www.cambridgewhoswho.com

M. Susan Haston
Title: Professor **Company:** Pensacola Christian College **Address:** 250 Brent Lane, Pensacola, FL 32503 United States **BUS:** College **P/S:** Higher Education **MA:** National **D/D/R:** Educating Future Teachers, Teaching Elementary Education, Educational Psychology, Child Growth and Development, Personal Community Health, Tests and Measurements **H/I/S:** Reading, Collecting Antiques **EDU:** Ph.D. in Elementary Education, Pensacola Christian College; Master's Degree in Psychology, University of West Florida; Coursework, Florida State University **C/VW:** Local Church
Email: marysusanh@aol.com
URL: http://www.cambridgewhoswho.com

Ilene E. Hatch, MD
Title: Physician **Company:** Fertility Center of Southern California **Address:** 2192 Martin Street, Suite 110, Irvine, CA 92612 United States **BUS:** Fertility Clinic **P/S:** Reproductive Endocrinology, Infertility Healthcare **MA:** International **D/D/R:** Fertility Patient Care **H/I/S:** Traveling, Skiing **EDU:** MD, University of Southern California **A/A/S:** American Society for Reproductive Medicine; Pacific Coast Fertility Society; Pacific Coast Fertility Society **C/VW:** All of Crest
Email: ihatchmd@aol.com

Dorothy W. Hatcher
Title: Retired Teacher, Activist for National Women of Achievement **Company:** Houston Independent School District **Address:** 3600 Richmond Avenue, Houston, TX **BUS:** School **P/S:** Education **MA:** Local **D/D/R:** Teaching Special Education **H/I/S:** Aerobics, Singing **EDU:** Bachelor of Arts in Religious Education, World Institute of Religious Education; College Coursework, Texas Southern University **A/A/S:** Gamma Sigma Sorority **C/VW:** Damascus Missionary Baptist Church, Ronald McDonald House, Crippled Veterans
URL: http://www.cambridgewhoswho.com

Al Hathy
Title: Director of Operations **Company:** Shuffle Master, Inc. **Dept:** Operations **Address:** 1106 Palms Airport Drive, Las Vegas, NV 89119 United States **BUS:** Manufacturing Company **P/S:** Card Shufflers, Electronic Table Games **MA:** International **EXP:** Mr. Hathy's expertise is in production. **D/D/R:** Managing Company Operations **H/I/S:** Spending Time with his Children, Golfing, Reading **EDU:** Bachelor of Science in Economics, Montana State University **CERTS:** Certified Product and Inventory Management, American Production and Inventory Control Society
Email: ahathy@shufflemaster.com
URL: http://www.shufflemaster.com

Sandra B. Hatley, MS.Ed.
Title: Teacher-Exceptional Children **Company:** Burke County Public Schools **Dept:** Forest Hill Elementary **Address:** 304 Ann Street, Morganton, NC 28655 United States **BUS:** Education School **P/S:** Public School Education from Kindergarten Through High School **MA:** Local **D/D/R:** Teaching Exceptional Children-Hearing, Visual, Orthopedic Impaired and Mentally Challenged **H/I/S:** Camping, Gardening, Reading **EDU:** University of Charlotte, MS-Education **A/A/S:** NCEA, NEA, Past Member of Council for Exceptional Children and Association of Curriculum
Email: shattley@burke.k12.nc.us.
URL: www.burke.k12.nc.us.

Brenda Jean Haught
Title: Chief Executive Officer, Minister **Company:** Assisted Living Ministry Services **Address:** 650 Saint Clair Avenue, East Liverpool, OH 43920 United States **BUS:** Assisted Living Ministry **P/S:** Assisted Living, Hospice Care **MA:** Pennsylvania, Ohio, West Virginia **EXP:** Ms. Haught's expertise is in ministry. **H/I/S:** Spending Time with her Family **EDU:** Bachelor of Science in Human Resources, Geneva College; Associate of Arts in Biblical Studies, Vision International University **CERTS:** Licensed Minister, Gospel Crusade Ministerial Fellowship; Certified in Early Childhood Development, Jefferson Community and Technical College **A/A/S:** East Liverpool Chamber of Commerce **A/H:** Honorary Chairwoman, Business Advisory Council, National Republican Congressional Committee; Businesswoman of the Year, Business Advisory Council, National Republican Congressional Committee, 2006 **C/VW:** Local Church, Trinity Broadcasting Network, Daystar, Leukemia & Lymphoma Society, American Cancer Society
Email: brenda_haught@msn.com

Cecelia Hauptman
Title: Owner **Company:** CT Maverick Wear **Address:** 195B Foxwood Drive, Grants Pass, OR 97527 United States **BUS:** Apparel Manufacturing Company **P/S:** Women's Hospital Scrubs, Service Aprons, Leisure Shirts **MA:** National **D/D/R:** Designing, Sewing **H/I/S:** Crocheting, Spending Time with her Family **EDU:** Diploma, Madonna High School, Aurora, Illinois **A/A/S:** Church **C/VW:** Local Church, Nursing Home
Email: celhauptman1333@charter.net
URL: http://www.ctmaverickwear.com

Shannon F. Hauser, RN, BSN
Title: Director of Nursing **Company:** Parkview Home **Address:** 1234 S. Park Boulevard, Freeport, IL 61032 United States **BUS:** Nonprofit Organization **P/S:** Long-Term Care Facility for Senior Citizens **MA:** Regional **D/D/R:** Her expertise is in overseeing staff, nursing services, monitoring policies and procedures, creating budgets, caring and planning for residents. **H/I/S:** Cooking, Hiking, Attending her Children's Sporting Events **EDU:** Bachelor of Science in Nursing, Marquette University (1986)
Email: jshauser@insightbb.com

Dr. Ray Ann D. Havasee
Title: Director **Company:** Center for Science Teaching and Learning **Address:** 1 Tanglewood Road, Rockville Centre, NY 11570 United States **BUS:** Nonprofit **P/S:** Science Education **MA:** National **EXP:** Dr. Havasee's expertise includes biology and science education. **H/I/S:** Traveling **EDU:** Doctor of Education in Biology and Science Education, Columbia University **A/A/S:** Association of Science-Technology Centers; American Association of Museums **C/VW:** Parent Center, World Conservatory Society, Worthy Wildlife Causes
Email: rayann@cstl.org
URL: http://www.cstl.org

Kristen T. Havnen
Title: Territory Manager **Company:** Salix Pharmaceuticals, Inc. **Address:** 1700 Perimeter Park Drive, Morrisville, NC 27560 United States **BUS:** Specialty Pharmaceutical Company **P/S:** Pharmaceutical Products for the Treatment of Gastrointestinal Disease **MA:** Regional **D/D/R:** Selling Gastroenterology Medications **H/I/S:** Movies, Running, Volleyball, Skiing **EDU:** Bachelor of Arts in Business Administration, Wisconsin-Madison (1996) **A/A/S:** Multiple Sclerosis Walk; Alzheimer's Association; Crohn's Colitis Foundation
Email: kthblonde1@wi.rr.com
URL: http://www.salix.com

Linda M. Hawk
Title: Owner **Company:** Hawk Research and Consulting Services **Address:** 396 Wunderlich Avenue, Barberton, OH 44203 United States **BUS:** Information Profession Consulting **P/S:** Research, Executive Reports, Home Based Business **MA:** Local **EXP:** Ms. Hawk's expertise is in architecture. **H/I/S:** Flute, Concert Band, Reading **EDU:** Master's Degree in Library and Information Science, Kent State University **A/A/S:** AIIP Association
Email: hawkresearch@sbcglobal.net
URL: http://www.cambridgewhoswho.com

Dianne Kendrick Hawkins
Title: Special Education Specialist **Company:** Dallas Independent School District **Address:** 408 N. Haskell, Dallas, TX 75214 United States **BUS:** School District **P/S:** Education **MA:** Dallas **EXP:** Ms. Hawking's expertise includes special education and administration. **H/I/S:** Traveling **EDU:** Pursuing Ph.D. in Exceptional Child Special Education, North Central University; Master of Education in Special Education, University of Texas, Tyler **A/A/S:** Association for Supervision and Curriculum Development; Council for Exceptional Children; Council of Administrators of Special Education; Texas Council of Administrators of Special Education **C/VW:** Local Public Television, Delta Sigma Theta Public Service Organization, Fundraising Drives for Public Television and Radio, Saint Anne Episcopal Church
Email: diannekhawkins@yahoo.com

Juliet V. Hawkins
Title: Licensed Psychotherapist and Behavioral Specialist **Company:** YAI/National Institute for People with Disabilities Network **Dept:** Centre for Specialty Therapy **Address:** 328 Beach 102nd Street, Rockaway Park, NY 11694 United States **BUS:** Sole Proprietorship **P/S:** Behavior Management and Parent Training Programs **MA:** National **D/D/R:** Organizing Behavioral Training Programs, Working with the Developmentally Disabled, Performing Psychotherapy, Writing, Consulting **H/I/S:** Sports, Creative Writing, Studying about the Universe, Cooking **EDU:** Master's Degree in Clinical Psychology, New York University (1988) **A/A/S:** The National Association for the Dually Diagnosed; American Psychotherapy Association
Email: julih1@aol.com
URL: http://www.yai.org

Tramaine Hawkins
Title: Legendary Gospel Artist **Company:** Lady Tramaine Hawkins Ministries **Address:** P.O. Box 2144, Rancho Cordova, CA 95741 United States **BUS:** Music and Entertainment Practice **P/S:** Gospel Music and Ministry **MA:** International **D/D/R:** Promoting Live Tours, Meeting her Fans, Singing Gospel Music, Hosting Vocal Technique Workshops **H/I/S:** Basketball, Football, Watching Movies and Opera **EDU:** Berkley High School **A/A/S:** Published; Gospel Hall of Fame **A/H:** Berkley Hall of Fame; Winner, Dual Grammy Awards
URL: http://www.ladytramainehawkinsministries.com

Karen Louisa Hawks
Title: Vice President of Supply Chain **Company:** Navesink Logistics, Inc. **Address:** 224 Commonwealth Circle, Grand Prairie, TX 75052 United States **BUS:** Virtual Network Consulting Firm **P/S:** Logistics and Supply Chain Consulting, Software Implementation and Integration, Recruiting **MA:** National **D/D/R:** Overseeing Business Development, Project Management and Recruiting **H/I/S:** Spending Time with Family and Friends, Going to the Movies **EDU:** Doctor of Business Administration, Rochville University; Master of Science in Professional Development, Amber University **A/A/S:** Former Member, Warehousing Education and Research Council
Email: kh@logjobs.com
URL: http://www.navesinklogistics.com

Sharon E. K Hawryluk
Title: Teacher **Company:** Manasquan High School **Dept:** Department of Social Studies **Address:** 162 Broad Street, Manasquan, NJ 08736 United States **BUS:** High School **P/S:** Secondary Education **MA:** Local **D/D/R:** Teaching Psychology, Organizing Advanced Placement Classes, Overseeing Curriculum Development, Instructing Classes, Managing Behavior **H/I/S:** Party Boat Fishing **EDU:** Master of Education in Counseling and Teaching, Monmouth College; Bachelor of Arts in Psychology, Monmouth College **A/A/S:** Teachers of Psychology in Secondary Schools; American Psychological Association
Email: shawryluk@manasquanboe.org
Email: shayrok@aol.com

Jon M. Hay

Title: Clinical Coordinator, Associate Professor, Certified Athletic Trainer **Company:** Nicholls State University **Address:** Athletic Training Science, P.O. Box 2090, Thibodaux, LA 70310 United States **BUS:** University **P/S:** Education **MA:** International **D/D/R:** Caring for Shoulder and Knee Injuries, Managing Rehabilitation, Athletic Training, Teaching **H/I/S:** Stargazing, Golfing, Fishing, Hiking **EDU:** Master of Education, Valdosta State College; Bachelor of Science in Education, Northwest Missouri State University **A/A/S:** National Athletic Trainers' Association; Louisiana Athletic Trainers' Association; McCue Society; Hughston Society
Email: jon.hay@nicholls.edu
URL: http://www.nicholls.edu/athletictraining

Lawrence J. Haye, MBA

Title: President, Chief Executive Officer **Company:** Haye Capital Group **Address:** 3914 Sunflower Circle, Mitchelville, MD 20721 United States **BUS:** Financial Service Provider **P/S:** Private Equity and Investments **MA:** National **D/D/R:** Managing Daily Business Operations, Establishing the Goals and Objectives for the Limited Liability Corporation, Ensuring All Set Goals Are Met, Exploring Investment Opportunities, Securing Potential Clients, Negotiating Major Contracts and Pricing, Developing and Maintaining Effective Business Relationships at the Highest Levels, Engineering Financial Solutions **H/I/S:** Boxing **EDU:** Keller Graduate School, University of Connecticut, Master of Business Administration, BS **A/A/S:** National Association of Black Engineers, National Piano Guild
Email: ljhaye@hayecapitalgroup.com
URL: www.hayecapitalgroup.com

Deborah L. Hayes

Title: Assistant Principal **Company:** Matt Kelly Elementary School **Address:** 1900 N. J Street, Las Vegas, NV 89106 United States **BUS:** School **P/S:** Education **MA:** Local **D/D/R:** Overseeing School Operations, Staff and Activities **H/I/S:** Making Jewelry **EDU:** Pursuing Doctorate in Educational Leadership, Nova Southeastern University; Master's Degree in Administration, University of Phoenix, 2002; Bachelor's Degree in Elementary Education, Minor in Music and Social Studies, Weber State University, 1992 **A/A/S:** Association for Supervision and Curriculum Development
Email: hayes0092@cox.net

Dorothy J. Hayes

Title: Teacher, Counselor, Dean, Retired **Company:** Los Angeles Unified School District **BUS:** School District **P/S:** Education **MA:** Los Angeles, California **D/D/R:** Directing the Chorus, Teaching, Counseling, Serving as the Dean of Students **EDU:** Master of Arts, Saint Louis University; Master of Science in Music Education, University of Southern California; Bachelor's Degree, Tennessee State University; Administrative Credential, Pepperdine University **A/A/S:** National Association of Negro Musicians; Scholarship Chairwoman, NANM, BEEM; Delta Sigma Theta; National Association for the Advancement of Colored People; Crenshaw United Methodist Church; Top Ladies of Distinction
URL: http://www.cambridgewhoswho.com

Justin Hayes

Title: Market Intelligence Analyst **Company:** The Timken Company **Address:** 1835 Dueber Avenue S.W., Canton, OH 44706 United States **BUS:** Manufacturing Company **P/S:** Bearings Products, Alloy Steel, Steel Components, Power Transmission Components and Systems, Lubrication, Seals and Motion Control Systems **MA:** International **D/D/R:** Conducting Market Research, Forecasting Information for Sales **EDU:** Master of Science in Integrated Marketing Communications, Walsh University, North Canton, OH; Bachelor of Science in Marketing Management, Walsh University **A/A/S:** The Canton Jaycees; American Marketing Association
Email: justin.hayes@timken.com
URL: http://www.timken.com

Kathryn M. Hayes-Pomeroy

Title: Special Education Teacher **Company:** Norfolk Public Schools-The Larrymore School **Address:** 7600 Halprin Drive, Norfolk, VA 23518 United States **BUS:** School **P/S:** Education **MA:** Local **D/D/R:** Teaching Children with Learning Disabilities and Emotional Disorders **H/I/S:** participating in Girl Scouts **EDU:** Master's Degree in Reading, Walden University(2006); Bachelor's Degree in Special Education, Northeastern Illinois University, Chicago (1997) **A/A/S:** National Education Association; American Federation of Teachers
Email: snoopygirl74@verizon.net

Lois A. Hayman

Title: Training Specialist **Company:** Philadelphia Corporation for Aging **Address:** 642 N. Broad Street, Philadelphia, PA 19130 United States **BUS:** Nonprofit Organization **P/S:** Community Services Including Raising Funds for Geriatric Centers, Organizing Meals on Wheels Programs, Transportation Services for Elderly People, Care for Disabled Young People **MA:** Regional **D/D/R:** Utilizing her Management Skills, Training Employees and Supervisors, Managing General Agency Orientation, Organizing Programs for the Treatment of Aged, Mentally Retarded Individuals **H/I/S:** Acting **EDU:** Master of Social Work, University of Pennsylvania (1974); Bachelor of Arts in Sociology, Hampton University, VA (1972) **CERTS:** Licensed Private Practitioner, State of Pennsylvania **A/A/S:** Board Member, Center on Ethnic and Minority Aging; Board Member, Resource Centers for Minority Aging Research; National Association of Black Social Workers **C/VW:** Older Adult Ministries, Presbyterian Church; American Society on Aging; Former Board Member, Little Brothers – Friends of the Elderly
Email: lhayman@pcaphl.org
URL: http://www.pcacares.org

Ellen Dean Haynes

Title: Realtor **Company:** All American Realty **Address:** 662 Sudderth Drive, Ruidoso, NM 88345 United States **BUS:** Real Estate Agency **P/S:** Real Estate **MA:** Local **D/D/R:** Advertising, Promoting, Residential and Commercial Sales, Open Houses **H/I/S:** Traveling **A/A/S:** National Association of Realtors; NWAR; Ambassador, Chamber of Commerce; Beta Sigma Phi **C/VW:** Local Church, Helping Senior Citizens
Email: EllenDean.Haynes@cwwemail.com
URL: http://www.cambridgewhoswho.com

Raymond J. Haynesworth

Title: Meter Services Division Manager **Company:** District of Columbia Water and Sewer Authority **Address:** 301 Bryant Street N.W., Washington, DC 20001 United States **BUS:** Utility Company **P/S:** Drinking Water and Wastewater Treatment **MA:** Regional **D/D/R:** Installing Water Meters, Testing and Ensuring the Accurate Registration of Water as it Passes through the Meters **H/I/S:** Listening to Music, Playing the Drums, Gardening **EDU:** Bachelor of Music, University of the District of Columbia (1979) **CERTS:** Diploma, Mendenhall School of Auctioneering, High Point, NC (1982) **A/A/S:** Eastern Meter Management Association **C/VW:** Central Union Mission
Email: raymond.haynesworth@dcwasa.com
URL: http://www.dcwasa.com

Nellie Hayse

Title: Self Employed **Company:** Retired From Scout Council of Colonial Coast as CEO **Address:** 932 Shoal Creek Trail, Unit B, Chesapeake, VA 23320 United States **BUS:** Your Travel Biz; Trading Stocks Online Home Business **P/S:** Your Travel Biz provides complete package and services used wide from booking flights and hotels to cruise packages. **MA:** National **D/D/R:** Stock Trading and Referring Travel Agent **H/I/S:** Loves to Sail, Hiking, Gardening, Symphony and Opera, Reading, Birding **EDU:** Wellesley College, Bachelor of Liberal Arts **A/A/S:** United States Power Squandrons, Rotary, Life Member Girl Scouts of The USA
Email: nellieh36@cox.net
URL: www.ytbtravel.com/nellieh

Dianne F. Hayward, RNC, MSN, WHNP, CLNC

Title: Legal Nurse Consultant **Company:** The Hayward Consulting Group **Address:** 4355 Sashabaw Road, Waterford, MI 48329 United States **BUS:** Private Consulting Firm **P/S:** Legal Medical Consulting **MA:** Regional **D/D/R:** Maternal/Child Legal Medical Consulting, Teaching at Oakland Community College, Experience as Nurse Practitioner in Women's Health **H/I/S:** Computers, Interior Design **EDU:** Master's Degree in Nursing, Wayne State University (1996) **A/A/S:** Sigma Theta Tau Lambda; Association of Women Obstetrical and Neonatal Nurses; Golden Key International Honour Society
Email: clnc.dhayward@yahoo.com
URL: http://www.cambridgewhoswho.com

Kristie E. Hazel, MBA

Title: Director of Audit **Company:** JT Walker and Subsidiaries **Address:** 203 Grove Circle S., Dunedin, FL 34678 United States **BUS:** Financial Services **P/S:** Home Products and Manufacturing **MA:** Florida **D/D/R:** Auditing, Offering Financial Services **H/I/S:** Snow Skiing, Spending Time with her Family **EDU:** Master of Business Administration, University of South Florida; Bachelor of Science, University of South Florida (2004) **A/A/S:** The Institute of Internal Auditors

Lisa C. Head

Title: Paraprofessional **Company:** Friendship Elementary School **Address:** 4450 Friendship Road, Buford, GA 30519 United States **BUS:** Elementary School **P/S:** Primary Education **MA:** Regional **D/D/R:** Organizing Reading Programs and Activities for the Literacy Center, Fundraising, Interacting with Parents, Introducing New Ideas to Children Including Sign Language **H/I/S:** Softball **EDU:** Coursework in Psychology; High School Diploma
Email: lisahead@hallco.org

Joyce M. Healy

Title: Educator **Company:** Washington School **Address:** 155 Washington Avenue, Nutley, NJ 07110 United States **BUS:** Elementary School **P/S:** Primary Education **MA:** Local **D/D/R:** Teaching All Subjects for First through Sixth-Grade Students **H/I/S:** Reading, Oil Painting **EDU:** Master of Arts in Teaching, Marygrove College, MI (1997); Bachelor of Arts in Elementary Education, Jersey City State College **A/A/S:** National Education Association; New Jersey Education Association; Education Association of Nutley; Highland Lakes Country Club & Community Association Ladies Auxiliary **C/VW:** Church
Email: jhealy@myway.com
URL: http://www.cambridgewhoswho.com

Amy L. Heaper

Title: Teacher **Company:** Sweet Springs R-7 School District **Address:** 105 Main Street, Sweet Springs, MO 65351 United States **BUS:** School District **P/S:** Education **MA:** Local **D/D/R:** Teaching Fourth-grade Students **H/I/S:** Interior Decorating, Camping, Reading, Crocheting, Needlepoint **EDU:** Master of Education, Central Missouri State University, 2003; Bachelor's Degree in Early Childhood Education, 1996 **A/A/S:** Missouri National Education Association; National Education Association **C/VW:** Central Christian Church Disciples of Christ
Email: aheaper@hotmail.com
URL: http://www.sweetsprings.k12.mo.us

Sabrina L. Heard

Title: Chief Executive Officer **Company:** Luantha **Address:** 4629 Sixth Street S.E., Washington, DC 20032 United States **BUS:** Merchandise Marketing **P/S:** Home Business, Inspirational Dolls, Novelty Items **MA:** Local **EXP:** Ms. Heard's expertise is in one-of-a-kind items. **H/I/S:** Family, Arts and Crafts **EDU:** Some College **A/A/S:** Womens Collectives, Rap Inc.
Email: luantha9@yahoo.com

Yasmin J. Hearon

Title: President **Company:** Extraordinary Women in Unity Conferences **Address:** P.O. Box 893177, Temecula, CA 92589 United States **BUS:** Nonprofit Organization for Women's Ministry **P/S:** Bringing Women Together to Achieve Their Visions and Goals **MA:** National **D/D/R:** Motivational Speaking **H/I/S:** Traveling, Reading **EDU:** Pursuing Registered Nurse License, Excelsior College **CERTS:** Licensed Practical Nurse, Merrick College (1999) **C/VW:** Church
Email: yasmin@unityofthefaith.com
URL: http://www.ewiuc.unityofthefaith.com

Melissa Heasley

Title: Therapist, Social Worker **Company:** Riverview Intermediate Unit 6, Clarion, PA United States **BUS:** Educational **P/S:** Counseling, Community Support, School-Based Counseling, Intensive Counseling **MA:** Local **D/D/R:** Counseling Emotional Support K-12, Independent and Group Counseling, Social Skills, Anger Management, Self-Esteem. **H/I/S:** Scrapbooking, Working Out, Reading **EDU:** Master of Science in Social Administration, Mandel School of Applied Social Sciences, Case Western Reserve University Bachelor of Arts, Psychology and Sociology, Thiel College, 2002 **A/A/S:** National Association of Social Workers
Email: melissaheasley@hotmail.com
URL: http://www.riu6.org

Tina Jacque Heath

Title: Educator **Company:** The Manor **Address:** 115 East Street, Jonesville, MI 49250 United States **BUS:** Nonprofit Residential Treatment and Special Education Facility **P/S:** Treatment for Developmentally Disabled Children with Behavioral Difficulties **MA:** Regional **EXP:** Ms. Heath's expertise is in the care of sexually-abused victims. **D/D/R:** Teaching All Subjects to Boys Between the Ages of 13 and 18, Including Job Skills and Personality Development **H/I/S:** Needlepoint **EDU:** Master's Degree in Emotionally Impaired Education, Eastern Michigan University (2003); Bachelor of Arts in Secondary Education and English, Spring Arbor University (1990) **A/H:** Award for Programming **C/VW:** Volunteer, Women's Pregnancy Crisis Centers; Volunteer, Church
URL: http://www.the-manor.org

Keri A. Hebert
Title: Registered Nurse **Company:** Lifespan (Rhode Island Hospital) **Address:** 2358 Providence Pike, North Smithfield, RI 02896 United States **BUS:** Nonprofit and Acute Care Hospital **P/S:** Comprehensive Diagnostic and Therapeutic Services to Inpatients and Outpatients **MA:** Regional **D/D/R:** Trauma 1 Medical-Surgical Nursing, Administering Medication, Assessing Patients, Completing Paperwork **H/I/S:** Playing Softball **EDU:** Bachelor of Science in Nursing, Endicott College (2006) **A/A/S:** Volunteer, Local Fire Station
Email: kahstars1784@cox.net
URL: http://www.lifespan.org/rih

Albert A. Hechme
Title: Vice President **Company:** CTA Corporation **Address:** 329 N. 13th Street, Allentown, PA 18104 United States **BUS:** Audio Visual Company **P/S:** Managing and Coordinating Meetings and Seminars **MA:** National **EXP:** Mr. Hechme's expertise includes photography and videography. **D/D/R:** Staging, Setting Up and Managing Meetings and Seminars **H/I/S:** Cross-Country Driving, Photography, Listening to Music, Playing on Computers **EDU:** Bachelor of Science in Business, College of Staten Island **C/VW:** St. Jude Children's Research Foundation
Email: ah@cta-corp.com
URL: http://www.cta-corp.com

Karla E. Heckaman
Title: Deputy Sheriff I **Company:** El Paso County Sheriffs Office **Address:** 2739 East Las Vegas, Colorado Springs, CO 80906 United States **BUS:** Law Enforcement, Sheriff **P/S:** Service to Protect the Community **MA:** Local **D/D/R:** Can Multi Task and Remain Calm Under Pressure **H/I/S:** Traveling, Hiking, Black and White Movies **EDU:** Pursuing Master of Arts in Criminal Justice, Colorado Technical University **A/A/S:** County Sheriff's Association
Email: kevg5@msn.com

Meredith A. Hedeen
Title: Director of Christian Education **Company:** Shadyside Presbyterian Church **Address:** 5121 West Minster Place, Pittsburgh, PA 15232 United States **BUS:** Church **P/S:** Education for Kindergarten through 12th-grade Students, Projects for Soldiers in Iraq and Walter Reed Hospital, Community Outreach to Pittsburgh Area, Developing Ministries and Religion in Individuals and Church **MA:** Local **D/D/R:** Teaching Second, Fourth and Sixth-grade Students, Communicating with Children to Meet Daily Classroom Needs, Developing Lesson Plans, Performing Student Evaluations, Oversee Two College Ministry Groups, One Young Adult Graduate Ministry Group, Youth Ministry, Child's Ministry, Adult Ministry Administrative Director **H/I/S:** Running, Swimming, Reading, Gardening **EDU:** Bachelor of Arts in Elementary Education, Emphasis in Science and Mathematics, Grove City College (2003) **CERTS:** Certification in Instructional Technology, Clarion University of Pennsylvania (2007) **A/A/S:** National Education Association; Pennsylvania State Education Association; Parent Teacher Association
Email: mhedeen@shadysidepres.org
URL: http://www.shadysidepres.org

Teresa L. Hedrick
Title: Co Owner **Company:** TNT Rentals LLC **Address:** 24252 B Canal Road, Orange Beach, AL 36561 United States **BUS:** Rentals Sports/Recreation **P/S:** Scooter Rentals, Motorcycle Rentals **MA:** Local **EXP:** Ms. Hedrick's expertise includes scooters and cycles. **H/I/S:** Golfing, Boating, Cycling **EDU:** North Western, Nursing **A/A/S:** Orange Beach Chamber of Commerce, Light House Diabetes Foundation, Veterans, State Troopers
Email: tntrentals@yahoo.com

Dianna H. Heeter
Title: Licensed Mortgage Broker **Company:** Landmark Mortgage of Tampa Bay **Address:** 3062 West Vinn Del Mar Boulevard, St. Pete Beach, FL 33706 United States **BUS:** Finance, Mortgages, Loans **P/S:** Loan Mortgages for Homes, Commercial Properties **MA:** State of Florida **EXP:** Ms. Heeter's expertise includes finance and credit repair. **H/I/S:** Spending Family Time **A/A/S:** Philanthropist for St. Jude's Hospital; Florida Association of Mortgage Brokers; National Professional Notary Association; St. Pete Beach Emergency Response Team; 'Beach Goes Pop' Committee Member; National Association of Mortgage Brokers
Email: diannaheeter@aol.com
URL: http://www.landmarkmorgage.net

Heidi Kristina Marie Hehnlin
Title: Realtor **Company:** Prudential Jack White/Vista Real Estate **Address:** 2422 Glacier Street, Anchorage, AK 99508 United States **BUS:** Real Estate Agency **P/S:** Real Estate Services Including Residential and Commercial Sales and Leasing, Multiple Unit or Income Property, Land Sales, Corporate and Residential Relocation, Property Management, Mortgage Loan Affiliates, Title Company Affiliates **MA:** National **EXP:** Ms. Hehnlin's expertise includes commercial real estate, residential foreclosures and sales. **D/D/R:** Selling New Construction Real Estate, Networking **H/I/S:** Figure Skating **EDU:** Associate Degree (2006); High School Education (1999) **CERTS:** Certification in Real Estate, Royse **A/A/S:** Alaska Association of Figure Skaters; Alaska Association of Realtors
Email: hsnyder@prudentialjackwhitevista.com
URL: http://www.prudentialjackwhitevista.com

Heather L. Heidenreich
Title: Structural Engineer **Company:** KJWW Engineering Consultants **Address:** 1771 W. Diehl Road, Suite 300, Naperville, IL 60563 United States **BUS:** Engineering Consulting Services **P/S:** Design, Construction **MA:** Regional **D/D/R:** Work with Architects and Contractors Doing Designs for Projects **EDU:** Milwaukee School of Engineers, Bachelor's Degree in Architectural Engineering
Email: heidenreichhl@kjww.com

Carole Currey Heim Whaley
Title: Independent Business Owner **Company:** Health Wholesale **Address:** 758 W. Shannon Road, Bridgeport, WV 26330 United States **BUS:** Online Retail Store **P/S:** Medical and Household Goods Including Goji Antioxidant Juices, Gemtek Personal Trackers and Melaleuca Products and Services **MA:** International **EXP:** Ms. Whaley's expertise includes operations and sales management. **D/D/R:** Managing Sales and Marketing, Recruiting, Acquiring and Maintaining Client Relationships, Overseeing Business Operations and New Business Developments **H/I/S:** Collecting Stained Glass, Making Bead-Works **EDU:** Master of Science in Vocational Administration, Marshall University (1986); Master of Science in Distributive Education, University of Pittsburgh (1973); Bachelor of Science in Business Studies, Carnegie Mellon University (1956) **A/A/S:** Toastmasters International; Scotch Heritage Festival
Email: whaleybc@verizon.net

Karen Bullock Heine
Title: Vice President **Company:** AM Best Company, Inc., Oldwick, NJ 08858 United States **BUS:** Credit Rating Agency **P/S:** Rating Financial Service Industries Including Banking and Insurance Sectors **MA:** National **EXP:** Ms. Heine's expertise includes information technology management and services. **H/I/S:** Running, Skiing **EDU:** Bachelor of Arts in English, University of Virginia **C/VW:** Local Church
Email: karen.heine@ambest.com
URL: http://www.ambest.com

Arleen M. Heintzelman
Title: Special Projects Coordinator **Company:** University of Great Falls **Address:** 1301 20th Street S., Great Falls, MT 59405 United States **BUS:** University **P/S:** Higher Education in Theatrical Arts **MA:** Local **D/D/R:** Acting, Writing **H/I/S:** Traveling, Playing Bridge, Acting **EDU:** Coursework, University of Great Falls; Various Acting Workshops **A/A/S:** Drama Camp; Boy Scouts of America
Email: aheintzelman7380@msn.com
URL: http://www.aweekinlondon.com

Lori A. Heiser
Title: Administrative Specialist **Company:** Aldevron, LLC **Address:** 3233 15th Street S., Fargo, ND 58104 United States **BUS:** Biotechnology Company **P/S:** Producing Plasmid DNA **D/D/R:** Organization, Purchasing **H/I/S:** Playing Racquetball **EDU:** Coursework, Moore State University **C/VW:** Relay for Life
Email: heiser@aldevron.com
URL: http://www.aldevron.com

Christy M. Heitger
Title: Freelance Writer and Editor **Address:** 3404 E. Winston Street, Bloomington, IN 47401 United States **BUS:** Writing and Editing **P/S:** Writing and Editing **MA:** National **D/D/R:** Editing and Copy Editing, Writing Magazine Articles **H/I/S:** Running, Spending Time with her Son **EDU:** Bachelor of Arts in English, Indiana University (1995) **CERTS:** Certificate in Writing, Florida State University
Email: cheitger@hotmai.com

Prudence E. Helders
Title: Direct Marketing Manager **Company:** All-State Legal **Address:** 1 Commerce Drive, Cranford, NJ 07016 United States **BUS:** Manufacturing Company **P/S:** Stationery and Office Supplies **MA:** National **D/D/R:** Overseeing Operations Related to Direct Mail, Collateral, the Company's Online Presence and Advertising **H/I/S:** Line Dancing, Scrapbooking, Reading **EDU:** Master of Business Administration, Concentration in Marketing, Montclair State University; Bachelor of Science in Marketing, Saint Peter's College **A/A/S:** American Marketing Association, New Jersey Chapter; Direct Marketing Association **C/VW:** Court Appointed Special Advocates
Email: phelders@yahoo.com
URL: http://www.aslegal.com

Sheila K. Helleson
Title: English as a Second Language Coordinator (Retired) **Address:** 505 Sunrise Drive, Tracy, MN 56175 United States **BUS:** Public School **P/S:** Secondary Education **MA:** Local **D/D/R:** Organizing and Ordering State Testing Materials, Teaching, Assigning Test Facilitators, Assessing Individual Students, Filing Data, Meeting with Parents, Making House Calls, Scheduling Translators for Parent-Teacher Conferences, Editing for the 'Minnesota Journal,' Teaching Kindergarten through 12th-Grade Students **H/I/S:** Reading **EDU:** Pursuing Master's Degree in English as a Second Language, Hamline University; Bachelor's Degree in Mathematics, Plus 60, Hamline University; Bachelor of Science, Gustavus Adolphus College (1969) **A/A/S:** Teachers of English to Speakers of Other Languages; Minnesota Education Association; American Federation of Teachers; National Education Association
Email: hellesos@iw.net
URL: http://www.cambridgewhoswho.com

Mr. Lee Helms
Title: Owner **Company:** Lee Helms Associates, LLC **Address:** 236 Town Mart, Clanton, AL 35045 United States **BUS:** Consulting Firm **P/S:** Business Development Consultations, Training Programs Including Emergency Operations, Homeland Security and Strategic National Stockpile, Human Resource Services, Motivational Strategy Consultations and Organizational Design **MA:** Local **D/D/R:** Reviewing Risk Assessments, Developing Emergency Plans, Training Employees, Evaluating Emergency Response, Consulting with Organizations **H/I/S:** Golfing **EDU:** Pursuing Bachelor's Degree in Business Management, Auburn University Montgomery, Alabama **A/A/S:** Alabama Emergency Management Council; Montgomery County Chamber of Commerce
Email: lee@leehelmsllc.com
URL: http://www.leehelmsllc.com

Shirley L. Helmuth
Title: 1) Owner, Bookkeeper 2) Minister **Company:** 1) Kalona Auto Used Cars 2) Private Ministry **Address:** 502 E. Avenue, Kalona, IA 52247 United States **BUS:** 1) Auto Sales and Rental Van Company 2) Private Ministry **P/S:** 1) Auto Sales and Van Rentals 2) Ministry **MA:** 1) Local 2) International **D/D/R:** Ministry **H/I/S:** Embroidery, Quilting, Tatting, Crafts, Spending Time with her Grandchildren **EDU:** High School Education **C/VW:** Summer Youth Camps
Email: helmuth@kctc.net
URL: http://www.kalonaauto.com

Robin Helton
Title: Massage Education Department Chair **Company:** Everest College **Address:** 6880 N. Frontage Road, Burr Ridge, IL 60527 United States **BUS:** College **P/S:** Education **MA:** Local **D/D/R:** Offering Massage Services Including Deep Tissue Massage, Swedish Massage, Chinese Medicine, Reflexology and Cranial Massage, Working as a Reiki Master **H/I/S:** Artwork, Jewelry, Quilting, Painting **CERTS:** Certifications in Lymphatic, Craniosacral, Lomi Lomi, Myofascial and Basic Massages; Certification in Muscle Activation Therapy, Certified Reiki Master
Email: rhelton@cci.edu
URL: http://www.cambridgewhoswho.com

Jerry A. Hemmer
Title: Investment Advisor **Company:** Alliance Financial Group **Address:** 14021 Metropolis Avenue, Fort Myers, FL 33912 United States **BUS:** Financial Firm **P/S:** Quality Financial Services, Addressing the Financial Concerns of Clients **MA:** National **D/D/R:** Creating Wealth, Offering Financial Advice **H/I/S:** Golfing, Participating in Water Sports, Teaching Economics Part-Time **EDU:** Bachelor's Degree in Political Science, SUNY Fredonia, 1998; Bachelor of Fine Arts, SUNY Fredonia, 1998 **A/A/S:** Million Dollar Round Table; Florida Association of Insurance and Financial Advisors
Email: jerry_hemmer@afgfl.com
URL: http://www.afgfl.com

Dr. Jennifer Hendershot
Title: Pediatric Dentist **Company:** Northern Valley Indian Health, Inc. **Address:** 207 N. Butte Street, Willows, CA 95988 United States **BUS:** Nonprofit Healthcare Organization **P/S:** Dental Care, Medical and Behavioral Healthcare for Women, Infants and Children, Outreach Programs **MA:** Local **EXP:** Dr. Hendershot's expertise is in pediatric dentistry. **D/D/R:** Managing Dental Care Services **H/I/S:** Practicing Yoga, Exercising **EDU:** Doctor of Dental Medicine, Harvard University; Master of Science in Oral Biology, University of Illinois; Bachelor of Science, The University of Scranton **CERTS:** Licensed Dentist, States of Michigan, Illinois and California; Board Certified Dentist, American Board of Pediatric Dentistry **A/A/S:** NCDA; Harvard Alumni Association; Genesee District Dental Society; Michigan Oral Health Coalition; California Society of Pediatric Dentistry; Northern California Dental Society; California Dental Association; Former Officer, Government Affairs Council; Systematized Nomenclature of Dentistry Committee; State Leader, Head Start Dental Home Project; Chairman, Council of Dental Benefits Programs, American Academy of Pediatric Dentistry; Fellow, Consultant, American Academy of Pediatric Dentistry; American Dental Association
Email: jennifer_hendershot@hotmail.com
URL: http://www.nvih.org

Denise Marie Henderson, DDS
Title: Doctor of Dental Surgery **Company:** Henderson Dental, Inc. **Address:** 2081 Forest Avenue, San Jose, CA 95128 United States **BUS:** Private Dental Healthcare Practice **P/S:** General and Cosmetic Dental Services **MA:** Regional **D/D/R:** Practicing General Family and Cosmetic Dentistry, Performing Standard Teeth Cleanings, Root Canals and Tooth Pulling, Administering X-Rays, Bleaching, Veneers and Fillings, Dentures, Crown and Invisalign **H/I/S:** Spending Time Outdoors, Camping, Hiking **EDU:** Doctor in Dental Surgery, University of Michigan (2003); Bachelor of Science in Ecology and Evolution, University of California, Santa Barbara (1998) **A/A/S:** American Academy of Cosmetic Dentistry; Santa Clara County Dental Society; California Dental Association; American Dental Association; Academy of General Dentistry
Email: dmhendu@gmail.com

Mr. Harry D. Henderson
Title: Owner, Operator **Company:** St. John Mine **Address:** 129 S. Main Street, Potosi, WI 53820 United States **BUS:** Tourism and Education **P/S:** Tours of Cave where Rich Veins of Lead Ore were Found and Mined **MA:** Local **D/D/R:** Conducting Tours of the Mines, Working with Local High School Students, Mentoring Students to become Tour Guides, Teaching Classes on Caves and Rivers, Managing Daily Operations, Overseeing Employees, Selling Merchandise, Lecturing on the Middle East and Africa for the University of Wisconsin **H/I/S:** Reading, Tourism, History, Working with Youth **A/A/S:** Local Chamber of Commerce; Former Member, President, Tri-State Tourism Council **C/VW:** Lions Club
Email: harryh@peii.net
URL: http://www.cambridgewhoswho.com

Sarah E. Henderson
Title: President **Company:** Custom Jewelry Design & Replacement **Address:** 3525 Vicksburg Lane N., Plymouth, MN 55447 United States **BUS:** Jewelry Repair and Manufacturing Company **P/S:** Fine Jewelry Repair, Jewelry Insurance Services **MA:** National **D/D/R:** Working with Insurance Companies to Replace Fine Jewelry, Appraising, Designing Custom Jewelry **H/I/S:** Shopping, Swimming, Taking Vacations, Volunteering **EDU:** Bachelor's Degree in Management and Marketing, Cardinal Stritch University, MN; Coursework in Gemology, Gemological Institute of America, CA **A/A/S:** West Metro Chamber of Commerce; Jewelers Board of Trade; Jewelers of America; Northwest Loss Association
Email: sarah@cjr1.com
URL: http://www.cjr1.com

Brenda Gail Henderson Waugh
Title: Nurse Manager **Company:** Huntington Veterans Administration Medical Center **Dept:** Intensive Care Unit **Address:** 1540 Spring Valley Drive, Huntington, WV 25704 United States **BUS:** Hospital **P/S:** Healthcare Services Including Nursing and Veteran Care **MA:** National **EXP:** Ms. Henderson Waugh's expertise includes case management and critical care nursing. **H/I/S:** Ballroom Dancing **EDU:** Master's Degree in Business Administration, Marshall University; Bachelor's Degree in Nursing
Email: bwaugh2@hotmail.com

Helene Y. Hendricks
Title: Call Center Manager **Company:** Department of Consumer and Regulatory Affairs **Address:** 941 N. Capitol Street N.E., Suite 9500, Washington, DC 20002 United States **BUS:** Government Regulatory Agency **P/S:** Regulates Businesses, Historic Preservation, Rental Housing and Real Estate, Issues Business and Alcoholic Beverage Licenses **MA:** National **D/D/R:** Training on Language Line, Working with Interpreters, Overseeing Properly Running Equipment, Running Data Reports, Meeting and Dealing with a Staff of Five, Dealing with Clients on the Phone, Contact Person for the Agency, Working with the Government Regarding Permits, Employee and Application Problems **H/I/S:** Movies, Dining Out, Bowling, Spending Time with her Son **EDU:** Two Years of College Coursework in Business Management, Washington Technical Institute
Email: helene.hendricks@dc.gov
URL: http://www.dcra.dc.gov

Mr. Ralph V. Hendrix
Title: Owner, Master Plumber **Company:** Hendrix Plumbing, LLC **Address:** P.O. Box 294, 444 Brodgon Road, Guyton, GA 31312 United States **BUS:** Plumbing Company **P/S:** Plumbing Services **MA:** Local **EXP:** Mr. Hendrix's expertise includes contract plumbing and reconstruction. **H/I/S:** Playing Darts, Watching Football, **EDU:** High School Graduate **CERTS:** Licensed Master Plumber, State of Georgia **A/A/S:** Georgia Plumbers' Trade Association; Home Builders Association of Georgia, National Small Business Alliance, Effingham County Farm Bureau Member, Georgia JC Member **C/VW:** Shriners of Savannah, Knights of Columbus, South Effingham High School
Email: r.v.hendrix@hotmail.com
URL: http://www.cambridgewhoswho.com

Carol Sue Henke
Title: Kindergarten Teacher **Company:** Forest Lane Elementary School **Address:** 222 Forest Lane, Montello, WI 53949 United States **BUS:** Public Elementary School **P/S:** Elementary Education **MA:** Local **D/D/R:** Teaching All Subjects Including Core Curriculum as Well as Curriculum and Technology Development **H/I/S:** Collecting Precious Moments Figurines, Working at the Church, Spending Time with her Family and Friends, Reading, Walking **EDU:** Master of Education, University of Wisconsin-Stevens Point; Bachelor of Science in Elementary Education, University of Wisconsin-Stevens Point **A/A/S:** Wisconsin Kindergarten Association; Wisconsin Mathematics Council; Montello Education Association; Wisconsin Education Association; T.R.U.E Unified Federation of Education; National Education Association; Christian Education Association, Circuit 17; Lutheran Women's Missionary League, Circuit 17; **A/H:** Teacher Nominee, Herb Kohl Education Foundation; Nominee, National Teacher Hall of Fame **C/VW:** Sunday School Superintendent and Teacher, Local Church; Vacation Bible School Teacher and Coordinator; Altar Guild; Evening Circle; Relay for Life
Email: chenke@montello.k12.wi.us
URL: http://www.cambridgewhoswho.com

Richard Hennagin
Title: Health, Safety and Environment Manager **Company:** Lynden Transport **Address:** 3027 Rampart Drive, Anchorage, AK 99501 United States **BUS:** Transport Company **P/S:** Transporting Products **MA:** Alaska **EXP:** Mr. Hennagin's expertise includes safety, department of transportation procedures and workers' compensation issues. **H/I/S:** Attending Alaska State Motocross Events **A/A/S:** American Trucking Association; Alaska Safety Advisory Council
Email: richardh@lynden.com
URL: http://www.lynden.com

Mary E. Hennen
Title: Owner, Stylist **Company:** Salon Depot **Address:** 38 Central Avenue South, Elbow Lake, MN 56531 United States **BUS:** Hair Salon and Spa **P/S:** Haircare, Massage Therapy, Skin Care, Nail Care, Tanning **MA:** Regional **D/D/R:** Manager and Stylist, Hair Cutting, Coloring, Perms, Overseeing All Daily Operations **H/I/S:** Spending Time with her Family **EDU:** High School Graduate **A/A/S:** Elbow Lake Chamber of Commerce
Email: maryhenn@runestone.net
URL: http://www.cambridgewhoswho.com

Barbara J. Hennings
Title: President **Company:** Hennings Financial, Inc **Address:** 1909 51st Street N.E., Cedar Rapids, IA 52402 United States **BUS:** Wealth Management Company **P/S:** Wealth Management, Design Income Stream for Retirees, Manage Retirement Plans **MA:** National **D/D/R:** Individual Retirement Plans **H/I/S:** Spending Time with her Family **EDU:** Bachelor's Degree in Education, University of Northern Iowa (1984) **CERTS:** Certified Senior Advisor **A/A/S:** Kirkwood Community College Foundation Board: Kirkwood Community College Investing and Auditing Committee: Jr. Achievement: Benton County Foundation Board: Church Council **C/VW:** Kirkwood Community College, Church
Email: bhennings@netinf.net

Jessie B. Henry
Title: Owner **Company:** Henry's Furniture Inc. **Address:** 325 Old Denton Road, Federalsburg, MD 21632 United States **BUS:** Furniture **P/S:** Buying and Selling of New and Used Furniture **MA:** Local **D/D/R:** Managing Business Operations **H/I/S:** Completing 3-D Puzzles **EDU:** High School Education

Lisa Q. Henry
Title: Loss Prevention Specialist **Company:** Sears **Address:** Brockton, MA 02301 United States **BUS:** One of the Largest Retail Organizations in the United States **P/S:** Retail Department Store **MA:** National **D/D/R:** Overseeing Loss Prevention, Ensuring Company Policies and Procedures are Followed, Handling Paperwork, Reports and Transactions, Conducting Investigations, Monitoring Refunds and Exchanges, Conducting Training on Safety and Fire Drill Procedures, Utilizing Former Experience at Strawberries, Wal-Mart, Laura Ashley and J-Crew **H/I/S:** Volunteering at her Daughter's Daycare **EDU:** Associate Degree in Liberal Arts, Massasoit Community College (1992) **CERTS:** Wicklander-Zulawski & Associate Certified (Certification to Conduct Interrogations and Investigations) **A/A/S:** Retailers Association of Massachusetts; Public Speaker, Trainings, Women's Seminars and Conferences **A/H:** District Loss Prevention Manager of the Quarter (2007); Winner, Regional Sales Award (2003)
Email: lquinny@comcast.net
URL: http://www.sears.com

Vicki A. Henry
Title: Registered Nurse **Company:** Memorial Medical Center **Address:** 13266 Welch Road, Waterford, CA 95386 United States **BUS:** Community Based and Nonprofit Organization that Exists to Maintain and Improve the Health Status of the Citizens of Greater Stanislaus County **P/S:** Cancer Services, Dialysis Center, Emergency Department, Family Birthing Center, Endoscopy Unit, Nuclear Medicine, Pharmacy, Same Day Surgery, Trauma Department **MA:** Regional **D/D/R:** Intermediate Level Two, Neonatal Nursery, Premature Births and Newborns Needing Extra Time and Care after Birth, General Patient Assessments, Organizing Patient Care, Teaching New Parents how to Take Care of their Newborn Children, Intensive Care Unit, Teaching for Critical Care Services **H/I/S:** Quilting, Traveling, Music **EDU:** Pursuing Bachelor of Science in Nursing, University of Phoenix; Associate Degree in Nursing, Excelsior College (1988) **A/A/S:** American Association of Critical Care Nurses; National Association of Neonatal Nurses
Email: tervic@sbcglobal.net
URL: http://www.memorialmedicalcenter.org

Gina K. Henson
Title: Professional Sales Representative **Company:** Actelion Biotechnology Company **Address:** 5000 Shoreline Court, Suite 200, San Francisco, CA 94080 United States **BUS:** Pharmaceutical Company **P/S:** Pharmaceutical Products **MA:** Regional **D/D/R:** Selling Specialty Pharmaceuticals for Genetic Disorders **H/I/S:** Spending Time with Family, Reading **EDU:** Bachelor in Biology, Oklahoma Christian University College of Arts and Sciences **C/VW:** St. Jude Children's Research Hospital
Email: gkat2@cox.net

Mr. Henry T. Hepner
Title: Independent Observer **Company:** VOICE **BUS:** Public Service **P/S:** Protect Environment and Wildlife, Improve Community Safety and Security **MA:** Regional **D/D/R:** Improving the Environment, Public Speaking, Offering Shelter for Wildlife, Independent Observer for the benefit protecting animals in their environment, environment (cleaning up the environment), Educating people on the need to clean up and keep clean the environment, Homeland Security Observer on Safety of our People, Safety for Community; Has Published his observances in local newspapers and on Public TV, Photo Journalism **H/I/S:** Environment, wildlife, nature and hiking, photography **EDU:** High School Education **C/VW:** Cleans up Streams, helps with Animals
Email: Henry.Hepner@cwwemail.com
URL: http://www.cambridgewhoswho.com

Amy Herbert
Title: Director of Children and Family Ministry **Company:** Central Baptist Church **Address:** 3100 W. Ralph Rogers Road, Sioux Falls, SD 57108 United States **BUS:** Religion **P/S:** Spiritual Services, Church **MA:** Local **EXP:** Ms. Herbert's expertise includes child and family ministry. **D/D/R:** Directing Programs **H/I/S:** Softball, Volleyball **EDU:** Bachelor of Arts; Master of Arts; Bachelor of Science (2007)
Email: amy@central-baptist.org
URL: http://www.central-baptist.org

Terese C. Herbig
Title: Senior Vice President of Consumer Goods **Company:** IAG Research **Address:** 345 Park Avenue S., 12th Floor, New York, NY 10010 United States **BUS:** Advertising Research Company **P/S:** Measuring of Television Advertising Effectiveness, Research Services, Consulting **MA:** National **D/D/R:** Business Management, Consumer Goods, Marketing, Advertising **H/I/S:** Spending Time with her Two Children, Playing Tennis, Reading **EDU:** Bachelor of Science in Business, Miami University, Oxford, Ohio **A/A/S:** American Marketing Association; Network of Executive Women
Email: therbig@iagr.net
URL: http://www.iagr.net

Catherine E. Herd
Title: Owner **Company:** TA and TI, LLC **Address:** 723 Dolphin Street, Baltimore, MD 21217 United States **BUS:** Housing Agency **P/S:** Short-Term Housing Services for Community Members **MA:** Regional **D/D/R:** Maintaining Eight Homes Including Painting, Installation of Phones and Cable, Carpeting, Furniture and Locks, Supervising Residents, Checking Properties Weekly, Managing Room Facilities for Low-Income Individuals **H/I/S:** Sewing, Fishing, Hunting, Spending Time with her Grandchildren, Caring for her Pets **EDU:** Coursework in Modeling; Diploma, Bel Alton High School (1962) **A/A/S:** Vice President, Dolphin Pool-Little Africa **C/VW:** Local Church
Email: vmdacat@yahoo.com

Erica M. Herkel-Ritsema
Title: Seventh and Eighth-Grade Special Education Teacher **Company:** Herscher School District 2 **Address:** 975 South Yates Avenue, Kankakee, IL 60901 United States **BUS:** School District **P/S:** Education for Kindergarten through Third-Grade and Sixth through Eighth-Grade Students **MA:** Local **D/D/R:** Assisting Children with Behavioral, Mental and Emotional Challenges **H/I/S:** Spending Time with her Daughter, Supporting her Daughter's Acting Career **EDU:** Master's Degree in Curriculum and Instruction, Olivet Nazarene University (2006); Bachelor's Degree in Elementary Education, Olivet Nazarene University (1996) **CERTS:** Certification in Special Education
Email: ritsemae@hsd2.k12.il.us
URL: http://www.hsd2.k12.il.us

Jennifer M. Herman
Title: Sales Relationship Representative **Company:** Wells Fargo Financial **Address:** 13216 Fountain Head Plaza, Hagerstown, MD 21742 United States **BUS:** Financial Services Company **P/S:** Retail Finance, Banking, Insurance, Investments, Mortgages, Loans, Credit Cards **MA:** National **D/D/R:** Studying Companies and Dealers to Determine the Best Finance Programs to Offer Customers, Maintaining Relationships with Clients, Offering Retail Finance Services to Consumers **H/I/S:** Participating in Outdoor Sports Activities, Snowboarding, Slalom Skiing, Water Sports **EDU:** Bachelor's Degree in Business, Concentration in Sales, Minor in Economics, Mount St. Mary's University (2003)
Email: jenniferherman@wellsfargo.com
URL: http://www.wellsfargo.com

Kathie L. Hermann
Title: President **Company:** Garden Argosy, Inc. **Address:** 361 Saint Armands Circle, Sarasota, FL 34236 United States **BUS:** Retail Home Accents Company **P/S:** Retail Home Accents, Crafts, Furniture **MA:** National **D/D/R:** Overseeing Company Operations **H/I/S:** Running, Exercising, Visiting the Beach, Gardening, Walking her Dog **EDU:** Associate Degree in Business, Milwaukee Area Technical College **A/A/S:** Chamber of Commerce **C/VW:** Florida Center for Children and Family Development
Email: gardenargo@aol.com
URL: http://www.gardenargosy.com

Anne Hermes
Title: Registered Nurse, Case Manager **Company:** Self-Employed **Address:** 5222 Wincroft Court, Houston, TX 77069 United States **BUS:** Sole Proprietorship **P/S:** Workers' Compensation Case Management **MA:** Local **D/D/R:** Handling Workers' Compensation Cases **H/I/S:** Playing Golf, Traveling, Reading, Swimming **EDU:** Associate of Science in Nursing, University of Albuquerque **C/VW:** Planned Parenthood
Email: afhermes@aol.com
URL: http://www.cambridgewhoswho.com

Diana L. Hernandez
Title: Teacher **Company:** Cascade Christian Academy **Address:** 600 N. Western Avenue, Wenatchee, WA 98801 United States **BUS:** Private Christian School **P/S:** Christian Education and Scholastic Opportunities for Students in Preschool through Senior High School, College Preparatory Programs, Community Service Components in Curriculum **MA:** Regional **D/D/R:** Teaching Mathematics and Science to Students in Sixth through Eighth-Grade, Developing Student Projects and Creating Lesson Plans **H/I/S:** Reading, Hiking, Art and Needlework **EDU:** Master's Degree in Science, Nutrition Specialization, Walla Walla College (1995); Bachelor's Degree in Nutrition, Loma Linda University (1985); Bachelor's Degree in Education, Union College (1974)
Email: dianalynnhernandez@hotmail.com
URL: http://www.ccawenatchee.org

Isabel P. Hernandez, BA
Title: Teacher **Company:** La Joya Independent School District **Address:** 200 W. Expressway 83, La Joya, TX 78560 United States **BUS:** School **P/S:** Education **MA:** Local **D/D/R:** Teaching Sixth through Eighth-Grade Mathematics, Coaching Volleyball, Baseball and Track and Field **H/I/S:** Reading, Playing Softball **EDU:** Pursuing Master of Arts in Guidance Counseling, University of Texas-Pan American; Bachelor of Arts in Special Education, University of Texas-Pan American **C/VW:** Young American Bowlers Alliance
Email: i.hernandez3@ljisd.com
URL: http://www.ljisd.com

Juana R. Hernandez
Title: Owner, Stylist **Company:** Ana's Hair Salon **Address:** 655 IL Route 68, Carpentersville, IL 60110 United States **BUS:** Beauty Salon **P/S:** Salon Services **MA:** Local **D/D/R:** Cutting, Coloring and Highlighting Hair, Facial Waxing **H/I/S:** Playing Tennis, Scrapbooking

Mara Hernandez
Title: Psychotherapist, Owner of Private Practice **Company:** Center for Attachment & Trauma **Address:** 1201 N. Mesa Street, Suite H, El Paso, TX 79902 United States **BUS:** Mental Healthcare Facility Center **P/S:** Treatment for Developmental Disturbances Produced by Traumatic Experiences **MA:** Regional **D/D/R:** Practicing Psychotherapy, Assisting Patients with Emotional Development Disturbances Caused by Trauma, Practicing Individual and Child Therapy, Treating Trauma and Attachment Disturbances **H/I/S:** Reading, Cleaning, Traveling, Practicing Yoga **EDU:** Master's Degree in Psychology, Chapman University (1998); Bachelor of Arts in Psychology, Saint Martin's University, Lacey, WA (1996) **A/A/S:** American Association of University Women
Email: marahernandez@sbcglobal.net

Michelle Mendoza Hernandez, MD
Title: Physician **Company:** Bien Vivir Senior Health Services **Address:** 2300 McKinley, El Paso, TX 79912 United States **BUS:** Hospice **P/S:** Geriatric Patient Care **MA:** Local **EXP:** Dr. Hernandez's expertise is in internal medicine. **H/I/S:** Practicing Yoga, Reading, Playing with her Daughter **EDU:** MD, Wright State University; Residency, Austin Medical Education Program, Austin, Texas **CERTS:** Board Certified in Internal Medicine **A/A/S:** Texas Medical Association; American College of Physicians **C/VW:** Alzheimer's Association, Susan G. Komen Breast Cancer Foundation
Email: michmendoza@hotmail.com

Vincent Hernandez Sr.
Title: Owner **Company:** Vinlan Home Improvements **Address:** 145 Kingsland Avenue, Brooklyn, NY 11222 United States **BUS:** Home Improvement Company **P/S:** Home Improvement Services including Contracting Services for Residential and Commercial Properties **MA:** Regional **D/D/R:** Remodeling Bathrooms, Kitchens and Floors, Plumbing, Hiring Contractors, Constructing Sidewalks, Designing Window Signs **H/I/S:** Collecting Antique Cars **EDU:** High School Education **CERTS:** Licensed Locksmith; License in Automatic Fire Sprinkler Installation; License in Automatic Standpipe Installation
Email: vinlanhomeimpro@aol.com

Darlene Y. Herndon
Title: Business Analyst, Entrepreneur **Company:** Herndon Enterprise **Address:** 2890A GA Highway 212, Suite 277, Conyers, GA 30094 United States **BUS:** Professional Consulting and Web Designing Company **P/S:** Consulting and Web Designing Services **MA:** Local **D/D/R:** Analyzing Business Systems and Processes, Strategically Offering Solutions that Add Value, Improve Business Operations and Increase Profitability, Designing Customized Websites for Small Businesses **H/I/S:** Traveling, Exercising, Reading, Shopping **EDU:** Bachelor of Science Degree in Public Administration, Central Michigan University; Associate of Science Degree in Financial Administration, Detroit College of Business **C/VW:** Hurricane Katrina, CMU Alumni
Email: dyherndo@yahoo.com
URL: http://www.herndonenterprise.com/

Cynthia W. Herold, MT (ASCP)
Title: Senior Consultant **Company:** Negley, Ott & Associates, Inc. **Address:** 4 Lakewood Court, Savannah, GA 31411 United States **BUS:** Healthcare **P/S:** Targeted Clinical Computing Services to Clients in the Healthcare Industry, Focusing on Achieving Defined Benefits from Clinical Information System Acquisition, Using a Best-Demonstrated Practices Approach **MA:** National **D/D/R:** Helping Clients Install Clinical Systems in Hospitals, Developing, Implementing and Supporting Clinical Software, Consulting in Clinical Computing **H/I/S:** Spending Time with her Grandchildren, Traveling **EDU:** Bachelor of Science in Medical Technology, Armstrong State University (1976); Registered Medical Technologist Certification, American Society of Clinical Pathology (1970) **A/A/S:** American Society of Clinical Pathology; Health Information Management Society
Email: cynthia.herold@noac.com
URL: http://www.noac.com

Anne E. Herrera
Title: Women's Healthcare Nurse Practitioner **Company:** Nutritional Weight Loss Center **Address:** 733 E. University Drive, Suite 3, Mesa, AZ 85203 United States **BUS:** Private Healthcare Practice **P/S:** Weight Loss Assessments and Counseling Services **MA:** Local **D/D/R:** Practicing Obstetrics and Gynecologic Nursing Care, Counseling Patients on Weight Loss Techniques and Maintenance, Working in Private Practices, County Clinics and Free Clinics, Teaching Bilingual Students, Teaching a Weight Loss and Nutrition Course in Spanish and English, Offering Women's Healthcare and Hospice Care, Managing Cases **H/I/S:** Collecting Rooster and Elephant Figurines, Collecting Red-Headed Dolls, Traveling **CERTS:** Registered Nurse, Los Angeles County-USC Medical Center (1966) **A/A/S:** Migrant Clinicians Network
Email: herrera@ieee.org
URL: http://www.ieee.org

Claudette B. Herring
Title: Past Missionary President, Hostess, Cashier **Company:** Hosley Chapel CME Church, McDonalds **Address:** 1109 South Grant Street, Fitzgerald, GA 31750 United States **BUS:** Religion, McDonald's Restaurant **P/S:** Missionary Services at Hosley Chapel, Restaurant Services **MA:** Local **D/D/R:** Leading the Missionary Society at Church, Customer Service **H/I/S:** Cooking **A/A/S:** Weekly Visits to Local Sick Seniors and Citizens

Anthony Charles Hersey
Title: Designer **Company:** O'Dell Associates, Inc. **Address:** 800 W. Hill Street, Charlotte, NC 28208 United States **BUS:** Architecture and Engineering Firm **P/S:** Architecture and Engineering Design Services **MA:** National **D/D/R:** Designing **H/I/S:** Singing in the Choir, Playing Basketball **EDU:** Bachelor's Degree in Architecture, University of Kansas **A/A/S:** American Institute of Architecture; Alpha Phi Alpha **C/VW:** Habitat for Humanity, Church, AIA
Email: herseya@odell.com
URL: http://www.odell.com

Ms. Hillary Herskowitz
Title: President **Company:** UPFront Communications Group, Inc. **Address:** 300 W. 55th Street, Suite 7F, New York, NY 10019 United States **BUS:** Public Relations Firm **P/S:** Publicity for Lifestyle Products and Services **MA:** National **D/D/R:** Overseeing Publicity for Lifestyle Products and Services, Representing Industries Including Food and Beverage, Entertainment and Children's Brands Such as Ringling Bros. and Barnum & Bailey and Disney On Ice **H/I/S:** Playing Tennis **EDU:** Bachelor's Degree in Journalism, New York University (1992) **A/A/S:** Pro Bono Program, The Life Lab
Email: hillary@upfrontnyc.com
URL: http://www.upfrontnyc.com

Cymbria L. Hess, IMFT
Title: Independent Marriage and Family Therapist **Company:** Anderson Hills Psychotherapy **Address:** 1060 Nimitzview Drive, Suite 215, Cincinnati, OH 45230 United States **BUS:** Counseling Center **P/S:** Counseling Services Including Psychotherapy **MA:** Cincinnati **D/D/R:** Offering Marriage and Adolescent Psychotherapy, Individual, Couples and Family Treatment, Addressing Teenage and Family Issues **H/I/S:** Spending Time with her Children, Hockey, Gymnastics, Scrapbooking **EDU:** Master's Degree in Developmental Psychology, University of Dayton, OH (1990) **CERTS:** Licensed Marriage and Family Therapist; License in Chemical Dependency Treatment; Licensed Social Worker **A/A/S:** American Association for Marriage and Family Therapy **C/VW:** World Vision; Local Church
Email: cymbria@ahpsych.com
URL: http://www.cambridgewhoswho.com

Reneé Hess
Title: Customer Service Technician **Company:** SSA **Address:** Wilkes-Barre, PA 18702 United States **BUS:** Consulting Company **P/S:** Telephone Service Including Customer Service **MA:** National **D/D/R:** Accessing Input Logs, Preparing Information Disclosure Statements, Verifying the Communications Network, Utilizing her Customer Service Skills **H/I/S:** Playing Play Station, Caring for her Pets, Reading, Working on Computers **EDU:** Associate Degree in Hotel and Restaurant Management, Luzerne County Community College, PA (1999); Associate Degree in Office Management, Luzerne County Community College (1998)
Email: nascakes@aol.com

Susan Rose Hetzer
Title: Clinical Coordinator **Company:** St. Mary's Hospital **Dept:** ICC Telemetry **Address:** 508 Comstock Drive, Lusby, MD 20657 United States **BUS:** Hospital Facility Dedicated to Excellence in Healthcare **P/S:** Full Array of Hospital Services **MA:** Regional **D/D/R:** Working in the Intensive Care Unit, Teaching Structured Classes in ICC and Telemetry Units, Supporting the Director Assisted Management, Helping with Scheduling and Supporting the Night Staff with Education **H/I/S:** Scuba Diving, Hiking, Outdoor Activities, Sailing **EDU:** Associate Degree in Nursing, Charles County Community College (1998); Bachelor's Degree in Biology, Frostburg State University (1991) **A/A/S:** AACN, CCRN
Email: suzzhd@yahoo.com
URL: http://www.smhwecare.com

Mrs. Barbara A. Heyder
Title: Owner, President **Company:** Aries Insurance Services, LLC dba Brooke Insurance **Address:** 9340 N. Florida Avenue, Suite A1, Tampa, FL 33612 United States **BUS:** Insurance Company **P/S:** Automobile, Home, Commercial, Life and Health Insurance **MA:** Statewide **D/D/R:** Offering Commercial and Personal Insurance Services **H/I/S:** Traveling **EDU:** College Coursework **C/VW:** Veterans of Foreign Wars; American Cancer Society
Email: barbara.heyder@brookeagent.com
URL: http://www.brookeagent.com

Martin F. Heyne
Title: Director, Group Sales **Company:** Church Mutual Insurance Company **Address:** 3000 Schuster Lane, Merrill, WI 54452 United States **BUS:** Insurance Company **P/S:** Property Insurance, Casualty Insurance **MA:** National **D/D/R:** Offering Property and Casualty Insurance in the Religious Market **H/I/S:** Golfing, Spending Time with Friends and Family, Exercising **EDU:** Bachelor of Arts in English, University of Wisconsin-Stevens Point **CERTS:** Pursuing Casualty and Property Insurance Underwriters Certification as well as a Certified Insurance Counselor Designation Bachelor's Degree, in 1990 **A/A/S:** Past Board Director Lincoln Community Theatre, Grace Lutheran Church **A/H:** e-Fusion Award, 2005 **C/VW:** Community Events
Email: mheyne@churchmutual.com
URL: http://www.churchmutual.com

Juliet Hibbs
Title: Teacher **Company:** Coconut Creek High School **Address:** 1400 N.W. 44th Avenue, Coconut Creek, FL 33066 United States **BUS:** Public High School **P/S:** Secondary Level Education for 2,700 Students **MA:** Regional **D/D/R:** Teaching Social Studies, Blending Styles to Appeal to All Students, Presenting Curriculum in an Interesting and Relative Way **H/I/S:** Computers **EDU:** Pursuing a Master's Degree in Brain Research, Nova Southeastern University; Bachelor of Science in Psychology, Nova Southeastern University (1999) **CERTS:** Certification in Social Studies Education (2007) **A/A/S:** Calvary Chapel; Hope Pregnancy Center; Public Speaking on Right To Life Issues
Email: juliet.hibbs@browardschools.com
URL: http://www.browardschools.com

Dr. Kathleen T. Hickey
Title: Cardiac Nurse Practitioner **Company:** Columbia University **Address:** 180 Fort Washington Avenue, New York, NY 10032 United States **BUS:** Public Healthcare Educational Facility **P/S:** Higher Education **MA:** Regional **D/D/R:** Conducting Research, Recruiting Patients, Seeing her Own Patients, Teaching Nurse Practitioner Students, Performing Clinic Duties in Cardiology, Lecturing for Companies for the American Heart Association **H/I/S:** Traveling **EDU:** Ed.D. in Education, Teachers College, Columbia University (2002) **A/A/S:** American Association of Critical-Care Nurses; Certified American Nurse Practitioner; Credentialing Center, American Nurses Association; Listed, Over 20 Journals
Email: kth6@columbia.edu
URL: http://www.columbia.edu

Ms. DeDe Hicks
Title: Vie President of Operations **Company:** Reluminate, Inc. **Address:** 1810 Buerkle Road, White Bear Lake, MN 55110 United States **BUS:** Electrical Contracting Company **P/S:** Interior Retrofitting, Maintenance, Repair and Exterior Upgrading for Commercial and Industrial Industries **MA:** Regional **D/D/R:** Making Emergency Calls, Managing Operations, Customer Service, Sales, Emergency Calls **EDU:** Diploma, Blaine High School (1987) **A/A/S:** Chamber of Commerce
Email: dede@reluminateinc.com
URL: http://www.reluminate.com

John D. Hicks
Title: Owner, Dental Laboratory Technician **Company:** Redemption Labs **Address:** 227 S. Sandbranch Road, Mount Hope, WV 25882 United States **BUS:** Manufacturing Company **P/S:** Manufacturing Dental Removable Prosthesis **MA:** Regional **D/D/R:** Repairing, Manufacturing, Realigning Dentures **H/I/S:** Watching Basketball and Football, Gardening, Farming **EDU:** Bachelor's Degree in Business Management, Mountain State University (2005); Associate Degree in Marketing, Mountain State University (2005) **CERTS:** Licensed Technician, National Board for Certification in Dental Laboratory Technology **A/A/S:** International Business Honor Society; Skills USA **A/H:** National Dean's List **C/VW:** Students in Free Enterprise
Email: johnhicks19@yahoo.com
URL: http://www.cambridgewhoswho.com

Kevin Patrick Hicks
Title: Assistant Vice President of Information Technology **Company:** M. J. Harris, Inc. **Dept:** Information Technology Department **Address:** 1 Riverchase Ridge, Suite 300, Birmingham, AL 35244 United States **BUS:** Construction Company **P/S:** Construction Services **MA:** National **EXP:** Mr. Hicks' expertise is in information technology management. **H/I/S:** Golfing, Racing, Running Triathlon, Bowling **EDU:** Master's Degree in Building Construction, Concentration in Information Technology, Auburn University **A/A/S:** Knights of Columbus; Rotary Club; Alpha Phi Omega; Auburn Alumni Association; Eagle Scout, Order of the Arrow
Email: kevinh@mjharris.com
URL: http://www.mjharris.com

Teresa C. Hicks
Title: Executive Director **Company:** Unitex, LTD **Address:** 1412 Broadway, Suite 1960, New York, NY 10018 United States **BUS:** Fashion Manufacturer **P/S:** Manufacturing Men's and Women's Clothing **MA:** International **D/D/R:** Designing Knitwear **H/I/S:** Rescuing Animals, Hiking, Skiing, Gardening **EDU:** Associate Degree, Fashion Institute of Technology, New York **C/VW:** Community Involvement
Email: thicks@unitexny.com
URL: http://www.fdmul.com

Kevin C. Hicok
Title: Manager and Scientist for Regenerative Therapeutics Research **Company:** Cytori Therapeutics **Address:** 3020 Callan Road, San Diego, CA 92121 United States **BUS:** Biotechnology Company **P/S:** Regenerative Cell Isolation System **MA:** International **D/D/R:** Stem Cell Research **H/I/S:** Performing Music with his Family, Playing Tennis **EDU:** Master's Degree in Cell and Developmental Biology, University of Minnesota **A/A/S:** International Federation of Adipose Therapeutics and Science **C/VW:** K-Love Christian Radio; Local Church
Email: khicok@cytoritx.com
URL: http://www.cytoritx.com

Anne Higgins
Title: Early Childhood Special Needs Educator **Company:** Grace Farrar Cole School **Address:** 81 High Street, Norwell, MA 02061 United States **BUS:** Public Elementary School Serving Residents of Norwell **P/S:** Public Elementary Education for Local Residents **MA:** Regional **D/D/R:** Teaching Special Needs Education and Reading Remediation, Working with Children with Autism and Asburger's, Training in General Education **H/I/S:** Working on Parrot Conservation **EDU:** Master's Degree in Early Childhood Education and Special Education, Bridgewater State College (1992); Bachelor's Degree in Elementary Education, Bridgewater State College (1990)
Email: ahiggins_395@comcast.net
URL: http://www.norwellschool.org

Brenda Higgonbotham
Title: Director of Clinical Education **Company:** Beverly Living Center **Address:** 301 S. Boundary Street, Magnolia, AR 71753 United States **BUS:** Long-Term Care Facility **P/S:** Long-Term Care **MA:** Local **D/D/R:** Psychiatric Nursing **H/I/S:** Reading (Two or More Weekly) **EDU:** Associate of Science in Nursing, Southern Arkansas University, Magnolia, Arkansas **CERTS:** Certification in Psychiatric Nursing
Email: brendahigginbotham@sbcglobal.net

Barbara L. Hightower
Title: Teacher **Company:** Lakeside Union School District **Address:** 9205 Lakeview Road, Lakeside, CA 92040 United States **BUS:** School District **P/S:** Education **MA:** Local **D/D/R:** Teaching, Identifying Students' Individual and Collective Learning Needs, Offering a Stimulating Learning Environment, Planning and Delivering Instruction Based on Student Needs, Evaluating and Communicating Student Progress **H/I/S:** Reading, Walking **EDU:** Master of Arts in Education, San Diego State University; Bachelor of Arts in Liberal Arts, San Diego State University; Associate Degree in Respiratory Therapy, Grossmont College **A/A/S:** San Diego Council on Literacy; California Teachers Association; CRCS; National Education Association
Email: blhightower@cox.net

Mercedes L. Hilbrecht
Title: Legal Administrator **Company:** Hilbrecht and Associates Law Firm **Address:** 723 S. Casino Center Boulevard, Las Vegas, NV 89101 United States **BUS:** Law Firm **P/S:** Administrative Law, General Civil and Appellate Practice, Transportation, Utility and Corporate, Business Law, Business Start-Ups, Probate Law, Trusts and Estates **MA:** National **D/D/R:** Managing Daily Office Operations Including Booking, Insurance Matters and Human Resources, Supervising Employees, Maintaining and Updating the Law Library, Proofreading Briefs **H/I/S:** Gardening, Reading, Traveling **EDU:** Graduate, Patricia Stevens Modeling School; Industry-Related Training **A/A/S:** Association of Legal Administrators; National Legal Administrators Association; Former President and Charter Member, Mercedes-Benz Club of America
Email: hilbrechtdaz@aol.com
URL: http://www.lawyers.com/hilbrecht

Janet L. Hildebrandt
Title: Teacher **Company:** Pinal Gila Community Child Services, Inc. **Dept:** Policy and Innovation Committee **Address:** 900 N. Plaza Drive, Apache Junction, AZ 85220 United States **BUS:** Nonprofit Organization **P/S:** Community Programs Including Child Care, Grandparents Raising Grandchildren Support and Conferences, Women's Empowerment Conference, Behavioral Health, Health and Nutrition Resources, Early Intervention and Lab Services **MA:** Local **D/D/R:** Creating Lesson Plans, Collaborating with Parents, Managing Operations, Overseeing Referrals for Parents with Learning Disabled Children **H/I/S:** Camping, Hunting **EDU:** Associate of Applied Science in Early Childhood Education, Central Arizona College (2005) **A/A/S:** National Association for the Education of Young Children; National Head Start Association
Email: janet1177@msn.com
URL: http://www.pgccs.org

Alison A. Hill
Title: Attorney **Company:** Reinhart Boerner van Deuren S.C. **Address:** 1000 N. Water Street, Milwaukee, WI 53202 United States **BUS:** Law Firm **P/S:** Legal Services, General Law Practice **MA:** National **D/D/R:** Practicing Product Distribution and Franchise Law, Managing Anti-Trust Cases, Litigation **H/I/S:** Playing Tennis, Reading, Attending Theater **EDU:** JD, University of Notre Dame (2006); Bachelor of Arts in History and French, Minor in English, Luther College **A/A/S:** National Association of Women Lawyers
Email: ahill@reinhartlaw.com
URL: http://www.reinhartlaw.com

Bonnie Jo Hill
Title: Owner **Company:** Tampa Bay Group Homes **Address:** 1100 Drew Street, Clearwater, FL 33755 United States **BUS:** Education Industry **P/S:** Homes to Stay in or Live in because of Illness or Death, or Home Circumstances **MA:** Local **D/D/R:** Caring for Children with Mental Retardation, from Profound to Autistic to Trainable, Overseeing Care for Eleven Children in Facility **H/I/S:** Golfing, Hiking **EDU:** Bachelor of Science Degree in Health and Physical Education; Attended NE High School
URL: http://www.cambridgewhoswho.com

Cecile L. Hill
Title: 1) Assistant Manager 2) Office Manager **Company:** 1) Bud Hills Security and Services 2) B-C and Sons Lawn Care **Address:** 123 W. State Highway 33, Tetonia, ID 83452 United States **BUS:** 1) Security Service Company 2) Lawn Care Company **P/S:** 1) Security Patrol, Residential and Commercial Property Protection, Courier Services 2) Lawn Maintenance, Lawn Care Services **MA:** Regional **D/D/R:** Overseeing Office Operations, Preparing Paperwork, Posting Checks, Billing, Picking up Deposits, Processing Payroll, Collecting Taxes **H/I/S:** Listening to Music **EDU:** Diploma, Skyline High School (1975) **A/A/S:** Better Business Bureau **C/VW:** Church of Jesus Christ of Latter-day Saints
Email: cecilehill99@hotmail.com

Major Doyle Hill II
Title: Registered Nurse **Company:** VA Medical Center **Address:** 1100 Tunnel Road, Asheville, NC 28805 United States **BUS:** Medical Center **P/S:** Healthcare **MA:** International **D/D/R:** Psychiatric Nursing **H/I/S:** Spending Time with Family and Friends, Wolf Hybrids Sanctuary **EDU:** Master of Science in Nursing, University of Phoenix; Bachelor of Science in Nursing, Western Carolina University **A/A/S:** North Carolina Chapter, American Nurses Association; Lifetime Member, Reserve Officers Association; AMSYS; NRA **A/H:** Military Awards **C/VW:** Local Community
Email: hillreid@hotmail.com

Harrison H. Hill
Title: Chief Executive Officer **Company:** Veritas LLC **Address:** 8418 Church Lane, Randell Town, MD 21133 United States **BUS:** Financial Insurance **P/S:** Insurance for Nonprofit Organizations **MA:** Local **D/D/R:** Managing Operations
Email: harrisonhill@verizon.net

Jo Ayn Hill
Title: Lead Administrative Specialist **Company:** Temple University **Address:** 3401 N. Broad Street, Philadelphia, PA 19140 United States **BUS:** University **P/S:** Education **MA:** International **EXP:** Ms. Hill's expertise is in administration. **H/I/S:** Traveling, Learning Chinese
Email: joayn.hill@tuhs.temple.edu
URL: http://www.temple.edu

Joy L. Hill

Title: Licensed Social Worker, Counsellor Intern **Company:** Avalon Correctional Facility **Address:** 1700 N. Horizon, El Paso, TX 79928 United States **BUS:** Halfway House **P/S:** Drug and Alcohol Counseling **MA:** Regional **D/D/R:** Assisting the Therapeutic Community, Outpatient Counseling, Conducting Assessments, Meeting with Clients Individually for Alcohol and Drug Abuse, Writing Treatment Plans and Assessments **EDU:** Bachelor of Arts in Social Work, New Mexico State University (1995) **CERTS:** Certified in Domestic Violence Counseling (2002) **A/A/S:** National Association of Social Workers
Email: joyhill43@hotmail.com
URL: http://www.cambridgewhoswho.com

Paula L. Hill, RN, BSN

Title: Registered Nurse **Company:** Georgetown University Hospital **Address:** 3800 Reservoir Road N.W., Washington, DC 20007 United States **BUS:** Hospital **P/S:** Healthcare, Education **MA:** National **D/D/R:** Nursing, Teaching Community Health Education **H/I/S:** Organizing Pampered Chef Parties **EDU:** Pursuing Master of Business Administration in Healthcare Management, University of Phoenix; Bachelor of Science in Nursing, Western Michigan University **A/A/S:** Greater Washington Vascular Nursing Chapter, American Indian Nurses Society **C/VW:** National Museum of the American Indian
Email: hotline49@hotmail.com
URL: http://www.pamperedchef.biz/hotline49

Shawn R. Hill

Title: Senior Vice President **Company:** Beacon Realty Capitol, Inc. **Address:** 549 Randolph Street, Suite 700, Chicago, IL 60661 United States **BUS:** Real Estate Firm **P/S:** Mortgage Banking **MA:** Local **D/D/R:** Renting Self-Storage Spaces, Offering Multi-Family and Commercial Properties, Ensuring Hospitality **H/I/S:** Boating, Skiing, Snowmobiling, Acquiring Wine Collectables **EDU:** Master's Degree in Urban Planning, Illinois University **A/A/S:** Mortgage Bank Association; University of Illinois Alumni Association, Chicago Real Estate Council, National Self Storage Association
Email: shill@beaconrealtycapital.com
URL: http://www.beaconrealty.com

Wilbur T. Hill

Title: Doctor of Osteopathy (Retired) **Address:** 218 Lakeside Drive, Liberty, MO 64068 United States **BUS:** Healthcare Center **P/S:** Healthcare Including Family Orthopedic Care **MA:** Regional **D/D/R:** Family Care Nursing, Performing Medical Therapy with Manipulative Techniques, Consulting with the American Osteopathic Association for the Evaluation of the Internship and Residency Training Program **H/I/S:** Golfing **EDU:** Doctor of Osteopathy, Kirksville College of Osteopathic Medicine **A/A/S:** Former President, MACPS; American Osteopathic Association **A/H:** Distinguished Award, FACGP (1999); Physician of the Year Award **C/VW:** District Governor, Lions Club
Email: wthilldo@sbcglobal.net
URL: http://www.cambridgewhoswho.com

Domenica D. Hillenbrand

Title: Police Officer **Company:** Las Vegas Metropolitan Police Department **Address:** 4750 W. Oakey Boulevard, Las Vegas, NV 89012 United States **BUS:** Police Department **P/S:** Law Enforcement **MA:** Regional **D/D/R:** Detective in Domestic Violence Unit **H/I/S:** Traveling, New York Jets **CERTS:** Eighteen Months of Police Training Licensed Cosmetologist
Email: domenica29@aol.com
URL: http://www.lvmpd.com

Margaret C. Hillman

Title: Owner, Operator **Company:** Maggie Mae's Styling Salon **Address:** 527 Fallonfield Avenue, Charleroi, PA 15022 United States **BUS:** Full-Service Hair Salon **P/S:** Hair Coloring and Cutting **MA:** Local **D/D/R:** Cutting and Coloring Hair, Donating Hair to Cancer Victims **H/I/S:** Football, White-Water Rafting **EDU:** High School Diploma, Pittsburgh Beauty School **A/A/S:** American Legion Auxiliary
Email: maggiemaes1@verizon.net

Betty J. Hilton

Title: General Manager **Company:** Amado Territory Inn **Address:** 3001 E. Frontage Road, P. O. Box 81, Building 6, Amado, AZ 85645 United States **BUS:** Proven Leader Committed to Excellence in the Hospitality Industry **P/S:** 17 Acre Ranch with 15 Rooms, Bed and Breakfast Services, Artist Studio and Restaurants **MA:** Regional **D/D/R:** Overseeing Entire Operations Including Restaurants, Bed and Breakfast, Artist Studio, Hosting Weddings, Family Reunions on Property, Handling Finances, Offering Employee Supervision, Managing Maintenance **H/I/S:** Dancing, Playing Cards, 'Enjoying Life' **EDU:** Coursework, Central Washington State College **A/A/S:** Chamber of Commerce; American Association of Businesswomen; Scottsdale Area Chamber of Commerce; Greater Phoenix Chamber of Commerce; Gilbert Chamber of Commerce and small business assoc. **A/H:** Hampton inn Hilton award, 'presidents award' 1998
Email: info@amado-territory-inn.com
URL: http://www.amado-territory.inn.com

Kimberly M. Hinderliter

Title: Budget Specialist **Company:** Indiana Army National Guard **Dept:** Finance **Address:** 402 Clark Street, Edinburgh, IN 46124 United States **BUS:** Government Agency **P/S:** Military Defense Services **MA:** Local **D/D/R:** Auditing Payable Accounts, Budgeting and Tracking Finances **H/I/S:** Golfing, Bowling, Coaching Baseball **EDU:** Pursuing Bachelor of Arts in Business Management, Indiana Wesleyan University **A/A/S:** Leader, Girl Scouts of the USA; Club Master, Boy Scouts of America
Email: kimberly.pinkston@us.army.mil
URL: http://www.inarng.org

Barbara Hine

Title: Teacher **Company:** Wilson Elementary **Address:** 985 S. Orange Boulevard, Sanford, FL 32771 United States **BUS:** Elementary School **P/S:** Primary Education **MA:** Regional **D/D/R:** Teaching All Subjects to First Grade Students **H/I/S:** Collect dolls from around the world; reading; biking; swimming **EDU:** Master's Degree in Elementary Education, The College of New Jersey (Formerly Trenton State College); Bachelor of Science in Elementary Education, Union College **A/A/S:** Florida Education Association; National Education Association
Email: barbara_hine@scps.k12.fl.us
URL: http://www.scps.k12.fl.us

Donna A. Hinkle

Title: Pre-Algebra Teacher, Leadership Advisor **Company:** Vail Ranch Middle School **Address:** 33340 Camino Piedra Rojo, Temecula, CA 92592 United States **BUS:** Middle School **P/S:** Secondary Education **MA:** Regional **D/D/R:** Designing Concepts to Facilitate Learning, Teaching Algebra to Seventh and Eighth-Grade Students, Overseeing Summer School Programs **H/I/S:** Spending Time with her Children, Crocheting **EDU:** Master's Degree in School Administration, Azusa Pacific University, with Honors **CERTS:** Certified Teacher **A/A/S:** Pi Lambda Theta
Email: hinklebaseball@aol.com
URL: http://www.tvusd.k12.ca.us

Mr. Richard Gene Hinkle Jr.

Title: Manager of Safety **Company:** Con-Way Freight **Address:** 8390 Hall Street, Saint Louis, MO 63147 United States **BUS:** Transportation **P/S:** Trucking, Less-Than-Truckload Freight **MA:** National **D/D/R:** Specializing in Safety Management **H/I/S:** Whitewater Canoeing, Kayaking, Fishing **EDU:** Coursework in Transportation Management and Physical Distribution, College of DuPage; Continuing Education Coursework **CERTS:** Certified in Hazwoper; Certification in Accident Reconstruction and Investigation **A/A/S:** Missouri Motor Carriers Association; Iowa Motor Truck Association; Trucking Driving Committee, Illinois Trucking Association **A/H:** Finalist, American Trucking Association America's Road Team (2001); Second Place Winner, Illinois Trucking Driving Championship (2001) **C/VW:** Cub Scouts
Email: hinkle.rick@con-way.com

Susan M. Hinrichs

Title: Director of Operations **Company:** Oklahoma Academy of Family Physicians **Address:** 1900 N.W. Expressway, Suite 501, Oklahoma City, OK 73118 United States **BUS:** Heathcare Organization **P/S:** Professional Organization for Family Physicians **MA:** Regional **D/D/R:** Writing Grants, Coordinating Meetings **H/I/S:** Spending Time with her Family, Reading, Traveling, Gardening, Wine Tasting **EDU:** Associate Degree in Executive Data Management, Harrisburg Community College **A/A/S:** Oklahoma Academy of Family Physicians; Campfire Association
Email: hinrichs@okafp.org
URL: http://www.okafp.org

Kimberly J. Hinshaw, CCIM

Title: Associate Broker **Company:** Anchor Commercial Real Estate **Address:** 126 Seven Farms Drive, Suite 110, Charleston, SC 29492 United States **BUS:** Real Estate Company **P/S:** Commercial Brokering **MA:** National **D/D/R:** Selling and Leasing Commercial Real Estate **H/I/S:** Boating **EDU:** General Business Degree, University of Oregon **CERTS:** Certified Commercial Investment Member **A/A/S:** South Carolina Association of Realtors; National Association of Realtors
Email: kimhinshaw@anchorcommercial.net
URL: http://www.anchorcommercial.net

June Hinton

Title: Director of Career Development **Company:** Molloy College, Career Development Center **Address:** 1000 Hempstead Avenue, Rockville Centre, NY 11571 United States **BUS:** College Career Counseling Center **P/S:** Career Counseling **MA:** Local **D/D/R:** Counseling, Managing Career Center and Career Development, Conducting Workshops **H/I/S:** Doing Yoga, Traveling, Reading, Cooking, Spending Time with Others, Music **EDU:** Master of Social Work, Fordham University; Professional Diploma in Counseling, Hofstra University; Master of Science in Counseling, Syracuse University; Bachelor of Science in English Education, Long Island University, C.W. Post Campus **A/A/S:** Secretary, Metropolitan New York College of Career Planning **C/VW:** Secretary, Metropolitan New York College of Career Planning
Email: jhinton@molloy.edu
URL: http://www.molloy.edu

Laura Hirsch

Title: Special Education Teacher Aide **Company:** Putnam Valley High School **Address:** 146 Peekskill Hollow Road, Putnam Valley, NY 10579 United States **BUS:** High School **P/S:** Education **MA:** Local **D/D/R:** Assisting the Special Education Teacher, Caring for High School Students with Special Needs **H/I/S:** Attending Sporting Events **EDU:** Associate of Arts in Business, Westchester Community College **CERTS:** Certified, Teaching Assistant, State of New York **C/VW:** Various High School Clubs
Email: lhirsch@pvcsd.org

Susan L. Hirshman

Title: Managing Director **Company:** JP Morgan Asset Management **Address:** 245 Park Avenue, New York, NY 10167 United States **BUS:** Finance Company **P/S:** Asset, Investment and Wealth Management **MA:** International **D/D/R:** Managing Assets and Personal Wealth **H/I/S:** Golfing, Traveling, Reading, Playing Tennis, Staying Active **EDU:** Master of Business Administration, Baruch College; Bachelor of Science in Business and Accounting, University at Buffalo **A/A/S:** Financial Planning Association; Chartered Financial Analyst Institute
Email: susan.l.hirshman@jpmorgan.com
URL: http://www.jpmorgan.com

Brenda C. Hiscox, BS

Title: Owner **Company:** Dalton Birds, LLC **Address:** 1530 N. Country Club Drive, Suite 4, Mesa, AZ 85201 United States **BUS:** Exceptional Retail Pet Shop **P/S:** Excellence in Retail Services, Pet Birds, Supplies, Grooming, Boarding, Consultations, Behavioral Advice, Corrective Grooming and Pet to Person Compatibility **MA:** Local **D/D/R:** Selling Parrots and Supplies, Grooming, Boarding, Consulting, Giving Behavioral Advice, Matching Personalities of Parrots to the Right Person, Running a Second Business with her Husband **H/I/S:** Creating Photography **EDU:** Bachelor of Science in Marketing, University of Colorado (1987) **A/A/S:** National Foundation for Infectious Diseases; National Rifle Association; SCI
Email: blhiscox1952@netzero.com

Cynthia J. Hitesman, M.Ed.

Title: Teacher **Company:** TBAISD, New Campus School **Address:** 1100 Red Drive, Traverse City, MI 49684 United States **BUS:** School District **P/S:** Education for Emotionally Impaired Students **MA:** Regional **H/I/S:** Reading, Swimming, Playing Water Sports **EDU:** Master of Education in Special Education, Michigan State University **A/A/S:** Michigan Association of Teachers of Children with Emotional Impairment; National Education Association; Michigan Education Association **C/VW:** National Cherry Festival; Director, Special Kids Day; Paralyzed Veterans Society
Email: chitesman@tbaisd.k12.mi.us
URL: http://www.cambridgewhoswho.com

Dena Hoban

Title: Human Resource Coordinator for Auxiliary and Substitutes **Company:** Wichita Falls Independent School District **Address:** 1104 Broad Street, Wichita Falls, TX 76308 United States **BUS:** School District **P/S:** Education **MA:** Local **EXP:** Ms. Hoban's expertise is in human resources. **H/I/S:** Scuba Diving **EDU:** Bachelor of Science in Management, Minor in Marketing, Midwestern State University **CERTS:** Professional Certification, Society of Human Resource Professionals, Alexandria, Virginia **A/A/S:** Local Chapter, Society of Human Resource Management; Local Midwestern State University Chapter of the Financial Management Association **C/VW:** Local Food Bank, North Texas State Hospital
Email: dhoban@wfisd.net
URL: http://www.wfisd.net

Judeth L. Hobbs

Title: Registered Nurse **Company:** Heritage Valley Health System **Address:** 1000 Dutch Ridge Road, Beaver, PA 15009 United States **BUS:** Healthcare System **P/S:** Medical, Surgical and Diagnostic Services **MA:** Local **D/D/R:** Offering Radiation Therapy and Cardiopulmonary Care **EDU:** Master of Science in Public Health, Columbia State University; Bachelor of Science in Public Health, Columbia State University; Associate Degree in Nursing, Community College of Beaver County **C/VW:** Hospice; Home Health Center
Email: judeth.hobbs@cwwemail.com
URL: http://www.cambridgewhoswho.com

Mary Ann V. Hoblock

Title: Teacher **Company:** Yonkers Public Schools **Address:** 481 E. Branch Road, Patterson, NY 12563 United States **BUS:** School District **P/S:** Education **MA:** Regional **D/D/R:** Teaching the Talented and Gifted **H/I/S:** Historical Traveling **EDU:** Master's Degree in Multicultural Education, Iona College (1990) **CERTS:** Certified Social Studies Teacher (7-12) Grades; Certified Teacher of Gifted and Talented Education; Certified Special Education Teacher; Certified Administrator **A/A/S:** Association for Supervision and Curriculum Development; National Education Association; Delta Mu Delta
Email: rayginia@aol.com
URL: http://www.yonkerspublicschools.org

Michelle Hock
Title: Owner **Company:** Shelley and Company **Address:** 1937 W. Palmetto Street, PMB 118, Florence, SC 29501 United States **BUS:** Giftware Retailer **P/S:** Unique Products, Giftware **MA:** National **EXP:** Ms. Hock's expertise is in Internet sales. **H/I/S:** Reading Mysteries, Traveling, Cooking **EDU:** Greece Olympia High School
Email: shelleyc1@aol.com
URL: http://www.cambridgewhoswho.com

Ilma O. Hodge
Title: Senior Partner, Vice President **Company:** R. I. Hodge & Associates **Address:** 3560 Patti Parkway, Decatur, GA 30034 United States **BUS:** Business and Tax Consulting **P/S:** Business Planning and Management, Tax Preparation and Financial Management **MA:** Regional **D/D/R:** Overseeing Tax Preparation and Consulting, Creating Business Plans, Generating Financial Statements, Preparing Tax Returns, Guiding New Businesses, Developing Financial Statements for Current Business Owners **H/I/S:** Gardening, Cooking, Interior Decorating, Meeting New People **EDU:** Master of Business Administration, University of the Virgin Islands (1992); Bachelor of Arts in Accounting, University of the Virgin Islands (1990) **A/A/S:** Association of Government Accountants; Toastmasters International
Email: ilma@bellsouth.net

Douglas D. Hodges
Title: Freelance Photographer and Writer **BUS:** Photography, Writing **P/S:** Photographs, Books **MA:** National **D/D/R:** Photography, Writing **H/I/S:** Using e-Bay, Doing Internet Research **EDU:** Coursework in Anthropology and Philosophy, University of Colorado at Colorado Springs **C/VW:** Mission Wolf, Colorado
Email: dhmoving2@aol.com
URL: http://www.cambridgewhoswho.com

Douglas Hodson
Title: First Vice President **Company:** Smith Barney **Dept:** Wealth Management **Address:** 129 Campbell Avenue S.E., Suite 100, Roanoke, VA 24011 United States **BUS:** Finance Company **P/S:** Financial and Investment Management Services **MA:** Regional **D/D/R:** Offering Wealth Management Services **H/I/S:** Coaching Youth Baseball and Amateur Athletic Union Basketball, Hunting, Fishing, Participating in Outdoor Activities **EDU:** Bachelor of Science in Business Administration, West Virginia University **A/H:** President's Council Producers, Smith Barney **C/VW:** Ducks Unlimited
Email: douglas.d.hodson@smithbarney.com
URL: http://www.fa.smithbarney.com/doughodson76608

Odes L. Hoehman
Title: Funer Dir, Emblmr, Preneed Cnsltnt **Company:** Criswell Funeral Home **Address:** 815 E. Arlington, Ada, OK 74820 United States **BUS:** Funeral Home and Pre-Need insurance Mortuary **P/S:** Funeral Services, Helping People in Time of Loss, Preneed consulting, Presenting the Deceased in a Comforting Manner **MA:** Local **D/D/R:** Funeral Direction/Embalming, selling of preneed insurance, US Army 1970-1995, Master Sgt.-Retired-Served in Desert Storm **H/I/S:** Church activities, Hunting and Fishing **EDU:** Dallas Institute of Mortuary Sciences, US Army November 1970 to May 1995, Mortuary Sciences, Master Sgt, Retired (Service in Desert Storm) **A/A/S:** Alliance Club, Morris Memorial Baptist Church, VFW, American Legion, Buckmasters, National Rifle Association, North American Hunting and Fishing Club
Email: hoehman@hotmail.com

Byron D. Hoenig
Title: Owner **Company:** Eagle Security Services, LLC **Address:** 1286 Macedonia Church Road, Stephens City, VA 22655 United States **BUS:** Security Company **P/S:** Residential and Commercial Electronic Security Systems **MA:** Virginia, West Virginia **D/D/R:** Overseeing Electronic Security Systems **H/I/S:** Coaching Basketball **CERTS:** Licensed Compliance, Installation and Sales Agent; Licensed Contractor; Licensed Firefighter II **A/A/S:** Winchester-Frederick County Chamber of Commerce; Winchester Fire Department **C/VW:** Virginia State Police Association; Frederick County National Little League
Email: byron.hoenig@cwwemail.com
URL: http://www.eaglesec.com

Arthur S. Hoffman, CRPC
Title: Assistant Vice President, Chartered Retirement Planning Counselor, Certified Financial Manager **Company:** Merrill Lynch **Address:** 2555 E. Camelback Road, Phoenix, AZ 85016 United States **BUS:** Financial Management Firm **P/S:** Financial Management and Advisory Services **MA:** International **EXP:** Mr. Hoffman's expertise includes portfolio implementation and management, asset modification and financial planning. **D/D/R:** Overseeing a 150 Million Dollar Clientèle Book, Demonstrating Leadership, Conducting Seminars and Web Presentations on 401K and Individual Retirement Account Rollovers, Financial Success and Debt Reduction Planning, Overseeing Retirement, Estate, Financial and Corporate Succession Planning, Helping Retiree's and Pre-Retiree's in Asset Planning, Consulting and Lecturing **H/I/S:** Playing Flag Football, Spending Time with his Family, Vacationing **EDU:** Bachelor of Arts in Liberal Arts and Social Sciences, Minor in Economics and Anthropology, Colorado State University **CERTS:** Certified Financial Manager; Certified Charter Retirement Planning Counselor, College of Financial Planning **A/A/S:** Arizona Employers' Council; Stock Market Challenge **A/H:** Junior Achievement Award **C/VW:** American Red Cross; Make-A-Wish; Habitat for Humanity
Email: arthur_hoffman@ml.com
URL: http://www.fa.ml.com/hoffman_herbert

Julia M. Hoffman
Title: Preschool Teacher **Company:** Fremont County School District 14 **Address:** 638 Blue Sky Highway, Ethele, WY 82520 United States **BUS:** School **P/S:** Education **MA:** Local **EXP:** Ms. Hoffman's expertise is in early childhood education. **H/I/S:** Walking, Hiking, Camping, Hunting, Reading, Participating in Church Activities **EDU:** Master of Education in Early Childhood Education, Lesley University **A/A/S:** National Education Association; ECTA; NCA **C/VW:** Church
Email: juliah@fremont14.k12.wy.us
URL: http://www.cambridgewhoswho.com

Paul Hoffman
Title: Owner **Company:** Paul'd Tree Service **Address:** Mesa, AZ 85201 United States **BUS:** Landscaping Service Provider **P/S:** Residential and Some Commercial Properties, Will Trim Trees and Haul Away Materials, Does Some Remolding and Painting **MA:** Local **D/D/R:** Working on All Types of Trees, All Natural, Started his Own Business at age of 10 Making and Selling Candles **H/I/S:** Fishing, Hunting **EDU:** Trinidad State University, CO, North East Senior High School, Associate in Aquaculture, Diploma **A/A/S:** Church

Lena J. Hoffmeier
Title: Owner, Licensed Massage Therapist **Company:** Center Massage **Address:** 1401 Keokuk Street, Iowa City, IA 52240 United States **BUS:** Private Massage Therapy Practice **P/S:** Several Forms of Massage Therapy Including the Milton Trager Method, Healing Touch and Reiki **MA:** Local **D/D/R:** Promoting Physical and Emotional Healing **H/I/S:** Gardening, Reading, Running **CERTS:** Licensed Practical Nurse; Licensed Massage Therapist; Certified Massage Therapist

Eric Hofmann
Title: Associate **Company:** Arquitectonica **BUS:** Architectural Firm **P/S:** Architectural Services **MA:** International **EXP:** Mr. Hofmann's expertise includes project management and the coordination of design documentation. **H/I/S:** Supporting the New York Urban Basketball League, Playing Baseball **EDU:** Master's Degree in Architecture, Chicago State University (2000); Bachelor of Arts in English, University of California, Riverside (1994)
Email: ehofmann@arquitectonica.com
URL: http://www.arquitectonica.com

Deborah E. Hogan, RN, MSN
Title: 1) Adjunct Clinical Instructor 2) Registered Nurse **Company:** 1) The University of Tennessee 2) The University of Tennessee Medical Center **Dept:** 1) College of Nursing **Address:** 312 Oak Park Drive, Knoxville, TN 37918 United States **BUS:** 1) University 2) Medical Center **P/S:** 1) Higher Education 2) Healthcare **MA:** Regional **D/D/R:** Teaching in a Clinical Setting for Nursing Students, Working as an Acute Care Registry and Critical Care Nurse, Nursing Practicing Oncology **H/I/S:** Interior Decorating, Gardening **EDU:** Master's Degree in Nursing, The University of Tennessee (2005) **A/A/S:** Sigma Theta Tau
Email: dhogan@utk.edu
URL: http://www.utk.edu

Ms. Barbara A. Hogue
Title: Chemist (Retired) **Company:** National Institutes of Health **Dept:** National Institute on Aging **Address:** 542 Westside Boulevard, Catonsville, MD 21228 United States **BUS:** Government Health Agency **P/S:** Medical Research, Health Information, Grants, Training, Scientific Resources **MA:** National **D/D/R:** Repairing DNA Pathways, Studying Oxidative Damage and Mitochondrial Repair, Administering Excision Repair, Researching **H/I/S:** Reading, Watching Movies, Traveling, Relaxing at the Beach **EDU:** Master's Degree in Biology, Towson University (2005) **A/A/S:** Kappa Delta Pi
Email: bahogue@msn.com
URL: http://www.nih.gov

Wayne Hogue Jr.
Title: Staff Registered Nurse **Company:** North Mississippi Medical Center **Address:** 830 S. Gloster Street, Tupelo, MS 38801 United States **BUS:** Hospital **P/S:** Healthcare **MA:** Mississippi, Eastern Alabama, Tennessee **D/D/R:** Critical-Care Nursing **H/I/S:** Listening to Music, Using the Computer **EDU:** Associate Degree in Nursing, Mississippi Delta Community College **CERTS:** Certified in Advanced Cardiac Life Support; Certified Critical-Care Registered Nurse **C/VW:** Church
Email: hwhlah1@bellsouth.net
URL: http://www.cambridgewhoswho.com

Christine M. Hojnacki
Title: Vice President, Special Promotions and Publicity **Company:** The Bon-Ton Stores, Inc. **Address:** 331 W. Wisconsin Avenue, Milwaukee, WI 53203 United States **BUS:** Proven Leader Committed to Excellence in the Retail Department Store Industry **P/S:** Fashion, Cosmetics, Home Furnishings, Women's, Children's and Men's Clothing, Shoes and Travel Accessories **MA:** National **D/D/R:** Handling Special Promotions, Publicity, Planning In-Store Events, Community Events and Grand Openings, Overseeing Marketing Plans, Supporting All Departments to Drive Sales, Managing Private Brand Marketing **H/I/S:** Working Out Enthusiastically, Cycling, Running, Swimming, Triathlete **EDU:** Pursuing Bachelor's Degree in Business and Marketing; Associate of Applied Science Degree in Business and Marketing **A/A/S:** TEMPO Women's Business Organization; United Way **A/H:** Named 'Woman of Influence', Community Supporter Category, Business Journal of Greater Milwaukee
Email: christine.knipple@bonton.com
URL: http://www.carsons.com

Kathi K. Holbert
Title: Teacher **Company:** Stamford Public Schools **Address:** 800 Washington Boulevard, Stamford, CT 06901 United States **BUS:** Public Elementary School **P/S:** Education for Kindergarten through Fifth-Grade Students **MA:** Regional **D/D/R:** Teaching All Subjects to First Grade Students, Reading Instruction **H/I/S:** Tennis **EDU:** Master of Arts in Elementary Education, University of Bridgeport (1987) **A/A/S:** Stamford Education Association
Email: kholbert@ci.stamford.us
URL: http://www.stamfordpublicschools.org

Tammy Jo Holcomb
Title: Special Education Teacher **Company:** Jefferson Elementary School **Address:** 22708 W. 182nd Street, Eagleville, MO 64442 United States **BUS:** Elementary School **P/S:** Primary Education **MA:** Local **D/D/R:** Teaching Special Education for Students with Autism, Various Levels of Retardation and Behavioral Disorders **EDU:** Pursuing Master's Degree in Educational Leadership, Morning side University; Bachelor of Arts in Special Education, Western Illinois University (1991) **CERTS:** Certified Therapy Dog Trainer **A/A/S:** Muscatine Education Association
Email: tjholcom@muscatine.k12.ia.us

Spencer Holden
Title: Founder, Executive Director **Company:** Marian Holden Theater and Drama Workshop, Inc. **Address:** 10 Hill Street, Apartment 11D, Newark, NJ 07102 United States **BUS:** Art Theater **P/S:** Art Performance, Show Production **MA:** National **D/D/R:** Performing at the Theater, Producing Original Plays and Musicals, Organizing Playwriting Workshops, Teaching Theater Acting, Speech and Rhyme Programs, Running the Art Education Program through the Theater **H/I/S:** Playing Basketball and Tennis, Producing Community Plays, Volunteering **EDU:** Bachelor's Degree in Political Science, CUNY Baruch (1975) **A/A/S:** Vice President, National Healthy Mothers, Healthy Babies Coalition; The Rhode Island Rhythm & Blues Preservation Society, Providence
Email: mholden3@optonline.net

Misty L. Holke
Title: President **Company:** One World One People **Address:** 137 N.W. 45th Avenue, Deerfield Beach, FL 33442 United States **BUS:** Nonprofit Organization **P/S:** Fundraising, Awareness about Children's Issues in Ghana **MA:** Local **D/D/R:** Making Documentary to Raise Funds, Creating Awareness, Informing People and Trying to Raise People, Consulting and Lecturing for her Private Shows, Nursing on Weekends, Teaching **H/I/S:** Traveling, Horseback Riding **EDU:** Bachelor's Degree in Elementary Education, Florida Atlantic University (1999); Bachelor's Degree in Psychology, Florida Atlantic University (2005); Master's Degree in Educational Psychology, Florida Atlantic University (2007) **A/A/S:** Golden Key International Honor Society **A/H:** Award for the Best Documentary Show 'What We Don't See' (2004)
Email: misty1427@aol.com
URL: http://www.cambridgewhoswho.com

Colleen C. Holland
Title: Visual Arts Specialist Company: Bartow Elementary Academy Address: 750 Wildwood Drive, Bartow, FL 33830 United States BUS: Magnet Elementary School P/S: Elementary Education for Students in Kindergarten through Fifth-Grade MA: Regional D/D/R: Composing Learning Grants for the Art Department, Teaching Kindergarten through Fifth-Grade students H/I/S: Horseback Riding EDU: Bachelor of Science in Art Education; Bachelor of Science in Graphic Design, Florida Southern College (2002); Associate Degree in Elementary Education, Polk Community College (1999) A/A/S: Florida Art Education Association; National Art Education Association; Polk Museum of Art; Bartow Art Guild
Email: colleen@hollandc.com
URL: http://www.bartowacademy.com

Julie Adele Holland
Title: Owner, Financial Mentor Company: The Perfect Home Budget, LLC Address: 505 High Street, Winston Salem, NC 27101 United States BUS: Finance Company P/S: Budget Planning Software, Household Budgeting, Cost Management, Personalized Budgets MA: Regional D/D/R: Managing Finances and Daily Office Operations, Educating Clients about Budgeting and Financial Savings H/I/S: Cooking, Participating in Outdoor Activities EDU: Associate Degree in Medical Assistant Studies, Virginia Polytechnic Institute and State University (1998) A/A/S: Winston-Salem Chamber of Commerce
Email: julie@theperfecthomebudget.org
URL: http://www.theperfecthomebudget.com

Steven W. Holland, PT
Title: Owner, Physical Therapist Company: Physical Therapy Clinic of Gulfport Address: 3506 Washington Avenue, Suite D, Gulfport, MS 39507 United States BUS: Physical Therapy Clinic P/S: Healthcare Including Orthopedic Physical Therapy MA: Local D/D/R: Overseeing Operations, Offering Sports Medicine and Orthopedic Treatments H/I/S: Sailing, Fishing, Golfing EDU: Pursuing Doctor of Physical Therapy; Bachelor of Science in Physical Therapy, The University of Mississippi Medical Center A/A/S: Missouri Physical Therapy Association; American Physical Therapy Association C/VW: Clinical Instructor, Local Clinics
Email: ptclinicgpt@yahoo.com
URL: http://www.cambridgewhoswho.com

Mr. Charles Holley
Title: Owner Company: Cakes by Charles Address: P.O. Box 133, Claremont, VA 23899 United States BUS: Bakery P/S: Baked Goods, Cake Decorating Services MA: Regional D/D/R: Baking, Creating Elaborate Weeding Cakes H/I/S: Golfing EDU: Pursuing Bachelor of Arts in Philosophy and Religion, Saint Leo University A/H: Gold Medal and Best in Show Awards, Culinary Society
Email: chefcharles1@hotmail.com

Mr. Jeremy L. Hollinger
Title: Special Education Teacher Company: Mobile County Public School System Address: 2815 Government Boulevard, Mobile, AL 36606 United States BUS: Public School System P/S: Challenging, Relevant, Multicultural and Integrated Curriculum Taught by a Caring, Competent, Motivated and Accountable Staff MA: Local D/D/R: Teaching Fifth-Grade Inclusion Class Reviewing Regular Class Work, Preparing Different Grade Level Assignments, Modifying Tests, Ensuring Students Understand the Material EDU: Pursuing Master's Degree in Psychometry; Bachelor's Degree in Special Education, University of South Alabama (2001) A/A/S: Who's Who Among American High School Students; Who's Who Among American College Students; Mobile County Education Association; National Education Association
Email: jlh9530@aol.com
URL: http://www.mcpss.com

Gwendolyn J. Hollinquest
Title: Registered Nurse Company: Veterans Administration Hospital Address: 11301 Wilshire Boulevard, West Los Angeles, CA 90073 United States BUS: Hospital P/S: Healthcare MA: Local D/D/R: Intensive Care Nursing, Subspecialty Clinics, Home Healthcare, Radiology Nursing, GI Nursing H/I/S: Reading, Spending Time on the Internet EDU: Bachelor's Degree in Nursing, University of Phoenix, 2006
Email: gwen1948@email.uophx.edu

Nancy L. Holloway
Title: Literacy Leader Company: Roane County Schools Dept: Kingston Elementary School, Midway Elementary School Address: 412 W. Rockwood Street, Rockwood, TN 37854 United States BUS: Elementary School Facility Committed to Excellence in Education P/S: Regular Core Curriculum Including Reading, Mathematics, Science, Social Studies, Art, Music and Writing MA: Regional D/D/R: Tutoring Individuals and Small Groups, Identifying Developmental Needs and Strategies to Match Kindergarten Needs in Reading, Creating Model Lessons, Handling Assessments, Identifying At-Risk Students in Reading, Overseeing Parent-Teacher Workshops, Training Teachers H/I/S: Reading EDU: Master's Degree in Curriculum and Instruction, University of Tennessee (1993) A/A/S: Tennessee Reading Association; International Reading Association; Delta Kappa Gamma A/H: Teacher of the Year (1998)
Email: nholloway@roaneschools.com
URL: http://www.roaneschools.com

Ms. Margaret I. Hollywood
Title: First Vice President Company: Morgan Stanley Dept: Global Wealth Management Address: 1200 Mt. Kemble Avenue, Second Floor, Morristown, NJ 07962 United States BUS: Internationally Renowned Investment and Financial Firm that merges its global reach with a strong emphasis on a local presence P/S: Investment and Financial Services including institutional and personal money management, alternative and structured investments, retirement and estate planning and variable annuities MA: New Jersey and New York D/D/R: A commitment to personalized client service and individualized asset allocations based upon client's goals and risk tolerance H/I/S: Socializing, Enjoying Musical Events, Working with Children's Charities, Golfing and Traveling EDU: Bachelor of Arts in Communications, Seton Hall University (1983) A/A/S: 9/11 Charity Organization, Make-A-Wish Foundation and Morgan Stanley's President's Circle
Email: margaret.hollywood@morganstanley.com
URL: http://www.morganstanley.com

Belden E. Holmes
Title: Telecommunications Laboratory Manager Company: Northrop Grumman Address: 3540 E. Dream Catcher Way, Sierra Vista, AZ 85635 United States BUS: Information Technology and Global Defense Company P/S: Telecommunications Testing for the United States Air Force, Military Plane Design and Maintenance and Ship Yard Management MA: International D/D/R: Managing Teleconferencing Units, Offering Certification for Military Units, Trouble Shooting, Testing Products, Collaborating and Advising in Product Design, Overseeing Video Telecommunications Testing H/I/S: Participating in Track and Field Events, Practicing Building and Carpentry EDU: Bachelor's Degree in Business, Specializing in Computer Science, Wayland Baptist University (1998); Associate Degree in Business, Wayland Baptist University (1995) A/A/S: Arizona Interscholastic Association; Elder, Sierra Vista Church of God and Christ; Retired Soldier, United States Army
Email: holmesb@cox.net
URL: http://www.northropgrumman.com

E. Jeff Holmes
Title: Senior Workers' Compensation Consultant Company: Allegheny Energy Address: 800 Cabin Hill Drive, Greensburg, PA 15601 United States BUS: Electric Utility Company P/S: Generating and Supplying Electricity MA: Regional D/D/R: Consultation Service for Workers' Compensation H/I/S: Exercising, Walking EDU: Bachelor of Arts in Human Resources, Seton Hall University (1990) CERTS: Workers' Compensation Certification, Michigan State University A/A/S: Industry Workers' Compensation Reform; Pennsylvania Self-Insurers' Association; Workers' Compensation Association; West Virginia Self-Insurers Association C/VW: Toastmasters
Email: eholmes@alleghenyenergy.com

Melissa K. Holmes
Title: Owner Company: Lucky Dog Resort, LLC Address: Snohomish, WA 98290 United States BUS: Pet Daycare Facility P/S: Daycare and Boarding for Pets, Beds and Kennels, Grooming MA: Local D/D/R: Managing Daily Business Operations, Maintaining the Website, Bookkeeping, Scheduling, Feeding and Exercising Pets, Dispensing Medications, Pet Sitting EDU: Coursework in Computer Programming, Renton Vocational Technical College (1988) CERTS: Certified Petcare Technician, American Boarding and Kennel Association A/A/S: American Boarding and Kennel Association
Email: melissa@luckydogresort.com
URL: http://www.luckydogresort.com

Joan B. Holmgren
Title: Partner, Esthetician Company: Leisure Time Day Spa Address: 564 Glatt Circle, Woodburn, OR 97071 United States BUS: Full-Service Day Spa and Cosmetology Practice P/S: Manicures, Pedicures, Facials, Haircuts in a Calm Relaxing Atmosphere MA: Regional D/D/R: Performing Full-Body Waxings and Facials, Creating Brow Design, Offering Complete Client Satisfaction H/I/S: Dancing, Clogging EDU: Graduate, Phagans School of Beauty (1998) A/A/S: Chamber of Commerce; Look Good Feel Better
Email: joanbh1942@yahoo.com
URL: http://www.ltdspa.com

Cassia M. Holt, RN, CLM, CNLCP
Title: Owner Company: Medical Intervention Services Address: P.O. Box 1058, Kailua, HI 96734 United States BUS: Healthcare Service Provider P/S: Nurse care management CMSA, CNLCP MA: International D/D/R: W/C Long term care, life planning H/I/S: Swimming, Walking, hiking, biking, dogs, grand children EDU: Kapiolani Community College, Associate Degree in Nursing CERTS: Certified Case Management, Certified Nurse, Life Care Planner A/A/S: CMSA, ANA, Life care planning
Email: medintserv@hawaii.rr.com

Mr. Michael J. Holt
Title: Industrial Sales Manager Company: Mayer Electric Supply Company, Inc. Address: 3405 Fourth Avenue S., Birmingham, AL 35222 United States BUS: Distribution P/S: Electrical Supplies MA: National D/D/R: Overseeing Operation of Three Departments with Approximately 20 Employees, Managing Electrical Engineering, Products and Robotics H/I/S: Scuba Diving, Skydiving EDU: Master's Degree in Business Administration, University of Alabama at Birmingham (1994) A/A/S: Institute of Electrical and Electronics Engineers, Inc.
Email: mholt@mayerelectric.com
URL: http://www.mayerelectric.com

Jill G. Holton
Title: Owner Company: Cowboy's Golf Carts Address: 9346 Florida Boulevard, Walker, LA 70785 United States BUS: Golf Carts Dealer Franchise P/S: Sales, Leasing, Service for Golf Carts MA: Local D/D/R: Sales, Leasing, Overseeing Contracts and Service Department, Hiring, Bookkeeping, advertising and Delegating, Working full Time as Administrative Coordinator H/I/S: Traveling EDU: Pursuing Pre-Law, Northwestern State University A/A/S: Better Business Bureau; Chamber of Commerce; National Association of Legal Secretaries
Email: jill@cowboysgolfcarts.com

Rebecca C. Holton
Title: Prekindergarten Teacher Company: Memphis City Schools, Magnolia Elementary School Address: 2061 Livewell Circle, Memphis, TN 38114 United States BUS: School P/S: Education MA: Regional D/D/R: Teaching Early Childhood Education and Prekindergarten self contained classroom, all content matter H/I/S: Reading, Cross-Stitching, Swimming, Dog, Foster Parenting EDU: Bachelor's Degree in Early Childhood Education, Mississippi University for Women CERTS: Columbus certified teacher mentor, state of Tennessee A/A/S: Local Education Association; Memphis Education Association; National Education Association; Phi Kappa Phi; American Association of Home-based Early Interventions C/VW: Tennessee Foster and Adoptive Care Association, Church, Tennessee Infant Parent School friends of the library; yucca; animal rescue
Email: rcholton@comcast.net

Jan Holwegner
Title: Safety Program Supervisor of Training, Development and Outreach Company: Seattle Children's Hospital, Research & Foundation Address: 4800 Sand Point Way N.E., Seattle, WA United States BUS: Hospital P/S: Healthcare MA: Regional D/D/R: Safety Risk Assessment Training, Developing Training Sessions and Programs for Emergency Response Teams, Supervising the Staff, Planning and Overseeing Events H/I/S: Reading, Hiking, Enjoying the Arts, Traveling, Spending Time with her Family and Friends EDU: Coursework in Emergency Management, University of Washington; Associate Degree in General Social Science, Mt. Hood Community College CERTS: Certified CPR Instructor; Certified Basic Life Support Instructor; Incident Command System Certifications; ERTI Certified Decontamination Trainer, Washington State Hospital Association A/A/S: Washington State Crime Prevention Association; Washington State Hospital Association; International Association for Healthcare Security & Safety A/H: Excellence Award (2006) C/VW: Children's Hospital Guild Association, Seattle Children's Hospital, Research, Foundation; Susan G. Komen for the Cure; Progressive Animal Welfare Society; United Way of America
Email: jholwe6876@aol.com
URL: http://www.seattlechildrens.org

Sarah M. Homer
Title: Personal Trainer, Freelance **Address:** 9408 Blue Falls Court, Elk Grove, CA 95624 United States **BUS:** Health Fitness Club **P/S:** Promote Healthy Habits, Fitness Programs **MA:** Regional **D/D/R:** Personal Training **H/I/S:** Running, Team Sports **EDU:** Bachelor of Arts in Physical Education, California State University at Stanislaus (2000) **CERTS:** Certified Personal Trainer, National Academy of Sports Medicine (2006); Certified Personal Trainer, National Academy of Sports Medicine (2005); Certified Personal Trainer, National Academy of Sports Medicine (2003); Certified, APEX Nutrition Systems **A/A/S:** National Academy of Sports Medicine
Email: sarah_homer@comcast.net
URL: http://wwww.cambridgewhoswho.com

Tina M. Honey
Title: Residential Real Estate Appraiser **Company:** Jymar Appraisal Group, Inc. **Address:** P.O. Box 246, Morrow, GA 30260 United States **BUS:** Real Estate Services **P/S:** Real Estate Valuations for the Mortgage Lending Marketplace **MA:** Regional **D/D/R:** Reducing Lenders' Time, Efforts and Costs in Managing the Appraisal Process, Dealing with Loan Officers, Real Estate Appraisals **H/I/S:** Jogging, Lifting Weights **EDU:** Master's Degree in Information Technology, University of Detroit (1996); Bachelor's Degree in Information Technology, Morris Brown College (1994) **A/A/S:** Founder and President, Tina M. Honey Foundation; National Association of Realtors
Email: jymarappraisals@gmail.com
URL: http://www.jymarappraisals.com

James D. Hong
Title: Director of Junior Golf **Company:** Harbor Links Golf Course **Address:** 1 Fairway Drive, Port Washington, NY 11050 United States **BUS:** Junior Golf Development Program Company **P/S:** Golf Instruction **MA:** Regional **D/D/R:** Instructing Competitive Junior Golfers **H/I/S:** Spending Time with Family **EDU:** Bachelor of Arts in English Writing, Trinity College **A/A/S:** Apprentice, Professional Golfers' Association of America
Email: jhong@palmergolf.com
URL: http://www.harborlinks.com

Naomi Hood
Title: Registered Nurse, Surgery Coordinator **Company:** Riverview Regional Medical Center **Address:** 600 S. Third Street, Gadsden, AL 35901 United States **BUS:** Hospital **P/S:** Healthcare **MA:** Regional **EXP:** Ms. Hood's expertise is in surgical nursing. **D/D/R:** Assisting Doctors, Coordinating Surgeries **H/I/S:** Reading, Traveling **EDU:** Associate of Science in Nursing, Gadsden State Community College **CERTS:** Certified Operating Room Nurse; Advanced Cardiac Life Support Instructor; Registered Nurse, State of Alabama **A/A/S:** Association of periOperative Registered Nurses **C/VW:** American Heart Association; American Cancer Society
Email: nhoodrn@yahoo.com

Bonetta R. Hoogeveen
Title: Director **Company:** Creative Memories **Address:** 3001 Clearwater Road, St. Cloud, MN 56302 United States **BUS:** Creative Scrapbooking Company **P/S:** Photo Albums, Frames, Consultations, Storybooks and Digital Storybooks **MA:** International **D/D/R:** Direct Sales, Consulting, Selling Quality Albums, Advising Customers on How to Document Family Memories, Conducting Classes on Photographs Preserving, Selling New Product Lines of Frames and Storybooks **H/I/S:** Quilting, Spending Time with her Family **EDU:** Associate Degree in Secretarial Science, Dordt College, Sioux City, Iowa (1976) **A/A/S:** Blandin Foundation
Email: bonnicm@willmarnet.com
URL: http://www.mycmsite.com/bhoogeveen

Robert D. Hooks
Title: Pastor, Founder **Company:** New Beginnings Baptist Church **Address:** 9491 Railroad Drive, El Paso, TX 79924 United States **BUS:** Church **P/S:** Christian Education **MA:** Regional **D/D/R:** Teaching Christian Education **H/I/S:** Attending Educational Conferences **EDU:** Bachelor of Science in Christian Education Biblical Studies, Indiana Bible College; Coursework in Medical Management, West Technical College, El Paso; Fellowship in Human Resources and Management Administration, Fort Ben Harris University, Indiana **CERTS:** Licensed Practical Nurse, Academy of Health and Science, San Antonio, Texas **A/A/S:** Chaplain, Alliance National Ministries; Vice President, African American Baptist Conventions; Chairman, Baptist District Association; National Dean, Christian Advocate; National Baptist, Inc.
Email: hookie@att.net

Lolita Y. Hoorfar
Title: Chiropractor **Company:** Lolita's Chiropractic **Address:** 10801 National Boulevard, Suite 340, Los Angeles, CA 90064 United States **BUS:** Chiropractic Practice **P/S:** Chiropractic Healthcare **MA:** Local **D/D/R:** Practicing Chiropractic Work and Alternative Healthcare, Administering Cold Laser Therapy for Pain **H/I/S:** Spending Time with Family, Watching Movies, Traveling **EDU:** Doctor of Chiropractic, Cleveland Chiropractic College; Bachelor of Science in Biology, Cleveland Chiropractic College
Email: chiroloi26@yahoo.com
URL: http://www.cambridgewhoswho.com

Charles O. Hoover
Title: Area Sales Manager **Company:** DuPont **Address:** 1426 Highway 51 S., Senatobia, MS 38668 United States **BUS:** Chemical Manufacturing **P/S:** Crop Protection Products, Agricultural Chemicals **MA:** International **D/D/R:** Selling Crop Protection Products and Chemicals to Distributors, Managing Sales Personnel **H/I/S:** Football, Woodworking, Hunting **EDU:** Bachelor of Arts in Marketing, Delta State University, Cleveland, Mississippi (1981) **A/A/S:** Southern Crop Production Association
Email: charles.hoover@usa.dupont.com
URL: http://www.dupont.com

Paul Hopgood
Title: Executive Director **Company:** Children Against Abortion, Pornography and Molestation **BUS:** Nonprofit Christian-Based Organization **P/S:** Child Abuse Prevention Education **MA:** National **D/D/R:** Mr. Hopgood's expertise is in creating public awareness of children's values, conducting seminars, offering spiritual advice and overseeing television broadcasting of methods to prevent abuse. **H/I/S:** Swimming **EDU:** Bachelor's Degree in Computer Science, Notre Dame College (1987) **A/A/S:** Toastmasters International **C/VW:** Doctors Without Borders; Council of Indian Nations
Email: paul.hopgood@cwwemail.com
Email: director@children-aapm.org
URL: http://www.children-aapm.org

Jennifer Hopkins
Title: Art Educator **Company:** Lakeshore Elementary School **Address:** 252 Lakeshore School Road, Mooresville, NC 28117 United States **BUS:** Public School **P/S:** Education **MA:** Iredell County **D/D/R:** Teaching Art **H/I/S:** Horseback Riding **EDU:** Pursuing Master's Degree in Education, Mansfield University; Bachelor of Art in K-12 Education and Visual Arts, Nazareth College
Email: jhopkins@iss.k12.nc.us

Donna J. Hoppe
Title: Information Technology Specialist **Company:** Kansas City VA Medical Center **Address:** 4801 E. Linwood Boulevard, Kansas City, MO 64128 United States **BUS:** Medical Center **P/S:** Healthcare for Agent Orange, Blind Rehabilitation, Cancer, Cold Injury, Diabetes, Flu like Influenza-Pandemic, Gulf War Illnesses, Hepatitis C, Homelessness, HIV/AIDS, Kidney Diseases, Mental Health, Weight Program, Poly-Trauma, Post-Traumatic Stress Disorder, Public Health, Recreation Therapy, Vet Center, Readjustment Counseling, Veterans Health Initiative, Women's Health **MA:** Regional **D/D/R:** Maintaining Medical Records, Overseeing All System Functionality for Vista Applications Systems, Clinician-Based Training, Confirming Reports and Record Accuracy of High-Risk Patient Data, Assisting with Program to All Hospital Staff Members with a Background in Nursing **H/I/S:** Skiing, Waterskiing, Hiking **EDU:** Bachelor of Science in Nursing, Saint Mary's University (1993); Associate Degree in Nursing, Kansas City Kansas Community College (1974) **A/A/S:** Air Force Association; Reserve Officers Association
Email: hopped@hughes.net
URL: http://www.va.gov

Brenda F. Hopperton
Title: Registered Nurse, Licensed Clinical Nurse **Company:** Saint Elizabeth Medical Center **Address:** 1 Medical Village Drive, Edgewood, KY 41017 United States **BUS:** Catholic Healthcare System Sponsored by the Diocese of Covington **P/S:** Quality Healthcare and Wellness Services for All People in the Tri-State Area **MA:** Regional **D/D/R:** Working as a Charge Nurse and Patient Advocate, Ensuring the Timeliness of Schedules, Overseeing Eight Nurses, Legal Nurse Consultant **H/I/S:** Hiking, Attending Auctions **EDU:** Bachelor of Science in Nursing, Thomas More College (1985); Associate of Science, Soloman University (2001) **A/A/S:** American Nurses Association; Order of the Eastern Star; Member, Local Church
Email: bhopperton@zoomtown.com

Thomas P. Hörger, LUTCF-CLU
Title: Agent and Financial Consultant **Company:** RBC Insurance **Address:** 100 Verdae Boulevard, Suite 402, Greenville, SC 29607 United States **BUS:** Insurance Provider for Middle-Income Families in Canada and the United States **P/S:** Wide Range of Insurance Protection and Wealth Management Solutions to More than Five Million North American Clients **MA:** International **D/D/R:** Offering Life Insurance Sales and Service with an Emphasis on Customer Satisfaction **H/I/S:** Enjoying Football and Baseball, Golfing **EDU:** Coursework in Pre-Med, Presbyterian College **CERTS:** Licensed Life and Health Agent **A/A/S:** National Association of Insurance and Financial Advisors; National Association of Local Underwriters
Email: tommy.horger@libertyagency.com
URL: http://www.rbcinsurance.com

Patti Van L. Horn
Title: Sole Proprietor, Owner and Operator **Company:** Patti's Patch Work **Address:** 3622 Mount Diablo Boulevard, LaFayette, CA 94549 United States **BUS:** Leather Apparel Alterations and Equestrian Network **P/S:** Leather Alterations and Repairs Geared Toward Motorcycle Horse Riding Industry, Patch Work, Motorcycle Seat, Home Furnishing and Boat Interior Repairs, Alterations to Riding Gear Including Chaps, Leather Pants or Jackets, Horse Riding Boots and Saddles **MA:** International **D/D/R:** Making Alterations, Working with Leather **H/I/S:** Bowling, Golfing, Traveling, Cruises, **EDU:** Los Madonnas College, PA, College Courses-Computer Technology, CA, Notary Public **A/A/S:** Harley Davidson Co, Cycle Gear, Suzuki, All Motorcycle Groups, Companies and Apparel Stores
Email: pattispatchwork@comcast.net
URL: http://www.cambridgewhoswho.com

Wendy L. Hornack
Title: President **Company:** AIBS, Inc. **Address:** 300 Ohukai Road, Suite C322, Kihei, HI 96753 United States **BUS:** Consulting Firm **P/S:** Consulting Services Including Troubleshooting, Technical Support **MA:** Maui **D/D/R:** Managing Business Operations and Projects, Promoting Relationships **H/I/S:** Spending Time with her Family **EDU:** Coursework in Computer Science, Minor in English, West Texas State University and University of Las Vegas **A/A/S:** Better Business Bureau; Maui Chamber of Commerce **C/VW:** Community Services
Email: whornack@aibshi.com
URL: http://www.aibshi.com

Cleola Horne
Title: Science Coordinator **Company:** Miami-Dade County Public Schools **Address:** 2981 N.W. 171st Street, Miami Gardens, FL 33056 United States **BUS:** Public School **P/S:** Education for Students in Kindergarten through Twelfth-Grade, Primary Learning Center, Specialized Programs **MA:** Regional **D/D/R:** Coordinating the Science Department, Teaching Fourth and Fifth-Grade Students, Coaching Cheerleading **EDU:** Master of Arts in Human Service Management, St. Thomas University (1999) **A/A/S:** Phi Delta Kappa; Association for Supervision and Curriculum Development; National Association for the Advancement of Colored People; American Federation of Labor-Congress of Industrial Organizations; Future Educator of America Health and Society Patrol
Email: chorne@dadeschool.net
URL: http://www2.dadeschools.net/index.htm

William H. Horne
Title: Chief Executive Officer **Company:** Echo Logistics Company, LLC **Address:** 474 Ockley Drive, Shreveport, LA 71105 United States **BUS:** Transportation Company **P/S:** Transportation and Logistic Services **MA:** National **D/D/R:** Arranging Transportation and Logistics for Customers throughout the United States, Lowering Transportation Costs **H/I/S:** Golfing, Hunting, Fishing, Spending Time with his Wife and Son **EDU:** Bachelor of Science in Environmental Science, University of Louisiana Lafayette **A/A/S:** United States Golf Association; Sigma Alpha Epsilon/Louisiana Alpha Chapter 1985; Coastal Conservation Association; NRP; Delta Waterfowl Association **C/VW:** CCA; Church Saint Mary's Episcopal Goodwill; Saint Jude's Children's Hospital
Email: echologi@comcast.net

Diana S. Horowitz
Title: Managing Director, Corporate Advertising **Company:** Business Development for Recruiting Advertising **Address:** 620 Eighth Avenue, New York, NY 10018 United States **BUS:** Media Firm **P/S:** New York Times Newspaper **MA:** International **D/D/R:** Advertising, Creating New Platforms for Advertising, Managing Business Development and Business Strategies **H/I/S:** Traveling, Biking, Riding **EDU:** Bachelor's Degree in French Studies, The George Washington University **A/A/S:** Business Marketing Association
Email: diana.horowitz@nytimes.com
URL: http://www.nytimes.com

Tina J. Horsey, RT, RM
Title: Lead Technologist **Company:** Alliance Imaging **Address:** 2004 Apache Trail, Hammonton, NJ 08037 United States **BUS:** Diagnostic Imaging Center **P/S:** Diagnostic and Medical Imaging Services **MA:** National **EXP:** Ms. Horsey's expertise includes computed axial tomography scanning and radiology. **D/D/R:** Performing Three-Dimensional and Magnetic Resonance Imaging **CERTS:** Certification in Mammographic Radiologic Technology **A/A/S:** American Society of Radiologic Technologists
Email: tinahorsey@comcast.net
URL: http://www.allianceimaging.com

Joni J. Hortert
Title: Third-Grade Teacher **Company:** Seneca Valley School District **Address:** 410 McCalmont Road, Renfrew, PA 16053 United States **BUS:** School District Committed to Excellence in Education **P/S:** Regular Core Curriculum for Grades K-6 Including English, Mathematics, Science, Social Studies, Language **MA:** Regional **D/D/R:** Teaching Mathematics, Language Arts, Science, Health, Spelling and Handwriting to Third-Grade Students in a Self-Contained Classroom, Coordinating Third-Grade District, Managing Goals and Curriculum for All Third-Grade Teachers in Four Elementary Schools **H/I/S:** Scrap-Booking, Remodeling Old Homes, Jazzercise Aerobics **EDU:** Master's Degree in Elementary Mathematics and Elementary Science, Dean's List, Slippery Rock University, Slippery Rock, Pennsylvania; Bachelor's Degree in Education, Dean's List (1992) **CERTS:** Certified in Special Education and Elementary Education, Slippery Rock University **A/A/S:** National Education Association; Pennsylvania Education Association; Former Instructor in Act 48 (2003-2005)
Email: jhortert@zoominternet.net
URL: http://www.svsd.net

Doreth M. HoSang
Title: Registered Nurse **Company:** Harris County Hospital District **Address:** 7550 Office City Drive, Houston, TX 77012 United States **BUS:** Hospital System **P/S:** Family Practice Healthcare, Triage Nursing, Community Health Clinic **MA:** Local **D/D/R:** Handling Triage, Seeing Patients, Urology and Orthopedic Nursing, Home Health Nursing **H/I/S:** Reading, Gardening **EDU:** Associate of Science in Nursing, Houston Community College, 2002 **C/VW:** Veterans Administration Association, Good Samaritan, Back to the Bible
Email: doreth_hosang@hchd.tmc.edu

George P. Hoskins
Title: Minister, Third District **Company:** Christian Union **Address:** 136 N. Vine Street, Vaughnsville, OH 45893 United States **BUS:** Christian Organization **P/S:** Preaching the Living Word **MA:** Local **D/D/R:** Friendly, Outgoing Help, Serving as a Minister at Low Gap Christian Union, Washington Hall Christian Union and Pount Pleasant Christian Union **H/I/S:** Fishing **EDU:** Ordained Minister **A/A/S:** Association of American Veterans **C/VW:** Hospice Work, St. Regis Hospital of Lima
Email: ghoskins@bright.net
URL: http://www.cambridgewhoswho.com

Patricia T. Hottinger
Title: Teacher **Company:** Rappahannock County Public Schools **Address:** 34 Schoolhouse Road, Washington, VA 22747 United States **BUS:** School District **P/S:** Education **MA:** Local **D/D/R:** Teaching Special Education **H/I/S:** Painting **EDU:** National Educational Technology Standards Certificate; Master's Degree in Education, Shenandoah University; Bachelor's Degree in Special Education, James Madison University; Associate Degree in Education, Shenandoah University **A/A/S:** Virginia Education Association; National Education Association; Rappahannock County Education Association; Council for Exceptional Children **C/VW:** American Cancer Society, School Charities
Email: pgarden@shentel.net
URL: http://www.cambridgewhoswho.com

Misti Houck Bailey, Pharm.D.
Title: PharmD, Pharmacy Resident **Company:** United States Public Health Service, Indian Health Service, Whiteriver PHS Indian Hospital, Whiteriver, AZ 85941 United States **BUS:** Community Pharmacy, Hospital **P/S:** Public Health Services, Prescription Drugs **MA:** Regional **D/D/R:** Counseling Patients, Dispensing Medications and Processing Patient Information, Studying Infectious Diseases, Medicinal Chemistry, Physiology, Biochemistry, Pharmacology, Therapeutics, Hospital and Retail Pharmacy Law, Managing Inpatients and Outpatients, Participating in Hospital Rotations **H/I/S:** Traveling, Exercising, Basketball **EDU:** Doctor of Pharmacy, Samford University, Birmingham, Alabama (2007); Bachelor of Arts in Interdisciplinary Sciences, Lincoln Memorial University, Tennessee (2007) **A/A/S:** American Pharmaceutical Association; The American Society of Health-System Pharmacists; Academy of Managed Care Pharmacy; National Community Pharmacists Association; Phi Lambda Sigma; Kappa Psi Pharmaceutical Fraternity
Email: misti.bailey@ihs.gov
URL: http://www.ihs.gov

Dr. Joan Houghton
Title: Director **Company:** Kansas State Department of Education, Kansas Project for Children and Young Adults who are Deaf and Blind **Address:** 120 S.E. 10th Avenue, Topeka, KS 66612 United States **BUS:** State Department of Education, Student Support Services **P/S:** General Education, Special Education, Technical Assistance for Students who Are Deaf-Blind, Training for Educators, Families and Students, Project Development and Dissemination **MA:** State, Regional and National **D/D/R:** Comprehensive School Reform, Single Subject Research, Positive Behavior Supports Studentws with Severe Disabilities and Complex Healthcare Needs, Qualitative Research **H/I/S:** Horseback Riding, Gardening, Collecting Antiques, Water Color, Acrylics, Wire Collecting, Theatre, Music, Playing the Piano **EDU:** Ph.D. in Special Education, Minor in Psychological Research and Evaluation, Emphasis on Severe Disabilities, The University of Kansas (2004), Master's in Cognitive Disabilities, Deaf-Blindness (1986); Bachelor's in General Education (1977); Bachelor's in Speech Pathology and Audiology (1976) **A/A/S:** The Association for Persons of Severe Handicaps; Council for Exceptional Children; Phi Lamda Theta; Association For Supervision and Curriculum Development; Academic Evaluation Report; National Association for Developmental Education; American Association on Intellectual and Developmental Disabilities
Email: jhinv25@hotmail.com
URL: http://www.ksde.org

Wendy Jo Houle
Title: District Service Manager **Company:** Agilent Technologies, Inc. **Address:** 3601 Minnesota Drive, Suite 800, Edina, MN 55435 United States **BUS:** Measurement Instrumentation **P/S:** Measurement Company **MA:** International **EXP:** Ms. Houle's expertise includes life sciences and chemical analysis. **EDU:** Bachelor's Degree in Business, University of Minnesota, Carlson School of Management **C/VW:** Youth Sailing Group, Church, Girls Scouts of the USA
Email: whoule@comcast.net
URL: http://www.agilent.com

James Michael House
Title: Chief Executive Officer, Founder **Company:** Squank Entertainment **Address:** P.O. Box 130, Junction City, OR 97448 United States **BUS:** Record Label Company **P/S:** Distribution of CD, DVD, Music Production **MA:** International **D/D/R:** Mr. House's expertise is in creative business planning, overseeing music production and composition. **H/I/S:** Spending Time Outdoors, Traveling, Practicing Yoga, Conducting Research in Philosophy and Quantum Physics, Creative Writing **A/A/S:** ACIC; Alumni Association, University of Oregon; American Civil Liberties Union
Email: james@squank.com
Email: squanksound@yahoo.com
URL: http://www.squank.com

Nicole T. Houston
Title: Director of Education **Company:** Cottage Hospital **Address:** 90 Swiftwater Road, Woodsville, NH 03785 United States **BUS:** Hospital **P/S:** Anesthesia, Pain Management, Birthing Center, Cardiac Rehabilitation, Day Surgery, Dietary Services, Emergency Department, Intensive Care Unit, Oncology, Cancer Management Program **MA:** Local **D/D/R:** Overseeing New Hire Orientation, Staff Development and Compliance, Teaching Registered Nursing Programs **H/I/S:** Downhill Skiing, Waterskiing, Jogging, Coaching Basketball and Softball **EDU:** Bachelor of Science in Nursing, University of Phoenix (2005) **CERTS:** Certification in Advanced Cardiac Life Support; Certification in Pediatric Advanced Life Support; Certification in Basic Life Support; Certified Emergency Nurse; Certification in Trauma Nursing Core Course **A/A/S:** Emergency Nursing Association; National Nursing Staff Development Organization; Sigma Theta Tau
Email: nhouston@cottagehospital.org
URL: http://cottagehospital.org

Nathan Houtsma
Title: Chef **Company:** Dick and Harry's **Address:** 370 Horizon Court, Cumming, GA 30041 United States **BUS:** Full Service Restaurant and Bar **P/S:** New American and Upscale Contemporary Cuisine, Food Including Crab Cakes, Lamb Chops, Drinks **MA:** Regional **D/D/R:** Organizing Standard and Weekly Specials Menus, Supervising Staff, Overseeing Financial and Marketing Operations **H/I/S:** Sailing, Yachting, Painting, Cooking **EDU:** Master's Degree in Fine Arts, San Francisco State University(2002); Coursework in Graphic Arts; Graduate Cordon Blew (2004) **A/A/S:** American Culinary Federation **A/H:** Best Outside Perimeter, Atlanta Magazine (2006,2007); Voted Top 100 Restaurants Jezebel Magazine (2007); Voted Top 100 Wine Enthusiast in the County (2007)
Email: n.houtsma@mac.com
URL: http://www.dickandharrys.com

Nancy T. Hovanic
Title: Eastern Regional Manager **Company:** Fisher & Paykel Healthcare, Inc. **Address:** 22982 Alcalde Drive, Laguna Hills, CA 92653 United States **BUS:** Manufacturing **P/S:** Medical Equipment Manufacturing **MA:** Local **D/D/R:** Manufacturing and Distribution of Respiratory Humidifiers and Infant Warmers, Communications **H/I/S:** Painting with Oils and Water Colors **EDU:** Associate of Science in Respiratory Therapy, Fairleigh Dickinson University **A/A/S:** American Association for Respiratory Care
Email: nthovanic@aol.com
URL: http://www.cambridgewhoswho.com

Carol S. Howard
Title: Teacher **Company:** East Cobb Middle School **Address:** 380 Holt Road, Marietta, GA 30068 United States **BUS:** Education Education/Secondary Education **P/S:** Moderately and Mildly Disabled Students **MA:** Local **D/D/R:** Teaching Disabled Children **EDU:** North Georgia College and State University, Master's Degree in Special Education **A/A/S:** ACEI, NEA, Wesley Foundation
Email: carolhoward@cobb.k12.org

David M. Howard
Title: Founder, Risk Manager **Company:** CST Risk Management **Address:** 7155 W. Campo Bello Drive, Suite C120, Glendale, AZ 85308 United States **BUS:** Risk Management Company **P/S:** Regulatory Compliance **MA:** Regional **EXP:** Mr. Howard's expertise includes regulatory and employment law compliance. **H/I/S:** Spending Time Outdoors, Riding his Harley-Davidson **EDU:** Associate Degree in Survival Operations, The University of Texas (1994) **A/A/S:** Risk and Insurance Management Society
Email: dhoward@cstrm.com
URL: http://www.cstrm.com

Kandice D. Howard
Title: Director of Case Management **Company:** Devine and Associates, Inc. **Address:** 321 High School Road, Bainbridge, WA 98110 United States **BUS:** Nursing **P/S:** Telephone Case Management **MA:** Regional **EXP:** Ms. Howard's expertise includes oncology and cardiac nursing. **H/I/S:** Skiing, Camping, Hunting, Fishing **EDU:** Associate Degree in Registered Nursing **A/A/S:** CMSA; ACCN
Email: kanhoward@clearwater.net
URL: http://www.devinecasemanagement.com

Mrs. Sara W. Howard
Title: President, Chief Executive Officer **Company:** Howard & Associates, Inc. **Address:** 201 Winn Cay Drive, Tallahassee, FL 32312 United States **BUS:** Marketing Company for Original Books **P/S:** Scientific Informational Services, Science Consulting, Public Speaking on Astronomy, Geology **MA:** International **D/D/R:** Working with Scientists and Apollo Astronomers on Government Projects, Writing Science-Based Children's Books Specializing in Astronomy and Aerospace, Conducting Research in Mental Healthcare **H/I/S:** Participating in the Music Chorus, Painting, Re-Enacting Civil War Scenes, Showing Horses and Dogs, Flying, Sailing, Volcano Watching, Studying Astronomy, Public Speaking **EDU:** Pursuing Master's Degree in Geology; Bachelor of Science in Mathematics, Minor in Astronomy, Louisiana State University **A/A/S:** Founder, First President, Shreveport Astronomical Society; One of the First Female Aerospace Engineers, Boeing on the S1C Stage of the Saturn V, Apollo Lunar Program; Worker (1990 and 2000 Census); Tour Guide, Great Britain; Executor of Three Estates
Email: sarawhoward@comcast.net
URL: http://www.sarastellarscience.com

Gayle L. Howard-Rolli
Title: President **Company:** Eden Trucking Services, Inc. **Address:** 2815 135th Circle N.W., Andover, MN 55304 United States **BUS:** Trucking Company **P/S:** Transportation Services **MA:** National **D/D/R:** Utilizing Leadership Skills, Managing the Company **H/I/S:** Boating, Fishing, Bowling, Gardening, Landscaping **CERTS:** Certification in Architecture **A/A/S:** Better Business Bureau
Email: gayle@edentrucking.com

Elizabeth C. Howell
Title: Director of Therapy Services **Company:** Palms of Pasadena Hospital (Iasis Healthcare) **Address:** 2020 Rutherford Drive, Dover, FL 33527 United States **BUS:** Healthcare Hospital **P/S:** Healthcare Services, Administration **MA:** Local **EXP:** Ms. Howell's expertise includes management, respiratory and neonatal care. **H/I/S:** Piano, Reading **EDU:** University of Phoenix, College of Health Science in Virginia, Associate in Respiratory, BA, Healthcare Administration, Master of Business Administration, Health **A/A/S:** AARC, American Heart Association, Recipient 2006 National Leadership Award
Email: ehowell@iasishealthcare.com
Email: behowe@verizon.net

Larry Howell
Title: Business, Manager Company: Artistic Plumbing, Inc Address: 6349 Quebec Avenue N., Brooklyn, MN 55428 United States BUS: Plumbing Contracting P/S: Service, Remodeling MA: Local D/D/R: Residential and Commercial Plumbing H/I/S: Driving my Corvette, Hot Rods-Won the 'Old Times International Motorcross Championship' EDU: Plumbers and Pipe Fitters National Association Apprenticeship School, Plumbers Contractors License, Comp Card St Paul, MN A/A/S: BNI

Victoria Ann Howell
Title: Teacher Company: Sardis Elementary School Address: 2805 Sardis Road, Gainesville, GA 30506 United States BUS: Elementary School P/S: Education MA: Local D/D/R: Teaching Academic Subjects to Elementary School Children H/I/S: Swimming, Photography EDU: Educational Specialist Degree in Teacher Leadership, North Georgia College A/A/S: Georgia Association of Educators; National Education Association; Association for Supervision and Curriculum Development C/VW: American Red Cross; American Cancer Society; United Way Email: email2you2@yahoo.com
URL: http://www.cambridgewhoswho.com

Kelli Ann Howie
Title: Artist Company: Kelli's Blue Mesa Studio Address: 1055 Landscale Drive, Duncaville, TX 75116 United States BUS: Fine Art instructor at visual expressions, lecturer, art collector P/S: Water Colors, Oil, Sculpture, Photography, Drawing MA: International EXP: Ms. Howie's expertise includes instruction, sculpture and indigenous artifacts from remote cultures in the Amazon. H/I/S: Traveling EDU: Texas Southern Methodist, Master of Fine Arts A/A/S: Texas Visual Arts Association, Chamber of Commerce (Duncanville), Promoter of the Arts, Supplier of public Art, Chaca International Museum of Cultures Email: kelliannhowie@aol.com
URL: www.kellihowiestudio.com

Tara Marie Hoxeng
Title: Youth Counselor Company: State of South Dakota Address: 44867 303rd Street, Yankton, SD 57078 United States BUS: Mental Healthcare Agency P/S: Mental Healthcare Services MA: South Dakota D/D/R: Offering Adolescent, Family and Group Counseling, Helping Patients to Develop Social Skills, Specializing in Conflict Resolution and Nonviolent Crisis Intervention, Deescalating Intense Situations H/I/S: Traveling, Boating, Hiking EDU: Bachelor's Degree in Psychology, University of South Dakota A/A/S: National Society of Collegiate Scholars; Psi Chi, the National Honor Society in Psychology Email: tara.hoxeng@state.sd.us
URL: http://www.cambridgewhoswho.com

Keith A. Hruska
Title: Director of Pediatric Nephrology, Professor of Pediatrics, Professor of Medicine Company: Washington University Address: 660 S. Euclid Street, Saint Louis, MO 63110 United States BUS: University P/S: Higher Education MA: International D/D/R: Conducting Research, Identifying Complications of Chronic Disease Including Skeletal and Muscular Leading to Cardiovascular Mortality H/I/S: Gardening, Snowboarding EDU: Residency, Cornell University; Internship, Cornell University; MD, Creighton University (1969); Bachelor's Degree in Art, Creighton University (1965) A/A/S: ASCI; American Academy of Pediatrics; American Society of Nephrology; American Society for Cell Biology; APS; Secretary, Treasurer, American Society for Bone and Mineral Research; American Society for Biochemistry and Molecular Biology; International Society of Nephrology Nexxus Email: hruska_k@kids.wustl.edu

Helen T. Hsueh
Title: Chief Financial Officer, Publisher Company: Las Vegas Chinese Daily News Address: 4215 Spring Mountain Road, Suite B206A, Las Vegas, NV 89102 United States BUS: Publishing Company P/S: Publishing Newspaper MA: Local D/D/R: Marketing, Building Public Relations H/I/S: Spending Time with her Family and Friends EDU: Industry-Related Training A/A/S: Chinese Community Email: helen@lvcdn.com
URL: http://www.lvcdn.com

Helen Hubbard
Title: 1) Community Health Care Consultant and Educator 2) Nurse Consultant Specialist Company: 1) Department of Health Care Services 2) Hubbard's Health Care Consultation and Education, Inc. Address: 4655 E. Tyler Avenue, Fresno, CA 93702 United States BUS: 1) Government Organization 2) Healthcare and Education Consulting Firm P/S: 1) Healthcare Educator 2) Healthcare Consulting MA: 1) Local 2) San Joaquin Valley, Northern CA EXP: Ms. Hubbard's expertise includes prevention oversight, the promotion of the awareness of chronic diseases and the organization of healthcare seminars and workshops. D/D/R: Working within the Community to Educate Diverse Targeted Populations on Female, Male and Infant Health Issues Including Nutrition and Chronic Disease Self-Management, Ensuring Community Health Care Services H/I/S: Reading, Gardening, Traveling, Shopping, Playing Basketball and Football EDU: Pursuing Ph.D. in Public Health and Education, California State University; Master of Science in Nursing, University of Phoenix (2007); Master of Healthcare Administration, Chapman University (1999); Bachelor of Science in Nursing and Health Science, Chapman University (1998) A/A/S: Member, Former President, Central Valley Black Nurses Association; California Nurses Association; American Nurses Association; Board of Directors, Central Valley Coalition of Nursing Organizations; Omicron Delta Chapter, Sigma Theta Tau International; American Cancer Society; California Transplant Donor Network; National Association for the Advancement of Colored People A/H: Community Health Black Image Award, National Association for the Advancement of Colored People; Registered Nurse of the Year, Central Valley Coalition of Nurses Association; Volunteer Service Award, Central Valley Black Nurses; Masonic Dedication Award for Community Service, Prince Hall Free and Accepted Masons; Board of Directors Service Award, American Cancer Society; President's Recognition Award, American Cancer Society C/VW: American Cancer Society; American Heart Association; American Lung Association; California Transplant Donor Network Email: hhubbard02@yahoo.com
Email: helen.hubbard@dhcs.ca.gov
URL: http://www.cambridgewhoswho.com

RubyeMae Annen Hubbard-Musser
Title: Registered Occupational Nurse (Retired) Company: Reasonable Affordable Health Management Address: 3148 Waterside Drive, Arlington, TX 76012 United States BUS: Healthcare Center P/S: Healthcare Services MA: Regional D/D/R: Nursing Experience, Managing Employee Healthcare Policies, Training Nursing Staff for Surgical Procedures H/I/S: Cooking, Swimming, Walking, Biking, Reading EDU: St. Paul's School of Nursing, Dallas, Texas (1957) A/A/S: President and Activities Director, North Texas Region Cadillac Club; President, Meadowbrook Business and Professional Woman's Club; Former President and Present Director, The American Association of Occupational Health Nurses

Ronda L. Huber
Title: Assistant to the Director Company: Hood County Library Address: 222 N. Travis Street, Granbury, TX 76048 United States BUS: Library P/S: Enrichment and Education for the Community MA: Regional D/D/R: Research and Statistics, Computer Management, Assist in Presentation of Annual Reports to County Commissioners H/I/S: Gardening, Cooking, Professional Cake Decorating for Weddings EDU: College Coursework for Two Years in General Business Studies, Tarleton State University A/A/S: Christmas for Children; Habitat for Humanity; Adopt-A-Soldier Email: rhuber@co.hood.tx.us
URL: http:co.hood.tx.us

Celena Hudak
Title: Finance Director Company: Greater Johnstown Community YMCA Address: 100 Haynes Street, Johnstown, PA 15901 United States BUS: Nonprofit Organization P/S: Meeting the Health and Human Services Needs of the Community MA: National D/D/R: Overseeing All Aspects of Finance for the Organization, Budgets, Financial Reports, Accounts Payable, Payroll H/I/S: Spending Time with her Daughters and Husband EDU: Master of Business Administration University of Phoenix; Bachelor of Science in Business Administration in Accounting, University of Pittsburgh, Pennsylvania A/A/S: Portage Women's Club C/VW: United Way, YMCA, American Cancer Society Email: celenahudak@yahoo.com

Jane H. Huddleston
Title: Realtor Company: Bob Parks Realty Address: 198 E. Main Street, Franklin, TN 37064 United States BUS: Real Estate Agency P/S: Residential Sales MA: Local D/D/R: Working with Buyers and Sellers in Residential, Investment, Land Development and New Construction H/I/S: Horses, Traveling EDU: Bachelor's Degree in Business, Stephens College, Missouri A/A/S: National Association of Realtors; Williamson County Association of Realtors C/VW: Make-A-Wish, Bridges Email: janehuddleston@realtracs.com
URL: http://www.bobparks.com

Rev. James H. Hudson, Ph.D.
Title: Pastoral Associate Company: Superior Emmanuel Church Address: 735 Brown Avenue, Erie, PA 16502 United States BUS: Religion Church P/S: Religion/Ministry MA: Local EXP: Rev. Hudson's expertise includes ministry studies and religious education. H/I/S: Reading, Fishing EDU: Northwood University, Penn State, Ministerial Training Institute Bible College, Bachelor of Business Administration, Master of Business Administration, Master's Degree, Church Administration, Ph.D. in Religious Education A/A/S: United States Chaplain Institute Email: drjhudson2003@yahoo.com

Ms. Patricia A. Hudson
Title: Coordinator, Administrator Company: AstraZeneca Pharmaceuticals, Inc. Address: 1800 Concord Pike, Wilmington, DE 19803 United States BUS: Pharmaceutical Company P/S: Pharmaceuticals Products MA: International D/D/R: Performing Administrative Duties, Scheduling and Fixing Appointments H/I/S: Spending Time with her Grandchildren EDU: Bachelor's Degree in Leadership and Business Development A/A/S: International Association of Administrative Professionals Email: pat.hudson@astrazeneca.com

Amy L. Huebner
Title: Nurse Company: Garden City Hospital Dept: Critical Care Unit Address: 6245 Inkster Road, Garden City, MI 48135 United States BUS: Hospital P/S: Healthcare MA: Local D/D/R: Working in the Intensive Care Unit, Practicing Critical Care Nursing, Caring for Major Surgery Patients, Monitoring Patients H/I/S: Reading Murder Mystery Novels, Crocheting, Caring for her Cats EDU: Associate Degree in Nursing, Rhodes State College, Lima, OH (1989) CERTS: Certification in Medical Surgery (1996); Licensed in Nursing, States of Michigan and Ohio Email: amyrnc7@aol.com

Jolinn A. Huebotter
Title: Registered Nurse, Patient Care Supervisor Company: Blessing Hospital Address: 927 Broadway Street, Quincy, IL 62301 United States BUS: Hospital P/S: Healthcare MA: Tristate Area EXP: Ms. Huebotter's expertise includes inpatient care and oncology. H/I/S: Playing Softball, Wedding Planning EDU: Bachelor of Science in Nursing, Blessing-Rieman College of Nursing A/A/S: Sigma Theta Tau; Oncology Nursing Society; Academy of Medical-Surgical Nurses C/VW: United Way Email: huebotter@sbcglobal.net
URL: http://www.cambridgewhoswho.com

Cynthia G. Huewitt
Title: Teacher Company: Quitman Elementary School Address: 2200 Moultine Road, Quitman, GA 31643 United States BUS: School P/S: Elementary Education MA: Local D/D/R: Teaching H/I/S: Reading, Cooking, Sewing EDU: Master of Science in Elementary Education, Valdosta State University C/VW: Drug Awareness Program Email: revbud@peoplepc.com
URL: http://www.cambridgewhoswho.com

Raymond D. Huff
Title: Owner, President Company: Details Masters Address: 2700 S. Broadway, Tyler, TX 75701 United States BUS: Automotive Customer Service P/S: Top Quality Auto Detailing Mechanical Work, Service Station, Uhaul Rentals MA: Local D/D/R: Auto Detailing and Excellent Customer Service H/I/S: Four Wheeling, Dune Buggies, Hunting EDU: High School A/A/S: BBB, Chamber of Commerce, Baptist Church, Shriners Email: raymonddhuff@hotmail.com

Linda S. Huffman, LPN
Title: 44883 Company: Pathology Labs Address: 2497 W. Market Street, Tiffin, OH 44883 United States BUS: Healthcare Laboratory P/S: Professional Pathology Laboratory Services MA: Local D/D/R: Licensed Practical Nurse and Phlebotomist, Draws Blood and Obtains Urine H/I/S: Hunting, Fishing, Outdoor Activities EDU: Marion General Hospital, LPN Degree A/A/S: LPNAO Email: builtfordtuff@yahoo.com

Trent E. Huffman
Title: Civil Engineer Company: Moffatt & Nichol Address: 1616 E. Millbrook Road, Raleigh, NC 27609 United States BUS: Engineering Firm P/S: Designing and Engineering Services MA: National EXP: Mr. Huffman's expertise is in civil engineering. H/I/S: Fishing, Spending Time with his Family EDU: Bachelor of Science in Civil Engineering, North Carolina State University CERTS: Registered Professional Engineer, States of Georgia and North Carolina A/A/S: Westminster Theological Seminary; American Society of Highway Engineers; American Society of Civil Engineers; Women's Transportation Seminar C/VW: American Cancer Society; Relay for life Email: thuffman@moffattnichol.com
URL: http://www.moffattnichol.com

Charles 'Sam' Hughes
Title: Food and Nutrition Services Director **Company:** Aramark Corporation **Dept:** Saint Vincent Healthcare **Address:** 1233 N. 30th Street, Billings, MT 59101 United States **BUS:** Catering Company **P/S:** Food Services for Hospitals **MA:** National **D/D/R:** Teaching Culinary Cost Containment and Nutrition **H/I/S:** Skiing, Traveling, Wine Tasting **EDU:** Bachelor of Arts in Communication, City University of New York, City College of New York **A/H:** Hospital Caring Award, Saint Clare Medical Center, Wisconsin (1990) **C/VW:** Board of Director, United Way **Email:** hughes-sam@aramark.com

Donna G. Hughes
Title: Secretary, Treasurer **Company:** H & H Wireline Service, Inc. **Address:** 8 Road 3452, Flora Vista, NM 87415 United States **BUS:** Oil and Gas Company **P/S:** Oil and Gas Services **MA:** New Mexico, Colorado, Utah, Arizona **D/D/R:** Managing Company Finances, Bookkeeping, Accounting **H/I/S:** Boating, Fishing, Crocheting, Knitting, Collecting and Creating Porcelain Dolls, Gardening **EDU:** Coursework, San Juan College
Email: donna.hughes@gobrainstorm.net
URL: http://www.cambridgewhosho.com

Karen H. Hughes
Title: Medical Doctor **Company:** G.V. (Sonny) Montgomery VA Medical Center **Address:** 1500 E. Woodrow Wilson Drive, Jackson, MS 39201 United States **BUS:** Veterans Affairs Medical Center **P/S:** Anatomic Pathology and Clinical Laboratory Services **MA:** Statewide **EXP:** Ms. Hughes' expertise is in anatomic clinical pathology. **H/I/S:** Spending Time with her Two Children and their School Activities, Riding Horses, Gardening **EDU:** MD, Mississippi State Medical Center; Bachelor of Science in Biology, Minor in Mathematics, University of Mississippi **A/A/S:** Centers for Medicare and Medicaid Services; American Society of Clinical Pathologists; CAP; MAP; Compliance Advisory Board Member, Executive Committee for Operations **A/H:** Secretary's Hero Award, Hurricane Katrina; American Top Physician, 2006 **C/VW:** Leukemia & Lymphoma Society, American Cancer Society, St. Jude Children's Research Hospital
Email: karen.hughes@med.va.gov

Ms. Lynn J. Hughes
Title: Senior Therapist **Company:** Lake County Behavioral Health **Address:** 3012 Grand Avenue, Waukegan, IL 60085 United States **BUS:** Healthcare Facility **P/S:** Medical Services **MA:** National **D/D/R:** Seeing Patients from Ages 18 to 65, Offering Anxiety and Mental Health Therapy, Counseling for Depression and Workers' Depression **H/I/S:** Collecting Jewelry **EDU:** Master of Social Work in Clinical Supervision, University of Wisconsin-Milwaukee (1989); Bachelor of Social Work in Social Work and Mental Health, University of Wisconsin-Milwaukee (1979) **A/A/S:** National Association of Social Workers; Dr. Reddy Association
Email: lhughes@co.lake.il.us
URL: http://www.co.lake.il.us

Sonya K. Hughes
Title: President **Company:** Circle Star Consulting, LLC **Address:** 612 Carl Avenue, Glen Burnie, MD 21060 United States **BUS:** Website Design Company **P/S:** Nonprofit Donation Collection Services, eCommerce Solutions, Online Store and Online Donations Management, Branding and Logo Development, Website Hosting, Website Layout and Graphic Development, Content Development and Inclusion, E-mail List-Serve Creation and Management, E-mail Campaign Services, Support for Content Services, Oracle and People Soft Consulting **MA:** National/International **EXP:** Ms. Hughes' expertise is in software development. **D/D/R:** Designing, Developing and Integrating Websites **H/I/S:** Kayaking, Traveling **EDU:** Master's Degree in World Politics, The Catholic University of America (2007); Bachelor's Degree **A/A/S:** Maryland ColdFusion User's Group **A/H:** National Honor Society
Email: shughes@circlestarconsulting.com
URL: http://www.circlestarconsulting.com

Terrie A. Hughes
Title: Teacher **Company:** Blytheville Middle School **Address:** 1561 US Highway 61 N., Luxora, AR 72358 United States **BUS:** School **P/S:** Secondary Education **MA:** Regional **D/D/R:** Preparing Lesson Plans, Facilitating Projects, Overseeing Literature Comprehensive Science Strategies, Teaching Seventh-Grade Science **H/I/S:** Reading, Traveling, Listening to Music, Shopping, Watching Basketball, Olympics, Tracking, Practicing Gymnastics **EDU:** Pursuing Master's Degree in Curriculum and Instruction, William Woods University, Steele, MO; Coursework in English as a Second Language, Henderson State University, AR (2007); Bachelor's Degree in Elementary Education, Emphasis in Science and Social Studies, Arkansas State University, Jonesboro, AR (2001)
Email: thughes@bps.k12.ar.us

Mr. William Hugus
Title: Supervisor **Company:** Duquesne Light Company **Address:** P.O. Box 255, Wildwood, PA 15091 United States **BUS:** Leader in the Transmission and Distribution of Electric Energy **P/S:** Superior Customer Service and Reliability to More Than Half a Million Customers in Southwestern Pennsylvania **MA:** Regional **D/D/R:** Working with Equipment, Machines and Tools, Developing Course Curriculum, Teaching Lineman **H/I/S:** Listening to Music **EDU:** Self-Taught **CERTS:** Multiple Certifications **A/A/S:** Veteran, United States Navy; Mason; Firefighter
Email: whugus@duqlight.com
URL: http://www.duquesnelight.com

Jenifer R. Hulfish
Title: Field Operations Leader **Company:** Pearson Digital Learning **Address:** 6710 E. Camelback Road, Scottsdale, AZ 85251 United States **BUS:** Software Development Company **P/S:** Educational Software **MA:** National **D/D/R:** Overseeing Field Support for Elementary Educational Software **H/I/S:** Spending Time with her Family and Friends, Playing Tennis, Listening to Music, Traveling **EDU:** Bachelor of Science in Business Management, Arizona State University
Email: jenifer.hulfish@pearson.com
URL: http://www.pearsondigital.com

Mrs. Lindsi J. Hull
Title: Process Engineer **Company:** Intel **Address:** 4500 S. Dobson Road, Chandler, AZ 85248 United States **BUS:** Manufacturing Company **P/S:** Design, Manufacturing and Marketing Microcomputer Components for Desktop and Server Systems **MA:** International **EXP:** Mrs. Hull's expertise is in semiconductor design. **H/I/S:** Traveling, Hiking **EDU:** Master of Science in Electrical and Computer Engineering, Minor in Semiconductor Device Physics, University of Florida (2005); Bachelor of Science in Electrical Engineering, Kansas State University (2004)
Email: ljg7444@hotmail.com
URL: http://www.cambridgewhoswho.com

Allison Huly
Title: ITR Specialist **Company:** Children's Network of Southwest Florida **Address:** 2232 Altamont Avenue, Fort Meyers, FL 33901 United States **BUS:** Lead Agency for the Department of Children and Families **P/S:** Child Welfare, Safety and Stability **MA:** Regional **D/D/R:** Transferring Files from the Child Protective Investigator to the Social Worker **H/I/S:** Traveling, Shopping **EDU:** Bachelor's Degree in Psychology, Sonoma State University (1999)
Email: allisonhuly@comcast.net
URL: http://www.childnetswfl.org

Mr. Donald K. Hummel, D.Min.
Title: Director of Ongoing Formation and Continuing Education of Priest **Company:** Archdiocese of Newark (Roman Catholic) **Address:** 171 Clifton Avenue, P.O. Box 9500, Newark, NJ 07104 United States **BUS:** Clergy **P/S:** Future Priest Training **MA:** Regional **D/D/R:** Working with Priests, Organizing Retreats for Spiritual Direction, Training New Priests, Offering Leadership Development and Continuing Education **H/I/S:** Traveling, Theater, Watching Sports **EDU:** Doctorate in Pastoral Ministry **CERTS:** Certified Pastoral Addiction Counselor; Certified Thanatologist; Certified Master Police Chaplain; Certified Pastoral Psychotherapist **A/A/S:** American Counseling Association; American Association of Christian Counselors; National Catholic Committee of Scouting; Chaplain to Union County; Chaplain to New Jersey Association of Chief Police; International Conference of Police Chaplains; The National Organization for Continuing Education of Roman Catholic Clergy
Email: hummeldo@rcan.org
URL: http://rcan.org

Mrs. Aliceson B. Humphries
Title: Assistant Superintendent **Company:** Lorain City Schools **Address:** 2350 Pole Avenue, Lorain, OH 44052 United States **BUS:** School District **P/S:** Public Education **MA:** National **EXP:** Mrs. Humphries' expertise includes administration, staff curriculum and professional development. **H/I/S:** Golfing, Playing Tennis, Traveling, Reading **EDU:** Master of Education, Bowling Green State University (2000); Bachelor of Science in Education, Bowling Green State University **CERTS:** Certified Superintendent, Bowling Green State University (2005); Licensed Administrator, Bowling Green State University **A/A/S:** Lorain County Alliance of Black School Educators; Ohio Association of Elementary School Administrators; Ohio Education Association; National Education Association; Association for Supervision and Curriculum Development; Ohio Alliance of Black School Educators; Falcon Club **C/VW:** Susan G. Komen for the Cure
Email: ahumph@lorainschools.org
URL: http://www.lorainschools.org

Kathleen G. Hundley
Title: Adjunct Professor **Company:** Central Carolina Community College **Address:** 136 Rocky Fells, Sanford, NC 27330 United States **BUS:** Public Institution of Higher Education **P/S:** Higher Education **MA:** Regional **D/D/R:** Developing Programs and Curriculum Including Tests and Outside Activities, Overseeing Educational Management and Design, Conducting Outside Consulting Work **EDU:** Ph.D. in Psychology, Minor in Medical Education, North Carolina State University; Master's Degree in Adult Education, North Carolina State University **A/A/S:** American Society for Training and Development; Vice President, Secretary, Friends of the Rocky Rive and Rocky River Heritage

Thomas H. Hunkele
Title: Assistant Athletic Trainer **Company:** Minnesota Vikings **Address:** 952 Vikings Drive, Eden Prairie, MN 55344 United States **BUS:** Football Team **P/S:** Football, National Football League **MA:** National **D/D/R:** Athletic Training and Physical Therapy for Professional Football Players **H/I/S:** Playing Football **EDU:** Master of Science in Physical Therapy, Duquesne University; Bachelor of Science in Physical Therapy, Duquesne University; Certification from NASMPS; Bachelor of Science in Athletic Training; Certification, NASM-PE **A/A/S:** North American Trainers Association; Sports Physical Therapy Section
Email: hunkelet@vikings.nfl.net

Celeste L. Hunt
Title: President **Company:** Orlando Packaging and Shipping **Address:** 1001 Virginia Drive, Orlando, FL 32803 United States **BUS:** EBay Internet Sales **P/S:** Will Sell Your Items on EBay also Crating and Shipping **MA:** National **D/D/R:** Internet Sales of Items Specializing in Antiques and Hard to Package Goods **H/I/S:** Tennis, Golf, House Horses **EDU:** Madison Wisconsin Area Technical College, Associate Degree in Business Administration
Email: mrsskippey43@aol.com

Kristyn E. Hunt
Title: Lecturer **Company:** Lamar University **Address:** P.O. Box 10050, Beaumont, TX 77710 United States **BUS:** Higher Education: College, University **P/S:** Graduate and Undergraduate Programs **MA:** Regional **EXP:** Ms. Hunt's expertise includes communications education and public speaking. **H/I/S:** Traveling, Shopping and Reading **EDU:** Master's Degree, University of Georgia **A/A/S:** National Communication Association; National Association of Black Journalists; Public Relations Society of America; Association for Women in Communications
Email: kehunt@my.lamar.edu
URL: http://www.lamar.edu

Alicia C. Hunter
Title: Educator **Company:** Bryan Station High School **Address:** 201 Eastin Drive, Lexington, KY 40505 United States **BUS:** High School **P/S:** Education **MA:** Local **D/D/R:** Teaching English and Language Arts to High School Students **H/I/S:** Photography, Reading, Writing, Spending Time with her Family **EDU:** Master's Degree in Instructional Leadership, 2007; Master's Degree in English Education, Georgetown College, 2004; Bachelor's Degree in English Education, University of Kentucky 1992 **CERTS:** Certification in English and Language Arts 9-12; Endorsement in Reading **A/A/S:** International Reading Association; National Council for Teacher Education; Kentucky Education Association **C/VW:** Church
Email: alicia.hunter@fayette.kyschools.us
URL: http://www.cambridgewhoswho.com

Carolyn L. Hunter
Title: Second-Grade Teacher **Company:** Shelby County Schools **Dept:** E.A. Harrold Elementary School **Address:** 4943 W. Union Road, Millington, TN 38053 United States **BUS:** School District **P/S:** Education **MA:** Local **D/D/R:** Teaching Second-Grade Students **H/I/S:** Reading, Crocheting **EDU:** Master of Education, University of Memphis **A/A/S:** National Education Association; Kappa Delta Pi **C/VW:** St. Jude Children's Research Hospital; Disabled American Veterans; Arthritis Foundation; American Cancer Society
Email: hunterc@comcast.net
URL: http://home.midsouth.rr.com/huntersk5site

Diana E. Hunter
Title: Senior Associate Business Manager **Company:** Kraft Foods **Address:** 1 Kraft Court, Glenview, IL 60025 United States **BUS:** Global Leader in Branded Foods and Beverages, Largest Food and Beverage Company Headquartered in North America and the Second Largest in the World **P/S:** Beverages, Snacks, Cereals, Grocery, Convenient Meals, Cheese, Foodservice **MA:** National **D/D/R:** Developing New Products **H/I/S:** Reading, Tennis, Working Out **EDU:** Master's Degree in Marketing, Roosevelt University (2001); Bachelor's Degree in Industrial Psychology, University of Illinois at Chicago (1996) **A/A/S:** Inroads in Chicago; Working on Internships for Minority Groups to Enter Corporate America
Email: desh1974@hotmail.com
URL: http://www.kraft.com

Karey B. Hunter
Title: Owner **Company:** Jerky Direct **Address:** 764 E. Elva Street, Idaho Falls, ID 83401 United States **BUS:** Health Snacks Supplier **P/S:** Internet Jerky Sales **MA:** International **D/D/R:** Utilizing her Entrepreneurial Skills **H/I/S:** Reading **EDU:** College Coursework **C/VW:** Group Leader, Boy Scouts of America, Girl Scouts of the USA
Email: hunter_764@msn.com
URL: http://www.jerkyhunter.com

Cheryl J. Huntington
Title: Teacher **Company:** Leesylvania Elementary School **BUS:** Education **P/S:** Elementary School **MA:** Regional **D/D/R:** Teaching Second-Grade Education, Teaching all Subjects, Working on Curriculum and Staff Development **H/I/S:** Collecting Children's Books, Cooking, Spending Time with her Five Grandchildren **EDU:** Bachelor's Degree in Human Development (With Honors), University of Mary Washington (1992) **A/A/S:** Prince William Education Association
Email: Cheryl.Huntington@cwwemail.com
URL: http://www.pwcs.edu

Jamalee D. Huntley, Pharm.D.
Title: Clinical Pharmacy Specialist **Company:** St. John's Mercy Health Systems **Address:** 1235 E. Cherokee Street, Springfield, MO 65804 United States **BUS:** Hospital **P/S:** Healthcare **MA:** Regional **EXP:** Ms. Huntley's expertise is in pediatrics. **EDU:** Doctor of Pharmacy, The University of Kansas **A/A/S:** The American Society of Health-System Pharmacists **C/VW:** Pediatric Pharmacy Advocacy Group
Email: jamalee.huntley@mercy.net
URL: http://www.stjohns.com

Daniel J. Huovinen
Title: President **Company:** Daniels Company **Address:** P.O. Box 16759, Essex, MD 21221 United States **BUS:** Beverage Company **P/S:** Installation of Remote Draft Beer, Water and Fountain Soda Systems for McDonald's, Hooters and the Macaroni Grill **MA:** MD, VA, DE, NJ, PA, DC **EXP:** Mr. Huovinen's expertise includes time management and efficiency. **H/I/S:** Camping **EDU:** College Coursework **A/A/S:** Local Chamber of Commerce **C/VW:** Vietnam Veterans of America, Veterans of Foreign Wars
Email: huovinen1@comcast.net

Kay W. Hurd
Title: Nurse Practitioner Manager (Retired) **Company:** Somerset Medical Center **Address:** 110 Rehil Avenue, Somerville, NJ 08876 United States **BUS:** Acutecare Hospital **P/S:** Healthcare **MA:** Local **D/D/R:** Managing Community Program to Provide Healthcare and Insurance, Partnering with Faith Communities **H/I/S:** Painting **EDU:** Master's Degree in Nursing, Seton Hall University (1979) **CERTS:** Certified Pediatric Nurse Practitioner **A/A/S:** Healthy Congregations (2005) **A/H:** Women of the Year in Social Services (2001)
Email: khurd@somerset-healthcare.com
Email: kwhurd@msn.com

Barbara A. Hurleigh
Title: Associate Director **Company:** Columbia University **Address:** 615 W. 131st Street, Third Floor, New York, NY 10027 United States **BUS:** University **P/S:** Higher Education **MA:** International **D/D/R:** Accounting **H/I/S:** Spending Time with her Son, Reading, Traveling **EDU:** Bachelor of Science, Bryant & Stratton College **CERTS:** Certified Public Accountant **A/A/S:** New York State Society of Certified Public Accountants; American Institute of Certified Public Accountants; Association for Financial Professionals **C/VW:** St. John's Church; St. Mary's Church
Email: bh2152@columbia.edu
URL: http://www.columbia.edu

Rachel L. Hurley, MS
Title: Elementary Classroom Teacher **Company:** Clinton Avenue School **Address:** 293 Clinton Avenue, New Haven, CT 06513 United States **BUS:** Elementary School **P/S:** Primary Education **MA:** Local **D/D/R:** teaching, utilizing activities with the curriculum to build students social skills, confidence and self-esteem, teaching social awareness, empathy and compassion, involving parents in students lives and preparing students for the Connecticut mastery test. **H/I/S:** Swimming, Walking, Caring for her Dog, Reading Classic Literature, Scrapbooking **EDU:** Master of Science in Special Education, Southern Connecticut State University
Email: hurley@snet.net

Anne Hurst
Title: Brokerage Associate **Company:** Daniel Crapps Agency, Inc **Address:** 2806 W. U.S. Highway 90, Lake City, FL 32055 United States **BUS:** Real Estate Broker **P/S:** Residential, Lake Front, New Construction, Condos, Gated, Golf Homes, Acreage **MA:** National **EXP:** Ms. Hurst's expertise is in residential properties. **H/I/S:** Likes To Travel **A/A/S:** Florida Association Of Realtors, National Association of Realtors
Email: hurstann17@yahoo.com
URL: www.myhome40.com

Thomas Hurst
Company: WMGM-TV 40 **Address:** P.O. Box 145, Pleasantville, NJ 08232 United States **BUS:** Broadcasting Company **P/S:** Television Series, Talk Shows, Commercials, News Coverage **MA:** Regional **D/D/R:** Adjusting Light Schemes, Repairing Media Controls, Maintaining Television Network Broadcasts **H/I/S:** Cooking, Gardening, Landscaping **EDU:** Bachelor of Science in Physics, The Richard Stockton College of New Jersey (1985); Associate Degree in Science and Electronics, Atlanta Community College, New Jersey (1979) **A/A/S:** Society of Physics Students; American Radio Relay League
Email: n2zaw@juno.com
URL: http://www.nbc40.net

Mr. Steven E. Hurt
Title: President, Chief Executive Officer **Company:** The TSM Company, Inc. **Address:** 3256 University Drive, Suite 35, Auburn Hills, MI 48326 United States **BUS:** Consulting Firm **P/S:** Executive Searches, Consulting Services **MA:** National **D/D/R:** Overseeing All Daily Operations of his Company Including Consulting and the Recruiting of Directors in the Industries of Automotives and Commercial Vehicles, Pharmaceutical and Medical Devices, Managing Executive Level Recruiting **H/I/S:** Skiing, Golfing **EDU:** Master's Degree in Finance, Kent State University, OH (1983) **A/A/S:** American Society of Mechanical Engineers; Chairman of the Board, Auburn Hills Economic Development Corporation; Society of Automotive Engineers
Email: shurt913@tsmcoinc.com
URL: http://www.tsmcoinc.com

Hadi Husani
Title: Executive Officer **Company:** Focus Humanitarian Assistance **Address:** 7777 Leesburg Pike, Suite 3035, Falls Church, VA 22043 United States **BUS:** Disaster Risk Management Organization **P/S:** Disaster Risk Management **MA:** International **D/D/R:** Overseeing Relations Management, Quality Assurance **H/I/S:** Traveling **EDU:** Master of Business Administration Temple University **C/VW:** AKF Foundation
Email: hhusani@focushumanitarian.org

Adeline E. Huss
Title: Faculty of Preparatory and Continuing Education Theory (Retired) **Company:** Cleveland Institute of Music **Address:** 11021 East Boulevard, Cleveland, OH 44106 United States **BUS:** Music Academy **P/S:** Music Education **MA:** Cleveland **D/D/R:** Teaching Music Theory, Playing the Organ **H/I/S:** Reading, Needlework, Attending Concerts, Watching Baseball and Basketball **EDU:** Master of Music, with a Concentration in Organ, Cleveland Institute of Music (1966); Bachelor of Music, Cleveland Institute of Music (1964) **A/A/S:** American Guild of Organists; Mu Phi Epsilon; Pi Kappa Lambda
Email: adeline.huss@cwwemail.com
URL: http://www.cambridgewhoswho.com

Judy Hutcheson
Title: Director of Network Integration Services **Company:** Descartes Systems Group **Address:** 2030 Powers Ferry Road, Suite 520, Atlanta, GA 30339 United States **BUS:** Information Technology Company **P/S:** Software, Electronic Data Interchange Services, Logistics, Applications for Subscriptions, Shipment Tracking, Transportation, Warehouse Management, Movement of Freights and Goods **MA:** International **D/D/R:** Managing a Team of Eight Employees, Supervising Engineers **H/I/S:** Researching Genealogy
Email: jhutcheson@decartes.com
URL: http://www.decartes.com

Laura L. Hutchins
Title: Art Educator **Company:** Newfound Regional High School **Address:** 95 Abbott Road, Concord, NH 03303 United States **BUS:** High School Facility Dedicated to Excellence in Education **P/S:** Regular Core Curriculum Including Reading, Mathematics, English, Science, Social Studies, Art, Music, History, Language Arts, Physical Education, Computers **MA:** Regional **D/D/R:** Art Education, Art Advocacy, Arts Leadership, Handling Art Budget and Curriculum, Portfolio Prep Coach, Public Speaking Nationally **H/I/S:** Photography, Rubber Stamping **EDU:** Bachelor's Degree in Photography, Maine College of Art (1986) **CERTS:** Certification in Art K-12 **A/A/S:** President, New Hampshire Art Education Association; President, New Hampshire Alliance for Arts Education; New Hampshire Citizens for the Arts; New Hampshire Forest Society; National Art Education Association
Email: hutchmuch@aol.com
URL: http://www.nhaea.org

Janet C. Hutchison
Title: Computer Routing Center Supervisor **Company:** Los Angeles Unified School District **Address:** 2710 Media Center Drive, Suite 100, Los Angeles, CA 90065 United States **BUS:** School **P/S:** Education for Kindergarten through 12th-Grade Students **MA:** Regional **D/D/R:** Analyzing Efficiency, Organizing School Bus Routes, Arranging Picking Up and Dropping Off Students, Handling Transportation Issues, Complying with Routing Laws **H/I/S:** Golfing **EDU:** Bachelor's Degree in Elementary Education, University of La Vernet **A/A/S:** Chapter President, California Association of School Transportation Officials
Email: janet.hutchison@lausd.net
URL: http://www.lausd.net

Susan Carol Hyde
Title: Teacher **Company:** West Clermont Local School District **Address:** 4639 Vermona Drive, Cincinnati, OH 45245 United States **BUS:** School District **P/S:** Education **MA:** Local **D/D/R:** Teaching Reading and Language Arts **H/I/S:** Reading, Traveling **EDU:** Master of Arts in Education, Northern Kentucky University; Bachelor of Arts in Education, Northern Kentucky University **A/A/S:** Kappa Delta Pi; National Education Association **C/VW:** Secretary, Parent-Teacher Organization
Email: schyde1073@aol.com
URL: http://www.cambridgewhoswho.com

Mindy F. Hylton
Title: Clinical Specialist **Company:** Medtronic, Inc. **Address:** 1 Summit Square, Langhorne, PA 19047 United States **BUS:** Medical Device Company **P/S:** Lifelong Solutions, Products, Therapies and Services to Enhance or Extend the Lives of Millions of People with Chronic Disease **MA:** International **D/D/R:** Attending to Patients with Implanted Defibrillators and Pacemakers Prior to and During Surgery, Holding In-service Presentations for Nurses and Doctors About the Use of Medical Devices **H/I/S:** Bowling **EDU:** Bachelor's Degree in Electrical and Computer Engineering, New Jersey Institute of Technology (2006); Internship, Devorah Heart and Lung Medical Center
Email: mindy.f.hylton@metronic.com
URL: http://www.medtronic.com

Henrique Hyndman
Title: Marketing, Sales Executive **Company:** Select Shopping USA **Address:** 1795 North Avenue, Apartment 5, Bridgeport, CT 06604 United States **BUS:** Retail Store **P/S:** Retail Sales and Affiliate Products Online **MA:** National **EXP:** Mr. Hyndman's expertise includes sales, marketing, Web designs, computer system designs and graphic design. **D/D/R:** Maintaining the Company Website Remotely, Offering Customer Service for Pens and Calendars **H/I/S:** Woodworking **EDU:** Master's Degree in Education, University of Bridgeport (1982); Bachelor's Degree in Economics, University of Colorado, Denver (1975) **A/A/S:** Former President, American Legion Post; Alumni Association, University of Bridgeport; Financial Officer, Society of 40&8; Third District Vice Commander, The American Legion Department of Connecticut; Parade Committee, Fairfield, Connecticut **C/VW:** United Service Organizations
Email: hyndmanhenrique@sbcglobal.net
URL: http://www.selectshoppingusa.com

Robert Iannacone Jr.
Title: Network Operations Manager **Company:** Carousel Industries **Address:** 10 Petra Lane, Albany, NY 12205 United States **BUS:** Network Solutions Company **P/S:** Telecommunications, Network Solutions **MA:** National **EXP:** Mr. Iannacone's expertise is in network operations. **D/D/R:** Converse Network Engineering, Large Internet Protocol Telephony Design **H/I/S:** Spending Time with his Family, Golfing **EDU:** Associate Degree in Engineering, Ira A. Fulton School of Engineering, Arizona State University **A/A/S:** Institute of Electrical and Electronics Engineers, Inc. **C/VW:** Knights of Columbus; Local Church Groups
Email: riannacone@carouselindustries.com
URL: http://www.carouselindustries.com

Andrew C. Iannone
Title: President **Company:** SoCal Kitchens and Baths, Inc. **Address:** 4588 Clairemont Drive, San Diego, CA 92117 United States **BUS:** Design and Remodeling Company **P/S:** Kitchen and Bath Remodeling and Designs Including Cabinets and Counter Tops, Hood Vents, Sinks and Faucets, Tile, Stone and Wood Flooring, Handicap Bathrooms, Condominium Conversions **MA:** Local **EXP:** Mr. Iannone's expertise includes operations and project management. **D/D/R:** Managing Customer Service, Overseeing Kitchen and Bath Remodeling **H/I/S:** Horseback Riding, Practicing Martial Arts, Going to the Beach, Swimming, Dancing **EDU:** College Coursework **A/A/S:** National Kitchen and Bath Association; AATA; USTA; Better Business Bureau **C/VW:** Second Chance; Junior Theater
Email: andrew@socalkb.com
URL: http://www.socalkb.com

Asako T. Ichiuji
Title: Federal Employee (Retired) **Company:** United States Government **BUS:** Government Administration **P/S:** Working for Various Sectors of the Federal Government **MA:** National **D/D/R:** Administration, Liaison to various government agencies **H/I/S:** Traveling, Arts and Crafts, Bridge **EDU:** Industry-Related Training and Experience **A/H:** Honored for School Support, Montgomery County Public School **C/VW:** National Japanese-American Memorial Foundation, Japanese-American Citizen's League, Montgomery County Public Schools, Volunteers Time to Assist the Elderly
Email: joe.ichiuji@verizon.net
URL: http://www.cambridgewhoswho.com

Robin I. Ide
Title: Director of Sales **Company:** Turtle Bay Resort **Address:** 57-091 Kamehameha Highway, Kahuku, HI 96731 United States **BUS:** Resort **P/S:** Hospitality **MA:** International **EXP:** Ms. Ide's expertise includes sales and marketing. **H/I/S:** Wine Tasting **EDU:** Coursework, University of Hawaii **C/VW:** Susan G. Komen for the Cure
Email: ride@benchmarkmanagement.com
URL: http://www.turtlebayresort.com

Sharighih Ighani
Title: Mortgage Specialist **Company:** National City Mortgage **Address:** 7125 Thomas Edison Drive, Columbia, MD 21046 United States **BUS:** Mortgage Lending Company **P/S:** Commercial and Residential Mortgages **MA:** National **EXP:** Ms. Ighani's expertise is in mortgages. **D/D/R:** Offering Financial Advice **H/I/S:** Traveling, Reading, Spending Time with Family **EDU:** Degree in Psychiatric Nursing, Earned in Iran; Degree in Financing, Earned in Iran **C/VW:** Institute for Health and Education, Costa Rica; Orphanage, Ecuador
Email: sharighih.ighani@ncmc.com

Robin Ilac
Title: Eighth-Grade Social Studies Teacher **Company:** Kermit Mc Kenzie Junior High School **Address:** P.O. Box 788, Guadalupe, CA 93434 United States **BUS:** Junior High School **P/S:** Education **MA:** Local **D/D/R:** Teaching Early American History **H/I/S:** Scrapbooking **EDU:** Bachelor's Degree in Social Sciences, Azusa Pacific University, 1997 **A/A/S:** National Council for the Social Studies; National Education Association **C/VW:** March of Dimes
Email: rgalyen@aol.com

Theodore A. Iliff
Title: Executive Vice President **Company:** NBCC International **Address:** Three Terrace Way, Greensboro, NC 27403 United States **BUS:** Counseling Support Organization **P/S:** International Counseling Development **MA:** International **EXP:** Mr. Iliff's expertise includes international business and media. **D/D/R:** Consulting on Counseling Programs, Offering Career Guidance **H/I/S:** Golfing, Traveling, Writing, Barbershop Singing, Studying the History of the Military **EDU:** Bachelor of Science, State University of New York **A/A/S:** American Counseling Association; International Association for Educational and Vocational Guidance; Tarheel Chorus of Greensboro; International Association of Counseling
Email: iliff@nbcc.org
URL: http://www.nbccinternational.org

Michelle P. Impellizeri
Title: Teacher, Administrator **Company:** 1) Saint Joseph School 2) Broker Connections Consulting Inc. **Address:** 1 Woodedge Road, Manhasset, NY 11030 United States **BUS:** School **P/S:** Education **MA:** Local **D/D/R:** Teaching English to Seventh and Eighth-Grade Students, Preparing Students for Tests, Managing Operations, Substituting for the Principal and Assistant Principal **EDU:** Master's Degree in Administration, Adelphi University (2005); Master's Degree in Education, St. John's University; Bachelor's Degree in English and Education, St. John's University **A/A/S:** National Teachers Association; English Teachers Association; Phi Kappa Beta; Middle States Accreditation; Concord Private Jet
Email: mpi712@aol.com

Joseph A. P. Imperlino
Title: Technical Writer **Company:** SCC Soft Computer **Address:** 5400 Tech Data Drive, Clearwater, FL 33760 United States **BUS:** Information Technology Firm **P/S:** Medical Software Programming and Development **MA:** National **EXP:** Mr. Imperlino's expertise is in software systems analysis. **D/D/R:** Acting as a Software Systems Analyst **H/I/S:** Walking **EDU:** Bachelor of Science in Computer Systems, Tampa Technical Institute
Email: jgapimperlino@msn.com
URL: http://www.softcomputer.com

David R. Indermill
Title: Realtor **Company:** Team Indermill **Address:** 4444 Mission Boulevard, San Diego, CA 92109 United States **BUS:** Realtor **P/S:** Residential, Executive, High-End Homes, Ocean Front and Bay Front Homes, Condominiums, New Construction **MA:** National **D/D/R:** Specializing in Coastal Residential and Investment Properties Selling, Managing Development, Investments and Assets **H/I/S:** Surfing, Snow Boarding, Riding Harley-Davidson Motorcycles, Enjoying Outdoor Sports **EDU:** Point Loma College **A/A/S:** Mission Bay Association of Realtors; California Association of Realtors; National Association of Realtors
Email: david@teamindermill.com
Email: davidsbeachdeals@hotmail.com
URL: http://www.teamindermill.com

Dennis R. Ingamells
Title: Chief Financial Officer **Company:** JLM Wholesale **Address:** 3095 Mullins Court, Oxford, MI 48371 United States **BUS:** Commercial Door Hardware Wholesaler **P/S:** Commercial Door Hardware **MA:** International **D/D/R:** Accounting, Financing **H/I/S:** Golf, Fishing **EDU:** Master of Arts in Finance, Walsh College, 1995
Email: dennisi@jlmwholesale.com

Tiffany A. Ingram
Title: Senior Accounting Supervisor **Company:** Covanta Energy **Address:** 155 River Road, Clifton, NJ 07014 United States **BUS:** Energy Firm **P/S:** Waste-To-Energy Power Generation, Waste Disposal **MA:** International **EXP:** Ms. Ingram's expertise is in accounts management. **D/D/R:** Supervising Accounts Payable, Forecasting Cash Flow, Budgeting for Projects, Managing Inventories **H/I/S:** Watching Baseball and Football, Reading **EDU:** Bachelor of Arts in Accounting, Saint Mary's College of California (1994)
Email: tiffy1972@optonline.net
URL: http://www.cambridgewhoswho.com

Brenda J. Inouye
Title: Resource Advisor **Company:** Sante **Address:** Los Angeles, CA **BUS:** Business Education **P/S:** Education **MA:** Local **D/D/R:** Advising Teachers, Assisting Principal, Hosting Career Day **H/I/S:** Reading, Playing Tennis, Exercising, Participating in Outdoor Activities **EDU:** Pursuing Master's Degree in Business, Marketing and Public Relations; Master of Education, University of La Verne **C/VW:** Freelance Legal Aid, California State University at Los Angeles, Haitian Child
Email: brenda.inouye@lausd.net

Miss Jessica L. Ippoliti
Title: Sports Massage Therapist **Address:** 500 Tamal Plaza, Suite 507, Corte Madera, CA 94925 United States **BUS:** Sole Proprietorship **P/S:** Sports Massage Therapy Including Active Release Techniques, Sports Massage, Deep Tissue Massage, Myofacial Therapy, Neuromuscular Therapy, Medical Massage **MA:** National **D/D/R:** Performing Massage Therapy **H/I/S:** Spending Time at the Beach with her Dog **EDU:** Coursework in Vocational Education, Space Coast Health Institute (2001) **CERTS:** Licensed Massage Therapist **A/A/S:** American Massage Therapy Association
Email: jess_lmt@hotmail.com
URL: http://www.sportstherapybyjess.com

Vicki Irey
Title: Director, Information Technology **Company:** City of Overland Park **Address:** 8500 Santa Fe Drive, Overland Park, KS 66212 United States **BUS:** Technology Government **P/S:** Information Technology **MA:** Local **EXP:** Ms. Irey's expertise is in information technology. **H/I/S:** Reading **EDU:** Long View Community College, Associate in Business **A/A/S:** Public Technology Institute
Email: vicki.irey@opkansas.org

Mr. David B. Irthum, LPN, LVN
Title: Licensed Practical Nurse, Licensed Vocational Nurse **Company:** Vista Ridge Comprehensive Adult Care **Dept:** Nursing **Address:** 700 E. Vista Ridge Mall Drive, Lewisville, TX 75067 United States **BUS:** 1) Rehabilitation and Nursing Center 2) Clinical instructor for AGAPE Health Care School in Dallas, Tax. **P/S:** Long-Term Care and Rehabilitation for Seniors blending positive care for body mind and spirit. Reverence and respect for our senior population and their family. **MA:** Regional **D/D/R:** Long-Term Nursing Care in Geriatric, Dementia and Alzheimer Care **H/I/S:** Spending Quality Time with his Family, Traveling, Hiking, Watching Hockey Games, Nature Photography. **CERTS:** Licensed Practical Nurse, Orleans Vocational Technical School, 1978 **C/VW:** World Vision; Lions Club International; United Way of America; Red Cross; Feed The Children
Email: shylaei_2000@yahoo.com

Deborah A. Irwin
Title: Secretary, Treasurer **Company:** Thompson Station United Methodist Church **Address:** 1532 Thompson Station Road W., Thompsons Station, TN 37179 United States **BUS:** Church **P/S:** Religious, Spreading Spiritual Services **MA:** Local **D/D/R:** Supporting Church Members, Taking Notes at Meetings, Organizing Fundraising, Budgeting, Working for the Bone and Joint Clinic, Billing **H/I/S:** Gardening, Quilting, Scrapbooking, Sewing **EDU:** Diploma, Franklin High School, TN **A/A/S:** Event Chairwoman, American Cancer Society, Williamson County **C/VW:** Avon Walk for Breast Cancer; Multiple Sclerosis Walk; Leukemia & Lymphoma Society; Walk For A Cure
Email: deborah.irwin@gmail.com
Email: dirwin@bonenjoint.com
URL: http://www.cambridgewhoswho.com

Peter C. Irwin
Title: Director of Development **Company:** Friends of Jowonio **Address:** 3049 E. Genesee Street, Syracuse, NY 13224 United States **BUS:** Nonprofit Organization **P/S:** Early Childhood Development, General and Special Education Programs, Therapy Services, Child Care, Social Work, Fundraising **MA:** Local **D/D/R:** Managing Daily Operations and Charitable Donations, Organizing Fund Raisers **H/I/S:** Singing, Attending Theater, Listening to Music **EDU:** Bachelor of Arts in Music, Syracuse University (1987)
Email: pirwin@jowonio.org
URL: http://www.jowonio.org

Herbert L. Isaac II, MD
Title: Owner, Physician **Company:** Herbert L. Isaac II, MD Family Practice Physician **Address:** 989 University Drive, Suite 101, Pontiac, MI 48342 United States **BUS:** Private Medical Practice **P/S:** Diagnostic and Treatment Services in Family Medicine **MA:** Local **D/D/R:** Caring for Infant, Children and Adult Patients with a Large Range of Illnesses Including Diabetes and Hypertension, Women's Health at St. Joseph's Mercy Hospital in Pontiac, Michigan and Oakwood Hospital in Dearborn, Michigan **EDU:** MD, Wayne State University School of Medicine (1994) **A/A/S:** Michigan Chapter, American Academy of Family Physicians; North Oakland Medical Center; Detroit Medical Center

Marla Joan Isaac
Title: Director **Company:** New England Reptile and Raptor Exhibits **Address:** 25 Floyd Avenue, Taunton, MA 02780 United States **BUS:** Educational Wildlife Programs in a Variety of Formats **P/S:** Presentation of Educational Wildlife Programs and Exhibits to Schools, County Fairs, Science Fairs, Festivals, Clubs, Special Events, Conferences, Organizations and Expositions **MA:** New England **D/D/R:** Working as a Naturalist and Artist, Lecturing, Offering Public Speaking, Working as a Falconer, Practicing Herpetology, Acting as Conservation Commissioner for the City of Taunton **H/I/S:** Collecting Books, Creating Art, Studying and Working with Nature **EDU:** Coursework in Art, Swaine School of Design, New Bedford, MA **A/A/S:** Member, International Wildlife Rehabilitation Association; Member, Science Advisory Board, Bristol County Agricultural High School; Member, North American Falconers Association; Massachusetts Educational Ecological Society
Email: nereptile@verizon.net
URL: http://www.nereptile.com

Andrea G.P. Isaacs
Title: Physician **Company:** Andrea G.P. Isaacs, MD, SCCP **Address:** 12 E. Palisade Avenue, Englewood, NJ 07631 United States **BUS:** Pulmonology Practice **P/S:** Critical-Care Medicine **MA:** Local **EXP:** Ms. Isaacs' expertise includes pulmonary care and internal medicine. **H/I/S:** Reading, Going to the Movies, Traveling **EDU:** Fellowship in Pulmonology, Cornell University **A/A/S:** American Association Chest Physicians **C/VW:** Local Church, Redeeming Love Christian Center
Email: aisaacs@att.net
URL: http://www.cambridgewhoswho.com

Cindy H. Isenhour
Title: Itinerant Resource Teacher **Company:** M.W. Howe Pre-K **Address:** 1020 Meares Street, Wilmington, NC 28401 United States **BUS:** School **P/S:** Education **MA:** Local **D/D/R:** Teaching Students with Special Needs; Employs a Variety of Teaching Methods to Meet the Needs of Autistic Students **H/I/S:** Reading, Swimming, Crocheting, Needle Pointing, Cross-Stitching **EDU:** Bachelor of Arts, University of North Carolina at Wilmington **A/A/S:** Council for Exceptional Children; National Association for the Education of Young Children; North Carolina Association for the Education of Young Children; North Carolina Association of Educators **C/VW:** Lower Cape Fear Hospice
Email: cisenhou@nhcs.net
URL: http://www.cambridgewhoswho.com

Bettye J. Isom
Title: Mission Outreach Ministries (MDM **Address:** 2713 Kelner Drive, Hyattsville, MD 20785 United States **BUS:** Christianity Mission Outreach **P/S:** Mission Outreach Ministries **MA:** Local **D/D/R:** Nursing Home Missionary, Hospital Missions, Ministries, Retired Nurse, Girl Scout Leader, Senior Citizen **H/I/S:** Reading, Crossword Puzzles, **EDU:** Washington Bible College **A/A/S:** Progressive National, DC Baptist Convention Inc, Southern Baptist Convention

Stephanie D. Iuliano
Title: Teacher **Company:** Northside Independent School District, John Glenn Elementary School **Address:** 5900 Evers Street, San Antonio, TX 78238 United States **BUS:** Elementary School **P/S:** Education **MA:** Local **D/D/R:** Teaching Second-Grade Students, Focusing on Biological Science, Writing Science Curriculum, Training Teachers in Computers **H/I/S:** Playing Piano and Guitar **EDU:** Bachelor of Science in Education, Minor in Biology, University of Texas at Austin; Trained in W.I.N. Writing **A/A/S:** Texas State Teachers Association
Email: siuliano@aol.com

Philip Ives
Title: Technical Support Representative **Company:** Renaissance Learning, Inc. **Address:** 2911 Peach Street, Wisconsin Rapids, WI 54494 United States **BUS:** Software Manufacturing **P/S:** Educational Software **MA:** International **EXP:** Mr. Ives' expertise is in server integration. **H/I/S:** Traveling, Participating in Outdoor Activities **EDU:** Associate Degree in Business Administration and Human Resources, Mid-State Technical College, Wisconsin Rapids **A/A/S:** Former Member, JA Titan **C/VW:** Volunteer, Wisconsin Community Theatre
Email: philip_ives@charter.net

Walter Warren Ivey
Title: Doctor of Audiology **Company:** Costco Hearing Aid Center **Address:** 4901 Gate Parkway, Jacksonville, FL 32246 United States **BUS:** Hearing Healthcare **P/S:** Hearing Aids, Hearing Counseling **MA:** National **EXP:** Mr. Ivey's expertise is in audiology. **H/I/S:** Golfing, Playing the Guitar and Bag Pipes **EDU:** Doctor of Audiology, Pennsylvania College of Optometry; Master's Degree, University of Florida; Bachelor's Degree, University of Florida **A/A/S:** American Academy of Audiology; Florida Academy of Audiology Jacksonville Hearing Loss Association **C/VW:** Donor, Local Religious Ministries, Volunteer City Rescue
Email: wwivey3@bellsouth.net
URL: http://www.hearingstation.com

Ms. Nila Kay Ivy
Title: Information Systems Services Coordinator **Company:** Department of Human Services of Oklahoma **Address:** 2405 Mercer Drive, Enid, OK 73701 United States **BUS:** Government Agency **P/S:** Adult Protective Services, Adoption Assistance, Children and Youth Services **MA:** Regional **D/D/R:** Installing and Maintaining Equipment and Software, Training Staff on the Usage of Microsoft Office, Overseeing Web Design for Local Offices **H/I/S:** Listening to Music, Singing, Playing Handbells **EDU:** Diploma, Frederick High School, OK (1966) **CERTS:** Pursuing Certification as a Microsoft Certified Desktop Support Technician; Technical Training, Enid and OU Training Center, Autry Vo-Tech School, Norman, OK; A Plus Certified; Dell Certified **A/A/S:** First Southern Baptist Church, Enid, OK; Charter Member, The Singing Church Women of Oklahoma
Email: fruitloop47@suddenlink.net
URL: http://www.okdhs.org

Rachel C. Izzo
Title: Marketing Supervisor **Company:** McDonald's Corporation **Address:** 1 Kroc Drive, Oak Brook, IL 60523 United States **BUS:** Fast Food Corporation **P/S:** Quick Service Restaurant **MA:** International **D/D/R:** Family Marketing **H/I/S:** Making Jewelry **EDU:** Bachelor's Degree in Journalism and Communications, Grand Valley State University, Michigan, 2002 **C/VW:** Various Charities, Special Olympics
Email: rachel.izzo@us.mcd.com
URL: http://www.mcdonals.com

Theresa Jacksis-Bonazzo
Title: 1) Teacher 2) Adjunct Professor **Company:** 1) Fairfield Public Schools 2) Sacred Heart University **Address:** 1625 Mill Plain Road, Fairfield, CT 06824 United States **BUS:** 1) School 2) University **P/S:** 1) Education 2) Higher Education **MA:** 1) Local 2) National **D/D/R:** Teaching Reading and Writing **H/I/S:** Reading, Exercising, Spending Time with her Children **EDU:** Coursework in Reading, Sacred Heart University **CERTS:** Pursuing Ed.D. in Teacher Leadership, Walden University **A/A/S:** Pi Lambda Theta; Connecticut Education Association; National Education Association; Language Arts Committee **C/VW:** Cystic Fibrosis Foundation
Email: bonazzo@optonline.net
URL: http://www.cambridgewhoswho.com

Arletta J. Jackson
Title: Nurse Manager, Medical-Surgical **Company:** Tanner Medical Center, Villa Rica **Address:** 601 Dallas Highway, Villa Rica, GA 30180 United States **BUS:** Medical Center **P/S:** Healthcare **MA:** Local **D/D/R:** Managing Medical-Surgical Nursing Group, Scheduling, Counseling, Ordering Supplies and Equipment, Monitor, Documenting Issues with Patients and Employees, Monitoring Compliance with National Standards **H/I/S:** Reading, Cooking, Walking, Church **EDU:** Pursuing Master's Degree in Nursing Administration, University of West Georgia; Bachelor of Nursing, Bear University **CERTS:** Certified in Advanced Life Support; Certified Entrepreneur **A/A/S:** American Nursing Association **C/VW:** Church
Email: jackson6431@bellsouth.net
URL: http://www.cambridgewhoswho.com

Brenda G. Jackson
Title: Teacher **Company:** Atlanta Public Schools, Adamsville Elementary School **Address:** 286 Wilson Mill Road S.W., Atlanta, GA 30331 United States **BUS:** Elementary School **P/S:** Education **MA:** Local **EXP:** Ms. Jackson's expertise includes elementary education and reading. **H/I/S:** Theater, Biking, Reading, Traveling **EDU:** Master of Arts in Elementary Education, Central Michigan University; Bachelor's Degree in Early Childhood Education, Elementary Education and Sociology, CUNY Hunter College **CERTS:** Certification in Teaching K-12 Education **A/A/S:** Alumni Association, Hunter College; American Federation of Teachers **A/H:** Teacher of the Year, 2006-2007 **C/VW:** Community Based Charities
Email: heytherbj@aol.com
URL: http://www.cambridgewhoswho.com

Deborah Denise Jackson
Title: Special Education Educator **Company:** Pearland School District **Address:** P.O. Box 7, Pearland, TX 77584 United States **BUS:** School **P/S:** Special Education **MA:** Regional **D/D/R:** Implementing Individual Education, Creating and Incorporating Student Curriculum, Accommodating Students, Parent and Teacher Meetings **H/I/S:** Golfing, Painting **EDU:** Master's Degree in Educational Technology, Nicholls State University (2003)
Email: askmyteacher1@yahoo.com

Don H. Jackson
Title: President **Company:** Don Diesel Services **Address:** 732 Redwood Highway, Grants Pass, OR 97527 United States **BUS:** Diesel Fuel/Thoroughbred Horses Retail, Kennel, Pet Care, Grooming **P/S:** Nationwide Fueling Stations, Horse Farm **MA:** Local **D/D/R:** Thoroughbred Horse Farm **H/I/S:** Fishing, Hunting, Racetrack **A/A/S:** Thoroughbred Association **A/H:** Nationally Known Sire Flying Lark

Elijah T. Jackson
Title: 1) President 2) Bishop **Company:** 1) J. Conway Construction Company 2) New Creation Christian Center **Address:** 1016 Main Street, Palatka, FL 32177 United States **BUS:** 1) Construction Company 2) Ministry **P/S:** 1) Construction Services for Commercial and Residential Properties 2) Spreading Spiritual Services **MA:** 1) Regional 2) Regional **EXP:** Ms. Jackson's expertise includes construction services, community support and outreach services. **H/I/S:** Attending Community Church **EDU:** Coursework in Accounting, Minor in Elementary Education, Greater Hartford Community College **C/VW:** March of Dimes; Shriners; T.D. Jakes Ministry; FIFA Ministry
Email: eajackson@gbso.net
URL: http://www.newcreationccinc.com

Jabari N. Jackson Sr.
Title: Owner, President **Company:** Pure Platinum Properties **Address:** 3257 Rolling Hills Lane, Apopka, FL 32712 United States **BUS:** Real Estate Company **P/S:** Residential Real Estate and Townhouses **MA:** Regional **D/D/R:** Managing the Office, Supervising Three Sales Agents, Training New Employees, Marketing, Overseeing Real Estate Sales and Financing **H/I/S:** Basketball, Spending Time with his Family **CERTS:** Licensed Broker (2006); Licensed Mortgage Broker (2003); Licensed in Real Estate (2001) **A/A/S:** Orange County NAACP; National Association of Realtors; Orlando Regional Realtors Association; Orlando Chamber of Commerce; African American Chamber of Commerce; Florida Association of Realtors
Email: jayjacksoncb@hotmail.com
URL: http://www.actionjacksonhomes.com

Jill Jackson
Title: Case Teacher **Company:** Cumberland County Schools **Address:** 7370 Clinton Road, Stedman, NC 28391 United States **BUS:** School **P/S:** Education **MA:** Local **D/D/R:** Teaching Learning Disabled Students and Reading **H/I/S:** Shopping, Gardening, Attending Antique Shows **EDU:** Bachelor of Science in Special Education, Concentration in Mental Retardation, Learning Disabled and Academically Gifted Education **A/A/S:** Professional Educators of North Carolina; Youth Council Pianist, Concord Baptist Church **C/VW:** Very Special Arts Festival, Church
Email: bunce9191@yahoo.com
URL: http://www.cambridgewhowho.com

Kristin Blair Jackson
Title: Chemistry Instructor **Company:** Harrisonville High School **Address:** 1504 E. Elm Street, Harrisonville, MO 64701 United States **BUS:** High School **P/S:** Education **MA:** Local **D/D/R:** Teaching All Subjects to High School Students **H/I/S:** Traveling, Camping, Canoeing, Cooking, Gardening **EDU:** Bachelor's Degree in Biology, Minor in Chemistry, Missouri State University **A/A/S:** National Education Association; Science Teachers of Missouri; National Science Teachers of America **A/H:** District Teacher of the Year, 2007-2008 **C/VW:** Local Animal Shelter, Church, Relay for Life
Email: jacksonkr@harrisonville.k12.mo.us
URL: http://www.harrisonschools.org

LeWanda R. Jackson
Title: Commercial Loan Accountant **Company:** Citigroup **Address:** 400 South Dupont Highway, Unit 118, New Castle, DE 19720 United States **BUS:** Financial Bank **P/S:** Global Loans **MA:** Local **D/D/R:** Trading Both Domestic/International **H/I/S:** Read, Go To Movies, Spend Time with Her Daughter **EDU:** Wesley College (Delaware), BA in Business Administration
Email: lewanda.jackson@citigroup.com

Mr. Mario J. Jackson
Title: Technical Account Manager **Company:** Hewlett-Packard Development Company **Address:** 305 Rockrimmon Boulevard S., Colorado Springs, CO 80919 United States **BUS:** Computer Company **P/S:** Computers and Related Products and Services **MA:** International **D/D/R:** Overseeing Customer Service Accounts **H/I/S:** Watching Sports, Hunting, Playing Chess and Computer Games **EDU:** Bachelor's Degree in Information Technology Management, Colorado Technical University; Associate Degree in Computer Information Systems, Colorado Technical University **C/VW:** Hillside Community Center; Big Brothers Big Sisters of America
Email: mjack2309@yahoo.com
URL: http://www.hp.com

Mary Kate Jackson
Title: Nurse, Supervisor **Company:** Village of Skyline **Address:** 3238 Atrium Point, Colorado Springs, CO 80906 United States **BUS:** Healthcare **P/S:** Assisted Living for Seniors **MA:** International **D/D/R:** Overseeing Staff Nurses, Patients and Facility Staff of Six, Ensuring that the Night Shift is Running Correctly from Day to Day **H/I/S:** Hiking **CERTS:** Licensed Practical Nurse, Indiana Vocational Technical School (1984) **A/A/S:** Former Member, United States Figure Skating Association
Email: northendbase@hotmail.com

Misty G. Jackson
Title: Senior Reliability Engineer **Company:** Honeywell Technology Solutions, Inc. **Address:** 1110 Bayfield Drive, Colorado Springs, CO 80906 United States **BUS:** Technology and Manufacturing Company **P/S:** Aerospace Products and Services, Control Technologies for Buildings, Homes and Industries, Automotive Products, Turbochargers **MA:** National **D/D/R:** Engineering Technology, Product Development, Project Development, Public Relations **EDU:** Bachelor of Science in Mechanical Engineering, Colorado School of Mines (2001) **A/A/S:** Society of Women Engineers; American Society of Mechanical Engineers
Email: misty.jackson@afscn.com
URL: http://www.honeywell.com

Randi J. Jackson
Title: Horse Consigner, Ranch Owner **Company:** CJ's Ranch **Address:** 8008 Woodyard Road, Clinton, MD 20735 United States **BUS:** Horse Ranch **P/S:** Horseback Riding Lessons, Equestrian Consignments **MA:** National **D/D/R:** Caring for Horses, Seeing that their Nutritional Needs are Met, Educating People on Riding, Matching People to the Right Horse **H/I/S:** Equestrian Activities **A/A/S:** Tennessee Walking Horse Association; National Spotted Saddle Horse Association; American Quarter Horse Association
Email: whispercj1@verizon.net
URL: http://www.cambridgewhoswho.com

Rosemary R. Jackson
Title: Medical Records Manager **Company:** University of South Florida **Address:** 4202 E. Fowler Avenue, Tampa, FL 33620 United States **BUS:** University **P/S:** Education, Student Healthcare **MA:** Regional **EXP:** Ms. Jackson's expertise is in medical records management. **H/I/S:** Traveling, Shopping, Making Crafts **EDU:** College Coursework **A/A/S:** Sigma Gamma Rho; Member, Greater Bethel Baptist Church **C/VW:** American Heart Association, American Lung Association
Email: saintrrj@msn.com
URL: http://www.usf.edu

Russell E. Jackson Sr.
Company: Central Delivery **Address:** 11240 Perry Road, Suite 17, Houston, TX 77064 United States **BUS:** Real Estate Finance **P/S:** Private Real Estate Financial Services **MA:** Worldwide **D/D/R:** Offering Private Financing to Real Estate Sellers, Listing Notes, Serving as liaison Between Sellers and Buyers **H/I/S:** Traveling **EDU:** Associate Degree in Criminology, Navarro College
Email: rustyjackson53@yahoo.com
URL: http://www.cash4cashflows.com/rjackson32

Suoliver W. Jackson
Title: Registered Nurse Supervisor **Company:** Orchard Healthcare Center **Address:** 629 State Highway 21 S., Hayneville, AL 36040 United States **BUS:** Public Healthcare Facility **P/S:** Nursing Home Services **MA:** Regional **D/D/R:** Supervising Certified Nursing Assistants and Licensed Practical Nurses, Overseeing 72 Patients, Dispensing Medication per Doctors' Orders, Offering Quality Care to Residents, Assisting in Hands On Care **H/I/S:** Attending All Church Activities, Enjoying Spectator Sports **EDU:** Diploma in Nursing, Ida V. Moffett School of Nursing (1972) **A/A/S:** Alabama State Nursing Association; American Nurses Association; Dallas County Nurses Association; Mount Zion Christian Church; Member, Tipton High School Alumni (1970)
Email: susieqj52@msn.com

Tandrea L. Jackson
Title: Registered Nurse, Student **Company:** Hawaii Pacific University **Address:** 1164 Bishop Street, Honolulu, HI 96813 United States **BUS:** University **P/S:** Education **MA:** International **D/D/R:** Nursing **H/I/S:** Singing, Spending Time with her Family **EDU:** Bachelor of Science in Psychology, University of South Carolina **A/A/S:** United States Army; Beta Beta Beta **C/VW:** City of Refuge Christian Church
Email: tandreaj@hotmail.com

Yvonne Jackson
Title: Counselor **Company:** Oakgrove-Jack Weaver School **Address:** 24275 Jefferson Avenue, Murrieta, CA 92562 United States **BUS:** Accredited School Facility **P/S:** Treatment and Education for At-Risk Children, Preservation of the Family through the Understanding of the Importance of Moving to the Mainstream **MA:** Regional **D/D/R:** Preventing Child Abuse, Offering Educational Assistance, Monitoring the Behavior of Special Needs, Autistic, Attention Deficit Disorder and Attention Deficit Hyperactivity Disorder, Keeping Students Focused **H/I/S:** Reading, Golfing, Sunning, Decorating, Acting as a Foster Parent, Spending Time with her Daughter **EDU:** Master's Degree Plus 60 in Behavioral Science, University of Arizona, Tucson; Bachelor's Degree **A/A/S:** Harvis Member **A/H:** Nominated, Coach of the Year
Email: yvonnepeace7@aol.com

Ms. Trina Jackson-Gaspard
Title: President, Owner **Company:** Sam's Professional Cleaning Service, Inc. **Address:** P.O. Box 470646, Brooklyn, NY 11247 United States **BUS:** Cleaning Services Company **P/S:** Residential and Commercial Cleaning Services **MA:** Local **D/D/R:** Specializing in Cleaning, Accounting, Managing Employee Payroll, Scheduling, Hiring, Consulting with Clientèle, Training Employees, Marketing the Business, Overseeing Company Estimates **H/I/S:** Interior Design. Writing a Novel **EDU:** Pursuing Master of Business Administration CUNY Baruch College; Bachelor of Art in English, University at Albany (1997) **A/A/S:** Eastern Star
Email: tj_samspcs@yahoo.com

Sam Jacob
Title: Diagnostic Imaging Manager **Company:** M.D. Anderson Cancer Center **Address:** 1515 Holcombe Boulevard, Houston, TX 77030 United States **BUS:** Cancer Hospital **P/S:** Cancer Patient Care **MA:** International **EXP:** Ms. Jacob's expertise is in MRI administration. **EDU:** Master of Business Administration, University of Phoenix **A/A/S:** American Healthcare Radiology Administrators **C/VW:** Church
Email: thyiljacob@earthlink.net
URL: http://www.cambridgewhoswho.com

Elizabeth M. Jacobs
Title: Director of Marketing **Company:** Siemens Building Technologies **Address:** 1000 Deerfield Parkway, Buffalo Grove, IL 60089 United States **BUS:** Commercial Building Development **P/S:** Building Automation Controls and Systems **MA:** International **D/D/R:** Product Branding, Packaging, Market Research **H/I/S:** Fly Fishing, Hiking, Hunting **EDU:** Bachelor of Arts Degree in Journalism, Southern Illinois University (1982) **A/A/S:** Business Marketing Association; Federation of Fly Fishermen
Email: getliz@sbcglobal.net
URL: http://www.siemens.com

Dr. Judy Bonita Jacobs
Title: Counselor **Company:** Christian Family Counseling **Address:** 1320 Central Park Boulevard, Fredericksburg, VA 22445 United States **BUS:** Christian Counseling Practice **P/S:** Marriage and Family Counseling **MA:** Local **D/D/R:** Marriage and Family Counseling **H/I/S:** Reading, Attending Plays, Traveling, Sports **EDU:** Pursuing Ph.D. in Christian Psychology from Christian Educational Center; Certified Through International Board of Christina Counselors **A/A/S:** American Association of Christina Counselors **C/VW:** A Can Can Make a Difference
Email: drjb55@aol.com
URL: http://www.fredcfc.tripod.com

Mary Gloria Jacobs
Title: Daycare Provider, Owner **Company:** Jacobs Family Childcare **Address:** 3522 Todd Avenue, Commerce, CA 90040 United States **BUS:** Daycare Center **P/S:** Daycare for Children from Infancy through Seven Years Old **MA:** Local **EXP:** Ms. Jacobs' expertise is in child care. **H/I/S:** Swimming, Walking on the Beach **EDU:** Diploma, Oxnard High School **A/H:** Caregiver of the Week Award, KCET **C/VW:** Eucharistic Minister, St. Gertrude's Church; Choir Member, Our Lady of Perpetual Health
Email: mary.jacobs@cwwemail.com

Mr. Russell L. Jacobs
Title: Owner **Company:** Chenango Apartments **Address:** 4 Maplewood Drive, Binghamton, NY 13901 United States **BUS:** Apartment Complex **P/S:** Apartment Rentals Including Four Four-Person Apartments and One Two-Person Apartment with Maintenance, Heat, Washer and Dryer **MA:** Regional **D/D/R:** Managing the Facilities and Daily Operations of the Building, Performing Maintenance and Repairs, Bookkeeping, Supervising the Professional Golf Course **H/I/S:** Fishing, Spending Time with his Grandchildren **EDU:** Coursework in Water Sewage Maintenance, Syracuse University **A/A/S:** National Golf Course Superintendent Association of America; Elks Club; Moose Club **A/H:** Award Recipient, New York State Golf Course Association (2002)
URL: http://www.cambridgewhoswho.com

Yvonne Jacobs
Title: Owner **Company:** My Homestyle Café **Address:** 523 Marin Street, Vallejo, CA 94590 United States **BUS:** Proven Leader in the Food Service and Restaurant Industry **P/S:** Food Services and Quality Home-style Cooking **MA:** Regional **D/D/R:** Cooking, Greeting, Customers, Handling All Menu Specialties, Creating Menus, Responsible for All Employees, Wait Staff, Bookkeeping, All Financial and Marketing Aspects of the Business **EDU:** Business Administration Coursework, The California State University; High School Education **A/A/S:** Mount Calvary Baptist Church Fairfield
URL: http://www.myhomestylecafe.com

Amy Jacobson
Title: Executive Chef **Company:** The Grill **Address:** 13744 Highway 27, Ferryville, WI 54628 United States **BUS:** Restaurant **P/S:** Food Service **MA:** Local **D/D/R:** Culinary Arts **H/I/S:** Playing Music, Exercising **EDU:** Bachelor of Arts, Radio and Television Production, University of Montana, Missoula
Email: oopy2@hotmail.com

Regina A. Jacques
Title: Teacher **Company:** St. Paul's Lutheran Early Childhood Development Center **Address:** P.O. Box 17374, Anaheim, CA 92817 United States **BUS:** Early Childhood Education **P/S:** Loving and Safe Atmosphere for the Encouragement of Learning, Self-Discovery and Independence through Jesus Christ as a Role Model **MA:** Regional **D/D/R:** Educating 2-Year-Olds, Bible Studies, Potty Training, Caregiving **H/I/S:** Swimming, Ballet, Theater, Ice Skating **EDU:** Associate of Arts in Liberal Arts, Fullerton College (1985) **CERTS:** Certification in Teaching, Fullerton College (2004); Certified in Christian Education, Concordia University (2004) **A/A/S:** National Association for Female Executives; Emeritus; National Association for the Education of Young Children; Association for Supervision and Curriculum Development
Email: reginaj99@yahoo.com
URL: http://www.st-paul.org/cdc

Bruce H. Jaffee
Title: Owner **Company:** Bruce's Handyman Service **Address:** P.O. Box 36692, Las Vegas, NV 89133 United States **BUS:** Home Improvement Company **P/S:** Residential Handyman Services Including Plumbing, Electrical, Drywall Installation and Repairing Services **MA:** Regional **D/D/R:** Ensuring Customer Satisfaction, Working with Realtors and Homeowners **EDU:** Coursework, West Valley Occupational Center **CERTS:** Certification in Automotive Repair, Trade School **C/VW:** Local Police Department
Email: bruce.jaffee@cwwemail.com
URL: http://www.cambridgewhoswho.com

Joshua T. Jahnish-Maltese
Title: Tutor **Company:** The Tutoring Club **Address:** 22 Chipperfield Drive, Effort, PA 18330 United States **BUS:** Tutoring Center **P/S:** Education **MA:** Local **D/D/R:** Tutoring Mathematics from First Grade to College Students, Assisting Students to Improve their Study Skills **H/I/S:** Wrestling, Golfing, Playing Ping Pong Game **EDU:** Pursuing Bachelor's Degree in Business Economics and Finance, Pennsylvania State University; Associate Degree in Business, Northampton College, Tannersville (2007) **A/A/S:** Phi Theta Kappa; Golden Key International Honour Society **A/H:** National Dean's List
Email: infinitytradingco@mac.com

Cheryle A. Jakinovich
Title: Registered Nurse Case Manager **Company:** Select Specialty Hospital **Address:** 159 Kercheval Avenue, Grosse Pointe Farms, MI 48236 United States **BUS:** Hospital **P/S:** Case Management, Long-Term Acute Care Patients **MA:** National **D/D/R:** Cardiac Treatment, Home Care and Discharge Planning **H/I/S:** Swimming, Boating, Traveling, Reading **EDU:** Associate Degree in Nursing, MaComb College **A/A/S:** Michigan Nurses Association **C/VW:** Salvation Army; Church; Purple Heart; American Cancer Society; American Heart Association
Email: cajboat@yahoo.com
URL: http://www.selectmedicalcorp.com

Joseph Patrick Jakubal
Title: Director of Information Technology **Company:** JKL Company **Address:** 1217 Victoria Avenue, Windsor, Ontario, INTL N8X 1N8 United States **BUS:** Medical Records Company **P/S:** Hospital and Government Agencies, Transcription **MA:** International **D/D/R:** Metrology, Micro-electronics, Physics, Submarine Tracking Systems, Magnetics, EMI testing, Leadership, Environmental testing, Manufacturing supervisor. **H/I/S:** Self-Improvement, Motivating Others, Writing, Guitar Skating, Cycling **EDU:** College Coursework, Degree in Precision Measurement Electronics, Random Vibration, Environmental Testing, Medical terminology **A/A/S:** Exemplary Recommendation from U.S. Air Force **C/VW:** Leprosy Foundation
Email: joe@JKLCompany.com
URL: http://www.jklcompany.com

Kyle R. Jamaitis
Title: Senior Sales Consultant **Company:** St. Jude Medical, Inc. **Address:** 4 Thackery Road, Hainesport, NJ 08036 United States **BUS:** Manufacturing Company **P/S:** Medical Devices Including Implantable Cardioverter Defibrillators, Cardiac Resynchronization Therapy Devices, Pacemakers, Electrophysiology Catheters Device, Mapping and Visualization Systems, Vascular Closure Devices, Heart Valve Replacement and Repair Products and Neurostimulation Devices **MA:** International **D/D/R:** Maintaining Customer Relationships, Managing the Sales Division, Marketing, Supporting Engineers, Educating Surgeons and Patients on Medical Devices, Consulting for Cardiac Device Implants **H/I/S:** Golfing, Sports, Supporting The New York Yankees **EDU:** Bachelor's Degree in Pre-Medical Studies, Villanova University (1995) **A/A/S:** Association of State Personnel Executives; Heart Failure Society of America; Heart Rhythm Society; Adjunct Professor of Philosophy, Villanova University
Email: kjamaitis@sjm.com
URL: http://www.sjm.com

Amy C. James
Title: Staff Accountant **Company:** Archon Group **Address:** Irving, TX 75039 United States **BUS:** Investment Management and Support Services Company **P/S:** Accounting, Real Estate, Investment Management and Support Services **MA:** International **D/D/R:** Accounting, Reviewing Client Taxes, Troubleshooting, Problem Solving Applications **H/I/S:** Going to the Symphony, Seeing Musicals **EDU:** Pursuing Bachelor's Degree in Accounting, Dallas Baptist University; Associate Degree in Accounting, Mountain View College **C/VW:** Make-A-Wish Foundation
Email: ajames6531@yahoo.com
URL: http://www.cambridgewhoswho.com

Dee L. James
Title: Cardiology Account Executive **Company:** Siemens Medical Solutions **Address:** 51 Valley Stream Parkway, Malvern, PA 19355 United States **BUS:** Medical Technology Company **P/S:** Imaging Equipment, Information Technology, Management Consulting, Clinical and Financial Solutions, Customer Service **MA:** International **D/D/R:** Managing Radiology and Cardiology Capital Equipment, Assisting Clients with Equipment **H/I/S:** Gardening, Playing with her Dogs, Spending Time with her Grandson **EDU:** Associate Degree in Business, Cameron University (1976)
Email: dee.james@siemens.com
URL: http://www.medical.siemens.com

Karen E. James

Title: Registered Nurse **Company:** Griffin Hospital **Dept:** ICU **Address:** Derby, CT 06418 United States **BUS:** Hospital **P/S:** Healthcare **MA:** Local **D/D/R:** Intensive Care Unit **H/I/S:** Playing Tennis, Exercising, Spending Time with her Family **EDU:** Bachelor's Degree in Nursing, Quinnipiac University; Bachelor's Degree in Elementary Education/Counseling Psychology, Keene State College **A/A/S:** Sigma Theta Tau; Psi Chi
Email: karenjames25@yahoo.com
URL: http://www.griffinhealth.org

Michael William James

Title: President, Chief Executive Officer **Company:** Jamko Technical Solutions, Inc. **Address:** 1105 Driving Park Avenue, Newark, NY 14513 United States **BUS:** Nuclear Power Company **P/S:** Nuclear Engineering **MA:** International **D/D/R:** Robotic Application, Overseeing All Operations of the Company **H/I/S:** Snowmobiling **EDU:** Bachelor of Science in Propulsion Engineering, Navy Nuclear Power School **A/A/S:** Electric Power Research Institute; U.S. Navy **C/VW:** Various Local Charities
Email: mjames@jamkosolutions.com
URL: http://www.jamkosolutions.com

Richard C. James

Title: Agent, Owner **Company:** American Family Insurance **Address:** 3100 W. Higgins Road, Suite 190, Hoffman Estates, IL 60169 United States **BUS:** Insurance Company **P/S:** Insurance Services Including Automotive, Home, Business, Health, Variable Annuity and Universal Life Insurance **MA:** National **D/D/R:** Overseeing Operations, Developing Marketing Strategies, Establishing Business Contacts, Retaining Clients, Performing Community Service, Public Speaking at Churches and Community Organizations Regarding Insurance Coverage **H/I/S:** Sports **CERTS:** Licensed, Health, Property, Life and Casualty Insurance Agent, Illinois, Indiana, Wisconsin, Arizona; Certification in 6 and 63 Series **A/A/S:** Streamwood Chamber of Commerce
Email: rjame1@amfam.com
URL: http://www.richardcjames.com

Troy James, Ph.D., DAPA

Title: Clinical Psychologist, Assistant Professor **Company:** Argosy University **Address:** 980 Hammond Drive, Building 2, Atlanta, GA 30328 United States **BUS:** Private Institution of Higher Education **P/S:** Professional Educational Programs at the Doctoral, Master's, Bachelor's and Associate Degree Levels **MA:** Regional **D/D/R:** Teaching Students About Complex Complicates Post-Traumatic Stress Disorders, Addictive Disorders, Promoting Individual, Group and Couples Psychotherapy, Teaching Personality Assessment, Conducting Psychotherapy Diagnostic Programs **H/I/S:** Theater **EDU:** Ph.D. in Adult Clinical Psychology, Southern Illinois University Carbondale (2004) **A/A/S:** American Psychological Association; American Psychotherapy Association; Georgia Psychology Association
Email: trjames@argosyu.edu
URL: http://www.argosyu.edu

Linda Jamison-Brown

Title: Administrative Assistant to the President **Company:** St. Vincent's Midtown Hospital **Address:** 426 W. 52nd Street, New York, NY 10019 United States **BUS:** 150-Bed Community Hospital **P/S:** Dave DeBusschere Cardiovascular Center, Older Adults Program, Family Health Center, Ambulatory Surgery, Spellman HIV Center and Many Other Services **MA:** Regional **D/D/R:** Responsible for President's Calendar, Scheduling Conference Calls, Meetings, Travel Arrangements, Handling Correspondence, Triage Phone Calls, Preparing Board of Directors Books for Board Meetings, Ordering Office Supplies, Front Desk Reception Duties **H/I/S:** Worshipping the Lord, Bible Study, Attending Family Reunions, Photography, Softball, Sewing, Traveling, Basketball, Tennis, Coordinating Trips, Coordinating Plays **EDU:** College Courses in Business Administration, Kings College, Charlotte, North Carolina; Graduate, Grace Down Airline School, New York, New York; Diploma, Blaney High School, Elgin, South Carolina **A/A/S:** Correspondence Secretary, United Missionary Baptist Association
Email: librown@svcmcny.org
URL: http://www.stvincentsmidtown.org

Rick T. Jandron

Title: President, Manager **Company:** Ponds and Mountain Streams, Inc. **Address:** 50 Jackrabbit Lane, Bozeman, MT 59718 United States **BUS:** Construction Company **P/S:** Designing and Building Custom Ponds, Waterfalls, Indoor Fountains and Wetlands **MA:** Regional **D/D/R:** Designing and Building Ponds, Waterfalls, Indoor Fountains and Wetlands, Planning Appropriate Aquatic and Upland Planting **H/I/S:** White Water Canoeing **EDU:** College Coursework in Business Management, Union County College; Landscape Design, Montana State University **A/A/S:** Dry Stone Conservancy; Walls, Bridges, Arches
Email: pondsandmountainstreams@Q.com
URL: http://www.pondsandmountainstreams.com

Billie Grey Janise

Title: Vice President, Co-Owner **Company:** J&B Industrial Fan Services, Inc. **Address:** 1124 Indy Court, Evansville, IN 47725 United States **BUS:** Industrial Construction **P/S:** Industrial Fans, Technical Service, Trouble-Shooting, Maintenance, Repair, Replacement Parts, Balancing Alignment **MA:** Regional **D/D/R:** Managing her daughter is her spokes model **H/I/S:** Working Out with a Trainer at a Gym, Spending Time with her Daughter **EDU:** Certified in Cosmetology, Miss Audrie's School of Beauty; Coursework in General Studies, University of Southern Indiana **A/A/S:** Chamber of Commerce; Daughters of the Nile; Masonic Order **C/VW:** Sisters of the Poor, The Humane Society, Church, Feed the Hungry; TBN
Email: billie@jbfanserv.com
URL: http://www.jbfanserv.com

Sally West Janke

Title: Vice President, Treasurer **Company:** 1) Ajax Oil Corporation 2) QTIP 3) MHW Family Corp, LLC **Address:** 810 Rue Bourbon, Metairie, LA 70005 United States **BUS:** Energy Firm **P/S:** Refining Oil and Gas **MA:** Nicaragua, LA, MS, TX, OK **EXP:** Ms. Janke's expertise is in accounting. **H/I/S:** Conducting Research in Family Tree, Painting, Playing Electronic Games **EDU:** Bachelor of Arts in Accounting, University of Oklahoma **C/VW:** Nebraska Animal Shelters; Best Friends Animal Society; DELTA Rescue; Make-A-Wish Foundation; The Humane Society of the United States; North Shore Animal League America; World Wildlife Fund
Email: bigredwon@aol.com

Doreen E. Jantz-Makofski

Title: Clinical Nurse Manager **Company:** Rush Copley Medical Center **Address:** 2000 Ogden Avenue, Aurora, IL 60504 United States **BUS:** Healthcare Hospital **P/S:** Medical Care Surgery **MA:** Local **D/D/R:** Nursing in Ambulatory Surgery and Recovery/GI-LAB, DSU and the Pain Center **H/I/S:** Biking, Fishing, Outdoors **EDU:** Harper Rainey College, Northern Illinois University, Roosevelt University, ASS in Nursing, BS in Community Health, Master in Public Administration **A/A/S:** CAPA, ASPAN, Surgical Care Improvement Project, Breast Cancer Society, Former Chairwoman for Pain Management Committee
Email: djantz@rsh.net

Regina K. Jaquess

Title: Pharmacy Student **Company:** University of Louisiana **Address:** 413 Eason place, Monroe, LA 71201 United States **BUS:** University **P/S:** Education **MA:** National **D/D/R:** Managing Clinical Pharmacy **H/I/S:** Water Skiing **EDU:** Pursuing Doctorate of Pharmacy, University of Louisiana, Monroe **A/A/S:** Louisiana Society for Pharmacy; American Society for Pharmacy; Water Ski Team, The University of Louisiana, Monroe; USA Water Ski **C/VW:** Manatee Club
Email: rjaquess@bellsouth.net
URL: http://www.ulm.edu

Janene Monica Jaramillo

Title: 1) Owner 2) Senior Account Manager **Company:** Destination Spa & Salon, Rainer Title **Address:** 15600 N.E. Eighth Street, Bellevue, WA 98008 United States **BUS:** 1) Spa and Salon 2) Title Agency **P/S:** 1) Beauty Treatment, Waxing, Facials, Massage, Full Spectrum Hair Service, Nails, Spray Tanning, Body Wraps, Body Evolution 2) Training, Processing Title and Escrow Orders **MA:** Local **D/D/R:** Customer Service, Marketing, Training **H/I/S:** Camping, Playing Soccer, Spending Time with her 11-Year-Old Daughter **CERTS:** Certified 12th-Grade Clock Hour Instructor **A/A/S:** President, Children's Cancer Foundation; Bellevue Professional Warrens Club; Award for Helping Children with Cancer; Former Cheerleader, Atlanta Falcons **C/VW:** Cancer Research
Email: janene@rainiertitle.com
Email: janene@destinationspaandsalon.com
URL: http://www.destinationspaandsalon.com

Yavanne C. Jaramillo

Title: 1) Artist 2) Owner **Company:** 1) Y.C. Jaramillo Southwest Art 2) Jaramillo's Cleaning Service **Address:** P.O. Box 1973, Ranchos de Taos, NM 87557 United States **BUS:** 1) Southwest Art Dealer 2) Commercial Janitorial Work **P/S:** 1) Southwestern Painting, Chili Peppers, Landscaping, Churches, Stain Glass Work, Welder 2) Commercial Cleaning **MA:** National **D/D/R:** 1) Painting, Landscapes, Southwest Art, Making Wooden Crosses 2) Commercial Cleaning **H/I/S:** Fishing, Camping, Gardening, Playing Racquetball **EDU:** Associate Degree in Business, University of New Mexico; Certified Welder **C/VW:** Hospice, AIDS Foundation, Disabled American Veterans, St. Jude Children's Hospital
Email: ycmillo@taosnet.com

Jacet Anseicha Jarrett

Title: Registered Nurse **Company:** Winthrop-University Hospital **Dept:** Acute Dialysis **Address:** 259 First Street, Mineola, NY 11501 United States **BUS:** Hospital **P/S:** Healthcare **MA:** Long Island, NY **EXP:** Ms. Jarrett's expertise includes pediatric and adult dialysis nursing. **D/D/R:** Assessing Patient History, Caring for Patients, Administering Medications, Educating on Patient Survival, Counseling **H/I/S:** Attending the Theater and Broadway Shows, Listening to Music, Reading **EDU:** Bachelor's Degree in Nursing, Earned in Jamaica, West Indies; Registered Nurse, York College **A/A/S:** American Nephrology Nurses' Association **A/H:** Dean's List (2007); All American Scholar in Nursing Award, Nurses Service Organization **C/VW:** St. Jude Children's Research Hospital; March of Dimes Foundation; American Heart Association
Email: jayjarr@aol.com
URL: http://www.cambridgewhoswho.com

Sadie D. Jarvis

Title: Director of Counseling **Company:** Claflin University **Address:** 400 Magnolia Street, Orangeburg, SC 29115 United States **BUS:** University **P/S:** Higher Education **MA:** Regional **EXP:** Ms. Jarvis' expertise is in counseling. **H/I/S:** Gardening, Reading, Solving Crossword Puzzles, Community Service **EDU:** Master of Education in Educational Administration and Counseling, South Carolina State University **A/A/S:** Empire Who's Who; American Counseling Association; Phi Delta Kappa **C/VW:** American Red Cross; The Salvation Army; Habitat for Humanity
Email: sjarvis@claflin.edu
URL: http://www.claflin.edu

Scott A. Jasch

Title: Building Manager **Company:** Northwest Community Hospital **Address:** 901 W. Kirchhoff Road, Arlington Heights, IL 60005 United States **BUS:** Hospital **P/S:** Healthcare **MA:** Local **D/D/R:** Managing Facilitation, Ensuring Customer Satisfaction **H/I/S:** Fishing **C/VW:** Muscular Dystrophy Association
Email: dunbar_320@yahoo.com
URL: http://www.cambridgewhoswho.com

Ms. Melanie R. Jasontek-Rubenstein

Title: Construction Coordinator **Company:** D.I. Construction Services, Inc. **Address:** 8 Shady Creek Lane, Amelia, OH 45102 United States **BUS:** General Contracting Company **P/S:** Hotels **MA:** National **D/D/R:** Writing Contracts, Ordering Materials, Purchasing Agreements, Cutting Checks **H/I/S:** Camping, Coaching Soccer **EDU:** Master of Science in Construction Management, Northern Kentucky University (2006); Bachelor of Science in Construction Management, Northern Kentucky University (2004) **A/A/S:** Professional Land Surveyors of Ohio; American Society of Civil Engineers; Master's Dissertation was Published ' The Need for Investing in the Safety of a Company'
Email: coordinator@di-construction.com
Email: melanie2712@yahoo.com
URL: http://www.di-construction.com

Mr. Joesph G. Javier, LNHA

Title: Licensed Nursing Home Administrator **Company:** Lexington Health Care **Address:** 730 W. Hintz Road, Wheeling, IL 60090 United States **BUS:** Health care organization with a commitment to quality and an innovative approach. Since 1984, Lexington has identified the health and social needs of individuals within the community and has responded to meet those needs. **P/S:** Products, Services and Management of Luxury Communities, Personal Care, Home Health Care and the Lexington Health Care Centers **MA:** Regional **D/D/R:** Directing departments such as client services, operations management, food service sanitation, social services, human resources and nursing. Licensed Nursing Home Administrator, Food Service Sanitation, Certified Nursing Assistant and Accident/Life Insurance Producer. **H/I/S:** I enjoy going to the gym to relieve stress, playing sports, working on the house and spending time with friends and family. Recently you will see me hitting the books as I work on my MBA. **EDU:** Bachelor of Arts in Psychology and Sociology, University of Illinois at Chicago **A/A/S:** Illinois Health Care Association, Alzheimer's Association
Email: josephgjavier@gmail.com
URL: http://josephgjavier.tripod.com

Kimberly L. Jay

Title: Fourth-Grade Teacher **Company:** Lawnwood Elementary School **BUS:** Elementary School with the Goal of Increasing Achievement in Writing, Reading and Mathematics **P/S:** Elementary Education in a Title I School, Curriculum Development, Mandatory Uniform for Kindergarten through Fifth-Grade Students, Full-Time Gifted Program, Reading Renaissance Program, an Average of Six Computers with Internet Access in all Classrooms **MA:** Regional **D/D/R:** Teaching All Subjects, Promoting Exceptional Student Education in the Classroom, Writing, Mentoring New Teachers, Certified to Have Student Teachers and Teaching Assistants, Team Teaching with Exceptional Student Education Teacher for Reading and Writing **H/I/S:** Running **EDU:** Pursuing Master's Degree in Education Leadership, Florida Atlantic University; Bachelor's Degree in Elementary Education, English for Speakers of Other Languages Endorsement, Florida Atlantic University (1997) **A/A/S:** National Education Association; Florida Education Association; American Cancer Society Relay for Life; National Board Certified Teacher; Walt Disney World Half Marathon; Disney's Minnie Marathon
Email: jayk@stlucie.k12.fl.us
URL: http://www.stlucie.k12.fl.us

Jean Jaynes

Title: Case Manager **Company:** CAB Health and Recovery Services, Inc. **Address:** 111 Middletown Road, Danvers, MA 01923 United States **BUS:** Nonprofit Substance Abuse Treatment Center **P/S:** Healthcare, Substance Abuse Treatment **MA:** Statewide **D/D/R:** Case Management, Education for the Heroin Education and Awareness Task Force **H/I/S:** Traveling, Reading, Swimming, Walking, Biking, Camping, Spending Time with her Two Daughters **EDU:** Bachelor of Arts in Criminal Justice, Minor in Youth Work, University of Massachusetts, Boston **C/VW:** Morgan Memorial, Big Brothers Big Sisters, CAB Health and Recovery Services, Inc.
Email: jjaynes02@comcast.net
URL: http://www.cabhealth.org

Fabienne Renelus Jean-Louis

Title: Employment Counselor **Company:** Jowanio **Address:** 142 Little Road, New City, NY United States **BUS:** Disability Agency **P/S:** Working with the Disabled to Enhance Independence **MA:** Local **D/D/R:** Finding Jobs, Job Coaching, Job Skill and Interview Preparation **H/I/S:** Reading, Writing **EDU:** Bachelor of Science in Education, CUNY City College of New York **A/A/S:** HAPA **C/VW:** Rockland Family Shelter, Care Net Pregnancy Center, Church
Email: lafsoie@verizon.net

Christina Jeannetti

Title: President **Company:** New York Crew Power, Inc. **Address:** 10220 159th Road, Howard Beach, NY 11414 United States **BUS:** Entertainment Production **P/S:** Production and Technical Crew Services **MA:** Regional **D/D/R:** Transforming a Venue into a Production Location, Utilizing Lighting Designers and Board Operators for Events Including Fashion Shows, Corporate Events, Meetings and Entertainment Program Productions, Overseeing Customer Satisfaction, Hiring New Personnel **H/I/S:** Spending Time with her Family, Traveling **EDU:** Coursework in Business Administration and Secretarial Studies, Berkeley College
Email: nycrewpower@aol.com
URL: http://www.newyorkcrewpower.com

Jeremy C. Jeffers

Title: Business Development Manager, Senior Consultant **Company:** Terracon Consulting Engineers and Scientists **Address:** 11849 W. Executive Drive, Suite G, Boise, ID 83713 United States **BUS:** Consulting Engineering Firm **P/S:** Geotechnical Construction Materials, Facilities and Engineering Services **MA:** Regional **D/D/R:** Managing Business Development, Project Management for Commercial and Retail Development **H/I/S:** Showing and Racing Cars **EDU:** Bachelor of Architecture, University of Idaho (1981) **CERTS:** Licensed Architect, States of Washington, Idaho, Montana, Utah and Nevada **A/A/S:** Director, Idaho Chapter, Construction Specifications Institute; Idaho District Council, Urban Land Institute; Building Owners and Managers Association of Boise; Idaho Chapter, United States Green Building Council; American Institute of Architects; International Code Council; International Conference of Shopping Centers; Institute of Store Planners; National Council of Architectural Registration Board **C/VW:** American Red Cross; United Way
Email: jcjeffers@terracon.com
URL: http://www.terracon.com

Shiou Jefferson

Title: President **Company:** Twin Dragon Restaurant **Address:** 3021 S. Broadway, Englewood, CO 80113 United States **BUS:** Restaurant **P/S:** Fine Dining, Mandarin-Style Cuisine, Gift Shop Including Imported Beers **MA:** Regional **D/D/R:** Managing Business Operations **H/I/S:** Gardening, Reading **EDU:** Master of Science in Economics, Kinki University, Japan (1975); Bachelor of Science in Education, National Taiwan University (1972) **A/A/S:** Chamber of Commerce
Email: joejefferson2002@yahoo.com
URL: http://www.twindragontrading.com

Dawn C. Jeffery

Title: Sales Account Director **Company:** Evans Distribution Systems **Address:** 28077 Roan Drive, Warren, MI 48093 United States **BUS:** Logistic Company **P/S:** Warehousing, Distribution and Pallet Delivery Service of Hazardous and Non-Hazardous Chemicals **MA:** National **EXP:** Ms. Jeffery's expertise is in sales. **D/D/R:** Making Appointments, Composing Contracts and Insurance for Start-up Business, Managing Follow-up Service Issues **EDU:** Associate Degree in Marketing, Macomb Community College (2007)
Email: dawn.jeffery@velocityexp.com
URL: http://www.velocityexpress.com

Douglas M. Jendras

Title: Senior Vice President **Company:** Above Net Communications **Address:** 360 Hamilton Avenue, White Plains, NY 10601 United States **BUS:** Telecommunications Company **P/S:** Optical Networks **MA:** International **EXP:** Mr. Jendras' expertise includes operations and finance. **H/I/S:** Playing Basketball, Softball, Reading, Hiking, Camping **EDU:** Master of Business Administration in Financial Management, Pace University; Bachelor's Degree in Social Science, Concentration in Psychology, SUNY Albany **C/VW:** Volunteer Basketball and Softball Coach
Email: djendras@above.net
URL: http://www.above.net

Brenda G. Jenkins

Title: Master Teacher **Company:** DC Public Schools **Dept:** C. Melvin Sharpe Health School **Address:** 4300 13th Street N.W., Washington, DC 20011 United States **BUS:** Nonprofit Organization **P/S:** Education for Children with Disabilities **MA:** Regional **D/D/R:** Teaching Children Ages Three through 18 with Disabilities Including Blindness, Deafness and Cerebral Palsy **H/I/S:** Cooking, Sewing, Singing, Teaching Aerobics, Dancing, Writing Poetry, Cheerleading **EDU:** Advanced Certificate of Graduate Studies in Special Education (1975); Master of Education in Early Childhood Education, Howard University (1972) **A/A/S:** Bison Foundation, Inc.; Theta Alpha Chapter, Kappa Delta Pi; Council for Exceptional Children; Pi Lambda Theta; Association for Supervision and Curriculum Development **A/H:** Teacher of the Year (1998); Howard University Athletic Hall of Fame (1995)
URL: http://www.boundlessplaygrounds.org

Gwendolyn D. Jenkins

Title: Director **Company:** 1) First Missionary Baptist Church Child Care Center 2) Pre-School **Address:** 200 Avenue R N.W., Winter Haven, FL 33881 United States **BUS:** 1) Church 2) Elementary School **P/S:** 1) Ministry Services 2) Primary Education **MA:** Local **EXP:** Ms. Jenkins' expertise is in elementary education. **D/D/R:** Creating Preschool Programs, Teaching Children from Ages 2 through 5, Utilizing the A Beka Program **H/I/S:** Walking, Jogging, Traveling **EDU:** Associate of Science in Early Childhood Education, Polk Community College, FL (2006) **A/A/S:** Association of Christian Schools International
Email: ngjenkins3@verizon.net

Lynn M. Jenkins

Title: Owner, Director **Company:** Magnolia Connections-Childcare, Education, Support Center **Address:** 18930 Green Meadow, Magnolia, TX 77355 United States **BUS:** Childcare Nonprofit **P/S:** Free Childcare for Teen Mothers, Support, Counseling and Education and Offers Discounted Rates for Other Members of the Community **MA:** Local **D/D/R:** Intervention Specialist, Works Directly with Junior High and High School Students at the Discipline Campus, At Risk Youth that are Having Problems with Drugs and Alcohol, Performs a Full Assessment after 30 Days of the Initial Program, Teaches Alcohol, Tobacco and Drug Classes as the Discipline Campus **H/I/S:** Spending Time with her Son and Daughter, Cats and Likes to Garden **EDU:** Bachelor of Science in Business, University of California, Santa Barbara **CERTS:** Certified Intervention Specialist, LCDC **A/A/S:** Member of the Counselor Association, Teaches a Class Called Reconnecting Youth and is also a Chemical Dependency and Intervention Specialist for the Magnolia ISD DEAP, Involved with the Society of Samaritans and also works with Baby and ME, offering a Home for Teen Mothers

Ronald D. Jenkins

Title: Doctor, Cardiologist **Company:** Heart Clinics Northwest **Address:** 700 Ironwood Drive, Suite 350, Coeur D Alene, ID 83814 **BUS:** Group Cardiology Practice **P/S:** Healthcare **MA:** Regional **EXP:** Dr. Jenkins' expertise includes cardiology, cardiac catheterization and cardiac services. **H/I/S:** Skiing **EDU:** MD, University of Utah; Bachelor of Science Chemistry, University of Utah **CERTS:** Board Certified in Internal Medicine, Cardiovascular Disease and Nuclear Medicine **A/A/S:** American College of Cardiology
Email: ronjenkins@hcnw.com
URL: http://www.hcnw.com

Mrs. Valerie A. Jenne

Title: Manager, Carrier Operations **Company:** Ball Corporation **Address:** 9300 W. 108th Circle, Broomfield, CO 80021 United States **BUS:** Manufacturing Company **P/S:** Aluminum Beverage Cans, Food Cans, Aerosol Products and Plastics **MA:** International **EXP:** Mrs. Jenne's expertise includes logistics and mediation. **H/I/S:** Drawing Cartoons, Writing, Illustrating **A/A/S:** Denver Transportation Club **C/VW:** United Way
Email: vjenne@comcast.net
Email: valerie.jenne@cwwemail.com

Mark G. Jennings

Title: Executive Director, Founder **Company:** Foundation of Character Development **Address:** 6116 Misty Way, Longmont, CO 80503 United States **BUS:** Nonprofit Organization **P/S:** Community Services Including Promoting Ethical Integrity for Adults, Youths and Children **MA:** National **D/D/R:** Managing Executive Operations **H/I/S:** Traveling, Making and Designing Cabinets, Scuba Diving, Attending the Theater **EDU:** Master of Education; Bachelor's Degree in Industrial Arts, Colorado State University **A/A/S:** Capital Area Metropolitan Planning Organization; Blacktie-Colorado; American Counseling Association; Metro Volunteers; ICF; U.S. Life Coach Association **C/VW:** World Wildlife Foundation; Doctors Without Borders; Botanical Gardens; Denver Art Museum
Email: ethics@ffcd.us
URL: http://www.ffcd.us

Stephanie Jennings-Stratford

Title: Chief Executive Officer, Realtor **Company:** Stratford Group/Long Foster Realty **Address:** 6315 Elmhurst Street, District Heights, MD 20747 United States **BUS:** Ministry/Real Estate Consulting/Broker **P/S:** A Consulting firm for the organizational design for small churches/Residential Real Estate **MA:** Local **D/D/R:** Consulting in ministry/Residential Real Estate **H/I/S:** Interior Design **EDU:** Coursework, Howard University
Email: thestratfordgroup@yahoo.com
URL: www.freewebs.com

Mr. Mark D. Jensen

Title: President **Company:** Mark's Lawn Service, Inc. **Address:** 10484 Maple Valley Drive, Maple Grove, MN 55369 United States **BUS:** Landscaping Company **P/S:** Thorough Property Maintenance Including Mowing, Snow Removal Lawn and Landscaping Services for Residential and Commercial Properties **MA:** Regional **D/D/R:** Maintaining and Designing Landscapes for Private Homes and Business Properties, Running the Daily Operations of the Company, Offering Exceptional Individualized Customer Service, Overseeing Landscaping Design, Installation and Irrigation **H/I/S:** Football, Camping, Boating, Snowmobiling **EDU:** Associate Degree in Business, Brainerd Community College (1976)
Email: mardoujen@earthlink.net

Susan Dinkel Jensen

Title: Assistant News Director, Anchor **Company:** WTHI-TV 10 **Address:** 918 Ohio Street, Terre Haute, IN 47807 United States **BUS:** Broadcast Media Company **P/S:** Television News **MA:** Local **D/D/R:** Reporting News, Anchoring Midday Newscasts, Supervising Anchors **EDU:** Bachelor's Degree in Mass Communications, DePaul University (1995); Bachelor's Degree in Sociology and Geography, DePaul University 1995)
Email: sdinkel@wthitv.com
URL: http://www.wthitv.com

Michael Jereb

Title: Owner **Company:** Creative Drywall **Address:** 2067 Mount Oso Court, Antioch, CA 94531 United States **BUS:** Drywall Company **P/S:** Drywall, Custom Design Textures **MA:** Local **D/D/R:** Overseeing Company Operations, Project Estimating and Proposals, Hiring **H/I/S:** Remodeling his Home **EDU:** Seminar on Leadership Skills, University of Notre Dame; Pursuing Contractor License **C/VW:** Childhood Leukemia Foundation, Make-A-Wish Foundation
Email: michaeljereb@sbcglobal.net

Julie A. Jernigan

Title: Senior Officer's Assistant **Company:** Commerce Bank **Dept:** Commercial Real Estate **Address:** 1701 Marlton Pike E., Cherry Hill, NJ 08003 United States **BUS:** Financial Institution **P/S:** Personal Banking Services, Business Banking Services, Investment Services, Personal and Business Insurance, Checking and Savings Accounts, Loans, Mortgages, Consulting Services **MA:** National **D/D/R:** Commercial Real Estate Lending Administration, Overseeing Event Management, Training and Development of New Employees and Work Flow Control. **H/I/S:** Art, Dancing **EDU:** Bachelor's Degree in Education, Gwynedd-Mercy College (1998) **A/H:** Commerce Bank WOW awards winner for Top Commercial Real Estate Administrative Assistant for 2007
Email: julie.jernigan@yesbank.com
URL: http://bank.commerceonline.com

William F. Jesse

Title: Supervisor of Operations **Company:** Herb Kilmer and Sons Flagstone **Address:** P.O. Box 18, Kingsley, PA 18826 United States **BUS:** Natural Science Manufacturer **P/S:** Natural Stone/Transportation **MA:** Local **D/D/R:** Supervising Operations **H/I/S:** Automobiles-Mustangs

Eric W. Jessiman

Title: Consultant **Company:** Solutions and Alternatives **BUS:** Transportation Consultancy **P/S:** Developing Alternatives to Idling Engines, Consulting, Information **MA:** Northeast **D/D/R:** Field Experience, Reducing Global Warming, Idle Reduction **H/I/S:** Traveling, Skiing, Caring for his Horses, Restoring Tractors, Spending Time with his Grandchildren, Sailing **EDU:** Associate Degree in Business, Niagara County Community College, 1968 **A/A/S:** Former Member, Maintenance Council, Society of Automotive Engineers **C/VW:** Bakersfield Historical Society, New York State School Districts
Email: jessiman@ncctv.net

Nilesh Kumar Jethwa

Title: Broker **Company:** RE/MAX Coastal Properties **Address:** 353 Military Cutoff Road, Wilmington, NC 28405 United States **BUS:** Real Estate Agency **P/S:** Residential and Commercial Property Sales **MA:** Regional **D/D/R:** Marketing and Selling Residential Real Estate **H/I/S:** Soccer, Golfing
Email: nileshjethwa@ec.rr.com
URL: http://www.dianeperryco.com

Kenneth L. Jewel

Title: President, Medical Doctor **Company:** Montclair Radiology **Address:** 1140 Bloomfield Avenue, West Caldwell, NJ 07006 United States **BUS:** Full Service Radiology Office **P/S:** MRI and CT Scanning, Ultrasound, Bone Density **MA:** Regional **EXP:** Mr. Jewel's expertise is in diagnostic radiology. **D/D/R:** Conducting MRI Scans **H/I/S:** Playing Tennis **EDU:** MD, SUNY at Buffalo; Fellowship, Columbia-Presbyterian Medical Center **C/VW:** Columbia Presbyterian Medical Center
Email: kjjewel1@aol.com
URL: http://www.montclairradiology.com

Claudia E. Jimenez

Title: Respiratory Therapist **Company:** United Medical Consultants **Address:** 10039 Umberland Place, Boca Raton, FL 33428 United States **BUS:** Private Healthcare Center **P/S:** Consulting Services, Treatments for Terminally Ill Patients Including Cystic Fibrosis and Other Congenital Diseases **MA:** Local **D/D/R:** Caring for Patients in their Homes, Treating Patients from Birth, Evaluating Patients with Respiratory and Other Cardiopulmonary Disorders **H/I/S:** Reading, Playing Volleyball, Swimming, Listening to Music **CERTS:** Certified Respiratory Therapist, Miami Respiratory Therapy Institute (1987) **A/A/S:** American Association for Respiratory Care
Email: clausjimenez@yahoo.com

Waleska Jimenez

Title: Human Resource Specialist **Company:** Biovail Laboratories **Address:** Call Box 1352, Dorado, PR 00646 United States **BUS:** One of the World's Leading Specialty Pharmaceutical Companies **P/S:** Anti-Depressant and Diabetes Medication **MA:** International **D/D/R:** Overseeing Recruitment and Staffing, Working on Policy Development, Creating Profiles of Employees **H/I/S:** Volunteering with Animal Shelters and Community Organizations **EDU:** Bachelor of Arts in Computer Science and Mathematics, University of Puerto Rico (1998) **CERTS:** Certified Professional in Human Resources, Society for Human Resource Management (2006) **A/A/S:** Society for Human Resource Management
Email: waleska.jimenez@biovail.com

Nancy Jiosa

Title: Notary Public **Company:** Independent Notary **Address:** 1205 Marguerite Way, Newberg, OR 97132 United States **BUS:** Financial, Mobile Notary **P/S:** Finance **MA:** Local **EXP:** Ms. Jiosa's expertise is in loan documents. **H/I/S:** Traveling **EDU:** College Coursework; Mounthood Community College; High School Graduate
Email: jiosa02@msn.com
URL: http://www.cambridgewhoswho.com

Hyun S. Jo

Title: Interior Decorator **Company:** Jo's Draperywork Room **Address:** 11006 Washington Street, Omaha, NE 68137 United States **BUS:** Sole Proprietor of Decorating Business **P/S:** Interior Decorating **MA:** Regional **D/D/R:** Interior Decorating and Sewing for Window Treatments **H/I/S:** Music, Singing **EDU:** Pursuing Associate Degree in Interior Design, Metro Community College **CERTS:** Certification, International Associate (2006) **A/A/S:** Faith Presbyterian Church; Chancel Choir
Email: moogoongwha1@yahoo.com

Tommie M. Jobe

Title: Public Health Educator **Company:** New York City Education & Community Partnership Unit **Address:** 253 Broadway, 12th Floor, New York, NY 10007 United States **BUS:** Government Agency **P/S:** Public Health Education, Counseling and Marketing **MA:** Local **D/D/R:** Educating Families and Pregnant Women, Training New Staff Members, Counseling **H/I/S:** Reading, Cooking, Traveling, Listening to Smooth Jazz, Traveling on Jazz Cruises, Attending Jazz Festivals **EDU:** Master's Degree in Marketing and Public Relations, New York University **A/A/S:** Black Women's Health Study; American Marketing Association **C/VW:** Alvin Ailey Dance Theater of Harlem; American Cancer Society
Email: tjobe@health.nyc.gov
URL: http://www.cambridgewhoswho.com

Charmaine L. Jodeh, BSN, ACRN

Title: Director of Nursing **Company:** Health in Home Services, Inc. **Address:** 1673 Fillmore Street, Denver, CO 80206 United States **BUS:** Residential Care Center **P/S:** Residential Care Services **MA:** Regional **D/D/R:** Caring for AIDS Patients, Consulting with Hospitals, Supervising the Staff, Treating Patients with Spinal Cord Injuries, Overseeing Geriatric Care Nursing **H/I/S:** Walking, Bicycling, Knitting, Crocheting **EDU:** Bachelor's Degree in Health Administration, Saint Francis Medical Center College of Nursing, IL **CERTS:** Certified HIV Nurse **A/A/S:** Home Care Association of Colorado; Association of Nurses in AIDS Care; The American Nurses Association; National Association for Home Care and Hospice
Email: cjodeh771@aol.com

Carol A. John

Title: Nurse Practitioner, Marriage and Family Therapist **Company:** Peace Health Medical Group **Address:** 4010 Aerial Way, Eugene, OR 97402 United States **BUS:** Medical Center **P/S:** Healthcare Including Mental Healthcare Services **MA:** Local **EXP:** Ms. John's expertise is in psychiatric. **H/I/S:** Woodworking, Traveling, Gardening **EDU:** Master's Degree in Marriage and Family Therapy, Newslines College; Bachelor of Science in Social Work, University of Oregon **A/H:** Nurse Practitioner of the Year Award (2001) **C/VW:** Local Church
Email: lencarol1@yahoo.com
URL: http://www.cambridgewhoswho.com

Ms. Barbara A. Johns

Title: Customer Sales Representative, Agent **Company:** Bilhartz Allstate Agency **Address:** 4100 S. E. Adams Road, Suite F 104, Bartlesville, OK 74006 United States **BUS:** Insurance Agency **P/S:** Insurance **MA:** National **D/D/R:** Overseeing Customer Satisfaction **H/I/S:** Exercising, Reading, Collecting Antiques, Collecting Cookery Books **EDU:** College Coursework; High School Diploma **A/A/S:** President Xi Theta Chapter Beta Sigma Phi, Past President, BMPW Organization, ABWA, Stillwater Credit Women's Club
Email: barbarajohns@allstate.com

Adrienne Johnson

Title: Managing Director of Operations, Partner **Company:** Recovery Management Advisors, Inc. **Address:** 31 High Street, New Britain, CT 06051 United States **BUS:** National Subrogation and Collection Services Company **P/S:** Claims Subrogation and Debt Collection Programs for Insurance Companies **MA:** Regional **D/D/R:** Managing Premium Audit Recovery; Overseeing Property, Auto, Medical Insurance and Reinsurance, Communicating with Insurance Companies **H/I/S:** Scrapbooking, Traveling, Golfing **EDU:** Bachelor of Arts in Legal Services, Bay Path College (2003) **A/A/S:** Member National Association of Subrogation Professionals; American Cancer Society; Volunteer, United Way; Northwest Connecticut Arts Council; Former Leader, Mentor and Trainer, Girl Scouts of the USA; Toastmasters International
Email: arienne@rmadvisors.com
URL: http://www.rmadvisors.com

Alma L. Johnson

Title: Lead Teacher **Company:** P4K P.S. 81 **Address:** 530 Stanley Avenue, Brooklyn, NY 11207 United States **BUS:** School **P/S:** Education **MA:** Local **D/D/R:** Teaching Special Education, Monitoring All Classrooms, Teaching All Programs that are Available to Special Education Students, Covering All Curriculum Areas, Helping Students Pass State Tests, Making Assessments **H/I/S:** Designing and Building New Homes, Fishing, Shooting Targets **EDU:** Master of Arts in Elementary Education, Adelphi University; Master of Arts in Special Education, Adelphi University; Bachelor of Science in Elementary Education, Medgar Evers College; Associate of Applied Science in Liberal Arts, New York City Community College **A/H:** Mother of the Year Award (1985); Medgar Evers Outstanding Teacher Award (1984); Effie Brown Award for Outstanding Teaching (1977)
Email: sendb@aol.com
URL: http://www.cambridgewhoswho.com

Dr. Arla Janeen Johnson

Title: Executive Administrative Assistant **Company:** American Federation of Government Employees **Address:** 6800 Park Ten Boulevard, Suite 296W, San Antonio, TX 78213 United States **BUS:** Government Agency **P/S:** Union for Federal Employees **MA:** National **EXP:** Dr. Johnson's expertise is in fiduciary management. **H/I/S:** Singing, Reading, Traveling **EDU:** Master of Arts in Arts Administration, University of the Incarnate Word **A/A/S:** Alpha Kappa Alpha **C/VW:** Local Church
Email: arlajaneen@aol.com
Email: johnsa@afge.org
URL: http://www.afgedistrict10.org

Barbara M. Johnson, Esq.

Title: Attorney at Law, Partner (Retired) **Company:** Choate, Hall and Stewart, LLP **Address:** 2 International Place, Boston, MA 02110 United States **BUS:** Law Firm **P/S:** Legal Services Including Investment Consulting, Litigating for Corporate, Intellectual Property, Wealth Management and Real Estate Law **MA:** International **D/D/R:** Practicing Corporate and Security Law, Assisting Information Technology Companies, Consulting on Equity and Financing **EDU:** JD, Boston College Law School, Magna Cum Laude (1993) **A/A/S:** Boston Bar Association; Massachusetts Bar Association; American Bar Association; MIT Sloan School of Management; Former Judge, Business Plan Competition
Email: tammy@gypsiesinthepalace.net
URL: http://www.choate.com

Beverly J. Johnson

Title: Abstractor, Researcher **Company:** Quality Research Services **Address:** 814 Barbara Drive, Craig, CO 81625 United States **BUS:** Title Research Company **P/S:** Land and Mineral Title Research **MA:** Regional **EXP:** Ms. Jonhson's expertise includes oil and gas mineral research. **H/I/S:** Golfing, Boating, Hunting, Hiking **A/A/S:** President, Quality Research; National Notary Association; Notary Agents Online; PRRN **C/VW:** United Way
Email: bjohnson@gctal.net

Carla J. Johnson

Title: President **Company:** Water Wellness Workouts, Inc **Address:** 3085 Sycamore Spring Road, Mountain Home, AR 72653 United States **BUS:** Fitness Internet **P/S:** Water Workout, Exercise CD ROMs **MA:** National **EXP:** Ms. Johnson's expertise includes water and personal fitness. **H/I/S:** Spending Time with Nature **EDU:** LSUS, Master of Education **A/A/S:** Member of Aquatic Exercise Association, 4 Certifications-US Water Fitness Association, CPR Certified
Email: carla@waterwellnessworkouts.com
URL: www.waterwellnessworkouts.com

Coleathia A. Johnson, LVN

Title: Licensed Vocational Nurse, Charge Nurse **Company:** Oak Groves Nursing Home **Address:** 5718 Myrtle Street, Orange, TX 77630 United States **BUS:** Nursing Home **P/S:** Healthcare **MA:** Regional **D/D/R:** Monitoring Heart Patients, Overseeing Staff, Coordinating Hospice Care for Geriatrics Patients **H/I/S:** Reading, Spending Time Outdoors, Participating in Fishing Tournaments **EDU:** Pursuing Associate Degree **CERTS:** Licensed Vocational Nurse, Lamar University (1999); Certification in Personal Financial Planning, West Jefferson Hospital (1985); Certification in 12 Lead Electrocardiogram Training, Delgado Community College, Louisiana; Certification in CPR **C/VW:** Volunteer, Band and Athletics Booster Clubs; Volunteer, First Responder, Local Fire Department
Email: cajunbayounurses5@yahoo.com
Email: cajunbayounurses5@aol.com

Ms. Darla J. Johnson

Title: Inspector **Company:** Waltek, Inc. **Address:** 14310 Sunfish Lake Boulevard, Ramsey, MN 55303 United States **BUS:** Manufacturing Company **P/S:** Aluminum and Steel Casting **MA:** International **D/D/R:** Accounting, Utilizing her People Management and Learning Skills **C/VW:** Volunteer, University of Minnesota; United Way
Email: darla.johnson@cwwemail.com
URL: http://www.cambridgewhoswho.com

Deana M. Johnson

Title: Orchestra Director **Company:** Rudder Middle School and Youth Orchestra of San Antonio **Address:** 7754 Oakhill Park Ride, San Antonio, TX 78249 United States **BUS:** Music Education **P/S:** Youth Orchestras **MA:** Regional **D/D/R:** Directing an Orchestra of 125 Kids with a Strong Emphasis on Reading, Performing with the San Antonio Symphony **H/I/S:** Gardening, Baseball **EDU:** Bachelor of Arts in Performance, University of Rochester (1982); Bachelor of Arts in Education, University of Rochester **A/A/S:** Texas Orchestra Directors Association; Former Educator, Texas State University at San Marcos
Email: deannajohnson@nisd.net
URL: http://www.nisd.net

Dudley C. Johnson
Title: Coordinator Community Programs **Company:** Aurora College **Address:** 10 Mackenzie Road, Norman Wells, X0E0V0 Canada **BUS:** School **P/S:** Professor of Biology **MA:** International **D/D/R:** Coroner, Liquor Inspector, Marriage Commissioner, Justice of the Peace, Notary Public **EDU:** Master's Degree in Administration, Bachelor of Science, Bachelor's Degree in Education, University of Newfoundland

Eleanor L. Johnson
Title: American History Teacher **Company:** Jamesville-DeWitt High School **Address:** P.O. Box 606, Syracuse, NY 13214 United States **BUS:** High School **P/S:** Secondary Education **MA:** Local **D/D/R:** Teaching American History for Seventh through 12-Grade Students **H/I/S:** Traveling, Reading, History, Researching the Early Settlers in Upstate NY, **EDU:** Master's Degree in Asian Studies, Syracuse University (1963); Bachelor of Art in American History, University of Rochester (1954) **A/A/S:** DeWitt Historical Preservation Committee; Town of Onondaga Historical Society; National Teachers' Association; New York State Retired Teachers' Association; DeWitt-Logan Retired Teachers Association **C/VW:** Local Church
Email: EleanorL.Johnson@cwwemail.com
URL: http://www.cambridgewhoswho.com

Ellen K. Johnson
Title: Learning Specialist **Company:** Andover Public Schools **Address:** 30 Bartlet Street, Andover, MA 01810 United States **BUS:** Public School System **P/S:** General Elementary and Secondary Curriculum, Arts, Music, Physical Education, Foreign Language Instruction, Special Programs, Learning Resources, Student Support Services, Athletics, Extracurricular Activities, Student Clubs and Organizations **MA:** Local **D/D/R:** Working with at-Risk Students, Managing Reading, Phonological Awareness Study, Skill Development and Achievement Programs, Overseeing Curriculum Development Plans, Meeting with the Student Success Team, Creating and Developing Plans to Assist Academically-Challenged Students, Assessing and Implementing Curriculum Initiatives **H/I/S:** Reading, Gardening **EDU:** Master's Degree in Speech Science and Communication Disorders, Emerson College, Boston, Massachusetts (1997); Bachelor of Arts in Special Education, Keene State College, Keene, New Hampshire (1979) **CERTS:** Pursuing Certificate of Advanced Graduate Study in Educational Leadership, Salem State College **A/A/S:** American Speech-Language-Hearing Association
Email: ejohnson@aps1.net
URL: http://www.aps1.net

Ms. Georgia L. Johnson
Title: Educational Aide III **Company:** Lausd Barrett Elementary School **Address:** 419 W. 98th Street, Los Angeles, CA 90003 United States **BUS:** Elementary School **P/S:** Education **MA:** Local **D/D/R:** Teaching First-Grade Mathematics, English and Social Studies, Babysitting, Tutoring Privately **H/I/S:** Reading Novels, Spending Time with her Family, Helping Children **EDU:** Coursework in General Education, Los Angeles City College
Email: jsjemjson5@sbcglobal.net

Hazel M. Johnson, GRI, CRS
Title: Realtor **Company:** Edina Realty, Inc **Address:** 990 Elm Street E., Suite 100, Annandale, MN 55302 United States **BUS:** Real Estate Broker **P/S:** Residential and Commercial Real Estate **MA:** Local **A/A/S:** National Realtors Association, St Cloud MLS

James E. Johnson
Title: Exclusive Agent **Company:** Allstate Offices of James Johnson **Address:** 2839 Suncrest Drive, Suite D, Jackson, MS 39212 United States **BUS:** Insurance Financial **P/S:** All Insurance Products and Services **MA:** Local **D/D/R:** Overseeing All Operations **H/I/S:** Chess and Traveling **EDU:** Mississippi College, University of New Orleans, NOBTS, Master's in Mathematics Education, Doctorate in Mathematics, Master's in Music **A/A/S:** Life Underwriters Association, National Life Underwriting Association
Email: a084484@allstate.com

Janet D. Johnson
Title: Administrative Assistant **Company:** Verizon Communications **Address:** 2171 Madison Avenue, New York, NY 10037 United States **BUS:** Verizon Communications/Media **P/S:** Public Services for Telephone, Computer, Etc **MA:** National **EXP:** Ms. Johnson's expertise is in cultural affairs. **EDU:** Lehman College, NYC Tech College, Bachelor of Art, Associate Degree

Jhamal D. Johnson
Title: Senior Systems Engineer **Company:** Raytheon Missile Systems **Address:** 7825 N. Coltrane Lane, Tucson, AZ 85743 United States **BUS:** Government Defense and Aerospace Systems Supplier **P/S:** Defense and Government Electronics, Space, Information Technology, Technical Services and Business Aviation and Special Mission Aircraft **MA:** International **D/D/R:** Testing and Supporting Communication System Specifications, Flight Testing Support, Requirement Analysis **H/I/S:** Golfing, Outdoor Sports **EDU:** Bachelor of Science Degree in Electrical Engineering, Tuskegee University (1998) **A/A/S:** National Society of Black Engineers; Eta Kappa Nu Electrical Engineer Honor Society
Email: jhamal74@msn.com

Juanita M. Johnson
Title: Elementary Educator **Company:** Boston Public Schools, J.F.K. Elementary School **Address:** 7 Bolster Street, Boston, MA 02130 United States **BUS:** Elementary School **P/S:** Elementary Education **MA:** Local **D/D/R:** Teaching All Subjects to Students in Grades Three to Five **H/I/S:** Traveling, Reading, Dancing, Singing in Choir **EDU:** Bachelor of Science in Education, Bishop College, 1971; Associate Degree in Archaeological Studies, Boston University, 1974 **A/A/S:** National Education Association; Massachusetts Education Association; American Federation of Teachers; Stepping Stones; Awarded the Hewlett Packard Scholarship Award for Graduate Studies **C/VW:** Girl Scouts of the USA, People's Baptist Church of Boston; Earth Watch, Inc.; New England Conservatory Millennium Choir
URL: http://www.cambridgewhoswho.com

Judy C. Johnson
Title: Broker **Company:** Re/Max United **Address:** 18 Atlantic Avenue, Benson, NC 27504 United States **BUS:** Real Estate Broker **P/S:** Residential, Executive Homes, Lake Front Homes, New Construction, Gated, Seniors, Horse Properties **MA:** National **D/D/R:** Selling Residential and Commercial Land **H/I/S:** Sings in Choir at Church **EDU:** Bachelor of Science in Business Administration, Campbell University **A/A/S:** North Carolina Association of Realtors, National Association of Realtors
Email: j.johnson@charter.net
URL: www.realtor.com/judyjohnson

Keith E. Johnson
Title: Research Fellow **Company:** University of Regina **Address:** 3737 Wascana Parkway, Regina, S4S 0A2 Canada **BUS:** University **P/S:** Education and Research **MA:** International **D/D/R:** Writing Research Papers and Reviews Regarding Ionic Liquids **H/I/S:** Walking, French Music, Classical Music, Particularly by Saint-Saens **EDU:** Doctor of Science in Chemistry, London, England **A/A/S:** Fellow, Canadian Institute of Chemistry; American Chemical Society; Electrochemical Society
Email: keith.johnson@uregina.ca

Kevin P. Johnson
Title: General Engineer, HVAC/R Technician, Teacher **Company:** Kanakanuk Hospital **Address:** P.O. Box 130, Dillingham, AK 99576 United States **BUS:** Hospital **P/S:** Healthcare **MA:** Local **D/D/R:** Hospital Ventilation, Air Conditioning and Refrigeration Technician and Maintenance **H/I/S:** Sports Fishing **CERTS:** Certified HVAC/R Technician, Trade School
Email: kpjohnson@bbahc.org
URL: http://www.cambridgewhoswho.com

Linda W. Johnson
Title: Owner, President **Company:** Designs by L. Wallace, Inc. **Address:** 8 Ribera Way, Hot Springs Village, AR 71909 United States **BUS:** Interior Design Firm **P/S:** Furniture, Fabric Finishes, Residential, Commercial **MA:** Regional **EXP:** Ms. Johnson's expertise includes residential and commercial designs and interior decoration. **D/D/R:** Redecorating for People who have Lived in their Homes for a While, Overseeing Four Employees, Consulting, Lecturing **H/I/S:** Golfing, Traveling **A/A/S:** Hot Springs Village Rotary
Email: designsby1wallac@aol.com
URL: http://www.cambridgewhoswho.com

Mark L. Johnson, BS
Title: President **Company:** Maleko Built, Inc. **Address:** 73-1397 Hamiha Street, Kailua Kona, HI 96740 United States **BUS:** Construction Company **P/S:** Commercial and Residential Construction Services **MA:** Local **D/D/R:** Inspecting Sites, Remodeling and Interior Designing for Commercial and Residential Buildings, Overseeing Construction Projects **H/I/S:** Scuba Diving **EDU:** Bachelor of Science in Business Administration, California State University, Fresno (1983) **A/A/S:** United States Chamber of Commerce; Better Business Bureau **C/VW:** Volunteer, Food Basket; Local Blood Bank
Email: mark_johnson@malekobuilt.com

Marlene Alberta Johnson
Title: Chairwoman **Company:** Huna Heritage Foundation **Address:** 9301 Glacier Highway, Juneau, AK 99801 United States **BUS:** Nonprofit Cultural and Heritage Restoration and Preservation Organization **P/S:** Long Term Financial Support for Cultural and Educational Programs through Investment Earnings **MA:** Regional **D/D/R:** Utilizing Knowledge of Indian Clan Culture, Conducting Workshops to Preserve, Record and Protect Culture of Huna People, Overseeing Youth Leadership Projects, Both Modern and within the Community, Handling Education Assistant Grants for Higher Education, Cultural and Vocational Education **H/I/S:** Gardening, Fishing, Skating **EDU:** Diploma, Juneau High School (1953) **A/A/S:** Trustee, Sealaska Heritage Institute; Former Director, Huna Totem Corporation; Board of Trustees, Alaska Chapter, Nature Conservatory; Native Affairs Committee, Robert Wood Johnson Foundation
Email: seagulls@acsalaska.net
URL: http://www.hunaheritage.org

Melinda Johnson
Title: Physician Assistant **Company:** South Gulf Coast Emergency Physicians **Address:** 13681 Doctor's Way, Fort Myers, FL 33912 United States **BUS:** Medical Center **P/S:** Healthcare Including Emergency Room Care **MA:** Regional **D/D/R:** Assisting Physicians, Treating Emergency Room Patients **EDU:** Master's Degree in Physician Assistant Studies, Barry University (2004) **CERTS:** Certified Physician Assistant **A/A/S:** Florida Academy of Physician Assistants; American Academy of Physician Assistants
Email: melindajean33@hotmail.com

Meredith S. Johnson
Title: Former Assistant to the Management Program Chair, Adjunct Faculty **Company:** Hodges University **Dept:** Kenneth Oscar Johnson School of Business **Address:** 4501 Colonial Boulevard, Fort Myers, FL 33966 United States **BUS:** University **P/S:** Higher Education **MA:** International **D/D/R:** Reading and Reviewing Student Submissions Including Research Papers, Case Analysis and Essays, Checking Papers for Spelling, Grammar, Punctuation, Format and APA Style, Teaching Management and Success Courses **H/I/S:** Playing Outdoors with Dogs, Riding Bike with NASCAR **EDU:** Pursuing Ph.D. in Applied Management and Design Science, Walden University; Master's Degree in Business Management, with a Concentration in Human Resources, Hodge University (2005) **A/A/S:** American Civil Liberties Union
Email: msjohnson10764@embarqmail.com
URL: http://www.internationalcollege.edu

Morris E. Johnson
Title: Owner **Company:** Mom's Electric and Repair **Address:** 2423 Fifth Street, Great Bend, KS 67530 United States **BUS:** Generators Retail **P/S:** Generators, Press Wash, Air Computers, Sales and Service **MA:** Local **EXP:** Mr. Johnson's expertise includes service and management. **H/I/S:** Houses **EDU:** Junior College, High School Diploma **A/A/S:** EJSA, Generator Repair Association, 40 Charities Donates to: Indian Preservations

Dr. Omolola O. Johnson
Title: Physician **Company:** Complete Healthcare, LLC **Address:** 809 N. Hammonds Ferry Road, Suite C, Linthicum, MD 21090 United States **BUS:** Medical Center, Private Practice for Internal Medicine and Pediatrics **P/S:** Healthcare **MA:** Local **EXP:** Dr. Johnson's expertise includes internal medicine and pediatrics. **H/I/S:** Listening to Jazz Music, Baking **EDU:** MD, University of Ibadan, Nigeria **A/A/S:** American Academy of Pediatrics **C/VW:** Disabled American Veterans
Email: aramidelola@aol.com

Priscilla Johnson
Title: Insurance Services Representative **Company:** Penn Prime **Address:** 414 N. Second Street, Harrisburg, PA 17101 United States **BUS:** Two Separate and Distinct Insurance Trusts **P/S:** Cost Effective Coverage for Property, Liability and Workers' Compensation to Pennsylvania Municipal Entities **MA:** Regional **D/D/R:** Customer Retention, First Point of Contact for Customers, Assisting the Director, Marketing Manager and Loss Control Managers, Working in Property, Casualty and Workers Compensation, Formerly Worked at an Insurance Company in Health Insurance **H/I/S:** Basketball Fan (76ers), Reading **EDU:** Pursuing Bachelor's Degree in Marketing; Industry-Related Coursework **A/A/S:** American Insurance Marketing and Sales Society; Insurance Professionals of Greater Harrisburg; Handling Presentations and Trainings for Work Place Safety Committees
Email: pjohnson@plcm.org
URL: http://www.pennprime.com

Renee A. Johnson
Title: President, Designer **Company:** Homes2Love **Address:** 4102 E. Indian School Road, Phoenix, AZ 85018 United States **BUS:** Home Staging Company **P/S:** Home Staging with Interior Design and Furniture Sales **MA:** Regional **EXP:** Ms. Johnson's expertise is in interior design. **D/D/R:** Overseeing Operations, Buying and Selling of New and Used Furniture, Staging Homes for Sales **H/I/S:** Home Decorating, Spending Time with her Family **EDU:** Bachelor of Fine Arts in Graphic Design, Northern Arizona University (1982) **CERTS:** Home Staging Certification, Association of Home Staging Professionals (2005) **A/A/S:** International Association of Home Staging Professionals
Email: reneeaj@hotmail.com
URL: http://www.homes2love.biz

Ricky Johnson
Title: President **Company:** Gulf Coast Centrifuge **Address:** 26343 Anderson Road, Magnolia, TX 77354 United States **BUS:** Global Leader in Centrifuge Manufacturing and Repairing **P/S:** Comprehensive Range of Flexible, Customized Product Solutions **MA:** International **D/D/R:** Overseeing All Employee Work, Handling the Day-to-Day Operations of a Facility, Speaking on New Products at Chemical Plants **H/I/S:** Hunting **EDU:** Coursework in Drafting and Engineering, University of Houston
Email: ricky@gulfcoastcentrifuge.com
URL: http://www.gulfcoastcentrifuge.com

Rosalind R. Johnson
Title: Special Police Officer **Company:** Hawk One Security **Address:** 1729 Alabama Avenue S.E., Unit 301, Washington, DC 20020 United States **BUS:** Security Service Provider **P/S:** Offering CCTV, Cameras an ID Check **MA:** Local **EXP:** Ms. Johnson's expertise is in the security of educational facilities. **H/I/S:** Reading, Games

Sandra Johnson
Title: Onsite Manager **Company:** Staffmark **Address:** 601 Memory Lane, York, PA 17402 United States **BUS:** Placement Service Company **P/S:** Placement Services **MA:** Regional **D/D/R:** Human Resources Staffing, Overseeing Applicant Tracking Systems, Networking with Companies, Sourcing for Candidates, Handling Training and Orientation, Tracking Applicants **H/I/S:** Spending Time with her Family, Reading **EDU:** Bachelor of Science in Management Information Systems, King's College (1994); Associate of Science in Business Administration, Raritan Valley Community College (1992) **A/A/S:** Human Resources Professionals Association
Email: sjohnson2570@yahoo.com
URL: http://www.cambridgewhoswho.com

Saundra K. Johnson
Title: Registered Nurse, Nurse Clinician III **Company:** Johns Hopkins Hospital-Sidney Kimmel Comprehensive Cancer Center **Address:** 401 N. Broadway, Baltimore, MD 21231 United States **BUS:** Hospital **P/S:** Healthcare, Hematology, Oncology **MA:** National **EXP:** Ms. Johnson's expertise includes team leadership, vascular access, PICC placement and bone marrow transplants. **H/I/S:** Traveling, Dining, Hiking **EDU:** Master of Science in Health Sciences and Healthcare Administration, Towson University, 2004; Bachelor of Science in Nursing, Towson University, 2007 **A/H:** 2007 Clinical Excellence Award **C/VW:** Volunteer, The Chocolate Affair; Healthcare for the Homeless
Email: johnssa@jhmi.edu

Steven M. Johnson, Ph.D.
Title: Human Resource Research Director **Company:** J.C. Penney **Address:** P.O. Box 10001, Dallas, TX 75031 United States **BUS:** Retail **P/S:** Department Store **MA:** National **D/D/R:** Industrial and Organizational Psychology, Community Services **H/I/S:** Spending Time with Family, Playing Sports such as Softball, Bowling **EDU:** Ph.D., Bowling Green State University; Master's Degree in Philosophy, Bowling Green State University; Bachelor of Science in Psychology, Denison University **A/A/S:** The Miracle League of Frisco, Texas; Society of Industrial Organizational Professionals; American Psychological Association; President, Frisco Soccer Youth Association **C/VW:** Soccer Youth Association of Frisco, Miracle League of Frisco
Email: smjohnso@jcpenney.com

Tanja Y. Johnson
Title: Full Time Student **Company:** Cleveland State Ubiversity **Address:** 3398 West 131st Street, Cleveland, OH 44111 United States **BUS:** Human Resources and Benefits Service Provider **P/S:** Health and Welfare Plans for Fortune 500 Companies **MA:** Local **EXP:** Ms. Johnson's expertise includes health and welfare administration. **H/I/S:** Jazz, Volleyball, Shooting Pool **EDU:** Pursuing Bachelor of Arts in Communications Management and Health Communications, Cleveland State University **A/A/S:** SHRM, WEB, Insurance Licenses-Accident & Health, Life and Variable Annuities
Email: tyjwvb@sbcglobal.net

Thais D. Johnson
Title: Speech and Language Pathologist **Company:** Westminster School District, Jessie Hayden Elementary School **Address:** 14127 Cedarwood Avenue, Westminster, CA 92683 United States **BUS:** School District **P/S:** Education **MA:** Local **D/D/R:** Speech and Language Pathology **H/I/S:** Practicing Yoga, Reading **EDU:** Master's Degree in Communicative Disorders, San Francisco State University; Bachelor's Degree in Communicative Disorders, California State University, Northridge **CERTS:** Certificate of Clinical Competency-Speech-Language Pathology **A/A/S:** American Speech-Language-Hearing Association; California Speech-Hearing-Language Association
Email: tdjohnson@wsd.k12.ca.us
URL: http://www.wsd.k12.ca.us

Pastor Trevor L. Johnson
Title: Pastor **Company:** Christ Tabernacle MBC **Address:** 2493 Atlantic Avenue, Long Beach, CA 90806 United States **BUS:** Religion Religion/Spiritual Services **P/S:** Pastoral Ministries and Marriage Ministries **MA:** Local **EXP:** Mr. Johnson's expertise includes leadership and community development. **A/A/S:** Southern Baptist Association
Email: revtj@hotmail.com

Wayne A. Johnson
Title: Executive Chef **Company:** Mayflower Park Hotel **Address:** 405 Olive Way, Seattle, WA 98101 United States **BUS:** Hotel **P/S:** Hospitality **MA:** Pacific Northwest **D/D/R:** Cooking Mediterranean Cuisine **H/I/S:** Reading, Traveling, Taking Cooking Courses, Caring for his Children, Cooking for Corporate Events and Weddings, Bowling, Hiking, Camping, Playing Softball **CERTS:** Certification, International Association of Culinary Professionals; Certification, Chef Collaboration **A/A/S:** International Association of Culinary Professionals, Chef Collaboration **C/VW:** March of Dimes, Providence Elder Center and Heritage House, Farmers' Coalition, African American Kidney Foundations, Pike Place, Food as Art, Auction for Washington Wines
Email: chefwaj@andaluca.com
URL: http://www.andaluca.com

Blanche Johnson Davis
Title: President **Company:** Trinity Theological Seminary of South Florida **Address:** 6255 33rd Manor, Vero Beach, FL 32966 United States **BUS:** Theological School **P/S:** Religious Education **MA:** Regional **D/D/R:** Overseeing All Seminary Sites, Developing Curriculum and Teaching **EDU:** Bachelor's Degree in Elementary Education and Early Childhood Education, Florida A&M University (1965) **A/A/S:** Pastor, Faith Temple Assembly Of God **A/H:** Nominee, Who's Who Among the Finest Teachers (Twice)
Email: blanchedavis@bellsouth.net
URL: http://www.trinitytheological-sfla.org

Ms. Alicia Johnson-Reed
Title: Director of Marketing and Communications **Company:** Alabama Shakespeare Festival **Address:** 1 Festival Drive, Montgomery, AL 36117 United States **BUS:** Theater Company **P/S:** Theater Productions, Festivals **MA:** Regional **D/D/R:** Marketing, Communications, Audience Development **H/I/S:** Gardening, Writing, Traveling **EDU:** Master's Degree in Arts Administration and Theater Management, University of Alabama **A/A/S:** Leader, Birmingham Chapter, Theatre Communications Group; Southeastern Theatre Conference; Delta Sigma Theta; Americans for the Arts **C/VW:** Magic City Art Connection
Email: ajohnson@asf.net
URL: http://www.asf.net

Donald B. Johnston
Title: Regional Manager **Company:** Los Angeles Baptist City Mission Society **Address:** 3325 Wilshire Boulevard, Suite 800, Los Angeles, CA 90010 United States **BUS:** Religious Society **P/S:** Administrative, Training and New Church Development Services **MA:** Regional **D/D/R:** Overseeing Company Finances and Human Resources **H/I/S:** Hiking in the Mountains of North California **EDU:** Master of Business Administration, California State University, Long Beach; Bachelor of Science, California State University, Long Beach **A/A/S:** Christian Management Association
Email: djb@abcla.org

Mary Selina Johnston
Title: Author, Realtor (Retired) **Address:** 1885 Courtyard Way, Apartment A105, Naples, FL 34112 United States **BUS:** Private Writing Practice **P/S:** Writing Children's Books and Memoirs **MA:** Local **D/D/R:** Writing Children's Books and Memoirs **H/I/S:** Photography, Reading, Writing, Swimming, Studying Opera **CERTS:** Registered Nurse; Licensed Realtor, State of Florida; Certification, American Red Cross **A/H:** Bronze Medallion Certificate, Granite Golf Club, Toronto **C/VW:** Branton Curling Club; Galt Curling Club; Calgary Horse Club
Email: maryselina.johnston@cwwemail.com

Rosalee D. Johnston
Title: Hearing Instrument Specialist **Company:** AVADA Hearing Care Center **Address:** Aberdeen, WA 98520 United States **BUS:** Medical Retail **P/S:** Hearing Instruments **MA:** National **D/D/R:** Checking Ear Canals, Administering Hearing, Speech and Bone Conduction Tests, Assessing the Comfort Level of Instruments, Explaining Uses and Maintenance of Products, Making Adjustments to Instruments **H/I/S:** Reading, Visiting Casinos, Spending Time with Family **CERTS:** Certified Hearing Instrument Fitter Dispenser (2003) **A/A/S:** Moose International

Willa I. Johnston
Title: General Partner **Company:** Putney Family Limited Partnership **Address:** 2700 S. Tabor Drive, Silver City, NM 88061 United States **BUS:** Construction Management Company **P/S:** Real Estate Acquisition and Renovation **MA:** CA, NM **D/D/R:** Real Estate Renovation, Interior Design, Making Decisions on Buying and Selling Property **H/I/S:** Golfing, Gardening, Reading, Interior Design **EDU:** Coursework in Real Estate, Computers and Interior Design; High School Education **CERTS:** Licensed Life and Health Insurance Broker
Email: willa.johnston@cwwemail.com
URL: http://www.cambridgewhoswho.com

Cedar Joiner
Title: President **Company:** Joiner Marketing & Promotions **Address:** 4706 Shavano Oak, Suite 102, San Antonio, TX 78249 United States **BUS:** Advertising, Marketing and Public Relations Agency **P/S:** Promotional Items Pens, Clothing, etc) Marketing Programs **MA:** National **EXP:** Ms. Joiner's expertise includes promotions and corporate marketing programs. **H/I/S:** Children's Hospital, Workout, Bicycling, Children **EDU:** University of Texas (San Antonio), State of Texas, Bachelor of Arts in Education, Teacher Certification **A/A/S:** American Cancer Society, Small Hispanic Women's Organization, San Antonio North Chamber of Commerce
Email: cedar@joinerpromotions.com
URL: www.joinerpromotions.com

Brandi L. Jolly
Title: Nurse, IGN **BUS:** Healthcare OB/GYN **P/S:** Emergency and ICU Care **MA:** Local **EXP:** Ms. Jolly's expertise is in patient care. **H/I/S:** Sleeping
Email: cjcjsmom@comcast.net

David L. Jonas
Title: Manager of Special Events **Company:** The United States Navy Memorial **Address:** 701 Pennsylvania Avenue N.W., Washington, DC 20004 United States **BUS:** Memorial Organization **P/S:** United States Navy Memorial **MA:** National **D/D/R:** Fundraising, Planning Events **H/I/S:** Singing in the Choir **EDU:** Bachelor of Arts in English and History, Ripon College **C/VW:** Human Rights Campaign, Whitman-Walker Clinic
Email: djevents@aol.com
URL: http://www.cambridgewhoswho.com

Albert Jones
Title: Civil Engineer, Masonry Instructor, Building Construction Technologist **Company:** California Department of Corrections and Rehabilitation **Address:** Sacramento, CA United States **BUS:** Government Department **P/S:** Correctional Facilities, Rehabilitation **MA:** California **D/D/R:** Building Construction Technology, Civil Engineering and Training, Rehabilitation of Human Resources **EDU:** Master of Art Degree, Smart Navy Education Training Center, Pensacola, FL; Graduate Coursework in Education, University of California at Los Angeles; Bachelor of Art in Human Resource Management, Pepperdine University, Malibu, California; Bachelor of Science in Liberal Arts, CUNY Excelsior College; Vocational Education Credentials in Building Construction Technology, Brick Masonry, Painting, Carpentry, Plastering, Business Administration, Human Resource Management, Industrial Management, Business **A/A/S:** CUCM United States Navy Seabeas (Retired); American Society of Civil Engineers **C/VW:** Minister; Scholarship Donations, Blythe High School
Email: albarber@aol.com

Anthony C. Jones
Title: Senior Vice President **Company:** State Department Federal Credit Union **Address:** 1630 King Street, Alexandria, VA 22314 United States **BUS:** Finance Credit Union **P/S:** Financial Service **MA:** International **EXP:** Mr. Jones' expertise is in executive management. **EDU:** Master's Degree in Human Resource Management, University of St Louis, Executive Master of Business Administration University of Maryland, Bachelor of Art in Marketing, South Carolina University **A/A/S:** AMA, National Black MBA Association, CUNA-Council Member, BPub Credit Union
Email: acjones@sdfcu.org
URL: www.sdfcu.org

Rev. Antonia L. Jones

Title: Pastor **Company:** Good Shepherd United Methodist Church **Address:** 6226 Arlington Boulevard, Richmond, CA 94805 United States **BUS:** Religion Church **P/S:** Pastorial Services, Mentoring, Counseling, Gospel **MA:** Local **D/D/R:** Ministering, Marriage and Family Counseling, Mentoring **H/I/S:** Music, Piano, Sports **EDU:** National University, City University, American Baptist Seminary of the West, Bell Grove Theological Seminary, Bachelor of Art in Business Administration, Master of Art in Human Behavior, Master of Art in Marriage and Family Counseling, Master's Degree in Divinity, Doctorate in Divinity, Doctorate in Ministries **A/A/S:** Zeta Phi Beta Sorority
Email: antonia517@aol.com

Belinda R. Jones

Title: Licensed Practical Nurse **Address:** 5 W. Locke Street, Ashdown, AR 71822 United States **BUS:** Sole Proprietorship **P/S:** Healthcare **MA:** Regional **H/I/S:** Reading, Traveling, Gardening **CERTS:** Licensed Practical Nurse, Cossatot Vocational School (1986) **A/A/S:** National Association for the Advancement of Colored People **C/VW:** Local Church
Email: belinda.jones00@cwwemail.com
URL: http://www.cambridgewhoswho.com

Betty A. Jones

Title: Executive Assistant **Company:** Cleveland School District **Address:** 305 Merritt Drive, Cleveland, MS 38732 United States **BUS:** School District **P/S:** Education for Kindergarten through 12th-Grade Students **MA:** Regional **D/D/R:** Offering Administrative Support, Assisting the Superintendent **H/I/S:** Working with Computers **EDU:** Bachelor of Arts in Business Administration, Delta State University (1987) **CERTS:** Certified Telecommunications Specialist, Alcatel-Lucent (2000) **A/A/S:** President-Elect, Mississippi Association of Administrative Assistants and Board Clerks; Bolivar County Leadership Class of 2003; National School Boards Association; Mississippi School Boards Association
Email: msjones639@yahoo.com
URL: http://www.cleveland.k12.ms.us

Byron Kent Jones

Title: Entrepreneur **Company:** 1) Kendor, LLC 2) KMark, LLC **Address:** 351 N. 650 E., Orem, UT 84097 United States **BUS:** Real Estate **P/S:** Real Estate Investments, Private Lending **MA:** Statewide **D/D/R:** Residential Real Estate, 'Fix and Flips', Private Lender, Coaching Students to get into the Real Estate Field **EDU:** Diploma, Richfield High School **A/A/S:** Lions Club; Chamber of Commerce; Church of Latter Day Saints
Email: bkentjones646@msn.com

Carrie B. Jones

Title: Assistant Director **Company:** Childcare Network **Address:** 780 Sutton Place, Monroe, NC 28112 United States **BUS:** Educational Organization **P/S:** Childcare, Education **MA:** Regional **D/D/R:** Coordinating Events, Creating Lesson Plans, Managing Classroom Ratio Control, Maintaining State Nutrition Program Guidelines **EDU:** Associate Degree in Early Childhood Education, South Piedmont Community College (2007) **C/VW:** Bennett Heights Church of God
Email: cbh52182@juno.com
URL: http://www.childcarenetwork.net

Christina Renee Jones, MS, LPC-I

Title: Clinical Specialist **Company:** Mental Health Department of Tarrant County **Address:** 1527 Hemphill Street, Fort Worth, TX 76104 United States **BUS:** Mental Health Facility **P/S:** Mental Health Services **MA:** Local **D/D/R:** Practicing Adolescent Psychology **H/I/S:** Spending Time with her Family **EDU:** Master's Degree in Psychology, Texas Wesleyan University **A/A/S:** American Association for Marriage and Family Therapy; American Counseling Association **C/VW:** Society for the Prevention of Cruelty to Animals
Email: christj@mhmrtc.org
URL: http://www.mhmrtc.org

Crystal J. Jones, M.Ed.

Title: Therapist, Owner **Company:** Jovon's Consulting and Therapeutic Services **Address:** 604 Arbor Drive, Cedar Hill, TX 75104 United States **BUS:** Healthcare Consulting **P/S:** Cognitive and Developmental Speech and Behavioral Therapy **MA:** Local **EXP:** Ms. Jones' expertise includes cognitive and developmental delays in children and adolescents. **H/I/S:** Exercise, Going to Church, Spending Time with Family **EDU:** Nova University-FL, Texas A&M, New Mexico State University, Pursuing Doctorate, MEd-Counseling/Education, BS-Communication Disorders **CERTS:** Texas Licensed-Foster Parent
Email: cjovon_jones@sbcglobal.net

David L. Jones

Title: 1) Biomedical Equipment Technician 2) Owner **Company:** 1) GE Healthcare 2) J & D's Wildlife & Woodwork **Dept:** 1) Portneuf Medical Center **Address:** 777 Hospital Way, Pocatello, ID 83201 United States **BUS:** 1) Healthcare Center 2) Manufacturing Company **P/S:** 1) Healthcare 2) Custom Woodwork and Taxidermy **MA:** Regional **D/D/R:** Overseeing Medical Equipment Service Including Ventilators, Anesthesia Machines, Balloon Pumps, Cardiothoracic Equipment and All Heart-Related Equipment, Patient Monitoring Systems and Bird Taxidermy **H/I/S:** Hunting, Fishing, Spending Time Outdoors with his Family **EDU:** Associate of Applied Science, Texas State Technical College, Waco **A/A/S:** North Texas Biomedical Association **A/H:** National Dean's List **C/VW:** Local Church
Email: david.x.jones@ge.com
URL: http://www.cambridgewhoswho.com

Debra A. Jones

Title: Classroom Teacher **Company:** Central Heights Independent School District, Central Heights Elementary School **Address:** 10317 U.S. Highway 259, Nacogdoches, TX 75965 United States **BUS:** Elementary School **P/S:** Education **MA:** Local **EXP:** Ms. Jones' expertise includes early childhood education, reading and language arts. **H/I/S:** Playing Piano, Sewing, Reading, Spending Quality Time with her Family **EDU:** Bachelor of Science in Elementary Education, Stephen F. Austin State University, with Honors **CERTS:** Certified Reading Specialist K-8 **A/A/S:** Delta Kappa Gamma; Alpha Chi; Texas Classroom Teachers Association; Association for Childhood Education; Christian Educators Association International; Texas and National Association for the Education of Young Children **C/VW:** Habitat for Humanity, Relay for Life, March of Dimes, Disabled American Veterans, New Hope Congregational Methodist Church, Missions Worldwide
Email: jmtexjones@yahoo.com

Erma J. Jones

Title: Owner **Company:** Mshonday Services **Address:** P.O. Box 55, Wichita, KS 67201 United States **BUS:** Bookkeeping Company **P/S:** Bookkeeping Using Peachtree, QuickBooks and Quicken Computer Software **MA:** Local **D/D/R:** Bookkeeping **H/I/S:** Traveling, Spending Time with her Family **EDU:** Diploma, Marquette High School **C/VW:** Local Church
Email: mshonday@earthlink.net

Gail A. Jones

Title: Gifted And Talented Education Teacher **Company:** Weaverville Elementary School **Address:** P.O. Box 1000, Weaverville, CA 96093 United States **BUS:** Elementary School Dedicated to Excellence in Special Education **P/S:** Special Education Curriculum Including Reading, Art, Music, History, Science, Social Studies **MA:** Regional **D/D/R:** Teaching Gifted and Talented Students and Physical Fitness Junior College Classes **H/I/S:** Running, Bicycling, Reading, Hiking **EDU:** Bachelor of Arts, Chico State University of California (1976) **CERTS:** Certified in Gifted and Talented Education (2007) **A/A/S:** National Education Association; California Teachers Association; California Association for the Gifted; Association for Supervision and Curriculum Development; AHPER
Email: differedgail@yahoo.com

Gerri L. Jones

Title: Realtor **Company:** RE/MAX Unlimited **Address:** 9563 Montgomery Road, Cincinnati, OH 45242 United States **BUS:** Real Estate Agency **P/S:** Real Estate Sales **MA:** International **D/D/R:** Listing and Selling Historic Homes, Residential Properties, Condos and Townhouses, Relocating Corporations **H/I/S:** Gardening, Traveling, Reading, Practicing Yoga, Interior Design **EDU:** Bachelor of Science in Business and Accounting, Indiana University **CERTS:** License in Real Estate, 1989 **A/A/S:** National Association of Realtors; Ohio Association of Realtors; Kentucky Association of Realtors; Cincinnati Board of Realtors; North Kentucky Board of Realtors; President Sales Club; Circle of Excellence **C/VW:** Newport School System, Youth Groups, Youth Sports Programs
Email: gljones@zoomtown.com
URL: http://www.gerrijones.com

Gwendolyn M. Jones

Title: Senior Human Resources Group Manager for Diversity **Company:** Target **Address:** 1000 Nicollet Mall, Minneapolis, MN 55411 United States **BUS:** Retail Firm **P/S:** Consumer Merchandise, Discount Products **MA:** National **D/D/R:** Managing Human Resources **H/I/S:** Bowling, Dancing, Attending Art Fairs **EDU:** Coursework in Business, Chicago State University, Bryant Stratton Business College **A/A/S:** Society for Human Resource Management **C/VW:** United Way; Susan G. Komen for the Cure; American Diabetes Association; American Red Cross
Email: gwen.jones@target.com
URL: http://www.target.com

Jason S. Jones

Title: President **Company:** Direct Buy of Dallas **Address:** 610 E. Highway 80, Sunnyvale, TX 75182 United States **BUS:** Buyers Club, Wholesale Retailer **P/S:** Furniture, Home Improvement Products **MA:** International **D/D/R:** Sales, Marketing, Overseeing Company Activities **EDU:** Graduate, Palmetto High School **A/A/S:** Freemasons **C/VW:** Texas Scottish Rite Hospital for Children
Email: jjones7477@yahoo.com
URL: http://www.directbuyfranchising.com

Jenni L. Jones

Title: Clinical Dietitian **Company:** Charleston Area Medical Center **Address:** 501 Morris Street, Charleston, WV 25301 United States **BUS:** Medical Center **P/S:** Healthcare **MA:** Regional **EXP:** Ms. Jones' expertise is in clinical nutrition. **H/I/S:** Spending Time with her Two Young Sons **EDU:** Master of Science in Human Nutrition, West Virginia University **A/A/S:** American Dietetic Association
Email: jennijns2@aol.com

Jill E. Jones

Title: Science Teacher **Company:** Norwell Middle School **Address:** 1100 E. U.S. 224 Highway, Ossian, IN 46777 United States **BUS:** Middle School Facility Dedicated to Excellence in Education **P/S:** Regular Core Curriculum Including Reading, Mathematics, English, Science, Social Studies, Art, Music, History **MA:** Regional **D/D/R:** Teaching Four Science Classes to 105 Students, Teaching One Collaboration Class to Help Enrich Student Skills, Team Leader for Other Teachers for Student Growth and Development **H/I/S:** Traveling **EDU:** Bachelor of Arts Degree in Secondary Education, Indiana University (1980's) **A/A/S:** National Education Association
Email: jill.jones@nwcs.k12.in.us
URL: http://www.nwcs.k12.in.us

Joyce F. Jones, RN

Title: Registered Nurse **Company:** World Harvest Ministries, Nursing Health Department **Address:** 3347 Londonderry Road, North Charleston, SC 29420 United States **BUS:** Health Education Facility **P/S:** Health Ministry **MA:** Regional **D/D/R:** Working in the Intensive Care Unit, Directing Nursing in the Health Ministry, Conducting Health Fairs for the Community, Taking Blood Pressure Tests, Engaging in Monthly Health Awareness Seminars, Discussing Health Issues with the Congregation, Taking Care of Emergencies **H/I/S:** Playing the Piano, Watching Basketball **EDU:** Bachelor of Science in Nursing Degree, Medical University of South Carolina(1985); Bachelor of Science in Biology, Wofford College
Email: thejoyfull777@yahoo.com

Kathy S. Jones, M.Ed.

Title: Reading Coordinator **Company:** Ector County Independent School District **Dept:** Curriculum and Instruction **Address:** 802 N. Sam Houston Avenue, Odessa, TX 79761 United States **BUS:** Public School District **P/S:** Public Education for Local Students **MA:** Statewide **D/D/R:** Teaching Dyslexia Education **H/I/S:** Scrapbooking, Tracing Genealogy **EDU:** Pursuing Doctorate Degree; Master's Degree in Reading Specialist Studies, Abilene Christian University (2001) **A/A/S:** Texas Classroom Teachers Association; International Reading Association; Irlen
Email: jonesks@ector-county.k12.tx.us
URL: http://www.cambridgewhoswho.com

Linda M. Jones

Title: President, Owner **Company:** LJ Promotional Modeling Agency **Address:** P.O. Box 6391, Ellicott City, MD 21242 United States **BUS:** Promotional Agency **P/S:** Mixed Media, Retail Promotions, Trade Shows, Fashion Shows, Makeup Artistry, Hosting and Greeting for Events **MA:** Regional **D/D/R:** Promotional Modeling, Demonstrating the Benefits and Features of Products **H/I/S:** Spending Time with Family, Real Estate **EDU:** High School Education **CERTS:** Real Estate License, 2007 **A/A/S:** Baltimore Area Chamber of Commerce; BACVA **A/H:** Givenchy Award **C/VW:** Joyce Meyer Ministries, Local Church
Email: ljmodelsink@comcast.net
URL: http://www.modelsink.bizland.com

Martina Jones

Title: Recruiter **Company:** US Airways Express/Piedmont Airlines **Address:** 499 Lethbridge Court, Millersville, MD 21108 United States **BUS:** Airline Travel **P/S:** Recruiter **MA:** National **D/D/R:** Working as a Certified Notary Public in the State of Maryland **EDU:** Annearunder University, Associate of Business Management **A/A/S:** United Way, Avon, State of Maryland Notary Rep.
Email: martina_jones@usairways.com
URL: www.usairways.com

Michael R. Jones, MS, RN

Title: Senior Business Consultant **Company:** Perot Systems **Address:** 2300 W. Plano Parkway, Plano, TX 75075 United States **BUS:** Healthcare Consulting Firm **P/S:** Health Information and Management Systems, Consulting **MA:** International **D/D/R:** Assisting Hospitals, Physicians, Clinicians and Other Stakeholders to Plan, Implement and Adopt an Electronic Health Record System **H/I/S:** Attending the Theater and Symphony **EDU:** Pursuing Doctor of Health Administration Degree, University of Phoenix; Master of Science in Health Administration, Capella University (2002); Bachelor of Science in Nursing, University of Maryland (1999) **A/A/S:** American Nurses Association; Health Information and Management Systems Society
Email: nursemjones@comcast.net

Pamela A. Jones

Title: Early Childhood Student Teacher Supervisor **Company:** Ohio University **Address:** 45425 National Road W., Saint Clairsville, OH 43950 United States **BUS:** University **P/S:** Higher Education **MA:** Regional **EXP:** Ms. Jones' expertise is in education. **D/D/R:** Conducting Workshops, Supervising Students and Teachers, Lecturing, Participating in Local School Board Meetings, Evaluating Students and Teachers **H/I/S:** Spending Time with her Family, Walking, Spending Time at the Beach **EDU:** Master's Degree in Early Childhood Education, West Virginia University (1976); Bachelor's Degree in Elementary Education, Ohio University (1970) **A/A/S:** Ohio School Board; Ohio Education Association; Board Member, St. Clairsville-Richland City School District; National Education Association; National Association for the Education of Young Children **A/H:** Achievement Award, Ohio School Board Association (2008)
Email: jonesp@ohio.edu
URL: http://www.eastern.ohiou.edu

Paula E. Jones

Title: Owner and Operator **Company:** Paula's Hair Unlimited **Address:** 729 Lakeside Drive W., Mobile, AL 36693 United States **BUS:** Beauty Salon **P/S:** Hair Salon **MA:** Regional **D/D/R:** Specializing in all Types of Services for Men, Women and Children, Nails, Hair-Color, Cutting, **H/I/S:** Reading, Working Out, Volunteering **CERTS:** Master Cosmetology License, Charles Academy **A/A/S:** Hair Dresser's Association; Chamber of Commerce **A/H:** Women's Eagle Award, 2007 **C/VW:** Volunteer Work with the Elderly, Sunday School Teacher, Greater Zion Tabernacle Choir Baptist Church
Email: paulae_jones@yahoo.com
URL: http://www.cambridgewhoswho.com

Roch S. Jones

Title: HR Coordinator **Company:** Tropical Hawaiian Products **Address:** P.O. Box 210, Keaau, HI 96749 United States **BUS:** Food Service Transportation Services Log **P/S:** Fruit Shipping **MA:** International **D/D/R:** Coordinating Human Resources, Accounting **H/I/S:** Theater, Choir, Art, Paint, Make Jewelry **EDU:** Associate of Arts, East Wyoming College **A/A/S:** Kilauea Drama and Entertainment Network, Volcano Festival
Email: rochjones@aol.com

Seymour Jones, CPA

Title: Clinical Professor **Company:** Stern School of Business NYU **Address:** 44 W. Fourth Street, New York, NY 10012 United States **BUS:** Education University **P/S:** Teaching, Accounting **MA:** Local **D/D/R:** Auditing, Forensic, International Accounting **H/I/S:** My Family, Theater, Dining Out, Reading, Traveling **EDU:** Stern School of Business, New York University, Master of Business Administration **A/A/S:** AICPA, NYSSCPA
Email: sjones@stern.nyu.edu

Susan K. B. Jones

Title: Clinical Nurse Specialist, Clinical Researcher **Company:** Integris Baptist Medical Center **Dept:** Department of Nursing Education and Research **Address:** 3300 N.W. Expressway, Suite 602, Oklahoma City, OK 73112 United States **BUS:** Nonprofit Healthcare Organization **P/S:** Healthcare Including Cardiology, Oncology, Diabetes Care, Fertility, Orthopedic Care Services **MA:** Regional **D/D/R:** Managing the Research and Development Process, Working with Researchers and Patients' Families, Overseeing the Pediatric and Critical Care Unit **H/I/S:** Traveling, Gardening **EDU:** Master of Science, University of Oklahoma (2002) **CERTS:** Registered Nurse; Certified Clinical Nurse Specialist **A/A/S:** Society of Critical Care Medicine; National Association of Clinical Nurse Specialists
Email: susan.jones@integris-health.com
URL: http://www.integris-health.com

Treva J. Jones, LE

Title: Owner, Professional Esthetician **Company:** The Center Day Spa **Address:** 1641 Commercial Street, Warsaw, MO 65355 United States **BUS:** Spa and Fitness Center **P/S:** Skin Therapy and Wellness Services **MA:** Regional **D/D/R:** Running the Wellness Spa and Fitness Center, Performing Microdermabrasions, Light Therapy Facials, Reflexology and Revitalizing Services, Working with the Ionic Cleanser, Maintaining Order Inventory, Creating and Selling her Skin Care and Cosmetics Line, Working on Public Relations at the Local Hospital, Selling Demagogical and Jane Iredele Cosmetic Lines **H/I/S:** Reading, Working with Clay, Pilot **EDU:** College Coursework **CERTS:** Licensed in Skin Care, Loria's College of Cosmetology
Email: trevajjones@earthlink.net
URL: http://www.cambridgewhoswho.com

William Jones Jr.

Title: Chief Executive Officer, Founder **Company:** Reclaim the Streets Ministries **Address:** 1801 State Street, Harrisburg, PA 17103 United States **BUS:** Church Ministry **P/S:** Community Services **MA:** Regional **D/D/R:** Ministering, Coordinating Outreach Programs, Overseeing the Activities of Anti-Violence Workshops, Performing Administrative Duties, Satisfying the Emotional, Social and Spiritual Needs of Others **H/I/S:** Watching Movies, Reading Leadership Journals **EDU:** Master of Science in Bioengineering, Central Missouri State University (1982); Bachelor of Science in Engineering and Biology, United States Air Force Academy (1980) **A/A/S:** National Commission for Scheduled Castes; National Christian Conference Center; Willow Creek Association; Creflo Dollar Ministerial Association; Ministers Association
Email: williej57@att.net
URL: http://www.reclaimthestreetsministries.org

Loreatha Jones Williams, LPN

Title: Licensed Practical Nurse, Charge Nurse **Company:** The Jewish Home of Greater Harrisburg **Address:** 4000 Linglestown Road, Harrisburg, PA 17112 United States **BUS:** Residential Nursing Home **P/S:** Exceptional Services and Gracious Amenities to Enhance Quality of Life, Preserve Dignity and Encourage Physical and Spiritual Well-Being **MA:** Regional **D/D/R:** Working as a Geriatric Charge Nurse in the Evenings, Making Sure Medications and Lab Workups are Prepared for the Following Day, Patient Care, Showing Respect and Care for All her Patients **H/I/S:** Cooking, Spending Time with her Grandchildren **CERTS:** Licensed Practical Nurse Degree, Harrisburg Vocational School of Nursing (1977) **A/A/S:** Former Delegate, Nurses Union; Muscular Dystrophy Association-Volunteer; Karate Club-Secretary; Medical Personnel, Little League
URL: http://www.jewishhomeharrisburg.org/

Lalitha Jonnavithula

Title: Clinical Operations Manager **Company:** Abbott Vascular **Address:** 3200 Lakeside Drive, San Jose, CA 95054 United States **BUS:** Medical Device Company **P/S:** Cardiac Devices **MA:** International **EXP:** Ms. Jonnavithula's expertise includes quality, operations, safety assurance and project management. **H/I/S:** Traveling, Swimming, Spending Time with her Child **EDU:** Master of Business Administration in International Business, McGill University; Bachelor of Science in Microbiology and Genetics, Mount Allison University **A/A/S:** Endocrine Society; Association of Clinical Research Professionals; American College of Cardiology **C/VW:** United Way, Disaster Relief
Email: lalitha.jonnavithula@av.abbott.com
URL: http://www.cambridgewhoswho.com

Barbe J. Jordan

Title: Salon Owner **Company:** Barbe's Facial Salon, LLC **Address:** 1426 Lime Street, Suite 2, Fernandina Beach, FL 32034 United States **BUS:** Beauty Salon **P/S:** Skin Treatments and Facials **MA:** Regional **D/D/R:** Booking Appointments, Greeting Clients, Budgeting, Performing All Facial Procedures, Accepting Referrals **EDU:** General Educational Development Diploma (1974); **CERTS:** Certification in Cosmetology, Jacksonville Cosmetology School (2000); Certification in Particle Skincare and Resurfacing; Certification in Training Research in Plastic Surgery; Certification in Particle Skin Resurfacing **A/A/S:** Associated Bodywork and Massage Professionals
Email: hookedonfacials@yahoo.com
URL: http://www.hookedonfacials.com

Emily A. Jordan

Title: Team Advisor **Company:** Schreiber **Address:** 1585 N. 400 E., Apartment 624, North Logan, UT 84341 United States **BUS:** Retail Dairy Company **P/S:** Private Label Dairy Products **MA:** International **D/D/R:** Leading and Managing the Yogurt Line of Private Label Products, Working with 12-15 Partners, Overseeing Employee and Equipment Safety, Completing Projects to Help Optimize Productivity **H/I/S:** Mountain Biking, Playing Volleyball, Running **EDU:** Bachelor of Science in Chemical Engineering, Ohio State University, Columbus, OH (2006) **A/A/S:** Alpha Omicron Pi Alumni Association; Ohio State Alumni Association, Salt Lake City; Assistant Coach, Mountain West Volleyball Club
Email: emilyjor@gmail.com

Kathleen M. Jordan

Title: Supervisor of Recruitment and Appointment **Company:** Moffitt Cancer Center and Research Institute **Dept:** Human Resources **Address:** 12902 Magnolia Drive, Tampa, FL 33612 United States **BUS:** Cancer Hospital and Research Center **P/S:** Healthcare for Oncology Patients **MA:** National **EXP:** Ms. Jordan's expertise is in recruitment. **H/I/S:** Reading, Gardening, Bike Riding, Walking **EDU:** Master of Business Administration in Management, Indiana University (2001)
Email: kathleen.jordan@moffitt.org
URL: http://www.moffitt.org

Rinata M. Jordan

Title: Branch Manager **Company:** Sun Trust Bank **Address:** 5350 Poplar Avenue, Suite 100, Memphis, TN 38119 United States **BUS:** Bank **P/S:** Banking and Finance **MA:** National **D/D/R:** Managing Finances **H/I/S:** Reading, Volunteer Work **EDU:** High School **A/A/S:** NCBW
Email: RinataJordan@aol.com

Mr. Douglas Jorgenson

Title: President **Company:** North American Energy Group **Address:** 4660 Slater Road, Suite 248, Eagan, MN 55122 United States **BUS:** Service Provider, Distributor **P/S:** Lighting Products for Commercial Buildings **MA:** National **D/D/R:** Distributing Long Lasting, Energy Efficient Lighting Fixtures, Bulbs and Other Products to Businesses **H/I/S:** Golfing **EDU:** Associate Degree in Business, Anoka-Ramsey Community College (1970)
Email: d.jorgenson@naeg.como
URL: http://www.naeg.com

Deborah Joseph

Title: Educator **Company:** Fremont Unified School District **Address:** 43 Trestle Drive, Hayward, CA 94544 United States **BUS:** Public School District **P/S:** Education for Students in Ninth through 12th-Grade, Art, Music, Athletics **MA:** Regional **D/D/R:** Teaching Precalculus, Advanced Placement and Honors Calculus **H/I/S:** Working on Sudoku Puzzles and Crossword Puzzles **EDU:** Master's Degree in Curriculum, University of Phoenix (2007) **A/A/S:** National Council of Teachers of Mathematics
Email: djrchrdsn@sbcglobal.net
URL: http://www.fremont.k12.ca.us

Ms. Zelna E. Joseph

Title: President, Chief Executive Officer **Company:** SET Family Medical Clinics **Address:** 2080 Farnsworth Drive, Colorado Springs, CO 80916 United States **BUS:** Nonprofit Medical Center **P/S:** Healthcare for Low-Income and Uninsured People **MA:** Regional **EXP:** Ms. Joseph's expertise is in healthcare management. **H/I/S:** Traveling, Hiking, Reading, Horseback Riding **EDU:** Master's Degree in Communication, Regis University (1993) **A/A/S:** National Council of Negro Women; Community Health Partnership **C/VW:** Colorado Homeless Charity; The Colorado Health Foundation; Governor's Council on Homelessness
Email: zelnajoseph@centura.org
URL: http://www.setofcs.org

Claire C. Joubert

Title: Physician Assistant in Pre-Liver Transplant **Company:** Tufts-New England Medical Center **Address:** 750 Washington Street, Boston, MA 02111 United States **BUS:** Medical Center **P/S:** Healthcare **MA:** Regional **D/D/R:** Transplanting Livers, Managing Liver Disease **H/I/S:** Reading, Walking on the Beach **CERTS:** Certified Physician Assistant, Northeastern University **A/A/S:** American Association for the Study of Liver Diseases
Email: cjoubert@tufts-nemc.org

Darryl Joyce

Title: Senior Pastor **Company:** Exouisia Ministries, Inc. **Address:** 22407 Goshen School Road, Laytonsville, MD 20882 United States **BUS:** Religious Teaching and Healing Ministry **P/S:** Religious and Spiritual Services **MA:** Local **D/D/R:** Running the Children's Learning Zone Program, Teaching and Preaching **H/I/S:** Running, Reading, Spending Time with her Grandchildren **EDU:** Master's Degree in Business Administration, Howard University
Email: exouisiaministriesinc@yahoo.com
URL: http://www.cambridgewhoswho.com

Gail Joyiens-Salam

Title: Owner **Company:** JS Transcription Service **Address:** 1334 Pierce Street, Rahway, NJ 07065 United States **BUS:** Medical and Business Transcription Service **P/S:** One-on-One Personal Care **MA:** National **D/D/R:** Medical Report Transcription, IMEs, Preparing Progress Notes and Assessments **H/I/S:** Swimming, Reading **A/A/S:** Animal Activist; Habitat for Humanity **C/VW:** Animal Activist, Habitat for Humanity, Humane Society
Email: salam13341@verizon.net

Emily R. Joyner
Title: Financial Officer **Company:** Texas Cancer Associates, LLP **Address:** 8440 Walnut Hill Lane, Suite 600, Dallas, TX 75231 United States **BUS:** Private Medical Practice Dedicated to Excellence in Healthcare **P/S:** Oncology, Hematology, Physician's Group **MA:** Regional **D/D/R:** Handling All Financial Collections, Managing All Vendor Accounts, Payroll, Cashflow Analysis, Performance Analysis, Communicating with Company's Attorneys **H/I/S:** Football, Baseball, Reading, Exercise **EDU:** Master of Business Administration in Healthcare Administration, Texas Women's University (2001); Master's Degree in Healthcare Administration, Texas Women's University (2005) **A/A/S:** Association of Community Cancer Centers; Medical Group Managers Association
Email: ejyner@txcan.com
URL: http://www.txcan.com

Katarzyna L. Juchas
Title: Supervisor **Company:** TCF National Bank **Address:** 6430 W. Irving Park Road, Chicago, IL 60634 United States **BUS:** Bank **P/S:** Banking Services **MA:** Regional **EXP:** Ms. Juchas' expertise is in sales management. **H/I/S:** Attending Theater, Learning Psychology and Philosophy, Writing Poems, Working with Computers **EDU:** Pursuing Bachelor's Degree in Management and International Business, Loyola University; Associate of Applied Science in International Business **A/A/S:** Phi Theta Kappa **A/H:** The National Dean's List **C/VW:** Local Charitable Organizations
Email: kjuchas@sbcglobal.net
URL: http://www.cambridgewhoswho.com

Joan S. Judge, CBR
Title: Broker **Company:** Kelley Real Estate **Address:** 138 Main Street, Ludlow, VT 05149 United States **BUS:** Real Estate Broker **P/S:** Residential, Lake Front Condos, Townhomes, Gulf Homes, Vacant Land, Horse Properties **MA:** National **EXP:** Ms. Judge's expertise includes residential and commercial properties and vacant land. **H/I/S:** Skiing **A/A/S:** Vermont Association of Realtors, National Association of Realtors
Email: joan@kelleyrealestate.com
URL: www.kelleyrealestate.com

Andrew V. Juettner
Title: Executive Director **Company:** Windsor County Youth Services **Address:** 6 Mill Street, Ludlow, VT 05149 United States **BUS:** Nonprofit Youth Services **P/S:** Homeless Shelters for Adolescents **MA:** Local **EXP:** Mr. Juettner's expertise is in transitional-age youths. **EDU:** Bachelor of Arts, College of Saint Joseph **A/A/S:** Vermont Coalition of Runaway and Homeless Youth; Vermont Coalition of Residential Providers; New England Network for Child, Youth & Family Services **C/VW:** United Way
Email: wcys.juettner@tds.net
URL: http://www.wcys.org

Mrs. Marlyn M. Jules
Title: Director of Patient Care Assessment and Quality Improvement **Company:** Radius Specialty Hospital **Address:** 59 Townsend Street, Roxbury, MA 02169 United States **BUS:** Hospital **P/S:** Healthcare **MA:** Local **EXP:** Mrs. Jules' expertise is in quality control. **H/I/S:** Gardening **EDU:** Master's Degree in Primary Care, Northeastern University **A/A/S:** Sigma Theta Tau **C/VW:** Local Church, Boys and Girls Club of America
Email: mjules@radiushospital.com
URL: http://www.cambridgewhoswho.com

Christophe Julliard
Title: Vice President in Quality and Strategy Planning **Company:** Accor North America **Address:** 4001 International Parkway, Carrollton, TX 75007 United States **BUS:** Hospitality **P/S:** Hospitality Services **MA:** National **D/D/R:** Marketing, Research, Quality Assurance, Guest Satisfaction, Energy and Environment, Strategy Planning **H/I/S:** Playing Tennis, Cooking, Wine **EDU:** Master's Degree in Hotel Management, Cornell University; Ecole Supérieure des Sciences Économiques et Commerciales **C/VW:** Children's Leukemia Society; Texas Scottish Rite Hospital for Children; Smile Train; Texas Campaign for the Environment
Email: cjulliard@sbcglobal.net
URL: http://www.cambridgewhoswho.com

William F. Juris
Title: Environmental Supervisor **Company:** Ohio Environmental Protection Agency **Address:** 50 W. Town Street, Suite 700, Columbus, OH 43215 United States **BUS:** Environmental Regulatory Agency **P/S:** Air Pollution Control, Hazardous Waste Management, Emergency and Remedial Response, Environmental and Financial Assistance **MA:** Regional **D/D/R:** Supervising Environmental Activities, Managing Industrial VOC Air Pollution Standards and Industrial Sources, Overseeing Air Quality Control Projects **H/I/S:** Bowling, Participating in Church Activities **EDU:** Bachelor of Science in Chemical Engineering, Case Western Reserve University (1970) **CERTS:** Licensed Professional Engineer, State of Ohio
Email: bill.juris@epa.state.oh.us
URL: http://www.epa.state.oh.us

Christina Ann Justice
Title: Teacher of Exceptional Children **Company:** Bonlee Elementary School **Address:** 153 Bonlee School Road, Bonlee, NC 27213 United States **BUS:** Elementary School **P/S:** Elementary Education **MA:** Local **D/D/R:** Teaching Exceptional Children **H/I/S:** Playing with her Cat **EDU:** Pursuing Master's Degree in Reading, University of North Carolina at Greensboro; Bachelor of Science in Special Education, Greensboro College **A/A/S:** North Carolina Association of Educators **C/VW:** Multiple Sclerosis Society
Email: cjustice@chatham.k12.nc.us
URL: http://www.cambridgewhoswho.com

Jaelene K. Kaaa
Title: Assistant Director of Finance **Company:** Hilton Hawaiian Village **Address:** 2005 Kalia Road, Honolulu, HI 96815 United States **BUS:** Hotel Resort **P/S:** Spa, Catering Facility, Restaurants, Recreational and Cultural Activities, Nightly Entertainment **MA:** Regional **D/D/R:** Accounting, Financing, Overseeing Financial Statements, Annual and Capital Budgets and Forecasts **H/I/S:** Reading, Doing Puzzles, Swimming, Shopping, Hunting, Fishing, Camping, Spending Time with Family and Friends **EDU:** Master of Business Administration in Accounting and Finance, Chaminade University of Honolulu (2002); Bachelor's Degree in Accounting, Minor in Sociology, Chaminade University of Honolulu (2000) **A/A/S:** Delta Mu Delta
Email: jaelene_kaaa@hilton.com
URL: http://www.hiltonhawaiianvillage.com

Barbara Sue Kachadurian
Title: Esthetician, Spa Coordinator **Company:** Kenneth Cote Renewal Center **Address:** 333 Main Street, East Greenwich, RI 02818 United States **BUS:** Beauty and Day Spa **P/S:** Demagogical Products, Waxing, Facials, Makeup Application **MA:** Rhode Island **EXP:** Ms. Kachadurian's expertise includes facials, body treatments and spa management. **H/I/S:** Gardening, Spending Time with her Family and Dogs **EDU:** Degree, Costin's Warwick Beauty Academy; Coursework, International Dermal Institute
Email: barbara@kennethcote.com
URL: http://www.kennethcote.com

Capt. Charles F. Kaczynski
Title: Chief Pilot, Partner **Company:** Atlanta Air Charter, Inc. **Address:** 1723 McCollum Parkway, Suite 460, Kennesaw, GA 30144 United States **BUS:** Air Charter Company **P/S:** Aviation and Charter Services **MA:** Caribbean, Southeast U.S. **D/D/R:** Overseeing Flight Operations, Business Development and Aviation Consulting **H/I/S:** Swimming, Boating, Skiing, Spending Time with his Family **EDU:** Bachelor of Science in Aviation Management, Florida Institute of Technology; Bachelor of Arts (1987) **CERTS:** Licensed Pilot, United States Air Force **A/A/S:** Reserve Officers Association; National Business Aviation Association; Pi Kappa Alpha **A/H:** Air Medal; Aerial Achievement Medal; Humanitarian Service Medal **C/VW:** Chairman, Children Helping Children; Mt. Zion United Methodist Church; American Cancer Society; American Cancer Society; Habitat for Humanity
Email: chipski@atlantaaircharter.com
Email: chipski@bellsouth.net
URL: http://www.atlantaaircharter.com

Pamela J. Kaffer
Title: Language Arts Teacher **Company:** Belleville Public School District No. 18, West Junior High **Address:** 840 Royal Heights Road, Belleville, IL 62226 United States **BUS:** School **P/S:** Education **MA:** Local **D/D/R:** Seventh-Grade Language Arts and Literature Character Education **H/I/S:** Boating, Swimming, Reading **EDU:** Master's Degree in of Educational Administration, Southern Illinois University, Edwardsville **A/A/S:** Kappa Delta Pi
Email: pjkaffer@stclair.k12.il.us
URL: http://www.cambridgewhoswho.com

Ms. Emily G. Kahn
Title: Photographer **Address:** 1 Fitchburg Street, Somerville, MA 02142 United States **BUS:** Sole Proprietorship **P/S:** Fine Arts Photography **MA:** Regional **D/D/R:** Creating Documentary Work, Abstract and Fine Arts, Managing a Website to Market her Products, Handling Independent Projects **EDU:** Bachelor of Arts, Harvard University (1989) **A/A/S:** Board Member, Rose Art Museum, Brandeis University; Photographic Resource Center, Boston University **A/H:** Travel Scholar Award
Email: nhakep@aol.com
URL: http://www.emilykhan.com

Shari L. Kain
Title: Financial Manager, Physics and Astronomy **Company:** The John Hopkins University **Address:** 3701 San Martin Drive, Baltimore, MD 21218 United States **BUS:** University **P/S:** Higher Education **MA:** National **D/D/R:** Managing the Finances for the Physics and Astronomy Departments **H/I/S:** Gardening, Spending Time with her Family **EDU:** College Coursework **C/VW:** American Cancer Society, Outreach for Students, Physics Fairs
Email: skain2@jhu.edu
URL: http://physics-astronomy.jhu.edu/

Linda J. Kaiser
Title: Care Manager, Registered Nurse **Company:** Meritain Health **Address:** 5825 Royalton Center Road, Gasport, NY 14067 United States **BUS:** One of the Nation's Largest Administrators of Self-Funded Benefits, Leading Independent Provider of Consumer-Directed Health Plans **P/S:** Services and Resources for Clients Managing the Long-Term Costs of Health Benefit Programs **MA:** National **EXP:** Ms. Kaiser's expertise is in occupational clinical therapy. **D/D/R:** Overseeing Pre-Certification for Hospital Admissions or X-Rays and MRIs, Determining the Medical Necessity and Appropriateness for Admission, Evaluating Durable Medical Equipment **H/I/S:** Participating in Home Winemaking Competitions, Collecting Wizard of Oz Paraphernalia, Antiques **EDU:** Associate of Science in Nursing (1974) **CERTS:** Certified in Gerontology, American Nurses Credentialing Center **A/A/S:** Volunteer, American Heart Association
URL: https://www.meritain.com/

Troy A. Kaiser
Title: National Technical and Warranty Operations Manager **Company:** Toyota Material Handling USA **Address:** 5559 Inwood Drive, Columbus, IN 47201 United States **BUS:** Material Handling Company **P/S:** Material Handling Equipment **EXP:** Mr. Kaiser's expertise includes after-market customer and dealer support. **H/I/S:** Spending Time Outdoors **EDU:** Bachelor's Degree in Applied Science, Minor in Business Administration, Pittsburgh State University; Certified, Association For Manufacturing Excellence
Email: troy.kaiser@thmu.com
URL: http://www.tmhu.com

Meredith M. Kalisz
Title: Pharmacy Manager **Company:** Walgreens **Address:** 3701 N. Kings Highway, Myrtle Beach, SC 29577 United States **BUS:** Pharmacy **P/S:** Pharmaceuticals **MA:** National **EXP:** Ms. Kalisz's expertise includes diabetes education, medication therapy, Medicare Part D management and hypertension education. **D/D/R:** Assisting Students on their Clinical and Introductory Rotations, Consulting, Lecturing, Ensuring Customer Satisfaction, Educating Patients, Blood Pressure Screening **H/I/S:** Dancing, Traveling **EDU:** Doctor of Pharmacy, Duquesne University **CERTS:** Immunization Certification **A/A/S:** Duquesne University; Southern California Public Health Association; Pharmacy Fraternity; APAJ; National Community Pharmacists Association
Email: mkalisz@mailpicnic.com
URL: http://www.cambridgewhoswho.com

Tiffanie Kalisz
Title: Director **Company:** Dance USA, Inc. **Address:** 1930 Village Center Circle, Suite 3-395, Las Vegas, NV 89134 United States **BUS:** Dance Training Institution **P/S:** Educational Training through Dance and Songs **MA:** International **D/D/R:** Directing and Organizing Events **H/I/S:** Poker, Skiing **A/A/S:** Radio City Music Hall; Carnegie Hall Corporation **A/H:** World Championship Award (Five Times) **C/VW:** Fueled By The Fallen
Email: danceusatk@yahoo.com
URL: http://www.danceusadance.com

Christo A. Kamara
Title: Pastor **Company:** Victor Christian Assembly of God **Address:** 870 Cummins Highway, Boston, MA 02126 United States **BUS:** Church **P/S:** A Christian Church **MA:** Local **D/D/R:** Adult Ministry, Youth Ministry and Community Outreach **H/I/S:** Soccer **EDU:** Attended School in Africa, BS **A/A/S:** Assembly of God
Email: spvcag712@aol.com

Stacie M. Kammer
Title: Speech-Language Pathologist **Company:** Western Ohio Therapy Associates **Address:** 1498 N. Broadway Street, Greenville, OH 45331 United States **BUS:** Therapy Center **P/S:** Speech-Language Pathology Therapy **MA:** Local **EXP:** Ms. Kammer's expertise includes speech and language therapy. **H/I/S:** Spending Time with her Children **EDU:** Master's Degree in Speech-Language Pathology, Miami University, Oxford, OH **CERTS:** Vita Stim Provider **A/A/S:** Ohio Speech-Language-Hearing Association; American Speech-Language-Hearing Association **C/VW:** Local Church
Email: skammer@woh.rr.com
URL: http://www.cambridgewhoswho.com

Cynthia K. Kamphaus, PT

Title: Physical Therapist, Owner **Company:** Solo Pro Physical Therapy **Address:** P.O. Box 351, Payson, AZ 85547 United States **BUS:** Physical Therapy Center **P/S:** Physical Therapy Services Including Rehabilitation, Fitness Tips, Golf Fitness, Professional Seminars **MA:** Regional **D/D/R:** Treating Patients with Spinal Cord Injuries, Amputees and Stroke Victims, Utilizing Modalities, Ultrasound, Crunch, Traction, Laser, Massage, Soft Tissue Mobilizations and Mobilization Techniques, Assisting Horseback Riders and Golfers with Performance Improvement Techniques, Collaborating with Chiropractors, Conducting Workshops, Treating Patients with Traumatic Brain Injuries, Complex Soft Tissue Defects and Orthopedic Patients **EDU:** Bachelor's Degree in Physical Therapy, The University of Kansas Medical Center, Kansas City (1971) **A/A/S:** American Physical Therapy Association
Email: solopropt@npgcable.com
URL: http://www.solopropt.com

Deborah J. Kandahari

Title: Administrator **Company:** Cancer and Blood Specialists of Northern Virginia, P.C. **Address:** 2280 Opitz Boulevard, Suite 220, Woodbridge, VA 22191 United States **BUS:** Time-Honored Medical Office **P/S:** Full Range of Healthcare Services for Cancer Patients **MA:** Local **D/D/R:** Overseeing the Research Coordination of the Hematology and Oncology Practice, Handling the Administrative Duties of the Office Including Finances, Negotiations, Contracting and Taxes, Owning a Separate Business in the Stonework Industry **H/I/S:** Enjoying Basketball, Football, Swimming, Cooking **EDU:** Pursuing Graduate Degree, George Mason University **A/A/S:** Virginia Association of Hematology Oncology Managers
Email: dkandahari@aol.com
URL: http://www.cambridgewhoswho.com

Kathleen T. Kane

Title: Commercial Department Manager **Company:** Madison Title Agency **Address:** 1125 Ocean Avenue, Lakewood, NJ 08701 United States **BUS:** Real Estate Financial **P/S:** Real Estate Title Insurance **MA:** Local **D/D/R:** Communicating with Clients, Management **H/I/S:** movies, roller skating **CERTS:** New Jersey, Title License
Email: kathleen@madisontitle.com

Rolfe Kanefsky

Title: Filmmaker **Company:** Valkhn Films **Address:** 11855 Magnolia Boulevard, Apartment 31, North Hollywood, CA 91607 United States **BUS:** Film Studio **P/S:** Film Production **MA:** National **D/D/R:** Making Independent Films, Horrors and Comedy **EDU:** Coursework, Hampshire College
Email: rolfe30@yahoo.com
URL: http://www.rolfekanefsky.com

Jason Kaniper

Title: Owner **Company:** Prolific Landscape **Address:** 615 W. Mauch Chunk Street, Nazareth, PA 18064 United States **BUS:** Landscaping Company **P/S:** Landscaping **MA:** Local **D/D/R:** Installation and Design, Contracting **H/I/S:** Snowmobiling, Four-Wheeling
Email: prolificlandscape@rcn.com
URL: http://www.cambridgewhoswho.com

Gaurav Kapur, MD

Title: Associate Staff, Spine Institute **Company:** Cleveland Clinic **Address:** 9500 Euclid Avenue, Cleveland, OH 44195 United States **BUS:** Nonprofit Organization, Medical Center **P/S:** Healthcare, Research and Education **MA:** Regional **D/D/R:** Overseeing Diagnosis Units, Caring for Patients Experiencing Back and Spinal Problems for Various Reasons Including Injuries, Assisting Doctors **H/I/S:** Traveling **EDU:** MD, Earned in India (1995); Fellowship in Spine Medicine (2002) **CERTS:** Certification in Physical Medicine and Rehabilitation **A/A/S:** American Board of Physical Medicine and Rehabilitation
Email: kapurg@ccf.org
URL: http://www.ccf.org

Myron S. Karasik, CPA, CMC

Title: Partner **Company:** Tatum, LLC **Address:** 1 Embarcadero Center, Suite 500, San Francisco, CA 94111 United States **BUS:** Consulting Firm **P/S:** Consulting Services **MA:** Regional **D/D/R:** Managing Property and Casualty Insurance, Overseeing Operations Including Accounting, Finance, Strategic Planning, the Sale of Medical Services, Manufacturing and Distribution **H/I/S:** Studying Scientific Endeavors, Artwork, Reading Poetry, Painting **EDU:** Master's Degree in Business Administration, Kellogg School of Management (1975); Master's Degree in Electronic Engineering, Purdue University (1972) **CERTS:** Certified Public Accountant, State of New York; Certified Management Consultant **A/A/S:** Illinois Certified Public Accountants Society
Email: myron.karasik@tatumllc.com
URL: http://www.tatumllc.com

Lena D. Karkalas, DDS

Title: Dentist, Owner **Company:** Lena D. Karkalas, DDS **Address:** 151 Waterman Street, Providence, RI 02906 United States **BUS:** Dental Office **P/S:** All Phases of Dentistry Including Cleanings and Prevention, Cosmetic Procedures, Periodontal Disease Diagnosis and Treatment, Restorations, Veneers and Laser Whitening **MA:** Regional **D/D/R:** Practicing Cosmetic Dentistry, Performing Laser Whitening and Veneer Treatments **H/I/S:** Spending Time with her Children, Traveling **EDU:** Doctor of Dental Surgery, New York University College of Dentistry (1992); Bachelor of Science, Clark University **A/A/S:** American Academy of Cosmetic Dentistry; Fellow, Academy of International Dentistry; Academy of General Dentistry; Holistic Dental Association **A/H:** Nominee, Best Dentist, Rhode Island
Email: drllena@confidentsmiles.net
URL: http://www.confidentsmiles.net

Bonnie Karl-Meacham

Title: Registered Nurse, CARN **Company:** Mission Vista Behavioral Health **BUS:** Behavioral Health Facility **P/S:** Chemical Dependency Treatments **MA:** Local **D/D/R:** Charge Nursing, Addictions Nursing, Planning, Administering Medications **H/I/S:** Working for Charities **EDU:** Associate of Science in Nursing, Howard College **CERTS:** Certified Registered Nurse **A/A/S:** INSA; National Nurses Organizing Committee **C/VW:** Homeless Ministries
Email: rmeachum@satx.rr.com
URL: http://www.cambridgewhoswho.com

Marianne Karol

Title: Social Worker **Company:** Fam Care **Address:** 270 Chestnut Road, Bridgeton, NJ 08302 United States **BUS:** Social Services Agency **P/S:** Adolescent and Parenting Programs **MA:** Regional **D/D/R:** Counseling Pregnant Adolescents, Visiting Homes to Provide Support Services, Teaching Stress Education to Girls Under the age of 18, Educating Adolescents about Employment and Parenting Skills **EDU:** Bachelor of Arts in Sociology, Rowan University (1978) **CERTS:** Certified Social Worker (2007) **A/A/S:** Jersey Cape Shell Club

Emilie L. Karpiuk

Title: Oncology Pharmacist **Company:** Wheaton Froedtert Hospital **Address:** 9200 W. Wisconsin Avenue, Wauwautosa, WI 53213 United States **BUS:** Hospital **P/S:** Healthcare, Patient Care **MA:** Regional **EXP:** Ms. Karpiuk's expertise includes adult medicine and oncology. **H/I/S:** Music, Gardening, Reading, Golf, Mission Work **EDU:** PharmD Degree, University of Texas Health Science Center (1984); Bachelor's Degree in Pharmacy, University of Michigan (1973) **CERTS:** Board Certified in Oncology Pharmacy Therapy **A/A/S:** American College of Clinical Pharmacy; American Society of Health System Pharmacists; Pharmacy Society of Wisconsin; Public Speaking Locally; Published Articles and Abstracts
Email: ekarpiuk@gmail.com

Betty Lou Kary-Khan, LPN

Title: Licensed Practical Nurse **Company:** Saint Alexius Medical Center **Address:** 1722 E. Avenue D, Bismarck, ND 58501 United States **BUS:** Medical Center **P/S:** Healthcare **MA:** National **EXP:** Ms. Kary-Khan's expertise includes geriatric healthcare and in-home care. **H/I/S:** Reading, Gardening, Spending Time with her Children and Grandchildren, Caring for her Cats and Dogs **CERTS:** Licensed Practical Nurse, North Dakota State College of Science, Wahpeton **C/VW:** American Cancer Society
Email: bkarykhan_1@hotmail.com
URL: http://www.cambridgewhoswho.com

Barbara Kashinski

Title: Lead Provider Liaison **Company:** ValueOptions of New Mexico **Address:** P.O. Box 30650, Albuquerque, NM 87190 United States **BUS:** Behavioral Healthcare Company **P/S:** Behavioral Healthcare Statewide combining Public and Private Funding **MA:** New Mexico **D/D/R:** Maintaining Provider Relations, Contracting, Coding (ICD-9, CPT, HCPCS), Training, Quality Management **H/I/S:** Baroness in the Society for Creative Anachronism **EDU:** Pursuing Ph.D. in Psychology, Northcentral University; Bachelor of Arts in History, University of New Mexico **CERTS:** Certified Professional in Healthcare Quality, National Association for Healthcare Quality **A/H:** First Employee of the Month, July 2005, Value Options of New Mexico
Email: barbara.kashinski@valueoptions.com

Mr. Mark C. Kasmarek, BS, PG

Title: Ground-Water Hydrologist **Company:** U.S. Geological Survey **Address:** 19241 David Memorial Drive, Suite 180, Shenandoah, TX 77385 United States **BUS:** Government Agency **P/S:** Collection, Archival and Presentation of Scientific Data of Landscapes and Natural Resources Including Biological and Mineral Resources and Water **MA:** Texas **EXP:** Mr. Kasmarek's expertise includes the study and collection of data on groundwater, water quality and levels, and land subsidence. **D/D/R:** Operating and Maintaining 13 Extensometers at 11 Sites, Monitoring and Evaluating the Groundwater, Reporting Results, Designing 2 Groundwater Flow Models using Modflow, Consulting with Federal, State and Local Agencies **H/I/S:** Hunting, Fishing, Studying Herpetology, Repairing Automobiles, Air Conditioners and Refrigerators, Scuba Diving, Bicycling, Reading Military World History, Collecting Rocks, Minerals and Fossils, Flying Airplanes **EDU:** Bachelor's Degree in Geological Sciences, The University of Texas (1982) **CERTS:** Certified Scuba Diver, National Association of Scuba Diving Schools (1974) **A/A/S:** School of Public Health, The University of Texas; Houston Geological Society **A/H:** U.S. Geological Survey Superior Service Award (2008)
Email: mckasmar@usgs.gov
URL: http://www.usgs.gov

Nancy L. Kasprzyk

Title: Pet Groomer **Company:** Crestway Animal Clinic **Address:** 6636 Crestway Drive, San Antonio, TX 78239 United States **BUS:** Grooming Veterinarian **P/S:** Pet Grooming, Clipping Nails, Cleaning Teeth and Ears, Cutting Hair and Bathing **MA:** International **D/D/R:** Offering Dog and Cat Grooming **H/I/S:** Traveling, Reading, Arts, Crafts, Photography, Computers **EDU:** South West Texas University-TX, St Edwards University-TX, San Antonio College-TX, College Courses-Art (Commercial)
Email: kaspr1986@yahoo.com

Renata Katayev

Title: Pharmacist **Company:** Walgreens Pharmacy **Address:** 3007 Aventura Boulevard, Aventura, FL 33180 United States **BUS:** Retail Pharmacy **P/S:** Pharmaceuticals **MA:** National **EXP:** Ms. Katayev's expertise is in diabetes. **H/I/S:** Spending Time with her Family **EDU:** Doctor of Pharmacy, Nova Southeastern University **A/A/S:** American Pharmacists Association; Florida Pharmacists Association **C/VW:** St. Jude Children's Research Hospital
Email: renatka17@aol.com

Suneel Katragadda, MD

Title: Medical Doctor, Children and Adolescent Psychiatrist **Company:** AVITA Community Partners **Address:** 2318 Brown Bridge Road, Gainesville, GA 30504 **BUS:** Community Practice **P/S:** Education, Healthcare **MA:** Regional **D/D/R:** Offering Adult, Child and Adolescent Psychiatry **H/I/S:** Traveling, Playing Tennis **EDU:** MD, Earned in India; Residency Training in Psychiatry, University of Alabama, Birmingham; Fellowship Training in Child and Adolescent Psychiatry, University of Alabama, Birmingham **CERTS:** Board Certification in Psychiatry, American Psychiatry Association, 1993 **A/A/S:** American Psychiatric Association; American Medical Association; American Academy of Child and Adolescent Psychiatry **C/VW:** National Alliance for the Mentally Ill
Email: suneelbk@yahoo.com

Joleen R. Katula

Title: Director of Operations **Company:** Health Spring **Address:** 9701 W. Higgins Road, Suite 360, Rosemont, IL 60018 United States **BUS:** Health Maintenance Organization **P/S:** Medicare Advantage Program **MA:** National **D/D/R:** Managing Memberships **H/I/S:** Traveling, Reading **EDU:** Bachelor of Science in Business Management, 1996, Millikin University **C/VW:** Y-Me, Access Community Health
Email: joleenk@healthspring.com
URL: http://www.cambridgewhoswho.com

Paula Markgraf Katz

Title: Director of Human Resources **Company:** The Los Angeles Times **Address:** 202 W. First Street, Los Angeles, CA 90012 United States **BUS:** Media Company **P/S:** Newspaper, Website **MA:** Local **EXP:** Ms. Katz's expertise includes employee relations, compensation, organizational effectiveness, staffing and recruitment. **H/I/S:** Playing the Piano, Listening to Music, Gardening, Practicing Yoga, Studying Politics, Walking **EDU:** Master of Arts in Ethnomusicology, University of Wisconsin; Bachelor of Music, University of Wisconsin **A/A/S:** Society for Human Resource Management; Lacoba **C/VW:** United Way, Planned Parenthood Federation of America
Email: paula.katz@latimes.com
URL: http://www.latimes.com

Angela Renee Kauffman
Title: Director of United States Marketing Operations **Company:** AON Corporation **Address:** 200 E. Randolph Street, 19th Floor, Chicago, IL 60601 United States **BUS:** Consulting Agency **P/S:** Risk Consulting, Insurance and Financial Services Including Insurance Brokerage **MA:** International **EXP:** Ms. Kauffman's expertise is in marketing. **H/I/S:** Planning her Wedding, Caring for her Two Greyhounds **EDU:** Master of Business Administration in Marketing and Management Strategy, Kellogg School of Management, Northwestern University (2005); Bachelor's Degree in Public Relations, Purdue University (1998) **A/A/S:** American Business Women's Association
Email: angela.kauffman@aon.com
URL: http://www.aon.com

Kirsten J. Kauffman-Perrelli
Title: Owner **Company:** Ginger Root Hair Salon **Address:** 524 W. State Street, Unit 1, Geneva, IL 60134 United States **BUS:** Aveda Concept Hair Salon **P/S:** Hair Styling, Waxing, Nails and Make-Up **MA:** Local **D/D/R:** Coloring and Installing Hair Extensions **H/I/S:** Classic Cars, Painting **EDU:** Hair Professional Beauty School (1991) **A/A/S:** Geneva Chamber of Commerce
Email: kirstenperrelli@hotmail.com
URL: http://www.gingerroothairsalon.net

Kerry Kaullen
Title: Program Administrator **Company:** Department of Agriculture **Address:** P.O. Box 630, Jefferson City, MO 65102 United States **BUS:** Regulatory State Petroleum Program **P/S:** Inspection Programs for Safety and Accuracy of Petroleum Services **MA:** Statewide **D/D/R:** Managing Field Staff of 25 Employees and Two Clerical Employees, Administrative Duties **H/I/S:** Swimming, Biking, Spending Time with Family **EDU:** High School Education **A/A/S:** Zonta International; National Conference of Weights and Measures; Central Conference Weights and Measures; Volunteer for RACS **C/VW:** United Way
Email: kerry.kaullen@mda.mo.gov
URL: http://www.mda.mo.gov

Kathryn A. Kavanagh
Title: Chief Financial Officer **Company:** Southbay Vending **Address:** 80556 Apricot Lane, Indio, CA 92201 United States **BUS:** Food Service Industry **P/S:** Vending, Food Preparation **MA:** Regional **D/D/R:** Overseeing All Payroll, Bills, Accounts Receivable and Payable, Hiring, Interviewing, Employee Paperwork, Offering Food Service to Two Prisons in the Indio Area, Liaison with Officials at the Facilities, Supplying All the Vending for Guards and Visitors, Has a San Francisco Vending Services Location, Formerly Cosmetic Retail Background **H/I/S:** Wine Tasting **EDU:** Bachelor of Arts in Interior Design, Illinois State University (1986) **A/A/S:** Parent Teachers Association
Email: katykav@dc.rr.com

Sophia Kaveti
Title: Vice President **Company:** Asterix Consulting, Inc. **Address:** 303 Fifth Avenue, Suite 1301, New York, NY 10016 United States **BUS:** Consulting Firm **P/S:** Information Technology Management, Clinical Research, Consulting **MA:** International **EXP:** Ms. Kaveti's expertise is in information technology. **H/I/S:** Reading, Watching Television **EDU:** Master's Degree in Computer Information, Kingston College **C/VW:** American Cancer Society, Paralyzed Veterans of America
Email: sri@asterixusa.com
URL: http://www.asterixusa.com

Rebecca Moore Kay
Title: Music Specialist (Retired), Hospice Volunteer Musician, Professional Organist **Company:** Hickory Grove Baptist Church **Address:** 1713 Landsdale Drive, Charlotte, NC 28205 United States **BUS:** Music **P/S:** Piano and Organ Instruction and Performance **MA:** Statewide **D/D/R:** Utilizing her Expertise as a Music Specialist **H/I/S:** Reading, Knitting, Crocheting and Painting **EDU:** Bachelor of Art in Music, Furman University **A/A/S:** Hickory Grove Baptist Church; Union County Board of Education **C/VW:** Hospice; Music Performances, Assisted Living Homes
Email: rebec1713@aol.com

Mr. Soroush Kazemi
Title: Corporate Manager **Company:** AT&T **Address:** P. O. Box 642795, Los Angeles, CA 90064 United States **BUS:** Telecommunications Company **P/S:** Telecommunication Services **MA:** National **D/D/R:** Managing Network Planning and Engineering, Overseeing Financial Planning **H/I/S:** Playing Racquetball, Swimming **EDU:** Master's Degree in Telecommunications, French Institute of Telecommunications, Paris, France (1992)
Email: Soroush-Kazemi@hps07.com
URL: http://www.att.com

Seems Z. Kazmi
Title: Pharmacist **Company:** Rite Aid Corporation **Address:** 6912 New Falls Road, Levittown, PA 19057 United States **BUS:** Retail Pharmacy **P/S:** Prescription Medications, Herbals, Vitamins, Over-the-Counter Remedies **MA:** National **EXP:** Dr. Kazmi's expertise includes ambulatory care, over-the-counter remedies, herbals, medication adherence, patient consultation and customer service. **H/I/S:** Listening to Music, Walking **EDU:** Doctor of Pharmacy, University of the Sciences in Philadelphia, Philadelphia College of Pharmacy, Magna Cum Laude **A/A/S:** American Pharmacists Association; American College of Clinical Pharmacy; Rho Chi Pharmaceutical Honor Society **A/H:** President's Choice Award, Student Government Association, USP; Top Ten Finalist APhA Local Patient Counseling Competition, USP
Email: seema137@gmail.com

Carolyn A. Keane
Title: Chief Executive Officer **Company:** Perket Technologies, Inc. **Address:** P.O. Box 492323, Lawrenceville, GA 30049 United States **BUS:** Network Security Consulting **P/S:** Security, Consulting, Informational Technology **MA:** National **EXP:** Ms. Kearney's expertise is in business operational administration. **H/I/S:** Golfing, **EDU:** Bachelor's Degree in Political Science, University of Georgia **C/VW:** Various Civic Organizations
Email: ckeane@perket.com
URL: http://www.perket.com

Dr. Donna J. Kearns
Title: Professor **Company:** University of Central Oklahoma **Address:** 100 N. University Drive, Edmond, OK 73034 United States **BUS:** Institution of Higher Learning Dedicated to Excellence in Education **P/S:** College of Arts, Media and Design, College of Business Administration, College of Education, College of Liberal Arts, College of Mathematics and Sciences and Many Other Programs and Degrees **MA:** Regional **EXP:** Dr. Kearns' expertise includes special education, transition issues, research and class supervision. **H/I/S:** Reading **EDU:** Doctorate of Education, University of Missouri **A/A/S:** Council of Exceptional Children; Children with Disabilities Association; Children and Adults with Attention Deficit Disorders
Email: dkearns@ucok.edu
URL: http://www.ucok.edu

Patricia 'Trish' Keaton
Title: Program Manager, Business Development Lead **Company:** Northrop Grumman Corporation **Address:** 1800 Glenn Curtiss Street, Carson, CA 90746 United States **BUS:** Aerospace and Defense Company **P/S:** Defense Systems **MA:** National **D/D/R:** Overseeing the Development and Marketing of Sensor and Networking Systems, Managing Leadership, Creating, Identifying, Qualifying, Shaping and Capturing New Business Targets, Implementing Business Developments, Managing Acquisition Processes, Managing Business Operations, Principle Investigating, Inventing, Managing Project Programs, Working as a Marketing Representative, Developing Proposals and Software **H/I/S:** Snowboarding, Listening to Music **EDU:** Pursuing Doctorate in Electrical Engineering, California Institute of Technology; Master of Science, Electrical Engineering, University of Texas, El Paso, with Honors; Bachelor of Science, Electrical Engineering, University of Texas, El Paso, Summa Cum Laude **A/A/S:** Institute of Electrical and Electronics Engineers; Association for Computing Machinery **C/VW:** Pet Adoption Fund
Email: trish.keaton@gmail.com

Elaine A. Keefe, RN
Title: Registered Nurse **Company:** Cambridge Health Alliance-Whidden Memorial Hospital **Address:** 1 Cedar Hill Drive, Danvers, MA 01923 United States **BUS:** Health System **P/S:** Primary Care, Family Medicine, Breast Center, Pediatrics, Cardiology, General Surgery, Senior Health, Dermatology, Endocrinology, Dental Services, Gastroenterology, Eye Care Center, Geriatrics, Ophthalmology, Emergency Medicine and Many Other Services **MA:** Regional **D/D/R:** Emergency Room Nursing, Rapid Response Unit, Intensive Care Nursing, Clinical Resource Nursing **EDU:** Master Level Program in Healthcare Science, Nursing and Leadership, Cambridge College **A/A/S:** Massachusetts Nursing Association; Emergency Nursing Association
Email: ekeefe@verizon.net
URL: http://www.challiance.org

Anne M. Keegan
Title: Special Educator **Company:** Adlai E. Stevenson High School **Address:** 1980 Lafayette Avenue, Bronx, NY 10473 United States **BUS:** Public High School **P/S:** High School Education, Special Education **MA:** Local **D/D/R:** Teaching 9 through 12 Grade Students with Mental Developmental Problems, Teaching All Subjects and Life Skills **H/I/S:** Playing Guitar, Singing **EDU:** Master's Degree Plus 30 in Special Education, Concentration in Students with Emotional Handicaps, College of New Rochelle, New York (1981) **A/A/S:** Council for Exceptional Children; School Treasurer, Former Department Assistant for Special Education; Former, Adjunct Professor at The College of Mount St. Vincent (1998-2004) **A/H:** Bronx 'Teacher of the Year' Award (1992)
Email: akeegan713@yahoo.com

Elizabeth J. Keeler, Ph.D.
Title: Community Resource Program Manager, Social Worker, Director of Networking and Education (Retired) **Company:** Washington State Department of Social & Health Services **Dept:** Helping Ourselves Means Education 'HOME' **BUS:** Nonprofit Public, Social and Health Service Organization **P/S:** Social Services, Education, Program Development, Resource Development, Job-Seeking Workshops for Welfare Recipients, Internship Programs, Newsletters and Workshops for Single Parents, Resource Center for Parents, Support for Parents Overcoming Challenges **MA:** Regional **EXP:** Ms. Keeler's area of expertise is resource center management. **D/D/R:** Organizing Workshops, Counseling and Teaching Fifth and Sixth-Grade Students, Offering Social Services to Single Parents, Overseeing the Development of a Resource Center for Single Parents, Collaborating with Local Social Service Agencies to Identify Service Gaps and Develop Programs to Serve Unmet Needs, Overseeing the Job-Seeking Workshops for Welfare Recipients, Offering Informational Workshops and Free Newsletters for those Wanting to Escape Poverty, Assisting those Seeking Higher Education through the Program 'Helping Ourselves Means Higher Education' **H/I/S:** Traveling, Skiing, Reading, Studying Genealogy, Writing, Serving on Boards and Committees of Nonprofit Social Service Programs **EDU:** Ph.D. in Leadership Studies, Gonzaga University; Master of Public Administration, Eastern Washington University; Master of Social Work, Eastern Washington University; Master's Degree in Applied Behavioral Science, Whitworth University; Master's Degree in Home Economics, Washington State University; Bachelor's Degree in Home Economics, Washington State University **A/A/S:** National Association of Social Workers; Eastern Washington Genealogical Society; Daughters of the American Revolution; Spokane Authors and Self-Publishers; Co-Founder, Former Board Member, Support for Parents Overcoming Challenges **A/H:** Woman of Achievement Award for Community Service, Young Women's Christian Association **C/VW:** Strategy Team, Spokane Alliance; Board Member, Eastern Washington Home; Family Empowerment Committee, Local Church
Email: kae3@q.com

Melissa M. Keen
Title: Corporate HIM Internal Auditor **Company:** St. Vincent's Health System **Address:** 810 St. Vincent's Drive, Birmingham, AL 35205 United States **BUS:** Hospital **P/S:** Acute Healthcare **MA:** Local **D/D/R:** Medical Coding **H/I/S:** Drawing, Reading **EDU:** Master of Business Administration, University of Southern Mississippi; Bachelor of Science in Health Information Management, University of Alabama, Birmingham; Bachelor of Science in Zoology, Louisiana State University **A/A/S:** American Health Information Management Association; Board of Directors, Alabama Association of Health Information Management; Local Chapter, American Health Information Management Association
Email: mkeen3348@charter.net

Ann N. Keenan
Title: Owner **Company:** Pine Needle Farm **Address:** P.O. Box 216, Kila, MT 59920 United States **BUS:** Farm **P/S:** Hand Spun Cashmere Yarn, Goat Milk Soap **MA:** International **EXP:** Ms. Keenan's expertise is in fiber artistry. **H/I/S:** Reading, Hiking, exercising **A/A/S:** North West Cashmere Association
Email: pineneedlefarm@yahoo.com
URL: http://www.pnfcashmeres.com

Rhoda J. Keener
Title: Executive Director **Company:** Mennonite Women, USA **Address:** 5207 Heisey Road, Shippensburg, PA 17257 United States **BUS:** Church Administration Church **P/S:** Denominational Women's Organization, Women's Ministry Resources, Retreats Publications **MA:** International **EXP:** Ms. Keener's expertise includes sister-link connections and global connections. **H/I/S:** Family Time, Co-Editor-'She has done a good thing' **EDU:** St Francis, Master's Degree in Health and Counseling, Denominational Women's Organization **A/A/S:** Women's Ministry Resources, Retreats, Publications
Email: Rhodak@mennonitewomenusa.org
URL: www.mennonitewomenusa.org

Krista J. Keeton, MSPT
Title: Physical Therapist **Company:** Hook Rehabilitation Center at Community Hospital East **Address:** 1500 N. Ritter Avenue, Indianapolis, IN 46219 United States **BUS:** Rehabilitation Facility **P/S:** Rehabilitation Services for Patients with Brain Injuries **MA:** Regional **D/D/R:** Working with Brain Injury Patients, Training Family Members **H/I/S:** Sports, Watching and Playing Basketball, Softball, Bike Riding, Spending Time with Family **EDU:** Master of Science in Physical Therapy, Krannert School of Physical Therapy, University of Indianapolis; Bachelor of Science in Biology and Chemistry, University of Indianapolis **C/VW:** Hook Athletic Program
Email: ksquared0605@aol.com
URL: http://www.cambridgewhoswho.com

Gail A. Kegolis
Title: Partner Company: Millgate Capital, Inc. Address: 500 Fifth Avenue, Suite 5200, New York, NY 10110 United States BUS: Hedge Fund P/S: International Equity Hedge Fund MA: International D/D/R: Trading, Client Services H/I/S: Reading EDU: Bachelor of Arts in Liberal Arts, Villanova University A/A/S: New Presbyterian Hospital; NDSS C/VW: Operation Smile Email: gail@millgateinc.com
URL: http://www.cambridgewhoswho.com

Edward J. Kehrer
Title: Electrician Company: IBEW Local 309 Address: 205 N. Broadway, Albers, IL 62215 United States BUS: Electrician Service Provider P/S: Electrical Work, Construction MA: Local EXP: Mr. Kehrer's expertise includes service and installation. EDU: Associate Degree in Technology A/A/S: Knights of Columbus
Email: ekehrer@yahoo.com

Mr. Dennis J. Keitel
Title: Senior Project Manager Company: Camp Dresser & McKee, Inc. Dept: Public Services Group Address: 12501 World Plaza Lane, Building 51, Fort Myers, FL 33907 United States BUS: Engineering Firm P/S: Private, Residential, Commercial, Industrial and Municipal Engineering MA: Regional EXP: Mr. Keitel's expertise includes water supply and distribution, and wastewater collection and management. H/I/S: Rowing, Scuba Diving, Sailing, Camping EDU: Master of Business Administration, University of Iowa; Bachelor of Science in Civil Engineering, Iowa State University A/A/S: American Society of Civil Engineers; Society of American Military Engineers; Old Capitol Rowing Club C/VW: Boy Scouts of America
Email: keiteldj@cdm.com
Email: djkeitel@juno.com
URL: http://www.cdm.com

Donna M. Keith
Title: President, Owner Company: Advanced Insurance Group, Inc. Address: 918 Grey Fox Avenue, Sebring, FL 33875 United States BUS: Insurance Agency P/S: Employer-Based Health Benefit Plans MA: Regional EXP: Ms. Keith's expertise includes business management. H/I/S: Swimming, Exercising, Home Remodeling EDU: Bachelor of Arts in Biology, Gocher College, Towson, Maryland C/VW: 4-H Clubs, Local County Fairs, Local Schools
Email: dmkins@embarqmail.com
URL: http://www.cambridgewhoswho.com

Renee Keith
Title: Treasurer, Secretary Company: Water Flow Productions, Inc. Address: 781 Highway 589, Purvis, MS 39475 United States BUS: Garden Center and Feed Store P/S: Garden Products MA: Regional EXP: Ms. Keith's expertise includes operations management and administration. H/I/S: Spending Time with Family EDU: Associate of Science in Computer Science, Pearl River Community College, Poplarville, Mississippi A/A/S: Mississippi Nursery and Landscape Association; Southern Nursery Association; Better Business Bureau; Economic Development Partnership C/VW: Special Olympics, Local Charities
Email: rolling20@comcast.net
URL: http://www.waterflowproductions.com

Karen A. Keleman
Title: Health Sewers Support Admin-D Company: The Boeing Company Address: 7755 E. Marginal Way S., Seattle, WA 98108 United States BUS: Aerospace P/S: Manufacture of Airplanes MA: International EXP: Ms. Keleman's expertise includes medical records confidentiality and data entry. D/D/R: Working EMR H/I/S: Egyptology EDU: Hyland Community College; Associate Degree, University of Washington A/A/S: AHIMA

Julia Kellaway
Title: Radio Announcer Company: Family Life Ministries Network Address: 7634 Campbell Creek Road, Bath, NY 14810 United States BUS: Nonprofit Christian Radio Ministry P/S: Christian Radio, Drama, Dinner Concerts and Theater MA: International D/D/R: Interviewing and Editing, Overnight Announcer, Sharing to Churches and Retreats of the Influence of God on her Life H/I/S: Hiking, Piano, Music, Singing, Theater, Biking EDU: Bachelor of Arts in Speech Communications, Roosevelt University (1991) A/A/S: Alpha Lambda Delta; Cum Laude; Who's Who Among American High School Students
Email: jkellaway@stny.rr.com
URL: http://www.fln.org

Dawn M. Keller
Title: Vice President of Strategic Sales Company: IES, Ltd. Address: 445 Godwin Avenue, Midland Park, NJ 07432 United States BUS: Software Company P/S: Document Software for Logistics Industry MA: International EXP: Ms. Keller's expertise is in sales. D/D/R: Managing the Warehouse and Inventory H/I/S: Traveling, Playing Sports, Playing Basketball, Running, Playing Golf EDU: Bachelor of Arts in Accounting, College of Saint Elizabeth A/A/S: Organization of Women in International Trade; Foreign Commerce Club; Council of Supply Chain Management Professionals; World Cargo Alliance C/VW: Cancer and Disability Charities
Email: dawn@iesltd.com
URL: http://www.iesltd.com

Rev. Mary L. Keller
Title: Pastor Company: First Divine Science Church Address: 16 Fox Creek Road, Belleville, IL 62223 United States BUS: Church P/S: Religious and Spiritual Services MA: Regional D/D/R: Spiritual Counseling, Teaching, Lecturing, Caring for People, Organizing Outreach Programs H/I/S: Reading, Writing, Listening to Music, Watching College Plays, Spending Time with her Grandchildren EDU: College Coursework CERTS: Ordained, Crestwood Church of Divine Science (1995) A/A/S: Church Women United; Zonta International; American Business Women's Association A/H: Zonta of the Year Award
Email: marygeok@sbcglobal.net
URL: http://www.cambridgewhoswho.com

Beverly D. Kelley
Title: Senior Event Director Company: Agility Event Planning Address: 311 28th Street, Old Hickory, TN 37138 United States BUS: Corporate Event Planning P/S: Coordinates All Facets of Occasions, Corporate Meetings, Meetings, Sales Meetings, Trade Shows, Weddings, Birthdays and Anniversaries MA: National D/D/R: Exceptional Attention to Detail in Handling All Aspects of Planning for Corporate Events, Training Classes for Companies on Trade Show Etiquette, Assessing Needs to Create the Perfect Final Products H/I/S: Horseback Riding CERTS: Certified Corporate Meeting Planner; Certified Trade Show Manager A/A/S: President, Old Hickory Chamber of Commerce; Nashville Chamber of Commerce
Email: bkagility@bellsouth.net
URL: http://www.agilityeventplanning.com

Diane Kelley
Title: Book Writer Company: Happiness is Reading and Exercising BUS: Writer P/S: Writing Books, Child Care MA: International D/D/R: Writing, Helping Others H/I/S: Writing, Exercising EDU: Bachelor's Degree in Business Administration, College of Alameda CERTS: Certification, Institute of Children's Literature C/VW: Volunteer, Kaiser Permanente
Email: dianekelley28179@sbcglobal.net

Kristie Lee Kelley
Title: Radiologic Technologist Company: Cary Medical Center Address: 10 Dudley Street, Presque Isle, ME 04769 United States BUS: Medical Center P/S: Healthcare MA: Regional EXP: Ms. Kelley's expertise includes outpatient services with X-rays and CAT scans. D/D/R: Managing Operations of the Emergency Room, X-raying and Performing CAT Scans EDU: Associate Degree in Medical Radiology, Eastern Maine Community College, Bangor, ME (2006); Associate Degree in Liberal Studies, University of Maine, Presque Isle (2004) A/A/S: American Society of Radiologic Technologists
Email: kristie.kelley@maine.edu
URL: http://www.cambridgewhoswho.com

Michael Garhart Kelley
Title: Professor of History (Retired) BUS: Higher Education P/S: Historian, Environmentalist MA: Local EXP: Mr. Kelley's expertise includes medieval Scottish history, the American Shakers, human rights activism and feminism. H/I/S: Genealogy EDU: Ph.D. in Medieval Scottish History, 1973, University of Edinburgh, Scotland; Master's Degree in European History, 1967, Boston University, Boston, Massachusetts; Bachelor's Degree in History, 1966, Boston University; Magna Cum Laude A/A/S: Phi Beta Kappa; Political Campaigns for Nancy Pelosi and Barbara Boxer in the 1980s; Marquis Who's Who in America C/VW: Sierra Club, World Wildlife Fund, Senior Center, Salvation Army, Various Church Organizations
URL: http://www.cambridgewhoswho.com

James K. Kellough
Title: Owner Company: Details Unlimited, LLC Address: 917 W. Quartz Street, Butte, MT 59701 United States BUS: Construction Company P/S: Construction MA: Local D/D/R: Restoring Old Buildings, Managing Construction H/I/S: Professional Stuntman A/A/S: Exchange Club of Butte, Montana C/VW: Volunteer, Big Brothers Big Sisters of America; Breast Cancer Society
Email: jmpinjames@aol.com

Annita Kelly
Title: Owner Company: Nita's Place Address: 212 S. Main Street, Fort Atkinson, WI 53538 United States BUS: Gallery Gift Shop P/S: Gifts, Woodwork, Handmade Jewelry, Pottery, Fine Crafts, Art MA: Local D/D/R: Making Jewelry, Creating Artwork from Wrought Iron H/I/S: Reading, Painting EDU: Bachelor's Degree in Political Science, University of Wisconsin-Milwaukee
Email: akelly@jetnet.com

Dorothy O. Kelly
Title: Special Education Teacher-Retiree Company: Onondaga-Cortland-Madison BOCES Address: 17 Hickory Park Road, Cortland, NY 13045 United States BUS: School District P/S: Education for the Developmentally Delayed MA: Regional D/D/R: Working with At-Risk Children from Infant to Three Years-Old with Special Needs, Conducting Home Visits with Children with Special Needs as a Special Instructor, Working with a Team of Therapists and Families to Assist Children in Achieving their Goals, Teaching Functional Academics and Daily Living Skills, Managing Developmentally Delayed Programs EDU: Bachelor of Arts in Elementary Education and Special Education, Marywood University, Scranton, PA (1964) CERTS: Permanent Certification in Elementary and Special Education, State of New York A/A/S: New York State United Teachers Union; Former Leader, Girl Scouts Of America; Former Assistant, Boy Scouts of America C/VW: Cortland County Retired Senior Volunteer Program
Email: dkelly40@twcny.rr.com
URL: http://www.ocmboces.org

Kelly Kelly
Title: Manager of Operations Company: Archery Trade Association Address: P.O. Box 253, Comfrey, MN 56019 United States BUS: Nonprofit Archery and Bow Hunting Trade Association P/S: Promoting and Growing the Sport of Archery MA: National D/D/R: Assisting the Chief Executive Officer, Working with Board Members, Assisting with Setting Up Exhibits at Trade Shows, Coordinating Events and Meetings H/I/S: Hunting, Volleyball, Children's Activities EDU: Diploma in Accounting, South Central Technical College (1990)
Email: kellykelly@archerytrade.org
URL: http://www.archertrade.org

Nancy Kelly
Title: Nurse Company: Mary Immaculate Hospital Address: 152-11 89th Avenue, Jamaica, NY 11436 United States BUS: Hospital P/S: Level One Trauma and Cardiac Units MA: Regional D/D/R: Ensuring Job Flow, Monitoring and Supporting Staff, Troubleshooting, Patient Care, Intervention H/I/S: Watching the New York Yankees Baseball Team EDU: Master's Degree in Nursing, Lehman College (2000); Bachelor's Degree in General Studies, Excelsior College (1997) A/A/S: Adjunct Professor in Nursing, City University of New York; Emergency Nurses Association
Email: mkelly6801@aol.com

Noreen A. Kelly-Najah
Title: Attorney Company: Latham & Watkins, LLP Address: 885 Third Avenue, New York, NY 10022 United States BUS: Law Firm P/S: Legal Services MA: Regional EXP: Ms. Kelly-Najah's expertise includes white collar criminal defense and securities litigation. EDU: JD, New York University A/A/S: Second Criminal Federal Court of Appeals; New Jersey State Bar Association; New York State Bar Association; Southern District of New York Bar Association; Eastern District of New York Bar Association; District of New Jersey Bar Association
Email: noreen.kelly-najah@lw.com
URL: http://www.lw.com

Susan J. Kempfer
Title: Nurse Reviewer Company: United Health Care Address: 550 Warrenville Road, Lisle, IL 60532 United States BUS: Insurance Company P/S: Insurance MA: National D/D/R: Reviewing Cases H/I/S: Making Art, Traveling, Eating in Restaurants, Watching Theater and Opera EDU: Bachelor of Science, Loyola University A/A/S: CMFA C/VW: American Heart Association; American Red Cross
Email: susan_j_kempfer@unitedhealthcare.com

Sherie L. Kendall, Ph.D.
Title: Assistant Professor in Biology **Company:** Midway College **Address:** 512 E. Stephens Street, Midway, KY 40347 United States **BUS:** Private Women's College **P/S:** Undergraduate Degree Programs, Career Development Programs, Learning Resources, Student Support Services, Student Clubs and Organizations **MA:** Local **D/D/R:** Teaching Biology to Students Enrolled in the Division of Nursing and Science, Conducting Brain Research, Researching Neurobiology and Life Planning **EDU:** Ph.D. in Medical Neurobiology, Indiana University School of Medicine (2001); Bachelor's Degree in Biology, with Distinction, Indiana University (1993) **CERTS:** Certification in Career Training, Therapeutic and Transitional Research, Indiana University **A/A/S:** Recording Secretary, Faculty Leadership Council, Midway College; Chairwoman, Faculty Development Committee, Midway College; Director of Research, Foundation for Life Care Planning Research; American Association for the Advancement of Science; Society for Neuroscience; Beta Beta Beta National Biological Honor Society; The Kentucky Academy of Science
Email: skendall@midway.edu
URL: http://www.midway.edu

Mr. Brian C. Kennedy
Title: Realtor **Company:** Re/Max North Coast **Address:** 1225 W. Morse Avenue, Suite 100, Chicago, IL 60626 United States **BUS:** Real Estate Brokerage **P/S:** Condominium Conversions **MA:** National **D/D/R:** Negotiating with Clients, Conducting Buyer Seminars, Marketing and Financing Property Sales, Managing Residential Property Sales **EDU:** Post-Doctorate Degree in Information and Technology (1987) **A/A/S:** Rogers Park Builders Group; DevCorp North; Illinois Association of Realtors; Chicago Association of Realtors; National Association of Realtors
Email: Brian@CallMyAgentBrian.com
Email: Brian@LivingInLakeView.com
URL: http://www.CallMyAgentBrian.com
URL: http://www.LivingInLakeView.com

Derek B. Kennedy
Title: Teacher **Company:** Teach for America, Markham Middle School **Address:** 1650 E. 104th Street, Inglewood, CA 90002 United States **BUS:** Public School **P/S:** Education **MA:** Local **D/D/R:** Teaching Life Science, Mentoring **H/I/S:** Playing Sports, Reading, Watching Movies **EDU:** Bachelor of Arts in Cultural Anthropology, Duke University; Master's Degree in Secondary Science Education, Loyola University **A/A/S:** Phi Eta Sigma; Teach for America **C/VW:** Teach for America, Local Hospitals
Email: derek.kennedy@gmail.com
URL: http://www.cambridgewhoswho.com

John W. Kennedy
Title: President **Company:** John W. Kennedy Consultants **BUS:** Consulting Firm **P/S:** Consulting Services for Companies Obtaining Clearances from U.S. Environmental Protection Agency **MA:** International **D/D/R:** Researching for Cancer and Other Diseases, Writing Novels and Technical Manuals, Consulting **H/I/S:** Scuba Diving **EDU:** Master's Degree in Biological Science and Entomology, Major in Advanced Studies, NY; Bachelor's Degree in Botany and Natural Science, University of Wisconsin-Madison (1962) **A/A/S:** The Rescue Squad, Maryland; AFIS; Entomological Society of America **A/H:** Distinguished Alumni Award, University of Wisconsin (2002); Distinguished Alumni Award, D.C. Everest High School
Email: John.Kennedy@cwwemail.com
Email: johnwaynekennedy@hotmail.com

Mary Ann Kennedy, MAE
Title: Sixth-Grade Science Instructor **Company:** Fredericktown R-1 School District **Address:** 501 South Park Drive, Fredericktown, MO 63645 United States **BUS:** Public School System **P/S:** Primary and Secondary Education **MA:** Regional **D/D/R:** Teaching Sixth-Grade Level Science, Using a Hands-On and Standard Curriculum **H/I/S:** Embroidery, Crocheting, Sign Painting, Reading **EDU:** Master's Degree in Education, Webster University (2001); Bachelor of Arts in General Education K-8, Central Methodist University (1995); Associate of Arts in General Education K-12, Mineral Area College (1992) **CERTS:** Certified Library Media Specialist (2005); Accounting Certificate in Bookkeeping, Scranton, Pennsylvania (1977) **A/A/S:** Missouri State Teachers Association; Volunteer, Literacy Coordination, Southwestern Bell Telephone (1998)
Email: kennedya@fredericktown.k12.mo.us
URL: http://www.fredericktown.k12.mo.us

Tiffany H. Kennedy
Title: Local Manager **Company:** Verizon **Address:** 820 Macbeth Drive, Monroeville, PA 15146 United States **BUS:** Telecommunications Company **P/S:** High-Speed Data Network for Homes, Small and Large Businesses, Wireless, Television, Entertainment, Communications **MA:** National **D/D/R:** Managing High Speed Data TI, T3, DS3, OC12s and Dial Tones, Installations, Overseeing Maintenance, 15 Technicians and Job Inspections, Meeting with Clients **H/I/S:** Playing Softball, Traveling **EDU:** Pursuing Master of Business Administration; Master's Degree in Management and Technology, Carlow University (2005); Bachelor of Science in Information Management, Carlow University (2002); Bachelor of Science in Business Management, Carlow University (2002)
Email: tiffany.h.kennedy@verizon.com
URL: http://www22.verizon.com

Daryl J. Kenney
Title: Insurance Agent **Company:** American Family Insurance **Address:** 1523 W. U.S. 30 Highway, Merrillville, IN 46410 United States **BUS:** Financial Insurance **P/S:** The Owner of the Office Operating Under AFI Umbrella, Acts as Manager, Handles all the Business and Financial Aspects, Also is an Agent Himself, Educating Clients on Insurance Needs and Products Available, Only One Focus for his Business-Making Sure Clients Needs are Met and They Understand their insurance-Auto, Life, Home and Health, Business and Commercial Insurance Available as well **MA:** International **D/D/R:** Meeting Clients Needs, Educating Clients on Various Insurance Products **H/I/S:** Football, Weight Training, 7 Days a week 2 hours per day, Reading Traveling **EDU:** University of Iowa, Served on Frontline of Desert Storm, BA-Architecture/Commercial Arts, College Football Running Back **A/A/S:** Church, Merrillville High School Football Team-Helps Coach and Gives Pointers to Running Backs
Email: dkenney@amfam.com
URL: www.amfam.com

Karen L. Kenney
Title: Vice President of Educational Development **Company:** Sephora **Dept:** Education and Development **Address:** 425 Market Street, Floor 2, San Francisco, CA 94105 United States **BUS:** Retail **P/S:** Beauty Care Products **MA:** National **D/D/R:** Educating, Servicing Customers, Selling Products, Supervising Through Sephora University, Educating Employees, Vendor Partners and Clients on Products, Application Selling Skills and Leadership **H/I/S:** Reading Mystery Novels **EDU:** Bachelor of Arts in Education, University of Kansas **A/A/S:** American Society for Training and Development **C/VW:** American Heart Association; Habitat for Humanity
Email: karen.kenney@sephora.com
URL: http://www.sephora.com

Mr. James O. Kennon
Title: President **Company:** Sevier Citizens for Clean Air and Water **Address:** 146 N. Main Street, Richfield, UT 84701 United States **BUS:** Nonprofit Organization **P/S:** Environmental Protection Services **MA:** Local **D/D/R:** Representing Private Citizens in Energy-Related Issues Affecting the Public **H/I/S:** Hunting, Fishing, Spending Time Outdoors **EDU:** Bachelor of Science in Liberal Studies, Sonoma State University (1979); Vocational Degree in Woodworking, San Francisco State University (1979); Associate of Arts in Fire Science, College of Marin (1970)
Email: sccaw@yahoo.com
URL: http://www.seviercitizens.com

Cheryl S. Kent
Title: Pacific Pride Office Manager **Company:** Tri-Star Energy, LLC **Address:** 1740 Ed Temple Boulevard, Nashville, TN 37208 United States **BUS:** Energy Firm **P/S:** Commercial Fuel, Sales, Marketing, Gasoline, Diesel and Bio Fuels **MA:** Regional **EXP:** Ms. Kent's expertise is in fleet management consulting. **D/D/R:** Overseeing Sales, Marketing and Public Relations, Training, Offering Customer Service **H/I/S:** Playing Football, Gardening, Fishing, Boating **EDU:** Associate Degree in Computer Science, University of Tennessee, Chattanooga **A/A/S:** Davidson County Chamber of Commerce; Williamson County Chamber of Commerce; Spring Hill Chamber of Commerce; Nashville Chamber of Commerce; The Humane Society of the United States
Email: ckent@tri-starenergy.com
URL: http://www.tri-starenergy.com

Yani Rose Keo
Title: Co-Founder **Company:** Alliance for Multicultural Community Services **Address:** 6440 Hillcroft, Suite 411, Houston, TX 77081 United States **BUS:** Community Service Social Service Provider **P/S:** To help refugees, immigrants and low income residents of Harris County become self sufficient and improve their quality of life **MA:** National **D/D/R:** Fund raiser and Public Relations **H/I/S:** Traveling, Gardening, Dancing and Swimming **EDU:** Texas State, Bachelor's **A/A/S:** Refugee Women Network, International Toast Master, united Way Project Blue Print, Citizen's Fire Academy Alumni, Texas Department of Agriculture and Mental Health and Mental Retardation **A/H:** Miss Houston Senior in December 2005, Received Award from KHWB TV as a Houston WB Asian Pacific American Unsung Hero 2006
Email: yanikeo@allianceontheweb.org
URL: www.allianceontheweb.org

Contance M. Kepner
Title: Staff Engineer **Company:** Butler County Department of Environmental Services **Address:** 130 High Street, Fifth Floor, Hamilton, OH 45011 United States **BUS:** Public Utility Company **P/S:** Water and Sanitary Services **MA:** Butler County, Ohio **D/D/R:** Engineering, Project Management **H/I/S:** Golfing, Cooking, Baking **EDU:** Bachelor's Degree in Chemical Engineering, Villanova University **A/A/S:** Speaker at National and Statewide Conferences
Email: mkepner@cinci.rr.com
URL: http://www.cambridgewhoswho.com

Mary E. Kerby
Title: SPMH Teacher and Team Leader **Company:** Hillsborough County Public Schools **Address:** 2600 W. Humphrey Avenue, Tampa, FL 33614 United States **BUS:** Public School District **P/S:** General Education, Special Education **MA:** Regional **D/D/R:** Teaching Severely and Profoundly Handicapped Children to be Independent and Communicate More Effectively **H/I/S:** Christian Counseling **EDU:** Master's Degree, University of South Florida (1993)
Email: mary.kerby@sdhc.k12.fl.us
URL: http://www.sdhc.k12.fl.us

Andrew J. Kern
Title: Industry Technical Consultant **Company:** Nalco Company **Address:** 1601 W. Diehl Road, Naperville, IL 60563 United States **BUS:** Water Chemical Company **P/S:** Water Treatment Company in the Electric Utility Industry **MA:** International **D/D/R:** Electric Consulting **H/I/S:** Reading, Boating, Fishing, Golfing **EDU:** Bachelor of Science in Chemistry, Bradley University (1968) **A/A/S:** American Nuclear Society; Cooling Technology Institute
Email: akern@nalco.com
URL: http://www.nalco.com

Ms. Jean T. Kerr
Title: Special Education **Company:** Albert Leonard Middle School, New Rochelle **Address:** 515 North Avenue, New Rochelle, NY 10801 United States **BUS:** Secondary Education for Students, Grades 6 through 8 **P/S:** Comfortable Learning Environment with an Excellent Staff, Newly Renovated Facility and Diverse and Talented Student Body **MA:** Regional **D/D/R:** Teaching Students with Learning Disabilities in a Self-Contained Setting Using the Same Curriculum but in Individual and Small Group Tutoring, Focusing on Reading and Writing **H/I/S:** Tennis, Skiing **EDU:** Master's Degree in Education, Long Island University (2003)
Email: jeannietk@msn.com
URL: http://www.albertleonard.nred.org

Lisa H. Kerr
Title: Administrative Professional **Company:** Durham College, University of Ontario Institute of Technology **Address:** 2000 Simcoe Street N., Oshawa, L1H7K4 Canada **BUS:** University **P/S:** Higher Education **MA:** International **EXP:** Ms. Kerr's expertise is in software programming. **H/I/S:** Spending Time Outdoors, Biking, Hiking, Sports **EDU:** Associate Degree, Durham College; Coursework in Office Administration
Email: lisa.kerr@dc-uoit.ca
URL: http://www.durhamcollege.ca

William G. Kerr
Title: President, Owner **Company:** Gerald Ag Center LLC **Address:** 14-782 County Road U, Napoleon, OH 43545 United States **BUS:** Agriculture Retail **P/S:** Fertilizers, Pesticides, Seeds, Custom Applications **MA:** Local **D/D/R:** Crop Consulting CCA **H/I/S:** Ohio State Football

Wendy A. Kersey
Title: Teacher **Company:** North Harlem Elementary School **Address:** 525 Fairview Drive, Harlem, GA 30814 United States **BUS:** Public Elementary School **P/S:** Basic Elementary School Classes **MA:** Regional **D/D/R:** Teaching Fourth and Fifth-Grade Mathematics and All Third-Grade Subjects **H/I/S:** Softball, Directing Choir **EDU:** Master of Science in Integrating Technology into Curriculum, Walden University (2005) **A/A/S:** Professional Association of Georgia Educators
Email: wkersey@ccboe.net
URL: http://www1.ccboe.net/nhe/index.htm

Hans B. Kersten
Title: MD, Assistant Professor of Pediatrics **Company:** St Christophers Hospital for Children **Address:** Front Street at Erie Avenue, Philadelphia, PA 19134 United States **BUS:** Healthcare Hospital **P/S:** General Academic Pediatrics **MA:** Local **EXP:** Dr. Kersten's expertise is in evidence-based medicine. **H/I/S:** Biking, Hiking **EDU:** Temple University, MD **A/A/S:** American Academy of Pediatrics, Ambulatory Pediatric Association
URL: www.schc.com

Rhonda A. Kesler
Title: Property Manager **Company:** Chester Village Green Apartment **Address:** 11001 Chester Garden Circle, Chester, VA 23831 United States **BUS:** Property Management Company **P/S:** Property Management Services Including Apartment Leasing **MA:** Regional **EXP:** Ms. Kesler's expertise includes property management and customer satisfaction. **H/I/S:** Spending Time with her Family **EDU:** High School Education **C/VW:** Local Charitable Organizations
Email: rkesler@plusmgt.com
URL: http://www.cambridgewhoswho.com

Anukware K. Ketosugbo
Title: President, Chief Executive Officer **Company:** Anukware Ketosugbo, MD, PC **Address:** 20 Plaza Street E., Brooklyn, NY 11238 United States **BUS:** Healthcare Firm **P/S:** Surgery, Diagnostic Testing **MA:** Local **EXP:** Dr. Ketosugbo's expertise includes cardiothoracic and cardiovascular surgery, and vascular diagnostics. **H/I/S:** Scuba Diving **EDU:** MD, Albert Einstein College of Medicine, Yeshiva University; Master of Arts in Molecular Biology **A/A/S:** Association of Black Cardiologists; Association of Black Cardiothoracic Surgeons; Society of Black Academic Surgeons; Fellow, American College of Surgeons; Medical Society of the State of New York **C/VW:** March of Dimes, United Negro College Fund
Email: anuketo@yahoo.com

Mr. David W. Kettley, MSN, RN
Title: Clinical Liaison **Company:** Clinical Business Solutions, Inc. **Address:** 89 Blackberry Trail, Aurora, IL 60506 United States **BUS:** Variety of Clinical and Marketing Support Services to the Pharmaceutical Industry **P/S:** Clinical Research, Clinical Call Center, Clinical Services, Medical Liaisons, Data Management, Continuing Education Program, Parkinson's Disease Education and Treatment **MA:** National **D/D/R:** Practicing Neuroscience, Teaching Clinical Education, Introducing Methods to Optimize Patient Treatment and Education Especially for Parkinson's Disease Patients **H/I/S:** Traveling, Reading, Gardening, Camping **EDU:** Master of Science in Nursing Degree, University of Phoenix (2004); Pursuing Doctorate Degree **A/A/S:** Sigma Theta Tau; American Society of Neurological Nurses; American Association for Critical Care Nurses; Infusion Nurses Society; National Speaker of Symposia and Presentations
Email: kettley@gmail.com
URL: http://www.accredocbs.com

Mary E. Keyser
Title: Social Worker **Company:** KVC Behavioral Health Care **Address:** 300B Prestige Park Drive, Hurricane, WV 25526 United States **BUS:** Social Work Facility **P/S:** In-Home Behavioral Healthcare **MA:** Local **D/D/R:** Supportive Counseling, Case Management, Working with Children, Adolescents and Adults **H/I/S:** Reading, Spending Time with her Parents and her Boyfriend's Grandmother **EDU:** Bachelor's Degree in Education, Marshall University **CERTS:** Licensed Social Worker, State of West Virginia **C/VW:** Girls Scouts of the USA
Email: keyser69@juno.com
URL: http://www.cambridgewhoswho.com

Dr. Fatima S. Khan
Title: Assistant Professor of Pediatrics, MD, FAAP, FACP **Company:** Rush Copley Medical Group **Address:** 2060 Ogden Avenue, Suite A, Aurora, IL 60504 United States **BUS:** Medical Practice **P/S:** Healthcare **MA:** Local **D/D/R:** Practicing Adult Internal Medicine and Pediatric Medicine, Focusing on Preventive Care, Treating Asthma and Allergies, Cholesterol and Women's Health **H/I/S:** Exercising, Bicycling, Golfing, Traveling, Reviewing Restaurants, Watching Plays and Shows **EDU:** MD, University of Illinois (1999); Bachelor of Arts in Biology, University of Chicago, with Honors (1995); Residency Program, Yale University **A/A/S:** American Academy of Pediatrics; American College of Physicians; American Medical Association
Email: fskyalemd@hotmail.com
URL: http://www.rushcopley.com/davinefamilymedicine

Rohini Khanduri
Company: Cloud Blue **BUS:** Information Technology Company **P/S:** Information Technology and Real Estate Outsourcing Services **MA:** National **EXP:** Ms. Khanduri's expertise includes application software development, project integration and information technology management. **H/I/S:** Traveling, Gardening, Reading, Exercising, Practicing Yoga and Pilates **EDU:** Bachelor of Arts in English Literature, University of Delhi, India **C/VW:** Children International
Email: rkhanduri@cloudblue.com
URL: http://www.cambridgewhoswho.com

Helen Anders Kho
Title: Musician, Teacher **Company:** Piano Studio **Address:** 28 Lorraine Street, Plattsburgh, NY 12901 United States **BUS:** Piano Studio **P/S:** Teaching Piano Lessons **MA:** Local **D/D/R:** Her expertise is in singing, teaching, accompanying and playing the piano. **H/I/S:** Photography, Watercolor Painting, Writing Short Stories **EDU:** Master of Science in Humanities, SUNY Plattsburgh (1987); Bachelor of Science in Music Education, West Chester University of Pennsylvania (1955)
Email: helenakho@verizon.net

Andria Kay Kidd
Title: Owner **Company:** Andria Kidd Training Center **Address:** 308 Chambersburg Road, Fillmore, CA 93015 United States **BUS:** Equestrian Training, Competition, Management **P/S:** Equestrian Training for Halter, Showmanship, Western, Saddle-Seat, Side-Saddle, Hunter Under Saddle, Handicapped and Special Needs Riders, Lessons for All Ages and Skill Levels, Equestrian Appraisals, Judging, Sales, Facility Design Consultation **MA:** International **D/D/R:** Teaching the Principles of Classical Horsemanship and Building Positive Communications and Partnerships Between Horse and Rider **H/I/S:** Antiquing, Collecting Western Memorabilia, Photography **EDU:** College Coursework; Studies in Horsemanship with a Member of the Spanish Riding School **CERTS:** Licensed Real Estate Agent **A/A/S:** Lifetime Member, American Society of Equine Appraisers; Former President, Various Equestrian Organizations; Special Needs and Handicapped Therapeutic Riding Program, Highlighted in a Book, 'Special Needs, Special Horses' by Naomi Scott; Learn to Horse Show Riding Clinics **C/VW:** Founder, Project Kids Helping Kids, Soroptimist International; Charity Horse Shows, National Bone Marrow Foundation
Email: sunfox@sbcglobal.net
URL: http://www.andriakidddtrainingcenter.com

Debra E. Kiefer
Title: Owner **Company:** Heart of Gold Independent Living Home **Address:** 2097 S.W. Beekman Street, Port Saint Lucie, FL 34953 United States **BUS:** Homecare Center **P/S:** Healthcare, Personal Care, Companionship, Assisted Living Services **MA:** Regional **EXP:** Ms. Kiefer's expertise is in operations management. **D/D/R:** Managing Operations of the Senior Living Facility, Assisting the Elderly in Retaining their Independence, Offering Personal Care and Companionship **H/I/S:** Boating **CERTS:** Certified Nursing Assistant; Certified Home Health Aide; Assisted Living Facility License; Certified in Alzheimer's II **A/A/S:** Chamber of Commerce **C/VW:** American Red Cross
Email: kiefer_debra@yahoo.com
URL: http://www.cambridgewhoswho.com

Anne Marie Kieft
Title: Realtor **Company:** Alloway Associates Realtors **Address:** 2 Retreat Road Route 206, Vicentown, NJ 08088 United States **BUS:** Real Estate Broker **P/S:** Residential, Executive, Water View Homes, Condos, Golf Homes, Senior, Gated, Vacant Land **MA:** National **EXP:** Ms. Kieft's expertise is in residential property. **H/I/S:** Skiing **A/A/S:** New Jersey Association of Realtors, National Association of Realtors
Email: amkieft626@aol.com
URL: www.allowayrealtors.com

Amy Kienast
Title: Director of Career Services **Company:** Michigan Institute of Aviation and Technology **Address:** 47884 D Street, Belleville, MI 48111 United States **BUS:** Aviation School **P/S:** Technical Education **MA:** National **D/D/R:** Assisting Students with Career Services and Job Placements **H/I/S:** Traveling, Fishing, Gardening, Analyzing Handwriting **EDU:** Bachelor's Degree in Education, University of Wisconsin, Oshkosh **CERTS:** Certified Human Resources Professional; Global Career Development Facilitator Certification **A/A/S:** Board of Directors, Michigan Career Development Association; Women in Aviation International; National Career Development Association; Experimental Aircraft Association; Planning Committee Member, Great Lakes International Aviation Conference; Advisory Board Member, Schoolcraft College; Guest Lecturer, Eastern Michigan University; Guest Online Instructor, Schoolcraft College
Email: akienast@miat.edu
URL: http://www.miat.edu

Marilyn Kiesel
Title: Realtor, Broker Associate **Company:** RE/MAX Professionals **Address:** 655 Main Street, East Greenwich, RI 02818 United States **BUS:** Real Estate Agency **P/S:** Residential Real Estate Sales, Marketing **MA:** Regional **EXP:** Ms. Kiesel's expertise is in real estate sales. **H/I/S:** Traveling, Photography **EDU:** Bachelor of Science in Nursing, University of Michigan **A/A/S:** KWAOR; Rhode Island Association of Realtors; National Association of Realtors **C/VW:** Various Local Organizations, Children's Miracle Network
Email: marilyneg@aol.com
URL: http://www.sellri.com

Betty M. Kievit
Title: Artist, Painter **Company:** B.M. Kievit **BUS:** Sole Proprietorship **P/S:** Painting Portraitures **MA:** National **D/D/R:** Painting Portraitures in Oils, Pastels and Water Colors **H/I/S:** Painting **A/A/S:** The Ridgewood Art Institute; Fair Lawn Art Association **C/VW:** Local Charitable Organizations
Email: betty.kievit@cwwemail.com

Patrick L. Kil
Title: General Contractor, Consultant **Company:** Kil Construction Company **Address:** 4909 Cumbre Del Sur Court N.E., Albuquerque, NM 87111 United States **BUS:** Construction Company **P/S:** Construction and Consulting Services **MA:** Local **EXP:** Mr. Kil's expertise is in new home constructions. **D/D/R:** Structural Framing, Consulting **H/I/S:** Exhibiting Quarter Horses, Wilderness Trail Riding **EDU:** Bachelor's Degree in General Studies, University of New Mexico **A/A/S:** Consultant, UBuildIt; Professional Singer, New Mexico Symphony Orchestra **C/VW:** Local Church; Motivational Speaker, Prisons
Email: patjudi@aol.com

Bill T. Kilfeather
Title: Territory Manager, Builder Specialist **Company:** Shaw Inc. **Address:** 1515 Winston Road, Anaheim, CA 92806 United States **BUS:** Manufacturing Company **P/S:** Manufacturing and Selling Ceramic Tile, Carpet, Area Rugs **MA:** International **D/D/R:** Building Customer Relationships, Territory Management **H/I/S:** Golfing, Going to Vegas **EDU:** Associate Degree in Theater Arts, Santa Anna College **A/A/S:** Brick Industry Association; SCFA **C/VW:** Young Men's Christian Association
Email: wkilfeather@msn.com
URL: http://www.cambridgewhoswho.com

Michelle M. Kilgore
Title: Interrelated Special Education Teacher **Company:** North Dodge Elementary School **Address:** 5125 Eighth Avenue, Eastman, GA 31023 United States **BUS:** Public Elementary School Serving Residents of Eastman **P/S:** Public Elementary Education for Local Students **MA:** Regional **D/D/R:** Teaching Reading and Language Arts to Special Needs Students, Following Georgia Performance Standards **H/I/S:** Spending Time with her Children, Traveling **EDU:** Master's Degree in Interrelated Special Education, Georgia Southern University (2005); Coursework in Autism Education, Enrichment Studies, Science and Mathematics **A/A/S:** Phi Kappa Phi; Georgia Association of Educators; Lecturer, Structured Reading Academy; Mentor, Teachers at a Local University; Model Classroom for Reading Education
Email: pkilgore50@hotmail.com

Ligia M. J. A Kilinski Cevasco, MSc
Title: Senior Manager, Epidemiologist **Company:** Elan Pharmaceuticals, Inc. **Dept:** Biometrics **Address:** 700 Gateway Boulevard, South San Francisco, CA 94080 United States **BUS:** Neuroscience-Based Biotechnology Company **P/S:** Research and Development of Advanced Therapies in Neurology, Autoimmune Diseases and Severe Pain **MA:** International **D/D/R:** Performing Research in Epidemiology, Managing Clinical Trails and Projects **H/I/S:** Spending Time Outdoors, Snowboarding, Whitewater Rafting, Rollerblading, Snorkeling, Swimming, Exercising, Dancing, Jet skiing, Camping, Traveling **EDU:** Master of Science in Epidemiology, University of London School of Hygiene and Tropical Medicine, London, UK; Master of Science in Medicine, Major in Cardiothoracic Surgery, University of Cape Town Medical School, South Africa; Bachelor of Science in Medical Microbiology, with Honors, University of Cape Town Medical School, South Africa; Bachelor of Science in Microbiology and Biochemistry, University of Cape Town, South Africa **CERTS:** Certified Project Manager, Simon Fraser University, Vancouver, BC, Canada; Certification in Radionucleotide Safety and Methodology, University of British Columbia (2003); Certification in Workplace Hazardous Materials Information System (2002); Certification in Medical Representative Sales, Solutions Human Development Consultants (1998) **A/A/S:** Association for Professionals in Infection Control and Epidemiology; Member, Clinical Research Professionals of British Columbia; Member, Pre-Clinical Network of British Columbia; BC Biotech Association; Canadian Red Cross (2003) **C/VW:** American Society for the Prevention of Cruelty to Animals
Email: ligiakilinski@yahoo.ca
URL: http://www.elan.com

Mr. Dennis M. Killmer
Title: Workflow Associate **Company:** Computer Sciences Corporation (CSC) **Address:** 6504 Hickock Drive, Unit C, Fort Worth, TX 76116 United States **BUS:** Computer Outsourcing Corporation **P/S:** Outsourcing Information Technology, Defense, Telephony, Computer Network, Desktop and Help Desk Services **MA:** International **D/D/R:** Managing Desktop Configurations, Information Technology, Trouble Tickets and Servicing Agreements, Communicating with Clients, Delivery Management **H/I/S:** NASCAR, Hockey, Photography, Researching Family Genealogy, Web Site Building **EDU:** Pursuing Associate Degree in Business Management, Ashworth University (Formerly Ashworth College) **CERTS:** Certification in Computers **A/A/S:** Disabled American Veterans
Email: dennismk1@earthlink.net
URL: http://www.cambridgewhoswho.com

Koni Kim

Title: Chief Executive Officer **Company:** Koni Corporation **Address:** 9654 Siempre Viva Road, San Diego, CA 92154 United States **BUS:** Distribution Company **P/S:** Distinctively Designed Bed Covers, Window Treatments, Fabrics, Linens, Bath Accessories **MA:** Regional **D/D/R:** Creating Design, Managing the Sales Department, Overseeing Business Operations **H/I/S:** Scuba Diving, Skiing, Rollerblading, Bicycling **EDU:** Master of Applied Arts, University of California, Los Angeles **A/A/S:** Network of Executive Women in Hospitality; Smithsonian **C/VW:** Crystal Cathedral; Juvenile Diabetes Research Foundation International
Email: koni@konicorp.com
URL: http://www.konicorp.com

Mr. Steven E. Kim, MBA

Title: Director of Business Development **Company:** UPS **Address:** 165 Chubb Avenue, Lyndhurst, NJ 07071 United States **BUS:** World's Largest Package Delivery Company **P/S:** Leading Global Provider of Specialized Transportation and Logistics Services **MA:** International **D/D/R:** Overseeing Supply Chain Management, Logistics Consulting, Specializing in the High Technology Sector **H/I/S:** Practicing Tae Kwon Do, Volleyball, Baseball, Football, Basketball, Golf **EDU:** Master's Degree in Business Administration, Emphasis in Finance and Investments, Baruch College (2001); Bachelor's Degree in English, Syracuse University (1995)
Email: sekim01@aol.com
URL: http://www.ups.com

Michael Alexander Kimbell

Title: Sole Proprietor **Company:** Michael & Edith Kimbell **Address:** 314 Clifton Road, Pacifica, CA 94044 United States **BUS:** Sole Proprietorship **P/S:** Write and Publish of Sheet Music **MA:** Regional **D/D/R:** Publishing Music, Tuning and Repairing Pianos, Composing Music, Performing Symphonic Works **H/I/S:** Reading, Hiking **EDU:** Doctor of Musical Arts in Composition, Cornell University (1973); Diploma, Niles Bryant School of Piano Tuning (1979) **CERTS:** Registered Piano Technician, Piano Technicians Guild **A/A/S:** Piano Technicians Guild; The National Association of Composers
Email: 2m4e7k@sbcglobal.net
URL: http://www.kimbellmusic.com

Clifford Leon Kimbrough Jr., Bishop, B.Th.

Title: Bishop, Pastor **Company:** Jonas Temple/Church of God in Christ, Inc **Address:** 10623 Lee Avenue, Cleveland, OH 44106 United States **BUS:** Religion Church **P/S:** Oversees Congregation and Ministries: 40 Churches in Ohio **MA:** Local **D/D/R:** Preaching, Teaching and Leadership Development, Ministries Include Adult, Youth, Children, Singles, Bible Study Programs, Counseling for Cancer Patients, Leadership Programs, Nursing Programs, Bible College in Progress for 2007 in Ohio, Striving for a More Affordable Education **H/I/S:** Reading, Bowling, Fishing, Traveling **EDU:** Walsh University, Ashlamb Theological Seminary, BA-Theology, MA-Christian Ministries (Pending) **A/A/S:** Ministerial Interdenominational Alliance
Email: cliffo.jr9555@sbcglobal.net

Tara J. Kimmins

Title: Western Regional Sales Representative **Company:** Kerr Corporation **Address:** 1717 W. Collins Avenue, Orange, CA 92867 United States **BUS:** Dental Products Manufacturer **P/S:** Dental Restorative Materials **MA:** Statewide **D/D/R:** Selling Dental Restorative Materials **H/I/S:** Golfing, Running, Traveling, Hiking, Biking, Rock Climbing **EDU:** Bachelor of Science in Business, Salve Regina University, Newport Rhode Island; Bachelor of Arts (1995) **A/A/S:** Mariner's Church; Susan G. Komen Race for the Cure **C/VW:** Mariner's Church, Junior High Ministry, Group Events, Dog Therapy Training; Big Brothers Big Sisters
Email: tkimmins@hotmail.com
URL: http://www.kerrdental.com

Judith Kinard-Wright

Title: Special Education Teacher **Company:** The New York City Department of Education **Address:** 985 Rockaway Avenue, Brooklyn, NY 11212 United States **BUS:** Department of Education **P/S:** Education **MA:** Regional **D/D/R:** Training, Teaching and Developing Social Skills for Emotionally and Developmentally Challenged Children **H/I/S:** Playing Tennis, Biking **EDU:** Master's Degree in Administration and Supervision, Brooklyn College (1993); Master's Degree in Special Education, Brooklyn College (1989) **CERTS:** Advanced Certification in Administration (1993) **A/A/S:** Who's Who in American Education **A/H:** Outstanding Women in America Award
Email: judkinwright11@aol.com

Mr. Emil Thomas Kindelberger

Title: Special Education Teacher **Company:** Southwestern Randolph High School **Address:** 1641 Hopewell Friends Road, Ashboro, NC 27205 United States **BUS:** High School **P/S:** Secondary Education **MA:** Local **D/D/R:** Teaching and Training Young Adults with Behavioral and Emotional Disabilities **H/I/S:** Officiating High School Sports, Hiking, Volunteering **EDU:** Master of Special Education, Appalachian State University **A/A/S:** North Carolina Association of Educators; National Education Association **C/VW:** Local Charitable Organizations; Special Olympics
Email: kindelbergertom@yahoo.com
URL: http://www.cambridgewhoswho.com

Sherry Y. Kinder

Title: Mobile DJ, Owner, MC **Company:** eSkay Music Inc **Address:** 1901 E. Lake Woodlands Parkway, Oldsmar, FL 34677 United States **BUS:** Musical Entertainment **P/S:** Only Mother/Daughter Team **MA:** Regional **D/D/R:** Weddings and Commitment Ceremonies **H/I/S:** Interior Decorating, Gardening **EDU:** Baldwin Wallace Community College **A/A/S:** Upper Tampa Bay Chamber of Commerce, American Disc Jockey Association, Tampa Bay Business Guild
Email: eskaymusic@tampabay.rr.com
URL: www.eskaymusic.com

Carroll W. King, Jr., D.Min.

Title: Director **Company:** Brazilian Free Methodist Seminary **Address:** 25 N.E. Second Avenue, Deerfield Beach, FL 33441 United States **BUS:** Religious Organization **P/S:** Training for Future Pastors, Evangelism, Church Growth **MA:** Local **D/D/R:** Teaching **H/I/S:** Collecting Stamps, Coins and Keychains **EDU:** Doctor of Ministry, Asbury Theological Seminary, 1990; Master of Theology in Biblical Literature, Asbury Theological Seminary, 1975; Master's Degree in Religious Education, Southern Baptist Theological Seminary, 1962; Bachelor of Divinity, Asbury Theological Seminary, 1953; Bachelor of Arts in History, Seattle Pacific University, 1950 **A/A/S:** International Society of Theta Thi
URL: http://www.cambridgewhoswho.com

Deanne C. King

Title: Physical Education Instructor **Company:** Midland Independent School District, Quanah Parker Elementary **Address:** 3800 Norwood Street, Midland, TX 79707 United States **BUS:** Elementary School **P/S:** Education **MA:** Local **D/D/R:** Teaching Physical Education and Health **H/I/S:** Swimming **EDU:** Master's Degree in Kinesiology, University of Texas, 2005; Bachelor's Degree in Kinesiology, Permian Basin **A/A/S:** Texas Association for Health, Physical Education, Recreation and Dance **C/VW:** Church, Youth Basketball
Email: dcking@esc18.net
URL: http://www.cambridgewhoswho.com

Jerry E. King

Title: President **Company:** Carpet King, Inc **Address:** 1007 Ross Street, Graham, NC 27253 United States **BUS:** Cleaning Service Provider **P/S:** Carpet Cleaning, Commercial/Residential **MA:** Local **D/D/R:** Oriental Rug Cleaning **H/I/S:** Traveling, Gardening, Yard Work, Working on Cars **A/A/S:** Mid South Professional Cleaners Association-MSPCA, ICRC
Email: carpetkinginc@aol.com

Lillie M. King

Title: Owner **Company:** Serving Spoon **Address:** 2109 Buena Vista Road, Columbus, GA 31906 United States **BUS:** Restaurant **P/S:** Breakfast, Lunch **MA:** Central Georgia **D/D/R:** Cooking Country Food **H/I/S:** Church **EDU:** High School Education **C/VW:** Church, Breast Cancer Survivors
URL: http://www.cambridgewhoswho.com

Michael P. King

Title: Partner **Company:** King, Chapman & Broussard **Address:** 700 Louisiana Street, Suite 4550, Houston, TX 77002 United States **BUS:** Management Consulting Firm **P/S:** Strategy Implementation for Fortune 500 Companies **MA:** International **D/D/R:** Consulting with Clients, Conducting Specialized Training **H/I/S:** Reading, Walking, Golfing **EDU:** Bachelor of Science, Rutgers University
Email: mikek@kcbcg.com
URL: http://www.kcbcg.com

Robbin L. King

Title: Owner **Company:** Rooms Made Simple **Address:** 7618 Old Bicycle Road, Panama City, FL 32404 United States **BUS:** Counseling Center **P/S:** Counseling on Professional Development **MA:** National **D/D/R:** Space Management, Life Coaching **H/I/S:** Photography, Cooking, Sewing, Writing **CERTS:** Certified Professional Organizer, National Association of Professional Organizers **A/A/S:** National Scholars Honor Society (2007); National Association of Professional Organizers **C/VW:** Rescue Mission; Mission House; Hunger and Homeless Coalition
Email: organizeitnow@comcast.net
URL: http://www.roomsmadesimple.com

Susan M. King, MA

Title: Teacher, Coach **Company:** Kaiser High School **Address:** 11155 Almond Avenue, Fontana, CA 92346 United States **BUS:** High School **P/S:** Secondary Education, Athletics, Physical Education, Biology and Student Services **MA:** Statewide **D/D/R:** Teaching Physical Education to Ninth through 12th-Graders, Coaching Tennis, Teaching Football, Soccer, Volleyball, Basketball, Softball **EDU:** Master's Degree in Administration, Azusa Pacific University, California (1989) **A/A/S:** Fontana Teacher's Association; California Teacher's Association
Email: kingsm@fusd.net
URL: http://www.fusd.net/schools/HighSchool/Kaiser/index.stm

Xaneve Penny King

Title: Chief Financial Officer **Company:** Empire Entity, Inc. **Address:** 24 Lincoln Street, Elmont, NY 11003 United States **BUS:** Marketing Company **P/S:** Marketing, Promotions for Small Business and Other Companies **MA:** Local **D/D/R:** Handling All Budgetary Concerns, Financial Issues, Payroll, Accounts Payable and Accounts Receivable for All Vendors **EDU:** Bachelor's Degree in Finance, Lehigh University (2003) **C/VW:** American Breast Cancer Foundation
Email: xpenny.king@gmail.com
URL: http://www.empireentity.com

Betty Kingery

Title: Special Education Teacher **Company:** 1) Lorena High School 2) Rio Brazos Education Cooperative **Address:** 1 Leopard Lane, Lorena, TX 76655 United States **BUS:** 1) High School 2) Educational Cooperative **P/S:** Education **MA:** Local **EXP:** Ms. Kingery's expertise is in special education. **D/D/R:** Teaching Adult Life Skills **H/I/S:** Sewing, Cooking, Making Crafts, Baking, Horseback Riding **EDU:** Master of Science in Physical Education and Health, Minor in Special Education, Baylor University (1973); Bachelor of Arts in Physical Education, Health and Recreation, Baylor University (1972) **A/A/S:** Association for Retarded Citizens; Special Olympics of Texas **A/H:** Pathfinder Award **C/VW:** Community-Based Charities
Email: bettykingery@lorenaisd.net
URL: http://www.lorenaisd.net

Paul J. Kingstrom

Title: Administrative Executive (Retired) **Company:** Amerock, A Newell Rubbermaid Company **Address:** 2970 Cotswold Circle, Rockford, IL 61114 United States **BUS:** Manufacturing Company **P/S:** Cabinet and Window Hardware **MA:** International **D/D/R:** Overseeing Business Development, Mentoring Employees **H/I/S:** Golfing, Gardening **EDU:** Bachelor of Arts in Liberal Arts and Business, School of Business and Nonprofit Management, North Park University, Chicago **A/A/S:** User Systems Incorporated; Former Regional President, National Office Management Association; Honeywell International
Email: pkingstrom@aol.com

Zena M. Kinne

Title: Director of Clinical Services **Company:** Washington Association of Community and Migrant Health Centers **Address:** 2120 State Avenue N.E., Olympia, WA 98506 United States **BUS:** Nonprofit Organization **P/S:** Healthcare and Human Services **MA:** Washington **EXP:** Ms. Kinne's expertise includes emergency preparedness, ambulatory care and quality improvement. **D/D/R:** Overseeing Healthcare Activities, Coaching **H/I/S:** Traveling, Boating, Gardening **EDU:** Master of Nursing, University of Washington
Email: zkinne@wacmhc.org
URL: http://www.wacmhc.org

Gustavo Kinrys, MD

Title: Medical Doctor **Company:** East Cambridge Clinic **Dept:** Depression and Anxiety Disorders Research Program **Address:** 1493 Cambridge Street, Cambridge, MA 02139 United States **BUS:** Clinic **P/S:** Healthcare Including Psychopharmacology, Psychiatric Services for Patients Suffering from Anxiety Disorders and Depression **MA:** Regional **EXP:** Mr. Kinrys' expertise is in healthcare. **D/D/R:** Supervising Staff, Conducting Research on Images of the Brain to Assess the Effects of Medication, Organizing and Directing Programs **H/I/S:** Playing Soccer and Basketball **EDU:** MD in Psychiatry, Concentration in Psychopharmacology, The Federal University of Rio de Janeiro, Brazil (1996); Coursework in Premedical Studies, The Federal University of Rio de Janeiro, Brazil (1993) **A/A/S:** American Psychiatric Association; Brazilian Psychiatric Association **C/VW:** Anxiety Disorders Association of America
Email: gkinrys@challiance.org

Heather K. Kinzie, SPHR
Title: Owner **Company:** A Leading Solution **Address:** P.O. Box 222682, Anchorage, AK 99522 United States **BUS:** Human Resources Consulting Agency **P/S:** Human Resource Consulting **MA:** Local **D/D/R:** Training, Development, Employee Relations **H/I/S:** Volunteer Prep Course Teacher **EDU:** Bachelor's Degree in Communication, Training and Development, Towson University, Maryland (1992) **A/A/S:** Society for Human Resource Management; Local Association for Human Resource Management; Member of Chapter in Anchorage **C/VW:** Alaska Rush
Email: heather@aleadingsolution.com
URL: http://www.aleadingsolution.com

Katherine L. Kirbo
Title: Executive Director **Company:** Reef Ball Foundation **Address:** 890 Hill Street, Athens, GA 30606 United States **BUS:** Environmental Nonprofit Organization **P/S:** Preserving the Ocean and Ecosystem, Restoring Coral Reefs **MA:** International **D/D/R:** Organizing and Managing Projects, Fund Raising **H/I/S:** Listening to Music, Horseback Riding, Playing Tennis, Diving **EDU:** Bachelor of Arts in Psychology, University of Georgia (1989) **A/A/S:** Board of Community Connections; Athens Area Community Foundation
Email: kathy@reefball.com
URL: http://www.reefball.org

Laurel Young Kirchmeyer
Title: Sales Professional **Company:** Genetech **Address:** 1 DNA Way, South San Francisco, CA 94080 United States **BUS:** Manmade DNA Company **P/S:** Biotechnology, Immunology, Oncology **MA:** International **EXP:** Ms. Kirchmeye's expertise is in clientele sales. **H/I/S:** Gardening, Entertaining **EDU:** Bachelor's Degree in Art, Minor in Marketing, Appalachian State University, Boone, North Carolina **A/H:** Top Salesperson in the Company, 2003 **C/VW:** Chairwoman, Sponsorship Committee, American Arthritis Foundation; American Diabetes Association
Email: laurelk@gene.com
URL: http://www.genetech.com

Debra K. Kirk
Title: Registered Nurse **Company:** Lutheran Hospital **Address:** 8300 W. 38th Street, Wheat Ridge, CO 80033 United States **BUS:** Hospital **P/S:** Healthcare **MA:** Local **D/D/R:** Critical-Care Nursing **H/I/S:** Mountaineering, Rock Climbing, Gardening, Reading, Trail Running, Advanced Racing **EDU:** Master of Arts in Therapeutic Recreation, University of Iowa; Bachelor of Science, University of Iowa; Bachelor of Science in Nursing, Denver School of Nursing **CERTS:** Licensed in Therapeutic Recreation **A/A/S:** Wilderness Medical Society; American Alpine Club **C/VW:** Colorado Mountain Club
Email: debra.kirk@yahoo.com

Jane Kirkland
Title: Teacher **Company:** John I. Leonard High School **Address:** 4701 10th Avenue N., Greenacres, FL 33463 United States **BUS:** Public High School **P/S:** Advanced Placement Courses for College Credit, Computer Technology Academy, Academy of Finance, International Spanish Academy, Dual Language English Spanish Program, Cooperative Programs Where Work and Education can be Combined, Dual Enrollment Options with Local Colleges and Technical Schools **MA:** Local **D/D/R:** Teaching Ninth through 12th-Grade Health, Fitness, Adapting Physical Education for Special Needs Students, Teaching over 200 Students, Teaching Tennis Classes and Coaching Girl's Tennis **H/I/S:** Tennis **EDU:** Master of Business Administration, University of Phoenix (2007); Bachelor of Science in Physical Education and Health Education, University of West Florida **A/A/S:** Phi Delta Kappa; Florida Education Association; California Teachers Association; National Education Association; ASLCIO; Alpha Sigma Tau; Florida Alliance for Health, Physical Education Recreation and Dance
Email: millironsj@bellsouth.net
URL: http://www.palmbeach.k12.fl.us/JohnILeonardHS/main/index.htm

Trevor L. Kirkwood
Title: Assistant Program Director **Company:** KTPK-FM **Address:** 2121 S.W. Chelsea Drive, Topeka, KS 66614 United States **BUS:** Radio Station **P/S:** Conducting Programs **MA:** Regional **EXP:** Mr. Kirkwood's expertise includes music programming and station-Website management. **H/I/S:** Working in his Home, Spending Time Outdoors, Exercising **EDU:** Pursuing Broadcast Journalism Degree, Washburn University (2007) **A/A/S:** Collegiate journalists, National Honors Society **C/VW:** Children's Miracle Network; American Lung Association; Multiple Sclerosis Society
Email: trevor@countrylegends1069.com
URL: http://www.countrylegends1069.com

Mr. Zachary Jarboe Kirsh
Title: Telesales Manager **Company:** Insight Communications **Dept:** Call Center **Address:** 4701 Commerce Crossings Drive, Suite 200, Louisville, KY 40229 United States **BUS:** Cable Multimedia Company **MA:** International **EXP:** Mr. Kirsh's expertise includes sales coaching and process innovation. **D/D/R:** Training, Coaching and Developing the Sales Staff, Generating Feedback to Help Improve Sales Skills, Standardizing Business Processes, Ensuring Products and Value are Clearly Communicated to the Community, Monitoring Calls Side by Side **H/I/S:** Poetry, Creative Writing, Listening to Digital Music, Traveling **EDU:** Master's Degree in Business and Technical Writing, University of Louisville (1996); Bachelor's Degree in English, University of Louisville (1994) **CERTS:** Certified Webtop Author, Documented and Information Mapping; Certified in Insurance Principles, America's Health Insurance Plans; Certification in Targeted Selection and Zenger-Miller Front Line Management **A/A/S:** Newspaper Association of America **A/H:** Visual Art Shows, Louisville, KY (2004, 2005, 2006); Student Prize for the Story 'Without Resistance,' Louisville Magazine; Short Story Prize in Fiction, 'In Other Words' (1996)
Email: kirsh.z@insightcom.com
URL: http://www.linkedin.com/in/zacharyjarboekirsh
URL: http://www.valueclick.com/

Tiffany L. Kiser
Title: Respiratory Care Practitioner, Level 4 **Company:** Children's National Medical Center **Address:** 111 Michigan Avenue N.W., Washington, DC 20010 United States **BUS:** Children's Hospital **P/S:** Pediatric Healthcare, Surgery, Intensive Care, Oncology **MA:** International **D/D/R:** Intensive Care, Respiratory Care, Rapid Deployment Extracorporeal Membrane Oxygenation **H/I/S:** Traveling **EDU:** Bachelor's Degree in Biology, The George Washington University **A/A/S:** American Association of Respiratory Care; Maryland/District of Columbia Society for Respiratory Care **C/VW:** International Order of the Rainbow for Girls
Email: tiffanylkiser@yahoo.com
URL: http://www.cnmc.org

S. Scott Kissinger
Title: President **Company:** Kissinger Investments **Address:** 3172 Bay Lane, Clearwater, FL 33759 United States **BUS:** Investment Firm **P/S:** Financial Services **MA:** National **EXP:** Mr. Kissinger's expertise is in wealth management. **D/D/R:** Overseeing Equity Investments **H/I/S:** Golfing, Camping, Playing Tennis, Flying Airplanes **EDU:** Master of Business Administration in Marketing and Finance, University of Florida (2004) **A/A/S:** American Marketing Association **C/VW:** National Brain Tumor Foundation
Email: scott@kissingerinvestments.com
URL: http://www.cambridgewhoswho.com

Gennene A. Kitsmiller
Title: General Manager **Company:** Kitsmiller RV, Inc. **Address:** 1211 N. Cedar Road, Mason, MI 48854 United States **BUS:** Automotive Dealership Agency **P/S:** Recreational Vehicle **MA:** Local **D/D/R:** Marketing, Advertising, Overseeing Departments, Managing the Dealership **H/I/S:** Traveling **EDU:** Associate Degree in Business, Lansing Community College (2001) **A/A/S:** Recreational Vehicle Industry Association; Recreation Vehicle Dealers Association of America; Recreation Vehicle Rental Association **C/VW:** Local Church
Email: kitsmiller@aol.com
URL: http://www.kitsmillerrv.com

Lori Kittle
Title: Director of Operations **Company:** Occupational HealthLink, Inc. **Address:** 1942 Broadway, Suite 501, Boulder, CO 80302 United States **BUS:** Medical Data Management Company **P/S:** Occupational Medicine Information System Services **MA:** National **EXP:** Ms. Kittle's expertise includes operations and business management. **D/D/R:** Training Employees **H/I/S:** Traveling, Photography, Spending Time Outdoors **EDU:** Bachelor's Degree in Microbiology, Colorado State University
Email: lkittle@occhealthlink.com
URL: http://www.occupationalhealthlink.com

Renee S. Kivikko
Title: Director of Education **Company:** Land Trust Alliance **Address:** 6869 S. Sprinkle Road, Portage, MI 49002 United States **BUS:** Land Conservation Organization **P/S:** Promotes Voluntary Private Land Conservation to Benefit Communities and Nature, Training, Publications, Census of Land Trusts, Lobbying, Digital Library, Grants, Regional Program Offices, Liability Insurance for Land Trusts **MA:** National **D/D/R:** Coordinating Development and Management of Education **H/I/S:** Raising and Training Dogs **EDU:** Bachelor's Degree in Anthropology, Beloit College, Wisconsin (1986) **A/A/S:** Natural Areas Association; Phi Beta Kappa Society
Email: rkivikko@lta.org
URL: http://www.lta.org

Carol A. Klacking
Title: Clinical Nurse Liaison, Marketing Director **Company:** HCR-Manorcare **BUS:** Healthcare Company **P/S:** Geriatric Long-Term and Short-Term Rehabilitation **MA:** National **D/D/R:** Critical-Care Nursing, Geriatric Nursing, Sales, Marketing **H/I/S:** Spending Time Outdoors, Hiking, Boating, Snow Skiing, Water Skiing, Reading **EDU:** Bachelor of Science in Education, University of Nevada, Reno **CERTS:** Licensed Practical Nurse, State of Florida, 1976; English Comprehensive, Sacramento, California, 1972; Registered Nurse, 1991 **A/A/S:** American Cancer Society; Relay for Life **A/H:** Chairman Award, Mariner Healthcare **C/VW:** Humane Society, Wildlife Society, American Cancer Society, Relay for Life, Underwriter
Email: caklacking2@aol.com
URL: http://www.cambridgewhoswho.com

Loreen L. Klauser
Title: Owner **Company:** Hunter's Nest **Address:** S80W14401 Schultz Lane, Muskego, WI 53150 United States **BUS:** Bar and Grill Restaurant **P/S:** Bar and Grill **MA:** Local **EXP:** Ms. Klauser's expertise is in management. **H/I/S:** Trap Shooting **EDU:** Diploma, Bayview High School, Milwaukee **A/A/S:** Local Gun Clubs; National Rifle Association; World Champion Trap Shooter

Mary Ellen Fleck Kleiman
Title: Associate General Counsel **Company:** National Association of Chain Drug Stores **Address:** 413 N. Lee Street, Alexandria, VA 22314 United States **BUS:** Trade Association **P/S:** Chain Drug Stores **MA:** National **D/D/R:** Legal Counseling **H/I/S:** Running **EDU:** JD, Cum Laude, Catholic University of America Columbus School of Law **A/H:** Larry M. Simonsmeier Award, American Society of Pharmacy Law, 2007 **C/VW:** Juvenile Diabetes Research Foundation International
Email: fleck_kleiman@msn.com

Tanya C. Kleinhenz, CMT, CST
Title: Owner, Massage Therapist, Craniosacral Therapist **Company:** Rainbow Ray's Healing Touch, LLC **Address:** 1617 W. Court Street, Janesville, WI 53548 United States **BUS:** Therapy Center **P/S:** Mobile Massage Therapy Services Including Therapeutic Massage, Craniosacral Therapy, Reiki Sessions and Training, Ear Candling and Young Living Essential Oils **MA:** South Central Wisconsin, Northern Illinois **D/D/R:** Paying Bills, Overseeing Business Operations, Organizing Monthly Meetings for a Parish Education Committee, Performing Therapeutic Massage Including Craniosacral Therapy, Reiki Training, Teaching **H/I/S:** Spending Time with her Family, Cooking Wheat, Gluten and Dairy-Free Foods, Walking, Biking, Gardening, Beading Jewelry with Healing Stones, Traveling, Swimming, Dancing, Singing, Meditating, Admiring Nature **CERTS:** Licensed Massage Therapist, State of Wisconsin (2005); Certified Reiki Master, Helping Hands Wellness Center (2005); Certified Craniosacral Therapist Level I and II, The Upledger Institute; Certification, Lakeside School of Massage Therapy, National Board Certification for Therapeutic Massage & Bodywork; Certification in SomatoEmotional Release Therapy, The Upledger Institute (2005-2007); Certification in Pediatrics, The Upledger Institute (2005-2007) **A/A/S:** American Massage Therapy Association; National Certification Board for Therapeutic Massage & Bodywork; The International Association of Healthcare Practitioners **C/VW:** Advocate for Rock County Autism and SPD Parent Connection Group, Chairwoman, The Education Committee, St. William Parish; La Leche League of Wisconsin; Troop Leader, Troop 492, Girl Scouts of the United States of America; Annual Health Fair, Blackhawk Technical College; Multiple Sclerosis Support Group, Mercy Medical Center
Email: tanyateejay@att.net
URL: http://www.cambridgewhoswho.com

Mary L. Kleis
Title: Registered Occupational Therapist, Certified Hand Therapist **Company:** Holland Hospital **Address:** 4553 Hidden Ridge, Hudsonville, MI 49426 United States **BUS:** Premier Hospital Serving West Michigan's Lakeshore Communities **P/S:** Expert and Experienced Medical Staff, State-of-the-Art Technology, Exceptional Patient Care **MA:** Regional **D/D/R:** Hand Therapy, Rehabilitation, Treating Amputations, Replantation of Limbs, Arthritis, Tendon and Nerve Injuries **H/I/S:** Animals, Photography, Crafts, Traveling **EDU:** Bachelor of Science Degree in Occupational Therapy, Western Michigan University (1986)
Email: maisyridge@sbcglobal.net
URL: http://www.hollandhospital.org

Ms. Kyle Louise Kleyn van de Poll
Title: Business Development Manager **Company:** Holland America Line Inc. **Dept:** Sales **Address:** 300 Elliot Avenue W., Seattle, WA 98119 United States **BUS:** Transportation Company **P/S:** Shipping Services **MA:** International **D/D/R:** Overseeing the Marketing of Cruises to Travel Agencies and Businesses, Training Agents and Businesses on Product Knowledge, Features and Benefits, Overseeing Sales Development in Southwest Florida **H/I/S:** Golfing, Cooking **EDU:** Coursework, Ramsey High School **A/A/S:** The American Society of Travel Agents
Email: kkleynvandepoll@hollandamerica.com
URL: http://www.hollandamerica.com

Julie M. Klimko
Title: Medical Transcriptionist, Editor **Company:** Medical Transcription Corporation **Address:** 1425 Tarkiln Road, Harrisville, RI 02830 United States **BUS:** Medical Transcription Company **P/S:** Medical Transcription Services **MA:** Regional **EXP:** Ms. Klimko's expertise is in medical transcription. **D/D/R:** Maintaining Surgical Records, Developing the Voice Recognition Process **H/I/S:** Gardening, Painting **CERTS:** Certified Medical Assistant, The Sawyer School (1984) **A/A/S:** American Association for Medical Transcription
Email: jul610mt@yahoo.com

Ann Toepel Klipstine
Title: Consultant **Company:** ATM Consultants **Address:** 3103 Saddlebrook Crossing, Valparaiso, IN 46385 United States **BUS:** Consulting Company **P/S:** Employee Development, Customer Service Skills Training **MA:** Local **D/D/R:** Consulting, Coordinating Staff Development and Enrichment Programs, Making Presentations, Focusing on Customer Service and Self Improvement, Developing Healthy Mindset and Attitude **H/I/S:** Listening to Music, Supporting the La Porte County Symphony, Traveling **EDU:** Bachelor of Arts in Social Science, Valparaiso University, IN **CERTS:** Licensed Social Worker **A/A/S:** La Porte County Symphony; Indiana State Leaders in Healthcare **C/VW:** Local Church
Email: atklipstine@comcast.net
URL: http://www.cambridgewhoswho.com

Shirley M. Kloiber
Title: Office Manager **Company:** Geo A Reppert & Sons Garage, LLC **Address:** 1934 Lincoln Avenue, Northampton, PA 18067 United States **BUS:** Automotive **P/S:** General Auto Repair **MA:** Local **D/D/R:** Office Management, Scheduling, Inventory, Billing **H/I/S:** Crafting **A/A/S:** American Heart Association, American Cancer Society
Email: reppert@enter.net

Keith Klotsche
Title: Special Education Teacher **Company:** Hicksville Union Free School District **Address:** Division Avenue, Hicksville, NY 11801 United States **BUS:** School **P/S:** Special Education **MA:** Local **D/D/R:** Teaching Students with Special Needs **H/I/S:** Watching Sports **EDU:** Master's Degree in Special Education, C.W. Post Campus, Long Island University; Bachelor's Degree in Sociology, Queens College, CUNY **A/A/S:** Educator, Religion; Coach, Baseball and Basketball Teams
Email: pklotsche@msn.com

Suzi G. Kluth
Title: Operations Manager **Company:** Rinker Materials **Address:** 3640 S. 19th Avenue, Phoenix, AZ 85009 United States **BUS:** Concrete Construction **P/S:** Concrete, Ready Mix **MA:** Local **D/D/R:** Supervises 5 Operators, 1 Mechanic, 40 Drivers and 6 Dispatchers **H/I/S:** Fish, Traveling, Hunting, Skiing **A/A/S:** Women in Construction
Email: sgkluth@rinker.com
URL: www.rinker.com

Julie Thomas Knap
Title: Director of Promotions, In-Game Marketing **Company:** Vivendi Games **Dept:** Integrated Marketing **Address:** 6060 Center Drive, Fifth Floor, Los Angeles, CA 90045 United States **BUS:** Global Developer, Publisher and Distributor of Multi-Platform Interactive Entertainment, Leader in the Subscription-Based Massively Multi-Player Online Games Category **P/S:** Blizzard Entertainment, Creation of Games Including World Of Warcraft, Diablo, Starcraft and Warcraft **MA:** International **D/D/R:** Overseeing All Promotions and Marketing of Dynamic Placement for Video Games, Working with Online, Trade Marketing and Brand Teams, Generating Awareness for Video Games **H/I/S:** Competing in Triathlons, Traveling, Cooking **EDU:** Bachelor's Degree in History of Public Policy, University of California (1994) **A/A/S:** Leukemia & Lymphoma Society
Email: julie.knap@vgames.com
URL: http://www.sierra.com

Laurie A. Knapp
Title: Owner **Company:** LAK Health **Address:** 446 Two Knotch Road, Lot 3, Lexington, SC 29073 United States **BUS:** Health and Nutrition Company **P/S:** Nutritional Supplements **MA:** International **EXP:** Ms. Knapp's expertise is in healthy weight loss. **H/I/S:** Caring for Horses **A/A/S:** Lexington Chamber of Commerce **C/VW:** Rescue Group for Retired Greyhounds
Email: lakhealth@yahoo.com
URL: http://www.shopherbalife.com/lakhealth

Vanesa M. Kneeskern, RN, BSN
Title: Registered Nurse, Case Manager **Company:** Prairie River Home Care, Inc. **Address:** 933 37th Avenue N.W., Rochester, MN 55901 United States **BUS:** Licensed, Medicare-Certified Home Health Agency **P/S:** Professional Medical and Non-Medical Caregiving Services, Education, Consulting and Treatment for Patients with Various Health Conditions, Nursing, Wound Care, Intravenous Therapy, Palliative Care, Physical, Speech and Occupational Therapy, Home Health Aides, Personal Care, Meal Preparation and Feeding, Companionship, Housekeeping **MA:** Regional **D/D/R:** Admitting, Diagnosing and Caring for Patients, Supplying Case Managers with Patients' Plans, Supervising more than 200 Clients, Educating Patients with Diabetes and Renal Diseases, Trauma Nursing **H/I/S:** Reading Romance Novels, Quilting **CERTS:** Registered Nurse, Riverland Community College (1999) **A/A/S:** Phi Beta Kappa Honor Society
Email: nessrn30@yahoo.com
URL: http://www.prhomecare.com/index.html

Donalyn P. Knight
Title: 1) Teacher 2) Owner, Founder **Company:** 1) Seminole High School 2) The Spirited Athlete, Inc. **Address:** 2557 S. Palmetto Avenue, Sanford, FL 32773 United States **BUS:** 1) High School 2) Consultation Service **P/S:** 1) General High School Curriculum, Arts, Music, Physical Education, Athletics, Extracurricular Activities 2) College-Bound Athlete Consultations, Seminars, Motivational and Inspirational Products for Coaches and Athletes **MA:** Regional **D/D/R:** Teaching Grades Life Management and Personal Fitness to Grades 10 through 12, Consulting, Product Speaking, Coaching Athletic Teams, Counseling and Advising High School Students, Assisting High School Students with College Transitions **H/I/S:** Traveling, Windsurfing, Sports **EDU:** Master's Degree in Administration and Supervision, Stetson University, DeLand, Florida (1980); Bachelor's Degree in Health and Physical Education, Stetson University (1974) **A/A/S:** Fellowship of Christian Athletes; Fellowship of Christian Airline Personnel
Email: spiritedathlete@aol.com
URL: http://www.thespiritedathlete.com

Katherine D. Knight
Title: Certified Athletic Trainer **Company:** DePaul University **Address:** 2323 N. Sheffield Avenue, Chicago, IL 60614 United States **BUS:** University **P/S:** Education **MA:** International **D/D/R:** Athletic Training **H/I/S:** Caring for her Dog, Walking, Participating in Outdoor Activities, Hiking, Reading **EDU:** Bachelor of Science in Kinesiology, University of Wisconsin-Madison **A/A/S:** National Athletic Trainers' Association; Illinois Athletic Trainers Association; Phi Kappa Phi **C/VW:** CPR Instructor, American Red Cross
Email: kknight4@depaul.edu

Michael D. Knight
Title: Member **Company:** McDowell Knight Roedder & Sledge, LLC **Address:** 63 S. Royal Street, Suite 900, Mobile, AL 36602 United States **BUS:** Law Firm **P/S:** Litigation Services Including Civil Law, Personal Injury and Medical Liability Cases **MA:** National **D/D/R:** Practicing Defense of Personal Injury Law, Property and Death Claims, Litigating Product Liability and Commercial Cases **H/I/S:** Fly Fishing **EDU:** Bachelor of Law, The University of Alabama School of Law (1964) **A/A/S:** American College of Trial Lawyers; International Academy of Trial Lawyers; Products Liability Advisory Council; President, Mobile Bar Association (2003); Board of Bar Commissioners, Alabama Bar Association; American Bar Association; Alabama State Bar Instituteís Continuing Legal Education Program; Alabama Defense Lawyers Association; American Board of Trial Advocacy; Federation of Defense and Corporate Counsel; International Academy of Trial Lawyers; Atlanta Claims Association
Email: mknight@mcdowellknight.com
URL: http://www.mcdowellknight.com

Wendy Knight
Title: Executive Director **Company:** TNHA TN Development Corporation **Address:** P.O. Box 409, Barrow, AK 99723 United States **BUS:** Housing Development **P/S:** Affordable Housing Projects, Programs, Community Development Projects, Program Management **MA:** Local **D/D/R:** Planning, Development, Affordable Housing, Consulting, Nonprofit Organization **H/I/S:** Travel, Renovating a 1940's School, Pottery, Teaching on the Side **EDU:** University of Chicago, BA-History, BA-Sociology **A/A/S:** Past Involvement with Habitat for Humanity, Mental Health Development Association, Also Involved with Cold Climate Research Program, Homeless Coalition
Email: wendy.knight@TNHA.net

Susan J. Knoblauch aka Salomé
Title: Artistic Director **Company:** Raks Shadan Troupe **Address:** 3435 Scottwood Road, Columbus, OH 43227 United States **BUS:** Dance Company **P/S:** Belly Dancing, Dance Seminars, Oriental Dancing **MA:** National **D/D/R:** Teaching Oriental and Middle Eastern Dance, Promoting Middle Eastern Cultures, Creating New Choreography, Specializing in Planning Performances, Lecturing on Dance, Scouting and Training Dancers **H/I/S:** Dancing **EDU:** Diploma, Rosary High School, Columbus, OH (1960) **CERTS:** Industry-Related Training with Ibrahim Farrah, New York **A/A/S:** Columbus International Festival
Email: maria@huffcpa.com
URL: http://www.cambridgewhoswho.com

Lisa M. Knoerr
Title: Pharmacy Manager **Company:** Walgreens **Address:** 2990 Bay Road, Saginaw, MI 48603 United States **BUS:** Drug Store **P/S:** Household Items, Prescriptions **MA:** National **D/D/R:** Managing the Pharmacy, Servicing Customers **H/I/S:** Hiking, Skiing, Playing Golf, Spending Time Outdoors **EDU:** Bachelor of Science in Pharmacy, Ferris State University **C/VW:** Nursing Homes; Relay For Life
Email: lmkfarms@charter.net
URL: http://www.walgreens.com

Lori Knopf Santora
Title: Speech and Language Therapist **Company:** San Lorenzo Unified School District, Lorenzo Manor School **Address:** 18250 Bengal Avenue, Hayward, CA 94541 United States **BUS:** Leading Kindergarten through Fifth-Grade Public School **P/S:** Developing Critical and Creative Thinkers who are Knowledgeable, Responsible, Caring Participants who Contribute to a Changing World **MA:** Local **D/D/R:** Specialty in Spanish Speech and Language Assessment of Children, In Charge of Assessing All Spanish Students throughout District **H/I/S:** Scuba, Travel, Photography, Needlepoint, Crossword Puzzles, Scrabble, Mah Jong **EDU:** Master of Science in Speech and Language Pathology, San Francisco State University (1983); Bachelor of Science in Linguistics, University of California at Los Angeles (1976)
Email: lsantora@slzusd.org
URL: http://www.sanlorenzousd.k12.ca.us

Mr. Jeffery Kevin Knowles
Title: Deputy Director of Public Works **Company:** City of Vacaville **Address:** 650 Merchant Street, Vacaville, CA 95688 United States **BUS:** Government Organization **P/S:** Transportation and Consulting **MA:** Local **D/D/R:** Traffic Engineering, Consulting **H/I/S:** Running Marathons, Mountain Climbing, Skiing, Scuba Diving **A/A/S:** Institute of Transportation Engineers; American Society of Civil Engineers
Email: jknowles@cityofvacaville.com
URL: http://www.cityofvacaville.com

Mrs. Roxanne E. Knox
Title: Owner, Broker **Company:** Sunshine Mortgage Company, LLC **Address:** 300 S. Washington Avenue, Titusville, FL 32796 United States **BUS:** Mortgage Broker Company **P/S:** Loan Options Including Purchases, Refinances, Lot, Construction, Permanent and Reverse Mortgages for Senior Citizens, Commercial Loan Division Including Churches, Golf Courses, Shopping Malls and Housing Developments **MA:** Local **D/D/R:** Lending to First-Time Home Buyers and the Credit-Challenged Buyer, Helping Everyone he can to Achieve the America Dream **H/I/S:** Riding Horses, Spending Quality Time with her Two Children and Husband **EDU:** Coursework in Banking, Brevard Community College **CERTS:** Pursuing Continuing Education as a Licensed Mortgage Broker **A/A/S:** Treasurer, North Brevard Horseman's Club (2004-2007); Titusville Area Chamber of Commerce; Financial Banker Industry **C/VW:** Volunteer, North Brevard Horseman's Club; Local Church Events
Email: roxanne_ssmc@yahoo.com
URL: http://www.sunshinemortgageco.com
URL: http://www.cambridgewhoswho.com

Daniel C. Knust
Title: Associate Minister **Company:** West Park Church of Christ **Address:** 926 Cherokee Road, Portsmouth, VA 23701 United States **BUS:** Religion Church **P/S:** Works a Three Fold Position-Administrative Duties, Education and Assimilation, Works Along Side the Pastor, Conducting and Writing Sermons, Visitations, Counseling and Spiritual Guidance as well as Training Ministry Leaders and Teachers of Bible Study, Also Available for Leadership and Personal Training to Congregation and Community, Oversees the Men's and Senior Ministry. Helps Organize the 24Plus Ministries the Church Supports **MA:** International **D/D/R:** Church is Expanding and Looking Forward to Introducing a Recreation Center on the Grounds-Youth Programs, Mentoring, Sports, Full Gym, Senior Groups and Activities, Teaching and Administration, Writing-Plenty of Articles Published, Currently Working on a New Book, His Writing is Mostly Spiritual Driven, Does some Fiction **H/I/S:** Time with his Family-Two Sons and Wife, Golfing and Camping **EDU:** Bachelor of Science in Religious Studies, Great Lakes Bible College-MI, Master's Degree in Practical Ministries, Cincinnati Christian University-OH **A/A/S:** Board Member of Campus Ministry at Virginia Technical University and Virginia Vision Ministry
Email: dknust@wpfamily.org
URL: www.wpfamily.org

Tracy Kobelt-Danosky
Title: New York State Hearing Specialist, Owner **Company:** Pearl River Hearing Center **Address:** Six E. Central Avenue, Pearl River, NY 10965 United States **BUS:** Hearing Center **P/S:** Assisted Listening Technology and Devices **MA:** Local **D/D/R:** Overseeing Patients, Answering Phones, Editing Book Work, Conducting Seminars, Educating Public on Hearing Loss **H/I/S:** Riding Motor Cycles, Spending Time with her Grandchildren **EDU:** Pursuing Associate Degree in Audiology, Phoenix Online College **A/A/S:** Pearl River Chamber of Commerce; Pearl River Lions Clubs; International Institute for Hearing Institute Studies; American Speech Language Hearing Association **C/VW:** Cancer Society
Email: pearlriverhearingcenter@verizon.net

Jerry A. Koble
Title: Special Education Teacher **Company:** Fort Madison Community School District **Address:** 1930 Avenue M, Fort Madison, IA 52627 United States **BUS:** School District **P/S:** Education **MA:** Local **D/D/R:** Teaching Students with Special Needs **H/I/S:** Traveling **EDU:** Bachelor of Arts in Art Education and Special Education, Iowa Wesleyan College **A/A/S:** Local Teachers Union; American Legion; National Education Association **C/VW:** American Society for the Prevention of Cruelty to Animals, Doris Day Animal League, Animal Shelters

Gail M. Koch, CPP
Title: Payroll Manager **Company:** Japs-Olson Company **Address:** 7500 Excelsior Boulevard, Saint Louis Park, MN 55426 United States **BUS:** Payroll **P/S:** Payroll, Commercial Printing **MA:** Local **EXP:** Ms. Koch's expertise includes payroll, benefits and taxes. **H/I/S:** Traveling, Boating, Biking, Cross Country Skiing **A/A/S:** American Payroll Association (Hot Line Referral Service), Northstar Chapter (Secretary, Membership Chair)
Email: gkoch@japsolson.com

R. Michael Koch, MD
Title: Physician **Company:** New York Group for Plastic Surgery **Address:** 155 White Plains Road, Suite 105, Tarrytown, NY 10591 United States **BUS:** Company of Gifted, Board-Certified Plastic Surgeons and Specialists **P/S:** Aesthetic and Reconstructive Surgery Including Laser Surgery, Microsurgery, Hand Surgery, Pediatric Plastic Surgery, Skin Cancer Surgery, Breast Augmentation, Breast Reduction, Breast Reconstruction, Wound Healing and Burn Care **MA:** Regional **D/D/R:** Practicing Micro-Surgery, Cancer Reconstruction and Aesthetic Surgery, Teaching Medical Students Breast, Orthopedic and Cosmetic Surgery **H/I/S:** Bicycling **EDU:** MD, Ottoman University (1993); Bachelor's Degree in Biology, University of California, Santa Barbara (1989) **A/A/S:** Partner, Private Practice; Fellow, Diplomat, American Council of Certified Podiatric Physicians and Surgeons; American Board of Plastic Surgery
Email: rmichaelkoch@msn.com
URL: http://www.nygplasticsurgery.com

Tracey M. Koch
Title: Practice Director **Company:** G2 Dental **Address:** 1068 South Lake Street, Suite 209, Forest Lake, MN 55025 United States **BUS:** Healthcare: Dentistry **P/S:** Healthcare Management Dental Office **MA:** Local **EXP:** Ms. Koch's expertise is in dental healthcare. **H/I/S:** Consulting, Traveling, Golf, Boating **EDU:** University of St Thomas, Master of Business Administration **A/A/S:** Humane Society, Home for Life
Email: tkoch@g2dental.com
URL: www.g2dental.com

Tara T. Kochis
Title: Executive Vice President of Business Development **Company:** Slone and Associates **Address:** 5705 Locust Branch Court, Centreville, VA 20120 United States **BUS:** Leading Privately Held Executive Search Firm **P/S:** Identification, Evaluation and Recruitment of Professional Talent in the Diagnostic Industry **MA:** National **D/D/R:** Recruiting Professionals in the Executive Laboratory Field **H/I/S:** Doing Yoga and Fitness Activities, Spending Time with her Family and Friends **EDU:** Bachelor's Degree in Human Resource Management, Boston College (1986) **A/A/S:** Academy of Clinical Healthcare Executives; Clinical Laboratory Management Association; Presenter, American Academy of Clinical Chemistry
Email: tara@sloneandassociates.com
URL: http://www.sloneandassociates.com

Mr. John D. Kocur
Title: Owner **Company:** Kocur Business Solutions **Address:** 935 Newtown Road, Warminster, PA 18974 United States **BUS:** Consulting Firm **P/S:** Business Development and Business Strategy Consulting Services **MA:** National **D/D/R:** Increasing Business Revenue through Marketing and Sales Strategies **H/I/S:** Golfing, Sports **EDU:** Bachelor's Degree in Finance, Minor in Information Systems and Statistical Analysis, Pennsylvania State University **A/A/S:** Chamber of Commerce; Southampton Business and Professional Association
Email: john-kocur@kocurbs.com
URL: http://www.kocurbusinesssolutions.com

Donna J. Koechig, LCSW, Ph.D.
Title: Associate Vice President of Diversity Community Outreach and Professional Organizational Development **Company:** Lane Community College **Address:** 4000 E. 30th Avenue, Eugene, OR 97405 United States **BUS:** Community College **P/S:** Higher Education for Students, Student Affairs, Innovative Instruction **MA:** Regional **D/D/R:** Organizational Development Student Services and Instruction **H/I/S:** Water Coloring and Fused Glass Art, Playing the Guitar and Bass **EDU:** Ph.D. in Counseling Psychology, University of Missouri-Columbia (1993); Master of Social Work, University of Missouri-Columbia (1980); Bachelor's Degree in Interdisciplinary Studies, Southeast Missouri State University (1976) **CERTS:** Licensed Psychologist; Licensed Clinical Social Worker **A/A/S:** Joint Boards Articulation Commission; President, Oregon Joint Boards Articulation Commission: Council Services; American Association for Women in Community Colleges; National Council of Instructional Administrators; National Institute for Leadership Development; Oregon Council of Student Services Administrators
Email: koechigd@lanecc.edu
URL: http://www.lanecc.edu

Suzanne B. Koenig
Title: Reading Specialist **Company:** Peoria School District **Address:** 11232 N. 65th Avenue, Glendale, AZ 85304 United States **BUS:** School District **P/S:** Education **MA:** Local **D/D/R:** Reading Instruction **H/I/S:** Reading, Hiking **EDU:** Master of Arts in Reading Education, Arizona State University **A/A/S:** National Education Association; Arizona Education Association; Phoenix West Reading Council **C/VW:** Eye Dog Foundation
Email: skoenig@peoriaud.k12.az.us
URL: http://www.cambridgewhoswho.com

Patricia J. Koepsel
Title: Teacher (Retired) **Company:** Fairfax County Public Schools **Address:** Fairfax County Public Schools, McLean, VA 22102 United States **BUS:** Elementary School Facility Dedicated to Excellence in Education **P/S:** Regular Core Curriculum Including Reading, Mathematics, English, Science, Social Studies, Art, Music, History, Physical Education **MA:** Regional **D/D/R:** Teaching CCD and Kindergarten **H/I/S:** Traveling **EDU:** Master's Degree Plus 60 Credits in Education, Texas A&M University (1965) **A/A/S:** Lifetime Member of the National Education Association, Fairfax Education Association and Virginia Education Association; Delta Kappa Gamma; Phi Delta Kappa; Ran Volunteer Intervention Program for Kindergarten; Retired Teachers Association; Council of CIVITAN International; Junior CIVITAN Coordinator
Email: pkoepsel@cox.net
URL: http://www.fcps.edu

Cindy C. Kohl
Title: Administrator **Company:** Christian Life Center Church Academy **Address:** 55 County Road 55, Piedmont, AL 36272 United States **BUS:** Private School **P/S:** Christian-Based Kindergarten through Twelfth-Grade Education **MA:** Regional **D/D/R:** Administration, Mentoring Students, Coordinating Class Schedules, Acting as a Liaison to the Board of Directors and Families **H/I/S:** Crocheting, Knitting, Embroidery **EDU:** Pursuing Bachelor's Degree in Ministry and Education, Patriot Bible University **A/A/S:** Chamber of Commerce; Volunteer, American Red Cross; Volunteer, Girl Scouts of the USA; Volunteer, 4-H Club
Email: ckohl@tds.net
URL: http://www.clccahomeedu.com

Chris Marie Kokesh
Title: Restaurant and Lounge Manager **Company:** Veterans of Foreign Wars, Post 7319 **Address:** 113 Second Street S.W., Wagner, SD 57380 United States **BUS:** Nonprofit Organization **P/S:** Food and Beverages for Veterans **MA:** Local **D/D/R:** Managing Operations, Bartending, Ordering Supplies **A/A/S:** South Dakota Retail Liquor Dealers Association; Secretary, Chamber of Commerce; Retail Promotion Committee; Ladies Auxiliary, Veterans of Foreign Wars **C/VW:** Ladies Altar Society, St. John the Baptist Catholic Church
Email: chrismarie.kukesh@cwwemail.com
URL: http://www.cambridgewhoswho.com

Bettie Kollock-Wallace
Title: Principal (Retired) **Company:** New York City Board of Education **Address:** 417 Amboy Street, Basement, Brooklyn, NY 11212 United States **BUS:** Board of Education **P/S:** Education **MA:** Local **D/D/R:** Supervision, Administration, Personal Training Coordinating Fitness Programs **H/I/S:** Going to the Gym, Gardening, Sewing, Surfing the Internet **EDU:** Master's Degree in Supervision and Administration, City College (1979); Master's Degree in Education, Long Island University (1975); Bachelor's Degree, CUNY Brooklyn College (1973); **A/A/S:** Second Vice President, Community Board 16; Personal Trainer and Group Fitness Coordinator, Water Instructor for Brownsville Recreation Center; Lambda Kappa Mu **C/VW:** Gym, Church, Community Planning Board
Email: betkwall@verizon.net
URL: http://www.cambridgewhosho.com

Sarah Ann Kolterman
Title: Educator **Company:** Schaumburg Christian School **Address:** 200 N. Roselle Road, Schaumburg, IL 60194 United States **BUS:** Christian School **P/S:** Education for Students in Preschool through Twelfth-Grade, Child Care, Fine Arts, Activity Center, Gymnasium **MA:** Regional **D/D/R:** Supervising, Heading Department, Mentoring 3rd-Grade Teachers, Teaching Bible Studies, Science, English, Mathematics, Reading to Third-Grade Students, Summer Tutoring for Students in English and Mathematics, Overseeing 121 Children **H/I/S:** Reading, Traveling, Photography **EDU:** Master of Science in Counseling, Bob Jones University (2003)
Email: sarahkolterman@bethelministries.org
URL: http://www.bethelministries.org

Cathleen C. Kononchuk
Title: Teacher **Company:** Lyman High School **Address:** 865 S. Ronald Reagan Boulevard, Longwood, FL 32750 United States **BUS:** High School **P/S:** Secondary Education **MA:** Local **EXP:** Ms. Kononchuk's expertise includes home economics and early childhood education. **D/D/R:** Teaching Ninth through 12th-Grade Students **H/I/S:** Reading, Spending Time with her Family **EDU:** Bachelor of Science in Early Childhood Education, Central Michigan University **CERTS:** Certified Teacher (Ninth-12th-Grade); Certified Mathematics Teacher (Sixth-12th-Grade); Certified CPR Instructor; Certified First Aid Instructor **A/A/S:** Department of Education and Curriculum Affairs **C/VW:** College Preparatory Mathematics; Lifestyle Health Club; Arnold Palmer Foundation; Ronald McDonald House
Email: cathleen_kononchuk@scps.k12.fl.us
URL: http://www.cambridgewhoswho.com

Derrick T. Koo
Title: Optometrist **Company:** Vision First Optometry **Address:** 10525 S. De Anza Boulevard, Cupertino, CA 95014 United States **BUS:** Optometry Center **P/S:** Optometry Services, Eyeglasses and Lenses, Eye Disease Diagnosis, Contact Lens Evaluation and Fitting, Pediatric and Comprehensive Eye Examinations **MA:** San Jose **D/D/R:** Pediatric Optometry, Ocular Disease, Corneal Refractive Therapy, Handling Gas Permeable Lenses **H/I/S:** Playing Basketball, Exercising, Wakeboarding **EDU:** Doctor of Optometry, Southern California College of Optometry; Master's Degree in Psychological Science, Concentration in Business Management, University of California, Los Angeles **A/A/S:** American Optometric Association; Santa Clara County Optometric Society
Email: derrick.koo@gmail.com
URL: http://www.svoptometry.com

Duangphat Koomsub
Title: Fund Accountant **Company:** Swiss Financial **Address:** 280 Shuman Boulevard, Suite 190, Naperville, IL 60563 United States **BUS:** Financial Services Company **P/S:** Fund Administration **MA:** National **EXP:** Ms. Koomsub's expertise is in hedge funds. **H/I/S:** Going to the Gym, Playing Tennis, Watching Movies, Traveling **EDU:** Master of Science in Accounting, University of Illinois; Bachelor of Science in Accounting, Chulalongkorn University, Thailand **A/A/S:** Illinois CPA Society; University of Illinois Alumni Association
Email: aomduangpat@yahoo.com

Laurie A. Koontz, NMNP
Title: Assistant to DGM, Director of Operations Company: Protection Technology Los Alamos Dept: Operations Division Address: P.O. Box 1400, Los Alamos, NM 87544 United States BUS: Contracting Company P/S: Security Services MA: International D/D/R: Managing Operations, Overseeing National Security and Criminal Justice Services, Managing Administrative Duties and Records Management H/I/S: Traveling, Singing, Writing, Sports, Basketball, Sewing, Creating Art, Making Crafts, Hiking EDU: Pursuing Bachelor's Degree in Criminal Justice, Northern New Mexico College and Santa Fe Community College; Diploma, Rifle High School, CO (1982) CERTS: Certified Administrative Professional; DOE Basic Instructor Trainer, ASIS Physical Security Professional Study Group; Certified Notary Public for the State of New Mexico A/A/S: Los Alamos National Laboratory Foundation Scholarship Review Committee; Association of Records Managers and Administrators; American Management Association; National Notary Association; National Rifle Association; Rocky Mountain Elk Foundation A/H: Certificate of Appreciation, Chapter 224, Security Professional Program (2004); Certificate of Appreciation, Cerro Grande Fire, American Red Cross C/VW: Local Church; Ronald McDonald House; St. Jude Children's Research Foundation; Locks of Love; Coats for Kids; United Way; American Red Cross; Crisis Center of Northern New Mexico
Email: lkoontz@lanl.gov
URL: http://www.cambridgewhoswho.com

Jane D. Kopperl
Title: Associate Landscape Architect Company: EDAW/AECOM Address: 1809 Black Street, Suite 200, Denver, CO 80202 United States BUS: Design Firm P/S: Landscape Architecture and Design MA: International EXP: Ms. Kopperl's expertise includes landscape architecture, ecological restoration, project management, construction documentation, construction administration, design and implementation. H/I/S: Reading, Equestrian Sports, Skiing, Hiking, Mountain Biking EDU: Bachelor of Science in Landscape Architecture, Colorado State University (1990); Bachelor of Science in Natural Resource Management, Colorado State University(1990) CERTS: Registered Landscape Architect, States of Wyoming and Colorado
Email: jayne.kopperl@edaw.com
URL: http://www.edaw.com

Marion Korin, RN, CEN
Title: Assistant Nurse Manager Emergency Room Company: UC Davis Medical Center Address: 2315 Stockton Boulevard, Sacramento, CA 95817 United States BUS: Healthcare P/S: Level 1 Trauma Center Hospital MA: Regional D/D/R: Emergency Room Charge Nurse in a Level I Trauma Center, Directly Responsible for Scheduling, Orientation and Mentoring Other Emergency Room Nurses, Handling Communication with Physicians and Other Hospital Officials, Overseeing Allocation of Emergency Room Nurses Time and Resources, Making Assessments, Handling Emergency Patient Treatment, Formerly Legal Nurse Consulting Services H/I/S: Golfing, Working Out, Yoga EDU: Associate Degree in Registered Nursing, Ramapo Valley College (1984) CERTS: Board Certified Emergency Nurse A/A/S: Emergency Nurses Association
Email: mkorin1952@yahoo.com

Robin M. Korner, RN
Title: Registered Nurse Company: Sebastian River Medical Center Address: 5041 Park Lake Drive, Unit 4, Melbourne, FL 32901 United States BUS: High Quality Hospital P/S: Wide Range of Medical Services MA: Local D/D/R: Pre-Operative Holding Area, Critical Recovery and Preceptor Nursing H/I/S: Bowling, NASCAR EDU: Diploma, Albany Medical Center, School of Nursing (1979) A/A/S: Member, Professional Practice Council; American Society of PeriAnesthesia Nurses; Florida Association of Post Anesthesia Nurses A/H: Nurse of the Quarter (2006)
Email: rkorner@cfl.rr.com
URL: http://www.srmcenter.com/index.html#

Joyce A. Korschqen, LPC, EAP
Title: Executive Director Company: Alliance Counseling Center, Inc. Address: 818 N.W. 17th Avenue, Suite 3, Portland, OR 97209 United States BUS: Proven Leader in the Counseling Industry P/S: Wide Range of Psychotherapy Services MA: Regional D/D/R: Owning and Running the Company, Overseeing the Payroll, Treating Eating Disorders H/I/S: Horseback Riding EDU: Master of Arts in Psychology, Portland State University (1983); Bachelor of Art, University of Hawaii (1978) CERTS: Nationally Certified Counselor A/A/S: Academy of Eating Disorders; American Mental Health Counseling Association
Email: joyce@alliancecounselingcenter.org
URL: http://www.alliancecounselingcenter.org

Sean P. Koscielniak
Title: Licensed Practical Nurse Company: Mount St. Francis Nursing Center Address: 7550 Assisi Heights, Colorado Springs, CO 80919 United States BUS: Long-Term Care Center P/S: Nursing, Healthcare MA: Local D/D/R: Overseeing Long-Term Care Nursing H/I/S: Spending Time Outdoors, Reading, Camping, Playing Hockey CERTS: Licensed Practical Nurse, Pikes Peak Community College (2006); Certification in Intravenous Therapy
Email: quikiebowhunter711@gmail.com

Rhonda M. Koska
Title: Facilities Manager Company: Avatar Pharmaceutical Services, Inc. Address: 257 Simarano Drive, Marlborough, MA 01752 United States BUS: Pharmaceutical Company P/S: Analytical Laboratory Testing Services MA: International D/D/R: Stability Studies H/I/S: Camping, Running, Gardening EDU: Bachelor of Science in Food Science and Technology, Framingham State College, Massachusetts C/VW: Girl Scouts of the USA
Email: rhondakoska@yahoo.com
URL: http://www.avatarps.com

Alicia D. Koster
Title: District Purchasing Agent Company: Kingston City School District Address: 61 Crown Street, Kingston, NY 12401 United States BUS: School District P/S: Education MA: Local EXP: Ms. Koster's expertise includes time and fiscal management. D/D/R: Reviewing Compliance with State Regulations, Negotiating Contracts, Managing the Procurement Process, Coordinating and Overseeing Purchasing Processes, Strategic Planning H/I/S: Spending Time with her Family, Exercising, Sports EDU: Pursuing Master of Business Administration, with a Concentration in Dual Global Management, Walden University; Bachelor of Science in Business Administration, SUNY Empire State College (2007) A/A/S: New York State Association of School Business Officials; State Association of Municipal Purchasing Officials A/H: Nominee, Leadership Academy (2007-2008) C/VW: Volunteer, Local Charitable Organizations
Email: ad_koster@yahoo.com
URL: http://www.kingstoncityschools.org

Christine A. Kosydar
Title: Partner Company: Stoel Rives LLP Address: 900 S.W. Fifth Avenue, Portland, OR 97204 United States BUS: Law Firm P/S: Law and Business Litigation for Major Businesses MA: National D/D/R: Offering Legal Services to Businesses Including Creditors' Rights, Insolvency and Real Estate H/I/S: Skiing, Hiking, Golfing, Backpacking EDU: JD, Northwestern University School of Law (1981); Master's Degree in Mathematics, Reed College (1977); Bachelor's Degree in Mathematics with High Honors, Portland State University (1973) CERTS: Licensed Attorney, States of Oregon and Idaho A/A/S: Oregon State Bar; American Bar Association
Email: cakosydar@stoel.com
URL: http://www.stoel.com

Kimberly C. Kouka
Title: Registered Nurse Company: Community Memorial Hospital Address: 147 N. Brent Street, Ventura, CA 93003 United States BUS: Hospital P/S: Healthcare MA: Local D/D/R: Intensive Care Nursing, Caring for Patients H/I/S: Traveling, Spending Time with Friends, Reading, Watching College Basketball and Football Games EDU: Bachelor of Science in Nursing, University of Tennessee at Knoxville C/VW: Alpha Rhi Omega
Email: kckouka@yahoo.com
URL: http://www.cambridgewhoswho.com

Demetrios M. Koutsouras
Title: President Company: Vezandio Contracting Corp Address: P.O. Box 860, New Hyde Park, NY 11040 United States BUS: Construction Contractor P/S: Construction Services MA: Local EXP: Mr. Koutsouras' expertise includes management and design services. H/I/S: Basketball EDU: New York Institute of Technology, Bachelor's Degree in Science, Bachelor's Degree in Architecture
Email: demetrios@vezandio.com
URL: www.vezandio.com

Sheryll Alene Kovell
Title: Educator Company: Marysville Charter Academy for the Arts Address: 1917 B Street, Marysville, CA 95901 United States BUS: High School P/S: Art Education for Seventh Thorough 12th-Grade Students MA: Local D/D/R: Teaching Honors English, Creative Writing and Public Speaking H/I/S: Writing EDU: Bachelor of Science, South Dakota State University; Bachelor of Arts in English, South Dakota State University (1964) A/A/S: National Council of Teachers for English; National Education Association; California Teachers Association; Council on Teacher Education A/H: Nominated Blue Ribbon School (2007); California Distinguished School Award (2006); Teacher Employer Award (2005); Outstanding Teacher Award (2000) C/VW: Teacher, Newspaper in Education (2007); California Association of Teachers of English

Ms. Barbara Ann Kowalczyk
Title: Manager, Chief Executive Officer, Treasurer Company: Upstate Telco Federal Credit Union Address: 137 Harrison Street, Gloversville, NY 12078 United States BUS: Credit Union P/S: Financial Services Including Accounting, Investments, Credit and Loans for Members MA: Local EXP: Ms. Kowalczyk's expertise includes the management of credit union operations and accounting. H/I/S: Riding her Motorcycle, Playing Eight-Ball and Nine-Ball Pool EDU: Associate Degree in Accounting, Fulton-Montgomery Community College (1990) A/A/S: Notary Public; Presidential Who's Who, American Poolplayers Association Pool League A/H: Phi Thetta Kappa (1987-1988, 1990)
Email: upstatetelcofcu@frontiernet.net
URL: http://www.upstatetelcofcu.org

Gina M. Koyer
Title: Third-Grade Teacher Company: Villa Park School District 45 Address: 208 S. Euclid Avenue, Villa Park, IL 60181 United States BUS: Elementary School P/S: Regular Core Curriculum Including Reading, Mathematics, English, Science, Social Studies, Art, Music, History and Physical Education MA: Regional D/D/R: Teaching Six Subjects to Third-Grade Class, Offering Accelerated Mathematics and Art in After School Enrichment Program H/I/S: Cooking, Exercising EDU: Master's Degree in Curriculum and Instruction, Plus 63, University of Illinois (1995) A/A/S: Mentor Teacher Program; Cadet Teaching Program; Vice President, Villa Park Education Association; Illinois Education Association A/H: State Winner, Invent America (1989)
Email: gkoyer@yahoo.com
URL: http://www.d45.dupage.k12.il.us

Debra Jane Kozar
Title: 1) Personal Trainer, Fitness Instructor 2) Fitness Instructor Company: 1) New Canaan Community YMCA 2) Norwalk Community College Address: 1) 564 South Avenue 2) 188 Richards Avenue, 1) New Canaan, CT 06840 2) Norwalk, CT 06854 BUS: 1) Nonprofit Organization 2) Community College P/S: 1) Health and Wellness 2) Education MA: 1) Local 2) Local D/D/R: Functional Fitness, Empowering the Elderly to Stay Fit; H/I/S: Reading, Spending Time with her Family, Spending Time Outdoors EDU: Associate of Science in Exercise Science, Norwalk Community College-2006 CERTS: AFAA Certified Group Fitness (2000) and Personal Training Certification (2008) A/A/S: Aerobics and Fitness Association of America; Marcia LaMote Scholarship for Exercise Science A/H: First Recipient, Marcia LaMoult Scholarship-2000 C/VW: Marcia LaMoult Scholarship, Missionary Donations
Email: debkozy55@aol.com

Pete Kozminsky
Title: Project Manager, Heavy Equipment Operator, Stone Setter Address: 2794 Old Calhoun Falls Road, Abbeville, SC 29620 United States BUS: Real Estate Site Development P/S: Site preparation for building residential homes using natural resources either on site or brought in. Large stone, railroad ties, trees. Maximizing full use of property. MA: Regional D/D/R: Building or lining streams, ponds, waterfalls. Retaining driveways for access to building site. Creating level area for pools, tennis courts, patios. If running water, possible hydro power. The transplanting of large trees on site or importing large trees for on site landscaping. The use and placement of large stone (boulders) for retaining, structural or aesthetics landscaping on property. Overseeing crews and equipment operators to create architects plans. H/I/S: Anything to do with water outdoors. EDU: Northern Westchester Technology Auto Mechanics. General Motors Training Center Diesel Engines. U.S. Marine Corps Track Vehicle Repair School. Marine Corps Institute Construction Blueprint Reading. New York C.D.L. Class A Driver
Email: PeteKozminsky@cww.com

John R. Kramer
Title: Fire Chief Company: Monitor Township Fire Department Address: 2483 Midland Road, Bay City, MI 48706 United States BUS: Fire Department P/S: Fire Suppression, Public Safety, Fire Prevention MA: Local D/D/R: Budget, Training, Supervising Rescue Scenes and Accident Scenes, Working with the Town to Better Stabilize the Fire Department, Conducting Staff Meetings, Answering Questions from the Community, Permits, Routine Maintenance H/I/S: Hockey, Woodworking EDU: High School Diploma, Mount Pleasant High School (1979) CERTS: Certified Fire Instructor, Fire Fighters Training Academy (2006); Certified Fire Inspector I; Fire Officer's Certificate I, II, III; Fire Inspectors Certification A/A/S: Michigan Fire Chiefs Association; Michigan State Fireman's Association; Michigan Society of Fire Inspectors
Email: monitorchief@charterinternet.com

Suzan M. Kramp
Title: DB2 Systems Programmer Company: Nationwide Insurance Address: 275 Marconi Boulevard, MR 02-101, Columbus, OH 43215 United States BUS: Insurance Company P/S: Financial Services Including, Investments, Retirement, Automobile, Property, Life and Health Insurance, Mortgages, Banking Services, Small Business Insurance, Liability Coverage MA: National EXP: Ms. Kramp's expertise is in database administration. D/D/R: Business Data Processing, Managing the Company's Mainframe, Assisting Internal Customers, Updating Current Technologies, Programming H/I/S: Playing Chess, Bird watching, Playing Euchre, Watching the Cincinnati Reds and Ohio State Buckeyes EDU: Associate Degree in Business Data Processing, Columbus State University (1987); Master of Music, Ohio State University (1977); Bachelor of Arts in Music Education, Susquehanna University (1975)
Email: birdcatlady@aol.com
URL: http://www.nationwide.com

Viktor Krasnitsky
Title: President Company: Moderno Design Studio Address: 78 Tomlinson Road, Huntington Valley, PA 19006 United States BUS: Manufacturing and Design Company P/S: Custom Furniture MA: Regional EXP: Mr. Krasnitsky's expertise includes the installation and design of custom residential and commercial furniture, kitchen cabinets and entertainment centers. H/I/S: Water Diving, Traveling EDU: Bachelor of Arts in Mechanical Engineering, Ukraine University (1975) A/A/S: The Pennsylvania State Building and Construction Trades Council; New Jersey Building and Construction Trades Council C/VW: Local Charitable Organizations
Email: vk@modernodesignstudio.com
URL: http://www.modernodesignstudio.com

Kimberly J. Kratz
Title: President, Owner, Founder Company: KJK, Inc. Address: 1279 Browning Court, Lansdale, PA 19446 United States BUS: Property Enhancement Company P/S: Property Enhancement for the Resale Housing Market MA: Regional D/D/R: Updating Outdated Residential Designs, Working for Real Estate Professionals, Preparing Homes for Resale, Working with Hand-Picked Contractors, Consulting, Ensuring Optimal Design for Marketing H/I/S: Golfing, Playing the Piano EDU: Bachelor's Degree in Classical Piano Performance, Cleveland Institute of Music (1974) CERTS: Certified Instructor for Continuing Education, Schlicher-Kratz Institute of Real Estate, PA A/A/S: Accredited Staging Professional; County Horticulture Society; Montgomery County Association of Realtors; Bucks County Association of Realtors; Montgomery County Association of Realtors; Pennsylvania Horticulture Society; International Association of Home Staging; International Furnishings and Design Association
Email: kjkinc@msn.com
URL: http://www.kjkinc.com

Gail S. Krauthoff
Title: Chief Executive Officer, President Company: STREAMS, Inc. Address: 286 Mt. Highway 28, P.O. Box 730, Plains, MT 59859 United States BUS: Real Estate Investing Firm P/S: Single and Multi-Family Residences, Outdoor Advertising MA: Regional EXP: Ms. Krauthoff's expertise includes marketing, sales and administration. H/I/S: Volunteering, Word Puzzles, Reading, Animals EDU: Coursework in General Studies, Arizona State University A/A/S: President, Clark Fork Valley Hospital Auxiliary; Former Vice President, Plains Woman's Club C/VW: American Cancer Society's Relay for Life
Email: flowingdollars@blackfoot.net

Timothy S. Krehbiel
Title: Manager Company: Nick Alexander Restoration Address: Los Angeles, CA 90013 United States BUS: Automotive Service Provider P/S: Automotive Restoration MA: National EXP: Mr. Krehbiel's expertise is in vintage car restoration. D/D/R: Overseeing All Individual Projects EDU: Southern California Institute of Architecture, Master's and Bachelor's of Arts in Architecture
Email: t.s.krehbiel@gmail.com

Kimberly A. Kreissig
Title: 1) Partner 2) Vice President, Partner Company: 1) K & K Builders, Inc. 2) Stonewood Development Corporation Address: P.O. Box 882078, Steamboat Springs, CO 80488 United States BUS: 1) Construction 2) Real Estate Development Company P/S: 1) Building High-End Residential Housing and Single Family Homes 2) Developing Real Estate MA: Regional D/D/R: Overseeing All Projects, Managing Transactions and Sales Team, Interacting with Clients, Supervising Staff, Advertising H/I/S: Skiing, Water Skiing, Biking, Hiking, Running EDU: Bachelor of Arts in Business, University of Colorado (1992) CERTS: Licensed Broker, State of Colorado
Email: kim@kreissighomes.com
URL: http://www.kreissighomes.com

Dr. Josef Kren
Title: Tenured Professor Company: BryanLGH College of Health Sciences Address: 5035 Everett Street, Lincoln, NE 68506 United States BUS: Medical Center, College P/S: Education for Healthcare Professionals MA: International D/D/R: Specializing in Physiology, Pathophysiology, Neurophysiology, Bird Vocalization H/I/S: Traveling, Bird watching, Entering Photography Competitions EDU: Doctor of Science in Physiology, Masaryk University, Czech Republic; Ph.D. in Evolutionary Biology, University of Nebraska, Lincoln; Master's Degree in Biology, Masaryk University; Bachelor's Degree in Biology and Chemistry, Masaryk University A/A/S: American Ornithologists Union, British Ornithologists Union A/H: Who's Who Among American Teachers, 2006, 2007 C/VW: National Audubon Society
Email: josef.kren@bryanlgh.org
URL: http://www.cambridgewhoswho.com

April Kressley
Title: Executive Sales Representative Company: GlaxoSmithKline BUS: Pharmaceutical Research and Development Company P/S: Innovative Medicines and Products that Help Millions of People Around the World MA: International D/D/R: Working on Pharmaceutical Sales with a Focus on Medications Geared for Sufferers of Diabetes and Asthma, Educating and Updating Healthcare Professionals on Product Lines H/I/S: Oil Painting, Hiking, Traveling, Reading EDU: Bachelor of Science in Communications, Central Connecticut State University (1987) A/A/S: Rotary Club
Email: april_kressley@yahoo.com
URL: http://www.gsk.com

Mr. John A. Krier
Title: Senior Sales Associate Company: Exit Realty Alaska Address: 1575 H Street, Anchorage, AK 99501 United States BUS: Real Estate Agency P/S: Residential and Commercial Real Estate Services MA: Regional D/D/R: Representing Buyers, Sellers and Investors in Commercial and Residential Properties H/I/S: Fishing EDU: Coursework in Government Affairs A/A/S: Former Member, Rotary International; Former Member, Board of Realtors; Anchorage Block Grant Committee; Anchorage Senior Citizen Committee; Anchorage Budget Committee
Email: krierestate@hotmail.com
URL: http://www.exitrealtyalaska.com

Gabriella M. Krill
Title: Teacher Company: Public School 140X Address: 916 Eagle Avenue, Bronx, NY 10456 United States BUS: Public Elementary School P/S: Primary Education MA: Local D/D/R: Educating Kindergarten Students, Teaching Language Arts, Poetry, Reading, Mathematics, Social Studies, Science and Special Education H/I/S: Dancing EDU: Master's Degree in Elementary Education, Queens College (1984); Bachelor of Science in Sociology and Elementary Education, Queens College (1974) A/A/S: Who's Who Among American Teachers (2007); United Federation of Teachers; National Education Association; Pelham Promenaders Square Dance Club C/VW: Member, St. Lucy's Church, Bronx, NY
Email: gabriella.krill@cwwemail.com

Kevin Kriz
Title: Owner, Manager Company: Isanti Pizza Man Address: 404 Whiskey Road N., Isanti, MN 55040 United States BUS: Restaurant P/S: Food Services Including Pizza MA: Local EXP: Mr. Kriz's expertise includes cooking and operations management. H/I/S: Attending Concerts CERTS: Industry-Related Training C/VW: Local Charitable Organizations
Email: isantipizzaman@msn.com
URL: http://www.pizzamanpizza.net

Linda F. Kroger
Title: Owner, Pet Stylist Company: Happy Tails to You Address: 77-371 Evening Star Circle, Indian Wells, CA 92210 United States BUS: Mobile Pet Grooming Salon P/S: Mobile Pet Grooming for Primarily Dogs and Disabled Animals MA: Regional D/D/R: Gentle Grooming for all Breeds and Sizes H/I/S: Gardening, Home Decorating, Interior Design EDU: Associate Degree in Business Administration, Shasta College (1976); University of California at Riverside for Interior Design (1999-2001) CERTS: Coursework, California School of Dog Grooming (2007) A/A/S: Chamber of Commerce; Wine Women C/VW: Volunteer Groomed at Shelters
Email: chilindie@aol.com

Henry F. Kroll
Title: Writer, Publisher Company: Alaska Publishing Address: 513 Peninsula, Kenai, AK 99611 United States BUS: Publishing Company P/S: Writing, Publishing MA: National D/D/R: Collaborating Biology, Physics and Stellar Orbit to Make Science Publications He has written about 10 publications on Advanced Science H/I/S: Playing the Piano at Concerts, Fishing, Boating EDU: College Coursework CERTS: Licensed Master Pilot
Email: hankkroll@gmail.com
URL: http://www.alaskapublishing.com

Anita L. Kronk
Title: Data Quality Manager Company: Carroll Hospital Center Address: 200 Memorial Avenue, Westminster, MD 21157 United States BUS: Full Service Hospital P/S: Healthcare, Medical Services MA: Local EXP: Ms. Kronk's expertise includes anesthesiology and chronic pain management. H/I/S: Gourmet Cooking, Horseback Riding, Scuba Diving CERTS: Certified Registered Health Information Technician, Certified Coding Specialist, Medical Records Technician A/A/S: American Health Information Management Association
Email: anitak@carrollhospitalcenter.org

Melissa J. Krueger, BS
Title: Educator Company: Educational Consultant Address: Route 148, Zeigler, IL 62999 United States BUS: School P/S: Education MA: Local D/D/R: Teaching Music and Elementary Education H/I/S: Playing Five Different Musical Instruments EDU: Bachelor's Degree in Elementary Education, Southern Illinois University (2005) A/A/S: Pi Lambda Theta
Email: mlssajo@yahoo.com

Michael H. Krul
Title: Attorney Company: Ruden McClosky Address: 200 E. Broward Boulevard, Fort Lauderdale, FL 33301 United States BUS: Corporate Law Firm P/S: Legal Services MA: Local EXP: Mr. Krul's expertise includes corporate and financial law.
Email: mhk@ruden.com
URL: http://www.ruden.com

Mr. David A. Kruzner
Title: Senior Executive Vice President Company: BSG Concours Address: 800 Rockmead Drive, Kingwood, TX 77339 United States BUS: Next Generation Enterprise Research and Consulting Firm P/S: Creation of the Next Generation on Demand MA: International D/D/R: Overseeing Global Sales, Executive Research, Education and Business, Information Technology and Human Resource Strategy H/I/S: Playing Professional Soccer EDU: Bachelor of Science in Accounting and Finance, Minor in Economics, California State University, Hayward (1982)
Email: dakruzner@concoursgroup.com
URL: http://www.concoursgroup.com

Peter W. Kryworuk, LLB
Title: Partner, Practice Group Leader Company: Lerners, LLP Address: 80 Dufferin Avenue, London, N6A 4G4 Canada BUS: Legal Services Law Firm P/S: Legal Services MA: International EXP: Mr. Kryworuk's expertise includes civil litigation, health law, insurance and personal injury, commercial litigation, and medical and personal negligence. H/I/S: Wine Collecting, Reading, Travel and Sports EDU: University of Windsor, Bachelor of Law/LLB A/A/S: CBA, ATLA, TAS, MLA, LSUC
Email: pkryworuk@lerners.ca
URL: http://www.learners.ca

Lynette Kuberski
Title: Registered Nurse Company: Covenant Health Care Address: 900 Cooper Avenue, Saginaw, MI 48602 United States BUS: Hospital P/S: Healthcare MA: Regional D/D/R: Emergency Room Nursing for the Trauma Center, Specializing in Pediatrics, Gynecology and Emergency Treatment for Psychology Patients, Working as a Charge Nurse in the Emergency Room H/I/S: Golfing, Playing Tennis, Traveling, Reading EDU: Bachelor of Science in Nursing, Saginaw Valley State University
Email: laniedzw@yahoo.com
URL: http://www.cambridgewhoswho.com

Carol Ann Kucharski
Title: Teacher Company: Tyler County Board of Education, A.I. Boreman Elementary School Address: P.O. Box 299, Middlebourne, WV 26149 United States BUS: Elementary School P/S: Elementary Education MA: Local D/D/R: Teaching Third-Grade H/I/S: Reading, Scrapbooking, Camping, Gardening EDU: Master's Degree Plus45 in Learning Disabilities, West Virginia University; Bachelor of Arts in Elementary Education and Special Education, West Liberty State College A/A/S: National Education Association; West Virginia Education Association; Tyler County Education Association A/H: Teacher of the Year, Tyler County, West Virginia; Teacher Excellence Award; Disney Teacher Award C/VW: President, Tyler County Public Library; Sunday School Teacher, Church
Email: joslean@verizon.net
URL: http://www.cambridgewhoswho.com

Keith U. Kuder

Title: General Counsel **Company:** ACN, Inc. **Address:** 32991 Hamilton Court, Farmington Hills, MI 48334 United States **BUS:** Consumer Telecommunications Services **P/S:** Consumer Telecommunications Services **MA:** International **D/D/R:** Practicing Commercial Law **H/I/S:** Playing Tennis, Watching Improvisational Comedy and Movies, Waterskiing **EDU:** JD, University of Virginia; Bachelor's Degree in Political and Social Thought, University of Virginia **A/A/S:** Phi Beta Kappa; Order of the Coif; Association of Corporate Counsel; The In-house Lawyers' Association; The District of Columbia Bar Association; American Bar Association **C/VW:** State Police; Member, Public Interest Research Group
Email: kkuder@acninc.com
URL: http://www.acninc.com

Sarah Kugelman

Title: President, Founder **Company:** Skyn Iceland **Address:** 136 E. 57th Street, Fourth Floor, New York, NY 10022 United States **BUS:** Manufacturer **P/S:** Solutions for Stressed Skins **MA:** International **D/D/R:** Marketing **H/I/S:** Exercising, Attending Movies, Reading, Traveling, Giving Back to her Community **EDU:** Master of Business Administration, Columbia University, 1987; Bachelor's Degree in English and French, Tufts University, 1985 **A/A/S:** Cosmetic Executive Women; Fashion Group International; Women in Film **A/H:** Cosmetic Executive Women 2007 Indie Brand Award **C/VW:** American Cancer Society, Sanctuary for Families
Email: sarahk@skyniceland.com
URL: http://www.skyniceland.com

Mr. Mark E. Kuhne, MBA

Title: Community Bank President **Company:** MidCountry Bank **Dept:** Commercial Banking **Address:** 5085 Yume Lane North, Plymouth, MN 55446 United States **BUS:** Community Banking Institution Committed to Excellence in the Financial Industry **P/S:** Personal and Business Checking, Personal and Business Savings, Personal HSAs, Personal CDs, Personal and Business Loans, Safe Deposit Boxes, Construction Loans, Land Development Loans, Mortgage Loans, Remodeling Loans, Home Equity Loans, Retail Banking, Leasing and Insurance Services **MA:** Twin Cities Metro Area **D/D/R:** Working in Commercial Banking, Working with Industrial and Commercial Real Estate, Developing Positive Client Relationships **H/I/S:** Scuba Diving, Traveling **EDU:** Master of Business Administration in Finance, University of St. Thomas (1992) **A/A/S:** Chamber of Commerce; Boy Scouts of America; Northwestern Health Sciences University Fundraising Program
Email: rockfordmark@yahoo.com
Email: mark.kuhne@midcountrybank.com
URL: http://www.midcountrybank.com

Julie Ann Kuksa

Title: Health Systems Specialist, Accreditation Manager **Company:** The DuPage County Sheriff's Office **Address:** 501 N. County Farm Road, Wheaton, IL 60187 United States **BUS:** Government Agency **P/S:** Law Enforcement **MA:** Local **D/D/R:** Overseeing Compliance **H/I/S:** Reading **EDU:** Bachelor's Degree in Teaching, Williams College **CERTS:** Certified Teacher (K-12 Grades); Certification in Law Enforcement
Email: julie.kuksa@dupageco.org
URL: http://www.cambridgewhoswho.com

Robert J. Kuletsky

Title: English Teacher **Company:** New York City Board of Education, High School for Service and Learning **Address:** 66 Summit Drive, Smithtown, NY 11787 United States **BUS:** Public High School Serving Residents of Smithtown **P/S:** Public Secondary Education for Local Students **MA:** Regional **D/D/R:** Teaching Three English Classes Including a Remedial Course, Participating in an Afterschool Program for Struggling Students in Need of Credits to Pass, Mentoring and Building Relationships with Students, Using a Rewards Program **H/I/S:** Golfing, Skiing, Reading **EDU:** Pursuing Master's Degree in School Building Leadership, St. John's University; Bachelor's Degree in English and Secondary Education, Salve Regina University (2006) **A/A/S:** Sigma Phi Sigma; Sigma Tau Delta; National Council of Teachers of English; Former Summer School Educator in SAT Preparation, Tuerton High School; Former Summer School Educator in SAT Preparation, High School, Harlem, NY
Email: robert.kuletsky@gmail.com

Thomas A. Kull

Title: Registered Nurse **Company:** Mercy General Health Partners **Address:** 1500 E. Sherman Boulevard, Muskegon, MI 49442 United States **BUS:** Healthcare Company Dedicated to Improving the Health of the Community **P/S:** Bypass Surgery, Surgical Medicine, Intensive Care and Open Heart Surgery Services **MA:** Local **D/D/R:** Caring, Evaluating and Treating Inpatients, Meeting the Special Needs of Intensive Care Patients **H/I/S:** Fishing, Camping, Boating **EDU:** Bachelor of Science in Nursing, University of Wisconsin (1990)
URL: http://www.mghp.com

Myra Kumarova, Ph.D.

Title: Chief Executive Officer **Company:** Myra Pro, Inc. **Address:** 2800 N. Palm Aire Drive, Apartment 305, Pompano Beach, FL 33069 United States **BUS:** Translation Company **P/S:** Translation and Software Localization Services **MA:** International **D/D/R:** Overseeing Translation Services **H/I/S:** Traveling, Playing Tennis **EDU:** Ph.D. in Linguistic Quality of Translation, Moscow State Linguistic University
Email: myrapro@yahoo.com
URL: http://www.cambridgewhoswho.com

Kimberly A. Kuncl

Title: Obstetrician, Gynecologist **Company:** Douglas Women's Center **Address:** 880 Crestmark Drive, Suite 200, Lithia Springs, GA 30122 United States **BUS:** Health Center **P/S:** Healthcare **MA:** Local **EXP:** Dr. Kuncl's expertise is in minimally invasive surgery. **H/I/S:** Reading, Traveling, Hiking **EDU:** MD, Morehouse School of Medicine, Atlanta; Board Certified Fellow, American College of Obstetricians and Gynecologists **A/A/S:** American College of Obstetricians and Gynecologists; American Association of Gynecologic Laparoscopists; American Medical Association **C/VW:** Porsche Foxx Community Force
Email: smith2kuncl@aol.com
URL: http://www.cambridgewhoswho.com

Phyllis Kupferstein

Title: Lawyer **Company:** McDermott Will & Emery, LLP **Address:** 2049 Century Park E., Suite 3800, Los Angeles, CA 90067 United States **BUS:** Law Firm **P/S:** Legal Services **MA:** International **EXP:** Ms. Kupferstein's expertise is in business litigation. **D/D/R:** Directing Labor Employment Group **EDU:** JD, Loyola Law School, Loyola Marymount University (1982); Bachelor of Arts, University of California, Los Angeles (1978) **A/A/S:** American Bar Association; California Bar Association; Los Angeles County Bar Association **C/VW:** Trustee, Greater Los Angeles Zoo Association
Email: pkupferstein@mwe.com
URL: http://www.mwe.com

Cheryl Ann Kurtz

Title: Marine Ecologist **Company:** Space and Naval Warfare Systems Center San Diego **Dept:** Environmental Sciences Branch **Address:** 53475 Strothe Road, Room 238, San Diego, CA 92152 United States **BUS:** Government Organization **P/S:** Scientific and Marine Environmental Support Services **MA:** International **D/D/R:** Managing the Database, Typing, Faxing, Photocopying, Writing Articles and Other Technical Documents, Developing Business Strategies, Conducting Research, Ensuring Environmental Compliance, Implementing Laboratory Safety Protocol, Investigating, Solving Problems, Overseeing Environmental Field Work and Bench Chemistry **H/I/S:** Scuba Diving, Snorkeling, Playing Hockey **EDU:** Master of Science in Marine Science, University of San Diego (2003); Bachelor of Science in Environmental Science, St. John's University, Jamaica, NY (1995) **CERTS:** Pursuing Certification in Geographic Information System, Environmental Systems Research Institute; Certification in Watershed Management, United States Environmental Protection Agency (2001) **A/A/S:** American Chemical Society; Roger Bacon Scientific Honor Society; Golden Key International Honour Society **C/VW:** Fundraiser, Susan G. Komen For the Cure
Email: cheryl.kurtz@navy.mil
URL: http://environ.spawar.navy.mil/compliance/index.html

Natalie Kurtzman

Title: President, Founder **Company:** Majestic Trophies **Address:** 288 Third Avenue, Brooklyn, NY 11215 United States **BUS:** Trophy and Award Manufacturer **P/S:** Creative Designs for Engraving Awards, Trophies and Plaques **MA:** National **D/D/R:** Overseeing Office Duties and Customer Service **H/I/S:** Reading, Taking Trips to Atlantic City, Walking, Using the Internet **EDU:** Diploma, Tilden High School **C/VW:** American Cancer Society
Email: nkurtzman100@yahoo.com
URL: http://www.cambridgewhoswho.com

Stevie Kushner

Title: Branch Administrative Manager **Company:** Wells Fargo Investments **Dept:** Licensed Banker Program **Address:** 3300 W. Sahara Avenue, Las Vegas, NV 89102 United States **BUS:** Brokerage Firm **P/S:** Brokerage Products and Services **MA:** Regional **D/D/R:** Overseeing Operations Including Brokerage, Training, Licensed Bankers and the Tracking of Employee Performance **H/I/S:** Traveling, Genealogy, Reading, Hiking **CERTS:** Licensed in Series 7, 8, 63 and 65, Financial Industry Regulatory Authority **C/VW:** Las Vegas Metropolitan Police Department; Police Athletic League; Board of Directors, Las Vegas Nebraskans
Email: hskrkush@cox.net
URL: http://www.cambridgewhoswho.com

Joseph S. Kusy

Title: Manager, Mechanical Division (Retired) **Company:** Stockton Unified School District **Address:** 1932 El Pinal Drive, Stockton, CA 95205 United States **BUS:** School District, Mechanical Division **P/S:** Education, Facilities Services Including Plumbing, Heating and Ventilation **MA:** Regional **D/D/R:** Overseeing All Aspects of Electrical Repair for Office Buildings, Observing Fire Codes, Maintaining Compliance, Plumbing, Fire Sprinklers, Installation HVAC Equipment **H/I/S:** Powerboat Racing **EDU:** Pursuing Bachelor's Degree in Business Management, Colorado Technical University
Email: jkusy@stockton.k12.ca.us
URL: http://www.stockton.k12.ca.us

Julie A. Kutruff

Title: Operations Superintendent **Company:** Northern Virginia Regional Park Authority **Address:** 5400 Ox Road, Fairfax Station, VA 22039 United States **BUS:** Recreation and Conservation **P/S:** Water Park, House Museum, Nature Center, Waterfront Park, 4000-Acre Campground **MA:** Alexandria, Fairfax City, Falls Church, Virginia **EXP:** Ms. Kutruff's expertise is in natural resource management. **H/I/S:** Canoeing **EDU:** Master of Arts in Education, George Washington University; Bachelor of Science in Biology, Virginia Polytechnic Institute and State University **A/A/S:** National Association for Interpretation
Email: jkutruff@nvrpa.org
URL: http://www.nvrpa.org

Ms. Elizabeth J. Kuzell

Title: Fundraiser **Address:** 2300 Pacific Avenue, Apartment 405, San Francisco, CA 94115 United States **BUS:** Nonprofit Organization **P/S:** Philanthropy and Fundraising Services for Various Charitable Organizations **MA:** International **EXP:** Ms. Kuzell's expertise includes the development of innovative and creative ideas for organizations. **D/D/R:** Solving Problems and Fundraising for Charitable Organizations **H/I/S:** Relaxing, Watching Movies, Spending Time with her Friends, Traveling **EDU:** Pursuing Master of Business Administration, Golden Gate University; Bachelor of Arts in History, University of California, Santa Barbara; Coursework in Computer Activities, City College of San Francisco; Coursework, Barat College **A/H:** Opera Guild Award **C/VW:** Opera Guild of San Francisco; Susan G. Koman for the Cure; Junior League of San Francisco; Metropolitan Club; Commonwealth Club; San Francisco Symphony; St. Dominic's Catholic Church; Epilepsy Foundation
Email: elizabeth.kuzell00@cwwemail.com

Mary F. Kwak

Title: First Grade Teacher **Company:** Vernon Township School District **Address:** P.O. Box 190, Route 517, Vernon, NJ 07462 United States **BUS:** Quality Leader in Public Education **P/S:** Learning for All Students Through Strong Remedial, Enrichment and Academic Programs Such as Mathematics, Social Studies, Language Arts and Sciences **MA:** Regional **D/D/R:** Teaching the First Grade as well as One Inclusion Class **H/I/S:** Reading, Walking **EDU:** Bachelor of Arts in Child Development and Sociology, St. Joseph's College (1967) **A/A/S:** National Education Association; New Jersey Education Association; Virginia Technology Education Association; Teacher Scholar in Residence Award; Governor Teacher Recognition Award; Faculty Senator
Email: kwakfam@hotmail.com
URL: http://www.vtsd.com

Robert S. Kwok

Title: JD, Owner **Company:** Robert Kwok & Associates, LLP **Address:** 6588 Corporate Drive, Suite 300, Houston, TX 77036 United States **BUS:** Law Firm **P/S:** Legal Services **MA:** National **D/D/R:** Litigating Personal Injury Cases, Representing Clients, Using the Highest Level of Skill and Integrity **H/I/S:** Golfing, Traveling **EDU:** JD, University of Houston Law Center (1993); Bachelor of Business Administration, Baylor University (1991) **CERTS:** Board Certification in Personal Injury Trial Law **A/A/S:** Houston Bar Association; Texas Trial Lawyers Association; Former President, Asian American Bar Association; AU Rated, Martindale-Hubbell; Million Dollar Advocate Forum; Law Dragon
Email: Robert.Kwok@cwwemail.com
Email: rkwok@kwoklaw.com
URL: http://www.kwoklaw.com

Mr. Michael J. La Burt

Title: President **Company:** Firefly Productions, Inc. **Address:** 218 Commercial Boulevard, Suite 201Q, Lauderdale by the Sea, FL 33308 United States **BUS:** Entertainment Company **P/S:** Film Production, Experimental Filmmakers, Independent Filmmaking **MA:** International **D/D/R:** Directing, Editing, Acting, Producing, Writing **H/I/S:** Traveling, Learning About New Cultures, Particularly Eastern Cultures and Traditions **EDU:** Coursework in Chinese Linguistics, Cornell University; Coursework in Mandarin, Beijing, China; Research and Development, India
Email: info@fireflyproductions.biz

Mary Jane LaBelle
Title: Chief Executive Officer **Company:** Data Metrix, Inc. **Address:** 455 Fifth Street, Port Orford, OR 97465 United States **BUS:** Finance Company **P/S:** Financial Audits for the Medical Industry **MA:** National **D/D/R:** Performing Medical Audits **H/I/S:** Weaving, Swimming, Skiing **EDU:** Bachelor of Arts in Classics, Mills College, Oakland, CA **CERTS:** Registered Nurse, Massachusetts General Hospital, Boston **A/A/S:** Association of Hospital Internal Auditors; American Association of Medical Audit Specialists **C/VW:** Friends of St. John's; Port Oxford Community Ambulance
Email: mj.labelle@data-metrix.com
URL: http://www.data-metrix.com

Rynette Labostrie-Barr
Title: President **Company:** Lagniappe Accounting, Inc. **Address:** 9852 Katella Avenue, Suite 290, Anaheim, CA 92804 United States **BUS:** Accounting Firm **P/S:** Small Business Accounting, Payroll Processing, Tax Preparation, Notary Public **MA:** National **D/D/R:** Preparing and Filing Taxes, Processing Payroll, Managing Accounts, Offering Notary Public Services **H/I/S:** Boating, Sewing, Dining Out **EDU:** Pursuing Master's Degree in Business Administration, University of Phoenix; Bachelor of Science in Accounting, Los Angeles, CA (1998) **A/A/S:** Better Business Bureau; Madison Who's Who
Email: rynette@lagniappeacct.com

Carol Ann Lacher, RN
Title: Clinical Nursing Director **Company:** Anne Arundel Medical Center **Dept:** Pediatrics and Neonatal Intensive Care Unit **Address:** 2001 Medical Parkway, Annapolis, MD 21401 United States **BUS:** Nonprofit Medical Center **P/S:** Healthcare **MA:** Regional **D/D/R:** Overseeing Administrative Duties of the Pediatric and Neonatal Intensive Care Units, Teaching Clinical Education and Facilitating a New NICU Nursing Transport Team with the NICU Medical Team for Critically-Ill Premature Infants **H/I/S:** Spending Time at the Beach, Bicycling, Spending Time with her Family **EDU:** Master of Science in Nursing Administration, University of Maryland **CERTS:** Certification in Leadership **A/A/S:** Teacher, Pediatric Advanced Life Support Program; National Association of Neonatal Nurses; American Association of Critical Care Nurses **A/H:** Nursing Excellence Award (2003) **C/VW:** Goodwill; Purple Heart Association (Now Military Order of the Purple Heart); United Way
Email: clacher@aahs.org
URL: http://www.aamc.org

Susan M. LaCroix
Title: Teacher **Company:** Norwood School District No. 63 **Address:** 6521 W. Farmington Road, Peora, IL 61604 United States **BUS:** School District **P/S:** Education **MA:** Local **D/D/R:** Teaching Mathematics to Fifth and Sixth-Grade Students **H/I/S:** Cooking, Reading **EDU:** Master of Science in Mathematics Education, Illinois State University **A/A/S:** Association of Mathematics Teacher Educators; State-Commissioned Board for Fourth-Grade Testing Exam Creation; SAMS **A/H:** Teacher of the Year, 2007 **C/VW:** St. Jude Children's Research Hospital
Email: lacroix13@insightbb.com
URL: http://www.cambridgewhoswho.com

Tracie Ladner
Title: Payroll Manager **Company:** Trinity Yacht, LLC **Address:** 13085 Seaway Road, Gulfport, MS 39503 United States **BUS:** Manufacturing Company **P/S:** Motor Boats and Yachts **MA:** International **EXP:** Ms. Ladner's expertise is in payroll management. **H/I/S:** Reading **EDU:** College Coursework; High School Diploma **C/VW:** Habitat for Humanity
Email: tracie219@aol.com
URL: http://www.cambridgewhoswho.com

Elizabeth M. Laffan-Costa, PMP
Title: Senior Solutions Manager **Company:** Xactly Corporation **Dept:** Client Services **Address:** 8410 East Twisted Leaf Drive, Gold Canyon, AZ 85218 United States **BUS:** Software Company **P/S:** On-Demand-Software as a Service (SaaS), Project Management, Enterprise Incentive Management **MA:** International **D/D/R:** Acting as the Liaison Between Implementation Partners and the Software Company, Quality Assurance, Troubleshooting, Supporting the Partners **H/I/S:** Golf, Travel **EDU:** Bachelor of Science in Computer Information Systems, Accounting, Dominican College; Certified Project Management Professional **A/A/S:** Project Management Institute, American Association of University Women **A/H:** 2005 Business Woman of the Year
Email: bcosta0918@msn.com
Email: bcosta@xactlycorp.com
URL: http://www.cambridgewhoswho.com

Christine LaFrenier
Title: Kitchen Manager **Company:** Steaksmith Restaurant **Address:** 3802 Maizeland Road, Colorado Springs, CO 80909 United States **BUS:** Steak and Seafood Restaurant **P/S:** Food and Beverages **MA:** Local **D/D/R:** Creating Pastries, Managing Kitchen Staff and Lunch Line, Purchasing Food and Cleaning Products
Email: christine@steaksmith.com
URL: http://www.steaksmith.com

Tammy G. Lagoski
Title: Director **Company:** Beardstown Houston Memorial Library **Address:** 13 Boulevard Road, Beardstown, IL 62618 United States **BUS:** Books Library **P/S:** Books, research Resources of Library **MA:** Local **EXP:** Ms. Lagoski's expertise includes Spanish language outreach, youth programs and human services. **H/I/S:** Reading, School **EDU:** Quincy University, Bachelor's Degree in Human Services **A/A/S:** Hispanic Networking Council, Local Inner Agency Council, Spanish Language Outreach
Email: tgynell@hotmail.com
URL: www.beardstown.lib.il.us/lib

Kelly LaHuis
Title: Owner **Company:** Balloon Beautiful **Address:** 4435 Friesian Court, Dorr, MI 49323 United States **BUS:** Event Decorator **P/S:** Rental and Sale of Balloon Decorations, Centerpieces, Lights **MA:** National **D/D/R:** Offering Balloon Decorations for All Types of Events, Working One-on-One with Clients, Showcasing at Bridal Shows, Sending Out Mailers, Managing the Daily Operations of the Company **H/I/S:** Volleyball, Outdoor Activities **EDU:** Pursuing Associate Degree, Grand Rapids Community College
Email: kalahuis@netzero.net
URL: http://www.balloonbeautiful.com

Judyann M. Laidley
Title: Registered Nurse **Company:** Kings County Hospital **Address:** 1594 President Street, Brooklyn, NY 11213 United States **BUS:** Hospital **P/S:** Healthcare **MA:** Local **D/D/R:** Overseeing Medical Surgical Nursing and Rehabilitation Units, Managing Staff, Offering Therapeutic Communication with Patients and their Families **H/I/S:** Reading **EDU:** Bachelor of Science in Nursing, Long Island University, with Honors (2007) **C/VW:** Volunteer, Local Hospital
Email: judyalail@aol.com

Mr. Michael J. Lair
Title: Actor **Company:** Michael Lair **Address:** P.O. Box 530, Mathews, VA 23109 United States **BUS:** Entertainment Service **P/S:** Performances, Live and Film Entertainment **MA:** National **D/D/R:** Performing in Major Motion Pictures Including Westerns and Television Productions **H/I/S:** Traveling **EDU:** College Coursework **A/A/S:** Screen Actors Guild
URL: http://www.cambridgewhoswho.com

Rev. Steve R. Lake Sr.
Title: Senior Pastor **Company:** Eureka Missionary Baptist Church **Address:** 721 Gaines Avenue, Hot Springs, AR 71901 United States **BUS:** Religion Church **P/S:** Ministry, Spreading the Gospel **MA:** Local **D/D/R:** Serving as a Pastor for a Congregation of 100 to 150 Members **H/I/S:** Sports, Music, Dining Out

Lynette L. Lalliss
Title: President, Owner **Company:** La Jella, LLC **Address:** 1804 S. Rand Street, Boise, ID 83709 United States **BUS:** Internet Sales Company **P/S:** Various Internet Sales **MA:** Local **D/D/R:** Overseeing Internet Sales **H/I/S:** Spending Time with her Niece and Nephew **EDU:** Bachelor of Science in Criminal Justice, Boise State University; Associate of Arts in Liberal Arts; Coursework, College of Southern Idaho; Coursework, University of Nevada, Reno; Coursework, Truckee Meadows Community College **A/A/S:** Boise Young Professionals
Email: lajella@gmail.com
URL: http://www.cambridgewhoswho.com

Knicholaus D. LaLumière
Title: Research Associate Scientist **Company:** Mannkind Corporation **Address:** 1 Casper Street, Danbury, CT 06811 United States **BUS:** Pharmaceutical Company **P/S:** Inhaled Insulin, Oncology **MA:** National **D/D/R:** Researching Chemistry, Ensuring Quality Performance in Analytical Instrumentation, Researching Synthetic Methodologies and Target Compounds Online, Processing Optimization on Current Manufacturing Processes **H/I/S:** Music, Traveling, Family Time **EDU:** Master's Degree in Science, Sacred Heart University (2007); Bachelor's Degree in Chemistry, University of Connecticut (2003); Bachelor's Degree in Mathematics, University of Connecticut (2001) **A/A/S:** American Chemical Society
Email: klalumiere@mannkindcorp.com
URL: http://www.mannkindcorp.com

Tammie R. Lamarre
Title: Licensed Practical Nurse **Company:** Amedifys Home Health **Address:** 4502 Bream Avenue, Boynton Beach, FL 33426 United States **BUS:** Home Health Care Agency **P/S:** Individualized Home Health Care **D/D/R:** Inserting Intravenous Therapies, Performing Wound Care Procedures, Hydrating Patients, Offering General Health Therapy, Teaching CPR **H/I/S:** Bicycling **CERTS:** Licensed Practical Nurse Degree, Southern Florida Community College
Email: lamarregang4@earthlink.net

Dr. Mary J. Lamb
Title: Professor of Nursing, Doctor of Nursing Practice **Company:** Bob Jones University **Address:** 404 Cold Branch Way, Greenville, SC 29609 United States **BUS:** University **P/S:** Higher Education **MA:** International **D/D/R:** Training Nurses, Consulting for Nursing Schools **H/I/S:** Traveling, Hunting **EDU:** Doctor of Nursing Practice, Rocky Mountain University of Health Professions; Master of Science in Nursing, Florida State University; Bachelor of Science in Nursing, University of South Alabama; Bachelor of Arts in Education, Bob Jones University **A/A/S:** Chairman, International Committee of Nursing Educators
Email: mlamb@bju.edu

Lisa Lambert
Title: Staff Nurse, Field Nurse **Company:** Pediatric Services of America **Address:** 2051 Toms Creek Church Road, Pilot Mountain, NC 27041 United States **BUS:** Healthcare Center **P/S:** Pediatric Home Care Services **MA:** National **EXP:** Ms. Lambert's expertise is in pediatric nursing. **D/D/R:** Conducting Home Visits to Chronically Ill Children, Performing Routine Examinations, Maintaining Medical Equipments, Assisting Patients and their Families, Taking Care of Children **H/I/S:** Reading Medical Thrillers **EDU:** Bachelor of Science in Nursing, Winston Salem State University (2006) **CERTS:** Licensed Practical Nurse, Surry Community College (2001)
Email: l_lynne_2000@yahoo.com
URL: http://www.psahealthcare.com

Vanya M. Lambert
Title: Design Project Manager **Company:** MGM Mirage Design Group **Address:** 4882 Frank Sinatra Drive, Las Vegas, NV 89109 United States **BUS:** Construction Company **P/S:** Construction Services **MA:** Local **EXP:** Ms. Lambert's expertise includes interior and architectural design. **H/I/S:** Scuba Diving **EDU:** Bachelor of Architecture, Kansas State University **A/A/S:** Historic Preservation Society; National Council for Architecture **C/VW:** The Humane Society of the United States
Email: justvanya@aol.com

Miss Lauren R. Lambrecht
Title: Administrative Assistant **Company:** Lee County Parks and Recreation **Address:** 3410 Palm Beach Boulevard, Fort Myers, FL 33916 United States **BUS:** Government Organization **P/S:** Parks, Conduction of Recreational Facilities and Programs **MA:** Local **D/D/R:** Assisting with Administrative Duties, Overseeing Program Registrations **H/I/S:** Going to Disney World, Spending Time with her Family and Friends, Administering Government Education **EDU:** Pursuing Master's Degree in Public Administration, Hodges University; Bachelor of Arts in History, Florida Gulf Coast University **CERTS:** Pursuing Certified Park and Recreation Professional, National Recreation and Park Association **A/A/S:** Phi Alpha Theta; Florida Recreation and Park Association **C/VW:** Candlelighters Childhood Cancer Foundation
Email: llambrecht@leegov.com
URL: http://www.leeparks.org

Dale Rene Laminack
Title: Special Education and Behavior Inclusion Focus Teacher **Company:** Ball Elementary School **Address:** 620 W. Krezdorn Street, Seguin, TX 78155 United States **BUS:** Elementary School **P/S:** Education **MA:** Local **EXP:** Mr. Laminack's expertise includes elementary special education, inclusion and behavior. **H/I/S:** Fishing, Jet Skiing, Hiking **EDU:** Bachelor of Arts in Business Plus300, Special Education Certification, Texas Tech University **A/A/S:** LD Online; SES; PTC; Seguin Education Association; Parents and Teachers Community **C/VW:** Child Bereavement Center, Local Schools, Church, Medina Valley Children's Home
Email: h2ogus@aol.com
URL: http://www.cambridgewhoswho.com

Patricia Lamm
Title: Senior Mortgage Advisor **Company:** Colonial National Mortgage **Address:** 7310 N. 16th Street, Suite 160, Phoenix, AZ 85020 United States **BUS:** Mortgage Company **P/S:** Mortgages, Home Equity Loans **MA:** Regional **D/D/R:** Advising Clients on Mortgages, Customizing Services for Each Client, Overseeing Cultural Fair Committee **H/I/S:** Traveling, Reading **EDU:** Coursework, Glendale Community College **A/A/S:** Presidents Club; Women's Council of Realtors
Email: patl@colonialsavings.com
URL: http://www.teamphx.com

Rebecca Lamp, RN, MSN, C-FNP
Title: Family Nurse Practitioner **Company:** Richwood Area Community Hospital **Address:** 139 Derwood Drive, New Cumberland, WV 26047 United States **BUS:** Primary Healthcare Services for a Small Rural Community **P/S:** Emergency and Acute Care, Laboratory and Radiology Services, Long-Term Care, Wide Variety of Patient Education Resources **MA:** Regional **D/D/R:** Working in the Family Practice Clinic for the Underserved Population in West Virginia, Emergency Room Nursing, Performing Examinations, Diagnosing and Treating Patients, Patient Education, Referring Patients to Other Community Resources as Needed **H/I/S:** Therapeutic Horseback Riding, Distance Running, Partial Marathons **EDU:** Master of Arts in Nursing, Franciscan University of Steubenville (2006); Training in General Disaster Emergency Preparedness **CERTS:** Certified Therapeutic Horseback Riding Instructor **A/A/S:** Sigma Theta Tau; Phi Theta Kappa; The Medical Reserve Corps; The Hancock-Brooke County Disaster Preparedness Team; Executive Director and Instructor, Hope-4-Us
Email: BRICELAMP@yahoo.com
URL: http://www.rach.yourmd.com

Olivia J. Lampert
Title: Registered Professional Nurse **Company:** Advantage RN **Address:** 8892 Beckett Road, West Chester, OH 45069 United States **BUS:** Nursing Recruitment Company **P/S:** Placing Registered Nurses in Hospitals with Nursing Shortages **MA:** Regional **D/D/R:** Labor, Delivery, Evaluating Expectant Mothers, Delivering Babies when Necessary, Administering Medications, Intravenous, Assessing Labor and Comfort of Patients **H/I/S:** Rollerblading **EDU:** Bachelor of Science in Nursing, St John's Hospital, Department of Nursing (2004)
Email: ojlamp@hotmail.com
URL: http://www.cambridgewhoswho.com

Deborah S. Lancaster
Title: Chief Executive Officer **Company:** DS Labels **Address:** 1359 General George Patton Road, Nashville, TN 37221 United States **BUS:** Printing Company **P/S:** Printing and Design Services Including Hot Stamping, Overlaminating and UV Coatings **MA:** National **EXP:** Ms. Lancaster's expertise includes customer satisfaction and operations management. **D/D/R:** Printing Labels and Decals, Overseeing the Package of Pressure Sensitive Products, Creating Decorative Tracking Solutions **H/I/S:** Golfing, Traveling, Painting **EDU:** Coursework in American History and Secondary Education, University of Memphis; Coursework in Court Reporting, Stenotype Institute, Jacksonville **CERTS:** Certification, Stenotype Institute **A/A/S:** eWomenNetwork
Email: debl@dslabels.net
URL: http://www.dslabels.net

Marita Landaveri
Title: Consul General, Diplomat **Company:** Consulate General of Peru in Denver **Address:** 1001 S. Monaco Parkway, Suite 210, Denver, CO 80224 United States **BUS:** Government **P/S:** Consul, Community Affairs **MA:** International **EXP:** Ms. Landaveri's expertise is in diplomacy. **H/I/S:** Traveling, Gourmet Dining **EDU:** Master's Degree in International Relations, Diplomatic Academy, Peru **A/A/S:** University of Oxford and Cambridge Consul; Welcome to Colorado International Club; WTC-Denver; AAA Denver Art
Email: mlandaveri@consuladoperu.net
URL: http://www.consuladoperu.com

Mickey Landesberg
Title: Vice President of Sales Operations **Company:** Sony Pictures Home Entertainment **Dept:** Domestic Sales **Address:** 10202 W. Washington Boulevard, Culver City, CA 90232 United States **BUS:** Entertainment and Picture Studio **P/S:** Home Entertainment Products Including DVD, Blu-ray, UMD **MA:** Domestic **EXP:** Mr. Landesberg's expertise includes retail marketing, operations and home entertainment. **H/I/S:** Watching Sports, Guitar **EDU:** Bachelor of Arts, George Brown College, 1986 **C/VW:** American Cancer Society
Email: mickey_landesberg@spe.sony.com
URL: http://www.sonypictures.com

Fely E. Landingin, RN
Title: Registered Nurse **Company:** Community Hospital of the Monterey Peninsula **Dept:** Oncology, Hematology Department **Address:** 258 Cosky Drive, Marina, CA 93933 United States **BUS:** Healthcare **P/S:** Hospital Services, Healthcare Services, Patient Care **MA:** Regional **D/D/R:** Working as an Oncology Nurse, Nursing Care, Starting IVs, Checking Vitals, Assessments, Following Up on Chemotherapy Treatments **H/I/S:** Gardening, Knitting, Cooking **EDU:** Bachelor of Science in Nursing, Philippines; Associate Degree in Nursing, Professional Health College (1977) **A/A/S:** American Cancer Society; Oncology Nursing Society
Email: chumjay@yahoo.com
URL: http://www.cambridgewhoswho.com

Raejean Landis, MA
Title: Resource Teacher **Company:** Baxter Elementary School **Address:** 1625 Linda Avenue, Cookeville, TN 38506 United States **BUS:** Primary School with Approximately 775 Students Enrolled **P/S:** All Core Academic Classes Including Social and Emotional Development **MA:** Regional **D/D/R:** Teaching Students from Kindergarten to Fifth-Grade with Learning Disabilities Reading, Mathematics and Written Expression, Consulting for SRA McGraw-Hill in Reading and Language to Teachers and Special Education Teachers **H/I/S:** Bowling, Singing **EDU:** Master's Degree in Special Education, Tennessee Technical University (1987); Bachelor of Science in Special Education, Tennessee Technical University (1985) **A/A/S:** Alpha Delta Kappa; Association for Direct Instruction; Christian Education Association International **A/H:** Teacher of the Year; Putnam County Teacher of the Year
Email: landisr@k12tn.net
URL: http://www.k12tn.net

Tonya M. Landry
Title: Director of Rehabilitation **Company:** Healthbridge **Address:** 395 Cherry Farm Road, Harrisville, RI 02830 United States **BUS:** Skilled Nursing and Rehabilitation Facility **P/S:** Skilled Rehabilitation Services **MA:** Regional **EXP:** Ms. Landry's expertise is in occupational therapy rehabilitation. **H/I/S:** Spending Time With Family, Reading, Outdoors activities, Travel **EDU:** Master's Degree, University of Phoenix **A/A/S:** American Occupational Therapy Association
Email: tland3@cox.net
URL: http://www.cambridgewhoswho.com

Laura Nelms Lane
Title: Teacher, Youth Coordinator, Executive Board Chairman, Secretary **Company:** Ensley Church of Christ **Address:** 1156 Grand Boulevard, Birmingham, AL 35214 United States **BUS:** Church **P/S:** Religious Services Including Seminars in Public Schools, Anti-Drug Programs **MA:** Local **D/D/R:** Public Speaking on the Bible, Addressing Young People, Substance Abuse and Domestic Violence Issues, Teaching Elementary and Special Education, Building Relationship with Sponsors, Helping People, Coordinating and Conducting Bible Classes for Women **H/I/S:** Listening to Music, Traveling, Spending Time with her Children, Innovating New Techniques in her Projects **EDU:** Master's Degree in Elementary Education and Special Education, University of Montevallo (1972); Bachelor of Arts in History and Sociology, Alabama A&M University (1969) **A/A/S:** Alabama Federation of Women's Clubs; National Sorosis Study Club Federation; National Pan-Hellenic Council; National Education Association; Zeta Phi Beta **A/H:** Youth Advisor of the Year Award (2006-2008); Alabama Hall of Fame for Outstanding Accomplishments (2005); Woman of the Year Award, National Sorosis Study Club Federation (1993); Zeta of the Year Award (1986) **C/VW:** Local Church; North Alabama Sickle Cell Foundation; March of Dimes
Email: sweetlaura72@aol.com

Penny H. Lane
Title: Teacher **Company:** Pulaski County Public Schools **Address:** 650 Giles Avenue, Dublin, VA 24084 United States **BUS:** School District **P/S:** Education **MA:** Local **D/D/R:** Teaching Mathematics and Science **H/I/S:** Raising her Eight-Year-Old Triplets **EDU:** Bachelor's Degree in Education, Bradford University **A/A/S:** Pulaski County Education Association; Virginia Education Association; National Education Association **C/VW:** Children's Miracle Network, Ronald McDonald House Charities, United Way
Email: plane@pcva.us
URL: http://www.pcva.us

Tana M. Lane
Title: Architect **Company:** Exempla Healthcare **BUS:** Healthcare Facility **P/S:** Addiction and Chemical Dependency, Behavioral Health and Mental Health Services, Birthing and Prenatal Services, Bone, Muscle and Joint Care, Medical Center, Breast Care Center, Cardiac, Vascular and Pulmonary Diagnostic Services, Cosmetic Surgery, Diabetes and Endocrine Center, Emergency Medical Services, Respiratory Therapy, Sleep Disorder Laboratory, Spiritual Care, Women's Health **MA:** Regional **D/D/R:** Managing Projects, Assisting with Designs for Rebuilding **H/I/S:** Spending Time with Family, Reading, Hiking, Biking **EDU:** Degree in Architecture, University of Oklahoma (1988) **A/A/S:** Colorado Association of Healthcare Engineers and Directors, ARA
Email: lanet@exempla.org
URL: http://www.exempla.org

Allison C. Lang
Title: Firefighter, Paramedic **Company:** Miami-Dade Fire Department **Address:** 1300 N.W. 41st Street, Miami, FL 33142 United States **BUS:** Fire Department **P/S:** Professional and Humanitarian Fire Rescue Services **MA:** Regional **D/D/R:** Answering Fire, Injury and Medical Emergency Calls **H/I/S:** Fishing, Scuba Diving, Kayaking, Caring for Animals **EDU:** Pursuing Bachelor's Degree in Fire Science; Associate Degree in Emergency Medical Services, Broward Community College, Florida (2007) **A/A/S:** Volunteer, Wildlife Center
Email: dreams1823@yahoo.com
URL: http://www.miamidade.gov/mdfr

Peggy A. Lang
Title: Manager **Company:** Vacations Travel **Address:** 430 E. Wood, Troy, MO 63379 United States **BUS:** Travel Service Provider **P/S:** Travel Services **MA:** International **EXP:** Ms. Lang's expertise includes destination weddings and honeymoons. **H/I/S:** Antiquing, Gardening **EDU:** High School Graduate **A/A/S:** ASTA, CLIA, IATAN, IATA, BNI
Email: langpeggy@hotmail.com
URL: www.takeatrip.net

Dorothy Lang-Wilson
Title: Grand Princess Captain of Florida and Nassau **Company:** Most Worshipful Union Grand Lodge **Address:** 410 Broad Street, Jacksonville, FL 32202 United States **BUS:** Religious and Educational Organization **P/S:** Educational Services, Religious Studies **MA:** National **D/D/R:** Managing the Organizational Guilds of Florida and Nassau, Bahamas, Teaching **H/I/S:** Listening to Music, Playing Football, Supporting the Jacksonville Jaguars Football Team, Singing, Playing the Piano **EDU:** Educational Specialist, Florida A&M University (1972); Master of Science in Education, Clark University; Bachelor of Science in Education, Clark University **A/A/S:** United Methodist Women; Imperial Court Daughters of Isis; Ladies of the Circle of Perfection; Order of the Eastern Star; Sigma Gamma Rho Sorority **A/H:** Teacher of the Year, Temple Crusades
Email: 638@bellsouth.net
URL: http://www.mwuglflorida.org
URL: http://www.floridacrusaders.org

Jeffery V. Lange
Title: Chief Operations Officer **Company:** Meeting and Conference Rentals International **Address:** 600 Corporate Court, South Plainfield, NJ 07080 United States **BUS:** Event Management Company **P/S:** Event Management Services Including Onsite Management, Staging, Lighting, Event Capture Services, Video, Teleconferencing and Rental Services **MA:** International **D/D/R:** Working with Subcontractors, Coordinating Events, Negotiating Contracts, Supervising Employees, Managing Rentals, Overseeing Advertising Services, Marketing **H/I/S:** Baseball, Basketball, Tennis, Soccer, Volleyball, Golfing **EDU:** Bachelor's Degree in Communications, The College of New Jersey (1994)
Email: jlange@mcrirents.com
URL: http://www.mcrirents.com

Carol A. Langelli
Title: Assistant Director of Central Service Materials Management **Company:** Brookhaven Memorial Hospital Medical Center **Address:** 101 Hospital Road, Patchogue, NY 11772 United States **BUS:** Community Hospital **P/S:** Healthcare, Sterilization, Internal Medicine, Surgery, Trauma, Emergency Care, Behavioral and Mental Health, Maternity **MA:** Regional **D/D/R:** Managing Central Service Purchasing, Distribution, Sterilization, Specialty Beds, Restocking Hospital Supplies, Overseeing Quality Assurance Invoices, Organizing Department Meetings **H/I/S:** Cooking **EDU:** Training in Lawson Software; Diploma, New Field High School (1973); Fema Training **CERTS:** Certificate, International Association of Healthcare Central Service Material Management, Purdue University (1995)

Mrs. Tamara H. Langhoff, RN, MSN, CPNP
Title: RN, MS, Certified Pediatric Nurse Practitioner **Company:** Medical College of Wisconsin **Address:** 9000 W. Wisconsin Avenue, Milwaukee, WI 53201 United States **BUS:** Hospital, Outpatient Clinic **P/S:** Full Array of Hospital Services and Programs Including Pediatrics **MA:** Regional **D/D/R:** Developing Programs for Pediatric Headaches, Working in Development, Transition and Neurology, Speaking at National Conferences **H/I/S:** Competing in Triathlons **EDU:** Master of Science, University of Wisconsin-Madison (1997); Bachelor of Science in Nursing, University of Wisconsin-Milwaukee (1988) **A/A/S:** Sigma Theta Tau; Society of Pediatric Nurses; Board Member, National Association of Pediatric Nurse Practitioners; Board Member, Association of Child Neurology Nurses
Email: tfennig@mcw.edu
URL: http://www.mcw.edu

Tammi B. Langley
Title: Information Technology Systems Analyst **Company:** Super Shoes Macro Retail Inc. **Address:** 10365 Mount Savage Road, Cumberland, MD 21502 United States **BUS:** Shoe and Clothing Retailer **P/S:** Writing Computer Programs, Installing Computers **MA:** East Coast **D/D/R:** Programming, Databases, Hardware, Software **H/I/S:** Traveling, Playing Texas Hold 'Em, Fishing, Home Remodeling **EDU:** Bachelor of Science in Computer Science, Frostburg State University **C/VW:** Maryland State Fraternal Order of Police, American Red Cross
Email: langleyt@hhbrown.com

Tia Langston

Title: Records Review Coordinator **Company:** LifeNet **Address:** 1864 Concert Drive, Virginia Beach, VA 23453 United States **BUS:** Organ, Tissue Bank **P/S:** Organ, Tissue Procurement **MA:** National **EXP:** Ms. Langston's expertise is in quality assurance. **H/I/S:** Playing Basketball, Cooking, Playing with her Pets, Spending Time with her Family **EDU:** Bachelor of Science in Health Science, Minor in Management, Old Dominion University **A/A/S:** Women in Military Services for America
Email: trmjl@cox.net

Frances L. Lanier

Title: Purchasing Manager **Company:** Gaster Lumber & Hardware, Inc. **Address:** 15010 Abercorn Street, Savannah, GA 31419 United States **BUS:** Distribution Company **P/S:** Building Materials, Lumber **MA:** Regional **D/D/R:** Overseeing Administrative Duties Including Mill Workers, Buyers and Products **H/I/S:** Fishing **EDU:** High School Education **A/A/S:** Epsilon Sigma Alpha **C/VW:** Local Church; St. Jude Children's Research Hospital; Easter Seals
Email: f.lanier@gasterlumber.com
URL: http://www.cambridgewhoswho.com

Elma M. Lannager

Title: Rehabilitation Counselor **Address:** P.O. Box 298, Roulette, PA 16746 United States **BUS:** Mental Health Practice **P/S:** Mental Health, Mental Retardation and Developmental Disabilities and Job Consulting and Counseling for Handicapped Individuals **MA:** National **D/D/R:** Training People with Disabilities for the Workforce by Finding Individual Talents **EDU:** Master's Degree in Rehabilitation Counseling **CERTS:** Certified, Commission on Rehabilitation Counselor Certification
Email: forrestnymph2005@yahoo.com
URL: http://www.cambridgewhoswho.com

Paulette Lanneaux

Title: Registered Nurse **Company:** Bellevue Hospital **Address:** 141 McKinley Avenue, Laurence Harbor, NJ 08879 United States **BUS:** 800-Bed Hospital Serving Residents of New Jersey and New York **P/S:** Comprehensive Inpatient and Outpatient State-of-the-Art Care, City-Wide Medical Specialty Referral Source **MA:** International **D/D/R:** Assessing Patients, Creating Treatment Plans, Collaborating with Physicians, Delegating Responsibilities, Working with Ancillary Departments, Educating Patients, Administering Medications, Discharging Plans **H/I/S:** Oil Painting, Fishing **EDU:** Pursuing Graduate Degree in Adult Healthcare, University of Medicine and Dentistry of New Jersey; Certified Legal Nurse Consultant; Bachelor of Science in Nursing, Seton Hall University (1999); Bachelor of Arts in Psychology, Rutgers, The State University of New Jersey (1994) **CERTS:** Certified in Trumpet and Cello, Preparatory Division, Manhattan School of Music (1978); Certified Real Estate Salesperson, Sierra School and Spencer School of Real Estate (2004); Certified Optometry Specialist **A/A/S:** Honorable Discharge, United States Air Force; Honorable Discharge, National Guard (1985)
Email: paulette7@optonline.net

Sarah Lanory

Title: Owner **Company:** The Beaded Fish **Address:** 4590 N.W. University Place, Suite 1, Corvallis, OR 97330 United States **BUS:** Gemstone Supply Company **P/S:** Gemstone Beads, Gemstone Chips **MA:** National **D/D/R:** Distributing Various Types of Nuggets, Chips, Rounds and Tumbles **H/I/S:** Fishing, Hiking, Riding, Walking, Going to the Coast **EDU:** Coursework, Western State College, Gunnison, Colorado
Email: thebeadedfish@gmail.com
URL: http://www.thebeadedfish.com

Pamela LaPage

Title: Owner, Artistic Director **Company:** Always Dancing **Address:** 76 East Genesee Street, Baldwinsville, NY 13027 United States **BUS:** Dance Company **P/S:** Dance Instruction and Performances **MA:** Local **D/D/R:** Teaching Tap, Jazz, Panimimi, Choreographing Recitals, Overseeing Daily Operations, Award Winning Dance Competition Teams **H/I/S:** Spending Time with Family, Friends and her Dogs, Photography, Writing **EDU:** Bachelor's Degree in English, SUNY **C/VW:** Multiple Sclerosis, Breast Cancer Relay for Life, Juvenile Diabetes, Local Charities
Email: alwaysdancing422@yahoo.com
URL: http://www.alwaysdancing.org

Linda Stella Laplume-Dean

Title: Paralegal, Real Estate Investor **Company:** Dean Enterprises **Address:** 1228 Johnson Street, Hollywood, FL 33019 United States **BUS:** Marine Engine Repair, Paralegal Services **P/S:** Real Estate, Paralegal **MA:** International **D/D/R:** Yacht Repairs, Paralegal Services, Real Estate Investment **EDU:** Associate Degree in Paralegal Studies, Dade Community College **CERTS:** Certified Paralegal
Email: lindaplume@comcast.net
URL: http://www.cambridgewhoswho.com

Donna Marie LaPorte, MHA, RN

Title: Clinical Medical Auditor **Company:** Lucile Packard Children's Hospital, Stanford **Address:** 2690 Hanover Street, Suite 5500, Palo Alto, CA 94304 United States **BUS:** Hospital **P/S:** Healthcare Includes Pediatric, Neonatology, Cardiology, Neurology Services **MA:** National **D/D/R:** Pediatric Nursing, Performing Concurrent Review on Blue Shield Accounts, Reviewing Reports for Insurance Companies **H/I/S:** Reading, Walking, Traveling, Watching Movies, Playing **EDU:** Master's Degree in Hospital Administration, California State University, Long Beach (1997); Bachelor's Degree in Healthcare Administration, California State University, Fullerton (1985); Associate Degree in Nursing (1967) **A/A/S:** The American Association of Medical Audit Specialists **C/VW:** Beginning Experience; Disabled American Veterans
Email: dlaporte@lpch.org
URL: http://www.lpch.org

Sue E. Larkin

Title: Teacher **Company:** Women's Housing and Economic Development Corporation **Address:** 50 E. 168th Street, Bronx, NY 10452 United States **BUS:** Nonprofit Dedicated to Alleviating Poverty **P/S:** Beautiful, Award-Winning Housing and Uniquely Integrated Programs in the Areas of Childcare, Education, Job-Training and Small Business Development to Narrow the Divide Between Rich and Poor **MA:** Regional **D/D/R:** Teaching 30 Head Start Students Preacademic and Social Skills to Prepare Them for Elementary School **H/I/S:** Watching Baseball, Reading **EDU:** Master's Degree in Early Childhood Education, Hunter College (2005); Bachelor's Degree in Elementary Education and Special Education, Dowling College **A/A/S:** National Education Association; New York Education Association; Choir Member, All Saints Episcopal Church
Email: suelarkin8@aol.com
URL: http://www.cambridgewhoswho.com

Bernadette Hanrahan LaRocca

Title: Executive Director **Company:** Addison Chamber of Commerce & Industry **Address:** 777 W. Army Trail Boulevard, Suite D, Addison, IL 60101 United States **BUS:** Chamber of Commerce **P/S:** Business Services **MA:** Local **D/D/R:** Organization, Planning, Direction of Chamber of Commerce **H/I/S:** Playing Golf, Traveling, Visiting Arizona **EDU:** College Coursework
Email: addisonchamber@sbcglobal.net
URL: http://www.addisonchamber.org

David A. Larrabee

Title: Executive Director **Company:** YMCA Camp Winona **Address:** 898 Camp Winona Road, De Leon Springs, FL 32130 United States **BUS:** Nonprofit Organization **P/S:** Resident Camping Including Outdoor Education and Rope Course Programs **MA:** Local **D/D/R:** Overseeing Group and Youth Camping Services, Managing Finance, Fundraising, Scheduling, Managing Group Facilities, Hiring Employees, Coordinating Educational Programs **H/I/S:** Sports, Traveling, Skiing, Snorkeling **EDU:** Bachelor's Degree in Business and Marketing, Bowling Green State University (1986) **A/A/S:** American Camp Association; Association of YMCA Professionals **A/H:** Cool Camp Award, FOX 35 **C/VW:** University YMCA; Christian Church, DeLeon Springs; American Youth Philharmonic Orchestras; United Way; Rotary International
Email: dslarr@bellsouth.net
URL: http://www.campwinona.org

Wayne L. Larrow, Ph.D.

Title: Owner **Company:** Larrow Investments, LLC **Address:** 1679 Cady Street, Erie, MI 48133 United States **BUS:** Consulting, Engineering and Management Company **P/S:** Consulting, Management **MA:** International **D/D/R:** Consulting, International Organization for Standardization, QS-9000 **H/I/S:** Buying and Selling Guns, Fishing, Camping, Motorcycles, Gourmet Cooking, Photography **EDU:** Ph.D., University of California **A/A/S:** SAE; ASQC; SME; PMA; American Legion; NRA-MCRG; OGCA; MPGO **C/VW:** Damascus House
Email: waynefromerie@charter.net
URL: http://www.cambidgewhoswho.com

Debra L. Larson

Title: Vice President, Clinical Applications **Company:** Healthsouth Corporation **Address:** 429 Old Brook Circle, Birmingham, AL 35242 United States **BUS:** Proven Leader in the Healthcare Industry **P/S:** Operation of Inpatient Rehabilitation Hospitals **MA:** Regional **D/D/R:** Running the Billing Offices, Calling Patients, Performing Clinical Documentation, Managing Remote and Internal Employees, Overseeing Application Support and Implementation **H/I/S:** Golfing, Sewing, Cooking **EDU:** Bachelor's Degree in Accounting, University of Iowa (1984) **A/A/S:** Health Information Management Systems Society; Youth Group Advisor
Email: deb.larson@healthsouth.net
URL: http://www.healthsouth.net

George R. Lartigue

Title: Clinical Social Worker **Company:** California Department of Corrections **Address:** 3400 Sillect Avenue, Bakersfield, CA 93308 United States **BUS:** Government Organization **P/S:** Correctional Services, Public and Community Safety, Victim and Survivor Services **MA:** Regional **D/D/R:** Organizing Individual Group and Family Psychotherapy Sessions, Entering Data, Scheduling Appointments for Parolees, Overseeing Mental Health Services for Parolees, Conducting Workshops, Seminars and Speaking to the Media **H/I/S:** Traveling, Public Speaking **EDU:** Master of Social Work, West Virginia University (1964); Bachelor's Degree in Social Work, Grambling State University (1962) **CERTS:** Licensed Clinical Social Worker, State of California (1985); Certified Domestic Violence Professional; Certified Anger Management Professional **A/A/S:** National Association of Social Workers; Academy of Certified Social Workers
Email: george.lartigue@cdcr.ca.gov
URL: http://www.cdcr.ca.gov

Juan A. Lasanta-Camacho, CPA

Title: Audit Manager **Company:** Williams, Adley & Company, LLP **Dept:** Audit Department **Address:** 1250 H Street N.W., Suite 1150, Washington, DC 20005 United States **BUS:** Accounting and Management Consulting Firm **P/S:** Financial Management and Assurance, Accounting, Advisory and Auditing Services **MA:** National **D/D/R:** Accounting, Management Consulting, Performing Audits for Federal, State, Local, Government and Nonprofit Organizations, Reviewing Procedures, Ensuring Quality, Overseeing Staff and Operations **H/I/S:** Practicing Martial Arts, Reading, Playing Chess **EDU:** Bachelor of Business Administration, Major in Accounting, American University of Puerto Rico, Summa Cum Laude (1990); Coursework, Finance School **CERTS:** Certified Public Accountant (1999) **A/A/S:** Who's Who in Accounting (2002-2007); Association of Certified Fraud Examiners; Association of Government Accountants; American Institute of Certified Public Accountants; Association of Certified Fraud Examiners **A/H:** Dean's List, American University of Puerto Rico **C/VW:** Children's International
Email: jlasanta@dcwacllp.com
URL: http://www.williamsadley.com

Thomas A. Lash

Title: Senior Partner **Company:** Saxon, Gilmore, Carraway, Gibbons, Lash and Wilcox, PA **Address:** 201 E. Kennedy Boulevard, Suite 600, Tampa, FL 33602 United States **BUS:** Law Firm **P/S:** Legal Services **MA:** Regional **D/D/R:** Business Structuring, Financing and Reconstructing, Partnering Businesses, Managing Creditors and Case Loads, Structuring Public-Private Partnership **H/I/S:** Sailing, Golfing, Playing with his Children **EDU:** JD, University of Virginia (1988); Bachelor's Degree in Law, University of Virginia Law School (1988); Bachelor of Science in Administration, Magna Cum Laude, University of Richmond **CERTS:** Certified Public Accountant, Virginia (1985) **A/A/S:** Executive Council, Business Law Section, Florida Bar Association; Tampa Bay Bankruptcy Bar Association
Email: tlash@saxongilmore.com
URL: http://www.saxongilmore.com

Diane Lass

Title: Domestic Violence Therapist **Company:** Family Justice Center **Address:** 4448 Granger Street, San Diego, CA 92107 United States **BUS:** The Most Comprehensive Facility in the Nation for Victims of Family Violence and their Children **P/S:** Advocacy, Childcare, Clothing, Counseling, Court Support, Deaf and Hard-of-Hearing Assistance, Food, Forensic Documentation of Injuries, Internet Access, Law Enforcement, Legal Assistance, Locksmith Services, Medical Services, Military Assistance, Telecommunications, Restraining Orders, Support Groups, Safety Planning, Spiritual Support, Transportation, Victim Compensation Assistance **MA:** Regional **D/D/R:** Conducting Clinical Risk Assessments, Offering Group and Individual Counseling, Safety Planning and Resource Referrals, Offering Expert Witness Testimony for Domestic Violence Cases **H/I/S:** Weight Training, Watching Football and Basketball, Cooking, Reading, Writing **EDU:** Ph.D. in Clinical Psychology, Alliant International University (2007); Master's Degree, California School of Professional Psychology (2002); Bachelor of Arts, Point Loma Nazarene University **A/A/S:** American Psychological Association
Email: lassoct1015@aol.com
URL: http://www.familyjusticecenter.org

Carlos H. Lasso

Title: Owner, Painter **Company:** Detail Painting **Address:** 8 Diane Court, Greenwood Lake, NY 10925 United States **BUS:** Painting and Construction Company **P/S:** Residential Construction, Painting **MA:** Regional **D/D/R:** Painting, Restoring, Constructing **H/I/S:** Trying Golf **EDU:** High School Education
URL: http://www.cambridgewhoswho.com

Terri A. Lastovka, CPA, JD, ASA
Title: Business Appraiser **Company:** Valuation and Litigation Consulting, LLC. **Address:** 600 East Granger Road, Independence, OH 44131 United States **BUS:** Financial Advisory Firm **P/S:** Business Valuation and Dispute Advisory Services **MA:** Regional **D/D/R:** Evaluating Businesses, Consulting in the Areas of Estate Planning, Probate, Family Law, Shareholder Disputes, Economic Damages, Forensic Accounting **H/I/S:** Water-Skiing, Snow Skiing **EDU:** JD, Cleveland-Marshall College of Law, Cleveland State University (1995) **CERTS:** Certified Public Accountant; Accredited Senior Appraiser **A/A/S:** American Society of Appraisers; Center for Principled Family Advocacy; Cleveland Bar Association; Lorain County Bar Association; Akron Bar Association; Cuyahoga County Bar Association; Ohio Bar Association
Email: lastovka@valueottio.com
URL: http://www.valueottio.com

Kathleen A. Latch
Title: Owner **Company:** The Yorkshire Inn Bed & Breakfast **Address:** 1135 Route 96, Phelps, NY 14532 United States **BUS:** Bed and Breakfast **P/S:** Two Hundred-Year-Old Restored Federalist Colonial Home, Bed and Breakfast Accommodations, Charming Rooms, Satellite Television Service, Wireless Internet Service, Craft and Vintage Quilts, Local Fishing and Golf Courses, Area Wineries **MA:** Regional **D/D/R:** Preparing Breakfast, Organizing Entertainment, Ensuring Clients' Comfort, Creating Brochures, Marketing **H/I/S:** Tennis **EDU:** Bachelor of Arts in Journalism, University of Denver (1983); Bachelor of Arts in History, University of Denver (1983) **A/A/S:** Seneca Lake Wine Trail; American Bed and Breakfast Association; Youth Leader, The Seneca Castle United Methodist Church
Email: innkeeper@theyorkshireinn.com
URL: http://www.theyorkshireinn.com

Maria G. Lathrop
Title: Teacher **Company:** Geneseo Central School **Address:** 4050 Avon Road, Geneseo, NY 14454 United States **BUS:** School **P/S:** Education **MA:** Local **D/D/R:** Teaching Reading, Writing and Mathematics for First-Grade Students **H/I/S:** Sewing, Swimming, Traveling, Spending Time Outdoors **EDU:** Master's Degree in Elementary Education, SUNY Geneseo (1971); Bachelor's Degree in Elementary Education, SUNY Geneseo (1970) **A/A/S:** National Storytelling Network **C/VW:** Local Church; Local Schools
Email: bandits@frontiernet.net
URL: http://www.cambridgewhoswho.com

Svetlana Latkovic
Title: Co-Owner **Company:** Cricket Mowing, Inc, **Address:** P.O. Box 361304, Strongsville, OH 44136 United States **BUS:** Landscaping Company **P/S:** Landscaping Design Services, Grounds Work, Weekly Grounds Maintenance, Snow Plowing **MA:** Local **D/D/R:** Specializing in Landscape Design and Maintenance **H/I/S:** Reading, Gardening **EDU:** Bachelor of Arts in Communications, Cleveland State University **CERTS:** Certified Medical Assistant, State of Ohio; Certification in Phlebotomy **A/A/S:** National Landscape Association
Email: cricketmowing@sbcglobal.net

Harvey H. Latson III
Title: Senior Lecturer **Company:** Texas State University San Marcos **Address:** 133 Watts Lane, Canyon Lake, TX 78133 United States **BUS:** University **P/S:** Higher Education **MA:** Regional **D/D/R:** Lecturing and Instructing Undergraduate Students in Exercise and Sports, Teaching Four Classes a Day with 30-35 Students in Strength and Conditioning, Instructing Racquetball **H/I/S:** Golfing, Making Golf Clubs **EDU:** Master's Degree in Physical Education, Texas State University (2002); Master's Degree in Public Administration, Webster University (1997); Bachelor's Degree in Criminal Justice, Tarleton State University (1976) **CERTS:** Certified Strength and Conditioning Specialist (2002); Certified Personal Trainer, National Academy of Sports Medicine **A/A/S:** Former Boy Scout Leader; Texas Association for Health, Physical Education, Recreation and Dance; Military Officers Association of America; American Society of Industrial Security
Email: harvelatson@aol.com
URL: http://www.txstate.edu

Jeanie Borlaug Laube
Title: Director of Community Service **Company:** 1) St. Mark's School of Texas 2) Hockaday School **Address:** 10600 Preston Road, Dallas, TX 75320 United States **BUS:** School **P/S:** Education **MA:** Local **D/D/R:** Teaching Spanish, Mentoring Students **H/I/S:** Spending Time with her Family **EDU:** Master of Arts in Spanish Literature, Texas A&M University (1993) **A/A/S:** Board of Genesis; American Association of Teachers of Spanish and Portuguese **C/VW:** Local Charitable Organizations; Shelter for Abused Women and Children; Board Member, The Salvation Army
Email: laube@smtexas.org
URL: http://www.cambridgewhoswho.com

Joanne Lauchman
Title: Language Arts Coordinator, Second-Grade Teacher **Company:** Immaculate Conception School **Address:** 101 N. Peter Street, New Oxford, PA 17350 United States **BUS:** School **P/S:** Education for Prekindergarten through Eighth-Grade Students Including Teaching Art, Athletics, Academics, Instrumental and Vocal Music **MA:** Local **D/D/R:** Teaching Language Arts and Reading, Developing New Programs, Preparing Students to Receive Sacraments, Training Teachers in Basic Early Literacy Skills Program **EDU:** Pursuing Master's Degree in Reading; Bachelor's Degree in Elementary Education, Concentration in Early Childhood Education, Millersville University (1981) **A/A/S:** National Catholic Education Association; Chairman, Middle States Steering Committee
Email: latchgjg@aol.com
URL: http://www.icsbvm.org

Sandra L. Laufersweiler
Title: Assistant Vice President, Pricing Support **Company:** National City Mortgage **Address:** 3232 Newmark Drive, Miamisburg, OH 45342 United States **BUS:** Mortgage Banking Company **P/S:** Mortgage Banking **MA:** National **D/D/R:** Pricing Analysis, Supporting 150 to 170 Branches for Loan Pricing, Product Guidelines and Closing Reports **H/I/S:** Gardening, Doing Crafts, Sports Enthusiast **EDU:** Associate of Arts in General Studies, St. Clair County Community College **C/VW:** Habitat for Humanity, The Humane Society, The Society for the Improvement of Conditions for Stray Animals
Email: sandra.laufersweiler@ncmc.com

Janis R. Launer, RN
Title: Registered Professional Nurse (Precept Specialist) **Company:** Memorial University Medical Center **Address:** 4700 Waters Avenue, Attention: Enterprise Wide Scheduling, Savannah, GA 31404 United States **BUS:** Medical Facility Dedicated to Excellence in Education **P/S:** Hemodialysis, Inpatient Surgery, Lithotripsy, Obstetrics, Psychiatric, Rehabilitation, Cardiovascular Services, Rehabilitation, Physical Therapy, Emergency Department **MA:** Regional **D/D/R:** Practicing Critical Care Nursing, Working as a Precept Specialist, Handling Commercial Insurance, Medicare and Medicaid Issues in the Accounting and Finance Department **H/I/S:** Antiquing, Hiking, Watching Movies, Traveling Across the Country and Abroad, Attending Symphonies and Ballets **EDU:** Associate Degree in Nursing, Floyd University **A/A/S:** Jaycees; Volunteer, Make-A-Wish Foundation; Public Speaking; Preceptor, Hospital; Volunteer, Local Community Worthy Causes
Email: launeja1@memorialhealth.com
URL: http://www.memorialhealth.org

Mr. Ronnie P. Lauranoff
Title: NACE Certified Coatings Inspector **Company:** Lauranoff Inspections **Address:** 145 Huisache Street, Lake Jackson, TX 77566 United States **BUS:** Inspection Company **P/S:** Inspection Services **MA:** Regional **D/D/R:** Conducting Industrial Inspections at Chemical Plants, Refineries, Oil and Nuclear Plants **H/I/S:** Fishing **EDU:** College Coursework **CERTS:** Certified Coatings Inspector, National Association of Corrosion Engineers
Email: sono502@aol.com

Hans G.D. Laursen
Title: Family Medicine Physician **Company:** South Central Family Health Center **Address:** 4425 S. Central Avenue, Los Angeles, CA 90011 United States **BUS:** Healthcare Center **P/S:** Nonprofit General Medicine Family Practice **MA:** Regional **EXP:** Dr. Laursen's expertise includes family medicine, prenatal care coordination, prenatal care and quality improvement. **H/I/S:** Skiing, Scuba Diving, Playing the Bagpipe **EDU:** Doctor of Osteopathy, Kirksville College of Osteopathic Medicine, 2003; Residency, Harbor-UCLA Medical Center **A/A/S:** American Academy of Family Physicians; American Osteopathic Association; American College of Osteopathic Family Physicians **C/VW:** Ruth B. Laursen Registered Nurse Urban Undeserved Primary Care Memorial Scholarship
Email: gatordoc99@hotmail.com
URL: http://www.scfhc.org

Patricia E. Lavan, ICPE
Title: Registered Nurse, Perinatal Grief Counselor **Company:** Somerset Hospital **Address:** 2832 Glade Pike, Somerset, PA 15501 United States **BUS:** Hospital **P/S:** Healthcare, Behavioral Health, Cardiac, Surgical, Women's Health and Emergency Services **MA:** Regional **D/D/R:** Labor and Delivery Nursing **H/I/S:** Spending Time with Children, Reading, Ghost Hunting **EDU:** Associate Degree in Nursing, Mount Aloysius College (1982)
Email: lavanshouse@aol.com
URL: http://www.somersethospital.com

Marcia M. Lavely, Ph.D.
Title: Chairwoman of English Department **Company:** Creek Wood High School **Address:** 3499 Highway 47 N., Charlotte, TN 37036 United States **BUS:** High School **P/S:** High School Education **MA:** Regional **D/D/R:** Teaching Senior English Education and Advanced Composition Classes **H/I/S:** Football, Baseball, Reading **EDU:** Ph.D. in Secondary Education English, The University of Mississippi (1991) **CERTS:** Certification in English, History, Psychology and Sociology Education **A/A/S:** Tennessee Education Association; National Education Association; Dickson County Education Association; The National Council of Teachers of English
Email: mlavely@dcbe.org
URL: http://www.dicksoncountyschools.org/CWHS

Kathleen E. Laverty-Segrest
Title: Educational Student Aide **Company:** New Jersey State Federation of Teachers **Address:** 114 Prospect Road, Sicklerville, NJ 08081 United States **BUS:** School District **P/S:** Education **MA:** Local **D/D/R:** Teaching, Working with Special Needs Children, Advocating for Students **H/I/S:** Spending Time at the Beach, Reading **EDU:** Associate Degree in Radiologic Technology **A/A/S:** President, Local Chapter 6171, Winslow Township Paraprofessionals Organization; American Federation of Labor-Congress of Industrial Organizations **C/VW:** American Foundation for Suicide Prevention
Email: alkat30@yahoo.com

Jon B. Law
Title: Owner **Company:** Arizona Copier Outlet **Address:** 26 W. Lone Cactus Drive, Suite 400, Phoenix, AZ 85027 United States **BUS:** Digital Business Machine Company **P/S:** Sales, Leasing, Service, Parts and Supplies for Digital Business Machines, Copiers, Printers, Network Scanners, Fax Machines **MA:** Metro Phoenix **D/D/R:** Overseeing All Aspects of the Company, Marketing **H/I/S:** All Sports, Traveling **EDU:** Bachelor of Art in Speech and Business Communications, Morningside College **A/A/S:** Better Business Bureau; Industrial Technology Association **C/VW:** American Cancer Society, American Heart Association, Muscular Dystrophy Association, Local Police and Fire Departments
Email: jon@copieroutlet.net
URL: http://www.copieroutlet.net

Cindy G. Lawhorn
Title: Claims Examiner **Company:** Virginia Department of Veteran Services **Address:** 270 Franklin Road S.W., Room 503, Roanoke, VA 24011 United States **BUS:** Government Agency **P/S:** Assists Veterans and their Families in Obtaining State, Federal and Local Benefits **MA:** National **D/D/R:** Writing Appeals on Denied Claims, Assisting Veterans to Receive Appropriate Compensation **H/I/S:** Gardening **EDU:** Associate Degree in Business Management, American International University (2004) **C/VW:** Veterans of Foreign Wars; American Legion; American Red Cross; U.S. Marine Corps
Email: cindy.lawhorn@dvs.virginia.gov
URL: http://www.dvs.virginia.gov

Richard Lawlor
Title: Superintendent of Golf Courses **Company:** Town of Yarmouth-Golf **Address:** 635 W. Yarmouth Road, West Yarmouth, MA 02673 United States **BUS:** Golf Course **P/S:** Golf **MA:** East Coast Resort **D/D/R:** Fine Turf-Maintenance, Operations **H/I/S:** Boating, Reading **EDU:** Master's Degree in Education, Assumption College; Bachelor's Degree in Sociology, Assumption College; Associate Degree in Plant and Soil Science, University of Massachusetts **A/A/S:** Golf Course Superintendents Association of America; Golf Course Managers Association of Cape Cod
Email: rickstang302@yahoo.com
URL: http://www.golfyarmouthcapecod.com

Bruce E. Lawrence Jr.
Title: President **Company:** Aagape Drywall Systems, Inc. **Address:** 104 Waverley Way, Suite 7, Athens, TX 75752 United States **BUS:** Construction Firm **P/S:** Commercial Dry Wall, Framing, Insulation and Doors **MA:** Regional **D/D/R:** Overseeing the Administration of Business, Managing the Employees, Performing Contract Negotiations, Supervising Material Purchases **H/I/S:** Practicing Archery **EDU:** Associate Degree in Business Administration, Dallas Community College (1992) **A/A/S:** Published, Walls and Ceilings Magazine
Email: brulawr@yahoo.com
URL: http://www.cambridgewhoswho.com

Fitzroy Lawrence Sr.
Title: Grants Analyst, Budget Analyst **Company:** New York City Department of Education **Address:** 1 Fordham Plaza, Bronx, NY 10438 United States **BUS:** Department of Education **P/S:** Education **MA:** Citywide **D/D/R:** Budget and Grant Analysis Allocation projects **H/I/S:** Reading, Traveling, Participating in Outdoor Recreational Activities **EDU:** Bachelor of Arts in Accounting, Mercy College **A/A/S:** Mercy College Alumni Association **C/VW:** Right Solutions
Email: bivgroy@aol.com
URL: http://www.cambridgewhoswho.com

Marcie L. Lawrence
Title: Reading Teacher **Company:** Brasher Falls Central School District, St. Lawrence Central Middle School **Address:** P.O. Box 307, Brasher Falls, NY 13613 United States **BUS:** Middle School **P/S:** Public Education **MA:** Local **D/D/R:** Teaching Reading Skills to Students in Kindergarten through 12, Making real life connections to students' learning **H/I/S:** Knitting, Spending Time with her Family, Playing Volleyball on a Women's League, Dancing, Singing **EDU:** Master of Science in Reading, SUNY Potsdam; Bachelor of Science in Elementary Education, SUNY Plattsburgh **A/A/S:** Kappa Delta Pi; Omicron Delta Kappa, Whos Who Among America's Teachers (2004-2005) NYSARC, Inc.
Email: mlawrence@bfcsd.org

Teresa N. Lawrence
Title: Service Consultant **Company:** Koeppel Volkswagen **Address:** 5701 Northern Boulevard, Woodside, NY 11377 United States **BUS:** Automotive Company **P/S:** Automotive Dealership Including Volkswagen Cars **MA:** Regional **D/D/R:** Performing Administrative Duties, Ensuring Customer Satisfaction, Verifying Information from Clients, Consulting, Lecturing **H/I/S:** Playing Baseball, Basketball and Tennis, Biking, Rollerblading, Rock Climbing **EDU:** Associate of Arts in Liberal Arts and Science, Queensborough Community College **A/H:** Award, Domestic Violence and Rape Crisis Center, Mount Sinai Hospital
Email: tee.1414@hotmail.com
URL: http://www.cambridgewhoswho.com

Annette L. Lawson
Title: Registered Staff Nurse (Retired) **Company:** New Jersey Health Care System **Dept:** Department of Veterans Affairs **Address:** 151 Knollcroft Road, Lyons, NJ 07939 United States **BUS:** Government Organization **P/S:** Healthcare of Veterans **MA:** Regional **D/D/R:** Working with Geriatric, Mental Illness and Alzheimer's Patients, Performing Reality Orientation, Behavior Modification, Music and Exercise Therapy, Managing Staff **H/I/S:** Gardening, Reading History, Playing the Organ and Piano, Remodeling Home **EDU:** Pursuing Coursework in Computer Applications; Bachelor of Science in Nursing, Kean University, NJ (1994); Associate Degree in Applied Science, Essex County College, Newark, NJ (1973) **CERTS:** Licensed Practical Nurse, Jersey City School System (1968) **A/H:** Golf Leaf Customer Service Award **C/VW:** Local Church
Email: vzeue0yu@verizon.net
URL: http://www.va.gov/visns/visn03/lyonsinfo.asp

Sheryl Nachbar Lawson
Title: Marketing Associate **Company:** Sysco Food Services of Kansas City **Address:** 1915 E. Kansas City Road, Olathe, KS 66061 United States **BUS:** Food Service Company **P/S:** Groceries, Food Service-Related Items **MA:** National **EXP:** Ms. Lawson's expertise is in customer relations. **H/I/S:** Weight Toning, Spending Time with Family and Friends, Watching Basketball and Softball Games **EDU:** Associate Degree, Johnson County Community College, Kansas City, Kansas **A/A/S:** Industry-Related Organizations **A/H:** Fred Nachbar Award, 1988; Torch Bearer Award **C/VW:** The Leukemia & Lymphoma Society, American Cancer Society
Email: lawson.sheri@kc.sysco.com
URL: http://www.sysco.com

Tracy J. Lay
Title: Administrative Coordinator **Company:** Humana **Address:** 1100 Employees Boulevard, Green Bay, WI 54344 United States **BUS:** Proven Leader in the Healthcare Industry **P/S:** Health Benefits and Services **MA:** National **D/D/R:** Reporting to the Vice President, Seeing to Administrative Duties, Assisting Charities, Handling All Functions **H/I/S:** Family **EDU:** Bachelor's Degree in Business Administration and Marketing, Lakeland College (2001) **A/A/S:** Volunteer, Big Brothers Big Sisters; Volunteer, United Way
Email: hay@humana.com
URL: http://www.humana.com

Dr. Sergio R. Lázaro
Title: 1) Chief Executive Officer 2) Owner, Chairman **Company:** 1) Psych4U 2) SRL, Inc. **Address:** 16950 Gramercy Place, Space 69A, Gardena, CA 90247 United States **BUS:** 1) Mental Health Practice 2) Finance Company **P/S:** 1) Healthcare Including Counseling and Stress Management Services 2) Financial Services Including Personal Loans and Life Insurance Policies **MA:** Local **D/D/R:** Counseling Clients with Domestic, Professional, Stress and Relationship Problems **H/I/S:** Supporting Argentina's Soccer Team, Poetry, Tango Dancing **EDU:** Ph.D. in Psychology, University of California, LA (1998); Master's Degree in Engineering, California State University, LA (1991)
Email: srl_4@yahoo.com
URL: http://psych4u.com

Alene T. Le
Title: Orthodontist **Company:** Arlene Le, DDS, MS, Inc. **Address:** 15455 Jeffrey Road, Suite 310, Irvine, CA 92618 United States **BUS:** Dental Office **P/S:** Dentistry **MA:** Local **EXP:** Dr. Le's expertise is in orthodontics. **H/I/S:** Swimming, Restoring Vintage Bicycles **EDU:** Master of Science in Craniofacial Biology and Dentofacial Orthopedics, University of Southern California **CERTS:** Certificate in Orthodontics **A/A/S:** Diplomate, American Board of Orthodontics; Pacific Coast Society of Orthodontics; American Dental Association; American Association of Orthodontists
Email: drle@sensationalsmyles.com
URL: http://www.sensationalsmyles.com

Tuan Tommy Le
Title: Senior Consultant **Company:** RSM McGladrey **Address:** 1954 Greenspring Drive, Suite 400, Lutherville Timonium, MD 21093 United States **BUS:** Regulatory Solvency and Insurance Consulting **P/S:** Information Technology Audit, Sarbanes-Oxley (SOX) Compliances, Governance and Risk Management **MA:** Domestic **D/D/R:** Information Technology Audit, Sarbanes-Oxley (SOX) Compliances, Governance and Risk Management, Corporate Transactions, Mergers and acquisitions, Hardware and Software Upgrades and Implementations **H/I/S:** Traveling, Soccer, Golfing, Fishing Favorite business publications are ISACA, Forbes, Money and Entrepreneur **EDU:** Bachelor of Arts in Management Information Systems and Finance, University of Memphis (2002) **A/A/S:** President, Association of Information Technology Professionals; Information Systems Audit and Control Association
Email: tommyle1@gmail.com
URL: http://www.rsmmcgladrey.com

Dana M. Leach
Title: CFO **Company:** Baseball Mentoring Program INC **Address:** 1513 Sports Drive, Unit 400, Sacramento, CA 95834 United States **BUS:** Baseball Mentoring **P/S:** Baseball Lessons, Mentoring, Recruiters **MA:** Local **EXP:** Ms. Leach's expertise is in controller administration. **EDU:** American River College **A/A/S:** Little League
Email: jdleachy@msn.com
URL: www.bmp.com

Jillian F. Leadley
Title: Graphic Designer **Company:** Kornerstone Signs **Address:** 725 Armstrong Drive, Buffalo Grove, IL 60089 United States **BUS:** Sign and Graphics Company **P/S:** Sign Design and Production **MA:** Chicago, Southern Wisconsin **D/D/R:** Designing, Producing and Installing Signage for Companies **H/I/S:** Camping, Bicycling, Working Out, Staying Fit **C/VW:** Member of Nickie C & the Auctionettes, Singing at Charity Auctions
Email: dragonhead13@msn.com
URL: http://www.ksigns.net

Mrs. Karen Maria Leak Simmons
Title: Teacher **Company:** Ocean Lakes High School **Address:** 885 Schumann Drive, Virgina Beach, VA 23454 United States **BUS:** Public High School **P/S:** Education **MA:** Regional **D/D/R:** Teaching Family and Consumer Sciences Education, Resource Management for Independent Living, Financial Management, Personal Skills and Child Development, Introducing Students to Design Occupations, Administrative and Supervision, Curriculum Writing, Technical and Career Education, Computer Technology and Culinary Occupations **H/I/S:** Traveling, Decorating, Handiwork, Softball, Meeting Inspiring and Motivational People, Designing Innovative Activities and Projects **EDU:** Pursuing Ph.D. in Instructional Technology and Distant Living, Nova Southeastern University; Master's Degree in Adult and Community Education, Appalachian State University (1983) **A/A/S:** National Honorable Mention in the Practice Money Skills for Life Educator Challenge (2005); Who Who's Among American Teachers (2002-2005); Discipline Association; National Education Association; Alumni, North Carolina Agricultural and Technical State University and Appalachian State University; Presenter at the Virginia Association for Teachers of Family and Consumer Sciences Conference (2005); Presenter at Technical and Career-FCCLA, Special Education (ALOHA) Conference (2002); Evaluator for FCCLA State Conference (2001) (2005-2007); Member of the Virginia Association for Teachers of Family and Consumer Sciences Association **A/H:** Wrote and Received a Mini Grant 'Multimedia Technology in the Classroom' (1995); Recieved the Rufus Beamer Award; First Place Group Winners (1996); Teacher of the Quarter, Great Neck Middle School, Virginia Beach, VA (1998); Total Quality Management Monthly Superintendent Award (03/1999); Nominated by a Student for Teacher of the Quarter, Ocean Lakes High School, Virginia Beach, VA (2006)
Email: karenstudioroom@cox.net
URL: http://www.oceanlakeshs.vbschools.com

Linda I. Leal
Title: Sales Representative **Company:** Charlotte Supply **Address:** 40 Bruce Place, Charlotte, TX 78011 United States **BUS:** Retail **P/S:** Ranch, Welding, Plumbing and Lumber Supplies, Construction Supplies **MA:** Local **D/D/R:** Selling Ranch Supplies, Plumbing and Welding Materials, Lumber **H/I/S:** Reading, Gardening **EDU:** Diploma, High School

Douglas M. Leary
Title: Owner **Company:** Leary and Wilson Builders, LLC **Address:** 30 Pearl Street, Essex Junction, VT 05452 United States **BUS:** Construction Company **P/S:** Stick-Frame and Pre-Fabricated Building **MA:** Regional **EXP:** Mr. Leary's expertise includes construction and real estate development. **H/I/S:** Fishing, Boating **EDU:** Bachelor's Degree in Zoology, University of Vermont **C/VW:** Step Up for Women, Rosie's Girls, Youth Build, Vermont Job Corps, Vermont Community High School, Local Youth Organizations
Email: dleary@learywilson.com
URL: http://www.learywilson.com

John Mike Leaver
Title: General Manager **Company:** Back to Eden **Address:** P.O. Box 661, Kaneohe, HI 96744 United States **BUS:** Landscape Construction Company **P/S:** Landscape Design and Construction Services, Consulting **MA:** Regional **D/D/R:** Landscape Designing, Consulting **H/I/S:** Fishing, Reading **A/A/S:** Honolulu Executive's Association; American Legion
Email: mike_backtoeden@hotmail.com
URL: http://www.cambridgewhoswho.com

Michele C. Leavitt
Title: Fine Artist **Company:** Michele C. Leavitt **Address:** 25 Waterway Drive, Sauderstown, RI 02874 United States **BUS:** Privately Owned Company Committed to Excellence in Art Work Production and Sales **P/S:** Fine Art Including Drawing, Painting, Collage, Quilts, Mixed Media and Limited Editions of Hand-Woven Rugs Knotted in Turkey to the Artist's Specifications, Art Education **MA:** International **EXP:** Ms. Leavitt's expertise is in fine art. **D/D/R:** Buying and Selling Original Art **H/I/S:** Tap Dancing, Distance Swimming, Buying, Renovating and Selling Real Estate Apartment Properties **EDU:** Bachelor of Fine Arts Degree, Rochester Institute of Technology; Master of Fine Arts, Cornell University (1985) **A/A/S:** Selected for Exhibition, American Embassy in Lithuania; Board of Artists League of Rhode Island Summer Program; Art Museum of the University of Virginia; Reviewed Favorably, Art Publications and Newspapers; Featured, Pictorial Quilting, Nina Holland (1978); Educator in Foundation Drawing, Rhode Island School of Design Summer Studies, Community College of Rhode Island; Lecturer on Art History; Selected, Numerous Juried Shows; Solo Exhibitioner, Newport Art Museum, University of Virginia Museum of Art, Community College of Rhode Island
Email: leavitt25@cox.net
URL: http://www.artleagueri.org

Linda F. Leazar
Title: Independent Landman **Company:** ConocoPhillips **Address:** 3300 N. A Street, Midland, TX 79705 United States **BUS:** Energy Firm **P/S:** Oil and Gas Exploration, Refining, On-and Off-Shore Drilling, Marketing **MA:** International **EXP:** Ms. Leazar's expertise is in contract negotiation. **D/D/R:** Dealing with Oil and Gas Leases, Supervising Field Workers, Working with the Upstream Team like Exploration Team Land, Geology and Engineering, Reviewing Legal Titles **H/I/S:** Painting, Photography, Reading, Traveling **EDU:** Master's Degree in Legal Studies, South Texas College of Law (1979); Bachelor of Arts in English and Religious Studies, Rice University (1975) **CERTS:** Certified Professional Landman (1991) **A/A/S:** Midland Arts Association; Texas Watercolor Society; Permian Basin Landman's Association; American Association of Professional Landmen
Email: lfleazar@bigfoot.com

David J. LeBeau
Title: W New England Representative **Company:** Bonhams Auctioneer and Appraisers **Address:** 119 S. Main Street, Sheffield, MA 01257 United States **BUS:** Auctioneers and Appraisers International Auction Company founded in London 1793 **P/S:** Auctions and Appraisals **MA:** International **D/D/R:** USPAP certified appraiser 2006. American Society of Appraisers Accredited Senior Appraiser of antiques and residential contents since 1976 **H/I/S:** Volunteer at the Sandisfield (MA) Arts Center **EDU:** Carnegie Institute of Technology, Master's Degree in Fine Arts **A/A/S:** American Society of Appraisers, Western England Representative for Bonhams Auctioneers & Appraisers 2005, AOA, Boy Scouts Council, Cancer Society
Email: ejlebeau@verizon.net
URL: www.appraisalbylebeau.com

JoMarie LeBlanc
Title: Controller **Company:** Coldwell Banker Alfonso Realty **Address:** 5379 Red Creek Road, Long Beach, MS 39560 United States **BUS:** Real Estate Agency **P/S:** Real Estate Leasing and Sales, Marketing, Residential and Commercial **MA:** Local **D/D/R:** Accounting, Responsible for All Financial Aspects of the company **H/I/S:** Bird Watching **EDU:** Bachelor's Degree in Accounting, University of Southern Mississippi **C/VW:** Audubon Society
Email: jo@alfonso.com
URL: http://www.coldwellbankalfonso.com

Diana M. Leccese
Title: Senior Sales Engineer Company: Merced Systems Address: 26 Colonial Avenue, Waltham, MA 02453 United States BUS: Software Vendor P/S: Performance Management Software MA: International EXP: Ms. Leccese's expertise is in performance management. D/D/R: Analyzing Statistics H/I/S: Boating, Playing the Piano, Traveling EDU: Master of Business Administration, Boston University; Bachelor of Science in Mechanical Engineering, University of Massachusetts A/A/S: American Society of Mechanical Engineers
Email: dleccese@mercedsystems.com
URL: http://www.mercedsystem.com

Mr. Thomas J. LeClerc
Title: Behavior Consultant II Company: Dual Diagnosis Treatment and Training Services Address: 2601 Gabriel Avenue, Parsons, KS 67357 United States BUS: Statewide Resource for Persons with a Dual Diagnosis of Developmental Disability and a Mental Health Disorder P/S: Short-Term Residential Assessment and Treatment, Development of Individual Education Plans (IEPS), Behavioral Services, Social Work and Intake Services, Licensed Physicians and Nursing Staff Provide and Monitor Medical Services, Speech and Language Therapy and Consultation Services MA: Regional D/D/R: Developing Programs for Persons with All Types of Disabilities for Independent Living, Conducting Behavior Functional Analysis H/I/S: Quilting EDU: Master's Degree in Arts, Indiana State University (1972); Master's Degree in Divinity, Iliff School of Theology, Denver, Colorado (1978) A/A/S: Who's Who in University Graduate Schools (1972)
Email: tjl@pshtc.ks.gov
URL: http://www.pshtc.org

Jerry O. Ledbetter
Title: Director of Information Technology Company: Franklin County Court of Common Pleas Address: 373 S. High Street, Columbus, OH 43215 United States BUS: Court P/S: Justice MA: Countywide EXP: Mr. Ledbetter's expertise is in information technology. H/I/S: Spending Time with his Wife and Daughter EDU: Bachelor's Degree in Information Management, Otterbein College; CMP Certification
Email: jledbetter@dublin.oh.us
URL: http://www.cambridgewhoswho.com

Nadine Lederfine
Title: Owner Company: Lederfine Nutrition Address: 3503 N. Bellflower Boulevard, Long Beach, CA 90808 United States BUS: Nutritionist P/S: Nutritional Services, Supplements MA: Local D/D/R: Assistant Patients with Nutritional Guidance and Supplements H/I/S: Wine Tasting, Real Estate Investor EDU: Two-Year Degree, International of Clinical Nutrition (2005) A/A/S: Children's Hunger Fund
Email: nadine@usana.com
URL: http://www.2usana.usana.com

Lisa Ledesma
Title: Home Mortgage Consultant Company: Wells Fargo Home Mortgage Address: 4365 Kukui Grove Street, Suite 101, Lihue, HI 96766 United States BUS: Real Estate Lending Office P/S: Mortgages for Homeowners/investor/2nd home MA: National D/D/R: Keeping Lifelong Customers H/I/S: Running, Biking CERTS: Certified in Financial Consulting, Hawaii Business College A/H: Customer Service Awards C/VW: Hawaii Children's Theatre/MDA
Email: lisa.ledesma@wellsfargo.com
URL: http://www.homeloans.com/lisa.ledesma

Linda Sue Ledger
Title: Pre-Planning Director Company: Boecker Pre-Need Preston Henley Address: 1918 Highwood Avenue, Pekin, IL 61554 United States BUS: Family Owned Funeral Home P/S: Funeral Services MA: Local D/D/R: Selling Insurance for Pre-need, Helping People Plan their Funerals H/I/S: Reading, Traveling, Spending Time with her Children and Grandchildren EDU: High School Diploma CERTS: Licensed Life Insurance Broker, State of Illinois
Email: lledger@insightbb.com

Barbara Lee
Title: Administrative Assistant Company: St. John's County Health and Human Services Address: 1955 U.S. 1 S., Suite C2, Saint Augustine, FL 32086 United States BUS: Government Agency P/S: Drug Abuse and Mental Health Recovery Services MA: National D/D/R: Assisting Clinical and Professional Staffs H/I/S: Gardening, Reading Non-Fiction EDU: Coursework in Cultural Competency C/VW: American Veterans; Vietnam Veterans; Humane Society
Email: blrat@bellsouth.net
URL: http://www.cambridgewhoswho.com

Dawn V. Lee, RN
Title: Nurse Manager Company: Dialysis Clinic, Inc. Address: 1417 Burrell Road, Clover, SC 29710 United States BUS: Privately Owned Clinic Facility Committed to Excellence in Healthcare P/S: Dialysis Nursing MA: Regional D/D/R: Oversees Two Nurses in Dialysis Unit, Specializing in Acute Patient Care H/I/S: Cooking, Reading EDU: Registered Nurse Degree, Central Piedmont Community College (1991) A/A/S: American Nurses Association
URL: http://www.cambridgewhoswho.com

Elaine D. Lee
Title: Budget Analyst Company: 81st RSC, Army Reserve Address: 255 W. Oxmoor Road, Birmingham, AL 35209 United States BUS: Government Organization P/S: Defense Services MA: Southeastern Region EXP: Ms. Lee's expertise is in operations management. D/D/R: Coordinating and Implementing Budget Procedures and Policies H/I/S: Reading, Bowling EDU: Bachelor's Degree in Management, Miles College, Birmingham A/A/S: Childhood Association A/H: Letter of Accommodation (2005); Meritorious Service Medal (1998) C/VW: Homeless Missions; Children's Missions
Email: lee_2003@bellsouth.net
URL: http://www.cambridgewhoswho.com

Jean A. Lee
Title: Senior Lecturer Company: The University of Akron Address: Summit College, Akron, OH 44325 United States BUS: University P/S: Higher Education, Undergraduate and Graduate Degree Programs Including Polymer Science and Engineering Programs MA: Regional D/D/R: Organizing Developmental Programs H/I/S: Walking, Collecting Antique Jewelry, Reading the Bible EDU: Master's Degree in Higher Education and Administration, The University of Akron (1991); Bachelor of Science in Higher Education Teaching and Administration (1991); Associate Degree in Criminal Justice; Licensed Social Worker A/A/S: Ohio Association for Developmental Education; Ohio Counselor, Social Worker and Marriage and Family Therapist Board, Ohio
Email: rlee62.rr.neo.com
URL: http://www.uakron.edu

Kendall L. Lee
Title: President, Owner Company: Altamont Custom Homes, LP Address: 1330 N. White Chapel Boulevard, Suite 200, Southlake, TX 76092 United States BUS: Construction and Development Company P/S: Construction of Commercial Office Spaces, Light Industrial Spaces and Warehouses, Residential Construction Services MA: Regional EXP: Mr. Lee's expertise includes commercial and residential construction. D/D/R: Overseeing Real Estate Development H/I/S: Traveling EDU: Coursework in Business Administration, Columbia Southern University A/A/S: Chamber of Commerce C/VW: Local Charitable Youth Organizations
Email: kendall-lee@sbcglobal.net
URL: http://www.altamontcustomhomes.com

M. Michael Lee
Title: Fire Protection Specialist Company: University of Virginia Address: Emmet House Station No. 1, Charlottesville, VA 22904 United States BUS: University P/S: Education, Fire Protection MA: International D/D/R: Repairing, Maintaining and Inspecting Fire Alarm Systems H/I/S: Waterskiing, Playing Darts, Slow Pitch Softball CERTS: Certified Fire Protection Specialist for the National Fire Protection Agency A/A/S: Journeyman Electrician, State of Virginia; Recognition, Southeastern Association of Housing Officers; Community Emergency Response Team A/H: Pride and Service Award, Housing Division Recognition Division; Shining Star Award, UVA Housing Division C/VW: University of Virginia
Email: mml2n@virginia.edu

Mary Anne Scott Lee
Title: Registered Nurse, Instructor Company: Medical Learning Center Address: 1840 Wilson Boulevard, Arlington, VA 22201 United States BUS: Medical Education Center P/S: Educating Nurses MA: Local D/D/R: Nursing Education H/I/S: Gardening, Watching Sports, Swimming, Bicycling, Bowling, Culinary Arts, Skating, Skiing, Tennis, Hiking EDU: Bachelor of Science in Nursing CERTS: Certified Public Health Nurse, St. Catherine College; Certification, Neonatal Resuscitation, Inova Fairfax Hospital; Registered Nurse, Commonwealth of Virginia A/A/S: Outstanding Service and Commitment to Patient Care, Inova Fairfax Hospital and Inova Fairfax Hospital for Children C/VW: Local Church, Ministering to the Ill
Email: maslbsn@yahoo.com

Nancy Strickland Lee
Title: Dental Hygiene Instructor Company: Wayne Community College Address: Wayne Memorial Drive, Goldsboro, NC 27534 United States BUS: College P/S: Higher Education MA: Local D/D/R: Teaching Dental Health, Coordinating Infection Control H/I/S: Reading, Boating, Skiing EDU: Bachelor of Science in Dental Hygiene, The University of North Carolina at Chapel Hill A/A/S: American Dental Hygienists Association; North Carolina Dental Hygiene Association C/VW: Greenville Learning Center
Email: nsl@suddenlink.net
URL: http://www.cambridgewhoswho.com

Paulette Y. Lee
Title: Medical Records Nurse Company: Montgomery Village Healthcare Center Dept: Nursing Address: 19042 Mills Choice Road, Montgomery Village, MD 20886 United States BUS: Healthcare P/S: Medical Records MA: Recognition D/D/R: Handling All Admissions and Discharges, Creating New Charts, Dealing with Doctors and Lawyers, Offering Patient Care H/I/S: Playing the Piano EDU: Associate Degree in Healthcare Management, Ashford College (2005) A/H: Employee of the Month (2006); Employee of the Year (2006)
Email: leep121@verizon.net

Shirley R. Lee, RN
Title: Owner, Founder, Administrator Company: Lee's Personal Care Home Address: 361 Murray Hill Avenue N.E., Atlanta, GA 30317 United States BUS: Home Health Care Facility P/S: Home Care for the Elderly MA: Regional D/D/R: Directing, Planning, Coordinating, Implementing All Activities, Overseeing Staff and Compliance, Ensuring Facility Policies, Caring for Mentally and Physically Ill People H/I/S: Playing the Piano, Spending Time at the Church, Singing in the Choir EDU: College Coursework CERTS: Registered Nurse, Dekalb Community College (1972) A/A/S: Who's Who Among Women in Business; President, Metropolitan Home Providers Association A/H: National Dean's List
Email: shirley.lee@cwwemail.com
URL: http://www.cambridgewhoswho.com

Theresa Lee
Title: Pastor Company: New Birth International Address: 443 Highland Avenue, Pontiac, MI 48341 United States BUS: Church P/S: Religious Services MA: Regional D/D/R: Focusing on Community, Volunteering at Youth Shelters, Public Speaking, Mentoring H/I/S: Skiing, Bowling, Fishing EDU: Diploma, Kingdom Faith Bible College A/A/S: Heart for Missions; Internationally Restoring Outreach Centers in Nigeria; Building Churches in Africa, Indonesia and the Philippines
Email: globalwoman2001@sbcglobal.net
URL: http://www.cambridgewhoswho.com

Wook Lee
Title: Chief Technology Officer Company: Peconic Partners, LLC Address: 350 Park Avenue, 30th Floor, New York, NY 10022 United States BUS: Investment Company P/S: Investment Advising, Financial Services, Hedge Funds MA: International D/D/R: Managing Budgets for Technology Products, Creating and Implementing Infrastructures, Maintaining the Technological Means for the Company H/I/S: Running EDU: Bachelor's Degree in Computer Information Systems, University of Massachusetts Boston (1997) A/A/S: Institute of Electrical and Electronics Engineers
Email: wlee@peconic.com
URL: http://peconic.com

Deidre Lee-McNeill, Pharm.D
Title: Pharmacist I Company: Wasco State Prison Pharmacy Address: 601 Scofield Avenue, Wasco, CA 93280 United States BUS: Minimum Custody Prison Pharmacy P/S: Pharmaceutical Healthcare Services for the Inmate Population MA: Regional D/D/R: Reviewing Doctors' Orders and Prescriptions, Dispensing Medications, Offering Therapy Treatment, Performing Hospital Services H/I/S: Coin Collecting, Stamp Collecting, Family, Travel, Reading EDU: Doctor of Pharmacy, University of the Pacific (1991); Bachelor of Science in Chemistry 1980 and Biology 1978, California State University at Long Beach
Email: dndleemcneill@aol.com
URL: http://www.cdcr.ca.gov/Visitors/fac_prison_WSP.html

Teresa M. Leezer
Title: Vice President Company: MetaCyte Business Lab, LLC Address: 201 E. Jefferson Street, Louisville, KY 40202 United States BUS: Manufacturing Company P/S: Health and Life Science Business Incubator, Consulting and Assisting Biomedical or Biotech Industries MA: National D/D/R: Marketing, Overseeing Business Development, Raising Venture Capital H/I/S: Running, Hiking, Bicycling EDU: Master of Business Administration, University of Louisville, KY (1989); Bachelor's Degree in Applied Science, University of Louisville, KY (1986) CERTS: Industry-Related Training, Columbia University (2005); Certification in Executive Management, The Wharton School of Business, University of Pennsylvania (2003) A/A/S: Board Member, Ronald McDonald House; Board Member, Louisville Health Information Exchange
Email: tleezer@metacyte.biz
URL: http://www.metacyte.biz

Marsha Leffridge

Title: Respiratory Supervisor **Company:** Community Hospital of San Bernardino **Address:** 1805 Medical Center Drive, San Bernardino, CA 92411 United States **BUS:** Hospital **P/S:** Healthcare **MA:** Local **EXP:** Ms. Leffridge's expertise includes child, respiratory and subacute care. **H/I/S:** Swimming, Fishing, Camping, Watching Movies, Spending Time with her Family, After-School Activities **EDU:** Associate of Science in Health Sciences, California College of Health Sciences **C/VW:** American Lung Association, American Red Cross
Email: marsha.leffridge@chw.edu
URL: http://www.cambridgewhoswho.com

Valarie Legacy

Title: Owner **Company:** Valarie's Vanity **Address:** 345 Miracle Mile, Lebanon, NH 03766 United States **BUS:** Time-Honored Community Beauty Salon **P/S:** Full Array of Cosmetic, Hair, Tanning and Nail Services **MA:** Regional **D/D/R:** Consulting, Offering Nail, Hair, Cosmetic, Skin Care and Tanning Services, Running the Day-to-Day Operations of the Business **H/I/S:** Snowmobiling, Shopping, Traveling **CERTS:** Certification, New England School of Hair Design (1990)
Email: vanity2@earthlink.net
URL: http://www.cambridgewhoswho.com

Nathalie D. Legault

Title: Office Manager, Dental Hygienist **Company:** Gentle Dental Care of Rochester, PC **Address:** 295 Monroe Avenue, Rochester, NY 14607 United States **BUS:** Dental Clinic **P/S:** Dental Care **MA:** Local **EXP:** Ms. Legault's expertise includes dental hygiene and the production of equipment. **D/D/R:** Managing Office Operations, Advertising, Marketing **H/I/S:** Spending Time with her Daughter **EDU:** Master of Public Administration and Healthcare Management, SUNY Brockport; Bachelor's Degree in Healthcare Administration, University of Brockport; Associate Degree in Dental Hygiene, Community College **A/A/S:** Chairwoman, Continuing Education Association; Dental Hygienists of New York, Rochester
Email: nlegault@rochester.rr.com
URL: http://www.cambridgewhoswho.com

William W. Leggett

Title: Fire Chief (Retired) **Company:** Hobgood Volunteer Fire Department **Address:** P.O. Box 374, Hobgood, NC 27843 United States **BUS:** Volunteer Fire Department **P/S:** Emergency Rescue Services, Public Safety **MA:** Regional **D/D/R:** Managing Fire Emergency Services, Educating the Public Regarding Fire Safety Awareness **H/I/S:** Hunting, Fishing **EDU:** College Coursework; High School Education **A/A/S:** Scottish Knights Templar; Freemasonry
Email: fluffone@earthlink.net
URL: http://www.townofhobgood.com/fire%20department.htm; http://www.glenoitfabrics.com

Ms. Nadine C. LeGrand

Title: Entrepreneur, Owner **Company:** N.C. LeGrand LLC **Address:** 926 T Street N.W., Suite A, Washington, DC 20001 United States **BUS:** Beauty and Personal Care Company **P/S:** Selective Information, Products and Services Associated with Beauty and Personal Care **MA:** International **EXP:** Ms. LeGrand's expertise includes beauty culture and business management. **H/I/S:** Reading, Socializing, Listening to Music **CERTS:** Licensed Cosmetologist Manager, States of Maryland and Virginia; Licensed Manager in Beauty Culture **A/A/S:** Cosmetic Index
Email: nadine@nclegrandbeauty.com
Email: nadine.legrand@verizon.net
URL: http://www.nclegrandbeauty.com

James A. Lehmann

Title: Treasurer **Company:** Board of Education, Eastern Local Schools **Address:** 1170 Tile Mill Road, Beaver, OH 45613 United States **BUS:** Public School District **P/S:** School District Financial Operations, $9.5 Million Budget **MA:** Local **D/D/R:** Managing All District Accounting Functions, Budgeting Federal Grants, Supplies, Sports Programs and Student Activities **H/I/S:** Sports Including Baseball **EDU:** Master's Degree in School Finance, Ashland University, Ohio (2002); Bachelor's Degree in Accounting, Bowling Green University (1975) **A/A/S:** Buckeye Association of School Administrators; Legislative Committee, Eastern Local Schools Board of Education; Accountability Committee, Eastern Local Schools Board of Education
Email: jlehmann_ep@scoca-k12.org
URL: http://www.el.k12.oh.us

Mrs. Deborah L. Lehrer

Title: Teacher **Company:** Racine Unified School District **Address:** 2220 Northwestern Avenue, Racine, WI 53404 United States **BUS:** School District **P/S:** Education **MA:** Local **EXP:** Ms. Lehrer's expertise is in early childhood education. **D/D/R:** Teaching, Coaching, Volunteering **H/I/S:** Reading **EDU:** Master of Education in Classroom Guidance and Counseling, Carthage College; Bachelor of Science in Psychology, University of Wisconsin-Parkside **A/A/S:** Parent-Teacher Association; Family Service of Racine; Racine Education Association/Racine Educational Assistants Association; Wisconsin Education Association Council; National Education Association; Phi Lambda Theta **A/H:** Family of the Year Award (1996); Wisconsin PTA Elementary Teacher of the Year Award (1985-1986) **C/VW:** Big Sisters of Greater Racine Inc.; Calvary Memorial Church, Awana Clubs International
Email: debbielehrer@wi.rr.com
URL: http://www.cambridgewhoswho.com

Cynthia L. Leidy

Title: Teacher **Company:** Pennridge School District, P.A. Guth Elementary School **Address:** 601 N. Seventh Street, Perkasie, PA 18944 United States **BUS:** Elementary School **P/S:** Elementary Education **MA:** Perkasie **D/D/R:** Teaching **EDU:** Master's Degree in General Studies, Kutztown University; Bachelor's Degree in Elementary Education and Early Childhood Education, Kutztown University **A/A/S:** National Education Association; TEA; Pennsylvania State Education Association; Who's Who Among American Teachers **C/VW:** American Legion Auxiliary, Church
Email: rcleidy@yahoo.com
URL: http://www.cambridgewhoswho.com

Theresa Leimkuehler

Title: Manager **Company:** Hops **Address:** 1106-2103, Morrison, MO 65061 United States **BUS:** Food Restaurant **P/S:** Dining **MA:** Local **D/D/R:** Managing the Restaurant and Bar **H/I/S:** Grandchildren **A/A/S:** Retired Postman Association
Email: hops@socket.net

Karen Pezza Leith

Title: Associates Director **Company:** Catholic Commission of Summit County **Address:** 795 Russell Avenue, Akron, OH 44307 United States **BUS:** Catholic Charities **P/S:** Education, Advocacy, Charity, Justice **MA:** Local **D/D/R:** Educating the General Public about Justice, War, Peace, Poverty and Criminal Issues **H/I/S:** Reading, Quilting, Needlepointing, Working with Watercolors **EDU:** Ph.D. in Social Psychology, Case Western Reserve University; Master of Science in Experimental Psychology, Case Western Reserve University; Master of Science in Religious Studies, John Carroll University; Bachelor of Arts in Mathematics and Economics, Brown University **A/A/S:** APA; APS **C/VW:** Lounge of Women; Catholic Charities; Save Darfur
Email: kpl7@aol.com

Kerstin Lemaster

Title: Lab Supervisor **Company:** Tri-State Hematology, Oncology **Address:** 617 23rd Street, Ashland, KY 41102 United States **BUS:** Oncology and Hematology Practice **P/S:** Healthcare **MA:** Regional **D/D/R:** Supervising (6) Nurses-Annual Employee Reviews, Sending Labs to Laboratory, Maintaining Accreditation, Responsible for the Operations of (4) Labs, OSHA Compliance. **H/I/S:** I enjoy reading the Medical Lab Observer. **EDU:** Associate Degree in Medical Assisting, Huntington Junior College
Email: lemo9430@windstream.net
URL: http://www.cambridgewhoswho.com

Louiselle L. Lemay

Title: Licensed Nursing Assistant **Company:** Greensboro Nursing Home **Address:** 2706 Orton Road, East Hardwick, VT 05836 United States **BUS:** Nursing Home **P/S:** Excellent Patient Care, Friendly Staff, Recreational Activities, Thirty Beds **MA:** Local **D/D/R:** Caring for and Communicating with Patients **H/I/S:** Cross Stitching, Working on Puzzles, Crafts **EDU:** General Education Diploma (1981) **CERTS:** Certified Nursing Assistant

Rev. Evelyn M. Lemons

Title: Pastor **Company:** Faith United Methodist Church **Address:** P.O. Box 205, Walnut Cove, NC 27052 United States **BUS:** Church **P/S:** Religious Services, Worship, Spiritual Growth, Community Outreach, Christian Fellowship **MA:** Local **D/D/R:** Revival Preaching **H/I/S:** Listening to Music, Reading, Walking, Gardening **EDU:** Master of Science in Agricultural Education, North Carolina State University (1990); Master of Divinity, Duke University (1993); Bachelor of Science in Agricultural Education, North Carolina State University (1987) **A/A/S:** The North Carolina Conference of The United Methodist Church
Email: faithumcpreacher@aol.com
URL: http://www.faithumcws.org

Judith M. Lenart, M.Ed.

Title: Physical Education and Health Teacher **Company:** Tremper High School **Address:** 8560 26th Avenue, Kenosha, WI 53143 United States **BUS:** High School **P/S:** Education **MA:** Regional **D/D/R:** Teaching Health and Physical Education **H/I/S:** Cooking, Canning Homemade Sauces, Biking, Gardening **EDU:** Master of Education, Olivet Nazarene University **A/A/S:** National Education Association; Wisconsin Education Association **C/VW:** Kenosha Human Development Services; Coach, Lincoln Middle School Track and Field
Email: jlenart@kusd.edu
URL: http://www.cambridgewhoswho.com

Jennifer D. Lengyel

Title: Director **Company:** Jay Nolan Community Services **Address:** 1190 S. Bascom Avenue, Suite 240, San Jose, CA 95128 United States **BUS:** Human Support Services Organization **P/S:** Inclusion Services for People with Disabilities **MA:** Statewide **D/D/R:** Supporting Adults to Realize their Dreams, Coordinating Services for Individuals with Development Disabilities Choosing to Live in the Community **H/I/S:** Avid Reader, Watching Football and Basketball, Traveling, Singing, Spending Time with Family **EDU:** Master's Degree in Management and Disability Services, University of San Francisco; Bachelor's Degree in Liberal Arts, California Lutheran University **A/A/S:** Association for Persons with Severe Handicaps; Steering Committee; California Supported Living Network **C/VW:** Local Organizations
Email: jenlen@comcast.net
URL: http://www.jaynolan.org

Lisa A. Leny

Title: Registered Nurse **Company:** Sturgis Hospital **Address:** 916 Myrtle Avenue, Sturgis, MI 49091 United States **BUS:** Hospital **P/S:** Hospital **MA:** Local **D/D/R:** Obstetric Nursing **H/I/S:** Reading, Camping, Spending Time with Family **EDU:** Associate of Science in Nursing, Kellogg Community College **A/A/S:** FFA
Email: angel_03leny@yahoo.com
URL: http://www.cambridgewhoswho.com

Mr. Chad W. Leonard

Title: Sheriff **Company:** Dallas County Sheriff's Office **Address:** 201 N. Nile Kinnick Drive, Adel, IA 50003 United States **BUS:** Law Enforcement Agency **P/S:** Protective Services **MA:** Local **D/D/R:** Protecting the Community, Patrolling, Overseeing Dispatch Team **H/I/S:** Coaching Baseball, Football and Wrestling **A/A/S:** The American Legion; National Rifle Association
Email: clemard@co.dallas.ia.us
URL: http://www.co.dallas.ia.us

Jennifer L. Leone

Title: Administrative Assistant **Company:** Consumer Credit Counseling Service **Address:** 1515 Market Street, Philadelphia, PA 19102 United States **BUS:** Credit Counseling Company **P/S:** Counseling Services for Consumers Who are in Debt and Behind their Mortgage Repayments, Credit Education Programs **MA:** Local **D/D/R:** Assisting the Management Team, Preparing Bank Reconciliation Statements, Generating Reports, Maintaining All Employee Records, Managing Human Resources Payroll, Accounts Payable and Paid Leave Time **H/I/S:** Coaching a Grade School Basketball Team **EDU:** College Coursework
Email: jj20604@msn.com

Jackie R. Leopard

Title: Clinical Educator of PeriOperative Services **Company:** Riverside Community Hospital **Address:** 1308 Cinnabar Avenue, Hemet, CA 92545 United States **BUS:** Hospital **P/S:** Healthcare **MA:** Regional **D/D/R:** Medical-Surgical Nursing, Overseeing Emergency Care, the Pre and Postoperative Unit and the Operating Room, Overseeing Staff Development, Troubleshooting, Assuring Quality Care and Safety Audit, Overseeing Policy Changes **H/I/S:** Scrapbooking, Horseback Riding, Nursing **EDU:** Associate of Science in Nursing, Cypress College; Bachelor of Science in Nursing, University of Phoenix (2004); Master of Science in Nursing, with a Concentration in Education, University of Phoenix (2007) **A/A/S:** Association of periOperative Registered Nurses; Sigma Theta Tau International
Email: jckleopard@yahoo.com
URL: http://www.rchc.org

Shirley J. Leow

Title: Vice President of Clinical Operations and Project Management **Company:** AVI BioPharma **Address:** 4575 S.W. Research Way, Corvallis, OR 97333 United States **BUS:** Pharmaceutical Company **P/S:** Pharmaceuticals, Oncology Research, Development of Novel Drugs **MA:** International **EXP:** Ms. Leow's expertise includes clinical product development and project management. **H/I/S:** Skiing, Photography, Listening to Music, Hiking, Kayaking, Bicycling, Sports **EDU:** Doctorate in Leadership, Franklin Pierce University; Master of Science in Biomedical Science, Western Michigan University **A/A/S:** Healthcare Businesswomen's Association; Scientific Steering Committee; National Institutes of Health **A/H:** W.E. Upjohn Leadership Award, National Science Foundation **C/VW:** St. Jude Children's Research Hospital; Friends of Boston's Homeless; The Nature Conservatory; Kenyon College; American Cancer Society
Email: sleow@earthlink.net
URL: http://www.antisoma.com

Michael M. Lerch

Title: Executive Director **Company:** Community Association Institute **Address:** 2221 W. Baseline Road, Suite 101, Tempe, AZ 85283 United States **BUS:** Nonprofit Educational Resource Company **P/S:** Educational and Networking Resources for Homeowners and Community Associations **MA:** Regional **D/D/R:** Directing Operations, Fundraising, Event Planning **H/I/S:** Outdoor Hiking and Climbing, Reading, Spending Time with his Family **EDU:** Bachelor of Arts in Political Science, University of Arizona **C/VW:** Phoenix Children's Hospital; Phoenix Alumni Board, University of Arizona
Email: mike@cai-az.org
URL: http://www.cai-az.org

Ranae S. Lesink

Title: Swimming Pool Designer **Company:** Anthony & Sylvan Pools **Address:** 2890 E. Tropicana Avenue, Las Vegas, NV 89121 United States **BUS:** Construction Company **P/S:** In-Ground Swimming Pools **MA:** Local **D/D/R:** Designing and Building in-Ground Swimming Pools **H/I/S:** Teaching Ballroom Dancing and Line Dancing, Horseback Riding, Spending Time with her Family **CERTS:** Licensed Life Insurance Agent **A/A/S:** Women in Networking; National Dance Teachers Association **C/VW:** American Caner Society, Humane Society, United Way
Email: rlesink@anthonysylvan.com
URL: http://www.anthonysylvan.com

William J. Leslie

Title: Clinical Research Coordinator **Company:** SNBL Clinical Pharmacology Center **Address:** 800 W. Baltimore Street, Baltimore, MD 21201 United States **BUS:** Pharmaceutical Industry **P/S:** Clinical Pharmacology Research and Phase I, Phase II, Phase III Clinical Trials **MA:** International **D/D/R:** Clinical Research Coordination of Trials **EDU:** Bachelor of Science in Health Science, Towson University
Email: wleslie@snbl-cpc.com
URL: http://www.snbl-cpc.com

Deborah R. Lesser Linder

Title: Life, Health Insurance Expert **Address:** 16 Colonial Drive, Waterford, CT 06385 United States **BUS:** Sales Firm **P/S:** Life and Health Insurance **MA:** Regional **D/D/R:** Working with Clients Mostly for Life Insurance Including Long-Term Care, Medicare, Supplemental and Health-Related **H/I/S:** Writing, Poetry, Cooking, Spending Time with Children **EDU:** JD, Quinnipiac University School of Law (1990) **A/A/S:** Phi Alpha Delta; International Society of Poetry; Local Sisterhood; Who's Who of Poetry
Email: lindyslhagent@sbcglobal.net

Mr. Arnold G. Leto

Title: President **Company:** Integrated Aircraft Services **Address:** 2915 Redhill Avenue, Suite C101, Costa Mesa, CA 92626 United States **BUS:** Aviation Aerospace/Aviation **P/S:** Aircraft Management and Pilot Services, Pilot Related Seminars and Training **MA:** National **D/D/R:** Instruction on Flying, Owner, Care and Maintenance of Individual Planes **H/I/S:** Scuba Diving, Golf **EDU:** Metropolitan State College of Denver, BS-Aviation Technology **A/A/S:** AOPA, MMOPA, NBAA, EAA, COPA
Email: arnie@iaircraftservices.com
URL: www.aircraftservices.com/www.pilotnetwork.com

Meegan K. Letourneau

Title: Office Manager **Company:** Banfield, The Pet Hospital **Address:** 9450 S.E. 82nd Avenue, Portland, OR 97086 United States **BUS:** Full-Service Pet Hospital **P/S:** Pet Healthcare **MA:** Local **D/D/R:** Managing Business Operations, Educating Clients on Managing their Pet's Health, Training Team Members, Scheduling, Managing Customer Service **H/I/S:** Rescuing Animals, Gardening, Crafts **EDU:** Attend Avertt College and Portland Community College **A/A/S:** The American Society for the Prevention of Cruelty to Animals; Best Friends Animal Society; The Humane Society of the United States **C/VW:** Best Friends Animal Society HSUS ASPCA
Email: om0385@banfield.net
Email: meegiescritters@comcast.net
URL: http://www.banfield.net

Mr. Theodore W. Leung

Title: Marketing Manager **Company:** CM Packaging **Address:** 800 Ela Road, Lake Zurich, IL 60047 United States **BUS:** Manufacturing Company **P/S:** Aluminum and Plastic Food Containers **MA:** National **D/D/R:** Marketing, Management **H/I/S:** Spending Time with his Children **EDU:** Master of Business Administration Keller Graduate School of Management, DeVry University **A/A/S:** United Fresh Produce Association; American Bakery Association; American Pie Council **C/VW:** Habitat for Humanity
Email: tleung@cmpackaging.com
URL: http://www.cmpackaging.com

Chanda M. LeVasseur

Title: Executive Services Analyst of Small Claims Support **Company:** Sprint Nextel Corporation **Address:** 2001 Edmund Halley Drive, Reston, VA 20191 United States **BUS:** Telecommunication Company **P/S:** Wireless Services **MA:** International **D/D/R:** Supporting the Legal Team and Senior Executives, Overseeing Projects **H/I/S:** Spending Time at the Church, Spending Time with her Family **EDU:** Bachelor of Arts in Business Administration, Southern New Hampshire University **A/A/S:** Local Committee of Small Claims **A/H:** President Award (2002); Customer Service Award; Quality Award **C/VW:** Local Church; National Breast Cancer Organization
Email: chanda.levasseur@sprint.com
URL: http://www.cambridgewhoswho.com

Debra K. Levens

Title: Global Sourcing Director **Company:** Cummins Power Generation **Address:** 1400 73rd Avenue N.E., Minneapolis, MN 55432 United States **BUS:** Energy Company **P/S:** Power Generation, Energy Supply, Distributed Power **MA:** International **D/D/R:** Figuring Cost Reductions for Internal Customers, In Time Lining For Manufacturers **H/I/S:** Gardening, Reading **EDU:** Bachelor of Arts in Marketing, Concordia University, Saint Paul, Minnesota **CERTS:** Certified Purchase Manager, Institute of Supply Management **A/A/S:** Institute of Supply Management **C/VW:** Local Homeless Shelters
Email: debra.levens@cummins.com
URL: http://www.cummins.com

Mr. Allen J. Levesque, DDS

Title: Dentist, Owner **Company:** The Smile Shapers **Address:** 3959 Telegraph Road, Ventura, CA 93003 United States **BUS:** Private Dental Practice **P/S:** Cosmetic and Family Dentistry **MA:** Local **D/D/R:** Performing Cosmetic, General and Family Dentistry **H/I/S:** Tennis, Snow Skiing, Vacationing in Hawaii **EDU:** Doctor of Dental Surgery, University of California, Los Angeles; Bachelor of Biology, Pre-Dentistry, Long Beach University **A/A/S:** American Dental Association; California Dental Association; Santa Barbara-Ventura County Dental Society; American Academy of Cosmetic Dentistry
Email: info@thesmileshapers.com
URL: http://www.thesmileshapers.com

Jason W. Levin

Title: Publisher, Chief Executive Officer **Company:** Steps for Recovery, Inc **Address:** 15130 Ventura Boulevard, Unit 300, Sherman Oaks, CA 91403 United States **BUS:** Nonprofit Publishing **P/S:** Recovery Lifestyle Newspaper **MA:** National **EXP:** Mr. Levin's expertise is in media-based communication. **A/A/S:** Board of Alcoholics and Chemical Dependency, National Council of Alcoholism and Drug Dependency
Email: mail@steps4recovery.org
URL: www.steps4recovery.org

Georgine J. Levine

Title: Chief Executive Officer **Company:** Southern Lakes Credit Union **Address:** 3000 80th Street, Kenosha, WI 53142 United States **BUS:** Bank **P/S:** Banking Services **MA:** Southeast Wisconsin **D/D/R:** Overseeing Operations, Administrative Duties, New Products and Services, Budgeting, Planning and Managing Employees **H/I/S:** Traveling, Reading, Walking **EDU:** Coursework in Business, Alverno College, WI **A/A/S:** Wisconsin Credit Union League; Credit Union Executive Society; Board Member, Milwaukee Credit Bureau **C/VW:** Goodfellows; The Giving Tree
Email: levine@southernlakescu.org
URL: http://www.southernlakescu.com

Marge Levine

Title: Painter, Free Lance Artist **Company:** Self-Employed **Address:** 108 Wesley Avenue, Atlantic Highlands, NJ 07716 United States **BUS:** Art **P/S:** Quality Pastel Painting **MA:** National **D/D/R:** Painting Landscapes in Pastel, Working with Four Galleries to Showcase her Art, Working Full Time in Studio, Entering National Art Shows, Teaching through Private Gallery, Workshops and Giving Demos **H/I/S:** Painting Outdoors **EDU:** Associate of Arts in Textile Designs, Fashion Institute of Technology and Design, New York (1956) **A/A/S:** International Society of Pastel Artists; Signature Member and Scholarship Winner, Pastel Painters Society of Cape Cod; Pastel Society of America; Degas Pastel Society; Plain Art Painters of the Jersey Coast; American Impressionist Society; International Landscape Painters Society; Illustrator of Several Books Including The Menorah, Life Birds, The Big Troll Book; Featured, American Artist Magazine; Featured, International Artist Magazine **A/H:** Recipient, Six Honorable Mentions in Shows' Recipient, Two Honorable Mentions, American Impressionist Society
Email: artmarge1@gmail.com
URL: http://www.mlevine.artspan.com

Avi Levy

Title: President **Company:** Saunders Interiors, Inc **Address:** 227 E. Main Street, Pullman, WA 99163 United States **BUS:** Construction Architecture/Design **P/S:** New Construction, Remodeling of Individual Homes or Large/Small Commercial Enterprises **MA:** Regional **D/D/R:** Specializing in the Fabrication of Solid Surfaces **H/I/S:** Skiing, Golf **EDU:** Master of Education **A/A/S:** North West Home Builders, Spokane Builders Association, ISFA, WFCA, NTCA
Email: avi@saundersinterior.com
URL: www.saundersinteriors.com

Stacia A. Levy, Ed.D.

Title: College Professor **Company:** 1.) University of California at Davis, 2.) University of the Pacific **Address:** 1 Shields Avenue, Davis, CA 95616 United States **BUS:** University **P/S:** Education, Undergraduate and Graduate Studies, Research, Libraries, International Programs, Teaching Resources, Arts and Culture, Athletics, Recreation, Student Organizations **MA:** Local **D/D/R:** Teaching English as a Second Language, Linguistic Studies and Writing, Educating Cultural Diversity, Writing, Lecturing **H/I/S:** Writing, Traveling, Dining Out **EDU:** Doctor of Education, University of the Pacific (2003) **A/A/S:** American Association for Applied Linguistics; Teachers of English to Speakers of Other Languages; National Association for Bilingual Education
Email: callmesal@msn.com
URL: http://www.ucdavis.edu

Andrea R. Lewis, BFA, MA

Title: Executive Director **Company:** The Dairy Barn Arts Center **Address:** 8000 Dairy Lane, Athens, OH 45701 United States **BUS:** Art/Cultural Organization **P/S:** Exhibitions, Educational Programming **MA:** Local **D/D/R:** Educational Programming, Event Planning, Fundraising, Management, Giving Classes, Overseeing Staff of Seven, Former Manager of a Biotech Company **H/I/S:** Cooking **EDU:** Bachelor of Fine Arts, Ohio University (1997); Master of Arts in Art History (2007) **A/A/S:** Farm Bureau Member; Rotary Club; Americans for the Arts; Visitors Center Board of Directors; AAOM
Email: andrea@dairybarn.org
URL: http://www.dairybarn.org

C. Preston Lewis, RN, MSN, CCRN

Title: Director of Hospital Education and Employee Development **Company:** Pikeville Medical Center **Address:** 911 Bypass Road, Pikeville, KY 41501 United States **BUS:** Premier Medical Center **P/S:** 16 Intensive Care Unit Beds, 16 Operating Suites, 40-bed Inpatient Rehabilitation Hospital and 1,300 Employees, Neurosurgery, Heart Institute with Philips Allura Interventional Catheterization Labs, Family Practice Clinic, Home Health, Medical Detoxification Unit, MedFlight of East Kentucky, Sleep Disorders Clinic, The Birth Place, Pediatric Transitional Care Unit, PET Scanning, State of the Art Diagnostic Department **MA:** Regional **D/D/R:** Ensuring Professional Employee Development and Nursing Education, Managing the Hospital's Leadership Training for Middle and Higher Managers and Supervisory Staff, Overseeing Program Curriculum and Organizational Development, Promoting Continuing Education, Coordinating All Education Affiliation Agreements with the Hospital, Developing and Coordinating Department Specific Orientation Training Programs and Leadership Programs for Hospital, Offering Nursing Administration **H/I/S:** Attending Church Regularly **EDU:** Master of Science in Nursing in Advanced Practice, Eastern Kentucky University (2004) **A/A/S:** American Association of Critical Care Nursing; Nursing National Staff Development Organization; Sigma Theta Tau
Email: preston.lewis@pikevillehospital.org
URL: http://www.pikevillehospital.org

Edythe G. Lewis, LPN

Title: Licensed Practical Nurse **Company:** Preferred Home Care **Address:** P.O. Box 42031, Philadelphia, PA 19101 United States **BUS:** Leader in Healthcare **P/S:** Nursing, Healthcare Services, Pediatric Services **MA:** Regional **EXP:** Ms. Lewis' expertise includes pediatrics, the in-home program of skilled visit nursing and private duty for disabled children. **H/I/S:** Collecting Basketball, Football and Baseball Cards, Playing Tennis **CERTS:** Licensed Practical Nurse Degree (1970) **A/A/S:** President, Willing Workers Club; Saint John's Catholic Church **A/H:** Employee of the Year Award (1998)
URL: http://www.cambridgewhoswho.com

Jo Elaine Lewis

Title: Director **Company:** Gila County Traffic Survival School **Address:** P.O. Box 1692, Claypool, AZ 85532 United States **BUS:** Traffic School **P/S:** Driving Education for People from 14 to 85-Years-Old **MA:** Regional **D/D/R:** Managing Operations, Teaching Eight-Hour Driving Classes, Instructing Defensive Driving Course, Managing School Facilities, Bookkeeping, Overseeing Accounts Payable **H/I/S:** Photography, Traveling, Reading **EDU:** General Equivalency Diploma (1990) **CERTS:** Certified Driving Instructor, Arizona Department of Education, Arizona Supreme Court **A/A/S:** Landmark Forum
Email: elewis36@hotmail.com
URL: http://www.cambridgewhoswho.com

Lori M. Lewis
Title: President, Chief Executive Officer **Company:** Lewis & Lewis Painting, Inc. **Address:** 658 N. Ridgewood Avenue, Ormond Beach, FL 32174 United States **BUS:** Residential, New Construction and Commercial Painting Company **P/S:** Painting, Waterproofing, Faux Finishing, Chattahoochee Decks **MA:** Flagler and Volusia County **EXP:** Ms. Lewis' expertise includes corporate management and business intensification. **H/I/S:** Spending Time with her Family, Beautifying her Neighborhood, Keeping Fit **EDU:** Diploma, Bald Eagle Nittany High School **A/A/S:** Volusia Home Builders Association; Florida Home Builders Association; National Association of Home Builders; Better Business Bureau; Dun & Bradstreet
Email: lewis_painting@yahoo.com
URL: http://www.cambridgewhoswho.com
URL: http://www.lewisandlewispaintinginc.com

Mary L. Lewis
Title: Director of Nursing **Company:** Palm Beach Shores **Address:** 1101 54th Street, West Palm Beach, FL 33407 United States **BUS:** Nursing and Sub-Acute Center **P/S:** Healthcare **MA:** Local **EXP:** Ms. Lewis' expertise is in nursing. **EDU:** Pursuing Master's Degree in Nursing, University of Phoenix; Bachelor of Science in Nursing, University of Phoenix **A/A/S:** Director, Nursing Association; Student Nursing Association
Email: marylew65@yahoo.com
URL: http://www.cambridgewhoswho.com

Stephanie J. Lewis
Title: MS OTR/L **Company:** Independent Contract Work **Address:** 2110 Fourth Street N.E., Jamestown, ND 58401 United States **BUS:** Healthcare Service Provider **P/S:** Occupational Therapy **MA:** Local **D/D/R:** Holistic Approach to OT Practicing on a Broadscope and Ability to Help Patients in all Settings, Versatility is a Specialty **H/I/S:** Travel, Outdoorsman, Hiking, Volleyball and Swimming **EDU:** University of Mary Bismark North Dakota, MS in OT **A/A/S:** AOTA
Email: SJohnsonOTR@hotmail.com

Valerie M. Lewis
Title: Teacher **Company:** Ps 29 Melrose School **Address:** 758 Courtlandt Avenue, Bronx, NY 10451 United States **BUS:** Public School **P/S:** Education **MA:** Local **D/D/R:** Teaching Reading for Fifth through Seventh-Grade Students **H/I/S:** Traveling, Shopping, Participating in Church Activities **EDU:** Master of Education, The City College of New York **C/VW:** Child's Memorial Temple; Church of God in Christ
Email: valeriem.lewis@cwwemail.com

Mattie A. Lewis-Bynum
Title: Director of Sales **Address:** 5500 Tuxedo Road, Tuxedo, MD 20170 United States **BUS:** Tourism Transportation Services/Logistics **P/S:** Transportation, Client Services, Responsible for Team of 6 **MA:** Local **D/D/R:** Sales/Marketing **H/I/S:** Reading, Friends **EDU:** Eastern Illinois University, BS-Computer Science and Personnel Management, Master's Degree in Business Administration **A/A/S:** National Black MBA Association

Alla Leybinsky
Title: Paralegal **Company:** Mega Consulting, LLC **Address:** 2377 E. 18th Street, Brooklyn, NY 11279 United States **BUS:** Paralegal Firm **P/S:** Paralegal Services **MA:** Regional **D/D/R:** Overseeing Disability in Social Security, Uncontested Divorces and Immigration **EDU:** Master's Degree in Special Education, Touro College (2004); Master's Degree in Social Work, Earned in Russia (2000)
Email: allaleybinsky@netzero.com

Dr. Qing-Shan Li
Title: Principal Scientist, Research and Development Manager **Company:** OxThera, Inc. **Address:** 13709 Progress Boulevard, Alachua, FL 32615 United States **BUS:** Biopharmaceutical Company **P/S:** Enzyme and Bacteria Drugs **MA:** International **EXP:** Dr. Li's expertise includes recombinant protein production, preformulation and oral enzyme drug formulation. **H/I/S:** Traveling **EDU:** Ph.D., East-China University of Science and Technology **A/A/S:** American Society of Chemistry; American Association of Pharmaceutical Scientists; Japanese Society for Agricultural Chemistry; Chinese Association for Biotechnology
Email: qingshan.li@oxthera.com
URL: http://www.oxthera.com

Zhenhua Li
Title: Postdoctoral Scholar **Company:** University of California of Los Angeles, Department of Urology **Address:** P.O. Box 951738, 12-948 Factor, Los Angeles, CA 90095 United States **BUS:** University Pharmaceutical and Cancer Research Department **P/S:** Education, Cancer and Pharmaceutical Research **MA:** National **D/D/R:** Conducting Pharmaceutical Research **H/I/S:** Traveling **EDU:** Ph.D. in Pharmaceuticals, China Pharmaceutical University **A/A/S:** American Association for Cancer Research; American Association of Pharmaceutical Scientists
Email: nkuzhli@hotmail.com
URL: http://www.cambridgewhoswho.com

Jill Libman
Title: Senior Associate Broker **Company:** Douglas Elliman Prudential **Address:** 75 E. End Avenue, Apartment 5G, New York, NY 10028 United States **BUS:** Real Estate Broker **P/S:** Residential and Commercial Sales **MA:** National **EXP:** Ms. Libman's expertise is in residential sales. **H/I/S:** Skiing, The Arts, Theater, Cooking, Entertainment (Hostess) **EDU:** Bachelor of Art in Education, University of Michigan, Master's in Education **CERTS:** Certified, Real Estate Institute of New York **A/A/S:** President's Circle, NNAA, RBNY
Email: jlibman@elliman.com

Rebekah E. Lichenstein
Title: Regional Clinical Research Associate **Company:** RPS Research Pharmaceuticals Services **Address:** 3424 52nd Avenue, N.E., Tacoma, WA 98422 **BUS:** Pharmaceuticals **P/S:** Cardiovascular, Psychiatric, Oncology and Pain Medications Research **MA:** International **D/D/R:** Overseeing Conduct of Clinical Trials at Research Facilities, Hospitals and Private Health Organizations, Analyzing Data and Documentation **H/I/S:** Outdoor Activities, Running, Sailing, Spending Time with her Rottweilers **EDU:** Bachelor of Science Degree in Biology, University Houston (1993); Coursework Studied at Sam Houston Certified Research Monitor **CERTS:** Certified Marine Naturalist in Washington State **A/A/S:** Association of Clinical Research Professionals; Member, Sierra Club
Email: rebekah.lichenstein@astrazeneca.com
URL: http://www.astrazeneca.com
URL: www.rpsweb.com

R. Michael Liddy
Title: Owner **Company:** Geauga Rebuilders **Address:** 10815 Clark Road, Chardon, OH 44024 United States **BUS:** Mechanical Rebuilding Shop **P/S:** Repair, Replacement and Service of Automobile Parts, Rebuilding Starters, Alternators and Generators **MA:** Local **D/D/R:** Servicing Starters, Generators and Alternators for All Types of Automobiles and Industrial Equipments **H/I/S:** Stock Car Racing **EDU:** Coursework, The Ohio State University; Diploma, Kirtland High School **A/A/S:** Veterans of Foreign Wars **C/VW:** Jerry's Kids
Email: michael.liddy@cwwemail.com

David Liebowitz
Title: Chief Science Officer **Company:** Vivaldi Bioscience **Address:** 1790 Marina Way, San Jose, CA 95125 United States **BUS:** Biomedical Products Manufacturers **P/S:** Influenza Vaccine **MA:** Local **D/D/R:** Overseeing All Scientific Functions, Framing Marketing Strategies, Financing **H/I/S:** Fly Fishing, Motorcycling **EDU:** MD in Hematology, University of Chicago; Ph.D. in Virology, University of Chicago **A/A/S:** American Society of Hematology, Clinical Oncology, Microbiology; American Society of Advancement of Science
Email: liebowitzd@mac.com

Linda K. Liew
Title: Chief Operating Officer **Company:** AOSS Medical Supply, Inc. **Address:** 4971 Central Avenue, Monroe, LA 71203 United States **BUS:** Distribution Company **P/S:** Medical and Disposable Equipment **MA:** International **D/D/R:** Managing Operations, Motivating People **H/I/S:** Gardening, Dancing, Artwork, Spending Time with her Family **EDU:** Associate of Arts, The University of Louisiana, Monroe **C/VW:** Twin City Ballet; ARCO
Email: lpruettaoss@aol.com
URL: http://www.aossmedical.com

Nina M. Lightfoot
Title: Senior Healthcare Consultant **Company:** Hayes Management Consulting **Dept:** Business Services **Address:** 1320 Centre Street, Suite 402, Newton Center, MA 02459 United States **BUS:** Consulting Firm **P/S:** Consulting Services Including Integrated Healthcare Solutions and Management **MA:** National **EXP:** Ms. Lightfoot's expertise includes the implementation of billing and managing accounts receivable, electronic data exchange and billing claims. **D/D/R:** Overseeing Electronic Billing Services for Primary and Secondary Payers, Implementing the National Provider Identifier for Billing Claims **H/I/S:** Composing Music for Devotional Songs, Preaching, Bowling **EDU:** Coursework in Office Management, Cuyahoga Community College **C/VW:** Deaconess, Messiah International Ministries
Email: n_lightfoot@yahoo.com
URL: http://www.favorstoreonline.com

Michael C. Lill
Title: Director of Blood and Marrow **Company:** Cedars-Sinai Medical Center **Address:** 8700 Beverly Boulevard Room, Unit AC1070, Los Angeles, CA 90048 United States **BUS:** Healthcare **P/S:** Professional in Research and Education of Stem Cell Application **MA:** National **EXP:** Mr. Lill's expertise is in the transplant program including the stem cell of the heart muscle. **H/I/S:** Marshall Arts **EDU:** Australia, UCLA, MBBS **A/A/S:** UCLA (on Faculty)

Christine Dawn Liloia
Title: Mental Health Therapist **Company:** Medallion Care Behavioral Health **Address:** 470 Colfax Avenue, Clifton, NJ 07013 United States **BUS:** Mental Health Center **P/S:** Counseling Services Including Case Management, Conducting Behavioral Health Programs **MA:** Local **D/D/R:** Counseling, Performing Mental Health Therapy **EDU:** Pursuing Master's Degree in Counseling, Fairleigh Dickinson University; Bachelor of Science in Psychology, William Paterson University
Email: chrissyd24@aol.com

Thomas Lim
Title: Director of Planning and Management Systems **Company:** University of Hawaii at Manoa **Dept:** College of Tropical Agriculture & Human Resources **Address:** 3050 Maile Way, Gilmore 215B, Honolulu, HI 96822 United States **BUS:** University **P/S:** Education **MA:** Local **D/D/R:** Academic Planning, Facilities Management **H/I/S:** Track, Volleyball, Cognitive Sciences **EDU:** Master's Degree in Architecture, University of Hawaii **A/A/S:** National Academy of Sciences
Email: limt@cthr.hawaii.edu

Doris K. Limbrick, Ph.D.
Title: Principal **Company:** Acts Christian Academy **Address:** 1034 66th Avenue, Oakland, CA 94621 United States **BUS:** Private School **P/S:** Christian Education for Prekindergarten through Eighth-Grade Students **MA:** Regional **D/D/R:** Overseeing School Functions Including Administration, Disciplinary Action and Building Maintenance, Training Teachers, Organizing Christian Curriculum **H/I/S:** Traveling, Spending Time with Family **EDU:** Ph.D., Sacramento School of Theology; Ordained Minister **A/A/S:** Association of Christian Schools International
Email: drlimbrick@actsfullgospel.org
URL: http://www.actsfullgospel.org/actschristianacademy

Winston T. Lin, Ph.D.
Title: Professor **Company:** The State University of New York at Buffalo **Dept:** School and Management **Address:** 325A Jacobs Management Center, Buffalo, NY 14260 United States **BUS:** Comprehensive and Research-Intensive Public University Dedicated to Academic Excellence **P/S:** Higher Education for Students, Post-Doctorate Students and Visiting Scholars in International Finance, Business Forecasting, IS and Production **MA:** International **D/D/R:** Researching Business Forecasting, Sales, Stock, Foreign Exchange Rates, Multinational Finances and Information Systems, Publishing Papers in Journals, Conducting Evaluations **H/I/S:** Playing Ping Pong, Fishing **EDU:** Ph.D. in Economics, Northwestern University (1976) **A/A/S:** Decision Sciences Institute; American Economic Association; Eastern Finance Association; American Mathematical Society; Econometric Society
Email: mgtfewtl@buffalo.edu

Wanda Lee Lind
Title: Chief Executive Officer, Founder **Company:** A Child Remembered, Inc. **Address:** P.O. Box 416, Amherst, OH 44001 United States **BUS:** Nonprofit Organization **P/S:** Social Services Including Child Care **MA:** Regional **EXP:** Ms. Lind's expertise is in social services. **D/D/R:** Overseeing the Food Distribution and Clothing for Underprivileged and Abused Children **H/I/S:** Playing Tennis, Golfing, Reading, Singing, Socializing with People from Diverse Groups **EDU:** Diploma, Admiral King High School **C/VW:** Feed The Children; Easter Seals; Veterans of Foreign Wars
Email: childremembered@yahoo.com
URL: http://www.achildremembered.org

Dr. Beverly J. Linde
Title: Associate Clinical Professor **Company:** Indiana University School of Nursing **Address:** 1111 Middle Drive, Office 419, Indianapolis, IN 46202 United States **BUS:** Indiana's Urban Research and Academic Health Sciences Campus **P/S:** Distinctive Range of Bachelor's, Master's, Professional and Ph.D. Degrees, Promotion of the Educational, Cultural and Economic Development of Central Indiana and Beyond through Innovative Collaborations, External Partnerships and a Strong Commitment to Diversity **MA:** International **D/D/R:** Emergency Room Nursing, Teaching Freshmen Pre-Nursing and Sophomores Introduction to the Discipline, Teaching History of Nursing, Mathematics, Mentor to Honor Students, Clinical Specialist in Cardiovascular, Formerly Teaching Clinical, Conducting Research Relating to Characteristics of Students Relating to Diversity, Culture and Service Learning, Legal Consulting **H/I/S:** Crafting, Water Aerobics, Making Cards **EDU:** Ph.D., University of Michigan (1989); Martens Clinical Specialist, University of Michigan (1971) **CERTS:** Certification, TCNN, ASLC, BCLS, ENPC, Cardiovascular Nursing **A/A/S:** Published in 12 to 15 Reference Journals; Emergency Room Nurses Association; Sigma Theta Tau; Member, Midwest Nurses Research Society; Member, National League for Nursing; Emergency Nurses Association; Member, Various Alumni Associations; Presenter at Three Conferences (2006) **A/H:** Recipient, Outstanding Section Leadership Award, Midwest Nurses Research Society
Email: blinde@iupui.edu
URL: http://nursing.iupui.edu

Krystyna M. Lindenmuth, MD

Title: Medical Doctor **Company:** Kaiser Permanente Medical Group, PC **Address:** 10350 E. Dakota Avenue, Denver, CO 80247 United States **BUS:** Medical Center **P/S:** Healthcare **MA:** Local **D/D/R:** Practicing Family Medicine **H/I/S:** Exercising **EDU:** MD **A/A/S:** American Medical Association; American Academy of Family Physicians; Colorado Academy of Family Physicians **C/VW:** Local Charitable Organizations
Email: nolinden@aol.com
URL: http://www.cambridgewhoswho.com

Linda S. Lindquist

Title: President **Company:** Seasonal Rental **Address:** 19233 Tuckaway Court, North Fort Myers, FL 33903 United States **BUS:** Property Management Firm **P/S:** Home Rental Services **MA:** National **EXP:** Ms. Lindquist's expertise is in property management. **D/D/R:** Managing Business Operations, Proposals and Rental Contracts, Computer Coaching for Seniors **H/I/S:** Volunteering, Dancing, Reading, Attending the Theater **EDU:** Bachelor of Arts in Mathematics, Millersville University **CERTS:** Certified Lead Assessor; Certification in Software Process Improvement **A/A/S:** Software Engineering Institute; Board Member, Homeowners Association **A/H:** Chairwoman Award (Five Times) **C/VW:** The Hunger Project; The Pachamama Alliance; Administrator, Good Shepherd United Methodist Church
Email: linda.lindquist@yahoo.com
Email: seasonalrentals@yahoo.com
URL: http://www.cambridgewhoswho.com

Mr. Channing R. Lindsay

Title: Vice President **Company:** Capitol Pacific Mortgage **Dept:** Administration **Address:** 2532 Dupont Drive, Irvine, CA 92612 United States **BUS:** Mortgage Brokerage **P/S:** Strategic Equity, Purchase Transactions, Real Estate Financing **MA:** Southern California **D/D/R:** Purchase Transactions, Overseeing Operations, Managing Partners **H/I/S:** Outdoor Sports, spending time with family and volunteering with community events **EDU:** Bachelor's Degree in Communications and Fine Arts, Loyola Marymount University **A/A/S:** City Events Committee; National Association of Mortgage Brokers; California Association of Mortgage Brokers; CMPS Institute **C/VW:** Children's Hospital of Orange County
Email: clindsay@capitolpacificmtg.com
URL: http://www.capitolpacificmtg.com

SueZane Lindsay

Title: Human Resource Manager **Company:** Oscar Renda Contracting, Inc. **Address:** 522 Benson Lane, Roanoke, TX 76262 United States **BUS:** Construction Company **P/S:** Utilities, Construction, Pipelines **MA:** National **EXP:** Ms. Lindsay's expertise includes public relations, safety, employee benefits, employment law and compliance. **H/I/S:** Spending Time with her Family, Attending her Children's Activities **EDU:** Associate Degree in Business, North Central Texas College **A/A/S:** North Texas Society for Human Resource Management
Email: slindsay@oscarrenda.com
URL: http://www.oscarrenda.com

Deborah L. Lindsey

Title: Registered Nurse **Company:** Wishard Health Services **Address:** 1001 W. 10th Street, Indianapolis, IN 46202 United States **BUS:** Hospital **P/S:** Healthcare **MA:** Local **D/D/R:** Cardiac Intensive Care Nursing, Post-Operative Care, Educating Patients on Treatment Plans **H/I/S:** Reading, Spending Time with her Family **EDU:** Associate Degree in Nursing, Ivy Tech Community College, Indiana **C/VW:** Former Board of Directors Member, Special Olympics; World Vision
Email: 05dlindsey@earthlink.net

Margaret L. Lindsey

Title: Legal Assistant **Company:** The Rex Carr Law Firm, LLC **Address:** 412 Missouri Avenue, East St. Louis, IL 62201 United States **BUS:** Law Firm **P/S:** Experience in the Areas of Personal Injury, Medical Malpractice, Product Liability, Workers' Compensation (IL/MO), Social Security Disability and Criminal Law **MA:** Regional **D/D/R:** Performing Administrative Duties for One Partner and One Associate on a Daily Basis **H/I/S:** Traveling, Camping, Shopping, Skating, Church and Family Activities, Soccer Mom **EDU:** Associate Degree in Legal Studies, Stratford Career Online University (2005) **A/A/S:** Member of West End M.B. Baptist Church; Grant Middle School PTA
Email: missie1107@aol.com
URL: http://www.rexcarr.com

Vanessa W. Ling

Title: Choir Teacher **Company:** Paul Revere Middle School **Address:** 1450 Allenford Avenue, Los Angeles, CA 90049 United States **BUS:** Middle School **P/S:** Secondary Education **MA:** Local **D/D/R:** Overseeing Six Choirs, Coordinating Concerts, Planning Festivals, Teaching Piano, Singing **H/I/S:** Reading, Playing Tennis, Spending Time at the Beach, Traveling, Spending Time with her Friends **EDU:** Bachelor of Arts in Music Education, University of California, Los Angeles (2003) **A/A/S:** Chorus Manager, District Middle School Honor Society; Southern California Vocal Association; The California Association for Music Education; American Choral Directors Association; Music Educators National Conference; Music Teachers National Association; Institute for Advanced Science & Engineering; School Safety Committee, International Development Association **C/VW:** Insight For Living; Harvest Ministry; Campus Crusade for Christ International
Email: msvanessaling@yahoo.com

David J. Link

Title: Neuromodulation Professional, Oncologist **Company:** Codman & Shurtleff, Inc. **Address:** 325 Paramount Drive, Raynham, MA 02767 United States **BUS:** Manufacturing Company **P/S:** Diagnostic and Therapeutic Products Including Pain Management and Neuron Critical Care Products, Implantable Infusion Pumps and Advanced Neuro-Monitoring Systems **MA:** International **EXP:** Mr. Link's expertise is in interventional pain management. **D/D/R:** Promoting Inflatable Infusion Pumps for Chronic Pain and Colon Cancer, Communicating with Pain Surgeons and Surgical Oncologists **H/I/S:** Walking, Biking **EDU:** Bachelor of Science in Marketing, University of Pittsburgh, PA (1990)
Email: dlinks@dpyus.jnj.com
URL: http://www.codman.com

Betty Link-Ettel, MS

Title: Manager, President **Company:** Agri-Service **Address:** 3096 Mount Ridge Road, St. Paul, MN 55113 United States **BUS:** Agriculture and Food Service **P/S:** Agriculture Services **MA:** Regional **D/D/R:** Leasing Properties and Service Contracts on Agricultural Properties, Consultant for all Agricultural Related Questions, Teaching, Extension for Adults at the University of Minnesota, Reading, Writing Lessons for the Extension for Adult Programs on Health, Food and Nutrition **H/I/S:** Reading, Teaching, Fishing **EDU:** Master's Degree in Education, University of Wisconsin (1991)
Email: bralink@juno.com
URL: http://www.agri-service.com

Larry L. Linkogle

Title: Founder, Owner **Company:** Metal Mulisha **Address:** 41720 Calle Cabrillo, Temecula, CA 92592 United States **BUS:** Clothes Apparel Beverages Men's/Women's Clothing **P/S:** Sports Apparel, Freestyle Motorcycle Riding **MA:** International **D/D/R:** Creating Freestyle Motocross Racers, Establishing Companies, Overseeing Innovations **H/I/S:** Motorcycles **EDU:** High School Education
Email: link1488@msn.com
URL: http://www.metalmulishadrink.com

Mrs. Deana Linstead

Title: Teacher **Company:** John L. Prueitt Elementary School **Address:** 600 Griffith Avenue, Wasco, CA 93280 United States **BUS:** Elementary School **P/S:** Primary Education for Students in Kindergarten through Sixth-Grade **MA:** Regional **D/D/R:** Teaching 20 Students in a Self-Contained First Grade Classroom, Mentoring Teachers in the District, Teaching an Extended Day Program, Developing and Managing the Tutoring Program, Writing the School Safety Program, Teaching Reading on a High School Level **H/I/S:** Going to Sea World, Riding Motorcycles and Dirt Bikes, Spending Time with her Children **EDU:** Master of Education, University of La Verne (1995); Bachelor's Degree in Liberal Studies, California State University at Fresno (1989) **CERTS:** CLAD Certification (2007) **A/A/S:** California Teachers Association; 4-H Club **A/H:** Teacher of the Year (1999)
Email: delinstead@wuesd.org
URL: http://www.wuesd.org/schools/prueitt

Kathleen E. Linville

Title: Administrative Technician **Company:** USA TACOM-TARDEC **Address:** 6501 E. 11 Mile Road, Warren, MI 48397 United States **BUS:** Government **P/S:** Army, Technology **MA:** National **D/D/R:** Performing Administrative Duties, Overseeing 100 Engineers and Scientists, Keeping Accurate Record of Employee Hours, Training Staff, Offering Security, Scheduling Travel **H/I/S:** Creating Crafts, Baking **EDU:** Pursuing Bachelor's Degree in Business Management, Baker College; Coursework, Baker College **A/A/S:** American Management Association Publications
Email: kathy.linville@us.army.mil
URL: http://www.cambridgewhoswho.com

Bruce Lioliadis

Title: Owner **Company:** Solar Photonics, LLC **Address:** 2478 S. 15th Place, Milwaukee, WI 53215 United States **BUS:** Information Technology Company **P/S:** Machine Vision Systems Integration, Programming, Lighting, Product Evaluations for Pharmaceutical and Automotive Companies **MA:** National **EXP:** Mr. Lioliadis' expertise is in electronics. **D/D/R:** Working on Computers, Creating Programs, Managing Accounts, Designing Machine Vision Systems **H/I/S:** Riding his Motorcycle and ATV, Listening to Music **CERTS:** Certified Non-Destructive Tester (1985) **A/A/S:** Ocean Spray Cranberries; Catalent Pharma Solutions
Email: blio311@hotmail.com

Amy B. Lipniarski

Title: Owner **Company:** Tea Time Antiques, Gifts and Travel **Address:** 6608 Shawnee Road, North Tonawanda, NY 14120 United States **BUS:** Retail **P/S:** Unique Gifts and Books, Accessories, Antique Furniture and Travel Agent **MA:** Local **EXP:** Ms. Lipniarski's expertise is in customer service. **H/I/S:** Antiquing, Theater, Reading, Travel **CERTS:** Certified Travel Consultant **A/A/S:** AIDS Benefits, Boston Varity Club
Email: teatimeantiques@frontiernet.net
URL: www.dreamscapes.joystar.com

Roger L. Lipscomb Jr.

Title: President, Executive Director **Company:** Ohio Utilities Protection Service **Address:** 4740 Belmont Avenue, Youngstown, OH 44505 United States **BUS:** One Call Service for call before you dig in the state of Ohio, in an ongoing effort to protect the underground infrastructure. **P/S:** Public Safety, Protecting Underground Infrastructure and the Environment, Public Education and Outreach Programs **MA:** Regional **D/D/R:** Acting as a Liaison between Excavators and Operators of Underground Utilities and Facilities, Interfacing with Government Officials, Public Utilities Commission and Trade Organizations on Safety Precautions in Excavating Underground Facilities **EDU:** College Coursework in Electrical Engineering **A/A/S:** Board Member, One-Call Systems International; Board Member, One Calls of America; Common Ground Alliance; Best Practices Committee
Email: rogerL@ohiooonecall.org
URL: http://www.oups.org

Mary Lou Lisic

Title: 1) Business Management Teacher 2) Adjunct Instructor **Company:** 1) Wayne County Schools Career Center 2) Wayne College **Address:** 518 W. Prospect Street, Smithville, OH 44677 United States **BUS:** 1) School District 2) College **P/S:** 2) Education 2) Higher Education **MA:** 1) Regional 2) Regional **D/D/R:** Teaching Vocational Programs to College Students and Technology Education to High School Students, Teaching Entrepreneurship, Business, Law, Economics and Cultural Studies programs **H/I/S:** Spending Time with her Family **EDU:** Bachelor's Degree in Education, The University of Akron, OH (1972); Coursework, Ashland University; Coursework, Kent State University **CERTS:** Certification in Business Management, The Ford Partnership for Advanced Studies **A/H:** Teacher of the Year, Wal-Mart; Teacher Award, Best Buy; Nominee, Ohio Teacher of the Year; Certificate of Commendation, Superintendent of Public, State of Ohio
Email: mlisic@wcscc.org
URL: http://www.wayne-jvs.k12.oh.us

Robert Liszeo

Title: 1) Licensed Massage Therapist 2) Flight Attendant **Company:** United Airlines **Address:** 800 W. Rand Road, Arlington Heights, IL 60004 United States **BUS:** Healthcare **P/S:** Massage Therapy **MA:** Local **D/D/R:** Deep Tissue Work, Stress Relief, Therapeutic Massage **H/I/S:** Traveling **EDU:** Coursework, Center for Therapeutic Massage and Wellness (1999) **A/A/S:** Associated Bodywork and Massage Professionals
Email: massager22@aol.com
URL: http://www.cambridgewhoswho.com

Angela Little

Title: Planner **Company:** National Oilwell Varco, Monoflo **Address:** 10529 Fischer Road, Houston, TX 77041 United States **BUS:** Industrial and Municipal Equipment Company **P/S:** Pumps, Munchers, Grinders, Screens, Packaged Solutions, Macerators, Project Capability, Service Exchange, On-Site Laboratory, Maintenance **MA:** International **D/D/R:** Inside Sales, Giving Quotes, Planning, Bringing Orders Together for Shipping, Customer Service, Handling Work with International Shipping Documents, Inventory, Equipment Attached to Pump and Muncher **H/I/S:** Outdoor Activities, Shopping **EDU:** Associate Degree in Computer Science, North Harris College (2005)
URL: http://www.monoflo.com

Drusilla H. Little

Title: Owner **Company:** Little Family Investments **Address:** 262 W. Elm Street, Rockmart, GA 30153 United States **BUS:** Investment Firm **P/S:** Property and Rental Investment Management **MA:** Local **EXP:** Ms. Little's expertise is in operations management. **H/I/S:** Fishing, Spending Time with her Family, Watersports **A/A/S:** Rockmart Business Alliance; Rockmart Chamber of Commerce
Email: drusillaemail@yahoo.com

Stephen J. Little
Title: Massage Therapist, Owner Company: A Little Massage, Inc. Address: 391 Aragon Avenue, Coral Gables, FL 33134 United States BUS: Massage Therapy P/S: Massage Therapy, Specialized Therapeutic Deep Tissue Massage MA: South Florida D/D/R: Experience since 2002 Performing Specialized Therapeutic Deep Tissue and Thai Medical Massages, Managing Client Referrals, Making House Calls, Physical Therapy H/I/S: Rock Climbing, Skydiving, Scuba Diving, Practicing Martial Arts, fine arts, culinary arts, EDU: Pursuing Doctor of Physical Therapy, University of Miami; Coursework in Massage Therapy, Emphasis in Eastern Modalities, Reidman College CERTS: Certification in Advanced Traditional and Medical Thai Massage (2005); Certification in Advanced Deep Tissue Massage (2003); Certification in Advanced Swedish Massage (2002) A/A/S: National Society of Collegiate Scholars, AKBAN, AMTA
Email: stephen@alittlemassage.com
URL: http://www.alittlemassage.com

Babette J. Littlefield
Title: Catering Director Company: 1) Valparaiso Country Club 2)Old Style Inn Address: 1) 2501 Country Club Road 2) 5 Lincolnway, 1) Valparaiso, IN 46383 2) Valparaiso, IN 46383 BUS: 1) Country Club 2) Inn P/S: 1) Country Club 2) Bar and Restaurant MA: Regional D/D/R: Custom Menu Planning EDU: Coursework in Hospitality and Restaurant Management CERTS: Food Service Certification
Email: puppypaws50@hotmail.com
URL: http://www.cambridgewhoswho.com

Miss Chia Yu Liu
Title: MBA Graduate MA: National D/D/R: Strong Background in Administration, Sales, Marketing, Customer Service, Management, Real Estate, Education, Law and Strong Presentation Skills, Promoting Cultural Diversity, Utilizing her Experience as an Assistant Manager, Running a Property Management Company H/I/S: Reading, sight-seeing, movie theatres, beach, spending quality time with loved ones EDU: Master's Degree in International Business, Summa Cum Laude, Florida Metropolitan University (2006); Bachelor's Degree in Management and Marketing, Queensland University of Technology (2004) A/A/S: Advisory Committee, Master of Business Administration; Former Secretary, Cultural Diversity Advisory Committee; Student Mentor of International Students
Email: L.Chiayu@gmail.com

Xinming Liu
Title: Doctor of Research Company: University of Nebraska Medical Center Address: Department of Pharmacy Science, COP 3026, 986025 Nebraska Medical Center, Omaha, NE 68198 United States BUS: Hospital Medical Facility P/S: Dentistry, Cardiology, Internal and Family Medicine, Pediatrics, Plastic Surgery, Psychiatry, Pulmonary, Critical Care, Sleep and Allergy Medicine, Radiation Oncology, Radiology, Drug Formulations, Pharmacy Services, Rheumatology and Immunology, Transplant Programs, Research and Many Other Services MA: Regional D/D/R: Researching Drug Formulations for Hospital Use and the Curing of Bone Diseases H/I/S: Traveling, Reading EDU: Ph.D. in Organic Chemistry, China (2004) A/A/S: Controlled Release Society; American Association of Pharmacological Scientists
Email: xmliu0618@yahoo.com
URL: http://www.unmc.edu

Lourdes Corbo Livas
Title: Manager, Owner Company: The Livas Apartment Buildings Address: 180 Wood Street, Inverness, IL 60010 United States BUS: Real Estate Agency P/S: Apartment Rentals MA: Local D/D/R: Managing Apartment Buildings and Medical Private Practice of her Husband H/I/S: Ballroom Dancing, Photography, Practicing Aerobics and Pilates EDU: Bachelor of Science in Commerce; Major in Banking and Finance, Southwestern University, Cebu City, Philippines (1973) CERTS: Certified Landlord; Certification in Real Estate and Investing, INVESCO A/A/S: Joy Dance Club of Chicago, Inc.; Philanthropist, Philippino Organizations; Mrs. Philippines Pageant A/H: Hall Of Fame Award
Email: gavelivas@yahoo.com

Jerry L. Livers
Title: Vice President of Annuity Sales Company: AIG American General Life Insurance Company Address: 2929 Allen Parkway, A10-20, Houston, TX 77019 United States BUS: Insurances Company P/S: Annuities, Retirement Planning, Insurance Plans MA: National D/D/R: Managing Sales, Overseeing Operations A/A/S: Board of National Fixed Annuities
Email: jerry_livers@aigag.com
URL: http://www.aigag.com

Rose M. Livingston
Title: Electronic Funds Coordinator Company: State of Delaware Division of Revenue Address: 820 N. French Street, Wilmington, DE 19801 United States BUS: Finance, Tax Collection Agency P/S: Business Taxes MA: Local D/D/R: Withholdings, Payment Verification, Assessments H/I/S: Reading EDU: Bachelor's Degree in Business Management, Wesley College C/VW: Big Brothers Big Sisters
Email: rose.livingston@state.de.us
URL: http://www.revenue.delaware.gov

Kellie A. Liwanag
Title: Nurse Therapist Company: South Beach Psychiatric Center Address: 777 Seaview Avenue, Staten Island, NY 10305 United States BUS: Mental Health Center P/S: Mental Healthcare MA: Statewide D/D/R: Nursing, Giving Patients Daily Injections and Medications, One-on-One Consulting, H/I/S: Shopping, Reading, Caring for her Dog EDU: Associate Degree in Nursing, Union County College, 1993 A/A/S: NYSNA C/VW: Local Charities
Email: kelster71@hotmail.com

Barbara Weaver Lloyd
Title: Senior Vice President, Benefit Consultant Company: Aon Consulting Worldwide Address: 806 Oxford Way, Benicia, CA 94510 United States BUS: Consulting Company P/S: Consulting Services for Employees Compensation, Benefits and Change Management MA: International D/D/R: Offering Benefit Consulting Services, Overseeing Human Resource Functions H/I/S: Skiing, Gardening, Home Renovation, Spending Time with her Daughter EDU: Bachelor of Arts in Mathematics, University of Washington, Seattle (1976); Bachelor of Arts in Physics, University of Washington, Seattle (1976) A/A/S: Local and National Human Resource Benefits Organizations
Email: barbara_weaver_lloyd@aon.com
URL: http://www.aon.com

Rebecca S. Lloyd
Title: Owner Company: Frankly Scarlet Address: 40 W. 25th Street, Gallery 115, New York, NY 10010 United States BUS: Art Gallery P/S: Ethnic Art Pieces MA: International D/D/R: Procuring Unusual African Art H/I/S: Working EDU: College Coursework C/VW: Women's Abuse Center, Albuquerque, New Mexico
Email: frankly.scarlet@att.net
URL: http://www.cambridgewhoswho.com

Phyllis L. Lober
Title: President Company: Learning Educational Study Services Address: 50 Skyline Drive, Coram, NY 11727 United States BUS: Educational Study Skills Company P/S: Educational Materials MA: New York and Florida EXP: Ms. Lober's expertise includes language arts skills and development. H/I/S: Gardening, Reading, Exercising EDU: Master of Science in Educational Administration, Long Island University, C.W. Post Campus; Bachelor of Arts in History and English, Hofstra University A/A/S: New York State English Council; New York State Council for the Social Studies A/H: Awards for Outstanding Teacher (2002); Star Award from Cornell University C/VW: Cinema Arts Center of Huntington, Darfur Organizations
Email: phyllob34@hotmail.com
URL: http://www.cambridgewhoswho.com

Ms. Tina Lochner
Title: Medical Lead Auditor Company: TUV Rheinland of North America, Inc. Dept: Medical Division Address: 3041 Sedgwick Street N.W., Washington, DC 20008 United States BUS: Independent Testing and Assessment Company P/S: Non-Active Medical Devices MA: International D/D/R: Certification, Testing H/I/S: Reading, Studying Art, Listening to Music EDU: Master of Science in Biotechnology, University of Maryland; Bachelor of Science in Biotechnology Engineering, Earned in Hamburg, Germany A/A/S: Phi Kappa Phi
Email: biotinloc@yahoo.com
URL: http://www.us.tuv.com

Jennifer Lockard
Title: Owner Company: Pink Rose Events Address: 3413 Gennene Lane, Fort Washington, MD 20744 United States BUS: Wedding and Event Planning Company P/S: Wedding and Event Planning MA: Tri-State Area D/D/R: Planning Weddings and Events EDU: Associate Degree, Prince George's Community College, Largo, Maryland A/A/S: Association of Bridal Consultants
Email: pinkroseevents@yahoo.com
URL: http://www.pinkroseevents.com

Alice Kay Locklear
Title: Mental Health Director, Clinical Social Worker Therapist Company: Health Care Connections Dept: Self Employed BUS: Hospital P/S: Healthcare Including Mental Health Services MA: Regional D/D/R: Overseeing the Staff and Social Work, Practicing Family, Child, Individual and Group Therapy H/I/S: Creative Writing, Writing Poems EDU: Master of Social Work, East Carolina University A/A/S: The National Association of Social Workers; Alpha Pi
Email: locktazz@embarq.com
URL: http://www.healthcare.com

Jennifer M. Lockwood
Title: Regional Coordinator and Legal Assistant Company: Council of Community Services of New York, Inc. Address: 85 Cannon Street, Poughkeepsie, NY 12603 United States BUS: Nonprofit Organization P/S: Community Technical Assistance MA: New York D/D/R: Legal Services, Membership Support, Marketing, Assisting and Reviewing Grant Applications EDU: Master of Public Administration, Marist College A/A/S: Chamber of Commerce; Chairwoman, Local Programs
Email: jlockwood@ccnys.org
URL: http://www.ccsnys.org

Cheryl A. Lodge
Title: Registered Nurse Company: Exeter Hospital Address: 5 Alumni Drive, Exeter, NH 03833 United States BUS: Hospital P/S: Healthcare MA: National EXP: Ms. Lodge's expertise includes maternal child home visits, neonatal intensive care obstetrics, pediatrics and patient education. H/I/S: Traveling, Dancing, Reading, Spending Time with her Children EDU: Bachelor of Science in Nursing, Saint Anselm College A/A/S: American Nurses Association
Email: csoucy44@verizon.net

Sara Loeppke
Title: Owner Company: The Silver Tulip Address: 5166 Remington Drive, Brentwood, TN 37027 United States BUS: Retail P/S: Selling and Buying Formal Wear MA: Regional D/D/R: Buying and Selling Merchandise, Managing Inventory H/I/S: Running, Reading EDU: Bachelor's Degree in Entrepreneurship, Belmont University (2007) A/A/S: President, Entrepreneur Club, Delta Kappa Epsilon
Email: thesilvertuliponline@gmail.com
URL: http://www.thesilvertuliponline.com

Ms. Cara L. Loeser, CPhT
Title: Sole Owner Company: Pilates by Cara Address: 5122 Likini Street, Suite 307, Honolulu, HI 96818 United States BUS: Physical training for individuals with physical challenges P/S: Fitness instruction for physically challenged individuals MA: Honolulu, Hawaii D/D/R: Pilates, Kickboxing, Step Aerobics all taught on land and/or in water. H/I/S: Ai Chi Aqua Moves, Light-weight Boxing EDU: Coursework in Office Administration CERTS: Fitness and Training Certification Workshops Including USA-YMCA Land and Water Fitness, Aquatic Education Association, Certified 'Client TV Producer/Editor/Camera' by Honolulu Olelo TV A/A/S: American Society of Health-System Pharmacists. C/VW: I regularly contribute to various abuse shelters.
Email: pilatesbycara@yahoo.com
URL: http://tinyurl.com/yt6vq

Kathleen Logan
Title: Pediatric Nurse Practitioner, Lactation Consultant Company: Kaiser Permanente, Washington Hospital Center Address: 1011 N. Capitol Street N.E., Washington, DC 20002 United States BUS: Healthcare Company P/S: Healthcare MA: National D/D/R: Pediatric Nursing, Consulting on Lactation H/I/S: Reading, Practicing Yoga, Dancing Swing, Walking, Running, Boating, Spending Time Outdoors, Going to the Beach, Playing with her Dog, Cooking, Traveling Internationally EDU: Master of Science in Nursing, The Catholic University of America; Bachelor of Science in Nursing, Northeastern University
Email: kathleen.logan@kp.org
URL: http://www.cambridgewhoswho.com

Jeanann Loiacono
Title: Mathematics Teacher Company: Kings Park High School Address: 200 Route 25A, Kings Park, NY 11754 United States BUS: Public High School P/S: Education for Ninth through 12th-Grade Students MA: Regional D/D/R: Teaching Advanced Placement Mathematics Courses Including Pre-Calculus and Trigonometry, Tutoring Students in Science, Instructing Advanced Placement Computer Courses H/I/S: Skiing, Boating EDU: Master's Degree in Mathematics, SUNY Stony Brook University (1982); Bachelor of Science in Mathematics and Economics, SUNY Stony Brook (1978) A/A/S: President, Suffolk County Mathematics Teachers Association; National Council of Teachers of Mathematics A/H: Association of Mathematics Teachers of New York State
Email: jaloiacono@optonline.net
URL: http://www.kpcsd.k12.ny.us

Nathaniel Lokey
Title: Project Manager **Company:** Logistics 2020, Inc **Address:** 9602 Iron Bridge Road, Chesterfield, VA 23832 United States **BUS:** Contractor Government **P/S:** Government Contractor **MA:** Local **D/D/R:** Working as a Budget Analyst **H/I/S:** Golf, Bowling, Working Out **EDU:** Associate Degree in Liberal Arts
Email: finelocke@yahoo.com
URL: www.logistics2020.com

Debra A. Lombard
Title: Energy Engineer **Company:** United Illuminating **Address:** 157 Church Street, Sixth Floor, New Haven, CT 06510 United States **BUS:** Electric Utility Company **P/S:** Public Utility **MA:** Regional **D/D/R:** Promoting the Conservation of Efficient Energy by Offering Financial Incentives to Commercial Users, Front Lines to Architects and Commercial Developers in order to Achieve Optimal Construction Results and Sustainable Design **EDU:** Bachelor of Science Degree in Civil Engineering, Tulane University (1988) **CERTS:** Certified Energy Manager **A/A/S:** Connecticut Green Building Council; Published Several Professional Articles and Co-Authored Two Publications
Email: dlombard@earthlink.net
URL: http://www.uinet.com

Linda S. Lombari
Title: Clinical Social Worker, Clinical Director **Company:** Lighthouse Counseling **Address:** 2520 Virginia Street N.E., Suite 200, Albuquerque, NM 87110 United States **BUS:** Counseling Center **P/S:** Counseling Services for Personality Disorders and Anxiety Patients **MA:** Regional **D/D/R:** Counseling Individuals Including Multiple Personalities Disorder, Trauma and Anxiety Patients, Fundraising, Coordinating Plans **H/I/S:** Watching Movies, Dining Out, Reading, Sewing, Skiing, Spending Time with her Children **EDU:** Master's Degree in Clinical Social Work, California State University, Sacramento (1982); Bachelor's Degree in Mental Health, Metropolitan State College of Denver (1976) **CERTS:** Licensed Independent Social Worker
Email: lcouncili@aol.com
URL: http://www.lighthouseabqnm.com

Elizabeth M. Loncar
Title: Owner, Real Estate Broker **Company:** Best Realty Group, Inc. **Address:** 331 N. Gun Barrel Lane, Gun Barrel City, TX 75156 United States **BUS:** Full-Service Real Estate **P/S:** Resort Properties, Lakefront and Residential Homes, Retirement Homes, Commercial Property **MA:** Regional **D/D/R:** Representing Clients Buying and Selling Residential Properties and Second Homes, Maintains Listings, Arbitrating Property Tax **H/I/S:** Water Skiing, Jet Skiing **CERTS:** Certification in Luxury Home Marketing, The Institute for Luxury Home Marketing **A/A/S:** Texas Association of Realtors; North Texas Real Estate Information Systems; Real Estate Buyer's Agent Council
Email: sethandliz@brgccl.com
URL: http://www.brgccl.com

Roger David London
Title: Chief Medical Officer **Company:** Touchstone Health Inc. **Address:** 185 Wilson Park Drive, Tarrytown, NY 10591 United States **BUS:** Healthcare Center **P/S:** Healthcare **MA:** International **EXP:** Mr. London's expertise includes clinical operations management and business development. **H/I/S:** Gardening, Practicing Martial Arts **EDU:** MD, Mount Sinai Medical Center; Master of Business Administration, Columbia University; Bachelor of Arts in History, Cornell University **A/A/S:** The New York Academy of Medicine; Renal Physicians Association; American College of Physician Executives **C/VW:** National Kidney Foundation; American Heart Association
Email: rlondon@optonline.net

Andrea C. Long
Title: Attorney **Company:** Boone, Beale, Cosby and Long **Address:** 27 N. 17th Street, Richmond, VA 23219 United States **BUS:** Law Attorneys **P/S:** Criminal Domestic Relations, Traffic Defense Law, Personal Injury **MA:** Local **D/D/R:** Offering Legal Services **H/I/S:** Gospel Music **EDU:** Virginia State University, University of Richmond, BA **A/A/S:** Metropolitan Richmond Juvenile and Domestic Relations, Richmond Criminal Bar Association, Old Dominion Bar Association
Email: aclatbbc189@aol.com

Jason M. Long
Title: Owner **Company:** Compu-Pro Communications **Address:** 3905 Sanderson Lane, Texarkana, AR 71854 United States **BUS:** Information Technology Communications Company **P/S:** Telecommunication Services **MA:** Regional **D/D/R:** Working with Fiber Optics and MCBE on Info Structure and Telecommunications Including Home Theater, Car Audio, Web Development, Web Pages and Graphic Design, Creating Software and Hardware **H/I/S:** Creating Custom Computers **CERTS:** Certification in Material Safety Data Sheets; Certification in MCBE; Certification in A+ Hardware Networking
Email: jasonlong818@cableone.net
URL: http://www.compupro-it.net

Joshua Earl Long
Title: Fifth-Grade Science Teacher **Company:** Robert E. Lee Elementary School **Address:** 7415 Brock Road, Spotsylvania, VA 22553 United States **BUS:** Elementary School **P/S:** Education **MA:** Local **D/D/R:** Kindergarten through Fifth-Grade Curriculum, Third and Fifth-Grade Mathematics and Science **H/I/S:** Golfing, Playing Video Games **EDU:** Master of Education in Instruction Curriculum and Technology, George Mason University; Bachelor's Degree in Elementary Education, Bloomsburg University **A/A/S:** National Education Association; Spotsylvania Education Association; International Society for Technology in Education; Virginia Society for Technology in Education **C/VW:** United Way
Email: jelong@es.spotsylvania.k12.va.us
URL: http://www.cambridgewhoswho.com

Marie E. Long
Title: Rancher **Company:** Long Ranch **Address:** P.O. Box 237, Ridgeview, SD 57652 United States **BUS:** Ranch **P/S:** Ranching, Raising Livestock **MA:** Local **EXP:** Ms. Long's expertise is in ranching. **H/I/S:** Gardening, Playing the Guitar and the Piano **A/A/S:** Cheyenne River Sioux Tribe **C/VW:** Local Church; Local Charitable Organizations
Email: marie.long@cwwemail.com
URL: http://www.cambridgewhoswho.com

Robert M. Long
Title: Associate in Research **Company:** Washington State University **Dept:** Institute of Biological Chemistry **Address:** Washington State University, 387 Clark Hall, Pullman, WA 99164 United States **BUS:** University **P/S:** Education **MA:** International **D/D/R:** Conducting Research on Protein Chemistry, Natural-Product Biosynthetic Pathways and Taxol, Studying Mechanisms by which the Yew Tree Produces Taxol, Identifying the Specific Enzymes that the Yew Tree Uses to Facilitate the Production of Taxol and the Genes that Encode those Enzymes **H/I/S:** Photography, Mountaineering, Hiking, Spending Time Outdoors **EDU:** Master's Degree in Biological Chemistry, Washington State University (1999); Bachelor of Science in Geology, Washington State University (1996) **A/A/S:** GSA; Southern Utah Wilderness Alliance **C/VW:** Sierra Club; Center for Biological Diversity
Email: rlong@mail.wsu.edu
URL: http://www.cambridgewhoswho.com

Mr. Steven M. Long
Title: Training Officer, Firefighter, Paramedic, Emergency Management Director **Company:** City of Kaw City **Dept:** Fire Department, Emergency Management **Address:** P.O. Box 30, 900 Morgan Square E., Kaw City, OK 74641 United States **BUS:** Emergency Services Company **P/S:** Fire, Rescue and Medical Emergency Services **MA:** Regional **D/D/R:** Overseeing All Emergency Medical Care, Acting as Training Officer, Working as a Paramedic, Operating Apparatus, Managing Hazardous Materials **H/I/S:** Spending Time with his Family, Playing Fire Department Basketball and Softball **EDU:** Fire Officer I, Oklahoma State University (2007); Firefighter II, Oklahoma State University (2007); Associate of Art, Northern Oklahoma College (1999); Firefighter 1, Oklahoma State University (2000) **CERTS:** Certified Emergency Services Instructor, Oklahoma State University (2006); Registered Paramedic (2006); Certification in Technical Rescue, Oklahoma State University (2002) **A/A/S:** Emergency Management Director; Director, Citizens Corp Council; Community Emergency Response Team; Local Emergency Planning Council; National Association of Emergency Medical Technicians; National Board of Fire Service Professional Qualifications; International Association of Firefighters **C/VW:** MDA, Salvation Army
Email: kawcityoem@yahoo.com

Diana Lynn Longacre
Title: Ultra Sonographer **Company:** Children's Hospital and Research Center Oakland **Address:** 2227 Serrano Way, Pittsburg, CA 94565 United States **BUS:** Children's Hospital **P/S:** Pediatric Healthcare **MA:** Local **D/D/R:** Specializing in Pediatric Ultrasound Imaging **H/I/S:** Reading, Spending Time with her 11-year-old Son, Spending Time at Mountain Lake Almanor **EDU:** Certified Radiologist, Peninsula Hospital at Burlington (1979) **A/A/S:** California Society of Radiologic Technologists; American Society of Radiologic Technologists **C/VW:** Arc, Hospice Thrift Shop
Email: danlongacre@comcast.net
URL: http://www.cambridgewhoswho.com

Glenda M. Longo
Title: National Sales Manager **Company:** Crider, Inc. **Address:** 1 Plant Avenue, Stillmore, GA 30464 United States **BUS:** Food Manufacturing **P/S:** Food Service Distribution and Poultry Reprocessing for Industries Across the United States **MA:** National **EXP:** Ms. Longo's expertise includes schools and USDA commodities. **H/I/S:** Reading, Going to the Beach, Spending Time with her Family **EDU:** Coursework in Business and Psychology, Coastal Carolina Community College and Cape Fear Community College **A/A/S:** American Commodity Distribution Association; School Nutrition Association; People for the Ethical Treatment of Animals; St. Jude Children's Research Hospital; United Way; Victory Junction Gang Camp; Domestic Violence Shelters of Wilmington of North Carolina
Email: glongo@criderinc.com
URL: http://www.cridercorp.com

Christine C. Loomie
Title: Vice President **Company:** Resources Plus Inc **Address:** 3904 Fulton Avenue, Seaford, NY 11783 United States **BUS:** Financial Service Provider **P/S:** Taxes and Paralegal **MA:** Local **EXP:** Ms. Loomie's expertise is in litigation. **H/I/S:** Travel, Sing in Multiple Choirs Including the Seaford Women's Chorale **EDU:** CW Post Long Island University, College of New Rochelle, Master's Degree inEducation, Bachelor of Art-History of Art **CERTS:** Certified Paralegal **A/A/S:** Long Island Paralegal Association
Email: thezloomie_12@msn.com

Jillian T. Lopardo
Company: Merrill Lynch, Pierce, Fenner and Smith **Address:** 59 Roff Street, Staten Island, NY 10304 United States **BUS:** Trading Company **P/S:** Stock Exchange **MA:** International **D/D/R:** Working as a Liaison between Representatives and Customers **H/I/S:** Attending the Theater, Working with Local Community Television Firm **EDU:** Bachelor of Arts in Film Production, Brooklyn College (2002)
Email: jilllopar@aol.com
URL: http://www.cambridgewhoswho.com

Belinda J. Lopes, Ph.D.
Title: Psychologist **Company:** Belinda Jo Lopes, Ph.D. **Address:** 1460 Maria Lane, Suite 310, Walnut Creek, CA 94596 United States **BUS:** Psychological Services **P/S:** Teaching and Supervising Interns, Clinical Psychology, Marriage and Family Therapy for individuals, couples, families, adolescent girls and the elderly. Clinical approaches used are psychodynamic, family systems, solution focused, cognitive-behavioral, narrative therapies and EMDR. **MA:** Regional **D/D/R:** Addictions and recovery; depression and anxiety; marital issues and infidelity; divorce recovery; the treatment of post-traumatic stress disorder with EMDR; issues of aging; stages of cancer survival and treatment; loss and grief; adolescent issues of depression, cutting, peer pressure, drug use, self-esteem, parent-child conflict; caring for elderly parents; work stress; finding your balance between personal and professional life; and spirituality. **H/I/S:** Reading Murder Mysteries, Cycling, Swimming, Rollerblading, Traveling abroad, gardening, playing with my companion dog 'Charlie' and going to the A's games. **EDU:** Ph.D. in Clinical Psychology, California School of Professional Psychology (1996); Master's Degree in Counseling Psychology, St. Mary's College (1987); Bachelor's Degree in General Psychology, University of California at Berkeley (1985) **A/A/S:** American Psychological Association; California Psychological Association; California Association of Marriage and Family Therapists; California Community College Instructors Credential-Psychology; Christ the King Catholic Church
Email: bjlopes28@sbcglobal.net
URL: http://www.cambridgewhoswho.com

Dara J. Lopez
Title: Business Owner **Company:** Paradise Consignment **Address:** 1055 Lakeview Avenue, Dracut, MA 01826 United States **BUS:** Private Company Committed to Excellence in the Consignment Industry **P/S:** Furniture and Home Furnishings, Pick-Up and Delivery Services **MA:** Regional **D/D/R:** Working within Sales, Operations, Management and Administration as well as in Advertising and Customer Service **H/I/S:** Watching Movies Out and at Home **CERTS:** Certified Medical Assistant, University of Massachusetts (2004) **A/A/S:** Published Article in the 'Lowell Sun' on September 28, 2006
Email: paradiseconsignments@comcast.net
URL: http://www.paradiseconsignments.com

Juanita Sema Lopez
Title: General Manager **Company:** Mission Roofing **Address:** 4580 E. Carey Avenue, Las Vegas, NV 89115 United States **BUS:** Roofing Contracting **P/S:** Roofing Installations, Repairs, Contracting, Deck Certifications, Gutters **MA:** Local **EXP:** Ms. Lopez's expertise includes estimates and sales. **H/I/S:** Spending Time with her Family **C/VW:** Fire and Police Department
Email: missionroofing@aol.com

Miriam G. Lopez
Title: Realtor **Company:** Sellstate Achievers Realty, Inc **Address:** 7431 College Parkway, Ft Meyers, FL 33907 United States **BUS:** Real Estate Broker **P/S:** Residential, Executive, Hi End, Beachfront, Golf Homes **MA:** National **EXP:** Ms. Lopez's expertise includes residential, executive, high-end, beachfront homes, waterfront condominiums, townhomes, golf homes, senior and gated communities. **H/I/S:** Cooking **A/A/S:** Florida Association of Realtors, National Association of Realtors
Email: miriamlopez0313@hotmail.com
URL: www.miriamruiz.com

Patricia Lopez
Title: Secretary, Manage **Company:** Dreams Recycling **Address:** 15401 W. California, Kerman, CA 93630 United States **BUS:** Recycling Waste Management/Recycling **P/S:** Plastic and Glass Recycling, Certified Recycler **MA:** Local **D/D/R:** Bookkeeping
Email: patrlop7@aol.com

Sher Lopez
Title: Business Outreach Manager **Company:** Blue Springs Economic Development Corp **Address:** 1600 N.E. Coronado Drive, Suite 221, Blue Springs, MO 64014 United States **BUS:** Community Outreach Nonprofit **P/S:** Business Retention and Expansion, Nonprofit Economic Development **MA:** Local **D/D/R:** Working as a Certified Business Retention Center **H/I/S:** Travel to Mexico **EDU:** Longview Community College, Business Retention and Expansion International, Applied Science Degree, BRE Project Coordinator Designation **A/A/S:** Blue Springs Chamber of Commerce, Partnership with the City of Blue Springs, Kansas City Chamber if Commerce, Kansas City Hispanic Chamber of Commerce, Missouri Economic Council
Email: slopez@bluespringsedc.com
URL: www.bluespringsedc.com

Mercedes Lopez Cabrera
Title: Owner **Company:** Mercedes Tax Services **Address:** 200 W. Expressway 83, Suite I, San Juan, TX 78589 United States **BUS:** Finance Company **P/S:** Financial Services Including Tax Preparation and Accounting **MA:** Regional **D/D/R:** Accounting, Managing Operations, Educating Clients on Taxes, Bookkeeping, Balancing Checks, Overseeing Reports **H/I/S:** Traveling, Hiking, Sight Seeing **EDU:** Coursework in Accounting **A/A/S:** National Federation of Independent Business
Email: cmercedes47@sbcglobal.net

Laura Lopez-Marino
Title: Special Education Teacher **Company:** Plainview-Old Bethpage School District, Old Bethpage Elementary and Middle School **Address:** 1191 Round Swamp Road, Old Bethpage, NY 11804 United States **BUS:** Public School **P/S:** Education **MA:** Local **D/D/R:** Teaching Special Education **H/I/S:** Playing Volleyball, Playing the Violin, Reading, Traveling **EDU:** Master's Degree in Special Education, Adelphi University, 2003 **A/A/S:** Who's Who Among American Teachers, 2006; Phi Beta Kappa
Email: lmlopez680@yahoo.com
URL: http://www.pob.k12.ny.us

Cynthia Loraas
Title: Master Sergeant **Company:** U.S. Army **Address:** 440 Union Street, Sun Prairie, WI 53590 United States **BUS:** Military Organization **P/S:** Defense Services **MA:** National **D/D/R:** Evaluating Locations for the Deployment of Medical Units, Lecturing **EDU:** Pursuing Ph.D.; Master's Degree in Healthcare Management, Lindenwood University, St. Charles, MO (2003) **A/A/S:** American Legion Association; Parents Without Partners; American Association of Tissue Banks; National Association of Emergency Medical Technicians
Email: cindy.loraas@usar.army.mil
Email: cloraas923@yahoo.com

Patricia A. Lorentz
Title: Administrative Assistant **Company:** Haskell Indian Nations University **Dept:** USDOL, Bureau of Indian Affairs **Address:** 155 Indian Avenue, Suite 5028, Lawrence, KS 66046 United States **BUS:** University **P/S:** Higher Education **MA:** National **D/D/R:** Managing Institutional Budgets, Administration, Involvement in Native American Higher Education and Healthcare **H/I/S:** Gardening, Reading **EDU:** Associate of Arts in Political Science and Sociology, Haskell Indian Nations University **A/A/S:** Former Member, Native American Indian Women's Association **C/VW:** Native American-Related Charities
Email: plorentz@haskell.edu
URL: http://www.haskell.edu

Felix A. Lorenz
Title: Minister **Company:** Saint Paul United Church of Christ **Address:** 26550 Cherry Hill Road, Dearborn Heights, MI 48127 United States **BUS:** Church, Ministry **P/S:** Religious Services, Worship, Guidance, Encouragement **MA:** Local **D/D/R:** Preaching **H/I/S:** Gardening **EDU:** Master's Degree in Public Relations, American University, Washington, DC **A/A/S:** Mensa International; Intertel **C/VW:** Habitat for Humanity; Church World Service; Interfaith Group
Email: norfelix@aol.com
URL: http://www.felixlorenz.com

Susan Loring, Ph.D.
Title: Clinical Psychologist **Company:** Loring Psychological Services **Address:** 225 Redfield Parkway, Suite 104, Reno, NV 89509 United States **BUS:** Private Practice **P/S:** Psychological Services and Assessments **MA:** Local **D/D/R:** Dialectical Behavior Therapy and Treatment for Trauma Issues, Making Neuro Psychological Assessments **H/I/S:** Riding and Training Horses **EDU:** Bachelor of Arts in General Psychology, California State University; Master of Arts in Experimental Psychology, California State University; Ph.D., Loma Linda University **A/A/S:** American Psychological Association; Nevada Psychological Association; NAPP **C/VW:** Various Charitable Organizations
Email: drsloring@yahoo.com

Mary M. Lorms
Title: Vice President of Underwriting **Company:** Safe Auto Insurance **Address:** 3883 E. Broad Street, Columbus, OH 43213 United States **BUS:** Insurance Company **P/S:** Auto Insurance **MA:** National **D/D/R:** Insurance Underwriting **H/I/S:** Traveling, Spending Time with her Children and Husband, Boating, Skiing **EDU:** Pursuing Bachelor's Degree in Business Management and Finance, Ohio Dominican University **C/VW:** Various Charitable Organizations, School, Church Activities
Email: mpuskus@safeauto.com

Jessica J. Loscalzo
Title: Severe and Profound Special Education Teacher **Company:** Bethel Board of Education **Address:** 500 Whittlesey Drive, Bethel, CT 06801 United States **BUS:** School District **P/S:** Education **MA:** Local **D/D/R:** Overseeing Five Children on Different Management Plans, Teaching Daily Life Skills Including Feeding, Oral, Motor and Social Skills, Coordinating Therapy-Based Programs **H/I/S:** Exercising, Letterboxing, Hiking, Volunteering, Reading, Writing Poetry **EDU:** Bachelor's Degree in Special Education and Elementary Education **A/A/S:** Connecticut Education Association; Council for Exceptional Children; Connecticut Council on Developmental Disabilities; Phi Delta Kappa; Kappa Delta Pi **A/H:** Rookie Teacher of the Year (2006) **C/VW:** Relay for Life, American Cancer Society; Easter Seals; March of Dimes
Email: loscalzoj@bethel.k12.ct.us

Gen. Bradley M. Lott
Title: President **Company:** True North Logistics **Address:** 3730 Riverview Terrace N., East China, MI 48054 United States **BUS:** Consulting Firm **P/S:** Business Consulting and Training Services **MA:** International **EXP:** Mr. Lott's expertise is in government acquisitions management. **D/D/R:** Business Consulting for Small and Mid-Sized Companies, Working with Companies to Hire Government Contracts, Helping Companies with Access to High Levels with the Government, Lecturing Centered Around Logistics and Contracting with the Federal Government **H/I/S:** Traveling, Boating, Spending Time with his Family **EDU:** Master of Arts in Logistics, National Defense University (1993); Master of Business Administration, University of Southern California (1988) **CERTS:** Certification in National and International Securities, Harvard University **A/A/S:** National Defense Industry Association **C/VW:** United Way; Coast Guard Auxiliary; Boy Scouts of America
Email: admin@truenorthco.com
URL: http://www.truenorthco.com

Randal E. Loubier
Title: Chief Financial Officer **Company:** Crotched Mountain Foundation **Address:** 1 Verney Drive, Greenfield, NH 03047 United States **BUS:** Healthcare **MA:** Regional **D/D/R:** Managing Finances **H/I/S:** Creating Artwork, Oil Painting, Palette Knife Paintings, Painting Landscapes, Exhibiting his Work in Galleries, Snowboarding **EDU:** Master of Business Administration in Finance, Golden Gate University; Bachelor's Degree in Business Administration, University of New Mexico **A/H:** Named 'Best Company to Work for in New Hampshire,' Business NH Magazine (2005) **C/VW:** United Way, State Troopers Association, Local Firefighters Organization
Email: randy.loubier@crotchedmountain.org
URL: http://www.pinktomatoes.com

John William Lough Jr.
Title: Customer Development Manager **Company:** French Meadow Bakery **Address:** 25462 Kalmia Avenue, Moreno Valley, CA 92557 United States **BUS:** Organic Bread **P/S:** Manufacture and Distribution of Organic Breads-Creator of Functional Foods **MA:** National **D/D/R:** Sales, New Customer Development, Gaining Display Space on Retailers Shelves, Advertising and Budgeting **H/I/S:** Football, Basketball **A/A/S:** All Things Organic, Promise Keepers, Union Rescue Mission, Olive Crest
Email: john@frenchmeadow.com
URL: www.frenchmeadowbakery.com

Josephine Louis Foley
Title: Teacher **Company:** Sojourner Truth Middle School **Address:** 116 Hamilton Street, East Orange, NJ 07017 United States **BUS:** Education **P/S:** Middle School for Grades 6-8, Special Education program **MA:** Regional **D/D/R:** Teaching 7th-Grade Earth Science to 80 Students, Mainstreaming Special Education Students in Classes, Has a Background in Physics **H/I/S:** Baseball (Yankees), Music **EDU:** Pursuing Doctorate Degree; Master's Degree, St. Peters College; Bachelor's Degree in Natural Science with an Emphasis in Physics, St. Peters College (2002) **CERTS:** Principal's License for State of New Jersey (2006); Elementary Education Certification, State of New Jersey (2005) **A/A/S:** Kappa Delta Pi Honor Society; Who's Who in High School and College; Pursuing Ph.D. Program
Email: joiejojo21@aol.com

Anthony L. Love
Title: Property Managers **Company:** C+R Properties, Inc **Address:** 2504-16 Avenue East, Palmetto, FL 34221 United States **BUS:** Lodging Management **P/S:** Apartment housing, Rental Company **MA:** National **EXP:** Mr. Love's expertise is in management. **H/I/S:** Listening to Jazz, Bicycling, Exercising **EDU:** Florida A&M University at Tallahassee Florida, BS-Business Management **A/A/S:** Tri-City Association, National Apartment Association, Kappa Alpha Psi
Email: loveaaacd@aol.com

Nadia M. Love
Title: Second-Grade Teacher **Company:** Peter S. Ogden Elementary School, Vancouver School District **Address:** 8100 N.E. 28th Street, Vancouver, WA 98662 United States **BUS:** Elementary School **P/S:** Education **MA:** Local **D/D/R:** Teaching Elementary School, English as a Second Language and Special Education **H/I/S:** Fishing, Reading **EDU:** Master of Education, University of Portland **CERTS:** Certified Cooperating Teacher, University of Portland **A/A/S:** Kappa Delta Pi
Email: nadialove@comcast.net
URL: http://www.cambridgewhoswho.com

Sheryl D. Love-Johnson
Title: President **Company:** Extraordinary Gifts & Beyond **Address:** P.O. Box 387, New York, NY 10150 United States **BUS:** Retail Store **P/S:** Stationary Items, Kosher Baskets, Bridal Party Gifts, Aromatherapy, Baby and Pet Products **MA:** International **EXP:** Ms. Love-Johnson's expertise includes the creation of unique gift baskets and products for weddings, bridal parties and babies. **D/D/R:** Selling Pet Products **H/I/S:** Cooking, Biking, Photography, Working on Computers **EDU:** High School Education **CERTS:** Licensed Notary Public **A/A/S:** National Notary Association
Email: sheryl@gift-extras.com
Email: info@gift-extras.com
URL: http://www.gift-extras.com

Plez Lovelady Jr., Ph.D.
Title: Senior Pastor **Company:** Southside Baptist **Address:** 39064 CR 16, Elkhart, IN 46515 United States **BUS:** Religious Religion/Spiritual Services **P/S:** Church, Education **MA:** National **D/D/R:** Teaching, Motivating, Author **EDU:** Freelandia University, 4 Doctorates, Ph.D.-Human Resources **A/A/S:** NAPMF of America, AAAS
Email: pllovela@aol.com

Cheryl L. Lovell
Title: Administrator, Chief Operations Officer **Company:** Cascade Occupational Medicine **Address:** 4000 Kruse Way Place, Lake Oswego, OR 97035 United States **BUS:** Compensation **P/S:** Preventative Healthcare and Care for Injured Workers **MA:** Portland Metropolitan Area, Central Oregon **EXP:** Ms Lovell's expertise includes operations management, business development and finance. **H/I/S:** Spending Time with her Family **EDU:** Bachelor of Business Administration with an Emphasis on Healthcare Administration, Webster University **A/A/S:** American College of Occupational Medicine; National Association for Home Care and Hospice; National Association of Health Professionals **C/VW:** Portland Rescue Mission, Alzheimer's Association
Email: lovell@cascadeoccmed.com
URL: http://www.cambridgewhoswho.com

Laura E. Lovett
Title: Regional Care Manager **Company:** Neighborhood Health Plan **Address:** Summer Street, Boston, MA 02110 United States **BUS:** Managed Care Organization **P/S:** Health Insurance **MA:** Regional **D/D/R:** Managing Patient Care, Reviewing Individual Cases, Advising Patients, Explaining Benefits and Procedures, Assisting Patients with Accessing Benefits **H/I/S:** Singing in Renaissance Fairs **EDU:** Bachelor of Science in Nursing, Russel Sage College, Troy, New York (2001) **A/A/S:** The American Legion; Disabled American Veterans; Sigma Theta Tau International
Email: laura_lovett@nhp.org
URL: http://www.nhp.org

Josephine Chu Low, RN, BSN, CLRN
Title: Registered Nurse **Company:** Cardiovascular Surgery Clinic, PLLC **Address:** 2695 Halle Parkway, Collierville, TN 38017 United States **BUS:** Leader in the Healthcare Industry **P/S:** Variety of Quality Healthcare Services Including Cardiovascular and Thoracic Surgery **MA:** Local **D/D/R:** Cardiothoracic, Assisting in Office and Clinic, Calling Patients for Review, Assisting in Surgery, Lung Resections, Vascular Bypasses, Ventricular Devices **H/I/S:** Football, Playing Piano **EDU:** Bachelor of Science in Nursing, Registered Nurse Studies, University of Tennessee (1987) **CERTS:** Certified Critical Care Registered Nurse (1994) **A/A/S:** Speaks about Devices for the American Association of Critical Care Nurses
Email: jolow@midsouth.com
URL: http://www.cvsclinic.com

Lozetta E. Lowe
Title: Certified Nursing Assistant **Company:** Galleria Woods, Brookdale Senior Living Community **Address:** 3850 Galleria Woods Drive, Birmingham, AL 35244 United States **BUS:** Senior Living Community **P/S:** Retirement Facility **MA:** Regional **D/D/R:** Caring for Patients, Nursing **H/I/S:** Sewing Children's Clothes, Participating in Various Community Outreach Programs **EDU:** Associate in Physical Therapy, Lawson State Community College **CERTS:** Certified Nursing Assistant, Half Care Nursing Facility; Licensed Cosmetologist **A/A/S:** Deacon, New Pilgrim Baptist Church; Volunteer Chaperone, Ramsey High School Field Trips

Mr. Michael A. Lowis
Title: Fourth-Grade Teacher **Company:** Sachem Central School District at Holbrook **Address:** 245 Union Avenue, Holbrook, NY 11741 United States **BUS:** Proven Leader in Education **P/S:** Instruction and Curriculum **MA:** Regional **D/D/R:** Teaching Mathematics, Social Studies, English, Language Arts, Science and Health Socialization **H/I/S:** Reading, Studying Military-Related Topics **EDU:** Master's Degree in Education, Dowling College (2002) **A/A/S:** Historical Society; Post Commander, American Legion; Kappa Delta Pi; Sports and Scholarships Committee; Who's Who Among American Teachers
Email: att.low@verizon.net
URL: http://www.sachem.edu

John P. Lowry
Title: Proprietor, President **Company:** John P. Lowry and Associates, Inc. **Address:** 2219 Luzerne Avenue, Silver Spring, MD 20910 United States **BUS:** Beverage Broker and Marketing Company **P/S:** Sales and Marketing of Alcoholic Beverages **MA:** National **D/D/R:** Distributing Beverages, Managing Sales, Overseeing the Marketing and Brokerage **H/I/S:** Riding Bikes **EDU:** Bachelor's Degree in Liberal Arts, Bellarmine University (1968)

Mary A. Loyer
Title: President **Company:** Natural Source Printing, Inc. **Address:** 108 Roswell Avenue, Apartment 6, Long Beach, CA 90803 United States **BUS:** Consulting Company **P/S:** Advisory Services on Printing, Packaging and Marketing Materials **MA:** International **D/D/R:** Coordinating All Facets of Business, Lecturing, Managing Operations, Ensuring Customer Satisfaction, Billing, Training, Negotiating Discounts for Large Companies, Troubleshooting, Analyzing Business Strategies, Managing Projects, Consulting for Marketing and Packaging Materials **H/I/S:** Spending Time at the Beach, Painting, Visiting Museums, Traveling, Acting, Watching Movies **EDU:** Coursework, Fullerton University, CA (1997); Coursework, Cyprus College, CA; Diploma, Loara High School, Anaheim, CA (1993) **C/VW:** Carbon Fund
Email: mary.loyer@staples.com
URL: http://www.carbonfund.org

Jaime Alfonzo Lozano
Title: Environmental Professional **Company:** Earth Resource Management, Inc. **Address:** 1829 E. Killen Place, Compton, CA 90221 United States **BUS:** Consulting Company **P/S:** Environmental Consulting Services **MA:** International **D/D/R:** Implementing Business Programs, Regulating Compliance for Solid and Hazardous Waste **H/I/S:** Studying History, Playing Sports, Practicing Judo **EDU:** Bachelor of Science in Political Science and Pre-Law, University of Oklahoma; Coursework in Law, Oklahoma City University School of Law **A/A/S:** Board Chairwoman, South Bay Business Environmental Coalition; Founding Trustee, California Resource Management Training Institute; California Resource Recovery Association **C/VW:** Boys & Girls Clubs of America
Email: jalozano1@ca.rr.com
URL: http://www.sbbec.com

Timothy Lubniewski
Title: President **Company:** Stream-N-Stone, Inc. **Address:** 54 Excelsior Avenue, Staten Island, NY 10309 United States **BUS:** Construction Company **P/S:** Construction Services for In-ground Pool Installation and Design **MA:** NY, NJ, Westchester County **D/D/R:** Installing and Designing in-Ground Pools and Patios **H/I/S:** Playing Baseball, Golfing **EDU:** Bachelor's Degree in Finance and Economics, SUNY Albany (2001) **A/A/S:** Interlocking Concrete Pavement Institute; Northeast Spa and Pool Association
Email: tim@stream-n-stone.com
URL: http://www.stream-n-stone.com

Cristina Lucas
Title: Hedge Fund Accountant **Company:** Opis Fund Services, LLC **Address:** Park 80 E., Third Floor, Saddle Brook, NJ 07663 United States **BUS:** Accounting for Hedge Funds **P/S:** Hedge Fund Accounting **MA:** Administration, Audit, Taxation **EXP:** Ms. Lucas' expertise is in hedge funds. **H/I/S:** Independent Films, Traveling, Reading, Soccer, Basketball **EDU:** Bachelor of Science in Accounting, Lehman College; Master's Degree in Information Science, Indiana University **A/H:** Hispanic Business Group Award
Email: clucas@opisfundservices.com
URL: http://www.opisfundservices.com

Gregory G. Lucas
Title: District Sales Leader **Company:** Frito-Lay, Inc. **Address:** 7170 Industrial Avenue, El Paso, TX 79915 United States **BUS:** Food Production Company **P/S:** Salty Snacks, Micro Snacks **MA:** International **EXP:** Mr. Lucas' expertise is in sales management. **D/D/R:** Utilizing his Leadership Skills **EDU:** College Coursework **A/H:** Top Performing District Sales Leader (2001); Top Performing District Sales Leader (2004); Top Performing District Sales Leader (2007)
Email: greg.lucas@fritolay.com
URL: http://www.cambridgewhoswho.com

Kenneth N. Lucas
Title: STTE Sergeant Major **Company:** United States Marine Corps **Address:** Mag-49 Box 24 NAS JRB, Willow Grace, PA 19090 United States **BUS:** Marine Aircraft Military **P/S:** Supporting and defending the constitution of the USA **MA:** Local **D/D/R:** Working as a Senior Advisor **H/I/S:** Fixing cars **EDU:** High School Graduate, Newark Vocational Technical High School, Taking Online Courses with Granthon University **A/A/S:** Bethel Deliverance International Church, Deliverance Evangelist Center

Debra Ann Lucente, RMC
Title: Office Manager **Company:** Ney Centers For Epilepsy Care **Address:** 45-18 Little Neck Parkway, Little Neck, NY 11362 United States **BUS:** Healthcare Neurology **P/S:** Epilepsy and sleep neurology **MA:** Local **D/D/R:** Managing Business Operations, Billing **H/I/S:** Scrapbooking, Baseball, Football **EDU:** New York Institute of Technology, Computer Science **A/A/S:** Association of Registered Health Care Professional
Email: debmed718@yahoo.com
URL: www.neycenters.com

Gisele Luci-Spencer
Title: Chief Executive Officer **Company:** Best In Shop (Formally Go Shop America, LLC) **Address:** Interlocken Tech Center, 11001 W. 120th Avenue, Suite 400, Broomfield, CO 80021 United States **BUS:** Internet Company **P/S:** Online Advertising **MA:** International **D/D/R:** Comparison Shopping and FCPC Advertising **H/I/S:** Traveling and Sports **EDU:** Bachelor of Arts, English, Santa Clara University; Master's Degree in English, Georgetown University **A/A/S:** Alpha Phi Alpha Sorority
Email: gluci@bestinshop.com
URL: http://www.bestinshop.com

Veronica M. Ludensky
Title: Business Operations Manager **Company:** PAREXEL International, Perceptive Informatics, Inc. **Address:** 900 Chelmsford Street, Lowell, MA 01851 United States **BUS:** Pharmaceuticals, Biotechnology Company **P/S:** Clinical Trail Services for Pharmaceutical Companies **MA:** International **D/D/R:** Offering Technology Solutions for Clinical Trials **H/I/S:** Traveling, Scuba Diving, Cooking **EDU:** Bachelor of Science in Molecular Biology, Boston University (2000)
Email: veronidca.ludensky@perceptive.com
URL: http://www.perceptive.com

Laura Maureen Ludwig
Title: Doctor of Osteopathic Medicine **Company:** Lehigh Valley Hospital and Health Network **Address:** P.O. Box 689, Cedar Crest and I-78, Allentown, PA 18105 United States **BUS:** Hospital **P/S:** Healthcare **MA:** Regional **EXP:** Dr. Ludwig's expertise includes laparoscopic, bariatric and general surgery. **H/I/S:** Drawing, Painting, Playing the Piano **EDU:** Doctor of Osteopathic Medicine, Chicago College of Osteopathic Medicine, Midwestern University (1998) **A/A/S:** American College of Osteopathic Surgeons; Association of Women Surgeons; American Medical Association; American Osteopathic Association; Chicago College of Osteopathic Medicine Alumni Association; American Society for Metabolic and Bariatric Surgery; Society of American Gastrointestinal and Endoscopic Surgeons; Society of Laparoendoscopic Surgeons; Michigan Osteopathic Association
Email: ludwiglaura@hotmail.com
URL: http://www.cambridgewhoswho.com

Carl A. Lueck
Title: Owner, Operator **Company:** Calco Development Company **Address:** 2475 S. W. Third Avenue, Fruitland, ID 83619 United States **BUS:** Real Estate Company **P/S:** Real Estate Investment and Construction Services **MA:** Regional **D/D/R:** Project Management and Planning **H/I/S:** Hunting, Fishing, Camping **EDU:** Pursuing Bachelor's Degree in Computer Science and Business Management, Northern Arizona University
Email: calueckiny@msn.com

Kimberli Luft-Pepelea
Title: Case Manager Supervisor **Company:** Hamilton Center, Inc. **Address:** 620 Eighth Avenue, Terre Haute, IN 47804 United States **BUS:** Community Mental Health Center **P/S:** Healthcare for Mentally Disabled **MA:** Local **D/D/R:** Working with Case Managers, Caring for Clients **H/I/S:** Reading, Cross-Stitching, Spending Time with her Family **EDU:** Master's Degree in Social Work, Indiana University **A/A/S:** Virgo County Homeless Collation; Board Member, People with Disabilities **C/VW:** Lighthouse Mission, The Alzheimer's Association
Email: kpepelea@sbcglobal.net
URL: http://www.cambridgewhoswho.com

Teresa M. Lugo
Title: Unit Leader, Independent Sales Representative **Company:** Avon **Address:** 1324 Graylyn Road, Virginia Beach, VA 23464 United States **BUS:** Cosmetics and Skin Care **P/S:** Cosmetics and Skin Care Products **MA:** Local **D/D/R:** Managing and Leading Sales Representatives, Recruiting, Training, Sales **H/I/S:** Reading, Bowling **EDU:** Three Years of College Coursework **A/A/S:** National Council De la Raze **C/VW:** Relay for Life Committee, American Cancer Society
Email: tere0118@yahoo.com
URL: http://www.youravon.com/tlugo

Ms. Alma Estella Lujan
Title: Hispanic SEPM **Company:** Kirtland Air Force Base **Dept:** Affirmative Employment **Address:** 4279 Hangar Road S.E. Building 1018, Room 112, Kirtland AFB, NM 87117 United States **BUS:** Department of Defense **P/S:** Helicopter Maintenance for the aircraft that train the Combat Rescue Officer Technical Training school (Special Ops), Managing the Hispanic Special Emphasis Program **MA:** International **D/D/R:** Managing the Hispanic Special Emphasis Program **H/I/S:** Vacationing, Window Shopping, Walking **EDU:** Associate of Science in Computer Programming **A/A/S:** Hispanic Round Table de Nuevo México **A/H:** Civilian of the Quarter Award (2007, 2006, 2005, 2000) Employee Recognition Award (1996) Department of Energy Honor Program Scholarship (1982-1984)
Email: estella.lujan@kirtland.af.mil

Pat E. Lum
Title: Millworks Specialist **Company:** Lowes Companies, Inc. **Address:** 75-5611 Hale Kapili Street, Kailua Kona, HI 96740 United States **BUS:** Home Improvement Company **P/S:** Home Improvement Services Including Millworks Supplies **MA:** Regional **D/D/R:** Contacting the Customers to Close the Sales, Explaining and Selling Products, Placing Orders for Windows and Doors, Designing Windows, Tracking Orders, Stocking Shelves **H/I/S:** Home Remodeling, Artwork **EDU:** College Coursework **A/H:** Public Speaking Award; Number One Salesperson Award
Email: lupal009@hawaii.rr.com
URL: http://www.cambridgewhoswho.com

Thomas L. Lumpkin
Title: Manager of Corporate Security **Company:** JM Family Enterprises, Inc. **Dept:** Corporate Security Department **Address:** 1751 Talleyrand Avenue, Jacksonville, FL 32206 United States **BUS:** Distribution Company **P/S:** Toyota Cars **MA:** National **EXP:** Mr. Lumpkin's expertise is in corporate security management. **D/D/R:** Overseeing Security Management of Multiple Corporate Sites of Jacksonville, FL, Including JM Family Enterprises, Inc., Southeast Toyota Distributors, LLC, Southeast Toyota Parts Distribution, LLC, Southeast Toyota Distributors, Southeast Toyota Distributors LLC, Commerce, GA, World Omni Financial Corporation, Mobile, AL **H/I/S:** Golfing, Attending Sporting Events **EDU:** Master's Degree in Business Management, Webster University; Bachelor's Degree, University of North Florida; Associate Degree, Florida Community College, Jacksonville **A/A/S:** Board Member, First Coast Crime Stoppers; City of Jacksonville Retired Employees Association; American Society for Industrial Security **C/VW:** Morocco Shrine Center (2008); Volunteer, Local Charitable Organizations; Youth Automotive Training Center; Deliver the Dream
Email: thomas.lumpkin@jmfamily.com
Email: tlumpkin@bellsouth.net
URL: http://www.jmfamily.com

M. Kathryn Lunday
Title: Owner, Operator **Company:** Lunday Farm and Cattle **Address:** 1710 Lundy Lane, Friendswood, TX 77546 United States **BUS:** Agricultural **P/S:** Cattle Farming **MA:** Regional **D/D/R:** Cattle Farming and Sales **H/I/S:** Collector of Trinkets and Novelties **A/A/S:** YMCA

Shelby-Lynne Lunn
Title: Registered Nurse **Company:** Woodridge Nursing Home **Address:** Berlin, VT 05641 United States **BUS:** Nursing Home **P/S:** Healthcare, Rehabilitation **MA:** Local **D/D/R:** Making Decisions, Planning Patient Care **H/I/S:** Hiking, Swimming, Traveling **CERTS:** Registered Nurse, Vermont Technical College **C/VW:** American Heart Association; Special Olympics
Email: sexybeautiful@msn.com
URL: http://www.cambridgewhoswho.com

Anthony Luparello
Title: Vice President **Company:** Luparello & Sons Lighting **Address:** 84 Toledo Street, Farmingdale, NY 11735 United States **BUS:** Distribution Company **P/S:** Supplying Lighting Services to Office Buildings, Residential High-Risers, Hospitals, Schools, Airport Terminals and Street Lights **MA:** Local **D/D/R:** Managing New Construction Projects Including High-Rise Buildings, Condominiums and Co-Operatives, Estimating Labor Price, Negotiating, Bidding **H/I/S:** Playing Basketball and Ice Hockey, Supporting the Mets and Jets **EDU:** College Coursework **A/A/S:** National Electrical Contractors Association
Email: tony@luparello.com
URL: http://www.luparello.com

Carla J. Lussier
Title: Wedding Consultant and Coordinator, Owner **Company:** Creative Weddings and More, Inc. **Address:** 4553 Poole Street, New Port Richey, FL 34652 United States **BUS:** Wedding Consulting Firm **P/S:** Wedding Planning and Consulting **MA:** Local **D/D/R:** Wedding Consulting and Coordinating, Negotiations, Overseeing Bride Budgets, Overseeing Vendors **H/I/S:** Reading, Writing Poetry, Spending Time with her Dogs **EDU:** Associate of Arts in Paralegal Studies **CERTS:** License in Cosmetology; License and Certified Travel Agent; Certified Wedding Planner **A/A/S:** International Poet Society
Email: carla@creativeweddingandmore.net
URL: http://www.creativeweddingandmore.net
URL: http://www.coordinatorscorner.com; http://www.weddingbeautifulworldwide.com

Dr. Nicholas Lutfi
Title: Assistant Professor of Anatomy **Company:** Nova Southeastern University, Health Professions Division, College of Medical Sciences **Address:** 3200 S. University Drive, Suite 1351, Fort Lauderdale, FL 33328 United States **BUS:** University **P/S:** Higher Education **MA:** International **D/D/R:** Performing Foot and Ankle Surgery, Teaching Anatomy **H/I/S:** Going to the Beach, Yoga, Spinning **EDU:** MD, Barry University, 1997 **A/A/S:** American Association of Anatomists **C/VW:** Who's Who Among American Teachers, 2006
Email: doclutfi1@bellsouth.net

Christine A. Lutz
Title: Teacher **Company:** Oconomowoc Area School District, Greenland Elementary School **Address:** 440 Coolidge Street, Oconomowoc, WI 53066 United States **BUS:** Elementary School **P/S:** Education **MA:** Local **D/D/R:** Teaching Elementary Education in All Subjects **H/I/S:** Traveling, Reading, Walking Dogs **EDU:** Master of Arts in Elementary Education, Aurora University; Bachelor of Science in Education, University of Wisconsin-Whitewater, 1973 **CERTS:** Certification in Safety Education; Certification in All Subjects 1-8, Emphasis in Upper Elementary Education **A/A/S:** National Education Association
Email: choclady@wi.rr.com
URL: http://www.cambridgewhoswho.com

Sam A. Lybarger
Title: Owner **Company:** Safety S.A.M. & Associates **Address:** 1306 W. Craig Road, Suite 200, North Las Vegas, NV 89032 United States **BUS:** Occupational Safety Service **P/S:** Occupational Training and Development, Consulting **MA:** Regional **D/D/R:** Consulting for Small and Middle-Sized Businesses, Offering Occupational Training and Safety to Prevent Accidents **H/I/S:** Football, Basketball **EDU:** Educational Specialist, University of Nevada (1988) **CERTS:** Certified Safety Professional; Professional Expert Witness **A/A/S:** Former Vice President, American Society of Safety Engineers; National Safety Council; National Fire Protection Association
Email: safetysam1@cox.net

Brian J. Lynch
Title: Respiratory Therapy Supervisor **Company:** Children's Specialized Hospital **Address:** 229 King George Road, Warren, NJ 07059 United States **BUS:** Hospital **P/S:** Healthcare Including Respiratory Therapy **MA:** Local **D/D/R:** Supervising Acute Care and Pediatric Rehabilitation Services **H/I/S:** Hiking, Playing the Guitar, Practicing Martial Arts **EDU:** Associate of Applied Science in Respiratory Care, Union County College **CERTS:** Registered Respiratory Therapist **A/A/S:** American Association for Respiratory Care
Email: dperaspirations@optonline.net
URL: http://www.cambridgewhoswho.com

Jennifer J. Lynch
Title: Center Director **Company:** KinderCare Learning Center **Address:** 496 Boston Post Road E., Marlborough, MA 01752 United States **BUS:** Learning Center **P/S:** Early Childhood Education Programs for Infants, Toddlers, Preschool, Prekindergarten and Kindergarten Children, Day Care **MA:** Regional **D/D/R:** Maintaining Quality Control, Managing Finances, Marketing, Supervising Staff and Classrooms, Performing Human Resources Duties **H/I/S:** Running, Gardening, Reading, Art **EDU:** Coursework in Early Childhood Education and Fine Arts, University of Massachusetts Amherst; Coursework in Fine Arts, University of Massachusetts Amherst **A/A/S:** Chamber of Commerce
Email: 301700@klcorp.com
URL: http://www.kindercare.com

Leif Sullivan Lynch
Title: Licensed Massage Therapist **Company:** Complexions **Address:** 811 E. Las Olas, Fort Lauderdale, FL 33301 United States **BUS:** Skin Care, Massage Studio **P/S:** Quality Spa Services **MA:** Local **D/D/R:** Quality Swedish Deep Tissue Massage, Hot Stone Massage, Reflexology **H/I/S:** Acting, Spending Time with his Dog, Watching Movies **EDU:** Bachelor of Fine Arts in Media and Performing Arts, Savannah College of Art and Design, 2003 **CERTS:** Certification, Boulder College of Massage Therapy, 2005 **A/A/S:** American Massage Therapy Association
Email: leiflynch@hotmail.com
URL: http://www.leiflynch.com

Marjorie S. Lynch
Title: District Ombudsman, Manager **Company:** Florida Department of Elder Affairs **Address:** 210 N. Palmetto Avenue, Daytona Beach, FL 32114 United States **BUS:** Government Organization **P/S:** Public Services, Healthcare **MA:** Florida **D/D/R:** Volunteering, Geriatric Nursing **H/I/S:** Traveling, Gardening **EDU:** Master of Science in Healthcare Management and Mental Health Counseling, Long Island University (1998); Bachelor of Science in Nursing (1961) **CERTS:** Registered Nurse, Columbia University **A/A/S:** Florida Nurses Association **C/VW:** Local Charitable Organizations
Email: lynchm@elderaffairs.org
URL: http://www.cambridgewhoswho.com

Crystal D. Lynes, CRCST
Title: Sterile Processing Technician **Company:** Northwest Medical Center Oro Valley **Address:** 1551 E. Tangerine Road, Oro Valley, AZ 85755 United States **BUS:** High Quality Hospital **P/S:** Private Care **MA:** Local **D/D/R:** Operating Room Technician, Teaching and Certifying Operating Room Technicians at Purdue University, Past Experience as a Department Supervisor **H/I/S:** Basketball, Running, Movies **EDU:** Pre Medical Degree, Maricopa University **A/A/S:** I-HCCMM
Email: wtsg@yahoo.com
URL: http://www.nmcorovalley.com

Beverly Lynshue-Chung
Title: Director **Company:** Little Stars Daycare, Inc. **Address:** 24 Whaley Street, Freeport, NY 11520 United States **BUS:** Daycare Serving Local Residents **P/S:** Preschool Education for Toddlers **MA:** Regional **D/D/R:** Running Four Daycare Sites with her Daughter, Overseeing a Staff of 17 People, Planning Trips, Enforcing Rules and Regulations **EDU:** Coursework, Beverly College, Jamaica; Coursework, Gloria Kay School **A/A/S:** Community Outreach
Email: littlestars123@aol.com
URL: http://www.littlestars.com

Victoria Lane Lyon
Title: Principal **Company:** Victoria Lyon Fine Interior Design and Decoration, LLC **Address:** 1140 Stillwater Road, Stamford, CT 06902 United States **BUS:** Interior Design Firm **P/S:** Interior Design and Decoration **MA:** Regional **D/D/R:** Renovating and Constructing High-End Luxury Homes **H/I/S:** Photography, Gardening, Traveling **EDU:** Bachelor of Arts, Smith College **C/VW:** Local Church, Smith College Club
Email: lyoninter@aol.com
URL: http://www.victorialyoninteriordesign.com

Margaret J. Lyons, PE
Title: Director **Company:** RCC Consultants, Inc **Address:** 100 Woodbridge Center Drive, Suite 201, Woodbridge, NJ 07095 United States **BUS:** Engineering **P/S:** Consulting RF Engineering, Public Safety, Communications **MA:** International **EXP:** Ms. Lyons' expertise is in public safety communications. **H/I/S:** Skiing, Baking, Beach **EDU:** Purdue University, BS-Electrical Engineering and Computers **CERTS:** Licensed Professional Engineer in New Jersey, New York, Connecticut, Delaware and Virginia **A/A/S:** Society of Women Engineers Life Member and Fellow, IEEE, Fellow of Radio Club of America, National Society of Professional Engineers, APCO
Email: mlyons@rcc.com

Carolyn J. Lytle
Title: Property Manager **Company:** L&R Management **Address:** 1451 Colqit Road, Apartment 102, Terrell, TX 75160 United States **BUS:** Real Estate Management **P/S:** Rental Apartments and Condominiums **MA:** Local **D/D/R:** Accounting **H/I/S:** Horseback Riding, Watching Soap Operas and 'Deal or No Deal,' Fishing, Visiting her In-Laws **EDU:** Master's Degree in Educational Administration and Supervision, Shenandoah University
Email: sidswife2004@yahoo.com

Jerry A. Maatman
Title: Owner **Company:** Jerry's Junk Hauling **Address:** 720 Ottawa Avenue, Holland, MI 49423 United States **BUS:** Waste, Junk Removal Company **P/S:** Hauling Furniture, Appliances, Equipment, Televisions, Carpets **MA:** Local **D/D/R:** Overseeing Operations of the Business, Customer Service **H/I/S:** Visiting Casinos, Fishing, Bowling **EDU:** High School Education **A/A/S:** VAW **C/VW:** Good Will
Email: dmctaf@juno.com
URL: http://www.cambridgewhoswho.com

Maria Theresa Canete Macalde
Title: Special Education Teacher **Company:** New York City Board of Education, P.S. 286 **Address:** 2525 Haring Street, Brooklyn, NY 11235 United States **BUS:** Board of Education **P/S:** Education **MA:** Regional **D/D/R:** Teaching Students with Special Needs **H/I/S:** Baking **EDU:** Master's Degree in Childhood Education, Touro College; Bachelor of Science in Elementary Education, St. Mary's College, Quezon, Philippines **CERTS:** Pursuing Certification in Special Education; Certification in Childhood Education **A/A/S:** United Federation of Teachers; Association of Filipino Teachers of America; FAME **C/VW:** Philippines Maneki Central Learning Center
Email: mtcmsped@yahoo.com
URL: http://schools.nyc.gov

Marsha J. MacBride
Title: Executive Vice President of Legal and Regulatory Affairs **Company:** National Association of Broadcasters **Address:** 1771 N. Street N.W., Washington, DC 20036 United States **BUS:** Trade Association **P/S:** Communications and Broadcasting **MA:** National **D/D/R:** Specializing in Communications Law and Policies **H/I/S:** Spending Time with her Family, Traveling, Golfing, Reading, Writing, Listening to Music, Biking **EDU:** JD, The George Washington University; Bachelor of Arts in History, Rutgers, The State University of New Jersey **A/A/S:** Bar Association of the District of Columbia; Pennsylvania State Bar Association; Federal Communications Bar Association **C/VW:** Leukemia and Lymphoma Society, Lance Armstrong Foundation
Email: mmacbride@nab.org
Email: marsha.macBride@cwwemail.com
URL: http://www.nab.org

Cecily Macdonald
Title: Owner **Company:** Nautical Adventures **Address:** 7132 Bandera Road, Unit 11, San Antonio, TX 78238 United States **BUS:** Travel Agency **P/S:** Travel Packages, Cruises and Tours **MA:** International **D/D/R:** Arranging Cruise and Tour Packages, Overseeing Operations and Management **H/I/S:** Traveling **EDU:** College Coursework **A/A/S:** Ambassador, Greater San Antonio Chamber of Commerce; Cruise Line International Association, Inc.; The Outside Sales Support Network; The National Association of Commissioned Travel Agents
Email: cecily@nautical-adventures.com
URL: http://www.nautical-adventures.com

Mr. Gregory A.J. MacDougall
Title: Operations Manager **Company:** Florida Environmental Compliance Corporation **Address:** 2418 Silver Star Road, Orlando, FL 32804 United States **BUS:** Multi-Disciplinary Environmental Remediation Company **P/S:** Industrial and Hazardous Waste Management, Site Remediation, Initial Response, Remedial Field Services, Technical and Regulatory Compliance Services, Tank, Hazardous and Non-Hazardous Waste Management, Compliance and Disposal, Environmental Compliance Audits, SARA Title III Compliance Assistance, Tier I and Tier II Reporting, Industrial Water Treatment Systems, Contingency Plan Preparation, Vacuum Truck Services, Lab Packs and Waste Consolidation Storage, Tank Removal, Installation, Service and Maintenance **MA:** International **D/D/R:** Managing Waste Disposal, Transportation and Soil Remediation, Heading Management Information Systems (MIS, CSIT), Overseeing Projects, Estimates and Five People **H/I/S:** Guitar, Piano **EDU:** Diploma, East Providence High School (1978); Pursuing Bachelor's Degree in Electronic Engineering, ITT Technical Institute **A/A/S:** St. Vincent DePaul Society
Email: gmacdougall@feccorporation.com
URL: http://www.feccflorida.com/index.html

Cynthia MacFarland
Title: Owner Company: Cyndi's Luvin Pet & House Care Address: 38 Giralda Walk, Long Beach, CA 90803 United States BUS: Pet Sitting Services P/S: Pet-Sitting MA: Local D/D/R: Running Business Operations H/I/S: Camping, Outdoor Activities, Horseback Riding, Swimming, Reading EDU: Coursework, Junior College A/A/S: Former Member of Long Beach Chamber of Commerce, Ambassador of the 2nd Quarter of June 2001 A/H: Chairwoman for The Month of April of 2001, Awarded The Ambassador of the Year 2002
Email: cyndipetcare@dslextreme.com
URL: http://www.cyndipetcare.com

Karen E. Machado
Title: Resource Specialist Program and Special Services Coordinator Company: Sundale Union Elementary School Address: 13990 Avenue 240, Tulare, CA 93274 United States BUS: Public Elementary School P/S: Education MA: Local D/D/R: Ensuring the Satisfaction that the Needs of all Special Education Children are Met, Overseeing Special Education Paraprofessionals H/I/S: Traveling, Reading, Gardening EDU: Master of Arts Equivalency in Special Education from Fresno Pacific University CERTS: Certified Resource Specialist; Certification Multiple Subjects; Certified in Mild-Moderate Learning Handicapped A/A/S: Kappa Delta Pi
Email: bluewilo56@yahoo.com
URL: http://www.cambridgewhoswho.com

Andrew Macijowsky
Title: Owner Company: Andrew Macijowsky Landscaping Address: RR 3 Box 113, Dalton, PA 18414 United States BUS: Landscaping Company P/S: Paving, Retaining Walls, Planting MA: Local D/D/R: Overseeing Operations of the Company H/I/S: Spending Time on Farms, Gardening, Spending Time with Friends and Family, Reading, Bowling, Going to the Movies EDU: Bachelor of Science in Horticulture, Pennsylvania State University; Bachelor of Science in Landscaping Management, Pennsylvania State University
URL: http://www.cambridgewhoswho.com

Darvi L. Mack
Title: Diversity Manager Company: Weyerhaeuser Address: P.O. Box 9777, Federal Way, WA 98063 United States BUS: Forest Products Manufacturer P/S: Manufacture of Forest Products for Use in Building Materials MA: International D/D/R: Diversity Management-Diversity Outreach, Work Life Strategies and Business Networks H/I/S: Reading, Writing Poetry, Published 2 Poems in National Anthology EDU: City University, South Illinois University, MA in Organizational Development and Leadership, BA in Education A/A/S: SHRM, National Speaker Association, Pacific NW Speakers Association, Training in Cultural Development
Email: darvi.mack@weyerhaeuser.com
URL: www.weyerhaeuser.com

Kevin Mack
Title: United States Army Sgt 1st Class Company: Us Army Address: 2102 N.E. 36th Street, Oklahoma City, OK 73111 United States BUS: Military Military/Defense/Armed Services P/S: Tactical Operation, Train Deploying Soldiers MA: National EXP: Mr. Mack's expertise is in equipment maintenance. H/I/S: Motorcycles EDU: Online School, Criminal Justice A/A/S: Combat Operations Military
Email: kevin.net@usarmy.mail

Susan K. Mack
Title: Branch Administrator Company: Wachovia Securities, LLC Address: 2400 E. Katella Avenue, Unit 1000, Anaheim, CA 92806 United States BUS: Financial Institution P/S: Securities, Investments, Stocks, Bonds MA: International EXP: Ms. Mack's expertise is in administrative management. H/I/S: Sewing EDU: Associate of Arts in Business, San Diego State University C/VW: The Leukemia & Lymphoma Society; American Cancer Society
Email: sewwhatcc@cox.net
URL: http://www.wachovia.com

Karen J. Mackay
Title: National Account Manager Company: Emser Tile Address: 8431 Santa Monica Boulevard, Los Angeles, CA 90069 United States BUS: Leading Supplier of the World's Finest Tile and Natural Stone P/S: Exclusive Programs That Help Dealers, Homebuilders, Commercial Builders, Contractors, Architects And Designers Exceed the Expectations of their Customers, While Keeping Projects on Schedule and within Budget MA: National D/D/R: Working with Branch Sales, Training Sales Representatives, Liaison between Customers and Contractors for 52 Branches Nationwide; Supervising Sales Representatives H/I/S: Surfing, Sailing, Listening to Music, Art EDU: Coursework in Art History, University of Houston (1970) A/A/S: Board of Advisors, Surf Rider Foundation A/H: Former United States Women's Surfing Champion (1977)
Email: karenmackay@emser.com
URL: http://www.emser.com

Rudy M. Mackey
Title: Program Manager Company: Project Home Address: 1401 72nd Avenue, Philadelphia, PA 19126 United States BUS: Nonprofit Outreach Residence P/S: Street Outreach, Supportive Housing, Comprehensive Services Neighborhood-Based Affordable Housing, Economic Development, Environmental Enhancement Programs, Access to Employment Opportunities, Adult and Youth Education, Healthcare MA: Regional D/D/R: Running Day-to-Day Operations, Overseeing Budgets and Reports, Supervising a Staff of 11, Ensuring that Residents Abide by Rules and Regulations, Maintaining an Atmosphere of Therapeutic Recovery H/I/S: Watching and Playing Basketball and Football EDU: Master's Degree in Counseling, Alvernia College (2007); Bachelor of Arts Degree in Behavioral Health Studies, Alvernia College (2002); Associate Degree in Liberal Arts, Philadelphia Community College (2000) A/A/S: American Counseling Association; Volunteer, Advocacy Committee, Shape It
Email: rudymc38@aol.com
URL: http://www.projecthome.org

Barbara E. MacLaughlin
Title: Teacher Company: Earhart Middle School Address: 16775 Orange Lane, Riverside, CA 92503 United States BUS: Middle School P/S: Education MA: Local D/D/R: Teaching Science to Gifted and Eighth-Grade, at-Risk Students H/I/S: Reading, Hiking, Gardening EDU: Doctoral Degree in Leadership, La Sierra University; Master of Education, Francis Marion University, SC (1985); Bachelor of Arts in English, Francis Marion University, SC (1982) A/A/S: Association for Supervision and Curriculum Development; California County Superintendents Educational Services Association; National Science Teachers Association C/VW: United Way
Email: bmaclaughlin@gmail.com
URL: http://www.sciencehawk.com

Paul A. MacLeod
Title: Attorney Company: Barrister and Solicitor Address: 32 Elm Street, Grimsby, INTL L3M1H3 Canada BUS: Attorney Services P/S: Custody, Divorce MA: Local EXP: Mr. MacLeod's expertise is in family law. H/I/S: Golf and Renovating Homes EDU: Bachelor of Arts, Honors, University of Guelph; Bachelor of Laws, University of Ottawa A/A/S: Member, Former President, Lincoln Law Association; Hamilton Law Association; Legal Aid Ontario; Counsel, Foundation of Resources for Texas
Email: office@macleod_barr.com
URL: http://www.cambridgewhoswho.com

Michael Vincent Macri, MD
Title: Physician Company: Michael V. Macri, MD, P.C./MD Aesthetics Address: 10 Fairview Avenue, Westwood, NJ 07675 United States BUS: Private Medical Practice P/S: Healthcare Services Including Physician Services MA: Local D/D/R: Family Practice Medicine, Pediatric Medicine and Aesthetics, Medicine Performing Minor Surgical Procedures, Treating Dermatological and Gynecological Patients H/I/S: Skeet Shooting, Hunting, Dogfield Trialing, Outdoor Activities EDU: MD, Chicago Medical School (1988); Bachelor of Science in Biology, Manhattan College (1981); Residency, Lenox Hill Hospital A/A/S: American Medical Association; American Society for Laser Medicine and Surgery; Academy of Aesthetic Medicine; American Board of Family Medicine; American Society of Laser Medicine and Surgery
Email: drmvm@aol.com
URL: http://www.mymdaesthetics.com

Vinetta L. Madaffari
Title: Special Education Teacher Company: Belmont Hills Elementary School Address: 200 School Street, Bala Cynwyd, PA 19004 United States BUS: Elementary School P/S: Primary Education MA: Local D/D/R: Teaching Autistic Students and Kindergarten through Fifth-Grade Students H/I/S: Traveling, Skiing, Spending Time with her Family, Cooking EDU: Master's Degree in Special Education, Saint Joseph's University, Philadelphia; Bachelor of Arts in Psychology, Saint Joseph's University A/A/S: Autism Society of America; ASCEND Group, Inc.; National Alliance for Autism Research; Autism Speaks; Order Sons of Italy in America C/VW: Autism Speaks
Email: vinettamadaffari@hotmail.com
URL: http://www.cambridgewhoswho.com

Frances G. Madden
Title: Elementary Teacher (Retired) Company: Passaic Board of Education Address: 101 Passaic Avenue, Passaic, NJ 07055 United States BUS: School District P/S: Education MA: Local D/D/R: Helping Children Recognize their Own Worth and Realize that Nothing is Unattainable, Making Learning Meaningful and Exciting, Emphasizing the Value of Reading H/I/S: Art, Reading, Traveling, Gardening EDU: Master's Degree in Administration, Kean University, 1988; Bachelor's Degree in Elementary Education, William Paterson University, 1966 CERTS: Principal and Supervision Certification, 1988 A/A/S: Red Hat Society C/VW: Church, Red Hat Society
Email: fgm617@optonline.net
URL: http://www.cambridgewhoswho.com

Cynthia G. Maddox
Title: Educator Company: Mount Vernon City Public School District Address: 165 N. Columbus Avenue, Mount Vernon, NY 10553 United States BUS: School District P/S: Education Including Self-Esteem Development Programs MA: Local D/D/R: Teaching Special Education, Overseeing Computer-Integrated Learning Systems and Curriculum Development H/I/S: Singing, Reading, Crocheting EDU: Master's Degree in Special Education, The College of New Rochelle; Bachelor of Arts, CUNY Lehman College; Coursework, The College of Arts and Science, New York University CERTS: Certified Teacher (K-12); Certified English Teacher (K 7-12) A/A/S: National Education Association; Council for Exceptional Children; American Seminar Leaders Association; Westchester PTA League; New York State United Teachers; SAS; American Educational Research Association C/VW: American Heart Association; Local Food Kitchen
Email: cynthiam009@yahoo.com
URL: http://www.cambridgewhoswho.com

Katherine B. Madison
Title: Teacher's Assistant Company: University of South Carolina Address: 192 Springway Drive, Columbia, SC 29209 United States BUS: Institution of Higher Learning Dedicated to Excellence in Education P/S: Full Array of Academic Programs MA: Regional D/D/R: Teaching Classes on Medieval Literature Using Professor's Syllabus, Teaching Freshman Composition and the British Literature Survey H/I/S: Hiking, Gardening EDU: Pursuing Ph.D. in Medieval Literature; Pursuing Master's Degree in in British and American Literature A/A/S: National Society of Collegiate Scholars; Alpha Kai; Sigma Tau Delta; Graduate English Association
Email: heisalive2@juno.com
URL: http://www.sc.edu

Carol Madrid
Title: Technology Trainer Specialist Company: Jones Day Address: 555 California Street, 26th Floor, San Francisco, CA 94104 United States BUS: Law Firm P/S: Computer Training MA: San Francisco D/D/R: Technical Training and Support H/I/S: Traveling, Reading EDU: Coursework in Computer Science, Skyline College, San Bruno, California CERTS: Certified Paralegal A/A/S: International Legal Technology Association C/VW: Jehovah's Witness Public Ministry
Email: carolmadrid@gmail.com

Ms. Rebecca Anne Madura
Title: Associate Director, Clinical Research Associate Company: Pharmanet Address: 10150 Mallard Creek Road, Suite 500, Charlotte, NC 28262 United States BUS: Pharmaceutical Company P/S: Pharmaceuticals Including Drug Development Services, Biotechnology, Generic Drug and Medical Devices MA: International D/D/R: Assisting with Clinical Research for Drug Approval, Food and Drug Administration Compliance Assurance, Working with Companies to Perform Clinical Research Trials EDU: Master of Science in Biology, Brown University (2000); Bachelor of Science in Biomedical Research, Syracuse University (1992) CERTS: Certification in Clinical Research, The Society of Clinical Research Associates A/A/S: Society of Clinical Research Associates
Email: ram7383@hotmail.com
URL: http://www.cambridgewhoswho.com

Jyoti Maewall
Title: President Company: Computer Data Circuit, Inc. Address: 69 Milk Street, Suite 220, Westborough, MA 01581 United States BUS: Software Consulting and Development P/S: Software Consulting and Development MA: International EXP: Ms. Maewall's expertise includes business management and immigration. H/I/S: Reading, Yoga, Cooking, Spending Time with Family EDU: Bachelor's Degree in Economics and Commerce, University of Bombay (Now University of Mumbai) CERTS: Post Bachelor's Certificate in Computer Programming, North Carolina State University C/VW: American Cancer Society, Police Departments, Veterans Organizations, Church
Email: jyoti@computerdatacircuit.com
URL: http://www.computerdatacircuit.com

Fleur Magbanua
Title: Clinical Resource Nurse, Cardiology Nurse, Mayo Clinic, MSN, RN Company: Valley Home Care Address: 8636 N. 59th Avenue, Glendale, AZ 85302 United States BUS: Home Health Agency P/S: Healthcare MA: Statewide D/D/R: Home Health and Cardiovascular Nursing H/I/S: Reading, Spending Time with Friends and Family EDU: Master of Science in Nursing, University of Phoenix; Bachelor of Science in Nursing, San Juan de Dios College A/A/S: Treasurer, Philippine Nurses Association of Arizona; Philippine Nurses Association of America; BARANGAY; Lion's Club C/VW: Starting a Scholarship for Nursing Students
Email: fleur_m@valleyhomecareaz.com
URL: http://www.cambridgewhoswho.com

Geri Magee

Title: Owner **Company:** National Discovery Network, Inc. **Address:** 4096 State Route 981, Saltsburg, PA 15681 United States **BUS:** Advertising Agency **P/S:** Advertisements Including Event Planning and Marketing Services **MA:** National **EXP:** Ms. Magee's expertise includes marketing and promotional management. **D/D/R:** Planning Events, Building Public Relationships, Conducting Talent Search Programs, Applying Paramedical and Fashion Makeup **H/I/S:** Playing Volleyball, Reading, Spending Time with her Family **EDU:** Coursework in Liberal Arts, Pennsylvania State University **CERTS:** Certified Personal Trainer Certification; Certified Yoga Instructor; Licensed Fashion and Medical Makeup Artist **A/A/S:** National Guild of Community Schools of the Arts **A/H:** Company of the Year Award, Pageantry (2007); Professional Event Planner of the Year Award, Conventions Health Magazine (2005)
Email: gerimagee@hotmail.com
URL: http://www.nationaldiscoveryinc.com

Velma J. Magill

Title: Art Instructor **Company:** Lancaster Mennonite School **Address:** 2176 Lincoln Highway E., Lancaster, PA 17602 United States **BUS:** School **P/S:** Education **MA:** International **EXP:** Ms. Magill's expertise is in art instruction. **H/I/S:** Spending Time with her Grandchildren, Walking, Hiking, Reading, Going to Art Galleries **EDU:** Bachelor of Arts Plus 30 in Art and Education, Millersville University **A/A/S:** National Education Association; Christians in the Visual Arts (CIVA) **C/VW:** Hospice of Lancaster County, Friendship Community, Ladies Auxiliary
Email: vj@lancastermennonite.org
URL: http://www.lancastermennonite.org

Pamela F. Magnuson

Title: Owner **Company:** Pam Magnuson Copywriting **Address:** 19710 S.W. Cascadia Street, Aloha, OR 97007 United States **BUS:** Copywriting Company **P/S:** Nutraceutical Copywriting **MA:** National **D/D/R:** Nutraceutical Copywriting, Ordering Supplements, Working in a Virtual Office, Building Client Relationships, Writing Books, Researching **H/I/S:** Landscaping, Flower Gardening, Reading **EDU:** Bachelor's Degree in Journalism, Minor in History and Literature, University of Colorado **CERTS:** Certified Hypnotherapist **A/A/S:** Oregon Hypnotherapy Association; American Marketing Association; American Botanical Council; Project Management Institute
Email: pam@pammagnusoncopywriting.com
URL: http://www.pammagnusoncopywriting.com

Michael F. Magsig

Title: Managing Director **Company:** Korn Ferry International **Address:** 200 Park Avenue, 37th Floor, New York, NY 10616 United States **BUS:** Consulting **P/S:** Executive Search **MA:** International **EXP:** Mr. Magsig's expertise includes all aspects of insurance. **EDU:** Huntington University, Bachelor of Arts **A/A/S:** FLMI, LLIF, LIMRA, AESC, IIS

Indira Maharaj-Mikiel

Title: Student **Company:** Medical University of the Americas **Address:** 9 Spruce Road, Hyde Park, NY 12538 United States **BUS:** University **P/S:** Higher Education **MA:** International **D/D/R:** Coordinating with Departments Including Blood Pressure, Cardiopulmonary Resuscitation, Diabetes, Phlebotomy and Suture Clinics, Teaching General Practice Including Vaccinations, Mentoring Students, Conducting Acute Immune Deficiency Syndrome Research Workshops **H/I/S:** Crocheting, Reading, Traveling **EDU:** Pursuing MD, Medical University of the Americas, West Indies; Master's Degree in Psychology, Marist College; Bachelor's Degree in Psychology, Marist College **A/A/S:** Upward Bound Program; Psi Chi; Alpha Phi **A/H:** Who's Who Among Students in American Colleges and Universities Awards (2002); Premier's Award for Community Involvement (2001)
Email: indira.maharajmikiel@cwwemail.com
Email: indiramikiel@gmail.com
URL: http://www.cambridgewhoswho.com

Stephanie M. Maher

Title: Staff Engineer **Company:** Geomatrix Consultants **Address:** 510 Superior Avenue, Newport Beach, CA 92663 United States **BUS:** Civil, Environmental Engineering Firm **P/S:** Consulting, Remediation **MA:** National **D/D/R:** Engineering, Managing Operations, Supervising Project Maintenance, Visiting Sites, Working with Project Managers **H/I/S:** Relaxing, Traveling **EDU:** Bachelor's Degree in Environmental Engineering, California Polytechnic State University, San Luis Obispo, California (2006) **A/A/S:** American Society of Civil Engineers
Email: smaher@geomatrix.com
URL: http://www.geomatrix.com

Andrea Mahoney

Title: Employee Benefits Manager **Company:** Brown and Brown Insurance of Florida, Inc **Address:** 17757 U.S. Highway 19 N., Suite 660, Clearwater, FL 33764 United States **BUS:** Financial **P/S:** Oversee employee benefits, manage insurance policies, meet with new clients and owners **MA:** Local **D/D/R:** Was and employee benefits manager for American Airlines, used to be client service manager for PEO, good with communication with staff and clients employee benefits **H/I/S:** Golf, Cooking, Reading and crafting **EDU:** RHU, Life and Health Insurance **A/A/S:** FLWC employee benefits council, member of the espirit santo catholic church
Email: amahoney@bbpinelleas.com

Mary A. Mahoney

Title: Associate Director Human Resources **Company:** Ernst & Young LLP **Address:** 925 Euclid Avenue, Suite 1300, Cleveland, OH 44115 United States **BUS:** Accounting Firm **P/S:** Accounting, Auditing, Tax Reporting and Operations, Business Risk, Technology and Security Risk Services, Transaction Advisory and Human Capital Services **MA:** International **D/D/R:** Offering Human Resources, Managing Budgets and Compensation, Creating Strategy, Training and Implementation **H/I/S:** Reading, Wine Tasting **EDU:** Master of Business Administration, Concentration in Human Resource Policy, Case Western Reserve University, Ohio (1993) **A/A/S:** Society for Human Resource Management
Email: mary.mahoney@ey.com
URL: http://www.ey.com

Brenda K. Maiden, MLS

Title: Library Media Specialist **Company:** Carver High School of Engineering and Sciences **Address:** 1600 W. Norris Street, Philadelphia, PA 19121 United States **BUS:** Education School **P/S:** Educating and Nurturing High School Students **MA:** Local **D/D/R:** Teaching Library Skills and Research **H/I/S:** Travel, Reading, Computers, Smooth Jazz, Shopping, Plays and Movies, Gardening
Email: bmaiden@phila.k12.pa.us

Toni Woods Maignan, BSN, RN

Title: Registered Nurse **Company:** Easton Hospital **Address:** 250 S. 21st Street, Easton, PA 18042 United States **BUS:** Private Small Community General Hospital **P/S:** Healthcare **MA:** Regional **D/D/R:** Emergency Room and Critical-Care Nursing in the Triage Area, Determining the Level of Urgency for Patients, Offering Quality Patient Care, Educating Families on Diagnosis and Rehabilitation **H/I/S:** Writing Poetry, Reading, Spending Time with her Husband and Children **EDU:** Bachelor of Science in Psychology, New York Institute of Technology (1996); Bachelor of Science in Nursing, Seton Hall University **A/A/S:** Sigma Theta Tau; Nu Epsilon Tau; Volunteer, Greater Shiloh Church
Email: towoods@gmail.com

M. Barry Mair

Title: Sales Person **Company:** Coldwell Banker Gundaker **Address:** 2 Crossroads Plaza, O'Fallon, MO 63368 United States **BUS:** Real Estate Agency **P/S:** Real Estate Sales **MA:** Local **EXP:** Mr. Mair's expertise is in residential real estate. **H/I/S:** Golfing **A/A/S:** National Association of Realtors; Missouri Association of Realtors **A/H:** Rookie of the Year, Coldwell Banker Gundaker, St. Louis Metro, 2006; Rookie of the Year, St. Charles County Board of Realtors, 2006; Rookie of the Year, CBG Highway K and N Office
Email: mmair@dogundaker.com
URL: http://www.cambridgewhoswho.com

Peggy A. Makemson

Title: Chief Executive Officer **Company:** Howatt Company, Inc. **Address:** 12212 Cyrus Way, Mukilteo, WA 98275 United States **BUS:** Heavy Truck Industry **P/S:** Manufacturing Interior Components for Heavy Truck Industry **MA:** United States, Canada, Mexico **D/D/R:** Managing Operations **H/I/S:** Spending Time with her Sons **EDU:** College Coursework in Computers, Edmonds Community College, Edmonds, WA **C/VW:** Local schools
Email: peggy.m@howattcoinc.com

Dorothy Makram Morgos, Ph.D.

Title: Post Doctorate Fellow **Company:** Yale School of Medicine, Child Study Center **Address:** 53 College Street, New Haven, CT 06510 United States **BUS:** Department of Higher Education Bringing Together Multiple Disciplines to Further the Understanding of the Problems of Children and Families **P/S:** Efforts with the Police Department for Acute Response to Domestic Violence Involving Children, Child Psychiatry, Pediatrics, Genetics, Neurobiology, Epidemiology, Psychology, Nursing, Social Work, Social Policy, Research, Clinical Services, Training Programs and Policy Work **MA:** International **D/D/R:** Treating Traumatized Children and Families, Including Refugees in War Zones **EDU:** Pursuing Degree in Criminal Justice, Boston University; Ph.D., Master's Degree in Clinical Psychology, Rosemead School of Psychology, Master's Degree in Theology, Talbot School of Theology; Master's Degree in Education and Psychology, University of Beirut **A/A/S:** American Psychological Association; Volunteer, Global Aid Network; Educator, Daystar University, Kenya
Email: dorothymorgos@gmail.com
Email: dorothy.morgos@yale.edu
URL: http://www.info.med.yale.edu/chldstdy

Liliana Malaut

Title: Owner, Dealer **Company:** Lily Socrates **Address:** 10810 El Plano Avenue, Fountain Valley, CA 92708 United States **BUS:** Private Advertising Company **P/S:** Advertising on Fitzsi Coffee Mugs **MA:** Regional **D/D/R:** Selling Advertising Space on Mugs to Local Small Businesses and Restaurants, Managing All Financial Aspects of the Business **H/I/S:** Traveling, Attending the Opera **EDU:** Bachelor's Degree in Business Administration, National University of La Jolla, San Diego County (2006) Bachelor in Business Administration with a concentration on Accounting-, National University of La Jolla (2006) **A/A/S:** Pinnacle Society for Higher Education **C/VW:** Community involvement, food banks
Email: livianamp@aol.com

Ann Malec

Title: Mathematics Teacher **Company:** Fairfax County Public Schools, Franklin Middle School **Address:** 3300 Lees Corner Road, Chantilly, VA 22042 United States **BUS:** Public School **P/S:** Middle School Education **MA:** Local **D/D/R:** Teaching Mathematics **H/I/S:** Traveling, Reading, Crocheting, Knitting **EDU:** Bachelor of Arts in Education, Virginia Polytechnic Institute and State University **A/A/S:** Department Chairwoman; Nominee, Disney Teacher of the Year, 2005
Email: malec4@verizon.net

Dr. Tara Devi Malhotra

Title: President **Company:** Malhotra Acupuncture Center **Address:** 2700 S. Tamiami Trail, Suite 3, Sarasota, FL 34239 United States **BUS:** Acupuncture Clinic **P/S:** Oriental-Based Healthcare Services **MA:** Regional **D/D/R:** Practicing Traditional Chinese Pharmacy Relating to Obstetrics, Gynecology, Pregnancy and Menopause, Performing Acupuncture, Managing Women's Health Issues **EDU:** Doctor of Oriental Medicine, East West College of Natural Medicine, Florida (2002); Diplomat in Oriental Medicine; Diplomat in Chinese Aerobiology
Email: drtaradevi@yahoo.com

Rozanne Malivuk

Title: Teacher **Company:** Kent City Schools **Address:** 1175 Hudson Road, Kent, OH 44240 United States **BUS:** School **P/S:** Education **MA:** Local **D/D/R:** Teaching Literature, Language Arts and Social Studies **H/I/S:** Traveling, Taking Walks with her Labrador Retriever **EDU:** Master of Education, Concentration in Reading Supervision for K-12, Kent State University; Bachelor's Degree in Education, University of Akron **CERTS:** Certification in Physical Education, K-8; Certified in Early Childhood Education; Certified in Elementary Education **A/A/S:** Delta Kappa Gamma; Social Studies Educators of America **C/VW:** The Humane Society of Greater Akron; First Christian Church; MS Society
Email: ke_rmalivuk@kentschools.net

Kim Mallory

Title: President **Company:** Events Concierge, Inc. **Address:** P.O. Box 270, Chester, MD 21619 United States **BUS:** Event Planning Company **P/S:** Full and Partial Event Planning **MA:** Regional **D/D/R:** Planning Corporate Meetings, Seminars, Weddings and Fundraisers, Coordinating Fashion and Trade Shows **H/I/S:** Boating, Acting, Spending Time with her Three Children **EDU:** High School Graduate; Coursework, Oakland Community College and Anne Arundel Community College **A/A/S:** Talbot County Chamber of Commerce; International Television and Video Association; Anne Arundel Chamber of Commerce **C/VW:** Hospice of Queen Ann County, Local Fire Department
Email: kim@eventsconcierge.com
URL: http://www.eventsconcierge.com

Sheila C. Malmanis
Title: Chief Executive Officer, Owner **Company:** MS Skintechnical, Inc. **Address:** 2501 W. Behrend Drive, Suite 1, Phoenix, AZ 85027 United States **BUS:** Cosmetics Company **P/S:** Derma MD Skincare Products **MA:** International **D/D/R:** Researching and Developing New Products, Training, Managing Operations, Production and Accounts Receivable and Payable, Working with Chemists, Overseeing Staff, Selling Products to Doctors' Offices and Spas, Lecturing Nationally and Internationally **H/I/S:** Playing Tennis, Exercising, Reading, Skiing, Watching Old Movies **EDU:** College Coursework **CERTS:** Certification in Paramedical Aesthetics **A/A/S:** Better Business Bureau; ISA; National Society of Paramedical Esthetic Professionals
Email: smalmanis@aol.com
URL: http://www.dermamdskincare.com

John T. Malone
Title: Owner, Operator **Company:** J.T. Malone Equipment **Address:** 15733 N. 141st E. Avenue, Collinsville, OK 74021 United States **BUS:** Distribution Company **P/S:** Buying, Selling and Rebuilding Pumping Units **MA:** National **D/D/R:** Rebuilding Equipment, Overseeing Oilfield Pumping Units and Pump Jack Systems **H/I/S:** Relaxing **EDU:** High School Education
Email: john.malone@cwwemail.com

Stephanie Malone
Title: Exercise Technician **Company:** The Health Club **Address:** 3720 W. Robinson Street 124, Norman, OK 73072 United States **BUS:** Physical Fitness Center **P/S:** Physical Fitness **MA:** Regional **D/D/R:** Personal Training, Teaching Classes, Body Composition, Program Development, Administrative Duties **H/I/S:** Competing in Fitness Competition, Wakeboarding, Running, Cooking **EDU:** Master's Degree in Exercise Physiology, University of Oklahoma (2006) **A/A/S:** National Strength and Conditioning Association; Phi Kappa Phi Honor Society
Email: stephanie.malone@ou.edu
URL: http://www.normanregional.com

Lisa M. Maloney
Title: Senior Vice President, Senior Counselor **Company:** Capmark Finance, Inc. **Address:** 116 Welsh Road, Horsham, PA 19044 United States **BUS:** Finance Company **P/S:** Financial Services for Commercial Real Estate **MA:** International **D/D/R:** Analyzing Corporate Structuring and Capital Markets, Studying European Banking, Domestic Banking and Legal Affairs, Advising on General Corporate and Banking Law, Overseeing Regulatory Compliance, Securitization, Syndication Programs, Staff Development and Crisis Management **H/I/S:** Traveling, Spending Time with her Daughter, Exercising **EDU:** JD, School of Law, Villanova University, PA (1992); Bachelor of Arts in Politics, Fairfield University, CT (1988) **A/A/S:** Association of Corporate Counsel; Irish American Business Chamber & Network; Chairwoman, Young Lawyers Division, Philadelphia Bar Association; Philadelphia Judicial Commission; American Bar Association **C/VW:** Junior Achievement; Saint Denis Catholic Church; Interfaith Hospitality Network
Email: lisamaloney29@yahoo.com
URL: http://www.cambridgewhoswho.com

Mr. Shawn M. Maloney
Title: Director of Product Management **Company:** ISGN Technologies **Address:** 3550 Engineering Drive, Suite 200, Norcross, GA 30092 United States **BUS:** Information Technology Company **P/S:** Information Technology and Software Solutions for the Mortgage Banking and Financial Services Industries **MA:** National **EXP:** Mr. Maloney's expertise includes software development and product management. **D/D/R:** Product Management, Ensuring Quality, Managing Release Cycles, Sales and Marketing Campaigns **H/I/S:** Listening to Music, Playing Basketball and Football **EDU:** Bachelor of Business Administration in Finance, Georgia Southern University (1992) **A/A/S:** Certificate of Recognition for Product and Project Management; Outstanding Customer Service, Attitude and Leadership Award
Email: shawnmaloney01@gmail.com
URL: http://www.cambridgewhoswho.com

Zachary F. Malveaux
Title: Director of Cardiopulmonary Services **Company:** Conerstone Hospital **BUS:** Healthcare Hospital **P/S:** Respiratory Care **MA:** Local **EXP:** Mr. Malveaux's expertise includes outpatient care and respiratory care. **H/I/S:** Football, Handball, Swimming **EDU:** DeBakey School of Health Professionals, Houston Community College, AA Respicare **A/A/S:** AARC
Email: zapppmannn@yahoo.com

Ying Sing Man
Title: Electrical Protection Engineer **Company:** AT&T **Address:** 2600 Camino Ramon, San Ramon, CA 94583 United States **BUS:** Utility **P/S:** Telecommunications **MA:** International **EXP:** Ms. Man's expertise includes electrical protection and power safety. **H/I/S:** Graphic Design, Photography **EDU:** Bachelor of Science in Electrical and Electronic Engineering, California State University at Sacramento **CERTS:** Certified Engineer in Training; Master of Science in Multimedia, California State University at East Bay **A/A/S:** Institute of Electrical and Electronics Engineers **C/VW:** OxFam, Toastmaster
Email: ym3273@att.com
URL: http://www.cambridgewhoswho.com

Evelyn A. Mancilla-Moore
Title: Elementary School Teacher **Company:** San Francisco Unified School District **Address:** 431 Capitol Avenue, San Francisco, CA 94112 United States **BUS:** Public School **P/S:** Education for Kindergarten through Eighth-Grade **MA:** State of California **D/D/R:** Teaching Education for Kindergarten through Eighth-Grade, Conducting Reading and Gifted Programs, Working with Gifted Children, Attending Workshops **H/I/S:** Gardening, Cooking, Traveling, Real Estate, Admiring Nature, Spending Time with Children **EDU:** Bachelor of Arts in Business and Anthropology, San Francisco State University (1967) **A/A/S:** American Federation of Teachers
URL: http://portal.sfusd.edu/template/default.cfm

Naomi-Sadi Mandel
Title: 1) Owner 2) Owner **Company:** 1) Ethos Environmental NW 2) Meadow Muffin Ranch **Address:** P.O. Box 530, Cal Nev Ari, NV 89039 United States **BUS:** Wholesale and Retail Company, Solar Panels, Wind Generators, Freelance Photography from Forensic to Wildlife **P/S:** Alternative Fuel, Freelance Photography **MA:** International **D/D/R:** Environmental Activism, Freelance Photography **H/I/S:** Geocashing, Four Wheeling, Quading, Fishing, Water Skiing, Wave Running, Monster Trucking **EDU:** College Coursework **CERTS:** Certified Written English Professional **C/VW:** National Council of Jewish Women
Email: hippiemams@msn.com
URL: http://www.ethosnw.com
URL: http://www.meadowmuffinranch.ran

Amber M. Manes
Title: Marketing Director **Company:** Outlets at Loveland **Address:** 5661 McWhinney Boulevard, Loveland, CO 80538 United States **BUS:** Retail Outlet Center **P/S:** Brand Name Merchandise at Discounted Prices **MA:** Local **D/D/R:** Hosting Events **H/I/S:** Dancing **EDU:** Bachelor of Arts in Marketing, Focus on Industrial Psychology **A/A/S:** Loveland Chamber of Commerce; Shop America; Rocky Mountain Shopping Center Association **C/VW:** Engaging Loveland
Email: amber@outletsatloveland.com
URL: http://www.outletsatloveland.com

Vincent Mangano
Title: Teacher, Trainer, Emergency Medical Technician **Company:** Southampton Union Free School District **Address:** 141 Narrow Lane, Southampton, NY 11968 United States **BUS:** School District **P/S:** Education **MA:** Local **D/D/R:** Teaching Mathematics and Calculus, Coaching High School Students for Football **H/I/S:** Golfing, Traveling, Reading **EDU:** Master's Degree in Mathematics Education, Stony Brook University **A/A/S:** National Athletic Trainers' Association; Eastern Athletic Trainers' Association; New York State Athletic Trainers Association; Suffolk County Training Association; New York State United Teachers **C/VW:** Lions Clubs International
Email: Vincent.Mangano@cwwemail.com
URL: http://www.cambridgewhoswho.com

Kim Manigault
Title: President **Company:** Keep Savannah Beautiful **Address:** 5 Bridgeport Road, Savannah, GA 31419 United States **BUS:** Nonprofit Organization **P/S:** Keeping a Clean, Litter-Free City, Enhancing the Quality of Life through Programs and Education for the Community **MA:** Local **D/D/R:** Promoting Education for Recycling and Beautification of the City, Marketing, Managing Public Relations **H/I/S:** Golfing **EDU:** Diploma, Washington Irving High School, New York **A/H:** Top Ladies of Distinction Award (2007) **C/VW:** Boys Scouts of America
Email: gwcloud@bellsouth.net

Stephen Manko
Title: Senior **Company:** Ernst and Young **Address:** 5842 Eastview Street N.E., Louisville, OH 44641 United States **BUS:** Finance Accountant **P/S:** Public Accounting, Assurance and Advisory Services **MA:** International **D/D/R:** Auditing of Financial Institutions **EDU:** University of Akron, Malone College-OH, Master of Business Administration, BA-Accounting, BA-Business Administration **A/A/S:** Ohio Society of CPA's American Institute of CPA's Torch Bearers
Email: stephen.manko@ey.com
URL: www.ey.com

Monica Nicole Manley
Title: Mortgage Closer **Company:** Saxon Home Mortgage, Inc. **Address:** 917 Bogart Road, Richmond, VA 23223 United States **BUS:** Residential Mortgage Organization Dedicated to Excellence in the Lending Industry **P/S:** Purchasing, Securing and Servicing Mortgage Loans **MA:** Regional **D/D/R:** Sub-Prime Residential Mortgage Lending, Closing Loans and Complying with HMDA and RESPA **H/I/S:** Tennis **EDU:** Bachelor of Science in Business Administration, Virginia Union University (1997) **A/A/S:** Sigma Gamma Rho
Email: manleym@saxonhomemortgage.com
URL: http://www.saxonhomemortgage.com

Jacquelyn J. Mann
Title: Owner **Company:** A Little Attitude Salon **Address:** 4127 Jackson Road, Ann Arbor, MI 48103 United States **BUS:** Retail Health and Cosmetology Cosmetics/Beauty/Spa **P/S:** Variety of Cosmetology Services **MA:** Local **D/D/R:** Specializing in Developing Cosmetologists into Business Owners Where They Can Run Their Own Companies Effectively and Proficiently **H/I/S:** Doing Whatever **EDU:** Northwest Missouri State University, BS-Environmental Biology **A/A/S:** Local Board Member of the Mothers and More Organizations, Very Active with the Salon School County Program

Mario J. Manna, DO, FAAFP
Title: Physician **Company:** Mario J. Manna, D.O., F.A.A.F.P. **Address:** 7318 13th Avenue, Brooklyn, NY 11228 United States **BUS:** Family Medicine **P/S:** Healthcare **MA:** Local **EXP:** Dr. Manna's expertise is in family medicine. **EDU:** Doctor of Osteopathic Medicine, New York College of Osteopathic Medicine **A/A/S:** American Academy of Family Physicians
Email: mmdo24@yahoo.com

Benjamin W. Manning
Title: Vice President of Development **Company:** Palm Desert Development Company **Address:** 427 Ninth Avenue, Suite 1003, San Diego, CA 92101 United States **BUS:** Real Estate Development Company **P/S:** Multi-Family Housing Services **MA:** Southwestern United States **D/D/R:** Working on Concept Development and Land Acquisitions, Assisting with the Entitlement Process, Overseeing Finances and Construction **H/I/S:** Playing Lacrosse, Traveling **EDU:** Bachelor of Arts in Business Administration, Whittier College (2001)
Email: bmanning@pddc.net
URL: http://www.pddc.net

Jeanette Anne Manning
Title: Skin Instructor **Company:** Loraines Academy **Address:** 1012 58th Street N., Saint Petersburg, FL 33707 United States **BUS:** Beauty School **P/S:** Beauty Education **MA:** Local **D/D/R:** Skin Care, Waxing, Make Up, Microderm Abrasion, Photo Rejuvenation, Make Up Artistry, Cosmetic Application and Retail **H/I/S:** Jet Skiing, Working Out, Fishing, Riding Motorcycles **EDU:** Advanced Training, Loraines Academy **C/VW:** Cancer Walk, Children's Hospital
URL: http://www.cambridgewhoswho.com

Phyllis W. Manning
Title: Teacher **Company:** Sweetwater High School **Dept:** Mathematics **Address:** 414 S. High Street, Sweetwater, TN 37874 United States **BUS:** High School **P/S:** Secondary Education **MA:** Regional **D/D/R:** Teaching Mathematics, Grading Papers, Tutoring, Promoting Credit Recovery, Utilizing Visual Aids and Hands-on Work, Developing Curriculum **H/I/S:** Walking, Soccer **EDU:** Bachelor's Degree in Joint Elementary and Secondary Mathematics Education, The University of Tennessee (1980) **CERTS:** Certified Elementary Teacher; Certified Mathematics Teacher (K12) **A/A/S:** National Education Association; Tennessee Education Association
Email: manningp@monroe.k12.tn.us
URL: http://www.monroe.k12.tn.us

Dawn M. Mannion
Title: Office Manager Paralegal **Company:** Mannion & Gray Co., LPA **Address:** 1300 E. Ninth Street, Suite 1625, Cleveland, OH 44114 United States **BUS:** Private Law Practice **P/S:** Product Liability, Medical Malpractice, Pharmaceutical Legalities and Personal Injury. **MA:** National **D/D/R:** Paralegal Office Manager, maintain books, human resources and administrative functions of Mannion & Gray Co., L.P.A. **H/I/S:** My twin boys and working with my husband. **EDU:** Associate Degree in Paralegal Studies, Cuyahoga Community College (1996 graduate)
Email: dmannion@manniongray.com
URL: http://www.manniongray.com

Edward A. Manolio
Title: Sales Coordinator **Company:** Aarrow Promos, Inc **Address:** 69 Hampton Place, Freeport, NY 11520 United States **BUS:** Embellishing Retail **P/S:** Screen Print/Embroidery **MA:** Local **EXP:** Mr. Manolio's expertise is in sales. **H/I/S:** Tennis, Antique Shopping, Novice Piano Player, Pets **EDU:** Boston Universities, Master's **A/A/S:** Ad Specialty Ind (ASI), Prompt Product Specialty Ind (PPSI)
Email: oded2002@optonline.net

Debra D. Mansell

Title: 1) Director, Sales Trainer 2) Physical Education Teacher **Company:** 1) The Pampered Chef, Ltd. 2) Pomfret Community School **Address:** 101 Woodland Road, Storrs Mansfield, CT 06268 United States **BUS:** 1) Online Shop 2) Community School **P/S:** 1) Kitchen Tools Including Organizing Shows and Cooking Lessons 2) Education **MA:** 1) National 2) Local **H/I/S:** Camping, Bicycling, Reading, Cooking, Spending Time Outdoors **EDU:** Master's Degree in Special Education and Physical Education, University of Connecticut; Bachelor's Degree in Physical Science, University of Connecticut (1977) **CERTS:** Certified Physical Education Instructor (K-12) **A/A/S:** Connecticut Education Association; Planning Committee Member, State Delegate, Assembly Representative, National Education Association **C/VW:** American Cancer Society; Relay for Life; American Heart Association
Email: debral101311@aol.com
URL: http://www.pamperedchef.biz/debmansell

Rachel Whitfield Manspeaker, RN, MSN, MBA, HCM

Title: 1) Registered Nurse 2) Vice President **Company:** 1) Registered Nurse 2) Whitfield Steel Recycling **Address:** 12905 N.W. Service Road 20, Bristol, FL 32321 **BUS:** 1) Healthcare Agency 2) Recycle Center **P/S:** Healthcare **MA:** Regional **D/D/R:** Maintaining Public Health, Performing Administrative Duties **H/I/S:** Creating Stained Glass Windows **EDU:** Master of Science in Nursing, University of Phoenix; Master of Science in Business Administration, University of Phoenix; Master of Science in Healthcare Management, University of Phoenix; Bachelor of Science in Nursing, Florida State University **A/A/S:** Liberty County Health Council; Liberty County Hospice Board; Board Member, Calhoun-Liberty Hospital; Florida Leadership Institute **C/VW:** Local Youth Programs
Email: rmanspeaker@gtcom.net

Danita J. Mantz

Title: Fire Services Specialist **Company:** Bay County Emergency Services **Address:** 644 Mulberry Avenue, Panama City, FL 32401 United States **BUS:** Government **P/S:** Public Safety and Services **MA:** Regional **D/D/R:** Managing 10 Fire Departments, Offering Emergency Measures, Overseeing Operations, Procuring **H/I/S:** Sports, Football, Boating **EDU:** Diploma, Scott High School, Madison, WV **A/A/S:** Chamber of Commerce; Toastmasters International **C/VW:** Church of Christ
Email: jbfiremantz@comcast.net

Richard A. Manzo

Title: Attorney **Company:** Law Offices of Manzo & Associates, PA **Address:** 5095 S. Washington Avenue, Suite 104, Titusville, FL 32780 United States **BUS:** Legal Profession Attorney **P/S:** Law Firm, Legal Representation, Criminal, DUI, Personal Injury, Real Estate, Family Law, Will and Probate, Corporate and Business Law, Wrongful Death **MA:** Local **EXP:** Mr. Manzo's expertise includes civil and criminal trial litigation. **H/I/S:** Travel **EDU:** South Texas College of Law, The University of Notre Dame Law School and The Advanced National Institute of Trial Advocacy, JD **A/A/S:** Florida Bar Board Certified Civil Trial Lawyer, Florida Bar Board Certified Criminal Trial Lawyer, Licensed to Practice in Florida and Texas, Academy of Florida Trial Lawyers, Association of Trial Lawyers of America, American Bar Association, Brevard County Bar Association, National Association of Criminal Defense Lawyers, US Navy League, Judge Advocate, Salvation Army Board of Directors
Email: manzolaw@cfl.rr.com

Maggie Marano, MA

Title: Accounts Manager **Company:** Matria Healthcare **Address:** 1850 Parkway Place S.E., Suite 1100, Marietta, GA 30067 United States **BUS:** Healthcare Center **P/S:** Medical Services Including Disease Management and Wellness Programs **MA:** National **EXP:** Ms. Marano's expertise is in accounts management. **H/I/S:** Traveling, Tennis, Watching Movies, Reading **EDU:** Master of Arts in Advertising, The University of Texas at Austin; Bachelor of Arts in History, University of Virginia
Email: maggie.marano00@cwwemail.com
Email: maggiemarano@hotmail.com
URL: http://www.matria.com

Barbarita Marbelt

Title: Market Research Manager **Company:** HJ Heinz **Dept:** Ketchup Condiments and Sauces **Address:** 2076 Powell Road, Cranberry Township, PA 16066 United States **BUS:** Consumer Products Manufacturer **P/S:** Heinz Ketchup, Condiments and Sauces **MA:** International **D/D/R:** Consumer Insights and Strategy, Innovations, New Product Development, Packaging and Delivery Systems, Communication, Positioning, Targeting **H/I/S:** Traveling, Gourmet Cooking, Learning about Cultures, Painting, Listening to Music **EDU:** Master of Business Administration in Marketing, Rutgers Business School (2006); Bachelor's Degree in Biological Basis of Behavior, University of Pennsylvania (1997) **A/A/S:** Hispanic MBA; Public Speaker, HJ Heinz
Email: barbarita.marbelt@us.hjheinz.com
Email: bmarbelt1@hotmail.com

Jeanne L. Marciano, RN

Title: Registered Nurse **Company:** Monmouth Medical Center **Address:** 300 Second Avenue, Long Branch, NJ 07740 United States **BUS:** Medical Center **P/S:** Healthcare Including Lasik-Refractive Surgery, Neurosurgery, Obstetrics and Gynecology, Pediatric Cardiology, Positron Emission Tomography, Radiation Oncology, Cardiology, Cardiac Surgery, Emergency, Home Health and Hospice Care Services **MA:** Regional **D/D/R:** Examining Patients, Managing Operations, Prescribing Medications **H/I/S:** Reading, Making Crafts, Scrapbooking **EDU:** Associate Degree in Nursing, Felician College of New Jersey **CERTS:** Certified CPR Instructor; Certification in Pediatric Advanced Life Support **A/A/S:** Juvenile Diabetes Association
Email: Jeann353@yahoo.com
URL: http://www.sbhcs.com/hospitals/clara_maass

Laurie A. Marcovitz

Title: Office Manager **Company:** Wyoming Outfitters and Guides Association **Address:** 128 W. Midwest, Casper, WY 82602 United States **BUS:** Outfitting Service Provider **P/S:** Promote Conservation and Restoration of Wildlands Fish and Wildlife **MA:** Local **EXP:** Ms. Marcovitz's expertise includes legal assistance, sales and public relations. **H/I/S:** Spending Time With my Daughter Mackenzie, Family, Friends, Traveling and being outdoors **EDU:** Associate Degree in Business, Casper College **A/A/S:** Safari Club International, SCISF, Who's Who Among American High School Students, Sportsman For Fish & Wildlife, Who's Who Among American High School Students
Email: wyoga@wyoga.org
URL: www.wyoga.org

Mary Octavia Marden

Title: Triage Nurse **Company:** Horizon Hospice **Address:** 103 W. Cascade Way, Spokane, WA 99208 United States **BUS:** Hospice **P/S:** Healthcare **MA:** Regional **D/D/R:** Domestic Violence Nursing, Overseeing Pain Therapy **H/I/S:** Exercising, Quilting, Gardening, Reading **EDU:** Master of Science in Nursing, Washington State University; Bachelor of Science in Nursing, Washington State University **A/A/S:** Sigma Theta Tau **C/VW:** Habitat for Humanity, Millennium Project
Email: mary_marden@peoplepc.com

Miss Kristen Margiotta

Title: 1) Illustrator 2) Artist **Company:** 1) Kristen Margiotta Illustration 2) Cherry's Closet **Address:** 38 Drexel Drive, Newark, DE 19711 United States **BUS:** 1) Freelance Illustration Company 2) Handmade Merchandise Company **P/S:** 1) Freelance Illustrations 2) Handmade Apparel and Various Merchandise **MA:** 1) Regional 2) International **EXP:** Ms. Margiotta's expertise includes freelance illustration and merchandise design. **H/I/S:** Visiting Museums, Attending Music Concerts, Studying History, Traveling **EDU:** Bachelor of Fine Arts in Visual Communications, Concentration in Illustration, University of Delaware. **A/A/S:** The Center for the Creative Arts, Yorklyn, DE; Glubdub.com; Surrealismnow.com; Imaginarybooks.com **A/H:** First Place, Professional Category, Wilmington National Arts Program (2008); Solo Exhibition, Delaware Division of the Arts, Mezzanine Gallery, Wilmington, DE (2007); Award for Creative Excellence in Illustration, University of Delaware (2005); Gallery Award, University of Delaware (2001)
Email: kristenmargiotta@aol.com
URL: http://www.kristenmargiotta.com

Ms. Frescia Margot Vasquez

Title: 1) Owner, Founder 2) President **Company:** 1) Restaurant Salones Doña Rosita 2) Fresciamargot.com (Nusta, Inc.) **Address:** 1118 Third Street, Apartment 502, Santa Monica, CA 90403 United States **BUS:** 1) Restaurant 2) Retail Merchandise Company **P/S:** 1) Food Services Including Cuisine, Peruvian Food, Creole, Seafood and Continental Dishes 2) Jewelry, Cosmetology Products, Fashion **MA:** 1) International 2) International **D/D/R:** Offering Jewelry Design, Cosmetology and Makeup Artistry Services, Spiritual and Energy Consultations, Fashion Consultations, Running a Restaurant in Peru, South America, Managing Operations, Budgeting, Marketing, Hiring **H/I/S:** Bicycling, Dancing, Working, Vacationing in Europe and Mexico **EDU:** Coursework in Cosmetology, University of New York; Coursework in Business, University of California, Los Angeles **CERTS:** Certification in Cosmetology, Make-up Business **A/H:** Medal of Honor, City of Lambayeque-Peru
Email: fresciamargot@yahoo.com
Email: info@fresciamargot.com
URL: http://www.restaurantsalonesdonarosita.com
URL: http://www.fresciamargot.com

Dolores Jean Marier, MS, LPC, LMST

Title: Mental Health Specialist III, Private Practice Therapist **Company:** Counseling Associates **Address:** 255 Bayard Drive, Grants Pass, OR 97527 United States **BUS:** Counseling Center **P/S:** Counseling Services Including Mental Health Counseling for Individuals, Groups and Couples **MA:** Local **D/D/R:** Counseling Patients with Depression, Relationships, Self-Esteem Issues, Bipolar, Anxiety, Post-Traumatic Stress, Mental, Personality and Dissociative Identity Disorders **H/I/S:** Reading, Cooking **EDU:** Master of Science in General Studies, with Concentration in Psychology and Counseling, Southern Oregon University (1985); Plus 4000 in Sexual Abuse and Trauma; Bachelor of Science in Psychology and Humanities, Southern Oregon University (1981) **CERTS:** Licensed Professional Counselor, State of Oregon (1999); Licensed Marriage and Family Therapist, State of Oregon; Certified Pre-Commitment Supervisor, State of Oregon; Certified Court Mental Health Examiner, State of Oregon **C/VW:** Pro-Bono Counseling
Email: dee@ammcor.com

Cara Maria Marino

Title: Department Chairman of Business, Technology for Bishop McDezih, Curriculum Chairman for Business, Technology for Archdiocese of Philadelphia **Company:** Archdiocese of Philadelphia **Address:** 125 Royal Avenue, Wyncote, PA 19095 United States **BUS:** Private Catholic Institution **P/S:** General High School Curriculum, Religious Instruction, Fine Arts, Music, Foreign Language Instruction, Physical Education, Student Support Services, Athletics, Extracurricular Activities, Student Clubs and Organizations **MA:** Regional **D/D/R:** Teaching Business and Technology Courses, Conducting Workshops for Educators, Coordinating and Creating Curriculum for Business Education Courses, Maintaining Educational Formulated Standards in Conjunction with National Standards for the Archdiocese of Philadelphia **H/I/S:** Fashion, Walking, Exercising **EDU:** Master's Degree in Education, Saint Joseph's University; Bachelor's Degree in Business Education, Gwynedd Mercy College **CERTS:** National Board Certification in Education **A/A/S:** National Business Education Association; National Catholic Educational Association; Eastern Business Education Association; Curriculum Committee, Archdiocese of Philadelphia
Email: marinocara@aol.com
URL: http://www.archdiocese-phl.org

Peggy Marker

Title: Director of Community Relations **Company:** The Marker Group, LLC **Address:** 309 Sunset Drive, Suite 1, Fort Lauderdale, FL 33301 United States **BUS:** Humanitarian Organization **P/S:** General Contracting in Construction and Development, Charitable Work **MA:** South Florida **EXP:** Ms. Marker's expertise includes community relations and business development. **H/I/S:** Spending Time with her Family **EDU:** Bachelor of Arts in Political Science, University of Vermont **A/A/S:** Pi Beta Phi; Fort Lauderdale Museum of Discovery and Science; Board Member, SPARK; Heart Gallery; Builder's Olympics; Hearts 4 Kids; Hospice 100; Diamond Collar Society
Email: peg@themarkergroup.com
URL: http://www.themarkergroup.com

Marsha Marko

Title: Student Health Services Director, Director of Residential Life **Company:** Woodlands Academy of the Sacred Heart **Address:** 760 E. Westleigh Road, Lake Forest, IL 60045 United States **BUS:** Boarding School **P/S:** High School Education **MA:** Local **D/D/R:** Caring for the Students' Mental and Physical Health, Overseeing the Residential Life Program for the Boarding School **H/I/S:** Reading, Walking, Traveling **EDU:** Bachelor of Arts in Psychology, Bard College **CERTS:** Certified Registered Nurse, Sacred Heart Nursing School **A/A/S:** LEAD; Independent Schools Association **C/VW:** Women's Residential Services, Darfur
Email: mmarko@woodlandsacademy.org
URL: http://www.woodlandsacademy.org

Ms. Gail Marlene-Püetz

Title: Educator **Company:** Valley View Public Schools District 365U, Romeoville High School **Address:** 100 N. Independence Boulevard, Romeoville, IL 60446 United States **BUS:** Public School **P/S:** Education **MA:** Local **D/D/R:** Teaching English **H/I/S:** Traveling, Reading, Pursuing Metaphysics **EDU:** Master of Science in Special Education, University of Dubuque; Master's Degree in Leadership, Aurora University **A/A/S:** American Federation of Teachers **C/VW:** Scholarship for Students who are Becoming Educators
Email: marleneg@usd.org

Juliette Marotta
Title: District Art Chairwoman, Magazine Publisher **Company:** South Country Central School District **Address:** 189 N. Dunton Avenue, East Patchogue, NY 11772 United States **BUS:** School District **P/S:** Education **MA:** Local **D/D/R:** Teaching Art Education **H/I/S:** Spending Time with her Family, Drawing, Painting, Traveling, Golfing **EDU:** Master of Arts in Liberal Studies, SUNY Stony Brook; Bachelor of Science in Art Education, Specialization in Art, Hofstra University **A/A/S:** Long Island Art Teachers Association; New York State Art Teachers Association; Patchogue Woman's Club; East End Arts Council; Who's Who Among American Teachers, 1998, 2003, 2003 **A/H:** 1999 South County Service Award **C/VW:** Society of St. Vincent de Paul, Big Brothers Big Sisters of America
Email: jmarotta331@aol.com
URL: http://www.teentrendmagazine.com

Delia Marquez
Title: Owner **Company:** Mission Medical Billing **Address:** 8305 Vickers Street, Suite 210, San Diego, CA 92111 United States **BUS:** Medical Billing Company **P/S:** Healthcare Billing **MA:** California **EXP:** Ms. Marquez's expertise includes oncology and billing. **H/I/S:** Reading, Traveling **EDU:** Pursuing Certification in Medical Billing **A/A/S:** Industry-Related Publications
Email: deliam@mcrmedbilling.com
URL: http://www.cambridgewhoswho.com

Marie B. Marquis
Title: Vice President **Company:** R + M Small Engine, Inc **Address:** 219 Liberty Street E, Osyka, MS 39657 United States **BUS:** Lawn and Forest Equipment Retail **P/S:** Sales and Service of Lawn Mowers, Chain Saws, STIHL, Exmark Snapper **MA:** Regional **D/D/R:** Bookkeeping Sales **H/I/S:** Gardening, Reading, Traveling **CERTS:** Certified Bookkeeper, Certified Engine Expert
Email: mbmarquis@bellsouth.net
Email: rmsmallengine@bellsouth.net
URL: www.randmsmallengine.com

Candace Marrast
Title: Registered Nurse **BUS:** Healthcare Company **P/S:** Home Healthcare Services **MA:** Regional **D/D/R:** Supervising Field Nurses, Conducting Assessments, Creating Reports and Schedules, Conducting Performance Appraisals, Patient Advocacy **H/I/S:** Singing, Cooking, Sewing, Playing Basketball **EDU:** Master of Science in Nursing, Phoenix University Online (2007); Bachelor of Science in Nursing, SUNY Downstate (1999); Associate Degree in Nursing, Kingsborough Community College (1996) **A/A/S:** Sigma Theta Tau; Nursing Honors Society; Volunteer, United Church of God
Email: blossom620@optonline.net

Lee M. Marriott
Title: Functional Behavioral Support Consultant **Company:** ABC Educational Services **Address:** 224 S. Hanover Street, Carlisle, PA 17013 United States **BUS:** Consulting and Training Services **P/S:** Education Services, Functional Behavioral Assessment, Behavioral Intervention Plans **MA:** Regional **D/D/R:** Offering Functional Behavioral Assessments, Preparing Behavioral Intervention Plans, Training and Consultation **H/I/S:** Skiing, Horseback Riding, Ballet Dancing, Traveling, Reading, Spending Time with Family and Friends **EDU:** Master's Degree in Special Education, Shippensburg University (2005); Master's Degree in Elementary Education, Shippensburg University (1991); Bachelor's Degree in Elementary Education, Minor in Psychology, Shippensburg University (1986) **CERTS:** Certification in Elementary Education and Special Education **A/A/S:** Phi Kappa Phi; Kappa Delta Phi **C/VW:** American Red Cross
Email: lmarriott@abcedservices.net
URL: http://www.abcedservices.net

Malikah D. Marrus
Title: Social Worker, Researcher **Company:** Center for Children, Law and Policy, University of Houston Law Center **Address:** 100 Law Center, Houston, TX 77204 United States **BUS:** Research Training Center and Affiliate of the National Juvenile Defender Center Offering Child Advocacy **P/S:** Research Training and Efforts to Bring Together Juvenile Defenders, Mental Health Professionals, Educators, Legislators and Other Juvenile Justice Professionals **MA:** Regional **D/D/R:** Conducting Research and Scholarship Training, Mentoring **H/I/S:** Playing Basketball **EDU:** Master's Degree in Social Work, University of Houston **A/A/S:** National Association of Social Workers; Board of Trustees, Shlenker School
Email: mmarrus@uh.edu
URL: http://www.law.uh.edu/juveniledefender

David N. Marsh
Title: Director of Organizational Improvement for Budget and Finance **Company:** Vonhabsburg-Marsh Consulting **Address:** 3034 Maybank Highway, John's Island, SC 29455 United States **BUS:** Consulting Firm **P/S:** Consulting Services Including Organizational Development for Failing Business Entities **MA:** International **EXP:** Mr. Marsh's expertise includes troubleshooting for failing businesses, interim business management and operational improvement. **H/I/S:** Golfing, Sailing, Raising Horses **EDU:** Ph.D. in Theoretical Physics, Canterbury College; Doctor of Laws, Canterbury College **CERTS:** Six Sigma Black Belt Certification **A/A/S:** Association of Inspectors General; Justice of the Peace Association; American Bar Association; Federation of American Scientists; International Bar Association **C/VW:** My Sister's House, South Carolina; Ronald McDonald House Charities; Carolina Youth Development Center; American Society for the Prevention of Cruelty to Animals
Email: marsh@vonhabsburg-marsh.com
URL: http://www.cofc.edu

Donna J. Marsh
Title: Musician, Teacher **Address:** 343 Heather Heights Court, Monrovia, CA 91016 United States **BUS:** Sole Proprietorship **P/S:** Music Education **MA:** Los Angeles **D/D/R:** Playing and Teaching the Violin and Viola **H/I/S:** Traveling, Spending Time with her Family **EDU:** Bachelor of Arts in Music, University of California, Irvine **A/A/S:** Bohemian Club, NY; Music Teachers' Association of California; Music Teachers National Association; American String Teachers Association; University of California, Irvine Alumni Association
Email: pmarsh1@roadrunners.com

Marjorie Marsh
Title: Registered Pharmacy Technician **Company:** Midland Memorial Hospital **Address:** 2200 W. Illinois Avenue, Midland, TX 79701 United States **BUS:** Hospital **P/S:** Healthcare **MA:** Local **D/D/R:** Overseeing Hospital Pharmacy **H/I/S:** Playing Bunko, Spending Time at the Church, Listening to Classical Music, Collecting Angels, Antiques, Salt, Butter Pat Dishes and Music Boxes, Cooking, Spending Time with her Family, Watching Hummingbirds, Caring for her Dog, Traveling, Vegetable and Rose Gardening, Watching Y and R, Wheeling and Dealing For Bargains **CERTS:** Registered Pharmacy Technician; Certified Pharmacy Technician **C/VW:** American Cancer Society; American Diabetes Association
Email: mmarsh@grandecom.net

Betty Marshall
Title: Teacher of Exceptional Student Education **Company:** Duval County Public Schools **Address:** 2139 W. 15th Street, Jacksonville, FL 32209 United States **BUS:** Public School District **P/S:** General and Special Education **MA:** Local **EXP:** Ms. Marshall's expertise is in special education. **H/I/S:** Arts and Crafts, Cooking, Football **EDU:** Bachelor of Arts in Early Childhood Education, Everwaters College, Jacksonville (1988)
Email: marshallb@dreamsbeginhere.com

Phyllis Ann Marshall
Title: Retired Teacher **BUS:** Primary School **P/S:** Primary Education **MA:** Local **D/D/R:** Teaching **H/I/S:** Attending Horse Shows, Dancing, Playing Golf, Reading **EDU:** Master's Degree in Reading and Supervision, Union Methodist College **A/A/S:** Board of Education; REA; National Education Association; Texas Education Agency Board of Education; REA; National Education Association; Texas Education Agency

Stephenie J. Marshall, MS, RD, LDN, SSC, CCHC
Title: Regional Nutrition Administrator **Company:** Louisiana Department of Health and Hospitals, Office of Public Health, Region 1 **Address:** 1010 Common Street, Suite 700, New Orleans, LA 70131 United States **BUS:** Public Health Agency **P/S:** Public Health, Nutrition Programs **MA:** Regional **D/D/R:** Overseeing the Nutrition Services for Supplemental Food Program, Working with Three of the Most Devastated Parishes after Katrina, Training Staff, Overseeing Programs, Technical Assistance to Other States on Nutrition Education, Scheduling Patients Services, Monitoring Vendors **H/I/S:** Watching Football **EDU:** Master's Degree in Institutional Administration, University of South Mississippi (1988) **A/A/S:** American Dietetic Association; Louisiana Dietetic Association; New Orleans Dietetic Association; Published in Local Newspaper and Magazines and School Service Research Review
Email: sbmarsha@dhh.la.gov
URL: http://www.dhh.la.gov

Millie Marshall Smith
Title: Kindergarten Teacher **Company:** Saint Joseph Catholic Elementary School **Address:** 501 Cardinal Drive, Thibodaux, LA 70301 United States **BUS:** Catholic Elementary School **P/S:** Educating the Youth of the Area Spiritually, Morally, Academically and Socially, in a Safe, Catholic, Christ-Centered Environment **MA:** Regional **D/D/R:** Teaching Children the Basics of Reading, Writing, Mathematics and Logical Thinking, Creating an Endless Desire for Learning **H/I/S:** Traveling, Reading, Playing the Piano, Enjoying Spectator Sports **EDU:** Bachelor of Arts in Kindergarten Education, Nicholls State University, Thibodaux, Louisiana (1970); Certified Teacher, K-8 **A/A/S:** National Association for the Education of Young Children
Email: stjoekb@htdiocese.org
URL: http://www.stjosephcatholicschool.net

Millie Martelino
Title: President, Chief Executive Officer **Company:** The Karyn Ashley Collection, Inc **Address:** P.O. Box 145, Nokesville, VA 20182 United States **BUS:** Internet Company **P/S:** House and Garden Products, Personal Items and Miscellaneous Merchandise **MA:** National **D/D/R:** Overseeing Company Operations **H/I/S:** Writing, Reading, Playing the Piano **EDU:** Postgraduate Coursework in Guidance and Counseling; Bachelor of Arts in Journalism **CERTS:** Licensed Financial Adviser, U.S. Securities and Exchange Commission
Email: info@karynashley.com

Mr. T. Christian Martens
Title: Owner **Company:** Pramar Creative Arts, North Pole Home Inspections **Address:** 2738 Georgette Place, Simi Valley, CA 93063 United States **BUS:** Project Management Consultant and Independent Home Inspection Agency **P/S:** Project Management Consulting in the Design and Construction of Entertainment Theme Parks and the Inspection of Private Residences and Commercial Properties, Working to Identify Material Defects in the Structure and Systems of a Building **MA:** Regional **D/D/R:** Overseeing Planning and Scheduling for Construction Projects in Project Management, Managing the Entire Business, Marketing, Accounting, Maintaining a Referral-Based Clientele, Working with Real Estate Agents and Private Clients with Respect to Home Inspections **H/I/S:** Boating, Working as Santa Claus **EDU:** Post Graduate Work, Columbia College, Los Angeles; Master's Degree in Santa Claus Studies, International University of Santa Claus; Bachelor of Arts in the Liberal Arts, University of California at Los Angeles **CERTS:** Certification in Home Inspections, National Association of Certified Home Inspectors; Cell Claims Adjusters License, State of Texas **A/A/S:** National Association of Certified Home Inspectors; Board Member, The Amalgamated Order of Real Bearded Santas; Gerson Lehman Group; Board of Directors, Simi Valley YMCA
Email: pramar@earthlink.net
URL: http://www.trustyourhome.biz

Aleta Kay Martin
Title: Clinical Educator **Company:** Children's Medical Center of Dallas **Address:** 1935 Motor Street, Dallas, TX 75227 United States **BUS:** Healthcare Hospital **P/S:** Healthcare Provider **MA:** Local **EXP:** Ms. Martin's expertise is in pediatrics. **H/I/S:** Football **EDU:** Pursuing Bachelor's in Respiratory Care **A/A/S:** AARC, NBRC, TSRC
Email: akmartdleearn@yahoo.com

Andrew J. Martin
Title: Consultant **Address:** 506 E. Browning Street, Marion, IL 62959 United States **BUS:** 618-993-5920 Consulting **P/S:** All Regimens Clinical Lab, Research Projects **MA:** Local **EXP:** Mr. Martin's expertise is in chemistry. **H/I/S:** Woodworking **EDU:** Associate of Science, US Army, Washington University **A/A/S:** NCA Emeritus
Email: kamcare38@clearwave.com

Barbara J. Martin
Title: Owner **Company:** Barbara's Cleaning Service **Address:** 7440 Varsity Lane N.E., Bremerton, WA 98311 United States **BUS:** Janitorial Company **P/S:** Cleaning Service **MA:** Local **D/D/R:** Professional Cleaning **H/I/S:** Gardening **EDU:** Coursework in Food Service, Vocational School **C/VW:** Mothers Against Drunk Driving
Email: migual@sinclair.net

Carol J. Martin
Title: Assistant Program Consultant **Company:** Education Professional Standards Board **Address:** 100 Airport Road, Third Floor, Frankfort, KY 40601 United States **BUS:** Government Agency **P/S:** Recruitment of Qualified Teachers, Issuance and Renewal of Certifications for Teachers **MA:** Regional **D/D/R:** Paying Teachers Who Supervise Student Teachers, Handling Inquires from Educators, Monitoring Teachers' Eligibility to Receive These Stipends **H/I/S:** Collecting Statues, Reading, Participating in Church Activities **EDU:** Master of Science in Education Plus 30 Credits, Eastern Illinois University (1967) **CERTS:** Certified Teacher, Eastern Illinois University **A/A/S:** Illinois and Kentucky Retired Teachers' Associations; Delta Kappa Gamma Society International; Anderson County Historical Society in Lawrenceburg, Kentucky
Email: cjmart@adelphia.net
Email: carol.martin@ky.gov

Debbie A. Martin
Title: President, Owner **Company:** Trimark Screen Printing **Address:** 710 Western Avenue, Lombard, FL 60148 United States **BUS:** Design Printing Service Provider **P/S:** Screen Printing and Embroidery **MA:** Local **D/D/R:** Offering Customer Service **H/I/S:** Gardening, Reading **EDU:** Associate Degree, College of DuPage **A/A/S:** Chamber of Commerce
Email: trimarkspat@sbcglobal.net

Donalva Andrea Martin
Title: Registered Nurse **Company:** Stamford Health Systems, William & Sally Tandet Center **Address:** 54 Ponus Avenue, Norwalk, CT 06850 United States **BUS:** Long-Term Care Facility **P/S:** Healthcare **MA:** Stamford, Lower Fairfield **EXP:** Ms. Martin's expertise is in geriatrics. **H/I/S:** Traveling, Reading **EDU:** Associate Degree in General Studies and Nursing, Norwalk Community College, 2001; Bachelor's Degree in General Studies and Social Science, University of Bridgeport, 2007 **CERTS:** Certificate in Gerontology, University of Bridgeport; Registered Nurse, Degree in Nursing, Norwalk Community College, 2002 **A/A/S:** Church **C/VW:** Church, Feeding the Elderly, Helping her Family in Jamaica
Email: donmart330@yahoo.com
URL: http://www.cambridgewhoswho.com

Geraldine B. Martin
Title: Assistant Superintendent **Company:** Southern County Department of Education **Address:** 1429 Senate Street, Columbia, SC 29201 United States **BUS:** Public School System **P/S:** Education for Students in Grades K Through 12 **MA:** Regional **D/D/R:** Planning, Strategizing and Working with a Team in Addressing the Needs of Underperforming Schools **H/I/S:** Gardening **EDU:** MST, Clemson University (1975) **A/A/S:** Association for Supervision and Curriculum Development; National Council of Teachers of Mathematics; South Carolina Association of School Administrators
Email: gmartin@ed.sc.gov

Mr. Harold Boyd Martin, DDS, MPH
Title: Professor Emeritus, Associate Dean for Advanced Education and Research (Retired) **Company:** Howard University, College of Dentistry **Address:** 600 W. Street N.W., Washington, DC 20059 United States **BUS:** University **P/S:** Higher Education Including Post-Graduate Programs on Surgery, Periodontal and Pediatric Dentistry **MA:** National **D/D/R:** Conducting Dental Research, Consulting on Public Health Issues, Managing Operations **H/I/S:** Golfing, Traveling **EDU:** Master of Public Health, Johns Hopkins University (1971); Doctor of Dentistry, Howard University (1957); Bachelor of Arts in Biological Science, Lincoln University (1950) **A/A/S:** American College of Dentists; International College of Dentists **C/VW:** Metropolitan Police Sports Club; American Cancer Society
Email: harold.martin@cwwemail.com

Jane L. Martin
Title: Magnet Coordinator **Company:** Atlanta Public Schools, Frederick Douglass High School **Address:** 225 Hamilton E. Holmes Drive N.W., Atlanta, GA 30318 United States **BUS:** High School **P/S:** High School Education **MA:** Local **D/D/R:** Helping Students and Adults to Realize their Potential, Teaching, Taking Care of Attendance **H/I/S:** Traveling, Spending Time with her Family **EDU:** Master's Degree in Curriculum and Instruction, North Adams College, Massachusetts **CERTS:** Certification in Administrative, New York City College **A/A/S:** Alpha Phi Sigma; National Association of State Boards of Education; National Association of Black School Educators **C/VW:** St. Jude Children's Research Hospital; New Birth South Church, Mount Zion, GA; St. Marx Roman Catholic Church, New York, NY
Email: jlmartin@atlanta.k12.ga.us

Jeannie L. Martin
Title: Certified Massage Therapist **Company:** Spa Meridian **Address:** 137 Keokuk Street, Unit A, Petaluma, CA 94952 United States **BUS:** Health and Fitness Club **P/S:** Health and Fitness Training **MA:** Local **D/D/R:** Performing Massage Therapy for Athletes and Health Spa Clients, Offering Hydrotherapy Treatment **H/I/S:** Hiking, Swimming, Singing **CERTS:** Certification in Massage Therapy, Western Institute of Science and Health (Now Sonoma State University) **A/A/S:** American Massage Therapy Association
Email: jeannieleemartin@comcast.net

Juanita Martin
Title: Elementary School Teacher **Company:** Alexandre Dumas Elementary School **Address:** 6650 S. Ellis Avenue, Chicago, IL 60637 United States **BUS:** Elementary School **P/S:** Primary Education **MA:** Local **D/D/R:** Teaching Mathematics, Reading **H/I/S:** Bowling, Watching Movies, Attending Theater **EDU:** Bachelor's Degree in Elementary Education, Roosevelt University **A/A/S:** Woodlawn Baptist Church
Email: jmartin@cps.edu

Linda Martin
Title: President **Company:** Community Connection **Address:** 408 Kellogg, Suite 200, Ames, IA 50010 United States **BUS:** Marketing **D/D/R:** Marketing And Fund Raising

Marilyn Marie Martin
Title: Registered Nurse **Company:** Hurley Medical Center **Address:** 1 Hurley Plaza, Flint, MI 48501 United States **BUS:** Healthcare **P/S:** Neurotrauma **MA:** Local **D/D/R:** Neurotrauma Nursing **H/I/S:** Reading, Bead Work **EDU:** Bachelor of Science in Nursing, Ferris University **C/VW:** Soup Kitchen, Genesee Free Clinic, Church
Email: nursemartin@comcast.net
URL: http://www.cambridgewhoswho.com

Nancy A. Martin
Title: Director, Resource Group **Company:** RRB Inc. dba Livingston Moving and Storage **Address:** 21207 Coffeen Street, Watertown, NY 13601 United States **BUS:** Moving, Storage Company **P/S:** Moving, Storage **MA:** National **EXP:** Ms. Martin's expertise includes finance, human resources and nursing. **H/I/S:** Spending time with my friends and family, Running, Walking my Jack Russell 'Zoe', Reading, Candles **EDU:** College Coursework **CERTS:** Certified Aerobics Instructor; Licensed Practical Nurse **A/A/S:** Society for Human Resource Management **C/VW:** MS Resources, ACS
Email: nancymartin@twcny.rr.com

Peter Martin
Title: Owner **Company:** Musicraft Productions **BUS:** Music Production Company **P/S:** Musical and Technical Production Services, Internet Music Products **MA:** International **D/D/R:** Offering Music Instruction, Publishing, Recording Music, Developing Educational Children's Products, Working with School Systems, Giving Performances **H/I/S:** Reading Non-Fiction History Books, Conducting Online Music Research, Speaking Ukrainian **EDU:** Coursework, Navy School of Music; Coursework in Architecture, Pasadena City College; Coursework in Liberal Arts, Sierra College **A/A/S:** Board Member, Sacramento Traditional Jazz Society; President Emeritus, Northern California Accordion Society; Board Member, Adjudicator, Clinician, The American Society of Composers, Authors and Publishers **A/H:** Second Place, ATG Art Van Damme International Jazz Accordion Competition, Dallas, TX (2005)
Email: petermartinjazz@pacbell.net
URL: http://www.petermartinjazz.com

Rose M. Martin
Title: Owner **Company:** American Flag Sales **Address:** 106 Florence Lane, P.O. Box 790, Cosmopolis, WA 98537 United States **BUS:** Marketing Company **P/S:** Flags, Flag Pole **MA:** Regional **EXP:** Ms. Martin's expertise is in sales management. **D/D/R:** Utilizing her Customer Service Skills **H/I/S:** Shopping, Collecting Antiques, Dining Out, Spending Time at the Beach, Gardening, Studying about Birds' Behavior **EDU:** High School Education **A/A/S:** Board of Elections, Town of Cosmopolis; Assembly of God Christian Center; Christian Women's Club **C/VW:** The Salvation Army; Union Gospel Mission; Billy Graham Evangelistic Association
Email: rosem@techline.com
URL: http://www.cambridgewhoswho.com

Stephen R. Martin
Title: Driver, Part Owner **Company:** Martin Excavation **Address:** 236 McComb Street, Saranac Lake, NY 12983 United States **BUS:** Construction Company **P/S:** Construction Services, Foundations and Septic Systems for Residential and Commercial Properties **MA:** Local **EXP:** Mr. Martin's expertise is in equipment direction. **D/D/R:** Helping in Running the Family Business, Overseeing Work Sites **EDU:** Diploma, Saranac Lake High School (1996) **A/A/S:** Local Chamber of Commerce **C/VW:** National Guard, Special Olympics
Email: stephen.martin@cwwemail.com
URL: http://www.cambridgewhoswho.com

Christie Martin-Gray
Title: President **Company:** Martin-Gray Communications, LLC **Address:** 1873 Birmingham Court, Hillsborough, NC 27278 United States **BUS:** Advertising Company Dedicated to Quality Services **P/S:** Design, Advertising and Marketing, Communications **MA:** National **D/D/R:** Creative Management, Director, Hiring Contractors **H/I/S:** Outdoor Activities, Music **EDU:** Bachelor's Degree in Fine Arts, Wake Forest University, North Carolina (1979)
Email: christie@martin-gray.net
URL: www.martin-gray.net

Adriana Martinez
Title: Quality Assurance Manager **Company:** Kimberly Clark Agent **Address:** 14 Finegan Road, Del Rio, TX 78840 United States **BUS:** Healthcare **P/S:** Manufacturing Medical Devices **MA:** Local **EXP:** Ms. Martinez's expertise includes quality assurance and Lean Six Sigma Black Belt Techniques. **H/I/S:** Travel, Reading, Golf **EDU:** Master's Degree, UANE
Email: adriana.c.martinez@kcc.com

Christine Martinez
Title: Quality Assurance Engineer **Company:** BI Technologies **Address:** 4200 Bonita Place, Fullerton, CA 92835 United States **BUS:** Manufacturing Manufacturing/Production/Machinery **P/S:** Automotive Sensors, Micro Circuit Hybrids and Potentiometers **MA:** National **D/D/R:** Specializing in Internal Audits, TS 16949 Certifications and Customer Audits **H/I/S:** Reading **EDU:** California Polytechnic at Pomona, BS-Manufacturing Engineering **A/A/S:** ASQ, St Josephs Catholic Church

Esteban A. Martinez, MD
Title: Chief of Staff **Company:** The Schumacher Group **Dept:** Hospital Medicine Division **Address:** 200 Corporate Boulevard, Lafayette, LA 70508 United States **BUS:** Privately-Owned Healthcare Center **P/S:** Healthcare **MA:** National **D/D/R:** Overseeing Medical Affairs for the Hospital Medical Division **H/I/S:** Golfing, Playing the Guitar **EDU:** MD, Universidad Central del Este, Dominican Republic (1980) **CERTS:** Board Certification in Internal Medicine, Nephrology and Emergency Medicine **A/A/S:** American Medical Association; American College of Emergency Physicians; American College of Physicians; FAAC **C/VW:** Volunteer, Hospice of Arcadia
Email: al_martinez@tsged.com

Kari I. Martinez
Title: Head Athletic Trainer, Physical Education Instructor **Company:** Casper College **Address:** 125 College Drive, Casper, WY 82601 United States **BUS:** College **P/S:** Higher Education **EXP:** Ms. Martinez's expertise includes sports management, athletic training and rehabilitation. **H/I/S:** Reading, Playing the Piano, Coaching a Rugby Team **EDU:** Bachelor's Degree in Executive Sports Science **A/A/S:** National Athletic Trainers' Association
Email: lmartinez@caspercollege.edu
URL: http://www.caspercollege.edu

Kathryn M. Martinez
Title: Owner, Personal Trainer **Company:** Empowering Bodies Personal Training, LLC **Address:** 4685 S. Ash Avenue, Suite H1, Tempe, AZ 85283 United States **BUS:** Personal Training Company **P/S:** Movement, Exercise, Nutrition **MA:** Local **EXP:** Ms. Martinez's expertise includes exercise and nutrition. **H/I/S:** Walking Dogs, Working Out **EDU:** Associate of Arts in Paralegal Studies, University of New Mexico **CERTS:** Certified Personal Training; Pursuing Certification for Personal Training through Level 2 Certified Z-Health Performance Training
Email: kathy@empoweringbodies.com
URL: http://www.empoweringbodies.com

Luisa Martinez
Title: Owner **Company:** Little Stars Daycare **Address:** 432 E. 105th Street, Apartment 5A, New York, NY 10029 United States **BUS:** Childcare Center **P/S:** Childcare **MA:** Local **D/D/R:** Offering a Safe and Comfortable Environment for Children During the Day **H/I/S:** Traveling, Spending Time with her Family **EDU:** Coursework in the Dominican Republic **CERTS:** Certified Licensed Childcare Provider **C/VW:** Goodwill, Church
Email: lmartinezt@yahoo.com
URL: http://www.cambridgewhoswho.com

Maria M. Martinez
Title: Instructional Assistant **Company:** Bonnie Branch Middle School **Address:** 4979 Ilchester Road, Ellicott City, MD 21043 United States **BUS:** HCPSS Serving Residents in HC **P/S:** Public Secondary Education for Local Students **MA:** Regional **D/D/R:** Working with Middle School-Special Education Department, Working Helping Students One-on-One, Working with Children with Emotional Issues, Severe Problems, Amyotrophic Lateral Sclerosis and Speech Issues, Hosting Workshops, Incorporating Music into her Classes, Assisting with Subjects, Acts as an Interpreter English-Spanish for Several Outside Companies **EDU:** Coursework, Howard Community College **A/A/S:** Associated and Volunteer in the Fire Department; Volunteer in the Boy Scout of America; Involved with PreMarital Counseling though Church; Notary Public
Email: martinez21075@yahoo.com

Nancy M. Martinez
Title: Director of Special Education **Company:** Prescott Unified School District 1 **Address:** 146 S. Granite Street, Prescott, AZ 86303 United States **BUS:** School **P/S:** Education **MA:** Local **EXP:** Ms. Martinez's expertise is in special education. **H/I/S:** Quilting, Gardening, Spending Time with her Two Cats **EDU:** Master's Degree in Special Education, Northern Arizona University; Bachelor of Arts in Elementary Education, University of Arizona **A/A/S:** Association for Supervision and Curriculum Development; Council for Exceptional Children; SEAA **C/VW:** Kiwanis Club of Prescott
Email: nancy.martinez@prescottschools.com
URL: http://www.prescottschools.com

Rachel Martinez
Title: Co-Owner, Manager **Company:** Martinez Roofing **Address:** 101 Spring Meadow, Bastrop, TX 78602 United States **BUS:** Roofing Company **P/S:** Residential and Commercial Roofing, Modifications, Compositions, Metal Roofing, Replacing Rotten Wood, Building Patios **MA:** Regional **D/D/R:** Roofing, Managing Paperwork for Business, Delivering Materials, Ordering Materials, Bookkeeping, Overseeing Marketing **H/I/S:** Exercising, Gardening **EDU:** High School Diploma
Email: martinezroofing@sbcglobal.net
URL: http://www.cambridgewhoswho.com

Ms. Sabrina Michelle Martinez
Title: President **Company:** Martinez Footers Inc. **Address:** 549 Wellon Avenue, Orlando, FL 32833 United States **BUS:** Construction Company **P/S:** Residential and Corporate Construction Services **MA:** Regional **D/D/R:** Offering Excavation, Setting, Refurbishing and Steel Services, Overseeing the Accounts Payable and Receivable, Building Small Homes **H/I/S:** Raising Birds, Sheep and Goats **EDU:** General Educational Development (1994)
Email: tippea@cfl.rr.com

Vidal V. Martinez
Title: President, Graphic Artist **Company:** VMTZ Gel Coat & Aztec Graphics, LLC **Address:** 3652 Swordfish Drive, Lake Havasu, AZ 86406 United States **BUS:** Printing Graphics **P/S:** Design, Banners, Screen Printing **MA:** Local **D/D/R:** Gel Coating **H/I/S:** Design Clothes **A/A/S:** Jehovah Witness
Email: vidalnirma@hotmail.com

Col. Jeffry Martini
Title: Director, Associate Publisher, Writer **Company:** Superfriends Marketing and Promotions Group **Address:** 226 N. Crescent Drive, Apartment 303, Beverly Hills, CA 90210 United States **BUS:** Marketing and Promotions Agency **P/S:** Marketing, Promotions, Radio Advertising, Microsoft Beta Testing-Vista, Silverleaf and other Windows Media Programs **MA:** International **D/D/R:** Mentoring, Helping People Launch New Products and Services **H/I/S:** Reading, Collecting First-Edition Ernest Hemingway Books, Watching Movies **A/A/S:** Board Member, Order of the Arrow; Direct Marketing Association; Electronic Retailing Association; Marketing Director, The Beverly Hills Courier **A/H:** CINE Golden Eagle Award; Emmy Award
Email: drymartini@earthlink.net
URL: http://www.superfriendsmarketing.com

Kathleen M. Martinoff
Title: Project Manager **Company:** QBE Regional Insurance **Address:** 1 General Drive, Sun Prairie, WI 53596 United States **BUS:** Insurance Company **P/S:** Property and Casualty Insurance **MA:** International **EXP:** Ms. Martinoff's expertise includes information technology, project management, package acquisition and budgeting. **D/D/R:** Managing Projects and Deliverables, Scheduling **H/I/S:** Ballroom Dancing **EDU:** Bachelor of Arts in Data Processing, Ferris State University, MI **CERTS:** Certified Project Management Professional, Project Management Institute (2001) **A/A/S:** Project Management Institute
Email: kathleen.martinoff@qbeamericas.com
URL: http://www.qberegional.com

Lea J. Martone
Title: Director of Finance **Company:** Marina Del Rey Marriott **Address:** 4100 Admiralty Way, Mafina Del Rey, CA 90292 United States **BUS:** Hotel **P/S:** Hotel Services **MA:** International **D/D/R:** Managing Finances **EDU:** Bachelor of Science in Accounting, University of Maryland (1997) **CERTS:** Certified Public Accountant, State of California (2004) **A/A/S:** California Society of Certified Public Accountants
URL: http://www.marriott.com

Dave Marty
Title: Owner **Company:** Dave Marty Entertainment **Address:** 205 Rockport Way, Novato, CA 94947 United States **BUS:** Entertainment Company **P/S:** Musical and Comedy Entertainment **MA:** Central California **EXP:** Mr. Marty's expertise is in musical entertainment. **H/I/S:** Practicing Music **EDU:** Coursework in Liberal Arts Studies, City College of San Francisco **A/A/S:** American Federation of Musicians; Fretted Instrument Guild of America **C/VW:** Various Charitable Organizations
Email: dbanjoman@comcast.net
URL: http://www.tekedmusic.info/dave.marty

Brian Marvin Sr.
Title: Owner **Company:** Tainter Construction **Address:** N8793 610th Street, Colfax, WI 54730 United States **BUS:** Construction Company **P/S:** General Contracting, Home Improvement, Home Remodeling **MA:** Local **EXP:** Mr. Marvin's expertise includes business management, accounting and customer service. **H/I/S:** Camping with his Family, Community Volunteering, Hunting **EDU:** Coursework, Chippewa Valley Technical School **CERTS:** Certified in Lead Removal; Licensed Contractor **C/VW:** Stat Patrol, 4-H Camp, Community Recovery Organization
Email: brimarv@hotmail.com

Sherine O. Marzouk, BA, JD
Title: Director, In-House Counsel **Company:** Infotek Consulting Services **Address:** 900 Wilshire Drive, Suite 202, Troy, MI 48084 United States **BUS:** Contract Professional Services of Outstanding Quality, Competence, Performance and Objectivity Provided by Highly Skilled Information Technology Professionals at a Competitive Price **P/S:** Information Technology Consulting Services, Legal Counsel, Sales Manager, Resource Augmentation and Solutions Delivery **MA:** International **D/D/R:** Co-Managing the Company, Attending Informal Hearings, Negotiating Contracts, Drafting and Handling Legal Documents, Overseeing Auditory Functions Including Recruitment, Marketing and Sales Activities, Consulting, Handling Client Negotiations **H/I/S:** Tennis, Swimming, Soccer **EDU:** JD, Wayne State University (2003); Bachelor's Degree in Film and Philosophy, Scripps College (1997) **A/A/S:** State Bar of Michigan; Work-Related Lecturing; Public Speaker
Email: smarzouk@infotek-consulting.com
URL: http://www.infotek-consulting.com

Linda F. Mask, RN II
Title: Registered Nurse II **Company:** Department of Aging and Disabilities Services for the State of Texas **Address:** 505 S. John Redditt Drive, Lufkin, TX 75904 United States **BUS:** Public Medical Center **P/S:** Public Healthcare **MA:** Regional **D/D/R:** Offering Rehabilitative, Orthopedic and Medical-Surgical Nursing, Working on the Campus Hospital, Handling Admissions, Conducting Assessments, Observations and Treatments, Performing Monthly Reviews on Health States and Annual Staff Reviews **H/I/S:** Crocheting, Reading, Participating in Church as a Speaker with the Youth Group and in the Choir **EDU:** Associate of Science in Nursing, Angelina Junior College **CERTS:** Certified in Advanced Cardiac Life Support **A/A/S:** Member, Simpson Chapel Baptist Church; United Way; Numerous Christian Organizations
Email: jehova1955@yahoo.com

Brenda Barrett Mason
Title: Artist, Instructor **Address:** 8693 National Road S.W., Pataskala, OH 43062 United States **BUS:** Sole Proprietorship **P/S:** Art Education Including Stained Glass and Watercolor Art **MA:** Local **D/D/R:** Teaching Stained Glass and Watercolor Art **H/I/S:** Photography, Reading **EDU:** Bachelor of Fine Arts **A/A/S:** Monarch Gallery, Lancaster, OH
Email: masonjar@insight.rr.com
URL: http://www.cambridgewhoswho.com

Joseph A. Mason, MA
Title: Assistant Director, Instructor **Company:** Howard Community College **Address:** 10901 Little Patuxent Parkway, Columbia, MD 21044 United States **BUS:** Community College **P/S:** Higher Education **MA:** Local **EXP:** Ms. Mason's expertise includes human development, stress management, personal counseling and health science. **H/I/S:** Reading, Exercising **EDU:** Master of Arts in Counseling, Michigan State University **A/A/S:** American Counseling Association **C/VW:** Various Local Black Charities
Email: jmason@howardcc.edu
URL: http://www.howardcc.edu

Sharon L. Mason
Title: Teacher **Company:** Heartland Christian Homeschool Center **Address:** 3327 Kenora Drive, Spring Valley, CA 91977 United States **BUS:** Christian School **P/S:** Education **MA:** Local **D/D/R:** Teaching Kindergarten and First Grade Students to Read Phonetically **H/I/S:** Gardening, Walking, Music (violin) **EDU:** Bachelor of Arts in Biblical Studies, Southern California Seminary **A/A/S:** Association of Christian Schools International
Email: massha@cox.net
URL: http://www.cambridgewhoswho.com

Harold Masse
Title: Captain District Commander **Company:** Illinois State Police **Address:** 1154 Shawnee College Road, Ullin, IL 62992 United States **BUS:** Government Organization **P/S:** Law Enforcement, Security Services **MA:** Local **D/D/R:** Overseeing Operations of the State Police and Seven Counties in Illinois **H/I/S:** Traveling **A/A/S:** National Academy Association; Asian American Law Enforcement Association; Federal Bureau of Investigation; Illinois State Police Command Officers Association; Illinois Association of Chiefs of Police; Fraternal Order of Police
Email: harry_masse@isp.state.il.us

Mrs. Janan L. Massey, RN
Title: Coordinator, Registered Nurse **Company:** Sansum Clinic **Dept:** Clinical Research Department **Address:** P.O. Box 1200, Santa Barbara, CA 93102 United States **BUS:** Healthcare Clinic **P/S:** Clinical Services and Specialty Medicine **MA:** Regional **D/D/R:** Specializing in Cardiology, Performing Medical Surgery, Offering Clinical and Intensive Care Services, Practicing Clinical Research in Endocrinology, Pharmacy and General Medicine **H/I/S:** Snow Skiing, Bicycling **EDU:** Degree in Registered Nursing, Methodist Kahler School of Nursing, The Mayo Clinic, Rochester, MN (1970) **CERTS:** Certification in Critical Care Nursing **A/A/S:** Association of Clinical Research Professionals
Email: jmassey@sansumclinic.org
URL: http://www.sansumclinic.org

Leah L. Mastaglio
Title: Director of Event Services **Company:** Reliant Park **Address:** 1 Reliant Park, Houston, TX 77054 United States **BUS:** Event Management Company **P/S:** Sports Events and Marketing **MA:** National **EXP:** Ms. Mastaglio's expertise is in sports marketing. **H/I/S:** Playing Tennis, Golfing **EDU:** Bachelor's Degree, Texas A&M University **C/VW:** Special Olympics
Email: lmastaglio@reliantpark.com
URL: http://www.cambridgewhoswho.com

Erin E. Masters
Title: Attorney **Company:** Nadler, Pritikin and Mirabelli **Address:** 130 E. Randolph Drive, 12th Floor, Chicago, IL 60601 United States **BUS:** Family Law Services **P/S:** Family Law, Divorce, Custody, Prenuptial Agreements, Adoption **MA:** Chicago and Surrounding Counties **D/D/R:** Practicing Family Law Including Pre-Decree and Post-Decree Matters **H/I/S:** Running **EDU:** JD, Loyola University; Bachelor of Arts in Psychology, University of California, San Diego **A/A/S:** American Bar Association; Illinois Bar Association; Chicago Bar Association
Email: e.masters@npmfamlaw.com
URL: http://www.npmfamlaw.com

Thomas A. Mastrobuoni, CPA
Title: Controller **Company:** Palladium Equity Partners **Address:** 1270 Avenue of the Americas, Suite 2200, New York, NY 10020 United States **BUS:** Finance Company **P/S:** Investments **MA:** Regional **D/D/R:** Managing Private Equity Investments, Accounting, Reporting, Securing Assets, Auditing Tax Compliances, Communicating with Investors and Fund Accounting to Investors **H/I/S:** Playing Softball, Volunteering Community Services **EDU:** Bachelor's Degree in Accounting, Villanova University (2000) **CERTS:** Certified Public Accountant (2006) **A/A/S:** American Institute of Certified Public Accountants; New York State Society of Certified Public Accountants; New Jersey Society of Certified Public Accountants **C/VW:** Local Church; Harlem RBI
Email: tmastrobuoni@palladiumequity.com
URL: http://www.palladiumequity.com

Christine Faith Mata
Title: Captain **Company:** City of Los Angeles Department of Transportation **Address:** 100 S. Main Street, Los Angeles, CA 90012 United States **BUS:** Government Organization **P/S:** Public Transportation Services **MA:** Regional **D/D/R:** Working with the Communication Centers, Coordinating with Outside Agencies, Supervising Traffic Officers who Issue Tickets and Direct Traffic, Overseeing special events, training crossing guards, coordinating and supervising **H/I/S:** Golfing, Watching Car Racing **EDU:** Coursework, California State University (1978); High School Education (1978)
Email: christine.mata@lacity.org
URL: http://www.lacity.org

Cristina Matera, MD
Title: Physician **Company:** Madison Women's Health and Fertility **Address:** 50 E. 77th Street, New York, NY 10075 United States **BUS:** Medical Clinic **P/S:** Women Healthcare Services Including Gynecology, Reproductive Endocrinology and Infertility Treatment **MA:** Regional **D/D/R:** Overseeing Gynecological Patient Care, Laproscopy, Hysteroscopy and Menopausal Treatments, Reproductive Endocrinology and Infertility Treatments, Teaching Clinical Obstetrics and Gynecology, Working in the Operating Room **EDU:** MD, School of Medicine, New York University (1986) **A/A/S:** Surgical Site Infections Committee; Health Information Management Committee, American College of Obstetricians and Gynecologists; American Society for Reproductive Medicine
Email: cmateramd@mac.com

Evalee A. Matheson
Title: Teacher **Company:** Shelley School District No. 60 **Address:** 475 W. Center Street, Shelley, ID 83274 United States **BUS:** School **P/S:** Education **MA:** Shelley, Idaho **D/D/R:** Teaching Fourth-Grade Students **EDU:** Bachelor's Degree in Elementary Education, Plus 60, Southern Utah University **A/A/S:** National Education Association; Idaho Education Association
Email: remeam8@quixnet.net
URL: http://www.cambridgewhoswho.com

Rainey R. Mathews
Title: Senior Pastor **Company:** New Life Complete in Christ Baptist Church **Address:** 1035 E. Annie Street, Fort Worth, TX 76104 United States **BUS:** Religion Religion/Spiritual Services **P/S:** Saving Souls and Helping the Needy **MA:** National **D/D/R:** Counseling and Painting **H/I/S:** Boxing **A/A/S:** NAACP, Former Heavy Weight Prize Fighter
Email: pastorrainey@yahoo.com

Ervin M. Mathias Jr.
Title: 1) Principal 2) Partner **Company:** 1) Mathias Real Estate, LLC 2) T&M Farms **Address:** 837 Wells Branch Road, Ulmer, SC 29849 United States **BUS:** 1) Real Estate Company 2) Farm **P/S:** 1) Resort Real Estate 2) Agriculture **MA:** Regional **D/D/R:** Managing Residential and Resort Sales, Marketing, Managing the Farm **H/I/S:** Hunting, Fishing, Spending Time with Grandchildren, Outdoor Sports **EDU:** Bachelor of Science in Business Administration, Newberry College, South Carolina (1967) **CERTS:** Licensed in Real Estate, States of South Carolina, North Carolina and Georgia **A/A/S:** South Carolina Board of Realtors; Kappa Alpha Order
Email: emmathias@bellsouth.net

Jennifer R. Mathis
Title: Manager **Company:** Rupee Rental **Address:** 1505 Cherokee Avenue, Giaffney, SC 29340 United States **BUS:** Real Estate Company **P/S:** Commercial and Residential Rental Properties **MA:** Local **D/D/R:** Accounting Services, Collecting Rent **H/I/S:** Spending Time with her Son, Reading, Scrapbooking, Spending Time with her Two Dogs **EDU:** Associate of Arts in Marketing, Spartanburg Community College (1996) **CERTS:** Certification in Cosmetology, Piedmont College of Hair Design (1994)
Email: mathis2006@netscape.com

George Raymond Matland
Title: Pastor-President **Company:** Signs of Victory Ministries **Address:** 620 Cleveland Street, Albany, OR 97321 United States **BUS:** Religion Ministries **P/S:** Preaching Word of God **MA:** Local **D/D/R:** Offering Praise to the Lord **H/I/S:** Preaching the Word of God **EDU:** Mt Sac College of California **A/A/S:** Church
Email: virginasov@aol.com
URL: www.sovretail.com

Maricelis G. Matsinger
Title: Second-Grade Spanish Immersion Teacher **Company:** Liberty Bell Elementary School **Address:** 3360 Muirfield Road, Center Valley, PA 18034 United States **BUS:** Public Elementary School Serving the Residents of Center Valley **P/S:** Standards-Based Education Program Developed to Meet the Needs of All Students through Content Areas Including Reading, Writing, Mathematics, Social Studies, Culture, Science and Technology, Life Assets and Work Skills **MA:** Local **D/D/R:** Working with 29 Second-Grade Students in a Completely Spanish-Immersed Learning Environment, Teaching Spanish as a Second Language to Students **H/I/S:** Walking, Traveling, Listening to Music **EDU:** Master's Degree in Early Childhood, Chestnut Hill College, Philadelphia (1986)
Email: matsingerm@sisd.org
URL: http://www.sisd.org

Janette Mattas
Title: Supply Technician **Company:** Field Support Services, Inc. **Address:** 601 Tasechee Drive, Sebring, FL 33870 United States **BUS:** Government Contractor **P/S:** Quality Services for the United States Air Force **MA:** International **D/D/R:** Purchasing Supplies, Overseeing Accounts Payable and Transportation Management **H/I/S:** Golfing, Gardening, Boating, Fishing, Traveling **EDU:** Bachelor of Science in Business Administration, Almeda University (2002) **A/A/S:** Veterans of Foreign Wars Auxiliary; Moose Auxiliary; COA
Email: janette.mattas@avonpark.macdill.af.mil

Carol Diefenderfer Matthews
Title: President **Company:** Life Extension Health Center **Address:** 416 Cambridge Boulevard, Winter Park, FL 32789 United States **BUS:** Healthcare Education and Products **P/S:** Health Supplements, Equipment, Research **MA:** National **D/D/R:** Health Consulting, Bookkeeping **H/I/S:** Spending Time with her Cats, Dancing, Gardening **EDU:** High School Education; Theocratic Ministry School **A/A/S:** Organization of Jehovah's Witnesses; Life Extension Foundation; Environmental Working Groups; Nutrition for Optimal Health Association, PETA **C/VW:** The Humane Society, People for the Ethical Treatment of Animals
Email: lehealthcenter@aol.com

Mr. James Matthews, MD
Title: Medical Director **Company:** Family Medicine of Gaithersburg **Address:** 981 Russell Avenue, Gaithersburg, MD 20879 United States **BUS:** Private Medical Practice **P/S:** Advanced Integrative Medicine **MA:** International **D/D/R:** Treating Occult Infections, Morgellon's Syndrome, Chronic Fatigue, Gulf War Syndrome, Lyme Disease, Conducting Research **H/I/S:** Practicing Yoga **EDU:** MD, SUNY Downstate (1999); Bachelor of Science in Biological Chemistry, SUNY Stony Brook (1993) **A/A/S:** Board Member, Life Medical Technologies, Inc.
Email: JasMatthews@msn.com
URL: http://www.familymedgaithersburg.com

Rev. Lee T. Matthews
Title: President **Company:** Feed My Sheep Food Bank Ministry of Eastern North Carolina, Inc. **Address:** 3430 Faircloth Freeway, Clinton, NC 28328 United States **BUS:** Food Bank Ministry **P/S:** Food Bank Ministry to All Surrounding Counties in Eastern North Carolina, Donations for Food Restocking **MA:** Regional **D/D/R:** Elder Rev. Matthew's expertise is in performing missionary work, Replenishment of Donations, Organizing Donations in the Proper Category, Ensuring Goods Are Safe to Eliminate Illnesses **H/I/S:** Football, Baseball **EDU:** Diploma in Practical Theology, International Seminary (2003); Associate in Psychology, Otero Junior College, La Junta, CO; Diploma in Theology, International Seminary (2002); Coursework in Supervision and Development, United States Marine Corps (1981); Associate Degree in Textiles, Eastern Kentucky University (1980); Degree in Law Enforcement, Coastal Carolina Community College (1972) **CERTS:** Ordained Elder; Ordained Preacher; Certificate of Completion in Postal Service Skills, United States Postal Service (1991) **A/A/S:** Retired Gunnery Sergeant, United States Marine Corps **A/H:** Certificate of Achievement in Personnel Management in Setting Performance Standards, Veterans Administration (1980); Certificate in Setting Performance Standards, Federal Deposit Insurance Corporation (1977); Letter of Appreciation, United States Marine Corps (1973)
Email: leemat@intrstar.net
URL: http://www.cambridgewhoswho.com

Regina T. Matthews
Title: President, Chief Executive Officer **Company:** Torek Development, Inc. **Dept:** Aqua Tech Dive Center **Address:** 1800 Logan Avenue, San Diego, CA 92113 United States **BUS:** Distribution Firm **P/S:** Scuba Diving and Marine Equipment; Scuba Diving Lessons **MA:** International **D/D/R:** Accounting, Managing Human Resources and Employee Relations, Processing Payroll **H/I/S:** Horseback Riding, Breeding Arabian Horses, Traveling **EDU:** College Coursework **A/A/S:** Former Chairwoman, 4-H Club, California State Project **C/VW:** The Ocean Foundation; Make-A-Wish
Email: accounting@divecenter.com
URL: http://www.diveusa.com

Sonya K. Matthies
Title: President **Company:** General Federation of Women's Clubs **Dept:** De Anza District, California Federation of Women's **Address:** 20345 Grand Avenue, Wildomar, CA 92595 United States **BUS:** Nonprofit Organization **P/S:** Services to Women and their Communities **MA:** International **D/D/R:** Overseeing Women's Clubs in the De Anza District **H/I/S:** Swimming, Walking, Playing Golf, Traveling **EDU:** College Coursework **A/A/S:** Heifer International; California Federation of Women's Clubs, General Federation of Women's Clubs
Email: shmatthies@aol.com
URL: http://www.cambridgewhoswho.com

Mr. Ivan O. Mattox Sr.
Title: Financial Advisor **Company:** Mattox Financial Services **Address:** 1516 Hill Top Circle, Maidens, VA 23102 United States **BUS:** Finance Company **P/S:** Financial Services **MA:** VA, MD, NC **EXP:** Mr. Mattox's expertise is in financial advising. **D/D/R:** Meeting the Needs of Clients in Planning, Estate Planning, Investments, Life and Health Insurance, Long Term Care, Group and Disability Insurance **EDU:** Coursework in Economics, Virginia Military Institute **A/H:** Top Six in Pension Sales, Ohio National **C/VW:** Goochland Fellowship; Goochland Christmas Mother
Email: mattoxfinancial@aol.com
URL: http://www.cambridgewhoswho.com

Rosanna Matucan-Carson
Title: Human Resources Manager **Company:** Bausch & Lomb **Address:** 21 Park Place Boulevard N., Clearwater, FL 33759 United States **BUS:** Manufacturing Company **P/S:** Eye Health and Eye Care Products **MA:** International **D/D/R:** Human Resources, Salary Planning, Performance Evaluations and Hiring, Overseeing Employee Interactions **H/I/S:** Spending Time with her Children **EDU:** Master's Degree in Human Resources, Chapman University; Master of Business Administration, Keller Graduate School of Management, DeVry University **A/A/S:** Society for Human Resource Management
Email: rosanna.matucan-carson@bausch.com
URL: http://www.cambridgewhoshwo.com

Walter 'Wally' O. Maul Jr.
Title: Commercial Closing Administrator **Company:** Bridgeview Bank Group **Address:** 407 Franklin Avenue, Apartment 4E, River Forest, IL 60305 United States **BUS:** Financial Banking **P/S:** Financial Service Provider **MA:** Local **EXP:** Mr. Maul's expertise includes the commercial process and closings. **H/I/S:** Bridge, Cooking, Traveling, Theater **EDU:** Southwest State University, BS
Email: wally.maul@bridgeviewbank.com

Marcella J. Maurepas
Title: Educator **Company:** Lake County Schools **Address:** 11607 Layton Street, Leesburg, FL 34788 United States **BUS:** School District **P/S:** Education **MA:** Local **D/D/R:** Working with Students with Emotional and Behavioral Disabilities **H/I/S:** Working with Children, Listening to Music, Spending Time with her Sons **EDU:** Bachelor's Degree in Organizational Management, Warner Southern College **A/A/S:** National Education Association; National Association of State Textbook Administrators; Safe Climate Committee **A/H:** Rookie Teacher of the Year **C/VW:** Helping Other Students; Child Abuse Task Force; Tribe of Benjamin; It's Great to Wait
Email: maurepasm@fl.lake.k12.us
URL: http://www.cambridgewhoswho.com

Roxanne Maurey
Title: Optometrist **Company:** RM Vision **Address:** 5555 U.S. Highway 41, Terre Haute, IN 47802 United States **BUS:** Vision Care Center **P/S:** Optical Care **MA:** Local **EXP:** Ms. Maurey's expertise includes optical and primary care. **H/I/S:** Making Stained Glass, Playing Soccer **EDU:** Bachelor of Arts in Biology, Indiana State University; Bachelor of Arts in Chemistry, Minor in Russian, Indiana State University **A/A/S:** American Optometric Association **C/VW:** Clothe-A-Child
Email: roxeye@broadreach.net

Denise G. Maxwell
Title: Office Manager **Company:** Orepac Building Products **Address:** 30160 S.W. Orepac Avenue, Wilsonville, OR 97070 United States **BUS:** Wholesaler **P/S:** Building Products **MA:** Western Oregon, Utah, Nevada, Washington **D/D/R:** Accounting **H/I/S:** Spending Time with her Daughters, Participating in their School Activities **EDU:** High School Graduate **C/VW:** Relay for Life, Habitat for Humanity
Email: dmaxwell@orepac.com
URL: http://www.cambridgewhoswho.com

Ellery B. May Jr.
Title: Systems Engineer Office, Deputy Manager of the Space Shuttle Project Office, Manager (Retired) **Company:** National Aeronautics and Space Administration, Marshall Space Flight Center **Dept:** Saturn Program **BUS:** Aeronautics Research Agency **P/S:** Scientific Spacecraft Research and Instruments, Large Complex Systems, Applied Materials and Manufacturing Processes **MA:** Regional **D/D/R:** Managing Apollo and Saturn Projects, Launching Vehicles, Developing Designs, Managing Space Shuttle Propulsion Elements and Science, Pursuing Scientific Breakthroughs in Space to Improve Life on Earth, Developing Transportation and Propulsion Systems for Space Infrastructure **H/I/S:** Gardening, Golfing, Reading **EDU:** Bachelor's Degree in Aeronautical Engineering, Auburn University (1947) **A/A/S:** Marshall Space Flight Center Retiree Association; Exceptional Service Award, NASA; Distinguished Services Medal, NASA
Email: gilerymay8@knology.net

Nora Baggaley May
Title: Special Education Teacher, Publication Advisor **Company:** Loudoun County Public Schools **Dept:** Park View High School **Address:** 400 W. Laurel Avenue, Sterling, VA 20164 United States **BUS:** High School **P/S:** Secondary Education **MA:** Local **D/D/R:** Teaching Students with Emotional Disabilities, Mentoring New Teachers, Advising for the Literary and Art Magazine 'Illusions,' Teaching Including a Photography Course to Adults **H/I/S:** Photography, Writing, Traveling **EDU:** Master's Degree in Special Education, The College of New Jersey (1985); Bachelor's Degree in Arts, Psychology, Boston University (1973); Associate of Applied Science and Photography, Northern Virginia Community College (1995) **CERTS:** Certified Teacher, NJ (K-8); Certified Teacher in Special Education (PreK-12) **A/A/S:** Association for Supervision and Curriculum Development; President, Virginia Chapter, Alpha Delta Kappa; Alpha Tau Kappa; International Reading Association **C/VW:** American Cancer Society; National Wildlife Federation
Email: norabmay@aol.com

Virginia A. Mayberry
Title: Management Assistant to General Counsel **Company:** U.S. Securities and Exchange Commission **Dept:** Office of the General Counsel **Address:** 100 F Street N.E., Washington, DC 20549 United States **BUS:** Government Organization **P/S:** Business Development, Law Enforcement, Marketing Strategy Implementation Service **MA:** National **D/D/R:** Overseeing Administrative Duties **H/I/S:** Traveling, Cooking, Skiing, Scuba Diving, Caring for her Dog **EDU:** Master's Degree in Business, Salve Regina University; Bachelor's Degree, University of Maryland; Coursework, U.S. Army War College **A/H:** Meritorious Civilian Service Award; Superior Civilian Service Award **C/VW:** Combined Federal Campaign
Email: mayberryv@sec.gov
URL: http://www.sec.gov

Jessica Maye
Title: Technology Support Analyst **Company:** UnitedHealth Group **Dept:** Department of Information Technology **Address:** 4316 Rice Lake Road, Duluth, MN 55811 United States **BUS:** Healthcare Center **P/S:** Healthcare Including Healthcare Management Services **MA:** International **D/D/R:** Overseeing Information Technology Services **H/I/S:** Traveling, Skiing **EDU:** Master of Business Administration, with a Concentration in Information Security; Master's Degree in Information Systems Management, with a Concentration in Information Security; Bachelor of Science in Technical Management, with a Concentration in Information Technology **C/VW:** Our Lady of the Rosary Church
Email: jessica_maye@uhc.com
URL: http://www.cambridgewhoswho.com

Dr. Andrea Mayfield
Title: Special Education Consultant **Company:** Department of Education State of Tennessee **Address:** 7529 Delta Lakes Boulevard, Walls, MS 38680 United States **BUS:** Education **P/S:** Adjunct Professor, Graduate, Undergraduate Education, Special Education **MA:** Regional **D/D/R:** Principles, Parent Counseling, Special Education, School System Paper Work **H/I/S:** Avid Reader, Historical, Biography, Bible **EDU:** University of Mississippi, Alcorn State University, DO in Curriculum and Instruction in Education, 2003, Master's Degree in Special Education 1997, Bachelor of Science in Special Education 1991 **A/A/S:** Counsel of Exceptional Children, Alpha Kappa Alpha, Department of Education of TN

Jeanne Mayfield
Title: Human Resources Manager **Company:** Baumann Springs North America **Address:** 3075 N. Great S.W. Parkway, Grand Prairie, TX 75050 United States **BUS:** Spring Manufacturer **P/S:** Springs **MA:** International **D/D/R:** Handling All Payroll, Times and Attendance, Data Entry, Maintaining Human Resource Database, Overseeing All Human Resource Issues Including Hiring, Termination, Behavior, Grievance Issues **H/I/S:** Hockey **EDU:** Coursework in Accounting and Computer Science **A/A/S:** American Payroll Association; Society for Human Resource Management; Orientation Leader for New Employees
Email: jeanne.mayfield@baumann-springs.com
URL: http://www.baumann-springs.com

Betty B. Mayo
Title: Youth Education Assistant (Retired) **Company:** University of Missouri Extension **Address:** 100 Sparks Avenue, Moberly, MO 65270 United States **BUS:** University **P/S:** Higher Education **MA:** Regional **D/D/R:** Enhancing Child Development **H/I/S:** Making Crafts, Flower Gardening **EDU:** Associate Degree in Administrative and Secretarial Services, Draughons Business College **A/A/S:** Missouri Association of Youth Workers; National Association of Youth Workers; Missouri Association for Family & Community Education; National Association for Family & Community Education **A/H:** Hall of Fame Award, Missouri 4-H Foundation **C/VW:** University of Missouri Extension Council; Youth Director, Church; 4-H Club Leader, Missouri 4-H Foundation; Community Work
Email: rcmayo@missvalley.com

Bethany J. Mays
Title: Kindergarten Teacher **Company:** Washington Elementary School **Address:** 1031 Fifth Avenue, Belvidere, IL 61008 United States **BUS:** Public Elementary School **P/S:** Education in an Atmosphere of Excellence which Develops Healthy, Responsible, Life-Long Learners and Problem Solvers **MA:** Regional **D/D/R:** Teaching Reading, Writing, Mathematics and Social Studies to Kindergarten Level Students, Focusing on Building Character Skills **H/I/S:** Reading, Cooking, Playing the Piano **EDU:** Pursuing a Master's Degree in Reading, Rockford College; Bachelor of Arts in Elementary Education, Rockford College (2002) **CERTS:** Certification in Elementary Education K-9 **A/A/S:** International Reading Association; Phi Delta Kappa; Recipient Middle School Endorsement; Northern Chapter, Illinois Reading Council; Pi Lambda Theta; International Reading Association; Northern Illinois Reading Council
Email: bjmays@aol.com
URL: http://www.district100.com

Lance S. Mayster
Title: President **Company:** Dwinn-Shaffer and Company **Address:** 30 W. Monroe Street, Suite 1610, Chicago, IL 60603 United States **BUS:** Mortgage Bunker **P/S:** Mortgage Banking, Real Estate **MA:** National **EXP:** Mr. Mayster's expertise is in finance. **H/I/S:** Reading, Playing Tennis, Spending Time with his Family, Boating, Caring for his Horses **EDU:** Bachelor of Science in Finance, University of Illinois, 1976 **CERTS:** Licensed Real Estate Broker **A/A/S:** Real Estate Investment Association; CREF; Illinois Mortgage Bankers Association; Mortgage Bankers Association **C/VW:** JUF, Children's Memorial Hospital
Email: lmayster@dwinn.com
URL: http://www.dwinn.com

Shola C. Mazgaj, RN, MS
Title: Staff Nurse **Company:** In Home Infusion **Address:** 90 N. Fourth Street, Martins Ferry, OH 43935 United States **BUS:** Pharmaceutical Suppliers Affiliated with East Ohio Regional Hospital **P/S:** Intravenous Medications and Supplies for Healthcare Professionals and Patients for Home Use **MA:** Regional **D/D/R:** Specializing in Labor, Delivery, Nursery and Intensive Care Unit Nursing, Administering IVs, Receiving Referrals from Hospitals for In-Home Patients, Assessing Patient Status via Phone and On-Site Examination, Reporting Status to Doctors and the Pharmacy **EDU:** Master's Degree in Health Services Administration, Ohio University (1991); Bachelor of Science Degree in Zoology, Ohio University (1988) **CERTS:** Registered Nurse, West Virginia Northern Community College (1992) **C/VW:** Volunteer, Health Clinic, United States Army Reserves
Email: smazgaj@myfam.com
URL: http://www.cambridgewhoswho.com

Debra Poller Mazon
Title: Human Resource Director **Company:** RAM Medical Inc. **Address:** 4 Haul Road, Wayne, NJ 07470 United States **BUS:** Medical Sales Company **P/S:** Wholesales Medical, Dental, Hospital Equipment and Supplies **MA:** NJ, NY, CT **EXP:** Ms. Mazon's expertise is in human resources. **H/I/S:** Exercising **EDU:** Master's Degree in Media and Computer Technology, Montclair State University; Bachelor of Arts in Drama, Speech and English, Douglas College **A/A/S:** Past President, Hadassah; Chamber of Commerce **C/VW:** Hadassah
Email: debby77548@aol.com
URL: http://www.cambridgewhoswho.com

Nicole A. Mazzei-Williams
Title: Account Executive **Company:** Maryland Hospital Association **Dept:** Prime **Address:** 6820 Deerpath Road, Elkridge, MD 21075 United States **BUS:** Nonprofit Organization **P/S:** Purchasing Contacts and Executive Services **MA:** Local **D/D/R:** Representing Maryland Hospitals and Health Systems through Leadership, Education, Information, Communication and Collective Action in the Public Interest **H/I/S:** Spending Time with her Children, Traveling, Exercising **EDU:** Master of Arts in Healthcare Administration, University of Maryland; Master of Business Administration, University of Maryland **A/A/S:** Maryland Association of Health Care Executives; American College of Healthcare Executives; Maryland Society of Healthcare Materials Managers **C/VW:** United Way; American Cancer Society
Email: nmazzei-williams@mhaonline.org

Ms. Beverly A. McAllister
Title: Laboratory Administrative Director **Company:** Ephrata Community Hospital **Address:** 169 Martin Avenue, Ephrata, PA 17522 United States **BUS:** Hospital **P/S:** Healthcare and Laboratory Medicine **MA:** Local **D/D/R:** Testing Patient Care and Healthcare Quality Management, Specializing in Clinical Chemistry, Overseeing Approximately 100 Employees, Checking Accreditations, Budgeting, Evaluating, Interacting with All Departments within a Hospital, Overseeing Laboratory Renovation, Facilitating for Hospital Teams, Mediating Employee Issues, Serving as the Purchasing-Agent for a Laboratory, Working with the Information Technology Department **H/I/S:** Gardening, Hiking, Biking, Swimming **EDU:** Master of Science in Administration, Western Connecticut State University (1993); Bachelor of Science in Medical Technology, Western Connecticut State University (1987) **CERTS:** Certification, American Society of Clinical Pathologists (1987) **A/A/S:** American Society of Clinical Pathologists; National Association of Healthcare Quality; American Society for Quality **C/VW:** Sunday School, Local Church
Email: beverlymcallister@ephratahospital.org

Mary E. McAsey
Title: Director of Research **Company:** Southern Illinois School of Medicine, Department of Obstetrics and Gynecology **Address:** P.O. Box 19672, Springfield, IL 62794 United States **BUS:** College Education **P/S:** Anatomy, Anesthesiology, Biochemistry and Molecular Biology, Family and Community Medicine, Information and Communication Sciences, Medical Education, Medical Humanities, Neurology, Obstetrics and Gynecology, Pediatrics, Pharmacology, Physicians Assistant Program, Physiology, Psychiatry, Radiology, Surgery **MA:** International **D/D/R:** Working with Residents and Medical Students, Writing Grants, Researching the Effects of Estrogen on the Brain, Overseeing Reproductive Endocrinology and Women's Health, Writing for the Board of Bioanalysis **EDU:** Ph.D. in Anatomy and Cell Biology, University of Arizona (1994) **A/A/S:** American Board of Bioanalysis; Co-Founder, College of Reproductive Biology; Society for Study of Reproduction
Email: mmcasey@siumed.edu
URL: http://www.siumed.edu

Joseph A. McBreen
Title: Branch Manager **Company:** National City Mortgage **Address:** 200 E. Delaware Place, Chicago, IL 60611 United States **BUS:** Mortgage Company **P/S:** Financial Services Including Mortgage **MA:** National **D/D/R:** Writing Loans, Managing Employees, Loan Officers and Mortgage Writers, Offering Construction Loans for Custom Residential Properties, Overseeing the Purchase and Refinance of Residential Mortgages **H/I/S:** Golfing **EDU:** Coursework in Business, National University of Ireland, Galway (1994)
Email: joseph.mcbreeen@ncmc.com
URL: http://www.ncmc.com

Gloria Dawn McBride
Title: Licensed Physical Therapist Assistant **Company:** Sava Senior Care **Address:** 800 Skyland Drive, Pisgah Forest, NC 28768 United States **BUS:** Healthcare **P/S:** Medical Services **MA:** Regional **D/D/R:** Rehabilitation for People who had a Stroke, Neurological Problems, Working on Time Management, Treating 12 to 15 Patients a Day, Different Diagnostics, Emotional and Psychological Problems, Daily Notes, Teaching Mobility to Stroke Victims, Bed Mobility, Sitting, Balance **H/I/S:** Psychology **EDU:** Pursuing Master's Degree in in Clinical Counseling; Bachelor's Degree in Psychology, Regions University(2007); Associate Degree in Physical Therapy, Walter State College (1992)
Email: gdmcbride@citcom.net
URL: http://www.savaseniorcare.com

Antoinette McBurney-Washington
Title: Correctional Sergeant **Company:** Miami-Dade County Corrections and Rehabilitation **Address:** 2525 N.W. 62nd Street, Miami, FL 33147 United States **BUS:** Correctional Institution **P/S:** Correctional Services **MA:** Regional **D/D/R:** Accommodating Juveniles, Supervising Female Offenders, Escorting Juveniles to Homes and Shelters, Interacting with Police Officers and Counselors **H/I/S:** Reading, Volunteering **EDU:** Bachelor of Science in Criminal Justice, Florida International University (2006) **A/A/S:** Delta Epsilon Iota; National Association for Female Executives; American Association of University Women **C/VW:** Foster Care Review; Make-A-Wish; American Red Cross; Big Brothers Big Sisters; Golden Key International Honour Society
Email: scoobsez@netzero.net
URL: http://www.miamidade.gov

Elizabeth J. McCain

Title: Kindergarten Teacher **Company:** Sierra Sands Unified School District **Address:** 113 W. Felspar Avenue, Ridgecrest, CA 93555 United States **BUS:** School District **P/S:** Education **MA:** Local **D/D/R:** Teaching Students in Kindergarten **H/I/S:** Collecting Stamps, Camping, Traveling, Reading, Scrapbooking **EDU:** Pursuing Master's Degree in Reading Education, California State University at San Bernardino; Bachelor's Degree in Reading Education, Eastern Washington University **A/A/S:** International Reading Association; California Teachers Association; Kappa Delta Pi
URL: http://www.cambridgewhoswho.comn

Michele M. McCallion

Title: Science Teacher **Company:** Overbrook School for the Blind **Address:** 6333 Malvern Avenue, Philadelphia, PA 19151 United States **BUS:** School for the Visually Impaired **P/S:** Education for the Visually Impaired **MA:** Regional **D/D/R:** Teaching Science to Visually Impaired Students, Coaching the Swim and Track Teams **H/I/S:** Reading, Gardening, Teaching Tae Kwon Do, Scuba Diving, Lifeguarding **EDU:** Master of Science in Rehabilitation Counseling, The University of Scranton; Plus 35 in Biology Sciences, Immaculate University; Dual Bachelor of Science in Special Education and Visually Impaired K-12 and Elementary Education, Kutztown University **A/A/S:** National Science Teachers Association; Third Degree Black Belt **C/VW:** Respite Care, Susan G. Komen for the Cure
Email: michele@obs.org
URL: http://www.obs.org

Kristy R. McCandless

Title: Administrative Assistant **Company:** Jacobs Technology **Address:** 6703 Odyssey Drive, Suite 304, Huntsville, AL 35806 United States **BUS:** Technology Company **P/S:** Information Technology for Military **MA:** International **D/D/R:** Offering Administrative Support for Upper Management, Technical Directors and Project Leaders **H/I/S:** Playing Tennis and Volleyball, Coaching Junior Varsity Volleyball **EDU:** Pursuing Bachelor's Degree in Human Resources, Athens State University; Associate Degree in Business, Calhoun Community College **C/VW:** Junior Varsity Volleyball Coach, Catholic High
Email: gymratfive@knology.net
URL: http://www.cambridgewhoswho.com

Rachel McCann

Title: Second-Grade Teacher **Company:** Pittsfield Public Schools-Morningside Community School **Address:** 100 Burbank Street, Pittsfield, MA 01021 United States **BUS:** Elementary School **P/S:** Instruction in Reading, Mathematics, English, Science, Social Studies, Art, Music, History, Physical Education **MA:** Regional **D/D/R:** Reading/Language Arts Instruction; Public Relations; Administrative Duties; Technology Integration Facilitator; New Teacher Mentor; Summer Learning Academy Program Coordinator; Berkshire Reading Council Board Member; Expanded School Day Steering Committee **H/I/S:** Swimmer; Musician; Outdoor Sport Enthusiast **EDU:** Associate Degree, Berkshire Community College; Bachelor of Science, Massachusetts College of Liberal Arts **CERTS:** Licensed in Early Childhood and Elementary Education **A/A/S:** Alpha Chi National Honor Society
Email: rmccann@pittsfield.net
URL: http://www.mail.pittsfield.net/~rachel_mccann

Alexis B. McCarthy

Title: 1) Human Resources Manager 2) Paralegal **Company:** 1) Home Depot 2) Alexis McCarthy, LDP **Address:** P.O. Box 1093, Alta Loma, CA 91701 United States **BUS:** 1) Home Improvement Retail 2) Civil Law Firm **P/S:** 1) Remodeling Services, Interior Designing 2) Paralegal Services **MA:** Regional **D/D/R:** Managing Human Resource Department, Overseeing Employee Benefits Plans, Offering Paralegal Services **H/I/S:** Spending Time with her Family **EDU:** Pursuing Law Degree; Master's Degree in Human Resources (2002); Coursework in Business Administration, University of Cambridge (1999) **A/A/S:** Professional Secretaries Association
Email: alexmc49@netzero.com

Janie E. McCarthy

Title: Speech-Language Pathologist **Company:** North Platte Public Schools **Address:** 301 W. F Street, North Platte, NE 69101 United States **BUS:** School District **P/S:** Education **MA:** Local **EXP:** Ms. McCarthy's expertise is in speech-language pathology. **H/I/S:** Spending Time with her Family, Golfing **EDU:** Master's Degree in Speech-Language Pathology, University of Nebraska **A/A/S:** North Platte Education Association; Nebraska Education Association **C/VW:** Church, Local Hospital
Email: jmccarth@nppsd.org
URL: http://www.cambridgewhoswho.com

Linda P. McCarthy, MA, CCC-SLP

Title: Speech-Language Pathologist **Company:** Prospect Child and Family Center **Address:** 133 Aviation Road, Queensbury, NY 12804 United States **BUS:** Nonprofit School for Developmentally Disabled Children **P/S:** Occupational, Speech, Physical and Developmental Therapy **MA:** Regional **EXP:** Ms. McCarthy's expertise includes preschool evaluations, assessments and therapy. **H/I/S:** Quilting **EDU:** Master's Degree in Speech-Language Therapy, SUNY Plattsburgh, 1986 **A/A/S:** American Speech-Language-Hearing Association; Capital Area Speech and Hearing Association **C/VW:** Local Environmental Organizations
Email: mccarthy.w@verizon.net

Timothy P. McCarthy, Ph.D.

Title: Professor and Lecturer on History, Literature and Public Policy **Company:** Harvard University **Address:** 58 Plympton Street, Cambridge, MA 02138 United States **BUS:** University **P/S:** Higher Education **MA:** Regional **D/D/R:** Teaching in a Joint Appointment to Harvard College Undergraduates in Political Speech Making and American Protest Literature, Conducting History and Literature Seminars, Teaching at the Kennedy School of Government and the Art of Political Communications **H/I/S:** Basketball, Tennis, Football **EDU:** Ph.D., Columbia University (2006); Master of Arts in History, Columbia University (1996); Master of Philosophy, Columbia University (1997); Bachelor of Arts in History and Literature, Harvard University (1993) **A/A/S:** Society for Historians of the Early American Republic; American Historical Association; Organization of American Historians; Modern Language Association; American Studies Association; Author, 'The Radical Reader,' Published by New Press (2003); Author, 'Profits of Protest,' Published by New Press
Email: mccarth3@fas.harvard.edu
URL: http://www.ksgfaculty.harvard.edu/timothy_mccarthy

Mr. Kelly Dale McCarty

Title: Executive Vice President **Company:** Brokers International, LTD **Address:** 1200 East Main Street, Panora, IA 50216 United States **BUS:** Premier Insurance Marketing Company **P/S:** One of the Largest National Providers of Distribution of Fixed Index Annuities **MA:** National **D/D/R:** Creating Activities with Marketing Partners, Assisting Clients in Achieving New Levels of Success, Designing Annuities to Actuaries and Developing Proprietary Products, Activity Direction **EDU:** Coursework in Business and Finance, Western State College **A/A/S:** Public Speaking Nationally, Motivational Speaker **A/H:** Certified Annuities Advisor Association
Email: kmccarty@theimg.net
URL: http://www.biltd.com

Michelle R. McCaskill

Title: Chief, Public Affairs Team **Company:** U.S. Army Material Command **Address:** AMCPC, 9301 Chapek Road, Fort Belvoir, VA 22060 United States **BUS:** Military **P/S:** Defense, Material Readiness **MA:** International **EXP:** Ms. McCaskill's expertise is in public affairs. **H/I/S:** Showing Dogs, Exercising, Running, Going to the Gym **EDU:** Master's Degree in Communications, University of Oklahoma; Bachelor's Degree in History, University of Missouri **C/VW:** American Society for the Prevention of Cruelty to Animals
Email: michelle.mccaskill@us.army.mil
URL: http://www.amc.army.mil

Barbara B. McClain

Title: Retired Director of Guidance **Company:** Lexington School District **Address:** 120 Heidelberg Circle, Columbia, SC 29036 United States **BUS:** Education School **P/S:** Helping students plan for future **MA:** Local **D/D/R:** Teaching, Counseling, Plus Administration, Also part of first year duties were to integrate high school under freedom choice act, which was the voluntary integration of students **H/I/S:** Reading **EDU:** UCLA, MA-English **A/A/S:** SEA, SCEA, NEA
Email: barbaramcclain@earthlink.net

Martha J. McClarnon

Title: Teacher (Retired) **Company:** Richardson Independent School District **Address:** 400 S. Greenville Avenue, Richardson, TX 75081 United States **BUS:** School District **P/S:** Education **MA:** Local **D/D/R:** Teaching Elementary Education and Reading **H/I/S:** Scrapbooking, Making Crafts, Gardening, Reading Mystery Books, Spending Time with her Grandchildren **EDU:** Master of Education in Reading, with Concentration in Commerce, Texas A&M University (1989); Bachelor of Science in Education, Brian College (1975) **A/A/S:** Texas State Teachers Association; National Education Association; Parent-Teacher Association; Texas Retired Teachers Association **C/VW:** The Heights Baptist Church
Email: tlmac03@verizon.net
URL: http://www.cambridgewhoswho.com

Cecilia McClendon

Title: Senior Vice President, Urban and Rhythm Promotion **Company:** Sony BMG/Columbia Music **Address:** 550 Madison Avenue, 26th Floor, New York, NY 10022 United States **BUS:** Music and Entertainment Company **P/S:** Music, Entertainment **MA:** National **EXP:** Ms. McClendon's expertise is in radio promotions. **H/I/S:** Cooking, Sewing, Making Jewelry **EDU:** Associate Degree in Computer Fashion, Wayne County Community College **C/VW:** Helped Raise $10,000 for Revlon Run/Walk
Email: cecilia@max.com
URL: http://www.cambridgewhoswho.com

Mr. John McClimon

Title: Supply Chain Director **Company:** Purcell International Group **Address:** 9635 Granite Ridge Drive, Suite 120, San Diego, CA 92123 United States **BUS:** Executive Search Company **P/S:** Executive Search **EXP:** Mr. McLimon's expertise includes distribution, logistics, engineering and human resources. **H/I/S:** Golfing, Traveling, Coaching, Woodworking **EDU:** Bachelor's Degree in Recreation, San Diego State University **A/A/S:** Sierra Club; Coach, High School Football and Baseball
Email: jmclimon@purcellintl.com
URL: http://www.cambridgewhoswho.com

Cindy Close McClure

Title: Owner **Company:** Have Gloves Will Travel, Inc. **Address:** 2315 Natalie Avenue, Las Vegas, NV 89169 United States **BUS:** Marine Detailing **P/S:** Cleaning and Detailing Boats in National Park Marinas, Color Restoration, Polishing Waxing, Butler Service **MA:** Arizona, Nevada **D/D/R:** Running Crews, Acquiring New Business, Customer Service, Marine Detailing and Cleaning, Sales, Accounting, Bookkeeping, Specialty Items **H/I/S:** Enjoying Water Sports, Dancing **A/A/S:** U.S. Coast Guard Auxiliary; FIN; Lake Yacht Club
Email: boatdetailing4u@yahoo.com
URL: http://www.cambridgewhoswho.com

Jonna K. McClure

Title: Director **Company:** Boone Guest Home **Address:** 3010 Farabaugh Lane, Pueblo, CO 81005 United States **BUS:** Human Services **P/S:** Developmental Disabilities Residential Facilities **MA:** Local **D/D/R:** Behavioral Technologies, Organizing Staff Activities and Training **H/I/S:** Spending Time with Family, Community Service Activities **EDU:** Bachelor of Science in Social Work, University of Southern California, 1993 **A/A/S:** American Association on Mental Retardation **C/VW:** Youth Group, Local Church, Special Olympics
Email: jjzmcclure@hotmail.com
URL: http://www.cambridgewhoswho.com

Nathan D. McClure III

Title: Public Safety Consultant **Company:** CTA Communications **Address:** 20175 Timberlake Road, Lynchburg, VA 24502 United States **BUS:** Communications Company **P/S:** Communications Engineering, Consulting Services **MA:** International **EXP:** Mr. McClure's expertise is in operations management. **D/D/R:** Overseeing Public Safety **H/I/S:** Sailing, Amateur Radio **EDU:** Master of Public Administration, Western Michigan University **A/A/S:** The Association of Public-Safety Communications Officials; 9-1-1 National Emergency Number Association; National Fire Protection Association **C/VW:** The Rotary Club of Lynchburg; American Red Cross; Campbell County Rescue Squad
Email: nmcclure@ctacommunications.com
URL: http://www.ctacommunications.com

Betty Susan McCollaum

Title: Teacher (Retired) **Company:** Carlsbad Municipal Schools, Eddy Elementary School **Address:** 700 W. Stevens Street, Carlsbad, NM 88220 United States **BUS:** Elementary School **P/S:** Education **MA:** Local **D/D/R:** Working in a Reading and Mathematics Computer Lab with First through Fifth-Grade Students **H/I/S:** Reading, Spending Time with her Family and Friends **EDU:** Master of Education, Emphasis in Reading and Mathematics, Western University; Bachelor of Science in Elementary Education, New Mexico State University **A/A/S:** National Education Association; New Mexico Education Association; Former Member, New Mexico Reading Association
Email: ed-r-us@mywdo.com
URL: http://www.cambridgewhoswho.com

Charles G. McCombs Jr.

Title: Certified Registered Nurse Anesthetist **Company:** Latrobe Anesthesia Associates **Address:** 121 W. Second Avenue, Latrobe, PA 15650 United States **BUS:** Healthcare Company **P/S:** Anesthetic Services, Research and Review Board for Nurse Anesthetists **MA:** National **D/D/R:** Teaching Anesthesiology **H/I/S:** Researching Military History, Reenacting Historical Events **EDU:** Bachelor of Science in Anesthesiology **A/A/S:** American Society Of Anesthesiology **A/H:** Alumni Anesthetist of the Year **C/VW:** Civil War Trust; Gettysburg National Park Foundation; American Diabetes Association; American Veterans Association
Email: chuckm9166@aol.com

Angela Marie McConnell
Title: Special Education Teacher **Company:** New Castle Area School District **Address:** 420 Fern Street, New Castle, PA 16101 United States **BUS:** Public School **P/S:** Education to Students in Grades K-12th **MA:** Local **D/D/R:** Offering Learning Support and Individual Attention to Ninth-Grade Mathematics Students **H/I/S:** Traveling, Spending Time with Grandchildren **EDU:** Pursuing Master of Education, Slippery Rock University; Bachelor's Degree in Education in Special Education and Elementary Education, Slippery Rock University, 1984 **C/VW:** American Cancer Society
Email: amcconnell@ncasd.com
URL: http://www.ncasd.com

Deborah A. McConnell
Title: Manager **Company:** Pipestone Veterinary Clinic **Address:** 1300 S. Highway 75, Pipestone, MN 56164 United States **BUS:** Veterinary Clinic **P/S:** Animal Care **MA:** Local **EXP:** Ms. McConnell's expertise include breeding gestation and nursery finishing. **H/I/S:** Practicing Yoga, Tae Kwon Doe, Reading **EDU:** High School Diploma **CERTS:** Certified Manager **A/H:** Minnesota Pork Production Swine Manager of the Year Award (2000)
Email: debmccnnll@yahoo.com

Ken J. McConnell
Title: Vice President of Finance **Company:** Garrett Law Office **Address:** 111 W. Fifth Street, Suite 800, Tulsa, OK 74103 United States **BUS:** Law Firm **P/S:** Personal Injury Representation, Workers Compensation Law, Social Security Disability Law, Medical Malpractice, Nursing Home Negligence, Commercial Negligence, Mass Tort, Criminal Law, Consulting Services, Resources, Financial Services **MA:** National **EXP:** Mr. McConnell's expertise includes finance, human resources and risk management law. **H/I/S:** Tennis **EDU:** Master of Arts in Finance, University of Phoenix (2002)
Email: kemmcconnell@cox.net
URL: http://www.garrettlawoffice.com

Ms. Denise McCool-Vogel
Title: President, Owner **Company:** Quality Home Healthcare **Address:** 545 Washington Boulevard, Second Floor, Sea Girt, NJ 08750 United States **BUS:** Home Healthcare Center **P/S:** Healthcare **EXP:** Ms. McCool-Vogel's expertise includes gerontology and cardiology. **D/D/R:** Overseeing Home Healthcare **H/I/S:** Playing Tennis, Skiing **EDU:** Pursuing Bachelor of Science in Nursing; Associate Degree in Nursing, Community College of Philadelphia **CERTS:** Registered Nurse; Certified Medical-Surgical Nurse; Certification in CPR; Certification in Telemetry; Certification in Venipuncture **A/A/S:** Sea Girt Chamber of Commerce; Howell Chamber of Commerce **A/H:** Club Champion in Tennis (2004); Good Citizens Award (1974) **C/VW:** Breast Cancer Society; American Lung Association
Email: dvogel@qualityhomecarenj.com
URL: http://www.qualityhomecarenj.com

Mr. David R. McCormack, Esq.
Title: Attorney **Company:** Law Office of David R. McCormack **Address:** 6025 Heards Lane, Suite 4W, Galveston, TX 77551 United States **BUS:** Criminal Law Firm **P/S:** Legal Services **MA:** National **D/D/R:** Consulting in Civil, Criminal and Racketeer Influenced and Corrupt Organizations Matters **H/I/S:** Reading, Sports **EDU:** JD, Southern Methodist University; Master's Degree in Political Science, Northwestern University; Bachelor's Degree in Political Science, Yale University **A/A/S:** State Bar of Texas; State Bar of Arizona; American College of Forensic Examiners **C/VW:** American Friends Service Committee, Planned Parenthood, Southern Methodist University
Email: davidrmccormack@aol.com
URL: http://www.davidrmccormack.com

Eugene R. McCormick
Title: Assistant Vice President, Editorial Director **Company:** Peoples Education **Address:** Peoples Education, Inc., 299 Market Street, Saddle Brook, NJ 07663 United States **BUS:** Publishing and Distribution Company **P/S:** Supplemental Materials for Grades One through 12 **MA:** National **D/D/R:** Conducting Programs, Working with Diverse Groups of Authors, Consultants, Editors, Designers and Programmers to Develop Instructional and Assessment Products to Cover State Standards in Print and Electronic Media Including Interactive Lessons, Activities, Games, Animations, Tests and Videos **EDU:** Master of Science in Marine Biology, C.W. Post Campus, Long Island University (1979) **A/A/S:** Association for Supervision and Curriculum Development; Beta Beta Beta National Biological Honor Society
Email: emccormick@peoplesed.com
URL: http://www.peopleseducation.com

Nerissa McCormick
Title: Service Coordinator **Company:** Elliot Health and Community Services **Address:** Lexington, MA United States **BUS:** Leading Human Services Organization Working with Numerous State and Local Agencies throughout the Country in the Delivery of Human Services Programs **P/S:** Residential Psychiatric Rehabilitation for Adults **MA:** National **D/D/R:** Rehabilitating Adults with Mental Illness, Helping Patients with Vocational and Life Skills, Managing Administration, Overseeing the Intake and Discharge of Patients, Supervising Counselors, Running Billing, Processing Notes and Correspondence with Corporate Headquarters on Patient Progress **H/I/S:** Traveling, Hiking **EDU:** Master's Degree in Psychiatric Rehabilitation, Boston University (2006); Bachelor's Degree in Rehabilitation, University of Maine at Farmington (2003) **CERTS:** Certified Rehabilitation Counselor
Email: nerissamccormick@nafi.com

Kelly B. McCowen
Title: Account Executive **Company:** Colour One O One **Address:** 1661 Defoor Avenue N.W., Atlanta, GA 30318 United States **BUS:** Marketing and Branding Agency **P/S:** Commercial Printing **MA:** Local **EXP:** Ms. McCowen's expertise includes account management, sales and artistic direction. **H/I/S:** Ballet Dancing, Listening to Music, Creating Art **EDU:** Pursuing Nursing Assistant Certification, North Metro Technical College; Pursuing Associate of Science in Radiology, North Metro Technical College **A/A/S:** Printing Industry Association of Georgia **C/VW:** Georgia Ballet, Metropolitan Hospice
Email: kelly@colour101.com

Cameron J. McCoy
Title: Regional Director **Company:** Simon Property Group **Address:** 2350 W. Airport Parkway, Suite 310, Bedford, TX 76022 United States **BUS:** Retail Real Estate Investment Trust **P/S:** Retail Real Estate **MA:** National **D/D/R:** Marketing **H/I/S:** Traveling, Golfing, Reading, Watching College Football **EDU:** Bachelor's Degree in History, Washington State University; Bachelor's Degree in Social Studies, Washington State University; Bachelor's Degree in Architectural Studies, Washington State University **C/VW:** Operation Kindness
Email: cjmccoy@gocougs.wsu.edu
URL: http://www.simon.com

James L. McCoy
Title: President **Company:** R & M Professional Development **Address:** 4502 W. Bridalwood Drive, Peoria, IL 61615 United States **BUS:** Professional Development Company **P/S:** Self and Business Enhancement **MA:** Local **EXP:** Mr. McCoy's expertise is in evaluation. **H/I/S:** Golfing, Basketball **EDU:** Bachelor of Science in Pre-Law Studies, Western Illinois University (1991) **A/A/S:** Vice President, Afro American Fire Fighters; Omega Psi Phi
Email: qdog4life@sbcglobal.net
URL: http://www.jaireneetravel.com

Annie K. McCracken
Title: Accounts Payable Clerk **Company:** Caraustar Industries **Address:** 5000 Austell-Powder Springs Road, Austell, GA 30106 United States **BUS:** Manufacturing **P/S:** Recycled Paper and Paperboard **MA:** International **D/D/R:** Paying Invoices, Handling Phone Communications with Clients and Vendors, Ordering All Supplies for Mill Group **H/I/S:** Automobile Restoration, Collecting Swords from the Medieval and Napoleonic Time Periods **EDU:** Bachelor of Arts Degree in International Affairs, Kennesaw State University, Georgia (2003) **A/A/S:** Safety Committee, Iron Mountain Representative for Mill Group
Email: annie.mccracken@caraustar.com
URL: http://www.caraustar.com

Nicole L. McCracken
Title: Owner, Stylist **Company:** Salon Kymneco's **Address:** 1008 W. Roosevelt Boulevard, Suite F, Monroe, NC 28110 United States **BUS:** Cosmetology **P/S:** Hair Cutting, Coloring, Weaving, Extensions, Fusion **MA:** Local **D/D/R:** Hair Cutting and Maintaining Healthy Hair, she comes in and opens the salon, full time stylist, manages the salon, paperwork, scheduling, payroll, consulting and lecturing, wings and wine to clients at the salon and answered the questions clients would have regarding hair care they do this for the clients twice a month, most rewarding aspect of her job is customer satisfaction and clients being excited about their new look, goals for the future is to expand and become bigger and better and become one of the leading salons in the nation **H/I/S:** Travel **EDU:** Wingate University, Brunswick Community College, B-Business Administration **CERTS:** Licensed Cosmetologist **A/A/S:** RHA House, Center for Disabled Children
Email: nlmccrac@aol.com
URL: www.mysalononline.com/kymnecos

Ann McCraw-Orlando
Title: Teacher, Director **Company:** St. Joseph the Carpenter School **Address:** 140 E. Third Avenue, Roselle, NJ 07203 United States **BUS:** Proven Leader in Education and Child Care **P/S:** Highest Quality of Educational Services for Students in Elementary School, After School Care Program **MA:** Regional **D/D/R:** Coordinating Science Program, Teaching Mathematics and Science, Directing After School Programs **H/I/S:** Dancing **EDU:** Bachelor of Arts Plus 18 Credits in Psychology and Instruction Curriculum, Kean University (1972) **A/A/S:** National Science Teachers Association; New Jersey Science Teachers Association
Email: orlando@stjosephsroselle.org
URL: http://www.stjosephsroselle.org

Herbert L. McCrea
Title: Chief Executive Officer **Company:** Royalty Automobile Services **Address:** 5530 N.W. 17 Avenue, Miami, FL 33142 United States **BUS:** Automobile Finance Company **P/S:** Automobile Financing and Credit Restoration **MA:** National **D/D/R:** Handling Automobile Financing, Helping Credit Repair and Restoration **H/I/S:** Playing Tennis, Basketball, Lifting Weights **EDU:** Coursework in Business, University of South Florida (1992) **A/A/S:** Neighbors to Neighbors; Liberty City Trust
Email: herbm38@yahoo.com
URL: http://www.royaltycreditsolutions.com

Patricia A. McCuin, RPH
Title: Pharmacist **Company:** CVS Pharmacy **Address:** 2674 S. 31st, Temple, TX 76504 United States **BUS:** Healthcare Retail Pharmacy Army Medical Center **P/S:** Offering Clinic Prescription Services to our Military Service Members, their Families, Centers and the Surrounding Communities **MA:** Local **D/D/R:** Working as a Pharmacy Manager, Preceptor, Technician and Pharmacist Trainer, Clinical Pharmacist and Student Mentor **H/I/S:** Devotional Reading, Basketball, Fishing, Student Mentor **EDU:** Bachelor of Science in Pharmacy, Texas Southern University **A/A/S:** National Cancer Association, State Trooper Association, CPS,National Community Pharmacists
Email: cedar6999@yahoo.com

Shannon L. McCulloch
Title: Owner, Operator **Company:** Shannon's Tranquility for Health and Beauty **Address:** P.O. Box 145, 1600 Broadway, Dakota City, NE 68731 United States **BUS:** Full-Service Salon and Spa **P/S:** Hair Care, Tanning, Massage Therapy, Spa Treatments, Nail Care **MA:** Local **D/D/R:** Overseeing Daily Operations, Administering Hair Care Treatments, Tanning, Massage Therapy and Spa Treatments **H/I/S:** Hunting, Fishing, Hiking, Participating in Outdoor Activities **CERTS:** Licensed in Cosmetology (1990); Licensed in Massage Therapy (2004) **A/A/S:** The National Certification Board for Therapeutic Massage and Bodywork
Email: shannon07@peoplepc.com

Brenda L. McCully
Title: Patient Care Mgr of Mental Health **Company:** Sunnybrook Health Sciences Centre **Address:** 2075 Bayview Avenue, Toronto, M4N3M5 Canada **BUS:** Healthcare Hospital **P/S:** Hospital for Adolescence, Adults and Geriatrics **MA:** Local **EXP:** Ms. McCully's expertise includes mental health and mood disorders. **H/I/S:** Family **EDU:** Ryerson University, Durham College, Bachelor Science Nursing, Post Grad Course Psychiatry **A/A/S:** RNAO, PNIG, CON, Certified Mental Health

Jennifer L. McCutcheon, Esq.
Title: President **Company:** Russell L Reineman Stable, Inc **Address:** 3355 W. 31st Street, Chicago, IL 60623 United States **BUS:** Equestrian Gaming **P/S:** Thoroughbred Breeding **MA:** International **D/D/R:** Racing **H/I/S:** Reading, Volleyball **EDU:** Miami of Ohio University, North Illinois University, University of Aberdeen, JD **A/A/S:** ITHA, ICA, ICTY, ABA, IBA
Email: jennifer@rlrstables.com
URL: www.rlrstable.com

Ms. Karen E. McDaniel, LPN
Title: Licensed Practical Nurse **Company:** Internal Medicine Clinic **Address:** 42078 Veterans Boulevard, Suite C, Hammond, LA 70403 United States **BUS:** Podiatrist **P/S:** Foot Care **MA:** Local **D/D/R:** Wound Care, Diabetic Care, Helping and Counseling Women who have Lost a Child to Suicide **H/I/S:** Reading, Selling Aloette Skin Care Products, Activities with Youth at Church **CERTS:** Certified IV, CPR, LPN, South Coast Junior College (1980)
Email: maclane53@wildblue.net

Rhonda G. McDaniel

Title: Aesthetician, Owner **Company:** A Caring Touch Skin Therapy, Inc. **Address:** 1308 E. Lumsden Road, Brandon, FL 33511 United States **BUS:** Skin Care Company **P/S:** Skin Care Treatments **MA:** Local **D/D/R:** Treating Acne, Microdermabrasion, Rosacea treatments, Customized Chemical and Non-Chemical Peels **H/I/S:** Reading, Scrapbooking **EDU:** Bachelor of Science in Accounting, Louisiana State University, Shreveport (1998) **CERTS:** FL Licensed Aesthetician and Clinical Certified **A/A/S:** Greater Brandon Chamber of Commerce; Riverview Chamber of Commerce; Better Business Bureau **C/VW:** American Cancer Society, Veterans of America
Email: skincare@actskintherapy.com
URL: http://www.actskintherapy.com

Mac McDermitt

Title: President **Company:** Southern States Lighting, Inc. **Address:** 1133 Heron Point Way, Deland, FL 32724 United States **BUS:** Manufacturing Company **P/S:** Acom Lighting and Steel Traffic Poles **MA:** Regional **D/D/R:** Managing the Sale of Aluminum Parts for Traffic Poles **H/I/S:** Golfing, Traveling, Spending Time with his Family **EDU:** Coursework in Business; High School Diploma **A/A/S:** Former Member, Traffic Engineering Society **C/VW:** Boys Town, Omaha; The Danny Thomas Show
Email: mac29@cfl.rr.com
URL: http://www.cambridgewhoswho.com

Angela J. McDonald

Title: Lab Tech, Medical Assistant **Company:** Commonwealth Free Clinic **Address:** 740 E. 10th Street, Bowling Green, KY 42101 United States **BUS:** Healthcare Clinic **P/S:** Free Healthcare for Working Poor **MA:** Local **EXP:** Ms. McDonald's expertise is in internal medicine. **H/I/S:** Reading Medical Coding **EDU:** Western Kentucky University/Johns Jr College, Bachelor's Degree in History and Library Service/Associate Degree in Health Info and Associate in Medical Assistant **A/A/S:** AHEMA, AAPC, AMT, AAMA
Email: ajmcdon_108@hotmail.com

Kimberley S. McDonald

Title: Correctional Lieutenant **Company:** Arizona Department of Corrections **Dept:** ASPC-Florence/East Unit **Address:** 2179 E. Butte Avenue, ASPC-F/East Unit, Florence, AZ 85232 United States **BUS:** Department of Corrections **P/S:** Minimum to Maximum Custody and Correctional Supervision for Incarcerated Inmates **MA:** Statewide **D/D/R:** Ensuring the Appropriate Number of Staff Members Are on Duty to Maintain a Safe, Secure Institution, Managing and Supervising Sergeants and Officers, Overseeing the Security and Custody of the Inmates, Developing and Scheduling Rosters, Maintaining Discipline and Order, Mentoring and Training Subordinate Officers and Future Sergeants, Preparing the Inmates to Develop their Social Skills **H/I/S:** Hiking, Scuba Diving, Reading, Walking **EDU:** Pursuing Associate Degree in Criminal Justice, Ashworth University; Coursework, Correctional Officer Training Academy (1995); Crisis Intervention Training **A/A/S:** Arizona Conference of Police and Sheriffs; Critical Incident Response Team
Email: kmcdonal@azcorrections.gov
Email: kmax_mac@hotmail.com
URL: http://www.azcorrections.gov

Raymond G. McDonald

Title: Firefighter **Company:** New Beaver Borough Volunteer Fire Department **Address:** Wampum New Galilee Road, Wampum, PA 16157 United States **BUS:** Volunteer Fire Department **P/S:** Firefighting **MA:** Local **D/D/R:** Fighting Fires, Fundraising **H/I/S:** Camping, Spending Time with Family and Friends **EDU:** Industry-Related Training and Experience **CERTS:** Certification in Vehicle Rescue **A/A/S:** Industry-Related Affiliations **C/VW:** Community Fundraising Events

Barbara E. McDonnaugh-Reece

Title: Lactation Educator, Registered Nurse, CNM **Company:** Barbara McDonnaugh-Reece **Address:** 4877 Patterson Avenue, Las Vegas, NV 89104 United States **BUS:** Independent Lactation Educator **P/S:** Midwifery, Education **MA:** Las Vegas Area, New York **D/D/R:** Assisting Low-Income Teenagers with Pregnancy Issues **H/I/S:** Gardening, Knitting, Reading **EDU:** Pursuing Bachelor's Degree, College of Santa Fe, NM; Associate of Arts, Community College of Southern Nevada (2007); Bachelor's Degree in Midwifery **A/A/S:** Phi Beta Kappa; Midwifery Organizations; Breastfeeding Task Force **A/H:** Dean's List **C/VW:** March of Dimes
Email: bmcdonnaugh1@aol.com
URL: http://www.cambridgewhoswho.com

Julia L. McDowell

Title: 1) Notary 2) Entrepreneur **Company:** Nanashands **Address:** 2736 Driftwood Road S., Saint Petersburg, FL 33705 United States **BUS:** 1) Licensed Notary Working with Local Real Estate Agents 2) Home-Based Company Making Gift Baskets and Cards for Business Accounts and Individuals **P/S:** 1) Licensed Notary Working with Local Real Estate Agents 2) Gift Baskets and Personalized Gift Cards **MA:** National **D/D/R:** 1) Notarizing Public Documents 2) Creating Personalized Baskets and Cards for Gifts **H/I/S:** Reading, Sewing, Attending the Theater **EDU:** Bachelor's Degree in Education, Rutgers, The State University of New Jersey, Newark (1972)
Email: nanashands245@yahoo.com
URL: http://www.cambridgewhoswho.com

Karen Y. McEldowney-Hay

Title: Dental Hygienist **Company:** Steven Thurn, DMD, General Dentistry **Address:** 222 Sixth Street, Springfield, OR 97477 United States **BUS:** Dental Clinic **P/S:** Dental Care **MA:** Local **D/D/R:** Performing Periodontal Therapy and Preventive Care Treatment **H/I/S:** Biking, Hiking, Scrapbooking, Attending Sporting Events **EDU:** Associate of Science in Dental Hygiene, Lane Community College, Eugene, OR **C/VW:** Volunteer, Local Children's Dental Clinic, Lane County; John Serbu Juvenile Justice Center, Eugene, OR
Email: sandrdc1@comcast.net
URL: http://www.cambridgewhoswho.com

Martha L. McElroy

Title: 1) President and Founder 2) Professor of Engineering Technology (Retired) 3) Custom Home Designer **Company:** 1) Congregation of YHWH, Inc. at Jacksonville FL Inc 2) Florida Community College 3) Technidraft **Address:** Jacksonville, FL 32216 United States **BUS:** 1) Religious Congregation 2) Community College 3) Architectural Design **P/S:** 1) Religious Publications based on Research 2) Engineering Education 3) Architectural Designs **MA:** 1) National 2) Local 3) Local **EXP:** Ms. McElroy's expertise includes religious and scriptural research, architectural and engineering education, and custom home design. **H/I/S:** Writing, Art, Painting, Biblical Research. **EDU:** Master of Education, University of North Florida; Bachelor's Degree in Education, University of North Florida; Associate of Arts, Paducah Community College; Diploma in Commercial Art **A/A/S:** Emeriti Alumni Association, UNF; Alpha Beta Honor Society; Phi Kappa Honor Society, Paducah Community College; Kappa Delta Pi Honor Society, UNF. **A/H:** First Prize, Paducah Centennial Seal Design; First Prize, John Latham Foundation Poster Award **C/VW:** Congregation of YHWH, Educational Outreach Program
Email: Truth_Search@Comcast.net
URL: http://www.cambridgewhoswho.com

Nancy M. McElveen

Title: Director of Institutional Assessment and Research **Company:** Greensboro College **Address:** 815 W. Market Street, Greensboro, NC 27401 United States **BUS:** College **P/S:** Higher Education **MA:** International **EXP:** Ms. McElveen's expertise includes French, institutional assessment and research. **H/I/S:** Reading, Needlework **EDU:** Ph.D. in French, University of North Carolina at Chapel Hill **A/A/S:** North Carolina Chapter, American Association of Teachers of French; Foreign Language Association of North Carolina; Association for Institutional Research; North Carolina Association of Institutional Research
Email: mcelveenn@gborocollege.edu
URL: Http://www.gborocollege.edu

Mariann McEniry

Title: Contracts Manager **Company:** Northrop Grumman **Address:** 1 Space Park Boulevard, Redondo Beach, CA 90278 United States **BUS:** Military and Defense Equipment Manufacturer **P/S:** Defense Equipment, Government Contracting **MA:** National **EXP:** Ms. McEniry's expertise is in government contracts. **H/I/S:** Traveling, Animals **EDU:** Bachelor of Science in Business Administration, University of Redlands **A/A/S:** National Contract Management Association **C/VW:** Veterans Administration Fund, Guide Dogs for the Blind, South Bay Rape Crisis Center
Email: mariann.mceniry@ngc.com
URL: http://www.cambridgewhoswho.com

Rev., Dr. Jacqueline R. McEwan

Title: Senior Pastor **Company:** Higher Place of Praise Ministries **Address:** 7973 Parston Drive, Forestville, MD 20747 United States **BUS:** Ministry **P/S:** Religious Services and Christian Values **MA:** Regional **D/D/R:** Mentoring, Preaching, Teaching, Managing Church Operations, Counseling, Teaching Sunday School **H/I/S:** Listening to Music, Reading, Writing **EDU:** Ph.D. in Theology and Counseling, Word of Faith Christian College (2005) **A/A/S:** Collective Banking Group; Kingdom Fellowship Covenant Ministry; Royal Priesthood Global Ministry; Pastors Strengthening Pastors; Clergy United
Email: royalpriesthood1@verizon.net
URL: http://www.cambridgewhoswho.com

Gladys G. McFadden

Title: Lead Vocalists, Music Director **Company:** The Loving Sisters **Address:** 2624 South Cross Street, Little Rock, AR 72206 United States **BUS:** Entertainment Singers **P/S:** Singing Gospel Music **MA:** National **EXP:** Ms. McFadden's expertise is in music. **H/I/S:** Songwriter, Travel **EDU:** University of Arkansas, Bachelor of Arts **A/A/S:** BMI, American Association of Gerontology

Tracy McFadden

Title: Traffic Manager **Company:** Operational Support Airlift Agency **Address:** 6970 Britten Drive, Building 3165, Quality Assurance Branch, Fort Belvoir, VA 22060 United States **BUS:** Airlifts **P/S:** Operational Support for Department of Defense **MA:** International **EXP:** Ms. McFadden's expertise includes traffic and quality control. **H/I/S:** Sports, Dancing **EDU:** College Coursework **A/A/S:** National Descent Transportation Association
Email: tracy.l.mcfadden@us.army.mil.
URL: http://160.147.9.92

Linda McFarland

Title: Owner, Designer **Company:** Sizzor Magic Salon **Address:** 796 E. Kiowa Avenue, Suite H-9, Elizabeth, CO 80107 United States **BUS:** Full-Service Beauty Salon **P/S:** Hair Styling, Skin and Nail Services Including Hair, Skin and Beauty Products **MA:** Local **D/D/R:** Highlighting and Coloring Hair, Sales and Finance Management **H/I/S:** Skiing, Snowmobiling, Camping, Boating **EDU:** College Coursework, Colorado Beauty College **CERTS:** Certified Barber, Capital City Barber College (1987) **A/A/S:** High Prairie Business Women's Association; Feel Better, American Cancer Society
Email: sizzormagic@juno.com

Harry E. McFee

Title: Owner **Company:** McFee's Auto Parts, Inc **Address:** 12 Hook Street, Southbridge, MA 01550 United States **BUS:** Automobiles Retail **P/S:** Full Service-Car Quest, Auto Parts, All Employees Area ASE Certified **MA:** Local **D/D/R:** Overseeing a Staff of 10, Offering Customer Service **H/I/S:** Antique Cars **A/A/S:** ASE

Keith A. McGaugh

Title: Sales Engineer **Company:** Carlton-Bates Company **Address:** 8900 Cameron Road, Austin, TX 78754 United States **BUS:** Manufacturing Company **P/S:** Electronics, Sensors, Automation, Safety Systems, Switches, Connectors, Wiring Devices **MA:** International **EXP:** Mr. McGaugh's expertise is in the development of new generation components. **D/D/R:** Overseeing Production of Sub-Assemblies for Electronics Distribution, Communicating with Engineering Directors **H/I/S:** Golfing, Fishing **EDU:** Bachelor's Degree in Communication, Abilene Christian University, TX (1989) **A/A/S:** ODBA
Email: kmcgaugh@austin.rr.com
URL: http://www.carlton-bates.com

Paulette R. McGee

Title: Owner, Director **Company:** Miracle Home Care Services, LLC **Address:** 5736 N. Tryon Street, Suite 130, Charlotte, NC 28213 United States **BUS:** In-Home Care Agency **P/S:** Caring for the Elderly and Disabled **MA:** Regional **D/D/R:** Overseeing Agency Operations and Staff **H/I/S:** Spending Time at the Beach, Water Activities **EDU:** Associate Degree in Business, Westchester Business Institute **A/H:** Dean's List, Westchester Business Institute **C/VW:** Missionary Work Through Church
Email: mspmiracle@yahoo.com

Bryana J. McGill, MBA

Title: Senior Partner **Company:** Gateway Healthcare Resources **Address:** 5142 Bent Oak Drive, House Springs, MO 63051 United States **BUS:** Consulting Company **P/S:** Healthcare Consulting **MA:** National **D/D/R:** Healthcare Compliance and Revenue Cycle Consulting **H/I/S:** Horseback Riding, Hiking and Spending Time with her Family and Friends **EDU:** Bachelor of Arts in Healthcare Administration and Master of Business Administration, Webster University **A/A/S:** Healthcare Compliance Association; National Association of Female Executives; National Association of Hospital Access Management, Medical Management Association; Healthcare Financial Management Association; AAPC **C/VW:** Leukemia & Lymphoma Society, CFS
Email: bjmgateway@yahoo.com
URL: http://www.gatewayhealthcareresources.com

Mr. Richard A. McGill

Title: Fire Chief **Company:** City of North Vernon Fire Department **Address:** 2000 N. Madison Avenue, North Vernon, IN 47265 United States **BUS:** Government Organization **P/S:** Fire Rescue Services, Inspection and Investigation **MA:** Regional **D/D/R:** Training **H/I/S:** Sports **EDU:** Bachelor's Degree in Public Safety Technology, Northwood University (2005); Associate Degree in Fire Science Technology, Indiana University-Purdue University, Indianapolis (1975) **CERTS:** Certification in Fire Investigations; Certification in Hazardous Material Operations; Licensed Helicopter Pilot **A/A/S:** Indiana Volunteer Fireman's Association; Indiana Fire Chief's Association; National Fire Protection Association; International Association of Fire Investigators **A/H:** Two Firefighter of Year Awards (1978, 1995); Silver Flight Award for Humanitarian Service (2001)
Email: rmcgill@northvernon-in.gov
URL: http://www.northvernon-in.gov

Jennifer Jorgensen McGinnis

Title: Preschool Teacher **Company:** Sunshine Day Care and Preschool **Address:** 3801 Glenwood Drive, Charlotte, NC 28208 United States **BUS:** Day Care, Preschool **P/S:** Quality Care, Early Childhood Development and Education **MA:** Local **D/D/R:** Teaching Special Needs Children **H/I/S:** Writing Children's Literature, Reading, Attending the Movies **EDU:** Master's Degree in Special Education, University of North Carolina at Charlotte **CERTS:** Certified in Early Childhood Education, University of North Carolina at Charlotte **C/VW:** St. Mark United Methodist Church
Email: jajmcg@carolina.rr.com
URL: http://www.cambridgewhoswho.com

Linda Leepard McGirr

Title: Owner **Company:** Dream Weddings by Linda **BUS:** Medical Office **P/S:** Healthcare **MA:** Local **D/D/R:** Patient Care, Making House Calls **H/I/S:** Decorating for Weddings **EDU:** Post-Graduate Coursework; Bachelor of Science in Zoology, Minor in Nutrition **A/A/S:** American Academy of Physician Assistants; National Commission on Certification of Physician Assistants; United States Air Force, 1975-1979 **C/VW:** Local Community Charities, Girl Scouts of the USA
Email: lleepardmcgirr@yahoo.com

D. Michael McGlone

Title: Owner **Company:** Zaremba Claims Services, Wenatchee **Address:** 509 N. Western Avenue, Suite 105, Wenatchee, WA 98801 United States **BUS:** Multi-Line Independent Adjusting Firm Licensed in the States of Washington and Oregon **P/S:** Independent Insurance Adjusters Serving Insurers, Commercial, Corporate and Governmental Self-Insurers, Risk Retention Pools, Third Party Claims Administrators and Risk Managers **MA:** Local **D/D/R:** Overseeing Property and Liability Insurance **H/I/S:** Volunteering, Collecting Coins, Reading **EDU:** Bachelor's Degree in Business Administration, San Jose State University **A/A/S:** AAI; International Association of Arson Investigators, Inc; Society of Registered Professional Adjusters
Email: wenatchee@zclaims.com
URL: http://www.zclaims.com

Dr. Daniel P. McGovern

Title: Podiatrist **Company:** United States Department of Veterans Affairs **Address:** 621A Maury Avenue, Norfork, VA 23517 United States **BUS:** Government Agency **P/S:** Patient Care and Federal Benefits for Veterans **MA:** National **EXP:** Dr. McGovern's expertise is in podiatry. **D/D/R:** Performing Foot and Ankle Surgery for Veterans in Virginia **H/I/S:** Mountain Biking, Hiking, Fishing, Playing with his Dog **EDU:** Doctor of Podiatric Medicine, Barry University, Miami Shores, FL (2001) **CERTS:** Fellow, American Board of Lower Extremity Surgeons; Board Certified Diplomate, Association of the American College of Foot and Ankle Surgery **A/A/S:** In-House Speaker for Veterans Affairs
Email: danmcgovern@cox.net
URL: http://www.cambridgewhoswho.com

Ruth S. McGowan

Title: Shift Supervisor **Company:** CVS Pharmacy **Address:** 401 N. Duval Street, Claxton, GA 30417 United States **BUS:** Pharmacy **P/S:** Pharmaceuticals **MA:** National **D/D/R:** Ensuring Customer Satisfaction, Overseeing 10 Employees, Performing Administrative Duties **H/I/S:** Reading, Listening to Music, Rescuing Animals, Collecting Porcelain Dolls **EDU:** Coursework in Technical Education
Email: ruth.mcgowan@cwwemail.com
URL: http://www.cvs.com

Ann V. McGrath

Title: Insurance and Billing Coordinator **Company:** Tri-State Audiology LLC **Address:** 485 Colliers Way, Suite F, Weirton, WV 26062 United States **BUS:** Audiology Practice **P/S:** Hearing Evaluation, Diagnostic Services **MA:** Regional **D/D/R:** Handling Insurance, Medical Billing and Coding **H/I/S:** Traveling, Spending Time with her Grandchildren **EDU:** Associate Degree in Medical Insurance and Coding, Jefferson Community College **C/VW:** South Carolina State Firefighters Association; Autism Speaks
Email: ann.mcgrath1@sbcglobal.net
URL: http://www.cambridgewhoswho.com

Michael McGraw

Title: Operations Manager **Company:** Visteon Corporation North Penn Plant **Address:** 2750 Morris Road, Lansdale, PA 19446 United States **BUS:** Automotive Component Supplier **P/S:** Climate Control Products, Electronics, Lighting, Interiors, Powertrain Controls, Engine Induction, Chassis, Powertrain, Aftermarket Products **MA:** International **D/D/R:** Electrical Engineering, Manufacturing, Managing Operations for all Electronic Products Produced Including Automobile Electrical Devices at North Penn Plant **H/I/S:** Bicycling, Running Track, Exercising, Participating in Duathlons **EDU:** Master's Degree in Manufacturing Systems Engineering, Lehigh University (1994)
Email: mmcgraw3@visteon.com
URL: http://www.visteon.com

D. Scott McGregor

Title: Founder **Company:** Wentworth Publishing, Inc. **Address:** 200 W. Midway Drive, Unit 101, Anaheim, CA 92805 United States **BUS:** Publishing Company **P/S:** Book and Internet Publishing **MA:** International **D/D/R:** Managing the Business **EDU:** Bachelor's Degree, Brigham Young University **CERTS:** Certified Financial Planner; Certified Securities Analyst **A/A/S:** Mortgage Bankers Association; CTIA-The Wireless Association; President's Council on Fraud; Association of American Publishers; Market Publishers Association
Email: scott@scottmcgregor.com
URL: http://www.wentworthpublishing.com

Camille H. McGuire

Title: Second-Grade Teacher **Company:** Mobile County Public School System **Dept:** Dauphin Island Elementary School **Address:** 1501 Bienville Boulevard, Dauphin Island, AL 36528 United States **BUS:** Outstanding Public School System **P/S:** Educational System which Produces Literate, Life-Long Learners **MA:** Regional **D/D/R:** Teaching Second-Grade Students, Focusing on the Reading Renaissance Program and Creative Expression in All Areas of School Curriculum Including Music, Dance, Cooking and Arts, Currently Writing Children's Books **H/I/S:** Reading, Skiing, Playing Piano, Cooking, Biking, Spending Quality Time with her Family and Friends **EDU:** College Coursework in Reading, University of San Diego; Master's Degree in Education, University of South Alabama **A/A/S:** National Education Association; Mobile County Education Association **A/H:** Mobile County Teacher of the Year (1999); O'Rourke Elementary Teacher of the Year (1999); Dauphin Island Teacher of the Year (2006)
Email: cmcguire@mcpss.com
URL: http://www.mcpss.com

Melanie L. McGuire

Title: Director of Faculty Services **Company:** Oral Roberts University **Address:** 7777 S. Lewis Avenue, Tulsa, OK 74171 United States **BUS:** University **P/S:** Education **MA:** International **D/D/R:** Planning and Coordinating Events **EDU:** Bachelor of Arts, Oral Roberts University **A/A/S:** Regional Director, Region 7, Association of Collegiate Conference and Events Directors-International **C/VW:** Local Church
Email: mmcguire@oru.edu
URL: http://www.oru.edu

Roger D. McGuyer

Title: Painter **Company:** Painters Plus **Address:** 241 E. Arch Street, Madisonville, KY 42431 United States **BUS:** Painting Contractor **P/S:** Interior and Exterior Painting of Residential and Commercial Properties **MA:** Regional **D/D/R:** Painting, Ensuring Customer Satisfaction, Offering Estimates **H/I/S:** Hunting and Fishing with his Son **EDU:** High School Education

Marilyn A. McIntosh

Title: Staff Therapist **Company:** Berger Health Systems **Address:** 600 N. Pickaway Street, Circleville, OH 43113 United States **BUS:** Healthcare Center **P/S:** Healthcare **MA:** Regional **D/D/R:** Caring for Patients, Practicing Respiratory Therapy **H/I/S:** Reading, Needlepoint, Gardening **EDU:** Coursework, California College for Respiratory Therapy **A/A/S:** American Association for Respiratory Care; National Board for Respiratory Care **C/VW:** Fairhope Hospice and Palliative Care Inc.
Email: mamcintosh@roadrunner.com
URL: http://www.bergerhealthsystems.com

Amy M. McIntyre

Title: Senior Account Executive **Company:** Time Warner Telecom **Address:** 4625 W. 86th Street, Indianapolis, IN 46268 United States **BUS:** Leading National Provider of Managed Network Services for Businesses, Organizations and Communication Services Companies **P/S:** Telecommunications, Ethernet and Transport Data Networking, Internet Access, Local and Long Distance Voice, VoIP and Security **MA:** National **D/D/R:** Data Internet and Voice Services, Selling New Customers Data Related Services including Internet, Fiber Optic Services, Overseeing Accounts and Company Acquisitions **H/I/S:** Gardening, Her Children's Activities **EDU:** Bachelor of Arts Degree in Psychology, Franklin College (1981) **A/A/S:** Delta Delta Delta
Email: amy.mcintyre@twtelecom.com
URL: http://www.twtelecom.com

Tina E. McIntyre

Title: National Accounts Supervisor **Company:** A.O. Smith Water Products Company **Address:** 500 Tennessee Waltz Parkway, Ashland City, TN 37015 United States **BUS:** Water Heaters Manufacturing **P/S:** Emergency Water Heaters **MA:** National **EXP:** Ms. McIntyre's expertise is in hot water system compliance. **H/I/S:** Reading, Helping the Underprivileged **A/A/S:** National Society of Professional Engineers; American Society of Plumbing Engineers; Association of Hotel and Lodging **C/VW:** Community Service
Email: tmcintyre@hotwater.com
URL: http://www.aosmith.com

Kelo J. McKay, MBA, RN, BSN

Title: Administrative Director **Company:** HCA Lakeview Regional Medical Center **Address:** 95 E. Fairway Drive, Covington, LA 70433 United States **BUS:** Full-Service, Acute Care Hospital **P/S:** Therapeutic Centers for the Diagnosis and Treatment of AIDS, Allergies, Diabetes, Kidney Disease, Pain Management, Skin Cancer, Skin and Sleep Disorders, Smoking, Stress, Stroke, Trauma, Weight Management, Women's Self Care, Emergency, Urgent Care, Radiology Outpatient Rehabilitation, Bone Density Screenings **MA:** Local **D/D/R:** Managing All Staffing and House Supervisors, Managing Bed Control, Overseeing Dialysis Service, Telemetry and Medical-Surgical Units, Fiscal Management of Department Budgets **H/I/S:** Horseback Riding, Spending Time with Three Sons **EDU:** Master of Business Administration, University of Phoenix (2004); Bachelor of Science in Nursing, Southeastern University, Louisiana (1997); Associate Degree in Science and Nursing, Louisiana State University (1994) **CERTS:** Certification in Nursing Administration **A/A/S:** American Organization of Nurse Executives
Email: kelo.mckay@hcahealthcare.com
URL: http://www.lakeviewregional.com

Wanda W. McKay

Title: Management, Program Analyst **Company:** Pension Benefit Guaranty Corporation **Address:** 1200 K Street N.W., Washington, DC 20005 United States **BUS:** Department of Labor **P/S:** Protection of Retirement Incomes for Workers with Defined Benefit Pension Plans **MA:** National **D/D/R:** Conducting Compliance Analysis **H/I/S:** Sewing, Fishing, Rollerblading, Relaxing **EDU:** Coursework in Business Management, Columbia Union College (2003) **A/A/S:** Feed the Children/Homeless Network; Neighborhood Watch; Shelter for Abused Women & Children
Email: wiley.wanda@pbgc.com
URL: http://www.pbgc.gov

Erin-Michelle McKee

Title: English Teacher, Department Chairwoman **Company:** North Tahoe High School **Address:** 2945 Polaris Road, Tahoe City, CA 96161 United States **BUS:** High School **P/S:** Education **MA:** Local **D/D/R:** Teaching English **H/I/S:** Skiing, Spending Time with Family, Reading **EDU:** Pursuing Master of Education in English, University of Nevada, Reno; Bachelor of Arts Plus 60 in English, Bachelor of Arts in Liberal Studies, California State University at Chico **A/A/S:** California Teachers Association; Tahoe-Truckee Association; Nominee, Who's Who Among American Teachers **C/VW:** Coach, Volleyball
Email: mckee-e@hotmail.com

Nicole A. McKelvy

Title: Library Director **Company:** Hidalgo Public Library **Address:** 710 E. Texano Drive, Hidalgo, TX 78557 United States **BUS:** Public Library **P/S:** Publications, Education, Information, Entertainment and Library Services **MA:** Regional **D/D/R:** Handling Reference Library Materials **H/I/S:** Knitting, Spending Time with her Granddaughter **CERTS:** Certified Library Director, Texas State Library and Archives Commission **A/A/S:** Texas Library Association **C/VW:** Vanguard Academy
Email: nicole@hidalgo.lib.tx.us
URL: http://www.hidalgo.lib.tx.us

Denise B. McKendry

Title: Teacher **Company:** Chesterfield County Public Schools **Address:** 15501 Harrowgate Road, Chester, VA 23831 United States **BUS:** Public Schools **P/S:** Elementary Education **MA:** Local **D/D/R:** Teaching third-Grade Students all Subjects **H/I/S:** Reading, Traveling, Art **EDU:** Master's Degree in Reading, Longwood University; Bachelor's Degree in Elementary Education, Piedmont Baptist College **A/A/S:** Phi Kappa Phi **A/H:** Nominee, Teacher of the Year 2007
Email: denisemckendry@gmail.com

Janet M. McKenna

Title: Third-Grade Teacher **Company:** Storm Lake School District **Address:** 1001 W. Sixth Street, Storm Lake, IA 50588 United States **BUS:** School District **P/S:** Education **MA:** Local **D/D/R:** Reading **H/I/S:** Reading, Walking, Spending Time with her Grandson **EDU:** Master of Education, Buena Vista University **A/A/S:** National Education Association; Storm Lake Education Association; Quiat **C/VW:** American Heart Association, Multiple Sclerosis Society, PEO International
Email: jmckenna@evertek.com
URL: http://www.cambridgewhoswho.com

Alison G. McKenzie

Title: Licensed Physical Therapist Assistant **Company:** Ortho-Sports Physical Therapy **Address:** 11808 Kingston Pike, Suite 185, Knoxville, TN 37934 United States **BUS:** Physical Therapy Practice **P/S:** Healthcare **MA:** Local **D/D/R:** Treating Orthopedic and Sports Injuries, Managing the Office and Daily Operations **H/I/S:** Performance Boating **EDU:** Bachelor of Science in Biology, Bowling Green University, 1998; **CERTS:** Certified Physical Therapist Assistant **A/A/S:** ATA; Who's Who Among American Students; American Physical Therapy Association **C/VW:** Children and Adults with Disabilities; Police and Fire Fighters; Meals on Wheels
Email: ospt@tds.net
URL: http://www.cambridgewhoswho.com

Megan R. McKenzie

Title: Pharmacy Intern **Company:** Walgreens **BUS:** Retail Pharmacy **P/S:** Pharmaceuticals **MA:** Local **EXP:** Ms. McKenzie's expertise is in clinical pharmacy. **H/I/S:** Running, Spending Time Outdoors, Reading, Studying **EDU:** Pursuing Doctor of Pharmacy, South University; Coursework in Psychology, Tulane University; Coursework in Pre-Pharmacy, University of Mississippi **A/A/S:** Kappa Epsilon; American Pharmacists Association; ASHP
Email: mrmckenz@gmail.com

Laurel McKenzie-Thompson

Title: Provider **Company:** Eagle Family Home **Address:** 119 S.W. Eighth Avenue, Delray Beach, FL 33444 United States **BUS:** Health Center **P/S:** Geriatric Healthcare **MA:** Statewide **EXP:** Ms. McKenzie-Thompson's expertise is in healthcare. **H/I/S:** Writing, Listening to Music, Reading, Nursing, Gardening **EDU:** Associate of Applied Sciences in Education, Jamaica; Associate of Arts in Education, Jamaica **A/A/S:** National League of Nursing **A/H:** American Staffing Outstanding Caregiver Award, 2001, 2002
Email: laurelmack@msn.com
URL: http://www.cambridgewhoswho.com

Mr. Scott J. McKeon

Title: Founder, Personal Wine Consultant **Company:** Wine God Collections, Inc. **Address:** 4441 Ashfield Terrace, Syracuse, NY 13215 United States **BUS:** Wine Consulting and Personal Wine Shopping Company **P/S:** Wine Tasting, Event Planning and Hosting, Wine Cellar, Closet and Fridge 'Stocking' Service, Wine Gift Baskets, Monthly, Semi-Monthly and Quarterly Wine Club, Wine Education, Wine Appreciation Seminars, Wine Cellar Design, Creation and Consultations, Personal Wine Consultations and Shopping Services **MA:** International **D/D/R:** Offering Wine Tastings for Corporate Events, Weddings, Cocktail Parties, Restaurants and Homes, Creating Custom-Selected Wine Collections Representing All Grape Varieties and All Regions of the World, Managing the Wine Cellar, Closet and Fridge 'Stocking' Service, Building Custom-Selected Three to Six Bottle Gift Baskets with Optional Add-Ons Including Gourmet Cheeses, Wine Accessories and More, Signing People with the Wine God Wine Club, Making Cellaring and Storing Recommendations and Food Pairing Suggestions, Holding Wine Education and Wine Appreciation Seminars, Planning Special Event Seminars and Tastings Hosted by Wine Makers and Vineyard Owners, Consulting on Wine Cellar Design and Creation, Selling Wine and Marketing **H/I/S:** Golfing, Mountain Biking, Making Wine **EDU:** Pursuing Master of Business Administration, Syracuse University; Bachelor of Science in Business Administration and Marketing, Le Moyne College (1994) **CERTS:** Certified Wine Professional, University of Delaware **A/A/S:** Boston Wine School; New York State Winemakers Association; Better Business Bureau **C/VW:** President, Board of Directors, Marcellus Community Childcare Center
Email: Scott@WineGodCollections.com
Email: winegodcollections@yahoo.com
URL: http://www.WineGodCollections.com

Richard A. McKinley, CPCU

Title: Vice President, Product Manager **Company:** York Insurance Services Group, Inc. **Address:** 99 Cherry Hill Road, Suite 230, Parsippany, NJ 07054 United States **BUS:** Insurance Company **P/S:** Third Party Administrators and Independent Adjustor's for Property, Casualty and Workers' Compensation Claims **MA:** National **D/D/R:** Quality Assurance and Standards, Managing Auditing, Training, Overseeing Staff **H/I/S:** Listening to Music, Gardening **EDU:** Bachelor of Arts in Music, Ball State University, Muncie, Indiana (1963) **A/A/S:** Chartered Property Casualty Underwriter
Email: richard.mckinley@york-claims.com
URL: http://www.yorkclaims.com

Lokey Byron McKinney

Title: Funeral Director, Embalmer Apprentice **Company:** Hubert C. Baker Funeral Home **Address:** 7415 Hodgson Memorial Drive, Savannah, GA 31406 United States **BUS:** Funeral Home **P/S:** Funeral Services **MA:** Local **D/D/R:** Selling Caskets, Embalming **H/I/S:** Football **EDU:** High School Education **CERTS:** Certified Mortician **A/A/S:** Emmanuel Baptist Church; Masson; Scottish Rights; Shriner
Email: lokey.mckinney@sci-us.com
URL: http://www.dignitymemorial.com/

Sandra L. McKinzie

Title: Director of National Accounts **Company:** Matson Integrated Logistics **Address:** 1815 S. Meyers Road, Suite 700, Oakbrook Terrace, IL 60181 United States **BUS:** Shipping and Transportation Company **P/S:** Transportation Services and Solutions, Industry-Leading Customer Support Center, Management of Shipment Information Via the Internet, Multimodal Transportation **MA:** National **D/D/R:** Overseeing Sales and Large Accounts, Managing Programs and Supply Channel Logistics **H/I/S:** Painting, Spending Time with her Husband **EDU:** Coursework, Richland College (1984) **A/A/S:** President, National Defense Transportation Association, Dallas; Board Member, Council of Supply Chain Management Professionals, Chicago
Email: smckinzie@matson.com
URL: http://matson.com

James V. McKnight

Title: Owner, President **Company:** Starstruck Video, Inc. **Address:** 150 E. Oak Street, Suite 7, Conway, AR 72032 United States **BUS:** Video Rentals and Sales Company **P/S:** Movie Rentals, VHS and DVD Sales **MA:** Local **EXP:** Mr. McKnight's expertise is in management. **D/D/R:** Consulting **H/I/S:** Writing **EDU:** Master's Degree in Sociology, University of California, 1993; Bachelor's Degree in Journalism, University of Central Arkansas, 1993 **A/A/S:** Chamber of Commerce; American Civil Liberties Union; Prepaid Paralegal Service **C/VW:** Special Olympics, Arkansas; Best Friends Animal Society, Utah; Various Community Organizations
Email: jmac@cyberback.com
URL: http://www.starstruckvideo.com

Hannah P. McKoy

Title: Administrator **Company:** Juniper Springs Center, Inc. **Address:** 153 Springs Lane, Ivanhoe, NC 28447 United States **BUS:** Healthcare Service Company **P/S:** Long-Term Care **MA:** Regional **D/D/R:** Administrating Healthcare Services **H/I/S:** Playing Volleyball, Playing Table Tennis **EDU:** Master's Degree, Fayetteville State University **A/A/S:** Phi Delta Kappa
Email: krystalbelpelham@yahoo.com

William B. McLane

Title: President **Company:** McLane and Associates **Address:** 974 Vista Del Collados, San Luis Obispo, CA 93405 United States **BUS:** Nuclear Power Consulting Company **P/S:** Nuclear Power Consulting **MA:** International **D/D/R:** Managing the Nuclear Consulting Company **H/I/S:** Participating in Church Activities, Fishing **EDU:** Master's Degree in Nuclear Engineering, University of Missouri **A/A/S:** American Nuclear Society **C/VW:** Volunteer, Boy Scouts of America, Local Church
Email: wbmclane@aol.com
URL: http://www.cambridgewhoswho.com

Janice McLaughlin

Title: Statistical Modeling Analyst **Company:** AAA **BUS:** Pharmaceutical Company **P/S:** Pharmaceutical Products **MA:** National **D/D/R:** Statistical Forecasting, Modeling **H/I/S:** Watching Hockey and Football, Spending Time with her Family **EDU:** Master's Degree in Statistical Computing, University of Central Florida; Bachelor's Degree in Mathematics, Middle Tennessee State University **C/VW:** Local Church
Email: janicelwhite@yahoo.com

Jill A. McLean

Title: Owner, Designer **Company:** Designs by Jill **Address:** 410 Machelle Drive, Cary, IL 60013 United States **BUS:** Sole Proprietor **P/S:** Earrings, Pins, Ornaments, Figures **MA:** Regional **D/D/R:** Designing and Creating Polymer Clay Items **H/I/S:** Spending Time with her Many Varied Pets, Attending Craft Shows, Crafting, Helping Others in Church, Missions and the Community, Gardening **EDU:** Diploma, Wauconda High School **A/A/S:** Homemakers; Lake Colony Association for Home and Community Services **C/VW:** Church Prayer Team, Benevolence, Lake Colony Association for Home and Community Services, Hospitality, Aid in Missions
Email: designsbyjill@comcast.net
URL: http://www.cambridgewhoswho.com

Carolyn F. McLemore

Title: English-Language Arts Teacher **Company:** Blount County Schools **Address:** 920 Huffstetler Road, Maryville, TN 37803 United States **BUS:** School **P/S:** Education **MA:** Local **D/D/R:** Teaching English Language Arts with Experience Teaching Elementary through High School **H/I/S:** Reading, Traveling, Spending Time with her Family and Friends **EDU:** Master of Science in Curriculum Development; Lincoln Memorial University, Harrogate, TN; Bachelor of Arts in English, Maryville College, TN **A/A/S:** National Education Association; Tennessee Education Association; Blount County Education Association; Alpha Delta Kappa; Beta Eta Chapter
Email: carolyn.mclemore@blountk12.org

Arthur McLin Jr.

Title: Licensed Mental Health Professional Therapist **Company:** Life Strategies Counseling Agency **Address:** 1217 Stone Street, Jonesboro, AR 72401 United States **BUS:** Counseling Center **P/S:** Counseling Services **MA:** Local **D/D/R:** Counseling Exceptional Children **H/I/S:** Composing Music, Playing the Trumpet **EDU:** Doctorate Degree in Educational Leadership, with Concentration in Counseling and Psychology, Arkansas State University **A/A/S:** American Educational Research Association; American Counseling Association
Email: amclin@astate.edu

Isabel McMahel, DN, ND

Title: Founder, President **Company:** Whole Life International Foundation, DBA Whole Life Foundation **Address:** P.O. Box 13207, Phoenix, AZ 85004 United States **BUS:** Nonprofit Organization **P/S:** Social Services, Healthcare **MA:** International **D/D/R:** Counseling, Networking, Serving and Helping People **H/I/S:** Developing Nutritional Recipes, Researching on Wellness Health and Nutritional Recipes **EDU:** Coursework in Naprapathy; Coursework in Naturopathy
Email: Isabel.McMahel@cwwemail.com

Robert F. McMeekin

Title: 1) Sergeant of Police (Retired) 2) Real Estate Broker (Retired) **Company:** 1) Los Angeles Police Department 2) Mary Mac & Associates **Address:** 1) 150 N. Los Angeles Street 2) 9056 Santa Monica, 1) Los Angeles, CA 90012 2) West Hollywood, CA 90 **BUS:** 1) Police Department 2) Real Estate Agency **P/S:** 1) Law Enforcement 2) Real Estate **MA:** 1) Local 2) Local **EXP:** Ms. McMeeking's expertise includes law enforcement and real estate sales. **H/I/S:** Swimming, Writing Poetry **EDU:** Master's Degree in Health Safety, California State University Los Angeles; Bachelor's Degree in Criminal Justice, California State University Los Angeles **A/A/S:** The Republican Party; California State Hotel and Motel **A/H:** Top Producer Award, Mary Mac and Associates, Real Estate
URL: http://www.cambridgewhoswho.com

Amber M. McMillan

Title: First Grade Teacher **Company:** Mesquite Independent School District, Mackey Elementary **Address:** 14900 N. Spring Ridge Circle, Balch Springs, TX 75180 United States **BUS:** Elementary School **P/S:** Early Childhood Education **MA:** Local **D/D/R:** Teaching **H/I/S:** Scrapbooking **EDU:** Bachelor of Science in Applied Learning and Development, University of Texas at Austin **CERTS:** Certified Teacher, State of Texas **A/A/S:** Mesquite Education Association; Association of Texas Professional Educators **C/VW:** First Christian Church
Email: amcmillan@mesquiteisd.org
URL: http://www.mesquiteisd.org

Lynn Carter McMillan

Title: Director of Technology **Company:** Coffee County School System **Address:** 1311 S. Peterson Avenue, Douglas, GA 31533 United States **BUS:** School System **P/S:** Education **MA:** Local **EXP:** Ms. McMillan's expertise is in technology. **H/I/S:** Collecting Primitive Antiques, Raising Mules and Donkeys **EDU:** Maters Degree in Instructional Technology, 1998; Bachelor of Science in Business Education, Valdosta University, 1996 **A/A/S:** Professional Association of Georgia Educators **A/H:** Awarded 4-H Club Program Assistant, Southeast District
Email: lmcmillan@coffee.k12.ga.us

Ila M. McMillian, Ph.D.

Title: Pastor **Company:** Faith Tabernacle Oasis of love International Church **Address:** 8005 Rogers Road, Chapel Hill, NC 27516 United States **BUS:** Church **P/S:** Spiritual Services **MA:** International **EXP:** Mr. McMillan's expertise is in preaching. **H/I/S:** Cooking **EDU:** Ph.D., Trinity Christian University **C/VW:** Ministerial Alliance
Email: imacmill@bellsouth.net
URL: http://www.cambridgewhoswho.com

Michele K. McMurray

Title: Officer Manager **Company:** Fayette Home Health Care Supply, LLC **Address:** 110 E. Market Street, Washington C.H., OH 43160 United States **BUS:** Healthcare **P/S:** Excellent Healthcare Services, Durable Medical Equipment and Supplies **MA:** Regional **D/D/R:** Managing the Office, Overseeing Health Insurance, Billing, Marketing, Interacting with Physicians Offices **H/I/S:** Scrap Booking, Spending Time with her Grandchildren, Gardening, Reading **EDU:** Associate Degree in Medical Management, ICP (1993); Associate Degree in Interior Design, La Salle University (1973) **A/A/S:** National Notary Association **A/H:** Fayette County Chamber Ambassador of the Year (2005-2006)
Email: mkmcmurray@sbcglobal.net
URL: http://www.cambridgewhoswho.com

C. Lisa McNair

Title: Teacher, English Department Head **Company:** Tuloso Midway Middle School **Address:** P.O. Box 10900, Corpus Christi, TX 78460 United States **BUS:** School **P/S:** Education **MA:** Local **D/D/R:** Teaching Reading **H/I/S:** Reading, Horseback Riding, Swimming, Spending Time with her Husband and Grandchildren **EDU:** Pursuing Ph.D. in Curriculum and Instruction, Specialization in Reading, Texas A&M University; Master's Degree in Curriculum and Instruction, Specialization in Reading, Texas A&M University; Bachelor of Science in Elementary Education, Texas A&M University, Kingville, Texas **A/A/S:** International Reading Association; College Board Consultant; Theta Gamma; Association of Professionals for Teachers of Reading **C/VW:** Volunteer, After School Tutoring Program
Email: lmcnair@tmisd.esc2.net
URL: http://www.cambridgewhoswho.com

Dennis McNally, S.J., Ph.D.

Title: Department Chair, Professor of Fine Arts **Company:** St. Joseph's University **Dept:** Fine and Performing Arts **Address:** 5600 City Avenue, Department of Fine and Performing Arts, Philadelphia, PA 19131 United States **BUS:** Leading Higher Learning Institution **P/S:** Educating Students in Preparation for Future Careers **MA:** National **D/D/R:** Teaching Fine Arts, Working as an Acclaimed Artist and Painter of Large Environmental Pieces, Overseeing Full Time and Part Time Faculty, Hiring and Firing, Mentoring, Reviewing Curriculum **H/I/S:** Swimming **EDU:** Ph.D. in Studio, New York University (1982); Master of Divinity Degree, Western Jesuit School of Theology (1974); Master of Arts in Art Education, New York University (1970) **A/A/S:** AURA; Chaired College Council; Published Two Books
Email: dmcnally@sju.edu
URL: http://www.mcnallyscorpus.com

Wanda G. McNamara

Title: Assistant to the Register **Company:** County of Cheshire Registry of Deeds **Address:** 33 West Street, Keene, NH 03431 United States **BUS:** County Government Management **P/S:** Registry of Deeds **MA:** Local **D/D/R:** Office Management **H/I/S:** Politics **EDU:** Northern State College, Bachelor's Degree in Early Childhood Education
Email: wmcnamara@co.cheshire.nh.us
URL: http://www.nhdeeds.com

David C. McNeal

Title: Pastor **Company:** Greater New Bethel Church of God in Christ **Address:** 2801 E. Mobile Lane, Phoenix, AZ 85040 United States **BUS:** Church Religion/Spiritual Services **P/S:** Salvation **MA:** International **D/D/R:** Preaching the Gospel **H/I/S:** My Family, Fishing, Outdoor Activities, Reading **EDU:** Associate Degree, Phoenix College
Email: mcneal284@aol.com

Amanda M. McNease

Title: Radiologic Technologist **Company:** Stone County Hospital **Address:** P.O. Box 1, Foxworth, MS 39483 United States **BUS:** Hospital **P/S:** Healthcare Including Medical Diagnostic Services **MA:** Regional **D/D/R:** Practicing Diagnostic Radiology Services **H/I/S:** Fishing, Hunting, Bowling **EDU:** Associate Degree in Science, Pearl River Community College (2003) **CERTS:** Certified Radiologic Technologist **A/A/S:** The American Registry Of Radiologic Technologists **C/VW:** American Cancer Society
Email: hottemperedstang_01@yahoo.com

Karen L. McNeil

Title: Human Resources Analyst **Company:** City of Tempe **Address:** P.O. Box 5002, Tempe, AZ 85280 United States **BUS:** Municipality **P/S:** Community and Economic Development, Housing Services, Historic Preservation, Quality Life Service for the Community **MA:** Regional **D/D/R:** Managing Human Resources Including Recruitment and Selection of City Employees, Reviewing Existing Positions, Completing Annual Assessments **H/I/S:** Swing-Dancing **EDU:** Master's Degree in Public Administration, Concentration in Human Resources, Arizona State University, Tempe (1997) **A/A/S:** Society for Human Resource Management
Email: karen_mcneil@tempe.gov
URL: http://www.tempe.gov

Cynthia D. McNulty

Title: ISO 14000 Lead Assessor **Company:** Lloyds of London Regulatory Quality Association **Address:** 1401 Enclave Parkway, Unit 200, Houston, TX 77077 United States **BUS:** Certification Organization **P/S:** Environmental Management **MA:** International **D/D/R:** Environmental Management, Performing System Audits **H/I/S:** Painting, Graphic Arts, Golfing, Traveling **EDU:** Master of Business Administration, Thunderbird International School of Global Management; Master of Science in Biochemistry, University of Arizona; Bachelor's Degree in Biology, Scripps College **C/VW:** Schizophrenics Anonymous
Email: cynthia.mcnulty@lrqa.com
URL: http://www.cambridgewhoswho.com

Stephanie McPeak

Title: Senior Designer **Company:** Lexington Luxury Builders **Address:** 6688 N. Central Expressway, Dallas, TX 75206 United States **BUS:** Residential Development Company **P/S:** Single Family Custom Homes, High-End Luxury Town Homes, Estates **MA:** Regional **D/D/R:** Interior Designing for Single-Family Custom Homes and Luxury Town Homes, Space Planning **EDU:** Bachelor's Degree in Interior Design, Minor in Spanish, Texas Christian University (2003) **A/A/S:** American Society of Interior Designers; The Urban Land Institute
Email: smcpeak@lexingtoncompanies.com
URL: http://www.lexingtoncompanies.com

Micki G. McPherson, RN, WCC

Title: Hospice Nurse **Company:** Saad's Hospice Services **Address:** 1515 University Boulevard, Mobile, AL 36609 United States **BUS:** Residential Healthcare Services **P/S:** Specialized Nurses, Nurse Aides, Companions, Homemakers, Personal Care Service Professionals, Certified Therapists and Medical Social Workers **MA:** Regional **D/D/R:** Hospice Nursing, State Testing, Administration, In-service Education for Licensed Practical Nurses and the Continuing Education Unit, Home Healthcare with Compassion and Care **H/I/S:** Golfing **EDU:** Associate Degree in Nursing, Goshen University (1993) **CERTS:** Certification in Wound Care **A/A/S:** Local Public Speaking on Nursing; Alabama Nursing Association
Email: milkimc@yahoo.com
URL: http://www.saadshealth.com

Robert McQuese

Title: Owner **Company:** Bill's Painting **Address:** 204 Pattison Street, Aurora, IN 47001 United States **BUS:** Painting Company **P/S:** Interior Paint Jobs, Pressure Cleaning **MA:** Regional **D/D/R:** Painting Residential Homes and New Construction **H/I/S:** Fishing **C/VW:** Local Church
Email: billspainting@msn.com
URL: http://www.billspainting1.com

Ms. Christine McRandal

Title: President **Company:** V2K Window Fashions, LLC **Address:** 210 Carson Street, Springdale, PA 15144 United States **BUS:** Shop-At-Home Decor Franchise **P/S:** Custom Window Treatments for All Lifestyles **MA:** Regional **D/D/R:** Solutions, Projects, Consultations relating to custom window treatments for residential and commercial, bedding, pillow and table runners Real Estates Representing Buyers and Sellers, Residential and Commercial **H/I/S:** Traveling, Fine Dining, Wine Tasting, Decorating **EDU:** Bachelor's Degree in Chemistry and Business, University of Pittsburgh (1998) **CERTS:** Window Fashions Certified Professional-2005, Window Fashions Certified Professional and V2K Window Decor and More-2004; Licensed in Real Estate Sales-1986 **A/A/S:** Western Pennsylvania Window Treatment Association; Chamber of Commerce Board; Diversity Resource Center **C/VW:** Habitat for Humanity
Email: chrismcrandal@v2k.com
URL: http://www.v2kpittsburghnorth.com

Susan 'Edie' M. McTamaney

Title: Director of Sales, Catering **Company:** Sawmill Inn **Address:** 2301-S Highway 169, Grand Rapids, MN 55744 United States **BUS:** Food Service Provider **P/S:** Hotel/Convention **MA:** National **D/D/R:** Catering, Banquets **H/I/S:** Camping, Fishing, Traveling, Cooking **EDU:** Associate of Arts
Email: sawmill@uslink.net
URL: www.sawmillinn.com

Lynn H. McUmber

Title: Managing Director **Company:** Marsh & McLennan **Address:** 1255 23rd Street, Suite 400, Washington, DC 20037 United States **BUS:** Global Consulting and Insurance Firm **P/S:** Insurance and Consulting, Risk Management, Recognition, Credibility, Networking, Consulting **MA:** International **D/D/R:** Delivering Customer Service and Solutions, Managing Service Teams, Understanding Clients' Needs **H/I/S:** Walking **EDU:** Bachelor of Science in Psychology, Niagara University (1986) **A/A/S:** Capital Hospice; Volunteer, Point of Hope Camp; Montgomery County Chamber of Commerce
Email: lynn.e.mcumber@marsh.com

Catherine McVety

Title: Artist **Company:** Cassis **Address:** 55 Kings Highway, Congers, NY 28079 United States **BUS:** Art Studio **P/S:** Art in Watercolor **MA:** Local **D/D/R:** Watercolor Painting **H/I/S:** Traveling, Working Out, Rollerblading, Dancing **EDU:** Bachelor of Arts in Art History, New York University and SUNY Empire State College; Bachelor of Science in Psychology, SUNY Empire State College **A/A/S:** Very Special Arts Festival Honoree
Email: cassmcvet@optonline.net
URL: http://www.cambridgewhoswho.com

Celia P. McWilliams

Title: Artist **Company:** Celia's Palette **Address:** 515 Richlyn Drive, Adrian, MI 49221 United States **BUS:** Fine Arts Company **P/S:** Fine Arts, Oil Paintings, Exhibits **MA:** National **EXP:** Ms. McWilliams' expertise includes operations and management, oil paintings, fine arts and exhibits. **H/I/S:** Golfing, Spending Time with Family **EDU:** Coursework in Management, Wayne State University (1970) **A/A/S:** Toledo Art Guild; Toledo Art Club; Public Speaking; Published Works
Email: cpmcwilliams@comcast.net

Brian M. Mead

Title: Chief Executive Officer **Company:** Gulfstream Associates, LLC **Address:** 8480 Baltimore National Pike, Suite 278, Ellicott City, MD 21043 United States **BUS:** Real Estate Agency **P/S:** Real Estate Consulting and Investments **MA:** Regional **EXP:** Mr. Mead's expertise is in real estate consulting. **D/D/R:** Overseeing Construction, Portfolio Plans **H/I/S:** Boating, Teaching Business to High School Students **EDU:** Bachelor of Science in Business, Columbia Union College (2002) **CERTS:** Certified Architecture in Urban Design, Harvard University Graduate School of Design **A/A/S:** Maryland Real Estate Investor; Affordable Housing for Family in Urban Areas **C/VW:** Volunteer, High School Business Teacher
Email: gulfstreamllc@verizon.net
URL: http://www.cambridgewhoswho.com

Roy J. Meaders

Title: President **Company:** Meaders Enterprises **Address:** 106 Victoria Way Inc., Piedmont, SC 29673 United States **BUS:** Consulting Firm **P/S:** Textile Machinery Industry and General Home Repair Consulting **MA:** Local **D/D/R:** Offering Consulting and General Home Repair Services **H/I/S:** Woodworking, Salt Water Fishing **EDU:** Associate of Arts in Mechanical Design, Greenville Technical College **A/A/S:** American Association of Textile Chemists and Colorists
Email: meadersenterprise@aol.com

Dr. Joann Treadaway Meadows

Title: Special Education Teacher (Retired) **BUS:** Educational Institution **P/S:** Education **MA:** Gordon County, GA **EXP:** Dr. Meadow's expertise is in special education. **D/D/R:** Instructing Students with Learning Disabilities and Emotional Disturbances, Addressing Learning Disabilities **H/I/S:** Reading, Gardening, Spending Time with her Grandchildren, Participating in Social Activities **EDU:** Doctor of Education in Human Services and Counseling, University of Sarasota; Master of Science in Behavioral Disorders, University of West Georgia; Bachelor of Arts in Behavioral Science, Berry College; Associate of Art, Norman College **CERTS:** Certified Teacher (K-12); Certified Educational Specialist, Jacksonville State University **A/A/S:** First Vice President, Former President, Calhoun County Beautification Board; Calhoun-Gordon County Retired Educators Association; Red Hats Belles of the South; Former President, Hillhouse Garden Club; The Deep South Region, The Garden Club of Georgia; Former Board Member, The Garden Club of Georgia (2003-2004); Former Education Chairwoman, Southern Division, American Legion Auxiliary (2006-2007); Former President, Department of Georgia, American Legion Auxiliary (2005-2006); President, United Daughters of the Confederacy; President, Kappa Kappa Iota **A/H:** Award, Georgia Women of Achievement (1999); Teacher of the Year Award **C/VW:** First Baptist Church, Calhoun; Veterans of Foreign Wars
Email: joanntreadaway.meadows@cwwemail.com
URL: http://www.cambridgewhoswho.com

Richard N. Meadows

Title: Owner **Company:** Meadowhill Equine Facility **Address:** 1903 King Bee Road, Perkinston, MS 39573 United States **BUS:** Equine and Cattle Ranch **P/S:** Manage, Train, Breeding Horses and Cattle, Consultations **MA:** Local **D/D/R:** Quarter Horses, International Judge, Breeder/Trainer **H/I/S:** Horseback Riding **EDU:** Armed Forces College, Air Force Intelligence E-7 **A/A/S:** Chamber of Commerce, American Cattlemans Association

Teresa D. Meares

Title: President, Owner **Company:** DGG Taser, Inc. **Address:** 8725 Youngerman Court, Unit 305, Jacksonville, FL 32244 United States **BUS:** Retailer of Law Enforcement Tasers **P/S:** Sales and Distribution of Law Enforcement Tasers **MA:** National **H/I/S:** Spending Time with Family **EDU:** Bachelor's Degree in Criminal Justice, Minor in Psychology, Troy University; Master's Degree in Public Administration, Central Michigan University **A/A/S:** Jacksonville Chamber of Commerce **C/VW:** Children's Miracle Network, Shriners
Email: teresa@dggtaser.com
URL: http://www.dggtaser.com

JoAnn H. Mech
Title: Registered Nurse **Company:** Vanderbilt Heart Institute **Address:** Nashville, TN 37223 United States **BUS:** Cardiology **P/S:** Cardiology Diagnostic Testing **MA:** Local **D/D/R:** Cardiology Diagnostic Testing **H/I/S:** Traveling, Fishing, Gardening **EDU:** Bachelor of Science in Nursing with Critical Care Training, Tennessee State University **CERTS:** Certified in Basic Life Support and Advanced Cardiac Life Support **A/A/S:** Nursing Service Organization; American Cancer Society; American Heart Association; Multiple Sclerosis Society **C/VW:** Room at the Inn
Email: jmech@bellsouth.net
URL: http://www.vanderbilt.edu

Kathleen F. Mecum
Title: Computer Scientist **Company:** Computer Sciences Corporation **Address:** 9000 S. Rita Road, Tucson, AZ 85744 United States **BUS:** Outsourcing Company **P/S:** Consulting Services, SAP Software System Programming and Business Warehouse **MA:** National **D/D/R:** SAP Business Warehousing, Writing ABAP Programs, Creating Solutions for BEX Reporting, Creating DSOs and Infocubes, Working with the Aerospace and Defense Industry, Quality Reporting **H/I/S:** Traveling, Playing Softball with her Daughter, Spending Time with her Friends, Reading **EDU:** Master of Business Administration in Finance, The University of Arizona (1986); Bachelor of Science in Information Systems Management, The University of Arizona (1982) **CERTS:** Certification in SAP and ABAP (2006); Certified Project Manager (2001) **A/A/S:** Girl Scout Leader, Former Assistant, Girl Scouts of the United States of America; Blood Drive Recruiter, American Red Cross **C/VW:** American Red Cross
Email: kmecum@csc.com
URL: http://www.csc.com

Crystal D. Meddings
Title: Youth Service Worker **Company:** West Virginia Department of Health and Human Resources **Address:** P.O. Box 686, Bradley, WV 25818 United States **BUS:** Government Organization **P/S:** Social Services **MA:** Local **D/D/R:** Attending Court with Clients, Organizing Treatment Plans for Youths, Acting as a Liaison for Young Members **H/I/S:** Playing Basketball and Volleyball **EDU:** Bachelor of Social Work, Mountain State University (2004) **A/A/S:** National Association of Social Workers
Email: crystalmeddings@aol.com

Ms. Margarita Medero-Rodriguez
Title: Attorney **Company:** Bauza and Gandara **Address:** 1612 Avenue Ponce de Leon, Suite 302, San Juan, PR 00909 United States **BUS:** Private Law Practice **P/S:** Law Counseling and Representation **MA:** Regional **D/D/R:** Practicing Civil Law Including Employment Discrimination, Labor Disputes, Contract Consultations and Bankruptcy Law **H/I/S:** Reading, Dancing **EDU:** Coursework in Bankruptcy Law; JD, University of Puerto Rico School of Law (2006); Master of Art in English Literature, University of Puerto Rico (2003); Bachelor of Art in Criminal Justice, University of Puerto Rico, Carolina Campus **A/A/S:** Association for Lawyers and Law Students; Puerto Rican Bar Association, Inc.; American Bar Association
Email: margarita.medero@gmail.com
URL: http://www.cambridgewhoswho.com

Isabel L. Medina
Title: Realtor **Company:** Allstate Homes **Address:** 3291 North Hillard Street, Fresno, CA 93726 United States **BUS:** Real Estate Service Provider **P/S:** Residential Mortgage Loans **MA:** Local **EXP:** Ms. Medina's expertise is in residential loans. **EDU:** Fresno City College, AS **A/A/S:** NAR

Ricky R. Medina
Title: Owner **Company:** Eagle Technical Service, LLC **Address:** 6756 Bright View Road, Las Cruces, NM 88007 United States **BUS:** Aircraft Manufacturing Company **P/S:** 3D Tool Design, Product Design **MA:** National **D/D/R:** Using Computer-Aided Three-Dimensional Interactive Analysis V4, V5, UGII/NX2 software **H/I/S:** Rebuilding Cars
Email: eagle_techserv@yahoo.com

Sonia M. Medrano-Hernandez
Title: Owner **Company:** Wintergarden Mobility Repair and Supplies **Address:** 504 E. Haynes Avenue, Pearsall, TX 78061 United States **BUS:** Supply Company for Disabled and Sick People **P/S:** Counseling, Supplies for Disabled People **MA:** Local **D/D/R:** Counseling, Offering Information and Referrals **H/I/S:** Reading **EDU:** Associate of Arts in Community Health, Northwest Vista College **A/A/S:** Phi Delta Kappa **C/VW:** American Cancer Society, Ronald McDonald House
Email: soniah@granderiver.net
URL: http://www.cambridgewhoswho.com

Danita Meeks
Title: Owner **Company:** Danita Meeks **Address:** 7100 Cainsville Road, Lebanon, TN 37090 United States **BUS:** Publishing Design Company **P/S:** Typesetting and Design for Books and Magazines **MA:** Mid-Tennessee **EXP:** Ms. Meeks' expertise is in precision typography. **H/I/S:** Animal Rescue, Spending Time with her Two Grandchildren. **EDU:** Coursework, Middle Tennessee State University; Coursework in Graphic Design; Diploma, Western High School, Louisville, Kentucky **A/A/S:** Master Printers of America; Award, Cracker Barrel **C/VW:** Humane Society of Wilson County
Email: danitameeks@dtccom.net

Laura S. Meeks
Title: Co-Owner, Vice President, Chief Financial Officer, Operations Manager **Company:** Belle Enterprise and Technology, Inc. **Address:** 69723 Camino Pacifico, Rancho Mirage, CA 92270 United States **BUS:** Quality Management Company **P/S:** Quality Management Programs, Consulting, Training **MA:** International **D/D/R:** Managing Projects and Accounts **H/I/S:** Hiking, Reading, Traveling **EDU:** Bachelor of Science in Psychology, University of Puget Sound; Diploma, The Blake School **A/A/S:** Quality Management System of Integration Technology; Former Major, United States Air Force **C/VW:** Unity Church; Habitat for Humanity
Email: laura.meeks@betquality.com
URL: http://www.betquality.com

Mary A. Meggie
Title: Teacher, Author **Company:** East Hartford High School **Address:** 869 Forbes Street, East Hartford, CT 06118 United States **BUS:** High School **P/S:** Education **MA:** Local **D/D/R:** Teaching English, Writing, American Literature, British Literature and Ballroom Dancing, Ballet **H/I/S:** Ballroom Dancing, Writing, Horseback Riding, Gardening **EDU:** Master's Degree in Education, Central Connecticut College; Six-Year Bilingual Degree, University of Connecticut, Bachelor of Arts in English, Central Connecticut College **A/A/S:** National Council of Teachers of English; NRA; Connecticut Council of Teachers of English; Student Assistance Center **C/VW:** Church
Email: m.meggie@easthartford.org

Edward G. Mehrhof, MD
Title: Child, Adolescent and Adult Psychiatrist **Company:** 1) Cayuga Counseling Services 2) SUNY Cortland Counseling Center **Address:** Cortland, NY 13045 United States **BUS:** Counseling Center **P/S:** Mental Health and Outpatient Psychiatric Services **MA:** Regional **D/D/R:** Treating Mental Health Problems for Adults and Children, Working in Psychotherapy and Psychopharmacology **H/I/S:** Bicycling **EDU:** Fellowship in Child Psychiatry, Karl Menninger School of Psychiatry and Mental Health Sciences, Topeka, KS; Residency in Adult Psychiatry, Karl Menninger School of Psychiatry and Mental Health Sciences, Topeka, KS; MD, Upstate Medical Center (1962) **A/A/S:** Diplomat, International Association for Child and Adolescent Psychiatry; American Psychiatric Association; American Academy of Child Adolescent Psychiatry
Email: emehrhof@yahoo.com

Richard A. Meide
Title: President **Company:** Midwest Cam Solutions **Address:** 3300 Bass Lake Road, Suite 201, Brooklyn Center, MN 55429 United States **BUS:** Computers Manufacturer **P/S:** Software and Support **MA:** Regional **EXP:** Mr. Meide's expertise is in management. **H/I/S:** Farm **EDU:** Associate Degree in Education, University of Minnesota **A/A/S:** MBMA, Better Business Bureau
Email: rick@midwestcamsolution.com
URL: www.midwestcamsolution.com

Paul D. Meier
Title: Athletic Trainer **Company:** The Steadman Hawkins Clinics **Address:** 360 Peak One Drive, Suite 340, Frisco, CO 80443 United States **BUS:** Orthopedic Surgery Clinic **P/S:** Orthopedic Surgery, Rehabilitation **MA:** International **EXP:** Mr. Meier's expertise is in sports medicine. **D/D/R:** Educating **H/I/S:** Skiing, Hiking, Biking, Working Out **EDU:** Fellowship in Sports Medicine and Athletic Training, Steadman Hawkins Clinic; Master in Education, University of Virginia; Bachelor of Science in Sports Medicine, Norwich University **A/A/S:** Certified, Athletic Trainer, Strength and Conditioning Specialist, Orthopedic Technician; Performance Enhancement Specialist
Email: pmeier@steadman-hawkins.com
URL: http://www.steadman-hawkins.com

Ms. Neva L. Meisner, M.Ed.
Title: Physical Education, Health Teacher **Company:** Eaton School District **Dept:** Physical Education and Health **Address:** 225 Juniper Avenue, Eaton, CO 80615 United States **BUS:** Public School District **P/S:** Education for Kindergarten through 12th-Grade Students **MA:** Local **D/D/R:** Teaching Mathematics, Science, Language Arts, Writing, Computer Skills, Health, Technology and Physical Education to Sixth through Eighth-Grade Students **H/I/S:** Kayaking, Camping, Fishing, Tae Kwon Do **EDU:** Master's Degree in Education, Lesley University, Cambridge, Massachusetts (2003) Bachelor of Science Degree, University of Colorado (1979) **A/A/S:** Colorado Association for Health, Physical Education, Recreation and Dance; American Association for Health, Physical Education, Recreation and Dance; NEA **A/H:** Middle School Physical Education Teacher of the Year Award (2005)
Email: nmeisner@eaton.k12.co.us
URL: http://eatonsd.middle.schoolfusion.us/overview/classroom.phtml?sessionid=e0faa7536c68949eb07b54f2c50d6afe
URL: http://www.eatonsd/schoolfusion.us/

P. Turner Melanie
Title: President **Company:** Turner Appraisals **Address:** 15205 Highway 17, Chaton, AL 36518 United States **BUS:** Real Estate Appraisals **P/S:** Real Estate Appraisals **MA:** Regional **D/D/R:** Specializing in Residential, Commercial, Land Appraisal and Real Estate Sales **H/I/S:** Walking, Reading **CERTS:** Licensed Appraiser, Licensed Real Estate Agent **A/A/S:** American Cancer Society
Email: mpturner@millry.net

Mrs. Rosalie J. Melby
Title: Classroom Teacher (Retired) **Address:** P.O. Box 365, Bowbells, ND 58721 United States **BUS:** Public School **P/S:** Education **MA:** Local **D/D/R:** Teaching Kindergarten through 12th-Grade Students **H/I/S:** Listening to Music, Reading, Traveling **EDU:** Bachelor's Degree in Elementary Education, Minor in Music, Minot State University **A/A/S:** North Dakota Education Association; National Education Association **A/H:** Young Educator Award **C/VW:** Church
URL: http://www.cambridgewhoswho.com

Michael Martin Melendrez
Title: Owner **Company:** Trees That Please **Dept:** Soil Secrets Worldwide **Address:** 3084 State Highway 47, Los Lunas, NM 87031 United States **BUS:** Manufacturing Company **P/S:** Soil Amendment Products **MA:** International **D/D/R:** Overseeing Business Operations, Growing Plants **H/I/S:** Mountain Climbing, Back Packing, Camping, Hiking, Botanizing **EDU:** Master of Science in Physiology, University of New Mexico **A/A/S:** International Oak Society; International Humic Substances Society; New Mexico Chapter, United States Green Building Council; United States Department of Agriculture; Plant Research Committee; Rotary Club
Email: soilsecrets@aol.com
Email: treesthatplease@comcast.net
URL: http://www.soilsecrets.com
URL: http://treesthatplease.us

Paula D. Mello
Title: Volunteer in Patrol (Retired) **Company:** Sheriff's Office **BUS:** Government **P/S:** Police Services **MA:** Local **D/D/R:** Volunteer for the Witness and Victim Program **H/I/S:** Reading Mystery Novels **EDU:** Associate of Arts in General Studies, College of the Sequoias **A/A/S:** Various Portuguese Clubs; Sheriff's Office **C/VW:** Various Animal Charities and Veterans Charities; Volunteer, Sheriff's Office; Volunteer, District Attorney's Witness and Victim Program
Email: p_mello@sbcglobal.net
URL: http://www.cambridgewhoswho.com

Margaret Meloni
Title: President **Company:** Meloni Coaching Solutions, Inc. **Address:** 5318 E. Second Street, Suite 413, Long Beach, CA 90803 United States **BUS:** Coaching Firm **P/S:** Coaching and Developmental Services for Information Technology Professionals **MA:** National **D/D/R:** Coaching Information Technology Professionals to Gain a Professional Image, Building Relationships, Managing the Reputation of the Firm **H/I/S:** Walking, Cooking, Kayaking **EDU:** Master's Degree in Business, California State University **A/A/S:** Project Management Institute; Professional Convention Management Association; Professional Coaches And Mentors Association
Email: Margaret.Meloni@cwwemail.com
Email: margaret@melonicoaching.com
URL: http://www.melonicoaching.com

Mr. Douglas E. Melton, RN, ADON
Title: Registered Nurse **Company:** Wedgewood Nursing Home **Address:** 6621 Dan Danciger Road, Fort Worth, TX 76133 United States **BUS:** Nursing Home **P/S:** Healthcare Including Geriatric and Residential Care Services **MA:** Regional **EXP:** Mr. Melton's expertise includes operations and nursing management. **H/I/S:** Involving in Political Activities, Reading **EDU:** Associate Degree in Nursing, New Mexico Junior College (1984)
Email: md2guys@sbcglobal.net
URL: http://www.wedgewoodnursinghome.com

Jon M. Melvin
Title: Owner **Company:** JM Inspections **Address:** 1024 Ledgeview Lane, West Pittston, PA 18643 United States **BUS:** Home Inspection Company **P/S:** Home, Real Estate Inspection Service **MA:** Local **D/D/R:** Home Inspection Including Ventilation, Electrical, Heating, Exterior, Plumbing, Foundation, Roofing, Mold, Asbestos, Wood Destroying Insect Inspection, Lead and Water Testing **H/I/S:** Golfing, Reading Golf Digest, Landscaping, Consulting **EDU:** Coursework in Chemistry and Landscape Architecture, Wilkes University; Bachelor of Science in Ceramic Science Engineering, Pennsylvania State University (1986) **A/A/S:** American Society of Home Inspectors; North American Housing Inspectors; National Pest Management Association; Pennsylvania Pest Management Association; National Association of Widows in Ireland
Email: jminspections@verizon.net

Deborah L. Menard
Title: Principal **Company:** Twin Lakes Academy Elementary School **Address:** 8000 Point Meadows Drive, Jacksonville, FL 32256 United States **BUS:** National Model School for Americans **P/S:** Regular Elementary Curriculum **MA:** Regional **D/D/R:** Overseeing Entire School of More than 1,100 Students Speaking More than 50 Languages, Ensuring Standards are Insured, Managing Professional Development for Teachers **H/I/S:** Reading, Going to the Beach, Spending Time with her Family **EDU:** Master's Degree Plus 30 in Educational Leadership, McNeese University (1980) **A/A/S:** Alpha Lambda Delta; Phi Delta Kappa; Phi Kappa Phi; DESP **A/H:** Principal Achievement Award for Outstanding Leadership, Duvale County (2005)
Email: menardd@dreamsbeginhere.org
URL: http://www.dreamsbeginhere.org

Sharon L. Mendenhall
Title: Clinical Therapist **Company:** J.O. Combs Unified School District **Address:** 301 E. Combs Road, Queen Creek, AZ 85240 United States **BUS:** School District **P/S:** Education **MA:** National **D/D/R:** Supervising, Treating Traumatized Children and Clinical Therapy **H/I/S:** Traveling, Photography, Art **EDU:** Master's Degree in Social Work, Wayne State University (1998) **CERTS:** Licensed Trauma Consultant, Long Term Care Institute; Diplomate, American Psychotherapy Association **A/A/S:** American Psychotherapy Association; National Association of Cognitive-Behavioral Therapists
Email: slmend6@msn.com
URL: http://www.cambridgewhoswho.com

Iraida R. Mendez-Cartaya
Title: Administrative Director **Company:** Miami-Dade County Public Schools, Intergovernmental Affairs and Grants Administration **Address:** 1860 Biscayne Boulevard, Suite 239, Miami, FL 33132 United States **BUS:** School **P/S:** Education **MA:** Local **D/D/R:** Working as a Certified Public Accountant, Grant Funding **H/I/S:** Spending Time with Family, Outdoor Sports, Fishing, Rafting **EDU:** Bachelor of Science in Business Administration, Concentration in Accounting, University of Miami; Master of Science in Science Taxation, University of Miami **CERTS:** Certified Service and Educational Leadership, Urban Cities Leaders, Harvard University **A/A/S:** Florida Association of School Administrators; Florida Education Legislative Liaisons; Leadership Miami **C/VW:** Big Brothers Big Sisters, Take Stock in Children, American Cancer Society, St. Jude Children's Research Hospital
Email: imendez@dadeschools.net
URL: http://www.2.dadeschools.com

Cynthia P. Mendoza
Title: Pharmacy Manager **Company:** Farmacia Remedios **Address:** 3351 International Boulevard, Oakland, CA 94601 United States **BUS:** Pharmacy **P/S:** Prescription Drugs, Homeopathic Medicine, Latin Products from Mexico **MA:** Local **D/D/R:** Consulting with Patients on Drugs in Spanish and English **H/I/S:** Playing Volleyball and Tennis, Playing the Piano, Dancing, Visiting Art Galleries and Museums **EDU:** Doctor of Pharmacy, University of California, San Francisco **A/A/S:** American Pharmacists Association **C/VW:** Bay Fund; International Culture; Bolivian Dance Group
Email: cindy@farmaciaremedios.com
URL: http://www.farmaciaremedios.com

Amy E. Menginie
Title: Piano Instructor, Owner **Company:** Taylor's Music Studio **Address:** 18 Kimbelot Lane, Landenberg, PA 19350 United States **BUS:** Music Studio and Retailer **P/S:** Instrument Instruction, Sales and Repairs **MA:** Regional **EXP:** Ms. Menginie's expertise is in music instruction. **D/D/R:** Teaching Music Theory Courses, Holding Piano and Keyboard Lessons **H/I/S:** Swimming, Drawing **EDU:** Bachelor of Arts in Music Education, West Chester University, PA (2008); Associate Degree in General Studies, Delaware County Community College **A/A/S:** Pennsylvania Music Educators Association; The National Association for Music Education
Email: amy2216@hotmail.com
URL: http://taylorsmusic.com

Ms. Magda A. Menner
Title: Paramedic, Field Training Officer **Company:** Monoc Hospital Services Corporation **Address:** 4806 Megill Road, Wall Township, NJ 07753 United States **BUS:** Emergency Medical Services **P/S:** Paramedic and Emergency Medical Response Services **MA:** Essex County, NJ **D/D/R:** Working as a Paramedic, Conducting Field Training for New Hires and Students, Instructing International Trauma Life Support Classes **H/I/S:** Gardening, Using Telescopes **EDU:** Bachelor of Science in Biology, Rowan University (Now Glassboro State College) (1987) **A/A/S:** National Association of Emergency Medical Technicians; National Paramedic Society; National Society of Emergency Medical Services Instructors **A/H:** Award, Paramedic Team Excellence
Email: mmenner@verizon.net
URL: http://www.cambridgewhoswho.com

Tamatha S. Menzie
Title: Spanish Teacher **Company:** Holley High School **Address:** 3800 N. Main Street, Holley, NY 14470 United States **BUS:** High School **P/S:** Education **MA:** Local **D/D/R:** Teach Spanish to Ninth through Twelfth-Grades Students, Teaches Two College Classes, Specialize in Grammar, Teaches both the Language and the Culture **H/I/S:** Walking, Bowling, Spending Time with her Family of Six Children **EDU:** Master's Degree in Elementary Education with a Bilingual Extension, SUNY Brockport **A/A/S:** New York State Association of Foreign Language Teachers **C/VW:** United Way, Camp Good Days and Special Times
Email: tmenzie@holleycsd.org
URL: http://www.cambridgewhoswho.com

Lorraine Mercanti-Erieg
Title: Registered Nurse, Clinical Leader **Company:** Delaware County Memorial Hospital **Dept:** IV-PICC Team, Clinical Leader **Address:** 501 N. Lansdowne Avenue, Drexel Hill, PA 19026 United States **BUS:** Hospital **P/S:** Healthcare **MA:** Local **D/D/R:** Vascular Access Nursing, Teaching Intravenous Therapy, Coordinating the Picc Team, Emergency Room Nursing **H/I/S:** Biking, Reading, Gardening **EDU:** Diploma in Registered Nursing, Roxborough Memorial Hospital **CERTS:** Certification in Basic Life Support; Certification in CPR **A/A/S:** Lite Organization; Infusion Nurses Society; Infection Control Committee; Nurse Practice Council; Central Line Bundle; Value Analysis Committee; Association for Vascular Access **C/VW:** Alzheimer's Association; American Diabetes Association; Susan B. Komen for the Cure
Email: lorraine.erieg@crozer.org
Email: lorraine.mercanti@cwwemail.com

R. Suzanne Mercer
Title: Mathematics Learning Specialist **Company:** Charleston County School District **Address:** 1105 Stratford Road, Hanahan, SC 29406 United States **BUS:** Public School **P/S:** Education and Curriculum **MA:** Regional **D/D/R:** English and Mathematics, Writing, Reviewing Curriculum, Professional Development for District in Mathematics, Budgeting **H/I/S:** Running, Kayaking **EDU:** Master's in Mathematics, Citadel (2004); Master's in English, Citadel (1996) **A/A/S:** Delta Kappa Gamma; National Council of Teachers of Mathematics; SCLME; SCCTM; LCCTM; Association for Supervision and Curriculum Development; National Staff Development Council
Email: suzanne.mercer@comcast.net
URL: http://www.ccsdschools.com

Linda D. Merchain
Title: Teacher **Company:** Alhambra Unified School District, Garfield Elementary School **Address:** 110 W. McLean Street, Alhambra, CA 91801 United States **BUS:** Elementary School **P/S:** Education, Nutrition Awareness **MA:** Local **D/D/R:** Coordinating the Nutrition Network, Teaching Third and Fifth-Grade Students, After-School Intervention Program **H/I/S:** Hiking, Animals **EDU:** Master's Degree in Elementary School, California State University at Los Angeles, 1972 **A/A/S:** National Education Association; Nutrition Network **C/VW:** Church, Christian Children Foundation Fund
Email: lindaeatshealthy@yahoo.com

Sandra A. Mercurio
Title: Massage Therapist **Company:** Sandra Mercurio, LMT **Address:** 3972 Helene Street, Sarasota, FL 34233 United States **BUS:** Massage Salon **P/S:** Wide Range of Massage Therapy Services **MA:** Regional **D/D/R:** Practicing Palliative and Therapeutic Massage for All Ages Including the Elderly **H/I/S:** Rollerblading **EDU:** College Coursework, Indiana University (1976-1980); Sarasota School of Massage **CERTS:** Certified in Thai Massage; Nationally Certified in Massage Therapy **A/A/S:** Florida State Massage Therapy Association
Email: donax4me@aol.com
URL: http://www.cambridgewhoswho.com

Elizabeth Merlino
Title: Chief Billing Officer **Company:** MD Billing Inc. **Address:** 4701 Meridian Avenue, Level E Nichols Building, Miami Beach, FL 33140 United States **BUS:** Healthcare Service Specialist Company **P/S:** Accurate, High-Quality Medical Billing, Collection and Operations Management **MA:** Regional **D/D/R:** Managing Four Offices, Billing Services for 25 Physicians, Running all Daily Operations Including Setting Up and Closing, Point Check-In and Check-Out, Compliance, Meeting Planning, Contracting, Hiring, Training of All Personnel, Performing Payroll Duties, Composing Monthly Reports, Teaching Coding to Healthcare Professionals **H/I/S:** Camping, Cub Scout Den Leader **EDU:** Master's Degree in Business Administration, Florida International University (2001); Bachelor's Degree in Business Administration, Florida International University **CERTS:** Certified Professional Coder **A/A/S:** CPCH; CCP; American Academy of Professional Coders
Email: lizmerlino@aol.com
URL: http://www.cambridgewhoswho.com

Christopher D. Merrett Ph.D.
Title: Professor and Director **Company:** Illinois Institute for Rural Affairs **Address:** 518 Sipes Hall, Holcomb, IL 61455 United States **BUS:** Higher Education **P/S:** Research, Teaching, Undergraduate Programs **D/D/R:** Research, Technical Assisting, Promoting the Economic Development, Leading Science Projects, $3 Million Dollar Budget, Working with Communities and Elected Officials, Government Agencies **H/I/S:** Skiing, Soccer **EDU:** Ph.D. in Geography and Planning, University of Iowa (1994) **A/A/S:** Association for American Geographers; Community Development Society; Canadian Association of Geographers; National Council for Educators
Email: cd-merrett@win.edu
URL: http://www.iira.org

Christina B. Merrill, CSW
Title: Executive Director **Company:** The Bone Marrow Foundation **Address:** 337 E. 88th Street, New York, NY 10128 United States **BUS:** Charity **P/S:** Healthcare **MA:** National **D/D/R:** Assisting Children and Adults with Cancer **EDU:** Master of Social Work, Columbia; Bachelor's Degree in Psychology and Sociology, Drew University **CERTS:** Certified Clinical Social Worker, State of New York **A/A/S:** National Society of Fundraising Executives
Email: cbmerrill@bonemarrow.org
URL: http://www.bonemarrow.org

Prof. Cynthia A. Merriwether-de Vries
Title: Associate Professor **Company:** Juniata College **Dept:** Department of Sociology **Address:** 128 W. Prospect Avenue, State College, PA 16801 United States **BUS:** Liberal Arts College **P/S:** Higher Education **MA:** Regional **EXP:** Ms. Merriwether-de Vries' expertise includes popular culture, human race and ethnic relations. **D/D/R:** Teaching Sociology, Counseling Students, Conducting Faculty Seminars **H/I/S:** Gardening, Walking, Listening to Dave Matthews Band Music **EDU:** Ph.D. in Human Development and Family Studies, The Pennsylvania State University (2000) **A/A/S:** American Sociological Association **A/H:** Nominee, University Teachers Grant, Rotary International; Community Driven Grant Award, National Institute for Social Work Education (Gero-Ed) **C/VW:** Bama Works Foundation
Email: cynthia.devries@yahoo.com
URL: http://www.juniata.edu

William Alan Mertins
Title: Registered Principal **Company:** Mertins Investments Services, Inc. **Address:** 375A N. Ninth Avenue, Pensacola, FL 32502 United States **BUS:** Asset Management Firm **P/S:** Investment Advising and Managing Finances **MA:** Regional **D/D/R:** Investment Advising, Offering Asset Management and Wealth Preservation, Helping Clients' Assets Grow, Managing Individual Retirement Accounts and Financial Investments **H/I/S:** Photography **EDU:** Bachelor of Science in Marketing, Florida State University (1975)
Email: bmertins@yahoo.com
URL: http://www.william.mertins.sarep.com

Lisa L. Meso, MD
Title: MD, Owner **Company:** Fitness Together/Ambulatory A **Address:** 820, Birmingham, MI 48004 United States **BUS:** Healthcare Healthcare/Medical Services **P/S:** Ambulatory, Anesthesia Services **MA:** Local **EXP:** Dr. Meso's expertise is in anesthesia. **H/I/S:** Running **EDU:** Wayne State University, Michigan State University, MD, BS **A/A/S:** ASA, AMA
Email: 1

Diana Messer

Title: Physics Teacher **Company:** Mason High School **Address:** 6100 S. Mason-Montgomery Road, Mason, OH 45040 United States **BUS:** Four-Year Public High School Accredited by the North Central Association **P/S:** Serving 2,350 Students in Grades 9 Through 12 Supported by Classroom Teachers, Media Specialists, Technologists, Administrators, Counselors and an Array of Staff Members, Special Educators, Volunteers and Aides **MA:** Regional **D/D/R:** Chemistry, Physical Science, Physics, AP Physics, Creative Thought Going into Each Lesson with Objective to Make Difficult Subject Matter Easier to Grasp and Retain, Use of Demonstrations Relative to Student Lives Presented First, then the Actual Textbook Explanation Follows, Hands-On, Student Design Materials, Equipment and then Must Show They Can Teach it to Someone Else, Guest Speaker at Educational Workshops and Physics Fest, Just Became an Approved AP Reader, Hand Selected to Grade National Physics Exam **EDU:** Master's Degree in Education, Wright State University (2000) **A/A/S:** American Association of Physics Teachers; Westchester's Mother of Twins and Multiples; Charitable Work, United Way
Email: messerd@mason.k12.oh.us
URL: http://www.masonohioschools.com/highschool.aspx

Marlene A. Messin

Title: President, Chief Executive Officer **Company:** Plastic Products Co, Inc **Address:** 30355 Akerson Street, Lindstrom, MN 55045 United States **BUS:** Plastic Manufacturer **P/S:** Plastic Parts, Custom Plastic Injection Molding **MA:** Local **D/D/R:** Running Company **H/I/S:** Read, Travel, Needlework, Antiques **EDU:** Various Courses **A/A/S:** Society of Plastic Engineers, Past Board Member
Email: marlenemessin@plasticproducts.sco.com

Ralph J. Messner

Title: Owner, Operator **Company:** Messner Home, Inc. **Address:** 708 Hill Rise Court, Lexington, KY 40504 United States **BUS:** Veterans Home Care Facility **P/S:** Housing and Care for Disabled Veterans **MA:** Regional **D/D/R:** Dispensing Prescriptions to Residents, Evaluating and Allocating Allowance for the Residents, Supervising Eight Employees **H/I/S:** Piloting Aircraft, NASCAR, Skydiving, RV Riding **EDU:** Diploma, Portland High School (1952) **A/A/S:** Shriners of North America
Email: rjmessner@aol.com
URL: http://www.messnerhome.com

Carmen Metcalf

Title: President **Company:** Rail Source International, Inc. **Address:** 2485 Jennings Road, Olin, NC 28660 United States **BUS:** Railroad Travel Agency **P/S:** Customizing Travel Packages, Rail Travel, Specialty and Scenic Trains, Ski Groups and Tailor-Made Packages, First-Class Escorted Train Journey **MA:** International **D/D/R:** Customizing Travel Packages for Switzerland, South Africa and East Africa, Tailoring Itineraries and Accommodations, Selling Wholesale to Travel Agencies **H/I/S:** Spending Time with her Children, Hiking **EDU:** Degree in Business Administration, Altdorf, Uri, Switzerland **A/A/S:** Board Member, Switzerland Tourist
Email: carmen@rsiworld.com
URL: http://www.rsiworld.com

Jeanne Beryl Metz

Title: President **Company:** Federated Gardens Clubs of New York State, Inc. **Address:** 104 F Convent Gardens, Albany, NY 12220 United States **BUS:** Nonprofit Organization **P/S:** Landscaping and Design, Environmental Consulting, Education for Youth, Botanical Shows, Highway Beautification, Civic Beautification **MA:** National **D/D/R:** Overseeing 100 Women on Executive Board, Recruiting, Managing Administrative Duties **H/I/S:** Painting Stained Glass, Swimming, Water Sports **EDU:** Coursework in Landscape Design and Environment **CERTS:** Certification in Gardening Study and Horticulture; National Accredited Flower Show Judge **A/A/S:** Daffodil Society; Orchid Society; Designer Choice **A/H:** Flower Show Award, NY (2007)
Email: jbm51ban@aol.com
URL: http://www.gardencentral.org

Barbara K. Metzler

Title: Co-Owner **Company:** Koala Dreams **Address:** 218 N. Woods Road, Festus, MO 63028 United States **BUS:** eBay and Auction Retailer **P/S:** Antiques, Mid-Century and Home Decor **MA:** International **D/D/R:** Purchasing and Selling Antiques, Paintings and Vintage Items, Creating Listings, Managing Daily Operations **H/I/S:** Playing Guitar, Painting, Writing **EDU:** Coursework, Sawyer Business College (1975); Coursework, Maryville University (1989) Master of Business Administration, Almeda University (2004) **A/A/S:** American Cancer Society
Email: koaladreams@wildblue.net
URL: http://stores.ebay.com/koalaskoolstuff83

Jayne E. Meyer, RN

Title: Senior Clinical Trial Associate **Company:** Dendreon Corporation **Dept:** Clinical Affairs **Address:** 3005 First Avenue, Seattle, WA 98121 United States **BUS:** Biotechnology Company **P/S:** Discovery, Development and Commercialization of Novel Therapeutics that Harness the Immune System **MA:** International **D/D/R:** Acting as a Liaison for Multiple Clinical Research Organizations, Coordinating the Departmental Standard Operating Procedure Committee, Overseeing Multiple Projects, Coordinating Registration for Research Subjects, Preparing Materials to Initiate Clinical Trials, Offering Administrative Support to the Staff **H/I/S:** Gardening, Traveling, Cooking **EDU:** Bachelor of Arts in Nursing, Augustana College, Sioux Falls, SD(1974) **CERTS:** Certification, North American Transplant Coordinators' Organization; Certification in Advanced Cardiac Life Support
Email: jmeyer@dendreon.com
URL: http://www.dendreon.com

Laurel M. Meyer

Title: Owner **Company:** Self-Employed Legal Nurse Consulting **BUS:** Healthcare, Integrated Holistic Healthcare **P/S:** Healthcare **MA:** Regional **D/D/R:** Nursing, Legal Nurse Consulting, In-Home Assessments **H/I/S:** Listening to Music, Spending Time Outdoors **EDU:** Bachelor of Science in Nursing, State University of New York; Vicki Milazzo Institute **CERTS:** Certification in Legal Nurse Consulting **C/VW:** Church, Manna Food Bank, Salvation Army, Feed the Children, Local Animal Groups
Email: wakingraptor@charter.net
URL: http://www.cambridgewhoswho.com

Mark A. Meyer, CPCU

Title: Manager, Corporate Risk **Company:** Steelcase, Inc **Address:** 901 44th Street S.E., Grand Rapids, MI 49508 United States **BUS:** Furniture Manufacturer **P/S:** Office Furniture Management **MA:** International **EXP:** Mr. Meyer's expertise includes insurance, risk quantification and litigation process. **H/I/S:** Golf, Coaching **EDU:** Hope College, Bachelor's Degree in Business Administration **CERTS:** Certified Properties/Casualties Underwriter **A/A/S:** Board of Local Chapter of Risk/Insurance Management/Coaching
Email: mmeyer@steelcase.com

Roger J.C. Meyer, MD

Title: President, Doctor of Medicine **Company:** Child and Family Health Foundation **Address:** 3566 Ridgetop Court N.E., Bremerton, WA 98310 United States **BUS:** Medical Center **P/S:** Healthcare Including Teaching Research for Physicians and Medical Professionals **MA:** National **D/D/R:** Practicing Pediatric Medicine and Emporiatrics, Organizing and Identifying Programs, Conducting Research, Writing Articles and Books, Managing the Private Practice **H/I/S:** Sight Seeing, Rowing **EDU:** Fellowship (1961); Residency, Strong Children's Hospital (1958); Internship, St. Louis Children's Hospital (1956); MD, Washington University in St. Louis (1955) **A/A/S:** Fellow, American Academy of Pediatrics; Historian, Kitsap Chapter, Military Officers Association of America
Email: rjcmeyer@aol.com
URL: http://www.cambridgewhoswho.com

Donna L. Meyers

Title: Police Officer **Company:** North Carolina Department of Agricultural and Consumer Services **Address:** 505 W. Chapel Hill Street, Durham, NC 27701 United States **BUS:** Government Organization **P/S:** Public Services Including Law Enforcement **MA:** Regional **EXP:** Ms. Meyers' expertise is in law enforcement. **D/D/R:** Answering Telephone Calls, Investigating Criminal Activities, Assisting Citizens, Writing Reports, Training, Conducting Homicide Investigations, Testifying in Court, Profiling Suspects' Methods of Operations, Overseeing Chemical Processing, Tracing Fingerprints **H/I/S:** Reading, Cross-Stitching, Watching Movies **CERTS:** Certification in Criminal Justice, North Carolina Justice Academy **A/A/S:** Policemen's Benevolent Association; Fraternal Order of Police; North Carolina Homicide Investigators Association
Email: donna.meyers@durhamnc.gov
URL: http://www.durhamnc.gov

Jill E. Meyers

Title: Vice President of Human Resources **Company:** RGA Media Group, Inc. **Address:** 350 W. 39th Street, New York, NY 10018 United States **BUS:** Digital Advertising Company **P/S:** Digital Interactive Advertising **D/D/R:** Offering Strategic Human Resources and Human Resources, Training Development, Managing Employee Relations, Coaching **H/I/S:** Snow Skiing, Playing Outdoor Sports, Watching Movies, Going to the Theater **EDU:** Master's Degree in Social Work, Boston University (1986)
Email: jill.meyers@rga.com
URL: http://www.rga.com

Mary C. Meyers

Title: Principal's Secretary **Company:** Granite School District **Dept:** Spring Lane Elementary School **Address:** 5315 S. 1700 E., Salt Lake City, UT 84117 United States **BUS:** Elementary School **P/S:** Elementary Education **MA:** Regional **D/D/R:** Overseeing the Budget, Checking Accounts, Enrolling and Removing Students, Ordering Supplies for Teachers, Managing the Office, Performing Administrative Duties **H/I/S:** Gardening, Four-Wheeling, Camping, Writing Poetry **EDU:** College Coursework in Office Management, Accounting and Administration **A/A/S:** Granite Association of Educational Office Professionals; Utah Association of Educational Office Professionals; National Association of Educational Office Professionals
Email: mcmeyers@graniteschools.org
URL: http://www.graniteschools.org

Valentina Mezheritskaya, RN

Title: Registered Nurse **Company:** Visiting Nurse Service of New York **Address:** 1707 E. 14th Street, Apartment 8, Brooklyn, NY 11229 United States **BUS:** Largest Nonprofit Home Health Care Agency in the Nation **P/S:** Nursing Services for Homebound Patients including Senior Care, Private Care, Rehabilitation Therapy, After Hospital Care, Pediatric Care, Hospice Care **MA:** National **D/D/R:** Nursing Care to Disabled and Homebound Patients **H/I/S:** Traveling, Skiing, Reading **CERTS:** Registered Nurse Certification (2000)
Email: mvalentinam@aol.com
URL: http://www.vnsny.org

Amy H. Michael, M.Ed.

Title: Teacher **Company:** St. Stephens High School **Address:** 5545 Bethel Church Road, Hickory, NC 28602 United States **BUS:** High School Facility Dedicated to Excellence in Education **P/S:** Regular Core Curriculum Including Reading, Mathematics, English, Science, Social Studies, Art, Music, History, Language Arts, Computers, Physical Education **MA:** Regional **D/D/R:** Teaching Mathematics to All High School Grades, Working as a Student Intervention Team Member **H/I/S:** Hiking, Anything Outdoors **EDU:** Master's Degree in Middle Grades Education, Appalachian State University (2006); Pursuing Ed.D. in Curriculum and Instruction, Gardener Webb University **A/A/S:** North Carolina Council of Teachers of Mathematics; National Council of Teachers of Mathematics; North Carolina Middle School Association; National Middle School Association
Email: amy_michael@catawba.k12.nc.us
URL: http://www.catawba.k12.nc.us

Nicole Michaels

Title: Radio Frequency Engineering Manager **Company:** T-Mobile **Address:** 800 Lake Murray Boulevard, Irmo, SC 29063 United States **BUS:** Cellular Communications Company **P/S:** Cell Phone Service and Sales **MA:** Local **D/D/R:** Managing the Performance Team, Lecturing, Radio Frequency Engineering, Programming **EDU:** Pursuing Master's Degree, Southern Methodist University; Bachelor's Degree in Electrical Engineering, Purdue University **A/H:** EUG, T-Mobile performance reward in 2008 **C/VW:** American Society for the Prevention of Cruelty to Animals
Email: nicole.michaels4@t-mobile.com
URL: http://www.cambridgewhoswho.com

David R. Michel

Title: Chief Financial Officer, Treasurer **Company:** Eastwood Local Schools **Address:** 4800 Sugar Ridge Road, Pemberville, OH 43450 United States **BUS:** School **P/S:** Education **MA:** Local **D/D/R:** Preparing Budgets, Processing Payroll, Accounting **H/I/S:** Golfing, Playing Basketball **EDU:** Master of Business Administration, Major in Finance, Xavier University; Bachelor of Arts in Economics, University of Cincinnati **A/A/S:** Ohio School Boards Association; Northwest Ohio Association of School Business Officials; Ohio Association of School Business Officials; Association of School Business Officials
Email: dmichel@eastwood.k12.oh.us
URL: http://www.eastwood.k12.oh.us

Ruth Yvonne Michels

Title: Grant Writer **Company:** Michels & Michels **Address:** 2151 Hawthorne Avenue, Grand Junction, CO 81506 United States **BUS:** Freelance Grant Writing for Government Agencies **P/S:** Grant Writing **MA:** National **D/D/R:** Technical Writing, Consulting grant reviewer; researcher; author of technical articles and papers; patient advocacy; three patents for cytology related devices; hoping to write a book detailing the life of her mother **H/I/S:** Reading, Spending Time with her Family, Fishing, Outdoor Activities, Traveling, Researching **EDU:** Associate Degree, Mesa State College; Degree in Cytology Technology, International Academy of Cytology **A/A/S:** American Society for Clinical Pathology; International Academy of Cytology **C/VW:** Mesa County Underage Drinking Task Force, Build a Generation, Speaking at Local Schools
Email: rmichels@acsol.net
URL: http://www.cambridgewhoswho.com

Marchia L. Mickens
Title: Teacher, Pageant Director **Company:** U.S. United Pageant **Address:** P.O. Box 491, Conley, GA 30288 United States **BUS:** National Pageant Honoring Females for their Personal, Professional and Community Achievements **P/S:** A Showcase for Each Contestant on her Own Merits and Personality **MA:** National **D/D/R:** Building Self-Esteem in Young Women, Teaching Elementary School, Volunteering as the Executive Director of the Pageant, Recruiting and Advertising for the Pageant, Finding Sponsors, Securing Volunteers and Judges for the Pageant **H/I/S:** playing the piano, directing choirs **EDU:** Master's Degree in Elementary Education, American InterContinental University (2006) **A/A/S:** Association for the Advancement of Retired Persons; Professional Association of Georgia Educators
Email: usunitedpageant1@aol.com
URL: http://www.usunitedpageant.com

Jane Middelton-Moz
Title: Director **Company:** Middelton-Moz Institute, The Institute for Professional Practice **Address:** P.O. Box 1249, Montpelier, VT 05601 United States **BUS:** Private Nonprofit Organization **P/S:** Speaking, Consulting, Community Intervention **MA:** International **D/D/R:** Corporate Consulting with Focus on Training on Bullying and Negativity in the Work Place, Offering Community Intervention **H/I/S:** Writing, Quilting **EDU:** Master's Degree in Clinical Psychology, St. Michael's University (1976)
Email: jmoz@ippi.org
URL: http://www.ippi.org

Tina M. Midkiff
Title: Owner, Coach **Company:** Pennsylvania Elite All Star Gym **Address:** 212 S. Queen Street, Littlestown, PA 17340 United States **BUS:** Gym **P/S:** Cheerleading, Dance, Gymnastics **MA:** Local **D/D/R:** Coaching Boys and Girls aged Eight to 18 in Tumbling and Gymnastics, Overseeing Coaches, Managing Operations **H/I/S:** Horses, Exercising **EDU:** NCSSE Master Certification; High School Education **CERTS:** Safety Certified with USA Gymnastics **A/A/S:** Littlestown Chamber of Commerce
Email: mandtmidkiff@aol.com
URL: http://www.paelineallstars.com

Steven A. Mientkiewicz
Title: Educator **Company:** Lincoln Consolidated Schools, Lincoln High School **Address:** 37207 Menton Street, Romulus, MI 48174 United States **BUS:** High School **P/S:** Education for Ninth through 12th-Grade Students, Courses in American Government, World Geography, Economics and U.S. Constitution **MA:** Regional **D/D/R:** Teaching Social Studies to Ninth through 12th-Grade Students **H/I/S:** Fishing, Hunting, Photography, Reading, Sports **EDU:** Bachelor of Science in Secondary Education Social Studies, Eastern Michigan University (2005) **CERTS:** Certification in Teaching History and Social Studies, Michigan State University **A/A/S:** Kappa Delta Phi; Golden Key International Honour Society; Phi Alpha Theta; Alpha Phi Omega
Email: mientkiewicz@gw.lincoln.k12.mi.us
URL: http://www.lincoln.k12.mi.us

Katherine M. Might
Title: Registered Nurse **Company:** Eleanor Slater Hospital **Address:** 600 New London Avenue, Cranston, RI 02920 United States **BUS:** Hospital **P/S:** Healthcare Including Group Therapy, Counseling Adults with Phobias, Depression, Substance Abuse and Anxiety Disorder **MA:** Regional **D/D/R:** Treating Borderline Personality Disorder, Nursing, Caring for Patients, Treating Mentally Ill Patients **H/I/S:** Traveling **EDU:** Associate Degree in Nursing, Community College of Rhode Island (1996) **CERTS:** Registered Nurse; Certified Nursing Assistant
Email: katherine.might@cwwemail.com
URL: http://www.mhrh.state.ri.us

Desiree Migon
Title: Sales Representative **Company:** Office Resource Group **Address:** 1303 W. Beltline Road, Suite 201, Carrollton, TX 75006 United States **BUS:** Retail Store **P/S:** Designing and Installing Office Furniture **MA:** Local **D/D/R:** Accounting, Managing Business Operations, Working on Computer-Aided Design, Designing Office Cabinets and Cubicles **H/I/S:** Spending Time at the Carrollton-Farmers Branch Soccer Association, Traveling, Spending Time Outdoors **EDU:** Bachelor of Fine Arts, Texas Tech University; Bachelor's Degree in Spanish, Texas Tech University **A/A/S:** Dallas Human Resource Management Association; Richardson Chamber of Commerce; Metrocon
Email: DMigon@officeresourcegroup.com
URL: http://www.officeresourcegroup.com

Heather M. Mikes
Title: Vice President of Regional Operations **Company:** Wragg & Casas Public Relations, Inc. **Address:** 27499 Riverview Center Boulevard, Suite 115, Bonita Springs, FL 34134 United States **BUS:** Independent Public Relations Firm **P/S:** Full-Service Marketing, Advertising and Public Relations Services, Strategic Counseling Services, Multicultural Communications, Web Designs, Public Affairs Issues and Crisis Management Services **MA:** National **D/D/R:** Working on New Business Developments, Overseeing Account Management, Developing Comprehensive Marketing and Communications Strategies, Acting as the Liaison Between Community Organizations and Recruitment **H/I/S:** Spending Time with her Family **EDU:** Bachelor's Degree in Communications, Florida State University (2000) **A/A/S:** Leadership Bonita (2006); Economic Development Council of Collier County; Kappa Alpha Theta; District Director, Board Member, AG Institute **A/H:** Nominee, Top 40 Under 40, Harvard Business Review
Email: hmikes@wraggcasas.com
URL: http://www.wraggcasas.com

John Mikstay Jr., CEM
Title: Manager **Company:** BPA Worldwide **Dept:** Events Audits **Address:** 2 Corporate Drive, Ninth Floor, Shelton, CT 06484 United States **BUS:** Nonprofit Organization **P/S:** Auditing Services for Media Owners and Buyers **MA:** International **EXP:** Mr. Mikstay's expertise includes sales, marketing, operations management and collateral materials creation. **D/D/R:** Budgeting, Forecasting **H/I/S:** Golfing, Surfing, Gardening, Listening to Music **EDU:** Bachelor's Degree in Geography and Cartography, The University of Akron (1994) **CERTS:** Certification in Exhibition Management; Certification in Cartography **A/A/S:** Trade Show Exhibitors Association; International Association of Exhibitions and Events; International Exhibitors Association; Association of Business Managers Event Audit Council; Research Committee, Center for Exhibition Industry Research; Golden Key International Honour Society; Gamma Theta Upsilon Honor Society
Email: jmikstay@bpaww.com
URL: http://www.bpaww.com

Lisa A. Milazzo
Title: Process and Control Business Analyst **Company:** Dow Jones & Company **Address:** P.O. Box 300, Princeton, NJ 08543 United States **BUS:** Publishing Company **P/S:** Business News **MA:** International **D/D/R:** Analyzing Business Processes, Web Design **H/I/S:** Reading, Playing the Piano, Listening to Music, Playing Cards **EDU:** Bachelor of Arts in Early Childhood Education and English, Trenton State University (1997); Associate of Arts in Music, Mercer County Community College (1992) **A/A/S:** International Institute of Business Analysts; ISACA **C/VW:** Children's Home Society; Local Church
Email: lee.milazzo@dowjones.com
URL: http://www.cambridgewhoswho.com

Jason M. Milburn
Title: Visual and Marketing Manager **Company:** Limited Brands **Address:** 2 Limited Parkway, Columbus, OH 43230 United States **BUS:** Clothing **P/S:** Clothing and Beauty **MA:** National **D/D/R:** Purchasing **H/I/S:** My Family, Golfing and Outdoor Activities, Reading, Traveling **EDU:** Master of Business Administration, Dominican University **A/A/S:** ISM; NAPPA; Board of Directors, Salvation Army
Email: jmilburn@limitedbrands.com

Anne Marie Milewski
Title: Emergency Room Quality and Safety Nurse Clinician **Company:** WM Beaumont Hospital **Address:** 44201 Dequindre Road, Troy, MI 48085 United States **BUS:** Hospital **P/S:** Healthcare **MA:** Regional **D/D/R:** Working with Quality and Safety Measures in the Emergency Department, Managing the Leadership Role and Peer Reviews, Processing the Improvement Program **H/I/S:** Cycling, Swimming **EDU:** Pursuing Master of Education, University of Phoenix; Bachelor of Science in Nursing, Nazareth College School of Health and Human Services (1982) **A/A/S:** American Nurses Association; Michigan Nurses Association; Sigma Theta Tau; Alzheimer's Association; American Lung Association; American Heart Association **A/H:** The National Dean's List
Email: rmilewski@sbcglobal.net
URL: http://www.beaumonthospitals.com

Brenda Milk
Title: Senior Account Clerk, Typist **Company:** Chenango County Department of Public Works **Address:** 79 Rexford Street, Norwich, NY 13815 United States **BUS:** Department of Public Works **P/S:** Landfill Operations, Commercial and Residential Recycling, Waste Management **MA:** Local **D/D/R:** Accounting, Managing Credit Collection, Checks, Overseeing Accounts Receivable and Payable, Balancing Ledgers, Sending Out Past Due Bills, Invoicing for Parts and Equipment, Generating Reports **EDU:** College Coursework **C/VW:** Local Church
Email: milkyway97_13801@yahoo.com
URL: http://www.co.chenango.ny.us

Mr. Rafael E. Millares
Title: Attorney **Company:** The Bainbridge Companies, LLC. **Address:** 12765 West Forest Hill Boulevard, Suite 1311, Wellington, FL 33414 United States **BUS:** Full Service Real Estate Firm **P/S:** All Real Estate Products **MA:** National **D/D/R:** Completing All Phases of Real Estate Property Development and Pre-Development, Practicing Criminal and Real Estate Law **H/I/S:** Participating in Water Sports, Soccer, Body Building, Jogging, Traveling, Spending Time with his Family **EDU:** Juris Doctor, Notre Dame-2001; Master of Law-Real Property Development, University of Miami-2004; Bachelor of Arts in English, Holy Cross College-1998 **A/A/S:** Florida Bar Association; Founding Board Member of Next In Line; Notre Dame Alumni Association, Holy Cross College Alumni Association, University of Miami Alumni Association, Ransom Everglades School Alumni Association. **C/VW:** Creative Beginnings Organization
Email: rmillares@bainbridgere.com
URL: http://www.cambridgewhoswho.com

Amy Miller
Title: Owner **Company:** We Care Home Health, Inc. **Address:** P.O. Box 3690, Seminole, FL 33775 United States **BUS:** Healthcare **P/S:** Home Healthcare **MA:** Local **D/D/R:** Overseeing Day to Day Operations, Running the Business **H/I/S:** Camping **CERTS:** Licensed Paralegal **A/A/S:** APD
Email: chamill@knology.net

Carol Miller
Title: Broker, Realtor **Company:** Prudential Tropical Realty **Address:** 2539 Countryside Realty, Unit 3340, Clearwater, FL 33761 United States **BUS:** Real Estate Real Estate **P/S:** Residential, Executive Homes, Bay Front, Lake Front, Intercoastal Waterways, Golf Homes, Senior, Gated **MA:** National **EXP:** Ms. Miller's expertise includes residential properties, golf homes, gated and bay-front properties. **H/I/S:** Grows **EDU:** University of Michigan, Bachelor of Science in Dental Hygiene **A/A/S:** Florida Association of Realtors, National Association of Realtors, National Society of Arts and Letters

Charles E. Miller
Title: President **Company:** Rooftop Consultants, Inc. **Address:** 1753 E. Broadway Road, Route 1-291, Tempe, AZ 85282 United States **BUS:** Construction Consultation Firm **P/S:** Evaluating, Inspecting and Monitoring Roofing Projects/ **MA:** Arizona, Nevada, New Mexico and Southern California **D/D/R:** Roofing Evaluations and Project Management **H/I/S:** Deep Sea Fishing **EDU:** High School Education **CERTS:** RCI, Certified Registered Roof Observer; TRI, Certified Roof Tile Installer; NRCA; Certified Roof Inspection, Diagnosis and Repair **A/A/S:** Roof Consultants Institute; Community Associations Institute; National Roofing Contractors Association; Roofers Union Local 135 **C/VW:** Veterans Organizations
Email: charlie@rooftopconsultants.com
URL: http://www.rooftopconsultants.com

Cindy L. Miller
Title: Vice President **Company:** RBF Consulting **Address:** 14725 Alton Parkway, Irvine, CA 92618 United States **BUS:** Civil Engineering Consulting Company **P/S:** Civil Engineering Design **MA:** Regional **D/D/R:** Water Resources Engineering **H/I/S:** Traveling, Weightlifting, Doing Yoga, Running **EDU:** Bachelor of Science in Civil Engineering, University of California, Irvine **A/A/S:** American Society of Civil Engineers; Ocean County Water Association; University of California, Irvine Affiliates Group **C/VW:** American Red Cross, Habitat for Humanity; American Cancer Society
Email: cliller@rbf.com
URL: http://www.rbf.com

Dawn Miller, PA-C
Title: Physician Assistant **Company:** University of Michigan **Address:** Ann Arbor, Ann Arbor, MI United States **BUS:** University **P/S:** Higher Education Including Health Care **MA:** National **D/D/R:** Handling Admissions and Discharge, Emergency Care and Medical-Surgical, Emergency Room and Cardiac Intensive Unit Patients, Psychiatry and in Assisting Heart Failure or Heart Transplant Teams **H/I/S:** Tennis, Kayaking, Rollerblading **EDU:** Master's Degree in Physician Assistant Studies, Wayne State University (2005); Bachelor of Science in Health Sciences and Psychology, Wayne State University (2002) **A/A/S:** Michigan Academy of Physician Assistants; The Phi Beta Kappa Society; Psi Chi; American Academy of Physician Assistants
Email: dawn_miller08@hotmail.com
URL: http://www.umich.edu

Diane Miller
Title: Director of Medical Billing **Company:** Northern NJ Radiation Oncology Billing **Address:** 95 Old Short Hills Road, West Orange, NJ 07052 United States **BUS:** Healthcare Radiation Oncology Billing Service **P/S:** Medical Billing **MA:** Regional **D/D/R:** Offering Radiation Oncology Billing Services **H/I/S:** Traveling **EDU:** Associate Degree in Finance, Essex County Community College

Francesca Miller
Title: Historian, Scholar **Address:** 908 Fordham Drive, Davis, CA 95616 United States **MA:** National **D/D/R:** Writing Books, Scholarly Articles and Fiction, Teaching American History **H/I/S:** Traveling, Swimming, Sailing **EDU:** Ph.D., University of California, Davis; Master of Arts in History, University of California, Davis **A/A/S:** American Historical Association; Latin American Studies Association; Western Association of Women Historians **A/H:** Sierra Award; Professor IV Award
Email: fwmiller@ucdavis.edu
URL: http://www.cambridgewhoswho.com

Jean A. Miller, RNC, MSN
Title: Retired, Registered Nurse **Company:** Alta Vista Internal Medicine **Address:** 3140 E. Shasta Lane, Tucson, AZ 85641 United States **BUS:** Healthcare Nursing **P/S:** Nursing Services **MA:** Local **D/D/R:** Managing Pediatric Clinic Kino Hospital, Tucson, Arizona, Certified in Maternal and Newborn Nursing **H/I/S:** Cruising **EDU:** Bachelor of Science in Nursing, University of Arizona (1976); Master of Science in Nursing, University of Arizona (1982) **CERTS:** Registered Nurse Certified, University of Arizona **A/A/S:** American Nurses Association, Northern Arizona Council of Governments
Email: jeanmiller@gainbroadband.com

Jeannine D. Miller
Title: Teacher **Company:** Mamaroneck Public Schools **Address:** 1000 W. Boston Post Road, Mamaroneck, NY 10543 United States **BUS:** School **P/S:** Elementary Education **MA:** Local **D/D/R:** Teaching All Subjects to Second-Graders **H/I/S:** Ballroom and Latin Dancing **EDU:** Master of Education, Sarah Lawrence College; Bachelor's Degree in Anthropology, Barnard College **A/A/S:** National Education Association; New York State Education Association **C/VW:** Local and Community Charities
Email: jeannmill@aol.com

Jennifer E. Miller
Title: Controller, HR Director **Company:** MBF Clearing Corp **Address:** 1 N. End Avenue, Suite 1201, New York, NY 10282 United States **BUS:** Commodities Service Provider **P/S:** Trading Commodities **MA:** Local **D/D/R:** Professional at Multi-Tasking **H/I/S:** Brand New Jack Russel Puppy

Ms. Kelly Lynn Miller
Title: Owner **Company:** Cedarview Learning Center Too, Inc. **Address:** 9446 U.S. Highway 19, Port Richey, FL 34668 United States **BUS:** Early Childhood Learning Center **P/S:** Childcare, Early Childhood Education Program for 134 Children **MA:** Regional **D/D/R:** Managing Daily Operations Including Finances **H/I/S:** Scrapbooking, Spending Time with her Family **EDU:** Bachelor of Science in Finance, University of Florida (1996) **CERTS:** Certification in Child-Care Development, Marchman Technical Education Center (2006) **A/A/S:** National Association for the Education of Young Children; Florida Association for Child Care Management
Email: kellylmllr@verizon.net

Lettie M. Miller
Title: Registered Nurse, Nurse Manager **Company:** San Francisco Hospital **Address:** 1001 Potilero Avenue, Oakland, CA 94611 United States **BUS:** Public Hospital **P/S:** Inner City Level 1 Trauma Center **MA:** Regional **D/D/R:** Managing a Twenty-Six Bed Unit, Treating Brain and Heart Trauma, Overseeing Ninety People, Assessing the Vital Signs of Patients **H/I/S:** Sailing, Fishing **EDU:** Master's Degree in Nursing Administration, University of California (2007); Bachelor's Degree in Nursing, California State University (1997); Associate Degree in Nursing, Evergreen Junior College (1982) **A/A/S:** Association of California Nurse Leaders
Email: millereight03@yahoo.com
URL: http://www.cambridgewhoswho.com

Marilyn O'Connor Miller
Title: Sole Proprietor **Company:** The Puppet Connection **Address:** P.O. Box 178, Canton Center, CT 06020 United States **BUS:** Sole Proprietorship **P/S:** Creating Multimedia Stories with Puppets or Masks **MA:** National **D/D/R:** Storytelling with Puppets **H/I/S:** Knitting, Gardening, Listening to Music **EDU:** Bachelor's Degree in English and Music, Marygrove College, Detroit **C/VW:** Local Charitable Organizations
Email: marilyn@ctpuppetry.org
URL: http://www.puppetconnection.com

Melissa A. Miller
Title: Clinical Pharmacy Specialist **Company:** UMass Memorial Medical Center **Address:** 55 Lake Avenue N., Worcester, MA 01655 United States **BUS:** Medical Center **P/S:** Medical Center **MA:** Local **D/D/R:** Working for Clinical Pharmacy Specialist for Critical Care Patients **H/I/S:** Outdoors, Sports, Softball **EDU:** Doctor of Pharmacy, University of Nebraska Medical Center **A/A/S:** American College of Clinical Pharmacy; Society of Critical Care Medicine; Association of Critical Care Pharmacists
Email: millem02@ummhc.org
URL: http://www.cambridgewhoswho.com

Ralph G. Miller III
Title: Emergency Preparedness Coordinator **Company:** Kennedy Health System **Address:** 2 Regulus Drive, Suite D, Turnersville, NJ 08071 United States **BUS:** Health System **P/S:** Healthcare **MA:** Regional **EXP:** Mr. Miller's expertise includes project management, and safety and emergency preparedness. **H/I/S:** Spending Time with his Family **EDU:** Associate Degree in Fire Protection Engineering, Delaware Technical & Community College **A/A/S:** American Society for Healthcare Engineering; National Fire Protection Association **C/VW:** Volunteer, Local Fire Department
Email: r.miller@kennedyhealth.org
URL: http://www.kennedyhealth.org

Sandra K. Miller
Title: Office Manager **Company:** Coast Surgical Group **Address:** 855 Third Avenue, Unit 3340, Chula Vista, CA 92021 United States **BUS:** Healthcare and Medical Services **P/S:** General and Bariatric Surgery **MA:** Local **D/D/R:** Office Duties and Nursing **H/I/S:** Scuba Diving, Deep Sea Fishing **EDU:** LVN **A/A/S:** Runs Support Group for Bariatric Patients
URL: www.coastsurgicalgroup.com

Susan Kaye Miller, CSR
Title: Associate Vice President of Management Information Services **Company:** AXA Equitable Life Insurance Company **Address:** 10290 Alliance Road, Cincinnati, OH 45242 United States **BUS:** Insurance Company **P/S:** Life Insurance, Annuities **MA:** National **D/D/R:** Managing Information Services, Working with Programmers, Assisting with Testing Program Changes **H/I/S:** Machine Embroidering, Reading **EDU:** Fellow, Life Management Institute; Coursework in Pre-Medicine, Indiana University **A/A/S:** LOMA Society
Email: skmiller@mail.usfli.com
URL: http://www.cambridgewhoswho.com

William H. Miller
Title: Financial Adviser **Company:** AIG Retirement **Address:** 2114 N.W. 40th Terrace, Suite B1, Gainesville, FL 32605 United States **BUS:** Financial Company **P/S:** Financial Services Including Retirement Planning, Investments and Insurance Services **MA:** National **D/D/R:** Consulting, Setting up Retirement Plans **H/I/S:** Golfing, Traveling **EDU:** Fellow, Life Underwriter Training Council (1985); Coursework in Business, Jacksonville State University, AL (1971) **C/VW:** Volunteer, Marion County Sheriff's Department; Hospice of Marion County; United Way; March of Dimes; Lions Club, Ocala
Email: william.miller@aigretirement.com
URL: http://www.aigretirement.com

Steven M. Millheim, VMD
Title: Veterinarian **Company:** Healthy Pet Corporation **Address:** 5755 Sullivan Trail, Nazareth, PA 18064 United States **BUS:** Private Veterinarian Practice **P/S:** Small Animal Care and Soft Tissue Surgery **MA:** Regional **D/D/R:** Treating Small Animal and Exotic Animals, Performing Small Tissue Surgery, Routine Examinations and Vaccines **H/I/S:** Camping, Fishing **EDU:** Degree, University of Pennsylvania, School of Veterinary Medicine (1994)
Email: smokey717@msn.com

Iris T. Millner
Title: Registered Nurse **Company:** Virginia Department of Corrections **Address:** 7000 Courthouse Road, Chesterfield, VA 23832 United States **BUS:** Correctional Facility **P/S:** Healthcare **MA:** Statewide **D/D/R:** Nursing **EDU:** Associate of Science in Nursing, Regent College **A/A/S:** Union **C/VW:** Church; Volunteer, Local School
Email: iris.millner@vadoc.virginia.gov
URL: http://www.cambridgewhoswho.com

Ms. Connie R. Mills, RN, BSN, CCM
Title: Medical Case Manager **Company:** Medical Managed Care of MS **Address:** 28 Suncrest Circle, Hattiesburg, MS 39402 United States **BUS:** Healthcare Company **P/S:** Managed Care, Workers' Compensation **MA:** Statewide **EXP:** Ms. Mills' expertise is in medical case management. **H/I/S:** Swimming, Knitting, Crocheting **EDU:** Pursuing Master's Degree; Bachelor of Science in Nursing, Mississippi College **CERTS:** Certified Case Manager; Registered Nurse **A/A/S:** Case Management Society of America **A/H:** State Department of Health Award, 1978 **C/VW:** Relay For Life, Local Church
Email: cmills36@msn.com
URL: http://www.cambridgewhoswho.com

James Patrick Mills
Title: Web Designer **Company:** T.I.M.S. **Address:** 1415 Essie McIntyre Boulevard, Augusta, GA 30901 United States **BUS:** Web Design Company **P/S:** Designing Websites, Applications and Web Hosting **MA:** Local **D/D/R:** Designing Websites **H/I/S:** Reading, Woodworking **A/A/S:** Association of Information Technology Professionals
Email: patrimills@gmail.com
URL: http://www.cambridgewhoswho.com

Lorrie M. Mills
Title: Senior Clinical Research Coordinator **Company:** Medicis Pharmaceutical Corporation **Address:** 7720 N. Dobson Road, Scottsdale, AZ 85256 United States **BUS:** Pharmaceutical Company **P/S:** Pharmaceutical Products Including New Drugs and Devices **MA:** International **EXP:** Ms. Mills' expertise is in clinical research. **D/D/R:** Managing Projects, Marketing, Overseeing Clinical Study Development **H/I/S:** Hiking, Spending Time with her Family and Friends, Sports, Reading **EDU:** Bachelor of Science in Business Management, University of Phoenix **CERTS:** Certified Clinical Research Professional; Certification in Project Management **A/A/S:** Society of Clinical Research Associates **C/VW:** United Food Bank: United Blood Services; Special Olympics; American Heart Association; American Diabetes Foundation
Email: lmills@medicis.com
Email: lmills1226@gmaill.com
URL: http://www.cambridgewhoswho.com

Rosie E. Mills
Title: Director **Company:** William Hodson Community Center, Inc. **Address:** 1320 Webster Avenue, Bronx, NY 10456 United States **BUS:** Long-Term Senior Healthcare Center **P/S:** Meals, Social Education and Legal Services for Independent Seniors, Rehabilitation **MA:** Regional **D/D/R:** Running a Congregate Meals Program, Working on the Budget and Finances, Hosting Legal Workshops, Working with Alzheimer's Patients **H/I/S:** Reading, Traveling, Caribbean Music **EDU:** Ph.D. in Gerontology, Walden University (2005); Master's Degree, Fordham University (1996); Bachelor of Science, Bachelor of Arts, Audrey Cohen College (1994) **A/A/S:** National Association for Female Executives; American Association of University Women; Professional Women's Network
Email: rosie@voicenet.com
URL: http://www.cambridgewhoswho.com

Thomas A. Mills
Title: Senior Engineer **Company:** American Chemical Technologies, Inc. **Address:** 485 E. Van Piper Road, Fowlerville, MI 48836 United States **BUS:** Lubrication Business **P/S:** Lubrication **MA:** National **D/D/R:** Working with Companies Having Difficulties with Lubricants, Mainly Steel and Power Generator Companies **H/I/S:** Motorcycles **EDU:** Associate Degree in Biomedical Engineering, The Pennsylvania University **A/A/S:** Iron Workers Local 207
Email: arthur722@aol.com
URL: http://www.cambridgewhoswho.com

Kathryn M. Milner, MME
Title: Choral Director **Company:** District 130, Nathan Hall Intermediate School **Address:** 5312 135th Street, Crestwood, IL 60445 United States **BUS:** Intermediate School **P/S:** Education **MA:** Local **D/D/R:** Teaching Choral Music **H/I/S:** Tae Kwon Do, Singing **EDU:** Master of Music Education, University of Illinois; Bachelor's Degree in Music Education, Illinois State University **A/A/S:** American Choral Directors Association; National Association for Music Education; National Education Association; Illinois Education Association **C/VW:** Gilda Radner Club
Email: kmilner1@yahoo.com
URL: http://www.cambridgewhoswho.com

Margaret J. Milutin
Title: Teacher **Company:** Dickinson High School **Address:** 3800 Baker Drive, Dickinson, TX 77539 United States **BUS:** High School **P/S:** Education **MA:** Local **D/D/R:** Teaching Algebra and Pre-Calculus to Ninth through Twelfth-Grade **H/I/S:** Reading; Traveling **EDU:** Master's Degree in Education, Stephen F. Austin State University (1989); Bachelor's Degree in Education, Stephen F. Austin State University (1987) **A/A/S:** Texas Girls Coaches Association
Email: mjmilutin@yahoo.com
URL: http://www.dickinsonisd.org

Mr. Edwin E. Minard II
Title: Regional Director of Special Education **Company:** Great Prairie Area Education Agency **Address:** 3601 N. Avenue Road, Burlington, IA 52601 United States **BUS:** Proven Leader in the Education Industry **P/S:** Excellence in Leadership and Services to the School Districts **MA:** Regional **D/D/R:** Teaching Special Education, Working with Special Services with Children and Supervising the Team, Evaluating Students and Creating Intervention Plans, Working with Staff Members who Teach Hearing Impaired Students, Working with Social Workers, Acting as a Liaison Between Staff Members and Social Workers **H/I/S:** Photography, Golfing **EDU:** Master's Degree in Arts and Audiology, Western Illinois University (1975); Master's Degree in Arts and Speech, Western Kentucky University (1974); Bachelor of Arts in History and Government, Western Kentucky University (1973) **A/A/S:** School Administrators of Iowa; Optimists International; Optimists Local District; American Speech-Language-Hearing Association; American Academy of Audiology; Kentucky Colonel
Email: eminard@aea16.k12.ia.us
URL: http://www.hgpaea.k12.ia.us

Denise Mining
Title: Owner, Manager **Company:** Custom Cleaning Unlimited, LLC **Address:** 16573 State Hwy 00, Strafford, MO 65757 United States **BUS:** Janitorial/Maintenance LLC **P/S:** Commercial Cleaning Services **MA:** Local **D/D/R:** Stripping and Waxing **H/I/S:** Reading, Basketball, Volleyball **EDU:** St Joseph Hospital School of Nursing, Diploma
Email: customcleaningunlimited@yahoo.com

Michelle Minneman
Title: Office Manager **Company:** Stafford Dental **Address:** 559 E. Pikes Peak Unit 208, Colorado Springs, CO 80903 United States **BUS:** Healthcare: Dentistry **P/S:** Dental Care **MA:** Local **D/D/R:** Making Sure the Business Runs Smoothly, accounts receivable, insurance processing, patient services, payroll, credentialing, consulting with patients about treatment planning and reviewing their benefits. **H/I/S:** Spending Any/All Spare Time with her Two Children **A/A/S:** MADD
Email: michelle_minneman@q.com

Caroline Minnick-Miller
Title: Chief Executive Officer **Company:** CM2 Marketing **Address:** 7709 Orly Drive, Suite 100, Plano, TX 75025 United States **BUS:** Marketing **P/S:** Marketing for Small Businesses **MA:** Local **D/D/R:** Small Business Marketing **H/I/S:** Horseback Riding **EDU:** University of Arkansas, BS **A/A/S:** Race for the Cure, Habitat for Humanity
URL: www.cm2marketingedge.com

Robert Minor
Title: Chief Deputy Clerk **Company:** U.S. District Court **Address:** 1936 E. Gate Drive, Stone Mountain, GA 30087 United States **BUS:** Federal Court District Serving Residents of Northern Georgia **P/S:** Judicial Services for Local Residents **MA:** Regional **D/D/R:** Supervising Non-Judicial Functions, Working as a Court Room Deputy, Overseeing 220 People in Case Management, Managing the Intake **EDU:** GAD, University of Notre Dame (1980); Bachelor of Arts in Science, United States Military Academy at West Point (1974) **A/A/S:** Attorney, United States Army (1974-2006); American Bar Association; Federal Bar Association; Indiana State Bar Association; San Antonio Bar Association; Veterans of Foreign Wars
Email: minorrl@aol.com

Ron Minyard
Title: Director of Nursing **Company:** Good Samaritan Village **Address:** 1701 N. Turner Street, Hobbs, NM 88240 United States **BUS:** Nonprofit Organization **P/S:** Rehabilitation Including Pharmaceutical Services, Recreational Activities, Respite and Hospice Care, Housekeeping, Laundry and Nursing Staff Services **MA:** Regional **D/D/R:** Nursing, Directing the Nursing Staff, Creating New Procedures and Policies, Recruiting, Overseeing Inventory, Generating Reports **EDU:** Ph.D. in Theology, Universal Life Church Seminary (2001); Master's Degree in Psychology, Trinity College (2000); Bachelor of Science in Healthcare Administration, University of Southern California (1999) **C/VW:** Lions Clubs International
Email: ronminyard@hotmail.com
URL: http://www.good-samaritan.com

Nadine C. Miranda-Luis
Title: Children's Social Worker **Company:** Children and Family Services Division **Address:** P.O. Box 7054, Van Nuys, CA 91409 United States **BUS:** Government Agency **P/S:** Child Abuse Prevention Services **MA:** Local **D/D/R:** Investigating Child Abuse Crimes **H/I/S:** Walking, Listening to Jazz Music **EDU:** Master of Science in Psychology, Pacific Oaks College & Children's School (2001); Bachelor of Arts in Sociology, California State University (1990) **CERTS:** Pursuing License in Marriage and Family Therapy, State of California **A/A/S:** California Association of Marriage and Family Therapists **C/VW:** American Association of Christian Counselors
Email: nadine_miranda@hotmail.com

John Miret
Title: President **Company:** Ximen, LLC **Address:** 1330 Wadsworth Boulevard, Lakewood, CO 80214 United States **BUS:** Health Insurance Company **P/S:** Insurance Services **MA:** Statewide **EXP:** Mr. Miret's expertise includes small group and individual health insurance. **H/I/S:** Traveling, Playing Baseball **EDU:** Bachelor of Arts in Technical Journalism, Colorado State University **C/VW:** Volunteer, Denver Rescue Mission; Local Church
Email: jmiret@earthlink.net
URL: http://www.cambridgewhoswho.com

Tim Miscovich
Title: Managing Partner **Company:** Hospitality Asset Advisors, LLC **Address:** 8391 Ranch Estates, Clarkston, MI 48348 United States **BUS:** Asset Expense Minimization Consultants **P/S:** Tax Consulting for Hotels **MA:** Local **EXP:** Mr. Miscovich's expertise includes specialized areas of taxation. **H/I/S:** Travel **EDU:** Concordia, Master of Business Administration **A/A/S:** National Motel/Hotel Association, National Golf Course Owners Association
Email: tim.miscovich@comcast.net
URL: www.arespartners.com

Katherine Misko
Title: Producer, Director **Company:** Kat Misko Productions **BUS:** Entertainment **P/S:** Documentary Film, Television Production, Writing **MA:** National **D/D/R:** Writing, Directing **H/I/S:** Writing, Reading, Photography, Traveling, Tennis, Film, Art **EDU:** Bachelor of Arts in English, Minor in Film and Spanish, Boston College, 2001 **A/A/S:** Emmy Nominee; Associate Producer **C/VW:** Local Food Drives, Volunteer
Email: katmisko@aol.com

Doreen Mita-Juanitas
Title: Senior Reliability Engineer **Company:** Space Systems/Loral **Address:** 3825 Fabian Way, Stop H22, Palo Alto, CA 94303 United States **BUS:** Manufacturing Company **P/S:** Commercial Satellite Systems **MA:** International **EXP:** Ms. Mita-Juanitas' expertise includes electron microscopy science, electronic failure device analysis and destructive physical analysis. **D/D/R:** Overseeing Failure Device Analysis of Electronic Components and Flight Hardware, Maintaining Scanning Electron Microscopes and Keeping Them Operational, Reviewing Destructive Physical Analysis Reports **H/I/S:** Kendo and Iaido, Reading **EDU:** Associate of Arts, San Joaquin Delta College (1984) **A/A/S:** Electronic Failure Device Analysis Society; Microscopy Society of America; American Society for Metals
Email: mita-juanitas.doreen@ssd.loral.com
URL: http://www.ssloral.com

Anne Mitchell
Title: Real Estate Agent **Company:** RE/MAX Homestead Realty **Address:** 1301 E. 17th Street, Idaho Falls, ID 83404 United States **BUS:** Real Estate Firm **P/S:** Residential and Commercial Real Estate, Luxury Homes, Land, Farms, Ranches **MA:** Local **D/D/R:** Servicing Clients and their Needs, Specializing in Transferees and Relocations, Marketing **H/I/S:** Traveling, Golfing, Playing Bridge **EDU:** High School Education; Certification in Marketing **A/A/S:** American Business Women's Association; Chamber of Commerce; Women's Council of Realtors; team Leader, The Pacific Northwest Relocation Council; The Masters Club; ReMax Platinum Club; ReMax President's Club **A/H:** Quality Service Award
Email: bethandanne@if.rmci.net
URL: http://www.anneandbeth.com

Brooks G. Mitchell
Title: Director of Administration **Company:** Oklahoma Corporation Commission **Address:** 2101 N. Lincoln Boulevard, Oklahoma City, OK 73105 United States **BUS:** Government Agency **P/S:** Oil, Gas, Utility, Transportation Regulation **MA:** Oklahoma **EXP:** Mr. Mitchell's expertise includes tax law and accounting. **H/I/S:** Golfing, Traveling **EDU:** Bachelor's Degree in Business Administration and Accounting **CERTS:** Certified Public Accountant, University of Oklahoma **A/A/S:** The Oklahoma Society of CPAs, Capital Committee for Infant Crisis Services
Email: brooks@brooksmitchellcpa.com
URL: http://www.cambridgewhoswho.com

Deborah C. Mitchell
Title: Pastor **Company:** Love and Mercy Fellowship **Address:** 1420 Union Boulevard, Bay Shore, NY 11706 United States **BUS:** Church **P/S:** Biblical Teachings for Daily Living **MA:** Local **D/D/R:** Teaching, Singing **H/I/S:** Pottery, Antiques, Christmas Villages, Bike Riding, Traveling, Musical Instruments **A/A/S:** Jesus Alive Ministries, Women of Substance Ministries, Operation Homeless Hope for the Future Ministries
Email: tantedcm@hotmail.com

Felicia K. Mitchell, LVN
Title: Licensed Vocational Nurse, Private Duty Pediatric Nurse **Company:** Angels of Care Pediatric Home Health **Address:** P.O. Box 338, Howe, TX 75459 United States **BUS:** Home Healthcare Company **P/S:** Private Duty Pediatric Nursing for Children with Special Needs **MA:** Regional **D/D/R:** Caring for Children with Special Needs, Organizing Charts, Dispensing Medications, Feeding, Bathing, Dressing, Checking Vital Signs, Administering Intravenous Therapy, Offering One-on-One Care, Hiring Employees **H/I/S:** Horseback Riding, Riding ATVs, Walking along the Beach, Cooking **CERTS:** Licensed Vocational Nurse, Cooke County College (1989)
Email: fmpartygirl123@aol.com

John R. Mitchell Sr.
Title: Commander **Company:** Robert E. Newman VFW Post No. 3636 **Address:** 4809 Poplar Level Road, Louisville, KY 40213 United States **BUS:** Veterans Affairs VA **P/S:** Charitable and Veterans Affairs **MA:** National **D/D/R:** Assisting Veterans of Foreign Wars **H/I/S:** Family Chess, Gardening **EDU:** Durrett High School, High School Diploma **A/A/S:** Vietnam Veterans of American Chapter 454, Boys Haven, Thereto Care

Karin Mitchell
Title: pediatric Speech Pathologist **Company:** Children's Hospital of Orange County **Address:** 244 San Carlos Way, Placentia, CA 92870 United States **BUS:** State-of-the-Art Hospital Facility Children's hospital **P/S:** Over One Hundred Programs and Services to Nurture, Advance and Protect the Health and Well-Being of Children **MA:** Local **D/D/R:** Practicing Speech Pathology, Offering Speech Therapy for Neonatal Patients, Teaching Premature Babies How to Suck Slowly, Treating Children with Brain Injuries, Offering Pediatric Feeding and Swallowing Treatments and Children's Ventilator Tracheotomies **H/I/S:** Snow and Water Skiing, Water Boarding, Off-Roading, Reading **EDU:** Master of Arts in Communication Disorders, California State University at Fullerton (1995); Bachelor of Arts, Biola University, La Mirada, California (1990) **CERTS:** Adult and Pediatric Vitalstim; Certificate of Clinical Competencies; Certificate, Neonatal Assessment Scale; Certified, Vital Stem and Neonatal Developmental Treatment; Certified in Sensory Integration and Lactation Education **A/A/S:** American Speech-Language-Hearing Association; California Speech-Hearing Association
Email: ckmitchellinc@sbcglobal.net
URL: http://www.choc.org

Mike C. Mitchell
Title: President **Company:** Innovative Design and Construction **Address:** 124 Belle Ridge Drive, Madison, AL 35758 United States **BUS:** Construction Company **P/S:** New Home Building and Construction, Remodeling **MA:** Local **D/D/R:** Managing Daily Business Operations, Overseeing the Development of New Homes **H/I/S:** Boating, Going to the Beach **CERTS:** Pursuing Certification as a Graduate Builder **A/A/S:** National Association of Home Builders; Huntsville/Madison County Builders Association
Email: mikemitchellidc@yahoo.com

Paula L. Mitchell
Title: Sub-Contractor **Company:** Tom Keith and Associates **Address:** 1215 Cool Spring Street, Fayettville, NC 28301 United States **BUS:** Real Estate Appraiser **P/S:** Work with Lenders, Insurance, Individuals for Developing Opinions About Their Properties **MA:** Local **D/D/R:** Working as a Certified Residential Appraiser Covering Eight Counties **H/I/S:** Reading, Traveling, Skiing, Hiking **EDU:** Bachelor of Arts in Public Relations, Appalachian State University **A/A/S:** North Carolina Association of Professional Appraisers
Email: appraisal.lady@usa.com

Robert B. Mitchell
Title: Attorney, Equity Member **Company:** Pullman & Comley, LLC **Address:** 850 Main Street, Bridgeport, CT 06601 United States **BUS:** Law Firm **P/S:** Legal Services, Labor and Employment, General Civil Trial Work **MA:** Regional **EXP:** Mr. Mitchell's expertise includes civil litigation, labor and employment law admiralty. **H/I/S:** Sailing **EDU:** JD, Tulane University **A/A/S:** American Bar Association; Connecticut Bar Association; Past President, Bridgeport Bar Association; Fairfield County Bar Association; DRI; CTLA; Society of Human Resource Management; Defense Research Institute; Connecticut Trial Lawyer Association **C/VW:** Cardinal Sheehan Center, Soundwaters, Local Connecticut Zoological Society
Email: rbmitchell@pullcom.com
URL: http://www.pullcom.com

Stephanie S. Mitchell
Title: Operating Room Pharmacy Coordinator **Company:** Baptist Health Medical Center **Dept:** Pharmaceutical Services Department **Address:** 9601 I-630, Exit 7, Pharmaceutical Services Department, Little Rock, AR 72205 United States **BUS:** Healthcare Center **P/S:** Healthcare **MA:** Regional **D/D/R:** Attending Queries on Medication, Working with Critical Care Patients, Reviewing Charts, Ensuring Doses are Correct, Suggesting Different Medicines for the Patient, Coordinating Pharmacy Services with the Operating Room, Mixing and Supplying All Drugs to the Operating Room **H/I/S:** Reading, Yoga, Gardening **EDU:** Doctor of Pharmacy, University of Arkansas for Medical Sciences(1998) **A/A/S:** Rho Chi Society; Kappa Psi; Arkansas Society of Health-System Pharmacists; Arkansas Pharmacists Association; American Society of Health-System Pharmacists; American Pharmacists Association **A/H:** Staff Pharmacist of the Year Award, Arkansas Society of Health-System Pharmacists
Email: stephanie.s.mitchell@baptist-health.org
URL: http://www.baptist-health.org

Michèle Melinda Mitchum
Title: Applications Engineer **Company:** Howden Group Ltd. **Address:** 2029 W. Dekalb Street, Camden, SC 29020 United States **BUS:** Engineering Firm **P/S:** Custom Engineered Fans **MA:** International **D/D/R:** Working on Variable Inlet Vanes and Applications in Fans **H/I/S:** Running, Fencing **EDU:** Bachelor of Arts (2007); Bachelor of Science in Mechanical Engineering, University of South Carolina, Columbia; Associate Degree in Chemical Science, University of South Carolina, Lancaster (2003) **A/A/S:** American Society of Mechanical Engineers; American Institution of Chemical Engineers **C/VW:** Community Outreach; Mentor, Local University
Email: mmitchum@howdenbuffalo.com
URL: http://www.howdenbuffalo.com

Karen Mittenzwei
Title: Special Education Teacher **Company:** Stepping Stone Day School **Address:** 2826 Westchester Avenue, Bronx, NY 10461 United States **BUS:** School **P/S:** Special Education **MA:** Local **EXP:** Ms. Mittenzwei's expertise is in special education. **EDU:** Master of Education in Special Education, Queens College; Master's Degree in Elementary Education, College of Staten Island (2003)
Email: mittenzwei12@aol.com
URL: http://www.cambridgewhoswho.com

Luis Miyakawa
Title: Manager, President **Company:** USA Audio & Security Distributors **Address:** 801 N. State Road 7, Hollywood, FL 33021 United States **BUS:** Retail and Wholesale Electronics Dealer **P/S:** Car Alarms, Stereos, Televisions, DVDs, Boom Boxes **MA:** Local **D/D/R:** Working as a Sound and Security Advisor **H/I/S:** Traveling **EDU:** Coursework in International Business, Broward Community College **A/A/S:** Rotary Club; Music Authors Copyright Protection
Email: usaaudio@bellsouth.net

Dumisani Mlungwana
Title: Occupational Therapist **Company:** Indiana Fitness Works, Inc **BUS:** Healthcare Hospital **P/S:** Rehabilitation **MA:** Local **D/D/R:** Offering Geriatric Care **EDU:** South Africa, BS in Occupational Therapy **A/A/S:** NOTA

Colleen Mobley
Title: Pharmacist **Company:** Kroger Pharmacy **Address:** 1550 E. College Avenue, Normal, IL 61761 United States **BUS:** Pharmacy and Retail Store **P/S:** Pharmacy, Bakery, Groceries, Liquor, Butcher **MA:** Regional **D/D/R:** Poison Prevention, Prescribing for Asthma, Prescribing for Diabetes, Filling Prescriptions, Checking for Drug Interactions **EDU:** Doctor of Pharmacy in Pharmacy, Midwestern University (2006) **A/A/S:** Kappa Psi; American Pharmaceutical Association; American Legion Auxiliary **A/H:** Phi Lambda Sigma Unification Award (2005)
Email: pharmd_06@hotmail.com
URL: http://www.kroger.com

Anisa Mock
Title: Clinical Pharmacist **Company:** Mercy Hospital **Address:** 3663 S. Miami Avenue, Miami, FL 33133 United States **BUS:** Hospital **P/S:** Healthcare **MA:** Regional **D/D/R:** Reviewing Admission Orders, Overseeing Pre-Operatory Medication, Writing Orders, Educating and Interacting with Patients to Verify Medical History **H/I/S:** Singing, Making Invitations on Parchment Paper **EDU:** Doctor of Pharmacy (2003) **A/A/S:** Florida Society of Health-System Pharmacists; American College of Clinical Pharmacy; American Society of Health-System Pharmacists
Email: anisaflores@yahoo.com
URL: http://www.mercymiami.org

Connie Mockenhaupt-Jimena
Title: Owner, Artistic Director **Company:** 1) Mikon 2) Stage Nine Entertainment 3) Theater Production and Technical Academy **Address:** Folson, CA 95630 United States **BUS:** Technical Theater Academy **P/S:** Theater Education **MA:** Local **EXP:** Ms. Mockenhaupt-Jimena's expertise is in theater education. **D/D/R:** Overseeing the Revitalization Program for Folsom's Historic and All Operations **H/I/S:** Performing Arts **EDU:** Master of Education in Drama, California State University, Sacramento; Bachelor of Arts in Music **A/A/S:** Sacramento Regional Theater Alliance; League of Theaters; Folsom Historic District Association; Folsom Chamber of Commerce; El Dorado Hills Chamber of Commerce; El Dorado Hills Arts Association
Email: stageninefolsom@yahoo.com
URL: http://www.stageninefolsom.com

Laura J. Modisette
Title: Research Leader **Company:** Battelle **Address:** 505 King Avenue, Columbus, OH 43201 United States **BUS:** Technology Engineering **P/S:** Technical Information Design and Engineering, Contract Research **MA:** International **EXP:** Ms. Modisette's expertise includes the design of interface, usability, the viability of Interface Design and information design. **H/I/S:** Yoga, Competitive Race Walking, Gardening, Reading **EDU:** University of Wisconsin, University of Houston, Master's Degree in Political Science and International Studies/Master of Future Studies **A/A/S:** UPA, STC, OHISPI, PMI
Email: modisetl@battelle.org
URL: www.battelle.org

Miss Betty L. Moe
Title: Registered Nurse, DSD **Company:** Job Train **Address:** 1200 O'Brien Drive, Menlo Park, CA 94025 United States **BUS:** Nonprofit Organization **P/S:** Adult Education and Training **MA:** Local **D/D/R:** Teaching Acute Care Nursing, Nursing Courses and Certified Nursing Assistant Programs **H/I/S:** Swimming, Sailing, Spending Time at the Beach **EDU:** Associate of Science in Nursing, Evergreen Valley College, San Jose, CA (1983) **CERTS:** Certified Nursing Instructor (2001); Registered Nurse (1983) **A/A/S:** Friendship Degree, Former Chairwoman, Moosehaven **C/VW:** Moose Lodge
Email: bmoe@jobtrainworks.org

Mary Lou Moffitt
Title: Owner, Electrologist **Company:** The Carousel Electrolysis Clinic **Address:** RR 5 Box 2324, Altoona, PA 16601 United States **BUS:** Electrolysis Clinic **P/S:** Permanent Hair Removal **MA:** Regional **D/D/R:** Removing Hair Permanently **H/I/S:** Spending Time with her Family, Including 20 Grandchildren; Gardening, Going to the Art Gallery her Husband Owns, Catering at Events **EDU:** Associate of Science in Technology, Mount Aloysius College **CERTS:** Licensed Cosmetologist, State of Pennsylvania; Licensed Electrologist, State of Pennsylvania
Email: moffitteric@aol.com
URL: http://www.cambridgewhoswho.com

Richard Mohammed
Title: Service Manager, Business Manager **Company:** AHR Service Center **Address:** 194 Hargreaves Avenue, Teaneck, NJ 07666 United States **BUS:** Automotive Repair Company **P/S:** Automotive Repair for All General Motor Vehicles Including Foreign and Domestic Brands **MA:** Regional **D/D/R:** Repairing Audis and Hondas, Scheduling Shifts, Overseeing Billing, Ordering Vehicle Parts **H/I/S:** Attending Car Shows, Collecting Cars **EDU:** Coursework in General Studies; High School Graduate **CERTS:** Certified, Automotive Service Excellence for Mechanics (2005)

Carol Mohrbacher
Title: Founder, Chief Financial Officer **Company:** Patrons of Special Care for Special Seniors Foundation, Inc. **Address:** P.O. Box 2594, Valley Center, CA 92082 United States **BUS:** Nonprofit Public Charity **P/S:** Building State-of-the-Art Residential Care Centers for Patients with Alzheimers and Dementia **MA:** Regional **D/D/R:** Helping Design the Program, Working on Gaining Exposure for the Program, Coordinating Fundraising Events, Speaking with People to See what Issues and Experiences they had with their Family Members **H/I/S:** Riding Motorcycles, Working in Community Service **CERTS:** Certified Nuclear Engineering Technician; Certified Ceramic Tile Consultant **A/A/S:** Board of Directors, Ceramic Tile Institute; San Diego Alzheimer's Association; Toastmasters International; Valley Center Chamber of Commerce; Rotarian, Rotary Club
Email: patrons@vcweb.org
URL: http://www.pscssf.org

Sarah R. Molenaar
Title: 1) Owner 2) Owner, Artist **Company:** 1) Holistic Home Services 2) Thingamessugenahs **Address:** 4025 Debbie Lane, Kalamazoo, MI 49006 United States **BUS:** 1) Jewelry Company 2) Cleaning Services Provider **P/S:** 1) Jewelry 2) Cleaning Homes, Businesses, Rental Properties and New Construction, Gardening, Landscaping, House and Pet Sitting **MA:** Local **D/D/R:** Creating Unique, One-of-a-Kind Jewelry Pieces, Offering Cleaning Services, Ensuring Customer Satisfaction, Gardening, Landscaping, House and Pet Sitting, Overseeing Business Operations **H/I/S:** Hiking, Camping, Learning to Play Bluegrass Music, Gardening, Spending Time with her Son **EDU:** Pursuing Bachelor's Degree in Social Work, Western Michigan University; Associate Degree in Social Work, Kalamazoo Valley Community College **A/A/S:** Phi Kappa Phi; Planning Committee, Southwest Michigan Title I; Robert Barstow Scholarship; National Honor Society **A/H:** National Dean's List; Dean's List **C/VW:** Kalamazoo Gospel Mission; Volunteer, Vine Neighborhood Association; Volunteer, Wheatland Music Organization; Volunteer, Southwest Michigan Title I Planning Committee; Volunteer, National Vaccine Information Center
Email: sarah.molenaar@wmich.edu

Rosa E. Molina
Title: Mathematics and Science Teacher **Company:** The Episcopal Cathedral School **Address:** 309 Canals Street, Stop 20, Santurce, PR 00907 United States **BUS:** School **P/S:** Education **MA:** Local **D/D/R:** Teaching Mathematics, Science, Biology, Microbiology **H/I/S:** Painting, Cooking **EDU:** Pursuing Master's Degree, Caribbean University; Master's Degree in Mathematics Curriculum; Bachelor of Science in Microbiology, Louisiana State University **C/VW:** March of Dimes, Muscular Dystrophy Association, Make-A-Wish Foundation
Email: rosaemolina@yahoo.com

Paul F. Molokie
Title: Pharmacist **Company:** Partners Healthcare System, Inc. **Address:** 70 Jackson Drive, Cranford, NJ 07016 United States **BUS:** Healthcare System **P/S:** Healthcare **MA:** New Jersey **D/D/R:** Long-Term Care Nursing, Working in Nursing Homes, Entering Data for Physicians, Offering General Medications and Intravenous to 200 Nursing Homes **H/I/S:** Playing Baseball and Tennis **EDU:** Bachelor of Science in Pharmacy, Ernest Mario School of Pharmacy, Rutgers, The State University of New Jersey (1986) **A/A/S:** New Jersey Pharmacists Association
Email: pfmstilltraining@yahoo.com
URL: http://www.partners.org

Dr. Sky Monarch
Title: Chiropractor **Company:** Monarch Chiropractic Office **Address:** 553 W. Clapier Street, Philadelphia, PA 19144 United States **BUS:** Chiropractic Office **P/S:** Healthcare, Chiropractic Services **MA:** Regional **D/D/R:** Using a Directional Non-Force Technique, Neuroemotional Technique, Contact Reflect Analysis, Zero Balance **H/I/S:** Sewing, Practicing Feng Shui **EDU:** Doctor of Chiropractic, Pennsylvania College of Chiropractic **C/VW:** Various Charitable Organizations
Email: monarchsky@gmail.com
URL: http://www.cambridgewhoswho.com

Elsa V. Moncivais-Lafitte
Title: Executive Assistant **Company:** U.S. Department of Treasury, FedSource-San Antonio **Address:** 16414 San Pedro Avenue, Suite 910, San Antonio, TX 78232 United States **BUS:** Government **P/S:** Contracts between Government Agencies and Contractors **MA:** National **D/D/R:** Directing Clients to Proper Contacts, Answering Phones and Questions, Organizing Calendar, Keeping Office Morale High **H/I/S:** Training and Breeding Rottweilers **EDU:** Pursuing Bachelor's Degree in Business Management, The University of Texas **A/A/S:** Bexar County Kennel Club; Junior Reserve Officers Training Corps, Madison High School; Leadership Group, Federal Executives Board
Email: emoncivais-lafitte@san.fedsource.gov
URL: http://www.ustreas.gov

Sherry Monelyon
Title: President, Chief Executive Officer **Company:** Rich Home Mortgages **Address:** 2250 N.W. 78th Avenue, Suite 104, Pembroke Pines, FL 33024 United States **BUS:** Mortgage Brokerage Company **P/S:** Mortgage Financing for Loans Pertaining to Purchasing and Refinancing Properties **MA:** Florida **EXP:** Ms. Monelyon's expertise includes subprime loans and notary services. **H/I/S:** Walking Five Miles Every Day, Exercising at the Gym **EDU:** Associate Degree in Business Management, Stratton, Pennsylvania Education Direct **CERTS:** Licensed Mortgage Broker **A/A/S:** Better Business Bureau **C/VW:** Various Charitable Organizations
Email: richhomemtges@yahoo.com

Ana L. Monge
Title: Interior Designer **Company:** Ana Lagos Interior Design **Address:** 220 Quail Drive, Winston Salem, NC 27105 United States **BUS:** Interior Design Company **P/S:** Interior Architecture, Product Design, Interior and Exterior Design, Furniture, Accessories **MA:** International **D/D/R:** Managing Design Projects for Furniture and Accessories, Overseeing Architectural Design, Purchasing and Securing International Materials **H/I/S:** Participating in Badminton, Tennis and Yoga **EDU:** Pursuing Master of Arts, The University of North Carolina; Bachelor of Arts, The University of North Carolina at Greensboro **CERTS:** Certified Sustainable Designer **A/A/S:** Hispanic League of the Piedmont Triad
Email: almonge@hotmail.com

Kathleen W. Monn

Title: Pediatric Dentist **Company:** Pediatric Dentistry, PA **Address:** 420 The Parkway, Suite B, Greer, SC 29650 United States **BUS:** Dental Clinic **P/S:** Pediatric Dentistry **MA:** Regional **EXP:** Ms. Monn's expertise includes pediatric dentistry, and dentistry for young children and children with special needs. **H/I/S:** Spending Time with her Family and Friends, Reading, Traveling, Watching Movies **EDU:** Doctor of Medical Dentistry, Medical University of South Carolina; Bachelor of Science in Biology, Clemson University **CERTS:** Certified Pediatric Dentist **A/A/S:** American Academy of Pediatric Dentistry; American Dental Association; Southeastern Society of Pediatric Dentistry **C/VW:** Meals On Wheels Association of America; Smiles for a Lifetime; St. Michaels' Lutheran Church
Email: Kathleen.Monn@cwwemail.com
Email: kmonn@charter.net
URL: http://www.funteeth.com

Joel Monsky

Title: Independent Consultant **Company:** Information Engine **Address:** 163-20 86th Street, Howard Beach, NY 11414 United States **BUS:** Marketing Company **P/S:** Direct Marketing, Database Selection **MA:** National **D/D/R:** Direct Marketing, Building Databases **H/I/S:** Boating **EDU:** Bachelor's Degree in Marketing, New York University
Email: jmonsky@aol.com

Donald Montano

Title: President, Owner, Partner **Company:** The Health & Rejuvenation Center **Address:** 3345 Burns Road, Suite 206, Palm Beach Gardens, FL 33410 United States **BUS:** Healthcare Center **P/S:** Healthcare Including Hormone Replacement Therapy, Nutrition, Physical Fitness, Dietary Supplements, Consulting, Skin Rejuvenation and Laser Hair Removal **MA:** National **D/D/R:** Managing and Expanding the Company, Processing Changes in Law and Products, Working in Laser and Electron Beam Welding **H/I/S:** Playing Tennis, Boating **EDU:** Diploma, Wilbraham & Monson Academy (1956); Coursework in Art **A/A/S:** Society for Age Management, FL; ASM International
Email: dmontano@tharc.com
URL: http://www.tharc.com

Judith M. Monteith

Title: Substance Abuse Counselor **Company:** M.H.A., Assertive Community Treatment Team **Address:** Mental Health Association, 233 S. French Broad Avenue, Asheville, NC 28801 United States **BUS:** Human Services **P/S:** Substance Abuse Counseling **MA:** Local **EXP:** Ms. Monteith's expertise includes substance abuse and energy healing. **H/I/S:** Reading, Knitting, Walking with her Dog, Taking Courses **EDU:** Bachelor of Arts in Addiction Counseling, Westbrook University; Associate of Science in Mental Health, Northern Essex Community College, Haverhill, Massachusetts; Master Herbalist; Doctor of Naturopathy **CERTS:** Certified Substance Abuse Counselor **A/A/S:** Emotional Freedom Technique **C/VW:** Humane Society of the United States
Email: marju@charter.net
URL: http://www.cambridgewhoswho.com

Teresa Montemayor

Title: Special Education Teacher **Company:** School District No. 143 Central Park School **Address:** 3621 151st Street, Midlothian, IL 60445 United States **BUS:** School **P/S:** Academic Basics for Students in Kindergarten through Eighth-Grade **MA:** Regional **D/D/R:** Teaching Children with Emotional and Behavioral Disorders **H/I/S:** Helping Children Train for the Special Olympics **EDU:** Bachelor of Science in Education, Eastern Illinois University (2003) **A/A/S:** National Education Association; Illinois Education Association; Council for Exceptional Children; Coach for the Special Olympics
Email: tmontemayor@msa143.s-cook.k12.il.us
URL: http://www.villageofmidlothian.net/Community/Education.htm

Reina C. Montes

Title: 1) Owner, President, Chief Executive Officer 2) Distributor **Company:** 1) Smart Umbrella Language Services 2) Nu Skin **Address:** P.O. Box 582555, Elk Grove, CA 95758 United States **BUS:** 1) Language Translation Services Company 2) Manufacturing Company **P/S:** 1) Language Translation Services 2) Beauty Care Products, Wellness, Anti-Aging and Nutrition Products **MA:** International **EXP:** Ms. Montes' expertise is in business management. **D/D/R:** Overseeing Operations Including Assigning Translation and Interpretation Projects to Language Professionals, Budgeting, Preparing Letters and Proposal Requests, Educating and Mentoring Interpreters and Translators, Interacting with Agencies and Companies, Overseeing Public and Customer Relations and Language Translation Services **H/I/S:** Playing Tennis, Swimming, Dancing **EDU:** Master of Business Administration, University of Phoenix; Bachelor of Arts, San Francisco State University; Coursework in Computer Science and Business Administration, Contra Costa College in San Pablo, CA **CERTS:** Medical Interpreter Training, University of California, Davis; Bilingual Status Certification, Employment Development Department, CA; Real Estate Financial Training, University of California, Davis; Certification in Surveillance, United States Department of Justice **A/A/S:** Northern California Translators Association; Southern California Area Translators and Interpreters Association; California Healthcare Interpreters Association; eWomen's Network Foundation; American Translators Association; National Association for Female Executives **C/VW:** The American Society for the Prevention of Cruelty to Animals; Sacramento Society for the Prevention of Cruelty to Animals
Email: reinamontes08@comcast.net

Angela J. Montgomery

Title: Certified Bookkeeper **Company:** Patterson, Prince & Associates, PC **Address:** 475 S. Seminary Street, Florence, AL 35630 United States **BUS:** Accounting Firm **P/S:** Financial and Tax Services, Certified Public Accountants **MA:** Northwest Alabama **D/D/R:** Bookkeeping, Individual Tax **H/I/S:** Reading, Making Crafts **EDU:** Bachelor of Arts in Broadcasting and Journalism, University of North Alabama **A/A/S:** American Institute of Professional Bookkeepers; Board Member, Court Appointed Special Advocates **C/VW:** Church
Email: jmont@pattersonprince.com

James R. Montgomery

Title: Principal **Company:** Gaston County School System, John Chavis Middle School **Address:** 103 S. Chavis Drive, Cherryville, NC 28021 United States **BUS:** Middle School **P/S:** Education **MA:** Local **EXP:** Mr. Montgomery's expertise is in leadership administration. **H/I/S:** Music, Spending Time with his Children, Attending Church **EDU:** Master of School Administration, University of North Carolina at Charlotte; Bachelor's Degree in Music Education, Western Carolina University **A/A/S:** Association of North Carolina School Administrators **C/VW:** Church, Community Organizations
Email: jrmontgomery@gaston.k12.nc.us

Lois M. Montgomery

Title: Medical Transcriptionist **Company:** Virdi Eye Clinic **Address:** 2202 18th Avenue, Rock Island, IL 61201 United States **BUS:** Eye Clinic **P/S:** Eye Care, LASEK Correction **MA:** Regional **D/D/R:** Typing Reports for Doctors, Consulting with Low-Vision Patients **H/I/S:** Traveling **EDU:** Pursuing Degree in Spanish Language Studies; Associate Degree in Psychology, Black Hawk College (1973) **CERTS:** Certification in Medical Transcription, Black Hawk College (1998) **A/A/S:** National Federation of the Blind; Member, Phi Theta Kappa Honor Society; Member, Citizens Advisory Council on Urban Planning
Email: lmm3527@aol.com

David W. Moody

Title: Owner **Company:** Moody Packaging Company **Address:** 2662 Seven Knobs Road, Gainesboro, TN 38562 United States **BUS:** Packaging Company **P/S:** Bags and Bag Closers for the Animal Feed Industry **MA:** National **EXP:** Mr. Moody's expertise is in business management. **H/I/S:** Watching the Bristol Motor Speedway **A/A/S:** Kentucky Feed & Grain Association; Tennessee Feed & Grain Association
Email: bagman@twlakes.net
URL: http://www.cambridgewhoswho.com

Mr. Michael S. Moody, Ph.D.

Title: President, Chief Executive Officer **Company:** Insight Education Group, Inc. **Address:** 16130 Ventura Boulevard, Suite 300, Encino, CA 91436 United States **BUS:** Educational Consulting Company **P/S:** Professional Development and Curriculum Design **MA:** National **D/D/R:** Educational Consulting, Overseeing K-12 Professional Development, Training and Supporting School Leadership **EDU:** Ph.D. in Urban School Leadership, University of Southern California (2005) **A/A/S:** Association for Supervision and Curriculum Development; National Staff Development Council
Email: moody@insighteducationgroup.com
URL: http://www.insighteducationgroup.com

Rita M. Moon

Title: Owner **Company:** Full Moon Pottery **Address:** 510 Swicegood Waitman Road, Lexington, NC 27295 United States **BUS:** Pottery Company **P/S:** Functional and Decorative Pottery **MA:** Regional **D/D/R:** Creating and Selling Handmade Functional Pottery Including Dinnerware, Serving Platters, Pitchers, Bird Houses, Bird Feeders and Lamps, Selling Customized Products **H/I/S:** Attending Trade Shows **EDU:** College Coursework in Pharmaceutical Studies **A/A/S:** Arts United for Davidson County
Email: fullmoonpottery@yahoo.com
URL: http://www.fullmoonpottery.net

Ms. Gwen Minchue Mooney

Title: Managing Director **Company:** Gwen Mooney Funeral Home **Address:** 4389 Spring Grove Avenue, Cincinnati, OH 45223 United States **BUS:** Funeral Home Mortuary Funeral Services **P/S:** Funeral Home Pre planning, Managing a Funeral Home **MA:** Regional **D/D/R:** Funeral Home Preplanning, Funeral Directing **H/I/S:** Traveling **EDU:** Cincinnati College of Mortuary Science, BS Mortuary Science **A/A/S:** VP of ICCFA, OFDA, NFDA
Email: gmooney@springgrove.org
URL: www.springgrove.org

Becky M. Moore

Title: Dental Hygienist **Company:** Harlan L. Hassen, DDS **Address:** 4100 N.E. Vivion Road, Kansas City, MO 64119 United States **BUS:** Dental Office **P/S:** Dental Care **MA:** Local **D/D/R:** Dental Hygiene, Dental Cleanings, Setting Appointments **H/I/S:** Spending Time Outdoors, Hiking, Fishing **EDU:** Bachelor of Science in Dental Hygiene, University of Missouri at Kansas City School of Dentistry **A/A/S:** American Dental Association; American Dental Hygienists' Association; Missouri Dental Hygienists' Association **C/VW:** Nature Conservancy; American Red Cross; Goodwill
Email: wbecky23@hotmail.com

Brenda F. Moore

Title: Vice President **Company:** steller one **Address:** 2307 W. Beverly Street, Staunton, VA 24401 United States **BUS:** Retail Banking and Lending Company **P/S:** Banking and Lending Services **MA:** Statewide **EXP:** Ms. Moore's expertise includes customer service, lending, management and loan officers. **D/D/R:** Taking Care of Customer Needs, Applications for Loans, Supervising Eight Other Employees Including Six Tellers, One Customer Service Representative and One Assistant **H/I/S:** Reading, Spending Time with Family **EDU:** Coursework in Banking, Blue Ridge Community College; Bachelor of Business Administration Degree; Two Certifications in Consumer Lending, Virginia Bank; Coursework Competed, Financial Institute; Coursework Completed, Consumer Lending Class (1999); Coursework Completed, Consumer Lending School (1999) **A/A/S:** Virginia Financial Group **A/H:** 2000 Spirit Award, United Way **C/VW:** Kiwanis Baseball
Email: mooreb@stellerone.com
URL: http://www.stellerone.com

Mr. Carl Moore Jr.

Title: Registered Nurse (Retired) **Company:** Center For Sight **Address:** 3009 Kingsley Drive, Decatur, IL 62521 United States **BUS:** Eye Clinic **P/S:** Cataract Surgery, Treatment for Glaucoma and Other Eye-Related Problems **MA:** Local **D/D/R:** Supervising the Operating Room and Emergency Room Staff, Outpatient Surgical Nursing, Performing Refractions, Administering Medications **H/I/S:** Stamp Collecting, History, Antique Cars **EDU:** Coursework in Nursing, Millikin University, Decatur, Illinois **CERTS:** Registered Nurse, Decatur Memorial Hospital School of Nursing (1958) **A/A/S:** Allan County, Kentucky Genealogical Society; President, Illinois Precancel Stamp Club; Macon County Genealogical Society; National Chevelle Car Club; Boy Scouts of America (1974)

Cassandra Y. Moore

Title: Vice President, Pastor, Higher Dimension Family Workshop Center **Company:** Harvesting Ministries, Inc. **Address:** 11313 Los Comancheros Road, Austin, TX 78717 United States **BUS:** Church **P/S:** Spiritual Growth and Development **MA:** Regional **D/D/R:** Offering Women's Ministry Counseling, Training **H/I/S:** Fashion, Tennis, Traveling, Shopping, Reading, Owning and Running a Fashion Store Titled Charmain's Fashion's Designs **EDU:** High School Education
Email: rumexia@aol.com
URL: http://www.harvestingministries.org

Christopher M. Moore

Title: Executive Chef **Company:** The Toledo Club **Address:** 235 14th Street, Toledo, OH 43604 United States **BUS:** Entertainment Club **P/S:** Food and Entertainment Services **MA:** Local **D/D/R:** Planning Menus, Cooking **H/I/S:** Golfing, Spending Time with his Family **EDU:** Associate Degree, Scottsdale Culinary Institute **A/A/S:** American Culinary Federation **C/VW:** The Humane Society of the United States; Share Our Strength
Email: chrisandericka@hotmail.com
URL: http://www.cambridgewhoswho.com

Denise Moore
Title: Owner, Appraiser **Company:** Beach Cities Appraisal **Address:** 9601 Olympic Drive, Huntington Beach, CA 92646 United States **BUS:** Real Estate Appraisal Company **P/S:** Residential Real Estate Appraisals **MA:** Local **D/D/R:** Appraising Single-Family Residences **H/I/S:** Spending Time with her Family, Attending Sporting Events, Spending Time with their Dog **CERTS:** Licensed Appraiser, State of California **A/A/S:** National Association of Real Estate Appraisers **C/VW:** Board Member, Daughter's Cheerleading Team; Coach, Son's Little League Baseball Team
Email: beachcitiesappraisal@yahoo.com
URL: http://www.beachcitiesappraisal.com

E. Whitney Grandy Moore
Title: Head Coach, Founder **Company:** Moore Training **Address:** 901 W. Prince Road, Tucson, AZ 85705 United States **BUS:** Health and Fitness Center **P/S:** Athletic Training **MA:** Local **D/D/R:** Athletic Training for Youths and Adults **H/I/S:** Competing in Sports, Traveling **EDU:** Master of Science in Health, Exercise, Science and Nutrition, Colorado State University **CERTS:** Certified Strength and Conditioning Specialist with Distinction, National Strength and Conditioning Association **A/A/S:** National Strength and Conditioning Association **C/VW:** Local School Districts
Email: whiyeney@mooretraining.us
URL: http://www.getmooretraining.com

Geoffrey R. Moore
Title: Business Manager **Company:** Total Petrochemicals USA, Inc. **Address:** 1201 Louisiana Street, Houston, TX 77002 United States **BUS:** Petrochemical Company **P/S:** Petrochemicals **MA:** National **D/D/R:** Managing the Business **H/I/S:** Golfing, Skiing, Coaching Rugby **EDU:** Bachelor's Degree in Chemistry, London University **A/A/S:** National Petrochemical and Refiners Association; SIRC **C/VW:** Woodland Valley Theater
Email: geoffrey.moore@total.com
URL: http://www.totalpetrochemicalsusa.com

Jenna C. Moore
Title: Senior Technical Communication and Documentation Manager **Company:** SAS Institute **Address:** 411 Feldspar Way, Durham, NC 27703 United States **BUS:** Information Technology and Development **P/S:** Information Technology **MA:** International **EXP:** Ms. Moore's expertise includes information design and development, and documentation design. **H/I/S:** Writing **EDU:** Bachelor of Arts in English, North Carolina State University **A/A/S:** Society for Technical Communications **C/VW:** WCPE Classical Radio Station
Email: jenna.moore@earthlink.net
URL: http://www.mayhawk.com

John C. Moore
Title: Safety Officer **Company:** Methodist Health Systems **Address:** 8303 Dodge Street, Omaha, NE 68114 United States **BUS:** Healthcare Hospital **P/S:** Acute Care Hospital **MA:** Local **EXP:** Mr. Moore's expertise includes life safety and hazardous material. **H/I/S:** Fishing, Hunting, Golf **EDU:** BS **A/A/S:** World Safety Org
Email: jc.moore@nmhs.org

Margaret Moore
Title: Kindergarten Teacher **Company:** Newark Public Schools, George Washington Carver Elementary School **Address:** 2 Cedar Street, Newark, NJ 07102 United States **BUS:** School **P/S:** Education **MA:** Local **D/D/R:** Teaching Kindergarten Students **H/I/S:** Creating Crafts, Attending Church Activities, Working with Children, Teaching Bible Studies, Writing **EDU:** Master of Education in Special Education, Kean College, 1981 **CERTS:** Certified Teacher of the Handicapped, Educatable Retarded and Slow Learners; Bachelor of Arts in Home Economics and Early Childhood Education, Family and Childcare Services, Montclair State College, 1976; Certified Teacher of Nursery and Kindergarten Students **A/A/S:** Newark Teachers Union; New Jersey Education Association; Newark Public Schools; Oasis Christian Center **C/VW:** Oasis Christian Center, Church

Maureen Ann Moore
Title: Registered Nurse **Company:** Mercy Suburban Hospital **Address:** 2701 DeKalb Pike, Norristown, PA 19401 United States **BUS:** Hospital **P/S:** Healthcare **MA:** Local **EXP:** Ms. Moore's expertise is in progressive, intensive care nursing. **H/I/S:** Reading, Traveling, Cooking, Biking, Water Sports **EDU:** Associate Degree in Nursing, Montgomery Community College; Licensed Esthetician, Magnolia School of Beauty **CERTS:** Certified in Advanced Cardiac Life Support and Basic Life Support, American Association of Critical-Care Nurses **A/A/S:** Association of Medical Esthetic Nurses
Email: mamoorern@comcast.net

Nancy A. Moore
Title: High School English Teacher, Special Education Teacher **Company:** St. Mary's School for the Deaf **Address:** 2253 Main Street, Buffalo, NY 14214 United States **BUS:** School **P/S:** Deaf Education **MA:** Local **D/D/R:** Teaching English, Deaf Education **H/I/S:** Spending Time with Children, Watching Sports, Crafts, Reading, Environment and Wildlife Protection, Coaching Level 1 Hockey **EDU:** Master of Education and Special Deaf Education, Canisius College; Bachelor's Degree in Literature and English, Canisius College **A/A/S:** New York State Association of Educators of the Deaf; New York State Teachers Association **A/H:** Former Hockey Mom of the Year **C/VW:** Former Religious Education Teacher, Defenders of Wildlife, Fund for Animals, The Otter Project, St. Francis Friends of the Poor
Email: namoore13@aol.com

Patricia A. Moore
Title: President, Chief Executive Officer **Company:** Healing Hands Enterprises, Inc. **Address:** 33325 Westlake Drive, Sterling Heights, MI 48312 United States **BUS:** Home Healthcare Agency **P/S:** Home Healthcare **MA:** Local **EXP:** Ms. Moore's expertise includes private duty home healthcare and executive duties. **H/I/S:** Reading, Cooking, Traveling, Shopping **EDU:** Associate of Science in Nursing, Wallace State Community College, 1998
Email: hlnghndsp@aol.com
URL: http://www.cambridgewhoswho.com

Sandra Fife Moore
Title: President, Founding Director **Company:** The Fifes and Drums of Prince William III **Address:** 137 Winding River Drive, Murrells Inlet, SC 29576 United States **BUS:** Music Institute **P/S:** Patriotic Music, Music Performance and Education **MA:** National **D/D/R:** Managing Music Performance in Fife, Flute, Wooden Whistle and Voice **H/I/S:** Quilting, Traveling, Spending Time with her Sister **A/A/S:** National Society Daughters of the American Revolution; CAPs
Email: fifesanddrum@sccoast.net
Email: fifesanddrums@comcast.net

Sharon K. Moore
Title: Frontline Performance Leader **Company:** Allstate Insurance Company **Address:** 4705 N.W. Expressway, Oklahoma City, OK 73132 United States **BUS:** Insurance **P/S:** Personal Property, Casualty, Home and Automobile Insurance Claims **MA:** National **EXP:** Ms. Moore's expertise includes personal property and casualty insurance. **H/I/S:** Volunteering **EDU:** Bachelor of Arts in Business Administration, Central State University (Now University of Central Oklahoma), 1983 **A/A/S:** Dale Carnegie Training **C/VW:** Director, Sunday Elementary School; Volunteer, Canterbury Academy of the Vocal Arts; President, Parent-Teacher Association
Email: cd33r@allstate.com
URL: http://www.allstate.com

Toni M. Moore
Title: Owner **Company:** Moore Floors **Address:** 819 W. Houghton Lake Drive, Prudenville, MI 48651 United States **BUS:** Floor and Carpet Dealer **P/S:** Floor Covering, Installation and Sales, Various Flooring Including Vinyl, Carpet, Woods, Ceramic and Vinyl Composition Tile **MA:** Regional **D/D/R:** Managing Sales, Overseeing Daily Business Operations **H/I/S:** Spending Time with Grandchildren **EDU:** High School Education (1980)

W. John Moore
Title: President **Company:** Senior Finance Center **Address:** 3101 Concorde Drive, Suite A, McKinleyville, CA 95519 United States **BUS:** Finance Company **P/S:** Reverse Mortgages, Banking, Financing **MA:** Northern California **D/D/R:** Financing, Managing Reverse Mortgages for Seniors, Operating Daily Business Operations, Educating Customers about Contributions to Pensions **EDU:** Bachelor of Arts in Business Administration, Humboldt State University (1972) **CERTS:** Certified Senior Adviser **A/A/S:** Society of Certified Senior Advisors; National Reverse Mortgage Lenders Association; The Benevolent and Protective Order of Elks of the USA; Former President, Rotary Club, Southwest Region; The Ingomar Club
Email: srfinance@sbcglobal.net
URL: http://www.srfinance.com

Ms. Kathleen Moore Iliff-Darnell, RN
Title: Registered Nurse **Company:** Mid-Atlantic Home Health **Dept:** RN case manager **Address:** 3234 Railstop Road, P.O. Box 281, Markham, VA 22643 United States **BUS:** Home Health Care Agency specializing in acute care of primarily pediatric patients who are homebound either from terminal illness or disability. **MA:** Regional **D/D/R:** Offering Long-Term Care and Rehabilitation Services, Operating Room Nursing **H/I/S:** Collecting vintage pottery and jewlery, vintage mustangs, knitting and crochet, numerous pets, swimming and canoeing, the ocean, the art of magic and illusion **EDU:** Pursuing Degree in Nurse Practitioner Studies, Shenandoah University; Associate Degree in Nursing, Registered Nurse, Lord Fairfax Community College (2006)
Email: kdanell540@aol.com

Ellery J. A Moore-Mendez
Title: Chief Medical Technologist **Company:** NewYork-Presbyterian Hospital **Dept:** Transfusion Medicine and Cellular Therapy **Address:** 525 E. 68th Street, New York, NY 10065 United States **BUS:** Hospital **P/S:** Healthcare **MA:** National **D/D/R:** Performing Cellular Therapy Including the Manipulation, Cryopreservation and Characterization of Various Stem Cells, Immunology, Molecular Biology, Overseeing Peer Evaluation of Cellular Therapy Laboratories for the American Association of Blood Banks and College of American Pathologists **H/I/S:** Playing Soccer, Hiking, Dancing **EDU:** Master's Degree in Health Sciences, Hunter College (1991); Bachelor of Science in Medical Laboratory Science, Hunter College (1984) **CERTS:** Licensed Medical Laboratory Technologist, State of New York; Certification, The Institute of Bio-Medical Sciences, The National Credentialing Agency and The American Society for Clinical Pathology **A/A/S:** Association of the American Society of Pathologists; American Association of Blood Banks; American Association of Molecular Biology
Email: elbomor@msn.com

Beechard E. Moorefield, MAOM, MBA
Title: Executive Director, Pastor **Company:** Eagle's Nest Forum, New Life Family Worship Center **Address:** 5024 Mountain View Road, Winston Salem, NC 27104 United States **BUS:** Progressive and Proactive Leadership Development and Personal and Professional Coaching Enterprise **P/S:** Developing a Legacy of Excellence in Leadership in the Business, Church and Educational Communities **MA:** Regional **D/D/R:** Life Coaching, Leadership Development Courses for Church Pastors, Small Business Owners and High School Students Entering College **H/I/S:** Music, Horseback Riding, Martial Arts, Hunting, Second Degree Black Belt in Tae Kwon Do and Kempo **EDU:** Master's Degree in Organizational Development, University of Phoenix (2003); Master of Business Administration, Almeda University (2003); Bachelor's Degree in Science, Winston-Salem State University **A/A/S:** Ordained Minister, Assemblies of God
Email: ezcolonel@triad.rr.com
URL: http://www.eaglesnestforum.com

A. Moossa, MD, FRCS, FACS
Title: Professor of Surgery **Company:** University of California, San Diego **Address:** 9300 Campus Point Drive, La Jolla, CA 92037 United States **BUS:** Healthcare University/Hospital **P/S:** Academic Surgery **MA:** Local **D/D/R:** All Aspects of General Surgery and Oncology Healthcare, Co Author of Six Books and has Lectured all over the World **EDU:** MD, Earned in Europe (1966) **A/A/S:** AMA, American Surgical Association, European Surgical Association, Emeritus Chairman for Clinical Affairs, Associate Dean for Thornton Hospital

Mr. John Morabito
Title: Fire Chief **Company:** Border City Fire Department **Address:** 55 Border City Road, Geneva, NY 14456 United States **BUS:** Fire Rescue Government Service **P/S:** Emergency Rescue Services for Fire-Related Incidents **MA:** Regional **D/D/R:** Responding to 180 Emergency Calls a Year **H/I/S:** Spending Time with his Son **EDU:** Graduate, Police Academy (1985); Coursework in Liberal Arts, Monroe Community College **A/A/S:** Educator, Local Grammar Schools; New York State Association of Fire Chiefs; New York Chapter, International Association of Arson Investigators, Inc.
Email: bcfd261@yahoo.com

Lois A. Morales
Title: Owner, Agent **Company:** L.A. Morales Agency **Address:** 1930 Veterans Highway, Suite 13, Islandia, NY 11749 United States **BUS:** Insurance **P/S:** Insurance for Individual and Business **MA:** Statewide **D/D/R:** Financial Planning, Automobile, Home, Rent, Life, Commercial and Business Insurance, Oversee Two Insurance Agents, Handles All Day to Day Operations of Management, **H/I/S:** Traveling, Gardening, Reading **EDU:** College Coursework in Social Work, Suffolk County Community College; Licensed Insurance Agent, Property, Casualty, Health; Series 6 and 63 Licenses **A/A/S:** Local Chamber of Commerce; HIA
Email: loismorales@allstate.com
URL: http://www.allstate.com/loismorales

Maj. Christine Brighton Moran
Title: Major; Chief Nutrition Care Division **Company:** United States Army, DeWitt Healthcare Network **Address:** 9501 Farrell Road, Fort Belvoir, VA 22060 United States **BUS:** Armed Forces; Army Hospital **P/S:** Healthcare for the Armed Forces **MA:** International **EXP:** Maj. Moran's expertise includes medical and nutritional therapy, and combined operations. **H/I/S:** Reading, Attending Church, Teaching Sunday School, Bike Riding, Canoeing, Hiking, Swimming **EDU:** Master's Degree in Health Service Management, Webster University **A/A/S:** American Dietetic Association; Defense Acquisition University **C/VW:** Focus on the Family, Prison Fellowship, Masters Institute Concordia Seminar
Email: christine.moran@usarmy.mil

Patrick A. Moran

Title: Attorney **Company:** Law Offices of Patrick Alan Moran, LLC **Address:** 530 S. Main Avenue, Suite B, Tucson, AZ 85701 United States **BUS:** Law Firm **P/S:** Legal Services **MA:** Local **EXP:** Mr. Moran's expertise is in criminal defense. **H/I/S:** Golfing, Playing Softball, Being a Sports Fan **EDU:** JD, University of Wyoming **A/A/S:** American Bar Association; Arizona Bar Association; Pima County Bar Association **C/VW:** Make-A-Wish Foundation; Local Schools
Email: azpmoran@msn.com

Mark T. Moranville, RN

Title: Registered Nurse **Company:** St. Jude Medical Center **Address:** 368 S. Puente Street, Brea, CA 92821 United States **BUS:** Hospital **P/S:** Healthcare for Audiology Services, Breast Screening and Mammography, Congestive Heart Failure Program, Genetic Risk Assessment, Heart Institute, Brain Injury Center, Centers for Rehabilitation, Pain Management Center, Physical Therapy, Urology, Wound Care **MA:** Regional **D/D/R:** Emergency Room Staff Nursing, Triage Nursing, Mobile Intensive Care Nursing, Assisting Doctors, Ensuring Patients have Proper Supplies, Gastroenterology Nursing, First STEMI Receiving Center in Orange County **H/I/S:** Winetasting, Reading **EDU:** Associate Degree in Nursing, Cypress College (1993) **CERTS:** Certification in Emergency Pediatric Nursing; Certification in Mobile Intensive Care Nursing **A/A/S:** Emergency Nurses Association
Email: moranvilleone@aol.com
URL: http://www.stjudemedicalcenter.org

Deborah Ann Morefield

Title: Special Assistant for Sustainability **Company:** Department of the Navy **Address:** 1000 Navy Pentagon BF986, Washington, DC 20350 United States **BUS:** Federal Government **P/S:** Defense **MA:** National **EXP:** Ms. Morefield's expertise includes range and weapon systems, and environmental issues. **H/I/S:** Playing Sports, Spending Time Outdoors **EDU:** Bachelor of Science in Engineering, University of Central Florida **CERTS:** Certified Hazardous Materials Manager **A/A/S:** Society of American Military Engineers; Women In Defense; AWMA **C/VW:** Various Charitable Organizations
Email: deborah.morefield@navy.mil

Maritza Morell

Title: Pediatric Dentist **Company:** Harvard University **Dept:** Harvard School of Dental Medicine **Address:** 188 Longwood Avenue, Boston, MA 02115 United States **BUS:** University **P/S:** Higher Education **MA:** Local **EXP:** Ms. Morell's expertise is in pediatric dentistry. **EDU:** Doctor of Dental Medicine, University of Puerto Rico; Master of Public Health, University of Puerto Rico; Master of Science, Harvard School of Dental Medicine **A/A/S:** Hispanic Dental Association; American Dental Association; American Association for Dental Research; American Association of Public Health Dentistry; American Art Deco Dealers Association
Email: doctor.morell@verizon.net
Email: maritza_marell@hsdm.harvard.edu
URL: http://www.cambridgewhoswho.com

Marci L. Morelli

Title: Co-Owner **Company:** Design for the Times **BUS:** Interior Design Firm **P/S:** Interior Design Including Counter Tops, Renovation, Reorganization and Home Staging **MA:** Regional **EXP:** Ms. Morelli's expertise includes interior design, commercial photography, decision-making and home staging. **D/D/R:** Managing Operations, Fixing Appointments with Clients, Planning, Purchasing Items for Clients, Choosing Colors, Decision Making on Layouts **H/I/S:** Horseback Riding, Collecting Antiques **EDU:** High School Education
Email: mlbmorelli@yahoo.com
URL: http://www.cambridgewhoswho.com

Kelly Morenko

Title: Account Executive **Address:** 477 Anacapa Drive, Roseville, CA 95678 United States **BUS:** Electronics Distribution Company **P/S:** Computer Components and Subcomponents, Broadline Electronics Sales and Distribution **MA:** International **D/D/R:** Managing Sales and Marketing for Purchase Agents and Design Engineers **H/I/S:** Water Aerobics, Reading **EDU:** Bachelor of Science in Biological Sciences, University of California, Davis (1979)
Email: morenko1@comcast.net
URL: http://www.futureelectronics.com

Karina Moreno

Title: Principal **Company:** Dolores Mission School **Address:** 170 S. Gless Street, Los Angeles, CA 90033 United States **BUS:** Private School **P/S:** Education **MA:** Local **D/D/R:** Teaching **H/I/S:** Reading **EDU:** Master's Degree in Education, Loyola Marymount University **A/A/S:** Loyola Marymount University PLACE Corps; Bassett Unified School Board; California School Board; National School Boards Association; Young Elected Officials Network **C/VW:** St. Louis of France Catholic Church
Email: kmorenoplacer1@yahoo.com
URL: http://www.doloresmission.com

Laura O. Moreno-Chavez, Ph.D.

Title: Psychotherapist **Company:** Miami Children's Hospital **Address:** 3100 S.W. 62nd Avenue, Miami, FL 33155 United States **BUS:** Health Care: Mental Wellness **P/S:** Full Service Pediatric Hospital **MA:** Local **D/D/R:** Mental Health Counseling for Children and Families **EDU:** Ph.D. in Neuropsychology; Pursuing License, Psychology **A/A/S:** American Psychology Association; Former Secretary, Florida Career Professional Association; American Psychotherapy Association
Email: lmorenochavez@aol.com
URL: http://www.mch.com/

Edith Moreu-Agrait

Title: Admistrative Officer **Company:** University of Puerto Rico **Address:** Milnillas Industrial Park, Suite 170 Road 174, Bayamon, PR 00969 United States **BUS:** Education **P/S:** Higher Education, College **MA:** Local **D/D/R:** Counseling **H/I/S:** Reading, Music, Jogging **EDU:** MD, Inter American University of Puerto Rico **A/A/S:** American Counseling Association
Email: emoreu@uprb.edu

Amber N. Morgan

Title: Medical Office Assistant **Company:** WMHS Occupational Health **Address:** 915 Bishop Walsh Road, Cumberland, MD 21502 United States **BUS:** Laboratory Clinic **P/S:** Alcohol and Drug Screenings, Laboratory Work, Exams **MA:** Regional **D/D/R:** Overseeing Quality Control, Meeting with Patients, Managing Laboratory Duties, Hazardous Material, Finances and Testing **H/I/S:** Playing Musical Instruments, Sports **EDU:** Associate Degree in Medical Laboratory Technology, Allegany College of Maryland (2003)
Email: jammk7@hotmail.com

Diani M. Morgan, RN

Title: RN, Clinical Admission Coordinator **Company:** Frankford Hospital **Address:** 380 N. Oxford Valley Road, Langhorne, PA 19047 United States **BUS:** Healthcare, Hospital **P/S:** Healthcare **MA:** Local **H/I/S:** Loves Angels, Crafts **CERTS:** Registered Nurse, Saint Francis Medical Center; Certification in Intravenous Therapy **A/H:** Employee of the Month (Nov-Dec. 2005) **C/VW:** Administers Flu Shots to Senior and Squads

Frances A. Morgan

Title: Creative Director **Company:** Ragalia Arts **Address:** 241 S.E. Eagles Nest Drive, Shelton, WA 98584 United States **BUS:** Media Arts **P/S:** Video Production, DVD Authorizing, Graphics **MA:** Regional **EXP:** Ms. Morgan's expertise is in multimedia production. **H/I/S:** Traveling, Sailing **EDU:** Bachelor of Arts in Communication, Evergreen State College **C/VW:** Save Our County's Kids Community Center
Email: moraganfran@hotmail.com
URL: http://www.ragaliaarts.com

Mr. John F. Morgan Jr.

Title: President, Chief Executive Officer **Company:** Morgan Capital **Address:** 19 Shelter Cove Lane, Suite 202, Hilton Head Island, SC 29928 United States **BUS:** Real Estate Development **P/S:** Project Development **MA:** National **D/D/R:** Residential and Apartment Project Development **H/I/S:** Golfing, Playing Football, Basketball **EDU:** Bachelor of Arts in Finance, University of Alabama **A/A/S:** Urban Land Institute; Congress for the New Urbanism; Atlanta Society of Financial Analysts
Email: john_morgan@nargray.com

Kay Korin Morgan

Title: Attorney **Company:** The Ammons Law Firm, LLP **Address:** 3700 Montrose Boulevard, Houston, TX 77006 United States **BUS:** Law Firm **P/S:** Legal Services Including Litigating for Plaintiffs' Product Liability and Personal Injury Suits **MA:** National **D/D/R:** Writing Research Papers **H/I/S:** Reading, Swimming, Caring for her Pets **EDU:** JD, St. Mary's University; Bachelor of Arts in History, Baylor University
Email: kay@ammonslaw.com
URL: http://www.ammonslaw.com

Roxanne D. Morgan

Title: Teacher **Company:** San Diego County Office of Education **Address:** 210 W. Ash Street, San Diego, CA 92101 United States **BUS:** Government Organization **P/S:** Educational Services for At-Risk Youth **MA:** Local **D/D/R:** Teaching English Language Arts and Social Sciences **H/I/S:** Golfing, Exercising, Reading, Spending Time with her Family **EDU:** Master of Science in Instructional Leadership and Curriculum and Instruction, National University; Master of Science in Educational Administration, National University; Bachelor of Arts in Liberal Arts and Social Science, San Diego State University **A/A/S:** California Teachers Association; American Association of University Women; National Education Association; Association for Research and Enlightenment; Pi Lambda Theta **C/VW:** St. Vincent de Paul Village; Friends from the Inside Out; Foresters; The Palavra Tree; Dollars for Scholars
Email: roxym@sdcoe.net

Stephen D. Morgan

Title: Regional Manager **Company:** Kurarax Dental Company **Address:** 5209 97th Avenue Court W., University Place, WA 98467 United States **BUS:** Leading Dental Manufacturer of Dental Bonding and Restorative Products Worldwide **P/S:** Dental Consumables **MA:** Washington **D/D/R:** Overseeing Sales People in the North Central and Regional United States **H/I/S:** Golfing, Reading **EDU:** Coursework in Business Administration, East High School, Cheyenne, WY
Email: morgandentalsale@aol.com
URL: http://www.cambridgewhoswho.com

Bella Morgera

Title: President **Company:** Bella Advertising, Inc. **Address:** P.O. Box 24116, Huber Heights, OH 45424 United States **BUS:** Beauty Company **P/S:** George Michael Hair Products, Beauty **MA:** National **EXP:** Ms. Morgera's expertise includes public relations, productions, hair, fashion and beauty services. **H/I/S:** Playing Piano, Swimming **EDU:** Continuing Education, Business Organization, CRI Rhode Island **A/A/S:** Academy of Arts and Science and Television **C/VW:** Brain Injury Association
Email: bellaadvertising@aol.com
URL: http://www.cambridgewhoswho.com

John F. Moriarty

Title: Chaplain **Company:** MacNeal Hospital **BUS:** Hospital **P/S:** Healthcare **MA:** Regional **D/D/R:** Working with the Fire Department, Overseeing Emergency Medical Services **H/I/S:** Traveling **EDU:** Master's Degree in Theology, Saint Meinrad School of Theology; Bachelor of Science in Accounting, Elmhurst College **A/A/S:** Board of Directors, Cumberland Green Cooperative **C/VW:** Knights of Columbus
Email: jfm1@ix.netcom.com
URL: http://www.cambridgewhoswho.com

Emily A. Morin

Title: Physician, Ophthalmologist **Company:** Mitchell Eye Institute, PC **Address:** 8200 Wisconsin Avenue, Suite 100, Bethesda, MD 20814 United States **BUS:** Medical School **P/S:** Ophthalmology **MA:** National **EXP:** Dr. Morin's expertise is in inpatient care. **D/D/R:** Teaching Clinical and Surgical Skills to Students **H/I/S:** Equestrian Sports, Spending Time with her Children **EDU:** MD, Georgetown University; Bachelor's Degree in Engineering, Purdue University **A/A/S:** American Academy of Ophthalmology; DCSO **C/VW:** Junior League of Northern Virginia; Committee, Baltimore Washington Eye Center
Email: emily_a_morin@yahoo.com
URL: http://www.mitchelleyeinstitute.com

Cheryl N. Morita

Title: Vice Principal **Company:** Aiea High School **Address:** 98-1276 Ulune Street, Aiea, HI 96701 United States **BUS:** High School **P/S:** Secondary Education **MA:** Local **EXP:** Ms. Morita's expertise is in educational leadership. **D/D/R:** Speaking Hawaiian, Organizing Cultural Programs **H/I/S:** Writing Hawaiian Music and Chants **EDU:** Pursuing Master of Arts in Administration, University of Hawaii; Bachelor of Arts in Hawaiian Studies, University of Hawaii (1983); Professional Development in Secondary Education, University of Hawaii (1991) **A/A/S:** Association for Supervision and Curriculum Development; Who's Who Among American Teachers **A/H:** Outstanding Teacher of the Year Award (2000) **C/VW:** Fundraiser, Local School
Email: moritac@hawaii.rr.com
URL: http://www.cambridgewhoswho.com

Marilu Morreale

Title: Owner **Company:** 1) La Vita E' Bella 2) Marisu, Inc. **Address:** 1708 Vetal Parkway E., Vestal, NY 13850 United States **BUS:** 1) Italian Restaurant 2) Pizzeria **P/S:** Italian Restaurant **MA:** Vestal, NY **EXP:** Ms. Marilu's expertise includes homemade pastas, desserts and family-oriented cuisine. **H/I/S:** Singing **EDU:** Three Years Coursework, SUNY Binghamton; Diploma, Binghamton North High School **A/A/S:** Appeared on RAI (Major Italian Television Network) Singing Back-Up to Famous Singers **C/VW:** Cancer Research, Heart Foundation

Adele G. Morris
Title: Technology Director **Company:** Craig County Public Schools **Address:** P.O. Box 245, New Castle, VA 24127 United States **BUS:** School District **P/S:** Education **MA:** Local **EXP:** Ms. Morris' expertise includes technology-related professional development for certified staff, communication, collaboration and connectivity. **D/D/R:** Managing Student Information Systems, Maintaining the School Website **H/I/S:** Reading, Cooking **EDU:** Pursuing Doctoral Degree in Instructional Technology and Design, Old Dominion University; Master of Science in Biology, Northeastern Illinois University (1984); Bachelor of Science in Biology and Geography, Frostburg State University (1971) **A/A/S:** Chairwoman, Regional Schools Contract and Planning Committee (2006); Who's Who Among America's Teachers (2004-2006); Who's Who Among International Technology Leaders (2000); Board of Directors, Blue Ridge Public Broadcasting System; Alpha Xi Delta Fraternity; Daughters of the American Revolution; The Mayflower Society; Chairwoman, Technology Committee, Craig County Public Schools; Board of Directors, Virginia Educational Technology Advisory Committee; United Methodist Church **C/VW:** Fort Lewis Chapter, Daughters of the American Revolution
Email: amorris@craig.k12.va.us
URL: http://www.craig.k12.va.us

Brian C. Morris
Title: Operations Manager Process Improvement **Company:** ATC Logistics and Electronics **Address:** 13500 Independence Parkway, Fort Worth, TX 76177 United States **BUS:** Company Specializing in the Management of High Value, High Velocity, Serialized Devices in the Wireless and High Tech Industries Using 3PL and Electronic Repair Services **P/S:** Multi-Layered Logistics Services **MA:** National **D/D/R:** Utilizing Lean Process Techniques, Overseeing Process Improvement, Six Sigma **H/I/S:** Golfing, Spending Time with Family, Watching Oklahoma State Athletics **EDU:** Bachelor of Science in Industrial Engineering, Oklahoma State University (1997) **A/A/S:** Institute of Industrial Engineers; Black Belt Six Sigma
Email: bmorris@atcle.com
URL: http://www.atcle.com

Felecia C. Morris
Title: Registered Nurse, BSN **Company:** Baltimore Washington Medical Center **Address:** 301 Hospital Drive, Glen Burnie, MD 21061 United States **BUS:** Hospital **P/S:** Medical Services **MA:** Regional **EXP:** Ms. Morris' expertise is in surgical medicine. **H/I/S:** Walking, Listening to Music, Traveling **EDU:** Bachelor of Science in Nursing, University of Arkansas, Pine Bluff
Email: cajsgirl@netzero.net
URL: http://bwmc.umms.org/

Kathy Y. Morris
Title: Co-Owner, Vice President **Company:** Mocat J. Enterprises **Address:** P.O. Box 2335, Ewa Beach, HI 96706 United States **BUS:** Online Travel Store **P/S:** Travel Arrangements **MA:** International **D/D/R:** Training Staff, Overseeing All Aspects of the Business, Dealing with Customers and Creating Travel Packages **H/I/S:** Playing Golf, Traveling **EDU:** Bachelor of Arts in Communications, Broadcasting and Journalism, Towson State University **C/VW:** Church
Email: mocatj@hawaiiantel.net
URL: http://www.mocatjenterprises.com

Mrs. Kristen L. Morris
Title: Staff Developer **Company:** PS 19 Queens **Address:** 9802 Roosevelt Avenue, Corona, NY 11368 United States **BUS:** Elementary School **P/S:** Primary Education **MA:** Local **EXP:** Mrs. Morris' expertise is in early childhood education. **D/D/R:** Teaching Staff to Use Repetition in Concepts, Simple Language, Pictures, Gestures and Sensory Perception to Teach Students **H/I/S:** Rollerblading, Dancing, Playing Softball, Spending Time with her Family **EDU:** Master of Education in Educational Technology, Plus 30, New York Technical Institute, Manhattan Campus; Bachelor's Degree in English, University of Connecticut **CERTS:** National Board Certification in Early Childhood Education and Literacy **A/A/S:** Teachers College, Columbia University **C/VW:** The Leukemia & Lymphoma Society; American Red Cross
Email: kkleppel1@yahoo.com
URL: http://www.cambridgewhoswho.com

Michael J. Morris
Title: President **Company:** Take it to the Limit **Address:** 1052 Greenwood Springs Boulevard, Suite E-F, Greenwood, IN 46143 United States **BUS:** Girls' Fast Pitch Training Company **P/S:** Pitching, Hitting, Complete Player Development, Fitness Training **MA:** Local **D/D/R:** Training **EDU:** Coursework in Medic Training **C/VW:** Disabled Children in his Community
Email: mike@ttlsoftball.com

Sherrie Lee Morris
Title: Assistant Resident Director **Company:** Mission Teens, Inc. **Address:** 48 Northville Road, Bridgeton, NJ 08302 United States **BUS:** Christian Drug and Alcohol Rehabilitation Center **P/S:** Counseling, Rehabilitation **MA:** National **D/D/R:** Counseling Adults with Drug and Alcohol Issues and Eating Disorders **H/I/S:** Playing Sports, Exercising **EDU:** Bachelor of Science in Nursing, Hahnemann University; Associate Degree in Nursing, Hahnermann University **CERTS:** Certification in Oncology Nursing, Robert Wood Johnson University **C/VW:** Victory Assembly of God, Centerton, NJ
Email: info@cambridgewhoswho
URL: http://www.missionteens.com

Trudy Morris Stern
Title: Web Content Editor, Writer **Company:** South Florida Water Management District **Address:** 3301 Gun Club Road, West Palm Beach, FL 33406 United States **BUS:** Government Organization **P/S:** Water Distribution **MA:** Regional **D/D/R:** Coordinating Professional Presentations, Writing, Editing and Overseeing Graphic Design **H/I/S:** Playing the Guitar, Writing Songs **EDU:** High School Diploma **CERTS:** Industry-Related Training **C/VW:** Local Church
Email: trudymorris@bellsouth.net
URL: http://www.cambridgewhoswho.com

Jane A. Morrison
Title: Licensed Practical Nurse **Company:** Christopher East **Address:** 4200 Browns Lane, Louisville, KY 40220 United States **BUS:** Healthcare Facility **P/S:** Skilled Nursing, Professional Care, Alzheimer's-Related Dementia Care, Hospice Care, Intermediate Care, Intravenous Therapy, Rehabilitation Therapy, Respite Care, Special Care Unit **MA:** Regional **D/D/R:** Treating Primary Care and Long-Term Brain Injury Patients, Overseeing the Life Skills Unit, Managing Patients' Medications, Changing Dressings **H/I/S:** Hunting, Fishing **CERTS:** Licensed Practical Nurse (1984); Certification in Crisis and Prevention Instruction; Certification in Cardiopulmonary Resuscitation; Certification in Venipuncture **A/A/S:** North American Hunting Club

Tara Morrison, MD
Title: Oncologist **Company:** Fox Chase Cancer Center **Address:** 333 Cottman Avenue, Philadelphia, PA 19111 United States **BUS:** Cancer Institute **P/S:** Cancer Care, Higher Education, Research and Development **MA:** Local **EXP:** Dr. Morrison's expertise includes neurology and neuro-oncology. **D/D/R:** Teaching Students About Cancer Treatments and their Effects on the Nervous System **EDU:** MD, University of Ottawa (1995); Bachelor of Science, University of Ottawa (1991) **A/A/S:** American Academy of Neurology; Society for Neuro-Oncology
Email: tara.morrison@fccc.edu
URL: http://www.fccc.edu

Dr. Jennifer Ann Morrow
Title: Assistant Professor **Company:** University of Tennessee, Department of Education, Psychology and Counseling **Address:** 2750 Rushland Park Boulevard, Knoxville, TN 37924 United States **BUS:** University **P/S:** Education **MA:** National **D/D/R:** Evaluating Programs, Statistical Consulting, Writing Grants **H/I/S:** Traveling **EDU:** Ph.D. in Experimental Psychology, University of Rhode Island **A/A/S:** American Psychological Association; Virginia Psychological Association; American Evaluation Association
Email: jamorrow@utk.edu
URL: http://www.cambridgewhoswho.com

Shirley D. Morrow, CPESC
Title: Independent Consultant **Address:** 21755 S. Main Street, Spring Hill, KS 66083 United States **BUS:** Construction **P/S:** Compliance for the Occurrence of Storm Water **MA:** National **D/D/R:** Working as a Private Consultant and an Erosion Control Specialist, Training for State Agencies **H/I/S:** Gardening, Taking Care of Pets **EDU:** Master's Degree in Environmental Science, Oklahoma State University (1995) **CERTS:** Certified Professional Erosion Control Specialist **A/A/S:** International Erosion Control Association
Email: sdmorrow1960@yahoo.com

Lauren E. Morse
Title: Occupational Therapy Manager **Company:** Cottage Hospital **Address:** P.O. Box 2001, Woodsville, NH 03785 United States **BUS:** Hospital **P/S:** Rehabilitation, Therapy and General Hospital Services **MA:** Local **D/D/R:** Offering Hand Occupational Therapy, Overseeing a Staff of Five Therapists, Budgeting, Reviewing, Developing Staff, Attending Department Head Meetings **H/I/S:** Reading, Traveling, Hiking, Spending Time with Family **EDU:** Bachelor of Science in Occupational Therapy, University of New Hampshire-1997 **CERTS:** Certified in Physical Agent Modalities-2006 **A/A/S:** American Occupational Therapy Association **A/H:** Nominated Employee of the Quarter-2002 **C/VW:** March of Dimes, American Cancer Society
Email: lmorse@fairpoint.net
URL: http://www.cambridgewhoswho.com

Dyann L. Morton
Title: Payroll Manager **Company:** Miller Paint **Address:** 12812 N.E. Whitaker Way, Portland, OR 97230 United States **BUS:** Paint Retail **P/S:** Sale of Paint and Paint Products **MA:** International **D/D/R:** Managing Payroll **H/I/S:** Bowling, Line Dancing **EDU:** College Coursework, Portland Community **A/A/S:** American Payroll Association
Email: dyannmorton@millerpaint.com
URL: www.millerpaint.com

Gloria Monica Moseley
Title: Teacher **Company:** Malvern Preparatory School **Address:** 418 S. Warren Avenue, Malvern, PA 19355 United States **BUS:** Independent Catholic School **P/S:** Preparing Young Men for College, for Leadership and for Life **MA:** Regional **D/D/R:** Teaching Theology, Christian and Hebrew Scriptures, Working on the Admissions Team, Teaching Seventh to Twelfth-Grade, with a Background in Child Development, Created 'In Search of the Black Madonna' **H/I/S:** Reading, Step Aerobics, Public Lecturing **EDU:** Master of Arts in Moral Theology, St. Charles Borromeo Seminary (1993); Bachelor of Arts in Business, Immaculate College (1985); Bachelor of Arts in Family and Consumer Science, Immaculate College (1985) **CERTS:** Certification in Theology (1985) **A/A/S:** National Independent Association of Schools; Catholic Educators of Philadelphia
Email: gmoseley@malvernprep.org
URL: http://www.malvernprep.org

Dr. Robert C. Moseley
Title: Senior Pastor **Company:** Arbela Baptist Church **Address:** Route 1, P.O. Box 82, Arbela, MO 63432 United States **BUS:** Religion Religion/Spiritual Leadership **MA:** Local **D/D/R:** Saving Souls **EDU:** Doctoral Degree in School Administration, University of Missouri **A/A/S:** American School Administrators Association
Email: moseleyfr@yahoo.com

Jennifer L. Moser
Title: Interior Consultant **Company:** Jennifer L.M. & Company, Inc. **Address:** 9890 Laura Drive, Orange, TX 77630 United States **BUS:** Consulting Company **P/S:** Interior Decorating Consulting **MA:** Local **D/D/R:** Interior Decorating, New Construction and Remodeling, Staging **H/I/S:** Playing Softball, Coaching her Daughter **C/VW:** Church
Email: jenandcompany@sbcglobal.net
URL: http://www.cambridgewhoswho.com

Broderick D. Moses
Title: Optometrist **Company:** Wal-Mart Vision Care **Dept:** Moses Vision Care **Address:** 1501 Manhattan Boulevard, Harvey, LA 70058 United States **BUS:** Eyecare Center **P/S:** Eye Care Including Conducting Eye Examination, Treatments for Ocular Lenses, Color Contacts, Bifocals, Multifocals, Children's Eye Care, Common Eye Diseases, Assisting Patients for Eyeglasses and Frames **MA:** Regional **EXP:** Mr. Moses' expertise is in optometry. **D/D/R:** Conducting Eye Examinations, Overseeing Administrative Duties, Prescribing Medications, Eyeglasses and Contact Lenses, Treating Patients with Ocular Disease **H/I/S:** Basketball, Football **EDU:** Doctor of Optometry, University of Houston College of Optometry (2004) **A/A/S:** American Society of Ophthalmic Administrators; American Optometric Association; NOCC; Biomedical Engineering Honor Society; Social Chairman, Louisiana State Association of Optometrists
Email: bmoses24@hotmail.com
URL: http://www.walmart.com/catalog/catalog.gsp?cat=5432

Stacy M. Moses
Title: Special Education Teacher **Company:** Burke County Public Schools **Dept:** Freedom High School **Address:** 511 Independence Boulevard, Morganton, NC 28655 United States **BUS:** School District **P/S:** Education **MA:** Local **D/D/R:** Teaching Special Education and Self-Contained English **H/I/S:** Caring for Dogs **EDU:** Pursuing Master's Degree in Administration, Grand Canyon University; Bachelor of Arts in Special Education, University of North Carolina at Charlotte **A/A/S:** North Carolina Association of Educators **C/VW:** American Red Cross
Email: smoses@burke.k12.nc.us
URL: http://www.cambridgewhoswho.com

DeAnn M. Mosher
Title: Owner, Clinical Trials Manager **Company:** Medical Research Associates **Address:** 3074 N. U.S. 31 S., Traverse City, MI 49686 United States **BUS:** Clinical Research Company **P/S:** Conducting Research Trials for the Federal Drug Administration to Approve New Drugs **MA:** Northern Michigan **D/D/R:** Coordinating Clinical Research Trials, Research Management, Serving as a Medical Laboratory Technician and Emergency Registered Nurse **EDU:** Bachelor's Degree in Biochemistry, Northern Michigan University, Marquette; Registered Nurse, Northwest Michigan College, 1999 **A/A/S:** Association of Clinical Research Professionals; National Association of Emergency Medical Technicians; Michigan Nurses Association **C/VW:** Volunteer Emergency Medical Technician, Veterans Foundations, Search and Rescue Team
Email: medicalresearch@hotmail.com

Kimberly Ann Mosley
Title: Vice President **Company:** KC Travel **Address:** 137 Eastminster Drive, Verona, PA 15147 United States **BUS:** Travel Agency **P/S:** Traveling and Shopping Excursions in New York **MA:** National **D/D/R:** Public Relations, Receiving and Verbally Selling Trips, Ensuring that Trips Run Smoothly, Safely, Putting Together the Package, Arranging Shopping Trips and Broadway Play Trips **H/I/S:** Shopping, Traveling, Taking Part in Church Activities **EDU:** Associate Degree in Business, Willard Business School (1982) **C/VW:** United Way
Email: koffeencream1017@yahoo.com

Anita A. Moss
Title: Lead Writer, Editor **Company:** Tinker Air Force Base **Address:** 1833 Center Drive, Midwest City, OK 73110 United States **BUS:** United States Military **P/S:** Defense **MA:** International **D/D/R:** Writing, Editing, Overseeing Technical Orders and Manual **H/I/S:** Spending Time with her Family **EDU:** High School Diploma **CERTS:** Certification in Desert Storm Command **C/VW:** National Transplant Assistance Fund
Email: anita.moss@tinker.af.mil
URL: http://www.cambridgewhoswho.com

Cindy Moss
Title: Billing Supervisor **Company:** Philadelphia Veterans Administration Medical Center **Address:** 3900 Woodland Avenue, Philadelphia, PA 19104 United States **BUS:** Acute-Care Hospital for Veterans **P/S:** Healthcare **MA:** Regional **D/D/R:** Medical Claims, Accounting, Conducts Security Training, Narcotics Inspector and Auditor Preparing Income Taxes for H&R Block, Lecturing and Public Speaking for Local Venues **H/I/S:** Traveling, Studying the Bible **EDU:** Bachelor of Arts in Accounting, La Salle University (1996) **A/A/S:** Compliance Committee; President, CDC; Appointed to National Practitioner Committee
Email: cmoss232@aol.com

George T. Moss
Title: President **Company:** Baxter Vault Co., Inc. **Address:** Galena, KS 66739 United States **BUS:** Funeral Services Manufacturing/Production/Machinery **P/S:** Concrete Burial Vaults and Urns **MA:** Regional **D/D/R:** Working as a Licensed Funeral Director and Embalmer **H/I/S:** Fishing/Boating **EDU:** Dallas Institute of Mortuary Science, Associate in Mortuary Science **CERTS:** Licensed Embalmer and Funeral Director **A/A/S:** Masons, Shriners, Boy Scouts, Past President of Eastern Stars

Rick Moss
Title: Chief Curator **Company:** African American Museum and Library at Oakland **Address:** 659 14th Street, Oakland, CA 94612 United States **BUS:** Museum and Library Dedicated to the Preservation, Interpretation and Sharing of African American History in the West **P/S:** Preservation of Historical and Cultural Experiences of African Americans in California and the West for Present and Future Generations **MA:** Regional **D/D/R:** Overseeing Administration of the Facility Including a Staff of Eight, Managing Museum Functions and Archives, Setting Exhibit Schedules, Creating and Installing Exhibits, Creating Public Programming with a Focus on Public History Regarding African Americans in the West **H/I/S:** Reading, Fitness, Adding to his Extensive Jazz Collection **EDU:** Master's Degree in History, University of California, Los Angeles (1980); Master's Degree in Historic Resources Management, University of California, Riverside (1987); Bachelor of Arts in History, University of California, Los Angeles (1977) **A/A/S:** Board Member, California Chapter, National Council on Public History; Commissioner, State Historical Resources Commission of California; Member, Public Art Advisory Committee, City of Oakland
Email: rmoss@oaklandlibrary.org
URL: http://www.oaklandlibrary.org

Yolanda M. Moton
Title: Director of Community Relations and Member Services **Company:** Managed Health Services **Address:** 1099 N. Meridian Street, Suite 400, Indianapolis, IN 46204 United States **BUS:** Managed Health Care Provider **P/S:** Healthcare for Medicaid Patients **MA:** Indiana **D/D/R:** Offering Healthcare Benefits to the Medicaid Population **H/I/S:** Spending Time with her Family, Tending to her Salt Water Aquarium, Gardening, Catering, Cooking **EDU:** Bachelor's Degree in Marketing and Business Analysis, Indiana University; Coursework, Indianapolis Entrepreneur Academy **A/A/S:** Member, Covering Kids and Families; Minority Health Coalition; Indiana Black Expo; Board Member, Wheelers Boy and Girls Club; Board Member, SOBY; Do Outreach and Community Work **C/VW:** United Negro College Fund, Boys and Girls Club, State of Our Black Youth
Email: ymoton@centene.com
URL: http://www.managedhealthservices.com

Raed V. Moughabghab
Title: Director of Mixed Signal Engineering **Company:** Entropic Communications, Inc. **Address:** 513 Verbena Court, Encinitas, CA 92024 United States **BUS:** Manufacturing Company **P/S:** Fabless Semiconductors for Broadband Connection **MA:** International **D/D/R:** Designing Analog and Mixed-Signal Devices **H/I/S:** Playing Tennis, Reading **EDU:** Ph.D. in Electrical Engineering, with a Concentration in Analog Design; Master of Science in Electrical Engineering, with a Concentration in Microwave Techniques **CERTS:** Diploma in Analog Design Engineering **A/A/S:** American Communication Association; Integrated Systems Solutions Corporation
Email: rmoughabghab@entropic.com
URL: http://www.entropic.com

Peter Mourad
Title: Vice President **Company:** A.E. Mourad Agency, Inc. **Address:** 28277 Dequindre Road, Madison Heights, MI 48071 United States **BUS:** Insurance Agency **P/S:** Insurance Services Including Employee Benefits **MA:** National **D/D/R:** Managing Employee Benefit Insurance **H/I/S:** Golfing, Playing Hockey, Spending Time with his Dog **EDU:** Bachelor of Science in Marketing, Western Michigan University **C/VW:** The Humane Society; Ronald McDonald House
Email: prmourad@aemourad.com
URL: http://www.aemourad.com

Nick J. Mouring, RN
Title: Registered Nurse, Behavioral Health **Company:** University of Pittsburgh Medical Center McKeesport **Address:** 1500 Fifth Avenue, McKeesport, PA 15132 United States **BUS:** Division of the University of Pittsburgh Medical Center Serving the Mentally Ill of the McKeesport Area **P/S:** Improving the Lives of More Than Four Million People Each Year in Western Pennsylvania and Surrounding States Through Redefined Models of Health Care Delivery and Superb Clinical Outcomes **MA:** Local **D/D/R:** Administering Medication to Patients with Depression and Schizophrenia, Active Psychotics, Drug and Alcohol Abusers and Geriatric Patients, Working as Team Leader, Supervising the Staff and Mental Health Workers **H/I/S:** Playing Tennis **EDU:** Pursuing Bachelor of Science in Nursing, California University of Pennsylvania; Bachelor's Degree in Philosophy, University of Pittsburgh (1970)
Email: mouring1302@comcast.net
URL: http://www.cambridgewhoswho.com

Mrs. Ruth S. Mouzon
Title: Third-Grade Teacher (Retired) **Company:** White Knoll Elementary School **Address:** 132 White Knoll Way, West Columbia, SC 29170 United States **BUS:** Elementary School **P/S:** Primary Education **MA:** Local **D/D/R:** Teaching Third-Grade **H/I/S:** Traveling, Reading, Knitting **EDU:** Master's Degree in Early Childhood Education, University of South Carolina (1982); Bachelor's Degree in Elementary Education, Charleston Southern University (1971) **A/A/S:** NCTA
Email: ruth49@windstream.net
URL: http://www.cambridgewhoswho.com

Paola Moyano
Title: Project Manager **Company:** Labatt Anderson **Address:** Tyson, VA United States **BUS:** Government Consultant **P/S:** Service of Budget Analysis **MA:** International **EXP:** Ms. Moyano's expertise is in budget analysis. **H/I/S:** Volunteering with the Hispanic Community of Virginia **EDU:** Master's Degree in International Commerce and Policy, George Mason University, 2004 **C/VW:** St. Anthony's Church, Hispanic Community of Virginia
Email: pmoyanoguzman@yahoo.com

Amy S. Moyer
Title: Assistant Elementary Principal, District Federal Grants Supervisor **Company:** Newman Middle School **Address:** 355 S. Osage, Skiatook, OK 74070 United States **BUS:** Middle School **P/S:** Education **MA:** Local **D/D/R:** Teaching Advanced English, Coaching Track and Volleyball **H/I/S:** Painting, Reading, Landscaping, Watching Sports **EDU:** Master of Arts in Administration, Northeast State University; Bachelor of Science in Art Education, University of Tulsa; Endorsement in English, Oklahoma Wesleyan College **A/A/S:** NBA; Ohio Education Association; International Reading Association; Oklahoma Coaches Association; Coach, All State High School Volleyball, 1998 **A/H:** Teacher of the Year, Newman Middle School, 2006-2007 **C/VW:** Golden Hurricane Club
Email: amoyer@skiatook.k12.ok.us

Mrs. Melissa M. Moyer
Title: Lead Instructor for the Allied Health Programs **Company:** Daymar College **Address:** 76 Carothers Road, 2777 California Crossroad, California, KY 41007 United States **BUS:** Proven Leader in the Education Industry and in the Field of Nursing **P/S:** Higher Education, Career-Oriented College, Health Programs **MA:** Regional **D/D/R:** Supervising Health Programs at College, Ensuring Programs are Matching to ACICF to be Accredited, Hospice Care for Crisis Solving and Management, Long Term Care Charge Nurse and Supervisor at Several Facilities for Skilled Nursing and Independent Living **H/I/S:** Quilting, Writing, Dog Breeder, Restoration of Historic Vehicles with Spouse **EDU:** Associate Degree in Paralegal, Brown Mackie College (2005) **CERTS:** Licensed Practical Nurse, Northern Kentucky Health Occupational Center (1984); Licensed LPN IV Therapist; Three Licensures in Pharmacology **A/A/S:** National Health in Wellness Club; Advisor to the Student Advisory Board; Teacher of the Month Several Times
Email: mmoyer@daymarcollege.edu
URL: http://www.daymarcollege.edu

Mrs. Lucille A. Mozzillo
Title: Music Teacher **Company:** Coxsackie-Athens Central School District **Dept:** Edward J. Arthur Elementary School **Address:** 51 Third Street, Athens, NY 12015 United States **BUS:** School District **P/S:** Education **MA:** Regional **D/D/R:** Teaching Music **EDU:** Master's Degree in Music, SUNY Fredonia **A/A/S:** New York State School Music Association; Music Educators National Conference: The National Association for Music Education; Sigma Alpha Iota; American Orff-Schulwerk Association **C/VW:** American Legion Auxiliary
Email: mozzillol@coxsackie-athens.org

Maryann Y. Muccio Tully
Title: Staff Registered Nurse **Company:** Rapid City Regional Hospital **Address:** Fairmont Boulevard, Rapid City, SD 57701 United States **BUS:** Hospital **P/S:** Healthcare **MA:** Regional **EXP:** Ms. Muccio Tully's expertise includes orthopedic and neurology nursing. **H/I/S:** Reading, Traveling, Spending Time with her Grandchildren **EDU:** Coursework, Middlesex Memorial Hospital School of Nursing, Middletown, CT **A/A/S:** National Association of Orthopedic Nurses **C/VW:** Local Catholic Church; Diocese Catholic Committee on Scouting and Camp Fire, SD
Email: maryann.mucciotully@cwwemail.com
URL: http://www.cambridgewhoswho.com

Brigitte A. Muehlbauer
Title: Occupational Therapist, Certified Lymphedema Therapist **Company:** JFK Medical Center **Address:** Edison, NJ 08817 United States **BUS:** Healthcare Hospital **P/S:** Patient Care, Therapy **MA:** Local **EXP:** Ms. Muehlbauer's expertise includes all aspects of occupational therapy and lymphedema therapy. **H/I/S:** Cross Stitch **EDU:** College Misercordia, Master's Degree, Bachelor's Degree **A/A/S:** Outdoor Trainer for Girl Scouts

Christina L. Muggenburg
Title: Music Teacher **Company:** Laramie County School District No. 1 **Address:** 2810 House Avenue, Cheyenne, WY 82007 United States **BUS:** Elementary School **P/S:** Education for Kindergarten through Sixth-Grade Students **MA:** Local **D/D/R:** Teaching Music Including String and Band Instrument Instruction to Fourth and Fifth-Grade Students **H/I/S:** Horseback Riding **EDU:** Pursuing Ph.D. in Music Education; Master's Degree in Music, University of Wyoming (2000) **A/A/S:** Wyoming Education Association; The National Association for Music Education; International Association of Theatrical and Stage Employees
Email: cmuggenburg@excite.com
URL: http://www.laramie1.k12.wy.us

Dolores R. Muhich, Ph.D.
Title: Owner, Manager **Address:** 8611 Green Valley, Austin, TX 78759 United States **BUS:** Real Estate **P/S:** Real Estate Services Including Renting **MA:** Local **D/D/R:** Managing Property Rentals and Investments, Educating, Teaching Business and Statistics, Conducting Research **H/I/S:** Ballroom and Latin Dancing, Singing in the Choir **EDU:** Ph.D. in Educational Psychology, Southern Illinois University (1970); Post Doctorate Degree in Counseling, The University of Texas at Austin **A/A/S:** Dance International; National Scrabble Association; AAA Storage; Victoria Square Homeowners Association **C/VW:** St. Matthew's Episcopal Church
Email: dmuhich@austin.rr.com

Trejsi L. Mulac
Title: Owner **Company:** Solid Rock Surfaces, LLC **Address:** 525 S. McClintock Drive, Suite 103, Tempe, AZ 85281 United States **BUS:** Manufacturing Company **P/S:** Granite and Engineered Stone, Fabrication **MA:** Regional **EXP:** Ms. Mulac's expertise is in custom store design. **H/I/S:** Painting **EDU:** Master's Degree in Justice Studies, Arizona State University; Bachelor of Science in Forensic Science, Scottsdale College; Associate Degree in Justice Studies **A/A/S:** Chamber of Commerce; The Marble Institute Women's Contractor Association
Email: trejsi@solidrocktop.com
URL: http://www.solidrocktops.com

Marlynn Mulder

Title: Postmaster **Company:** United States Postal Service **Address:** 54 Zero Street, Granby, CO 80446 United States **BUS:** Post Office **P/S:** Mail **MA:** Local **D/D/R:** Utilizing her Organizational Skills **H/I/S:** Snowmobiling, Fishing, Hiking **EDU:** High School Education
Email: mildew121@msn.com

Carlos A. Mulero

Title: Environmental Engineering Consultant **Company:** Environmental and Engineering Services **Address:** P.O. Box 897, Guaynabo, PR 00970 United States **BUS:** Environmental Consulting Company **P/S:** Environmental Consulting and Compliance **MA:** Regional **D/D/R:** Consulting, Collaborating, Operational Imaging, Engineering Design, Consulting, Conducting Inspections, Performing Assessments, Maintaining Environmental compliance **H/I/S:** Exercising, Golfing **EDU:** Master's Degree in Civil Engineering, University of Puerto Rico **A/A/S:** National Registry of Environmental Professionals **C/VW:** Trainee, Local College of Engineers
Email: carlos.mulero@gmail.com
URL: http://www.cambridgewhoswho.com

Linda A. Mull

Title: Sole Proprietor **Company:** H.B. International **Address:** 7051 County Road 23, Archbold, OH 43502 United States **BUS:** Independent Distributor of Nutritional Supplements **P/S:** Herbalife Products **MA:** National **D/D/R:** Building her Herbalife Distributorship, Running a Retail Establishment, Overseeing Recruiting, Marketing **EDU:** Coursework in Medical Studies, Owens Community College **A/A/S:** Author, International Society of Poetry
Email: xtrdnarybizz@hotmail.com

Jessica P. Mullen, MPA, CHES

Title: Health Educator, Senior **Company:** Portsmouth Health Department **Address:** 1701 High Street, Suite 102, Portsmouth, VA 23704 United States **BUS:** Public Health Department **P/S:** Public Health Issues, Promoting, Protecting and Preserving a Healthy and Safe Community **MA:** Local **D/D/R:** Teaching Importance of Fighting Obesity, Promoting Physical Activity to Obtain Optimal Health **H/I/S:** Golfing, Traveling, Spending Time with Family and Friends **EDU:** Master of in Public Administration, Old Dominion University; Bachelor of Science in Exercise Science, East Carolina University **CERTS:** Certified Health Education Specialist, National Commission for Health Education **A/A/S:** American College of Sports Medicine; National Center for Health Education **C/VW:** Suffolk 60 Cares
Email: jessica.mullen@vhd.virginia.gov
URL: http://www.vdh.va.gov

Mr. Louis A. Muller

Title: Chief Financial Officer, Chief Information Officer **Company:** Independent Medical Expert Consulting Services, Inc. **Address:** 157 S. Broad Street, Lansdale, PA 19446 United States **BUS:** National Independent Review Organization **P/S:** High-Quality Medical Reviews, Extensive Panel of Experts and Responsiveness to Client and Regulatory Needs **MA:** National **D/D/R:** Performing Instruction in Information Technology, Designing and Developing Applications, Managing and Overseeing All Financial Aspects of the Company **H/I/S:** Golfing **EDU:** Associate Degree in Computer Science, Temple University (1978) **A/A/S:** National Association of Independent Review Organizations
Email: dmiller@imedecs.com
URL: http://www.imedecs.com

Tara Michele Mullin

Title: Administrative Assistant III **Company:** University of Nevada, Las Vegas **Address:** 4505 S. Maryland Parkway, P.O. Box 451017, Las Vegas, NV 89154 United States **BUS:** University **P/S:** Higher Education **MA:** International **EXP:** Ms. Mullin's expertise is in human resource management. **H/I/S:** Reading, Watching Movies, Playing Tennis and Baseball **EDU:** Bachelor of Science in Business Administration and Human Resource Management, University of Nevada, Las Vegas **A/A/S:** Alumni, University of Nevada, Los Angeles; Alpha Gamma Delta **C/VW:** Juvenile Diabetes Research Foundation
Email: tara.mullin@unlv.edu
URL: http://www.unlv.edu

Carol Ann Mullins

Title: Licensed Practical Nurse, Back Up MD's Coordinator **Company:** Village Care Center **Address:** 4211 Monnett New Winchester Road, Bucyrus, OH 44820 United States **BUS:** Health Care **P/S:** Long Term Nursing Care, Rehabilitation Services, Hospice and Respite Care **MA:** Regional **D/D/R:** Assessing Patients, Caring for Short- and Long-Term Residents, Working as a MD's Assistant, Taking Care of Infectious Control **H/I/S:** Dance, Ballet, Tap, Jazz **EDU:** Intravenous Therapy, Conrad House (2003); Pursuing Degree in Nursing, American College Network **CERTS:** Licensed Practical Nursing Certification, North Central State (2001)
Email: armsdancer@yahoo.com

Otis Dwayne Mullins

Title: Manager of Safety and Environmental Affairs **Company:** Clintwood Elkhorn Mining **Dept:** Safety **Address:** 61 Allen House Lane, London, KY 40741 United States **BUS:** Mining Company **P/S:** Coal Mining **MA:** International **D/D/R:** Protecting the Environment, Ensuring the Health and Safety of All Employees **H/I/S:** Motorcycling **EDU:** Coursework in Science; Coursework in Psychology; Associate Degree in Mine Technology, Pikeville College, Eastern Kentucky (1977) **A/A/S:** National Registry of Environmental Professionals **C/VW:** Masonic Lodge
Email: odmullins@tecoenergy.com
Email: ottisdm@yahoo.com
URL: http://www.tecocoal.com

Deborah L. Mundy

Title: Controller **Company:** Priority Partners **Address:** 1530 Caton Center Drive, Suite C, Baltimore, MD 21227 United States **BUS:** Information Technology Management Company **P/S:** Assistance for Customers Looking to Capitalize on the Tools of the Digital Age by Offering Leadership and Daily Operational Support of Clients' Business and Network-Related Systems **MA:** National **D/D/R:** Accounting, Functioning as Controller of the Company, Managing the Daily Operations of the Offices and Handling All Bookkeeping Responsibilities **H/I/S:** Sewing, Reading Fiction and Mysteries **EDU:** Associate Degree in Accounting, Catonsville Community College, Maryland
Email: dmundy@prioritypartners.com
URL: http://www.prioritypartners.com

Rev. Frederick L. Munford Sr., PD, MS, D.Min

Title: Consultant Pharmacist **Company:** FLM Enterprises **Address:** 8805 Junaluska Terrace, Clinton, MD 20735 United States **BUS:** Healthcare Pharmacist **P/S:** Consulting **EXP:** Rev. Munford's expertise is in nutritional support. **H/I/S:** Skiing, Chess, Jogging, Bike Riding **EDU:** Howard University, Master's Degree in Nutrition **A/A/S:** ASHP, NPA, Consultant Pharmacy Association

Javier Munoz

Title: Information Technology and Software Development Manager, Computer Science Engineer **Company:** Datamark, Inc. **Address:** 43 Butterfield Circle, El Paso, TX 79906 United States **BUS:** Information Technology Company **P/S:** Business Process Outsourcing Services, Data and Remote Remittance Processing, Document Storage and Destruction, Client System Interfacing **MA:** International **D/D/R:** Supervising Infrastructure of Six Plants, Data Processing **H/I/S:** Golfing **EDU:** Bachelor of Science in Computer Science, Instituto Tecnológico y de Estudios Superiores de Monterrey, Mexico (1990) **CERTS:** Certification in Professional Management; Certified Six Sigma Black Belt; Judo Black Belt **A/A/S:** Association of Engineers, Instituto Tecnológico de Estudios Superiores de Monterrey
Email: javier_munoz@datamark.net
URL: http://www.datamark.net

Sonia M. Munoz, Esq.

Title: President, Attorney **Company:** Immigration Legal Experts **Address:** 101 N.E. Third Avenue, Suite 1500, Ft Lauderdale, FL 33301 United States **BUS:** Legal Services Attorney **P/S:** Counsel on Immigration Law to Companies **MA:** National **EXP:** Ms. Munoz's expertise includes immigration law and business immigration matters. **EDU:** University of Miami, University of Florida, BA, JD **CERTS:** Certificate in International Commercial Law **A/A/S:** Florida Bar Association, American Bar Association, Inn of Court, Hispanic Bar Association
URL: www.immigrationlegalexperts.com

Sarah Munson

Title: Registered Nurse **Company:** Meriter Hospital **Address:** 202 S. Park Street, Madison, WI 53713 United States **BUS:** Hospital **P/S:** Healthcare **MA:** Local **D/D/R:** Medical and Surgical Care Nursing **H/I/S:** Coaching High School Softball Team **EDU:** Bachelor of Science in Nursing, Edgewood College
Email: munson17@gmail.com
URL: http://www.cambridgewhoswho.com

Marcia Reneé Murden-Taylor

Title: Director of Medical Oncology **Company:** Saint Francis Hospital **Address:** 2986 Kate Bond Avenue, Bartlett, TN 38133 United States **BUS:** Quality Healthcare **P/S:** Acute Care Services, Patient Care **MA:** Regional **EXP:** Ms. Murden-Taylor's expertise includes medical and surgical leadership for the oncology unit. **D/D/R:** Lecturing, Training, Mentoring, Continuing Education, Policies and Procedures, Continuously Improving Quality, Conducting Random Chart Audits **H/I/S:** Spending Time with Family, Going to Movies, Reading **EDU:** Master of Business Administration in Management, American Intercontinental University (2006); Master of Business Administration in Healthcare Administration, American Intercontinental University (2006); Bachelor's Degree in Organizational Management, Crichton College (2000) **A/A/S:** Oncology Nurse Society; National Association of Female Executives; Public Speaking; American College for Healthcare Executives
Email: murdenworld@bellsouth.net
URL: http://www.saintfrancisbartlett.com

Wadida Murib-Holmes

Title: Director of National and Major Accounts **Company:** Humana **Address:** 500 W. Main Street, Louisville, KY 40202 United States **BUS:** Healthcare Insurance **P/S:** Healthcare Insurance, Commercial, Medicare, Military, Self Insured Customers **MA:** National **EXP:** Ms. Murib-Holmes' expertise includes strategic consulting and healthcare transparency. **H/I/S:** Traveling, Gardening, Reading, Movies, Music, Art **EDU:** Master of Business Administration in International Business and Business Management, Xavier University (1963); Bachelor of Fine Arts in Advertising Graphic Design, Miami University (1981) **C/VW:** Local Food Shelters, United Way, Fund for the Arts, HALTER, American Council of the Blind, Kentucky Harvest, American Cancer Society, National Multiple Sclerosis Society; March of Dimes
Email: wmuribholmes@humana.com
URL: http://www.humana.com

Anthony J. Murphy

Title: Executive Director **Company:** Town Watch Integrated Services **Address:** 1441 Sansom Street, Second Floor, Philadelphia, PA 19102 United States **BUS:** Government Agency **P/S:** Law Enforcement Such Crime and Drug Prevention Programs, Emergency Response and Integrated Services **MA:** National **D/D/R:** Motivational Speaking, Conducting Workshops on Inter-Culturall and Multicultural, Relationships Traveling, Counseling about Conflict Resolution and Life Skills **H/I/S:** Reading, Playing Basketball, Tennis and Chess **EDU:** Bachelor of Arts in Human Services, Antioch University (1987) **A/A/S:** National Association of Blacks in Criminal Justice; Blacks in Social Work; National Association for the Advancement of Colored People **A/H:** Congressional Medal of Distinction, The Republican Party (2008); Community Service Award, National Association of Blacks in Criminal Justice (2007); Governor's Award, Community Engagement (2005) **C/VW:** Volunteer, Universal Negro Improvement Association; AARP
Email: anthony.murphy@phila.gov
URL: http://www.phila.gov/townwatch

Clara Reyes Murphy

Title: Sales Manager **Company:** United Healthcare **Address:** 4050 Rio Bravo Boulevard, El Paso, TX 79902 United States **BUS:** Insurance Company **P/S:** Managed Care, Health Insurance **MA:** International **D/D/R:** Explaining Benefits to Medicare-Eligible Patients, Managing Sales **H/I/S:** Motorcycling **EDU:** Associate Degree in Business Technology, University of New Mexico **A/A/S:** National Association of Health Underwriters; National Association of Insurance and Financial Advisors **C/VW:** Susan G. Komen Breast Cancer Foundation, Holy Cross Catholic Church
Email: murphyclarita@comcast.net
URL: http://www.cambridgewhoswho.com

Eunice C. Murphy

Title: President **Company:** Kidz World Child Care Inc **Address:** 94 Hillside Avenue, Mt Vernon, NY 10553 United States **BUS:** Social Services Social Services: Childcare **P/S:** Child Care and Foster Care **MA:** Local **EXP:** Ms. Murphy's expertise is in child development. **H/I/S:** Church, Casinos, Bowling **EDU:** Westchester Business Institute, Associate Degree in Secretarial Studies
Email: eunice1945@verizon.net

Linda D. Murphy

Title: Manager **Company:** Whee Care II **Address:** 2419 Ramblewood Drive, District Heights, MD 20747 United States **BUS:** Healthcare **P/S:** Assisting Care for Seniors, Residential Care, Long Term Care, At-Home Nursing **MA:** Local **D/D/R:** Caring for the Elderly **H/I/S:** Reading, Cooking, Singing in Church Choir **EDU:** Coursework, Basic Computer, Prince George's Community College **A/A/S:** Red Hot Society; Veterans Administration; Adelphy Nursing Home; Medicaid for Maryland Waiver Program
Email: murphlind@yahoo.com

Mercedes C. Murphy, JD

Title: Senior Trial Attorney **Company:** Seventh Judicial District Attorney's Office **Address:** 855 Van Patten Street, Truth or Consequences, NM 87901 United States **BUS:** Law Firm **P/S:** Legal Services Including Litigation for Criminal Law Cases **MA:** International **EXP:** Ms. Murphy's expertise is in criminal prosecution. **H/I/S:** Reading **EDU:** JD, Oklahoma City University **A/A/S:** Prosecutors' Division; New Mexico State Bar Association; American Bar Association; Phi Alpha Delta
Email: mmurphy@da.state-nm.us
URL: http://www.cambridgewhoswho.com

Shawn Murphy

Title: Civil Engineer **Company:** HNTB Corporation **Address:** 111 North Canal Street, Suite 1250, Chicago, IL 60606 United States **BUS:** Civil Engineering
Email: sjmurphy@hntb.com

Donna G. Murray
Title: Physical Education Teacher **Company:** Broken Arrow Elementary School **Address:** 4300 S. Juniper Place, Broken Arrow, OK 74011 United States **BUS:** Elementary School **P/S:** Primary Education **MA:** Regional **D/D/R:** Teaching Adaptive Physical Education and Regular Physical Education for Kindergarten through Fifth-Grade Students **H/I/S:** Practicing Tae Kwon Do, Fishing, Golfing **EDU:** Bachelor of Science in Physical Education, Northeastern University (1984) **A/A/S:** Texas Association for Health, Physical Education, Recreation, and Dance
Email: dmurray@baschools.org
URL: http://www.baschools.org

Judi Murray
Title: Teacher **Company:** Beaumont Unified School District **Address:** 500 Grace Avenue, Beaumont, CA 92223 United States **BUS:** School **P/S:** Education **MA:** Local **D/D/R:** Teaching Mathematics, Mentoring Other Teachers **H/I/S:** Reading, Singing, Spending Time with her Son **EDU:** Master of Arts in Administration, Azusa Pacific University, California **A/A/S:** Delta Kappa Gamma; Who's Who Among American Teachers **A/H:** District Teacher of the Year, 2006-2007 **C/VW:** Local Church
Email: tjbmurray@verizon.net
URL: http://www.jmurray.k12.ca.us

Mary K. Murray, MD
Title: Breast Surgical Oncologist, MD **Company:** Mary K. Murray **Address:** 3925 Embassy Parkway, Suite 275, Akron, OH 44333 United States **BUS:** Private Practice Committed to Excellence in Healthcare **P/S:** Breast Cancer Oncologist **MA:** Regional **D/D/R:** Practicing Breast Surgical Oncology, Working with Patients with a Family History and/or High Risk of the Disease, Taking Preventative Measures and Referrals from Primary Care Physicians **EDU:** General Surgery, Wright State Medical University (1998) **A/A/S:** American Society of Breast Disease; Society of Breast Surgery; Society of Oncologists, Fellowships and Surgeons
Email: drmkmurray@yahoo.com
URL: http://www.marykmurraymd.com

Reinette Powers Murray
Title: Registered Nurse, Assistant Professor of Nursing **Company:** Lake Superior State University **Address:** 650 W. Easterday Avenue, Sault Ste. Marie, MI 49783 United States **BUS:** University **P/S:** Education **MA:** National **D/D/R:** Emergency Room Nursing, Consulting, Offering End-of-Life Care **H/I/S:** Boating, Reading **EDU:** Master of Science in Nursing, Eastern Michigan University **A/A/S:** Sigma Theta Tau; Michigan League of Nurses; Speaker, Palliative Care International Symposium, Naples **C/VW:** Church
Email: lucy48154@yahoo.com
URL: http://www.cambridgewhoswho.com

Trudy J. Murray, RECS
Title: Realtor **Company:** Illustrated Properties Real Estate, Inc **Address:** 300 W. Indian Town Road, Jupiter, FL 33458 United States **BUS:** Real Estate Broker **P/S:** Residential, Executive Homes, Water Front, Condos, Town Homes, Gulf Homes, New Construction, Gated **MA:** National **D/D/R:** Specializing in Waterfront Properties, Golf Club Community Homes, condos, single family homes, Estate homes **H/I/S:** Golf, Boating **EDU:** Columbia College, Liberal Arts **A/A/S:** Florida Association of Realtors, National Association of Realtors, Christies greater estates
Email: tmur3225@bellsouth.net
URL: www.trudymurray.com

Tara Murrow
Title: Third-Grade Teacher **Company:** Tommy's Road Elementary School **Address:** 211 Ashby Lane, Goldsboro, NC 27530 United States **BUS:** Public School **P/S:** Regular Elementary Curriculum **MA:** Local **D/D/R:** Teaching All Subjects to Third-Grade Students **H/I/S:** Spending Time with her Three Children, Outdoor Activities, Doing Crafts **EDU:** College Coursework in Elementary Education, University of Florida (1994)
Email: jtmurrow@nc.rr.com

Mr. James B. Murtland III
Title: Vice President, Chief Financial Officer **Company:** Sloan Trends **Address:** 2958 Sunset Hills, Escondido, CA 92025 United States **BUS:** Research Firm **P/S:** Researching on Food and Beverages **MA:** National **EXP:** Mr. Murtland's expertise is in finance management. **D/D/R:** Overseeing Treasury, Processing Payroll, Managing Finance, Overseeing Industrial Engineering **H/I/S:** Boating, Flying Airplanes **EDU:** Master of Science in Advanced Management, National University; Bachelor of Science, Central Naval Academy **A/A/S:** Adjunct Professor, Accounting and Finance, University of Phoenix; Director, Southern California Yachting Association **C/VW:** Vestry, Trinity Episcopal Church
Email: jimmurtland@aol.com
URL: http://www.sloantrend.com

Marla Jane Musil
Title: Elementary Educator **Company:** Wilber-Clatonia Public Schools **Address:** 900 S. Franklin, Wilber, NE 68465 United States **BUS:** Elementary School **P/S:** Education **MA:** Local **D/D/R:** Teaching First Grade **H/I/S:** Doing Needlework, Reading, Spending Time with Family **EDU:** Bachelor's Degree in Elementary Education, University of Nebraska-Lincoln **A/A/S:** National Education Association; Nebraska State Education Association; Eastern Nebraska Reading Council **C/VW:** Local Church
Email: stitchinmom3@gmail.com
URL: http://www.cambridgewhoswho.com

Kathleen Ann Musson
Title: Associate Executive Director **Company:** Oklahoma State Medical Association **Address:** 601 N.W. Grand Boulevard, Oklahoma City, OK 73118 United States **BUS:** Healthcare Facility **P/S:** Wide Range of Medical Services, Associates for Medical and Osteopathic Doctors Affiliated with American Medical Association **MA:** Regional **D/D/R:** Overseeing Operational Issues, Hiring and Firing, Conducting Employee Reviews, Training, Dealing with Computer Problems, Contacting and Overseeing Information Technology Professionals, Writing Promotional Materials, Overseeing the Administration of the Database, Managing the Conversions to New Programs **H/I/S:** Tracing her Genealogy, Studying Computer Technology **EDU:** Bachelor's Degree in Organizational Leadership, Southern Nazarene University (1984) **CERTS:** Certified Association Executive, American Society of Association Executives (2002) **A/A/S:** American Society of Association Executives; Oklahoma Society of Association Executives; Executive, American Medical Society
Email: musson@osmaonline.org
URL: http://www.okmed.com

Omar A. Mustafa
Title: Chief Executive Officer, Owner **Company:** Magnoon Trucking Service **Address:** 2700 Holme Avenue, Philadelphia, PA 19152 United States **BUS:** Transportation **P/S:** Trucking Services **MA:** Regional **D/D/R:** Supervising Managers, Overseeing Contracts and Deadlines **EDU:** Associate Degree in Business Administration, Jersey City State University (1982)
Email: omarmusta7@aol.com

Srisailas Muthialu
Title: Research Associate **Company:** Chem-Master International, Inc. **Address:** 460 Old Town Road, Apartment 28N, Port Jefferson Station, NY 11776 United States **BUS:** Research and Development Company **P/S:** Custom Synthesis, Process Development and Chemical Research for the Chemical, Pharmaceutical and Biotechnology Industries **MA:** International **D/D/R:** Conducting International Chemical Research Including Cancer Molecule Research, Analyzing Molecules, Research Data and Study Findings **EDU:** Doctorate in Organic Chemistry, Earned in India (2003) **A/A/S:** American Chemical Society
Email: msrisailas@yahoo.com
URL: http://www.chemmasterint.com

Albert M. Muzikar
Title: Manager **Company:** Consolidated Edison Company of New York **Address:** 4 Irving Place, New York, NY 10003 United States **BUS:** Electrical **P/S:** Electrical Services for the City of New York **MA:** Regional **EXP:** Mr. Muzikar's expertise includes human resources and customer services. **D/D/R:** Updating Health, Environmental and Safety Records **H/I/S:** Tennis **EDU:** Master of Business Administration, Fordham University (1971) **A/A/S:** Society for Human Resource Management; National Register of Who's Who
Email: almuzikar@aol.com

Anthony P. Myatt
Title: Judicial Assistant **Company:** Los Angeles Superior Court **Address:** 42011 Fourth Street W., Lancaster, CA 93535 United States **BUS:** Court **P/S:** Legal Services **MA:** Local **D/D/R:** Practicing Criminal Law, Offering Technical Support **EDU:** Bachelor's Degree in Music, University of Southern California (1976) **A/H:** Judicial Assistant of the Year (2006)
Email: tmyatt1@gmail.com

Connie L. Myers
Title: Unit Leader **Company:** Avon **Address:** 4526 Yackey Drive N.W., Strasburg, OH 44680 United States **BUS:** Distribution Firm **P/S:** Cosmetics, Skin Care, Beauty and Body Products, Jewelry, Clothes for Women and Men **MA:** International **D/D/R:** Managing the Sale of Cosmetics, Beauty Products, Clothes and Shoes **H/I/S:** Playing Cards, Reading **EDU:** High School Education **A/A/S:** President's Club; Honor Society for Avon Sales; Dover Historical Society **C/VW:** Various Charitable Organizations; Elks Lodge
Email: myerscon57@roadrunner.com
URL: http://www.youravon.com

Jeffrey D. Myers
Title: Recreation Director **Company:** Town of Perinton **Dept:** Department of Recreation and Parks **Address:** 1350 Turk Hill Road, Fairport, NY 14450 United States **BUS:** Government Agency **P/S:** Recreational Activities and Facilities **MA:** Local **D/D/R:** Directing International Recreation Programs **H/I/S:** Golfing, Hiking, Spending Time in Adirondack Mountains **EDU:** Bachelor of Science in Recreation Management, SUNY Brockport **A/A/S:** Honorary Member, Rho Phi Lambda; Board Member, National Recreation and Park Association; Vice President, The New York State Recreation and Park Society; Executive Board Member, American Park and Recreation Society; Former President, Genesee Valley Recreation and Park Society **A/H:** Good Guy Award, New York State Recreation and Park Society (2005)
Email: jmyers@perinton.org
URL: http://www.perinton.org

Mary M. Myers
Title: Bookkeeper, Secretary **Company:** Chattahoochee Elementary School **Address:** 2800 Holtzclaw Road, Cumming, GA 30041 United States **BUS:** Elementary School **P/S:** Primary Education **MA:** Regional **EXP:** Ms. Myers' expertise is in bookkeeping. **D/D/R:** Purchasing, Laminating, Copying and Delivering Books **EDU:** Bachelor of Arts in Psychology, Minor in Sociology, University of West Georgia (1974) **A/A/S:** Treasurer, Relay for Life; Daughters of the American Revolution **C/VW:** Volunteer, Relay for Life
Email: mmyers@forsyth.k12.ga.us
URL: http://www.forsyth.k12.ga.us

Thomas Arthur Myers, OD
Title: Owner, OD **Company:** Myers Family Vision **Address:** 5208 E. Whitehall Lane, Colbert, WA 99005 United States **BUS:** Optometry Office **P/S:** Healthcare **MA:** Regional **D/D/R:** General Practice, Sees all Patients Including Children, Will Buy Larger Practice to Expand **H/I/S:** Fishing, Golf, Outdoor Sports **EDU:** Doctor of Optometry, Pacific University (2003) **A/A/S:** American Optometric Association
Email: myer1666@pacificu.edu
URL: http://www.pacificu.com

Walter L. Myles
Title: President **Company:** MYMC Holding and M&M Sports Wear, LLC **Address:** PO Box 4242, Baltimore, MD 21205 United States **BUS:** Finance, Banking, Credit Services **P/S:** Payroll Financing/Virtual Money, International Debt Care **MA:** International **D/D/R:** Accounting Business Finance and Management **H/I/S:** Travel **EDU:** University of Baltimore, BS Accounting, Master Agent for Virtual Money **A/A/S:** Alumni University of Baltimore, NABA, Phi Beta Sigma, On Board of Baltimore Freedom Academy
Email: wmyles03@cs.com

Jesus M. Nacanaynay
Title: Program Director **Company:** Integrated Living Services **Address:** 655 W. Smith Street, Suite 207, Northville, MI 48167 United States **BUS:** Healthcare Nonprofit **P/S:** Residential Care and Community Integration **MA:** Local **D/D/R:** Training and Education **H/I/S:** Reading, Running, Yoga, His Three Children **EDU:** Marquette University, St Louis University at Philippines, Master's Degree in Philosophy **A/A/S:** Holy Spirit Parish, AAPT
Email: dadhjr@yahoo.com

Marie G. Nadeau
Title: First Grade Teacher **Company:** West Broadway Elementary School **Address:** 29 Bainbridge Avenue, Providence, RI 02909 United States **BUS:** Public Elementary School **P/S:** Educating Students in Prekindergarten through Fifth-Grade, English as a Second Language, Special Education **MA:** Local **D/D/R:** Teaching Language Arts, Mathematics, Science, Social Studies and Reading Basics to First Grade Students **H/I/S:** Sewing, Walking **EDU:** Master's Degree in General Education, Rhode Island College (1988) **A/A/S:** Phi Delta Kappa; Union Delegate, American Federation of Teachers

Rosa M. Nagaishi, BS
Title: Academic Advisor, Science Coach **Company:** Urban Educational Partnership **Address:** 315 W. Ninth Street, Suite 110, Los Angeles, CA 90015 United States **BUS:** Consulting Firm **P/S:** Consulting Services for Professional Development for Teachers **MA:** Local **D/D/R:** Mentoring Elementary Teachers, Working with Students, Teaching Sewer Science Programs, Visiting the County High School Sanitation Department, Coaching Students on Chemistry and Physical Science **H/I/S:** Gardening, Spending Time with her Grandson **EDU:** Bachelor of Science in Chemistry, University of San Diego **A/A/S:** Board Member, Greater Los Angeles Science Teachers' Association; National Science Teachers Association
Email: tjmini281@yahoo.com
URL: http://www.targetscience.org

Herbert S. Nagy Sr.
Title: President **Company:** H.S. Nagy & Associates, Inc. **Address:** 676 S.E. Bayberry Lane, Suite 102, Lee's Summit, MO 64063 United States **BUS:** Manufacturing and Distribution Company for Food, Chemical and Pharmaceutical Industries **P/S:** Material Handling and Processing Equipment Including Mills, Sifters, Pneumatic Systems, Mechanical Conveying Systems **MA:** Regional **D/D/R:** Representing Food, Chemical and Pharmaceutical Companies, Regional Automobile Traveling to Meet Customers' Needs and Goals, Managing Employees **H/I/S:** Horseback Riding **EDU:** Coursework in Mechanical Engineering (1963-1965) **A/A/S:** Former Member, MANNA **A/H:** Top Sales Group for Williams W. Myers & Sons (2000)
Email: hsnagy@sbcglobal.net
URL: http://www.hsnagy.com

Phyllis S. Naiad
Title: Senior Field Representative **Company:** Washington Federation of State Employees Council 28 AFSCME **Address:** Hawthorne Court, Suite 308, 16710 Smokey Point Boulevard, Arlington, WA 98223 United States **BUS:** Government Agency **P/S:** Council Representation for the State of Washington **MA:** Regional **D/D/R:** Negotiating Contracts Between the Union and the Employees, Overseeing Relocations, Handling Higher Level Duties, Following up on Unfair Labor Practices, Training on Diversity and Gay and Lesbian Issues in the Workplace **H/I/S:** Playing Softball, Avid Motorcycle Rider **EDU:** Coursework in Police Science Administration and Foreign Language
Email: psntyche@aol.com

John Kirk Nail
Title: Area Manager **Company:** The CIT Group, Inc., Home Lending Division **Address:** 1540 W. Fountainhead Parkway, Tempe, AZ 85282 United States **BUS:** Financial Services Company **P/S:** Financial Services **MA:** International **D/D/R:** Sales, Marketing, Tactical Thinking, Executive Management **H/I/S:** Traveling, Attending NFL Events, Hiking, Camping, Golfing, Writing, Listening to Jazz, Spending Time with his Fiancée **EDU:** Master of Business Administration, Colorado State University **A/A/S:** Arizona Association of Mortgage Brokers; National Association of Mortgage Brokers; Masonic Fraternity; Scottish Rite Foundation; American Management Association; Sigma Iota Epsilon **C/VW:** Masonic Fraternity, Scottish Rite Foundation
Email: naileman@hotmail.com
URL: http://www.cit.com

Raymond D. Nalls
Title: President **Company:** Integrity Limousine Service **Address:** 9154 S. Laflin Street, Chicago, IL 60620 United States **BUS:** Transportation Company **P/S:** Ground Transportation **MA:** Regional **D/D/R:** Transporting People to and from Airports, Hotels and Private and Corporate Events **H/I/S:** Golfing, Fishing, Traveling **CERTS:** Licensed Chauffeur **C/VW:** Monument of Faith Evangelistic Church
Email: integritylimousine@att.net

Sanya Namboun
Title: Teacher **Company:** Garvey School District **Address:** 2730 Delmar Avenue, Rosemead, CA 91770 United States **BUS:** Public School System **P/S:** Primary and Secondary Level Education to a Multicultural and Diverse Student Population **MA:** Regional **D/D/R:** Molding Students in Kindergarten through Fourth-Grades for the Future, Teaching Speech-Language Education **H/I/S:** Crocheting **EDU:** Bachelor of Arts, Emphasis on Psychology and Education, University of California at Riverside (1995) **A/A/S:** Riverside Alumni Association; Garvey Education Association K-3 Representative for the District
Email: sanyan@garvey.k12.ca.us
URL: http://www.garvey.k12.ca.us

Leanne M. Nantais-Smith, Ph.D., NNP, RNC
Title: Clinical Assistant Professor **Company:** Wayne State University **Dept:** College of Nursing **Address:** 5777 Cass Avenue, Detroit, MI 48202 United States **BUS:** University **P/S:** Education, Neonatal Nurse Practitioner Programs **MA:** National **D/D/R:** Teaching, Coordinating Programs, Running Neonatal Nurse Practitioner Clinical Practice **H/I/S:** Playing the Harp **EDU:** Ph.D. in Nursing, Wayne State University; Master's Degree in Nursing, Wayne State University; Master's Degree in Russian Language and Literature, Michigan State University; Bachelor's Degree in Nursing, Michigan State University **A/A/S:** Sigma Theta Tau; Adjunct Professor, Department of Pediatrics and Human Development College of Human Medicine, Michigan State University; Neonatal Nurse Practitioner, Sparrow Hospital, Lansing, MI; Michigan Association of Neonatal Practitioners; Michigan Nurses Association; Florida Association of Neonatal Practitioners
Email: ar2446@wayne.edu

Margaret E. Napier
Title: President **Company:** Rev. Dr. Frank Napier, Jr. Memorial Scholarship Fund **Address:** P. O. Box 552, Paterson, NJ 07524 United States **BUS:** Nonprofit Community Charitable Organization **P/S:** Funding for College, Scholarships **MA:** Local **D/D/R:** Running the Organization, Helping Students of Three High Schools in Paterson, NJ **H/I/S:** Learning to Crochet, Vacationing in Hawaii and Africa **CERTS:** Certificate, MTI Business School

Tanya Napoli
Title: Teacher, Literacy Coach **Company:** Department of Education **Address:** 320 Manhattan Avenue, Brooklyn, NY 11211 United States **BUS:** Public Education **P/S:** Teaching and Counseling **MA:** Regional **D/D/R:** Working as a Literary Coach, Reading, Writing, Overseeing the Resource Room, Teaching Prekindergarten through Fifth-Grade Students, Training **H/I/S:** Scrapbooking, Spending Time Creating Albums of her Loved Ones, Friends and Students **EDU:** Master's Degree in Literacy, University of New England (2004) **CERTS:** Certified in Prekindergarten through Sixth-Grade
Email: teenteacher@aol.com
URL: http://www.schools.nyc.gov

Chandana Narayan, LEED AP
Title: Principal **Company:** Danalika LLC **Address:** 4139 Park Lane, Dallas, TX 75220 United States **BUS:** Interior Design Company **P/S:** Interior Design **MA:** International **EXP:** Ms. Narayan's expertise includes interior design for commercial and healthcare facilities. **H/I/S:** Playing Tennis, Playing the Piano, Photography, Physical Fitness **EDU:** Bachelor's Degree in Interior Design, The University of Oklahoma **A/A/S:** Texas Board of Architectural Examiners; National Council for Interior Design Qualifications; United States Green Building Council; International Interior Design Association **C/VW:** UNICEF
Email: cn@danalika.com
URL: http://www.cambridgewhoswho.com

Mr. Stephen E. Narigon
Title: President **Company:** Nexxus Healthcare Services **Address:** 101 Cherokee Drive, Thomasville, NC 27360 United States **BUS:** Medical Staffing Company **P/S:** Temporary Nursing Services, Supplemental Nursing Services **MA:** National **D/D/R:** Travel Nursing Industry, Contract With Hospitals And Sends in Temporary Nurses Nationally, Oversees Staff of 40 Nurses, **H/I/S:** Riding Motorcycles, Spending Time with his Son and Family **EDU:** Bachelor of Arts in General Studies, Oklahoma University (1993); Associate Degree in Nursing, Oklahoma University (1995); Pursuing Nurse Practitioner, University of North Carolina, Greensboro **A/A/S:** ASA **C/VW:** Church, Pentecostal
Email: snarigon@nexxushealth.com
URL: http://www.nexxushealth.com

Susan R. Nasir, MS, PT
Title: Director of Therapy Services **Company:** Saint Elias Specialty Hospital **Address:** 4800 Cordova Street, Anchorage, AK 99503 United States **BUS:** Hospital **P/S:** Healthcare, Physical Therapy, Cardiopulmonary and Rehabilitation Programs, Wound and Infectious Disease Care **MA:** Regional **D/D/R:** Assisting with Patient Care, Maintaining Policies and Procedures, Hiring, Firing, Acting as a Liaison between Doctors, Patients and their Families, Offering Acute Care Therapies **H/I/S:** Spending Time Outdoors **EDU:** Master of Arts in Science, Florida International University (1978) **A/A/S:** American Physical Therapy Association
Email: sklein@st-eliashospital.com
URL: http://www.st-eliashospital.com

Sylvia A. Natale, M.Ed.
Title: Elementary School Principal (Retired) **Company:** Woonsocket Education Department **Dept:** Governor Aram J. Pothier Elementary School **Address:** 54 Lewis Street, N. Providence, RI 02904 United States **BUS:** Public Elementary School **P/S:** Primary Education for Local Primary and Intermediate Level Students **MA:** Regional **D/D/R:** Teaching Behavior and Education Leadership, Supervising After-School Programs and Remedial Programs for Failing Schools, Ensuring Literacy-Based Programs **H/I/S:** Traveling, Dancing **EDU:** Master of Arts in Education, Concentration in English as a Second Language; Master of Arts in Administration of Education; Bachelor's Degree in Psychology and Elementary Education, Rhode Island College (1978)
URL: http://www.cambridgewhoswho.com

Bethanna Nation-Graves
Title: Registered Nurse **Company:** HCA Bayshore Medical Center **Dept:** Radiation Therapy **Address:** 4000 Spencer Highway, Pasadena, TX 77504 United States **BUS:** Hospital **P/S:** Healthcare **MA:** Local **EXP:** Ms. Nation-Graves' expertise is in radiation oncology nursing. **H/I/S:** Singing, Making Crafts, Reading **EDU:** Associate Degree in Nursing, Houston Community College (1983) **A/A/S:** Administrative Counsel **C/VW:** Holy Trinity United Methodist Church
Email: bng-gly@sbcglobal.net
URL: http://www.bayshoremedical.com

Dolores M. Navarro
Title: Guidance Counselor **Company:** Stockton Unified School District **Address:** 701 N. Madison Street, Stockton, CA 95204 United States **BUS:** School District **P/S:** Education **MA:** Local **D/D/R:** Guidance Counseling **H/I/S:** Reading, Hiking, Gardening **EDU:** Master's Degree in Social Work, Sacramento State University; Licensed Clinical Social Worker, Board of Behavioral Sciences, State of California; People Personnel Services Credential, Sacramento State University; Secondary Teaching Credentials in History, University of the Pacific **A/A/S:** American Association of University Women; People to People Ambassador's Program; Delegate, United States Education Conference **C/VW:** Eucharistic Minister; Catholic Church; Seminarian Sponsor, India
Email: 2prieta@comcast.net
URL: http://www.cambridgewhoswho.com

Ramon L. Navarro, CRNA
Title: Staff Nurse Anesthetist **Company:** D.W. Mcmillan Memorial Hospital **Dept:** Anesthesia **Address:** 1301 Bellville Avenue, Brewton, AL 36426 United States **BUS:** Hospital **P/S:** Healthcare **MA:** Local **D/D/R:** Specializing in Anesthesia **EDU:** Diploma in Nursing Anesthesia, The University of Tennessee, Knoxville **A/A/S:** American Association of Nurse Anesthetists
Email: ramon.navarro@cwwemail.com

Barbara L. Naydeck, MPH
Title: Senior Analyst **Company:** Regence Blue Cross Blue Shield **Dept:** Healthcare Informatics **Address:** 200 S.W. Market Street, Mail Stop E10C, Portland, OR 97201 United States **BUS:** Healthcare Insurer **P/S:** Healthcare Insurance **MA:** National **H/I/S:** Enjoying Music, Singing and Piano, Snow Skiing, Fly-fishing with Husband, Jewelry Collecting, Reading **EDU:** Bachelor's Degree in Economics, University of Pittsburgh (1985); Master's Degree in Public Health and Epidemiology, University of Pittsburgh (1995)
Email: bnaydeck@yahoo.com
URL: http://www.highmark.com

Michael Beth Nazimek
Title: President, Owner **Company:** Nazimek Appraisal Services, Inc. **Address:** 210 E. Broadway, Apartment 6F, Long Beach, NY 11561 United States **BUS:** Appraising and Consulting Company **P/S:** Real Estate Appraisals **MA:** Statewide **D/D/R:** Working as a Real Estate Appraisal Specialist, Offering Residential Real Estate Services **H/I/S:** Baseball, Volleyball **EDU:** Bachelor of Business Administration, Adelphi University, 2000 **C/VW:** Children's Cancer Society
Email: mnaz21@optonline.net

Mr. James Michael Neal, RN, BS
Title: Registered Nurse Administrator **Company:** Surgicore, Inc. **Address:** 10547 S. Ewing Avenue, Chicago, IL 60617 United States **BUS:** Ambulatory Surgery Center **P/S:** Outpatient Podiatry Center Specializing in Foot and Ankle Surgery **MA:** Local **EXP:** Mr. Neal's expertise includes nursing administration, and the organization and development of outpatient surgery centers. **D/D/R:** In-Service Training of Employees, Updating the Staff on Changes in the Industry, Processing Payroll, Overseeing Patient Admission and Discharge, Ensuring Doctor and Facility Compliance with State Credential Regulations **H/I/S:** Singing, Riding Bicycles **EDU:** Bachelor of Science in Health Administration, University of St. Francis (2004); Associate Degree in Nursing, Truman College **CERTS:** Registered Nurse Administrator **A/A/S:** Association of Operating Room Nurses
Email: jmikl@sbcglobal.net
URL: http://www.cambridgewhoswho.com

Sheila A. Neal
Title: Teacher, Coach **Company:** Central Junior High School **Address:** 2811 W. Huntsville Avenue, Springdale, AR 72762 United States **BUS:** School **P/S:** Learning Institution **MA:** Local **D/D/R:** Teaching **H/I/S:** Golfing, Handicapped Children **EDU:** Bachelor of Arts Plus 15 in Education, University of Tulsa **C/VW:** Salvation Army, Christmas Angel
Email: sneal@sdale.org

Mr. Tim Neary, BSW
Title: Manager **Company:** Club Q **Address:** 1213 S. Sixth Street W., Missoula, MT 59801 United States **BUS:** LGBT, Alternative Night Club. Open on Saturday Nights. Dance Music, Smoke-Free Bar and Dance Club, Drink Specials, Adjacent Smoking Lounge, Sharp Sound System and Brilliant Light-Show! Theme Nights, Community Spot-Nights and Shows (Live Concerts and Drag Functions). Hours: 9pm-2am Admission: Free: 21 and Up $5: 18-20 yrs. **P/S:** Entertainment. Dance Club Atmosphere. Live Concerts featuring LGBT Musicians. **MA:** Statewide **D/D/R:** Facilitating Gay/Lesbian Events on a Weekend Basis, Organizing Dances, Themed Parties and Community Events, Assisting in the Planning of the State Gay PRIDE Event **H/I/S:** Music, Traveling, Attending University of Montana Grizzly Football games. **EDU:** Bachelor of Social Work, University of Montana (1991) **A/A/S:** Board of Directors, Volunteer Coordinator, Western MT. Gay & Lesbian Community Center Treasurer; Elks Lodge Imperial Sovereign Court of the State of Montana; Gay PRIDE Planning Committee
Email: clubqtm@hotmail.com
URL: http://www.myspace.com/clubq1

Josephine Eli Ned
Title: Elementary Teacher Company: St. Francis of Assisi School Address: 5100 Dabney Street, Houston, TX 77026 United States BUS: Catholic School P/S: Education MA: Local D/D/R: Early Childhood Education, Teaching All Subjects to First and Second-Grade Students, Teaching English as a Second Language H/I/S: Horseback Riding, Playing Tennis EDU: Master's Degree in Education, University of Louisiana at Lafayette A/A/S: National Catholic Educational Association; Texas Education Association C/VW: Mothers Against Drunk Driving
Email: elighdun@aol.com

Robert T. Nees
Title: General Manager Company: Sunset Manufacturing Company Address: P.O. Box 308, Tualatin, OR 97062 BUS: Manufacturing Company P/S: Machined Parts MA: National EXP: Mr. Nees' expertise includes operations, customer relations and management. H/I/S: Skiing, Golfing, Spending Time with Family EDU: Bachelor's Degree in Psychology, University of Oregon A/A/S: Society of Manufacturing Engineers; Northwest High Performance Enterprise Consortium C/VW: Various Charitable Organizations
Email: robn@sunsetcorp.com
URL: http://www.sunsetcorp.com

Sheryl L. Neff
Title: Gifted and Talented Education Program Facilitator Company: Clark County School District Dept: Gifted and Talented Program Address: 2625 E. Saint Louis Avenue, Las Vegas, NV 89104 United States BUS: School District P/S: Education MA: Clark County, NV D/D/R: Identifying Minority Gifted Students H/I/S: Spending Time with her Four Horses, Rescuing South American Birds with her Husband, Playing the Harp, Spinning and Weaving EDU: Master's Degree in Educational Administration and Supervision, University of Phoenix A/A/S: National Association of Government Employees; Association for Supervision and Curriculum Development C/VW: Christian Organizations
Email: sheryl_l_neff@interact.ecsd.net

Trista M. Negele
Title: Plastic Surgeon, Owner Company: Aesthetic Profiles Address: 800 Biesterfield Road, Suite 2004, Elk Grove Village, IL 60007 United States BUS: Plastic Surgery Center P/S: Plastic Surgery MA: Local D/D/R: Performing Cosmetic and Reconstructive Surgery, Specializing in Breast Reconstruction H/I/S: Traveling, Speaking in Spanish EDU: MD, University of Missouri A/A/S: Candidate Association Women's' of Surgeon (AWS); American Medical Association; Illinois Medical Society
Email: drtrista@aol.com
URL: http://www.cambridgewhoswho.com

Janet S. Neice
Title: Registered Nurse, CTL, Preceptor Company: Carilion Giles Memorial Hospital Address: 1 Taylor Avenue, Pearisburg, VA 24134 United States BUS: Critical Assess Hospital P/S: Healthcare, Rehabilitation MA: Local EXP: Ms. Neice's expertise is in administration. D/D/R: Clinical Nursing, Offering Bedside Care H/I/S: Horseback Riding, Riding her Harley-Davidson EDU: Associate Degree in Nursing, Regents University CERTS: National Nursing Certification, 2003 A/A/S: American Nurses Association C/VW: Veterans of Foreign Wars Ladies Auxiliary
Email: luvmyhuggr@yahoo.com

Michele Neiman
Title: Director of Human Resources Company: Northrop Grumman IT Dept: Human Resources Address: 4805 Stonecroft Boulevard, Chantilly, VA 20151 United States BUS: Information Technology P/S: Planning and Implementing Information Technology Solutions in Order for Companies to Grow or Overcome Common Business Challenges MA: International D/D/R: Planning Strategic Business Operations, Recruiting and Staffing Personnel for a Company with More Than 5,000 Employees EDU: Bachelor of Science in Social Work, University of North Carolina, Greensboro, North Carolina (1997) CERTS: Certified SPHR, PHR, Human Resources Certification Institute A/A/S: Society of Women Engineers; Society for Human Resource Management
Email: michele.neiman@ngc.com
URL: http://www.it.northrupgrumman.co/itcareers.html149257

Russ Nelms
Title: Salesman Company: Caldwell Banker, Commercial, NRT Address: 2690 E. Main Street, Saint Charles, IL 60174 United States BUS: Real Estate Company P/S: Real Estate MA: National D/D/R: Mr. Nelms' expertise includes land acquisition, assemblage, and the sale and purchase of vacant land. H/I/S: Golfing, Hunting, Skiing, Spending Time at the Lake, Spending Time with his Five Children EDU: Accredited Land Consultant A/A/S: Realtors Land Institute; National Association of Realtors
Email: russ.nelms@cbexchange.com
URL: http://www.russnelms.com

Betty Nelson
Title: Owner, President Company: N2 Granite, Inc. Address: 127-C Cedar Pointe Drive, Mooresville, NC 28117 United States BUS: Fabrication P/S: Natural Stone Surfaces MA: Regional D/D/R: Selling, Fabricating and Installing Natural Stone Counter Tops and Other Products H/I/S: Horseback Riding, ATV Riding EDU: High School Diploma A/A/S: Mooresville Chamber of Commerce; Lake Norman Home Builders Association; Women's Council Association A/H: Best of the Lake Design Competition, 2006; Awards Winners of Homearama, 2006 C/VW: Olivet Baptist Church, Community Free Clinic, Camp Care/Children with Cancer
Email: bettynelson@n2granite.com
URL: http://www.n2granite.com

Gale Nelson
Title: Classroom Instructor Company: Mira Costa College Address: 1 Barnard Drive, Oceanside, CA 92056 United States BUS: College P/S: Higher Education MA: Regional D/D/R: Teaching Kindergarten to 12th-Grade Students, Conducting Computer Classes for Undergraduates, Teaching Web Page Design H/I/S: Fishing, Photography EDU: Master of Science in Education Technology, National University (1997)
Email: headache17@hotmail.com

James W. Nelson Jr.
Title: Generation Engineer Company: Tucson Electric Power Address: P.O. Box 2222, Springerville, AZ 85938 United States BUS: Electrical Utility Company P/S: Electricity, Engineering MA: Local EXP: Mr. Nelson's expertise includes civil engineering, construction and management. H/I/S: Watching and Playing Sports EDU: Bachelor of Science, Arizona State University (1998) A/A/S: American Society of Civil Engineers; American Concrete Institute
Email: jnelson@tep.com
URL: http://www.tep.com

John B. Nelson
Title: President, Chief Executive Officer Company: Media Marketing Services, Inc. Address: 31 Highway 12, Flemington, NJ 08822 United States BUS: Target Marketing for the Medical Field P/S: Micro Marketing Program, Sales Promotional Program MA: National D/D/R: Creating Targeted Marketing Programs for Pharmaceutical Physicians and Doctors with Educational Based Products H/I/S: Golfing, Scuba Diving, Running EDU: Bachelor of Arts in Psychology, Minor in Business, East Carolina University (1976) A/A/S: Healthcare Marketing and Communications Council
Email: jnelson@mediamarketingservices.com
URL: http://www.mediamarketingservices.com

Kathy L. Nelson
Title: Kindergarten Teacher Company: Southwest Calloway Elementary School Address: 3345 Sid Darnall Road, Benton, KY 42025 United States BUS: Elementary School P/S: Primary Education MA: Local D/D/R: Overseeing Textbook Procurement and Distribution, Working with Parent-Teacher Association Executive Board and Social Committee, Developing Curriculum, Supervising Student and Practicum Teachers, Teaching Beginning-Level Reading to Kindergarten Students H/I/S: Scuba Diving, Skiing EDU: Master's Degree in Elementary Education, Murray State University (1982); Bachelor of Fine Arts in Music, Murray State University (1974) CERTS: Rank 1 Certification in Primary Education, Murray State University (1994) A/A/S: Kentucky Education Association; National Education Association
Email: bnkn@wk.net
URL: http://www.calloway.k12.ky.us/Schools/southwest/southwestelementary.html

Kimberly S. Nelson
Title: Program Supervisor Company: Four Rivers Special Education District Address: 936 W. Michigan Avenue, Jacksonville, IL 62650 United States BUS: School District P/S: Special Education Program for 20 Districts MA: Regional D/D/R: Teaching Students with Autism H/I/S: Spending Time with her Family, Playing Volleyball, Attending her Children's Sporting Events EDU: Bachelor of Arts Plus 12 in EMH,TMH and Levels of Autism, Illinois State University CERTS: Certification in Physically and Mentally Handicapped; Trainer in Non-Violent Crisis Intervention, Crisis Prevention Institute; LBSI Certified A/A/S: Bill Russell Award for Bringing Technology into the Classroom C/VW: Special Olympics
Email: knelson@frsed.org

Lois A. Nelson
Title: Guidance Counselor Company: U.S. Air Force Dept: 5 Mission Support Squadron Address: 210 Missile Avenue, Minot Air Force Base, ND 58705 United States BUS: Government Agency P/S: Defense MA: National D/D/R: Counseling, Overseeing the Career Track Assistance Program, Performing Cliff Exam Assistance and Personality Testing H/I/S: Oil Painting, Volunteering EDU: Pursuing Master's Degree in Psychology Counseling, Liberty University, Lynchburg, VA; Bachelor of Arts in Psychology, Minot State University, ND (1981) A/H: Professional of the Year Award, Association for Counselors and Educators in Government (2007) C/VW: Air Force Aid Society; The Humane Society
Email: lois.nelson@minot.af.mil
URL: http://www.airforce.com

Matthew J. Nelson, MD
Title: MD Company: Orthopedic Associations of Fargo Address: 2301 25th Street S., Fargo, ND 58103 United States BUS: Healthcare Surgeon P/S: Orthopedic Surgery MA: Local EXP: Dr. Nelson's expertise includes orthopedic surgery and sports medicine. H/I/S: Golf EDU: University of North Dakota and North Dakota State University, MD and BS
Email: MNelsen@orthofargo.com

Retha J. Nelson
Title: Contract Writer of Regulatory Affairs Company: Blue Cross Blue Shield Address: 3535 Blue Cross Road, Eagon, MN 55122 United States BUS: Health Insurance Provider P/S: Health Insurance MA: National D/D/R: Working as a Copywriter, Writing Contracts H/I/S: Painting, Playing the Piano, Singing EDU: Bachelor of Arts in Education, University of Wisconsin Eau Claire (1973) A/H: Life Works Volunteer Award, 2005 C/VW: Children's Miracle Network, Gillette Children's Hospital, The Arc
Email: retha_nelson@msn.com
URL: http://www.cambridgewhoswho.com

Sherry Nelson
Title: Business Owner, Proprietor Company: Mumbo Jumbo Antiques & Habe Dashery Address: 4206 N. Seventh Avenue, Phoenix, AZ 85013 United States BUS: Retail Store P/S: Antiques, Gifts MA: Local D/D/R: Selling Antiques and Furniture H/I/S: Riding her Harley-Davidson, Taking Care of Animals EDU: Coursework in Travel and Tourism A/A/S: Seventh Avenue Merchants Association C/VW: Humane Society of the United States; Arizona Humane Society; Best Friends Animal Society
Email: wildwestlady1031@msn.com

Todd E. Nelson
Title: Chief Executive Officer Company: Advanced Rehab & Sports Medicine Services Address: 135 N. Williamsburg Drive, Bloomington, IL 61704 United States BUS: Healthcare Company P/S: Physical, Occupational and Speech Therapy, Athletic Training MA: Central Illinois, Eastern Iowa EXP: Mr. Nelson's expertise is in administrative management. EDU: Bachelor of Arts in Accounting, Monmouth College, Illinois A/A/S: American Medical Association; Bloomington Chamber of Commerce C/VW: American Red Cross, Various Organizations Involving Children
Email: tnelson@advrehab.com
URL: http://www.advrehab.com

Hooshang Nematollahi
Title: Operating Room Manager Company: University Medical Center Address: 1501 N. Campbell Avenue, Tucson, AZ 85724 United States BUS: Teaching Hospital P/S: Healthcare MA: International EXP: Mr. Nematollahi's expertise includes periOperative care and management. H/I/S: Gardening, Hiking EDU: Master of Business Administration, Adelphi University; Bachelor of Science in Nursing, University of Arizona; Bachelor's Degree in Construction Management A/A/S: Association of periOperative Registered Nurses; Arizona Organizational Nurse Executives C/VW: American Diabetes Association
Email: hnematollahi@umcaz.edu
URL: http://www.cambridgewhoswho.com

Eugene A. Nenni
Title: Code Enforcement Company: Town of Lockport Address: 6560 Dysinger Road, Lockport, NY 14094 United States BUS: Municipal Code Enforcement P/S: Codes Regulations, Code Enforcement MA: Regional D/D/R: Supervising Staff, Enforcing Municipal State Regulations Regarding Material Laws, Zoning, Planning, Fire, Building Construction and Development H/I/S: Hunting, Jogging, Golf EDU: Two Years College Coursework in Liberal Arts, Genesee Community College A/A/S: New York State Building Code Council; Niagara Frontier Building Association; Western New York Fire Marshals
Email: building_inspector@elockport.com
URL: http://www.elockport.com

Denise J. Nesbitt
Title: General Music Teacher **Company:** Berkeley County Schools **Address:** 149 Bedington Road, Martinsburg, WV 25401 United States **BUS:** Music School **P/S:** Music Education **MA:** Local **D/D/R:** Music Education for Children, Opera Singing, Performing, Teaching from Prekindergarten through College **H/I/S:** Gardening, Photography, Traveling **EDU:** Master's Degree in Music Performance, University of Redland (1988); Master's Degree in Teaching, Marshall University (2006); Bachelor's Degree in Musicology, University of California, Santa Barbara (1978); Associate Degree in Computer Programming, Los Angeles Valley College (1983) **A/A/S:** Trainer, CATA (1986-1988)
Email: denise_nesbitt@hotmail.com

Ann Ness
Title: Primary Teacher, Technology Coordinator **Company:** Anchorage School District, Chugiak Elementary **Address:** 19932 Old Glenn Highway, Chugiak, AK 99567 United States **BUS:** Elementary School **P/S:** Education **MA:** Local **D/D/R:** Teaching a First Grade Spanish Immersion Class and Chat Team, Coordinating Technology Use **H/I/S:** Snow Machining, Fishing, Boating, Berry Picking, Snowshoeing, Motor Home Traveling, Reading, Sewing **EDU:** Bachelor of Science in Psychology, University of Washington; Bachelor of Education, University of Alaska; Master of Education Equivalent **A/A/S:** National Education Association; Alaska Education Association; Alaska Society for Technology in Education; International Society for Technology in Education **C/VW:** American Cancer Society, Relay for Life
Email: ayayan@mtaonline.net
URL: http://www.asdk12.org/home.asp?num=100842

Anke Neu
Title: Pharmacy Manager **Company:** CVS **Address:** 4320 26th Street W., Bradenton, FL 34212 United States **BUS:** Retail Pharmacy Chain **P/S:** Pharmaceuticals, Household Items, Cards, Groceries, Photograph Developing **MA:** National **D/D/R:** Managing the Pharmacy and All Staff, Consulting with Physicians and Educating Customers on Medications, Filling Prescriptions, Scheduling, Managing Paperwork and Inventory, Ordering **H/I/S:** Reading, Softball, Swimming **EDU:** Bachelor of Science in Pharmacy, Auburn University (1993) **A/A/S:** American Pharmacists Association; Florida Pharmacy Association
Email: aneu1@tampabay.rr.com
URL: http://www.walgreens.com

Alexis L. Neumann
Title: Executive Director of Institutional Advancement **Company:** Texas State Technical College, Waco **Dept:** Institutional Advancement **Address:** 3801 Campus Drive, Waco, TX 76705 United States **BUS:** Coeducational Two-Year Institution of Higher Education Offering Courses of Study in Technical Vocation Education **P/S:** One Hundred Technical Associate Degree and Certificate Programs, Extensive Hands-On Laboratory Experiences **MA:** Regional **D/D/R:** Overseeing Marketing, Recruiting, Network and Telecommunication Operations, Maintaining Program Compliance, Offering Database Services, Development and Fund Raising, Upholding the President's Vision **H/I/S:** Working, Farming, Research **EDU:** Actively Pursuing a Ph.D.; Master of Business Administration, Texas Tech University (2003); Bachelor of Science in Animal Science, Texas Tech University (1999) **A/A/S:** Alpha Phi; Local and National Lecturer; Published in Local Paper
Email: alexisneumann@tstc.edu
URL: http://www.waco.tstc.edu

Georgeann G. Neuzil
Title: Clinical Nurse Specialist **Company:** Twin Valley Behavioral Healthcare Organization **Address:** 2200 W. Broad Street, Columbus, OH 43223 United States **BUS:** Healthcare Organization **P/S:** Healthcare Including Psychiatric Behavioral Healthcare Services **MA:** Regional **D/D/R:** Psychiatric Mental Healthcare Nursing, Working with Substance Abuse and Mental Illness Patients **H/I/S:** Reading, Gardening, Traveling **EDU:** Master's Degree in Nursing, Ohio State University **A/A/S:** Ohio Nurses Association; American Psychiatric Nurses Association; Sigma Theta Tau **C/VW:** National Alliance on Mental Illness
Email: neuzilg@yahoo.com
URL: http://www.cambridgewhoswho.com

Barbara Jean Nevers Scott
Title: Program Manager for Dead and Hard of Hearing Program **Company:** Mt. Diablo Unified School District **Address:** 1936 Carlotta Drive, Concord, CA 94521 United States **BUS:** School District **P/S:** Education **MA:** Regional **D/D/R:** Overseeing Administrative Duties, Supervising Students, Teaching Special Education, Teaching Deaf students, Supervising Interpreters, Conducting Infant and Preschool Assessments, Managing Compliance, Meeting Parents **H/I/S:** Dancing, Sports, Exercising, Attending the Ballet and Modern Dance Shows **EDU:** Master of Arts in Administration, California State University, Hayward (1986); Master of Arts in Deaf Education, San Francisco State University (1971); Bachelor of Arts in Social Welfare, San Francisco State University
Email: barbarajean39@astound.net
URL: http://www.mdusd.k12.ca.us

Carrie L. Nevills, MS
Title: Network Relation Consultant **Company:** Anthem BlueCross BlueShield of MO **Address:** 1831 Chestnut Street, St. Louis, MO 63103 United States **BUS:** Largest Provider of Healthcare Benefits in Missouri **P/S:** Administers Health Plans for Individuals and Groups **MA:** Regional **D/D/R:** Working as a Liaison between Insurance and Provider Group, Resolving Issues, Conducting Presentations to Large Groups, Making Office Visits **H/I/S:** Antiquing **EDU:** Bachelor of Science in Healthcare Administration, Sterling College (1994)
Email: cnevills@healthlink.com
URL: http://www.bcbsmo.com

Kevin B. Newbern
Title: President, Owner, Chief Executive Officer **Company:** Premier Signs Inc **Address:** 236 Paddlewheel Drive, Florissant, MO 63033 United States **BUS:** Maintenance Construction **P/S:** Installation and Maintenance With Regard to Signs, Billboards and Large Building Wraps **MA:** Local **EXP:** Ms. Newbern's expertise includes construction and electrical work. **H/I/S:** Bass Fishing **EDU:** Studied in the Field of Business Construction and Technology **A/A/S:** IBEW Local 1
Email: kevinpremier@signsinc.com
URL: www.premiersignsinc.com

Angela Newman
Title: Chief Executive Officer, Owner **Company:** Wholesale Lighting & Design **Address:** 11211 Sorrento Valley Road, Suite H, San Diego, CA 92121 United States **BUS:** Retail Lighting Store **P/S:** Interior and Exterior Lighting Fixtures and Bulbs **MA:** National **D/D/R:** Consulting with Clients and Contractors, Overseeing the Distribution of Lighting Fixtures and Bulbs **H/I/S:** Spending Time with her Children **EDU:** College Coursework **A/A/S:** American Lighting Association **C/VW:** California Children's Services; AIDS Foundation, Houston
Email: info@wholesalelite.com
URL: http://www.wholesalelite.com

Jimmy L. Newman Sr.
Title: Security Officer **Company:** Independent Security **Address:** 19250 Slate Creek Drive, Walnut, CA 91789 United States **BUS:** Armed Security Company **P/S:** Armed Security for the Television and Film Industry **MA:** Regional **D/D/R:** Securing Movie Productions, Working with at risk incarcerated youth. **H/I/S:** Swimming, Playing Volleyball, Training his Dog **EDU:** Master of Science in Music Education, Minor in Mathematics, Science and Social Studies, Pepperdine University (1973) **A/A/S:** Past Member, National Education Association; Los Angeles County Association (1988); Past President, Los Angeles County Teachers Union **A/H:** California State Teacher Award (1990)
Email: jimmylnewmansr@yahoo.com

Marjorie Newsome
Title: Co Pastor **Company:** St Albans Gospel Assembly **Address:** 257-58 148 Road, Rosedale, NY 11422 United States **BUS:** Ministry Church **P/S:** A Gospel Church **MA:** Local **D/D/R:** Counseling for Married Couples and Adults **H/I/S:** Reading, Walking **A/A/S:** ACAC
Email: evornew@myown.com

Heather Blair Newton
Title: Special Education Teacher **Company:** Henry County Schools **Address:** 1201 Old Conyers Road, Stockbridge, GA 30281 United States **BUS:** School District **P/S:** Education **MA:** Local **D/D/R:** Teaching Special Education, Overseeing Special Education Department Activities, Mentoring Teachers **H/I/S:** Reading, Singing at the Choir **EDU:** Master's Degree in Early Childhood and Special Education, Georgia State University **A/A/S:** Council for Exceptional Children; Professional Association of Georgia Educators; Who's Who in American Teachers **A/H:** Teacher of the Year Award; Certificate of Merit for Outstanding Scholarship and Service **C/VW:** American Cancer Society
Email: blair25@charter.net

Valerie Ney
Title: President **Company:** Certified Editing, Inc. **Address:** 427 Dunaway Drive, Valrico, FL 33594 United States **BUS:** Consulting Company **P/S:** Editing, Writing Services, Publishing, CEI **MA:** National **D/D/R:** Editing, Working on Websites and Corporate Accounts in Business and Politics Areas, Delivering what Promised on Time, CEI, Academic, Grant Writing and Business editing **H/I/S:** Going on Vacation, Traveling **EDU:** Graduate Cum Laude, Society of Human Resource Managers; Bachelor's Degree in Human Resource Management and Political Science, Ottawa University (1998) **CERTS:** Certified Expert Rating (2006) **A/A/S:** Society of Human Resource Managers
Email: valerien@certifiedediting.com
URL: http://www.certifiedediting.com

Doris Ng
Title: Owner, Co-Founder **Company:** GingeRootz, LLC **Address:** 4837 N. Fuji Drive, Appleton, WI 54913 United States **BUS:** Restaurant **P/S:** Dining and Catering Services **MA:** Local **D/D/R:** Overseeing Business Operations, Supervising and Training 23 Employees, Staffing, Consulting with Partners **H/I/S:** Traveling **EDU:** Bachelor of Arts in Journalism, University of Wisconsin-Madison **A/A/S:** Young Professionals; Chamber of Commerce **A/H:** Count Me in Award (2008) **C/VW:** Go Red for Women; Local Church; Volunteer, Local Charitable Organizations
Email: doris@gingerootz.com
URL: http://www.gingerootz.com

Lisa Vo Nguyen
Title: Dentist **Company:** Children's Dental Group **Address:** 2156 E. Lincoln Avenue, Anaheim, CA 92806 United States **BUS:** Pediatric Specialty Dental Office **P/S:** Healthcare **MA:** Regional **EXP:** Dr. Nguyen's expertise is in pediatric dentistry. **H/I/S:** Learning Languages, Traveling, Photography, Reading, Investing, Cooking, Interior Design, Healthy Living, Spending Time with her Family **EDU:** Doctor of Dental Surgery, University of California at San Francisco, 2004; Bachelor of Science in Biological Sciences, University of Irvine, 2000 **CERTS:** Certification in Dentistry, 2004 **A/A/S:** American Dental Association; California Dental Association; Orange County Dental Society; AAPD
Email: drlisa13@gmail.com
URL: http://www.childrensdentalgroup.com

Oanh N. Nguyen
Title: Pharmacy Manager **Company:** Rite Aid Pharmacy **Address:** 1035 E. Capitol Express Way, San Jose, CA 95121 United States **BUS:** Pharmaceuticals Pharmacy **P/S:** Pharmacy **MA:** National **D/D/R:** Working as a Pharmacist **H/I/S:** Jogging, Swimming **EDU:** Xavier College, Doctorate
Email: oanhngu@yahoo.com

P. Denise Nibbe
Title: General Manager **Company:** Cracker Barrel **Address:** 154 Stadium Drive, Kodak, TN 37764 United States **BUS:** Full Service Restaurant **P/S:** Food, Dining Services **MA:** National **D/D/R:** Managing Employees, Overseeing Restaurant Facilities **H/I/S:** Cross-Stitching, Spending Time with her Children **EDU:** Coursework in Pre-Med, St. Francis College, Fort Wayne, Indiana
Email: dnbirdlegs@yahoo.com

Glenda Nicholas
Title: Adult Education Teacher **Company:** Portage Township Schools **Address:** 6240 U.S. Highway 6, Portage, IN 46368 United States **BUS:** School District **P/S:** Education **MA:** Local **EXP:** Ms. Nicholas' expertise is in special education. **H/I/S:** Traveling, Gardening, Practicing Taekwondo **EDU:** Bachelor of Arts in Elementary Education, University of St. Thomas; Coursework, University of San Diego **A/A/S:** Indiana Association for Adult and Continuing Education **C/VW:** Local Church; Haitian Support Ministries; St. Jude Children's Research Hospital; Christian Children's Fund, American Heart Association
Email: 1glendanicholas@comcast.net
URL: http://www.cambridgewhoswho.com

E. Delores Nicholas-Cowherd
Title: District Director of Guidance **Company:** Willingboro Public Schools **Address:** 440 Beverly Rancocas Road, Willingboro, NJ 08046 United States **BUS:** Local School District Dedicated to Excellence in Education **P/S:** Regular Core Curriculum Including Reading, Mathematics, English, Social Studies, Science, Art, Music, History, Physical Education, Language Arts, Computers, Guidance and Counseling for Local School Students **MA:** Local **D/D/R:** Supervising 19 School Guidance Counselors, Holding Monthly Meetings with Guidance Counselors from Elementary, Middle and High Schools, Conducting Parent-Teacher Meetings Regarding State Testing, Conversing with the Director of State Testing **H/I/S:** Reading **EDU:** Master's Degree in Guidance and Counseling, Clemson University (1970); Bachelor's Degree in Music Education with a Minor in Social Studies, Saint Augustine's College, Raleigh, NC (1996) **CERTS:** Certified Substance Abuse Coordinator; Supervisor Certification **A/A/S:** Delta Sigma Theta; American Association of School Administrators; New Jersey Association of School Administrators; Director, Jersey City University; National Association for College Admission Counseling
Email: dcowherd@wboe.net
URL: http://www.willingboropublicschools.com

Mary Ruth Nichols
Title: French Teacher, Librarian **Company:** Easton School District **Address:** 162 Main Street, Fort Fairfield, ME 04742 United States **BUS:** Education Education/Secondary Education **P/S:** French Teacher, European Tour Director **MA:** Local **D/D/R:** Working as a Librarian, Teaching French at the High School Level **H/I/S:** Down Hill Skiing, Reading, Travelling, Candle Making **EDU:** University of Maine, Master's Degree in French and Library Science **A/A/S:** REFLECT, NEA
Email: nichm@eastonhs.easton.k12.me.us

Sandra E. Nichols

Title: 1) Manager of Palliative Care and Social Services 2) Director **Company:** 1)Trinity Pathway Hospice 2) Trinity Visiting Nurse and Homecare Association **Address:** 106 19th Avenue, Moline, IL 61265 United States **BUS:** Hospice Center **P/S:** Healthcare, Home Care **MA:** Local **D/D/R:** Offering Hospice Administration, Palliative Care, Overseeing Residential Hospice and Home Care Units, Developing New Palliative Care Programs, Caring for Patients **H/I/S:** Reading, Traveling **CERTS:** Certified Hospice Administrator; Master of Social Work, University of Iowa **A/H:** Trinity Model of Excellence Award **C/VW:** Trinity Health Foundation
Email: nicholss@ihs.org
URL: http://www.cambridgewhoswho.com

Mr. Bruce A. Nicholson

Title: Realtor, Associate **Company:** Coldwell Banker United Realtors **Address:** 1505 Heights Boulevard, Houston, TX 77008 United States **BUS:** Real Estate Agency **P/S:** Real Estate Services Including Single Family Homes, Townhouses, Condominiums, Land Sales, Relocation Services, Leasing, First Time Home Buyers **MA:** Regional **D/D/R:** Assisting Buyers and Sellers in the Purchase and Sale of Single-Family Homes, Condominiums, Townhouses and Land Sales, Working with First-Time Home Buyers, Managing Relocation and Leasing Services, Overseeing Construction of Old English Tudor-Style Estate Homes and Bungalow-Style Homes of the Early 1900s to 1960s **H/I/S:** Playing and Watching Football **EDU:** College Coursework **A/A/S:** Houston Association of Realtors; Great Autos of Yesteryear; National Chrysler Car Club; National Association of Realtors
Email: banicholson@coldwellbankerunited.com
URL: http://www.har.com/banicholson

Elnora J. Nicholson

Title: Engage Life Director **Company:** Atria Shaker **Address:** 345 Northern Boulevard, Albany, NY 12204 United States **BUS:** Senior Living Community **P/S:** Healthcare, Assisted Living Housing and Quality Care **MA:** National **D/D/R:** Encouraging Residents to Live Full Lives, Music, Planning Activities for Residents **H/I/S:** Spending Time with her Grandson, Swimming, Knitting, Reading **EDU:** Bachelor's Degree in Music Education, West Virginia Wesleyan College **C/VW:** Muscular Dystrophy Association, Cancer Research
Email: elnora.nicholson@atriaseniorliving.com
URL: http://www.atriaseniorliving.com

Richard Craig Nicholson

Title: Owner, President **Company:** Lake George Park Construction **Address:** 2997 Lake Shore Drive, Lake George, NY 12845 United States **BUS:** Construction Firm **P/S:** Construction, Remodeling, Additions, New Custom Homes and Boathouses, Repair Work **MA:** Local **EXP:** Mr. Nicholson's expertise includes residential and commercial construction, log homes, cedar log and twig work, historic Victorian restoration, mahogany decks and floors, log railings, stone chimneys, media rooms, and custom kitchen and bathrooms. **H/I/S:** Snowmobiling, Water Skiing, Boating, Camping **EDU:** High School **C/VW:** Jehovah's Witness, Disaster Relief, Local Shelters
Email: nicholsons@gmail.com
URL: http://www.lakegeorgeparkconstruction.com

Justin Nickel

Title: Civil Engineer I **Company:** City of Overland Park Public Works **Address:** 8500 Santa Fe Drive, Overland Park, KS 66213 United States **BUS:** Municipality **P/S:** Infrastructure **MA:** Local **D/D/R:** Civil Engineering **H/I/S:** Working on his Graduate Degree **EDU:** Pursuing Graduate Degree in Civil Engineering, University of Kansas; Bachelor of Science in Civil Engineering, Iowa State University **A/A/S:** Kansas Society of Professional Engineers; American Public Works Association
Email: justin.nickel@opkansas.org
URL: http://www.opkansas.org

Pamela J. Nickerson

Title: Co-Owner, Treasurer **Company:** Benjamin T. Nickerson, Inc. **Address:** 149 Commerce Park E., South Chatham, MA 02659 United States **BUS:** Waste Management Company **P/S:** Sanitation, Waste Management **MA:** Local **D/D/R:** Managing Operations, Dispatching Radio, Overseeing Payroll, Attending Telephone Calls **H/I/S:** Traveling, Reading, Gardening **EDU:** Pursuing Associate Degree in Business Management
Email: bennickerson@comcast.net
URL: http://www.nickersondisposal.com

Paula C. Nicolau

Title: Comptroller **Company:** Dominion Concrete and Masonry **Address:** 43053 Pemberton Square, S-120, Suite 301, South Riding, VA 20152 United States **BUS:** Licensed Commercial and Residential Contracting Company **P/S:** Installation of Driveways, Patios, Curbs, Gutters and All Types of Masonry Work **MA:** Regional **D/D/R:** Accounting, Overseeing All Business Decisions and Bookkeeping Processes **EDU:** High School Diploma
Email: pcnicolay@aol.com
URL: http://www.dcmcflatwork.com

Lisa Ann Nicotra

Title: Seventh-Grade Social Studies Teacher **Company:** Parker Junior High School **Address:** 2810 School Street, Flossmoor, IL 60422 United States **BUS:** Public Middle School Serving the Residents of Flossmoor **P/S:** Public Secondary Education for Local Students **MA:** Regional **D/D/R:** Teaching Seventh and Eighth-Grade History Classes, Assisting in the Publication of the Sixth, Seventh and Eighth-Grade Social Studies Curriculum, Tutoring Students Privately **H/I/S:** Reading, Writing Poetry **EDU:** Bachelor's Degree in Secondary Education, History and English (2000) **A/A/S:** National Education Association; Lecturer, Community Groups; Mentor
Email: midnite_bonc@yahoo.com

Ms. Esther M. Niedzwiecki

Title: Vice President **Company:** Friends of the Old School **Address:** 101 W. Third Street, P.O. Box 102, Owen, WI 54460 United States **BUS:** Nonprofit Organization **P/S:** Community Center, Preservation of Heritage and Local History, Displays of Artwork and Historical Artifacts **MA:** Local **D/D/R:** Preservation **H/I/S:** Painting, Hunting, Gardening, Spending Time with Family and Friends **A/A/S:** Owen Chamber of Commerce; The Historical Society

Lorelei R. Nielsen

Title: Owner **Company:** Omnia Bona-All the Good Things **BUS:** Event Production Company **P/S:** Event Planning, Unique Weddings, Fundraisers, Charities, Funerals, Baby Showers **MA:** National **D/D/R:** Developing Unique Ideas and Event Themes, Planning All Aspects of Events, Accommodating 300 to 1000 Guests, Marketing, Managing Human Resources **H/I/S:** Running, Kayaking, Rock Climbing **EDU:** Pursuing Master's Degree in Public Administration, University of California; Bachelor's Degree in Public Relations and Communications, California State University (1978) **A/A/S:** Ronald McDonald House Charities; American Cancer Society; Children's Hospital Society; President, Parent Teacher Association
Email: loreleirozell@cox.net

Nicole Niemann

Title: Director of Training **Company:** Z Gallerie **Address:** 1855 W. 139th Street, Gardena, CA 90249 United States **BUS:** Retail Store **P/S:** Home Furnishings and Accessories, Bedding, Pillows, Candles, Clocks, Frames, Decorative Accessories, Dinnerware, Flatware, Glassware, Area Rugs, Drapery Panels, Lighting, Art, Employee Development **MA:** National **D/D/R:** Training and Educating Retail Associates on Products and Customer Service, Developing Associates' Leadership and Management Skills **H/I/S:** Golfing, Show Jumping **EDU:** Master's Degree in Organizational Development, University of Salzburg (1995); Bachelor's Degree in International Communication and Relations **A/A/S:** American Society for Training and Development; International Association of Facilitators; Alpha Phi
Email: dvpoftp@hotmail.com
URL: http://www.zgallerie.com

Dolores Nieto

Title: Vice President **Address:** 116 E. Hidalgo, Raymondville, TX 78580 United States **BUS:** Community Service, Financial **P/S:** Financial Services to Community **MA:** Local **D/D/R:** Lending/Loan Officer, Overseeing Operations **H/I/S:** Coaches Football **A/A/S:** Chamber of Commerce, American Cancer Society, Alliance International
Email: deenieto@yahoo.com
URL: http://www.cambridgewhoswho.com

Monique L. Nieves

Title: Corporate Product Development Chef **Company:** Philips Foods, Inc. **Address:** 1215 E. Fort Avenue, Baltimore, MD 21230 United States **BUS:** Restaurant **P/S:** Food Services, Seafood, Signature Crab Cakes, Research and Development **MA:** International **D/D/R:** Researching and Developing Various Dishes, Modifying Existing Recipes **H/I/S:** Exercising, Reading, Bowling **EDU:** Bachelor's Degree in Culinary Nutrition, Johnson & Wales University **A/A/S:** research chefs association () **C/VW:** March of Dimes
Email: mnieves@philipsfoods.com
URL: http://www.philipsfoods.com

Hania Niklas

Title: President **Company:** Audio Lab, Inc. **Address:** 36 JFK Street, Cambridge, MA 02138 United States **BUS:** Electronics Store **P/S:** Residential and Commercial Sales, Installation and Service **MA:** International **D/D/R:** Electronic Repairs, Selling Hi-Fi Equipment, On-Site Repairs, Installations **H/I/S:** Swimming, Basketball, Running, Boating **EDU:** Bachelor's Degree, Wellesley College; Master of Business Administration, University of Massachusetts **C/VW:** American Cancer Society, Leukemia & Lymphoma Society, Big Brothers Big Sisters, Vietnam Veterans of America, WWZN Charities, American Lung Association
Email: theaudiolab@hotmail.com
URL: http://www.theaudiolab.com

Katherina A. Nikzad

Title: Therapist **Company:** Family Counseling Services **Address:** 1321 Trent Boulevard, Building 1, Lexington, KY 40517 United States **BUS:** Nonprofit Counseling Agency **P/S:** Counseling for Adults, Couples, Families, Adolescents and Children **MA:** Regional **EXP:** Ms. Nikzad's expertise is in gerontology. **D/D/R:** Counseling Adults **H/I/S:** Spending Time with her Family, Singing in the Church Choir, Attending the Local Women's Bible Study Group, Playing the Flute, Scrapbooking, Crocheting, Reading **EDU:** Master of Social Work, University of Kentucky; Bachelor of Arts in Psychology, Otterbein College **A/A/S:** National Association of Social Workers; Alumni Member, Mortar Board National College Senior Honor Society; American Psychological Association; The Gerontological Society of America; Society for Social Work Research **C/VW:** Winged-Women Inc, Alzheimer's Association, Cornelia de Lange Syndrome Foundation Outreach, Helping Hands Foundation, Local Daycare Center
Email: kanikz2@uky.edu
URL: http://www.mc.uky.edu/gerontology

Timothy C. Nininger

Title: Vice President **Company:** Bug Man Exterminating, Inc. **Address:** 1918 Orange Avenue, Roanoke, VA 24012 United States **BUS:** Professional Pest Control Company **P/S:** Termite and Pest Control Services **MA:** Local **D/D/R:** Offering Management Services **H/I/S:** Golfing **EDU:** Bachelor of Science, Clemson University **A/A/S:** Christian Church; National Pest Management Association; National Association of Home Builders; National Association of Realtors
Email: tim@bugmanext.com
URL: http://www.bugmanext.com

Midori Nishida

Title: Naturopathic Doctor **Company:** Natural Health Medical Center **Address:** 11695 National Boulevard, Los Angeles, CA 90064 United States **BUS:** Natural Healthcare **P/S:** Natural and Holistic Medicine **MA:** Regional **EXP:** Dr. Nishida's expertise includes naturopathic medicine, herbal medicine, body work and energetic medicine, nutritional medicine, and homeopathy. **H/I/S:** Traveling, Attending Concerts, Watching Theater Productions, Playing the Piano, Reading **EDU:** Degree in Naturopathic Medicine, National College of Naturopathic Medicine (National College of Natural Medicine) (2001) **A/A/S:** American Association of Naturopathic Physicians; California Naturopathic Doctors Association
Email: deiyamato@hotmail.com
URL: http://www.cambridgewhoswho.com

Sonia Nistal

Title: Licensed Massage Therapist, Wellness Coach **Company:** Medical Wellness Center, University of Miami **Address:** 1503 127st Street, North Miami Beach, FL 33161 United States **BUS:** Healthcare Facility **P/S:** Fitness Programs, Personal Training, Massage Therapy, Yoga **MA:** Regional **D/D/R:** Sports Medicine, Deep Tissue, Reflexology, Yoga, Preparing a Fitness Program with Functional Training, Using a Figure Assessment LAB to Determine Clients' Needs, Educating Clients on all Phases of a Healthy Life, Nutrition, Exercise, Massage and Yoga **H/I/S:** Triathlon, Biking, Swimming, Running, Weight Training, Yoga **EDU:** Bachelor of Arts in Physical Education, American University, Puerto Rico (1996) **CERTS:** Licensed Massage Therapist, Florida State University (2002) **A/A/S:** American Massage Therapy Association; Disney World Triathlon (2005-2006); Multiple Sclerosis and Leukemia Society
Email: nistalfitness@aol.com
URL: http://wellness.med.miami.edu/x188.xml#

Cherie A. Nixon, PE

Title: Senior Civil Engineer **Company:** Arup **Address:** 12777 W. Jefferson Boulevard, Suite 200, Los Angeles, CA 90066 United States **BUS:** Civil Engineering **P/S:** Land Development **MA:** International **EXP:** Ms. Nixon's expertise includes land development, drainage, water resources and sustainability. **H/I/S:** Friends, Travel, Photography, Movies, Music, Rollerblading, Reading, Fine Food and Drink **EDU:** University of Sydney, University of Waterloo, Graduate Diploma in Molecular Biology, Bachelor of Applied Science in Civil Engineering **A/A/S:** ASCE
Email: cherie.nixon@arvp.com

Florence O. Nnebe, MD

Title: Attending Physician **Company:** University Physicians Group **Address:** 242 Mason Avenue, Suite 1, Staten Island, NY 10305 United States **BUS:** Healthcare Pediatrician **P/S:** Patient Care, Clinical Education **MA:** Local **EXP:** Ms. Nnebe's expertise is in pediatrician. **H/I/S:** Reading **EDU:** University of Nigeria, MBBS **A/A/S:** Doctors without Borders, Residency at Harlem Hospital Center of Columbia University
Email: fnnebe@siuh.edu

Jenny F. Noble

Title: Pre-Operation and Post-Operation Nurse **Company:** Children's Hospitals and Clinics of Minnesota **Address:** 345 Smith Avenue N., Second Floor, Saint Paul, MN 55102 United States **BUS:** Hospital **P/S:** Child Healthcare **MA:** Local **EXP:** Ms. Noble's expertise includes pre and post-operative nursing. **D/D/R:** Educating Patients on Surgical Procedures **H/I/S:** Traveling, Attending Antique Car Shows, Reading **EDU:** Bachelor of Science in Nursing, Augsburg College (1979) **A/A/S:** Minnesota Nurses Association
Email: jennynoble11@hotmail.com
URL: http://www.cambridgewhoswho.com

Kimberly P. Noblett, RDA

Title: Registered Dental Assistant **Company:** Dr. Allen Chance, DDS, MDS, PLLC **Address:** 520 S. Main Street, Sweetwater, TN 37885 United States **BUS:** Dental Clinic **P/S:** Orthodontia Services **MA:** Local **D/D/R:** Treating Children and Adults **H/I/S:** Reading Self-Help Books, Whiteboarding, Boating, Tennis **CERTS:** Registered Dental Assistant, Anderson County Dental Assistant Program (2006)
Email: kpnoblett2885@yahoo.com

Lois G. Nogoda

Title: Executive Vice President **Company:** People's Federal Credit Union **Address:** 419 First Avenue S., Nitro, WV 25143 United States **BUS:** Community Credit Union **P/S:** Financial Services **MA:** Putnam, Mason and Kanawha Counties **D/D/R:** Accounting **H/I/S:** Traveling **EDU:** High School Graduate **A/A/S:** President, Kanawha Valley Chapter of Credit Unions **C/VW:** Make-A-Wish Foundation, Children's Miracle Network
Email: lnogoda@peoplesfcu.com
URL: http://www.peoplesfcu.com

Wendy W. Nole

Title: Owner, Dental Technician **Company:** Nole Dental Lab **Address:** 117 Reeves Street, Dunmore, PA 18512 United States **BUS:** Dental Lab **P/S:** Orthodontic Appliances **MA:** Regional **D/D/R:** Manufacturing and Fabrication of Dental Appliances **H/I/S:** Traveling, Practicing Karate **EDU:** Associate of Science, Luzerne County Community College, 1981 **A/A/S:** Parent Teach Association **C/VW:** March of Dimes, American Cancer Society
Email: wnole@verizon.com

Mary E. Nondorf

Title: Social Worker **Company:** Cornerstone Hospital of Houston **Address:** 5314 Dashwood Drive, Houston, TX 77081 United States **BUS:** Hospital **P/S:** Healthcare Including Long-Term Acute Care **MA:** Local **EXP:** Ms. Nondorf's expertise includes case management and social service. **H/I/S:** Collecting Antiques, Dancing, Reading, Attending Ballet Shows **EDU:** Bachelor of Arts in Sociology and Social Work **A/A/S:** SSWLA; National Association of Social Workers; HGS
Email: menondorf@hotmail.com
URL: http://www.cambridgewhoswho.com

Melina L. Norberto

Title: Realtor **Company:** Fortune Global Realty **Address:** P. O. Box 771078, Orlando, FL 32877 United States **BUS:** Privately Owned Company Committed to Excellence in the Real Estate Industry **P/S:** Buying Selling Residential and Commercial Properties, Referrals, Land Sales, Relocations, First Time Home Buyers **MA:** Regional **EXP:** Ms. Norberto's expertise includes residential sales, referrals, land sales, commercial properties and relocations. **H/I/S:** Skiing, Snowboarding **EDU:** Associate of Arts Degree in Marketing, Valencia Community College (2005) **A/A/S:** National Association of Realtors; Florida Association of Realtors; Orlando Regional Realtors Association
Email: melina.fgrealty@gmail.com
URL: http://www.melina.directhomes.com

Ronald D. Nordenbrock

Title: Fire Chief **Company:** Poplar Springs Fire Department **Address:** 3400 Moore Duncan Highway, Moore, SC 29369 United States **BUS:** Fire Department **P/S:** Fire and Rescue **MA:** Regional **D/D/R:** Managing Fire Scenes, Overseeing Daily Operations for Three Stations, Managing Volunteer Fire Fighters and Personnel Issues, Responding to Fire Calls, Overseeing Budgetary Concerns and Maintenance of Equipment, Ordering New Equipment, Maintaining Knowledge of Current Developments in the Industry, Administering Building Inspections **H/I/S:** Motorcycling, Woodworking **EDU:** Bachelor's Degree in Mechanical Engineering, University of Dayton (1969); Coursework, South Carolina Fire Academy **CERTS:** Nationally Certified Firefighter II, National Fire Protection Association **A/A/S:** National Fire Protection Association; Spartanburg County Fire Chief's Association; Spartanburg County Forestry Commission; Adjunct Professor, South Carolina Fire Academy
Email: chief@poplarspringsfd.com
URL: http://poplarspringsfd.com

Brett Norgaard

Company: Four51 **Address:** 8300 Norman Center Drive, Suite 1275, Minneapolis, MN 55437 United States **BUS:** E-Commerce Company **P/S:** Intelligence Projects and Programs, Customized Research and Market Intelligence Agenda, Advantages to Sales, Marketing and Consulting Professionals **MA:** National **D/D/R:** Applying Intelligence to Win Deals, Writing about Branching Out and Differentiating **H/I/S:** Spending Time with his Family, Golfing, Skiing **EDU:** Bachelor's Degree in Science, St. Olaf College, MN (1982) **A/A/S:** Minnesota High Tech Association; Branch Productivity Institute; Sales and Marketing Executives International
Email: Brett@wirethemarket.com
URL: http://www.wirethemarket.com

Ms. Ellen R. Norman

Title: Chief Executive Officer **Company:** No Stress for Nurses **Address:** 801 N. Federal Street, Apartment 2133, Chandler, AZ 85226 United States **BUS:** Counseling Center **P/S:** Seminars, Workshops, Lectures, e-Books and other Informational Tools, Stress Relieving Services for Nurses and Caregivers **MA:** International **EXP:** Ms. Norman's expertise is in nursing. **H/I/S:** Attending Book and Chess Clubs, Wine Tasting, Cooking, Writing, Racquetball **EDU:** Associate of Arts, Austin Community College **CERTS:** Licensed Practical Nurse, Western Massachusetts Hospital, School of Practicing Nurses **A/A/S:** National Hospice and Palliative Care Organization; Phi Beta Kappa **C/VW:** Hospice of the Valley; American Cancer Association; Amnesty International USA
Email: ellie_norman2006@yahoo.com
Email: ellen@nostress4nurses.com
URL: http://www.nostress4nurses.com

Susie Norman

Title: Teacher **Company:** New Albany-Plain Local School District **Address:** 87 N. High Street, New Albany, OH 43054 United States **BUS:** Elementary School **P/S:** Education **MA:** Local **D/D/R:** Reading and Gifted Education **H/I/S:** Traveling, Working Out, Spending Time with her Husband and her Golden Retriever **EDU:** Master of Education in Reading Education, Bowling Green State University; Endorsement in Gifted Education and Reading Education **A/A/S:** International Reading Association; American Reading Forum **C/VW:** Mid-Ohio Food Bank
Email: skauffman@new-albany.k12.oh.us
URL: http://www.new-albany.k12.oh.us

Gerald J. Norris

Title: Executive Director **Company:** UBS **Dept:** P and S Consulting **Address:** 325 N. Old Woodward Avenue, Suite 200, Birmingham, MI 48009 United States **BUS:** Financial Firm **P/S:** Financial Services, Wealth Management Consulting **MA:** International **EXP:** Mr. Norris' expertise includes retirement and estate planning. **H/I/S:** Boating, Golfing **EDU:** Bachelor of Science in Pharmaceuticals, Ferris State University **A/A/S:** CEMA **C/VW:** American Cancer Society; Leader Dogs for the Blind
Email: gerald.norris@ubs.com
URL: http://www.ubs.com

William M. Norris

Title: Owner, Manager **Company:** Norris Landscape Services **Address:** 3901 Days End Road, Wimberley, TX 78676 United States **BUS:** Landscaping Lawn Care/Landscaping **P/S:** Landscape Construction, Custom Rock, Transport and Trucking **MA:** Local **EXP:** Mr. Norris' expertise includes custom rock, outdoor barbecue pits and custom lighting. **H/I/S:** Motorcycle Riding-Harley Davidson **EDU:** San Jose State University, Botany Degree **A/A/S:** Masonic Lodge, Scottish Right Hospital, St Judes, 700 Club
Email: texasnsl@verizon.net

JoAnne North Goetz

Title: Author, Speaker **Company:** Hey Who **Address:** 190 Ashton Place Circle, Winston Salem, NC 27106 United States **BUS:** Publishing Company **P/S:** Novels **MA:** National **D/D/R:** Publishing her First Book March 2007, 'Longtime Coming' **H/I/S:** Bowling, Track, Basketball, Softball, Coaching Volleyball **EDU:** Master's Degree, Appalachian State University (1956) **A/A/S:** Lions Club; America's Success Coach; Rhododendron Society at Appalachian State University **A/H:** Teacher of the Year, State of Georgia (1994); Teacher of the Year, State of North Carolina (1985); Long Leas Pine Award, Highest Civilian Honor in Education, State of North Carolina; Award, Appalachian State University **C/VW:** serve on the institute for dismantling racism and tolerance at AME Zion church, friendship-vision house, Darryl hunt project for freedom and justice.
Email: jrvgoetz@hotmail.com
URL: http://www.joannegoetz.com

Laurie M. Northey

Title: Apartment Manager **Company:** Holiday Builders **Address:** 1051 E. Park Street, Grants Pass, OR 97527 United States **BUS:** Housing for Seniors, Handicapped and Disabled Individuals **P/S:** Housing **MA:** Local **D/D/R:** Managing, Doing Paperwork, Handling the Issues of a 124 Unit Complex **H/I/S:** Quilting, Crabbing, Swimming, Canning **EDU:** College Coursework **A/H:** Oregon Manager of the Year (2005) **C/VW:** Volunteer, Salvation Army
Email: lnorthey@charterinternet.com
URL: http://www.cambridgewhoswho.com

Dr. Honora A. Norton, ABD

Title: Parish Manager **Company:** The Community of the Blessed Sacrament **Address:** 11300 N. 64th Street, Scottsdale, AZ 85254 United States **BUS:** Religion **P/S:** Spiritual Services, Religious Services, Youth Task Force, Administrative Services **MA:** Local **D/D/R:** Overseeing Stewardship, Building an Adult Day Care, Managing the Financial Council **H/I/S:** Breeding and Training Yorkshire Terriers, Vacationing in Ireland **EDU:** Doctorate in Ministry, Wisdom University (2007); Master of Science in Management, Cardinal Stritch University, Milwaukee, Wisconsin; Bachelor of Arts in Business Administration, University of Wisconsin, Madison, Wisconsin **A/A/S:** Interface Network of Scottsdale; City of Scottsdale Youth Task Force; Rotary International; Christian Business Women's Association; starlight starbright Arizona leadership council
Email: mike.honora@cox.net
URL: http://www.drnortonconsulting.com

Doris A. Norval

Title: Secretary, Treasurer **Company:** Riverview Bible Church **Address:** 5715 S.W. 1001 Road, El Dorado Springs, MO 64744 United States **BUS:** Church **P/S:** Religious Programs and Activities **MA:** Regional **D/D/R:** Managing All Church Finances, Assisting the Pastor **H/I/S:** Four Wheeling, Fishing, Reading **EDU:** High School Education **A/A/S:** PEO **A/H:** Twentieth Century Club Award, Outstanding Woman in her Community
Email: doty@lpa.net

Francine M. Norwood

Title: Senior Flight Test Engineer **Company:** Sikorsky Aircraft **Address:** W101 E., P.O. Box 109610, 101 West Court, West Palm Beach, FL 33410 United States **BUS:** Engineering Company **P/S:** Helicopter Manufacturing, Development Flight Center **MA:** International **D/D/R:** Handling Qualities, Briefing Pilots on Flight Tests, Monitoring Flight in Telemetry Room, Gathering Data, Writing Reports for Clients to Support Certification on Aircraft **H/I/S:** Volunteering, Guest Speaking at the Jupiter-Tequesta Athletic Association **EDU:** Master of Science in Mathematics, Nova Southeastern University (2004); Bachelor of Science in Aerospace Engineering, Texas A&M University (1988) **A/A/S:** Former Member, Aerospace Industries Association of America, Inc.; American Institute of Aeronautics and Astronautics; American Helicopter Society; Minority Americans in Engineering and Science; Junior Engineering Technical Society
Email: fnorwood@sikorsky.com
URL: http://www.sikorsky.com

Rodney E. Norwood

Title: Technical Coordinator **Company:** Telecom Technology Services, Inc. **Dept:** RF Engineering Department **Address:** 6140 Stoneridge Mall Road, Suite 365, Pleasanton, CA 94588 United States **BUS:** Telecommunication Company **P/S:** Telecommunication Services Including Consulting, Software Development and the Implementation of Radio Frequency Telecommunication Solutions **MA:** National **EXP:** Mr. Norwood's expertise includes the management and coordination of technical projects, purchasing, and test and measurement equipment oversight. **H/I/S:** Collecting Trains, Old Telecommunications and Optical Equipment **CERTS:** Certification in General Educational Development **C/VW:** Shepherd's Gate; Battered Women's Shelter
Email: rnorwood@ttswireless.com
URL: http://www.ttswireless.com

Holly Novacich
Title: Salon Owner, Head Stylist Company: Josef and Mari's Salon and Spa Address: 822 Ridge Road, Munster, IN 46321 United States BUS: Beauty and Wellness Salon and Spa P/S: Full Service Beauty Salon and Spa Run by Holly, a National Platform Artist and Educator, She Does all Hiring, Runs Daily Operations, Subjects all New Hires, Out of School or From Another Salon to Intense Training and Evaluation of Technical and Art Skills, Ensuring Nothing but the Best for her Clients, Does Educational Seminars Incorporating Other Stylists and Massage Therapists Making Them the Best they Can Be and Enabling them to Teach MA: International D/D/R: All Aspects from Cutting Hair, Coloring and Chemicals to Nails, Teaching the Industry, The Salon Features Massage Therapy for Relaxation and Pampering, Make Up Artists, Nail Technicians for Gel Nails, Natural Manicures and Pedicures, Skin Treatments, Facials, Practice Ear Candling, a European Practice for Sinus Issues and of Course all Treatments for your Hair. The Focus is Health Wellness and Beauty CERTS: Charles Allen Academy of Beauty Culture, Provanna International, Rusk International, Mazzani, Licensed Esthetician, Licensed Cosmetologist, Certified Colorist, Certified Platform Artist, Certified Cutting and Chemicals A/A/S: Chamber of Commerce, Community Outreach, Donating Services for People Looking for Work or Financial Issues
Email: hnovacich4680@wowway.com

Jason Novich
Title: Owner Company: TRA Computers Address: 32 Park Terrace, Spring Valley, NY 10977 United States BUS: Technology Service Provider P/S: Technologist for Small Businesses MA: Local D/D/R: Offering Technology H/I/S: Movie Buff and Loves to Read EDU: Master of Arts in Technology Management, MD A/A/S: IEEE, AIMP
Email: jasonnovich@tracomputers.net
URL: www.tracomputers.net

Gail A. Nowaskey
Company: Self-Employed Address: 1358 Reserve Drive, Venice, FL 34285 United States BUS: Sole Proprietorship P/S: High-End Fashion Consulting MA: Regional D/D/R: Consulting on Fashion, Participating in Regional Couture Shows H/I/S: Golfing, Painting, Writing
Email: cambridgewhoswho.com
URL: http://www.cambridgewhoswho.com

Monica D. Nuckols
Title: Second-Grade Teacher Company: R.M. James Elementary School Address: 701 W. 18th Street, Portales, NM 88130 United States BUS: Public Elementary School P/S: Education MA: Local D/D/R: Teaching Reading H/I/S: Reading, Gardening, Taking Care of her Children EDU: Bachelor of Science in Education, Emphasis in Language Arts, Eastern New Mexico University
Email: mnuckols@portalesschools.com
URL: http://www.jamesschools.com

Kenneth Lloyd Nulle
Title: Electrical Contractor/Owner Company: Kenn's Electric Address: 48 Sun Valley Road, Tularosa, NM 88352 United States BUS: Construction Contracting P/S: Residential and Commercial Wiring MA: Local D/D/R: All Electrical Work H/I/S: Bowling EDU: Associate Degree in Electronics, DeVry A/A/S: IEC, US Air Force
Email: kennselectric@tularosa.net

Laura Nunemaker-Bynum
Title: Senior Public Relations Specialist Company: American Society for Training and Development Address: 1640 King Street, Alexandria, VA 22314 United States BUS: Nonprofit Educational Institution P/S: Vocational Education MA: International D/D/R: Building Public Relations H/I/S: Collecting Antiques, Caring for her Dog, Spending Time with her Children EDU: Master of Arts in Public Relations and Mass Communications, University of South Florida, Tampa A/A/S: Public Relations Society of America; National Association for Female Executives C/VW: Inova HealthPlex, Springfield, VA
Email: lbynum@astd.org
URL: http://www.astd.org

William A. Nutini
Title: Vice President of Sales Company: Toshiba America Electronic Components, Inc. Address: 19900 MacArthur Boulevard, Irvine, CA 92612 United States BUS: Electronics Company P/S: Electronic Components MA: International EXP: Mr. Nutini's expertise includes sales and executive management. H/I/S: Ice Hockey, Traveling EDU: Bachelor of Science in Marketing, Psychology and Mathematics, Loyola University, Chicago, Illinois A/A/S: Corporate Partners Program, University of California at Irvine C/VW: Various Local Charities
Email: bill.nutini@taec.toshiba.com

Sally C. Nyhan
Title: Teacher, Team Leader Company: King Philip Middle School Address: 100 King Philip Drive, West Hartford, CT 06117 United States BUS: Middle School P/S: Education MA: Local D/D/R: Teaching American History, Developing Lesson Plans, Coaching Mock Trial Team, Assisting the Drama Club H/I/S: Traveling, Reading, Watching Sports EDU: Master of Arts in Teaching, Quinnipiac University; Master of Arts in Medieval History, University of Kent at Canterbury; Bachelor of Science in Journalism CERTS: Certified Teacher of English to Speakers of Others Languages, Pilgrims Language School A/A/S: Organization of American Historians; Connecticut Council for the Social Studies; National Council for the Social Studies
Email: sally_nyhan@whps.org
URL: http://www.whps.org

Christine Jeannine O'Brien
Title: Bankruptcy Paralegal Company: Fein, Such, Kahn and Shepard, PC Address: 7 Century Drive, Suite 201, Parsippany, NJ 07054 United States BUS: Law Firm P/S: Legal Services MA: National EXP: Ms. O'Brien's expertise is in bankruptcy law. H/I/S: Reading EDU: Associate Degree in Paralegal Studies, Berkeley College (2001); Associate Degree in Early Childhood Education, Berkeley College (1999) A/A/S: National Association of Legal Assistants C/VW: Local Charitable Organizations
Email: cobby24@hotmail.com
URL: http://www.cambridgewhoswho.com

Joanne O'Brien
Title: Group Account Director Company: Secret Weapon Marketing Address: 1653 10th Street, Santa Monica, CA 90404 United States BUS: Marketing Company P/S: Marketing, Advertising MA: National D/D/R: Advertising Account Management, Strategic Marketing Management H/I/S: Spending Time with Family, Volunteering at her Children's School EDU: Bachelor's Degree in Marketing, Bryant University A/A/S: Ad Club; The Association of Accredited Advertising Agents C/VW: American Heart Association, American Cancer Society, Salvation Army, American Red Cross
Email: joanne@secretweapon.net
URL: http://www.secretweapon.net

Mrs. Michelle A. O'Brien
Title: Senior Business Manager Company: Global Financial Services Address: 212 S. Tryon Street, Charlotte, NC 28281 United States BUS: Interim Staffing to Bank, Brokerage and Trust Firms P/S: Staffing MA: National D/D/R: Securities Operations Processing, Processing All Financial Transactions after a Trade H/I/S: Traveling, Reading, Running, Scrapbooking, Acting EDU: Bachelor of Arts in Public Relations, Purdue University-1990 A/A/S: SOD-Security Operations Division of SIA; Securities Industry Financial Markets Association
Email: mobrien@g-f-s.com
URL: http://www.g-f-s.com

Patricia J. O'Brien Townsend, RN, BSN, CWOCN
Title: Clinical Coordinator, Nurse, Wound Care Specialist Company: Bozeman Deaconess Hospital Dept: Wound and Lymphedema Center Address: 915 Highland Boulevard, Suite 4350, Bozeman, MT 59715 United States BUS: Community Based Nonprofit Hospital P/S: Inpatient and Outpatient Services, Inpatient Nursing Services through Obstetrics and Nursery Units, Medical Unit, Surgical Unit and Intensive Care Unit and a 24-Hour Support Staff Involved in Diagnostic and Therapy Services MA: Local EXP: Ms. O'Brien Townsend's expertise is in clinical coordination. D/D/R: Counseling and Advising Patients, Nursing Patients who have Wounds, Infections, Non-Healing Wounds, Diabetic Ulcers and Poor Blood Circulation H/I/S: Gardening, Quilting EDU: Bachelor of Science in Nursing, Montana State University, Bozeman (1975); Coursework in Nursing, St. John's McNamara School of Nursing, Rapid City, SD (1972) CERTS: Specialty Training in Wound and Ostomy Care, Barnes-Jewish Hospital, Washington University, St. Louis, MO (1980) A/A/S: Montana Nurses Association; Wound Ostomy and Continence Nurses Society; American Nurses Association; Sigma Theta Tau C/VW: Volunteer, Local Charitable Organization
Email: pobrien@bdh-boz.com
URL: http://www.bozemandeaconess.org

Jennifer J. O'Connor
Title: Clinical Engineering Director Company: Trinity Health, Mercy General Health Partners Dept: Clinical Engineering Address: 1500 E. Sherman Boulevard, Muskegon, MI 49444 United States BUS: Healthcare P/S: Medical Equipment MA: Regional D/D/R: Clinical Engineering EDU: Master of Business Administration, Baker College of Graduate Studies (2008), Bachelor of Business Administration in Management, McKendree College (2004), Associate of Applied Science in Biomedical Equipment Technology, College of the Air Force (2003) A/A/S: Chairman for House of Wishes
Email: oconnje@trinity-health.org

Tiffany O'Connor-Triana
Title: Speech-Language Pathologist Address: 4130 S. Cordia Court, Gold Canyon, AZ 85218 United States BUS: Sole Proprietorship P/S: Speech and Language Therapy MA: Local EXP: Ms. O'Connor-Triana's expertise is in augmentative communication. H/I/S: Mountain Hiking, Scrapbooking EDU: Master of Science in Speech-Language Pathology, Northern Arizona University (2005); Bachelor of Arts in Speech and Hearing Science, Edinboro University of Pennsylvania (1993) CERTS: Certification in Clinical Competency-Speech-Language Pathology A/A/S: American Speech-Language-Hearing Association C/VW: Foundation for Blind Children
Email: triana97@msn.com

Mr. Terrance P. O'Donal
Title: Owner Company: Terry's Fixit Service Address: 453 Powers Road, Caribou, ME 04736 United States BUS: Appliance Service and Repair P/S: Residential and Commercial Refrigeration and Air Conditioning, Major Household Appliance Service and Repair, Both Gas and Electric, Automobile Air Conditioning Service MA: Regional D/D/R: Company Management, Repairing Commercial and Residential Appliances, Budgeting H/I/S: Skiing, Camping, Outdoor Activities EDU: Various Military Education Primarily in Service and Repair, Vocational Degree in HVACR A/A/S: Retired Army Veteran
Email: todonal@earthlink.net
URL: http://www.cambridgewhoswho.com

Mary E. O'Donnell-Mongelli
Title: School Psychologist Company: Mary Mongelli Address: 414 Beach 124th Street, Belle Harbor, NY 11694 United States BUS: Premier Provider of Educational Services P/S: Excellence in Education, Student Services, Behavior Modification, Parent Training, Special Education, English Language Learners, Testing and Assessment, Food and Nutrition Services, Student Health Services MA: Local D/D/R: Working with Autistic Children and Individuals with Behavioral Problems H/I/S: Swimming EDU: Master's Degree in Psychology, St. John's University (1985); Master's Degree in Special Education, St. John's University (1980); Bachelor of Arts Degree in Psychology with a Minor in Education and Business, College of Mount St. Vincent (1978) A/A/S: American Psychology Association; NCPA; Council for Exceptional Children
URL: http://www.cambridgewhoswho.com

Barbara D. O'Hearn
Title: Teacher Company: South Kitsap School District Address: 1962 Hoover Avenue S.E., Port Orchard, WA 98366 United States BUS: School District P/S: Education MA: Local D/D/R: Teaching Kindergarten through 12th-Grade Students H/I/S: Altering and Sewing Gowns, Crocheting, Making Crafts EDU: Master's Degree in Education and Curriculum, University of Connecticut A/A/S: Pi Lambda Theta C/VW: Local Church
Email: barbohearn@hotmail.com

Patricia O'Leary
Title: Vice President of Human Resources Company: Zoots Address: 153 Needham Street, Building 1, Newton, MA 02464 United States BUS: Dry Cleaning Company P/S: Dry Cleaning MA: National D/D/R: Organizing and Overseeing Employee Benefits and Employee Relations H/I/S: Reading, Gardening, Traveling A/A/S: National Rifle Association C/VW: Juvenile Diabetes Foundation, Susan G. Komen for the Cure, American Lung Association
Email: trish_oleary@zoots.com
URL: http://www.zoots.com

John R. O'Malley
Title: Superintendent-Maintenance Company: BP West Coast Products, LLC Address: 2350 E. 223rd Street, Carson, CA 90810 United States BUS: Petroleum Refining Company P/S: Energy EXP: Mr. O'Malley's expertise includes operations and maintenance. H/I/S: Doing Woodwork, Playing Golf EDU: Bachelor of Business Administration, University of Phoenix A/A/S: Institute of Electrical and Electronics Engineers, Inc.; Industry Applications Society; Petroleum and Chemical Industry Committee C/VW: Local Church
Email: john.omalley@bp.com
URL: http://www.cambridgewhoswho.com

Mary P. O'Mara
Title: Professional Educator Company: Buffalo Public Schools Address: 281 Heath Street, Buffalo, NY 14214 United States BUS: Public School P/S: Education MA: Local D/D/R: Teaching Early Childhood Education H/I/S: Playing Bass in a Band called 'Right Back Atcha' EDU: Master's Degree in Education, Canisius College (1990); Bachelor's Degree in Elementary Education, Buffalo State College (1986) A/A/S: Buffalo Teachers Federation C/VW: Girl Scouts of the United State of America
Email: rehcor07@msn.com
URL: http://www.buffaloschools.org

Alice F. O'Neill
Title: Principal **Company:** Performance Resources **Address:** 524 Columbus Avenue, Suite 1, Boston, MA 02118 United States **BUS:** Professional Development Training **P/S:** Corporate Training Regarding Sales, Management, New Business Development **MA:** National **D/D/R:** Specializing in Training Management, Training, Consultation and New Business Development and Customer Service **H/I/S:** Traveling **EDU:** Master of Science in Management **A/A/S:** New England Human Resources Association
Email: alice.oneill@performanceresources.net

Penny O'Neill
Title: Educator **Company:** Holy Cross High School **Address:** 5035 Route 130 South, Delran, NJ 08075 United States **BUS:** Education Facility **P/S:** Instruction and Curriculum **MA:** Regional **EXP:** Ms. O'Neill's expertise includes business arts and technology. **D/D/R:** Teaching Computer Application, General Business Entrepreneurship and Aided Drawing **H/I/S:** Jewelry Making **EDU:** Bachelor's Degree Plus 106 Credits in Business, College of New Jersey (1989) **CERTS:** Certified Business Teacher, Ninth through 12th-Grade
Email: penny.oneill@hclance.org
URL: http://www.sp.holycrossingschool.org

Nancy Elizabeth O'Reilly
Title: Rehabilitation Coordinator **Company:** Lincoln National Corporation **Address:** 6201 Powers Ferry Road N.W., Atlanta, GA 30339 United States **BUS:** Insurance and Financial Services Company **P/S:** Insurance and Financial Services **MA:** National **D/D/R:** Handling Medical and Workman's Compensation Cases **H/I/S:** Spending Time with her Two Sons, Mountain Biking, Skiing, Running, Rollerblading, Golfing **EDU:** Master of Science in Rehabilitation Counseling, Boston University; Bachelor of Science in Rehabilitation Counseling, Boston University **CERTS:** Certified Rehabilitation Counselor and Case Manager **A/A/S:** Former Member, National Business Group on Health; Case Management Society of America **C/VW:** Kids' Chance
Email: noreilly@bellsouth.net
URL: http://www.lfg.com

Laura J. O'Toole
Title: Vice President of Global Sourcing **Company:** First Consulting Group **Address:** 111 W. Ocean Boulevard, Long Beach, CA 90802 United States **BUS:** Healthcare Consulting Company **P/S:** Consultations, Implementation of Healthcare Solutions **MA:** International **D/D/R:** Recruiting, Outsourcing, Operations **H/I/S:** Reading, Traveling, Softball **EDU:** Pursuing Master's Degree in Hospital Administration, Nova Southeastern University **A/A/S:** Society for Human Resource Management; ERE; Parent-Teacher Association; Church **C/VW:** Cystic Fibrosis Foundation, March of Dimes, Morris County Homeless Shelter
Email: lotoole@fcg.com
URL: http://www.fcg.com

Danielle Assunta Oakes
Title: Lab Technician **Company:** Internist of Central Pennsylvania **Address:** 108 Lowther Street, Lemoyne, PA 17043 United States **BUS:** Internal Medicine Practice **P/S:** Internal Medicine **MA:** Regional **D/D/R:** Phlebotomy, Analyzing Blood **H/I/S:** Playing Volleyball and Softball **EDU:** Pursuing Bachelor of Science in Nursing, York College; Associate Degree in Nursing **C/VW:** Softball Tournament for Charities
Email: dasoakes@aol.com
URL: http://www.cambridgewhoswho.com

Dan C. Oana
Title: Medical Doctor **Company:** Semel Oana Goldenring Chua Costeas **Address:** 22 Old Short Hills Road, Livingston, NJ 07039 United States **BUS:** Healthcare Center **P/S:** Healthcare **MA:** Local **EXP:** Dr. Oana's expertise is in pediatric healthcare. **H/I/S:** Traveling, Reading **EDU:** MD, University of Romania **A/A/S:** Essex County Medical Society; American Medical Association; ADP
Email: agnesdan@aol.com
URL: http://www.cambridgewhoswho.com

Imad Makram Obeid, MD
Title: Medical Doctor **Company:** Henry Ford Hospital **Address:** 2799 West Grand Boulevard, Detroit, MI 48202 United States **BUS:** Hospital **P/S:** Healthcare **MA:** Regional **EXP:** Dr. Obeid's expertise includes pulmonary care and critical care. **H/I/S:** Traveling, Reading, Playing Racquetball **EDU:** MD, Damascus University, Syria (1999) **A/A/S:** American College of Physicians; American Medical Association
Email: obeidmd2001@yahoo.com

Laurie D. Oberhoff
Title: President **Company:** NAPM Houston, Inc. **Address:** 1120 Tobola Street, Rosenberg, TX 77471 United States **BUS:** Nonprofit Organization **P/S:** Education, Supply Chain Management **MA:** Houston **D/D/R:** Communicating, Negotiating, Managing Procurement and Education **H/I/S:** Volunteering **EDU:** College Coursework; High School Diploma **A/A/S:** Institute for Supply Management **A/H:** James O. Cox Award for Outstanding Member (2002); Secretary Person of the Year Award (2000-2001); President's Award (2007-2008) **C/VW:** Lifetime Member, Houston Livestock Show And Rodeo; Volunteer, Fort Bend County Fair Association, Rosenberg, TX
Email: loberhoff@tecmag.com
URL: http://www.napmhou.org

Joshua Obie
Title: Office Manager **Company:** CAPE, SEIU **Address:** 1720 S. Bellaire Street, Suite 605, Denver, CO 80222 United States **BUS:** Nonprofit Organization **P/S:** Union Organization for State Employees **MA:** Regional **D/D/R:** Managing Office Operations Including Finances, Ordering Equipment, Organizing Projects **H/I/S:** Playing Billiards **EDU:** Bachelor's Degree in Business Administration, Emphasis in Management, University of Northern Colorado (2005)
Email: jobie@ecape.net
URL: http://www.ecape.net

Heather A. Ochalek
Title: Owner **Company:** Music Showcase, Inc. **Address:** 402 Oakfield Drive, Brandon, FL 33511 United States **BUS:** Music Retail Store and Education Center **P/S:** Instrumental Rentals and Sales, Private Lessons, Group Classes, Show Choir, Theater Productions, Instrument Repairs **MA:** Pasco County, Sarasota County, Polk County, Hillsborough County, Manatee County, Florida **EXP:** Ms. Ochalek's expertise includes music therapy, voice and piano lessons, and business management. **H/I/S:** Spending Time with her Family **EDU:** Master of Business Administration and Master of Music Therapy, Shenandoah University, The University of Tampa **A/A/S:** Brandon Chamber of Commerce; National Association of Music Merchants; National Association of School Music Dealers; American Music Coalition; Founding Member, Independent Music Retailers Association; Retail Print Music Distributors Association **C/VW:** Brandon Care Pregnancy Center, The Spring, Joshua House, Local Churches; Board Member, Brandon Arts Council; Center Place
Email: mso@musicshowcaseonline.com
URL: http://www.musicshowcaseonline.com

Rebecca M. Ochs
Title: Registered Nurse **Company:** Central Kansas Medical Center **Address:** 3515 Broadway Avenue, Great Bend, KS 67530 United States **BUS:** Medical Center **P/S:** Healthcare **MA:** Regional **EXP:** Ms. Ochs' expertise is in nursing. **D/D/R:** Caring for Orthopedic and all Medical Patients **H/I/S:** Reading **CERTS:** Registered Nurse, Fort Hayes University (2006); Certification in Basic Life Support; Certification in CPR; Training in First Aid Treatment **A/A/S:** Who's Who Among American High School Students (1997-2001); College Who's Who
Email: beccamj116@hotmail.com
URL: http://www.cambridgewhoswho.com

Slavica Octenjak
Title: Designer **Company:** Lowe's **Address:** 5258 S. Wadsworth Boulevard, Littleton, CO 80123 United States **BUS:** Home Improvement Center **P/S:** Home Improvements, Retail, Installations **MA:** National **D/D/R:** Designing Cabinets, Kitchens and Baths, Fashion **H/I/S:** Reading, Art, Cooking, Gardening **EDU:** Bachelor's Degree in Interior Design and Furniture Design, Zagreb Art School, Croatia; Degree in Fashion Design **A/A/S:** Denver Art Gallery; Botanical Gardens **C/VW:** Disabled American Veterans
Email: slavicaoctenjak@lowes.com
Email: slavica.octenjak@store.lowes.com
URL: http://www.lowes.com

Susan E. Oderwald
Title: Executive Director, Chief Executive Officer **Company:** Society of Plastics Engineers **Address:** 14 Fairfield Drive, Brookfield, CT 06804 United States **BUS:** Professional Scientific Society **P/S:** Professionals Services, Journals, Magazines, Conferences **MA:** International **D/D/R:** Nonprofit Management, Fundraising, General Executive Management **EDU:** Master of Business Administration, Loyola College; Bachelor's Degree in International Relations and Russian, Wheaton College **A/A/S:** American Society of Association Executives; Connecticut Society of Association Executives; Association of Fundraising Professionals; Thomas Watson Fellow **C/VW:** Society of Plastics Engineers Foundation, Episcopal Church
Email: seoderwald@4spe.org
URL: http://www.4spe.org

William C. ODonnell Jr.
Title: Physician **Company:** WC ODonnell, Jr, MD, PA **Address:** 708 Hill Country Drive, Building 300 A, Kerrville, TX 78028 United States **BUS:** Family Practice **P/S:** Family Practice Medicine with Focus on Treating the Whole Patient **MA:** Local **D/D/R:** Excellent Patient Care with Focus on Younger Patients with ADD, Learning and Behavioral Disorders **H/I/S:** Golf, Photography of Golf Courses and Gardening **EDU:** University of Southwest Texas, Dallas, University of Texas, Austin, MD, BA in Zoology **A/A/S:** AMA, Tri County Medical Society, TMA, TAFP
Email: wcodon@ktc.com

George M. Oehlsen
Title: DO **Company:** University Medical Center Quick Care **Address:** 1769 E. Russel Road, Las Vegas, NV 89119 United States **BUS:** Healthcare Clinic **P/S:** Walk in Health Clinic **MA:** Local **EXP:** Dr. Oehlsen's expertise includes internal medicine, sports medicine and urgent care medicine. **H/I/S:** Traveling and Reading **EDU:** DeMoine University, Degree in Osteopathic Medicine
Email: goehlsen@aol.com

Kayce N. Ofodile
Title: Apostle **Company:** Lively Stones Ministries International, Inc. **Address:** 1799 Cooper Lakes Drive, Grayson, GA 30017 United States **BUS:** Ministry **P/S:** Mentoring Services, Help for Families, Therapy **MA:** International **D/D/R:** Preaching the Gospel of Jesus Christ, Offering Marriage and Family Therapy and Addiction Treatment, Performing Trauma Specialties **H/I/S:** Reading, Praying, Traveling, Playing Soccer **EDU:** Doctorate in Christian Clinical Counseling and Religious Arts, Cornerstone University **CERTS:** Advanced Certification, National Christian Counselors Association **A/A/S:** American Counseling Association; American Association of Christian Counselors; American Counsel Association; International Association of Traumatic Stress; Diplomat Member, Clinical Supervisor, National Board of Christian Clinical Therapists; United Way; Black Festival of Arts
Email: apostlekayce@yahoo.com

Byron T. Ogburn
Title: Senior Pastor **Company:** Living Waters Ministry Center, CMC **Address:** 11187 S.E. 41 North, White Springs, FL 32096 United States **BUS:** Church **P/S:** Religious Services **MA:** Local **D/D/R:** Offering Prayer and Worship Services, Counseling **H/I/S:** Golf, Softball, Hunting, Fishing
Email: ogburn99@alltell.net

Prof. Thomas Warren Ogletree
Title: Frederick Marquand Professor of Ethics and Religious Studies **Company:** Yale University **Dept:** Divinity School **Address:** 409 Prospect Street, New Haven, CT 06511 United States **BUS:** University **P/S:** Theological Education **MA:** International **EXP:** Mr. Ogletree's expertise is in theological education. **D/D/R:** Teaching Theology and Christian Social Ethics **H/I/S:** Spending Time with his Family **EDU:** Honorary Doctor of Laws, Livingstone College, Hood Theological Seminary (1995); Honorary Doctor of Divinity, Birmingham-Southern College (1991); Honorary Master of Arts, Yale University (1990); Post-Doctoral Study, Christian Social Teaching (1987); Post-Doctoral Study, Phenomenology, Herneneutics and the Moral Life, Seminar for Advanced Studies, The Sorbonne, Paris, France (1973-1974); Post-Doctoral Study, Marxist-Christian Dialog, Free University. West Berlin, German Federal Republic (1968-1969); Ph.D. in Theological Studies, Vanderbilt University, Nashville, TN (1963); Bachelor of Divinity, Garrett Theological Seminary, Evanston, IL, Summa Cum Laude (1959); Bachelor of Arts, Birmingham-Southern College, Birmingham, AL, Valedictorian, Summa Cum Laude (1955) **A/A/S:** Former Member, Selection Committee, Faculty Fellowships Program, Association of Theological Schools (1990-1994); Former Member, Accreditation Team, Review of University of Chicago Divinity School, Association of Theological Schools (1993); Former Member, Accreditation Team, Review of Duke Divinity School, Association of Theological Schools (1994); Former Consultant on Theological Scholarship, Association of Theological Schools (1993-1994); Conference, Basic Issues in Theological Education, Association of Theological Schools (1989); Former President, Society of Christian Ethics (1983-1984); Former Member, Board of Directors, Executive Committee Board, Society for Values in Higher Education (1978-1984); Former Vice-President. Society of Christian Ethics (1982-1983); Former Executive Committee Member of the Board of Directors, Society of Christian Ethics (1982-1984); Former Chairman, Publications Committee, Society of Christian Ethics (1980-1981); Founding Editor, The Annual of the Society of Christian Ethics (Now The Journal of the Society of Christian Ethics) (1981); Former Member, North American Academy of Ecumenists (1968); Former Chairman, Central Committee for Program Planning, Society for Values in Higher Education **C/VW:** Local Church
Email: thomas.ogletree@yale.edu
URL: http://www.cambridgewhoswho.com

Karen L. Ohlsen
Title: President **Company:** Muddy River Training Center, LLC **Address:** 30957 T Road, Netawaka, KS 66516 United States **BUS:** Private Career School **P/S:** Education for Heavy Equipment Operators **MA:** Regional **D/D/R:** Teaching **H/I/S:** Traveling the Back Roads of Kansas, Missouri and Nevada **EDU:** Master's Degree Plus 48 in Education, Kansas State University **C/VW:** Local Church, Orphanage in Mexico
Email: klohlsen@mrivertraining.com
URL: http://www.mrivertraining.com

Jeffrey W. Ohmes
Title: Distributor, Sales Manager **Company:** Kirchner Block and Brick, Inc. **Address:** 12901 St. Charles Rock Road, Bridgeton, MO 63044 United States **BUS:** Distribution Firm **P/S:** Concrete Masonry and Landscape Building Products **MA:** Regional **EXP:** Mr. Ohmes' expertise includes sales and operations management. **H/I/S:** Traveling, Scuba Diving, Fishing, Water Sports, Snow Skiing **EDU:** Bachelor of Science in Business, Missouri State University **A/A/S:** Board Member, Department of Public Works, Saint Charles **C/VW:** Board Member, Academy of the Sacred Heart
Email: johmes@kirchnerblock.com
URL: http://www.kirchnerblock.com

Mr. Luis Antonio Ojeda
Title: President **Company:** High Living Developers & Management Group **Dept:** Management **Address:** P.O. Box 378, Angeles, PR 00611 United States **BUS:** Construction Management and Engineering Consulting **P/S:** Construction Management, Engineering, Inspection, Land Surveying, Consulting, Home Inspection, ARPE Permits **MA:** Puerto Rico **D/D/R:** Inspecting Civil Engineering Projects **H/I/S:** Music, basketball, baseball and Theology **EDU:** Bachelor of Arts in Civil Engineering, Polytechnic University of Puerto Rico (1985) **CERTS:** Certification in Special Preparation and Structural Design (1985) **A/A/S:** National Society of Professional Engineers (NSPE); American Society of Civil Engineers (ASCE); American Concrete Institute (ACI); Professional college and land surveyors of Puerto Rico (CIAPR) **C/VW:** We Determined this freely during the year.
Email: luisojeda@ciaprmail.org
Email: luis_ojeda1@yahoo.com
URL: http://webmail.ciaprmail.org/
URL: http://www.cambridgewhoswho.com

Celina C. Okpaleke
Title: Chief Executive Officer, President **Company:** Faith Home Health, Inc **Address:** 2508 W. Tampa Bay Boulevard, Tampa, FL 33607 United States **BUS:** Healthcare Rehab **P/S:** Home Health Services, Rehabilitation Services **MA:** Local **D/D/R:** Working as a Physician Assistant **H/I/S:** Choir, Sing **EDU:** Bachelor of Science in Medicine, University of Florida at Gainesville **A/A/S:** AAPA, Association of Home Health Industry of Florida
Email: cokpaleke@faithhomehealth.org
URL: www.faithhomehealth.org

Omotayo T. Okusanya
Title: Equity Research Analyst **Company:** UBS **Address:** 1285 Avenue of the Americas, New York, NY 10019 United States **BUS:** Financial Firm **P/S:** Investment Banking **MA:** National **EXP:** Mr. Okusanya's expertise includes financial equities, real estate research and investment banking. **H/I/S:** Playing Tennis **EDU:** Master of Business Administration, Harvard University; Bachelor's Degree in Accounting and Computer Science, Rutgers, The State University of New Jersey **CERTS:** Certified Public Accountant; Certified Senior Accountant **A/A/S:** New York Society of Security Analysts; New Jersey Society of Certified Public Accountants
Email: omotayo.okusanta@ubs.com
URL: http://www.ubs.com

Alicia Olea-Bell, MS
Title: Bilingual Teacher (Retired) **Company:** Beacon New York School District **Address:** 58 Crosstree Drive, Hilton Head Island, SC 29926 United States **BUS:** Art Company **P/S:** Landscape and Seascape Paintings in Oil, Watercolors, Ink, Pastels and Charcoal **MA:** Local **D/D/R:** Exhibiting Art, Painting in Oils, Pastels and Charcoal, Showing in Local Galleries, Publishing her Poetry, Translating in Spanish **H/I/S:** Sailing, Gardening, Bicycling, Playing Tennis, Swimming, Playing the Guitar, Singing, Writing Poetry **EDU:** Master of Science in Spanish Education, New Paltz (1985); Bachelor of Science in Education **CERTS:** Certification in Elementary Middle and High School Spanish and Bilingual Education **A/A/S:** Soba Art Gallery; Tennis Player, United State Tennis Association; Cultural Arts Center; Saint Francis by the Sea Catholic Church **A/H:** Award, Juried Show 2007, Hilton Head Island Art Gallery, Bluffton; Former President, First Place Award, Federated Garden Clubs of New York State, Inc.
Email: lichab34@aol.com

Reagan Harris Oles
Title: Elementary School Principal **Company:** Claude Independent School District **Address:** 509 High Street, Claude, TX 79019 United States **BUS:** Education **P/S:** Education **MA:** Local **EXP:** Mr. Oles' expertise includes children's education and administration. **H/I/S:** Spending Time with her Husband and Three Children **EDU:** Master's Degree in Educational Administration; Bachelor's Degree in Interdisciplinary Studies, West Texas A&M University **A/A/S:** Texas Education Association; Texas Elementary Principals and Supervisors Association **C/VW:** First Baptist Church of Claude, 4-H Club
Email: reagan.oles@region16.net
URL: http://www.cambridgewhoswho.com

Mrs. Virginia A. Olive
Title: Reading and Literacy Coach **Company:** Leonard Dober Elementary School **Dept:** Department of Education **Address:** 44-46 Kongens Gade, St. Thomas, 00802 United States **BUS:** Elementary School **P/S:** General Elementary Curriculum, Arts, Music, Reading and Literacy Program, Physical Education, Learning Resources, Student Support Services, Athletics, Extracurricular Activities **MA:** Regional **D/D/R:** Overseeing Reading and Literacy Program for Students in Kindergarten through Sixth-Grade, Teaching Writing, Coaching Teachers **H/I/S:** Cooking, Reading **EDU:** Bachelor's Degree in Elementary Education, University of the Virgin Islands (1987) **A/A/S:** American Federation of Teachers; North American Reading Program; No Child Left Behind Act **A/H:** Outstanding Educator Award, Leonard Dober Elementary School (2000-2001) **C/VW:** Board Member of Sts. Peter & Paul School Board Religious Education Teacher, Our Lady of Perpetual Help Church, St. Thomas, V.I. Volunteer/Chaperone, Sts. Peter & Paul Cathedral Altar Servers
Email: volive@sttj.k12.vi
URL: http://www.sttj.k12.vi/SCH-SITES/Dober/Index.htm

Charles R. Oliver
Title: (Retired) **Company:** Fluor Corporation **Dept:** Washington Group International, Inc. **Address:** P.O. Box 1681, Hamilton, MT 59840 United States **BUS:** Engineering and Construction Company **P/S:** Engineering, Construction and Technical Services for Public Agencies **MA:** International **D/D/R:** Civil Engineering, Managing Sales and Operations Including Mining, Handling Petroleum Chemicals, Finance and Strategic Planning **H/I/S:** Traveling, Fly Fishing, Horseback Riding, Golfing **EDU:** Doctoral Degree, California State University, with Honors; Bachelor of Science in Civil Engineering, Auburn University, AL **A/A/S:** American Society of Civil Engineers; Advisory Board Member, Davidson Honors College, University of Montana; Trustee, The University of Montana Foundation; Grizzly Riders International
Email: oliverchar@aol.com

Ms. Lisa A. Oliver, M.S.Ed., ATC/LAT
Title: Athletic Trainer **Company:** Klein Oak High School **Address:** 16334 Morning Mist Drive, Houston, TX 77090 United States **BUS:** High School **P/S:** Education, Allied Health Provider **MA:** Local **D/D/R:** Preventing Injuries, Rehabilitation, Educating Athletes on Nutrition and the Prevention and Treatment of Injuries **H/I/S:** Reading, Movies, Gardening, Sports, Cultural Events **EDU:** Bachelor of Arts, Baylor University Master's Degree in Education, Baylor University **A/A/S:** National Athletic Trainers' Association; Southwest Athletic Trainers' Association; Association of Texas Professional Educators, Greater Houston Athletic Trainer's Society **C/VW:** Good Will, Special Olympics, Susan G. Komen for the Cure, Salvation Army, Nature Conservancy
Email: silvanone@sbcglobal.net
Email: loliver@kleinisd.net
URL: http://www.cambridgewhoswho.com

Dustin Oliverson
Title: Director of Marketing **Company:** Neotone Records, Inc. **Address:** 2104 37th Street, Des Moines, IA 50310 United States **BUS:** Music Production Company **P/S:** CDs, Records, Music Production **MA:** International **D/D/R:** Overseeing Distribution, Licensing and Publishing **H/I/S:** Cycling, Traveling, Attending Concerts **C/VW:** Des Moines Music and Coalition
Email: dustyo@neotone-records.com
URL: http://www.neotone-records.com

Peter E. Ollen
Title: Attorney at Law **Company:** Paul, Hastings, Janofsky & Walker LLP **Address:** 75 E. 55th Street, 16th Floor, New York, NY 10022 United States **BUS:** Legal Services **P/S:** Civil Representation/Corporate Clients **MA:** International **EXP:** Mr. Ollen's expertise includes private equity, and corporate and private mergers and acquisitions,. **H/I/S:** Political Philosophy, Tennis **EDU:** Oxford University, Oxford, England, MA Juris Prudence **A/A/S:** NY State Bar Association; Solici for England and Wales
Email: peterollen@paulhastings.com

Kevin Olmstead
Title: Environmental Engineer **Company:** Tetra Tech **Address:** 710 Avis Drive, Ann Arbor, MI 48108 United States **BUS:** Engineering and Consulting Firm **P/S:** Engineering and Consulting Services **MA:** International **D/D/R:** Consulting on Wastewater Treatments **EDU:** Ph.D. in Environmental Engineering, University of Michigan **A/A/S:** American Society of Civil Engineers; American Institute of Chemical Engineers; Water Environment Federation **A/H:** Award, Who Wants to be a Millionaire **C/VW:** Toastmasters International
Email: kevinolmstead76@yahoo.com
URL: http://www.tetratech.com

Charlene Marie Olsen
Title: First Grade Teacher **Company:** South School Elementary School **Address:** 710 N. Webb Avenue, Reedsburg, WI 53959 United States **BUS:** School District **P/S:** Education **MA:** Local **D/D/R:** Designing First Grade Curriculum, Teaching all subjects **H/I/S:** Outdoor Activities, Camping, Spending Time with her Children **EDU:** Pursuing Master's Degree, University of Wisconsin-Platteville; Bachelor's Degree in Elementary Education, University of Wisconsin-Platteville **CERTS:** Pursuing Reading Licenses **A/A/S:** Phi Kappa Phi **C/VW:** Feed the Children, Multiple Sclerosis
Email: jccn@mchsi.com

Joy E. Olsen, LMT
Title: Licensed Massage Therapist **Company:** A-Touch of Light Therapeutic Massage **Address:** 837 Daisy Street, Sandy, UT 84094 United States **BUS:** Massage Spa **P/S:** Massage Therapy **MA:** Regional **D/D/R:** Educating Clients on Wellness and its Relationship to Massage, Emphasizing the Importance of Stretching and Range of Motion Exercises, Offering Deep Tissue, Swedish and Therapeutic Massages, Practicing Muscle Release Techniques, Pressure Point Therapy and Energy Work **H/I/S:** Bowling, Golfing, Working with Leather, Beading **CERTS:** Licensed Massage Therapist, Utah College of Massage Therapy (2000) **A/A/S:** American Massage Therapy Association; Better Business Bureau **A/H:** Sterling Club Award (2008); Leadership Conference Award (2008)
Email: magichands6699@msn.com

Brad M. Olson
Title: Fire Fighter, Emergency Medical Technician **Company:** Grays Harbor Fire District 5 **Address:** 73 McCleary Road, McCleary, WA 98557 United States **BUS:** Fire Department **P/S:** Emergency Medical Technician Services, Fire Suppression **MA:** Regional **D/D/R:** Doing Rigorous Checks in the Morning, Going on Calls, Making Sure the Firehouse is Clean **H/I/S:** Hunting, Snowboarding **EDU:** Emergency Medical Technician, Gray's Harbor Emergency (2007)
Email: olson_2@hotmail.com

Julie Ann Olson
Title: Channel Manager **Company:** Wells Fargo Bank, NA **Address:** 255 Second Avenue S., Minneapolis, MN 55479 United States **BUS:** Bank **P/S:** Banking, Investments **MA:** Local **EXP:** Ms. Olson's expertise is in technology. **H/I/S:** Spending Time with her Family, Visiting their Cabin **EDU:** Bachelor of Science in Business and Psychology, Concordia College **A/A/S:** Women in Technology **C/VW:** Girl Scouts of the USA, Junior Achievement, Habitat for Humanity
URL: http://www.cambridgewhoswho.com

Mrs. Marian Olson
Title: Partner **Company:** Suburban Feed & Supply **Address:** 1404 Main Street, Hopkins, MN 55343 United States **BUS:** Retail Store **P/S:** Food and Supplies for Pets and Wildlife **MA:** Twin Cities and Surrounding Area **D/D/R:** Working with Minnesota Human Society Fostering Cats for Adoption, Managing the Nutrition of Dogs and Cats with Dietary Allergies and Sensitivities **H/I/S:** Phenology, Wild Bird Watching, Studying and Volunteering Work **EDU:** Bachelor's Degree in French, Lawrence University
Email: tolson7515W@aol.com
URL: http://www.cambridgewhoswho.com

Thomas J. Olson
Title: Owner **Company:** Olson Landscaping and Garden Design **Address:** 2909 Livingston Street N.E., Salem, OR 97301 United States **BUS:** Landscaping Company **P/S:** Landscape Design, Maintenance **MA:** Local **D/D/R:** Designing Landscapes, Pruning, Residential Communities **H/I/S:** Working on his Backyard
Email: olsonmur@comcast.net

Sharon M. Ondreyco, MD
Title: Lead Physician, President, Founder **Company:** Palo Verde **Address:** 10460 N. 92nd Street 402, Scottsdale, AZ 85258 United States **BUS:** Medical Practice **P/S:** Hematology and Oncology Medical Services **MA:** Regional **D/D/R:** Specializing in all Aspects of Hematology and Oncology Healthcare as well as Coordinating the Overall Business Functions and Maintaining Quality Patient Service **EDU:** Ohio State University School of Medicine, University of Utah, Fellowship in Hematology and Oncology in 1978, MD in 1975 **A/A/S:** The American Society School of Clinical Oncology, American College of Physician Executives, American Society of Breast Disease

Emelie M. Ongcapin, MD
Title: Pathologist **Company:** St. Barnabas Medical Center **Address:** 94 Old Short Hills Road, Livingston, NJ 07039 United States **BUS:** Non-Sectarian Health Care Institution Primary, Secondary and Tertiary Health Services **P/S:** Ambulatory Surgery Center, Anesthesiology, Behavioral Health Network, Breast Center, Burn Center, Cancer Programs and Services, Dialysis, Emergency Department, Epilepsy Center, Adult and Pediatric, Hospice Services, Imaging Center, Obesity and Weight Management Center, Obstetrics/Gynecology, The Pain Management Institute, Pathology, Pediatrics, Peritoneal Dialysis, Physical Medicine and Rehabilitation, Plastic and Reconstructive Surgery, Pulmonary Rehabilitation, Outpatient Radiation Oncology, Radiology Department and Many Other Services **MA:** Regional **EXP:** Dr. Ongcapin's expertise includes pathology, geriatrics and gynecological pathology. **H/I/S:** Jogging, Tennis **EDU:** MD, Far East University (1964) **A/A/S:** United States/Canadian International Association of Pathologists; American Association of Clinical Pathologists; Academy of Medicine of New Jersey; Article Published in Clinical Journal of Human Oncology
Email: eongcapin@sbhcs.com
URL: http://www.sbhcs.com

Mr. Rick C. Onstott
Title: Parking Director **Company:** Anchorage Community Development Authority **Address:** 700 W. Sixth Avenue, Suite 206, Anchorage, AK 99501 United States **BUS:** Government Agency **P/S:** Public Parking and Resources **MA:** Regional **EXP:** Managing, Developing and Controlling Public Parking Facilities. **H/I/S:** Sports, Football, Hunting, Fishing, Taxidermy **EDU:** Bachelor of Arts in Education, St. Mary's College, Dodge City, KS (1981) **A/A/S:** Anchorage Downtown Partnership; Northwest Parking Association; International Parking Institute
Email: rickonstott@acda-ap.com
URL: http://www.anchorageparking.com

Beverly M. Opalka
Title: 1) Deputy Probation Officer II 2) College Instructor 2) Psychology Instructor **Company:** 1) LA County Probation Department 2) Chapman University **Address:** 1) 42011 Fourth Street W., Suite 1900 2) 40015 Sierra, 1) Lancaster, CA 93534 2) Palmdale, CA 93550 **BUS:** 1) Corrections and Law Enforcement 2) Education **P/S:** 1) County Probation Department 2) Private University **MA:** 1) Regional 2) International **D/D/R:** Juvenile and Adult Probation, Collaborating with Courts, Law Enforcement Officials, Social Services and Schools **H/I/S:** Traveling, Watching Movies, Painting, Biking, Playing with Cats and Dogs, Tinkering with her Classic Car **EDU:** Master's Degree in Psychology, Phillips Graduate Institute, 2003; Bachelor's Degree in Criminal Justice, Long Beach State University, 1985 **A/A/S:** Department Safety; California Narcotic Association **C/VW:** Former Member, Lions Club, Antelope Valley Children's Center, 2001-2003
Email: chillydawgg62@yahoo.com
URL: http://www.cambridgewhoswho.com

Thomas H. Ophardt
Title: Optometrist **Company:** Dr. Tom Optometry **Address:** 15 Market Street, Brockport, NY 14420 United States **BUS:** Private Clinic **P/S:** Eye Care Services Such as Eye Testing Prescribing Contact Lenses, Fashion Glasses **MA:** Local **EXP:** Mr. Ophardt's expertise is in general optometry. **H/I/S:** Square Dancing, Country Dancing, Painting, Photography, Traveling, Two-Stepping **EDU:** Doctor of Optometry, Southern California College of Optometry; Bachelor of Arts in German, Hartwick College; Coursework in Biology, University of Wuerzburg, Germany **C/VW:** Local Church
Email: thomaso510@mac.com
URL: http://www.eyefinity.com/drtomoptometry

Mollie M. Oram
Title: Manager, Owner **Company:** Country Roads Tree Farm **Address:** 9647 Taberg Florence Road, Taberg, NY 13471 United States **BUS:** Family-Owned Tree Farm **P/S:** Christmas Trees, Logs, Firewood, Finished Wood Products **MA:** International **D/D/R:** Offering Business Management, Planning, Woodworking, Skidding, Replanting **H/I/S:** Traveling, Woodworking **EDU:** Diploma, Rome Free Academy High School (1964) **A/A/S:** Christmas Tree Growers of New York; American Tree Farmer
Email: molliemoram@yahoo.com
URL: http://www.cambridgewhoswho.com

Gioconda A. Orellana, RN
Title: Registered Nurse **Company:** Jackson Memorial Hospital **Address:** 18464 N.W. 21st Street, Pembroke Pines, FL 33029 United States **BUS:** Hospital **P/S:** 1,550 Licensed Bed Hospital and Referral Center, Medical Research Center, Adult and Pediatric Level 1 Trauma Center, Teaching Facility for the University of Miami Leonard M. Miller School of Medicine **MA:** Regional **D/D/R:** Post-Surgical Patient Care, Charge Floor Nursing, Educating Patients on Procedures, Chemotherapy, Administration **H/I/S:** Bowling, Playing Basketball **EDU:** Master of Arts in Business Administration, University of Colorado (2007); Bachelor of Science in Economics, Universidad Inca Garcilaso de la Vega, Peru (1981) **CERTS:** Registered Nurse, Miami Dade College (2005); Certification in Preventive Healthcare; License in Chemotherapy Treatment; **A/A/S:** In-service for Cultural Diversity, Saint Edward Catholic Church; ADVANCE for Nursing (2007); Radio Show **A/H:** Featured, Best Nursing Team (2007-2008) **C/VW:** United Baptist Church
Email: gioco212@aol.com
URL: http://www.cambridgewhoswho.com

Jeanne L. Ormsby
Title: Owner **Company:** Jeanne Ormsby Marketing Communications **Address:** 18355 Jefferson Park Road, Suite 204, Middleburg Heights, OH 44130 United States **BUS:** Advertising Agency **P/S:** Advertising Consulting **MA:** Local **D/D/R:** Advertising Consulting for Small Businesses and Nonprofit Organizations **H/I/S:** Playing Golf, Playing Bridge **EDU:** Bachelor of Arts in English, Political Science and History, Case Western Reserve University **A/A/S:** First Woman President, Cleveland Chapter, Public Relations Society of America; President, Zonta Club of Cleveland **C/VW:** United Way, Easter Seals, Amnesty International, Various Native American Charities

Peter Oroszlany
Title: Principal **Company:** Mott Hall V School **Address:** 2055 Mapes Avenue, Bronx, NY 10460 United States **BUS:** School **P/S:** Education **MA:** Local **D/D/R:** Supervising Staff and Student Body to Assure Quality Education, Overseeing Budget, Making Modifications to Student Behavior, Preparing Courses in Mathematics, Science and Technology **H/I/S:** Canoeing, Spending Time Outdoors, Maintaining Cars **EDU:** Master's Degree in Urban and Multicultural Education, College of Mount Saint Vincent, Riverdale; Master's Degree in Administration and Supervision, The College of New Rochelle **A/A/S:** National Middle School Association
Email: poroszl@schools.nyc.gov
URL: http://www.cambridgewhoswho.com

Kaylie Orr
Title: Occupational Therapist **Company:** San Diego County Office of Education **Address:** 6401 Linda Vista Road, San Diego, CA 92111 United States **BUS:** Health Care **P/S:** Education **MA:** Local **EXP:** Mr. Orr's expertise includes sensory integration therapy and school-based occupational therapy. **H/I/S:** Surfing, Practicing Yoga, Reading, Hiking **EDU:** Master of Arts in Occupational Therapy, University of Southern California, 2001; Bachelor of Science in Human Development, University of California at Davis, 1997 **A/A/S:** American Occupational Therapy Association
Email: kaylieorr@hotmail.com

Jennifer Kaye Orr-Williams
Title: Social Worker **Company:** Burlington House **Address:** 2222 Springdale, Cincinnati, OH 45231 United States **BUS:** Social Worker Nursing Home **P/S:** Long Term Care Facility **MA:** Local **EXP:** Ms. Orr-Williams' expertise includes mental assessments. **D/D/R:** Working with Alzheimer's Patients, Advocating for Seniors **H/I/S:** Reading, Singing, Dancing **EDU:** Master's Degree in Science Social Work **A/A/S:** NASW, American Red Cross, Boy Scouts
Email: jenniferwilliams@fuse.net

Rafael Orta
Title: Owner, Chief Information Officer **Company:** OraProfessionals **Address:** 12 Longbridge Drive, Mount Laurel, NJ 08054 United States **BUS:** Information Technology Consulting Company **P/S:** Consulting **MA:** National **D/D/R:** Databases Project Management, Custom Development, Data Mining, Operations and Management, Consulting Services for Small Businesses **H/I/S:** Playing Tennis, Beach, Researching about Artificial Intelligence and expert systems. **EDU:** Master of Science in Computer Science, Earned in the USA at New Jersey Institute of Technology; Bachelor of Science in Computer Engineering earned at IUNP in Caracas, Venezuela. **A/A/S:** New Jersey Oracle Users Group, IOUG, Philadelphia Oracle Users Group, First State Oracle Users Group Vice President, NJOUG (2007) **C/VW:** Saint Joan of Arc center for integral Development (JACID)
Email: Rafael.Orta@oraprofessionals.com
URL: http://www.oraprofessionals.com

Tracy C. Ortega
Title: Vice President, Controller **Company:** Campos & Sons Trucking, Inc. **Address:** 5002 A National Parks Highway, Carlsbad, NM 88220 United States **BUS:** Transportation Company **P/S:** General Trucking Services Including Fork Lifts, Flatbed Trucks, Pipe Hauling for Oilfield Industry **MA:** Regional **D/D/R:** Managing Business Operations **H/I/S:** Reading, Spending Time with her Daughter **EDU:** High School Education
Email: campostrucking@yahoo.com

Angela Ortiz
Title: Intake Officer **Company:** Cuyahoga County Court of Common Please Juvenile Division **Address:** 12650 Detriot Ave, Lakewood, OH 44107 United States **BUS:** Juvenile Court Government **P/S:** Services for Children and Family Under Court Jurisdiction **MA:** Local **D/D/R:** Community Resource Referral, Legal Intake Services, Mediation Hearing Officer **H/I/S:** Bowling, Golf, Spending time with friends and family **EDU:** The University of Akron, Bachelor of Science in Psychology, Adorned Training in Mediation Through the Court System **A/H:** Winner on the First Extra Mile Away by Cuyahoga Court System
Email: aortiz1@marykay.com
URL: http://www.marykay.com/aortiz1

Gerardo F. Ortiz Jr.
Title: Electrical Instructor **Company:** Home Builders Institute **Address:** 1205 15th Street N.W., Sixth Floor, Washington, DC 20005 United States **BUS:** Educational Institution **P/S:** Craft Education and Training Programs **MA:** National **EXP:** Mr. Ortiz's expertise includes wiring and circuitry management. **H/I/S:** Playing Tennis **EDU:** Coursework, University of Sacramento; Coursework, University of Arizona
Email: ortiz.gerard@jobcorps.org
Email: gortiz47@hotmail.com
URL: http://www.cambridgewhoswho.com

Jose R. Ortiz
Title: Drug and Alcohol Therapist **Company:** Eagleville Hospital **Address:** 1463 Meadowview Drive, Pottstown, PA 19464 United States **BUS:** Hospital **P/S:** Healthcare Services, Geriatric Psychiatry Program, Drug and Alcohol Counseling Services **MA:** Regional **D/D/R:** Counseling Mental Health Patients, Individuals with Drug and Alcohol Dependencies, Group Therapy, Performing Emergency Room Assessments, Managing Cases **H/I/S:** Entertaining Guests **EDU:** Pursuing Master's Degree; Bachelor of Arts in Criminal Justice, Temple University (1992) **A/A/S:** The National Notary Association
Email: mousecaspers@yahoo.com
URL: http://www.eaglevillehospital.org

Sara Ortiz
Title: Early Childhood Educator **Company:** Chicago Public Schools **Address:** 9735 S. Exchange Avenue, Chicago, IL 60617 United States **BUS:** Public School System **P/S:** General Primary and Secondary School Curriculum, Early Childhood Programs, Arts, Music, Physical Education, Athletics, Extracurricular Activities, Student Organizations and Clubs **MA:** Regional **D/D/R:** Teaching 5 and 6-Year-Old Students, Teaching Mathematics, Science, Social Science and Social Development **H/I/S:** Gardening, Arts and Crafts **EDU:** Bachelor's Degree in Early Childhood Education, Chicago State University (2001) **CERTS:** Certification in Type IV Teaching **A/A/S:** The Missionettes
Email: sortiz3@cps.k12.il.us
URL: http://www.cps.k12.il.us

LeRoy D. Ortopan
Title: Librarian (Retired) **Company:** University of California **Address:** 387 Soda Hall, Berkeley, CA 94720 United States **BUS:** University **P/S:** Higher Education **MA:** National **EXP:** Mr. Ortopan's expertise is in information cataloging. **H/I/S:** Reading, Attending the Theater, Listening to Music **EDU:** Master's Degree in English, Case Western Reserve University; Master's Degree in Library Science, Case Western Reserve University **A/A/S:** California Library Association; American Library Association; Northern California Technical Processing Group **C/VW:** AIDS Hospice; Glide Memorial Church
Email: ortopan@comcast.net

Ise O. Osaghae
Title: Registered Nurse **Company:** Greater Baltimore Medical Center **Dept:** Obstetrics Department **Address:** 6701 N. Charles Street, Baltimore, MD 21204 United States **BUS:** Medical Center **P/S:** Healthcare **MA:** Regional **D/D/R:** Overseeing Mothers and Babies in the Nursery, Assuring a Combined Effort for Patients, Filling Patients' Needs **H/I/S:** Listening to Music, Shopping **EDU:** Bachelor of Science in Nursing, University of Maryland (2008); Associate Degree in Nursing, Wesley College (2003) **C/VW:** Greater Baltimore Medical Center
Email: iosagha1@yahoo.com
URL: http://www.gbmc.org

Ana Paulino Osborne
Title: President, Executive Director **Company:** Multi-Language Solutions, Inc. **Address:** 2 Canal Street, Suite 2222, New Orleans, LA 70130 United States **BUS:** Language Services, Classes **P/S:** Language Classes, Interpretation and Translation, Staff-Independent Contractors 27-30, Roughly 80 Students in Language Classes, 50 in Business Interpretation **MA:** International **D/D/R:** Managing the Office, Handles all Finances, Hiring Staff, Client Relations **H/I/S:** Travel **EDU:** Certification in English Composition; Master's Degree in English Literature, Warick University in England (2000); Bachelor's Degree in Modern Language, Earned in Portugal and Germany (1998)
Email: anapaulino@multi-languagesolutions.com
URL: http://www.multi-languagesolutions.com

Donald L. Osborne
Title: Owner **Company:** Don Osborne and Son, LLC **Address:** 76 Circle Drive, Oak Ridge, NJ 07438 United States **BUS:** Construction Company **P/S:** Construction Services **MA:** Regional **EXP:** Mr. Osborne's area of expertise is in construction. **D/D/R:** Overseeing Residential and Commercial Carpentry Work, Brick Pavement Repair, Sidewalks and Patio Work, Ensuring Customer Satisfaction **H/I/S:** Exercising **CERTS:** Black Seal Boiler License **A/H:** Educational Support Staff Award; Second Place, Education Support Professional of the Year Award
Email: dogo5@verizon.net
URL: http://www.cambridgewhoswho.com

Shea W. Osborne
Title: Special Educator **Company:** McKinley Middle School **Address:** 3000 Kanawha Terrace, Saint Albans, WV 25177 United States **BUS:** Public Middle School **P/S:** Education **MA:** Local **D/D/R:** Teaching Students with Special Needs **H/I/S:** Playing Baseball and Softball **EDU:** Master's Degree in Special Education, Emphasis in Behavior Disorders, Marshall University; Bachelor's Degree in Social Studies Education, K-12, West Virginia State University; Educational Specialist in Learning Disabilities and Learning Impaired, West Virginia State University **A/A/S:** American Federation of Teachers
Email: osborne51@marshall.edu
URL: http://www.cambridgewhoswho.com

Pastor José Luis Oseguera
Title: Pastor **Company:** Iglesia Vigilancia Cristiana **Address:** 3906 W. Hadley Street, Phoenix, AZ 85009 United States **BUS:** Church **P/S:** Preaching the Gospel of Jesus Christ, Counseling **MA:** International **D/D/R:** Teaching, Preaching Marriage Consulting Youth Consulting **H/I/S:** Spending Time with Family **EDU:** Bachelor of Divinity, Alameda University; Ministry Degree, Iglesia Vigilancia Cristiana (1988); Credentials, Christian Vigilance Church **A/A/S:** El Monitor Hispano **C/VW:** Helping Hands, American Red Cross
Email: phoenixcvc@hotmail.com
URL: http://www.vigilanciacristiana.com

Sandra L. Oshiro
Title: Educator **Company:** Momilani Elementary School **Address:** 2130 Hookiekie Street, Pearl City, HI 96782 United States **BUS:** Elementary School **P/S:** Education for Elementary School Students **MA:** Regional **D/D/R:** Teaching General Education **H/I/S:** Anything Outdoors Including Camping, Hiking, Fishing **EDU:** Sixth Year Professional Diploma in Elementary Education, University of Hawaii (1989) **A/A/S:** Hawaii State Teachers Association; National Education Association
Email: sloshiro@yahoo.com
URL: http://www.k12.hi.us

Josef Oskar
Title: General Sales Manager **Company:** ACC USA, LLC **Address:** 113 Jetplex Circle, Suite B1, Madison, AL 35758 United States **BUS:** Manufacturer **P/S:** Compressors for Refrigeration **MA:** United States, Canada and Mexico **D/D/R:** Sales Engineering **H/I/S:** Listening to Classical Music, Reading **EDU:** Master of Science in Engineering, Master of Business Administration in Operations Management, Polytechnic School of Milan, Italy; Matriculated Bachelors Diploma, Nautical College, Akko, Israel **A/A/S:** Association of Engineers, Italy
Email: josef.oskar@hotmail.it

Lucy L. Osorio
Title: Administrator, Psychotherapist **Company:** Sunrise Medical, PC **Address:** 4039 Junction Boulevard, Corona, NY 11368 United States **BUS:** General Medical Practice **P/S:** Healthcare, Psychology. Psychotherapy **MA:** Local **D/D/R:** Performing Administrative Duties, Psychotherapy, Treating Private Patients **EDU:** Master's Degree in Mental Health and Social Work, Columbia University (1993) **A/A/S:** National Association of Social Work
Email: losorio@sunrisemedicalpc.com

Josephine A. Osterkamp
Title: 1) Financial Management Officer 2) Co-Owner 3) Manager **Company:** 1) Minnesota Veterans Homes 2) Dan's Ailing Auto Clinic 3) Summit Mini Storage, LLC **Address:** 1629 Highway 96 E., White Bear Lake, MN 55110 United States **BUS:** 1) Nursing Home 2) Auto Repair Company 3) Storage Facility **P/S:** 1) Healthcare 2) Auto Repair and Service 3) Storage **MA:** Local **EXP:** Ms. Osterkamp's expertise includes management and finance. **D/D/R:** Accounting, Managing Business Operations, Handling Payrolls, Maintaining Budgets **EDU:** Bachelor's Degree (2003) **CERTS:** Licensed Notary Public, Minnesota
Email: joosterk@mpls.mvh.state.mn.us
URL: http://www.mvh.state.mn.us/

Mr. Noah S. Ostroff
Title: Owner, Vice President of Operations **Company:** Strategic Logistics Staffing, LLC **Address:** 449 S. Pennsylvania Avenue, Morrisville, PA 19067 United States **BUS:** Transportation Company **P/S:** Driver Leasing, Staffing, Transportation Management **MA:** National **D/D/R:** Overseeing Daily Operations of Pennsylvania, Virginia and Indiana, Managing Payroll and Employee Records, Hiring Employees, Terminating Employees, Reviewing Driver Contracts with Subcontractors, Maintaining Employee Relationships, Training **H/I/S:** Football, Basketball, Baseball, Spending Time with his Family, Golfing **EDU:** Bachelor of Science in Business, Minor in International Studies, The Pennsylvania State University (2003)
Email: noah@slsdrivers.com
URL: http://www.slsdrivers.com

Charlene Hoffman Oswald
Title: Special Education Teacher **Company:** Glen Cove School District **Dept:** Gribbin Elementary School, Daisy Elementary School **Address:** Seaman Road, Glen Cove, NY 11542 United States **BUS:** Elementary School **P/S:** Education **MA:** Local **EXP:** Ms. Oswald's area of expertise is in special education. **D/D/R:** Working with Physically and Learning Disabled Students Individually and Within Groups, In and Out of a Regular Classroom Setting, Creating a Clubhouse Environment for the Children to Learn in, Teaching an Inclusion Class **H/I/S:** Reading, Walking, Gardening **EDU:** Post-Master's Degree in Education, Plus 75, Various Graduate Institutions; Master's Degree in Special Education, Long Island University **A/A/S:** Secretary, Special Education Parent Teacher Association; Council for Exceptional Children; International Dyslexia Association; Northshore Historical Society **C/VW:** Children's Cancer Research Organizations
Email: bunky123@aol.com

Rosa D. Otero-Walsh
Title: Detective Specialist (Retired) **Company:** New York Police Department **Address:** 1 Police Plaza, New York, NY 10038 United States **BUS:** Police Department **P/S:** Law Enforcement **MA:** Statewide **EXP:** Ms. Otero-Walsh's expertise includes community crime prevention and immigration. **D/D/R:** Overseeing Operations **H/I/S:** Spending Time with her Family **A/A/S:** Community Solutions Advisory Board **A/H:** Women of the Year Award, Puerto Rican Day Parade (2006)
Email: tuff4u88@yahoo.com
URL: http://www.cambridgewhoswho.com

Theresa Otten
Title: Owner **Company:** Design Trust, LLC **Address:** 579 D'Onofrio Drive, Suite 1, Madison, WI 53719 United States **BUS:** Interior Design Company **P/S:** Commercial and Residential Interior Design **MA:** National **D/D/R:** Specializing in Commercial and Residential Interior Design, Overseeing Operations Including Billing and Scheduling Appointments, Communicating with Clients **H/I/S:** Spending Time with Family **EDU:** Associate Degree in Interior Design, The Sheffield College, New York (1993) **A/A/S:** International Interior Design Association; National Association of Home Builders; Madison Area Builders Association; Wisconsin Builders Association; The Wisconsin Greenbuilding Alliance
Email: theresao@design-trust.com

Shannon J. Otto
Title: Social Worker **Company:** Springer Municipal School **Address:** P.O. Box 308, Springer, NM 87747 United States **BUS:** School **P/S:** Education, Counseling, Therapy **MA:** Local **D/D/R:** Play Therapy **H/I/S:** Traveling, Hiking, Spending Time with her Children **EDU:** Master's Degree in Social Work, New Mexico Highlands University **A/A/S:** National Association of Social Workers **C/VW:** Volunteer, National Honor Society
Email: shannotto@yahoo.com
URL: http://www.myspace.com/shannotto

J. Charles Oubre
Title: Senior Accountant **Company:** St. Charles Parish **Address:** P.O. Box 302, Hahnville, LA 70057 United States **BUS:** Government Organization **P/S:** Community Services **MA:** National **EXP:** Mr. Oubre's area of expertise is in accounting. **D/D/R:** Budgeting, Processing Payroll, Managing Finance, Overseeing Investments and Office Operations **H/I/S:** Sports, Coaching **EDU:** Bachelor of Science in Accounting, Louisiana State University **A/A/S:** Association of Government Accountants; Government Finance Officers Association **C/VW:** Knights of Columbus
Email: jco3@bellsouth.net
URL: http://www.cambridgewhoswho.com

Helen May Outt
Title: School Guidance Counselor (Retired) **Company:** Indianapolis Public Schools **Address:** 120 East Walnut Street, Indianapolis, IN 46204 United States **BUS:** Public School with Emphasis on Boosting the Reading Skills of all Children **P/S:** Reading Initiative, Mathematics and Science Education **MA:** Regional **D/D/R:** Counseling Elementary and Middle School Students **H/I/S:** Photography **EDU:** Master in Elementary Education, West Chester University of Pennsylvania (1971); Bachelor of Science in Elementary Education, West Chester University of Pennsylvania (1964) **A/A/S:** National Education Association; American Counseling Association; American Mental Health Counselors Association; SCA
Email: opoppy1@sbcglobal.net
URL: http://www.ips.k12.in.us

Paulette Oven
Title: Special Education Teacher **Company:** Alexandria School District **Address:** 720 22nd Avenue E., Suite 209, Alexandria, MN 56308 United States **BUS:** School **P/S:** Special Education **MA:** Regional **D/D/R:** Teaching and Advising Students, Tending to Children with Behavioral Issues **H/I/S:** Playing Volleyball, Running, Swimming, Reading **EDU:** Pursuing Master's Degree in Special Education, Minnesota State University; Bachelor's Degree in Special Education, Minnesota State University Moorehead (2006) **A/A/S:** Council for Exceptional Children; Minnesota Educators Association
Email: poven@alexandria.k12.mn.us

Mrs. Aaron A. Overlin
Title: Licensed Practical Nurse **Company:** Sunbridge Care Center & Rehabilitation Center **Dept:** Alzheimer's Unit **Address:** 640 Filer Avenue W., Twin Falls, ID 83301 United States **BUS:** Long-Term Care and Rehabilitation **P/S:** Healthcare **MA:** Statewide **D/D/R:** Geriatric Alzheimer Nursing **H/I/S:** Listening to Music, Riding Four-Wheelers with Family, Camping, Water skiing **EDU:** Associate Degree, College of Southern Idaho **A/A/S:** National Student Nurses Association
Email: dnaerin@cableone.net
URL: http://www.cambridgewhoswho.com

Jan Lynn Owen
Title: State and Local Government and Industry Relations Manager **Company:** Washington Mutual **Address:** 801 K Street, Suite 110, Sacramento, CA 95814 United States **BUS:** Bank **P/S:** Financial Services **MA:** National **D/D/R:** Financial Services **H/I/S:** Singing, Playing Piano, Traveling, Coaching Children's Basketball, Reading About Politics **EDU:** Bachelor of Science in Economics, California State University at Fresno **A/A/S:** Public Policy Advisory, California Mortgage Bankers Association; Policy Advisor, California Chamber of Commerce **C/VW:** March of Dimes, Adoptive Services
Email: jan.owen@wamu.net
URL: http://www.wamu.com

Barrett Owens
Title: President **Company:** Maverick Residential Mortgage, Inc. **Address:** 2401 Internet Boulevard, Suite 103, Frisco, TX 75034 United States **BUS:** Residential Mortgage Company **P/S:** Residential Mortgage Banking Services **MA:** National **D/D/R:** Mortgages **H/I/S:** Playing Golf, Skiing, Hunting **EDU:** Bachelor of Business Administration **A/A/S:** National Association of Mortgage Brokers; Texas Association of Mortgage Brokers **C/VW:** The Leukemia & Lymphoma Society; Susan G. Komen for the Cure
Email: barrett@maverickmortgage.com
URL: http://www.maverickmortgage.com

Craig S. Owens
Title: President, Owner **Company:** Internet Group Business **Address:** 759 Creston Avenue, Marion, OH 43302 United States **BUS:** Online Group Business **P/S:** Real Estate Services, Discount Travel Vacations, Gaming, Retail Products through Online Services **MA:** International **EXP:** Mr. Owens' expertise includes computer technology and online business management. **H/I/S:** Fishing, Watching Football and Basketball Games, Playing Football and Basketball, Spending Time with his Friends **EDU:** Bachelor of Arts in Sociology and Psychology, University of Virginia's College, Wise (1993)
Email: craigowens@yahoo.com

Jeffrey M. Owens

Title: President **Company:** The Business Planning Group **Address:** 305 NE 102nd Avenue, Suite 270, Portland, OR 97220 United States **BUS:** Financial Insurance **P/S:** Insurance and Investments, Financial Planning **MA:** Local **D/D/R:** Financial Planning for business owners and their key people **H/I/S:** Outdoors, Fishing, Hunting **EDU:** Bachelor of Arts in Business, Linfield College **A/A/S:** NAFP, SEC, NASD, NAIC, MDRT
Email: jowens@jhnetwork.com

Nancy S. Owens

Title: Owner **Company:** A Cut Above **Address:** 1153 Cummings Street, Abingden, VA 24211 United States **BUS:** Beauty Cosmetology Cosmetics/Beauty/Spa **P/S:** Perms, Cuts, Color and Nails **MA:** Local **D/D/R:** Perms and Color **H/I/S:** Golf, Reading, Travel, Crochet **CERTS:** Licensed Cosmetologist

Sandra J. Owens

Title: Teacher **Company:** Oregon Middle School **Address:** 601 Pleasant Oak Drive, Oregon, WI 53575 United States **BUS:** Public Middle School **P/S:** Education **MA:** Local **D/D/R:** Teaching United States History to Eighth-Grade Students **H/I/S:** Gardening, Reading, Watching Movies, Spending Time with her Mother, Children and Grandchildren, Following Union Affairs **EDU:** Master's Degree in Educational Administration, University of Wisconsin-Madison **CERTS:** National Board Certified Teacher **A/A/S:** National Council for the Social Studies; Wisconsin Council for the Social Studies; National Education Association; Wisconsin Education Association; Oregon Education Association; National Geographic Society; CAUS-N; Wisconsin Geographic Alliance **C/VW:** Church, Habitat for Humanity
Email: sowens7978@yahoo.com
URL: http://www.cambridgewhoswho.com

Zena Elizabeth Owens

Title: Clerk **Company:** Bethlehem Temple Church, Inc. **Address:** 958 E. 52nd Street, Los Angeles, CA 90011 United States **BUS:** Church **P/S:** Religious Services, Spiritual Guidance **MA:** Local **D/D/R:** building relationships with people **H/I/S:** Watching the 'I Love Lucy' Reruns **EDU:** Bachelor of Arts in Christian Education, Aenon Bible College; Associate of Arts in Child Development, Los Angeles Southwest College; Associate of Science in Sign Language, El Camino Community College **A/A/S:** Ministers and Deacons Wives **C/VW:** Hope for Children
Email: zenaowens@hotmail.com
URL: http://www.cambridgewhoswho.com

Iris A. Oxendine

Title: Assistant City Assessor **Company:** Portsmouth City Assessor's Office **Address:** 801 Crawford Street, Portsmouth, VA 23704 United States **BUS:** City Government, Real Estate Division **P/S:** Real Estate Assessments **MA:** Local **D/D/R:** Assessing Real Estate **H/I/S:** Reading, Singing, Taking Care of her Mother **EDU:** Bachelor of Arts in Business, Norfolk State University; Associate Degree in Secretarial Science, Norfolk State University; Business Degree, Kee Business College (1985) **A/A/S:** International Association of Assessing Officers; Virginia Association of Assessing Officers
Email: oxendinei@portsmouth.va.gov
URL: http://www.cambridgewhoswho.com

Meredith K. Oyler

Title: Registered Nurse, Owner **Company:** Meri Oyler RN **Address:** 201 W. Park Avenue, Durango, CO 81301 United States **BUS:** Healthcare Center **P/S:** Healthcare **MA:** Regional **D/D/R:** coordinating staff, scheduling, assisting and consulting patients and determining level of nursing care and training staff **H/I/S:** Walking, Jogging, Biking **EDU:** Associate Degree in Nursing, Community College of Denver (1991) **A/A/S:** American Nurses Association; La Plata Search and Rescue **C/VW:** Volunteer, 9Health Fair; American Cancer Society; Rocky Mountain PBS
Email: meri@bresnan.net

Keith R. Pace

Title: Operations Manager **Company:** Kohl's Department Store **Address:** Stoughton, MA 02072 United States **BUS:** Retail Departmental Store **P/S:** Clothes, Domestic Products **MA:** National **EXP:** Mr. Pace's area of expertise is in sales management. **D/D/R:** Overseeing Operations and Human Resources, Processing Payroll, Managing Freight Operations, Keeping the Facility Up to Standards, Ensuring Customer Satisfaction **H/I/S:** Golfing **EDU:** Master's Degree in Management, University of Phoenix (2007) **A/H:** District Performance Award, Sears (Twice); Regional Performance Award, Sears (Twice)
Email: keith.pace@kohls.com
Email: paceman316@hotmail.com
URL: http://www.kohls.com

Yvette M. Pace

Title: Attorney **Company:** Kubicki Draper, PA **Address:** 201 S Orange Avenue, Suite 475, Orlando, FL 32801 United States **BUS:** Legal Services Legal Services **P/S:** Legal Services, Civil Defense **MA:** Regional **D/D/R:** Civil Defense **H/I/S:** Dance, Exercise **EDU:** JD, St. Thomas University School of Law; Bachelor of Science in Political Science, University of South Florida **A/A/S:** Florida Bar Association; Middle District, Federal Bar Association
Email: yp@kubickidraper.com
URL: http://www.kubickidraper.com

Ann C. Packard

Title: Owner, Designer **Company:** Yes Ma'am **Address:** 6903 Lyre Lane, Dallas, TX 75214 United States **BUS:** Jewelry and Interior Design Firm **P/S:** Jewelry and Interior Design Services **MA:** Local **EXP:** Ms. Packard's expertise includes interior and jewelry design. **H/I/S:** Reading, Gardening **EDU:** Bachelor of Science in Nursing **C/VW:** Volunteer, Local Community; Wilkinson Center; Arboretum Society
Email: ann.packard@cwwemail.com
URL: http://www.cambridgewhoswho.com

Carlos Mauricio Padilla

Title: Sales Manager **Company:** Liberty Mutual **Address:** 6101 Executive Boulevard, Suite 100, Rockville, MD 20852 United States **BUS:** Insurance Company **P/S:** Life Insurance, Automobile Insurance, Home Insurance, Disability Insurance **MA:** National **D/D/R:** overseeing sales, personal and affinity markets and in assisting Spanish speaking customers **H/I/S:** Traveling, Sports **EDU:** Bachelor of Business Administration in Finance and International Business, James Madison University (2001) **A/A/S:** National Association of Insurance and Financial Advisors; Gaithersburg-Germantown Chamber of Commerce
Email: c.mauricio.padilla@libertymutual.com
URL: http://www.libertymutual.com

Gary Pagan

Title: Title Examiner **Company:** New Vision Abstract **Address:** 1054 52nd Street, Brooklyn, NY 11219 United States **BUS:** Real Estate Company **P/S:** Title Report and Abstracts, Real Estate **MA:** Regional **D/D/R:** Managing Real Estate Title Abstracts **EDU:** Bachelor's Degree in Business, Fairleigh Dickinson University (1997)
Email: garpag6@aol.com

Dr. Jean Pagano

Title: President **Company:** Circle Consulting Services **Address:** 3180 Fallen Oaks Court, Suite 813, Rochester Hills, MI 48309 United States **BUS:** Information Technology **P/S:** Tandem Platform and Microsoft Support Services **MA:** Regional **D/D/R:** Consulting on Hardware and Software, Offering Support Services for Windows Platform and Tandem, Developing Systems, Interfacing with Customers **H/I/S:** Running **EDU:** Ph.D. in Metaphysics, American Institute of Holistic Theology (2007) **CERTS:** Microsoft Certified Professional; Microsoft Certified Small Business Specialist **A/A/S:** Association for Computing Machinery; Institute of Electrical and Electronics Engineers, Inc.
Email: circleconsultingservices@comcast.net

Vita Marie Pagano-Lusk

Title: Student Services Teacher **Company:** Livonia Public Schools **Address:** 6217 Lynn Court, West Bloomfield, MI 48323 United States **BUS:** School District **P/S:** Education **MA:** Local **D/D/R:** Teaching Special Education to Kindergarten through Eighth-Grade Students **H/I/S:** Running **EDU:** Master's Degree in Behavior and Learning Disabilities, Wayne State University **A/A/S:** Council for Exceptional Children **C/VW:** The Friendship Circle
Email: vlusk@livonia.k12.mi.us
URL: http://www.livonia.k12.mi.us

John Edward Page, Esq.

Title: Attorney **Company:** Kluger, Peletz, Kaplan and Berlin, PL **Address:** 2385 N.W. Executive Center Drive, Suite 300, Boca Raton, FL 33431 United States **BUS:** Local Law Firm **P/S:** Commercial Bankruptcy Law for Mid-Size Companies and Corporations Including Court Litigation **MA:** National **D/D/R:** Practicing Commercial Bankruptcy and Business Law **H/I/S:** Traveling, Running, Hiking, Spending Time Outdoors, Playing Sports **EDU:** JD in Law, Magna Cum Laude, University of Miami, Florida; Bachelor of Science in Economics, Summa Cum Laude, George Washington University **A/A/S:** Brower County Bar Association; Florida State Bar Association; Bankruptcy Bar Association of the Southern District of Florida
Email: jpage@kpkb.com
URL: http://www.kpkb.com

Ruth A. Paige

Title: Information Technology Manager **Company:** Horizon Blue Cross Blue Shield of New Jersey **Address:** 1427 Wycoff Road, Wall Township, NJ 07753 United States **BUS:** Insurance Company **P/S:** Health Insurance **MA:** National **EXP:** Ms. Paige's expertise includes information technology management, imaging and data capture. **H/I/S:** Motorcycling, Traveling, Watching Movies, Studying Spanish **EDU:** Master's Degree in Information Systems **CERTS:** Certified Document Imaging Architect **A/A/S:** The Association of Word Processing Imaging; Association of Imaging Management; Central Jersey Club; National Association of Negro Business and Professional Women's Club **C/VW:** Juvenile Diabetes Research Foundation
Email: ruth_paige@horizonblue.com
URL: http://www.cambridgewhoswho.com

John C. Painter

Title: Superintendent, Special Assistant, Advisor **Company:** Lee County Board of Education **Address:** P.O. Box 233, Salem, AL 36874 United States **BUS:** Board of Education **P/S:** Education **MA:** Local **D/D/R:** overseeing personnel and school safety, communicating information, managing strategic and fiscal planning **H/I/S:** Walking, Admiring Nature **EDU:** ABD, Auburn University (1982); Master of Education, Louisiana State University (1976); Bachelor of Arts in Social Work, Southeastern Louisiana University (1970) **A/A/S:** American Association of School Administrators; Phi Delta Kappa
Email: painter.johnc@gmail.com
URL: http://www.lee.k12.al.us

Howard M. Pakosh

Title: Director **Company:** Elliptic Semiconductor **Address:** 1770 Massachusetts Avenue, Suite 183, Cambridge, MA 02140 United States **BUS:** Security Intellectual Property Company **P/S:** Security Software, Semiconductor Intellectual Property **MA:** International **D/D/R:** Sales, Marketing **H/I/S:** Playing Tennis, Biking, Wine Collecting **EDU:** Bachelor's Degree in Electrical Engineering, George Brown College, Toronto, Canada **A/A/S:** ITECH, Canada; TIE Atlantic; Board Member, Elliptic
Email: hpakosh@ellipticsemi.com
URL: http://www.ellipticsemi.com

Denise C. Palacios-Vulchev

Title: Occupational Therapist (Self-Employed) **Company:** Denise Palacios-Vulchev, OTR **Address:** 3934 Mediterranean Street, Rockwall, TX 75087 United States **BUS:** Home Healthcare Company **P/S:** Home Healthcare **MA:** Local **D/D/R:** Geriatrics **H/I/S:** Traveling Internationally, Snorkeling **EDU:** Bachelor of Science, Texas Womans University **CERTS:** Registered Occupational Therapist, State of Texas **C/VW:** United Church of God
Email: denisevulchev@hotmail.com
URL: http://www.cambridgewhoswho.com

Vikki Yvonne Palazzari

Title: Director of Web Products and Services **Company:** eRepublic, Inc. **Address:** 2745 King Richard Drive, El Dorado Hills, CA 95762 United States **BUS:** Business Technology Company **P/S:** Business Technology Distribution for State and Local Governments, Education Markets, Website Education, Publishing the Market's Leading Periodicals, Facilitating Intergovernmental Conferences, Custom Events Productions, Research and Market Advisory Services **MA:** National **D/D/R:** Managing Digital Communities, Programs, Projects, Accounts and Business, Creating Systems, Procedures and Policies, Managing Delivery for Web Advertising and Products, Overseeing Performance Levels, Customer Service, Supervising Employees **H/I/S:** Sketching, Creating Art, Painting, Writing Poetry **EDU:** Industry-Related Training; High School Education
Email: vikpalvi@yahoo.com
URL: http://www.govtech.com

Ilona M. Paley

Title: President **Company:** Impact International **Address:** 322 Culver Boulevard, Suite 250, Playa Del Rey, CA 90293 United States **BUS:** Personality Development Company **P/S:** Tools for Transformation, Self-Empowerment, Motivation, Self-Help **MA:** International **D/D/R:** writing articles of leading edge discoveries and jewelry making through symbolism and sacred geometry **H/I/S:** Painting **EDU:** Bachelor of Business Administration, Earned in Hungary (1971) **A/A/S:** National Association for Female Executives; International Association of Counselors and Therapists
Email: ilonamp@yahoo.com
URL: http://www.cambridgewhoswho.com

Cynthia L. Palka
Title: Chief Human Resources Officer and VP of Global Special Projects **Company:** Bilcare GCS **Address:** 300 Kimberton Road, Phoenixville, PA 19450 United States **BUS:** Pharmaceutical and Biotechnology Company **P/S:** Clinical Supplies, Clinical Trial Services, Research, Packaging Systems **MA:** International **D/D/R:** Managing Human Resources and Recruitment, Monitoring Performance **H/I/S:** Traveling, Wine Tasting **EDU:** Master of Science in Chemistry, Princeton University (1995); Bachelor of Science in Chemistry **CERTS:** Pursuing Executive Certification in International Management, Garvin School; Certified Professional Coach, International Coach Federation **A/A/S:** International Coach Federation; Society for Human Resource Management; Regulatory Affairs Professionals Society
Email: cynthia.palka@bilcare.com
URL: http://www.bilcaregcs.com

Mark L. Palmatier
Title: Project Manager **Company:** Cornerstone Construction **Address:** 5050 Cordova Street, Anchorage, AK 99503 United States **BUS:** General Contractors **P/S:** Commercial Contracting Services **MA:** Alaska **D/D/R:** Managing Projects **H/I/S:** Golfing, Bowling, Traveling **CERTS:** Certified Project Management Professional **C/VW:** Board Member, Society of American Military Engineers; The Associated General Contractors of America; Sub-Committee Member, United States Army Corps of Engineers, Alaska District
Email: mpalmatier@cornerstone.ak.com

J. Brian Palmer
Title: Chief Accounting Officer **Company:** White Mountains Insurance Group, Ltd. **Address:** 1 Beacon Street, Fifth Floor, Boston, MA 02108 United States **BUS:** Insurance Company **P/S:** Property and Casualty Insurance Services **MA:** International **D/D/R:** accounting, managing financial operations, generating reports, overseeing merger and acquisition support activities and cash management **H/I/S:** Playing Softball and Poker, Reading **EDU:** Bachelor of Science in Accounting, University of Massachusetts **A/A/S:** American Institute of Certified Public Accountants; Massachusetts Society of Certified Public Accountants **C/VW:** Lance Corporal Eric Paul Valdepenas Scholarship; The Devon Nicole House Foundation
Email: bpalmer@whitemountains.com
URL: http://www.whitemountains.com

Kim M. Palmer
Title: Mental Health Counselor **Company:** Utah State Prison, Department of Corrections **Address:** 14425 S. Bitterbrush Lane, Draper, UT 84020 United States **BUS:** Correctional Institution **P/S:** Correctional Services **MA:** Local **EXP:** Ms. Palmer's area of expertise is in mental health counseling. **H/I/S:** Reading, Cooking, Walking, Running **EDU:** Master's Degree in Mental Health, Wright State University, Dayton, OH (1989) **A/A/S:** Association for the Advancement of Mental Health; National Christian Counselors Association
Email: kimpalmer@utah.gov
URL: http://www.cambridgewhoswho.com

Nancy M. Palmer
Title: Owner, Operator, Administrator **Company:** S&N Palmer Enterprises, Inc. **Address:** 432 E. Idaho Street, Suite C404, Kalispell, MT 59901 United States **BUS:** Transportation Company **P/S:** Transportation Services for National Military Bases **MA:** National **D/D/R:** performing administrative duties and ensuring delivery of military equipment **H/I/S:** Singing, Crocheting, Painting, Traveling, Reading, Spending Time with her Family **EDU:** Diploma, GAR Memorial Junior Senior High School, Wilkes-Barre, PA (1967) **C/VW:** Local Sheriff Organization
Email: sid002@centurytel.net

Deborah W. Palmisano, MSW, LISW
Title: Social Worker II **Company:** Cincinnati Children's Hospital **Address:** 3333 Burnet Avenue, Cincinnati, OH 45229 United States **BUS:** Hospital **P/S:** Healthcare **MA:** International **EXP:** Ms. Palmisano's expertise includes pediatric palliative care, pediatric brain and spinal cord injuries, individual and family therapy, child welfare and medical social work. **H/I/S:** Reading, Scuba Diving, Boating, Gardening, Traveling **EDU:** Master of Social Work, University of Cincinnati **A/A/S:** National Association of Social Workers
Email: palw9v@cchmc.org
URL: http://www.cambridgewhoswho.com

Merisa A. Palovcak
Title: Speech-Language Pathologist **Company:** Pennsylvania Hospital **Address:** 800 Spruce Street, Philadelphia, PA 19107 United States **BUS:** Hospital **P/S:** Healthcare **MA:** Local **D/D/R:** Speech-Language Pathology **EDU:** Master's Degree in Speech-Language Pathology, LaSalle University **A/A/S:** American Speech-Hearing Association (ASHA)
Email: palovcakm@uphs.upenn.edu
URL: http://www.cambridgewhoswho.com

Linda A. Panaccione
Title: President **Company:** Campus Catering, Inc. **Address:** 10617 Tallahassee Drive, Frisco, TX 75035 United States **BUS:** Proven Leader Dedicated to Excellence in the Food Service Industry **P/S:** All Aspects of Food Service for Christian Schools **MA:** Regional **D/D/R:** Menu Planning, Administrative Responsibilities, Training Staff on Cooking and Service, Working with Parents, Administrators, Teachers and Students, Putting on Demonstrations such as Cooking Shows, Taste Testing with Students **H/I/S:** Traveling, Sewing, Dancing, Enjoying Life, Spending Time with her Adult Children **EDU:** College Coursework; Self Taught **A/A/S:** Texas Association for School Nutrition; the Board of Boys and Girls Club; Youth Programs at Church
Email: linda_campuscatering@comcast.net

Ms. Lily Y. Pang
Title: Labor and Delivery Charge Nurse **Company:** Swedish Medical Center **Address:** 747 Broadway, Seattle, WA 98122 United States **BUS:** Medical Center **P/S:** Labor and Delivery for High Risk OB **MA:** Regional **D/D/R:** Labor and Delivery Nursing **H/I/S:** Sewing, Reading, Hiking **EDU:** Certified Registered Nurse (2004); Bachelor of Science in Nursing, Linfield College (1991) **A/A/S:** Children Nursing Association
Email: pangster@msn.com

Gina M. Pangione
Title: Owner **Company:** Premier Enoteca, Inc. dba Jamie's Fine Wine and Spirits **Address:** 100 N. Main Street, Carver, MA 02330 United States **BUS:** Neighborhood Wine and Spirits Boutique **P/S:** Large Selection of Quality Wine and Spirits **MA:** Regional **D/D/R:** Running the Daily Operations of the Store, Marketing, Writing Newsletters, Overseeing All Inventory and Supplies, Developing and Maintaining the Website **H/I/S:** Reading, Writing, Traveling, Attending her Children's Sports Events **EDU:** JD, Western New England School of Law (1996); Bachelor of Arts in Marketing, Buffalo University, Buffalo **A/A/S:** Mom's Club of Carver; Carver Chamber of Commerce; Won Writing Contest
Email: vinorasso1@netzero.com
URL: http://www.jamiesfws.com

Tanya M. Panizzo
Title: Owner/Instructor **Company:** Midwest Tae Kwon Do, LLC **Address:** 251 N Main Street, Plymouth, MI 48170 United States **BUS:** Sports Service Provider **P/S:** Martial Arts **MA:** Local **D/D/R:** Tae Kwon Do Instruction **H/I/S:** Spending Time With Daughter **EDU:** Bachelor of Science **A/A/S:** World Tae Kwon Do Federation
URL: http://www.midwesttaekwondo.com

Kimberly W. Pannell
Title: Marketing Director **Company:** Darby Bank & Trust Co. **Address:** 300 Bull Street, Savannah, GA 31401 United States **BUS:** Bank **P/S:** Banking Services **MA:** Local **D/D/R:** Marketing **H/I/S:** Playing Tennis **EDU:** Bachelor's Degree in Marketing; Bachelor of Arts, Meredith College (2000) **A/A/S:** American Bankers Association; Georgia Bankers Association; Community Bankers Association of Georgia; Board Member, Telfair Musician of Ari Junior League **C/VW:** Junior League of Savannah; Local Senior Citizens Organization
Email: kpannell@darbybank.com
URL: http://www.darbybank.com

Wayne S. Panter
Title: Resource Language Teacher **Company:** Franklin County Board of Education **Address:** 215 S. College Street, Winchester, TN 37398 United States **BUS:** Board of Education **P/S:** Education **MA:** Franklin County, Tennessee **D/D/R:** Supporting Elementary Resources **H/I/S:** Golfing, Hunting, Fishing **EDU:** Master's Degree in Middle Tennessee State University; Bachelor's Degree in Elementary Education, University of Alabama in Huntsville **A/A/S:** Tennessee Education Association
Email: wayne1@tnets.net
URL: http://www.cambridgewhoswho.com

Dr. Benjamin J. Paolucci
Title: President, General Surgeon **Company:** Dr. Benjamin J. Paolucci, PC **Address:** 27483 Dequindre Road, Madison Heights, MI 48071 United States **BUS:** Surgical Practice **P/S:** Healthcare **MA:** Local **D/D/R:** General Surgery, Sports Medicine **H/I/S:** Playing Handball, Working Out, Spending Time with his Grandchildren **EDU:** Master's Degree in Surgical Education, Oakland University **A/A/S:** National Medical Association; National Basketball Association; American Osteopathic Association; Michigan Osteopathic Association; Osteopathic College Association; American Society for Orthopaedic Sports Medicine
Email: bjp30537@yahoo.com

Gina M. Pappalardo
Title: President **Company:** Fireside Staffing, Inc. **Address:** 17 Guadet Lane, Pelham, NH 03076 United States **BUS:** Healthcare Staffing Agency **P/S:** Staffing Agency for Healthcare Industry **MA:** Statewide **D/D/R:** Recruiting for Long-Term Care Facilities and Hospitals **H/I/S:** Antiquing **EDU:** Industry-Related Coursework
Email: gpappalardo@verizon.net

Maria A. Pappas
Title: Paralegal, Legal Assistant **Company:** Law Offices of Robert E. Slota **Address:** 801 Old Lancaster Road, Bryn Mawr, PA 19010 United States **BUS:** Law Office **P/S:** Medical Malpractice **MA:** Eastern Pennsylvania **D/D/R:** Overseeing Legal Operations **H/I/S:** Swimming, Gardening, Crocheting, Traveling **EDU:** Coursework, Duquesne University **CERTS:** Paralegal Certification, Manor College (2004)
Email: maria_pappas@hotmail.com
URL: http://www.cambridgewhoswho.com

Antoinette 'Toni' C. Parada
Title: Activity Director Certified **Company:** Lockport Presbyterian Home **Address:** 327 High Street, Lockport, NY 14094 United States **BUS:** Nursing Home **P/S:** Healthcare **MA:** Local **D/D/R:** Creating Activities for Senior that Promote Activity and Socialization **H/I/S:** Knitting, Traveling, Golfing, Gardening **CERTS:** Nationally Certified Activity Director **A/A/S:** Western New York Association of Activity Professionals; New York State Association of Activity Professionals **C/VW:** Volunteer, Lockport Presbyterian Home
Email: tparada@pscwny.org
URL: http://www.pscwny.org

Raymond J. Parana
Title: Owner, Operator **Company:** Parana's Contracting and Cleaning Service **Address:** 172 Glen Mayo Road, Johnsonburg, PA 15845 United States **BUS:** Construction **P/S:** Home Repairs, Roofing, Siding, Running the Job Sites, Designing New Constructions **MA:** Regional **D/D/R:** Owner, Operating, Running and Overseeing the Jobs, Architectural Designs **H/I/S:** Fishing. Hunting, Oil painting, Cooking **EDU:** General Studies, High School Diploma, Johnsonburg High School
Email: emp1@alltel.net

Maria Parente
Title: 1) New York City School Teacher 2) Consultant **Company:** 1) New York City Department of Education, I.S. 281 2) EMC Paradigm **Address:** 8787 24th Avenue, Brooklyn, NY 11214 United States **BUS:** 1) Middle School 2) Educational Consulting Company **P/S:** 1) Education 2) Consulting **MA:** 1) Local 2) Local **D/D/R:** 1) Teaching Arts and Humanities 2) Working with English as a Second Language Teachers to Incorporate Textbooks into Lessons **H/I/S:** Traveling, Reading **EDU:** Master's Degree in Administration, Mercy College (2007); Master's Degree in Elementary and Middle School Education, University of Phoenix (2004) **A/A/S:** Economics Bowl **C/VW:** Columbia Children's Presbyterian Hospital
Email: miagirl@verizon.net
URL: http://nylearns.org/mpariente

Lenora T. Parham
Title: Owner/CEO **Company:** LTP Enterprises **Address:** 1224 Lockburne, Columbus, OH 43206 United States **BUS:** Education Consulting **P/S:** Education and Finances **MA:** Local **D/D/R:** Finance Education **H/I/S:** Traveling **EDU:** Bachelor of Science, Capitol University

Megan B. Paris
Title: Teacher **Company:** Delran Intermediate School **Address:** 4030 Brown Street, Philadelphia, PA 19104 United States **BUS:** School **P/S:** Elementary Education **MA:** Local **EXP:** Ms. Paris' expertise is in reading education. **D/D/R:** Teaching all Subjects, Managing Leadership Team and Language Arts Committee, Working with Staff on Curriculum and Professional Development **H/I/S:** Reading, Scrapbooking, Spending Time with her Family **EDU:** Master of Education in Reading, University of La Verne, CA; Bachelor of Science in Elementary Education, University of Pennsylvania **A/A/S:** National Council of Teachers of English; International Reading Association; ASCV
Email: dnmparis@mac.com
URL: http://www.cambridgewhoswho.com

Mrs. Ashley Summerlyn Park
Title: Senior Manager **Company:** WellPoint, Inc. **Dept:** Technology **Address:** 6002 W. Club Lane, Richmond, VA 23226 United States **BUS:** Insurance Company **P/S:** Health Insurance **MA:** National **D/D/R:** Managing the Information Technology Department, Inspecting Software, Ensuring Quality **H/I/S:** Traveling, Cooking **EDU:** Bachelor of Arts in Political Science, The University of North Carolina at Chapel Hill **C/VW:** United Way of America
Email: ashpark@verizon.net
URL: http://www.wellpoint.com

Elizabeth K. Park
Title: Early Childhood Education and Montessori Teacher Education Director **Company:** Chaminade University of Honolulu **Address:** 3140 Waialae Avenue, Honolulu, HI 96816 United States **BUS:** University **P/S:** Higher Education Including Collaborative Learning Environment with Many Academic Programs, Partnerships with the Community and the Church, Educational Support **MA:** National **D/D/R:** overseeing programs, developing quality control and early childhood education **H/I/S:** Swimming, Painting, Cooking **EDU:** Pursuing Ph.D. in Educational Technology, University of Hawaii; Master's Degree in Early Childhood Education, Chaminade University of Honolulu (2002) **CERTS:** Montessori Certification **A/A/S:** National Association for the Education of Young Children; American Montessori Society **C/VW:** Volunteer, The Humane Society of the United States
Email: epark@chaminade.edu
URL: http://www.chaminade.edu

Terry J.S. Park
Title: Owner, Chiropractor **Company:** Dr. Terry Park, Chiropractic **Address:** 586 US 41 E., Negaunee, MI 49866 United States **BUS:** Chiropractic Practice **P/S:** Healthcare **MA:** Regional **D/D/R:** Restoring Nerve Flow, Helping Patients Maintain Good Health, Specializes in Sports Injuries and Proletarians **H/I/S:** Spending Time with her Family, Participating in Outdoor Activities, Running, Bicycling **EDU:** Doctor of Chiropractic, Palmer College of Chiropractic; Bachelor of Arts in Biology, New England College **A/A/S:** ACA; Board of Directors, Preferred Chiropractors; PSAS; Certified Clinical Scientist Chiropractor **C/VW:** Blood Drives, Local Charities
Email: tpark_28@yahoo.com
URL: http://www.cambridgewhoswho.com

Bonita L. Parker, Ph.D.
Title: Senior Research Associate **Company:** James Bell Associates **Address:** 1001 19th Street, Suite 1500, Arlington, VA 23209 United States **BUS:** Research Consulting **P/S:** Research and Evaluating, Government **MA:** Local **D/D/R:** Child Welfare, Foster Care **H/I/S:** Reading, Genealogy **EDU:** Ph.D., University of North Carolina at Chapel Hill **A/A/S:** APA, NBCDI, NCNW
Email: BLParker1@excite.com

Denise N. Parker
Title: School Nurse **Company:** Christina School District **Address:** 600 Lombard Street, Wilmington, DE 19801 United States **BUS:** School **P/S:** Education **MA:** Local **D/D/R:** Pediatric Nursing **H/I/S:** Reading, Poetry **EDU:** Bachelor of Science in Nursing
URL: http://www.cambridgewhoswho.com

Jane Parker
Title: Biology Teacher **Company:** Lewisville High School North **Address:** 1301 Summit Avenue, Lewisville, TX 75077 United States **BUS:** School District **P/S:** Regular Core Curriculum Including Reading, Mathematics, English, Science, Social Studies, Art, Music, History and Physical Education **MA:** Local **D/D/R:** Teaching Secondary Biology, Using Original Models and Demonstrations, Illustrating Abstract Biological Concepts, Training other Teachers **H/I/S:** Traveling, Practicing Photography, Writing **EDU:** Bachelor of Arts in Psychology, University of Texas (1978) **CERTS:** Certification in Biology Education, University of Texas (1978); Certification in Psychology Education, University of Texas (1978); Certification in Sociology and Computer Literacy, State Testing; Certified Technology Enhanced Student Assessment Teacher Trainer **A/A/S:** Teacher of the Year (1983, 2003); Service Award, Regional Parent Teacher Association; Psi Chi
Email: parkerj@lisd.net
URL: http://www.lisd.net

Jody Parker
Title: Engineering Director of Lean Six Sigma **Company:** Lockheed Martin **Address:** 5600 Sand Lake Road, Orlando, FL 32819 United States **BUS:** Aerospace Defense Company **P/S:** Navigating and Targeting Systems, Missiles **MA:** International **D/D/R:** Engineering, Lean Six Sigma **H/I/S:** Flying **EDU:** Bachelor of Science in Engineering, University of Virginia **C/VW:** Junior Achievement, Local Church
Email: jody.a.parker@mco.com

Maxwell V. Parker
Title: MD **Address:** 1501 S Airport Drive, Lot 403, Weslaco, TX 78596 United States **BUS:** Healthcare /Doctor **P/S:** OB/GYN **MA:** Local **D/D/R:** Reconstructive Vaginal Surgery **EDU:** Bachelor of Science, University of Medicine-Galveston; Trinity University **A/A/S:** American Medical Society

Pamela P. Parker
Title: Instructor **Company:** Point Arena High School **Address:** 270 Lake Street, Paint Arena, CA 95468 United States **BUS:** High School **P/S:** Education **MA:** Local **D/D/R:** Teaching Computer Literacy, Desktop Publishing, Microsoft Office Application, Webpage Design, Animation, Spanish and History to High School Students **H/I/S:** Exercising, Skiing, Bicycling **EDU:** Bachelor of Arts in History, Minor in Spanish, University of the Pacific **CERTS:** Vocational Credential in Microsoft Office Applications; CISCO System Certification in Web Design **A/A/S:** California Teachers Association; Point Arena High School Teachers' Association **C/VW:** Lions Club, Local Charities
Email: pamador@mcn.org

Rhonda M. Parker
Title: President **Company:** Virtually Yours 9-2-5 **Address:** 44 Wallflower Drive, Rexford, NY 12148 United States **BUS:** Virtual Assistance **P/S:** Virtual Assistance to Entrepreneurs, Staffing, Professional Support Services **MA:** National **D/D/R:** Administering, Assisting Senior Level Executives and Managers in Computer Technology, Software Management, Organizing Events, Handling Communications **H/I/S:** Boating, Reading, Gardening, Traveling, Working with Computers, Entertaining, Swimming, Walking, Tai Chi, Baseball, Basketball, Amusement Parks and with her Pets **EDU:** Bachelor of Arts in Business Administration, Wiltshire University (2000); Associate in Applied Science in Secretarial Science, SUNY Cobleskill (1976) **A/A/S:** Southern Saratoga County Chamber of Commerce; International Virtual Assistants Association; Digital-Women; Virtual Assistant Networking Association; Directory of Virtual Assistants; Virtual Assistant Directory Canada; Chairwoman, High School Reunion; Strathmore's Who's Who; Merchant Circle **C/VW:** Crohn's and Colitis Foundation; Salvation Army
Email: rhonda@virtuallyyours925.com
Email: info@nevaa.org
URL: http://www.virtuallyyours925.com
URL: http://www.nevaa.org

Jacqueline A. Parkes
Title: Dir of Performance Development **Company:** Healthnow NY **Address:** 30 Century Hill Drive **BUS:** Healthcare : Medical Services **P/S:** Health Insurance **MA:** Local **D/D/R:** Process, Customer Management **H/I/S:** 3 Year Old Son **EDU:** Pursuing MPA; Bachelor of Science in Economics, SUNY Albany **A/A/S:** ASQ
Email: jap3a1@nycap.rr.com

Cindy A. Parkinson
Title: Mortgage Professional **Company:** Allied Home Mortgage **Address:** 67 Franklin Street, Annapolis, MD 21401 United States **BUS:** Mortgage Banking Company **P/S:** Mortgages **MA:** Maryland, Delaware, Virginia **D/D/R:** Lending, Subprime Credit, Credit Restoration **H/I/S:** Reading, Spending Time with her Son **EDU:** Bachelor of Science in Criminology and Criminal Justice, University of South Carolina **A/A/S:** Anne Arundel County Association of Realtors; Queen Anne County Chamber of Commerce **C/VW:** Local Church
Email: cindyaparkinson@gmail.com

Donald W. Parks
Title: VP Sales and Marketing/Retired **Company:** Central Texas Corrugated, LP **Address:** 7200 Mars Drive, Waco, TX 76710 United States **BUS:** Corrugated Sheets Manufacturer **P/S:** Manufactured Corrugated Sheets **MA:** Local **D/D/R:** Sales, Marketing, Management **H/I/S:** Golf **EDU:** Associate Degree in Marketing, Miami University **A/A/S:** Waco Symphony Orchestra-Hippodrone
Email: donparks1@aol.com

Elena Adriana Parlea, MD
Title: Medical Doctor **Company:** CAP Anesthesia **Address:** 736 Cambridge Street, Brighton, MA 02135 United States **BUS:** Healthcare Center **P/S:** Anesthesiology, Pain Management **MA:** Regional **EXP:** Ms. Parlea's expertise includes pain management and anesthesia. **D/D/R:** Administering Anesthesia, Lecturing on Interventional Pain Management for Residents and Fellows **H/I/S:** Artwork, Photography, Playing the Piano, Reading Literature and History, Spending Time Outdoors **EDU:** Fellowship in Pain Management (2006); Residency in Anesthesiology (2005); Internship in Surgery (2002); MD, University of Medicine and Pharmacy, Iasi, Romania (1992); Bachelor of Science in Mathematics and Physics, Ferdinand I College, Romania (1986) **CERTS:** Certification, American Board of Anesthesiology; Certification, American Board of Pain Medicine; Certified ACLS Instructor **A/A/S:** Massachusetts Society of Anesthesiologists; American Society of Anesthesiologists; American Academy of Pain Physicians; American Medical Association; European Society of Anesthesiology; European Society of Regional Anesthesia & Pain Therapy
Email: adria3009@yahoo.com

Eva Ann Paroly
Title: Co-Owner **Company:** Monograms Plus **Address:** 1819 State Street, Schenectady, NY 12304 United States **BUS:** Customized Sportswear and Apparel Retailer **P/S:** Embroidery and Screen Printing Garments, Graphic Design, Display Business Logo or School Name, Monograms and Screen Printing for Clothing, Gear and Accessories **MA:** National **D/D/R:** Graphic Design, Bookkeeping, Managing the Office and Daily Operations, Dividing Work between her and her Partner **H/I/S:** Hiking, Skiing, Biking **EDU:** Associate Degree in Science, Valedictorian, SUNY, Sullivan County Community College (1977)
Email: mplus@nycap.rr.com
URL: http://www.monograms-plus.com

David C. Parris
Title: Fitness Director **Company:** Cardio Kinetics **Address:** 52 N. Chapel Street, Newark, DE 19711 United States **BUS:** Preventative Medicine Company **P/S:** Personal Training, Echocardiogram Services **MA:** Regional **D/D/R:** Exercise Physiologist **H/I/S:** Spending Time with his Girlfriend, Singing, Dancing, Playing Paintball, Traveling **EDU:** Bachelor of Science in Exercise Physiology, Temple University **CERTS:** Certified Strength and Conditioning Specialist **A/A/S:** American Council on Exercise; National Strength & Conditioning Association
Email: eboniman2@aol.com
URL: http://www.cardiokinetics.com

Susannah Parrish
Title: Owner **Company:** TexaSUS Design **Address:** 216 Maple Drive, Franklin, TN 37064 United States **BUS:** Graphic Design Firm **P/S:** Graphic Designing Services Including Printing **MA:** National **EXP:** Ms. Parrish's expertise includes graphic and Web design. **D/D/R:** Designing for Music Industry Related Products, designing posters, composing Christian music, overseeing print production, producing compact discs and publishing magazines **H/I/S:** Reading, Listening to Music, Attending the Theater, Watching Movies **EDU:** Bachelor of Business Administration, with a Concentration in Music Business, Belmont University (1995) **A/H:** Regional Addy Award **C/VW:** Local Christian Radio Station; Big Brothers Big Sisters of America; American Society for the Prevention of Cruelty to Animals
Email: sus@texasusdesign.com
URL: http://www.texasusdesign.com

Sean C. Parry
Title: President **Company:** Pegasus Technology, Inc. **Address:** 1486 Glencrest Drive, San Marcos, CA 92078 United States **BUS:** Manufacturing Company **P/S:** Consumer Electronic Entertainment Products **MA:** International **D/D/R:** Managing Sales Teams, Accounting, Marketing, Strategic Planning, Overseeing Business Development and Financial Communications Operations, e-Marketing, Managing Public Relations, Promoting and Launching New Products, analyzing market segmentation, traditional media and cutting edge marketing trends, ensuring personal development of team members **H/I/S:** Cycling, Spending Time with his Family **EDU:** Bachelor's Degree in Marketing, Brigham Young University **A/A/S:** Software & Information Industry Association; ExecuNet; American Marketing Association **C/VW:** Volunteer, San Diego Fire Relief (2007); Escondido Clergy Association; Coach, Youth Soccer and Basketball
Email: sean@parryweb.com

Donald Parsley
Title: Senior Technical Trainer **Company:** Valero Refining **Address:** 1202 Loop 197 S., Texas City, TX 77592 United States **BUS:** Oil Refining Company **P/S:** Gasoline, Diesel and Kerosene **MA:** International **EXP:** Mr. Parsley's expertise is in the professional instruction of process technology. **D/D/R:** Managing Unit Operations Including Fluidized Catalytic Cracking Unit, Crude Unit, Distillation and Hydrotreaters, Working as Reformer, teaching in college **H/I/S:** Swimming, Fishing, Reading Novels **EDU:** Bachelor of Arts in English and Religion, East Texas Baptist University (1970) **CERTS:** Certified Trainer, Xavier University; Certification in Collaborative Training and Development **A/A/S:** Gulf Coast Process Technology Alliance; CAPT; President, Board of Directors, College of the Mainland; Board President, College of the Mainland Foundation; Former President, Process Technology Advisory Committee, College of the Mainland; Co-Chairman, Educational Sub Committee of the Gulf Coast Process Technology Alliance
Email: don.parsley@valero.com
Email: dpars19966@aol.com
URL: http://www.valero.com

Wendy S. Parsley
Title: Founder, President **Company:** Quint Strategies **Address:** 511 Avenue of the Americas, Suite 368, New York, NY 10011 United States **BUS:** Consulting Firm **P/S:** Consulting Services, Marketing **MA:** International **EXP:** Ms. Parsley's area of expertise is in revenue generation. **H/I/S:** Running, Spending Time with her Family, Watching Movies, Reading, Hiking **EDU:** Bachelor of Business Administration, Florida State University **A/A/S:** Business Marketing Association; Meeting Professionals International **C/VW:** Toastmasters International
Email: wparsley@quintstrategies.com
URL: http://www.quintstrategies.com

Veronica L. Parsons
Title: Occupational Therapist **Company:** Sunbelt Staffing **BUS:** Staffing Agency **P/S:** Staffing **MA:** Local **D/D/R:** Occupational Therapy **H/I/S:** Working Out, Reading, Spending Time Outdoors Camping and Hiking **EDU:** Bachelor's Degree in Occupational Therapy, Pennsylvania State University **A/A/S:** American Occupational Therapy Association
Email: vpars524@yahoo.com
URL: http://www.cambridgewhoswho.com

Dr. Kameron B. Partridge
Title: Program Director **Company:** Civitan International Research Center **Dept:** University of Alabama at Birmingham **Address:** 1719 Sixth Avenue S., Birmingham, AL 35294 United States **BUS:** University Affiliated Clinic **P/S:** Enhancing the Quality of Life for Adults with Disabilities by Supervising and Assisting Individualized Support Services **MA:** Local **D/D/R:** Developmental Psychology, Treating Adults 23 to 50 Years of Age, Offering Community Support Services, Teaching a University Child Development and Research Methods Course **H/I/S:** Cooking, Decorating, Spending Quality Time with Friends **EDU:** Ph.D. in Developmental Psychology, University of Alabama at Birmingham (2006) **A/A/S:** American Psychological Association; American Association on Intellectual and Developmental Disabilities
Email: kameron@uab.edu
URL: http://www.circ-uab.edu

Joann A. Paschal
Company: K-States Research and Extension, Russell County **Address:** 401 Main Street, Russell, KS 67665 United States **BUS:** Research Center **P/S:** Integrated Research, Analysis and Education Including Cooperative Extension and Food Safety **MA:** Local **D/D/R:** ensuring food safety **H/I/S:** Woodworking, Writing, Painting **EDU:** Bachelor of Science, Kansas State University; Bachelor of Arts in Human Ecology (1976) **A/A/S:** Kansas Educators Association; National Extension Association of Family and Consumer Sciences; FCS; AFCS **A/H:** National Excellence Award, National Extension Association of Family and Consumer Sciences (2007)
Email: jpaschal@ksu.edu
URL: http://www.cambridgewhoswho.com

Gloria Pascual
Title: Fiscal Specialist Supervisor **Company:** University of Washington **Dept:** Department of Genome Sciences **Address:** Campus Box 355065, Foege Building S250, Seattle, WA 98905 United States **BUS:** University **P/S:** Higher Education **MA:** Local **D/D/R:** overseeing staff and operations **H/I/S:** Performing Polynesian Cultural Programs **EDU:** Associate Degree in Office Administration, Edmonds Community College, Lynnwood, WA **C/VW:** Make-A-Wish Foundation
Email: glomarie@hotmail.com
URL: http://www.gs.washington.edu

Mark Paskowitz
Title: Senior Consulting Partner **Company:** The Ken Blanchard Companies **Address:** 3935 Kendall Street, San Diego, CA 92109 United States **BUS:** Consulting Firm **P/S:** Business Management Consulting Services **MA:** International **D/D/R:** Working with Individual Contributors, Introducing New Professionals to Advanced Levels of Management, Consulting on Business strategy for Professionals **H/I/S:** Practicing Martial Arts, Listening to Music, Traveling, Reading, Snow Skiing **EDU:** Bachelor's Degree in Speech Communications, Missouri State University (1984) **CERTS:** Certified Coach **A/A/S:** Coachville
Email: mark.paskowitz@kenblanchard.com
URL: http://www.professionalcoach4u.com

Jim Pass, Ph.D.
Title: Founder **Company:** Astrosociology Research Institute **Address:** P.O. Box 1129, Huntington Beach, CA 92647 United States **BUS:** Research Institute **P/S:** Astrosociological Research, Education **MA:** International **D/D/R:** conducting astrosociology research and coordinating conferences **H/I/S:** Playing Tennis, Jogging, Researching **EDU:** Ph.D. in Sociology, University of Southern California, Los Angeles (1991); Master's Degree in Sociology, University of Southern California (1984); Master's Degree in Criminal Justice, California State University, Long Beach (1984); Bachelor's Degree in Sociology and Criminal Justice, California State University, Long Beach (1979) **A/A/S:** California Sociological Association; American Institute of Aeronautics and Astronautics; American Sociological Association; Space Technology and Applications International Forum; Pacific Sociological Association
Email: jpass@astrosociology.org
URL: http://www.astrosociology.org

Mr. Jason A. Patacsil
Title: Lieutenant Commander **Company:** U.S. Navy **Address:** 1321 Buttermilk Lane, Griffin, GA 30224 United States **BUS:** Government Organization **P/S:** Conserving the National Freedom of the United States, Healthcare **MA:** National **D/D/R:** Nursing, Administering Anesthesia to Patients **H/I/S:** Spending Time with Family, Renovating his Home, Playing Tennis **EDU:** Bachelor of Science in Nursing; Certified Nurse Operating Room **A/A/S:** Sigma Theta Tau; American Association of Nurse Anesthetists; Association of Preoperative Registered Nurses
Email: japatacsil@yahoo.com

Dorothy J. Patch
Title: Chef, Owner **Company:** Culinary Creations, LLC **Address:** P.O. Box 257, Plainfield, CT 06374 United States **BUS:** Catering Company **P/S:** Catering Services **MA:** Regional **D/D/R:** catering to all types of parties including cocktail, designing wedding cakes, dinners and family parties **H/I/S:** Gardening, Exercising, Practicing Yoga, Hiking, Spending Time Outdoors **EDU:** Associate of Applied Science in Culinary Arts, Johnson & Wales University, Providence, RI **A/A/S:** American Culinary Federation; World Wildlife Fund; The American Society for the Prevention of Cruelty to Animals; American Diabetes Association; Multiple Sclerosis Association **C/VW:** American Cancer Society; Little League Football and Baseball; Various Charitable Organizations
Email: culinarycreations_1@msn.com
URL: http://www.cambridgewhoswho.com

Pastor Thurman M. Pate
Title: Senior Pastor **Company:** Faith Free Will Baptist Church **Address:** 4531 Bruhin Road, Knoxville, TN 37912 United States **BUS:** Religion **P/S:** Spreading Gods Gospel and Counseling **MA:** Local **D/D/R:** Preparation of Sermons and Bible Studies Geared Towards Educating all in the Word of God **H/I/S:** Walk-A-Thon for Foreign Missions **EDU:** Bachelor of Arts in Bible Studies, Johnson Bible College **A/A/S:** Tennessee State and National Associations of Free Will Baptist Churches

Hiral Patel, DO
Title: Doctor of Osteopathy **Company:** Montgomery County Asthma and Lung Center, P.C. **Address:** 1330 Powell Street, Suite 508, Norristown, PA 19401 United States **BUS:** Private Medical Practice **P/S:** Pulmonary Healthcare Services **MA:** Local **EXP:** Dr. Patel's area of expertise is in osteopathy. **D/D/R:** Treating Patients with Pulmonary Disorders and Sleep Apnea, Practicing Critical Care **EDU:** Doctor of Osteopathy in Pulmonary Care, Philadelphia College of Osteopathic Medicine (2001) **A/A/S:** American Osteopathic Association; American College of Chest Physicians
Email: hiralp8@hotmail.com

Neena Patel
Title: Practice Administrator **Company:** Wills Diagnostic Clinic **Address:** 2000 Crawford Street, Suite 900, Houston, TX 77002 United States **BUS:** Healthcare and Wellness Center Service Provider **P/S:** Medical Office, Wellness Center **MA:** Local **D/D/R:** Healthcare Administration, Business Administration **H/I/S:** Cook, Skiing, Outdoor Activities **EDU:** Bachelor of Arts, University of Texas at Austin; Master's Degree in Healthcare Administration, University of Houston; Master of Business Administration **A/A/S:** American Diabetes Association, Muscular Dystrophy, BAPS Temple
Email: neenaap71@yahoo.com

Arthur E. Paton, Ph.D.
Title: Senior Learning Consultant **Company:** Motorola, Inc. **Address:** 1303 E. Algonquin Road, Schaumburg, IL 60196 United States **BUS:** Telecommunications Company **P/S:** Consumer Devices, Communications Solutions for Businesses, Governments and Service Providers **MA:** International **EXP:** Mr. Paton's area of expertise is in telecommunications services. **D/D/R:** Strategic Learning and Development, e-Learning Applications, License Management, Researching and Developing Software **H/I/S:** Bicycling **EDU:** Ph.D. in Biological Physics and Biological Chemistry, The University of Tennessee **A/A/S:** Sigma Si; American Society for Training & Development
Email: atec77@motorola.com
URL: http://www.cambridgewhoswho.com

Jessie L. Patrick
Title: Owner, Operator **Company:** Patrick Adult Residential Care **Address:** 731 Pickerell Avenue, Corcoran, CA 93212 United States **BUS:** Residential Care Center **P/S:** Residential Healthcare Including Long-Term Care for Mentally Challenged Adults **MA:** Regional **D/D/R:** caring for mentally challenged adults **H/I/S:** Sewing, Fishing **EDU:** Coursework in Interior Decoration, Jefferson Davis Community College **CERTS:** Licensed Homecare Provider **A/A/S:** Order of the Eastern Star; Prince Hall Grand High Court of Heroines of Jericho
Email: jessiesundaybest@yahoo.com
URL: http://www.cambridgewhoswho.com

Mr. Richard H. Patt, MD
Title: Principal **Company:** RadMD **Address:** 90 Oak Grove Road, Ottsville, PA 18942 United States **BUS:** Consulting and Management Service Company **P/S:** Expert Consulting and Radiology Services to Biotechnical and Pharmaceutical Companies and Professionals **MA:** Regional **D/D/R:** Pharmaceutical and Medical Device Research, Consulting for Many Pharmaceutical Companies and Regulatory Groups, Using Medical Imaging, Overseeing Operations **EDU:** Post Graduate Coursework, Georgetown University; MD, Georgetown University (1985); Bachelor of Science in Biology, George Washington University (1980) **A/A/S:** American College of Radiology; Society for Magnetic Resonance Imaging; Radiology Society of North America; Pennsylvania Radiology Society
Email: rpah@rad-md.net
URL: http://www.rad-md.net

Rachel M. Patten, Ph.D.
Title: Director of Undergraduate Teacher Education **Company:** Johnson Bible College **Address:** 7900 Johnson Drive, Knoxville, TN 37998 United States **BUS:** College **P/S:** Education **MA:** Local **D/D/R:** Specializing in Elementary Education and English as a Second Language **H/I/S:** Traveling, Scrap Booking **EDU:** Ph.D. in Elementary Education, University of Tennessee (2003) **A/A/S:** Teachers of English to Speakers of Other Languages **C/VW:** Faith Hospitality Network; Missions
Email: rpatten@jbc.edu
URL: http://www.cambridgewhoswho.com

Jeanie Lynn Patterson
Title: Owner **Company:** Daily Grind 419 **Address:** 3549 Electric Road, Suite A, Roanoke, VA 24018 United States **BUS:** Cafe **P/S:** Coffee and Drinks, Baked Goods, Sandwiches, Soups, Gelato, Desserts **MA:** Local **EXP:** Ms. Patterson's expertise includes management and customer service. **D/D/R:** Catering, Managing Operations **H/I/S:** Spending Time with her Family, Boating, Fishing, Waterskiing, Biking, Hiking, Playing Tennis **EDU:** Associate Degree, Community College, Winston-Salem **CERTS:** Registered Nurse **A/A/S:** National Association for Female Executives; RWCC; Christian Rescue Mission Church; Hispanic Representative, CHIP; BNI **A/H:** Nominee, Small Business Award, Chamber of Commerce **C/VW:** Volunteer, Local Middle School
Email: jpatterson@dailygrindunwind.com
URL: http://www.dailygrindunwind.com

Dena Marie Patton
Title: Owner, Chief Executive Officer **Company:** Chat Chew & Chocolate, LLC **Address:** 4340 E. Indian School Road, Suite 21143, Phoenix, AZ 85018 United States **BUS:** Women's Social Group and Inspirational Events Company **P/S:** Special Events, Retails and Speaking Engagements **MA:** National **EXP:** Ms. Patton's expertise is women's inspiration and empowerment. **D/D/R:** Planning Private Events and Retreats, Selling Chapters, Marketing **H/I/S:** Ballroom Dancing, Photography **CERTS:** Certified Life Coach **A/A/S:** National Association of Women Business Owners **A/H:** Athena Award Nominee (2008); Award, Arizona Foothills Magazine (2008); Woman of The Year (2007); New Member of the Year, Clear Channel Radio (2007); Phoenix Event of the Year, National Association of Women Business Owners (2007); Best Of Award, AzTec Awards (2007); Top 50, New Times Magazine Platinum Awards **C/VW:** Fresh Start Women's Foundation; Girl's Rule Foundation
Email: dena@chatchewandchocolate.com
URL: http://www.chatchewandchocolate.com

Michelle B. Patty
Title: Chief Executive Officer **Company:** Michelle B. Patty **Address:** 109 Rosana Drive, Brandon, FL 33511 United States **BUS:** Consulting Firm **P/S:** Consulting Services including Legal and Medical; Advice, Referral Service **MA:** Local **D/D/R:** consulting **H/I/S:** Swimming, Playing Tennis, Traveling, Shopping, Spending Time with her Husband **EDU:** Bachelor's Degree in Theology, Blessed Hope Bible College, FL **A/A/S:** Better Business Bureau; Board Member, Mountain Pleasant Standard Base Charter School **C/VW:** Brooke Boxers, Sickle Cell Foundation; Susan G. Komen for the Cure; American Heart Association
Email: bootpatty@yahoo.com
URL: http://www.michellebpattyreferralservice.net

Dr. De'Borah G. Paul
Title: Chief Executive Officers **Company:** De'Borah's Dynasty & Wedding & Designs **Address:** 7198 N.W. 48th Court, Lauderhill, FL 33319 United States **BUS:** Bridal Planning Company **P/S:** Complete Wedding Planning and Consulting **MA:** National **D/D/R:** Preparing Floral Arrangements, Catering Services, Overseeing All Bridal Needs, Working with Vendors, Negotiating Bridal Pricing, Creating Wedding Color Schemes, Performing Ceremonies, Pre-Counseling for Couples, decorating event facilities using floral arrangements **H/I/S:** Traveling, Cooking, Pastoring Church and Bible reading **EDU:** Bachelor of Arts in Business Administration, Broward Community College **CERTS:** Ordained Pastor; Licensed Marriage Counselor **A/A/S:** Pastor, Ordained TABERNACLE OF THE MOST HIGH MINISTRIES. founder of Jehovah Shammah Christian Academy. Founder of International Christian women on the battle field. **C/VW:** Good will and salvation
Email: deborahdynasty@aol.com
URL: http://www.deborahdynasty.com

Mary T. Paul
Title: Proprietor **Company:** Mary's Tax and Accounting **Address:** 2350 S. 23rd Street, Lot 1091, Manitowoc, WI 54220 United States **BUS:** Accounting and Tax Preparation Firm **P/S:** Accounting and Tax Preparation Services **MA:** Regional **D/D/R:** preparing tax returns **H/I/S:** Photographing Eagles **EDU:** Coursework, Technical School **A/A/S:** Trout Unlimited **C/VW:** Local Church; Wisconsin Jaycees
Email: maryt@lakefield.net
URL: http://www.cambridgewhoswho.com

Marlene G. Paulick
Title: Art Teacher **Company:** North Allegheny School District **Dept:** Ingomar Middle School **Address:** 3 Camden Drive, Pittsburgh, PA 15215 United States **BUS:** Suburban School District **P/S:** Primary and Secondary Education in All Core Subjects, Arts and Technology, Athletic Programs, Special Programs, Afterschool Programs **MA:** Regional **D/D/R:** Teaching Scholastic Art and Writing to Students in Sixth through Eighth-Grades, Supervising 120 Teachers in the Region, Incorporating Writing in the Form of Self-Evaluation **H/I/S:** Sailing **EDU:** Master's Degree in Art Education, The Pennsylvania State University (1966) **A/A/S:** Pennsylvania Art Education Association; Delta Kappa Gamma; Supporter, Carnegie Museum of Art
Email: mpaulick@northallegheny.org
URL: http://www.northallegheny.org

Mr. Daniel W. Paulson
Title: President **Company:** InVision Business Development and Marketing, LLC **Address:** 628 Jamie Street, Dodgeville, WI 53533 United States **BUS:** Organizational Development Consulting Firm **P/S:** Training and Development to Become Highly Successful through Balance, Communication, Creativity and Teamwork **MA:** National **D/D/R:** Strategic Planning and Leadership, Business Development, On-Site Sales Coaching, Working with Businesses to Develop New Skills and Build Relationships **H/I/S:** Golfing **EDU:** Bachelor's Degree in Business Administration, University of Wisconsin (1992) **CERTS:** Certification in Attribute Assessment
Email: dan@invisionbusinessdevelopment.com
URL: http://www.invisionbusinessdevelopment.com

Terry Pawlowski
Title: Project Engineer **Company:** Obayashi/PSM JV **BUS:** Civil Construction Company **P/S:** Civil Construction, Structural Engineering **MA:** International **D/D/R:** Overseeing a Staff of Six Field Engineers, Designing Bridges, Managing Quality Control Issues Nationally and Internationally, Finalizing Contracts **H/I/S:** Hunting, Fishing **EDU:** Bachelor's Degree in Civil Engineering, Montana State University (1999) **A/A/S:** American Society of Civil Engineers
Email: terryp@obayashi-usa.com

Pamela M. Payne, Ed.D.
Title: Assistant Professor **Company:** Grambling State University **Address:** Grambling, LA 71270 United States **BUS:** University **P/S:** Honors College, Two Professional Schools, Graduate School, Division of Continuing Education, Excellent Nursing, Computer Science and Teacher Education Programs, Honor Societies, Greek Organizations **MA:** Regional **D/D/R:** teaching composition courses to freshman students, acting as a liaison between the English and education departments and supervising student teachers **H/I/S:** Reading **EDU:** Doctor of Education in Developmental Education, Grambling State University (2004); Master's Degree in Curriculum and Instruction, Louisiana Tech University (1992); Bachelor of Science in Education, Columbus State University (1985) **A/A/S:** Kappa Delta Phi; Association for Supervision and Curriculum Development **C/VW:** Newsletter Producer, Zion Traveler Baptist Church
Email: paynepm@gram.edu
URL: http://www.gram.edu

Patricia Payne Lunka
Title: Managing Director **Company:** JP Morgan Private Bank **Address:** 345 Park Avenue, New York, NY 10154 United States **BUS:** Financial Institution **P/S:** Financial Services, Banking **MA:** Local **D/D/R:** Risk and Insurance Management, Handling Public and Private Real Estate, Developing Wealth Plans and Investment Policies for Clients **H/I/S:** Golfing, Playing Tennis, Exploring the Cultural Arts **EDU:** Master of Business Administration, University of Chicago (1986); Bachelor's Degree in Business, with Concentration in Accounting, Lake Forest College (1979) **A/A/S:** New York Junior League; Assistant Treasurer, Finance Committee, Wine Society; Advisory Board, Calloway School of Business and Accountancy; Financial Planning Association; Featured, Barron's Top 100 Women Financial Advisers; Board Member, East 71st Street Corporation
Email: patricia.lunka@jpmorgan.com

Nikole A. Payton
Title: Realtor, Sales Manager **Company:** Intergulf Development **Address:** 650 First Avenue, San Diego, CA 92101 United States **BUS:** Leader in the Real Estate Industry **P/S:** High Quality Real Estate Services, Residential Condominiums **MA:** Regional **D/D/R:** Working for a Developer Company, Previously Involved in Selling all Four Major Projects with this Company, Handling Residential High-Rise Condominium Sales, Chief Executive Officer of Plern Corporation **H/I/S:** Watching Sports, Playing Basketball, Reading, Listening to Music **EDU:** Real Estate License (2000); Bachelor of Science Degree in Criminology, Law and Society, University of California at Irvine (1999) **CERTS:** Real Estate Brokers License (2006) **A/A/S:** National Association of Realtors; California Association of Realtors
Email: elokin32@yahoo.com
URL: http://www.intergulf.com

Christine K. Peach
Title: Research Biologist **Company:** Center for Disease Control and Prevention **Address:** 102 W. Fourth Street, Meta, MO 65058 United States **BUS:** Research Company **P/S:** DNA Extraction **MA:** Regional **EXP:** Ms. Peach's expertise includes molecular biology and DNA extraction. **H/I/S:** Hiking, Gardening **EDU:** Bachelor's Degree in Biology, Minor in Chemistry, Lincoln University at Missouri (1997) **A/A/S:** American Society of Microbiology
Email: christine.peach@dhss.mo.gov

Geri Lynn Peak
Title: Independent Consultant **Company:** Two Gems Consulting Services **Address:** 1016 Lenton Avenue, Baltimore, MD 21212 United States **BUS:** Program Evaluation **P/S:** Technical Support **MA:** International **D/D/R:** Program Evaluation, Consulting **H/I/S:** Spinning, Weaving, Knitting, Dancing, Performing African and Modern Dance **EDU:** Doctor of Public Health, Johns Hopkins University, Bloomberg School of Public Health; Master of Arts in Public Health, University of California at Los Angeles, School of Public Health; Bachelor of Arts, Mount Holyoke College **A/A/S:** American Public Health Association; American Evaluation Association; Elected Official, Spiritual Assembly **C/VW:** Virtues Project; Facilitator, Fellowship of Lights; Crimson Ark Regional; Training Institute Board; Spiritual Assembly
Email: geri@twogemsconsulting.com
URL: http://www.twogemsconsulting.com

Rita J. Pearce
Title: 1) Executive Vice President 2) Owner **Company:** 1) Moby Theatrical Company 2) Sweet Talk **BUS:** 1) Professional Theater and Entertainment Company 2)Voice-Over Production Company **P/S:** 1) Live Theatrical Productions, Talented Actors, Actresses, Directors, Technically Skilled Performers and Workshops 2) Voice Over Artistry for Radio, Television and the Internet **MA:** National **D/D/R:** Handling Public Relations and Marketing Campaigns, Advising on Technical Support, Constructing Theater Setting, Producing and Directing Actors and Actresses, Working as an Actress and Vocalist, Conducting Voice Over Artistry for Television, Radio and the Internet **H/I/S:** Quilting, Creating Art **EDU:** Master's Degree in Curriculum and Administration, Southern Illinois University, Plus 23, Carbondale (1974) **A/A/S:** Paradise Valley Players; Lifetime Member, National Education Association; Lifetime Member, Southern Illinois University Alumni Association **C/VW:** New Hope Church
Email: mobytheatrical@hotmail.com

Rev. Debra A. Pearson
Title: Reverend **Company:** Prayer Lighthouse Ministries **Address:** 1531 E Mullet Lake Road, Indian River, MI 49749 United States **BUS:** Religion Ministry **P/S:** Evangelist Ministry Services **MA:** Local **D/D/R:** Weddings, Baptism, Funerals, In Home Worship Services **H/I/S:** Snowmobile, Hiking
Email: info@cambridgewhoswho.com
URL: http://www.prayerlighthouseministries.com

Keyia A. Pearson
Title: Director of Education **Company:** Bethany Child Care and Preschool **Address:** 3305 Longlois Drive, Lafayette, IN 47904 United States **BUS:** Childcare Center **P/S:** Childcare, Preschool **MA:** Local **D/D/R:** Enhancing Young Minds, Caring for Children **EDU:** Associate Degree in Business, Ivy Tech Community College **C/VW:** St. Jude Children's Research Hospital
Email: keyiap@hotmail.com
URL: http://www.cambridgewhoswho.com

Tarasha Pearson, DDS
Title: Dentist **Company:** Ozark Dental Care **Address:** 927 N Business 71, Anderson, MO 64831 United States **BUS:** Healthcare /Dentistry **P/S:** General Dentistry **MA:** Local **D/D/R:** Oral Healthcare **H/I/S:** Jogging **EDU:** University of Tennessee, Doctor of Dental Surgery **A/A/S:** American Dental Association, NDA
Email: pearson0604@yahoo.com

Beverly A. Peck
Title: Massage Therapist, Reiki Master and Teacher, Certified Reflexologist **Company:** Therapeutic Massage for Humans and Equines **Address:** Williamsville, NY 14221 United States **BUS:** Massage Therapy Services for Humans, Equines and Dogs **P/S:** Deep Tissue Massage and Reflexology **MA:** Regional **D/D/R:** Offering Massage Therapy for Humans and Animals, Reiki Teacher, Licensed Massage Therapist and Certified Registered Reflexologist **H/I/S:** Driving a Horse and Carriage **EDU:** Associate Degree in Occupational Therapy, Erie Community College (1972) **A/A/S:** American Occupational Therapy Association; National Certification Board for Therapeutic Massage and Body Work; Association of Body Work and Massage Professionals
Email: lstunicorn@hotmail.com

Jonnae C. Peck
Title: Realtor **Company:** Keller Williams Realty **Address:** 3502 Henderson Boulevard, Tampa, FL 33609 United States **BUS:** Full Service Real Estate Company **P/S:** Residential Real Estate, Historical Home Sales **MA:** Regional **D/D/R:** Historical Homes **EDU:** Associate Degree in Pharmaceutical Skin Care, Local Community College
Email: jonnae.peck@kw.com
URL: http://www.jonnaepeck.com

Renee A. Pederson, CPA
Title: Manager **Company:** CBIZ & Mayer Hoffman McCann, P.C. **Address:** 2301 Dupont Drive, Suite 200, Irvine, CA 92612 United States **BUS:** Accounting Firm **P/S:** Accounting Services **MA:** Regional **D/D/R:** auditing for property management companies, real estate departments, overseeing staff and compliance **H/I/S:** Playing Volleyball, Attending the Theater, Reading, Vacationing **EDU:** Bachelor's Degree in Accounting, Azusa Pacific University (2001) **CERTS:** Certified Public Accountant, State of California (2004)
Email: rpederson@cbiz.com
URL: http://www.cbiz.com

Becky W. Pedrick
Title: Teacher **Company:** Cleveland Municipal School District **Address:** 1380 E. Sixth Street, Cleveland, OH 44113 United States **BUS:** High School **P/S:** Education **D/D/R:** Special Education, Teaching Troubled Children with Disciplinary Problems, Teaching Grammar, Reading, Writing, Life Skills **H/I/S:** Coaching Tennis, Bowling, Crocheting **EDU:** Bachelor of Arts in Secondary Education, History and English, Bob Jones University (1971) **A/A/S:** National Education Association; Welcome Wagon
Email: pedrick_becky@sbcglobal.net
URL: http://www.cmsdnet.net

Carole A. Peery
Title: Teacher **Company:** Edgemere Elementary School **Address:** 3200 N. Walker Avenue, Oklahoma, OK 73118 United States **BUS:** Elementary School **P/S:** Education for Prekindergarten through Fifth-Grade Students **MA:** Local **D/D/R:** Teaching First Grade, Students Developing Curriculums, Acting as an Accreditation Task Force Representative **H/I/S:** Playing Sports and Football, Playing in a Band, Pottery, Needlework, Reading, Scrapbooking, Photography, Water Skiing, Fishing, Boating, Gardening, Cooking, Writing Children's Books **EDU:** Bachelor of Science in Education, University of Central Oklahoma **A/A/S:** Oklahoma Education Association; National Education Association; American Federation of Teachers **C/VW:** President, Oklahoma Children's Cancer Association; Local Schools; Local Church; World Vision International; Feed The Children
Email: cpeery@cox.net

Nicole M. Pegues
Title: Senior Communications Specialist **Company:** OfficeMax, Inc. **Dept:** Global Communications and Enterprise Project Manager **Address:** 263 Shuman Boulevard, Naperville, IL 60563 United States **BUS:** Supply Chain Store **P/S:** Office Supplies and Services **MA:** International **EXP:** Ms. Pegues' expertise includes graphic design, visual and communication media. **H/I/S:** Traveling, Reading **EDU:** Master of Science, Northwestern University; Bachelor of Science, University of Illinois at Urbana-Champaign **C/VW:** Local Charitable Organizations
Email: nicolepegues@officemax.com
Email: nicole.pegues@gmail.com
URL: http://www.officemax.com

Ms. Annah C. Pelin
Title: Concierge **Company:** St. Regis Hotel **Address:** 2 E. 55th Street, New York, NY 10022 United States **BUS:** Hotel **P/S:** Accommodations, Dining, Concierge Services **MA:** International **D/D/R:** Booking Dining Reservations, New York Tours, Theater Tickets, Managing Travel Arrangements, Customer Service **H/I/S:** Attending Theater, Spending Time with her Two-Year-Old Daughter **EDU:** College Coursework **A/A/S:** New York Association of Hotel Concierges
Email: annahinnyc@hotmail.com

Donna Lynn Pellegrini
Title: Executive Director **Company:** Hunger Mountain Children's Center **Address:** 123 South Main Street, Waterbury, VT 05676 United States **BUS:** Education **P/S:** Pre School Child Care Services **MA:** Local **D/D/R:** Leadership **H/I/S:** Scrap Booking, Decorating **EDU:** Bachelor of Science in Early Childhood Education with a Minor in Child Psychology, Toccoa Falls
Email: hmcc@verizon.com

Michael Pellegrino
Title: Attorney **Company:** Law Office of Michael Pellegrino, Esq. **Address:** 1259 Richmond Avenue, Staten Island, NY 10314 United States **BUS:** Legal Services Attorney **P/S:** Law Services **MA:** Local **D/D/R:** Elder Law, Estate Planning, Real Estate, Entertainment Law **H/I/S:** Spectator Sports and Music, Plays Guitar, Bass and Keyboard **EDU:** Bachelor of Arts, St. Johns University; JD, New York Law School **A/A/S:** New York State Bar Association, Richmond County Bar Association, Seminars to Seniors and Nursing Homes on Elder Law and Medicaid, Supports Cancer Society, ASPCA, Alzheimer's Association
Email: mpelle7@aol.com

Vicki J. Pelleymounter
Title: Registered Nurse **Company:** Boone County Hospital **Address:** 1015 Union Street, Boone, IA 50036 United States **BUS:** Hospital **P/S:** Healthcare **MA:** Local **EXP:** Ms. Pelleymounter's expertise is in intensive care nursing. **H/I/S:** Gardening, Sewing, Quilting, Attending Red Hat Events **EDU:** Associate Degree in Nursing, North Iowa Area Community College **A/A/S:** American Association of Critical Care Nurses **C/VW:** St. John's Church; Volunteer, Boone County Hospice; The Humane Society of the United States; Local Schools; The Salvation Army; American Cancer Society; American Red Cross
Email: pelley@opencominc.com
URL: http://www.cambridgewhoswho.com

Debra J. Peltier
Title: Owner **Company:** Trout Bums **Address:** 408 Rock Creek Road, Clinton, MT 59825 United States **BUS:** Vacation Rental Company **P/S:** Fly Shop, Vacation Cabin Rentals **MA:** International **D/D/R:** Helping People Plan Fishing Vacations **H/I/S:** Spending Time with her Nine Grandchildren, Participating in Outdoor Activities **EDU:** Diploma, Superior High School **A/A/S:** National Federation of Independent Businesses **C/VW:** Christian Life Center
Email: troutbums@blackfoot.net
URL: http://www.rockcreektroutbums.com

Irma A. Peña
Title: Fine Arts Teacher **Company:** Brownville Independent School District, Vermillion Road Elementary School **Address:** 6895 FM 802, Brownsville, TX 78526 United States **BUS:** Elementary School **P/S:** Education for Students in Kindergarten through 12th-Grade **MA:** Brownsville **D/D/R:** Teaching Fine Arts, Teaching Students in Kindergarten through Fifth-Grade, Conducting the Choir for Fourth and Fifth-Grade Students **H/I/S:** Using Seashells to Create Crafts **EDU:** Master's Degree in Secondary Education, Stephen F. Austin State University (1994); Bachelor of Science in Education, University of Texas-Pan American (1985) **C/VW:** Activities through School and Church, Colleges

Rosalinda Pena
Title: Teacher **Company:** San Antonio Independent School District, Ball Elementary School **Address:** 343 Koehler Court, San Antonio, TX 78223 United States **BUS:** Public School **P/S:** Education **MA:** Local **D/D/R:** Training Teachers, Teaching Bilingual Education **H/I/S:** Scrapbooking, Reading, Traveling, Dancing **EDU:** Master's Degree in Education, University of Texas at San Antonio; Bachelor's Degree in Elementary Education, St. Mary's University, San Antonio **A/A/S:** National Education Association; American Federation of Teachers; Future Teachers of America **C/VW:** The Unforgettable Sixties, Metro Alliance
Email: rpena4@saisd.net
URL: http://www.cambridgewhsowho.com

Jason Pendergist
Title: Senior Vice President **Company:** Washington Mutual **Address:** 3200 Park Center Drive, Suite 200, Costa Mesa, CA 92626 United States **BUS:** Bank **P/S:** Commercial Real Estate **MA:** National **D/D/R:** Multi-Family, Office, Industrial and Retail Real Estate Finance **H/I/S:** Traveling, Golfing, Tennis **EDU:** Master of Business Administration, University of Colorado; Bachelor's Degree in Communication **C/VW:** Orange County Rescue Mission
Email: jason.pendergist@wamu.net
URL: http://www.cambridgewhoswho.com

Heather M. Pendley
Title: Teacher, MA **Company:** Walnut Grove Elementary School **Address:** 6103 N.E. 72nd Avenue, Vancouver, WA 98661 United States **BUS:** Elementary School **P/S:** Elementary Education, Instruction and Curriculum **MA:** Regional **D/D/R:** Teaching all Academics, Reading Program, Arranging Meetings, Writing, Discussing with Students **H/I/S:** Spending Time with her Family, Cooking, Practicing Yoga **EDU:** Master's Degree in Elementary Education, Reading and Literacy, Walden University (2006) **A/A/S:** National Education Association; Washington Education Association
Email: heather.pendley@vansd.org

Peggy A. Penn
Title: Management Services Specialist **Company:** Directorate of Human Resources, AG **Address:** 5450 Strom Thurmond Boulevard, Columbia, SC 29207 United States **BUS:** Recruitment Firm **P/S:** Military Administrative Services Including Recruitment **MA:** Regional **D/D/R:** paying attention to detail and managing administrative duties **H/I/S:** Directing the Choir **EDU:** Coursework in Accounting and Business Management
Email: butrflypeggy@bellsouth.net
URL: http://www.cambridgewhoswho.com

Larry R. Pennington, MD
Title: Professor of Surgery, General Surgeon **Company:** Oklahoma University Medical Center **Address:** 920 S.L. Young Boulevard, Oklahoma City, OK 73104 United States **BUS:** Public Medical Center for Local Residents **P/S:** Medical and Educational Services **MA:** Regional **D/D/R:** Working as a Professor of General Surgery and Private Practice in General Surgery, Focusing on Transplantation and Surgery of the Liver **H/I/S:** Golfing, Spending Time with her Family **EDU:** MD, University of Oklahoma (1975) **A/A/S:** Southwestern Surgery Associates; Southern Surgical Association; Transplantation Society; American Society of Transplant Surgeons; American Association for the Study of Liver Diseases; Public Speaker
Email: larry-pennington@ouhsc.edu

Robin Pensyl
Title: Licensed Practical Nurse **Company:** UPMC Bedford Memorial Hospital **Address:** 10455 Lincoln Highway, Everett, PA 15537 United States **BUS:** Hospital **P/S:** Nursing **MA:** National **D/D/R:** Seeing Patients, Checking IVs, Bathing Hygiene, Helping Patients **H/I/S:** Playing Piano, Golfing, Playing Soccer **A/A/S:** Nurses Student Organization **C/VW:** Phi Theta Kappa
Email: robin_pensyl@yahoo.com

Donna M. Peoples
Title: Human Resources Consultant **Company:** Verizon Wireless **Dept:** Human Resources **Address:** 100 Southgate Parkway, Morristown, NJ 07960 United States **BUS:** Telecommunication Company **P/S:** Cell Phone Plans and Accessories **MA:** National **D/D/R:** utilizing her communication skills, managing human resources, training, overseeing employee's activities and salary requirements **H/I/S:** Shopping, Relaxing **EDU:** College Coursework **CERTS:** Certified Human Resource Consultant **A/A/S:** Society for Human Resource Management
Email: donna.peoples@verizonwireless.com

Jean Paul Pepin
Title: Automation Engineer **Company:** PACIV **Address:** 807 Fernandez Juncos Avenue, Second Floor, San Juan, PR 00907 United States **BUS:** Pharmaceutical **P/S:** Manufacturing **MA:** National **D/D/R:** Systems Automation, Validation, Calibrating of Pharmaceutical and Manufacturing Equipment, Training **H/I/S:** Bike Riding, Sailing, Boating **EDU:** Bachelor of Science in Electrical Engineering, Polytechnic College of Puerto Rico (2002) **A/A/S:** Free Mason
Email: pepinj@paciv.com
URL: http://www.paciv.com

Susan Queen Pepper
Title: Health and Safety Specialist II **Company:** Novo Nordisk Delivery Technologies, Inc. **Address:** 3920 Point Eden Way, Hayward, CA 94545 United States **BUS:** Pharmaceutical Device Company **P/S:** Pharmaceutical Medical Devices **MA:** International **D/D/R:** Environmental Health and Safety **H/I/S:** Camping, Hiking **EDU:** Bachelor of Arts in Biology and German, The Johns Hopkins University, Baltimore, Maryland **A/A/S:** American Chemical Society; American Society of Safety Engineers
Email: spep@novonordisk.com
URL: http://www.novonordisk.com

Donna T. Perchatsch, RN
Title: Registered Nurse **Company:** Edward Hospital **Address:** 801 S. Washington Street, Naperville, IL 60540 United States **BUS:** Hospital **P/S:** Healthcare **MA:** Local **D/D/R:** Medical-Surgical Nursing **H/I/S:** Shopping for Antiques, Reading **EDU:** Pursuing Bachelor of Science in Nursing, Benedictine University; Associate Degree in Nursing, College of DuPage, Illinois (2006); Associate of Arts, University of Maryland University College; Coursework in Liberal Arts, Earned in Mannheim, Germany (2001) **A/A/S:** Phi Theta Kappa
Email: dperchatsc@aol.com
URL: http://www.edward.org

Carrie S. Perdue
Title: Licensed Practical Nurse **Company:** Washington Christian Village **Address:** 900 Centennial Drive, East Peoria, IL 61611 United States **BUS:** Nursing Home, long-term care facility **P/S:** Long-Term Nursing **MA:** Mid-West Region **D/D/R:** Geriatric Nursing **H/I/S:** Cooking, Gardening, Traveling, Spending Time with her Two Dogs **EDU:** Training in Nursing, Carl Soundburg College, Illinois **A/A/S:** Illinois Nurses Association **C/VW:** Breast Cancer Foundation, Kid's Wish Foundation
Email: info@cambridgewhoswho.com
URL: http://www.cambridgewhoswho.com

Luz M. Pereira
Title: Owner **Company:** Luz's Spa **Address:** 116 Madison Street, Newark, NJ 07105 United States **BUS:** Beauty Spa **P/S:** Anti-Stress Therapy **MA:** International **EXP:** Ms. Pereira's expertise includes bone and aromatherapy. **H/I/S:** Spending Time with her Family **EDU:** Coursework in Medical Massage Therapy **CERTS:** Certification in Swedish Massage Therapy; Certification in General Medical Therapy **A/A/S:** International Massage Association
Email: lcpcarlos@yahoo.com
URL: http://www.luzdayspa.com

Armando Perez
Title: Owner **Company:** J&A Masonry, Inc. **Address:** 247 Founders Boulevard, Lexington, SC 29073 United States **BUS:** Masonry Construction **P/S:** Masonry for Residential **MA:** Local **D/D/R:** Masonry Work **H/I/S:** Travel with his Wife and Three Children **EDU:** High School Graduate **A/A/S:** SC Home Builders Association
Email: lauraesq@alltell.net

Emilio I. Perez
Title: Doctor **Company:** St. Luke's-Roosevelt Hospital Center **Address:** 515 W. 59th Street, Apartment 12H, New York, NY 10019 United States **BUS:** Hospital **P/S:** Board Certified Physicians, Residency Training Program, Level 1 Trauma Center, 24-Hour Cardiac Catheterization Laboratory, Obstetrics and Gynecology, Rapid Triage and Care, Fasttrack for Non-Critical Care **MA:** National **D/D/R:** Internal Medicine **H/I/S:** Playing Tennis, Photography **EDU:** MD, Earned in Dominican Republic (1999) **A/A/S:** American Medical Association; American College of Physicians; Dominican Red Cross; Dominican Hospital Society; Dominican Medical College
Email: emil_ivan@hotmail.com
URL: http://www.skmed.org

Josh Perez
Title: Professional Life Coach **Company:** Morph Coaching **Address:** 5242 17th Place S.W., Naples, FL 34116 United States **BUS:** Professional Coaching Service **P/S:** Professional and Personal Coaching **MA:** National **D/D/R:** Business and Life Coaching **H/I/S:** Golfing, Snow, Skiing **EDU:** Associate Degree in Ministry, Christian Leadership University **CERTS:** Certified Professional Life Coach, PCCCA **A/A/S:** Pastor with New Hope Ministries
Email: info@morphcoaching.com
URL: http://www.morphcoaching.com

Luis Martin Perez
Title: Quality Assurance **Company:** Saint Dominic's Home **Address:** 500 Western Highway, Blauvelt, NY 10913 United States **BUS:** Healthcare Center **P/S:** Healthcare **MA:** Regional **D/D/R:** staffing, accounting, auditing and assuring quality **H/I/S:** Playing the Trumpet **EDU:** Master's Degree in Education, Mercy College; Bachelor's Degree in Fine Arts, City College **A/A/S:** Alpha Delta Pi **C/VW:** American Red Cross
Email: lperez@stdominicshome.org
URL: http://www.cambridgewhoswho.com

Rachel L. Perez
Title: Ambulatory Nurse Clinician **Company:** The Cleveland Clinic Foundation **Address:** 7832 Debonarie Drive, Mentor, OH 44060 United States **BUS:** Nonprofit Organization **P/S:** Healthcare Including Emergency Room, Pediatric, Geriatric, Women's Health, Bariatric Surgery, Pain Management, Heart and Vascular, Cancer and Nursing Care Services **MA:** Regional **D/D/R:** Nursing, Treating Patients Recovering from Neurosurgery, Reviewing Patients' Medical History, Conducting Physical Training Programs, Consulting, Overseeing Homecare Nursing for Post-Surgical Patients, Removing Sutures, Discharging Patients **H/I/S:** Exercising, Spending Time Outdoors, Hiking, Swimming, Playing Tennis **EDU:** Pursuing Master's Degree in Family Practice, Ursuline College; Bachelor's Degree in Nursing, Ursuline College (2002) **A/A/S:** American Academy of Ambulatory Care Nursing; The American Association of Neuroscience Nurses
Email: rperez9179@sbcglobal.net
URL: http://www.clevelandclinic.org

Stephanie Nicole Perez, Pharm.D.
Title: Registered Pharmacist **Company:** Osco Drug **Address:** 615 Wheeler Street, Griffith, IN 46319 United States **BUS:** Retail Pharmacy Industry **P/S:** Prescriptions, Over-the-Counter Medications, Medical Products, Women's, Men's and Children's Products, Seasonal Products **MA:** Regional **D/D/R:** Filling Prescriptions, Calling Doctors and Nurses, Counseling Patients on their Prescriptions, Performing Interaction Reviews **H/I/S:** Traveling **EDU:** Doctor of Pharmacy, Purdue University (2006) **A/A/S:** American Pharmacists Association; American Society of Healthcare Professionals
Email: perez.stephanie@gmail.com
URL: http://www.jewel.osco.com

Gregg A. Perich
Title: Vice President **Company:** Higher Images, Inc. **Address:** 510 Washington Avenue, Carnegie, PA 15106 United States **BUS:** Internet Marketing Company **P/S:** Internet Marketing, Pay Per Click Advertising, Search Engine Optimization, Website Design **MA:** National **D/D/R:** Local and National Search Marketing, Working with Companies with Multiple Locations in Various Markets Throughout the United States. **H/I/S:** Coaching Softball, Golf, Fishing, Spending Time with Family **EDU:** University of Central Florida
Email: gregg@higherimages.com
URL: http://www.higherimages.com

Valerie A. Perino
Title: Associate Broker **Company:** Key Properties, GMAC **Address:** 6002 Route 130 N., Delran, NJ 08075 United States **BUS:** Real Estate Agency **P/S:** Real Estate Sales and Listings **MA:** Burlington and Camden Counties **D/D/R:** Selling Residential Property, Representing Home Buyers **H/I/S:** Professional Painting, Art, Listening to Music, Playing Piano **EDU:** Associate of Science, Pierce College, Philadelphia **A/A/S:** GMAC Premier Club; President, Mount Laurel, N.J. Business Association, Eight Years; Owner, President, Valerie's Village Ice Cream Incorporated, 22 Years **C/VW:** American Cancer Society, Progressive Animal Welfare Society
Email: lakodafree@msn.com
URL: http://www.homesinmtlaurel.com

Julie Helton Perkins
Company: Ramey-Estep High School **Address:** 18958 State Route 854, Rush, KY 41168 United States **BUS:** School **P/S:** Education, Technical Coursework in Agriculture and Horticulture **MA:** Regional **D/D/R:** Horticulture Education, Running a Green House to Grow and Sell Produce, Organizing Landscaping Programs, Teaching Job Skills to Young Adults, Teaching Equine Classes **H/I/S:** Riding and Caring for her Quarter Horses, Reading **EDU:** Master's Degree in Education and Guidance Counseling, Morehead State University (2001) **CERTS:** Rank I, National Board Certification **A/A/S:** National Education Association; Agriculture Teachers Association; Boyd County Conservation Board; Farm Bureau
Email: julie.perkins@boyd.kyschool.us
URL: http://www.boyd.kyschools.us

Rex M. Perkins
Title: Technical Staff Engineer **Company:** Microchip **Address:** 2355 W. Chandler Boulevard, Chandler, AZ 85224 United States **BUS:** Microcontroller Manufacturer **P/S:** Semiconductors **MA:** International **D/D/R:** Designing, Test Engineering, New Part Development, Fabrication **H/I/S:** Sound Engineering, Video Editing **EDU:** Bachelor of Science in Computer Engineering, University of New Mexico (1995) **A/A/S:** Grove Bible Church (Sound Team Ministry) **C/VW:** Grove Bible Church
Email: rex.perkins@microchip.com
URL: http://www.microchip.com

Laura Perlman
Title: Music Editor, Educator, Composer, Musician **Address:** 8932 Wonderland Avenue, Los Angeles, CA 90046 United States **BUS:** Education, Music Editing, Composing, Musician. **P/S:** Education, Music Editing, Composing, Songwriting, Performing. **MA:** Local **D/D/R:** Music Editing. Educating, Composing, Writing Songs **H/I/S:** Music, Sculpting, Pets, Travel. **EDU:** Pursuing Master's Degree in Commercial Music; Bachelor of Music Degree, Berklee College of Music (1981) **A/A/S:** Motion Picture Editors Guild; Musicians Union; International Association for Jazz Education; University Film and Video Association. Nominated for 2 Golden Reel Awards for: 'Backdraft' and 'The Preacher's Wife'
Email: ljperl@earthlink.net

Candice Lee Perrillo
Title: Student **Company:** Extreme **Address:** 98 New Street, Pittston, PA 18640 United States **BUS:** Healthcare Service Provider **P/S:** Dance Instruction and Exercise **MA:** Local **D/D/R:** Teaching Cheerleading, Dance, Fitness **H/I/S:** Traveling, Cheerleading, Dancing **EDU:** Coursework, Luzerne County Community College **A/A/S:** The Phi Beta Kappa Society; National Honor Society
Email: candicep6@student.luzerne.edu
URL: http://www.cambridgewhoswho.com

Mrs. April R. Perrine
Title: Early Childhood Specialist **Company:** Manzanita Preschool **Address:** 2901 Detroit Avenue, Kingman, AZ 86401 United States **BUS:** Preschool **P/S:** Early Childhood Education **MA:** Local **D/D/R:** Developing the Curriculum, Adapting and Modifying Materials, Evaluating Team Performance, Working with Severely Disabled Children, Identifying Children for Early Intervention, Utilizing her Communication Skills **H/I/S:** Mountain Biking **EDU:** Master of Arts in Early Childhood Education, Northern Arizona University (2007); Bachelor of Science in Elementary and Special Education, Northern Arizona University **A/A/S:** National Association for the Education of Young Children
Email: aperrine@kusd.org

Juliet Perrucci
Title: President, Appraiser **Company:** Buckhead Real Estate Appraisals, Inc. **Address:** 150 Dogwood Court, Dallas, GA 30157 United States **BUS:** Real Estate Appraising Company **P/S:** Selling Residential Property **MA:** Regional **D/D/R:** Specializing in Real Estate, Appraising Various Residential Properties **H/I/S:** Outdoors, Spending Time with Family and Dogs **EDU:** Coursework in Real Estate and Appraisal Classes, Kennesaw State University **CERTS:** Realtors License (2007); Appraisers License (2000)
Email: gaappraiser@yahoo.com
URL: http://www.erabuckheadrealty.com

Cindy A. Perry
Title: Auditor, Consultant **Company:** Axolotl Corporation **Address:** 1322 S.W. Hamilton Road, Mountain Home, ID 83647 United States **BUS:** Provider of Web-based tools **P/S:** Healthcare Information **MA:** National **D/D/R:** Ensuring the Quality of Medical Records, Analyzing Patient Data, overseeing auditing and interim management **H/I/S:** Skiing, Fishing **EDU:** Associate of Arts, Rose State College; Associate in Applied Science, Rose State College; Registered Health Information Technician

Donald D. Perry
Title: Steelworker (Retired) **Company:** Allegheny Ludlam Steel **Address:** 100 River Road, Brackenridge, PA 15014 United States **BUS:** Steel Manufacturing Company **P/S:** Clad Metal, Various Steel Products **MA:** International **D/D/R:** Pipe Fitting Clad Metal **H/I/S:** Singing, Reading, Woodworking, **EDU:** Apprenticeship, Metal Industry; Coursework in Woodworking, Trade School **A/A/S:** Crossroads Vineyard Church **C/VW:** American Legion Volunteer, Volunteer doing Hymn Sings at local nursing homes

Nancy M. Perry
Title: General Partner **Company:** The Perry Law Firm, LLP **Address:** 5608 Malvey, Suite 109, Fort Worth, TX 76107 United States **BUS:** Law Firm Law Firm **P/S:** family Law, Wills, Trust, Probate, Legal Services **MA:** Local **D/D/R:** Family Law, Divorce, Estate Planning, Probate, General Civil Law, Collaborative Law **H/I/S:** Spending time with the kids **EDU:** JD, Oklahoma City **A/A/S:** Tarrant County Bar Association, Tarrant County Family Law Bar Association, Collaborative Law Institute of Texas, IACP Association
Email: nancy@texaslaw4u.com
URL: http://www.TexasLaw4U.com

Sara L. Perry, RN, BSN
Title: Registered Nurse **Company:** Harborview Medical Center **Address:** 325 9th Avenue, Seattle, WA 98104 United States **BUS:** Medical Center **P/S:** Healthcare Services Including Intensive Care and Clinical Care, Neuroscience, Trauma, Reconstruction and Rehabilitation Services for Mentally Ill and Medically Vulnerable People, Acquired Immune Deficiency Syndrome and Sexually Transmitted Diseases Treatment **MA:** Regional **EXP:** Ms. Perry's area of expertise is in nursing. **D/D/R:** Following Doctors' Orders, Accompanying Doctors on their Rounds, Generating Patient's Reports, caring for patients and overseeing intensive care unit **H/I/S:** Rock Climbing, Teaching Guitar Lessons, Supporting the Chicago Cubs **EDU:** Bachelor of Science in Nursing, Syracuse University (2000) **A/A/S:** American Association of Critical-Care Nurses **C/VW:** Northwest Burn Foundation
Email: slperry72@comcast.net
URL: http://www.uwmedicine.org/facilities/harborview.com

Wanda K. Perry
Title: Owner, Licensed Massage Therapist **Company:** Gentle Hand with a Healing Touch, LLC **Address:** P.O. Box 663, Greensburg, LA 70441 United States **BUS:** Massage Therapy Office **P/S:** Massage Therapies, Including Reflexology, Neuromuscular, Reiki, Swedish Massage **MA:** Regional **D/D/R:** Reflexology, Neuromuscular Therapy **H/I/S:** Crafts, Gardening, Tending to her Tree Nursery **EDU:** Massage Therapy Diploma, Blue Cliff College of Baton Rouge; Second Degree Reiki Level II **A/A/S:** American Massage Therapy Association; National Certification in Massage Therapy and Body Work, International Institute of Reflexology **C/VW:** Cystic Fibrosis Foundation, Girl Scouts of the USA, Church
Email: wkp.massage@yahoo.com

Jane E. Person
Title: Teacher **Company:** Ocean Beach School **Address:** 400 Washington Street S., Long Beach, WA 98631 United States **BUS:** School **P/S:** Education **MA:** Local **D/D/R:** Teaching Reading **H/I/S:** Making Jewelry, Singing, Playing Piano, Sewing **EDU:** Master of Education, Specialization in Reading, Whitworth College **A/A/S:** Nominee, Who's Who Among American Teachers **C/VW:** Hospice, American Breast Cancer Society
Email: jane.person@ocean.k12.wa.us
URL: http://www.cambridgewhoswho.com

Gerri Peters
Title: Activity Director **Company:** Brian Center/Health and Rehab **Address:** 105 Clonce Street, Gate City, VA 24251 United States **BUS:** Healthcare Facility Nursing Home **MA:** Local **D/D/R:** Activity Director/Volunteer Coordinator **H/I/S:** Church, 4-H Club, Car Shows **EDU:** University of Southern Indiana, Bachelor of Science **A/A/S:** American Association of Respiratory Care
Email: rt35stack@yahoo.com

Dr. Robert E. Peters
Title: Senior Pastor **Company:** New Haven Church of God in Christ **Address:** 7426 S Hoover, Los Angeles, CA 90262 United States **BUS:** Church **P/S:** Multi Faceted Outreach Ministry **MA:** Local **D/D/R:** Biblical interpretation **H/I/S:** Golf, Travel, Reading **EDU:** Doctor of Divinity, Canterbury University; Master of Science in Biblical Studies, Roxville University; Bachelor of Science in Biblical Studies, Southern Trinity University **A/A/S:** Fraternal Order of Police, Northridge State University
Email: rpeterssr@aol.com
URL: http://www.newhavenministries.org

Sharon K. Peters
Title: Assistant Director of Nursing **Company:** Shiawassee County Medical Care Facility **Address:** 729 Norton Street, Corunna, MI 48817 United States **BUS:** Healthcare Center **P/S:** Healthcare **MA:** Local **EXP:** Ms. Peters' expertise is in psychiatric nurse management. **D/D/R:** Managing the Department of Infection Control, In-Service Education, Overseeing Audit Accident Reports, Caring for Patients, Managing Assessment, Overseeing Administrative Duties, Attending Emergency Calls, Training, Conducting Skill Testing **H/I/S:** Golfing, Writing, Swimming **EDU:** Master's Degree **C/VW:** Local Church; March of Dimes; Feed the Children; Association of Administrative Law Judges; Alliance Defense Fund
Email: skpeters49@charter.net
URL: http://www.cambridgewhoswho.com

Ms. Tia M. Peters
Title: Teacher Liaison for Special Ed/Special Education Teacher-9th-Grade **Company:** Binghamton City School District, Binghamton High School **Address:** 31 Main Street, Binghamton, NY 13905 United States **BUS:** School District **P/S:** Education **MA:** Local **D/D/R:** Teaching Students with Special Needs responsible for student IEP's, Parental contact, CSE meetings member, modify and adapt all core content for academics, testing, writes annual reviews, does educational testing, provides specialized services. **H/I/S:** Life Long Learning, Skiing, Traveling, Reading **EDU:** SUNY Cortland; Master of Education in Curriculum and Instruction, University at Buffalo (2005); Bachelor's Degree in Elementary and Special Education for Kindergarten through 12th-Grade, University at Buffalo (2003) **CERTS:** Pursuing Certificate in Advanced Studies and Administration School District and Building Leader **A/A/S:** Omicron Delta Kappa; Sigma Delta Kappa Sigma alpha Pi, national honor society of leadership and success, **C/VW:** Race for the Cure, March of Dimes, Special Olympics Judy's walk local cancer walk
Email: petemt92@gmail.com
URL: http://www.binghamtoncityschools.org

Ralph R. Petersen, LPN
Title: Licensed Practical Nurse **Company:** Gaylord Hospital **Address:** Gaylord Farm Road, Box 400, Wallingford, CT 06492 United States **BUS:** Hospital **P/S:** Healthcare **MA:** Local **D/D/R:** Rehabilitation **H/I/S:** Automobiles **EDU:** Associate Degree in Nursing, San Bernardino Valley College **A/A/S:** Licensed Practical Nurses Association **C/VW:** Salvation Army
Email: oneringbarrer@aol.com
URL: http://www.cambridgewhoswho.com

David J. Peterson, PE
Title: President, Chief Executive Officer **Company:** Watershape Consulting, Inc., Watershape Products, Inc. **Address:** 3830 Valley Centre Drive, Suite 705-316, San Diego, CA 92130 United States **BUS:** Engineering and Construction Company **P/S:** Design, Engineering and Construction of Watershapes, Including Pools, Spas and Water Features **MA:** International **D/D/R:** dealing with pool related issues, overseeing the design and engineering of multiple projects, consulting and running forensics **H/I/S:** Golfing, Spending Time with his Son **EDU:** Bachelor of Science in Civil Engineering, California Polytechnic Institute (1995 **CERTS:** Professional Engineer (1998) **A/A/S:** American Society of Civil Engineers; Construction Specifications Institute
Email: dave@watershapeconsulting.com
URL: http://www.watershapeconsulting.com

Mary Ann Peterson
Title: Founder, Director **Company:** Joy Center **Address:** 225 W. Broadway Street, P.O. Box 485, Monticello, MN 55362 United States **BUS:** Nonprofit Organization **P/S:** Public Services **MA:** Regional **D/D/R:** supervising parenting time **H/I/S:** Photography **EDU:** Master of Business Administration, University of St. Thomas; Bachelor of Arts in Child and Family Development, University of Minnesota, Saint Paul **C/VW:** Local Church; Volunteer, 4-H Program; Kiwanis International
Email: joy.center@hotmail.com
URL: http://www.joycenteronline.com

Ms. Nancy Ann Peterson
Title: Physical Therapist Assistant **Company:** Life Care Center of Chattanooga **Address:** 455 N. Highland Park Avenue, Chattanooga, TN 37404 United States **BUS:** Nursing Home **P/S:** Long-Term Care Services, Sub-acute Healthcare Services, Rehabilitation Services **MA:** Regional **D/D/R:** Treating Patients with Physical Therapy **H/I/S:** Traveling **EDU:** Associate Degree in Physical Therapy, Davenport University (2001) **A/A/S:** American Physical Therapy Association; Tennessee Physical Therapy Association
Email: redrosesandivy@yahoo.com

Mr. Pete Peterson
Title: RN, BSN **Company:** Tweedpeaches, Inc. **Address:** 2911 Gayridge Street, Pomona, CA 91767 United States **BUS:** Healthcare **P/S:** Provider of Healthcare, Quality Assurance, Risk Management, Development of Policy and Procedure, Development of Active Patient Advocate **MA:** Regional **D/D/R:** Registered Nursing in Critical Care, Hospital Supervisor, Offering Healthcare and Direct Patient Care **H/I/S:** Gardening, Traveling, Gym **EDU:** Doctorate Degree in Health Science, Trinity Southern University (2003); Master's Degree in Public Health, Wilshire University, United Kingdom (2002); Bachelor of Science Degree in Nursing Administration; Associate of Science in Nursing **A/A/S:** California Nurses Association; American Association of Critical Care Nurses; Unofficial Compliance Officer for the Department of Health, Joint Commission on Accreditation of Healthcare Organizations; American Heart Association; California Nurses Association
Email: rhpeaches@aol.com
URL: http://www.cambridgewhoswho.com

Tiffany L. Peterson
Title: Paralegal, Office Manager **Company:** Kent T. Perry & Company, L.C. **Address:** 8551 Gabriel Lane, Lenexa, KS 66227 United States **BUS:** Law Firm **P/S:** Legal Advice and Representation, Legal Matters in Business, Securities, Taxation, Civil Litigation, Probate and Estate Planning **MA:** Regional **D/D/R:** Managing Client Files, Accounts Payable and Accounts Receivable, Overseeing Office Personnel, Managing Drafts and Press Pleas, Communicating with Clients, Performing Legal Duties for Attorneys **H/I/S:** Drag Racing, Water Sports **EDU:** Associate Degree in Legal Studies, Washburn University (2002) **CERTS:** Certified Legal Office Manager; Certified Bookkeeper
Email: perry_reuter@msn.com
URL: http://www.lawyers.com/perreulaw

Helen M. Petho
Title: Accountant III **Company:** State of Louisiana, Department of Civil Service **Address:** P.O. Box 94111, Baton Rouge, LA 70704 United States **BUS:** State Agency **P/S:** Human Resources **MA:** Statewide **D/D/R:** Budgeting, Accounting, Auditing **H/I/S:** Photography, Videography **EDU:** Bachelor of Science in Accounting, Louisiana State University **CERTS:** Certified Internal Auditor **A/A/S:** Association of Governmental Accountants; Institute of Internal Auditors **C/VW:** Youth Group Leader, Photographer, Videographer, Albany Hungarian Presbyterian Church; Louisiana Public Broadcasting
Email: hpetho@eatel.net

Donna Petree
Title: Music Specialist (Retired) **Company:** Wausau School District **Address:** 415 Seymour Street, Wausau, WI 54403 United States **BUS:** School District **P/S:** Education, Kindergarten through Eighth **MA:** Local **D/D/R:** Teaching Music from Levels K-12, Directing the High School Choir **H/I/S:** Reading, Traveling **EDU:** Bachelor's Degree in Music Education, Baylor University **A/A/S:** Wisconsin Music Association; Wisconsin School Music Association; Wisconsin Music Educators Association; Worcester Regional Transit Authority **C/VW:** Plays the Organ at her Local Church, American Cancer Society
Email: dlpetree@charter.net
URL: http://www.cambridgewhoswho.com

Ann R. Petrosky
Title: Owner **Company:** Ann's Collectible Plates **Address:** P.O. Box 3, Masury, OH 44438 United States **BUS:** Antique Collectible China Store **P/S:** Antiques **MA:** International **D/D/R:** collecting antiques and overseeing business operations **H/I/S:** Writing **EDU:** Master of Science in Education, University of Westminster; Bachelor of Science in Education, Youngstown State University **A/A/S:** Retired Teachers Association **C/VW:** Local Church
Email: petrosky@infonline.net
URL: http://www.cambridgewhoswho.com

Randy Kae Petrucci
Title: Registered Nurse **Company:** St. John Hospital **Address:** 22101 Moross Road, Detroit, MI 48236 United States **BUS:** Referral Teaching Hospital Affiliated with Wayne State University, 607 Licensed Beds, a 700-Member Medical Staff and More than 50 Medical and Surgical Specialties **P/S:** Surgical Specialties and Subspecialties Healthcare **MA:** Regional **D/D/R:** Level III Hospital Nursing, Working with Patients with High-Risk Pregnancy and Post-Partum Issues, Labor and Delivery **H/I/S:** Golfing, Bowling **EDU:** Associate of Science in Nursing, Macomb Community College **A/A/S:** Service Excellence Program
Email: floridafishpink@yahoo.com
URL: http://www.cambridgewhoswho.com

Derek Petry
Title: Director of Research and Development **Company:** Triumph Foods **Address:** 5302 Stockyards Expressway, Saint Joseph, MO 64505 United States **BUS:** Agricultural Company **P/S:** Premium Pork Products **MA:** International **D/D/R:** Conducting Research and Development to Improve Product Quality, Conducting Studies on the Shelf Life and Genetic Improvement of TR4 Sire Line, Analyzing Data for Value Models, Validating Product Specifications, Predicting Yields **H/I/S:** Golfing, Watching College Football **EDU:** Ph.D. in Quantitative and Molecular Genetics, Minor in Statistics, University of Nebraska (2005); Master of Business Administration, University of Nebraska (2005); Master of Science in Quantitative Genetics (2001); Bachelor of Science, Texas A&M University (1996) **A/A/S:** American Society of Animal Science; Gamma Sigma Delta; Sigma Xi
Email: dpetry@triumphfoods.com
URL: http://www.triumphfoods.com

Jason T. Pettet
Title: Master of Oriental Medicine **Company:** Primary Health Care P.C. **Address:** 494 W. 17th Street, Holland, MI 49423 United States **BUS:** Healthcare Facility **P/S:** Healthcare **MA:** Western Michigan **D/D/R:** Acupuncture, Oriental Medicine **H/I/S:** Traveling, Swimming **EDU:** Master of Oriental Medicine, Tai Hsuan Foundation, Hawaii **CERTS:** National Certification in Oriental Medicine **A/A/S:** Michigan Association of Acupuncture and Oriental Medicine; National Certification in Oriental Medicine; Diplomat, National Certification Commission for Acupuncture and Oriental Medicine **C/VW:** Church
Email: dreamreacher_inc@hotmail.com
URL: http://www.cambridgewhoswho.com

Linda T. Pettit
Title: Teacher **Company:** Memphis City Schools **Dept:** Treadwell Elementary School **Address:** 3538 Given Avenue, Memphis, TN 38122 United States **BUS:** Largest School System in the State of Tennessee **P/S:** Primary and Secondary Education for Students in Kindergarten through Twelfth-Grades **MA:** Regional **D/D/R:** Teaching First Graders Reading, Mathematics, Science, English, Health and Social Studies Using the Reading First Program **H/I/S:** Gardening, Painting **EDU:** Bachelor of Science in Elementary Education K-8; Mississippi State College for Women (1972) **A/A/S:** Honors Day Committee; First Grade Chairman; Two Rotary Grants, The Rotary Club
Email: pettitlindat@mcs.k12.net
URL: http://www.mcsk12.net/

Chere L. Petty
Title: Microscopist, Manager, Keith R. Porter Imaging Facility **Company:** University of Maryland, Baltimore County **Address:** 1000 Hilltop Circle, Baltimore, MD 21250 United States **BUS:** University Combining an Emphasis on Teaching with the Innovation of a Research University **P/S:** Bachelor, Masters and Doctoral Degree Programs, Research, Professional Studies, Clubs and Organizations, Health Services, Athletics **MA:** National **D/D/R:** Working with Electron and Light Microscopes, Organizing the Facility, Maintaining and Servicing Machines, Acquiring New Equipment through Grant Writing, Teaching Graduate and Undergraduate Students how to use the Equipment **H/I/S:** Classical Ballet, Reading, Skiing, Waterskiing, Going to Spas, Wine Tasting **EDU:** Master's Degree in Biological Sciences, University of Maryland, Baltimore County (2004); Bachelor's Degree in Biology and Biological Sciences, University of Maryland, Baltimore County **A/A/S:** Direct Donation Program, National Institute of Health; Local Public Speaker, AAAS, National Cell Society
Email: cpetty1@umbc.edu
URL: http://www.umbc.edu

Lisa Petzinger
Title: Computer Teacher, Former Athletic Director, Librarian **Company:** Our Lady of Sorrows **Address:** 3690 Thomas Street, Memphis, TN 38127 United States **BUS:** Catholic School Dedicated to Excellence in Education **P/S:** Fosters the Spiritual, Intellectual, Emotional and Physical Development of the Students in Keeping with the Teaching of the Catholic Church **MA:** Regional **D/D/R:** Teaching Computer Classes in Computer Lab for Students from Pre-K to Eighth-Grade, Classroom Involvement, Administrator of the Network System in the School, Holding Computer Classes for Parishioners of the Church and for Spanish Speaking Population, Librarian **H/I/S:** Mowing the Lawn, Spending Time with Family **EDU:** Bachelor of Science in Early Childhood Education and Elementary Education with Kindergarten Endorsement, Texas Christian University (1983) **A/A/S:** National Association for Educators of Young Children
Email: lisa.petzinger@ols.cdom.org
URL: http://www.olos.schoolfusion.us

Michelle Hill Pfeifer
Title: Science Teacher **Company:** Reservoir Middle School **Address:** 516 Sunderland Terrace, Chesapeake, VA 23322 United States **BUS:** Middle School **P/S:** Education for Sixth through Eighth-Grade Students **MA:** Local **D/D/R:** Teaching Science to Sixth through Eighth-Grade Students, Coordinating Science Programs **H/I/S:** Irish Dancing **EDU:** Master's Degree in Secondary Education, Old Dominion University, VA (2007) **A/A/S:** Parent-Teacher Association
Email: michelle.pfeifer@nn.k12.va.us

Tracy L. Pfeiffer
Title: Kindergarten Teacher **Company:** Whitney Point Central School District **Address:** 52 Kales Hill Road, Whitney Point, NY 13862 United States **BUS:** School District **P/S:** Education **MA:** Regional **D/D/R:** Instructing Prekindergarten through Eighth-Grade Students, Teaching Early Literacy, Preparing Students' Social, Reading and Writing Skills, Overseeing Literary Leader Group **H/I/S:** Walking, Taking Vacations, Cooking, Reading, Basketball, Football, Soccer **EDU:** Master of Arts in Literacy, SUNY Cortland (2005); Bachelor of Science in Elementary Education, East Stroudsburg University (1988)
Email: tpfeiffer@stny.rr.com
URL: http://www.wpcsd.org

Diana Wood Pfenning, M.Ed.
Title: Executive Director of the Tapestry Program **Company:** Rutland Public Schools **Address:** 6 Church Street, Rutland, VT 05701 United States **BUS:** School **P/S:** Education Including Summer Program for Students **MA:** Local **D/D/R:** managing operations, conducting afterschool and summer programs, supervising, writing Grants **H/I/S:** Crafting, Reading, Spending Time with her Grandchildren **EDU:** Master of Education, Wheelock College (1991); Bachelor of Science in Education, Castleton State College (1969) **A/A/S:** Former Chairwoman, Vermont School Age Care Network; National Afterschool Association (NAA) **C/VW:** The Humane Society
Email: dpfenning@rutlandhs.k12.vt.us
URL: http://www.rutlandhs.k12.vt.us

Mr. Christian W. Pfister
Title: Contract Specialist **Company:** CPS Energy **Address:** 214 Laramie Drive, San Antonio, TX 78209 United States **BUS:** One of the Nation's Second Largest Utilities Company in the Nation, Municipally Owned **P/S:** Electric Gas Services to the City of San Antonio, Texas, Offering Contacts all Over National and Regional Areas, Commercial Goods and Services **MA:** National **D/D/R:** Working within the Legal Department Reviewing all Contracts Over $100,000, Approving Contracts **H/I/S:** Playing Piano, Sailing **EDU:** Master of Business Administration, University of Texas (1982) **A/A/S:** Toast Masters International; Public Speaking and Lecturing
Email: cwpfister@cpsenergy.com
URL: http://www.cpsenergy.com

Mi Kyong Pham
Title: Owner **Company:** My Nail Spa and My Bella Spa & Supply **Address:** 7116 Brighton Brook Road, Charlotte, NC 28212 United States **BUS:** Retail **P/S:** Sells all Nail Supply, Tanning, Waxing Equipment **MA:** Local **D/D/R:** Nail Care, Nail Care Distributors **EDU:** High School Graduate
Email: bellsaly@yahoo.com

Betty Pharris
Title: Writer **Address:** 913 S. Redbud Avenue, Broken Arrow, OK 74012 United States **BUS:** Sole Proprietorship **P/S:** Writing Articles and Columns for Publications Including Decision, International Literature, Christian Life, The Secret Place **MA:** National **D/D/R:** writing inspirational and religious articles and columns **H/I/S:** Spending Time with her Family **EDU:** Coursework in Writing; Diploma, Will Rogers High School (1951)
Email: bpharris1@cox.net
URL: http://www.cambridgewhoswho.com

Mr. Joel W. Phelps
Title: Vice President of Livestock Services **Company:** Meadowbrook Farms Cooperative **Address:** 10 S. Jackson Street, Belleville, IL 62220 United States **BUS:** Pork Processing Company **P/S:** Pork Products, Swine Genetics, Production, Marketing, Management **MA:** North America **D/D/R:** Procurement of Animals, Assessing Agri-Business Risks, Strategic Planning, Livestock Production Management, Swine Genetics, Business Leadership, Setting up Strategies Focusing on Profitability **H/I/S:** Hunting, Fishing **EDU:** Pursuing Master's Degree in Agri-Business, Kansas State University; Bachelor's Degree in Business Management, University of Phoenix (2005); Two-Year Degree in Agri-Business Management, Ridgewater College (1985) **A/A/S:** IACUC
Email: jphelps@farms.coop
URL: http://www.farms.coop

Susan Oglesby Phelps
Title: Teacher **Company:** Southampton County Schools **Address:** 23350 Southampton Parkway, Courtland, VA 23837 United States **BUS:** School **P/S:** Education **MA:** Local **D/D/R:** Teaching, Motivating Students, Overseeing the Department, Academic Coaching, Inclusion Classes **H/I/S:** Reading, Community Service **EDU:** Master's Degree in Reading, Virginia State University (1987); Bachelor of Arts in English and History, University of North Carolina at Greensboro (1976) **A/A/S:** Phi Beta Kappa **C/VW:** American Red Cross, NCTE
Email: sphelpseng@yahoo.com

Nikki Philipopoulos
Title: Teacher **Company:** Taper Avenue Elementary School **Address:** 1621 Cadding Drive, Rancho Palos Verdes, CA 90275 United States **BUS:** Elementary School Facility Dedicated to Excellence in Education **P/S:** Regular Core Curriculum Including Reading, Mathematics, English, Science, Social Studies, Music, Art, Physical Education **MA:** Regional **D/D/R:** Teaching Second-Grade All Core Subjects **EDU:** Bachelor of Arts in Psychology, Long Beach State University **A/A/S:** National Education Association
Email: philipopoulos@aol.com

Carl Maxey Phillips
Title: Owner **Company:** Carl Maxey Phillips, EA **Address:** 1081 Wall Avenue, Cookeville, TN 38501 United States **BUS:** Taxation Firm **P/S:** Tax Preparation, Bookkeeping and Consulting Services **MA:** Regional **H/I/S:** Watching Movies, Reading **EDU:** Master's Degree in Journalism; Master's Degree in Instructional Media; Coursework, The University of Alabama; Coursework, Jacksonville State University **A/A/S:** National Association of Enrolled Agents; National Society of Accountants; National Federation of Independent Business
Email: frznrth@juno.com
URL: http://www.frznrth.com

Mr. David S. Phillips
Title: Owner, Manager **Company:** Sunset Fossils & Minerals **Address:** 575 Beaumont Drive, Morgantown, WV 26508 United States **BUS:** Mining Company **P/S:** Retail Mining Company **MA:** West Virginia **D/D/R:** Discovering Local Minerals, Fossils and Rocks, Promoting Rockhounding on Television, Lecturing, Producing the 'Gem and Fossil Show', Educating the Public on the Industry **H/I/S:** Paleontology **EDU:** College Coursework in Chemistry, Fairmont State University **A/A/S:** President, Society of Prehistoric West Virginia
Email: wvfossils@aol.com

Frances T. Phillips, MS
Title: Educator **Company:** Broadalbin-Perth Intermediate School **Dept:** Broadalbin-Perth Central School **Address:** 1870 County Highway 107, Amsterdam, NY 12010 United States **BUS:** School **P/S:** Fourth, Fifth and Sixth-Grade Education **MA:** Local **D/D/R:** Teaching Elementary Education **H/I/S:** Swimming, Biking, Traveling, Reading, Writing **EDU:** Master of Science in Elementary Education, SUNY Oneonta; Bachelor's Degree in Elementary Education, SUNY Oneonta **A/A/S:** New York State United Teachers; National Education Association
Email: phillipsf@bpcsd.org
URL: http://www.bpcsd.org

Janet L. Phillips
Title: Massage Therapist **Company:** A Touch of Massage **Address:** 234 Riviera Drive, Newport, TN 37821 United States **BUS:** Massage Therapy Center **P/S:** Massage, Relaxation Therapy **MA:** Local **EXP:** Ms. Phillips' expertise is in deep tissue massage. **H/I/S:** Scrapbooking, Singing with her Church Choir **EDU:** High School Education **A/A/S:** Tennessee Massage Therapy Association; American Massage Therapy Association **C/VW:** Shriner's; The Humane Society of the United States
Email: janet.phillips@cwwemail.com
URL: http://www.cambridgewhoswho.com

Nancy E. Phillips
Title: Realtor **Company:** Michael Saunders & Company **Address:** 8325 Lakewood Ranch Boulevard, Bradenton, FL 34202 United States **BUS:** Real Estate Agency **P/S:** Real Estate **MA:** Florida **D/D/R:** Selling Residential Real Estate, Golf Communities, Bay Relocation Specialist **EDU:** Master of Education in Reading, Rhode Island College; Bachelor's Degree in Special Education and Sociology, Salve Regina University, Newport, Rhode Island **A/A/S:** National Association of Realtors; Florida Association of Realtors; Manatee Board of Realtors; Sarasota Association of Realtors **C/VW:** Special Olympics, Habitat for Humanity
Email: nancyphillips@michaelsaunders.com
URL: http://www.michaelsaunders.com

Ramona Lisa Phillips
Title: Supervisor **Company:** Baylor All Saints Medical Center **Address:** 1400 Eighth Avenue, Fort Worth, TX 76104 United States **BUS:** Private, Nonprofit Hospital with Over 200 Beds **P/S:** Advanced Patient Care in a Family-Centered Environment **MA:** Regional **D/D/R:** Creating Nutrition Plans to Ensure Proper Diet Intake for Diabetic Patients, Checking the Trays and Making Sure of Nutritional Fitness, Giving Daily Meetings to Staff **H/I/S:** Writing Poems **EDU:** Pursuing Degree in Medical Transcription; Coursework in Physical Therapy; Coursework in Medical Transcription, Professional Career Development School **CERTS:** Certified in Type Clerk **A/A/S:** Safety Award, Keystone Community Outreach, Keystone Baptist Church (2007); Member, Safety Meeting Committee, Baylor All Saints Medical Center
Email: ramonap@baylorhealth.edu
URL: http://www.baylorhealth.edu

Susan L. Phillips, EFO
Title: Deputy Fire Chief, Fire Marshall **Company:** Town of Menasha Fire Department **Address:** 1326 Cold Spring Road, Neenah, WI 54956 United States **BUS:** Premier Town Fire Department **P/S:** Top Quality Public Fire Safety **MA:** Regional **D/D/R:** Teaching Fire Prevention **H/I/S:** Jewelry Making, Knitting **EDU:** Associate Degree in Public Safety; Executive Fire Officer Certification, National Fire Academy (2005) **A/A/S:** International Association of Fire Chiefs; Women's Fire Chief Association; Wisconsin Fire Chief Association; Wisconsin Fire Inspectors Association
Email: sphillips@town-menasha.com
URL: http://www.town-menasha.com

Janell I. Phillmon, RN
Title: Registered Nurse (Retired) **Company:** Florida State Hospital **Address:** 100 N. Main Street, Chattahoochee, FL 32324 United States **BUS:** Hospital **P/S:** Healthcare for the Mentally Ill, Recovery Skills and Support Needed to Live, Work and Learn in the Community **MA:** Local **D/D/R:** Offering Psychiatric Nursing, Caring for Patients in Convalescent Homes **H/I/S:** Reading **EDU:** Degree in Nursing, South Mississippi Charity Hospital **A/A/S:** American Nurses Association
URL: http://www.dcf.state.fl.us/institutions/fsh

Thuy-Jennifer Phung
Title: Permanent Makeup Artist, Owner **Company:** Touch of Beauty **Address:** 103 Park Street S.E., Vienna, VA 22180 United States **BUS:** Beauty Salon **P/S:** Beauty Care Services **MA:** Local **D/D/R:** Performing Permanent Cosmetic, Lash Extension, Lash Tinting and Lash Curling Procedures **EDU:** Bachelor of Science in Microbiology, University of Maryland, College Park (2002)
Email: jennifer@mytouchofbeauty.com
URL: http://www.mytouchofbeauty.com

Nancy J. Piatt
Title: Director **Company:** Advanced Medical Solutions **Address:** 19544 Fisher Avenue, Poolesville, MD 20837 United States **BUS:** Privately Owned Company Dedicated to Offering Home Care Patients/Clients with Quality Healthcare Equipment and Services **P/S:** Rentals, Sales, and Service of a Wide Variety of Respiratory Products Including Oxygen Therapy Products, Home Medical Equipment, Respiratory Therapy Products, Physical Therapy Aids, Daily Living Aids, Prosthetic and Orthotic Products, Other Supplies **MA:** Regional **D/D/R:** Medical Administration, Consulting to Doctors, Hospitals, Helps Start Medical Practices for Physicians, Handling Medical, Hospital and Audit Medical Billing, Handling Fraud Investigations, Overseeing All Human Resource Functions and All Aspects of Medical Practice Administration **H/I/S:** Sailing, Gardening, Swimming **EDU:** Bachelor of Arts in Liberal Arts, California University of Pennsylvania (1981) **A/A/S:** Association of Professional Coders
Email: advmedsolutions@aol.com
URL: http://www.amsdme.com

Sandra Picasso
Title: Branch Operations Manager **Company:** California National Bank **Address:** 1611 W. Beverly Boulevard, Montebello, CA 90640 United States **BUS:** Leading Consumer, Business and Commercial Real Estate Bank **P/S:** Customer Service, Quality Financial Solutions and Genuine and Lasting Client Relationships **MA:** Regional **D/D/R:** Monitoring All Operations of the Branch Including Loss of Branch, Immediate Credit to Customers, Proper Holds, Controlling Teller Losses, Compiling Reports, Auditing Day-to-Day Activities and New Accounts, Overseeing All Required Documentation, Follow Up and Verification, Maintaining Bank Sales, Open Accounts and Loans **H/I/S:** Watching the Lakers, Dodgers and USC, Spending Time with her Family **EDU:** High School Graduate; Continuing Education, California National Bank; Public Notary **A/A/S:** Operation Hope; Presenter, In-services to Employees and Customers
Email: spicasso@calnationalbank.com
URL: http://www.calnationalbank.com

Judith C. Pick
Title: Owner, Audioprosthologist **Company:** Center for Better Hearing Aids **Address:** 5589 Winfield Boulevard, Suite 100, San Jose, CA 95123 United States **BUS:** Hearing Aids **MA:** Local **D/D/R:** Hearing Aid Specialist **H/I/S:** Building Miniature Room Boxes **EDU:** Associate Degree in Hearing Services **A/A/S:** Hearing Health Care Professionals of California; International Hearing Association; Girl Scouts **C/VW:** American Cancer Society
Email: hearingaidsca@aol.com

Cynthia Pickett, Esq.
Title: Of Council **Company:** Doyle Restrepo Harvin & Robbins, LLP **Address:** 600 Travis Street, Suite 4700, Houston, TX 77002 United States **BUS:** Law Firm **P/S:** Legal Services Including Business Litigation, Securities and Arbitration, Oil, Gas and Petrochemical Litigation, Insurance Coverage, Sports Law, Family Law and Consulting **MA:** Regional **D/D/R:** managing oil and gas, real estate and construction litigation, complex multi-district litigation, arbitration practice, commercial security, product liability defense, corporate, employment and environmental law, international trade and real estate law **H/I/S:** Fishing, Exercising **EDU:** JD, South Texas College of Law (1980) **CERTS:** Licensed Attorney, U.S. Supreme Court; Licensed Attorney, Fifth and 11th Circuit, United States Court of Appeals **A/A/S:** State Bar of Texas; Houston Bar Association; Center for Excellence in Education **C/VW:** Galveston Bay Foundation
Email: cpickett@drhrlaw.com
URL: http://www.drhrlaw.com

Stephanie A. Pickren
Title: Physical Therapist **Company:** Anew Physical Therapy **Address:** 1401 Main Avenue, Suite C, Durango, CO 81301 United States **BUS:** Healthcare **P/S:** Physical Therapy **MA:** Regional **D/D/R:** Working as a Physical Therapist, Orthopedic Manual Physical Therapy, Working in Multiple Locations **H/I/S:** Dancing **EDU:** Bachelor's Degree in Physical Therapy, University of Hartford (2002) **A/A/S:** American Physical Therapy Association
Email: anewphysicaltherapy@hotmail.com
URL: http://www.cambridgewhoswho.com

Elizabeth L. Pidgeon
Title: Vice-President Human Resources **Company:** Supervalu, Inc. **Address:** 11840 Valley View Road, Eden Prairie, MN 55344 United States **BUS:** Leader in the Grocery Retailing Industry **P/S:** Research and Analysis, Store Design and Engineering, Merchandising and Marketing, Retail Technology **MA:** International **D/D/R:** Overseeing Business Marketing, Human Resources and Finance **H/I/S:** Reading, Traveling, Yoga **EDU:** Bachelor's Degree in Education, SUNY Buffalo **A/A/S:** Society of Human Resource Management
Email: libby.l.pidgeon@supervalu.com
URL: http://www.supervalu.com

Charles Pierce Jr.
Title: Pastor **Company:** Peace Tabernacle Revival Center **Address:** 420 Pinhurst Drive, Meridian, MS 39305 United States **BUS:** Church **P/S:** Religion, Worship **MA:** Local **D/D/R:** Counseling for Spiritual Growth, Teaching and Studying Prophecy, Ministering Faith and Deliverance, Teaching and Guiding the Congregation, Preaching the Word of God, Visiting the Sick and Injured **H/I/S:** Collecting Old Cars, Coins and World War II Medals, Reading, Golfing **EDU:** Master's Degree in Theology, Jackson College of Ministries **A/A/S:** Bill Pierce Evangelistic Association
Email: shawngrayl@yahoo.com
URL: http://www.cambridgewhoswho.com

Joan H. Pierce
Title: Owner **Company:** Preferred Pets **Address:** 3810 148th Street S.W., Lynnwood, WA 98087 United States **BUS:** Pet Care and Sitting Service **P/S:** Pet Care, Pet Sitting **MA:** Local **D/D/R:** Paying Special Attention to Cats and Dogs **H/I/S:** Reading, Golfing, Cooking **EDU:** Associate Degree in Horticulture, Edmonds Community College, Washington **A/A/S:** The Humane Society **C/VW:** Heritage Park in Lynnwood, Washington
Email: joan.pierce@cwwemail.com

Levy E. Pierce
Title: Principal/Teacher **Company:** Country Club Hills Tech and Trade Center **Address:** 8741 West 183rd Street, Country Club Hills, IL 60478 United States **BUS:** Education **P/S:** Offering Education in Multimedia, Video/Film Education **MA:** Local **D/D/R:** Working with Grants and Funding to Expand the Centerto Students **EDU:** Masters in Education **A/A/S:** Chairman Trustee, Who's Who in American Teachers

Sally K. Pierce
Title: Director **Company:** Jackson Public Library **Address:** 100 N. Missouri Street, Jackson, MO 63755 United States **BUS:** Library **P/S:** Books **MA:** Regional **D/D/R:** Overseeing the Automation of Cataloging System of Books from the Dewey Decimal System to Computers, overseeing staff, ordering books, book cataloging and purchasing, hiring, supervising staff and training new employees **H/I/S:** Caring for her Pets, Playing and Coaching Football, Reading Biographies and Non-Fiction Books **EDU:** Master's Degree in Library Science, University of Oklahoma (1972); Bachelor of Science in English, with Minor in Library Science, Southwest Missouri State College (Now Southwest Missouri State University) (1965) **A/A/S:** Missouri Library Association
Email: skpierce@charter.net
URL: http://www.jackson.lib.mi.us

Lorene Pierce Shapiro, Ph.D.
Title: Writer **Company:** Daydee Books **Address:** P. O. Box 265, Cardwell, MO 63829 United States **BUS:** Author **P/S:** Children's Books **MA:** National **D/D/R:** Writing Children's Books on Bullying, Racial Harmony, Formerly Taught Teachers How to Teach Special Education **EDU:** Ph.D. in Special Education (1975) **A/A/S:** Lectures on How to Teach Children
Email: docwriter29@rittermail.com
URL: http://www.cambridgewhoswho.com

Patricia Elizabeth Pierson
Title: Chief Executive Officer **Company:** PowerSurge Enterprise, Inc. **Address:** 22920 Timberline Drive, Southfield, MI 48033 United States **BUS:** Prepaid Legal Services **P/S:** Legal Services **MA:** National **D/D/R:** Identity Theft, Classroom Management, Mentoring Teachers **H/I/S:** Traveling, Gardening, Home Decorating **EDU:** Master of Education in Curriculum and Development, University of Michigan (1970) **A/A/S:** Alpha Kappa Alpha; National Education Association
Email: pepup5@sbcglobal.net
URL: http://www.cambridgewhoswho.com

Claudia Allen Pieters
Title: Vice President NW Regional Mgr **Company:** US Bank **Address:** 111 S.W. Fifth Avenue, T-4, Portland, OR 97204 United States **BUS:** Bank **P/S:** Financial Services **MA:** National **D/D/R:** Financial Solutions and Depository Services for the Real Estate Closing Industry **H/I/S:** Skiing, Tennis **EDU:** Foreign Language Studies, Portland State University and Oregon State University **A/A/S:** Portland Executive Association, Estate Planning Council of Portland, Speaker, Oregon State Bar 'Administering Trusts in Oregon'; Speaker, Lorman, 'Trust Administration in Oregon'; Member, OR/WA/ID Land Title Association **C/VW:** New Avenues for Youth, Boys and Girls Aids Society
Email: claudia.pieters@usbank.com
URL: http://www.usbank.com

Rose Marie Pietras
Title: Senior Planner **Company:** Contra Costa County **Address:** 651 Pine Street, Martinez, CA 94553 United States **BUS:** Community Development Organization **MA:** San Francisco Bay Area **D/D/R:** Land Development **H/I/S:** Walking, Reading, Traveling, Visiting Museums, Watching Films **EDU:** Master of Arts in Urban Policy and Administration, San Francisco State University; Bachelor of Arts in History and Political Science, University of California at Berkeley; Certification in Land Use and Development Planning **C/VW:** Church
Email: pietras_rose@comcast.net

James M. Piggee
Title: Assistant Principal **Company:** Gary Community School Corp **Address:** 620 E Tenth Street, Gary, IN 46407 United States **BUS:** Education **P/S:** Education and Development of Children **MA:** Local **D/D/R:** Assistant Principal **H/I/S:** Sports Fan, Teaches Swimming **EDU:** Master's Degree in Special Education, Indiana State; Master's Degree in Administration and Supervision, Indiana University **A/A/S:** Indiana Black Educators, CEO of Historical Black College Tour
Email: jamesp915@aol.com

Robin J. Pikscher
Title: Owner, Graphic Artist, Web Design **Company:** Pikscher Perfect Graphics **Address:** 8282 Lake Ridge Drive, Burr Ridge, IL 60527 United States **BUS:** Freelance Graphic Artist **P/S:** Graphic Design and Web Design **MA:** Regional **D/D/R:** Designing Websites, Greeting Cards, Letterheads and Logos, Coordinating On-Line Products **H/I/S:** Drawing, Painting **EDU:** Bachelor of Science in Web Design, Westwood College (2005); Bachelor of Science in Graphic Arts, Robert Morris College, Illinois (2001)
Email: robin@rpikscher.com
URL: http://www.rpikscher.com

Patricia A. Pilshaw
Title: Director, Information Technology **Company:** SAFC Biosciences **Address:** 9900 Skyview Lane, Lenexa, KS 66220 United States **BUS:** Biotechnology Company **P/S:** Developing and Producing Biopharmaceuticals Using Mammalian and Insect Cell Culture Methods **MA:** International **D/D/R:** aligning information technology solutions at strategic levels and overseeing staff who implement solutions **H/I/S:** Bowling, Watching Football
Email: pat.pilshaw@sial.com
URL: http://www.sigmaaldrich.com/SAFC/Biosciences

Jeanne Pincha-Tulley
Title: Forest Fire Chief **Company:** USDA Forest Service **Dept:** Tahoe National Forest **Address:** 631 Coyote Street, Nevada City, CA 95959 United States **BUS:** Forestry Agency of the U.S. Department of Agriculture **P/S:** Wild Land Fire Protection, Maintaining and Improving Mobilization and Tracking Systems, Using Aircraft for Operational Personnel Transport, Research, Forest Rehabilitation, Law Enforcement Support, Aerial Photography, Infrared Detection and Fire Prevention and Suppression **MA:** International **D/D/R:** Managing Incidents, Directing Protection for 1.6 Million Acres of Land, Managing Fire Suppression, Overseeing Aviation and National Response **EDU:** Bachelor of Science, Forest Management, University of Washington (1980) **A/A/S:** Society of American Foresters; National Wildfire Suppression Association; California Fire Chiefs Association
Email: jpinchatulley@fs.fed.us
URL: http://www.fs.fed.us/r5/tahoe

Jennifer M. Pineda
Title: Finance Clerk **Company:** The Salvation Army **Address:** 2946 S. Canal Street, Chicago, IL 60616 United States **BUS:** International Organization Dedicated to Helping People **P/S:** Disaster Relief, Rehabilitation, Counseling and Community Service **MA:** National **D/D/R:** Overseeing Accounts Payable, Accounts Receivable, Budgeting and Banking, Maintaining Correspondence with Corporate Headquarters on Properties, Keeping Track of Accounts **H/I/S:** Volleyball, Softball, Sewing **EDU:** Associate Degree in Executive Accounting, Northwestern Business College (2006) **CERTS:** Notary Public (2006)
Email: kokomana84@aol.com
URL: http://www.salvationarmyusa.org

Mary Beth Pinette
Title: Program Manager, Account Implementation Manager **Company:** Humana, Inc. **Dept:** Senior Products Strategy and Product Development **Address:** 417 Wood Stprings Road, LaGrange, KY 40031 United States **BUS:** Health Insurance Company Serving Seniors, Military Members and Self-Employed Individuals **P/S:** Health Insurance **MA:** National **D/D/R:** Implementing All Policies, Working as a Leading Player in the Medicare Market, Offering Life, Dental and Ancillary Insurance to Consumers **H/I/S:** Traveling, Reading **EDU:** Bachelor of Arts in Literature, Minor in Business, Central State University (1988)
Email: m.pinette@insightbb.com

Lori A. Pinjuh
Title: Attorney, Senior Associate **Company:** Margaret W. Wong & Associates Company, LPA **Address:** 3150 Chester Avenue, Cleveland, OH 44114 United States **BUS:** Law Firm **P/S:** Legal Services **MA:** National **D/D/R:** Managing Immigration and Naturalization Cases, Preparing Criminal Defenses for Immigrants, litigating for immigration and citizenship law **H/I/S:** Traveling, Exercising **EDU:** JD, Law School, Syracuse University (1996) **A/A/S:** Cleveland Metropolitan Bar Association; Maryland Bar Association; American Immigration Lawyers Association **A/H:** Best Lawyer in America Award (2007); Rising Star Award (2005) **C/VW:** Former Member, Muscular Dystrophy Association; Legal Aid Society
Email: pinjuh@imwong.com
URL: http://www.imwong.com

Melinda Pinon
Title: Assistant Speech-Language Pathologist **Company:** Children First Pediatric Rehabilitation **BUS:** Rehabilitation Center **P/S:** Healthcare **MA:** Regional **EXP:** Ms. Piñón's area of expertise is in speech-language pathology. **H/I/S:** Spending Time Outdoors **EDU:** Bachelor's Degree in Communication Disorders, The University of Texas-Pan American (2001) **C/VW:** Go Red For Women
Email: melinda.pinon@cwwemail.com
URL: http://www.cambridgewhoswho.com

Beulah T. Piper
Title: Executive Director, Owner **Company:** Wilbert Tross Tutorial Center **Address:** 418 7th Street, Unit 22, Gretna, LA 70053 United States **BUS:** Nonprofit Organization, Mentoring Center **P/S:** Tutoring and Extra-Help Programs for First through 12th-Grade Students **MA:** Regional **D/D/R:** Mentoring and Tutoring Students, Organizing Afterschool Programs for Underprivileged Children **H/I/S:** Spending Time with Children, Attending Church, Volunteering in the Community **EDU:** Master's Degree in Special Education, Minor in Speech Pathology, Southeastern Louisiana University (1979); Bachelor's Degree in Speech Pathology, Southern University and A&M College (1967) **A/A/S:** Association for Supervision and Curriculum Development; Louisiana Speech-Language-Hearing Association; National Black Association for Speech-Language and Hearing
Email: thetrosscenter@yahoo.com
URL: http://www.cambridgewhoswho.com

Joanne Pipkin
Title: Principal **Company:** State Street Global Advisors **Address:** 1 Lincoln Street, 24th Floor, Boston, MA 02111 United States **BUS:** Financial Company **P/S:** Investment Management **MA:** International **D/D/R:** Client Service, Managerial Leadership **H/I/S:** Golfing, Playing Tennis, Cycling **EDU:** Master's Degree in Administrative Science and Finance, The Johns Hopkins University **A/A/S:** The Johns Hopkins Alumni Council; The Johns Hopkins Executive Council; Governor's Program for Gifted Children; PGGNY; Georgia Planned Giving Council; Advisory Board for Futures; Portsmouth High School; Arthritis Foundation **C/VW:** Boston Partners in Education
Email: jpw603@comcast.net

Vesna Pirec
Title: MD, Ph.D. **Company:** Vesna Pirec, Ltd. **Address:** 655 W. Irving Park Road, Suite 206, Chicago, IL 60613 United States **BUS:** Private Women's Mental Health Practice **P/S:** Psychiatry **MA:** Regional **D/D/R:** Psychiatric Care for Pregnant Women, Evaluating Women who have Lost Children Due to Mental Health **EDU:** Ph.D. in Neural Pharmacology, University of Illinois (1993); MD, Belgrade University School of Medicine (1988) **A/A/S:** American Psychiatric Association; NAPSOG
Email: vpirec@sbcglobal.net

Joseph E. Piskulic
Title: Paramedic **Company:** St James Ambulance District **Address:** 203 S Louise, St James, MO 65559 United States **BUS:** Pre-hospital Healthcare 911 Advanced Life Support **P/S:** Healthcare **MA:** Local **D/D/R:** Pre-Hospital Emergency Care **H/I/S:** Working on his Own Business 'Herbal Life' **EDU:** Paramedicine **A/A/S:** National Association of EMT, EMP
Email: medic63010@yahoo.com
URL: http://www.herbal.nutrition.net/joepiskulic

Josette Pitardi
Title: Professional Educator **Company:** Alpine School District **Dept:** Vineyard Elementary School **Address:** 575 N. 100 E., American Fork, UT 84003 United States **BUS:** Elementary School **P/S:** Primary Education **MA:** Local **D/D/R:** Developing Curriculum, Teaching Character Education **H/I/S:** Spending Time Outdoors, Landscaping, Reading, Attending the Ballet and Symphony **EDU:** Master of Arts in Organizational Management, University of Phoenix; Bachelor's Degree in History, Brigham Young University **A/A/S:** National Education Association; Utah State Education Association; Alpine Education Association **C/VW:** Community Committees
Email: josettewins@yahoo.com
URL: http://www.cambridgewhoswho.com

Kenneth D. Pittman
Title: Maintenance Coordinator **Company:** Heritage Properties **Address:** 7570 Old Canton Road, Madison, MS 39110 United States **BUS:** Property Management Company **P/S:** Multifamily Housing, Conventional Apartment Communities **MA:** Regional **EXP:** Mr. Pittman's expertise is in maintenance training. **D/D/R:** coordinating approximately 10,000 units **H/I/S:** Hunting, Fishing
Email: kpittman@heritageproperties.com
URL: http://www.cambridgewhoswho.com

Bertha Pizarro-Wilson
Title: Director **Company:** Montgomery Village Day Care Center **Address:** 9845 Lost Knife Road, Montgomery Village, MD 20886 United States **BUS:** Proven Leader in the Day Care Industry **P/S:** Outstanding Day Care Services, Cares for Children 6 Weeks Old to 5 Years Old, Treats Children with Respect, Love and Understanding **MA:** Regional **D/D/R:** Caring for Children, Running Entire Operation of the Center, Teaching Mathematics, Reading and English, Handling the Bookkeeping, Accounts Payable, Accounts Receivable, Scheduling, Day Care Curriculum **EDU:** Bachelor's Degree in Political Science, Long Island University (1982)
URL: http://www.cambridgewhoswho.com

Janet L. Pladson
Title: Assistant Superintendent for Academic Services **Company:** Bloomington Public Schools **Address:** 1350 W. 106th Street, Bloomington, MN 55437 United States **BUS:** Public School District Dedicated to Offering Students with the Best Education **P/S:** Elementary Education, Secondary Education, Transportation, Athletics, Multicultural Opportunities, Summer Programs, Before and After School Programs, Media Centers, Community Education, Volunteer Opportunities **MA:** Regional **D/D/R:** Overseeing Curriculum and Instruction, Strategic Planning, Building Operations, Information Technology, Data Analysis, Goal-Setting and Continuous Improvement and Professional Development, Managing Academic Volunteers, Organizing Athletics **H/I/S:** Hiking, Camping, Reading **EDU:** Doctorate in Education, The University of North Dakota (1986) **A/A/S:** Phi Delta Kappa International; Association for Supervision and Curriculum Development; Minnesota Elementary School Principals' Association; National Distinguished Principal (1995); Milken National Educator Award (1997)
Email: jpladson@bloomington.k12.mn.us
URL: http://www.bloomington.k12.mn.us

Dale Plank
Title: Realtor, ABR, GRI **Company:** Realty One Group **Address:** 10750 W. Charleston, Suite 180, Las Vegas, NV 89135 United States **BUS:** Real Estate Company **P/S:** Real Estate Services **MA:** National **D/D/R:** Offering Residential Real Estate Services **H/I/S:** Weight Lifting, Fitness, Spending Time with his Family **CERTS:** Graduate Realtor Institute (2006); Licensed Real Estate Agent (2004); Accredited Buyer Representative (2004) **A/A/S:** Nevada Association of Realtors; National Association of Realtors
Email: dplanklasvegas@aol.com
URL: http://www.daleplank.com

Robert J. Plath, Ph.D.
Title: Academic Professor, Statistician, Economist, Mathematician **Company:** National University **Address:** 9159 Firelight Way, Sacramento, CA 95826 United States **BUS:** University **P/S:** Education, Graduate Research, Undergraduate Courses **MA:** National **D/D/R:** Mathematical and Statistical Economics, Research and Development of Online Learning Systems **H/I/S:** Skiing, Swimming, Playing Chess, Speaking Six Languages **EDU:** Ph.D. in Education, Statistical Research and Design of Online Systems, Capella University (2006); Master's Degree in Statistical Economics, Washington State University (1972); Bachelor's Degree in Mathematics, Washington State University, With Honors (1971) **A/A/S:** Association of American Statisticians; Sacramento Association of Statisticians; Master Chess Player **C/VW:** Local High School District; Volunteer, Programs in Mathematics and Distance Education
Email: rplath@comcast.net
URL: http://www.cambridgewhoswho.com

Rose M. Platt
Title: President **Company:** Platt Enterprises **Address:** 3185 Cowilng Road, Sanger, TX 76266 United States **BUS:** Real Estate Rent Property **P/S:** Houses **MA:** Local **D/D/R:** Accounts Receivable, Billing, Collecting **H/I/S:** Church Activities, Fishing, Being with Family, Dealing with Farm animals, Gardening and Cooking **EDU:** University of North Texas **A/A/S:** ASPCA, Kiwanis
URL: http://www.jackplatt.com

Ms. Kathy J. Pleiness
Title: Owner, Operator **Company:** Pleiness Tree Moving **Address:** 3016 S. Scottville Road, Scottville, MI 49454 United States **BUS:** Tree Service **P/S:** Moving trees **MA:** Local **D/D/R:** Creating Privacy Lines with Trees, Owning and Operating the Company **H/I/S:** Riding her Horse, Basket Weaving **EDU:** Bachelor of Science in Dairy Science, Michigan State University **C/VW:** County Fair Grounds; Historical Society; White Pine Village
Email: barryp@t-one.net

Carol A. Plodzien
Title: Teacher, Athletic Coordinator (Retired) **Company:** William Fremd High School **Address:** 1000 S. Quentin Road, Palatine, IL 60067 United States **BUS:** High School **P/S:** Secondary Education **MA:** Local **EXP:** Ms. Plodzien's area of expertise is in physical education. **D/D/R:** coordinating athletic programs, scheduling athletic contests, supervising athletic trainer, budgeting and hiring officials for contests for all athletic events **H/I/S:** Writing Poetry, Camping, Coaching Girls Basketball Team **EDU:** Master's Degree in Athletic Administration, Roosevelt University (1989); Master's Degree in Environmental Education, George Williams College (1979); Bachelor of Science in Physical Education, Northern Illinois University (1971) **CERTS:** Certified Physical Education Teacher (K-12) **A/A/S:** Illinois Coaches Association; Illinois Basketball Coaches Association; National Audubon Society; National Wildlife Federation; Who's Who Among American Women; Who's Who Among American Teachers **A/H:** Outstanding Achievement Award for Poetry, International Society of Poets (2008) **C/VW:** Save-A-Pet; Rotary International; International Crane Foundation
Email: cplod@comcast.net
URL: http://www.cambridgewhoswho.com

Michael D. Plummer
Title: Retired Chief of Police **Company:** Lovelock Tribal Police **Address:** Lovelock, NV 89419 United States **BUS:** Police Department **P/S:** Law Enforcement **MA:** Local **D/D/R:** Child Abuse, Sexual Assault Investigations **H/I/S:** Camping, Pistol Shooting, Animals, Dogs, Horses **EDU:** Bachelor's Degree in Criminal Justice, Texas Tech University **A/A/S:** FBI Law Enforcement Executive Development Association; Fraternal Order of Police **C/VW:** Pershing County Sheriff's Department, Pershing County Public School District
Email: mplummerp42@hotmail.com
URL: http://www.cambridgewhoswho.com

Megan A. Podolsky, DMD
Title: Periodontist **Company:** Contemporary Periodontics and Implant Dentistry **Address:** 2722 Hendrickson Street, Brooklyn, NY 11234 United States **BUS:** Dental Office **P/S:** Implantology Periodontics, Plastic Surgery **MA:** Local **D/D/R:** Periodontics, Implant Dentistry, Treats gum disease, oral conditions, replace missing teeth, periodontal cosmetic surgery, bone grafting **H/I/S:** Traveling, skiing, theater, opera and philharmonic **EDU:** Doctor of Medical Dentistry, The University of Pennsylvania (2003); Residency in Periodontics (2003-2006) **A/A/S:** American Dental Association; American Academy of Periodontology; Nassau County Dental Society; New York State Dental Association; Delaware Valley Academy of Osseointegration; Northeastern Society of Periodontists **C/VW:** Ronald McDonald House; Boys & Girls Clubs of America
Email: meg1211@gmail.com

Ms. Jane Stuart Vander Poel
Title: President (Retired) **Company:** Greeting Card Company and Graphic Arts Company **BUS:** Greeting Card and Graphic Arts Company **P/S:** Art **MA:** International **D/D/R:** Commissioned Sculpting and Calligraphy, Graphic Arts, Watercolor Painting, Line Drawings **H/I/S:** Writing a Cookbook **EDU:** Coursework, The Master's School **A/A/S:** Puppies Behind Bars **C/VW:** Pet Therapy in Hospitals
Email: jsvp@mac.com
URL: http://www.cambridgewhoswho.com

James H. Pogue
Title: Chief Executive Officer, Physician **Company:** 1) Belmont Medical Group 2) Novus Institute **Address:** 5552 Franklin Pike, Suite 100, Nashville, TN 37220 United States **BUS:** 1) Medical Center 2) Therapy Center **P/S:** 1) Healthcare 2) Spiritual Healing and Psychotherapy **MA:** Regional **D/D/R:** practicing family medicine, performing laser surgery, overseeing dermatology and geriatric treatments, pain management and consulting **EDU:** MD, Vanderbilt University School of Medicine **A/A/S:** American Academy of Hospice and Palliative Medicine; American Medical Association; American Academy of Family Physicians; American Legion **A/H:** Air Force Commendation Medal; Top Family Doctor Award; America's Top Physician Award, Consumers' Research Council of America
Email: poguemd@yahoo.com
URL: http://www.viphealthplans.com

René T. Poinsette
Title: Training Director, Realtor **Company:** Century 21 Platinum **Address:** 11721 Woodmore Road, Mitchellville, MD 20721 United States **BUS:** Real Estate Agency **P/S:** Real Estate Services **MA:** Local **D/D/R:** Training, Educating **H/I/S:** Gardening **EDU:** Master's Degree in Education, Trinity University (1975); Bachelor of Arts in Education, Major in English Literature, Iona College (1973); Associate Degree in Education, Trinity University **A/A/S:** NCRW; NBR; ASTD; Founder, Septima Poinsette Clark Foundation **C/VW:** Church
Email: rene.poinsette-realtor@juno.com
URL: http://www.spcfoundation.org

Ms. Melissa M. Poisson
Title: Director of Sales **Company:** MARS Petcare U.S. **Address:** 315 Cool Springs Boulevard, Franklin, TN 37067 United States **BUS:** Manufacturing Company **P/S:** Pet Care Food, Snack Food, Main Meal Food, Drinks, Name Brand Products and Treats **MA:** International **EXP:** Ms. Poisson's expertise includes sales management, customer marketing and strategy and internal details, idea implementation, product promotion and the oversight of packing and deliveries. **EDU:** Bachelor's Degree in Communication Management, University of Dayton (1988) **CERTS:** Pursuing Certification in Leadership, Scarlett Leadership Institute, Belmont University
Email: melissa.poisson@effem.com
URL: http://www.marspetcare.com

Ms. Ilona Poka
Title: Real Estate Specialist **Company:** Call Realty **Address:** 1757 E. Baseline Road, Suite 133, Gilbert, AZ 85233 United States **BUS:** Real Estate Agency **P/S:** Residential Property Sales **MA:** Regional **D/D/R:** Marketing Residential Properties, Overseeing Open House Listings and Strategies, Assisting Clients with Financial Aspects **H/I/S:** Photography, Traveling **EDU:** Bachelor's Degree in Psychology, Marymount College, Tarrytown, New York (2000) **A/A/S:** National Association of Realtors; Arizona Association of Realtors; SouthEast Valley Regional Association of Realtors
Email: ilona@ilonapoka.com
URL: http://www.ilonapoka.com

Rosa E. Pol
Title: Senior Pastor **Company:** Segunda Iglesia Bautista **Address:** 1920 E. Columbus Drive, Chicago, IN 46312 United States **BUS:** Church **P/S:** Spiritual Services Including Sunday School, Bible Teachings and Children's Ministry **MA:** Local **EXP:** Ms. Pol's area of expertise is in Bible studies. **D/D/R:** Managing Administrative Duties, Offering Counseling, Teaching Bible Study and Sunday School for Adults and Children, Preaching **H/I/S:** Traveling, Reading, Writing Poems in Spanish **EDU:** Pursuing Bachelor's Degree in Bible Studies; Pursuing Bachelor's Degree in Social Studies, Moody Bible Institute; Bachelor's Degree in Sociology, Calumet College of St. Joseph (1991); Associate Degree in Social Work, Calumet College of St. Joseph (1989) **C/VW:** Local Nursing Home
Email: RosaE.Pol@cwwemail.com
URL: http://www.cambridgewhoswho.com

Patricia Polak
Title: Writer **Company:** Self-Employed **Address:** 405 E. 56th Street, Apartment 10A, New York, NY 10022 United States **BUS:** Writer **P/S:** Poetry **MA:** National **D/D/R:** History, Political Science, Eastern European Studies **H/I/S:** Horseback Riding, Traveling, Collecting Art and Antiques **EDU:** Pursuing Master of Fine Arts, CUNY Hunter College; Bachelor of Arts, SUNY Empire State College, with Outstanding Honors **A/A/S:** The Academy of American Poets; Poets House
Email: ejplppolak@gmail.com

Lisa Renne Polaskey
Title: First Grade Teacher **Company:** Watervliet South Elementary School **Address:** 433 Lucinda Lane, Watervliet, MI 49098 United States **BUS:** Elementary School **P/S:** Primary Education Including Hearing-Impaired Students **MA:** Local **D/D/R:** teaching reading, writing, mathematics, social studies and science for first grade students **H/I/S:** Scrapbooking, Reading **EDU:** Master's Degree in Elementary Education, Western Michigan University (2000); Bachelor's Degree in Elementary Education, Michigan State University (1992) **A/H:** Finalist, PAC Excellence in Education Award (2007)
Email: lpolaskey@watervliet.k-12.mi.us
URL: http://www.watervliet.k12.mi.us/south

Andrea L. Policicchio
Title: Owner **Company:** Andrea's Restaurant **Address:** 320 Main Street, Boswell, PA 15531 United States **BUS:** Restaurant **P/S:** Breakfast, Lunch **MA:** Boswell **D/D/R:** Running the Restaurant, Waiting Tables, Cooking, Bussing Tables **H/I/S:** Spending Time with her Children, Red Hat Society, Historical Society **EDU:** High School Education **A/A/S:** Red Hat Society **C/VW:** Food Pantry
Email: andrealed@aol.com

Christine M. Politis
Title: Principal **Company:** Communication Insights **Address:** 11114 Albury Park, Tomball, TX 77375 United States **BUS:** Marketing, Consulting **P/S:** Corporate Communications **MA:** International **D/D/R:** Corporate Communications for Fortune 100 Companies, Acquisition Communications, Project Management **H/I/S:** Tennis, Traveling **EDU:** Bachelor of Business Administration in Journalism, Texas A&M University **A/A/S:** International Association of Business Communicators; AMA
Email: christine@comminsights.com
URL: http://www.comminsights.com

Raymond D. Pollard
Title: President, Owner **Company:** A Glass Act, Inc. **Address:** P.O. Box 693, Sagle, ID 83860 United States **BUS:** Professional Window Cleaning Company **P/S:** Commercial and Residential Window Washing **MA:** Statewide **D/D/R:** Overseeing Company Daily Operations **H/I/S:** Playing Golf **EDU:** Bachelor of Science in Recreation and Leisure, Emphasis on Commercial, University of Utah **A/A/S:** International Window Cleaners Association **C/VW:** The Community Cancer Center
Email: glassact@gotsky.com

Joseph A. Pollock
Title: Owner **Company:** J. A. Pollock Enterprises **Address:** 12625 Frederick Street, Suite F 13 and14, Moreno Valley, CA 92553 United States **BUS:** Retailer, Wholesale **P/S:** Wholesale and Retail Outlets **MA:** Local **D/D/R:** Merchandising, Promoting, Buying Products, Running Company Operations **H/I/S:** Golfing, Bowling, Developing a Professional Development Computer Course, Working with a Consulting Firm **EDU:** Coursework in Business, Citrus Community College; Diploma, Azusa High School; Monrovia High School **A/A/S:** Chamber of Commerce
Email: joepollock_59@msn.com
URL: http://www.jpelectronicsandmore.com

Joseph C. Polujan
Title: Owner/Master Plumber **Company:** Husky Plumbing **Address:** 301 Center Street, Baden, PA 15005 United States **BUS:** Construction Plumbing **P/S:** Plumbing Services **MA:** Local **D/D/R:** Commercial and Residential Services **H/I/S:** Hunting, Fishing **EDU:** Conley Technical College, 5 Years Tech School **A/A/S:** BBB
Email: jpolujan1968@yahoo.com

Ms. Lindsay W. Pomeroy
Title: Owner, Principal Consultant **Company:** The Wine Smarties **Address:** San Diego, CA 92101 United States **BUS:** Wine Consulting Firm **P/S:** Wine Classes, Private Parties, Consulting for Restaurants and Retail Wine Shops **MA:** Regional **D/D/R:** Planning and Hosting Classes and Private Wine Events, Educating Customers about Wine, Consulting for Restaurants and Retail Stores, Purchasing Wines, Developing Wine Programs **H/I/S:** Traveling, Yoga **EDU:** Bachelor of Arts in American Studies and Anthropology, Lafayette College (1999) **A/A/S:** Society of Wine Educators
Email: lindsay@winesmarties.com
URL: http://www.winesmarties.com

Brandy L. Ponka
Title: Administrative Assistant **Company:** Northwestern Ontario Infection Control Network **Address:** 289 Munro Street, Thunder Bay, P7A2N3 Canada **BUS:** Healthcare Hospital **P/S:** Coordinating Meetings and Conferences, Distribute Documentation, Putting Together Presentations and Taking Minutes, Answering Phones, Responding to Inquires, Managing Network Coordinators Schedule and Calendar, Daily Reporting, Data and Analytical Work **MA:** International **D/D/R:** Conference Planning **H/I/S:** Traveling, reading, Dolphins, Time with 3 Year Old Son **EDU:** Diploma, Legal Secretary, Diploma, Office Administration Executive, Ontario Business College, Confederation College **CERTS:** Certified Medical Terminology **A/A/S:** IAAP, Association of Administrative Assistants
Email: ponkab@tbh.net

Debra LeAnn Pontious
Title: 1) Chief Executive Officer for E-Commerce 2) Speech-Language Pathologist **Company:** 1) D.P. Motivation 2) Savi-Annah's Experience **Address:** 9077 E. 28th Street, Tulsa, OK 74129 United States **BUS:** 1) Retail Store 2) Speech and Language Therapy Center **P/S:** 1) Health and Beauty Care Products 2) Medical and Educational Speech Therapy **MA:** Local **EXP:** Ms. Pontious' expertise is in pediatric dysphagia. **D/D/R:** treating people with communication disorders **H/I/S:** Traveling, Reading, Spending Time with her Daughter **EDU:** Master's Degree in Speech, with a Concentration in Speech Pathology, Oklahoma State University **A/A/S:** American Speech-Language-Hearing Association
Email: debrapontious@katewwdb.com
URL: http://www.dpmotivation.wwdb.biz

Crystal A. Poole, RN
Title: RN, BSN **Company:** St Francis Hospital **Address:** 900 Hyde Street, San Francisco, CA 94109 United States **BUS:** Healthcare Hospital **P/S:** Offering Care to Critically Ill Patients **MA:** Local **D/D/R:** Intensive Care Unit Nursing **H/I/S:** Travel, Art, Music **EDU:** University of Southern Mississippi, Bachelor of Science in Nursing **A/A/S:** CCRN Classes, Support Local Charities
Email: pkris@aol.com

Karen L. Poor
Title: President, Owner **Company:** Posh Palate Caterers and Events **Address:** 64 Arnold Avenue, West Babylon, NY 11704 United States **BUS:** Catering and Event Planning **P/S:** Custom Event Planning, Themed Parties, Food Stations **MA:** International **D/D/R:** Overseeing Destination Weddings, Planning Events, Corporate Events, Seeking Out Interesting Venues, Supervising Staff, Discussing Ideas with Two Chefs and 22 Staff Members **H/I/S:** Shopping, Vacationing **EDU:** Associate Degree in Fashion Toby Colburn (1985)
Email: mrsposh1@aol.com
URL: http://www.poshpalatecaterers.com

Dawn K. Popadics
Title: Owner **Company:** The Carriage House Coffee Shop **Address:** 34 N. Main Street, Jasper, GA 30143 United States **BUS:** Restaurant Previously Office manager of Pediatricians Office and Oral Surgeons Office **P/S:** Homemade Pies, Cakes, Quiches, Soups. Special attention to customer service. **MA:** Local **D/D/R:** Customer Service, Operations of Business **H/I/S:** Traveling, Reading, Movies **EDU:** College Coursework in Business, Appalachian Technical College, Jasper, Georgia **A/A/S:** Board Member, Chamber of Commerce Leadership Pickens **C/VW:** Donate Life Organization, American Red Cross, Good Samaritan, The Joy House
Email: mycarriagehouse@etcmail.com
URL: http://www.cambridgewhoswho.com

Judith A. Pope
Title: North Texas Market Administrative Manager **Company:** Wachovia Securities **Address:** 8115 Preston Road, Suite 300, Dallas, TX 75225 United States **BUS:** Securities and Investment Company **P/S:** Financial Services **MA:** International **D/D/R:** Quality Assurance, Compliance, Supervising 140 Financial Advisers **H/I/S:** Traveling, Walking, Reading Unabridged Writings, Spending Time with her Family **EDU:** Diploma, Kilgore High School; Coursework in Business, Accounting and Law, Kilgore College, Kilgore, Texas; Coursework, Tyler Junior College **C/VW:** Susan G. Komen For the Cure, American Red Cross, Various Charities and Organizations
Email: judith.pope@wachoviasec.com
URL: http://www.wachoviasec.com

Mark C. Popovich
Title: Assistant County Attorney **Company:** Isle of Wright County **Address:** 17090 Monument Circle, Suite 128, Isle of Wright, VA 23397 United States **BUS:** Local Government Agency **P/S:** Legal Services **MA:** Local **D/D/R:** Promoting a General Practice **H/I/S:** Going to the Beach **EDU:** Master's Degree in Law, McGeorge School of Law **A/A/S:** American Bar Association; Virginia Bar Association; Washington Bar Association
Email: mpopovich@verizon.net

Dr. Ronald J. Portell
Title: Assistant Pastor, Principal **Company:** Mount Pisgah Baptist Church **Address:** 20243 Alabama Highway 99, Athens, AL 35614 United States **BUS:** Baptist Church School **P/S:** Education **MA:** Local **D/D/R:** Teaching **H/I/S:** Hunting **EDU:** Doctor of Education, Faith Baptist Bible College and Theological Seminary **C/VW:** Church
Email: drrjpcsp@wmconnect.com
URL: http://www.cambridgewhoswho.com

Clyde Porter
Title: Associate Vice Chancellor for Facilities Management, Distribution Architect **Company:** The Dallas County Community College **Address:** 4343 I-30, Desoto, TX 75115 United States **BUS:** College **P/S:** Higher Education **MA:** Regional **EXP:** Mr. Porter's expertise includes facilities management and district architecture. **H/I/S:** Traveling, Tennis **EDU:** Master's Degree in Architecture, Prairie View A&M University, TX **CERTS:** Registered Interior Designer, National Organization of Minority Architects **A/A/S:** American Institute of Architects; Association of Physical Plant Administrators; National Green Building Council
Email: cxp1161@bcccd.edu
URL: http://www.cambridgewhoswho.com

Laurie Porter
Title: Headmaster **Company:** Cornerstone Christian School **Address:** 24975 Highway 25, Columbiana, AL 35051 United States **BUS:** Private Christian School Offering Quality Educational Services **P/S:** Education for Kindergarten through Twelfth-Grade Students, Academics, Athletics, Student Organizations **MA:** Regional **D/D/R:** Overseeing Administration, Kindergarten through Twelfth-Grade Education, Working on the Budget Policy, Discipline, Hiring and Firing Employees **H/I/S:** Crafting, Rodeo Activities **EDU:** Bachelor's Degree in Secondary Education, Samford University (1987)
Email: tellbirdy@aol.com
URL: http://www.ccschargers.us

Peggy Porter
Title: Teacher **Company:** Forestville Elementary School, Forestville Union School District **Address:** 56321 Highway 116, Forestville, CA 95436 United States **BUS:** Elementary School Facility Dedicated to Excellence in Education **P/S:** Regular Core Curriculum Including Reading, Mathematics, English, Science, Social Studies, Art, Music, History, Physical Education **MA:** Regional **D/D/R:** Teaching First Grades All Core Subjects Including Music and Technology in a Low-Income District **H/I/S:** Swimming, Bicycling, Working Out, All Leisure Activities **EDU:** Bachelor of Arts plus 72 Credits in Recreation Administration, University of the Pacific Stockton, California (1979) **A/A/S:** National Education Association; California Education Association; California Teachers Association
Email: pporter@forestville.k12.ca.us
URL: http://www.forestville.k12.ca.us

Ms. Stella Porto

Title: Director of Assistive Technology **Company:** New York City Department of Education **Dept:** Technology Solutions Department **Address:** 2525 Haring Street, Brooklyn, NY 11235 United States **BUS:** Department of Education **P/S:** Assistive Technology Consulting Services **MA:** New York, New Jersey **D/D/R:** integrating technology Into the special education curriculum **H/I/S:** Coaching College Softball **EDU:** Bachelor of Science in Psychology, College of Staten Island; Bachelor of Science in Special Education, College of Staten Island **CERTS:** Certification in Educational Administration, College of Saint Rose **A/A/S:** International Society for Technology; NYCSCAPE
Email: sporto@schools.nyc.gov
URL: http://www.ablenet.com

Carolyn D. Poskey

Title: Speech-Language Pathologist, Independent Contractor **Company:** Elite Rehabilitation, Independent Contractor **Address:** 801 Regency Street, Monroe, LA 71201 United States **BUS:** Healthcare Contracting Company **P/S:** Nursing Services and Therapy for Nursing Homes and the Geriatric Population **MA:** Regional **D/D/R:** Offering Speech-Language Pathology and Restorative Nursing, Caring for Patients in their Homes, Treating Stroke Victims and Patients with Congestive Heart Failure, Parkinson's Disease and Swallowing Issues **H/I/S:** Painting, Watching Movies, Walking, Dining with Friends **EDU:** Master of Arts in Communicative Disorders, The University of Louisiana at Monroe (1990); Bachelor of Arts in English and Library Science, The University of Louisiana at Monroe (1974) **A/A/S:** American Speech-Language-Hearing Association; Louisiana Speech-Language-Hearing Association; Omicron Delta Kappa; All American Scholar Award (1990); Best Graduate Speech Clinician (1989-1990)
Email: cposkey@comcast.net

Mrs. Christina Lynn Posta

Title: Owner **Company:** Posno Heating & Air **Address:** 260 Avery Road, New Bern, NC 28560 United States **BUS:** Heating and Air Conditioning Company **P/S:** Residential and Commercial Installations **MA:** Local **EXP:** Mrs. Posta's area of expertise is in customer service. **H/I/S:** Gardening, Riding her Bike, Skiing, Traveling, Spending Time with her Family, ATV Riding **EDU:** Bachelor of Arts (2007); Bachelor of Science in Criminal Justice, Mount Olive College **A/A/S:** Chamber of Commerce; New Bern Home Builders Association; Highway Patrol Association **C/VW:** St. Jude Children's Research Hospital; Shrines
Email: thepostamom@yahoo.com

Cindy Postlethwait

Title: Supervisor, Work Lead **Company:** ACS **Address:** 6400 Flank Drive, Suite 500, Harrisburg, PA 17112 United States **BUS:** Customer Care Center **P/S:** Customer Care Services for Pennsylvania Department of Transportation **MA:** Regional **D/D/R:** Managing Operations, Payroll, Attendance, Technical Problems, Assisting Customers, Handling Supervisory Calls **H/I/S:** Touring on her Motorcycle **EDU:** Bachelor of Science in Management and Computer Science, California University of Pennsylvania (1992) **A/A/S:** Board Member, Susquehanna Valley Collie and Sheltie Rescue
Email: cindy_postlethwait@comcast.net

Leah M. Poston, CTBS

Title: Question and Answer Risk and Safety Manager **Company:** Southeast Tissue Alliance **Address:** 6241 NorthWest 23nd Street, Suite 400, Gainesville, FL 32653 United States **BUS:** Tissue Banking **P/S:** Tissue Banking **MA:** Local **D/D/R:** Medical Records, Auditors, and Questions and Answers **EDU:** Associate of Science in Business Management, Santa Fe Community College **CERTS:** Certificate in Tissue Banking **A/A/S:** AATB
Email: leah_p@bellsouth.net

Mary Frances Postupack

Title: Chief Operating Officer **Company:** East Stroudsburg University of Pennsylvania **Dept:** Center for Research and Economic Development **Address:** 200 Prospect Street, E. Stroudsburg, PA 18301 United States **BUS:** University **P/S:** Sponsored Research Entrepreneurship, Workforce Training **MA:** International and Regional **D/D/R:** Directing Economic Development and Entrepreneurship Programs **H/I/S:** Traveling, Practicing Yoga, Walking, Reading, Gardening **EDU:** Master of Education in Educational Administration, East Stroudsburg University of Pennsylvania **A/A/S:** University Economic Development Association; Pennsylvania Angel Network; National Business Incubation Association; Association of University Research Parks; Ben Franklin Technology Partners of Northeast Pennsylvania; Economic Development Committee, Pennsylvania System of Higher Education; Rotary Club of the Stroudsburg; Recipient, ATHENA Award **C/VW:** United Way of Monroe County
Email: mpostupack@po-box.esu.edu
URL: http://www.esu.edu

Gary S. Potter

Title: Realtor **Company:** ERA Advantage Realty **Address:** 528 N. Main Street, Logan, UT 84321 United States **BUS:** Real Estate Agency **P/S:** Residential Properties Including Executive Homes, Golf Homes, Condos, Senior, Gated, Horse Properties and Development **MA:** National **EXP:** Mr. Potter's area of expertise is in property development. **D/D/R:** selling residential, commercial and recreational properties **H/I/S:** Fishing **A/A/S:** Utah Association of Realtors; National Association of Realtors
Email: gary.potter@era.com
URL: http://www.era.com

John H. Potvin

Title: Emergency Medical Services Director **Company:** East Providence Fire Department **Address:** 913 Broadway, East Providence, RI 02914 United States **BUS:** Fire Department **P/S:** Fire Suppression, Emergency Medical Services **MA:** Local **D/D/R:** Emergency Medical Services **H/I/S:** Leading a Boy Scout Troop, Spending Time with Family **EDU:** Hazardous Materials Technician; Storm Officer; Fire Officer; Fire Instructor **A/A/S:** International Association of Fire Chiefs; International Association of Fire Fighters **C/VW:** Boy Scouts of America
Email: emsofficer@eastprovfire.com

Kim E. Poutré

Title: Licensed Esthetician, Owner **Company:** Special Event Beauty **Address:** Bridgewater, MA 02324 United States **BUS:** Beauty Spa **P/S:** Skincare and Makeup Artistry **MA:** Regional **D/D/R:** Performing Facials and Massages at Weddings, Television and Events, Instructing for Young Estheticians and Make-up Artists at Lisa Marie's Day Spa, Consulting to a Wholesale Company Called Luxlash, administering, airbrush, applying makeup and chemical peels for advanced extractions and other skin, hairstyling and nails procedures for proms, threading, waxing, facials, skin care and makeup seminars **H/I/S:** Artwork, Reading, Spending Time with her Family **EDU:** Coursework, Catherine Hinds Institute of Esthetics (1981) **CERTS:** Certification in Eyelash Extensions, Microdermabrasion and Photo Light Therapy **C/VW:** Fundraising Director, Keeping Pace with Multiple Miracles
Email: specialeventbeauty@comcast.net
URL: http://www.specialeventbeauty.com

Arlisa H. Powell

Title: Music Specialist **Company:** Newport News Public Schools **Dept:** R.O. Nelson Elementary School **Address:** 826 Moyer Road, Newport News, VA 23608 United States **BUS:** School District **P/S:** Education **MA:** Regional **D/D/R:** teaching vocal music and general music education including private piano lessons and mentoring teachers **H/I/S:** Listening to Music **EDU:** Bachelor of Science in Music Education, Old Dominion University (1989) **CERTS:** Certified Music Specialist (K-5) **A/A/S:** Virginia Music Educators Association; Virginia Education Association; The National Association for Music Education; National Association for the Study and Performance of African American Music; Music Educators National Conference **C/VW:** Local Charitable Organization; Volunteer, First Baptist Church Denbigh
Email: arlisapowell@aol.com
URL: http://nelson.nn.k12.va.us

Shandrika W. Powell

Title: Owner, Designer **Company:** Shandrika's Decorating and Design **Address:** 580 Primrose Lane, Benicia, CA 94510 United States **BUS:** Interior Design Consultant **P/S:** Indoor and Outdoor Coloring, Paint, Moldings, Purchasing of Furniture and Accessories, Holiday Decor **MA:** Regional **D/D/R:** Residential and Commercial Interior Design Consulting, Assisting Clients in Completing Projects with a Step-by-Step Process to Create a Finished and Complete Look which Reflects the Client's Taste, Budgeting, Making Referrals for Installation Work **H/I/S:** Decorating, Design **EDU:** College Coursework; Business License; Wholesale License **A/A/S:** Chamber of Commerce
Email: shandrikasdecor@pacbell.net
URL: http://www.shandrikasdecor.com

Marcia P. Powell-McGregor

Title: Director of Nursing, Registered Nurse **Company:** Newark Beth Israel Medical Center **Address:** 201 Lyons Avenue, Newark, NJ 07112 United States **BUS:** Medical Center **P/S:** Healthcare **MA:** Regional **D/D/R:** cardiac nursing and working in the cardiac telemetry unit, Overseeing Employees **EDU:** Bachelor of Science in Nursing, New Jersey City University (1998); Associate Degree in Nursing, Jamaica (1982) **CERTS:** Certified Medical-Surgical Registered Nurse; Certified Nursing Administrator; Registered Nurse, State of New Jersey **A/A/S:** New Jersey State School Nurses Association; Organization of Nurse Executives of New Jersey; American Nurses Association; American Association of Critical-Care Nurses
Email: mmcgregor@sbhcs.com
URL: http://www.sbhcs.com

Amanda Powers

Title: Director Account Service **Company:** Greater Than One, Inc **Address:** 395 Hudson Street, Fifth Floor, New York, NY 10014 United States **BUS:** Business Services Advertising, Marketing, Public Relations **P/S:** Interactive Advertising, Digital Advertising **MA:** International **D/D/R:** Account Services **H/I/S:** Horseback Riding, Travel **A/A/S:** HBA, IAB, I-Media, Greater Good, ASPCA
Email: amanda@greaterthanone.com

Mary L. Powers

Title: Mathematics Department Head, Teacher **Company:** Waxahachie Independent School District, Turner Middle School **Address:** 614 N. Getzendaner Avenue, Waxahachie, TX 76065 United States **BUS:** Middle School **P/S:** Education **MA:** Local **D/D/R:** Teaching Mathematics **H/I/S:** Fishing **EDU:** Bachelor of Science, Dallas Baptist University **A/A/S:** Teacher of the Year (2002); Church's League; Coordinator, University Interscholastic League; Walk Across Texas **C/VW:** United Way
Email: mpowers@wisd.org

Donna Pozzuoli

Title: Real Estate Agent **Company:** Maole Mills Realty **Address:** 460 S. 100 E., Bountiful, UT 84010 United States **BUS:** Real Estate Broker **P/S:** Real Estate Sales **MA:** Local **D/D/R:** Residential Homes **H/I/S:** Horseback Riding **A/A/S:** National Association of Realtors, Salt Lake Board of Realtors, Davis County Association of Realtors
Email: pozdon@wfrmls.com
URL: http://www.donnahomesales.com

Karla V. Prado, MA

Title: Fifth-Grade Inclusion Teacher **Company:** Perrine Elementary Expressive Arts School **Address:** 8851 S.W. 168th Street, Village of Palmetto Bay, FL 33157 United States **BUS:** Elementary School **P/S:** Elementary Education, Expressive Arts Education **MA:** Regional **D/D/R:** Teaching a Self-Contained Classroom Including Special Education Students, Average Students and Gifted Students, Teaching Each Group Using Similar Strategies and Tools, Challenging Gifted Students with More Difficult Work, Accommodating Special Education Students' Individual Needs **H/I/S:** Drawing, Bowling, Basketball **EDU:** Master of Arts in Reading, Nova Southeastern University (2006) **A/A/S:** The United Teachers of Dade; International Reading Association; National Education Association; Florida Education Association; Nominee, Teacher of the Year, Perrine Elementary Expressive Arts School (2007-2008) **C/VW:** Sunday School Program, Local Church
Email: kprado@dadeschools.net
URL: http://perrineelementary.dadeschools.net

Dina S. Prak

Title: Payroll and Accounting Administrator **Company:** SelectBuild **Address:** 3401 Etiwanda Avenue, Building Unit 831 C, Mira Loma, CA 91752 United States **BUS:** Proven Leader in the Building and Construction Industries **P/S:** Framing **MA:** Local **D/D/R:** Developing and Implementing Payroll Procedures and Processes, Analyzing and Processing Employer Federal and State Tax Returns, Troubleshooting **H/I/S:** Reading, Spending Quality Time with Family **EDU:** Bachelor of Arts in Human Development, Minor in Psychology, California State University at San Bernardino (2001)
Email: dina.prak@selectbuild.com
URL: http://www.selectbuild.com

Cathy Pratt, Ph.D.
Title: Director **Company:** Indiana Institute on Disability and Community **Dept:** Indiana Resource Center for Autism **Address:** 2853 E. 10th Street, Bloomington, IN 47408 United States **BUS:** Resource Center for Autism **P/S:** Outreach Training and Consultations, Research, Development and Dissemination of Information Focused on Building the Capacity of Organizations that Support Children and Adults Across the Autism Spectrum in Typical Work, School, Home and Community Settings **MA:** National **D/D/R:** Public Speaking, Training, Publishing Articles, Consulting, Assisting People with Autism Spectrum Disorders **H/I/S:** Gardening, Traveling **EDU:** Ph.D. in Special Education and Public Management, Indiana University (1992) **A/A/S:** Teacher, Indiana University; Advisory Board Member, College Internship Program; New York Families for Autistic Children; Advisory Board Member, Map Services; Public Review Committee, Research Roadmap, Interagency Autism Coordination Committee; Advocate, Institute on Rehabilitation Issues; Co-Director, Network of Autism Training and Technical Assistance Programs; Advisory Board Member, Autism Spectrum Quarterly Programs; Guest Editor, Journal of Autism and Developmental Disorders; Association for Persons in Supported Employment; Chairwoman, Autism Society of America; Advisory Board Member, Chairwoman, Conference Committee, Panel of Professional Advisors, Autism Society of America; Advisory Board Member, The National Professional Development Center on Autism Spectrum Disorders; Scientific Advisory Board Member, International Meeting for Autism Research **A/H:** Princeton Fellowship Award (2005); Certificate of Recognition, New York City Council; Certificate of Recognition, New York State Senate; Individual Achievement Award, Autism Society of America; Certificate of Recognition, United States House of Representatives
Email: prattc@indiana.edu
URL: http://www.iidc.indiana.edu

Guillermo Jose Hoyos Precssas
Title: Chief Executive Officer **Company:** The Hato Rey Center **Address:** 268 Avenue Ponce De Leon, Suite 501, San Juan, PR 00918 United States **BUS:** Medical Center **P/S:** Healthcare **MA:** National **D/D/R:** Forensics, Child Psychiatry **H/I/S:** Swimming, Jogging, Listening to Music, Traveling **EDU:** MD, University of Madrid **A/A/S:** Medical Association of Puerto Rico; American Psychiatric Association **C/VW:** World Vision
Email: psychmd@prtc.net

Jennifer Dawn Presley
Title: Chief Executive Officer **Company:** Professional Paralegal Services, Inc. **Address:** 737 Arnoldsville Road, Waterville, GA 30683 United States **BUS:** Legal Firm **P/S:** Real Estate Abstracts, Private Investigations, Process Serving **MA:** Local **D/D/R:** Title Abstractors, Private Investigations, Process Serving **H/I/S:** Traveling, Private Investigating **EDU:** Bachelor of Science in Business Administration, Almeda University; Associate Degree in Accounting, Athens Technical College **CERTS:** Licensed Private Investigator, Gwinnett Technical College
Email: presley_jennifer@yahoo.com

Bernice A. Pressley
Title: Executive Unit Leader **Company:** Avon **Address:** 306 Driftwood Drive, Piedmont, SC 29673 United States **BUS:** The World's Largest Beauty and Direct Sales Company **P/S:** Cosmetics, Skin Care Products, Hair Care and Nail Care Products, Perfumes, Jewelry, Toys, Clothing, Lingerie, Spa Products, Vitamins, Men's Brochure, Fund-Raiser Programs **MA:** International **D/D/R:** Recruiting, Training and Developing Independent Sales Representatives, Motivating People and Inspiring Them to Make their Dreams Come True, Offering Excellent Customer Service to Customers, Working with Any Sized Organization to Raise Money with a Customized Fund-Raiser Programs **H/I/S:** Spending Time with her Family, Collecting Glassware **EDU:** High School Diploma **A/H:** Number One in Division Unit Sales Volume Award; Number One in Division Unit Sales Increase Award; Number One in Division in the Number of Recruits Brought to Avon in a Year; Spirit of Avon, Top Achiever in District for Personal Sales and Sales Increase
Email: mrsavonmon@aol.com
URL: http://www.youravon.com/bpressley

William L. Prester
Title: President, Managing Principal **Company:** HNI Risk Services **Address:** 1621 W. Colonial Parkway, Inverness, IL 60067 United States **BUS:** Insurance and Risk Management Company **P/S:** Business Insurance, Employee Benefits, Personal Insurance Services to the Transportation, Manufacturing and Construction Industries **MA:** National **D/D/R:** developing designs for insurance and risk management products for the trucking industry **H/I/S:** Coaching Youth Sports, Running **EDU:** Master of Business Administration, Lake Forest College, IL (1990); Bachelor of Arts in Science and Economics, Illinois State University (1984); Bachelor of Arts in Psychology (1984) **A/A/S:** Illinois Trucking Association; Truckload Carriers Association; Executive Member, Operating Committee, American Trucking Associations; American Trucking Association
Email: wprester@hni.com
URL: http://www.hnitruckgroup.com

Ms. Cheryl J. Preston
Title: President/Owner **Company:** Preston Design and Co, Inc **Address:** 10120 S.W. Numbus C-5, Tigard, OR 97223 United States **BUS:** Cosmetology Cosmetics, Beauty, Spa **P/S:** Beauty Services and Products **MA:** Local **D/D/R:** Hair Coloring **H/I/S:** Traveling **EDU:** Associate Degree, CO Community College
Email: cjp1of7@earthlink.net

Sherry A. Preston
Title: Owner, Founder **Company:** Island Wolf Furs **Address:** P.O. Box 99921, Craig, AK 99921 United States **BUS:** Taxidermy Company **P/S:** Trophy Mounts **MA:** National **D/D/R:** delivering the highest quality deer head mounts **H/I/S:** Photography, Making Crafts **EDU:** High School Education **A/A/S:** American Taxidermists Association; Alaska Historical Society **C/VW:** Local Charitable Organizations; International Association of Fire Fighters; Local Troopers Association
Email: dugout@aptalaska.net

Stacey L. Prestridge
Title: Controller's Assistant **Company:** GI Associates of SWLA **Address:** 555 S. Ryan Street, Lake Charles, LA 70601 United States **BUS:** Healthcare **P/S:** GI Specialty Medicine **MA:** Regional **D/D/R:** Accounting, Bookkeeping, Assisting with Computer Problems, Billing, Accounts Payable, Overseeing Business, Handling of Employees **H/I/S:** Softball, Woodworking **EDU:** College Coursework, McNeese State University **A/A/S:** HRC
Email: stacey.prestridge@suddenlinkmail.com

Arlene Price
Title: President, Owner **Company:** A&A WIG and Hairpiece Supplies Corporation **Address:** 3167 Saint Johns Bluff Road S., Suite 102, Jacksonville, FL 32246 United States **BUS:** Manufacturing Company **P/S:** Canvas Block Heads, Styrofoam Heads, Supplies for Wigs and Hair Pieces, Wig Stands, Mustaches, Beard Blocks **MA:** International **D/D/R:** overseeing operations **H/I/S:** Traveling, Reading, Shopping **EDU:** Coursework, Tilden High School
Email: hairreplace@earthlink.net
URL: http://www.wigandhairpiecesupply.com

Crystal D. Price
Title: Vice President **Company:** Gulf Coast Siding, Inc. **Address:** 21797 Ridgeview Drive, Saucier, MS 39574 United States **BUS:** Construction Company **P/S:** Vinyl Siding, Stucco **MA:** Gulf Coast **D/D/R:** Management, Oversee All Aspect of Business **H/I/S:** Spending Time with her Family **EDU:** Bachelor's Degree in Medical Transcription, Mississippi Gulf Coast Community College
Email: cpncp02@bellsouth.net
URL: http://www.cambridgewhoswho.com

Fern Rainsberger Price
Title: 1) Secretary 2) Owner **Company:** 1) Share the Asphalt Road Safely Forever, Inc. 2) Catering Establishment **Address:** 7037 Sylvan Oak Drive, Las Vegas, NV 89147 United States **BUS:** 1) Nonprofit Organization 2) Catering Company **P/S:** 1) Assisting Families Who Have Lost Loved Ones in Roadway Accidents 2) Catering for All Needs **MA:** 1) International 2) Local **D/D/R:** 1) Administration 2) Cooking, Catering **H/I/S:** Cooking, Hiking, Fishing, Working Out at the Gym **EDU:** Associate of Occupational Science; Graduate, Le Cordon Bleu College of Culinary Arts, Magna Cum Laude **A/A/S:** Vice President, Fraternal Order of Eagles Auxiliary **C/VW:** Share the Asphalt Road Safely Forever
Email: fandd@cox.net
URL: http://www.starsforeverinc.com

Jennifer L. Price
Title: Owner **Company:** Cartridge World-Delavan **Address:** 1741 E. Geneva Street, Delavan, WI 53115 United States **BUS:** Remanufacturer Company **P/S:** Refilling and Remanufacturing Toner and Ink Cartridges **MA:** International **D/D/R:** Sales, Marketing, Accounting, Customer Service **H/I/S:** Attending Church and School Events, Community Fundraisers **EDU:** Certified Medical Executive Secretary, Minor in Modeling, Patricia Stevens College **CERTS:** Certified Phlebotomist, Elgin Community College **A/A/S:** Chamber of Commerce **C/VW:** Smiles Ranch, Local Community Organizations
Email: cartridge.world.delavan@gmail.com
URL: http://www.cartridgeworldusa.com

Mr. Marc J. Price
Title: Construction Manager **Company:** Tishman Realty and Construction **Address:** 215 Coral Lane, Reading, PA 19606 United States **BUS:** Construction Firm **P/S:** Construction, Building and Engineering Services **D/D/R:** overseeing funds, delivering on and designing projects, establishing budgets, studying technology, coordinating scheduling and working on contracts and data communications **H/I/S:** Golfing, Spending Time with Children **EDU:** Coursework in Construction Technology and Management **A/A/S:** Congress of Industrial Organizations; American Federation of Labor
Email: mprice@tishman.com
URL: http://www.tishman.com

Seraphia L. Price
Title: Manager of Talent Management **Company:** Caremark **Address:** 750 W. John Carpenter Freeway, Irving, TX 75039 United States **BUS:** Pharmaceutical Company **P/S:** Pharmacy Benefits Management **MA:** National **D/D/R:** Acquiring and Managing Talent, Overseeing Leadership Development and Employee Relations Performance Management **H/I/S:** Traveling, Going to the Beach **EDU:** Master's Degree in Human Resource Development Leadership, University of Texas at Austin; Bachelor of Arts in Psychology, Texas State University **A/A/S:** Dallas Chapter, Society for Human Resource Management; American Society for Training and Development **C/VW:** Vice President, Delta Sigma Theta
Email: seraphia@yahoo.com

Arlene Ann Pricer
Title: Physical Therapist Assistant, Wound Care Certified **Company:** Daybreak Corporation **Address:** 3600 Angle Avenue, Fort Worth, TX 76106 United States **BUS:** Nursing and Rehabilitation Center **P/S:** Therapy Rehabilitation Services **MA:** Regional **D/D/R:** caring for wounded patients and performing skilled therapy **H/I/S:** Genealogy **EDU:** Associate of Applied Science in Physical Therapy, Tarrant County College **CERTS:** Wound Care Certification **A/A/S:** Phi Theta Kappa; Daughters of American Revolution; The Society of Mayflower Descendants; American Physical Therapy Association; Advanced Proficiency of Wound Care
Email: scarlet-lpta@sbcglobal.net

Sally Priebe
Title: Teacher for Self-Contained Behavior Disorder **Company:** Waterloo East High School **Address:** 702 Home Park Boulevard, Waterloo, IA 50701 United States **BUS:** Public High School **P/S:** Secondary Education in Academics, Athletics, Arts, Computer Science, Special Education, Gifted and Talented Programs, Afterschool Programs **MA:** Local **D/D/R:** Education of High School Students with Behavior Disorders, Managing Behavior, Developing and Implementing Programs for Specific Individual Needs, Working with Community Leaders, Church Officials and the Probation Department, Utilizing a Proactive Approach, Fundraising, Conducting Home Visits, Consulting with Parents of Problem Children **H/I/S:** Playing the Piano, Watching Sports, Fundraising, Spending Time with her Dog **EDU:** Pursuing Master's Degree in Counseling and Psychology, University of Phoenix; Master's Degree in Behavior Disorders, St. Ambrose University (1994): Bachelor of Arts in Special Education, University of Northern Iowa (1979) **A/A/S:** National Education Association; Fraternal Order of Eagles; City Council
Email: priebesally9@aol.com
URL: http://www.cedarnet.org/easthigh/index.htm

Tatiana M. Prihodko
Title: Skin Care Professional, Esthetician **Company:** Sasha Salon and Spa **Address:** 23 Arrow Street, Cambridge, MA 02138 United States **BUS:** Salon **P/S:** Skin Care, Facials, Microdermabrasions, Intense Pulsed Light Treatments and Waxing **MA:** Local **EXP:** Ms. Prihodko's expertise includes ultrasonic facials, microdermabrasion and intense pulsed light treatment. **D/D/R:** Performing Ultrasonic Facials, Pulsed Light Treatments, Waxing, Organic Pumpkin Peel Procedures **H/I/S:** Reading, Listening to Music, Traveling, Walking, Spending Time Outdoors **EDU:** Master's Degree in Language, Earned in Soviet Republic (1989); Master's Degree, Bojack Academy of Beauty Culture, MA **CERTS:** Licensed Esthetician (2002) **C/VW:** Commonwealth of Independent States, Soviet Republic
Email: tmp6695@verizon.net
URL: http://www.cambridgewhoswho.com

Kristen M. Prince, BSN, RN
Title: Nurse **Company:** Hospital of the University of Pennsylvania **Address:** 205 Candlebrook Road, King of Prussia, PA 19406 United States **BUS:** Hospital and Healthcare System **P/S:** Allergy and Immunology, Anesthesia, Behavioral Health, Neonatology, Obstetrics and Gynecology, Occupational Therapy, Ophthalmology, Cardiology and Cardiac Surgery, Pediatrics, Endocrine and Oncologic Surgery and Many Other Services **MA:** Local **D/D/R:** Nursing in Neonatal Intensive Care, Nursing at Patient's Bedside, Caring for One-Three Sick and Premature Babies, Collaborating with Doctors and Social Workers **H/I/S:** Reading, Vacationing **EDU:** Bachelor of Science in Nursing, University of Pennsylvania (1997)
Email: kristensquire@netscape.net
URL: http://www.pennhealth.com/hup

Judith M. Priniski
Title: Owner, Registered Nurse, Consultant **Company:** A Peaceful Nature **Address:** 1817 17 1/2 Street N. W., Rochester, MN 55901 United States **BUS:** Health and Wellness Center **P/S:** Information, Education, Consultation **MA:** Regional **D/D/R:** Nursing, Scheduling, Consulting, Developing Personalized Health Plan, Educating the Patients, Acupuncture **H/I/S:** Crafts, Scrapbooking, Reading, Listening to Music **EDU:** Pursuing Coursework in Natural Health, Craiton College; Registered Nurse, Henry Ford Hospital (1980)
Email: jmpriniski@hotmail.com

Helen M. Pritchett
Title: Owner **Company:** The House of Hope Daycare **Address:** 1010 S. 10th Avenue, Maywood, IL 60153 United States **BUS:** Child Care Center **P/S:** Day Care Services for Children **MA:** Local **D/D/R:** Utilizing Musical Games for Infants, Experimenting with Toys and the Animal Recognition Method **H/I/S:** Softball, Volleyball, Baseball, Bowling, Basketball **EDU:** Coursework in Early Childhood Education, Triton College **A/A/S:** Childcare Network
Email: bigyellow1@msn.com

Karen P. Procaccino
Title: Owner, President **Company:** Sport Tan USA **Address:** 954 S. Lake Boulevard, Mahopac, NY 10541 United States **BUS:** Tanning Salon **P/S:** Tanning Services, Tanning Lotions, Sterling Silver Jewelry, Ear-Piercing Services **MA:** Local **D/D/R:** Managing Business Operations **H/I/S:** Working Out at the Gym, Dancing, Going to the Casino, Shopping, Gardening, Traveling **EDU:** Diploma, St. Barnabas High School **A/A/S:** Indoor Tanning Association, Inc.

Laura E. Profilio
Title: PTA President **Company:** Medfield Heights Elementary School **Dept:** Parent Teachers Association **Address:** 4300 Buchanan Avenue, Baltimore, MD 21211 United States **BUS:** Elementary Education **P/S:** Education and Support for School, Family and Community **MA:** Regional **D/D/R:** Organizing Fund-Raising Events to Meet Teachers, Students and School's Needs, Educating Community on Safety and Drug Prevention, Producing and Directing School Plays; Managing a Home Day Care Service **H/I/S:** Making Crafts **EDU:** Diploma, Western Senior High School, Maryland (1982)
Email: unonachos@msn.com
URL: http://www.medfieldheights.com/pta.html

Mrs. Cathy A. Prokash
Title: Director of Procurement **Company:** Royal Office Products **Dept:** Purchasing **BUS:** Dealer **P/S:** Office Products, Printing Services, Furniture, Coffee, ASI **MA:** National **D/D/R:** Managing Product Procurement, Managing Expansion, Accruing Staff, Inventory Control, Operations and Supply Chain, Training at All Levels **H/I/S:** Spending Time with Children, Basketball, Bowling **A/A/S:** Employee of the quarter in two different companies.
Email: cathyprokash@yahoo.com

Meg Proskey
Title: Business Development Director **Company:** Maritz Travel Company **Address:** 1395 N. Highway Drive, Fenton, MO 63026 United States **BUS:** Incentive and Business Travel Agency **P/S:** Travel Arrangements **MA:** National **D/D/R:** Process Improvement **H/I/S:** Playing Golf, Running, Spending Time with her Three Children **EDU:** Bachelor's Degree, University of Maryland, College Park **A/A/S:** Standing Ovation Award **C/VW:** Dress for Success, Church, Local School Fundraisers
Email: meg.proskey@maritz.com

Charles R. Proudfoot
Title: Teacher **Company:** Taylor County Board of Education **Address:** 1 Prospect Street, Grafton, WV 26354 United States **BUS:** School District **P/S:** Special Education **MA:** Local **D/D/R:** Special Education, Teaching the Profoundly Handicapped **H/I/S:** Sports **EDU:** Master of Arts Plus 45 in Severe and Profound Handicapped Education, West Virginia University; Endorsement in Autism, Marshall University **A/A/S:** Alternate Access Community; West Virginia Education Association; National Education Association; Committee to Develop Tests for Mentally Handicapped Students **C/VW:** Special Olympics
Email: crproudf@access.k12.wv.us
URL: http://www.access.k12.wv.us

Heather C. Proveaux, RN
Title: Registered Nurse **Company:** South Carolina Heart Center **Address:** 506 North Street, Bamberg, SC 29003 United States **BUS:** Cardiology Center **P/S:** Healthcare **MA:** Regional **D/D/R:** Office Management, Patient Care **H/I/S:** Playing Softball, Walking, Spending Time with Family **EDU:** Pursuing Bachelor of Science in Nursing, University of South Carolina Upstate; Associate of Science in Nursing, Orangeburg-Calhoun Technical College **A/A/S:** American Nurses Association **C/VW:** Home for Children, Compassion International
Email: hcproveaux@uscupstate.edu

Michael V. Provinzino
Title: Realtor Associate, CNC **Company:** Century 21 Lullo **Address:** 16 W. Lake Street, Addison, IL 60101 United States **BUS:** Real Estate Brokerage Firm **P/S:** Residential and Commercial Real Estate **MA:** Regional **D/D/R:** Selling Commercial and Residential Real Estate, Devoting Full Attention to All Clients, Assisting Clients with Relocation, Teaching First Time Home Buyers **H/I/S:** Consumer Educator in Wine Tasting **A/A/S:** National Association of Realtors; Illinois Association of Realtors; Multiple Listing Service of Northern Illinois; Realtor Association of the West/South Suburban Chicagoland; Historical Commissioner of Addison, Trustee Knights of Columbus
Email: mprovinzino@c21lullo.com
URL: http://www.cambridgewhoswho.com

Mr. Glenn P. Pruitt
Title: Quality Technologist **Company:** DSM Thermoplastic Elastomers **BUS:** Manufacturing **P/S:** Pharmaceuticals, Raw Materials, Sports Drinks **MA:** International **D/D/R:** Managing Quality Assurance, Testing and Research **EDU:** Associate Degree in Medical Science Studies, Colorado University **A/A/S:** American Society of Quality
Email: glenn.pruitt@dsm.com

Marsha D. Pruitt
Title: Realtor **Company:** GSH Real Estate **Address:** 11844 Rock Landing Drive, Newport News, VA 23606 United States **BUS:** Real Estate Company with Listed Properties on the Internet **P/S:** High Quality of Real Estate Services **MA:** Local **D/D/R:** Overseeing Retail Management, Selling Residential and Rental Real Estate **H/I/S:** Traveling, Spending Time with her Dogs
Email: mpruitt@gsh.com
URL: http://www.gsh.com

Kristine R. Pruy
Title: Telecommunication Specialist **Company:** United States Secret Service **Address:** 950 H Street N.E., Suite 2000, Washington, DC 20002 United States **BUS:** Government Agency **P/S:** Law Enforcement **MA:** International **D/D/R:** managing telecommunications including cellular and blackberry communications, overseeing satellite phones, secure calls and radios **H/I/S:** Fitness Snowboarding, Traveling, Spending Time at the Beach **EDU:** Pursuing Bachelor's Degree **A/A/S:** The United States Army **C/VW:** Local Charitable Organizations
Email: kristine.pruy@usss.dhs.gov
URL: http://www.dhs.gov

Ms. Alicia Pucci
Title: Owner, Sole Proprietor **Company:** Sew-It-All **Address:** 15 Libra Drive, Novato, CA 94947 United States **BUS:** Sewing Company **P/S:** Custom Sewing, Sewing Classes, Product Development **MA:** San Francisco Bay Area **D/D/R:** Teaching the Art of Sewing, Custom Sewing and Design **H/I/S:** Playing Tennis, Hiking, Cooking, Traveling **EDU:** Bachelor of Science in Home Economics, California Polytechnic State University, San Luis Obispo **CERTS:** Single Subject Teaching Credential; SDAIE Certificate Credential **A/A/S:** Home Economics Teachers Association of California; American Federation of Teachers; California Teachers Association; Assistant to Sandra Betzina; Bay Area Business Women **C/VW:** Local Church and School Fundraising Events; Team in Training, Leukemia & Lymphoma Foundation, FIDM Scholarship Foundation
Email: alicia@sew-it-all.com
URL: http://www.sew-it-all.com

Margarita Puckett
Title: Owner/Photographer **Company:** Simple Reflections **Address:** 10536 Via Como Court, Clermont, FL 34711 United States **BUS:** Photography, Digital Art **P/S:** Digital Photography for All Occasions **MA:** Regional **D/D/R:** Weddings, Portraiture, Special Events, Children Portraits **H/I/S:** Photography, Painting, Spending Time with her Family **EDU:** Community and Human Services; Coursework in Photoshop **A/A/S:** Professional Photographers of America; Now I Lay Me Down to Sleep Foundation **C/VW:** United Way; Coalition for the Homeless; Clothesline Annual Event; Public Speaker, Women's Support Group for Domestic Violence
Email: margarita@simplereflectionsbympuckett.com
URL: http://www.simplereflectionsbympuckett.com

Barbara A. Pugh
Title: Owner, Agent **Company:** Night and Day Travel & Cruises **Address:** P.O. Box 25050, Portland, OR 97298 United States **BUS:** Travel Company **P/S:** Complete Range of Travel Services Including Airline Tickets and Cruises **MA:** Regional **D/D/R:** Managing Travel Arrangements for Trips to Latin America, Western Europe and Hawaii, Advertising **H/I/S:** Cooking, Wine Tasting, Gardening, Traveling **EDU:** Bachelor's Degree in Mathematics, Portland State College (1964) **A/A/S:** The National Association of Commissioned Travel Agents.; Volunteer, The National Peace Corps Association
Email: night_daytravel@msn.com

Mr. John M. Pugliese
Title: Vice President, Sales and Marketing **Company:** The Network Support Company **Address:** 7 Kenosia Avenue, Danbury, CT 06810 United States **BUS:** Information Technology Company **P/S:** Networking Services, Desktop, Voice, Security, Cabling and Wireless Data Services **MA:** Regional **D/D/R:** Building Relationships with Client CEOs and COOs to Meet their IT Needs **H/I/S:** Golfing **EDU:** Bachelor of Science in Business and Marketing Management, Western Connecticut State University (1981) **CERTS:** Certifications in Project Management, Time Management and Disaster Recovery **A/A/S:** Hospitality Financial and Technology Professionals; Greater Danbury Chamber of Commerce; Stanford Chamber of Commerce/Lincoln County
Email: jpugliese@network-support.com
URL: http://www.network-support.com

Debra Puglisi Sharp
Title: Registered Nurse, Author, Inspirational Speaker **Company:** Debra Puglisi Sharp **Address:** P.O. Box 365, Millsboro, DE 19966 United States **BUS:** Sole Proprietorship **P/S:** Inspirational and Public Speaking, Seminars and Consulting Services **MA:** International **D/D/R:** conducting programs for victims of violence and rape on education and awareness for law enforcement, public speaking, volunteering and nursing **H/I/S:** Traveling with her Husband, Reading at the Book Club, Researching Different Cultures, Dancing, Spending Time with her Pets, Reading about Bills and Legislation of Victim's Rights **EDU:** Associate Degree in Nursing, Delaware Technical and Community College **CERTS:** Registered Nurse, Delaware Board of Nursing (1989) **A/A/S:** Crime Law Enforcement Network, Mid-Atlantic Great Lakes; Criminal Justice Advisory Board, Wilmington College; Volunteer, Delaware Contact Lifeline Rape Crisis; Board of Directors, National Coalition for Victims in Action **A/H:** United States Attorney General's Award of Special Courage (2007) **C/VW:** Various Charitable Organizations
Email: deb9033@aol.com
URL: http://www.puglisisharp.com

Judith Pullar
Title: Vice President **Company:** Cannon Design **Address:** 360 Madison Avenue, New York, NY 10017 United States **BUS:** Design Firm **P/S:** Architectural and Engineering Services, Interior Design **MA:** International **EXP:** Ms. Pullar's area of expertise is in business development. **H/I/S:** Attending her Son's Baseball Games **EDU:** College Coursework **CERTS:** Certification in Construction Management, New York University **A/A/S:** Board Member, Society for Marketing Professional Services **A/H:** 40 Under 40 Award (2006) **C/VW:** West Paterson Boys and Girls Club; American Heart Association; New Windsor Little league
Email: jpullar@cannondesign.com
URL: http://www.cannondesign.com

Bertha V. Pulliam, MS, CSW
Title: Administrator **Company:** First Choice Outreach Services, Inc. **Address:** 5250 N. 68th Street, Milwaukee, WI 53218 United States **BUS:** Nonprofit **P/S:** Case Management, Budget Management, Counseling **MA:** Regional **D/D/R:** Teaching, Empowering Clients, Developing Programs, Financial Management, Arranging Guardianships of Person and Estates, Offering Case Management Services **H/I/S:** Riding Horses, Biking, Playing Golf, Jogging, Exercising, Teaching Sunday School, Playing Tennis **EDU:** Master of Social Work, Springfield University; Bachelor's Degree in Social Work, University of Wisconsin, Milwaukee **A/A/S:** Sojourner of Truth Institute **C/VW:** American Red Cross; Salvation Army; Domestic Violence; Police Department; Veterans, Mission for the Homeless
Email: fcos95@yahoo.com
URL: http://www.fcos.gov

Diane T. Pulse
Title: Owner **Company:** Diane T Pulse and Associates Ltd **Address:** 114 North Commerce Street, Ripley, MS 38663 United States **BUS:** Social Security and Disability Advice Consulting **P/S:** Social Security and Disability Advice **MA:** Local **D/D/R:** Social Security/Disability **H/I/S:** Fly Fishing **EDU:** University of Mississippi, Administrative Law **A/A/S:** Chamber of Commerce
Email: dianepulse@ripleycable.net

Monica A. Purcell
Title: President **Company:** Alpha Medical Billing Associates, Inc. **Address:** 1662 W. Breese Road, Suite G, Lima, OH 45806 United States **BUS:** Medical Billing Company **P/S:** Medical Billing, Coding and Healthcare Management Consulting Services **MA:** Regional **EXP:** Dr. Purcell's expertise includes internal, emergency and family medicine. **D/D/R:** specializing in anesthesia, orthopedics, urology, physical therapy, performing general surgeries, caring for pediatric, chiropractic, pediatric otolaryngology, neuropsychiatric patients **H/I/S:** Studying, Spending Time with her Family **EDU:** Associate Degree in Healthcare Administration, Daytona Beach Community College **CERTS:** Registered Medical Coder, American Academy of Professional Coders; Certified Health Unit Coordinator, Daytona Beach Community College; Certification in Medical Billing **C/VW:** Local Church
Email: monica@alphamedbilling.com
URL: http://www.alphamedbilling.com

Kimberly B. Purdy
Title: Office and Account Manager **Company:** Dr. Cavanaugh Medical Office **Address:** 51 Main Street, Hyannis, MA 02601 United States **BUS:** Healthcare Private Practice **P/S:** General Medical Practice **MA:** Local **D/D/R:** Community Relations, Very Involved **H/I/S:** Reading, Outdoors, Nature, Animals, Spending Time with Daughter 'Ashley' **EDU:** Fisher Junior College, Vocational, Business **A/A/S:** Humanity for Habitats, ASPCA, Troop Leader for the 'Daisies'
Email: kim@doctorcavanaugh.com
URL: http://www.doctorcavanaugh.com

Patricia Purnell
Title: Speech-Language Pathologist Company: Centralia School District Address: 6625 La Palma Avenue, Buena Park, CA 90620 United States BUS: School District P/S: Education MA: Local D/D/R: Speech-Language Pathology H/I/S: Traveling EDU: Master of Science in Speech-Language Pathology; Chapman University (1977); Master of Science in Communication Disorders, Chapman University (1977) A/A/S: California Speech-Language-Hearing Association; American Speech-Language-Hearing Association
Email: pmpurnell@hotmail.com

Mr. John E. Pusey III
Title: Director Company: Graphics III Advertising, Inc. Dept: Development and Hosting Address: 832 L Oregon Avenue, Linthicum, MD 21090 United States BUS: Internet Advertising Company P/S: Web Designs and Hosting, Commercial Printing MA: National D/D/R: Developing Web Applications and Web Hosting H/I/S: Swimming EDU: Master of Science in Instructional and Interactive Technology, Bloomsburg University of Pennsylvania; Bachelor of Business Administration in Political Science, Bloomsburg University of Pennsylvania A/A/S: American Society for Training and Development C/VW: Orthodox Church in America; Children's Cancer Foundation
Email: johnp@g3group.com
Email: john@nightgazing.com
URL: http://www.g3group.com
URL: http://www.nightgazing.com

Ruth M. Putnam
Title: Administrator Company: Natrona County School District 1 Address: 970 N. Glenn Road, Casper, WY 82601 United States BUS: Public Schools P/S: Education, Administration MA: Local D/D/R: Managing Student Support Services, Administering Waivers for Home-Bound Students and Students Displaced from Hurricane Katrina, Consulting with Parents, Assisting Other Departments with Typing and Office Responsibilities, Coordinating Athletic Activities, Acting as a Liaison between the Community and the School H/I/S: Watching NFL Football, Golfing EDU: Bachelor of Science Degree in Physical Education, Minor in Business, University of South Dakota (1972) CERTS: Certification K-12 for Physical Education and High School Business A/A/S: National Association of Educational Office Professionals; Wyoming Association of Educational Office Professionals; National and Local Association of Educational Support Staff; Philanthropic Educational Organization
Email: ruthputnam@yahoo.com

Desiree J. Puzio, RN
Title: Nurse Manager Company: Ozana Hall Nursing Home Address: 4241 201 Street, Bayside, NY 11361 United States BUS: Nursing Home P/S: Wide Range of Nursing Services MA: Local D/D/R: Managing a 50 Bed Unit in a Nursing Home, Special Care, Writing a Policy on Hickman Catheter H/I/S: Crocheting, Arts and Crafts, Traveling EDU: Bachelor of Science in Nursing (1996); Registered Nurse, Queensborough Community College (1992) A/A/S: President, New York State Nurses Association C/VW: Disabled American Veterans; Veterans of Foreign Wars; American Red Cross; Easter Seals
URL: http://www.ozanamhall.org

Larry R. Pyle
Title: Medical Doctor Company: Larry R. Pyle, MD, FAAFP Address: 2701 Eureka Way, Suite 1C, Redding, CA 96001 United States BUS: Doctor's Office P/S: Family Medical Practice MA: Local D/D/R: Family Practice, Sole Practice H/I/S: Golfing EDU: MD, Universidad Autónoma de Guadalajara, Mexico (1978); Residency, New York Medical College (1979-1983) A/A/S: American Academy of Family Physicians; American Medical Association; CMA
Email: lrpyle@yahoo.com

Stephen Quackenbush
Title: Fire Chief Company: Green Acres Rural Fire Protection District Address: 93449 Green Acres Lane, Coos Bay, OR 97420 United States BUS: Fire Department P/S: Offering Fire and Emergency Medical Services MA: Local D/D/R: Commanding Emergencies of All Types H/I/S: Golfing EDU: Coursework, Southwest Oregon Community College A/A/S: Local Fire Chiefs Association C/VW: Fire Department
Email: grfpd@aol.com
URL: http://www.cambridgewhoswho.com

Louis G. Quartararo, MD
Title: Orthopedic Spine Surgeon Company: Spine and Trauma Institute Address: 663 Palisades Avenue, Cliffside Park, NJ 07010 United States BUS: Medical Center P/S: Healthcare Including Orthopedic and Rehabilitative Care, Diagnosing of Diseases and Injuries of Bones, Muscles, Tendons, Nerves and Ligaments, Surgical and Non-Surgical Treatments of Sports Injuries of the Knee, Shoulder, Fracture and Trauma Care, Same Day Surgery, Physical Medicine and Rehabilitation MA: Regional D/D/R: treating complex traumas and performing surgery H/I/S: Collecting Coins EDU: Fellowship, Johns Hopkins University; MD, Mount Sinai School of Medicine (1993) A/A/S: Orthopedic Trauma Association; North American Spine Society; American Academy of Orthopedic Surgeons
Email: spineoncall@hotmail.com
URL: http://premortho.com

Lara A. Queen
Title: Teacher Company: Fort Gay Elementary School Address: 8600 Orchard Street, Fort Gay, WV 25514 United States BUS: Elementary School P/S: Education MA: Local D/D/R: Teaching Reading H/I/S: Gardening EDU: Master of Arts in Reading, Marshall University; Bachelor of Science in Multi-Subject K-8 Education, Marshall University CERTS: Certified Reading Specialist A/A/S: Beta Kappa Phi C/VW: St. Jude Children's Research Hospital
Email: lpc93@lycos.com

Gina F. Quesada
Title: Director of ICU Company: Lea Regional Medical Center Address: 7916 N Piedras Drive, Hobbs, NM 88242 United States BUS: Healthcare Hospital P/S: Oversees all Functions of Intensive Care Unit MA: International D/D/R: Critical Care, Cardiology H/I/S: Spending Time with Family EDU: Associate of Science of Nursing, Carlsbad, New Mexico A/A/S: Hispanic Chamber of Commerce
Email: gina.quesada@triadhospitals.com

Emma B. Quimbley
Title: County Coroner Company: Dougherty County Coroners Office Address: 225 Pine Avenue, Room 105-2, Albany, GA 31702 United States BUS: Government P/S: Examining Deceased Persons to Determine the Cause, Method and Manner of Death in Cases Involving Homicide, Suicide, Accident, Suspicious or Unusual Manner and/or When Unattended by a Physician MA: Statewide D/D/R: Investigating Homicides, Suicides, Prevention Counseling H/I/S: Fishing, Reading EDU: Diploma, Mitchell County High School, Georgia (1973) A/A/S: Board of Directors, Albany Area Health Association; Board of Directors, Albany State University, Forensics
Email: equimbley@dougherty.ga.us
URL: http://www.dougherty.ga.us

Ms. Heather A. Quinn
Title: Elementary Teacher Company: Virginia Beach City Public Schools, North Landing Address: 1900 N. Great Neck Road, Virginia Beach, VA 23454 United States BUS: Elementary School P/S: Education MA: Local D/D/R: Elementary Education with Emphasis on Reading Specialization H/I/S: Traveling, Playing Tennis, Spending Time with her Family and Friends EDU: Certified Reading Specialist, State of Virginia; Master's Degree in Reading, East Stroudsburg University; Bachelor's Degree in Elementary Education, Pennsylvania State University
Email: buggyb21@yahoo.com

Texlin Quinney
Title: Financial Executive Company: Robert Half International Dept: Management Resources Address: 3424 Peachtree Road NE, Suite 2000, Atlanta, GA 30326 United States BUS: Staffing Company of Senior-Level Accounting and Finance Professionals on a per Project and Interim Basis P/S: Staffing Assistance for Clients in a Variety of Industries and Interim Positions MA: National D/D/R: Consulting on Various Financial Projects, Public and Project Accounting, Payroll, Corporate Spending, Budget Forecasting, Systems Analysis, External Reporting, SOX Business, Business Process Improvement Initiatives and Documentation of Internal Controls H/I/S: Basketball, Swimming, Running, Cycling, Individual/Team Basketball Skills Training, Biblical Study EDU: Certified Public Accountant; Master of Business Administration in Business Management; Bachelor of Science in Accounting and Mathematics, Seton Hall University (1996-1998) A/A/S: American Institute of Certified Public Accountants; Beta Alpha Psi; Speaker, AICPA Student Leadership Conference (2007); Former Basketball Player, Women's National Basketball Association; Inducted in the Hall of Fame, Sacred Heart Academy, Buffalo, New York; RSM Servant Leader at New Birth Missionary Church, Lithonia, Georgia
Email: texlin.quinney@rhmr.com
URL: http://www.roberthalfmr.com

Wanda I. Quinones
Title: Medical Office Manager Company: Carlos H. Loubriel, MD, PA Address: 4242 Hondo Pass, Suite 101, El Paso, TX 79904 United States BUS: Healthcare P/S: Private OB/GYN Practice MA: Local D/D/R: Supervising a Private OB/GYN Practice, Bilingual Patient Services H/I/S: Children, Cooking EDU: Bachelor of Science in Secretarial Science, University of Puerto Rico A/A/S: Project Management Institute

Mr. Joseph Quintana
Title: Front Office Supervisor Company: Courtyard Marriott Miami Dadeland (MG Hospitality Group) Dept: Front Office Address: Courtyard Marriott Miami Dadeland, 9075 South Dadeland Boulevard, Miami, FL 33156 United States BUS: Hotels and Resorts P/S: Hotel Guest Rooms, Customer Service MA: Local D/D/R: Guest Services, Hospitality H/I/S: Traveling EDU: Master's Degree in Hospitality, Florida International University
Email: joseph.quintana@mdmusa.com
Email: jquintana07@bellsouth.net
URL: http://www.marriott.com/hotels/travel/miacy-courtyard-miami-dadeland/

Mayra C. Quintero
Title: Owner Company: Mayra's Personal Touch Catering Address: 1432 N.W. Ninth Street, Dania Beach, FL 33004 United States BUS: Catering Company P/S: Catering Services for Weddings, Private and Corporate Functions MA: Local D/D/R: managing business operations H/I/S: Dancing, Exercising A/A/S: Marine Industries Association of South Florida
Email: landi914@comcast.net
URL: http://www.mayracatering.com

Alanna G. Quirk
Title: Owner, Manager Company: Milano Salon & Spa Address: 282 Washington Street, Stoughton, MA 02072 United States BUS: Spa P/S: Manicure and Pedicure Services, Skin Care Treatments, Nail and Skin Care Products MA: Local D/D/R: performing skin care treatments including firming, chemical peel, lymphonic drainage, electric muscle stimulation and microdermabrasion, overseeing operations, bookkeeping and communicating with clients EDU: Associate Degree in Liberal Arts, Fisher College (1998) CERTS: Licensed Esthetician A/H: Dean's List, Phi Beta Kappa
Email: agq1977@yahoo.copm
URL: http://www.milanoskincare.com

Beth Quitadamo, BS, MS
Title: Chief of Safety and Training Company: General Dynamics, American Overseas Marine Corporation Address: 100 Newport Avenue Extension, Quincy, MA 02171 United States BUS: Government Marine Contractor P/S: Ship Operations MA: International D/D/R: Managing All Human Resource Records, Training All Mariners Sent to Sea H/I/S: Running, Cooking, Avid Boston Red Sox Fan EDU: Master of Science in Marine Safety and Environmental Health, Maria College (2006); Bachelor of Science Degree, Master of Arts Degree, Maritime Academy (2002)
Email: bquitadamo@gdamsea.com
URL: http://gdamsea.com

Cynthia A. Raber
Title: Educator Company: P.S. 123 Address: 14501 119th Avenue, Jamaica, NY 11436 United States BUS: Public Elementary School Serving Residents of Jamaica P/S: Public Elementary Education for Local Students MA: Jamaica D/D/R: Teaching an Inclusion Third-Grade Class, Working with the Special Education Teacher H/I/S: Horseback Riding EDU: Master's Degree in Elementary Education, CUNY Queens College (1998) A/A/S: Certified in Common Branches; Certified and Licensed Educator, State of New York
Email: eraber@optonline.net
URL: http://www.cambridgewhoswho.com

Carollee M. Race
Title: RPT, CRT Company: Boswell Memorial Hospital Address: Sun City, AZ United States BUS: Hospital P/S: Healthcare, Geriatric Care MA: Local D/D/R: Respiratory Care H/I/S: Reading EDU: Associate of Science, Long Technical College A/A/S: American Association for Respiratory Care C/VW: Upward Foundation
Email: czcar@aol.com
URL: http://www.cambridgewhoswho.com

Cheryl C. Rachford
Title: Teacher Company: Pulaski County Education System, Southern Middle School Address: 200 Enterprise Drive, Somerset, KY 42501 United States BUS: Public Middle School P/S: Education MA: Local D/D/R: Teaching Dance, Music, Visual Arts and Drama to Eighth-Grade Students H/I/S: Antiquing EDU: Master's Degree in Special Education, Eastern Kentucky University (1997)
Email: cherylcrachford@hotmail.com
URL: http://www.pulaski.k12.ky.us

Wanda J. Rackley
Title: Lead Teacher, Facilitator **Company:** Sheltering Arms Child Early Education & Family Center **Address:** 529 Flint Trail, Jonesboro, GA 30236 United States **BUS:** Child Development Center **P/S:** Education **MA:** Regional **EXP:** Ms. Rackley's area of expertise is in early childhood education. **D/D/R:** Overseeing 20 Teachers, Infants and Toddlers, Teaching, Training, Consulting, Lecturing **H/I/S:** Cooking **EDU:** Bachelor of Arts in Sociology, Fayetteville State University (1995) **A/A/S:** National Head Start Association **A/H:** Award of Excellence, Sheltering Arms Child Early Education & Family Center **C/VW:** Divine Faith Church
Email: wrackley@shelteringarmsforkids.com
URL: http://www.shelteringarmsforkids.com

John B. Radcliffe
Title: Director **Company:** Christian Children's Home of Ohio **Address:** 2685 Armstrong Road, Wooster, OH 44691 United States **BUS:** Social Services Social Services **P/S:** Christian Counseling **MA:** Local **D/D/R:** Counseling, Mentoring **H/I/S:** Playing with his Children, Archery, Reading, Canoeing **EDU:** Master of Arts in Counseling, Cincinnati Bible Seminary **A/A/S:** APT, American Association of Christian Counseling, Ohio Counseling Association
Email: radcliffej@ccho.org
URL: http://www.ccho.org

Peter Rademacher
Title: Public Relation Sales **Company:** North Gateway Tire Co **Address:** 4001 North Court St, Medina, OH 44256 United States **BUS:** Automotive Distributor **P/S:** All Size tire distribution and retail Sales, Tire and Automotive Services **MA:** National **D/D/R:** Sales and Public Relations **H/I/S:** Mechanically Inclined, Motorcycling, Family time, Boxing and wrestling **EDU:** Yakima Valley Junior College and Washington State, Major-Animal Sciences **A/A/S:** Heavyweight and Gold Medalist (1956)

Rhonda Radloff
Title: Photographer, Owner **Company:** R-Images **Address:** 2485 Perry Street, Apartment 2, Madison, WI 53713 United States **BUS:** Proven Leader in the Photography Industry **P/S:** High Quality Freelance Photography Services for Clients **MA:** National **D/D/R:** Working with all Types of Photography including Personal Portraits, Weddings, Commercial and Print **H/I/S:** Golf, Tennis **EDU:** Associate Degree in Photography, Madison Technical College, Wisconsin (2002)
Email: r_images@yahoo.com
URL: http://www.r-imagesphotography.com

Allen Raducha
Title: Financial Consultant **Company:** Wachovia Securities **Address:** 4 Main Street, Farmington, CT 06032 United States **BUS:** Financial Company **P/S:** Full-Service Investment Firm **MA:** National **D/D/R:** Financial Consulting, Asset Management, Retirement Planning **H/I/S:** Playing Golf, Traveling **EDU:** Bachelor's Degree in Finance and Marketing, Babson College **CERTS:** Accredited Asset Managed Specialist, The College for Financial Planning **C/VW:** Various Charities
URL: http://www.agedwards.com

Danielle T. Rafols, DVM
Title: Associate Veterinarian **Company:** McAfee Animal Hospital **Address:** 651 Eastport Centre Drive, Valparaiso, IN 46383 United States **BUS:** Animal Hospital **P/S:** Veterinary Medicine **MA:** Regional **D/D/R:** working with small animals, taking care of hospitalized patients in clinics, seeing patients, performing surgery and treating sick, injured and orphaned wildlife **H/I/S:** Playing the Piano, Skiing **EDU:** Doctor of Veterinary Medicine, Purdue University (2005) **A/A/S:** Research Committee, Talltree Arboretum; American Veterinary Medicine Association; AAHA **C/VW:** Morraine Wildlife Center
Email: lucycries@yahoo.com
URL: http://www.mcafeeah.com

Charles Ragonese
Title: Owner **Company:** Charles Ragonese Insurance and Investment Services **Address:** 199 S. Monte Vista Avenue, Suite 1, San Dimas, CA 91773 United States **BUS:** Financial Company **P/S:** Retiring Planning Strategies **MA:** California **D/D/R:** Retirement Planning **H/I/S:** Golfing, Horseback Riding, Trimaran Boating, Traveling, Cigars **EDU:** College Coursework **A/A/S:** National Alliance for Information Assurance; Court of the Table, Million Dollar Round Table; CFS; CLTC; CRPC **C/VW:** Alicia Rose Victorious Foundation, Society of Saint Vincent de Paul
Email: crcfs@yahoo.com
URL: http://www.charlesragonese.com

John R. Rainbow
Title: Owner **Company:** Rainbow Value **Address:** 41 East 7th Street, Apartment 19, New York, NY 10003 United States **BUS:** Entertainment Provider **P/S:** Balladeer Extraordinaire **MA:** Local **D/D/R:** Baritone Singer **H/I/S:** Music, Traveling **EDU:** Bachelor's Degree in Music and Voice, WV
Email: rainbowvalue@aol.com

Mr. Russell S. Rains
Title: Patient Accounts Team Leader **Company:** Northwest Health Systems **Address:** 2007 Robyn Road, Springdale, AR 72762 United States **BUS:** Healthcare Facility **P/S:** Cardiac Diagnosis and Treatment Center, Neonatal Intensive Care Unit, Intravascular Ultrasound with Virtual Histology Services **MA:** Regional **D/D/R:** Managing Patient Accounts, Overseeing Finances and Customer Service, Reviewing Explanation of Benefit Reports, Acting as Liaison between the Patients and Insurance Companies **H/I/S:** Sports **EDU:** Pursuing Bachelor's Degree in Psychology, University of Phoenix
Email: rrains@nw-health.com
URL: http://www.northwesthealth.com

Niraja Rajan, MD
Title: Medical Director **Company:** Hershey Outpatient Surgery Center **Address:** Cherry Drive, Hershey, PA 17033 United States **BUS:** Outpatient Surgery Center **P/S:** Outpatient Surgery, Ambulatory Surgery, General Urology, Plastic Surgery, Pediatrics, Gynecology, Anesthesiology **MA:** Regional **D/D/R:** Specializing in Pediatric Anesthesia, Managing Anesthesia Services, Overseeing Daily Operations, Ensuring Medical Center is in Compliance with Standards **H/I/S:** Reading, Listening to Music, Biking, Hiking, Tennis **EDU:** MD, University of Pennsylvania (2001); Fellowship in Pediatric Anesthesiology (2001); Bachelor of Science in Biology, Maulana Azad Medical College, New Delhi (1993) **A/A/S:** Diplomate, The American Board of Anesthesiology; Fellow, The American Board of Pediatrics
Email: nrajanmd@yahoo.com
URL: http://www.cambridgewhoswho.com

Bruce F. Rajwasser
Title: Assistant Principal **Company:** New York City Department of Education **BUS:** Government Organization **P/S:** Education **MA:** Regional **D/D/R:** creating and developing business technologies and teaching business education **H/I/S:** Spending Time with his Family **EDU:** Master of Science, CUNY Baruch (1997); Bachelor of Science in Business Education and Finance, College of Staten Island (1989); Coursework in Biology and Food Service **A/A/S:** Innovation First; Technical Education Association, NY; National Council for Technical Education, NJ
Email: brajwasse@msn.com
URL: http://www.cambridgewhoswho.com

Cynthia Ralliford
Title: Counselor **Company:** Garner Department of Corrections **Address:** 50 Nunnawauk Road, Newton, CT 06470 United States **BUS:** Correctional Facility **P/S:** Corrections **MA:** Regional **D/D/R:** Counseling, Mental Health Counselor for a Maximum Level Four Correctional Facility, Motivational Speaker and Help Prepare Inmates Getting Back into Society **H/I/S:** Fishing **EDU:** Pursuing Ph.D. in Criminal Justice; Master's Degree in Criminal Justice Counseling, University of New Haven; Bachelor's Degree in Criminal Justice, University of New Haven **C/VW:** Program Coordinator, The Epiphany
Email: davis4980@sbcglobal.net
URL: http://www.cambridgewhoswho.com

Melvin L. Rambo
Title: President, Chief Executive Officer **Company:** Equitable Reserve Association **Address:** 116 S. Commercial Street, Neenah, WI 54956 United States **BUS:** Financial Planning Company **P/S:** Life Insurance, Annuities **MA:** Regional **D/D/R:** Management, Actuarial Analysis **H/I/S:** Traveling **EDU:** Master of Business Administration, Drake University; Bachelor's Degree, Drake University (1976) **A/A/S:** Fellow, Society of Actuaries; American Academy of Actuaries **C/VW:** United Way, Junior Achievement
Email: rambom@equitablereserve.com
URL: http://www.equitablereserve.com

Delynn C. Ramirez
Title: Realtor **Company:** Realtron, Inc. **Address:** 13276 Research Boulevard, Suite 105, Austin, TX 78750 United States **BUS:** Real Estate Agency **P/S:** Real Estate Sales, Residential **MA:** Austin, Texas **D/D/R:** Marketing Real Estate, Selling Real Estate **H/I/S:** Spending Time with her Family **CERTS:** Real Estate License (2004) **A/A/S:** National Association of Realtors; Texas Association of Realtors **C/VW:** Church
Email: delynnrealtron@hotmail.com
URL: http://www.realtroninc.com

Irma Ramirez
Title: Business Director **Company:** Titan Technologies International **Address:** 9001 Jameel Road, Suite 180, Houston, TX 77040 United States **BUS:** Manufacturing Company **P/S:** Torque Products **MA:** International **D/D/R:** International Business Development for Latin America **H/I/S:** Golfing, Playing Piano **EDU:** Master's Degree in International Business Management, Earned in Mexico **C/VW:** Lions Club
Email: iramirez@titan.com

Thelma L. Ramirez
Title: Teacher **Company:** Lamar Consolidated Independent School District **Address:** 1811 Runaway Scrape Court, Richmond, TX 77469 United States **BUS:** Public School District **P/S:** Education for Low-Income and At-Risk Children **MA:** Local **D/D/R:** Teaching Dual Languages, Instructing Students in Bilingual Studies **H/I/S:** Spending Time with Family, Reading, Exercising, Gardening, Archaeology, Volunteering **EDU:** Associate Degree, Dominican College of Houston; Bachelor's Degree, University of Houston; Master's Degree, University of Houston **A/A/S:** Texas Association for Bilingual Education; Texas Classroom Teachers Association

Nora Ramirez-Shoultz
Title: President **Company:** Naradex Enterprises **Address:** 283 Chimney Rock, Beaumont, CA 92223 United States **BUS:** Real Estate **P/S:** Real Estate **MA:** Regional **D/D/R:** Buying and Selling Real Estate Properties Including Condominiums **H/I/S:** Growing Flowers, Traveling, Reading, Landscaping in the Community **EDU:** Bachelor of Science in Biology, Earned in Puerto Rico; Ordained Non-Denominational Minister, Lighthouse Madonna Ministry **A/A/S:** Beta Beta Beta; California Association for Medical Laboratory Technology; American Society for Microbiology; American Investors Network **C/VW:** Colina Hospital
Email: noraschoultz@yahoo.com

Alex Ramos
Title: Owner **Company:** Ramos Maintenance Service, Inc. **Address:** 12022 Hemlock Avenue, Brookwood, AL 35444 United States **BUS:** Construction Company **P/S:** Commercial and Residential Construction **MA:** National **D/D/R:** Painting, Sheetrock Repair, Working on New and Existing Homes **H/I/S:** Spending Time with his Family and Friends **A/A/S:** Home Builders Association of Alabama **C/VW:** Local Schools, Salvation Army, Local Soccer Team
Email: zanjon@bellsouth.net

Crisabel T. Ramos, RN, BSHCM
Title: Outpatient Consult Review Nurse **Company:** Naval Medical Center **Address:** 7248 Zest Street, San Diego, CA 92139 United States **BUS:** Military Health System Department of the Navy **P/S:** Managed Care Nursing, Utilization Review **MA:** San Diego County **D/D/R:** Utilization Review, Managing Outpatient Referrals, Military Health System **H/I/S:** Movies, Karaoke, Singing, Walking **EDU:** Bachelor of Science Degree in Healthcare Management, Southern Illinois University (2003); Nurse Educator, University of California, San Diego (2001); RN Diploma, Baguio General Hospital School of Nursing (1974) **CERTS:** Certified Managed Care Nurse; Certified Professional Utilization Review; Certified Professional Coder **A/A/S:** Community Service Award, PNASD (2005); Philippine Nurses Association, San Diego; American Association of Managed Care Nurses; American Academy of Professional Coders; Baguio General Hospital School of Nursing Alumni Association of Southern California
Email: crisabelr@yahoo.com
URL: http://www.nmcsd.med.navy.mil

Matt Ramos
Title: Photographer Studio Owner **Company:** Matt Ramos Photography, LLC **Address:** 1720 Guilderland Avenue, Schenectady, NY 12306 United States **BUS:** Professional Photography **P/S:** Commercial, Corporate, Portraits, Weddings Wedding planning **MA:** Regional **D/D/R:** General Photography (Most Known For Weddings), Presentations, Album Design, Training and Workflow **H/I/S:** Photography, Sports, Cars, Computers **EDU:** Coursework in Computer Science, University of Maryland As Well As Various Photography-Type Seminars. **A/A/S:** Top Ranked Wedding Photographer in the NY Capital Region; Professional Photographers of America; Wedding & Portrait Photographers International, Better Business Bureau
Email: matt@mattramosphotography.com
URL: http://www.mattramosphotography.com

Maricela A. Ramos-Rodriguez
Title: Spanish Instructor, Interpreter **Company:** United States Army **Address:** Fort Bragg, Fayetteville, NC 28310 United States **BUS:** Government **P/S:** Security on an International Level **MA:** International **D/D/R:** Commercial Law and Spanish Language Instruction for Special Operations in the United States Army **H/I/S:** Traveling, Keeping Fit, Running, Watching Movies **EDU:** Master in Commercial Law, Université Paris Sorbonne, France; Bachelor's Degree in Criminal Law, Pontificia Universidad Catolica Madre y Maestra, Dominican Republic **A/A/S:** Catholic Church
Email: maricela-rodriguez@hotmail.com
URL: http://www.cambridgewhoswho.com

Marcia J. Ramsay
Title: Broker Company: Windermere Investor Address: 609 E. Jackson Street, Medford, OR 97504 United States BUS: Real Estate Firm P/S: Residential and Commercial Property Sales MA: Local D/D/R: Overseeing Commercial Investments, Marketing Residential Properties Including Ranches and Farms, High-End River Homes, Land and Commercial Property H/I/S: Sailing, Fishing, Outdoor Activities EDU: Diploma, High School Education CERTS: Certified Residential Investor; Certified Residential Specialist; Licensed Graduate Real Estate Institute
Email: marcia@imrealestate.com
URL: http://www.windermere.com

Paul Ramseur II
Title: Vice President Company: Siemens Financial Services, Inc. Address: 170 Wood Avenue, South Iselin, NJ 08830 United States BUS: Financial Company P/S: Commercial Financial Services MA: International EXP: Mr. Ramseur's area of expertise is in risk management. H/I/S: Spending Time with his Family, Playing Sports Including Football EDU: JD, Syracuse University; Bachelor of Arts in Telecommunications Management, Howard University A/A/S: Equipment Leasing and Finance Association C/VW: Board of Directors, March of Dimes
Email: paul.ramseur@siemens.com
URL: http://www.cambridgewhoswho.com

Nancy I. Ramsey
Title: Secretary Company: Southeastern Community College Address: 1500 W. Agency Road, West Burlington, IA 52655 United States BUS: Institution of Higher Education P/S: Lifelong Learning Opportunities, Innovative Responsive Programs and Services, Promotes Professional, Personal, Social and Economic Development MA: Regional D/D/R: Handling Administrative Duties in the Finance Department Including Accounts Receivable, Handling Federal Funds and working with students in the federally funded program of Trio called Student Support Services H/I/S: Bowling, Crafts, Boating EDU: Associate of Arts, Southeastern Community College, West Burlington, Iowa (2006) A/A/S: Southeastern Community College Alumni Association; ISEA ESA Excellence Award, National Education Association; Education Support Professionals (2006)
Email: nramsey@wildblue.net
URL: http://www.scciowa.edu

Mary B. Randall
Title: President of Offices in Edwards and Vail, Colorado Company: Millennium Bank Address: 2111 N. Frontage Road W., Suite A, Vail, CO 81657 United States BUS: State Chartered Bank P/S: Financial Services Including Brokerage, Leasing, Insurance, Consumer Real Estate and Settlement Services MA: Regional D/D/R: Developing Products, Overseeing Trust Operations, Distributing Proxies, managing bank and financial operations, marketing and overseeing administrative duties H/I/S: Skiing, Hiking, Watching the Qi Chong EDU: Master of Business Administration, Northwestern University, IL (1993) A/A/S: President, Founder, Shaw Outreach Team A/H: Banker of the Year Award, Independent Bankers of Colorado (2003)
Email: maryr@millenniumprivatebank.com
URL: http://www.mymillenniumbank.com

Neva C. Randolph
Title: Manager of Cardiopulmonary Care Company: Scott Memorial Hospital Address: 1430 N. Gardner Street, Scottsburg, IN 47170 United States BUS: Hospital P/S: Healthcare MA: Countywide D/D/R: Managing Neurology, Cardiology and Respiratory Departments and Sleep Labs H/I/S: Quilting, Scrap Booking, Spending Time with her Grandchildren EDU: Bachelor of Science in Health Sciences, California College A/A/S: AART; ASSET C/VW: United Way, Various Community Events
Email: neva.randolph@smh1.org

Debra Rangel
Title: Literacy Specialist Company: Bullock Elementary School Address: 3909 Edgewood Drive, Garland, TX 75042 United States BUS: Elementary School P/S: Primary Education MA: Local D/D/R: Teaching Kindergarten through Fifth-Grade Reading, Teaching Reading Fluency and Comprehension Strategies in Spanish to Kindergarten through 2nd-Grade Students, Teaching TAKS and Comprehension Strategies to Third through Fifth-Grade Students H/I/S: Traveling EDU: Bachelor of Arts in Interdisciplinary Studies, Texas A&M University, Commerce (1999) A/H: Exemplary Leadership Award, United States Department of Education (2003-2004) C/VW: Garland Independent School District
Email: cypres1215@aol.com

Chris Ransom
Title: Consulting Engineer Company: AmerenUE Address: 34 Thrasher Court, Saint Charles, MO 63303 United States BUS: Electric Utility Company P/S: Relay Protection, Automated Relay Testing MA: Local D/D/R: Relay Protection, Automated Relay Testing H/I/S: Playing Basketball and Softball EDU: Bachelor of Science in Electrical Engineering, University of Missouri; Bachelor of Arts, Roll Phelps County University of Missouri (1981) A/A/S: Institute of Electrical and Electronics Engineers; Missouri Society of Professional Engineers C/VW: United Methodist Church
Email: ctransom@sbcglobal.net

Hema K. Rao
Title: Executive Director Company: Harita TVS Technologies, Inc. Address: 165 Kirts Boulevard, Suite 600, Troy, MI 48084 United States BUS: Engineering Design Company P/S: Automotive, Industrial Equipment and Energy Solutions and Networking Domains MA: International D/D/R: Engineering Design Services EDU: Pursuing Master of Business Administration in Engineering A/A/S: Society of Automotive Engineers
Email: k.hemarao@haritatvs.com
URL: http://www.haritatvs.com

Susana Galicia Rapido
Title: Designer Company: Susana Galicia Rapido Address: 1332 Woolner Avenue, Fairfield, CA 94533 United States BUS: Architecture and Structural Engineering Design Firm P/S: Architectural and Structural Design Services MA: Regional D/D/R: overseeing residential and commercial architectural design services H/I/S: Gardening EDU: Master's Degree in Structural Engineering, University of the Philippines A/A/S: Philippine Institute of Civil Engineers; American Society of Civil Engineers
Email: jsconstruction@gmail.com
URL: http://www.cambridgewhoswho.com

Karolina Rasa
Title: Interim Co-Executive Director Company: The Maurer Foundation for Breast Health Education Address: 114 Old Country Road, Suite 400, Mineola, NY 11501 United States BUS: Nonprofit Organization P/S: Breast Health Education and Training Programs MA: International D/D/R: conducting breast health education programs, evaluating and overseeing the management EDU: Master's Degree in Community Health Education, Adelphi University (2007); Bachelor of Arts in Communication, St. John's University (2002) A/A/S: National Breast Cancer Coalition; American Public Health Association; American Society for Training and Development
Email: karolinarasa@aol.com
URL: http://www.cambridgewhoswho.com

Christina M. Rasiewicz
Title: 1) Social Worker 2) Adjunct Professor Company: 1) New Jersey Department of Law and Public Safety 2) Brookdale Community College Dept: 1) Juvenile Justice Commission Address: P.O. Box 585, Farmingdale, NJ 07727 United States BUS: Government Agency P/S: Law Enforcement and Public Safety Including Juvenile Detention, Probation and Court Services MA: Regional D/D/R: Screening Residents, Preparing Social Histories for Diagnostic and Rehabilitative Purposes, Co-Facilitating the Planning and Implementation of Program Design, Acting as a Co-Chairwomen at HOC Treatment Teams, Mentoring, Supervising Clinical Internship Programs, Mentoring, Coordinating and Planning Meetings, Leading Champion Team, Hiring, Conducting Statewide Training Program on Curriculum, Acting as a Social Security Liaison as well Bloodbourne Pathogens Representative, Consulting, Lecturing, Teaching Sociology and Intercultural Communications H/I/S: Artwork, Listening to Music, Traveling EDU: Master of Social Work, Columbia University; Master of Business Administration, Fairleigh Dickinson University; Bachelor's Degree in Social Work, Georgian Court College; Bachelor's Degree in Sociology, Georgian Court College CERTS: Certified Police Training Commission Instructor (2008); Certified School Social Worker; Certified Disaster Response Crisis Counselor, State of New Jersey; Certified Child Behavioral Health Services Needs Assessment Screener; Certified Human Participant Researcher, National Institutes of Health; Certified Life Skills Instructor; Certified Life Skill Instructor A/A/S: Zeta Nu Chapter, Phi Alpha; American Scholars National Honor Society A/H: Mayoral Proclamation, Lakewood, NJ; Community Service Leadership Award, Georgian Court College
Email: cstarr619@yahoo.com
URL: http://www.cambridgewhoswho.com

Vicki J. Raspa
Title: Real Estate Broker Owner Company: SunQuest Realty Address: Tampa, FL 33603 United States BUS: Full Service Brokerage P/S: Quality Real Estate Services in Residential and Commercial properties including Single Family New Construction, Luxury, Waterfront, Multi-Family and Condominium. MA: International D/D/R: Directing Sales, Marketing, Financing and Administration H/I/S: Fitness, Running, Cycling, Outdoors EDU: Bachelor's Degree in Economics, University of Ottawa, Canada (1985) A/A/S: National Association of Realtors; Florida Association of Realtors; Greater Tampa Association of Realtors; GTAR International Council; National Association of Mortgage Brokers; Florida Association of Mortgage Brokers, West Coast Chapter; RECS
Email: Vicki@FloridaSunSearch.com
URL: http://www.FloridaSunSearch.com

Mr. William B. Ratcliff
Title: Owner, Private Investigator Company: Cape Fear Investigative Services, Inc. Address: 401-C Chestnut Street, Wilmington, NC 28401 United States BUS: Licensed Investigative Agency Serving the Wilmington, North Carolina Area P/S: Full Range of Private Investigation Services to the Legal Profession, Government Agencies, Insurance Companies, Small Businesses Homicides and Private Individuals MA: Regional D/D/R: Running All Aspects of the Business H/I/S: Football, Dolphins Fan A/A/S: North Carolina Association of Private Investigators; NAPIS; Profiled in Wilmington State (2006)
Email: bill@capefearinvestigative.com
URL: http://www.capefearinvestigative.com

Pamela Sue Rathke
Title: Teacher Company: Ridgeview High School Address: 202 E. Wood Street, Colfax, IL 61728 United States BUS: High School P/S: Education MA: Local D/D/R: Teaching Art, Photography and Graphic Design H/I/S: Spending Time with her Children, Educating Teachers, Making Regional Office Presentations EDU: 39 Credits of Postgraduate Coursework; Bachelor of Fine Arts in Art, Illinois Wesleyan University A/A/S: Illinois Education Association; Illinois Art Education Association; Nominee, Illinois Teacher of the Year (2004) C/VW: Adopt-A-Family
Email: prathke@ridgeview19.org
URL: http://www.ridgeview19.org

Mildred J. Ratzloff
Title: Executive Director, Community Liaison Company: Pregnancy Care Center Connection Address: 510 East Washington Boulevard, Crescent City, CA 95531 United States BUS: Crisis Pregnancy Center, Resource Center P/S: Pregnancy center Preschool, Daycare, Family Resource Center, Conferences, Training with Nonprofit agencies MA: Local/Regional D/D/R: Education, Social Work, Nonprofit, Public Speaking H/I/S: Photography, Traveling EDU: Bachelor's Degree in History and Political Science; California Baptist University; Pepperdine University; Simpson College CERTS: Teaching Credentials, Pre-K through Adult A/A/S: NorthCoast Baptist Association, Women's Director; Del Norte County Vice-President Local Childcare Planning Council; Del Norte County Economic Development-Education/Workforce Cluster; Del Norte County Ministerial Alliance-Publicity; Crescent City Business and Professional Women; Heart Call Speaker on Women's Issues C/VW: Disabled American Veterans, American Cancer Society
Email: eaglevizzion@yahoo.com
URL: http://www.cambridgewhoswho.com

Peter J. Rauen
Title: Director, Sales Specialist Company: US Food Service Address: 11955 E. Peakview Avenue, Centennial, CO 80111 United States BUS: Food Service Distribution Company P/S: Food and Non-Food Product Sales, Marketing Services for Restaurants, Hotels and Hospital MA: National D/D/R: Food Preparation, Sales H/I/S: Playing Golf, Fishing EDU: Coursework, University of Colorado A/A/S: American Culinary Federation C/VW: Denver Children's Home
Email: peterrauen@comcast.net
URL: http://www.cambridgewhoswho.com

Ms. Patricia M. Raven
Title: Owner, Manager, Stylist **Company:** Town & Country Beauty Salon **Address:** 10005 N. Raven Road, Hayward, WI 54843 United States **BUS:** Beauty Salon and Skin Treatment **P/S:** Spa and Beauty Care Services, Microderm Facial Machine that Removes Dead Skin and Rejuvenates Without Scarring and Scraping **MA:** Regional **EXP:** Ms. Raven's expertise includes salon management and skin care treatments in oxygen botanical and oxygen mineral lines. **D/D/R:** Managing Hair Care Services Including Permanent Coloring and Cutting, Overseeing Spa Services Including Pedicures and Acrylic and Gel Nails, Performing Facials, Tanning, Waxing, Offering Special Non-Invasive Microdermabrasion Skin Care through the SkinBella System **H/I/S:** Photography, Making Jewelry, Kayaking, Canoeing, Boating, Scrapbooking, Exercising, Traveling **CERTS:** Certified Cosmetologist, Accredited School of Cosmetology and Beauty Culture (1970) **A/A/S:** Curves Fitness Club; National Cosmetology Association; National Health and Wellness Club; Fashion Group International **C/VW:** American Cancer Society; Breast Cancer Research Organization, Participate and Contribute to many community benefits.
Email: praven@cheqnet.net
URL: http://www.townandcountryspa.com

Lynette Irene Rawlings
Title: Owner **Company:** Rawlings Concessions **Address:** P.O. Box 1096, Atwater, CA 95301 United States **BUS:** Food Services Company **P/S:** Food Concession Stands for Fairs and Events **MA:** Regional **EXP:** Ms. Rawlings' expertise is in food service management. **H/I/S:** Collecting Classic Cars **EDU:** College Coursework **A/A/S:** Outdoor Amusement Business Association; Western Fairs Association; NICA **C/VW:** Various Charitable Organizations
Email: goombah@elite.net

Jackie L. Ray
Title: Sales Manager **Company:** Omni Corpus Christi Hotel **Address:** 900 N. Shoreline Boulevard, Corpus Christi, TX 78401 United States **BUS:** Hotel **P/S:** Food and Hospitality Service **MA:** International **EXP:** Ms. Ray's area of expertise is in sales. **D/D/R:** negotiating, imparting training on convention services and business development, supervising entertainment activities and considering government issues **H/I/S:** Spending Time with her Family, Reading, Traveling **EDU:** Coursework, Western Texas College **A/A/S:** Society of Government Meeting Professionals; Executive Women International **C/VW:** Family Outreach of Corpus Christi
Email: jray@omnihotels.com
URL: http://www.omnihotels.com

Sylvian R. Ray
Title: Professor of Computer Science **Company:** University of Illinois **Address:** 201 N. Goodwin Avenue, Urbana, IL 61801 United States **BUS:** University **P/S:** Research **MA:** National **D/D/R:** Neural Networks **H/I/S:** Reading **EDU:** Ph.D. in Electrical Engineering, University of Illinois **A/A/S:** International Neural Network Society
Email: ray@cs.uiuc.edu
URL: http://www.cambridgewhoswho.com

Carole L. Rayes
Title: Senior Portfolio Manager **Company:** Harris Bank **Address:** 6720 N. Scottsdale Road, Suite 111, Scottsdale, AZ 85253 United States **BUS:** Bank **P/S:** Wealth Management **MA:** International **D/D/R:** Portfolio Management **H/I/S:** Playing Tennis, Maintaining Physical Fitness and Wellness **EDU:** Master of Business Administration, Arizona State University; Bachelor's Degree in Business Administration, Arizona State University **A/A/S:** Industry-Related Affiliations; Internal Awards for Going Above and Beyond the Call of Duty **C/VW:** Susan G. Komen Race for the Cure
Email: carole.christakis@harrisbank.com
URL: http://www.harrisbank.com

Renée M. Raymundo
Title: Educator **Company:** Public Schools of the Tarrytowns **Dept:** Washington Irving School **Address:** 103 S. Broadway, Tarrytown, NY 10591 United States **BUS:** Elementary School **P/S:** Education Including Writing Workshops, Enrichment Programs **MA:** Local **D/D/R:** teaching all subjects, conducting summer school, and after-school programs **H/I/S:** Dancing, Exercising, Scrapbooking **EDU:** Master of Education in Early Childhood and Elementary Education, The College of New Rochelle (2004); Bachelor of Arts in Communication, Fordham University (1996) **A/A/S:** Discipline Committee; Curriculum Coordinator, Fine Art Committee **C/VW:** St. Mary's Church; The Salvation Army
Email: rraymundo@tufsd.org
URL: http://www.cambridgewhoswho.com

Kathy I. Razavi
Title: Realtor **Company:** Century 21 Alliance **Address:** 1528 S El Camino Real, San Mateo, CA 94402 United States **BUS:** Real Estate Broker **P/S:** Residential, Executive, BayView Homes, Condos, TownHomes, Gulf Homes **MA:** National **D/D/R:** Residential, Condos, Commercial, Shopping Centers, Office Buildings **H/I/S:** Painting, Decorating **EDU:** Bachelor of Science in Business Administration, Nova Southeastern University **A/A/S:** California Association of Realtors, National Association of Realtors
Email: kathy.razavi@century21.com

Brenda Ready
Title: Owner **Company:** A Better Buzz LLC **Address:** 8914 Aurora Avenue N., Seattle, WA 98103 United States **BUS:** Cafe **P/S:** Biker-Friendly Espresso Bar, Deli, Free Wi-Fi Games, Megaforce Games, Pool Table and Pin Ball Machine, Open Mic Nights, Live Music **MA:** Regional **D/D/R:** managing operations and promotions, marketing, contacting motorcycle clubs to encourage patronage, supervising and training staff **H/I/S:** Gardening, Motorcycling, Flying Air Planes **EDU:** College Coursework **A/A/S:** Board Member, Alcoholics Anonymous; Boys & Girls Clubs of King County **C/VW:** Sponsor, Local Baseball Team
Email: brendaready@aol.com

Jo Ann Ream
Title: Consultant **Company:** Pepsico Business Solutions Group **Address:** 5600 Headquarters Drive, Plano, TX 75024 United States **BUS:** Manufacturing, Food and Beverage Consumer Goods **P/S:** Pepsico and Frito Lay Products **MA:** National **D/D/R:** Software Quality Assurance, Project Management, Supervising Employees, Software Questions and Answers, Ensuring Software is Up to Date and Upgrades Training as Needed **H/I/S:** Movies, Reading, Traveling **EDU:** Bachelor's Degree in Education, University of Texas, Arlington (1975); Master's Degree in Software Design and Development, Texas Christian University (1986) **A/A/S:** Justin United Methodist Church; Joy Circle Member; Community Involvement
Email: JoAnn.Ream@pbsg.com

André Reams
Title: President and Chief Executive Officer **Company:** Essential Momentum Group, Inc. **Address:** 7477 W. Lake Mead Boulevard, Unit 170, Las Vegas, NV 89128 United States **BUS:** Management Company **P/S:** Corporate Projects, Personal Management and Consulting Including Creative Facilitation **MA:** International **EXP:** Mr. Reams' expertise includes project creation, execution and management. **H/I/S:** Reading Science Fiction, Sailing, Photography **C/VW:** Enrich Amerifund
Email: dzmc@juno.com
URL: http://www.cambridgewhoswho.com

Jessica S. Reardon
Title: High School and Junior High Physical Education Teacher, Assistant Volleyball Coach, Head Basketball Coach **Company:** Winchester High School **Address:** P.O. Box 451, Benson, IL 61516 United States **BUS:** High School **P/S:** Education **MA:** Regional **D/D/R:** Physical Education and Development on the Secondary Level, Coaching Volleyball and Basketball **H/I/S:** Gardening, Traveling, Keeping Fit, Spending Time with her Dog **EDU:** Pursuing Master's Degree; Bachelor of Science in Physical Education and Teaching, Eureka College; Several Teaching Endorsements **A/A/S:** National Fastpitch Coaches Association; IFT; American Alliance for Health, Physical Education, Recreation and Dance **C/VW:** Special Olympics, Eureka College Alumni
Email: ilearnbyteaching@yahoo.com

Lewis Paul Reavis
Title: Minister of Music/Educator **Company:** Live Oak First Baptist Church **Address:** 11560 Toepperwein Road, San Antonio, TX 78233 United States **BUS:** Church **P/S:** Ministry/Offering Professional Education, I 35 Live Quartet **MA:** Local **D/D/R:** Choir Direction/Soloist **H/I/S:** Tennis **EDU:** Bachelor of Science in Music, LaMar University; Master of Religious Education, South Western Baptist Theological Seminary **A/A/S:** Texas Choral Association, Texas Music Education Association

Mr. Samuel Recenello
Title: Chief Financial Officer **Company:** Aegis Media Americas-Carat Americas **Address:** 3 Park Avenue, 32nd Floor, New York, NY 10016 United States **BUS:** Media, Advertising, Entertainment, Public Accounting, Professional Services and Marketing Services. **P/S:** Earnings Performance, Balance Sheet Management, Operations, Leadership, Financial and Tax Strategy, Mergers and Acquisitions, Integration, Accounting, Compliance, and, Directorships, Professional Business Consulting Services. **MA:** National **D/D/R:** Managing Strategic Financial Planning, Mergers and Acquisitions, Integration, Financial Operations and Reporting, Information Technology, Financial Systems, Legal, Tax, Treasury, Human Resources, and Investor Relations in Public and Private Companies **H/I/S:** Outdoor Enthusiast, Amateur Chef. **EDU:** Bachelor of Science in Accounting, Kean University (1983) **CERTS:** Certified Public Accountant (1988) **A/A/S:** NYS Society of Certified Public Accountants; New Jersey Society of Certified Public Accountants; American Association of Advertising Agencies; American Institute of Certified Public Accountants; Financial Executives International
Email: samrecenello@gmail.com

Patricia B. Recker
Title: Biology Teacher **Company:** East Central Independent School District, East Central High School **Address:** 7173 FM 1638, San Antonio, TX 78263 United States **BUS:** High School **P/S:** Education **MA:** Local **D/D/R:** Teaching Ninth-Grade AP Biology **H/I/S:** Black and White Photography, Traveling **EDU:** Master's Degree in Biology, University of the Incarnate Word, San Antonio **CERTS:** Certification in Biology Education **A/A/S:** Texas Classroom Teachers Association; National Science Teachers Association; National Association of Biology Teachers; Science Teachers Association of Texas; Texas Association of Biology Teachers **C/VW:** Parent-Teacher-Student Association, Special Olympics
Email: patrecker@nisd.net
URL: http://www.cambridgewhoswho.com

Ronda L. Redden
Title: Strategic Planner **Company:** Oklahoma Gas and Electric **Address:** P. O. Box 321, Oklahoma City, OK 73101 United States **BUS:** Electric Utility Company **P/S:** Generator Assessment **MA:** Regional **D/D/R:** Various Projects and Studies on Resource Planner, Generation Assessment as Far as Out as 30 Years, Studies Current Future Needs **H/I/S:** Golf **EDU:** Bachelor of Science in Electrical Engineering, University of Oklahoma (1986) **A/A/S:** National Society of Professional Engineers
Email: reddenrl@oge.com
URL: http://www.oge.com

Eileen Alannah Reddy
Title: Teacher **Company:** Governor John Carver Elementary School **Address:** 3 Carver Square Boulevard, Carver, MA 02330 United States **BUS:** Public Elementary School **P/S:** Education for Third through Fifth-Grade Students **MA:** Regional **D/D/R:** Facilitating Fun Educational Programs to Help Students Prepare for State Examinations **H/I/S:** Cooking, Gardening **EDU:** Master of Education, Fitchburg State College (1994); Bachelor of Science in Early Childhood Education, Lesley University (1979) **A/A/S:** National Education Association; Massachusetts Teachers Association
Email: eileenreddy@yahoo.com
URL: http://www.carver.org/elementary_school/elementary.htm

Diana L. Redman
Title: Psychotherapist **Company:** Genesys Hillside Center **Address:** 8435 Holly Road, Grand Blanc, MI 48439 United States **BUS:** Mental Health Facility **P/S:** Outpatient Therapy for Adults, Adolescents and Children, Individual and Group Therapy, Psychiatry **MA:** Regional **D/D/R:** Leading Group Therapy, Developing Programs, Counseling Patients with Depression, Treating a Variety of Mental Illnesses **H/I/S:** Exercising, Dancing, Cross-Country Skiing, Boating, Fishing, Swimming, Art **EDU:** Master of Social Work, Michigan State University (1987); Bachelor's Degree in Psychology, Central Michigan University (1984) **CERTS:** Licensed Master Social Worker, Academy of Certified Social Workers **A/A/S:** National Association of Social Workers; American Academy of Medical Hypnoanalysts
Email: dianalou421@yahoo.com
URL: http://www.mhweb.org/midmichigan/genesys.htm

Gretchen Kris Reece
Title: President **Company:** Nutra Products, Inc. **Address:** 4376 Edinburg Court, Fairfield, CA 94534 United States **BUS:** Distribution Company **P/S:** Ingredient Supply, Nutraceutical Garlic, High Allicent Buffered Garlic, Comfortese-Antacid, Acqua Lite-Liquid and Powder Forms-Electrolyte **MA:** National **D/D/R:** overseeing product development, generating garlic supplements and distributing products **H/I/S:** Water Sports, Exercising, Skiing **EDU:** Bachelor of Science in History, University of California, Berkeley (1987)
Email: greece@nutraproductsinc.com
URL: http://www.nutraproductsinc.com

Dennis T. Reed
Title: Paramedic (Retired) **Company:** Nashville Fire Department-Paramedic/ALS Div. **Address:** 1417 Murfreesboro Road, Nashville, TN 37217 United States **BUS:** Fire Department **P/S:** Pre-Hospital Emergency Care **MA:** Local **D/D/R:** Healthcare, Mangement, EMS **H/I/S:** Stock Car Driving, Dirt Track Racing, Gardening **EDU:** Bachelor's Degree in Healthcare Administration-Human Resource Management, Warren National University (2007) **CERTS:** Certification in CPR Instruction, American Heart Association **A/A/S:** Board of Directors, Williamson County Res. Sq. **C/VW:** Elks Club, Rescue Squad
Email: dreed1195@bellsouth.net

Kathlyn L. Reed, Ph.D., OTR, MLIS
Title: Associate Professor **Company:** Texas Woman's University Houston Center **Address:** 6700 Fannin, Houston, TX 77030 United States **BUS:** University **P/S:** Higher Education **MA:** National **D/D/R:** Occupational Therapy **H/I/S:** Collects Playing Cards **EDU:** Bachelor of Science, University of Wisconsin; Master of Arts, Kansas University; Master of Library and Information Science, Western Michigan University, University of Oklahoma; Ph.D., University of Washington at Seattle **A/A/S:** American Occupational Therapy Association, Texas Occupational Therapy Association, World Federation of Occupational Therapists, Council for Exceptional Children, Medical Library Association, RESNA, Neurodevelopment Therapy Association, Associate Professor, Writes Text Books on Occupational Therapy, Physical Therapy and Speech Therapy

Naomi E. Coleman Reed
Title: Licensed Practical Nurse **Company:** Beckley Appalachian Regional Hospital, Inc. **Address:** 306 Stranaford Road, Beckley, WV 25801 United States **BUS:** Hospital **P/S:** Healthcare **MA:** Regional **D/D/R:** Nursing and Rehabilitation for Troubled Adolescents and Youth with Alcoholic Dependencies **H/I/S:** Making Ceramic Crafts, Freelance Artwork **CERTS:** Licensed Practical Nurse **A/A/S:** West Virginia Licensed Practical Nurse Association **C/VW:** American Red Cross
Email: info@cambrigdewhoswho.com

Vicki L. Reed
Title: Manager, Corporate Relationships **Company:** Renaissance **Address:** 6100 W. 96th Street, Suite 100, Indianapolis, IA 46278 United States **BUS:** Charitable Planning **P/S:** Charitable Trust Administration **MA:** National **D/D/R:** Managing Corporate Relationships, Contacting Broker Dealers, Maintaining Corporate Relationships **H/I/S:** Reading, Watching Movies, Spending Time with Family, Decorating **EDU:** Bachelor's Degree in Management, Ball State University **C/VW:** Dress for Success
Email: reedvl@comcast.net
URL: http://www.charitabletrust.com

Mark D. Reede
Title: President **Company:** Reede's Custom Curb LLC **Address:** 5906 Hilgemann Street, Weston, WI 54476 United States **BUS:** Landscape, Lawncare **P/S:** Decorative Concrete **MA:** Regional **D/D/R:** Running the Company, Overseeing Operations and Management, Estimating and Installing, Billing, Overseeing Three Employees, Performing Seasonal Work, Installing Decorative Concrete Edging **H/I/S:** Golf, Fishing, Boating, Skiing, Snow Mobiling **EDU:** License Airframe and Power Plant **A/A/S:** Wausau Builders Association, Knights of Columbus Mosinee Area Chamber, Marshfield Area Chamber GOLDEN SANDS BUILDER ASSOCIATION.
Email: reedescustomcurb@charter.net
URL: http://www.reedescustomcurb.com

Mrs. Anita D. Reedy
Title: Activity Director **Company:** Community Care Health Services **Address:** 144 Washington Road, Edgewater, MD 21037 United States **BUS:** Healthcare Center **P/S:** Healthcare **MA:** Regional **D/D/R:** Developing Programs for Residents to Improve the Quality of their Life, Assisting Residents, Managing Sensory Activities **H/I/S:** Painting, Collecting Angels **EDU:** Coursework, Anne Arundel Community College **CERTS:** Licensed Geriatric Nurse Assistant; Certified Activity Director **A/H:** Morris Hechtlinger Memorial Certificate of Honor
Email: anita.reedy@cwwemail.com
URL: http://www.cambridgewhoswho.com

Beth A. Reeseman
Title: Medical Technologist **Company:** University of Pittsburgh Medical Center **Address:** 200 Lothrop Street, Pittsburgh, PA 15213 United States **BUS:** Integrated Nonprofit Healthcare System Affiliated with the University of Pittsburgh Schools of the Health Sciences **P/S:** Healthcare Services for Local Residents **MA:** Regional **D/D/R:** Analyzing Body Fluids, Working in Hematology and Chemistry, Conducting Laboratory Testing to Find Patient Diagnosis' **H/I/S:** Weight Training, Singing, Gardening **EDU:** Bachelor of Science, La Roche College (1989) **A/A/S:** Institute of Children's Literature
Email: beth1205@alltel.net

Dennis John Reeve
Title: CAD Administrator **Company:** Jacobs Engineering **Address:** 2600 Federal Avenue, Everett, WA 98201 United States **BUS:** Paper Manufacturer **P/S:** Pulp and Paper Manufacturing **MA:** Local **D/D/R:** Specializing in Overseeing the Historic Database of Records that Pertains to the Design Team Regarding Auto Cam Applications and Hybrid Documents, Also Makes Sure Archive Practices Adhere to Standards **EDU:** Clover Park College, Certificate in Machine Design (1987) **A/A/S:** New Beginnings Inner City Church Where he Supports Many Missions, Served in the US Army for Three and a Half Years
Email: dennis.reeve@jacobs.com

Kimberly K. Reeves
Title: Production Coordinator **Company:** Varsity Spirit Fashions **Address:** 6745 Lenox Center Court, Suite 300, Memphis, TN 38115 United States **BUS:** Manufacturing Company **P/S:** Uniforms for Cheerleaders, Dance Team and Booster Club **MA:** National **D/D/R:** Helping Manufacturers, Acting as a Liaison between Contractors and the Manufacturer, producing cheerleading apparel, scheduling production programs **H/I/S:** Spending Time with her Family **EDU:** Bachelor of Arts in Spanish, Middle Tennessee State University (1999) **A/A/S:** National Association for Female Executives **C/VW:** Second Baptist Church
Email: kreeves@varsityspirit.com
URL: http://www.varsity.com

Shirlee J. Reeves
Title: Nurse Manager, Intensive Care Unit **Company:** Central Arkansas Veterans Healthcare System John L. McClellan Memorial Veterans Hospital **Address:** 4300 W. Seventh Street, Little Rock, AR 72205 United States **BUS:** Healthcare **P/S:** General Medical Facility, Outpatient Clinics, Research Facilities, Broad Spectrum of Inpatient and Outpatient Healthcare Services Ranging from Disease Prevention through Primary Care, to Complex Surgical Procedures, to Extended Rehabilitative Care **MA:** Regional **D/D/R:** Charge Nurse for Medical Intensive and Coronary Care Unit, Managing Scheduling, Educational Staff Development and Proficiencies, Ensuring All Nurses have the Skills and Education Necessary to Perform their Jobs, Teaching Competency Skills Classes, Overseeing Safety Program and Gold Sharing Team, Checking on New Equipment and Ensuring Proficiency of Nurses on New Equipment **H/I/S:** NASCAR **EDU:** Bachelor of Science in Nursing and Biology, Southeastern Louisiana University (1994) **A/A/S:** Received Going the Extra Mile Award (2004); American Association of Nurses; Critical Care Journal Club; Critical Care Team; CPR Committee; Committee for Nursing Professional Standards Board; Leadership Committee; Nurse Recruiter Team
Email: reeves.shirlee@little-rock.med.va.gov
URL: http://www.geriatrics.uams.edu/clinical/CAVHS.asp

Christopher M. Regan
Title: Personal Trainer, Strength Coach **Company:** Advanced Training Principals **Address:** 271 Spruce Court, Bensalem, PA 19020 United States **BUS:** Fitness Center **P/S:** Yoga, Pilates, Kickboxing, Cardio Vascular Machinery, Weight Training Classes **MA:** Local **D/D/R:** training elderly with medical conditions, flexibility, strength and cardio vascular machines **EDU:** Bachelor's Degree in Sports Science, Temple University (2006) **A/A/S:** National Strength and Conditioning Association
Email: mrprez7883@yahoo.com
URL: http://www.cambridgewhoswho.com

Chantal Regibeau
Title: Chief Executive Officer **Company:** Laurel International **Address:** 3938 Old Hanover Road, Westminster, MD 21158 United States **BUS:** Consulting Firm **P/S:** Defense and Homeland Security Consultation **MA:** International **EXP:** Ms. Regibeau's expertise includes international marketing and sales management. **D/D/R:** Troubleshooting, Organizing Oil and Gas Trade Shows **H/I/S:** Reading, Swimming, Playing Tennis, Watching Movies, Listening to Music **EDU:** Bachelor's Degree in Conference Interpretation, Psychology Teaching, University of Mons, Belgium (1975)
Email: chantal.regibeau@laurelinternational.com
URL: http://www.laurelinternational.com

Linda R. Regulski
Title: Human Resources Manager **Company:** American Distribution, Inc. **Address:** 2 Brick Plant Road, South River, NJ 08882 United States **BUS:** Manufacturing Company **P/S:** Manufacturing and Distributing of Electronic Components **MA:** Local **D/D/R:** Supervising **H/I/S:** Reading, Making Crafts **EDU:** High School Diploma, Bayonne, NJ **A/A/S:** Honored Member, Former Den Leader, Boy Scouts of America
Email: lregulski@aol.com
URL: http://www.cambridgewhoswho.com

Felisha A. Reich
Title: Office Manager, Legal Assistant **Company:** Law Office of Jennifer P. Bierly **Address:** 315 S. Allen Street, Suite 416, State College, PA 16801 United States **BUS:** Law Firm **P/S:** Adoption, Divorce, Custody, Support, Guardianship, Children and Youth Services Child Protection Actions, Protection from Abuse Actions, Name Changes **MA:** Local **D/D/R:** Running the Office, Overseeing Customer Service, Volunteering as a Teacher's Assistant at Dale Carnegie **H/I/S:** Traveling, Reading, Working with Dogs **EDU:** Coursework, Dale Carnegie **A/A/S:** Chamber of Business and Industry of Centre County
Email: fdib@centrefamilylaw.com
URL: http://www.centrefamilylaw.com

Rae Ann Reichmuth
Title: President **Company:** Peninsula Parking, Inc. **Address:** 1139 San Carlos Avenue, Suite 304, San Carlos, CA 94070 United States **BUS:** Valet Parking Company **P/S:** Valet Parking Services, Parking Management, Traffic Control, Van Shuttle Services, Complete Insurance Coverage, Uniformed Attendants **MA:** Regional **D/D/R:** Overseeing Daily Operations, Organizing Parking Services for Special Events, Private Events and Political Fundraisers, Managing Valet Parking for Restaurants and Business Daily Valet Service, Overseeing Shuttle Service with Vans and Limousines **H/I/S:** Wave Boarding, Boating, Snowboarding, Traveling, Scrapbooking, Interior Home Remodeling **A/A/S:** San Carlos Chamber of Commerce; Better Business Bureau **C/VW:** Various Charities
Email: raeann@peninsulaparking.com
URL: http://www.peninsulaparking.com

Mr. David J. Reid
Title: Owner **Company:** Action Wolf Exteriors **Address:** 350 N. Draper Lane, Provo, UT 84601 United States **BUS:** Home Improvement Company for Commercial and Residential Structures **P/S:** Residential and Commercial Stucco, Stone and Brick Work, Siding, Hardy Planking **MA:** Regional **D/D/R:** Running the Day-to-Day Operations of the Business **EDU:** College Coursework, University of Puget Sound; Diploma, United States Military **A/A/S:** Served in the United States Army (Eight Years); SBA
Email: actionwolfexteriors1@yahoo.com
URL: http://actionwolfexteriors.tripod.com/

Romeo R. Reid
Title: HSE Coordinator **Company:** Conoco Phillips, Marine Division **Address:** 600 N. Dairy Road, Houston, TX 77079 United States **BUS:** Oil Company **P/S:** Health, Safety and Environmental Management **MA:** International **D/D/R:** Enforcing Company Protocols and Polices **H/I/S:** Reading, Participating in Outdoor Activities, Camping, Fishing **EDU:** Master of Business Administration, ITT Technical Institute at Indianapolis (2006); Bachelor's Degree in Marine Engineering, Massachusetts Maritime Academy (1992) **A/A/S:** U.S. Merchant Marine Officer; Unites States Propeller Club, Port of Boston; SNAME; National Technical Honor Society; The National Board of Boiler and Pressure Vessel Inspectors; PMI **C/VW:** Coach, Son's Soccer Team; Cub Scout Leader, Boy Scouts of America; Boston Latin School High School Alumni Association; Massachusetts Maritime Academy Alumni Association
Email: romeo.r.reid@conocophillips.com
URL: http://www.conocophillips.com

Elizabeth J. Reidy, RD
Title: Clinical Dietitian (Retired) **Company:** Kaiser Foundation Hospital **Address:** 450 Peralta Avenue, Long Beach, CA 90803 United States **BUS:** Hospital **P/S:** Healthcare **MA:** Regional **D/D/R:** Treating Gestational Diabetes Patients, Creating Individualized Menus for Patients **H/I/S:** Reading, Walking, Gardening, Watching Documentaries **EDU:** Internship, University of Michigan; Bachelor's Degree in Food and Nutrition, Minor in Chemistry, University of Oklahoma (1947) **A/A/S:** California Dietetic Association; American Dietetic Association **C/VW:** Covenant Presbyterian Church
Email: elizabeth.reidy@cwwemail.com

Audrey L. Reilly
Title: Administrative Assistant **Company:** Allegro Micro Systems, Inc. **Address:** 115 Northeast Cutoff, Worcester, MA 01606 United States **BUS:** Semiconductor Manufacturing Company **P/S:** Semiconductor Manufacturing **MA:** International **D/D/R:** Administration, Marketing **H/I/S:** Art, A-Capella Singing, Playing the Oboe, Woodcarving **EDU:** Pursuing Master of Business Administration in Economics and International Business, Nichols College; Bachelor's Degree in Liberal Arts, Assumption College; Associate Degree in Graphic and Visual Arts, Quinsigamond Community College **A/A/S:** American Society for Quality **C/VW:** American Cancer Society

Donald H. Reimann

Title: Director **Company:** Colliers Parrish International **Address:** 450 W. Santa Clara Street, San Jose, CA 95113 United States **BUS:** Industrial Real Estate Company **P/S:** Lease and Sale of Office and Industrial Property **MA:** National **D/D/R:** Office and Industrial Real Estate Brokerage and Consultation **H/I/S:** Playing Golf **EDU:** Master of Business Administration in Management Sciences, Bryant University (1976) **A/A/S:** Society of Industrial and Office Realtors **C/VW:** NAIOP
Email: dreimann@colliersparrish.com
URL: http://www.colliersparrish.com

Kimberly S. Reimschisel

Title: Registered Dental Hygienist **Company:** Stetzel Dental Group **Address:** 10010 Dupont Circle Court, Fort Wayne, IN 46825 United States **BUS:** Dentists Office **P/S:** Dental Care **MA:** Local **D/D/R:** All Office Responsibilities, Evaluations, All Services **H/I/S:** Playing Racquetball, Tennis and Dodgeball **EDU:** Associate Degree in Dental Hygiene, University of Indiana **A/A/S:** University of Indiana; Board Member, Cinema Center

Joann M. Reis, RN

Title: Associate Director **Company:** Pfizer, Inc. **Address:** 50 Pequot Avenue, New London, CT 06320 United States **BUS:** Pharmaceutical Company Committed to Helping People Improve their Health by Discovering and Developing Medicines **P/S:** Services in the Medical Sciences Field, Global Research of New Drugs, Discovers and Develops Medicines, Informs Consumers and Healthcare Providers about Medicines and the Medical Conditions they Treat **MA:** International **D/D/R:** Clinical Research in Diabetes and Pulmonary Condition Medications, Mentoring New Team Members, Answering Questions, Explaining Trial System to Doctors Offices Involved in Drug Studies and Trials, Gathering Information from other Groups in Company who are Working on the Same Project, Dealing with Medical and Scientific Issues with Drug Studies **H/I/S:** Reading, Motorcycle Riding, Grandchildren **CERTS:** Registered Nurse Certification, Joseph Lawrence School of Nursing (1970) **A/A/S:** Does Presentations at American Diabetes Association Meetings; Former Instructor in PERI Courses on Source Document Verification and On-Site Selection
Email: joann.m.reis@pfizer.com
URL: http://www.pfizer.com

Nicole A. Reisdorfer

Title: Account Manager **Company:** Allied Purchasing **Address:** 1334 18th Street S.W., Mason City, IA 50401 United States **BUS:** Purchasing Cooperative **P/S:** Purchasing for the Bottled Water, Dairy and Beverage Industries **MA:** National **D/D/R:** Accounting, Invoicing, Budgeting, Promoting Sales, Projections, Helping Customers **EDU:** Bachelor of Arts in History and Business, Buena Vista University **A/A/S:** international bottled water association; water quality association
Email: ntrousdale@alliedpurchsing.com

Sarah E. Reising

Title: Registered Nurse **Company:** St. Mary's Medical Center **Address:** 3700 Washington Avenue, Evansville, IN 47714 United States **BUS:** Hospital **P/S:** Outpatient and Inpatient Care **MA:** Local **D/D/R:** Working in the Newborn Nursery of the Hospital Aiding in taking Care of Well Baby, Assessments, Vital Signs, New Admission and Discharged **H/I/S:** Reading, Making Crafts **EDU:** Bachelor of Science in Nursing, University of Southern Indiana (2006); Associate Degree in Nursing, Ivy Tech State College, Evansville, Indiana (1999) **A/A/S:** 4H Club **C/VW:** Coaches the Local Youth Softball Team
Email: sarahreising@yahoo.com
URL: http://www.cambridgewhoswho.com

James L. Reissner

Title: Chief Executive Officer **Company:** Activar, Inc. **Address:** 7808 Creekridge Circle, Minneapolis, MN 55439 United States **BUS:** Manufacturing Company **P/S:** Metal and Plastic Products Including Fire Protection Products **MA:** National **D/D/R:** Managing Leadership and Finance, Overseeing Management **H/I/S:** Golfing, Boating, Hunting **EDU:** Master's Degree in Banking and Finance, Rutgers University; Bachelor in Business Administration, Macalester College **A/A/S:** National Association of Corporate Directors
Email: jim@activar.com
URL: http://www.activar.com

Mr. Michael V. Remer

Title: Director of Business Development **Company:** Barr Systems, LLC **Address:** 4500 N.W. 27th Avenue, Gainesville, FL 32606 United States **BUS:** Information Technology **P/S:** Computer Software, Hardware, Output Management, Communication Software and Hardware Solutions in Mainframe Environments **MA:** International **D/D/R:** Managing Major Accounts, Developing New Business, Offering Day-to-Day Management of Large Accounts Including IBM and Advaati **H/I/S:** Golfing, Cruising, Loves Working Out, Spending Time with his Granddaughter **EDU:** Bachelor's Degree in Electrical Engineering, Trent State College dba College of New Jersey (1976) **A/A/S:** International Electrical and Electronic Engineering Association
Email: mike.remer@barrsystems.com
URL: http://www.barrsystems.com

Cynthia Rendeiro-Lontrao

Title: Child Care Specialist **Company:** Pasco County Schools **Address:** 7227 Land O Lakes Boulevard, Land O Lakes, FL 34638 United States **BUS:** School District **P/S:** Education **MA:** Regional **D/D/R:** communicating with others and overseeing cultural activities **H/I/S:** Dancing, Attending the Theater **EDU:** Bachelor of Arts in Social Welfare, Adelphi University **A/A/S:** National School-Age Child Care Alliance; Florida Association of School Administrators; North Central Ohio Computer Cooperative; ENSACA **C/VW:** North Shore Animal League America
Email: crendeir@msn.com
URL: http://www.pasco.k12.fl.us

Sonny Renken

Title: Ambulance Coordinator, EMS Educator **Company:** Jersey Community Hospital **Address:** 400 Maple Summit Road, Jerseyville, IL 62052 United States **BUS:** Hospital Offering People-Focused Primary Care-Plus Stressing Preventative Services and Public Accountability **P/S:** Provides a Wide Array of Quality Healthcare Services Such as Obstetrics, Physical Therapy, Radiology, Inpatient and Outpatient Surgery, Emergency Medical Services and Community Health Education Programs, Among Many Others **MA:** Regional **D/D/R:** Pre-hospital Care, Training **H/I/S:** Spending time with his Four Grandchildren **CERTS:** Certified EMS Instructor **A/A/S:** National Association of EMTs; Bio-terrorism Team; Illinois Association of EMTs; Local Emergency Planning Committee; National Safety Council; Domestic Violence Council; American Ambulance Association
Email: srenken@jch.org
URL: http://www.jch.org

Debra S. Rennick

Title: Director of Radiology **Company:** Minnesota Valley Health Center **Address:** 621 S. Fourth Street, Le Sueur, MN 56058 United States **BUS:** Health Center **P/S:** Healthcare **MA:** Local **D/D/R:** Offering Radiology Services, Performing Managerial Duties, Ensuring Policy and Procedures and Occupational Safety and Health Administration Compliance **H/I/S:** Traveling, Spending Time with her Family **EDU:** Associate of Arts in Radiology, Argosy University **A/A/S:** Michigan Society of Radiologic Technologists; American Registry of Radiologic Technologists; Susan G. Komen Foundation **C/VW:** Saint Jude Children's Research Hospital
Email: mvhc@mvhc.org
URL: http://www.mvhc.org

Mildred E. Replogle

Title: Licensed Practical nurse **Company:** InteliStaf **Address:** 1810 Lakeland Hills Boulevard, Lakeland, FL 33805 United States **BUS:** Lower Correctional Facility **P/S:** Healthcare, Inmate Patient Care **MA:** Local **D/D/R:** Prison Nursing **EDU:** Licensed Practical Nurse Degree, Central Florida Community College
Email: dizzylady53@aol.com
URL: http://www.cambridgewhoswho.com

Bonnie J. Retalic

Title: Owner **Company:** K & B Excavating, Inc. **Address:** 915 Diplomat Drive, Suite 101F, Debary, FL 32713 United States **BUS:** Multifaceted Class V Fire Protection Contractor **P/S:** Installation of Underground Water Mains for Fire Line Piping, Ductile Iron and PVC, Backflow Preventers, Fire Hydrants, Post Indicator Valves, FDCs and All Related Appurtenances, Full Range of Earthwork **MA:** Regional **D/D/R:** Handling the Day-to-Day Operations of the Company Including Invoicing, Billing, Accounts Receivables and Payables, Scheduling, Purchasing, Job Costing, Customer Relations, Human Resources and Offering Job Estimates **H/I/S:** Gardening, Fishing, Boating **EDU:** Coursework in Business Administration, Broome Community College
Email: bonnie@knbexcavating.com
URL: http://www.knbexcavating.com

Shirley K. Retzlaff, RN, MSN

Title: Associate Professor **Company:** Bryan LGH College of Health Sciences **Address:** 1905 S. 148th Street, Walton, NE 68461 United States **BUS:** Education, Healthcare **P/S:** Educates Nursing Students, School of Nursing, School of Allied Health, School of Nurse Anesthesia, General Education Courses, Center for Advancing Nursing Practice **MA:** Regional **D/D/R:** Critical Care, Health Assessment, Issues Involving the Bachelor of Science in Nursing Program, Instructing and Teaching Nursing Students **H/I/S:** Watching Sporting Events **EDU:** Master of Science in Nursing, University of Nebraska Medical Center (1992) **A/A/S:** American Nurses Association; Nebraska Nurses Association; Sigma Theta Tau International; National League for Nursing; Nebraska League for Nursing
Email: sretzlaff@bryanlgh.org
URL: http://www.bryanlghcollege.org

Susan R. Reuter

Title: Owner **Company:** Nightingales Nursing Uniforms and Supplies **Address:** 129 S. Main Street, Bellefontaine, OH 43311 United States **BUS:** Healthcare Retailer **P/S:** Nursing Uniforms and Equipment **MA:** National **D/D/R:** Nursing and Equipments **H/I/S:** Reading **EDU:** Ohio Highpoint Vocation School, LPN
Email: nightingaleuniforms@hotmail.com

John D. ReVeal

Title: Partner **Company:** Powell Goldstein LLP **Address:** 901 New York Avenue N.W., Third Floor, Washington, DC 20001 United States **BUS:** Law Firm **P/S:** Legal Services **MA:** National **EXP:** Mr. ReVeal's area of expertise is in legal services. **D/D/R:** Overseeing the Regulation of Financial Institutions, Managing Mergers and Acquisitions **EDU:** JD, University of California, Berkeley; Joint Degree Program, Harvard Law School
Email: jreveal@pogolaw.com

Manuela Naidas Rex

Title: Staff Pharmacist **Company:** CVS Pharmacy **Address:** 1812 Valentine Avenue, Cleveland, OH 44109 United States **BUS:** Retail Pharmacy **P/S:** Prescription Medication for In-Store Pick-Up **MA:** National **D/D/R:** Building and Maintaining an Accurate Dispensing and Counseling Base for Patient Health **H/I/S:** Gardening, Music (Both Classical and Pop), Tennis **EDU:** Bachelor of Science in Pharmacy, University of the Philippines **CERTS:** License Holder, Ohio Pharmacist (1996); Certificate, Foreign Pharmacy Graduate Examination Commission (1987) **A/A/S:** Roman Catholic of St. Michael's Parish; Secretary, Holy Cross, Inc.; Household Head, Handmaids of the Lord; Certificate Holder, Disabled Veterans; Charitable Organizations
URL: http://www.cvs.com

Beatriz R. Reyelts

Title: First-Grade Teacher **Company:** Trinity Valley School **Address:** 7500 Dutch Branch Road, Fort Worth, TX 76132 United States **BUS:** Private School **P/S:** Education **MA:** Local **D/D/R:** Teaching Reading and Language Arts to First-Grade Students **H/I/S:** Reading, Watching Spanish Soap Operas **EDU:** Bachelor of Science, Plus 12, Texas State University **A/A/S:** National Education Association **C/VW:** Boys & Girls Clubs of Greater Fort Worth
Email: breyelts@charter.net

Rebeca G. Reyes

Title: Teacher **Company:** Martin High School **Address:** 2002 San Bernardo Avenue, Laredo, TX 78040 United States **BUS:** High School **P/S:** Education **MA:** Local **D/D/R:** Teaching Mathematics, Calculus **H/I/S:** Spending Time with her Family, Traveling, Reading **EDU:** Bachelor of Science in Mathematics, Texas Woman's University (1988) **A/A/S:** Association of Texas Professional Educators **C/VW:** Church
Email: rreyes4@sbcglobal.net

Dorothy L. Reyna

Title: Library Media Specialist **Company:** Elk City Public Schools, Grandview 5th and 6th Center **Address:** 800 N. Pioneer Road, Elk City, OK 73644 United States **BUS:** Middle School **P/S:** Education for Fifth and Sixth-Grade Students, Learning and Gifted Programs **MA:** Regional **D/D/R:** Managing Checkout and Returns, Teaching Library and Informational Skills Including the Dewey Decimal Classification System **H/I/S:** Drawing, Painting, Crocheting **EDU:** Master's Degree in Library Media, Southwestern Oklahoma State University (2000); Bachelor of Education, Southwestern Oklahoma State University (1997); National Teacher Certification
Email: dlreyna@itlnet.net
URL: http://www.elkcityschools.com/Grandview

Adelle M. Reynolds

Title: Building Commissioner **Company:** Town of Douglas **Address:** 29 Depot Street, Douglas, MA 01516 United States **BUS:** Municipal Government **P/S:** New Construction, Inspection **MA:** Local **D/D/R:** Building Construction **H/I/S:** Coach Soccer, Oktoberfest, Football, Time with Kids **EDU:** Associates in Building Construction, Yava Pai College **A/A/S:** Massachusetts Building, Construction and Inspection Association
Email: areynolds@douglasma.org

Carol Reynolds

Title: Director of Auxiliary Human Resources **Company:** 1) Carol J. Reynolds Personal Fitness Trainer 2) Bryan Independent School District **Address:** 1202 Todd Trail, College Station, TX 77845 United States **BUS:** 1) Fitness Company Committed to Offering Quality Services 2) School District Committed to Excellence in Elementary, Middle and High School Education **P/S:** 1) Fitness, Personal Training, Health and Wellness 2) Curriculum Development, Special Education, After-School Programs, Library and Media Services **MA:** Local **D/D/R:** Performing Human Resource Duties **H/I/S:** Biking, Former Runner **EDU:** Master's Degree in Exercise Physiology, Texas A&M University (1983) **CERTS:** Certified Personal Trainer **A/A/S:** BVHRMA; American Council on Exercise
Email: reynolds@bryanisd.org
URL: http://www.bryanisd.org

Geneva B. Reynolds
Title: Director of Special Education **Company:** South Central Community Services, Inc. **Address:** 7550 S. Phillips Avenue, Chicago, IL 60649 United States **BUS:** Social Service Agency **P/S:** Education, Day Treatment Programs for Third through 12th-Grade Students with Emotional and Behavioral Disorders **MA:** Regional **D/D/R:** Overseeing Treatment Programs, Assisting the Principal, Upholding State Requirements, managing school policies and procedures **H/I/S:** Attending the Theater, Participating in Church Activities **EDU:** Master's Degree in Educational Administration, Chicago State University (2000); Bachelor's Degree in Education, Chicago State University (1986) **A/A/S:** Council for Exceptional Children **C/VW:** Mount Pisgah Baptist Church
Email: mgm.reynolds@sbcglobal.net
URL: http://www.sccsinc.org

Ms. Hope Yvonne Reynolds
Title: Administrative Manager **Company:** Columbia University **Dept:** Department of Dermatology **Address:** 161 Fort Washington Avenue, New York, NY 10032 United States **BUS:** University **P/S:** Education **MA:** International **D/D/R:** Human Resources **H/I/S:** Playing Tennis **EDU:** Bachelor of Arts in Business Administration, Minor in Human Resources, Baruch College **A/A/S:** Society for Human Resource Management **C/VW:** Salvation Army
Email: hr9@columbia.edu

Mr. Kevin A. Reynolds, RCDD
Title: Project Manager **Company:** Baker Electric, Inc. **Dept:** Baker Cabling Systems **Address:** 111 Jackson Avenue, Des Moines, IA 50315 United States **BUS:** Contracting Company **P/S:** Electrical Services **MA:** Regional **EXP:** Mr. Reynolds' expertise is in project management. **D/D/R:** Managing Home Improvement Projects, consulting clients, designing and installing information transport and procurement systems **H/I/S:** Reading, Motorcycling **EDU:** High School Diploma **CERTS:** Registered Communications Distribution Designer, Building Industry Consulting Services International; Certified Trainer, Building Industry Consulting Services International **A/A/S:** Building Industry Consulting Services International
Email: kreynolds@bakerelectric.com
URL: http://www.bakerelectric.com

Melby Ed Reynolds Jr.
Title: Principal **Company:** Reynolds Inspections, Inc DBA Inspect it First **Address:** 1517 E Bluebird Court, Gilbert, AZ 85296 United States **BUS:** Real Estate Inspector **P/S:** Residential and Commercial Inspections **MA:** Local **D/D/R:** Management **H/I/S:** Computer Gaming **EDU:** Bachelor of Science, University of Phoenix, Granite Computer Institute **A/A/S:** LDS, FREA, BNI
Email: edreynolds@cox.net
URL: http://www.ereynoldsinspects.com

Stephen L. Reynolds
Title: Coordinator **Company:** Sumner Mental Health Center **Address:** 1601 W. 16th Street, Wellington, KS 67152 United States **BUS:** Behavioral Health Center **P/S:** Psychotherapy and Drug Addiction Counseling **MA:** Local **D/D/R:** Coordinating Programs for Adolescents and Adults with Drug Addictions and Post-Traumatic Stress Disorder and Depression, Oppositional Defiant Disorder, Traumas **H/I/S:** Teaching Martial Arts, Goju-Ryu and Karate, Crafting Stained Glass Lamps **EDU:** Pursuing Ph.D.; Master of Arts in Clinical Psychology, Wichita State University, Kansas (1977) **A/A/S:** Kansas Association of Addict Professionals
Email: sreynolds@sumnermentalhealth.org
URL: http://www.sumnermentalhealth.org

Ms. Sara G. Rheault, RN, BSN
Title: Registered Nurse **Company:** Mercy Medical Center **Dept:** Department of Nursing **Address:** 271 Carew Street, Springfield, MA 01102 United States **BUS:** Medical Center **P/S:** Healthcare **MA:** Regional **D/D/R:** caring for patients with chest tubes, postoperative pain, tracheotomy and with various types of respiratory problems **H/I/S:** Reading, Traveling, Shopping **EDU:** Bachelor of Science in Nursing, Saint Joseph College, CT (2006) **A/A/S:** Massachusetts Nurses Association
Email: srheault@sjc.edu
URL: http://www.mercycares.com/pages

Carlene Rhodes
Title: President **Company:** Brookwood Foster Care **Address:** 19696 S.W. Stacey Street, Aloha, OR 97006 United States **BUS:** Foster Care Home **P/S:** Foster Care Services **MA:** National **D/D/R:** ensuring quality foster care services for mentally disabled adults **H/I/S:** Painting, Racing Motocross, Spending Time with her Twin Daughters **CERTS:** License, University of Idaho **C/VW:** Volunteer, Mix and Mingle a Friendship
Email: hyland_subway@hotmail.com

David W. Rhodes
Title: Police Officer, K-9 Handler **Company:** Albemarle County Police Department **Address:** 1600 Fifth Street Extension, Charlottesville, VA 22902 United States **BUS:** Police Department **P/S:** Law Enforcement, State and Federal Laws, Comprehensive Crime Prevention **MA:** Regional **EXP:** Mr. Rhodes' expertise includes patrol and narcotics detection. **H/I/S:** Spending Time with his Family **EDU:** Coursework, Piedmont Virginia Community College **A/A/S:** Eastern Police Canine Association; Southern State Police Benevolent Association; Fraternal Order of Police; National Association of Professional Canine Handlers
Email: rhodesd@albemarle.org
URL: http://www.albemarle.org

Violet E. Rhodes, BA, M.Ed.
Title: Teacher **Company:** McIntosh County Academy **Address:** 200 Pine Street, Darien, GA 31305 United States **BUS:** High School **P/S:** Education for Sixth through Eighth-Grade Students **MA:** Regional **D/D/R:** Teaching Secondary Mathematics, Managing Homeroom, Offering Conflict Mediation, Assisting with Staff and Curriculum Development, Conducting Work Ethics Workshops, Head of Mathematics Department, Leadership Team for School Improvement **H/I/S:** Cooking **EDU:** Master of Arts in Secondary Education, Concentration in Mathematics, Troy University (2006); Bachelor of Arts in Sociology and Applied Relations, Eastern Connecticut State University (2003) **CERTS:** Certified Teacher of Gifted and Exceptional Children; Certification in Secondary Mathematics **A/A/S:** Lions Club; Jamaica Teachers Association; Teacher, Sunday School **C/VW:** Leukemia Lymphoma Society; Teenage Mother's Program at her Church
Email: violetrhodes@hotmail.com

Leonard R. Ricchiuti Jr.
Title: Executive Director **Company:** Albany Police Athletic League **Address:** 165 Henry Johnson Boulevard, Albany, NY 12210 United States **BUS:** Nonprofit Organization **P/S:** Juvenile Crime Prevention Program that Assists Approximately 4000 Children Annually **MA:** National **D/D/R:** Managing a staff of 15 and 700 Children a Week in After School Programs, Organization Management, Youth Services, Operations, Marketing, Financials, Public Speaking, Training **H/I/S:** Spending Time with his Family, Golfing, Playing Basketball **EDU:** Associate Degree in Criminal Justice, Hudson Valley Community College (1980) **A/A/S:** New York State Afterschool Coalition; National Association of School Resource Officers; Sons of Italy; Knights of Columbus; Board Member, National Association of Police Activities; Recipient, Jefferson Award, National Public Service Award; Police Officer of the Year; Award New York State Afterschool Coalition **C/VW:** Epilepsy Foundation; Special Olympics, U.S. Olympic Committee; National Law Enforcement Endowed Memorial; Local Youth Advocate, Little League Baseball, Board of Director Natiional Association of Police Athlete League
Email: lennyalbpal@nycap.rr.com
URL: http://www.albanypal.org

Brittany Renee Amos Rice
Title: Teacher **Company:** North Side Middle School **Address:** 300 Lawrence Street, Elkhart, IN 46514 United States **BUS:** Middle School **P/S:** Education **MA:** Local **D/D/R:** Teaching Mathematics to Middle School Students **H/I/S:** Scrapbooking, Photography **EDU:** Master of Education, Indiana University South Bend; Bachelor of Arts in Education, Adrian College **A/A/S:** National Council of Teachers of Mathematics; Local Union **C/VW:** Autism Society of America Foundation
Email: BrittanyReneeAmos.Rice@cwwemail.com

Jody D. Rice
Title: Resource Manager **Company:** Panola State Conservation **Address:** 2600 Highway 155, Southwest Stockbridge, GA 30281 United States **BUS:** State Park **P/S:** Outdoor Wilderness Education and Research **MA:** United States, Canada **D/D/R:** Technical Tree Climbing, Researching Primitive Skills, Training Staff **H/I/S:** Church, Traveling, Spending Time with Family and Friends **EDU:** Bachelor of Science in Special Education, Georgia Southwestern State University (2003); Bachelor of Science in Outdoor Therapy and Counseling, Georgia Southwestern State University (2002) **A/A/S:** National Association for Interpretation; Tree Climber Coalition; Association of Experienced Educators **C/VW:** Church, Boy Scouts of America
Email: jody_rice@dnrstate_ga.us
URL: http://www.cambridgewhoswho.com

Lois R. Rice
Title: Executive Vice President (Retired) **Company:** Wells Fargo **Address:** 333 S. Grand Avenue, Los Angeles, CA 90071 United States **BUS:** Bank **P/S:** Banking Services **MA:** International **EXP:** Ms. Rice's area of expertise is in her people management skills. **D/D/R:** Overseeing Division Managers, Retail Banking and All Business Operations, Integrating Offices, Initiating Projects **H/I/S:** Golfing, Fly Fishing, Cooking, Spending Time with her Grandchildren **EDU:** Diploma, Grossmont High School **A/A/S:** President, National Advisory Council, Gene Autry Western Heritage Museum; First Chairwoman, President, Junior Achievement, Los Angeles, CA; Board Member, West County Museum; Board Member, Thomas Rivera Center; Board Member, Los Angeles County Museum of Art; Los Angeles Sports Council; Los Angeles Area Chamber of Commerce; Ketchum Downtown Area, Young Men's Christian Association; Los Angeles Town Hall **A/H:** Albert Schweitzer Award (1997); Citizen of the Year Award, International Visitor's Council (1995); Banking Creative Retailer Award, City of Los Angeles (1995) **C/VW:** Local Community-Based Organizations; Autry National Center
Email: loisrice@aol.com
URL: http://www.cambridgewhoswho.com

Mrs. Shelly Cathryn Rice, Ed.S.
Title: Teacher **Company:** Magdalena Elementary School **Address:** 200 Duggins Drive, Magdalena, NM 87801 United States **BUS:** Elementary School **P/S:** Primary Education **MA:** Local **D/D/R:** overseeing professional development, teaching elementary education and English as a second language **H/I/S:** Swimming, Traveling, Walking, Spending Time with her Family **EDU:** Educational Specialist Degree in Administration, University of New Mexico; Master of Arts in English as a Second Language, University of New Mexico; Bachelor's Degree in Elementary Education, New Mexico State University **C/VW:** First Baptist Church
Email: srice@magdalena.k12.nm.us
Email: shellyr@socorro.com

Gretchen G. Rich
Title: Assistant Professor of English **Company:** Dakota Wesleyan University **Address:** 1200 W. University Avenue, Mitchell, SD 57301 United States **BUS:** University **P/S:** Higher Education **MA:** Regional **D/D/R:** Writing Grants for Students with Disabilities, Overseeing Assessment Plans, Consulting, Working with Graduate Students in Dissertations, Lecturing, teaching foundational English, composition and English history, grammar and structure principles and organizing seminars **H/I/S:** Reading, Poetry, Knitting, Walking **EDU:** Master's Degree in American Literature, The University of South Dakota (1981); Bachelor's Degree in Speech and Theater, Yankton College (1977) **A/A/S:** College English Association; National Council of Teachers of English; Delta Kappa Gamma; Toastmasters International
Email: grrich@dwu.edu
URL: http://www.dwu.edu

Maisha K. Richard
Title: Realtor, Broker, Property Manager **Company:** Eastern Carolina Realty, Keystone Property Management **Address:** 3105 S. Evans Street, Suite E, Greenville, NC 27858 United States **BUS:** Real Estate Agency **P/S:** Real Estate Sales **MA:** Local **D/D/R:** Buying and Selling Residential Real Estate **H/I/S:** Reading **EDU:** Master of Business Administration, East Carolina University; Bachelor's Degree in Business Administration, Emphasis in Marketing, East Carolina University **CERTS:** Licensed Broker, State of North Carolina (2006) **A/A/S:** National Association of Realtors; North Carolina Association of Realtors
Email: maisha_richard@hotmail.com

Teresa E. Richard
Title: Special Education Teacher **Company:** Hartford Board of Education **Address:** 17 David Drive, East Windsor, CT 06088 United States **BUS:** Education **P/S:** Special Needs Curriculum **MA:** Regional **D/D/R:** Teaching Special Needs Students Language and Reading **EDU:** Master's Degree in Early Childhood Education, American International College (2004); Bachelor of Science in Business, Charter Oak State College (2001); Associate of Science, Asnuntuck Community College, Enfield, Connecticut (1999)
Email: trichard18@cox.net

Christina C. Richards
Title: Marketing and Sales Representative **Company:** Working Rx **Address:** 4225 Lake Park Boulevard, Suite 400, Salt Lake City, UT 84120 United States **BUS:** Workers' Compensation Claims Management Company **P/S:** Essential Financial Services to Over 22,000 Independent and Chain Pharmacies Nationwide **MA:** National **D/D/R:** Direct Marketing for Pharmacies, Computer System Tracking, Training, Billing, with a Focus on Workers' Compensation, Working as a Sales Representative for Over 1,000 Independent Pharmacies **H/I/S:** Hiking, Swimming, Sky Diving, Enjoying All Outdoor Activities **EDU:** Associate Degree, Salt Lake City Community College (2006)
Email: christinarichards@workingrx.com
URL: http://www.workingrx.com

Francoise Richards
Title: Director Company: Couple Communication Address: 30 Lincoln Plaza, New York, NY 10023 United States BUS: Marriage Counseling Organization P/S: Counseling, Running Groups for Couples MA: Local D/D/R: Practicing Jungian Psychology, Counseling Couples H/I/S: Playing Sports, Reading EDU: Master of Science in Psychology, The C.J. Jung Institute of New York and Switzerland A/A/S: The C.J. Jung Institute C/VW: Maurey Institute
Email: psychefrancoise@aol.com
URL: http://www.cambridgewhoswho.com

Kathy D. Richards
Title: Owner, Self-Entrepreneur Company: First Class Cleaning Service Address: 400 Cottontail Lane, Weatherford, TX 76088 United States BUS: Customized Cleaning Company P/S: Specialized, Detailed and Customized Cleaning Services for Residential and Commercial Buildings MA: Regional D/D/R: Developing Relationships with Customers, Creating her Own Cleaning Products Specifically for Individual Clients, Educating Owners H/I/S: Working on Crafts, Fishing EDU: Coursework in Business Administration; High School Degree
Email: krichards@itexas.net

Misty Y. Richards, RN, BSN
Title: Registered Nurse Company: Banner Baywood Heart Hospital Dept: Telemetry Unit Address: 6750 E. Baywood Avenue, Mesa, AZ 85206 United States BUS: Heart Hospital P/S: Full Complement of Diagnostic, Catheterization and Surgical Technologies Including, Diagnostic Testing and Surgical Procedures MA: Regional D/D/R: Working with Patients Who have Cardiac and Vascular Diseases H/I/S: Camping, Spending Quality Time with her Family EDU: Bachelor's Degree in Nursing, Arizona State University (1992) A/A/S: Alumni Association, Arizona State University, College of Nursing; Arizona Nurses Association, Chapter 30; American Nurses Association
Email: misty.richards@bannerhealth.com
URL: http://www.bannerhealth.com

Christina D. Richardson
Address: 42 N. Ruby Street, Philadelphia, PA 19139 United States BUS: Pharmaceuticals/Biotechnology Industry P/S: Pharmaceuticals MA: International D/D/R: Overseeing Clinical Trail and Drug Development Information, Knowledge of Sales and Marketing in the Pharmaceutical and Biotechnology Industry H/I/S: Skiing, Planning for her Wedding (2009) EDU: Master of Business Administration, Concentration in Pharmaceutical Business, University of the Sciences, Philadelphia, PA; Bachelor of Arts in Psychology, Temple University; Master of Science in Psychology, Virginia State University A/A/S: Psi Chi; American Pharmacists Association, Academy of Student Pharmacists
Email: mricha3818@aol.com

Eleanor M. Richardson
Title: Prep Room Supervisor and Embalmer Company: Todd Memorial Chapel Address: 570 N Garey Ave, Pomona, CA 91767 United States BUS: Funeral Home P/S: Provides Final Arrangement for Deceased MA: Local D/D/R: Embalming, Make-Up, Hair H/I/S: Word Puzzles, Reading the Bible EDU: Associate of Science in Mortuary Science, Cypress College CERTS: Licensed Embalmer (1981) A/A/S: Epsilon Meu Delta Mortuary Fraternity, Inc

James M. Richardson
Title: Partner/Attorney Company: Bankston & Richardson, LLP Address: 400 West 15th Street, Suite 710, Austin, TX 78701 United States BUS: Legal Services P/S: Business and Commercial Litigation MA: National D/D/R: Civil Cases, Contracts, Trial Law, General Litigation H/I/S: Boating, Water Skiing EDU: JD in Law and Political Science, Minor in Economics, University in Tulsa, Oklahoma, University of California, LA A/A/S: US District Court, Southern Western District of Texas, Supreme Court, US Court of Appeals; Texas Bar Foundation, Wine Fellow, Austin Bar Wine Foundation; Named Super Lawyer, Texas Magazine (2006-2008)
Email: jrichardson@bankrichardson.com
URL: http://www.bankrichardson.com

Kimberly L. Richardson
Title: Second-Grade Teacher Company: P.S. 64 Queens, New York Dept: Department of Education Address: 8201 101st Avenue, Ozone Park, NY 11416 United States BUS: Public School P/S: Education MA: Local D/D/R: Teaching Mathematics, Reading, Social Studies and English as a Second Language to Second-Grade Students, Creating Lessons, Tutoring Students H/I/S: Bowling, Reading About History and Politics, Watching Classic Movies, Exercising EDU: Master of Science in Education, with a Concentration in Reading and Literature, Fordham University (2003); Bachelor's Degree in Elementary Education, SUNY Oneonta (2000) A/A/S: Phi Kappa Phi; Parish Scholarship Luncheon; U.S. Capital Historical Society A/H: Local Charitable Organizations
Email: kimmyqueens@yahoo.com
URL: http://www.uschs.org

Virginia Cooper Richardson
Title: Educator Company: Carvers Bay Middle School Address: 914 Ray Road, Hemingway, SC 29554 United States BUS: Middle School P/S: Education MA: Georgetown County D/D/R: Teaching Reading and Language Arts to Middle School Students, Academic Coach H/I/S: Reading, Spending Time with her Cats EDU: Master's Degree in Language Arts, University of South Carolina (1989); Bachelor's Degree in Sociology, Francis Marion University A/A/S: Social Studies Association; International Reading Association; National Education Association; South Carolina Education Association; Social Studies Teachers Association; Who's Who Among American Teachers; National Honor Roll; Outstanding American Tea C/VW: Various Local Charities
Email: vir154864913@aol.com

Jennifer I. Richman
Title: Occupational Therapist Company: NYS Psychiatric Institute Address: 262 Prospect Place, Suite 4, Brooklyn, NY 11238 United States BUS: Rehabilitation P/S: Rehabilitation with Autism and Schizophrenia MA: National D/D/R: Rehabilitation Through Music, Autism and Mental Health Rehabilitation H/I/S: Professional Music, Dance, Songwriting, Singing, Wilderness Walking, Spending time on the beach EDU: Bachelor of Science, Brooklyn College and SUNY Down State A/A/S: AOTA-American Occupational Therapy Association
Email: jenrichmn@yahoo.com
URL: http://www.jenniferrichman.com

Michelle S. Ricker
Title: Supervisor of Therapeutic Milieu Team Company: Bethanna Residential Treatment Address: 55 Laurel Road, Southampton, PA 18966 United States BUS: Residential Treatment Facility P/S: Servicing Children and Families, Staff and Clinical Work for Home for Boys, Supporting At-Risk Children, Youth and Families, Social and Mental Health Services MA: Regional D/D/R: Supervising Residential Services for Boys with Issues Including Attention Deficit Disorder, Bipolar Syndrome, Behavioral Issues, Servicing Children and Families, Offering Supervision of Staff and Clinical Work for Home for Boys, Supporting At-Risk Children, Youth and Families, Offering Social and Mental Health Services H/I/S: Social Work, Reading, Writing EDU: Master's Degree in Social Work, West Chester University of Pennsylvania (2005); Bachelor of Art in Social Work, West Chester University of Pennsylvania (2002) A/A/S: Phi Alpha Honor Society
Email: mricker@bethanna.org
URL: http://www.bethanna.org/

Mr. Bobby J. Riddell
Title: Co-Owner Company: Riddell Boiler Service, LLC Address: 195 Taylor Street, Monterey, KY 40359 United States BUS: Boiler and Heating Services P/S: Boilers, Burners for Commercial and Industrial Contracts MA: Regional D/D/R: Specializing in Oil Burners and Waste Oil Recycling for Heating in Other Units, Exclusive Service, Offering Parts for Boiler Room Systems or Power Plants, Service Maintenance, Handling Customer Service, Repair Any System, HVAC Licensed H/I/S: Fishing, Spending Time with his Family EDU: One Year of Coursework in Electronic Engineering, Bell and Howell Technical College CERTS: Certified Master Electrical Contractor, Lexington Vocational School (1968-1970) A/A/S: HVAC Mechanical Contractors Association; Chamber of Commerce, Owen County, Kentucky; Former Member of JC's Vocational National Association
Email: lyriddell@aol.com

Sheryl L. Ridens
Title: Vice President, Branch Manager, Dean of Academics Company: Coleman College Address: 8888 Balboa Avenue, San Diego, CA 92123 United States BUS: College P/S: Education MA: Regional D/D/R: Academics Management H/I/S: Reading, Watching Old Movies EDU: Master of Science in Management Information Systems, Coleman College; Bachelor of Science in Computer Engineering Technology, Coleman College A/A/S: Vistage International; Women in Technology C/VW: Coleman Cares
Email: sridens@coleman.edu
URL: http://www.coleman.edu

Mildred Ridgway, MD
Title: Physician Company: Jackson Gynecologic Oncology Address: 971 Lakeland Drive, Suite 750, Jackson, MS 39216 United States BUS: Medical Center P/S: Healthcare, Medicine, Pelvic Surgery, Diagnosis and Treatment of Ovarian, Uterine, Cervical, Vaginal and Fallopian Tube Cancers MA: Regional D/D/R: Practicing Gynecologic Oncology, Treating Malignancies in Female Genital Tracts, Performing Minimally Invasive Laparoscopic and Robotic Surgery H/I/S: Running, Spending Time with Family EDU: Fellowship in Gynecologic Oncology (2005); Residency in Obstetrics and Gynecology, Duke University (2002); MD, Tulane University (1998) A/A/S: Fellow, American College of Obstetricians and Gynecologists; Candidate Member, Society of Gynecologic Oncologists
Email: mridgwayjgo@yahoo.com
URL: http://www.jacksongynoncology.com

Mr. Robert C. Riegel
Title: Owner Company: Oak View Homes, LLC Address: 1140 Beaumont Avenue, Suite D, Beaumont, CA 92223 United States BUS: Privately Owned Real Estate Company P/S: Investing MA: Regional D/D/R: Dentist (Retired), Handling Foreclosures, Finding New Homes, Saving Credit, Real Estate Investing and Internet Sales H/I/S: Aviation EDU: Doctor of Dental Surgery, University of Missouri (1985); Graduate, Graduate Program (1983); Degree (1968) A/A/S: American Dental Association; Local Better Business Bureau; Chamber of Commerce
Email: rriegel2@verizon.net

Jana R. Rieker
Title: Sales Development Manager Company: Meredith Corp. Address: 13310 Hickory Avenue, Clive, IA 50325 United States BUS: Marketing Publisher P/S: Development and Marketing Sales, National Sales MA: International D/D/R: Development Sales Market H/I/S: Lady's Journal, Golfing, Children, and Reading EDU: Master of Business Administration in Organizational Development, Iowa University A/A/S: NAMA
Email: j.rieker@meredith.com
URL: http://www.meredith.com

Amy René Riessland
Title: Early Childhood Mental Health Specialist, Registered Play Therapist Company: Horizon Family Group Specialized Address: 300 W. Broadway, Suite 7, Council Bluffs, IA 51503 United States BUS: Nonprofit Organization P/S: Public Services Including International and Domestic Adoption and Foster Care Services MA: Regional EXP: Ms. Riessland's expertise is in social services. D/D/R: screening children, consulting with parents, counseling, overseeing mental heath day care for behavioral problems and collaborating with homeless shelters H/I/S: Spending Time with her Daughter EDU: Master's Degree in Social Work, University of Nebraska (2003); Bachelor's Degree in Psychology, University of St. Thomas (1998) CERTS: Pursuing Certification in Play Therapy A/A/S: National Association of Social Workers; Association for Play Therapy
Email: amymail1713@yahoo.com
URL: http://www.lfsneb.org

Frank S. Riggi Jr.
Title: Owner Company: Riggi Paving, Inc. Address: 456 Walker Street, Fairview, NJ 07022 United States BUS: Contracting Company P/S: Contracting Services Including Asphalt, Concrete, Interlocking Block Walls, Belgian Block Curbs and Paving Stones MA: Regional D/D/R: overseeing construction of pavement using asphalt, concrete, interlocking block walls, Belgian block curbs and paving stones A/A/S: 200 Club of Bergen County; Ridgefield Manufacturers Association; Golf Course Superintendent Association; Former Board Member, Palisades Amusement Park Historical Society C/VW: Volunteer, Local Police Department
Email: frank.riggi@cwwemail.com
URL: http://www.riggipaving.com

Bonnie Riggs
Title: Assistant Director, Institutional Research Company: Chattanooga State Technical Community College Address: 4501 Amnicola Highway, Chattanooga, TN 37406 United States BUS: Community College P/S: Higher Education MA: Statewide D/D/R: State and Federal Reporting, Statistical and Otherwise, Gathering Data for Surveys, Tracking Graduates H/I/S: Traveling EDU: Master of Business Administration, The University of Tennessee at Chattanooga A/A/S: Tennessee Association for Institutional Research; National Association for Institutional Research; Southern Association for Institutional Research
Email: bonnie.riggs@chattanoogastate.edu
URL: http://www.chattanoogastate.edu

David Rigney
Title: Realtor Company: RE/MAX Properties Northwest Address: 37 S. Prospect Avenue, Park Ridge, IL 60068 United States BUS: Real Estate P/S: Residential Real Estate MA: Local D/D/R: Marketing, Consulting H/I/S: Playing Golf, Enjoying Time with his Family EDU: Pursuing Bachelor's Degree in Fire Science, Southern Illinois University A/A/S: National Association of Realtors; Chicago Northwest Board of Realtors C/VW: Habitat for Humanity
Email: david.rigney@remax.net
URL: http://www.davidrigney.com

Roy J. Rike Sr.
Title: Owner Company: Roy's Sharpening Service Industrial and Domestic Address: 1796 Pacific Avenue, Norco, CA 92860 United States BUS: Sharpening Blades Service Provider P/S: Blade Sharpening Industrial and Domestic Products MA: Local D/D/R: Precision Grinder H/I/S: Watching News on TV, Shopping, Working Out EDU: High School, Alpha Beta College, Rehab School, Business Degree, Business Courses A/A/S: County Works Development Board, Chamber of Commerce

Debbie L. Riley

Title: President **Company:** Through The Pages **Address:** 121 1/2 E. Sealy Avenue, Monahans, TX 79756 United States **BUS:** Bookstore **P/S:** New and Used Books **MA:** National **EXP:** Ms. Riley's area of expertise is in operations management. **H/I/S:** Reading, Gardening **A/A/S:** The Ward County Civic Theater Association; Desert Sands Garden Club **C/VW:** Local Schools; Ward County Community Endowment Foundation; Reading Program for Odessa American Newspaper; Relay for Life; MDA
Email: throughthepages@sbcglobal.net
URL: http://www.throughthepages.com

Joshua M. Riley

Title: Student **Company:** Norwich University **Address:** 40 Haynes Road, Deerfield, NH 03037 United States **BUS:** University **P/S:** Higher Education, Architecture Programs **MA:** Local **D/D/R:** Studying Architecture, Art and Design **H/I/S:** Golfing, Snowboarding **EDU:** Pursuing Master's Degree in Architecture, Norwich University; Bachelor of Science in Architectural Studies, Norwich University (2007)
Email: joshriley2000@yahoo.com

Mr. Matthew Riley

Title: Executive Chef, President **Company:** Riley Restaurant Corporation, DBA Matthews at the Airport & Matthews **Address:** 1215 Spring Street, Paso Robles, CA 93446 United States **BUS:** Restaurant **P/S:** Food and Beverage Service **MA:** Local **D/D/R:** Wine Country Cuisine **H/I/S:** Cooking, Horseback Riding **CERTS:** Certified Executive Chef, Culinary Institute of America **A/A/S:** American Culinary Federation
Email: Cateringbyrc@aol.com
URL: matthewsattheairport.com

Shannon S. Riley, CHMM

Title: President, Chief Executive Officer **Company:** One Stop Environmental, LLC **Address:** 4924 First Avenue N., Birmingham, AL 35222 United States **BUS:** Environmental Contracting Company **P/S:** Waste Management, Industrial Cleaning, Maintenance and Remediation **MA:** National **EXP:** Ms. Riley's area of expertise is in waste management. **D/D/R:** assessing, packaging, transporting and disposing waste **H/I/S:** Sports, Spending Time Outdoors, Driving Cars, Camping **EDU:** Master's Degree in Chemistry, The University of Alabama; Bachelor's Degree in Chemistry, Furman University **CERTS:** Certified Hazardous Materials Manager **A/A/S:** American Chemical Society; National Association of Women Business Owners
Email: sriley@onestopenv.com
URL: http://www.onestopenv.com

Tom Jeom Taek Rim

Title: President **Company:** T & R Produce Wholesale & Trucking, Inc. **Address:** 1300 S. French Avenue, Suite 8C, Sanford, FL 32771 United States **BUS:** Wholesale and Trucking Company **P/S:** Fruits, Vegetables Wholesale and Trucking Services **MA:** Regional **D/D/R:** managing business operations, overseeing employees, and the grocery and produce supplies **H/I/S:** Golfing **EDU:** Associate Degree in Business Administration, Dong Seoul College, South Korea (1984)
Email: tandrproduce@hotmail.com

Mr. Ender Rincón

Title: Inspections Manager **Company:** BIVAC North America (Bureau Veritas) **Address:** 20511 Cedar Rain Drive, Katy, TX 77449 United States **BUS:** Trade Industry **P/S:** Import and Export Services **MA:** International **D/D/R:** Running Inspections, Overseeing 200 Inspectors, Consulting, Specializing in Quality and Quantity Assurance and Customer Relations **H/I/S:** Enjoying Music, Playing the Piano **EDU:** Bachelor's Degree in International Accounting
Email: ender.rincon@us.bureauveritas.com
URL: http://www.bureauveritas.com

Clarence L. Rinehart

Title: 1) Firefighter (Retired) 2) Advertisement Compositor (Retired) **Company:** 1) Citizens Truck Company 2) Frederick News-Post **Address:** 9 S. Court Street, Frederick, MD 21701 United States **BUS:** 1) Fire Department 2) Newspaper **P/S:** 1) Fire Fighting 2) Newspapers **MA:** 1) Local 2) Local **D/D/R:** 1) Fire Prevention **H/I/S:** Traveling, Collecting Fire Department Memorabilia **EDU:** High School Education **A/A/S:** Frederick County Volunteer Fire and Rescue Association (2007); Maryland State Firemen's Association **C/VW:** Church
Email: clarence.rinehart@cwwemail.com
URL: http://www.cambridgewhoswho.com

Cynthia E. Ringenary

Title: Owner, President **Company:** Paint N' Pottery & Bead Bazaar **Address:** 15 W. Oakland Avenue, Doylestown, PA 18901 United States **BUS:** Retail Store **P/S:** Ceramic Painting, Bead Crafting, Birthday Parties, Workshops, Custom Made Items **MA:** Local **D/D/R:** Painting, Floral Designs, Gardening, Beading **H/I/S:** Gardening, Reading, Outdoor Adventures **EDU:** Bachelor's Degree in Ornamental Horticulture Design, Delaware Valley College (1993); Associate Degree in Small Business Management, Northampton County Community College (1989) **A/A/S:** Chamber of Commerce; Doylestown Merchants; First Fridays Doylestown; Best of Bucks Montgomery County (2007)
Email: info@doylestownpaintandbead.com
URL: http://www.doylestownpaintandbead.com

Susan T. Rioux

Title: Peer Counseling Coordinator **Company:** Westglades Middle School **Address:** 11000 Hulmberg Road, Parkland, FL 33076 United States **BUS:** Education **P/S:** Education **MA:** Broward County **D/D/R:** Peer Counseling Program, Conflict Mediation, Counseling, Tutoring **H/I/S:** Spending Time with her Family, Hiking, Gardening, Reading, Sailing **EDU:** Master of Education, University of Georgia; Bachelor in Science **A/A/S:** National Education Association; Teacher of the Year (2000, 2005) **C/VW:** Jerry's Kids, American Heart Association, American Cancer Society, United Way
Email: susan.rioux@browardschools.com
URL: http://www.browardschools.com

Josephine Barbara Rippey

Title: Supreme Court Family Mediator, Registered Marriage and Family Therapist **Company:** J. Rippey Mediation **Address:** 3070 Blanding Boulevard, Middleburg, FL 32068 United States **BUS:** Family Mediation **P/S:** Dispute Resolutions and Mediation **MA:** Statewide **D/D/R:** Family and County Mediator; Registered Marriage and Family Therapist Intern **H/I/S:** Horseback Riding, Skating, Sewing **EDU:** Supreme Court Certification in Family and County Mediation; Master's Degree in Marriage and Family Therapy, St. Thomas University; Bachelor of Science in Psychology, Barry University **A/A/S:** Author of It's Ok to be a Pre-Mie **C/VW:** Jackson Memorial Hospital, Miami; Substance Abuse Ministry, Church
Email: jrippeymediation@bellsouth.net

Sara F. Risser

Title: Executive Director **Company:** 1) Foundation for Community Action 2) Global Outreach International **Address:** FUNDACO Casilla 17-17-1727, Quito, Ecuador **BUS:** Nonprofit Organization **P/S:** Services for Nursing Students and Orphans **MA:** International **D/D/R:** Missionary Nursing, Facilitating Logistics for Visitation Groups, Fundraising, Supplying Refurbished Wheelchairs to Ecuadorian Citizens, caring for abandoned and abused children **H/I/S:** Riding Horses, Sports, Traveling **EDU:** Master's Degree in Nursing Service Administration, Minor in Labor and Management, The Catholic University of America, Washington, DC (1970); Bachelor's Degree in Nursing Education, Bob Jones University (1960) **CERTS:** Registered Nurse, Lancaster General Hospital (1957) **A/A/S:** International Lecturer; Educator, Ecuador's National School of Nursing; Mission Groups, Global Outreach International; Author, Mini-Autobiography; Former Director, The village health worker program
Email: sararisser123@hotmail.com
URL: http://www.cambridgewhoswho.com

Barbara M. Rito-Bodkin

Title: President, Owner, Founder **Company:** Bodkin Unlimited, Inc. **Address:** 37309 N. Fairview Lane, Lake Villa, IL 60046 United States **BUS:** Mortuary Facility **P/S:** Mortuary, Cosmetology for the Deceased, Assisting 250 Funeral Homes and Directors **MA:** Regional **D/D/R:** Hairdressing, Applying Theatrical Makeup for the Deceased, Attending to Funeral Directors **H/I/S:** Boating, Raising Poodles, Spending Time with her Husband, Son and his Wife and Three Grandchildren **EDU:** Licensed in Cosmetology, Vogue School of Beauty Culture; Coursework in Business, Roosevelt University; Apprenticeship in Cosmetology **A/A/S:** Chairwoman, Women of the Moose; Secretary, Homeowners Association; Received International Co-Worker of the Year **C/VW:** Moose Fraternal Organization; American Legion Auxiliary; The Humane Society; Cancer Society; Girl Scouts
Email: shelion728@aol.com
URL: http://www.cambridgewhoswho.com

Barbara Jo Rittgers

Title: Owner **Company:** Rittgers Rentals **Address:** 16483 Cox Road, Logan, OH 43138 United States **BUS:** Time-Honored Real Estate Rental Company **P/S:** Maintenance and Rental of Residential Properties **MA:** Regional **D/D/R:** Running the Family Business, Buying, Improving and Maintaining Houses for Rental, Funding Locations, Performing Repair Work, Acting as a Hands-On Owner, Working as a Co-Owner of 33 Shake Shoppe, an Ice Cream Parlor, Assisting with All Aspects of the Operations of the Business **H/I/S:** Fishing, Quilting, Enjoying Wildlife **EDU:** Coursework, Realtor School **A/A/S:** National Wildlife Association
Email: bricecream@aol.com

Elsie L. Ritzenhein

Title: President, Chief Executive Officer **Company:** Creative Sources **Address:** 54570 Monarch Drive, Shelby Township, MI 48316 United States **BUS:** Education Consulting Company **P/S:** Consulting and Facilitation Services **MA:** National **D/D/R:** Strategy and Processes for Leadership and Change in Education **H/I/S:** Walking, Reading, Nature **EDU:** Educational Specialist in Administration, Wayne State University; Master of Arts in Teaching, Oakland University; Bachelor of Science in Music Education, Capital University **A/A/S:** Association for Supervision and Curriculum Development; National Staff Development Conference **C/VW:** The Humane Society
Email: elsieritz07@comcast.net
URL: http://www.creativesources.org

Catalina Rivera

Title: Senior Administrative Assistant to Executive Staff **Company:** Marine Corps Association **Address:** 715 Broadway Street, P.O. Box 1775, Quantico, VA 22134 United States **BUS:** Preeminent Professional Association for All Marines **P/S:** Professional Development and Special Services for Members of the U.S. Marines, Awards Program, Informative Forum Lectures, Reading Program **MA:** National **D/D/R:** Serving as Administrative Assistant for 200 Marines, Data Analysis Operations, Converting Word Documents to Excel for more Efficient Analyses, Acting as Correspondent to the President of the Association **EDU:** Pursuing Bachelor of Science in Science Education, North Virginia Community College, George Mason University
Email: c.rivera@mca-marines.org
URL: http://www.mca-marines.org

Marlene Rivera, MD, MPH

Title: MD, MPH **Address:** 2735 Henry Hudson Parkway, Suite 204, Bronx, NY 10463 United States **BUS:** Private Healthcare Practice **P/S:** Pediatric Care **MA:** Local **D/D/R:** Pediatrics **H/I/S:** Travel, Exercise **EDU:** Bachelor of Science in Biology, Fordham; MD, MPH, SUNY Health and Science Center at Brooklyn **A/A/S:** AMA, AAP
Email: mardoc98@aol.com
URL: http://www.cambridgewhoswho.com

Robert Rivera

Title: Account Executive **Company:** Nuestra Casa **Address:** 808 Greenwood Street, Evanston, IL 60201 United States **BUS:** Advertising Company **P/S:** Publication for Hispanic Realty, Mortgages for Latinos **MA:** National **D/D/R:** Sales, Customer Service **H/I/S:** Golfing **EDU:** College Coursework **A/A/S:** Hispanic Chamber of Commerce **C/VW:** Church
Email: rrivera@nuestracasainc.com

Ms. Shanina Rivera

Title: Owner **Company:** Movements **Address:** 3125 Glendale Boulevard, Los Angeles, CA 90039 United States **BUS:** Retail Boutique **P/S:** Women's Boutique Featuring Trendy Accessories and Clothing **MA:** Regional **D/D/R:** Marketing and Sales in the Boutique, Creating Websites for the Business, Handling Financial Aspects of the Business, Property Manager and Singer, Acting as an Independent Contractor with Price Waterhouse Coopers Assisting with Latino Diversity Events **H/I/S:** Singing, Working with Young Children at a Talent Boot Camp **EDU:** College Coursework in Business Studies, Baruch College (1997) **A/A/S:** Former Vice President, Association of Latino Professionals in Finance and Accounting
Email: movementsboutique@yahoo.com
Email: movementsclothing@sbcglobal.net
URL: http://www.movementsboutique.net

Noemy Rivera-Gutierrez

Title: President/Manager **Company:** Sabor Catering and Café **Address:** 6209 Georgia Avenue N.W., Washington, DC 20011 United States **BUS:** Restaurant **P/S:** Full Service Restaurant, Catering Services, A Mixture of Foods to Choose From Such as Latin American, French, Italian, and American Cuisine, Available for Weddings and All Special Occasions **MA:** International **D/D/R:** Staying on Top of USDA Regulations, Offering Balanced and Healthy Menus, Business Management **H/I/S:** Traveling, Involved with Community, Coaches Baseball for Two of her Children, Her Husband Coaches Soccer for the Other Two Children **EDU:** Associate of Science in Business Administration, Strayer University **A/A/S:** Minority Business Owners Association, Chamber of Commerce
Email: saborcatering@aol.com

Dr. Harry Rodriguez Rivero
Title: Executive Director **Company:** Instituto de Banca y Comercio **Address:** Los Altos Escorial, Carolina, PR 00987 United States **BUS:** Vocational Institute **P/S:** Commercial, Technical and Vocational Courses **MA:** Regional **D/D/R:** Supervising and Coordinating of Faculty Duties and Activities of the Academy, Administering Faculties and Personnel **H/I/S:** Spending Time at the Gym, Weight Lifting, Reading, Jogging **EDU:** Doctor in Educational Administration, Inter American University (2005); Master of Business Administration, Inter American University, Puerto Rico (1993); Bachelor's Degree in Management, Inter American University, Puerto Rico **A/A/S:** Association of Christians in Student Development; Association of Supervision and Development Curriculum; Golden Key International Honor Society
Email: harryr5@yahoo.com

Carl A. Rizza
Title: Program Manager (Retired) **Company:** Lockheed Martin **Address:** 19316 N. 62nd Avenue, Glendale, AZ 85308 United States **BUS:** Lead Systems Integrator and Information Technology Company **P/S:** Research, Design, Development, Manufacture and Integration of Advanced Technology Systems, Products and Services **MA:** International **D/D/R:** Overseeing Program Management, Consulting in the Field **H/I/S:** Traveling **EDU:** Master's Degree in Business Management, Golden Gate University (1978)
Email: azrizza@cox.net
URL: http://www.cambridgewhoswho.com

Helaine Andrea Rizzo
Title: Special Education Teacher, Education Coordinator **Company:** Yonkers Board of Education **Dept:** Roosevelt High School **Address:** 11 Sentry Place, Scarsdale, NY 10583 United States **BUS:** School **P/S:** Education **MA:** Local **EXP:** Ms. Rizzo's area of expertise is in special education. **H/I/S:** Spending Time with her Family, Decorating, Going to the Theater, Performing Charity Work, Fundraising, Traveling **EDU:** Master's Degree in Special Education, College of New Rochelle (1986); Dual Bachelor of Arts in Psychology and Gerontology, Iona College (1982) **C/VW:** Volunteer, Richmond Children's Center; Volunteer, Richmond Senior Residential Facility
Email: helair9@gmail.com

Cheol G. Ro
Title: Operations Manager **Company:** Stanley **Address:** 1538 Highway 2, Two Harbors, MN 55616 United States **BUS:** Heavy Equipment Manufacturing Plant **P/S:** Production of Five Different Families of High End Motorcycle Models and Recreational Vehicles Customized for Style and Comfort, Shears **MA:** International **D/D/R:** Operation Manager for Heavy Duty Tools Manufacturer, Launching Future Models of the Sportster Motorcycle Model, Running the Entire Manufacturing Process from the Fabrication of Designs to Painting to Assembly Line Production, Relaying Manufacturing Information to Upper Management throughout the Entire Corporation **H/I/S:** Running, Bicycling, Enjoying Off-Course Motorcycling **EDU:** Master's Degree in Mechanical Engineering, University of Illinois at Chicago (1994); Master's Degree in Finance, Emphasis on Operations, University of Wisconsin-White Water (1998); Bachelor's Degree in Mechanical Engineering and Mathematics, University of Wisconsin (1990) **A/A/S:** American Society Of Mechanical Engineers
Email: cro@stanleyworks.com
URL: http://www.stanleyworks.com

Tonya Elizabeth Robak
Title: Regional Director of Clinical Services **Company:** EmCare **Dept:** Clinical Services, South West Region **Address:** 16019 Biscayne Shoals Drive, Friendswood, TX 77546 United States **BUS:** Consulting Firm **P/S:** Consulting Services for Healthcare Including Emergency Nursing and Leadership **MA:** National **EXP:** Ms. Robak's expertise includes emergency nursing and legal nurse consulting. **D/D/R:** Overseeing Quality Management, Staff Development and Process Improvement, Educating Patients, Analyzing Patients Output **H/I/S:** Traveling, Snorkeling, Spending Time Outdoor, Writing, Cooking **EDU:** Bachelor of Science in Nursing, Jacksonville University, Jacksonville, Florida **A/A/S:** Emergency Nurses Association; American Association of Legal Nurse Consultants **C/VW:** The Leukemia & Lymphoma Society; American Cancer Society
Email: toni.robak@comcast.net
Email: toni.robak@gmail.com
URL: http://www.emcare.com

Dana J. Robbins
Title: Senior Software Consultant **Company:** Icarus Innovations **Address:** 3215 N.E. 184th Street, Apartment 14209, Aventura, FL 33160 United States **BUS:** Consulting Firm **P/S:** Consulting Services Including Enterprise Resource Planning Implementations, Project Management, Business Process Re-Engineering, Strategic Planning, User Procedures and Training Materials, Payroll Testing, Performance Analysis and Tuning **MA:** International **D/D/R:** software consulting, working with oracle, managing human resources, software implementation, implementing public and private sector enterprise resource planning and processing payroll **H/I/S:** Snowboarding, Golfing, Playing Outdoor Sports **CERTS:** Fast Forward Program in Computer Networking and Security, The Chubb Institute (1992) **A/A/S:** National Speaker, Oracle Human Capital Management Users Group
Email: dana.robbins@icarus-innovations.com
URL: http://www.icarus-innovations.com

Susan E. Robbins
Title: Senior Asset Manager **Company:** Prudential Asset Resources **Address:** 2200 Ross Avenue, Suite 4900 E, Dallas, TX 75201 United States **BUS:** Commercial Mortgage Company **P/S:** Commercial Mortgage Back Securities **MA:** National **D/D/R:** Commercial Asset Management **H/I/S:** Playing Tennis **EDU:** Bachelor's Degree in Business and Finance, Southern Methodist University **A/A/S:** Junior League of Dallas **C/VW:** Gilda's Club of North Texas
Email: serobbins@charter.net

Joyce M. Roberson
Title: Teacher **Company:** Milby Senior High School **Address:** 1601 Broadway Boulevard, Houston, TX 77012 United States **BUS:** Public High School **P/S:** Secondary Level Education **MA:** Regional **D/D/R:** Teaching English and Reading to Ninth and Tenth-Grade Students, Working with English as a Second Language Students, Writing Lesson Plans **H/I/S:** Reading, Outdoor Activities **EDU:** Bachelor of Science in English, Southern University Baton Rouge (1977) **A/A/S:** Area Language Arts Association; Peace Club
Email: jroberso@houstonisd.org
URL: http://hs.houstonisd.org/milbyhs

Barbara J. Roberts
Title: Special Education Teacher **Company:** Bucks County Intermediate Unit 22 **Address:** 705 Shady Retreat Road, Doylestown, PA 18901 United States **BUS:** Intermediate School **P/S:** Education **MA:** Local **D/D/R:** Literacy, Dyslexia **H/I/S:** Gardening **EDU:** Master of Education in Childhood Education, Arcadia University **CERTS:** Certified Reading Specialist; Certificate in Dyslexia **A/A/S:** Association for Supervision and Curriculum Development; International Reading Association
Email: broberts@bucksiu.org
URL: http://www.bucksiu.org

Mr. Christopher Roberts
Title: Dispatcher **Company:** Polly Express **Address:** 565 Dave Smith Road, Prospect Hill, NC 27314 United States **BUS:** Logistic Company **P/S:** Logistic Services **MA:** International **D/D/R:** scheduling shipments for raw materials and components to New Mexico plant, expediting shipping of finished goods, training individuals and overseeing transportation security administration **EDU:** Pursuing Associate Degree in Global Logistics, Guilford Technical Community College
Email: gsoguy3000@earthlink.net
URL: http://www.takata.com

Doreen C. Roberts, RMC
Title: Coder, Billing Manager, Registered Medical Coder **Company:** Hot Springs Health Program **Dept:** Accounts Receivable **Address:** 590 Medical Park Drive, Marshall, NC 28753 United States **BUS:** Healthcare Center **P/S:** Healthcare **MA:** Regional **EXP:** Ms. Roberts' expertise includes the management of accounts receivable, accounting and billing. **D/D/R:** Addressing Patient Needs, Overseeing Electronic Monitoring Systems and Data Entry Operations, Maintaining Records, Managing Accounting Information Quality, Acting as a Liaison **H/I/S:** Reading, Boating, Crocheting, Fishing, Camping, Spending Time with her Family **CERTS:** Certified Medical Coding Specialist, Association of Registered Health Care Professionals (2005) **C/VW:** Relay for Life, American Cancer Society
Email: droberts@hotspringshealth-nc.org
URL: http://www.hotspringshealth-nc.org

Mr. Josef B. Roberts
Title: DJ **Company:** Fever Entertainment **Address:** 1266 Sutter Avenue, Apt. 6G, Brooklyn, NY 11208 United States **BUS:** Music, Entertainment **P/S:** Disc Jockey **MA:** Local **D/D/R:** Weddings, Retirement Parties, Birthday Parties, Working with the New York City Transit Authority **H/I/S:** Motorcycles, Boxing **CERTS:** Licensed and Registered Professional Disc Jockey, State of New York
Email: jobroa@feverentertainment.com

Laura Helena Roberts
Title: Educator **Company:** Columbus Public Schools, Clinton Middle School **Address:** 270 E. State Street, Columbus, OH 43215 United States **BUS:** Middle School Committed to Excellence in Academics **P/S:** Elementary Education First through Eighth, Areas of Study Include Pre-Algebra, Language Survey, Reading, Language Arts, Mathematics, Science, Social Studies, Health **MA:** Regional **D/D/R:** Teaching Mathematics and Pre-Algebra to Sixth, Seventh and Eighth-Grade Students, Social Studies, Reading Language Arts, Tutoring, Professional Development **H/I/S:** Reading, Church Activities, Missionary Work, Singing **EDU:** Pursuing Master's Degree in Education Administration, Ashland College; Bachelor of Science in Education Plus 120, Southern Illinois University (1970) **A/A/S:** Estella R. Davis Charity Club; Christian Women's Auxiliary of Ohio; Eastern Star; National Education Association; Ohio Education Association; Columbus Education Association; Board of Directors, United Way; Habitat for Humanity
Email: helenaroberts1@columbus.rr.com
URL: http://www.columbus.k12.oh.us

Ms. Linda L. Roberts
Title: Manager **Company:** Colette's Dunkin Donuts **Address:** 319 Main Street, Lewiston, ME 04240 United States **BUS:** Retail Food and Beverage Outlet **P/S:** Coffee, Coffee Drinks, Specialty Sandwiches, Doughnuts, Bagels **MA:** Regional **D/D/R:** Scheduling Food and Beverage Delivery, Calculating Payroll, Managing 35 Employees, Managing Employee Issues Including Write-ups and Warnings, Bookkeeping **H/I/S:** Gardening, Golf, Showing Rottweiler Dogs, Rescuing Animals **EDU:** College Coursework in Business Management and Secretarial Studies (1974) **CERTS:** Certification in Basic Business Management; Certification in Safe Serve; Certification in Nurse Aide
Email: LRoberts326@adelphi.net
URL: http://www.cambridgewhoswho.com

Mel Roberts
Title: Aquatic Supervisor **Company:** Leigh Pratt Aquatic Center **Address:** 55 N. 200 W., Tooele, UT 84074 United States **BUS:** Recreational Center **P/S:** Aquatic Activities, Sports Facilities, Swimming Pools, Education **MA:** Regional **D/D/R:** Teaching Competitive Swimming **H/I/S:** Swimming, Coaching **EDU:** Bachelor's Degree in Mathematics, The University of Utah (1969)
Email: melr@tooelecity.org
URL: http://www.tooelecity.org

Randal W. Roberts
Title: Managing Partner, Attorney **Company:** Simone, Roberts & Weiss, PA **Address:** 1120 Lomas Boulevard N.E., Suite 210, Albuquerque, NM 87112 United States **BUS:** Law Firm **P/S:** Insurance Defense **MA:** Regional **D/D/R:** Product Liability, Insurance Law **H/I/S:** Flying Airplanes, Hot Air Ballooning, Photography **EDU:** JD, University of Colorado at Boulder (1976); Bachelor of Arts in Economics, University of Colorado at Boulder, Summa Cum Laude (1973) **A/A/S:** American Board of Trial Advocates; Defense Research Institute; Phi Beta Kappa; The Order of the Coif
Email: rroberts@srw-law.com

Suzanne Roberts
Title: Teacher (Retired) **Company:** Oak Grove Elementary School **Address:** Lewisburg, TN 37091 United States **BUS:** Elementary School **P/S:** Primary Education **MA:** Local **EXP:** Ms. Roberts' expertise is in teaching. **H/I/S:** Horseback Riding, Practicing Martial Arts **EDU:** Bachelor of Science in Early Childhood Education, Montana State University; Associate of Science, Columbia State Community College **C/VW:** Volunteer, Oak Grove Elementary School; Volunteer, Church Street Church of Christ; Girl Scouts of the USA
Email: susur@bellsouth.net

Julia A. Roberts Guttman
Title: Project Supervisor (Retired) **Company:** Rochester City School District **Address:** 131 W. Broad Street, Rochester, NY 14614 United States **BUS:** School District **P/S:** Education **MA:** Local **EXP:** Ms. Roberts Guttman's expertise includes parent and early childhood education. **H/I/S:** Spending Time Outdoors, Gardening, Reading, Involving in Politics **EDU:** Master of Arts in Social Psychology and Labor Economics, University of Wisconsin; Bachelor of Arts in Sociology and Philosophy, Cedar Crest College, Allentown, PA **CERTS:** Certified School Administrator **A/H:** Award, Rochester Association for the Education of Young Children (2008) **C/VW:** Local Charitable Organizations; Children's Zone; Emmanuel Temple Church; United Way
Email: julia.robertsguttman@cwwemail.com
URL: http://www.cambridgewhoswho.com

Diane G. Robertson, BA
Title: Director of Broadcast Services **Company:** WHUT-Howard University Television **Address:** 2222 Fourth Street, N.W., Washington, DC 20059 United States **BUS:** The First African-American Owned and Operated Noncommercial Television Station in the United States **P/S:** Public Television, Diverse Programming, Broadcasts more than 3,500 Hours of Public Affairs and Educational Programming per Year **MA:** National **D/D/R:** Programming for Varied Televised Subjects, Lectures in an International Program **H/I/S:** Dancing, Watching Movies **EDU:** Bachelor of Arts, School of Communications, Magna Cum Laude, Howard University (2000) **A/A/S:** Women in Film and Video; Invited to Join Golden Key
Email: diane_robertson@whut.pbs.org
URL: http://www.howard.edu/tv/

Ms. Jessica Robertson
Title: Business Analyst **Company:** Broadcast Music, Inc. **Address:** 320 W. 57th Street, New York, NY 10019 United States **BUS:** Performing Rights Organization **P/S:** Music License Service **MA:** International **D/D/R:** Managing Projects, Assessing Business Processes, Writing Proposals and Manuals **H/I/S:** Playing Music, Internet Profiling, Advertising, Updating the Web-Site
Email: jrobertson@bmi.com
URL: http://www.bmi.com

Linda B. Robertson
Title: Associate Director of Cancer Control Services **Company:** University of Pittsburgh Medical Center **Address:** 5150 Centre Avenue, Pittsburgh, PA 15232 United States **BUS:** University Medical Center **P/S:** Higher Education, Healthcare **MA:** National **EXP:** Ms. Robertson's area of expertise is in oncology nursing. **H/I/S:** Knitting, Walking, Reading **EDU:** Doctor of Public Health, Graduate School of Public Health, University of Pittsburgh; Master of Science in Nursing, with a Concentration in Oncology, University of Pittsburgh **A/A/S:** Oncology Nursing Society; American Public Health Association **C/VW:** Community Presbyterian Church of Ben Avon
Email: robertsonlk@upmc.edu
URL: http://www.upmc.edu

Patricia Robertson
Title: Licensed Practical Nurse (Retired) **BUS:** University **P/S:** Education **MA:** National **D/D/R:** Healthcare, Geriatrics, Rehabilitation, Teaching Sunday School **H/I/S:** Knitting, Crocheting, Cross-Stitching, Quilting, Cooking, Gardening, Raising Goats **EDU:** Associate Degree in Business, Finance, Accounting, Agriculture and Farm Management **C/VW:** Mission for Bible Babies
Email: robertson@otelco.net

Cameron D. Robinson
Title: Chief Executive Officer **Company:** Campus Connection Media **Address:** 23900 Lyons Avenue, Suite A, Newhall, CA 91321 United States **BUS:** Digital Broadcast and Advertising Company **P/S:** Digital Broadcast and Advertising Services **MA:** National **D/D/R:** Designing and Selling Signage **H/I/S:** Watching Soccer, Playing Video Games, Wakeboarding, Snowboarding **EDU:** Bachelor of Science in Computer Information Systems, California Lutheran University **A/A/S:** Chamber of Commerce **C/VW:** American Veterans; Firemen's Association; California Lutheran University
Email: cameron@campusconnectionmedia.com
URL: http://www.campusconnectionmedia.com

Christina B. Robinson
Title: Instructor, Department of Dental Hygiene **Company:** Wake Technical Community College **Address:** 2901 Holston Lane, Raleigh, NC 27610 United States **BUS:** College **P/S:** Higher Education **MA:** Local **D/D/R:** teaching periodontics, pharmacology, clinical dental hygiene and orofacial anatomy **H/I/S:** Gardening, Needlework, Collecting Antiques **EDU:** Master of Science in Dental Hygiene, The University of North Carolina **A/A/S:** Greater Raleigh Dental Hygiene Association; North Carolina Dental Hygiene Association; North Carolina Dental Hygiene Educators Association; American Dental Hygiene Association
Email: cbrobinson@waketech.edu
URL: http://www.waketech.edu

Cynthia M. B Robinson
Title: Master Provider III **Company:** Mrs. Cynthia's Munchkin Romper Room **Address:** 5430 Germantown Avenue, Philadelphia, PA 19144 United States **BUS:** Professional Family Childcare Center **P/S:** Family Childcare **MA:** Local **D/D/R:** Teaching, Offering Pre-Kindergarten Day Care for Students, Leadership Instructor **H/I/S:** Crafting, Reading **EDU:** Associate Degree in Early Childcare, Montgomery Community College **A/A/S:** Philadelphia Early Childhood Collaborative; Pennsylvania Association of Notaries; Pennsylvania Child Care Association; NASCC; Instructor of Module One Associate Development; Delaware Valley Association for the Education of Young Children; National Association for the Education of Young Children; National Association for Family Child Care
Email: robinsoncmb12@aol.com
Email: robinsoncmb12@verizon.net

Ms. Elda L. Robinson
Title: Teacher **Company:** Monte Vista Christian School **Address:** 2 School Way, Watsonville, CA 95076 United States **BUS:** Boarding School **P/S:** Education **MA:** International **EXP:** Ms. Robinson's area of expertise is in curriculum development. **D/D/R:** teaching science and bible studies **H/I/S:** Reading, Whale Watching, Spending Time Outdoors **EDU:** Master's Degree in Computer Technology Curriculum Development, University of Phoenix **A/A/S:** Curriculum Writer, Association of Christian Schools International **C/VW:** Pianist, Local Church
Email: eldarobinson@nvcs.org

Jeffrey R. Robinson
Title: Professional Scout **Company:** Minnesota Vikings **Address:** 9520 Viking Drive, Eden Prairie, MN 55344 United States **BUS:** National Football League **P/S:** Football Games, Vikings Paraphernalia and Newsletters **MA:** International **D/D/R:** Assisting with College Scouting, Managing Time, Evaluating League Talent, Managing Public Relations and Team Operations **EDU:** Bachelor's Degree in Business, Northwestern University (1989)
Email: robinsonj@vikings.nfl.net
URL: http://www.vikings.com

Karen V. Robinson
Title: Clinical Dietitian **Company:** St. John's Hospital **Address:** 967 North Broadway, Yonkers, NY 10701 United States **BUS:** Premier 407-Bed Community Hospital **P/S:** Medical Services **MA:** Regional **D/D/R:** Overseeing Patients in Orthopedics, Medical-Surgical, New Stroke Unit, On Weekends, Covering Entire Hospital, Covering when Needed in Outpatient Clinic, Family Practice, Maternity Patients and In-House Substance Abuse Patients, Nutrition Assessments, Offering Plans of Care, Giving Nutritional Education to Patients and Family Members, Helping Co-Workers as a Resource Person, Started as a Candy Striper, Worked with Dietitian and Realized Proper Nutrition Can Prevent Medical Conditions from Getting Worse, Focus on Changing Eating Habits, Worked in Public Health and Food Management Supervision, Community Services Instructor, Westchester Community College (2001), **H/I/S:** Travel, Antiquing, Exercise, Quiet Time with Husband and Pet Rabbit **EDU:** Master's Degree in Health Science with Minor in Dietetics, James Madison University (1992) **A/A/S:** American Dietetic Association, Dietetic Practice Groups, Nutrition Entrepreneurs, Consulting Dietitians; Secretary, Westchester-Rockland Dietetic Associations; Regional Public Speaker, Lecturer, Writer, ADA Association in Washington, DC
Email: kvrobinson@aol.com
URL: http://www.riversidehealth.org

Kristin L. Robinson, PHR
Title: Human Resource Generalist **Company:** DeVry University **BUS:** University **P/S:** Education **MA:** Regional **H/I/S:** Playing and Coaching Soccer, Skydiving, Wakeboarding **EDU:** Bachelor's Degree in Global Business, Arizona State University (2004) **CERTS:** Professional in Human Resources **A/A/S:** Society for Human Resource Management
Email: heykristin@cox.net
URL: http://www.cambridgewhoswho.com

Paul A. Robinson, MSN, FNP, AACRN
Title: Regional Medical Scientist **Company:** Boehringer Ingelheim Pharmaceuticals, Inc. **Address:** 947 Edgewood Avenue N.E., Atlanta, GA 30307 United States **BUS:** Pharmaceutical Company **P/S:** HIV and Virology Pharmaceuticals **MA:** International **D/D/R:** Speaking with HIV Specialist Providers who Care for Patients and Conduct Research, Answering Questions, Gathering Information for the Company, Discussing Disease State Issues, Products and how Products can be Combined to Treat Patients more Effectively, Offering Group Presentations **H/I/S:** Traveling, Boating **EDU:** Master of Science in Nursing, Emory University (2000); Bachelor's Degree in Biology, The University of Georgia (1987); Registered Nurse, Armstrong Atlantic State University (1993) **CERTS:** Advanced Certified AIDS Nurse (2006); Certified Specialist, The American Academy of HIV Medicine (2001); Board Certified Family Nurse Practitioner, Emory University (2000) **A/A/S:** Sigma Theta Tau International; Association of Nurses in AIDS Care; The American Academy of HIV Medicine; Board Member, HIV/AIDS Nursing Certification Board
Email: paulrobinsonnp@earthlink.net
URL: http://www.boehringer-ingelheim.com

Rhonda Robinson
Title: Associate Engineer **Company:** D.R. Griffin & Associates **Address:** 141 Elk Street, Rock Springs, WY 82901 United States **BUS:** Engineering and Surveying Company **P/S:** Survey Work, Pipeline Design **MA:** Local **D/D/R:** drafting and designing **H/I/S:** Spending Time with her Children, Sewing, Caring for Horses **EDU:** Pursuing Bachelor's Degree in Engineering, California National University; Master's Degree in Education, Washington State University; Bachelor's Degree in Home Economics, Pacific Union College **A/A/S:** Technical Team, North Dakota Association **C/VW:** Volunteer, Forage for Horses
Email: robinson.rhonda@hotmail.com
URL: http://www.cambridgewhoswho.com

Scott N. Robinson
Title: Director Retail Management **Company:** Amerisource Bergen **Address:** 1300 Morris Drive, Chesterbrook, PA 19087 United States **BUS:** Pharmaceutical Wholesale Company **P/S:** Pharmaceutical Distribution, Healthcare Service **MA:** National **D/D/R:** Offering Information and Education to the Pharmaceutical Network, Developing Marketing Plans and Concepts, Researching, Training **H/I/S:** Running Marathons and Triathlons **EDU:** Bachelor of Business Administration, Colorado State University (1991) **A/A/S:** American Pharmacists Association
Email: srobina4@yahoo.com
URL: http://www.amerisourcebergen.com

Susan Robinson
Title: Funeral Director **Company:** All Souls Mortuary **Address:** 4400 Cherry Avenue, Long Beach, CA 90807 United States **BUS:** Mortuary, Funeral Home Funeral Services **P/S:** Working Closely with the bereaved **MA:** Local **D/D/R:** Working with People **EDU:** Golden West College, Association Degree **A/A/S:** Lakewood Chamber of Commerce
Email: sarobinson@stei.com
URL: http://www.stei.com

Belinda Denise Robinson Garcia
Title: Professor **Company:** Kean University **Address:** 1000 Morris Avenue, Union, NJ 07083 United States **BUS:** University **P/S:** Higher Education, Undergraduate Studies, Graduate Studies **MA:** Regional **D/D/R:** Teaching Registered Nursing Health Classes, Working as an Adjunct Professor **H/I/S:** Scrapbooking **EDU:** Registered Nurse; Master's Degree in Health Administration, New Jersey City University (2001) **A/A/S:** American Nurses Association; National Association of School Nurses
Email: bdrgarci@online.net
URL: http://www.kean.edu

Deborah C. Robitaille
Title: Chief Executive Officer, Owner **Company:** Robo's Cleaning Service **Address:** 9327 Castle Falls Circle, Fayetteville, NC 28314 United States **BUS:** Cleaning Business **P/S:** Commercial and Residential Cleaning and Janitorial Services **MA:** Local **D/D/R:** Management **H/I/S:** Spending Time with her Family, Outdoor Activities, Traveling **EDU:** Pursuing Bachelor's Degree in Elementary Education, Fayetteville State University; Associate Degree in Criminal Justice, Fayette Technical Community College; Diploma, 71st High School **A/A/S:** Fayetteville Technical Community Alumni Association; Mothers Against Drunk Driving; Crimestoppers **C/VW:** Crimestoppers; Mothers Against Drunk Driving
Email: horsesense45@aol.com

Rosalie G. Robles
Title: Hospice Chaplain Spiritual Director **Company:** 1) Rosalie G. Robles 2) Skagit Hospice **Address:** 1224 S. 16th Street, Mount Vernon, WA 98274 United States **BUS:** Christian Ministry and Guidance **P/S:** Ministry for Weddings, Funerals, Spiritual Direction and Counseling and Motivational Speaking, Baptism **MA:** Regional **D/D/R:** Spiritual Direction and Counseling for Individuals, Couples and Families, Hospice Counseling **H/I/S:** Playing Volleyball, Playing the Guitar, Creating Art **EDU:** Master's Degree in Theology and Religious Studies, Canterbury University (1995) **A/A/S:** Federation Christian Ministries; Institutional Review Board, Skagit Hospital; Author, Football for Women Doesn't Have to Be a Bad Word
Email: robl@nwlink.com
URL: http://www.nwlink.com/~robl

Catherine Rose Roche
Title: Middle School Teacher **Company:** Beacon Country Day School **Address:** 6100 E. Belleview Avenue, Greenwood Village, CO 80111 United States **BUS:** Private School **P/S:** Education **MA:** Local **D/D/R:** Teaching **H/I/S:** Making Arts and Crafts **EDU:** Bachelor of Arts in Sociology, University of Denver; Master's Degree in Regional Planning, Syracuse University **C/VW:** Girl Scouts of the USA
Email: croseroche@aol.com

Richard R. Rock
Title: Chairman of the Board **Company:** Rockgate Management **Address:** 6705 S. Granite Avenue, Tulsa, OK 74136 United States **BUS:** Hotel Management Company **P/S:** Hotel Management Services **MA:** National **D/D/R:** managing business operations **H/I/S:** Golfing, Reading, Writing his Autobiography, Traveling **EDU:** JD, Washburn University, Topeka, KS (1950); Bachelor of Science in Political Science, Washburn University (1947) **A/A/S:** Kansas Bar Association **C/VW:** Local Church
Email: richard_rock@att.net
Email: r.r.rock@att.net
URL: http://www.rockgatehotels.com

Randall Hilton Rockwood
Title: Certified Senior Advisor Company: Georgia Association of Planning Partners Address: 1352 Main Street, Suite 1, Young Harris, GA 30582 United States BUS: Membership Organization P/S: Financial Services Including Estate Planning, Elder Law, Business Continuation Planning, Long-Term Care, Retirement and Investment Strategies MA: National EXP: Ms. Rockwood's area of expertise is in financial planning for seniors. H/I/S: Teaching Snowboard and Ski Lessons, Flying, Writing Poetry EDU: Bachelor's Degree in Computer Science Engineering, Minor in Business Finance, The University of Utah A/A/S: Society of Certified Senior Advisors, American Association of Snowboard Instructors C/VW: Meals on Wheels; Legacy Link
Email: estatehelp@alltel.net
URL: http://www.fillthegapps.org

Clarence J. Roddy
Title: President Company: Fast & Clean, Inc. Address: 233 Western Boulevard, Suite J, Jacksonville, NC 28546 United States BUS: Retail Store P/S: High Performance Parts and Equipment, Automobile Accessories, Car Care Products MA: Regional D/D/R: selling automotive products to car dealers and government agencies, Repairing Racing Cars, Overseeing Operations H/I/S: Drag and Autocross Racing, Entering Corvette Shows EDU: Associate Degree in Business Administration, Coastal Carolina Community College (1989) A/A/S: Jacksonville Chamber of Commerce; National Federation of Independent Business; North Carolina Business Bureau; Veteran, United States Marine Corps A/H: Small Business Person of the Year Award, Wachovia Bank Chamber of Commerce C/VW: Kiwanis Club of Jacksonville
Email: crody@earthlink.net
URL: http://www.fastandcleaninc.com

Mr. Keith A. Rodenberger
Title: Owner Company: The Palms Tanning Resort Address: 8577 E. Arapahoe Road, Suite A, Greenwood Village, CO 80112 United States BUS: Leading Tanning and Beauty Operation P/S: Elegantly Prepared Private Bungalows for Tanning Including Tanning Amenities such as Fresh Towels, Protective Eyewear, Bottled Water and Private AM/FM/CD/Cassette Stereo with Personal Stereo Headsets MA: Regional D/D/R: Overseeing the Operations of an Exclusive Tanning Salon, Successful Entrepreneur Since the Age of 16 H/I/S: Boating, Camping, Skiing EDU: Bachelor of Arts in Economics, University of Southern California, Los Angeles (1990) A/A/S: Chamber of Commerce; ITA; Smart Tan Association, Best Image Award (2003); Best Decor Award (2004), Featured in Today's Image Magazine and Tanning Trends Magazine, The Palms is the Official Tanning Resort of the Denver Broncos Cheerleaders
Email: keith@thepalmstanningresort.com
URL: http://www.thepalmstanningresort.com

Jean M. Rodgers
Title: Job Coach Company: Lifeworks Services Address: 7040 Lakeland, Brooklyn Park, MN 55429 United States BUS: Private Nonprofit Organization Started by Families who have Children with Disabilities P/S: Offering People with Disabilities Opportunities that Lead to Personal Growth and Meaningful Experiences through Work and Learning Opportunities, Ensuring Families and Individuals Receive Fiscal Support Services that Help Make their Lives Easier MA: Regional D/D/R: Serving 17 Caseloads, Supervising Clients and their Supervisors to Ensure Jobs are Secure and Clients are Successful H/I/S: Card Making, Scrap Booking, Golfing EDU: Bachelor of Science Degree in Human Services with a Concentration in Deafness, Metro State University (1987); Two-Year Degree in Occupational Therapy
Email: jrodgers@lifeworks.org
URL: http://www.lifeworks.org

Mary Elizabeth Rodman
Title: Owner Company: Rodman Farms Address: 154 Blanche Road, Taft, TN 38488 United States BUS: Farm P/S: Breeding and Raising Cattle, Producing Calves for Market, Cutting Hide MA: Local D/D/R: Producing Calves for Market, Monitoring, Feeding and Caring for Animals H/I/S: Horseback Riding, Sewing, Cooking, Bush Hogging EDU: Industry-Related Training; High School Education A/A/S: Tennessee Cattlemen's Association
Email: rodman02@bellsouth.net

David P. Rodrigues
Title: Master Electrician Company: D. R. Electric Address: 23 Desmarais Avenue, Pawtucket, RI 02861 United States BUS: Electrical Service P/S: Electrical Work MA: Regional D/D/R: Specializing in Electrical Additions and Replacements, Consulting and Upgrading Commercial, Residential, New and Old Construction H/I/S: Boating, Fishing, Reading, Watching the Boston Red Sox, Spending Time with his Wife and Three Children EDU: Diploma, Tolman High School (1996)
Email: dreletric@cox.net
URL: http://www.cambridgewhoswho.com

Alexandro Rodriguez
Title: Realtor Company: AMCAP Realty Address: 4764 Kelton Way, Sacramento, CA 95838 United States BUS: Real Estate Broker P/S: Residential, Executive, New Construction, Town Homes, Condos, Golf Homes, Senior, Gated, House Properties MA: National D/D/R: Residential Real Estate H/I/S: Gym A/A/S: California Association of Realtors, National Association of Realtors
Email: alex740@comcast.net
URL: http://www.amcaprealty.com

Angela Rodriguez
Title: RE Loan Consultant Company: Buy America Real Estate and Loans Address: 3620 Pacific Coast Highway, Torrance, CA 90505 United States BUS: Real Estate Consultant P/S: Real Estate Mortgage Financing MA: Local D/D/R: Financing

Dolores Dee Rodriguez
Title: Coordinator Company: Winslow Children's Theater Address: 521 E. Maple Street, Winslow, AZ 86047 United States BUS: Nonprofit Theater P/S: Performing Arts for Children MA: Local D/D/R: Coordinating Production, Hiring and Training Volunteers, Fundraising, Directing H/I/S: Painting, Working with Ceramics and Stained Glass EDU: Diploma, Winslow High School (1961) A/A/S: City Council (12 Years); Arizona Clean and Beautiful Committee
Email: deeluzi@msn.om

Francisco J. Rodriguez, MD, FACS
Title: MD Company: Sussex Surgical Associates Address: 808 Middleford Road, Seaford, DE 19973 United States BUS: Healthcare Facility P/S: General Surgery, Surgical Center MA: Regional D/D/R: Laproscopic Surgery, Breast Surgery, Cancer, Vein Treatments, Advanced Wound Care H/I/S: Scuba Diving, Watersports, Boating EDU: Bachelor of Arts, University of Pennsylvania; Master of Science, University of Kansas; Ph.D., State University of NY; MD, Health and Science Center at Brooklyn A/A/S: Medical Society of Delaware, American Board of Breast Surgery

Mrs. Josefa N. Rodriguez
Title: Special Education Teacher Company: Miami-Dade County Public Schools-Miami Edison Sr. High Address: 40 N.E. 52nd Street, Miami, FL 33137 United States BUS: School District P/S: Education MA: Local D/D/R: Special Education, Teaching English to Speakers of Other Languages, Learning Disabilities, Spanish, Childcare Trainer H/I/S: Attending the Opera, Giving Piano Lessons, Playing Tennis, Painting EDU: Master's Degree in Exceptional Student Education, Barry University (1992); Bachelor's Degree in Professional Studies-Barry University (1981) CERTS: Certified in Teaching the Mentally Handicapped, Grades K-12; Certified in Teaching Children with Specific Learning Disabilities; Certified in Teaching Spanish, Grades K-12; ESOL Certified A/A/S: National Education Association; American Federation of Teachers; United Teachers of Dade; Art Association of Dade County; Barry Alumni Association; Who's Who in American; Who's Who in the World (2007); Who's Who in American Education (2007-2008)
Email: jrodriguez@dadeschools.net

Maurilia 'Molly' Rodriguez
Title: Diabetes Educator Company: Certified Diabetic Services, Inc. Address: 10111 N.W. Park Drive, Houston, TX 77086 United States BUS: Distribution Company P/S: Supplying Diabetes Medical Products, Testing, Education and Information MA: Regional EXP: Ms. Rodriguez's expertise includes diabetes education and consulting. H/I/S: Reading, Listening to Audio Books, Gardening, Spending Time with her Grandchildren EDU: Ph.D. in Nursing, Texas Woman's University (1991); Master's Degree in Nursing, Texas Woman's University (1980); Bachelor's Degree in Nursing, Texas Woman's University (1965) CERTS: Certified Diabetes Educator; National Certification Board of Diabetes Educators A/A/S: American Association of Diabetes Educators; American Association of Diabetes Nurses; National Association of School Nurses; Diabetes Interactive C/VW: The Leukemia & Lymphoma Society; St. Jude Children's Research Hospital; American Diabetes Association
Email: mo3lly@sbcglobal.net
URL: http://www.mydiabetespartner.org/blog

Nancy Rodriguez
Title: Physical Therapist, Clinical Manager Company: Select Medical Corporation Address: 600 El Paseo, Lakeland, FL 33805 United States BUS: Rehabilitation Center P/S: Healthcare, Physical and Occupational Therapy MA: Statewide D/D/R: Managing Business Operations, Physical Therapy H/I/S: Reading, Traveling EDU: Bachelor of Science in Physical Therapy, University of Puerto Rico A/A/S: American Physical Therapist Association C/VW: Church
Email: nrr098@msn.com
Email: narodriguez@selectmedical.com
URL: http://www.cambridgewhoswho.com

Ruby E. Rodriguez
Title: Principal Company: Ector County Independent School District Address: P.O. Box 3912, Odessa, TX 79760 United States BUS: School District P/S: Education MA: Local D/D/R: Counseling At-Risk Students H/I/S: Gardening, Spending Time with her Grandchildren EDU: Master of Arts in Counseling, University of Texas of the Permian Basin A/A/S: Texas Association of Secondary School Principals; Administrator of the Year (2003)
Email: rodrigre@ector-county.k12.tx.us

Angel Santos Rodriguez-Morales
Title: Billing Director Company: Advanced Cardiology Center Address: P.O. Box 1838, Mayaguez, PR 00681 Puerto Rico BUS: Hospital Healthcare P/S: Cardiology MA: International D/D/R: Patient Accounting Currently working as Billing Director for Advanced Cardiology Center in Mayaguez, Puerto Rico H/I/S: Reading, Photography and Contemplative Mediation EDU: Master of Science, Wassard University; Bachelor of Science, Catholic University A/A/S: Treasurer of the Dr. Betances Health Foundation HFMA affiliate (Healthcare Financial Management Association) AFAMEP affiliate (Puerto Rico Medical Billers Association)
Email: angel.rodriguez@advancedcardiology.com

Evelyn M. Rodriquez
Title: Account Manager Company: Parish Pay Address: 50 Broadway, 21st Floor, New York, NY 10004 United States BUS: Financial Company P/S: Fund Collection for Churches MA: National D/D/R: Pharmaco Epidemiologist, Pediatrician, Expert in Public Health, Clinical Trials, Drug Safety, Risk Management, Quick Prevention Medicine H/I/S: Traveling, Playing the Guitar, Painting, Sketching EDU: Master's Degree in Public Health Administration, Major in Epidemiology; Bachelor of Science in Applied Economics and Management, Cornell University A/A/S: Board Member, Fluid Motion Theater and Film Company; International Society For Pharmacoeconomics and Outcomes Research; CDC, ISPOR, CDC, Epidemic Intelligence Service, Class of 1995 C/VW: Preparatory School; Eagle Hill School; International Dyslexia Association
Email: evelyn.rodriquez@gmail.com
URL: http://www.parishpay.com

Deone M. Roe
Title: Vice President Company: All Texas Grubbing Inc. Address: 3401 Sanco Road, Robert Lee, TX 76945 United States BUS: Brush Clearing Company P/S: Dozer and Excavation MA: Texas, New Mexico D/D/R: Administration, Legal Paperwork, Advertising H/I/S: Artwork, Ranching EDU: Associate Degree in Commercial Art and Advertising, Texas State Technical College, Waco C/VW: 64 Study Club; District Officer, United Methodist Woman's Club
Email: alltexas@wtxs.net
URL: http://www.alltexasgrubbing.com

Ms. Rachel A. Roebuck
Title: Senior Ceramic Engineer Company: PCC Airfoils, LLC Address: 8607 Tyler Boulevard, Mentor, OH 44060 United States BUS: Manufacturing Company P/S: Industrial Gas Turbine Blades MA: National D/D/R: Leading Projects on Upgrades, Preparing Ceramic Shell Mix H/I/S: Playing Volleyball, Golf and Softball, Spending Time Outdoors, Reading Ceramics Magazine EDU: Bachelor of Science in Chemistry, Mount Union College (1996)
Email: rachel.roebuck@pccmentor.com
URL: http://www.cambridgewhoswho.com

Kathleen L. Roehrs
Title: Speech-Language Pathologist Company: c/o Dudley-Charlton Regional School District Address: 19 Indian Lane, Webster, MA 01570 United States BUS: School District P/S: Education, Language Therapy MA: Local D/D/R: Children's Language Therapy, Communication Therapy H/I/S: Reading, Traveling, Spending Time with Family and Friends, Visiting Museums EDU: Bachelor's Degree in Communication Disorders, The Ohio State University, Wooster; Master's Degree in Counseling Psychology, Anna Maria College A/A/S: American Speech-Language-Hearing Association; Massachusetts Teachers Association C/VW: American Cancer Society
Email: rohehrsdesign@msn.com

Frances A. Rog
Title: Retired Teacher, Volunteer Company: Le Lande School Address: 207 E Walnut, Blue Springs, MO 64014 United States BUS: School P/S: Volunteer, Spanish Teacher MA: Local D/D/R: Teaching, Volunteering for Books for Peace and Youth Friends H/I/S: Gardening, Family Time, Cooking, Museums, Library EDU: Master of Arts and Curriculum, Leslie College, Cambridge, MA CERTS: Certified for Life to Teach K-12; Certified for Life to Teach Deaf and Hard of Hearing C/VW: Church

Barbara Rogers
Title: 1) Owner 2) Author **Company:** 1) B & J Sales 2) How to Make Boxes of Cash with Self Storage Auctions **Address:** P.O. Box 3205, Saratoga, CA 95070 United States **BUS:** 1) Self-Storage Auction 2) Online Book Store **P/S:** 'How To' Book for Self Storage Auctions **MA:** National **D/D/R:** Self-Storage Auctions, Writing Books **H/I/S:** Spending Time with her Husband and Two Children, Traveling, Going on an Annual Trip to Las Vegas **EDU:** College Coursework **A/A/S:** All Experts.com **C/VW:** Joel Osteen Ministries, Anthony Robbins Foundation
Email: bcrogers1970@selfstorageauctioncash.com
URL: http://www.selfstorageauctioncash.com

Felicia A. Rogers
Title: Administrative Marketing Assistant **Company:** Dominion Video Satellite, Inc. **Address:** 3050 Horseshoe Drive N., Suite 290, Naples, FL 34104 United States **BUS:** Christian Television Service **P/S:** Marketing and Advertising Services **MA:** International **D/D/R:** Marketing, Advertising, Offering Materials to Promote Dominion Including Web Banners, Printing Advertisements, Creating Weekly, Monthly and Quarterly Market Analysis Reports **H/I/S:** Playing Volleyball, Softball and Soccer, Enjoying the Outdoors, Reading **EDU:** Bachelor of Arts in Business Administration, Mount Vernon Nazarene University (2004); Bachelor of Arts in Spanish, Mount Vernon Nazarene University (2004) **A/A/S:** Naples Christian Church
Email: felicia.rogers@skyangel.com
URL: http://www.skyangel.com

Jeana S. Rogers
Title: Third-Grade Teacher **Company:** Keppel Union School District, Alpine Elementary School **Address:** 8244 Pearblossom Highway, Littlerock, CA 93543 United States **BUS:** School **P/S:** Education **MA:** Local **D/D/R:** Teaching Grades Kindergarten through Six **H/I/S:** Reading, Spending Time with Family **EDU:** Master of Arts in Curriculum and Instruction, Chapman University; Bachelor of Arts in Elementary Education, Doane College **CERTS:** CLAD Certified; EDI Certified **A/A/S:** National Education Association; Keppel Union Teachers Association; District Teacher of the Year (2000) **C/VW:** American Red Cross, Salvation Army
Email: jrbr77777@aol.com
URL: http://www.cambridgewhoswho.com

Joseph Paul Rogers
Title: Senior Director **Company:** Cisco **Address:** 400 Carillon, Suite 220, Saint Petersburg, FL 33716 United States **BUS:** Networking and Technology Company **P/S:** Communication Devices and Systems **MA:** International **D/D/R:** Technological Products and Services **H/I/S:** Boating, Spending Time with his Family **EDU:** Bachelor of Science in Business Administration, University of Maryland (1984) **C/VW:** Knights of Columbus
Email: jorogers@cisco.com

Mrs. Leticia I. Rogers
Title: Senior International Financial Analyst **Company:** Driscoll's Strawberry Associates **Dept:** International Finance Department **Address:** 345 Westridge Drive, Watsonville, CA 95076 United States **BUS:** Agricultural Company **P/S:** Organic Strawberries, Raspberries and Blackberries **MA:** International **D/D/R:** Analyzing Financial Transactions, Supporting International Entities, Reviewing Processes, Interacting with Employees **H/I/S:** Kickboxing, Practicing Yoga, Mountain Biking, Walking **EDU:** Pursuing Master of Business Administration; Bachelor of Arts in Accounting, Earned in Mexico (1994) **CERTS:** Certified Public Accountant, Earned in Mexico
Email: leticia.rogers@driscolls.com
URL: http://www.driscolls.com

Marjorie A. Rogers
Title: Owner **Company:** Marge's China and Gifts **Address:** P.O. Box 431, Woonsocket, SD 57385 United States **BUS:** Art Retail Company **P/S:** Hand-Painted Porcelain and China, Education **MA:** Regional **D/D/R:** Selling Hand-Painted Porcelain, Teaching Home Classes about the Art of China Painting, Producing Cast Molds, Developing Art Pieces, Shipping **H/I/S:** Yard Work, Attending Auction Sales, Shopping **EDU:** Coursework in Business, South Dakota State University; High School Education (1955) **A/A/S:** Ceramic Manufacturers Association; The World Organization of China Painters; South Dakota Organization of China Painters; Woonsocket Area China Painters
Email: mrchina@santel.net
URL: http://www.santel.net/~mrchina

Sheila J. Rogers
Title: Sales Administration Manager **Company:** Fujitsu Ten Limited **Address:** 19600 S. Vermont Avenue, Torrance, CA 90502 United States **BUS:** Manufacturing Company **P/S:** Head Units, Signal Processors and Amplifiers, Car Navigation 6ps **MA:** International **D/D/R:** maintaining customer relations, overseeing sales administration and the manufacturing of car audio products **H/I/S:** Hiking, Reading, Spending Time Outdoors, River Rafting, Houseboating, Spending Time with her Children **EDU:** Coursework in Business Administration, University of Nevada, Reno
Email: rogers@lao.ten.fujitsu.com

Tala Rogers
Title: Owner **Company:** Distinctive Design **BUS:** Architecture and Design Home Improvement **P/S:** Interior Design **MA:** Local **D/D/R:** Design **H/I/S:** Mountain Biking, Photography **EDU:** Bachelor's Degree in Architecture, Ohio State University **A/A/S:** LIDA
Email: tala@wideopenwest.com

Darlene E. Rogge
Title: Owner, Chef **Company:** K & D's Dutch Korner, Inc. **Address:** 13935 St. Wendel Road, Evansville, IN 47720 United States **BUS:** Restaurant **P/S:** Fine Dining **MA:** Posey County **D/D/R:** Preparing Steak and Chicken, Financial Business Operations **H/I/S:** Playing on her Computer, Cooking **EDU:** High School Education **C/VW:** Smile Train

Ms. Cynthia Rohret
Title: Executive Director **Company:** Wesley Community Services **Address:** 9013 Ridgeview Drive, Johnston, IA 50131 United States **BUS:** Hospice Center **P/S:** Elderly Care and Retirement Services **MA:** Regional **EXP:** Ms. Rohret's area of expertise is in palliative care nursing. **H/I/S:** Walking **EDU:** Bachelor of Science in Nursing, Jacksonville University (2005) **CERTS:** Certified Hospice Nurse (2000) **A/A/S:** Iowa Nurses Association; Iowa Hospice Organization; Infusion Nurses Society; National Hospice and Palliative Care Organization; National Association for Home Care and Hospice; American Nurses Association; Sigma Theta Tau
Email: crohret@wesleyservices.org

Eneida O. Roldan
Title: Medical Doctor, Chief Executive Officer **Company:** Metropolitan Hospital **Address:** 5959 N.W. Seventh Street, Miami, FL 33126 United States **BUS:** Hospital **P/S:** Short-Term Acute Care **MA:** Local **D/D/R:** Turn Around Bankruptcy, Administration, Endocrinology, Nutrition, Metabolism **H/I/S:** Traveling, Boating **EDU:** MD, Ross University School of Medicine; Master of Public Health, University of South Florida; Master of Business Administration, University of Tennessee **A/A/S:** American College of Healthcare Executives; American College of Physician Executives; American Society of Bariatric Physicians; Beta Gamma Sigma **C/VW:** American Cancer Society
Email: eroldanmd@aol.com

Pamela Jo Roller
Title: Teacher **Company:** Galveston Elementary School **Address:** 401 S. Maple Street, Galveston, IN 46932 United States **BUS:** Elementary School **P/S:** Primary Education **MA:** Regional **D/D/R:** Teaching All Subjects for Second-Grade Students, Developing Curriculum, Presenting Workshops at State Level Science Teachers Associations, Traveling, Delivering Speeches on her Traveling Experience **H/I/S:** Practicing Hawaiian Entertainment, Traveling, Reading, Interviewing Veterans for the Library of Congress **EDU:** Bachelor of Science in Elementary Education, Indiana University-Purdue University (1976); Bachelor of Science in Elementary Education (1974) **CERTS:** Certification in Aerospace Education (K-12), Purdue University (1991); Certified Lay Speaker, United Methodist District **A/A/S:** Pi Lambda Theta (2006-2007); Advisory Council, Dewey Dooits (2005-2007); Pals Program, Trucker Buddy International (1995-2007); Workshop Presenter, Hoosier Association of Science Teachers (1994-2007); School on Saturday Program (1994-2007); National Science Teachers Association (1994-2007); Founder, Coordinator of Mentoring Program, Tender Loving Care (1989-2007); Founder, Coordinator, Young Astronauts Program (1988-2007); Teacher Participant, Japan Fulbright Memorial Fund (2005); Educator, International Aerospace Education, Russian Space Science Internet (1994); National Science Teachers Association (1993); Educator, International Aerospace Education, Soviet Union (1991); Space Orientation, Washington, DC (1990); Educator, Space Camp for Professional Educators, Huntsville, AL (1988) **A/H:** Who's Who Among American Women (2006-2008); Who's Who in America (2006-2008); Honoree, Make a Difference Day, U.S.A. Weekend Magazine (2006-2007); Who's Who Among America's Teachers (2003-2007); Nominee, NASA's Educator Astronaut Program (2004); Honoree, Disney's American Teacher Awards (2003) **C/VW:** Red Cross Volunteer, Logansport Memorial Hospital, IN (1987-2004)
Email: proller1@verizon.net
Email: rollerp@sesc.k12.in.us
URL: http://www.cambridgewhoswho.com

Richard L. Rollins
Title: Sales Manager, United States Navy Fighter Pilot (Retired) **Company:** Townson Holding **BUS:** Marketing Company **P/S:** Marketing Services **MA:** National **D/D/R:** selling promotional products **H/I/S:** Surfing **EDU:** Coursework in Business Administration, Florida Institute of Technology; Bachelor of Science in Aerospace Engineering, United States Naval Academy (1975) **C/VW:** Dr. Seuss Literacy; The Church of Jesus Christ of Latter-day Saints; Boy Scouts of America; Local Charitable Organizations
Email: varollins@aol.com

Greta Jo Romain
Title: President, Chief Executive Officer **Company:** Montana Candle Scentsations **Address:** 22029 Montana Highway 223, Fort Benton, MT 59442 United States **BUS:** Candle Manufacturer **P/S:** Homemade Candles **MA:** Regional **D/D/R:** Hand Pouring Candles, Specialize in Unique Montana Fragrances **H/I/S:** Horseback Riding, Backpacking, Camping with her Grandchildren, Ranching **A/A/S:** Board of Directors, Liberty County Arts Council **C/VW:** Opportunities Incorporated of Great Falls, Montana; Former 4-H Leader
Email: mtcandle@mtintouch.net
URL: http://www.cambridgewhoswho.com

Mr. Dan G. Romano, MBA
Title: President, Chief Executive Officer **Company:** Granny Mo's, Inc. **Address:** P.O. Box 7524, Gulfport, MS 39506 United States **BUS:** Retail Firm **P/S:** American Indian Baskets, Charter Boating, High End Excursion Charters **MA:** Regional **D/D/R:** Hand Weaving Baskets, Guiding Three Hours Trips in Southern Mississippi, Incorporating Mohegan History, Practices and Traditions into Excursions, Accounting, Scheduling, Guiding, Conducting Maintenance, Crafting, Consulting in Business, Offering Finance Management, Targeting Small and Medium Sized Businesses **H/I/S:** Swimming, Camping, Fishing, Hunting **EDU:** Master's Degree in Business Administration, Norwich University (2007); Bachelor's Degree in Electrical Engineering Technology, University of Southern Mississippi (1987) **A/A/S:** Mohegan Tribal Member; Air Force Reserve Captain (1983-2005); Merchant Mariner Captain; Mississippi Gulf Coast Captains Association; Indian Arts and Crafts Association; National Charter Boat Captains Association
Email: mohegan1@msn.com

Maureen A. Romboldi
Title: Store Manager **Company:** Jasmine Sola **Address:** 92 Derby Street, Hingham, MA United States **BUS:** Fashion **P/S:** High End Denim Clothes **MA:** Local **D/D/R:** Fashion Merchandising and Management **H/I/S:** Exercise **EDU:** Associate Degree, Fisher College
Email: mromboldi62@hotmail.com

Richard T. Romer, PE, PTOE
Title: Principal **Company:** Orth-Rodgers and Associates, Inc **Address:** 1140 Town Center Drive 190, Las Vegas, NV 89144 United States **BUS:** Engineering Consulting Services **P/S:** Consulting Services, Engineering, Civil Transportation **MA:** Local **D/D/R:** Civil and Transportation Engineering and Planning **H/I/S:** Golfing, Boating, Traveling **EDU:** Master of Science in Civil Engineering, University of Nevada, Las Vegas (1995); Bachelor of Science in Management, University of Nevada, Las Vegas (1981) **A/A/S:** ITE, APWA
Email: rromer@orth-rodgers.com
URL: http://www.orth-rodgers.com

Debi J. Romero
Title: Box Office Manager **Company:** Oklahoma State Fair Park **Address:** 500 Land Rush Street, Oklahoma City, OK 73107 United States **BUS:** State Fair **P/S:** Entertainment for the Residents of Oklahoma **MA:** Oklahoma **D/D/R:** Business Administration, Finance, Retail, Ticketing, Supervision of Employees **H/I/S:** Reading, Gardening **EDU:** High School Graduate **C/VW:** Mothers Against Drunk Driving
Email: dromero@statefair.com
URL: http://www.statefair.com

Virginia Romero-Batista
Title: Teacher **Company:** El Rancho Unified School District **Address:** 7250 Citronell Avenue, Pico Rivera, CA 90660 United States **BUS:** Elementary School **P/S:** Elementary Education **MA:** Local **EXP:** Ms. Romero-Batista's area of expertise is in education. **H/I/S:** Scrapbooking, Reading, Spending Time with her Family **EDU:** Master's Degree in Elementary Education, Major in Mathematics, California State University (2002); Bachelor's Degree in Liberal Arts, Bilingual Education, California Polytechnic State University (1992) **A/A/S:** National Council of Teachers of Mathematics **C/VW:** Boystown; United Way
Email: varomista@hotmail.com
URL: http://www.cambridgewhoswho.com

Danielle K. Ronquille, MOT, LOTR
Title: Occupational Therapist, Certified Lymphedema Therapist **Company:** Gulfport Memorial Hospital **Address:** 4500 13th Street, South Building, Gulfport, MS 39502 United States **BUS:** Therapy Healthcare Center **P/S:** Inpatient and Outpatient Rehabilitation Services, Physical and Speech Therapy **MA:** Local **D/D/R:** Caring for Patients with Hand and Upper Extremities, Strokes, Traumatic Brain Injuries, Patient Education, Teaching Occupational Therapy, In-service **H/I/S:** Boating, Shopping **EDU:** Master of Occupational Therapy, Texas Woman's University (2003); Bachelor of Science in Child and Family Studies, University of Louisiana at Lafayette (2000) **CERTS:** Certified Lymphedema Therapist (2005) **A/A/S:** Team Leader, American Cancer Society
Email: dkrll377@hotmail.com
URL: http://www.cambridgewhoswho.com

Thomas Rooney Jr.
Title: Principal **Company:** Cardinal Dougherty High School **Address:** 6301 N. Second Street, Philadelphia, PA 19120 United States **BUS:** High School **P/S:** Secondary Education **MA:** Regional **EXP:** Mr. Rooney's expertise includes supervision, curriculum and staff development. **H/I/S:** Reading, Traveling, Teaching College Level Courses **EDU:** Doctor of Education, Immaculata University; Master's Degree in Education Administration, Villanova University; Master's Degree in Soviet History, Niagara University; Bachelor's Degree in History, Saint Francis University **A/A/S:** Association for Supervision and Curriculum Development; National Catholic Educational Association; Phi Delta Kappa **A/H:** Who's Who Among American College Students, Immaculata University (1996) **C/VW:** Volunteer, Local College Alumni Association
Email: cdprin@adphila.org
URL: http://www.cambridgewhoswho.com

Katha L. Root
Title: WIC Director **Company:** Opportunities for Chenango, Inc. **Address:** 44 W. Main Street, Norwich, NY 13815 United States **BUS:** Community Action Agency **P/S:** Human Services for Low-Income Residents **MA:** Countywide **EXP:** Ms. Root's area of expertise is in nutrition. **D/D/R:** Overseeing Nutrition Programs **H/I/S:** Sewing, Making Crafts **EDU:** Bachelor's Degree in Home Economics, SUNY Oneonta; Bachelor's Degree in Organizational Management and Development, Bluefield College, VA **A/A/S:** Headstart Advisory Council; Former Chairwoman, Greene Township for United Way **C/VW:** Volunteer, Greene Open-Door Soup Kitchen, Chenango County Hunger Coalition
Email: kroot@ofcinc.org
URL: http://www.ofcinc.org

Mr. Robert Ropars
Title: Senior Account Manager **Company:** SubscriberMail **Address:** 3333 Warrenville Road, Suite 530, Lisle, IL 60532 United States **BUS:** Service Provider, Marketing, Consulting, Strategy, Business to Business, Business to Consumer **P/S:** Email Services **MA:** International **D/D/R:** Service Provider, Email Marketing, Marketing, Consulting, Strategy, Business to Business, Business to Consumer **H/I/S:** Writing, Reading, Taking Photographs, Watching Independent Foreign Films, Hiking, Spending Time Outdoors **EDU:** Bachelor of Arts in English, North Central College, Naperville, Illinois **C/VW:** Associations Supporting Breast Cancer and Prostate Cancer Patients, American Red Cross
Email: ropars@subscribermail.com
URL: http://www.subscribermail.com/?ti=70140000000H0of

Rosalee Ropp
Title: Owner, President **Company:** Dallas Watch and Jewelry **Address:** 12801 Midway Road, Suite 505, Dallas, TX 75244 United States **BUS:** Jewelry and Watch Store **P/S:** Fine Swiss Watches and Jewelry **MA:** Regional **D/D/R:** Working with Fine Swiss and Pre-Owned Rolex Watches, Jewelry
Email: texasrose1217@aol.com
URL: http://www.cambridgewhoswho.com

James E. Rosa Jr.
Title: 1) President, Owner 2) Regional Director **Company:** 1) J. Rosa Consulting 2) Western Loehmann's Stores **Address:** 2742 Fremont Lane, Costa Mesa, CA 92626 United States **BUS:** 1) Consulting Firm 2) Retail Store **P/S:** 1) Consulting Services 2) Retail Sales **MA:** Regional **D/D/R:** Overseeing 23 Store Operations, organizing management training for retail establishments, assessing issues, implementing improvements, overseeing customer service and business strategies **H/I/S:** Playing Tennis, Golfing **EDU:** Bachelor of Arts in Economics, California State University, Sacramento (1975) **A/A/S:** Honorary Chairman, Business Advisory Council, National Republican Congressional Committee (2006) **A/H:** National Leadership Award (2006)
Email: jameserosa@yahoo.com

Adalberto Rosado-Nieves
Title: President **Company:** Pro Clean Tech, Inc. **Address:** 61 N. Calle Dr. Ramon E. Betances S., Mayaguez, PR 00680 United States **BUS:** Dry Cleaning Company **P/S:** Dry Cleaning, Laundry **MA:** Regional **D/D/R:** Dry Cleaning, Sales, Marketing **H/I/S:** Visiting Aquariums, Traveling, Bicycling **EDU:** Bachelor of Science in Biology, University of Puerto Rico **A/A/S:** Dry Cleaning Association; International Fabricare Institute **C/VW:** Cancer Foundation, Christian Aid Mission
Email: arosado61@gmail.com
URL: http://www.procleantech.com

Danielle A. Rosario
Title: Educator **Company:** Somerset Academy Charter School **Address:** 18491 S.W. 134th Avenue, Miami, FL 33177 United States **BUS:** Public Elementary Charter School Dedicated to Holding High Standards for Student Education and Parent Involvement Serving Residents of Miami **P/S:** Public Elementary Education for Local Students **MA:** Regional **D/D/R:** Teaching Fifth-Grade at a Charter School, Specializing in Elementary Education Including Mathematics, Reading, Writing, Science and Social Studies, Encouraging Manners and Etiquette in the Students **H/I/S:** Kickboxing, Cheerleading, Hiking, Writing **EDU:** Bachelor's Degree in Elementary Education and Psychology, University of Miami (2002) **A/A/S:** Volunteer, Ronald McDonald House Charities; SCAT Scores Award (2006,2007)
Email: darosario3@aol.com

Dr. Ernesto Rosario-Hernandez
Title: Professor of Industrial Psychology **Company:** Ponce School of Medicine **BUS:** Medical School **P/S:** Medical Education **MA:** Regional **EXP:** Mr. Rosario-Hernandez's expertise is in industrial-organizational psychology. **D/D/R:** Performing Psychological Assessments, Professional Statistics, Research and Test Construction, Consulting for the Marshall Administration Office, Teaching at The Catholic University of America and the Inter American University of Puerto Rico **H/I/S:** Reading, Golfing, Going to the Beach, Watching Movies **EDU:** Ph.D. in Industrial-Organizational Psychology, Carlos Albizu University, Puerto Rico (1996) **A/A/S:** American Psychological Association; Society for Industrial and Organizational Psychology; Division 14, Puerto Rican Psychology Association **A/H:** Recognition of Excellence as a Professor, Ponce School of Medicine (2008); American Psychological Foundation Awards, Caribbean (2007); Student Appreciation Award (2002) **C/VW:** SER de Puerto Rico
Email: ernestor@coqui.net
URL: http://www.cambridgewhoswho.edu

Carmela Rose
Title: Owner **Company:** Carmela's Fashion **Address:** 600 Fischer Boulevard, Toms River, NJ 08753 United States **BUS:** Retail Store **P/S:** Eveningwear, Sportswear, Cruise Wear **MA:** Regional **D/D/R:** Women's Fashions, Expert Tailoring, Mother-of-the-Bride Gowns **H/I/S:** Going to the Beach, Exercising **C/VW:** Local Charities, New Lisbon Development Center
Email: csrfashion@aol.com

Judith B. Rose
Title: Innkeeper, Owner **Company:** Rose Farm Inn **Address:** 1005 Roslyn Road, Block Island, RI 02807 United States **BUS:** Farm Inn **P/S:** Hospitality Services, Planning Beverage and Food Menus for Wedding Receptions, Wedding Guest Accommodations, Floral Designing **MA:** Regional **EXP:** Ms. Rose's area of expertise is in hospitality services. **D/D/R:** managing finance, supervising nine employees, delegating duties and ordering supplies **H/I/S:** Ballroom Dancing **EDU:** Bachelor's Degree in Medical Technology, University of Colorado (1963) **A/A/S:** Chamber of Commerce; Rhode Island Hospitality and Tourism Association
Email: rosefarm@riconnect.com
URL: http://www.rosefarminn.com

Mr. Richard S. Rose
Title: President **Company:** R & R Loss Prevention Associates **Address:** 21 Rensselaer Drive, Spring Valley, NY 10977 United States **BUS:** Loss Prevention Firm **P/S:** Fraud Investigation **MA:** National **D/D/R:** Investigating Corporate Fraud, Ensuring Security **EDU:** Bachelor of Arts in Retail, New York University (1952); Bachelor of Arts in Accounting, New York University (1952) **A/A/S:** New Jersey Food Council; American Society for Industrial Security
Email: rsrosesv@cs.com

Mr. Martin Rosen
Title: Partner **Company:** Sharff, Wittmer, Kurtz & Jackson, CPA **Address:** 4627 Ponce de Leon Boulevard, Coral Gables, FL 33146 United States **BUS:** Accounting Firm **P/S:** Auditing, Taxation, Estate and Trust Planning **MA:** Local **D/D/R:** Tax Planning, Estate, Trust Planning and Auditing **H/I/S:** Reading, Playing Scrabble **EDU:** Bachelor of Science in Biology, Dalhousie University **A/A/S:** Florida Institute of Certified Public Accountants; American Institute of Certified Public Accountants
Email: mrosen@swkj-cpa.com
URL: http://www.swkj-cpa.com

Clara Mae Rosenberger
Title: CEO/Creative Director **Company:** Rosie's Graphics **Address:** 1729 Maple Street, Wickliffe, OH 44092 United States **BUS:** Graphic Design Arts/Fine Arts/Visual/Graphic Design **P/S:** Creative Designs, Branding, Creative Concepts **MA:** Local **D/D/R:** Creative Design and Renaissance Professional **H/I/S:** Poetry, Writing **A/A/S:** American Society of Poets

Joyce M. Rosenfield
Title: Founder, President, Author, Composer **Company:** California Spiritual Harp Institute **BUS:** Nonprofit Music Company **P/S:** Music Performance and Composition, Entertainment, Inspiration, Parapsychology 'Healing Harp' Music **MA:** National **D/D/R:** Playing Inspirational Harp, Performing at Carnegie Hall and the Oklahoma, Baltimore, Virginia and North Carolina Music Symphonies, Teaching Harp and Piano Playing, Teaching Beginners Piano for Seniors through Intermediate Level **EDU:** Coursework in Conservatory of Music, Oberlin College; Coursework, Curtis Institute of Music; Diploma, LaGuardia High School of Music and Art and Performing Arts **A/A/S:** Music Teachers' Alliance of California; World Harp Congress; American Harp Society; Free Thinkers Religion; Former Member, Music Teachers' Association; World Harp Congress
Email: lilacmuse@sbcglobal.net
URL: http://www.audioadventuresplus.com

Sandra L. Rosenthal
Title: Owner **Company:** Crossroads of Fashion, LLC **Address:** 9646 Allisonville Road, Indianapolis, IN 46250 United States **BUS:** Fashion Boutique **P/S:** Clothing, Casual Dresses, Business Attire **MA:** Local **D/D/R:** overseeing business operations and ensuring customer satisfaction **H/I/S:** Traveling, Ballroom Dancing **A/A/S:** Fishers Chamber of Commerce; Better Business Bureau **C/VW:** Autism Society of Colorado; Shelter for Battered Women and Children; Muscular Dystrophy Association; National Parkinson Foundation
Email: sandrarosenthal@sbcglobal.net
URL: http://www.crossroadsoffashion.com

Annethra Faith Ross
Title: Special Education Teacher **Company:** Little Axe Public Schools **Address:** 2000 168th Avenue N.E., Norman, OK 73026 United States **BUS:** School District **P/S:** Education **MA:** Local **D/D/R:** Special Education **H/I/S:** Fishing, Going to the Beach, Participating in Outdoor Activities **EDU:** Master's Degree in Counseling, East Central University (2007) **A/A/S:** Oklahoma Education Association; National Education Association; Council for Exceptional Children; District Teacher of the Year (2006); Elementary Teacher of the Year (2006) **C/VW:** Special Olympics
Email: ross45acp@sbcglobal.net
URL: http://www.cambridgewhoswho.com

Mr. Chapman M. Ross
Title: Project Environmental Engineer **Company:** Geosyntec Consultants **Address:** 289 Great Road, Suite 105, Acton, MA 01720 United States **BUS:** Engineering Consulting Firm **P/S:** Environmental Engineering Consulting **MA:** International **D/D/R:** Conducting Soil and Groundwater Investigations, Designing Remediation Systems **H/I/S:** Mountain Biking, International Travel, Cooking, West African Drumming **EDU:** Master of Science in Environmental Engineering, Clemson University; Bachelor of Science in Civil Engineering, Clemson University **A/A/S:** American Society of Civil Engineers (ASCE)
Email: cross@geosyntec.com
URL: http://www.geosyntec.com

Doris J. Ross
Title: District Librarian, Text Book Coordinator **Company:** Carlisle Independent School District **Address:** 8960 FM 13 W., Henderson, TX 75654 United States **BUS:** School District **P/S:** Education **MA:** Local **D/D/R:** Overseeing State Reading Programs, Establishing Reading Programs, Mentoring Teachers, managing library functions, coordinating text books for district, managing inventory and overseeing purchasing **H/I/S:** Reading, Cooking, Solving Puzzles, Spending Time with her Grandchildren **EDU:** Master's Degree in Public School Administration, University of Alaska **CERTS:** Certified Elementary Teacher (K-8); Certified Special Education Teacher **A/A/S:** Texas School Classroom Teachers Association; Texas Library Association; Texas Public School Library Association; President, Local Chapter, Delta Kappa Gamma **A/H:** Teacher of the Year Award
Email: rossbooklady@aol.com
URL: http://www.cambridgewhoswho.com

Ms. Jane Arlene Diamond Ross

Title: Director of Music Ministries **Company:** First Christian Church **Address:** 116 E. Boyer Street, Wadsworth, OH 44281 United States **BUS:** 1) School 2) Church **P/S:** 1) Public Education, Board-Approved Elementary and Junior High Curriculum, Vocal and General Music Methods 2) Religious Services Including Worship, Fellowship, Youth, Music and Choirs **MA:** 1) Local 2) Local **EXP:** Ms. Ross' expertise includes music education including general organ music, choral, handbells, piano and voice instruction, leadership, management and curriculum development. **D/D/R:** Teaching Music Education **H/I/S:** Needlework, Travel, Reading, Collecting Bells **EDU:** Post Master's Degree, University of Akron, Oberlin College and Ashland University; Master of Music, The University of Akron (1985); Bachelor of Science in Music Education, Major in Piano, Minor in Voice, Indiana University of Pennsylvania, Indiana, PA (1967); Academic Diploma, Albert Gallatin Senior High School, Point Marion, PA (1963); Numerous Workshops and Seminars in Music Education **A/A/S:** Medina City Teachers Association; Northeast Ohio Education Association; Lifetime Member, Ohio County Retired Teachers Association; Lifetime Member, Medina County Retired Teachers Association; Ohio Education Association; Ohio Music Education Association; National Education Association; Music Educators National Conference; American Guild of English Handbell Ringers; American Guild of Organists; Lifetime Member, Delta Omicron International Honorary Music Fraternity for Women **A/H:** Who's Who of American Women (2002); Nationally Registered Music Educator, Music Educators National Conference (1991); Martha Holden Jennings Scholar Award (1987-1988); Distinguished Service Award, Medina City Schools (1989); Excellence in the Fine Arts $10,000 Grant Award, Rockefeller Brothers Fund (1984); Keynote Speaker, Regional Symposium of Fine Arts, National Endowment of the Arts (1984) **C/VW:** Local Charitable Organizations; Kappa Mu; Retired Medina Teachers Service Organization
Email: jross@wadsnet.com
URL: http://www.fccwadsworth.org

Kimberly A. Ross, RN, BSN

Title: Case Management Supervisor **Company:** HCA Twin Cities Hospital **Address:** 2190 Highway 85 N., North College Boulevard, Niceville, FL 32578 United States **BUS:** Hospital **P/S:** Healthcare **MA:** Regional **D/D/R:** acting as resource for staff and physicians on many regulatory issues both managed care and private insurance, overseeing department functions which includes discharge planning, UR, quality, benchmarking and social work, participating and initiating nursing educational sessions, community education concerning a variety of subjects **H/I/S:** Karate, Reading, Cross-Stitching **EDU:** Bachelor of Science in Nursing, University of South Alabama (1993) **CERTS:** Certification in Case Management; Registered Nurse **A/A/S:** Sigma Theta Tau
Email: kimberly.ross@hcahealthcare.com
URL: http://www.tchealthcare.com

Megan N. Ross

Title: Pharmacy Intern **Company:** CVS **Address:** 6007 Allentown Boulevard, Harrisburg, PA 17112 United States **BUS:** Retail Pharmacy **P/S:** Retail Pharmacy Goods **MA:** Local **D/D/R:** General Pharmacy Services **H/I/S:** Playing Soccer, Boating, Traveling **EDU:** Coursework in Pharmacy, Shenandoah University, Bernard J. Dunn School of Pharmacy **A/A/S:** Phi Delta Chi; American Pharmacists Association **C/VW:** American Red Cross
Email: mross@su.edu
URL: http://www.cambridgewhoswho.com

Robert J. Ross

Title: Principal Engineer **Company:** Ross Engineering, Inc. **Address:** 10400 Griffin Road, Suite: 206, Cooper City, FL 33328 United States **BUS:** Proven Leader in the Engineering Industry **P/S:** Professional Engineering Services **MA:** National **D/D/R:** Practicing Civil and Water Resource Engineering **H/I/S:** Golfing, Enjoying Watersports, Traveling **EDU:** Master of Science in Civil Engineering, Florida International University (2003); Bachelor of Science in Civil Engineering, Florida International University (2000); Bachelor of Science in Engineering Technology, University of Central Florida (1994) **A/A/S:** American Society of Civil Engineers; National Society of Professional Engineers; American Water Resources Association; Florida Institute of Consulting Engineers; Florida Engineering Society; NRP **C/VW:** American Breast Cancer Society; Kids in Distress
Email: rross@rossengineers.com
URL: http://www.rossengineers.com

Nancy R. Rossi, CPA

Title: Accountant **Company:** Goldburg & Zuffelato **Address:** 445 Boston Post Road, Orange, CT 06477 United States **BUS:** Accounting Firm **P/S:** Accounting **MA:** Eastern United States **EXP:** Ms. Rossi's area of expertise is in tax management. **H/I/S:** Volunteering **EDU:** Bachelor of Science in Accounting, Charter Oak State College **A/A/S:** Connecticut Society of Certified Public Accountants **C/VW:** City Council Member, West Haven; Board Member, Ward-Heitmann Museum House
Email: raeetta@aol.com

Mrs. Tara A. Rosso-McGee

Title: Assistant Principal **Company:** Medlock Bridge Elementary School **Address:** 10215 Medlock Bridge Parkway, Alpharetta, GA 30022 United States **BUS:** Elementary School **P/S:** Primary Education **MA:** Local **D/D/R:** teaching elementary education, scheduling, grading students, overseeing staff and students discipline **H/I/S:** Traveling, Spending Time Outdoors **EDU:** Master's Degree in Administration, University of St. Thomas, Houston, TX; Bachelor's Degree in Elementary Education, Minor in Mathematics, Texas A&M University **A/A/S:** Association for Supervision and Curriculum Development; Professional Association of Georgia Educators **C/VW:** Young Texans Against Cancer
Email: mcgee@fultonschools.org

Audrey I. Roth

Title: Sixth-Grade Mathematics Teacher (Retired) **Company:** Claude Brown Intermediate **Address:** 209 Lincoln Trail, Hawk Point, MO 63349 United States **BUS:** Middle School **P/S:** Intermediate School Instruction and Curriculum **MA:** Regional **EXP:** Ms. Roth's area of expertise is in education. **D/D/R:** teaching mathematics, reading, social studies, a wide range of abilities and special education **H/I/S:** Gardening, Fishing, Spending Time with her Two Grandchildren **EDU:** Master's Degree in Elementary Education, Southwest Baptist University, Bolivar, MO (2000) **A/A/S:** California Teachers Association; PTO; Missouri State Teachers Association
Email: faroth@centurytel.net
URL: http://www.troy.k12.mo.us/cbi

Lisa K. Roth

Title: Principal **Company:** Belcher Elementary School **Address:** 1839 S. Belcher Road, Clearwater, FL 33764 United States **BUS:** Public Elementary School **P/S:** Education for Kindergarten through Fifth-Grade Students **MA:** Regional **D/D/R:** Overseeing Staff and Students, Organizing Curriculums and Instruction Programs, Maintaining Safety Compliance **H/I/S:** Reading, Bicycling **EDU:** Master's Degree in Educational Leadership, University of South Florida (1997) **A/A/S:** Association for Supervision and Curriculum Development; Alpha Delta Kappa; Phi Delta Kappa International; International Reading Association
Email: rothli@pcsb.org
URL: http://www.belcher-es.pinellas.k12.fl.us

Ms. Lizzy Rothouse

Title: Broker, Owner **Company:** Fleur de Liz Realty, LLC **Address:** 3110 Magazine Street, Suite 145, New Orleans, LA 70115 United States **BUS:** Real Estate Sale and Lease Company **P/S:** Real Estate Sales and Leases, Luxury Condos, Property Management, Historic Neighborhoods, Investment Properties **MA:** New Orleans Metro Area, Uptown, Garden District, Lower Garden District, Irish Channel, Warehouse District/CBD, French Quarter, Marigny, Bywater, Holy Cross, Mid-City, Lakeview, Central City, Broadmoor **EXP:** Ms. Rothouse's expertise includes the sale of condominiums, historic homes and investment properties as well as property management. **D/D/R:** Managing a Real Estate Brokerage Company, Managing Property, Accounting, Managing Transactions, Marketing, Prospecting, Advertising **H/I/S:** Traveling, Listening to Live Music, Cats, Swimming **EDU:** Master's Degree in International Public Health, Tulane University; Bachelor's Degree in Anthropology, Minor in Business, Indiana University **CERTS:** Real Estate Broker's License, Donaldson Education **A/A/S:** Women's Council of Realtors; National Council of Realtors; NOMR; Rex Condo Association; BNI; Krewe of King Arthur **A/H:** RE/MAX Team Player Award; Cooperative Spirit Award, Mid-States and Dixie Region **C/VW:** Habitat for Humanity; 90.7 WWOZ Guardian of the Groove
Email: erothouse@yahoo.com
URL: http://www.fleurdelizrealty.com

Mary Ellen Rotolo

Title: Physical Therapy Assistant **Company:** Comprehensive Home Care **Address:** 6472 Bonnie Bay Circle, Pinellas Park, FL 33781 United States **BUS:** Homecare Service for Patients **P/S:** In-Home Physical Therapy **MA:** Regional **D/D/R:** Practicing Healthcare in Multiple Settings and Treatment Programs in Multiple Healthcare Areas, Balloons, Magic, Games, Storytelling, Poetry, Buffoonery **H/I/S:** Reading **EDU:** Buffoonery Degree, Clowns Galore (1997); Associate Degree in Physical Therapy, St. Petersburg College (1991) **A/A/S:** Former President, Clown Galore Association (2005-2005); Former Member, Fools for Christ; American Physical Therapy Association; Children and Adults with Attention Deficit Disorders; New Journey Fellowship **C/VW:** Relay For Life
Email: mrotolo@tampabay.rr.com
URL: http://www.cambridgewhoswho.com

Amanda M. Roulston

Title: Area Credit Manager **Company:** The Reynolds Company **Address:** 2861 Merrell Road, Dallas, TX 75229 United States **BUS:** Electrical Supply Company **P/S:** Connectors and Terminations, Electrician Supplies, Line Hardware, Mechanical Equipment, Wiring Devices, Distribution Equipment, Fuses and Accessories, Lighting, Material Handling Equipment, Pipe, Tube, Hose and Fittings **MA:** Regional **D/D/R:** Handling $8.5 Million Portfolio Package, Determining Credit Limits Based on Information from Dun and Bradstreet, Filing Bonds and Liens' Claims, operating credit collections **H/I/S:** Spending Time with her Children **EDU:** Coursework in Media Communications, Tarrant County College, Fort Worth, TX; High School Education (1996) **A/A/S:** National Association of Credit Management **C/VW:** Mentor, Local Charitable Organizations
Email: aroulston@reynco.com
URL: http://www.reynoldsonline.com

Amandia K. Rouse

Title: Unit Director **Company:** Boys & Girls Club of America, Jackson and George Counties **Address:** P.O. Box 1903, Lucedale, MS 39452 United States **BUS:** Youth Development Organization **P/S:** Afterschool Programs, Summer Programs **MA:** Local **D/D/R:** Overseeing Activities **H/I/S:** Attending Antique Car Shows, Traveling, Fishing **EDU:** Master's Degree in Education, William Carey University; Bachelor of Science in Political Science and History, University of Southern Mississippi; Associate Degree, Mississippi Gulf Coast Junior College **C/VW:** American Red Cross, Disaster Relief
Email: arouse@bgcjc.org
URL: http://www.bgcic.org

John F. Rousseau

Title: Chief Executive Officer **Company:** Mainely Trim, Inc. **Address:** 213 County Line Auburn Road, Auburn, GA 30011 United States **BUS:** Construction Company **P/S:** Installation and Design of Residential Constructions, Consulting Services **MA:** Regional **D/D/R:** overseeing carpentry work and layout and construction of stairways and rails **H/I/S:** Watching Falcons, Braves and Gladiators, Snow Skiing, Horseback Riding **EDU:** Associate Degree in Business, DeKalb County Community College **A/A/S:** National Association of Home Builders **C/VW:** Local Charitable Organizations
Email: john.rousseau@cwwemail.com
URL: http://www.cambridgewhoswho.com

Melissa M. Rowe

Title: Teacher **Company:** South Bend Community School Corporation **Address:** 1021 Blaine Avenue, South Bend, IN 46616 United States **BUS:** Elementary Education **P/S:** Core Curriculum Including Reading, Mathematics, English, Science, Social Studies, Art, Music, History, Physical Education **MA:** Regional **D/D/R:** Teaching Literacy and Reading Framework to Inner-city Children **H/I/S:** Teaching **EDU:** Bachelor's Degree in Elementary Education, Indiana University, South Bend (1999) **A/A/S:** National Educators Association; State Teaching Association; Apostolic Temple Church; Teacher of the Year
Email: mrowe@sbcsc.k12.in.us
URL: http://www.sbcsc.k12.in.us

Richard Rowehl Jr.

Title: Vice President, Eastern Regional Director **Company:** Oppenheimer and Co., Inc. **Dept:** Retirement Services **Address:** 200 Park Avenue, Floor 25, New York, NY 10166 United States **BUS:** Investment Company **P/S:** Corporation Retirement Plans **MA:** National **EXP:** Mr. Rowehl's expertise includes corporate defined contribution, defined benefits, non-qualified deferred compensation and executive benefits. **H/I/S:** Automobile Racing, Golfing, Listening to Music, Spending Time with his Family **EDU:** Bachelor of Arts in Management and Finance **A/A/S:** American Society of Pension Professionals and Actuaries **C/VW:** Cubmaster, Boy Scouts of America; Huntington Chamber of Commerce; East Northport Chamber of Commerce
Email: richard.rowehl@opco.com
URL: http://www.cambridgewhoswho.com

Susan F. Rowland

Title: Director of Adult Education **Company:** Delaware Area Career Center **Address:** 4565 Columbus Pike, Delaware, OH 43015 United States **BUS:** School **P/S:** Post Secondary Vocational School, Training for Healthcare, Law, EMT, Etc **MA:** Local **D/D/R:** Leadership Training **H/I/S:** Cooking, Reading, Travel, Painting, Quilting **EDU:** Master's Degree in Early and Mid-School Education, Otterbein College; Bachelor of Science in Education, Ohio State University **CERTS:** Principal Administration Certificate; Superintendent License **A/A/S:** Rotary International, Ohio Association Career and Technical Educators, American Association of Career and Technical Educators
Email: rowlands@delawareareacc.org
URL: http://www.delawareareacc.org

Carol Ann Roy
Title: Registered Nurse Company: Androscoggin Valley Hospital Address: 59 Page Hill Road, Berlin, NH 03570 United States BUS: Hospital P/S: Healthcare MA: Local D/D/R: Home Health and Hospice Nursing H/I/S: Scrapbooking, Spending Time with Family EDU: Associate Degree in Nursing, New Hampshire Vocational Technical College A/A/S: China Adoptive Families from Association
Email: mccroy2002@yahoo.com
URL: http://www.cambridgewhoswho.com

Kevin C. Roy
Title: President Company: Bayline Media Address: 35 Maple Street, Suite 2, South Hamilton, MA 01982 United States BUS: Full-Service Web Design and Development Company P/S: Website Design and Development MA: National D/D/R: Building and Developing Websites and Search Engines, Creating Complex Databases, Utilizing the Discovery Process, Teaching Businesses to Maximize Online Visibility and Revenue H/I/S: Surfing, Working as a Cross Fit Gym, Enjoying All Outdoor Activities EDU: Master's Degree in International Business and Marketing, Bentley College (1998) A/A/S: Business Networking International
Email: kroy@baylinemedia.com
URL: http://www.baylinemedia.com

Michelle M. Roy
Title: Registered Pharmacist Company: Paradise Shop 'N' Save Address: 62 W. Main Street, Fort Kent, ME 04743 United States BUS: Private Retail Pharmacy P/S: Dispensing Pharmaceuticals to Retail Customers and Long Term Care Facilities MA: Local D/D/R: Counseling Patients, Dispensing Medication, Reviewing Interactions H/I/S: Running EDU: Bachelor's Degree in Pharmacy, Northeastern University A/A/S: American Pharmacists Association C/VW: Edgar Paradis Cancer Foundation
Email: mjroy22@hotmail.com

Tamika M. Roy
Title: Senior Marketing Manager Company: Amgen Address: One Amgen Center Drive, Thousand Oaks, CA 91320 United States BUS: Leading Human Therapeutics Company in the Biotechnology Industry P/S: Entrepreneurial, Science-Driven Enterprise Dedicated to Helping People Fight Serious Illness MA: International D/D/R: Expertise is Overseeing all Marketing, Overseeing Marketing Access and Rehabilitation; Biotechnology, Research and Development Products, Biologist H/I/S: Traveling, Tennis, Golf EDU: Bachelor's Degree in Marketing, Arkansas State University A/A/S: Spoken to Audiences at Payer-Ad
Email: tamikaroy@gmail.com
URL: http://www.amgen.com

Elizabeth H. Royse
Title: Eastern Procurement Manager Company: US GreenFiber, LLC Address: 14606 Arcadia Street N.W., Canal Fulton, OH 44614 United States BUS: Manufacturing and Commodity Company P/S: Insulation, Fire and Sound Products, 100 Percent Recycled Paper for Products, Green Building Manufacturer MA: International D/D/R: Overseeing Recycling Commodity Market, Managing Recycled Material Procurement EDU: Dual Bachelor's Degrees in International Business and Logistics, The University of Akron, International School, Holland (1995) A/A/S: Mu Kappa Tau; Beta Gamma Sigma; Golden Key International Honor Society
Email: beth.royse@us-gf.com
URL: http://www.greenfiber.com

Miss Debra A. Rubatt
Title: Founder, Executive Director, Missouri President Company: Fun Active Senior Toy's Organization Address: 337 Mach Lane, Rockaway Beach, MO 65740 United States BUS: Nonprofit Seniors' Charity P/S: Fundraising and Charity Events for Seniors, Toy for Seniors Including Glass Bead Necklaces, Giant Remote Controls, Cards, Books and Bibles MA: International D/D/R: Fundraising, Managing Operations, Creating Toys for Seniors, Developing Events that Seniors will Enjoy, Focusing on the Forgotten Elderly, Developing Therapy Dog Programs H/I/S: Gardening, Watching Movies, Camping, Fishing, Boating, Music, Playing the Flute, Visiting Nursing Homes with her Dog, Honey Bear, Helping People CERTS: Certification in Secretarial Administration, St. Petersburg Vocational and Technical Institute (1986); Certified Nursing Aid (1976); Certification in CPR A/A/S: Phi Beta Lambda; The Humane Society; Future Business Leaders of America; Angel for the Hospice Volunteers A/H: Food Service Cash Award and Letter of Appreciation for Sales and Service C/VW: F.A.S.T.; Twilight Foundation; Hospice; Volunteer Firefighters; United Way; Local Food Banks
Email: debrarubatt@centurytel.net
Email: F.A.S.T@centurytel.net

Mary-Jo W. Rubin
Title: Physical Therapist, Acupuncture Physician Company: Physical Therapy Specialties, Inc. Address: 4360 Northlake Boulevard, Suite 104, Palm Beach Gardens, FL 33410 United States BUS: Physical Therapy Practice P/S: Physical Therapy, Acupuncture MA: Local D/D/R: Treating Pediatric and Geriatric Neurological Conditions Such as Cerebral Palsy, Cerebral-Vascular Accidents, Multiple Sclerosis, Pain Control H/I/S: Reading EDU: Master's Degree in Education, West Virginia University; Certification, Physical Therapy, University of Pittsburgh CERTS: Licensed Physical Therapist A/A/S: APTA; Florida Physical Therapy Association C/VW: American Society for the Prevention of Cruelty to Animals

Mata E. Rubino
Title: President Company: Rubino Enterprises, Inc. Address: 710 N. Hammonds Ferry Road, Linthicum, MD 21090 United States BUS: Construction, Project and Contract Management Company P/S: General Construction, Project and Contract Management Services MA: Local EXP: Ms. Rubino's area of expertise is in contract administration. D/D/R: Developing the Business H/I/S: Spending Time with her Daughters EDU: Diploma, Maryvale High School A/A/S: Maryland Minority Business Association; Building Trade Association C/VW: Maryland Small Business Reserve Program; Make-A-Wish; American Cancer Society
Email: mrubino@rubinoenterprises.com
URL: http://www.rubinoenterprises.com

Paul Rucker
Title: Real Estate Manager Company: Bankers Hill Property Mgt, Inc Address: 1940 Fifth Avenue, Suite 201, San Diego, CA 92101 United States BUS: Real Estate and Property Management P/S: Property Management Services/Variety of Management Specialties MA: Local D/D/R: Metropolitan Property Management of Multi-Income Properties H/I/S: Tennis, Travel, Cross Country EDU: Associate of Science in Real Estate and Business, San Diego Mesa College A/A/S: San Diego Apartment Association, IREM-Institute of Real Estate Management, Phi Theta Kappa
Email: paulinsky77@yahoo.com

Mary K. Rudd
Title: Lead Senior Speech-Language Pathologist Company: East Alabama Medical Center Address: 2000 Pepperell Parkway, Opelika, AL 36801 United States BUS: Medical Center P/S: Medical Services MA: Regional D/D/R: Restoring Communication and Swallowing Functions to People who are Neurologically Impaired H/I/S: Studying Genealogy EDU: Master's Degree in Communication Disorders, Auburn University; Bachelor of Science in Speech and Hearing Disorders, Auburn University A/A/S: American Speech-Language-Hearing Association C/VW: Daughters of the American Revolution
Email: jrmr97@bellsouth.net
URL: http://www.cambridgewhoswho.com

Lynda Rudge-Esposito
Title: Business Development Manager Company: MidCo, Inc. Address: 16 W. 221 Shore Court, Burr Ridge, IL 60527 United States BUS: Distribution Firm P/S: Business Telephone and Security Systems MA: National D/D/R: Selling Telecommunications Systems H/I/S: Golfing, Traveling EDU: Bachelor of Fine Arts in Graphic Design, Bradley University
Email: lespostio@midcosystems.com
URL: http://www.midcosystems.com

Lana Rudym
Title: Owner, Interior Designer Company: Lana Rudym Interiors Address: 35 Tudor Street, Suite 15, Lynn, MA 01902 United States BUS: Interior Design Company Serving Residents of Lynn P/S: Interior Decor and Design Services for Commercial and Residential Properties MA: National D/D/R: Overseeing Interior Design for Residential and Commercial Properties, Wellness Spas, Medical Offices and Boutiques H/I/S: Traveling, Working on Interior Design, Enjoying Outdoor Activities, Spending Time with her Children EDU: Ph.D. in Psychology, Kharkov State University, Russia (1986) A/A/S: International Furnishings and Design Association; North Shore Women and Boutique Business Groups; Featured, Room for Improvement, Channel 7
Email: lana.interiors@comcast.net
URL: http://www.lanarudyminteriors.com

Rodney D. Ruff
Title: Technical Writer Address: 6522 Blondo Street, Omaha, NE 68104 United States BUS: Technical Writing P/S: Writing, Editing and Proofreading Help Files and User Manuals MA: Local D/D/R: Technical and Creative Writing, Editing and Proofreading Help Files and User Manuals H/I/S: Reading, Writing Articles EDU: Bachelor of Science, University of Nebraska at Omaha A/A/S: American Mensa C/VW: Local Homeless Shelters
Email: manoftrivia@hotmail.com
URL: http://www.myspace.com/rodneyruff

Tricia Ruggiero
Title: Director of Finance Company: Insider Advantage, Inc. Address: 4401 Northside Parkway N.W., Suite 100, Atlanta, GA 30327 United States BUS: Online News Agency P/S: Online News, Consulting Services on Politics and Polling MA: National D/D/R: managing finances H/I/S: Spending Time with her Family EDU: High School Diploma
Email: tricia@insideradvantage.com
URL: http://www.insideradvantage.com

Denise Ruiz
Title: Production Manager Company: Millar Instruments Address: 6001 Gulf Freeway, Suite A, Houston, TX 77023 United States BUS: Medical Device Manufacturer P/S: Pressure Sensor Technology to Accurately Measure Heart Pressure, Flow and Volume in Humans MA: National D/D/R: Overseeing the Clean Room for Manufacturing Catheters, Managing Production Schedules H/I/S: Hosting Parrot Rescues
Email: druiz@millarmail.com
URL: http://www.millarinstruments.com

Martha E. Ruiz
Title: General Manager Company: Denny's Restaurant Address: 1390 S. First Street, San Jose, CA 95110 United States BUS: Quality Family Dining P/S: Good Food and Service in a Casual Dining Atmosphere MA: National D/D/R: Overseeing Staff, Ordering Inventory and Supplies, Strong Sales Skills, Community Relations, Hiring and Firing for Store, Scheduling for Employees and Managers, Human Resources, Payroll, Training managers and Employees H/I/S: Fine Dining EDU: General Dentist, Mexico
Email: mruizc@sbcglobal.net
URL: http://www.dennys.com

Ms. Annette Ruizesparza
Title: Financial Aid Specialist, Foster Youth Liaison Company: Evergreen Valley College Address: 3095 Yerba Buena Road, San Jose, CA 95135 United States BUS: Community College P/S: Higher Education MA: National EXP: Ms. Ruizesparza's expertise is in financial aid services. D/D/R: Managing Financial Aid H/I/S: Biking, Traveling EDU: Associate Degree in General Studies, San Jose Community College C/VW: Various Outreach Programs
Email: annette.ruiz-esparza@evc.edu
URL: http://www.cambridgewhoswho.com

Jennifer C. Rummel
Title: Director of Human Resources Company: East Texas Medical Center, Athens Address: 2000 S. Palestine Street, Athens, TX 75751 United States BUS: Medical Center P/S: Healthcare MA: Local EXP: Ms. Rummel's area of expertise is in human resource management. D/D/R: Overseeing Administrative Duties for Two Healthcare Organizations, Consulting, Lecturing EDU: Master's Degree in Human Resources, University of Texas A/A/S: Tennessee Society for Healthcare Human Resources Administration; Society for Human Resource Management C/VW: American Heart Association
Email: jrummel@etmc.org
URL: http://www.cambridgewhoswho.com

Carolyn Sue Taylor Rumsfeld
Title: Court Reporter, Singer, Songwriter Company: Self-Employed Address: New Orleans, LA BUS: Court Reporting P/S: Court Reporting Services MA: National D/D/R: Traveling to Regional Destinations Including Texas Deposition Transcripts, Court Proceedings, Symposiums, Arbitration and Meeting Conferences H/I/S: Cooking, Fishing, Listening to Music, Singing EDU: Bachelor's Degree in Music and Classical Piano, Trinity University, San Antonio, Texas; Bachelor of Arts in Teaching Music, Trinity University (1976) A/A/S: Past President LCRA, Board Member NCRA, A/H: Certified RPR, CCR, CSR
Email: staylorrum@aol.com

Jason Runnels
Title: Assistant Music Librarian Company: Southwestern Baptist Theological Seminary Address: 2001 W. Seminary Drive, Fort Worth, TX 76115 United States BUS: Seminary, Library P/S: Education, Research MA: National D/D/R: Sacred Music, Musicology H/I/S: Choirmaster at Episcopal Church, Singing, Oil Painting, Reading, Spending Time with his Family EDU: Pursuing Ph.D. in Musicology, Southwestern Baptist Theological Seminary; Master's Degree in Church Music, Emphasis in Music History, Southwestern Baptist Theological Seminary A/A/S: American Musicological Society; American Theological Library Society C/VW: St. Andrew Episcopal Church
Email: jrunnels@swbts.edu
URL: http://www.cambridgewhoswho.com

Donna L. Ruokonen
Title: Quality Manager Company: Northeast Laboratories, Inc. Address: 129 Mill Street, Berlin, CT 06037 United States BUS: Scientific Laboratory P/S: Laboratory Testing Services MA: International D/D/R: ensuring quality H/I/S: Horseback Riding EDU: Master of Business Administration, Sacred Heart University A/A/S: Environmental Laboratory Advisory Committee, CT; American Society for Quality
Email: donna@nelabsct.com
URL: http://www.nelabsct.com

Margaret A. Rupert
Title: Teacher **Company:** Thornridge High School **Address:** 6529 E. Illiniwick Road, Oreana, IL 62554 United States **BUS:** Public High School **P/S:** Education for Students in Ninth through Twelfth-Grade, Business, Engineering, Natural Resources and Technology, Art and Communications, Freshman Academy, Health and Human Services, Athletics **MA:** Regional **D/D/R:** Teaching Family and Consumer Sciences, Teaching Freshman Courses Including a Sewing Workshop and Survey Courses about Cooking, Fashion and Working, Teaching Professional Culinary Courses **H/I/S:** Creating Ornaments, Quilting, Sewing, Cooking **EDU:** Master's Degree in Vocational and Technological Relations, University of Illinois (1982); Master's Degree in Home Economics Education, University of Illinois (1982) **A/A/S:** Illinois Family and Consumer Sciences Teachers' Association; Illinois Association for Career and Technical Education; American Association of Family and Consumer Sciences; Kappa Delta Pi
Email: mrupert@excite.com

Denise Ann Rurka
Title: Owner, Child Care Provider **Company:** Dew Drops and Day Dreams **Address:** 66 Mechanic Street, Winchester, NH 03470 United States **BUS:** Child Care Organization **P/S:** High Quality Child Care Services in a Family Environment **MA:** Regional **D/D/R:** Offering Quality Child Care from Infancy to Age Six, Preschool, Working on Arts and Crafts, Walking, Cooking, Teaching Science **H/I/S:** Traveling, Camping, Quilting, Reading **EDU:** Paraprofessional Certification (1996); College Coursework **CERTS:** Licensed in Child Care, New Hampshire **A/A/S:** National Association for the Education of Young Children
Email: mrdr2@comcast.net

Darla P. Rushing
Title: Owner **Company:** Rush Inn **Address:** 1026 State Route 127, Nashville, IL 62263 United States **BUS:** Tavern **P/S:** Hospitality Services Including Alcoholic Beverages and Entertainment **MA:** Regional **EXP:** Ms. Rushing's area of expertise is in accounting. **D/D/R:** Managing Accounts Payable and Receivable, Bookkeeping **H/I/S:** Walking **EDU:** Diploma, Nashville High School
Email: darla.rushing@cwwemail.com

Sandra Kay Russ
Title: Owner **Company:** Kays Hair and Beauty Supplies **Address:** 1829 Highway 46 S., Suite B, Dickson, TN 37055 United States **BUS:** Hair Salon **P/S:** Human Hair Wigs and Extensions, Beauty Products **MA:** Local **D/D/R:** Shampooing, Conditioning, Hairspray, Fitting Adult and Children Hairpieces, Attaching Extensions **H/I/S:** Reading **EDU:** Coursework in Secretarial School; High School Diploma **C/VW:** Rotary Club; Community-Based Charities; The Elderly
Email: skayjusttalk@comcast.net

Brenda S. Russell
Title: Teacher **Company:** Salem County Special Services School District **BUS:** School District **P/S:** Education **MA:** Local **D/D/R:** teaching disabled students **H/I/S:** Camping, Traveling, Reading, Scrapbooking, Writing **EDU:** Master of Arts in Teaching; Bachelor's Degree in Special Education **CERTS:** Certification in Elementary Education (K-5) **A/A/S:** Institute of Children's Literature **C/VW:** Local Charitable Organizations
Email: dbs1996@verizon.net
URL: http://www.cambridgewhoswho.com

Deborah J. Russell
Title: Registered Nurse **Company:** Marietta Memorial Hospital **Address:** 401 Matthew Street, Marietta, OH 45750 United States **BUS:** Healthcare Hospital **P/S:** Nursing **MA:** Local **D/D/R:** Chemical Dependency, Detoxification Unit **H/I/S:** Playing Piano, Arts and Crafts **EDU:** Associate of Science in Nursing, Owens Technical College

Jodi Russell
Title: Teacher **Company:** Galena Middle School **Address:** 702 E. Seventh Street, Galena, KS 66739 United States **BUS:** Public Middle School **P/S:** Middle School Education **MA:** Local **D/D/R:** Teaching Science and Social Studies **H/I/S:** Reading, Leading Bible Studies, Spending Time with her Two Teenage Daughters **EDU:** Bachelor's Degree, Missouri Southern State University; Continuing Education Coursework **A/A/S:** Kansas National Education Association; National Science Teachers Association; Chairwoman, Social Studies Curriculum Development; Kansas State Board of Education, School Site Social Studies Contact Person **C/VW:** American Cancer Society, Children's Miracle Network, St. Jude Children's Research Hospital
Email: jrussell@usd499.org

Ray L. Russell
Title: President **Company:** ExecuTrends-Executive Education and Leadership **Address:** 1550 N. Stapley Drive, Unit 21, Mesa, AZ 85203 United States **BUS:** Speaking, Coaching, Training **P/S:** Professional Speaking, Executive Coaching, Management Consulting **MA:** International **D/D/R:** Personal Leadership **H/I/S:** Scouting **EDU:** Doctor of Veterinary Medicine, Kansas State University; Master of Business Management, Human Relations and Organizational Behavior, University of Phoenix; Bachelor of Science, Kansas State University; Bachelor of Arts, Purdue University; Certificate in Administration, Krannert School of Management, Purdue University; Certified Professional Attitudes, Values and Attributes Index Analyst, TTI International, Inc.; Undergraduate Coursework **CERTS:** Certified Professional Behavioral Analyst, TTI International, Inc. **A/A/S:** National Speakers Association; Arizona Speakers Association; Former Member, Arizona State Community College Board; Former Advisory Board Member, Desert Samaritan Hospital; Former Vice President, Southside District Hospital Board; Former President, Mesa Chamber of Commerce **C/VW:** President, Several Professional, Business and Civic Organizations
Email: ray@executrends.com
URL: http://www.executrends.com

Jennifer Russo
Title: Manager, Owner **Company:** The Wet Spot **Address:** 950 Spencer Street, Syracuse, NY 13204 United States **BUS:** Restaurant, Bar and Club **P/S:** Food, Alcohol **MA:** Regional **D/D/R:** Managing All Inventory and Finances, Hiring and Firing Employees, Organizing Daily Food and Drink Specials **H/I/S:** Skiing, Boating, Camping, Hiking and Traveling **EDU:** High School Education **A/A/S:** Syracuse Chamber of Commerce
Email: jmrusso@twcny.rr.com
URL: http://www.cambridgewhoswho.com

Pamela S. Rutecki
Title: Registered Nurse, Clinical Nursing Supervisor **Company:** Roswell Park Cancer Institute **Address:** Elm & Carlton Streets, Buffalo, NY 14263 United States **BUS:** Cancer Institute **P/S:** Oncology Healthcare **MA:** Local **D/D/R:** Surgical Oncology Nursing **H/I/S:** Traveling **EDU:** Associate Degree in Nursing, Trocaire College
Email: p.rutecki@verizon.net
URL: http://www.cambridgewhoswho.com

Bonnie L. Rutherford
Title: Owner, Screenwriter **Company:** My Script Needs Help! **Address:** 18653 Ventura Boulevard, PMB 441, Tarzana, CA 91356 United States **BUS:** Screenplay Critique and Ghostwriting Service **P/S:** Analyzing and Ghostwriting Scripts **MA:** International **D/D/R:** Critiquing Film Scripts **H/I/S:** Participating in Animal Rights Activism Groups **EDU:** Master of Business Administration, Averett University; Bachelor of Arts in English Literature, University of Virginia **C/VW:** People for the Ethical Treatment of Animals, The Humane Society
Email: service@myscriptneedshelp.com
URL: http://www.myscriptneedshelp.com

Frank Zane Ruttenberg
Title: Partner **Company:** Bracewell & Giuliani, LLP **Address:** 106 S. Saint Marys Street, Suite 800, San Antonio, TX 78205 United States **BUS:** Law Firm **P/S:** Legal Services **MA:** Local **D/D/R:** litigating for real estate, water and partnership law and preparing briefs **H/I/S:** Playing Racquetball **EDU:** JD, Saint Mary's Law School, San Antonio, TX (1979); Master's Degree, New York University (1982); Bachelor of Business Administration in Finance, University of Texas, Austin (1976) **A/A/S:** Executive Board Member, Treasurer, San Antonio Zoological Society; Business Law Section, State Bar of Texas; Real Property Trusts and Probate, American Bar Association
Email: frank.ruttenberg@bgllp.com
URL: http://www.bgllp.com

Carl Ruzycki
Title: Chief Executive Officer **Company:** Holistic Security dba GiftBats.biz **Address:** 2024 Seebeck Court, Suite 3, San Jose, CA 95132 United States **BUS:** Online Store **P/S:** Handmade Customized Designer Baseball Bats **MA:** International **EXP:** Mr. Ruzycki's expertise includes sales, marketing, business and new market development. **H/I/S:** Golfing **A/A/S:** Institute of Electrical and Electronics Engineers, Inc.
Email: carl@giftbats.biz
URL: http://www.giftbats.biz

John Edward Ryan Jr.
Title: President **Company:** Program Management Consulting, Inc. **Address:** P.O. Box 9548, Louisville, KY 40209 United States **BUS:** Consulting Firm **P/S:** Consulting Services Including Project Management **MA:** Louisville, Southern Indiana **D/D/R:** Ensuring Customer Satisfaction, Managing Sales, Conducting Research **H/I/S:** Golfing, Swimming, Playing Basketball **EDU:** Pursuing Ph.D. **C/VW:** Optimist Club of Louisville
Email: rockynavy@yahoo.com

Mary E. Ryan
Title: Special Education Teacher **Company:** Oswego County BOCES **Address:** 179 County Route 64, Mexico, NY 13114 United States **BUS:** School **P/S:** Education **MA:** Local **D/D/R:** Teaching Students with Special Needs **H/I/S:** Reading, Running, Swimming, Gardening **EDU:** Master of Science in Education, SUNY Oswego; Bachelor of Science in Education, SUNY Geneseo; Associate in Arts, Jefferson Community College **A/A/S:** Council for Exceptional Children; Girl Scouts of the USA, Southern Poverty Law Center; New York State United Teachers; Special Olympics **C/VW:** Ronald McDonald House, Andrews Memorial United Methodist Church
Email: mryan@oswegoboces.org
URL: http://www.cambridgewhoswho.com

Laurie A. Ryba
Title: Deputy Sheriff **Company:** Brevard County Sheriffs Office **Address:** 700 Park Avenue, Titusville, FL 32780 United States **BUS:** Law Enforcement Agency **P/S:** Law Enforcement **MA:** Local **D/D/R:** Victim Advocacy, Crisis Intervention **H/I/S:** Traveling, Golfing, Riding for Motorcycle Benefits **EDU:** Graduate, Police Academy of Medina County, Ohio **CERTS:** Certified in Crisis Intervention **C/VW:** Special Olympics, Domestic Violence Center, Rape Crisis Center
Email: laurieryba@msn.com
URL: http://www.brevardsheriff.org

Ms. Carolyn M. Ryder
Title: Owner **Company:** Isler Medford, LLC **Address:** 1555 E. McAndrews Road, Suite 301, Medford, OR 97504 United States **BUS:** Certified Public Accountancy Firm **P/S:** Tax Returns and Government Audits **MA:** Local **D/D/R:** Preparing Estate, Corporate and Personal Tax Returns, Conducting Municipal, Government, Schools, Pension Plans, Small Government Audits, Mentoring and Lecturing for the Oregon Society of Certified Public Accountants **H/I/S:** Gardening, Riding Horses, Reading, Raising Cattle, Spending Time with her Family **EDU:** Bachelor's Degree in Business Administration and Accounting, South Oregon College (1984) **A/A/S:** Oregon Society of Certified Public Accountants; American Institute of Certified Public Accountants; Government Finance Office Association; Oregon Barrel Races Association; Southern Oregon Barrel Race Association
Email: cryder@islermedford.com
URL: http://www.islermedford.com

Kelly Ryner
Title: Vice President of New Business Development **Company:** Thinkwell Design & Production **Address:** 695 South Glenwood Place, Burbank, CA 91506 United States **BUS:** Project Development **P/S:** Designing Theme Parks, Museums, Destination Resorts and Innovative Consumer Experience **MA:** International **D/D/R:** Art Directing, Guest Experience **H/I/S:** Developing Ideas **EDU:** Bachelor's Degree in Theatre, Virginia Technology **A/A/S:** Themed Entertainment Association; Ryman Arts Foundation; International Association of Amusement Park Attractions; American Association of Museums
Email: kryner@thinkwelldesign.com
URL: http://www.thinkwelldesign.com

Urve Saarse
Title: Owner **Company:** U.S.'s Land Properties **Address:** 2385 Kalkaska Drive, Henderson, NV 89044 United States **BUS:** Real Estate Company **P/S:** Real Estate, Land Properties **MA:** International **D/D/R:** Buying and Selling Land **H/I/S:** Nourishing her Spirituality, Nature, Traveling **EDU:** Bachelor of Science, University of Pennsylvania (1960) **A/A/S:** Unity Church of Sedona; Assist in Emergency Preparedness **C/VW:** Catholic Healthcare West, St. Rose Dominican Hospitals, Local Assisted Living Homes
Email: urve3@yahoo.com
URL: http://www.cambridgewhoswho.com

Jessica Horstman Sabatini
Title: Life Coach and Trainer **Company:** Prosper with Purpose Coaching **Address:** 2376 33rd Street, Astoria, NY 11105 United States **BUS:** Personal and Professional Coaching Practice **P/S:** Practical, Reliable Strategies for Accomplishing Goals and Living Life Fully through Sessions Conducted by Phone, Goal-Setting Seminars, Free Bi-Monthly Ezine with Practical Tools for Creating Effective Strategies and Reaching Goals **MA:** International **D/D/R:** Remaining on Top of the Latest Developments in Neuroscience and Metaphysics, Offering Life Direction Coaching to Help People Clarify their Priorities and Speed Up the Time Line Between Where Clients are Now and Where They Really Want to Be **H/I/S:** Theatre, Art, Science, Travel, Health, Spending Time in the Great Outdoors **EDU:** RCS Certified Life Coach; Bachelor's Degree in Theater Management, East Carolina University (2001) **A/A/S:** Toastmasters International
Email: jessica@prosper-with-purpose.com
URL: http://www.prosper-with-purpose.com

Hani Sabbour

Title: Doctor **Company:** Cardiology Associates, Inc. **Address:** 25 John A. Cummings Way, Suite 4, Woonsocket, RI 02895 United States **BUS:** Medical Center **P/S:** Healthcare, Cardiology Care, Pacer Implantation, Clinical Cardiac Electrophysiology and Internal Medicine **MA:** Local **D/D/R:** treating cardiology patients, educating doctors and medical students on cardiac health procedures and medicine, teaching continuing medical education for clinics and overseeing operations **H/I/S:** Building Model Airplanes, Reading **EDU:** Fellowship in Cardiology, SUNY Stony Brook **CERTS:** Board Certification in Cardiac Arrhythmia, Massachusetts General Hospital; Board Certification in Cardiology; Certification in Continuing Medical Education, Roger Williams University; Board Certification in Nuclear Cardiology
Email: hanisabbour1@aol.com

Mr. Antonia R. Sacchetti, MD

Title: Medical Director **Company:** Mission Neighborhood Health Center **Dept:** Administration and Pediatrics Department **Address:** 240 Shotwell Street, San Francisco, CA 94110 United States **BUS:** Federally-Qualified Community Healthcare Center **P/S:** Healthcare **MA:** Regional **EXP:** Dr. Sacchetti's expertise includes pediatrics, quality control and the medical management of preventive care, acute and chronic care for all life cycles including prenatal, pediatrics, teen, adult, elders and specialized populations including patients with HIV and homeless patients. **D/D/R:** Overseeing Clinical Operations **H/I/S:** Kayaking, Skiing, Hiking **EDU:** Residency, University of California, San Francisco, CA (1968-1969); Moffitt Hospital, San Francisco, CA (1968-1969); East Bay Children's Hospital, Oakland, CA (1968-1969); Rotating Internship, St. Luke's Hospital, San Francisco, CA (1964-1965); MD, University of Michigan Medical School (1964); Bachelor of Arts, University of Michigan (1957); Coursework, Fordham Graduate School of Economics, New York (1957); Pediatric First Year Resident, Internal Medicine, University of California, San Francisco **A/A/S:** Phi Beta Kappa (1957); Phi Kappa Phi (1953); San Francisco Medical Society; Founding Member, Western Clinicians Network; San Francisco Health Plan; Quality Improvement Committee, Physicians Advisory Committee, National Association of Community Health Centers, Inc.; California Primary Care Association; California Medical Association; American Medical Association **A/H:** High Honors, Economics (1957); Summa Cum Laude (1957) **C/VW:** Food for the Poor; United Nations Educational, Scientific and Cultural Organization; Doctors Without Borders; Women's Breast Cancer Research
Email: antoniasacchetti@mnhc.org
URL: http://www.mnhc.org

Melisa M. Saccucci

Title: Pastor **Company:** First United Methodist Church **Address:** 415 N. Seminary Street, Florence, AL 35630 United States **BUS:** Methodist Church **P/S:** Religious Services and Activities **MA:** Local **D/D/R:** Preaching, Spiritual Formation **H/I/S:** Reading **EDU:** Master of Divinity, Arizona State University; Asbury Theological Seminary (2003) **C/VW:** Community Outreach, Church
Email: msaccucci@bellsouth.net

Dianna M. Saelens

Title: Provider Specialist **Company:** Community Action of Eastern Iowa **Address:** 500 E. 59th Street, Davenport, IA 52807 United States **BUS:** School **P/S:** Childcare Education **MA:** Local **D/D/R:** Mentoring and Training Day Care Providers **H/I/S:** Reading, Collecting Lady Bugs **EDU:** Master of Science in Organizational Leadership, St. Ambrose University (2008); Bachelor of Arts in Early Childhood Education, St. Ambrose University **A/A/S:** National Association for the Education of Young Children
Email: dsaelens@iowatrain.org
URL: http://www.cambridgewhoswho.com

Mr. Barry Safarpoormonfared

Title: President **Company:** Asbestos Environmental Consultants **Address:** 70 Austin Street, Suite 15, Lowell, MA 01854 United States **BUS:** Consulting Firm **P/S:** Consulting Services for Construction Company **MA:** National **D/D/R:** Traveling to Construction Sites, Ensuring Customer Satisfaction, Meeting Clients, Rehabilitating Properties, Lecturing **H/I/S:** Playing Chess and Backgammon, Motorcycling, Bicycling **CERTS:** Accredited Asbestos Inspector, State of Massachusetts; Asbestos Project Monitor, State of New Hampshire **A/A/S:** Minority Award, AIHA **C/VW:** Boston Marathon Jimmy Fund Walk; Dana-Farber Cancer Institute
Email: aec.barry@comcast.net

Barbara A. Sager

Title: District School Nurse **Company:** North Boone School District 200 **Address:** 17641 Poplar Grove Road, Poplar Grove, IL 61065 United States **BUS:** School District **P/S:** Education **MA:** Northern Boone County, IL **EXP:** Ms. Sager's area of expertise is in emergency medicine. **D/D/R:** reviewing immunization records **H/I/S:** Farming, Gardening, Spending Time with her Children **EDU:** Bachelor of Science in Nursing, University of Phoenix; Associate Degree in Nursing, Rock Valley College, Rockland, IL **A/A/S:** Illinois School Nurses Association; National School Nurses Association **A/H:** Education Excellence Award; Community Service Award **C/VW:** 4-H Club
Email: sagerbarb@nbcusd.org
URL: http://www.cambridgewhoswho.com

Cheryl A. Saher

Title: Owner **Company:** Professional Connections **Address:** 135 Madison Lane N., Newport News, VA 23606 United States **BUS:** Employment Placement Agency **P/S:** International Recruiting **MA:** International **D/D/R:** Recruiting and Placing Individuals in Chemical-Related and Business-Related Positions, Being in contact with people and locating candidates for her clients via phone interviews and face to face interviews, negotiating offers. **H/I/S:** Golfing, Scuba Diving, Traveling, Reading, Gardening **EDU:** College Coursework
Email: cheryl@chemicalrecruiter.com
URL: http://www.chemicalrecruiter.com

Katherine A. Sahlas

Title: (Retired) **Company:** Pasture to Plate **Address:** 5105 W. Ogden, Cicero, IL 60804 United States **BUS:** Food Distributor **P/S:** Specialty and High-End Meats, Game and Fish **MA:** National **D/D/R:** Liaison to Owners, Organizing the Office, Help to Set Up Food and Beverages Shows, Areas Hiring, Prior Middle School Science Teacher for all Outdoor Education at Inner City School, Writer Programs for School Children to Learn and Educate on Animal Presentation and Conservation at Brookfield Zoo Education **H/I/S:** Traveling, Playing Golf, White Water Kayaking, Biking, Sky Diving, Cross Country Skiing, Gardening **EDU:** Master's Degree in Guidance Counseling, Concordia University; Master's Degree in the Educational Teaching of Science, Concordia University; Bachelor of Science in Education, Illinois State University; Post Graduate Coursework at Elmhurst University, Northwestern University and Northern Illinois University **A/A/S:** AAUW **C/VW:** Multiple Sclerosis Walk, Heart Society Walk, HELP Shelter for Battered Women and Children
Email: kate_sahlas@sbcglobal.net
URL: http://www.cambridgewhoswho.com

Ritu Saini

Title: Dermatologist **Company:** University of Miami, Miller School of Medicine **Address:** 1600 NW 10th Avenue, Miami, FL 33136 United States **BUS:** Dermatology Office **P/S:** Dermatology **MA:** National **D/D/R:** Dermatology **H/I/S:** Traveling **EDU:** MD, New York University; Residency, University of Miami **A/A/S:** American Medical Association; American Society of Dermatology; American Society for Dermatological Surgery; Women's Dermatological Society; American Society for Mohs Surgery **C/VW:** Skin Cancer Foundation
Email: rsaini@optonline.net

Susan G. Saintz

Title: Director of Marketing and Admission **Company:** Assisted Living Facility **Address:** 2100 Bent Creek Boulevard, Mechanicsburg, PA 17050 United States **BUS:** Geriatric Center **P/S:** Care for Elderly **MA:** Local **EXP:** Ms. Saintz's expertise includes nurse and finance management. **H/I/S:** Making Jewelries, Gardening **CERTS:** Licensed Practical Nurse, Harrisburg Area Community College **A/A/S:** Student Nurse, Excelsior College; National Association of Insurance and Financial Advisors **C/VW:** Breast Cancer Organizations
Email: sgs@concast.com
URL: http://www.cambridgewhoswho.com

Scott Salatich

Title: Senior Project Manager **Company:** Gray Construction **Address:** P.O. Box 8001, Auburn, CA 95604 United States **BUS:** General Contractor **P/S:** Custom Homes **MA:** Regional **D/D/R:** General Relations, Oversee Entire Relations for Construction Site **H/I/S:** Playing Softball **EDU:** High School Diploma
Email: scott@grayconstruction.com
URL: http://www.grayconstruction.com

Ligia T. Salazar

Title: President **Company:** Nu-Way Cleaning Inc **Address:** 41-07 42nd Street, Apartment 2A, Sunnyside, NY 11104 United States **BUS:** Cleaning Service **P/S:** Office/Business Cleaning Service **MA:** National **D/D/R:** Pride in Quality Cleaning, People Skills **H/I/S:** Salsa Dancing, Watching Movies, Spending Time with the Family **A/A/S:** Save the Children, Homeless Helper, Columbia Children
Email: drscar10@aol.com

Delia H. Saldaña, Ph.D.

Title: Associate Professor **Company:** University of Texas Health Science Center at San Antonio **Dept:** Department of Psychiatry **Address:** 7703 Floyd Curl Drive, San Antonio, TX 78229 United States **BUS:** University Health Science Center **P/S:** Higher Education, Teaching University, Medical, Dental, Nursing and Psychology Programs and Degrees **MA:** Local **D/D/R:** Working with Community-Based Organizations, Offering Services to Adults and Children, Training Individuals and Organizations in Evidence-Based Practices, Formerly Taught Undergraduates Bilingual English and Spanish at Trinity University in San Antonio **H/I/S:** Enjoying Gardening, Outdoor Sports **EDU:** Ph.D. in Clinical Psychology, University of California, Los Angeles (1988); Master of Science in Clinical Psychology, Trinity University, San Antonio, Texas (1980); Bachelor of Arts, Double Major in Psychology and Sociology, Two Years at Wellesley College, Massachusetts, Two Years at Trinity University, San Antonio, Texas (1976) **A/A/S:** Received a Dissertation Award, American Psychological Association of the Southwest (2002); Member, Rural Task Force of the American Psychological Association; American Psychological Association; National Science Network on Substance Abuse
Email: saldana@uthscsa.edu
URL: http://www.uthscsa.edu

Dr. Robert D. Saler

Title: Owner, Operator **Company:** Saler's Christian Rest Home **Address:** 5739 Bon Secour Highway, Bon Secour, AL 36511 United States **BUS:** Assisted Living Facility **P/S:** Healthcare Services Including 24-Hour Care, Prescription Management and Transportation **MA:** Regional **EXP:** Mr. Saler's area of expertise is in operations management. **D/D/R:** Overseeing Daily Operations, Supervising Staff of Eight, Maintaining Patients' Records, Creating Menus **H/I/S:** Golfing, Playing Baseball and Hockey **EDU:** Associate Degree in Psychology, Moody Bible Institute (1948)
Email: info@cambridgewhoswho.com
URL: http://www.cambridgewhoswho.com

Sandra F. Salgado

Title: Human Resources Manager **Company:** Pioneer Center for Human Services **Address:** 4001 Dayton Street, McHenry, IL 60050 United States **BUS:** Nonprofit Disability Resource Center **P/S:** Vocational Services for Clients with Developmental Disabilities, Mental Health Services for Sexual Assault Victims, Supported Living Arrangement Programs **MA:** Local **D/D/R:** Overseeing Human Resources Department, Runs PADS Division (Public Action to Deliver Shelter) for the Homeless Population **H/I/S:** Reading to Children **EDU:** Master's Degree in Industrial Psychology, Roosevelt University (2006) Bachelor's Degree in Psychology, Columbia College Chicago **A/A/S:** McHenry County Board Society for Human Resource Management
Email: sandefay@yahoo.com
URL: http://www.pioneercenter.org

Michelle C. Sallee

Title: Apartment Manager **Company:** Stern Hendy Properties, Inc. **Address:** 750 Grand Avenue, Cincinnati, OH 45202 United States **BUS:** Quality Housing for Senior Citizens **P/S:** Leaders in Assisted Living Services, High Quality Housing Services, Residential Care, Senior Care **MA:** Regional **D/D/R:** Maintaining 184 Units, Interaction with the Elderly, Managing the Facility **H/I/S:** Reading **EDU:** Graduated Bracken High School (1973)

Eileen M. Salsman

Title: President **Company:** e-Solutions and Systems, LLC **Address:** P.O. Box 2756, Monument, CO 80132 United States **BUS:** Information Technology Company **P/S:** Education Technology, Systems Integration and Software Sales for Education of Kindergarten through 12-Grade Students **MA:** Regional **D/D/R:** managing sales, marketing and solution-based consulting **H/I/S:** Snorkeling, Scuba Diving, Hiking, Bicycling **EDU:** High School Education **A/A/S:** Association for Supervision and Curriculum Development
Email: esalsman@esolandsys.com
URL: http://www.esolutionsandsystems.com

Barbara A. Salvatore

Title: President/Owner **Company:** Beyond Design Inc. **Address:** 807 Pine Brook Road, Walton, NY 13856 United States **BUS:** Art, Design and Fabrication Corporation **P/S:** Scenery Fabrication, Mold Making, Displays, Retail and Museum Displays, Film **MA:** Local **D/D/R:** Paint, Color, Small Sculpture, Administration **H/I/S:** Team of Draft Horses, Writing, Riding, Illustrating Young Adult Novels, Herbology and Native American Studies **EDU:** Bachelors, School of Visual Arts **A/A/S:** SCBWI (Society of Children's Book Writers and Illustrators)UPS (United Plant Savers)
Email: b16horsewomen@frontiernet.net
URL: http://www.beyonddesigninc.com

Erin Salzano
Title: Owner **Company:** Erin Salzano Design **Address:** 297 Cypress Lane, Hamilton, NJ 08619 United States **BUS:** Graphic Design Company **P/S:** Custom Wedding Invitations, Corporate Identity Packages, Business Cards, Logo Designs, Outdoor Signage and More **MA:** Regional **D/D/R:** Working One-on-One with Clients to Design Products to Suit their Specific Needs, Designing Unique and Exceptional Logos and Letterheads for All Industries, Custom Invitations and Design **H/I/S:** Spending Time with New Baby **EDU:** Bachelor of Arts in Graphic Design, The College of New Jersey (2001)
Email: erinsalzanodesigns@mac.com
URL: http://www.cambridgewhoswho.com

Fred Samandari
Title: Senior Design Center Manager **Company:** ChipX, Inc. **Address:** 1910 Cochran Road Manor Oak Two, Suite 482, Pittsburgh, PA 15220 United States **BUS:** Semiconductor Networking, Wireless **P/S:** ASIC, SOC and IP development **MA:** International **D/D/R:** IC, Board design and Management **H/I/S:** Squash, Racquetball **EDU:** University of Southern California (USC), MSEE, BSEE, Executive Master of Business Administration Essentials **A/A/S:** TGC, ECG
Email: fredsamandari@yahoo.com

Pompillo John Sambogna
Title: Owner **Company:** Pompillo Pizzeria and Italian Restaurant **Address:** 223 Westwood Avenue, Westwood, NJ 07675 United States **BUS:** Food Restaurant **P/S:** Italian Restaurant and Pizzeria, A Variety of Italian Dishes **MA:** Local **D/D/R:** Specializing in Personal Hands-On Customer Service, Overseeing the Quality and Presentation of the Food and Overall Financial Operations **EDU:** Diploma, Palisades Park High School (1977) **A/A/S:** Westwood Recreation Association

Ann Samler
Title: Vice President of Technology Development **Company:** Genco Marketplace **Address:** 100 Papercraft Park, Pittsburgh, PA 16066 United States **BUS:** Logistics Solutions Company **P/S:** Third-Party Logistics Solutions and Services **MA:** International **D/D/R:** Working in the Technology Development, Managing Online Marketplace and Warehouse, Marketing Websites **EDU:** Doctoral Degree in Engineering Technology Management, University of Southern California (2003)
Email: samlera@genco.com
URL: http://www.genco.com

Marguerite A. Samples, M.Ed.
Title: Teacher **Company:** Tucson Unified School District, Dunham Elementary School **Address:** 9850 E. 29th Street, Tucson, AZ 85748 United States **BUS:** Elementary School **P/S:** Education **MA:** Local **D/D/R:** Teaching Early Childhood, Reading, certified to teach k-8 English language learners (ESL); Teaches Professional Development Science Classes for Teachers in 3 school districts **H/I/S:** Watching Movies **EDU:** Master's Degree in English Reading and Literature, University of Arizona (1998); Endorsed as a Reading Specialist k-12; Early Childhood, ESL and SEI; Candidate for National Board Certification of an Early Childhood Generalist **A/A/S:** National Science Teachers' Association; Who's Who Among American Teachers
Email: marguerite.samples@tusd1.org

Gareth M. Sampson
Title: Patent Agent **Company:** Meyertons, Hood, Kivlin, Kowert & Goetzel **Address:** 700 Lavaca Street, Suite 800, Austin, TX 78701 United States **BUS:** Intellectual Property Law Firm **P/S:** Legal Services for Patents, Copyrights, Trademarks, Trade Secrets, Unfair Competition and Domain Names **MA:** National **EXP:** Mr. Sampson's area of expertise is in patents prosecution. **D/D/R:** writing patents and assisting clients **H/I/S:** Mountain Biking, Playing Volleyball, Golfing **EDU:** Ph.D. in Chemical Engineering, The University of Texas (1998) **CERTS:** Certified Patent Agent (2002)
Email: gsampson@intprop.com
URL: http://www.intprop.com

Phyllis Morrow Sams
Title: English Teacher, Department Chairperson **Company:** Charles County Public Schools, La Plata High School **Address:** 6035 Radio Station Road, La Plata, MD 20646 United States **BUS:** High School **P/S:** Education **MA:** Local **D/D/R:** Teaching American Literature **H/I/S:** Reading **EDU:** Pursuing Master's Degree, University of Maryland; Bachelor of Science in Education, Indiana University of Pennsylvania **CERTS:** Advanced Certification **A/A/S:** National Council of Teachers of English; National Education Association; Maryland State Teachers Association **C/VW:** American Cancer Society, Donates to the Indiana University of Pennsylvania Alumni Fund
Email: psama@ccboe.com
URL: http://www.cambridgewhoswho.com

Marta C. Samuelson
Title: Sales Director **Company:** CA, Inc. **Address:** 6150 Oaktree Boulevard, Independence, OH 44131 United States **BUS:** Computer Software Company **P/S:** Enterprise Software **MA:** International **D/D/R:** Sales Management, Security Solutions **H/I/S:** Reading, Working Out **EDU:** Master of Business Administration in General Management, Ashland University **A/A/S:** Kent State University Business Development Relations Group **C/VW:** Leukemia & Lymphoma Society
Email: marta.samuelson@gmail.com

Sandra Bonilla San Miguel
Title: Lead School Social Worker **Company:** Seminole County Public Schools **Address:** 1722 W. Airport Boulevard, Sanford, FL 32771 United States **BUS:** Public School **P/S:** Education **MA:** Local **D/D/R:** dealing with all aspects of social work, case working with migrant workers, crisis intervention, inmates and social work in education **H/I/S:** Reading History, Biographies, Science Fiction, Politics, Arts, Listening to Classical Music **EDU:** Master of Social Work, Columbia University; Bachelor of Arts in Education, Saint Joseph's College **CERTS:** Certification in School Social Work; Florida Teacher Certification in School Social Worker **A/A/S:** Board of Directors, Seminole Community Mental Health Center; Board Member, Florida Association of Social Workers; President, Florida Association of Student Services Administrators; School Social Work Association of America; National Association of Social Workers; National Network for Social Work Manage **A/H:** Presidential Award at the State Conference, Florida Association of School Social Workers (2007); District Level Teacher of the Year Award, Seminole County, FL (2000); Social Work Administrator of the Year Award, Florida Association of School Social Workers (1999); Outstanding Hispanic Achievement Award, Casa de Puerto Rico, Orlando, FL (1999); Outstanding Contributions to Student Services Certificate, Florida Department of Education (1995); Outstanding Leadership Award, Florida Association of School Social Workers (1994); Juan Ponce de Leon Award for Distinguished Services to Hispanic Community, Orlando, FL (1992); Outstanding Services Award, Seminole Community Mental Health Center (1991); Distinguished Community Service Award, University of Central Florida (1991)
Email: sanmiguel1969@earthlink.com
URL: http://www.scps.k12.fl.us

Antonia Sanchez
Title: Human Resource Business Partner **Company:** Lloyds TSB Bank **Address:** 2 S. Biscayne Boulevard, One Biscayne Tower, Suite 3200, Miami, FL 33131 United States **BUS:** Trustee Savings Bank **P/S:** Private Banking Services **MA:** International **D/D/R:** Recruiting **H/I/S:** Traveling, Scuba Diving **EDU:** Master of Arts in Economics, University of Lausanne (1999) **C/VW:** Career Women's Forum
Email: asanchez@lloydstsb-usa.com

Leticia Sanchez
Title: Teacher **Company:** Riverside Elementary School **Address:** 1414 S. 51st Avenue, Phoenix, AZ 85043 United States **BUS:** Elementary School **P/S:** Education **MA:** Local **D/D/R:** Teaching Kindergarten through Eighth-Grade **H/I/S:** Spending Time with her Children **EDU:** Bachelor's Degree in Elementary Education, Arizona State University, West Campus **C/VW:** Church
Email: lettysanchez@cox.net
URL: http://www.cambridgewhoswho.com

Richard Sanchez
Title: Real Estate Consultant **Company:** At Properties **Address:** 3101 E Greenview, Chicago, IL 60657 United States **BUS:** Real Estate **P/S:** Residential Homes, New Construction, Condos, Lofts **MA:** National **D/D/R:** Strictly Concentrates on New Construction and Lofts **H/I/S:** Riding Motorcycles **EDU:** Bachelor of Science in Business Management, Roosevelt University **A/A/S:** Illinois Association of Realtors, Nationals Association of Realtors
URL: http://www.@Properties.com

Donna R. Sandberg
Title: Charge Nurse, RN **Company:** Golden Ours Convalescent Home **Address:** 900 Lincoln Avenue, Grant, NE 69140 United States **BUS:** Geriatric Care Facility **P/S:** Long-Term Geriatric Care **MA:** Local **D/D/R:** Geriatric Nursing **H/I/S:** Reading, Scrapbooking **EDU:** Associate of Applied Science in Nursing, North Platte Community College **A/A/S:** President, Church Women's Club **C/VW:** Church
Email: donnasandberg@nebnet.net

Jenifer LaDonna Sanders
Title: Managing Member **Company:** JR Theatres, LLC **Address:** 109 West Avenue D, Copperas Cove, TX 76522 United States **BUS:** Movie Theater and Live Theater **P/S:** Renovation of Dilapidated, Historic Theaters **MA:** Regional **D/D/R:** Renovations, Organizational Management, Ministry **H/I/S:** Vacationing, Traveling **EDU:** Bachelor's Degree in Political Science and Business Administration, Texas A&M University **A/A/S:** International Rotary Foundation; Minister, Extreme Youth Ministry **C/VW:** Heritage of Faith Ministry, Extreme Youth Ministry
Email: jenifer@covetheatre.com
URL: http://www.covetheatre.com

Theresa Sanders
Title: Ambulatory Care Technician **Company:** Mount Sinai Medical Center **Address:** One Gustaval Elvy Place, New York, NY 10029 United States **BUS:** Teaching Hospital **P/S:** Clinical Care Services, Education, Scientific Research, Neurology, Ambulatory Healthcare Services **MA:** Regional **D/D/R:** Sterilizing Treatment Rooms, Performing Electrocardiograms, Drawing Blood, Assisting Physicians, Overseeing the Inventory of Medical Supplies **H/I/S:** Creating Gift Baskets, Crocheting, Attending Church **EDU:** Diploma, Northwestern High School (1962)
Email: theresasandrs@yahoo.com
URL: http://www.mountsinai.org

Kathleen E. Sanderson
Title: Business Development manager **Company:** Steptoe and Johnson, LLP **Address:** 1330 Connecticut Avenue N.W., Washington, DC 20036 United States **BUS:** Law Firm **P/S:** Legal Services **MA:** International **EXP:** Ms. Sanderson's expertise is in business management. **D/D/R:** Managing Six Practice Groups, Handling all Legal Marketing, Focusing on Marketing Strategies, Expanding on Current Client Relationships, Drafting Marketing Pitch Proposals, Writing Web site Content **H/I/S:** Playing Tennis, Dancing **EDU:** Pursuing Master of Arts in International Relations, American University, School of International Service; Bachelor of Arts in Spanish and Foreign Affairs, University of Virginia **A/A/S:** Legal Marketing Association; People to People International; International Club of DC **C/VW:** Volunteer, Children International
Email: ksanderson@steptoe.com
URL: http://www.cambridgewhoswho.com

Marnita E. Sandifer, Ph.D.
Title: Spa Director, Owner **Company:** AJ's Spa Millennium **Address:** 3365 Richmond Road, Suite 120, Beachwood, OH 44122 United States **BUS:** Day Spa and Skin Clinic **P/S:** Manicure Services, Artificial Enhancements, Pedicure Services, Hair Removal, Specialty Skin Care Services, Designer Peels, Specialty Masks, Cosmetics Applications, Massage Therapy, Aromatherapy, Permanent Cosmetic Procedures, Permanent Cosmetic Classes, Skincare Information Services, Body Wraps, Salt Scrubs, Continuing Education Classes **MA:** Regional **D/D/R:** Formulating Skin Care Products, Overseeing Spa Operations, Overseeing Facials, Manicures, Pedicures, Body Treatments and Hair Cutting **EDU:** Ph.D. in Chemistry, Case Western Reserve University (1994); Master of Science, Case Western Reserve University (1992); Bachelor of Science, Baldwin Wallace College (1988) **A/A/S:** Universal Sisters of Cleveland Honoree, Cleveland Clinic Foundation; Alumni Wall of Fame Inductee, Cuyahoga Community College; Gold Star Award, Cuyahoga County; World Class Esthetician, Cleveland Plain Dealer; Society of Cosmetic Chemists; National Colition of 100 Black Women, Greater Cleveland Chapter2008 Honoree woman of vision award
Email: marnita@ajsspamillennium.com
URL: http://www.ajsspamillennium.com

Donna Sandoli
Title: President **Company:** Eagle & Dove Ministries **Address:** 954 Washington Street, Gloucester, MA 01930 United States **BUS:** Ministry **P/S:** Spiritual Services Including Education and Judah's Roar Meeting **MA:** International **D/D/R:** managing operations, preaching, artwork, counseling, teaching and composing music **H/I/S:** Gardening, Sailing, Walking **EDU:** Coursework, Morningstar Ministries, SC; High School Diploma **A/A/S:** Massachusetts Audubon Society; Gloucester Garden Society; Apostolic Resource Center; Society for the Encouragement of the Arts; Gloucester County Chamber of Commerce **C/VW:** MorningStar Ministries
Email: eagleanddove@comcast.net
URL: http://www.eagledove.com

Hector M. Sandoval
Title: Senior Manager, Aero Engineer **Company:** Lockheed Martin **Address:** P.O. Box 748, Fort Worth, TX 76101 United States **BUS:** Manufacturing and Technology Company **P/S:** Fighter Aircrafts **MA:** International **D/D/R:** modifying and upgrading **EDU:** Ph.D. in Management, with Concentration in Leadership; Master of Business Administration, The California State University; Bachelor's Degree in Business Administration, University of Redlands; Bachelor's Degree in Engineering, Northrop State University **CERTS:** Certified Professional Manager, James Madison University **A/A/S:** Fort Worth Chapter, Society of Hispanic Professional Engineers; Lockheed Martin Leadership Association; Toastmasters International; Adjunct Professor, The University of Texas, Arlington; Adjunct Professor, University of Phoenix-Dallas Fort Worth **A/H:** Aero Star Award, Lockheed Martin **C/VW:** Local Charitable Organizations; Chairperson, Director, High School Speech Contest; Marine Toys for Tots Foundation; Lockheed Martin Leadership Association
Email: hector.sandoval@lmco.com
URL: http://www.lockheedmartin.com

Nicole J. Sanfilippo
Title: Teacher **Company:** New York City Department of Education, I.S. 61 **Address:** 98-50 50th Avenue, Corona, NY 11368 United States **BUS:** Department of Education **P/S:** Education **MA:** Local **D/D/R:** Teaching Science and English as a Second Language **H/I/S:** Skiing, Going to the Beach and the Poconos, Spending Time with Family and Friends **EDU:** Master of Science in Education, Touro College (2006); Bachelor's Degree in Social Control and Disobedience, John Jay College of Criminal Justice (2002)
Email: moonster42@aol.com
URL: http://www.cambridgewhoswho.com

Mr. Kyle Sanford
Title: Systems Administration **Company:** VF Outdoor **Dept:** Product Development Services **Address:** 2013 Farllon Drive, San Leandro, CA 94577 United States **BUS:** Apparel, Equipment and Footwear Supplier and Retail **P/S:** Accessories, Equipment, Footwear, Outerwear, Snow Sports and Sportswear **MA:** International **D/D/R:** Managing Product Development Systems, Project Management **H/I/S:** Horseback Riding **EDU:** Associate of Arts in Business Management; Reid State Technical College **A/A/S:** Project Management Institute; Product Development and Management Association. Systems Management from Gerber Technology. **C/VW:** Lee National Denim Day, SF Aids Walk
Email: KSanford61@aol.com
URL: VFC.com

Melissa R. Sanniota
Title: Owner/Mortgage Broker **Company:** Reliable Mortgage Group **Address:** 611 S Federal Highway, Suite D, Stuart, FL 34994 United States **BUS:** Finance Broker **P/S:** Residential and Commercial Mortgage Loans **MA:** National **D/D/R:** Ownership and Mortgage Broker **H/I/S:** Home Decor **EDU:** IFREC, Mortgage Broker and Biz School **CERTS:** Realtor License/Mortgage
Email: ms_rmg@bellsouth.net
URL: http://www.reliablemortgagegroupllc.com

Karen A. Santagata
Title: Litigation and Compliance Specialist **Company:** American Greetings Corporation **Address:** 1 American Road, Cleveland, OH 44144 United States **BUS:** Manufacturing and Distribution Company **P/S:** Social Expression Products **MA:** International **D/D/R:** Legal Litigation, Immigration, Employment, Insurance Defense, Compliance, Product Safety, Paralegal Mentoring and Teaching **H/I/S:** Gardening, Reading **CERTS:** Paralegal Certificate and Advanced Certificate in Litigation and ADR, American Institute of Paralegal Studies, Inc. **A/A/S:** National Federation of Paralegal Associations; Board Member, Cleveland Paralegal Association **C/VW:** Susan G. Komen for the Cure
Email: karen.santagata@amgreetings.com
URL: http://www.amgreetings.com

German Santana
Title: Owner **Company:** Santana Custom Refinishing **Address:** 37530 Los Alamos Road, Murrieta, CA 92563 United States **BUS:** Furniture Refinishing Company **P/S:** Furniture Refinishing, Color Matching **MA:** Regional **D/D/R:** Furniture Refinishing, Color Matching **H/I/S:** Hunting, Fishing, Collecting Antiques Cars
Email: santanarefinishing@msn.com
URL: http://www.cambridgewhoswho.com

Scott T. Santarella
Title: Executive Director, Chief Operations Officer **Company:** Multiple Myeloma Research Foundation **Address:** 383 Main Avenue, Norwalk, CT 06851 United States **BUS:** Nonprofit Cancer Research Foundation **P/S:** Nonprofit Research to Prolong Cancer Patients' Lives **MA:** Local **D/D/R:** Planning, Fundraising, Programming, Managing the Staff and Directors **H/I/S:** Golfing **EDU:** Bachelor of Arts in Journalism, University of Massachusetts Amherst **C/VW:** Multiple Myeloma Research Foundation
Email: santarellas@thgmmrf.org
URL: http://www.multiplemyeloma.org

Dr. Maria I. Sante
Title: Pathologist **Company:** University of Puerto Rico School of Medicine **Address:** El Senorial Mail Station Box 660, San Juan, PR 00926 Puerto Rico **BUS:** Education University **P/S:** Professor of Pathology, Teacher, Laboratory Director **MA:** International **D/D/R:** Clinical Pathology **H/I/S:** Travel, Cooking, Enjoys Playing Volleyball **EDU:** Bael Basco in Spain, Doctorate in Pathology **A/A/S:** Alpha Omega Alpha, College of Pathology, Medical Association of Spain, PR
Email: mariasantepr@yahoo.com

Lori L. Santiago
Title: Guest Manager **Company:** Hilton Garden Inn **Address:** 1565 Crossways Boulevard, Chesapeake, VA 23320 United States **BUS:** Hotel **P/S:** Hospitality Services **MA:** International **D/D/R:** ensuring customer satisfaction **H/I/S:** Reading, Spending Time with her Family, Artwork, Making Crafts **EDU:** Coursework, Bryant & Stratton College **CERTS:** Diploma, Blue Mountain Academy, Hamburg, PA **A/H:** Catch Me At My Best Award, Hilton Hotels Corporation; Spirit of Pride Award, Hilton Hotels Corporation; Teacher of the Year Award
Email: lori.santiago@hilton.com
URL: http://www.hilton.com

William J. Santini
Title: Staff Accountant **Company:** Greene, Rubin, Miller and Pacino, CPAs **Address:** 1340 Soldiers Field Road, Boston, MA 02135 United States **BUS:** Certified Public Accountant Firm **P/S:** Accounting, Financial Statements, Taxation **MA:** Regional **D/D/R:** Accounting, Auditing, Financial Statements, Taxation **H/I/S:** Movies, Beach, Spending Time with Friends and Family **EDU:** Bachelor of Science in Accounting, Western New England College (2001) **CERTS:** Pursuing Certification in Public Accounting **A/A/S:** New Hampshire Society of Certified Public Accountants
Email: bsstrr1@msn.com
URL: http://www.cabridgewhoswho.com

Barbara Santora
Title: Teacher, Owner **Company:** Santora Tutoring **Address:** 5155 State Highway, Suite 206, Bainbridge, NY 13733 United States **BUS:** Tutoring Company **P/S:** Tutoring in All Areas of Study for Kindergarten through Eighth-Grade Students, Educational Services **MA:** Regional **D/D/R:** Calling to Make Contacts, Scheduling Tutoring Sessions, Traveling to Teach Students, Meeting with Students, Operations Management, Working as a Substitute Teacher for Mathematics, History, Science, Gym and Home Economics **H/I/S:** Bowling, Reading, Playing Card Games, Playing Board Games **EDU:** Bachelor of Education, Felician College (1980) **A/A/S:** National Catholic Educational Association
Email: disneylover22@aol.com
URL: http://www.cambridgewhoswho.com

Larry G. Santos
Title: United Auto Workers International Representative (Retired) **Company:** UAW-DaimlerChrysler National Training Center **Address:** 2211 E. Jefferson Avenue, Detroit, MI 48207 United States **BUS:** Automobile Company **P/S:** National PEL, Employee Assistance Program, Diversity Programs **MA:** National **D/D/R:** Training Union Members, Leadership **H/I/S:** Fishing, Spending Time with his Eight Grandchildren **EDU:** High School Graduate **A/A/S:** Democratic Party **C/VW:** Leukemia & Lymphoma Society, St. Jude Children's Research Hospital

Jackie M. Sapp
Title: Owner **Company:** Underwater Service Associates **Address:** P.O. Box 3041, High Springs, FL 32655 United States **BUS:** Contracting Company **P/S:** Component Cleaning, Repairing, Traveling Water Screen Maintenance and Service, Trash Rack Maintenance, Condenser Line Cleaning and Inspections, Underwater Video Inspections, De-watering Services, Hydraulic Dredging, Air Lifting Services
Email: usa_jmsapp@att.net
URL: http://www.cambridgewhoswho.com

Cindy-Kaye Saraceno
Title: Registered Nurse **Company:** Good Samaritan Hospital **Address:** 1000 Montauk Highway, West Islip, NY 11795 United States **BUS:** Healthcare **P/S:** Hospital **MA:** Regional **D/D/R:** Medical Surgical Nursing, Palliative Care, Hospice Care **H/I/S:** Gardening, Doing Creative Yard Work **EDU:** Pursuing Bachelor of Science in Nursing; Registered Nurse, Suffolk Community College; Licensed Practical Nurse, BOCES Brookhaven **CERTS:** Pursuing Certification in Palliative Care; Certified in Advanced Life Support and Pediatric Advanced Life Support **A/A/S:** Hospice and Palliative Nurses Association; Professional Nurses of Suffolk County **A/H:** Bernstein Humanitarian Award (1999)
Email: cindiblonde317@yahoo.com
URL: http://www.cambridgewhoswho.com

Dr. Hakan Sarbanoglu
Title: Director of Knowledge Center **Company:** Kalido **Address:** One Wall Street, 5th Floor, Burlington, MA 01803 United States **BUS:** Enterprise Data Warehousing and Master Data Management Software **P/S:** Management and Software Services **MA:** Local **D/D/R:** Creating Business Modeling and Solution Architecture **H/I/S:** Hiking **EDU:** Ph.D. in Geographical Info Systems, Bosphorus University (1995)
Email: hakan.sarbanoglu@kalido.com
URL: http://www.kalido.com

Anne E. Saro
Title: Director of Development **Company:** San Diego Institute for Policy Research **Address:** La Jolla, CA 92037 United States **BUS:** Fundraising Nonprofit **P/S:** Public Policy, Fundraising Events **MA:** Local **D/D/R:** Fund Raising, Event Specialist **EDU:** Bachelors, St Josephs University **A/A/S:** FRWF
Email: annesaro@gmail.com

Stella Marie P. Sasing
Title: Industrial Engineer **Company:** United Parcel Service **Address:** 610 N. Campus Avenue, Upland, CA 91786 United States **BUS:** World's Largest Package Delivery Company **P/S:** Specialized Transportation and Logistics Services **MA:** International **D/D/R:** Industrial Engineering, Planning Forecasts for Six Centers, Staffing, Employee Production Analysis, Performing Service Audits **EDU:** Bachelor of Science in Industrial Engineering, Cal Poly Pomona (2004)
Email: ssasing@ups.com
URL: http://www.upser.com

Alicia C. Sasser
Title: Economist **Company:** Federal Reserve Bank of Boston **Address:** 600 Atlantic Avenue, Boston, MA 02210 United States **BUS:** Bank **P/S:** Labor and Health Economics **MA:** Regional **D/D/R:** Economic Research **H/I/S:** Skiing, Mountain Biking, Running **EDU:** Ph.D. in Economics, Harvard University **A/A/S:** Women in the Committee of Economics; American Economic Association
Email: alicia.sasser@bos.frb.org
URL: http://www.bos.frb.org/economic/neppc

M. Scott Satterfield
Title: Deputy Director **Company:** Jefferson County Emergency Management **BUS:** Emergency Rescue Service **P/S:** Emergency Medical Services, Advanced Life Support, Pediatric Advanced Life Support, Basic Trauma Life Support, Basic Life Support, Training and Education **MA:** Regional **D/D/R:** Overseeing Staff, Performing Human Resources Duties, Hiring, Managing Daily Operations, Dispatching **H/I/S:** Golfing, Bowling, Supporting College Football **EDU:** Pursuing Master's Degree; Bachelor's Degree in Organizational Management, Tusculum College, Greenville, Tennessee (2003) **A/A/S:** Freemasons
Email: bsfd2@yahoo.com
URL: http://www.r2ems.com/agency/jeffersoncounty

Daniel J. Sauer
Title: Area Director **Company:** American Youth Soccer Organization **Dept:** Youth Soccer **Address:** 1921 Vondron Road, Madison, WI 53716 United States **BUS:** Sports **P/S:** Youth Soccer Program **MA:** Local **D/D/R:** Operations and Management **H/I/S:** Hockey **EDU:** Associate Degree in Marketing, Madison Area Technical College (1979) **A/H:** Achievement Award for Area 6, Section 6, St. Dennis Parish (2006)
Email: djsauer58@hotmail.com
URL: http://www.soccer.org

Tom J. Sauerwein
Title: Endocrine Fellowship Program Director **Company:** United States Air Force **Address:** 2200 Bergquist Drive, Suite 1, Lackland Air Force Base, TX 78236 United States **BUS:** Air Force **P/S:** National Defense, Healthcare, Education **MA:** National **D/D/R:** Training Future Endocrinologists **H/I/S:** Spending Time with his Daughter **EDU:** MD, Uniformed Services University of the Health Sciences; United States Air Force **A/A/S:** American Association of Clinical Endocrinologists; American College of Physicians; The Endocrine Society **C/VW:** Board Member, Camp Independence
Email: tom.sauerwein@lackland.af.mil

Johnny Sauls
Title: Safety and Training Manager **Company:** Norbord Mississippi, Inc. **Address:** 1194 Highway 145 N., Guntown, MS 38849 United States **BUS:** Proven Leader in the Engineering Industry **P/S:** Manufacture of Oriented Strand Board, Lumber and Wood Products **MA:** International **D/D/R:** Ensuring Occupational Safety and Health Compliance and Environmental Compliance **H/I/S:** Golfing, Motorcycles **EDU:** Diploma, Byram High School (1988) **A/A/S:** American Society of Safety Engineers; Occupational Health and Safety Technician
Email: johnny.sauls@guntown.norbord.com
URL: http://www.cambridgewhoswho.com

Deborah M. Saunders, RN
Title: Army Nurse (Retired) **Company:** Nurses Health Auxiliary **Address:** P.O. Box 7155, Roanoke, VA 24019 United States **BUS:** Government Healthcare Organization **P/S:** Education, Counseling, Health Fairs, Screenings **MA:** Regional **D/D/R:** Visiting Homes of the Disabled, Sick and Elderly, Coordinating Educational Programs, Overseeing Psychiatric Treatment **H/I/S:** Cooking, Attending Church, Going to the Theater **EDU:** Bachelor's Degree in Nursing, Hampton University (1981); Registered Nurse **A/A/S:** Delta Sigma Theta; Chi Eta Phi; The National Association for the Advancement of Colored People; Founder, Nurses Health Auxiliary
Email: deborahforjustice@cox.net
URL: http://www.cambridgewhoswho.com

Jimmy D. Saunders
Title: President **Company:** Posillipo, Inc. **Address:** 9601 Highway 29 W., Georgetown, TX 78628 United States **BUS:** Aviation Company **P/S:** Research and Development of Missile Systems, Hydrographic Surveys and Autonomous Robotic Vehicles **MA:** National **D/D/R:** missile defense consulting, testing for instrumentation system, program management and troubleshooting **H/I/S:** Golfing **EDU:** Master's Degree in Physics; Bachelor of Science in Mathematics; Coursework, United States Naval Academy; Coursework, The University of Mississippi **A/A/S:** Former Commander, U.S. Navy; American Physical Society **C/VW:** Institute of Electrical and Electronics Engineers; Sigma Chi
Email: jimmy.saunders@j3s.us
URL: http://www.cambridgewhoswho.com

Patricia D. Saunders
Title: Travel Agent **Company:** VLP Travel **Address:** Bronx, NY 10462 United States **BUS:** Online Travel Agency **P/S:** Travel Arrangements and Packages **MA:** National **D/D/R:** Making Travel Arrangements **H/I/S:** Traveling, Reading, Photography **EDU:** Bachelor of Arts in Economics and Business Education, CUNY Lehman College
Email: vlptravel@hotmail.com
URL: http://www.ythexpress.com/101318

Aerica L. Savage
Title: Certified Registered Nurse Practitioner **Company:** Tennessee Valley Cardiovascular Center **Address:** 541 W. College Street, Florence, AL 35630 United States **BUS:** Physician's Office **P/S:** Healthcare **MA:** Local **D/D/R:** Cardiology **EDU:** Master's Degree in Cardiology, University of Alabama in Huntsville **A/A/S:** Alabama State Nurses Association; American Academy of Nurse Practitioners; North Alabama Nurse Practitioner Association; American College of Cardiology **C/VW:** Salvation Army
Email: asavage@tvccpc.com
URL: http://www.cambridgewhoswho.com

Vicky Savage
Title: President, Owner **Company:** UptoDate Bookkeeping, Inc. **Address:** 179 Lake Street S., Suite 210, Forest Lake, MN 55025 United States **BUS:** Bookkeeping Firm **P/S:** Write-up (Bookkeeping) Services for Small to Medium size Companies, QuickBooks **MA:** Local **EXP:** Ms. Savage's area of expertise is in bookkeeping. **D/D/R:** Installing, Setting Up and Training Clients on QuickBooks, Doing Write-Up Work, Answering Clients' Questions Managing the Office, Networking **EDU:** Diploma, Park Center High School (1980) **CERTS:** Certified QuickBooks ProAdvisor (2000); Certified Notary (1987) **A/A/S:** American Institute of Professional Bookkeepers; Board Member, Chamber of Commerce; Better Business Bureau
Email: vsavage@uptodatebookkeeping.com
URL: http://www.uptodatebookkeeping.com

Danielle R. Savona
Title: Special Education Teacher, Department Chairwoman **Company:** Redlands Unified School District **Address:** 20 W. Lugonia Avenue, Redlands, CA 92373 United States **BUS:** Public School District **P/S:** Education **MA:** Local **D/D/R:** Teaching Special Education **H/I/S:** Photography, Traveling, Reading **EDU:** Master's Degree in Special Education **A/A/S:** Redlands Educational Partnership Foundation; Redlands Teachers Association **A/H:** Teacher of the Year, Redlands Unified School District **C/VW:** United Way
Email: daniellesavona@hotmail.com
URL: http://www.redlands.k12.ca.us

Edward A. Sawada
Title: Medical Physician **Company:** Edward A. Sawada **Address:** P.O. Box 9814, Towson, MD 21284 United States **BUS:** Medical Practice **P/S:** Prevention of Cervical Cancer and Human Papillomavirus **MA:** Regional **D/D/R:** Treating Cervical Cancer, Human Papillomavirus and Genital Tract Pre-Cancer **H/I/S:** Spending Time with Family and his Grandson **EDU:** Coursework Georgetown University and University of Virginia **A/H:** Lifetime Achievement Award, State of Maryland
URL: http://www.cambridgewhoswho.com

Rebekah A. Sawyer, RRT
Title: Respiratory Therapist **Company:** Hacienda Healthcare **Address:** 16806 S Magenta Road, Phoenix, AZ 85048 United States **BUS:** Healthcare Center **P/S:** Respiratory Therapy **MA:** Local **D/D/R:** Pediatric Long Term Care **H/I/S:** Working Out, Reading **EDU:** Beckly College, Associate of Arts **A/A/S:** AARC
Email: rasaw77@msn.com
URL: http://www.csuewalker.stemtechhealth.com

Cindy Sayakomarn
Title: Owner **Company:** Sayakomarn's **Address:** 419 16th Street, Canyon, TX 79015 United States **BUS:** Restaurant **P/S:** Thai and Lao Cuisine **MA:** Local **D/D/R:** Customer Service, Thai and Lao Cuisine **EDU:** Bachelor's Degree in Finance, West Texas A&M University **A/A/S:** Chamber of Commerce
Email: csayakomarn@hotmail.com
URL: http://www.cambridgewhoswho.com

Terri Lewis Sayre
Title: President **Company:** Sayre and Associates **Address:** 2200 Ormond Boulevard, Destrehan, LA 70047 United States **BUS:** Consulting Company **P/S:** Consulting Services Including Legal Nurse Consulting, Medical Case Management and Life Care Planning **MA:** National **EXP:** Ms. Sayre's expertise includes medical and legal consulting. **D/D/R:** offering expert testimony in case management and life care planning **H/I/S:** Caring for her Dogs **CERTS:** Certified Legal Nurse Consultant; Certification in Medical Case Management; Certification in Life Care Planning Program; Diploma in Nursing, St. Joseph's Hospital School of Nursing **C/VW:** St. Jude Children's Research Hospital
Email: info@sayrelnc.com
URL: http://www.sayrelnc.com

Valerie R. Scales
Title: Assistant Director of Operations **Company:** Boston Centers for Youth and Families **Address:** 1483 Tremont Street, Boston, MA 02120 United States **BUS:** Community Center **P/S:** Programs and Services for Preschool Children to Senior Citizens **MA:** Regional **D/D/R:** Organizing a Vast Variety of Programs for Pre-School Children to Senior Citizens, Supervising, Managing, Overseeing the Implementation of Federal Grants, Organizing, Monitoring, Designing Programs for New Community Centers, Offering Training Opportunities for Staff, Overseeing 17 Facilities **H/I/S:** Exercising, Walking, Watching Movies and Sports, Traveling **EDU:** Master's Degree in Management, Cambridge College (1994); Master of Education, Cambridge College (1989); Bachelor of Science in Therapeutic Recreation, York College, PA (1982); Associate Degree in Community Recreation, Lasell College (1980) **A/A/S:** Former Member, Recreation Association **A/H:** Parkman Award, Exceptional Work and Dedication, City of Boston; Distinguished Award for Exceptional Work and Dedication, City of Boston
Email: valerie.scales@cityofboston.gov
URL: http://www.cityofboston.gov/bcyf

Deborah Scaling Kiley
Title: Publisher, Author, Chief Executive Officer **Company:** NVOS Publishing **Address:** 504 Alta Drive, Fort Worth, TX 76107 United States **BUS:** Private Publishing Company **P/S:** Books Including 'No Victims, Only Survivors' and 'The Sinking' **MA:** International **D/D/R:** Speaking Motivationally, Writing Books on Survival Skills and Life Experiences **H/I/S:** Showing Horses **EDU:** Coursework, University of Texas **A/A/S:** The Authors Guild; Alliance for Children; Juvenile Diabetes Research Foundation International; American Cancer Society
Email: dskioi@charter.net
URL: http://www.novictimsonlysurvivors.com

Michele L. Scamoffa
Title: Postmaster **Company:** United State Postal Service **Address:** 5624 Route 9, New Gretna, NJ 08224 United States **BUS:** Government Regulated Postal Service **P/S:** Postal Services Including Mailing, Shipping and Postage **MA:** Regional **D/D/R:** Overseeing Non-Delivery Office with a Second Other Employee, Distributing Mail, Handling Customer Service and Administrative Responsibilities **H/I/S:** Playing the Guitar in a Country Band, Traveling, Spending Time with her Family **EDU:** College Coursework **A/A/S:** Officer, Order of the Eastern Star; National Association of Postmasters of the United States; Former State Secy Treasurer (2005-2006); Presenter on E-Travel Coordination, District Level Training
Email: michele.l.scamoffa@usps.gov

Sigyn K. Scarangella
Title: Owner **Company:** Sunny Escape Tanning **Address:** 924 Atlantic Avenue, Baldwin, NY 11510 United States **BUS:** Distribution Firm **P/S:** Tanning Lotions, Skincare Products, Bathing Suits, Sunglasses and Pet Grooming Services **MA:** Local **D/D/R:** ensuring customer satisfaction, overseeing operations, maintaining and ordering inventory **H/I/S:** Swimming, Reading, Playing Tennis, Spending Time with her Two Children **EDU:** College Coursework **C/VW:** The National Children's Cancer Society; Breast Cancer Research; North Shore Animal League America; Autism Speaks
Email: psa02@optonline.net

Lynn Elizabeth Scarengos, RDH
Title: Registered Dental Hygienist **Company:** Audubon Dental **Address:** 4508 Rebecca Boulevard, Metaire, LA 70003 United States **BUS:** Healthcare **P/S:** Dentures, Extractions, Relines, Cleanings, Checkups, Polishing, Sealants, Bleaching, Bonding, Contouring, Veneers, Crowns, Bridges, Fillings, Partials, Implants and Root Canals, Full Mouth Reconstruction, Treatment for TMJ Disorders **MA:** Regional **EXP:** Ms. Scarengos' areas of expertise include dental education for patients. **D/D/R:** Promoting Oral Hygiene, Educating Patients on the Importance of Good Oral Hygiene and Healthcare, screening for gastroesophageal reflux disease, diabetes and oral cancer detection, performing non-surgical treatments and practicing general dental healthcare **H/I/S:** Working Out, Genealogy, Scrapbooking, Research **EDU:** Associate Degree in Dental Hygiene, Loyola University, New Orleans (1973) **A/A/S:** President, New Orleans Area Dental Hygiene Association; Jefferson Genealogical Society; LDHA **C/VW:** Veterans of Foreign Wars; Local Seminars
Email: rscareng@bellsouth.net
URL: http://www.affordablesmiles.net

Ms. Pamela M. Scarpelli
Title: Owner **Company:** Runners **Address:** 380 Sunrise Avenue, Kingman, AZ 86409 United States **BUS:** Concierge Service **P/S:** Assistance for Elderly, Disabled and Home-Bound Individuals **MA:** Regional **D/D/R:** Serving the Community, Running Errands for Elderly, Disabled and Home-Bound Individuals Including Assisting in their Banking Needs, Grocery Shopping, Filling Prescriptions and Public Transportation **H/I/S:** Hand and Machine Sewing **EDU:** Coursework in Interior Design, College of DuPage
Email: pamscarpelli@yahoo.com

Frank Anthony Scattaregia
Title: President, Owner **Company:** Frank A. Scattaregia, MD **Address:** 786 W. Second Street, Weston, WV 26452 United States **BUS:** Medical Center **P/S:** Healthcare Services Including Cardiology, Geriatric Medicine and Internal Medicine Treatments **MA:** Local **D/D/R:** treating patients for non-invasive cardiology and internal medicine, advising patients in preventing heart disease and stroke and overseeing nursing for clinical cardiology care **H/I/S:** Golfing, Playing Tennis, Swimming, Hiking, Biking **EDU:** MD, University of Bologna, Italy (1975); Master of Arts in Public Health, University of Pittsburgh (1976); Bachelor of Arts in Chemical Engineering, Carnegie Mellon University (1969) **A/A/S:** Former President, American Heart Association; West Virginia Medical Association; West Virginia Geriatrics Society **A/H:** Volunteer of the Year Award (1990)
Email: fascattaregia@hotmail.com

Tina Marie Schaare
Title: Licensed Vocational Nurse **Company:** Spanish Meadows Rehabilitation and Nursing Home **Address:** 1480 Katy Flewellen Road, Katy, TX 77494 United States **BUS:** Rehabilitation and Nursing Home **P/S:** Elderly Rehabilitation, Nursing Home Care, Skilled Nursing Care **MA:** Statewide **D/D/R:** Geriatric Care **H/I/S:** Traveling, Gardening, Taking Care of her Child, Running a Day Care **CERTS:** Licensed Vocational Nurse Certification, North Country Community College, New York; Certified in CPR, Certified IV Nurse
Email: tschaare@yahoo.com
URL: http://www.spanishmeadows.com

Deborah J. Schad
Title: Reading Specialist **Company:** District School Board of Collier County **Dept:** Village Oaks Elementary **Address:** 511 Shadyside Street, Lehigh Acres, FL 33936 United States **BUS:** School District **P/S:** Education Including Organizing Cultural, Social and Academic Pursuits, Athletics, Afterschool and English as a Second Language Programs **MA:** Florida **D/D/R:** Reading, Teaching Mathematics, Organizing Classes for Students with Reading Disabilities, Preparing Students for Comprehensive Assessment Testing Programs, Utilizing her Visual, Oral and Critical Thinking Skills **H/I/S:** Reading, Sewing, Making Crafts, Running a Holiday Workshop for Children **EDU:** Master of Arts in Mathematics, University of South Florida (1986); Master of Arts in Curriculum Instruction, Emphasis in Reading, University of South Florida (1982); Bachelor of Arts in Education, University of South Florida (1978) **CERTS:** Certified Reading Specialist (1982) **A/A/S:** Kappa Delta Phi; International Reading Association
Email: schadde@collier.k12.fl.us
URL: http://www.collier.k12.fl.us

Suzanne R. Schaeffer
Company: Patton Boggs, LLP **Address:** 2550 M. Street N.W., Washington, DC 20037 United States **BUS:** International Law Firm **P/S:** Full-Service Firm with a National Presence in Every Major Area of Legal Representation **MA:** International **D/D/R:** Working with the Department of the Interior, the Native American Law Department and the Department of Justice Regarding Native American Land, Water Rights and Environmental Issues **H/I/S:** Singing with Choral Society, Gardening, Spending Time with her Family **EDU:** JD, University of Virginia (1990) **A/A/S:** District of Columbia Bar Association; American Bar Association
Email: sschaeffer@pattonboggs.com
URL: http://www.pattonboggs.com

Barbara A. Schaffer

Title: Psychotherapist, Coach, Mediator **Company:** Whitestar, LLC **BUS:** Mental Healthcare, Coaching and Mediation Center **P/S:** Mental Healthcare and Mediation Services Including Therapy, Hypnosis, Counseling, Coaching and Energy Psychology **MA:** Regional **EXP:** Ms. Schaffer's expertise includes individual, family, child and medical health counseling, the design and implementation of health education programs and services, divorce and life coaching, clinical hypnosis, energy psychology and mediation. **H/I/S:** Traveling, Photography, Art, Swimming, Snorkeling **EDU:** Master of Social Work, Arizona State University (1991); Bachelor of Science in Psychology, Northern Arizona University (1977) **A/A/S:** Institute of Noetic Science; Collaborative Law Group of Southern Arizona; National Association of Social Workers **A/H:** Dedicated and Outstanding Service Award for Excellence in Offering Meaningful Community Rehabilitation Services (1998) **C/VW:** Local Environmental Groups; Local Schools
Email: starlight247@cox.net

Jerry A. Schaffer

Title: President, Chief Executive Officer **Company:** Quality Cable Services, Inc. **Address:** 4908 Jasper Road, Emmaus, PA 18049 United States **BUS:** Telecommunications Contracting Company **P/S:** Cable Phone and Internet Installations **MA:** Local **D/D/R:** Offering Cable, Phone and Internet Wiring Services, Overseeing the Running of the Company Including Installations, Wiring and Wall Fishing **H/I/S:** Flying, Practicing Martial Arts
Email: qcsi@ptd.net

Sara Parks Schaffnit

Title: Second-Grade Teacher **Company:** Nelson Mandela Elementary School **Address:** 1800 N. 25th Street, East Saint Louis, IL 62204 United States **BUS:** Elementary School **P/S:** Education **MA:** Local **D/D/R:** Working with Underprivileged Children **H/I/S:** Training Dogs in Obedience and Confirmation **EDU:** Master's Degree Plus 16, Lindenwood University **C/VW:** Education Station, Tutoring After School

Wendy L. Scharf

Title: Teacher **Company:** Albany Public School 19 **Address:** 369 New Scotland Avenue, Albany, NY 12208 United States **BUS:** School **P/S:** Education **MA:** Local **D/D/R:** Teaching English **H/I/S:** Gardening, Exercising, Traveling, Visiting Friends **EDU:** Bachelor's Degree in English and Philosophy, Saint Lawrence University; Master's Degree in Childhood Education Grades 1-6, SUNY Potsdam **CERTS:** ; Certification in Special Education Grades 1-6
Email: wendylynnscharf@hotmail.com

Margaret Schatteles

Title: Administrative Assistant **Company:** Graduate Management Admission Council **Dept:** Communications **Address:** 1600 Tysons Boulevard, Suite 1400, Mc Lean, VA 22102 United States **BUS:** Nonprofit Organization **P/S:** Promotion of Graduate Management Education and Assistance on Obtaining a Master of Business Administration Degree, Developing GMAT Exam **MA:** International **D/D/R:** Working for Vice President of Communications, Setting Up Meetings, Managing Budget and Resource Library, Scheduling, Checking E-mails and Expense Reports, Offering Information to Schools Regarding Trends on Student Life after Graduation and Program Management **H/I/S:** Watching Ice Hockey **EDU:** Bachelor of Science in Economics, George Mason University (2005) **A/A/S:** American Society of Administrative Professionals
Email: mschatteles@gmac.com
URL: http://www.gmac.com

Donna L. Scheele

Company: Duroshed, Inc. **Dept:** Sales Department **Address:** 147 Seton Creek Drive, Oswego, IL 60543 United States **BUS:** Construction Company **P/S:** Constructing Sheds **MA:** Illinois **EXP:** Ms. Scheele's area of expertise is in sales management. **D/D/R:** does tradeshows twice a year, meet with customers and discuss their orders and purchases **H/I/S:** Golfing, Bowling, Hiking, Swimming, Artwork, Making Crafts and Jewelry, Sewing, Gemology **EDU:** College Coursework **CERTS:** Certified Emergency Medical Technician-Basic; Certification in Medical Transcription **A/A/S:** Citizens Police Academy **A/H:** Salutatorian Award; Award, U.S. Army **C/VW:** Fox Valley Animal Welfare League; Oswego Citizen's Police Academy
Email: ahtoday@comcast.net
URL: http://www.duroshedusa.com

Jennifer E. Scheid

Title: Field Manager **Company:** Info USA **Address:** 5711 S. 86th Circle, Omaha, NE 68127 United States **BUS:** Marketing Company **P/S:** Mailing Service **MA:** National **D/D/R:** formulating direct marketing strategies **H/I/S:** Reading **EDU:** Bachelor of Science in Sociology, Fort Hays State University; Bachelor of Science in Geology (2002)
Email: jennifer.scheid@infousa.com
URL: http://www.infousa.com

Chris T. Schellinger, DC

Title: Chiropractor **Company:** C-Schell Spine Specialists, Inc. **Address:** 1169 Walker Road, Dover, DE 19904 United States **BUS:** Private Practice Dedicated to Excellence in Physical Healthcare **P/S:** Chiropractic Services **MA:** Regional **D/D/R:** Specific Adjustments to the Spine, Specializing in the Gonstead System, Consulting with New Patients to Execute a Plan of Care, Handling Spinal Examinations **EDU:** Doctor of Chiropractic, Sherman Straight Chiropractic (2006); Bachelor of Science in Nutrition, University of Delaware (2002) **A/A/S:** Central Delaware Chamber of Commerce; Delaware Chiropractic Society
Email: cschell1223@gmail.com
URL: http://www.cschellchiro.com

Kathy Brechtel Scherer

Title: VP/MANAGER **Company:** Old Southern Bank **Address:** 1515 W. Highway 50, Clermont, FL 34711 United States **BUS:** Bank **P/S:** Financial Services **MA:** Local **D/D/R:** Financial Lending, Training, Sales **H/I/S:** Traveling, Gardening **EDU:** Associate Degree in Finance **C/VW:** Habitat for Humanity, Goodwill, Food for Family, Jr. Achievement, Ronald McDonald House, American Heart Association, United Way
Email: kscherer@oldsouthernbank.com
URL: http://oldsouthernbank

Jill M. Schiavone

Title: Senior Internal Auditor **Company:** McKesson **Address:** 1220 Senlac Drive, Carrollton, TX 75006 United States **BUS:** Pharmaceutical Distribution Company **P/S:** Pharmaceutical Distribution **MA:** National **D/D/R:** Auditing, Special Projects **H/I/S:** Traveling, Reading, Shopping, Watching Movies **EDU:** Master of Science in Accounting, Abilene Christian University; Bachelor of Business Administration of Accounting, Abilene Christian University **A/A/S:** American Institute of Certified Public Accountants; International Institute of Accountants; Association for Certified Fraud Examiners
Email: jill.schiavone@mckesson.com
URL: http://www.cambridgewhoswho.com

Mr. Christopher Schiermeier

Title: National Service Account Manager **Company:** Bancsource, Inc. **Address:** 9310 N. Walnut, Republic, MO 65738 United States **BUS:** Field Service Corporation **P/S:** Equipment Maintenance and Supplies **MA:** National **D/D/R:** Managing Large National Accounts, Project Management **H/I/S:** Fishing, Baseball **EDU:** Technical Training, Control Data Institute, Missouri
Email: chris.schiermeier@bancsourceinc.com
URL: http://www.bancsourceinc.com

Susan Schillaci

Title: Classroom Teacher **Company:** Rochester City School District, School of the Arts **Address:** 45 Prince Street, Rochester, NY 14607 United States **BUS:** School **P/S:** Education **MA:** Local **D/D/R:** Performing Arts, Teaching Sixth-Grade Reading, Mathematics, Science and Social Studies, Seventh-Grade English **H/I/S:** Reading, Dancing, Working Out, Traveling, Spending Time with the family, **EDU:** Master's Degree in Elementary Education, Nazareth College of Rochester; Bachelor of Arts, Marymount College (1981) **A/A/S:** Gifted and Talented Program **C/VW:** Visiting Nurse Service
Email: sschill1@rochester.rr.com
URL: http://www.cambridgewhoswho.com

Virginia A. Schinbeckler

Title: Teacher **Company:** Northern Heights Elementary School **Address:** 5209 N. State Road 109, Columbia City, IN 46725 United States **BUS:** Elementary School **P/S:** Elementary Education **MA:** Regional **D/D/R:** creating lesson plans for the state curriculum, involving in various school committees as well as teaching second-grade all subjects including health and level reading **H/I/S:** Walking, Collecting Antiques, Reading, Spending Time with her Grandchildren **EDU:** Bachelor's Degree in Elementary Education, Indiana University-Purdue University Indianapolis (1998)
Email: virginia.schinbeckler@cwwemail.com

Sandra F. Schirmer

Title: Perioperative Clinical Specialist **Company:** Danbury Hospital **Address:** 24 Hospital Avenue, Danbury, CT 06810 United States **BUS:** Hospital **P/S:** Healthcare **MA:** Local **D/D/R:** Training, Educating and Handling Peri Operative Orientation, Training Adjunct Faculty at the Charter Oak State College, Teaching an Online Course **H/I/S:** Boating **EDU:** Master of Science in Nursing, Western Connecticut State University (1991); Bachelor of Science in Nursing Western Connecticut State University (1978) **A/A/S:** Association of Peri Operative Registered Nurses; Sigma Theta Tau; Danbury Hospital Alumni Association Nurse Education/Clinical Nurse Specialist Specialty Assembly
Email: sandysch60@comcast.net

Sheryl A. Schlater

Title: Customer Service Manager **Company:** Wal-Mart **Address:** 1801 W. Main Street, Troy, OH 45373 United States **BUS:** Retail Store **P/S:** Retail Center **MA:** National **D/D/R:** Customer Service Management **H/I/S:** Hand Quilting, Reading **EDU:** Coursework in Banking, Sinclair Community College; Coursework, Legal Secretary Studies, Miami Jacobs College **A/A/S:** Troy Lions Club **C/VW:** Troy Lions Club
Email: sas5128@woh.rr.com
URL: http://www.cambridgewhoswho.com

Jan Schlegel, MFA

Title: Professor of Fitness, Exercise and Sports Department **Company:** New Jersey City University **Address:** 2039 John F. Kennedy Boulevard, Jersey City, NJ 07305 United States **BUS:** Vibrant, Exciting University Campus **P/S:** Combination of Liberal Arts and a Variety of Major Concentrations Including Media Arts, Business, Education, Nursing and Criminal Justice **MA:** Regional **D/D/R:** Teaching Fitness, Exercise, Sports, Weight Lifting, Flexibility, Posture and Pilates, Running Two Workshops **H/I/S:** Dancing, Olympic Weight Lifting **EDU:** Master of Science in Arts in Dance, New York University (1960's) **A/A/S:** National Academy of Sports Medicine; National Strength and Conditioning Association
Email: jschlegel@njcu.edu
URL: http://www.cambridgewhoswho.com

Linda J. Schlenker

Title: Medical Laboratory Technician **Company:** Cambridge Medical Center **Address:** 701 S. Dellwood, Cambridge, MN 55008 United States **BUS:** Medical Center **P/S:** Clinic and Hospital Laboratory Services **MA:** Local **D/D/R:** Hematology, Microbiology, Chemistry, Coagulation, Urinalysis, Blood Bank, Phlebotomy **H/I/S:** Scrapbooking, Making Crafts **EDU:** FEMA Certified; Hazmat Certified; Associate of Science, Lakeland Medical Academy **CERTS:** FEMA Certified; Hazmat Certified **A/A/S:** American Society of Clinical Pathologists
Email: lovefornoah@aol.com

Donald N. Schlosser

Title: President **Company:** Creative Dental Techniques, Inc **Address:** 600 S State Road, Marysville, PA 17053 United States **BUS:** Dental Lab Manufacturer **P/S:** Producing Crowns and Bridges for Over 50 Dental Offices **MA:** Local **D/D/R:** Known for Anterior Crown and Bridge Work **H/I/S:** Owns an '89 Red Corvette, Sports **EDU:** Coursework, Elizabethtown College, PA

Melva Haskins Schmeiser

Title: Teacher **Company:** Limon Public Schools **Dept:** Limon High School **Address:** 874 F Avenue, Limon, CO 80828 United States **BUS:** High School **P/S:** Education **MA:** Local **D/D/R:** Teaching Social Science Studies **H/I/S:** Reading, Gardening **EDU:** Bachelor's Degree in History and Psychology, Seattle Pacific University **CERTS:** Certificate in History and Psychology, Seattle Pacific University; Certified Teacher for Grades K-12 **A/A/S:** National Education Association; Colorado Education Association **C/VW:** Limon Historical Society
Email: mschmeis@hotmail.com

Brian A. Schmidt

Title: Broker, Owner **Company:** Camarillo Home Loans, Inc. **Address:** 370 N. Lantana, Unit 18, Camarillo, CA 93010 United States **BUS:** Mortgage Company **P/S:** Construction, Commercial and Home Equity Line of Credit Services **MA:** Regional **D/D/R:** Focusing on Primary County, Supervising Seven Employees, Continuous Education with Weekly Meetings, Hosting Training Seminars for Newly Licensed Agents, Overseeing All Functions of the Business **H/I/S:** Working as the Vice Chairman of the School Site Council **EDU:** Licensed Broker, State of California (2006); Bachelor's Degree in Business, Arizona State University (1999); California Real Estate Salesperson (1998) **A/A/S:** California Association of Mortgage Brokers; Camarillo Chamber of Commerce; Board of Directors, Good Samaritan Shelters
Email: brian@chlinc.net
URL: http://www.camarillohomeloans.com

Debra W. Schmidt

Title: Teacher, Mathematics Coordinator **Company:** Bradshaw Mountain High School **Address:** 6000 E. Long Look Drive, Prescott Valley, AZ 86314 United States **BUS:** Public High School **P/S:** Education **MA:** National **D/D/R:** Teaching Mathematics, Coordinating Secondary Mathematics Instruction for the District **H/I/S:** Hiking, Freshwater Fishing **EDU:** Master of Arts in Teaching Mathematics, Northern Arizona University **A/A/S:** Arizona Association of Teachers of Mathematics; National Council of Teachers of Mathematics; Alpha Delta Kappa **A/H:** Presidential Award for Excellence in Mathematics and Science Teaching from President Clinton and the National Science Foundation
Email: debra.schmidt@humboldtunified.com

Kathy J. Schmidt, LPN
Title: Supervisor **Company:** Women's Care **Address:** 1600 Coit Road, Suite 402, Plano, TX 75075 United States **BUS:** Healthcare Practice **P/S:** Feminine Healthcare Services **MA:** Local **D/D/R:** Obstetrics and Gynecology, Overseeing Pap Smears and Mammograms, Filing Insurance Claims, Supervising Employees, Coding **H/I/S:** Quilting, Playing Tennis **EDU:** Licensed Practical Nurse (1979); Coursework in Licensed Practical Nurse Studies (1979)
Email: kschjf2001@tx.rr.com

Mathilde Apelt Schmidt
Title: Author **Company:** Self-Employed **Address:** 18218 Walnut Road, Castro Valley, CA 94546 United States **BUS:** Author **P/S:** Literary Arts Including Writing Books and Articles **MA:** National **EXP:** Ms. Schmidt's area of expertise is in the literary arts. **H/I/S:** Gardening, Reading Biographies and Novels, Attending Opera Productions **EDU:** Master's Degree in Special Education **CERTS:** Credential for Severely Handicapped, Hayward (Now East Bay University of California); Credential in Teaching High School Students in German, Mathematics, Biology and Geography, University of Hayward **A/A/S:** American Association of University Women; Women's National Book Association; Member, Four Book Clubs **C/VW:** Castro Valley Library; Volunteer, Financial Supporter, Alameda County Library System
Email: mathildes@comcast.net
URL: http://www.mschmidtbooks.com

Paul J. Schmidt
Title: Owner, Production Director **Company:** UnoDeuce Multimedia Productions **Address:** 4921 Leafdale Boulevard, Royal Oak, MI 48073 United States **BUS:** Multimedia Production Company **P/S:** Producing Multimedia Materials for Small Businesses, Churches and Nonprofit Organizations **MA:** National **D/D/R:** Video and Television Production **H/I/S:** Watching Movies, Outdoor Activities **EDU:** Bachelor of Arts in Broadcasting and Cable Productions, Western Michigan University **A/A/S:** Detroit Regional Chamber of Commerce; Telly Award; Communicator Award
Email: pauls@unodeauce.com
URL: http://www.unodeuce.com

Elizabeth W. B Schmitt
Title: Upper School English and Theater Teacher **Company:** Lakehill Preparatory School **Address:** 2720 Hillside Drive, Dallas, TX 75214 United States **BUS:** Private Preparatory School **P/S:** Education **MA:** Local **D/D/R:** Teaching English Theater, Shakespeare and Directing **H/I/S:** Reading, Scrap Booking **EDU:** Master's Degree in English and European Renaissance Drama, University of Warwick, Coventry England; Bachelor of Arts in Drama, Vassar College, Poughkeepsie, New York **A/A/S:** Texas Educational Theater Association; Educational Theater Association; Thespian Troop; National Junior Honor Society **C/VW:** Local Temple
Email: eschmitt@lakehillprep.org
URL: http://www.lakehillprep.org

Elizabeth Hope Schmitt Lynn
Title: Naturopathist **Company:** Hopes Naturopathy Wellness Center **Address:** 1306 Devils Hollow Road, Frankfort, KY 40601 United States **BUS:** Wellness Center **P/S:** Natural Healing **MA:** National **EXP:** Ms. Schmitt Lynn's expertise includes acupressure, massage and reflexology therapy. **H/I/S:** Making Crafts, Fishing, Herbology **EDU:** Coursework in Naturopathic Medical Education, University of Arkansas; Coursework in Cosmetology, Kentucky Board of Hairdressers and Cosmetologists **CERTS:** Licensed Cosmetologist **A/A/S:** National Alliance on Mental Illness **C/VW:** Local Blood Bank
Email: drhopend@hotmail.com
URL: http://www.cambridgewhoswho.com

Martha Schmucker
Title: 1) Critical Care Registered Nurse 2) Owner **Company:** 1) Goshen General Hospital, Magnet Status 2) Auf Wiedersehen Shoppe **Address:** 121 S. Main Street, Topeka, IN 46571 United States **BUS:** 1) Healthcare Center 2) Retail Store **P/S:** 1) Healthcare 2) Books, Fresh Flowers, Educational Activities for Children **MA:** 1) National 2) Regional **EXP:** Ms. Schmucker's expertise includes critical-care nursing and medical-surgical nursing. **D/D/R:** Managing the Retail Store, working in the intensive care unit, caring for patients with cancer and developing healthcare plans for patients **H/I/S:** Reading, Gardening, Crafts **EDU:** Bachelor of Science in Nursing, Goshen College (1987) **CERTS:** Diploma in Business Management, Stratford Career Institute (2006); Diploma in Floral Design, Stratford Career Institute (2004)
Email: mutter7@earthlink.net
URL: http://www.cambridgewhoswho.com

Cindy Cureton Schneider
Title: Perinatal and Newborn Educator **Company:** United State Army Reserve Nurse Corps **Dept:** Florida Hospital **Address:** 601 E. Rollins Street, Orlando, FL 32803 United States **BUS:** Army Medical Center **P/S:** Healthcare, Acute Care **MA:** National **EXP:** Ms. Schneider's expertise includes critical care obstetric, prenatal and high-risk care. **H/I/S:** Spending Time with her Family, Spending Time Outdoors **EDU:** Pursuing Master of Science in Nursing, University of Florida; Bachelor of Science in Nursing, University of Phoenix **A/A/S:** American WWII Orphans Network; American Academy of Pediatrics; Code of Club Commission; ANCS; Phi Kappa Phi; Sigma Theta Tau **C/VW:** American Heart Association; Boy Scouts of America
Email: cindy.schneider@us.army.mil
URL: http://www.cambridgewhoswho.com

Mr. Edward L. Schneider
Title: Director of Pastoral Counseling **Company:** Concordia Lutheran Church **Address:** Huebner Road Route 1604, San Antonio, TX 78232 United States **BUS:** Ecclesiastical Industry **P/S:** Spiritual and Emotional Care **MA:** Local **D/D/R:** Civilian Pastorage, Clergyman Counseling, Training Counselors **H/I/S:** Fishing **EDU:** Master of Divinity, Concordia Seminary, St. Louis, MO; Master's Degree in Sacred Theology, Concordia Seminary, St. Louis, MO **A/A/S:** Legion of Merit; Full Colonel, Veteran, United States Army
Email: schneidere@sbcglobal.net
URL: http://www.cambridgewhoswho.com

Michele P. Schneider
Title: Managing Member, Owner **Company:** Mortgage Solutions de Santa Fe **Address:** 502 West Cordova Road, Suite A, Santa Fe, NM 87505 United States **BUS:** Mortgage Company **P/S:** Financial Services for Commercial and Residential Purposes Including Land Loans **MA:** National **EXP:** Ms. Schneider's expertise is in financial management. **H/I/S:** Writing Poetry, Acting in the Community Theater, Running **EDU:** Master's Degree in Special Education, C.W. Post Campus, Long Island University; Bachelor's Degree in Interdisciplinary Studies, SUNY Old Westbury **CERTS:** Certification, International Dyslexia Society (Now International Dyslexia Association); Certified Mortgage Broker, State of New Mexico **A/A/S:** International Dyslexia Association; Former Member, Commodities Exchange **C/VW:** Board Member, Challenge New Mexico
Email: mishpaula@aol.com
URL: http://www.msdesf.com

Diane M. Schnell
Title: Paraprofessional/Title 1 Reading **Company:** Lehighton Area School District **Address:** 200 Beauer Run Road, Lehighton, PA 18235 United States **BUS:** School District **P/S:** Education **MA:** Local **D/D/R:** Teaching Reading **H/I/S:** Spending Time with her Children, Soccer Mom **EDU:** Pursuing Bachelor's Degree; Associate Degree in Elementary Education, Lehighton County Community College **A/A/S:** Masonic Eastern Star **C/VW:** Local Church
Email: ges1@ptd.net
URL: http://www.cambridgewhoswho.com

Laura R. Schock
Title: 1) Head of Design and Production 2) Owner **Company:** 1) D&S Advertising, Inc. 2) Tempest FX **BUS:** 1) Advertising Company 2) Design Solution Company **P/S:** 1) Advertising Materials 2) Print/Website Design **MA:** 1) Long Island 2) National **D/D/R:** Designing, Consulting **H/I/S:** Traveling, Swimming, Hiking **EDU:** Pursuing Master's Degree in Education, Dowling College; Bachelor's Degree in Visual Communications, SUNY Farmingdale State College **A/A/S:** Contributed to Help Find Fugitives through Website Design, lifugitivefinder.com **C/VW:** Make-A-Wish Foundation
Email: schocky3xl@yahoo.com
URL: http://www.tempestfx.com

Dawn Metzger Schoenhalls
Title: Owner **Company:** Metzger's Pub **Address:** 4135 Seneca Street, West Seneca, NY 14224 United States **BUS:** Privately-Owned Tavern and Restaurant **P/S:** Music, Food, Beverages **MA:** Regional **D/D/R:** Serving Full Menu for Lunch and Dinner, Specializing in Buffalo Wings and Beef, Home Cooking, Live Music, Overseeing Staff of 25, Payroll, Customer Relations, Booking Bands, Managing Accounts Receivable and Payable **H/I/S:** Archery, Traveling, Fishing **EDU:** High School Education **A/A/S:** National Field Archery Association; New York Fellow Archery & Bow Association; ABATE **A/H:** Western New York Champion Archer (2007)
Email: archergirl1231@aol.com
URL: http://www.mymetzgerspub.com

Jolene R. Schonchin
Title: Public Information Officer, Editor **Company:** Comanche Nation Public Information Office, The Comanche Nation News **Address:** P.O. Box 908, Lawton, OK 73502 United States **BUS:** Newspaper Publishing Company **P/S:** Newspaper **MA:** Regional **D/D/R:** Acting as a Liaison Between the Tribe and the Media, Editing **H/I/S:** Reading, Swimming, Spending Time with her Family **EDU:** Bachelor of Arts in Liberal Arts, Oklahoma State University; Associate Degree in Computer Science, Southwestern Indian Polytechnic Institute **A/A/S:** National Journalists Association **C/VW:** Goodwill Ambassador, Tribal Princess
Email: comanche_news@yahoo.com

Leslie J. Schoolman
Title: Medical Billing Assistant Supervisor **Company:** SVA Healthcare Services, LLC **Address:** 434 S. Yellowstone Drive, Madison, WI 53719 United States **BUS:** Healthcare Management Consulting Firm **P/S:** Financial and Business, Healthcare Management Consulting Services Including Medical Billing and Coding Services, Accounting, Tax **MA:** National **EXP:** Ms. Schoolman's expertise includes the supervision of medical billing and coding operations. **D/D/R:** overseeing accounts receivable, reimbursements, patient's accounts, generating reports on client's payment, sending e-mails, managing client contact and training **H/I/S:** Selling Avon Products **CERTS:** Certified Professional Coding Training Program (2006)
Email: schoolmanlj@hotmail.com
URL: http://www.svaplanners.com

Peggy A. Schorsch
Title: Museum Director **Company:** City of Independence **Address:** 112 S. Third Street, Independence, OR 97351 United States **BUS:** Museum Preserving and Displaying the History and Culture of the River Town of Independence and Polk County Oregon **P/S:** Collections of Artifacts, Documents and Photographs Made Available to the Public by Means of Tours and Working with Other Historical Groups and Community Organizations **D/D/R:** Writing Educational Grants, Working with Donors and Volunteers for Funds, Recycling Exhibits, Directing the Museum **H/I/S:** Sewing, Quilting **EDU:** High School Diploma **A/A/S:** Heritage Museum Society; Polk County Cultural Coalition; Historic Preservation Commission; Chamber of Commerce
Email: heritagemuseum@minetfiber.com
URL: http://www.herimuseum.org

Michael E. Schrage
Title: Owner **Company:** Schrage Electric **Address:** 11585 River Hills Road, Festus, MO 63028 United States **BUS:** Electrical Contracting Company **P/S:** Electric **MA:** Local **D/D/R:** Electrical Contracting **EDU:** Associate Degree in Fire Science, Jefferson College **A/A/S:** Chamber of Commerce, Elks Club; Crystal City Fire Department; Festus Special Road District **C/VW:** Chamber of Commerce
Email: schrage_electric@sbcglobal.net
URL: http://www.cambridgewhoswho.com

Mr. Andrew Schreiber, Ph.D.
Title: Psychotherapist (Retired) **Company:** Andrew Schreiber, Ph.D., MFT **Address:** 1658 Via Laguna, San Mateo, CA 94404 United States **BUS:** Professional Office **P/S:** Psychotherapy Services **MA:** Regional **D/D/R:** Marriage and Family Therapy and Consulting **H/I/S:** Enjoying the Arts, Classical Music **EDU:** Ph.D. in Psychology, Heed University (1980s) **A/A/S:** American Psychiatric Association; American Association for Marriage and Family Therapy

Susan Schreiner Joyce
Title: 1) Registered Dental Hygienist 2) Social Worker II **Company:** 1) Dr. James Betancourt 2) Indian River Medical Center **Address:** 70 Royal Palm Pointe, Vero Beach, FL 32960 United States **BUS:** 1) Dentistry Office 2) Nonprofit Hospital **P/S:** 1) Periodontal Dental Care, Implants 2) Healthcare, Social Services **MA:** 1) Local 2) Indian River County, Florida **EXP:** Ms. Joyce's expertise includes orthodontics and periodontics, social services and case management. **D/D/R:** Counseling, Assisting with Dental Surgery **H/I/S:** Kayaking, Doing Pilates and Yoga, Fly Fishing, Horseback Riding, Reading, Traveling **EDU:** Master's Degree in Social Work, Barry University (2006); Bachelor of Arts in Liberal Studies, Concentration in Psychology, Barry University (2003); Associate Degree in Dental Hygiene, Pensacola Junior College (1978) **CERTS:** Pursuing Clinical Social Worker License, Florida Department of Health **A/A/S:** American Dental Hygienist Association; National Association of Social Workers **C/VW:** Volunteer, Dental Health Department; Former Board Member, Coalition for the Homeless; American Red Cross; Friends Committee, Vero Beach Museum of Art
Email: joyc1418@bellsouth.net
URL: http://www.cambridgewhoswho.com

David J. Schroeder
Title: Professor **Company:** Miami Dade College **Address:** 11011 S.W. 104th Avenue, Room 2217, Miami, FL 33176 United States **BUS:** State College **P/S:** Higher Education for Students, Undergraduate and Graduate Degree Programs **MA:** Local **D/D/R:** Teaching English Composition, Business and Creative Writing, Instructing a Class on Research Papers and Short Stories **H/I/S:** Sailing **EDU:** Master of Arts, University of Miami (1984); Bachelor's Degree in English Literature, University of Miami **A/A/S:** Advisor, Miambiance Student Literature Magazine, Miami Dade College; United States Disabled Sailing Team **A/H:** Excellence in Teaching Award, Miami Dade College
Email: david.schroeder@mdc.edu
URL: http://www.mdc.edu/home

Kristen A. Schroeder
Title: Gifted Program Coordinator, Lead Science Teacher **Company:** Keller Regional Gifted Center, Chicago Public Schools **Address:** 3020 W. 108th Street, Chicago, IL 60655 United States **BUS:** Specialty Learning Center Offering Education Services for First through Eighth-Grade Students **P/S:** Instruction for Gifted and Talented Students, Accelerated and Enriched Curriculums, Reading, Writing, Mathematics and Science Integrating Technology and Leadership Development **MA:** Local **D/D/R:** Coordinating the Gifted Student Program, Assisting in Writing State Grants for Funding, Mentoring Students, Specialist, Chicago Mathematics and Science Initiative **H/I/S:** Baseball **EDU:** Pursuing Master's Degree in Administration; Illinois State University (2003) **CERTS:** National Board Masters Teacher Certification **A/A/S:** Illinois State Physics Association; Specialist, Chicago Mathematics and Science Initiative; Kappa Delta Pi; National Science Foundation
Email: kaschroeder@cps.k21.il.us
URL: http://www.keller.cps.k12.il.us/

Pamela Renae Schroth
Title: Child Care Provider, Owner **Company:** Pam's Curtain Climbers **Address:** 207 N. Main Street, Accident, MD 21520 United States **BUS:** Childcare Provider **P/S:** Wide Range of High Quality Child Care Services **MA:** Regional **D/D/R:** Training in Pre-School Education, Overseeing Daily Care For Children, Infants through 13 Years Old, with 23 Children Enrolled **H/I/S:** Going Shopping, Singing Karaoke **EDU:** College Coursework, Pre-School Education **A/A/S:** Garrett County Day Care Association; Vice President, PTO Accident Elementary School
Email: pam8525@verizon.net

Mr. John E. Schudy
Title: Director of Operations **Company:** Bushwick Metals **Address:** 807 Rockland Avenue, Mamaroneck, NY 10543 United States **BUS:** Steel Distribution Company **P/S:** Service Center Handling All Shapes of Steel Including Beams, Decking, Wire Mesh, Guard Rails, High Strength Jumbo Beams, Fence Pipe, Fencing **MA:** National **D/D/R:** Directing Five Facilities and Warehouses, Overseeing Orders, Overseeing 150 Employees with 10 Direct Reports **H/I/S:** Sailing, Snow Skiing, **EDU:** Master of Business Administration in Industrial Distribution, Pace University (1998); Bachelor of Science in Engineering and Management, Clarkson University (1983) **C/VW:** Local Sports Organizations
Email: jschudy@marmonkeystone.com
URL: http://www.bushwickmetals.com

Gail L. Schuler
Title: Guest Services Agent **Company:** Harrison Group Resort Hotels **Dept:** Hilton Suites Oceanfront Hotel **Address:** 204 33rd Street, Suite 206A, Ocean City, MD 21842 United States **BUS:** Hotel **P/S:** Food Services Including Hospitality **MA:** International **EXP:** Ms. Schuler's expertise includes signal network and network wire service maintenance. **D/D/R:** ensuring guest reservations and customer satisfaction **H/I/S:** Baseball, Football **EDU:** Coursework in English and Foreign Languages; Diploma, Wheaton High School (1968) **A/H:** Women of the Moose Award
Email: markgails@comcast.net

Mr. Ryan E. Schulten
Title: Realtor **Company:** Heritage Homes Group **Address:** 101 E. Lancaster Avenue, Paoli, PA 19301 United States **MA:** Regional **D/D/R:** Traveling Primarily with Residential Buyers and Sellers in Suburban Counties around Philadelphia, Responsible for Home Staging and Open Houses, Renting Residential Properties **H/I/S:** Playing Football, Snowboarding, Going to the Gym **EDU:** Pursuing Associate Degree in Business Management, Montgomery County Community College **A/A/S:** National Association of Realtors; Former Member, Surburban West Realtors Association; Former Member, Million Dollar Club, Weichert Realty
Email: reschulten@gmail.com
URL: http://www.chooseheritage.com

Diane Lynn Schultz
Title: World Sales Shipping Agent **Company:** FedEx **Address:** 431 Richards Boulevard, Sacramento, CA 95814 United States **BUS:** Shipping Company **P/S:** Shipping **MA:** International **D/D/R:** Customer Service **H/I/S:** Gardening, Crocheting **A/H:** Outstanding Sales, Second Quarter (2007) **C/VW:** Susan G. Komen for the Cure

Mr. Robert E. Schultz Jr.
Title: President **Company:** Koffler Building Company, Inc. **Address:** P. O. Box 16061, Pittsburgh, PA 15242 United States **BUS:** General Contractor Company **P/S:** Commercial Property Renovations **MA:** Regional **D/D/R:** Interior Renovations for Commercial Properties **H/I/S:** Building Model Airplanes, Taking Vacations, Working on Landscapes **EDU:** Coursework in Business, Computer Technical Institute (1978)
Email: bobschkbc@aol.com

Kathleen P. Schulz
Title: Manager of Health and Wellness **Company:** Campbell Soup Company **Address:** 1 Campbell Place, Camden, NJ 08103 United States **BUS:** Food Manufacturer **P/S:** Food **MA:** International **D/D/R:** Strategic Direction for the Occupational Health Department of 13 Medical Clinics, Developing Corporate Wellness Strategies **H/I/S:** Running, Playing Soccer **EDU:** Master of Science in Organization and Administration, St. Joseph's University (2001); Post-Masters Diploma in Occupational Health, St. Joe's (2001); Bachelor of Science in Education, Northeastern University (1990) **CERTS:** Certified Health Specialist (2007) **A/A/S:** Former Member, American College of Sports Medicine **C/VW:** Journal of Occupational Environmental Health
Email: kathleen_schulz@campbellsoup.com

Valerie K. Schulze
Title: Eight Grade Teacher **Company:** Patrick Henry Middle School **Address:** 6-900 Street Route 18, Hamler, OH 43524 United States **BUS:** School Dedicated to Excellence in Education **P/S:** Instruction and Curriculum **MA:** Local **D/D/R:** Mathematics, Reading, Writing **H/I/S:** Snorkeling, Hiking, Nature, Singing, Reading **EDU:** Master's Degree in General Education, Bowling Green State University (1994); Bachelor of Arts in Elementary Education, Bowling Green State University **A/A/S:** Ohio Council of Mathematics Teachers; Woman of Church, Sunday School; St. John Lutheran Church; Public Speaking
Email: phe_aca_vs@nwoca.org

Erika L. Schumacher
Title: Marketing and Communication Manager **Company:** INC Research **Address:** 3636 Nobel Drive, Suite 430, San Diego, CA 92122 United States **BUS:** Pharmaceutical Company **P/S:** Pharmaceutical Sales and Services **MA:** International **D/D/R:** Business, Marketing, Public Relations, Creating Advertising Campaigns, Events, Trade Shows **H/I/S:** Reading, Skiing, Traveling **EDU:** Bachelor of Science in Marketing, Arizona State University **A/A/S:** American Marketing Association
Email: eschumacher@incresearch.com
URL: http://www.incresearch.com

Mr. Jeffrey A. Schuppe
Title: Fire Engineer, Paramedic **Company:** Sterling Fire & Rescue **Address:** 410 N. Fifth Street, Sterling, CO 80751 United States **BUS:** Government Municipality Dedicated to Excellence in Public Safety **P/S:** Firefighting, Rescue Services **MA:** Regional **D/D/R:** Medical Paramedics, Firefighting, Engineering for Fire Apparatuses, Instructing and Training Volunteers in Paramedics and Emergency Medical Procedures, Rescue Services **H/I/S:** Snow Skiing, Coaching Baseball **EDU:** Bachelor's Degree in Public Safety Administration, Grand Canyon University, Arizona (2007); Associate Degree in Pre-Medicine, Northeastern Junior College of Colorado (1993) **A/A/S:** International Association of Fire Fighters
Email: fire_medic_422@hotmail.com
URL: http://www.cambridgewhoswho.com

Melinda K. Schuster
Title: Accountant **Company:** McEagle Properties **Address:** 1001 Boardwalk Springs Place, O'Fallon, MO 63368 United States **BUS:** A Leading Design-Build and Development Company, Market-Driven Real Estate Development Company that is Supported By Employee Shared Values and Vision **P/S:** Unsurpassed Commitment to Customers in Identifying Needs and Delivering a Quality Product and Service for all Clients **MA:** Regional **D/D/R:** Accounting, Construction Draws, Handling Expenses for all Property Management, 60 Companies, Financial Statement **H/I/S:** Swimming, Reading, Exercise **EDU:** Master of Business Administration, Maryville University (2006); Bachelor's Degree in Accounting and Information Systems (2004)
Email: mkshuster@mc-eagle.com
URL: http://www.mc-eagle.com

Jason E. Schutz
Title: Owner **Company:** Schutz Creative Photography **Address:** 109 Main Street E., Sleepy Eye, MN 56085 United States **BUS:** Photography Studio **P/S:** Photography, Framing, Family Portraits, Commercial Photography **MA:** International **EXP:** Mr. Schutz's expertise includes commercial photography and aerial photography. **D/D/R:** designing portraits, products, interiors, exteriors, brochures and press kits **H/I/S:** Spending Time with his Family, Camping, Hiking, Collecting Cars **EDU:** Industry-Related Training and Experience; Coursework in Photography, Ridgewater College **CERTS:** Certified Professional Photographer **A/A/S:** Sleepy Eye Chamber of Commerce; Sleepy Eye JC's; Minnesota Professional Photographers Association; Professional Photographers of America
Email: jaschultz@sleepyeyetel.net
URL: http://www.schutzcreativephotography.com

Rita K. Schwalm
Title: Educator **Company:** Greenwich Elementary School, Kutztown Area School District **Address:** 50 Trexler Avenue, Kutztown, PA 19530 United States **BUS:** Education **P/S:** Elementary School Education **MA:** Local **D/D/R:** Teaching Kindergarten **H/I/S:** Reading, Traveling **EDU:** Master's Degree in Elementary Education, Kutztown University **A/A/S:** Pennsylvania State Education Association; National Education Association **C/VW:** United Way, American Heart Association

Karen Lynn Schwartz, RN, BSN, AE
Title: Allergy and Asthma Nursing Educator **Company:** Adult Pediatric Allergy-Asthma, Henry J. Kanarek, MD **Address:** 4601 W. 109th, Unit 350, Overland Park, KS 66212 United States **BUS:** Private Practice **P/S:** Healthcare for Allergies, Asthma and Immunology **MA:** Regional **D/D/R:** Offering clinical testing for the screening/detection of allergies and asthma. Empowering allergy/asthma patents with a greater sense of control over their disease entity to ensure a more positive outcome in their treatment regime. Offering pediatric/family practices the resources for implementing earlier screening/detection and treatment initiatives for allergies and asthma. **H/I/S:** Spending time with friends and family, Listening to music, Walking/Pilates Exercise, Reading, Gardening, Setting up bird sanctuaries, Playing with pets, Watching football (especially the Crimson Tide and the Chiefs) Searching for beautiful beaches Really into Scottish Terriers **EDU:** Bachelor of Science in Nursing, Avila University, Kansas City, Kansas (1974) **A/A/S:** American Lung Association; Allergy Asthma Foundation of America; Food Allergy Network Hadassah Nursing Council **A/H:** National Asthma Care Award (2006) **C/VW:** Kehilath Israel Synagogue, Jewish Federation, American Cancer Society, Hadassah
Email: kschwartz4@kc.rr.com

Rachel Schwartz-Wernick, Ph.D., MSW, MA
Title: Ph.D. Psychology, MSW, MA **Company:** Sole Proprietor **Address:** 23209 North 39th Terrace, Phoenix, AZ 85050 United States **BUS:** Proven Leader as a Physician's Office Dedicated to Excellence in Healthcare **P/S:** Psychologist Evaluations, Assessments and Treatments **MA:** Phoenix, AZ **D/D/R:** Admitting and Discharging in County Hospital, Offering One-on-One and Group Counseling, Assessments and Evaluations for Court-Ordered Adults, Offering Health Treatment for Mentally Ill Patients **H/I/S:** Jewelry Designing, Spending Time with her Children **EDU:** Doctorate Degree in Psychology, Argosy University (2003); Master of Science in Psychology, Argosy University (2002); Master's Degree in Social Work, Arizona State University (1997); Bachelor of Science in Psychology, Boston University (1994) **A/A/S:** National American Psychology Association; Arizona Psychology Association
Email: rwernick@cox.net
URL: http://www.cambridgewhoswho.com

Thérèse F. Schwarz
Title: Elementary Physical Education Teacher **Company:** Ingram Independent School District, Ingram Elementary School **Address:** 1115 Barbara Ann Street, Kerrville, TX 78028 United States **BUS:** Elementary School **P/S:** Education for Students in Kindergarten through Fifth-Grade **MA:** Regional **D/D/R:** Teaching Kindergarten through Fifth-Grade Students, Coordinating and Running the Physical Education Program, Coordinating the Duty Schedule for Teachers and Morning Assembly, Reviewing Plans and Lessons, Teaching Cooperative Games with the Younger Grades, Teaching In-Season Sports Including Soccer, Basketball, T-Ball and Baseball **H/I/S:** Spending Time with her Children, Sports, Reading **EDU:** Master's Degree in Education, Schreiner University (2007) **A/A/S:** Texas Association for Health, Physical Education, Recreation & Dance; Association of Texas Professional Educators
Email: sthscm@ktc.com
URL: http://www.ingramisd.net/

Bonnie S. Schwiger
Title: Owner **Company:** Bridal and Formal Wear by B **Address:** 564 N. Lex-Springmill Road, Mansfield, OH 44906 United States **BUS:** Bridal and Formal Wear Shop **P/S:** Tuxedos, Prom Gowns, Bridal Gowns, Bridesmaid Gowns, Special Occasion Dresses **MA:** Local **EXP:** Ms. Schwiger's expertise is in business operations management. **D/D/R:** Overseeing Fittings, Marketing, Hiring Staff **H/I/S:** Sewing, Crafting, Spending Time with her Family and Grandchildren **EDU:** Associate Degree in Bridal Consultation, Association of Bridal Consultants (1989) **CERTS:** Certified Medical Laboratory Technician (1964)
Email: c.schwiger@neo.rr.com
URL: http://www.bridalandformalwearbyb.com

Carisa A. Sciortino
Title: Speech Therapist **Company:** New York City Department of Education **Address:** 47 Humphrey Drive, Syosset, NY 11791 United States **BUS:** Department of Education **P/S:** Education **MA:** Regional **EXP:** Ms. Sciortino's area of expertise is in speech-language pathology for students in kindergarten through fifth-grade. **H/I/S:** Spending Time with her Friends and Family **EDU:** Master of Arts in Speech-Language Pathology, St. John's University (2007); Bachelor of Arts in Speech Pathology, Adelphi University **A/A/S:** American Speech-Language-Hearing Association **C/VW:** Walk for Autism
Email: carissssa@hotmail.com
URL: http://www.vclc.org

Angela Scott
Company: Divine Universal Sisterhood **Address:** 4629 Coleherne Road, Baltimore, MD 21229 United States **BUS:** Holistic Living Center of all Cultures **P/S:** Performing Moral and Cultural Presentations **MA:** International **D/D/R:** Teaching by Example **H/I/S:** Traveling **EDU:** Associate Degree in Public Relations, University of the District of Columbia; Associate Degree in International Public Relations, School of the Prophets, Dimona, Israel **A/A/S:** Sisters Place **C/VW:** Support a Child International
Email: yeshiyah@hotmail.com
URL: http://journeyuptojerusalem.com

Deborah M. Scott
Title: Business Owner **Company:** D&D's Dog House **Address:** 123 N. Raiford Street, Selma, NC 27576 United States **BUS:** Pet Needs **P/S:** Pet Supplies, Grooming, Boarding **MA:** Local **D/D/R:** Customer Service **H/I/S:** Mountain Hiking **EDU:** Diploma, Triple S Smithfield Selma Senior High School
Email: dhobbs10@nc.rr.com

Jerry A. Scott
Title: Vice President **Company:** Ed Street Development Company **Dept:** Finance Department **Address:** 2513 Wesley Street, Suite 4, Johnson City, TN 37601 United States **BUS:** Property Management Company **P/S:** Commercial Property Development **MA:** National **D/D/R:** managing finance and commercial development including big box, shopping centers and banks **H/I/S:** Traveling **EDU:** Master of Business Administration, East Tennessee State University
Email: jerry@edstreet.com

Lionel L. Scott
Title: General Manager **Company:** Bob Evans **Address:** 4122 South Way Lane, Suite 43, Triangle, VA 22124 United States **BUS:** Food Restaurant **P/S:** Food and Beverage **MA:** Local **D/D/R:** Managing People **H/I/S:** Reading, Swimming **A/A/S:** Church
Email: lionelmofire@hotmail.com

Nina R. Scott
Title: Director of Choral Activities **Company:** Renaissance High School **Address:** 6565 W. Outer Drive, Detroit, MI 48235 United States **BUS:** High School **P/S:** Education **MA:** Local **D/D/R:** Vocal Music **H/I/S:** Traveling, Cruising **EDU:** Master of Arts in Music Education, Eastern Michigan University; Bachelor of Arts in Music Education, Rust College **A/A/S:** American Choral Directors Association; National Association of Negro Musicians; Michigan School Vocal Music Association; Two-Time Conductor of State Honor Choirs **A/H:** Teacher of the Year in Vocal Music **C/VW:** Church, Nina R. Scott Preparatory School
Email: nina.scott@detroitk12.org

Terri L. Scott
Title: President **Company:** Robert Paul Homes, Inc. **Address:** 2511 Ventura Drive, League City, TX 77573 United States **BUS:** Family Owned Construction Company **P/S:** New Custom Homes Construction, New Construction Services **MA:** Regional **D/D/R:** Bookkeeping, Interior Designing Including Painting, Tiling and Quality Control, Designing Homes Post-Construction **H/I/S:** Oil Painting **EDU:** College Coursework **A/A/S:** Greater Houston Builders Association; National Association of Home Builders; International Society of Poets
Email: terriscottl123@hotmail.com

J. Scott Keene
Title: Funeral Director **Company:** Woodlawn Memorial Park **BUS:** Funeral Home **P/S:** Death and Interment Services **MA:** International **D/D/R:** Removing and Transporting Deceased Bodies, Embalming and Preparing Bodies for Burial and Cremation, Counseling and Consoling Grieving Families **H/I/S:** Traveling, Spending Time with his Family **EDU:** College Coursework, Chattanooga State Technical Community College; Associate of Science in Business Administration, John A. Gupton School of Mortuary Science; Associate of Science in Mortuary Science, John A. Gupton School of Mortuary Science **CERTS:** Licensed Funeral Director; Licensed Embalmer **A/A/S:** The Gideon; Masonic Order **C/VW:** Woodmont Baptist Church
Email: sk4nd@yahoo.com
URL: http://www.cambridgewhoswho.com

Karen L. Scribner
Title: Owner **Company:** Karen's Main Street Diner **Address:** 439 Main Street, Calais, ME 04619 United States **BUS:** Restaurant **P/S:** Food Services, Customer Service **MA:** Regional **D/D/R:** Cooking, Overseeing Restaurant Operations **H/I/S:** Traveling
Email: scribs70@hotmail.com
URL: http://www.cambridgwhoswho.com

Ms. Bobbie Scroggins
Title: Educator (Retired) **Company:** Board of Education **Dept:** Chicago Heights School District 170 **Address:** 228 Lee Bowden Drive, Huntsville, AL 35806 United States **BUS:** Public School District **P/S:** Administrative Services, General Elementary and Secondary School Curriculum, Special Education, Learning Resources, Support Services, Extracurricular Activities, Student Clubs and Organizations, Athletics **MA:** Regional **D/D/R:** Teaching Mathematics to Students in Kindergarten through Seventh-Grade, Organizing Mathematics Programs for Young Children **H/I/S:** Bowling, Decorating **EDU:** Bachelor of Science in Mathematics, Arkansas Baptist College (1962), Industry-Related Training, Sylvan Learning Center **A/A/S:** Newcomers Club **C/VW:** Program Volunteer, Peer Assistance and Leadership
Email: egobooster@charter.net

Pamela R. Scruggs
Title: Strategic Financial Analyst **Company:** Financial Intelligence, Inc **Address:** 400 Davis Street, Suite 303, San Leandro, CA 94577 United States **BUS:** Finance Consulting **P/S:** Meet with Clients to Plan, Evaluate and Analyze Finances, Specializing in Financial Engineering Technology **MA:** Local **D/D/R:** Portfolio Management, Investments and Securities, Very Detail Oriented **H/I/S:** Reading and Cooking, Attends Seminars Every Quarter **EDU:** UCLA-Berkley, University of Phoenix, California State, Masters in Financial Engineering, Masters in Accounting, Bachelor of Science in Computer Science, Minor in Accounting, Notary in Consumer Reporting **A/A/S:** UNCF, Mayors Committee, Director of Conservatory School of Music and Arts, Church
Email: pamela_scruggs@sbcglobal.net

Carrie Ann Scubert
Title: Vice President **Company:** Bearverton Bakery, Inc **Address:** 12375 SW Broadway, Beaverton, OR 97005 United States **BUS:** Baked Goods Bakery **P/S:** Baked Goods, Wholesale, Retail **MA:** Local **D/D/R:** Teaching and Outside Sales **H/I/S:** Local Musicians **A/A/S:** Board of Washington County Historical Society, Childrens Museum

Laura A. Scullin
Title: Owner **Company:** Lauras Golden Thread **Address:** 46 Last Road, Middletown, NY 10941 United States **BUS:** Embroidery Business **P/S:** Embroidery **MA:** National **D/D/R:** Embroidering Hats, Jackets and Quilts **H/I/S:** Attending Dog Shows, Going Out to Dinner with Friends and Family **C/VW:** American Cancer Society, Golden Retriever Rescue
Email: info@laurasgoldenthread.com
URL: http://www.laurasgoldenthread.com

Olive E. Seales
Title: Head Nurse **Company:** Interfaith Medical Center **Address:** 1545 Atlantic Avenue, Brooklyn, NY 11213 United States **BUS:** Hospital **P/S:** Healthcare **MA:** Local **D/D/R:** Psychiatric Nursing, Serving as the Head Nurse of the Psychiatric Emergency Room Unit **H/I/S:** Working Out Five Days a Week, Playing Tennis, Golfing, Playing Soccer, Watching Movies, Spending time with Family and Friends, Traveling **EDU:** Master of Public Administration, Long Island University, C.W. Post Campus, Brookville, New York; Bachelor of Science, Saint Josephs College, Brooklyn, New York **A/A/S:** New York State Nurses Association; ANA **C/VW:** Meals on Wheels, American Heart Association, American Diabetes Foundation, American Cancer Society, American Alzheimer's Association, Diabetes Association.
Email: oeseales@optonline.net
URL: http://www.interfaithmedicalcenter.com

Kenneth J. Searcy, RN
Title: President, Owner **Company:** Searcy Medical Solutions, Inc. **Address:** 606 Haley Meadows Drive, Romeoville, IL 60446 United States **BUS:** Medical Center **P/S:** Healthcare Including Emergency Medical Services **MA:** Regional **EXP:** Mr. Searcy's area of expertise is in critical care nursing. **D/D/R:** creating and maintaining emergency medical services for the community, training nurses and supplying medication **H/I/S:** Collecting Antique Medical Apparatus **EDU:** Associate Degree in Nursing, Joliet Junior College **A/A/S:** American Association of Critical Care Nurses; Emergency Nursing Association; American Heart Association; National Association of EMS Educators
Email: cprxprt@aol.com
URL: http://www.searcymedical.com

Joshua Sears
Title: Athletic Trainer **Company:** Menaul School **Address:** 301 Menaul Boulevard N.E., Albuquerque, NM 87107 United States **BUS:** Private School **P/S:** Private Education **MA:** Local **D/D/R:** Athletic Training, Physical Education **EDU:** Bachelor of Science in Athletic Training, University of New Mexico **CERTS:** Certified Athletic Trainer, National Athletic Trainers' Association **A/A/S:** New Mexico Athletic Trainers' Association; National Athletic Trainers' Association
Email: lobotrainer@yahoo.com
URL: http://www.menaulschool.com

Kathleen Seaton Cope
Title: Teacher **Company:** Clark County School District, J. Harold Brinkley Middle School **Address:** 2480 Maverick Street, Las Vegas, NV 89108 United States **BUS:** Dynamic School District Dedicated to Pupil Achievement **P/S:** General Education to Students of all Ages, Student Support Services, Guidance and Counseling, Student Athletics **MA:** Regional **D/D/R:** Teaching English, Drama and Theater, Mentoring Students **EDU:** Master's Degree in Theatrical Arts, Central Missouri State University (1980); Bachelor of Science in Education, Minor in English, Central Missouri State University (1972) **A/A/S:** National Education Association; NTE; American Association of University Women; Who's Who of American Teachers
Email: copewithit@cox.net
URL: http://www.ccsd.net

Stacy T. Sebro
Title: Academic/Guidance Counselor **Company:** Blair Christian Academy **Address:** 220 W. Upsal Street, Philadelphia, PA 19119 United States **BUS:** Christian School **P/S:** Education **MA:** Local **D/D/R:** Advising Students about College, Offering Career Guidance and Counseling **H/I/S:** Traveling, Listening to Music, Going to the Theater **EDU:** Pursuing Master's Degree in Clinical Counseling Psychology with a Concentration in Child and Adolescent Therapy, Chestnut Hill College; Bachelor's Degree in Psychology, Eastern University **A/A/S:** Psi Chi Honor Society; National Honor Society **A/H:** Service Award for Dedication, Commitment and Love, Blair Christian Academy (2007) **C/VW:** Youth Ministry, Local Church
Email: ssebro1@hotmail.com
URL: http://www.cambridgewhoswho.com

Mary J. Sederburg
Title: Art Teacher, Business Teacher **Company:** Van Buren Community Schools **Address:** 405 Fourth Street, Keosauqua, IA 52565 United States **BUS:** School District **P/S:** Education **MA:** Regional **D/D/R:** teaching art and business endorsement and advising students **H/I/S:** Painting, Photography, Drawing **EDU:** Master of Education, Viterbo University (2002) **CERTS:** National Board Certified Teacher (2003) **A/A/S:** Supervisor, Yearbook Club; National Education Association; National Art Education Association; Delta Kappa Gamma **C/VW:** Local Charitable Organizations
Email: mary.sederburg@gpaea.k12.ia.us
URL: http://www.van-buren.k12.ia.us

Anna L. Seedhill
Title: President **Company:** IFLEX Resource Management **Address:** P.O. Box 9724, Scottsdale, AZ 85252 United States **BUS:** Consulting Firm **P/S:** Develop and Maintain Policies, Documentation, Plans, Programs and Procedures to Comply with Company and Stakeholders Requirements **MA:** Regional **D/D/R:** Marketing, Consulting with Small Businesses, Training **H/I/S:** Reading, Traveling, Gardening **EDU:** Associate Degree, Earned in Sweden (2003) **A/A/S:** Swedish Women's Educational Association
Email: ais@iflexresource.com
URL: http://www.iflexresource.com

Janet G. Seefried
Title: President **Company:** Seefried and Associates, LLC **Address:** 3000 E. 13 Mile Road, Warren, MI 48092 United States **BUS:** Consulting Firm **P/S:** Consulting Services **MA:** National **D/D/R:** Managing Finance, Performance and Executive Management, Working with the Government, Energy and Software Companies, Strategic and Merger Integration Planning **H/I/S:** Cooking, Needlepointing, Silk and Metal Embroidery **EDU:** Master of Business Administration in Finance, University of Detroit Mercy; Bachelor of Science in Natural Science, Marygrove College **A/A/S:** Board Member, Institute of Management Accountants (2003-2005); Board Member, Accounting Aid Society, Detroit; Chairwoman, Ethics Committee; Budget Appropriations Committee; Jewish Vocational Society, Detroit **C/VW:** United Way
Email: seefriedaj@aol.com
URL: http://www.cambridgewhoswho.com

Eva M. Seftic
Title: Teacher Company: Forest Hills School District Dept: Early Childhood Address: 512 Corrigan Drive, Johnstown, PA 15904 United States BUS: Public Education, Special Education P/S: Education of Kindergarten through 12th-Grade in Core Academics in Health, Nutrition, Physical Activities and Physical Education MA: Regional D/D/R: Teaching All Subject Areas to Kindergartners and Formerly a First Grade Teacher H/I/S: Gardening, Listening to Music EDU: Bachelor's Degree in Elementary Education, Concentration in English, University of Pittsburgh (1982) A/A/S: National Education Association; Pennsylvania State Education Association
Email: jimseftic@atlanticbb.net
URL: http://www.fhsd.k12.pa.us

Diego A. Segatore
Title: Database Marketing Analyst Company: ZALE Corporation Address: 901 W. Walnut Hill Lane, Irving, TX 75038 United States BUS: Jewelry Company P/S: Retail Jewelry MA: International D/D/R: Marketing Analytics H/I/S: Practicing Karate EDU: Master of Science in Economics, North Texas University (2004); Bachelor of Arts in Economics, North Texas University; Bachelor of Arts in Spanish, North Texas University A/A/S: DMA
Email: dsegator@zalecorporation.com
URL: http://www.zale.com

Lia Segerblom
Title: Owner, Photographic Portrait Artist Company: Lia Photography Address: 24452 Caracas Street, Dana Point, CA 92629 United States BUS: Photo Studio P/S: Photography MA: International D/D/R: Creating lifestyle portraits H/I/S: Traveling, Scuba Diving, Sailing EDU: Master of Photography, Professional Photographers of America; Master Craftsman Degree, Professional Photographers of America; Bachelor of Fine Arts, with a Concentration in Painting, Massachusetts College of Art and Design, Boston; Bachelor's Degree in Photography, Brooks Institute of Photography; Associate of Applied Science, Santa Ana College CERTS: Certified Professional Photographer, Professional Photographers of America A/A/S: Professional Photographers of America C/VW: American Cancer Society; Make-A-Wish; Alzheimer's Foundation of America
Email: liaphotography@cox.net
URL: http://www.liaphotography.com

Denise K. Segovia
Title: Workers' Compensation Coordinator Company: Kohler Address: 444 Highland Drive, Kohler, WI 53044 United States BUS: Plumbing Company P/S: Plumbing Services MA: International D/D/R: Workers' Compensation, Working with the Program Coordinator to Ensure Environmental Safety and Health H/I/S: Spending Time with her Children CERTS: Certified Medical Assistant
Email: denise.segovia@kohler.com
URL: http://www.cambridgewhoswho.com

Anne Q. Segullo
Title: Emergency Medical Technician Company: Corona Community Ambulance Address: 75 Sprain Valley Road, Scarsdale, NY 10583 United States BUS: Ambulance Services P/S: Emergency Medical Services MA: Local D/D/R: Emergency Care H/I/S: Studying Art CERTS: Certified Emergency Medical Technician

Alexis B. Seibert
Title: Special Education Teacher Company: Oskaloosa Elementary School Address: Oskaloosa, IA 52577 United States BUS: Public Elementary School P/S: Elementary Education for Students in Kindergarten through Fifth-Grade MA: Local D/D/R: Teaching Reading, Mathematics and Verbal Special Education to Grades Second, Third and Fourth in an Inclusion Classroom H/I/S: Traveling Across America to Visit All 50 States EDU: Pursuing Master's Degree in Education; Bachelor of Arts in Elementary Education, Central College (2003) A/A/S: National Education Association; Iowa State Education Association
Email: seiberta@oskaloosa.k12.ia.us

Christine Seifert
Title: Owner, Physical Therapist Company: Well Within Physical Therapy and Magnetics Address: 3408 Niles Road, St. Joseph, MI 49085 United States BUS: Alternative Complimentary Wellness Solutions P/S: Physical Therapy, Rehabilitation and Wellness MA: Regional D/D/R: Treating Chronic Pain through Myofascial Release, Rehabilitation and Wellness, Holistic Treatment, Treating Neurologically Impaired Clients on All Age Levels, Independent Wellness Consulting for Nikken Corporation H/I/S: Baseball EDU: Bachelor's Degree in Physical Therapy, University of Pittsburgh (1973) CERTS: Neurodevelopment Certification (1996) A/A/S: National and Michigan Chapters, American Physical Therapy Association
Email: cjs2kwellwithin@sbcglobal.net
URL: http://www.nikken.com

Ms. Jerry L. Seiler, M.Ed.
Title: Sixth-Grade Teacher Company: St. Peter's School Address: 51 W. Maple Avenue, Merchantville, NJ 08109 United States BUS: Private Catholic Elementary School P/S: Regular Core Curriculum Including Reading, Mathematics, English, Science, Social Studies, Language Arts, Physical Education, Music, Art MA: Regional D/D/R: Teaching Sixth-Grade Language Arts and Religion, Dealing with Curriculum, Overseeing Training and Staff Development EDU: M.Ed., Holy Family University (2005) CERTS: Certified K-8 Reading Specialist A/A/S: Alpha Upsilon Alpha; International Reading Association; National Catholic Educational Association; WJRC
Email: jsdutch@aol.com

Marlene Elizabeth Sekaquaptewa
Title: Hopi Customary Law Consultant Company: Nakatsvewat-Hopi Dispute Resolution Services Address: P.O. Box 724, Hotevilla, AZ 86030 United States BUS: Consulting Firm P/S: Consulting Services MA: Local D/D/R: Training Hopi Mediators, Overseeing Culture, Language and Traditions, consulting regarding property disputes, divorce disputes, child custody and land dispute H/I/S: Quilting, Gardening, Spending Time with her Grandchildren EDU: Associate Degree in Tribal Management, Scottsdale Community College (1984) A/A/S: Former President, National Indian Council on Aging; Chairman, Hopi Foundation; Board Member, Hopi Education Endowment Fund C/VW: Bacavi Elderly Adult Program
Email: marlenesek@yahoo.com
URL: http://www.cambridgewhoswho.com

Jonathan S. Selgas
Title: Grand Master Trainer, MOD Company: Complete Health and Fitness Address: 420 Alton Road, Miami Beach, FL 33139 United States BUS: Healthcare: Fitness and Wellness P/S: Personal Training, Spa, Massage Therapy MA: Local D/D/R: Tai Chi Instructing H/I/S: Martial Arts
Email: iwan2@aol.com
URL: http://www.imagroupmembers.com/jonathoanselgas

Mr. Jay Seller
Title: Chapter Director Company: Colorado State Thespians Address: 200 S. Dexter Street, Denver, CO 80246 United States BUS: Nonprofit Educational Theater Program P/S: Educational Workshops for High School Students in Theater and the Performing Arts, Sponsoring Thespian Festivals and Theater Workshops, Producing Educational Materials, Offering College Scholarship Opportunities for Students MA: Regional D/D/R: Directing Daily Operations of the Theater, Planning Conferences, Completing Contracts, Negotiating Funding with the State H/I/S: Enjoying the Theater EDU: Pursuing Ph.D. in Leadership K-12, Walden University; Master of Arts in Education, Lesley College (1985) CERTS: Licensed High School Instructor, State of Colorado; Nationally Certified Educator A/A/S: Educational Theater Association; Alliance for Colorado Theater Educators; National Education Association
Email: jay@cothespians.com
URL: http://www.cothespians.com

Mr. Robert J. Sellers Jr.
Title: Owner Company: RJS Woodworks Address: 133 Coolspring Drive, Windber, PA 15963 United States BUS: Manufacturing Company P/S: Custom Woodwork MA: Local EXP: Mr. Sellers' expertise is in business management. D/D/R: Estimating, Overseeing Administrative Duties, Creating Custom Woodwork H/I/S: Fishing, Volunteering, Hunting A/A/S: Handyman Club of America; North American Hunting Club C/VW: Firefighter, Windber Fire Department
Email: rjswoodworks@hotmail.com

Ashley M. Selman
Title: Owner, Personal Trainer Company: Evolution Trainers Address: 1235 Pear Avenue, Suite 101, Mountain View, CA 94043 United States BUS: Largest Private Training Facility in the Bay Area P/S: Sports and Fitness Training MA: Regional D/D/R: Overseeing Private, Personal and Independent Trainers in Both Sports and Fitness, Training Athletes, Seeing Clients, Recruiting, Marketing, Ordering Catering Services H/I/S: Spending Time Outdoors, Hiking, Mountain Bicycling, Traveling EDU: Master's Degree in Sports Psychology, John F. Kennedy University (2006) A/A/S: National Strength and Conditioning Association
Email: ashley@evolutiontrainers.com
URL: http://www.evolutiontrainers.com

Lawrence M. Seman
Title: Owner Company: Larry's Landscaping Service Address: 14521 Summit Avenue, Maple Heights, OH 44137 United States BUS: Landscaping Company P/S: Landscaping MA: Local D/D/R: Grounds Maintenance H/I/S: Traveling with his Wife, Reading EDU: Coursework in Mathematics, John Caroll University, Ohio C/VW: Church
Email: info@cambridgewhoswho
URL: http://www.cambridgewhoswho.com

Ann Semler
Title: Teacher, Student Council Advisor Company: Galena Park Independent School District, North Shore Senior High School Address: 353 N. Castlegory Drive, Houston, TX 77049 United States BUS: School P/S: Education MA: Local D/D/R: Teaching Economics, Coordinating Fundraisers H/I/S: Reading, Bowling EDU: Master's Degree in Secondary Education, University of Houston A/A/S: Association of Texas Professional Educators A/H: School Sweepstakes Winner C/VW: Susan G. Komen Breast Cancer Foundation, Radio Lollipop, Texas Children's Hospital
Email: asemler@galenaparkisd.com
URL: http://www.cambridgewhoswho.com

John E. Senffner
Title: Chief Building Inspector Company: City of Chandler Arizona Address: P.O. Box 4008, Mail Stop 306, Chandler, AZ 85244 United States BUS: Government Organization P/S: Public Service MA: National D/D/R: overseeing building safety, fire protection and safety inspections in heavy industrial and commercial construction H/I/S: Spending Time Outdoor, Camping, Fishing EDU: Bachelor's Degree in Business Administration (1967)
Email: john.senffner@chandleraz.gov
URL: http://www.chandleraz.gov

Diane J. Senn
Title: Music Teacher Company: Sage Elementary Elko County School District Address: 208 Boyd Kennedy Road, Spring Creek, NV 89815 United States BUS: Education P/S: Elementary Education MA: Local D/D/R: Vocalist, General Music Instruction H/I/S: Golfing, Walking, Song leader for the church EDU: Bachelor's Degree in Elementary Education and Music, Dickinson State University (1982)
Email: DLadyDi76@netscape.net
URL: http://www.cambridgewhoswho.com

Joelle C. Senter
Title: Owner, General Manager Company: Keller Williams-Fox Valley Realty Address: 1450 W. Main Street, Suite G, Saint Charles, IL 60174 United States BUS: Real Estate Agency Marketing and Promotions P/S: Residential and Commercial Real Estate Brokerage, Real Estate Services MA: North America D/D/R: Career Development, Overseeing Business Operations, Training; Public Speaking H/I/S: Boating, Biking, Interior Decorating, Staging, Hunting EDU: Bachelor's Degree in Business Administration and Business Law, Illinois State University A/A/S: Agent Technology Council; Agent Leadership Council C/VW: Anderson Animal Shelter, American Cancer Society, National Wildlife Federation
Email: jsenter@kw.com
URL: http://www.kw-fvr.com
URL: http://www.foxvalley-homes.com

Christopher P. Sepanski
Title: Chiropractic Doctor Company: Oxford Valley Chiropractic and Sports Injuries Address: 100 N. Buckstown Road, Suite E200, Langhorne, PA 19047 United States BUS: Chiropractic Office P/S: Chiropractic and Physical Therapy MA: Local D/D/R: Physical Therapy H/I/S: Playing Hockey, Personal Training EDU: Doctor of Medicine in Chiropractic Studies, Palmer College of Chiropractic, San Jose, California A/A/S: Pennsylvania Chiropractic Association C/VW: The Leukemia & Lymphoma Society; Local Fire Department; Children Burn Centers
URL: http://www.ovcsportsinjuries.com

Tracy J. Seremak
Title: AVID Director Company: Waukegan High School Address: 2325 Brookside Avenue, Waukegan, IL 60085 United States BUS: Public High School P/S: Education, College Preparatory Program MA: Local D/D/R: Coordinating and Directing the Program H/I/S: Reading, Practicing Yoga, Jogging, Camping, Bowling, Spending Time Outdoors EDU: Master's Degree in Educational Leadership, Northeastern Illinois University (2007); Bachelor's Degree in Secondary Mathematics Education, DePaul University, Chicago (1998) A/A/S: National Council of Teachers of Mathematics; Illinois Federation of Teachers; Advancement Via Individual Determination C/VW: Vietnam Veterans of America, La Casa, Church Organizations
Email: tseremak@hotmail.com
URL: http://www.waukeganschools.org

Kathryn L. Serna
Title: RNC, Nurse Manager Company: Holy Cross Hospital Address: 1327 Weimer Road, Taos, NM 87175 United States BUS: Acute Care Facility P/S: Emergency Services, Internal Medicine, Obstetrics, Family Practice, Women's Services, Surgical Services, Orthopaedics, Radiology, Ophthalmology, Laboratory Services, Pediatrics MA: Regional D/D/R: Registered Nursing, Neonatal Re-visitation Instructor, Fetal Monitor Instructor, Labor, Delivery, Recovery and Postpartum Nursing H/I/S: Artist, Painting EDU: Master's Degree in Obstetrics CERTS: Neonatal Inpatient Certification A/A/S: Association of Women's Health
Email: kserna@taoshospital.org
URL: http://www.taoshospital.org

Nancy J. Serozynsky, BSN, RN

Title: MDS Coordinator **Company:** Life Care Center of North Shore **Address:** 111 Birch Street, Lynn, MA 01902 United States **BUS:** Nursing Home **P/S:** Long-Term Care, Rehabilitation Services **MA:** Regional **D/D/R:** coordinating the wound and intensive care units, Reviewing Charts, Assessing Residents' Needs, Communicating with Department Heads, Determining Proper Payments through Medicare and Medicaid **H/I/S:** Knitting, Sewing, Crocheting **EDU:** Bachelor of Science in Nursing, University of Connecticut (1972) **CERTS:** Registered Nurse
Email: nurserusty77@yahoo.com

Melinda D. Service, MT, ASCP

Title: Medical Technologist **Company:** Gateway Medical Center **Dept:** Laboratory **Address:** P.O. Box 782, Elkton, KY 42220 United States **BUS:** Hospital **P/S:** Laboratory Services, Healthcare **MA:** Regional **D/D/R:** Hematology, Laboratory Services **H/I/S:** Traveling, Swimming, Reading, Scrap Booking, Spending time with family **EDU:** Bachelor of Science in Biology, Austin Peay State University **CERTS:** Certified ASCP **A/A/S:** President's, Emerging Leader's Scholarship Program at APSU (1993-1997) **A/H:** Medical Technologist of the Year, Gateway Medical Center (2003); Voted 'Most Likely to Succeed' **C/VW:** St. Jude Children's Research Hospital and the ASPCA
Email: melinda.service@yahoo.com
URL: http://www.cambridgewhoswho.com

Deidre E. Sessoms

Title: Acting Supervisor and Director of Parking Enforcement **Company:** Village of Spring Valley, Municipality **Address:** 200 N. Main Street, Spring Valley, NY 10977 United States **BUS:** Local Government Agency **P/S:** Local Government **MA:** Local **D/D/R:** Supervising Parking Law Enforcement Department **H/I/S:** Spending Time with her Grandchildren **EDU:** Mount Vernon High School **C/VW:** Local Church
URL: http://www.villageofspringvalley.org

Michael W. Sette, MBA

Title: 1) Operations Director 2) Business Professor **Company:** 1) TVR Communications, LLC 2) Briarcliffe College **Dept:** 1) Operations Department 2) Business Department **BUS:** 1) Distribution Company 2) College **P/S:** 1) Hospital Patient Video and Voice Products, Interactive Patient Education and Services, Entertainment and Communication Systems Technology 2) Higher Education **D/D/R:** Overseeing Organizational Development, Working with Business Analytics, Strategic Planning, Managing Operations, Implementing Training Programs **H/I/S:** Spending Time with his Family and Friends, Traveling, Working Out, Mentoring, Dinning Out **EDU:** Master of Business Administration in Total Quality Management, Dowling College (2002); Bachelor's Degree in English, Dowling College (1993) **A/A/S:** American Society for Quality
Email: msette@bcl.edu
Email: mwsette@gmail.com
URL: http://www.tvrc.com

Amy Severson

Title: District Manager **Company:** Barr Laboratories **Address:** 606 Beech Hanger Drive, Morrisville, NC 27560 United States **BUS:** Pharmaceutical Company **P/S:** Pharmaceutical and Medical Devices **MA:** International **D/D/R:** Managing Five States and 10 Sales Professionals **H/I/S:** Traveling, Playing the Violin and Piano, Biking, Swimming, Skiing **EDU:** Bachelor's Degree in Organizational Speech Communications and Journalism, Concordia College **A/A/S:** American Management Association; Certified Medical Representatives Institute **A/H:** Highest Production Award **C/VW:** Volunteer, Food Bank
Email: southernbound@juno.com
URL: http://www.barrlabs.com

Susan M. Seward

Title: Supervisor of Inside Sales **Company:** Thomson Tax and Accounting **Dept:** Research and Guidance **Address:** 5400 Data Court, Suite 100, Ann Arbor, MI 48108 United States **BUS:** Tax Publishing Company **P/S:** Tax and Legal Publishing **MA:** National **D/D/R:** Sales, Management **H/I/S:** Exercising **EDU:** Pursuing Master of Business Administration; Received Bachelor of Science in English Literature and Psychology, East Michigan University **C/VW:** Susan G. Komen Breast Cancer 3-Day Walk
Email: susan.seward@thomson.com
URL: http://www.ria.thomson.com

Jerri A. Sewell, RDH

Title: Registered Dental Hygienist **BUS:** Private Dentistry Practice **P/S:** Dental Hygiene **MA:** Local **D/D/R:** Assisting Patients with Dental Hygiene **H/I/S:** Spending Time with her Family **EDU:** Associate Degree in Dental Hygiene, Amarillo College **A/A/S:** Church
Email: jjts03@suddenlink.net

Alessandra Sgubini, LLM

Title: CEO **Company:** Bridge Mediation, LLC **Address:** 964 Fifth Avenue, Suite 216, San Diego, CA 92101 United States **BUS:** Mediation Consulting **P/S:** International Dispute Consulting Company and Negotiation **MA:** International **D/D/R:** International Law, Mediation and Negotiation **H/I/S:** Swimming **EDU:** JD, University of Milano, University of California **A/A/S:** Italian Bar Association and San Diego University Club
Email: alessandra@bridgemediation.com
URL: http://www.bridge-mediation.com

Jihada S. Shabazz

Title: Project Manager **Company:** Lifebridge Health, Sinai Hospital **Address:** Baltimore, MD **BUS:** Hospital **P/S:** Healthcare **MA:** Statewide **D/D/R:** Accounting, Management **H/I/S:** Listening to Jazz Music, Reading, Traveling **EDU:** Bachelor of Arts in Business Administration and Accounting, University of Baltimore; Bachelor's Degree in Chemistry, University of Maryland **A/A/S:** CPA; National Association for the Advancement of Colored People
Email: jshabazz@msn.com
URL: http://www.cambridgewhoswho.com

Deborah L. Shacklock

Title: Physical Education Teacher **Company:** Anne Arundel County Public Schools, Fort Smallwood Elementary School **Address:** 1720 Poplar Ridge Road, Pasadena, MD 21122 United States **BUS:** Elementary School **P/S:** Education **MA:** Regional **D/D/R:** Coaching Team Sports, Teaching Physical Education **H/I/S:** Traveling, Playing Sports of All Kinds, Reading, Swimming, Gardening **EDU:** Master of Science in Sports Physiology, West Virginia University; Bachelor of Arts in Physical Education, Frostburg State University **A/A/S:** Maryland Association for Health, Physical Education, Recreation and Dance; TA; MPSSAA **C/VW:** American Cancer Society, Relay For Life; American Heart Association
Email: dshacklock@aacps.org
URL: http://www.cambridgewhoswho.com

Mr. Amir Shafaee

Title: Quality Assurance, Quality Control Manager **Company:** Berkeley Farms **Address:** 25500 Clawiter Road, Hayward, CA 94545 United States **BUS:** Continuous Milk Processor **P/S:** Dairy Products, Milk, Butter, Ice Cream **MA:** National **D/D/R:** Overseeing Quality of Plant, Working to Ensure Highest Quality, Involved in Production and Sanitation **EDU:** Bachelor's Degree in Science and Biology, University of California at Davis (2002)
Email: auramazda@gmail.com
URL: http://www.berkeleyfarms.com

Stephen D. Shafer

Title: Rehabilitation Counselor **Company:** Young Adult Institute **Address:** 147 Deep Hollow Drive, Greentown, PA 18426 United States **BUS:** Employment Readiness, Rehabilitation and Education Facility **P/S:** Advocacy and Rehabilitation Services for Young Adults **MA:** Regional **D/D/R:** Promoting Job Development for Disabled Adults, Accepting Referrals from County, State and Federal Organizations, Teaching Abilities to Adults Entering the Workforce **H/I/S:** Collecting Coins, Football **EDU:** Master's Degree in Rehabilitation Psychology, Minor in Philosophy and Religion, University of Scranton (2006); Bachelor's Degree in Human Services, University of Scranton (1998) **A/A/S:** American Counsel Association; National Rehabilitation Association; American Association of Spirituality and Values in Counseling
Email: stephenshaf01@yahoo.com

Mary Ann Shaffer

Title: Medical Office Coordinator **Company:** Arthritis Specialists of Nashville **Address:** 507 Decherd Lane, Smyrna, TN 37167 United States **BUS:** Medical Clinic **P/S:** Healthcare Specializing in Treating Arthritis, Autoimmune Diseases and Rheumatology **MA:** National **D/D/R:** Specializing in Healthcare, Medical Billing and Coding, Managing the Front Office, Scheduling More than 20 Employees **EDU:** Diploma, North High School, Akron (1965) **CERTS:** Certified Medical Biller; Certified Professional Coder **A/A/S:** American Academy of Professional Coders; Nashville Chapter, Medical Group Management Association
Email: maryann.shaffer@hcahealthcare.com
URL: http://www.arthritisspecialistsofnashville.com

Bimal Shah

Title: President **Company:** Rajparth Advisory Group, LLC **Address:** 55 N.E. Fifth Avenue, Suite 402, Boca Raton, FL 33432 United States **BUS:** Financial Firm **P/S:** Financial Services Including Insurance, Taxation, Financial Consultation and Investment Services **MA:** International **EXP:** Mr. Shah's expertise is in financial planning. **D/D/R:** Meeting Clients and Making a Positive Difference in their Lives Financially, Utilizing Creative Strategies and Ideas in Business Planning to Help Increase Profitability, Retain Key Employees, and Leave Behind a Legacy, Offering a Successful Financial Network that Encompasses Several Arenas to Make a One-Stop Shop for All of his Clients Needs, Speaking at Presentations for Various Events Including Physician Association Meetings, Asian Indian Cultural Events, Business Associations and Networking Meetings **H/I/S:** Horseback Riding **EDU:** Bachelor of Commerce, Bombay University, India, with Honors; Bachelor of Science in Advertising, University of Florida, Gainesville **CERTS:** Pursuing Chartered Advisor for Senior Living Certification; Chartered Life Underwriter, The American College; Chartered Financial Consultant, The American College; Certified Advisor for Seniors **A/A/S:** Broward Association of Insurance and Financial Advisors; National Association of Insurance and Financial Advisors; Court of the Table, The Million Dollar Round Table; Talk Radio Host, 'Money Matters,' 980 AM; National Association of Securities Dealers; America's Who's Who **A/H:** A Plus Rating, National Ethics Award; National Quality Award; National Sales Achievement Award
Email: bimalshah@bellsouth.net
URL: http://www.buildmyfinancialfuture.com

Sara Shahim

Title: Deputy Executive Director **Company:** Lincoln Medical and Mental Health Center **Address:** 25 Rockledge Avenue, White Plains, NY 10601 United States **BUS:** Nonprofit Medical Center **P/S:** Emergency Room Services, Treatment Services for Asthma, Obesity, Cancer, Diabetes and Tuberculosis, Stroke Center, Ambulatory Care Services, Educational Programs **MA:** Regional **D/D/R:** Treating Patients, Managing the Infectious Disease Control Department, Ensuring Patient Safety and Quality Care, Overseeing Risk Management, Patient Complaints Department, Medical Staff Credentialing, Privileging and Utilization Management Department. **H/I/S:** Watching Movies, Reading **EDU:** Doctoral Degree in Education, Boston University (1978); Registered Nurse
Email: shahim421@aol.com
URL: http://www.linmed.org

Vera A. Shamis

Title: Owner **Company:** Allegro Music School **Address:** 550 Pilgrim Drive, Foster City, CA 94404 United States **BUS:** Music School **P/S:** Music Education Including Piano, Voice, Strings, Woodwinds and Percussion Instruments, Music Theory and Chorus **MA:** Regional **D/D/R:** teaching how to play the piano and music, conducting private lessons and judging local competitions **H/I/S:** Sewing, Knitting, Traveling, Admiring Nature **EDU:** Master of Arts in Performing Arts, Ural State Conservatory, Russia (1981) **A/A/S:** President, Music Teachers Association of California, San Mateo
Email: verashamis@hotmail.com
URL: http://www.fcallegro.com

Mrs. Barbara R. Shanders

Title: Independent Business owner **Company:** Direct Sales in Ameriplan USA & Tastefully Simple **Dept:** Sales **Address:** 4030 Bahia Isle Circle, Wellington, FL 33449 United States **BUS:** Direct Sales in Ameriplan, Tastefully Simple **P/S:** Affordable Dental, Prescription and Healthcare Plans for People who have no Coverage, are Underinsured, Uninsurable or Just Want a Supplemental Policy **MA:** National **D/D/R:** Helping Customers by Determining their Needs and Offering Excellent Services **H/I/S:** Spending Time with her Family, Fishing, Gardening, Spending Time Outdoors **EDU:** Degree in Marketing; Licensed in Real Estate, State of Florida. Personal Financial Representative. Washington Mutual Bank **C/VW:** Church, Humane Society
Email: Shanders@helloworld.com
URL: http://www.DentalForLess.org
URL: http://www.SaveTimeCooking.com

Dorothy M. Shanks

Title: President **Company:** Dot's Boutique **Address:** 9879 Elmar Avenue, Oakland, CA 94603 United States **BUS:** Retail Store **P/S:** Retail Services Including Art, Clothing, Hats, Handbag and Collectables **MA:** Local **EXP:** Ms. Shanks expertise is in communications management. **H/I/S:** Swimming, Horseback Riding **EDU:** Master of Science, Nova Southeastern University **A/A/S:** Oakland Education Association **C/VW:** Community Outreach; Local Church
Email: dorothy.shanks@cwwemail.com
URL: http://www.cambridgewhoswho.com

Nancy J. Shannon
Title: Special Education Teacher **Company:** Davenport North High School **Address:** 626 W. 53rd Street, Davenport, IA 52806 United States **BUS:** Public High School **P/S:** Education **MA:** Local **D/D/R:** Special Education, Working with Mentally Disabled Students **H/I/S:** Reading, Sports **EDU:** Master's Degree in Special Education, University of Northern Iowa **A/A/S:** Davenport Education Association; Iowa State Education Association; National Education Association **C/VW:** Special Olympics
Email: nsshannon@aol.com

Edith Shapira, MD
Title: Psychiatrist **Company:** Edith L. Shapira, MD **Address:** 401 Shady Avenue, A-205, Pittsburgh, PA 15206 United States **BUS:** Healthcare **P/S:** Treatments, Evaluations, Adult Psychiatry **MA:** Local **D/D/R:** General Adult Psychiatry **EDU:** MD, University of Pittsburgh School of Medicine; Bachelor of Science in Psychology and Biology, Oberlin College **A/A/S:** ACMS; PMS; American Medical Association; APA; PSS
Email: eshapira@city-net.com

Peggy R. Shapiro
Title: Owner **Company:** Shapiro Billing & Payroll Services **Address:** P.O. Box 7330, Stockton, CA 95267 United States **BUS:** Billing Services Company **P/S:** Medical Billing and Payroll for Medical Professionals and Facilities **MA:** Regional **D/D/R:** Managing Receivables Collections, Pick-Ups and Deliveries, Obtaining Clients' Medical Records and Reports for Insurance Companies **H/I/S:** Reading, Riding Harley-Davidson Motorcycles **EDU:** Associate of Arts in Business, Delta College (2007) **A/A/S:** Women's Business Network; Alpha Gamma Sigma
Email: shapirobilling@yahoo.com

Maj. Donald Sharp
Title: Major, Uniformed Patrol **Company:** St Tammany Parish Sheriffs Office **Address:** 2070 Collins Boulevard, Covington, LA 70434 United States **BUS:** Parish Sheriff's Office Service Provider **P/S:** Protect and Serve the Citizenry of Parish **MA:** Local **D/D/R:** Nurse for a Total of 185 Officers, With Border Patrol, Search and Rescue, and Swat and Dive Teams, Patrolling 951 Miles of Coast Line **H/I/S:** Golf, Traveling, Fishing **EDU:** Covington High School with Studies at LSU, and DelGato, Associate of Science, Criminology Courses and Management **A/A/S:** FBI National Academy Graduate, Louisiana Sheriff Association, Louisiana Deputy Association, Louisiana Peace Office Association
Email: donaldsharp@stpso.com
URL: http://www.stpso.com

Louise A. Sharp
Title: Organizer, Co-Owner **Company:** Sharp Floor Co., LLC **Address:** 741 W. Dallas Street, Buffalo, MO 65622 United States **BUS:** Flooring, Retailer **P/S:** Floor Care. Laminate, Vinyl, Hardwoods, Carpets, Tile **MA:** Local **D/D/R:** Floor Care, Accounting, Deliveries, Supplies, Orders, Organizing **H/I/S:** Boating, Camping, Attending Bible Studies, Antique Sales **EDU:** Graduate of Buffalo High School, Buffalo, Missouri **A/A/S:** Buffalo First Free Will Bible Study Fellowship International **C/VW:** Coordinator, Ladies Auxiliary in Springfield, Missouri; First Free Will Church of Springfield
URL: http://www.cambridgewhoswho.com

Tiffany Sharp
Title: Lead Quality Assurance Analyst **Company:** Phoenix Life Insurance **BUS:** Life Insurance Company **P/S:** Life Insurance **MA:** Regional **D/D/R:** Lead Quality Assurance Analyst, Technology **H/I/S:** Reading, Running **EDU:** Bachelor of Art in Secondary Education and Mathematics, The College of Saint Rose
Email: yankee2111@yahoo.com
URL: http://www.cambridgewhoswho.com

Vernice V. Sharpe
Title: Assistant Principal, Literacy Coach **Company:** Carminati School **Address:** 820 E. Cullumber Street, Gilbert, AZ 85234 United States **BUS:** Elementary School **P/S:** Education **MA:** Local **D/D/R:** Curriculum, Instruction, Supervising Teachers and Classified Personal **H/I/S:** Hiking, Reading, Housework **EDU:** Master of Education in Educational Administration and Supervision, University of Phoenix **A/A/S:** American Evaluation Association; Association for Supervision and Curriculum Development **C/VW:** Deputy Director, Pathfinder Club, Beacon of Light Seventh-Day Adventist Church
Email: vsharpe@tempeschools.org

Glenda Shaver
Title: Licensed Practical Nurse, Staff Nurse **Company:** Life Care Center for Rochester **Address:** 316 Tyler Avenue, Peru, IN 46970 United States **BUS:** Healthcare Center **P/S:** Long-Term Care **MA:** Regional **EXP:** Ms. Shaver's area of expertise is in geriatric care. **CERTS:** Licensed Practice Nurse, Ivy Tech Community College **A/H:** Nurse of the Year Award, Life Care Center of Rochester
Email: g.shaver@att.net
URL: http://www.cambridgewhoswho.com

James R. Shaw
Title: Owner **Company:** Shaw Auto Repair **Address:** 113 S. Third Street, Paducah, KY 42003 United States **BUS:** Automotive Service Center **P/S:** Automotive Repair Services Including Engine and Transmission Exchange, Brakes, Heat and Air Conditioning, Basic Maintenance **MA:** Regional **EXP:** Mr. Shaw's area of expertise is in operations management. **D/D/R:** Overseeing Electrical Services, Budgeting, Supervising Staff, Advertising, Marketing **H/I/S:** Sports, Playing Baseball **CERTS:** Certified Master Technician, Ford Motor Company (2001); General Equivalency Diploma, Washington State University (1979) **C/VW:** Various Veterans Organizations
Email: jshaw@hics.net
URL: http://www.cambridgewhoswho.com

Noma H. Shaw
Title: Attorney **Company:** Noma H. Shaw, PC **Address:** 1420 Locust Street, Suite 10J, Philadelphia, PA 19102 United States **BUS:** Law Firm **P/S:** Legal Services **MA:** Local **D/D/R:** Social Security and Tort Law, Legal Advocacy **H/I/S:** Swimming, Computer Technology, Walking, Reading, Writing **EDU:** JD, Widener School of Law; Doctor of Education, Temple University **A/A/S:** Pennsylvania Bar Association **C/VW:** Pro Bono Legal Work
Email: nhshaw@msn.com
URL: http://www.cambridgewhoswho.com

Albert W. Shay
Title: Attorney **Company:** Sonnenschein Nath & Rosenthal, LLP **Address:** 1301 K Street N.W., Washington, DC 20005 United States **BUS:** Law Firm **P/S:** Legal Services **MA:** National **EXP:** Mr. Shay's area of expertise is in healthcare law. **H/I/S:** Scuba Diving, Golfing, Spending Time with his Family **EDU:** JD, Saint Louis University; Master of Hospital Administration, Saint Louis University; Bachelor of Arts in Government and Politics, University of Maryland; Bachelor of Arts in Psychology, University of Maryland **A/A/S:** American Health Lawyers Association; Valedictorian, Saint Louis University **C/VW:** Rockville Family Center
Email: ashay@sonnenschein.com
URL: http://www.sonnenschein.com

Carolina L. Shea
Title: Graphic Design, Fine Arts **Address:** 47 Coachlight Square, Montrose, NY 10548 United States **BUS:** Advertising and Web Design Company **P/S:** Web and Print Design and Advertising **D/D/R:** Creating Product Layout and Illustration, Advertising Design, Web Design, Print Design and Freelance Graphic Art **H/I/S:** Painting, Exercising **EDU:** Bachelor's Degree, Mercy College (2003)
Email: carolinashea@carolinashea.com
URL: http://www.carolinashea.com

Lauren T. Shears
Title: Public Information Officer **Company:** County of Essex **Address:** 25 Fulton Street, East Orange, NJ 07017 United States **BUS:** Government Organization **P/S:** Maintenance of 17 Parks, Five Reservations, Ice Skating Rink, Roller Skating Rink, Minor League Baseball Stadium, 15-Acre Zoo and Three Golf Courses **MA:** Regional **D/D/R:** Supporting State Officials, Managing Public Relations, Overseeing Park Services, Organizing Press Conferences and Events **H/I/S:** Coaching Volleyball **EDU:** Pursuing Master of Business Administration, Strayer University; Bachelor's Degree in Communications, William Paterson University (2006) **A/A/S:** National Association of Black Journalists
Email: tiffroc@aol.com
URL: http://www.essex-countynj.org

Quanna L. Sheehan
Title: Licensed Practical Nurse, Clinical Care Coordinator, Restorative Nursing Supervisor **Company:** Tri-County Extended Care Center **Address:** 5200 Camelot Drive, Fairfield, OH 45014 United States **BUS:** Healthcare Center **P/S:** Nursing Staff Services, Long-Term Care Treatment **MA:** Regional **D/D/R:** Overseeing Resident and Patient Statuses, Supervising the Nursing Staff, Recruiting **H/I/S:** Riding her Motorcycle, Gardening, Exercising **CERTS:** Pursuing Registered Nurse, Miami University; Licensed Practical Nurse, Butler Technical College (1992)
Email: quanna.sheehan@cwwemail.com

Pamela S. Sheets
Title: Chief Executive Officer **Company:** Sheets Home Health Care, Inc. **Address:** 404 W. Decatur Street, Apt. 105, Madison, NC 27025 United States **BUS:** Privately Owned Facility Dedicated to Excellence in Healthcare **P/S:** Daily Living Services **MA:** Florida **D/D/R:** Traveling to Homes Offering Grocery Shopping, Pet Therapy, Cooking, Cleaning, Bathing, Light Maintenance Work, Scheduling Doctors Appointments on a 24-Hour, 7-Day a Week Basis, Licensed in North Carolina and Florida **H/I/S:** Water Skiing, Riding Sea Doos **EDU:** Pursuing Associate Degree; College Coursework **A/A/S:** Humane Society; Fire Department Board of Directors; Secretary and Treasurer, Ladies Auxiliary; Supports the Rockingham County Fire and Rescue Department; Volunteers, Rockingham County Fire and Rescue Department

Sarajean A. Sheinin, RN
Title: Registered Nurse **Company:** Mercy Medical Center **Address:** 1000 N. Village Avenue, Rockville Center, NY 11570 United States **BUS:** Medical Center **P/S:** Healthcare **MA:** Local **D/D/R:** overseeing the maternity unit operations and in obstetrics gynecology nursing **H/I/S:** Spending Time with her Family and Friends. Spending Time at the Beach, Spending Time Outdoors, Gardening, Helping People **EDU:** Bachelor of Science in Nursing, Molloy College; Associate of Science in Nursing, Nassau Community College **A/A/S:** Sigma Theta Tau; Phi Epsilon Kappa **C/VW:** St. Jude Children's Research Hospital
Email: dss119@msn.com

Paula J. Sheldon
Title: Mental Health Counselor II **Company:** State of Nevada Youth Parole Bureau **Address:** 7028 Desert Clover Court, Las Vegas, NV 89129 United States **BUS:** Parole Bureau **P/S:** Family and Marriage Counseling, Parole Services **MA:** Regional **D/D/R:** Counseling Juveniles and their Families, Lecturing on Mental Health Conditions **H/I/S:** Traveling, Fishing, Reading, Playing Bridge **EDU:** Master of Arts in Counseling Physiology, Mount St. Mary's College, CA (1985) **CERTS:** Certification in Teaching Social Studies, Mount St. Mary's College; Certification in Teaching College Social Studies, Mount St. Mary's College; Certified Mental Health Specialist **A/A/S:** American Association of Marriage and Family Therapists; American Association of Counseling; American Red Cross Disaster Relief Program
Email: sheldon@dcfs.state.nv.us
URL: http://www.dcfs.state.nv.us

Arnita F. Shelton
Title: Registered Nurse **Company:** Prince George's Hospital Center **Address:** 3001 Hospital Drive, Cheverly, MD 20785 United States **BUS:** Hospital **P/S:** Hospital-Based Healthcare **MA:** Regional **D/D/R:** Medical Surgical Nursing, Specializing in Post Partum, Lactation and Sexual Assault Nurse Exams **H/I/S:** Traveling, Making Crafts **EDU:** Associate Degree in Nursing, Prince George's Community College; Clinical Nurse Ladder I, Prince George's Hospital Center; Bereavement Coordinator, Price George's Hospital Center; Registered Nurse, Prince George's Community College **A/A/S:** Sexual Assault Forensic Examiner; American Nurses Association; International Association of Forensic Nurses; Maryland Network Against Domestic Violence; Association of Women's Health; Obstetric and Neonatal Nurses **C/VW:** Earth Baptist Church; Leader, Daisy Girl Scout, 10 Years; Friends of Largo Library; Member, Former Secretary, Millwood-Waterford Citizens Association; Sisters in Discipleship
Email: arnita.f.sheton@verizon.net
URL: http://www.princegeorgeshospital.org

Emily Shelton McElfresh
Title: Owner **Company:** 1) The Crafty Pelican 2) Pelican Cay Harbor Marina, Inc **Address:** 7625 S.W. 167th Street, Miami, FL 33157 United States **BUS:** 1) Stained Glass Shop 2) Marina **P/S:** 1) Custom Made Stained Glass Sales 2) Marina Boat Docking Services **MA:** Regional **D/D/R:** 1) Working on Crafts, Creating Silk Flower Arrangements through Custom Work, Teaching Elementary School, Middle High School English and Drama, Offering High and Middle School Counseling, Teaching Magnet Classes, Overseeing 11 Teachers and 600 Students, Maintaining Curriculum in Art, Dance, Drama, Photography and Music, Recruiting 2) Managing the Marina with 26 Boat Ships and Trailers for Rent, Private Rental Properties to Dockery Only **H/I/S:** Boating, Fishing, Visiting Home in the Keys **EDU:** Master's Degree in Guidance and Counseling, Florida Atlantic University; Bachelor of Arts in Elementary Education and English, Minor in History and Drama, Longwood College (1961) **A/A/S:** Lifetime Member, Alpha Psi Omega Drama Society; Boerc eh Thorn (English Honor Society); 20 Publications
Email: pelicancayharbor@aol.com
URL: http://www.cambridgewhoswho.com

Julie L. Shepard
Title: Special Education Teacher **Company:** Greenville County Schools, Fountain Inn Elementary School **Address:** 608 Fairview Street, Fountain Inn, SC 29644 United States **BUS:** School **P/S:** Education **MA:** Local **D/D/R:** Teaching Students with Learning Disabilities **H/I/S:** Sports, Reading **EDU:** Master's Degree in Emotionally Disabled Education, Furman University Bachelors in Science Early Childhood Education Erskine College; Bachelor's Degree in Early Childhood Education, Erskine College **A/A/S:** Honored as an Educator **C/VW:** Samaritan's Purse
Email: jshepard@greenville.k12.sc.us

Christina N. Shepherd
Title: Co-Owner **Company:** Korean Institute of Martial Arts **Address:** 1342 42nd Street, Woodward, OK 73801 United States **BUS:** Martial Arts School **P/S:** Martial Arts Education and Training **MA:** Oklahoma **D/D/R:** Working as the Office Manager, Bookkeeping, Working with Children and Adults **H/I/S:** Horseback Riding, Camping, Fishing **EDU:** Pursuing Bachelor's Degree in Business, High Plains Institute Of Technology; Associate of Applied Science, High Plains Institute of Technology (2008) **A/A/S:** Business Publications of America
Email: shepette_68@sbcglobal.net
URL: http://www.cambridgewhoswho.com

Jean A. Shepherd, CRM, MHA
Title: Director of Loss Prevention **Company:** East Jefferson General Hospital **Address:** 4200 Houma Boulevard, Metairie, LA 70006 United States **BUS:** Hospital **P/S:** 454 Bed Facility Offering Expert Patient Care for Citizenry **MA:** Local **D/D/R:** Responsible for Risk Management, Guest Services, Security and Claims Handling **H/I/S:** Motorcycling, Gardening **EDU:** University of Phoenix, University of Alabama-Birmingham, Master's Degree in Hospital Administration, Bachelor's Degree in Human Resources **A/A/S:** LASociety for Human Resource Management, National Alliance of Insurance Education and Research
Email: jshepher@ejgh.org
URL: http://www.ejgh.org

Rosemary T. Shepherd
Title: Massage Therapist **Company:** Ambiance Day Spa **Address:** 1380 Central Park Boulevard, Fredericksburg, VA 22401 United States **BUS:** Healthcare **P/S:** Massage **MA:** Local **D/D/R:** Massage and Energy Therapies **H/I/S:** Skiing, Dancing, Yoga, Pilates, Chinese Brush Painting **CERTS:** Licensed Massage Therapist **A/A/S:** American Massage Therapist Association **C/VW:** American Cancer Society; Best Friends Animal Society
Email: rs-gs@adelphia.net
URL: http://www.cambridgewhoswho.com

Gloria Ann Sheppard
Title: Consultant **Company:** Candor Consulting, LLC **Address:** 9208 Foxcroft Avenue, Clinton, MD 20735 United States **BUS:** Consulting Company **P/S:** Consulting Services **MA:** Local **D/D/R:** budgeting, accounting and overseeing real estate exchange **H/I/S:** Sewing **EDU:** Bachelor's Degree, Columbia University
Email: sheppardga@verizon.net

Mary E. Sheppard
Title: County Planning Commissioner **Company:** Manatee County, Florida **BUS:** County Planning Organization **P/S:** County Planning **MA:** Manatee County **D/D/R:** Recommending Citizen Land Usage to the Commissioner, Planning Projects **H/I/S:** Gardening, Hiking, Camping, Traveling **EDU:** Bachelor of Science in Elementary Education and Social Studies, Florida State University (1952) **A/A/S:** Executive Board Member, Sierra Club; Executive Committee, Manatee Sarasota Group of Florida; Sierra Club **A/H:** Bradenton Herald Outstanding Person of the Year (2003); Person of the Year (1997); Sierra Outstanding Worker for Conservation (1986) **C/VW:** Sierra Club; National Audubon Society
Email: mecomary@aol.com
URL: http://www.manatee.fl.us

Irene Sherba
Title: Pharmaceutical Information Analyst **Company:** GlaxoSmithKline **Address:** 200 N. 16th Street, Philadelphia, PA 19102 United States **BUS:** Pharmaceutical Company **P/S:** Pharmaceuticals **MA:** Regional **D/D/R:** analyzing information sources **H/I/S:** Reading, Traveling **EDU:** Master's Degree in Information Science, Drexel University (1985) **A/A/S:** American Pharmaceutical Association **C/VW:** Choir Member, Local Church; Ukrainian Culture Center
Email: irene.sherba@cwwemail.com
URL: http://www.cambridgewhoswho.com

Kevin D. Sheridan
Title: Owner **Company:** Rutgers Painting **Address:** 863 Valley Street, Vauxhall, NJ 07088 United States **BUS:** Home Improvement Company **P/S:** Exterior Painting **MA:** Local **D/D/R:** Exterior Painting **H/I/S:** Martial Arts, Surfing **EDU:** Bachelor of Arts in History, Rutgers, The State University of New Jersey **A/A/S:** Painting and Decorating Contractors of America; Personal Dynamics, Life Coaching
Email: kevinsheridan8@aol.com
URL: http://www.rutgerspainting.com

Bonnie L. Sherman
Title: Owner **Company:** Db Services **Address:** 732 N. Cherokee Trail, Benson, AZ 85602 United States **BUS:** Real Estate Agency **P/S:** Buying, Renting and Selling Residential Homes **MA:** Local **EXP:** Ms. Sherman's expertise is in property management. **D/D/R:** accounting and selling residential homes **H/I/S:** Horseback Riding, Writing, Hiking **EDU:** Bachelor's Degree, Chaparral University **A/A/S:** Hogan School of Real Estate; The Arizona Bankers Association; Tucson Association of Realtors; Arizona Association of Realtors; National Association of Realtors
Email: bls63@msn.com
URL: http://www.cambridgewhoswho.com

Deidre Sherman
Title: Chief of Police **Company:** Spring City Police Department **Address:** 6 S. Church Street, Spring City, PA 19475 United States **BUS:** Police Department **P/S:** Public Safety and Law Enforcement **MA:** Local **D/D/R:** defending people from child abuse and domestic violence **H/I/S:** Crocheting, Singing **EDU:** Bachelor of Arts in French and Sociology, Lake Erie College; Coursework in Criminal Justice, West Chester University of Pennsylvania **A/A/S:** Red Hat Society **C/VW:** Local Chapter, Queen Mother; Relay for Life; Susan G. Komen for the Cure
Email: chiefdeescpd@hotmail.com
URL: http://www.cambridgewhoswho.com

Laura Kathryn Sherman, MD
Title: Psychiatrist **Company:** Laura Kathryn Sherman, MD **Address:** 14539 W. Indian School Road, Suite 800, Goodyear, AZ 85338 United States **BUS:** Mental Healthcare **P/S:** Private Psychiatric Practice, Counseling, Diagnosis, Treatment **MA:** Regional **D/D/R:** Specializing in Treating Chronic Pain, Mental Illness, Neurological Problems, Diabetes Management, Depression, Cancer Patients, Medically and Terminally Ill Population **H/I/S:** Cooking, Archeology, Spectator Sports, Exercise, Traveling **EDU:** MD in Psychiatry, University of Illinois (1995) **A/A/S:** Diplomat, American Board of Psychiatry and Neurology
Email: beatlsherm@aol.com
URL: http://www.cambridgewhoswho.com

Patricia A. H Sherman, GRI, SRES
Title: Realtor **Company:** Coldwell Banker Walter Williams Realty **Address:** 4701 US Highway 17, Suite 107, Orange Park, FL 32003 United States **BUS:** Real Estate Broker **P/S:** Residential, Executive, Hi End, Water Front, Ocean Front, Lake Front, New Construction, Condos, Gated **MA:** National **D/D/R:** Residential, Executive Homes, New Construction, Gulf Homes, Gated **H/I/S:** Camping, Sewing **EDU:** Florida Community College, Art **A/A/S:** Florida Association of Realtors, National Association of Realtors
Email: psherman1@coldwellbanker.com
URL: http://www.patriciasherman.com

Faye M. Sherrill
Title: Interface Programmer **Company:** MEDHOST **Address:** 5055 Keller Springs Road, Suite 400, Addison, TX 75001 United States **BUS:** Software Solutions Company **P/S:** Emergency Department Information Management System and Software, Laboratory and Radiology Systems, Computerized Applications **MA:** National **D/D/R:** Specializing in Customers to Implement Interfacing Systems, Tracking Patient Information **H/I/S:** Boating, Racquetball **EDU:** Bachelor's Degree in Business Administration, Catawba College (1999)
Email: faye71@ctc.net
Email: fmsherrill@ctc.net
URL: http://www.medhost.com

Cynthia L. Sherwood
Title: Administrative Assistant **Company:** The Wesleyan Church **Address:** P.O. Box 50434, Suite 207, Indianapolis, IN 46250 United States **BUS:** Ministry **P/S:** Spiritual Support, Education, Community Service, Financial Services **MA:** Regional **D/D/R:** Assisting the General Director of Evangelism and Church Growth, Overseeing Finances and Accounting Duties, Organizing Travel Arrangements, Managing Correspondence, Planning Events **H/I/S:** Cooking, Music **EDU:** Pursuing Bachelor's Degree in Christian Counseling, John Wesley Honors College, Indiana Wesleyan University
Email: sherwoodc@wesleyan.org
URL: http://wesleyan.org

Derek Shields
Title: 1) Co-Founder 2) Creative Director **Company:** 1) The Arterie 2) Skwibble **Address:** 3211 Cahuenga Boulevard W., Los Angeles, CA 90068 United States **BUS:** 1) Advertising Agency 2) Online Store **P/S:** 1) Advertisements Including Visuals for Movie Posters and Brands 2) Online Invitation Cards **MA:** International **D/D/R:** advertising, designing and overseeing operations and business development **H/I/S:** Reading, Caring for her Dog **EDU:** Associate Degree, El Camino College, CA **A/A/S:** Industry-Related Associations **C/VW:** Local Charitable Organizations
Email: dshields@thearterie.com
URL: http://www.thearterie.com

Katherine D. Shiflett
Title: President, Owner **Company:** DAME Construction Inc. **Address:** 2916 Jackson Drive, Haymarket, VA 20169 United States **BUS:** General Contractor **P/S:** Office, Warehouse, Retail Construction **MA:** Local **D/D/R:** Construction Management General Contractor, Blueprints, Permits, Interior Tenant Fit-Up, Estimates, Bids. **H/I/S:** Reading, Quilting, Needlepoint, Spending Time at Home **EDU:** High School Education; Blueprint Reading Classes, Melville North Virginia Community College **A/A/S:** Board of Directors, DIDLAK **C/VW:** DIDLAK-Organization Helping the Disabled Find Work
Email: dameinc1@msn.com
URL: http://www.cambridgewhoswho.com

Nancy L. Shilts
Title: Kennel Owner **Company:** Windy Ridge Kennel **Address:** 8881 W. C Avenue, Kalamazoo, MI 49009 United States **BUS:** Dog Kennel Housed in a 700 Square Foot Building with Bath Facilities **P/S:** Breeding and Sale of Quality Puppies Including Labrador Retrievers, Jack Russells, Corgis, Pugs **D/D/R:** Breeding and Selling Quality Puppies, Grooming Dogs, Removing Claws, Administering Shots, Training Puppies **H/I/S:** Exercising, Walking, Working on Crafts, Spending Time in Nature **EDU:** Coursework in Medical Assistant Studies, Olympia Technical Institute (2005) **A/A/S:** American Kennel Club; United Kennel Club
Email: puppybreeder@charter.net

Diane L. Shinault
Title: Licensed Practical Nurse, Certified Surgical Technician, Instrument Room Coordinator **Company:** Riverside Regional Medical Center **Address:** 500 J. Clyde Morris Boulevard, Newport News, VA 23601 United States **BUS:** Hospital **P/S:** Healthcare **MA:** Virginia, North Carolina **D/D/R:** General Surgery, Cardiac surgery **H/I/S:** Spending Time with her Children and Grandchildren, Attending Church **CERTS:** Licensed Practical Nurse, Riverside Regional Medical Center; Certification in Surgical Technology, Association of Surgical Technologists; Instrument Room Coordinator **A/A/S:** Association of Surgical Technologists **C/VW:** Church
Email: dshine80@cox.net
URL: http://www.riversideonline.com/rrme

Cornelia J. Shipley
Title: Partner, Senior Vice President Coaching **Company:** 3 C Consulting **Address:** P.O. Box 20212, Ferndale, MI 48220 United States **BUS:** Executive and Life Coaching Company **P/S:** Professional Coaching and Human Resource Consulting **MA:** International **D/D/R:** Offering Executive, Life, Strategy and Entrepreneurial Coaching, Promoting Diversity Training **H/I/S:** Ballroom, Liturgical and Chicago Step Dancing, Reading, Leading a Book Club, Watching Movies, Serving on the Liturgical Board **EDU:** Master of Business Administration, Southern Methodist University **A/A/S:** Michigan Association for Female Entrepreneurs; Coach, Society for Human Resource Management
Email: cornelia@3cconsult.com
URL: http://www.3cconsult.com

Mrs. Margo C. Shipp
Title: Literacy Specialist **Company:** West Central Higher Regional School Improvement Team **Address:** 1045 Dearbaugh Avenue, Suite 1, Wapakoneta, OH 45895 United States **BUS:** Higher Department of Education **P/S:** Literacy Professional Development Programs for Teachers **MA:** Regional **D/D/R:** working with teachers to improve literacy practices in reading and writing, conducting workshops, professional development and teaching elementary grades **H/I/S:** Reading, Gardening, Traveling **EDU:** Master's Degree in Teaching and Learning in Language, Literacy and Culture with a Concentration in Reading, Ohio State University (2001) **A/A/S:** International Reading Association; Phi Kappa Phi
Email: mshipp@n-union.k12.oh.us
URL: http://www.noacsc.org/rsit

Sheila Renee Shirk
Title: Office Manager, Paralegal **Company:** Law Office of Donna Keene Holt **Address:** P.O. Box 10307, Knoxville, TN 37939 United States **BUS:** Law Firm **P/S:** Legal Services, Complex Litigation **MA:** Local **EXP:** Ms. Shirk's expertise is in medical records management. **D/D/R:** accounting and preparing case files for trial and litigation **H/I/S:** Playing Softball, Exercising **EDU:** Associate Degree in Paralegal Science, Pellissippi State University **CERTS:** Certified Notary Public **A/A/S:** Alumni Board, Pellissippi State University; Phi Beta Kappa **C/VW:** Lost Sheep
Email: sheilafreestyle@bellsouth.net
Email: shirk06@comcast.net
URL: http://www.cambridgewhoswho.com

Jonathan Y. Shirley
Title: Librarian **Company:** Shanksville-Stonycreek School District **Address:** P.O. Box 128, Shanksville, PA 15560 United States **BUS:** School **P/S:** Librarian **MA:** Local **D/D/R:** Education **EDU:** Bachelor of Science in Sociology, Frostburg State University; Master's Degree in Library Science, Kutztown University
Email: jysh@sprynet.com

Janine M. Shively, RN
Title: Registered Nurse, Nurse Specialist in Ortopedics **Company:** Leesburg regional Medical Center **Address:** 3241 S.W. 34th Street, Ocala, FL 34471 United States **BUS:** Ambulatory Surgery Center **P/S:** Outpatient Surgical Services, Skilled Nursing Services **MA:** Regional **D/D/R:** Nursing, Managing the Operating Room and Staff Schedule, Supervising the Nursing Staff, Circulating between Patients, Collaborating with Doctors and Nurses, Treating Patients, Controlling Infections **H/I/S:** Running, Fishing for Bass **EDU:** Associate Degree in Nursing, Central Florida Community College (1995) **CERTS:** Registered Nurse; Certified Operating Room Nurse; Certification in Advanced Critical Life Support **A/A/S:** Association of Perioperative Registered Nurses; Quality Control Committee
Email: jshively@symbion.com
Email: janines54@embarqmil.com
URL: http://www.symbion.com

Dolores Cooper Shockley
Title: Professor/Chairman **Company:** Meharry Medical College **Address:** 4141 West Hamilton, Nashville, TN 37218 United States **BUS:** College **P/S:** Education, Pharmacology **D/D/R:** Private College **H/I/S:** Photography, Reading **A/A/S:** Society Neuro Science
Email: dshockley@mmmc.edu
URL: http://www.mmc.edu

Jeffery M. Shoemaker
Title: Corporate Account Manager **Company:** PolyOne Corporation **Address:** 80 N. Street, Norwalk, OH 44857 United States **BUS:** Manufacturing Company **P/S:** Automotive Plastics, Colorants, Polymer Compounds **MA:** International **EXP:** Mr. Shoemaker's expertise includes automotive sales and marketing. **H/I/S:** Golfing, Traveling **EDU:** Industry-Related Training **A/A/S:** Society of Plastics Engineers **A/H:** Chairman's Club Award (Twice)
Email: jeff.shoemaker@polyone.com
URL: http://www.polyone.com

Sheri L. Shon
Title: Group Exercise Director, Personal Trainer, Instructor Trainer **Company:** Bronson Athletic Club **Dept:** Group Exercise **Address:** 8841 Wendalyn Way, Kalamazoo, MI 49009 United States **BUS:** Athletic Club **P/S:** Group Exercise Director, Personal Trainer, Instructor Trainer **MA:** Regional **D/D/R:** Instructor Trainer and Personal Trainer. Master Gliding Trainer. **H/I/S:** Traveling, Visiting her Children and Grandchildren, Staying Updated in the Fitness Industry, Learning **EDU:** Coursework in Pre-Medical Studies in Health Science, Western Michigan University **CERTS:** ACE Certified Group Exercise Instructor (1988); Certified Master Gliding Trainer, ESA Step Instructor, Trainer; Specialty Certifications BLS Instructor for The American Heart Association (1988) **A/A/S:** American Council on Exercise; IDEA Fitness Association, ESA Step Safety Association, AEA Association, American College of Sports Medicine., The American Heart Association **A/H:** Several Awards **C/VW:** American Heart Association, American Cancer Society, Celiac Sprue Association
Email: shons@bronsonhg.org
Email: sherishon@charter.net
URL: http://www.cambridgewhoswho.com

Alexsondra M. Shore, Esq.
Title: Attorney **Company:** Mitchell Silberberg & Knupp, LLP **Address:** 11377 W. Olympic Boulevard, Los Angeles, CA 90064 United States **BUS:** Law Firm **P/S:** Legal Services **MA:** International **D/D/R:** representing large corporations, international firms and the entertainment industry in matters of immigration law, mergers and acquisition legal services, estate planning and assisting clients with visa issues **H/I/S:** Cooking, Skiing, Watching Movies **EDU:** JD, Loyola Law School, Los Angeles (2004) **A/A/S:** Women Lawyers Association of Los Angeles; American Immigration Lawyers Association; American Bar Association; Board of Barristers, Beverly Hills Bar Association
Email: axs@msk.com
URL: http://www.msk.com

Stephanie R. Shoulders
Title: Teacher **Company:** Los Angeles Unified School District **Dept:** Virginia Road Elementary School **Address:** 2925 Virginia Road, Los Angeles, CA 90016 United States **BUS:** School District **P/S:** Primary Education **MA:** Regional **D/D/R:** teaching and developing curriculum for fourth-grade students **H/I/S:** Reading, Listening to Jazz **EDU:** Bachelor of Arts in Psychology, California State University, Long Beach **A/A/S:** American Federation of Teachers
Email: srs152356797@yahoo.com

Ms. Mattie G. Shouse
Title: Avon Representative **Company:** Avon Products, Inc. **Address:** 1251 Avenue of the Americas, New York, NY 10020 United States **BUS:** Skincare and Cosmetic Company **P/S:** Cosmetics, Skincare, Clothing **MA:** International **D/D/R:** Customer Service **H/I/S:** Crocheting, Knitting **EDU:** Diploma, Irving High School **A/H:** gets awards from the honor society, president club **C/VW:** Various Charities
URL: http://www.cambridgewhoswho.com

Thomas W. Showalter, BA, MA, MBA
Title: Senior Vice President **Company:** First American Default Information Services **Address:** 1 First American Way, Westlake, TX 76262 United States **BUS:** Mortgage Company **P/S:** Mortgages, Information Services, Securities Data, Risk Analysis, Product Development and Pricing **MA:** Local **EXP:** Mr. Showalter's expertise is in distressed asset pricing. **D/D/R:** overseeing product management, developing sales, revenues, mortgage bond pricing and trading **EDU:** Master of Business Administration, Stanford University (1982); Master's Degree in Statistics, University of Virginia (1972); Coursework in Computer
Email: toshowalter@firstam.com

Angela C. Shrewsbury, MA
Title: Elementary Educator **Company:** Mercer County Board of Education **Dept:** Spanishburg School **Address:** P.O. Box 7, Spanishburg, WV 25922 United States **BUS:** Board of Education **P/S:** Education **MA:** Local **D/D/R:** teaching reading, language arts, elementary and special education **H/I/S:** Caring for her Pets, Walking, Reading, Spending Time Outdoors **EDU:** Master of Arts in Special Education, Marshall University; Bachelor of Science in Education (K-8), Bluefield State College **CERTS:** Certification in English as the Medium of Instruction (K-12) **C/VW:** Muscular Dystrophy Association; Special Olympics; Local Church; American Cancer Society; Local Charitable Organizations
Email: capeviewus@yahoo.com
URL: http://www.cambridgewhoswho.com

Todd A. Shulek
Title: Illustrator **Company:** Todd Shulek **Address:** 218 High Avenue, Masontown, PA 15461 United States **BUS:** Sole Proprietorship **P/S:** Art, Cartoon Illustrations **MA:** National **D/D/R:** drawing illustrations and cartoons **H/I/S:** Watching Old Black-and-White Movies, Marx Brother's and Godzilla Movies **EDU:** Coursework, Penn State Fayette Campus, Pennsylvania State University **CERTS:** Certification in Cartoon and Graphic Art, Joe Kubert School of Cartoon and Graphic Art **C/VW:** Goodwill; Society of St. Vincent de Paul; Helping Hands
Email: todd_shulek@hotmail.com
URL: http://www.toddshulek.com

Debra L. Shumar
Title: President, Founder **Company:** 3P Partners a DL Shumar and Associates Company **Address:** 5B Park Lane, Hilton Head Island, SC 29928 United States **BUS:** Consulting Firm **P/S:** Culture Change Services and Operations Management for Manufacturing and Healthcare Companies **MA:** International **D/D/R:** ensuring quality, transitioning culture and utilizing key partnerships **H/I/S:** Golfing, Running, Reading **EDU:** Bachelor of Arts in Business Administration, Malone College **A/A/S:** American Society for Quality; The Lean Enterprise Institute; Advisory Board, University of North Carolina, Charlotte, Engineering School **C/VW:** Charles and Ellen Taylor Prostate Cancer Partners of the Lowcountry; Susan G. Komen for the Cure
Email: dshumar@3ppartnersdls.com
URL: http://www.3ppartnersdls.com

Diane L. Shuster
Title: Teacher **Company:** Rahway Board of Education **Dept:** Madison Elementary School **Address:** 1138 Kline Place, Rahway, NJ 07065 United States **BUS:** School District **P/S:** Primary Education **MA:** Local **D/D/R:** teaching science and mathematics for fifth-grade students, mentoring and utilizing her leadership skills **H/I/S:** Reading, Making Cards, Gardening **EDU:** Master of Arts in in Liberal Studies, Plus 30, Kean University **A/A/S:** New Jersey Education Association; National Science Teachers Association; Safety Patrol Advisor; Character Education Committee; Bully Busters Program **A/H:** Recipient, Association of Science Technology Award for The Tri-State Area (1992) **C/VW:** Volunteer, Robert Woods Johnson University Hospital
Email: dlshuster@verizon.net
URL: http://www.cambridgewhoswho.com

Kathy C. Sicignano
Title: Payroll Clerk **Company:** State of Connecticut **Address:** 5 Mueller Drive, Hamden, CT 06514 United States **BUS:** Government Agency **P/S:** Public Services **MA:** Local **D/D/R:** Processing Payroll, Overseeing Administrative Duties **H/I/S:** Reading, Playing on the Computer **EDU:** Associate Degree in Secretarial Studies, GateWay Community College **CERTS:** Licensed Massage Therapist; Licensed Notary Public **A/A/S:** American Massage Therapy Association **C/VW:** Cure Autism Now
Email: ksicignano@aol.com

Ms. Julie Ann Sidelinger
Title: Physician Assistant **Company:** St. Joseph Mercy Hospitals **Dept:** Cardiothoracic Surgery **Address:** 5301 McAuley Drive, Suite 2509, Ypsilanti, MI 48197 United States **BUS:** Hospital **P/S:** Healthcare **MA:** Local **EXP:** Ms. Sidelinger's expertise includes cardiothoracic and vascular surgery. **D/D/R:** First-Assisting for Cardiothoracic and Vascular Surgeries, Harvesting Veins, Performing Invasive Procedures such as Thoracentesis, Thoracostomy Tube Placement, Central Line Placement, Intra-Aortic Balloon Pump Placement, and Arterial Line Placement, Offering Pre and Postoperative Patient Care and Education **H/I/S:** Playing Volleyball and Softball, Mountain Biking, Running, Water-Skiing, Snow Skiing, Adventure Racing, Playing the Piano, Reading, Photography, Spending Time with Family and Friends **EDU:** Master of Science in Medicine, Western Michigan University (2005); Bachelor of Science in Biology, Lake Superior State University (1999) **CERTS:** Licensed Paramedic, State of Michigan (2000); Licensed Physician Assistant, State of Michigan; Certified Physician Assistant, National Commission on Certification of Physician Assistants **A/A/S:** Fellow, Association of Physician Assistants in Cardiovascular Surgery; American Academy of Physician Assistants **C/VW:** Healthy Hearts 101
Email: juliesidelinger@yahoo.com
URL: http://www.cambridgewhoswho.com

Eunice E. Siedsma
Title: Registered Nurse, Consultant **Company:** Eunice E. Siedsma **Address:** 912 Quinn Street, Aplington, IA 50604 United States **BUS:** Consulting **P/S:** Healthcare, Consulting **MA:** Regional **D/D/R:** Assisting with Open Heart Surgeries and Labor and Delivery **H/I/S:** Creating Wreaths, Making Candles, Gardening, Arranging Dried and Fresh Flowers **EDU:** Diploma in Nursing, Evangelical School of Nursing (1968) **CERTS:** Licensed Registered Nurse, State of Iowa, CPR Certified, Standard First Aid **A/A/S:** Volunteer, American Red Cross; Special Olympics
Email: eunicern@iowatelecom.net

Michelle Siegel Nachman
Title: Teacher of Exceptional Student Education **Company:** Charlotte County School District **Dept:** Charlotte High School **Address:** 2722 Lucaya Avenue, North Port, FL 34286 United States **BUS:** School District **P/S:** Secondary Education **MA:** Regional **D/D/R:** teaching special education for ninth through 12th-grade students with autism, emotional disorders and developmental delays, teaching English, reading, social studies, life and communication skills for post-secondary students **H/I/S:** Watching Sports **EDU:** Educational Specialist Degree, Barry University (1997); Master's Degree in Education and Therapeutic Recreation for Special Population, The George Washington University (1980); Bachelor of Science in Physical Education and Health, University of Maryland **A/A/S:** Former Coach, Special Olympics; National Education Association; Council for Exceptional Children
Email: siegel123@aol.com

Roman Sierra
Title: Producer **Company:** Bloomberg TV **Address:** 731 Lexington Avenue, New York, NY 10022 United States **BUS:** Financial News Publication Company **P/S:** Financial and Economic News **MA:** International **D/D/R:** Conducting Interviews and Early Shows **H/I/S:** Reading **EDU:** Bachelor's Degree in Broadcast Journalism, Lehman College (2000) **A/A/S:** National Association of Hispanic Journalism; Journalists
Email: rsierral@bloomberg.net
URL: http://www.bloomberg.com

Ellen S. Siff
Title: Paralegal Administrator **Company:** Becker & Poliakoff, P.A. **Address:** 3111 Stirling Road, Fort Lauderdale, FL 33312 United States **BUS:** Law Firm **P/S:** Asset Protection, Wealth and Business Preservation, Civil and Complex Commercial Litigation, Entertainment and Sports Law, Insurance Law and Risk Management, Personal Injury and Product Liability Litigation, Real Estate Law **MA:** Regional **D/D/R:** Preparing Closings for Residential and Commercial Real Estate Clients, Drafting Legal Documents Including Deeds, Bills of Sales, Affidavits and Closing Statements, Supervising Paralegals and Closers **H/I/S:** Spinning **EDU:** Master's Degree in Psychology, New York University (1982)
Email: esiff@becker-poliakoff.com
URL: http://www.becker-poliakoff.com

Sandra J. Sigmon
Title: Director **Company:** North Family Community School **Address:** 4651 Savannah Highway, P.O. Box 309, North, SC 29112 United States **BUS:** Adult Education Facility **P/S:** Adult Special Education **MA:** Western Orangeburg County **D/D/R:** Helping Adults with Learning Disabilities, Reading and Writing, Practicing Photography, Offering Leadership Training **H/I/S:** Writing Poetry, Developing Computer Art, Gardening, Fishing **EDU:** Coursework in Liberal Arts, University of California **A/A/S:** National Association for Community-Based Programs **A/H:** Special Services Award **C/VW:** North Family Community School
Email: sasigmon@tds.net

Yvette M. Sikorsky
Title: Owner **Company:** Yvette Sikorsky Studio **Address:** 223 Locust Avenue, Cortlandt Manor, NY 10567 United States **BUS:** Studio **P/S:** Artwork **MA:** International **D/D/R:** designing upholstery fabrics and fine artwork **H/I/S:** Reading, Listening to Music **CERTS:** Certificate of Professional Aptitude, School of Design, Paris **A/A/S:** Honorable Member, Committee of Salon Violet, Paris **A/H:** Award of Excellence in Manhattan Arts, Edward Rubin and Rene Phillips; Bronze Medal, Paris **C/VW:** Various Charitable Organizations; The Association of Indians in America; American Soldiers Overseas
Email: yvette.sikorsky@cwwemail.com

Maureen W. Sileo
Title: Chief Executive Officer **Company:** Sileo and Associates Medical Legal and Forensic Consultants **Address:** Huntington, NY 11743 United States **BUS:** Medical Legal Forensic Consulting **P/S:** Consulting Education, Screen Medical Cases to Determine Merit, Review and Analyze Medical Records, Research Medical and Nursing Standards of Care, Research Hospital Policies and Procedures, Prepare Reports, Clarify Medical Data, Identify and Locate Medical Expert Witnesses, Assistance in Exhibit Preparation, Conduct Forensic Investigations **MA:** Regional **D/D/R:** Offering Medical Services as an Registered Nurse and Paramedic, Medical Care, Forensic Nursing, Educating Attorneys and Insurance Companies on Nursing Practices, Investigating Cases of Sexual Assault, Child Abuse, Elder Abuse, Domestic Violence, Homicide Cases and Crime Scenes **H/I/S:** Gardening, Fitness Training **EDU:** Master Degree in Healthcare Administration, C.W. Post Campus of Long Island University (1991) **CERTS:** Certified Forensic Nurse, Kaplan University (2006); Board Certified Emergency Nurse; Certified Trauma Nurse **A/A/S:** Emergency Nurses Association; National Alliance of Certified Legal Nurse Consultants; United States Coast Guard Auxiliary
Email: sileoassociates@verizon.net
URL: http://www.sileoconsultants.com

Kate L. Sill
Title: Fourth-Grade Teacher **Company:** Cobleskill-Richmondville Central Schools, Golding Elementary School **Address:** 177 Golding Drive, Cobleskill, NY 12043 United States **BUS:** Elementary School **P/S:** Elementary Education **MA:** Local **D/D/R:** Teaching Elementary Education **H/I/S:** Spending Time with Family, Camping, Traveling, Reading **EDU:** Master's Degree in Curriculum Development and Instructional Technology, SUNY Albany; Bachelor's Degree in Childhood Education-Birth through Age Six, SUNY Oneonta; Associate Degree in Liberal Arts and Humanities, SUNY Morrisville **A/A/S:** Association of Supervision and Curriculum Development **C/VW:** 4-H, National FFA, Past State Officer
Email: silk@crcs.k12.ny.us
URL: http://www.cambridgewhoswho.com

Donald W. Silva
Title: Senior Systems Analyst **Company:** Blue Cross and Blue Shield of Rhode Island **Address:** 444 Westminster Street, Providence, RI 02903 United States **BUS:** Health Insurance Company **P/S:** Health Insurance **MA:** National **D/D/R:** Ergonomics **H/I/S:** Lecturing at the National Ergonomic Conference, Coaching Girls' Softball **EDU:** Master's Degree in Education Computing, Johnson and Wales University; Bachelor of Arts in Data Systems Management, Johnson and Wales University; Bachelor of Science in Accounting, Roger Williams University **A/A/S:** Veteran, United States Navy **C/VW:** Special Olympics; Leukemia & Lymphoma Society; Muscular Dystrophy Association; Hasbro Children's Hospital
Email: silva.dw@bcbsri.org
URL: http://www.bcbsri.org

Adriana Silva Strunk
Title: Clinical Social Worker **Company:** Children's Hospital at Scott & White **Address:** 2401 S. 31st, Temple, TX 76508 United States **BUS:** Healthcare Hospital/Outpatient **P/S:** Counseling, Social Work **MA:** Local **D/D/R:** Counseling, Working with Children, Adolescents and their Families, Working with the Chronically Ill **H/I/S:** Quilting, Traveling, Reading **EDU:** University of Mary Hardin-Baylor, Belton, Texas; University of Texas-Austin, Texas, Bachelor of Science in Behavioral Science, Masters, Master of Science in Social Work **A/A/S:** National Association of Social Workers; Advisory Board, UMHB Social Work Program; Institutional Review Board, Scott & White (1999) **A/H:** Social Worker of the Year, NASW Central Texas Branch
Email: aslmsw@hot.rr.com
URL: http://www.sw.org

Kevin J. Silverang
Title: Managing Member **Company:** Silverang & Donohue, LLC **Address:** 595 Lancaster Avenue, St Davids, PA 19087 United States **BUS:** Real Estate Real Estate **P/S:** Real Estate Law and Real Estate Development **MA:** Local **H/I/S:** Playing Guitar, Rugby, Cooking **EDU:** Boison College, University of Southern Florida, Associate of Arts in Liberal Arts **CERTS:** Certified Esthetician **A/A/S:** Pennsylvania and Philadelphia Bar Associations
Email: skincareteacher@aol.com
URL: http://www.sanddlawyers.com

Jonathan A. Silverstein
Title: Senior Vice President of Business Development, Account Director **Company:** GSD&M Idea City **Address:** 828 W. Sixth Street, Austin, TX 78703 United States **BUS:** Advertising Agency **P/S:** Advertisements, Brand Marketing and Retail Communications **MA:** National **D/D/R:** Handling Communications for Management Groups, Managing the Finance Department, Healthcare, Consumer-Packaged Goods and the Telecom Industries **H/I/S:** Spending Time with his Children, Golfing, Skiing **EDU:** Master of Business Administration, Fordham University **A/A/S:** Former Member, Advertising Club of New York **C/VW:** Jewish Community Association; Marketing & Business Development Association
Email: jonathan.silverstein@ideacity.com
URL: http://www.ideacity.com

Lisa E. Sim
Title: Owner **Company:** Future Green **Address:** 2352 S. Kinnickinnic Avenue, Milwaukee, WI 53207 United States **BUS:** Eco-Conscience Retailer **P/S:** Organic, Fair Trade, Re-Created and Eco-Conscience Building and Interior Decorating Tools. We carry a full selection of exquisite organic cloths, bedding, body care, Fair Trade and rare artisan crafts from all over the world. Remodel your home with the best in Eco-Friendly interior decorating tools and building supplies. **MA:** International **D/D/R:** Implementing the Best Eco-Friendly Designs, Specializing in Chemical Sensitivity **H/I/S:** Practicing Falun Gong Qi Gong and Meditation, Inventing products for the store, Biking, Horse Riding, Swimming, Kayaking, Traveling **EDU:** Culinary Arts, Graphic Arts, Milwaukee Area Technical College (1987) **A/A/S:** Reporter for the Epoch Times News paper, National Audubon Society; World Wildlife Fund; Amnesty International Member
Email: lisa@futuregreen.net
URL: http://www.futuregreen.net

Dr. Ernest D. Simela
Title: President **Company:** Simela Medical Arts PC **Address:** Hempstead, NY 11550 United States **BUS:** Healthcare Service Provider **P/S:** Patient Services **MA:** Local **D/D/R:** Pediatrics **H/I/S:** Reading, Traveling, Photography **EDU:** MD in Pediatric, Albert Einstein College of Medicine; Bachelor of Science in Chemistry and Biology, Hamline University
Email: esimela@aol.com
URL: http://www.cambridgewhoswho.com

Debra A. Simmons
Title: Respiratory Therapist CRT **Company:** Pinecrest Developmental Center **Address:** 60 Pinecrest Drive, Pineville, LA 71360 United States **BUS:** Healthcare Center **P/S:** Healthcare **MA:** Local **D/D/R:** Breathing Treatments **H/I/S:** Reading, Scrapbooking **CERTS:** Certified Respiratory Therapist, California State University
Email: simmonsone@suddenlink.net

Michael R. Simmons
Title: Real Estate Salesperson **Company:** Western Homes **Address:** 3639 Inyokern Road, Ridgecrest, CA 93555 United States **BUS:** Real Estate Company **P/S:** Property Listing Services, On Location Agent Presence, Marketing and Sales Services **MA:** Local **D/D/R:** Assisting Clients with Purchasing and Selling Commercial and Residential Real Estate Properties Including Vacant Land, Subdivisions and Remodeling Projects, In-depth Experience in Wireless Cable, Hybrid Fiber Coaxial Cable Systems and Broadcast Television, Designing Cable Systems, Handling Facility Design, Designing and Drafting Transmission Site Constructions, Overseeing Personnel, Operations Manager, Conducting Marketing and Demographic Studies **H/I/S:** Scuba Diving **EDU:** College Coursework in Liberal Arts, Santa Ana College; NCTI Graduate **CERTS:** Pursuing Brokers License; Hughes Microwave Certification; Magnavox CATV Systems Certification; Scientific Atlanta Digital Systems; U.S. Marine Corps, Real Estate Law Principles, Private Pilot License **A/A/S:** Society of Cable Television Engineers
Email: paygemichael@hotmail.com
URL: http://www.westernhomesridgecrest.com

Scott Simmons
Title: Owner/CEO **Company:** Simmons Construction **Address:** 106 Circle V Drive, Montezuma, IA 50171 United States **BUS:** Concrete Contractor **P/S:** Poured Basement Walls & Decorative Concrete **MA:** Local **D/D/R:** Supervising **H/I/S:** Hunting, Boating, Fishing **EDU:** Associates, Applied Science, Criminal Justice **A/A/S:** BBB
URL: http://www.simmonsconstruction

Cynthia Simon
Title: Vice President, Change Consultant **Company:** Bank of America **Address:** 9000 Southside Boulevard, Jacksonville, FL 32256 United States **BUS:** Bank **P/S:** Banking Services **MA:** National **D/D/R:** monitoring associates' engagement and their satisfaction, Coordinating Innovation Campaigns and Community Involvement Program, Developing Associate Programs, Lecturing at Universities for Adult Learning Models **H/I/S:** Writing **EDU:** Doctor of Education in Organizational Leadership, with a Concentration in Conflict and Dispute Resolution, Nova Southeastern University; Master's Degree in Organizational Management, University of Phoenix **A/A/S:** Black Data Processing Associates; League of Black Women; Society for Human Resource Management **A/H:** Instructor of the Year Award, INROADS **C/VW:** Dignity U Wear; United Way; Habitat for Humanity
Email: ccol126@aol.com
URL: http://www.cambridgewhoswho.com

Lorena Simon
Title: Owner **Company:** Universal Light **Address:** 13526 W. Young Street, Surprise, AZ 85374 United States **BUS:** Psychic Center **P/S:** Clairvoyant Services, Psychic Readings Including Entertainment for Conventions and Large and Small Parties **MA:** International **EXP:** Ms. Simon's expertise includes psychic and business consultation and Website updates. **H/I/S:** Traveling, Dancing, Spending Time at the Beach, Talking, Watching Mad Money and Movies, Caring for Dogs **EDU:** Coursework, Highline Community College
Email: lorenasimon@cox.net
Email: mshuggers1@yahoo.com
URL: http://www.lorenasimon.com

Louise R. Simonelli
Title: Inventor, Artist **Company:** Head Lights **Address:** 9101 Shore Road, Apartment 208, Brooklyn, NY 11209 United States **BUS:** Sole Proprietorship **P/S:** Scientific Innovations **MA:** International **EXP:** Ms. Simonelli's expertise is in scientific innovation. **H/I/S:** Visual Art, Sculpting, Gourmet Cooking **C/VW:** The American Society for the Prevention of Cruelty to Animals; Special Olympics
Email: louroe89@yahoo.com

Joy N. Simons
Title: Owner, Manager **Company:** Belle Casa Bed & Breakfast **Address:** 180 Verde Street, Clarkdale, AZ 86324 United States **BUS:** Proven Leader Committed to Excellence in the Hospitality Industry **P/S:** Bed and Breakfast Facility, Overnight Accommodations, Gourmet Cuisine **MA:** National **D/D/R:** Hotel Accommodations, Overseeing Marketing, Upkeep and Booking Guests **H/I/S:** Baseball, Crocheting, Hiking, Reading Fiction and Biographies, Music, Singing **EDU:** Master's Degree in Music, Northern Arizona University (2001); Bachelor's Degree in Music, James Madison University (1981) **A/A/S:** Local PEO
Email: joy@commspeed.net
URL: http://www.bellecasabandb.com

Lucille J. Simotes, ABR
Title: Realtor **Company:** Apple Tree **Address:** 90 Pond View Way, Fitchburg, WI 53711 United States **BUS:** Real Estate Agent Serving Residents in the Madison Area **P/S:** Sale of Residential and Commercial Real Estate **MA:** Regional **D/D/R:** Showing Residential and Commercial Real Estate Properties in Wisconsin, Building Personal Relationships with her Clients **H/I/S:** Hiking, Skiing, Attending the Theater **EDU:** High School Diploma **A/A/S:** National Association of Realtors; South Central Wisconsin Board of Realtors; Wisconsin Realtors Association; Real Estate Buyers Agent Council **A/H:** Rookie of the Year (2005); Executive Club Top Producer (2005); Achievement Award (2006)
Email: lucy@appletree-homes.com
URL: http://www.appletree-homes.com

Amber D. Simpson
Title: Vice President of Global Trade Services **Company:** US Bank **Address:** 1 U.S. Bank Plaza, Saint Louis, MO 63101 United States **BUS:** Sixth Largest Commercial Bank in the United States **P/S:** Comprehensive Line of Banking, Brokerage, Insurance, Investment, Mortgage, Trust and Payment Services Products to Consumers, Businesses and Institutions **MA:** International **D/D/R:** Identifying Quality Imports and Exports, Navigating Businesses in High Risk Situations, Opening Accounts and Letters of Credit **H/I/S:** Dancing, Vacationing, Photography **EDU:** Master of Business Administration in International Business, Saint Louis University (2007) **A/A/S:** Midwest International Trade Association; United States Hispanic Chamber of Commerce
Email: amber.simpson@usbank.com

Dawn M. Simpson, RN, BSN
Title: Nurse Manager, Registered Nurse **Company:** Peggy V. Helmerich Women's Center **Address:** 1120 S. Utica Avenue, Tulsa, OK 74101 United States **BUS:** Healthcare Center **P/S:** Newborn and Maternity Services Including Neonatal Intensive Care Unit, Women's Care Services, Exercise Programs, Breast Health Services, Breast Cancer Awareness and Breast Examinations **MA:** Regional **D/D/R:** Acting Nurse Manager of the Women's Care, Gynecological, Mothers and Babies Care Unit, Managing 90 Employees, Overseeing Quality Improvement Projects and Patient Safety Initiatives, practicing labor and delivery, postpartum nursing, creating procedures and policies, hiring and firing, conducting yearly staff evaluations, managing discipline issues, assisting with charts and orders, performing patient care, obtaining new equipment for units, promoting the education and orientation of staff **H/I/S:** Crocheting, Cross-Stitching, Reading **EDU:** Bachelor of Science in Nursing, University of Minnesota (1990) **A/A/S:** A1 Fetal Monitor Instructor, Association of Women's Health, Obstetric and Neonatal Nurses
Email: dawnsrn@yahoo.cox
URL: http://www.hillcrest.com

Geok H. Simpson
BUS: University **P/S:** Higher Education **EXP:** Dr. Simpson's expertise includes economics and finance. **EDU:** Ph.D., Mississippi State University; Master of Business Administration, Mississippi State University; Bachelor of Science, The University of Iowa **C/VW:** American Cancer Society; American Diabetes Association; Make-A-Wish Foundation; Smile Train; USO
Email: ghching@yahoo.com
URL: http://www.cambridgewhoswho.com

Mrs. Marva D. Simpson
Title: Senior Project Manager **Company:** Christus Health **Address:** 2600 N. Loop W., Houston, TX 77092 United States **BUS:** Nonprofit Healthcare Center **P/S:** Healthcare **MA:** National **EXP:** Mrs. Simpson's expertise includes programming, project and administrative management. **H/I/S:** Singing in the Choir, Bowling, Collecting Dolls **EDU:** Associate Degree in Computer Science, University of Illinois **A/A/S:** Information Technology Infrastructure Library; Project Management Institute
Email: marva.donelson@christushealth.org
URL: http://www.cambridgewhoswho.com

Pamela K. Simpson
Title: Recreation Program Supervisor **Company:** Leavenworth Parks and Recreation **Address:** 123 S Esplanade, Leavenworth, KS 66048 United States **BUS:** Recreation Service Provider, City Government **P/S:** Recreation, Sports, Leisure Activities **MA:** Local **D/D/R:** Aquatics International **H/I/S:** Reading, Travel **EDU:** Eastern New Mexico University, Bachelor's Degree -Spanish **A/A/S:** Lions Club, Red Cross, ABWA, USWFA, Kansas Recreation and Parks Association, National Recreation and Parks Association
Email: psimpson@firstcity.org

Tina M. Simpson-Price
Title: Attorney at Law **Company:** Hoffert, Huckabee & Weiler, PC **Address:** 537 Court Street, Reading, PA 19603 United States **BUS:** Legal Services Legal Services **P/S:** Provides Legal Council on family **MA:** Local **H/I/S:** Working Out, Shopping **EDU:** JD, Dickenson School of Law; Bachelor of Science in Human Development, Penn State **A/A/S:** PBA, American Bar Association, Pennsylvania Bar Association

Erin Sims, MBA, MISM, CBM, LIFA, DCFS
Title: Chief Executive Officer **Company:** Cameron Funding Company, LLC **Address:** 7201 Archibald Avenue, Suite 4333, Alta Loma, CA 91701 United States **BUS:** Financial Company **P/S:** Financial Services, Accounting and Strategic Planning Services **MA:** Regional **D/D/R:** Overseeing Financial Reporting, Creating Business Plans and Development, Conducting Investigation Fraud **H/I/S:** Spending Time with her Son **EDU:** Master of Information Systems Management, Keller Graduate School of Management; Master of Business Administration, West Coast University (1989) **CERTS:** Certified in Business Management; Licensed International Financial Analyst **A/A/S:** Association of Certified Fraud Examiners; IRA; Association of Professionals in Business Management; American Cash Flow Association; American Accounting Association; Diversified Cash Flow Specialist; CRTP
Email: info1@camfunding.com
URL: http://www.camfunding.com
URL: http://www.erinsims.com

Ralph W. Sims
Title: Security Manager **Company:** Dassault Falcon Jet **Address:** P.O. Box 967, Little Rock, AR 72203 United States **BUS:** Aviation Company **P/S:** Manufacturing Aircrafts **MA:** International **D/D/R:** managing 60 officers, overseeing security services and performing administrative duties, Lecturing **H/I/S:** Spending Time Outdoors **CERTS:** Certified Security Supervision Manager, International Foundation for Protection Officers **A/A/S:** Regional Vice President, American Society for Industrial Security; Air Force Security Police Association; ASIS International; International Foundation for Protection Officers **C/VW:** Boy Scouts of America; Goodwill Industries International; American Legion
Email: ralph.sims@falconjet.com
URL: http://www.dassaultfalcon.com

Jessica M. Sinaly
Title: Client Service Associate **Company:** Smith Barney **Address:** 6357 76th Street, Middle Village, NY 11379 United States **BUS:** Global, Full-Service Financial Firm **P/S:** Brokerage, Investment Banking and Asset Management Services to Corporations, Governments and Individuals Around the World **MA:** International **D/D/R:** Opening Accounts, Offering Client Services, Making Wire Transfers for Clients **H/I/S:** Dancing, Practicing Ballet, Tap and Jazz **EDU:** Bachelor of Business Arts in Finance, St. John's University (2005) **A/A/S:** Pi Lambda Phi, St. John's University
Email: jsprep824@aol.com

Asha Singh
Title: Senior Training Specialist **Company:** Customs Border Protection **Address:** 3801 Beauregard, Alexandria, VA 22311 United States **BUS:** Security Company **P/S:** Security **MA:** International **D/D/R:** Managing Training and Projects, **H/I/S:** Dancing, Jogging, Going to the Health Club **EDU:** Master's Degree in Communication and Organizational Development, Clarion State University; Master's Degree in English Literature, Earned in India **A/A/S:** Member, Project Management Institute
Email: asha.singh@associates.dhs.gov

Jacquiline R.G. Singletary
Title: Community Coordinator **Company:** New York City Housing Authority **Address:** 1553 University Avenue 174th Street, Bronx, NY 10451 United States **BUS:** Community Operations Government/Municipal **P/S:** School Age Child Care, Community Centers **MA:** Regional **D/D/R:** Child Care Professional **H/I/S:** Reading Novels, Plays Music, Arts, Off-Broadway Shows, Gospel, Sewing **EDU:** Coursework in School Age Child Care, New York (2007); Graduate, Child Care (2006); Leighman College, Bronx Community College (1982); Associate of Science in Psychology, Bronx Community College (1978); Bachelor of Science in Psychology **A/A/S:** Child Care Inc, PaceUniversity, NCAAS, HousingAuthority, Road Runners
Email: jacquiline.singletary@cwwemail.com

Diane Singleton
Title: Elementary Teacher **Company:** Baldwin-Whitehall School District **Address:** 4900 Curry Road, Pittsburgh, PA 15227 United States **BUS:** Public School District **P/S:** Education for Kindergarten through 12th-Grade Students **MA:** Local **D/D/R:** Instructing Second and Fifth-Grade Students, Teaching Social Skills, Adhering with Pennsylvania Learning Standards **H/I/S:** Walking, Camping **EDU:** Master's Degree in Elementary Education, California University (1992); Bachelor's Degree in Psychology Edinboro University **A/A/S:** Pennsylvania State Education Association; National Education Association
Email: dsingleton@bwschools.net
URL: http://www.bwschools.net

Ms. Krista M. Siniscarco
Title: Instr. Tech./Graphic Designer **Company:** Hamilton College **Dept:** Information Technology Services **Address:** 198 College Hill Road, Clinton, NY 13323 United States **BUS:** Education College **P/S:** Undergraduate Courses **MA:** Local **D/D/R:** Graphic Design, Digital Art **H/I/S:** Digital Artist **EDU:** SUNY Empire State, Bachelor of Art in Arts/Multimedia **A/A/S:** AIGA
Email: ksinisca@hamilton.edu
URL: http://www.kristasiniscarco.com
URL: http://www.hamilton.edu

Elissa Siony, Psy.D.
Title: Clinical Psychologist **Company:** Elissa Siony, Psy.D. **Address:** 45 N. Station Plaza, Suite 307, Great Neck, NY 11021 United States **BUS:** Self-Owned Private Medical Practice **P/S:** Clinical Mental Health Therapy and Psychology **MA:** Local **D/D/R:** Treating Patients with Eating Disorders, Anxiety and Depression **H/I/S:** Exercising, Reading, Spending Time with Children **EDU:** Doctor of Clinical Psychology **A/A/S:** American Psychological Association; New York State Psychological Association
Email: lissimon@aol.com

Mr. Matthew W. Siro
Title: Oncology Sales Specialist **Company:** Novartis Oncology **Address:** 6A Caldwell Avenue, Summit, NJ 07901 United States **BUS:** Pharmaceutical Sales **P/S:** Pharmaceutical Products Including Zometa **MA:** Local **D/D/R:** Updating Physicians and Continuously Calling Upon Physicians Regarding New Drugs and Products Including Zometa **H/I/S:** Displaying Electric Trains **EDU:** Master of Business Administration, Fairly Dickinson University, Teaneck, New Jersey (1997); Bachelor of Arts, Centenary College New Jersey, Hackettstown, New Jersey (1995)
Email: matthew.siro@novartis.com
URL: http://www.novartis.com

Robert W. Sisak
Title: Woodworker **Company:** F.G. Lancia Custom Woodworking **Address:** 813 N. Skinker Boulevard, Saint Louis, MO 63130 United States **BUS:** Woodworking Company **P/S:** Custom Cabinets, Woodwork **MA:** International **D/D/R:** Woodworking, Cabinet Making, Builds, Installs and Finishes Furniture **EDU:** Trade School **A/A/S:** Carpenter's Union **C/VW:** Locks for Love, Children's Hospital
Email: sisak06@netzero.net
URL: http://www.cambridgewhoswho.com

Timothy W. Sisk
Title: Project Manager **Company:** Chestnut Flats Preserve **Address:** 681 Pot Leg Road, Waynesville, NC 28785 United States **BUS:** Residential Gated Community **P/S:** Planned Community Facilities, Access to Mountains, Hiking, Biking and Equestrian Trails, Camping Pavilions, New Home Constructions **MA:** Regional **EXP:** Mr. Sisk's expertise is in project management. **D/D/R:** Coordinating All Aspects of Field Development, Hiring and Supervising Contractors, Land Surveyors and Engineers **H/I/S:** Camping **EDU:** High School Education **CERTS:** Licensed Electrical Contractor, State of North Carolina; Licensed General Contractor, State of North Carolina **A/A/S:** Jonathan Creek Volunteer Fire Department **C/VW:** Volunteer Firefighter, Waynesville Fire Department
Email: tsisk1@bellsouth.net
URL: http://www.chestnutflatspreserve.com

Collins Sita
Title: Director of Pharmacy **Company:** Fawcett Memorial Hospital, Port Charlotte **Address:** 51 Rotonda Circle, Rotonda West, FL 33947 United States **BUS:** Community Hospital **P/S:** Healthcare Services Including Pain Management, Total Parenteral Nutrition **MA:** Regional **EXP:** Mr. Sita's expertise includes pain management, oncology, clinical monitoring and total parenteral nutrition. **D/D/R:** Reviewing, Preparing Study Materials, Ordering Antibiotics Needed by the Physicians, implementing and managing pharmaceutical programs **H/I/S:** Playing Music, Spending Time at the Beach, Riding his Motorcycle, Flying Airplanes, Watching Jimmy Buffet Concerts **EDU:** Doctor of Pharmacy, Samford University **A/A/S:** The Aircraft Owners and Pilots Association; Investigational Review Board, Charlotte **C/VW:** Mote Marine Laboratory
Email: ifrflyboy@aol.com
URL: http://www.cambridgewhoswho.com

Carol M. Sivley
Title: Technical Coordinator **Company:** Integrated Concepts and Research Corporation **Address:** Huntsville, AL United States **BUS:** Diversified Technical and Management Services Company **P/S:** Information Technology, Advanced Vehicle Technology, Aerospace, Engineering and Transportation Infrastructure **MA:** International **D/D/R:** Working to Launch Vehicle for NASA, Resources Determining How Many People for Project and Budget, Keeping Up with Presentations, Operating Web Meetings **H/I/S:** Raising Dogs **EDU:** Master of Business Administration in Management, The University of Alabama (2006); Bachelor's Degree in English and Secondary Education (1976) **A/A/S:** Phi Kappa Phi Society
Email: csivley@nehp.net
URL: http://www.icrcsolutions.com

Kristen A. Skaricich
Title: Teacher **Company:** Champion Local Schools **Address:** 5759 Mahoning Avenue N.W., Warren, OH 44483 United States **BUS:** School District **P/S:** Education **MA:** Local **D/D/R:** Sixth-Grade Mathematics. Wrote 'Math Attacks with Songs, Stories and Funky Raps' to help students have fun while learning concepts in mathematics, Tutors mathematics in her community and after school. The after school mathematics tutorial helps students about to take their state achievement test. **H/I/S:** Reading, Working Out, Running, Cooking **EDU:** Master of Education in Mathematics, Grades 6-8, Walden University (2007) **A/A/S:** National Education Association; Ohio Education Association; North Eastern Ohio Education Association; Cheerleading Advisor for Champion Middle School **A/H:** Tribute Chronical Teacher Award (2007) **C/VW:** Believers Christian Fellowship
Email: kristen.skaricich@neomin.org
URL: http://www.champion.k12.oh.us

Patricia E. Skelton
Title: Fifth-Grade Teacher **Company:** Opelika City Schools **Address:** 8 Morris Avenue, Opelika, AL 36801 United States **BUS:** School System **P/S:** Primary and Secondary Education **MA:** Regional **D/D/R:** Teaching Self-Contained Classes in All Subjects, Hosting an Advanced Reading Group **H/I/S:** Reading, Singing, Exercising **EDU:** Bachelor of Science in Elementary Education, Auburn University (1995); National Board Certification (2006) **A/A/S:** National Education Association; Alabama Education Association
Email: patricia.skelton@opelikaschools.org
URL: http://www.opelikaschools.org/

Mrs. Melissa B. Skinner
Title: Physician Assistant, Certified **Company:** Vaidhyaa Paediatrix, PLLC **Address:** P.O. Box 748, Weston, WV 26452 United States **BUS:** Healthcare **P/S:** Medical Services **MA:** Local **D/D/R:** Pediatrics, Seeing Patients, Diagnostics, Treatment, Consultations **H/I/S:** Running, Movies **EDU:** Master's Degree in Science, Marietta College (2006); Bachelor of Arts Degree in Exercise Physiology, West Virginia University (2004) **A/A/S:** American Academy of Physician Assistants
Email: melissabrookeskinner@hotmail.com
URL: http://www.cambridgewhoswho.com

Sarah Skipper
Title: Head Secretary **Company:** Garfield Elementary School **Address:** 121 W. Walnut Street, Garden City, KS 67846 United States **BUS:** Elementary School **P/S:** Primary Education **MA:** Local **D/D/R:** Managing Time Clocks, Assisting the Principal, Ordering Supplies, Keeping the Office in Order, performing administrative tasks and budgeting **H/I/S:** Reading, Quilting, Spending Time with her Children **EDU:** Pursuing Bachelor's Degree, University of Missouri-Kansas City; Coursework in Piano Performance, Bethel College **A/A/S:** GCAOP **C/VW:** Local Church
Email: sskipper@gckschools.com
URL: http://www.gckschools.com

Mr. Matthew B. Skoog
Title: Owner **Company:** e-MotionMedia, Inc. **Address:** 715 Latteridge Drive, Austin, TX 78748 United States **BUS:** Web Design Corporation **P/S:** Multimedia, Web and Print Design **MA:** National **D/D/R:** Performing Flash Design and Development Services, Layouts and Web Pages **H/I/S:** Enjoying All Sports **EDU:** Associate Degree in Multimedia Design, Art Institute of Houston (2002)
Email: mskoog@em2group.com
URL: http://www.em2group.com

Constance C. Slack, CISA, CBM
Title: Senior Information Systems Auditor **Company:** Ingram Micro, Inc. **Address:** 1600 E. Saint Andrew Place, Santa Ana, CA 92705 United States **BUS:** Distribution Company **P/S:** Distributing Computer Products and System Solutions **MA:** International **D/D/R:** Auditing, Overseeing Risk Management, Information Technology Governance **H/I/S:** Visiting Spas **EDU:** Bachelor's Degree in Mathematics, California State University; Certified Business Manager **A/A/S:** Information Systems Audit and Control Association; Association of Professionals in Business Management **C/VW:** Society for the Prevention of Cruelty to Animals, Los Angeles Philharmonic, Science Museum
Email: cslack@gmail.com

Tiffany Slade
Title: Homemaker **Company:** Visiting Nurse Association of Central Connecticut **Address:** 122 Rossi Drive, Bristol, CT 06010 United States **BUS:** Nurses Association **P/S:** Home Health Nursing Aides **MA:** Local **EXP:** Ms. Slade's expertise is in home healthcare nursing. **H/I/S:** Playing the Trombone and Baritone, Singing **EDU:** Bachelor's Degree in Science and Marketing, Central Connecticut State University (2006) **C/VW:** National Museum of Women in the Arts; Americans for the Arts Action Fund
Email: lsladetia@yahoo.com
URL: http://www.vnacc.org

Jacob M. Slania
Title: Attorney Partner **Company:** Kirby Noonan Lance and Hoge, LLP **Address:** 600 W. Broadway, Suite 1100, San Diego, CA 92101 United States **BUS:** Law Firm **P/S:** Civil Litigation Attorney **MA:** Local **D/D/R:** Practicing Probate Litigation, Civil Litigation **H/I/S:** Golfing, Reading, Spending Time at the Beach **EDU:** JD (1998); Bachelor of Arts, University of San Diego (1995) **A/A/S:** Association of Business Trial Lawyers; American Trial Lawyers Association; California Bar Association; Advisory Board of Second Chance San Diego **C/VW:** Second Chance Sheltie Rescue; Breast Cancer Awareness Program, Leukemia Society; Little League
Email: jslania@knlh.com
URL: http://www.cambridgewhoswho.com

Timothy J. Slate
Title: Manager of Application Development **Company:** C&S Wholesale Grocers **Address:** 10 Poitical Avenue, Keene, VT 03431 United States **BUS:** Wholesale Grocery Distributor **P/S:** Food **MA:** National **D/D/R:** Mainframe and Mid Range Application Development, Deployment and Support **H/I/S:** Playing Poker, Writing Screenplays **EDU:** Associate Degree in Computer Science, Vermont Technical College **A/A/S:** Institute of Certified Professional Managers
Email: wjstarder@verizon.net
URL: http://www.cswg.com

Denise M. Slater
Title: enterprise Fleet Manager **Company:** Textron, Inc. **Address:** 40 Westminster Street, Providence, RI 02903 United States **BUS:** Multi-Industry Company **P/S:** Multi Services **MA:** International **D/D/R:** Fleet Management **EDU:** Certification in Auto and Diesel Mechanics, Trade School (1988); High School Diploma **A/A/S:** National Association of Fleet Administrators **C/VW:** Mentoring Children
Email: dslater@textron.com
Email: dslater@textcon.com
URL: http://www.textcon.com

Deborah J. Slattery
Title: Teacher **Company:** Adrian R-III Schools **Address:** P.O. Box 98, Adrian, MO 64720 United States **BUS:** Elementary School **P/S:** Education **MA:** Local **D/D/R:** Teaching Social Studies and Communication Arts **H/I/S:** Reading, Writing Poetry, Creating Stories, Painting **EDU:** Master of Science in Education, Curriculum and Instruction, Missouri State University **A/A/S:** Certified Teacher Association; President, Missouri State Teachers Association; Who's Who Among Elementary Teachers; Sponsor, Future Teachers of America **A/H:** Teacher of the Year (1999); Veterans of Foreign Wars Citizenship Education Award (2006) **C/VW:** Special Olympics, American Cancer Society, Veterans of Foreign Wars
Email: slattery@adrian.k12.mo.us
URL: http://www.cambridgewhoswho.com

Michelle L. Slawiak
Title: Development and Special Event Associate **Company:** Buffalo Philharmonic Orchestra **Address:** 499 Franklin Street, Buffalo, NY 14202 United States **BUS:** Entrainment Company **P/S:** Entertainment Including Event Management Services **MA:** National **D/D/R:** overseeing project development **H/I/S:** Wine Tasting **EDU:** Master's Degree **A/A/S:** Buffalo Niagara Event Professionals Network; Miscellaneous Book Club
Email: msiawiak@bpo.org
URL: http://www.bpo.org

Gail Patricia Sledge
Title: Fund Administrator **Company:** Lord Abbett & Co. **Address:** 90 Hudson Street, Jersey City, NJ 07302 United States **BUS:** Investment Firm **P/S:** Investment Management and Strategic Growth for Clients' Assets **MA:** Statewide **D/D/R:** Handling 25 Mutual Funds, Checking Each Clients' Portfolio for Accuracy **H/I/S:** Exercising **EDU:** Bachelor of Arts in Economics, Montclair State University (1997)
Email: gps4772@aol.com

Emily Slicer-Smith
Title: Human Resources Generalist **Company:** The College of William & Mary **Address:** 303 Richmond Road, Williamsburg, VA 23185 United States **BUS:** College **P/S:** Education **MA:** National **D/D/R:** Human Resources Recruitment, Employee Relations **H/I/S:** Reading, Gardening, Taking Weekend Trips, Watching Football **EDU:** Bachelor of Arts in History, Christopher Newport University; Certified by the Society for Human Resource Managers **A/A/S:** Society for Human Resource Management **C/VW:** Boy Scouts of America
Email: emslic@wm.edu
URL: http://www.wm.edu

Brenda L. Sloan
Title: CEO **Company:** Brenda's Marketing, Inc **Address:** 2800 Watkinstown Road, Raleigh, NC 27616 United States **BUS:** Advertising Marketing **P/S:** Sampling Products, setting up mystery shoppers for restaurants, Hotels, Trade Shows and Character Role Play, Survey costumer base and Figure Demographics **MA:** International **D/D/R:** Marketing and Advertising **H/I/S:** Traveling, Reading, Time with her two sons **EDU:** Associate of Science in Business Management, Daneville Community College **A/A/S:** BBB, NADC
Email: brendasmarketing@aol.com

Mikhail Slobodskoi, PT, Ph.D.
Title: Ph.D., Physical Therapist **Company:** Infinity of Care, Inc **Address:** 2 Park Lane, Suite 104, Feasterville, PA 19053 United States **BUS:** Physical Therapy Facility **P/S:** Physical Therapy/Sports Rehabilitation **MA:** Regional **D/D/R:** Physical Therapy **H/I/S:** Travel, Reading **EDU:** Ph.D., Tashkent Medical School, Russia **CERTS:** Certified Physical Therapist **A/A/S:** Cystic Fibrosis Association
Email: service@infinityofcare.com

Rich Slugoski
Title: Human Resources Administrator **Company:** William Morris Agency, LLC **Dept:** Human Resources Department **Address:** 1 William Morris Place, Beverly Hills, CA 90212 United States **BUS:** Talent Agency **P/S:** Represents Literary-Gifted and Talented People **MA:** International **D/D/R:** Interacting with People, utilizing his communication skills **H/I/S:** Watching Movies, Traveling, Spending Time with his Friends and Family, Hiking, Swimming, Exercising **EDU:** High School Diploma
Email: richslugo@yahoo.com

Heather Small
Title: Certified Massage Therapist **Company:** Maharishi Ayur Veda Medical Center **Address:** 679 George Hill Road, Lancaster, MA 01523 United States **BUS:** Health Spa **P/S:** Authentic Ayurvedic Treatments **MA:** Local **EXP:** Ms. Small's expertise includes relaxation and Thai massage with ayurvedic treatments. **D/D/R:** Training New Technicians, Purchasing Orders, Consulting **H/I/S:** Spending Time with her Family **CERTS:** Certified Massage Therapist, The Salter School of Massage Therapy **A/A/S:** Tracy Watson Cancer Care Research; American Massage Therapy Association **C/VW:** National Multiple Sclerosis Society
Email: moonflowermassage@yahoo.com
URL: http://www.lancasterhealth.com
URL: http://www.worcester.globalcountry.net

Brian K. Smallwood
Title: President **Company:** B.K. Enterprises of Southwest Florida, Inc. **Address:** 4104 N.W. 12th Street, Cape Coral, FL 33993 United States **BUS:** Building and Remodeling Company **P/S:** Real Estate **MA:** Regional **D/D/R:** Building and Investment Real Estate **H/I/S:** Traveling, Fishing **EDU:** High School Education **A/A/S:** Florida Home Builders Association;National Association of Realtors **A/H:** Double Diamond Achiever Award (2004-2006) **C/VW:** National Cancer Association, Little League
Email: briansmallwoodrealtor@yahoo.com

Donna W. Smart
Title: Pharmacist **Company:** Walgreens, Inc. **Address:** 3005 Emmorton Road, Abingdon, MD 21009 United States **BUS:** Retail Pharmacy **P/S:** Retail Products, Pharmacy **MA:** National **D/D/R:** Counseling Patients, Customer Service, Filling Prescriptions, Chemist, Water Treatment Plant **H/I/S:** Traveling, Learning French and Spanish Cultures **EDU:** Doctor of Pharmacy, University of Maryland; Bachelor of Science in Chemistry, University of West Indies, Trinidad; Licensed Real Estate Sales Person **A/A/S:** American Pharmacist Association
Email: sdmsmart1@aol.com
URL: http://www.dsmart.qhealthbeauty.com

Mr. Ryan Preston Smart
Title: 44B/Metal Worker **Company:** BC 47th BSB **Address:** 2507 Skeel Street, Brighton, CO 80601 United States **BUS:** Army National Guard Military Branch of the U.S. Government **P/S:** Manufacturing, Production, Machinery **MA:** National **D/D/R:** Performing Welding, Working with Metals **H/I/S:** Reading History, Going to the Beach **EDU:** Attending Baker University; Graduate, Aberdeen Metal School

Linda Smedshammer
Title: Executive Director **Company:** Suncatcher Therapeutic Riding Academy **Address:** P.O. Box 3975, Rapid City, SD 57709 United States **BUS:** Nonprofit Organization **P/S:** Equine Facilitated Therapy, Special Olympic Equestrian Training, Improvement of Cognitive Abilities, Enhancement of Social Interaction and Spiritual Services **MA:** Regional **D/D/R:** training and breeding horses, instructing therapeutic riding for children and individuals with disabilities **H/I/S:** Landscaping, Gardening, Horseback Riding **CERTS:** Certified Therapeutic Riding Instructor **A/A/S:** North American Riding for the Handicapped Association
Email: suncatchertra@aol.com
URL: http://www.suncatchertra.org

Jo Anne Smiley
Title: 1) Mayor 2) Owner **Company:** 1) City of Clarksville, Missouri 2) B.T. Dove Antiques & Gifts **Address:** Clarksville, MO 63336 United States **BUS:** 1) Government Organization 2) Retail Store **P/S:** 1) Administration of a Cultural City Amass with Artisans, Potters, Glass Blowers, Jewelry Designers, Antique Dealers, Furniture Makers and Specialty Craftsmen 2) Antiques and Gifts **MA:** Regional **EXP:** Ms. Smiley's expertise is in administration. **D/D/R:** Rebuilding the Town after Storm, Developing the Town with latest Technology, Ensuring Customer Service, Acquiring Inventory, selling fine antiques and gifts **H/I/S:** Playing Piano, Listening to Music, Singing in the Choir **EDU:** Bachelor of Music in Music Education, Southern Methodist University (1962) **A/A/S:** Department of Tourism; Department of Natural Resources; Missouri Municipal League; P.E.O. International **C/VW:** Lions Club
Email: jsmiley@tcip.net
URL: http://www.clarksvillemo.us

Amber K. Smith
Title: President, Owner **Company:** Elite Business Administration **Address:** 1624 Ninth Street N.W., Cedar Rapids, IA 52405 United States **BUS:** Consulting Company **P/S:** Small Business Administration **MA:** National **D/D/R:** Assisting Small Businesses with Bookkeeping, Management, Marketing, Budgeting, Debt Management, Hiring, Training, Organization, Automation, Event Planning **H/I/S:** Gardening, Shopping, Training her Dog **EDU:** Certified in Business Management, Kirkwood College **A/A/S:** Professional Women's Network **C/VW:** The Humane Society; Volunteer, Local Senior Citizen Groups
Email: eliteba@yahoo.com

Angela S. Smith
Title: Senior Vice President, Director of Check Education **Company:** PaymentsNation **Address:** P.O. Box 47085, Windsor Mill, MD 21244 United States **BUS:** Financial Institution **P/S:** Financial Education **MA:** National **D/D/R:** Conducting Training Program for Financial Institutions, Overseeing Process and Regulations, Ensuring Customer Satisfaction **H/I/S:** Singing, Spending Time with her Granddaughter **EDU:** Bachelor of Science in Organizational Management, Columbia Union College, Takoma Park, MD; Associate of Arts in Computer Studies; Coursework in Christian Counseling in Mentoring; Coursework, Merlin Banking School; Coursework, National Payments Institute **CERTS:** Certified Pastoral Counselor Specializing in Women's Issues; Accredited ACH Professional **A/A/S:** On the Steering Committee for the Electronic Check Council; Board of Regions for the National Payment Institute; Eccho Operations Committee **C/VW:** Local Church
Email: angie.smith@paymentsnation.com
URL: http://www.paymentsnation.com

Arloa I. Smith
Title: Retired Insurance Agent **Company:** The Abott & Filmore Agency, Inc. **Address:** 105 W Main Street, Stockbridge, MI 49285 United States **BUS:** Financial Insurance **P/S:** Offering Insurance Services **MA:** International **D/D/R:** Office Management, Procedure **H/I/S:** Gardening, Reading, Time with her grand daughters **EDU:** Coursework in Elementary Education, Eastern Michigan University **CERTS:** Licensed in Property and Casualty Insurance, States of MI and IN **A/A/S:** Church Garden Club

Mr. Barry C. Smith
Title: Owner, Luthier **Company:** String Haven Luthiery and Woodworks **Address:** 1640 S.W. Broadway Drive, Portland, OR 97201 United States **BUS:** Manufacturing Business **P/S:** Woodworking, Luthiery, Stringed Musical Instruments, Acoustic Guitars, Ukuleles and Dulcimers **MA:** Regional **D/D/R:** Building Guitars and Stringed Musical Instruments **H/I/S:** Practicing Martial Arts, Oil Painting **EDU:** Coursework, Junior College
URL: http://www.cambridgewhoswho.com

Bonnie Hurd Smith
Title: Founder, Chief Executive Officer **Company:** Hurd Smith Communications **Address:** 15 Winter Street, Apartment 2, Salem, MA 01970 United States **BUS:** Public Relation Company **P/S:** Media Relations, Project and Organizational Management **MA:** Local **D/D/R:** Performing Administrative Duties, Being Creative, Administrative and Public Relations **H/I/S:** Attending Museums, Visiting Historic houses, Walking, Spending Time Outdoors, Gardening, Exploring **EDU:** Master's Degree in Communications Management, Simmons College, Boston (1993) **A/A/S:** New England Museum Association; North of Boston Convention and Visitors Bureau; Commissioner, Essex National Heritage Commission
Email: bonnie@hurdsmith.com
URL: http://www.hurdsmith.com

Bruce A. Smith
Title: Principal **Company:** Smith Sales Group, LLC **Address:** 259 Kensington Road, River Edge, NJ 07661 United States **BUS:** Book Sales and Marketing Company **P/S:** Book Sales, Marketing **MA:** Regional **D/D/R:** Selling Books to Bookstores and Museum Stores **H/I/S:** Golf, Coaching his Daughter's Softball Team, Gardening **EDU:** Bachelor of Arts in Linguistics, CUNY Queens College **A/A/S:** Association of Book Travelers
Email: basmith428@optonline.net

Carol K. Smith
Title: Registered Nurse, Case Manager **Company:** Action Healthcare Management Services **Address:** 6245 N. 24th Parkway, Suite 112, Phoenix, AZ 85016 United States **BUS:** Healthcare Management Company **P/S:** Healthcare Management Services **MA:** National **D/D/R:** managing telephone cases, coordinating and evaluating management programs **EDU:** Master of Science in Nursing, Arizona State University (1994); Bachelor of Science in Nursing, Thomas Jefferson University (1980) **CERTS:** Certified Case Manager, American Nurses Credentialing Center (2000) **A/A/S:** Arizona Nurses Association; Content Expert Panel; Case Management Society of America; American Nurses Credentialing Center; American Nurses Association
Email: ckingsmith@hughes.net

Catherine M. Smith
Title: Science Teacher **Company:** New Canaan High School **Address:** 11 Farm Road, New Canaan, CT 06840 United States **BUS:** High School **P/S:** Education **MA:** Local **D/D/R:** teaching biology, marine science, chemistry and medical technology **H/I/S:** Car Racing, Training Dogs **EDU:** Master of Business Administration, Sacred Heart University (1994); Bachelor of Medical Technology, University of Bridgeport (1980) **A/A/S:** Connecticut Science Teachers Association; National Science Teachers Association
Email: catherine.smith@newcanaan.k12.ct.us

Cheryl K. Smith
Title: Owner/Manager **Company:** Total Home Care Services **Address:** 6709 Bankert Road, Ava, NY 13303 United States **BUS:** Home Care Service Provider **P/S:** Cleaning, Remodeling, in Home Pet Care **MA:** Local **D/D/R:** Coordinating Color and Style **H/I/S:** Home Time **EDU:** High School Graduate
Email: smitty842@verizon.net

Corinne M. Smith
Title: Owner and Designer **Company:** Panacea Event Floral Design **Address:** 2894 Shadowbrook Lane, San Luis Obispo, CA 93405 United States **BUS:** Retail, Floral Design **P/S:** Gifts and Favors for Events **MA:** National **D/D/R:** Design **H/I/S:** Amateur Photography, Writing, Traveling **EDU:** Bachelor of Science, Marketing, Walla Walla College **A/A/S:** Chamber of Commerce; Society of American Florists; Central Coast Wedding Professionals
Email: cmspanacea@msn.com
URL: http://www.panaceaflowers.com

David R. Smith
Title: Head Women's Basketball Coach **Company:** Bellarmine University **Address:** 2001 Newburg Road, Louisville, KY 40205 United States **BUS:** University **P/S:** Education **MA:** Local **D/D/R:** Coaching Basketball **H/I/S:** Collecting Sports Memorabilia **EDU:** Master's Degree in Health and Physical Education, Indiana State University(1971); Bachelor of Science in Health and Physical Education, Indiana State University(1969) **A/A/S:** Women's Basketball Coaches Association; National Association of Basketball Coaches; Kiwanis Club; Metrobon of Louisville; Optimist Club of Louisville **C/VW:** Mom's Closet
Email: dsmith@bellarmine.edu
URL: http://www.bellarmine.edu

Denise N. Smith
Title: Vice President, Emerging Markets Business Development Manager **Company:** JP Morgan Chase Bank **Address:** 10 S. Dearborn Street, Chicago, IL 60603 United States **BUS:** Bank **P/S:** Financial Services **MA:** International **D/D/R:** Emerging Markets Business Development, Sales **EDU:** Master of Public Administration, Roosevelt University
Email: denise.n.smith@chase.com
URL: http://www.chase.com

Dionne R. Smith
Title: Pharmacy Manager **Company:** Walgreens **Address:** 800 Wilmont Road, Deerfield, IL 60613 United States **BUS:** Retail Pharmacy **P/S:** Pharmaceuticals **MA:** National **D/D/R:** Overseeing Pharmacy **H/I/S:** Reading, Shopping **EDU:** Doctor of Pharmacy, Xavier University of Louisiana **C/VW:** Kera.org
Email: pharmdee@hotmail.com

Elizabeth A. Smith
Title: Licensed Practical Nurse, Certified Pharmacy Technician **Company:** Boydton Healthcare on the Square **Address:** 380 Washington Street, Boydton, VA 23917 United States **BUS:** Independent Healthcare Facility **P/S:** Healthcare **MA:** Local **D/D/R:** Patient Care, Pharmacy **H/I/S:** Reading, Skeet Shooting, Refinishing Furniture **EDU:** Licensed Practical Nurse, Southside Community College; Certified Pharmacy Technician **A/A/S:** Alpha Beta **A/H:** Rescue Volunteer of the Year; Community Leader of the Year **C/VW:** Volunteer Rescue Squad
Email: epseas2@wmconnect.com

Mr. Geoffrey L. Smith
Title: Artist, Gallery Owner **Company:** Aries East Gallery **Address:** 2805 Main Street, Brewster, MA 02631 United States **BUS:** Private Gallery Committed to Excellence in the Art Industry **P/S:** Artwork, Pictures and Sculpture Sales, Paintings **MA:** National **D/D/R:** Running the Art Gallery, Painting Award Winning Oil Paintings, Landscapes and Sports-Themed Works, Overseeing a Full Service Art Gallery Including Selling Paintings, Sculptures and Pictures, Creating Art Shows and Exhibits **H/I/S:** Skiing, Golfing, Enjoying Water Sports and Any Boating Sports **EDU:** Bachelor of Arts in American Literature and Art, University of New Hampshire (1972) **A/A/S:** Former Member, Copley Society of Boston; Cape Cod Art Association; Boston Museum of Fine Art; Public Speaking Locally
Email: rebecca.smith114@verizon.net
URL: http://www.cambridgewhoswho.com

Gloria D. Smith
Title: Director **Company:** Minority Health Coalition of South Hampton Roads, Inc. **Address:** 5215 Colley Avenue, Norfolk, VA 23508 United States **BUS:** Health Education Center **P/S:** Community Health Education **MA:** Local **D/D/R:** Organizational Duties fundraising; grant writing **H/I/S:** Reading, Spending Time with her Grandchildren **A/A/S:** American Heart Association; American Cancer Association **C/VW:** Church; District President, Women's Ministry
Email: gdrs39@cavtel.com

Heather Malynne Smith
Title: Physical Therapist **Company:** Claiborne County Hospital, Outpatient Rehabilitation Center **Address:** 1750 Old Knoxville, Tazewell, TN 37879 United States **BUS:** Hospital **P/S:** Healthcare, Rehabilitation, Orthopedic Care, Wound Care, Lyphedema Physical Therapy **MA:** Regional **D/D/R:** Orthopedic and Manual Therapy **H/I/S:** Riding her Motorcycle, Sports **EDU:** Pursuing Certification in Manual Therapy, University of St. Augustine; Master's Degree in Physical Therapy, University of Tennessee, Health Sciences Center; Associate of Science, Walter State Community College (1998) **A/A/S:** American Physical Therapy Association; Phi Theta Kappa; Epsilon Nu Eta **C/VW:** East Tennessee Children's Hospital
Email: volgirl_pt@yahoo.com
URL: http://www.cambridgewhoswho.com

Jaclyn Marie Smith
Title: Clinical Coordinator **Company:** The Center for Urban Community Services **Address:** 530 W. 178th Street, New York, NY 10033 United States **BUS:** Social Services Organization **P/S:** Social Services, Permanent Housing for Low-Income Families **MA:** Local **D/D/R:** Mental Health, Supportive Housing **H/I/S:** Reading **EDU:** Master of Social Work, Columbia University
Email: jsmith@cucs.org
URL: http://www.cambridgewhoswho.com

Janet M. Smith
Title: Title Agent-Owner **Company:** Community Title Agency **Address:** 1115 Canton Road N.W., Suite A-1, Carrollton, OH 44615 United States **BUS:** Real Estate Insurance **P/S:** Real Estate Title Insurance **MA:** Local **H/I/S:** Knitting, Needlepoint, Schooling, Jewelry, Crafts **EDU:** Associates in Fine Arts **A/A/S:** Ohio Land Title Association, American Land Title Association, Chamber of Commerce
Email: janet@community-title.net
URL: http://www.community-title.net

John H. Smith
Title: Owner **Company:** Smith's Painting and Construction, Inc. **Address:** 624 Cameron Road, Jesup, GA 31545 United States **BUS:** Contracting Company **P/S:** Painting, Construction **MA:** Local **D/D/R:** Business Operations **H/I/S:** Traveling **EDU:** Industry-Related Training and Experience **A/A/S:** Industry-Related Affiliations **C/VW:** American Cancer Society, Local Police and Fire Departments
Email: smiths01@bellsouth.net
URL: http://www.cambridgewhoswho.com

Kara L. Smith
Title: President **Company:** Karasma Media **Address:** 15 W. 120Th Street, Apartment 5, New York, NY 10027 United States **BUS:** Publicity and Public Relations **P/S:** Regional **MA:** National **D/D/R:** New Media Marketing Campaigns **H/I/S:** Running, Cooking, Singing. Film and Music **EDU:** Master of Arts in Media, The New School **A/A/S:** PRSA, New York Women in Communications
Email: Karasma@karasmamedia.com
URL: http://www.karasmamedia.com

Katharine R. Smith
Title: Education Coordinator **Company:** Pee Dee Regional EMS, Inc. **Address:** 1314 W. Darlington Street, Florence, SC 29501 United States **BUS:** EMS Training School **P/S:** Pre-Hospital and Hospital Emergency Medical Service Training **MA:** Regional **D/D/R:** Teaching American Heart Association Courses, Paramedic Instruction **H/I/S:** Volunteering, Spending Time with her Family **EDU:** Associate of Science in Emergency Medicine, Florence-Darlington Technical College (2006) **A/A/S:** National Registry of Emergency Medical Technicians; South Carolina Emergency Medical Services Association **C/VW:** Timmonsville Rescue Squad; West Florence Rural Volunteer Fire Department
Email: ksmith@pdrems.com
URL: http://www.pdrems.com

Kenneth Smith Jr.
Title: GSM **Company:** KBMT-TV **Address:** 512 Interstate 10, Beaumont, TX 77702 United States **BUS:** Television Station **P/S:** Television Station **MA:** National **D/D/R:** Sales Manager **H/I/S:** Studying Astronomy **EDU:** Bachelor of Science in Mass Communications, La Mar University **A/A/S:** NAB; TVB; ASTRA **C/VW:** Church
Email: ksmith@kbmt12.com
URL: http://www.kbmt12.com

Kirby N. Smith, DVM, MSPH
Title: Senior Clinical Writer II **Company:** Wyeth Pharmaceuticals **Address:** 45 Sheridan Street, Woburn, MA 01801 United States **BUS:** Pharmaceutical Company **P/S:** Over-the-Counter Pharmaceutical Products, Prescription Medications, Animal Health Products, Therapy Areas, Research and Clinical Trials **MA:** International **D/D/R:** Clinical Research Writing, Preparing Documents for International Regulatory Agencies **H/I/S:** Hiking, River Rafting, Skiing **EDU:** Doctor of Veterinary Medicine, Washington State University (1977); Master of Science in Public Health **A/A/S:** New England Chapter, Mensa International; Drug Information Association; American Medical Writers Association
Email: kirbysmith45@comcast.net
URL: http://www.wyeth.com

Laura D. Smith
Title: OTR **Company:** Rehab Care **Address:** 210 Hickory Road, Bullard, TX 75757 United States **BUS:** Healthcare Rehab **P/S:** Rehabilitation, Nursing Facility **MA:** Local **D/D/R:** Geriatrics **H/I/S:** Camping, Kayaking **EDU:** Texas Womens University, Bachelor of Arts of Science
Email: deedyotr@yahoo.com

Lisa A. Smith
Title: Administrative Nursing Supervisor **Company:** Banner Good Samaritan Medical Center **Address:** 1111 E. McDowell Road, Phoenix, AZ 85006 United States **BUS:** Medical Center **P/S:** Healthcare **MA:** Regional **EXP:** Ms. Smith's expertise is in disaster management. **D/D/R:** Overseeing Leadership and Staff Development Programs **H/I/S:** Reading, Walking, Skiing **EDU:** Bachelor of Science in Nursing, CUNY College of Staten Island **A/A/S:** American Nurses Association **C/VW:** The Jesus Film Project; Happiness Foundation
Email: lisa.smith@bannerhealth.com

Louise A. Smith
Title: Registered Nurse **Company:** Robert Wood Johnson University Hospital **Address:** 1 Hamilton Health Place, Hamilton, NJ 08690 United States **BUS:** University Hospital **P/S:** Healthcare **MA:** Local **D/D/R:** Cardiac Nursing **H/I/S:** Reading, Sewing, Walking **CERTS:** Registered Nurse, St. Helier School of Nursing, England **C/VW:** Local Church
Email: louisern@verizon.net
URL: http://www.cambridgewhoswho.com

Mamie L. Smith
Title: Middle School Educator **Company:** Chicago Public Schools **Address:** 3232 Chestnut Drive, Flossmoor, IL 60422 United States **BUS:** Outstanding Urban Public School System **P/S:** Educating Students in Prekindergarten through 12th-Grades in All Core Subjects Including Special Education, Physical Education, Gifted Programs and After-School Programs **MA:** Regional **D/D/R:** Teaching Sixth-Grade Students with a Focus on Language Arts and Writing, Coordinating Programs, Staff Development, Developing Young Minds in Preparation for Secondary Education and Life-Long Growth and Learning, Overseeing Staff Development, Speaking Motivationally, Writing Grants, Conducting Program Evaluations, Mentoring Teachers, Educational Consulting., School Improvement Planning, Program Evaluation **H/I/S:** Traveling, Reading, Collecting Blue and White China **EDU:** Pursuing a Doctorate Degree, Master's Degree in Reading and Curriculum, Chicago State University (1981); Bachelor's Degree in Elementary Education, Northern Illinois University (1972) **CERTS:** Real Estate License **A/A/S:** Grant Recipient; Union Delegate Representative; Alpha Phi Alpha; United Negro College Board; Former Member, Toastmasters International; Alpha Kappa Alpha Sorority **A/H:** Top Ladies of Distinction Award
Email: smithflssmr@aol.com

Marilyn P. Smith
Title: Director **Company:** Woodbridge Community Church **Dept:** Children's Ministries **Address:** 5000 Barranca Parkway, Irvine, CA 92604 United States **BUS:** Community Church **P/S:** Personal Counseling, Spiritual Growth, Foundations of Scripture, Biblical Instruction **MA:** Local **D/D/R:** Overseeing Children and Family Ministries, Paid and Volunteer Teachers, Selecting, Writing and Distributing Curriculum for Children's Programs, Acting as a Liaison between Church and Community **H/I/S:** Reading, Traveling **EDU:** Master's Degree in Children and Family Ministry, Bethel University Seminary; Bachelor of Social Science in Social Work **A/A/S:** Community Chamber Music Association; THINK Together: Mentor ME Ministries; Children's Christian Ministry Association
Email: msmith@woodbridgechurch.org
URL: http://www.woodbridgechurch.org

Mary P. Smith
Title: Organizer, Ex-Officio Director **Company:** Pettis Memorial CME Church Day Care and Learning Center **Address:** 121 S. Coanza Street, West Helena, AR 72390 United States **BUS:** Religious-Affiliated Day Care **P/S:** Education **MA:** Local **D/D/R:** Nurturing and Training Children **H/I/S:** Reading, Visiting the Elderly in Nursing Homes and Hospitals **EDU:** Master's Degree in Education, University of Arkansas; Bachelor of Science in Mathematics, Jackson State University **A/A/S:** American Council of Educators International; National Council of Teachers of Mathematics **C/VW:** CME Day Care
Email: mpsmith1937@sbcglobal.net
URL: http://www.cambridgewhoswho.com

Michael L. Smith
Title: Owner **Company:** M.L. Smith Blacksmithing, LLC **Address:** N. 4960 Highway TT, Columbus, WI 53925 United States **BUS:** Sole Proprietorship **P/S:** Blacksmith Services Including Ironwork **MA:** Regional **EXP:** Mr. Smith's expertise is in hand-forged railing sales. **H/I/S:** Camping, Caring for Bees and Pigeons **EDU:** Diploma, Beaver Dam High School **A/A/S:** State Pigeon Association
Email: michaell.smith@cwwemail.com
URL: http://www.mlsmithblacksmithing.com

Michelle M. Smith, Pharm.D., BCPS
Title: Regional Manager, Clinical Pharmacy Services **Company:** Adventist Midwest Health **Address:** 120 N. Oak Street, Hinsdale, IL 60521 United States **BUS:** Largest Nonprofit Protestant Healthcare Provider in the Nation **P/S:** Pharmacy Services in a Hospital Setting **MA:** National **D/D/R:** Overseeing Pharmaceutical Therapy, Performing Clinical Services with Physicians and Nurses on the Clinical Committee, Putting CPOE in Practice, Reviewing Procedures with Physicians to Update Practices in Prescribing Practices **H/I/S:** Cooking, Walking, Dancing, Bicycling **EDU:** Pharm.D. in Pharmacy, University of Illinois at Chicago (1991); Bachelor of Science in Pharmacy, University of Iowa (1987) **A/A/S:** American Society of Health-System Pharmacists
Email: michelle.smith@ahss.org
URL: http://www.ahss.org

Mr. Nathan S. Smith
Title: Lead Health Physics Supervisor **Company:** New World Environmental, Inc. dba New World Technology **Address:** 448 Commerce Way, Livermore, CA 94551 United States **BUS:** Native American-owned Small Disadvantaged Business **P/S:** Radioactive Waste Management, Decontamination, Radioactive and Hazardous Site Remediation, Waste Brokerage, and Unexploded Ordnance Range Decontamination Services **MA:** Regional **D/D/R:** Offering Radiological Protection, Environmental Remediation and Radioactive Safety **H/I/S:** Managing Money **EDU:** College Coursework
Email: nathans@newworld.org
URL: http://www.newworld.org

Rev. Philip W. Smith
Title: Pastor **Company:** IDA Baptist Church **Address:** 7656 FM 697, Sherman, TX 75090 United States **BUS:** Local Church **P/S:** Religion and Spiritual Services **MA:** Texas **D/D/R:** Equipping and Sharing Gospel **H/I/S:** Boating, Fishing **EDU:** Master's Degree in Religious Studies, Southern Baptist Seminary **A/A/S:** Southern Baptist Convention

Rachel K. Crane Smith, MS, PES, CSCS
Title: Exercise Physiologist **Company:** Terrio Therapy-Fitness **Address:** 4101 Easton Drive, Bakersfield, CA 93309 United States **BUS:** Physical Therapy and Fitness Training Center **P/S:** Physical Therapy, Weight Management, Sports Conditioning **MA:** Local **D/D/R:** Weight Management, Children's Fitness, Cardiopulmonary Rehabilitation **H/I/S:** Traveling, Swimming, Teaching, Prenatal Yoga, Playing Tennis **EDU:** Master of Science in Exercise Science and Health Promotion, California University of Pennsylvania (2005); Bachelor of Science in Exercise Science; University of California at Bakersfield (2001); Performance Enhancement Specialist; Certified, National Association of Sports Medicine; CSCS, PES **A/A/S:** National Academy of Sports Medicine; Certified National Strength and Conditioning Association
Email: mrcjbs3@yahoo.com
URL: http://www.terrio-therapyfitness.com

Rene E. Smith
Title: Program Manager **Company:** Tephinet, Inc. **Address:** 2872 Woodcock Boulevard, Suite 211, Atlanta, GA 30341 United States **BUS:** Nonprofit Healthcare Company **P/S:** Epidemiology Training Programs for Foreign Countries for Surveillance and Outbreak Investigations **MA:** International **D/D/R:** Budgetary Concerns, Overseeing Contractors and Epidemiology Development **H/I/S:** Hiking, Playing Tennis, Biking **EDU:** Master's Degree in Healthcare, Ohio State University; Master of Public Health Epidemiology, Ohio State University; Bachelor's Degree in Psychology and Premedicine, Michigan State University **A/A/S:** Sierra Club, Conservation Societies, Georgia Public Health Association **C/VW:** Energy Conservatory
Email: livingmore@gmail.com
URL: http://www.tephinet.org

Robert A. Smith
Title: Founder, President **Company:** Robert A. Smith Ministries, Inc. **Address:** P.O. Box 14101, Huntsville, AL 35815 United States **BUS:** Ministry **P/S:** Music, Spiritual Services, Revivals, Concerts, Conventions **MA:** International **D/D/R:** Music **H/I/S:** Golf **EDU:** Master's Degree, New Orleans Baptist Theological Seminary; Bachelor's Degree, Athens State University **A/A/S:** Conference of Southern Baptist Evangelists; Pi Tau Chi National Association Society in Religion
Email: bobsmithmusic@knology.net
URL: bsmithministries.org

Scott D. Smith
Title: Owner, President **Company:** Scott's Painting Inc. **Address:** 270 Littleton Road, Trailer 178, Chelmsford, MA 01824 United States **BUS:** Painting Company **P/S:** Residential, Commercial Interior and Exterior Painting Services **MA:** Regional **D/D/R:** managing daily operations, ensuring customer satisfaction, interior and exterior painting, estimating and communicating with clients **H/I/S:** Camping **EDU:** Bachelor of Arts in Management Information Systems, Minor in Computer Science, University of Massachusetts, Lowell (1985)
Email: scottspainting@comcast.net
URL: http://www.cambridgewhoswho.com

Stacey Lynn Smith
Title: Financial Manager **Company:** Caterpillar, Inc. **BUS:** Manufacturing Company **P/S:** Construction and Mining Equipment Including Diesel and Natural Gas Engines, Excavators, Track Type Tractors and Wheel Loaders **MA:** International **EXP:** Ms. Smith's expertise is in financial management. **D/D/R:** Handling Accounting **H/I/S:** Traveling, Reading **EDU:** Master's Degree in Accounting, Virginia Polytechnic Institute and State University **CERTS:** Pursuing Certification in Management Accountancy; Certified Public Accountant **A/A/S:** Institute of Management Accountants **C/VW:** Local Church; St. Jude Children's Research Hospital; Juvenile Diabetes Research Foundation International; United Way
Email: smith_stacey@cat.com
URL: http://www.cat.com

Ms. Susan A. Smith
Title: Activity Director **Company:** John Knox Village of Central Florida **Dept:** Oak View Suites **Address:** 101 W. Lake Drive, Orange City, FL 32763 United States **BUS:** Retirement Home **P/S:** Assisted Living Residence, Healthcare **MA:** Local **D/D/R:** Taking Care of a Diverse Group of Clientele Including Alzheimer's and Dementia Patients, Psychiatric and Developmentally Challenged Patients and Abused and Neglected Residents, Coordinating Activity Programs, Setting Up Educational Programs for the State of Florida's Healthcare Activity Coordinators Association **H/I/S:** Cooking, Baking, Making Arts and Crafts Items, Traveling, Reading **EDU:** Associate Degree in Sociology, Daytona Beach Community College; Coursework in Psychology, University of Central Florida; Nationally Certified Activity Director; Coursework in Professional Activity, 90 Hours; Coursework in Advance Management, 90 Hours **A/A/S:** LAC, National Association of Activity Professionals (2008); Conference Chairperson, National Association of Activity Professionals (2006); Connecticut Association of Therapeutic Recreational Directors; President, District 14, Florida Health Care Activity Coordinators Association; State Membership Chairperson, Budget and Finance and Long Range Committees, Florida Health Care Activity Coordinator's Association **A/H:** Member of the Year, Florida Health Care Activity Coordinators Association (2006); Award of Excellence, Healthcare Foundation of Florida (2006) **C/VW:** First Baptist Church, Orange City, FL
Email: mhurn@cfl.rr.com

Sylvia O. Smith
Title: Residential Placement, Foster Care **Company:** Arizona Department of Economic Security, Division of Developmental Disabilities **Address:** 2602 S. 24th Street, Phoenix, AZ 85034 United States **BUS:** Child Placement, Child Care and Foster Care Department **P/S:** Foster Care **MA:** Local **D/D/R:** Placing Developmentally Disabled Children **H/I/S:** Reading, Traveling **EDU:** Bachelor's Degree in Special Education, University of Wisconsin Waldorf College **A/A/S:** NBRTC; Inner Agency Case Management Project for Child Welfare for Regular as Well as Disabled Children
Email: sylviasmith@azdes.gov

Ms. Treair E. Smith
Title: Plant Engineering Supervisor **Company:** United Parcel Service of America **Address:** 4455 Seventh Avenue S., Seattle, WA 98108 United States **BUS:** Shipping Company **P/S:** Package Shipping **MA:** International **D/D/R:** Mechanical, Plant and Chemical Engineering, Project Estimating, Managing 4 Staff, Administration, Project Management, **H/I/S:** Hiking, Fishing, Working on her 1969 Mustang **EDU:** Bachelor of Science in Chemical Engineering, Montana State University (2000) **A/A/S:** Parent-Teacher Association, **C/VW:** Habitat for Humanity, United Way
Email: treair_smith@hotmail.com

Veronica L. Smith
Title: Mail Center Coordinate, Supervisor Company: Belmont University Address: 1900 Belmont Boulevard, Nashville, TN 37212 United States BUS: University P/S: Education MA: Local D/D/R: Overseeing Mail Operations Central Receiving, Coordinating Mail, Shipping H/I/S: Reading EDU: Certified Mail Manager, In-Plant Printing and Mailing Association A/A/S: International Print and Mail Association; College and University Mailing Association C/VW: First Baptist Nashville Church; Teacher, Sunday School
Email: smithv@mail.belmont.edu
URL: http://www.belmont.edu/mailcenter

William Clark Smith
Title: Respiratory Therapist Company: Kindred Hospital Address: 4722 Market Street, Apartment 4, Oakland, CA 40202 United States BUS: Hospital P/S: Healthcare MA: National EXP: Mr. Smith's expertise is in respiratory therapy. H/I/S: Traveling, Playing Tennis EDU: Bachelor of Science in Health Science, San Francisco State University CERTS: Registered Respiratory Therapist; Certified Respiratory Therapist A/A/S: American Association for Respiratory Therapy; National Board for Respiratory Therapy C/VW: Local Charitable Organizations
Email: willclark555@sbcglobal.net
URL: http://www.cambridgewhoswho.com

William R. Smith
Title: Chief Pilot Company: U.S. Jet Address: Venango Regional Airport, Franklin, PA 16323 United States BUS: U.S. Energy P/S: Natural Gas MA: National D/D/R: Flight Instructor, Flying Planes H/I/S: Building, Flying, Participating in Air Shows, Spending Time with his Family EDU: Diploma, E.G. Glass High School A/A/S: National Business Aviation Association, Inc.; Experimental Aircraft Association
Email: monocoupe@csonline.net
URL: http://www.cambridgewhoswho.com

Amelia Yvonne Smith-Cayton
Title: Founder Company: Tulsa Booker T. Washington High School Dept: West Coast Alumni Social Organization Address: P.O. Box 5065, Carson, CA 90749 United States BUS: Alumni Organization P/S: Social Assistance, Charity MA: West Coast D/D/R: Social Assistance H/I/S: Exercising, Playing Tennis, Reading, Traveling, Spending Time with her Grandchildren EDU: Associate Degree in Nursing, Compton Community College A/A/S: Secretary, Women's Congressional Council for the late Congresswoman; Juanita Millender McDonald 37th District; Barahobarmer the Audacity of Hope A/H: Employee of the Year Award; Perfect Attendance Award
Email: 2amelia@sbcglobal.net
URL: http://www.cambridgewhoswho.com

Lovie D. Smith-Schenk
Title: President Company: Houston Professional Musicians Association Address: 609 Chenevert, Houston, TX 77003 United States BUS: Music Union P/S: Labor Relations MA: National D/D/R: Percussion H/I/S: Woodworking EDU: Master of Arts, Rice University A/A/S: Baptist Church; AFOEM; PAS
Email: lss@afmhouston.com
URL: http://www.afmhouston.com

Rhonda Mattingly Smolenski
Title: Sales Manager, Drag Racer Company: Rapid Automotive Address: 1480 N. Dixie Boulevard, Radcliff, KY 40160 United States BUS: Wholesale Autoparts Company P/S: Sales of Basic Auto Parts MA: Regional D/D/R: Counter Sales Person, Hiring, Firing, Billing, Administrative Duties, Drag Racing, Managing Store H/I/S: Drag Racing, Fishing EDU: High School Graduate A/A/S: Ohio Valley Dragway A/H: Wally Drag Racing Trophy (2003)
Email: sixpack@bbtel.com
URL: http://www.luvracin.com

John E. Smothergill
Title: Chief Executive Officer Company: New Fibrin DNA Glassing Address: 7310 150 Street S.W., Suite 30, Lakewood, WA 98439 United States BUS: Manufacturing Company P/S: Manufacture of Industrial Teleportation, DNA Regents and Chips Replication, DNA Exchanges MA: International EXP: Mr. Smothergill's expertise is in binary energy of DNA. D/D/R: Maintaining the Web Site, Working with the DNA Sequencer, Public Speaking, Consulting and Lecturing H/I/S: Surfing the Internet EDU: Associate of Arts in Business and Information Technology Management, Western Governor University A/A/S: Friends of Lakewood Public Library; Roll Back Malaria Partnership; Berkeley Lab Friends of Science C/VW: Christian Children's Fund; The Salvation Army
Email: congressionalpermit@hotmail.com
URL: http://www.dnaglassing.org

Dawn M. Snead
Title: 1) Bookkeeper, Tax Preparer, Paralegal 2) Office Administrator, Bookkeeper Company: 1) Ogden Services, Inc. 2) Law Office of Robert L. Frugé, PC Address: 8030 Spouse Drive, Suite A, Prescott Valley, AZ 86314 United States BUS: 1) Accounting Firm 2) Law Firm P/S: 1) Accounting and Tax Preparation Services 2) Legal Services Including Personal Injury and Defense Litigation MA: Regional D/D/R: preparing tax returns, bookkeeping, performing administrative duties, billing and accounting H/I/S: Crystal Beading, Playing Baseball EDU: High School Diploma CERTS: Certified Legal Document Preparer, Arizona State Supreme Court A/A/S: National Association of Tax Professionals; National Association of Legal Assistants
Email: ogdenpv2@commspeed.net

Tami Blake Snell
Title: Director of Operations Company: Grace Presbyterian Church Address: 10221 Ella Lee Lane, Houston, TX 77042 United States BUS: Church P/S: Religious Services, Education MA: Local D/D/R: Directing Daily Operations H/I/S: Reading, Spending Time with her Family, Music EDU: Coursework in Accounting and Food Service, Eastern Kentucky University A/A/S: National Food Service Association C/VW: Star of Hope, West Houston Assistance Ministries, Mission Trips to Kenya
Email: tsnell@gpch.org
URL: http://www.gpch.org

Gwenda L. Snoddy, M.Ed.
Title: Mathematics Department Chairwoman Company: Madison Academy Address: 325 Slaughter Road, Madison, AL 35758 United States BUS: Co-Educational Prekindergarten through 12th-Grade Christian-Based Private School P/S: Quality Primary and Secondary Level Education in a Christian Environment MA: Regional D/D/R: Teaching Mathematics, Acting as Chairperson of the Department, Educating Students in High School Level Mathematics, Calculus and Pre-Calculus EDU: Master of Education in Mathematics, Mississippi State University (1975)
Email: gsnoddy@macademy.org
URL: http://www.macademy.org

Mary Jo Snorek
Title: Neonatal Nurse Practitioner Company: Children's Hospital of Wisconsin Address: 9000 W. Wisconsin Avenue, Milwaukee, WI 53226 United States BUS: Children's Hospital P/S: Healthcare MA: Local D/D/R: Intensive Neonatal Nursing H/I/S: Reading, Restoring Old Farm Houses EDU: Master of Science in Nursing, Rush University A/A/S: National Association of Neonatal Nurses; American Association of Critical-Care Nurses; The Academy of Neonatal Nursing C/VW: Children's Hospital, March of Dimes
Email: msnorek@aol.com
URL: http://www.cambridgewhoswho.com

Matthew A. Snow
Title: Account Executive Company: Tanenbaum-Harber Co., Inc. Address: 320 W. 57th Street, New York, NY 10019 United States BUS: Risk Management and Insurance Brokerage Firm P/S: Bonds, Consulting, Emerging Business Services, Estate Planning, Individual Life Insurance, Disability Insurance, Marine and Transit Insurance, Real Estate Insurance, Risk Management, Construction Insurance MA: National D/D/R: Specializing in Construction and Real Estate Insurance H/I/S: Football, Baseball EDU: Bachelor of Arts in Communication, SUNY Oswego (2002) A/A/S: Delta Sigma Phi
Email: snowm@tanhar.com
URL: http://www.tanhar.com

Dr. Vicki R. Snowden-Jackson
Title: Learning Center Director Company: Table Mountain Rancheria Address: 23736 Sky Harbor Road, Friant, CA 93626 United States BUS: Learning Center P/S: Education MA: Regional D/D/R: helping teachers and overseeing education programs for kindergarten children through adults H/I/S: Reading, Baking, Making Candy, Scrapbooking EDU: Ph.D. in Educational and Organizational Leadership (2007) A/A/S: Alumni Association, California State University; American School Counselor Association C/VW: Susan G. Komen for the Cure; Habitat for Humanity
Email: vsjackson@tmr.org
URL: http://www.cambridgewhoswho.com

Helenka L. Snyder, BS
Title: Principal, Vice President of Corporate Design Pier Management Group Company: Lotus Interior Design Studio Address: 1405 San Juan Hills Drive, Unit 101, Las Vegas, NV 89134 United States BUS: Design Firm P/S: Interior Design MA: International D/D/R: creating commercial design conceptions, developing, constructing and designing EDU: Bachelor's Degree in Interior Architecture, Kansas State University (1994)
Email: helenka@lotusids.com

Meredith L. Snyder
Title: Teacher Company: Fleetwood Area School District, Andrew Maier Elementary School Address: 355 Andrew Maier Boulevard, Blandon, PA 19510 United States BUS: Elementary School P/S: Education MA: Local D/D/R: Teaching First Grade Students All Subjects, Helping Lower Level Students Reach their Goals H/I/S: Coaching, Playing Basketball and Volleyball, Traveling, Spending Time at the Beach, Reading EDU: Bachelor of Science in Education, Millersville University A/A/S: National Education Association; Pennsylvania State Education Association C/VW: Habitat for Humanity
Email: msnyder@fleetwoodasd.k12.pa.us
URL: http://www.cambridgewhoswho.com

Michael Soares
Title: Vice President of Business Development Company: Thomson Address: 6200 S. Syracuse Way, Suite 200, Greenwood Village, CO 80111 United States BUS: Leading Global Provider of Integrated Information-Based Solutions to Business and Professional Customers P/S: Value-Added Information with Software Tools and Applications to Help Customers Make Better Decisions MA: International D/D/R: Working as the Vice President for an Eight Billion Dollar Company, Offering Data Bases to Information Technology Systems in Finance and Healthcare H/I/S: Skiing, Riding Motorcycles EDU: Bachelor of Science in Pharmacy, Massachusetts College of Pharmacy and Health Sciences (1985) A/A/S: American Society of Health-System Pharmacists; Healthcare Information and Management Systems Society
Email: michael.soares@thomson.com
URL: http://www.thomson.com

Maria Del S. Socorro Agado
Title: Educator Company: San Benito Consolidated Independent School District Dept: Sullivan Elementary School Address: 900 Elizabeth Street, San Benito, TX 78586 United States BUS: School District P/S: Elementary Education MA: Local D/D/R: teaching kindergarten students H/I/S: Baking, Traveling EDU: Bachelor of Science in Education, Minor in Art, The University of Texas-Pan American CERTS: Endorsement in Bilingual Education; Certification in Gifted and Talented Education A/A/S: Texas State Teachers Association; Parent-Teacher Association A/H: Campus Teacher of the Year Award (2005-2006); Who's Who Among American Teachers Award (2003-2006) C/VW: Co-Captain, Relay for Life
Email: magado@email.sanbenito.k12.tx.us

Lurline Alice Boué Soignet
Title: Artist Company: Independent Artist Address: 655 Sharp Lane, Apartment 101, Baton Rouge, LA 70815 United States BUS: Artist P/S: Artwork MA: International D/D/R: Creating Paintings H/I/S: Traveling, Painting, Running, Collecting Antiques A/A/S: L'Union Francaise; 11th Ward Social Club C/VW: Canon Hospice, Father Seelos Center

Stacy J. Sola
Title: Fitness Director Company: YMCA Address: 1761 W. University Avenue, St. Paul, MN 55104 United States BUS: Community/Charities/Nonprofit Organization Health and Fitness Management P/S: Health and Fitness MA: National D/D/R: Fitness Management, Operations Management, Human Resources, Organizational Wellness and Photography organizing activities, maintaining budget, oversee weight room, group fitness instructors, personal training staff, active older adult program H/I/S: Social Functions, Photography, Fitness, Aerobics, Running, Walking, Swimming, Volleyball, Ice Skating, Skiing EDU: Master's Degree in Business Management, University of Wisconsin-Green Bay; Bachelor of Arts in Communication, Media and Theatre, Minor in Art, Emphasis Graphic Design and Photography, St. Norbert College, De Pere, Wisconsin A/A/S: AFAA; IDEA; SilverSneakers A/H: St. Norbert College JFK Academic Scholarship (1998-2002); Student-Faculty Development Endowment (2001); Student Art Exhibit Third Place and Honorable Mention (2001)
Email: solasjonline@yahoo.com
Email: stacy.sola@ymcastpaul.org

Alexandra Solano
Title: Financial Aid Processor Company: Barry University Address: 11300 N.E. Second Avenue, Miami Shores, FL 33161 United States BUS: University P/S: Higher Education MA: International D/D/R: Managing Accounts, Preparing Tax Returns H/I/S: Reading, Traveling EDU: Bachelor's Degree in Accounting, Barry University A/A/S: Alumni, Students in Free Enterprise C/VW: Goodwill
Email: alexandrasolano@bellsouth.net

Gaylord H. Solem
Title: Salesman Company: Dahlstrom Motors, Inc. Address: 1200 Main Street, Oslo, MN 56744 United States BUS: Automotive Sales P/S: Chevrolet, Ford, Honda, Hyundai, Oldsmobile, Pontiac and Toyota Car Dealership MA: Regional D/D/R: Selling Cars H/I/S: Golfing, Fishing EDU: High School Education A/A/S: Mark of Excellence Award, Legion of Leaders
URL: http://www.dahlstrommotors.com

Mary Soliven
Title: Human Resources Manager Company: Designer Greetings, Inc. Address: 250 Arlington Avenue, Staten Island, NY 10303 United States BUS: Greeting Card Company P/S: Greeting Card Design and Manufacture MA: International D/D/R: Managing Human Resources Duties, Leading Staff Development H/I/S: Reading, Playing Badminton EDU: Bachelor of Arts in Business Management, Earned in the Philippines (1986) A/A/S: Staten Island Leukemia Foundation
Email: mary.soliven@designergreetings.com
URL: http://www.designergreetings.com

Barry P. Solomon
Title: Transportation Manager Company: Toys 'R' Us Address: 1110 W. Merrill Avenue, Rialto, CA 92376 United States BUS: Retail Store P/S: Toys, Baby Products MA: International D/D/R: managing customer compliance and overseeing transportation services and product distribution H/I/S: Spending Time with his Family EDU: Master of Business Administration, University of Phoenix (1992) CERTS: Certification in California Transportation Plan; Certified Transportation Professional (2006)
Email: solomonb@toysrus.com
URL: http://www.toysrus.com

Stephen J. Solomon, Ph.D.
Title: Independent Statistical Consultant Company: Stephen J. Solomon Address: 301 Fox Lane, Perkasie, PA 18944 United States BUS: Sole Proprietorship P/S: Clinical Statistical Consulting Services MA: Regional D/D/R: consulting, analyzing clinical trials, setting up database, assisting programmers on performance analysis, writing statistical analysis plans, lecturing and training upper level management on interpreting analysis results H/I/S: Yard Work, Dining Out EDU: Ph.D. in Psychology, CUNY Queens College (1979) A/A/S: American Statistical Association; American Psychological Association; Drug Information Association
Email: stephenjsolomon@comcast.net
URL: http://www.cambridgewhoswho.com

Susan F. Somers
Title: Registered Nurse Company: Shore Memorial Hospital Address: Sunny Avenue, P.O. Box 217, Somers Point, NJ 08244 United States BUS: Hospital P/S: Full Service Healthcare MA: Local D/D/R: Maternal Child Health H/I/S: Spending Time with Children and Family, Traveling EDU: Bachelor of Science in Nursing, Stockton State College, New Jersey A/A/S: Certified Lactation Consultant; Certified School Nurse; Sigma Theta Tau C/VW: Industry-Related Charities
Email: cbclass1@comcast.net
URL: http://www.shorememorial.org

Allison E. Sommerhalter
Title: Designated Broker Company: Sonora West Development, Inc. Address: 14269 N. 87th Street, Suite 105, Scottsdale, AZ 85260 United States BUS: Real Estate Agency P/S: Real Estate Sales Including Luxury Homes MA: Regional D/D/R: managing real estate sales H/I/S: Scuba Diving, Traveling, Reading EDU: Bachelor's Degree in Criminal Justice, Wichita State University A/A/S: Scottsdale Area Association of Realtors A/H: Young Salesperson of the Year
Email: allison@sonorawestdev.com
URL: http://www.sonorawestdev.com

Irene J. Song
Title: Business Analyst (Retired) BUS: Finance Company P/S: Financial Services Including Equity Swaps and Trading MA: International D/D/R: Learning about Finance Optimization and Pricing Models, analyzing delta one business H/I/S: Playing Tennis EDU: Pursuing Ph.D., Columbia University; Bachelor's Degree in Mathematics, Smith College; Bachelor's Degree in Literature, Smith College C/VW: Save the Children; Children International
Email: irene.j.song@gmail.com
URL: http://www.cambridgewhoswho.com

George E. Soper, Ph.D.
Title: Senior Vice President Company: Memorial Health System Address: 615 N. Michigan Street, South Bend, IN 46601 United States BUS: Full-Service Hospital P/S: Center for Occupational Health, Clinical Research, Heart Surgery, Lung Center, Heart and Vascular Center, Newborn Intensive Care Unit, Orthopedic Neurosurgery, Pain Control Center, Cancer Center, Childbirth Center, Rehabilitation Services, Sleep Disorders Center, Sports Medicine, Outpatient Services, Radiology, Trauma Services, Weight Loss and Geriatric Surgery Center, Home-Care MA: Local D/D/R: Overseeing Administration Responsibility for Clinic Service and Human Resources H/I/S: Sailing EDU: Ph.D. in Physical Therapy, The University of Iowa (1976)
Email: gsoper@memorialsb.org
URL: http://www.qualityoflife.org

Ms. Sandi L. Sorensen
Title: Director of Finance Company: Four Seasons Hotel Dept: Accounting Address: 98 San Jacinto Boulevard, Austin, TX 78701 United States BUS: Hospitality Chain P/S: Luxury Hotels and Condominiums MA: Regional D/D/R: Forecasting Renovations, Maintaining the Budget, Compiling the Yearly Budget, Moving the Company Forward H/I/S: Scuba Diving, Dancing, Enjoying Water Sports, Water Skiing EDU: Bachelor of Science in Business, Concentration in Accounting, California Polytechnic State University (1994) A/A/S: Delta Sigma Pi; Hospitality Financial and Technology Professionals
Email: sandi.sorensen@fourseasons.com
URL: http://www.fourseasons.com

Diana Sorges-Alkana
Title: Group Leader, Advisor Company: First Assembly of God Church Support Group Address: 534 N. Alameda Avenue, Azusa, CA 91702 United States BUS: Nonprofit Organization P/S: Spiritual Services, Counseling MA: Local D/D/R: Counseling H/I/S: Caring for her Pets and Foster Pets, Photography EDU: Coursework in Social Sciences, Pasadena City College A/A/S: President, Democratic Club, Azusa; Azusa Woman's Club; Oblate Member, Saint Andrew's Abbey A/H: Recognized, Democrat of the Year Award C/VW: Clowning Around Charity Foundation; Veteran's Memorial Committee
Email: d.sorgesalkana@yahoo.com

Anthony Sorrentino Jr.
Title: In-Charge Auditor Company: Feeley and Driscoll, PC Address: 200 Portland Street, Boston, MA 02114 United States BUS: CPA Firm P/S: Financial Services MA: National D/D/R: Consulting, Auditing, Tax Preparation, Doing ERISA Pension Audits H/I/S: Golfing, Participating in Recruiting Events for the Bentley Alumni Association EDU: Pursuing CPA; Master's Degree in Accounting, Northeastern University; Bachelor of Science in Accounting, Bentley College A/A/S: Boston Young Professionals Association
Email: anthonys@fdcpa.com

Maria Gabriela Sosa
Title: Vice President Company: BG Consulting, Inc. Address: 121 S. Alfred Street, Alexandria, VA 22314 United States BUS: Consulting Company P/S: Consulting in the Private Sector and Government MA: International D/D/R: Trade and Business Promotion H/I/S: Running EDU: Master's Degree in Law, Harvard University (1994) A/A/S: United States Chamber of Commerce; Global Intelligence Alliance; Greater Washington Ibero American Chamber of Commerce C/VW: Alzheimer's Association, UNICEF
Email: mariasosa@bg-consulting.com
URL: http://www.bg-consulting.com

Paul Sotherland
Title: Lawyer Company: Sotherland Law Firm, LLC Address: 17 Dexter Avenue, Birmingham, AL 35213 United States BUS: Full-Service Law Firm Serving Residents of Birmingham P/S: Personal Insurance Defense MA: Regional D/D/R: Practicing Civil Defense Law H/I/S: Running EDU: 8 Years Post-Graduate Schooling, Cumberland School of Law, Samford University (1985) A/A/S: National Association of Civil Defense Lawyers; Litigation Council of America
Email: pls@sotherlandlaw.com
URL: http://www.sotherlandlaw.com

Elias P. Soto Sr.
Title: 1) Owner, Chief Executive Officer Company: GG Express Address: 8515 W. Cavalier Drive, Glendale, AZ 85305 United States BUS: Transportation Company P/S: Transportation Services, Trucks, Flat Beds and Building Products MA: Local D/D/R: Driving, Offering Education and Counseling H/I/S: Restoring Cars, Attending and Showing in Car Shows, Traveling EDU: Doctorate Degree in the Theology of Bible, California Christian University; Doctorate of Pneumatics, California Christian University A/A/S: Local Church; Ugandan Orphanage; Love Kitchen International; Churches in Nayarit, Mexico and Walla Walla, Washington
Email: eliassoto@cox.net
URL: http://www.cambridgewhoswho.com

Mary Joy Soto
Title: Teacher Company: Nadaburg Elementary School Address: 21419 W. Dove Valley Road, Wittmann, AZ 85361 United States BUS: Elementary School P/S: Primary Education MA: Local EXP: Ms. Soto's expertise includes reading and early childhood education. D/D/R: helping the disabled in learning H/I/S: Spending Time with her Son, Reading, Traveling EDU: Master's Degree in Education and Reading, Arizona State University (1994); Bachelor of Science in Education, Northern Arizona University (1986) A/A/S: National Education Association; Arizona Education Association C/VW: Local Church
Email: hmjsoto@aol.com
URL: http://www.cambridgewhoswho.com

Sandra R. Soto-Carlo
Title: President Company: Benefit Consulting Group of Puerto Rico, Inc. Address: 109 Isabel Andreu, Second Floor, San Juan, PR 00918 United States BUS: Consulting Firm P/S: Consulting Services on Retirement Planning MA: Puerto Rico D/D/R: Assisting Clients on Retirement, 401K, KEOGH, Target and Profit Sharing Plans, consulting, overseeing compliance, ensuring and qualifying plans H/I/S: Reading, Spending Time with her Family EDU: Master's Degree in Industrial Management, Universidad Interamericana de Puerto Rico; Bachelor's Degree, University of Puerto Rico, Carolina A/A/S: American Society of Pension Professionals & Actuaries; Association of Retirement Benefit Professionals of Puerto Rico
Email: sandra@benefitconsultingpr.com
URL: http://www.benefitconsultingpr.com

Carissa M. Soucie, BSN
Title: Staff Registered Nurse, Emergency Company: Marlborough Hospital Address: 69 Grove Street, Leicester, MA 01524 United States BUS: Outstanding Hospital Facility P/S: Convenient Access to High Quality Medical Care MA: Local D/D/R: Bedside, Private Duty Nursing, Working in the Intensive Care Unit and Emergency Room, Pain Management, Acting as a Patient Advocate, Performing Orientation for New Nurses H/I/S: Exercising, Walking, Watching Sports EDU: Bachelor of Science in Nursing, Worcester State College (1997) A/A/S: Massachusetts Nurses Association; Former Member, Emergency Nurses Association
Email: inangelc@ummhc.org
URL: http://www.ummhc.org

Stephanie Souder
Title: Product Marketing Manager Company: Verizon Business Address: 22001 Loudon County Parkway, Ashburn, VA 20147 United States BUS: Telecommunications Company P/S: Access Solutions for Businesses MA: International D/D/R: Developing, Enhancing and Maintaining Products, Training Staff, Developing Marketing Materials for Internal and External Communications H/I/S: Participating in Outdoor Activities EDU: Bachelor of Science in Communications, Old Dominion University (1994)
Email: stephanie.souder@verizonbusiness.com
URL: http://www.verizonbusiness.com

Mr. Pierre J. Souraty, MD
Title: MD Company: Harbor UCLA Medical Center C-I Annex Address: 2700 Arlington Avenue, Suite 112, Torrance, CA 90501 United States BUS: Hospital P/S: Healthcare MA: Local D/D/R: Facilitating Clinical Work and Inpatient Consulting, Conducting Dialysis Rounds H/I/S: Flying Private Planes, Skiing, Playing the Guitar EDU: Fellowship in Nephrology (2008); Residency (2003); MD, Saint-Joseph University, Lebanon (1992) A/A/S: American Medical Association; American Society of Nephrology; American College of Physicians
Email: merlinpi@hotmail.com
URL: http://www.cambridgewhoswho.com

Pamela L. Southard
Title: Assistant Vice President, Bank Card Information Technology Manager Company: Fifth Third Bank Address: 38 Fountain Square, MD 10AT61, Cincinnati, OH 45202 United States BUS: Bank P/S: Banking Services Including Information Technology Customer Support and Great Customer Relationships MA: National D/D/R: issuing debit and credit card and programming H/I/S: Camping, Boating EDU: Bachelor of Arts in Business, Thomas Moore College C/VW: American Heart Association
Email: pl_southard@hotmail.com
URL: http://www.53.com

Ms. Ellen R. Sowards
Title: Fifth-Grade Teacher Company: South-Western City Schools Address: 1831 Finland Avenue, Columbus, OH 43223 United States BUS: School District P/S: Education MA: Local D/D/R: teaching mathematics and science to sixth-grade students H/I/S: Reading EDU: Master's Degree in Supervision and Management, John Carroll University (1996) A/A/S: National Council of Teachers of Mathematics; National Education Association; Oklahoma Education Association
Email: lnbushek@aol.com
URL: http://www.cambridgewhoswho.com

Clara O. Soyoola, RPH
Title: Pharmacist Company: Wal-Mart Dept: Pharmacy Address: 1742 Brittany Dawn Drive, Snellville, GA 30078 United States BUS: Retail Chain P/S: Retail Services, Pharmacy Services MA: Regional D/D/R: Filling Prescriptions, Counseling Customers, Assisting Customers with Over-the-Counter Medications H/I/S: Reading, Shopping EDU: Master of Pharmacy, Auburn University (1990); Bachelor of Pharmacy, Nigeria (1984) A/A/S: Minister, Abundant Life Church for All Nations; Phi Kappa Phi; American Pharmacists Association
Email: clarasoyoola@bellsouth.net
URL: http://www.walmart.com

Tonya Spada-Dixon
Title: Registered Dietitian, Clinical Nutrition Manager **Company:** Conemaugh Memorial Medical Center **Dept:** Food and Nutrition **Address:** 1086 Franklin Street, Johnstown, PA 15905 United States **BUS:** Hospital **P/S:** Healthcare, Level I Trauma Center **MA:** Western Pennsylvania **D/D/R:** Overseeing All Aspects of Nutrition with an Emphasis in Oncology and Cuticle Care Nutrition, Offering Food Service Management **H/I/S:** Spending Time with her Family, Bicycling, Reading **EDU:** Bachelor of Science in Dietetics **A/A/S:** Pennsylvania Dietetic Association; American Dietetic Association **A/H:** Gold Star Award **C/VW:** Outstanding Young Women, Relay for Life
Email: tns_d@hotmail.com

Sonya A. Spady, M.Ed.
Title: Special Education Teacher **Company:** William B. Ward Elementary School **Address:** 311 Broadfield Road, New Rochelle, NY 10805 United States **BUS:** School **P/S:** Education **MA:** Regional **D/D/R:** Teaching All Subjects to Kindergarten through Sixth-Grade Students, Teaching Children with Learning Disabilities **H/I/S:** Rollerblading, Listening to Music, Cooking, Going to the Movies, Reading Junra Poetry **EDU:** Master of Science in Special Education, College of New Rochelle (2004) **A/A/S:** National Association for the Advancement of Colored People; Park Chester Kiwanis Club; West Chester Alliance of Black School Educators
Email: sas1105@optonline.net
URL: http://www.ward.nred.org

Susan Spagnoli
Title: Owner, President **Company:** Stone Surfaces, LLC **Address:** 4136 Clemson Boulevard, Anderson, SC 29621 United States **BUS:** Countertop Construction Company **P/S:** Silestone, Granite and Quartz Countertops **MA:** Regional **D/D/R:** Kitchen and Bath Interior Designing **H/I/S:** Reading, Attending Hunter Jump Horse Riding Competitions, Spending Time at the Lake **EDU:** Associate of Science in Management, Gwinnett Technical College, Georgia **A/A/S:** Anderson Home Builders Association **C/VW:** Local Recreation Center; Sponsor, Local Sport Teams
Email: susanspagnoli@bellsouth.net
URL: http://www.cambridgewhoswho.com

Cynthia A. Spanier, Ph.D.
Title: Chief Executive Officer **Company:** Independent Distributor for Herbalife International **Address:** 530 Brookdale Drive, Pittsburgh, PA 15215 United States **BUS:** Distribution Company **P/S:** Health, Nutrition and Weight Loss Products **MA:** International **D/D/R:** assisting clients on their health issues, coaching and training clients **EDU:** Ph.D. in Psychology, University of Pittsburgh (1997); Master of Science in Communication Disorders, Marquette University (1982); Bachelor of Science in Communication, Marquette University (1981) **A/A/S:** Women's Board of Pittsburgh
Email: cswilson.hlife@verizon.net
URL: http://www.health4you-hli.com

Mr. Joshua H. Sparber
Title: System Engineer **Company:** Defense Contract Management Agency **Address:** 3370 E. Miraloma Avenue, Building 250, Mail Stop 31-ABO2, Anaheim, CA 92806 United States **BUS:** Government Defense, Aerospace **P/S:** Satellite Communications, Government Contracts, Defense Systems **MA:** International **D/D/R:** Organizing Engineering Across Very Large Programs Involving Multiple Platforms, Managing Systems Electrical Engineering in Special Communications and Signal Conditioning, Offering Training, Reviewing Large Defense Industry and Government Contracts in Aerospace and Satellite Communications **H/I/S:** Playing Tennis, Swimming, Hiking **EDU:** Master's Degree in Electrical Engineering, California State University (1999) **A/A/S:** The International Council on Systems Engineering
Email: joshua.sparber@dcma.mil

Mary Sparks
Title: Owner/Operator **Company:** Budget Car and Truck **Address:** 5414 Clinton Highway, Knoxville, TN 37912 United States **BUS:** Automotive Rentals **P/S:** Car and Truck Rentals **MA:** Local **D/D/R:** Running All Aspects, Rental Cars and Trucks **H/I/S:** Softball **EDU:** Career Community College, Computer Science **A/A/S:** Community Charities/DARE

Susan J. Spaulding
Title: Service Associate I **Company:** Liberty Bank **Address:** 77 Salem Turnpike, Suite 101, Norwich, CT 06360 United States **BUS:** Bank **P/S:** Financial Services and Diversified Financial Consulting **MA:** National **EXP:** Ms. Spaulding's expertise is in money marketing. **D/D/R:** overseeing customer service including investments, mortgage and loan department, completing transactions for customers, ensuring accuracy with transactions, balancing general ledger, rectifying errors **H/I/S:** Reading, Boating, Hiking **EDU:** Associate Degree in Accounting, Three Rivers Community College (1995) **CERTS:** Consumer Lending Certificate, Center for Financial Training Services (2006) **C/VW:** Volunteer, Occum Fire Department; National Association of Emergency Medical Technicians
Email: sspaulding@liberty-bank.com
URL: http://www.liberty-bank.com

Keila M. Speakman
Title: Co-Owner **Company:** Odd Ball Cleaning Services **Address:** 1301 1/2 W. Story Street, Bozeman, MT 59715 United States **BUS:** Janitorial Service **P/S:** Residential Cleaning Services **MA:** Regional **D/D/R:** Assisting in the Management of the Daily Operations, Cleaning, Maintaining Supplies, Distributing Paychecks, Generating Paperwork **H/I/S:** Outdoor Activities, Camping, Hiking **EDU:** Coursework in Microbiology, Montana State University **A/A/S:** The National Society of Collegiate Scholars
Email: kms0347@msn.com

Zephia Spears, RN
Title: Registered Nurse, Director of Pediatrics **Company:** Interim Health Care **Address:** 6601 W. Interstate 40, Suite 500, Amarillo, TX 79106 United States **BUS:** Home Healthcare Company **P/S:** Home Care Nursing Services, Medical Staffing **MA:** Regional **D/D/R:** scheduling and coordinating nurses for in-home care of special needs children **H/I/S:** Reading, Bowling, Swimming **EDU:** Associate Degree in Nursing, Amarillo College (1996) **CERTS:** Registered Nurse; Certification in Pediatric Care, Interim Healthcare **A/A/S:** America's Registry for Outstanding Professionals
Email: dees@interimwesttex.com
URL: http://www.interimhealthcare.com

Alison S. Speight
Title: Program Supervisor **Company:** Johns Hopkins Bayview Medical Center **Dept:** Addiction Treatment Services **Address:** 5200 Easter Avenue, MFL Building, E. Tower, Sixth Floor, Baltimore, MD 21224 United States **BUS:** Hospital **P/S:** Substance Abuse Treatment and Rehabilitation, Pediatric Healthcare, New Medical Technologies **MA:** National **D/D/R:** Leadership **H/I/S:** Skiing, Traveling **EDU:** Master of Science in Psychology, Calston University (2000); Bachelor of Science in Psychology, Wofford College; Licensed in Substance Abuse, State of Maryland Talseson **A/A/S:** American Counseling Association; American Psychology Association **C/VW:** Hospital Charities, Local Community
Email: aspeigh1@jhmi.edu
URL: http://www.jhbmc.org

Kisha B. Spellman-O'Bannon
Title: Administrator **Company:** Ascending Roots Scholastic & Athletic Premise **Address:** 7310 N. 27th Avenue, Phoenix, AZ 85051 United States **BUS:** Charter School **P/S:** Education **MA:** Local **D/D/R:** Educating, Administrative Duties, Discipline **H/I/S:** Basketball, Vacationing **EDU:** Bachelor's Degree, Arizona State University; Associate Degree in Business Administration, Yauapai College **A/A/S:** Network-Based Education, Charter Association; NABE **C/VW:** Community Network and Fellowship
Email: arsap2002@yahoo.com
URL: http://www.ascendingroots.com

Faun Spencer
Title: Owner, RN **Company:** Twilight Care, Inc. dba Stevens Residence **Address:** 3704 Cardinal Road, Minnetonka, MN 55345 United States **BUS:** Healthcare Facility **P/S:** Mental Healthcare, Home for Alzheimer's Patients, Dementia Care **MA:** Local **D/D/R:** Dementia Care **H/I/S:** Reading, Making Stained Glass Windows **EDU:** Associate of Science in Business Management, Ashworth University (1998); Associate of Science, Normandale Community College **A/A/S:** Board of Directors, Care Providers of Minnesota; Board of Directors, National Center for Assisted Living
Email: caregiverfms@juno.com
URL: http://www.cambridgewhoswho.com

Margaret K. Spencer
Title: Teacher (Retired) **Company:** Battle Ground High School **Address:** 300 W. Main Street, Battle Ground, WA 98604 United States **BUS:** School **P/S:** Education **MA:** Local **D/D/R:** Teaching English, Social Studies, Writing **H/I/S:** Quilting **EDU:** Master's Degree in Teaching, Lewis & Clark College
Email: spencer.kenni@bgsd.k12.wa.us

Christopher Spera
Title: Licensed Sales Agent **Company:** RE/MAX Showcase **Address:** 1919 Deer Park Avenue, Deer Park, NY 11729 United States **BUS:** Real Estate Agency **P/S:** Real Estate Sales **MA:** Regional **D/D/R:** Real Estate Sales **H/I/S:** Golfing, Playing with Gas Powered Remote Control Cars, Fishing, Going to the Beach, Watching the Yankees Baseball Games **EDU:** College Coursework **A/A/S:** Long Island Board of Realtors; National Association of Realtors; New York State Association of Realtors
Email: weloanny@yahoo.com
URL: http://www.housesrusrealty.com

Marc T. Spess
Title: Owner **Company:** Animate Clay **Address:** 2612 W. Blackburn Drive, Springfield, MO 65807 United States **BUS:** Stop Motion and Clay Animation Educational Website and Retail Store **P/S:** Stop Motion and Clay Animation Services and Tutorials **MA:** International **D/D/R:** Creating and Selling Instructional and How To Videos and E-Books, Updating the News on their Web Page, Sculpting, Searching for New Ideas to Offer Members, Creating Cartoon Commercials, Building Web Pages, Writing Books **H/I/S:** Working on Animation and Sculpting **EDU:** Coursework in in Drawing and Sculpting, St. Charles Community College
Email: marc@animateclay.com
URL: http://www.animateclay.com

Mrs. Keitha Spiekerman
Title: Realtor, ABR, e-PRO, GRI **Company:** Keller Williams **Address:** 801 N. Ware Road, McAllen, TX 78501 United States **BUS:** Real Estate Company **P/S:** High Quality Real Estate Sales, Residential Homes, Multi-Family Work, Investments **MA:** Hidalgo Country **D/D/R:** Sharyland Plantation, McAllen, Mission and Edinburg Texas, the Rio Grande Valley **H/I/S:** Fishing **EDU:** High School Graduate **A/A/S:** Texas Association of Realtors; National Association of Realtors, The Greater McAllen Association of Realtors; ABR; e-PRO; GRI
Email: keitha@keithaandalma.com
URL: http://www.keithaandalma.com

Stefanie L. Spieth-Woolford
Title: Executive Director **Company:** Maumee Senior Center **Address:** 2430 Detroit Avenue, Maumee, OH 43537 United States **BUS:** Nonprofit Senior Center **P/S:** Encouraging Older Adults to Remain Independent and Helping them Stay Involved in their Community Through Education, Socialization, Information and Referral and Supportive Services **MA:** Countywide **D/D/R:** Gerontology **H/I/S:** Boating, Watching NASCAR **EDU:** Master of Public Administration, University of Toledo; Bachelor's Degree in Sociology, Minor in Gerontology, Miami University of Ohio **A/A/S:** Maumee Rotary; Zonta Club of Toledo I; Maumee Chamber of Commerce; National Institute of Senior Centers; NOVA **C/VW:** Jail & Bail, Lions Clubs International
Email: sspieth@maumeeseniorcenter.com
URL: http://www.maumeeseniorcenter.com

Jeanette G. Spinelli
Title: Owner **Company:** The Red Barn **Address:** 28336 Clayton Street, Route 26, Dagsboro, DE 19939 United States **BUS:** Retail Establishment Selling Furniture, Household Items and Antiques **P/S:** New and Antique Furniture, Household Items, Dolls and Bears **MA:** National **D/D/R:** Buying and Selling Merchandise, Assisting Customers in Buying Merchandise, Seeking Out Original Products to Buy **EDU:** High School Graduate (1962)

Felix Martin Spitelle
Title: Records Storage Analyst **Company:** EI Dupont De Nemours & Co, Inc. **Address:** 4417 Lancaster Pike, Wilmington, DE 19805 United States **BUS:** Manufacturing Company **P/S:** Commercial Products Including Chemicals, Plastics, Bioproducts and Specialty Products **MA:** International **D/D/R:** managing records and inventory **H/I/S:** Gardening, Traveling, Working in Fixup Projects **EDU:** Bachelor of Science in Business Administration, University of Delaware **A/A/S:** Local Chapter, Association of Records Managers and Administrators **C/VW:** Local Charitable Organizations; Local Soup Kitchens; Knights of Columbus
Email: felix.m.spitelle@usa.dupont.com
URL: http://www.cambridgewhoswho.com

Claude B. Spivey
Title: CEO/Founder **Company:** Visions-Innervisions, LLC **Address:** 4710 Lincoln Highway, Suite 140, Matteson, IL 60443 United States **BUS:** Entertainment Productions **P/S:** Concert Productions, Calle Broadcasting **MA:** International **D/D/R:** Historic Preservation of Musical Artists **H/I/S:** Golf **EDU:** Livingston College, Rutgers University, Bachelor of Arts **A/A/S:** Christian Church
Email: visionsinnervisions@helloworld.com

Patricia E. Spoerri, MSM
Title: Director of Organization Development **Company:** City of Boynton Beach **Address:** 13320 Four Willows Drive, Frisco, TX 75035 United States **BUS:** Organization and Strategic Development Company **P/S:** Citizen Services **MA:** Local **D/D/R:** Training, Developing and Building Programs for Employees to Increase their Skills and Productivity, Designing All Management and Administrative Training, Technical Training, Computer and Safety Training, Ensuring U.S. Equal Employment Opportunity Commission Compliance, Creating Partnerships with Local Universities **H/I/S:** Reading, Researching, Bicycling **EDU:** Master's Degree in Management, University of St. Thomas (1992); Graduate Certificate in Human Resources **CERTS:** Certified Executive Coach **A/A/S:** NSOD; Lecturer, Barry University; Lecturer, Broward Community College; Lecturer, University of St. Thomas
Email: pspoerri@tx.rr.com

Stephen Spooner
Title: Senior Merchant **Company:** Home Depot **Address:** 2455 Paces Ferry Road S.E., Atlanta, GA 30339 United States **BUS:** World's Largest Home Improvement Specialty Retailer with Stores in All 50 States, the District of Columbia, Puerto Rico, U.S. Virgin Islands, 10 Canadian Provinces, Mexico and China **P/S:** Home Improvement Products **MA:** International **D/D/R:** Working as a Buyer for Kitchens, Countertops and Flooring, Traveling Internationally to Find New Products, Training Employees at Different Stores for Training to Ensure Quality Assurance **H/I/S:** Enjoying All Sports **EDU:** Bachelor of Arts in Business Administration, University of Miami (1971) **A/A/S:** National Kitchen and Bath Association **A/H:** Innovation Award (2006); Runner Up, Innovation Award (2005)
Email: steve_spooner@homedepot.com
URL: http://www.homedepot.com

Frank A. Sprecace
Title: Roman Catholic Priest (Retired) **Company:** Roman Catholic Diocese of Camden **Address:** 856 Palermo Road, Saint Augustine, FL 32086 United States **BUS:** Church **P/S:** Spiritual Services **MA:** Regional **D/D/R:** Teaching Children, Visiting Sick People, Giving Sacraments, Fundraising for Carnivals, Conducting Bingo Games **H/I/S:** Spending Time with his Pet **EDU:** Bachelor of Theology, St. Bonaventure University (1955)
Email: frank.sprecace@cwwemail.com

Rachel R. Spring
Title: Kennel Supervisor, Pet Bereavement Counselor **Company:** Valley Inn for Pets **Address:** 320 Russell Street, Hadley, MA 01035 United States **BUS:** Veterinary Hospital **P/S:** Veterinary Care, Comprehensive Boarding **MA:** Local **D/D/R:** Coordinating Boarding of Pets **H/I/S:** Writing, Traveling, Hiking **EDU:** Master of Arts in Counseling Psychology, Pacifica Graduate Institute; Bachelor of Arts in Early Childhood Education, University of Detroit Mercy, Detroit, Michigan **A/A/S:** American Boarding Kennels Association
Email: rspring878@aol.com

Joni B. Springer
Title: Owner **Company:** Sabine Healthcare Management, LLC **Address:** 610 Nabours Street, Many, LA 71449 United States **BUS:** Medical Management Company **P/S:** Medical Transcription, Coding, Billing, Collections **MA:** Local **EXP:** Ms. Springer's expertise is in medical management. **H/I/S:** Playing Bingo, Traveling **EDU:** Associate Degree in Medical Administration, Corinthians College **C/VW:** Volunteer, Local Fire Department
Email: jonispringer@yahoo.com
URL: http://www.cambridgewhoswho.com

Brian E. Springett
Title: Principal **Company:** Fingerprint Advisors **Address:** 4620 Chestnut Lane, Boulder, CO 80301 United States **BUS:** Digital Printing Company **P/S:** Electrophotographic Materials, Digital Printing **MA:** International **D/D/R:** Business Development, Consulting, Tutorials **H/I/S:** Exercising, Photography **EDU:** Ph.D. in Physics, University of Chicago; Master of Science in Physics and Mathematics, Cambridge University **A/A/S:** Society for Imaging Science and Technology **C/VW:** Doctors Without Borders, OxFam
Email: fingerpost@juno.com

Cindy K. Sproles
Title: Office Administrator **Company:** Comfort Keepers **Address:** 377 Woodcrest Drive, Kingsport, TN 37663 United States **BUS:** Healthcare Residential Care/Nursing Home/Long Term Care **MA:** Local **D/D/R:** Running the Office, Billing, Human Resources **H/I/S:** Creative Writing **EDU:** University of Phoenix, Bachelors **A/A/S:** Bellevue Christian Church
Email: trycity@comfortkeepers.com
URL: http://www.comfortkeepers.com

Richard J. Spurlin Jr.
Title: President, Owner, Founder **Company:** Justright Awnings & Signs **Address:** 2 Industrial Park Drive, Dover, NH 03820 United States **BUS:** Manufacturing Company **P/S:** Awnings, Signs **MA:** Local **D/D/R:** designing, fabricating and installing awning systems and signs **H/I/S:** Motocross Racing **EDU:** High School Education **A/A/S:** Republican National Committee **C/VW:** Special Olympics
Email: justrightawnings@aol.com
URL: http://www.justrightawnings.net

Connie Jo Squires
Title: Teacher, Psychologist (Retired 1998) **Company:** Spokane School District, Mead School District, West Valley School District **Address:** Spokane, WA 99208 United States **BUS:** Public School System **P/S:** Primary and Secondary Education, Academics, Athletics, Arts and Sciences, Special and Gifted Programs, After-School Programs, Guidance **MA:** Regional **D/D/R:** Working as a School Psychologist with a Reading Specialist Background, Private Counseling and Counseling Students within the School System **H/I/S:** Flower Gardening, Sewing **EDU:** Master's Degree in Psychology, Seattle Pacific University **A/A/S:** National Association of School Psychologists; Washington State Psychological Association **A/H:** Washington State Psychologist of the Year Award (1995)
Email: cdjs33@earthlink.net
URL: http://www.cambridgewhoswho.com

Nagarajan Sridhar
Title: Project Manager **Company:** Texas Instruments **Dept:** HPA **Address:** 12500 TI Boulevard, Dallas, TX 75243 United States **BUS:** Electronic Company **P/S:** Design and Manufacturing of Analog Technologies, Digital Signal Processing and Microcontroller Semiconductors, Computers, Automotive and Consumer Electronic Applications **MA:** International **EXP:** His expertise includes product development and improvement. **H/I/S:** Playing the Violin and Cricket **EDU:** Ph.D. in Materials Science, SUNY Buffalo **C/VW:** United Way; Local Charitable Organizations
Email: n-sridhar1@ti.com
URL: http://www.cambridgewhoswho.com

Gregg St. Clair
Title: Vice President **Company:** Salt River Materials Group **Address:** 3000 W. Cement Plant Road, Clarkdale, AZ 86324 United States **BUS:** Cement Manufacturing Company **P/S:** Cement Supplies **MA:** Western United States **D/D/R:** Executive Operations for Cement Manufacturing **H/I/S:** Golfing, Camping, Fishing, Traveling **EDU:** Bachelor's Degree in Civil Engineering, University of Tucson, AZ **A/A/S:** The Portland Cement Association; Institute of Electrical and Electronics Engineers
Email: gwstclair@srmaterials.com
URL: http://www.srmaterials.com

Darlene M. St. John
Title: Photographer **Company:** The Main Event Photography, LLC **Address:** 4011 Caddoa Drive, Loveland, CO 80538 United States **BUS:** Photography **P/S:** All Major Events, Fundraising, Weddings, Other Events, Photo Journalism **MA:** International **D/D/R:** Fine Art, Weddings, Special Events, Fund Raising, Social Awareness, Charity Events **H/I/S:** Loves Wild Horses **EDU:** Two Years of College, High School Graduate **A/A/S:** Hearts & Horses Therapeutic Riding Center
Email: darstjohn@mac.com
URL: http://www.themaineventphotography.com

Jean St. Pierre
Title: Vice President, Owner **Company:** Broadway Costume **Address:** 273 Summer Street, Boston, MA 02210 United States **BUS:** Theatrical Costumes and Cosmetic Sales **P/S:** Theatrical Costumes Adult and Children Rentals and Sales **MA:** Local **D/D/R:** Operations **H/I/S:** Cooking Healthy Nutritious Foods **EDU:** Coursework in Liberal Arts, Dean Junior College **A/A/S:** Archdiocese Catholic Women **C/VW:** Archdiocese Cardinal Appeal
Email: info@broadwaycostume.com
URL: http://www.broadwaycostume.com

Joy A. Stackhouse
Title: Lead Physical Therapist **Company:** Virtua Home Care **Address:** 215 Courtney Drive, Barrington, NJ 08007 United States **BUS:** Home Care Agency **P/S:** Healthcare, Physical Therapy **MA:** Southern New Jersey **D/D/R:** Home Care Clinician **H/I/S:** Camping, Children's Sporting Events **EDU:** Bachelor's Degree in Physical Therapy, University of Delaware **C/VW:** Muscular Dystrophy Walk, Church
Email: joyastack@comcast.net

Cecilia D. Stafford
Title: Director of Library Services **Company:** New Mexico State University **Address:** 1500 Third Street, Grants, NM 87020 United States **BUS:** Education University **P/S:** Secondary Education **MA:** Local **D/D/R:** Library Science **H/I/S:** Gardening, Traveling **EDU:** Master's Degree in Library Science, University of Alabama **A/A/S:** American Library Association
Email: stafford@nmsu.edu
URL: http://www.grants.nmsu.edu/gr_lid/lib.htm

Velma A. Stafford
Title: RN **Company:** Intermountain Healthcare **Address:** Salt Lake City, UT United States **BUS:** Hospital **P/S:** Women's and Childbirth Programs, Strong Inpatient and Outpatient Surgery Services, Sleep Disorders Clinic, Advanced Imaging Services and a Cardiac Catheterization Laboratory **MA:** Local **D/D/R:** Directing Women's Services, Managing Payroll, Ordering Inventory, Quality Control, Supervising a Staff of Over 50 Employees Including Certified Nurse Assistants, Licensed Practical Nurses and Registered Nurses, Coordinating Staff Meetings Gyn Surgery, Antepartum, Post Partum Unit, 60 Bed Maternity unit, Charge Nurse, Staff Nurse, Preceptor, **H/I/S:** Reading Novels and Autobiographies, Shopping, ATVing, Spending Time with her Seven Children, more than 20 Grandchildren **EDU:** Pursuing Master's Degree in Nursing and Health Administration, University of Phoenix; Bachelor's Degree in Nursing, California State University (1999); Bachelor of Arts in Business, California State University (1996); Associate of Science in Liberal Arts (1993) **A/A/S:** Sigma Theta Tau **A/H:** Perseverance Award, California State University (1999)
Email: VelmaA.Stafford@cwwemail.com

Carla A. Stahl
Title: Registered Nurse, Certified Pediatric Nurse **Company:** Aberdeen Pediatrics **Address:** Physician Plaza, 201 S. Lloyd Street, Aberdeen, SD 57401 United States **BUS:** Pediatric Healthcare Center **P/S:** Comprehensive Preventive Medical Services for Infants, Children and Adolescents Including Regular Physical Examinations, Health Screening and Immunizations **MA:** Regional **D/D/R:** Administering State Immunizations, Scheduling Surgical Procedures, Evaluating Patients, Approving Referrals, Practicing Pediatric Hematology and Oncology **H/I/S:** Knitting, Gardening **EDU:** Associate Degree in Nursing (1985)

Steven J. Stahl
Title: Director of Technical Operations **Company:** Cable News Network, Washington Bureau **Address:** 820 First Street N.E., Washington, DC 20002 United States **BUS:** Broad-Casting Company **P/S:** Broad-Casting Services for all CNN Broad-Casting Networks and Production of Shows **MA:** International **EXP:** Mr. Stahl's expertise includes show production, direction and technical staff management. **D/D/R:** Overseeing the Studio and Control Room, Working with Audio and Graphic Designers, Directing the Floor, Producing 'Larry King Live' and CNN's 'Wolf Blitzer' **H/I/S:** Golfing, Biking, Caring for his Dog **EDU:** Bachelor of Science, Southern Illinois University (1984) **A/H:** Emmy Awards
Email: steve.stahl@cnn.com
URL: http://www.cnn.com

Mr. Ronald J. Stalica
Title: Medical Care Representative **Company:** Astrazeneca **Address:** 58-30 71st Street, Maspeth, NY 11378 United States **BUS:** Pharmaceutical Company **P/S:** New Medicines Designed to Improve the Health and Quality of Life of Patients Around the World **MA:** Regional **D/D/R:** Managing Cardiovascular and Anatomy, Physiology, Administering Pathology Medications, Calling on Physicians, Working as an Office-Based and Hospital Representative, Coordinating Programs **H/I/S:** Competitive Weight-Lifting **EDU:** Bachelor's Degree in Mechanical Technology, New York Institute of Technology (1992) **A/A/S:** Delegate, National Convention, American College of Cardiology; Delegate, National Convention, American Diabetes Association
Email: ronniechest@aol.com
URL: http://www.astrazeneca.com

Brandy Stallings
Title: PMO Assistant HP Account **Company:** Hewlett Packard **Address:** 3000 Hanover Street, Palo Alto, CA 94304 United States **BUS:** Technology Company **P/S:** Technology Products and Services **MA:** World Wide Business **D/D/R:** Program Management, Process Outsourcing, Office Management, Data Management, Web Development **H/I/S:** Cooking, Gardening, Trap Shooting, Mountain Biking **EDU:** Diploma, James Lick High School, Certified in Web Publishing, Ongoing Business Education **C/VW:** United Way
Email: brandy.stallings@hp.com
URL: http://www.hp.com

George K. Stambouloglou
Title: Wholesale Account Executive **Company:** JPMorgan Chase & Co. **Address:** P.O. Box 493, Waterbury, CT 06720 United States **BUS:** Banking and Finance Company **P/S:** Wholesale Mortgages, Small Mixed Use **MA:** Regional **D/D/R:** Managing Credit Analysis Reports **H/I/S:** Basketball, Soccer, Golfing **EDU:** College Coursework; Certification in Banking; Connecticut School of Finance and Management (2001) **A/A/S:** President Club Member, Mortage Lenders Network USA, Inc. (2005)
URL: http://www.chaseb2b.com

Amy L. Stamps
Title: Owner **Company:** Sliced Right, LLC **Dept:** Caruso's Sandwich Company **Address:** 15310 E. Marietta Avenue, Suite 4, Spokane Valley, WA 99216 United States **BUS:** Deli **P/S:** Food Products, Sandwich **MA:** Local **EXP:** Ms. Stamps' expertise is in customer satisfaction assurance. **H/I/S:** Horseback Riding, Traveling
Email: slicedright@gotsky.com

Haley Stancil-Mitchell
Title: Curriculum and Exceptional Children Coordinator **Company:** South Smithfield Elementary **Address:** 201 W. Sanders Street, Smithfield, NC 27577 United States **BUS:** Elementary School **P/S:** Elementary Education **MA:** Local **D/D/R:** Teaching, Administration **H/I/S:** Reading, Going to the Beach **EDU:** Master's Degree in School Administration, Fayetteville State University; Master's Degree in Special Education, Fayetteville State University; Bachelor of Science in Elementary Education, Campbell University **A/A/S:** Bright Ideas Grant **C/VW:** Autism Society of America
Email: hstancilmi@bellsouth.net
URL: http://www.cambridgewhoswho.com

John R. Standley
Title: Executive Director **Company:** Housing Authority of the City of Buffalo **Address:** P.O. Box L, Buffalo, TX 75831 United States **BUS:** Government Organization **P/S:** Housing for Low-Income Families **MA:** Buffalo **EXP:** Mr. Standley's expertise is in operations management. **H/I/S:** Collecting Coins and Stamps, Masonry **EDU:** Bachelor of Business Administration in Industrial Production Management, Southern Methodist University **CERTS:** Diploma in Transportation, Shirley Hill Traffic College; Diploma in Transportation, North Texas Commerce School **A/A/S:** Sigma Iota Epsilon; Delta Nu Alpha **C/VW:** Masonic Order; Shriners Hospital for Children
Email: bhatx@hotmail.com
URL: http://www.cambridgewhoswho.com

Debbie K. Stanford
Title: Vice President **Company:** AquaTest, Incorporated **Address:** 400 W. Midland Avenue, P.O. Box 1905, Woodland Park, CO 80866 United States **BUS:** Utility Service **P/S:** Operations and Management of Water Systems **MA:** Regional **D/D/R:** Managing All Administrative and Financial Aspects of the Office water and waste water utilities **H/I/S:** Knitting, Snowmobiling, Attending Hockey Games **EDU:** College Coursework in Early Childhood Education, Southern Colorado University (One Year) **A/A/S:** Faith Lutheran Church; Special District Association of Colorado; Colorado Rural Water Association; Lutheran Women's Missionary League
Email: h2o@h2oconsultants.biz
URL: http://www.h2oconsultants.biz

Judith A. Stang
Title: Program Director, Strategic Leadership Program **Company:** Neumann College **Address:** 1 Neumann Drive, Aston, PA 19014 United States **BUS:** College **P/S:** Education **MA:** National **D/D/R:** Developing a Masters Level Strategic Leadership Program, Developing Online and Hybrid Programs **EDU:** Doctor of Public Administration, Nova Southeastern University **A/A/S:** American Diabetes Association, Sustainability Christian Housing Authority, Prison Society, Zonta
Email: stangj@neumann.edu
URL: http://www.neumann.edu

Ms. Andrea C. Stanley
Title: Owner **Company:** Andrea's Touch, C.A.R.E., Inc. **Address:** 409 Woodward Street, Amory, MS 38821 United States **BUS:** Bath and Body Works and Youth Outreach Program **P/S:** Soap Products to Benefit Outreach **MA:** Local **D/D/R:** Makes and Sells Baskets, Homemade Soap and Aromatherapy **H/I/S:** Scrapbooking, Antiquing, Collecting Coins, Stamps and Dolls, Embroidering **EDU:** Pursuing Bachelor of Arts; Associate Degree, Ashford University (1970) **A/A/S:** AARP; WWF; Save a Tree; Outreach Missionary Youth Groups; Little Friends; Public Speaking to Teens
Email: handyandy3269@yahoo.com

Dr. Denise S. Stanley
Title: Pharmacist for Medicare Policy **Company:** Center's for Medicare and Medicaid Services **Address:** 190 Southwood Court, Fayetteville, GA 30214 United States **BUS:** Medicare Prescription Drug Coverage **P/S:** Medicare and Medicaid Policy Issues **MA:** Regional **D/D/R:** Resolving Medicare Part D Inquiries, Keeping the Process of Medicare Moving and Abreast of Any Changes and Policy Issues with Weekly Staff Meetings, Negotiating with Disgruntled Physicians and Patients, Traveling to Eight Southeast States, Talking to Beneficiaries **EDU:** Doctor of Pharmacy, Southern School of Pharmacy, Mercer University (1987) **A/A/S:** American Public Health Association
Email: denise.stanley@cms.hhs.gov
URL: http://www.cms.hhs.gov

Niolene E. Stanley
Title: Dental Hygienist **Company:** Millennium Dental **Address:** 2827 E. Millennium Place, Suite 3, Fayetteville, AR 72703 United States **BUS:** Dental Office **P/S:** Dental Healthcare **MA:** Regional **D/D/R:** Oral Health, Dental Hygiene **H/I/S:** Playing Tennis, Basket-Weaving, Scrap Booking, Knitting, Spending Time with her Three Dogs **EDU:** Associate Degree in Dental Hygiene and Health Science, University of Tennessee **A/A/S:** American Dental Hygenist Associiation Razor Back Study Club **A/H:** Selected by the church secretary to perform hygene services for mission fields. **C/VW:** Church, New Heights Church
Email: niolene@cox.net
URL: http://www.cambridgewhoswho.com

Virna D. D. Stanley
Title: Manager **Company:** Bankruptcy Services **BUS:** Bankruptcy Solutions Company **P/S:** Bankruptcy Solutions and Consulting Services **MA:** National **D/D/R:** Managing the Business **H/I/S:** Attending Musical Concerts, Boating, Four-Wheeling, Spending Time with her Family **EDU:** Diploma, Allen High School
Email: Virna.Stanley@cwwemail.com
Email: dd_stanley@yahoo.com

Duane C. Stanton
Title: Electrician **Company:** Stanton Electric **Address:** 807 N. Canty Avenue, New Hampton, IA 50659 United States **BUS:** Electronic Equipment Retailer **P/S:** Residential and Commercial High Voltage Electronic Equipment **MA:** Local **D/D/R:** Business Management, Working and Repairing Electronic Equipment, Repairing Electronic Equipment **H/I/S:** Hunting, Fishing **EDU:** College Coursework **A/A/S:** Local Gun Organizations; Local Golf Clubs **C/VW:** Volunteer, Local Rescue Squad
Email: Duane.Stanton@cwwemail.com
URL: http://www.cambridgewhoswho.com

Iowa Gay Stapleford
Title: Office Manager **Company:** Capital Kia **Address:** 13573 N. Highway 183, Austin, TX 78750 United States **BUS:** Automotive **P/S:** Kia Dealership **MA:** Statewide **D/D/R:** Accounting and Managing Business Office **C/VW:** Family Readiness Group
Email: igstapleford@capitolkia.net
URL: http://www.capitolkia.net

Shelly Starbuck
Title: Occupational Therapy for Special **Company:** Old National Trial Special Services **Address:** 4754 Milton Street, Toacsville, IN 46121 United States **BUS:** School **P/S:** Occupational Therapy for Special Children **MA:** Local **EDU:** Indiana University, Bachelor/Occupational Therapy **A/A/S:** Indiana Occupational Therapy Association, American Occupational Therapy Association

Britta M. Starke
Title: Clinical Social Worker, Addiction Therapist **Company:** Equine Reflections, Inc. UNC hospital **Address:** P.O. Box 52678, Durham, NC 27713 United States **BUS:** Social Worker, Nonprofit **P/S:** Social Work with Families and Children **MA:** Local **D/D/R:** Offering Individual, Family and Group Therapy to Recovering Addicts, Training for the National Association of Social Workers, Performing Social Work **H/I/S:** Reading, Horseback Riding **EDU:** Master of Social Work, University of North Carolina at Chapel Hill; Substance Abuse Certified **A/A/S:** National Association of Social Workers
URL: http://www.cambridgewhoswho.com

Hugh Benjamin Andre Starks, MD
Title: Medical Director **Company:** Counseling Solutions of Alaska **Address:** 701 E. Tudor Road, Anchorage, AK 99503 United States **BUS:** Mental Health Practice **P/S:** Healthcare, Outpatient Mental Health, Medicine Management, Psycho-Education **MA:** Local **D/D/R:** Adult, Child and Adolescent Psychiatry **H/I/S:** Playing Tennis, Swimming, Biking, Playing Racquetball, Hiking, Walking **EDU:** MD, University of Nebraska Medical Center College of Medicine; Bachelor of Arts in Psychology, Creighton University; Bachelor of Science in Radiologic Technology, Creighton University; Board Certification in Child and Adult Psychiatry **A/A/S:** American Academy of Child and Adolescent Psychiatry; American Psychiatric Association; National Medical Association; American Group Psychiatry Association; Retired, American Registry of Radiologic Technologist **C/VW:** American Red Cross, Blood Bank of Alaska
Email: blye12@aol.com

Mrs. Cassandra L. Starner
Title: Partner **Company:** P3 Photography **Address:** 13100 Taylor Wayne Lane, Oklahoma City, OK 73165 United States **BUS:** Photography Company **P/S:** Photography **MA:** Regional **D/D/R:** Business Development, Administration, Photography **H/I/S:** Spending Time with her Family **EDU:** Bachelor Science in Management, Oklahoma City University **A/A/S:** Professional Photographers of Oklahoma, Inc. **C/VW:** North Shore Animal League
Email: p3photography@excite.com
URL: http://www.printroom.com/pro/p3photography

Willie Mae Starr-White
Title: Customer Operations Manager **Company:** Pitney Bowes Legal Solutions **Address:** 500 Grant Street, OMC 31st Floor, Pittsburgh, PA 15219 United States **BUS:** Leading Provider of Mainstream Solutions and Facilities Management **P/S:** Cross Border Shipping Services, Document Creation, Document Distribution, Document Production, Document Storage and Retrieval, Education and Training, Federal Government Solutions, Installation and Relocation, Legal Solutions, Optimization Services, Postage Payment Options and Presort and Mail Consolidation Services **MA:** Regional **D/D/R:** Managing Facilities, Overseeing Legal Accounts, Faxing and Scanning Documents, Managing Several Sites, Renegotiating Contracts, Handling Human Resource Duties **H/I/S:** Spending Time with Family **EDU:** Bachelor of Arts in Science, Minor in Mathematics, Carlow College (1994)
Email: williemae.starr-white@pb.com
URL: http://www.pb.com

Daniel L. Staton
Title: Concrete, Aggregate Technician **Company:** Charles W. Barger and Son **Address:** 1309 Walnut Avenue, Buena Vista, VA 24416 United States **BUS:** Manufacturing Company **P/S:** Concrete and Stone **MA:** Regional **D/D/R:** Designing for the Highway and Residential Industry, Stone Testing for Materials Used on Individual Folios, Conducting Safety Classes at Work **H/I/S:** Racing **EDU:** College Coursework in Business Management, Ferrum College (1981-1982) **A/A/S:** Virginia Ready Mix Advisor Council
Email: danemdjtim@netlos.net

Lonna M. Stauffer
Title: Owner, Garden Designer **Company:** Junebug Artistic Garden Design, Inc. **Address:** 193A 32nd Street, Suite 1, Brooklyn, NY 11232 United States **BUS:** Garden Design Company **P/S:** Garden Designs for Urban Locations **MA:** Local **D/D/R:** Designing and Installing Gardens in Plazas, Interiors and Roofs **H/I/S:** Studying **EDU:** Pursuing Master of Science in Natural Medicine; Bachelor's Degree in Natural Medicine, Clayton College of Natural Health **A/A/S:** Farm Bureau of New York
Email: mattlonn@verizon.net
URL: http://www.junebuggardens.com

Bettie J. Stayton
Title: Office Manager, Training Director **Company:** Total Home Health **Address:** 780 S McLean Boulevard, Elgin, IL 60123 United States **BUS:** Healthcare **P/S:** Oxygen, Ventilators, CPAP, Durable Medical Equipment, Sleep Apnea Devices, Respiratory Equipment, Ventilators, All Mobility Hospital Beds **MA:** Regional **D/D/R:** Billing, Collections and Training **H/I/S:** I enjoy playing pool, water skiing, boating, camping, fishing **EDU:** Capital City Junior College, Associates **A/A/S:** Dale Carnegie Services; Women in Management; Chamber of Commerce
Email: Bstayton@totalhomehealth.com
URL: http://www.totalhomehealth.com

Keith E. Steadham
Title: Superintendent **Company:** ARCO Design/Build **Address:** 4406 Windchime Way N.W., Kenneshaw, GA 30152 United States **BUS:** Construction Management Firm **P/S:** Construction Management of Industrial Projects Including Manufacturing Companies, Cold Storage and Food Distribution Companies, Warehouses, Commercial Buildings and Offices, Site Selection Service, Design Services, Competitive Lump-Sum Pricing, Value Engineering, Zoning, Permit and Code Expertise, General Contracting Services **MA:** National **D/D/R:** Overseeing Hazardous Material Storage and Containment, Supervising Production, Design and Construction Projects, Traveling, Ensuring Coding Standards, Consulting **H/I/S:** Bow Hunting, Boating, Fishing **EDU:** Bachelor's Degree in Construction Management, The University of Alabama (1980) **A/A/S:** National Association of Home Builders
Email: kes01@msn.com
URL: http://www.arcodb.com

Tina M. Stearns
Title: Human Resources Technician **Company:** Wood County Board of Mental Retardation and Developmental Disabilities **Address:** 11160 E. Gypsy Lane Road, Bowling Green, OH 43402 United States **BUS:** Nonprofit Agency **P/S:** Education and Adult Services for Individuals with Mental Retardation and Developmental Disabilities **MA:** Local **D/D/R:** Human Resources **H/I/S:** Collecting Baskets, Traveling **C/VW:** Wood County Board of Mental Retardation and Developmental Disabilities
Email: tstearne@woodmrdd.org

Ms. Diane M. Stecher
Title: President **Company:** Alobars Incorporated **Address:** 716 Hanley Industrial Court, Saint Louis, MO 63144 United States **BUS:** Rental, Service and Installation Company **P/S:** Sound, Lighting and Audiovisual **MA:** Regional **D/D/R:** Overseeing All Day-to-Day Operations, Lighting and Audiovisual Equipment to Schools, Churches, Nightclubs and Works with Fitness Centers, Managing Special Events for Corporate Businesses, Accounts Receivable and Payable, Bookkeeping, Marketing and Advertising, Working with Fitness Centers **H/I/S:** Bicycling, Gardening **EDU:** Bachelor's Degree in Accounting, University of Missouri-Saint Louis (1987) **A/A/S:** International Special Events Society; NAMM; Better Business Bureau; Brentwood Chamber of Commerce; National Director Officer, Delta Zeta
Email: diane@alobars.net
URL: http://www.alobors.com

Susan L. Stedman
Title: Writer, Proofreader, Editor **Address:** 2134 Happy Valley Drive, Medford, OR 97501 United States **BUS:** Writer, Editor, Court Reporter **P/S:** Writings, Court Reports **MA:** National **D/D/R:** Court Reporting, The Arts **H/I/S:** Traveling **EDU:** Coursework, Wheaton College, Illinois; Coursework, Southern Oregon University **A/A/S:** Phi Kappa Phi **C/VW:** Heifer International
Email: susanstedman2@hotmail.com
URL: http://www.victoriachristian.com

Lynne Steele
Title: President **Company:** Reid's Decorating Inc. **Address:** 334 Canyon Trail, Charlotte, NC 28270 United States **BUS:** Interior Design Service Provider **P/S:** Window Treatments, Wall Paper **MA:** Local **D/D/R:** Draperies **EDU:** Bachelor of Arts in Science, Northwestern University **A/A/S:** IDS
Email: lynnewsteele@aol.com
URL: http://www.reidsdecorating.com

Diane L. Stefancin
Title: Merchandise Manager **Company:** Hy-Ko Products **Address:** 60 Meadow Lane, Northfield, OH 44067 United States **BUS:** Manufacturing Company **P/S:** Numbers, Letters, Signs, Keys, Key Accessories **MA:** International **D/D/R:** Developing Merchandising **H/I/S:** Playing Golf, Spending Time with Family **EDU:** Bachelor's Degree in Marketing, Pennsylvania State University **A/A/S:** Trade Show Exhibitors Association; Point-Of-Purchase Advertising International **C/VW:** Parent Teacher Association
Email: dstefancin@hy-ko.com
URL: http://www.hy-ko.com

Carrie J. Steffens
Title: President **Company:** Well Being Center **Address:** 1360 S. Wadsworth Boulevard, Suite 114, Lakewood, CO 80226 United States **BUS:** Wellness Center **P/S:** Wellness **MA:** Local **D/D/R:** Healing Arts **H/I/S:** Traveling, Hiking, Outdoor Activities **EDU:** Associate Degree in Business, Brooks College **A/A/S:** American Massage Therapy Association **C/VW:** Susan G. Komen for the Cure
Email: wellbeingcenter@earthlink.net
URL: http://www.wellbeinginfo.com

Marti J. Steger
Title: Programs Manager **Company:** Denver Center for the Performing Arts **Address:** 1101 13th Street, Denver, CO 80204 United States **BUS:** Nonprofit Organization **P/S:** Educational Theater **MA:** Regional **D/D/R:** Production Coordination **H/I/S:** Moderating Groups for Professional Women, Leading her Daughter's Girl Scout Troop, Camping, Horseback Riding **EDU:** Associate Degree in Audio Engineering, The Art Institute of Colorado
Email: msteger@dcpa.org
URL: http://www.denvercenter.org

William J. Stehlin
Title: Nutritional Service **Company:** Woman's and Children's Hospital **Address:** 140 Bryant Street, Buffalo, NY 14222 United States **BUS:** Hospital **P/S:** Healthcare **MA:** Local **D/D/R:** Offering the Nutritional Needs of Over 200 Patients **H/I/S:** Movies, Pool Player **EDU:** Pennsylvania Culinary **A/A/S:** Union SEIU 1199
Email: willydawg20g2003@yahoo.com

Paul G. Stein
Title: President **Company:** PGS Engineering **Address:** 12 Eastview Drive, Simsbury, CT 06070 United States **BUS:** Aircraft Industry **P/S:** Aircraft Fuel Efficiency Enhancement, Environmental Control Systems, Engine Start Systems, Turbo Machinery **MA:** International **D/D/R:** Designing Aircraft Environmental Control Systems on 95 Percent of Commercial Aircraft Flying in the United States **H/I/S:** Photography, Traveling **EDU:** Master of Science, California Institute of Technology **CERTS:** Registered Professional Engineer, Arizona and California **A/A/S:** American Society of Mechanical Engineers; The New York Academy of Sciences **A/H:** NASA Apollo Achievement Award
Email: paulbettystein@comcast.net

S. Keven Steinberg
Title: Principal, Attorney **Company:** Steinberg Law Offices **Address:** 11500 Olympic Boulevard, Suite 316, Los Angeles, CA 90064 United States **BUS:** Law Office **P/S:** Legal Services **MA:** Southern California **D/D/R:** Business Transactions, Litigation, Employment Law, Real Estate **H/I/S:** Spending Time with Family, Enjoying Nice Cars, Collecting sports memorabilia **EDU:** JD, Southwestern Law School **A/A/S:** California Bar Association; AIA; American Trial Lawyers Association; Encino Chamber of Commerce; Professor, Los Angeles Valley College **C/VW:** Temple
Email: ksteinburg@steinburg-lawoffices.com
URL: http://www.steinburg-lawoffices.com

Susan K. Steinhauser
Title: Owner **Company:** Rebecca's Cottage **Address:** 114 Woods End Road, Huntsville, AL 35806 United States **BUS:** Art and Gift Shop **P/S:** Hand-Painted Treasures and Unique Home Decor **MA:** National **D/D/R:** Creating Customized Artwork for Clients, Eclectic Hand-Painted Glassware, Metalware, Flower Arrangements, Holiday Items, Gift Baskets **H/I/S:** Cooking, Enjoying Music, Art, Football, Traveling **EDU:** Bachelor of Science in Business Administration, University of Alabama in Huntsville (1984) **A/A/S:** Hunstville Art League; Huntsville Literary Association; Public Speaking Nationally
Email: rebeccascottage@knology.net
URL: http://www.rebeccas-cottage.com

John R. Steinmann
Title: Vice President **Company:** King Architectural Products, Inc **Address:** 31 Simpson Road, Bolton, L7E 1E4 Canada **BUS:** Architecture Marketing **P/S:** Electronic Directories, Signage, Way Finding **MA:** International **D/D/R:** International Marketing **H/I/S:** Woodworking, Hiking **EDU:** Bachelor of Science in Chemistry, University of Manitoba; Master of Business Administration, University of Western Australia **A/A/S:** SCGD
Email: jsteinmann@kingarchitecturalproducts.com
URL: http://www.kingarchitecturalproducts.com

Terri Lyn Stephan
Title: Instructional Facilitator for Intermediate Language Arts **Company:** Laramie County School District 1 **Address:** 2810 House Avenue, Cheyenne, WY 82001 United States **BUS:** School **P/S:** Education **MA:** Local **D/D/R:** Teaching Language Arts, Coaching Teachers in Professional Development, Creating Model Lessons, Implementing Strategies, Organizing Conferences with Teachers **H/I/S:** Traveling **EDU:** Master's Degree Plus 62 in Reading and Elementary Education, University of Wyoming; Bachelor's Degree in Deaf Education, University of Northern Colorado **A/A/S:** National Reading Association; National Council of Teachers of Mathematics **C/VW:** Board Member, Animal Shelter
Email: stephant@laramie1.k12.wy.us

Dianne F. Stephens
Title: Visual Arts Teacher **Company:** Fitzgerald High School **Address:** 601 W. Cypress Street, Fitzgerald, GA 31750 United States **BUS:** High School **P/S:** Education **MA:** Local **D/D/R:** Teaching Visual Arts **H/I/S:** Riding her Motorcycles **EDU:** Master's Degree, University of Georgia **A/A/S:** Association of American Educators; Georgia Association of Educators
Email: mdfirwin@netscape.net
URL: http://www.ben-hill.k12.ga.com

Julie Stephens
Title: Principal, Architect **Company:** J.R. Stephens Architects **Address:** 3119 Methacton Avenue, Eagleville, PA 19403 United States **BUS:** Architecture Firm **P/S:** Design Drawing, Three-Dimensional Modeling, Construction Administration, Project Development, Design Build, Structural Drawings, Mechanical Drawings, Electrical Drawings, Planning Commission Testimony, Zoning Board Testimony, Residential Additions, Custom Homes, Kitchen Renovations, Bathroom Renovations **MA:** Regional **D/D/R:** Overseeing Daily Operations Including Bookkeeping, Designing Residential and Commercial Structures, Additions and Renovations **EDU:** Bachelor of Architecture, Philadelphia University (1998) **A/A/S:** Women's Referral Network; The American Institute of Architects
Email: julie.stephens@cambridgewhoswho.com
URL: http://www.jrstephensarchitects.com

Tana M. Stephens
Title: Closing Officer **Company:** Key Bank National Association **Address:** 1675 Broadway, Suite 300, Denver, CO 80202 United States **BUS:** Bank **P/S:** Mortgages, Loans, Closings for Commercial Real Estate **MA:** Regional **D/D/R:** performing real estate closings **H/I/S:** Traveling, Reading, Spending Time with her Family **EDU:** Pursuing Bachelor's Degree in Accounting, University of Phoenix
Email: tana_m_stephens@keybank.com
URL: http://www.keybank.com

Gregory N. Stepp
Title: Band Director **Company:** Royal Springs Middle School **Address:** 332 Champion Way, Georgetown, KY 40324 United States **BUS:** Middle School **P/S:** Education **MA:** Local **EXP:** Mr. Stepp's expertise is in instrumental music education. **D/D/R:** Teaching Middle School Band Classes for 22 to 75 Students **H/I/S:** Golfing, Fishing **EDU:** Master's Degree in Secondary Education, University of Kentucky **CERTS:** Certified Teacher, National Board for Professional Teaching Standards **A/A/S:** National Band Association; Music Educators National Conference; Phi Nu Alpha **C/VW:** First United Methodist Church, Frankfort, KY; The Salvation Army; American Red Cross; Boy Scouts of America
Email: greg.stepp@scott.kyschools.us
URL: http://www.cambridgewhoswho.com

Ms. Julie L. Sterling
Title: Director of Human Resources **Company:** Zane State College **Address:** 1555 Newark Road, Zanesville, OH 43701 United States **BUS:** State College **P/S:** Education, Associates Degree Programs, Certificate Programs, Occupational Skills Programs, Training Modules, Computer Workshops, Pathways to Engineering and Human Resources **MA:** Regional **D/D/R:** Managing Human Resources, Hiring Associates, Conducting Orientation Programs, Training Employees, Evaluating and Developing Staff, Attending to General Personnel Matters, Managing Employee Benefit Plans and Insurance Policies for 280 Employees **H/I/S:** Walking, White-Water Rafting, Reading, **EDU:** Master of Arts in Public Administration, Concentration in Human Resource Management, The Ohio State University (1997); Master of Arts in Leadership Development and Administration, Ohio University (1996); Bachelor of Specialized Studies, Ohio University (1986) **A/A/S:** The Society for Human Resource Management; College and University Personnel Association for Human Resources; National Association of College and University Business Officers; Human Resources Director, Ohio Association of Community Colleges; Muskingum Valley Human Resouce Management Association **A/H:** Presented at Midwest CUPA Human Resouce Conference-Balancing Employee Satifaction with Increasing Costs (2008) **C/VW:** Habitat for Humanity, Salvation Army, Christ's Table Volunteer
Email: jsterling@zanestate.edu
URL: http://www.zanestate.edu

George Frederick Sterne
Title: President **Company:** George Sterne Agency **Address:** 254 E grand Ave, Escondido, CA 92025 United States **BUS:** Mailing Lists Financial **P/S:** Mailing lists, E-mails, Direct Mailing **MA:** National **D/D/R:** Financial Services in Insurance, Life Insurance **H/I/S:** Travel, Golf, Gold trader **EDU:** Western Ontario, Bachelor of Arts **A/A/S:** CRu, CLI, DSMA, GF-Sterns and Sons, Sales and Marketing
Email: gfs97@yahoo.com
URL: http://www.georgesterneagency.com

Ms. Dorothy Fahrner Sterrett
Title: Professor **Company:** Broward College **Address:** 3501 S.W. Davie Road, Davie, FL 33314 United States **BUS:** College **P/S:** Higher Education **MA:** Regional **D/D/R:** motivating students, teaching freshman student success classes and skills **H/I/S:** Exercising, Gardening **EDU:** Master of Science in Elementary Education, Barry University (2002) **CERTS:** Certified Teacher in Exceptional Student Education; Certification in Teaching English as a Second Language; Certification in Life Success Skills
Email: dsterret@broward.edu
URL: http://www.broward.edu

Clifford Stevens II
Title: Owner **Company:** Superior Hardwood Floors **Address:** 119 Dyer Street, Columbia, TN 38401 United States **BUS:** Hardwood Flooring Company **P/S:** Bamboo, All Types of Hardwood Flooring, Carpet, Tile Floor Coverings **MA:** Local **D/D/R:** Custom Borders, In-Lays, Sand and Finishing **H/I/S:** Golfing, Spending Time at Church, Spending Time with his Family **EDU:** Certified, National Oak Flooring Manufacturers Association; Awarded Congressional Honor of Merit **A/A/S:** Members, National Oak Flooring Manufacturers Association
Email: superiorhardwoodfloor@yahoo.com
URL: http://www.superiorhardwoodfloor.com

Holly R. Stevens
Title: Associate Attorney **Company:** Segal McCambridge Singer & Mahoney **Address:** 330 N. Wabash Avenue, Suite 200, Chicago, IL 60611 United States **BUS:** Law Firm **P/S:** Litigation Services Including Commercial Law, Insurance, Labor and Employment Law, General Litigation, Products Liability, Toxic and Hazardous Substances Litigation, Consumer Litigation, Business Immigration and Business Counseling **MA:** National **EXP:** Ms. Stevens' expertise includes business and product litigation, consumer claim, employment and truck defenses, personal injury lawsuits, breach of warranty for claims and consumer actions. **D/D/R:** writing an employment newsletter and insurance coverage newsletter **EDU:** JD, John Marshall Law School (2000); Bachelor of Arts in Psychology, University of Michigan (1994) **A/A/S:** The Chicago Bar Association; Illinois State Bar Association; Women's Bar Association of Illinois; National Defense Research Institute
Email: hstevens@smsm.com
URL: http://www.smsm.com

Joey Ann Stevens, BS
Title: Founder, Inventor **Company:** The Earring-Aid Company **Address:** 1860 Sandy Plains Road, Marietta, GA 30066 United States **BUS:** Online Store **P/S:** Earrings, Jewelry Accessories **MA:** International **D/D/R:** designing and selling earrings **H/I/S:** Caring for Animals **EDU:** Bachelor of Science in Business, Auburn University (1972) **C/VW:** Environmental Volunteer Programs
Email: earringaidmail@comcast.net
URL: http://www.earring-aid.com

Mrs. Marilyn Ann Stevens
Title: Joint Owner **Company:** LynAnn's Specialty Shoppe **Dept:** Department of Administration **BUS:** Distribution Company **P/S:** Air Purifying, Water Filtration and Odor and Smoke Removal Products **MA:** International **D/D/R:** Overseeing the Distribution of Company Products, Managing Business Operations **H/I/S:** Watching Sports, Antiquing, Traveling, Working on Computers **A/A/S:** Alliance to Save Florida's Trauma Care; Coalition to Protect Healthcare Access; National Kidney Foundation of Florida; National Kidney Foundation **A/H:** Making Lives Better Award, National Kidney Foundation; Jefferson Award for Outstanding Public Service; Certificate of Excellence **C/VW:** United Church of God
Email: terencestevens@verizon.net
Email: terence@ecoquestintl.com
URL: http://www.ecoquestintl.com/terence
URL: http://www.myabcspace.com/airandwaterpurifiers

Nancy M. Stevens
Title: Licensed Real Estate Broker Associate **Company:** Century 21 Mac Levitt **Address:** 652 Sunrise Highway, Baldwin, NY 11510 United States **BUS:** Real Estate **P/S:** Real Estate Agency **MA:** Local **D/D/R:** Residential Specialist, Marketing Specialist **H/I/S:** Spending Time with her Four Grandchildren **EDU:** Licensed Real Estate Agent, State of New York; Licensed Broker, State of New York **A/A/S:** Consultant, Mary Kay Cosmetics
Email: c21nms@aol.com
URL: http://www.marykay.com/nstevens82

Patricia R. Stevens
Title: Licensing Administrator **Company:** BWX Technologies, Inc. **Address:** 1570 Mount Athos Road, Lynchburg, VA 24504 United States **BUS:** Leader in Developing Nuclear Technologies and Premier Manager of Complex, High-Consequence Nuclear and National Security Operations **P/S:** Nuclear Innovations and Manufacturing Capabilities to Commercial and Government Customers **MA:** Regional **D/D/R:** Making All Facility Changes, Ensuring Licensing Applicability, Working on All Administration **H/I/S:** Playing Softball, Reading, Swimming **EDU:** Pursuing Bachelor's Degree in Business Administration, Averett University **A/H:** National Dean's List
Email: prstevens@bwxt.com

Stacie L. Stevens
Title: Event Consultant **Company:** Lakeshore Events, LLC **Address:** 509 Buena Vista Drive, Spring Lake, MI 49456 United States **BUS:** Event Planning Company **P/S:** Planning Services and Event Management for Corporate Events, Fundraisers, Funerals, Social Occasions, Expositions, Birthday Parties, Theme Parties, Holiday Festivals, Boat Shows, Charitable Events and Weddings, Promotions, Consultation Services **MA:** Regional **D/D/R:** Event Planning and Consulting, Managing Public Relations, Advertising through Radio, Television and Newsprint to Promote Events, Finding Caterers, Entertainment, Vendors and Brokers, Consulting with Website Designer, Overseeing Finances **H/I/S:** Boating, Bicycling, Gardening, In-Line Skating, Practicing Yoga, Gourmet Cooking **EDU:** Bachelor of Business Management, Davenport University (1999); Associate Degree in Legal Applied Science, Davenport University (1988) **CERTS:** Licensed Realtor, State of Michigan (1992); Notary Public State of Michigan **A/A/S:** President, Lakeshore Chapter, Alliance of Women Entrepreneurs, Michigan; Board of Directors, The Central Business District Development Authority; Hollard Area Chamber, Muskegon Chamber; Grand Haven Chamber of Commerce; Inforum, Michigan
Email: stacielstevens@yahoo.com
URL: http://www.lakeshore-events.com

Wendy Stevens
Title: Pres of Info Security Sys Assoc **Company:** Credant Technologies **Address:** 17915 Windtop Lane, Dallas, TX 75287 United States **BUS:** IT Security Consultant **P/S:** IT Security Software/IT Security Account Manager **MA:** International **D/D/R:** Sales/Consultant **H/I/S:** Bike Racing, Hiking and Travel **EDU:** Bachelor's Degree, Nursing Degree, VA **A/A/S:** RSA, Board for Members and Professionals in Corporations
Email: wsteve008@aol.com

Leanne L. Stevenson
Title: Manager Natural Resources and Policy Division **Company:** Wyoming Department of Agriculture, State of Wyoming **Address:** 2219 Carey Avenue, Cheyenne, WY 82001 United States **BUS:** Government **P/S:** Managing Programs, Developing Natural Resources **MA:** National **D/D/R:** Managing Livestock Range, Researching Natural Resource Conservation, Studying Drought Issues and Terrestrial Carbon Sequestration **H/I/S:** Spending Time with her Grandchildren, Horseback Riding, Sewing, Cooking **EDU:** Master of Science in Agronomy, Kansas State University; Bachelor of Animal Science, Colorado State University **A/A/S:** 4-H Program, Local Church
Email: leanne.stevenson@cwwemail.com

Alice Louise Stewart
Title: Office Manager **Company:** Shirley Water Supply Corporation **Address:** 6684 FM 1567 W., Sulphur Springs, TX 75482 United States **BUS:** Water Supply Corporation **P/S:** Water Supply **MA:** Local **D/D/R:** Office Management **H/I/S:** Cooking **EDU:** Coursework in Bookkeeping, Business College **A/H:** Office Manager of the Year, Texas Rural Water Association (2004) **C/VW:** Wesley Methodist Church; Secretary, Sunday School; Sulfur Springs Community Center
Email: shirleywater@bluebonnet.net

Cathy Arlene Stewart
Title: Systems Principal **Company:** Communications Anonymous Systems **Address:** 1400 Elliston Road, Memphis, TN 38106 United States **BUS:** Publishing Company **P/S:** Business Invitations, Stationary, Program Design **MA:** Local **D/D/R:** printing, designing programs and personal greeting cards **H/I/S:** Traveling **EDU:** Bachelor of Arts in English Literature, Minor in Journalism, The LeMoyne-Owen College **C/VW:** Former Motivational Speaker, Memphis City School System
Email: cas_sys@yahoo.com
URL: http://www.myspace.com/casprintbuff

Dana Morgan Stewart
Title: Community Manager **Company:** Metric Property Management **Address:** 1475 Sawdust Road, Spring, TX 77380 United States **BUS:** Management Company **P/S:** Multimillion Dollar Asset Management **MA:** Local **D/D/R:** Performing Management and Administrative Tasks, Budgeting, Reviewing Paperwork, Leasing Units, Customer Service **H/I/S:** Spending Time with her Daughter, Going on Family Outings **EDU:** Coursework, Sam Houston State University **CERTS:** cert CAM **A/A/S:** Chamber of Commerce **A/H:** Customer Service Excellence Award (2006) **C/VW:** The Crossing Church
Email: woodridgepark@metricproperties.com
URL: http://www.cambridgewhoswho.com

Drucilla Stewart
Title: Cosmetologist, Owner **Company:** Dionne's Hair Salon **Address:** 8888 Jennings Station Road, Jennings, MO 63136 United States **BUS:** Hair Salon **P/S:** Hair Growth, Beauty, Hair Styling **MA:** Local **D/D/R:** Managing Shop, Seeing Clients, Offering Customer Service **H/I/S:** Reading, Playing Darts, Singing **C/VW:** Church, Gospel Choir Courses, Veterans Association

Jenelle Stewart
Title: Human Resource Administrator **Company:** North American Lighting, Inc. **Address:** 2277 S. Main Street, Paris, IL 61944 United States **BUS:** Light Manufacturing Company **P/S:** Automobile Head and Tail Lights **MA:** International **D/D/R:** Human Resources, Benefits **H/I/S:** Working in her Yard, Playing Softball, Going to the Lake, Walking with her Golden Retriever **EDU:** Bachelor's Degree in Park and Recreation Administration, Illinois State University **A/A/S:** Kiwanis International; P.E.O. International; Home Extension **C/VW:** Relay for Life, SHRINE
Email: jstewart@nal.com

John R. Stewart
Title: President **Company:** Hue Color Systems, LLC **Address:** 48 Lawrence Avenue, Bedford Hills, NY 10507 United States **BUS:** Supplier to Commercial Printers **P/S:** Ink Dispensers, Color Software, Press Room Products **MA:** International **D/D/R:** Importing Machinery Including Ink Dispensers, Mixers for the Blending of Print Inks **H/I/S:** Fishing, Tennis, Sail Boating **EDU:** Associate of Applied Science in Marketing and Communication, Brookdale College (1976) **A/A/S:** Printing Industries of America; GATF
Email: info@huecolorsystem.com
URL: http://www.huecolorsystem.com

Mr. Kirk Stewart
Title: Owner, Graphic Designer **Company:** Digital Design Solutions **Address:** 1354 Eisenhower Circle, Apartment 304, Woodbridge, VA 22191 United States **BUS:** Graphic Design **P/S:** Custom Graphic Designs and Corporate Branding, Logo Creations, Brochure Designs **MA:** National **D/D/R:** Managing Corporate Projects, Creating Illustrations, Working with Photographs in Photoshop **H/I/S:** Snowboarding **EDU:** Diploma, Lawrence High School (1998); Pursuing Associate Degree in Graphics Design, Westwood College **A/A/S:** American Institute of Graphic Artists
Email: kirk_stewart@digitaldesignsolutions.net
URL: http://www.digitaldesignsolutions.net

Marion Stewart
Title: Liver Transplant Coordinator **Company:** Duke University Medical Center **Address:** Box 3876, Durham, NC 27710 United States **BUS:** University Hospital **P/S:** Inpatient and Outpatient Care **MA:** Regional **D/D/R:** Managing Liver Transplantations and the Transportation List, Assisting Patients **H/I/S:** Hiking, Walking, Reading **EDU:** Pursuing Master's Degree; Bachelor of Science in Nursing, The University of Texas; Certified Nephrology Nurse; Certified Clinical Transplant Coordinator **A/A/S:** Sigma Theta Tau; International Transplant Nurses Society; American Nephrology Nurses Association
Email: marionkstweart@aol.com
URL: http://medschool.duke.edu

Rosalind Hydie Stewart
Title: Pediatric Office Manger, Certified Pharmacy Technician **Company:** Heartland Pediatrics **Address:** 805 West Deyoung, Marion, IL 62959 United States **BUS:** Healthcare **P/S:** Pediatric Healthcare **MA:** Local **D/D/R:** Healthcare Office Management, Pharmaceuticals **H/I/S:** Fishing, Traveling **EDU:** Certified Pharmacy Technician; Certified Phlebotomist; Associate of Science in Psychology, John A. Logan College; Pursuing Certified Medical Assistant **A/A/S:** Beta Sigma Phi **C/VW:** Volunteer, Special Olympics
Email: hydie@hughes.net
URL: http://www.cambridgewhoswho.com

Noelle A. Stewart-Sullivan
Title: Physical Education Teacher **Company:** Tuscan Elementary School **Address:** 25 Harvard Avenue, Maplewood, NJ 07040 United States **BUS:** Elementary School **P/S:** Primary Education **MA:** Regional **D/D/R:** Physical Fitness Testing, Teaching Nutrition and Healthy Living to students and special needs children in a self-contained classroom, Acting as a Liaison between the Students and the Teachers on Health and Fitness, Working with the Community Against Obesity in Children and Academic Achievement, Improving the Self-Esteem of Children **H/I/S:** Exercising, Playing Softball, Volunteering **EDU:** Master's Degree in Adapted Physical Education, Ohio State University (1994) **CERTS:** Certification in Elementary Physical Education **A/A/S:** New Jersey Alliance for Health, Physical Education, Recreation and Dance; New Jersey Education Association; National Education Association; American Alliance for Health, Physical Education, Recreation and Dance **A/H:** Cambridge VIP Award **C/VW:** Local Charitable Organizations
Email: nstewart1969@aol.com

Alicia A. Stiffler
Title: Owner **Company:** Stiffler Contracting, LLC **Address:** 818 17th Street, Washougal, WA 98671 United States **BUS:** Construction Company **P/S:** Parking Lot Maintenance, Asphalt Resurfacing **MA:** Regional **D/D/R:** Managing the Business, Laying Down Asphalt **H/I/S:** Gardening, Camping, Spending Time with Family **EDU:** Associate Degree in General Studies, Clark College
Email: stifflercontracting@comcast.net

Heather D. Stiltner
Title: Paramedic **Company:** Beacon of Life Ambulance Service **Address:** P.O. Box 608, Saint Paul, VA 24283 United States **BUS:** Emergency Services **P/S:** Advanced Life Support **MA:** National **D/D/R:** Paramedic, Firefighter, Emergency Medical Technician Instruction **H/I/S:** Spending Time with Family and Friends **EDU:** Associate of Applied Science in Emergency Medical Services, Southwest Virginia Community College (2006); Continuing Education Classes **A/A/S:** National Association of Emergency Medical Technicians; National Registry of Emergency Medical Technicians; Town of Tazewell Fire Department **C/VW:** Community Organizations
Email: pyrochic_620@yahoo.com

Winnie C. Stine
Title: Teacher **Company:** Governor's Ranch Elementary **Address:** 5354 S. Field Street, Littleton, CO 80123 United States **BUS:** Elementary School **P/S:** Education **MA:** Local **D/D/R:** Teaching **H/I/S:** Watching Tennis, Golfing **EDU:** Master's Degree, University of Colorado **A/A/S:** Colorado Council International Reading Association **C/VW:** Race for the Cure, Goodwill, American Red Cross, Disabled American Veterans
Email: wstine@jeffco.k12.co.us

Penelope Stinney
Title: Inventor/Owner **Company:** The Baby Bank **Address:** 105 Stinney Lane, Summerville, SC 29483 United States **BUS:** Inventor Retail **P/S:** Invented a Baby Bank to Help Children Learn and Have Fun Saving Money **MA:** International **D/D/R:** Created the Baby Bank **H/I/S:** Cooking, Spending Time with Family **CERTS:** Certified Medical Office Assistant, Rutledge College

Herb Stinson
Title: Teacher, Coach **Company:** Bayfield High School, Aztec High School **Address:** 106 Willow Lane, Aztec, NM 87410 United States **BUS:** Public High School **P/S:** Education for Students in Ninth through 12th-Grade, Sports **MA:** Regional **D/D/R:** Teaching Physical Education, Coaching Wrestling and Football, Speaking Nationally at Wrestling Clinics **H/I/S:** Traveling, Motorcycle Riding **EDU:** Bachelor of Arts in History and Social Sciences, Southern Utah University (1975) **A/A/S:** Coach, US Tourde Mond Team against Canada (1989); Coach, USA Wrestling All Star Team against Iowa All Star Team (1998); National Education Association **A/H:** National Coach of the Year (1991, 1995, 2000); Teacher of the Year (1991); Coaching Hall of Fame, Southern Utah University; New Mexico Coaching Hall of Fame; New Mexico Wrestling Hall of Fame
Email: herb_stinson@hotmail.com
URL: http://www.bayfield.k12.co.us/hs

Geraldine S. Stith
Title: Author **Company:** Self Employed **Address:** 500 Madisonville Street, Princeton, KY 42445 United States **BUS:** Writing **P/S:** Books **MA:** International **D/D/R:** Writing Books **H/I/S:** Reading **EDU:** High School Education
Email: gstith@hotmail.com
URL: http://www.allienlegacy1955.com

Mr. Charles E. Stocker
Title: Tech Service Manager **Company:** McElroy Metal, Inc. **Address:** 1500 Hamilton Road, Bossier City, LA 71111 United States **BUS:** Leading Manufacturer of Metal Roofing, Metal Siding and Sub-structural Components **P/S:** Product Line Includes a Wide Variety of Architectural Standing Seam Roofing Systems as well as Many Industrial and Commercial Wall and Roof Panels **MA:** National **D/D/R:** Overseeing the Employees, Project Management, Estimating and Detailing Management **H/I/S:** Fishing **EDU:** Associate Degree in Architecture, ICS (1975); Associate Degree in Drafting and Design Technology, Ryder Technical College (1972); Associate Degree in Grafting Programming, Hampton County Community College
Email: cstocker@mcelroymetal.com
URL: http://www.mcelroymetal.com

Veda A. Stockland
Title: Registered Nurse **Company:** Meeker County Memorial Hospital **Address:** 612 South Sibley Avenue, Litchfield, MN 55355 United States **BUS:** Healthcare Hospital **P/S:** All Aspects of Hospital Healthcare Services **MA:** Local **D/D/R:** Specializing in all Areas of Critical Care Nursing as well as Ambulance Service Coordination **H/I/S:** Spending Time With Family and Friends **EDU:** Normandale College, Associate Degree in Nursing (1978); Certified in BIS, ACLS, TNCC, EMT, ACLS Instructor **A/A/S:** American Nurses Association; Minnesota Nurses Association; Immanuel Lutheran Church; Volunteer Fire Department; Minnesota Ambulance Association

Mary Ann Stockwell
Title: Faith Community Nurse Coordinator **Company:** Henry Ford Macombs Hospital **Address:** 43421 Garfield Road, Clinton Township, MI 48038 United States **BUS:** Hospital **P/S:** Healthcare Including Patient Care, Health Education, Consultation, Program Development, Training, Support Network for Faith Community Services and Parish Nurses **MA:** Tri-County **EXP:** Ms. Stockwell's expertise includes gerontology and faith community nursing. **H/I/S:** Reading, Gardening, Making Crafts **EDU:** Master of Social Work, Wayne State University; Bachelor of Science in Nursing, University of Detroit Mercy **CERTS:** Certified Gerontological Nurse; Certified Professional Geriatric Care Manager **A/A/S:** Prince George's County Municipal Association; National Association of Social Workers **C/VW:** Saint Matthias Catholic Church
Email: senior_connections@yahoo.com
URL: http://www.sjmparishnursing.org

Dr. Ron Stoffer
Title: Owner **Company:** Lewis-Clark Care Center, LLC **Address:** 1633 10th Avenue, Lewiston, ID 83501 United States **BUS:** Residential Care Center **P/S:** Healthcare Assisted Living for the Elderly **MA:** Local **D/D/R:** Managing Operations, Overseeing Seven Staff Members and Residents **H/I/S:** Mushroom Hunting **EDU:** Ph.D. in Biochemistry, University of Idaho (1973); Master's Degree in Plant Physiology, University of Nebraska (1962); Bachelor of Science in Agriculture, Washington State University (1960) **A/A/S:** Idaho Assisted Living Association; Idaho Health Care Association; Former President, The Idaho Academy of Science; Former Member, American Chemical Society **A/H:** Outstanding Professor of the Year Awards **C/VW:** Disabled American Veterans
Email: lccc@cableone.net
URL: http://www.cambridgewhoswho.com

Mr. Richard J. Stoicsitz
Title: President, Chief Executive Officer **Company:** Patriot Energy Savings Company **Address:** 2613 Woodstream Drive, Hatfield, PA 18440 United States **BUS:** Energy Company **P/S:** Energy Saving Services **MA:** National **D/D/R:** managing new business operations, overseeing the contract management development programs and building federal division **H/I/S:** Golfing, Fishing **EDU:** Bachelor of Science in Business Management, Delaware College of Science (1989) **A/A/S:** Green Building Council; National Contracts Management Association; Society of American Military Engineers; American Energy Engineers
Email: richard.stoicsitz@patriotenergy.us
URL: http://www.patriotenergy.us

Ms. Heather M. Stokes
Title: Information Technology Analyst and Assistant Database Administrator **Company:** Oklahoma County Clerk's Office **Address:** 320 Robert S. Kerr Avenue, Suite 105, Oklahoma City, OK 73102 United States **BUS:** Government **P/S:** Public Service **MA:** Local **D/D/R:** Informational Technology, Database Technologies **H/I/S:** Reading, Horseback Riding **EDU:** Bachelor of Science in Management Informational Systems, University of Central Oklahoma; Microsoft Certified Systems Engineer (MCSE); Microsoft Certified Systems Administrator (MCSA); Microsoft Certified Professional (MCP) **A/A/S:** Court Appointed Special Advocate; Oracle Users Group **C/VW:** Church
Email: email2hms@yahoo.com
URL: http://www.cambridgewhoswho.com

Mary Ann Stoll
Title: Reading Coach, Educator **Company:** Morris Avenue Intermediate School **Address:** 310 Lee Drive, Auburn, AL 36832 United States **BUS:** School **P/S:** Education **MA:** Regional **D/D/R:** teaching students from third through fifth-grade, assisting students with improving reading skills **H/I/S:** Reading, Camping, Spending time with her Grandchildren **EDU:** Master of Education, University of Wisconsin-Eau Claire (1989); Bachelor of Arts in Elementary Education, Oakland City University, IN (1973) **CERTS:** Certified Elementary Teacher, State of Alabama **A/A/S:** National Education Association; Alabama Education Association; Delta Zeta
Email: mary.annstoll@opelikaschools.org
URL: http://www.opelikaschools.org

Brian A. Stoller
Title: Regional Business Director of Asia Pacific **Company:** MindShare **Dept:** Interaction **Address:** 36/F PCCW Tower, Taikoo Place, Quarry Bay, Hong Kong, Hong Kong **BUS:** Advertising Company **P/S:** Global media strategy and buying **MA:** International New Media Specialist **D/D/R:** Specializing in Strategy, Marketing, New Media **EDU:** Bachelor of Arts in Chinese and Advertising, University of Massachusetts (1996) **A/A/S:** IAB; Mobile Marketing Association **C/VW:** Tutors Mandarin
Email: postmaster@brianstoller.com
URL: http://www.mindshareworld.com
URL: http://www.brianstoller.com

James 'Ed' E. Stolze Jr.
Title: Director of Information Systems and Technology **Company:** Creighton School District **Address:** 2702 E. Flower Street, Phoenix, AZ 85016 United States **BUS:** School District **P/S:** Education, Integrating Computer Technology **MA:** Arizona **D/D/R:** Managing Information Systems and Technology **H/I/S:** Golfing, Traveling **EDU:** Master's Degree in Human Relations and Organizational Behavior, University of Oklahoma; Bachelor of Science in Computer science and Sociology; Microsoft Certified Systems Engineer; Microsoft Certified Professional; Certified Project Manager, Villanova University **A/A/S:** Arizona Technology and Education Association **C/VW:** Shriners of North America
Email: jstolze@cox.net

Mr. Brian Stone
Title: Assistant Head of Information Technology **Company:** Scranton Public Library **Address:** 500 Vine Street, Scranton, PA 18509 United States **BUS:** Professionals in Library Services **P/S:** Full Service Library with Internet and Reference Access, Computer Lab, Genealogy Section, Government Documents, Reference Department **MA:** Regional **D/D/R:** Networking Computer Support, Programming and Maintenance **H/I/S:** NASCAR Racing **EDU:** Bachelor of Science in Computer Science, University of Scranton (2001)
Email: bstone@albright.org
URL: http://www.albright.org

David Stone
Title: Manufacturing Supervisor **Company:** L-3 Tinsley **Dept:** Computer Controlled Optical Surface Division **Address:** 4040 Lakeside Drive, Richmond, CA 94806 United States **BUS:** Manufacturing Company **P/S:** Large Optical Lenses **MA:** Regional **D/D/R:** overseeing the manufacture of optical lenses and aviation production **H/I/S:** Boating **EDU:** Bachelor of Arts in Aeronautical Engineering; Bachelor of Science in Professional Aeronautics **A/A/S:** American Association of Airport Executives; United States Air Force
Email: david.stone@l-3com.com
URL: http://www.ssginc.com

Elizabeth A. Stone
Title: Executive Director **Company:** The Baby Hui **Address:** P.O. Box 10826, Honolulu, HI 96816 United States **BUS:** Nonprofit **P/S:** Positive Parenting Help for Parents of Young Children **MA:** Statewide **D/D/R:** Program Development, Grant Writing, Reporting to the State, Fund Raising, Serving as Liaison Between Various Agencies **H/I/S:** Community Theater, Reading, Traveling **EDU:** JD, Law University of Hawaii (1990); Bachelor of Science in Political Science, University of Oregon (1986) **A/A/S:** Junior League of Hawaii; KEIKI Caucus
Email: executive_director@thebabyhui.org
URL: http://www.thebabyhui.org

Lorrie B. Stone
Title: Adult Case Manager II **Company:** SEABHS **Address:** 185 S. Moorman Avenue, Sierra Vista, AZ 85635 United States **BUS:** Mental Health Facility **P/S:** Mental Healthcare **MA:** Southeast Arizona **D/D/R:** Advocating Adult Education for the Mentally Ill, Case Management, Facilitating Outreach Therapy Groups **H/I/S:** Spending Time with her Daughter, Hiking, Horseback Riding **EDU:** Industry-Related Training and Experience **C/VW:** Forgach House
Email: hstockel@cox.net

Mr. Nathan Stone
Title: Credit Accountant **Company:** Crane Fencing Solutions **Address:** 894 Prairie Avenue, Wilmington, OH 45177 United States **BUS:** Creating and Manufacturing Vinyl Fencing **P/S:** Vinyl Fencing Products **MA:** Ohio **D/D/R:** Reviewing Customer Accounts, Collecting and Conferring with Sales **H/I/S:** Soccer, Lacrosse **EDU:** Bachelor's Degree in Accounting, Wheeling Jesuit University, West Virginia (2006)
Email: nathans@cranefencing.com
URL: http://www.cranefencing.com

Rebecca Claire Stone, APRN, BC, FNP
Title: Family Nurse Practitioner **Company:** Access Family Health Services, Inc. **Address:** 10103 Highway 178 E., Tremont, MS 38876 United States **BUS:** Family Healthcare Organization **P/S:** Superior Healthcare Services **MA:** Regional **D/D/R:** Offering Family, Children and Women's Health Nursing, Managing Chronic Disease Management, Working with Uninsured Patients Full-Time **H/I/S:** Reading, Playing the Piano, Traveling **EDU:** Master's Degree in Nursing, Vanderbilt University for Women (2006); Certified Family Nurse Practitioner, Vanderbilt University for Women(2006); Bachelor's Degree in Nursing, Mississippi University (2004); American Nurses Credentialing Center **A/A/S:** Sigma Theta Tau; American Academy of Nurse Practitioners; Mississippi Nurses Association
Email: cstone@accessfamilyhealth.com
URL: http://www.accessfamilyhealth.com

Pauline E. Stoneburner
Title: Elementary Teacher **Company:** Prince William County Public Schools **Address:** 751 Norwood Lane, Woodbridge, VA 22191 United States **BUS:** Proven Leader in the Education Industry **P/S:** High Quality Educational Services for Students **MA:** Regional **D/D/R:** Teaching Fourth-Grade, Working with English for Speakers of other Languages Students **EDU:** Bachelor of Science in Education Plus 15, Virginia Commonwealth University; Certified to Teach Gifted Children **A/A/S:** National Education Association; Virginia Education Association; Prince William Education Association; Retired Safeway Employees Association
Email: stonebpe@pwcs.edu
URL: http://www.pwcs.edu

Bob Stoops
Title: Head Football Coach **Company:** University of Oklahoma **Address:** 180 W. Brooks Street, Suite 320, Norman, OK 73019 United States **BUS:** University **P/S:** Undergraduate and Graduate Program, Athletics **MA:** Regional **D/D/R:** Coaching Football, Managing Staff and Group Meetings, Evaluating Practices, Preparing for Games, Recruiting **H/I/S:** Golfing **EDU:** Bachelor's Degree in Business Administration and Marketing, The University of Iowa (1983) **A/A/S:** National Football League Coaches Association
URL: http://soonersports.com

Anne M. Stores
Title: Co-Owner **Company:** Chief Sabael Cottages **Address:** P.O. Box 1031, Sabael, NY 12864 United States **BUS:** Rental Company **P/S:** Cottage Rentals **MA:** International **EXP:** Ms. Stores' expertise is in business management. **D/D/R:** Overseeing Guest Relations and Rentals, Maintaining the Cottages and Grounds, Managing Operations **H/I/S:** Spending Time with her Family **EDU:** Master of Education in Elementary Education, Cambridge College; Bachelor of Arts in Education, SUNY Plattsburgh **A/A/S:** Indian Lake Area Chamber of Commerce **C/VW:** American Legion; Marist Mission Centre
Email: chiefsabael@frontiernet.net
URL: http://www.chiefsabael.com

Edmund Storms
Title: President **Company:** Energy K Systems, Inc **Address:** 2140 Paseo Ponderosea, Santa Fe, NM 87501 United States **BUS:** Science Consulting Services **P/S:** Research **MA:** Local **D/D/R:** Cold Fusion **H/I/S:** Wood Working **EDU:** Penn State, Washington University, Bachelor of Science, Master of Science, Ph.D. **A/A/S:** Society of Scientific Inspiration, American Society of Advancement Science

Alex Stotler
Title: Chef De Cuisine **Company:** Due Mari **Address:** 1449 Irving Street, Rahway, NJ 07065 United States **BUS:** Contemporary Italian Restaurant **P/S:** Fine Dining, Lunch and Dinner Menu, Seafood and Italian Based Dishes, Appetizers, Dessert **MA:** Regional **D/D/R:** Preparing Cuisine Including Braised Short Ribs, Steamed Eggs, Sausage and Terrines, Collaborating with Head Chef to Create New Menu Offerings, Overseeing Staff of 20, Managing and Ordering Supplies Including Produce **EDU:** Associate Degree in Liberal Arts, Emphasis on Business, Union County College (1999) **C/VW:** Local charity for Abused Women
Email: alexstotler@hotmail.com
URL: http://www.daviddrakes.com

Patricia A. Stoudt
Title: Program Assistant **Company:** Kean University **Address:** 1000 Morris Avenue, Union, NJ 07083 United States **BUS:** University **P/S:** Higher Education **MA:** Statewide **D/D/R:** Cooperative Education, Internships **H/I/S:** Spending Time with her Family **EDU:** Bachelor's Degree in Management Science, Kean University **A/A/S:** New Jersey Cooperative Education and Internship Association **C/VW:** Volunteers at a Local Martial Arts School
Email: pstoudt@kean.edu

Russell P. Stover
Title: Dealer Operator **Company:** BMW-MINI of Nashville **Address:** 4040 Armory Oaks Drive, Nashville, TN 37204 United States **BUS:** Car Dealership **P/S:** Luxury Automobiles, Service, Parts **MA:** Regional **D/D/R:** Promoting Cooperation Between Associates and Customers **H/I/S:** Traveling; Playing Sports, Especially Water Sports **EDU:** College Coursework **A/A/S:** Board of Directors, YMCA; Chamber of Commerce; Former President, National Franchise of Auto Dealers; BMW Dealer Council; BMW-MINI Dealer Council **C/VW:** YMCA, American Cancer Society, Vanderbilt Children's Hospital
Email: rstover@bmwofnashville.com
URL: http://www.bmwofnashville.com

Maria D. Stradley
Title: Owner **Company:** Altitude Analysis Inc. **Address:** 2528 Foothill Boulevard, Rock Springs, WY 82901 United States **BUS:** Clinical Laboratory **P/S:** Testing for Blood, Drugs, Alcohol and Wellness **MA:** Local **D/D/R:** Overseeing Clinical Lab Scientists, Handling Bills, Quality Assurance, Marketing **H/I/S:** Coaching Volley Ball **EDU:** Bachelor's Degree in Clinical Laboratory Science, University of Wyoming (2000) **A/A/S:** American Society for Clinical Laboratory Science **C/VW:** Local Various Charities
Email: maria.stradley@gmail.com

Donna K. Strait
Title: Realtor **Company:** Coldwell Banker 1st Choice Realty **Address:** 18401 E. Highway 24, Woodland Park, CO 80863 United States **BUS:** Proven Leader in Real Estate **P/S:** Full Service Real Estate Company **MA:** Regional **EXP:** Ms. Strait's expertise is in residential real estate. **H/I/S:** Horseback Riding, Sewing, Crafts **EDU:** Real Estate Degree from Jones Real Estate College **A/A/S:** NAR; CAR; Pikes Peak Association of Realtors
Email: donna@1stchoicerealtycb.com
URL: http://www.thestraitway.com

Ebony Strange
Title: Director of Resource Development **Company:** MENTOR/National Mentoring Partnership **Address:** 1600 Duke Street, Suite 300, Alexandria, VA 22314 United States **BUS:** Nonprofit Organization **P/S:** Youth Mentoring **MA:** National **D/D/R:** Special Events, Campaigns **H/I/S:** Relaxing, Watching Movies, Entertaining, Traveling **EDU:** Bachelor's Degree in Sociology, University of Mary Washington **A/A/S:** ISES, Meeting Planners International
Email: estrange@mentoring.org
URL: http://www.mentoring.org

Mr. Walter Stratford III
Title: Owner **Company:** Stratford Small Remodels **Address:** 1813 Sharon Drive, Albany, GA 31707 United States **BUS:** Contracting **P/S:** Cosmetic Renovations, Residential and Commercial Buildings, Remodeling **MA:** Regional **D/D/R:** Bidding, Measuring, Organizing, Scheduling, Communicating with Clients, Fixing and Redoing Floors, Tiles, Carpet, Painting **H/I/S:** Playing Soccer, Collecting Stamps and Coins, Traveling **EDU:** Trade School Diploma in Auto Refinishing, Albany Technical College (2004)

Barbara Ann Straub
Title: Elementary Teacher (Retired) **Company:** Montgomery County Public Schools **Address:** 301 North Drive, Blacksburg, VA 24060 United States **BUS:** Elementary School **P/S:** Regular Core Curriculum Including English, Mathematics, Science, History, Social Studies, Music, Art **MA:** Regional **D/D/R:** Teaching Third-Grade Mathematics, Science and Integrated Language Arts, Writing Grants, Conducting Workshops in Mathematics and Science for Elementary Teachers **H/I/S:** Swimming, Gardening, Flower Arranging **EDU:** Master's Degree in Education, Michigan State University (1973); Certified Activities Involving Mathematics and Science Trainer **A/A/S:** Montgomery County Education Association; National Education Association; Leadership Team, Activities Involving Mathematics and Science Foundation **A/H:** Nominee, Presidential Award for Excellence in Mathematics and Science Teaching
Email: bsannerik@yahoo.com
URL: http://www.mcps.org

Lillian Streeter
Title: Addictions Counselor, Director of Substance Abuse Program **Company:** 1) Echo House Multi-Service Center 2) Bethel A.M.E. Church Freedom Now **Address:** 1705 W. Fayette Street, Baltimore, MD 21223 United States **BUS:** Out-Patient Facility **P/S:** Substance Abuse Programs **MA:** Local **D/D/R:** Addictions Counseling **H/I/S:** Traveling, Dining Out **EDU:** Master's Degree in Christian Education; Saint Mary's Seminary **C/VW:** Freedom Now
URL: http://www.cambridgewhoswho.com

Sandra Deniece Strickland
Title: Professional Model **Company:** US Postal Service **Address:** 7001 S Central Avenue, Los Angeles, CA 90051 United States **BUS:** Modeling Fashion **P/S:** Modeling, Commercials, Talent, Singing **MA:** National **D/D/R:** Availability for Immediate in Modeling and Commercial **H/I/S:** Paint and Arts/Crafts, Singing **EDU:** Barbizon Modeling School **A/A/S:** Ministering Haul Ministry with Homeless on Skid Row
Email: Sandra.Strickland@cwwemail.com

Emmalene Stroble Pearson
Title: President **Company:** Emmalene's Discount Shop **Address:** 1801 Thomas Road, Fort Washington, MD 20744 United States **BUS:** Privately Owned Company Committed to Excellence in the Discount Clothing Industry **P/S:** Internet Sales, Apparel, Accessories, Automobile Accessories, Camping and Outdoors, Electronics, Fragrances, General Merchandise, Gift Ideas, Health and Beauty, Home Decor, Jewelry, Kitchen and Dining, Music Equipment, Remote Control Cars, Small Household Appliances, Sports Items, Toys, Games and Videos, Shoes **MA:** Regional **D/D/R:** Running a Travel Service, Buying Wholesale, Selling Under Retail, Working for Otolaryngology and Associates, Approving Workmen's Compensation in Virginia **H/I/S:** Swimming, Reading, Traveling **A/A/S:** Boys Club; Girls Club; Volunteer America
Email: epearson1234@hotmail.com
URL: http://www.emmalenesdiscountshop.com

Elika Elise Stroman
Title: Serving and Sports Ministries Coordinator **Company:** Trinity Church **Address:** 3355 Dunckel Road, Lansing, MI 48911 United States **BUS:** Church **P/S:** Religious Ministries **MA:** International **D/D/R:** Coordinating Ministry Events and Sporting Leagues and Events Based on Season, Recruiting and Leading Volunteer Teams, Managing and Coordinating Large Events, Outreach to the Community relating to events and sports leagues **H/I/S:** Traveling, Watching Sports, Going to the Movie Theater, Playing Games **EDU:** Bachelor of Science in Discipleship Ministries, Minor in Leadership Development, Crown College (2006) **A/H:** Recognition for Execellent Academics in Christian Education (2006)
Email: elika.stroman@trinitywired.com
URL: http://www.trinitywired.com

Michael O. Strong
Title: Owner **Company:** Denny Landscaping **Address:** 22315 Currie Road, Northville, MI 48167 United States **BUS:** Landscaping Company **P/S:** Landscape Design, Maintenance Services **MA:** National **EXP:** Mr. Strong's expertise includes landscape design and contracting. **H/I/S:** Weightlifting, Golfing **EDU:** Coursework in Business, University of Michigan, Dearborn **C/VW:** Local Church
Email: strongermike@aol.com

Mr. Tom Strottner
Title: Engineer, Realtor **Company:** Century 21 at the Rockies **Address:** 1220 E. 7800 S., Sandy, UT 84094 United States **BUS:** Real Estate Agency **P/S:** Commercial and Residential Real Estate Exchange **MA:** National **EXP:** Mr. Strottner's expertise includes mechanical and architectural design and residential real estate sales. **D/D/R:** Overseeing New Construction Sites, Pre-Existing Structures, Land Development and Consulting **H/I/S:** Playing Soccer, Camping, Spending Time Outdoors **CERTS:** Certification in Drafting Technology, American Design Drafting Association (1991) **A/A/S:** American Design Drafting Association; National Association of Realtors **C/VW:** Chairman, School Community Councils
Email: strottnergroup@c21rockies.com
URL: http://www.strottnergroup.com

Ricardo T. Stroud
Title: Medical Laboratory Technician **Company:** Hawthorn Medical Associates **Address:** 237A State Road, North Dartmouth, MA 02747 United States **BUS:** Outpatient Clinic **P/S:** Clinical Services Including Allergy Care, Audiology and Hearing-Aid Services, Coumadin Clinic, Cancer Center, Diabetes Management Center, Endoscopy Center, Orthopedic and Arthritis Center, Physical Therapy, Sleep Center and Urgent Care Center, Diagnostic Services Including Digital Mammography, Magnetic Resonance Imaging, Computed Tomography and Positron Emission Tomography Scan Services, Nuclear Medicine Services, Ultrasound Services, X-ray Services **MA:** Regional **D/D/R:** Calibrating Controls, Testing Blood and Body Fluids, Training and Mentoring Interns **H/I/S:** Hiking, Bicycling, Motorcycling **EDU:** Associate Degree in Medical Lab Science, Bristol Community College (1999); Certified Nursing Assistant (1997); Associate Degree in Business, Bristol Community College (1991)
Email: brendenrs28@yahoo.com
URL: http://www.hawthornmed.com

Ivy B. Strozier
Title: Kindergarten Teacher **Company:** LaSalle Parish School Board **Address:** P.O. Box 90, Jena, LA 71342 United States **BUS:** School **P/S:** Elementary Education **MA:** Local **D/D/R:** Teaching Kindergarten **H/I/S:** Reading, Square Dancing **EDU:** Bachelor of Arts in Kindergarten Education, University of Southwestern Louisiana (Now University of Louisiana at Lafayette); Certification in Elementary Education **A/A/S:** Louisiana Early Childhood Association; President, Louisiana Square Dance Association; Delta Kappa Gamma **A/H:** Teacher of the Year, LaSalle Parish (1992) **C/VW:** Operation Smile, Louisiana Methodist Children's Home
Email: istrozier@lasallepsb.com
URL: http://www.cambridgewhoswho.com

Shirley Ann Strusz, LPN, HHA
Title: Licensed Practical Nurse, Home Health Aide (Retired) **Company:** Zumbrota Health Care **Address:** 433 Mill Street, Zumbrota, MN 55992 United States **BUS:** Nursing Home **P/S:** Senior Home Healthcare Services **MA:** Regional **D/D/R:** Overseeing All Patient Treatments and Medications, Performing Administrative Duties, Assessing Patients, Performing Personal Care for Clients Including Shopping, Cleaning and Administering Medication **H/I/S:** Gardening, Crafts **EDU:** Licensed Practical Nurse, Red Wing School of Practical Nursing (1955); Home Health Aide **A/A/S:** Home Council Member; County Extension Program
Email: elroystrusz@realtyexecutive.com

Edward J. Strzelecki
Title: Executive Director of Engineering **Company:** Expert Corporation **Address:** 900 Wilshire Drive, Troy, MI 48084 United States **BUS:** Engineering Management **P/S:** Automotive Components, Evaporative Emissions, Chassis Structural Components **MA:** International **D/D/R:** Operation, Engineering Management **H/I/S:** Riding Dirt Bikes **EDU:** Master's Degree in Mechanical Engineering, Rensselaer Polytechnic Institute **A/A/S:** Society of Mechanical Engineers; Society of Automotive Engineers
Email: estrzelecki@expertna.com
URL: http://www.expertna.com

Ms. Joy Stubbs
Title: President, Chief Executive Officer Company: Joybies LLC, Joybies Pet Specialties Dept: Corporate Administration Address: Joybies Pet Specialties, P.O. Box 97004, Lakewood, WA 98497 United States BUS: Pet Attire and Supplies Manufacturing P/S: Patented Pet Garment Designs and Products, Piddle Pants(TM) MA: International D/D/R: Tailoring; Design; Designing Pet Garments H/I/S: Designing, music, golf EDU: Real Estate Appraisal, Design A/H: Annual Editor's Choice Award, Cat Fancy Magazine C/VW: World Vision
Email: joybies@aol.com
Email: JoybiesLLC@aol.com
URL: http://www.joybies.com
URL: http://www.piddlepants.com

Mr. Bobby G. Stucker
Title: Quality Manager Company: Wright Metal Products Dept: Quality Address: 550 Emily Lane, Piedmont, SC 29673 United States BUS: Fabrication, Manufacturing, Assembly and Metal Packaging P/S: Metal Packaging Solutions MA: International D/D/R: Nondestructive Testing of Specialty Shipping Crates, Managing the Production Line, Returns and Customer Contacts, Supervising and Training Personnel, Performing Design 3-D Work, Ensuring Overall Quality Control H/I/S: Computing, Gaming, Hiking, Fishing EDU: Master of Business Administration in Technology Management, University of Phoenix (2004) A/A/S: American Society for Nondestructive Testing; American Society of Mechanical Engineers
Email: bstucker@wrightmetalproducts.com
Email: bobbys73@charter.net
URL: http://www.wrightmetalproducts.com

Carol Stukes
Title: Pension Trustee Company: City of Philadelphia Dept: Board of Pension and Retirement Address: 1500 John F. Kennedy Boulevard, Two Penn Center, 16th Floor, Philadelphia, PA 19102 United States BUS: Municipal Office P/S: Pension Funds, Retirement System MA: National D/D/R: Responding to Investors' Pension and Benefits Questions, Keeping Up to Date on New and Changing Information, Addressing Policy Issues H/I/S: Dancing, Reading EDU: Pursuing Master of Science in Administration, Lincoln University; Bachelor of Science in Accounting, La Salle University; Associate Degree in Accounting, Community College of Philadelphia A/A/S: Executive Board Member, National Conference on Public Employee Retirement Systems; National Association of Security Professionals; Chairwoman, Mid-Atlantic Plan Sponsor C/VW: Mercy Neighborhood Ministries; Our Lady of Hope Church
Email: carol.stukes@phila.gov
URL: http://www.cambridgewhoswho.com

Sharyn A. Stumpf
Title: District Language Arts, Reading Resource Teacher (Retired) Company: Madison Metropolitan School District Address: 545 W. Dayton Street, Madison, WI 53703 United States BUS: School District P/S: Education MA: Local D/D/R: Teaching Literacy, English Literature and Art H/I/S: Spending Time with her Family, Traveling EDU: Master's Degree in Spirituality, Loyola University (1993); Master's Degree in Curriculum, University of Wisconsin-Madison (1969) A/A/S: International Reading Association; Wisconsin State Reading Association; National Education Association C/VW: American Cancer Society, American Heart Association, United Way, March of Dimes, Habitat for Humanity
Email: fastumpf@charter.net
URL: http://www.madison.k12.wi.us

Brent D. Sturgill
Title: Vice President, Financial Consultant Company: Merrill Lynch Address: 1416 Winchester Avenue, Ashland, KY 41101 United States BUS: Investment Firm P/S: Financial Management MA: Kentucky D/D/R: overseeing client investments and assisting retirement planning H/I/S: Spending Time with his Family EDU: Bachelor of Arts in Finance and Business, Brigham Young University A/A/S: Quincy International C/VW: Boy Scouts of America, Church of Jesus Christ of Latter-Day Saints
Email: brent.sturgill@cwwemail.com
URL: http://www.cambridgewhoswho.com

Michelle Stux Ramirez
Title: Owner Company: Stux Management, RG Medical Address: 633 Third Avenue, Eighth Floor, New York, NY 10017 United States BUS: Healthcare Staffing Company P/S: Staffing MA: National D/D/R: Staffing Healthcare Facilities, Consulting H/I/S: Traveling, Playing Tennis, Reading EDU: Master of Business Administration in Management and Finance, Fairleigh Dickinson University A/A/S: National Human Resources Association; EWA C/VW: Community Organizations; Vice President, Little League, Football League
Email: mstux1202@aol.com

Alison Styles
Title: Accountant Company: Northwestern Mutual Financial Network Address: 720 Olive Way, Suite 1900, Seattle, WA 98101 United States BUS: Financial Company P/S: Insurance Investments, Wealth Management MA: Regional D/D/R: Keeping Financial Records, Tracking Money Accounts, Commissions, Coordinating Technology H/I/S: Soccer, Spending Time with Family and Friends EDU: Bachelor of Arts in Finance, Western Washington University (2006); Bachelor of Arts in Economics, Western Washington University (2006) A/A/S: Washington Society of Certified Public Accountants
Email: astyles11@gmail.com
URL: http://www.nmfn.com

Joan Styles
Title: Director of School Age Services Company: U.S. Army Address: Fort Stewart BUS: Military Facility Committed to Excellence in Education P/S: Accredited After School Services MA: Regional D/D/R: Before and Afterschool Educational and Recreational Programs for First through Fifth-Grade Students H/I/S: Reading EDU: Bachelor's Degree in Education, Fort Valley State University (1981)
Email: joan.styles@us.army.mil
URL: http://www.us.army.mil

Susan I. Sublette, RD
Title: Chief Clinical Dietitian Company: Columbus Regional Hospital Address: 2400 E. 17th Street, Columbus, IN 47201 United States BUS: Regional Referral Hospital P/S: Bariatric Center, Joint Replacement Center, Birthing Center, Laboratory Services, Breast Health Center, Mental Health Services, Cancer Center, Radiology Services, Children's Services, Rehabilitation Center, Diabetes Services, Respiratory Services, Dialysis Services, Sleep Disorders Center, Emergency Services, Stroke Center, Heart Center, Surgical Services, Home Services, Women's Services, Intensive Care MA: Regional D/D/R: Patient Care, Nutrition Counseling for Cardiac and Diabetic Patients, Teaching Cardiac Rehabilitation Classes, Outpatient and Inpatient Services, Leading Registered Dietitians, Respiratory Care, Teaching Classes in Respiratory Nutrition H/I/S: Traveling, Music, Singing EDU: Bachelor of Science Degree in Dietetic Food Science and Nutrition, Northern Illinois University (1971); Internship, Good Samaritan Hospital (1972) A/A/S: American Dietetic Association; Clinical Nutrition Manager, Indiana Dietetic Association; Sandy Hook United Methodist Church
Email: ssublette@crh.org

Robert J. Suco
Title: President Company: Suco Ventures, Inc., dba Tel Efficient Address: 7370 S.W. 152nd Avenue, Miami, FL 33193 United States BUS: Consulting Firm P/S: Telecommunication Consulting Services, Phone Systems MA: South Florida, Central America EXP: Mr. Suco's expertise includes project management and telecommunications industry consultation. H/I/S: Camping, Reading, Researching EDU: Bachelor of Fine Arts, New York University (1985) A/A/S: Doral and Airport West Chamber of Commerce; New York University Alumni Association; Business Network International; Building Industry Consulting Service International
Email: rsuco@tel-efficient.com
URL: http://www.tel-efficient.com

Kathleen J. Suesz
Title: Educational Advisor Company: Educational Talent Search, Lewis-Clark State College Address: 500 Eighth Avenue, Lewiston, ID 83501 United States BUS: State College P/S: Education MA: Local D/D/R: Working with At-Risk and Retention-Challenged Middle School Students H/I/S: Raising Poodles EDU: Bachelor's Degree in Elementary Education, Lewis-Clark State College; Master's Degree in Adult and Organizational Learning, University of Idaho A/A/S: Pi Lambda Theta
Email: ksuesz@lcsc.edu

Ms. Beth Suggs-Wyatt
Title: Operations Supervisor Company: American Medical Response Address: 2905 Sixth Street, Tuscaloosa, AL 35401 United States BUS: Emergency Medical Company P/S: Emergency Medical Services, Advanced and Basic Life Support, Para-Transit MA: Local D/D/R: Management, Serving as a Paramedic H/I/S: Boating EDU: Certification in Emergency Medicine, Alabama Fire College A/A/S: Tuscaloosa Chamber of Commerce; Alabama Ambulance Association; Kid 1 Transport C/VW: Kid 1 Transport
Email: tsuggs@amr-ems.com
URL: http://www.amr.net

Alma J. Sullivan
Title: Owner Company: A.J. Sullivans Pilot/Escort Service Address: 1500 S. Main Street, Hope, AR 71801 United States BUS: Escort Service Company P/S: Transporting Large Loads Across the Country MA: National D/D/R: Business Management H/I/S: Collecting Ceramics, Taking Care of a Handicapped Child C/VW: St. Jude Children's Research Hospital
Email: alma_massey2000@yahoo.com

Carol E. Sullivan
Title: Music Specialist Company: Irving Independent School District Dept: M.C. Lively Elementary School Address: 1800 Plymouth Street, Irving, TX 75061 United States BUS: Public Education P/S: Educational Services, Curriculum, Athletics and Extracurricular Activities MA: Regional D/D/R: Teaching Varied Music Activities to Kindergarten through Fifth-Grade H/I/S: Singing in the Irving Chorale, Golfing, Traveling EDU: Master of Education in Elementary Education, University at Buffalo (1976); Bachelor of Science in Music Education, The Crane School of Music, SUNY Potsdam A/A/S: National Association for Music Education (Formerly Music Educators National Conference); Association of Texas Professional Educators; Texas Music Educators Association; Alpha Delta Kappa; TMAC
Email: csullivan@irvingisd.net
URL: http://www.irvingisd.net

James J. Sullivan
Title: Senior Engineer Company: Tectonic Engineering and Surveying Consultants Address: 70 Pleasant Hill Road, Mountainville, NY 10953 United States BUS: Civil Engineering Firm P/S: Residential and Commercial Development Permitting MA: National D/D/R: Project Management H/I/S: Working Out, Traveling, Playing Sports, Watching Sports and Concerts EDU: Bachelor of Science in Civil Engineering, Manhattan College A/A/S: American Society of Civil Engineers; National Society of Professional Engineers C/VW: American Society for the Prevention of Cruelty to Animals, Catholic Charities, Franciscan Friars of Atonement
Email: jimjsully77@yahoo.com
URL: http://www.tectonicengineering.com

John L. Sullivan
Title: CEO/President Company: Sullivan Home Interior Products Company, Inc. Address: 55 Algiers Lane, Greenwood, DE 19950 United States BUS: New Construction P/S: Development MA: Local D/D/R: Updating Homes

Michelle Sullivan
Title: Choral Director Company: North Wilkes High School Address: 2986 Traphill Road, Hays, NC 28635 United States BUS: High School P/S: Secondary Education MA: North Carolina D/D/R: teaching vocal music, sight reading, theoretical music, history of music and singing techniques H/I/S: Watching Comedies and Thriller Movies, Exercising, Traveling EDU: Master of Music, Appalachian State University, NC; Bachelor of Music, Appalachian State University, NC A/A/S: Kappa Delta Pi; Music Educators National Conference; National Education Association; North Carolina Music Educators Association C/VW: Local Church
Email: sullivanj@wilkes.k12.nc.us
URL: http://www.wilkes.k12.nc.us

Dale Summers
Title: Real Estate Agent Company: HER Real Living Address: 190 E. Broad Street, Pataskala, OH 43062 United States BUS: Real Estate Agency P/S: Residential Real Estate Sales MA: National D/D/R: Negotiating Homes Sales for both Buyers and Sellers, Relocation H/I/S: Fishing, Coordinating Events, Spending Time with Grandchildren, Home Staging and Design EDU: Graduate of Honduras College; Industry-Related Training A/A/S: Affordable Housing Committee; National Association of Realtors; Ohio Association of Realtors; Columbus Board of Realtors C/VW: Relay for Life, April Marie Foundation, Kidney Foundation
Email: dale.summers@realliving.com
URL: http://www.dalesummers.com

Ramona J. Summers
Title: Special Education Teacher Company: Willamette Leadership Academy Address: 87230 Central Road, Eugene, OR 97402 United States BUS: Educational Institution P/S: Education, Training Program MA: Regional D/D/R: teaching special education students with autism, working with middle and high school students with discipline problems, helping students H/I/S: Golfing, Waterskiing, Reading CERTS: Certification in Special Education, Chicago State University (1986) A/A/S: Spay and Neuter Team of Atlanta; Toastmaster, Toastmasters International C/VW: Volunteer, Reading Program; Honorary Lifetime Member, Parent-Teacher Association
Email: grammysummers@aol.com
URL: http://www.cambridgewhoswho.com

Mrs. Paula Hamada Summit
Title: Former President **Company:** New York State Association for Health, Physical Education, Recreation, and Dance **Address:** 555 Harvard Street, Rochester, NY 14607 United States **BUS:** Nonprofit Educational Facility **P/S:** Advocation and Promotion of Physically Active and Healthy Lifestyles through Schools and Community Programs **MA:** Local **D/D/R:** Teaching Elementary Level Physical Education **H/I/S:** Garth Fagan Dance, Photography, Lacrosse, Skiing **EDU:** Bachelor of Science in Physical Education, Springfield College (1968) **A/H:** United States Lacrosse Greater Rochester Hall of Fame (2004); Lottery Educator of the Week New York State (2001); Amazing Person Award, New York State Association for Health, Physical Education, Recreation, and Dance (2001); Elementary Teacher of the Year, New York State Association for Health, Physical Education, Recreation and Dance (2000)
Email: summit5@aol.com
URL: http://www.nysahperd.org

Maxine Sumner-Clark
Title: Chief Executive Officer **Company:** JMAX **Address:** 121 V Street N.W., Washington, DC 20001 United States **BUS:** Proven Leader in the Field of Home Improvement **P/S:** High Quality Home Improvement, Excavation and Masonry Services to Clients **MA:** Regional **D/D/R:** Interacting with Clients and Workers, Making sure all Materials are up to Standard, Marketing, Advertising, Decorating **H/I/S:** Decorating **EDU:** High School Graduate **A/A/S:** National Association of Retired Federal Employees
Email: sam1906@msn.com
URL: http://cambridgewhoswho.com

Gia Sun
Title: Jewelry Designer **Company:** Gia Sun Designs **Address:** Los Angeles, CA **BUS:** Fine Jewelry **P/S:** Jewelry, Rare Gems and Stones **MA:** National **D/D/R:** Creating and Designing Jewelry Collections **EDU:** Bachelor's Degree in Psychology, California State University at Northridge **A/A/S:** Small World Convention **C/VW:** IPA
Email: gia@raregems.net
URL: http://www.giasundesigns.com

Alice M. Sunderman
Title: Home Healthcare Provider **Company:** Independent **Address:** 617 Melody Lane, Eagle Lakes, TX 77434 **BUS:** Home Health Care Service **P/S:** In-Home Healthcare **MA:** Local **D/D/R:** Offering Personal Home Care and Hospice Training **H/I/S:** Reading, Playing Bridge, Spending Time with her Children, Grandchildren, Great-Grandchildren and Husband **EDU:** Licensed in Real Estate, State of Texas; Hospice Training; Banking Courses; Coursework, Wharton County Junior College; Coursework, Victoria College; Diploma, Flatonia High School **A/H:** Conservation Homemaker Award **C/VW:** Study Club, Eagle Lake United Methodist Women; Chair, The Prayer Chain; Lifetime Pink Lady, Rice Community Hospital; Former Volunteer, Hospice; Former Sunday School Teacher; Former Youth Leader; Former Chairwoman, Former Administrative Board Member, Christian Education; Former Cub Scout Leader
Email: sundermanha@sbcglobal.net
URL: http://www.cambridgewhoswho.com

Bryan A. Sunisloe, JD, BA
Title: Attorney **Company:** Bryan A. Sunisloe, Attorney at Law **Address:** 66 Market Street, Mt Clemens, MI 48043 United States **BUS:** Attorney **P/S:** Legal Service **MA:** Local **D/D/R:** Civil and Criminal Trial Attorney **H/I/S:** Golf, Boating **EDU:** Wayne State, Detroit College of Law, Bachelor of Arts, JD **A/A/S:** Michigan Bar Association; NASCAR; Care House; March of Dimes
Email: bsunisloeatty@hotmail.com
URL: http://www.baslaw1.com

Dr. William G. Suratt
Title: Pastor/Administrator **Company:** Temple Baptist Church/Old Dominion **Address:** P.O. Box 888, Kosciusco, MS 39090 United States **BUS:** Church **P/S:** Offering Counseling, Ministry and Education to a Baptist Congregation **MA:** Local **D/D/R:** Pastor, Counselor **H/I/S:** Sports **EDU:** Louisiana Baptist University, Doctors Education
Email: olddominion@bellsouth.net

April Surprenant, MS
Title: Owner **Company:** MMARK, Inc. **Address:** 9030 W. Sahara Avenue, Suite 685, Las Vegas, NV 89117 United States **BUS:** Proven Leader in the Real Estate Industry **P/S:** Eco-Friendly Homes, High Quality Real Estate Services for Clients **MA:** National **D/D/R:** Building Eco-Friendly Homes, Handling Operations **H/I/S:** Tennis, Hiking **EDU:** Master of Science in Urban Planning, University of Pennsylvania (1994); Bachelor of Science in Architecture, Suburban University (1991) **A/A/S:** American Institute of Certified Planners; American Institute of Architects; Greater Las Vegas Association of Realtors
Email: april@mmarkinc.com
URL: http://www.mmarkinc.com

Mr. Rick C. Susong
Title: President **Company:** Fisher Performance, Inc. **Address:** 716 Bridge Road, Akron, OH 44312 United States **BUS:** Auto Racing Company **P/S:** Automotive Sales and Repair **MA:** Local **D/D/R:** Customer Service **H/I/S:** Golfing, Car Racing **EDU:** High School Education
Email: fisherperforick@neo.rr.com
URL: http://www.fisherperformance.net

Deborah Cardwell Suter
Title: Line Assembly **Company:** Akebono Brake Corporation **Address:** 300 Ring Road, Elizabethtown, KY 42701 United States **BUS:** Manufacturing Corporation **P/S:** Brakes for New Automobiles **MA:** International **D/D/R:** Production, Quality Control **H/I/S:** Flower Gardening **A/A/S:** Master Gardener Program

Dr. Susan E. Sutherland
Title: Director of Research **Company:** Mission Health and Hospitals **Address:** 509 Biltmore Avenue, Asheville, NC 28801 United States **BUS:** Nonprofit Community Hospital System **P/S:** Provides Treatment, Promotes Prevention of Illness **MA:** International **D/D/R:** Performing Healthcare Research Administration, Offering Epidemiology and Biostatistical Consultation **EDU:** Ph.D. in Epidemiology; Master of Science Degree in Biostatistics; Bachelor of Science in Nursing **A/A/S:** Fellow, American Heart Association; Adjunct Professor, Medical University of South Carolina; FACE
Email: susan.sutherland@msj.org
URL: http://www.missionhospitals.org

Wendy E. Suto
Title: President, Chief Executive Officer **Company:** Search Circus **Address:** P.O. Box 33604, North Royalton, OH 44133 United States **BUS:** Website Marketing Firm **P/S:** Search Engine Optimization, Website Promotion and Online Marketing Solutions **MA:** International **EXP:** Ms. Suto's expertise includes search engine marketing, business and network administrative operations. **D/D/R:** performing initial analysis of websites, managing sales, assigning projects to staff, generating reports, coaching **H/I/S:** Exercising, Playing Tennis **EDU:** Bachelor's Degree in Print Journalism, Bowling Green State University, with Honors (2000) **A/H:** Dean's List, Bowling Green State University
Email: wendy@searchcircus.com
URL: http://www.searchcircus.com

Dr. Janice M. Sutton
Title: Principal **Company:** George Washington Carver High School for the Sciences **Address:** 14310 Springfield Boulevard, Springfield Gardens, NY 11413 United States **BUS:** High School **P/S:** Secondary Education **MA:** Local **D/D/R:** teaching, overseeing administrative duties **H/I/S:** Playing Tennis, Golfing **EDU:** Doctor of Education, Teachers College, Columbia University, NY (1999); Master of Science in Secondary School Science, Teachers College, Columbia University, NY (1997); Master of Science in Science Education, Queens College CUNY (1989); Bachelor of Arts in Biology, Minor in Chemistry and Biochemistry, Queens College CUNY (1985) **CERTS:** Certified Principal, New York City Board of Education (2002); State Certified School District Administrator (1999); Certification in Administration and Supervision (1998); Certification in Biology and General Science, State of New York (1992) **A/A/S:** National Science Supervisors Association; National Science Teachers Association; The Council of School Supervisors and Administrators; American Federation of School Administrators; National Association of Biology Teachers; Association for Supervision and Curriculum Development; The United Federation of Teachers; New York State United Teachers; American Federation of Teachers **C/VW:** Susan G. Komen for the Cure; American Institute for Cancer Research; Williston Park Emergency Rescue Squad; Williston Park Fire Department; Nassau County Police Activity League; Mineola Volunteer Ambulance Corps
Email: jmsutton1@gmail.com

Ms. Michelle Suzuki
Title: President **Company:** MSC **Address:** 16500 Shamhart Drive, Granada Hills, CA 91344 United States **BUS:** Consulting Company **P/S:** Consulting Services Including Strategic Marketing and Communications Counseling to Businesses and Nonprofit Organizations, Combining Public Relations and Marketing Expertise in the Areas of General Consumer Branding, Technology, Entertainment, 12-Volt, Consumer Products and Packaged Goods, Telecommunications, Electronics, Automotive and Grass Roots Marketing **MA:** National **EXP:** Ms. Suzuki's expertise includes marketing management and public relations. **D/D/R:** Overseeing All Aspects of Agency, Functioning as the Primary Contact for Corporate Communications, Building Media and Ethnic Relations, Coordinating Outreach for Nonprofit Organizations, Managing Marketing of Consumer Electronics **H/I/S:** Scuba Diving, Watching Football, Auto Racing **EDU:** Bachelor of Arts Degree in English, University of California at Los Angeles (1991) **A/A/S:** Executive Board Member, Former President, Diseiweek; Student Alumni Association, University of California at Los Angeles
Email: michelle@msc-pr.com
URL: http://www.msc-pr.com

Craig Lamar Swan
Title: Real Estate Investor **Company:** Good News Investment **Address:** 733 Basil Court, Lemoore, CA 93245 United States **BUS:** Real Estate Agency **P/S:** Affordable Homes for Moderate to Low Income Families, Real Estate Investing **MA:** National **D/D/R:** Working with Multifamily and Single Family Homes, Purchasing and Reselling Homes, Overseeing Reconstruction of Properties, Managing Rental Properties, Managing and Overseeing Maintenance Department **H/I/S:** Basketball **EDU:** Master of Business Administration (1997); Master of Business Administration, Embry-Riddle Aeronautical University, Florida (1992)
Email: goodnewsinvestment@sbcglobal.net

Rev. Leon E. Swanson Sr.
Title: Founder, Ministry Director **Company:** Bema Outreach Ministries **Address:** P.O. Box 2731, Upper Marlboro, MD 20773 United States **BUS:** Para-church Organization **P/S:** Community Outreach Services through Prison, Nursing Home and Music Ministries **MA:** Local **EXP:** Rev. Swanson's expertise is in humanitarian work. **D/D/R:** Attending Phone Calls from Ex-Offenders and Family Members, Networking with Affiliated Ministries, Personal and Marital Counseling **H/I/S:** Writing, Bowling, Listening to Classical Music, Traveling **EDU:** Pursuing Master of Pastoral Counseling; Bachelor of Christian Ministry **CERTS:** Diploma in General Bible Studies, Liberty University; Certification in Ministerial Ordination, AME Zion Church **A/A/S:** Chesapeake Bible College & Seminary; Advisor, Aglow Women's Ministry, Camp Springs, MD; Advisory Board Member, Coalition of Prison Ministries, Washington, DC; Life Member, Disabled American Veterans **A/H:** Humanitarian Award, Scriptures for Daily Living; Certificate of Appreciation, Good News Jail & Prison Ministry, Prince George's County; Certificate of Appreciation, Bible Study Ministry; Certificate of Appreciation, District of Columbia Department of Corrections; Certificate of Appointment to Conference Evangelist, AME Zion Church; Certificate of Promotion to Coordinator of Prison Ministry, Star of Bethlehem COGIC; Certificate of Completion, L.D.S. Institute of Christian Counseling and Biblical Studies, Certificate of Completion in Practical Biblical Theology and Old Testament Survey, Family Radio School of the Bible; Certificate of Completion, District of Columbia Department of Corrections **C/VW:** Future Care, Clinton, MD; Healthy Mentoring Matters Program, Laurel, MD; Volunteer, Prison Minister, Maryland Correctional Training Center
Email: bema_song@hotmail.com
URL: http://www.bemaoutreachministries.com

Candace M. Swartz
Title: Childcare Provider **Company:** Sweet Dreams Childcare **Address:** 540 N. Pine Street, Reedsburg, WI 53959 United States **BUS:** Daycare Center **P/S:** Kindergarten Readiness Programs **MA:** Local **D/D/R:** Educating Young Children **H/I/S:** Camping **EDU:** Master of Arts in Education, American InterContinental University; Bachelor of Arts in Communicative Arts, Editing and Publishing, Wisconsin Lutheran College **A/A/S:** Wisconsin Early Childhood Association; National Association for the Education of Young Children; Wisconsin Family Child Care Association
Email: candy@merr.com

Jerry D. Sweatt
Title: Area Manager **Company:** Multi-Chem Production Chemicals **Address:** 5301 Knickerbocker Road, Suite 200, San Angelo, TX 76904 United States **BUS:** Oil and Gas **P/S:** Specialty Chemicals **MA:** International **D/D/R:** Operations Management of 62 People in Sales, Service and Delivery of Liquid Chemical Products, Overseeing Finances, Budgeting **H/I/S:** Fishing, Spending Time with his Boys **EDU:** Bachelor's Degree in Chemistry, University of Kansas **C/VW:** Leukemia & Lymphoma Society
Email: jerrydon_sweatt@multi-chemgroup.com
URL: http://www.multi-chemgroup.com

D. Jeanne Sweet
Title: Director of Housekeeping and Laundry (Retired) **Company:** Peralta Hospital **Address:** Oakland, CA 94610 United States **BUS:** Private Hospital **P/S:** Healthcare **MA:** Local **D/D/R:** Housekeeping **H/I/S:** Making Crafts, Cooking **EDU:** Bachelor of Science in Elementary Education, Nyack College **A/A/S:** Phi Kappa Beta **C/VW:** Volunteer, Local Community Events
URL: http://www.cambridgewhoswho.com

Tammy Sweet-Merrihew
Title: Practice Administrator **Company:** Women's Cancer Care Associates **Address:** 319 S. Manning Boulevard, Suite 301, Albany, NY 12208 United States **BUS:** Group Practice **P/S:** Healthcare Including Gynecologic Oncology Program **MA:** Mid-Hudson Valley **EXP:** Ms. Sweet-Merrihew's expertise is in administration. **D/D/R:** Performing Administrative Duties, Processing Payroll, Recruiting, Staffing, Purchase Orders, Managing Accounts Payable and Accounts Receivable **H/I/S:** Reading, Acrylic Painting, Cooking **EDU:** Associate of Science in Finance, Hudson Valley Community College **C/VW:** St. Jude Children's Research Hospital
Email: tsweet@womenscancercareassociates.com
URL: http://www.cambridgewhoswho.com

Robyn J. Sweinhart
Title: Site Director, Quality **Company:** Alkermes, Inc. **Address:** 265 Olinger Circle, Wilmington, OH 45177 United States **BUS:** Pharmaceutical Company **P/S:** Pharmaceuticals **MA:** Local **D/D/R:** Quality Control **H/I/S:** Spending Time with her Family **EDU:** Bachelor's Degree in Biology, University of North Carolina **A/A/S:** Parenteral Drug Association **C/VW:** Local Church
Email: robyn.sweinhart@alkermes.com

Athena T. Swentzell-Steen
Title: Co-Director **Company:** The Canelo Project **Address:** HC1 Box 324, Elgin-Canelo, AZ 85611 United States **BUS:** Small Nonprofit Organization Dedicated to the Exploration and Development of Living Systems, Including Growing Food and Building that Creates Friendship, Beauty and Simplicity **P/S:** Education and Development **MA:** International **D/D/R:** Sustainable Living and Building Practices, Baskets, Houses, Thatch Roofs, Field Trips, University Groups, Inspired by the Culture of Mexico, Spain and Japan **EDU:** Bachelor's Degree in Philosophy, St. John's College (1983)
Email: absteen@dakotacom.net
URL: http://www.caneloproject.com

Todd J. Swick, MD
Title: MD **Company:** Sleep Medicine Consultants of Houston **Address:** 7500 San Felipe, Suite 525, Houston, TX 77063 United States **BUS:** Healthcare **MA:** Regional **D/D/R:** Sleep-Wake Disorders **H/I/S:** Boating **EDU:** Stony Brook University, Bachelor of Science -Sleep Specialist
Email: Todd.Swick@cwwemail.com

Jonathan D. Swindle
Title: Orthopaedic Surgery Resident **Company:** Genesys Regional Medical Center **Address:** 1 Genesys Parkway, Grand Blanc, MI 48439 United States **BUS:** Medical Center **P/S:** Healthcare **MA:** Regional **D/D/R:** Orthopaedic Surgery **H/I/S:** Staying Fit, Playing Golf, Reading, Spending Time with his Family **EDU:** Doctor of Osteopathic Medicine, Chicago College of Osteopathic Medicine **A/A/S:** American Osteopathic Association; Christian Medical and Dental Association **C/VW:** Local Church
Email: jonswindle@yahoo.com

Pastor Steven L. Swisher
Title: Pastor **Company:** Living Word Revival Center **Address:** 1762 Highway 64 E, Hayesville, NC 28904 United States **BUS:** Religion **P/S:** Reaching out to the Community for Christ **MA:** Local **D/D/R:** Biblical Studies **H/I/S:** Boating, Golf **A/A/S:** Church on the Rock International, Women in Crisis
Email: azsealy@aol.com

Wade G. Swormstedt
Title: Publisher, Editor **Address:** 407 Gilbert Avenue, Cincinnati, OH 45202 United States **BUS:** Magazine Publisher **P/S:** Writing Editorials, Publishing **MA:** National **D/D/R:** Publishing, Editing, Legislation, Public Speaking **H/I/S:** Plays on 3 Softball Teams, Choir Singer, Sunday School Teacher **EDU:** Bachelor of Arts in Journalism, Boston University

Malcolm P. Sykes
Title: Product Manager **Company:** Southern Tile Distributors **Address:** 4590 Village Avenue, Norfolk, VA 23502 United States **BUS:** Wholesale Flooring Distributor **P/S:** Flooring Wholesale, Retail **MA:** Statewide **D/D/R:** Sales, Marketing **H/I/S:** Sailing, Racing **EDU:** Bachelor's Degree in Economics, St. Paul's Collegiate School, New Zealand **A/H:** National Sales Manager of the Year, Wilsonart (2005) **C/VW:** Lifetime Member, Republican Party
Email: sykesm2005@comcast.net

Kenrick Sylvester
Title: Operations Complex Superintendent **Company:** Hovensa LLC **Address:** 1 Estate Hope, St. Croix, USVI 00820 **BUS:** Crude Oil Processing **P/S:** Top Professional Crude Oil **MA:** International **D/D/R:** Operations Complex Superintendent, Specialty in Vacuum and Crude Units **H/I/S:** Swimming in the Ocean, Fishing **EDU:** Associate Degree in Mechanical Engineering, Vocational Institute of Tobago, Republic of Trinidad; Bachelor of Science in Chemical Engineering; Re-Certification Paralegal **C/VW:** St. Croix Red Cross
Email: ksylvester_2@yahoo.com
URL: http://www.hovensa.com

Heather Diane Szabo
Title: Marketing Manager **Company:** Westlake Village Costco **Address:** 5700 Lindero Cyn Road, Westlake Village, CA 91362 United States **BUS:** Retail Store **P/S:** Selling Brand Name Merchandise **MA:** National **D/D/R:** Marketing, Business Management **H/I/S:** Exercising, Swimming, Playing Tennis **EDU:** Bachelor of Arts in Business Management, California Lutheran University **A/A/S:** Westlake Village Chamber of Commerce **C/VW:** Los Angeles Children's Hospital; Children's Miracle Network
Email: hdszabo@yahoo.com
Email: heather.szabo@cwwemail.com
URL: http://www.cambridgewhoswho.com

Pamela A. Szczesniak, CIC, CRM
Title: Account Executive, Financial Services **Company:** Jenkins Athens Insurance Services **Address:** 1455 Response Road, Suite 260, Sacramento, CA 95815 United States **BUS:** One of the Largest and Well-Respected Independent Insurance Services Firms in Northern California **P/S:** Business Insurance, Risk Management, Property and Casualty Claims Management, Safety and Loss Protection, Contract and Lease Review, Management and Professional Liability and Bonding and Surety Services **MA:** California **D/D/R:** Selling Insurance to Commercial Lines, Zoos and Aquariums, Overseeing Claims Administration, Benefits, Professional and Management Liability **H/I/S:** Gardening, Scuba Diving **EDU:** Certified Insurance Counselor; Certified Risk Manager
Email: pszczesniak@jenkinsathens.com
URL: http://www.jenkinsathens.com

Amanda J. Szot
Title: Registered Dietitian **Company:** South Coast Hospitals Group **Address:** 363 Highland Avenue, Fall River, MA 02720 United States **BUS:** Hospital **P/S:** Healthcare **MA:** Maine **D/D/R:** Cardiac Nutrition **H/I/S:** Working Out, Sewing, Reading **EDU:** Pursuing Master's Degree in Applied Nutrition, Northeastern University; Bachelor of Science in Science Nutrition, Minor in Exercise Science, University of Rhode Island
Email: szota@southcoast.org
URL: http://www.southcoast.org

Suzanne Szumigalski, Psy.D.
Title: Clinical Psychologist, Owner **Company:** Psychological Wellness Center, Inc. **Address:** 1030 S. La Grange Road, Suite 8, La Grange, IL 60525 United States **BUS:** Rehabilitation Center **P/S:** Rehabilitation Services **MA:** Regional **D/D/R:** conducting individual, marriage and family counseling, performing psychological evaluations, administering mediation, mentoring, offering life and business coaching **H/I/S:** Gardening, Spending Time with her Friends **EDU:** Doctorate Degree in Clinical Psychology, Adler School of Professional Psychology (2004); Master of Arts, Governors State University (1994); Bachelor of Arts, Trinity Christian College (1992); Associate of Arts, Moraine Valley Community College (1991) **CERTS:** Nationally Certified Clinical Mental Health Counselor **A/A/S:** American Psychological Association; American Counseling Association; International Association of Marriage and Family Therapists **C/VW:** American Red Cross
Email: mtwmtm@comcast.net
URL: http://www.cambridgewhoswho.com

Denise L. Tabacheck
Title: Occupational Therapist **Company:** Epic Healthcare **Address:** 3300 4th Avenue, Conway, SC 29579 United States **BUS:** Healthcare Service Provider **P/S:** Nursing Home, Rehabilitation Center **MA:** Local **D/D/R:** Geriatric Rehabilitation **H/I/S:** Reading, Swimming, Gardening, Going to the Beach **EDU:** Bachelor of Science Degree **A/A/S:** South Carolina Occupational Association
Email: tabacheck@msn.com

Paul E. Taboada
Title: 1) Chief Executive Officer, Chairman 2) President, Chairman **Company:** 1) Charles Morgan Securities 2) PCM Industries 3) Mandalay Industries **Address:** 120 Wall Street, New York, NY 10005 United States **BUS:** Finance Company **P/S:** Investment Consulting and Advice, Broker and Dealer **MA:** National **D/D/R:** Financial Securities, Investment Banking **H/I/S:** Playing the Classical Guitar **EDU:** Executive Program, Wharton School; Bachelor of International Business, American College of Switzerland; Bachelor of Foreign Language, American College of Switzerland **A/A/S:** PCM Industries, Mandalay Industries
Email: pthbw@aol.com
URL: http://www.charlesmorgansecurities.net

Michael Tabor
Title: Owner **Company:** NightHawk Security and Investigations, LLC **Address:** P.O. Box 760, Wayne, WV 25570 United States **BUS:** Security Service Company **P/S:** Security Services, Armed and Unarmed Security Guards and Investigation **MA:** Regional **D/D/R:** overseeing operations including security services for schools, armed sites and companies, patrolling **H/I/S:** Motorcycling, Climbing **A/A/S:** West Virginia State Police; Veterans of Foreign Wars; American Legion
Email: nighthawk78@myway.com
URL: http://www.cambridgwhoswho.com

Linda B. Tafone
Title: Director of Quality Management **Company:** Brooklyn Hospital **Dept:** Internal Medicine **Address:** 339 Hicks Street, Brooklyn, NY 11201 United States **BUS:** Hospital **P/S:** Healthcare **MA:** Local **D/D/R:** Overseeing Administration and Education **H/I/S:** Traveling, Reading **EDU:** Master's Degree in Adult and Community College Education; Master's Degree in Healthcare Administration **C/VW:** Breast Cancer Charities; AIDS Walk
Email: ltafone@chpnet.org

M. Taheri, DDS
Title: DDS **Company:** Syosset Dental Works **Address:** 573 Underhill Boulevard, Suite 105, Syosset, NY 11791 United States **BUS:** Healthcare Dentistry **P/S:** Surgical Dentistry, Dentistry **MA:** Local **D/D/R:** Specializing in Dentistry **EDU:** NYU, Doctor of Dental Surgery **A/A/S:** AGD, AOA, AOT, Orthopedic Association

Lynette C. Tait
Title: Teacher **Company:** Taylor Middle School **Address:** 350 E. Shirley Avenue, Warrenton, VA 20186 United States **BUS:** Middle School **P/S:** Education **MA:** Local **D/D/R:** Teaching Foreign Language and Culture to High School Students **H/I/S:** Traveling, Meeting New People **EDU:** Master of Education, Universidad Federal Fluminense, Rio de Janeiro, Brazil **A/A/S:** Recipient Recognition and Awards, Taylor Middle School
Email: lcdmt8@worldnett.att.net

Judy A. Takeuchi
Title: Investment Coordinator, Administration Manager **Company:** Arcano Capital USA, Inc. **Address:** 641 Lexington Avenue, Suite 1530, New York, NY 10022 United States **BUS:** Private Equity Firm **P/S:** Equity Ownership Advising, Management of Mutual Funds and Investments **MA:** International **D/D/R:** Managing Administrative Aspects of the Office, Working with the U.S. Chief Investment Officer, Filling out Subscription Documents, Coordinating Investments of Clients **H/I/S:** Yoga, Reflexology **EDU:** Bachelor of Science in Business Administration, California Coast University
Email: jtakeuchi@arcanocapital.com
URL: http://www.arcanocapital.com

Elizabeth Talamonti
Title: Vice President **Company:** Public Sector Personnel Consultants **Address:** 4110 N. Scottsdale Road, Scottsdale, AZ 85251 United States **BUS:** Consulting Services **P/S:** Classification and Compensation Consulting Services Specializing in Public Sector Clients **MA:** Regional **D/D/R:** Classification and Compensation **H/I/S:** Gardening, Traveling **EDU:** Bachelor's Degree in Business, Arizona State University; Certified Compensation Professional, World at Work **A/A/S:** WorldatWork
Email: ltalamonti@compensationconsulting.com
URL: http://www.compensationconsulting.com

Marc A. Talbert
Title: Psychotherapist, Private Practice **Company:** Inner Space Therapy, LLC **Address:** P.O. Box 847, Santa Fe, NM 87504 United States **BUS:** Children and Adolescent Psychology **P/S:** Counseling **MA:** Local **D/D/R:** Psychotherapy, Writing Novels **H/I/S:** Running in the Mountains, Cooking **EDU:** Master of Arts in Counseling, Pacifica Graduate Institute (2006) **A/A/S:** American Psychological Association; Authors Guild; PEN; SCBWI **C/VW:** Local Schools, Santa Fe Preparatory School
Email: marc@marctalbert.com
URL: http://www.marctalbert.com

Darla Talerico
Title: Owner, Cook **Company:** Talerico's Bar and Grill **Address:** 2300 Duss Avenue, Ambridge, PA 15003 United States **BUS:** Restaurant, Bar and Grill **P/S:** Home Cooked Food **MA:** Local **D/D/R:** Overseeing the Operations, Cooking **H/I/S:** Shooting, Playing Pool, Gambling **EDU:** High School Diploma **A/A/S:** Chamber of Commerce **C/VW:** Church
Email: karaokemichele@hotmail.com

Laura Lee J. Talley
Title: Program Specialist (Retired) **Company:** U.S. Army **Address:** 789 Vermont National Guard Road, Colchester, VT 05446 United States **BUS:** Government Organization **P/S:** Defense Services **MA:** National **EXP:** Ms. Talley's expertise is in referral service for families. **H/I/S:** Participating in Girl Scouts Activities **EDU:** Pursuing Coursework in Business, Saint Michael's College; Coursework, Sergeant Majors Military Academy (2004) **A/A/S:** National Amateur Athletic Union Basketball League; Girl Scouts of the United States of America; Veterans of Foreign Wars **C/VW:** Girl Scouts of the United States of America
Email: laura.lee.talley@us.army.mil

Dr. John A. Tallmadge Jr.
Title: Professor of Chemical Engineering (Retired) **Company:** Drexel University **Address:** 3141 Chestnut Street, Philadelphia, PA 19104 United States **BUS:** University **P/S:** Education, Research **MA:** International **D/D/R:** Chemical Engineering, Specializing in Fluid Dynamics, Processing of Thin Films, Powder Metallurgy, Managing Waste Water Treatment, Polymer Processing, Working with Non-Newtonian Liquids **H/I/S:** Playing Tennis, Traveling, Reading History and Geography **EDU:** Ph.D. in Chemical Engineering, Carnegie Mellon University, Pittsburgh, Pennsylvania; Master's Degree in Chemical Engineering, Carnegie Mellon University; Bachelor of Science in Chemical Engineering, Lehigh University **A/A/S:** Former President, New Haven, Connecticut Chapter; American Institute of Chemical Engineers; President, Philadelphia Chapter; Chemical Heritage Foundation
Email: john.tallmadge@cwwemail.com
URL: http://www.drexel.edu

Nina L. Tam

Title: Chief Executive Officer **Company:** Shining Star Records **Address:** P.O. Box 1611, Huntington, NY 11743 United States **BUS:** Entertainment Company **P/S:** Music and Entertainment **MA:** International **D/D/R:** Management **H/I/S:** Traveling **EDU:** Ph.D. in Hypnotherapy, Albert University; Ph.D. in Alternative Medicine, Albert University; Interfaith Minister, The Sanctuary of Peace and Harmony
Email: ninakoo@thekungfugirls.com
URL: http://www.myspace.com/thekungfugirls

Keat C. Tan

Title: AIA, Principal, Director of Design **Company:** Klipp **Address:** 1512 Larimer Street, Bridge Level, Denver, CO 80202 United States **BUS:** Full-Service Architectural, Programming, Planning, Design and Construction Administration **P/S:** Public, Commercial and Educational Facility Design **D/D/R:** Directing Teams, Overseeing Universal Design Services **H/I/S:** Soccer **EDU:** Bachelor's Degree in Architecture, Syracuse University (1981); Interior Design, London South Bank University (1976)
Email: keat@klipparch.com
URL: http://www.klipparch.com

Insuk Tanaka

Title: Owner **Company:** Fashion Gal **Address:** 9684 Bruceville Road, Suite 109, Elk Grove, CA 95757 United States **BUS:** Women's Apparel Retail **P/S:** Wedding and Formal Dress **MA:** Local **D/D/R:** Customer Service/Management **H/I/S:** Golf
Email: fashiongalplus@hotmail.com
URL: http://www.naomissummerwear.com

Michael J. Tangen

Title: Manager **Company:** Tangen Financial, LLC **Address:** 9 Birchwood Drive, Blue Grass, IA 52726 United States **BUS:** Financial Services **P/S:** Planning, Stocks, Bonds, Mutual Funds, Medical, Life and LTC Insurances **MA:** Local **D/D/R:** Financial Planning **EDU:** Bachelor of Science in Finance, Drake University **C/VW:** YMCA, Camp Abraham Lincoln
Email: planmjt@aol.com
URL: http://www.planmjt.com

Dr. Dayalal D. Tank

Title: Psychiatrist **Company:** Sunset Psychiatric Medical Center **Address:** 933 S. Sunset Avenue, Suite 105, West Covina, CA 91790 United States **BUS:** Medical Center **P/S:** Healthcare and Psychiatric Care Services **MA:** Local **EXP:** Mr. Tank's expertise includes psychiatric disorder treatment and bipolar disorder treatment. **H/I/S:** Traveling **EDU:** MD, Earned in India **CERTS:** Training in Psychiatric, Drew University, Los Angeles **A/A/S:** California Medical Association; LAMA; American Psychiatric Association; American Medical Association
Email: tikusweetu@yahoo.com
URL: http://www.cambridgewhoswho.com

Karla Tankersley

Title: Director of Engineering **Company:** Gap, Inc. **Address:** 8009 State Road, Cincinnati, OH 45255 United States **BUS:** Specialty Retailer in Men's and Women's Fashions **P/S:** Men's and Women's Clothing and Accessories **MA:** International **D/D/R:** Leading and Guiding 12 Distribution Centers in their Engineering Resources, Overseeing Distribution for the North American Operations with the Council for Leadership Team **H/I/S:** Running **EDU:** Master's Degree in Engineering, University of Cincinnati (2008); Bachelor's Degree in Industrial Engineering, University of Cincinnati (2000) **A/A/S:** Society of Women Engineers; Institute of Industrial Engineers; Speaking Locally and Nationally
Email: pilotank@fuse.net
URL: http://www.cambridgewhosgap.com

Karen E. Tanner

Title: Athletic Trainer, Personal Trainer **Company:** Five Seasons Sports Club **Address:** 1300 E. 96th Street, Indianapolis, IN 46240 United States **BUS:** Sports Club **P/S:** Healthcare, Fitness **MA:** Local **D/D/R:** Fitness Training, Exercise, Rehabilitation, Creating Individualized Programs **H/I/S:** Participating in Outdoor Activities, Hiking **EDU:** Master of Arts in Wellness Management, Ball State University; Bachelor's Degree in Athletic Training, Taylor University; Certified Athletic Trainer, National Athletic Training Association; Performance Specialist, National Academy of Sports Medicine; Licensed Athletic Trainer, State of Indiana **A/A/S:** National Athletic Training Association
Email: karentanner78@yahoo.com
URL: http://www.trainingbytanner.com

Semra Tanrikulu Erguven

Title: Esthetician **Company:** Semra Skin Care **Address:** 3623 R Street N.W., Washington, DC 20007 United States **BUS:** Privately Owned Company Committed to Excellence in the Beauty Spa Industry **P/S:** Skincare, Waxing, Facials, Makeup **MA:** Regional **D/D/R:** Renting her Own Space, Performing Facials, Waxing, Permanent Makeup, Eyebrow Shaping, Eyelash Extensions, Skin Care **H/I/S:** Running, Traveling **EDU:** Bachelor of Science Degree in Business, Yvonne de Bel Air School, France (1997)
Email: semra4skin@gmail.com

Diane Tappan Horst, ABR

Title: Realtor **Company:** Dauphin Realty **Address:** 29674 S. Bayshore Drive, Orange Beach, AL 36561 United States **BUS:** Real Estate Industry **P/S:** Real Estate Sales of Residential, Commercial and Historic Properties **MA:** Regional **D/D/R:** Handling Buying and Selling of Residential Homes, Commercial Historic Properties and Land Investment, Investment Homes, Waterfront Resort Properties **H/I/S:** Sailing, Fishing, Traveling, Historic Property Development and Reconstruction **EDU:** Coursework in Interior Design, Bell Haven College and University Alabama; Licensed Realtor, Alabama; Accredited Buyers Representative **A/A/S:** National Association of Realtors; Alabama Association of Realtors; Mobile Area of Realtors; Mobile Historic Development Commission; Representative, Gunston Hall Plantation (500 Acre Property that Belonged to George Mason); Board, Conde-Charlotte Museum House; Board of Regents Representative, State of Alabama
Email: dth1944@gulftel.com
URL: http://www.dauphinrealty.com

Tracy Tarantino

Title: Teacher **Company:** Tryon Hills Pre-K Center **Address:** 2600 Grimes Street, Charlotte, NC 28206 United States **BUS:** Pre-School **P/S:** Pre-School Education **MA:** Local **D/D/R:** coordinating child and family development classes, teaching early childhood education **H/I/S:** Reading, Spending Time at the Lake **EDU:** Bachelor of Arts in Child and Family Development, University of North Carolina, Charlotte **C/VW:** Local Church
Email: tracy23ann@yahoo.com
URL: http://www.cambridgewhoswho.com

Pamela G. Tarr

Title: Chief Executive Officer, President, Author **Company:** Tarr & Associates Insurance Management **Address:** 10210 289th Street E., Myakka City, FL 34251 United States **BUS:** Insurance Brokerage Agency **P/S:** Individual and Group Insurance, Life, Health and Disability Insurance, Recruitment of Agents **MA:** International **EXP:** Ms. Tarr's expertise includes sales and product training. **D/D/R:** marketing, training and managing agents, conducting meetings, overseeing daily business operations **H/I/S:** Swimming, Traveling, Fishing, Camping, Spending Time with her Family and Friends, Writing, Journaling, Public Speaking, Reading, Playing the Cello **EDU:** College Coursework; Coursework in Leadership **A/A/S:** American Health Underwriters; Florida Chapter, National Association of Life Underwriters; Board Chairwoman, First Christian Church, Sarasota, FL **A/H:** Woman of the Year Award (2007) **C/VW:** The Salvation Army, American Cancer Society; Myasthenia Gravis Foundation of America
Email: pam.tarr@tarrassociates.com
URL: http://www.tarrassociates.com

Betty G. Tarver

Title: Elementary Music Teacher **Company:** Bear Branch Elementary School **Address:** 8909 FM 1488, Magnolia, TX 77354 United States **BUS:** Elementary School **P/S:** Primary Education **MA:** Regional **D/D/R:** teaching music lessons, conducting the choir **H/I/S:** Traveling, Playing the Piano **EDU:** Bachelor's Degree in Music Education, Plus 80, Sam Houston State University **CERTS:** Certified Kindergarten Teacher **A/A/S:** Texas Music Education Association; Association of Texas Professional Educators; Who's Who Among America's Teachers; Who's Who of American Women; Who's Who in America **A/H:** Teacher of the Year Award (2007) **C/VW:** The Salvation Army; Good Will
Email: btarver@magnoliaisd.org
URL: http://www.cambridgewhoswho.com

Dawn M. Tasher

Title: Owner/Head Teacher **Company:** Montessori Academy **Address:** 3602 West 80th Lane, Merrillville, IN 46410 United States **BUS:** School **P/S:** Preschool 3-6 Year Old Education **MA:** Local **D/D/R:** Preschool Education **H/I/S:** Ballroom Dancing **EDU:** Montessori Society, Certified Teacher **A/A/S:** Montessori Society
URL: http://www.montessorinwi.com

Jeanne B. Tassis

Title: President **Company:** Circle of Hope Lymphedema Foundation, Inc. **Address:** 36 Woodcrest Drive, Prospect, CT 06712 United States **BUS:** Nonprofit Agency **P/S:** Professional Education, Awareness and Treatment Information to Medical Professionals and Patients with Lymphedema **MA:** National **D/D/R:** Running Circle of Hope Lymphedema Foundation **H/I/S:** Arts and Crafts, Scrapbooking, Reading, Traveling, Arranging Flowers, Ceramics, Reiki **EDU:** Bachelor's Degree in Education, Eastern Connecticut State University; Certified Lebed Method Focus on Healing Instructor, Southern Connecticut State University; Graduate Courses, Sedona Method **A/A/S:** Lymph Science Advocacy Program; National Lymphedema Network; Vodder Association of North America; Lebed Method Focus on Healing; CLMC; Connecticut Coalition for Lymphedema Legislation; St. Anthony's Ladies Guild **C/VW:** Donating Time to Lymphedema Support Groups and Organizations
Email: jtlymphedema@aol.com
URL: http://www.lymphedemacircleofhope.org

William L. Tate

Title: Owner **Company:** Tate's Enterprise **Address:** P.O. Box 1774, Junction City, KS 66441 United States **BUS:** Accounting Firm **P/S:** Accounting and Financial Services Including Accounting, Tax Preparation, Computer Service, Mobile Tax Services, Investments and Annuities **MA:** Regional **EXP:** Mr. Tate's expertise is in annual tax form preparation. **D/D/R:** Marketing, Participating Business Expo, Consulting for Customers Expo, Training New Employees, Teaching Clients to Use QuickBooks for Accounting, Consulting with People to Start their Own Business, training clients on tax filing, offering mobile tax services and new financial planning services including investing and annuities **EDU:** Bachelor of Science in Business Administration, with a Concentration in Money and Banking, Kansas State University (1998) **A/A/S:** United States Army
Email: wlt7007@yahoo.com
URL: http://www.cambridgewhoswho.com

Anna Tattan

Title: Teacher **Company:** Public School 40 **Address:** 265 Ralph Avenue, Brooklyn, NY 11233 United States **BUS:** Public School **P/S:** Elementary Education **MA:** Regional **D/D/R:** Teaching Kindergarten in the Inner City **H/I/S:** Running **EDU:** Bachelor's Degree in Elementary Education, University of Michigan (2006) **A/A/S:** National Education Association; United Federation of Teachers
Email: ATattan@schools.nyc.gov

Sarah J. Taub

Title: Special Education Teacher **Company:** School of the Arts **Address:** 29 Farrington Place, Rochester, NY 14610 United States **BUS:** Middle and High School Facility **P/S:** Full Academic Course Load as well as a Fine Arts Sequence **MA:** Regional **D/D/R:** Childhood Literacy for First through Sixth-Graders, General and Special Education, Teaching Four Inclusion Classes and Two Resource Classes **H/I/S:** Playing Softball, Dancing, Ballet **EDU:** Master's Degree in Early Childhood Literacy, SUNY Genesee (2005) **A/A/S:** Phi Delta Kappa
Email: sarahtaub25@yahoo.com
URL: http://www.rcsdk12.org/schools/secondary/sota.htm

Betty A. Taucher

Title: Teacher, Poet **Company:** St. Mary of the Assumption School **Address:** 8540 Mentor Avenue, Mentor, OH 44068 United States **BUS:** Middle School **P/S:** Regular Core Curriculum Including Reading, Mathematics, English, Science, Social Studies, Art, Music, History, Physical Education **MA:** Regional **D/D/R:** Teaching Reading, Health and Family Life to Sixth, Seventh and Eighth-Grades **H/I/S:** Reading, Astronomy, Listening to the Beatles, Writing Poetry, Undertaking Historical Recreations **EDU:** Bachelor of Arts Degree in History, Cleveland State University (1973); Certified in Secondary Education for 6th-12th-Grades **A/A/S:** St. Mary's Book Group; TSR-St. John Vianney; Public Speaking; Virtus Trainer; International Poets of the Year, International Poets Society (2006); Who's Who Among American Educators; Who's Who Among American Professional Women **C/VW:** Peace Committee Missions for School Charities
Email: mccartneymaniac@pepperland.zzn.com
URL: http://www.cambridgewhoswho.com

Alexandra P. Tavlarides

Title: President, Chief Executive Officer **Company:** Atav Appraisals **Address:** P.O. Box 309, Syracuse, NY 13214 United States **BUS:** Real Estate Appraisal Company **P/S:** Residential Real Estate Appraisals **MA:** Onondaga, Oswego and Madison Counties **D/D/R:** Overseeing Estate, New Construction and Relocation Appraisals, 1-4 Units Income Properties, Assessing Tax, Sales, Reverse Mortgages, Equity Loans **H/I/S:** Swimming, Hiking, Camping Canoing, Traveling, Listening to Classical and Opera Music, Cooking, Singing in Church Choir **EDU:** SRA Designation, Appraisal Institute; Bachelor of Science in Mathematics, University of Pittsburgh **A/A/S:** The Appraisal Institute; Greater Syracuse Association of Realtors; New York State Association of Realtors; National Association of Realtors; Employment Relocation Council; Federal Housing Administration; Former President, Top Hats Dance Club; Daughters of Penelope and Syracuse Friends of Chamber Music **C/VW:** Syracuse Friends of Chamber Music; Program Ad Committee; Ladies Auxiliary; Camp Good Days; Special Times; Daughters of Penelope
Email: atavlar2@twcny.rr.com
URL: http://www.atavappraisals.com

Allison Taylor

Title: Fifth-Grade Teacher **Company:** Holy Savior-St. John Fisher School **Address:** 122 E. Ridge Road, Linwood, PA 19061 United States **BUS:** School **P/S:** Education **MA:** Local **D/D/R:** Mathematics, Technology **H/I/S:** Spending Time with her Family **EDU:** Bachelor's Degree in Early Childhood and Elementary Education, Neumann College
Email: hssjfmrstaylor@gmail.com
URL: http://www.cambridgewhoswho.com

Betty R. Taylor
Title: Registered Nurse **Company:** Cherokee Women's Wellness Center **Address:** 876 Acquoni Road, Cherokee, NC 28719 United States **BUS:** Wellness Center **P/S:** Women's Healthcare **MA:** Local **D/D/R:** Women's Health, Case Management **H/I/S:** Gardening, Bird Watching **EDU:** Nursing Diploma, Bluefield State College; Associate of Science in Nursing, Bluefield State College **C/VW:** Harris Regional Hospital Auxiliary, REACH Program
Email: beml123@aol.com

Carol A. Taylor
Title: Author, Publisher **Company:** Carol Taylor Books **Address:** 5408 4th Avenue S., Great Falls, MT 59405 United States **BUS:** Publishing Company **P/S:** Non-Fiction Historical Works **MA:** International **D/D/R:** Writing Grants, Writing Proposals, Editing, Proofreading, Interviewing, Publication of Many Articles in Major Magazines **H/I/S:** Caring for her Two Horses, Dogs and Two Cats, Reading, Landscaping, Playing the Cello **EDU:** Bachelor of Science in Human Services, Metropolitan State College, Magna Cum Laude (1976); Associate Degree in Applied Science, Metropolitan State College (1974); Coursework in Journalism, English and Public Administration, University of Wyoming **A/A/S:** Former Secretary of Drug and Alcohol Task Force, Denver; All-State Orchestra and Choir **A/H:** Two-Time Beauty Contestant; Winner of Many Essay Contests
Email: carol@meanestwinter.com
Email: caataylor@hotmail.com
URL: http://www.meanestwinter.com
URL: http://www.caroltaylorbooks.com

Charmaine R. Taylor
Title: Director, North America Operations and Owner Relations **Company:** Starwood Hotels & Resorts Worldwide, Inc. **Address:** 1111 Westchester Avenue, White Plains, NY 10604 United States **BUS:** Hotel and Resorts **P/S:** Hospitality and Food Services **MA:** International **EXP:** Ms. Taylor's expertise is in business management. **D/D/R:** Overseeing Benchmarking and Capital Prioritization Processes, Organizational Designing, Analyzing Finances, Implementing Business Initiatives Across Different Brands, Developing All Communication Deliverables for Owners and Real Estate Development Groups, Strategic Consulting **H/I/S:** Traveling, Photography, Biking, Snow Skiing, Scuba Diving, Playing the Violin and Piano, Pastry Cooking **EDU:** Master of Business Administration in General Management, Harvard University (2006); Bachelor of Arts in Organizational Behavior and Psychology, University of Pennsylvania (2000) **A/A/S:** National Black MBA Association; National Association for Female Executives; American Management Association
Email: charmaine.taylor@starwoodhotels.com
URL: http://www.starwoodhotels.com

Danyelle M. Taylor
Title: Attorney **Company:** Law Offices of Danyelle M. Taylor **Address:** 1065 Muller Parkway, Suite A, Westwego, LA 70094 United States **BUS:** Law Firm **P/S:** Legal Services **MA:** Local **EXP:** Ms. Taylor's expertise includes civil and family law litigation. **D/D/R:** Practicing Law before the Appellate and State Supreme Court **H/I/S:** Scrapbooking, Plays the Guitar **EDU:** JD, Loyola University School of Law; Bachelor of Arts, Loyola University School of Law; Associate of Science, Loyola University School of Law **A/A/S:** Nichols Bar Association; New Orleans Bar Association; Co-Founder, Jefferson Parish Family Law Association; Westwego Civic Association; Harvey Canal Industrial Association; New Orleans Bowl Foundation **C/VW:** Cornerstone Christian Center; The Metro Club; The Women's National Republican Club
Email: danytay1@bellsouth.net
URL: http://www.cambridgewhoswho.com

Ellen Taylor
Title: Controller **Company:** Joele Frank, Wilkinson Brimmer Katcher **Address:** 140 E. 45th Street, 37th Floor, New York, NY 10017 United States **BUS:** Strategic, Financial and Corporate Communications Firm **P/S:** Public and Investor Relations Services, Crisis Management, Mergers and Acquisitions Transactions, Financial and Regulatory Matters **MA:** International **EXP:** Ms. Taylor's expertise is in money management. **D/D/R:** Managing Operations including Financial Reporting, Budgeting, Utilizing Analytical and Organizational Skills, Creating Auditor Packages, Streamlining Internal Procedures **H/I/S:** Attending Museums, Theater, Concerts, Tennis Matches **EDU:** Bachelor's Degree in Economics and Accounting(1972) **A/A/S:** Museum of Modern Art; Metropolitan Museum of Art; Carnegie Hall; Joyce Theater; Lincoln Center
Email: etaylor50@earthlink.net
URL: http://www.joelefrank.com

Ila Darlene Taylor
Title: Property Manager **Company:** JLE Properties **Address:** 312 E. Orangeburg Avenue, Modesto, CA 95350 United States **BUS:** Multi-Housing Unit Company **P/S:** Coordination, Marketing, Leasing **MA:** Central and Northern California **D/D/R:** Designing Interiors, Managing Properties **H/I/S:** Cooking Gourmet Meals, Wine-tasting **A/A/S:** Multi-Housing Anti-Crime Program; Fresh Outdoors **C/VW:** Valley Children's Hospital
Email: silverice@juno.com

Joanne M. Taylor
Title: Teacher **Company:** Olathe School District 233, Scarborough Elementary **Address:** 2000 S. Lindenwood Drive, Olathe, KS 66062 United States **BUS:** School **P/S:** Education **MA:** Local **D/D/R:** Teaching Deaf and Hard of Hearing Children **H/I/S:** Riding her Bike, Reading **EDU:** Master of Science in Deaf Education, University of Kansas; Bachelor of Science in Education and Speech Pathology, North East Missouri State University **A/A/S:** Council of Exceptional Children; American Annals of the Deaf **C/VW:** Special Olympics
Email: jtaylorsc@olatheschools.com
URL: http://www.cambridgewhoswho.com

Mrs. Laura R. Taylor
Title: Regional Manager **Company:** Mississippi Real Estate Closing, Inc. **Address:** 1576 Moriteith Avenue, Suite A, Hemando, MS 38632 United States **BUS:** Real Estate Firm **P/S:** Real Estate **MA:** Regional **D/D/R:** Marketing Residential and Commercial Property Sales **H/I/S:** Skeet Shooting, Pistol Shooting, Hunting, Horseback Riding **EDU:** College Coursework; High School Graduate **A/A/S:** Chamber of Commerce **C/VW:** Junior Auxiliary of Greenwood; American Heart Association
Email: laura.taylor@msclosings.com
URL: http://www.msclosings.com

Marge R. Taylor
Title: Administrative Manager **Company:** Eastern Michigan University **Address:** 586 Ridge Lane, Tecumseh, MI 49286 United States **BUS:** Public University **P/S:** Undergraduate and Graduate Degree Programs, Research, Athletics and Recreation, Student Support Services, Clubs and Organizations **MA:** Regional **D/D/R:** Overseeing Daily Operations Including Records and Budgeting, Assisting the Dean, Managing the Work-Study Program **H/I/S:** Playing French Horn, Performing with Community Band **EDU:** Master's Degree in Special Education, The University of Toledo (1994); Bachelor's Degree in Physical Education, The University of Toledo (1975) **A/A/S:** Phi Kappa Phi
Email: marge.taylor@gmail.com
URL: http://www.emich.edu

Mrs. Nicole Taylor
Title: Independent Representative **Company:** Silpada Designs **Address:** Springfield, MO 65802 United States **BUS:** Jewelry Shop **P/S:** Direct Sales for High Quality Handcrafted Sterling Silver Jewelry **MA:** National **D/D/R:** selling jewelry, recruiting new representatives, creating partnerships, building relationships with representatives and clients, hosting home parties and organizing fundraising events **H/I/S:** Writing, Reading, Photography, Shopping, Creating Photo Albums **EDU:** Bachelor's Degree in Communication Management, Southwest Missouri State University (1991) **A/A/S:** Association for Women in Communications **A/H:** Top Recruiter Award (2006); Second Best Business Developer Award (2006); National Conference Lecturer Award (2006); Top Rookie Recruiter Award (2001); Top Recruiter Award (2001); Career Recruiter Award
Email: nicole@silversuccess.com
URL: http://www.silversuccess.com

Pearline Taylor
Title: Laboratory Analyst **Company:** Lucite International **Address:** 2665 Fite Road, Memphis, TN 38127 United States **BUS:** Chemical Manufacturing Company **P/S:** Chemical Manufacturing of Acrylic-Based Products, Monomers and Polymers **MA:** International **D/D/R:** Laboratory Quality Control **H/I/S:** Hand Quilting, Reading One Book Every Day **EDU:** Master's Degree in Science, University of Memphis (Formerly Memphis State University) **A/A/S:** Society of Women Engineers **A/H:** Congressional Citation for Community Service (1976) **C/VW:** Various Charities
Email: chip5ee@aol.com
URL: http://www.cambridgewhoswho.com

Ronald W. Taylor
Title: Director of RF Engineering **Company:** Equity Media Holding Corporation **Address:** 1 Shackleford Drive, Suite 400, Little Rock, AR 72211 United States **BUS:** Commercial Broadcast Television **P/S:** Commercial Broadcast Television **MA:** National **D/D/R:** RF Engineering **H/I/S:** Designing Sound System, Running Live Sound Events **EDU:** Coursework in Broadcast Engineering, Bob Jones University **A/A/S:** Master Engineer, National Association of Radio and Telecommunication Engineers, Inc. **C/VW:** Bible Baptist Church
Email: rtaylor@ebcorp.net
URL: http://www.cambridgewhoswho.com

Sandra L. Taylor
Title: Office Manager, Co-Owner **Company:** EST Enterprises, Inc. **Address:** 43220 N. 22nd Street, New River, AZ 85087 United States **BUS:** Weed Control Company **P/S:** Weed Control, Fertilizing Grass, Trees and Shrubs, Grass and Plant Insect Control, Kill Grass for Rock Installations, Olive Tree Fruit Control, Mauget Injections, Free Consultations and Educational Seminars **MA:** Regional **EXP:** Ms. Taylor's expertise is in operations management. **D/D/R:** Bookkeeping, Training Employees, Maintaining Status of Certifications, Managing Human Resource Issues **H/I/S:** Bowling, Horseback Riding **EDU:** High School Diploma **CERTS:** Certified Medical Assistant **A/A/S:** Better Business Bureau **C/VW:** Local Church; Volunteer, BMX Tracks
Email: staylor@estentinc.com
URL: http://www.estenterprisesinc.com

Svetlana Y. Taylor
Title: Teacher **Company:** Sandia High School **Address:** 7801 Candelaria School, Albuquerque, NM 87100 United States **BUS:** Public High School **P/S:** Education **MA:** Local **D/D/R:** Teaching Special Education **H/I/S:** Gardening, Reading, Traveling, Writing Poetry, Participating in International Walk for the Livable World from Los Angeles to New York **EDU:** Master of Arts in Special Education, University of New Mexico (2000); Master of Arts in Linguistics, Belorussian University of Linguistics (1977); Gifted Certification **A/A/S:** Association for Supervision and Curriculum Development **A/H:** Who's Who Among American Teachers (2000, 2001, 2002, 2006) **C/VW:** ARCHA
Email: taylor_51919@comcast.net
URL: http://www.sandimatadors.com

Thomas Taylor Jr.
Title: Field Clinical Specialist, Sales Representative **Company:** Biotronik **Address:** 6024 Jean Road, Lake Oswego, OR 97035 United States **BUS:** Manufacturing Company **P/S:** Manufacturing Pacemakers and Related Products **MA:** International **D/D/R:** Sales, Implantable Cardiac Devices **H/I/S:** Traveling, Supporting Education Grants **EDU:** Several Years of Professional Development at Various Institutions **A/A/S:** HRS **C/VW:** Central Christian Church
Email: ttaylor638@cox.net

Kathryn Taylor Reynolds
Title: President, Photographer **Company:** Kathryn Reynolds Photography, Inc. **Address:** P.O. Box 148, Clemmons, NC 27012 United States **BUS:** Internationally Renowned and Award-Winning Commercial and Fine-Art Photographer **P/S:** Wide Range of Photographic Services **MA:** International **D/D/R:** Creating Commercial Photography and Fine Art Photography **H/I/S:** Horseback Riding. Practicing Yoga, Mountain Climbing, Skiing, Playing Tennis **EDU:** Bachelor of Arts in Commercial Photography, Randolph Community College (1996); Bachelor of Arts in English, University of Georgia; Coursework, Thames Valley University, London, England **A/A/S:** Association of Media Photographers **A/H:** Recipient, Advertising Photographer of the Year; Recipient, Honorable Mentions, 'Lucie Awards'
Email: kathryn@kathrynreynoldsphotography.com
URL: http://www.kathrynreynoldsphotography.com

Darlene Taylor-Hooper
Title: Nurse (Retired) **Company:** Los Angeles County **Address:** 12440 E. Imperial Highway, Suite 522, Norwalk, CA 90650 United States **BUS:** Department of Healthcare **P/S:** Healthcare Including Medical, Surgical and Emergency Neonatal Intensive Care and Psychiatric Services **MA:** Regional **EXP:** Ms. Taylor-Hooper's expertise is in nursing. **D/D/R:** inspecting healthcare facilities, ensuring compliance with federal and state laws, investigating departmental complaints, issuing licenses and certificates, training nurse evaluators, ensuring patients' health and safety **H/I/S:** Antiquing **EDU:** Bachelor's Degree in Nursing, The California State University (1985); Associate Degree in Nursing, Compton Community College (1973) **A/A/S:** American Nurses Association
Email: glh417@aol.com
URL: http://www.ladhs.org

Bambi Teague
Title: Chief of Resource Management, Science Supervisor **Company:** Blue Ridge Parkway **Address:** 199 Hemphill Knob Road, Asheville, NC 28803 United States **BUS:** National Park Service for Recreation and Tourism **P/S:** Science and Ecological Programs, Tourism, Recreation **MA:** Local **D/D/R:** Managing and Supervising Staff, Protecting Ecological and Cultural Resources **H/I/S:** Working for the Church, Protecting the Environment **EDU:** Master's Degree in Liberal Arts, University of North Carolina, Asheville **C/VW:** Church
Email: bambi_teague@nps.gov
URL: http://www.cambridgewhoswho.com

Anita K. Tedesco
Title: Professor Company: Union County College Address: 1033 Springfield Avenue, Cranford, NJ 07016 United States BUS: College P/S: Higher Education MA: Local D/D/R: Attending Cultural Events in New York and New Jersey, supervising department operations, teaching Spanish, humanities, Italian bilingual and cultural studies H/I/S: Attending the Theater and Opera Shows, Walking, Exercising EDU: Doctoral Degree in Education, Walton University; Education Specialist Degree, Seton Hall University; Master's Degree in Education, with a Concentration in Spanish, Seton Hall University; Bachelor of Arts in Spanish, College of Saint Elizabeth; Coursework, University of Madrid, Spain A/A/S: National Education Association C/VW: A Special Wish Foundation
Email: atede50413@aol.com
URL: http://www.ucc.edu/default.htm

Bryan A. Teel
Title: Senior Engineer Company: City Water and Light Address: 400 E. Monroe Avenue, Jonesboro, AR 72401 United States BUS: Utility Company P/S: Control of Electrical Grid, Power and Water Supply, Sewer Construction MA: Local D/D/R: controlling and designing electrical substation systems, Managing Engineering Projects and the Electrical Grid of the City, Mapping H/I/S: Traveling EDU: Bachelor of Arts in Electrical Engineering, Arkansas State University CERTS: Licensed Professional Engineer A/A/S: National Society of Professional Engineers; The American Society of Plumbing Engineers C/VW: United Way of America
Email: bteel@jonesborocwl.org
URL: http://www.jonesborocwl.org

Mary Teets
Title: President Company: Don Teets Contracting, Inc. Address: 12570 Tamiami Trail, Punta Gorda, FL 33955 United States BUS: Construction and Contracting P/S: High-End Residential and Commercial Remodeling MA: Regional D/D/R: Running the Office, Coordinating Clients, Consulting, Sales and Marketing, Overseeing All Operations of the Company H/I/S: Fishing, Traveling, Reading EDU: Associate of Science in Business, Oakland Community College A/A/S: Charlotte DeSoto Building Industry Association; Better Business Bureau; Business Network International; Punta Gorda Chamber of Commerce; Premier Builder, Punta Gorda C/VW: Church, FBA, CDBIA
Email: maryteets@donteets.com
URL: http://www.donteets.com

Gwen Teixeira
Title: Professional Clown Company: Cotton Candy's Clown Circus Address: 25 Aulike Street, Apartment 226, Kailua, HI 96734 United States BUS: Circus P/S: Entertainment Services Including Magic MA: Regional D/D/R: performing at parties, community fundraising, booking, managing finances, marketing H/I/S: Spending Time at the Beach A/A/S: Clowns of America International; Paradise Clown Club; The International Brotherhood of Magicians; Former Member, The Society of American Magicians C/VW: Local Charitable Organizations
Email: Sagapopanagiopis@Juno.com
URL: http://cc_clowns.tripod.com

Jonathan V. Telesca
Title: Special Education Teacher Company: Springfield Public Schools Address: 75 S. Springfield Avenue, Springfield, NJ 07081 United States BUS: School District P/S: Public Education MA: Local D/D/R: Special Education, Reading, Writing H/I/S: Reading, Writing, Jogging EDU: Master's Degree in Education, Fairleigh Dickinson University; Bachelor's Degree in Communications, Fairleigh Dickinson University; Certification in Supervision, Rutgers University A/A/S: New Jersey Education Association C/VW: Pennies for Patients, Toys for Tots
Email: jvtelesca@yahoo.com
URL: http://www.cambridgewhoswho.com

Henry Tellez, MD
Title: Neurologist Company: Sandhills Neurologists Address: 295 Olmsted Boulevard, Pinehurst, NC 28374 United States BUS: Healthcare Neurologists P/S: Healing MA: Local D/D/R: Neurology H/I/S: Tennis EDU: Valley University, St. Louis University, University of North Carolina, MD, Internship and Residency, Fellowship A/A/S: American Academy of Neurology, American Society of Neuro Imaging
Email: shneurol1@earthlink.net

Collis B. Temple III
Title: Regional Vice President Company: Primerica Financial Services Address: Sherwood Forest Tower, 3636 S. Sherwood Forest Boulevard, Baton Rouge, LA 70816 United States BUS: Financial Services Provider P/S: Income Protection, Debt Elimination, Asset Management, Personalized Financial Needs Analysis, Education Savings, Educational Brochures, Customized Programs for Short and Long-Term Expenses MA: International D/D/R: Recruiting, Training and Developing New Business Brokers, Advising Clients How to Become Debt-Free H/I/S: Basketball, Reading EDU: Master's Degree in Business Management, Louisiana State University (2002) A/A/S: Tiger Athletic Foundation; Chairman, Greater Baton Rouge Court; Former Basketball Player, Detroit Pistons, National Basketball Association
Email: bjvr6@primerica.com
URL: http://www.primerica.com

Gen. Merdith W. B. Temple, PE
Title: Director of Military Programs Company: United States Army Corps of Engineers Address: 441 G Street N.W., Washington, DC 20314 United States BUS: Federal Defense Agency P/S: Military Defense and Engineering Services MA: International D/D/R: Managing Civil Engineering and Construction Projects, Managing Policy, Program and Technical Functions H/I/S: Traveling to Historic Sites EDU: Master of Science in Civil Engineering; Bachelor of Science in Civil Engineering A/A/S: SAME, Army Engineers Organization A/H: Army Superior Unit Award; Master Parachutist Badge; Army Meritorious Service Medal; Defense Meritorious Service Medal; Joint Service Commendation Medal; The Legion of Merit
Email: bo.temple@usace.army.mil

Dr. Svetlana Ten
Title: Director Company: Infants and Children's Hospital of Brooklyn at Mailmonides Address: 977 48th Street, Brooklyn, NY 11225 United States BUS: Healthcare P/S: Pediatrics MA: Local D/D/R: Endocrinology Pediatrics H/I/S: Traveling EDU: MD, Minsk Medical School
Email: tenlana@aol.com
URL: http://www.cambridgewhoswho.com

Beth A. Tenney
Title: Respiratory Therapist Company: Southcrest Hospital Address: 6225 E King Pl, Tulsa, OK 74115 United States BUS: Healthcare Hospital P/S: Respiratory Therapy 2 Patient Service MA: Local D/D/R: Caring for Patients, Respiratory Therapy H/I/S: E Commerce Business, Through EBay Scrapbooking EDU: Oklahoma Baptist, Social Work A/A/S: AARC, OSRC
Email: Bettergurls@aol.com

Kenneth E. Tepe, MD
Title: Medical Director Company: Community Behavioral Health, Inc. Address: 210 S. Second Street, Hamilton, OH 45011 United States BUS: Nonprofit Corporation P/S: Healthcare, Psychiatric Services MA: Local D/D/R: Specializing in Adult Psychiatry and Chemical Dependency, Offering Dual Diagnosis, Overseeing Forensic Staff, Giving Testimony in Several Courts Including Substance Abuse, Chemical Dependency on Felony Level, Consulting and Overseeing Case Managers and Nurses in Offering Free Services to Indigent Persons Emerging from Hospitalization or Incarceration, Directing the Mental Health Treatment of 1500 Inmates in County Jails, Teaching Judges, Magistrates, Probation Officers and Clinical Staff through the Supreme Court of the State of Ohio, the Ohio Department of Mental Health and the Ohio Department of Drug Addiction and Alcoholism Services EDU: Residency in Adult Psychiatry, University of Cincinnati Medical Center; MD, University of Cincinnati College of Medicine; Bachelor of Science, Magna Cum Laude, Xavier University A/A/S: Ohio Supreme Court Judicial College; Affiliate, Cleveland Clinic; Fellow, American College of Forensic Examiners; Diplomat, American Board of Forensic Medicine; Diplomat, American Board of Law Enforcement Experts C/VW: Company-Affiliated Charities
Email: kentepe@aol.com
URL: http://www.cambridgewhoswho.com

Kathryn Marie Terlikowski
Title: Registered Operating Room Nurse Company: Henry Ford Hospital Address: 2799 W. Grand Boulevard, Detroit, MI 48202 United States BUS: Hospital P/S: Healthcare MA: Detroit EXP: Ms. Terlikowski's expertise is in operating room nursing. D/D/R: Assisting in Surgeries Including Robotic, Cardiovascular, Trauma Care, Gynecology, Orthopedic, Urology, Vascular, Transplant and General Surgery, Procuring Organs for Transplantation H/I/S: Traveling, Watching Baseball, Listening to Music, Reading, Photography, Spending Time with her Friends and Family, Attending Concerts, Yoga, Volunteering for Holistic Health and Medicine EDU: Bachelor of Science in Nursing, University of Phoenix CERTS: Certified Level II Reiki Practitioner C/VW: Volunteer, Animal Shelters; Clean Water Act, MI; National Wildlife Federation; Wild Animal Rescue Mission
Email: kterlikowski@sbcglobal.net
URL: http://www.henryfordhealth.org

Mr. Patrick Terraglio
Title: President Company: Terraglio Homes, LLC Address: 625 N. Central Avenue, Oviedo, FL 32765 United States BUS: Custom Homes Construction Company P/S: Building and Developing High-Quality Individual Homes and Communities, Interior and Exterior Design and Construction MA: Regional D/D/R: Building Homes, Working with Brick and Stone, Ensuring Code Compliance, Overseeing Organizational Planning, Running the Operations of the Business with his Wife EDU: Bachelor's Degree in Business, Long Island University (1961)
Email: pat@terragliohomes.net
URL: http://www.terragliohomes.net/

Theresa A. Terrebonne
Title: Attorney Company: Miller & Terrebonne Address: 8778 Helena Road, Pelham, AL 35124 United States BUS: Law Firm P/S: Legal Representation MA: Regional D/D/R: Practicing Criminal Defense, Personal Injury, Family and Probate Law H/I/S: Siberian Hockey, Traveling, Spending Time with Family EDU: Coursework, Birmingham State University (1996) A/A/S: American Bar Association; Shelby County Bar Association; Alabama State Bar Association; Birmingham Bar Association; Criminal Act Panel
Email: tterrebonne@charterinternet.com

Amanda Terrones
Title: Teacher Company: The McClelland School Address: 415 E. Abriendo Avenue, Pueblo, CO 81004 United States BUS: School P/S: Physical Education, Coaching MA: Local D/D/R: Managing Enrichment Programs H/I/S: Traveling, Reading, Cooking, Taking Nature Walks, Running, Gardening, Spending Time with her Family and Friends, Practicing Calligraphy EDU: Bachelor of Science in Art, University of Southern Colorado (1984); Certified K through 12th-Grade Teacher A/H: Award, Outstanding Middle School Physical Educator, Colorado Association for Health, Physical Education, Recreation and Dance (1991) C/VW: Former Council President, Local Church Parish
Email: a_terrones@mcclellandschools.org

Tamee Terry
Title: Chief Executive Officer Company: Office Two Go Address: 482 Singing Waters Lane, Purlear, NC 28665 United States BUS: Outsourcing Firm P/S: Bookkeeping and Taxation Services, Medical Billing, Claims Processing and Office Assistance MA: National D/D/R: Assisting Companies Lacking Efficient Time and Staff to Perform Office Functions, Taking Phone Dictation, Handling Medical Billing Registration H/I/S: Caring for her Animal Farm, Gardening EDU: High School Education A/A/S: American Institute of Professional Bookkeepers; Internal Revenue Service
Email: tamee@officetwogo.com
URL: http://www.officetwogo.com

Theresa L. Testa
Title: Owner Company: Treasure Time, LLC Address: 4810 Old Post Road, Charlestown, RI 02813 United States BUS: Retail Company P/S: Antiques, Gifts, New and Estate Furniture MA: Southern CT, RI D/D/R: Antique Stemware, Estate Pieces H/I/S: Antiquing, Traveling, Golfing EDU: Master's Degree in Education, Central Connecticut State University A/A/S: Phi Delta Kappa C/VW: Church; Local Soup Kitchen
Email: tjtesta@comcast.net

Katherine Elizabeth Teuton
Title: Teacher Company: Evergreen Elementary School Address: 400 W. Anthony Road, Ocala, FL 34475 United States BUS: School P/S: Education MA: Local D/D/R: Teaching Mathematics, Reading, Science and Language Arts to Approximately 18 to 20 Students H/I/S: Reading, Singing in a Choir EDU: Bachelor of Science in Elementary Education, Nova Southeastern University; Master of Science in Exceptional Student Education; Endorsement in English to Speakers of Other Languages A/A/S: National Education Association; Florida Education Association C/VW: Church
Email: ketjet2222@yahoo.com
URL: http://www.cambridgewhoswho.com

Phillip N. Thai
Title: Supervisor Company: Duane Reade Pharmacy Address: 441 9th Avenue, New York, NY 10001 United States BUS: Pharmacy P/S: Medications, Prescriptions, Health and Beauty Aids, Photography Center, Baby and Home Care Items MA: Regional D/D/R: Dispensing Prescriptions, Maintaining Customers' Health, Offering Customer Service, Overseeing Quality Assurance and Health Insurance Issues, Educating Patients on Prescription Side Effects and Interactions H/I/S: Basketball, Golfing, Boating EDU: Bachelor of Science in Pharmacy, St. John's University, College of Pharmacy and Applied Health Professions (1999)
Email: philmaria646@hotmail.com
URL: http://www.duanereade.com

Jodi L. Thanner
Title: Vice President Company: Ice Cream and More Address: 3419 Mexicali Street, New Port Richey, FL 34655 United States BUS: Wholesale Frozen Foods Distribution Company P/S: Ice Cream Novelties, Pints, Half Gallons, Tasty Cake, Sandwiches and Cones, Giant Van Sandwiches, Good Humor Brand Products, Barq's Root Beer Float Squeeze, Klondike Products, Pretzels MA: Central Florida, Tampa Bay Area D/D/R: Managing Daily Operations, Marketing, Accounting, Sales, Distribution H/I/S: Traveling, Scuba Diving EDU: College Coursework in Science, Essex Community College (1980-1981); Diploma, Parkville Senior High School, Baltimore, Maryland A/A/S: Supporter, Weeki Wachee Theme Park
Email: jodi@icecreamandmore.com
URL: http://www.icecreamandmore.com

Katherine E. Tharin
Title: Child and Adolescent Counselor Company: Ogeechee Behavioral Health Services Address: 305 Park Drive, Waynesboro, GA 30830 United States BUS: Counseling Service P/S: Counseling MA: Local D/D/R: Specializing in Diagnostic Intakes on Children and Adolescents with Behavioral Issues, Individual and Group Counseling in Schools, Clinic Aids with Coping Skills, Anger Management Skills, Peer Pressure, Bullies, Teasing Issues, Specializes in Counseling Single Parent Families and Blended Families H/I/S: Reading, Participating in Church Activities EDU: Master's Degree in Education, Augusta State University, Georgia (2004) A/A/S: Licensed Associate Professional Counselors Association of Georgia; Board Eligible NCC C/VW: Volunteer, Domestic Violence Charity; Co-Facilitator, Women's Support Group
Email: KatherineE.Tharin@cwwemail.com
URL: http://www.cambridgewhoswho.com

Mr. Michael J. Tharp
Title: General Manager Company: Boarder to Boarder Trucking, Inc. Address: P.O. Box 328, Edinburg, TX 78540 United States BUS: Logistics Firm P/S: Transportation Services MA: National D/D/R: managing operations, dealing with insurance regulations, dispatching, overseeing maintenance works and work schedules, supervising employees and budgeting H/I/S: Fishing, Collecting Coins, Hunting, Photography EDU: Coursework in Architecture, University of Texas A/A/S: President, Hidalgo Coin Club, TX
Email: mtharp@btbtrucking.com
URL: http://www.btbtrucking.com

Cynthia L. Theiss, MD
Title: Physician Company: Mind Matters Address: 5606 PGA Boulevard, Suite 113, Palm Beach Gardens, FL 33418 United States BUS: Private Practice Dedicated to Excellence in Healthcare P/S: Outpatient Psychiatric Service for Adults and Children MA: Florida D/D/R: Psychiatry for Adults and Children, Promoting the Private Outpatient Service, Overseeing Expansion with Premier Products in Health and Beauty H/I/S: Snow Skiing, Bicycle Riding, Going to the Beach EDU: MD in Psychiatry, University of Miami (1995); Board Certified (1995); Internship and Residency at Thomas Jefferson University, Philadelphia, Pennsylvania (1990); Master's Degree in Physical Education, University of Florida (1984); Bachelor of Arts in English Literature, University of Florida (1976)
Email: ctheiss118@aol.com

Athena Theodosatos
Title: Family Medicine Resident Company: Florida Hospital Address: 2501 N. Orange Avenue, Orlando, FL 32804 United States BUS: Christian Hospital Committed to Offering High Quality Healthcare Services P/S: Acute Healthcare System, Internationally Recognized for Cardiology, Cancer, Diabetes, Digestive Health, Women's Medicine, Neurology, Neurosurgery, Orthopedics and Rehabilitation, Outpatient and Inpatient Care MA: Regional D/D/R: Completing Residency in Family Medicine, Doing Monthly Rotations in Obstetrics and Gynecology, Pediatrics, Family Medicine, Geriatrics, Specializing in Dermatology, Preparing to Take Step Three Board Exams, Undergoing Training in the Community and Office as well H/I/S: Running, Arts and Crafts EDU: Doctor of Medicine Degree, University of Medicine and Dentistry of New Jersey (2006); Master's Degree in Public Health, University of South Florida College of Public Health (2002) A/A/S: American Osteopathic College of Family Physicians; American College of Family Physicians
Email: athenatheo@hotmail.com
URL: http://www.flhosp.org

Mrs. Patricia Theriault
Title: Owner Company: DPT Unlimited Dept: Finance Department BUS: Logistics Company P/S: Logistics and Transportation Services MA: National EXP: Mrs. Theriault's expertise is in freight claims management. D/D/R: Performing Administrative Duties, Ensuring Customer Satisfaction H/I/S: Cooking, Shopping, Training her Dogs, Camping EDU: Coursework in Legal Studies and Bookkeeping, International Business College A/H: Patriot of the Year Award, TX; Letters of Appreciation for Outstanding Customer Service; Certificate of Appreciation, Easter Seals; Certificate of Appreciation, Boys Town C/VW: Cal Farley's; Help Hospitalized Veterans; St. Joseph's Indian School; West Texas Food Bank; Texas Narcotic Officer's Association; Easter Seals; National Fallen Firefighters Foundation; Boys Town; National Children's Cancer Society; Paralyzed Veterans of America; Food For The Poor
Email: dtheriault@elp.rr.com
Email: dptunlimited@elp.rr.com
URL: http://www.cambridgewhoswho.com

Dianne L. Thibault
Title: Office Manager Company: Family Physicians Group Address: 2191 Ninth Avenue N., Saint Petersburg, FL 33713 United States BUS: Healthcare Center P/S: Family Medicine, Healthcare MA: Local EXP: Ms. Thibault's expertise includes EKG telemetry, pharmacology, phlebotomy, diabetic teaching, gate training, wound care nursing and cast work and pacemaker tracks management. D/D/R: Acting as a Medical Assistant, Scheduling, Managing Patient Referrals H/I/S: Scrapbooking, Spending Time with her Grandchildren, Knitting, Crocheting EDU: Master's Degree, The University of Tampa (1983); Coursework, Van Dyke University CERTS: Certified Nursing Assistant; Certified Notary Public; Certified CPR Instructor A/A/S: RMAAHS; ACNA; HHC
Email: dthibault@fpg-florida.com
URL: http://www.fpg.com

Mary L. Thibodeaux
Title: Railroad Engineer Company: BNSF Railway Address: 110 Sunbeam Lane, Lafayette, LA 70506 United States BUS: Private Railroad Delivery System P/S: Cross-Country Transportation for Products MA: Regional D/D/R: Maintaining Continuous On-Call Status, Working in the Railroad Yard, Driving the Freight Train H/I/S: Enjoying Outdoor Activities EDU: High School Education
Email: mlthib1@aol.com

Nicole P. Thiel, O.Md., Psy.D., MAOM, L.Ac., MFT
Title: Director, Clinician, Owner Company: A Turning Point Center of Oriental Medicine and Integrated Therapy Address: 29 Meadow Park Circle, Belmont, CA 94002 United States BUS: Alternative Healthcare P/S: Comprehensive, Gentle and Compassionate Care Relevant to the Client's Health and Well Being through the Integration of Oriental Medicine's Disciplines, Western Bioscience, Psychology and Meditative Practices MA: National D/D/R: Chinese Medicine, Women's Health Care, Gynecology, Treatment for Psychology Disorders H/I/S: Sailing, Walking, Music EDU: Doctorate in Psychology, Naropa University (1989); Master's Degree in Psychology, Pacific College (1986); Bachelor of Science in Humanities, University of California at Berkeley (1972) A/A/S: Humanistic Society; Association of Marriage and Family Relationships
Email: ntspiritmedicines@comcast.com
URL: http://www.acufinder.com/Acupuncturist/59484

Tamara R. Thoel
Title: Owner/Webmaster Company: Creating Images Address: 4472 Kilgore, Kenockee, MI 48006 United States BUS: Website Designer, Retail Sales P/S: Web Design, Banner Design, Logo Design, Retail Sales MA: International D/D/R: Website Design H/I/S: Riding Horses, Reading EDU: College Coursework
Email: webdesign@creatingimages.biz
URL: http://www.creatingimages.biz

Adam D. Thomas
Title: Owner Company: A2Z Paint & Body Shop Address: 704 Miller Avenue, Westlake, LA 70669 United States BUS: Automotive Company P/S: Automotive Repair and Painting Services MA: Louisiana EXP: Mr. Thomas' expertise includes operations management and leadership. H/I/S: Fishing, Motorcycling, Traveling, Spending Time with his Family EDU: High School Diploma (1990) C/VW: Bellview Baptist Church
Email: adamt777@hotmail.com

Arculious R. Thomas
Title: Delivery Driver and Sales Company: R and H Supply, Inc Address: 1109 Raney Street, Longview, TX 75602 United States BUS: Gas Supply Company P/S: Valves, Vibrator Hoses, Connection Liners MA: Regional D/D/R: Deliveries, Sales, Customer Service H/I/S: Traveling, Watching Movies, Comedy Shows EDU: Bachelor's Degree in General Business, McMurry University in Texas (2003)
Email: thomasarculious@yahoo.com
URL: http://www.cambridgewhoswho.com

Brenda Thomas
Title: Chief Executive Officer Company: Thomas Transportation Services, Inc. Dept: MDH Transportation, Inc. Address: 2654 Northvale Drive N.E., Apartment 201, Grand Rapids, MI 49525 United States BUS: Transportation Company P/S: Transportation Services MA: National D/D/R: bookkeeping, supervising drivers, ensuring customer satisfaction EDU: High School Diploma A/A/S: Michigan Trucking Association; Michigan Association of Police; Michigan State Firemen's Association C/VW: Joyce Meyer Ministries; Nell Trotter Ministries
Email: mdhtrucking@comcast.net

Connie J. Thomas
Title: President Company: Quality-Time Visitation Group, Inc. Address: 678 S. Indian Hill Boulevard, Suite 124, Claremont, CA 91711 United States BUS: Court-Ordered Child Visitation Agency P/S: Supervising Parental and Family Visitation with Children when Abuse or Neglect has been Reported MA: Regional D/D/R: Monitoring and Assessing Child Visitation Sessions, Reporting to Court Agencies and Counsel, Consulting with Therapists, Determining the Validity of Claims EDU: Certified Supervised Visitation Organization, State of California; Business License to Operate, City of Claremont
Email: gvisit@qualitytimevisitation.com
URL: http://www.qualitytimevisitation.com

Ms. Dianne C. Thomas
Title: Owner Company: Lady Di's Restaurant and Catering Address: 332 E. Cap Wisdon Road, Duncanville, TX 75116 United States BUS: Restaurant P/S: Hospitality Services MA: National D/D/R: Purchasing, Cooking, Managing Staff, Budgeting H/I/S: Reading A/A/S: SDBPW; Business and Professional Women A/H: Quest for Success Award (2005) C/VW: Local Church; Local Charitable Organizations
Email: diannec4242@sbcglobal.net
URL: http://www.ladydirestaurant.com

Eddie R. Thomas
Title: Registered Respiratory Therapist Company: Deborah Heart and Lung Center Address: 200 Trenton Road, Browns Mills, NJ 08015 United States BUS: Hospital P/S: Healthcare Including Cardiac, Pulmonary and Electrophysiology Services, Comprehensive Vascular Program, Sleep Medicine, Respiratory Therapy, Fellowship Program MA: Regional D/D/R: supervising the staff, scheduling, overseeing operations and patients' treatments, caring for asthma and emphysema patients, managing medical equipment including respirators and oxygen therapy equipment H/I/S: Playing Football, Basketball and Baseball EDU: Associate Degree in Applied Science, CA (1986) CERTS: Registered Respiratory Therapist; Neonatal and Pediatric Respiratory Care Specialist
Email: thomase@deborah.org
URL: http://www.deborah.org

Mr. Harold W. Thomas Jr.
Title: Arizona Water Resource Practice Leader Company: Brown and Caldwell Address: 201 E. Washington Street, Suite 500, Phoenix, AZ 85004 United States BUS: Engineering and Consulting Firm P/S: Engineering and Consulting Services MA: Arizona, Southwestern United States D/D/R: managing water resources, overseeing two regional coalitions of public and private water and waste water agencies H/I/S: Traveling, Riding his Motorcycles, Exercising, Collecting Indian Pottery EDU: Bachelor of Science in Chemical Engineering, Arizona State University A/A/S: Vice Chairman, Committee on Concentrate Management, Environmental & Water Resources Institute; Arizona Water & Pollution Control Association; Central Arizona Salinity Study; Colorado River Water Users Association; West Valley Central Arizona Project Subcontractors; Water Environment Federation; Water Reuse Association; Western Coalition of Arid States; Western Maricopa Coalition; American Membrane Technology Association; American Society of Civil Engineers; American Water Works Association; Former Chairman, City of Phoenix Water and Wastewater Rate Advisory Committee A/H: Distinguished Performance Award, Western Coalition of Arid States (2005); Community Service Award, Water Committee Chairman, Western Maricopa Coalition (1997); Golden Cactus Special Recognition Award, Western Coalition of Arid States (1995); Special Recognition Award, Salt River Project (1995); Board Member, Western Coalition of Arid States C/VW: Water for People; Patriot Guard
Email: hwthomasjr@cox.net
URL: http://www.cambridgewhoswho.com

Jack W. Thomas, PDMC
Title: Safety Director **Company:** Robert Bowden, Inc. **Address:** 850 White Circle Court N.W., Marietta, GA 30060 United States **BUS:** Manufacturing Company **P/S:** Building Material and Manufacturing Services **MA:** Georgia **D/D/R:** managing occupational health and safety administration, environmental protection agency and department of transportation, ensuring regulatory compliance regarding safety, developing strategies for political advocacy, maintaining worker's compensation, ensuring paramedic services **H/I/S:** Traveling, Horseback Riding **EDU:** Coursework in Emergency Management, Federal Emergency Management Agency; Bachelor of Science in Business Management, Roger Williams University **CERTS:** Certified Police Officer; Certified Paramedic; Certified Firefighter **C/VW:** American Cancer Society; Autism Society of America
Email: jthomas@robertbowden.com
URL: http://www.robertbowden.com

Jody Thomas
Title: Chief Executive Officer **Company:** CISCorp **BUS:** Insurance Brokerage Firm **P/S:** Insurance for Both Small and Large Businesses Including Benefit Packages **MA:** National **D/D/R:** Overseeing Company Public Relations, Experience in Multi-Insurance Areas, Creating Solutions for Problem Areas, Accommodating All Client Needs, Creating and Running her Business **H/I/S:** Baseball, Tap Dancing **EDU:** Bachelor of Fine Arts, Georgia Southern University, Statesborough (1970) **A/A/S:** Los Angeles Association of Health Underwriters; West Side Professionals Group; California Chamber of Commerce; Santa Clara Chamber of Commerce; Valley Community Clinic; Mothers of Motion Pictures; Wheels for Humanity; SHAMBALA
Email: jt@inshelper.com
URL: http://www.inshelper.com

Karen S. Thomas
Title: President **Company:** KST Consulting, LLC **Address:** 8525 Avonlea Lane, Port Tobacco, MD 20677 United States **BUS:** Business Consulting Firm **P/S:** Consulting Services, Interim Chief Executive Officer Services, Group Facilitation, Strategic Planning, Team Building, Leadership Development, Executive Coaching, Transition Consulting, Workshops **MA:** National **D/D/R:** Consulting for Nonprofit, Healthcare and Educational Organizations **H/I/S:** Going to the Beach, Boating, Reading, Spending Time with her Family **EDU:** Bachelor of Business Administration, University of Missouri (1989); Certified Association Executive **A/A/S:** American Society of Association Executives; Fellow, National Speakers Association; Maryland Society of Association Executives; BoardSource
Email: karen@kstconsulting.net
URL: http://www.kstconsulting.net

Kim Thomas
Title: Teacher **Company:** Village Elementary School **Address:** 2100 N. W. 70th Avenue, Sunrise, FL 33313 United States **BUS:** Elementary School **P/S:** Education **MA:** Local **D/D/R:** Teaching Behavioral Curriculum and Anger Control **H/I/S:** Traveling, Reading **EDU:** Master's Degree in Educational Leadership, University of Phoenix (2007); Bachelor's Degree in Business Education, Bethune-Cookman College, Florida (1978) **A/A/S:** Alpha Kappa Alpha; Christian Life Center
Email: zelena8@bellsouth.net
Email: kimthomas@browardschools.com
URL: http://www.cambridgewhoswho.com

Lincy Thomas
Title: Associate Director of Regulatory Affairs **Company:** Novartis Pharmaceuticals **Address:** 1 Health Plaza, Building 104, East Hanover, NJ 07936 United States **BUS:** Pharmaceutical Company **P/S:** Pharmaceuticals **MA:** International **D/D/R:** overseeing drug regulatory affairs **H/I/S:** Singing **EDU:** Doctor of Pharmacy, Rutgers, The State University of New Jersey **A/A/S:** Regulatory Affairs Professional Society; Drug Information Association; American Society of Health System Pharmacists **C/VW:** Indian Orthodox Church; The Leukemia and Lymphoma Society; American Cancer Society
Email: lincyt@gmail.com
URL: http://www.novartis.com

Maria D. Thomas
Title: Behavioral Health Specialist **Company:** Department of Education **Address:** 335 S Papa Avenue, Kahului, HI 96732 United States **BUS:** Education **P/S:** Counseling for Youth and Families **MA:** Local **D/D/R:** Counseling **H/I/S:** Travel, Reading, Spending Time with 10 Month Old Daughter **EDU:** Masters in Professional Counseling, American School of Professional Psychology; Cert Gerontology From University of Hawaii Manoa **A/A/S:** Alpha Delta Kappa
Email: mariamaui@hawaii.rr.com

Mary Stella Thomas
Title: Chief Executive Officer **Company:** Charles Bus Service, LLC **Address:** 6633 Thrush Drive, Houston, TX 77087 United States **BUS:** Transportation Service Provider **P/S:** Provide School Bus Transportation For Students in Public, Parochial and Charter School **MA:** Local **D/D/R:** Oversee Employers and Fleet of Buses as Well as Administrative Office Duties **H/I/S:** Traveling **EDU:** St Peter Clairborne, Gulf Coast College, Houston Community College, Business Study **A/A/S:** Association of Private Bus Owners

Nancy L. Thomas
Title: Coordinator of Health Programs **Company:** First Coast Technical College **Address:** 2980 Collins Avenue, Saint Augustine, FL 32084 United States **BUS:** Educational Institute **P/S:** Vocational Education **MA:** Local **D/D/R:** overseeing administrative duties and health programs including phlebotomy, nursing and medical assistance, teaching practical nursing, pediatrics and career skills to students, practicing massage therapy and organizing dental assisting programs **H/I/S:** Reading, Traveling, Spending Time with her Grandchildren **EDU:** Master of Education, University of North Florida; Bachelor of Science in Nursing, Ohio State University **A/A/S:** American Nurses Association; Florida Nurses Association; Association of Practical Nurse Educators of Florida **C/VW:** Local Church
Email: tphillip211@aol.com
URL: http://www.cambridgewhoswho.com

Patrice C. Thomas
Title: Event Planner, Party Coordinator **Company:** Cherished Moments **Address:** 15 Ninth Avenue, Farmingdale, NY 11735 United States **BUS:** Party Planning and Coordinating Company **P/S:** Events Planning, Wedding Planning, Decorating **D/D/R:** Planning Parties and Events from Start to Finish, Decorating Venues **H/I/S:** Playing Volleyball **C/VW:** Long Island Team Challenge, Freedom Chapel Assembly of God, American Red Cross
Email: pctpbw@gmail.com
URL: http://www.cambridgewhoswho.com

Rieanne Thomas
Title: Lead Outpatient Coder **Company:** Kent County Memorial Hospital **Address:** 455 Tollgate Road, Warwick, RI 02886 United States **BUS:** Hospital **P/S:** Healthcare Services **MA:** Regional **D/D/R:** Outpatient Coding **H/I/S:** Spending Time with her Daughters, Traveling, Reading **A/A/S:** American Health Information Management Association
Email: rthomas@kentri.org

Ruby Casco Thomas
Title: Manager/Owner **Company:** Holistic Health Center **Address:** 1356 Route 51, Jefferson Hills, PA 15025 United States **BUS:** Healthcare Service Provider **P/S:** Holistic Healthcare and Nutrients **MA:** National **D/D/R:** Massage Therapist, Naturopath **H/I/S:** Gardening **EDU:** University of Manilla, Bachelor of Arts **A/A/S:** Catholic Church, Lions Club-Past President
URL: http://www.rubyshealthcenter.com

Susan E. Thomas
Title: Owner **Company:** Thomas Financial Services **Address:** P.O. Box EC, Pacific Grove, CA 93950 United States **BUS:** Finance Company **P/S:** Tax Assessments, Property Management, Bookkeeping Related Services **MA:** International **D/D/R:** Offering Tax Assessments and Property Management Services, Utilizing Accounting Software, Reviewing Financial Statements, Preparing Taxes **H/I/S:** Personal Training **EDU:** Bachelor's Degree in Arts, San Jose State University (1988) **A/A/S:** National Association for the Self-Employed **C/VW:** United Way Community Hospital
Email: sjjthomas@msn.com

Tyrone H. Thomas
Title: Therapist, Senior Research Coordinator **Company:** University of Pennsylvania **Address:** 3451 Walnut Street, Philadelphia, PA 19104 United States **BUS:** University **P/S:** Higher Education **MA:** National **D/D/R:** performing relapse prevention therapy and cognitive behavioral therapy, conducting addiction research, consulting **H/I/S:** Breeding Tropical Fish, Playing Basketball and Football, Participating in Sports **EDU:** Pursuing Bachelor's Degree in Behavioral Health Counseling; Master's Degree in Human Services, Lincoln University; Associate Degree in General Studies, Community College of Philadelphia **CERTS:** Certified Associate Addiction Counselor **A/A/S:** Victim Witness Association; Pennsylvania Recovery Association
Email: thtomas@aol.com

Andrea Thomas Murphy
Title: Educator **Company:** Nantucket Public Schools, Nantucket Elementary School **Address:** 30 Surfside Road, Nantucket, MA 02554 United States **BUS:** Elementary School Facility Committed to Excellence in Education **P/S:** Regular Core Curriculum Including Reading, Writing, Mathematics, Science, Social Studies, Art, Music, History **MA:** Regional **D/D/R:** Teaching All Subjects to Third-Grade Students, Experience in Teaching Fifth-Grade through High School Students **H/I/S:** Swimming, Traveling, Reading, Walking, Community Involvement, Spending Time with Family and Friends **EDU:** Master's Degree, Lesley University (1980); Bachelor of Science Degree, The University of Vermont (1976) **A/A/S:** Who's Who in America's Teachers; National Education Association; Nantucket Teachers Association; Massachusetts Teachers Association; President, Tristrams' Long Pond Association; Vice President, Nantucket Civic League; Secretary, Nantucket Teachers' Association; Taconic Lake Association; Nantucket Chamber of Commerce; Nantucket Theatre Workshop
Email: admurphack@comcast.net
URL: http://www.nantucket.k12.ma.us

Laverne K. Thomason
Title: Owner **Company:** Merle Norman Cosmetics **Address:** 608 S. Union Street, Opelousas, LA 70570 United States **BUS:** Cosmetic Company **P/S:** Selling Cosmetics and Gifts **MA:** Local **D/D/R:** Training Professionals on the Proper Way to Apply Cosmetics **H/I/S:** Traveling, Reading **EDU:** Coursework in Cosmetology, Trade School; High School Education **A/A/S:** Chamber of Commerce; Order of the Eastern Star **A/H:** Awarded for wning the business for over 40 years. **C/VW:** Salvation Army, Masonic Children's Fund
Email: Laverne K. Thomason
URL: http://www.merlenorman.com

Arcelia Lawson Thompson
Title: 1) Co-Owner 2) Teacher **Company:** 1) Kidz Clothing 2) Washington DC Public School Systems **Address:** 1050 21st Street, Washington, DC 20036 United States **BUS:** 1) Clothing Store 2) Elementary School **P/S:** 1) Clothing and Accessories 2) Education **MA:** 1) Local 2) Local **D/D/R:** Designing Displays, Teaching Core Subjects to Elementary Students **H/I/S:** Reading, Shopping, Traveling **EDU:** Master's Degree in Education, Trinity College; Bachelor's Degree in Early Childhood Education, A&T State University; Bachelor's Degree in Home Economics, A&Y State University; Post-Graduate Coursework, Pan African University, Washington, DC (1992) **A/A/S:** Positive Behavioral Interventions and Supports; Stevens Personal Committee; LSRT Team; International Day Committee, Black History Committee **C/VW:** Volunteer Work with her Church, Teaches at Bible College
Email: sbedney@hotmail.com
URL: http://www.cambridgewhoswho.com

Cheryl A. Thompson
Title: Teacher **Company:** Pacific High School **Address:** 425 Indian Warpath Drive, Pacific, MO 63069 United States **BUS:** School **P/S:** Education **MA:** Local **D/D/R:** Teaching Students Necessary Life Skills, Teaching Special Education to Students with Developmental Disabilities, Reading Specialist **H/I/S:** Reading, Spending Quality Time with her Son **EDU:** Master of Science in Classroom Teaching, Missouri Baptist University; Certified Reading Specialist, Missouri Baptist University **A/A/S:** National Education Association **C/VW:** National President, Society of Government Meets Professionals
Email: cthompson@mvr3.k12.mo.us
URL: http://www.mvr3.k12.mo.us

Debra L. Thompson
Title: Owner **Company:** Debra Thompson, CPA **Address:** 1400 McLain Street, Newport, AR 72112 United States **BUS:** Certified Public Accountant Office **P/S:** Tax Returns, Accounting, Financial Planning **MA:** National **D/D/R:** Making Retirement Plans, College Plans, Accounting for Small Businesses **H/I/S:** Puppeteering, Chalk Drawing, Performing as a Gospel Illusionist, Spending Time with her Grandchildren **EDU:** Bachelor of Arts in Accounting, Arkansas State University **A/A/S:** Kiwanis International; Arkansas Society of Certified Public Accountants; National Society of Accountants; Newport Chamber of Commerce **C/VW:** New Life Church, Project New Start
Email: debra@dltcpa.com
URL: http://www.dltcpa.com

Emily Anne Thompson
Title: Producer **Company:** Theatre Bristol **Address:** 512 State Street, Bristol, TN 37620 United States **BUS:** Live Theatre Education **P/S:** Mainstage Musicals, Children's Theatre **MA:** Regional **D/D/R:** Producing, Theatre Management, Writing Grants, Overall Production Experience, of Cast Members **EDU:** College Coursework in History, Kings College (1986)
Email: info@theatrebristol.org
URL: http://www.theatrebristol.org

James Thompson Jr.
Title: Writer Player, Vice President **Company:** Jath Music Co. **Address:** 522 Parish Street, Philadelphia, PA 19123 United States **BUS:** Publishing Company, Producing **P/S:** Music **MA:** International **D/D/R:** Music Publishing, Musical Composition and Lyrics, Musical Recording **H/I/S:** Music, Enjoys Reading the Sports Pages, Cross Word Puzzles **A/A/S:** Musicians Union; Harry Fox Agency
Email: sunnyt11@msn.com

Ms. Kathie H. Thompson
Title: Finance Specialist, Payroll **Company:** Family Development Services, Inc. **Address:** 3637 N. Meridian Street, Indianapolis, IN 46208 United States **BUS:** Daycare Center **P/S:** Head Start and Early Head Start Educational Programs **MA:** Local **D/D/R:** processing payroll, managing garnishments and direct deposits **H/I/S:** Caring for her Pets, Reading **EDU:** Pursuing Bachelor of Science in Business Administration, with a Concentration in Accounting, Kaplan College; Associate of Applied Science in Administrative and Business Administration, Kaplan College (2006) **CERTS:** Certification in Fundamental Payroll **A/A/S:** American Payroll Association
Email: kthompson@fds.org
Email: kathawkes@comcast.net
URL: http://www.fds.org

Lane A. Thompson
Title: Project Manager, Engineer **Company:** G. C. Wallace, inc. **Address:** 1555 S. Rainbow Boulevard, Las Vegas, NV 89146 United States **BUS:** Civil Engineer **P/S:** Land Development **MA:** Regional West Coast **D/D/R:** Residential Subdivisions **H/I/S:** Boating, Hiking **EDU:** Bachelor of Science in Architectural Engineering, University of Wyoming **A/A/S:** American Society of Civil Engineering
Email: lthompson@gcwallace.com
URL: http://www.gcwallace.com

Lorin Thompson Jr.
Title: Vice Chairman of the Board **Company:** Feather River Recreation and Park District **Address:** 1200 Myers Street, Oroville, CA 95965 United States **BUS:** Local Park and Recreational Office **P/S:** Public Parks, Recreational Programs **MA:** Local **D/D/R:** Governing the Board **H/I/S:** Reading, Fishing **EDU:** College Coursework **A/A/S:** Native Sons of the Golden West; Knights of Columbus; The American Legion
Email: venehelen@earthlink.net
URL: http://www.frrpd.com

Marie Thompson
Title: Registered Nurse **Company:** Saint Joseph's Hospital **Address:** 5673 Peachtree Dunwoody Road, Atlanta, GA 30342 United States **BUS:** Hospital **P/S:** Healthcare **MA:** Local **D/D/R:** Wound Care and Ostomy Nursing, Training in Ostomy, Teaching **H/I/S:** Reading, Walking, Working Out, Cooking, Playing Card Games **EDU:** Bachelor of Science in Nursing, Memphis State University (Now University of Memphis); Certified Wound, Ostomy and Continence Nurse, Emory University WOCN Nursing Education Center **A/A/S:** Wound, Ostomy and Continence Nurses Society **A/H:** Phillips College Outstanding Nurse of the Year (1981); WOC/ET Nurse of the Year (1996) **C/VW:** Health Ministry, Outreach Ministry, Church; Olympic Committee (1996); Board Member, SER (2000, 2004-2006); Conference Planning Comission, WOCN (2000)
Email: math4178@bellsouth.net

Paula M. Thompson
Title: Regional Sales Manager **Company:** Covidien **Address:** 4280 Hacienda Boulevard, Pleasanton, CA 94588 United States **BUS:** Medical Sales **P/S:** Respiratory Products **MA:** International **D/D/R:** Teaching, Training, Management **EDU:** Bachelor of Science in Respiratory Care, University of Kansas; Coursework, University of Kansas Medical Center **A/A/S:** American Association of Respiratory Care **C/VW:** American Lung Association
Email: paula.thompson@covidien.com
URL: http://www.nellcor.com

Rosina Thompson
Title: Deputy Sheriff Private First Class **Company:** Fairfax County Sheriff's Office **Address:** 14095 Red River Drive, Centreville, VA 20121 United States **BUS:** Law Enforcement Agency **P/S:** Public Safety, Adult Detention Services, Court Security, Alternative Incarceration, Community Relations, Civil Enforcement, Volunteer Services **MA:** Regional **D/D/R:** Ms. Thompson's expertise is in law enforcement. Monitoring, Transporting and Managing the Classification of Inmates, Teaching in the Academy, Instructing Field Training **H/I/S:** Crafting, Scrapbooking, Swimming **EDU:** College Coursework **CERTS:** Certified Field Trainer; Certified Law Enforcer; Certified Law Enforcement Instructor **A/A/S:** Fairfax County Sheriff's Association
Email: rosinalak@yahoo.com
URL: http://www.fairfaxcounty.gov/sheriff

Shelly K. Thompson
Title: Performance Improvement Coordinator **Company:** Rusk County Memorial Hospital **Address:** 900 College Avenue W., Ladysmith, WI 54848 United States **BUS:** Hospital and Nursing Home **P/S:** Inpatient and Outpatient Healthcare **MA:** Regional **D/D/R:** Managing Performance Improvement, Performing Peer Reviews and Evaluations, Collaborating with Various Departments Independently and as a Whole, Developing Performance Quality for All Hospital Operations **H/I/S:** Writing, Gardening, Traveling, Reading **EDU:** Pursuing Master's Degree in Healthcare Management, University of Phoenix; Bachelor of Science in Social Work, University of Wisconsin-Superior (1991) **A/A/S:** Rural Wisconsin Health Cooperative; W.K. Kellogg Foundation; Writer's Exchange
Email: sthompson@ruskhospital.org
URL: http://www.ruskcounty.org/economicprofile

Troy Roland Thompson
Title: Owner **Company:** Roland's Rod Shop **Address:** 211 S.E. 136th Avenue, Portland, OR 97233 United States **BUS:** Automotive Steel Reproduction Company **P/S:** Garnish Moldings, Coupe Steel Doors, Steel Parts, Restoration Services **MA:** International **D/D/R:** Restoring Automobiles, Shaping Steel Parts for Coupe Automotive Bodies, Reproducing Quality Factory-Original Steel Parts **H/I/S:** Cars **EDU:** High School Education; Licensed Remodeling Contractor (1989)
Email: rolandrodshop@hotmail.com
URL: http://www.rolandsrodshop.com

Barbara Thompson McKinnon
Title: Product Line Director **Company:** Accredo Nova Factor **Address:** 1640 Century Center Parkway, Memphis, TN 38134 United States **BUS:** Leading Specialty Pharmacy **P/S:** Dispensing Expensive Biopharmaceuticals for the Treatment of Chronic Diseases **MA:** National **D/D/R:** Product Management, Acting as a Liaison Between the Manufacturers and Drug Companies for the Distribution and the Marketing **H/I/S:** Spending Time with Family **EDU:** Pharm.D., University of Tennessee (1984) **A/A/S:** American Society of Health Systems Pharmacies; Tennessee Society of Health Systems Pharmacies
Email: bmckinnon@novafactor.com
URL: http://www.accredohealth.com

Shawn R. Thomson
Title: General Manager, Artist **Company:** Twisted Spoke **Address:** 4022 N. Milwaukee Avenue, Second Floor, Chicago, IL 60641 United States **BUS:** Restaurant, Bar **P/S:** Food Service Management **MA:** Local **D/D/R:** Painting in Oil, Acrylic and Watercolor **H/I/S:** Playing Softball and Basketball **EDU:** Bachelor of Arts in Theology and Philosophy, Trinity University (1991) **A/A/S:** Local Church, USN
Email: shawnot@hotmail.com

Thomas Thornburg II
Title: Vice President **Company:** Liberty Title & Escrow **Address:** 1575 S. County Trail, East Greenwich, RI 02818 United States **BUS:** Nationwide Title Insurance Company **P/S:** Title Insurance **MA:** National **D/D/R:** Foreclosures, Real Estate Owned **H/I/S:** Playing Golf, Traveling, Fishing, Spending Time with his Family **EDU:** High School Education **A/A/S:** National Notary Association; Mortgage Bankers Association **C/VW:** Make-A-Wish Foundation
Email: thomasthornburg@libtitle.com
URL: http://www.libtitle.com

Christina G. Thornton
Title: Consultant **Company:** Mission City Management, Inc. **Address:** 8122 Datapoint Drive, Suite 1000, San Antonio, TX 78229 United States **BUS:** Public Policy Consulting **P/S:** Education and Grassroots Advocacy **MA:** Local **D/D/R:** Managing Applicable Funding, Creating Vouchers, Managing Company **H/I/S:** Boating **EDU:** Bachelor's Degree in Government Studies, Patrick Henry College, Virginia (2004)
Email: christina.thornton@gmail.com
URL: http://www.texansforschoolchoice.com

Sonja Thornton
Title: Professional Recruiter **Company:** Future Step, A Korn/Ferry Company **Address:** 2929 Allen Parkway, Suite 1450, Houston, TX 77019 United States **BUS:** Executive Recruiting Company **P/S:** Recruitment Outsourcing **MA:** International **D/D/R:** Building Relationships with Clients **H/I/S:** Spending Time Outdoors, Reading, Golfing, Going to Concerts, Attending Plays, Watching Films **EDU:** Bachelor of Science in Business Administration, LeTourneau University **A/A/S:** National Black MBA Association **C/VW:** Education Committee, Houston Livestock Show and Rodeo Scholarship Fund; Various Community Nonprofit Organizations
Email: sonja.thornton@futurestep.com
URL: http://www.futurestep.com

Lisa M. Thorstenberg
Title: Human Resources Director, Health, Safety and Environmental Director **Company:** Mertz Manufacturing, LLC **Address:** 1701 N. Waverly, Ponca City, OK 74601 United States **BUS:** Manufacturing Company **P/S:** Trailers and Mountain Movers for the Oil Field Service Industry **MA:** National **D/D/R:** Overseeing Human Resources, Specializing in Environmental Safety, Interviewing Perspective Welders for the Welding School **H/I/S:** Writing, Traveling, Cooking, Watching Movies, Bowling **EDU:** JD, Loyola School of Law (1983); Bachelor of Science in Political Science, Oklahoma State University (1979) **A/A/S:** Deacon, The First Presbyterian Church of Ponca City (2008) Lions Club, Ponca; Phi Delta Phi **C/VW:** Board of Directors, The United Way, Ponca City
Email: lthorstenberg@mertzok.com
URL: http://www.mertzok.com

Mrs. Jacqueline L. Thrash
Title: Owner, Occupational Therapist **Company:** Jacqueline Thrash **Address:** 1317 N. San Fernando Boulevard, Suite 198, Burbank, CA 91504 United States **BUS:** Private Practice Committed to Excellence in Healthcare **P/S:** Occupational Therapy Services for Geriatric Patients, Book for use by Occupational Therapists, Physical Therapists and Speech Therapists with Spanish Speaking Clients **MA:** International **D/D/R:** Occupational Therapy Services for Geriatric Patients in Nursing Homes, Rehabilitation Centers and Clinics, Wrote an Educational Program Manual for Activity Managers at Activity Centers, Written in Spanish and English with 40 Complete Volumes for International Use **H/I/S:** Photography, Quilting, Culture and Language, Family **EDU:** Bachelor's Degree in Occupational Therapy, San Jose State University; Master's Degree in Progress in Occupational Therapy, San Jose State University; Licensed in California as a Registered Therapist (1986); Nationally Registered Therapist **A/A/S:** American Occupational Therapy Association; Occupational Therapy Association of California; Linguistics Society of America; American Anthropology Association; Southwestern Anthropology Association
Email: thrash@pinkiemae.com
URL: http://www.livingskillstherapy.com

Steven R. Thulin
Title: Captain **Company:** Bass Kikker Charters **Address:** 8 Budd Avenue, Budd Lake, NJ 07828 United States **BUS:** Charter Boat and Fishing Vessel **P/S:** Fishing Trips **MA:** Lower Manhattan, New Jersey **D/D/R:** Fly-Fishing **H/I/S:** Fly-Fishing, Camping **EDU:** Diploma, Ramapo High School **A/A/S:** Fisherman Conservation Association; American Inventor **C/VW:** Fisherman Conservation Association
Email: Bassikkercharters@verizon.net

Bobby R. Thurman
Title: President **Company:** Nelson Funeral Service **Address:** 202 E. Madison Avenue, Berryville, AR 72616 United States **BUS:** Funeral Services Company **P/S:** Funeral Services and Arrangements **MA:** Local **EXP:** Mr. Thurman's expertise is in funeral services. **D/D/R:** Arranging and Conducting Funeral Services, Preparing and Performing the Embalming Process, Ensuring Client Satisfaction, Approving Operational Expenditures within Established Parameters **EDU:** Associate Degree in Funeral Services **A/A/S:** Northwest Arkansas Funeral Directors Association; Arkansas Funeral Directors Association; National Funeral Directors Association; Independent Order of Odd Fellows **C/VW:** Kiwanis International
Email: bobby.thurman@cwwemail.com
URL: http://www.nelsonfuneral.com

Mary Joy Yagin Tibay
Title: Associate Engineer **Company:** Parsons Corporation **Address:** 50 Fremont Street, San Francisco, CA 94105 United States **BUS:** Engineering and Construction Company **P/S:** Infrastructure, Industrial Construction, Transportation and Other Consulting Services **MA:** International **D/D/R:** Civil Engineering, Traffic Control Design, Transportation **H/I/S:** Playing Tennis, Reading **EDU:** Bachelor of Science in Civil Engineering, University of Nevada, Reno
Email: maryjoy.tibay@parsons.com
URL: http://www.parsons.com

Susan J. Tice
Title: Owner, President **Company:** Lynneville Hotel, Inc. **Address:** 8148 Bausch Road, New Tripoli, PA 18066 United States **BUS:** Hospitality **P/S:** Guest Hotel with Restaurant and Bar, Guest Rooms, Food, Beverage and Liquor Services **MA:** Local **D/D/R:** Owning, Managing, Supervising and Overseeing Complete Hotel, Restaurant, Bar Operations, Overseeing Guest Services **H/I/S:** Animal Lover and Activist, Actively Helps in the Capture of Stray Cats, Nurturing and Adoption of Dogs, Humane Society Volunteer, Especially Loves Horses, Avid Horseback Rider **EDU:** High School Education **A/A/S:** Treasurer, Lehigh County Tavern Association **C/VW:** Actively Volunteers Time and Donates Charitably to Humane Society
Email: suej1939@aol.com
URL: http://www.cambridgewhoswho.com

Steven G. Tietel
Title: General Manager Company: Lake Elmo Inn Address: 848 New Century Boulevard S., Saint Paul, MI 55119 United States BUS: Restaurant, Food Service P/S: Serving Lunch and Dinner, Group and Large Party Reservations, Catering Services MA: Local D/D/R: Food and Beverage Manager H/I/S: Golf, Gardening EDU: Bachelors, Restaurant Management, University of Wisconsin; Associates, Business Management, Inverhill Community College
Email: ltietel@comcast.net
URL: http://www.lakeelmoinn.com

Andrea Tighe, AA, RN, CPTC
Title: Procurement Manager Company: Life-Source, Upper Midwest Organ Procurement Organization Address: 2250 University Avenue W., Suite 315 South, St. Paul, MN 55114 United States BUS: Nonprofit, Federally Designated Organization Dedicated to Saving Lives through Organ and Tissue Recovery and Donation in the Upper Midwest Covering Minnesota, North Dakota, South Dakota and Portions of Western Wisconsin P/S: Managing All Aspects of Organ and Tissue Donation, from Identifying Potential Donors to Matching Organs with Needy Recipients, Coordinating Clinical Activities, Arranging Surgical Recovery Teams, Linking the Stages of the Donation and Transplantation Processes MA: Regional D/D/R: Clinical Manager, Overseeing a Staff of 16-17 People, Coordinating Clinical Activities and Stages of Donations and Transplantation Processes H/I/S: Gardening, Spending Quality Time with Family EDU: Pursuing Bachelor of Science in Nursing, Michigan State University; Certified PTC A/A/S: Association of Organ Procurement Organizations; American Association of Critical-Care Nurses; North American Transplant Coordinators Organization
Email: atighe@life-source.org
URL: http://www.life-source.org

Catherine M. Tijerina
Title: Executive Director, Co-Founder Company: RIDGE Project, Inc. Address: 1935 E. Second Street, Suite D, Defiance, OH 45312 United States BUS: Nonprofit Organization P/S: Social Services and Education for Vulnerable Youths and Families MA: Regional D/D/R: Developing Evaluations, Writing Grants, Training and Overseeing the Staff, Speaking at School Assemblies H/I/S: Camping, Reading, Spending Time with Family EDU: Associate Degree in Legal Assistant Studies, Blackstone Career Institute (1998) A/A/S: National Abstinence Education Association; Ohio Hispanic Youth Development Outreach Program
Email: catherine@theridgeproject.com
URL: http://www.theridgeproject.com

Amy L. Tillett
Title: Owner Company: T's Barber Shop Address: 7018 Maynardville Pike, Knoxville, TN 37918 United States BUS: Salon P/S: Hair Cutting and Styling MA: Regional D/D/R: Cutting and Styling Hair H/I/S: Riding her Harley-Davidson, Spending Time with her Family A/A/S: Certified Cosmetologist; License in Cosmetology, Tennessee School of Beauty C/VW: Special Olympics; St. Jude Children's Research Hospital
Email: amy.tillett@cwwemail.com
Email: nosierosie05@yahoo.com

Nakita L. Tillman
Title: Wage Specialist Company: Sears Holdings Corporation, Human Resources Support Center Address: 4740 Hugh Howell Road, Tucker, GA 30084 United States BUS: Retail Company P/S: Clothing, Footwear, Home Goods MA: National D/D/R: Processing Payroll, Managing Human Resource Operations H/I/S: Reading, Watching Football, Supporting the Atlanta Falcons, Traveling EDU: Coursework in Medical Transcription
Email: ntillma@searshc.com
URL: http://www.searsholdings.com

Suzanne Timko
Title: Assistant Manager Company: Burger Federal Credit Union Address: 3201 Belmont Street, Suite 702, Bellaire, OH 43906 United States BUS: Credit Union P/S: Loans, Titles, Liens, Insurance MA: Regional D/D/R: Management H/I/S: Crafts, Reading, Farm EDU: Associate of Applied Science in Computer Programming and Accounting, Belmont Technical College
Email: suzieandbud@windstream.net
URL: http://www.burgercu@sbcglobal.net

Elizabeth M. Tingey
Title: Educator, Art and French Company: South Davis Junior High, Davis School District Address: 60 S. 200 W., Kaysville, UT 84037 United States BUS: Public Education P/S: Instruction and Curriculum MA: Regional D/D/R: Educational Trips in France and Spain for Twenty-Eight Students and Parents, Ninth-Grade Studio Art, Professional Artist H/I/S: Traveling EDU: Master's Degree in Education Psychology, University of California (1976); Bachelor of Art, Santa Barbara Art Institute A/A/S: Board Member, Utah Education Association; Utah Educational Association; Davis Educational Association; National Educational Association
Email: bitngey2@yahoo.com
URL: http://www.davis.k12.ut.us/home/schools.html

Vivian V. Tinsley
Title: Subscription Coordinator Company: American Public Health Association Address: 800 I Street N.W., Fourth Floor, Washington, DC 20001 United States BUS: Public Health Association P/S: Assistance with Racial and Ethnic Health Disparities, International Child Health Priorities, Contemporary Environmental and Occupational Health Issues MA: National D/D/R: Communicating with Agencies, Members and Subscribers Regarding Occupational Health Issues, Locating Underpaid Accounts, Initiating Payments, Promoting Marketing Tactics to Increase Subscriptions H/I/S: Reading Poetry, Traveling, Cooking, Photography EDU: Bachelor of Arts in Journalism, Pennsylvania State University (1999) CERTS: ; Certificate, Diversity in Journalism A/H: Achievement Award, District Channel 28
Email: ortiz1000@lycos.com
URL: http://www.apha.org

Michael J. Tirak
Title: Owner Company: Affordable Electric Services Address: 38539 Lemsford Avenue, Palmdale, CA 93550 United States BUS: Electrical Contracting Company P/S: Electrical Contracting Services MA: Regional D/D/R: Specializing in Electrical Engineering and Wiring New Homes and Room Additions, Overseeing All Day-to-Day Operations, Handling All Financial, Marketing and Advertising Aspects of the Business H/I/S: Basketball EDU: Coursework in Electronics, Antelope Valley College (1974)
Email: mtirak@sbcglobal.net

Merryl H. Tisch
Title: Vice Chancellor Company: New York State Board of Regents BUS: State Education Department P/S: Education Policies and Laws, Assessment Systems, Federal Agendas, Annual Reports, Legislative and Budget Proposals MA: Regional D/D/R: Contributing to State Education Policies, Licensing 45 Professions, Chartering Libraries, Museums, Archives and Public Television Shows H/I/S: Golfing EDU: Doctor of Education, Teachers College, Columbia University; Master of Education, New York University (2005) A/A/S: Chairwoman, Metropolitan Council on Jewish Poverty
Email: mhtisch@aol.com
URL: http://www.regents.nysed.gov

Debra A. Titsworth
Title: Owner, Chief Executive Officer Company: Green Country Wholesale Florist, Inc. Address: P.O. Box 397, Chouteau, OK 74337 United States BUS: Wholesale and Retail Flower Business P/S: Fresh Cut Flowers and Supplies D/D/R: Designing Floral Arrangements H/I/S: Traveling, Fishing, Horseback Riding EDU: Certification in Biblical Studies (2007); Certification in Biblical Studies, Domata School of Leadership (2006); High School Diploma A/A/S: Word Fellowship Bible School; National Republican Congressional Committee
Email: ldtitsworth@fairpoint.net
URL: http://www.cambridgewhoswho.com

Marietta E. Toal
Title: Clinical Data Manager Company: Wellstat Therapeutics Address: 930 Clapper Road, Gaithersburg, MD 20878 United States BUS: Pharmaceuticals MA: Local D/D/R: Clinical Data Management H/I/S: Reading EDU: Bachelor of Science in Biology, St. Norbert College C/VW: Church
Email: mtoal@wellstattherapeutics.com
URL: http://www.cambridgewhoswho.com

Evelyn G. Tobey, M.Ed.
Title: Third-Grade Teacher Company: Cynthia Mann Elementary School Address: 5401 Castle Drive, Boise, ID 83703 United States BUS: School P/S: Education MA: Local D/D/R: Teaching Mathematics, Language, Critical and Creative Thinking H/I/S: Traveling, Swimming, Singing, Canoeing, Reading EDU: Master of Education, Concentration in Critical and Creative Thinking, Plymouth State University (1987); Bachelor of Science in Elementary Education, Keene State College (1982) A/H: Who's Who Among American Teachers (2006, 2007) C/VW: Boys and Girls Town, Idaho Food Bank, Rescue Mission, St. Jude Children's Research Hospital
Email: evelyn.tobey@boiseschools.org
URL: http://www.cambridgewhoswho.com

William G. Toburen
Title: Dentist, Owner Company: Bayshore Dental Group, SC Address: 316 E. Silver Spring Drive, Suite 243, Whitefish Bay, WI 53217 United States BUS: General Dentistry P/S: Wide Range of Dental Services MA: Regional D/D/R: Practicing General Dentistry and Cosmetic Dentistry, Treating Children and Adults, Implant Restoration, Preventive Oriented Practice Serving Children Through Adulthood H/I/S: Tennis, Reading, Travel, Gardening EDU: Doctor of Dental Surgery, Marquette University Dental School; Bachelor of Science in Zoology, University of Wisconsin-Madison A/A/S: Alpha Omega International Dental Fraternity; Omicron Kappa Epsilon; Alpha Sigma Nu; American Academy of Cosmetics Dentistry
Email: wgtsmile@aol.com
URL: http://www.cambridgewhoswho.com

Mr. Daniel J. Todd
Title: Owner Company: Todd Enterprises Address: 7420 N. Woods Drive, Semmes, AL 36575 United States BUS: Event Planning P/S: Decorating, Event Consulting, Pyrotechnics, Firework Display, Fund Raising, Balloon Decor MA: Regional D/D/R: Overseeing All Operations, Creating 90 Percent of the Designs, Translating Customer's Needs into a Creative Vision to be Executed by Team, General Manager of 'Mobile Sharks' H/I/S: Football, Announcing Baseball Games A/A/S: Recording Secretary, Pharaohs Mystical Society; Mobile Chamber of Commerce; Mobile Bay Convention and Visitors Bureau; General Manager of the Year for Minor League Football (2004)
Email: toddente@netscape.net
URL: http://www.cambridgewhoswho.com

Mirium Jackson Todd
Address: 28 Long Bow Drive, Sewell, NJ 08080 United States BUS: Federal Government Regulatory Agency P/S: Compliance Ensurance with Federal Statutes MA: National D/D/R: Conducting Investigations and Program Analysis, Overseeing Management and Organization, Utilizing Information Technology H/I/S: Reading Non-Fiction Literature, Creating Graphic Presentations, Writing EDU: Master of Education in Counseling Psychology, Howard University; Bachelor of Science in Psychology, Howard University A/A/S: American Counseling Association; Kappa Delta Pi; Association for Multicultural Counseling and Development; Howard University Alumni Association
Email: mirium.todd@comcast.net

Mr. Albert Todesca III
Title: Vice President Company: AJT Supplies, Inc. Address: 4945 Washington Street, West Roxbury, MA 02132 United States BUS: Masonry and Landscape Supply Company P/S: Masonry Work, Supplies, Stones, Walkways, Driveways, Stairs, More than 100 Masonry Supply Products and More than 80 Landscape Supply Products MA: Regional D/D/R: Managing Daily Operations, Scheduling, Ensuring Effective Disbursement of Materials EDU: Associate Degree in Civil Engineering, Wentworth Institute of Technology (2005)
Email: alberttodesca@yahoo.com
URL: http://www.ajtsupplies.com

Anne M. Toewe, MFA
Title: Head of Design and Technology, Resident Costume Designer Company: University of Northern Colorado Dept: School of Theatre Arts and Dance Address: 105 Frasier Hall, Greeley, CO 80631 United States BUS: Leader in the Education Industry, Colorado Program of Excellence by the Colorado Commission on Higher Education P/S: Higher Education, Pre-Professional Training for Students who Plan to Pursue Careers in Professional Theatre, or as Teachers of Theatre Arts MA: Local D/D/R: In Charge of Overall Design Program for Undergraduates, Geared Towards Preparing Students to Continue on to Graduate School, Daily Scholastic Advising, Developing Design Assignments, In Charge of Technical and Dress Rehearsals, Acting as Resident Costume Director for Students Majoring in Costume Design, Monitoring the Work in the Costume Shop, Handling Recruiting and Internships H/I/S: Theatre, Traveling EDU: Ph.D. in Theatre, University of Colorado (2008); Master of Fine Arts in Costume Design, Tulane University (1991); Bachelor of Science in Biology, College of William and Mary (1987) A/A/S: United States Institute for Theatre Technology; Costume Society of America; United Scenic Artists, Number 829; Attended Oxford Round Table; Association for Theater in Higher Education; Kemmedy Center; American College Theatre Festival A/H: Meritorious Achievement Award for Costume Design, Jeckyll and Hyde (2004)
Email: anne.toewe@unco.edu
URL: http://www.unco.edu

Sue E. Tokarz
Title: Second-Grade Teacher Company: Millcreek-West Unity Schools Address: 113 S. Defiance Street, West Unity, OH 43570 United States BUS: School P/S: Education MA: Local D/D/R: Teaching All Subjects to Second-Graders H/I/S: Walking, Basketball EDU: Master's Degree in Elementary Education, University of Toledo (1998) A/A/S: National Education Association; Ohio Education Association
Email: wun_aca_st@nwoca.org
URL: http://www.hilltop.k12.oh.us

Mr. Anthony M. Tolle
Title: Technical Writer **Company:** B/E Aerospace, Inc. **Address:** 1455 Fairchild Road, Winston Salem, NC 27105 United States **BUS:** B/E Aerospace is the World's Leading Manufacturer of Cabin Interior Products for Commercial Aircraft and Business Jets **P/S:** Cabin Interior Equipment and Furnishings for Commercial and Business Jet Aircraft, Including Passenger Seating Products (First, Business, and Coach Class), Beverage Maker Products, Oven Products, Oxygen System Products, Refrigeration Products, Galley Products and Inserts, Lighting Products, De-Icing Systems, Business Jet Cabinetry and Super-First Class Seats and Aircraft Interior Reconfiguration Engineering Services **MA:** International **D/D/R:** Technical Writing of B/E's Seating Products Group Component Maintenance Manuals, specializing in the management and production of Temporary Revisions to same. Initial investigator (in the Technical Publications group) of customer requests and claims about changes needed to the manuals. **H/I/S:** Football (NFL's Pittsburgh Steelers) **EDU:** Master of Science Degree in Technology, University of Texas at Tyler (1992); Bachelor of Science Degree in Physical Science, United States Naval Academy (1987) **A/A/S:** Honorably Discharged as a USAF Aircraft Maintenance Officer (Senior Captain), U.S. Air Force; Lifetime Member, American Legion; Member, National Rifle Association and National Air and Space Museum (Smithsonian Institute)
Email: tony_tolle@beaerospace.com
URL: http://www.beaerospace.com

Hollis C. Tomashek, M.Ed.
Title: Teacher (Retired) **Company:** Valley View School District **Dept:** Irene King Elementary School **Address:** 755 Luther Drive, Romeoville, IL 60446 United States **BUS:** Elementary School **P/S:** Education for Kindergarten through Fifth-Grade Students **MA:** Local **D/D/R:** Teaching First Through Fifth-Grade Students **H/I/S:** Traveling, Singing, Writing **EDU:** Master of Education in Curriculum, National-Louis University (1988); Bachelor of Science in Music Education, University of Illinois (1973)
Email: holly_tomashek@msn.com

Stephanie and Papa Tomatis and Fall
Title: Co-Owners **Company:** Boga Fashion **Address:** 32 Biltmore Avenue, Asheville, NC 28801 United States **BUS:** Retail Franchise Store **P/S:** Imported Fashion Apparels like Denim, Casual and Sports Wear, Jewelry **MA:** International **D/D/R:** overseeing business operations **H/I/S:** Discovering New Culture and Fashion Trends **EDU:** College Coursework **CERTS:** Certification in Micro-Enterprise in Global Markets; Certified in Global Trade Professional, North Carolina State University **A/A/S:** MMF
Email: stomatis@bogaonline.com
URL: http://www.bogafashion.com

Nancy B. Tomlin
Title: Compliance and Quality Assurance Officer **Company:** University of Alabama School of Dentistry, Birmingham **Address:** 1001 Lake Shore Drive, Cropwell, AL 35054 United States **BUS:** University **P/S:** Higher Education Includes General Dentistry, Oral Surgery and Periodontics, Clinics, Hospital Dental Programs **MA:** Regional **EXP:** Ms. Tomlin's expertise includes dental hygiene, compliance assurance, quality assurance, student rotation and annual infection control, chart auditing. **D/D/R:** lecturing and conducting research on infection control **H/I/S:** Cooking, Studying Nutrition, Gardening, Edible Landscaping **EDU:** Bachelor of Science in Dental Hygiene, The University of Alabama (1984) **A/A/S:** Organization for Safety and Asepsis Procedures
Email: ntomlin@uab.edu
URL: http://www.dental.uab.edu

Jane B. Tompkins
Title: Teacher **Company:** Assumption High School **Address:** 1020 W. Central Park Avenue, Davenport, IA 52804 United States **BUS:** High School **P/S:** Secondary Education **MA:** Local **D/D/R:** teaching advanced placement English and British literature **H/I/S:** Gardening, Walking, Golfing, Reading **EDU:** Pursuing Ph.D., The University of Iowa; Master's Degree in Educational Leadership, Plus 30, St. Ambrose University **C/VW:** Local Church
Email: zteachu@aol.com

Yunxia Tong
Title: Research Fellow **Company:** National Institutes of Health **Address:** 9000 Rockville Pike, Building 10, Room 3C103, Bethesda, MD 20892 United States **BUS:** Medical Research Facility **P/S:** Disease Prevention, Causes, Treatments and Cures for Common and Rare Diseases, Financial Support to Researchers, Psychology and Neuroscience Departments, Collecting, Disseminating and Exchanging Information in Medicine and Health, 27 Institutes and Centers, Laboratory of Hygiene, Marine Hospital **MA:** Regional **D/D/R:** Conducting Research about Cognitive Neuroscience, Managing Neuroimaging, Analyzing Data **H/I/S:** Spending Time with Family **EDU:** Ph.D. in Psychology, Purdue University **A/A/S:** Society for Neuroscience
Email: yunxia@mail.nih.gov
URL: http://www.nih.gov

Shantie Toolsie
Title: President, Founder **Company:** Plato Home Day Care **Dept:** Plato Home Day Care **Address:** 3712 N. Broadway Street, Suite 260, Chicago, IL 60613 United States **BUS:** Day Care Center and Preschool **P/S:** Day Care for Children Below Three Years Old, Education **MA:** Local **D/D/R:** Customer Service, Educating Children, Handling All Changes in School Systems, Handling Administration and Marketing, Statistical Analyst **H/I/S:** Traveling, Entertaining the Children, Baking, Watching Movies, Sports, Volunteering **EDU:** Master's Degree in Statistics, Michigan State University (1997); Bachelor of Arts in Mathematics, Pace University (1994) **A/A/S:** Lincoln Park Chamber of Commerce; Statistical Association; National Association for the Education of Young Children
Email: math165@platodaycare.com
URL: http://www.platodaycare.com

Beatrice F. Tooten, LPN
Title: Licensed Practical Nurse **Company:** Coral Gables Convalescent Rehabilitation Center **Address:** 7060 S.W. Eighth Street, Miami, FL 33144 United States **BUS:** Nursing Home **P/S:** Healthcare **MA:** Regional **D/D/R:** scheduling, generating reports, nursing patients and administering medication to patients **H/I/S:** Watching Baseball **EDU:** Associate Degree in Nursing, Miami Dade College (1996) **CERTS:** Licensed Practical Nurse, Broward Nursing and Rehabilitation Center
Email: beatricef.tooten@cwwemail.com

Maria-Elena Torales
Title: Spanish Instructor **Company:** Imperial Valley College **Address:** 380 E. Aten Road, Imperial, CA 92251 United States **BUS:** College **P/S:** Higher Education **MA:** Local **D/D/R:** Teaching Spanish and Spanish-American Literature **H/I/S:** Reading **EDU:** Master's Degree in Spanish American Literature, San Diego State University **C/VW:** Oasis Del Nino
Email: mariaelena.torales@imperial.edu
URL: http://www.cambridgewhoswho.com

Mr. John J. Torneo, LPN
Title: Licensed Practical Nurse **Company:** Beacon Hospice **Address:** 54 Pleasant Street, Bristol, CT 06010 United States **BUS:** Hospice Center **P/S:** Healthcare Including Physical and Occupational Therapy, Speech and Language Pathology and Residential Care Services **MA:** Regional **EXP:** Mr. Torneo's expertise includes case management, real estate investment, medical-surgical, pre and post operative care nursing. **D/D/R:** Assisting in Telemetry and Emergency Room Nursing, Certifying Nurse Aides in Cardiopulmonary Resuscitation, Admitting and Caring for Patients **H/I/S:** Investing in Real Estate **CERTS:** Diploma in Nursing, Prince Regional Vocational Technical School (1996)
Email: jjtorneo@snet.net
URL: http://www.beaconhospice.com

Dr. Sheryl Torr-Brown
Title: Company Principle **Company:** Spiral 5 Consulting, LLC **Address:** 91 Spring Valley Road, Mystic, CT 06355 United States **BUS:** Leader in Healthcare **P/S:** Health Writing, Health Business Consulting, Health Information **MA:** International **D/D/R:** Running and Overseeing the Entire Company, Looking for Projects along with Working on Projects, Knowledge, Management and Healthcare Consulting **H/I/S:** Bike Riding, Traveling, Cooking, Drawing, Piano, Guitar, Reading, Writing Fiction **EDU:** Ph.D. in Medicine, London University, United Kingdom (1991) **A/A/S:** Institute of Noetic Sciences; New York Academy of Sciences; Society of Competitive Intelligence Professionals
Email: srtorr@gmail.com
URL: http://web.mac.com/spiral5

Felix Torres
Title: President **Company:** Torres Aerospace Consulting **Address:** P.O. Box 777130, Henderson, NV 89077 United States **BUS:** Aerospace Consultant **P/S:** Analyzing Organizational Structure Feasibility Studies, Set Up Companies, Proposals **MA:** National **D/D/R:** Network Analysis Negotiations, Aerospace Professionals, Aircraft, Missiles Systems and Space Programs **H/I/S:** Family **EDU:** Southwest Electrical Institute of San Antonio Texas, Bachelors **A/A/S:** Church, Quality Engineering

Mrs. Heather C. Torres
Title: Executive Assistant **Company:** Spring International Language Center **Address:** 900 Auraria Parkway, Tivoli Building, Suite 454, Denver, CO 80204 United States **BUS:** Education Center **P/S:** Teaching English as a Second Language to International Students, Quality Teachers, University Partnerships **MA:** International **D/D/R:** Managing Correspondence, Administration, Bookkeeping, Student Services, Acting as Liaison with Government Institutions, Speaking Spanish and English **H/I/S:** Foreign Languages, Sports/Fitness, Reading, Learning about different cultures, Travelling **EDU:** Bachelor of Arts in Spanish, University of Colorado (2006)
Email: heather@spring-usa.com
URL: http://www.spring-usa.com

Kenny J. Torres
Title: Assistant Plant Manager **Company:** B & W Quality Growers, Inc. **Address:** 17825 79th Street, Fellsmere, FL 32948 United States **BUS:** Food Packing Company **P/S:** Arugula, Watercress **MA:** National **D/D/R:** Overseeing Production and Manufacturing, Supervising the Staff, Handling Machine and Product Control **H/I/S:** Playing Computer Games, Playing Football, Hockey, Baseball and Soccer **EDU:** Pursuing Degree in Computer Science
Email: kennytorres@watercress.com

Lucrecia C. Torres-Suarez
Title: Bilingual Special Education Teacher **Company:** Don Pedro Albizu Campus **Dept:** Public School 161 **Address:** 499 W. 133rd Street, New York, NY 10027 United States **BUS:** School District **P/S:** Education **MA:** Local **EXP:** Ms. Torres-Suarez's expertise is in bilingual special education. **H/I/S:** Dancing, Playing the Piano, Reading, Traveling **EDU:** Master's Degree in Special Education, Plus 30, City College; Bachelor of Arts in Bilingual Education, City College **C/VW:** Local Church
Email: lucreciatorres1@netzero.com
URL: http://www.cambridgewhoswho.com

Rosa M. Torruellas
Title: Senior Validation Scientist III **Company:** Bristol Myers Squibb **Address:** 345 Park Avenue, New York, NY 10154 United States **BUS:** Pharmaceutical Company **P/S:** Tablets, Healthcare Products **MA:** International **D/D/R:** validating products **H/I/S:** Photography **EDU:** Master of Business Administration, University of Turabo **A/A/S:** Puerto Rico Society for Microbiologists
Email: rosa.torruellas@bms.com
URL: http://www.bms.com

Rhonda A. Toston
Title: VP **Company:** Jones Long La Salle **Address:** 3424 Peachtree Road, Atlanta, GA 30326 United States **BUS:** Real Estate Management **P/S:** Project Management **MA:** International **D/D/R:** Commercial **H/I/S:** Cooking, Gardening **EDU:** University of Wisconsin, Bachelors **A/A/S:** Cornette Global
Email: rhonda.toston@am.ll.com
URL: http://www.joneslonglasalle.com

Lynn M. Toub, LPN
Title: Therapeutic Aphaeresis Specialist **Company:** HemaCare Corporation Blood Services **BUS:** Therapeutic Aphaeresis Company **MA:** Local **D/D/R:** Nursing for Therapeutic Aphaeresis **H/I/S:** Spending Time Outdoors, Hiking, Running **EDU:** Licensed Practical Nurse, Bucks County Technical School; Diploma, Quaker Town Community Senior High School **A/A/S:** Appalachian Service Project through her Church **C/VW:** American Cancer Society
Email: lynntoub@dejazzd.com

Irma V. Tovar
Title: Chief Executive Officer **Company:** Christ for Mexico **Address:** 3213 Dublin Road, El Paso, TX 79925 United States **BUS:** Nonprofit Organization **P/S:** Humanitarian Services **MA:** International **D/D/R:** overseeing feeding programs for children, clothing drives and education programs **H/I/S:** Scrapbooking **EDU:** Coursework, El Paso Community College; Coursework in Interior Design, Sacramento City College. CA **A/A/S:** Kiwanis Club; Hispanic Medical Association **C/VW:** Various Charitable Organizations
Email: ivtovar@sbcglobal.net
URL: http://www.cambridgewhoswho.com

Jackie F. Towler, GBR, CRS, CLHMS
Title: Realtor **Company:** Re/Max Action Realty **Address:** 1126 Horsham Road, Maple Glen, PA 19002 United States **BUS:** Real Estate Broker **P/S:** Residential, Executive homes, New Construction **MA:** National **D/D/R:** Residential Real Estate, Does Relocation and is a Producer **H/I/S:** Walking, Traveling **EDU:** Master of Science in Guidance Counseling, University of Virginia; Bachelor of Science in Education, University of Virginia **A/A/S:** PAR; National Association of Realtors; Institute of Luxury Home Marketing Specialist
Email: jackie@hjtowler.com
URL: http://www.ipahomesales.com

Hope C. Townsend
Title: Director of Field Services **Company:** Muscular Dystrophy Association **Address:** 3300 E. Sunrise Drive, Tucson, AZ 85718 United States **BUS:** Nonprofit Organization **P/S:** Medical and Community Services Including Professional and Public Health Education, Research and Programs for Neuromuscular Diseases **MA:** National **D/D/R:** Managing Operations, Processing Human Resource Request Forms, Budgeting and Purchasing All Operational Equipments **H/I/S:** Biking, Swimming **EDU:** Bachelor's Degree in Business Management, Queens University of Charlotte, NC (1996)
Email: htownsend@mdausa.org
URL: http://www.mda.org

Sherry Ann Townsley
Title: Graduate Teacher Assistant **Company:** Tarleton State University **Dept:** Education **Address:** Box T-0290, Stephenville, TX 76402 United States **BUS:** University **P/S:** Computer Information Systems, Computer Science, Communications, Criminal Justice, Economics, Educational Leadership and Policy Studies, Engineering Technology, English and Languages, Environmental Science, Finance, Fine Arts and Communications, Management Marketing and Administrative Systems, Military Sciences, Music, Nursing, Physics, Psychology and Counseling, Social Sciences, Sociology, Social Work and Theater **MA:** Local **D/D/R:** Reading **H/I/S:** Practicing Needle Crafts, Reading **EDU:** Pursuing Master's Degree; Bachelor of Science, Howard Payne University (1992); Certification in Teaching Kindergarten through Eighth-Grade **A/A/S:** Texas Classroom Teachers Association; Pi Gamma Mu
Email: townsleyjewelers@earthlink.net
URL: http://www.tarleton.edu

Christie P. Tracey
Title: Administrator **Company:** Trapic Bath Improvements, LLC **Address:** 4623 Clyde Park Avenue S.W., Grand Rapids, MI 49509 United States **BUS:** Bathroom Remodeling Company **P/S:** Bathroom Remodeling, Bath and Shower Accessories, Acrylic Bath Shower, Bath Tub Refinishing Services **MA:** Local **D/D/R:** overseeing office administration, accounting, advertising, payroll, hiring and scheduling **H/I/S:** Walking, Singing, Spending Time with her Family **EDU:** Diploma, Absegami High School (1995) **A/A/S:** Local Chamber of Commerce; Home & Building Association of Greater Grand Rapids **C/VW:** Local Federation of Police; Various Cancer Societies
Email: cptracey@sbcglobal.net
URL: http://www.bathfitter.com

Thomas J. Tracy III
Title: President **Company:** Trade Winds Power Corp **Address:** 5820 N.W. 84th Avenue, Miami, FL 33166 United States **BUS:** Generators Manufacturer **P/S:** Diesel Power Generator Sets **MA:** International **D/D/R:** Psychology **H/I/S:** Travel, Reading, Surfing, Snowboarding, Hunting, Fishing **EDU:** Bachelor of Arts in Psychology, West Virginia University
Email: ttracy@tradewindspower.com
URL: http://www.tradewindspower.com

Catherine Trahan
Title: Realtor **Company:** Bradley Real Estate **Address:** 1701 Novato Boulevard, Suite 100, Novato, CA 94947 United States **BUS:** Real Estate Agency **P/S:** Homes, New Construction, Land Development **MA:** Countywide **D/D/R:** Residential Real Estate, Townhouse, Condos, Vacant Land, Corp Relocation **H/I/S:** Gardening, Reading, Spending Time with Family, Snow Skiing, Hiking **EDU:** Bachelor of Arts in Business, Rhodes College (1989); Licensed Realtor in the State of California (1997) **A/A/S:** Real Estate CyberSpace Society; Marin Chapter, Women's Council of Realtors; Marin Association of Realtors; National Association of Realtors **C/VW:** Cancer Care, Son's School
Email: ctrahan@sprintmail.com
URL: http://www.catherinetrahan.com

Barbara A. Trainor
Title: Director of Curriculum and Instruction **Company:** Exploration Summer Programs **Dept:** Educational Curriculum **Address:** 932 Washington Street, PO Box 368, Norwood, MA 02062 United States **BUS:** Summer Enrichment Program **P/S:** Summer Education Enrichment **MA:** International **D/D/R:** Designing Curriculum, Classroom Instruction, Mentoring New Teachers, designing and delivering educational professional development **EDU:** Master of Education, New England College; Bachelor's Degree in Biology and Nutrition, Cornell University; Certification in Teaching, State of New Hampshire **A/A/S:** National Council of Teachers of Mathematics; Association for Supervision and Curriculum Development
Email: btrainor@explo.org
URL: http://www.explo.org/

Michelle Trammell
Title: President **Company:** The Securities Groups, LLC **Address:** 6465 N. Quail Hollow Road, Suite 400, Memphis, TN 38120 United States **BUS:** Healthcare Securities Broker **P/S:** Investments, Health Care Private Placement Offerings **MA:** National **D/D/R:** Physician Joint Ventures **H/I/S:** Motorcycling, Hiking, Roller Blading, Snow Skiing, Water Skiing **EDU:** Bachelor of Science in Marketing, University of Memphis; Master of Arts in Business Administration; Master of Business Administration Management
Email: mtrammell@thesecuritiesgroup.com
URL: http://www.thesecuritiesgroup.com

Jacqueline V. Tran, MD
Title: Doctor of Neurology **Address:** 16259 Sylvestor Road S.W., Suite 503, Burien, WA 98166 United States **BUS:** Healthcare Neurology **P/S:** General Neurology **MA:** Local **D/D/R:** General Neurology **H/I/S:** Cooking, Reading **EDU:** MD in Neurology, Dartmouth School of Medicine; Bachelor of Science in Biology, University of California, Los Angeles **A/A/S:** Make-A-Wish Foundation
Email: jakhlyki@earthlink.net

Don Traphagan
Title: Authorized Dealer **Company:** Magic Kids Inc **Address:** 7039 Nelda Way, Redding, CA 96002 United States **BUS:** Children's Clothing Retail **P/S:** Wholesale/Retail Children's Clothing **MA:** National **D/D/R:** Designer Kids Wear **H/I/S:** Reading **A/A/S:** Chamber of Commerce
URL: http://www.magickidsusa.com

Catalina Valdez Trasporte
Title: 1) Administrator 2) Director **Company:** 1) C Cares 4U 2) X Power Saves-EBill **Address:** 1719 Richardson Street, San Bernardino, CA 92408 United States **BUS:** Home Health Service **P/S:** Home Healthcare **MA:** California **D/D/R:** Overseeing Patient Care **H/I/S:** Writing Stories, Playing the Piano and Flute **EDU:** Master of Arts in Public Health, Adventist University of the Philippines; Bachelor of Arts in Secretarial Science, Mountain View College; RCFE and ARF Licensed **C/VW:** Community Service
Email: ading7461@yahoo.com
URL: http://www.cambridgewhoswho.com

Mr. Kenneth A. Travers
Title: Senior Vice President **Company:** ABS Consulting EQECAT **Address:** 5301 Limestone Road, Suite 210, Wilmington, DE 19808 United States **BUS:** Independent Global Provider of Risk Management Services **P/S:** Risk Modeling, Practical Engineering and Technology Based Solutions **MA:** International **D/D/R:** Engineering, Risk Management, Catastrophe Remodeling, Managing All Corporate Market Responsibilities, Business Development and Strategic Planning, Developing Software Products, Speak to Reinsurance and Risk Management Professional at Conferences **H/I/S:** Digital Video Projects, Playing Guitar, Golfing **EDU:** Master's Degree in Business Administration, Goldey-Beacom College (1998) **A/A/S:** Risk and Insurance Management Society; National Fire Protection Association
Email: ktravers@absconsulting.com
URL: http://www.absconsulting.com

Christine Travis
Title: Administrative Specialist **Company:** Delaware Technical & Community College **Address:** 100 Campus Drive, Dover, DE 19904 United States **BUS:** College **P/S:** Higher Education Including Applied Agriculture, Architectural Engineering, Biotechnology, Business Administration, Civil Engineering, Criminal Justice, Electromechanical, Engineering, Fire Protection Engineering, Mechanical Engineering and Visual Communications **MA:** Local **D/D/R:** managing finances, monitoring budgets, payouts and incumbent positions, overseeing instructional and travel reconciliations, managing the daycare system and monitoring professional development **EDU:** Pursuing Bachelor's Degree in Human Resources, Delaware State University; Associate Degree, Delaware Technical & Community College (2004); Associate Degree in Business Management, Delaware Technical & Community College (2004) **CERTS:** Certified Microsoft Office Specialist
Email: ctravis@dtcc.edu
URL: http://www.dtcc.edu

Ms. Michelle S. Travis
Title: Director of Groups, Events and Media **Company:** Stinson Brand Innovation **Dept:** GEM Division **Address:** 3910 Hill Road, Suite 103, Boise, ID 83703 United States **BUS:** Advertising and Brand Consulting Company **P/S:** Branding **MA:** International **D/D/R:** Groups, Events and Media **H/I/S:** Running Marathons, White Water Rafting, Spending Time with her Family and Friends **EDU:** Bachelor of Business Administration in Marketing, Boise State University **A/A/S:** Boise Metro Rotary Club; Boise Advertising Federation **C/VW:** Family Advocate Program
Email: michelle@stinsonbrandinnovation.com
URL: http://www.stinsonbrandinnovation.com

Danita L. Traxinger, RNAC
Title: MDS Coordinator **Company:** Castle Rock Convalescent Center **Address:** 1445 Uinta Drive, Green River, NY 82935 United States **BUS:** Rehabilitation Facility **P/S:** Geriatric Care, Rehab Facility **MA:** Local **D/D/R:** Certified MDS Coordinator **H/I/S:** Reading, Gardening **EDU:** Western Wyoming Community College, RNACC **A/A/S:** ANACC, Fraternal Order of Eagles, VFW, United Way
Email: danitatraxinger@lycos.com
URL: http://www.crhd.org

Karen Trefz
Title: Vice President **Company:** Western Truck School **Address:** P.O. Box 980393, West Sacramento, CA 95798 United States **BUS:** Training School **P/S:** Truck Driving Training Programs **MA:** Regional **D/D/R:** Recruiting and Promoting Staff, Ensuring Health Insurance Benefits, managing human resources **H/I/S:** Boating **EDU:** Coursework in Pre-Medicine, Kansas Wesleyan University, Salina; Coursework in Pre-Medicine, University of Colorado (1967); Coursework in Human Resources, University of Phoenix
Email: karent@westerntruckschool.com
URL: http://www.westerntruckschool.com

Loree L. Tremeling-King
Title: Special Education **Company:** Sandy Valley Jr/Sr High School **Address:** State Route 183, Magnolia, OH 44624 United States **BUS:** School **P/S:** Teaching Children Requiring Individual Attention in a Regular Classroom Setting, Accompanied by a Regular Education Teacher, She Provides Attention to the Students in Need, Same Materials, different Formats and Strategies **MA:** Local **D/D/R:** Caring, Patient and Understanding While Working Through Academic Challenges **H/I/S:** Boating, Traveling, Antiquing, Sports **EDU:** Bachelor of Arts in Municipal Recreation, Special Education, Concentration in Autism, Kent State University, OH
Email: atwoodlou@yahoo.com

Paula Medley Hernandez Trent
Title: Contracts Manager **Company:** Luminator Mark IV **Address:** 2201 K. Avenue, Plano, TX 75074 United States **BUS:** Environmental Engineering Company **P/S:** Environmental Engineering **MA:** International **D/D/R:** Contract Management, Natural Resources **H/I/S:** Studying Native American Archeology and Cultural Resources **EDU:** Master's Degree in Liberal Studies, Southern Methodist University(2007); Bachelor of Arts Degree in Humanities, University of Texas at Dallas(2002) **A/A/S:** National Contract Management Association **C/VW:** Lions Club
Email: pdtrent@hotmail.com
URL: http://www.cambridgewhoswho.com

America Trevino
Title: Breast Feeding Coordinator, Supervisor of Nursing **Company:** North Central Bronx Hospital **Address:** 3424 Kossuth Avenue, Bronx, NY 10467 United States **BUS:** Hospital **P/S:** Healthcare **MA:** Local **EXP:** Ms. Trevino's expertise is in childbirth education. **H/I/S:** Reading, Traveling, Watching Movies **EDU:** Bachelor of Science in Nursing, CUNY Lehman College **CERTS:** Registered Nurse **A/A/S:** La Leche League; International Childbirth Education Association **C/VW:** Memorial Sloan-Kettering, Children's Hospital
Email: trevino359@aol.com
URL: http://www.cambridgewhoswho.com

Michael J. Trevis
Title: Chief of Police **Company:** Huntington Park Police Department **Address:** 6542 Miles Avenue, Huntington Park, CA 90255 United States **BUS:** Police Department **P/S:** Law Enforcement **MA:** Local **D/D/R:** planning, managing public relations and overseeing public safety **H/I/S:** Traveling, Reading **EDU:** Pursuing Doctorate Degree; Master's Degree in Organizational Leadership and Management **C/VW:** Local Charitable Organizations
Email: mtrevis@huntingtonparkpd.org
URL: http://www.cambridgewhoswho.com

David B. Tribble, MD, ABHPM, FAAFP
Title: Chief Medical Officer **Company:** The Center for Hospice and Palliative Care **Address:** 111 Sunnybrook Court, South Bend, IN 46637 United States **BUS:** Medical Center **P/S:** Healthcare **MA:** Regional **EXP:** Mr. Tribble's expertise is in family medicine. **D/D/R:** overseeing hospice and palliative care services **H/I/S:** Woodworking, Photography **EDU:** MD, Temple University, Philadelphia, PA **CERTS:** Board Certification in Family Medicine, American Board of Hospice and Palliative Medicine **C/VW:** World Vision; Local Church
Email: tribbled@centerforhospice.org
URL: http://www.centerforhospice.org

Ms. Linda Tribby
Title: Vice President, Business Banking Relationship Manager **Company:** Wachovia **Dept:** Business Banking **Address:** 611 E. Main Street, Purcellville, VA 20132 United States **BUS:** Financial Institution **P/S:** Personal and Business Financial Services, Business Banking Relationship Management, Credit and Small Business Association Lender Services **MA:** National **EXP:** Ms. Tribby's expertise is in business banking relationships. **D/D/R:** Promoting Business Banking and Relationship Building, Overseeing Client Portfolios, Maintaining Client Business Relationships, Ensuring that Clients Receive all Available Financial Opportunities, Managing New Business Acquisitions and Relationships, Small Business Administration Lending, Helping to Develop Successful Start-up Companies **H/I/S:** Farming, Golfing, Antiquing **EDU:** Bachelor of Science in Finance, Shepherd University (1996); Associate Degree in Marketing, Northern Virginia Community College (1991) **CERTS:** Licensed in Series 6, 63, Life and Health, American Institute of Banking (1990); Licensed Real Estate Agent (1988) **A/A/S:** Network Referral Group; Women's Leadership Society **A/H:** National Honor Society **C/VW:** Mount Olive Methodist Church; Rotary Club; Juvenile Diabetes PTD
Email: linda.tribby@wachovia.com
URL: http://www.wachovia.com

Luis A. Trigo Jr.
Title: Warehouse Manager **Company:** BrandsMart USA **Address:** 5000 Motors Industrial Way, Doraville, GA 30360 United States **BUS:** Appliance and Electronic Store **P/S:** Consumer Appliances and Electronics **MA:** National **D/D/R:** Shipping and Receiving of Items in the Warehouse, Oversee the Whole Warehouse, Employee Relations, Human Resource Responsibilities, Hire/Fires, Payroll, Customer Service Issues with Customers Directly, Inventory the Warehouse, Drives Forklifts and other Related Vehicles, Managing Shipments, Organizing Merchandise, Hiring and Training New Employees **H/I/S:** Traveling, Spending Time Outdoors, Reading **EDU:** Pursuing Bachelor's Degree in Business Management, Georgia State University **CERTS:** Certified in Driving Warehouse Vehicles **C/VW:** Volunteers With Adopt a Road Program
Email: saintshank@gmail.com

Joyce Trinder
Title: Owner, Founder **Company:** Boer's Store (AKA NA Collectables) **Address:** P.O. Box 1641, Auburn, WA 98071 United States **BUS:** Embroidered Apparel and Gifts, Family Owned and Operated Apparel Business **P/S:** Embroidery, Screen Printing and Digitizing for Apparel. Embroidered Specialty Gifts for Birthdays, Anniversaries, Holidays, Babies and other occasions. (Aprons, Picture Frames, Travel Mugs, Coasters and More) Customized Company Logos, No Minimums. Bids give upon request. **MA:** International **D/D/R:** Creating Custom Designs for Customers Including Stock Designs, Owning and Operating the Home-Based Internet Business, Marketing, Handling Accounts Payable and Receivable. Doing Shows in Washington and Oregon. **H/I/S:** Sewing, Embroidery, Spending Time with her husband, children and Grandchildren, Traveling, **EDU:** Coursework, Renton Technical College **A/A/S:** Contributor, Widows' Fund; Seattle's Union Gospel Mission; Local Firefighters Association; Retired Police Department Fund; 4-H: Seattle Emergency Shelter
Email: jc@boersstore.com
URL: http://www.boersstore.com

Dianne Tritica
Title: Spanish Teacher **Company:** Harvard, Westlake School **Address:** 3700 Coldwater Canyon, North Hollywood, CA 91604 United States **BUS:** School **P/S:** Education **MA:** Local **D/D/R:** Teaching Second Language Acquisitions **H/I/S:** Reading Prose Fiction, Traveling, Watching Movies, Going to the Theater **EDU:** ABD, Hispanic Linguistics, University of Southern California **A/A/S:** Modern Classics Language of Southern California: AATSP **C/VW:** University of Southern California, Norris Cancer Center
Email: dtritica@hw.com
URL: http://www.hw.com

Ester L. Trivino, PG
Title: Environmental Group Manager **Company:** ATC Associates **Address:** 791 E. Washington Boulevard, Los Angeles, CA 90021 United States **BUS:** Consulting Firm **P/S:** Environmental and Geotechnical Services **MA:** International **D/D/R:** Quality Control, Client Meetings, Environmental Geology **H/I/S:** Opera Singing, Sports, Kayaking, Bicycling **EDU:** Master's Degree in Geology, Loma Linda University **A/A/S:** Association of Environmental and Engineering Geologists; AIDS Organizations, Ground Water
Email: ester.trivino@atcassociates.com

Vladimir Troitsky
Title: Film Producer **Company:** G-Effect, LLC **Address:** 405 Avenue L, Brooklyn, NY 11230 United States **BUS:** Film and Television Production Company **P/S:** Movies, Film Production **MA:** International **D/D/R:** Acting, Writing **H/I/S:** Traveling, Playing Sports **EDU:** New York University Tisch School of the Arts, major Film and Television production. Industry-Related Training and Experience **A/A/S:** Screen Actors Guild
Email: oneway-films@att.net
URL: http://www.sag.com

Constance J. Trompeter-Lindeman
Title: President **Company:** Constance T. Lindeman OTR, Inc. **Address:** P.O. Box 189, Saint Michaels, MD 21663 United States **BUS:** Therapy Center **P/S:** Occupational Therapy **MA:** Regional **D/D/R:** Performing Occupational Therapy and Pediatric Habilitation and Rehabilitation, Coordinating Home Healthcare Programs and Clinical Work with Children and Adults, Guiding Patients to Achieve the Highest Possible Level of Physical, Developmental and Psychosocial Functions **H/I/S:** Sailing, Knitting, Gardening, Skiing, Traveling, Listening to Choral Music **EDU:** Bachelor of Science, Colorado State University (1957) **CERTS:** Registered Occupational Therapist (1959); Certification in Therapeutic Listening **A/A/S:** Former Member, Board of Education, Rumson-Fair Haven Regional High School; Secretary and Treasurer, Shrewsbury Conference; Maryland Occupational Therapy Association; The American Occupational Therapy Association; Easton Choral Arts Society; SPURS National Honor Society; Kappa Alpha Theta **A/H:** Who's Who of American Women (1976) **C/VW:** Christ Church; Tred Avon Yacht Club; Former President, Junior League of Monmouth County, NJ
Email: constance.trompeterlindeman@cwwemail.com
URL: http://www.cambridgewhoswho.com

Beth E. Trotter
Title: Sales Officer **Company:** Nationwide Insurance **Address:** 1651 Exposition Boulevard, Sacramento, CA 95815 United States **BUS:** Insurance Company **P/S:** Insurance **MA:** Local **D/D/R:** Sales **EDU:** Master of Business Administration, Queens University; Registered Insurance Representative; Series 6, 63 and 26 Licenses **A/A/S:** National Association of Insurance and Financial Advisors; Women in Business **C/VW:** Local Organizations
Email: trotteb@nationwide.com
URL: http://www.nationwide.com

Mr. James G. Trout
Title: President, Chief Executive Officer **Company:** Trout's Trucking, LLC **Address:** 5527 Greenridge Drive, Toledo, OH 43615 United States **BUS:** Trucking Company **P/S:** Transportation Services **MA:** Regional **D/D/R:** hiring and terminating employees, equipment maintenance and negotiating contracts **H/I/S:** Listening to Music, Playing the Drums **EDU:** Associate Degree in Criminal Justice, The University of Toledo (1976) **A/A/S:** Jazz Trio; Toledo Jazz Society; National Federation of Independent Business
Email: clues91255@sbcglobal.net

Toy L. True., RN, BS, MBA, CCM, FAACM
Title: Manager of Care Management **Company:** Lakeland Regional Medical Center **Address:** 1234 Napier Avenue, Saint Joseph, MI 49085 United States **BUS:** Hospital **P/S:** Acute-Care Healthcare **MA:** Regional **D/D/R:** Overseeing 35 Social Workers and Registered Nurse Case Managers **H/I/S:** Dancing with the National Sacred Dance Company, Fine Art **EDU:** Master of Business Administration, Breyer State University; Master of Care Management and Business Administration, Breyer State University; Certified Case Manager **A/A/S:** Case Management Society of America; National Institute for Case Management; American Case Management Association; Fellow, American Academy of Case Management **C/VW:** Church
Email: dancewithtoy@aol.com
URL: http://www.cambridgewhoswho.com

Craig D. Truitt
Title: Partner **Company:** Private Advisors, LLC **Address:** 8029 Riverside Drive, Richmond, VA 23225 United States **BUS:** Investment and Asset Management Firm **P/S:** Investing, Marketing, Funds of Funds **MA:** International **D/D/R:** Marketing, Specializing in Client Services **H/I/S:** Golfing, Fly Fishing, Reading **EDU:** Bachelor of Science in Finance, Virginia Tech
Email: ctruitt@privateadvisors.com

Rosemarie Helen Truman
Title: Partner **Company:** PRTM **Address:** 1700 Pennsylvania Avenue N.W., Washington, DC 20006 United States **BUS:** Management Consulting Company **P/S:** Consulting Services Including Innovation, Business Strategy, Information Technology, Research and development and Corporate Strategy **MA:** International **D/D/R:** managing international financial services, consulting, utilizing industrial, high-tech, communications and wireless strategies **H/I/S:** Golfing, Traveling **EDU:** Ph.D. in Software Engineering, Oxford University; Executive Master of Business Administration, Harvard University **A/H:** Innovation Patents Award; Samuel Bowles Prize
Email: rtruman@prtm.com

Terry L. Trundle
Title: 1) President, Owner 2) Director of Sports Medicine **Company:** 1) Athletic Rehabilitation Institute 2) Velocity Spine & Sports Physical Therapy Clinic **Address:** 2529 Eden Ridge Lane, Acworth, GA 30101 United States **BUS:** 1) Athletic Injury Consultant Company 2) Private Group Practice **P/S:** 1) Provides Athletic Injury Services to Christian Schools, Consulting Services to Several Olympic Development Teams 2) Training Programs, Personal Attention from the Coach, Video Analysis System, Improves Muscle Speed, Stamina, Joint Strength, Balance, Agility and Flexibility **MA:** Regional **D/D/R:** Training Olympic Athletes, Researching, Preventing Knee and Shoulder Injury, Overseeing Rehabilitation Services, Consulting with Clientele, Teaching Athletes Health Education, Lecturing Regionally, Nationally, Internationally, Conducting 40 Seminars in a Year on Rehabilitation of Knees and Shoulders, Producing DVD's on Seminars **H/I/S:** Golfing, Baseball **EDU:** Certified Athletic Trainer; Licensed Athletic Trainer; Bachelor's Degree in Health, Physical Education and Recreation, University of Tennessee, Chattanooga; Associate Degree in Physical Therapy **A/A/S:** Chairman, Advisory Board of Rehabilitation Summit; National Athletic Trainers' Association; American Physical Therapy Association
Email: Kneeman14@hotmail.com
URL: http://www.kneeman.net/index.htm

William Trutt
Title: Account Executive **Company:** Carnall Insurance, Inc. **Address:** 67 Wall Street, Norwalk, CT 06850 United States **BUS:** Insurance Company **P/S:** Commercial and Personal Insurance, Life and Health Insurance, Employee Benefits **MA:** Regional **D/D/R:** managing the commercial line of property and casualty insurance and ensuring customer satisfaction **H/I/S:** Golfing, Playing Softball **EDU:** Bachelor's Degree in Communication, Mount St. Mary's College(1994)
Email: wtrutt@carnallinsurance.com
URL: http://www.carnallinsurance.com

Cynthia Tsang
Title: Help Desk Team Lead **Company:** Wolverine Trading, LLC **Address:** 175 W. Jackson Boulevard, Suite 200, Chicago, IL 60604 United States **BUS:** Trading Firm **P/S:** Hardware, Software, Accounting, Intranet **MA:** International **D/D/R:** Managing Information Technology, Project Planning **H/I/S:** Traveling, Biking **EDU:** Bachelor's Degree in Computer Science and Information Systems, DePaul University (2001) **A/A/S:** National Honor Society **C/VW:** Metro Squash Holy Trinity
Email: ctsang@wolve.com
URL: http://www.wolve.com

Donna M. Tsubochi
Title: Registered Physical Therapist **Company:** Glendale Advantis Home Health Agency **Address:** 23928 Arroyo Park Drive, Unit 113, Valencia, CA 91355 United States **BUS:** Home Healthcare Agency **P/S:** Home Healthcare Services **MA:** Regional **EXP:** Ms. Tsubochi's expertise is in orthopedics. **D/D/R:** treating patients with neurological disorders **H/I/S:** Playing Basketball, Attending the Theater **EDU:** Master of Arts in Anatomy, University of Southern California (1971); Bachelor of Science in Physical Therapy, Loma Linda University (1969) **CERTS:** Certification Program in Orthopedics, Neurology and Scoliosis, American Physical Therapy Association **A/A/S:** American Physical Therapy Association
Email: donnam.tsubochi@cwwemail.com

Noel E. Tuazon
Title: President **Company:** Net Enterprises, Inc **Address:** 23441 Golden Springs Drive, Suite 480, Diamond Bar, CA 91765 United States **BUS:** Payroll Services **P/S:** Company Payroll Execution, Finance **MA:** National **D/D/R:** Specializing in Maintaining Business Growth, Interacting and Enlightening New Businesses about the Company **EDU:** Bachelor of Science in Industrial Engineering **A/A/S:** Living Waters Christian Fellowship, Compassion International
URL: http://www.cambridgewhoswho.com

Sandee Tuck
Title: Owner **Company:** Sandee's Candee's, Creator of SPUD Fudge **Address:** 28 Industrial Lane, Salmon, ID 83467 United States **BUS:** Food Production Company **P/S:** Creamy Sugarless Potato Fudge **MA:** International **EXP:** Ms. Tuck's expertise is in operations management. **H/I/S:** Traveling, Spending Time with her Grandchildren, Volunteering **EDU:** High School Diploma **A/A/S:** Local Chamber of Commerce; Special Guest, Every Woman's Conference **A/H:** Nominee, Business Woman of the Year Award, ID; Most Popular Dessert Made with Potatoes, Potato Bowl **C/VW:** City Lights; Boise Rescue Mission
Email: sandee@spudfudge.com
URL: http://www.spudfudge.com

Mr. Chuck E. Tucker
Title: Grounds Supervisor, Security Manager **Company:** Willamette View **Address:** 12705 S.E. River Road, Portland, OR 97222 United States **BUS:** Congenial Continuing Care Residential Community Dedicated to Excellence in Senior Retirement **P/S:** Independent Living, Assisted Living, Skilled Nursing Facilities, Sports Center, Putting Greens, Tennis Courts, Koi Ponds, Theater, Shopping, Furniture Stores, Pools, Saunas **MA:** Regional **D/D/R:** Offering Public and Customer Service, Acting First Responder for Any and All of the 625 Residents for Any Needs, Managing Security System, Tracking Census Reports of Residents, Daily Scheduling for Landscapers, Overseeing Six Direct Reports for Groundskeepers and Six Direct Reports for Armed Security, Speaking to Residents Bi-Annually on Landscaping Projects and Security Techniques **H/I/S:** Golfing, Tennis, Beach Combing **EDU:** Graduated Gresham High School (1973); Certified with the Department of Public Safeties and Standards for Oregon (2005); Certified by MEDICO in High Security Locks (1999) **A/A/S:** Volunteer, Annie Ross Halfway House in the Community
Email: chuckt@willametteview.org
URL: http://www.williametteview.org

Mrs. Karen Lavon Tucker
Title: Registered Nurse **Company:** JPS Health Network **Dept:** Cancer Care Center **Address:** 229 E. Cunningham Avenue, Crowley, TX 76036 United States **BUS:** Healthcare Center **P/S:** Healthcare and Medical Education **MA:** Regional **D/D/R:** Treating Patients who have Cancer, Performing Chemotherapy Infusions, Writing Reports, Administering Medications **H/I/S:** Camping, Country Western Dancing, Spending Time with her Grandchildren **EDU:** Bachelor's Degree in Registered Nursing, Hardin-Simmons University, Methodist School of Nursing (1970) **A/A/S:** Oncology Nursing Society
Email: ptucker251@sbcglobal.net
URL: http://www.jpshealthnet.org

Rosita Tucker
Title: Chief Executive Officer **Company:** Chemphase Corporation, Inc. **Address:** P.O Box 495513, Garland, TX 75049 United States **BUS:** Electrical Company **P/S:** Semiconductor Equipments **MA:** International **D/D/R:** Marketing, Overseeing Daily Operations Including Accounts Payable and Accounts Receivable, Managing All Human Resource Functions, Supervising Staff **H/I/S:** Listening to Music **EDU:** Bachelor's Degree in Civil Engineering, University of Bologna, Italy (1994)
Email: sat.tucker@comcast.net

Maribeth Tuckerman
Title: Operations Manager **Company:** Clair David Interiors **Address:** 6540 W. Central Avenue, Toledo, OH 43617 United States **BUS:** Office Furnishing and Design Company **P/S:** Contemporary and Traditional Office Furnishings Designed to Meet Both Individual and Complete Office Needs **MA:** Regional **D/D/R:** Overseeing Marketing and Advertising, Working in Sales, Entering Orders, Bookkeeping, Invoicing, Managing All Back End Functions **H/I/S:** Spending Time with her Expanding Family **EDU:** College Coursework in Marine Biology **A/A/S:** Women's Entrepreneurial Network
Email: mtuckerman@clairdavid.com
URL: http://www.clairdavid.com

Stephen M. Tulli
Title: Science and Technology Education Instructor **Company:** Ayer Public School, Ayer High School **Address:** 141 Washington Street, Ayer, MA 01432 United States **BUS:** Public High School **P/S:** General Secondary Curriculum, Science and Technology Programs, Arts, Music, Physical Education, Learning Resources, Student Support Services, Athletics, Extracurricular Activities, Student Clubs and Organizations **MA:** Regional **D/D/R:** Teaching Chemistry, Technology, Engineering and Transportation, Designing Technology Preparation Program for College-Bound Students, Sponsoring School Programs, **H/I/S:** Golfing, Tennis, Coaching Soccer **EDU:** Master of Science in School Administration, Fitchburg State College (1995); Bachelor of Science in Chemistry, Fitchburg State College (1991) **A/A/S:** National Education Association; Massachusetts Teachers Association; Ayer Education Foundation; Sponsor, Ayer High School Leadership Program; Sponsor, Ayer Highs School Broadcasting Club; Massachusetts Army National Guard; Sponsor, Ayer High School Broadcasting Club; Air Public Access Corporation
Email: stullie@ayer.k12.ma.us
URL: http://www.ayer.k12.ma.us/hs/hs_home.cfm

Tinmar Tun
Title: MD **Company:** Tun Pediatric Center **Address:** 450 76th Street, Brooklyn, NY 11209 United States **BUS:** Medical Office Solo Practice **P/S:** Multi-Cultural Pediatric Services **MA:** Local **D/D/R:** Pediatrics **H/I/S:** Being with Her Children **EDU:** MD in Pediatrics, Brooklyn Medical Center **A/A/S:** Pediatric Association, Buddhist Temple
Email: timitun@yahoo.com

Glenn Tunstull
Title: Fine Artist **Company:** Tunstull Studio **Address:** P.O. Box 264, Claverack, NY 12513 United States **BUS:** Art Studio **P/S:** Creating Artwork, Publishing Prints and Note Cards **MA:** International sales and exhibitions **D/D/R:** Oil Painting, Fine Art Painting, Publishing Prints and Note Cards, Illustrating Water Colors **H/I/S:** Gardening, Movies, International Travel, Cards **EDU:** Associate Degree Program in Fashion Illustration, Parsons The New School for Design **A/A/S:** Berkshire County Craft Guild; FIT; CCCA Kent Art Assoc; Oil Painters of America **C/VW:** Local Schools, Teaching Art Classes, Pratt Institute teach at marist college
Email: tunstullstudio@aol.com
URL: http://www.tunstullstudio.com

Andrew R. Turcotte, RN, CFRN, CCEMT-P, FP-C, EMS-I
Title: Flight Paramedic, Registered Nurse **Company:** Lifeflight of Maine **Address:** 44330 Mercure Circle, Suite 260, Dulles, VA 20166 United States **BUS:** Nonprofit Organization **P/S:** Healthcare Services **MA:** Regional **D/D/R:** educating physicians, nurses and emergency medical technicians on emergency medical services, overseeing patient management, public relations, triage education, critical care nursing and air medical services **H/I/S:** Playing Baseball **CERTS:** Registered Nurse, Excelsior College, Albany, NY (2005)
Email: aturcotte@phihelico.com
URL: http://www.phihelico.com

Caprice Turek
Title: Sales Manager **Company:** Palecek **Address:** Fort Meyers, FL 33908 United States **BUS:** Wholesale Import Business **P/S:** Home Furnishings, Furniture, Lighting and Accessories, Natural Materials Including Wicker, Rattan, Leather, Wood and Bamboo **MA:** National **D/D/R:** Importing Wicker and High-End Home Furnishing Products, Consulting with Buyers **H/I/S:** Boating **EDU:** College Coursework
Email: turek321@comcast.net
URL: http://www.palecek.com

Mrs. Donna Sue Turk
Title: Behavior Health Case Manager **Company:** Wellmark Blue Cross and Blue Shield of Iowa **Dept:** Health Management **Address:** 3012 340th Street, Anita, IA 50020 United States **BUS:** Health Insurance Company **P/S:** Health Insurance Services **MA:** IA, SD **D/D/R:** Registered Nurse with Extensive Experience in Working with Patients of all Ages, Skilled in Complex Assessment of the Whole Individual, Complex Discharge Planning, Cost-Effective Management of Inpatient, Outpatient and Alternative Services, Admirable Background Practice in Child, Adolescent Day Treatment School, Inpatient Services, Adult Outpatient Mental Health and Chemical Dependency Services, Emergency Room Evaluations, Utilization Review of Services, Community Education, Evaluations, Marketing, Telephonic Utilization and Case Management and Managing Inpatient Geriatric Behavioral Health Services, Facilitating a Team-Centered Culture, Behavioral Health Management **H/I/S:** Gardening, Landscaping, Antiquing **EDU:** Pursuing Master of Business Administration, Capella University; College Coursework, Bellevue, NE (1999); Associate Degree in Registered Nursing, Southwestern Community College (1992); Practical Nursing Degree, Iowa Western Community College (1991) **A/A/S:** American Psychiatric Nurses Association
Email: donnasueturk@yahoo.com
URL: http://www.wellmark.com

Cassandra Turner
Title: English Teacher **Company:** Paul Robeson High School **Address:** 6835 S. Normal Boulevard, Chicago, IL 60621 United States **BUS:** High School **P/S:** Secondary Education **MA:** Local **D/D/R:** teaching English with an emphasis on vocabulary skills **H/I/S:** Reading, Attending the Health Club, Roller Skating, Swimming, Walking **EDU:** Bachelor of Arts in English, Chicago State University; Master of Art in Education, with a Concentration on Curriculum and Instruction, Olivet Nazarene University **A/A/S:** Association for Supervision and Curriculum Development; National Council of Teachers of English **C/VW:** Local School
Email: cturner696@aol.com
URL: http://www.cambridgewhoswho.com

Deborah F. Turner
Title: Deputy Director **Company:** Montgomery County Emergency Communication District 911 **Address:** P.O. Box 1830, Conroe, TX 77305 United States **BUS:** Public Safety Agency **P/S:** Emergency Services **MA:** Local **D/D/R:** Accounting, Purchasing, Human Resources, 911 Networking, Maintaining the Equipment Behind the Scenes **H/I/S:** Camping, Hiking, Fishing, Alternative Medicine, Cooking, Gardening **EDU:** Bachelor's Degree in Business Administration, Minor in Accounting and Law, Sam Houston State University; Certified Texas Purchasing Manager **A/A/S:** National Emergency Number Association; Associated Public Communications Officer; Professional of Human Resource; American Records Management Association; Public Funds Investment; Lions Club; Committee Member, Texas NENA Group
Email: dturner@mc911.org

Florida Lillian Turner, LD, MBA
Title: Independent Business Owner **Company:** AmeriPlan **Address:** 23805 S. Kurt Lane, Crete, IL 60417 United States **BUS:** Discount Medical Plan Organization **P/S:** Medical, Vision, Prescription, Dental and Chiropractic Supplemental Benefit Plans **MA:** National **D/D/R:** Offering Health Savings for Clients and Opportunities for Future Business Owners, Offering People Discount Health Plans for Medical, Dental, Vision, Prescriptions and Chiropractic Care **H/I/S:** Reading, Walking, Traveling **EDU:** Master of Business Administration, Roosevelt University, Chicago, IL (1978); Bachelor of Science in Foods and Nutrition, Southern University, Baton Rouge, LA **A/A/S:** United Methodist Church; Board President, CCA Academy
Email: flturner12@yahoo.com
URL: http://www.iboplus.com/fturner
URL: http://www.iboplus.com/11077906

Kelli R. Turner
Title: President **Company:** Heavenly Touch Day Spa, Inc **Address:** 500 S Grandstaff Drive, Auburn, IN 46706 United States **BUS:** Massage Therapy Spa **P/S:** Offers and Provides Full Service **MA:** Local **D/D/R:** Massage, Deep Tissues, Nail Tech, Tanning, Hot Tubs **H/I/S:** Gardening **EDU:** Center for Vital Living, Southern Ohio College

Mary V. Turner
Title: House Manager, Caregiver **Company:** Turner Rentals and Cleaning Service **Address:** 316 Branded Boulevard, Kokomo, IN 46901 United States **BUS:** Caregiving Facility **P/S:** Caregiving **MA:** Local **D/D/R:** Caring for the Elderly, House Cleaning **H/I/S:** Quilting **EDU:** College Coursework, Certified Public Accountant, Clearly College
Email: mvturner1@juno.com
URL: http://www.cambridgewhoswho.com

Rebecca Turner
Title: Pharmacist **Company:** 1) Bedford Regional Medical Center 2) Pharmacy Systems, Inc. **Address:** 3009 Illinois Street, Apartment A, Bedford, IN 47421 United States **BUS:** 1) Medical Center 2) Pharmacy **P/S:** 1) Healthcare 2) Pharmaceuticals **MA:** Regional **D/D/R:** Reviewing All Drug Orders from Doctors, Clarifying Questions Regarding Orders, Ensuring that Patient's Receive the Proper Medicine at the Proper Dose, Filling Prescriptions, Educating Patients, overseeing Pharmaceutical Operations **H/I/S:** Reading, Biking **EDU:** Doctor of Pharmacy, Purdue University (2005) **A/A/S:** American Pharmaceutical Association; American Society of Health-System Pharmacists
Email: purdueurx@yahoo.com
URL: http://www.cambridgewhoswho.com

Teddi Lane Turner
Title: Campus Dean **Company:** Strayer University **Address:** 100 Mansell Court E., Suite 100, Roswell, GA 30076 United States **BUS:** University Adult Education **P/S:** Higher Education **MA:** International **D/D/R:** Law and Business, Managing Operations **EDU:** Doctorate Degree in Law, Faulkner University; Master's Degree in Education, University of Phoenix (2004)
Email: tturner@strayer.edu
Email: teddi.turner@cwwemail.com
URL: http://www.strayer.edu

Sue Turteltaub
Title: Senior Systems Analyst, Programmer, Supervisor **Company:** Hydranautics **Address:** 401 Jones Road, Oceanside, CA 92058 United States **BUS:** Manufacturing Company **P/S:** Water Filter Manufacturing **MA:** International **EXP:** Ms. Turteltaub's expertise includes information technology and AS/400 system analysis. **H/I/S:** Gardening, Camping, Fishing **EDU:** Associate Degree in Accounting, Miramar College; Diploma, Mira Mesa High School **A/A/S:** Oceans **A/H:** Employee of the Year Award **C/VW:** Temecula United Methodist Church; Bread from Heaven Food Pantry
Email: sturtletaub@hydranautics.com
URL: http://www.hydranautics.com

John Tussey
Title: Professional Musician, Private Music Instructor, Composer, Recording Artist **Company:** Keyboard Artistry **Address:** P.O. Box 860688, Wahiawa, HI 96786 United States **BUS:** Music Company **P/S:** Music Instruction, Entertainment Services Including Background Tracks, Recording, Professional Song Writing, Music Publication, Relaxation, Gospel, Contemporary Christian, Blues, Pop, Rock and Jazz Music **MA:** International **EXP:** Mr. Tussey's expertise includes piano playing, music theory, improvisation and contemporary music composition. **H/I/S:** Exercising, Hiking, Traveling, Fishing **EDU:** College Coursework **A/A/S:** Filipino Chamber of Commerce of Hawaii; Honolulu Piano Teachers Association; The American Society of Composers, Authors and Publishers **C/VW:** Local Church
Email: keyboardhawaiiblue@yahoo.com
URL: http://www.myspace.com/johntussey

Katherine L. Tuttle
Title: Instructor **Company:** Alief Elsik High School **Address:** 12601 High Star Drive, Houston, TX 77072 United States **BUS:** Public School **P/S:** Education **MA:** Regional **D/D/R:** English III Team Leader, Advanced Placement Language & Composition **H/I/S:** Working with Stained Glass, Painting, Reading, Traveling **EDU:** Bachelor of Arts in Liberal Arts, English and History, University of Houston; Teaching Certification, University of Houston at Victoria **A/A/S:** Phi Kappa Phi Honors Fraternity **C/VW:** Church
Email: katherine.tuttle-garcia@aliefisd.net

Alison Z. Twersky, MS
Title: Teacher, Counselor **Company:** Palmdale School District **Address:** 39149 10th Street E., Palmdale, CA 93552 United States **BUS:** Public School District **P/S:** Educational Services **MA:** Regional **D/D/R:** Teaching Seventh and Eighth-Grade Literature **H/I/S:** Knitting, Reading, Traveling, Spending Time with her Family **EDU:** Pursuing Doctorate in Education; Master of Science in General Education, University of La Verne (1996) **A/A/S:** American Counseling Association; American School Counselors Association
Email: alistars@yahoo.com
URL: http://www.psd.k12.ca.us

Mr. John D. Tye
Title: Manager **Company:** Bishop's Store House **Address:** 4400 Presidential Place N.E., Albuquerque, NM 87109 United States **BUS:** Food Service Company **P/S:** Canned Goods and Produce **MA:** Regional **D/D/R:** Educational Leadership and Administration **H/I/S:** Hiking, Camping **EDU:** Bachelor's Degree in Education, University of New Mexico (1971)
Email: heyjudetee@aol.com

Cynthia M. Tyler
Title: Kindergarten Educator **Company:** Unified School District of Antigo **Address:** W11141 County Road HH, Antigo, WI 54409 United States **BUS:** School District **P/S:** Education **MA:** Local **D/D/R:** Working with 22 Students in Kindergarten Subject Matter and Specialties, Reading K-12 **H/I/S:** Playing Golf, Practicing Archery, Gardening, Spending Time Outdoors **EDU:** Master's Degree in Reading, University of Tulsa; Bachelor's Degree in Early Childhood Development and Elementary Education, Rockford College **A/A/S:** National Education Association; Wisconsin Education Association; National Board Certification Association **A/H:** Blue Ribbon for her School, No Child Left Behind; Two-Time Wisconsin New Promise School
Email: ctyler@antigo.k12.wi.us
URL: http://www.cambridgewhoswho.com

Jera G. Tyler
Title: High School English Teacher **Company:** Hominy High School **Address:** 200 S. Pettit, Hominy, OK 74035 United States **BUS:** High School **P/S:** Education **MA:** Local **D/D/R:** Teaching English, Teaching Bible History Studies **H/I/S:** Traveling, Reading **EDU:** Bachelor of Science in English and Theology, Mid-America Bible College **A/A/S:** Who's Who Among American Teachers (2003-2004) **A/H:** Nominatee, Who's Who Among American Teachers (2004-2006) **C/VW:** Calvery Worship Center
Email: tylerjair@aol.com
URL: http://www.cambridgewhoswho.com

Erin L. Tyner
Title: Financial Aid Officer, Assistant Business Manager **Company:** Vistamar School **Address:** 737 Hawaii Street, El Segundo, CA 90245 United States **BUS:** Independent High School Facility Dedicated to Excellence in Education **P/S:** Regular Core Curriculum including Reading, Mathematics, Science, Social Studies, Art, Music, History, Languages, Accounting, Finance **MA:** National **D/D/R:** Financial Aid Officer Handling Accounts Payable, Accounts Receivable, Legal Situations, Purchasing, Building Loans, Personal Finances, Taxes, Employee Insurance Benefits, Workers' Compensation, Student Screening, Audits, Accounting, Retirement Plans, Finger Printing Laws for Students, Personal Finances for Students **H/I/S:** Reading **EDU:** Bachelor's Degree in English Literature and Irish Studies, Pitzer College (2004); One Year of Graduate School, Claremont Graduate University; Pursuing Online Courses in Accounting **A/A/S:** National Association of Independent Schools; Creative Writing in College; Lecturing to Small Groups of Students and Parents Occasionally
Email: erintyner@vistamarschool.org
URL: http://www.vistamarschool.org

Jane Tyree Lowe
Title: High School History Teacher **Company:** Hamilton County High School **Address:** 12020 CR 137 N, Wellborn, FL 32094 United States **BUS:** High School **P/S:** Education **MA:** Regional **D/D/R:** Mentoring and Teaching High School Children, Mentoring Young Teachers **H/I/S:** Reading, Traveling, Gardening **EDU:** Bachelor of Science in History Education **A/H:** District Teacher of the Year (2003); Echol's Company Teacher of the Year (1980)
Email: lowe_j@firn.edu
URL: http://www.cambridgewhoswho.com

Karen K. Tyznik
Title: Emotional and Behavioral Difficulties Teacher **Company:** Colby High School **Address:** 705 N. Second Street, Colby, WI 54421 United States **BUS:** High School **P/S:** Education **MA:** Local **D/D/R:** Teaching Special Needs High School Students, Specializing in Reading **H/I/S:** Reading, Gardening, Watching Sports **EDU:** Bachelor of Science Plus 24 in Emotional and Behavioral Difficulties, University of Wisconsin-Eau Claire; Bachelor's Degree in Elementary Education, University of Wisconsin-Eau Claire **A/A/S:** Wisconsin Indian Education Association **C/VW:** Library Board, Local Fire Department, Emergency Medical Technician Volunteer
Email: chris101@centurytel.net
URL: http://www.cambridgewhoswho.com

Dr. Valentina Ugolini
Title: Founding Partner **Company:** Willowbrook Cardiovascular Associates **Address:** 13300 Hargrave Road, Suite 500, Houston, TX 77070 United States **BUS:** Healthcare Center **P/S:** Healthcare **MA:** Regional **D/D/R:** Preventing Cardiovascular Disease and Sudden Death, Cardiac and Vascular Diagnostic Imaging, Specializing in Congestive Heart Failure and Cardiovascular Diseases in Women, Offering General Non-Invasive Cardiology, Reading Ultrasounds, Making Hospital Rounds, Seeing Patients in the Clinic and in the Intensive Care Unit **H/I/S:** Walking, hiking, bike riding Travel, photography, art, science and technology **EDU:** MD, Earned in Italy; Board Certified in Internal Medicine; Board Certified in Cardiology; Licensed Medical Practitioner, States of Texas and California **A/A/S:** Fellow, American College Cardiology; Fellow, American College of Physicians; Member, Harris County Medical Society; Fellow, Texas Chapter of the American College of Cardiology **C/VW:** Chairman of the Texas Arrhythmia Institute, a Nonprofit foundation dedicated to research and education to fight heart rhythm disorders and sudden death Member of the DeBakey Heart Center Council, The Methodist Hospital
Email: vugolini@gmail.com

Heather L. Ujhely
Title: Physical Therapist **Company:** Genesis Rehab **BUS:** Rehabilitation Center **P/S:** Rehabilitation Services **MA:** Eastern U.S. **D/D/R:** Offering General Rehabilitation, Physical Therapy **H/I/S:** Watching Sports **EDU:** Master of Science in Physical Therapy, Richard Stockton College; Bachelor of Science in Biology, Richard Stockton College **A/A/S:** American Physical Therapy Association
Email: bsktbal78@aol.com

Nnene O. Ukoha
Title: Certified Registered Nurse Practitioner **Company:** Stella Maris, Inc. **Address:** 6523 Redgate Circle, Baltimore, MD 21228 United States **BUS:** Nursing Home **P/S:** Sub-Acute and Long-Term Nursing Care, Hospice Care **MA:** Local **EXP:** Ms. Ukoha's expertise is in nursing. **H/I/S:** Spending Time with her Family, Traveling **EDU:** Master of Science in Nursing, Salisbury University; Geriatric Nurse Practitioner, Baltimore, Maryland **A/A/S:** American Nurses Association; Sigma Theta Tau **C/VW:** Local Charitable Organizations; The Salvation Army; Veterans of Foreign Wars; Disabled American Veterans
Email: nneneu@netzero.net
URL: http://www.cambridgewhoswho.com

John A. Ulibarri
Title: Owner **Company:** Long John Silver Turquoise Treasure Chest of Santa Fe **Address:** 115 E. San Fransisco Street, Santa Fe, NM 87501 United States **BUS:** Retail Store **P/S:** Native American Items Including Jewelry, Rugs, Antiques and Pottery **MA:** National **EXP:** Mr. Ulibarri's expertise is in sales management. **D/D/R:** Selling Indian Jewelry, Traveling around the Country for Trade Shows **H/I/S:** Fishing, Swimming **EDU:** College Coursework **A/A/S:** Santa Fe Fiesta Council; The Benevolent and Protective Order of Elks of the USA **C/VW:** Local Charitable Organization; Boy Scouts of America; Girl Scouts of the United States of America
Email: silvercomp@msn.com
URL: http://www.cambridgewhoswho.com

Craig C. Ullock
Title: Physical Therapist **Company:** Physical Therapy Professionals **Address:** 66 Stanley Street, Mt Morris, NY 14510 United States **BUS:** Healthcare Orthopedics **P/S:** Physical Therapy Outpatient **MA:** Local **D/D/R:** Physical Therapy **H/I/S:** Sports, Spending Time with Family **EDU:** Bachelor of Science in Physical Therapy, Daemen College
Email: cullock@rochester.rr.com

Dawnya Underwood
Title: Licensed Social Worker, Founder **Company:** Underwood Consulting Group **Address:** P.O. Box 8006, Chicago, IL 60680 United States **BUS:** Social Service, Family Support and Mental Health Services Organization **P/S:** Individual and Family Counseling with Specialties in Trauma and Loss; Treating Children Aged 0-6 Years; Programs Offered: Parent Mentoring, My Creative Voice, and Toys, Books, And Games; Services Offered: Comprehensive Clinical Mental Health Assessments, Client-Center Treatment Planning, Individual, Family and Group Therapy, Parent Mentoring, Quarterly Progress Reports, Training and Workshops, and Referrals and Linkages **MA:** Local **EXP:** Ms. Underwood's expertise includes child and family health, adolescent health, child welfare system, teen parenting, foster parenting, case management and home-based therapy for children. **H/I/S:** Traveling, Reading, Poetry, Health, Fitness, Sports **EDU:** Pursuing Certification, Irving B. Harris Infant Mental Healt, Erikson Institute in Chicago, IL; Masters of Social Work from the George Williams College of Social Work at Aurora University (2001); Bachelors of Criminal Justice from the University of Illinois at Chicago; Licensed Social Worker in the State of Illinois; Over Two Years of Postgraduate Clinical Experience in Social Work **A/A/S:** National Association of Social Workers; Illinois Association of Social Workers; Delegation Group- "People to People" Ambassador; Guest Speaker at DePaul University and Chicago State University on Sociology and Social Work; Full Time Practitioner at Metropolitan Family Services; Program Coordinator for the Chicago Safe Start Project; Conducts Workshops on Infant Mental Health, Children's Exposure to Violence, Social Work Practice, Family Support and Mental Health Services for Children Exposed to Violence and Trauma
Email: dawnya@underwoodconsultinggroup.com
URL: http://www.underwoodconsultinggroup.com

Joyce D. Underwood
Title: Art Teacher **Company:** Englewood Elementary **Address:** 900 Engle Drive, Orlando, FL 32807 United States **BUS:** Education **P/S:** Elementary School, Visual Arts, Music, World Culture, Humanities **MA:** Regional **D/D/R:** Teaching Basics of Drawing, Objectives and Elements of Art, Shapes, Textures, Multicultural Humanities Style of Teaching Including African, Celtic, Students to Critiques of Famous Artworks, Teaching Cartooning, Special Effects Make-Up Artist **H/I/S:** Theater, Ballet, Ballroom Dancing, Teaching Ballroom Dancing, Belly Dancing, Reading Books About Different Cultures **EDU:** Bachelor of Fine Arts, University of Central Florida (1975); Certified Visual Arts K-12 (1975) **A/H:** Peter Fetzer Award, Metropolitan Family Services (2005)
Email: darlenjoy1@aol.com

Cyndi A. Unger, GRI, CRS
Title: Realtor **Company:** United Real Estate Solutions **Address:** 835 Gordon Drive, Sioux City, IA 51101 United States **BUS:** Real Estate Broker **P/S:** Residential, Executive, Hi-End, Lake Front, New Construction, Condos, Gulf Homes, Gated **MA:** National **D/D/R:** Residential Real Estate **H/I/S:** Remodeling **A/A/S:** Iowa Association of Realtors; National Association of Realtors
Email: c21unger@aol.com
URL: http://www.realtor.com/cyndiunger

Shashank Upadhye
Title: VP-Head of Intellectual Property **Company:** Sandoz, Inc **Address:** 506 Carnegie Center, Princeton, NJ 08540 United States **BUS:** Intellectual Property: Patients and Trademarks Pharmaceuticals/Biotechnology **P/S:** Responsible for Managing the Portfolio of the Generic Drug Strategy for Sandoz's Domestic and Global Market **MA:** International **D/D/R:** Patents and Intellectual Property **H/I/S:** Skiing, Traveling, Spending Time with the Family **EDU:** Bachelor of Science in Bio Chemistry, Master of Business Administration, JD in Law, Brock University, John Marshall School of Law **CERTS:** Registered to Practice Law in New York, Illinois, Massachusetts and Indiana; Registered Patent Attorney **A/A/S:** AIPLA
Email: shashank.upadhye@novartis.com
URL: http://www.us.sandoz.com

Janet H. Upton
Title: Supply Chain Manager **Company:** AT&T **Address:** 2200 Glenview Avenue, Louisville, KY 40222 United States **BUS:** Telecommunications Company **P/S:** Telecommunications **MA:** International **D/D/R:** Managing Operations, Overseeing Telecommunications **H/I/S:** Riding her Motorcycle, Boating **EDU:** Licensed Pilot, Birmingham Flight School; Certified Scuba Diver **A/A/S:** Business and Professional Women, Louisville **C/VW:** Exploited Children's Help Organization
Email: jhupton@bellsouth.net
URL: http://www.cambridge.whoswho.com

Ethel M. Urbina
Title: Realtor **Company:** Sapphire Realty **Address:** 707 Mabbette Street, Kissimmee, FL 34741 United States **BUS:** Real Estate Real Estate **P/S:** Residential, Executive, Lakefront, Town Homes, Condos, Golf Homes, Senior, Gated **MA:** National **D/D/R:** Residential, Executive Homes, Lakefront, Town Homes, Golf Homes, Senior, Gated **H/I/S:** Gardening, Cooking **EDU:** San Francisco City College, CA, Bachelor of Science Accounting **A/A/S:** Florida State Association of Realtors, National Association of Realtors
Email: eurbina02@hotmail.com
URL: http://www.ethelurbina.com

Mr. Mark Allen Urquhart
Title: Vice President of Facilities, Design and Construction **Company:** University of Chicago Medical Center **Dept:** Facilities, Design and Construction Support Service **Address:** 5841 South Maryland Avenue, Chicago, IL 60637 United States **BUS:** Healthcare Provider **P/S:** Healthcare **MA:** International **D/D/R:** Working With Disadvantaged Youth, Responsible for Business Diversity/Construction Compliance **H/I/S:** Physical Fitness, Basketball, Track and Field **EDU:** Master of Business Administration, University of Chicago Graduate School of Business; Bachelor of Science, Indiana University of PA Chicago Urban League Beautiful People Award (2004); Chicago Cosmopolitan Chamber of Commerce 'E. Johnson' Service Excellence Award (2005); Black Contractors United (2006); Who's Who in Black Chicago (2007), Chicago Defender Men of Excellence Award(2007), Chicago United Business Leader of Color award (2007) **A/A/S:** American College of Healthcare Executives; Member, Chicago United; Certified Fire Protection Specialist, NFPA; Fellow, Leadership Greater Chicago; Member, American College of Healthcare Executives; Member, Lambda Alpha International, Ely Chapter, Land Economics Society; Member, National Association of Health Services Executives; Board Member, Ronald McDonald Charities, Chicago land/Northwestern IN Chapter; Board Member, Southside YMCA; Board Member, Chicago United Board **C/VW:** Ronald McDonald House Charters, South Side YMCA,,Uhlich Children's Advantage Network,University of Chicago Forefront Fund
Email: maurq1@aol.com
Email: mark.urquhart@uc.hospitlas.edu
URL: http://www.cambridgewhoswho.com

Ms. Marissa B. Usman
Title: Healthcare Coordinator **Company:** The Jefferson, Sunrise Senior Living **Address:** 7315 Farr Street, Annandale, VA 22003 United States **BUS:** Senior Living Center **P/S:** Healthcare, Hospice Care, Nursing and Rehabilitative Care for Senior Citizens **MA:** Local **D/D/R:** Administration, Management, Budgeting, Human Resources, Caring for Patients **H/I/S:** Swimming, Camping, Walking **EDU:** Bachelor's Degree in Nursing, Quezon Memorial Hospital School of Nursing, the Philippines; Registered Nurse **A/A/S:** Vice President, Philippine Nurses Association of Metropolitan Washington; American Nurses Association
Email: sanandmis2@cox.net
URL: http://www.sunriseseniorliving.com

Raymond M. Uttaro
Title: Emergency Service Coordinator **Company:** County of Nelson **Address:** 98 Courthouse Square, Lovinston, VA 22949 United States **BUS:** Emergency Response **P/S:** Search and Rescue, Emergency First Response **MA:** Regional **D/D/R:** Law Enforcement Communications, Search and Rescue Department **H/I/S:** Fresh Water Fishing **EDU:** High School Education; Hazardous Weather Preparedness Certification; First Response Medical Certification; Infection Control Certification; Certified Public Information Officer; Certified in Radiological Emergency Management; Certified in Hazardous Material for Medical Personnel; Certified Basic Thermographer **A/A/S:** American Society of Protection from Cruelty to Animals; Central Virginia Criminal Justice Society; Thomas Jefferson Emergency Medical Services
Email: ruttaro@nelsoncounty.org
URL: http://www.nelsoncounty.org

Sunday Uwubiti
Title: President **Company:** Nursing resources Network, LLC **Address:** 8133 N. 107th Street, Unit R, Milwaukee, WI 53224 United States **BUS:** Staffing Agency **P/S:** Recruitment Services **MA:** Statewide **EXP:** Mr. Uwubiti's expertise includes administration, marketing, web design, hosting, computer repair, tax filing and preparation. **H/I/S:** Traveling **EDU:** Master of Business Administration in Finance, New York University; Bachelor of Science in Nursing, Bellin College of Nursing **A/A/S:** American Nurses Association
Email: myafrospace@yahoo.com
URL: http://www.cambridgewhoswho.com

Gaylene T. Uyemura
Title: Third-Grade Teacher **Company:** Running Creek Elementary School **Address:** 900 S. Elbert Street, P.O. Box 550, Elizabeth, CO 80107 United States **BUS:** Elementary School **P/S:** Primary Education and Extracurricular Activities **MA:** Regional **D/D/R:** Teaching Third-Grade Students, Organizing Social Development Classes **H/I/S:** Reading, Traveling, Sports, Supporting the Denver Broncos **EDU:** Bachelor's Degree in Elementary Education and Speech Communication, University of Southern Colorado (1976) **A/A/S:** Cultural Arts Committee; Science Committee; Language Arts Committee; Yearbook Committee
Email: gayluym@aol.com
URL: http://www.cambridgewhoswho.com

Margaret F. Vail
Title: Professor of English (Retired) **Company:** Xavier University of Louisiana **Address:** 1 Drexel Drive, New Orleans, LA 70130 United States **BUS:** University **P/S:** Education **MA:** National **D/D/R:** Teaching Renaissance and Victorian Literature **H/I/S:** Caring for Animals **EDU:** Doctorate, Latin and 19th Century British Literature, Tulane University **A/A/S:** Various Organizations **C/VW:** Various Charitable Organizations
Email: mvail7@aol.com
URL: http://www.trafford.com

Laura M. Valdez
Title: First Grade Teacher **Company:** Paramount Unified School District, Harry Wirtz School **Address:** 137 Beach Street, Montebello, CA 90640 United States **BUS:** Single Track Year-Round School **P/S:** Education for Students in Kindergarten through Eighth-Grade, Development of Young Minds in Preparation for Secondary Schooling **MA:** Regional **D/D/R:** Teaching Open Court Reading Programs, Working on Mathematics and English Language Development, Monitoring and Reporting Attendance, Meeting with Parents, Running the Afterschool Student Assistance Program, Administering WRAT Tests Learning about the Cooperative Group Called the Professional Learning Collaboration **H/I/S:** Watching Movies, Attending her Children's Sporting Events, Walking **EDU:** Master of Science in Liberal Arts, Mount Saint. Mary's College; Bachelor's Degree in Liberal Arts, Minor in English (1990), Mount St. Mary's College; Certification in Administration, California State University at Fullerton (2006); Teaching Credentials, California State University at Dominguez Hills (1997) Master of Science **A/A/S:** California Teachers Association; Student Needs Program; Leadership Team; Student Review Team **A/H:** Teacher of the Year (2000)
Email: lvaldez@paramount.k12.ca.us
URL: http://www.paramount.k12.ca.us/schools/wirtz.html

Jaime P. Valdivieso
Title: Quality Engineer **Company:** Balseal Engineering **Address:** 19650 Pauling, Foothill Ranch, CA 92610 United States **BUS:** Manufacturing **P/S:** High Precision Seals **MA:** International **D/D/R:** Quality Engineering **H/I/S:** Reading Science Fiction **EDU:** Dual Associate of Arts Degree in CAD/CAM and Machine Technology, Santa Ana College; Certified Quality Engineer, American Society of Quality; Black Belt Six Sigma-Six Sigmnius **A/A/S:** American Society of Quality
Email: jvaldivieso@balseal.com
URL: http://www.balseal.com

Maricza Valentin
Title: Vice President, Artistic Director **Company:** Latin Rhythms Academy of Dance and Performance **Address:** 210 N. Racine Avenue, Chicago, IL 60607 United States **BUS:** Dance Academy **P/S:** Latin Dance Instruction for All Ages, Performing Arts **MA:** Regional **D/D/R:** Dance Education **H/I/S:** Making Jewelry, Walking Dogs **EDU:** Bachelor's Degree in Dance, Columbia College **A/A/S:** West Loop Organization; Chicago Latino Network **C/VW:** American Society for the Prevention of Cruelty to Animals, People for the Ethical Treatment of Animals
Email: maricza@latinrhythmsdance.com
URL: http://www.latinrhythmsdance.com

Ms. Mary Jo Valentine
Title: Oncology Clinical Nurse Specialist **Company:** Memorial Hospital of South Bend **Address:** 615 N. Michigan Street, South Bend, IN 46601 United States **BUS:** Hospital **P/S:** Healthcare **MA:** Regional **D/D/R:** Monitoring and Educating Patients and Staff, Treating Patients Using Evidence-Based Practice Issues, Scheduling, budgeting, managing human resources, conducting training for chemotherapy and biotherapy treatments **H/I/S:** Reading, Spending Time with her Family **EDU:** Master of Science in Nursing, Indiana University-Purdue University Indianapolis (2005); Bachelor's Degree in Nursing, Indiana University South Bend (1996) **CERTS:** Certified Oncology Nurse; Clinical Nurse Specialist **A/A/S:** Oncology Care Committee; Clinical Nurse Specialist Group; Oncology Nursing Society; National Association of Clinical Nurse Specialists
Email: mvalentine@memorialsb.org
URL: http://www.qualityoflife.org

Mr. Michael S. Valik
Title: Manager **Company:** V-Centrum Dental, LLC **Dept:** Administrative **Address:** 1225 Vine Street, Suite 401, Philadelphia, PA 19107 United States **BUS:** General Dentistry Company **P/S:** General Dentistry Services to Small Businesses and Unions **MA:** Local **D/D/R:** Overseeing Staff, Offering Scheduling, Ordering of Supplies, Managing Payments, Ensuring Customer Satisfaction, **H/I/S:** Camping, Reading, Writing, Photography, Music studies, Dining. **EDU:** Bachelor's Degree in Philosophy and Religion, Temple University (2006) **A/A/S:** Golden Key International Honor Society
Email: vcentrumdental@comcast.net

Margaret Vallhonrat
Title: Registered Nurse, Advanced Legal Nurse Consultant, Administration **Company:** New Health Care **Address:** 10825 S.W. 75th Street, Miami, FL 33173 United States **BUS:** Home Healthcare Agency **P/S:** Home Healthcare Aides, Skilled Nursing **MA:** Local **EXP:** Ms. Vallhonrat's expertise is in nursing. **D/D/R:** overseeing administrative duties, daily operations, paralegal duties and medical transcription, treating geriatric patients, processing claims including insurance billing, Medicare and Medicaid billing **H/I/S:** Reading, Traveling, Spending Time with her Family **EDU:** Bachelor of Science in Nursing, University of Miami (1983) **CERTS:** Pursuing License in Medical Transcription; Certified Legal Nurse Consultant (2007); Registered Nurse **A/A/S:** Sigma Theta Tau; American Association of Legal Nurse Consultants
Email: bottm@bellsouth.net

Nicole J. Valliere
Title: Manager, Practice Development **Company:** REM Medical **Address:** 10611 N. Hauden Road, Building G Suite 102, Scottsdale, AZ 85260 United States **BUS:** Leader in Sleep Services **P/S:** Full Service Sleep Medicine Clinics to Diagnose and Treat the entire Range of Sleep-Wake Disorders **MA:** Regional **D/D/R:** Specializing in Marketing, Sales and Business Development **H/I/S:** Cycling, Hiking, Running **EDU:** Bachelor of Science in Business Management, University of Colorado **A/A/S:** Medical Marketers Association; Public Speaking on a Local Level
Email: nvalliere@remmedical.com
URL: http://www.remmedical.com

Maria Valverde
Title: Community Alternative Sentencing **Company:** Help of Southern Nevada **Address:** 1640 E. Flemingo Road, Suite 100, Las Vegas, NV 89119 United States **BUS:** Nonprofit Organization **P/S:** Human Services, Community Alternative Sentencing **MA:** Nevada **D/D/R:** Checking Clients Report, Managing nonprofit Organization, Handling Community Service Compliance **H/I/S:** Reading **EDU:** Industry-Related Training; High School Diploma **A/A/S:** Las Vegas Chamber of Commerce; Human Trafficking; Volunteer, Senior Locations and Various Events
Email: mvalverde@helpsonv.org
URL: http://www.helpsonv.org

Agnes Marie Van De Weghe, CNA
Title: General Partner **Company:** Higher Endeavors **Address:** W4640 Center Road W., Winter, WI 54896 United States **BUS:** Home Care Agency **P/S:** Holistic Healing **MA:** Local **D/D/R:** Hands-On Healing, Working with Herbs, Preventative Care, Spiritual Healing **H/I/S:** Walking, Spending Time Outdoors, Gardening, Reading **EDU:** Certified Nurses Assistant, Northcentral Technical College (2006); Coursework, Lombard East College
Email: av.higherndeavors@yahoo.com

Elizabeth Van Duyne
Title: Marketing Manager **Company:** Hypertherm, Inc. **Address:** 2 Technology Drive, West Lebanon, NH 03784 United States **BUS:** Manufacturing Company **P/S:** Plasma Metal Cutting Equipment **MA:** International **D/D/R:** Marketing, Advertising, Handling Communications, Demonstrating Vehicles, Channel Partner Training, Managing Sales Promotions and Programs **H/I/S:** Reading, Exercising **EDU:** Bachelor's Degree in Business, Norwich University, Northfield, VT **A/A/S:** American Marketing Association; Trade Show Exhibitors Association; American Welding Society; Canadian Welding Association **C/VW:** March of Dimes; Special Olympics; Philanthropy Team, Hypertherm; Everybody Wins; Reading Program
Email: betsy.vanduyne@hypertherm.com
URL: http://www.hypertherm.com

Colleen F. Van Egmond-Avila
Title: Associates **Company:** Thayer Harvey Greyerson Hedberg and Jackson **Address:** 1100 Fourteenth Street, Suite F, Modesto, CA 95353 United States **BUS:** Legal Firm Legal Services **P/S:** Legal Services **MA:** Local **D/D/R:** Insurance Litigation/Business Litigation **H/I/S:** Playing Piano **EDU:** JD, Bachelor of Science in Managerial Economics, UC Davis, McGeorge School of Law **A/A/S:** Modesto County Bar Association, American Bar Association Volunteer Judge for Youth Court of Modesto, Board of Trustees for Center for Human Services

Mr. Andrew P. Van Hook
Title: Executive Vice President, Realtor **Company:** Four Seasons Realty **Address:** 2439 W. Main Street, Millville, NJ 08332 United States **BUS:** Real Estate Company **P/S:** Residential and Commercial Real Estate Services **MA:** Southern New Jersey **D/D/R:** Overseeing Accounting, Selling Real Estate, Specializing in Commercial Real Estate **EDU:** Bachelor's Degree in Accounting, Rowan University (2007) **A/A/S:** Cumberland County Board of Realtors; New Jersey Association of Realtors; National Association of Realtors
Email: andrewvanhook@gmail.com

Anna Van Matre
Title: Artist **Company:** Art Studio and Gallery **Address:** 4051 Clifton Ridge Drive, Cincinnati, OH 45220 United States **BUS:** Art Gallery **P/S:** Art Presentations **MA:** International **D/D/R:** Creating Paintings, Installations, Collages and Silk Prints **H/I/S:** Traveling in Europe, Listening to Jazz and Classical Music, Attending Ballet Performances **EDU:** Master of Fine Arts, Academy of Arts, Warsaw, Poland **A/A/S:** Polish Art History Association; Art Association of America; World Art Media **C/VW:** Francis CCM Society
Email: vanmatre@cinci.rr.com
URL: http://www.annavanmatre.com

Catherine A. Van Nort
Title: Music Teacher, Musician **Company:** Scranton School District, Robert Morris Elementary School **Address:** 1824 Boulevard Avenue, Scranton, PA 18509 United States **BUS:** Elementary School **P/S:** Education **MA:** Local **D/D/R:** Playing the Piano, Singing, Teaching Music to Prekindergarten and Fifth-Grade Students, Mentoring Young Musicians, Teaching the Violin **H/I/S:** Reading, Going on Cruises, Dining with her Friends **EDU:** Bachelor of Music in Music Education, Plus 30 Graduate Credits, Marywood University **A/A/S:** Scranton Federation of Teachers; Elected Board Member of American Federation of Musicians; Local 120 Scranton Women's Teachers Club **C/VW:** Humane Society of Lackawanna County
Email: cathy.vannort@scrsd.org
URL: http://www.scrsd.org

Nancy A. Van Rikxoord
Title: Community Outreach **Company:** Namaste Comfort Care Hospice **Address:** 1633 Fillmore Street, Suite 300, Denver, CO 80206 United States **BUS:** Healthcare **P/S:** Hospice **MA:** Regional **D/D/R:** Working with HIV, Hepatitis B and C, Young and Disabled Patients, Coordinating Health Services, Working in Hospice and Home Health, Geriatrics **EDU:** Bachelor of Arts in Political Science (1984) **A/A/S:** East Coalition of Services for Seniors; Hospice Organization; Board of Directors, Comfort Fund; Fundraising
Email: nvanrikxoord@comfortnow.org
URL: http://www.namastecomfortcare.com

Wayne Van Wart
Title: Managing Partner **Company:** Impact-Retail, LLC **BUS:** Consulting Firm **P/S:** Consulting, Technology, Field Force Automation, Manpower Deployment **MA:** Local **D/D/R:** Retail Execution **H/I/S:** Swimming, Outdoor Activities, Sailing **EDU:** Bachelor of Science in Business Administration, Boston University **C/VW:** American Cancer Society
Email: wayne.vanwart@impact-retail.com
URL: http://www.impact-retail.com

Judith S. VanAlstyne
Title: Writer, Owner **Company:** VanAlstyne and Associates **Address:** 1688 S. Ocean Lane, Suite 265, Fort Lauderdale, FL 33316 United States **BUS:** Writing **P/S:** Research on Technical Writing and Travel **MA:** International **D/D/R:** Writing College Technical Writing Textbooks, Poetry and Travel Articles **H/I/S:** Traveling, Writing, Attending Cultural Events, Attending the Theater, Opera and Symphony, Working Out, Swimming **EDU:** ABD in English Literature, Florida Atlantic University; Master of Arts in English Literature, Florida Atlantic University **C/VW:** Former Board Member, Fort Lauderdale Museum of Art
Email: ladyvanj@aol.com
URL: http://www.cambridgewhoswho.com

Linda J. VanArtsdalen
Title: Owner, Manager **Company:** Dynamite Stitches **Address:** P.O. Box 464, Cape May Court House, NJ 08210 United States **BUS:** Retail Store **P/S:** Crafts, Supplies, Yarns, Embroidery, Plastic Canvas, Cross Stitch Kits **MA:** National **EXP:** Ms. VanArtsdalen's expertise includes needle pointing, cross-stitching, embroidery and knit design. **H/I/S:** Gardening, Fishing, Traveling, Hand Painting Tiny Ornaments, Spending Time at the Church, Singing, Creating Design **EDU:** High School Education **C/VW:** Love of Linda Cancer Fund; March of Dimes; American Cancer Society
Email: dynamitestitches@yahoo.com
URL: http://www.dynamitestitches.com

Deb Vande Loo
Title: Professional Organizer **Company:** The Professional Organizer **BUS:** Professional Organizing Company **P/S:** Professional Organizing **MA:** Local **D/D/R:** Teaching Organization for Professional and Residential, Emphasis on Home Offices and Clutter Management **H/I/S:** Golfing, Photo Scrapbooking **EDU:** Bachelor's Degree in Criminal Justice, University Wisconsin (1981) **A/A/S:** National Association of Professional Organizers; Local Association of Professional Organizers **C/VW:** Local Church
Email: organizerdeb@charter.net
URL: http://www.organizerdeb.com

Patricia E. Vanden Heuvel
Title: Owner **Company:** Pro Plumbing Services **Address:** 535 S. Gilbert Street, Castle Rock, CO 80104 United States **BUS:** Plumbing **P/S:** Plumbing and Heating **MA:** Regional **D/D/R:** Commercial, Residential, Plumbing and Heating, Basement Remodeling **H/I/S:** Being a Grandmother **EDU:** College Coursework, North Arizona University, Maricopa College
Email: pevandenheuvel@ppstotherescue.com
URL: http://www.ppstotherescue.com

J. Eric Vander Arend
Title: Partner **Company:** Hughes Socol Piers Resnick & Dym **Address:** 70 W Madison Street, Suite 4000, Chicago, IL 60602 United States **BUS:** Law Firm Legal Services/Attorney/Partner/Judge **P/S:** Legal Services **MA:** Local **D/D/R:** Commercial Litigation, Contractual Matters **H/I/S:** Bike to Work, 25 Miles Round Trip Everyday **EDU:** Philadelphia College of Art, Northwest University, Bachelor of Fine Arts, JD **A/A/S:** Illinois State Bar
Email: evanderarend@hsplegal.com
URL: http://www.hsplegal.com

Rick W. Vander Veen
Title: Events Director **Company:** Grand Rapids Community College **Address:** 143 Bostwick Avenue N.E., Grand Rapids, MI 49503 United States **BUS:** Community Junior College **P/S:** Training in Manufacturing, Auto Service, Building and Construction Trades, Liberal Arts and Occupational Courses, Academic, Physical Education, Wellness and Sports Programs, Seminars, Workshops, Training Classes and Distance Learning Options **MA:** Regional **D/D/R:** Managing Sports and Wellness Events **H/I/S:** Spending Time Outdoors, Grand Rapids Convention and Visitors Bureau **EDU:** Pursuing Master of Arts in Public Administration, Western Michigan University; Bachelor of Arts in Business Administration, Emphasis on Operations, Human Resources and Public Relations, Aquinas College **A/A/S:** International Association of Assembly Managers
Email: rvanderv@grcc.edu
URL: http://www.grcc.edu

Lonnie J. Vandergriff
Title: Owner/Master Mason **Company:** Vandergriff Construction **Address:** 290 CR 1774, Chico, TX 76413 United States **BUS:** Construction Building/Construction **P/S:** Custom Home Builder **MA:** Local **D/D/R:** Brick and Stone Mason **H/I/S:** Cutting Horses **EDU:** Texas A&M University **A/A/S:** Mason, BBB, Help a Child Fund, AQHA
Email: sleppyd@ntws.net

Patricia M. Vanderwall
Title: Career Agent **Company:** MassMutual Financial Group **Address:** 3152 Peregrine Drive N.E., Grand Rapids, MI 49525 United States **BUS:** Insurance Company **P/S:** Insurance, Financial Solutions, Cost and Investment Management for Individuals and Businesses, Financial Protection, Accumulation and Income Management **MA:** National **D/D/R:** selling long-term care, disability and life insurance to clients including annuities, investments and retirement plans **H/I/S:** Gardening, Golfing, Collecting Antiques **EDU:** Bachelor of Science in Secondary Education, Eastern Michigan University (1972) **CERTS:** Pursuing Life Underwriting Training Council Certification; License in Series 6 and 63; Licensed Life Insurance Agent; Licensed Health Insurance Agent; Licensed Variable Insurance and Securities Agent; Corporation for Long-Term Care Certification **A/A/S:** Local Chamber of Commerce; Secretary, Treasurer, Heritage Homes; Ambassador Group, Holland Area Chamber of Commerce; Women in Insurance and Financial Services **C/VW:** Loan Executive, Treasurer, Audiow County, United Way; Volunteer, Greater Ottawa County, United Way
Email: pvanderwall@finsvcs.com
URL: http://www.massmutual.com

Natalie E. VanDrongelen, RN
Title: Registered Nurse, Nursing Student **Company:** Dakota Wesleyan University **Address:** 1200 University Avenue, Mitchell, SD 57301 United States **BUS:** Liberal Arts College Dedicated to Developing the Whole Person through Opportunities to Explore Leadership Potential in Service to God and the Community **P/S:** Education Enabling Students to Identify and Develop their Individual Talents for Successful Lives in Service to God and the Common Good **MA:** Regional **D/D/R:** Critical-Care Nursing, Working in All Aspects of Patient Care, Hands-On Clinical Training at Local Hospitals **H/I/S:** Horseback Riding, Playing Softball **EDU:** Pursuing Bachelor's Degree in Nursing, Dakota Wesleyan University; Associate Degree in Nursing, Dakota Wesleyan University (2007); Bachelor of Science in Counseling, South Dakota State University (1997); Certified Nursing Assistant **A/A/S:** National Student Nurses' Association; South Dakota Student Nurses' Association; Volunteer, Local Helping Hands; Speaker on Conflict Resolution; Former Mental Health Counselor
Email: dnlvan@santel.net
URL: http://www.cambridgewhoswho.com

Jennifer L. VanMatre
Title: Teacher **Company:** Sidney Middle School **Address:** 980 Fair Road, Sidney, OH 45365 United States **BUS:** Public Middle School Serving Resident of Sidney **P/S:** Public Secondary Education for Local Students **MA:** National **D/D/R:** Teaching Eighth-Grade Language Arts **H/I/S:** Spending Time with her Family, Researching and Authoring a Book on Misconceptions and Methods of Preparation by Teachers for the Assessment Tests **EDU:** Master's Degree Plus 15 in Special and Gifted Education, Wright State University (1983); Bachelor's Degree in Elementary Education, Miami University (1983) **A/A/S:** National Association for Gifted Children; Ohio Association for Gifted Children; National Middle School Association; Speaker, National Middle School Association; Ohio Middle School Association
Email: gvanmatre2@woh.rr.com

Melissa E. VanWijk
Title: Founder **Company:** Signing Up, LLC **Address:** 811 Walton Avenue, Apartment B18, Bronx, NY 10451 United States **BUS:** Educational Company **P/S:** Dance Education, Special Needs Education, American Sign Language and Deafness, Teaching Families to Communicate with Their Infants Through Sign Language **MA:** Regional **D/D/R:** Teaching Families to Communicate with their Infants through Sign Language, Choreography, Special Education, American Sign Language and Deafness, Instructing Dance **H/I/S:** Traveling, Watersports, Dance, Attending the Theater **EDU:** Certified Sign2Me Presenters Network; Master's Degree in Dance Education, New York University; Bachelor of Fine Arts in Theater Arts, Hofstra University; Bachelor of Arts in Dance, Hofstra University **A/A/S:** National Dance Education Organization; Phi Beta Kappa; Golden Key Honor Society **C/VW:** American Red Cross; National Resource Defense Council; Defenders of Wildlife; Childreach; Amnesty International
Email: mvanwijk1@optonline.net
URL: http://www.cambridgewhoswho.com

Mr. Valentine Varga III
Title: Transportation Director **Company:** Manchester Schools **Address:** 323 Dorsey Lane, Bayville, NJ 08721 United States **BUS:** Public School System **P/S:** Primary and Secondary Education **MA:** Regional **D/D/R:** Directing the Transportation for the School District, Managing and Coordinating the Drivers Transporting 4,000 Students **H/I/S:** Volunteering as a Fireman, Serving on the First Aid Squad **EDU:** Degree in Law Enforcement, Richard Stockton College of New Jersey (1971); Certification in Transportation **A/A/S:** President, Kappa Psi Sigma
Email: vvarga@manchestertwp.org
URL: http://www.manchestertwp.schools.com

George Varghese
Title: Affiliate Broker **Company:** Crye-Leike Realtors **Address:** 1510 Gunbarrel Road, Chattanooga, TN 37421 United States **BUS:** Real Estate Company **P/S:** Residential Real Estate Sales **MA:** National **D/D/R:** Residential and Commercial Real Estate **H/I/S:** Spending Time Outdoors, Photography **EDU:** Bachelor of Science in Biology, University of Kerala, India **A/A/S:** National Association of Realtors; Tennessee Association of Realtors
Email: alpha4omega4@yahoo.com
URL: http://www.crye-leike.com

Richard W. Varner
Title: Owner **Company:** Varner Sight & Sound **Address:** 227 E. St. John Road, Phoenix, AZ 85022 United States **BUS:** Electronics Company **P/S:** Audio and Video Integration **MA:** Regional **D/D/R:** Audio Engineering, Performing High-End Automobile and Home Installations **H/I/S:** Biking **EDU:** High School Diploma **CERTS:** Certification, Industry-Related Training Program **A/A/S:** Custom Electronic Design and Installation Association **A/H:** Nominee, Top 50 Installers in the World; Third Place for International Installation and Design
Email: varnersightandsound@cox.net

Grace M. Vascone-Pareira
Title: MD, DO **Company:** Grace M Vasconez-Pereira, MD, DO **Address:** 162 Street, New York, NY 10011 United States **BUS:** Medical Office **P/S:** Medicine **MA:** Local **D/D/R:** Family Physician **H/I/S:** Hockey Outside Sports **EDU:** New York College of Medicine, St Barnibus Hospital, MD, Doctor of Osteopathy **A/A/S:** AMA
Email: gvpdo@mindspring.com

Liliana Vasquez-Macias
Title: Third-Grade Teacher **Company:** Austin Independent School District **Address:** 1111 W. Sixth Street, Austin, TX 78703 United States **BUS:** School **P/S:** Education **MA:** Local **D/D/R:** Teaching Third-Grade **H/I/S:** Jogging, Participating in Outdoor Activities **EDU:** Master's Degree in Education **C/VW:** St. Jude Children's Research Hospital
Email: lvazque1@austinisd.org

Kenda S. Vasturo
Title: Office Manager **Company:** Century Roofing, Inc. **Address:** 4486 Davie Road, Davie, FL 33314 United States **BUS:** Roofing Company **P/S:** Shingle and Flat Roofs **MA:** South Florida **D/D/R:** Overseeing All Jobs, Invoicing, Contracts and Customer Service **H/I/S:** Spending Time with her Family, Gardening **EDU:** Associate Degree in Nursing, Broward Community College **A/A/S:** American Heart Association
Email: centuryroofing3@aol.com
URL: http://www.cambridgewhoswho.com

W. Glaze Vaughan, MD
Title: President/Pediatric Surgeon **Company:** Pediatric Surgical Associates of Fort Worth **Address:** 901 7th Avenue, Suite 210, Fort Worth, TX 76104 United States **BUS:** Healthcare Company **P/S:** Pediatric Surgery entails the general, thoracic and minimally invasive surgery of infants, children and adolescents. **MA:** Regional **D/D/R:** Working in Clinical Practice, Offering General Surgical Care for Infants, Children and Adolescents **H/I/S:** Playing the Guitar, Outdoor Activities, Camping, Spending Time with Family **EDU:** Fellowship, Pediatric Surgery, J. W. Riley Hospital for Children, Indiana University School of Medicine (1993-1995); Residency, The University of Texas Southwestern Medical Center at Dallas and Affiliated Hospitals (1987-1993); MD, Medical College of Georgia (1987) **A/A/S:** Fellow, The American College of Surgeons; Fellow, Surgical Section, American Academy of Pediatrics; American Pediatric Surgical Association; American Medical Association; American College of Physician Executives; Medical Group Management Association; Alpha Omega Alpha; Texas Medical Association; Parkland Surgical Society; Fort Worth Surgical Society **C/VW:** The local church, christian school, mission work
Email: gvaughan@cookchildrens.org
URL: http://www.pedisurgdfw.com

Glenda F. Vaughn
Title: Teacher **Company:** Pearl River Valley Opportunity, Inc. **Address:** P.O. Box 188, Columbia, MS 39429 United States **BUS:** Education Company **P/S:** Education for Children Between Three and Five Years Old **MA:** Local **D/D/R:** Early Childhood Education **H/I/S:** Baking, Cooking, Traveling, Reading, Completing Puzzles, Shopping, Spending Time with her Grandchildren **EDU:** Bachelor of Science in Child Care and Family Services, Jackson State University; Certified Child Development Associate **A/A/S:** Mississippi Education Association **C/VW:** Boys & Girls Clubs of America
Email: g.vaughn1030@bellsouth.com

Eric K. Vaught
Title: Program Assoc Div of Agriculture **Company:** University of Arkansas **Address:** 1260 W Maple, Fayetteville, AR 72701 United States **BUS:** University **P/S:** Nutritional Laboratory Testing for People **MA:** International **D/D/R:** Specializing in Minerals and New Protein Analysis **EDU:** The University of Arkansas, MS in Physiology **A/A/S:** Calvary Baptist Church of Fayetteville, The Watch Dogs, Volunteer Fathers Group, The Arkansas Wind Ensemble

Anna Vaul
Title: Owner **Company:** Studio 520 Salon **Address:** 816 Belvedere Drive, Kokomo, IN 46901 United States **BUS:** Hair Salon **P/S:** Cosmetology **MA:** Central Indiana **D/D/R:** Hair Styling, Educating **H/I/S:** Sewing, Snowboarding, Gardening, Spending Time with Gretchen **EDU:** Coursework in Fine Arts and Visual Design, Purdue University, West Lafayette, Indiana; Professional License in Cosmetology **A/A/S:** National Federation of Independent Businesses **C/VW:** Angels for Kids, Donating Hair Supplies to Women's Shelter
Email: annav520@sbcglobal.net

Dr. Aman A. Vazir
Title: Physician **Company:** Aman Vazir, LLC **Address:** 999 McBride Avenue, Suite 201-C, West Paterson, NJ 07424 United States **BUS:** Medical Practice **P/S:** Medical Direction of Sleep Lab for Sleep Disorders **MA:** Local **D/D/R:** Pulmonary, Sleep Medicine **H/I/S:** Golfing, Playing Tennis, Skiing, Reading, Doing Activities with Children **EDU:** MD in Pulmonology, Saint George's University, Granada; Bachelor of Arts in Biochemistry, Columbia University **A/A/S:** American Thoracic Association; American College of Chest Physiology; American Sleep Society Medicine; Associate Professor, Mount Sinai, New York; Residency Review Committee **C/VW:** Clinic for Indigent Care; Emergency Medical Services, Chatham, New Jersey; County TB Clinic; Medical Director, Sleep Lab
Email: avazir@msn.com
URL: http://www.cambridgewhoswho.com

Gonzalo A. Vazquez-Casals, Ph.D.
Title: Neuropsychologist **Company:** North East Regional Epilepsy Group **Address:** 333 Westchester Avenue, Suite 104, White Plains, NY 10604 United States **BUS:** Mental Health **P/S:** High Quality Interventions **MA:** Tri-State Area **D/D/R:** Neuropsychological Assessment, Cognitive Rehabilitation, Psychotherapy **H/I/S:** Spending Time with his Wife and Two Children, Playing Classical and Rock Music **EDU:** Doctorate Degree in Counseling Psychology, Lehigh University; Master's Degree in Clinical Psychology, Earned in Mexico; Bachelor's Degree in Psychology, Earned in Venezuela; Clinical Neuropsychology Fellowship, Belleview Hospital (1999-2001) **A/A/S:** American Psychological Association; Society for Personality Assessment; National Register of Health Service Providers in Psychology
Email: gavc@worldnet.att.net
URL: http://www.epilepsygroup.com

Israel 'Izzy' Vega
Title: President **Company:** Race Track Chaplaincy of California **Address:** P.O. Box 8245, Anaheim, CA 91791 United States **BUS:** Nonprofit Organization **P/S:** Counseling Including Religious and Social Services **MA:** International **D/D/R:** Fundraising, Training, Delivering Motivational Speeches, Consulting, Lecturing, Managing Sales **H/I/S:** Reading, Golfing, Fishing, Traveling **EDU:** Coursework in Communications, California State University, Fullerton; Bachelor of Arts in Religion and Education, Vanguard University of Southern California **CERTS:** Certified Trainer, Outreach Ministries; Certified Trainer, Bible League **A/A/S:** Assemblies of God Church, Willow Creek Association **C/VW:** Local Church; Local Community Organizations
Email: israelgracevega@msn.com
URL: http://www.cambridgewhoswho.com

Mr. Nicholas P. Velardi
Title: Director of Operations **Company:** Ehrhart and Schaefer Gardens **Address:** 100 Francis Court, Union, NJ 07083 United States **BUS:** Senior Housing Developments **P/S:** Senior Citizen Apartment Complexes **MA:** Local **D/D/R:** Mechanical Engineering, Property Management **H/I/S:** Traveling, Hiking, Fishing **EDU:** College Coursework **A/A/S:** New Jersey Housing Authority; United States Department of Housing and Urban Development **C/VW:** Various Charities
Email: nvelardi66@hotmail.com
URL: http://www.cambridgewhoswho.com
URL: http://www.nj.gov/dca/hmsa

Sandra Velasco
Title: Realtor **Company:** Tarbell Realtors **Address:** 315 Magnolia Avenue, Corona, CA 92879 United States **BUS:** Real Estate Agency **P/S:** Property Sales and Purchase, Resources, Advertising, Financial Services, Consulting, Specialized Marketing, Preferred Properties **MA:** Regional **D/D/R:** Selling Residential Properties, Single-Family Homes, Townhouses, Condominiums and Commercial Properties, Overseeing Property Listing Services, Showing Properties to Clients **H/I/S:** Running Marathons, Dancing, Singing in Church Choir, Volunteering in the Community **EDU:** Real Estate License, The State of California (2006); High School Education **A/A/S:** Samantha's Pride Committee
Email: sundravelasco@tarbell.com
URL: http://www.tarbell.com

Juan D. Velez
Title: Professional Painter **Company:** Velez Professional Painting **Address:** 8607 W. Greenfield Avenue, Apartment 3, West Allis, WI 53214 United States **BUS:** Painting Company **P/S:** Professional Painting, Texture, Drywall, Refinishing and Staining Services for Residential and Commercial Buildings **MA:** Regional **D/D/R:** managing color coordination, restoring interior and exterior buildings through staining and refinishing decks and contracting with other workers **H/I/S:** Spending Time with his Family **A/A/S:** Better Business Bureau; National Association for the Self-Employed
Email: juan.velez@cwwemail.com
URL: http://www.cambridgewhoswho.com

Roberta T. Veloso
Title: Dental Consultant **Company:** Staff Driven Practices **Address:** 40 Galesi Drive, Wayne, NJ 07470 United States **BUS:** Consulting Company **P/S:** Dental Practice Development **MA:** Regional **D/D/R:** Professional Coaching, Consulting **H/I/S:** Practicing Yoga and Tai Chi, Reading, Cooking **EDU:** Associate Degree in Dental Hygiene, New York University; Bachelor's Degree in Psychology, Universidad Federal de Minas Gerais, Brazil, Certified Dental Hygienist **A/A/S:** American Dental Association; American Dental Hygienists Association **C/VW:** Leader for Troop 96, Ridgefield, Boy Scouts of America
Email: rvdentrix@hotmail.com
Email: robertat.veloso@cwwemail.com
URL: http://www.cambridgewhoswho.com

Sandra L. Vencill
Title: Co-Owner **Company:** Vencill Consulting, LLC **Address:** 8293 Redford Way, Sacramento, CA 95829 United States **BUS:** Consulting Firm **P/S:** Information Technology Consulting Services **MA:** Local **EXP:** Ms. Vencill's expertise is in project management. **D/D/R:** Working with the State and County Governments, Overseeing HIPA Compliance and Business Analysis, Programming, Working with Clients to Stage their Homes for Quick Resale in a Sluggish Real Estate Market **H/I/S:** Interior Decorating **EDU:** Bachelor of Arts in Business Administration, Trinity College **CERTS:** Certified Interior Designer; Certified Project Management Professional; Microsoft Project Orange Belt Certification (2007); Licensed Cosmetologist; Licensed Notary Public **A/A/S:** Project Management Institute; Sacramento Chapter Institute; National Notary Association **C/VW:** Local Charitable Organizations
Email: svencill@comcast.net

Ryan Venis
Title: Certified Emergency Physician **Company:** St. Vincent Emergency Physicians, Inc. **Address:** 5989 E. Boulder Drive, Crawfordsville, IN 47933 United States **BUS:** Emergency Medical Center **P/S:** Emergency Medical Services **MA:** National **D/D/R:** practicing emergency medicine, treating minor and major medical conditions including heart attacks, trauma, strokes and accident victims, treating transferred patients from other hospitals **H/I/S:** Listening to Music, Collecting Beatles Memorabilia, Jogging, Exercising **EDU:** Pursuing Master's Degree in Public Health, University of Massachusetts; Residency, Indiana University; MD, Indiana University (2002) **CERTS:** Certified Emergency Physician, American Board of Emergency Medicine **A/A/S:** American Academy of Emergency Medicine; American College of Emergency Physicians; Diplomat, American Board of Emergency Medicine **C/VW:** Christian Mission, South Haiti
Email: ryan_venismd@yahoo.com

Carla A. Venteicher
Title: Band Director **Company:** Agwsr High School **Address:** 918 4th Avenue, Ackley, IA 50601 United States **BUS:** High School Facility Dedicated to Excellence in Education **P/S:** Regular Core Curriculum Including Reading, Mathematics, English, Science, Social Studies, History, Art, Music, Languages, Physical Education **MA:** Regional **D/D/R:** Directing the Band, Coordinating Concerts, Overseeing the Jazz Band, Marching Band, Pep Band and Color Guard, Arranging Instrumental Music **H/I/S:** Crocheting **EDU:** Bachelor's Degree in Music Education, University of Northern Iowa (2002) **A/A/S:** Iowa Music Educators Association; Iowa Bandmasters Association; NCIBA; MENC
Email: c_venteicher@agwsr.k12.ia.us
URL: http://www.high-schools.com

Alfredo Vera Jr.
Title: Senior Financial Analyst **Company:** Valley Baptist Health System **Address:** 2101 Pease Street, Harlingen, TX 78550 United States **BUS:** Hospital **P/S:** Community-Based Healthcare System **MA:** Local **D/D/R:** Accounting **H/I/S:** Reading, Golfing, Hunting **EDU:** Master of Business Administration, University of Texas at Brownsville **A/A/S:** Healthcare Financial Management Association; American College of Healthcare Executives
Email: alfredo.vera@valleybaptist.net
URL: http://www.cambridgewhoswho.com

Carl F. Verbeke
Title: Engineer, Emergency Medical Treatment **Company:** Americus Fire & Emergency Services **Address:** 119 S. Lee Street, Americus, GA 31709 United States **BUS:** Public Safety **P/S:** Rescue Specialist in Extrication, High Angle, Water and Collapse **MA:** Local **D/D/R:** Fire Rescue, Medical Emergency Services **H/I/S:** Traveling, Motorcycling **EDU:** Associate Degree in Business, Darton College **A/A/S:** Civil War Preservation Society **C/VW:** Disabled Veterans Association; Chrone's Colitis of America
Email: carlverbeke@cwwemail.com

Mrs. Mamta Verma

Title: Special Education Teacher **Company:** Hilliard Elementary School **Address:** 8115 E. Houston Road, Houston, TX 77028 United States **BUS:** Education **P/S:** Elementary Education, Special Education, ESL, Bilingual Education, Guidance and Counseling, Early child Education **MA:** International **D/D/R:** Teaching Reading and Language Arts, Teaching Resource Students, Special Education, Guidance and Counseling, School Administration **H/I/S:** Stress Management through Yoga, Vastu (Indian Geomancy) **EDU:** Master's Degree in Administration, Texas Southern University (2006); Master's Degree in Curriculum, Earned in India (1996); Master's Degree in Guidance and Counseling, Earned in India (1997); Master's Degree in English and Language Arts, Earned in India (1983) **A/H:** Outstanding Educator by Lion Club, Delhi, India (2003,2004); Outstanding Educator, National Women of Achievement, Houston, Texas (2006)
Email: vermamamta@hotmail.com

Lisa M. Verrocchi, M.Ed.

Title: Teacher **Company:** Central School in Stoneham **Address:** 9 Thomas Circle, Stoneham, MA 02180 United States **BUS:** Private Elementary School **P/S:** Education **MA:** Local **D/D/R:** Teaching in a Self-Contained Classroom, Creating Innovative and Hands-On Games and Strategies for Active Learning, Differentiated Instruction with IEP Students, Tutoring, Mentoring **H/I/S:** Exercising **EDU:** Master's Degree in Literacy, Lesley University (2006); Bachelor's Degree in Psychology, Minor in Education, Merrimack College (2003) **A/A/S:** National Honor Society; Massachusetts Teachers Association; Discipline Committee
Email: missverrocchi@yahoo.com
URL: http://www.cambridgewhoswho.com

Pauline L. Verstraete

Title: Owner **Company:** Paula's Cleaning Service **Address:** 25434 Mandarin Court, Loma Linda, CA 92354 United States **BUS:** Cleaning Service **P/S:** Residential and Commercial Cleaning **MA:** Local **D/D/R:** Customer Satisfaction, Cleaning Kitchens and Bathrooms **H/I/S:** Spending Time with her Grandchildren, Shopping **A/A/S:** Better Business Bureau **C/VW:** Supporting Police and Fire Personnel, Foster Children, March of Dimes, American Veterans

Kathleen L. Vezza

Title: Piano Teacher **Company:** Self-Employed **Address:** 40 Gales Drive, Apartment 2, New Providence, NJ 07974 United States **BUS:** Musical Instruction **P/S:** Music Education, Music Therapy **MA:** Local **D/D/R:** Teaching Music Theory and History, Ear Training, Singing Music Therapy, Psychology with Children and Music **H/I/S:** Gardening, Photography, Cooking, Socializing with Family, Playing Piano, Attending Concerts-New Jersey Symphony **EDU:** Coursework in Music Education, University of Cincinnati, Emery School of Music; Coursework in Visual Communication, Kean University **A/A/S:** Red Hat Society; Fulbright Society; Volunteer, Runnells Hospital **C/VW:** St. Jude Children's Research Hospital, Seeing Eye Dogs, Religious Missions, Wildlife, Church
Email: kathypiano10@msn.com

Jennifer S. Vice

Title: Corporate Chemist **Company:** Sanderson Farms, INC. **Dept:** Analytical Chemistry Laboratory **Address:** 225 N. 13th Avenue, Laurel, MS 39440 United States **BUS:** Agricultural Company Marketing United States Department of Agriculture Grade A Chill-Pack Chicken **P/S:** Produce, Process, Market and Distribute Top-Quality Fresh, Frozen and Further Processed Chicken Products and Other Processed and Prepared Food Items **MA:** International **D/D/R:** Overseeing Lab Floor Personnel, Insuring Proper Safety Procedures are in Place/Practiced, Ordering Supplies, Equipment and Chemicals, Chemical Analysis of Chicken and Feed Products **H/I/S:** Traveling, Reading, Pets, Sports **EDU:** Bachelor's Degree in Biological Sciences, Mississippi State University (2002); Associate of Arts, Jones County Junior College (1996) **A/A/S:** JCJC Alumni Association; MSU Alumni Association **A/H:** Beta Beta Beta National Biological Honor Society; Phi Theta Kappa International Honor Society; Golden Key Honor Society; Letter 'J' Award; The National Dean's List; MSU Presidential Scholarship; JCJC ACT and Band Scholarships
Email: jvice@sandersonfarms.com
URL: http://www.sandersonfarms.com

Rosalina L. Vicencio

Title: Registered Nurse **Company:** Coast Plaza Doctors Hospital **Address:** 9114 Baysinger Street, Downey, CA 90241 United States **BUS:** Hospital **P/S:** Reconstructive Surgery, Pain Management, Arthroscopic Surgery, Podiatry **MA:** Local **D/D/R:** Executing Doctor's Pre-Operation and Post-Operation Orders, Performing Lab Work **H/I/S:** Traveling, Bicycle Riding, Spending Time with her Family **EDU:** Doctor of Dental Surgery, Centro Escolar University (1987); Bachelor of Science in Nursing, De Ocampo Memorial College (2004) **A/A/S:** Supervisor, Medical Dental Mission **C/VW:** Volunteer, St. Jude Children's Research Hospital
Email: dr_sallangay@yahoo.com
URL: http://www.cambridgewhoswo.com

Travis W. Vickerson

Title: Fire Fighter **Company:** City of Durham Fire Department **Address:** 1009 E. Club Boulevard, Durham, NC 27704 United States **BUS:** Fire and Emergency Services **P/S:** Firefighting, Emergency Medical Services, Public Safety **MA:** City of Durham, North Carolina **D/D/R:** Technical Rescue **H/I/S:** Participating in Outdoor Activities, Going to the Theater and Opera **EDU:** Pursuing Bachelor's Degree in Emergency Management Preparedness, University of North Carolina at Charlotte; Associate Degree in Emergency Management Preparedness and Associate Degree in Fire Protection Technology, Durham Technical Community College **A/A/S:** Durham City Fire Union; Durham Fraternal Order of Firefighters; United States Army Reserve Team **C/VW:** Youth Group Leader, Young Life
Email: t_vickerson@yahoo.com
URL: http://www.durhamfire.net

Dane C. Victory

Title: Office Manager **Company:** Barrett's Wrecker Service, Inc. **Address:** 1307 Dawson Place, Murfreesboro, TN 37129 United States **BUS:** Towing and Recovery Service **P/S:** Towing and Recovery of Freight Hauling Vehicles **MA:** National **D/D/R:** Budgeting, Analyzing Finances, Taxes, Payroll, Accounts Payable and Receivable, Tags and Registration for States **H/I/S:** Spending Time with her Dogs, Attending NASCAR Races, Spending Time with her Two Grandchildren **EDU:** College Coursework; Industry-Related Training and Experience **C/VW:** True Vine Free Will Baptist Church, Assisting the Underprivileged with Doctors Appointments and Medications
Email: danish43@bellsouth.net

Joseph Viera

Title: Quality Engineer **Company:** Stryker Orthopaedics **Address:** 325 Corporate Drive, Mahwah, NJ 07430 United States **BUS:** Medical Manufacturing Company **P/S:** Medical Devices, Orthopedic Implants and Instruments for Surgery **MA:** International **D/D/R:** Handling New Equipment, Managing Process Improvement and Troubleshooting, Overseeing Validation, Maintaining Compliance **H/I/S:** Playing the Guitar, Piano and Percussion Instruments **EDU:** Bachelor of Arts in Mechanical Engineering, New Jersey Institute of Technology; Six Sigma Black Belt Certification **A/A/S:** American Society of Mechanical Engineers; American Society for Quality; Society of Hispanic Professional Engineers; Former President, Lambda Theta Phi
Email: joseph.viera@stryker.com
URL: http://www.stryker.com/orthopaedics

S. Marea Vigil

Title: Medical Transcriptionist, Owner **Company:** Valley Star Transcription **Address:** 6255 Emma Lane, Colorado Springs, CO 80922 United States **BUS:** Medical Transcription Company **P/S:** Records Documentation **MA:** National **D/D/R:** Medical Transcription **H/I/S:** Reading, Painting, Drawing **EDU:** High School Graduate, Wyoming **A/A/S:** American Medical Transcriptionist Association; Citizenship Award **C/VW:** Adventist Disaster Relief Agency, Disabled American Veterans
Email: vmarea@hotmail.com

Cristin A. Vignola

Title: Special Education Teacher **Company:** Manassas Park Elementary School **Address:** 101 Tremont Street, Manassas Park, VA 20111 United States **BUS:** Elementary School **P/S:** Education **MA:** Local **D/D/R:** Inclusion Special Education, Working with Special Needs Children in a General Education Environment **H/I/S:** Spending Time Outdoors **EDU:** Pursuing Master's Degree in Special Education, George Mason University; Bachelor of Arts in Special Education, Clemson University **A/A/S:** Council for Exceptional Children; Leadership Team
Email: cvignol@hotmail.com
URL: http://www.cambridgewhoswho.com

Kimberly A. Vilardi

Title: President **Company:** One 2 One Programming & Design, Inc. **Address:** 1423 Water Wheel Drive, Bethlehem, GA 30620 United States **BUS:** Communications Company **P/S:** Design and Programming of Personalized Marketing Collateral **MA:** Local **D/D/R:** Pageflex, VIPP, Graphic Designing, Consulting **H/I/S:** Painting, Horses **C/VW:** Local Charities
Email: kvilardi@one2one-programming.com
URL: http://www.one2one-programming.com

Connie Croslin Villalobos, Ph.D.

Title: 1) Master Graphologist 2) Teacher 3) Minister **Company:** Self-Employed **Address:** 2010 Stein Way, Carrollton, TX 75007 United States **BUS:** Master Cryptologist **P/S:** Cryptological Analysis, Forensic and Educational Consulting, Graphological Analysis **MA:** Local **D/D/R:** Handwriting Analysis **H/I/S:** Reading, Sewing **EDU:** Ph.D. in Comparative Religion; Master of Arts in Handwriting Analysis; Master of Arts in Counseling; Bachelor of Arts in Graphology; Bachelor of Arts in Metaphysics **A/A/S:** Former President of the Texas Institute of Graphology; Regional Director, Institute of Graphologists; Worked with Children's Medical Center for Thirteen Years; Red Cross **A/H:** Prism Award for Improving Life of People with Mental Illness and Promoting Public Understanding about Mental Health Issues
Email: wisdomstar@msn.com

Veronica E. Villalobos

Title: Attorney **Company:** U.S. Equal Employment Opportunity Commission **Address:** 1801 L Street N.W., Washington, DC 20036 United States **BUS:** Government Organization **P/S:** Legal Services **MA:** National **EXP:** Ms. Villalobos' expertise is in labor and employment law including Title VII of the civil rights act of 1964, Americans with disabilities, equal pay, age discrimination in employment and genetic information nondiscrimination acts. **D/D/R:** Advising on Hispanic Issues, Working with Relationship Management Team, Supervising Attorneys **H/I/S:** Hiking, Golfing, Reading **EDU:** JD, Washington College of Law, American University (2000); Bachelor of Arts in Political Science and Psychology, Saint Mary's College **A/A/S:** Maryland State Bar Association; State Bar of Michigan; Chairwoman, Equal Employment Opportunity Commission Forms Federal Hispanic Work Group; Excel Annual Conference, National Council of Hispanic Employment Program Managers **A/H:** Chair's Excellence in Leadership Award (2007); Chair's Opportunity to Reward Excellence Award (2005) **C/VW:** Hispanic Youth Symposium; The National Organization for Mexican American Rights
Email: vev1973@yahoo.com

Jennifer Villaneueva

Title: Retail Store Manager **Company:** T-Mobile USA, Inc. **Address:** 4830 N. Pulaski Road, Suite 106, Chicago, IL 60630 United States **BUS:** Telecommunications Company **P/S:** World Wide Communication Services Including Cell Phones, Service and Communication Products **MA:** International **EXP:** Ms. Villaneueva's expertise includes retail management and employee training. **H/I/S:** Dancing **EDU:** Pursuing Bachelor's Degree in Marketing and Communications, Columbia College; High School Education
Email: jennifer.villanueva@t-mobile.com
URL: http://www.cambridgewhoswho.com

Benny Villarreal

Title: Instructional Technology Trainer **Company:** San Benito C.I.S.D. **Address:** 240 N. Crockett Street, San Benito, TX 78586 United States **BUS:** School District **P/S:** Education **MA:** Local **D/D/R:** Supporting Teacher to Integrate Technology into their Lesson Plans **H/I/S:** Basketball, Soccer **EDU:** Bachelor's Degree in Kinesiology and Computer Science, University of Texas; Pursuing Master's Degree in Education Technology, University of Texas
Email: bvillarreal@sbcisd.net
URL: http://www.sbcisd.net

Irene T. Vincelette-Jones

Title: LSSP (School Psychology) **Company:** East Williamson Community Cooperative **Address:** 2500 North Drive, Taylor, TX 76574 United States **BUS:** Special Educational Services **P/S:** Special Educational Services **MA:** Local **D/D/R:** Behavior and Autism, Foster Parent for Special Needs Children **H/I/S:** Family Time, Camping, Farm **EDU:** New Mexico State University, Texas State University, Bachelor of Science Psychology, MED, Behavior and Autism, Behavior Coach **A/A/S:** NASP, TASP, Blue Bonnet Trails; MHMR
Email: ijones@taylor.isd.tenet.edu

Don Vincent

Title: Composer, Pianist **Company:** Music By Design **Address:** 838 N. Doheny Drive, Suite 1107, Los Angeles, CA 90069 United States **BUS:** Music and Film Composer, Movies, Television **P/S:** Music Performance, Pianist, Songs in Movies, Recordings **MA:** National **D/D/R:** Composing and Conducting, Directing Music for the Sands Hotel and Casino Orchestra, Operating a Recording Studio **H/I/S:** Music, Tennis, Travel, Hiking **EDU:** Master's Degree in Music Composition, Carnegie Mellon University (1957); Bachelor's Degree in Music Composition, Carnegie Mellon University (1956) **A/A/S:** Played at White House for Presidents Gerald Ford and Ronald Regan; Plays with Wayne Newton at Shows in Las Vegas; Owner, Multi Media Music Studio, Toluca Lake, CA; Recipient, BMI Award for Film Composing
Email: mmmuzik@adelphia.net
URL: http://www.cambridgewhoswho.com

Tanya D. Vincent, BFA

Title: Owner **Company:** Atlantic Coast Academy of Dance **Address:** 49 John Maki Road, West Barnstable, MA 02668 United States **BUS:** Dance Studio **P/S:** Classical Ballet Instruction for Students Age 2 through Adult **MA:** Local **D/D/R:** Teaching Classical Ballet, Artistic Directing, Managing Daily Operations **H/I/S:** Going to Movies, Traveling **EDU:** Bachelor of Fine Arts in Dance, California State University at Long Beach **A/A/S:** Coastal Dance Society; President and Artistic Director, The Cultural Council; Special Olympics, United Way
Email: acaofdance@yahoo.com
URL: http://www.acad-dance.com

Joselito F. Vinluan, MD
Title: Doctor of Medicine Company: Danbury Hospital Address: 24 Hospital Avenue, Danbury, CT 06810 United States BUS: Hospital P/S: Healthcare MA: Regional D/D/R: Cardiac Anesthesia H/I/S: Golfing, Fishing, Traveling EDU: MD, University of the East Ramon Magsaysay Memorial Medical Center, Philippines (1990) A/A/S: American Society of Appraisers; SCA A/H: Robert D. Dripps Memorial Award; Outstanding Resident Award (1999-2000)
Email: yolan2@mac.com
URL: http://www.cambridgewhoswho.com

William F. Vinson III
Title: Owner Company: William F. Vinson Address: 266 Hubert Boulevard, Apartment 41, Hubert, NC 28539 United States BUS: Stucco Enhancement Company P/S: Home Improvement, Specialty Stucco, Dressing Homes MA: Local D/D/R: Specialty Stucco H/I/S: Gardening EDU: High School Graduate A/A/S: Sheriffs' Association
Email: stuccoman1958@yahoo.com
URL: http://www.cambridgewhoswho.com

Elizabeth C. Violago
Title: Clinical Coordinator, Clinical Information Systems Company: Montefiore Medical Center Dept: Emerging Health Information Technology Address: 12 Remsen Street, Williston Park, NY 11596 United States BUS: Medical Center P/S: Healthcare Including Cardiology and Cardiac Surgery, Cancer, Tissue and Organ Transplantation, Children's Health and Women's Healthcare Services MA: National D/D/R: nursing, implementing applications, updating the curriculum, managing ambulatory care, creating training manuals for employees and online documentation for healthcare providers H/I/S: Horseback Riding, Shopping, Hiking EDU: Master of Science in Health Administration and Education, Hofstra University (2001); Bachelor of Science in Nursing, St. Paul College of Manila, Philippines CERTS: Registered Nurse
Email: eviolago@montefiore.org
URL: http://www.emerginghealthit.com

Doris P. Virginia Hoffman
Title: Head Volunteer, Third and Fourth-Grade Teacher (Retired) Company: Reisterstown Library Dept: Department of History and Genealogy Address: 21 Cockeys Mill Road, Reisterstown, MD 21136 United States BUS: Library P/S: Library Services Including Family and Local History Books MA: Regional D/D/R: Volunteering for the Town Library, managing library books including history and social studies, meeting the public, delivering speeches, reorganizing the library, rendering free services for all persons inquiring about their roots, fundraising, conducting lectures on the local history H/I/S: Sports, Traveling EDU: Master's Equivalency in Education and Special Education, Board of Education, Towson, MD (1974) A/A/S: Franklin High School Alumni C/VW: Women's Club
Email: doris.hoffman@cwwemail.com
URL: http://www.cambridgewhoswho.com

Anna Laura Visger
Title: Kindergarten Teacher Company: Canyon Rim Elementary School Address: 3045 S. Canyon Rim, Mesa, AZ 85212 United States BUS: Elementary School P/S: Primary Education MA: Regional D/D/R: Teaching All Subjects and Early Childhood Education H/I/S: Riding her Motorcycle, Spending Time with her Family, Camping, Hiking, Playing Games EDU: Pursuing Master's Degree in Early Childhood, Arizona State University; Internships, Plus 150, Arizona State University; Bachelor of Arts in Early Childhood Education, with a Concentration in Structured English Immersion Endorsement and Sign Language, Arizona State University (2006) CERTS: Diploma, Chandler High School, AZ (1994) A/A/S: Phi Theta Kappa (2002-2006); Society for Creative Anachronism A/H: National Dean's List (2002-2006); Student Teacher of the Year Award, Arizona State University (2006)
Email: mikey_the_monkey06@yahoo.com

Mrs. Jennifer A. Viteritto
Title: QA Manager Company: Pegasus Technologies, Inc. Address: 932 Pilot Drive, Green Cove Springs, FL 32043 United States BUS: Aviation P/S: New Aviation Products, Aircraft Airworthiness MA: International D/D/R: Specializing in Quality Assurance aircraft certification H/I/S: Her Dog, Walking, Cooking, Listening to Charles Stanley EDU: Licensed Air Frame and Power-plant, Inspection Authorization; Designated Airworthiness Representative
Email: jviteritto@ptifl.com
URL: http://www.ptifl.com

Peter Vits
Title: President Company: Wing Partners, LLC Address: 147 W. 24th Street, Third Floor, New York, NY 10011 United States BUS: Furniture Importer P/S: Importing European Office Furniture and Glass Office Fronts MA: International D/D/R: Overseeing Company Operations H/I/S: Golfing, Traveling EDU: Associate of Science in Economics, Earned in Belgium
Email: pvits@wingpartners.com
URL: http://www.wingpartners.com

Ms. Diana Vivanco-Castillo, BS
Title: Project Manager Company: Pharmaceutical Services Corporation Address: 81 N. Mentor Avenue, Pasadena, CA 91106 United States BUS: Biotechnology Company P/S: Consulting, Validation and Audit Services, Technical Management, Compliance MA: National D/D/R: Addressing Pharmaceutical and Validation Compliance Issues, Attending High School and College Conferences to Promote the Chemical Engineering Field H/I/S: Marathon Running EDU: Bachelor of Science in Chemical Engineering, University of Illinois at Urbana-Champaign (1999) A/A/S: Scholarship Recipient, American Chemical Society
Email: diana.vivanco@gmail.com
URL: http://www.biotech.com

Michelle C. Viviel
Title: Owner, Manager Company: Chelly's Kitchen, Inc., dba Market Street Deli and Salads Address: 76 N. Market Street, Charleston, SC 29401 United States BUS: Restaurant P/S: Food Services Including Catering MA: Local H/I/S: Going to Beach and Ocean EDU: Associate Degree, Johnson & Wales University A/A/S: Charleston Jaycees
Email: mcv12266@hotmail.com
URL: http://www.marketstreetdeliandsalads.com

Jennifer L. Vizzo
Title: Director, Retail Finance Company: Allianz Global Investors Address: 1345 Avenue of the Americas, New York, NY 10105 United States BUS: One of the World's Top Five Asset Management Groups P/S: Financial Services MA: International D/D/R: Overseeing Business Accounting, Finance, Budgeting, Forecasting and Commissions H/I/S: Volleyball, Basketball, Softball EDU: Bachelor of Science in Accounting, Roger Williams University (1994)
Email: jennifer.vizzo@allianzinvestors.com
URL: http://www.allianzglobalinvestors.com

Crisanta Vogan
Title: Pharmacist Company: Rite Aid Address: 2580 Lake Avenue, North Muskegon, MI 49445 United States BUS: Retail Pharmacy P/S: Prescription Medications, Over-the-Counter Medications, Consulting Services, Household Goods, Personal Care Products, Beauty Supplies, Nutrition and Wellness Products MA: National D/D/R: Specializing in Pharmaceutics, Administering Prescription and Refills, Overseeing Daily Operations and Staff, Counseling and Educating Patients, Consulting with Doctors Regarding Medications H/I/S: Playing Softball and Football, Camping, Swimming EDU: Doctor of Pharmacy, Ferris State University, College of Pharmacy (2004); Associate of Science, Ferris State University (1999) A/A/S: Michigan Pharmacists Association; American Pharmacists Association; National Community Pharmacists Association
Email: spif36v@yahoo.com
URL: http://www.riteaid.com

Patricia L. Vogt
Title: Project Manager Company: Blue Cross Blue Shield of Massachusetts Address: 21 Oakdale Avenue, Dedham, MA 02026 United States BUS: Insurance Company P/S: Health Insurance MA: National D/D/R: Hosting Meetings and Presentations, Reporting to Upper Management with Projects, Working on Progress for New Products H/I/S: Boating, Basketball EDU: Master's Degree in Healthcare Management, Cambridge College (2004); Bachelor of Science in Management Information Systems, Northeastern University (1996) A/A/S: Sigma Epsilon Rho Honor Society
Email: plvogt@yahoo.com
URL: http://www.bluecrossma.com/common/en_US/index.jsp

M. Kathleen Volle
Title: RCP, II, RRT Company: St Louise Regional Hospital Address: 9400 N. Name Uno, Gilroy, CA 95020 United States BUS: Healthcare Hospital P/S: Acute Care MA: Local D/D/R: Adult Critical, Emergency Care H/I/S: Family EDU: Rogue Community College, Deanza College, Courses, Associates

Dianne T. Volpe
Title: Reading and Intervention Specialist Company: Jefferson County Public School Dept: Newburg Middle School Address: 8403 Happiness Way, Louisville, KY 40291 United States BUS: Public Middle School P/S: Education in Preparation for Secondary Level Schooling MA: Regional D/D/R: Working with At-Risk Sixth through Eighth-Grade Students on Reading Skills, Dealing with Low Achievers or Children with Behavioral Issues, Empowering them with Independence, Pride and Integrity, Using Stress Reduction through Alternative Methods Including Music, Water Fountains, Aromatherapy and Yoga H/I/S: Writing Poetry, Creating Art and Visiting Art Galleries EDU: Bachelor's Degree in Psychology and Art, Spaulding University (2002) A/A/S: Alumni Association of Spaulding University; Visual Artist in All Media
Email: phillygirltf@bellsouth.net
URL: http://www.jefferson.k12.ky.us/

Arthur von der Linden Jr.
Title: Executive Vice President Company: Wingate Financial Group Inc. Address: 450 Bedford Street, Lexington, MA 02420 United States BUS: Wealth Management Company P/S: Retirement and Estate Planning, Wealth Management Services MA: National D/D/R: Retirement Planning, Estate Planning H/I/S: Skiing, Golfing, Sailing, Participating in Outdoor Activities EDU: Master's Degree in Taxation, Bentley College; Master of Business Administration, University of Pennsylvania, Wharton School of Business; Bachelor of Science in Mechanical Engineering, Rensselaer Polytechnic Institute A/A/S: Financial Pros Association
Email: artvdl@yahoo.com
URL: http://www.wingatefinancialgroup.com

Mr. Lewis William Vondy
Title: Director of Aviation Company: SMDC Health System Address: 407 E. Third Street, Duluth, MN 55805 United States BUS: Nonprofit Healthcare Organization P/S: Healthcare Including Emergency Medical Services, Helicopter and Airplane Transportation MA: Regional EXP: Mr. Vondy's expertise is in aviation administration. H/I/S: Spending Time with his Family, Homeowner Management EDU: Bachelor of Science in Aviation Administration, University of Wisconsin-Superior (2007) CERTS: Licensed Helicopter and Airplane Pilot; Certification, Helicopter Association International
Email: lvondy@smdc.org
URL: http://www.smdc.org

Liudmila A. Vorontsova
Title: Scientist I Company: Diosynth RTP Address: 3000 Weston Parkway, Cary, NC 27513 United States BUS: Biotechnology Company P/S: Scientific Research, Pharmaceuticals MA: International EXP: Ms. Vorontsova's expertise is in scientific studies. H/I/S: Gardening, Hiking EDU: Ph.D., Earned in Russia (1991) A/A/S: American Chemical Society
Email: lstrelet@msn.com
Email: vorontsoval@bellsouth.net
URL: http://www.diosynthbiotechnology.com

Judith Voufo
Title: Registered Nurse Company: Massachusetts General Hospital Address: 173 Oak Street, Apartment 101, Newton, MA 02464 United States BUS: General Hospital P/S: Inpatient and Outpatient Healthcare MA: Regional D/D/R: Working in the Neurosurgical Department, Preparing Patients for Procedures, Monitoring Patient Treatment and Progress, Managing Wounds and Dressings, Administering Medications, Checking Vital Signs, Assisting with Phlebotomies and Electrocardiograms H/I/S: Music, Meditation, Bicycling, Running EDU: Bachelor's Degree in Nursing, Simmons College (2006); Registered Nurse Certification (2006); Certified Nursing Assistant, American Red Cross (2001); Certified in Phlebotomy and Electrocardiograms A/A/S: Sigma Theta Tau; Phi Beta Kappa; One Family, Inc.
Email: awoum13@hotmail.com
URL: http://www.massgeneral.org/

Peter J. Vrabel
Title: Dean Company: Metropolitan Education Address: 2084 Shiloh Avenue, Milpitas, CA 95035 United States BUS: School P/S: Education MA: Regional D/D/R: Administration, Overseeing Registration, Discipline, Enrollment H/I/S: Scouting, Camping, Biking EDU: Master of Education, San Jose State University A/A/S: CAROCP; ACSA; ACTE; Boy Scouts of America; CACP C/VW: President, Kiwanis Association
Email: pvrabel@metroed.net
URL: http://www.metroed.net

Fayth K. Vuong
Title: President, Co-Owner Company: Three Petals and Linens Address: 3001 Red Hill Avenue, Suite 5-104, Costa Mesa, CA 92626 United States BUS: Flower and Linen Service P/S: Wedding and Event Decor MA: Local D/D/R: Flowers, Linens, Chair Covers EDU: Bachelor's Degree in Human Services, California State University
Email: fayth@threepetals.com
URL: http://www.threepetals.com

Kim L. Wachtelhausen
Title: Project Leader for Beginning Educator Support and Training Program Company: Connecticut State Department of Education Address: 165 Capitol Avenue, Hartford, CT 06106 United States BUS: Board of Education P/S: Education MA: Connecticut D/D/R: Organizing Teacher Education Programs, Preparing a Portfolio H/I/S: Reading, Listening to Books on Tape, Spending Time with Family and Friends EDU: Pursuing Coursework in Administration and Educational Leadership, University of Connecticut; Master's Degree in Elementary Education, Central Connecticut State University; Bachelor of Science in Elementary Education, Central Connecticut State University A/A/S: Association for Supervision and Curriculum Development; National Council of Teachers of English; National Council of Teachers of Mathematics; International Reading Association; Phi Delta Kappa C/VW: St. Jude Children's Research Hospital
Email: wachtelhausen@aol.com

Margo C. Waddell
Title: Director for Programs **Company:** Women 4 Women **Address:** 5302 Schureck Court, Lagrange, KY 40031 United States **BUS:** Nonprofit Organization **P/S:** Program Development, Training and Technical Assistance Family Literacy and Early Childhood Programs, Encouraging Parents and Children to Achieve their greatest Academic Potential **MA:** National **D/D/R:** Overseeing the Staff, Raising Funds for Welfare Programs, Developing Financial Education and Welfare Programs **H/I/S:** Swimming, Hiking **EDU:** Bachelor of Arts in Social Work, Adelphi University (2001) **CERTS:** Early Childhood Training Credential, State of Kentucky (2005); Certified Trainer, National Center for Family Literacy (2002) **A/A/S:** Louisville Asset Building Coalition; Family Literacy Alliance; National Association for Education of Young Children; Keynote Speaker, National Center for Family Literacy
Email: margo.waddell@insightbb.com
URL: http://www.w4w.org

Darin K. Wade
Title: General Sales Manager **Company:** Rich Ford Sales **Address:** 8601 Lomas Boulevard NE, Albuquerque, NM 87112 United States **BUS:** Automotive Dealership **P/S:** New and Used Ford Vehicle Sales, Pre-Owned Inventory, New Vehicle, Parts and Service Specials, Fleet Specials, Service Scheduling, Parts, Accessories, Wholesale, Power Stroke Center, Body Shop **MA:** Regional **D/D/R:** Automotive Management, Hiring, Firing, Selling **H/I/S:** Playing Soccer, Playing Tennis, Billiards **EDU:** Bachelor of Business Administration in Automotive Studies, Northwood University (2005); Bachelor of Business Administration in Human Resource Management, The University of New Mexico (1995) **A/A/S:** Phi Kappa Phi
Email: dwade@rich-ford.com
URL: http://www.rich-ford.com

Ms. Kathy M. Wadleigh
Title: Co-Owner **Company:** Paper-n-Clay, LLC **Address:** 340 Stillwater Avenue, Bangor, ME 04401 United States **BUS:** Art Gallery **P/S:** Scrapbooking and Painting Including Bridal Showers, Classes on Paper Crafting **MA:** Local **D/D/R:** Organizing Events, educating patrons on making crafts, managing operations **H/I/S:** Attending Children's Sporting Events **EDU:** Associate Degree in Recreation Management, University of Maine (1985) **A/A/S:** CCSA **C/VW:** Arthritis Foundation
Email: kath@papernclay.com
URL: http://www.papernclay.com

Betty D. Waggoner
Title: Postmaster **Company:** United States Postal Service **BUS:** Postal Service **P/S:** Mail and Package Delivery, Postage Stamps, First-Class Mail Service, Express Mail Service, Registered Mail, Address Changes, Boxing and Packaging, Bulk Mail, Business Tools, Carrier Pickup, Certified Mail Service, Delivery Confirmation, Customized Postage, Electronic Postmark, Envelopes, Global Delivery, Ground and Air Transport, Insurance Services, Post Office Box Service, Money Orders, Passports, Postage Meters, Postal Supplies **MA:** International **D/D/R:** Supervising Clerks in Office, Preparing Inventory, Sorting Mail, Assisting Customers, Managing Postal Reports **H/I/S:** Skiing, Scrapbooking, Walking **EDU:** Diploma, Tyrone High School (1971) **A/A/S:** National Association of Postmasters of the United States
Email: waggonerhaven@hotmail.com
URL: http://www.usps.com

Carlton L. Wagner
Title: Owner **Company:** Wagner Trucking **Address:** P.O. Box 1331, Chickasha, OK 73023 United States **BUS:** Trucking Company **P/S:** Trucking Services Including Food Product Transportation **MA:** National **EXP:** Mr. Wagner's expertise is in business operations management. **H/I/S:** Fishing **EDU:** College Coursework **A/A/S:** American Legion; Local Chamber of Commerce **C/VW:** Fraternal Order of Eagles
Email: truck53268@yahoo.com
URL: http://www.cambridgewhoswho.com

Dr. Julie D. Wagner
Title: Advanced Clinical Educator, Medical-Surgical **Company:** St. Mary's Regional Medical Center **Address:** St. Mary's Medical Center, 235 West Sixth Street, Reno, NV 89503 United States **BUS:** Medical Center **P/S:** 1) Education 2) Healthcare **MA:** 1) Regional 2) Local **D/D/R:** 1) Online and Classroom Education 2) Medical-Surgical Nursing 3) Gerontology **H/I/S:** Walking Dogs, Archiving Family History, Fishing, Hiking, Cooking **EDU:** Pursuing Master of Science in Nursing, University of Nebraska Methodist College; Ph.D. in Adult Education and Gerontology, University of Nebraska, Lincoln; Master of Science in Health Education, University of Nebraska-Omaha; Bachelor of Science in Health Sciences, College of St. Francis **A/A/S:** American Medical-Surgical Nursing Society; Nevada Nurses Association; American Nurses Association; Nevada Pain Initiative Committee; Sigma Theta Tau **C/VW:** Nursing Scholarships, Clothing Drives, Gerontological Educator
Email: julie.wagner@chu.edu
URL: http://www.saintmarysreno.org

Timothy A. Wagner
Title: Chiropractor **Company:** Wagner Family Chiropractic **Address:** 3023 S Harvard B, Tulsa, OK 74114 United States **BUS:** Healthcare Facility **P/S:** Chiropractic Service **MA:** Local **D/D/R:** Chiropractic Health **H/I/S:** Hunting and Fishing, Riding Horses **EDU:** Palmer College, Doctorate Medicine **A/A/S:** Unified Chiropractic Society
Email: wagnerfamilychiropractic@yahoo.com

Richard D. Wahnetah
Title: Office Assistant **Company:** City of Hattiesburg **Address:** 103 Fulkner Road, Hattiesburg, MS 39401 United States **BUS:** City Council **P/S:** Public Services **MA:** City of Hattiesburg, Mississippi **D/D/R:** Telecommunications, Ensuring the Safety of Hattiesburg Citizens by Offering Drainage Improvements and Street Repairs, Operating Heavy Equipment, Dispatch **H/I/S:** Working on his Home, Fishing **EDU:** Diploma, Trenton High School, Trenton, New Jersey **A/A/S:** Cherokee Nation Eastern Band Tribe; National Rifle Association **A/H:** Acclamation, Mayor; Acclamation for Hard Work and Group Work, Wells Fargo **C/VW:** United Way
Email: crazzymonya@yahoo.com
Email: nsrwahnetah@aol.com

Saiqua A. Waien
Title: Director of Internal Medicine and Nephrology **Company:** Carolina Kidney and Endocrine Centers **Address:** 2809 McLamb Place, Goldsboro, NC 27534 United States **BUS:** Nephrology Practice **P/S:** Healthcare **MA:** Eastern North Carolina **D/D/R:** Nephrology Dialysis, Kidney Transplants, Consulting **H/I/S:** Working Out at the Gym, Gardening, Traveling **EDU:** MD, St. George University, Grenada **A/A/S:** American Medical Association; American Society of Nephrology
Email: waiensa@yahoo.com
URL: http://www.cambridgewhoswho.com

David B. Wait
Title: Director of Operations 4 Corners **Company:** CH2M Hill Trigon inc **Address:** 150 Tech Center Drive, Durango, CO 81303 United States **BUS:** Engineering Consulting Services **P/S:** Engineering Consulting **MA:** International **D/D/R:** Engineering **H/I/S:** Skiing, Hiking, Custom Furniture **EDU:** Bachelor of Science in Structural Engineering, Colorado School of Mines **A/A/S:** ACE
Email: dwait@trigon-epc.com
URL: http://www.cambridgewhoswho.com

Victoria Wakelee
Title: Certified Veterinary Technician, Registered Veterinary Technician **Company:** Animal Health Services **Address:** 37555 N. Cave Creek Road, Cave Creek, AZ 85331 United States **BUS:** Veterinary Clinic **P/S:** Veterinary Healthcare and Medicine **MA:** Local **D/D/R:** Managing Animal Behavior, Radiology **H/I/S:** Photography **EDU:** Associate Degree in English, San Diego State University; Associate Degree in Veterinary Technology, San Joaquin **A/A/S:** American Veterinary Society of Animal Behavior; American Veterinary Medical Association
Email: wakelee53@yahoo.com

Leonard L. Walch III
Title: Sales **Company:** Audi Henderson **Address:** 210 N. Gibson Road, Henderson, NV 89014 United States **BUS:** Automobile Company **P/S:** Automobiles **MA:** Statewide **D/D/R:** Home Theater Systems **H/I/S:** Playing Golf, Playing with his Scottish Terrier **EDU:** Bachelor's Degree in Hotel Administration and Marketing, University of Nevada **CERTS:** Certification, Rapport Leadership Institute; Certification in Senior Executive Management, Hughes International; Certification in Executive Management, Hilton Hotels Corporation **A/H:** Full Golf Scholarship, University of Nevada **C/VW:** Catholic Charities
Email: m3lenny@yahoo.com
URL: http://www.cambridgewhoswho.com

Lana Waldman Zukovski
Title: Human Resources Manager **Company:** Da Vinci Dental Studios, Inc. **Address:** 22135 Roscoe Boulevard, West Hills, CA 91304 United States **BUS:** Manufacturer of Superior Dental Prosthetics **P/S:** Dental Prosthetics and Veneers **MA:** Regional **D/D/R:** Human Resources Manager, Maintaining Employee Records, Medical Benefits and Promotional Reviews, Keeping in Tune with Compliance and Regulations Information and Laws, Administrator of 401 Plans, Posting Employee Recruitment Advertisements and General Human Resources Performance, Administrative Assistant to the Chief Executive Officer **H/I/S:** Auto Racing, Frequenting Museums and Cultural Events **EDU:** College Coursework **CERTS:** ADP Certified **A/A/S:** National Notary Association
Email: lana@davincilab.com
URL: http://www.davincilab.com

Carolyn J. Waldvogel
Title: Teacher **Company:** New York City Department of Education, Public School 155Q **Address:** 130-02 115th Avenue, South Ozone Park, NY 11420 United States **BUS:** Public Elementary School **P/S:** Elementary Education **MA:** Regional **D/D/R:** Educating Children, Teaching First Grade Students Reading, Mathematics, Writing, Spelling **H/I/S:** Crocheting, Camping **EDU:** Master's Degree in Elementary Education, CUNY Queens College (1991)
URL: http://schools.nyc.gov/OurSchools/Region5/Q155

Lorraine A. Waling
Title: Teacher **Company:** Waveland Elementary School **Address:** 506 E. Green Street, Waveland, IN 47989 United States **BUS:** Elementary School **P/S:** Primary Education **MA:** Local **D/D/R:** teaches reading, language arts, special studies, teach all subjects except music, art and gym, most rewarding aspect of her job is being around the children, dealing with first graders teaching them how to read **H/I/S:** Reading, Walking, Gardening, Horseback Riding **EDU:** Coursework in Continuing Education, Purdue University; Master of Education, Indiana State University; Bachelor's Degree in Elementary Education, Indiana State University **CERTS:** Certified K-8 Teacher **A/A/S:** South Montegamary Community Education Association; Indiana State Teacher Association; American Quarter Horse Association **C/VW:** Volunteer, New Hope Christian Church
Email: l.waling@southmontk12.in.us

Ann L. Walker
Title: President **Company:** Carl G. Jung Study Center of Southern California **Address:** 1011 Pico Boulevard, Unit 16, Santa Monica, CA 90404 United States **BUS:** Analytic Psychology Training Center **P/S:** Psychological Education for Licensed Mental Health Professionals **MA:** Southern California **D/D/R:** Jungian Analysis **H/I/S:** Staying Fit, Gardening **EDU:** Ph.D. in Clinical Psychology, University of North Texas; Master of Arts in Psychology, University of North Texas **A/A/S:** American Psychological Association; International Association of Jungian Analysts; North American Society of Jungian Analysts; Editor, Psychological Perspective
Email: annwalker@speakeasy.net
URL: http://www.cambridgewhoswho.com

Carol A. Walker
Title: Vice President of Quality Assurance **Company:** Siemens Medical Solutions Diagnostics **Address:** 333 Coney Street, East Walpole, MA 02032 United States **BUS:** Diagnostic Solutions Company **P/S:** Diagnostic Laboratory Equipment **MA:** International **D/D/R:** Overseeing the Quality Assurance Sector **H/I/S:** Golfing, Traveling, Entertaining Friends and Family **EDU:** Bachelor of Science in Medical Technology, Rochester Institute of Technology (1984) **A/A/S:** American Quality Controllers **C/VW:** United Way; Big Brothers, Big Sisters
Email: carol.walker@siemens.com
URL: http://www.cambridgewhoswho.com

Cheryl Walker
Title: Nurse Anesthetist, Owner **Company:** Valley Nurse Anesthesia LLC **Address:** 231 Beechwood Estates, Scott Depot, WV 25560 United States **BUS:** Healthcare Service Provider **P/S:** Relief Services WV, AANA **MA:** National **D/D/R:** Anesthesia **EDU:** Master's Degree in Health Administration, Marshall University Graduate College **A/A/S:** American Anesthesia of Nurses Association

Doretha C. Walker, MPA
Title: Resins Production Planner **Company:** DAK Americas, LLC **Address:** 1209 Llewellyn Road, Mount Pleasant, SC 29464 United States **BUS:** Manufacturing Company **P/S:** Chemical and Plastic Pet Resin for Soda Bottles, Low-Cost Production of Commodity Products **MA:** Regional **EXP:** Ms. Walker's expertise is in the manufacture of chemical resin. **D/D/R:** Overseeing Production Scheduling, Ordering Raw Materials, Managing Rail Car Fleet for Distribution **H/I/S:** Playing Sports, Running **EDU:** Pursuing Residency in Public Policy and Administration, Walden University; Master's Degree in Public Administration, Ball State University; Bachelor's Degree in Education, The University of Alabama **A/A/S:** Board of Directors, Center for Women; National Association of Professional Women; Association for the Study of African-American Life and History
Email: dwimages@hotmail.com

Gwendolyn V. Walker
Title: Office Manager **Company:** Mills Cardiology and Gastroenterology **Address:** 8515 Delmar, St. Louis, MT 63124 United States **BUS:** Healthcare **P/S:** Healthcare **MA:** Local **D/D/R:** Office Healthcare Management **EDU:** Attended Southern Illinois University **A/H:** Outstanding Ambassador Award **C/VW:** Local Police Department
URL: http://www.cambridgewhoswho.com

Jennifer M. Walker
Title: Teacher **Company:** Broadoaks Children's School of Whittier College **Address:** 134 Philadelphia Street, Whittier, CA 90608 United States **BUS:** Elementary School **P/S:** Elementary School for Preschool through Sixth-Grade Students **MA:** Local **D/D/R:** Co-Teaching third-Grade Students, Supervising Pre-Service Teachers and College Students, Administration **H/I/S:** Serving her Community, Cooking **EDU:** Master of Education, Whittier College (2007); Bachelor of Arts in Child Development, Whittier College (2003) **A/A/S:** Delta Phi Epsilon
Email: jwalker@whittier.edu
URL: http://www.whittier.edu

Judy D. Walker
Title: 1) Respiratory Therapist 2) Home Healthcare Specialist **Company:** 1) Alleghany Memorial Hospital 2) Lincare **Address:** 233 Doctors Street, Sparta, NC 28675 United States **BUS:** 1) Hospital 2) Residential Healthcare Center **P/S:** 1) Healthcare 2) Home Healthcare **MA:** Local **D/D/R:** performing respiratory care, mechanical ventilation nebulizer and home care treatments **H/I/S:** Traveling, Spending Time with her Family **EDU:** Associate Degree in Medical Science, California College of Health Sciences; Coursework, Wilkes Community College (1992)
Email: impressionsjwalker@yahoo.com
URL: http://www.cambridgewhoswho.com

Lynnda D. Walker
Title: Co-Owner, Manager **Company:** A Slender You **Address:** 292 Ridge Road, Suite 6A, Lafayette, LA 70506 United States **BUS:** Licensed Provider of the Victoria Morton Body Wrap **P/S:** Victoria Morton Mineral Body Wraps **MA:** Regional **D/D/R:** Offering Treatments of Various Conditions with Mineral Body Wraps, Promoting Weight Loss and Detoxification Benefits **H/I/S:** Watching Professional Football, Bicycling, Swimming, Enjoying Water Aerobics **EDU:** Coursework in Business Education, Cloud County Community College **A/A/S:** Better Business Bureau
Email: aslenderyoula@hotmail.com
URL: http://www.aslenderyoula.com

Marsha S. Walker
Title: Exceptional Student Education Resource Teacher **Company:** Buddy Taylor Middle School **Address:** 4500 Belle Terre Parkway, Palm Coast, FL 32164 United States **BUS:** Leader in Education **P/S:** Quality Educational Services for Students **MA:** Regional **D/D/R:** Educating Students with Physical and Emotional Learning Disability, Overseeing the Resource Science Program, Preparing for Florida Comprehensive Assessment Test **H/I/S:** Golfing, Working Out, Swimming **EDU:** Bachelor's Degree in Physical Education, Minor in English **A/A/S:** National Education Association; NTA
Email: mswalker46@hotmail.com
URL: http://www.flaglerschools.com/btms

Michael Walker
Title: President **Company:** TBK Services Inc. dba VIP Property Services **Address:** 42022 Fillmore Street, Belleville, MI 48111 United States **BUS:** Home and Business Improvement Company **P/S:** Home Improvement **MA:** Local **D/D/R:** Property Service **H/I/S:** Golfing, Fishing **EDU:** Coursework in Business Management, Washtenaw Community College **A/A/S:** Detroit Metropolitan Apartment Association; Washtenaw Area Apartment Association; Snow Plowing Institute and Management; National Lighting Institute Association
Email: vipcc@aol.com
URL: http://www.vippropertyservices.com

Patricia A. Walker
Title: Teacher **Company:** Children's Community School **Address:** 31 Wolcott Street, Waterbury, CT 06702 United States **BUS:** Community School Dedicated to Excellence in Education **P/S:** Elementary Education, Student Services **MA:** Regional **D/D/R:** Teaching Preschool Children, Encouraging Children to Read and Write, Guiding Students in Regards to Nutrition and Health, Teaching Third-Grade Students **H/I/S:** Collecting Hummels **EDU:** Master's Degree in Elementary Education, Central Connecticut State University (1982) **A/A/S:** National Education Association; Connecticut Education Association

Paul J. Walker
Title: Owner **Company:** Touch of Grace Outfitters **Address:** 105 Gower Circle, Garner, NC 27529 United States **BUS:** Clothing Store **P/S:** Clothing, Custom Logos **MA:** National **D/D/R:** Developing Advertising **EDU:** General Equivalency Diploma **C/VW:** Boys Youth Group, Macedonia Apostolic Church
Email: deconpaul@yahoo.com
URL: http://www.cambridgewhoswho.com

Thomas E. Walker
Title: Pastor **Company:** The Main Street Church of the Living God **Address:** 2000 N. Main Street, Decatur, IL 62526 United States **BUS:** Church **P/S:** Community Outreach Programs **MA:** Local **D/D/R:** Overseeing Church's Day to Day Operations, Assisting with the Youth Ministry, Overseeing After School Programs, Tutoring **H/I/S:** Traveling **EDU:** Associate Degree in Theology, Lincoln Christian Center **A/A/S:** Partner with School District to Business Students; MIA; Divine Group
Email: info@cambridgewhoswho.com
URL: http://www.themainstreetchurch.com

Amy Walker Gatta
Title: Senior Account Executive **Company:** Direct Media **Address:** 200 Pemberwick Road, Greenwich, CT 06830 United States **BUS:** Direct Marketing Advertising **P/S:** Provide Direct Marketing, Advertising for Clients on a National Stage **MA:** National **D/D/R:** Insert Management for Companies Such as Omaha Steaks **H/I/S:** Dancing, Traveling **EDU:** Bachelor of Arts in Hotel Management, Pennsylvania State University
Email: walker@directmedia.com

Sarah T. Walkowicz
Title: Teacher **Company:** St. Anthony of Padua Catholic School **Dept:** Early Childhood **Address:** 46 N. Old Cedar Circle, The Woodlands, TX 773382 United States **BUS:** Catholic School **P/S:** Instruction and Curriculum **MA:** Regional **D/D/R:** Creating Curriculum, Communicating with Parents on the Children's Developments **H/I/S:** Scrapbooking, Dancing, Reading and Traveling **EDU:** Bachelor of Science in Early Childhood Education, Franciscan University of Steubenville (2004) **A/A/S:** Music Ministry; Fundraising
Email: swalkowicz@staopcs.org
URL: http://www.staopcs.org/chuch/schoolwebsite2/index.htm

Jennifer L. Walla, BA
Title: Owner **Company:** Cowboy Catering Company & Mesa Market **Address:** 525 McGregor Drive, Gypsum, CO 81637 United States **BUS:** Catering Company **P/S:** Catering Services, Party Planning and Execution **MA:** Regional **EXP:** Ms. Walla's expertise is in food service. **D/D/R:** overseeing daily operations, catering, using organic and natural products for cooking and organizing wedding events and parties **H/I/S:** Fly-Fishing, Snowboarding, Wakeboarding, Skiing, Caring for her Dogs **EDU:** Bachelor of Arts in Communications, Western Michigan University (1991) **A/A/S:** Meals on Wheels Association of America; Chamber of Commerce
Email: jen@mesamarket.net
URL: http://www.mesamarket.net

Mrs. Detrice Maria Wallace
Title: Manager **Company:** Bowhead **Dept:** Organizational Management **Address:** 4900 Seminary Road, Suite 1000, Alexandria, VA 22311 United States **BUS:** Wholly Owned Ukpeagvik Inupiat Corporation Subsidiary **P/S:** Technical and Professional Services, Government Contracting **MA:** International **D/D/R:** Overseeing Strategic Planning and Process Re-Engineering **H/I/S:** Reading **EDU:** Master's Degree in Information Technology, American InterContinental University Online **C/VW:** Lupus Foudation
Email: detrice.wallace@bowheadsupport.com
Email: dmwallace@hughes.net
URL: http://www.bowheadsupport.com

John F. Wallace
Title: President **Company:** IGES, Inc. **Address:** 4153 Commerce Drive, Salt Lake City, UT 84107 United States **BUS:** Consulting Firm **P/S:** Consulting Services Including Geoenvironmental Consulting, Geotechnical Engineering, Waste Management **MA:** Regional **EXP:** Mr. Wallace's expertise is in geotechnical engineering. **H/I/S:** Golfing, Traveling **EDU:** Master's Degree in Civil Engineering, West Virginia University **A/A/S:** American Society of Civil Engineers; Geo Institute; American Society for Testing and Materials **C/VW:** Volunteer, Local Church
Email: johnw@igesinc.com
URL: http://www.igesinc.com

Robert Duncan Wallace, MD
Title: Medical Director, Psychiatrist **Company:** Copper Hills Youth Center **Address:** 2972 Devonshire Circle, Salt Lake City, UT 84108 United States **BUS:** Healthcare Center **P/S:** Healthcare **MA:** National **EXP:** Dr. Wallace's expertise includes adult and adolescent psychiatry including a continuum of outpatient, partial, inpatient, and residential treatment plus consultation and liaison medical and surgical services. **D/D/R:** Working Extensively with Adolescents and their Families, Treating Adults, Couples, Individuals, Groups, Geriatric Patients, the Physically Disabled with Psychiatric Problems, and the Chemically Dependent, Fulfilling Medical Directorships while Working Up to 35 Hours Weekly **H/I/S:** Golfing, Fly-Fishing **EDU:** Adolescent Visiting Fellowship, Albert Einstein College of Medicine of Yeshiva University, Bronx, NY (1967); Residency in Psychiatry, University of Utah (1967); Rotating Internship, San Diego County Hospital (1964); MD, University of Utah College of Medicine (1963); Bachelor of Science, University of Utah (1961) **A/A/S:** Board of Trustees, Drug Crisis Center, Salt Lake City, UT (1969-1972); Psychiatric Consultant to Peace Corps (1969-1971); Psychiatric Consultant, Champus; Former President, Utah Psychiatric Association; Utah Medical Association; American Psychiatric Association; American Medical Association; Pi Kappa Alpha; Salt Lake County Medical Society; **A/H:** America's Top Psychiatrists, Consumer's Research Council of America (2007); Intern of the Year Award, San Diego County General Hospital, San Diego, CA (1963-1964); Graduation Speaker, East High School (1956); Four Time Award Recipient as Hospital Programs Medical Director, Joint Commission on Accreditation
Email: gerriewallace@comcast.net
URL: http://www.cambridgewhoswho.com

Jakia L. Waller, MA, CCC-SLP
Title: Speech-Language Pathologist **Company:** Columbus Public Schools **BUS:** Public School District **P/S:** Primary Education, Speech Pathology **MA:** Regional **D/D/R:** Offering Speech-Language Pathology, Articulation, Phonology, and Language Evaluations and Treatment, Offering Speech Therapy for Kindergarten through 12th-Grade Students with Multiple Disabilities, Cerebral Palsy and Global Development Delay, Treating Handicapped and Autistic Students, Collaborating with Teachers, Parents, Occupational Therapists and Social Workers **H/I/S:** Reading, Studying Health and Nutrition, Fitness, Advocating for Children with Speech-Language Disabilities **EDU:** Master of Arts in Speech-Language Pathology, University of Cincinnati (2002); Certificate of Clinical Competency-Speech-Language Pathology **A/A/S:** American Speech-Language-Hearing Association; Ohio Speech-Language-Hearing Association
Email: walfaw10@aol.com

Victoria Wallette
Title: Owner **Company:** Vicky's Candles **Address:** 591 N. 25th Road, Suite B3, Grand Junction, CO 81505 United States **BUS:** Candle Manufacturer **P/S:** Candles, Air Fresheners, Show Dog Products, Jewelry **MA:** International **D/D/R:** Making Candles, Hand Making Jewelry, Store Operations **H/I/S:** Making Jewelry, Fishing, Hiking, Camping **EDU:** Coursework, Mesa State College **A/A/S:** Botanical Society; Board Member, Farmers Market **C/VW:** National Multiple Sclerosis Society
Email: vicky@summitsensations.com
URL: http://www.summitsensations.com

Anita M. Walls, CRTS
Title: Owner, Manager **Company:** Family Touch Moving **Address:** Plano, TX 75023 United States **BUS:** Consulting Company **P/S:** Consulting Services for Senior Citizens **MA:** Local **D/D/R:** Helping Seniors in Transition to a Senior Living Community, Assisting Seniors and their Families on Stress and Emotional Issues **H/I/S:** Traveling, Reading **EDU:** High School Diploma **CERTS:** Certified Relocation and Transition Specialist **A/A/S:** National Association of Senior Move Managers; National Association of Professional Women
Email: anita@familytouchmoving.com
URL: http://www.familytouchmoving.com

Louise K. Walls, MSW
Title: Director **Company:** Noble Care Corporation **Address:** 1070 West Schafer Drive, Tucson, AZ 85705 United States **BUS:** Healthcare Facility **P/S:** Residential, Respite, Day Programs for the Developmentally Disabled **MA:** Tucson **D/D/R:** Overseeing Services for the Developmentally Disabled **H/I/S:** Reading **EDU:** Master of Social Work, Purdue University (1979) **A/A/S:** Advocacy Resource Center for the Handicapped; Quality Alliance **C/VW:** Foster Mother, Ronald McDonald House, Disabled American Veterans
Email: noblecarecorp@msn.com
URL: http://www.noble-care.com

Richard P. Walmsley
Title: Operations Manager Company: Propel Schools Address: 24 S. 18th Street, Pittsburgh, PA 15203 United States BUS: High-Performance Public Charter School P/S: High-End Education MA: Local D/D/R: Overseeing Operations of Five Schools, Contacting Vendors, Managing Safety, School Safety, Food, Technology and Online Services, Hiring Staff H/I/S: Remodeling Classic Cars, Gardening EDU: Bachelor of Arts, Indiana University at Pennsylvania (1987); Associate of Applied Science in Criminal Justice and Business Safety (1985); Certified Asbestos Inspector A/A/S: Pennsylvania Association of School Business Officials; Association of Industry Security; Instructor, American Saftety and Health Insituite
Email: rwalmsley@propelschools.org

Sylvia M. Walsh
Title: Owner, Chief Executive Officer Company: The Spa at Traditions Address: 4101 Watson Boulevard, Johnson City, NY 13790 United States BUS: Resort, Spa P/S: Food Services Including Hospitality, Spa Services, Golf Course, Banquet Halls MA: International D/D/R: Managing Clients, Delivering Customer-Oriented Service H/I/S: Playing Tennis, Traveling EDU: Associate Degree in Secretarial Studies, SUNY Broome Community College; Diploma, Binghamton North High School A/A/S: Vestal High School Hall of Fame Community; United States Tennis Association; International Spa Association; NYSPA C/VW: Vestal High School; Vestal School Foundation
Email: sylvia.walsh@traditionsresort.com
URL: http://www.traditionsresort.com

James M. Walter
Title: Manager of Materials Company: Bioserv Corporation Address: 5340 Eastgate Mall, San Diego, CA 92121 United States BUS: Contract Manufacturer P/S: Contract Manufacturing MA: International D/D/R: Managing Materials and Facilities H/I/S: Bicycling, Golfing EDU: Bachelor of Science in Biotechnology, Concentration in Biochemistry, Worcester Polytechnic Institute C/VW: Worcester Polytechnic Institute
Email: jkwalter@cox.net
URL: http://www.bioservcorp.com

Prof. Clifford A. Walters, MD
Title: Doctor of Medicine, Executive Master of Business Administration Company: Loma Linda University Address: Loma Linda University, Chan Shun Pavilion Room 21015, Loma Linda, CA 92354 United States BUS: Nonprofit Religious University P/S: Higher Education for Undergraduate and Graduate Students MA: Local D/D/R: Directing Graduate Core Curriculum and Online Programs, Teaching Students Professionalism and Communications Courses EDU: Coursework in Gynecology, Claremont University (2002); Fellowship in Reproductive Medicine, University of Connecticut (1984) A/A/S: American Medical Association; Honor Society Beta Gamma Sigma
Email: cwalters@llu.edu
URL: http://www.llu.edu

Scott H. Walters
Title: Director of Tax Technology Company: The Gagnon Group, LLC Address: 184 High Street, Suite 400, Boston, MA 02110 United States BUS: Taxation Services Company P/S: Multi-State Tax Consulting MA: National D/D/R: ERP Applications, Oracle and SAP Software, Developing Tax Systems, Integration, Handling Manufactures and Retail, Managing Relationships with Companies Including Virtex, Sabrex and Tax Ware Systems H/I/S: Traveling, Dining Out EDU: Bachelor of Science in Business Administration and Economics, Illinois State University A/A/S: Institute for Professionals in Taxation C/VW: Special Olympics
Email: swalters@thegagnongroup.com
URL: http://www.thegagnongroup.com

Holly Lynne Walthers
Title: Business Owner Company: Vail Doggie Day Spa and Lodging Address: 2448 Garmisch Drive, Suite 5, Vail, CO 81657 United States BUS: Dog Day Spa P/S: Dog Boarding, Day Care Center, Dog Grooming MA: International D/D/R: caring for dogs, working with rescue organizations who foster dogs H/I/S: Hiking, Skiing, Running EDU: Master of Science in Special Education, Ball State University; Bachelor of Science in Education, Ball State University A/A/S: American Boarding and Kennel Association C/VW: Muscular Dystrophy Association; American Cancer Society
Email: holly_walthers@yahoo.com
URL: http://www.vaildoggie.com

David W. Walton
Title: Owner Company: David Walton Enterprises, LLC Address: 2589 Kingston Street, Newton, NC 28658 United States BUS: Real Estate Construction P/S: Beautification of Custom Homes as well as Commercial Work MA: National D/D/R: Customer Satisfaction, Believes in the Importance of a Job Well Done and That His Dedication to his Craft Speaks for Itself H/I/S: Spending Time with his Daughter
Email: dwenterprisesllc@hotmail.com

Myrtle R. Walton, GRI
Title: Realtor Company: JB Jochum and Associates, LLC Address: 2155 W. Highway 89A, Suite 213, Sedona, AZ 86336 United States BUS: Real Estate P/S: Residential, Executive, High-End, Creek Front, New Construction, Town Homes, Condos, Golf Homes, Gated MA: National D/D/R: Residential Properties H/I/S: Golfing A/A/S: Arizona Association of Realtors; National Association of Realtors
URL: http://www.jbjochum.com

Elizabeth M. Wanersdorfer
Title: Clinical Staff Registered Nurse, Clinical Instructor Company: Memorial Hospital Address: 1400 E. Boulder Street, Colorado Springs, CO 80909 United States BUS: Hospital P/S: Healthcare MA: Local D/D/R: teaching medical surgery nursing H/I/S: Cooking, Making Crafts, Running EDU: Master's Degree in Cardiovascular Nursing, The Catholic University of America A/A/S: American Association of Critical Care Nurses; Sigma Theta Tau C/VW: Silver Key
Email: jwanersdorfer@msn.com
URL: http://www.cambridgewhoswho.com

Stephanie Wang
Title: Chief Operations Officer Company: Upright Mounts, Inc. Address: 5595 Daniels Street, Suite F, Chino, CA 91710 United States BUS: Wholesale and Distribution Company P/S: Motorized Lifts and Mounting Brackets For Flat Screen TV's MA: International D/D/R: Managing Operations H/I/S: Spending Time with her Children, Reading, Watching Movies EDU: Bachelor of Business Arts, University of Iowa
Email: stephaniewang@urmounts.com
URL: http://www.urmounts.com

Maureen Wanner
Title: Owner Company: Timeless Salon Spa Address: 605 E Broadway Avenue, Bismarck, ND 58501 United States BUS: Cosmetology Salon P/S: One Location, Hair Care, Skin Care, Body Care MA: Local D/D/R: Advanced Skin Care, Chemical Peels, Microderm Abrasion H/I/S: Quality Time With Family, Sing EDU: Joseph School of Hair Design, Cosmetology Degree, Diplomas in Advanced Skin Care A/A/S: NCA
Email: in2skincare@bis.midco.net

Larry A. Warch
Title: Special Investigator Company: FBI Address: 2670 Walston Road, Mount Airy, MD 21771 United States BUS: Government FBI P/S: Background Investigator MA: National D/D/R: CFE, FCIS, CIA Insurance Fraud and Claims EDU: University of Maryland, Associate of Arts A/A/S: International Association ofAuto Theft Investigators
Email: lwarch@leo.gov

Glenda H. Ward
Title: Social Worker III Company: Swanson Center for Youth Address: 5119 Highland Road, Monroe, LA 71202 United States BUS: Juvenile Correction Facility P/S: In-House Juvenile Correctional Facility for Youths 12 to 21 Year Old, Adjudicated for Crimes Committed in the Community MA: Regional D/D/R: Conducting Group and Individual Sessions, Family Therapy, Working with the Purpose of Integrating Youth back into Society, Representing Youth in Court to Report on Progress Made H/I/S: Watching her Children Play Sports EDU: Master of Social Work, Grambling State University(1992) A/A/S: Board Member, Volunteers of America; National Association of Social Workers; Church Activities
Email: harris349578@bellsouth.com
URL: http://www.cambridgewhoswho.com

Linda M. Ward
Title: Teacher Company: El Paso Independent School District Dept: Green Elementary School Address: 5430 Buckley Drive, El Paso, TX 79912 United States BUS: School District P/S: Education MA: Local D/D/R: teaching early childhood literacy. organizing programs for veterans and their families H/I/S: Skiing, Playing Water Sports, Hiking, Reading, Spending Time with her Family EDU: Master of Arts in Education and Diverse Learning, University of Phoenix (1999); Bachelor of Science in Geology, The University of Texas of the Permian Basin A/A/S: Texas Classroom Teachers Association C/VW: Local Charitable Organizations; Local Church; Make-A-Wish
Email: lward@elp.rr.com

Nadine J. Ward
Title: Pressman, Realtor, Business Entrepreneur Company: Newsday Address: 235 Pinelawn Road, Melville, NY 11747 United States BUS: Publishing Company P/S: Newspaper MA: Metropolitan New York D/D/R: managing operations of the printing press H/I/S: Reading, Cooking, Spending Time with her Family, Entertaining EDU: Coursework in Real Estate Services, Long Island Board of Realtors; Diploma, Central Commercial High School CERTS: Licensed Realtor A/A/S: Keystone Realty USA C/VW: United Way
Email: njkward1@aol.com
URL: http://www.nadineward.com

Wanda L. Ward
Title: Educational Consultant (Retired) Company: Pittsford Public Schools BUS: Consulting Firm P/S: Education MA: Regional D/D/R: Educational Consulting, Directing the Teacher Center, Staff Development, Administration, Time Management Workshops for Teachers, Teaching Reading Techniques H/I/S: Golfing, Painting with Oils, Listening to Classical Music, Spending Time with her Family EDU: CAS, SUNY Brockport; Master's Degree in Young Childhood Education, SUNY Geneseo; Bachelor's Degree in Education, McMurry College A/A/S: Delta Kappa Gamma; Women in Education; International Regional Director, Banquet Speaker, Stockholm, Sweden
Email: wanaward@rochester.rr.com
URL: http://www.cambridgewhoswho.com

Carlanna Ward-Zygowicz, Ph.D.
Title: Advocate, Psychologist Company: Court Appointed Special Advocate Address: P.O. Box 880, Belvidere, IL 61008 United States BUS: Advocate for Abused Children P/S: Guardians for Abused and Neglected Children MA: Local D/D/R: Psychological Profiling H/I/S: Reading, Traveling EDU: Ph.D. in Education, Administration and Psychology, Pacific Western University, Los Angeles C/VW: Board Member, Lutherans in Medical Missions; Voice of Care; Lutheran Woman's Missionary League; Extra Mile Ministry
Email: czygowicz@hotmail.com
URL: http://www.cambridgewhoswho.com

Cynthia A. Ware
Title: Teacher Company: Stinesville Elementary Address: Stinesville, IN United States BUS: Public Elementary School P/S: Education MA: Local D/D/R: Teaching Language Arts H/I/S: Scrapbooking, Reading EDU: Master of Arts in Education, Indiana Wesleyan University A/A/S: Northeast Youth Association; National Education Association; Central Committee; Class Committee
Email: warec@bluemarble.net
URL: http://www.bluemarble.net

Harlena Elsie Warford
Title: Owner Company: Gut' Shu wu, Inc. Address: P.O. Box 273, Hoonah, AK 99829 United States BUS: Pharmacy P/S: Pharmaceutical Products including Skookem Ointment to Restore Damaged Muscles, Broken Bones, Neuropathy, Fibromyalgia and Other Degenerative Conditions, Devils Club Ointment for Eczema, Psoriasis, Dry Skin and Chapped Lips MA: International EXP: Ms. Warford's expertise is in native medicine. H/I/S: Cedar Basket Weaving, Ravens Tail Weaving, Designing Jewelry, Cooking, Singing EDU: High School Diploma CERTS: Certification in Native Arts A/A/S: Hoonah Indian Association; Hoonah Tandem Corporation; Honah Heritage Foundation; Sealaska Corporation; Sealaska Heritage Foundation A/H: Sealaska Heritage Foundation Award; Alaska Native Brotherhood Award
Email: gutshuwu@yahoo.com
URL: http://www.gutshuwu.com

Lenoria A. Warmack
Title: Community Resource Analyst Company: State of Michigan Address: 6821 Medbury, Detroit, MI 48211 United States BUS: Government Organization P/S: Social Services MA: Local D/D/R: Information Resources H/I/S: Reading EDU: Bachelor of Arts in Business Admin Management, Inster HS, Cleary Business College A/A/S: SD Sheba, YWCA, Work Forces Program, Vanguard Community Development
Email: warmackl@mich.gov
URL: http://www.mich.gov

Susan Q. Warner, CMP
Title: Director of Conferences Company: The Scientific Consulting Group, Inc Address: 656 Quince Orchard Road, Suite 210, Gaitheburg, MD 20878 United States BUS: Government Consulting P/S: Management Planning, Graphic Design MA: National D/D/R: Government Meeting Planning H/I/S: Golfing EDU: Pursuing Master of Public Health, Washington State University; Bachelor of Arts in Speech Communications, Penn State A/A/S: SGMP, MPI, Leukemia-Lymphoma Society
Email: swarner@scgcorp.com
URL: http://www.scgcorp.com

Barbara Warren
Title: Nurse Education Specialist Company: Baylor University Medical Center Address: 3801 Main Street, Second Floor, Dallas, TX 75226 United States BUS: Educational Healthcare System P/S: Preparing Students for the Medical Field and a Resource for Professional Education MA: Regional D/D/R: Nursing, Nursing Education, Performing Orientation of Unlicensed Assistive Personnel H/I/S: Crocheting, Knitting EDU: Master of Science in Nursing, Catholic University of America in Washington, D.C. (1972) A/A/S: Sigma Theta Tau; Academy of Medical-Surgical Nurses
Email: barbarwa@baylorhealth.edu
URL: http://www.baylorhealth.edu

Joyce S. Warren
Title: Community Care Specialist **Company:** Walgreens **Address:** 1410 Clearbrook Street, North Charleston, SC 29405 United States **BUS:** Retail Pharmacy **P/S:** Pharmacy, Photography Laboratory, Cosmetics, General Merchandise **MA:** Regional **D/D/R:** Filling Prescriptions, Combining Medicines, Consulting with Patients **H/I/S:** Reading, Shooting Pool, Rollerblading **EDU:** Bachelor of Science in Pharmacy, Medical University of South Carolina (1996) **A/A/S:** American College of Clinical Pharmacy; American Society of Health-System Pharmacists; The South Carolina Pharmacy Association; American Society of Consultant Pharmacists
Email: warrenjs@comcast.com
URL: http://www.walgreens.com

Whitney L. Warren
Title: Family and Primary Therapist **Company:** Four Winds Ranch Recovery Center **Address:** 501 N. Santa Fe Road, Guthrie, OK 73044 United States **BUS:** Private, Inpatient Treatment Center **P/S:** Rehabilitation Facility for Adolescent Young Women Suffering from Drug Addiction **MA:** Regional **D/D/R:** Combined Marital and Family Therapy with an Emphasis on Drug and Alcohol Addiction Issues, Acting as the Lead Clinician of the Facility, Mentoring and Overseeing Interns, Conducting Group Therapy Meetings Daily, Individual Therapy Sessions with Residents, Keeping in Contact with the Residents' Parents **H/I/S:** Wakeboarding, Lifting Weights **EDU:** Master of Science in Marriage and Family Therapy, Oklahoma State University (2005); Bachelor's Degree in Psychology, Oklahoma State University (2000); Associate Degree in Psychology, Cowley College (1998); Pursuing Licensure in Drug and Alcohol Counseling; Licensed Marriage and Family Candidate Program **A/A/S:** American Association of Marriage and Family Therapists; Oklahoma Chapter of Marriage and Family Therapists
Email: wwarren@atlinkwifi.com
URL: http://www.fourwindsranchrtc.com

Mark B. Washauer
Title: Owner, President **Company:** MBW Properties LLC and Washauer Development LLC **Address:** 1650 Cameron Avenue, Baton Rouge, LA 70806 United States **BUS:** Real Estate Development Company **P/S:** High-Density Condominiums, Office Buildings, Shopping Centers, Residential Sub-Division Development **MA:** National **D/D/R:** Residential and Commercial Land Development **H/I/S:** Working **EDU:** Bachelor of Science in Construction Management and Structural Architecture, Louisiana State University (1973) **A/A/S:** Home Builders Association
Email: mbw@washauerdevelopment.com
URL: http://www.cambridgewhoswho.com

Barry M. Washington Sr.
Title: Director **Company:** New Jersey Transit **Address:** 601 Doremus Avenue, Newark, NJ 07105 United States **BUS:** Public Transportation Agency **P/S:** Public Transit Services includes Buses and Trains, Airport Connections, Schedules, Online Trip Planner, Online Ticketing **MA:** Local **EXP:** Mr. Washington's expertise is in public transportation services. **D/D/R:** overseeing machine shop, overhaul shop, electronic shop and fleet of 3000 buses, managing daily repairs, building and rebuilding buses, repairing and rebuilding engines and transmissions, furnishing buses, supervising staff of 17 managers and 200 mechanics, managing 60 million dollar budget **EDU:** Coursework in Transportation **A/A/S:** Former President, Executive Board Member, Eastern Maintenance Bus Conference (1990-2008)
Email: cbopbmn@njtransit.com
URL: http://www.njtransit.com

Kate Washington
Title: Realtor **Company:** RE/MAX Benchmark Realty Group **Address:** 65-67 Main Street, Warwick, NY 10990 United States **BUS:** Real Estate Agency **P/S:** Residential and Commercial Real Estate Exchange Including Purchase and Sales of Residential, Executive, Lake Front, Newly Constructed and Gated Properties and Vacant Lands **MA:** National **D/D/R:** buying and selling residential, executive, lake front and gated properties and vacant lands **H/I/S:** Interior Design **A/A/S:** New York State Association of Realtors; National Association of Realtors
Email: katewashington@hotmail.com
URL: http://www.katewashington.com

Mary R. Washington, MLS
Title: Director of Library **Company:** Darton College **Address:** 2400 Gillionville Road, Albany, GA 31707 United States **BUS:** College **P/S:** Higher Education, Undergraduate and Graduate Degree Programs, Library **MA:** Regional **D/D/R:** Supervising Three Librarians and Three Lab Assistants, Attending Meetings **H/I/S:** Crocheting, Playing Tennis **EDU:** Master of Library Science, Florida State University (1973) **A/A/S:** Southern Rural Black Women's Initiative; Georgia Library Association; Secretary, AIMWM
Email: mary.washington@darton.edu
URL: http://www.darton.edu

Deborah A. Wasko
Title: Director of Orchestras **Company:** Blue Springs School District **Address:** 2000 Ashton Drive, Blue Springs, MO 64015 United States **BUS:** Public School District **P/S:** Primary and Secondary Level Education in General Studies, Arts, Music and Physical Education, After-School Programs **MA:** Regional **D/D/R:** Directing the Middle and High School Orchestras, Teaching Beginner and Advanced Strings, Developing Original Arrangements, Playing the Violin and Viola **H/I/S:** Playing in a String Quartet and Mariachi Band **EDU:** Bachelor of Arts in Music Education, University of Kansas City Conservatory (1991) **A/A/S:** The National Association for Music Education; American String Teachers Association
Email: dwasko@bssd.net
URL: http://www.bluesprings-schools.net

Donna Arlene Wassilchalk
Title: First Grade Teacher **Company:** Perry Elementary **Address:** 142 Constitution Street, Perryopolis, PA 15473 United States **BUS:** Elementary School **P/S:** Education **MA:** Local **D/D/R:** Teaching Children on an Elementary Level, Prior Teacher in Elementary Emotional Support Kindergarten through Fifth **H/I/S:** Baton Twirling, Dancing, Reading, Swimming **EDU:** Master's Degree in Reading, California University of Pennsylvania; Bachelor's Degree in Elementary Education, California University of Pennsylvania **A/A/S:** Kappa Delta Pi; Belle Vernon Area Twirling Corp, Assistant Director and Instructor; Yough Hish School Marching Band, Majorette Instructor; Kappa Kappa Psi, Sigma Phi Epsion Delta **A/H:** Nomination for Disney's Creativity in Teaching Award **C/VW:** Church Youth Group, Leader
Email: dwassilchalk@frazierschooldistrict.org
URL: http://www.frazierschooldistrict.org

Dr. Wayne Watanabe
Title: Chiropractor **Company:** Acupuncture Healthcare Clinic, PC **Address:** 3695 Alamo Street, Suite 205, Simi Valley, CA 93063 United States **BUS:** Healthcare Center **P/S:** Healthcare **MA:** Regional **EXP:** Dr. Watanabe's expertise is in chiropractic care. **D/D/R:** Offering Chiropractic Care to Patients Using Directional Non-Force Zone Healing and Neurovascular Dynamic Techniques **EDU:** Doctor of Chiropractic, Southern California University of Health Sciences; Bachelor of Science in Human Biology, California State University, Dominguez Hills **CERTS:** Certified Athletic Trainer, California State University, Dominguez Hills **A/H:** America's Top Chiropractor Award (2007) **C/VW:** World Wildlife Foundation
Email: waynewatanabe@sbcglobal.net

Adrian Waters
Title: Owner **Company:** Waters Property Management Services, LLC **Address:** P.O. Box 239, Randallstown, MD 21133 United States **BUS:** Property Management Firm **P/S:** Property Management, Tenant Placement, Property Maintenance, Rent Payment and Collections **MA:** Regional **D/D/R:** Recruiting, Project Management, Overseeing Daily Operations, Managing the Staff, Renovating Properties **H/I/S:** Golfing, Playing Billiards, Basketball and Football **EDU:** College Coursework, Morgan State University **A/A/S:** National Association of Residential Property Managers
Email: awaters@wpmsinc.com
URL: http://www.wpmsinc.com

Nancy L. Waters
Title: Licensed Practical Nurse **Address:** 2802 Parental Home Road, Suite 119A, Jacksonville, FL 32216 United States **BUS:** Hospital **P/S:** Healthcare **MA:** Regional **D/D/R:** Helping the Sick, Needy and Psychiatric Patients **H/I/S:** Needlepoint, Playing Scrabble, Bowling, Gardening, Spending Time with her Children **EDU:** Licensed Practical Nurse, Florida Community College, Jacksonville, FL (1991)
Email: nancy.waters@cwwemail.com
URL: http://www.cambridgewhoswho.com

Lisa R. Watkins
Title: Nursing Academic Division Administrator **Company:** Tulsa Community College, Nursing Division **Address:** 10300 E. 81st Street, Tulsa, OK 74133 United States **BUS:** Community College **P/S:** Associate in Arts, Associate in Science, Associate in Applied Science, Performing Arts Center, Accounting, Business, Child Development, Electronics, Healthcare Administration, Interior Design, Nursing, Stage Production Technology, Transportation Management, Veterinary Technology **MA:** Regional **D/D/R:** Geriatric Nursing, Managing New Facility, Teaching Programs Including Level I and II Foundation, Acute Care, Patient Care Technical Certification and Geriatric Technical Certification **H/I/S:** Antiquing, Traveling **EDU:** Master of Science in Nursing and Gerontology, The University of Oklahoma (1997); Bachelor of Science in Nursing, Northeastern State University (1991); Associate Degree in Nursing, Tulsa Community College (1982); Registered Nurse **A/A/S:** Aging and Disabilities Scholar Program, University of Oklahoma (2003); Oklahoma Gerontological Nursing Association; Oklahoma Nurses Association; Board Member, Oasis Adult Care Services
Email: lwatkins@tulsacc.edu
URL: http://www.tulsacc.edu

Judy Watkins-Tull
Title: Secretary, Treasurer **Company:** Devil's Shores Water Supply Corporation **Address:** P.O. Box 421535, Del Rio, TX 78840 United States **BUS:** Water Utility Company **P/S:** Water Supply **MA:** Local **D/D/R:** Handcrafting Gifts and Novelties, Secretarial Skills, Money Management **H/I/S:** Making Ceramic Pieces and Pottery, NASCAR, Fishing **EDU:** Trade Certifications **A/A/S:** Elected to Numerous Posts and Various Committees
Email: thetulls@rionett.coop

Becky L. Watson, Ed.D.
Title: Director of Public Relations and Marketing **Company:** Central Washington University **Address:** 400 E. University Way, Barge Hall, Room 406, Ellensburg, WA 98926 United States **BUS:** Public University **P/S:** Higher Education **MA:** National **D/D/R:** Designing Visual Communications, Graphics and Photography, Writing and Editing Media Relations, Working as the Voice of the University for External and Internal Media Messages, News Outlets and Campus News Forums, Working in Campus Public Relations **H/I/S:** Hiking, Bicycling, Volunteering with the Maya Research Program, Diggs Community Service **EDU:** Doctorate in Higher Education Leadership Administration, University of Nevada, Las Vegas (2000); Master of Arts in Graphic Design, Central Washington University; Bachelor Arts in Graphic Design, Central Washington University **A/A/S:** Publications Specialist, University of Nevada, Las Vegas, NV; Wakima Rotary; CASE, University and College Designers Association; Alumni Association, University of Nevada, Las Vegas; Alumni Association, Central Washington University; Maya Foundation; Kittitas Valley Community Hospital
Email: blwatson@charter.net
URL: http://www.cwu.edu

Damon T. Watson
Title: Chief Executive Officer **Company:** Elite Synergy, LLC **Address:** 7437 Maplewood Drive, Erie, PA 16510 United States **BUS:** Marketing Firm **P/S:** Provides Strategic Plans and Implementations for Developing Business, Advertising, Business Consulting, Financial Planning **MA:** National **D/D/R:** recruiting employees, advertising, fundraising, consulting, marketing, training employees and overseeing finance **H/I/S:** Mentoring, Four-Wheeling, Snowmobiling **EDU:** Associate of Arts in Electricity, Triangle Tech (1997)
Email: damon@linkmedia.com
URL: http://www.elitesynergy.com

Delores Watson
Title: School Director **Company:** Pat Goin's Beauty School **Address:** 3138 Louisville Avenue, Monroe, LA 71201 United States **BUS:** Beauty School **P/S:** Beauty Education **MA:** Statewide **D/D/R:** Teaching Beauty Education, Overseeing Four Schools **H/I/S:** Traveling, Spending Time with her Grandson **EDU:** Beauty Instructor (1989); License, Bastrop Beauty School (1979) **A/A/S:** Evaluator for NACCAS; Lady Auxiliary Treasurer; ASCS; Morehouse Parish, Louisiana; Cosmetology Association; Cosmetology Educators of America **C/VW:** Mothers Against Drunk Driving, Missionary in Mexico
Email: mdcwatson1@aol.com
URL: http://www.cambridgewhoswho.com

Joseph E. Watson
Title: Bishop, Overseer **Company:** United Christian Fellowship Community Ministries **Address:** 6200 S.W. 62nd Street, South Miami, FL 33143 United States **BUS:** Church **P/S:** Community Services **MA:** National **D/D/R:** overseeing pastors and all church operations, Managing Church Records **H/I/S:** Fishing, Football **EDU:** Master's Degree in Theology, Andersonville Theological Seminary (2005); Bachelor's Degree in Theology, Manhattan Bible College **A/A/S:** African-American Council of Christian Clergy; Mentor, Role Model of Excellence Program, Miami Dade County Public School
Email: josephesrwatson@bellsouth.net
URL: http://www.cambridgewhoswho.com

Peggy L. Watson
Title: Manager of Contracts and Pricing **Company:** Amgen, Inc. **Address:** One Amgen Center Drive, MS 27-4A, Thousand Oaks, CA 91320 United States **BUS:** Pharmaceutical Company **P/S:** Biopharmaceuticals **MA:** International **D/D/R:** Medicaid Rebate Program, Managing Government Contracts, Giving Medicaid Rebate Program Seminars **H/I/S:** Hot Air Ballooning, Boating, Sailing, Scuba Diving **EDU:** Coursework, St. Mary-of-the-Woods, Indiana **A/A/S:** Advisory Board Member, International Institute of Research Data
Email: pwatson@amgen.com
URL: http://www.amgen.com

Rev. Shirley McCoy Watson
Title: Owner **Company:** Health and Wellness Fitness **Address:** 10972 Acorn Park Drive E., Jacksonville, FL 32218 United States **BUS:** Healthcare Center **P/S:** Nutritional Drinks and Supplements for Health **MA:** Local **D/D/R:** Offering Business Operations **H/I/S:** Reading, Taking Walks, Watching Television and Action Movies **EDU:** Doctoral Degree in Pastoral Counseling, Golden State School of Theology **A/A/S:** NAACP **C/VW:** Florida Highway Patrol; American Cancer Society
Email: smw7@att.net
URL: http://www.cyberwize.com/4418276

Angela D. Watson-Cozier
Title: Fourth-Grade Teacher **Company:** Public School 114 **Address:** 1077 Remsen Avenue, Brooklyn, NY 11236 United States **BUS:** Elementary School **P/S:** Education **MA:** Local **D/D/R:** Teaching Fourth-Grade, Managing 23 Students **H/I/S:** Sports **EDU:** Master's Degree Plus 30 in Teaching and Reading, Long Island University, Brooklyn Campus; Master's Degree in Elementary Education, Long Island University; Bachelor's Degree in Elementary Education, Long Island University
Email: terry191@optonline.net

Monica DeLarie Watt
Title: Staff Nurse **Company:** Coral Spring Medical Center **Address:** 4245 N.W. 115th Avenue, Fort Lauderdale, FL 33323 United States **BUS:** Hospital **P/S:** Medical Services **MA:** Regional **EXP:** Ms. Watt's expertise includes labor and delivery. **H/I/S:** Dancing, Traveling **EDU:** Master's Degree in Nursing, University of Phoenix (2000); Bachelor's Degree in Nursing, Florida International University (1995) **CERTS:** Registered Nurse and Midwife, London, England **A/A/S:** Sigma Teacher
Email: monica.watt@cwwemail.com
URL: http://www.cambridgewhoswho.com

Ginger D. Watts
Title: District Sales Manager **Company:** American Family Mutual Insurance Company **Address:** 260 E. Horsetooth Road, Suite 103, Fort Collins, CO 80525 United States **BUS:** Insurance Company **P/S:** Auto, Home, Life, Business and Health Insurance **MA:** Local **EXP:** Ms. Watts' expertise includes agency development and consulting. **H/I/S:** Distance Cycling, Hiking, Exercising, Practicing Tae-Bo **EDU:** Coursework, Colorado State University **CERTS:** Certified Life Underwriter Training Council Fellow; Certification in Auto, Home and Health Insurance **A/A/S:** National Association of Insurance and Financial Advisor's; GMAA **A/H:** Athena Award **C/VW:** United Way
Email: gwatts@amfam.com
URL: http://www.amfam.com

Wylene S. Watts
Title: Executive Director **Company:** WellStar Health System **Dept:** Rehabilitation Services **Address:** 3950 Austell Road, Austell, GA 30106 United States **BUS:** Medical Healthcare System **P/S:** Healthcare **MA:** Local **D/D/R:** Overseeing Rehabilitation Services for Five Hospitals, Integrating Acute Care, Inpatient Rehabilitation, Long-Term and Outpatient Rehabilitation Care **H/I/S:** Antiquing, Reading, Meeting New People, Interior Decorating **EDU:** Bachelor of Science in Physical Therapy, Georgia State University **A/A/S:** American Physical Therapy Association; American Management Association; Georgia Hospital Association; Metropolitan Atlanta Area Rehabilitation Directors Forum; WellStar Leadership Institute; Physical Therapy Association of Georgia **A/H:** WellStar Best of the Best **C/VW:** American Cancer Society; American Heart Association; American Diabetes Association; World Vision; Habitat for Humanity; WellStar Foundation; World Missions; MUST Ministries
Email: wylene.watts@wellstar.org
URL: http://www.wellstar.org

Mark D. Waugh
Title: Product Manager **Company:** Murata Electronics, NA Inc **Address:** 2200 Lake Park Drive, Smyrna, GA 30080 United States **BUS:** Technology **P/S:** Electronic Components **MA:** International **D/D/R:** Project Management in Electronics **H/I/S:** Kayaking, Skiing, Mountain Biking **EDU:** Penn State University, Bachelors in Science
Email: mwaugh@murata.com
URL: http://www.murata.com

Rev. James A. Way
Title: Senior Pastor **Company:** Buffalo Baptist Church **Address:** 6390 Lockhart Road, Kershaw, SC 29067 United States **BUS:** Church **P/S:** Changing Lives to Change Communities **MA:** Local **D/D/R:** Organizational Administration and Music-Piano, Violin, Fiddle and Guitar **H/I/S:** Kick Back in a Hammock, Yardwork, Bow Hunting, Wood Working, Spending Quality Time with Family, Music **EDU:** Master of Divinity, Concentration in Missions and Evangelism, Southwestern Baptist Theological Seminary; Bachelor of Arts in Church Music, Charleston Southern University **A/A/S:** AACC
Email: jamaway777@cs.com
URL: http://www.namb.org

Marianne B. Way
Title: Field Engineer Specialist III **Company:** Xerox Corporation **Address:** 1350 Jefferson Road, Suite 801-37A, Rochester, NY 14623 United States **BUS:** Distribution Firm **P/S:** Color Printers, Office Equipment and Services **MA:** International **EXP:** Ms. Way's expertise includes document management and technical support. **H/I/S:** Quilting, Gardening, Caring for her Dog **EDU:** Pursuing Master of Arts in Organizational Leadership **C/VW:** Local Churches
Email: marianne.way@xerox.com

Barbara Joyce Marvin Wayne
Title: Author Of Tales **Company:** Tales From Moonfire **Address:** 23852 Pacific Coast Highway 349, Malibu, CA 90265 United States **BUS:** Private Publishing **P/S:** Tales From Moonfire, Letters From Moonfire **MA:** National **D/D/R:** Handwritten Manuscripts **H/I/S:** Writing **EDU:** Bachelor of Arts in English Literature, Finch College, New York **A/A/S:** Who's Who Of American Woman **C/VW:** Los Angeles Public Library
Email: hernewgod@aol.com
URL: http://www.cambridgewhoswho.com

Jon Weast
Title: Assistant Manager **Company:** Circuit City Stores, Inc. **Address:** 9950 Mayland Drive, Richmond, VA 23233 United States **BUS:** Retail Store **P/S:** Consumer Electronic Products **MA:** National **D/D/R:** overseeing operations, training, performing administrative duties, budgeting, managing sales **H/I/S:** Traveling **EDU:** Industry-Related Training and Experience; Coursework, John A. Logan Community College **C/VW:** United Way; Williamsburg Community Center
Email: jon_weast@circuitcity.com
URL: http://www.circuitcity.com

Tammy L. Weatherstone
Title: Co-Manager **Company:** Wal-Mart **Address:** 135 Fairgrounds Memorial Parkway, Ithaca, NY 14850 United States **BUS:** Retail Store **P/S:** Selling Electronics, Toys, Home, Garden, Baby Products **MA:** Local **D/D/R:** Managing Daily Operations **H/I/S:** Spending Time with her Children, Spending Time Outdoors **A/H:** Store of the Year (2004); Manager of the Year (2002-2004); Vanguard Award (1996) **C/VW:** Children's Miracle Network; Relay for Life; United Way; Parent Teacher Association
Email: gftlbe@yahoo.com
URL: http://www.cambridgewhoswho.com

Kathleen A. Weaver
Title: Teacher **Company:** North Shore School District 112, Elm Place School **Address:** 2031 Sheridan Road, Highland Park, IL 60035 United States **BUS:** Middle School **P/S:** Education for Sixth through Eighth-Grade Students **MA:** Regional **D/D/R:** Family and Consumers Science Teacher **H/I/S:** Golfing, Baseball, Football, Sewing, Food Preparation, Arts and Theater **EDU:** Master's Degree in Administration and Supervision, Loyola University of Chicago (1994); Bachelor's Degree in Home Economics Education, Iowa State University (1984) **A/A/S:** American Association of Family and Consumer Science; Illinois Association of Family and Consumer Science; Member and Conference Speaker, National Middle School Association; Member and Conference Speaker, Illinois Middle School Association; Vice President, Family and Consumer Science Teacher's Network of Northern Illinois; Board Member, North Shore Baseball League (1992) **A/H:** Teacher of the Year, North Shore School District 112 (2001-2002); Recognition for Outstanding Teaching in the 'To those Who Excel' Contest, State Board of Education (2002)
URL: http://www.nssd112.org/elmplace

Robert Weaver
Title: President **Company:** O & M Propeller Service, Inc. **Address:** 101 Ellis Street, Suite F, Staten Island, NY 10307 United States **BUS:** Retail Marine Repair Company **P/S:** Marine Propeller Repair and Sale **MA:** East Coast **D/D/R:** Administering Pitch Changes, Welding Propellers, Selling, Making Repairs and Custom Fabrications **H/I/S:** Fishing, Driving Four-Wheelers, Learning Something New Everyday **EDU:** Diploma, High School **A/A/S:** Chamber of Commerce; Write Your Congressman **C/VW:** Special Olympics; Mother's Against Drunk Driving; Cancer Recovery; Children's Make a Wish Foundation; Vanished Children; Veterans of Foreign Wars; National Guard
Email: onmpropeller@aol.com

Alice L. Webb
Title: Adoptive and Foster Parent **Company:** Licensed by State of Nevada **Address:** 1843 Escondido Terrace, Henderson, NV 89074 United States **BUS:** Government Agency **P/S:** Childhood Adoption Services **MA:** Regional **H/I/S:** Arts and Crafts **EDU:** Associate Degree in Child Development, Michigan State University (1995)
Email: al2334@cox.net

David Webb
Title: Production Team Leader **Company:** The Boeing Company **Address:** 3855 N. Lakewood Boulevard, Long Beach, CA 90846 United States **BUS:** Manufacturing Company **P/S:** Commercial Jetliners and Military Aircraft **MA:** International **EXP:** Mr. Webb's expertise is in human resource management. **D/D/R:** overseeing the manufacturing of aircraft **H/I/S:** Traveling, Swimming, Biking, Watching Broadway Musicals, Attending Concerts, Gourmet Cooking **EDU:** Master of Business Administration, Major in Human Resource Management, University of Phoenix; Bachelor of Science in Business Management, University of Phoenix **C/VW:** Habitat for Humanity; River City Mission; Second Harvest Food Bank; Covenant House
Email: 5qeese@msn.com

Carolyn J. Weber
Title: Master Affiliate **Company:** Independent Reliv Distributor **Address:** 2219 Grandview Avenue, Wooster, OH 44691 United States **BUS:** Manufacturing and Distribution Firm **P/S:** Nutritional Supplements, Weight Loss Products, Sports Drinks, Fiber Restoratives, Cardio-Essentials, Energy Drinks and Skin Care Products **MA:** International **D/D/R:** promoting, marketing, selling and connecting clients to representatives with similar health issues **H/I/S:** Collecting Swarovski Crystals, Steiff Stuffed Animals and Bells, Spending Time with her Son **EDU:** High School Education **A/A/S:** Catholic Daughters of the Americas
Email: carrottop@sssnet.com
URL: http://www.reliv.com

Ms. Dee Weber
Title: Owner, Manager **Company:** Elegance Plus, LLC **Address:** 4702 Johnston Street, Suite J, Lafayette, LA 70503 United States **BUS:** Boutique **P/S:** Bridal Gowns, Bridesmaids and Prom Dresses, Debutante Gowns, Children's Formal Wear, Accessories, Jewelry, Hats, Lingerie, Alfred Angelo Gowns, Ball Gowns, Justin Alexander Wedding Dresses, Eternity, Ella Rose, Advance Bridal, Sincerity **MA:** Regional **D/D/R:** Selling Bridal Gowns, Bridesmaids Dresses, Formal Wear for Women and Ethnic Apparel, Overseeing Staff, Managing Business Operations Including Sales, Ensuring Customer Satisfaction, Marketing **H/I/S:** Traveling, Listening to Music, Horseback Riding, Singing in a Choir and in the Atlanta Symphony Orchestra Chorus **EDU:** Coursework in Elementary Education and Musical Instruction, Lewis and Clark Community College, Godfrey, IL **A/A/S:** Lafayette Chamber of Commerce; Business Network International **A/H:** Presidents Club, T-Mobile **C/VW:** Teen Ministry, Cathedral of St. John; St. Jude Children's Research Hospital; Muscular Dystrophy
Email: eleganceplus@hotmail.com
URL: http://www.eleganceplusllc.com
URL: http://www.theweddingmarket.com

Phillip H. Webster
Title: 1) Resource Specialist 2) Travel Agent Part-Owner and Director of Adrienne Cruises Inc. **Company:** 1) Farragut Primary School, Knox County Schools 2) Adrienne Cruises Inc. **Address:** 8321 Brightmoor Court, Knoxville, TN 37923 United States **BUS:** 1) Public Elementary School Serving Residents of Knoxville 2) Cruise Only Travel Agency **P/S:** 1) Public Elementary Education for Local Students 2) Cruise-Only Travel Services **MA:** 1) Local 2) International **D/D/R:** 1) Teaching Special Education and Early Intervention in a Pullout Program, Teaching Directed Reading and Mathematics to Kindergarten and First Grade Students with All Levels of Disabilities 2) Offering Cruise Vacations on Ships from 21 Cruise Lines Worldwide **H/I/S:** Playing Guitar, Boating, Traveling (Especially on Cruises), Watching College Sports Avidly **EDU:** Master's Degree Plus 85 in Developmental Psychology, University of Tennessee (1972); Accredited Cruise Counselor, Cruise Lines International Association **A/A/S:** Council for Exceptional Children; BUDDY'S Race Against Cancer; FISH Ministries; Honor Society of Phi Kappa Phi; Vice President, Phi Kappa Psi Fraternity
Email: webster8321@knology.net
URL: http://www.adriennecruises.com

Debbie L. Wedding, RN
Title: RN, Charge Nurse **Company:** Deaconess Hospital **Address:** 600 Mary Street, Evansville, IN 47747 United States **BUS:** Healthcare Hospital **P/S:** Cardiology **MA:** Local **D/D/R:** Cardiac Catheterization Lab **H/I/S:** Motorcycles and Boating **EDU:** Henderson Community College, RN **A/A/S:** American Heart Association, Chairman of the Education Committee in the Cath Lab, Chosen This Day as a Team Leader
Email: dwnurse@bellsouth.net

Dennis D. Weeks, Ph.D.
Title: President **Company:** SIVAL Corporation **Dept:** Sterile Intravenous Admixture Labs **Address:** 5411 W. Orange Drive, Suite 11, Glendale, AZ 85301 United States **BUS:** Pharmaceutical Company **P/S:** Pharmaceutical Services and Assisted Living Facilities for Hospitals, Nursing Homes and Veterans **MA:** Regional **EXP:** Mr. Weeks' expertise is in pharmaceuticals services. **D/D/R:** Managing Operations, Collaborating with the Licensing Board, Maintaining the Sterile Compound Room, Entering Data for Automated Logs, Calibrating Equipment, Training Employees and Residents from Professional Associations **H/I/S:** Golfing, Riding his Harley Davidson, Woodworking, Metalworking, Restoring Classic Cars, Caring for his Dogs and Parrots **EDU:** Doctor of Pharmacy, The Johns Hopkins University (1979); Bachelor of Science, Ferris University (1972)
Email: dennis@sival.net

Paul J. Wehner
Title: Senior Executive Search and Human Resources Consultant **Company:** The Human Capital Group **Address:** 5630 Windridge View, Cincinnati, OH 45243 United States **BUS:** Executive Search and Human Resources Consulting Firm **P/S:** Executive Recruiting, Talent Acquisition, Human Resources Consulting, Human Resources Leadership and Support, Assessment and Development, Coaching and Team Facilitation, Performance Management, Succession Planning **MA:** National **D/D/R:** Overseeing Financial Services and Education, Developing Business, Networking, Consulting, Leads Human Capital Groups Cincinnati, Ohio Region **H/I/S:** Spending Time with his Family **EDU:** Bachelor of Arts in Psychology, Xavier University (1969) **A/A/S:** Cincinnati Chamber of Commerce; Board Member, Greater Cincinnati Human Resources Association
Email: paul@humancapitalgroupinc.com
URL: http://www.humancapitalgroupinc.com

Ann J. Weikel
Title: Owner, Manager **Company:** Little Rockspring Farm **Address:** 20430 Salem Road, Blairs Mills, PA 17213 United States **BUS:** Dairy Farm **P/S:** Dairy Goat Milk, Breeding Top Quality LaMancha and Toggenburg Dairy Goats **MA:** National **D/D/R:** Management of Daily Operations **H/I/S:** Painting **EDU:** Bachelor of Science in Zoology and Entomology, Pennsylvania State University; Plus 30 in Art, Pennsylvania State University and Montgomery County Community College **A/A/S:** Licensed Judge, American Dairy Goat Association; Licensed Judge and Classifier, American Goat Society; Former President, Pennsylvania Dairy Goat Association; Honored, Dairy Goat Pioneer Program, American Dairy Goat Association
Email: lrockspring@innernet.net
URL: http://www.lrockspring.com

Sherry M. Weiner
Title: Materials Clerk **Company:** The Finley Hospital **Address:** 350 N. Grandview Avenue, Dubuque, IA 52001 United States **BUS:** Hospital **P/S:** Healthcare **MA:** National **D/D/R:** Logistics of Freight, Light Bookkeeping, Problem Solving **H/I/S:** Camping, Participating in Outdoor Activities, Hiking, Reading **EDU:** Diploma, Hempstead High School **A/A/S:** Boy Scouts of America; PCC
URL: http://www.cambridgewhoswho.com

Roy E. Weinheimer
Title: Ranch Manager **Company:** Weinheimer Ranch Inc **Address:** 1767 N RR 1623, Stonewall, TX 78671 United States **BUS:** Ranching Agriculture/Food Production **P/S:** Cattle, Sheep, Goats **MA:** Local **D/D/R:** Ranch Manager **H/I/S:** My Family, Traveling, Reading **A/A/S:** School Trustee, On the Hospital Board, Cattle Judge
Email: roy.weinheimer.cww@e-mail.com

Mr. André T. Weir
Title: Architecture Manager **Company:** D. R. Horton Homes, Inc. **Address:** 8200 Roberts Drive, Suite 400, Atlanta, GA 30350 United States **BUS:** Home Development Industry **P/S:** Single-family attached and detached units for sale **MA:** Souteast United States **D/D/R:** New Product Design, Maintaining Operations of Existing Designs, Consulting with Outside Vendors, Responsible for Products in Regional Marketplace, Selling Single and Multi-Family Homes, Overseeing Residential Design **H/I/S:** Piano, travel, football **EDU:** Bachelor's Degree in Architecture, Southern University of Baton Rouge, la **A/A/S:** Southern University Alumni Association Atlanta Homebuilders Association
Email: atweir@drhorton.com
URL: http://www.drhorton.com

Michele S. Weisberg
Title: Sixth-Grade Teacher **Company:** Fort Lee School District **Dept:** Fort Lee School No. 2 **Address:** 2047 Jones Road, Fort Lee, NJ 07024 United States **BUS:** School District **P/S:** Education **MA:** Local **D/D/R:** Teaching Sixth-Grade Students **H/I/S:** Spending Time with her Grandchildren, Horseback Riding, Riding Motorcycles, Traveling, Reading **EDU:** Bachelor of Arts in Communications **A/A/S:** Curriculum Mapping Committee; Character Committee; Environment Club; Cheerleading Club; New Jersey Education Association; Leader, People to People Student Ambassador Program **C/VW:** Charitable Organizations
Email: weisberm@fortlee-boe.net
URL: http://www.cambridgewhoswho.com

Anne Marie Weisman
Title: Broker Associate **Company:** RE/MAX Shores **Address:** 4110 Merrick Road, Massapequa, NY 11758 United States **BUS:** Real Estate **P/S:** Residential Real Estate Including Investment Properties **MA:** International **D/D/R:** Managing Short Sales and Foreclosures, Selling Homes and Investment Properties **H/I/S:** Fishing, Boating, Home Decorating **EDU:** Bachelor of Arts in Accounting, New York University (1977); Certified Buyer's Agent **A/A/S:** National Association of Realtors; Long Island Board of Realtors; Massapequa Chamber of Commerce
Email: amweisman@optonline.net

Ron R. Weiss
Title: Sales and Leasing Consultant **Company:** Plummer Cadillac Buick Pontiac GMC **Address:** 1333 E. Kettleman Lane, Lodi, CA 95240 United States **BUS:** Automobile Dealership **P/S:** Cadillacs, Buicks, Pontiacs, GMC **MA:** National **D/D/R:** Selling and Leasing Cars **H/I/S:** Golfing, Wine Tasting **EDU:** High School Graduate (1980)
Email: ronw@plummer.com
Email: weiss-w@sbcglobal.net
URL: http://www.plummer.com

Kristine K. Weitzell
Title: Assistant Deputy Director **Company:** Iowa Department of Corrections **Address:** 510 E. 12th Street, Des Moines, IA 50319 United States **BUS:** Correctional Department **P/S:** Correctional Facilities **MA:** Iowa **D/D/R:** Security, Training **H/I/S:** Spending Time with Family **EDU:** Master of Public Administration, Drake University, Des Moines, Iowa; Bachelor of Science in Sociology, Iowa State University, Ames **A/A/S:** American Correctional Association; Iowa Correctional Association; Association of Women Executives in Corrections; United States Deputy Warden Association **C/VW:** Special Olympics, Iowa
Email: kris.weitzell@iowa.gov

Mori G. Welborn
Title: Massage Therapist, Owner **Company:** Beneficial Massage by Mori **Address:** 9947 Wolf River Boulevard, Suite 105, Germantown, TN 38139 United States **BUS:** Healthcare Facility **P/S:** Mori Took Her Background in Physical Therapy and Combined it With the Art of Massage. She Works Primarily with Prenatal Massage Clients and Medical Massage Clients-Orthopedic Patients, Arthritis, Lower Back, Elbow and Joint Pain. She will not deny a Massage for Relaxation and Pampering purposes, but she focuses on the Healing and Alleviation power in Massage. **MA:** International **D/D/R:** Certified-Prenatal Massage, Reflexology, Medical Massage, Deep Tissue Massage and Therapeutic Massage. Mori works primarily with Medical Massage clients and Prenatal 'Pregnancy' Massage Clients. She Implements many techniques into each session to create a unique individual massage. She has worked with many orthopedic issues such as low back pain, neck pain, shoulder issues such as rotator cuff pain and stiffness, golf and tennis elbow, sciatica, and foot pain etc. Though she believes and focuses on the healing and alleviation power in massage therapy, she also knows that sometimes we all just need to get away from the world, relax, and pamper ourselves and massage therapy is a wonderful reprieve **H/I/S:** Spending Time with her Husband, Going to the Gym, Working Out, Making Pottery **EDU:** Associate of Science in Physical Therapy, South West Community College, TN **CERTS:** Certified, Prenatal Massage; Certified, Reflexology; Certified, Medical Massage; Certified, Deep Tissue and Therapeutic Massage; Licensed Massage Therapist
Email: mgwelborn@hotmail.com
URL: http://www.morismedicalmassage.com

Julie A. Welch
Title: Credit Manager **Company:** US Foodservice/Knoxville **Address:** 269 Kings Court, Alcoa, TN 37701 United States **BUS:** Wholesale Food Distributor **P/S:** Food Products, Restaurant Equipment and Supplies **MA:** National **D/D/R:** Divisional Credit Management **H/I/S:** Spending Time with her Family **EDU:** High School Education **A/A/S:** National Association of Credit Management **C/VW:** Chilhowee Baptist Center
Email: jwelch7917@charter.net
URL: http://www.cambridgewhoswho.com

Brian D. Welcker
Title: Vice President **Company:** Alliance Realty Services, Inc. **Address:** 150 Walnut Street, Suite 700, Philadelphia, PA 19102 United States **BUS:** Real Estate Broker **P/S:** Full Service Real Estate Management and Ownership **MA:** Local **D/D/R:** All Real Estate Operations **H/I/S:** Golf, Kayaking **EDU:** Fordham University, Master of Business Administration, Certified Property Manager, IREM **A/A/S:** Institute of Real Estate Management, BOMA, Toastmasters
Email: bwelcker@allianceservs.com
URL: http://www.alliancerealtyservices.com

Brett K. Wellman
Title: Assistant Director of Resident Life **Company:** Alfred University **Address:** 1 Saxon Drive, Alfred, NY 14802 United States **BUS:** University **P/S:** Education **MA:** Regional **D/D/R:** Assisting First-Year Residential Students **H/I/S:** Hiking, Camping, Reading, Watching Movies **EDU:** Master of Education, SUNY Oneonta (2003) **A/A/S:** ACHVO-I
Email: wellmanb@alfred.edu
URL: http://www.cambridgewhoswho.com

Allison E. Wells
Title: Student **Company:** Vanderbilt University School of Nursing **Address:** 3415 W. End Avenue, Apartment 210, Nashville, TN 37203 United States **BUS:** Nursing School **P/S:** Instruction and Curriculum **MA:** Regional **D/D/R:** Offering Pediatric Primary Care **H/I/S:** Horseback Riding, Playing Soccer **EDU:** Master of Science in Nursing, Vanderbilt University, School of Nursing (2007); Bachelor's Degree in History, Vanderbilt University (2004) **A/A/S:** National Honors Scholarship Society
Email: allison.e.wells@vanderbilt.edu
URL: http://www.vanderbilt.edu/nursing

Catherine D. Wells
Title: Inclusion Specialist **Company:** Stanislaus County Office of Education **Address:** 1100 H Street, Modesto, CA 95354 United States **BUS:** Board of Education **P/S:** Education **MA:** Regional **EXP:** Ms. Wells' expertise is in modifying curriculum to accommodate kindergarten through 12th-grade students with disabilities. **D/D/R:** Overseeing 16 Schools **H/I/S:** Gardening, Swimming, Hiking **EDU:** Master's Degree in Special Education, San Francisco State University; Bachelor of Arts in Special Education, National University **A/A/S:** National Education Association
Email: cwells@stancoe.org
URL: http://www.stancoe.org

Mr. Joel Wells
Title: Physical Education Instructor **Company:** Frederic High School **Address:** 1437 Clam Falls Drive, Frederic, WI 54837 United States **BUS:** High School **P/S:** Education **MA:** Local **D/D/R:** Physical Education Instruction, Coaching Football, Wrestling, Track and Basketball **H/I/S:** Sports, Hunting, Fishing, Spending Time with his Three Daughters **EDU:** Bachelor of Arts in Physical Education, Ripon College, Ripon, WI; Certification for Bigger, Faster, Stronger (2007) **A/A/S:** Wisconsin Football Coaches Association; WBCA
Email: wellsj@frederic.k12.wi.us
URL: http://www.frederic.k12.wi.us

Sammie W. Wells
Title: Chief Information Officer **Company:** Ammunition Terminal Group **Address:** 6280 Sunny Point Road, Southport, NC 28451 United States **BUS:** Branch of the United States Armed Forces **P/S:** Protecting America's Freedoms at Home and Abroad, Securing the Homeland and Defending Democracy Worldwide **MA:** International **D/D/R:** Managing and Forwarding Cargo Information and Documentation, Supervising Radio, Phone and Network Infrastructure of Ocean Terminal Operations **H/I/S:** Practicing Martial Arts, Motorcycling **EDU:** Pursuing Master of Business Administration, University of North Carolina, Chapel Hill; Bachelor of Arts in Political Science, Eastern Kentucky University (1988); Certified Unix Administrator; Certified Microsoft Trainer; **A/A/S:** United States Army; National Defense Transportation Association; American SeidoKan Association
Email: sammie.wells@us.army.mil
URL: http://www.goarmy.com

William H. Wells

Title: Director **Company:** 1 John 2:6 Ministries **Address:** 6408 Welch Court, Arvada, CO 80004 United States **BUS:** Church Health and Growth Ministry Training and Consulting **P/S:** Small/medium sized church consulting, workshops, equipping church members for more effective ministry/service both in the church as well as in the community **MA:** Local **D/D/R:** Leadership Development, Teaching Church Members how to Become More Effective Servants of Jesus Christ **H/I/S:** Model Building, Reading **EDU:** Regis University **A/A/S:** National Network of Youth Ministries, Mentor Youth, Office of Reconciliation Ministries (Chapter Director-Denver Metro Area), Arvada Citizen's Police Academy Alumni Association
Email: holmesww@aol.com
URL: In Progress

Dr. Changhe Wen

Title: Assistant Director **Company:** 1) Rhodes Technologies 2) Purdue Pharma, LP **Dept:** Analytical Research and Development **Address:** 498 Washington Street, Coventry, RI 02816 United States **BUS:** Pharmaceutical Company **P/S:** Pharmaceuticals **MA:** International **EXP:** Dr. Wen's expertise includes analytical chemistry in pharmaceutical research and development. **EDU:** Ph.D. in Chemistry, University of Massachusetts Amherst **A/A/S:** American Chemical Society; American Association of Pharmaceutical Scientists
Email: changhe.wen@pharma.com
Email: cwen1@comcast.net
URL: http://www.pharma.com

Bertrum W. Wendell III

Title: President **Company:** Wendell Homes, LLC, Wendell Development LLC **Address:** 389 Edwin Drive, Suite 100, Virginia Beach, VA 23462 United States **BUS:** Real Estate Company **P/S:** Residential Building and Land Development **MA:** Regional **D/D/R:** Overseeing All Operations of the Construction Company, Supervising Accounting, Payroll, Budgeting, Advertising, Hiring and Firing, Visiting Sites, Making Sure Standards are Met and On Schedule, Collaborating on Designs and Architecture **H/I/S:** Hunting, Fishing **A/A/S:** Tidewater Builders Association; National Association of Home Builders
Email: wendellhomes@mchsi.com

Loni Wendt, M.Ed.

Title: Teacher **Company:** Waupun High School **Address:** 805 E. Lincoln Street, Waupun, WI 53963 United States **BUS:** Leader in Quality Public Education **P/S:** Optimum Learning Environment for a Diverse Population of Students, Developing a Positive Atmosphere in which Students can become Life-Long Learners **MA:** Regional **D/D/R:** Basic Skills and Special Education, Teaching, Mentoring and Monitoring 57 Students, Educating Freshmen, Assisting with Assignments, Helping with Homework, Using Alternative Curriculum to Assist with Projects in Areas of Interest, Personalizing Projects **H/I/S:** Crafts, Reading **EDU:** Master of Education in Curriculum and Instruction, Olivet Nazarene University (2002); Bachelor of Arts, University of Wisconsin, Eau Claire (1994) **A/A/S:** National Educators Association; Wisconsin Educators Association; Wisconsin Education Association Council; Winnebagoland UniServ; Waupun Educators Association; Instruction on Teenage Driving and Organ Donation in her Daughter's Memory; Melissa Hanson Foundation, Founded (2002)
Email: slwendt@charter.net
URL: http://www.waupun.k12.wi.us

Victor A. Wenger

Title: Clinical Manager, Therapist **Company:** District of Columbia Department of Mental Health **Address:** 1250 U Street, NNW, Third Floor, Washington, DC 20009 United States **BUS:** Mental Health Clinic **P/S:** Public Mental Healthcare **MA:** Regional **D/D/R:** Multi-Cultural Mental Healthcare, Spanish and American **H/I/S:** Relaxing, Watching Television, Reading **EDU:** Sciatica Comprehensive Development for Mental Illness, Drug Addiction and Alcoholism; Certified Dual-Diagnosis Therapist, American Academy of Health Care Providers; Certified Addictions Specialist, American Hypnosis Training Academy, Inc.; Art & Science of Clinical Hypnosis, Southwestern Academy of Crisis Intervention; Crisis Intervention-Advance Course, Nordestana University, Dominican Republic; Doctor of Medicine, St. Vincente del Paul Hospital, Dominican Republic; Medical Internship, St. Vincents del Paul Hospital **CERTS:** Certification in Crisis Intervention; Certified Diplomat in Clinical Hypnotherapy; Certified Cognitive Behavioral therapist; Certified Addiction Specialist **A/A/S:** Fellow American Psychotherapy Association; Brief Solution-Focused Psychotherapy; Master Neuro Linguistic Programming
Email: victordin@verizon.net
URL: http://www.cambridgewhoswho.com

Robin M. Wensel

Title: Registered Nurse, Certified Oncology Specialist **Company:** SUNY Upstate Medical University **Address:** 750 E. Adams Street, Syracuse, NY 13210 United States **BUS:** Hospital **P/S:** Healthcare **MA:** Regional **D/D/R:** Bone Marrow Transplant Nursing, Oncology Nursing **H/I/S:** Traveling, Enjoying Music, Playing in Two Jazz Bands and a Contemporary Christian Band **EDU:** Bachelor of Science in Nursing, D'Youville College **A/A/S:** Oncology Nursing Society; Contemporary Choir Worship Committee, Youth Choir Director, Director of Youth Groups and Programs, St. Paul's United Methodist Church **C/VW:** Church
Email: mochamist@usadatanet.net

Mary A. Wentzel

Title: Advanced Practice Registered Nurse **Company:** St. Francis Hospital and Health Centers **Address:** 5255 E. Stop 11 Road, Indianapolis, IN 46237 United States **BUS:** Hospital, Healthcare Center **P/S:** Acute Healthcare **MA:** Local **D/D/R:** Cardiology Nursing, Rehabilitation **H/I/S:** Traveling with her Family, Exercising **EDU:** Master of Science in Nursing, University of Indianapolis; Bachelor of Science in Nursing, Ball State University; Board Certified, American Nurses Credentialing Center **A/A/S:** Sigma Theta Tau International; Golden Key International Honour Society
Email: mwentzel1@sbcglobal.net
URL: http://www.stfrancishospitals.org

Aileen L. Werner

Title: Sales Representative **Company:** Stryker Corporation **Address:** 3800 E. Centre Avenue, Portage, MI 49002 United States **BUS:** Manufacturer of Medical Devices **P/S:** Critical Care Beds, Medical/Surgical Beds, Labor and Delivery Beds, Hospital and ER Stretchers and Hospital Furniture **MA:** International **D/D/R:** Key Account Management, New Business Development, Strategic Planning, Solution Selling, Sales Training and Development and Project Management **H/I/S:** Traveling, Wine Tasting, Cycling, Hiking/Walking, Alliance for Lupus Research (ALR) **EDU:** Bachelor of Arts in Business, Western Washington University (1988) **C/VW:** United Way, Alliance For Lupus, Guiding Eyes for the Blind, Humane Society, Mulitple Hospital Foundations
Email: aileen.werner@stryker.com
URL: http://www.stryker.com

John T. Wernette

Title: Surface Mount Engineer **Company:** Delphi **Address:** 7929 S. Howell Avenue, Oak Creek, WI 53154 United States **BUS:** Manufacturing Company **P/S:** Automotive Engineering **MA:** International **D/D/R:** Mechanical Engineering **H/I/S:** Staying Fit, Basketball, Golfing **EDU:** Bachelor's Degree in Mechanical Engineering, University of Wisconsin-Milwaukee (2002); Diploma, Heritage Christian School **C/VW:** Faith Builders
Email: jwernette@wi.rr.com
URL: http://www.delphi.com

Tasha K. Werry, M.Ed.

Title: Educator **Company:** Marietta City Schools **Address:** 401 Washington Street, Marietta, OH 45750 United States **BUS:** Public Educational System **P/S:** Teaching Students on the Primary and Secondary Levels of Schooling **MA:** Regional **D/D/R:** Teaching Fourth and Fifth-Grade Mathematics and Science, Acting as a Learn and Serve Building Representative for the School **H/I/S:** Painting, Exercising, Reading **EDU:** Master's Degree in Education, Ohio State University (1997) **A/A/S:** Women in the Sciences Summer Program; National Education Association; District Curriculum Council
Email: ma-ttwerry@seovec.org
URL: http://www.marietta-city.k12.ga.us/

Dawn R. Werts Philbin, MA, CCC-SLP

Title: Speech Language Pathologist **Company:** The Speech Language Dyslexia Clinic, PC **Address:** 100 Kellerman Lane, Waukee, IA 50263 United States **BUS:** Sole Proprietorship **P/S:** Speech Language Pathology **MA:** Regional **D/D/R:** Treating Dyslexia in Children and Adults, Assent Medication **H/I/S:** Spending Time with her Family, Reading **EDU:** Master of Science in Speech Language Pathology, Northwest Missouri State University; Master of Arts in Communications Disorder; Certified Dyslexia Therapist; Certified Dyslexia Diagnostician **A/A/S:** The International Dyslexia Association; Iowa Branch, The International Dyslexia Association; American Speech-Language-Hearing Association
Email: dawnphilbin@speech-language-dyslexia.com
URL: http://www.speech-language-dyslexia.com

Dona R. Wessels

Title: Administrative Assistant **Company:** FNBC Iowa **Address:** 383 Collins Road N.E., Suite 100, Cedar Rapids, IA 52402 United States **BUS:** Business Real Estate **P/S:** Buying and Selling Business Properties **MA:** Regional **D/D/R:** Overseeing Client/Broker Relations, Making Clients Feel Comfortable, Directing Clients to Appropriate Brokers, Managing All Advertising and Client Files, Connecting Business Buyers and Sellers **H/I/S:** Decorating, Exercising, Reading, Spending Time with her Family **EDU:** Attended Secretarial School, Northeast Iowa Community College, Peosta, Iowa **A/A/S:** Iowa State Representative for PostPartum Support International; Linn County Foster Care Review Board
Email: dwessels@fnbciowa.com
URL: http://www.fnbciowa.com

Ann Bell West

Title: 1) Administrator (Retired) 2) Teacher **Company:** 1) Tamalpais Union High School District 2) Oakland Unified School District **Address:** 227 Del Casa Drive, Mill Valley, CA 94941 United States **BUS:** School District **P/S:** Education **MA:** CA **D/D/R:** Teaching, Overseeing Administrative Duties **H/I/S:** Woodworking, Completing Construction Projects **EDU:** Master of Arts, San Francisco State University (1960); Bachelor of Arts, University of California (1953) **A/A/S:** Student Body President, Santa Rosa Junior College; The Associated Students of the University of California, Berkeley; Prytanean Women's Honor Society; California Teachers Association; Published Poet, Poetry.com **C/VW:** Various Charitable Organizations
Email: annbwest@earthlink.net

Jenny West

Title: Teacher **Company:** Liberty Elementary School **Address:** 11820 Liberty Road, Frederick, MD 21701 United States **BUS:** Elementary School **P/S:** Primary Education **MA:** Local **EXP:** Ms. West's expertise is in elementary education. **D/D/R:** Teaching Kindergarten Students **H/I/S:** Scrapbooking, Teaching, Camping, Traveling **EDU:** Master's Degree in Language Arts, Hood College; Bachelor's Degree in Home Economics, Hood College **A/A/S:** Frederick County Teachers Association; Maryland State Teachers Association; National Education Association Organizations: Treasurer, Frederick County Teachers Association, Former President, Thurmont Lions Club; Bereavement Facilitator, Compassionate Friends **A/H:** Agnes Meyer Outstanding Teacher Award, The Washington Post **C/VW:** Thurmont Historical Society; Thurmont Lions Club; Compassionate Friends
Email: jennywest229@msn.com
URL: http://www.cambridgewhoswho.com

Katherine Rose West Vallés

Title: Assistant Company Manager **Company:** New York City Opera **Address:** P.O. Box 20156, New York, NY 10021 United States **BUS:** Innovative Repertory, Theater **P/S:** American Opera, New Musicals, Avant-Garde Theater, Art Education and Outreach Programs **MA:** Regional **D/D/R:** Working as an Assistant Company Manager, Managing Human Resources, Insurance Claims, Workers Compensation and Payroll, Paying Stagehands, Selling Tickets, Hiring and Firing Staff **H/I/S:** Supporting the Pittsburgh Steelers, Making Independent Films **EDU:** Bachelor's Degree in Theater Arts, The Pennsylvania State University (1998) **A/A/S:** Actors' Equity Association; Production Manager, Prospect Theater Company (Five Years); Production Manager, 'Casi, Casi' Independent Film, Puerto Rico (2006); Stage Management Association
Email: kwestnyc@gmail.com
URL: http://www.nycopera.com

Raymond Westbrook II

Title: Physician **Company:** Arlington Medial Clinic **Address:** 3612 Matlock Road, Suite 104, Arlington, TX 76015 United States **BUS:** Physician's Office **P/S:** Healthcare **MA:** Local **D/D/R:** Internal Medicine **H/I/S:** Sailing **EDU:** Doctor of Osteopathy, University of North Texas; Residency in Internal Medicine, Methodist Hospital, Dallas **A/A/S:** American College of Physicians; American Medical Association; Texas Medical Association **C/VW:** Mission Arlington
Email: westbrook@sbcglobal.net
URL: http://www.arlingtonmed.calclinic.com

Orville A. Westlund

Title: Chaplain (Retired) **Company:** U.S. Navy **Address:** 2611 N. Busby Road, Oak Harbor, WA 98277 United States **BUS:** U.S. Navy **P/S:** Defense **MA:** Regional **D/D/R:** Preaching Christianity, Teaching Classes in the Community **H/I/S:** Reading **EDU:** Master's Degree in Divinity, Evangelical Theological Seminary (1956) **A/A/S:** Board Member, Nordic Lodge; Board Member, PBY Memorial Foundation **C/VW:** Sons of Norway; Presbyterian Church
Email: orville.westlund@cwwemail.com

Mrs. Jenifer R. Westphal

Title: President, Founder **Company:** Kyle Westphal Foundation **Address:** 1080 Stackhouse Mill Road, Newtown Square, PA 19073 United States **BUS:** Nonprofit Organization **P/S:** Community Services, Caring for Autism and their Families **MA:** International **D/D/R:** Organizing Programs, Assisting People with Autism Disorders and their Families **H/I/S:** Traveling, Cooking **EDU:** Bachelor of Arts in Political Science and History, Temple University; Bachelor of Arts in History, Temple University **C/VW:** Local Breast Cancer Organization; Local Homeschooling Resources; Young Presidents' Organization
Email: jenifer.westphal@cwwemail.com
Email: jrwestphal@kylestreehouse.org
URL: http://www.kylestreehouse.org

Eric C. Weydt

Title: Principal, Administrator **Company:** Holy Name Catholic Elementary School **Address:** 409 S. 22nd Street, Escanaba, MI 49829 United States **BUS:** Catholic Elementary School **P/S:** Education for Students in Prekindergarten through Eighth-Grade, Private Catholic Education **MA:** Regional **D/D/R:** Catholic Education, Administrator, Educational Leadership, Managing the School, Administering Meetings for All Employees, Supervising Faculty **H/I/S:** Walking, Reading, Music **EDU:** Pursuing Master of Science, St. John's University; Bachelor of Arts, University of Wisconsin (1986); Associate Degree, Marquette, Michigan **A/A/S:** Association for Supervision and Curriculum Development; National Catholic Educational Association; Michigan Association of Non-Public Schools
Email: holynameschool_1@hotmail.com
URL: http://www.cambridgewhoswho.com

Wendy B. Whang

Title: President **Company:** Bella Faccia Dental Spa **Address:** 12705 Monte Vista Road, Poway, CA 92064 United States **BUS:** Day Spa and Dental Practice **P/S:** Spa Treatments, Skin Care Products, Dental Services **MA:** Local **D/D/R:** Managing Business Operations **H/I/S:** Embroidering, Designing Home Decors **EDU:** Master of Business Administration University of California, Irvine; Bachelor of Engineering, University of California, Los Angeles **A/A/S:** California Dental Association; American Medical Spa Association **C/VW:** Rotary Club, California Chamber of Commerce, Local Schools
Email: ladybug81@mac.com
URL: http://www.bellafacciadentalspa.com

Hubert E. Wheatley

Title: Owner, Manager **Company:** Illiana Sports Timing, LLC **Address:** 429 Ravine Drive, Bedford, IN 47421 United States **BUS:** Electronics **P/S:** Sales, Services, Installation, Operating Equipment **MA:** Regional **D/D/R:** Industrial Electronics Engineering **H/I/S:** Yard Work **EDU:** Bachelor of Science in Engineering, University of Evansville; Certifications, Crane Naval Weapons, Support Center **A/A/S:** Indiana Swimming Team **C/VW:** Bedford-North Lawrence School District, Mitchell Community School, Knights of Columbus
Email: cormaz@insightbb.com

Janey Stewart Wheeler

Title: Assistant Director of Visitor Services **Company:** Oklahoma City University **Address:** 2501 N. Blackwelder Avenue, Oklahoma City, OK 73106 United States **BUS:** City University **P/S:** Higher Education **MA:** International **D/D/R:** Managing and Organizing the Student Ambassador Program, Recruiting, Training and Supervising, Student Retention, Acting as Liaison Between Students, Public and Community, In Charge of Campus Visiting Center On The University, Campus Visit Program and Ambassador Program **H/I/S:** Listening to Music, Watching Movies, Spending Time with her Grandchildren (4) **EDU:** Pursuing Master of Education in Behavioral Study, Oklahoma City University; Master of Liberal Arts in Leadership and Management, Oklahoma City University (2004); Bachelor of Arts in Psychology, Oklahoma City University (2001) **A/A/S:** Alpha Sigma Lambda; President, Collegiate Information and Visitor Services Association; National Association for College Admission Counseling
Email: jwheeler@okcu.edu
URL: http://www.okcu.edu

Kay J. Whelan

Title: Chief Operating Officer **Company:** Sawyer Design Associates, LP **Address:** 167 Turtle Creek Boulevard, Dallas, TX 75207 United States **BUS:** Commercial Interior Design Firm **P/S:** Interior Design Services, Furniture Sales **MA:** National **D/D/R:** Operations **H/I/S:** Reading, Exercising, Traveling **EDU:** Bachelor of Science, University of Texas at Austin
Email: kayw@sawyerdesignassoc.com
URL: http://www.sawyerdesignassoc.com

Lana Jo (Jody) Whicker

Title: Owner, President **Company:** The Common School, Inc. **Address:** 2084 S. County Road 125 W., Danville, IN 46122 United States **BUS:** Instructional Materials and Services **P/S:** Public Education and Instructional Materials for Educators and Students **MA:** International **D/D/R:** Creating Instructional Materials Including Lesson Plan Books, Primary Day Planners, Alphabet Books, Sky Writing, Lesson Plan books for Teachers, Lifelong Educator, Kindergarten Facilitator **H/I/S:** Restoring Historic Homes, Traveling, Reading **EDU:** Continuing Education, Indiana Wesleyan University; Master of Arts in English, Specialization in Lexicography, Indiana State University at Terra Haute (1989); Master of Arts in Teaching, Elementary Education, DePauw University (1973); Bachelor of Arts in Secondary Education, Concentration in German, English and Spanish, Purdue University; Bachelor of Arts in English, Butler University **A/A/S:** National Education Association; Indiana State Teachers Association; Indianapolis Educators Association; International English Association; International Education Association; Public Speaker on a National Level; Pilot Teacher, National Phonics, Language Arts and Reading Program; Wrote Children's Book in Pre-Publication; President, Whicker and Wallace Teachers, Inc., Offering Instructional Materials for Primary Grades
Email: ljwhicker@ccrtcblue.com
URL: http://www.cambridgewhoswho.com

Laverne A. Whisenant

Title: Aphaeresis Coordinator **Company:** Life Share Blood Center **Address:** 2051 N. Mall Drive, Alexandria, LA 71301 United States **BUS:** Blood Bank **P/S:** Quality Blood Components and Related Services for Use by Patients **MA:** Regional **D/D/R:** Automation of Blood, Creating a More Efficient Collection of Blood Components **H/I/S:** Traveling **EDU:** Licensed Practical Nurse, Alexandria Vocational Technical Institute **A/A/S:** American Society for Apheresis
Email: lavernw@lifeshare.org
URL: http://www.lifeshare.org

Mr. Ernest Whitaker

Title: Lead Science Teacher **Company:** Newark Public School **Address:** 150 Newton Street, Newark, NJ 07103 United States **BUS:** Public School District **P/S:** Education for Students in Pre-Kindergarten through High School, Supplemental Educational Services Program, Adult Education, English as a Second Language, Special Education **MA:** Regional **D/D/R:** Teaching Science to Students in Pre-Kindergarten through Eighth-Grade, Preparing Students for Grade Eight Proficiency Assessment, Teaching Summer Classes, Mentoring **EDU:** Pursuing National Board Certification; Master's Degree in Educational Administration, University of Phoenix (2006); Certified Supervisor **A/A/S:** New Jersey Science Teachers Association
Email: njwhit1.1@netzero.net
URL: http://www.nps.k12.nj.us/

Mary Katherine Whitbeck

Title: Teacher **Company:** Allendale Columbia School **Address:** 519 Allens Creek Road, Rochester, NY 14618 United States **BUS:** School **P/S:** Education **MA:** Local **D/D/R:** Teaching Language Arts **H/I/S:** Reading, Golfing, Swimming, Boating, Gardening **EDU:** Master's Degree in Education, Concentration in Early Childhood Education, Nazareth College, Rochester, NY (1992); Bachelor's Degree in Psychology, Concentration in Elementary Education, SUNY, Brockport (1990) **C/VW:** Young Men's Christian Association; New York State Association of Independent Schools
Email: mwhitbeck@allendalecolumbia.org

Barbara A. White, BSW, MA

Title: Social Worker **Company:** First Home Health and Hospice Inc. **Address:** 235 N. McPherson Church Road, Fayetteville, NC 28303 United States **BUS:** Private, Nonprofit Home Healthcare Agency **P/S:** First Home Health and Hospice, Hospice Care and Private Duty Services **MA:** Regional **D/D/R:** Completing Social Work in Home Healthcare and Hospice, Offering Bereavement Counseling **EDU:** Master's Degree in Counseling, Webster University, NC (2006) **A/A/S:** National Association of Social Workers

Brenda L. White

Title: Chief Executive Officer, Owner, Operator **Company:** Rocking B Farms **Address:** 7840 Blue Springs Road, Sweetwater, TN 37874 United States **BUS:** Farm **P/S:** Breeding Black Angus Cattle, Growing Tobacco **MA:** National **D/D/R:** Business Management **H/I/S:** Spending Time with her Grandchildren, Traveling **EDU:** Continuing Education Coursework in Business, Hiwassee College, Madisonville; Real Estate License, Hiwassee College, Madisonville (1985); Diploma, Madisonville High School **A/A/S:** National Cattlemen's Beef Association; Burley Tobacco Growers Cooperative Association; Monroe Burley Tobacco Growers Cooperative Association; Women's Cattle Association of America; Farm Bureau Association of Loudon County; Loudon County Cattlemans Association **C/VW:** St. Jude Children's Research Hospital, Loudon County Advocacy Agency
Email: blw02@netzero.com

Cynthia E. White

Title: Special Education Teacher **Company:** Hope School **Address:** 2031 Hope School Drive, Marianna, FL 32448 United States **BUS:** School for Special Needs Students **P/S:** Special Education **MA:** Local **D/D/R:** Teaching Special Needs Students, Special Education **H/I/S:** Playing Softball, Running, Exercising **EDU:** Bachelor's Degree in Elementary Education, Troy State University **A/A/S:** Chairwoman, Homecoming; Chairwoman, Harvest Day **C/VW:** Local High School
Email: cynthia.white@jcsb.org

Elizabeth D. White

Title: President **Company:** Betsy White Enterprises, Inc. **Address:** 22 New Shore Road, Waterford, CT 06385 United States **BUS:** Production Company **P/S:** Producing Films and Theater Shows **MA:** National **D/D/R:** Producing Films and Theater Shows **H/I/S:** Creating Jewelry, Sailing **EDU:** Industry-Related Training and Experience **A/A/S:** League of New York Theatre; League of Professional Theatre Women; The Cosmopolitan Club; Wadsworth Atheneum Museum of Art; United States Coast Guard Auxiliary **C/VW:** Founding Member, Eugene O'Neill Memorial Theater Center
Email: betsywhite@nyc.rr.com

Mr. Frederick Richard White

Title: President, Executive Chef **Company:** NWB Enterprises, Inc. dba Muffy's Mountain Burgers & Such **Address:** 364 Blue Ridge Street, Blairsville, GA 30512 United States **BUS:** Restaurant **P/S:** Casual Dining, Food and Catering Services **MA:** Regional **D/D/R:** Overseeing All Food Preparation and Cooking, Planning Menus, Offering Catering Services, Ensuring Customer Service, Creating Seasonal and Casual Upscale Dining Atmospheres **H/I/S:** Traveling, Playing Football **EDU:** Associate Degree in Business Administration, South Florida University (1984) **A/A/S:** Union County Chamber of Commerce
Email: wertlesnert@yahoo.com

Dr. Jess-Juanita White

Title: Third-Grade Educator **Company:** Washington School **Address:** 862 W. McHood Road, Winslow, AZ 86047 United States **BUS:** Public Elementary School Serving Residents of Winslow **P/S:** Public Elementary Education for Local Students **MA:** Local **D/D/R:** Teaching Remedial Reading in an Inclusion and Self-Contained Classroom, Creating Lesson Plans, Interacting Parents, Recording Student Progress, Mentoring New Teachers **EDU:** Doctorate Degree in Education, Montgomery College, Rockville (2003) **A/A/S:** National Education Association; American Federation of Teachers; Consortium on Reading Excellence
Email: jwhite@winslowsdk12.az.us

Lance A. White

Title: Owner **Company:** Whitedel dba Taken to The Cleaners **Address:** P.O. Box 5372, Lincoln, NE 68505 United States **BUS:** Dry Cleaning Company **P/S:** Dry Cleaning Services **MA:** Local **EXP:** Mr. White's expertise is in business management. **D/D/R:** Managing Operations Including Pick-ups and Deliveries, Training Employees, Ensuring Customer Satisfaction **EDU:** Bachelor of Arts in Journalism, University of Nebraska **A/A/S:** Better Business Bureau, Lincoln Chamber of Commerce; Loyola Institute of Business Administration
Email: takentothecleaners@windstream.net

Margaret White

Title: Founder **Company:** Sailors Remembrance Day **Address:** P.O. Box 2034, St. Augustine, FL 32085 United States **BUS:** Water and Boating Safety Skills Organization; Lifeguarding; and Community Service **P/S:** Sailors Remembrance Day Festival, Water, Boating and Safety Skills Education **MA:** National **D/D/R:** Advocating Water, Shark Awareness and Boating Safety Skills, Speaking Engagements with Public Officials **H/I/S:** Organizing Sailors Remembrance Day, Working with Children, Teaching Swimming, Boating **EDU:** 78 College credits JU FJC University of TN **A/A/S:** United States Coast Guard Auxiliary; World Ocean Day **C/VW:** Volunteer, Scenic Byway A1A Trash Pickup; SharkBait Foundation: all for festival of Sailors Remembrance Day
Email: shark_bait@bellsouth.net
URL: http://www.sharkb8.net

Michael W. White

Title: Repair Process Manager **Company:** Collision Plus **Address:** 1274 Central Park Drive, O'Fallon, IL 62269 United States **BUS:** Automobile Repair Business **P/S:** Autobody and Collision Repair for Damaged Cars, Local Pickup and Delivery, Claims Handling Assistance, Personally Signed Warranty **MA:** Regional **D/D/R:** Managing Insurance Claims and Damage Estimates, Writing Damage Reports, Keeping Customers Updated on their Vehicle Status **H/I/S:** Camping, NASCAR Racing, Four-Wheeling **EDU:** Associate Degree in General Studies and Survival Equipment Technology, Davis-Monthan Air Force Base (1999) **A/A/S:** Former Member, Elks Club; U.S. Military
Email: Michael.White@cwwemail.com
URL: http://www.collisionplus.com

Pam K. White

Title: Associate Director of Finance and Administration **Company:** City of Albuquerque **Dept:** Aviation Department **Address:** 2200 Sunport Boulevard S.E., Albuquerque, NM 87106 United States **BUS:** Government Organization **P/S:** Aviation Services **MA:** Albuquerque, NM **D/D/R:** Processing Payrolls, Managing Administration and Financial Support to the Aviation Department and Financial Team for Airport Revenue Bonds, Implementing Performance Based Measures, Preparing and Monitoring Budgets, Creating and Developing Business Policies, Promoting Team Efforts, Supervising Administrative and Financial Divisions Including Financial Manager and Auditors, Overseeing Capital Improvements, Debt Service, Rates, Charges Calculations Per Airline Agreements, Business Development, and Accounts Receivable and Payables, Purchasing, Refunding on Airport Revenue Bonds **H/I/S:** Working as an Amateur Radio Operator, Gardening, Maintaining Saltwater Aquariums **EDU:** Bachelor of Arts in Finance and Administration, University of Phoenix **A/A/S:** Women in Aviation; American Association of Airport Executives **C/VW:** Regional Treasurer, Gold Wing Road Riders Association
Email: pwhite@cabq.gov
URL: http://www.cabq.gov

Rebecca 'Susan' White

Title: Clinical Laboratory Scientist, Medical Technologist **Company:** Wake Forest University Baptist Medical Center (Downtown Health Plaza) **Address:** 3730 Derbyshire Road, Winston-Salem, NC 27104 United States **BUS:** One of the Nation's Preeminent Academic Medical Centers **P/S:** Acute Care, Rehabilitation and Long-Term Care Beds, Outpatient Services and Community Health and Information Centers **MA:** Regional **D/D/R:** Working as a Staff Technologist, Generalist, Working in the Main Hospital Laboratory, Outpatient Clinic and Cancer Center, Offering Hematology, Chemistry, Urinalysis, DNA Procedures and Central Processing, **H/I/S:** Walking, Traveling, Eating Out, Attending Family Events **EDU:** Moses Cone Hospital School of Medical Technology (1968); Bachelor of Science in Biology, Western Carolina University (1967) **A/A/S:** National Boards for Medical Technologist; Clinical Laboratory Scientist Credentials (1994, Re-Certified 2006); American Society of Clinical Pathologists; American Society of Clinical Laboratory Scientists; Former Professor of Medical Technology, The University of North Carolina at Greensboro; Chief Technologist, Veterans Affairs Outpatient Clinic; Assistant Chief Technologist, Teaching Technologist, Hospital Blood Bank; Generalists
Email: ewhite25@bellsouth.net
URL: http://www1.wfubmc.edu/dhp

Roberta J. White McCullough

Title: Office Manager, Human Resource Manager **Company:** Panel Processing of Texas, Inc. **Address:** 1010 S. Bolton Street, Jacksonville, TX 75766 United States **BUS:** Manufacturing Company **P/S:** Wood Store Fixtures Including Custom Finished and Fabricated Hardboards and Pegboards, Custom Fabricated Particleboards, Melamine Panel Components and Parts, Samples, Display and Tile Boards, Chalkboards and Marker boards **MA:** Statewide **D/D/R:** Purchasing, Offering Insurance, Processing Payroll, Hiring, Overseeing Invoices, Analyzing Labor Reports **H/I/S:** Reading, Traveling, Watching Movies **EDU:** Associate Degree in Business, Southwestern University, with Honors (1967) **A/H:** Daughters of the American Revolution Award
Email: rwhite@panel.com
URL: http://www.panel.com

Joyce M. Whited

Title: Respiratory Care Therapist **Company:** Smithville Regional Hospital **Address:** 800 Highway 71E, Smithville, TX 78616 United States **BUS:** Hospital **P/S:** Healthcare **MA:** Local **D/D/R:** Respiratory Care Therapy **H/I/S:** Reading **EDU:** Certified Respiratory Care Technician, Alvin Community College **A/A/S:** TSRC
Email: jyocewhited@yahoo.com
URL: http://www.cambridgewhoswho.com

Inga Whitehead

Title: Realtor Associate **Company:** RE/MAX Masters **Address:** 475 E. Badillo Street, Covina, CA 91723 United States **BUS:** Real Estate Agency **P/S:** Sales of Residential and Commercial Properties **MA:** Local **D/D/R:** Specializing in Residential Sales and Market Analysis, Assisting First Time Home Buyers and Sellers, Handling Investment Properties and Relocations **H/I/S:** Photography, Going to Church **CERTS:** Certification in Real Estate **A/A/S:** Citrus Valley Association of Realtors; California Association of Realtors; National Association of Realtors
Email: ingawhitehead@remax.net
URL: http://www.remaxmasters.com

Deborah Whitelaw

Title: Art Director **Company:** Quixtar, Inc. **Address:** 5101 Spaulding Plaza, Suite SC-2N, Ada, MI 49355 United States **BUS:** Business Opportunity Company **P/S:** Business Opportunities for Entrepreneurs, Web-Based Businesses, Multi-Level Marketing, Healthcare Products, Cosmetics **MA:** National **D/D/R:** Creating Conceptual Designs, Logos, Brochures and Advertising Campaigns **H/I/S:** Scuba Diving, Road Biking, Reading, Spending Time with her Dogs **EDU:** Bachelor of Fine Arts, University of Michigan, Magna Cum Laude (1976)
Email: deb_whitelaw@quixtar.com
URL: http://www.quixtar.com

Donna M. Whiteman

Title: Branch Manager **Company:** Finishmaster, Inc. **Address:** 300 Old Reading Pike, Stowe, PA 19464 United States **BUS:** Automotive Body Shop Supplier **P/S:** Body Shop Paints, Repair Supplies **MA:** National **D/D/R:** Overseeing Customer Service, Branch Management **H/I/S:** Spending Quality Time with her Son, Friends and Family, Competitive Swimming **A/H:** Multiple Customer Service Commondations and Awards **C/VW:** American Cancer Society
Email: donnadupont@aol.com
URL: http://www.finishmaster.com

Sandra A. Whiteside

Title: Registered Nurse, Teacher **Company:** Gulfport School District, Gulfport High School **Address:** 100 Perry Street, Gulfport, MS 39507 United States **BUS:** High School **P/S:** Healthcare Education **MA:** Local **D/D/R:** Student and Staff Development, Community Services, Accreditations **H/I/S:** Reading **EDU:** Specialist Degree in Education and Administration, University of Southern Mississippi; Master of Science in Technical Education, University of Mississippi; Bachelor of Science in Nursing, William Carey University **A/A/S:** American Nurses Association; Mississippi Nurses Association; Association for Career and Technical Education; Sponsor, Health Occupations Students of America; MSDA; Phi Kappa; Committee Member, Region 4 **C/VW:** American Red Cross, American Cancer Society
Email: sandra.whiteside@gulfportschools.org
URL: http://www.cambridgewhoswho.com

Debra J. Whitlatch, BA, MA

Title: English Teacher **Company:** Greenland Public Schools **Address:** P.O. Box 67, Greenland, AR 72737 United States **BUS:** Public School **P/S:** Education **MA:** Local **D/D/R:** Teaching Secondary Education, Teaching Reading, Serving as a Student Advocate **H/I/S:** Reading, Hiking, Traveling **EDU:** Master of Arts in Secondary Education, University of Arkansas **A/A/S:** Phi Kappa Phi; Golden Key International Honour Society; University of Arkansas Alumni Association; National Council of Teachers of English **C/VW:** Make-A-Wish Foundation, Alzheimer's Association, Arkansas Police Department
Email: debshelher@yahoo.com

Linda S. Whitley

Title: Designer in Sales **Company:** Food Equipment Specialists **Address:** 10460 S. Sam Houston Parkway W., Houston, TX 77071 United States **BUS:** Kitchen Design, Restaurant Equipment and Smallware Sales Store **P/S:** Specialized in Commercial Food Service Designs and Furnishing **MA:** Texas **D/D/R:** Kitchen and Furniture Design, Field Coordination, Managing Sales **H/I/S:** Reading, Traveling, Fishing, History **EDU:** College Coursework **C/VW:** American Diabetes Foundation; American Cancer Society
Email: linda.whitley@cwwemail.com
URL: http://www.foodequipspc.com

Ronni D. Whitman

Title: Academic Department Director **Company:** The Art Institute of California-Orange County **Address:** 3601 W. Sunflower Avenue, Santa Ana, CA 92704 United States **BUS:** Art Institute **P/S:** Interior Design Education **MA:** Local **D/D/R:** Safety, Security, Sustainable Design **H/I/S:** Traveling, Dancing, Painting **EDU:** Master of Interior Design, Florida State University **A/A/S:** American Society of Interior Designers; International Interior Design Association; Interior Design Educators Council; U.S. Green Building Council **C/VW:** Philharmonic Society, Child Abuse Prevention, Helping Hands, Painted a Mural for a Bed-Ridden Child through the Make-A-Wish Foundation
Email: rwhitman@aii.edu

Janice H. Whitmire-York

Title: Chief Executive Officer **Company:** JRD, Inc. **Address:** 245 Hominy Creek Road, Carrollton, GA 30116 United States **BUS:** Consulting Firm **P/S:** Consulting Services for International Government Operations **MA:** International **EXP:** Ms. Whitmire-York's expertise includes insurance, finance and trust operations management. **H/I/S:** Listening to Music, Playing the Piano, Reading, Fashion Design **EDU:** Coursework in Risk Management and Insurance, The University of Georgia **A/A/S:** Army Volunteer Corps; Military Aid and Assistance Organizations; Local Charitable Organizations, Washington, D.C.; American Solutions; Republican Presidential Task Force
Email: jw@lotus-finance.net
Email: oaks7zurich@yahoo.com
URL: http://www.cambridgewhoswho.com

Doris M. Whitt

Title: Registered Nurse Supervisor **Company:** Manor Care Health Services **Address:** 100 Abbyville Road, Lancaster, PA 17603 United States **BUS:** Healthcare Center **P/S:** Healthcare, Nursing and Rehabilitation **MA:** Local **D/D/R:** Geriatrics **H/I/S:** Camping, Traveling **EDU:** School of Nursing, RN Diploma **A/A/S:** YFC; Lebanon Valley Bible Church
Email: doris.whitt@cwwemail.com
URL: http://www.cambridgewhoswho.com

Dan E. Whitten, RN

Title: OR Nurse **Company:** Poplar Bluff Medical Partners **Address:** 14106 Allan Drive, Poplar Bluff, MO 63901 United States **BUS:** Healthcare Surgery Center Surgeon **P/S:** An Ambulatory Surgery Center **MA:** Local **D/D/R:** Emergency Medicine **H/I/S:** Camping, Hunting **EDU:** University of New Mexico, RN
Email: dewtew90@socket.net

Krista L. Whittleman

Title: Middle School Core Teacher **Company:** Granite City Community School District Suite 9, Grigsby Middle School **Address:** 1947 Adams Street, Granite City, IL 62040 United States **BUS:** School **P/S:** Education **MA:** Local **D/D/R:** Teaching Literature and Composition **H/I/S:** Spending Time with her Two Children, Reading **EDU:** Bachelor of Science in Elementary Education, Southern Illinois University, Edwardsville (1994) **A/A/S:** National Middle School Association
Email: krista.whittleman@gcsda.net
URL: http://www.gcsd9.net

Mary Ellen Wich

Title: Operations Support Manager **Company:** Unitus Community Credit Union **Address:** 1300 S.W. Sixth Avenue, Portland, OR 97201 United States **BUS:** Credit Union **P/S:** Financial Services **MA:** Local **D/D/R:** Overseeing Member Operations **H/I/S:** Traveling **EDU:** Associate Degree in Business Administration, Mt. Hood Community College (1984) **C/VW:** Local Church; Abundant Life Church
Email: mewich@unitusccu.com

Bonnie E. Wicker

Title: Owner, Manager **Company:** Bonnie's Snack Bar **Address:** 6705 Winton Blount Boulevard, Montgomery, AL 36119 United States **BUS:** Retail Food Company **P/S:** Snacks, Meals and Beverages **MA:** Local **D/D/R:** Running a Small Snack Bar with the Disability of Blindness **H/I/S:** Refinishing Antique Furniture, Growing Flower and Vegetable Garden, Sewing Clothes, Decorating Home, Woodworking **A/A/S:** Enterprise Program for the Blind
Email: busybon@mon-cre.net
URL: http://www.cambridgewhoswho.com

Ward T. Wicklund

Title: Cosmetologist, Owner, Operator **Company:** Tropix Salon **Address:** 1102 Finnegan Way, Bellingham, WA 98225 United States **BUS:** Salon **P/S:** Hair Coloring, Styling and Cutting, Waxing, Facials **MA:** Local **D/D/R:** Overseeing Business Operations, Cutting and Coloring Hair **H/I/S:** Scuba Diving, Spending Time Outdoors, Golfing, Playing Tennis, Traveling **EDU:** Coursework in Landscape Architecture, West Valley College **CERTS:** Certified Cosmetologist, State of Washington **A/A/S:** Bellingham Associations **C/VW:** Local Women's Shelters; Local Children's Museum; Young Men's Christian Association
Email: lordward58@yahoo.com
URL: http://www.cambridgewhoswho.com

Joseph R. Wiegand

Title: MOTR/L **Company:** St Barnabas Hospital **Address:** 603 Victory Road, Allison Park, PA 15101 United States **BUS:** Healthcare Nursing Home **P/S:** Occupational Therapy **MA:** Local **D/D/R:** Geriatrics **H/I/S:** Hockey, Football, Playing with his Children **EDU:** Master of Arts in Occupational Therapy, Duquesne University **A/A/S:** AOTA, Phi Kappa Epsilon
Email: wiegand0499@comcast.net

James W. Wielgolewski, MD
Title: Physician **Company:** Dupage Surgical Consultants **Address:** 120 Spalding Drive, Suite 100, Naperville, IL 60540 United States **BUS:** Medical Center **P/S:** Healthcare Including General, Vascular, Pediatric, Breast, Colon, Rectal, Bariatric and Advanced Laparoscopic Surgical Care **MA:** Regional **D/D/R:** Diagnosing, Performing Colon and Rectal Surgeries, Treating Patients **H/I/S:** Golfing, Fishing **EDU:** MD, Loyola University Medical School (1974); Bachelor's Degree in Premedical Studies, Loyola University, Chicago (1970) **CERTS:** Certified General Surgeon **A/A/S:** American Medical Association; Fellow, American Cancer Society; Fellow, American Society of Cataract and Refractive Surgery
Email: jwielgo@aol.com
URL: http://www.dupagesurgicalconsultants.com

Sandi L. Wiese
Title: Special Education Teacher **Company:** Alice Buffett Magnet Middle School **Address:** 14101 Larimore Avenue, Omaha, NE 68164 United States **BUS:** Departmentalized Middle School for Fifth through Eighth-Grade Students **P/S:** Special Education, Soar to Success Reading Redemption Program, Electronic Media, Communications Skills **MA:** Regional **D/D/R:** Teaching to Seventh and Eighth-Grade Students in an Inclusion Class, Teaching Pre-Algebra, Reading, Language Arts **H/I/S:** Football, Track **EDU:** Bachelor of Science in Special Education, Elementary Education, Chadron State College (2003) **A/A/S:** Nebraska State Education Association; Omaha Education Association
Email: sani.wiese@ops.org
URL: http://www2.ops.org/BUFFETT

Pamela R. Wiggins
Title: Associate Dean of Academic Affairs **Company:** ITT Technical Institute **Dept:** Academic Affairs **Address:** 6600 Youngerman Circle, Suite 10, Jacksonville, FL 32244 United States **BUS:** University **P/S:** Higher Education **MA:** National **D/D/R:** Higher Education Leadership; Child Welfare Law and Policy; **H/I/S:** Bike Riding, Walking, Traveling, Shopping, Bowling, Participating in Leisure Activities. **EDU:** Ed.D. (ABD), Organizational Leadership, Higher Education, Nova Southeastern University; M.A. Organizational Management, University of Phoenix; B.A. Psychology, Marymount University **A/A/S:** American Association of University Women; Association for Supervision and Curriculum Development **A/H:** Employee of the Month (2007); Adjunct Instructor of the Quarter (2006)
Email: pamela.wiggins@cwwemail.com
Email: prwiggins@comcast.net

Carl Dean Wike Jr.
Title: President **Company:** It's All About You Salon, Inc. **Address:** 427 Church Street N., Concord, NC 28025 United States **BUS:** Full-Service Salon **P/S:** Salon Services, Aveda Products **MA:** Local **D/D/R:** Customer Service **H/I/S:** Traveling **EDU:** Diploma, Southeastern Beauty School **A/A/S:** National Cosmetology Association of North Carolina
Email: mitchdean@carolina.rr.com
URL: http://www.itsallaboutyouconcord.com

Melanie Wilbur
Title: Guest Relations Coordinator **Company:** Victory Junction Gang Camp **Address:** 4500 Adam's Way, Randleman, NC 27317 United States **BUS:** Nonprofit Organization **P/S:** Camp for Children with Disabilities **MA:** International **D/D/R:** Guest Relations, Greeting VIP Members, Giving Tours to new Campers and Interested Observers **H/I/S:** Music, Movies, Football, NASCAR **EDU:** Bachelor's Degree in Business Administration, Focus in Music and Entertainment, Belmont University (2001)
Email: mwilbur@victoryfunction.org
URL: http://www.victoryfunction.org

Deborah C. Wilcox
Title: Paralegal, Bookkeeper **Company:** Bolton and Kearney, PA **Address:** 102 S. Parke Street, Aberdeen, MD 21001 United States **BUS:** Law Firm **P/S:** Estate, Family and Bankruptcy Law **MA:** Local **EXP:** Ms. Wilcox's expertise includes bankruptcy and estate law. **D/D/R:** Interviewing Clients, Preparing Documents, Doing Research, Bookkeeping for Approximately Seven Accounts **H/I/S:** Reading, Solving Crossword Puzzles, Participating in the Red Hat Society, Scrapbooking **EDU:** Paralegal Continuing Education Classes in Estate and Probate (2003) Coursework in Computers, Johns Hopkins University (1986); Coursework in Computers, Harford Community College (1985); Coursework in Paralegal Studies, Harford Community College (1980); Coursework in Property and Casualty Insurance, Cecil Community College (1974); Diploma, Rising Sun High School (1971); **CERTS:** Certified Paralegal, Harford Community College **A/A/S:** Camp Fire Girls; Secretary, Parent Teacher Association, William Paca/OPR School; New Life Baptist Church; Harford County Disabilities Commission; Harford County Women's Commission; American Legion Ladies Auxiliary; Red Hat Society; American Association of Retired Persons **C/VW:** Susan G. Komen for the Cure, Alzheimer's Foundation, American Heart Association, American Diabetes Association
Email: deborahwilcox@comcast.net

Marjorie S. Wilder
Title: Attorney **Company:** Pullman & Comley, LLC **Address:** 90 State House Square, Hartford, CT 06103 United States **BUS:** Legal Service Company **P/S:** Legal Services **MA:** Local **D/D/R:** Municipal Law, Property Assessments, Condemnations **H/I/S:** Reading, Bridge, Grandchildren and Family **EDU:** Tufts University, Smith, University of Connecticut, AB, Masters, JD with Highest Honors **A/A/S:** Connecticut Bar Association, Connecticut Bar Foundation, Pension Board of W Hartford, Past Town Attorney, Town of West Hartford, International Property Tax Organization
Email: mwilder@pullcom.com
URL: http://www.pullcom.com

Anne E. Wiles
Title: Senior Vice President of Data Process and Systems **Company:** AAIPharma **Address:** 2320 Scientific Park Drive, Wilmington, NC 28405 United States **BUS:** Pharmaceutical Company **P/S:** Clinical Research, Pharmaceutical Development **MA:** International **D/D/R:** Technology Application in Clinical Research **EDU:** Master's Degree in Statistics, University of Leeds **A/A/S:** DIA; Society for Clinical Data Management; United Kingdom Institute of Directors
Email: anne.wiles@aaipharma.com

Rev. Robert J. Wiley Jr.
Title: Pastor **Company:** Calvin Presbyterian Church **Address:** 126 Angell Road, Cumberland, RI 02864 United States **BUS:** Church **P/S:** Spiritual Services **MA:** Local **D/D/R:** Preaching, Biblical Theology **H/I/S:** Photography, Traveling **EDU:** Master of Divinity, Fuller Theological Seminary, Pasadena, CA; Bachelor of Arts in English Literature, California State University, East Bay
Email: pastorjud@juno.com
URL: http://www.calvinpres.org

Claire L. Wililam
Title: Senior Landscape Architect **Company:** Burgess & Niple **Address:** 3204 Tower Oaks Boulevard, Suite 200, Rockville, MD 20852 United States **BUS:** Land and Site Planning Architecture and Design **P/S:** Engineering Services **MA:** Regional **D/D/R:** Land/Site Planning, Land Architecture **H/I/S:** Gardening **EDU:** University of Michigan, Masters in Landscape Architecture **A/A/S:** American Association of Land Architecture
Email: cwilliams@burnip.com

Dr. Darline J. Wilke
Title: Professor Emeritus (Retired) **Company:** North Park University **Address:** 3225 W. Foster Avenue, Chicago, IL 60062 United States **BUS:** Private University **P/S:** Education **MA:** National **D/D/R:** Gerontology, Nursing **H/I/S:** Reading, Gardening, Traveling **EDU:** Doctor of Education in Education and Nursing, Loyola University **A/A/S:** American Nurses Association; Sigma Pheta Tau **C/VW:** Church
Email: darlinewilke@aol.com
URL: http://www.cambridgewhoswho.com

Cheryl Lynne Wilkerson
Title: Registered Nurse Medical Management **Company:** St. John's Health System Medical Management **Address:** 3229 W. Grayrock Drive, Springfield, MO 65810 United States **BUS:** Hospital Systems **P/S:** Healthcare **MA:** Regional **EXP:** Ms. Wilkerson's expertise includes clinical nursing and medical management. **D/D/R:** Administering Allergy Shots and Immunizations **H/I/S:** Gardening, Spending Time with her Grandchildren **EDU:** Bachelor of Science in Liberal Arts, Drury University (2005)
Email: cwilkerson@sprg.mercy.net
URL: http://www.stjohns.com

Mrs. Debbie C. Wilkins, RN
Title: Registered Nurse **Company:** Western Kentucky Ambulatory Center **Address:** 104 W. 18th Street, Hopkinsville, KY 42240 United States **BUS:** Regional Leading Healthcare Facility **P/S:** Same Day Surgery **MA:** Regional **D/D/R:** Registered Nurse in Recovery Room, Holding Room in Surgery, Overseeing Staff, Clinical Processing, Coordinating Procedures with Other Departments, Patient Care **H/I/S:** Gardening, Cooking, Cross-Stitching **EDU:** Registered Nurse, Austin Peay State University (1976) **A/A/S:** American Association of Operating Room Nurses
Email: swilkins@logantele.com

Amy L. Wilkinson
Title: Clinical Data Analyst **Company:** Theradex **Address:** East Windsor, NJ 08520 United States **BUS:** Oncology Research Facility **P/S:** Healthcare **MA:** International **D/D/R:** Analyzing Oncology Clinical Trials Data **H/I/S:** Sports, Coaching, Volunteering **EDU:** Pursuing Master's Degree in Biology; Bachelor of Science in Horticulture, Plant Science and Biotechnology, Delaware Valley College **A/A/S:** American Horticulture Society
Email: wilkinson_al@hotmail.com

Elisabeth LaSalle Wilkinson
Title: Certified Interior Designer **Company:** Chateau de La Salle Interiors, Inc **Address:** 804 Pollock Street, New Bern, NC 28562 United States **BUS:** Interior Design Architecture/Design **P/S:** Consultation, Estimates, Creating Window Treatments and Decorating **MA:** Local **D/D/R:** Certified Interior Designer **H/I/S:** Golfing, Traveling **EDU:** NY School for Interior Design, College of Mt St Vincent, Bachelors in Art History **A/A/S:** American Society of Interior Design
Email: lasalleinc@pconnect.net
URL: http://www.lasalleinc.net

Ruth M. Wilkinson
Title: Health and Physical Education Teacher, Department Chair **Company:** Roanoke City Public Schools **Dept:** Patrick Henry High School **Address:** 2102 Grandin Road S.W., Roanoke, VA 24015 United States **BUS:** Public School System **P/S:** Primary and Secondary Level Education **MA:** Local **D/D/R:** Teaching Driver's Education, Strength and Fitness Training, Health and Physical Education, Acting as the Chairperson of the Department **H/I/S:** Weightlifting, Enjoying Virginia Tech Football **EDU:** Master's Degree in Health and Physical Education, Virginia Polytechnic Institute and State University **A/A/S:** Department of Motor Vehicles Certified Instructor; Virginia Education Association; Roanoke Education Association
Email: wilky3@cox.net
URL: http://www.rcps.info

Carmen Wilks-Stanford
Title: Owner **Company:** Miracle Home Care **Address:** 1665 S.W. Gemini Lane, Port Saint Lucie, FL 34984 United States **BUS:** Homecare **P/S:** Health Care **MA:** Local **D/D/R:** Specializing in Elderly Healthcare, Feeding, Cleaning, Dressing, Shopping **H/I/S:** Dancing, Cooking, Traveling **EDU:** Certified Nurse Assistant, Certification in Home Health Care (1995); Certified Eke Technician (1990) **A/A/S:** Caribbean American Association
Email: miraclehomecare@bellsouth.net

Janet N. Willbanks
Title: Chief Executive Officer **Company:** Willbanks Connections, Inc. **Address:** 883 Santa Cruz Avenue, Menlo Park, CA 94025 United States **BUS:** Consulting Company **P/S:** Travel Consulting **MA:** Regional **D/D/R:** Overseeing Company Operations, Negotiating **EDU:** Bachelor's Degree in History and Political Science, University of San Diego **A/A/S:** Meeting Professionals International; Association of Corporate Travel Executives
Email: jan@connectionsww.com
URL: http://www.cambridgewhoswho.com

Michelle L. Willey
Title: Educator **Company:** Queen Anne's County Public Schools, Bayside Elementary School **Address:** 301 Church Street, Stevensville, MD 21666 United States **BUS:** Elementary Schools **P/S:** Education for Third through Fifth-Grade Students, Reading, Language Arts, Mathematics, Social Studies, Science, Music, Art, Physical Education **MA:** Local **D/D/R:** Elementary Education, Teaching Fourth-Grade Students **H/I/S:** Reading, Solving Logic Puzzles, Traveling, History **EDU:** Master of Administration, Wilmington College, Delaware (2004); Bachelor of Arts in Elementary Education, Salisbury University, Maryland (1993) **A/A/S:** National Education Association; Queen Anne's County Education Association
Email: willeym@qacps.k12.md.us
URL: http://www.qacps.k12.md.us/bes/teachers/willeym/willeym.htm

Alfred E. Williams Jr.
Title: Archaeologist, Egyptologist **Company:** Barr Institute and Replica Museum of Egyptian Archeology **Address:** 8787 E. Oglethorpe Highway, Midway, GA 31320 United States **BUS:** Museum **P/S:** Artifacts, Education **D/D/R:** Archeology, Egyptology, Giving Tours, Making Presentations **H/I/S:** Cooking, Practicing Martial Arts **EDU:** Degree in Egyptology, Concentration in Biblical Archeology, Vermont College of Union Institute University; Bachelor of Arts in Theology and History, Atlantic Union College **A/A/S:** Biblical Archeology Society; Founder, Journal of Biblical Archeology **C/VW:** Hinesville First Seventh-Day Adventist Church
Email: iba1@msn.com
URL: http://www.barrone.net

Amy J. Williams
Title: Mental Health Professional Trainer Company: National Alliance for Mental Illness Address: 307 Orchard City Drive, Suite 205, Campbell, CA 95008 United States BUS: Mental Health Organization P/S: Brain Disorder Treatment and Advocacy MA: National D/D/R: Training Healthcare Service Providers, Therapy for Children, Adults and Families, Advocacy for People Struggling with Brain Disorders, Running a Ten Week Program where each Week Another Topic is Discussed H/I/S: Traveling, Running, Reading, Yoga, Makeup Artistry, Keeping a Sense of Humor EDU: Bachelor of Arts Behavioral Sciences; Bachelor of Arts Psychology; Master of Social Work, San Jose State University; Therapist A/A/S: National Alliance for Mental Illness; National Association of Social Workers; Black Masque Honor Society, A.S. 55 Club; Delta Gamma; Panhellenic Council C/VW: Leukemia and Lymphoma Society, Special Olympics, Second Harvest Food Bank, Hill Haven Convalescent Hospital, Dominican Hospital, City of San Jose Youth Commission; Service for sight
Email: ajwilliamscc@yahoo.com
URL: http://www.cambridgewhoswho.com

Angelina R. Williams
Title: Licensed Vocational Nurse Company: Texas Home Health Address: 524 W. Waco Drive, Waco, TX 76701 United States BUS: Healthcare Center P/S: Healthcare Including Nursing Care, Home Healthcare and Healthcare Teaching MA: Statewide EXP: Ms. Williams' expertise includes geriatrics and home healthcare. D/D/R: Skilled and Charge Nursing, Overseeing Wound Care, Assessing and Teaching on Disease Processes H/I/S: Spending Time with her Son, Traveling, Gardening CERTS: Licensed Vocational Nurse, McLennan Community College; Certification in Intravenous Therapy A/H: Dean's List C/VW: The Bellmeade United Pentecostal Church
Email: Angelina.Williams@cwwemail.com
URL: http://www.cambridgewhoswho.com

Mr. Anthony Williams
Title: Environmental Engineer Company: MACTEC Engineering & Consulting Address: 401 E. State Street, P.O. Box 27, Trenton, NJ 08608 United States BUS: Consulting Firm P/S: Environmental Consulting Services MA: National EXP: Mr. Williams' expertise includes air quality regulation, environmental engineering, the preparation of air quality permits and the review of emission statements. H/I/S: Reading, Basketball, Listening to Jazz, Rhythm and Blues EDU: Bachelor of Science in Chemical Engineering, Howard University A/A/S: National Honor Society; National Society of Black Engineers C/VW: WBGO; United Negro College Fund
Email: aw1259@yahoo.com
URL: http://www.cambridgewhoswho.com

Barbara Sheppard Williams
Title: Co Director/Heather Williams Company: Kids' Workshop Training Institute Address: 126 DeSilliio Road, Bellvue, CO 80512 United States BUS: Healthcare Private Practice P/S: Psychotherapy, Consulting, Advisor MA: International D/D/R: Children, Humanistic Behaviors, Social Work, Psychohtherapy, Diversity and working with Navajo and Different cultures worldwide H/I/S: Travel, Pets, Hiking EDU: Masters in Social Work A/A/S: National Certified of Social Workers, International Humanistic Psychologists, NASW, Certified in Social Work, Int. Per-Centered Staff Member for the Institute of the Person Centered Approach in Italy and in France
Email: bkidsworkshop@aol.com
URL: http://www.kids-workshop.com

Bonita L. Williams
Title: President Company: The Tandem Group, Inc. Dept: Health and Annuities Address: 8336 Tifton Road, Charlotte, NC 28226 United States BUS: High Quality Insurance Agency P/S: Licensed in Life, Health, Long Term Care, Disability Income and Annuities, Group Insurance Programs with Various Benefits Premiums and Payment Options, Customized Insurance Programs, Outstanding Customer Service MA: North Carolina, South Carolina, Virginia, Pennsylvania D/D/R: Communicating with Clients, Business Development, Customer Service, Human Resource H/I/S: Football, Reading, Listening to Music, Gardening EDU: Bachelor's Degree in Psychology and Business, Immaculate University (2000) A/A/S: National Association of Insurance and Financial Advisers; Psi Chi National Honor Society in Psychology
Email: bonitawilliams@carolina.rr.com
URL: http://www.cambridgewhoswho.com

Brenda A. Williams
Title: Respiratory Company: Rehabilitation Institute of Chicago Address: 345 East Superior, Chicago, IL 60612 United States BUS: Healthcare Rehab P/S: Pulmonary Rehabilitation MA: Local D/D/R: Pulmonary Practitioner H/I/S: Sewing, Crochet, Volunteers w/Girl Scouts EDU: Malcolm X, Bachelors in Respiratory A/A/S: AARC, American Lung Association
Email: Redpieface@american.net

Bridgette D. Williams
Title: Teacher Company: Laburnum Elementary School Address: 500 Meriwether Avenue, Richmond, VA 23222 United States BUS: Elementary School P/S: Elementary Education MA: Local EXP: Ms. William's expertise is in early childhood education. H/I/S: Traveling, Reading EDU: Master of Arts in Teaching, Regent University; Bachelor of Social Work, Virginia Union University A/A/S: Association for Childhood Education International C/VW: Henrico County Historical Society
Email: bdwillia@henrico.k12.va.us
URL: http://www.henrico.k12.va.us

Catherine Jean Williams
Title: Owner, Hairstylist Company: 1) Shawn Michael Hair Studio 2) Cathy's Hair Salon & Boutique Address: 3825 Carpenter Road, Ypsilanti, MI 48197 United States BUS: 1) Hair Salon 2) Women's Clothing Boutique and Salon P/S: 1) Barber Shop and Salon 2) Women's Hair Salon and Clothing Boutique MA: 1) Washtenaw County 2) Washtenaw County D/D/R: 1) Cutting Hair, Weaving, Coloring 2) Cutting Hair H/I/S: Reading, Traveling, Swimming EDU: Licensed Cosmetologist, State College of Beauty A/A/S: Honored by Local Television Station for Giving Makeovers to Katrina Victims C/VW: Sunday School Teacher, Church; Counselor, Women's Group of New Beginnings
URL: http://www.cambridgewhoswho.com

Charles Ody Williams
Title: Cardiac Catheter Specialist III Company: Emory University Hospital, Cardiovascular Laboratory Address: 1364 Clifton Road N.E., Atlanta, GA 30322 United States BUS: Academic Medical Center P/S: Healthcare MA: Regional D/D/R: Invasive and Interventional Cardiology and Radiology Procedures H/I/S: Golfing, Restoring Vintage Automobiles, Writing. EDU: Pursuing Master's Degree in Health Sciences; Bachelor's Degree in Cardiovascular-Interventional Technology and Radiology Practitioner Assistant, Weber State University; Registered Radiologic Technologist in Radiology (ARRT); Advanced Certification in Cardiac-Interventional Studies (ARRT); Advanced Certification in Cardiovascular Interventional Studies (ARRT); Registered Cardiovascular Invasive Specialist (CCI); Certified Pulmonary Function Technologist (NBRC); Certified Cardiographic Technician (C A/A/S: National Society of Radiology Practitioner Assistants; Society of Invasive Cardiovascular Professionals; Consulting Editor, Cath Lab Digest, Fellow, Society of Invasive Cardiovascular Specialists C/VW: NSRPA, Republican National Committee
Email: cbrpa_cow@yahoo.com
URL: http://www.cambridgewhoswho.com

Connie A. Williams
Title: Owner, Operator Company: McDonald's Address: 4121 Hiawatha Avenue, Minneapolis, MN 55406 United States BUS: Restaurant P/S: Food Services MA: National D/D/R: Managing the Restaurant H/I/S: Traveling EDU: Associate Degree in Business, Delta School of Business C/VW: VOA Church
Email: connie.williams1406@hotmail.com

Cynthia M. Williams
Title: Elementary School Principal Company: LaSalle Avenue Elementary School Address: 8715 LaSalle Avenue, Los Angeles, CA 90047 United States BUS: Elementary School P/S: Education for Kindergarten through Fifth-Grade Students MA: Regional D/D/R: Supervising School Instruction, Training Staff, Evaluating Teachers, Ensuring Statewide Goals are Met, Educating Children Emotionally and Socially H/I/S: Reading, Traveling EDU: Master's Degree in Educational Administration, California State University (1989) A/A/S: Council of Black Administrators, Los Angeles Unified School District; The Links, Incorporated
Email: cwill5@lausd.net
URL: http://www.lasalleschools.net

Desiree Marie Williams
Title: Payroll, Human Resources Coordinator Company: The Parkes Companies, Inc. Address: 105 Reynolds Drive, Franklin, TN 37064 United States BUS: Construction Company P/S: Payroll and Human Resources Administration MA: Regional D/D/R: Processing Weekly Payroll for 150 Employees, Completing Tax Returns, Administering Health Plans H/I/S: Traveling, Reading EDU: Associate Degree in Criminal Justice, Central Lakes College A/A/S: American Payroll Association
Email: dwilliams@parkescompanies.com
URL: http://www.parkescompanies.com

Dixie L. Williams
Title: Controller Company: IU Health, Inc. dba IU Medical Group-Primary Care Address: 8910 Purdue Road, Suite 500, Indianapolis, IN 46268 United States BUS: Healthcare Center P/S: Healthcare MA: Local D/D/R: Managing Finance Including Accounting, Financial Healthcare, Budgeting, Accounts Payable, Banking Reconciliations, Preparing Financial Statements, Processing Payroll H/I/S: Singing in Indianapolis Symphonic Choir, Teaching Card Making, Singing in the Chamber EDU: Master of Business Administration, University of Indianapolis (2006); Bachelor of Science in Accounting, Southern College of Seventh Day Adventist (1983) A/A/S: Fellow, Academy of Healthcare Management; Delta Mu Delta C/VW: Local Church; Local Charitable Organizations
Email: dwilliams@iumg.com
URL: http://www.iumg.com

E. Keith Williams
Title: Chief Investigator, Trial Unit Company: Federal Public Defenders Office Address: 321 E. Second Street, Los Angeles, CA 90012 United States BUS: Legal Services P/S: Defending Criminals MA: Central District of California D/D/R: Representing Criminals with Federal Charges, Serving Subpoenas, Plea Arguments, Trial Work, Habeas Work at the Capital and Non-Capital Level H/I/S: Reading, Listening to Music, Art, Visiting Museums, Going to the Beach EDU: Coursework in Criminal Justice and Sociology, Bethune-Cookman College; Licensed Private Investigator; Bachelor of Science in Sociology, Bethune-Cookman College A/A/S: National Defender Investigator Association C/VW: KCET; Public Broadcasting Service; Veterans Affairs
Email: keith_williams@fd.org
URL: http://www.fd.org

Fannie M. Williams
Title: Missionary Company: Church of God in Christ Address: 2212 Vanderbilt Circle, Anchorage, AK 99508 United States BUS: Church P/S: Religious and Community Outreach MA: National D/D/R: Missionary H/I/S: Sewing, Reading and Traveling EDU: Bachelor of Science in Business Administration, Alaska University A/A/S: Church of God in Christ
Email: fanniemw@aol.com

Gene R. Williams
Title: Freelance Copywriter BUS: Copywriting Services MA: National D/D/R: Copy for the Self-Help Industry H/I/S: Watching NASCAR Races, Walking EDU: Coursework in Automotive Studies, Community College C/VW: Trinity Lutheran Church, Bloomington, Illinois
Email: copywritergene007@yahoo.com
URL: http://www.cambridgewhoswho.com

Gregory E. Williams
Title: Account Coordinator Company: Lloyd Bedford Cox, Inc. Address: 783 N. Street, Greenwich, CT 06831 United States BUS: Insurance Agency P/S: Property and Casualty Insurance Brokerage with Expertise in and Access to Chubb and Fireman's Fund Personal Insurance Products, Offering Insurance for High-Value Homeowners, Valuable Articles, Umbrella, Condominiums, Cooperatives, Yachts and other Watercraft, Flood MA: Regional D/D/R: Managing Personal Property Taxes and Casualty Insurance, Conducting Account Pricing, Managing General Agency, Retail Sales of Insurance Products, Company-Specific Product Knowledge, Offering Analysis and Solutions to Complex Personal Insurance Needs H/I/S: Skiing, Fishing, Boating, Riding his Motorcycle EDU: Bachelor of Arts in History, Middlebury College, VT (2002)
Email: greg@lbcinc.com
URL: http://www.lbcinc.com

Mr. James Henry Williams
Title: Founder, Owner Company: Renaissance Dept: Research and Education Address: P.O. Box 1692, El Cerrito, CA 94530 United States BUS: Publishing Company P/S: Reference Guide Calendars, Booklets, Postcards, Posters MA: International D/D/R: Creating and Publishing Calendars Used as Reference Guides, Offering Information about African-American Inventors, Distributing Booklets, Postcards and Posters H/I/S: Playing Football, Listening to Jazz Music, Keeping Fit, Reading, Researching EDU: Master of Science in Sociology, Southern Oregon University; Bachelor of Science in Sociology, Southern Oregon University (1972) A/A/S: Former President, Chief Justice, Contra Costa Community College Student Court; Screen Actors Guild; American Federation of Television and Radio Artists A/H: Who's Who Among Students in American Universities and Colleges (1971-1972) C/VW: Various Diabetes and Blood Donation Organizations
Email: james.williams@cwwemail.com
URL: http://www.cambridgewhoswho.com

Janet Williams
Title: Histologic Technician, Qualifications of Immunohistochemistry **Company:** Longmont United Hospital **Address:** 1950 W. Mountain View Avenue, Longmont, CO 80501 United States **BUS:** Hospital **P/S:** Healthcare, Surgical Pathology **MA:** Local **D/D/R:** Immunohistochemistry, Pathology **H/I/S:** Sewing, Cooking, Reading Mysteries, Traveling, Creating Various Types of Baskets **EDU:** Associate of Science in Chemistry and Biology, Estherville Junior College, Iowa (1962); Diploma, Dolliver High School, Iowa **A/A/S:** American Society for Clinical Pathology; National Society of Histotechnology; QIHC; American Society of Clinical Pathologists **A/H:** Employee of the Month (2007) **C/VW:** Health Fair, Vietnam Veterans; Volunteer, 4-H Foundation
Email: avenger@idcomm.com

Jeremy L. Williams
Title: Finance Manager **Company:** DC Public Charter School Board **Dept:** Finance **Address:** 3333 14th Street N.W., Suite 210, Washington, DC 20010 United States **BUS:** Education **P/S:** Charter School Oversight **D/D/R:** Analyzing Finances, Managing Budgets **H/I/S:** Jogging, Working Out, Reading **EDU:** Master of Business Administration in Finance, University of Virginia; Bachlelor of Science in Mechanical Engineering, Florida A&M University **A/A/S:** National Society of Black MBAs
Email: jerlorwil@aol.com
URL: http://www.cambridgewhoswho.com

Joyce Ann Turner Williams
Title: Guidance Counselor **Company:** Lee County School System **Address:** 5 Park Street, Jonesville, VA 24263 United States **BUS:** School District **P/S:** Education **MA:** Local **D/D/R:** Counseling Troubled Children who have Domestic Issues **H/I/S:** Decorating Cakes, Music, Singing **EDU:** Master's Degree in Elementary Guidance Counseling, Lincoln Memorial University (1994); Bachelor of Salutatorian in Elementary Education, Lincoln Memorial University (1976) **A/A/S:** National Education Association, Virginia Education Association **C/VW:** St. Jude Children's Research Hospital, American Heart Association
Email: dinahdog@hotmail.com
URL: http://www.cambridgewhoswho.com

Kari Cie Williams
Title: Owner **Company:** Mahogany Hair Revolution **Address:** 490 S. San Vicente, Suite 10, Los Angeles, CA 90048 United States **BUS:** Hair Salon **P/S:** Hair Styling, Trichology Services **MA:** Local **D/D/R:** Styling Hair, Textured Weaving **H/I/S:** Traveling, Relaxing, Eating Out **EDU:** Bachelor's Degree in Mass Communications, University of California at Berkeley **A/A/S:** Delta Sigma Beta Sorority, Inc. **C/VW:** Climb
Email: mahogany_will@yahoo.com
URL: http://www.mahoganyrevolution.com

Kevan E. Williams
Title: Paramedic **Company:** Penndel-Middletown Emergency **Address:** 616 E. Lincoln Highway, Langhorne, PA 19047 United States **BUS:** Pre-hospital Care **P/S:** Emergency Medical Services **MA:** Local **D/D/R:** Emergency Medical Services, Hazardous Materials, Education **H/I/S:** Traveling, Motor Sports **EDU:** Industry-Related Training and Experience **A/A/S:** Industry-Related Affiliations **A/H:** American Ambulance Stars of Life Award (1992)
Email: kwilliams@pmems.org
URL: http://www.cambridgewhoswho.com

Laura A. Williams
Title: Educator of Moderate Special Needs **Company:** City of Worchester, Norrback Avenue School **Address:** 23 Red Oak Street, Paxton, MA 01612 United States **BUS:** Public School **P/S:** Education for Prekindergarten through Sixth-Grade Students **MA:** Regional **D/D/R:** Teaching Kindergarten through Third-Grade Students with Special Needs, Utilizing Inclusion Learning Techniques, Helping Students Focus on their Assignments, Offering a Supportive Learning Environment **H/I/S:** Crocheting, Reading, Spending Time with Children **EDU:** Master's Degree in Special Education and Reading, K-9, Fitchburg State College; Bachelor's Degree in Elementary Education; Certificate of Advanced Graduate Studies, Reading K-9 Education **A/A/S:** Massachusetts Teachers Association
Email: williamsl@worc.k12.ma.us
URL: http://www.wpsweb.com/norrback

Leah G. Williams
Title: Human Resource Manager **Company:** Abengoa Bioenergy Corp. **Address:** 1827 Industrial Drive, Portales, NM 88130 United States **BUS:** Manufacturing **P/S:** Ethanol Manufacturing **MA:** International **D/D/R:** Human Resources **H/I/S:** Reading, Playing Piano, Watching Classic Movies **EDU:** Bachelor of Arts in Business Administration and Human Resources, Eastern New Mexico University; Professional in Human Resources Certification, Human Resource Certification Institute **A/A/S:** Society for Human Resource Management; Delta Mu Delta **C/VW:** Various Organizations
Email: leah.williams@bioenergy.abengoa.com
URL: http://www.abengoabioenergy.com

Marcella M. Williams
Title: Owner **Company:** Fashion Design and Poetry **Address:** 175 Mayflower Road, Kenbridge, VA 23944 United States **BUS:** Fashion Design and Poetry Service Provider **P/S:** Designed Clothing and poetic cards **MA:** National **D/D/R:** Writing Poetry and designing various clothing **H/I/S:** Helping Others, Writing Poetry, Sewing, Reading, Swimming, Basketball and Volleyball **EDU:** Mid Plains Community College, Certification **A/A/S:** International Library ofPoetry, Concerned ParentAssociation, NAACP
Email: williamsnL2@vcu.edu

Dr. Marlon S. Williams
Title: Chiropractic Physician **Company:** Williams Chiropractic Clinic **Address:** RRI, Box 10556, Kingshill, 00850 United States **BUS:** Physician's Office, Private Practice **P/S:** Chiropractic Services, Diagnosis and Treatment of Spine and Musculoskeletal System Disorders **MA:** Regional **D/D/R:** General Chiropractic Services, Treating Patients with Sports Injuries **H/I/S:** Marathon Running, Cooking, Volunteering for Charities **EDU:** Doctor of Chiropractic, Logan College of Chiropractic (1985) **A/A/S:** American Chiropractic Association; Board Member, Local Chiropractors Association **A/H:** Best Chirporactor in Saint Croix, Virgin Islands Daily News (2007)
Email: mswchirocare@hotmail.com
URL: http://www.cambridgewhowho.com

Michael P. Williams
Title: Executive Restaurant Chef **Company:** Borgata Hotel, Casino & Spa **Address:** 1 Borgata Way, Atlantic City, NJ 08401 United States **BUS:** Casino, Hotel **P/S:** Lodging, Gambling, Restaurant, Culinary **MA:** International **EXP:** Mr. Williams expertise includes French, Asian and Latin cuisine. **H/I/S:** Participating in Water Sports and Outdoor Activities, Collecting Wine and Art **EDU:** Graduate, Academy of Culinary Arts (Gold Medal); Coursework in Pastry and Cuisine, Le Cordon Bleu, Paris, France; Coursework in Cuisine, Alain Ducasse Formation, Argenteuil, France; Coursework in Cuisine, Blue Elephant School of Royal Thai Cookery, Bangkok, Thailand; Coursework in Sugar and Chocolate Work, International School of Confectionery Arts, Gaithersburg, MD **CERTS:** Certified Executive Chef, American Culinary Federation; Certified Food Service Manager; Certified Dietetic Assistant **A/A/S:** Over 41 Medals for Various Local and International Competitions
Email: maximnj@comcast.net
URL: http://www.cambridgewhoswho.com

Mimi Williams
Title: President of Medical Marketing **Company:** Mimi Williams and Associates **Address:** 9501 W. Sahara Avenue, Unit 1255, Las Vegas, NV 89117 United States **BUS:** Cosmetic Surgery **P/S:** Full Service Cosmetic Surgery **MA:** Regional **D/D/R:** Running Office, Billing, Paperwork, Communication and Marketing with Vendors, Patients' Needs, Helping Patients Understand All Aspects of Procedures and Financial Obligations **H/I/S:** Gourmet Cook **EDU:** College Coursework in Theatre, Minor in Languages, Carlton College **A/A/S:** Lectured Locally, 'Wall of Hope' in California and Las Vegas
Email: nvmimiw@yahoo.com
URL: http://www.jobbait.com/b/mimi/htm

Noel G. Williams
Title: Director of Cultural Diversity **Company:** Maysville Community and Technical College **Address:** 1755 US 68, Maysville, KY 41056 United States **BUS:** College **P/S:** Education **MA:** Local **D/D/R:** Cultural Diversity **H/I/S:** Woodcarving **EDU:** Master's Degree in Adult and High Education, Moorehead State University **A/A/S:** American Association of Affirmative Action; Society for Human Resource Management; CUAK; KSBLC; Human Resources Executive Council
Email: noel.williams@kctcs.edu
URL: http://www.ktcts.edu

Reba L. Williams, MBA
Title: President **Company:** Aberlyn Williams & Associates, LLC **Address:** 14 Boggs Lane, Suite 100, Bear, DE 19701 United States **BUS:** Financial Consulting Company **P/S:** Financial Aid Consulting Services **MA:** Local **D/D/R:** Managing Finance Including Analyzing and Interpreting Programs in Higher and Post-Secondary Education **H/I/S:** Reading, Jogging, Traveling, Listening to Jazz Music, Playing Basketball and Football **EDU:** Pursuing Ph.D., Walden University; Master of Business Administration, Kaplan University, FL (2007); Bachelor of Science in Finance, Wilmington College, DE (2005) **CERTS:** Certified Notary Public, State of Delaware **A/A/S:** Board of Directors, Stone Mill Maintenance Corporation; Pennsylvania Association of Student Financial Aid Administrators; National Association of Student Financial Aid Administrators; Civil Affairs Association, U.S. Army; Delta Epsilon Rho Honor Society
Email: rwilliams@aberlynwilliams.com
URL: http://www.aberlynwilliams.com

Sabrina R. Williams
Title: Executive Director, Founder **Company:** Excell Academy for Higher Learning **Address:** 6510 Zane Avenue N., Suite 107, Brooklyn Park, MN 55429 United States **BUS:** Public Charter School **P/S:** Education for Pre-kindergarten through Sixth-Grade Students **MA:** Local **D/D/R:** Overseeing 50 Employees **H/I/S:** Singing **EDU:** Master's Degree in Gifted Education, University of St. Thomas (1999) **A/A/S:** Minnesota Association of Charter Schools
Email: swilliams@excellacademy.org
URL: http://www.excellacademy.org

Shanin Williams
Title: Executive Director, Owner **Company:** Williams and Associates **Address:** 1124 N.W. D Street, Grants Pass, OR 97526 United States **BUS:** Guardianship Company **P/S:** Eldercare Advocates **MA:** National **D/D/R:** Eldercare Advocacy **EDU:** Bachelor of Science in Social Science, Maryhurst University; Associate of Science in Management, Portland Community College **C/VW:** Volunteer, Boys & Girls Club of America; Volunteer, Local Women's Crisis Team
Email: shanin@jeffnet.org

Shirley L. Williams
Title: Owner **Company:** Shirley's Merle Norman and Boutique **Address:** 8 N Lafayette Street, Valparaiso, IN 46383 United States **BUS:** Cosmetology Retail **P/S:** Merle Norman Cosmetics/Boutique **MA:** Local **D/D/R:** Custom Bra's and Wigs for Cancer Patients **H/I/S:** Opera **A/A/S:** NFIB

Stephen L. Williams
Title: President **Company:** Williams Windows and Siding, LLC **Address:** P.O. Box 654, Muncie, IN 47308 United States **BUS:** Home Improvement **P/S:** Windows, Siding, Gutter **MA:** Regional **D/D/R:** Managing Sales, Overseeing a Staff of Four **H/I/S:** Riding Bikes, Fishing **EDU:** Certified IUFY Technician, Indiana Technical Vocational College; Training in Sales and Marketing; Training in Production **A/A/S:** Building Trades Association
Email: williamswindows@yahoo.com
URL: http://www.williamswindowsandsiding.biz/splash.asp

Thomas E. Williams
Title: Owner **Company:** Superior Pool Service **Address:** 350 N. Bedford Street, East Bridgewater, MA 02333 United States **BUS:** Swimming Pool Company **P/S:** Swimming Pool Installation, Service and Maintenance **MA:** Local **D/D/R:** Swimming Pool Installation, Service and Maintenance **EDU:** High School Education
Email: superiorpool@comcast.net
URL: http://www.superiorpoolsvc.com

Tonja Williams
Title: Owner, Consultant **Company:** Williams Consulting **Address:** 45-13 Moss Spring Drive, Raleigh, NC 27616 United States **BUS:** Consulting Company **P/S:** Medical Consultations **MA:** Statewide **D/D/R:** Advising Physicians on the Operational Aspect of their Medical Practices **H/I/S:** Reading **EDU:** Master of Health Administration, Pfeiffer University **C/VW:** American Cancer Society
Email: drpsychbeh@aol.com

Vivian A. Williams
Title: Care Giver **Company:** Williams Home of Care **Address:** 8609 W. Roma Avenue, Phoenix, AZ 85037 United States **BUS:** Home Based Child Care **P/S:** Care to Children who are in Need **MA:** Local **D/D/R:** Caring for Children who are no Longer with their Parents or Family **H/I/S:** Reading Inspirational Books and Magazines **A/A/S:** Pentacostals of Phoenix Church
URL: http://www.cambridgewhoswho.com

Cecilia M. Williams-Nelson
Title: Dentist **Company:** Takoma Dental Clinic **Address:** 6480 New Hampshire Avenue, Suite 302, Takoma Park, MD 20912 United States **BUS:** Dental Clinic **P/S:** Dental Services **MA:** Regional **EXP:** Dr. Williams-Nelson's expertise includes general and cosmetic dentistry. **H/I/S:** Creative Writing **EDU:** Doctor of Dental Surgery, Howard University (1988); Bachelor's Degree in Zoology, Howard University (1981) **CERTS:** Licensed Dentist, State of Maryland, District of Columbia (1990) **A/A/S:** Who's Who Among American High School Students
Email: rayne16@verizon.net
URL: http://www.cambridgewhoswho.com

Emilie S. Williamson
Title: Kindergarten Teacher **Company:** South Wasco County School District, Maupin Elementary **Address:** 346 Deschutes Avenue, Maupin, OR 97037 United States **BUS:** Public Elementary School **P/S:** Elementary Education **MA:** Local **D/D/R:** Teaching Early Childhood Education, Mentoring Teachers **H/I/S:** Skiing, Making Outdoor Floral Arrangements **EDU:** Bachelor of Science, Oregon State University **A/A/S:** Wasco County Community College; Susan G. Komen Breast Cancer Foundation; Local Library

Donald D. Williford, Ph.D.
Title: Associate Provost, Professor of the New Testament Company: Hardin-Simmons University Address: 2200 Hickory Street, Abilene, TX 79698 United States BUS: University P/S: Higher Education MA: Regional D/D/R: Acting as a Reaccreditation Liaison between the University and the Southern Association of Colleges and Schools, Dealing with Student Issues Including Homework Complaints, Grading Appeals and Transfer Issues Including Faculty Issues and Concerns, Teaching the New Testament on the Undergraduate and Graduate Levels H/I/S: Reading, Carpentry, Golfing EDU: Ph.D. in the New Testament, Southwestern Baptist Theological Seminary (1981) A/A/S: Society of Biblical Literature; American Schools of Oriental Research; National Association of Baptist Professors of Religion C/VW: Local Church
Email: willifrd@hsutx.edu
URL: http://www.hsutx.edu

Jo Ann K. Willis
Title: Manager Company: Naomis Cottage Address: 728 Bush Street, Roswell, GA 30075 United States BUS: Social Services Social Services/Rehabilitation/Counseling P/S: Serving Women Who are in Life Transitions MA: Local D/D/R: Specializing in Diversity Training, Making Sure the Women Execute Their Duties and Helping Them in Their Quest to Find Work EDU: Lansingburg High School, Graduated A/A/S: Pleasant Hill Missionary Baptist Church

April M. Willis-Harper
Title: Migrant Advocate, English as a Second Language Coordinator Company: Barren County Schools Address: 1309 Roseville Road, Glasgow, KY 42141 United States BUS: School District P/S: Education for Students in Elementary School through High School MA: Regional D/D/R: Teaching and Assisting Migrant Students, Teaching English as a Second Language H/I/S: Public Speaking, Photography, Clogging EDU: Rank I Program, Counseling K-12, Western Kentucky University (2003) A/A/S: Kentucky Association of School Administrators; Kentucky Counseling Association; Kentucky Leadership Academy
Email: april.harper@barren.kyschools.us
URL: http://www.barren.k12.ky.us

Darlene R. Willson
Title: Sculptor, Owner Company: Darlene's Delights Address: 10950 Skyline Drive, Atlanta, MI 49709 United States BUS: Sculpture Design Company P/S: Clay Sculptures, Hand Sculptures and Personalized Sculptures MA: International D/D/R: Making Clay Sculptures, Hand Sculptures and Personalized Sculptures H/I/S: Crocheting A/H: Achievement Honor Roll Certification of Recognition, Michigan Commission for the Blind (2006)
Email: darlenesdelights@msn.com
URL: http://www.darlenesdelights.com

Avril R. Wilmot
Title: Occupational Health Nurse Company: Sanden International Address: 601 South Sanden Boulevard, Wylie, TX 75098 United States BUS: Compressors Manufacturer P/S: Occupational, Air Conditioner Compressors MA: International D/D/R: Occupational Health Nurse H/I/S: Reading EDU: South Africa, Bachelor of Science Nursing A/A/S: Occupational Nursing Society, AAOHN
Email: avril.wilmot@sbcglobal.net

Andrea L. Wilson
Title: Licensed Practical Nurse Company: Dr. Zelda Johnson & Associates, PLCC Address: 101 Cowardin Avenue, Suite 307, Richmond, VA 23224 United States BUS: Family Medical Practice P/S: Healthcare MA: Local D/D/R: Phlebotomy, Nursing H/I/S: Participating in Family Activities EDU: Licensed Practical Nurse, Richmond School of Health and Technology C/VW: Leukemia & Lymphoma Society
Email: candy4_2322@yahoo.com

Becky M. Wilson, BSN, RN
Title: Registered Nurse Company: The Regional Hospital for Respiratory and Complex Care Address: 12844 Military Road S, Tulcwila, WA 98168 United States BUS: Healthcare P/S: Hospital for Acute Care Facility Specializing in Ventilator Weaning and Intensive Care MA: National D/D/R: Registered Nurse in all Aspects of Healthcare in the Field H/I/S: Skiing, Snow Mobiling, Rock Climbing, Kayaking, Fishing EDU: Bachelor's Degree, Nursing, University of Washington A/A/S: National Ski Patrol C/VW: Special Olympics, Katrina

Colleen M. Wilson
Title: Job Developer Company: Sacramento City Unified School District Address: 5241 J Street, Sacramento, CA 95819 United States BUS: School District P/S: Education MA: Local D/D/R: Job Placement, Job Coaching H/I/S: Raising Farm Animals EDU: Master of Science in School and Career Counseling, California State University at Sacramento; Certified School Counselor; Certification in Substitute Teacher Kindergarten through 12th; Business License in Career Counseling A/A/S: Biltmore Who's Who
Email: cwhealey@abcglobal.net

Debora A. Wilson
Title: Manager Company: Saxon Drilling Dept: Human Resources Address: 1500 Museum Road, Suite 100, Conway, AR 72032 United States BUS: Oilfield Service Company P/S: Natural Gas Contract Drilling and Well Services MA: Regional D/D/R: Hiring and Supervising the Staff, Managing Human Resource Operations and Discipline Processes, Overseeing Policy Management and Implementation H/I/S: Scrapbooking, Writing EDU: Master's Degree in Interpersonal and Organizational Communications, University of Arkansas at Little Rock (1998) CERTS: Certified Professional in Human Resources, Human Resource Certification Institute A/A/S: Faulkner County Human Resource Association; Central Arkansas Human Resources Association; Society for Human Resource Management C/VW: Board of Directors, United Way of America; Woman, Inc.
Email: dwilson@saxonservices.com

Don J. Wilson
Title: Team Leader/Southern Region Company: Alberta Infrastructure and Transportation Address: Willow Glen Business Park 803 Manning Road N.E., Calgary, T2E 7M8 Canada BUS: Traffic Safety Government P/S: Licensing and Driving Safety MA: Regional D/D/R: Driver Programs and Licensing Standards H/I/S: Musician, Plays in a Band, Railway Coordination for Heritage Park, Calgary EDU: Bachelor of Arts in Education, University of Calgary A/A/S: Canadian Institute of Certified Administrators
Email: djwilson@shaw.ca

Gordon A. Wilson
Title: Systems Development Consultant Company: Electric Boat Division of General Dynamics Address: 404 Thames Street, Groton, CT 06340 United States BUS: Submarine Manufacturer P/S: Building Submarines MA: National D/D/R: Purchasing, Accounting H/I/S: Golfing at the Manchester Country Club EDU: Bachelor of Science, University of Hartford; Coursework, Bentley College A/A/S: Board of Directors, Disabled American Veterans C/VW: Center Congregation Church, Hartford Foundation
URL: http://www.cambridgewhoswho.com

Joseph Wilson Jr.
Title: President Company: Starchem, LLC Address: 10150 Greenville Highway, Wellford, SC 29385 United States BUS: Manufacturing Company P/S: Chemicals for the Textile, Pulp and Paper Industry MA: North America H/I/S: Sports, Collecting Antique Car EDU: Bachelor of Science in Chemical Engineering, Cornell University A/A/S: Technical Association of the Pulp and Paper Industry; American Chemical Society; American Institute of Chemical Engineers; Paper Industry Management Association
Email: joe.wilson@star-na.com
URL: http://www.cambridgewhoswho.com

Mrs. Judy G. Wilson
Title: Office Manager Company: Dr. Armin Abron DDS, MS, PA Dept: Business Office Address: 292 Commerce Avenue, Yadkin Park, Southern Pines, NC 28387 United States BUS: Dental Office P/S: Periodontics, Implantology MA: Regional D/D/R: Managing Business Office with Responsibilities Including but not limited to Processing Reports, Sending Necessary Information to Patients, Doctors and Accountant, Accounts Payable and Receivable, Inputting and Updating Data for Patient Files, Handling Patient and Staff Conflicts, Insurance Filing, Scheduling Appointments with Patients, Scheduling Staff Updates for HIPAA, OSHA and CPR, Organizing the Sandhills Study Club H/I/S: Reading, Spending Time with her Grandchildren EDU: Certified Dental Assistant; Continuing Education Certificates in Coronal Tooth Polishing and Nitrous Oxide Sedation; Certified Dental Practice Management Administrator A/A/S: A New Beginning Assembly Of God; Women of Faith Association; The Sandhills Study Club
Email: wilson1113@peoplepc.com
URL: http://www.dr.Abron.com

Kimberly J. Wilson
Title: Project Engineer Company: P.J. Dick, Incorporated Address: 1020 Lebanon Road, West Mifflin, PA 15122 United States BUS: Construction Company P/S: General Construction Services MA: Regional D/D/R: Construction Manager H/I/S: Running, Teaching Gymnastics EDU: Bachelor of Science in Civil Engineering, University of Pittsburgh; Bachelor of Arts in Architectural Studies, University of Pittsburgh A/A/S: American Society of Civil Engineers C/VW: Local Church; Board of Directors for the Lutheran Campus Ministry of Greater Pittsburgh
Email: kim.wilson@pjdick.com
URL: http://www.pjdick.com

LaChay Wilson
Title: Chief Executive Officer, President Company: Chaydylake Productions Address: 20284 Washtenaw Street, Harper Woods, MI 48225 United States BUS: Entertainment P/S: Event Planning, Design and Execution MA: Regional D/D/R: Planning Events Including Themes and Personalized Touches H/I/S: Traveling, Bowling, Shopping EDU: Master of Science in Administration, Concentration in Leadership
Email: chaydylakeproductions@comcast.net

Marc H. Wilson
Title: Coach Company: Maryland Crusaders Address: 9605 Juniper Drive, Mitchellville, MD 20721 United States BUS: Nonprofit Organization P/S: Nonprofit Youth Basketball Organization MA: Mid-Atlantic Regional D/D/R: Promoting Student Athletics H/I/S: Reading EDU: Pursuing Bachelor's Degree in Criminal Justice, Gibbs College C/VW: Bladensburg High School
Email: ball-coach@comcast.net

Nancy L. Wilson
Title: Occupational Therapist Company: Rehab Care Address: 5208 Oak Gate Court, Arlington, TX 76016 United States BUS: Rehabilitation Center P/S: Rehabilitation MA: Regional D/D/R: Treating Geriatric Patients, Discharging Certifications, OTA Screening, Scheduling H/I/S: Traveling EDU: Bachelor of Science in Occupational Therapy, Texas Women's University (1987)
Email: liltwirp361963@yahoo.com

Rebecca 'Becky' Wilson
Title: Co-Owner, Office Manager Company: Krooked River Ranch Outfitters Address: 2771 Hendrick Ranch Road, Haskell, TX 79521 United States BUS: Ranch P/S: Hunting and Lodging MA: International D/D/R: Managing Customer Relations H/I/S: Traveling, Hunting A/A/S: Lone Star Land Stewards Award

Ross E. Wilson
Title: Account Executive Company: CIA Financial Group Address: 45600 Village Boulevard, Shelby Township, MI 48315 United States BUS: Insurance Company P/S: Commercial, Life and Auto Insurance, Financial Advising MA: Local D/D/R: Commercial Insurance H/I/S: Golfing, Spending Time with his Family C/VW: Church, Community Charities, Salvation Army
Email: rwilson@ciafg.com
URL: http://www.ciafg.com

Sherry L. Wilson
Title: Certified Medical Transcriptions Company: Outsourcing Solutions, Inc. Address: Jupiter, FL 33478 United States BUS: Medical P/S: Healthcare and Medical Transcriptions, Documentation and Coding Solutions to Hospitals and Clinics, Time-Sensitive Reports and Innovative and Customized Solutions MA: National D/D/R: Documenting Medical Reports and Research, Typing Reports for Physicians and Hospitals H/I/S: Walking on the Beach EDU: Associate of Arts in Medical Secretarial Studies, Bucks County Community College (1975) CERTS: Certified Medical Transcriptionist, American Association for Medical Transcription (1988) A/A/S: Florida Association for Medical Transcription
Email: medtangel55@comcast.net
URL: http://www.ositranscription.com

Susanne M. Wilson
Title: Vice President of Development and Marketing Company: Southwest Indiana Network for Education Address: T23, Box 126, Oakland City, IN 47660 United States BUS: Nonprofit Educational Agency P/S: Consulting, Literacy Programs MA: Southwestern Indiana D/D/R: Marketing, Project Management and Development H/I/S: Teaching Kickboxing, Reading, Traveling, Playing Tennis and Basketball EDU: Master of Business Administration, Auburn University; Master of Science in Secondary Education, University of Southern Indiana; Bachelor of Science in Social Sciences, University of Southern Indiana A/A/S: Phi Kappa Phi; Rotary Club C/VW: Big Brothers Big Sisters of America; American Cancer Society
Email: swilson0206@yahoo.com
URL: http://www.sineonline.com

Tracy J. Wilson
Title: Healthcare Professional, Lab Technician **Company:** Wilson Care **Address:** Hawthorne, CA 90250 United States **BUS:** Healthcare Provider **P/S:** Healthcare for the Handicapped **MA:** Regional **D/D/R:** Caring for Patients with Special, Tube Feedings **H/I/S:** Spending Time with her Two Children **EDU:** Associate Degree in Health Science, Santa Monica American College of Medical Technology; Bachelor of Arts in Health Science, UCLA and California State at Northridge; Certified in Phlebotomy and Lab Technician, The American College of Medical Technology **C/VW:** American Red Cross
Email: tjwtko@ca.rr.com

Vivian P. Wilson-Beverly
Title: Independent Insurance Agent **Company:** Wilson-Beverly Insurance **MA:** Regional **D/D/R:** Caring for her Customers and Ensuring their Satisfaction, Making Telephone Calls, Consulting, Managing Medicare Supplemental Insurance Services **H/I/S:** Freshwater Fishing, Gardening, Spending Time Outdoors **EDU:** Coursework, Real Estate School; High School Education **CERTS:** Certification in Property Management; Licensed Insurance Agent **A/A/S:** JCs; Life Insurance Association; Real Estate Association **C/VW:** Volunteer, Local Hospital; Valley Grove Baptist Church; Happy Hills Farm; Boy Scouts of America; Girl Scouts of the United States of America
Email: longarm07@peoplepc.com
URL: http://www.cambridgewhoswho.com

Ericka C. Wilson-Kerr
Title: Regional Sales Director **Company:** CVS Pharmacy **Address:** 1616 Memorial Drive, Chicopee, MA 01020 United States **BUS:** Pharmacy **P/S:** Pharmaceuticals **MA:** National **EXP:** Ms. Wilson-Kerr's expertise includes operations and finance management. **D/D/R:** Developing the Pipeline of Talented Future Leaders, Overseeing Marketing in Five Different States **H/I/S:** Listening to Music **EDU:** Associate Degree in Music, University of Hartford (1985) **A/A/S:** Participant, Emerging Leadership Program; Mentorship Programs; Founding Member, Corporate Diversity Council
Email: eckerr@cvs.com
URL: http://www.cvs.com

Peter M. Wilusz, DPM, PC
Title: President, Podiatrist **Company:** Peter M. Wilusz DPM, PC **Address:** 6510 Town Center Drive, Suite C, Clarkston, MI 48346 United States **BUS:** Podiatry Clinic **P/S:** Podiatric Medicine and Surgery, Diabetic Limb Salvage, Conservative Care, Foot, Ankle and Wound Care **MA:** Regional **D/D/R:** Treating Podiatric Patients, Performing Surgery, Teaching Hospital Residents, Managing Hospital Rounds, Lecturing **H/I/S:** Spending Time with his Family **EDU:** Doctor of Podiatric Medicine, The Ohio College of Podiatric Medicine (2001) **A/A/S:** Diplomate, American Board of Podiatric Surgery; Fellow, American College of Foot and Ankle Surgeons
Email: peteandmarni@comcast.net
URL: http://www.towncenterfootandankle,com

Alease Winchester, MS
Title: Clinical Research Associate **Company:** Research Pharmaceutical Services, Inc. **Dept:** Clinical Research **Address:** 610 W. Germantown Pike, Suite 200, Plymouth Meeting, PA 19462 United States **BUS:** Pharmaceutical Company **P/S:** Clinical Research **MA:** International **D/D/R:** Monitoring Clinical Trials, Working with Doctors on Enrollment, Ordering Supplies, Collecting Data **EDU:** Master's Degree in Healthcare Administration, Eastern University (1992); Bachelor of Science in Nursing, Weidner University (1987)
Email: awinchester@rpsweb.com
URL: http://www.cambridgewhoswho.com

JoAnn B. Windham
Title: Reverse Mortgage Specialist **Address:** 1701 Hermitage Boulevard, Suite 101, Tallahassee, FL 32308 United States **BUS:** Sole Proprietorship **P/S:** Financial Services Including Banking, Insurance, Investments and Mortgage Services **MA:** National **EXP:** Ms. Windham's expertise is in reverse mortgage services. **D/D/R:** Meeting People at their Home and Office, Lecturing, Conducting Seminars and Consulting Services at the Senior Citizen Center and Kiwanis, Overseeing Mortgage Approval for Senior Citizens through Government-Funded Operations **H/I/S:** Spending Time with her Grandchildren, Attending the Church **EDU:** High School Diploma **C/VW:** First Baptist Church; Order of the Eastern Star
Email: joann.b.windham@wellsfargo.com
URL: http://www.wellsfargo.com

Mrs. Rhonda M. Winfield
Title: Rhonda M Winfield **Company:** Winfield and Winfield **Address:** 329 Hidden Creek Circle, Warner Robins, GA 31088 United States **BUS:** Religious Company **P/S:** Support Services for Families in Times of Need **MA:** Local **D/D/R:** Assisting her Husband in Various Administrative Outreach Ministry Duties such as Reaches out to homeless, nursing homes, reaches out to all people spreading the gospel of Jesus Christ **H/I/S:** Watching Movies, Dining, Entertaining **EDU:** Pursuing Bachelor of Arts in English, University of District of Columbia **A/A/S:** Peace Corps, Toastmasters **C/VW:** Macedonia Baptist Church, Revival Temple Church Youth Ministries
Email: winfieldstanley@bellsouth.net
URL: http://www.cambridgewhoswho.com

Marjorie H. Wingard
Title: Co-Owner (Retired) **Company:** Wingard's Nursery **Address:** 1403 N. Lake Drive, Lexington, SC 29072 United States **BUS:** Plant Nursery **P/S:** Plants, Gardening Supplies **MA:** Local **D/D/R:** Selling Shrubbery, Trees and Perennials

Angela K. Wingerter
Title: Teacher **Company:** Sacred Heart School **Address:** 416 W. Third Street, Sedalia, MO 65301 United States **BUS:** School **P/S:** Education **MA:** Local **D/D/R:** Teaching English and Science **H/I/S:** Spending Time with her Family and at the Lake **EDU:** Pursuing Master's Degree in Administration, William Woods University (2007); Bachelor's Degree in Elementary Education, Missouri Valley College **C/VW:** St. Jude Children's Research Hospital
Email: angelawingerter@hotmail.com
URL: http://www.gogremlins.com

Dr. Irma June Wink
Title: Managing Partner **Company:** Wink and Wink **Address:** P.O. Box 780142, San Antonio, TX 78278 United States **BUS:** Entertainment Company **P/S:** Choral Music, Musical Dramas, Melodies, Gospel Music **MA:** International **D/D/R:** Composing, Publishing **H/I/S:** Gardening, Attending Art Exhibitions and Museums, Attending Musical Concerts **EDU:** JD, University of Texas **A/A/S:** The American Society of Composers, Authors and Publishers; Dean's Roundtable, University of Texas Law School
Email: winkandwink@sbcglobal.net
URL: http://www.cambridgewhoswho.com

Alan R. Winn
Title: Corporate Counsel **Company:** Morgan Management Corporation **Address:** 2800 McCree Road, Garland, TX 75041 United States **BUS:** Building Company **P/S:** Manufactures Buildings, Spas and Pools **MA:** National **D/D/R:** Law **EDU:** Course Work; Texas Tech School of Law
Email: arwinn@morganusa.com
URL: http://www.morganusa.com

Monika R. Winn
Title: Bookkeeper **Company:** Foothill-De Anza Community College District **Address:** 21250 Stevens Creek Boulevard, Cupertino, CA 95014 United States **BUS:** Community College District **P/S:** Education **MA:** Statewide **D/D/R:** Financial Accounting **H/I/S:** Working on Electronics and Cars **EDU:** Diploma, Mountain View High School **A/A/S:** Oceanic Institute **C/VW:** Oceanic Institute
Email: winnmonika@fhda.edu
URL: http://www.fhda.edu

Dawn M. Winrow
Title: Terminal Manager **Company:** New Jersey Transit Rail Operations **Address:** 390 Seventh Avenue, Penn Station, NY 10001 United States **BUS:** Public Transportation Corporation **P/S:** Commuter Railway Services **MA:** Regional **D/D/R:** Station Facility Maintenance and Operations, Minor through Major Rehabilitation, Ensuring Facility Safety, Comfort and Cleanliness, Overseeing all Janitorial Services, 60 Facility Maintenance Engineers and Customer Assistance Services, Scheduling of Train Service **H/I/S:** Reading, Dancing, Traveling **EDU:** Business Degree, Associate Business Career School of Technology, Philadelphia (1981); Safety Training Courses, New Jersey Rail Operations
Email: dwinrow@njtransit.com
URL: http://www.njtransit.com

Lisa S. Winslow
Title: Executive Director **Company:** Pasquotank Arts Council **Address:** 609 E. Main Street, Elizabeth City, NC 27909 United States **BUS:** Arts **P/S:** Arts Council **MA:** Local **D/D/R:** Working with the Public **H/I/S:** Spending Time with her Two Grandchildren **A/A/S:** President, Downtown Business Association; Board Member, Arts North Carolina **C/VW:** Cystic Fibrosis Foundation
Email: lisaw@pastquotankarts.org
URL: http://www.pasquotankarts.org

Shelly R. Winston
Title: Director **Company:** Matria, Inc. **Dept:** Cancer Division **Address:** 1593 Spring Hill Road, Suite 410, Vienna, VA 22182 United States **BUS:** Provider of Comprehensive Cancer Treatment Support Programs **P/S:** Improving the Quality of Life for Cancer Patients, Cost Savings for Payers **MA:** National **D/D/R:** Acting as a Client Liaison, Interacting with Providers and Facilities, Performing Customer Service, Account Management, Educating Patients on the Program and its Services, Supervising Representatives **H/I/S:** Playing Tennis, Running **EDU:** Licensed in Insurance Sales (1999); Master's Degree in Health Administration, George Washington University (1981); Bachelor's Degree in English, Yeshiva University (1977)
Email: swinston@qualityoncology.com
URL: http://www.qualityoncology.com

Maureen T. Winter
Title: Senior Systems Engineer **Company:** Polycom, Inc. **Address:** 85 Nottingham Road, Raymond, NH 03077 United States **BUS:** Video Conferencing Company **P/S:** Video Conferences **MA:** International **D/D/R:** Offering Technical Support for a Team of Five Salespeople, Offering Customer Relations **H/I/S:** Scuba Diving, Knitting, Traveling **EDU:** Bachelor's Degree in Business Administration, Salem State College **A/A/S:** Delta Mu Delta; Time-Off Coordinator Volunteer, Polycom Andover Facility
Email: maureen.winter@polycom.com
URL: http://www.polycom.com

Kristy L. Wireman
Title: Nurse, Office Manager, Biller, Licensed Practical Nurse **Company:** Big Sandy Surgical **Address:** 5230 KY Route 321, Suite 2, Prestonsburg, KY 41653 United States **BUS:** Hospital **P/S:** Healthcare, Surgical Center for Gall Bladder, Appendix, Hernia and Lung Surgeries, Pre-Cancer Monitoring **MA:** Local **D/D/R:** Managing Office Operations, Nursing, Billing, Consulting, Counseling, Overseeing Patients with Special Needs **H/I/S:** Ballroom Dancing **EDU:** MD, Pikeville College School of Osteopathic Medicine; Associate Degree in Nursing, Prestonsburg Community College of Nursing (2005); Licensed Practical Nurse (2005); Coursework in Business Administration (1998) **A/A/S:** Who's Who Among Students
Email: kalzadon@bellsouth.net

Lilyan E. Wischnack
Title: Owner (Retired) **Company:** Lilyan Ent. Ltd. **Address:** 535 Pierce Street, Apartment 2216, Albany, CA 94706 United States **BUS:** Interior Design Firm **P/S:** Residential Interior Design **MA:** Local **D/D/R:** Managing Clients, Furnishing **H/I/S:** Oil Painting **EDU:** Diploma, The New School, NY
Email: lilywish@sbcglobal.net

Cheri L. Wise
Title: Assistant to the President **Company:** Butler Color Press **Address:** 119 Bonnie Drive, Butler, PA 16002 United States **BUS:** Printing and Publishing Company **P/S:** Four-Color Printing for Butler Eagle Newspaper **MA:** Local **EXP:** Ms. Wise's expertise includes human resource management and the maintenance of customer relationships. **H/I/S:** Reading, Needlepoint, Fishing, Skiing, Scuba Diving, Horseback Riding **EDU:** Coursework in Music Education, Florida State University **C/VW:** Local Charitable Organizations
Email: lapper3@aol.com
URL: http://www.butlercp.com

Roxane M. Wise
Title: RN **Company:** Schering-Plough **Address:** 74B Woodside Gardens, Roselle Park, NJ 07204 United States **BUS:** Pharmaceuticals Service Provider **P/S:** Drug Safety **MA:** Local **D/D/R:** Drug Safety Associate Manager **H/I/S:** Traveling and Reading **EDU:** Bachelor of Science in Nursing, Rutgers University **A/A/S:** Commission for Case Management Certification
Email: roxwise@aol.com

Spring M. Wishmeyer
Title: Owner, Licensed Massage Therapist **Company:** Simply Massage **Address:** 5121 69th Street, Lubbock, TX 79424 United States **BUS:** Massage Therapy Business **P/S:** Massage Therapy **MA:** Local **D/D/R:** Deep Tissue, Hot Stone, Mother-To-Be and Swedish Massage, Reflexology **H/I/S:** Playing Tennis, Traveling, Cooking, Eating **EDU:** Licensed Massage Therapist, Austin School of Massage **C/VW:** American Heart Association, Girl Power Happy Hour, Community Charities
Email: spring.wishmeyer@gmail.com

Robert M. Wisner
Title: Senior Vice President **Company:** HealthSouth Corporation **Address:** One Health South Parkway, Birmingham, AL 35242 United States **BUS:** Healthcare Hospital **P/S:** Healthcare **MA:** National **D/D/R:** Healthcare Reimbursement **H/I/S:** Golf, Scuba, Softball **EDU:** Mt St Mary College, Bachelor of Science - Accounting **A/A/S:** Federation of American Hospitals, American Hospital Association
Email: robert.wisner@healthsouth.com
URL: http://www.healthsouth.com

Ann C. Wiszynski
Title: Domestic Engineer **Company:** Annie's **Address:** 5190 Bennett Road, Jackson, MI 49201 United States **BUS:** Professional Housekeeping Service **P/S:** Home Cleaning **MA:** Local **D/D/R:** Home Organization and Cleaning **H/I/S:** Watching Soap Operas, Traveling, Playing Bingo **C/VW:** Church, Paralyzed Veterans of America, Easter Seals
URL: http://www.cambridgewhoswho.com

April B. Witherspoon
Title: Founder, Director **Company:** Zoë Behavior Health Services **Address:** 974 Woodleaf Court, Winston Salem, NC 27107 United States **BUS:** Mental Health Facility **P/S:** Mental Health Services **MA:** Winston Salem, Forsyth County **D/D/R:** Coordinating Mental Healthcare Programs, Overseeing Operations of the Facility, Behavior Management and Modification **H/I/S:** Taking Part in Church Activities, Attending Plays **EDU:** Bachelor of Arts in Sociology, Salem College **A/A/S:** SNPHA; PACNC; Piedmont Club **C/VW:** Union Baptist Church
Email: awitherspoon@zoebhs.com
URL: http://www.cambridgewhoswho.com

Gary B. Witt
Title: Executive Vice President **Company:** Colorado Telecommunications Association **Address:** 225 E. 16th Avenue, Suite 260, Denver, CO 80203 United States **BUS:** Telecommunications Association **P/S:** Advancement of the Interest of Rural Telecommunications **MA:** Regional **D/D/R:** Managing Media Relations, Advising on Legal Services to the Companies and Some Individuals, Overseeing Budgets, Working as Lead Representative to Public Utilities, Commissions, the Legislature and the Governor's Office **H/I/S:** Jogging, Playing Tennis **EDU:** JD, University of Denver (1978) **CERTS:** Licensed to Practice Law, States of District of Columbia, California and Colorado **A/A/S:** Speaker, National Cooperative Telephone Association
Email: gwitt@att.net
URL: http://www.gwitt.com

Kandace A. Wittry, OTR
Title: Occupational Therapist **Company:** Area Education Agency 267 **Address:** 3706 Cedar Heights Drive, Cedar Falls, IA 50613 United States **BUS:** State Education Organization **P/S:** Education **MA:** Local **D/D/R:** Pediatrics, Work within the Educational system for the benefit of Students with Special Needs, consults with teachers regarding individual students, specializing in relating to developmental skills, working part time in the geriatric field **H/I/S:** Traveling, Reading, Spending Time with her Nieces and Nephews **EDU:** Master's Degree in Occupational Therapy, St. Ambrose University (2005); Bachelor of Science in Therapeutic Recreation-Western Illinois University (1992) **A/A/S:** Board Member Iowa Occupational Therapy Association; American Occupational Therapy Association; Junior Chamber of Commerce **C/VW:** Up with Families
Email: kandyisland@hotmail.com
URL: http://www.cambridgewhoswho.com

Lisa M. Wobbema
Title: Director of Health Informational Management **Company:** Olmstead Medical Center **Address:** 210 Ninth Street S.E., Rochester, MN 55904 United States **BUS:** Hospital, Medical Clinic **P/S:** Healthcare Information Management **MA:** Local **D/D/R:** Health Information Management, Managing Hospital Medical Records, Privacy Compliance, Personnel Management, Maintaining Electronic Medical Records **H/I/S:** Reading, Playing the Piano, Spending Time with her Three Children **EDU:** Bachelor's Degree in Organizational Management, Viterbo University **A/A/S:** American Health Information Management Association; Minnesota Health Information Management Association
Email: lisa.wobbema@uplandhillshealth.org
URL: http://www.uplandhillshealth.org

Irma V. Woerner
Title: Senior Regulatory Affairs Specialist **Company:** Department of the Army **Address:** 8164 Clairborne Drive, Frederick, MD 21702 United States **BUS:** Government Organization **P/S:** Defensive Operations **MA:** International **D/D/R:** Administrative and Regulatory Support to FDA of Pharmaceutical Documents and Reports, Working Under Seven Trail Monitors, Coordinating all Travel Plans, Dealing with Travel Expenses, Proofing and Editing Field Data Reports and Submitting them to the Commanders of the Projects, Products, Relay Messages, Taking Care of Correspondence, Problem Remedy **H/I/S:** Sewing, Reading **A/A/S:** Paralegal, US Air Force (1978-1997)
Email: irma.woerner1@verizon.net
URL: http://www.army.mil

Cheryl A. Wohlmuth
Title: Teacher **Company:** Indianapolis Public Schools, William A. Bell School **Address:** 3330 N. Pennsylvania Street, Indianapolis, IN 46205 United States **BUS:** Elementary School **P/S:** Elementary Education **MA:** Local **D/D/R:** Teaching, Being Creative, Thinking Outside of the Box **H/I/S:** Quilting, Reading, Biking, Gardening **EDU:** Master's Degree Plus 40 in General Education, DePaul University **A/A/S:** Delta Kappa Gamma; State Board Nominee Committee **C/VW:** Gleaners Food Bank, Local Dog Shelter
Email: cwohlmuth7224@comcast.net
URL: http://www.cambridgewhoswho.com

Kelly Marie Wojcik
Title: Teacher **Company:** Thomas Metcalf Laboratory School **Address:** Campus Box 7000, Normal, IL 61790 United States **BUS:** School **P/S:** Education **MA:** Local **D/D/R:** Teaching Young Children who are Hard of Hearing **H/I/S:** Reading, Scrapbooking **EDU:** Post-Masters Coursework, Illinois State University; Master of Education, Illinois State University **A/A/S:** Council for Exceptional Children **C/VW:** Home Sweet Home Mission
Email: kmkriz@ilstu.edu
URL: http://www.cambridgewhoswho.com

Sally Roberta Wolberg
Title: Clinician **Company:** Intervention Specialists **Address:** 453 Morris Avenue, Elizabeth, NJ 07208 United States **BUS:** Mental Health, Offering psychotherapy in a Mental Health or Substance Abuse Treatment Center **P/S:** Outpatient Therapy **MA:** Central New Jersey **D/D/R:** Counseling People with Chemical Dependency and Co-Occurring Disorders **H/I/S:** Reading, Watching Movies, Going to the Theater in New York City, Fine Dining, Traveling, Listening to Music **EDU:** Master of Science Degree in Child Development, West Virginia University; Master of Arts Degree in Counseling, George Washington University. Post-Graduate Degree in Counseling with a Specialization in Marriage and Family Therapy, University of Bridgeport; Certified MICA Specialist (CMS) (mentally ill chemical abuser), Licensed Alcohol and Drug Counselor (LCADC); Licensed Professional Counselor (LPC) Criminal Justice Certification (CJC) **A/A/S:** New Jersey Counseling Association
Email: sararina@optonline.net
URL: http://www.cambridgewhoswho.com

Ronald E. Wolf
Title: President, Chief Executive Officer **Company:** Wolftracks Enterprises **Address:** 6 Timber Cove, Campbell, CA 95008 United States **BUS:** Business Services **P/S:** Tahoe Vacation Rental Retreats, Products and New Inventions, Home Lawn and Garden Services **MA:** National **D/D/R:** Assisting Clients with Products and New Inventions, Offering Home and Gardening Services, Selling Vacation Rentals **H/I/S:** Gardening, Softball, Skiing, Trout Fishing, Traveling **EDU:** Management and Marketing Coursework, Southwest Mississippi State University **A/A/S:** Sigma Pi
Email: wolftrx@earthlink.net
URL: http://www.home.earthlink.net/~wolftrx

Christopher Wolfe
Title: Tools Smith, Manager **Company:** Software Consulting Services, LLC **Address:** 630 Selvaggio Drive, Suite 420, Nazareth, PA 18064 United States **BUS:** Newspaper Systems Company **P/S:** Software **MA:** International **D/D/R:** Computational Mathematics **H/I/S:** Reading, Driving **EDU:** Bachelor of Science in Computer Science, The Pennsylvania State University
Email: cwolfe@newspapersystems.com
URL: http://www.newspapersystems.com

Beth C. Wolffe
Title: Attorney **Company:** The Wolffe Law Firm, LLC **Address:** 3204 N. Tacoma Street, Arlington, VA 22213 United States **BUS:** Employment defense lawyer for companies only. **P/S:** Employment Defense Litigation **MA:** MD, DC, VA **D/D/R:** Defending and Advising Companies in Cases Involving Discrimination, At-will Employment, Retaliation, Sexual Harassment, Non-Compete Agreements, Employment Contracts, Overtime Claims, Employee Handbooks and Traditional Union Charges and Grievances **H/I/S:** Tutoring disadvantaged students **EDU:** JD, Villanova University School of Law; Bachelor of Arts, University of Michigan **A/A/S:** Litigation, Labor and Employment Sections of the VA, DC, MD and American Bar Associations; Society for Human Resource Management **C/VW:** George Mason University College Education and Human Development
Email: wolffelaw@verizon.net
URL: http://www.wolffelaw.com

Debra Wolfrum
Title: Senior Analyst Biller **Company:** Chelsea Retirement Center **Address:** 8436 Ann Arbor Road, Grass Lake, MI 49240 United States **BUS:** Nonprofit Organization **P/S:** Community Services **MA:** Regional **D/D/R:** Managing Medical Billing Services and Response Mail **H/I/S:** Bowling **EDU:** Diploma, East High School, Des Moines, IA (1968)
Email: doneright8436@yahoo.com
URL: http://www.unitedmethodistretirementcommunity.com

Tim Wollesen
Title: President **Company:** Sales Midwest, Inc **Address:** 15350 South Keeler, Olathe, KS 66062 United States **BUS:** Farm Equipment Retail **P/S:** Farm and Industrial Equipment **MA:** Local **D/D/R:** Sales, People Management **H/I/S:** Dawn (Wife) Colton Son, Snow Mobiling **EDU:** Graduated HS
Email: salesmidwest@sbcglobal.net
URL: http://www.salesmidwest.com

Susan E. Wolz
Title: K-6 Counselor **Company:** Osage County R-1 Schools **Dept:** Chamois High School **Address:** 614 S. Poplar Street, Chamois, MO 65024 United States **BUS:** School District **P/S:** Education **MA:** Missouri **D/D/R:** Guidance Counseling, Assisting Students, Speech Coaching **H/I/S:** Reading, Spending Time with her Granddaughter **EDU:** Master of Education in Counseling, Lincoln University; Bachelor's Degree in English and Speech, Southwest Baptist University **A/A/S:** Mid-Missouri School Counselors Association; American School Counselors Association **C/VW:** Local Church; Local Charitable Organization
Email: wolz@chamois.k12.mo.us
URL: http://www.cambridgewhoswho.com

Reneé R. Womack
Title: Senior Public Health Advisor **Company:** New York City Department of Health and Mental Hygiene **Dept:** HIV Epidemiology Program **Address:** 346 Broadway, Room 706, New York, NY 10013 United States **BUS:** Government Agency **P/S:** Public Health Education, Epidemiology **MA:** Regional **D/D/R:** Answering Telephone Calls, Collecting Information from Medicine Providers, Overseeing 75 Locations, Conducting Surveys and Generating Reports on HIV Patients, Managing Medical Facilities, Acting as a Liaison for Testing Facilities, Coordinating Assistance Programs **H/I/S:** Reading, Shopping, Traveling **EDU:** Coursework in Community Health Education, CUNY York **CERTS:** Certification in Pre and Post Test Counseling in HIV, New York City Department of Health **A/H:** Employee of the Quarter Award (1992-1993) **C/VW:** Local Church; Community Baptist Church, Bayside, NY
Email: rwomack@health.nyc.gov
URL: http://www.nyc.gov

Anjanetta M. Wonderlick
Title: Dentist **Company:** Private Practice **Address:** 1112 S Washington, Suite 211, Naperville, IL United States **BUS:** Private Practice **P/S:** Dental Services **MA:** Local **EXP:** Dr. Wonderlick's expertise is in cosmetic dentistry. **H/I/S:** Exercise, Jogging, Interior Decorating, Golfing **EDU:** Doctor of Dental Surgery **A/A/S:** ADA, IDS, American Academy of Cosmetic Dentistry
Email: wonderglow@sbcglobal.net
URL: http://www.cambridgewhoswho.com

Mr. John Y. Wong
Title: Owner **Company:** Chinese and American Business Network, LLC **Address:** P. O. Box 471, Uncasville, CT 06382 United States **BUS:** Private Company Committee to Excellence in the Publishing Industry **P/S:** Monthly Magazine in English and Chinese **MA:** National **D/D/R:** Establishing a Chinese and American Business Network, Producing a Monthly Magazine in English and Chinese featuring Business and Professional Advertisements, Articles of Interest to Integrate the Chinese and American Communities, Distributing 5,000 Magazines Monthly to 15-20 Towns and Cities **H/I/S:** Painting **EDU:** High School Graduate **A/A/S:** Invited to become a Board Member, American Cancer Society; Norwich Newcomers Club; Board Member, Norwich Medical Center; Founder, Chinese Culture Existing Association Assisting Newcomers Integrate into the Community; Day Care, Educational Materials and Scholarships
URL: http://www.cambridgewhoswho.com

Mr. Michael C. Wong
Title: Registered Nurse **Company:** Hawaii Medical Center West **Address:** 91-2141 Fort Weaver Road, Ewa Beach, HI 96706 United States **BUS:** Healthcare Center **P/S:** Healthcare **MA:** Local **EXP:** Mr. Wong's expertise includes emergency room, trauma and disaster care nursing. **H/I/S:** Running Marathons **EDU:** Pursuing Bachelor's Degree, University of Phoenix; Coursework, Cerritos College, Coursework in Nursing, East Los Angeles College **A/A/S:** Dr. Adele Mitchell Nursing Honor Society; Hawaii Nurses' Association; National Healthcareer Association **C/VW:** Disabled American Veterans; American Cancer Society
Email: kapoleikids@aol.com
URL: http://www.cambridgewhoswho.com

Tamara L. Wong
Title: Teacher **Company:** Sacramento City Unified School District, Martin Luther King Jr. K-8 **Address:** 480 Little River Way, Sacramento, CA 95831 United States **BUS:** Elementary School **P/S:** Education **MA:** Local **D/D/R:** Teaching Primary Education **H/I/S:** Traveling with Family to Hawaii, Reading, Spending Time with Friends **EDU:** Master of Education, University of California, Davis; Bachelor of Science in Human Development, University of California, Davis **A/A/S:** Sacramento City Teachers Association; National Education Association **C/VW:** Susan G. Komen Breast Cancer Foundation; Local Church; Local Charities
Email: tamlyns8@yahoo.com
URL: http://www.cambridgewhoswho.com

Bethany A. Wood
Title: Owner **Company:** Health Partners Network, North Country Ltd. **Address:** 11 Riverglen Lane, Suite 125, Littleton, NH 03561 United States **BUS:** Occupational Healthcare Clinic **P/S:** Occupational Medicine **MA:** New Hampshire, Vermont **D/D/R:** Business Management **H/I/S:** Playing with her Children, Hiking, Reading **EDU:** College Coursework **A/A/S:** Best Doctors Group; National Association of Occupational Health Professionals **C/VW:** Relay for Life, March of Dimes, Affordable Housing and Educational Services
Email: bwood@hpnnc.com
URL: http://www.cambridgewhoswho.com

David J. Wood
Title: President **Company:** Wood Properties, LLC **Address:** 6015 42nd Street, Riverside, CA 92509 United States **BUS:** Real Estate Agency **P/S:** Real Estate, Tax Defaulted Properties, Selling Homes at Auctions **MA:** Regional **D/D/R:** Handling Phones and Computers, Contacting People, Checking Out Government Auctions, Searching Title and Property **H/I/S:** Fishing, Restoring Old Chevys, Motorcycling **EDU:** Coursework, Riverside Community College
Email: wddave@msn.com
URL: http://www.inlandgiftshop.com

Sister Helene Wood
Title: Director **Company:** Office of Worship, Diocese of Honolulu **Address:** 6301 Pali Highway, Kaneohe, HI 96744 United States **BUS:** Diocese **P/S:** Episcopal Functions, Workshops, Consultations, Resources and Guidelines for Liturgical Services **MA:** Statewide **D/D/R:** Coordinating Functions, Completing Administrative Tasks **H/I/S:** Hawaiian Quilting, Reading, Hawaiian Cultural Crafts **EDU:** Master of Pastoral Liturgy, Santa Clara University; Master of Science in Education, University of Hawaii **A/A/S:** Federation of Diocesan Liturgical Commissions; National Pastoral Musicians Association
Email: hwood@rcchawaii.org
URL: http://www.rcchawaii.org

Linda D. Wood
Title: President, Treasurer **Company:** Passion Products, Inc. dba Chatham Presence **Address:** 632 Main Street, Chatham, MA 02633 United States **BUS:** Retail Store **P/S:** Retail Furniture, Lamps, Gifts, Home Goods **MA:** National **D/D/R:** Overseeing Store Operations **H/I/S:** Breeding Arabian Horses **EDU:** Master of Business Administration in Finance, University of Lowell; Bachelor's Degree in Biochemistry, Brown University **A/A/S:** Chatham Chamber of Commerce; Chatham Merchants Association **C/VW:** American Cancer Society
Email: chatampresence@verizon.net
URL: http://www.chathampresence.com

Tim Wood
Title: Advisor **Company:** Deschutes Investment Advisors **Address:** 1211 SW Fifth, Suite 2830, Portland, OR 97204 United States **BUS:** Investment Service Company **P/S:** Qualified Plans Advise, Financial Planning **MA:** Local **D/D/R:** ERISA **H/I/S:** Golf **EDU:** Bachelor of Science in Political Science, Oregon State University, Louis and Clark College
Email: t@deschutesadvisors.com
URL: http://www.deschutesadvisors.com

Gwendolyn Wood-Tisdale
Title: Teacher, Poet **Company:** Gibbs Elementary School **Address:** 500 19th Street N.E., Washington, DC 20020 United States **BUS:** Elementary School **P/S:** Education **MA:** Local **D/D/R:** Literacy **H/I/S:** Reading, Writing, Community Service **EDU:** Master's Degree Equivalency, Howard University, Trinity College, The Catholic University of America; Bachelor of Science in Elementary Education, Alabama State College **C/VW:** Capitol Hill Seventh-Day Adventist Church, Forever Young Ministry
Email: tisdale202@aol.com
URL: http://www.cambridgewhoswho.com

Jennifer L. Woodard
Title: Registered Nurse, Clinical Nurse Specialist **Company:** Clarian Health **Dept:** Indiana University Hospital **Address:** 550 University Boulevard, Indianapolis, IN 46202 United States **BUS:** Hospital **P/S:** Healthcare Including Research Development **MA:** Local **EXP:** Ms. Woodard's expertise includes gastrointestinal and oncology surgery, and bedside care for post-operative patients. **D/D/R:** Ensuring Clinical Quality Services for Patient Care **H/I/S:** Playing Tennis, Reading **EDU:** Master's Degree in Clinical Nurse Specialist and Adult Health Studies, Indiana University; Bachelor's Degree in Biology, University of Evansville (1997) **A/A/S:** National Association of Clinical Nurse Specialists; Academy of Medical-Surgical Nurses
Email: jwoodard@clarian.org
URL: http://www.clarian.org

Shirley M. Woodard
Title: Bookkeeper **Company:** Shirley Woodard Bookkeeping **Address:** 1616 S. Platinum Avenue, P.O. Box 173, Deming, NM 88030 United States **BUS:** Accounting Firm **P/S:** Bookkeeping, Tax Preparation **MA:** Local **EXP:** Ms. Woodard's expertise includes bookkeeping, tax preparation and payroll. **H/I/S:** Reading Mysteries **EDU:** Coursework
Email: shirleym.woodard@cwwemail.com

Cynthia J. Woodburn
Title: Mathematics Professor **Company:** Pittsburg State University **Dept:** Mathematics Department **Address:** 1701 S. Broadway Street, Pittsburg, KS 66762 United States **BUS:** University **P/S:** Education **MA:** Local **EXP:** Ms. Woodburn's expertise is in mathematics. **D/D/R:** Teaching Computational Constructive Algebra, Mediating Instruction, Coordinating Mathematics, Music and 'Across the Curriculum' Programs **H/I/S:** Studying Mathematics **EDU:** Ph.D. in Mathematics, New Mexico State University (1994); Master of Science in Mathematics, Pittsburgh State University (1987); Bachelor of Science in Education, Pittsburgh State University (1986) **A/A/S:** Web master, Mathematics Department, Pittsburgh State University; Mathematics Committee, BSED, Pittsburgh State University; Arts and Sciences Academic Policies Committee, Pittsburgh State University; North Central Region, Kappa Mu Epsilon; Information Coordinator, Kansas Section of the Mathematical Association of America; Mathematical Association of America; American Mathematical Society; National Council of Teachers of Mathematics; Association for Women in Mathematics; National Treasurer; Kappa Mu Epsilon
Email: cwoodbur@pittstate.edu
URL: http://www.pittstate.edu/math/cynthia/cynthia.html

James Cameron Woodhead
Title: President **Company:** Woody's Custom Landscaping, Inc. **Address:** 13503 N.E. Mountain View Drive, Battle Ground, WA 98604 United States **BUS:** Landscape Construction Company **P/S:** Landscape Construction, Flat Stone Patios, Retaining Walls **MA:** Vancouver, Portland **D/D/R:** Working with Pavers, Hardscaping, Utilizing Flat Stone and Slate, Installing Water Features **H/I/S:** Working **EDU:** Bachelor of Science in Ornamental Horticulture, Minor in Business, California Polytechnic State University, San Luis Obispo, CA **A/A/S:** Washington Association of Landscape Professionals; Interlocking Concrete Pavement Institute **C/VW:** Catholic Church
Email: jmswoodhead@aol.com
URL: http://www.woodyscustomlandscaping.com

Lance R. Woodruff
Title: Land Specialist, Realtor **Company:** Windermere Real Estate/East, Inc. **Address:** 1810 15th Place N.W., Suite 100, Issaquah, WA 98027 United States **BUS:** Real Estate **P/S:** Land Sales of Vacant, Underdeveloped Rural and Urban Properties **MA:** Regional **D/D/R:** Managing and Selling Vacant Real Estate Properties **H/I/S:** Baseball, Golfing **EDU:** Bachelor's Degree in Marketing, Gonzaga University (1978)
Email: lwoodruf@windermere.com

Matthew Woodrum
Title: Cytotechnologist **Company:** LabCorp **Address:** 312 Sixth Avenue, South Charleston, WV 25301 United States **BUS:** Clinical Laboratory **P/S:** Clinical Research Services **MA:** National **EXP:** Mr. Woodrum's expertise includes cytotechnology and the screening of gynecology and non-gynecology specimens. **H/I/S:** Camping, White Water Canoeing, Mountain Biking **EDU:** Bachelor of Science in Biology **CERTS:** Certified Cytologist, Charleston Area Medical Center
Email: matcheswvu@gmail.com
URL: http://www.labcorp.com

Carol P. Woods, CRNA, MS, APN
Title: Nurse Anesthetist **Company:** University of Tennessee Medical Group **Address:** 66 N. Pauline Street, Memphis, TN 38105 United States **BUS:** Nonprofit, Non-Tax-Supported Group Practice **P/S:** Quality Patient Care, Medical Education and Medical Research **MA:** Regional **D/D/R:** Working in a Level I Trauma Center, Treating Life Threatening Injuries, Helping to Keep Patients Alive for Treatment from Doctors, Accepting Shock Trauma Calls and Emergencies, Intubating Patients, Conducting Anesthesia Follow-Ups **H/I/S:** Playing Tennis, Snow Skiing, Boating, Gardening, Traveling, Learning About Wine, Teaching Intensive Care Unit Nurses **EDU:** Master of Science in Biology, Southern Connecticut State University (2003) **A/A/S:** American Association of Nurse Anesthetists; American Nurses Association; Tennessee Association of Nurse Anesthetists; Featured, TN 24/7 (2005); Featured, Nursing America
Email: carolwoodscrna@hotmail.com

Cynthia Woods
Title: Marketing Asst **Company:** Master Builder Inc **Address:** 23700 Chagrin Boulevard, Beachwood, OH 44120 United States **BUS:** Concrete Industry **D/D/R:** Marketing

Marion D. 'Buzz' Woods
Title: President/CEO **Company:** Republic Mortgage Commercial, LLC **Address:** 4516 S. 700 E., Suite 350, Salt Lake City, UT 84107 United States **BUS:** Financial Finance/Banking/Credit Services **P/S:** Real Estate, Commercial Lending, Mortgage Banking **MA:** Regional **D/D/R:** Development Loans, Permanent Takeouts and Acquisitions **EDU:** Master of Business Administration **A/A/S:** Association of America
Email: bwoods@republiccommercial.com

Odell Woods
Title: Maintenance Manager **Company:** Spring Global **Address:** 2363 Baton Rouge Road, Chester, SC 29706 United States **BUS:** Textiles Service Provider **P/S:** Textiles Plant **MA:** International **D/D/R:** Designs and Specifications **EDU:** York Technical College, Associate of Arts **A/A/S:** Ordained Deacon
Email: odell.woods@springs.com
URL: http://www.springs.com

Terri D. Woods
Title: Teacher **Company:** Hosford Park School **Address:** 4735 Arthur Street, Gary, IN 46408 United States **BUS:** School **P/S:** Education **MA:** Local **D/D/R:** Differentiating Instruction to Meet the Needs of Each Individual Learner **H/I/S:** Spending Time with her Six Children and 13 Grandchildren, Reading, Watching Wrestling, Baseball and Football **EDU:** Reading License and Kindergarten Endorsement, Indiana University (1987); Master's Degree Plus 15 in Elementary Education, Indiana University; Bachelor's Degree in Elementary Education, Indiana University; Certification in K-5 Education; 7-8 Reading Endorsement; Kindergarten Endorsement **A/A/S:** Association for Supervision and Curriculum Development; National Education Association; Indiana State Reading Association
Email: woodssr9232@comcast.net
URL: http://www.cambridgewhoswho.com

Vicky R. Woods
Title: Eighth-Grade Mathematics and Science Teacher **Company:** St. Thomas the Apostle School **Address:** Newton, IL 62448 United States **BUS:** School **P/S:** Education **MA:** East Central Rural Illinois **D/D/R:** Teaching Mathematics, Algebra and General Science **H/I/S:** Reading, Making Jewelry, Polymer Clay, Wire Works **EDU:** Bachelor's Degree in Elementary Education, Eastern Illinois University; Endorsements in Mathematics and Science for Middle School
Email: vwoodsy9@hotmail.com
URL: http://www.cambridgewhoswho.com

Paul V. Woolley, MD
Title: Physician **Address:** 88 Osborne Street, Johnstown, PA 15905 United States **BUS:** Private Practice **P/S:** Treating Patients with Oncology and Hematology **MA:** Local **D/D/R:** Caring for Oncology and Hematology Patients **H/I/S:** Skiing, Scuba Diving, Playing the Piano, Spending Time Outdoors **EDU:** Fellowship, National Cancer Institute, MD (1975); Fellowship, National Cancer Institute, MD (1973); Fellowship in Internal Medicine, Roosevelt Hospital; MD, University of Michigan, Ann Arbor (1969); Bachelor of Arts in History, Cornell University (1961) **A/A/S:** Fellowship, American College of Physicians; American Society of Clinical Oncology; National Cancer Institute, MD
Email: woolleypv@atlanticbb.net

Jennifer M. Wooten
Title: Lead Teacher **Company:** Chatsworth Elementary School **Address:** 500 Green Road, Chatsworth, GA 30705 United States **BUS:** Elementary School **P/S:** Primary Education **MA:** Local **D/D/R:** Practicing For High-Stake Assessments, Teaching Reading and Mathematics to Second-Grade Students **H/I/S:** Scrapbooking, Spending Time with her Family, Hunting, Camping **EDU:** Pursuing Master's Degree in Elementary Curriculum, Instruction and Assessment, Walden University; Bachelor's Degree in Early Childhood Education, Shorter College **CERTS:** Work Study Program, Shorter College **C/VW:** United Way; North Broad Baptist Church
Email: cjw11075@alltel.net
URL: http://www.cambridgewhoswho.com

Charles N. Word
Title: General Manager **Company:** Ruth's Chris Steak House **Address:** 447 E. Cooper Street, Aspen, CO 81611 United States **BUS:** Restaurant **P/S:** Food Services **MA:** International **EXP:** Mr. Word's expertise includes management and customer service. **H/I/S:** Golfing, Hiking, Riding his Bike, Fishing **EDU:** Associate Degree in Engineering, Auburn University, AL (2002)
Email: normwardau@yahoo.com
URL: http://www.cambridgewhoswho.com

Jamie Worden
Title: Cosmetologist **Company:** Hair Connection **Address:** 106 S. Ninth Street, Williams, AZ 86046 United States **BUS:** Beauty Spa **P/S:** Hair Styling, Make-Up, Nail Manicure, Waxing **MA:** National **EXP:** Ms. Worden's expertise includes makeup application and skin care. **D/D/R:** Coloring Hair, Giving Manicures **H/I/S:** Reading, Attending the Church **CERTS:** Licensed Cosmetologist, Artistic Beauty College, AZ **A/A/S:** Arizona Chamber of Commerce **C/VW:** Local Church; Arizona Department of Transportation
Email: jamie.worden@cwwemail.com
URL: http://www.cambridgewhoswho.com

Kelvin D. Workman
Title: Electrical Service Technician **Company:** Kearney Electric, Inc. **Address:** 3609 E. Superior Avenue, Phoenix, AZ 85040 United States **BUS:** Electric and Communications Company **P/S:** Contract Lighting, Industrial Maintenance, Preventative Maintenance Including Infrared Scanning, High Voltage Installation and Maintenance, Instrumentation and Control Work, Design and Installation of Automation Programmable Systems, Installation and Maintenance of Uninterrupted Power Supplies, Fire Alarm Installation and Maintenance, Telecommunications Services, Standardization, Technology Design and Upgrades, Data Center Design, Installation and Maintenance, Fiber-Optic Installation, Outside Plant Distribution Cabling, Network Certification, Security Controls Cabling Audio/Visual Cabling, Electrical Contractor Construction **MA:** Regional **D/D/R:** Maintaining Commercial and Industrial Electrical and Communications Systems, Installing Power Outlets, Electrical Construction, Offering Technical Support **H/I/S:** Restoring his Classic Volkswagen and 1964 Dune Buggy **EDU:** Certified Industrial Technician (1991)
Email: kvworkman@cox.net
URL: http://www.kearneyelectric.com

Cynthia L. Worley
Title: Principal **Company:** Sheldon Independent School District **Dept:** C.E. King High School **Address:** C.E. King Parkway, Houston, TX 77044 United States **BUS:** High School **P/S:** Education **MA:** Local **D/D/R:** Teaching Mathematics, Overseeing Budget, Staff and Students **H/I/S:** Fishing, Playing Basketball **EDU:** Certified Principal; Master of Arts in Counseling, University of Houston **A/A/S:** Texas Association of Secondary School Principals; National Association of Secondary School Principals; National Association of Principal Partnership
Email: cworley@sheldon.k12.tx.us
URL: http://www.sheldonisd.com

Kate F. Worth
Title: Owner, Court Reporter **Company:** Worth Court Reporting **Address:** 820 Keshena Court, Fond du Lac, WI 54935 United States **BUS:** Court Reporting Firm **P/S:** Court Reporting Service **MA:** International **D/D/R:** Managing Lawyer's Offices, Government Offices and Corporations, Writing Verbatim Transcripts, Arbitrations, Depositions, Public Hearings and Workers' Compensation Hearings **H/I/S:** Playing Tennis, Gardening, Listening to Music **CERTS:** Registered Professional Reporter **A/A/S:** Wisconsin Court Reporters Association; National Court Reporters Association; National Association for Legal Professional; National Federation for Independent Businesses **C/VW:** United Methodist Church; United Methodist Women; National Alliance for the Mentally Ill; Republican Party
Email: k@worthreporting.com
URL: http://www.worthreporting.com

Lani Worthington Shaver
Title: President **Company:** A New View **Address:** 1407 E. Bayview Drive, Tempe, AZ 85283 United States **BUS:** Building and Construction Company Serving Residents of Tempe **P/S:** Building and Remodeling Services for Houses and Custom-Order Homes **MA:** Regional **D/D/R:** Creating Building Design, Offering Decorating Assistance, Running the Company, Supervising the Staff **H/I/S:** Gardening, Reading, Watching Basketball, Attending Family Events **EDU:** Master's Degree in Occupational Therapy, Texas Woman's University (1968); Master's Degree in Marriage and Family Counseling, Texas Woman's University (1987)
Email: lwsassoc@qwest.net

Samuel R. Wray, Ph.D.
Title: Professor, Director **Company:** Medical and Scientific Development Trust **Address:** 4453 N. San Andros, West Palm Beach, FL 33411 United States **BUS:** Research and Education **P/S:** Researching how Drugs Affect the Brain, Central Nervous System and Behavior **MA:** International **D/D/R:** Specializing in Neuropsychology **EDU:** Doctorate in Science, United Nations University; Ph.D. in Biochemistry of Mental Illness, University of Hull, United Kingdom; Bachelor of Science in Neuropsychology, University of London, United Kingdom **A/A/S:** American Psychological Association; British Association for Psychopharmacology **A/H:** Professorship and Knighthood (1990)
Email: sirsamuelr@aol.com

Suzanne P. Wren
Title: Social Science Department Chairwoman **Company:** Enterprise High School **Address:** 3411 Churn Creek Road, Redding, CA 96002 United States **BUS:** High School **P/S:** Education **MA:** Local **D/D/R:** Teaching United States History and American Government, Overseeing Functions of the Department **EDU:** Bachelor's Degree in English; Certified Secondary English and Social Science Teacher **A/A/S:** National Education Association; California Teachers Association
Email: swren@suhsd.net

Anthony J. Wright
Title: Vice President **Company:** Hewlett Packard **Dept:** Global Software Delivery Division **Address:** 599 N. Mathilda Avenue, Sunnyvale, CA 94085 United States **BUS:** Information Technology Corporation **P/S:** Software Development, Automation Technology **MA:** International **EXP:** Mr. Wright's expertise includes technology management and strategic development. **H/I/S:** Riding his Motorcycle, Skiing, Playing Chess, Reading **EDU:** College Coursework
Email: awright@opsware.com
Email: awright007@yahoo.com
URL: http://www.cambridgewhoswho.com

Dell Wright
Title: Founder-Past CEO **Company:** Wrights Adolescent Development Center, Inc **Address:** 274 S. Dallas Avenue, San Bernadino, CA 92410 United States **BUS:** Nonprofit Care Provider and Real Estate Investor **P/S:** Residential Adolescent Treatment and Care **MA:** Local **D/D/R:** Aerospace Engineering, Adolescent Care and Business Management **H/I/S:** Traveling, RV Camping, Fishing, Motorcycling **EDU:** Control Data Institute; Rochville University; Almeda College & University, Computer Technology, Master's Degree in Computer Science, Master of Business Administration in Business Management **A/A/S:** NASA, Department of Defense, AARP, Sierra Club, Veterans of America, Red Cross, ACLU. Provided Support to NASA Apollo, Soyuz Test Project (ASTP)and NASA Galileo Space Program, B-1 Bomber Aircraft and Ground to Air Stinger Missiles
Email: wdell29@sbcglobal.net
URL: http://www.dellwrightauthor.com

Josephine H. Wright
Title: Co-Pastor **Company:** Greater Grace Temple Apostolic Church **Address:** 914 S. Madison Avenue, Anderson, IN 46016 United States **BUS:** Pentecostal Church **P/S:** Pentecostal Church **MA:** International **D/D/R:** Women's Ministry, Spirituality, Preaching **H/I/S:** Walking, Reading, Taking Piano Lessons, Working on the Board of Ushers **EDU:** Bachelor's Degree in Theology, Calvary Theological Seminary **A/A/S:** Pentecostal Assembly of the World, Ministers Wives Auxiliary **C/VW:** Mission Board, Overseas Mission Work, American Cancer Association
Email: josiewri03@sbcglobal.net
URL: http://www.myspace.com/gracetempleapostolic

Mr. Kenneth E. Wright Jr.
Title: Attorney, Partner **Company:** Lake Martin Law Center **Address:** 125 W. Columbus Street, Dadeville, AL 36853 United States **BUS:** Proven Leader in the Law Industry **P/S:** Variety of High Quality Legal Assistance and Services to Clients **MA:** Regional **D/D/R:** Criminal and Civil Trials, Business Law, Real Estate, Mediation **H/I/S:** Tennis, Golf, Water Sports, Travel **EDU:** Degree in Law, Faulkner University (1997); Master's Degree in English, Florida International University; Bachelor's Degree in English and Journalism, Auburn University **A/A/S:** Lee County Association of Realtors; Alabama Bar Association; Vice President, Tallapoosa Bar Association; Lee County Chamber of Commerce Kiwanis
Email: kewlaw99@yahoo.com

Maude P. Wright
Title: Associate Broker **Company:** Home Sellers of Maine **Address:** 26 Atlantic Avenue, Booth Bay Harbor, ME 04538 United States **BUS:** Real Estate Broker **P/S:** Residential, Water Front, Lake Front, River Front, Town Homes, Condos, Gulf Homes, Relocation Specialist **MA:** National **D/D/R:** Hi End, Residential, But Expertise is in Water Front Properties **H/I/S:** Tennis **A/A/S:** Maine Association of Realtors, National Association of Realtors
Email: mwright@homesellersmaine.com
URL: http://www.mwrighthomesellers.com

Pamela Joy Wright
Title: Head Nurse, Adherence Counselor **Company:** DMR and Stamford Hospital **Address:** 146 Silvermine Avenue, Norwalk, CT 06850 United States **BUS:** Hospital **P/S:** Healthcare **MA:** Regional **D/D/R:** Caring for HIV-Positive Patients **H/I/S:** Cooking, Partying, Entertaining **EDU:** Associate Degree in Counseling, University of West Indies; Nursing Midwife, University Hospital, Jamaica, West Indies **CERTS:** Certified HIV Counselor and Tester, State of California **C/VW:** Local Church
Email: pwright@stamhgauth.com
URL: http://www.cambridgewhoswho.com

Shameka S. Wright
Title: Human Resource Generalist **Company:** County of Campbell **Address:** P.O. Box 1222, Rustburg, VA 24588 United States **BUS:** Government Agency **P/S:** Human Resource Generalist **MA:** Local **D/D/R:** human Resources **H/I/S:** Traveling, Reading, Exercising **EDU:** Master's Degree in Management and HR Management, University of Phoenix **A/A/S:** Society for Human Resources Management, IPMA-HR
Email: wright_s1@msn.com

Tara G. Wright
Title: Teacher **Company:** Tularosa Public Schools **Address:** 504 First Street, Tularosa, NM 88352 United States **BUS:** Public School **P/S:** Education **MA:** Local **D/D/R:** Teaching Science **H/I/S:** Reading, Walking **EDU:** Master's Degree in Elementary Education, Grand Canyon University; Bachelor's Degree in Elementary Education, Eastern New Mexico University **C/VW:** American Heart Association
Email: twright@tularosa.k12.nm.us
URL: http://www.cambridgewhoswho.com

William A. Wright
Title: Program Manager **Company:** Unisys Corporation **Address:** 2741 Gunter Park Drive W., Montgomery, AL 36109 United States **BUS:** Information Technology Company **P/S:** E-Business Solutions and Services **MA:** International **D/D/R:** Department of Defense Programs, Setting Goals for Staff, Training, Staffing, Overseeing Operations **H/I/S:** Reading, Golfing, Hunting Turkey and White Tail Deer, Bass Fishing **EDU:** Master of Public Administration, Golden Gate University **C/VW:** United Way
Email: william.a.wright@unisys.com
URL: http://www.unisys.com

Kristy L. Wrisinger
Title: Consultant **Address:** 321 N.W. Bradford Street, Lees Summit, MO 64064 United States **BUS:** Consulting Firm **P/S:** Creation and Establishment of Project Management Offices **MA:** National **D/D/R:** Working on Project Financials, Budgeting, Allocating Resources for Established Business Plans, Defining and Redefining Requirements for Various Projects **H/I/S:** Golfing **EDU:** Master of Business Administration, Baker University (2003) **A/A/S:** Project Management Institute
Email: rysinger@swbell.net

Mr. George F. L. Wu
Title: Senior Research Scientist (Retired) **Company:** Eastman Kodak Company **Address:** 343 State Street, Rochester, NY 14650 United States **BUS:** Film Company **P/S:** Photographic Products, Films and Emulsions **MA:** International **D/D/R:** Invented T-Grains, Photographic Chemistry of Silver Halide Crystal **H/I/S:** Attending Concerts, Conducting Research on Classical Music, Ballroom Dancing, Swing Dancing **EDU:** Master of Science in Material Science, University of Rochester **A/A/S:** Past President, Chinese Club **C/VW:** Church, Community Volunteering for the Chinese Community
Email: gwu@frontiernet.net
URL: http://www.cambridgewhoswho.com

Sheryl Wulkan, MD
Title: Internal Medicine Events Specialist **Company:** Pro Health Care Associates **Address:** 2 Ohio Drive, Lake Success, NY 11042 United States **BUS:** Medical Facility **P/S:** Consulting and Healthcare for Athletes Including Pain Management, Physical Therapy, Chiropractic, Neurology, Orofacial Pain, Sleep Disorders, Headaches and Medical Massages **MA:** National **D/D/R:** Working for National Collegiate Athletic Level Clients **H/I/S:** Practicing Martial Arts, Swimming, Playing Tennis, Reading **EDU:** Degree, SUNY, Stony Brook (1980) **A/A/S:** American College of Physicians; American Medical Association; American College of Sports Medicine; American Board of Internal Medicine; American Academy of Ringside Physicians **A/H:** Award, Consumers Research Council of America (2006)
Email: swsportsdoc@msn.com

Cheryl Wyatt
Title: Benefits Manager **Company:** JV Industrial Companies, Ltd. **Address:** 11807 N. D Street, La Porte, TX 77571 United States **BUS:** Petrochemical Construction Company **P/S:** Construction **MA:** International **D/D/R:** Human Resource Benefits Manager **H/I/S:** Spending Time with her Family, Reading **EDU:** Coursework, University of Phoenix **A/A/S:** Society for Human Resource Management
Email: cheryl.wyatt@jvic.com
URL: http://www.jvic.com

Mr. William E. Wyche Sr.
Title: Second Assistant Chief **Company:** Medford Fire Department **Address:** 171 Oregon Avenue, Medford, NY 11763 United States **BUS:** Fire Department, Government **P/S:** Firefighting, Public Safety **MA:** Regional **D/D/R:** Ordering Equipment, Ensuring Vehicles are Repaired, Interior Fire Rescue **H/I/S:** Hockey **EDU:** Certification in National Incident Management (2006); Certified Equipment and Machinery Extrication Technician (2006); Certified Extrication Technician (2005); Certification in Heavy Rescue (2001); Certification in Hazardous Materials (1999); Certification in Incident Command (1992); Certified Advanced Breathing Extrication Technician (1991); High School Education **A/A/S:** Suffolk County Volunteer Firefighters Emerald Society
Email: captwillie50@yahoo.com
URL: http://www.medfordfd.com

Heather A. Wylie
Title: Vice President of Marketing and Sales **Company:** Haddad-Wylie Industries, LLC **Address:** 4143 Brownsville Road, Pittsburgh, PA 15227 United States **BUS:** Design Builders for the Life Science Industries and Clean Room Consulting **P/S:** HWI Provides Aseptic 'Bio-Gard' Wall laminate or Sterile Environments, Clean Rooms for the Life Science Industry, Certifications of Clean Rooms and all Clean Room ProHWI's Expertise is Retrofitting Clean Rooms into Any Environment, Proven Ourselves to be the Top Provider to Hospital Pharmacies Around the Nation, Build State of the Art Clean Room Facilities for Pharmaceutical Companies, Hospital Pharmacies (USP 797), Medical Device Labs and Any Facility in Need of an Aseptic Environment. Nano Technology and Bio Technologies, Full Turn-Key Design Builders for Clean Rooms **MA:** National **D/D/R:** Marketing, designing, advertising, generating sales leads, Management of the marketing team of 5 nationally **H/I/S:** Bicycling, Reading, Dancing, Gardening, Spending Time with her Three Children **EDU:** Bachelor's Degree in Education, Carlow University, Pittsburgh, Pennsylvania (1996) **A/A/S:** Kappa Delta Epsilon Honor Society, **C/VW:** Auberle emergency housing
Email: hwylie@hwicleanrooms.com
URL: http://www.hwicleanrooms.com

Shirley R. Wynn
Title: Special Education Lead Teacher **Company:** Union Point Elementary School **Address:** 1401 Highway 77 N., Union Point, GA 30669 United States **BUS:** Public School **P/S:** Education **MA:** Local **D/D/R:** Special Education Lead Teacher, Supervising Five Special Education Teachers and Five Para-Professionals **H/I/S:** Reading, Walking **EDU:** Master's Degree in Mental Retardation, University of Georgia; Supervision Certificate in Interrelated Special Education, University of Georgia **A/A/S:** Organization for Exceptional Children **A/H:** Two-Time Recipient, Teacher of the Year Award **C/VW:** Church Choir, After-School Events with Children, After-School Tutorial Services
Email: shirley.wynn@greene.k12.ga.us

Barbara S. Wynne
Title: Founder, Coordinator **Company:** Washington Township Schools Tennis Program **Address:** 1805 E. 86th Street, Indianapolis, IN 46240 United States **BUS:** School Tennis Association **P/S:** Tennis Lessons, Local, Regional and National Level Tournaments **MA:** Local **H/I/S:** Playing Tennis and Table Tennis **EDU:** Bachelor of Science in Education, Northwestern University (1955) **A/A/S:** Officer, Indianapolis Tennis Association; Founder, President, Indianapolis Junior Tennis Development Fund; Former Officer, Midwest Section, United States Tennis Association; Founder, Indianapolis Chapter, National Junior Tennis League **A/H:** Award, International Table Tennis Federation (2007); Hall of Education Award, United States Tennis Association; Silver Service Bowl, United States Tennis Association; Indianapolis Woman of the Year Award (1980)
Email: bb@thewyness.com
URL: http://www.tennisprogram.com
URL: http://www.indyschild.com

Jeff G. Wyrick, EMT-P
Title: Paramedic **Company:** Heartland Regional Medical Center **Address:** 5325 Furaon, St Joseph, MO 64505 United States **BUS:** Healthcare Hospital **P/S:** Full Service Regional Hospital **MA:** Local **D/D/R:** Offering Quality Care for Patients in Emergency Situations **H/I/S:** Motorcycles and Weight Lifting **EDU:** Technical School, 1 Year for EMT and 1 and a Half Years for Paramedic
Email: jeffwyrick@hotmail.com

Diana Yacobi
Title: Educational Director **Company:** Temple Emanu-El **Address:** 180 Piermont Road, Closter, NJ 07624 United States **BUS:** Temple **P/S:** Hebrew School, Youth and Volunteer Programs, Temple Services **MA:** Regional **EXP:** Ms. Yacobi's expertise is in education. **D/D/R:** Offering Supplementary Jewish Education, Developing Curriculum, Managing School Administration, Mentoring Teachers **H/I/S:** Spending Time with her Family **EDU:** Master of Arts in Jewish Education, The Jewish Theological Seminary (1995); Bachelor's Degree in Social Studies, Ramapo College of New Jersey (1990) **A/A/S:** Jewish Educators Assembly; Network for Research in Jewish Education
Email: dyacobi@earthlink.net
URL: http://www.templeemanu-el.com
URL: http://www.sarahdavid.com

Tracy Lynn Yakutchik
Title: Station Manager **Company:** Delta Airlines Global Services **Address:** 2309 Barbara Way, Pottsdam, PA 19464 United States **BUS:** America's Fastest Growing International Airline Carrier in the Travel Industry **P/S:** Offering Flights to 458 Destinations in 99 Countries on Delta, Delta Shuttle, the Delta Connection Carriers and Worldwide Partners, Charter Flight Service, Logistics, Technical Services, Maximizing Corporate Travel Budget **MA:** National **D/D/R:** Handling Customer Service for Cross Counter and Administrative Connection Carriers **H/I/S:** Traveling **EDU:** Associate Degree in Travel and Tourism Management, Widener University (1985) **A/A/S:** New Castle Chamber of Commerce
Email: tracy.l.yakutchik@delta.com
URL: http://www.delta.com

Christine C. Yamashita
Title: Center Manager **Company:** Northrop Grumman Corporation **Dept:** Space Technology **Address:** 1 Space Park Drive, Redondo Beach, CA 90278 United States **BUS:** Global Defense and Technology Company **P/S:** Solutions in Information and Services, Electronics, Aerospace and Shipbuilding to Government and Commercial Customers Worldwide **MA:** International **D/D/R:** Managing Configuration, Planning, Overseeing the Daily Operations with a Staff of 60 Employees, Offering Aerospace and Commercial Experience **H/I/S:** Reading Fictional Novels, Watching Movies **EDU:** Master's Degree in Business, University of La Verne (2000); Bachelor's Degree in Business, University of La Verne (1990) **A/A/S:** American Production and Inventory Control Society
Email: christine.yamashita@ngc.com
URL: http://www.ngc.com

Elmira J. Yancey
Title: Technology Coordinator (Retired) **Company:** Morton Street Middle School **Address:** 17 Synott Place, Newark, NJ 07106 United States **BUS:** Middle School **P/S:** Education **MA:** Regional **EXP:** Ms. Yancey's expertise is in technology education. **D/D/R:** Coordinating Technology Programs, Teaching Computer Technology to Students and Teachers, Troubleshooting and Operating Computer Laboratories **EDU:** Master's Degree in Educational Administration and Supervision, Kean University (2002) **A/A/S:** Delta Sigma Theta **C/VW:** Bethany Baptist Church
Email: elmiray@yahoo.com

Mingdi Yang
Title: Chief Operating Officer **Company:** Chinese Media Net **Address:** 9 Park Place, Great Neck, NY 11021 United States **BUS:** Chinese Multi-Media News Group **P/S:** Daily Online Chinese News Source, Weekly Newspaper and Magazine **MA:** International **D/D/R:** Overseeing the Entire Operations of Business Including Business Development Projects, Sales and Marketing, Managing a Staff of 70 **H/I/S:** Practicing Yoga, Tap Dancing **EDU:** Master of Arts in Journalism, University of Wisconsin (1995)
Email: mdyang@chinesenewsnet.com
URL: http://www.dwnews.com

Megan Yankovich
Title: Personal Trainer **Address:** Indianapolis, IN 46237 United States **BUS:** Independent Contractor with Cardinal Fitness **P/S:** Exercise and Physical Fitness **MA:** Regional **D/D/R:** Offering Personal Training and One-on-One Fitness Training **H/I/S:** Rock Climbing, Working as an Environmental Activist **EDU:** Bachelor of Science in Exercise Science, Indiana Purdue University, Indianapolis, Indiana (2006) **A/A/S:** National Strength and Conditioning Association
Email: ma.yankovich@gmail.com
URL: http://www.cambridgewhoswho.com

J. Michelle Yarbrough
Title: Literacy Coach **Company:** Watson Primary School **Address:** 314 N. Gaskill, Huntsville, AR 72740 United States **BUS:** Public Elementary School **P/S:** Primary Level Education **MA:** Regional **D/D/R:** Teaching Reading and Writing Skills, Setting Up Laboratory Classrooms that Follow a Comprehensive Literacy Model, Instructing Teachers to Incorporate All Laboratory Components, Assisting Teachers with Lesson Plans and Implementing Programs Correctly, Performing Data Entry, Testing Student Progress, Ordering Supplies, Acting as a Praxis III Assessor for the State, Training and Evaluating New Teachers **H/I/S:** Driving Race Cars, Going to the Beach, Spending Time with her Family **EDU:** Pursuing Master's Degree in Reading, University of Arkansas, Little Rock; Bachelor of Arts in Elementary Education, Plus 21, University of Arkansas, Fayetteville (1992)
Email: myarbrou@hhs.nwsc.k12.ar.us
URL: http://eagle.nwsc.k12.ar.us/primary.html

Susan E. Yarger
Title: Geologist **Company:** TTL Associates, Inc. **Address:** 1915 N. 12th Street, Toledo, OH 43604 United States **BUS:** Engineering Firm **P/S:** Environmental Consulting, Testing, Geotechnical Engineering **MA:** National **EXP:** Ms. Yarger's expertise includes subsurface investigations and brownfield remediation. **H/I/S:** Photography **EDU:** Bachelor of Science in Geology, Ohio State University
Email: syarger@ttlassoc.com

Faith Hope Yascone
Title: Owner **Company:** Club Kid Production **Address:** 1335 S. Brook Street, Louisville, KY 40208 United States **BUS:** Production Company **P/S:** Event Promotions, Individual Consulting, Entertainment **MA:** National **D/D/R:** Promotions, Building Networks, Business Operations **H/I/S:** Traveling, Gardening **EDU:** Bachelor of Arts in Film and Television, Columbia College Chicago
Email: faithyascone@aol.com

Kimberly Yates, RN
Title: Registered Nurse, Charge Nurse, Staff Nurse **Company:** Spartanburg Regional Medical Center **Address:** 1887 Chase High Road, Forest City, NC 28043 United States **BUS:** Medical Center **P/S:** Trauma Care, Behavioral Healthcare, Bloodless Medicine, Health Sciences Library, Imaging Services, Neurology, Orthopedic Services, Palliative Care, Hospice, Rehabilitation Services, Sleep Services, Pediatrics, Surgical Weight Loss, Stroke Care, Urology, Wound Healing Center **MA:** Regional **D/D/R:** Nursing, Managing Neuro-Intensive Care Unit, Treating Patients with Head and Spinal Cord Injuries, Treating Pediatric Patients, Training Nursing Staff **H/I/S:** Reading, Shopping, Motorcycles, Four-Wheeling, Camping, Going to the Beach and Mountains, Enjoying Outdoor Activities **EDU:** Bachelor of Science in Nursing, University of South Carolina Upstate, Spartanburg, South Carolina (1991); Registered Nurse **A/A/S:** American Association of Critical Care Nurses
Email: kyatesrn@bellsouth.net
URL: http://www.srhs.com

Mr. Trevor B. Yates

Title: Vice President **Company:** Cambridge Education LLC **Address:** 178 Orchard Drive, Hanover, PA 17331 United States **BUS:** Global Education Services Company **P/S:** Helping Improve Education for Children and Young People through Quality Reviews Geared toward School District Improvement **MA:** International **D/D/R:** Running the United States Branch of the Company, Overseeing All Operations, Specializing in Leadership and Development **H/I/S:** Reading, Playing Sports **EDU:** Master's Degree in English, Leeds University, England (1972) **A/A/S:** Royal Society of Arts; Institute of Management; Fellow, Royal Society for the Encouragement of Arts; Fellow, Institute of Management Consultants
Email: trevor.yates@camb-ed-us.com
URL: http://www.camb-ed.com

Natalie Yearsley

Title: Certified Athletic Trainer **Company:** Sports Medicine Specialists, LLC **Address:** 425 S. Medical Drive, Suite 220, Bountiful, UT 84010 United States **BUS:** Medical Office **P/S:** Non Surgical Medical Care **MA:** National **D/D/R:** Patient Education **H/I/S:** Spending Time Outdoors **EDU:** Bachelor of Science in Lifestyle Management **A/A/S:** National Athletic Trainers' Association
Email: natalie@keepingactivepeopleactive.com
URL: http://www.keepingactivepeopleactive.com

Bryan J. Yeazel, Esq.

Title: Vice President, General Counsel and Secretary **Company:** Stock Building Supply Holdings **Address:** 8020 Arco Corporate Parkway, Raleigh, NC 27617 United States **BUS:** Manufacturing Company **P/S:** Construction Materials, Construction Services **MA:** National **D/D/R:** Corporate Law, Mergers, Acquisitions **H/I/S:** Reading **EDU:** JD, Magna Cum Laude, Wake Forest University, ND **A/A/S:** American Bankers Association; VBA; Cistu Church **C/VW:** Catholic Charities
Email: bjyeazel@yahoo.com
URL: http://www.stocksupply.com

Ray Yeh, DO

Title: President **Company:** AIM Hospitalist **Address:** P.O. Box 10347, Oakland, CA 94610 United States **BUS:** Healthcare Center **P/S:** Healthcare Including Regular Hospitalist Services, Hospitals and Six Full Time Physicians **MA:** National **D/D/R:** Having Set up Hospitalist Programs within Various Hospitals and Acts as a Hospitalist, Seven to 10 Hospitalist Programs already in Place throughout California, Developing New Hospitalist Group **H/I/S:** Musical Composition, Playing Violin, Art Shows, Drawing, Oil Painting, Skateboarding, Furniture-Making **EDU:** Doctor of Osteopathy, College of Osteopathic Medicine (1992) **CERTS:** Internship and Residency, Highland Hospital
Email: rayyeh@pacbell.net

Lisa K. Yerby

Title: Teacher **Company:** Southside Primary School **Address:** 303 Fort Worth Street, Cleveland, TX 77327 United States **BUS:** School **P/S:** Education **MA:** Local **D/D/R:** Teaching Kindergarten and First Grade, Teaching Gifted and Talented Students **H/I/S:** Making Crafts, Cooking **EDU:** Bachelor of Science in Education, Texas Tech University **A/A/S:** Delta Kappa Gamma; Texas Association for the Gifted and Talented **C/VW:** World Vision
Email: lyerby@sbcglobal.net

Rachel Yi

Title: Human Resources and Accounting **Company:** Rainbow Research Optics, Inc **Address:** 4880 Ironton Street Unit K, Denver, CO 80239 United States **BUS:** Laser Optics Manufacturer **P/S:** Manufactures Laser Optics **MA:** Local **D/D/R:** Account Manager, Human Resources **EDU:** Denver Technical University, Bachelor of Arts

Mr. Frank Yip

Title: President **Company:** Jam Mix Productions, Inc. **Address:** 2005 Merrick Road, Suite 348, Merrick, NY 11566 United States **BUS:** Disc Jockey Entertainment Company **P/S:** Disc Jockeys, Karaoke, Party Planning, Sound Reinforcement. **MA:** NY Tri-State and Metro Area **D/D/R:** Disc Jockeying **H/I/S:** All Sports **EDU:** Bachelor of Science in Architecture, New York Institute of Technology **A/A/S:** NYCC; Better Business Bureau; American Disc Jockey Association **C/VW:** Local Schools
Email: frank@jammix.com
URL: http://www.jammix.com

Sharon K. 'Mast' Yoder

Title: Kindergarten Teacher **Company:** Topeka Elementary School **Address:** 38 School Street, Topeka, IN 46571 United States **BUS:** Elementary School **P/S:** Education **MA:** Local **D/D/R:** Kindergarten, Teaching Amish Children **H/I/S:** Reading, Watching her Daughter Play Soccer **EDU:** Master's Degree in Elementary Education **A/A/S:** Nation Education Association; Westview Education Association **C/VW:** Local Library, Church, Daughter's Private School
Email: Dennis02@earthlink.net
URL: http://www.cambridgewhoswho.com

Georgiana Yonuschot

Title: Attorney **Company:** Womble, Carlyle, Sandridge & Rice, PLLC **Address:** One W. Fourth Street, Lobby, Winston-Salem, NC 27101 United States **BUS:** Law Firm **P/S:** Product Liability, Expert Witness Development **MA:** National **D/D/R:** Preparing Expert Witnesses for Testimony **EDU:** JD Degree, Marshall School of Law, Texas Southern University (2005); Master of Social Work, The University of North Carolina at Chapel Hill (1999); Bachelor of Science in Public Health, University of North Carolina at Chapel Hill (1993) **A/A/S:** American Bar Association; North Carolina Bar Association; Forsyth County Bar Association; Forsyth County Women Attorneys Association
Email: gyonuschot@wcsr.com

Sigrid A. Yorke

Title: 1) Aesthetician 2) Cosmetic Tattoo Artist C.D.T. **Company:** 1) Skintopia, Inc. 2) Beauty Gone Green Co. **Address:** 1515 North Carolina Highway 54 W., Suite 130, Durham, NC 27707 United States **BUS:** 1) Tattoo Parlor 2) Distribution Firm **P/S:** 1) Cosmetic Tattoo 2) Beauty Products **MA:** Regional **D/D/R:** Offering Skin Care Treatments, Chemical Peels and Makeup Artistry, Conducting Cosmetic Tattooing for Medical and Cosmetic Purposes **H/I/S:** Cycling, Practicing Martial Arts Aerobics, Hiking, Weight Lifting **EDU:** Licensed Aesthetician, Laure Conan Chicoutimi, Quebec (1982) **A/A/S:** North Carolina Aestheticians Association; Society of Plastic Surgical Skin Care Specialists **A/H:** Best Aesthetician Award, Herald Sun (2006)
Email: skintopia@msn.com
URL: http://www.beautygonegreen.com

Sylvia Youn, Pharm.D.

Title: Licensed Pharmacist **Company:** Fountain Valley Regional Hospital **Dept:** College of Pharmacy **Address:** Pomona, CA 91766 United States **BUS:** General Hospital **P/S:** Pharmacy Education **MA:** Local **D/D/R:** Bilingual Korean, Obtained Residency in General Medicine **H/I/S:** World traveling **EDU:** Pharm.D., Western University of Health Sciences School of Pharmacy (2007) **A/A/S:** American Society of Health-System Pharmacists; APhA; ASHP
Email: syoun@westernu.edu

Barbara Wiggs Young

Title: Teacher **Company:** Midland Independent School District, Emerson Elementary School **Address:** 2800 Moss Avenue, Midland, TX 79705 United States **BUS:** Elementary School **P/S:** Education for Kindergarten through Fifth-Grade Students **MA:** Local **D/D/R:** Teaching a Self-Contained Classroom, Promoting the Academic, Emotional and Social Growth of Students, Teaching Students Effective Communication Methods, Teaching All Non-Specialty Subjects **H/I/S:** Reading, Biking, Spectator Sports **EDU:** Bachelor's Degree in Education, Western Texas College (1961) **A/A/S:** Delta Kappa Gamma; Midland Area Reading Council; Texas Classroom Teachers Association
Email: jynby1@cox.net
URL: http://www.midlandisd.net/campus/emerson

Charlene G. Young, OTR-L

Title: President, Owner **Company:** Functional Abilities, LLC **Address:** 304 Clark Drive, London, KY 40741 United States **BUS:** Limited Liability Company **P/S:** Healthcare Education and Consultation Services **MA:** National **D/D/R:** Conducting Educational Seminars on Neurological Disorders, Designing New Programs, Workshops and Marketing Areas **H/I/S:** Stock Market, Traveling, Golfing, Basketball **EDU:** Bachelor of Science in Occupational Therapy and Psychology, Eastern Kentucky University (1993) **A/A/S:** Eastern Kentucky District Chair, Occupational Therapy Association; Lecturing Nationally on Life Skills **A/H:** Featured in Advance (2002)
Email: charotrl@yahoo.com
URL: http://www.cambridgewhoswho.com

Mr. Dax Q. Young

Title: Sole Proprietorship **Company:** Dax Q. Young **Address:** 1903 N. Hickory Street, Crest Hill, IL 60435 United States **BUS:** Construction Company **P/S:** Designing Building Construction, Concrete Work **MA:** Chicago **D/D/R:** Management **H/I/S:** Spending Time with his Family **EDU:** Bachelor of Arts in Psychology, Western Illinois University **A/A/S:** Environmental Building Association; Lions Club International
Email: young.dax@gmail.com

Donald G. Young

Title: Director of Talent Acquisition **Company:** Tesoro Companies, Inc. **Address:** 9601 McAllister Freeway, San Antonio, TX 78216 United States **BUS:** Refining and Marketing Company **P/S:** Gasoline **MA:** International **D/D/R:** Acquiring Talent, International Human Resources **H/I/S:** Golfing, Playing Tennis and Racquetball **EDU:** Bachelor of Arts (1983); Bachelor of Science in Economics, North Carolina Agricultural and Technical State University **A/A/S:** Society of Human Resource Management; The Human Resource Planning Society; National Association of Colleges and Employers **C/VW:** Various Charities
Email: dyoung2@tsocorp.com
URL: http://www.tsocorp.com

Elizabeth L. Young

Title: Town and County Supervisor **Company:** Town of Taghkanic **Address:** 977 Livingston Road, Elizaville, NY 12523 United States **BUS:** Town Government **P/S:** Local Services **MA:** Taghkanic, NY **D/D/R:** Acting as the Supervisor of the Community, Overseeing the Board of Administration **H/I/S:** Crocheting, Reading, Spending Time with her Family **EDU:** Registered Nurse **A/A/S:** Columbia County Association for Retarded Citizens; Chairwoman, Human Services Board; Deputy Chairwoman, Legal Committee; Chairwoman, Mental Health Committee; Chairwoman, Board of Health; Chairwoman, Agriculture Committee **A/H:** Recognition Award, Young Republican National Federation **C/VW:** World Association of Persons with Disabilities
Email: ell516yng16@netscape.net

Jamie M. Young

Title: Real Estate Agent **Company:** Guarantee Real Estate **Address:** 6710 N. West Avenue, Suite 108, Fresno, CA 93711 United States **BUS:** Real Estate Agency **P/S:** Commercial and Residential Real Estate Exchange **MA:** National **D/D/R:** Assisting Clients **H/I/S:** Exercising, Scrapbooking **EDU:** College Coursework
Email: jamie.young@cwwemail.com
URL: http://www.cambridgewhoswho.com

JoAnn W. Young

Title: Teacher **Company:** Miami-Dade County Public Schools **Address:** 600 Harbor Drive, Key Biscayne, FL 33149 United States **BUS:** Public School District **P/S:** Education for Kindergarten through Twelfth-Grade Students, Adult Education, Specialized Centers **MA:** Regional **D/D/R:** Teaching Art Education, Fine Arts and Computer Technology, Incorporating Computer Skills and Language Arts into Fine Arts Subjects, Teaching Students about Contemporary Artists, Working with Students in K-Eighth-Grade **H/I/S:** Golfing, Tennis, Collecting Art **EDU:** Master of Science in Computer Technology, Barry University; Bachelor of Fine Arts, University of Florida (1978); Certification in Teaching K-12 Art **A/A/S:** Elected to Key Biscayne Council (1989-1991); Young Artist Sponsor, Art Program; United Teachers Association; Dade Concert Association of Florida; National Association of Educators; National Education Association; United States Teachers Association; Chairperson, Fourth of July Committee; American Legion Auxiliary; Key Biscayne Yacht Club; Shanes Teaching Hospital; University of Florida Aligators Newspaper **A/H:** Citibank Grant (2004-2005); Citibank Grant (1993-1994)
Email: jawyoung@aol.com
URL: http://www2.dadeschools.net

K. C. Young

Title: Mgr of Spiritual Care Department **Company:** Empire Health Services **Address:** 800 W. Fifth, Spokane, WA 99210 United States **BUS:** Healthcare Service Provider **P/S:** Spiritual Care **MA:** National **D/D/R:** Chaplain, Counseling, Mentoring **H/I/S:** Gardening, Hiking, Reading **EDU:** University of San Francisco, State University of California, Masters in Spirituality, Certified in Substance Abuse Counseling **A/A/S:** NACC, Certified Chaplain, Donates to Interfaith Groups in Washington, Network, Catholic Society, Justice Lobby, Various Environmental Groups and Other Various Charities, Also Received 7 Units in Clinical Pastoral Education from Billings Montana Seattle, WA, Loves to Advocate for Others
Email: kcyoungop@comcast.net

Laura M. Young

Title: Lead Magnetic Resonance Imaging Technologist **Company:** InnerVision West Advanced Medical Imaging **Address:** 3482 McClure Avenue, Suite 100, West Lafayette, IN 47906 United States **BUS:** Imaging Center **P/S:** Outpatient Diagnostic Services **MA:** Regional **EXP:** Ms. Young's expertise is in magnetic resonance imaging. **D/D/R:** Training Technologists to Accurately Scan Patients, Monitor the Scans Performed at Another Imaging Center **H/I/S:** Reading the Holy Bible, Woodworking, Remodeling **EDU:** Associate Degree in Theology, The Way College of Biblical Research **A/A/S:** American Registry of Radiologic Technologists; International Society for Magnetic Resonance in Medicine **C/VW:** Spirit & Truth Fellowship International
Email: im4god2@verizon.net
URL: http://www.cambridgewhoswho.com

Mr. Marc A. Young, CIMA, CFP
Title: Certified Financial Planner, Wealth Management Advisor **Company:** Merrill Lynch **Address:** 101 Bullitt Lane, Suite 400, Louisville, KY 40222 United States **BUS:** Investment Company **P/S:** Financial Services **MA:** International **D/D/R:** Wealth Management **H/I/S:** Running in Marathons, Long-Distance Running, Cycling **EDU:** Master of Business Administration, Indiana University (2004); Certified Investment Management Analyst, Wharton School (2003); Bachelor of Science in Business Administration, Emphasis in Accounting, University of Louisville (1998); Bachelor of Science in Political Science, University of Louisville (1990); Certified Financial Planner **A/A/S:** Investment Management Consultants Association; Chartered Institute of Management Accountants; Certified Financial Planner Board of Standards, Inc. **C/VW:** Louisville Multiple Sclerosis Society; American Heart Association; United Way
Email: marc_young@ml.com
URL: http://fa.ml.com/wygroup

Michael E. Young
Title: Doctor of Optometry **Company:** United States Air Force **Address:** 1050 W. Perimeter Road, Andrews Air Force Base, MD 20762 United States **BUS:** United States Air Force **P/S:** Armed Forces **MA:** Military **D/D/R:** Overseeing Active Members, Overseeing Aero-Medical Evacuations, Optometry **EDU:** Doctor of Optometry, Pacific University of Oregon **A/A/S:** American Optometric Association; Armed Forces Optometric Society; Fellow, American Academy of Optometry **C/VW:** Combined Federal Campaign Fund
Email: young-fam@comcast.net
Email: michael.young@cwwemail.com
URL: http://www.cambridgewhoswho.com

Paul E. Young
Title: Supply Chain Director **Company:** Frankfort Regional Medical Center **Address:** 299 Kings Daughters Drive, Frankfort, KY 40601 United States **BUS:** Hospital **P/S:** Healthcare, Hospital Supplies, Resource Management **MA:** Local **D/D/R:** Managing Contracts, Supplying Medical Equipment, Budgeting, Setting up New Items for Charging and Reordering, Entering Data, Examining Back Orders, Finding Replacement Products or Suppliers, Assisting Departments, Ordering, Checking Contract Compliance **H/I/S:** Playing Various Sports, Hang Gliding **EDU:** Master of Business Administration, Marshall University Graduate College, Huntington, WV (1992) **A/A/S:** Association for Healthcare Resource and Materials Management; Society for Advancement of Management; Blue Key National Honor Fraternity; Kentucky Hospital Association
Email: paul.young@hcahealthcare.com

Steven F. Young, LCSW
Title: Need Assessment Counselor **Company:** Nix Health Care System **Address:** 4330 Vance Jackson, San Antonio, TX 78230 United States **BUS:** Healthcare, Hospital **P/S:** Psychiatric Services **MA:** Local **D/D/R:** Child, Adolescent **H/I/S:** Bonsai Trees, Astronomy **EDU:** Master's Degree in Counseling and Social Worker, Kansas State University
Email: socialsreve5@aol.com

Angela P. Young-Hill
Title: 1) President 2) Department Assistant **Company:** 1) Heavenly Bites & Decor, Inc. 2) Emory Crawford Long Hospital **Address:** 550 Peachtree Street N.E, Atlanta, GA 30238 United States **BUS:** 1) Food 2) Hospital **P/S:** 1) Weddings, Corporate Functions, Parties 2) Healthcare **MA:** 1) Local 2) Local **D/D/R:** 1) Cooking, Design 2) Administration **H/I/S:** Spending Time with Children, Watching Movies, Participating in Outdoor Activities **EDU:** Associate Degree in Medical Technology, Georgia Medical Institute (1982) **C/VW:** Sisters.By Choice, Inc.
Email: ayounghill@yahoo.com

Mr. Richard A. Youngs
Title: Owner, Senior Management Consultant **Company:** Richard A. Youngs **BUS:** Sole Proprietorship **P/S:** Management Systems for Nuclear Power Production, Nuclear Waste Storage and Aerospace Facilities, Quality Management Systems Services Including Technical Development, Site Implementation, Hardware Qualification and Field Audit, Quality Programs and Procedures Writing, Telecommute Evaluation of Program Manuals and Procedures **MA:** International **EXP:** Mr. Youngs' expertise includes aerospace, nuclear power, nuclear production, waste management, water desalination and quality assurance management systems. **D/D/R:** Monitoring Quality Assurance and Quality Control Requirements at All Levels, Audit Planning, Evaluating Performance and Reporting, Troubleshooting Management Systems, Preparing Quality Programs and Procedures, Overseeing Quality Management Training **H/I/S:** Writing **EDU:** Coursework, California State Polytechnic University, San Luis Obispo; Coursework, University of Alaska; Coursework, The University of Iowa **CERTS:** Licensed Professional Engineer; Quality Control Number 1026, American Society for Quality Control **A/A/S:** Former Member, American Nuclear Society; Former Member, American Society for Quality Control **C/VW:** Various Veterans Organizations; Various Children's Charitable Organizations
Email: jandratironmountains6@msn.com
URL: http://www.cambridgewhoswho.com

Catherine Liz Yrlas
Title: Audiologist **Company:** Newport-Mesa Audiology **Address:** 500 Old Newport Boulevard, Suite 101, Newport Beach, CA 92663 United States **BUS:** Audiology **P/S:** Private Audiology Practice **MA:** Local **D/D/R:** Hearing and Balance, Offering Testing and Assessment of Patients **H/I/S:** Traveling, Attending School **EDU:** Pursuing Doctorate Degree in Audiology, University of Florida; Master of Arts in Audiology, Ohio State University (2005)
Email: yrlascat@msu.edu
URL: http://www.bizziland.com

Jason Yudoff
Title: Musician, Singer, Songwriter **BUS:** Music Industry **P/S:** Music **MA:** International **D/D/R:** Playing Keyboard and Drums, Songwriting, Voice-Overs, Producing Industrial Shows **H/I/S:** Golfing, Playing Softball, Traveling **EDU:** Bachelor of Arts in Fine Arts, Montclair State University **A/A/S:** Broadcast Music, Inc., National Songwriter Hall of Fame; Screen Actors Guild; American Federation of Television and Radio Artists **C/VW:** Goodwill
Email: jason@jasonyudoff.com
URL: http://www.jasonyudoff.com

Rosa A. Yunes
Title: Senior Director of Supply Chain Management **Company:** McDonald's Corporation **Address:** 2915 Jorie Boulevard, Oak Brook, IL 60523 United States **BUS:** Food Service Retailer **P/S:** Fast Food **MA:** International **D/D/R:** Managing and Directing the Supply Chain of Food Packaging and Promotional Products for all of the McDonald's Fast Food Restaurants **H/I/S:** Reading, Enjoying Music **EDU:** Master of Business Administration in Food Technology, La Salle University, Mexico (1982); Bachelor's Degree in Chemical Engineering, La Salle University (1981)
Email: rosa_alicia.yunes@us.mcd.com
URL: http://www.mcdonalds.com/corp/

Christopher P. Zabbo
Title: Physician **Company:** Brown University, Rhode Island Hospital, **Address:**Providence, RI United States **BUS:** Hospital **P/S:** Healthcare, Level I Trauma Center **MA:** Regional **D/D/R:** Emergency Medicine, Trauma and Critical-Care Medicine **H/I/S:** Traveling, Downhill Skiing, Going to the Beach, Hiking, Kayaking, Spending Time Outdoors **EDU:** Doctor of Osteopathy, University of New England; Bachelor's Degree in Biology, Rhode Island College **A/A/S:** American College of Emergency Physicians; Society for Academic Emergency Medicine; Rhode Island Hospital Ethics Committee **C/VW:** Amos House, Crossroads Association
Email: cpzabbo@cox.net
URL: http://www.cambridgewhoswho.com

Joseph M. Zaccaria 'Zack'
Title: OSHA Coordinator and Facility Maintenance Supervisor **Company:** American Express Company **Address:** 1 Express Drive Stewart Airport, Newburgh, NY 12550 United States **BUS:** Aviation **MA:** International **D/D/R:** OSHA Safety Consulting **H/I/S:** Motorcycling, Horses, Boating **EDU:** Licensed Aircraft Mechanic, Certified Machinist **A/A/S:** JJ Keller and Associates, OSHA, NFPA, Knights of Columbus, Elks Lodge, Navy, Past Hydraulic Technician Instructor
Email: cody@aol.com

David Zaga
Title: President **Company:** Falcon Properties, Inc **Address:** 500 Fifth Avenue, Suite 2500, New York, NY 10110 United States **BUS:** Real Estate Management **P/S:** Commercial Real Estate Management **MA:** Local **D/D/R:** Finance and Management **H/I/S:** Reading, Opera, Museums, Bicycling **EDU:** Pursuing Master of Business Administration in Real Estate, NYU, Bachelor of Arts in Real Estate Management **A/A/S:** Real Estate Board of New York
Email: davidz@falconproperties.com
URL: http://www.falconproperties.com

Marcie E. Zaharee, Ph.D.
Title: Information Management and Practice Associate Department Head **Company:** Mitre Corporation **Address:** 202 Burlington Road, Bedford, MA 01730 United States **BUS:** Nonprofit Organization Chartered to Work in the Public Interest **P/S:** Application of Expertise in Systems Engineering, Information Technology, Operational Concepts and Enterprise Modernization to Address Sponsors' Critical Needs **MA:** International **D/D/R:** Utilizing Knowledge Management as the Associate Department Head for Policy Information, Overseeing Training, Management and Practice **H/I/S:** Practicing Fitness **EDU:** Ph.D. in Education, Nova Southeastern University (2005) **A/A/S:** Volunteer, Reading to the Blind; Educator, Webster University; Volunteer, Power Lunch Program (Reading to First, Second and Third-Graders); Volunteer, Visiting Nursing Homes with her Therapy-Trained Dogs
Email: marcie-zaharee@comcast.net
URL: http://www.scis.nova.edu

Maya J. Zahira
Title: Director, Owner **Company:** The Maya Zahira School of Belly Dance **Address:** Lawrence, KS 66044 United States **BUS:** Belly Dance Performance and Education **P/S:** Dance Classes, Performances, Outreach to Charitable Causes **MA:** Regional **D/D/R:** Teaching and Performing Dance **H/I/S:** Dancing, Alternative Healing **EDU:** Ongoing Independent Studies in Middle Eastern Studies; Bachelor of Arts in Education, Kansas State University **C/VW:** Topeka AIDS Project, Safeline
Email: info@mayazahira.com
URL: http://www.mayazahira.com

Mary Zahner
Title: Public Health and Lead Nurse, Case Manager **Company:** UG Wyandotte County Public Health Department **Address:** 619 Ann Avenue, Suite 321, Kansas City, KS 66101 United States **BUS:** Public Health Department **P/S:** Childhood Lead Poisoning Prevention Programs **MA:** Kansas **D/D/R:** Nursing, Educating Parents and Children on Lead Poisoning Prevention, Re-mediating and Removing Lead from the Body, Testing for the Presence of Lead in the Body, Consulting with Physicians, Delivering Speeches at Health Fairs, Events and Conferences **H/I/S:** Cross-Stitching, Fostering Kittens **EDU:** KOHE Certification; Kansas KDHE Certification; Bachelor of Science in Nursing, Avila University (1982) **A/A/S:** American Nurses Association
Email: mzahner@wychokck.org
URL: http://www.unleadedks.com

Karla Zak
Title: Manager **Company:** Becky's Carpet & Tile Super Store **Address:** 7301 N. Lindbergh, Hazelwood, MO 63042 United States **BUS:** Retail Store **P/S:** Carpet and Tiles **MA:** Missouri, Illinois **D/D/R:** Customer Service, Management **H/I/S:** Gardening, Traveling, Reading **EDU:** Associate Degree in Accounting and Computers, Sanford-Brown College (19920
Email: beckyshzman@yahoo.com
URL: http://www.beckyscarpet&tilesuperstore.com

Michelle S. Zale
Title: Owner, Licensed Massage Therapist **Company:** Hands of Health Massage Therapy **Address:** 291 Main Street, Milford, MA 01757 United States **BUS:** Massage Therapy Practice **P/S:** Massage Therapy **MA:** Local **D/D/R:** Deep Tissue Massage, Therapeutic Massage, Swedish Massage, Pregnancy, Reflexology, Working on Children and Adults, Oncology Massage **H/I/S:** Skiing, Hiking, Painting **EDU:** Licensed Massage Therapist, Spa Tech Institute (2006); Bachelor of Science in Early Childhood Education, Fitchburg State College (1996) **A/A/S:** Associated Bodywork & Massage Professionals **C/VW:** Various Charities
Email: zale58@yahoo.com
URL: http://www.hohmassagetherapy.com

Mr. Richard M. Zalusky
Title: Reporter **Company:** Willimantic Chronicle **Address:** 123 Boretz Road, Colchester, CT 06415 United States **BUS:** Daily Newspaper **P/S:** Local News and Sports Headlines, Weather, Classifieds, Obituaries, Opinions Columns **MA:** Regional **D/D/R:** High School Sports Editor. writing daily roundups and coverage of a variety of games. Since 2001-02, Beat writer for the University of Connecticut Women's Basketball Team and women's soccer team. Since 2004 Beat writer for the WNBA's Connecticut Sun (women's professional basketball). **H/I/S:** Tennis, Golf. Assistant camp coordinator, Tri-County Baseball School, Colchester CT Established 1983. **EDU:** Bachelor's Degree in Communications, Eastern Connecticut State University (1993) **A/A/S:** Charter Oak Conference High School Boys Soccer (2004) **A/H:** Writer of the Year; Finalist, Connecticut Boys Soccer
Email: rzalusky@thechronicle.com
URL: http://www.thechronicle.com

Joseph Zanfardino
Title: Senior Corporate Account Manager **Company:** Medtronic **Address:** 18000 Devonshire Street, Northridge, CA 91325 United States **BUS:** Medical Technology Manufacturer **P/S:** Insulin Pump Therapy, Continuous Glucose Monitoring **MA:** National **D/D/R:** Overseeing Contract Negotiation, Medical Policy Development, Work Efficiencies and Diabetes Disease Management **H/I/S:** Playing Basketball and Table Tennis, Cross-Country Biking, Attending his Children's Sporting Events **EDU:** Bachelor of Science in Marketing, University of Scranton; Bachelor of Arts in Philosophy, University of Scranton **A/A/S:** Garden State Association of Diabetes Educators; Corporate Member, Case Management Society of America; American Diabetes Association
Email: joe.zanfardino@medtronic.com
URL: http://www.minimed.com

Tony Zapata, MBA

Title: President, Owner **Company:** CTE Networks, Inc. **Address:** 120 S. Denton Tap Road, Suite 450-202, Coppell, TX 75019 United States **BUS:** Telecommunications Company **P/S:** Telecommunications Services, Collaborating with AT&T Wireless, Verizon Wireless and T-Mobile, Installation of Radios and Systems **MA:** International **D/D/R:** One Year of Experience, Installing Radios and Boxes for Companies, Offering Program Management Services **H/I/S:** Supporting the Dallas Cowboys **EDU:** Master of Business Administration in Information Systems and Computers, Tarleton State University (1999)
Email: tzapata@cte-networks.com
URL: http://www.cte-networks.com

Suzanne C. Zaremba

Title: United Stated History Teacher **Company:** Lucille Brown Middle School **Address:** 6300 Jahnke Road, Richmond, VA 23225 United States **BUS:** School **P/S:** Education **MA:** Local **D/D/R:** Teaching United States History **H/I/S:** Reading, Collecting Japanese Pottery **EDU:** Bachelor of Arts in Elementary Education, East Tennessee State University, 1991; Certification in Art, East Tennessee State University (1971); Certification in Education Grades 3-8 **A/A/S:** Keizai Koho Center Fellow; National Council for the Social Studies; Virginia Council for the Social Studies; Alpha Delta Kappa **A/H:** Keizai Koho Fellowship (1995) **C/VW:** Heart Fund, Cancer Research
Email: szaremba@comcast.net
URL: http://www.cambridgewhoswho.com

Jamie L. Zastrow

Title: Business Administrator **Company:** Kings Way United Methodist Church **Address:** 2401 S. Lone Pine Avenue, Springfield, MO 65804 United States **BUS:** Church **P/S:** Spiritual Services **MA:** Local **EXP:** Ms. Zastrow's expertise is in management. **D/D/R:** Overseeing Administration **H/I/S:** Decorating, Cooking, Spending Time with her Family, Home Remodeling, Reading **EDU:** Bachelor's Degree, Missouri State University **A/A/S:** National Association of Church Business Administrators
Email: jzastrow@kingsway-umc.org
URL: http://www.cambridgewhoswho.com

Betsy K. Zavakos

Title: Underwriting Trainer **Company:** National City Mortgage **Address:** 3232 Newmark Drive, Miamisburg, OH 45342 United States **BUS:** Mortgage Lending and Finance Company **P/S:** Mortgage Loans **MA:** National **D/D/R:** Developing Underwriting Training Programs, Reviewing Investment Quality, Testing the Top 10 Lenders in the United States **H/I/S:** Spending Time with her Three Grandchildren **EDU:** College Coursework, California State, Riverside, CA
Email: hzavakos@woh.rr.com

Elinor A. Zayas

Title: Music Teacher **Company:** Sachem Central School District **Dept:** Sequoya Middle School **Address:** 480 Ackerson Boulevard, Brightwaters, NY 11718 United States **BUS:** Large Suburban School District **P/S:** Educational Services, Athletics, Extracurricular Activities **MA:** Regional **D/D/R:** Working as a Music Teacher, Teaching Music Education, Offering Professional Performances Including Concerts in New York City, Overseeing Public and Private Music Studies, Functioning as an Adjunct Professor at Hofstra University and Five Towns College, Professional Pianist **H/I/S:** Traveling, Sailing, Art **EDU:** Master's Degree, Stony Brook University (2003); Master's Degree in Piano Performance, Manhattan School of Music (1978); Master's Degree in School District Administration **A/A/S:** National Association for Music Education; Suffolk County Music Educators Association; Art Director, Nepenthe Chamber Ensemble
Email: eazayas@optonline.net
URL: http://www.sachem.edu

Todd G. Zeiler

Title: President/Owner **Company:** DLS Flooring Systems **Address:** 3924 Harbor Drive, The Colony, TX 75056 United States **BUS:** Flooring Service Provider **P/S:** Garland Floor, Epoxy, Stain, Commercial Flooring **MA:** Local **D/D/R:** Floor Design, Epoxy **H/I/S:** Reading, Golfing **A/A/S:** Concrete Institute, OSHA
Email: tzeiler@dlsfloors.com
URL: http://www.dlsfloors.com

Daniel P. Zelesnikar

Title: Senior Analyst **Company:** Engineering Services Network, Inc. **Address:** 2450 Crystal Drive, Suite 1015, Arlington, VA 22202 United States **BUS:** Engineering and Technology Services Company **P/S:** Engineering Technical Support **MA:** National **D/D/R:** Overseeing Operations of Aircraft Carrier Computer, Electronic Command and Control Systems **EDU:** Bachelor of Arts in Sociology, State University of New York
Email: dandeb1@cox.net
URL: http://www.esncc.com

Leila J. M Zemke

Title: Director **Company:** Play of Life Therapies **Address:** 104 E. Main Street, Unit 316, Bozeman, MT 59715 United States **BUS:** Healthcare Facility **P/S:** Healing Arts for Adults and Children with Special Needs Utilizing Kinesthetic Neurological Therapies and Therapeutic Art **MA:** National **D/D/R:** Practicing and Teaching Occupational Therapy, Brain Gym(R), Managing Daily Operations, Working as a Sole-Proprietor **H/I/S:** Gardening, Camping, Traveling **EDU:** Bachelor of Science in Occupational Therapy, Barry University, Miami (1992); Coursework, Educational Kinesiology Foundation, Licensed Brain Gym(R) practitioner and consultant **A/A/S:** Educational Kinesiology Foundation
Email: zemlei@aol.com

Anthony Zeno

Title: Saiko Sensei **Company:** Kyo Kuninja Kan **Address:** Hopewell Junction, NY 12533 United States **BUS:** Martial Arts Education **P/S:** Specialized Martial Arts, Started Training in Hand-Hand Combat after High School, Developed into Kyo Kuninja Kan, Specialized Street Martial Arts, Using Practical Martial Arts and Military Style Combat, A Mix of Jiu Jitsu, Aikido, Karate and Smaller Martial Arts Referred to as a 'Hybrid' The Classes are Used to Build Strength, Ability to Protect Oneself **MA:** International **D/D/R:** 7 Dan Black Belt Kyo Kuninja Kan, 6th Dan Karate, 4th Dan Jiu Jitsu, 3rd Dan Aikido, Air Commander **H/I/S:** Time with Family, Seeing Students Prosper **EDU:** 48 Years Experience, Previous Military Combat Instructor for 7 Years
Email: knkdefense@frontiernet.net

Bonnie Zepf

Title: Owner **Company:** Zepf Textiles and Design **Address:** 267 W. Overlook Drive, Palm Springs, CA 92264 United States **BUS:** Textile and Design **P/S:** Manufacturing Active Sportswear **MA:** Statewide **D/D/R:** Garment Manufacturing **H/I/S:** Traveling, Skiing, Jogging **EDU:** Bachelor of Arts in Art
Email: bzepf@dc.rr.com
URL: http://www.cambridgewhoswho.com

Elaine L. Zevenbergen

Title: Fiscal Manager **Company:** Wahkiakum County Health and Human Services **Address:** 2651 Terry Avenue, Longview, WA 98632 United States **BUS:** Local Government Agency **P/S:** Health and Human Services **MA:** Countywide **EXP:** Ms. Zevenbergen's expertise is in financial management. **H/I/S:** Playing Tennis, Reading, Taking Care of Cats **EDU:** Bachelor's Degree in Accounting
Email: elainezevenbergen@yahoo.com
URL: http://www.cambridgewhoswho.com

J. Werner Ziegler

Title: Medical Doctor **Company:** Radiology and Imaging Consultants, P.C. **Address:** 155 Printers Parkway, Suite 100, Colorado Springs, CO 80910 United States **BUS:** Radiology Diagnostic Center **P/S:** Healthcare, Radiology Medical Consultants **MA:** Colorado Springs, South Denver **EXP:** Mr. Ziegler's expertise is in aortic aneurysm repair. **D/D/R:** Handling Vascular and Interventional Radiology **H/I/S:** Skiing, Tasting Wines, Spending Time with his Sons **EDU:** MD, University of Chicago **CERTS:** Board Certified Diagnostic Radiologist; Certification of Added Qualification, Interventional Radiology Training **A/A/S:** President, Rocky Mountain Vascular Center; Colorado Medical Society; Society of Interventional Radiology; World Aquaculture Society **C/VW:** Make-A-Wish Foundation
Email: wernerziegler@yahoo.com
URL: http://www.ricradiology.com

Tammy Ziegler

Title: Agency Owner **Company:** Allstate Insurance **Address:** 162 S. Virginia Avenue, Tifton, GA 31794 United States **BUS:** Insurance Company **P/S:** Automobile, Home and Life Insurance Policies, Individual Retirement Accounts, Financial Services **MA:** Local **EXP:** Ms. Ziegler's expertise includes sales management and marketing. **CERTS:** Licensed in Life and Health Insurance Series 6 and 63; Licensed in Property, Casualty and Variables **A/A/S:** Tifton Chamber of Commerce; National Association of Insurance and Financial Advisors
Email: tammyzeigler@allstate.com
URL: http://www.allstate.com

Malgorzata Ewa Zielonka, Pharm.D.

Title: Pharmacist **Company:** Loyola University Health System Hospital **Dept:** Pharmacy **Address:** 2160 S. First Avenue, Maywood, IL 60153 United States **BUS:** Medical Center **P/S:** Healthcare and Benefits for United States Veterans and their Families, Wide-Range of Inpatient and Outpatient Services Including Medicine, Surgery, Neurology, Physical Medicine, Rehabilitation, Mental Health Services and Geriatric Care, Anti-Coagulation Clinic **MA:** Regional **D/D/R:** Offering Wide-Range of Inpatient and Outpatient Services, Specializing in Pharmaceutical Services **H/I/S:** Jogging, Walking **EDU:** Pharmacy Practice Residency, S, Stratton Veterans Affairs Medical Center (2006); Doctor of Pharmacy, Midwestern University, Chicago College of Pharmacy (2005) **A/A/S:** Phi Theta Kappa International Honor Society of Two-Year Colleges (1999); Illinois Council of Health-System Pharmacists; American Pharmacists Association **A/H:** Dean's List, Chicago College (2005); The National Dean's List (1999-2005)
Email: malgorzatzielonka@sbcglobal.net
URL: http://www.daytonveteransadministrationmedicalcenter.gov

Maya A. Ziglar

Title: Lieutenant **Company:** Naples Community Hospital **Address:** 350 Seventh Street N., Naples, FL 34102 United States **BUS:** 390-Bed Hospital with More than 500 Physicians, 4,000 Highly Trained Employees and 1,000 Volunteers. **P/S:** Services Including Cardiology, Oncology, Inpatient and Outpatient Rehabilitation, Psychiatry, Pediatric Emergency Medicine, Surgery and Diagnostics **MA:** Local **D/D/R:** Supervising a Shift of Public Safety Officers for the Hospital **H/I/S:** Working as a Canine Handler to Track dangerous Felons and to ensure Public Safety, Boating, Snorkeling, Mountain Bicycling, Enjoying Music and Sports **EDU:** Bachelor's Degree in Public Administration, Barry University (2001); Certified Canine Handler; Police Officer, States of California and Florida **A/A/S:** Member, American Police Hall of Fame and Museum (1997); Artist; Professional Drummer **A/H:** Police Officer of the Year, Operational Excellence, Community Service, National Deans List (2002); President's List of Academic Honors Barry University (2001, 2002); Siver Medalist Police and Fire World Games, Silver Medalist California Police Olympics; Certification of Recognition, Inland Robbery and Homicide Associaton
Email: zigdpig@hotmail.com

Keith J. Zimmerman

Title: Attorney, Principal **Company:** Kahn, Smith & Collins, PA **Address:** 201 N. Charles Street, 10th Floor, Baltimore, MD 21201 United States **BUS:** Law Firm **P/S:** Labor Law **MA:** Maryland **D/D/R:** Representing Unions **H/I/S:** Cycling, Traveling, Reading **EDU:** JD, Antioch School of Law; Bachelor of Science. Cornell University School of Industrial and Labor Relations **A/A/S:** Maryland Bar Association; Member, Labor and Employment Section Council **C/VW:** Volunteer, High School Mock Trial Team, Baltimore City College
Email: zimmerman@kahnsmith.com
URL: http://www.kahnsmith.com

Sheri Ann Zimmerman

Title: Wealth Management Adviser **Company:** TIAA-CREF **Address:** 4205 Carillon Point, Kirkland, WA 98033 United States **BUS:** Financial Services Company **P/S:** Retirement and Investment Planning **MA:** National **D/D/R:** Investment Advice, Wealth and Estate Planning **H/I/S:** Traveling, Playing Volleyball **EDU:** Bachelor's Degree in Finance, Minnesota State University **C/VW:** Seattle Children's Hospital
Email: zimmerman@tiaa-cref.org
URL: http://www.tiaa-cref.org

Irene Zingg

Title: President/Owner **Company:** Sazingg **Address:** 2212 S.W. 22nd Avenue, Miami, FL 33145 United States **BUS:** Jewelry Retail **P/S:** Retail, Jewelry, Gifts **MA:** National **D/D/R:** Designer
Email: irenezingg@hotmail.com
URL: http://www.sazingg.com

Angela M. Zinno, MAT

Title: Teacher **Company:** Pendergast Elementary School District, Canyon Breeze Elementary School **Address:** 18330 N. 79th Avenue, Apartment 1052, Avondale, AZ 85308 United States **BUS:** Public Elementary School **P/S:** Regular Core Curriculum Including Reading, Mathematics, English, Social Studies, Science, Art **MA:** Local **D/D/R:** Teaching Third-Grade Reading Comprehension, Mathematics, Writing, Science, Behavior **H/I/S:** Yoga, Reading **EDU:** Bachelor of Science in Exercise Science, Major in Physical Education, Slippery Rock University of Pennsylvania (1998); Master of Education Degree, Chatham College (2002) **A/A/S:** American College Experts of Madison
Email: j25nad@yahoo.com
URL: http://www.azinno@pesd92.org

Melody L. Ziobro

Title: Assistant Nursing Professor **Company:** Morrisville State College **Address:** P.O. Box 901, Morrisville, NY 13408 United States **BUS:** Residential College Offering Hands-On Education to Students, the First College to Supply Students with Laptop Computers with High Speed Internet Access **P/S:** A Wide Range of Two-Year and Four-Year Programs in Agriculture, Business, Engineering Technologies, Health, Hospitality, Liberal Arts, Natural Resources, and Other Technologies **MA:** Local **D/D/R:** Lecturing and Teaching Across the Curriculum for Associate Degree Program, Working with Freshman Class in Evening Programs, Teaching Fundamentals of Nursing, Mental Health Nursing and Medical and Surgical Components, Teaching Psychiatric Nursing to Senior Classes, Clinical Rotation with Students in Local Hospitals, Teaching Part Time at Excelsior College **H/I/S:** Traveling, Swimming, Boating, Skiing, Animals, Going to the Adirondacks **EDU:** Post-Masters Certification, Rutgers University (2006); Master of Science in Nursing, Syracuse University (1993); Bachelor of Science in Nursing, SUNY Utica, Rome, NY (1983); Associate Degree in Nursing, Onondaga Community College (1974); Licensed Practical Nursing, Geneva School of Practical Nursing (1969) **A/A/S:** New York State Nurses Association; Chenango County and Delaware County New York State Nurses Association
Email: ziabrom2004@yahoo.com
URL: http://www.morrisville.edu

V. Betty Zisch-de la Rosa

Title: Executive National **Company:** Betty Zisch National **Address:** P.O. Box 13140, Chandler, AZ 85248 United States **BUS:** Networking Marketing Company **P/S:** Skin Care Consultation, Nutritional Education, Acne Treatment and Skin Analysis for Small Businesses **MA:** National **D/D/R:** Teaching Skin Care Techniques, Teaching Others how to Run their Skin Care Businesses **H/I/S:** Golfing, Traveling, Going on Cruises, Playing Outdoor Sports, Spending Time with her Grandchildren, Watching Tee Ball **EDU:** Coursework in Business, Arkansas University **A/A/S:** Business and Professional Women; Republication Co-Chairwoman, President Bush's Advisory Council **C/VW:** Our Savior's Lutheran Church, Sojourners Battered and Homeless Women's Shelter, Risen Saviors Lutheran Church
Email: bzdarbnvp@wbshi.net

Mr. Adrian K. Zitzmann

Title: Owner **Company:** Rowan Homes LLC **Address:** 2292 W. Magee Road, Suite 220, Tucson, AZ 85742 United States **BUS:** Preeminent Custom Home Builders **P/S:** Luxury Custom Homes Starting at Five Hundred Thousand Dollars and Up, Cottages, Cabins **MA:** National **D/D/R:** Building Custom Luxury Homes Primarily in the Tucson and Southern Tucson Areas, Running the Daily Operations of the Business, Owner of Mac Management (Property Management Company) Regional **H/I/S:** Architecture, Spending Time with his Children, Sports **EDU:** Pursuing Master's Degree in Business, University of Arizona; Bachelor's Degree in Psychology, University of Arizona (2000) **A/A/S:** Southern Arizona Home Builders Association; National Home Builders Association; Better Business Bureau
Email: rowanhomes@msn.com
URL: http://www.rowanhomesaz.com

Wojciech J. Zolcik, MD

Title: Psychiatrist **Company:** Campell County Memorial Hospital **Address:** 501 S. Buma, Gillette, WY 82716 United States **BUS:** Healthcare Hospital **P/S:** Healthcare Provider **MA:** Local **D/D/R:** Psychiatry **H/I/S:** Horse Back Riding Running **EDU:** Charlesten University, MD **A/A/S:** American Medical Association
Email: wozcik@hotmail.com

Sonja G. Zook

Title: Algebra and Special Education Teacher **Company:** Chesapeake Public Schools, Indian River High School **Address:** 1969 Braves Trail, Chesapeake, VA 23325 United States **BUS:** School **P/S:** Education **MA:** Local **D/D/R:** Teaching Mathematics **H/I/S:** Traveling, Spending Time with her Extended Family **EDU:** Master of Education in Special Education, Old Dominion University **C/VW:** Volunteer, Union Missions Feeding the Homeless; Supporting Pro-Life Organizations; Church Youth Group
Email: sonja_zook@yahoo.com

Rev. Dori Christine Zubizarreta

Title: Pastor **Company:** St. Boniface Episcopal Church **Address:** Comfort, TX 78013 United States **BUS:** Church **P/S:** Missionary Work, Community Service, Religious Services **MA:** Local **D/D/R:** Helping People in Crisis **H/I/S:** Playing Guitar and Trumpet, Swimming **EDU:** Master's Degree in Christian Counseling, Regent University, VA (1990); Master's Degree in Education, Regent University, VA; Bachelor's Degree in Music, University of Montana (1972); Bachelor's Degree in Education, University of Montana **A/A/S:** National Organization for Victim Assistance; Charter Member, American Association of Christian Counselors; Dean Valley Convocation of Episcopal Churches; Chaplain to the National President, Episcopal Churches **C/VW:** Missionary in Honduras; Our Little Roses Ministries
Email: doriolr@aol.com

Pam Zuckerman

Title: Associate Professor, Career Counselor **Company:** State University of New York **Dept:** Fashion Institute of Technology **Address:** Seventh Avenue 27th Street, New York, NY 10001 United States **BUS:** University **P/S:** Education in Fashion and Design, Business and Technology **MA:** International **D/D/R:** Offering Career Development Counseling, Conducting Seminars and Workshops, Advising on Job Search Strategies, Teaching Career Development Classes **H/I/S:** Traveling, Exercising, Making Jewelry, Watching Movies, Going to Museums **EDU:** Master's Degree in Arts, Columbia University (1979); Master's Degree in Education, Columbia University (1979) **A/H:** Chancellor's Award for Excellence in Professional Service (1997)
Email: pam_zuckerman@fitnyc.edu

Mr. Jim B. Zumwalt

Title: Owner, Contractor, Artist **Company:** JimKim Construction **Address:** 44526 Denmore Avenue, Lancaster, CA 93535 United States **BUS:** Residential Construction Company **P/S:** Residential Construction, Room Additions, Re-Modeling and Repair Services **MA:** Antelope Valley, Santa Clarita Valley **D/D/R:** Remodeling, Repairing, Room Additions and Renovations **H/I/S:** Painting, Sculpting, Spending Time with his Family **EDU:** College Coursework, Pepperdine University; High School Diploma **A/A/S:** Antelope Valley Allied Arts Association; Lancaster Chamber of Commerce; Rosamond Chamber of Commerce
Email: derzum4@yahoo.com

Jackie A. Zurl

Title: Medical Record Officer **Company:** The McGuire Group, Brookhaven Health Care Facility **Dept:** Medical Records Department **Address:** 35 Andreano Avenue E., Patchogue, NY 11772 United States **BUS:** Nursing Home **P/S:** Nursing Services Including Long-Term and Short-Term Skilled Nursing Care, Sub-acute Rehabilitation and Specialized Memory Care for Individuals with Dementia and Alzheimer's Disease **MA:** Regional **D/D/R:** Admitting and Discharging Patients, Scheduling Doctors' Appointments, Ordering Forms from the Corporate Office, Working with the Director of Nursing, Residents and Families, Thinning Charts, Keeping Medical Records and Coding within the New York State Department of Health, Care Planning, Training **H/I/S:** Reading, Antique Shopping, Working on Computers, Visiting Antique Shows **EDU:** Pursuing Coursework in Business Administration, Briarcliffe College **CERTS:** Pursuing Certification in Alcohol and Substance Abuse Counseling **A/H:** Employee of the Month Award (Thrice)
Email: jackiez4@yahoo.com
Email: jsatterley@mcguiregroup.com
URL: http://www.mcguiregroup.com

Mary Louise Zwaan

Title: Senior Professional in Human Resources **Company:** Wachovia Corporation **Address:** 123 S. Broad Street, Suite 1269, Philadelphia, PA 19109 United States **BUS:** Financial Firm **P/S:** Financial Services Including Personal Loans, Investment Planning, Insurance Policies, Online Retirement Services and Mortgages **MA:** National **D/D/R:** Overseeing the Human Resource Department, Monitoring the Performance of Programs, Coordinating Programs **H/I/S:** Reading, Baking, Playing Softball and Football **EDU:** Master of Science in Leadership, Rosemont College (2000); Bachelor of Science in Management, Rosemont College
Email: marylou.zwaan@wachovia.com
Email: marylouzwaan@wachovia.com
URL: http://www.wachovia.com

Brenda J. Zwilling

Title: Teacher **Company:** Maybury Elementary School, Columbus Public Schools **Address:** 6278 Upperridge Drive, Canal Winchester, OH 43110 United States **BUS:** Public Elementary School **P/S:** Primary Education **MA:** Regional **D/D/R:** Teaching First and Second-Grade Students English, Reading, Writing, Mathematics, Social Studies, Tutoring **H/I/S:** Photography **EDU:** Master's Degree in Elementary Education, Mary Grove (2005); Bachelor of Science in Education, East Carolina University (1971) **A/A/S:** National Education Association; Columbus Education Association; Ohio Education Association
Email: bjzmaz@aol.com
URL: http://www.columbus.k12.oh.us

DISCLAIMER